LITERARY MARKET PLACE™

LMP 2025

Literary Market Place™
85th Edition

Publisher
Thomas H. Hogan

Senior Director, ITI Reference Group
Owen O'Donnell

Managing Editor
Karen Hallard

Assistant Editor
Karen DiDario

Tampa Operations:

Manager, Tampa Editorial Operations
Debra James

Project Coordinator, Tampa Editorial
Carolyn Victor

Graphics & Production:

Production Manager
Tiffany Chamenko

Production
Dana Stevenson
Jackie Crawford

LITERARY MARKET PLACE™

LMP 2025

THE DIRECTORY OF THE AMERICAN BOOK PUBLISHING INDUSTRY WITH INDUSTRY INDEXES

Volume

Published by

Information Today, Inc.
143 Old Marlton Pike
Medford, NJ 08055-8750
Phone: (609) 654-6266
Fax: (609) 654-4309
E-mail (Orders): custserv@infotoday.com
Web site: www.infotoday.com
Copyright 2024, Information Today, Inc. All Rights Reserved

ISSN 0000-1155
ISBN 978-1-57387-604-9 (set)
Library of Congress Catalog Card Number 41-51571

COPYRIGHT ©2024 INFORMATION TODAY, INC. All rights reserved. No part of this publication may be reproduced, stored in a retrieval system, or transmitted, in any form or by any means, electronic, mechanical, photocopy, recording or otherwise without the prior written permission of the publisher.

Information Today, Inc. uses reasonable care to obtain accurate and timely information. However, Information Today, Inc. disclaims any liability to any party for any loss or damage caused by errors or omissions in *Literary Market Place*™ whether or not such errors or omissions result from negligence, accident or any other cause.

Information Today, Inc.
143 Old Marlton Pike
Medford, NJ 08055-8750
Phone: 800-300-9868 (Customer Service)
         800-409-4929 (Editorial)
Fax: 609-654-4309
E-mail (orders): custserv@infotoday.com
Web Site: www.infotoday.com

Printed in the United States of America

CONTENTS

VOLUME 1

Preface ix
Abbreviations & Acronyms xi

BOOK PUBLISHERS
U.S. Publishers 1
   U.S. Publishers — Geographic Index 239
   U.S. Publishers — Type of Publication Index 247
   U.S. Publishers — Subject Index 277
Imprints, Subsidiaries & Distributors 333
Canadian Publishers 395

EDITORIAL SERVICES & AGENTS
   Editorial Services — Activity Index 429
Editorial Services 435
Literary Agents 447
Illustration Agents 485
Lecture Agents 487

ASSOCIATIONS, EVENTS, COURSES & AWARDS
   Book Trade & Allied Associations — Index 489
Book Trade & Allied Associations 493
Foundations 525
   Calendar of Book Trade & Promotional Events — Alphabetical Index of Sponsors 527
   Calendar of Book Trade & Promotional Events — Alphabetical Index of Events 531
Calendar of Book Trade & Promotional Events 535
Writers' Conferences & Workshops 553
Courses for the Book Trade 561
Awards, Prize Contests, Fellowships & Grants 569

BOOKS & MAGAZINES FOR THE TRADE
Reference Books for the Trade 681
Magazines for the Trade 699

INDEXES
Company Index 709
Personnel Index 785
Publishers Toll Free Directory 1079
Index to Sections 1089

VOLUME 2

Preface ix
Abbreviations & Acronyms xi

ADVERTISING, MARKETING & PUBLICITY

Advertising Agencies 1099
   Promotional Printing & Allied Services — Activity Index 1101
Promotional Printing & Allied Services 1103
Public Relations Services 1107
Direct Mail Specialists 1115
Mailing, Duplicating & Fax Services 1117
Mailing List Brokers & Services 1119
   Columnists & Commentators — Subject Index 1123
Columnists & Commentators 1125
Book Review Syndicates 1127
Book Review & Index Journals & Services 1129
Book Exhibits 1139
Book Clubs 1141
Book Lists & Catalogs 1145
Serials Featuring Books 1147
News Services & Feature Syndicates 1189
Radio, TV & Cable Networks 1193
Radio Programs Featuring Books 1197
TV Programs Featuring Books 1201

BOOK MANUFACTURING

Complete Book Manufacturing 1207
   Prepress Services Index 1217
Prepress Services 1221
   Printing, Binding & Book Finishing Index 1235
Printing, Binding & Book Finishing 1247
   Manufacturing Materials Index 1263
Manufacturing Materials 1265
   Manufacturing Services & Equipment Index 1275
Manufacturing Services & Equipment 1277

SALES & DISTRIBUTION

Book Distributors & Sales Representatives 1285
   Wholesalers — Activity Index 1305
Wholesalers 1311
Prebinders to Schools & Libraries 1325
Book Exporters & Importers 1327
Export Representatives 1331
Shipping Services 1333
Shipping Suppliers 1337

SERVICES & SUPPLIERS

- *Consultants — Activity Index* 1339
- Consultants 1343
- Book Producers 1353
- *Publishing Systems, Services & Technology Index* 1359
- Publishing Systems, Services & Technology 1363
- Employment Agencies 1381
- Clipping Bureaus 1383
- Typing & Word Processing Services 1385
- *Translators & Interpreters — Source Language Index* 1387
- *Translators & Interpreters — Target Language Index* 1393
- Translators & Interpreters 1399
- *Artists & Art Services — Activity Index* 1407
- Artists & Art Services 1411
- Photographers 1419
- Stock Photo Agencies 1427

INDEXES

- Company Index 1433
- Personnel Index 1465
- Index to Sections 1541

Preface

The 2025 edition marks the 85th annual publication of *Literary Market Place*™—the leading directory of the American and Canadian book publishing industry. Covering publishers and literary agents to manufacturers and shipping services, *LMP* is the most comprehensive directory of its kind. The revised 2025 edition contains almost 7,500 entries. Of these listings 1,973 are publishers—including Canadian houses. Together with its companion publication, *International Literary Market Place*™, these directories cover the global book publishing industry.

Organization & Content
Volume 1 covers core publishing industry information: Book Publishers; Editorial Services and Agents; Associations, Events, Courses and Awards; and Books and Magazines for the Trade.

Volume 2 contains information on service providers and suppliers to the publishing industry. Advertising, Marketing and Publicity; Book Manufacturing; Sales and Distribution; and Services and Suppliers can be found in this volume.

Entries generally contain name, address, telephone and other telecommunications data, key personnel, company reportage, branch offices, brief statistics and descriptive annotations. Where applicable, Standard Address Numbers (SANs) have been included. SANs are unique numbers assigned to the addresses of publishers, wholesalers and booksellers. Publishers' entries also contain their assigned ISBN prefixes. Both the SAN and ISBN systems are administered by R.R. Bowker LLC.

Indexes
In addition to the numerous section-specific indexes appearing throughout, each volume of *LMP* contains four indexes that reference listings appearing in that volume. The Industry Indexes cover two distinct areas of data: a Company Index that includes the name, address, communications information and page reference for company listings and a separate Personnel Index that includes the main personnel associated with each entry as well as the page reference. Also included in each volume is an Index to Sections for quickly finding specific categories of information.

A Note to Authors
Prospective authors seeking a publisher should be aware that there are publishers who, as a condition for publishing and marketing an individual's work, may require a significant sum of money be paid to the publisher. This practice is known by a number of terms including author subsidized publishing, author investment, and co-operative publishing. Before entering an agreement involving such a payment, the author is advised to make a careful investigation to determine the standing of the publisher's imprint in the industry.

Similarly, authors seeking literary representation are advised that some agents request a nominal reading fee that may be applied to the agent's commission upon representation. Other agencies may charge substantially higher fees which may not be applicable to a future commission and which are not refundable. The recommended course is to first send a query letter with an outline, sample chapter, and a self-addressed stamped envelope (SASE). Should an agent express interest in handling the manuscript, full details of fees and commissions should be obtained in writing before the complete manuscript is sent. Should an agency require significant advance payment from an author, the author is cautioned to make a careful investigation to determine the agency's standing in the industry before entering an agreement. The author should always retain a copy of the manuscript in his or her possession.

Occasionally, the editors of *LMP* will receive complaints against publishers or agents listed in the work. If, after investigation and review, the editors determine that the complaints are significant and justified, we may exclude the company or individual in question. However, the absence of a listing in *LMP* for any particular publisher or agent should not be construed as a judgment on the legitimacy or integrity of that organization or individual.

Compilation
LMP is updated throughout the year via a number of methods. A request for updated information is sent to current entrants to corroborate and update the information contained on our database. All updates received are edited for the next product release. Those entrants who do not respond to our request may be verified through telephone interviews or online research. Entrants who cannot be verified or who fall short of entry criteria are dropped from the current edition.

Information for new listings is gathered in a similar method. Possible new listings are identified through ongoing research, or when a listing request is received either from the organization itself or from a third party. If sufficient information is not initially gathered to create a listing, a data collection form is provided to the organization to submit essential listing information.

Updated information or suggestions for new listings can be submitted by mail to:

Literary Market Place
Information Today, Inc.
121 Chanlon Rd, Suite G-20
New Providence, NJ 07974-2195

An updating method using the Internet is also available for *LMP* listings:

Visit the *Literary Market Place* web site to update an *LMP* listing. **Literarymarketplace.com** allows you the opportunity to provide new information for a listing by clicking on the "Update or Correct Your Entry" option. The Feedback option on the home page of the web site can be used to suggest new entries as well.

Related Services

Literary Market Place, along with its companion volume *International Literary Market Place*, is available through the Internet at **www.literarymarketplace.com**. Designed to give users simple, logical access to the information they require, the site offers users the choice of searching for data alphabetically, geographically, by type, or by subject. Continuously updated by Information Today's team of editors, this is a truly enhanced version of the *LMP* and *ILMP* databases, incorporating features that make "must-have" information easily available.

Arrangements for placing advertisements in *LMP* can be coordinated through Customer Service by telephone at 609-654-6266, or by e-mail at custserv@infotoday.com.

Your feedback is important to us. We strongly encourage you to contact us with suggestions or comments on the print edition of *LMP*, or its web site. Our editorial office can be reached by telephone at 800-409-4929 (press 3) or 908-219-0277, or by e-mail at khallard@infotoday.com.

The editors would like to thank those entrants who took the time to respond to our requests for current information.

Abbreviations & Acronyms

The following is a list of acronyms & abbreviations used throughout *LMP*.

AALA - Association of American Literary Agents
AB - Alberta
Acct(s) - Account(s)
Acctg - Accounting
Acq(s) - Acquisition(s)
Ad - Advertising
Admin - Administrative, Administration, Administrator
Aff - Affairs
AK - Alaska
AL - Alabama
appt - appointment
Apt - Apartment
AR - Arkansas
Assoc - Associate
Asst - Assistant
AV - Audiovisual
Ave - Avenue
AZ - Arizona

B&W - Black & White
BC - British Columbia
Bd - Board
bio - biography
BISAC - Book Industry Standards and Communications
Bldg - Building
Blvd - Boulevard
Br - Branch
Busn - Business

CA - California
CEO - Chief Executive Officer
CFO - Chief Financial Officer
Chmn - Chairman
Chpn - Chairperson
CIO - Chief Information Officer
Circ - Circulation
CN - Canada
CO - Colorado
Co(s) - Company(-ies)
Co-edns - Co-editions
Coll(s) - College(s)
Comm - Committee
Commun(s) - Communication(s)
Comp - Compiler
Compt - Comptroller
Cont - Controller
Contrib - Contributing
COO - Chief Operating / Operations Officer
Coord - Coordinator
Corp - Corporate, Corporation
Coun - Counsel
CT - Connecticut
Ct - Court
CTO - Chief Technical / Technology Officer

Ctr - Center
Curr - Current
Cust - Customer
CZ - Canal Zone

DC - District of Columbia
DE - Delaware
Dept - Department
Devt - Development
Dir(s) - Director(s)
Dist - Distributed, Distribution, Distributor
Div - Division
Dom - Domestic
Dr - Drive

ed - edition
Ed(s) - Editor(s)
Edit - Editorial
Educ - Education, Educational
El-hi - Elementary-High School
Elem - Elementary
Ency - Encyclopedia
Eng - English
Engg - Engineering
Engr - Engineer
Equip - Equipment
ESL - English as a Second Language
Est - Established
EVP - Executive Vice President
exc - except
Exec - Executive
Expwy - Expressway
ext - extension

Fed - Federal
Fin - Finance, Financial
fl - floor
FL - Florida
Freq - Frequency
Fwy - Freeway

GA - Georgia
Gen - General
Govt - Government
GU - Guam

HD - High-definition
HI - Hawaii
HR - Human Resources
HS - High School
Hwy - Highway

IA - Iowa
ID - Idaho
IL - Illinois
Illus - Illustrator
IN - Indiana
Inc - Incorporated

indiv(s) - individual(s)
Indus - Industrial, Industry
Info - Information
Instl - Institutional
Instn(s) - Institution(s)
Instrl - Instructional
Intl - International
ISBN - International Standard Book Number
ISSN - International Standard Serial Number
IT - Information Technology

Jr - Junior
Jt - Joint
Juv - Juvenile

K - Kindergarten
KS - Kansas
KY - Kentucky

LA - Louisiana
Lang(s) - Language(s)
Lib(s) - Library(-ies)
Libn - Librarian
Lit - Literature

MA - Massachusetts
MB - Manitoba
MD - Maryland
Mdse - Merchandise
Mdsg - Merchandising
ME - Maine
Med - Medical
memb(s) - member(s)
Metro - Metropolitan
Mfg - Manufacturing
Mgmt - Management
Mgr - Manager
MI - Michigan
Mkt(s) - Market(s)
Mktg - Marketing
MN - Minnesota
Mng - Managing
MO - Missouri
mo - month
MS - Mississippi
ms(s) - manuscript(s)
MT - Montana

Natl - National
NB - New Brunswick
NC - North Carolina
ND - North Dakota
NE - Nebraska
NH - New Hampshire
NJ - New Jersey
NL - Newfoundland and Labrador
NM - New Mexico
No - Number

ABBREVIATIONS & ACRONYMS

NS - Nova Scotia
NT - Northwest Territories
NU - Nunavut
NV - Nevada
NY - New York

Off(s) - Office(s)
Offr - Officer
OH - Ohio
OK - Oklahoma
ON - Ontario
Oper(s) - Operation(s)
OR - Oregon

PA - Pennsylvania
Pbk(s) - Paperback(s)
PE - Prince Edward Island
Perms - Permissions
Photo - Photograph
Photog - Photographer, Photography
Pkwy - Parkway
pp - pages
PR - Public Relations
PR - Puerto Rico
Pres - President
Proc - Processing
Prod(s) - Product(s)
Prodn - Production
Prodr - Producer
Prof - Professional, Professor
Prog(s) - Program(s)
Proj(s) - Project(s)
Promo(s) - Promotion(s)
Prop - Proprietor
Pub Aff - Public Affairs

Publg - Publishing
Publr - Publisher
Pubn(s) - Publication(s)
Purch - Purchasing

QC - Quebec

R&D - Research & Development
Rd - Road
Ref - Reference
Reg - Region
Regl - Regional
Rel - Relations
Rep(s) - Representative(s)
Res - Research
RI - Rhode Island
Rm - Room
Rte - Route
Rts - Rights

SAN - Standard Address Number
SASE - Self-Addressed Stamped Envelope
SC - South Carolina
Sci - Science
SD - South Dakota
Secy - Secretary
Serv(s) - Service(s)
SK - Saskatchewan
Soc - Social, Sociology
Spec - Special
Sq - Square
Sr - Senior
St - Saint, Street
Sta - Station
Ste - Sainte

Subn(s) - Subscription(s)
Subs - Subsidiary
Supv - Supervisor
SVP - Senior Vice President
Synd - Syndicated, Syndication

Tech - Technical
Technol - Technology
Tel - Telephone
Terr - Terrace
TN - Tennessee
Tpke - Turnpike
Treas - Treasurer
TX - Texas

UK - United Kingdom
Univ - University
unsol - unsolicited
UT - Utah

V - Vice
VA - Virginia
VChmn - Vice Chairman
VI - Virgin Islands
vol(s) - volume(s)
VP - Vice President
VT - Vermont

WA - Washington
WI - Wisconsin
WV - West Virginia
WY - Wyoming

yr - year
YT - Yukon Territory

Book Publishers

U.S. Publishers

Listed in alphabetical order are those U.S. publishers that have reported to *LMP* that they produce an average of three or more books annually. Publishers that have appeared in a previous edition of *LMP*, but whose output currently does not meet our defined rate of activity, will be reinstated when their annual production reaches the required level. It should be noted that this rule of publishing activity does not apply to publishers of dictionaries, encyclopedias, atlases or Braille books or to university presses.

The definition of a book excludes charts, pamphlets, folding maps, sheet music and material with stapled bindings. Publishers that make their titles available only in electronic or audio format are included if they meet the stated criteria. In the case of packages, the book must be of equal or greater importance than the accompanying piece. With few exceptions, new publishers are not listed prior to having published at least three titles within a year.

§ before the company name indicates publishers involved in electronic publishing.

The following indexes can be found immediately after the publishers' listings:

U.S. Publishers–Geographic Index
U.S. Publishers–Type of Publications Index
U.S. Publishers–Subject Index

See **Imprints, Subsidiaries & Distributors** for additional information on the companies listed herein. This section should also be checked for apparently active companies that are no longer listed in the U.S. Publishers section. In many cases, they have been acquired as an imprint or subsidiary of a larger entity and no longer have a discrete listing.

§A-R Editions Inc
1600 Aspen Commons, Suite 100, Middleton, WI 53562
Tel: 608-836-9000 *Toll Free Tel:* 800-736-0070 (North America book orders only) *Fax:* 608-831-8200
E-mail: info@areditions.com; orders@areditions.com
Web Site: www.areditions.com
Key Personnel
Pres & CEO: Patrick Wall *Tel:* 608-203-2575 *E-mail:* patrick.wall@areditions.com
Dir, Spec Projs: James Zychowicz *Tel:* 608-203-2580 *E-mail:* james.zychowicz@areditions.com
Founded: 1962
Scholarly critical editions of music for performance & study; computer music & digital audio professional books, electronics & Internet technology, online music anthology (www.armusicanthology.com) & co-published series with MLA: Index & Bibliography, Basic Manual & Technical Reports Series.
ISBN Prefix(es): 978-0-89579
Number of titles published annually: 25 Print
Total Titles: 500 Print
Imprints: Greenway Music Press
Distributor for AIM (American Institute of Musicology)

A 2 Z Press LLC
3670 Woodbridge Rd, Deland, FL 32720
Tel: 440-241-3126
E-mail: sizemore3630@aol.com
Web Site: www.a2zpress.com; www.bestlittleonlinebookstore.com
Key Personnel
CEO: Terrie Sizemore
Proofreader/Asst: Katherine O'Brien
Founded: 2016
Small publishing press that has the vision to receive submissions from writers who have quality titles that meet our submission guidelines but have been rejected by other publishing houses.
ISBN Prefix(es): 978-0-9976407; 978-1-946908; 978-1-954191; 978-1-962101
Number of titles published annually: 60 Print; 30 Online; 20 E-Book
Total Titles: 180 Print; 15 E-Book
Distribution Center: Ingram Wholesale
Membership(s): The American Library Association (ALA); Independent Book Publishers Association (IBPA); Society of Children's Book Writers & Illustrators (SCBWI)

AAAI Press
Imprint of Association for the Advancement of Artificial Intelligence
2275 E Bayshore Rd, Suite 160, Palo Alto, CA 94303
Tel: 650-328-3123 *Fax:* 650-321-4457
E-mail: publications21@aaai.org
Web Site: www.aaai.org/Press/press.php
Key Personnel
Exec Dir: Carol Hamilton
Pubns Chair: Stephen F Smith
Pubns Assoc: Emma Wischmeyer
Founded: 1989
Publishing books on all aspects of artificial intelligence.
ISBN Prefix(es): 978-0-929280; 978-1-57735
Number of titles published annually: 4 Print; 4 Online; 40 E-Book
Total Titles: 550 Print; 8 Online; 50 E-Book

AABB, see Association for the Advancement of Blood & Biotherapies

§AAPG (American Association of Petroleum Geologists)
1444 S Boulder Ave, Tulsa, OK 74119
Mailing Address: PO Box 979, Tulsa, OK 74101-0979
Tel: 918-584-2555 *Toll Free Tel:* 800-364-AAPG (364-2274) *Fax:* 918-580-2665
E-mail: info@aapg.org
Web Site: www.aapg.org
Key Personnel
Ed: Matthew Pranter
Founded: 1917
Peer-reviewed geological science tomes.
ISBN Prefix(es): 978-0-89181; 978-1-58861
Number of titles published annually: 10 Print; 10 CD-ROM
Total Titles: 100 Print; 80 CD-ROM
Distributed by Affiliated East-West Press Pvt Ltd; Canadian Society of Petroleum Geologists; Geological Society of London
Distributor for Geological Society of London
Shipping Address: 125 W 15 St, Tulsa, OK 74119

ABA Publishing, see American Bar Association Publishing

§Abbeville Press
Imprint of Abbeville Publishing Group
655 Third Ave, New York, NY 10017
Tel: 212-366-5585 *Toll Free Tel:* 800-ART-BOOK (278-2665); 800-343-4499 (orders)
E-mail: abbeville@abbeville.com; sales@abbeville.com; marketing@abbeville.com; rights@abbeville.com
Web Site: www.abbeville.com
Key Personnel
Cust Serv Mgr: Nadine Winns
Rts & Perms: David Fabricant
Founded: 1977
Fine arts publisher.
ISBN Prefix(es): 978-0-89659; 978-1-55859; 978-0-7892
Number of titles published annually: 25 Print
Distribution Center: W W Norton & Company Inc, 500 Fifth Ave, New York, NY

U.S. PUBLISHERS

10110-0017 *Tel:* 212-354-5500 *Fax:* 212-869-0856 *E-mail:* orders@wwnorton.com *Web Site:* books.wwnorton.com

Abbeville Publishing Group
655 Third Ave, New York, NY 10017
SAN: 211-4755
Tel: 646-375-2136
E-mail: abbeville@abbeville.com; rights@abbeville.com
Web Site: www.abbeville.com
Key Personnel
Publr: David Fabricant
Cust Serv Mgr: Nadine Winns *E-mail:* nwinns@abbeville.com
Founded: 1977
Publishers of high-quality, fine art books, nonfiction illustrated books, children's books, limited editions, prints, gift line.
ISBN Prefix(es): 978-0-89659; 978-1-55859; 978-0-89660; 978-0-7892
Number of titles published annually: 40 Print
Total Titles: 700 Print
Imprints: Abbeville Kids; Abbeville Press; Artabras
Foreign Rep(s): ACC Art Books (Europe, Ireland, UK); Gilles Fauveau (Japan, South Korea); Penguin Random House Canada (Canada); Peribo Pty Ltd (Eddie Coffey) (Australia); Wei Zhao (China, Hong Kong, Taiwan)
Foreign Rights: Bookbank SA (Latin America, Mexico, Spain); Motovun Tokyo (Japan); Ultreya SRL (Italy)
Orders to: Publishers Group Worldwide, 250 W 57 St, 15th fl, New York, NY 10107 *Tel:* 212-581-7839 *E-mail:* intlorders@pgw.com
Warehouse: Client Distribution Services, 193 Edwards Dr, Jackson, TN 38301 *Toll Free Tel:* 800-343-4499 *Toll Free Fax:* 800-351-5073
See separate listing for:
Abbeville Press

§ABC-CLIO
Subsidiary of Bloomsbury Publishing Inc
147 Castilian Dr, Santa Barbara, CA 93117
Tel: 805-968-1911 *Toll Free Tel:* 800-368-6868
 Toll Free Fax: 866-270-3856
E-mail: customerservice@abc-clio.com
Web Site: www.abc-clio.com
Key Personnel
Pres: Becky Snyder
Edit Specialist: Jennifer Hutchinson
Founded: 1955
A privately held corporation which has for many years enjoyed an international reputation for high quality & innovation. As an educational reference publisher, the company has received critical acclaim for its computer assisted abstracting & indexing services, world renowned book program & cutting-edge online products.
ISBN Prefix(es): 978-0-87436; 978-1-57607
Number of titles published annually: 300 Print; 300 Online; 300 E-Book
Total Titles: 20,000 Print; 15,000 Online; 15,000 E-Book
Imprints: Greenwood; Praeger

ABDO
Subsidiary of Abdo Consulting Group Inc (ACGI)
8000 W 78 St, Suite 310, Edina, MN 55439
Mailing Address: PO Box 398166, Minneapolis, MN 55439-8166
Tel: 952-698-2403 *Toll Free Tel:* 800-800-1312 *Fax:* 952-831-1632 *Toll Free Fax:* 800-862-3480
E-mail: customerservice@abdobooks.com; info@abdobooks.com
Web Site: abdobooks.com
Key Personnel
Pres: Jill Hansen *E-mail:* jhansen@abdobooks.com
EVP: Paul Abdo *E-mail:* pabdo@abdobooks.com
VP, Direct Sales & Content: Monte Kuehl *E-mail:* mkuehl@abdobooks.com
VP, Sales & Mktg: Paul Skaj *E-mail:* pskaj@abdobooks.com
Publr: Jim Abdo *E-mail:* jim@abdobooks.com
Assoc Ed: Tyler Gieseke *E-mail:* tgieseke@abdobooks.com
Founded: 1985
Children's PreK-12 educational publishing for school & public libraries.
ISBN Prefix(es): 978-1-56239; 978-1-57765
Number of titles published annually: 350 Print; 700 Online
Total Titles: 10,000 Print; 5,000 Online; 5,000 E-Book
Imprints: A&D Xtreme (grades 3-9 bold hi-lo nonfiction); Abdo & Daughters (grades 5-9 nonfiction); Abdo Digital (interactive products); Abdo Kids (grades PreK-2 beginning readers); Abdo Kids Jumbo (grades PreK-2 oversized nonfiction); Abdo Kids Junior (grades PreK-2 nonfiction); Abdo Publishing (grades PreK-12 educational nonfiction); Abdo Zoom (engaging nonfiction); Beginning Readers (grades PreK-4 early fiction); Big Buddy Books (grades 2-5 oversized nonfiction); Buddy Books (grades 2-5 nonfiction); Calico (grades 2-5 chapter books); Calico Kid (grades PreK-3 chapter books); Chapter Books (grades K-8 intermediate stories); Checkerboard Library (grades 3-6 curriculum-based nonfiction); Classics (grades 3-8 illustrated literature); Core Library (grades 3-6 Common Core nonfiction); Dash! (grades K-4 leveled books); Essential Library (grades 6-12 research & reference); Fly! (grades 2-8 hi-lo nonfiction); Graphic Novels (grades 2-12 comic book stories); Graphic Planet (grades 2-8 graphic novels); Launch! (grades PreK-2 beginning research); Leveled Readers (grades PreK-4 emerging readers); Looking Glass Library (grades PreK-4 picture books); Magic Readers (grades K-3 leveled readers); Magic Wagon (grades PreK-8 illustrated); Marvel Illustrated (grades 2-12); Marvel Picture Books (grades PreK-6 Marvel storytime favorites); Picture Books (grades PreK-6 storytime favorites); Pop! (web enhanced 4D nonfiction); Sandcastle (grades PreK-3 beginning nonfiction); Short Tales (grades 1-6 adapted stories); Spellbound (grades 2-8 hi-lo chapter books); SportsZone (grades 2-12); Spotlight (grades PreK-8 popular fiction); Super Sandcastle (grades K-4 oversized early nonfiction)
Warehouse: 1920 Lookout Dr, North Mankato, MN 56003

§Abingdon Press
Imprint of The United Methodist Publishing House
810 12 Ave S, Nashville, TN 37203
SAN: 201-0046
Toll Free Tel: 800-251-3320
E-mail: orders@abingdonpress.com; permissions@abingdonpress.com
Web Site: www.abingdonpress.com
Key Personnel
Pres & Publr: Brian Milford
Contractor for Pres & Publr: Tamara Crabtree *E-mail:* tcrabtree@umpublishing.org
Sr Exec Dir, Sales & Mktg: Jeff Barnes *E-mail:* jbarnes@umpublishing.org
Dir, Trade Sales: Robin Glennon *E-mail:* rglennon@abingdonpress.com
Founded: 1789
Religion/ecumenical Christianity; general interest, children's, family, church professional, academic, reference, lay spiritual; United Methodist history, doctrine, polity.
ISBN Prefix(es): 978-0-687; 978-1-4267; 978-1-63088; 978-1-5018
Number of titles published annually: 175 Print
Total Titles: 270 Print; 10 CD-ROM; 3 Online
Foreign Rep(s): Canaanland Distributors (Malaysia); CLC Wholesale (UK); KCBS (South Korea); MediaCom Education Inc (Australia); SKS Books (Singapore); Word Alive/Anchor (Canada)
Foreign Rights: Riggins International Rights Services
Returns: 700 Airtech Pkwy, Plainfield, IL 46168

Harry N Abrams Inc
Subsidiary of Media-Participations
195 Broadway, 9th fl, New York, NY 10007
SAN: 200-2434
Tel: 212-206-7715 *Toll Free Tel:* 800-345-1359 *Fax:* 212-645-8437
E-mail: abrams@abramsbooks.com; publicity@abramsbooks.com; sales@abramsbooks.com
Web Site: www.abramsbooks.com
Key Personnel
Exec Chair of the Bd: Michael Jacobs
Pres & CEO: Mary McAveney
CFO: Vandana Patel
Cont: Brian Pierson
Asst Cont: Dennis Sleater
SVP & Publr, Adult Trade: Michael Sand
SVP & Publr, Children's Books: Andrew Smith
SVP, Fin: John Quinn
SVP, Mktg & Publicity: Melanie Chang
SVP, People: Ayana Albert
SVP, Publg Opers: Anet Sirna-Bruder
SVP, Publg Servs: Josh Weiss
SVP, Sales: Christine Edwards
SVP, Strategic Devt: Steve Tager
SVP, Supply Chain: Frank Albanese
VP & Publr, Abrams ComicArts: Rodolphe Lachat
VP & Assoc Publr: Holly Dolce
VP & Creative Dir, Adult Art & Design: Deb Wood
VP, Busn & Legal Aff: Peggy Garry
VP, Children's & Adult Mktg: Kim Lauber
VP, Digital Publg Sales: Lindy Humphreys
VP, IT: Chris Raymond
VP, Sales: Monica Shah
VP, Subs Rts: Yulia Borodyanskaya
VP, Technol Devt: Phil DiSanto
Assoc Publr, Abrams Children's: Maggie Lehrman
Assoc Publr, Abrams ComicArts: Joseph Montagne
Exec Dir, Abrams Publicity: Taryn Roeder
Exec Dir, Publg Opers: Mary O'Mara
Exec Dir, Spec Sales: Nadine Sferratore
Sr Dir, Children's Publicity & School & Lib Mktg: Hallie Patterson
Sr Dir, Mktg: Kevin Callahan
Sr Dir, Mktg, Adult Books: Jessica Wiener
Sr Dir, Royalties & Fin System: Brian Alvarez
Creative Dir: Pam Notarantonio
Dir, Corp Events & Exec Asst to CEO: Merle Brown
Dir, Fin Planning & Analysis: Roberto Velez
Dir, Intl & Export Sales: Kathleen Spinelli
Dir, Mktg, Abrams ComicArts: Nicole Valdez
Dir, Prodn: Alison Gervais
Dir, Publicity: Gabby Fisher
Dir, Sales Natl Accts: Mark Harrington
Edit Dir, Abrams Press/The Overlook Press: Jamison Stoltz
Edit Dir, Cameron+Company: Pippa White
Edit Dir, Entertainment Publg & Content Devt: Anne Heltzel
Edit Dir, PreK, Abrams Children's: Meredith Mundy
Natl Accts Dir: Andy Weiner
Natl Accts Sales Dir, Mass Merchandisers: Elizabeth Frew
Publg Dir, Calendars: Miriam Tribble
Assoc Art Dir: Eli Mock
Assoc Art Dir, Amulet Books: Deena Fleming
Assoc Art Dir, Diary of a Wimpy Kid: Lora Grisafi

PUBLISHERS

Assoc Creative Dir, Mktg Design: Xander Hollenbeck
Assoc Dir, Children's Publicity: Mary Marolla
Assoc Dir, Integrated Mktg: Borana Greku
Assoc Dir, Digital & Soc Media Mktg, Children's: Trish McNamara O'Neill
Assoc Dir, Fin Planning & Analysis: Christine Geary
Assoc Dir, Prodn: Sarah Masterson Hally
Assoc Dir, Publicity: Natasha Martin
Assoc Dir, School & Lib Mktg: Kristen Luby
Assoc Dir, Subs Rts: Talia Behrend-Wilcox
Asst Art Dir: Heather Kelly
Ed-in-Chief: Rebecca Kaplan
Ed-in-Chief, Abrams ComicArts: Charles Kochman
Exec Ed: Laura Dozier
Exec Ed, Children's: Erica Finkel
Exec Ed, Graphic Novels, Children's: Charlotte Greenbaum
Sr Mng Ed, Adult: Lisa Silverman
Sr Mng Ed, Children's Books & ComicArts: Marie Oishi
Mng Ed: Ashley Albert
Mng Ed, Children's: Megan Carlson
Assoc Mng Ed: Kristy Keplinger
Asst Mng Ed: Nate Lee
Sr Ed: Zack Knoll
Sr Ed, Children's: Courtney Code
Sr Ed, Entertainment Publg, Children's: Diego Lopez
Ed: Soyolmaa Lkhagvadorj; Abby Muller
Ed, Abrams ComicArts: Kristi Iwashiro; Kristiina Korpus; Anita Okoye
Ed, Children's: Erum Khan; Claire Stetzer
Ed, Children's (Magic Cat): Mary Jones
Ed, Entertainment List: Connor Leonard
Ed-at-Large: Eric Himmel; Howard Reeves
Assoc Ed: Juliet Dore
Assoc Ed, Abrams Press: Sarah Robbins
Assoc Ed, Children's: Sara Sproull
Assoc Ed, Entertainment Publg & Content Devt, Children's Books: Ivan Taurisano
Asst Ed: Aria Devlin; Asha Simon
Asst Ed, Abrams ComicArts: Lydia Nguyen
Asst Ed, Children's: Angelica Busanet
Sr Mgr, Indie & Ingram Sales & Retail Mktg: Christian Westermann
Sr Mgr, Spec Sales: Wayne Gurreri
Sr Mktg Mgr: Kristen Milford
Sr Mktg Mgr, Children's: Jenna Lisanti
Sr Sales Mgr: Kay Makanju
Mgr, Spec Sales: Shelby Ozer
Mktg Mgr, Brand Partnerships & Consumer Engagement: Danielle Kolodkin
Mktg Mgr, Events & Consumer Engagement: Megan Evans
Prodn Mgr: Amanda Banci
Royalty Mgr: Hema Sukhram
Assoc Prodn Mgr: Maggie Moore
Asst Mgr, Spec Sales: Jay Salton
Design Coord: Madeline Morales
Mktg Coord, Children's Books: Lauren Moye
Sr Contracts Assoc: Heather Allen
Sr Designer, Mktg: Zoe Michaels
Sr Designer: Andrea Miller
Sr Graphic Designer: Brann Garvey
Designer: Jade Rector
Sr Fin Analyst: Evelyn Lema; Claude Williams
Sr Publicist: Andrew Gibeley; Tara Lehmann
Sr Publicist, Abrams ComicArts: Kyle Daileda
Publicist, Children's: Anneliese Merz
Assoc Publicist: Stephanie Keane
Assoc Publicist, Children's Books: Tayla Monturio
Assoc, Subs Rts: Abby Pickus
Digital & Soc Media Mktg Assoc: Victoria Reynolds
Mktg Assoc, E-Commerce & Consumer Engagement: Victoria Reynolds
Prodn Assoc: Hayley Earnest
Dist Sales Asst: Ryan Norris
Mktg Asst: Maddie Brock
Sales Asst: Shea Dunlop
Sales Asst, Trade & Intl: Julian Benayoun
Founded: 1949
Art & architecture, photography, natural sciences, performing arts & children's books, gifts, calendars & stationary.
ISBN Prefix(es): 978-0-8109
Number of titles published annually: 300 Print
Total Titles: 2,600 Print
Imprints: Abrams Appleseed; Abrams Books; Abrams Books for Young Readers; Abrams ComicArts; Abrams Image; Abrams Noterie; Abrams Plus (ebooks); Abrams Press; Amulet Books; Cameron+Company; Cernunnos; Magic Cat; The Overlook Press; Surely; Taunton Books
Distributed by Abrams & Chronicle Books (Great Britain); Ducasse Edition
Distributor for Blackwell & Ruth; Booth-Clibborn Editions; Bungie; Cameron+Company; Cernunnos; Ducasse Edition; Enchanted Lion; Familius; Getty Publications; Lucky Spool (Australia, New Zealand & North America); Milky Way Picture Books; The Museum of Modern Art; Red Comet Press; SelfMadeHero; Skittledog; Tate Publishing; Unruly; V&A Publishing; Vendome Press
Foreign Rep(s): Abrams & Chronicle Books (Europe, Middle East, South Africa, UK); Canadian Manda Group (Canada); Intermediaamericana Ltd (David Williams) (Caribbean, Latin America); Sino Publishing Services Ltd (Rance Ru) (China, Hong Kong, Taiwan); Thames & Hudson Australia (Australia, New Zealand)
Orders to: Hachette Book Group USA (North America) Toll Free Tel: 800-759-0190 Toll Free Fax: 800-286-9471 E-mail: customerservice@hbgusa.com
Membership(s): Association of American Publishers (AAP)
See separate listing for:
The Overlook Press
Stewart, Tabori & Chang
Taunton Books

§Academic Press
Imprint of Elsevier BV
50 & 60 Hampshire St, 5th fl, Cambridge, MA 02139
Web Site: www.elsevier.com/books-and-journals/academic-press
Founded: 1942
Scientific, technical & professional information in multiple media formats.
ISBN Prefix(es): 978-0-12
Number of titles published annually: 375 Print; 25 E-Book
Total Titles: 4,700 Print; 200 E-Book

Academica Press
1727 Massachusetts Ave NW, Suite 507, Washington, DC 20036
E-mail: editorial@academicapress.com
Web Site: www.academicapress.com
Key Personnel
Pres & Publr: Dr Paul du Quenoy
Founded: 2001
Publish scholarly research, monographs & collections in humanities, social sciences, education & law.
ISBN Prefix(es): 978-1-933146; 978-1-930901; 978-1-68053
Number of titles published annually: 40 Print
Total Titles: 600 Print; 200 Online
Imprints: Maunsel & Co Publishers (Dublin); W B Sheridan (law books)
Foreign Rep(s): Eurospan Group (London) (Asia-Pacific, Europe)
Orders to: Ingram Publisher Services, One Ingram Blvd, MS 512, La Vergne, TN 37086 E-mail: ips@ingramcontent.com SAN: 631-8630
Returns: Ingram Publisher Services, One Ingram Blvd, MS 512, La Vergne, TN 37086 E-mail: ips@ingramcontent.com SAN: 631-8630
Warehouse: Ingram Publisher Services, One Ingram Blvd, MS 512, La Vergne, TN 37086 E-mail: ips@ingramcontent.com SAN: 631-8630
Distribution Center: Ingram Publisher Services, One Ingram Blvd, MS 512, La Vergne, TN 37086 E-mail: ips@ingramcontent.com SAN: 631-8630
Membership(s): American Conference on Irish Studies (ACIS)

Academy Chicago Publishers
Imprint of Chicago Review Press
814 N Franklin St, Chicago, IL 60610
Tel: 312-337-0747 Toll Free Tel: 800-888-4741 (orders) Fax: 312-337-5110
E-mail: frontdesk@chicagoreviewpress.com
Web Site: www.chicagoreviewpress.com
Key Personnel
Publr & Acqs Ed: Cynthia Sherry
 E-mail: csherry@chicagoreviewpress.com
Founded: 1975
Fiction, nonfiction, history, mysteries, women's studies; emphasis on neglected classics & books for women.
ISBN Prefix(es): 978-0-915864; 978-0-89733
Number of titles published annually: 12 Print
Total Titles: 367 Print
Distribution Center: Independent Publishers Group (IPG), 814 N Franklin St, Chicago, IL 60610 Tel: 312-337-0747 Toll Free Tel: 800-888-4741 (orders) Fax: 312-337-5985

The Academy of Northwest Writers & Publishers, see Lost Horse Press

Academy of Nutrition & Dietetics
120 S Riverside Plaza, Suite 2190, Chicago, IL 60606-6995
Tel: 312-899-0040 (ext 5000) Toll Free Tel: 800-877-1600
E-mail: publications@eatright.org; sales@eatright.org
Web Site: www.eatrightstore.org
Key Personnel
Dir, Practice Pubns: Betsy Hornick
 E-mail: bhornick@eatright.org
Sr Mgr, Prodn: Erin Faley E-mail: efaley@eatright.org
Founded: 1917
Information on food, nutrition & fitness for dietitians & other allied health professionals.
ISBN Prefix(es): 978-0-88091; 978-0-9837255 (Eat Right Press)
Number of titles published annually: 10 Print; 10 E-Book
Total Titles: 70 Print; 60 E-Book
Imprints: eatrightPress
Foreign Rep(s): Eurospan (worldwide exc Canada & USA)
Foreign Rights: John Scott & Co (worldwide)
Warehouse: Publishers Storage & Shipping, Receiving, Fitchburg, MA 01420

ACC Art Books
Division of ACC Art Books (England)
6 W 18 St, Suite 4B, New York, NY 10011
Tel: 212-645-1111 Toll Free Tel: 800-252-5231 Fax: 212-989-3205
E-mail: ussales@accpublishinggroup.com
Web Site: www.accartbooks.com/us/
Founded: 1966
Books on fine & decorative arts, gardening, architecture & antiques, multicultural.
ISBN Prefix(es): 978-1-85149; 978-0-907462; 978-0-902028
Number of titles published annually: 300 Print
Total Titles: 1,500 Print
Imprints: ACC Editions; Garden Art Press
Divisions: ACC Distribution

U.S. PUBLISHERS

Foreign Office(s): Sandy Lane, Old Martlesham, Woodbridge, Suffolk 1P12 4SD, United Kingdom *Tel:* (01394) 389950 *Fax:* (01394) 389999 *E-mail:* sales@antique-acc.com *Web Site:* www.antiquecollectorsclub.com
Foreign Rep(s): Jenny Gosling (Belgium, London, Luxembourg, Netherlands); Lilian Koe (Malaysia); Clive & Moira Malins (Northeast England, Scotland); Michael Morris (Middle East, Near East); Penny Padovani (Italy, Portugal, Spain); David Pearson (France); Ian Pringle (Brunei, Indonesia, Singapore, Thailand); Ed Summerson (China, Hong Kong, Philippines, South Korea, Taiwan); Ralph & Sheila Sumners (Japan); Robert Towers (Ireland, Northern Ireland)

§ACM Books
Imprint of Association for Computing Machinery
1601 Broadway, 10th fl, New York, NY 10019-7434
SAN: 267-7784
Tel: 212-869-7440
E-mail: acmbooks-info@acm.org
Web Site: www.acm.org; books.acm.org
Key Personnel
Publg Dir: Scott Delman *Tel:* 212-626-0659
   E-mail: scott.delman@hq.acm.org
Asst Dir: Sara Kate Heukerott *Tel:* 212-626-0641
   E-mail: heukerott@hq.acm.org
Exec Ed: Sean Pidgeon *Tel:* 212-626-0675
   E-mail: pidgeon@hq.acm.org
Digital Lib Coord: Jillian Elkin *Tel:* 212-626-0658 *E-mail:* elkin@hq.acm.org
Admin Asst: Darshanie Jattan *Tel:* 212-626-0671
   E-mail: darshanie.jattan@hq.acm.org
Founded: 1947
Computer science.
ISBN Prefix(es): 978-0-89791; 978-1-58113; 978-1-59593; 978-1-60558; 978-1-4503; 979-8-4007; 978-1-947487
Number of titles published annually: 150 Print
Total Titles: 500 Print
Distribution Center: Eurospan, Gray's Inn House, 127 Clerkenwell Rd, London EC1R 5DB, United Kingdom (worldwide exc North America) *Tel:* (020) 3286 2420 *E-mail:* info@eurospan.co.uk *Web Site:* eurospan.co.uk
Membership(s): Society Publishers' Coalition (SocPC)

ACMRS Press
Imprint of Arizona Center for Medieval & Renaissance Studies (ACMRS)
Arizona State University, PO Box 874402, Tempe, AZ 85287-4402
Tel: 480-727-6503 *Toll Free Tel:* 800-621-2736 (orders) *Fax:* 480-965-1681 *Toll Free Fax:* 800-621-8476 (orders)
E-mail: acmrs@asu.edu
Web Site: acmrspress.com
Key Personnel
Mng Ed: Roy Rukkila *E-mail:* roy.rukkila@asu.edu
Founded: 2019
Scholarly/academic press. Specialize in Open Access titles.
ISBN Prefix(es): 978-0-86698
Number of titles published annually: 10 Print
Total Titles: 92 Print
Sales Office(s): Chicago Distribution Center, 11030 S Langley Ave, Chicago, IL 60628 *Tel:* 773-702-7000 *Toll Free Tel:* 800-621-2736 *Fax:* 773-702-7212 *Toll Free Fax:* 800-621-8476 *E-mail:* orders@press.uchicago.edu *Web Site:* www.press.uchicago.edu
Billing Address: Chicago Distribution Center, 11030 S Langley Ave, Chicago, IL 60628 *Tel:* 773-702-7000 *Toll Free Tel:* 800-621-2736 *Fax:* 773-702-7212 *Toll Free Fax:* 800-621-8476 *E-mail:* orders@press.uchicago.edu *Web Site:* www.press.uchicago.edu
Orders to: Chicago Distribution Center, 11030 S Langley Ave, Chicago, IL 60628 *Tel:* 773-702-7000 *Toll Free Tel:* 800-621-2736 *Fax:* 773-702-7212 *Toll Free Fax:* 800-621-8476 *E-mail:* orders@press.uchicago.edu *Web Site:* www.press.uchicago.edu
Returns: Chicago Distribution Center, 11030 S Langley Ave, Chicago, IL 60628 *Tel:* 773-702-7000 *Toll Free Tel:* 800-621-2736 *Fax:* 773-702-7212 *Toll Free Fax:* 800-621-8476 *E-mail:* orders@press.uchicago.edu *Web Site:* www.press.uchicago.edu
Distribution Center: Chicago Distribution Center, 11030 S Langley Ave, Chicago, IL 60628 *Tel:* 773-702-7000 *Toll Free Tel:* 800-621-2736 *Fax:* 773-702-7212 *Toll Free Fax:* 800-621-8476 *E-mail:* orders@press.uchicago.edu *Web Site:* www.press.uchicago.edu

Acres USA
Division of Acres USA Inc
603 Eighth St, Greeley, CO 80631
Mailing Address: PO Box 1690, Greeley, CO 80632-1690
Tel: 970-392-4464 *Toll Free Tel:* 800-355-5313
E-mail: info@acresusa.com
Web Site: www.acresusa.com
Founded: 1970
Books & a monthly periodical on organic & sustainable agriculture.
ISBN Prefix(es): 978-0-911311; 978-1-60173
Number of titles published annually: 6 Print; 10 Audio
Total Titles: 100 Print; 100 Audio

ACS Publications
Division of The American Chemical Society (ACS)
1155 16 St NW, Washington, DC 20036
SAN: 201-2626
Tel: 202-872-4600 *Toll Free Tel:* 800-227-5558 (US) *Fax:* 202-872-6067
E-mail: help@acs.org
Web Site: pubs.acs.org; publish.acs.org/publish
Key Personnel
Pres: James Milne, PhD
Publr: Sara Tenney *E-mail:* s_tenney@acs.org
Acq Ed: Beth Campbell *E-mail:* b_campbell@acs.org
Founded: 1876
Serials, proceedings, reprint collections, monographs & other professional & reference books; specializes in food chemistry, environmental sciences & green chemistry, analytical, inorganic, medicinal, organic & physical chemistries, biochemistry, polymer & materials science & nanotechnology.
ISBN Prefix(es): 978-0-8412
Number of titles published annually: 31 Print
Total Titles: 500 Print; 1 CD-ROM
Distributed by Oxford University Press USA
Distributor for Royal Society of Chemistry
Foreign Rep(s): Maruzen Co Ltd (Japan); Sonya Nickson (UK); Andrew Pitts (UK)
Membership(s): Association of American Publishers (AAP)

§ACTA Publications
7135 W Keeney St, Niles, IL 60714
Toll Free Tel: 800-397-2282
E-mail: actapublications@actapublications.com
Web Site: www.actapublications.com
Key Personnel
Pres & Publr: Gregory F A Pierce *Tel:* 773-590-3801 *E-mail:* gfapierce@actapublications.com
Founded: 1957
ACTA stands for "A Commitment to All." Books & media that are "gifts that compel" on a variety of topics.
ISBN Prefix(es): 978-0-87946; 978-0-914070; 978-0-915388
Number of titles published annually: 10 Print; 5 E-Book; 1 Audio
Total Titles: 300 Print; 25 E-Book; 10 Audio
Imprints: ACTA Sports; In Extenso Press
Foreign Rep(s): Veritas (Ireland, UK)
Membership(s): Association of Catholic Publishers Inc; Independent Book Publishers Association (IBPA)

ACU Press
Affiliate of Abilene Christian University
ACU Box 29138, Abilene, TX 79699
SAN: 207-1681
Tel: 325-674-2720 *Toll Free Tel:* 877-816-4455
E-mail: acupressoffice@groupmail.acu.edu
Web Site: www.acupressbooks.com; www.leafwoodpublishers.com
Key Personnel
Dir, Sales & Opers: Duane Anderson
Founded: 1984
Religion & ethics.
ISBN Prefix(es): 978-0-915547; 978-0-89112
Number of titles published annually: 20 Print; 20 E-Book
Total Titles: 620 Print; 300 E-Book
Imprints: Leafwood Publishers (Christian trade imprint)

Adams & Ambrose Publishing
1622 Capital Ave, Madison, WI 53705-1228
SAN: 655-5624
Tel: 608-572-2471
E-mail: info@adamsambrose.com
Key Personnel
Mktg Dir & Intl Rts: Joyce Harrington
   E-mail: jharrington@adamsambrose.com
Sr Ed: Jill Robinson Wren *E-mail:* jrwren@adamsambrose.com
Edit: Roger B Oakes *E-mail:* rboakes@adamsambrose.com
Founded: 1983
Publication of nonfiction books. Specialize in academic, professional & how-to books.
ISBN Prefix(es): 978-0-916951
Number of titles published annually: 6 Print
Total Titles: 6 Print
Returns: c/o United Parcel Service, 8350 Murphy Dr, Middleton, WI 53562 (hold for pick up)

§Adams Media
Division of Simon & Schuster, LLC
100 Technology Center Dr, Suite 501, Stoughton, MA 02072
Tel: 508-427-7100
Web Site: www.simonandschuster.com
Key Personnel
VP & Publr: Karen Cooper
Mktg & Publicity Dir: Beth Gissinger-Rivera
Ed-in-Chief: Brendan O'Neill
Dir of Mng Edit: Meredith O'Hayre
Sr Content Ed: Lisa Laing
Assoc Publr: Stephanie McKenna
Assoc Dir, Devt: Katherine Corcoran-Lytle
Exec Ed: Jacqueline Musser
Sr Devt Ed: Laura Daly; Brett Palana-Shanahan
Devt Ed: Sarah Doughty
Sr Ed: Eileen Mullan
Ed: Rebecca Tarr Thomas; Julia Belkas
Assoc Ed: Colleen Mulhern; Jennifer Kristal; Natalie McGregor
Edit Asst: Colby Yokell
Sr Publicist: Lydia Rasmussen
Publicist: Maria Orlandi
Sr Mktg Mgr: Gia Manalio-Bonaventura
Creative Dir & Design Mgr: Frank Rivera
Natl Sales Dir: Kaiya Muniz
Founded: 1980
General nonfiction publisher, with emphasis on business, self-help, careers, health, New Age, cooking, parenting, reference, & relationships.

ISBN Prefix(es): 978-0-937860; 978-1-55850; 978-1-58062; 978-1-59337; 978-1-59869; 978-1-60550; 978-1-4405; 978-1-5072
Number of titles published annually: 125 Print; 110 E-Book
Total Titles: 1,200 Print; 20 CD-ROM; 1,100 E-Book
Imprints: Adams Business (busn); Everything (series)
Foreign Rights: Bardon-Chinese Media Agency (China, Hong Kong, Taiwan); Graal Literary Agency (Poland); Imprima Korea Agency (South Korea); International Editors' Co - Yanez Agencia Literaria (Spain); Japan UNI Agency (Japan); Alexander Korzhenevski Agency (Russia); Michael Meller Literary Agency GmbH (Germany); Silkroad Publishers Agency (Jane Vejjajiva) (Thailand)

Addicus Books Inc
PO Box 45327, Omaha, NE 68145
Tel: 402-330-7493 *Fax:* 402-330-1707
E-mail: info@addicusbooks.com
Web Site: www.addicusbooks.com
Key Personnel
Publr: Rod Colvin *E-mail:* rod@addicusbooks.com
Assoc Publr: Jack Kusler *E-mail:* jack@addicusbooks.com
Founded: 1994
Independent press, publishing high-quality trade paperbacks. Submissions by e-mail or mail only. No phone inquiries.
ISBN Prefix(es): 978-1-886039; 978-1-936374; 978-1-938803; 978-1-940495
Number of titles published annually: 9 Print; 10 E-Book
Total Titles: 230 Print; 230 Online; 185 E-Book
Billing Address: IPG Books, 814 Franklin St, Chicago, IL 60610 *Tel:* 312-337-0747 *Toll Free Tel:* 800-888-4741 *Fax:* 312-337-5985 *Web Site:* ipgbook.com
Returns: IPG Warehouse, 600 N Pulaski, Chicago, IL 60624
Warehouse: IPG Warehouse, 600 N Pulaski, Chicago, IL 60624
Distribution Center: IPG Books, 814 Franklin St, Chicago, IL 60610 *Tel:* 312-337-0747 *Toll Free Tel:* 800-888-4741 *Fax:* 312-337-5985 *Web Site:* ipgbook.com
Membership(s): Independent Book Publishers Association (IBPA)

Adirondack Mountain Club (ADK)
4833 Cascade Rd, Lake Placid, NY 12946-4113
SAN: 204-7691
Tel: 518-837-5047 *Toll Free Tel:* 800-395-8080
E-mail: info@adk.org
Web Site: www.adk.org
Key Personnel
Pres: Tom Andrews
VP: Charles Kilbourne
Exec Dir: Michael Barrett *E-mail:* michael@adk.org
Founded: 1922
Wall calendar; trade, hiking, canoeing & skiing guidebooks & maps for New York State; cultural & literary works on the Adirondacks, members journals, *Adirondac*.
ISBN Prefix(es): 978-0-935272; 978-1-931951; 978-0-9896073
Number of titles published annually: 4 Print
Total Titles: 39 Print

Advance Publishing Inc
6950 Fulton St, Houston, TX 77022
SAN: 263-9572
Tel: 713-695-0600 *Toll Free Tel:* 800-917-9630 *Fax:* 713-695-8585
E-mail: info@advancepublishing.com
Web Site: www.advancepublishing.com
Key Personnel
VP: John Sommer
Founded: 1984
Publish children's picture books, junior biographies & general nonfiction, technical books & current events.
ISBN Prefix(es): 978-1-57537; 978-0-9610810
Number of titles published annually: 20 Print
Total Titles: 150 Print; 72 CD-ROM; 75 Online
Imprints: Another Great Achiever Series (biographies of men & women of inspiring accomplishment); Number Success (online video practical mathematics program for adult & children); Phonics Adventure (motivational phonics literature-based children's reading program); Quest for Success (short stories for upper elementary & reluctant middle & high school readers); Reading Success (adult intensive phonics literature-based reading program); Sommer-Time Story Classics Series (inspirational picture books with a fun & modern take on timeless folktales & fables); Sommer-Time Story Series (character-building books for children)
Membership(s): The Children's Book Council (CBC); Independent Book Publishers Association (IBPA)

AdventureKEEN
2204 First Ave S, Suite 102, Birmingham, AL 35233
SAN: 212-7199
Tel: 763-689-9800 *Toll Free Tel:* 800-678-7006 *Fax:* 763-689-9039 *Toll Free Fax:* 877-374-9016
E-mail: info@adventurewithkeen.com
Web Site: adventurewithkeen.com
Key Personnel
Owner: Robert W Sehlinger
Publr & COO: Molly Merkle
Pres: Richard Hunt
Sales Dir: Meredith Hutchins *E-mail:* meredith@adventurewithkeen.com
Mktg & PR: Liliane Opsomer *E-mail:* liliane@adventurewithkeen.com
Founded: 1988
General trade & regional.
ISBN Prefix(es): 978-0-934860; 978-1-885061; 978-1-59193
Number of titles published annually: 67 Print
Total Titles: 979 Print; 2 CD-ROM
Imprints: Adventure Publications; Clerisy Press; Menasha Ridge Press; Nature Study Guides; Shelter Publications; Unofficial Guides; Wilderness Press
Distributor for Kollath-Stensaas; Lake 7 Creative; Nodin Press
Distribution Center: Ingram Content Group LLC, One Ingram Blvd, La Vergne, TN 37086 *Tel:* 615-793-5000
See separate listing for:
Clerisy Press
Menasha Ridge Press

§Adventures Unlimited Press (AUP)
One Adventure Place, Kempton, IL 60946
Mailing Address: PO Box 74, Kempton, IL 60946-0074
Tel: 815-253-6390 *Fax:* 815-253-6300
E-mail: info@adventuresunlimitedpress.com
Web Site: www.adventuresunlimitedpress.com
Key Personnel
Pres & Intl Rts Contact: David H Childress
Mng Dir: Jennifer Bolm
Founded: 1983
Eclectic variety of books on mysteries of the past, alternative technologies & conspiracy theories.
ISBN Prefix(es): 978-0-932813; 978-1-931882; 978-1-935487; 978-1-939149
Number of titles published annually: 11 Print
Total Titles: 215 Print
Distributor for Eagle Wing Books; EDFU Books; Yelsraek Publishing
Foreign Rep(s): Brumby Books (Australia); Speaking Tree (UK)
Foreign Rights: Il Caduceo (Italy)

The AEI Press
Division of American Enterprise Institute
1789 Massachusetts Ave NW, Washington, DC 20036
SAN: 202-4527
Tel: 202-862-5800 *Fax:* 202-862-7177
Web Site: www.aei.org
Key Personnel
Mng Dir, Media Rel: Phoebe Keller *Tel:* 202-420-0155 *E-mail:* phoebe.keller@aei.org
Founded: 1943
Public policy economics, foreign affairs & defense, government & politics, law; research on education, energy, government regulation & tax policy.
ISBN Prefix(es): 978-0-8447
Number of titles published annually: 15 Print
Total Titles: 300 Print
Distributed by MIT (selected titles)
Foreign Rep(s): Eurospan
Orders to: c/o National Book Network, 4501 Forbes Blvd, Suite 200, Lantham, MD 20706 *Toll Free Tel:* 800-462-6420 *Toll Free Fax:* 800-338-4550 *E-mail:* custserv@nbnbooks.com

Africa World Press Inc
Affiliate of The Red Sea Press Inc
541 W Ingham Ave, Suite B, Trenton, NJ 08638
Tel: 609-695-3200 *Fax:* 609-695-6466
E-mail: customerservice@africaworldpressbooks.com
Web Site: www.africaworldpressbooks.com
Key Personnel
Owner: Kassahun Checole *E-mail:* kchecole@awprsp.com
Founded: 1983
Publisher of books on Africa & the African World (North America, the Caribbean, etc).
ISBN Prefix(es): 978-0-86543; 978-1-59221
Number of titles published annually: 100 Print
Total Titles: 2,350 Print; 10 Online; 10 E-Book
Foreign Rights: Turnaround Publisher Services Ltd (Europe, London)

§African American Images Inc (AAI)
3126 E Fruitvale Ct, Gilbert, AZ 85297
Tel: 480-621-8307 *Fax:* 480-621-7794
E-mail: customersvc@africanamericanimages.com
Web Site: africanamericanimages.com
Key Personnel
Founder: Dr Jawanza Kunjufu, PhD
Founded: 1983
Publish & distribute books of an Africentric nature that promote self-esteem, collective values, liberation & skill development.
ISBN Prefix(es): 978-0-913543; 978-0-9749000; 978-1-934155
Number of titles published annually: 8 Print
Total Titles: 130 Print; 2 CD-ROM

AGU, see American Geophysical Union (AGU)

§AICPA® & CIMA®
Subsidiary of American Institute of Certified Public Accountants
220 Leigh Farm Rd, Durham, NC 27707
SAN: 202-4578
Tel: 919-402-4500 *Toll Free Tel:* 888-777-7077 (memb serv ctr)
Web Site: www.aicpa-cima.com/cpe-learning
Key Personnel
Pres & CEO: Barry C Melancon
Founded: 2017
Technical guidance for accountants & auditors, books on practice management & specialized topics, research & practice development tools,

U.S. PUBLISHERS

magazines, newsletters, online & downloadable products.
ISBN Prefix(es): 978-1-119
Number of titles published annually: 150 Print; 10 CD-ROM; 20 Online; 100 E-Book
Total Titles: 600 Print; 20 CD-ROM; 50 Online; 200 E-Book
Branch Office(s)
1455 Pennsylvania Ave NW, Washington, DC 20004-1081 Tel: 202-737-6600
Princeton South Corporate Ctr, 100 Princeton S, Suite 200, Ewing, NJ 08628 Tel: 609-671-2902
1345 Avenue of the Americas, 27th fl, New York, NY 10105 Tel: 212-596-6200
Distributed by Practitioners Publishing Co; Thomson Reuters
Distributor for Wiley

AIHA (American Industrial Hygiene Association)
3141 Fairview Park Dr, Suite 777, Falls Church, VA 22042
Tel: 703-849-8888 Fax: 703-207-3561
E-mail: infonet@aiha.org
Web Site: www.aiha.org
Key Personnel
CEO: Lawrence D Sloan
Mng Dir, Mktg & Communs: Susan Marchese
Founded: 1939
Serves the needs of occupational & environmental health professionals practicing industrial hygiene in industry, government, labor, academic institutions & independent organizations.
ISBN Prefix(es): 978-1-931504
Number of titles published annually: 7 Print
Total Titles: 150 Print

AIP Publishing LLC
Subsidiary of American Institute of Physics
1305 Walt Whitman Rd, Suite 110, Melville, NY 11747
Tel: 516-576-2200
E-mail: help@aip.org; press@aip.org; rights@aip.org
Web Site: www.aip.org; publishing.aip.org
Key Personnel
CEO: Alexandra (Alix) Vance
CFO: Roy Levenson
Chief Publg Offr: Penelope Lewis
Chief Strategy Offr: Dean Sanderson
Chief Transformation Offr: Ann Michael
Head, Global Sales & Mktg: Kevin Steiner
Head, HR: Madelene Sutton
Head, Mktg & Communs: Sara Girard
Head, Prod Devt & Opers: Tracy Denien
Founded: 1931
Publisher of conference proceedings, professional journals, magazines & books.
ISBN Prefix(es): 978-0-88318; 978-1-56396; 978-0-7354
Number of titles published annually: 13 Print; 8 CD-ROM; 3 Online
Total Titles: 700 Print; 200 Online
Imprints: University Science Books (USB)
Distributed by Springer-Verlag
Membership(s): Association of American Publishers (AAP)
See separate listing for:
University Science Books

AK Press
Subsidiary of AK Press Inc
370 Ryan Ave, Unit 100, Chico, CA 95973
Tel: 510-208-1700 Fax: 510-208-1701
E-mail: info@akpress.org
Web Site: www.akpress.org
Founded: 1990
Specialize in publishing & distribution of radical & small press nonfiction.
ISBN Prefix(es): 978-1-873176; 978-1-902593; 978-1-904859
Number of titles published annually: 20 Print

Total Titles: 500 Print
Distributor for Arbeiter Ring; Autonomedia; Crimethinc; Freedom Press; Charles H Kerr; Kersplebedeb

§Akashic Books
232 Third St, Suite A115, Brooklyn, NY 11215
Tel: 718-643-9193
E-mail: info@akashicbooks.com
Web Site: www.akashicbooks.com
Key Personnel
Publr & Ed-in-Chief: Johnny Temple
Mng Ed & Dir, Foreign Rts: Johanna Ingalls
Prodn Mgr, Ebook Developer & Assoc Ed: Aaron Petrovich
Founded: 1997
Brooklyn-based independent publishers of literary fiction, crime fiction, music/pop culture books & political nonfiction.
ISBN Prefix(es): 978-1-888451; 978-0-9719206; 978-1-933354; 978-1-936070; 978-1-61775; 978-1-63614
Number of titles published annually: 35 Print; 35 E-Book
Total Titles: 500 Print; 500 E-Book
Imprints: Black Sheep Books for Young Readers; Edge of Sports (Dave Zirin's imprint); Gracie Belle (Ann Hood's imprint); Kaylie Jones Books; Open Lens
Distributed by W W Norton & Company Inc
Orders to: W W Norton & Company Inc, 500 Fifth Ave, 5th fl, New York, NY 10110 Toll Free Tel: 800-233-4830
E-mail: customerservice@wwnorton.com Web Site: wwnorton.com
Returns: W W Norton & Company Inc, 500 Fifth Ave, 5th fl, New York, NY 10110 Toll Free Tel: 800-233-4830 E-mail: customerservice@wwnorton.com Web Site: wwnorton.com
Warehouse: W W Norton & Company Inc, c/o National Book Co Inc, 800 Keystone Industrial Park, Scranton, PA 18512 Toll Free Tel: 800-233-4830 E-mail: customerservice@wwnorton.com Web Site: wwnorton.com
Distribution Center: W W Norton & Company Inc, 500 Fifth Ave, 5th fl, New York, NY 10110 Tel: 212-354-5500 Fax: 212-869-0856 E-mail: customerservice@wwnorton.com Web Site: wwnorton.com

ALA, see The American Library Association (ALA)

§ALA Neal-Schuman
Imprint of The American Library Association (ALA)
225 N Michigan Ave, Suite 1300, Chicago, IL 60601
Toll Free Tel: 800-545-2433 Fax: 312-280-5860
E-mail: editionsmarketing@ala.org
Web Site: www.alastore.ala.org
Key Personnel
Mktg Coord: Rob Christopher Tel: 312-280-5052 E-mail: rchristopher@ala.org
Founded: 1976
How-to manuals, technology, library & information science texts.
ISBN Prefix(es): 978-0-8389; 978-0-918212; 978-1-55570
Number of titles published annually: 65 Print; 30 E-Book
Total Titles: 320 Print; 300 E-Book
Billing Address: Chicago Distribution Center, 11030 S Langley Ave, Chicago, IL 60628
E-mail: alastore@ala.org

Aladdin Books, see Simon & Schuster Children's Publishing

Alaska Native Language Center (ANLC)
Division of University of Alaska Fairbanks

PO Box 757680, Fairbanks, AK 99775-7680
SAN: 692-9796
Tel: 907-474-7874
E-mail: uaf-anlc@alaska.edu (orders)
Web Site: www.uaf.edu/anlc
Key Personnel
Dir: Walkie Charles E-mail: swcharles@alaska.edu
Ed: Lillian Maassen E-mail: lmaassen@alaska.edu
Founded: 1972
Publish books in & about Alaska's 20 indigenous languages, including dictionaries, grammars & collections of folktales & oral history, language maps.
ISBN Prefix(es): 978-1-55500; 978-0-933769
Number of titles published annually: 3 Print
Total Titles: 200 Print; 3 Audio

Albert Whitman & Company
250 S Northwest Hwy, Suite 320, Park Ridge, IL 60068
SAN: 201-2049
Tel: 847-232-2800 Toll Free Tel: 800-255-7675 (orders) Fax: 847-581-0039
E-mail: mail@albertwhitman.com; orders@albertwhitman.com
Web Site: www.albertwhitman.com
Key Personnel
Pres & Co-Owner: John Quattrocchi
VP & Co-Owner: Pat McPartland
Publg Dir: Sue Tarsky
Sr Art Dir: Rick DeMonico
Dir, Sales & Mktg: Tom MacDonald
Ed: Josh Gregory
Sr Accounting Mgr: John Scully
Sr Mktg Specialist: Molly Fletcher
Mktg Specialist: Kiki Schotanus
Mktg Coord: Koraima Carrillo
Founded: 1919
Juveniles, language arts, fiction & nonfiction.
ISBN Prefix(es): 978-0-8075
Number of titles published annually: 50 Print
Total Titles: 800 Print
Foreign Rep(s): Canadian Manda Group (Canada)
Membership(s): Association of American Publishers (AAP)

Alexander Street, part of Clarivate PLC
789 E Eisenhower Pkwy, Ann Arbor, MI 48108
SAN: 858-5512
Toll Free Tel: 800-521-0600; 888-963-2071 (sales)
E-mail: sales@alexanderstreet.com; marketing@alexanderstreet.com; support@alexanderstreet.com
Web Site: alexanderstreet.com
Key Personnel
Sr Dir, Prod Mktg: Bradley Cigich E-mail: bradley.cigich@clarivate.com
Dir, Prod Mgmt: Nathalie Duval E-mail: nathalie.duval@clarivate.com
Founded: 2000
Publish large-scale digital collections of works in the humanities & social sciences.
ISBN Prefix(es): 978-1-4631; 978-1-5016; 978-1-5034
Number of titles published annually: 30 Print; 6 Online; 2,000 E-Book; 4 Audio
Total Titles: 34 Online; 10,000 E-Book; 6 Audio
Imprints: Filmakers Library; Insight Media; Microtraining Associates
Membership(s): The American Library Association (ALA)

§Alfred Music
285 Century Place, Louisville, CO 80027
Tel: 818-891-5999 (dealer sales, intl)
Toll Free Tel: 800-292-6122 (dealer sales, US & CN); 800-628-1528 (cust serv) Fax: 818-893-5560 (dealer sales); 818-830-6252 (cust serv) Toll Free Fax: 800-632-1928 (dealer sales)

E-mail: customerservice@alfred.com; sales@alfred.com
Web Site: www.alfred.com
Key Personnel
Chief Busn Devt Offr: Ron Manus
Pres: Greg Dell'Era
SVP, Content & Licensing: Heath Matthews
VP, Prodn & Edit: Derek Richard
Founded: 1922
Publisher of music education; music books & software, performance & instructional.
ISBN Prefix(es): 978-0-88284; 978-0-87487; 978-0-7390; 978-1-58951; 978-1-4574; 978-1-4706
Number of titles published annually: 500 Print
Total Titles: 150,000 Print
Imprints: Belwin; Highland/Etling; Kalmus; Music Inc; Warner/Chappell Music Inc
Foreign Office(s): Lutzerathstr 127, 51107 Cologne, Germany *Tel:* (0221) 933539 0 *E-mail:* info@alfredverlag.de *Web Site:* alfredverlag.de
20 Sin Ming Lane, No 05-54 Midview City, 5th fl, Singapore 573968, Singapore *Tel:* 6659 8919 *E-mail:* music@alfred.com.sg
Burnt Mill, Elizabeth Way, Harlow, Essex CM20 2HX, United Kingdom *Tel:* (01279) 828960 *E-mail:* music@alfred.uk.com *Web Site:* alfreduk.com
Distributor for Dover Publications Inc; Drum Channel; FJH; LudwigMasters; MakeMusic Inc; Faber Music Ltd; Penguin; WEA
Membership(s): News/Media Alliance

Alfred Publishing LLC, see Alfred Music

Algora Publishing
1632 First Ave, No 20330, New York, NY 10028-4305
Mailing Address: 500 Westover Dr, No 20330, Sanford, NC 27330
Tel: 212-678-0232 *Fax:* 212-202-5488
E-mail: editors@algora.com
Web Site: www.algora.com
Key Personnel
Publr: Claudiu A Secara
Ed: Martin De Mers
Author Rel: Andrea Secara
Founded: 1992
Books on subjects of history, international affairs, current issues, political economy, philosophy, etc in the tradition of independent progressive thinking.
ISBN Prefix(es): 978-0-87586; 978-0-9646073; 978-1-892941; 978-1-62894
Number of titles published annually: 25 Print; 25 E-Book
Total Titles: 600 Print; 600 E-Book
Imprints: Agathon Press
Membership(s): Association of American Publishers (AAP); Independent Book Publishers Association (IBPA)

§All About Kids Publishing
PO Box 159, Gilroy, CA 95021
Tel: 408-337-1152
E-mail: info@allaboutkidspub.com
Web Site: www.allaboutkidspub.com
Key Personnel
Ed: Linda L Guevara *E-mail:* lguevara@allaboutkidspub.com
Founded: 2000
Strives to set the standards in children's book publishing by creating innovative books of the highest quality with beautiful art work for children of all walks of life. See submission guidelines on web site.
ISBN Prefix(es): 978-0-9700863; 978-0-9710278; 978-0-9744446
Number of titles published annually: 6 Print
Total Titles: 20 Print
Imprints: Talking Donkey Press

Warehouse: 34 Production Ave, Keene, NH 03431 *Tel:* 603-357-0236 *Toll Free Tel:* 800-345-6665 *Fax:* 603-965-2181
Membership(s): Independent Book Publishers Association (IBPA)

§All Things That Matter Press
79 Jones Rd, Somerville, ME 04348
E-mail: allthingsthatmatterpress@gmail.com
Web Site: www.allthingsthatmatterpress.com
Key Personnel
CEO: Debra Harris
Founded: 2008
ISBN Prefix(es): 978-0-9966634
Number of titles published annually: 10 Print; 10 E-Book; 4 Audio
Total Titles: 245 Print; 245 E-Book; 70 Audio

Alloy Entertainment LLC
Member of Warner Bros Entertainment Group
30 Hudson Yards, 22nd fl, New York, NY 10001
Key Personnel
Pres: Leslie Morgenstein
EVP: Josh Bank
SVP, Edit: Sara Shandler
VP & Exec Ed: Lanie Davis
VP, Book Devt: Joelle Hobeika
Sr Ed: Viana Siniscalchi
Ed: Jess Harriton
Assoc Ed: Laura Barbiea
Edit Asst: Kat Jagai *E-mail:* kjagai@alloyentertainment.com
Founded: 1987
Hardcover, trade, mass market juvenile & young adult fiction & nonfiction; adult trade fiction & mass market fiction.
ISBN Prefix(es): 978-0-9850261; 978-1-939106
Number of titles published annually: 50 Print
Distributed by Avon Books; HarperCollins; Hyperion; Little, Brown and Company; Penguin Publishing Group; Penguin Random House LLC; Scholastic Books; Simon & Schuster, LLC
Foreign Rep(s): Rights People (UK)

§Allworth Press
Imprint of Skyhorse Publishing Inc
307 W 36 St, 11th fl, New York, NY 10018
Tel: 212-643-6816 *Fax:* 212-643-6819
Web Site: www.allworth.com
Key Personnel
Founder & Publr: Tad Crawford
  E-mail: tcrawford@skyhorsepublishing.com
Founded: 1989
Business & self-help books for artists, crafters, designers, photographers, authors & film & performing artists; books about business & law for the general public.
ISBN Prefix(es): 978-0-927629; 978-0-9607118; 978-1-880559; 978-1-58115; 978-1-62153
Number of titles published annually: 10 Print; 20 E-Book
Total Titles: 500 Print; 400 E-Book
Sales Office(s): Simon & Schuster Sales Division, 1230 Avenue of the Americas, New York, NY 10020
Distributed by Simon & Schuster, LLC
Foreign Rights: Jean V Naggar Literary Agency (worldwide)

AllWrite Publishing
PO Box 1071, Atlanta, GA 30301
Tel: 770-284-8983 *Fax:* 770-284-8986
E-mail: questions@allwritepublishing.com; support@allwritepublishing.com (orders & returns)
Web Site: allwritepublishing.com
Key Personnel
Pres & Publr: Annette R Johnson *Tel:* 770-284-8956 *E-mail:* annette@allwritepublishing.com
Founded: 2003

A conventional small press. Books that we do not decide to publish are given thorough feedback.
ISBN Prefix(es): 978-0-9744935
Number of titles published annually: 5 Print; 5 E-Book
Total Titles: 5 Print; 5 E-Book
Distribution Center: Ingram Content Group LLC, One Ingram Blvd, La Vergne, TN 37086-1986 *Tel:* 615-793-5000 *E-mail:* customerservice@ingramcontent.com *Web Site:* www.ingramcontent.com
Membership(s): Independent Book Publishing Professionals Group (IBPPG); Writers Guild of America, East (WGAE)

Amadeus Press
Imprint of Rowman & Littlefield Publishing Group
4501 Forbes Blvd, Suite 200, Lanham, MD 20706
Tel: 212-529-3888 *Fax:* 212-529-4223
Web Site: www.rowman.com
Key Personnel
Acqs Ed: Michael Tan
Founded: 1987
Full service publisher that produces books about classical music & opera.
ISBN Prefix(es): 978-1-57467
Number of titles published annually: 5 Print; 5 E-Book
Total Titles: 1,200 Print; 1,000 E-Book
Foreign Rep(s): Rowman & Littlefield (UK)

§Amakella Publishing
PO Box 9445, Arlington, VA 22219
Tel: 202-239-8660
E-mail: info@amakella.com
Web Site: www.amakella.com
Independent publisher interested in publishing books in areas such as social sciences, international development, environmental conservation, investing & current affairs.
ISBN Prefix(es): 978-1-63387
Number of titles published annually: 2 Print; 2 E-Book
Total Titles: 7 Print; 8 E-Book
Membership(s): Independent Book Publishers Association (IBPA)

§Ambassador International
Division of Emerald House Inc
411 University Ridge, Suite B14, Greenville, SC 29601
Tel: 864-751-4844
E-mail: info@emeraldhouse.com; publisher@emeraldhouse.com (ms submissions); sales@emeraldhouse.com (orders/order inquiries); media@emeraldhouse.com; design@emeraldhouse.com
Web Site: ambassador-international.com; www.facebook.com/AmbassadorIntl; x.com/ambassadorintl
Key Personnel
Pres & CEO: Dr Samuel Lowry
COO: Anna Raats *E-mail:* araats@emeraldhouse.com
Art Dir: Karen Slayne
Publicity Dir: Kimberly Davis
Sr Ed: Katie Cruice Smith *E-mail:* ksmith@emeraldhouse.com
Founded: 1980 (UK, 1996 US)
Christian publisher. Works with authors to create quality Christian literature of several genres - fiction, devotional & children's books. The company's vision has always been to create products that strengthen believers in their Christian walk & direct the lost to the way of salvation. New titles each year in both print & ebook format. Offices in the US & Northern Ireland, distribution partnerships on four continents & books in the hands of readers around the world.

U.S. PUBLISHERS

ISBN Prefix(es): 978-1-889893; 978-1-932307; 978-1-620202; 978-1-64960
Number of titles published annually: 45 Print; 45 E-Book; 45 Audio
Total Titles: 400 E-Book; 200 Audio
Foreign Office(s): Ambassador Books & Media, The Mount, 2 Woodstock Link, Belfast BT6 8DD, United Kingdom *Tel:* (028) 9073 0184 *Fax:* (028) 9073 0199 *Web Site:* www.ambassadormedia.co.uk
Distribution Center: Baker & Taylor, 2550 W Tyvola Rd, Suite 300, Charlotte, NC 28217 (US dist) *Tel:* 704-998-3100 *Toll Free Tel:* 800-775-1800 *Web Site:* www.baker-taylor.com
Ingram/Spring Arbor, One Ingram Blvd, La Vergne, TN 37086 (US dist) *Tel:* 615-793-5000 *Web Site:* www.ingramcontent.com
Membership(s): American Christian Fiction Writers (ACFW); Christian Small Publishers Association; Independent Book Publishers Association (IBPA); Professional Editors Network (PEN)

Amber Lotus Publishing
Imprint of Andrews McMeel Publishing LLC
PO Box 11329, Portland, OR 97211
SAN: 247-6819
Tel: 503-284-6400 *Toll Free Tel:* 800-326-2375 (orders only) *Fax:* 503-284-6417
E-mail: info@amberlotus.com; neworder@amberlotus.com
Web Site: www.amberlotus.com
Key Personnel
Co-Owner & Pres: Lawson Day
Co-Owner & Creative Dir: Leslie Gignilliat-Day
VP, Sales & Mktg: Tim Campbell
Mktg Dir: Dianne Foster
Founded: 1988
Calendars, greeting cards, journals & books.
ISBN Prefix(es): 978-1-885394; 978-1-56937; 978-1-60237; 978-1-63136
Number of titles published annually: 65 Print
Foreign Rep(s): Akasha Books & Gifts Ltd (New Zealand); Aurora Productions (Belgium, Holland, Luxembourg); Brumby Sunstate (Australia); Deep Books (Europe, Scandinavia, UK); Dempsey Distributing (Canada); Leecom Enterprises (Asia); New Horizon Distributors (South Africa); Quanta Distribution Inc (Canada); Tarots Del Mundo (Central America, South America); Vision Antics (Ireland, UK)

AMC Books, see Appalachian Mountain Club Books

American Academy of Environmental Engineers & Scientists®
147 Old Solomons Island Rd, Suite 303, Annapolis, MD 21401
Tel: 410-266-3311 *Fax:* 410-266-7653
E-mail: info@aaees.org
Web Site: www.aaees.org
Key Personnel
Exec Dir: Burk Kalweit *E-mail:* bkalweit@aaees.org
Mgr, Spec Projs: J Sammi Olmo
 E-mail: jsolmo@aaees.org
Mktg Mgr: Marisa Waterman
 E-mail: mwaterman@aaees.org
Pubns Mgr: Yolanda Y Moulden
 E-mail: ymoulden@aaees.org
Founded: 1955
Journals & textbooks for the environmental engineering & science professions.
ISBN Prefix(es): 978-1-883767
Number of titles published annually: 5 Print
Total Titles: 49 Print
Distributor for The ABS Group; CRC Press; McGraw-Hill; Pearson Education; Prentice Hall; John Wiley & Sons Inc

American Academy of Pediatrics
345 Park Blvd, Itasca, IL 60143
Toll Free Tel: 888-227-1770 *Fax:* 847-228-1281
Web Site: www.aap.org; shop.aap.org; publishing.aap.org
Key Personnel
VP, Publg: Mark Grimes *E-mail:* mgrimes@aap.org
Founded: 1930
Patient educational material, medical textbooks, professional textbook, patient education & practice management materials; pediatrics; family & emergency medicine.
ISBN Prefix(es): 978-0-910761; 978-0-87493; 978-0-915473; 978-0-87553; 978-0-553; 978-0-89707; 978-1-56055; 978-1-58110
Number of titles published annually: 40 Print; 5 CD-ROM; 10 Online; 120 E-Book
Total Titles: 400 Print; 10 CD-ROM; 10 Online; 120 E-Book
Foreign Rights: John Scott & Co
Orders to: PO Box 776442, Chicago, IL 60677-6442
Distribution Center: Independent Publishers Group (IPG), 814 N Franklin St, Chicago, IL 60610 *Toll Free Tel:* 800-888-4741 *E-mail:* orders@ipgbook.com *Web Site:* www.ipgbook.com

American Alpine Club
710 Tenth St, Suite 100, Golden, CO 80401
Tel: 303-384-0110 *Fax:* 303-384-0111
E-mail: info@americanalpineclub.org
Web Site: americanalpineclub.org
Key Personnel
Exec Ed: Dougald MacDonald
 E-mail: dmacdonald@americanalpineclub.org
Founded: 1902
Mountaineering: general, regional guides, safety, medical & scientific, annual journals & historical.
ISBN Prefix(es): 978-0-930410
Number of titles published annually: 3 Print; 6 E-Book
Total Titles: 57 Print
Distributed by Mountaineers Books
Foreign Rep(s): Mountaineers Books (worldwide)
Foreign Rights: Mountaineers Books (worldwide)

§American Anthropological Association (AAA)
2300 Clarendon Blvd, Suite 1301, Arlington, VA 22201
E-mail: pubs@americananthro.org
Web Site: www.americananthro.org
Key Personnel
Dir, Publg: Melissa Schmidt
Sr Mng Ed: Sean Mallin
Ed, Anthropology News: Natalie Konopinski
Founded: 1902
Publish scholarly journals.
ISBN Prefix(es): 978-0-913167; 978-1-931303; 978-0-9799094; 978-0-9826767; 978-0-9836822
Number of titles published annually: 100 Print
Distributed by Wiley-Blackwell
Membership(s): Association of American Publishers (AAP); World Council of Anthropological Associations (WCAA)

American Association of Collegiate Registrars & Admissions Officers (AACRAO)
1108 16 St NW, Washington, DC 20011
Tel: 202-293-9161 *Fax:* 202-872-8857
E-mail: pubs@aacrao.org
Web Site: www.aacrao.org
Key Personnel
Exec Dir: Melanie Gottlieb *E-mail:* gottliebm@aacrao.org
Assoc Dir, Pubns: Heather Zimar
 E-mail: zimarh@aacrao.org
Founded: 1910

Periodicals, monograph series, higher education-general, international, technology.
ISBN Prefix(es): 978-0-929851; 978-0-910054
Number of titles published annually: 4 Print; 4 E-Book
Total Titles: 118 Print; 13 E-Book
Distribution Center: AACRAO Distribution Center, PO Box 231, Annapolis Junction, MD 20701 *Tel:* 301-263-0292 *Fax:* 240-396-5986 *E-mail:* pubs@aacrao.org *Web Site:* www.aacrao.org/bookstore

American Bar Association Publishing
Division of American Bar Association (ABA)
321 N Clark St, Chicago, IL 60654
Tel: 312-988-5000 *Toll Free Tel:* 800-285-2221 (orders) *Fax:* 312-988-5850 (orders)
E-mail: service@americanbar.org
Web Site: www.americanbar.org/groups/departments_offices/publishing
Key Personnel
Dir, Publg: Donna Gollmer *E-mail:* donna.gollmer@americanbar.org
Founded: 1878
Books, magazines, journals, newsletters & AV materials.
ISBN Prefix(es): 978-1-57073; 978-1-59031; 978-1-60442; 978-1-63905
Number of titles published annually: 170 Print; 25 CD-ROM; 100 Online; 100 E-Book
Total Titles: 1,013 Print; 150 CD-ROM; 250 Online; 250 E-Book
Branch Office(s)
1050 Connecticut Ave NW, Suite 400, Washington, DC 20036 *Tel:* 202-662-1000
Returns: ABA Return Processing Unit, 545 Wescott Rd, Eagan, MN 55123
Membership(s): Independent Book Publishers Association (IBPA)

§American Bible Society
101 N Independence Mall E, 8th fl, Philadelphia, PA 19106-2112
SAN: 203-5189
Tel: 215-309-0900 *Toll Free Tel:* 800-322-4253 (cust serv); 888-596-6296
E-mail: info@americanbible.org
Web Site: www.americanbible.org
Key Personnel
Mng Dir, Opers: John Greco
Founded: 1816
Publisher, producer & distributor of Bibles, books, audio, video & software products emphasizing Christian, inspirational & family values.
ISBN Prefix(es): 978-1-58516
Number of titles published annually: 20 Print
Total Titles: 800 Print
Warehouse: PO Box 2854, Tulsa, OK 74101-9921
Toll Free Fax: 866-570-1777

§American Carriage House Publishing (ACHP)
PO Box 1900, Pen Valley, CA 95946
Tel: 530-432-8860 *Toll Free Tel:* 866-986-2665
E-mail: editor@carriagehousepublishing.com
Web Site: www.americancarriagehousepublishing.com
Founded: 2003
Focused on providing traditional & family values in a new fresh approach.
ISBN Prefix(es): 978-0-970
Number of titles published annually: 8 Print; 20 CD-ROM; 8 Online; 14 E-Book; 68 Audio
Total Titles: 16 E-Book; 240 Audio
Distribution Center: Amazon
Ingram Book Group
Quality Books Inc
Membership(s): The Association of Publishers for Special Sales (APSS); Independent Book Publishers Association (IBPA)

PUBLISHERS / U.S. PUBLISHERS

§American Catholic Press (ACP)
16565 S State St, South Holland, IL 60473
SAN: 162-4989
Tel: 708-331-5485 *Fax:* 708-331-5484
E-mail: acp@acpress.org
Web Site: www.acpress.org
Key Personnel
Exec Dir: Rev Michael Gilligan, PhD
Mktg Dir: Rosa Lynch
Off Mgr: Jeanine Zamiar
Founded: 1967
Christian liturgy, especially in the Roman Catholic Church including music resources for churches. No poetry or fiction.
ISBN Prefix(es): 978-0-915866
Number of titles published annually: 5 Print; 1 Audio
Total Titles: 25 Print; 1 CD-ROM; 4 Audio

§The American Ceramic Society
550 Polaris Pkwy, Suite 510, Westerville, OH 43082
Tel: 240-646-7054 *Toll Free Tel:* 866-721-3322
Fax: 240-396-5637
E-mail: customerservice@ceramics.org
Web Site: ceramics.org
Key Personnel
Exec Dir: Mark Mecklenborg
  E-mail: mmecklenborg@ceramics.org
Dir, Tech Content & Communs: Eileen De Guire
  E-mail: edeguire@ceramics.org
Mng Dir, Ceramics Publishing Co: Bill Janeri
  E-mail: bjaneri@ceramics.org
Founded: 1898
Dedicated to the advancement of ceramics, serving more than 8,000 members & subscribers. Members include engineers, scientists, researchers & others in the ceramics & materials industry. Provides the latest technical, scientific & educational information.
ISBN Prefix(es): 978-0-944904; 978-1-57498; 978-0-916094
Number of titles published annually: 25 Print
Total Titles: 250 Print; 8 CD-ROM

The American College of Financial Services
630 Allendale Rd, Suite 400, King of Prussia, PA 19406
SAN: 240-5822
Tel: 610-526-1000 *Toll Free Tel:* 866-883-5640
Web Site: www.theamericancollege.edu
Key Personnel
Pres & CEO: George Nichols, III
EVP & Provost: Gwen Hall, PhD
Founded: 1927
An independent, accredited nonprofit educational institution offering financial services texts & course guides online & life insurance for students in financial services programs at colleges & universities including American College programs: CLU, ChFC, CLF, LUTCF, RHU, REBC, CASL & CFP certification curriculum & MSFS degree for professionals in the financial services industry. Subject specialties: business, finance, insurance & securities.
ISBN Prefix(es): 978-0-943590; 978-1-57996; 978-1-932819; 978-1-58293
Number of titles published annually: 42 Print; 60 Online; 11 Audio
Total Titles: 42 Print; 15 CD-ROM; 60 Online; 11 Audio

American College of Surgeons
633 N Saint Clair St, Chicago, IL 60611-3211
Tel: 312-202-5000 *Fax:* 312-202-5001
E-mail: postmaster@facs.org
Web Site: www.facs.org
Key Personnel
Dir, Div of Integrated Communs: Natalie Boden
  Tel: 312-202-5219 *E-mail:* nboden@facs.org
Ed-in-Chief: Jennifer Bagley *E-mail:* jbagley@facs.org
Founded: 1913
Publishes reference books & manuals. Specialize in surgery, trauma, cancer & professional liability. Also publishes the *Journal of the American College of Surgeons* (monthly) & the *Bulletin of the American College of Surgeons* (monthly).
ISBN Prefix(es): 978-0-9620370
Number of titles published annually: 5 Print; 10 Online
Total Titles: 20 Print

American Correctional Association
206 N Washington St, Suite 200, Alexandria, VA 22314
Tel: 703-224-0000 *Toll Free Tel:* 800-222-5646
Fax: 703-224-0179
E-mail: publications@aca.org
Web Site: www.aca.org
Founded: 1870
Corrections professionals.
ISBN Prefix(es): 978-1-56991
Number of titles published annually: 6 Print
Total Titles: 200 Print

American Council on Education (ACE)
One Dupont Circle NW, Washington, DC 20036
Tel: 202-939-9300
Web Site: www.acenet.edu
Key Personnel
Chief Learning & Innovation Offr: Louis Soares
Pres: Ted Mitchell
SVP, Educ Futures: Derrick Anderson
  E-mail: danderson@acenet.edu
VP & Chief of Staff: Jessie Brown
  E-mail: jbrown@acenet.edu
VP & Gen Coun: Peter McDonough
Asst VP & Exec Dir, ACE Connect: Gailda Pitre Davis
Founded: 1917
Books, directories & handbooks in higher education, monographs.
ISBN Prefix(es): 978-0-8268; 978-0-89774
Number of titles published annually: 70 Print
Total Titles: 200 Print
Distributed by Rowman & Littlefield

American Counseling Association (ACA)
6101 Stevenson Ave, Suite 600, Alexandria, VA 22304
Tel: 703-823-9800 *Toll Free Tel:* 800-298-2276
Toll Free Fax: 800-473-2329
E-mail: orders@counseling.org (book orders)
Web Site: www.counseling.org
Key Personnel
Chief Communs & Mktg Offr: Stacy Brooks Whatley *E-mail:* swhatley@counseling.org
Dir of Publns: Christine Fruin
Dir of Mktg: Caressa Morris
Founded: 1952
More than 55,000 members from the school counseling, mental health & human development professions at all educational levels. Publishes 10 scholarly journals, a magazine & approximately 8-10 new professional book titles a year for members & nonmembers.
ISBN Prefix(es): 978-1-55620
Number of titles published annually: 10 Print; 10 E-Book
Total Titles: 100 Print; 60 E-Book
Imprints: ACA

§American Diabetes Association
2451 Crystal Dr, Suite 900, Arlington, VA 22202
Tel: 703-549-1500 *Toll Free Tel:* 800-342-2383
E-mail: booksales@diabetes.org; ada_pubs@diabetes.org
Web Site: diabetes.org; diabetesjournals.org/books; www.facebook.com/adapublications
Key Personnel
VP, Prof Pubns: Christian S Kohler
  E-mail: ckohler@diabetes.org
Mng Dir, Prof Pubns: Heather Norton Blackburn
  E-mail: hnorton@diabetes.org
Dir, Book Edit Opers: Victor Van Beuren
  E-mail: vvanbeuren@diabetes.org
Assoc Dir, Book Prodn: John Clark
  E-mail: jclark@diabetes.org
Assoc Dir, Prof Pubns, Prodn & Design: Keang Hok *E-mail:* khok@diabetes.org
Edit & Prodn Mgr, Prof Pubns: Meaghan Foley
  E-mail: mfoley@diabetes.org
Founded: 1945
Books, scholarly journals, handouts & collateral materials pertaining to diabetes for patients & health care professionals.
ISBN Prefix(es): 978-1-58040; 978-0-94544
Number of titles published annually: 20 Print; 15 E-Book
Total Titles: 180 Print; 80 E-Book
Distribution Center: Publishers Group West (PGW), 1700 Fourth St, Berkeley, CA 94710
Toll Free Tel: 800-788-3123 (cust serv)
SAN: 202-8522

American Federation of Arts
305 E 47 St, 10th fl, New York, NY 10017
Tel: 212-988-7700 *Toll Free Tel:* 800-232-0270
Fax: 212-861-2487
E-mail: pubinfo@amfedarts.org
Web Site: www.amfedarts.org
Key Personnel
Mgr, Pubns: Anna Kyoko Barnet
  E-mail: abarnet@amfedarts.org
Head, Communs & Mktg: Sarah Fonseca
  E-mail: sfonseca@amfedarts.org
Founded: 1909
Publisher of exhibition catalogues (books) that accompany art exhibitions organized by the American Federation of Arts; more information on AFA titles can be found on the web site & on AFA's social media channels @amfedarts.
ISBN Prefix(es): 978-0-917418; 978-1-885444
Number of titles published annually: 4 Print
Total Titles: 47 Print
Distributed by Harry N Abrams Inc; D Giles Ltd; Hirmer Publishers; Hudson Hills Press Inc; Rizzoli Electa; Scala Publishers; University of Washington Press; Yale University Press
Distribution Center: Distributed Art Publishers Inc, 75 Broad St, Suite 630, New York, NY 10004 *Tel:* 212-627-1999 *Fax:* 212-627-9484
Web Site: www.artbook.com

American Federation of Astrologers Inc
6535 S Rural Rd, Tempe, AZ 85283-3746
Tel: 480-838-1751 *Toll Free Tel:* 888-301-7630
E-mail: info@astrologers.com
Web Site: www.astrologers.com
Key Personnel
Exec Secy: Celeste Nash-Weninger
Founded: 1938
Astrology book publisher & membership organization.
ISBN Prefix(es): 978-0-86690
Number of titles published annually: 5 Print
Total Titles: 250 Print

American Fisheries Society
425 Barlow Place, Suite 110, Bethesda, MD 20814-2144
Tel: 301-897-8616; 703-661-1570 (book orders)
Fax: 301-897-8096; 703-996-1010 (book orders)
E-mail: main@fisheries.org
Web Site: fisheries.org/books-journals
Key Personnel
Dir, Pubns: Laura Hendee *Tel:* 301-897-8616 ext 227 *E-mail:* lhendee@fisheries.org
Founded: 1870
Fisheries science, aquaculture & management materials, aquatic ecology, fisheries law, fisheries history, conservation biology & publishing.

U.S. PUBLISHERS

ISBN Prefix(es): 978-0-913235; 978-1-888569; 978-1-934874
Number of titles published annually: 10 Print; 5 Online
Total Titles: 193 Print
Orders to: Books International, PO Box 605, Herndon, VA 20172 *Tel:* 703-661-1570 *Fax:* 703-996-1010 *E-mail:* bimail@presswarehouse.com

American Geophysical Union (AGU)
2000 Florida Ave NW, Washington, DC 20009
SAN: 202-4489
Tel: 202-462-6900 *Toll Free Tel:* 800-966-2481 (North America) *Fax:* 202-328-0566
E-mail: service@agu.org (cust serv)
Web Site: www.agu.org
Key Personnel
VP, Pubns: Matthew Giampoala
 E-mail: mgiampoala@agu.org
Dir, Pubns: Jenny Lunn *E-mail:* jlunn@agu.org; Jeanette Panning *E-mail:* jpanning@agu.org
Founded: 1919
International scientific society with more than 50,000 members in over 135 countries. For over 80 years, AGU researchers, teachers & science administrators have dedicated themselves to advancing the understanding of earth & its environment in space. AGU now stands as a leader in the increasingly interdisciplinary global endeavor that encompasses the geophysical sciences.
ISBN Prefix(es): 978-0-87590
Number of titles published annually: 15 Print; 23 Online
Total Titles: 500 Print
Membership(s): Council of Science Editors (CSE); Society for Scholarly Publishing (SSP)

§American Geosciences Institute (AGI)
4220 King St, Alexandria, VA 22302-1502
Tel: 703-379-2480 (ext 246)
E-mail: agi@americangeosciences.org
Web Site: www.americangeosciences.org; www.geosciencestore.org
Key Personnel
Exec Dir: Jonathan D Arthur *Tel:* 703-379-2480 ext 202 *E-mail:* jarthur@americangeosciences.org
Educ & Outreach: Edward C Robeck *Tel:* 703-379-2480 ext 245 *E-mail:* ecrobeck@americangeosciences.org
Geoscience Profession & Higher Educ: Christopher Keane *Tel:* 703-379-2480 ext 219 *E-mail:* keane@americangeosciences.org
Mktg & Pubns: John Rasanen *Tel:* 703-379-2480 ext 224 *E-mail:* jr@americangeosciences.org
Founded: 1948
Geoscience reference books.
ISBN Prefix(es): 978-0-922152; 978-0-913312; 978-1-941878
Number of titles published annually: 5 Print; 3 E-Book
Total Titles: 60 Print; 10 CD-ROM; 2 Online; 5 E-Book
Distributed by W H Freeman; It's About Time Inc; Prentice Hall

American Girl Publishing
Subsidiary of Mattel Inc
2330 Eagle Dr, Middleton, WI 53562
Tel: 608-830-4444 *Toll Free Tel:* 800-845-0005 (US & CN) *Fax:* 608-836-1999
Web Site: www.americangirl.com/pages/books; www.americangirl.com
Key Personnel
SVP & Gen Mgr: Jamie Cygielman
Founded: 1986
Children's fiction & nonfiction. No unsol submissions are accepted.
ISBN Prefix(es): 978-0-937295; 978-1-56247; 978-1-58485; 978-1-68337
Number of titles published annually: 10 Print; 10 Online; 10 Audio
Total Titles: 150 Print; 30 Online; 30 Audio
Imprints: American Girl
Distributed by Simon & Schuster, LLC
Membership(s): The Children's Book Council (CBC)

§American Historical Association (AHA)
400 "A" St SE, Washington, DC 20003
Tel: 202-544-2422
E-mail: info@historians.org; awards@historians.org
Web Site: www.historians.org
Key Personnel
Exec Dir: Jim Grossman
Founded: 1884
The umbrella organization for the history profession.
ISBN Prefix(es): 978-0-87229
Number of titles published annually: 5 Print; 3 Online
Total Titles: 100 Print

American Industrial Hygiene Association, see AIHA (American Industrial Hygiene Association)

§American Institute for Economic Research (AIER)
250 Division St, Great Barrington, MA 01230
Mailing Address: PO Box 1000, Great Barrington, MA 01230-1000
Tel: 413-528-1216 *Toll Free Tel:* 888-528-1216 (orders) *Fax:* 413-528-0103
E-mail: press@aier.org; submissions@aier.org
Web Site: www.aier.org
Key Personnel
Pubns Mgr: Alexander Gleason
Founded: 1933
Conducts independent, scientific, economic research to educate individuals, thereby advancing their personal interests & those of the nation.
ISBN Prefix(es): 978-0-913610; 978-1-63069
Number of titles published annually: 3 Print; 8 Online; 4 E-Book
Total Titles: 50 Print; 46 Online; 4 E-Book

§American Institute of Aeronautics and Astronautics (AIAA)
12700 Sunrise Valley Dr, Suite 200, Reston, VA 20191-5807
Tel: 703-264-7500 *Toll Free Tel:* 800-639-AIAA (639-2422) *Fax:* 703-264-7551
E-mail: custserv@aiaa.org
Web Site: www.aiaa.org; arc.aiaa.org (orders)
Key Personnel
VP, Prod Opers: Michele Dominiak *Tel:* 703-264-7531 *E-mail:* micheled@aiaa.org
Exec Dir: Daniel L Dumbacher
Dir, Communs: Rebecca B Gray *Tel:* 804-397-5270 (cell) *E-mail:* rebeccag@aiaa.org
Dir, Pubns Strategy & Acq: David Arthur *Tel:* 703-264-7572 *E-mail:* davida@aiaa.org
Sr Mgr, Pubns Opers: Karina Bustillo *Tel:* 703-264-7525 *E-mail:* karinab@aiaa.org
Founded: 1963
Professional technical books; member magazine; archival journals & technical meeting papers in the science & technology of aerospace engineering & systems; online delivery.
ISBN Prefix(es): 978-0-915928; 978-0-930403; 978-1-56347; 978-1-60086; 978-1-62410
Number of titles published annually: 20 Print
Total Titles: 600 Print
Foreign Rep(s): Accucoms (worldwide)

§American Institute of Chemical Engineers (AIChE)
120 Wall St, 23rd fl, New York, NY 10005-4020
Tel: 203-702-7660 *Toll Free Tel:* 800-242-4363
E-mail: customerservice@aiche.org
Web Site: www.aiche.org/publications
Key Personnel
Exec Dir & CEO: Darlene S Schuster, PhD
Founded: 1908
Chemical engineering books & journals, technical manuals, symposia proceedings, directories.
ISBN Prefix(es): 978-0-8169
Number of titles published annually: 15 Print
Total Titles: 300 Print; 4 CD-ROM
Distributed by John Wiley & Sons Inc
Distributor for ASM International (selected titles); John Wiley & Sons Inc; Engineering Foundation; IchemE (selected titles)
Orders to: 100 Mill Plain Rd, 3rd fl, Danbury, CT 06811 (cust serv ctr)

American Institute of CPAs®, see AICPA® & CIMA®

American Law Institute
4025 Chestnut St, Philadelphia, PA 19104-3099
SAN: 204-756X
Tel: 215-243-1600 *Toll Free Tel:* 800-253-6397
E-mail: custserv@ali.org
Web Site: www.ali.org
Key Personnel
Pubns Dir: Deanne Dissinger
Edit Mgr: Karen Van Gorder
Sr Ed: Todd David Feldman
Founded: 1923
Professional & scholarly legal books & treatises.
ISBN Prefix(es): 978-0-8318
Number of titles published annually: 10 Print

§American Law Institute Continuing Legal Education (ALI CLE)
Affiliate of American Law Institute
4025 Chestnut St, Philadelphia, PA 19104
Tel: 215-243-1600 *Toll Free Tel:* 800-CLE-NEWS (253-6397) *Fax:* 215-243-1664
E-mail: custserv@ali-cle.org; press@ali-cle.org
Web Site: www.ali-cle.org
Key Personnel
Pubns Mgr: Dara Lovitz *E-mail:* dlovitz@ali.org
Founded: 1947 (as ALI-ABA; reconstituted as ALI CLE in 2012)
Publish law books, legal periodicals & journals.
ISBN Prefix(es): 978-0-8318
Number of titles published annually: 2 Print; 2 Online

§The American Library Association (ALA)
225 N Michigan Ave, Suite 1300, Chicago, IL 60601
SAN: 201-0062
Tel: 312-944-6780 *Toll Free Tel:* 800-545-2433; 866-SHOP-ALA (746-7252, orders) *Fax:* 312-280-5275; 312-440-9374; 312-280-5860 (orders)
E-mail: ala@ala.org; alastore@ala.org
Web Site: www.alastore.ala.org; www.ala.org
Key Personnel
Chief IT Offr: Rebecca Headrick
Publr & Ed: George Kendall *Tel:* 800-545-2433 ext 5717 *E-mail:* gkendall@ala.org
Publr, ALA Editions/Neal-Schuman: Angela Gwizdala *Tel:* 800-345-2433 ext 1544 *E-mail:* agwizdala@ala.org
Mng Ed: Samantha Kundert *Tel:* 800-345-2433 ext 3244 *E-mail:* skundert@ala.org
Sr Acqs Ed: Rachel Chance *Tel:* 800-545-2433 ext 1548 *E-mail:* rchance@ala.org; Jamie Santoro *Tel:* 800-545-2433 ext 5107 *E-mail:* jsantoro@ala.org
Sr Mktg Mgr: Ramon Robinson *Tel:* 800-545-2433 ext 5840 *E-mail:* rrobinson@ala.org
Licensing & Perms Mgr: Mary Jo Bolduc *Tel:* 800-545-2433 ext 5418 *E-mail:* mbolduc@ala.org
Founded: 1876

Publisher of titles for librarians & educators; library & information science, professional books.
ISBN Prefix(es): 978-0-8389; 978-1-937589
Number of titles published annually: 36 Print; 30 E-Book
Total Titles: 400 Print; 300 E-Book
Imprints: ALA Editions; ALA Neal-Schuman
Divisions: American Association of School Librarians (AASL); Association for Library Service to Children (ALSC) (including ALSC Matters!); Association of College & Research Libraries (ACRL) (including ACRL Choice); Core: Leadership, Infrastructure, Futures; Public Library Association (PLA); Reference & User Services Association (RUSA); United for Libraries (Trustees, Friends, Foundations); Young Adult Library Services Association (YALSA) (including YA Forum)
Distributed by University of Chicago Press
Foreign Rep(s): Eurospan (Africa, Europe, Israel, UK)
Foreign Rights: Inbooks (James Bennett) (Australia); Ontario Library Association (Canada)
Orders to: Chicago Distribution Center (CDC), 11030 S Langley Ave, Chicago, IL 60628
Returns: Chicago Distribution Center (CDC), 11030 S Langley Ave, Chicago, IL 60628
Distribution Center: Chicago Distribution Center (CDC), 11030 S Langley Ave, Chicago, IL 60628 (North America) *Tel:* 773-702-7010 *Toll Free Fax:* 800-621-8476 *Web Site:* press.uchicago.edu/cdc
See separate listing for:
ALA Neal-Schuman
Association of College & Research Libraries (ACRL)

American Mathematical Society (AMS)
201 Charles St, Providence, RI 02904-2213
SAN: 201-1654
Tel: 401-455-4000 *Toll Free Tel:* 800-321-4267
Fax: 401-331-3842; 401-455-4046 (cust serv)
E-mail: ams@ams.org; cust-serv@ams.org
Web Site: www.ams.org
Key Personnel
Exec Dir: Dr Catherine A Roberts
Publr: Dr Sergei Gelfand
Assoc Exec Dir: Dr Robert M Harrington
Assoc Exec Dir, Washington, DC: Dr Karen Saxe
Founded: 1888
Membership society & publisher of mathematics.
ISBN Prefix(es): 978-0-8218; 978-0-8284; 978-1-4704
Number of titles published annually: 100 Print
Total Titles: 3,400 Print; 2 CD-ROM; 28 Online
Imprints: Chelsea Publishing Co Inc
Branch Office(s)
1527 18 St NW, Washington, DC 20036-1358 (govt rel & sci policy) *Tel:* 202-588-1100 *Fax:* 202-588-1853 *E-mail:* amsdc@ams.org
Mathematical Reviews®, 416 Fourth St, Ann Arbor, MI 48103-4820 (edit) *Tel:* 734-996-5250 *Fax:* 734-996-2916 *E-mail:* mathrev@ams.org
Secretary of the AMS - Society Governance, Dept of Computer Science, North Carolina State University, Box 8206, Raleigh, NC 27695-8206 *Tel:* 919-515-7863 *Fax:* 919-515-7896 *E-mail:* secretary@ams.org
Distributor for Annales de la faculte des sciences de Toulouse mathematiques; Bar-Ilan University Press; Brown University; European Mathematical Society; Hindustan Book Agency; Independent University of Moscow; International Press of Boston Inc; Mathematica Josephina; Mathematical Society of Japan; Narosa Publishing House; Ramanujan Mathematical Society; Science Press USA Inc; Societe Mathematique de France; Tata Institute of Fundamental Research; Theta Foundation of Bucharest; University Press; Vieweg Verlag Publications
Foreign Rep(s): Eurospan Australia (Australia, New Zealand, Oceania); Eurospan Group (Africa, Europe, Middle East, Southeast Asia); Hindustan Book Agency (India); IBH Book & Magazines Distributors Pvt Ltd (India); Maruzen Co Ltd (Japan); Neutrino Inc (Japan); Segment Book Distributors (India)
Returns: Pawtucket Warehouse, 35 Monticello Place, Pawtucket, RI 02861
Warehouse: Pawtucket Warehouse, 35 Monticello Place, Pawtucket, RI 02861, Contact: Donald Proulx *Tel:* 401-729-4184 *Fax:* 401-728-3564 *E-mail:* dap@ams.org
Distribution Center: Pawtucket Warehouse, 35 Monticello Place, Pawtucket, RI 02861, Contact: Donald Proulx *Tel:* 401-729-4184 *Fax:* 401-728-3564 *E-mail:* dap@ams.org
Membership(s): Society for Scholarly Publishing (SSP)

American Medical Association (AMA)
AMA Plaza, 330 N Wabash, Suite 39300, Chicago, IL 60611-5885
Tel: 312-464-5000; 312-464-4430 (media & edit)
Toll Free Tel: 800-621-8335
E-mail: media@ama-assn.org (media & edit); bookandonlinesales@ama-assn.org (volume book/ebook sales)
Web Site: www.ama-assn.org
Key Personnel
EVP & CEO: James L Madara, MD
SVP & Chief Mission Offr, Publg: Thomas J Easley
SVP & Ed-in-Chief, Scientific Pubns: Kirsten Bibbins-Domingo, PhD
Group VP & Publr: Brian Shields
Founded: 1847
Publisher of books & specialty journals for the latest research, medical news & ongoing advocacy efforts supporting patients & physicians.
ISBN Prefix(es): 978-0-89970; 978-1-57947; 978-1-60359; 978-1-62202
Number of titles published annually: 30 Print
Total Titles: 150 Print
Foreign Rep(s): Australasian Medical Publishing Co Pty Ltd (Australia, China, Far East, New Zealand); Eurospan Group (UK); Login Canada (Canada)
Advertising Agency: GSP Marketing Services Inc
Distribution Center: Rittenhouse Book Distributors, 511 Fehely Dr, King of Prussia, PA 19406 *E-mail:* customer.service@rittenhouse.com *Web Site:* rittenhouse.com
Membership(s): Association of American Publishers (AAP)

American Numismatic Society
75 Varick St, 11th fl, New York, NY 10013
Tel: 212-571-4470 *Fax:* 212-571-4479
E-mail: ans@numismatics.org
Web Site: www.numismatics.org
Key Personnel
Exec Dir: Dr Gilles Bransbourg
Ed, ANS Magazine: Dr Peter van Alfen
Founded: 1858
Scholarly materials.
ISBN Prefix(es): 978-0-89722
Number of titles published annually: 5 Print
Total Titles: 100 Print

American Philosophical Society Press
104 S Fifth St, Philadelphia, PA 19106
SAN: 206-9016
Tel: 215-440-3425 *Fax:* 215-440-3450
Web Site: www.amphilsoc.org
Key Personnel
Exec Offr: Robert M Hauser
Pres: Roger Bagnall
Dir, APS Press: Peter Dougherty *E-mail:* pdougherty@amphilsoc.org
Opers Mgr: Alison Beninato *E-mail:* abeninato@amphilsoc.org
Founded: 1743
Nonprofit educational institution for promotion of useful knowledge in humanities & sciences.
ISBN Prefix(es): 978-0-87169; 978-1-60618
Number of titles published annually: 13 Print
Total Titles: 1,150 Print
Imprints: APS Books; Proceedings; Transactions
Distributed by University of Pennsylvania Press

American Press
75 State St, Suite 100, Boston, MA 02109
SAN: 210-7007
Tel: 617-247-0022
E-mail: americanpress@flash.net
Web Site: www.americanpresspublishers.com
Key Personnel
Publr: R K Fox
Ed: Marci Taylor
Founded: 1911
College textbooks, study guides, lab manuals & handbooks.
ISBN Prefix(es): 978-0-89641
Number of titles published annually: 20 Print
Total Titles: 300 Print

§American Psychiatric Association Publishing
Division of American Psychiatric Association (APA)
800 Maine Ave SW, Suite 900, Washington, DC 20024
SAN: 293-2288
Tel: 202-459-9722 *Toll Free Tel:* 800-368-5777
Fax: 202-403-3094
E-mail: appi@psych.org
Web Site: www.appi.org; www.psychiatryonline.org
Key Personnel
Publr: Simone Taylor, PhD
Dir, Sales & Mktg: Patrick Hansard
Edit Dir, Journals Div: Michael Roy
Ed-in-Chief, Books: Laura Roberts, MD
Mng Ed, Books: Greg Kuny
Acqs Mgr: Erika Parker
Dir, Publg Busn Opers: Debra Eubanks
Licensing Coord: Samantha Kralstein
Founded: 1981
Professional, reference & general trade books, college textbooks; behavioral & social sciences, psychiatry, medicine.
ISBN Prefix(es): 978-0-88048; 978-0-89042; 978-0-87318; 978-1-58562; 978-1-61537
Number of titles published annually: 30 Print; 3 Online; 30 E-Book
Total Titles: 750 Print; 30 Online; 420 E-Book; 1 Audio
Distributor for Group for the Advancement of Psychiatry
Foreign Rep(s): Catamount (Latin America); CBS Publishers & Distributors Pvt Ltd (India); Eurospan (Central Asia, China, East Asia, Singapore, South Korea); Ingram Publisher Services UK (Europe, UK); International Publishers Representatives (Africa, Middle East); Login Canada (Canada); Nankodo Co Ltd (Japan); Oxford University Press (Southern Africa)
Foreign Rights: John Scott Agency
Warehouse: Ware-Pak, 2427 Bond St, University Park, IL 60484-3170
Membership(s): American Association of University Presses (AAUP); Association of American Publishers (AAP)

American Psychological Association
750 First St NE, Washington, DC 20002
Tel: 202-336-5510 *Toll Free Tel:* 800-374-2721
Fax: 202-336-5502
E-mail: order@apa.org; booksales@apa.org
Web Site: www.apa.org/books
Key Personnel
Exec Publr: Jasper Simons *Tel:* 202-336-5636 *E-mail:* jsimons@apa.org
Sr Dir, APA Style: Emily Ayubi *E-mail:* eayubi@apa.org

Dir, Book Sales: Kerry Cahill
Dir, Books Mktg: Jason M Wells *E-mail:* jwells@apa.org
Dir, Edit Acqs: Emily Ekle *E-mail:* eekle@apa.org
Dir, Edit Devt: Elise Frasier *E-mail:* efrasier@apa.org
Dir, Video Media: Ed Meidenbauer
 E-mail: emeidenbauer@apa.org
Edit Dir, Magination Press®: Kristine Enderle
Sr Acqs Ed: Christopher Kelaher
Books Mktg Mgr: Devon Renwick
 E-mail: drenwick@apa.org
Content Devt Mgr, APA Style: Hayley Kamin
Devt Mgr, APA Style: Samantha Denneny
Mgr, APA Style: Timothy McAdoo
Instrl Lead, APA Style: Chelsea Lee
Journal Content Coord: Sarah Fell
Founded: 1892
Scholarly & professional works on psychology & related fields, including books, journals, videos, databases; trade books for general audiences (LifeTools); children's books (Magination Press®); APA Style Central®, a suite of integrated services & tools for writing & teaching APA Style; *American Psychologist*® (flagship quarterly journal) & *Monitor on Psychology*, a monthly magazine.
ISBN Prefix(es): 978-0-912704; 978-1-55798; 978-0-945354; 978-0-9792125; 978-1-59147; 978-1-4338
Number of titles published annually: 45 Print
Total Titles: 900 Print
Imprints: APA Books®; APA Journals; APA Style; APA Video®; Educational Publishing Foundation (EPF); LifeTools; Magination Press®
Foreign Rep(s): China Publishers Services Ltd (Ben Bai) (China, Hong Kong); Eurospan Group (Africa, Europe, Middle East); Login Canada (Canada); Vital Books Korea (Moo-Seock Pyun) (Japan, South Korea, Taiwan); The White Partnership (Andrew White) (India, Indonesia, Malaysia, Pakistan, Philippines, Singapore, Sri Lanka, Thailand, Vietnam); Woodslane Pty Ltd (Australia, Fiji, New Zealand, Papua New Guinea)
Warehouse: APA Order Dept, PO Box 92984, Washington, DC 20090-2984

American Public Works Association (APWA)
1200 Main St, Suite 1400, Kansas City, MO 64105-2100
Tel: 816-472-6100 *Toll Free Tel:* 800-848-APWA (848-2792) *Fax:* 816-472-1610
Web Site: www.apwa.org
Key Personnel
Chief Growth Offr: Jared Shilhanek *Tel:* 816-595-5257 *E-mail:* jshilhanek@apwa.org
Mng Ed, APWA Reporter: Christie Dotolo
 Tel: 816-595-5258 *E-mail:* cdotolo@apwa.org
Founded: 1894
Public work related publications. Also publishes *APWA Reporter* magazine.
ISBN Prefix(es): 978-0-917084; 978-1-60675
Number of titles published annually: 12 Print; 3 E-Book
Total Titles: 50 Print; 12 E-Book
Branch Office(s)
25 Massachusetts Ave NW, Suite 500A, Washington, DC 20001 *Tel:* 202-408-9541

American Quilter's Society (AQS)
Division of Schroeder Publishing Co Inc
5801 Kentucky Dam Rd, Paducah, KY 42003-9323
Mailing Address: PO Box 3290, Paducah, KY 42002-3290
Tel: 270-898-7903 *Toll Free Tel:* 800-626-5420 (orders) *Fax:* 270-898-8890
E-mail: orders@americanquilter.com; info@aqsquilt.com
Web Site: www.americanquilter.com

Key Personnel
Pres & CEO: Bill Schroeder, III
Founded: 1983
Publish books & magazines, distributes books & operates quilting shows.
ISBN Prefix(es): 978-0-89145; 978-1-57432; 978-1-60460; 978-1-68339
Number of titles published annually: 20 Print; 10 CD-ROM; 4 E-Book
Total Titles: 300 Print; 20 CD-ROM; 7 E-Book

§American Society for Nondestructive Testing
1201 Dublin Rd, Suite G04, Columbus, OH 43215
Toll Free Tel: 800-222-2768
E-mail: customersupport@asnt.org
Web Site: www.asnt.org; source.asnt.org (orders); asntmediaplanner.com (ad & sponsored content)
Key Personnel
Dir, Pubns: Jill Ross *Tel:* 614-384-2484
 E-mail: jross@asnt.org
Dir, Mktg & Commun: Garra Liming
 E-mail: gliming@asnt.org
Founded: 1941
Nonprofit association producing educational materials for members & nonmembers engaged in nondestructive testing.
ISBN Prefix(es): 978-0-931403; 978-1-57117
Number of titles published annually: 12 Print; 12 E-Book
Total Titles: 250 Print; 200 E-Book
Distributed by American Ceramic Society (ACerS); American Society for Mechanical Engineers (ASME); American Society for Metals (ASM); The American Welding Society (AWS); ASTM; Edison Welding Institute; Mean Free Path

§American Society for Quality (ASQ)
600 N Plankinton Ave, Milwaukee, WI 53203
Mailing Address: PO Box 3005, Milwaukee, WI 53201-3005
Tel: 414-272-8575 *Toll Free Tel:* 800-248-1946 (US & CN); 800-514-1564 (Mexico)
E-mail: help@asq.org; books@asq.org
Web Site: www.asq.org
Founded: 1983
Publisher of technical books: quality, statistical process control, ISO9000, six sigma, QS9000, ISO14000, statistics, reliability, auditing, sampling, standards' supplier quality & quality costs. Also management topics: total quality management, human resources & teamwork, health care, government, education & benchmarking, quality tools.
ISBN Prefix(es): 978-0-87389
Number of titles published annually: 25 Print; 25 E-Book
Total Titles: 500 Print; 5 CD-ROM; 200 E-Book
Distribution Center: Bright Key, 60 West St, 3rd fl, Annapolis, MD 21401

§American Society of Agricultural & Biological Engineers (ASABE)
2950 Niles Rd, St Joseph, MI 49085-9659
Tel: 269-429-0300 *Toll Free Tel:* 800-371-2723
Fax: 269-429-3852
E-mail: hq@asabe.org
Web Site: www.asabe.org
Key Personnel
Exec Dir: Darrin Drollinger *Tel:* 269-932-7007
 E-mail: drollinger@asabe.org
Dir, Pubns: Joe Walker *Tel:* 269-932-7026
 E-mail: walker@asabe.org
Book & Journal Ed: Peg McCann *Tel:* 269-932-7019 *E-mail:* mccann@asabe.org
Journal Ed: Glenn Laing *Tel:* 269-932-7014
 E-mail: laing@asabe.org; Melissa Miller
 Tel: 269-932-7017 *E-mail:* miller@asabe.org
Pubns Asst: Jill Straub *Tel:* 269-932-7004
 E-mail: straub@asabe.org

Founded: 1907
Agricultural, biological & food systems, books & journals.
ISBN Prefix(es): 978-0-916150; 978-0-929355; 978-1-892769
Number of titles published annually: 4 Print
Total Titles: 150 Print; 1 CD-ROM; 2 Online

American Society of Agronomy (ASA)
5585 Guilford Rd, Madison, WI 53711-5801
Tel: 608-273-8080
E-mail: books@sciencesocieties.org
Web Site: www.agronomy.org
Key Personnel
CEO: Jim Cudahy *Tel:* 608-268-4973
Dir, Pubns: Matt Wascavage *Tel:* 608-819-3916
Mng Ed: Richard Easby *Tel:* 608-268-4991
 E-mail: reasby@sciencesocieties.org
Founded: 1907
Technical books for professionals in agronomy; crop science, soil science, environmental sciences & related fields.
ISBN Prefix(es): 978-0-89118
Number of titles published annually: 12 Print
Total Titles: 90 Print

§American Society of Civil Engineers (ASCE)
1801 Alexander Bell Dr, Reston, VA 20191-4400
SAN: 204-7594
Tel: 703-295-6300 *Toll Free Tel:* 800-548-ASCE (548-2723) *Toll Free Fax:* 866-913-6085
E-mail: ascelibrary@asce.org; pubsful@asce.org
Web Site: www.asce.org
Key Personnel
Publr & Mng Dir: Angela Cochran *Tel:* 703-295-6133
Dir, Pubns Busn Opers: Gina Lindquist
Dir, Pubns Mktg: William Nara
Founded: 1852
Books, technical journals, information products on civil engineering & related fields; online & print.
ISBN Prefix(es): 978-0-87262; 978-0-7844
Number of titles published annually: 60 Print; 25 E-Book
Total Titles: 1,400 Print; 425 E-Book
Imprints: ASCE Press
Foreign Rep(s): Aditya Books (P) Ltd (Bangladesh, Bhutan, India, Nepal, Pakistan, Sri Lanka); Allied Book Co (Pakistan); Apex Knowledge Sdn Bhd (Brunei, Malaysia); Areesh Education & Trading Sdn Bhd (Brunei, Malaysia); Booknet Co Ltd (Suphaluck Sattabuz) (Cambodia, Laos, Myanmar, Thailand, Vietnam); Capital Books Pvt Ltd (India); ChoiceTEXTS (Asia) Pte Ltd (Phillip Ang) (Indonesia, Singapore); Grupo Difusion Cientifica (Mexico, South America); Eurospan Group (Africa, Continental Europe, Middle East, UK); ICaves Ltd (Eddy Lam) (China, Hong Kong, Macau); International Book House Pvt Ltd (India); MegaTEXTS Phil Inc (Jean Tiu Lim) (Philippines); Multi-Line Books (Bangladesh, Bhutan, Nepal, Pakistan); PT Ina Publikatama (Indonesia); Shankar's Book Agency Pvt Ltd (India); Taiwan Publishers Marketing Services Ltd (George Liu) (Taiwan); Unique Sellers (India)
Orders to: PO Box 79162, Baltimore, MD 21279-0162
Returns: 9050 Junction Dr, Annapolis Junction, MD 20701

American Society of Electroneurodiagnostic Technologists Inc, see ASET - The Neurodiagnostic Society

§American Society of Mechanical Engineers (ASME)
2 Park Ave, New York, NY 10016-5990
SAN: 201-1379

Tel: 646-616-3100 *Toll Free Tel:* 800-843-2763 (cust serv-CN, Mexico & US) *Fax:* 973-882-1717 (orders & inquiries)
E-mail: customercare@asme.org
Web Site: www.asme.org
Key Personnel
Sr Dir, Publg Devt: Mary Grace Stefanchik *E-mail:* stefanchikm@asme.org
Founded: 1880
Publisher of codes & standards, journals, conference proceedings, professional references, *Mechanical Engineering* magazine, technical papers & reports.
ISBN Prefix(es): 978-0-7918; 978-0-9956762; 978-1-9993459; 978-0-9714081
Total Titles: 400 Print; 200 E-Book
Imprints: ASME Press
Warehouse: 150 Clove Rd, Little Falls, NJ 07424-2100

American Society of Plant Taxonomists
c/o Missouri Botanical Garden, 4344 Shaw Blvd, St Louis, MO 63110
SAN: 282-969X
E-mail: businessoffice@aspt.net
Web Site: www.aspt.net
Key Personnel
Busn Off Mgr: Theresa Smid
Founded: 1980
Botanical monographs.
ISBN Prefix(es): 978-0-912861; 978-1-943751
Number of titles published annually: 3 Print
Total Titles: 102 Print

American Technical Publishers
Division of The ATP Group Inc
10100 Orland Pkwy, Suite 200, Orland Park, IL 60467-5756
SAN: 206-8141
Toll Free Tel: 800-323-3471 *Fax:* 708-957-1101
E-mail: service@atplearning.com; order@atplearning.com
Web Site: www.atplearning.com; www.atpcanada.com (CN orders)
Key Personnel
Pres: Robert D Deisinger
Dir, Strategic Partnerships: Jonathan Gosse
Founded: 1898
Technical, industrial & vocational textbooks, reference books & related materials.
ISBN Prefix(es): 978-0-8269
Number of titles published annually: 8 Print; 2 CD-ROM; 25 Online; 3 E-Book
Total Titles: 200 Print; 10 CD-ROM; 25 Online; 3 E-Book
Distributor for Craftsman Book Co

American Traveler Press, see Golden West Cookbooks

§American Water Works Association (AWWA)
6666 W Quincy Ave, Denver, CO 80235-3098
Tel: 303-794-7711 *Toll Free Tel:* 800-926-7337
E-mail: service@awwa.org (cust serv); aws@awwa.org; books@awwa.org
Web Site: www.awwa.org/publications
Key Personnel
Dir, Publg: John Fedor
Founded: 1881
Water works technology & management. Books, journals, magazines & newsletters.
ISBN Prefix(es): 978-0-89867; 978-1-58321; 978-1-61300; 978-1-62576
Number of titles published annually: 50 Print
Total Titles: 500 Print; 12 CD-ROM; 2 Online
Imprints: AWWA
Foreign Rep(s): Aditya Books (P) Ltd (India); Apex Knowledge Sdn Bhd (Brunei, Malaysia); Booknet Co Ltd (Cambodia, Laos, Myanmar, Thailand, Vietnam); BSB Edge Pvt Ltd (India); Choice Texts Pte Ltd (Indonesia, Malaysia, Singapore); Elit Kitabevi Tic Ltd (Far East); ELOT (standards only, Greece) (Europe, UK); Eurospan Group (Africa, Continental Europe, Middle East, UK); Hakhen Books (Far East); Haward Publications (Far East); Infotech Standards (standards only) (India); Kabdwal Book International (India); Normdocs Inc (standards only) (Russia); Nortec (standards only) (South America); Putra Standards (Indonesia, Malaysia, Singapore); Techniz Books International (India)
Membership(s): AM&P Network; Publishers Association of the West (PubWest)

Amicus
PO Box 227, Mankato, MN 56002
Tel: 507-388-9357 *Toll Free Tel:* 800-445-6209 (cust serv/orders)
E-mail: info@thecreativecompany.us (gen inquiries); orders@thecreativecompany.us (cust serv)
Web Site: amicuspublishing.us
Key Personnel
Assoc Publr: Rebecca Glaser
Founded: 2010
Publish books for children that educate & inspire young readers. Our library imprints—Spot, Amicus Readers, Amicus Illustrated & Amicus High Interest—offer informational books in a variety of formats that make reading to learn fun & encourage life-long learning. Our trade imprint, Amicus Ink, features original picture books & board books, each sharing a child's-eye view of the world. Amicus: Friend of education. Friend for life.
ISBN Prefix(es): 978-1-60753; 978-1-68151; 978-1-68152; 978-1-64549
Number of titles published annually: 130 Print; 120 E-Book
Total Titles: 991 Print; 750 E-Book
Imprints: Amicus Ink (children's board books & picture books); Amicus Learning
Distributed by The Creative Co
Foreign Rights: Lorena Vazzola (worldwide)
Distribution Center: Saunders Book Co, PO Box 308, Collingwood, ON L9Y 3Z7, Canada
Tel: 705-445-4777 *Toll Free Tel:* 800-461-9120 *Fax:* 705-445-9569 *Toll Free Fax:* 800-561-1763 *E-mail:* info@saundersbooks.ca

AMMO Books LLC
3653 Primavera Ave, Los Angeles, CA 90065
Mailing Address: PO Box 412402, Los Angeles, CA 90041
Tel: 323-223-AMMO (223-2666) *Fax:* 323-978-4200
E-mail: weborders@ammobooks.com; orders@ammobooks.com
Web Site: ammobooks.com
Key Personnel
Co-Founder & Pres: Paul Norton *E-mail:* paul@ammobooks.com
Founded: 2006
Provocative, one-of-a-kind titles that highlight the best of the visual arts & pop culture.
ISBN Prefix(es): 978-0-9786076; 978-1-934429; 978-1-62326
Number of titles published annually: 50 Print

§Ampersand Inc/Professional Publishing Services
515 Madison St, New Orleans, LA 70116
Tel: 312-280-8905 *Fax:* 312-944-1582
E-mail: info@ampersandworks.com
Web Site: www.ampersandworks.com
Key Personnel
Pres & Publr: Suzanne Talbot Isaacs *E-mail:* suzie@ampersandworks.com
Founded: 1995 (began publishing in 2005)
Private publisher. Highly customized books, tailored to the author's specific objectives & developed by professionals with over 30 years of publishing experience. We take your ms to finished book in a matter of weeks, on time & on budget, support your marketing efforts, warehouse & distribute your book. Branch office in Chicago, IL.
This publisher has indicated that 90% of their product line is author subsidized.
ISBN Prefix(es): 978-1-7340; 978-1-4507; 978-0-9818126; 978-0-9761235; 978-0-873671; 978-1-4675; 978-0-9962525; 978-0-9722529; 978-0-9994; 978-0-9985; 978-0-9974; 978-0-9905
Number of titles published annually: 10 Print; 5 E-Book
Total Titles: 80 Print; 19 E-Book
Membership(s): Association of Independent Authors (AIA); The Association of Publishers for Special Sales (APSS); Independent Book Publishers Association (IBPA); Society of Children's Book Writers & Illustrators (SCBWI)

Anaphora Literary Press
1108 W Third St, Quanah, TX 79252
Tel: 470-289-6395
Web Site: anaphoraliterary.com
Key Personnel
Dir: Anna Faktorovich, PhD *E-mail:* director@anaphoraliterary.com
Founded: 2009
Publisher of paperback, hardcover & ebooks in poetry, fiction & nonfiction, scholarly & trade. Has released books by best-selling & award-winning novelists & academic books by top professors. Always welcoming to works by innovative new writers. 50/50 split of royalties. E-mail submission with ms, paragraph biography & summary. Anaphora helps with marketing via designed press releases, processing review copy submissions & exhibiting titles at conventions. Publisher of the British Renaissance Reattribution & Modernization series.
ISBN Prefix(es): 978-1-937536; 978-1-68114
Number of titles published annually: 30 Print; 30 E-Book
Total Titles: 300 Print; 300 E-Book
Distribution Center: Lightning Source, 1246 Heil Quaker Blvd, La Vergne, TN 37086
Membership(s): Community of Literary Magazines & Presses (CLMP); Independent Book Publishers Association (IBPA); Independent Book Publishing Professionals Group (IBPPG); Modern Language Association (MLA)

Ancient Faith Publishing
Division of Ancient Faith Ministries Inc
PO Box 748, Chesterton, IN 46304
Tel: 219-728-2216 *Toll Free Tel:* 800-967-7377
E-mail: general@ancientfaith.com; support@ancientfaith.com
Web Site: www.ancientfaith.com/publishing
Key Personnel
CEO: Melinda Johnson *E-mail:* mjohnson@ancientfaith.com
Founded: 1978
Books, booklets, brochures, greeting cards, icons.
ISBN Prefix(es): 978-0-9622713; 978-0-888212; 978-0-9822770; 978-1-936270; 978-1-944967
Number of titles published annually: 12 Print; 10 E-Book; 2 Audio
Total Titles: 160 Print; 133 E-Book; 6 Audio
Distributed by St Tikhon's; St Vladimir's
Foreign Rep(s): Crossroad Books (Australia)

Sara Anderson Children's Books
PO Box 47182, Seattle, WA 98146
Tel: 206-285-1520
Web Site: www.saraandersonchildrensbooks.com
Key Personnel
Founder & CEO: Sara Anderson *E-mail:* sara@saranderson.com
Founded: 2008
Specialize in colorful, innovatively designed early-concept books for babies & toddlers, picture books & a line of preschool bilingual

U.S. PUBLISHERS

(Spanish-English) children's board books. No unsol mss.
ISBN Prefix(es): 978-0-9702784; 978-0-9911933; 978-1-943459
Number of titles published annually: 5 Print
Total Titles: 18 Print

§Andrews McMeel Publishing LLC
Division of Andrews McMeel Universal
1130 Walnut St, Kansas City, MO 64106-2109
Tel: 816-581-7500 *Toll Free Tel:* 800-851-8923
Web Site: www.andrewsmcmeel.com; publishing.andrewsmcmeel.com
Key Personnel
Chmn, Andrews McMeel Universal: Hugh Andrews
CEO, Andrews McMeel Universal/Pres & Publr, Andrews McMeel Publishing: Kirsty Melville
VP, Cont & Dir, Opers: Brent Bartram
VP & Assoc Publr, Books: Betty Wong
VP, Corp Mktg & Communs: Kathy Hilliard
VP, Licensing: James Andrews
VP, Publg Servs, Books & Calendars: Shona Burns
VP, Sales, Books: Lynne McAdoo
Mng Art Dir, Calendars: Jenny Mohrfeld
Children's Mktg Dir: Diane Mangan
Prodn Dir, Books: Chuck Harper
Asst Art Dir: Sierra Stanton
Exec Ed: Patty Rice
Exec Ed, Calendars: Sarah Tobaben
Sr Ed, Books: Lucas Wetzel
Sr Ed, Children's Books: Erinn Pascal
Sr Prodn Ed: Julie Railsback; Brianna Westervelt
Prodn Ed: Jasmine Lim
Ed: Amanda Meadows; Marya Pasciuto; Melissa Rhodes Zahorsky
Assoc Ed, Calendars: Rebecca Ngo
Assoc Ed, Children's Books: Hannah Dussold
Prodn Mgr: Jeff Preuss
Assoc Prodn Mgr: Alex Alfano
Mktg Specialist: Alfonzo Fuller *Tel:* 816-581-7491 *E-mail:* afuller@amuniversal.com
Founded: 1973
Publish calendars, humor, poetry, interactive puzzles, children's books & series.
ISBN Prefix(es): 978-0-8362; 978-88-7407; 978-1-4494; 978-1-5248
Number of titles published annually: 300 Print
Imprints: Accord Publishing; Amber Lotus Publishing; Udig (ebooks)
Distributor for Gooseberry Patch (North America); Signatures Network; Sporting News; Universe Publishing Calendars; Vegan Heritage Press
Foreign Rep(s): Andrews McMeel Universal (Wendy Nyemaster) (Australia, Ireland, New Zealand, UK); Canadian Manda Group (Peter Hill-Field) (Canada); Simon & Schuster International (Martin Rino R Balatbat) (Japan, Micronesia, South Korea, Southeast Asia); Simon & Schuster International (Stanson Yeung) (China, Hong Kong, Taiwan); Simon & Schuster International (Lauren Weidner) (Caribbean, Latin America)
Orders to: Simon & Schuster, LLC, 100 Front St, Riverside, NJ 08075 (US orders) *Toll Free Tel:* 800-943-9839 *E-mail:* purchaseorders@simonandschuster.com SAN: 200-2442; Simon & Schuster, LLC, 100 Front St, Riverside, NJ 08075 (CN orders) *Toll Free Tel:* 800-268-3216 *E-mail:* canadianorders@simonandschuster.com SAN: 200-2442
Returns: Simon & Schuster, LLC, c/o Jacobson Logistics, 4406 Industrial Park Rd, Bldg 7, Camp Hill, PA 17011
Distribution Center: Simon & Schuster, LLC, 100 Front St, Riverside, NJ 08075 (US orders) *Toll Free Tel:* 800-943-9839 *E-mail:* purchaseorders@simonandschuster.com SAN: 200-2442
See separate listing for:
Amber Lotus Publishing

Andrews University Press
Division of Andrews University
Sutherland House, 8360 W Campus Circle Dr, Berrien Springs, MI 49104-1700
SAN: 241-0958
Tel: 269-471-6134 *Toll Free Tel:* 800-467-6369 (Visa, MC & American Express orders only) *Fax:* 269-471-6224
E-mail: aupo@andrews.edu; aup@andrews.edu
Web Site: www.universitypress.andrews.edu
Key Personnel
Dir: Ronald Knott *E-mail:* knott@andrews.edu
Assoc Dir: Scottie Baker *Tel:* 269-471-6133
Ed: Deborah L Everhart
Selected areas of theology, education, philosophy, science, faith & learning.
ISBN Prefix(es): 978-0-943872; 978-1-883925; 978-1-936337; 978-1-940980
Number of titles published annually: 3 Print; 1 E-Book
Total Titles: 85 Print; 1 CD-ROM; 1 Online; 30 E-Book

Angel City Press
2118 Wilshire Blvd, Suite 880, Santa Monica, CA 90403
Tel: 310-395-9982
E-mail: info@angelcitypress.com
Web Site: www.angelcitypress.com
Key Personnel
Co-Publr: Paddy Calistro; Scott McAuley
Founded: 1992
Publish books on California & Southern California social & cultural history.
ISBN Prefix(es): 978-1-883318; 978-1-62640
Number of titles published annually: 8 Print
Total Titles: 100 Print
Distributed by Gibbs Smith Publisher
Foreign Rep(s): Turnaround Publishing Services (London)

§Angelus Press
Subsidiary of The Society of Saint Pius X, Southwest District
522 W Bertrand St, St Marys, KS 66536
Mailing Address: PO Box 217, St Marys, KS 66536
Tel: 816-753-3150 *Toll Free Tel:* 800-966-7337
E-mail: support@angeluspress.org
Web Site: www.angeluspress.org
Key Personnel
Ed: James Vogel
Founded: 1978
Monthly journal of Catholic Tradition; traditional Roman Catholic books.
ISBN Prefix(es): 978-0-935952; 978-1-892331; 978-1-937843
Number of titles published annually: 10 Print
Total Titles: 175 Print
Imprints: Sarto House
Distributed by Fatima Crusader

Anhinga Press Inc
PO Box 3665, Tallahassee, FL 32315
E-mail: info@anhinga.org
Web Site: www.anhingapress.org; www.facebook.com/anhingapress
Key Personnel
Co-Dir: Carol Lynne Knight; Kristine Snodgrass *E-mail:* kristine.snodgrass@gmail.com
Founded: 1974
ISBN Prefix(es): 978-0-938078; 978-1-934695
Number of titles published annually: 8 Print
Total Titles: 70 Print
Membership(s): Community of Literary Magazines & Presses (CLMP)

Annual Reviews
1875 S Grant St, Suite 700, San Mateo, CA 94402
SAN: 201-1816
Mailing Address: PO Box 10139, Palo Alto, CA 94303-0139
Tel: 650-493-4400 *Toll Free Tel:* 800-523-8635 *Fax:* 650-424-0910; 650-855-9815
E-mail: service@annualreviews.org
Web Site: www.annualreviews.org
Key Personnel
CFO: Jonathan Michael *E-mail:* jmichael@annualreviews.org
Pres & Ed-in-Chief: Richard Gallagher
Dir, HR: Lisa Wucher *E-mail:* lwucher@annualreviews.org
Dir, Prodn: Jennifer Jongsma *E-mail:* jjongsma@annualreviews.org
Dir, Technol: Paul Calvi *E-mail:* pcalvi@annualreviews.org
Mktg Mgr: Jenni Rankin *E-mail:* jrankin@annualreviews.org
Founded: 1932
Scientific review literature, in print & online, in the biomedical, life, physical & social sciences.
ISBN Prefix(es): 978-0-8243
Number of titles published annually: 20 Print; 54 Online
Total Titles: 54 Online
Foreign Rep(s): Gazelle Book Services Ltd (Africa, Continental Europe, Ireland, Middle East, UK); SARAS Books (Bangladesh, India, Pakistan, Sri Lanka)
Returns: 526 N Earl Ave, PO Box 5685, Lafayette, IN 47903 (return authorization required)
Membership(s): The American Library Association (ALA); International Federation of Library Associations & Institutions (IFLA); Medical Library Association; National Information Standards Organization (NISO); Society for Scholarly Publishing (SSP); Special Libraries Association (SLA); STM

§ANR Publications University of California
Division of Agriculture & Natural Resources, University of California
2801 Second St, Davis, CA 95618
Tel: 530-400-0725 (cust serv) *Toll Free Tel:* 800-994-8849
E-mail: anrcatalog@ucanr.edu
Web Site: anrcatalog.ucanr.edu
Key Personnel
Dir, Publg: Rachel Lee *E-mail:* anrlee@ucanr.edu
Mktg Dir & Foreign Rts: Cynthia Kintigh *Tel:* 530-750-1217 *E-mail:* cckintigh@ucanr.edu
Founded: 1914
Peer-reviewed publications on agriculture, gardening, integrated pest management, nutrition, childhood obesity & natural resources.
ISBN Prefix(es): 978-0-931876; 978-1-879906; 978-1-60107
Number of titles published annually: 4 Print; 30 Online; 5 E-Book
Total Titles: 350 Print; 500 Online; 5 E-Book
Returns: Whiplash, 6935 W 2100 S, West Valley City, UT 84128 (contact mvcomtois@ucanr.edu for RA prior to making a return), Contact: Roger Alvey *Tel:* 801-977-0085 *E-mail:* roger_alvey@ryder.com
Warehouse: Whiplash, 6935 W 2100 S, West Valley City, UT 48128
Membership(s): Publishers Association of the West (PubWest)

AOTA Press
Imprint of The American Occupational Therapy Association Inc (AOTA)
6116 Executive Blvd, Suite 200, North Bethesda, MD 20852-4929
Tel: 301-652-6611 *Fax:* 770-238-0414 (orders)
E-mail: aotapress@aota.org; customerservice@aota.org
Web Site: store.aota.org; www.aota.org

PUBLISHERS

Key Personnel
Acqs & Devt Mgr: Ashley Hofmann
 E-mail: ahofmann@aota.org
Founded: 1917
Single titles, newsletters, journals & magazines.
ISBN Prefix(es): 978-1-56900
Number of titles published annually: 25 Print
Total Titles: 150 Print
Orders to: PO Box 49021, Baltimore, MD 21297-4921 *Toll Free Tel:* 800-729-2682

APC Publishing
PO Box 461166, Aurora, CO 80046-1166
Tel: 303-660-2158 *Toll Free Tel:* 800-660-5107 (sales & orders)
 E-mail: mail@4wdbooks.com; orders@4wdbooks.com
Web Site: www.4wdbooks.com
Key Personnel
Publr: Peter Massey
Mktg Dir: Jeanne Massey
Founded: 1999
ISBN Prefix(es): 978-0-930657; 978-0-9665675; 978-1-930193
Number of titles published annually: 5 Print
Total Titles: 70 Print
Imprints: Outdoor Books & Maps

Aperture Books
Division of Aperture Foundation Inc
548 W 28 St, 4th fl, New York, NY 10001
SAN: 201-1832
Tel: 212-505-5555 *Toll Free Fax:* 888-623-6908
 E-mail: customerservice@aperture.org
Web Site: aperture.org
Key Personnel
Creative Dir & Publr: Lesley Martin
Exec Dir: Sarah Meister
Dir, Sales & Mktg: Kellie McLaughlin
 E-mail: kmclaughlin@aperture.org
Sales Dir, Books: Richard Gregg
 E-mail: rgregg@aperture.org
Sr Ed: Denise Wolff
Communs Mgr: Lauren Van Natten
 E-mail: lvannatten@aperture.org
Founded: 1952
Quarterly magazine; books on photography as fine art, history of photography, photojournalism, environment.
ISBN Prefix(es): 978-0-89381; 978-0-15971
Number of titles published annually: 15 Print; 3 E-Book
Total Titles: 250 Print; 13 Online; 12 E-Book
Imprints: Aperture; Masters of Photography; Writers & Artists on Photography Series
Foreign Rep(s): Ingram International (worldwide exc Canada & USA)
Distribution Center: Ingram Publisher Services, 14 Ingram Blvd, Mail Stop 631, La Vergne, TN 37086 *Toll Free Tel:* 844-841-0255 *Web Site:* www.ingrampublisherservices.com

§APH Press
Imprint of American Printing House for the Blind Inc (APH)
1839 Frankfort Ave, Louisville, KY 40206
SAN: 203-5235
Tel: 502-895-2405 *Toll Free Tel:* 800-223-1839
 E-mail: press@aph.org
Web Site: aph.org/shop
Key Personnel
Dir: Heather Spence
Founded: 1859
Text & professional books in the fields of blindness & low vision.
ISBN Prefix(es): 978-0-89128; 978-1-95072
Number of titles published annually: 2 Print; 2 E-Book
Total Titles: 60 Print; 60 E-Book

The Apocryphile Press
1700 Shattuck Ave, Suite 81, Berkeley, CA 94709
Tel: 510-290-4349
 E-mail: apocryphile@me.com
Web Site: www.apocryphilepress.com
Key Personnel
Publr & Ed: John R Mabry
Assoc Ed: Michael Asteriou
Founded: 1994
Publishes edgy spirituality, liberal religious fiction & mystical poetry.
ISBN Prefix(es): 978-1-933993; 978-0-9747623; 978-0-9764025; 978-0-9771461; 978-1-937002; 978-1-940671
Number of titles published annually: 12 Print
Total Titles: 200 Print

Apogee Press
PO Box 10066, Berkeley, CA 94709
 E-mail: apogeelibri@gmail.com
Web Site: www.apogeepress.com
Key Personnel
Ed: Valerie Coulton; Edward Smallfield; Laura Walker
Founded: 1998
Publishes innovative poetry with an emphasis on West Coast writers.
ISBN Prefix(es): 978-1-7331375
Number of titles published annually: 3 Print
Total Titles: 43 Print; 2 E-Book
Membership(s): Community of Literary Magazines & Presses (CLMP)

§APPA - Leadership in Education Facilities
1643 Prince St, Alexandria, VA 22314-2818
Mailing Address: PO Box 29, Alexandria, VA 22313-0029
Tel: 703-684-1446; 703-542-3837 (bookshop)
 E-mail: webmaster@appa.org
Web Site: www.appa.org
Key Personnel
Dir, Knowledge Mgmt: Steve Glazner
 E-mail: steve@appa.org
Assoc Dir, Pubns: Anita Dosik *E-mail:* anita@appa.org
Founded: 1914
All titles seek to enhance the development of leadership & professional management applicable to the planning, design, construction & operation of higher education facilities.
ISBN Prefix(es): 978-0-913359; 978-1-890956
Number of titles published annually: 5 Print
Total Titles: 60 Print

Appalachian Mountain Club Books
Division of Appalachian Mountain Club
10 City Sq, Boston, MA 02129
SAN: 203-4808
Tel: 617-523-0655
 E-mail: amcbooks@outdoors.org; amcpublications@outdoors.org
Web Site: www.outdoors.org
Key Personnel
VP, Mktg & Communs: Rondi Stearns
Founded: 1897
Guidebooks, maps, outdoor recreation & conservation, mountain history, nature & travel for Northeast US.
ISBN Prefix(es): 978-0-910146; 978-1-878239; 978-1-929173; 978-1-934028; 978-1-62842
Number of titles published annually: 20 Print
Total Titles: 110 Print
Foreign Rep(s): Canadian Manda Group (Canada); Windsor Books Ltd (Europe)
Distribution Center: National Book Network (NBN), 15200 NBN Way, Blue Ridge Summit, PA 17214 *Tel:* 717-794-3800 *Toll Free Tel:* 800-462-6420 *Fax:* 717-794-3828 *Toll Free Fax:* 800-338-4550 *E-mail:* customercare@nbnbooks.com *Web Site:* www.nbnbooks.com

Applause Theatre & Cinema Books
Imprint of The Globe Pequot Press
64 S Main St, Essex, CT 06426
Tel: 973-223-5039
 E-mail: info@applausepub.com
Web Site: www.applausepub.com
Key Personnel
Sr Ed: Chris Chappell *Tel:* 484-477-2813
 E-mail: chappell@rowman.com
Acq Ed: John Cerullo *E-mail:* jcerullo@rowman.com
Founded: 1983
Plays, theatre books, cinema books, entertainment, television; including DVDs.
ISBN Prefix(es): 978-0-936839; 978-1-55783
Number of titles published annually: 25 Print; 20 E-Book; 10 Audio
Total Titles: 1,000 Print; 700 E-Book; 50 Audio
Sales Office(s): National Book Network, 15200 NBN Way, Blue Ridge Summit, PA 17214 *Toll Free Tel:* 800-462-6420
Distributor for The Working Arts Library; Glenn Young Books
Foreign Rep(s): Ingram Publisher Services UK (worldwide exc Canada, Ireland, UK & USA); Publishers Group UK (UK); Woodslane (Australia, New Zealand)
Foreign Rights: Rowman & Littlefield International Sales & Marketing (Rachel Twombly) (worldwide)
Orders to: National Book Network, 15200 NBN Way, Blue Ridge Summit, PA 17214 *Toll Free Tel:* 800-462-6420
Warehouse: National Book Network, 15200 NBN Way, Blue Ridge Summit, PA 17214 *Toll Free Tel:* 800-462-6420
Distribution Center: National Book Network, 15200 NBN Way, Blue Ridge Summit, PA 17214 *Toll Free Tel:* 800-462-6420

Applewood Books
Imprint of Arcadia Publishing Inc
210 Wingo Way, Suite 200, Mount Pleasant, SC 29464
Tel: 843-853-2070
 E-mail: retailers@arcadiapublishing.com; publishing@arcadiapublishing.com
Web Site: www.arcadiapublishing.com
Key Personnel
Publr: Banks Smither
Assoc Publr: Katie Parry
Mng Ed: Caitrin Cunningham
Founded: 1976
Americana reprints.
ISBN Prefix(es): 978-0-918222; 978-1-55709; 978-1-889833; 978-1-933212; 978-1-4290; 978-0-9819430; 978-1-60889; 978-0-9844156; 978-0-9836416; 978-1-938700; 978-0-9882885; 978-1-5162
Number of titles published annually: 500 Print
Total Titles: 2,500 Print

Appraisal Institute
200 W Madison, Suite 1500, Chicago, IL 60606
Tel: 312-335-4100 *Toll Free Tel:* 888-756-4624
 E-mail: aiservice@appraisalinstitute.org
Web Site: www.appraisalinstitute.org
Key Personnel
Sr Mgr, Pubns: Eliana Munro *E-mail:* emunro@appraisalinstitute.org
Founded: 1932
Professional real estate appraisal books, monographs, periodicals & education.
ISBN Prefix(es): 978-0-911780; 978-0-922154
Number of titles published annually: 6 Print
Total Titles: 60 Print
Distributed by Dearborn Trade
Foreign Rep(s): Royal Institution of Chartered Surveyors (Africa, Caribbean, Commonwealth, Ethiopia, Europe, Far East)

§Apress Media LLC
Division of Springer Nature
One New York Plaza, Suite 4600, New York, NY 10004-1562
Tel: 212-460-1500

U.S. PUBLISHERS

E-mail: editorial@apress.com; customerservice@springernature.com
Web Site: www.apress.com
Key Personnel
Mng Dir: Welmoed Spahr *E-mail:* welmoed.spahr@springer.com
Edit Dir: Susan McDermott *E-mail:* susan.mcdermott@apress.com
Devt Ed: Laura Berendson *E-mail:* laura.berendson@apress.com; Jim Markham *E-mail:* james.markham@apress.com
Technical publisher devoted to meeting the needs of IT professionals, software developers & programmers with books in print & electronic format.
ISBN Prefix(es): 978-1-893115; 978-1-59059; 978-1-4302
Total Titles: 3,000 Print

§APS PRESS
Imprint of The American Phytopathological Society (APS)
3340 Pilot Knob Rd, St Paul, MN 55121
Tel: 651-454-7250 *Toll Free Tel:* 800-328-7560 *Fax:* 651-454-0766
E-mail: aps@scisoc.org
Web Site: my.apsnet.org/apsstore
Key Personnel
EVP: Amy Hope *E-mail:* ahope@scisoc.org
Pubns Mktg Dir: Greg Grahek *Tel:* 651-454-7250 ext 141 *E-mail:* ggrahek@scisoc.org
Pubns Mktg Coord: Dawn Wuest *Tel:* 651-994-3838 *E-mail:* dwuest@scisoc.org
Founded: 1908
Publishers of key reference books, field guides, laboratory manuals & other scientific titles related to plant health.
ISBN Prefix(es): 978-0-89054
Number of titles published annually: 10 Print; 2 CD-ROM; 4 Online
Total Titles: 300 Print; 40 CD-ROM; 2 Online

APS Press, see American Philosophical Society Press

§Arbordale Publishing
612 Johnnie Dodds Blvd, Suite A2, Mount Pleasant, SC 29464
SAN: 256-6109
Tel: 843-971-6722 *Toll Free Tel:* 877-243-3457 *Fax:* 843-216-3804
E-mail: info@arbordalepublishing.com
Web Site: www.arbordalepublishing.com
Key Personnel
Publr: Mr Lee German *E-mail:* leegerman@arbordalepublishing.com
Ed: Donna German *E-mail:* donna@arbordalepublishing.com
Off Mgr: Elma Haley *E-mail:* elma@arbordalepublishing.com
Founded: 2005
Company on a mission to create picture books that will excite children's imagination, are artistically spectacular & have educational value. Most of our stories are fictional but relate to a nonfictional theme of science, nature or animals. Each book is seriously vetted for scientific accuracy before publication. We reserve 3-5 pages in the back of each book to add our "Creative Minds" section, loaded with fun facts, crafts & games to supplement the educational thread of the book. Ebooks with auto read, auto flip & selectable English & Spanish text in audio.
ISBN Prefix(es): 978-0-9777423; 978-1-60718; 978-1-62855; 978-1-934358; 978-0-9764943; 978-0-9768823
Number of titles published annually: 36 Print; 24 Online; 27 E-Book; 27 Audio
Total Titles: 228 Print; 303 Online; 303 E-Book; 303 Audio

Foreign Rep(s): Ediciones Enlace de PR (Puerto Rico)
Foreign Rights: Sylvia Hayes Literary Agency
Distribution Center: Follett School Solutions Inc, 1340 Ridgeview Dr, McHenry, IL 60050 *Tel:* 815-759-1700 *Toll Free Tel:* 888-511-5114 (cust serv) *Fax:* 815-459-9831 *Toll Free Fax:* 800-852-5458 *E-mail:* info@follettlearning.com *Web Site:* www.follettlearning.com SAN: 169-1902
Mackin Educational Resources, 3505 County Rd 42 W, Burnsville, MN 55306 *Tel:* 952-895-9540 *Toll Free Tel:* 800-245-9540 *Fax:* 952-894-8806 *Toll Free Fax:* 800-369-5490 *E-mail:* customerservice@mackin.com *Web Site:* www.mackin.com
The Booksource Inc, 1230 Macklind Ave, St Louis, MO 63110 *Toll Free Tel:* 800-444-0435 *Toll Free Fax:* 800-647-1923 *E-mail:* service@booksource.com *Web Site:* www.booksource.com
Baker & Taylor, 2550 W Tyvola Rd, Suite 300, Charlotte, NC 28217 *Toll Free Tel:* 800-775-1800 *Fax:* 704-998-3100 *E-mail:* btinfo@baker-taylor.com *Web Site:* www.baker-taylor.com
Ingram, One Ingram Blvd, La Vergne, TN 37086 *Tel:* 615-793-5000 *Toll Free Tel:* 800-937-8200 *E-mail:* customer.service@ingrambook.com *Web Site:* www.ingrambook.com
Membership(s): American Booksellers Association (ABA); BookSense Publisher Partner; The Children's Book Council (CBC); Florida Authors & Publishers Association Inc (FAPA); Independent Book Publishers Association (IBPA); International Literacy Association (ILA); National Association for Bilingual Education; National Association of Book Entrepreneurs (NABE)

Arcade Publishing Inc
Imprint of Skyhorse Publishing Inc
307 W 36 St, 11th fl, New York, NY 10018
Tel: 212-643-6816 *Fax:* 212-643-6819
E-mail: info@skyhorsepublishing.com (subs & foreign rts)
Web Site: www.arcadepub.com
Key Personnel
Pres & Publr: Tony Lyons
Ed: Stephan Zguta
Founded: 1988
Trade fiction & literary nonfiction-adult.
ISBN Prefix(es): 978-1-61145; 978-1-5107; 978-1-62872; 978-1-64821; 978-1-950691; 978-1-951627; 978-1-950994; 978-1-956763
Number of titles published annually: 25 Print; 25 E-Book
Total Titles: 700 Print
Imprints: Arcade CrimeWise
Distributed by Simon & Schuster, LLC

Arcadia Publishing Inc
210 Wingo Way, Suite 200, Mount Pleasant, SC 29464
SAN: 255-268X
Tel: 843-853-2070
E-mail: retailers@arcadiapublishing.com
Web Site: www.arcadiapublishing.com
Key Personnel
CEO: Brittain Phillips
COO: Matthew Gildea
Assoc Publr: Katie Parry
Dir, IT: William Brandt
Dir, Sales: Amy Kaneko
Publg Dir, Arcadia & The History Press: Adam Ferrell; Kate Jenkins
Publg Dir, Arcadia Children's Books: Nancy Ellwood
Mng Ed: David Mandel
Field Sales Mgr: Chuck Deane
Natl Sales Mgr: Aline Matushev
Founded: 1992
Local & regional content.

ISBN Prefix(es): 978-0-7385; 978-1-4396; 978-1-4671
Number of titles published annually: 500 Print
Total Titles: 17,000 Print; 6,000 E-Book
Imprints: Applewood Books; Arcadia Children's Books; Arcadia Publishing; Belt Publishing; Commonwealth Editions; The History Press; Pelican Children's Publishing; Pelican Publishing
See separate listing for:
Applewood Books
Commonwealth Editions
Pelican Publishing

Arcana Publishing, see Lotus Press

ARE Press
Division of The Association for Research & Enlightenment Inc (ARE)
215 67 St, Virginia Beach, VA 23451
Tel: 757-428-3588 *Toll Free Tel:* 800-333-4499
Web Site: www.edgarcayce.org
Key Personnel
Chief of Staff & Dir, Trade Sales/Rts & Perms: Cassie McQuagge *Tel:* 757-457-7210 *E-mail:* cassie.mcquagge@edgarcayce.org
Dir, IT & Public Info: Tim Duckworth *Tel:* 757-457-7199 *E-mail:* tim@edgarcayce.org
Founded: 1931
Holistic health & spiritual development, based on Edgar Cayce material.
ISBN Prefix(es): 978-0-87604
Number of titles published annually: 1 Print; 2 E-Book; 2 Audio
Total Titles: 88 Print; 120 E-Book; 12 Audio
Imprints: 4th Dimension Press

Ariadne Press
270 Goins Ct, Riverside, CA 92507
Tel: 951-684-9202
E-mail: ariadnepress@aol.com
Web Site: www.ariadnebooks.com
Key Personnel
Partner: Jorun Johns
Founded: 1988
Studies in Austrian literature, culture & thought.
ISBN Prefix(es): 978-0-929497; 978-1-57241
Number of titles published annually: 12 Print
Total Titles: 205 Print
Foreign Rep(s): Gazelle Book Services Ltd (UK); Schaden (Austria)
Foreign Rights: Gazelle Book Services Ltd (UK)

§Ariel Press
Subsidiary of Light
2317 Quail Cove Dr, Jasper, GA 30143
Mailing Address: PO Box 251, Marble Hill, GA 30148
Tel: 770-894-4226
E-mail: lig201@lightariel.com
Web Site: www.lightariel.com
Key Personnel
Pres & Publr: Carl Japikse
Art Dir: Nancy Maxwell
Founded: 1976
Nonfiction hardcover & paperbound books; essays & subscription series on personal growth, creativity, holistic health & psychic phenomena; esoteric fiction; reprints.
ISBN Prefix(es): 978-0-89804
Number of titles published annually: 11 Print; 10 E-Book
Total Titles: 200 Print; 25 E-Book
Imprints: Enthea Press; Kudzu House
Distributor for Enthea Press; Kudzu House

The Arion Press
Division of Lyra Corp
The Presidio, 1802 Hays St, San Francisco, CA 94129
SAN: 203-1361

PUBLISHERS

Tel: 415-668-2542 Fax: 415-668-2550
E-mail: arionpress@arionpress.com
Web Site: www.arionpress.com
Key Personnel
Mktg & Prog Assoc: Alice Lin
Founded: 1974
Fine, limited edition illustrated books of fiction, literature & poetry.
ISBN Prefix(es): 978-0-910457
Number of titles published annually: 3 Print
Total Titles: 110 Print
Divisions: M & H Type

Jason Aronson Inc
Imprint of Rowman & Littlefield Publishing Group
4501 Forbes Blvd, Suite 200, Lanham, MD 20706
SAN: 201-0127
Tel: 301-459-3366 Toll Free Tel: 800-462-6420 ext 3024 (cust serv) Fax: 301-429-5748
Toll Free Fax: 800-338-4550 (cust serv)
E-mail: orders@rowman.com; customercare@rowman.com
Web Site: www.rowman.com
Key Personnel
SVP & Publr: Julie E Kirsch Tel: 301-459-3366 ext 5309 E-mail: jkirsch@rowman.com
Exec Channel Mgr, Academic & Spec Libs: Kim Lyons Tel: 301-459-3366 ext 5602 E-mail: klyons@rowman.com
Perms & Alternate Format for Students with Disabilities: Rachel Twombly Tel: 301-459-3366 ext 5420 E-mail: rtwombly@rowman.com
Founded: 1965
Professional books in psychotherapy, psychoanalysis & psychology.
ISBN Prefix(es): 978-0-87668; 978-1-56821; 978-0-7657; 978-1-4425
Number of titles published annually: 25 Print; 25 E-Book
Total Titles: 1,700 Print
Foreign Rep(s): Academic Marketing Services Pty Ltd (Botswana, Namibia, South Africa, Zimbabwe); APD Singapore Pte Ltd (Brunei, Cambodia, Indonesia, Laos, Malaysia, Singapore, Thailand, Vietnam); Asia Publishers Service Ltd (China, Hong Kong, Philippines, South Korea, Taiwan); Avicenna Partnership Ltd (Afghanistan, Algeria, Armenia, Bahrain, Cyprus, Egypt, Iran, Iraq, Jordan, Kuwait, Lebanon, Libya, Morocco, Oman, Palestine, Qatar, Saudi Arabia, Sudan, Syria, Tunisia, United Arab Emirates, Yemen); Durnell Marketing Ltd (Austria, Baltic States, Belgium, Czechia, Denmark, Finland, France, Germany, Greece, Hungary, Iceland, Italy, Malta, Netherlands, Norway, Poland, Portugal, Slovakia, Slovenia, Spain, Sweden, Switzerland); Ingram Publisher Services UK; Overleaf (Bangladesh, Bhutan, India, Nepal, Sri Lanka); United Publishers Service Ltd (Japan, South Korea)

Art Image Publications
Division of Beauchemin International Inc
PO Box 160, Derby Line, VT 05830
Toll Free Tel: 800-361-2598 Toll Free Fax: 800-559-2598
E-mail: info@artimagepublications.com; customer.service@artimagepublications.com
Web Site: www.artimagepublications.com
Key Personnel
Pres: Yvan Boulerice
Secy: Francoise Desjardins
Founded: 1980
ISBN Prefix(es): 978-1-896876; 978-1-55292
Number of titles published annually: 12 Print
Total Titles: 52 Print

The Art Institute of Chicago
111 S Michigan Ave, Chicago, IL 60603-6404
SAN: 204-479X

Tel: 312-443-3600 Toll Free Tel: 855-301-9612
E-mail: aicshop@artic.edu
Web Site: www.artic.edu/print-publications; shop.artic.edu
Key Personnel
Pres & Eloise W Martin Dir: James Rondeau
Dir, Prodn: Lauren Makholm; Joseph Mohan
Mgr, Rts & Images: Katie Levi
Founded: 1879
Exhibition catalogues, popular & scholarly art books on the museum's permanent collection: African art & Indian art of the Americas; American art; Ancient & Byzantine art; architecture & design; Asian art; contemporary art; European painting, sculpture & decorative arts; photography; prints & drawings; textiles.
ISBN Prefix(es): 978-0-86559; 978-0-300
Number of titles published annually: 10 Print; 1 Online
Total Titles: 131 Print; 19 Online; 1 E-Book
Distributed by Yale University Press

§Art of Living, PrimaMedia Inc
1250 Bethlehem Pike, Suite 241, Hatfield, PA 19440
SAN: 299-8858
Tel: 267-421-7326
E-mail: info@artoflivingprimamedia.com
Web Site: artoflivingprimamedia.com
Key Personnel
CEO: Maria Liberati
Ed: Gia Carispat E-mail: primamedia12@yahoo.com
Billing: Joan Campo E-mail: primamedia40@gmail.com
Orders & Cust Serv: Sue Thomson
Orders & Returns: Sue Timmons Thomas
Contact: Katherine Rafter E-mail: primamedia4@yahoo.com
Founded: 2005
Multimedia content & boutique publishing company. Publisher of the award-winning book series *The Basic Art of Italian Cooking* & *The Basic Art*. Creates multimedia content in the genres of food, home, DIY, garden, art, culture, recipes & style. Orders are accepted by e-mail (preferred) or telephone.
ISBN Prefix(es): 978-1-928911
Number of titles published annually: 20 Print; 10 E-Book
Total Titles: 25 Print; 35 Online; 35 E-Book
Distribution Center: Amazon.com
Follett School Solutions Inc, 1340 Ridgeview Dr, McHenry, IL 60050 Tel: 815-759-1700 Toll Free Tel: 888-511-5114 (cust serv) Fax: 815-759-9831 Toll Free Fax: 800-852-5458 E-mail: info@follettlearning.com Web Site: www.follettlearning.com SAN: 169-1902
Lightning Source/Ingram, One Ingram Blvd, La Vergne, TN 37086 Tel: 615-793-5000 Web Site: www.ingramcontent.com

ArtAge Publications
PO Box 19955, Portland, OR 97280
Tel: 503-246-3000 Toll Free Tel: 800-858-4998
Web Site: www.seniortheatre.com
Key Personnel
Pres: Bonnie L Vorenberg E-mail: bonniev@seniortheatre.com
Founded: 1997
The Senior Theatre Resource Center has the largest collection of plays, books & information for older performers. We help older performers fulfill their theatrical dreams.
ISBN Prefix(es): 978-0-9669412
Number of titles published annually: 45 Print; 45 Online; 27 E-Book; 5 Audio
Total Titles: 400 Print; 300 Online; 275 E-Book; 11 Audio
Returns: 7845 SW Capitol Hwy, Suite 12, Portland, OR 97219

Arte Publico Press
Affiliate of University of Houston
4902 Gulf Fwy, Bldg 19, Rm 100, Houston, TX 77204-2004
Tel: 713-743-2998 (orders)
E-mail: appinfo@uh.edu; bkorders@uh.edu
Web Site: artepublicopress.com
Key Personnel
Publr: Dr Nicolas Kanellos
Founded: 1979
Books by American Hispanic authors.
ISBN Prefix(es): 978-0-934770; 978-1-55885; 978-1-61192 (ebooks); 978-1-5185 (ebooks)
Number of titles published annually: 20 Print
Total Titles: 630 Print; 1,500 E-Book
Imprints: Pinata Books
Foreign Rights: Agencia Literaria Virginia Lopez-Ballesteros (Spain); Villas-Boas & Moss Agencia Literaria (Brazil)
Membership(s): Association of American Publishers (AAP)

§Artech House®
Subsidiary of Horizon House Publications Inc
685 Canton St, Norwood, MA 02062
SAN: 201-1441
Tel: 781-769-9750 Toll Free Tel: 800-225-9977 Fax: 781-769-6334
E-mail: artech@artechhouse.com
Web Site: us.artechhouse.com
Key Personnel
COO: Christopher D Ernst E-mail: cernst@artechhouse.com
Publr: William M Bazzy E-mail: wmbazzy@artechhouse.com
Dir, Edit & Prodn: Darrell Judd
Exec Ed: Judi Stone
Acq Ed: Natalie McGregor E-mail: nmcgregor@artechhouse.com
Sr Mgr, Mktg: Ana Tobin E-mail: atobin@artechhouse.com
Founded: 1970
Technical & engineering.
ISBN Prefix(es): 978-0-89006; 978-1-58053; 978-1-59693; 978-1-60807; 978-1-60783; 978-1-63081
Number of titles published annually: 35 Print; 35 E-Book
Total Titles: 1,500 Print; 600 E-Book
Foreign Office(s): 16 Sussex St, London SW1V 4RW, United Kingdom, Sr Commissioning Ed: Keri Dickens Tel: (020) 7596 8750 Fax: (020) 7630 0166 E-mail: artech-uk@artechhouse.com Web Site: uk.artechhouse.com
Foreign Rep(s): Akateeminen (Finland); Anglo-American Book Co (Italy); Asian Books Pvt Ltd (India, Pakistan); C V Toko Buku Topen (Indonesia); Clarke Associates Ltd (Pacific Basin); Computer Press (Sweden); D A Book Pty Ltd (Australia, New Zealand); Dai-Iti Publications Trading Co Ltd (Japan); Diaz de Santos (Spain); Dietmar Dreier (Germany); DK Book House Co Ltd (Thailand); Freihofer AG (Switzerland); Kumi Trading Co Ltd (South Korea); Librairie Lavoisier (France); Login Canada (Canada); Julio Logrado de Figueiredo Lda (Portugal); The Modern Book Co (UK); Pak Book Corp (Pakistan); Polyteknisk (Denmark); Sejong (South Korea); Ta Tong Book Co Ltd (Taiwan); Tapir (Norway); Tecmedd (Brazil); UBS Library Services (Singapore); United Publishers Services Ltd (Japan, South Korea); L Wouters (Belgium)
Foreign Rights: ABE Marketing (Poland); BSB Distribution (Germany); Fleet Publications (Chile); Foyles (UK); Hoepli (Italy); Kuwkab (Mideast); Livraria Canuto (Brazil); Papsotiriou (Greece)
Returns: Ingram Publisher Services UK, One Deltic Ave, Rooksley, Milton Keynes MK13 8LD, United Kingdom Tel: (01752) 202301 E-mail: ipsuk.cservs@ingramcontent.com Web Site: www.ingrampublisherservices.co.uk; Pub-

U.S. PUBLISHERS

lishers Storage & Shipping Corp (US only), 231 Industrial Park, 46 Development Rd, Fitchburg, MA 01420 *Tel:* 978-345-2121 *Fax:* 978-348-1233
Warehouse: Publishers Storage & Shipping Corp (US only), 231 Industrial Park, 46 Development Rd, Fitchburg, MA 01420 *Tel:* 978-345-2121 *Fax:* 978-348-1233

ArtWrite Productions
1555 Gardena Ave NE, Minneapolis, MN 55432-5848
Tel: 612-803-0436
Web Site: artwriteproductions.com; adaptedclassics.com
Key Personnel
Owner: Jerome Tiller *E-mail:* jtiller@adaptedclassics.com
Founded: 2003
Publishes books using humorous storytelling to enhance lessons in natural & social sciences. Under the imprint, Adapted Classics, we adapt stories by the world's greatest authors, using gallery-worthy illustrations to entice young adults to discover & embrace classic literature.
ISBN Prefix(es): 978-1-939846; 978-0-9777693
Number of titles published annually: 2 Print; 2 E-Book
Total Titles: 12 Print; 9 E-Book
Imprints: Adapted Classics (illustrated literature for middle school)
Distribution Center: Follett School Solutions, 1340 Ridgeview Dr, McHenry, IL 60050, Contact: Liz Michmershuizen *Tel:* 708-884-6564 *Fax:* 815-759-9552 *E-mail:* lmichmershuizen@follett.com
Baker & Taylor Books, 2550 W Tyvola Rd, Suite 300, Charlotte, NC 28217, Sr Buyer: Ms Robin Bright *Tel:* 908-541-7425 *E-mail:* robin.bright@baker-taylor.com *Web Site:* btol.com
Membership(s): Independent Book Publishers Association (IBPA); Midwest Independent Publishing Association (MIPA)

ASBO International, see Association of School Business Officials International

§ASCD
2800 Shirlington Rd, Suite 1001, Arlington, VA 22206
Tel: 703-578-9600 *Toll Free Tel:* 800-933-2723 *Fax:* 703-575-5400
E-mail: member@ascd.org; books@ascd.org
Web Site: www.ascd.org
Key Personnel
Chief Content Offr: Anthony Rebora *Tel:* 703-575-5753 *E-mail:* anthony.rebora@ascd.org
Mng Dir, Book Acqs & Editing: Genny Ostertag *Tel:* 703-575-5469 *E-mail:* gostertag@ascd.org
Dir, Book Editing & Prodn: Mary Beth Nielsen *Tel:* 703-575-5702 *E-mail:* mnielsen@ascd.org
Founded: 1943
Professional books for educators.
ISBN Prefix(es): 978-0-87120; 978-1-4166
Number of titles published annually: 50 Print; 35 E-Book
Total Titles: 480 Print; 460 E-Book
Orders to: 905 Carlow Dr, Unit B, Bolingbrook, IL 60490

§Ascend Books LLC
11722 W 91 St, Overland Park, KS 66214
SAN: 856-3454
Tel: 913-948-5500
Web Site: www.ascendbooks.com
Key Personnel
Publr & CEO: Robert Snodgrass *E-mail:* bsnodgrass@ascendbooks.com
Pubn Coord: Molly Gore *Tel:* 913-948-7635 *E-mail:* mgore@ascendbooks.com
Founded: 2008
Publisher of books on sports & entertainment topics & children's books by celebrity authors & educators.
ISBN Prefix(es): 978-0-9830619
Number of titles published annually: 12 Print; 10 E-Book
Total Titles: 125 Print; 40 E-Book
Distribution Center: Cardinal Publishers Group, 2402 N Shadeland Ave, Suite A, Indianapolis, IN 46219, Sales Mgr: Tom Doherty *Tel:* 317-352-8200 *Toll Free Tel:* 800-296-0481 *E-mail:* tdoherty@cardinalpub.com *Web Site:* cardinalpub.com
Ingram Book Co, One Ingram Blvd, La Vergne, TN 37086, Contact: Kitti McConnell *Tel:* 615-213-5335 *Toll Free Tel:* 800-937-8200 *E-mail:* kitti.mcconnell@ingramcontent.com *Web Site:* www.ingrambook.com
Membership(s): Independent Book Publishers Association (IBPA)

Ascension Press
PO Box 1990, West Chester, PA 19380
Tel: 484-875-4550 (admin) *Toll Free Tel:* 800-376-0520 (sales & cust serv) *Fax:* 484-875-4555
E-mail: orders@ascensionpress.com; newsroom@ascensionpress.com; sales@ascensionpress.com
Web Site: ascensionpress.com
Key Personnel
Pres & CEO: Jonathan Strate
Religious educational publishers.
ISBN Prefix(es): 978-1-932645; 978-0-9742238; 978-0-9659228; 978-0-9744451; 978-1-932631; 978-1-932927; 978-1-934217; 978-1-935940; 978-1-954179; 978-1-954881; 978-1-954882; 978-1-896747
Number of titles published annually: 15 Print
Total Titles: 250 Print; 200 Online; 40 Audio

§ASCP Press
Subsidiary of American Society for Clinical Pathology
33 W Monroe St, Suite 1600, Chicago, IL 60603
SAN: 207-9429
Tel: 312-541-4999 *Toll Free Tel:* 800-267-2727 *Fax:* 312-541-4998
Web Site: www.ascp.org
Key Personnel
Publr: Joshua R Weikersheimer *Tel:* 312-541-4866 *E-mail:* joshua.weikersheimer@ascp.org
Founded: 1959
Books, multimedia, exam simulation, atlases, study guides, apps for pathologists & lab professionals. Cover pathology & laboratory medicine.
ISBN Prefix(es): 978-0-89189
Number of titles published annually: 14 Print; 22 Online
Total Titles: 416 Print; 112 Online; 28 E-Book
Warehouse: 7750 Zionsville Rd, Suite 500, Indianapolis, IN 46268, Contact: Rhonda Drexler *E-mail:* rhonda.drexler@ascp.org

ASCSA Publications
321 Wall St, Princeton, NJ 08540-1515
Tel: 609-683-0800
Web Site: www.ascsa.edu.gr/publications
Founded: 1881
Publishing office for the American School of Classical Studies at Athens, an advanced research & teaching institution focused on the history & culture of Greece & the wider Greek world.
ISBN Prefix(es): 978-0-87661 (print titles); 978-1-62139 (e-book titles)
Number of titles published annually: 5 Print; 5 E-Book
Total Titles: 300 Print; 44 E-Book
Imprints: American School of Classical Studies at Athens; Gennadeion Monographs; Hesperia
Orders to: Ian Stevens Distribution, 70 Enterprise Dr, Suite 2, Bristol, CT 06010 *Tel:* 860-584-6546 *E-mail:* orders@isdistribution.com *Web Site:* isdistribution.com
Returns: Ian Stevens Distribution, 70 Enterprise Dr, Suite 2, Bristol, CT 06010 *Tel:* 860-584-6546 *E-mail:* orders@isdistribution.com *Web Site:* isdistribution.com
Shipping Address: Ian Stevens Distribution, 70 Enterprise Dr, Suite 2, Bristol, CT 06010 *Tel:* 860-584-6546 *E-mail:* orders@isdistribution.com *Web Site:* isdistribution.com
Warehouse: Ian Stevens Distribution, 70 Enterprise Dr, Suite 2, Bristol, CT 06010 *Tel:* 860-584-6546 *E-mail:* orders@isdistribution.com *Web Site:* isdistribution.com
Distribution Center: Ian Stevens Distribution, 70 Enterprise Dr, Suite 2, Bristol, CT 06010 *Tel:* 860-584-6546 *E-mail:* orders@isdistribution.com *Web Site:* isdistribution.com
Membership(s): American Association of University Presses (AAUP); Association of American Publishers Professional & Scholarly Publishing Division

ASET - The Neurodiagnostic Society
402 E Bannister Rd, Suite A, Kansas City, MO 64131-3019
Tel: 816-931-1120 *Fax:* 816-931-1145
E-mail: info@aset.org
Web Site: www.aset.org
Key Personnel
Exec Dir: Kevin Helm *Tel:* 816-945-9226 *E-mail:* kevin@aset.org
Founded: 1959
Books on EEG, evoked potentials, nerve conduction studies, long-term monitoring for epilepsy, intraoperative neuromonitoring & polysomnography/sleep technology.
ISBN Prefix(es): 978-1-57797
Number of titles published annually: 8 Print
Total Titles: 100 Print; 75 CD-ROM

Ash Tree Publishing
PO Box 64, Woodstock, NY 12498
Tel: 845-246-8081 *Fax:* 845-246-8081
Web Site: www.ashtreepublishing.com
Key Personnel
Founder & Owner: Susun Weed *E-mail:* wisewoman@herbshealing.com
Orders: Michael Dattorre
Founded: 1985
ISBN Prefix(es): 978-1-888123; 978-0-9614620
Number of titles published annually: 3 Print; 2 Audio
Total Titles: 14 Print; 3 Audio
Distribution Center: New Leaf Distributing Co, 1085 E Lotus Dr, Silver Lake, WI 53170 *Tel:* 262-889-8501 *Toll Free Tel:* 800-326-2665 *Fax:* 262-889-8598 *E-mail:* orders@newleafdist.com SAN: 169-1449

§Ashland Creek Press
2305 Ashland St, Suite C417, Ashland, OR 97520
Tel: 760-300-3620
E-mail: editors@ashlandcreekpress.com
Web Site: www.ashlandcreekpress.com
Key Personnel
Founder & Ed: Midge Raymond *E-mail:* midge@ashlandcreekpress.com; John Yunker *E-mail:* john@ashlandcreekpress.com
Founded: 2011
Small, independent publisher of books with a world view. Our mission is to publish a range of books that foster an appreciation for worlds outside our own, for nature & the animal kingdom & for the ways in which we all connect.
ISBN Prefix(es): 978-0-9796475; 978-1-61822
Number of titles published annually: 3 Print; 3 E-Book; 3 Audio
Total Titles: 36 Print; 36 E-Book; 6 Audio

PUBLISHERS

Imprints: Byte Level Books
Membership(s): Association for the Study of Literature and Environment

The Ashland Poetry Press
Affiliate of Ashland University
Bixler Center for the Humanities, Ashland University, 401 College Ave, Ashland, OH 44805
E-mail: app@ashland.edu
Web Site: www.ashlandpoetrypress.com
Key Personnel
Dir & Ed: Chuck Carlisle
Assoc Ed: Jennifer Rathbun
Founded: 1969
Publish & promote poetry submitted by new & established authors writing in English, as well as translations of Spanish poetry into English.
ISBN Prefix(es): 978-0-912592
Number of titles published annually: 3 Print
Total Titles: 100 Print
Membership(s): Community of Literary Magazines & Presses (CLMP); Independent Book Publishers Association (IBPA)

ASIS International
1625 Prince St, Alexandria, VA 22314
Tel: 703-519-6200 *Fax:* 703-519-6299
E-mail: asis@asisonline.org
Web Site: www.asisonline.org
Founded: 1955
Organization for security professionals, with more than 33,000 members worldwide. Dedicated to increasing the effectiveness & productivity of security professionals by developing educational programs & certification reference materials that address broad security interests, such as the annual seminar & exhibits, as well as specific security topics. Also advocates the role & value of the security management profession to business, the media, government entities & the public.
ISBN Prefix(es): 978-1-887056
Number of titles published annually: 3 Print; 2 CD-ROM
Total Titles: 35 Print; 2 CD-ROM

ASIS&T, see Association for Information Science & Technology (ASIS&T)

§ASM International
9639 Kinsman Rd, Materials Park, OH 44073-0002
SAN: 204-7586
Tel: 440-338-5151 *Toll Free Tel:* 800-336-5152; 800-368-9800 (Europe) *Fax:* 440-338-4634
E-mail: memberservicecenter@asminternational.org
Web Site: www.asminternational.org
Key Personnel
Mgr, Prodn: Madrid Tramble *Tel:* 440-338-5151 ext 5241
Founded: 1913
Technical & reference books.
ISBN Prefix(es): 978-0-87170; 978-0-62708; 978-0-61503
Number of titles published annually: 10 Print; 1 CD-ROM; 35 Online
Total Titles: 210 Print; 1,000 Online

§ASM Publishing
Division of American Society for Microbiology
1752 "N" St NW, Washington, DC 20036-2904
Tel: 202-737-3600
E-mail: communications@asmusa.org; service@asmusa.org
Web Site: www.asm.org; journals.asm.org
Key Personnel
Exec Publr: Melissa Junior
Founded: 1899
Microbiology, cell biology, medicine, books, journals, proceedings & abstracts.
ISBN Prefix(es): 978-1-55581; 978-0-914826; 978-1-683
Number of titles published annually: 14 Print; 15 Online
Total Titles: 250 Print; 25 Online

§Aspatore Books
Division of Thomson Reuters
610 Opperman Dr, Eagan, MN 55123
Tel: 651-687-7000 *Toll Free Tel:* 844-209-1086
E-mail: globallegalproducts@thomson.com
Web Site: store.legal.thomsonreuters.com
Founded: 1999
Legal tips from leading executives & lawyers to help attorneys expand their practice.
ISBN Prefix(es): 978-0-314; 978-1-58762; 978-1-59622
Number of titles published annually: 150 Print
Total Titles: 500 Print

Aspen Publishers Inc, see Wolters Kluwer Law & Business

Associated Music Publishers Inc, see G Schirmer Inc/Associated Music Publishers Inc

Association for Information Science & Technology (ASIS&T)
673 Potomac Station Dr, Suite 155, Leesburg, VA 20176
Tel: 301-495-0900 *Fax:* 301-495-0810
E-mail: asist@asist.org
Web Site: www.asist.org
Key Personnel
Exec Dir: Lydia Middleton *Tel:* 301-495-0900 ext 1200
Mng Ed: Garrett Doherty *Tel:* 301-495-0900 ext 1400
Founded: 1937
Provides high-quality conference programs & publications for information systems developers, online professionals, information resource managers, librarians, records managers, academics & others who "bridge the gap".
ISBN Prefix(es): 978-0-87715
Number of titles published annually: 12 Print; 1 CD-ROM; 1 Online
Total Titles: 12 Print; 1 CD-ROM; 1 Online
Distributed by Information Today, Inc; John Wiley & Sons Inc

Association for Talent Development (ATD) Press
1640 King St, Box 1443, Alexandria, VA 22314-1443
SAN: 224-8972
Tel: 703-683-8100 *Toll Free Tel:* 800-628-2783 *Fax:* 703-299-8723; 703-683-1523 (cust care)
E-mail: customercare@td.org
Web Site: www.td.org
Key Personnel
Pres & CEO: Tony Bingham
Dir, Creative & Edit: Sarah Halgas
  E-mail: shalgas@td.org
Sr Mktg Mgr, Pubns: Kay Hechler
  E-mail: khechler@td.org
Founded: 1944
Internationally renowned source of insightful & practical information for professionals & general readers on workplace learning & performance topics, including training basics, evaluation & return-on investment, instructional systems development, e-learning, management, leadership & career development.
ISBN Prefix(es): 978-1-56286; 978-1-60728
Number of titles published annually: 12 Print; 1 CD-ROM
Total Titles: 250 Print
Distribution Center: Consortium Book Sales & Distribution, 34 13 Ave NE, Suite 101, Minneapolis, MN 55413 (US & CN) *Tel:* 612-746-2600 *Toll Free Tel:* 866-400-5351
  E-mail: cbsdinfo@ingramcontent.com *Web Site:* www.cbsd.com
Ingram Publisher Services International (Africa, Asia, Australia, Caribbean, Continental Europe, Ireland, Latin America, Middle East, New Zealand & UK) *E-mail:* orders@ingramcontent.com
Membership(s): AM&P Network; Association of American Publishers (AAP)

§Association for the Advancement of Blood & Biotherapies
North Tower, 4550 Montgomery Ave, Suite 700, Bethesda, MD 20814
Tel: 301-907-6977; 301-215-6499 (orders outside US) *Toll Free Tel:* 866-222-2498 (sales) *Fax:* 301-907-6895
E-mail: aabb@aabb.org; sales@aabb.org (ordering); publications1@aabb.org (catalog)
Web Site: www.aabb.org
Key Personnel
Dir, Pubns: Laurie Munk *E-mail:* laurie@aabb.org
Mgr, Pubns: Jennifer Boyer *Tel:* 301-215-6596
  E-mail: jboyer@aabb.org
Founded: 1947 (as American Association of Blood Banks)
Professional medical society publishing texts in blood banking standards, transfusion medicine, transplantation, biotherapies & cellular therapy.
ISBN Prefix(es): 978-1-56935
Number of titles published annually: 20 Print; 20 Online
Total Titles: 83 Print; 136 Online
Returns: BrightKey Inc, Attn: AABB Returns, 1780 Crossroads Dr, Odenton, MD 21113

Association of College & Research Libraries (ACRL)
Division of The American Library Association (ALA)
225 N Michigan Ave, Suite 1300, Chicago, IL 60601
Tel: 312-280-2523; 312-280-2516
Toll Free Tel: 800-545-2433 (ext 2523)
Fax: 312-280-2520
E-mail: acrl@ala.org; alastore@ala.org
Web Site: www.ala.org/acrl; alastore.ala.org
Key Personnel
Interim Exec Dir: Allison Payne
Sr Prodn Ed: Dawn Mueller *E-mail:* dmueller@ala.org
Content Strategist: Erin Nevius *E-mail:* enevius@ala.org
Founded: 1940
Higher education association for librarians. Representing more than 9,000 academic & research librarians & interested individuals, ACRL develops programs, products & services to help academic & research librarians learn, innovate & lead within the academic community. ACRL is the largest division of The American Library Association (ALA).
ISBN Prefix(es): 978-0-8389
Number of titles published annually: 15 Print; 15 E-Book
Total Titles: 125 Print; 70 E-Book
Foreign Rep(s): Baker & Taylor International; Booknet Co Ltd (Cambodia, Laos, Myanmar, Thailand); Broad River Books (Caribbean, Latin America); Eurospan (Africa, Europe, Israel, UK); iGroup (Asia-Pacific); Ontario Library Association (Canada); PMS Publishers Services Pte Ltd (Singapore)
Orders to: Chicago Distribution Center (CDC), Attn: ALA, 11030 S Langley Ave, Chicago, IL 60628
Returns: Chicago Distribution Center (CDC), Attn: ALA, 11030 S Langley Ave, Chicago, IL 60628
Distribution Center: Chicago Distribution Center (CDC), Attn: ALA, 11030 S Langley Ave, Chicago, IL 60628

Membership(s): The American Library Association (ALA); Association for Information Science & Technology (ASIS&T); Association of Research Libraries (ARL); Modern Language Association (MLA)

Association of International Certified Public Accountants, see AICPA® & CIMA®

Association of Research Libraries (ARL)
21 Dupont Circle NW, Suite 800, Washington, DC 20036
Tel: 202-296-2296 *Fax:* 202-872-0884
E-mail: webmgr@arl.org
Web Site: www.arl.org
Key Personnel
Exec Dir: Andrew K Pace
Sr Dir, Communs: Jessica Aiwuyor
 E-mail: jaiwuyor@arl.org
Founded: 1932
Serial, occasional paper series & special topics of interest.
ISBN Prefix(es): 978-0-918006; 978-1-59407
Number of titles published annually: 4 Print; 8 Online; 4 E-Book
Total Titles: 618 Print; 188 Online; 125 E-Book
Distribution Center: ARL Publications Distribution Center, PO Box 531, Annapolis Junction, MD 20701-0531 *Tel:* 301-362-8196 *Fax:* 240-396-2479 *E-mail:* arl@brightkey.net

Association of School Business Officials International
44790 Maynard Sq, Suite 200, Ashburn, VA 20147
Tel: 703-478-0405 *Toll Free Tel:* 866-682-2729 *Fax:* 703-478-0205; 703-708-7060 (membership)
E-mail: asboreq@asbointl.org; membership@asbointl.org
Web Site: www.asbointl.org
Key Personnel
Chief Busn & Leadership Offr: Sabrina Soto *Tel:* 866-682-2729 ext 7088 *E-mail:* ssoto@asbointl.org
COO: Siobhan McMahon *Tel:* 866-682-2729 ext 7076 *E-mail:* smcmahon@asbointl.org
Exec Dir: David Lewis *Tel:* 866-682-2729 ext 7061 *E-mail:* dlewis@asbointl.org
Dir, Educ & Res: Cristin Watson *Tel:* 866-682-2279 ext 7086 *E-mail:* cwatson@asbointl.org
Dir, Membership, Engagement & Outreach: Jackie Wallenstein *Tel:* 866-682-2729 ext 7082 *E-mail:* jwallenstein@asbointl.org
Exec Asst & Governance Rel: Angela Tombul *Tel:* 866-682-2729 ext 7063 *E-mail:* atombul@asbointl.org
Founded: 1910
Professional books co-published with Rowman & Littlefield Education.
ISBN Prefix(es): 978-0-910170; 978-0-810847; 978-1-1578860
Number of titles published annually: 8 Print
Total Titles: 40 Print

Asta Publications LLC
3 E Evergreen Rd, No 1112, New City, NY 10956
Tel: 678-814-1320 *Toll Free Tel:* 800-482-4190 *Fax:* 678-814-1370
E-mail: info@astapublications.com
Web Site: www.astapublications.com
Key Personnel
CEO: Assuanta Howard *E-mail:* ahoward@astapublications.com
Founded: 2004
Delivering first-class book publishing services for corporations, entrepreneurs & individuals who understand the power of being a published author.
This publisher has indicated that 30% of their product line is author subsidized.

ISBN Prefix(es): 978-0-9777060; 978-1-934947
Number of titles published annually: 200 Print; 200 Online; 200 E-Book
Total Titles: 500 Print; 500 Online; 500 E-Book
Membership(s): The Association of Publishers for Special Sales (APSS); The Imaging Alliance

§ASTM International
100 Barr Harbor Dr, West Conshohocken, PA 19428-2959
Mailing Address: PO Box C700, West Conshohocken, PA 19428-0700
Tel: 610-832-9500; 610-832-9585 (intl) *Toll Free Tel:* 877-909-2786 (sales & cust support) *Fax:* 610-832-9555
E-mail: sales@astm.org
Web Site: www.astm.org
Key Personnel
Pres: Katharine E Morgan *Tel:* 610-832-9721
 E-mail: kmorgan@astm.org
Dir, Communs: Dan Bergels *Tel:* 610-832-9602
 E-mail: dbergels@astm.org
Founded: 1898
Standards, technical publications, data series manuals & journals on engineering, science, materials testing, safety, quality control.
ISBN Prefix(es): 978-0-8031; 978-1-6822
Number of titles published annually: 176 Print; 125 CD-ROM
Total Titles: 1,500 Print; 125 CD-ROM; 80 Online
Branch Office(s)
1120 20 St NW, Suite 390, Washington, DC 20036, Contact: Jeffrey Grove *Tel:* 202-223-8505 *E-mail:* jgrove@astm.org
Foreign Office(s): Rue de la Loi 67, 1040 Brussels, Belgium, Contact: Sara Gobbi *Tel:* (02) 8405127 *E-mail:* sgobbi@astm.org
Suite EF02, Twin Towers E, B-12 Jianguomenwai Ave, Chaoyang District, Beijing 100022, China, Contact: H U Yanan *Tel:* (010) 5109-6033 *Fax:* (010) 5109-6039 *E-mail:* nhu@astm.org
EnginZone, Monterosa 233, of 402 Chacarilla del Estanque, Surco, Lima 33, Peru, Contact: Maria Isabel Barrios *Tel:* (01) 205-5502 *E-mail:* astmlatinamerica@astm.org
One Raffles Place, Tower 2, No 27-64, Singapore 048616, Singapore, Contact: Elvin Chia *E-mail:* echia@astm.org

Astra Books for Young Readers
Imprint of Astra Publishing House Inc
19 W 21 St, No 1201, New York, NY 10010
Tel: 646-844-3485
E-mail: ahinfo@astrahouse.com; permissions@astrapublishinghouse.com
Web Site: astrapublishinghouse.com
Key Personnel
COO: Ben Schrank
Pres & CFO: Leying Jiang *E-mail:* ljiang@astrapublishinghouse.com
VP, Publg/Publr, Kane Press, Calkins Creek & Wordsong: Juliana Lauletta *E-mail:* jlauletta@astrapublishinghouse.com
Asst Publr: Susan Dobinick
Sr Fin Dir: Paul Boccardi
Art Dir, Hippo Park/mineditionUS: Amelia Mack
Dir, Sales & Analytics: Jack W Perry
 E-mail: jperry@astrapublishinghouse.com
Edit Dir: Rebecca Davis *E-mail:* rdavis@astrapublishinghouse.com
Edit Dir, Calkins Creek: Carolyn P Yoder
 E-mail: cyoder@astrapublishinghouse.com
Edit Dir, Hippo Park: Jill Davis *E-mail:* jdavis@astrapublishinghouse.com
Edit Dir, Minerva: Maria Russo
Mktg Dir: Kerry McManus *E-mail:* kmcmanus@astrapublishinghouse.com
Exec Ed, Kane Press: Harold Underdown
Ed-at-Large, Astra Young Readers/mineditionUS: Leonard Marcus
Assoc Ed: Millie von Platen
Assoc Ed, Calkins Creek: Thalia Leaf

Asst Ed, Hippo Park/mineditionUS: Octavia Saenz
Asst Mktg & Publicity Mgr: Chelsea Abdullah
Founded: 2021
Books for children of all ages.
ISBN Prefix(es): 978-1-56397; 978-1-57565; 978-1-59078; 978-1-63592; 978-1-87809
Number of titles published annually: 40 Print
Total Titles: 800 Print
Imprints: Astra Young Readers (fiction & nonfiction); Calkins Creek (history); Hippo Park (illustrated books for children under 12); Kane Press (STEM/education fiction & nonfiction); Minerva; WordSong (poetry)
Foreign Rights: 2 Seas Agency
Returns: Penguin Random House, Attn Returns Dept, 1019 N State Rd 47, Crawfordsville, IN 47933; Penguin Random House of Canada Ltd, Attn Returns Dept, 6971 Columbus Rd, Mississauga, ON L5T 1K1, Canada
Distribution Center: Penguin Random House LLC, 400 Hahn Rd, Westminster, MD 21157 *Toll Free Tel:* 800-726-0600; 800-733-3000 *Toll Free Fax:* 800-659-2436 *E-mail:* csorders@penguinrandomhouse.com
Penguin Random House Canada, 320 Front St W, Suite 1400, Toronto, ON M5V 3B6, Canada *Toll Free Tel:* 888-523-9292 *Toll Free Fax:* 888-562-9924

Astragal Press
Imprint of The Globe Pequot Press
31 E Main St, New Kingstown, PA 17072
Mailing Address: PO Box 90, New Kingstown, PA 17072-0090
Tel: 717-590-8974
Web Site: astragalpress.com
Key Personnel
Publr, Globe Pequot Trade Div: Judith Schnell
 E-mail: jschnell@rowman.com
Founded: 1983
Early tools, trades & technology.
ISBN Prefix(es): 978-0-9618088; 978-1-879335; 978-1-931626; 978-1-4930; 978-0-904638
Number of titles published annually: 5 Print
Total Titles: 89 Print; 89 Online
Distribution Center: National Book Network (NBN), 15200 NBN Way, Blue Ridge Summit, PA 17214 *Tel:* 717-794-3800 *Toll Free Tel:* 800-462-6420 (orders) *Fax:* 717-794-3828 *Toll Free Fax:* 800-338-4550 (orders)
E-mail: customercare@nbnbooks.com

The Astronomical Society of the Pacific
390 Ashton Ave, San Francisco, CA 94112
Tel: 415-337-1100; 415-715-1414 (cust serv) *Toll Free Tel:* 800-335-2624 (cust serv) *Fax:* 415-337-5205
E-mail: service@astrosociety.org
Web Site: astrosociety.org
Key Personnel
Ed-in-Chief, PASP: Jeff Mangum
 E-mail: jmangum@nrao.edu
Mng Ed, ASPCS: Joseph Jensen
 E-mail: jjensen@aspbooks.org
Assoc Ed, ASPCS: Jonathan Barnes
 E-mail: jonathan@aspbooks.org
Pubns Mgr, ASPCS: Beth Wardeell
 E-mail: publicationmanager@aspbooks.org
Founded: 1889
Books, booklets, tapes, slide sets, software & other educational materials about astronomy; conference proceedings. Publisher of *Mercury Magazine*, *Publications of the Astronomical Society of the Pacific* journal & *Astronomical Society of the Pacific Conference Series*.
ISBN Prefix(es): 978-0-937707; 978-1-886733; 978-1-58381
Number of titles published annually: 20 Print; 1 CD-ROM; 20 E-Book; 1 Audio
Total Titles: 360 Print; 1 CD-ROM; 60 E-Book; 1 Audio

PUBLISHERS
U.S. PUBLISHERS

ATD Press, see Association for Talent Development (ATD) Press

Atheneum Books for Young Readers, see Simon & Schuster Children's Publishing

§Atlantic Publishing Group Inc
1210 SW 23 Place, Ocala, FL 34471
Tel: 352-622-1825
E-mail: sales@atlantic-pub.com
Web Site: www.atlantic-pub.com
Key Personnel
Pres: Douglas R Brown
VP: Sherri L Brown
Founded: 1982
Provides millions of readers information to jump-start their careers, start businesses, manage employees, invest, plan for retirement, learn technologies, build relationships & live rewarding, fulfilling lives.
ISBN Prefix(es): 978-0-910627; 978-1-60138; 978-1-62023
Number of titles published annually: 100 Print; 25 CD-ROM
Total Titles: 500 Print; 150 CD-ROM
Membership(s): American Booksellers Association (ABA); American Publishers Association; Association of American Publishers (AAP); The Association of Publishers for Special Sales (APSS); Florida Authors & Publishers Association Inc (FAPA); Independent Book Publishers Association (IBPA); Young Adult Library Services Association (YALSA)

§Atlas Publishing
16050 Circa de Lindo, Rancho Santa Fe, CA 92091
Tel: 858-790-1944
E-mail: permissions@atlaspublishing.biz
Web Site: www.atlaspublishing.biz
Key Personnel
Mng Ed: Brent D Tharp *E-mail:* brent@atlaspublishing.biz
Founded: 2011
Traditional publisher of children's & nonfiction titles. Author services also available for books not printed under our imprint. Please note that the only fiction titles that we print under our imprint are children's books. We provide editing services for all genres, but publish only children's books & nonfiction titles. Writers interested in submitting materials may do so directly, but initial submissions should be limited to query letters, sell sheets & synopses. Please do not submit full mss or attachments at the initial query stage as they will not be reviewed.
ISBN Prefix(es): 978-0-9969679; 978-1-945033
Number of titles published annually: 4 Print; 3 E-Book
Total Titles: 10 Print; 10 E-Book
Distribution Center: Ingram
Membership(s): Editorial Freelancers Association (EFA); Independent Book Publishers Association (IBPA)

Atria Books
Imprint of Atria Publishing Group
1230 Avenue of the Americas, New York, NY 10020
Tel: 212-698-7000 *Fax:* 212-698-7007
Web Site: www.simonandschuster.com
Key Personnel
SVP & Publr: Libby McGuire *Tel:* 212-698-7675 *E-mail:* libby.mcguire@simonandschuster.com
SVP & Ed-in-Chief, Emily Bestler Books: Emily Bestler *Tel:* 212-698-7685 *E-mail:* emily.bestler@simonandschuster.com
VP, Publr & Ed-in-Chief, Marysue Rucci Books: Marysue Rucci *E-mail:* marysue.rucci@simonandschuster.com
VP & Ed-in-Chief: Peter Borland *Tel:* 212-698-7569 *E-mail:* peter.borland@simonandschuster.com
VP & Ed-in-Chief, Simon Element: Doris Cooper *E-mail:* doris.cooper@simonandschuster.com
VP & Publr, One Signal Publishers: Alessandra Bastagli *E-mail:* alessandra.bastagli@simonandschuster.com
VP & Publr, Simon Element & Simon Acumen: Richard Rhorer *E-mail:* richard.rhorer@simonandschuster.com
VP & Assoc Publr, Primero Sueno Press/Atria Books: Michelle Herrera Mulligan *Tel:* 212-698-7696 *E-mail:* michelle.herreramulligan@simonandschuster.com
VP & Exec Ed, Simon Element: Justin Schwartz *E-mail:* justin.schwartz@simonandschuster.com
VP & Dir of Backlist Mktg: Suzanne Donahue *E-mail:* suzanne.donahue@simonandschuster.com
Assoc Publr & Dir, Mktg: Dana Trocker *E-mail:* dana.trocker@simonandschuster.com
Sr Mktg Dir: Karlyn Hixson *E-mail:* karlyn.hixson@paramount.com
Sr Mktg Dir, Simon Element: Elizabeth Breeden *E-mail:* elizabeth.breeden@simonandschuster.com
Mktg & Soc Media Dir: Morgan (Hoit) Pager *E-mail:* morgan.prager@simonandschuster.com
Sr Mktg Mgr, Simon Element: Alyssa diPierro *E-mail:* alyssa.dipierro@simonandschuster.com
Mktg Mgr: Maudee Genao *E-mail:* maudee.genao@simonandschuster.com; Zakiya Jamal *E-mail:* zakiya.jamal@simonandschuster.com; Dayna Johnson *E-mail:* dayna.johnson@simonandschuster.com
Mktg Mgr, Simon Element: Francesca Carlos *E-mail:* francesca.carlos@simonandschuster.com
Mktg Assoc, Simon Element & Marysue Rucci Books: Ingrid Carabulea *E-mail:* ingrid.carabulea@simonandschuster.com
Mktg & Soc Media Coord: Jolena Podolsky *E-mail:* jolena.podolsky@simonandschuster.com
Deputy Dir, Publicity: Joanna Pinsker *E-mail:* joanna.pinsker@simonandschuster.com
Sr Publicity Dir, Simon Element & Marysue Rucci Books: Jessica Preeg *E-mail:* jessica.preeg@simonandschuster.com
Publicity & Mktg Dir: David Brown *E-mail:* david.brown@simonandschuster.com
Assoc Dir, Publicity & Mktg, Primero Sueno Press: Maria Mann *E-mail:* maria.mann@simonandschuster.com
VP & Dir, Publicity: Lisa Sciambra *Tel:* 212-698-7086 *E-mail:* lisa.sciambra@simonandschuster.com
Deputy Dir, Publicity: Shida Carr *E-mail:* shida.carr@simonandschuster.com
Sr Publicity Mgr: Alison Hinchliffe *E-mail:* alison.hinchliffe@simonandschuster.com; Falon Kirby *E-mail:* falon.kirby@simonandschuster.com
Publicity Mgr, Simon Element: Stacy Reichgott *E-mail:* stacy.reichgott@simonandschuster.com
Publicity Mgr, Simon Element & Marysue Rucci Books: Clare Maurer *E-mail:* clare.maurer@simonandschuster.com
Sr Publicist: Gena Lanzi *E-mail:* gena.lanzi@simonandschuster.com; Holly Rice-Baturin *E-mail:* holly.ricebaturin@simonandschuster.com; Megan Rudloff *E-mail:* megan.rudloff@simonandschuster.com
Publicist, Simon Element: Nan Rittenhouse *E-mail:* nan.rittenhouse@simonandschuster.com
Assoc Publicist: Camila Araujo *E-mail:* camila.araujo@simonandschuster.com; Debbie Norflus *E-mail:* debbie.norflus@simonandschuster.com; Sierra Swanson *E-mail:* sierra.swanson@simonandschuster.com
Art Dir, Simon Element: Jenny Carrow *E-mail:* jenny.carrow@simonandschuster.com
Edit Dir, Nonfiction: Kate Napolitano *E-mail:* kate.napolitano@simonandschuster.com
Exec Ed: Laura Brown *E-mail:* laura.brown@simonandschuster.com; Kaitlin Olson *Tel:* 212-698-7342 *E-mail:* kaitlin.olson@simonandschuster.com; Emilia Rhodes *E-mail:* emilia.rhodes@simonandschuster.com; Yaniv Soha *E-mail:* yaniv.soha@simonandschuster.com
Exec Ed, Marysue Rucci Books: Anne Speyer
Exec Ed, Simon Acumen: Stephanie Hitchcock *E-mail:* stephanie.hitchcock@simonandschuster.com
Exec Ed, Simon Element & Marysue Rucci Books: Emily Graff *E-mail:* emily.graff@simonandschuster.com
Exec Ed, Simon Element: Samantha Weiner *E-mail:* samantha.weiner@simonandschuster.com
Mng Ed, Simon Element: Jessie McNiel *E-mail:* jessie.mcniel@simonandschuster.com
Sr Ed: Melanie Iglesias Perez *E-mail:* melanie.iglesiasperez@simonandschuster.com; Loan Le *E-mail:* loan.le@simonandschuster.com; Jenny Xu *E-mail:* jenny.xu@simonandschuster.com
Sr Ed, Emily Bestler Books: Sarah Grill *E-mail:* sarah.grill@simonandschuster.com
Sr Ed, Emily Bestler Books/Atria Books: Lara Jones *E-mail:* lara.jones@simonandschuster.com
Sr Ed, One Signal Publishers & Black Privilege Publishing: Nicholas Ciani *E-mail:* nicholas.ciari@simonandschuster.com
Sr Ed, Simon Element: Veronica (Ronnie) Alvarado *E-mail:* veronica.alvarado@simonandschuster.com
Ed: Sean deLone *E-mail:* sean.delone@simonandschuster.com
Ed, Primero Sueno Press: Maria Mann *E-mail:* maria.mann@simonandschuster.com; Yezanira Venecia *E-mail:* yezanira.venecia@simonandschuster.com
Ed, Simon Acumen: Kimberly Meilun *E-mail:* kimberly.meilun@simonandschuster.com
Assoc Ed, Simon Acumen: Karina Leon *E-mail:* karina.leon@simonandschuster.com
Asst Ed: Jade Hui *E-mail:* jade.hui@simonandschuster.com
Asst Ed, One Signal Publishers: Abby Mohr *E-mail:* abby.mohr@simonandschuster.com
Asst Ed, Simon Element: Maria Espinosa *E-mail:* maria.espinosa@simonandschuster.com; Emma Taussig *E-mail:* emma.taussig@simonandschuster.com
Assoc Ed, Primero Sueno Press: Norma Perez-Hernandez *E-mail:* norma.perezhernandez@simonandschuster.com
Publg Coord: Abby Velasco *E-mail:* abby.velasco@simonandschuster.com
Publg Coord, Marysue Rucci Books: Andy Jiaming Tang *E-mail:* jiaming.tang@simonandschuster.com
Founded: 2002
ISBN Prefix(es): 978-0-671; 978-0-7434; 978-0-7432
Imprints: Atria Books Espanol; Atria Trade Paperbacks; Emily Bestler Books; Beyond Words; Black Privilege Publishing; Howard Books; Keywords Press (in collaboration with United Talent Agency); Marble Arch Press™; One Signal Publishers; Primero Sueno Press; Simon Element (includes Marysue Rucci Books & Simon Acumen); Washington Square Press
Foreign Rights: Akcali Copyright Agency (Turkey); Bardon-Chinese Media Agency (China, Thailand); The Book Publishers' Association of Israel, International Promotion & Literary Rights Department (Israel); BookLab Literary Agency (Poland); The Italian Literary Agency Srl (Italy); JLM Literary Agency (Greece); Mohrbooks AG Literary Agency (Germany); La Nouvelle Agency (France); Andrew Nurnberg Associates Ltd (Bulgaria,

U.S. PUBLISHERS

Croatia, Estonia, Hungary, Latvia, Lithuania, Montenegro, North Macedonia, Romania, Russia, Serbia, Slovakia, Slovenia, Ukraine); Sane Toregard Agency (Denmark, Finland, Iceland, Norway, Sweden); Tuttle-Mori Agency Inc (Japan); Eric Yang Agency (South Korea)

§Augsburg Fortress Publishers, Publishing House of the Evangelical Lutheran Church in America
411 Washington Ave N, 3rd fl, Minneapolis, MN 55401
SAN: 169-4081
Mailing Address: PO Box 1209, Minneapolis, MN 55440-1209
Tel: 612-330-3300 *Toll Free Tel:* 800-426-0115 (ext 639, subns); 800-328-4648 (orders)
Fax: 612-330-3455
E-mail: info@augsburgfortress.org; copyright@augsburgfortress.org (reprint permission requests); customercare@augsburgfortress.org
Web Site: www.augsburgfortress.org; www.1517.media
Key Personnel
Pres & CEO: Tim Blevins *Tel:* 612-330-3300 ext 400 *E-mail:* blevinst@1517.media
Publr, Worship & Music: Suzanne Burke *E-mail:* burkes@augsburgfortress.org
Publg Dir: Andrew DeYoung *E-mail:* deyounga@1517.media
Ed-in-Chief, Fortress Press: Ryan Hemmer *E-mail:* hemmerr@fortresspress.com
Perms, Pubns: Michael Moore *E-mail:* moorem@1517.media
Founded: 1855
ISBN Prefix(es): 978-0-8066; 978-0-8006
Number of titles published annually: 100 Print
Total Titles: 4,600 Print; 1,700 E-Book; 3,500 Audio
Imprints: Augsburg Fortress; Beaming Books; Broadleaf Books; Fortress Press; Sparkhouse
Sales Office(s): PO Box 1209, Minneapolis, MN 55440-1209
Foreign Rep(s): Asian Trading Corp (India); Australian Church Resources (Australia); Canaanland Distributors Sdn Bhd (Malaysia); Cross Communications Ltd (Hong Kong); Durnell Marketing (Israel); John Garratt Publishing (Australia); Glad Sounds Sdn Bhd (Malaysia); Ingram Publisher Services UK (Europe, UK); KCBS Inc (South Korea); Kyo Bun Kwan Inc (Japan); Logos Publishers Ltd (Hong Kong); MediaCom Education (Australia); N-Online Co Ltd (Japan); Pustaka Sufes Sdn Bhd (Malaysia); SKS Books Warehouse (Singapore); Soul Distributors Ltd (New Zealand); Taosheng Publishing House (Hong Kong); Tecman Management Services (Singapore)
Foreign Rights: Rowman & Littlefield Publishing Group (worldwide exc South Korea)
Billing Address: PO Box 1209, Minneapolis, MN 55440-1209
Orders to: Books International, 22830 Quicksilver Dr, Dulles, VA 20166
Warehouse: Books International, 22830 Quicksilver Dr, Dulles, VA 20166
Distribution Center: Books International, 22830 Quicksilver Dr, Dulles, VA 20166

August House Inc
3500 Piedmont Rd NE, Suite 310, Atlanta, GA 30305
Tel: 404-442-4420 *Toll Free Tel:* 800-284-8784 *Fax:* 404-442-4435
E-mail: ahinfo@augusthouse.com
Web Site: www.augusthouse.com
Key Personnel
CEO: Steve Floyd *E-mail:* steve@augusthouse.com
EVP: Graham Anthony *E-mail:* graham@augusthouse.com
Dir, Devt: Rob Cleveland *E-mail:* rob@augusthouse.com
Founded: 1979
Folklore, multicultural folktales & storytelling.
ISBN Prefix(es): 978-0-87483
Number of titles published annually: 15 Print; 30 Online; 15 E-Book
Total Titles: 350 Print; 300 Online; 15 E-Book; 71 Audio
Imprints: August House Audio; August House Little Folk; August House Story Cove
Foreign Rights: The Fielding Agency (Whitney Lee)

AuthorHouse
Division of Author Solutions LLC
1663 Liberty Dr, Bloomington, IN 47403
Toll Free Tel: 833-262-8899; 888-519-5121
E-mail: sales@authorhouse.com; vip@authorhouse.com
Web Site: www.authorhouse.com
Key Personnel
CEO: Billy Elliot
COO: Bill Becher
CIO: Joe Steinbach
Exec Asst: Vickie Breeden
Founded: 1997
The leading provider of indie book publishing, marketing & bookselling services for authors around the globe. Committed to providing the highest level of customer service. Assign each author personal publishing & marketing consultants who provide guidance throughout the process.
This publisher has indicated that 100% of their product line is author subsidized.
ISBN Prefix(es): 978-1-58500; 978-0-9675669; 978-1-58721; 978-1-58820; 978-0-7596; 978-1-4033; 978-1-4107; 978-1-4140; 978-1-4184; 978-1-4208; 978-1-6655
Number of titles published annually: 7,500 Print
Total Titles: 96,000 Print
Distribution Center: Baker & Taylor LLC, 2550 W Tyvola Rd, Suite 300, Charlotte, NC 28217
Ingram Book Group, One Ingram Blvd, La Vergne, TN 37086-1986
Membership(s): American Booksellers Association (ABA)

Authorlink® Press
Imprint of Authorlink®
103 Guadalupe Dr, Irving, TX 75039-3334
Tel: 972-402-0101
E-mail: admin@authorlink.com
Web Site: www.authorlink.com
Key Personnel
Founder, CEO & Ed-in-Chief: Doris Booth *E-mail:* dbooth@authorlink.com
Founded: 1996
Provides production & consulting services for ebooks & print-on-demand titles for about 150 self-published & small press clients per year. The parent company's new Authorlink® Books N' Flix system offers an inexpensive big data research platform for authors & small presses. *Authorlink® Writers & Readers Magazine* provides news & information about the publishing & film industry. In addition, Authorlink® publishes & represents several leading authors but is not accepting new authors at this time.
ISBN Prefix(es): 978-1-928704
Number of titles published annually: 10 Print; 150 E-Book
Total Titles: 10 Print; 150 E-Book
Orders to: Lightning Source, 1246 Heil Quaker Blvd, La Vergne, TN 37086 *Tel:* 615-213-5815 *Fax:* 615-213-4426 *E-mail:* inquiry@lightningsource.com *Web Site:* www.lightningsource.com
Distribution Center: Lightning Source, 1246 Heil Quaker Blvd, La Vergne, TN 37086 *Tel:* 615-213-5815 *Fax:* 615-213-4426
E-mail: inquiry@lightningsource.com *Web Site:* www.lightningsource.com
Membership(s): Independent Book Publishers Association (IBPA)

Autumn House Press
5530 Penn Ave, Pittsburgh, PA 15206
Tel: 412-362-2665
E-mail: info@autumnhouse.org
Web Site: www.autumnhouse.org
Key Personnel
Ed-in-Chief: Christine Stroud *E-mail:* cstroud@autumnhouse.org
Founded: 1998
Nonprofit corporation with the mission of publishing poetry, fiction & nonfiction. Submissions should be through one of the annual contests. Guidelines are posted on the web site.
Publish the online journal *Coal Hill Review*.
ISBN Prefix(es): 978-0-9669419; 978-1-932870
Number of titles published annually: 8 Print; 4 E-Book
Total Titles: 100 Print; 50 E-Book
Distribution Center: Chicago Distribution Center (CDC), 11030 S Langley Ave, Chicago, IL 60628 *Tel:* 773-702-7010 *Toll Free Fax:* 800-621-8476

§Avant-Guide
Unit of Empire Press Media Inc
244 Fifth Ave, Suite 2053, New York, NY 10001-7604
Tel: 917-512-3881 *Fax:* 212-202-7757
E-mail: info@avantguide.com; communications@avantguide.com; editor@avantguide.com
Web Site: www.avantguide.com
Key Personnel
Dir: Laura Stone
Founded: 1999
Publisher of nonfiction books on marketing, keynote speakers, travel, business as well as handbooks for keynote speakers & trends by the global trends expert Daniel Levine.
ISBN Prefix(es): 978-1-891603
Number of titles published annually: 50 Print; 50 E-Book
Total Titles: 513 Print; 513 E-Book
Imprints: Empire; Keynote Speakers Today; Top Keynote Speakers; Trends Experts
Foreign Rep(s): Hi Marketing (Europe, UK)
Foreign Rights: Publishers Group West (PGW) (Canada)
Distribution Center: Publishers Group West, 1700 Fourth St, Berkeley, CA 94710 *Tel:* 510-809-3700 *Toll Free Tel:* 866-400-5351 *Fax:* 510-809-3777

Ave Maria Press Inc
Division of United States Province of the Congregation of Holy Cross
PO Box 428, Notre Dame, IN 46556
SAN: 201-1255
Toll Free Tel: 800-282-1865 *Toll Free Fax:* 800-282-5681
E-mail: avemariapress.1@nd.edu
Web Site: www.avemariapress.com
Key Personnel
Publr & CEO: Karey Circosta
VP & Creative Dir: Kristen Hornyak Bonelli
Dir, Sales & Mktg: Heather Glenn
Edit Dir: Josh Noem
Exec Ed: Michael Amodei
Exec Ed, Ministry Resources: Eileen M Ponder
Exec Ed, Trade: Kristi M McDonald
Sr Mng Ed: Susana J Kelly
Sr Acqs Ed: Heidi Hess Saxton
Data Mktg Mgr: Lori Goodline
Digital Mktg Mgr: Rachel Smith
Publicity Mgr: Mrs Erin Pierce *Tel:* 800-282-1865 ext 223 *E-mail:* epierce@nd.edu
Sales Mgr: Kay Luther
Founded: 1865

PUBLISHERS / U.S. PUBLISHERS

Adult paperback books of religious interest; prayer books & religious education materials, programs & textbooks.
ISBN Prefix(es): 978-0-87793 (Ave Maria Press); 978-0-939516 (Forest of Peace); 978-0-87061 (Christian Classics); 978-1-893732 (Sorin Books); 978-1-59471 (Ave Maria Press); 978-1-933495 (Sorin Books)
Number of titles published annually: 40 Print
Total Titles: 550 Print
Imprints: Christian Classics; Forest of Peace; Sorin Books
Foreign Rep(s): Bayard Novalis Distribution (Canada); Garratt Publishing (Australia); Pleroma Christian Supplies (New Zealand); Redemptorist Publishing (Europe)
Returns: 1865 Moreau Dr, Notre Dame, IN 46556
Distribution Center: Baker & Taylor, 2550 W Tyvola Rd, Suite 300, Charlotte, NC 28217 Tel: 704-998-3100 Toll Free Tel: 800-775-1800 E-mail: btinfo@baker-taylor.com
Ingram Content Group, One Ingram Blvd, La Vergne, TN 37086-3629 Toll Free Tel: 800-937-8000 E-mail: customerservice@ingramcontent.com

Avery
Imprint of Penguin Publishing Group
c/o Penguin Random House LLC, 1745 Broadway, New York, NY 10019
Tel: 212-366-2000
Web Site: www.penguin.com/avery-overview/
Key Personnel
SVP & Publr, Avery/TarcherPerigee: Tracy Behar
VP & Ed-in-Chief: Lucia Watson
Assoc Publr & Dir, Publicity & Mktg, Avery/TarcherPerigee: Lindsay Gordon
Sr Dir, Subs Rts: Ritsuko Okumura
Publicity Dir, Avery/TarcherPerigee: Anne Kosmoski; Casey Maloney
Mktg Dir, Avery/TarcherPerigee: Farin Schlussel
Asst Dir, Publicity, Avery/TarcherPerigee: Lillian Ball
Sr Ed: Jacob Surpin
Ed, Avery/TarcherPerigee: Hannah Steigmeyer
Assoc Ed, Avery/TarcherPerigee: Isabel McCarthy
Sr Mktg Mgr, Avery/TarcherPerigee: Neda Dallal
Mktg Mgr, Avery/TarcherPerigee: Roshe Anderson; Carla Iannone
Publicity Mgr, Avery/TarcherPerigee: Alyssa Adler; Jamie Lescht
Assoc Mktg Mgr, Avery/TarcherPerigee: Katie MacLeod-English
Founded: 1976 (acquired by The Penguin Group in the fall of 1999)
The imprint is dedicated to publishing books on health & nutrition with a complimentary, natural, or alternative focus.
Penguin Random House & its publishing entities are not accepting unsol submissions, proposals, mss, or submission queries via e-mail at this time.
Number of titles published annually: 35 Print
Total Titles: 247 Print

Avery Color Studios
511 "D" Ave, Gwinn, MI 49841
Tel: 906-346-3908 Toll Free Tel: 800-722-9925 Fax: 906-346-3015
E-mail: averycolor@averycolorstudios.com
Web Site: www.averycolorstudios.com
Key Personnel
Pres: Amy McKay
Founded: 1956
Regional publisher. Specialize in nautical books.
ISBN Prefix(es): 978-0-932212; 978-1-892384
Number of titles published annually: 4 Print
Total Titles: 50 Print

Avid Reader Press
Imprint of Simon & Schuster, LLC
1230 Avenue of the Americas, New York, NY 10020
Web Site: avidreaderpress.com
Key Personnel
VP & Publr: Jofie Ferrari-Adler; Ben Loehnen
VP & Assoc Publr: Meredith Vilarello
VP & Edit Dir: Caroline Sutton; Lauren Wein; Shannon Welch
VP & Exec Ed: Joy de Menil
Exec Ed: Margo Shickmanter
Ed: Julianna Haubner
Assoc Ed: Carolyn Kelly
Asst Ed: Amy Guay
Edit Asst: Megan Noes
Sr Dir, Publicity: David Kass
Assoc Dir, Publicity: Alexandra Primiani
Sr Art Dir: Alison Forner
Number of titles published annually: 30 Print

Avotaynu Books LLC
10 Sunset Rd, Needham, MA 02494
Tel: 781-449-2131
E-mail: info@avotaynubooks.com
Web Site: www.avotaynubooks.com
Key Personnel
Publr: Alexis Shapiro E-mail: alexis@avotaynubooks.com
Founded: 1984
Publisher of information & products of interest to persons researching their Jewish family history. This includes the journal & books.
ISBN Prefix(es): 978-0-9626373; 978-1-886223; 978-0-9836975
Number of titles published annually: 3 Print
Total Titles: 55 Print

Baby Tattoo Books
6045 Longridge Ave, Van Nuys, CA 91401
Tel: 818-416-5314
E-mail: info@babytattoo.com
Web Site: www.babytattoo.com
Key Personnel
Pres & Publr: Robert Self E-mail: bob@babytattoo.com
Founded: 2003
Publisher of art books by contemporary artists.
ISBN Prefix(es): 978-0-9729388; 978-0-9778949; 978-0-9793307; 978-0-9845210; 978-1-61404
Number of titles published annually: 4 Print
Total Titles: 30 Print
Orders to: SCB Distributors Inc, 15608 S New Century Dr, Gardena, CA 90248 Toll Free Tel: 800-729-6423
Returns: SCB Distributors Inc, 15608 S New Century Dr, Gardena, CA 90248 Toll Free Tel: 800-729-6423
Shipping Address: SCB Distributors Inc, 15608 S New Century Dr, Gardena, CA 90248 Toll Free Tel: 800-729-6423
Warehouse: SCB Distributors Inc, 15608 S New Century Dr, Gardena, CA 90248 Toll Free Tel: 800-729-6423
Distribution Center: SCB Distributors Inc, 15608 S New Century Dr, Gardena, CA 90248 Toll Free Tel: 800-729-6423

Back to Eden Books, see Lotus Press

Backbeat Books
Imprint of The Globe Pequot Press
PO Box 1520, Wayne, NJ 07042-1520
Tel: 973-987-5363
E-mail: submissions@halleonardbooks.com
Web Site: www.backbeatbooks.com
Key Personnel
Sr Exec Ed: John Cerullo E-mail: jcerullo@rowman.com
Dir, Rts: Sean McDonagh E-mail: smcdonagh@rowman.com
Founded: 1991
Books about popular music & musical instruments.
ISBN Prefix(es): 978-0-87930
Number of titles published annually: 30 Print; 20 E-Book
Total Titles: 400 Print; 300 E-Book
Foreign Rep(s): National Book Network (Europe, India, Latin America, Mexico, Middle East, Pacific Rim, Russia & former USSR, South America); Publishers Group UK (UK); Woodslane (Australia, New Zealand)
Distribution Center: National Book Network, 15200 NBN Way, Blue Ridge Summit, PA 17214

§Baen Books
PO Box 1188, Wake Forest, NC 27588
Tel: 919-570-1640 Fax: 919-570-1644
E-mail: info@baen.com
Web Site: www.baen.com
Key Personnel
Publr: Toni Weisskopf E-mail: toni@baen.com
Founded: 1984
Only science fiction & fantasy.
ISBN Prefix(es): 978-0-671; 978-0-7434; 978-1-4165
Number of titles published annually: 70 Print; 50 Online; 48 E-Book
Total Titles: 1,200 Print; 1,200 Online; 1,200 E-Book
Distributed by Simon & Schuster, LLC
Foreign Rep(s): EYA (South Korea); Lora Fountain Literary Agency (Lora Fountain) (France); Grayhawk Agency (China, Taiwan); Alex Korzhenevshi (Russia); Kristin Olson (Czechia); PNLA (Italy); Thomas Schlueck GmbH (Germany); Tuttle-Mori Agency Inc (Japan)

Baha'i Publishing Trust
Subsidiary of The National Spiritual Assembly of the Baha'is of the United States
1233 Central St, Evanston, IL 60201
Tel: 847-853-7899 Toll Free Tel: 800-999-9019 (orders)
E-mail: bds@usbnc.org; acquisitions@usbnc.org
Web Site: www.bahaibookstore.com
Founded: 1955
Religion (Baha'i).
ISBN Prefix(es): 978-0-87743; 978-1-931847
Number of titles published annually: 15 Print
Total Titles: 1,300 Print
Imprints: Baha'i Publishing
Divisions: Baha'i Distribution Service

§Baker Books
Division of Baker Publishing Group
6030 E Fulton Rd, Ada, MI 49301
Mailing Address: PO Box 6287, Grand Rapids, MI 49516 SAN: 299-1500
Tel: 616-676-9185 Toll Free Tel: 800-877-2665 (orders) Fax: 616-676-9573 Toll Free Fax: 800-398-3111 (orders)
E-mail: media@bakerpublishinggroup.com; orders@bakerpublishinggroup.com; sales@bakerpublishinggroup.com
Web Site: www.bakerpublishinggroup.com
Key Personnel
Pres & CEO: Dwight Baker
EVP, Academic Publg: Jim Kinney E-mail: jkinney@bakerpublishinggroup.com
EVP, Sales & Mktg: Dave Lewis E-mail: dlewis@bakerpublishinggroup.com
Dir, Rts & Contracts: Marilyn Gordon E-mail: mgordon@bakerpublishinggroup.com
Edit Dir: Brian Vos
Founded: 1939
Religion (Protestant).
ISBN Prefix(es): 978-0-8010
Number of titles published annually: 75 Print; 1 CD-ROM; 1 Audio
Total Titles: 1,000 Print
Imprints: Hamewith; Hourglass
Foreign Rep(s): Christian Art Distributors (South Africa); Manna Christian Stores (New Zealand); SPCK (Ireland, UK)

U.S. PUBLISHERS

Ballinger Publishing
21 E Garden St, Suite 205, Pensacola, FL 32502
Mailing Address: PO Box 12665, Pensacola, FL 32591-2665
Tel: 850-433-1166 *Fax:* 850-435-9174
E-mail: info@ballingerpublishing.com
Web Site: www.ballingerpublishing.com
Key Personnel
Owner & Publr: Malcolm Ballinger *Tel:* 850-433-1166 ext 27 *E-mail:* malcolm@ballingerpublishing.com
Exec Ed: Kelly Oden *Tel:* 850-433-1166 ext 23 *E-mail:* kelly@ballingerpublishing.com
Founded: 2001
Publishers of local & regional magazines. This publisher has indicated that 100% of their product line is author subsidized.
ISBN Prefix(es): 978-0-9791103
Number of titles published annually: 80 Print

Bancroft Press
4527 Glenwood Ave, La Crescenta, CA 91214
Tel: 818-275-3061 *Fax:* 410-764-1967
E-mail: bruceb@bancroftpress.com
Web Site: www.bancroftpress.com
Founded: 1992
General interest trade book publisher; has received special recognition & ranks among the nation's top 10 independent presses. Worldwide rights & distribution.
ISBN Prefix(es): 978-1-890862
Number of titles published annually: 7 Print; 1 Audio
Total Titles: 150 Print; 1 Audio
Returns: Baker & Taylor Publisher Services, 30 Amberwood Pkwy, Ashland, OH 44805 *Toll Free Tel:* 888-537-6727 *Web Site:* www.btpubservices.com
Distribution Center: Baker & Taylor Publisher Services, 30 Amberwood Pkwy, Ashland, OH 44805 *Tel:* 567-215-0030 *Toll Free Tel:* 888-814-0208 *E-mail:* info@btpubservices.com *Web Site:* www.btpubservices.com

B&H Publishing Group
Imprint of LifeWay Christian Resources
200 Powell Place, Suite 100, Brentwood, TN 37027-7707
SAN: 201-937X
Toll Free Tel: 800-251-3225 (retailers); 800-448-8032 (consumers); 800-458-2772 (churches) *Fax:* 615-251-3914 (consumers); 615-251-5933 (churches) *Toll Free Fax:* 800-296-4036 (retailers)
E-mail: customerservice@lifeway.com
Web Site: www.bhpublishinggroup.com
Founded: 1934
Religious trade publisher of nonfiction (Christian living, inspirational, devotional, contemporary issues); fiction; children's books; Bibles; Biblical reference; Biblical commentaries.
ISBN Prefix(es): 978-0-8054; 978-1-5359; 978-1-4300; 978-1-0877
Number of titles published annually: 95 Print
Total Titles: 700 Print; 5 Audio
Imprints: B&H Academic; B&H Espanol; B&H kids; B&H Publishing; Holman Bibles
Foreign Rights: Riggins International Rights Services Inc (worldwide exc USA)
Returns: LifeWay Christian Resources, 535 Maddox-Simpson Pkwy, Lebanon, TN 37090

Baptist Spanish Publishing House, see Casa Bautista de Publicaciones

Barbour Publishing Inc
1810 Barbour Dr, Uhrichsville, OH 44683
Tel: 740-922-6045 *Fax:* 740-922-5948
E-mail: info@barbourbooks.com
Web Site: www.barbourbooks.com
Key Personnel
Pres & COO: Mary Burns
VP, Edit: Kelly McIntosh *E-mail:* kmcintosh@barbourbooks.com
VP, Mktg: Shalyn Sattler
VP, Sales: William Westfall *E-mail:* bwestfall@barbourbooks.com
Founded: 1981
Christian books, Bibles, fiction, gift books, devotional journals, reference.
ISBN Prefix(es): 978-1-57748; 978-0-916441; 978-1-55748; 978-1-58660; 978-1-59310; 978-1-59789; 978-1-60260; 978-1-61626; 978-1-63058; 978-1-63409; 978-1-62416; 978-1-62836; 978-1-68322; 978-1-64352; 978-1-63609
Number of titles published annually: 244 Print
Total Titles: 793 Print
Imprints: Barbour Books; Barbour Espanol; Barbour Kidz; DayMaker

Barcelona Publishers LLC
10231 N Plano Rd, Dallas, TX 75238
Tel: 214-553-9785
E-mail: warehouse@barcelonapublishers.com
Web Site: www.barcelonapublishers.com
Key Personnel
Dir: Kenneth E Bruscia
Founded: 1989
Music therapy books & materials.
ISBN Prefix(es): 978-0-9624080; 978-1-891278; 978-1-937440; 978-1-945411
Number of titles published annually: 8 Print; 5 Audio
Total Titles: 95 Print; 70 Online; 70 E-Book
Foreign Rep(s): Eurospan Group (worldwide exc North America)
Distribution Center: Eurospan Group, Gray's Inn House, 127 Clerkenwell Rd, London EC1R 5DB, United Kingdom *Web Site:* www.eurospanbookstore.com/barcelona

Barefoot Books
23 Bradford St, 2nd fl, Concord, MA 01742
Tel: 617-576-0660 *Toll Free Tel:* 866-215-1756 (cust serv); 866-417-2369 (orders) *Fax:* 617-576-0049
E-mail: help@barefootbooks.com
Web Site: www.barefootbooks.com
Key Personnel
CEO: Nancy Traversy *E-mail:* nancy.traversy@barefootbooks.com
VP, Publg: Helen Kissler *E-mail:* helen.kissler@barefootbooks.com
VP, Global Sales: Suzanne Albert
Global Sales Dir: Liz Fleming *E-mail:* liz.fleming@barefootbooks.com
Sr Ed: Lisa Rosinsky *E-mail:* lisa.rosinsky@barefootbooks.com
Founded: 1993
Publishes high quality picture books & activity decks for children of all ages. Specialize in the work of authors & artists from many cultures.
ISBN Prefix(es): 978-1-898000; 978-1-901223; 978-1-902283; 978-1-84148; 978-1-84686; 978-1-905236; 978-1-78285; 978-1-64686; 979-8-88859
Number of titles published annually: 50 Print; 4 Audio
Total Titles: 420 Print
Returns: LSC Communications, 655 Brighton Beach Rd, Menasha, WI 54952
Warehouse: LSC Communications, 655 Brighton Beach Rd, Menasha, WI 54952
Membership(s): The American Library Association (ALA); The Children's Book Council (CBC)

Barranca Press
17 Rockridge Rd, Mount Vernon, NY 10552
Tel: 347-820-2363
E-mail: editor@barrancapress.com
Web Site: www.barrancapress.com
Key Personnel
Ed: Lisa Noudehou *E-mail:* lisa@barrancapress.com
Founded: 2012
Booklist includes photojournalism, novels, literary collections, children's books & memoirs. Unsol mss accepted March-August annually. E-mail submissions preferred.
ISBN Prefix(es): 978-1-939604
Number of titles published annually: 3 Print
Total Titles: 21 Print
Membership(s): Independent Book Publishers Association (IBPA)

Barringer Publishing
Division of Schlesinger Advertising & Marketing
16398 Barclay Ct, Naples, FL 34110
Tel: 239-920-1668
E-mail: schlesadv@gmail.com
Web Site: www.barringerpublishing.com
Key Personnel
Owner: Jeff Schlesinger *E-mail:* js@barringerpublishing.com
Founded: 2009
Full service: Cover & book design, editing, printing, marketing, advertising & public relations, web sites, graphics, displays & illustrations.
ISBN Prefix(es): 978-0-9825109
Number of titles published annually: 20 Print; 20 E-Book; 1 Audio
Total Titles: 208 Print; 203 E-Book; 1 Audio
Membership(s): Independent Book Publishers Association (IBPA)

Barrytown/Station Hill Press
120 Station Hill Rd, Barrytown, NY 12507
SAN: 214-1485
Tel: 845-758-5293
E-mail: publishers@stationhill.org
Web Site: www.stationhill.org
Key Personnel
Publr: George Quasha
Co-Publr: Susan Quasha
Dir: Sam Truitt
Founded: 1977
General trade books, quality paperbacks & fine editions; poetry, fiction & discourse; visual arts; studies in literature & psychology, classics, translations, theater, creative nonfiction, health/New Age.
ISBN Prefix(es): 978-0-930794; 978-0-88268
Number of titles published annually: 6 Print
Total Titles: 300 Print
Foreign Rep(s): Lora Fountain (France); Gara Media (Germany); Japanville (Japan); Kerrigan (Spain); Living Weary (Italy)
Distribution Center: Midpoint Trade Books, 814 N Franklin St, Suite 100, Chicago, IL 60610 *Tel:* 312-337-0747 *Toll Free Tel:* 800-888-4741 *Fax:* 312-337-5985 *E-mail:* orders@ipgbook.com *Web Site:* www.midpointtrade.com

Bartleby Press
Member of Jackson Westgate Publishing Group
8926 Baltimore St, No 858, Savage, MD 20763
SAN: 241-2098
Tel: 301-589-5831 *Toll Free Tel:* 800-953-9929
E-mail: inquiries@bartlebythepublisher.com
Web Site: www.bartlebythepublisher.com
Key Personnel
Publr: Jeremy Kay *E-mail:* publisher@bartlebythepublisher.com
Proj Ed: John Adams
Founded: 1981
ISBN Prefix(es): 978-0-910155; 978-0-9625963; 978-0-935437
Number of titles published annually: 7 Print; 8 E-Book; 1 Audio
Total Titles: 72 Print; 37 E-Book; 3 Audio
Imprints: Eshel Books
Distribution Center: Independent Publishers Group (IPG), 814 N Franklin St, Chicago, IL 60610 *Tel:* 312-337-0747 *Toll Free Tel:* 800-

888-4741 *Fax:* 312-337-5985 *Web Site:* www.ipgbook.com
Membership(s): Independent Book Publishers Association (IBPA)

§Basic Books Group
Division of Hachette Book Group Inc
1290 Avenue of the Americas, New York, NY 10104
Tel: 212-340-8100 *Toll Free Tel:* 800-343-4499 (cust serv) *Fax:* 212-340-8105
E-mail: customer.service@hbgusa.com; orders@hbgusa.com
Web Site: www.hachettebookgroup.com/imprint/basic-books/
Key Personnel
SVP & Publr: Lara Heimert *E-mail:* lara.heimert@hbgusa.com
VP & Ed-in-Chief, Basic Books: Brian Distelberg *E-mail:* brian.distelberg@hbgusa.com
VP & Edit Dir, Basic Books: Thomas Kelleher *E-mail:* thomas.kelleher@hbgusa.com
Publr, PublicAffairs: Clive Priddle *E-mail:* clive.priddle@hbgusa.com
Exec Ed, Basic Books: Brandon Proia *E-mail:* brandon.proia@hbgusa.com; Eric A Schmidt *E-mail:* eric.schmidt@hbgusa.com; Emily Taber *E-mail:* emily.taber@hbgusa.com
Exec Ed, PublicAffairs: Benjamin Adams *E-mail:* benjamin.adams@hbgusa.com
Edit Dir, PublicAffairs: Colleen Lawrie *E-mail:* colleen.lawrie@hbgusa.com
Assoc Ed, Basic Books: Michael Kaler *E-mail:* michael.kaler@hbgusa.com
Assoc Ed, PublicAffairs: Anu Roy-Chaudhury *E-mail:* anupama.roy-chaudhury@hbgusa.com
Asst Ed, Basic Books: Kristen Kim *E-mail:* kristen.kim@hbgusa.com
Exec Dir, Mktg, Basic Books: Jessica Breen *E-mail:* jessica.breen@hbgusa.com
Mktg Asst, Basic Books: Brianne Oliva *E-mail:* brianne.oliva@hbgusa.com
Publicist, Basic Books: Meghan Roberts *E-mail:* meghan.roberts@hbgusa.com
Exec Publicity Dir, Basic Books: Liz Wetzel *E-mail:* liz.wetzel@hbgusa.com
Assoc Publicity Dir, Basic Books: Angela Messina *E-mail:* angela.messina@hbgusa.com
Asst Publicity & Mktg Dir, Basic Books: Ivan Lett *E-mail:* ivan.lett@hbgusa.com
Asst Publicity Dir, PublicAffairs: Brooke Parsons *E-mail:* brooke.parsons@hbgusa.com
Publicity Mgr, PublicAffairs: Johanna Dickson *E-mail:* johanna.dickson@hbgusa.com
Creative Dir, Basic Books: Chin-Yee Lai *E-mail:* chin-yee.lai@hbgusa.com
Designer, Basic Books: Emmily O'Connor *E-mail:* emmily.oconnor@hbgusa.com
Imprint Sales Dir: Elizabeth Blue Guess *E-mail:* elizabeth.guess@hbgusa.com
Founded: 1950
ISBN Prefix(es): 978-0-201 (Basic Books); 978-0-465 (Basic Books); 978-0-7867 (Basic Books); 978-1-887178 (Basic Books); 978-0-941423 (Basic Books); 978-1-56858 (Basic Books); 978-1-56924 (Basic Books); 978-0-7382 (Basic Books); 978-0-931188 (Seal Press); 978-1-878067 (Seal Press); 978-0-86531 (Basic Books); 978-0-8133 (Basic Books); 978-1-56025 (Basic Books); 978-1-58243 (Basic Books); 978-1-58648 (PublicAffairs); 978-0-938410 (Basic Books); 978-1-891620 (PublicAffairs); 978-1-58005 (Seal Press); 978-1-61039 (PublicAffairs); 978-1-64503 (Bold Type Books); 978-1-5417 (PublicAffairs/Bold Type Books); 978-1-5416 (Basic Books); 978-1-4789 (Basic Books)
Imprints: Basic Books; Bold Type Books; PublicAffairs; Seal Press
Orders to: 1094 Flex Dr, Jackson, TN 38301 *Toll Free Tel:* 800-343-4499 *Toll Free Fax:* 800-351-5073
Membership(s): Association of American Publishers (AAP); National Book Foundation

Basic Health Publications Inc
Imprint of Turner Publishing Co LLC
4507 Charlotte Ave, Suite 100, Nashville, TN 37209
Tel: 615-255-2665
E-mail: marketing@turnerpublishing.com
Key Personnel
Mktg Mgr: Kaylon Hicks
Founded: 2001
ISBN Prefix(es): 978-1-59120; 978-1-68442
Number of titles published annually: 15 Print; 15 Online; 15 E-Book
Total Titles: 250 Print; 250 Online; 250 E-Book
Imprints: Basic Health Guides; User's Guides
Foreign Rights: Athena Productions Inc (worldwide)
Distribution Center: Ingram Content Group, One Ingram Blvd, La Vergne, TN 37086 *Tel:* 615-793-5000 *Web Site:* www.ingramcontent.com

Baylor University Press
Baylor University, One Bear Place, Waco, TX 76798-7363
SAN: 685-317X
Tel: 254-710-3164
E-mail: bup_marketing@baylor.edu
Web Site: www.baylorpress.com
Key Personnel
Dir: Dr Dave Nelson *E-mail:* dave_nelson@baylor.edu
Deputy Dir, Mktg, Sales & Publicity: David Aycock *E-mail:* david_aycock@baylor.edu
Assoc Dir, Digital Publg & Prodn Mgr: Jenny Hunt *E-mail:* jenny_hunt@baylor.edu
Assoc Dir, Fin & Opers/Rts Mgr: Michelle McCaig *E-mail:* michelle_mccaig@baylor.edu
Asst Dir & Mng Ed: Cade Jarrell *E-mail:* cade_jarrell@baylor.edu
Graphic Designer: Ely Encarnacion *E-mail:* ely_encarnacion@baylor.edu
Founded: 1897
Scholarly books & monographs.
ISBN Prefix(es): 978-0-918954; 978-1-932792; 978-1-481308; 978-1-602581; 978-1-481309
Number of titles published annually: 40 Print; 1 Audio
Total Titles: 650 Print
Shipping Address: 1920 S Fourth St, Waco, TX 76706
Distribution Center: Longleaf Services Inc, 116 S Boundary St, Chapel Hill, NC 27514-3808 *Toll Free Tel:* 800-848-6224 ext 1 *Fax:* 919-962-2704 *E-mail:* customerservice@longleafservices.org *Web Site:* www.longleafservices.org
Membership(s): American Association of University Presses (AAUP)

Beach Lane Books, see Simon & Schuster Children's Publishing

Beacon Hill Press of Kansas City
Subsidiary of The Foundry Publishing
PO Box 419527, Kansas City, MO 64141
SAN: 202-9022
Tel: 816-931-1900 *Toll Free Tel:* 800-877-0700 (cust serv) *Fax:* 816-531-0923
Toll Free Fax: 800-849-9827
E-mail: orders@thefoundrypublishing.com; customercare@thefoundrypublishing.com
Web Site: www.thefoundrypublishing.com
Key Personnel
CEO: Mark Brown
Dir: Bonnie Perry
Ministry Prod Line Ed: Richard E Buckner
Founded: 1912
Religion (Nazarene), ministry resources, Christian care & spiritual growth.
ISBN Prefix(es): 978-0-8341
Number of titles published annually: 30 Print
Total Titles: 700 Print

Beacon Press
24 Farnsworth St, Boston, MA 02210-1409
SAN: 201-4483
Tel: 617-742-2110 *Fax:* 617-723-3097
E-mail: production@beacon.org
Web Site: www.beacon.org
Key Personnel
CFO: Matt Davis
Assoc Publr: Sanj Kharbanda
Dir: Gayatri Patnaik
Contracts Dir: Melissa Nasson, Esq
Creative Dir: Carol Chu
Dir, Communs: Pamela MacColl
Edit Dir: Amy Caldwell
Prodn Dir: Marcy Barnes
Assoc Dir, Busn Opers: Jill Dougan
Assoc Dir, Mktg: Alyssa Hassan
Assoc Publicity Dir: Caitlin Meyer
Mng Ed: Susan Lumenello
Sr Ed: Joanna Green
Ed: Maya Fernandez; Haley Lynch; Rachael Marks
Assoc Ed: Catherine Tung
Edit Asst & Asst to Assoc Dir: Ruthie Block
Edit Asst: Nicole-Anne Keyton; Alison Rodriguez
Sr Mktg Mgr: Emily Powers
Digital Mktg Mgr: Christian Coleman
Prodn Mgr: Beth Collins
Reprint & Digital Prodn Mgr: Daniel Barks
Mktg & Sales Coord: Isabella Sanchez
Sales & Mktg Coord: Frankie Karnedy
Designer: Louis Roe
Busn Opers Analyst: Claire Desroches
Busn Opers Asst: Isabel Tehan
Sr Publicist: Bev Rivero
Publicist: Perpetua Charles
Asst Publicist: Priyanka Ray
Founded: 1854
General nonfiction, religion & theology, current affairs, anthropology, women's studies, history, gay & lesbian studies, African-American studies, Latino studies, education, hardcover, paperback, ebook & audio.
ISBN Prefix(es): 978-0-8070
Number of titles published annually: 60 Print; 35 E-Book
Total Titles: 800 Print; 350 E-Book; 5 Audio
Imprints: Concord Library; The King Legacy (writings of Dr Martin Luther King Jr)
Foreign Rep(s): NewSouth Books (Australia, New Zealand)
Foreign Rights: Akcali Copyright Agency (Mustafa Urgen) (Turkey); Eliane Benisti Literary Agency (Noemie Rollet) (France); Chinese Connection Agency (Mr Gending Fan) (China); The Deborah Harris Agency (Ms Geula Geurts) (Israel); Agence Hoffman GmbH (Uwe Neumahr); International Editors' Co - Yanez Agencia Literaria (Valentina Stefanini) (Portugal, Spain); Agenzia Internazionale Literaria (Federica Graceffa) (Italy); Maxima Creative Agency (Santo Manurung) (Indonesia); Prava i prevodi (Milena Kaplarevic) (Eastern Europe exc Estonia, Latvia, Lithuania & Russia, Greece); Agencia Riff (Roberto Matos) (Brazil); Sebes & Bisseling Literary Agency (Stephanie Nooteboom) (Netherlands, Scandinavia); Synopsis Literary Agency (Olga Zasetskaya) (Russia); Tuttle-Mori Agency Inc (Fumika Ogihara) (Japan); Eric Yang Agency (Jackie Yang) (South Korea)
Returns: Penguin Random House Returns Dept, 1019 N State Rd 47, Crawfordsville, IN 47933
Warehouse: Penguin Random House Publisher Services (PRHPS), 400 Hahn Rd, Westminster, MD 21157 *Toll Free Tel:* 800-733-3000 *Toll Free Fax:* 800-659-2436
E-mail: csorders@randomhouse.com *Web Site:* prhpublisherservices.com
Distribution Center: Penguin Random House Publisher Services (PRHPS), 400 Hahn Rd, Westminster, MD 21157 *Toll Free Tel:* 800-733-3000 *Toll Free Fax:* 800-659-2436

U.S. PUBLISHERS

E-mail: csorders@randomhouse.com Web Site: prhpublisherservices.com
Penguin Random House International Sales, 1745 Broadway, 6th fl, New York, NY 10019 (worldwide exc Australia, New Zealand & US) Tel: 212-572-6083 Fax: 212-572-6045 E-mail: internationalsales@penguinrandomhouse.com Web Site: prhinternationalsales.com
Membership(s): American Association of University Presses (AAUP); New England Independent Booksellers Association (NEIBA)

Beaming Books, see Augsburg Fortress Publishers, Publishing House of the Evangelical Lutheran Church in America

Bear & Bobcat Books
Imprint of Hameray Publishing Group Inc
5212 Venice Blvd, Los Angeles, CA 90019
Toll Free Tel: 866-918-6173 Fax: 858-369-5201
E-mail: info@hameraypublishing.com (cust serv); sales@hameraypublishing.com (sales)
Web Site: www.bearandbobcat.com
Founded: 2018
Bear & Bobcat Books feature works by internationally renowned authors & illustrators whose stories inspire laughter & a love of reading among children. As a part of the Hameray Publishing Group, Bear & Bobcat Books is dedicated to sparking imaginations & success of children through the powerful act of reading.
ISBN Prefix(es): 978-1-7324300
Number of titles published annually: 4 Print
Total Titles: 4 Print
Distributed by Hameray Publishing Group Inc

Bear & Co Inc
Imprint of Inner Traditions International Ltd
One Park St, Rochester, VT 05767
Mailing Address: PO Box 388, Rochester, VT 05767-0388
Tel: 802-767-3174 Toll Free Tel: 800-932-3277 Fax: 802-767-3726
E-mail: customerservice@InnerTraditions.com
Web Site: InnerTraditions.com
Key Personnel
Pres: Ehud C Sperling E-mail: prez@InnerTraditions.com
VP, Opers: Diane Shepard E-mail: dianes@InnerTraditions.com
Dir, Content & Consumer Sales: Rob Meadows E-mail: robm@InnerTraditions.com
Dir, Sales & Mktg: John Hays E-mail: johnh@InnerTraditions.com
Ed-in-Chief: Jeanie Levitan E-mail: jeaniel@InnerTraditions.com
Acqs Ed: Jon Graham E-mail: jong@InnerTraditions.com
Audiobook Mgr: Mahar Sperling E-mail: mahars@InnerTraditions.com
Print Mgr: Jon Desautels E-mail: jond@InnerTraditions.com
Foreign Rts & Perms: Maria Loftus E-mail: marial@InnerTraditions.com
Publicity: Manzanita Carpenter E-mail: manzanitac@InnerTraditions.com
Sales & Mktg: Andrea Raymond E-mail: andyr@InnerTraditions.com
Spec Sales: Jessica Arsenault E-mail: jessa@InnerTraditions.com
Founded: 1980
Mysticism, philosophy, spirituality & medieval studies, contemporary prophecy, earth sciences, indigenous wisdom, new thought, alternative healing.
ISBN Prefix(es): 978-1-879181; 978-0-939680; 978-1-59143
Number of titles published annually: 16 Print; 16 E-Book
Total Titles: 370 Print; 328 E-Book

Foreign Rights: Akcali Copyright Agency (Turkey); Big Apple Agency Inc (China, Taiwan); Blackbird Literary Agency (Netherlands); The Book Publishers' Association of Israel, International Promotion & Literary Rights Department (Israel); Graal Literary Agency (Poland); International Editors' Co - Yanez Agencia Literaria (Spain); The Italian Literary Agency Srl (Italy); Simona Kessler International Copyright Agency Ltd (Romania); Alexander Korzhenevski Agency (Russia); Ilidio Matos Agency (Portugal); George Millett Agency (Brazil); Andrew Nurnberg Associates (Baltic States, Bulgaria, Czechia, Hungary); Plima doo (Croatia); Read n Right Agency (Greece); Thomas Schlueck GmbH (Germany); Agence Schweiger (France); Tuttle-Mori Agency Inc (Indonesia, Japan, Thailand); Eric Yang Agency (South Korea)
Orders to: Inner Traditions International - Bear & Co, c/o Simon & Schuster, LLC, 100 Front St, Riverside, NJ 08075 Toll Free Tel: 800-223-2336 Toll Free Fax: 800-943-9831 E-mail: purchaseorders@simonandschuster.com
Returns: Simon & Schuster, LLC, c/o Jacobson Logistics, 4406 Industrial Park Rd, Bldg 7, Camp Hill, PA 17011 (truckload shipments must call for an appt: 800-967-3914 ext 5318)
Warehouse: Inner Traditions International - Bear & Co, c/o Simon & Schuster, LLC, 100 Front St, Riverside, NJ 08075 Toll Free Tel: 800-943-9831 E-mail: purchaseorders@simonandschuster.com

§BearManor Media
1317 Edgewater Dr, No 110, Orlando, FL 32804
Tel: 760-709-9696
Web Site: www.bearmanormedia.com
Key Personnel
Owner & Pres: Ben Ohmart E-mail: ben@bearmanormedia.com
ISBN Prefix(es): 978-0-9714570; 978-1-59393; 978-1-62933
Number of titles published annually: 70 Print; 90 E-Book; 20 Audio
Total Titles: 1,100 Print; 900 E-Book; 60 Audio
Imprints: BearManor Bare (adult film biographies); BearManor Fiction (fiction about or by Hollywood stars)
Membership(s): Independent Book Publishers Association (IBPA)

Bearport Publishing
5357 Penn Ave S, Minneapolis, MN 55419
Tel: 212-337-8577 Toll Free Tel: 877-337-8577 Fax: 212-337-8557 Toll Free Fax: 866-337-8557
E-mail: service@bearportpublishing.com
Web Site: www.bearportpublishing.com
Founded: 2003
Curriculum-aligned, high-interest content for the educational school & library market.
ISBN Prefix(es): 978-1-59716; 978-1-936087; 978-1-61772; 979-1-99568
Number of titles published annually: 200 Print; 1,200 E-Book; 200 Audio
Total Titles: 1,400 Print
Returns: Corporate Graphics International, 1885 Northway Dr, North Mankato, MN 56003 Toll Free Tel: 800-851-8767 (sales & mktg); 800-247-2751 (cust serv) E-mail: marketing@cgintl.com Web Site: cgintl.com
Membership(s): The American Library Association (ALA); The Children's Book Council (CBC)

Beaver's Pond Press Inc
939 Seventh St W, St Paul, MN 55102
Tel: 952-829-8818
E-mail: submissions@beaverspondpress.com
Web Site: www.beaverspondpress.com

Key Personnel
CEO: Lily Coyle E-mail: lily@beaverspondpress.com
Ed: Alicia Ester E-mail: alicia@beaverspondpress.com; Laurie Herrmann E-mail: laurieh@beaverspondpress.com
Coord: Evan Allgood E-mail: evan@beaverspondpress.com; Becca Hart E-mail: becca@beaverspondpress.com
Founded: 1998
Veteran-owned, woman-owned company for independent authors. Specialize in children's & coffee table books.
This publisher has indicated that 100% of their product line is author subsidized.
ISBN Prefix(es): 978-1-59298; 978-1-64343; 978-1-890676; 978-1-931646
Number of titles published annually: 60 Print; 20 E-Book
Total Titles: 1,300 Print; 550 E-Book
Orders to: Itasca Books, 210 Edge Place NE, Minneapolis, MN 55418, Contact: Mark Jung Tel: 952-223-8373 Toll Free Tel: 800-901-3480 ext 118 Fax: 952-920-0541 E-mail: orders@itascabooks.com Web Site: itascabooks.com
Returns: Itasca Books, 210 Edge Place NE, Minneapolis, MN 55418, Contact: Mark Jung Tel: 952-223-8373 Toll Free Tel: 800-901-3480 ext 118 Fax: 952-920-0541 E-mail: orders@itascabooks.com Web Site: itascabooks.com
Warehouse: Itasca Books, 210 Edge Place NE, Minneapolis, MN 55418, Contact: Mark Jung Tel: 952-223-8373 Fax: 952-920-0541 E-mail: mark@itascabooks.com Web Site: itascabooks.com
Distribution Center: Itasca Books, 210 Edge Place NE, Minneapolis, MN 55418, Contact: Mark Jung Tel: 952-223-8373 Toll Free Tel: 800-901-3480 ext 118 Fax: 952-920-0541 E-mail: orders@itascabooks.com Web Site: itascabooks.com
Membership(s): Dramatists Guild of America Inc; Independent Book Publishers Association (IBPA); Midwest Independent Booksellers Association (MIBA); Midwest Independent Publishing Association (MIPA); PEN America; Society of Children's Book Writers & Illustrators (SCBWI)

Bedford, Freeman & Worth Publishing Group, LLC, see Macmillan Learning

Bedford/St Martin's
Imprint of Macmillan Learning
One New York Plaza, 46th fl, New York, NY 10004
Tel: 212-576-9400; 212-375-7000
E-mail: press.inquiries@macmillan.com
Web Site: www.macmillanlearning.com/college/us
Founded: 1981
Humanities publisher specializing in English composition, literature, history, communication & college success.
ISBN Prefix(es): 978-0-312; 978-1-457
Number of titles published annually: 200 Print; 50 E-Book
Warehouse: MPS Distribution Center, 16365 James Madison Hwy (US Rte 15), Gordonsville, VA 22942 Toll Free Tel: 888-330-8477 Fax: 540-672-7540 (cust serv) Toll Free Fax: 800-672-2054 (orders) SAN: 631-5011
Membership(s): Association of American Publishers (AAP)

Beehive Books
4700 Kingsessing Ave, Suite C, Philadelphia, PA 19143
E-mail: beehivebook@gmail.com
Web Site: www.beehivebooks.net
Key Personnel
Co-Founder: Maelle Doliveux; Josh O'Neill
Founded: 2017

A boutique visual arts press specializing in the odd, inventive, lovely & quixotic. Artist's books, monographs, magazines, graphic novels, prints & more.
ISBN Prefix(es): 978-1-948886
Number of titles published annually: 5 Print
Total Titles: 8 Print
Foreign Rights: Sequential Rights (Amber Garza) (worldwide)
Distribution Center: Consortium Book Sales & Distribution, 34 13 Ave NE, Suite 101, Minneapolis, MN 55413 *Tel:* 612-746-2600

Begell House Inc Publishers
50 North St, Danbury, CT 06810
Tel: 203-456-6161 *Fax:* 203-456-6167
E-mail: orders@begellhouse.com
Web Site: www.begellhouse.com
Key Personnel
Pres: Yelena Shafeyeva *E-mail:* elena@begellhouse.com
Gen Mgr: Meghan Rohrmann *E-mail:* meghan@begellhouse.com
Founded: 1991
Science books & journals.
ISBN Prefix(es): 978-1-56700
Number of titles published annually: 43 Print; 43 Online
Total Titles: 200 Print; 135 E-Book
Subsidiaries: Begell-Atom LLC
Membership(s): American Society of Engineering Educators; Association of American Publishers (AAP)

Behrman House Inc
241B Millburn Ave, Millburn, NJ 07041
SAN: 201-4459
Tel: 973-379-7200 *Toll Free Tel:* 800-221-2755 *Fax:* 973-379-7280
E-mail: customersupport@behrmanhouse.com
Web Site: store.behrmanhouse.com
Key Personnel
Pres & CEO: David Behrman
Partner: Vicki Weber
Exec Ed: Dena Neusner
Founded: 1921
Jewish interest trade & educational books for children & adults.
ISBN Prefix(es): 978-0-87441; 978-1-69115; 978-0-87670; 978-0-80741
Number of titles published annually: 200 Print
Total Titles: 1,100 Print
Imprints: Apples & Honey Press
Distribution Center: Two Rivers Distribution, One Ingram Blvd, La Vergne, TN 37086 *E-mail:* busops@ingramcontent.com *Web Site:* www.ingramcontent.com

Frederic C Beil Publisher Inc
609 Whitaker St, Savannah, GA 31401
Tel: 912-233-2446
E-mail: fcb@beil.com
Web Site: www.beil.com
Key Personnel
Pres & Publr: Frederic C Beil
Founded: 1982
Biography, history & fiction.
ISBN Prefix(es): 978-0-913720; 978-1-929490
Number of titles published annually: 4 Print
Total Titles: 145 Print
Imprints: Hypermedia Inc; The Sandstone Press
Foreign Rep(s): Gazelle Book Services Ltd (Europe, UK)

Bell Pond Books, see SteinerBooks Inc

§Bella Books
PO Box 10543, Tallahassee, FL 32302
Tel: 850-576-2370 *Toll Free Tel:* 800-729-4992
E-mail: info@bellabooks.com; orders@bellabooks.com; ebooks@bellabooks.com
Web Site: www.bellabooks.com
Key Personnel
Publr & CEO: Linda Hill *E-mail:* linda@bellabooks.com
Founded: 1999
Primarily publishes fiction by, for & about women.
ISBN Prefix(es): 978-0-9628938; 978-1-883061; 978-1-959493; 978-1-642473
Number of titles published annually: 40 Print
Total Titles: 800 Print
Distribution Center: Two Rivers Distribution, 1400 Broadway, Suite 3200, New York, NY 10018 *Toll Free Tel:* 866-400-5351; 800-343-4499 *E-mail:* ips@ingramcontent.com *Web Site:* www.tworiversdistribution.com

BelleBooks
PO Box 300921, Memphis, TN 38130
Tel: 901-344-9024 *Fax:* 901-344-9068
E-mail: bellebooks@bellebooks.com
Web Site: www.bellebooks.com
Key Personnel
Pres & CEO: Debra Dixon
Edit Dir, ImaJinn: Brenda Chin
Opers Mgr: Pamela Ireland
Founded: 1999
ISBN Prefix(es): 978-0-9768760
Number of titles published annually: 100 Print
Total Titles: 750 Print
Imprints: Bell Bridge Books; ImaJinn Books
See separate listing for:
ImaJinn Books

Bellerophon Books
PO Box 21307, Santa Barbara, CA 93121-1307
SAN: 202-392X
Tel: 805-965-7034 *Toll Free Tel:* 800-253-9943 *Fax:* 805-965-8286
E-mail: sales.bellerophon@gmail.com
Web Site: www.bellerophonbooks.com
Key Personnel
Pres: Ellen Knill
Founded: 1969
Children's art & history.
ISBN Prefix(es): 978-0-88388
Number of titles published annually: 6 Print
Total Titles: 142 Print
Returns: 6685 El Pomar Dr, Templeton, CA 93465

§Bellevue Literary Press
90 Broad St, Suite 2100, New York, NY 10004
Tel: 917-732-3603
Web Site: blpress.org
Key Personnel
Publr & Edit Dir: Erika Goldman *E-mail:* erika@blpress.org
Asst Ed: Laura Hart *E-mail:* laura@blpress.org
Founded: 2007
A nonprofit, mission-driven press devoted to publishing literary fiction & nonfiction at the intersection of the arts & sciences because we believe that science & the humanities are natural companions for understanding the human experience. With each book we publish, our goal is to foster a rich, interdisciplinary dialogue that will forge new tools for thinking & engaging with the world.
ISBN Prefix(es): 978-1-942658; 978-1-934137; 978-1-954276
Number of titles published annually: 8 Print; 8 E-Book
Total Titles: 111 Print; 108 E-Book
Foreign Rights: Kaplan/DeFiore Rights (Linda Kaplan) (worldwide)
Distribution Center: Consortium Book Sales & Distribution, The Keg House, 34 13 Ave NE, Suite 101, Minneapolis, MN 55413-1007 *Tel:* 612-746-2600 *Toll Free Tel:* 866-400-5351 (cust serv, Jackson, TN) *E-mail:* cbsdinfo@ingramcontent.com *Web Site:* www.cbsd.com
SAN: 200-6049
Membership(s): Community of Literary Magazines & Presses (CLMP); PEN America

Ben Yehuda Press
122 Ayers Ct, No 1B, Teaneck, NJ 07666
E-mail: orders@benyehudapress.com; yudel@benyehudapress.com
Web Site: www.benyehudapress.com
Key Personnel
Owner & Edit Dir: Larry Yudelson *E-mail:* larry@benyehudapress.com
Founded: 2005
Pluralistic Jewish publisher. Accept agented & unagented material. Prefer to see queries of a short synopsis (less than a page), table of contents & complete ms by electronic submission in Word format.
ISBN Prefix(es): 978-0-9769862; 978-0-9789980
Number of titles published annually: 12 Print; 6 E-Book
Total Titles: 110 Print; 18 E-Book
Membership(s): Independent Book Publishers Association (IBPA)

§BenBella Books Inc
10440 N Central Expwy, Suite 800, Dallas, TX 75231-2264
Tel: 214-750-3600
Web Site: www.benbellabooks.com; www.smartpopbooks.com
Key Personnel
Chief Fin & Admin Offr: Aida Herrera *E-mail:* aida@benbellabooks.com
Publr: Glenn Yeffeth *E-mail:* glenn@benbellabooks.com
Deputy Publr: Adrienne Lang *E-mail:* adrienne@benbellabooks.com
Sr Mktg Dir: Jennifer Canzoneri *Tel:* 214-750-3600 ext 104 *E-mail:* jennifer@benbellabooks.com
Mktg Dir: Lindsay Marshall *E-mail:* lindsay@benbellabooks.com
Mktg Dir, Smart Pop: Heather Butterfield *E-mail:* heather@benbellabooks.com
Prodn Dir: Monica Lowry *E-mail:* monica@benbellabooks.com
Ed-in-Chief: Leah Wilson *E-mail:* leah@benbellabooks.com
Ed-in-Chief, Matt Holt Books: Matt Holt
Sr Ed: Rick Chillot; Claire Schulz *E-mail:* claire@benbellabooks.com
Sr Ed, Matt Holt Books: Katie Dickman *E-mail:* kdickman@benbellabooks.com
Ed & Acqs Mgr: Rachel Phares *E-mail:* rachel@benbellabooks.com
Prodn Ed: Kim Broderick *E-mail:* kim@benbellabooks.com
Asst Ed, Matt Holt Books: Lydia Choi *E-mail:* lydia@benbellabooks.com
Sr Mktg Mgr, Matt Holt Books: Mallory Hyde *E-mail:* mallory@benbellabooks.com
Vendor Content Mgr: Alicia Kania *E-mail:* alicia@benbellabooks.com
Deputy Prodn Mgr: Jessika Rieck *E-mail:* jessika@benbellabooks.com
Graphic Design & Prodn Assoc: Aaron Edmiston *E-mail:* aaron@benbellabooks.com
Mktg Assoc, Matt Holt Books: Kerri Stebbins *E-mail:* kerri@benbellabooks.com
Founded: 2001
The best of health & nutrition, pop culture & smart nonfiction.
ISBN Prefix(es): 978-1-932100; 978-1-933771; 978-1-935251; 978-1-935618; 978-1-936661; 978-1-937856; 978-1-939529; 978-1-940363; 978-1-941631; 978-1-942952; 978-1-944648; 978-1-946885; 978-1-948836; 978-1-950665
Number of titles published annually: 40 Print
Total Titles: 150 Print
Imprints: BenBella Vegan; Matt Holt Books; Smart Pop

U.S. PUBLISHERS

Distributed by Simon & Schuster, LLC
Foreign Rep(s): Jonathan Ball Publishers (South Africa); Canadian Manda Group (Canada); Edison Garcia (Asia); NewSouth Books (Australia); Penguin Books India Pvt Ltd (India)
Membership(s): Independent Book Publishers Association (IBPA)

Matthew Bender & Co Inc, see LexisNexis®
Matthew Bender®

John Benjamins Publishing Co
10 Meadowbrook Rd, Brunswick, ME 04011
SAN: 219-7677
Toll Free Tel: 800-562-5666 (orders)
Web Site: www.benjamins.com
Key Personnel
Consultant: Paul Peranteau *E-mail:* paul@benjamins.com
Founded: 1981
Linguistics, language studies, ESL, terminology & art; translation studies; literacy; scientific study of consciousness & communication.
ISBN Prefix(es): 978-1-55619; 978-0-915027; 978-90-272; 978-1-58811
Number of titles published annually: 120 Print; 1 CD-ROM; 1 Online; 165 E-Book
Total Titles: 4,800 Print; 10 CD-ROM; 4 Online; 4,800 E-Book
Imprints: B R Gruener Publishing Co
Subsidiaries: John Benjamins North America Inc
Foreign Office(s): Box 36224, 1020 ME Amsterdam, Netherlands
Orders to: John Benjamins, PO Box 960, Herndon, VA 20172 *E-mail:* benjamins@presswarehouse.com
Returns: Books International, 22883 Quicksilver Dr, Dulles, VA 20166
Shipping Address: Books International, 22883 Quicksilver Dr, Dulles, VA 20166, Contact: Todd Riggelman *E-mail:* benjamins@presswarehouse.com
Warehouse: Books International, 22883 Quicksilver Dr, Dulles, VA 20166 *Fax:* 703-661-1501
Distribution Center: Books International, 22883 Quicksilver Dr, Dulles, VA 20166

§Bentley Publishers
Division of Robert Bentley Inc
1734 Massachusetts Ave, Cambridge, MA 02138-1804
SAN: 213-9839
Tel: 617-547-4170
E-mail: sales@bentleypubs.com
Web Site: www.bentleypublishers.com
Key Personnel
Chmn & Pres: Michael Bentley
Dir, Publg: Janet Barnes
Founded: 1949
Technical automotive reference, automotive repair manuals, automotive history, automotive performance driving & motorsports.
ISBN Prefix(es): 978-0-8376
Number of titles published annually: 35 Print
Total Titles: 400 Print; 30 CD-ROM; 30 Online
Imprints: Bentley Pubs (alternate imprint, used in parallel with Bentley Publishers); Linnaean Press (general trade, history, education & nontechnical topics)

BePuzzled
Division of University Games
2030 Harrison St, San Francisco, CA 94110
Tel: 415-934-3705 *Toll Free Tel:* 800-347-4818
E-mail: info@ugames.com; consumer@ugames.com
Web Site: universitygames.com
Key Personnel
Pres: Bob Moog *E-mail:* moog@ugames.com
Gen Mgr: Craig Hendrickson *E-mail:* craigh@ugames.com
Founded: 1985

Puzzle Plus & Brain Teaser collections including Original 3D Crystal Puzzles, 3D Pixel Puzzles, Hanayama Cast Puzzles, Classic Mystery Jigsaw Puzzles & Preschool Jigsaw Puzzles.
ISBN Prefix(es): 978-1-57528; 978-1-57561
Number of titles published annually: 15 Print
Total Titles: 50 Print
Membership(s): American Specialty Toy Retailing Association (ASTRA); Toy International Association (TIA)

Berghahn Books
20 Jay St, Suite 512, Brooklyn, NY 11201
Tel: 212-233-6004 *Fax:* 212-233-6007
E-mail: info@berghahnbooks.com; salesus@berghahnbooks.com; editorial@journals.berghahnbooks.com
Web Site: www.berghahnbooks.com
Key Personnel
Publr & Ed-in-Chief: Dr Marion Berghahn *E-mail:* publisher@berghahnbooks.com
Publg Opers Dir, Books & Journals: Melissa Gannon *E-mail:* melissa.gannon@berghahnbooks.com
Mng Dir & Journals Edit Dir: Vivian Berghahn *E-mail:* vivian.berghahn@berghahnbooks.com
Mktg Mgr, Journals: Young Lee *E-mail:* young.lee@berghahnbooks.com
Sales & Mktg Mgr: Michelle Bayuk
Founded: 1994
Scholarly books & journals in humanities & social sciences.
ISBN Prefix(es): 978-1-57181; 978-1-84545
Number of titles published annually: 150 Print; 1,000 E-Book
Total Titles: 2,800 Print; 1,500 E-Book
Divisions: Berghahn Books Ltd (UK)
Foreign Office(s): 3 Newtec Place, Magdalen Rd, Oxford OX4 1RE, United Kingdom *Tel:* (01865) 250011 *Fax:* (01865) 250056
Foreign Rep(s): About3 Pty Ltd (Australia, New Zealand); Avicenna (Middle East, North Africa); Iberian Book Services (Peter Prout) (Portugal, Spain); Jacek Lewinson (Central Europe, Eastern Europe); MHM Ltd (Japan); Missing Link (Germany); Ian Taylor Associates Ltd (China); David Towle International (David Towle) (Scandinavia); Unifacmanu Trading Co Ltd (Celine Li) (Taiwan); Andrew White (India, Malaysia, Southeast Asia)
Foreign Rights: Afroditi Forti (worldwide)
Warehouse: Ingram, Jackson, TN

Berkley
Imprint of Penguin Publishing Group
c/o Penguin Random House LLC, 1745 Broadway, 19th fl, New York, NY 10019
Tel: 212-366-2000
Web Site: www.penguin.com/publishers/berkley/; www.penguin.com/ace-overview/
Key Personnel
Pres, Putnam/Dutton/Berkley: Ivan Held
EVP & Publr: Christine Ball
SVP & Exec Creative Dir, Putnam/Dutton/Berkley: Anthony Ramondo
VP & Deputy Publr: Jeanne-Marie Hudson
VP & Assoc Publr: Craig Burke
VP & Edit Dir: Amanda Bergeron; Tom Colgan; Cindy Hwang
VP & Ed-in-Chief: Claire Zion
Exec Dir, Ad & Promo, Berkley/Dutton/Plume/Putnam: Jaime Mendola-Hobbie
Dir, Mktg: Jin Yu
Publicity Dir: Erin Galloway
Assoc Dir, Digital Mktg: Bridget O'Toole
Assoc Dir, Mktg: Jessica Mangicaro
Asst Publicity Dir: Lauren Burnstein; Danielle Keir
Exec Ed: Tracy Bernstein; Kerry Donovan; Jen Monroe; Kate Seaver; Esi Sogah; Anne Sowards; Kristine Swartz; Michelle Vega; Jessica Wade
Sr Ed: Sarah Blumenstock

Ed: Lisa Bonvissuto; Sareer Khader; Angela Kim
Ed-at-Large: Leis Pederson
Assoc Ed: Liz Sellers
Asst Ed: Mary Baker; Candice Coote
Edit Asst: Carly James; Amanda Maurer; Annelise Odders; Gabrielle Pachon
Publg Assoc: Kiera Bertrand
Sr Mktg Mgr: Jessica Plummer
Assoc Mktg Mgr: Elisha Katz
Sr Publicist: Kristin Cipolla; Tina Joell; Tara O'Connor; Chelsea Pascoe
Publicist: Stephanie Felty; Dache' Rogers
Assoc Publicist: Yazmine Hassan
Digital Mktg Assoc: Alicia Ross
Mktg Assoc: Kim Salina-I; Hillary Tacuri
Founded: 1954
An industry leader in commercial & genre fiction, Berkley has a rich tradition of discovering new talent, defining emerging trends & building authors & series into global franchises. With Berkley's dedicated focus & guidance, many bestselling authors have grown into international brand names, including Nora Roberts, William Gibson, Laurell K Hamilton, Jim Butcher & Charlaine Harris. We're proud to publish Jasmine Guillory, Jayne Ann Krentz, Karen White, Patricia Briggs, Christine Feehan, Mark Greaney, Susan Meissner, Kristan Higgins & Chanel Cleeton, among others.
Number of titles published annually: 350 Print
Imprints: Ace Books; Berkley Books; Jove; Prime Crime; Signet Classics

Berkshire Publishing Group LLC
122 Castle St, Great Barrington, MA 01230
E-mail: info@berkshirepublishing.com; cservice@berkshirepublishing.com; rights@berkshirepublishing.com
Web Site: www.berkshirepublishing.com
Key Personnel
CEO: Karen Christensen
Founded: 2005
Specialize in international relations, cross-cultural communication, global business & economic information, environmental sustainability.
ISBN Prefix(es): 978-1-933782
Number of titles published annually: 7 Print; 6 E-Book
Orders to: Eurospan Group, Grays Inn House, 127 Clerkenwell Rd, London EC1R 5DB, United Kingdom (Continental Europe & UK) *Tel:* (020) 7240 0856 *Fax:* (020) 7379 0609 *E-mail:* info@eurospangroup.com *Web Site:* eurospanbookstore.com/berkshire

Bernan
Imprint of Rowman & Littlefield Publishing Group
4501 Forbes Blvd, Suite 200, Lanham, MD 20706
Mailing Address: PO Box 191, Blue Ridge Summit, PA 17214-0191
Tel: 717-794-3800 (cust serv & orders)
Toll Free Tel: 800-462-6420 (cust serv & orders) *Fax:* 717-794-3803 *Toll Free Fax:* 800-338-4550
E-mail: customercare@rowman.com; orders@rowman.com; publicity@rowman.com
Web Site: rowman.com/page/bernan
Key Personnel
Res Ed: Mary Meghan Ryan *Tel:* 301-459-3366 ext 5720 *E-mail:* mryan@rowman.com
Mktg Mgr: Veronica M Dove *Tel:* 301-459-2255 ext 5716 *Fax:* 301-459-0056 *E-mail:* vdove@rowman.com
Founded: 1952
Publishes original government-related reference works & provides a wide range of services to help librarians build their government information collections.
ISBN Prefix(es): 978-1-59888; 978-1-63671
Number of titles published annually: 45 Print
Total Titles: 336 Print

PUBLISHERS

Distribution Center: National Book Network, 15200 NBN Way, Blue Ridge Summit, PA 17214 *Tel:* 301-459-7666 *Toll Free Tel:* 800-865-3457 *Fax:* 301-459-6988 *Toll Free Fax:* 800-865-3450

§**Berrett-Koehler Publishers Inc**
1333 Broadway, Suite 1000, Oakland, CA 94612
Tel: 510-817-2277 *Fax:* 510-817-2278
E-mail: bkpub@bkpub.com
Web Site: www.bkconnection.com
Key Personnel
Founder & Sr Ed: Steve Piersanti
Publr & CEO: Praveen Madan
VP, Design & Prodn: Edward Wade
VP, Edit: Lesley Iura
VP, Sales & Mktg: Kristen Frantz
Mng Dir, Edit: Jeevan Sivasubramaniam
Art Dir: Ashley Ingram
Dir, Subs Rts: Catherine Lengronne
Edit Dir: Neal Maillet
Assoc Dir, Communs: Katie Sheehan
Assoc Dir, Data & Technol: Kenneth Cook
Sr HR Mgr: Sean Davis
Sr Mktg Mgr & Copywriter: Christy Kirk
    E-mail: ckirk@bkpub.com
Sr Sales Mgr: Leslie Crandell
Acctg Mgr: Accalia Calip
Prodn Mgr: Katelyn Keating
Royalty Mgr: Alison Knowles
Digital Mktg Strategist: Sarah Nelson
Mktg & Metadata Coord: Robert Fox
Founded: 1992
Publications on business, work, stewardship, leadership, management, career development, human resources, entrepreneurship & global sustainability for the trade, scholarly, text & professional reference markets.
ISBN Prefix(es): 978-1-881052; 978-1-57675; 978-1-887208; 978-1-56726; 978-1-62656; 978-1-5230; 978-1-58376; 978-1-60509; 978-1-60994
Number of titles published annually: 40 Print
Total Titles: 320 Print
Distribution Center: Penguin Random House International *Tel:* 410-848-1900 *Toll Free Tel:* 888-523-9292 (CN) *E-mail:* customerservice@penguinrandomhouse.com

§**Bess Press Inc**
3565 Harding Ave, Honolulu, HI 96816
Tel: 808-734-7159 *Fax:* 808-732-3627
E-mail: customerservice@besspress.com
Web Site: www.besspress.com
Key Personnel
Owner & Publr: Benjamin E Bess
Dir, Publg & COO: David DeLuca
    E-mail: deluca@besspress.com
Founded: 1979
Books about the Pacific Islands, with a special emphasis on Hawaii. Includes elementary & secondary level textbooks in Hawaiian & Pacific Island history, geography & environment, Hawaiian & Pacific bilingual language materials, popular regional trade paperbacks, cookbooks, anthologies, humor, Christmas, guides, how-to & children's books on Hawaii & Oceania.
ISBN Prefix(es): 978-0-935848; 978-1-880188; 978-1-57306; 978-1-949000
Number of titles published annually: 17 Print
Total Titles: 700 Print; 12 Audio
Distributed by The Islander Group

Bethany House Publishers
Division of Baker Publishing Group
11400 Hampshire Ave S, Bloomington, MN 55438
SAN: 201-4416
Tel: 952-829-2500 *Toll Free Tel:* 800-877-2665 (orders) *Fax:* 952-829-2568 *Toll Free Fax:* 800-398-3111 (orders)
Web Site: www.bethanyhouse.com; www.bakerpublishinggroup.com
Key Personnel
EVP & Dir: Jim Parrish
VP, Edit: David Horton
VP, Mktg: Steve Oates
Pres, Baker Publishing Group: Dwight Baker
EVP, Sales & Mktg, Baker Publishing Group: Dave Lewis
Natl Sales Mgr: Rod Jantzen
Founded: 1956
Religion (Evangelical).
ISBN Prefix(es): 978-0-87123; 978-1-55661; 978-0-7642; 978-0-76428
Number of titles published annually: 75 Print; 75 E-Book
Total Titles: 1,100 Print
Foreign Rep(s): Challenge Enterprises of Ghana (Nigeria); Christian Literature Center (Hong Kong); Christian Literature Crusade (Japan); Glad Sounds Sdn Bhd (Malaysia); Manna Christian Stores (New Zealand); Salvation Book Center (Malaysia); Scripture Union (Singapore); SPCK (Netherlands, Norway, Sweden, UK); Word of Life Press (Japan, South Korea)

Bethlehem Books
Affiliate of Bethlehem Community
10194 Garfield St S, Bathgate, ND 58216
Toll Free Tel: 800-757-6831 *Fax:* 701-265-3716
E-mail: contact@bethlehembooks.com
Web Site: www.bethlehembooks.com
Key Personnel
Pres: Jim Rasmussen
Gen Mgr & Publr: Daniel Rasmussen
    E-mail: dan@bethlehembooks.com
Founded: 1993
Children's & youth books.
ISBN Prefix(es): 978-1-883937; 978-1-932350
Number of titles published annually: 8 Print; 10 E-Book; 4 Audio
Total Titles: 100 Print; 100 E-Book; 22 Audio
Distributed by Ignatius Press
Foreign Rights: Canadian Home Education Resources (Canada); St Andrews Books (Canada); Saint Benedicts Book Centre (Australia); Sunrise Marian Distributors (Canada)
Distribution Center: Amazon.com

§**Bhaktivedanta Book Trust (BBT)**
9701 Venice Blvd, Suite 3, Los Angeles, CA 90034
Mailing Address: PO Box 341445, Los Angeles, CA 90034
Tel: 310-837-5283 *Toll Free Tel:* 800-927-4152 *Fax:* 310-837-1056
E-mail: store@krishna.com
Web Site: www.krishna.com
Founded: 1972
Books of Vedic culture & philosophy, vegetarianism, reincarnation & karma.
ISBN Prefix(es): 978-0-89213; 978-0-912776
Number of titles published annually: 3 Print; 2 CD-ROM
Total Titles: 96 Print; 2 E-Book; 84 Audio
Warehouse: 13569 Larwin Circle, Santa Fe Springs, CA 90670-5032, Contact: Efren Gonzalez *Tel:* 562-229-1234 *Fax:* 562-229-1080

BiG GUY BOOKS
6866 Embarcadero Lane, Carlsbad, CA 92011
SAN: 253-0392
Tel: 760-652-5360 *Toll Free Tel:* 800-536-3030 (booksellers' cust serv)
E-mail: info@greatbooksforboys.com
Web Site: www.bigguybooks.com
Key Personnel
Pres: Robert Gould *E-mail:* robert@bigguybooks.com

U.S. PUBLISHERS

Founded: 2000
Publishes high quality adventure stories for children. Combine cutting-edge graphics & old fashioned values to increase literacy as well as confidence & self-respect in young male readers.
ISBN Prefix(es): 978-1-929945
Number of titles published annually: 3 Print
Imprints: BiG STUFF™; Time Soldiers®
Membership(s): American Booksellers Association (ABA); The American Library Association (ALA); Independent Book Publishers Association (IBPA)

§**Biographical Publishing Co**
95 Sycamore Dr, Prospect, CT 06712-1011
Tel: 203-758-3661 *Fax:* 253-793-2618
E-mail: biopub@aol.com
Web Site: www.biopub.us
Key Personnel
Ed: John R Guevin
Founded: 1991
Pre-print, printing & marketing services.
ISBN Prefix(es): 978-0-9637240; 978-1-929882; 978-1-7338120; 978-0-9976028; 978-1-7369019
Number of titles published annually: 5 Print; 5 E-Book; 2 Audio
Total Titles: 150 Print; 110 Online; 50 E-Book; 5 Audio
Distributor for Eagles Landing Publishing; Spyglass Books LLC
Distribution Center: Pathway Book Service, 34 Production Ave, Keene, NH 03431, Serv Contact: Bob Zipoli *Tel:* 603-357-0236 *Toll Free Tel:* 800-345-6665 *Fax:* 603-357-2073 *E-mail:* pbs@pathwaybook.com *Web Site:* www.pathwaybook.com

Bird Dog Publishing, see Bottom Dog Press

§**George T Bisel Co Inc**
710 S Washington Sq, Philadelphia, PA 19106-3519
Tel: 215-922-5760 *Toll Free Tel:* 800-247-3526 *Fax:* 215-922-2235
E-mail: gbisel@bisel.com
Web Site: www.bisel.com
Key Personnel
Pres & CEO: Franklin Jon Zuch *E-mail:* fjzuch@bisel.com
Ed-in-Chief: Tony Di Gioia
Ed: Frank Coyne *E-mail:* fcoyne@bisel.com
Acctg: Nikolas Grupp *E-mail:* ngrupp@bisel.com
Order Fulfillment: Ron Black *E-mail:* rblack@bisel.com
Sales & Mktg: Paul Roberts *E-mail:* proberts@bisel.com
Founded: 1876
Publisher & resource for books on Pennsylvania law, legal information & procedures.
ISBN Prefix(es): 978-1-887024; 978-0-9970199; 978-0-9755281; 979-8-9858848
Number of titles published annually: 8 Print
Total Titles: 75 Print; 10 CD-ROM; 1 Audio

§**Bisk Education**
9417 Princess Palm Ave, Suite 400, Tampa, FL 33619
Tel: 813-621-6200
E-mail: media@bisk.com
Web Site: www.bisk.com
Key Personnel
CEO: Mike Bisk
EVP & CFO: Justin Sheppard
EVP & Gen Coun: Rob Abramson
SVP, Learning Design: Dr Richard Sites
VP, Mktg: Joseph Lapin
VP, Technol: Jordan Medlen
VP, Workforce & Educ: Dr Jennifer King
Assoc VP, Mktg: Chris Shindelbower
Assoc VP, Workforce & Educ: Clynton Hunt

U.S. PUBLISHERS

Dir, Workforce & Educ: Dr Brenda Berube; Matt Sargent
Founded: 1971
One of the leading providers of online degree & certificate programs to learners around the world. Support for universities such as Villanova University, Michigan State University, University of South Florida, Florida Institute of Technology, Emory University, Southern Methodist University, University of British Columbia, Vanderbilt University, Eastern Connecticut University & Columbia Law School.
ISBN Prefix(es): 978-1-57961
Number of titles published annually: 50 Print
Total Titles: 500 Print; 50 CD-ROM; 150 Online; 9 E-Book; 90 Audio

Bisk Publishing Co, see Bisk Education

§Bitingduck Press LLC
1262 Sunnyoaks Circle, Altadena, CA 91001
Tel: 626-507-8033
E-mail: notifications@bitingduckpress.com
Web Site: bitingduckpress.com
Key Personnel
Ed-in-Chief: Jay Nadeau *E-mail:* jay@bitingduckpress.com
Creative Dir: Dena Eaton *E-mail:* dena@bitingduckpress.com
Technol Dir: Chris Lindensmith *E-mail:* chris@bitingduckpress.com
Ed: Barbara Thompson *E-mail:* barbara.j.thompson@gmail.com
Acqs Ed: Marie Nadeau *E-mail:* marie@bitingduckpress.com
Founded: 2012
Quality electronic publishing for a digital world.
ISBN Prefix(es): 978-1-938463; 978-1-68553
Number of titles published annually: 4 Print; 6 E-Book
Total Titles: 150 Print; 200 E-Book
Imprints: Boson Books™
Distribution Center: Ingram Book Group, One Ingram Blvd, La Vergne, TN *Tel:* 615-793-5000
Membership(s): The Authors Guild; Independent Book Publishing Professionals Group (IBPPG)
See separate listing for:
Boson Books™

§BJU Press
Unit of BJU Education Group
1430 Wade Hampton Blvd, Greenville, SC 29609-5046
SAN: 223-7512
Tel: 864-770-1317; 864-546-4600
    Toll Free Tel: 800-845-5731
E-mail: bjupinfo@bju.edu
Web Site: www.bjupress.com
Key Personnel
Pres: Bill Apelian
Exec Asst: Jennifer Headley
Founded: 1974
El-hi textbooks & trade media.
ISBN Prefix(es): 978-0-89084; 978-1-57924; 978-1-59166
Number of titles published annually: 50 Print
Total Titles: 2,500 Print
Imprints: JourneyForth Books
Warehouse: 134 White Oak Dr, Greenville, SC 29607-1218

BkMk Press Inc
5 W Third St, Parkville, MO 64152
Tel: 816-200-7895
E-mail: info@bkmkpress.org
Web Site: www.bkmkpress.org
Key Personnel
Ed: Ben Furnish *E-mail:* ben@bkmkpress.org
Founded: 1971
Fine literature & essays.
ISBN Prefix(es): 978-0-933532; 978-1-886157; 978-0-197010

Number of titles published annually: 5 Print
Total Titles: 130 Print
Distribution Center: University of Arkansas Press, 11030 S Langley Ave, Chicago, IL 60628 *Tel:* 773-702-7000 *Toll Free Tel:* 800-621-2736 *Fax:* 773-702-7212
Membership(s): Community of Literary Magazines & Presses (CLMP)

Black Classic Press
3921 Vero Rd, Suite F, Baltimore, MD 21203-3414
SAN: 219-5836
Mailing Address: PO Box 13414, Baltimore, MD 21203-3414
Tel: 410-242-6954 *Toll Free Tel:* 800-476-8870
E-mail: email@blackclassicbooks.com; blackclassicpress@yahoo.com
Web Site: www.blackclassicbooks.com; www.agooddaytoprint.com
Key Personnel
Pres: W Paul Coates
Publr: Natalie Stokes-Peters
Digital Print Consultant: Damani Coates
Founded: 1978
Publishing obscure & significant works by & about people of African descent.
ISBN Prefix(es): 978-0-933121; 978-1-57478
Number of titles published annually: 20 Print
Total Titles: 135 Print
Imprints: Inprint Editions
Distributed by Publishers Group West (PGW)
Membership(s): Independent Book Publishers Association (IBPA)

Black Dome Press Corp
PO Box 64, Catskill, NY 12414
Tel: 518-577-5238
E-mail: blackdomep@aol.com
Web Site: www.blackdomepress.com
Key Personnel
Publr: Steve Hoare
Founded: 1990
Regional small press publishing New York State & New England histories & guidebooks.
ISBN Prefix(es): 978-1-883789; 978-0-9628523; 979-8-9856921
Number of titles published annually: 3 Print
Total Titles: 100 Print; 1 Audio

Black Heron Press
PO Box 614, Anacortes, WA 98221
Tel: 360-899-9335
Web Site: blackheronpress.com
Key Personnel
Publr & Lib Sales Dir: Jerry Gold
    E-mail: jgoldberon@aol.com
Founded: 1984
Literary fiction & nonfiction pertaining to independent publishing & the writing craft; literature, science fiction (not dungeons & dragons).
ISBN Prefix(es): 978-0-930773; 978-1-936364
Number of titles published annually: 4 Print; 2 E-Book
Total Titles: 100 Print; 12 E-Book
Foreign Rights: Eulama International Literary Agency (Pina von Prellwitz) (worldwide)
Distribution Center: Independent Publishers Group (IPG), 814 N Franklin St, Chicago, IL 60610 *Tel:* 312-337-0747 *Toll Free Tel:* 800-888-4741 *Fax:* 312-337-5985 *E-mail:* orders@ipgbook.com *Web Site:* www.ipgbook.com

§Black Mountain Press
Unit of Flood Gallery Fine Arts Center
PO Box 9907, Asheville, NC 28815
Tel: 828-273-3332
Web Site: www.theblackmountainpress.com
Key Personnel
Publr: Carlos Steward *E-mail:* carlos@theblackmountainpress.com
Founded: 1994

Literary press for emerging writers. Focus on poetry, creative novels & short story collections.
ISBN Prefix(es): 978-0-9700165; 978-1-940605; 978-0-9649020; 978-1-9774138; 978-1-902867
Number of titles published annually: 12 Print; 10 E-Book
Total Titles: 25 Print; 10 E-Book

Black Rabbit Books
2140 Howard Dr W, North Mankato, MN 56003
Mailing Address: PO Box 3263, Mankato, MN 56002-3263
Tel: 507-388-1609 *Fax:* 507-388-2746
E-mail: info@blackrabbitbooks.com; orders@blackrabbitbooks.com
Web Site: www.blackrabbitbooks.com
Key Personnel
Assoc Publr: Jen Besel
VP, Sales: Jonathan Strickland
Founded: 2006
Founded on the principle that quality books produce quality readers. Our list of K-12 books has a wide variety of topics, innovative approaches & multiple reading levels to serve all facets of the school library market.
ISBN Prefix(es): 978-1-84234; 978-1-84193; 978-1-59920; 978-1-58340; 978-1-59771; 978-1-59566; 978-1-59604; 978-1-93288; 978-8-86098; 978-1-93383; 978-1-93279; 978-1-84837
Number of titles published annually: 375 Print
Total Titles: 2,000 Print
Imprints: Bolt; Bolt Jr; Book House; Brown Bear Books; Hi Jinx; Smart Apple Media
Foreign Rep(s): Saunders Book Co (Canada)
Distribution Center: The Creative Co, PO Box 227, Mankato, MN 56002 *Toll Free Tel:* 800-445-6209 *Fax:* 507-388-2746 *E-mail:* sales@thecreativecompany.us *Web Site:* thecreativecompany.us
Saunders Book Co, PO Box 308, Collingwood, ON L9Y 3Z7, Canada *Tel:* 705-445-4777 *Toll Free Tel:* 800-461-9120 *Fax:* 705-445-9569 *Toll Free Fax:* 800-561-1763 *E-mail:* info@saundersbooks.ca

The Blackburn Press
PO Box 287, Caldwell, NJ 07006-0287
Tel: 973-228-7077 *Fax:* 973-228-7276
Web Site: www.blackburnpress.com
Key Personnel
Publr & Edit Dir: Frances Reed *E-mail:* freed@blackburnpress.com
Gen Mgr: Maryanne Kenny *E-mail:* mkenny@blackburnpress.com
Cust Serv & Mktg: Barbara Chmiel
    E-mail: bchmiel@blackburnpress.com
Founded: 1999
Book titles, largely reprints, of classics in science & technology. Worldwide distributors.
ISBN Prefix(es): 978-1-930665; 978-1-932846
Number of titles published annually: 20 Print
Total Titles: 100 Print

§Blair
905 W Main St, Suite 19 D-1, Durham, NC 27701
Tel: 919-682-0555
E-mail: customersupport@blair.com
Web Site: www.blairpub.com
Key Personnel
Publr: Lynn York
Assoc Publr & Sr Ed: Robin Miura
Founded: 2018 (combined list of Carolina Wren Press & John F Blair, Publisher)
Prose & poetry.
ISBN Prefix(es): 978-0-910244; 978-0-89587; 978-0-932112
Number of titles published annually: 9 Print
Total Titles: 159 Print
Distribution Center: Consortium Book Sales & Distribution, The Keg House, 34 13 Ave NE, Suite 101, Minneapolis, MN 55413-1007

Tel: 612-746-2600 *Toll Free Tel:* 866-400-5351 *E-mail:* cbsdinfo@ingramcontent.com *Web Site:* www.cbsd.com SAN: 200-6049

Blood Moon Productions Ltd
75 Saint Marks Place, Staten Island, NY 10301-1606
Tel: 718-556-9410
Web Site: bloodmoonproductions.com
Key Personnel
Pres & Publr: William Danforth Prince
 E-mail: danforthprince@gmail.com
Founded: 2004
A New York-based publishing enterprise dedicated to researching, salvaging & indexing the oral histories of America's entertainment industry.
ISBN Prefix(es): 978-0-9748118; 978-0-9786465; 978-1-936003
Number of titles published annually: 4 Print; 4 E-Book
Total Titles: 55 Print; 55 E-Book
Distribution Center: National Book Network (NBN), 4501 Forbes Ave, Suite 200, Lanham, MD 20706 (select older titles) *Tel:* 301-459-3366 *E-mail:* customercare@nbnbooks.com *Web Site:* nbnbooks.com
Ingram Book Co, One Ingram Blvd, La Vergne, TN 37086 *Tel:* 615-793-5000 *Toll Free Tel:* 800-937-8200 *Fax:* 615-213-4426 *E-mail:* customerservice@ingramcontent.com *Web Site:* www.ingramcontent.com
Membership(s): American Booksellers Association (ABA); Independent Book Publishers Association (IBPA); New Atlantic Independent Booksellers Association (NAIBA); Southern Independent Booksellers Alliance (SIBA)

Bloom's Literary Criticism
Imprint of Infobase Learning
132 W 31 St, 16th fl, New York, NY 10001
Toll Free Tel: 800-322-8755 *Toll Free Fax:* 800-678-3633
E-mail: custserv@infobase.com
Web Site: www.infobasepublishing.com; www.infobase.com (online resources)
Key Personnel
Pres & CEO, Infobase Learning: Paul Skordilis
Edit Dir, Infobase Learning: Laurie Likoff
Dir, Book & Ebook Sales: Justyna Pawluk
 Tel: 800-322-8755 ext 4255 *E-mail:* jpawluk@infobaselearning.com
Dir, Licensing & Busn Devt, Infobase Learning: Ben Jacobs *Tel:* 212-896-4268
 E-mail: bjacobs@infobaselearning.com
Dir, Mktg, Infobase Learning: Zina Scarpulla
 Tel: 800-322-8755 ext 4218
Dir, Publicity, Infobase Learning: Laurie Katz
 Tel: 800-322-8755 ext 4269 *E-mail:* lkatz@infobaselearning.com
Offers hundreds of volumes of literary criticism edited by Harold Bloom, focusing on the writers & works most often studied in high schools & universities.
ISBN Prefix(es): 978-0-7910; 978-1-4381
Number of titles published annually: 67 Print; 67 E-Book
Total Titles: 453 Print; 525 E-Book
Foreign Rep(s): EDU Reference Publishers Direct Inc (Canada)
Returns: c/o Maple Logistics Solutions Distribution Ctr, 704 Legionaire Dr, Fredericksburg, PA 17026

Bloomsbury Academic
Imprint of Bloomsbury Publishing Inc
1385 Broadway, 5th fl, New York, NY 10018
SAN: 213-8220
Tel: 212-419-5300
Web Site: www.bloomsbury.com/us/academic
Key Personnel
Publr, Fairchild Books: Emily Samulski
 E-mail: emily.samulski@bloomsbury.com
Publr, Film & Media Studies: Katie Gallof
 E-mail: katie.gallof@bloomsbury.com
Publr, Music & Sound Studies: Leah Babb-Rosenfeld *E-mail:* leah.babb-rosenfeld@bloomsbury.com
Academic Publg Dir, Digital: Kevin Ohe
 E-mail: kevin.ohe@bloomsbury.com
Dir, Scholarly & Student Publg US: Haaris Naqvi
 E-mail: haaris.naqvi@bloomsbury.com
Edit Dir, Bloomsbury Libraries Unlimited: David Paige *E-mail:* david.paige@bloomsbury.com
Edit Dir, Bloomsbury Reference: Kevin Downing
 E-mail: kevin.downing@bloomsbury.com
US A&P Sales Dir: Karen Treat *E-mail:* ktreat@abc-clio.com
Sr Acqs Ed, Bloomsbury Reference: Kevin Hillstrom *E-mail:* kevin.hillstrom@bloomsbury.com; Maxine Taylor *E-mail:* maxine.taylor@bloomsbury.com
Sr Devt Ed, Bloomsbury Libraries Unlimited: Emma Bailey *E-mail:* emma.bailey@bloomsbury.com
Acqs Ed, Bloomsbury Libraries Unlimited: Jessica Gribble *E-mail:* jessica.gribble@bloomsbury.com
Acqs Ed, Bloomsbury Reference: Thomas Krause *E-mail:* thomas.krause@bloomsbury.com; Fatima Policarpo *E-mail:* fatima.policarpo@bloomsbury.com
Acqs Ed, Literary Studies: Amy Martin
 E-mail: amy.martin@bloomsbury.com
Acqs Ed, Music & Sound Studies: Rachel Moore
 E-mail: rachel.moore@bloomsbury.com
Acqs Ed, Politics: Katherine De Chant
 E-mail: katherine.dechant@bloomsbury.com
Art Devt Ed, Fairchild Books: Edie Weinberg
 E-mail: edie.weinberg@bloomsbury.com
Devt Ed, Bloomsbury Reference: Nicole Azze
 E-mail: nicole.azze@bloomsbury.com
Devt Ed, Fairchild Books: Julie Vitale
 E-mail: julie.vitale@bloomsbury.com
Asst Ed, Film & Media Studies: Stephanie Grace-Petinos *E-mail:* stephanie.grace-petinos@bloomsbury.com
Asst Ed, Literary Studies: Hali Han *E-mail:* hali.han@bloomsbury.com
Asst Ed, Politics: Saville Bloxham
 E-mail: saville.bloxham@bloomsbury.com
Sr Mktg Mgr, Philosophy & History: Joe Kreuser
 E-mail: joseph.kreuser@bloomsbury.com
Devt Mgr, Fairchild Books: Joseph Miranda
 E-mail: joseph.miranda@bloomsbury.com
Mktg Mgr, Visual Arts & Drama: Paige Domantey *E-mail:* paige.domantey@bloomsbury.com
Publicity Mgr: Deirdre Kenney *E-mail:* deirdre.kennedy@bloomsbury.com
Asst Mktg Mgr: Ellie Scott
Mktg Assoc: Elizabeth Morris *E-mail:* elizabeth.morris@bloomsbury.com
Mktg Assoc, Area Studies: Celia Moore
 E-mail: celia.moore@bloomsbury.com
Edit Asst, Bloomsbury Reference & Bloomsbury Libraries Unlimited: Adriane Kong
 E-mail: adriane.kong@bloomsbury.com
Edit Asst, Fairchild Books: Maria Nunez
 E-mail: maria.nunez@bloomsbury.com
Founded: 1999 (result of a merger between The Continuum Publishing Company of NY & the academic & religious publishing programs of Cassell plc in London)
Hardcover & paperbacks; scholarly & professional & general interest; music, film, literature, media studies, the arts & popular culture; philosophy, religion, biblical studies, theology & spirituality, history, politics & contemporary issues, education; women's studies & reference.
ISBN Prefix(es): 978-0-304; 978-0-7201; 978-0-8264; 978-1-56338; 978-0-7136; 978-0-86012; 978-0-225; 978-0-264; 978-0-7185; 978-0-86187; 978-1-85567; 978-0-7220; 978-0-567; 978-0-485; 978-1-84127; 978-1-85805; 978-1-84371; 978-0-8044; 978-0-223
Number of titles published annually: 1,200 Print
Total Titles: 6,000 Print
Distributor for Paragon House; Spring Publications
Foreign Rights: Allen & Unwin Pty Ltd (Australia); APD (Brunei, Indonesia, Malaysia, Singapore, Thailand, Vietnam); APS Ltd (China, Hong Kong, Philippines, South Korea, Taiwan); Robert Barnett (USA); BCR University Bookstore (Jamaica); Bounty Press Ltd (Nigeria); Continuum (Africa exc North & South Africa, Caribbean, Germany, Israel, Netherlands, North America); Durnell Marketing Ltd (Europe); Horizon Books (Botswana, Lesotho, Namibia, South Africa, Swaziland); IPS (Middle East exc Israel, North Africa); Richard Lyle (London); Maya Publishers Pvt Ltd (Bangladesh, India, Sri Lanka); Richard McNeace (USA); Natoli Stefan & Oliva Literary Agency (Italy); Novalis (Canada); Nick Pepper (Northern England, Scotland); Publishers Consultants & Representatives (Pakistan); Jonathan Rhodes (England, Midlands); Andrew Toal (England); United Publishers Services Ltd (Japan)

Bloomsbury Libraries Unlimited, see Libraries Unlimited

Bloomsbury Publishing Inc
Subsidiary of Bloomsbury Publishing Plc
1385 Broadway, 5th fl, New York, NY 10018
Tel: 212-419-5300
E-mail: marketingusa@bloomsbury.com; adultpublicityusa@bloomsbury.com; askacademic@bloomsbury.com
Web Site: www.bloomsbury.com
Key Personnel
Pres: Sabrina McCarthy
VP, US Sales & Mktg: Valentina Rice
Sr Dir, Inventory & Opers: Donna Gauthier
Sr Dir, Mktg & Publicity, Children's Trade: Erica Barmash
Sr Dir, Mktg, Publicity & Communs: Marie Coolman
Sr Dir, School & Lib Mktg & Dom Subs Rts: Beth Eller
Mng Edit Dir: Laura Phillips
Academic Publg Dir, Digital Prods: Kevin Ohe
Academic Mktg & Publicity Dir: Elena McAnespie
Brand Dir: Angela Craft
Dir, Children's Publicity: Faye Bi
Dir, Mktg Design & Opers: Alona Fryman
Dir, Scholarly & Student Publg US: Haaris Naqvi
Edit Dir, Adult Trade: Callie Garnett
Edit Dir, Children's: Sarah Shumway
Mktg & Publicity Dir: Rachel Ewen
Mktg Dir, Adult Trade: Lauren Moseley
Mktg Dir, Bloomsbury Digital Resources: Michelle Kelly
Publg Dir, Adult Trade: Nancy Miller
Publg Dir, Children's Trade: Mary Kate Castellani
Sales Dir, US Academic & Prof: Daniel Bean
Assoc Art Dir, Children's: Jeanette Levy
Assoc Dir, Children's Mktg: Lily Yengle
Assoc Rts Dir: Jennifer Choi
Asst Art Dir: Katya Mezhibovskaya
Exec Ed, Adult Trade: Anton Mueller
Exec Ed, Children's: Noa Wheeler
Mng Ed: Barbara Darko
Sr Ed, Adult Trade: Grace McNamee; Amber Oliver
Sr Ed, Children's: Camille Kellogg
Sr Ed, Children's & Young Adults: Alex Borbolla
Sr Prodn Ed: Oona Patrick
Ed, Adult Trade: Mo Crist
Nonfiction Ed, Children's: Megan Abbate
Prodn Ed, Adult Trade: Akshaya Iyer; Rebecca McGlynn

U.S. PUBLISHERS

Assoc Ed, Adult Trade: Morgan Jones; Harriet LeFavour
Assoc Prodn Ed: Hannah Bowe
Asst Ed, Adult Trade: Ragav Maripudi
Asst Ed, Children's: Kei Nakatsuka; Hannah Rivera; Kate Sederstrom
Asst Prodn Ed, Adult Trade: Suzanne Keller
Sr Acct Mgr, Bloomsbury Digital Resources: Melissa Mazza
Sr Publicity Mgr, Adult Trade: Amanda Dissinger; Rosie Mahorter
Mktg Mgr, Adult Trade: Katie Vaughn
Publicity Mgr, Children's & Young Adult: Alexa Higbee
Sales Mgr, Trade: Jaclyn Sassa
Soc Media Mgr: Phoebe Dyer
Asst Rts Mgr: Andrew Nguyen
Children's Asst School & Lib Mktg Mgr: Kathleen Morandini
Sr Commercial & Fin Planning Analyst, Trade & Spec Interest: Daniel O'Connor
Sr Publicist, Adult Trade: Lauren Ollerhead Fries
Publicist, Adult Trade: Emily Fishman
Assoc Publicist, Children's: Ariana Abad
Mktg Assoc, Adult Trade: Kenli Young
Mktg Assoc, Children's: Briana Williams
Publicity Asst, Adult Trade: Lauren Wilson
Sales & Mktg Asst: Catherine Valdez
Exec Designer: Erica Chan
Designer, Children's Art Dept: Yelena Safronova
Founded: 1998
No unsol mss.
ISBN Prefix(es): 978-1-58234; 978-1-61963; 978-1-62040; 978-1-63286; 978-1-68119; 978-1-59691; 978-1-59990; 978-1-60819
Number of titles published annually: 100 Print
Imprints: Bloomsbury; Bloomsbury Academic; Bloomsbury USA (adult); Libraries Unlimited; Osprey Publishing
Subsidiaries: ABC-CLIO
Distributed by Macmillan
Orders to: MPS Distribution Center, 16365 James Madison Hwy, Gordonsville, VA 22942-8501 Toll Free Tel: 888-330-8477 Toll Free Fax: 800-672-2054
Returns: MPS Returns Center, 14301 Litchfield Rd, Orange, VA 22960
Distribution Center: MPS Distribution Center, 16365 James Madison Hwy, Gordonsville, VA 22942-8501 Toll Free Tel: 888-330-8477 Toll Free Fax: 800-672-2054
See separate listing for:
ABC-CLIO
Bloomsbury Academic
Libraries Unlimited

§BLR®—Business & Legal Resources
Division of Simplify Compliance LLC
5511 Virginia Way, Suite 150, Brentwood, TN 37027
Tel: 860-510-0100 Toll Free Tel: 800-727-5257 Toll Free Fax: 800-785-9212
E-mail: media@blr.com; sales@blr.com; service@blr.com; techsupport@blr.com
Web Site: blr.com
Key Personnel
Pres: Darin McMillan
VP, Client Experience: Beth Greene
Dir, Sales: Will Honeycutt
Busn Devt: Heather Payne
Founded: 1977
Business newsletters, books, booklets, films & CD-ROMs. Specialize in safety, human resource & environmental training & compliance.
ISBN Prefix(es): 978-1-55645
Number of titles published annually: 100 Print
Total Titles: 380 Print; 113 CD-ROM; 4 Online; 4 E-Book
Divisions: HCPro; HealthLeaders Media; M Lee Smith Publishers
Membership(s): NEPA

See separate listing for:
HCPro/DecisionHealth
M Lee Smith Publishers

Blue Book Publications Inc
PO Box 184, Eva, AL 35621
Tel: 952-854-5229 Toll Free Tel: 800-877-4867 Fax: 952-853-1486
E-mail: support@bluebookinc.com
Web Site: www.bluebookofgunvalues.com; www.bluebookofguitarvalues.com
Founded: 1989
Industry leader in up-to-date & accurate values & information for firearms, airguns, modern black powder replicas, amplifiers & fretted instruments. Publisher of reference books, consumer pricing guides, encyclopedias & coffee table books. Online information provider/appraisals.
ISBN Prefix(es): 978-1-936120
Number of titles published annually: 20 Print; 8 Online; 2 E-Book
Total Titles: 200 Print; 8 Online; 2 E-Book
Membership(s): American Booksellers Association (ABA); Midwest Independent Booksellers Association (MIBA); Outdoor Writers Association of America (OWAA)

Blue Crane Books Inc
36 Hazel St, Watertown, MA 02472
Tel: 617-926-8989
Key Personnel
Pres: Alvart Badalian
Secy: Mr Aramais Andonian
Founded: 1991
Publish adult trade fiction & nonfiction, history, political & social sciences, culture & art. Special line of adult & children's books in Armenian & English translations of Armenian originals. No unsol mss.
ISBN Prefix(es): 978-0-9628715; 978-1-886434
Number of titles published annually: 3 Print
Total Titles: 20 Print

Blue Mountain Arts Inc
PO Box 4549, Boulder, CO 80306-4549
SAN: 299-9609
Tel: 303-449-0536 Toll Free Tel: 800-525-0642 Toll Free Fax: 800-545-8573
E-mail: info@sps.com; bmpbooks@sps.com (submissions)
Web Site: www.sps.com
Founded: 1971
Publisher of trade books: inspirational, self-improvement, personal growth, gift books & sidelines.
ISBN Prefix(es): 978-0-88396; 978-1-58786; 978-1-59842; 978-0-98288; 978-1-68088
Number of titles published annually: 20 Print; 20 Online
Total Titles: 120 Print; 120 Online
Imprints: Artes Monte Azul; Blue Mountain Press®; Orphiflamme Press™; Rabbit's Foot Press™
Returns: 6455 Spine Rd, Boulder, CO 80301
Shipping Address: 6455 Spine Rd, Boulder, CO 80301
Membership(s): National Association of College Stores (NACS)

Blue Note Books, see Blue Note Publications Inc

Blue Note Publications Inc
721 North Dr, Suite D, Melbourne, FL 32934
Tel: 321-799-2583; 321-622-6289
 Toll Free Tel: 800-624-0401 (orders) Fax: 321-799-1942; 321-622-6830
E-mail: bluenotebooks@gmail.com
Web Site: bluenotepublications.com
Key Personnel
Pres: Paul Maluccio
Founded: 1988
Small press book publishing, production, printing, distribution, marketing.
ISBN Prefix(es): 978-1-878398; 978-0-9963066
Number of titles published annually: 25 Print; 20 Online; 15 E-Book
Total Titles: 180 Print; 2 CD-ROM; 80 Online; 40 E-Book
Imprints: Blue Note; Blue Note Books
Membership(s): Independent Book Publishers Association (IBPA)

§Blue Poppy Press
Division of Blue Poppy Enterprises Inc
4824 SE 69 Ave, Portland, OR 97206
Tel: 503-650-6077 Toll Free Tel: 800-487-9296 Fax: 503-650-6076
E-mail: info@bluepoppy.com
Web Site: www.bluepoppy.com
Founded: 1982
Books on acupuncture & Chinese medicine.
ISBN Prefix(es): 978-0-936185; 978-1-891845
Number of titles published annually: 20 Print; 3 E-Book
Total Titles: 100 Print; 100 E-Book
Distribution Center: China Books
New Leaf Books
Partner's Book Distributing Inc
Partner's/West Book Distributing Inc
Redwing Book Co
Satas

Blue Whale Press
237 Rainbow Dr, No 13702, Livingston, TX 77399-2037
SAN: 855-7004
Toll Free Tel: 800-848-1631
E-mail: info@bluewhalepress.com; sales@bluewhalepress.com
Web Site: www.bluewhalepress.com
Key Personnel
Content & Developmental Ed: Alayne Kay Christian E-mail: submissions@bluewhalepress.com
Publr: Steve Kemp E-mail: steve@bluewhalepress.com
Founded: 2008
ISBN Prefix(es): 978-0-9814938; 978-1-7328935
Number of titles published annually: 4 Print
Total Titles: 3 Print
Distribution Center: Follett School Solutions Inc, 1340 Ridgeview Dr, McHenry, IL 60050 Tel: 815-759-1700 Toll Free Tel: 888-511-5114 (cust serv) Fax: 815-759-9831 Toll Free Fax: 800-852-5458 E-mail: info@follettlearning.com Web Site: www.follettlearning.com SAN: 169-1902
Ingram Content Group LLC, One Ingram Blvd, La Vergne, TN 37086-1986 Tel: 615-793-5000 Web Site: www.ingramcontent.com

BlueBridge
Imprint of United Tribes Media Inc
8 Cottage Place, Katonah, NY 10536
Tel: 914-301-5901
Web Site: www.bluebridgebooks.com
Key Personnel
Founder & Publr: Jan-Erik Guerth E-mail: janguerth@bluebridgebooks.com
Founded: 2004
Independent publisher of international nonfiction based near New York City. Subjects include culture, history, biography, nature & science, inspiration & self-help.
ISBN Prefix(es): 978-1-933346; 978-0-9742405; 978-1-62919
Number of titles published annually: 4 Print
Total Titles: 40 Print
Distribution Center: Publishers Group West, 1700 Fourth St, Berkeley, CA 94710 Tel: 510-809-3700 Toll Free Tel: 866-400-5351 (cust serv) Fax: 510-809-3777 Toll Free Fax: 800-838-1149 E-mail: ips@ingramcontent.com Web Site: www.pgw.com

PUBLISHERS

Bluestocking Press
3045 Sacramento St, No 1014, Placerville, CA 95667-1014
SAN: 667-2981
Mailing Address: PO Box 1014, Placerville, CA 95667-1014
Tel: 530-622-8586 *Toll Free Tel:* 800-959-8586 *Fax:* 530-642-9222
E-mail: customerservice@bluestockingpress.com; orders@bluestockingpress.com
Web Site: www.bluestockingpress.com
Key Personnel
Owner & Pres: Jane A Williams *E-mail:* jane@bluestockingpress.com
Founded: 1987
Among subjects offered: free market economics, business, finance, justice, ancient Rome, World Wars, Mideast War. Sell on nonreturnable basis (except for books received damaged) to the reseller market.
ISBN Prefix(es): 978-0-942617
Number of titles published annually: 21 Print
Total Titles: 23 Print
Sales Office(s): PO Box 1014, Placerville, CA 95667-1014, Contact: Ann Marie *E-mail:* annmarie@bluestockingpress.com
Billing Address: PO Box 1014, Placerville, CA 95667-1014, Accts Payable: Jane Williams *E-mail:* jane@bluestockingpress.com
Orders to: PO Box 1014, Placerville, CA 95667-1014, Contact: Ann Marie *E-mail:* annmarie@bluestockingpress.com

BNi Building News
990 Park Center Dr, Suite E, Vista, CA 92081-8352
Tel: 760-734-1113 (pubn dept) *Toll Free Tel:* 888-BNI-BOOK (264-2665)
Web Site: www.bnibooks.com
Founded: 1946
Construction books, building codes, legal forms & contracts, cost estimating tools & other reference materials for the building trades.
ISBN Prefix(es): 978-1-55701; 978-1-878088; 978-1-58855
Number of titles published annually: 100 Print
Total Titles: 120 Print

BOA Editions Ltd
250 N Goodman St, Suite 306, Rochester, NY 14607
Tel: 585-546-3410 *Fax:* 585-546-3913
E-mail: contact@boaeditions.org
Web Site: www.boaeditions.org
Key Personnel
Publr: Peter Conners *E-mail:* conners@boaeditions.org
Devt Dir & Off Mgr: Kelly Hatton *E-mail:* hatton@boaeditions.org
Dir, Mktg & Prodn: Ron Martin-Dent *E-mail:* martindent@boaeditions.org
Founded: 1976
Publication of books of poetry, poetry in translation & fiction.
ISBN Prefix(es): 978-0-918526; 978-1-880238; 978-1-929918; 978-1-934414
Number of titles published annually: 12 Print; 12 E-Book
Total Titles: 215 Print; 100 E-Book
Orders to: Consortium Book Sales & Distribution, The Keg House, Suite 101, 34 13 Ave NE, Minneapolis, MN 55413-1007 *Tel:* 612-746-2600 *Toll Free Tel:* 866-400-5351 (cust serv, Jackson, TN) *E-mail:* cbsdinfo@ingramcontent.com *Web Site:* www.cbsd.com
SAN: 200-6049
Shipping Address: Consortium Book Sales & Distribution, The Keg House, Suite 101, 34 13 Ave NE, Minneapolis, MN 55413-1007 *Tel:* 612-746-2600 *Toll Free Tel:* 866-400-5351 (cust serv, Jackson, TN) *E-mail:* cbsdinfo@ingramcontent.com *Web Site:* www.cbsd.com
SAN: 200-6049
Warehouse: Consortium Book Sales & Distribution, The Keg House, Suite 101, 34 13 Ave NE, Minneapolis, MN 55413-1007 *Tel:* 612-746-2600 *Toll Free Tel:* 866-400-5351 (cust serv, Jackson, TN) *E-mail:* cbsdinfo@ingramcontent.com *Web Site:* www.cbsd.com
SAN: 200-6049
Distribution Center: Consortium Book Sales & Distribution, The Keg House, Suite 101, 34 13 Ave NE, Minneapolis, MN 55413-1007 *Tel:* 612-746-2600 *Toll Free Tel:* 866-400-5351 (cust serv, Jackson, TN) *E-mail:* cbsdinfo@ingramcontent.com *Web Site:* www.cbsd.com
SAN: 200-6049

§BoardSource
750 Ninth St NW, Suite 520, Washington, DC 20001-4793
Tel: 202-349-2500
E-mail: members@boardsource.org; mediarelations@boardsource.org
Web Site: www.boardsource.org
Key Personnel
Pres & CEO: Monika Kalra Varma
Chief of Staff: Judy Reckelhoff
VP, Fin: Joan Payne
Assoc VP, Foundation Rel: Stella Ford
Dir, Governance Networks & Innovation: Angelyn Frazer-Giles
Dir, Governance Strategy: Dani Robbins
Dir, Memb Engagement & Mktg: Mina Shin
Assoc Dir, Client & Memb Servs: Natalie Younger
Sr Mgr, Governance & Educ: Joy Folkedal
Mktg & Membership Mgr: Carson Jager
Technol & Integration Mgr: Jamii Roberson
Founded: 1988
Premier resource for practical information, tools & best practices, training & leadership development for board members of nonprofit organizations. Enables organizations to fulfill their missions by helping build effective nonprofit boards, offering credible support in solving tough problems.
ISBN Prefix(es): 978-0-925299; 978-1-58686
Number of titles published annually: 6 Print; 3 CD-ROM; 2 E-Book
Total Titles: 100 Print; 6 E-Book

§Bolchazy-Carducci Publishers Inc
1000 Brown St, Unit 301, Wauconda, IL 60084
SAN: 219-7685
Tel: 847-526-4344 *Fax:* 847-526-2867
E-mail: info@bolchazy.com; orders@bolchazy.com
Web Site: www.bolchazy.com
Key Personnel
Pres: Bridget Dean, PhD *E-mail:* bridget@bolchazy.com
Vice Chair of the Bd: Allan Bolchazy *E-mail:* abolchazy@bolchazy.com
Dir, Fin: David Fiedelman *E-mail:* dfiedelman@bolchazy.com
Ed: Donald Sprague *E-mail:* don@bolchazy.com; Amelia Wallace *E-mail:* amelia@bolchazy.com
Opers Mgr: Mr Rene Vela *E-mail:* rene@bolchazy.com
Prodn & E-Learning Mgr: Jody Cull *E-mail:* jcull@bolchazy.com
Founded: 1978
Scholarly books, textbooks, self-teaching Latin series, Latin music CDs & Slovak publications.
ISBN Prefix(es): 978-0-86516; 978-1-61041
Number of titles published annually: 3 Print
Total Titles: 450 Print; 5 Online; 250 E-Book; 20 Audio
Orders to: NBN International, 10 Estover Rd, Plymouth, Devon PL6 7PY, United Kingdom (Europe) *Tel:* (01752) 202301 *Fax:* (01752) 202333 *E-mail:* orders@nbninternational.com

U.S. PUBLISHERS

§Bold Strokes Books Inc
648 S Cambridge Rd, Bldg A, Johnsonville, NY 12094
Tel: 518-859-8965
E-mail: service@boldstrokesbooks.com
Web Site: www.boldstrokesbooks.com
Key Personnel
Pres: Len Barot *E-mail:* publisher@boldstrokesbooks.com
Sr Ed: Sandy Lowe
Founded: 2004
Independent publishing company publishing works of gay, lesbian & feminist themed fiction in all genres, including general, genre & young adult fiction. Readership is international & all titles are released in print & multi-format ebook version. Employs conventional distribution channels to bring products to the customers.
ISBN Prefix(es): 978-1-9331100; 978-1-60282; 978-1-62639
Number of titles published annually: 110 Print; 160 Online; 110 E-Book; 50 Audio
Total Titles: 2,200 Print; 2,500 Online; 2,500 E-Book; 450 Audio
Orders to: Bella Distribution, 1041 Aenon Church Rd, Tallahassee, FL 32304
Returns: Bella Distribution, 1041 Aenon Church Rd, Tallahassee, FL 32304
Shipping Address: Bella Distribution, 1041 Aenon Church Rd, Tallahassee, FL 32304
Warehouse: Bella Distribution, 1041 Aenon Church Rd, Tallahassee, FL 32304
Distribution Center: Bella Distribution, 1041 Aenon Church Rd, Tallahassee, FL 32304, Contact: Becky Arbogast *Toll Free Tel:* 800-533-1973 *Fax:* 850-576-3498 *E-mail:* info@belladistribution.com
Membership(s): Independent Book Publishers Association (IBPA); Romance Writers of America (RWA)

Book Marketing Works LLC
50 Lovely St (Rte 177), Avon, CT 06001
Mailing Address: PO Box 715, Avon, CT 06001-0715
Tel: 860-675-1344
Web Site: www.bookmarketingworks.com
Key Personnel
Pres: Brian Jud *E-mail:* brianjud@bookmarketingworks.com
Founded: 1990
ISBN Prefix(es): 978-1-928782
Number of titles published annually: 10 Print
Total Titles: 26 Print
Imprints: Strong Books
Subsidiaries: Book Marketing Works

Book Sales
Imprint of Quarto Publishing Group USA Inc
142 W 36 St, 4th fl, New York, NY 10018
SAN: 299-4062
Tel: 212-779-4972; 212-779-4971 *Fax:* 212-779-6058
Web Site: www.quartoknows.com
Founded: 1952
Publisher & supplier of books to wholesalers, mail order companies & retail stores.
ISBN Prefix(es): 978-0-89009; 978-1-55521; 978-0-7858
Number of titles published annually: 300 Print
Total Titles: 2,500 Print
Imprints: Blue & Gray; Castle Books; Chartwell Books; Crestline; Poplar Books
Orders to: Hachette Book Group Inc, 53 State St, Boston, MA 02109 *Toll Free Tel:* 800-759-0190
Returns: Hachette Book Group Inc, 322 S Enterprise Blvd, Lebanon, IN 46052 (accepted only with pre-approval prior to return)

Warehouse: Hachette Book Group Inc, 121 N Enterprise Blvd, Lebanon, IN 46052
Membership(s): American Booksellers Association (ABA)

The Book Tree
3316 Adams Ave, Suite A, San Diego, CA 92116
Mailing Address: PO Box 16476, San Diego, CA 92176
Tel: 619-280-1263 *Toll Free Tel:* 800-700-8733 (orders) *Fax:* 619-280-1285
E-mail: orders@thebooktree.com; info@thebooktree.com
Web Site: thebooktree.com
Key Personnel
Owner: Paul Willey
Founded: 1992
Metaphysical, spiritual & controversial books; do not accept, respond to or return unsol mss.
ISBN Prefix(es): 978-1-885395; 978-1-58509
Number of titles published annually: 10 Print
Total Titles: 300 Print
Membership(s): Independent Book Publishers Association (IBPA)

Bookhaven Press LLC
302 Scenic Ct, Moon Township, PA 15108
SAN: 668-7075
Tel: 412-494-6926
E-mail: info@bookhavenpress.com; orders@bookhavenpress.com
Web Site: bookhavenpress.com
Key Personnel
Pres & Publr: Dennis V Damp *E-mail:* ddamp@aol.com
Assoc Publr: Victor Richards *E-mail:* vrichards@bookhavenpress.com
Founded: 1985
Independent publishing house dedicated to producing award-winning business, career & finance books. *The Book of U.S. Government Jobs* was awarded "Best Career Title" by the Benjamin Franklin Awards Committee. Bookhaven's titles have been reviewed & recommended by Library Journal, Booklist, the New York Times & Washington Post, Career Opportunities News & over 100 magazines, newspapers & journals. We also publish comprehensive web sites for our titles.
ISBN Prefix(es): 978-0-943641
Number of titles published annually: 1 Print; 2 E-Book
Total Titles: 5 Print; 3 E-Book
Distribution Center: Independent Publishers Group (IPG), 814 N Franklin St, Chicago, IL 60610 *Tel:* 312-337-0747 *Toll Free Tel:* 800-888-4741 *Fax:* 312-337-5985 *E-mail:* orders@ipgbook.com *Web Site:* www.ipgbook.com
Membership(s): Independent Book Publishers Association (IBPA)

§BookLogix
1264 Old Alpharetta Rd, Alpharetta, GA 30005
SAN: 860-0376
Tel: 470-239-8547
E-mail: publishing@booklogix.com; info@booklogix.com; customerservice@booklogix.com
Web Site: www.booklogix.com
Key Personnel
CEO: Angela DeCaires
Founded: 2009
Nontraditional book publisher supporting writers & independent/small publishers to help them produce professional, high-quality books.
This publisher has indicated that 100% of their product line is author subsidized.
ISBN Prefix(es): 978-1-61005; 978-1-63183; 978-1-6653
Number of titles published annually: 150 Print; 100 E-Book

Total Titles: 2,500 Print; 1,000 E-Book
Imprints: Heavenly Light Press; Lanier Press; Mountain Arbor Press

Books In Motion
Division of Classic Ventures Ltd
9922 E Montgomery Dr, Suite 31, Spokane Valley, WA 99206
Tel: 509-922-1646 *Toll Free Tel:* 800-752-3199 *Fax:* 509-922-1445
E-mail: info@booksinmotion.com
Web Site: www.booksinmotion.com
Key Personnel
Pres: Gary Challender
Founded: 1980
Produce fiction books on CD & MP3. Does not accept unsol mss. Criteria is exceptionally high for acceptance. There is no cost to the authors. Currently seeking subsidiary audio rights on previously print published titles.
ISBN Prefix(es): 978-1-55686; 978-1-58116; 978-1-59607; 978-1-60548
Number of titles published annually: 24 Print; 60 Audio
Total Titles: 2,000 Audio

Books on Tape™
Imprint of Penguin Random House Audio Publishing Group
1745 Broadway, New York, NY 10019
Toll Free Tel: 800-733-3000 (cust serv)
Toll Free Fax: 800-940-7046
Web Site: PenguinRandomHouseLibrary.com
Key Personnel
Pres & Publr, Penguin Random House Audio Group: Amanda D'Acierno
SVP, Lib Sales & Digital Strategy/SVP & Dir, Sales Opers: Skip Dye
Mktg Dir: Cheryl Herman
Sr Ed, Listening Library®: Emily Parliman
Asst Acqs Ed, Listening Library®: Megan Mills
Publg Mgr: Lauren Diaz Morgan
Coord, Digital Opers, Listening Library®: Renee Watson
Founded: 1975
For over 40 years Books on Tape® has offered the best in unabridged audiobooks. Our best selling & award-winning titles are produced in NY & LA studios & read by the finest narrators in the industry. Select from over 3,000 titles available, durable library packaging & delivered with a complement of services tailored to meet special needs of librarians & educators. Flexible standing order plans, featuring the freedom to choose your titles & free lifetime replacement guarantees. Books on Tape® is proud to exclusively have Listening Library®, the premier audio book publisher of children's & young adult literature, as its children's imprint.
Number of titles published annually: 300 Audio
Total Titles: 3,000 Audio
Imprints: Listening Library®
Distributor for Listening Library®
Orders to: Penguin Random House Publisher Services (PRHPS), Library & School Services, 400 Hahn Rd, Westminster, MD 21157
Returns: Penguin Random House LLC, 1019 N State Rd 47, Crawfordville, NJ 47933
Membership(s): AASL; ALSC; The American Library Association (ALA); California Library Association; National Council of Teachers of English (NCTE); Public Library Association (PLA); Young Adult Library Services Association (YALSA)

BOOM! Studios
Imprint of Random House Publishing Group
5670 Wilshire Blvd, Suite 400, Los Angeles, CA 90036

E-mail: contact@boom-studios.com; customerservice@boom-studios.com; press@boom-studios.com
Web Site: www.boom-studios.com
Key Personnel
Founder & CEO: Ross Richie
Pres, Devt: Stephen Christy
Pres, Publg & Mktg: Filip Sablik
SVP, Film: Adam Yoelin
VP, Edit & Creative Strategy: Bryce Carlson
VP, Licensing & Mdsg: Lance Kreiter
Ed-in-Chief: Matt Gagnon
Sales Coord: Manny Castellanos
E-mail: mcastellanos@boom-studios.com
Founded: 2005
ISBN Prefix(es): 978-1-934506; 978-1-60886; 978-1-61398; 978-1-932386; 978-1-936393; 978-1-68159; 978-1-939867
Number of titles published annually: 80 Print
Imprints: Archaia Entertainment LLC; BOOM! Box; KaBOOM!
Distributed by Simon & Schuster, LLC

§Boson Books™
Imprint of Bitingduck Press LLC
1262 Sunnyoaks Circle, Altadena, CA 91001
Tel: 626-507-8033 *Fax:* 626-818-1842
Web Site: bitingduckpress.com
Key Personnel
Ed-in-Chief: Jay Nadeau *E-mail:* jay@bitingduckpress.com
Publr & Ed: Chris Lindensmith *E-mail:* chris@bitingduckpress.com
Founded: 1994
Publish ebooks & selected print books. First commercial general ebook publisher.
ISBN Prefix(es): 978-1-886420; 978-0-917990; 978-1-932482
Number of titles published annually: 8 Print; 13 E-Book
Total Titles: 100 Print; 350 E-Book
Distribution Center: Ingram Book Group, One Ingram Blvd, La Vergne, TN 37086 *Tel:* 615-793-5000
Membership(s): The Authors Guild

BoT, see Books on Tape™

Bottom Dog Press
813 Seneca Ave, Huron, OH 44839
SAN: 689-5492
Mailing Address: PO Box 425, Huron, OH 44839-0425
Tel: 419-602-1556 *Fax:* 419-616-3966
Web Site: smithdocs.net
Key Personnel
Dir & Publr: Larry Smith *E-mail:* lsmithdog@smithdocs.net
Assoc Ed: Susanna Sharp Schwacke; Laura Smith
Founded: 1985
ISBN Prefix(es): 978-0-933087; 978-1-933960; 978-1-947504
Number of titles published annually: 6 Print; 6 E-Book; 2 Audio
Total Titles: 210 Print; 2 CD-ROM; 18 E-Book; 4 Audio
Imprints: Bird Dog Publishing
Distribution Center: Baker & Taylor, 501 Gladiolus St, Momence, IL 60954
Ingram Publisher Services, 14 Ingram Blvd, Mail Stop 631, La Vergne, TN 37086 *Tel:* 615-793-5000 *Toll Free Tel:* 866-400-5351 (orders) *Web Site:* www.ingrampublisherservices.com
Membership(s): Appalachian Studies Association; Community of Literary Magazines & Presses (CLMP); PEN America; Working-Class Studies Association

R R Bowker LLC
Subsidiary of Cambridge Information Group
26 Main St, Suite 102, Chatham, NJ 07928

PUBLISHERS

Tel: 734-761-4700 *Toll Free Tel:* 888-269-5372 (edit & cust serv); 800-521-0600 *Toll Free Fax:* 877-337-7015 (US & CN) *E-mail:* isbn-san@bowker.com; isbn-san@proquest.com
Web Site: www.bowker.com
Founded: 1872
Leading provider of bibliographic information & management solutions designed to help publishers, authors & booksellers better serve their customers. Creators of products & services that make books easier for people to discover, evaluate, order & experience. The company also generates research & resources for publishers, helping them understand & meet the interests of readers worldwide. Bowker® is the official ISBN Agency for Australia & the US.
ISBN Prefix(es): 978-0-8352
Number of titles published annually: 14 Print; 8 Online
Total Titles: 8 Online
Editorial Office(s): PO Box 8134, Bridgewater, NJ 08807
Foreign Office(s): Thorpe-Bowker, Level One, 607 St Kilda Rd, Melbourne, Victoria 3004, Australia *Tel:* (03) 8517 8333 *Fax:* (03) 8517 8399 *E-mail:* customer.service@thorpe.com.au *Web Site:* www.bowker.com/en/thorpe-bowker
Bowker®, an affiliate of ProQuest, 3 Dorset Rise, 5th fl, London EC4Y 8EN, United Kingdom, VP, Strategic Partnerships & Licensing: Doug McMillan *Tel:* (020) 7832 1700 *E-mail:* doug.mcmillan@proquest.com
Distributed by Grey House Publishing Inc™
Membership(s): The American Library Association (ALA); Association of American Publishers (AAP); Book Industry Study Group (BISG); Evangelical Christian Publishers Association (ECPA); National Association of College Stores (NACS)

Boydell & Brewer Inc
Affiliate of Boydell & Brewer Ltd (UK)
668 Mount Hope Ave, Rochester, NY 14620-2731
Tel: 585-275-0419 *Fax:* 585-271-8778
E-mail: boydell@boydellusa.net
Web Site: www.boydellandbrewer.com
Key Personnel
Mng Dir: Sue Smith *Tel:* 585-273-2817 *E-mail:* smith@boydellusa.net
Edit Dir: Sonia Kane *Tel:* 585-273-5778
Founded: 1989
Publisher of scholarly books.
ISBN Prefix(es): 978-0-85115; 978-0-85991; 978-0-86193; 978-0-7293; 978-0-900411; 978-1-85566; 978-1-878822; 978-1-58046; 978-1-57113; 978-1-900639; 978-1-64014
Number of titles published annually: 200 Print
Total Titles: 3,100 Print
Imprints: Boydell Press; DS Brewer; Camden House; Companion Guides; James Curry Ltd; Early English Text Society; Plumbago Books; Royal Historical Society; Scholarly Digital Editions; Scottish Text Society; Suffolk Records Society; Tamesis Books; Toccata Press; University of Rochester Press; Victory History of the Counties of England; York Medieval Press
Foreign Office(s): Boydell & Brewer Ltd, Bridge Farm Business Park, Top St, Martlesham, Suffolk 1P12 4RB, United Kingdom, Mng Ed: James Powell *Tel:* (01394) 610600 *Fax:* (01394) 610316 *E-mail:* editorial@boydell.co.uk
Distributed by Ingram Academic (North & South America)
Orders to: Boydell & Brewer Ltd, Bridge Farm Business Park, Top St, Martlesham, Suffolk 1P12 4RB, United Kingdom *Tel:* (01394) 610600 *Fax:* (01394) 610316 *E-mail:* editorial@boydell.co.uk
Returns: Ingram Publisher Services, 210 American Dr, Jackson, TN 38301 *Tel:* 731-988-4440

Warehouse: Ingram Publisher Services, 210 American Dr, Jackson, TN 38301
College Farm, Forward Green, Stawmarket, Suffolk IP14 SEH, United Kingdom
Distribution Center: Ingram Publisher Services, 210 American Dr, Jackson, TN 38301 (CN, Caribbean, Latin America & US) *Toll Free Tel:* 866-400-5351

Boynton Bookworks, see Simon & Schuster Children's Publishing

Boys Town Press
Division of Father Flanagan's Boys' Home
13603 Flanagan Blvd, 2nd fl, Boys Town, NE 68010
Tel: 531-355-1320 *Toll Free Tel:* 800-282-6657 *Fax:* 531-355-1310
E-mail: btpress@boystown.org
Web Site: www.boystownpress.org
Key Personnel
Dir: Erin Green *E-mail:* erin.green@boystown.org
Sales & Mktg Mgr: Patricia Martens *Tel:* 531-355-1334 *E-mail:* patricia.martens@boystown.org
Founded: 1992
Publisher of books for counselors, children, educators, youth care professionals & parents. Also inspirational titles.
ISBN Prefix(es): 978-0-938510; 978-1-889322; 978-1-934490; 978-1-944882
Number of titles published annually: 14 Print; 10 E-Book
Total Titles: 120 Print; 2 CD-ROM; 80 E-Book; 9 Audio
Distributed by CSH Educational Resources Pte Ltd (Singapore); Deep Books Ltd (Europe & UK); Silvereye Learning Resources (NSW, Australia); University of Toronto Press (Canada)
Foreign Rights: DropCap (worldwide exc North America)
Returns: 250 Monsky Dr, Boys Town, NE 68010
Warehouse: 250 Monsky Dr, Boys Town, NE 68010
Distribution Center: Follett School Solutions Inc, 1340 Ridgeview Dr, McHenry, IL 60050 *Tel:* 815-759-1700 *Toll Free Tel:* 888-511-5114 (cust serv) *Fax:* 815-759-9831 *Toll Free Fax:* 800-852-5458 *E-mail:* info@follettlearning.com *Web Site:* www.follettlearning.com SAN: 169-1902
Bookazine, 75 Hook Rd, Bayonne, NJ 07002 *Tel:* 201-339-7778 *Toll Free Tel:* 800-221-8112 *E-mail:* lzarahn@bookazine.com *Web Site:* www.bookazine.com
Baker & Taylor, 2550 W Tyvola Rd, Suite 300, Charlotte, NC 28217 *Tel:* 815-802-2479 *Toll Free Fax:* 800-411-8433 *Web Site:* www.baker-taylor.com
Ingram Book Co, One Ingram Blvd, La Vergne, TN 37086-3650
Membership(s): Independent Book Publishers Association (IBPA)

BPC
415 Farm Rd, Summertown, TN 38483
Mailing Address: PO Box 99, Summertown, TN 38483-0099
Tel: 931-964-3571 *Toll Free Tel:* 888-260-8458 *Fax:* 931-964-3518
E-mail: info@bookpubco.com
Web Site: www.bookpubco.com
Key Personnel
Pres: Robert Holzapfel
Ed: Cynthia Holzapfel
Mktg: Anna Pope *E-mail:* annap@bookpubco.com
Founded: 1974
Community-owned independent press committed to promoting books that educate, inspire & empower. Topics include plant-based cooking

U.S. PUBLISHERS

& nutrition, sustainable living, natural health care, gardening, sci-fi & fantasy novels, Native American culture & hi-lo novels for young adults.
ISBN Prefix(es): 978-0-913990; 978-1-57067; 978-1-55312
Number of titles published annually: 8 Print
Total Titles: 450 Print; 2 Audio
Imprints: Books Alive; Botanica Press; GroundSwell; Healthy Living; Native Voices; Norwalk Press; 7th Generation
Distributor for Cherokee Publications; Crazy Crow; CRCS Publications; Critical Path; Gentle World; Hippocrates Publications; The Magni Co; Moon River Publishing; Second Nature; Sproutman Publications; Uproar Books
Foreign Rep(s): Brumby Books (Australia); Faradawn (South Africa); Publishers Group UK (England)

§Brandylane Publishers Inc
5 S First St, Richmond, VA 23219
Tel: 804-644-3090
Web Site: brandylanepublishers.com
Key Personnel
Publr: Robert H Pruett *E-mail:* robert@brandylanepublishers.com
Founded: 1985
Brandylane publishes almost all genres. Also provides editing, design, printing, ebook & audiobook services.
This publisher has indicated that 60% of their product line is author subsidized.
ISBN Prefix(es): 978-1-883911; 978-1-947860; 978-1-951565; 978-1-953021; 978-1-958754
Number of titles published annually: 40 Print; 40 Online; 35 E-Book; 10 Audio
Total Titles: 400 Print; 200 Online; 140 E-Book; 5 Audio
Imprints: Belle Isle Books (offers self publishing option)
Foreign Rights: PubMatch (worldwide)
Distribution Center: Ingram Book Group (US)
Membership(s): Independent Book Publishers Association (IBPA)

BRAVE Books
Imprint of Brave Books LLC
13614 Poplar Circle, Suite 302, Conroe, TX 77304
Tel: 932-380-5648
E-mail: info@brave.us
Web Site: bravebooks.us
Key Personnel
Founder & CEO: Trent Talbot
COO: Walker Jester
Chief Creative Offr: Eric Presley
Chief Strategy Offr: Zach Bell
Founded: 2021
Christian publishing company that makes books for kids (ages 4-12) that reinforce biblically-based, foundational values. Our mission is to be the brand parents trust with their children's imaginations by creating a world, characters, & stories that not only enthrall them but build their character while doing so.
ISBN Prefix(es): 978-1-955550
Number of titles published annually: 11 Print
Total Titles: 38 Print

§George Braziller Inc
90 Broad St, Suite 2100, New York, NY 10004
SAN: 201-9310
Tel: 212-260-9256
E-mail: editorial@georgebraziller.com
Web Site: www.georgebraziller.com
Key Personnel
Publr & Edit Dir: Michael Braziller
Secy-Treas & Dir, Perms: Joel Braziller
Dir, Publicity: Jonah Fried *E-mail:* jfried@georgebraziller.com
Founded: 1955

U.S. PUBLISHERS

Publishers of fine illustrated art books, serious literary works & works of art history, architecture & criticism.
ISBN Prefix(es): 978-0-8076
Number of titles published annually: 12 Print
Total Titles: 300 Print
Distributed by ACC Art Books; W W Norton & Company Inc
Foreign Rep(s): ACC Art Books (Australia, England, Europe, India, New Zealand)
Orders to: W W Norton & Company Inc, 500 Fifth Ave, New York, NY 10110 *Toll Free Tel:* 800-233-4830 *Toll Free Fax:* 800-458-6515

Breakaway Books
PO Box 24, Halcottsville, NY 12438-0024
E-mail: breakawaybooks@gmail.com
Web Site: www.breakawaybooks.com
Key Personnel
Publr: Garth Battista
Founded: 1994
Sports literature & books.
ISBN Prefix(es): 978-1-891369; 978-1-55821; 978-1-62124
Number of titles published annually: 10 Print
Total Titles: 100 Print; 1 E-Book
Distribution Center: Consortium Book Sales & Distribution, 34 13 Ave NE, Suite 101, Minneapolis, MN 55413-1007 *Tel:* 612-746-2600 *Toll Free Tel:* 866-400-5351 (cust serv, Jackson, TN) *E-mail:* cbsdinfo@ingramcontent.com *Web Site:* www.cbsd.com SAN: 200-6049

Breakthrough Publications Inc
3 Iroquois St, Emmaus, PA 18049
Tel: 610-928-4062
E-mail: dot@booksonhorses.com; ruth@booksonhorses.com
Web Site: www.booksonhorses.com
Key Personnel
Pres & Publr: Peter E Ognibene *E-mail:* peter@workkplace.com
Founded: 1980
Career & equestrian books & DVDs.
ISBN Prefix(es): 978-0-914327
Number of titles published annually: 30 Print
Total Titles: 50 Print
Imprints: Breakthrough Publications

Nicholas Brealey Publishing
Imprint of John Murray Press (UK)
53 State St, 9th fl, Boston, MA 02109
Tel: 617-523-3801
E-mail: sales-us@nicholasbrealey.com
Web Site: nbuspublishing.com
Key Personnel
Dir, Prodn: Michelle Morgan
Sales Mgr: Melissa Carl
Founded: 1992
Professional/trade business book (hardcover & original paperback) publisher. Additional subjects include: international business & culture, training & human resources.
ISBN Prefix(es): 978-0-89106 (Davies-Black); 978-1-85788; 978-1-90483
Number of titles published annually: 50 Print
Total Titles: 330 Print
Imprints: Davies-Black
Distributed by Hachette Book Group Inc
Membership(s): Association of American Publishers (AAP)

Brentwood Christian Press
PO Box 4773, Columbus, GA 31914-4773
Toll Free Tel: 800-334-8861
E-mail: brentwood@aol.com
Web Site: www.brentwoodbooks.com
Key Personnel
Owner: U D Roberts
Founded: 1982
Custom self-publishing of Christian books.
This publisher has indicated that 100% of their product line is author subsidized.
ISBN Prefix(es): 978-1-55630
Number of titles published annually: 150 Print
Total Titles: 10,000 Print

Brethren Press
Division of Church of the Brethren
1451 Dundee Ave, Elgin, IL 60120
SAN: 201-9329
Tel: 847-742-5100 *Toll Free Tel:* 800-441-3712 *Toll Free Fax:* 800-667-8188
E-mail: brethrenpress@brethren.org
Web Site: www.brethrenpress.com
Key Personnel
Publr: Wendy McFadden *Tel:* 847-742-5100 ext 307 *E-mail:* wmcfadden@brethren.org
Dir, Mktg & Sales: Jeff Lennard *Tel:* 847-742-5100 ext 321 *E-mail:* jlennard@brethren.org
Founded: 1897
Trade books, church school curriculum, tracts & pamphlets & various media resources. Specialize in Bible study, theology, church history, practical discipleship, personal lifestyle issues, social concerns, peace & justice, devotional life & personal growth.
ISBN Prefix(es): 978-0-87178
Number of titles published annually: 6 Print
Total Titles: 100 Print; 6 E-Book
Imprints: faithQuest
Membership(s): Protestant Church-Owned Publishers Association (PCPA)

Brewers Publications
Division of Brewers Association
1327 Spruce St, Boulder, CO 80302
Mailing Address: PO Box 1679, Boulder, CO 80306
Tel: 303-447-0816 *Toll Free Tel:* 888-822-6273 (CN & US) *Fax:* 303-447-2825
E-mail: info@brewersassociation.org
Web Site: www.brewersassociation.org
Key Personnel
Publr: Kristi Switzer *Tel:* 720-473-7660 *E-mail:* kristi@brewersassociation.org
Founded: 1986
Not-for-profit educational publishing house & the foremost publisher of books on the art, science, history & culture of brewing for professional & amateur brewers & serious beer enthusiasts. Must know at least 10 brewers to query.
ISBN Prefix(es): 978-0-937381
Number of titles published annually: 3 Print; 2 E-Book
Total Titles: 50 Print
Foreign Rep(s): Sylvia Hayse Literary Agency (Sylvia Hayse) (worldwide exc North America)
Foreign Rights: Sylvia Hayse Literary Agency (Sylvia Hayse) (worldwide exc North America)
Shipping Address: National Book Network, 15200 NBN Way, Blue Ridge Summit, PA 17214 *Toll Free Tel:* 800-462-6420 *Toll Free Fax:* 800-338-4550 *E-mail:* custserv@nbnbooks.com
Warehouse: National Book Network, 15200 NBN Way, Blue Ridge Summit, PA 17214 *Tel:* 717-794-3800 *Toll Free Tel:* 800-462-6420 *Toll Free Fax:* 800-338-4550 *E-mail:* custserv@nbnbooks.com

Brick Tower Press
Subsidiary of J T Colby & Co Inc
Manhanset House, PO Box 342, Shelter Island Heights, NY 11965-0342
Tel: 212-427-7139 *Toll Free Tel:* 800-68-BRICK (682-7425)
E-mail: bricktower@aol.com
Web Site: bricktowerpress.com
Key Personnel
Publr: John T Colby, Jr
Founded: 1993
ISBN Prefix(es): 978-1-883283; 978-0-9531737; 978-1-899694
Number of titles published annually: 20 Print; 10 E-Book
Total Titles: 150 Print; 50 E-Book
Foreign Rep(s): Gazelle Book Services Ltd (Europe, UK); Ingram Content Group LLC (Australia, Canada, European Union)
Foreign Rights: Creative Management Partners (Canada, USA); D4EO Literary Agency (Bob Diforio) (worldwide)
Warehouse: Ingram Content Group LLC, One Ingram Blvd, La Vergne, TN 37086 *Tel:* 615-793-5000
Distribution Center: Ingram Content Group LLC, One Ingram Blvd, La Vergne, TN 37086 *Tel:* 615-793-5000

Bridge Logos Inc
14260 W Newberry Rd, Newberry, FL 32669-2765
E-mail: info@bridgelogos.com
Web Site: www.bridgelogos.com
Key Personnel
Pres: Suzi Wooldridge *E-mail:* swooldridge@bridgelogos.com
Founded: 1967
Bibles, Christian classics, spirit-filled life, Christian books, parenting, family, Eschatological, evangelism, revival, children's bibles.
ISBN Prefix(es): 978-0-88270; 978-0-61036
Number of titles published annually: 20 Print
Total Titles: 216 Print
Imprints: Bridge; Haven; Logos; Open Scroll; Synergy
Distributor for Warboys LLC
Foreign Rights: Bluth Agency (Annie Sung)
Orders to: Anchor Distributors, 1030 Hunt Valley Circle, New Kensington, PA 15058 *Tel:* 724-334-7000 *Toll Free Tel:* 800-444-4484 *Fax:* 724-334-1200 *Toll Free Fax:* 800-765-1960 *E-mail:* anchor.customerservice@anchordistributors.com *Web Site:* www.anchordistributors.com
Returns: Anchor Distributors, 1030 Hunt Valley Circle, New Kensington, PA 15058 *Tel:* 724-334-7000 *Toll Free Tel:* 800-444-4484 *Fax:* 724-334-1200 *Toll Free Fax:* 800-765-1960 *E-mail:* anchor.customerservice@anchordistributors.com *Web Site:* www.anchordistributors.com
Shipping Address: Anchor Distributors, 1030 Hunt Valley Circle, New Kensington, PA 15058 *Tel:* 724-334-7000 *Toll Free Tel:* 800-444-4484 *Fax:* 724-334-1200 *Toll Free Fax:* 800-765-1960 *E-mail:* anchor.customerservice@anchordistributors.com *Web Site:* www.anchordistributors.com
Distribution Center: Anchor Distributors, 1030 Hunt Valley Circle, New Kensington, PA 15058 *Tel:* 724-334-7000 *Toll Free Tel:* 800-444-4484 *Fax:* 724-334-1200 *Toll Free Fax:* 800-765-1960 *E-mail:* anchor.customerservice@anchordistributors.com *Web Site:* www.anchordistributors.com

Bridge Publications Inc
5600 E Olympic Blvd, Commerce, CA 90022
SAN: 208-3884
Tel: 323-888-6200 *Toll Free Tel:* 800-722-1733 *Fax:* 323-888-6202
E-mail: info@bridgepub.com
Web Site: www.bridgepub.com
Key Personnel
Pres: Blake Silber
Dir, Trade Opers: Ann Arnow *E-mail:* annarnow@bridgepub.com
Independent Sales Mgr: Thatcher Stokes *E-mail:* tstokes@bridgepub.com
Founded: 1981
US & international nonfiction publisher of L Ron Hubbard's Dianetics & Scientology materials.
ISBN Prefix(es): 978-0-88404; 978-1-57318; 978-1-4031

Number of titles published annually: 3,200 Print; 400 CD-ROM; 52 Online; 5 Audio
Total Titles: 32,400 Print; 3,500 CD-ROM; 257 Online; 288 Audio
Imprints: BPI Records; Bridge Audio; Theta Books
Branch Office(s)
Bridge Publications Canada, 696 Yonge St, Toronto, ON M4Y 2A7, Canada, Contact: Emily Harris *Tel:* 416-964-8927 *Fax:* 416-964-3201
Foreign Office(s): Era Dinamica Editores SA de CV, Pablo U Cello, No 16, Colonia de los Deportes, 03710 Mexico, CDMX, Mexico, Contact: Irma Macias *Tel:* (0155) 5984487 *Fax:* (0155) 5984624
Foreign Rep(s): New Era Publications International (Copenhagen, Europe, Russia & former USSR)
Distribution Center: Amazon.com (house acct)
Follett School Solutions Inc, 1340 Ridgeview Dr, McHenry, IL 60050 *Tel:* 815-759-1700 *Toll Free Tel:* 888-511-5114 (cust serv) *Fax:* 815-759-9831 *Toll Free Fax:* 800-852-5458 *E-mail:* info@follettlearning.com *Web Site:* www.follettlearning.com
Baker & Taylor, 2550 Tyvola Rd, Suite 300, Charlotte, NC 28217 (house acct) *Tel:* 815-802-2479 *Fax:* 815-411-8433 *Web Site:* www.bakertaylor.com
Membership(s): Independent Book Publishers Association (IBPA)

Brigantine Media
211 North Ave, St Johnsbury, VT 05819
Tel: 802-751-8802 *Fax:* 802-751-8804
Web Site: brigantinemedia.com
Key Personnel
Edit Chief: Janis Raye *E-mail:* janis@brigantinemedia.com
Acqs Ed: Neil Raphel *E-mail:* neil@brigantinemedia.com
Founded: 1990
ISBN Prefix(es): 978-0-9826644
Number of titles published annually: 12 Print; 2 Online; 12 E-Book
Total Titles: 50 Print; 2 Online; 40 E-Book
Imprints: Compass (educational materials for teachers); Voyage (fiction, primarily from VT & regional authors)

§Brill Inc
Subsidiary of Koninklijke Brill NV
10 Liberty Sq, 3rd fl, Boston, MA 02109
Tel: 617-263-2323 *Fax:* 617-263-2324
E-mail: sales@brill.com
Web Site: www.brill.com
Key Personnel
Sales Dir, Americas: Sylvia Bonadio *E-mail:* sylvia.bonadio@brill.com
Founded: 1683
Publishes high-level, specialized, academic titles.
ISBN Prefix(es): 978-90-04
Number of titles published annually: 600 Print
Total Titles: 6,000 Print

Brilliance Publishing Inc
Subsidiary of Amazon Publishing
1704 Eaton Dr, Grand Haven, MI 49417
Tel: 616-846-5256 *Toll Free Tel:* 800-648-2312 (orders only)
E-mail: brilliance-publishing@amazon.com; customerservice@brilliancepublishing.com; media@brilliancepublishing.com; publicity@brilliancepublishing.com
Web Site: www.brilliancepublishing.com
Key Personnel
Dir, Sales & Opers: Natalie Fedewa
Dir, Studio & Edit Opers: Brian Pepera
Founded: 1984
Leading independent audiobook publisher.
ISBN Prefix(es): 978-0-930435; 978-1-56100; 978-1-56740; 978-1-58788; 978-1-59086; 978-1-59355; 978-1-59600; 978-1-59710; 978-1-59737; 978-1-4233; 978-1-4418; 978-1-61106; 978-1-4558
Number of titles published annually: 700 Audio
Total Titles: 6,500 Audio
Imprints: Brilliance Audio™
Membership(s): Audio Publishers Association

Bristol Park Books
252 W 38 St, Suite 206, New York, NY 10018
Tel: 212-842-0700 *Fax:* 212-842-1771
E-mail: info@bristolparkbooks.com
Web Site: bristolparkbooks.com
Key Personnel
Pres: Richard Alexander
Promotional hardcover reprints.
ISBN Prefix(es): 978-0-88365; 978-0-88486; 978-1-57866
Number of titles published annually: 50 Print
Total Titles: 200 Print
Orders to: National Book Network, 4501 Forbes Blvd, Suite 200, Lantham, MD 20706 *Tel:* 301-459-3366 *Web Site:* nbnbooks.com
Distribution Center: National Book Network, 4501 Forbes Blvd, Suite 200, Lantham, MD 20706 *Tel:* 301-459-3366 *Web Site:* nbnbooks.com

Broadleaf Books, see Augsburg Fortress Publishers, Publishing House of the Evangelical Lutheran Church in America

§Paul H Brookes Publishing Co Inc
PO Box 10624, Baltimore, MD 21285-0624
SAN: 212-730X
Tel: 410-337-9580 (outside US & CN)
Toll Free Tel: 800-638-3775 (US & CN)
Fax: 410-337-8539
E-mail: custserv@brookespublishing.com
Web Site: www.brookespublishing.com
Key Personnel
Chmn of the Bd: Paul H Brookes
Pres: Jeffrey D Brookes *E-mail:* jbrookes@brookespublishing.com
EVP: Melissa A Behm *E-mail:* mbehm@brookespublishing.com
EVP & Publr: George S Stamathis *E-mail:* gstamathis@brookespublishing.com
VP, Fin: Kathy Harris *E-mail:* kharris@brookespublishing.com
VP, Opers: Erika Kinney *E-mail:* ekinney@brookespublishing.com
Dir, Assessment & Content Solutions: Heather Shrestha *Tel:* 410-337-9580 ext 102 *E-mail:* hshrestha@brookespublishing.com
Dir, Mktg: Jessica Reighard *E-mail:* jreighard@brookespublishing.com
Dir, Prodn: Dana Battaglia *E-mail:* dbattaglia@brookespublishing.com
Dir, Sales: Robert Miller *E-mail:* rmiller@brookespublishing.com
Assoc Dir, Rts & Intellectual Property: Heather Lengyel *Tel:* 410-491-3311 *E-mail:* hlengyel@brookespublishing.com
Founded: 1978
Publishes professional books, textbooks, assessments, curricula & web-based products in the areas of: early childhood, early intervention, social-emotional development, literacy, learning disabilities, autism, behavior, special education, developmental disabilities, communication & language.
ISBN Prefix(es): 978-0-933716; 978-1-55766; 978-1-59857; 978-1-68125
Number of titles published annually: 50 Print; 5 CD-ROM; 5 Online; 40 E-Book
Total Titles: 642 Print; 20 CD-ROM; 10 Online; 107 E-Book
Imprints: Health Professions Press (specialist publisher focused on the broad range of issues in gerontology, long-term care & health administration)
Foreign Rep(s): Eurospan Ltd (Africa, Asia, Europe, Middle East, UK)
Returns: Maple Logistics Solutions, 60 Grumbacher Rd, I-83 Industrial Park, York, PA 17406
Warehouse: Maple Logistics Solutions, PO Box 15100, York, PA 17405 *Web Site:* www.maplelogisticssolutions.com
See separate listing for:
Health Professions Press

§The Brookings Institution Press
Division of The Brookings Institution
1775 Massachusetts Ave NW, Washington, DC 20036-2188
SAN: 201-9396
Tel: 202-797-6000
E-mail: permissions@brookings.edu
Web Site: www.brookings.edu
Key Personnel
Dir: Bill Finan
Asst Dir: Yelba Quinn
Mng Ed: Cecilia Gonzalez *Tel:* 202-238-3510 *E-mail:* cgonzalez@brookings.edu
Digital & Mktg Mgr: Steven Roman *Tel:* 202-536-3609 *E-mail:* sroman@brookings.edu
Prodn Mgr: Elliott Beard *Tel:* 202-797-6303 *E-mail:* cbeard@brookings.edu
Publicity Mgr: Robin Ceppos *E-mail:* rceppos@brookings.edu
Rts Mgr: Kristen Harrison *Tel:* 202-536-3604 *E-mail:* kharrison@brookings.edu
Founded: 1916
Economics, foreign policy & government affairs.
ISBN Prefix(es): 978-0-8157
Number of titles published annually: 35 Print; 35 E-Book
Total Titles: 1,650 Print; 1,450 E-Book
Distributed by Rowman & Littlefield
Foreign Rep(s): APD Singapore Pte Ltd (Brunei, Indonesia, Malaysia, Singapore, South Korea, Thailand, Vietnam); Eurospan Group (Africa, China, Europe, Hong Kong, Middle East, Taiwan, UK); Far Eastern Booksellers (Mr Nobuyuki Namekawa) (Japan); MHM Ltd (Japan); NewSouth Books (Australia, New Zealand); Publishers Group Canada (Canada); Viva Books Pvt Ltd (Bangladesh, India, Nepal, Pakistan, Sri Lanka)
Foreign Rights: Agency Literaria Internazionale (Italy); Big Apple Agency Inc (China); Tuttle-Mori Agency Inc (Japan)
Distribution Center: Ingram Academic Services, 210 American Dr, Jackson, TN 38301 (US) *E-mail:* ipsjacksonorders@ingramcontent.com
Membership(s): American Association of University Presses (AAUP); Association of American Publishers (AAP)

Brookline Books
8 Trumbull Rd, Suite B-001, Northampton, MA 01060
Fax: 413-584-6184
E-mail: brbooks@yahoo.com
Founded: 1985
Education, special needs, readings, general trade.
ISBN Prefix(es): 978-0-914797; 978-1-57129
Number of titles published annually: 5 Print
Total Titles: 125 Print

Brooklyn Publishers LLC
PO Box 248, Cedar Rapids, IA 52406
Tel: 319-368-8012 *Toll Free Tel:* 888-473-8521 *Fax:* 319-368-8011
E-mail: customerservice@brookpub.com; editor@brookpub.com
Web Site: www.brookpub.com
Key Personnel
Sr Ed: David Burton

ISBN Prefix(es): 978-1-930961; 978-1-931000; 978-1-931805; 978-1-932404; 978-1-60003
Number of titles published annually: 100 Print
Total Titles: 1,800 Print

Brown Books Publishing Group (BBPG)
16250 Knoll Trail, Suite 205, Dallas, TX 75248
Tel: 972-381-0009
E-mail: publishing@brownbooks.com
Web Site: www.brownbooks.com
Key Personnel
Publr & CEO: Milli Brown
Pres & COO: Tom Reale
Founded: 1994
Full service independent publisher. Committed to producing high quality books of all genres for authors who choose to retain the rights to their intellectual property.
This publisher has indicated that 85% of their product line is author subsidized.
ISBN Prefix(es): 978-1-933285; 978-1-934812; 978-1-61254
Number of titles published annually: 150 Print
Total Titles: 1,000 Print
Imprints: Brown Books; Brown Books Kids; Brown Christian Press
Subsidiaries: The Agency at Brown Books; Brown Books Distribution
Divisions: Brown Books Business; Brown Books Young Adult; The Education Press; The Medical Press; Military Division; The Political Press; Signature Books
Membership(s): Independent Book Publishers Association (IBPA)

Bucknell University Press
One Dent Dr, Lewisburg, PA 17837
Tel: 570-577-1049
E-mail: universitypress@bucknell.edu
Web Site: www.bucknell.edu/universitypress
Key Personnel
Dir: Suzanne Guiod *Tel:* 570-577-1552
  E-mail: suzanne.guiod@bucknell.edu
Mng Ed: Pam Dailey *Tel:* 570-577-3674
  E-mail: pad024@bucknell.edu
Edit Asst: Molly Clay *E-mail:* mmc022@bucknell.edu
Founded: 1968
ISBN Prefix(es): 978-0-8387; 978-1-61148
Number of titles published annually: 25 Print
Total Titles: 1,200 Print
Distributed by Rutgers University Press (www.rutgersuniversitypress.org/bucknell.org)
Membership(s): Association of University Presses (AUPresses)

§BuilderBooks
Division of National Association of Home Builders (NAHB)
1201 15 St NW, Washington, DC 20005
SAN: 207-7035
Toll Free Tel: 800-368-5242
E-mail: info@nahb.org
Web Site: builderbooks.com
Key Personnel
Sr Dir, Prod Mktg: Patricia Potts *Tel:* 800-368-5242 ext 8224 *E-mail:* ppotts@nahb.org
Dir, Mktg Opers: Stephanie Thomas *Tel:* 800-368-5242 ext 8125 *E-mail:* sthomas@nahb.org
Founded: 1943
Publish books about home construction & design, remodeling, land development, housing & construction management, sales & marketing of new homes, safety & seniors housing.
ISBN Prefix(es): 978-0-86718
Number of titles published annually: 7 Print
Total Titles: 150 Print
Orders to: Independent Publishers Group (IPG), 814 N Franklin St, Chicago, IL 60610 *Toll Free Tel:* 800-888-4741 *Fax:* 312-337-5985 *E-mail:* frontdesk@ipgbook.com *Web Site:* www.ipgbook.com

Returns: Independent Publishers Group (IPG), Returns Dept, 600 N Pulaski Rd, Chicago, IL 60624; c/o Fraser Direct Distribution, 124 Guelph St W, Acton, ON L7J 2M2, Canada

§Bull Publishing Co
PO Box 1377, Boulder, CO 80306
SAN: 208-5712
Tel: 303-545-6350 *Toll Free Tel:* 800-676-2855
E-mail: sales@bullpub.com
Web Site: www.bullpub.com
Key Personnel
CFO: Emily Sewell *E-mail:* emily@bullpub.com
Pres & Publr: James Bull
Dir, Mktg: Claire Cameron
Founded: 1974
Self-care, nutrition & health care, physical fitness, weight loss, mental health, parenting & child care, psychology, self-help.
ISBN Prefix(es): 978-0-915950; 978-0-923521; 978-1-933503; 978-1-945188
Number of titles published annually: 6 Print; 1 Audio
Total Titles: 70 Print; 6 Audio
Foreign Rep(s): Gazelle Book Services Ltd (UK & the continent)

§The Bureau for At-Risk Youth
40 Aero Rd, Unit 2, Bohemia, NY 11716
Toll Free Tel: 800-99YOUTH (999-6884)
  Toll Free Fax: 800-262-1886
Web Site: www.at-risk.com
Key Personnel
Owner: Carmine Russo
Founded: 1988
Educational materials on at-risk children's issues for educators, counselors, parents & children.
ISBN Prefix(es): 978-1-56688
Number of titles published annually: 15 Print
Total Titles: 250 Print

§Bureau of Economic Geology
Unit of University of Texas at Austin, Jackson School of Geosciences
c/o The University of Texas at Austin, 10100 Burnet Rd, Bldg 130, Austin, TX 78758
Mailing Address: c/o The University of Texas at Austin, PO Box X, University Sta, Austin, TX 78713-8924
Tel: 512-471-1534 *Fax:* 512-471-0140
E-mail: pubsales@beg.utexas.edu
Web Site: www.beg.utexas.edu
Key Personnel
Dir: Scott W Tinker
Mgr, Pubn Sales/The Bureau Store: Amanda Masterson *E-mail:* amanda.masterson@beg.utexas.edu
Founded: 1909
Scientific & technical books in geosciences.
ISBN Prefix(es): 978-1-970007
Number of titles published annually: 6 Print; 1 CD-ROM; 3 Online
Total Titles: 1,800 Print; 8 CD-ROM; 900 Online
Distributor for Gulf Coast Association of Geological Societies; Gulf Coast Section SEPM; Texas Memorial Museum (selected titles)
Orders to: The Bureau Store, c/o The University of Texas at Austin, PO Box X, University Sta, Austin, TX 78713-8924, Mgr: Amanda Masterson *Tel:* 512-471-3794 *Fax:* 512-471-0140 *Web Site:* store.beg.utexas.edu

Burford Books
101 E State St, No 301, Ithaca, NY 14850
Tel: 607-319-4373 *Fax:* 607-319-4373
  Toll Free Fax: 866-212-7750
E-mail: info@burfordbooks.com
Web Site: www.burfordbooks.com
Key Personnel
Pres: Peter Burford
Founded: 1997

Publisher of books on the outdoors, sports, food & wine, fitness, nature, travel, fishing, military, Finger Lakes area.
ISBN Prefix(es): 978-1-58080
Number of titles published annually: 6 Print; 6 E-Book
Total Titles: 125 Print; 54 E-Book
Foreign Rep(s): Gazelle Book Services Ltd (UK)
Distribution Center: National Book Network, 15200 NBN Way, Blue Ridge Summit, PA 17214 *Tel:* 717-794-3800
Membership(s): Independent Publishers Association

Burns Archive Press
Imprint of Burns Archive Photographic Distributors Ltd
140 E 38 St, New York, NY 10016
Tel: 212-889-1938
E-mail: info@burnsarchive.com
Web Site: www.burnsarchive.com
Key Personnel
Pres & CEO: Stanley B Burns, MD
Founded: 1979
Renowned for images of the darker side of life: death, disease, crime, racism, revolution & war. Provides a unique source of historic visual documentation containing over 700,000 vintage photographs. The Archive houses world-class holdings of African-American imagery & Judaica, as well as the foremost collection of early medical photography. More than a century of iconographic & historic photographs from the 1840s through the 1950s are available as stock photography. In addition, The Archive provides consultation, prepares exhibitions & publishes books on photographic history.
ISBN Prefix(es): 978-0-9612958; 978-0-9748688; 978-0-9748688; 978-0-9764495; 978-0-9764495; 978-1-934421; 978-1-936002
Number of titles published annually: 4 Print
Total Titles: 51 Print

Business & Legal Resources, see BLR®—Business & Legal Resources

Business Expert Press
222 E 46 St, Suite 203, New York, NY 10017-2906
Tel: 212-661-8810 *Fax:* 646-478-8107
E-mail: sales@businessexpertpress.com
Web Site: www.businessexpertpress.com
Key Personnel
COO: Sung Tinnie *E-mail:* stinnie@businessexpertpress.com
Mng Exec Ed: Scott Isenberg *E-mail:* scott.isenberg@businessexpertpress.com
Founded: 2008
Providing MBA level students, as well as practitioners & executive education classes, with applied, concise textbooks that can be used in & out of the classroom.
ISBN Prefix(es): 978-1-60649; 978-1-63157; 978-1-94784
Number of titles published annually: 100 Print; 100 Online; 100 E-Book
Total Titles: 1,300 Print; 1,300 Online; 1,300 E-Book
Foreign Rep(s): iGroup (Asia, Europe, Latin America, Middle East)
Membership(s): The American Library Association (ALA); Special Libraries Association (SLA)

Business Research Services Inc
PO Box 42674, Washington, DC 20015
SAN: 691-8522
Tel: 301-229-5561 *Toll Free Fax:* 877-516-0818
E-mail: brspubs@sba8a.com
Web Site: www.sba8a.com; www.setasidealert.com

Key Personnel
Pres & Publr: Thomas D Johnson
    E-mail: tjohnson@setasidealert.com
Founded: 1984
Directories/lists of minority & women's businesses; small business newsletters & contract opportunities services.
ISBN Prefix(es): 978-0-933527
Number of titles published annually: 2 Print; 1 Online
Total Titles: 7 Print; 1 Online
Distributor for Riley & Johnson

Bywater Books Inc
3415 Porter Rd, Ann Arbor, MI 48103
Tel: 734-662-8815
Web Site: bywaterbooks.com
Key Personnel
Publr & Ed-in-Chief: Salem West
    E-mail: salemwestbywater@gmail.com
Dir, Creative Servs: Ann McMan *E-mail:* ann.mcman@gmail.com
Dir, Opers: Marianne K Martin
    E-mail: mkmbywater@gmail.com
Mng Ed, Amble Press: Eric Peterson
    E-mail: eastendboy7@gmail.com
Founded: 1992
Bywater Books publishes top quality lesbian, sapphic, women loving women & feminist narrative fiction & nonfiction. Amble Press imprint publishes LGBTQ+ narrative fiction & nonfiction, with a primary though not exclusive emphasis on writers of color.
ISBN Prefix(es): 978-1-932859; 978-1-61294
Number of titles published annually: 20 Print; 20 E-Book
Total Titles: 250 Print; 255 E-Book
Imprints: Amble Press; Bloody Brits Press
Distribution Center: Consortium Book Sales & Distribution, 34 13 Ave NE, No 101, Minneapolis, MN 55413 *Web Site:* www.cbsd.com
Membership(s): Independent Book Publishers Association (IBPA); Independent Publishers Caucus (IPC)

§Cambridge University Press
Division of University of Cambridge
One Liberty Plaza, 20th fl, New York, NY 10006
SAN: 200-206X
Tel: 212-924-3900; 212-337-5000 *Fax:* 212-691-3239; 845-353-4141
E-mail: customer_service@cambridge.org; orders@cambridge.org; subscriptions_newyork@cambridge.org
Web Site: www.cambridge.org/us
Key Personnel
Exec Publr, Psychology: David Repetto
    E-mail: david.repetto@cambridge.org
Publr, Economics & Political Sci: Robert Dreesen
Publr, Law: Matthew Gallaway *E-mail:* matthew.gallaway@cambridge.org
Publr, Mathematical Sciences: Kaitlin Leach
    E-mail: kaitlin.leach@cambridge.org
Pubr, Religious Studies, Archaeology & Art History: Dr Beatrice Rehl *E-mail:* beatrice.rehl@cambridge.org
HR Dir: Giuseppe Rotella
Head, Retail Sales: Tom Willshire
Sr Ed, Soc Sci: Rachael Blaifeder
    E-mail: rachael.blaifeder@cambridge.org
Sr Ed, US & Latin American History: Cecelia Cancellaro
Journals Ed: Mark Zadrozny
Ed, Math & Computer Sci: Lauren Cowles
Journals Mktg Mgr: Susan Soule
Sr Publicist: Josh Hamel
Founded: 1534
Scholarly & trade books, college textbooks & journals.
ISBN Prefix(es): 978-0-521
Number of titles published annually: 2,400 Print
Total Titles: 45,000 Print; 160 Online

Foreign Office(s): The Edinburgh Bldg, Shaftesbury Rd, Cambridge CB2 8BS, United Kingdom *Tel:* (01223) 358331
Warehouse: One Ingram Blvd, La Vergne, TN 17202
Distribution Center: Ingram Academic Services (US & CN)
Membership(s): Association of American Publishers (AAP); Association of University Presses (AUPresses); Book Industry Study Group (BISG)

Camino Books Inc
PO Box 59026, Philadelphia, PA 19102-9026
Tel: 215-413-1917 *Fax:* 215-413-3255
E-mail: camino@caminobooks.com
Web Site: www.caminobooks.com
Key Personnel
Pres & Publr: Edward Jutkowitz
    E-mail: ejutkowitz@caminobooks.com
Founded: 1987
Regional trade books for the Mid-Atlantic states.
ISBN Prefix(es): 978-0-940159; 978-1-933822; 978-1-68098
Number of titles published annually: 10 Print; 10 E-Book
Total Titles: 90 Print; 85 E-Book
Returns: Maple Logistic Solutions, Lebanon Distribution Ctr, 704 Legionaire Dr, PA 17026, Contact: Jennifer Comly *Tel:* 717-865-7600
Warehouse: Maple Logistic Solutions, Lebanon Distribution Ctr, 704 Legionaire Dr, Fredericksville, PA 17026, Contact: Jennifer Comly *Tel:* 717-865-7600

Campfield & Campfield Publishing LLC
6521 Cutler St, Philadelphia, PA 19126
Toll Free Tel: 888-518-2440 *Fax:* 215-224-6696
E-mail: info@campfieldspublishing.com
Web Site: www.campfieldspublishing.com
Key Personnel
Publr: Charlene M Campfield
Founded: 2009
Publisher of Christ-centered books for children, teens & young adults.
ISBN Prefix(es): 978-0-9817025
Number of titles published annually: 2 Print; 2 Online
Total Titles: 10 Print; 10 Online; 4 E-Book
Membership(s): Independent Book Publishers Association (IBPA)

Candid
32 Old Slip, 24th fl, New York, NY 10005-3500
SAN: 207-5687
Tel: 212-620-4230 *Toll Free Tel:* 800-424-9836
    Fax: 212-807-3677
Web Site: candid.org
Key Personnel
CEO: Ann Mei Chang
Founded: 2019 (merger of Foundation Center & GuideStar)
Comprehensive data, tools & resources on philanthropic giving & nonprofit operations.
Number of titles published annually: 3 Online
Total Titles: 3 Online

Candied Plums
Imprint of Paper Republic LLC
7548 Ravenna Ave NE, Seattle, WA 98115
Mailing Address: 2301 N 65 St, Seattle, WA 98103
E-mail: candiedplums@gmail.com
Web Site: www.candiedplums.com
Key Personnel
Publr: Eric Abrahamsen *E-mail:* eric@candiedplums.com
Publg Consultant: Roxanne Feldman
    E-mail: roxannefeldman@gmail.com
Edit Coord: Lisa Lee *E-mail:* lisa.candiedplums@gmail.com

Ed: Nancy Zhang *E-mail:* nancy.candiedplums@gmail.com
Founded: 2016
ISBN Prefix(es): 978-1-945295
Number of titles published annually: 20 Print
Total Titles: 20 Print
Orders to: Pathway Book Service, 34 Production Ave, Keene, NH 03431, Contact: George Corrette *Toll Free Tel:* 800-345-6665 *Fax:* 603-965-2181 *E-mail:* george.corrette@pathwaybook.com
Returns: Pathway Book Service, 34 Production Ave, Keene, NH 03431, Contact: George Corrette *Toll Free Tel:* 800-345-6665 *Fax:* 603-965-2181 *E-mail:* george.corrette@pathwaybook.com
Warehouse: Global Union International Inc, 16801 Gale Ave, Unit C, City of Industry, CA 91745, Contact: Allen Wang *Tel:* 626-965-8878 *Fax:* 626-965-8877 *E-mail:* allenwang@globaluniontl.com
Distribution Center: Pathway Book Service, 34 Production Ave, Keene, NH 03431, Contact: George Corrette *Toll Free Tel:* 800-345-6665 *Fax:* 603-965-2181 *E-mail:* george.corrette@pathwaybook.com

§Candlewick Press
Subsidiary of Walker Books Ltd
99 Dover St, Somerville, MA 02144-2825
Tel: 617-661-3330 *Fax:* 617-661-0565
E-mail: bigbear@candlewick.com; salesinfo@candlewick.com
Web Site: candlewick.com
Key Personnel
CFO: Hilary Berkman
SVP, Commercial Opers: Susan Batcheller
SVP, Edit & Assoc Publr: Katie Cunningham
SVP, Global Integration & Planning: Derek Stordahl
SVP, Sales, Mktg & Busn Opers, US & CN: Mary Marotta
VP, Consumer & Brand Mktg: Karen Walsh
VP, Contracts, Rts & Royalties/Dir, Group Royalties & Biblio Info Systems: Becky S Hemperly
VP, Group HR Strategy, Walker Books Group/Candlewick Press: Jamie Ghaffar
VP, HR & Admin: Emily Marchand
VP, Publicity: Tracy Miracle
VP, Publicity & Mktg: Jennifer Roberts
VP, Trade Mktg: Michelle Montague
Exec Art Dir: Nancy Brennan
Exec Creative Dir: Ann Stott
Exec Dir, Educ/Lib Sales & Mktg: Kathleen Rourke
Exec Dir, Independent Retail & CN Sales: Elise Supovitz
Exec Dir, Prodn & Mfg: Kim Lanza
Exec Dir, Spec Mkts & Proprietary Sales: Alex Cotton Nash
Exec Edit Dir: Mary Lee Donovan
Exec Edit Dir, Walker Books US: Susan Van Metre
Sr Art Dir: Maria Middleton
Sr Dir, Graphic Prodn: Gregg Hammerquist
Art Dir/Design Mgr: Brandy Polay
Contracts Dir: Rich Paradis
Dir, Edit Opers & Sr Exec Ed: Kaylan Adair
Dir, Mktg, Publicity & Key Partnerships: Phoebe Kosman
Edit Dir: Kate Fletcher; Sarah Ketchersid
Inventory Dir: Andy Mott
Publg Dir-at-Large: Karen Lotz
Retail Dir, Sales: Jess Brigman
Assoc Art Dir: Maryellen Hanley; Heather McGee
Asst Art Dir: Amy Berniker; Pam Consolazio; Martha Kennedy; Hayley Parker; Lisa Rudden
Asst Art Dir, Fiction, Nonfiction & Graphic Novels: Rachel Wood
Sr Exec Ed: Andrea Tompa; Hilary Van Dusen
Exec Mng Ed: Sally Bratcher
Sr Mng Ed: Kate Hurley

U.S. PUBLISHERS

Sr Copy Ed/Proofreader: Jackie Houton
Sr Ed: Carter Hasegawa; Miriam Newman; Olivia Swomley
Ed: Lydia Abel; Melanie Cordova
Ed, MIT Kids Press/MITeen Press: Kristin Zelazko
Assoc Ed: Ainslie Campbell-Schwartz; Alex Robertson
Asst Ed: Juan Botero
Sr Contracts & Licensing Mgr: Melanie Blais
Sr HR Rep & Off Mgr: Kristin Seim
Sr Natl Acct Mgr, Amazon: Karen Menzie
Sr Prodn Mgr: Sarah Sherman
Sr Subs Rts & Royalties Mgr: Nancy Bruckman
Acct Mgr: Lindsey Macarthur; Charlotte Roth
Acctg Mgr: Frank Antippas
Commercial Opers Mgr: Katlyn Stokarski
Edit Servs Mgr: Pete Matthews
Educ Mktg Mgr: Anne Irza-Leggatt
Mgr, Lib Mktg: Sawako Shirota
Natl Accts Mgr & Natl Accts Licensing Mgr: Mary McCagg
Natl Accts Mgr: Johanna Schutter
Publicity Mgr: Jamie Tan
Soc Media Mgr: Salma Shawa
Typesetting Mgr/Sr Book Designer: Nathan Pyritz
Assoc Mktg & Publicity Mgr: Rachel Johnston
Consumer Mktg Coord: Neda Kamalhedayat
Contracts & Rts Coord: Breanna Cummings
Mktg Coord: Sofia Elbadawi
Publicity Coord: Kayla Phillips
Sales Coord, Spec Mkts & Proprietary Sales: Jaclyn Withers
Sr Accountant: Zachary Simpson
Sr Fiction Prodn Strategist: Angela Dombroski
Sr Publicist & CN Mktg Liaison: Laura Rivas
Sr Systems Admin: Tom Brennan
Systems Admin: Christos Spanos
Contracts & Rts Admin: Janella Angeles
Art Coordination Assoc/Contracts & Illustrator Liaison: Katherine Codega
Sr Book Designer: Rita Csizmadia; Carolynn DeCillo; Lauren Pettapiece; Jackie Shepherd; Maya Tatsukawa
Book Designer: Larsson McSwain; Vera Villanueva
Promos Designer: Nina Ellery; Rory Lake
Publicist: Stephanie Pando
Reprints Prodn Cont: Margaret Rosewitz
Mailroom Supv: Anderson Bass
Sales Asst: Lauren Bittrich; Cameron Moore
Trade Mktg Asst: Caitlyn Davis
Founded: 1992
ISBN Prefix(es): 978-1-56402; 978-0-7636
Number of titles published annually: 300 Print
Total Titles: 2,250 Print; 230 E-Book
Imprints: Big Picture Press; Candlewick Entertainment; Candlewick Studio (media-inspired imprint from the Walker Books Group); MIT Kids Press; MITeen Press; Templar Books
Divisions: Walker Books US
Foreign Rights: Walker Books Australia; Walker Books London
Returns: Penguin Random House LLC, 1019 N State Rd 47, Crawfordsville, IN 47933; Penguin Random House Canada, 6971 Columbus Rd, Mississauga, ON L5T 1K1, Canada
Distribution Center: Penguin Random House Publisher Services (PRHPS), 400 Hahn Rd, Westminster, MD 21157 Toll Free Tel: 800-733-3000 Toll Free Fax: 800-659-2436 E-mail: customerservice@randomhouse.com Web Site: prhpublisherservices.com
Penguin Random House Canada, 320 Front St W, Suite 1400, Toronto, ON M5V 3B6, Canada Toll Free Tel: 888-523-9292 Toll Free Fax: 888-562-9924 SAN: 201-3975
Membership(s): The Children's Book Council (CBC)

C&T Publishing Inc
1651 Challenge Dr, Concord, CA 94520-5206
Tel: 925-677-0377
E-mail: ctinfo@ctpub.com
Web Site: www.ctpub.com
Key Personnel
CEO: Todd Hensley
CFO: Tony Hensley
Publr: Amy Marson
Edit Dir: Gailen Runge
Founded: 1983
Specialize in fiber & paper craft books & products.
ISBN Prefix(es): 978-0-914881; 978-1-57120
Number of titles published annually: 45 Print
Total Titles: 700 Print
Imprints: Crosley-Griffith Publishing Co Inc; Fan-Powered Press; FunStitch Studio; Kansas City Star Quilts; Stash Books
Distribution Center: National Book Network (NBN), 15200 NBN Way, Blue Ridge Summit, PA 17214 Tel: 925-677-0377 (intl) Toll Free Tel: 800-462-6420 Fax: 717-794-3828 E-mail: customercare@nbn.com
Membership(s): Independent Book Publishers Association (IBPA)

§Capen Publishing Co Inc
Formerly Southwestern Publishing House Inc
4440 Edison St, San Diego, CA 92117
Toll Free Tel: 800-358-0560
E-mail: info@capenpublishingco.com
Web Site: capenpubco.com
Key Personnel
Pres: Christopher Capen Tel: 858-243-7515 E-mail: ccapen@capenpublishingco.com
Founded: 1855 (as Southwestern Publishing House Inc)
Custom book publisher.
ISBN Prefix(es): 978-1-935442; 978-1-941800; 978-1-943198; 978-0-9790769; 978-0-87197; 978-0-9796590
Number of titles published annually: 20 Print
Imprints: Beckon Books; Blue Sneaker Press; Favorite Recipes Press; Greenwich Publishing; Historic Hospitality Books; Quail Ridge Press; San Diego Zoo Wildlife Alliance Press
Membership(s): Independent Book Publishers Association (IBPA); International Association of Culinary Professionals (IACP)
See separate listing for:
Quail Ridge Press (QRP)

Capitol Enquiry Inc
1034 Emerald Bay Rd, No 435, South Lake Tahoe, CA 96150
Tel: 916-442-1434 Toll Free Tel: 800-922-7486 Fax: 916-244-2704
E-mail: info@capenq.com
Web Site: govbuddy.com
Key Personnel
Owner & Mktg Dir: Bruce Campbell
Founded: 1973
Professional directories primarily focused on state legislatures of CA & NY, online & printed.
ISBN Prefix(es): 978-0-917982
Number of titles published annually: 7 Print
Total Titles: 15 Print
Distributor for Center for Investigative Reporting

Capstone Publishers™
1710 Roe Crest Dr, North Mankato, MN 56003
Toll Free Tel: 800-747-4992 (cust serv)
 Toll Free Fax: 888-262-0705
E-mail: customer.service@capstonepub.com
Web Site: www.capstonepub.com
Key Personnel
Owner: Robert Coughlan
CEO: Randi Economou
Chief Revenue Offr: Haygood Poundstone
VP & Publr: Beth Brezenoff
Founded: 1991
Provides new & struggling readers with a strong foundation on which to build reading success. Our broad range of nonfiction titles for grades PreK-8 easily blends a world of books with the world children experience every day.
ISBN Prefix(es): 978-1-66904; 978-0-7565; 978-1-4846; 978-1-66901
Number of titles published annually: 450 Print
Total Titles: 10,000 Print
Imprints: Capstone Editions; Capstone Press; Pebble; Picture Window Books; Stone Arch Books
Distribution Center: 1905 Lookout Dr, North Mankato, MN 56003

Captain Fiddle Music & Publications
94 Wiswall Rd, Lee, NH 03861
Tel: 603-659-2658
E-mail: cfiddle@tiac.net
Web Site: captainfiddle.com
Key Personnel
Owner: Ryan J Thomson
Founded: 1985
ISBN Prefix(es): 978-0-931877
Number of titles published annually: 1 Print
Total Titles: 24 Print

Cardiotext Publishing
750 Second St NE, Suite 102, Hopkins, MN 55343
SAN: 852-2251
Tel: 612-925-2053 Fax: 612-922-7556
E-mail: info@cardiotext.com
Web Site: www.cardiotextpublishing.com
Key Personnel
Pres: Mike Crouchet E-mail: mike.crouchet@cardiotext.com
Founded: 2007
Independent print & digital publisher. Specialize in the field of cardiovascular medicine.
ISBN Prefix(es): 978-1-935395; 978-1-942909; 978-0-979016
Number of titles published annually: 10 Print; 10 Online; 10 E-Book
Total Titles: 35 Print; 35 Online; 35 E-Book
Foreign Rights: John Scott & Co (worldwide exc North America)
Distribution Center: Ingram Publisher Services UK, 10 Thornbury Rd, Plymouth PL6 7PP, United Kingdom Tel: (01752) 202301 E-mail: ipsuk.cservs@ingramcontent.com Web Site: www.ingrampublisherservices.co.uk
Membership(s): STM

Cardoza Publishing
1916 E Charleston Blvd, Las Vegas, NV 89104
Tel: 702-870-7200
E-mail: cardozaent@aol.com
Web Site: cardozapublishing.com
Key Personnel
Publr & Author: Avery Cardoza
Founded: 1981
Independent publisher. Specialize in gaming, gambling, poker, backgammon & chess titles.
ISBN Prefix(es): 978-1-58042
Number of titles published annually: 15 Print
Total Titles: 200 Print
Distributed by Simon & Schuster, LLC
Orders to: Simon & Schuster, 100 Front St, Riverside, NJ 08075, Order Processing Dept Toll Free Tel: 800-223-2336 Toll Free Fax: 800-943-9831 E-mail: order_desk@distican.com

Carlisle Press - Walnut Creek
2593 Township Rd 421, Sugarcreek, OH 44681
Tel: 330-852-1900 Toll Free Tel: 800-852-4482 Fax: 330-852-3285
E-mail: cpress@cprinting.com
Key Personnel
Publr: Marvin Wengerd
Founded: 1992
Amish books & cookbooks, *Keeper's at Home* Magazine.
ISBN Prefix(es): 978-1-890050; 978-0-9642548; 978-1-933753

Number of titles published annually: 6 Print
Total Titles: 60 Print

Carnegie Mellon University Press
5032 Forbes Ave, Pittsburgh, PA 15289-1021
SAN: 211-2329
Tel: 412-268-2861
E-mail: cmupress@andrew.cmu.edu
Web Site: www.cmu.edu/universitypress
Key Personnel
Dir: Gerald Costanzo *E-mail:* gc3d@andrew.cmu.edu
Sr Ed: Cynthia Lamb *E-mail:* cynthial@andrew.cmu.edu
Prodn Mgr: Connie Amoroso *E-mail:* camoroso@andrew.cmu.edu
Founded: 1974
ISBN Prefix(es): 978-0-915604; 978-0-88748
Number of titles published annually: 12 Print
Total Titles: 225 Print
Distribution Center: Chicago Distribution Center (CDC), 11030 S Langley Ave, Chicago, IL 60628 *Tel:* 773-702-7010 *Toll Free Fax:* 800-621-8476
Membership(s): Association of University Presses (AUPresses)

§Carolina Academic Press
700 Kent St, Durham, NC 27701
SAN: 210-7848
Tel: 919-489-7486 *Toll Free Tel:* 800-489-7486
Fax: 919-493-5668
E-mail: cap@cap-press.com
Web Site: www.cap-press.com; www.caplaw.com
Key Personnel
Publr: Keith R Sipe *Tel:* 919-489-7486 ext 120 *E-mail:* ksipe@cap-press.com
Assoc Publr, List Devt: Scott Sipe *Tel:* 919-489-7486 ext 129 *E-mail:* css@cap-press.com
Mng Ed: Ryland Bowman *Tel:* 919-489-7486 ext 133 *E-mail:* rbowman@cap-press.com
Sr Ed: Linda M Lacy *Tel:* 919-489-7486 ext 128 *E-mail:* linda@cap-press.com
Founded: 1974
Scholarly books & journals; anthropology, archaeology, criminal justice, economics, government, political science, history, reference, law, social science, African studies.
ISBN Prefix(es): 978-0-89089; 978-1-59460; 978-1-61163
Number of titles published annually: 150 Print; 150 E-Book
Total Titles: 1,250 Print; 450 E-Book

Carolrhoda Books Inc
Imprint of Lerner Publishing Group Inc
241 First Ave N, Minneapolis, MN 55401
Tel: 612-332-3344 *Toll Free Tel:* 800-328-4929
Fax: 612-332-7615 *Toll Free Fax:* 800-332-1132
E-mail: info@lernerbooks.com; custserve@lernerbooks.com
Web Site: www.lernerbooks.com; www.facebook.com/lernerbooks
Key Personnel
Chmn: Harry J Lerner
Pres & Publr: Adam Lerner
EVP & COO: Mark Budde
EVP & CFO: Margaret Thomas
EVP, Sales: David Wexler
VP & Ed-in-Chief: Andy Cummings
VP, Mktg: Rachel Zugschwert
Dir, HR: Maggie Wolfson *E-mail:* mwolfson@lernerbooks.com
Dir, Rts, Spec Sales & Intl Dist: Maria Kjoller
Edit Dir, Millbrook & Carolrhoda: Carol Hinz
Ed: Amy Fitzgerald
Founded: 1969
Children's picture books & middle grade fiction.
Number of titles published annually: 15 Print; 15 E-Book
Total Titles: 400 Print; 400 E-Book
Foreign Rep(s): Bounce Sales & Marketing Ltd (Europe, India, Middle East, Pakistan, Scandinavia, UK); CrossCan Education (Canada); Phambili Agencies (Botswana, Lesotho, Namibia, Southern Africa, Swaziland, Zimbabwe); Publishers Marketing Services (PMS) (Brunei, Malaysia, Singapore); Saunders (school & lib) (Canada); Walker Australia (Australia, New Zealand)
Foreign Rights: AC2 Literary (Italy); Sandra Bruna Literary Agency (Brazil, Portugal, Spain); CA-Link (Hong Kong, Macau, Mainland China, Taiwan); English Agency Japan Co Ltd (middle grade fiction) (Japan); Japan Foreign-Rights Centre (JFC) (exc middle grade fiction) (Japan); Korea Copyright Center Inc (KCC) (South Korea); Agence Michelle Lapautre (France); RightsMix (Eastern Europe, Greece, Israel, Netherlands, Russia, Scandinavia, UK); Literarische Agentur Silke Weniger (Germany)
Warehouse: CGC Fulfillment Warehouse, 150 Kingswood Dr, Mankato, MN 56001

Carolrhoda Lab™
Imprint of Lerner Publishing Group Inc
241 First Ave N, Minneapolis, MN 55401
Tel: 612-332-3344 *Toll Free Tel:* 800-328-4929
Fax: 612-332-7615 *Toll Free Fax:* 800-332-1132
E-mail: info@lernerbooks.com; custserve@lernerbooks.com
Web Site: www.lernerbooks.com; www.facebook.com/lernerbooks
Key Personnel
Chmn: Harry J Lerner
Pres & Publr: Adam Lerner
EVP & COO: Mark Budde
EVP & CFO: Margaret Thomas
EVP, Sales: David Wexler
VP & Ed-in-Chief: Andy Cummings
VP, Mktg: Rachel Zugschwert
Dir, HR: Margaret Wolfson *E-mail:* mwolfson@lernerbooks.com
Dir, Rts, Spec Sales & Intl Dist: Maria Kjoller
Edit Dir: Amy Fitzgerald
School & Lib Mktg Dir: Lois Wallentine
Founded: 2010
Dedicated to distinctive, provocative, boundary-pushing fiction for teens & their sympathizers.
Number of titles published annually: 5 Print; 5 E-Book
Total Titles: 80 Print; 80 E-Book
Foreign Rep(s): Bounce Sales & Marketing Ltd (Europe, India, Middle East, Pakistan, Scandinavia, UK); CrossCan Education (Canada); Phambili Agencies (Botswana, Lesotho, Namibia, Southern Africa, Swaziland, Zimbabwe); Publishers Marketing Services (PMS) (Brunei, Malaysia, Singapore); Saunders (school & lib) (Canada); Walker Australia (Australia, New Zealand)
Foreign Rights: AC2 Literary (Italy); Sandra Bruna Literary Agency (Brazil, Portugal, Spain); CA-Link (Hong Kong, Macau, Mainland China, Taiwan); English Agency Japan Co Ltd (young adult fiction) (Japan); Japan Foreign Rights Centre (JFC) (young adult nonfiction) (Japan); Korea Copyright Center Inc (KCC) (South Korea); Agence Michelle Lapautre (France); RightsMix (Eastern Europe, Greece, Israel, Netherlands, Russia, Scandinavia, UK); Literarische Agentur Silke Weniger (Germany)
Warehouse: CGC Fulfillment Warehouse, 150 Kingswood Dr, Mankato, MN 56001

Carson Dellosa Publishing LLC
PO Box 35665, Greensboro, NC 27425-5665
Tel: 336-632-0084 *Toll Free Tel:* 800-321-0943
Fax: 336-632-0084
E-mail: custsvc@carsondellosa.com
Web Site: www.carsondellosa.com
Key Personnel
CEO: Kelly Geer
Founded: 1976
Publishes supplementary educational materials, including activity books, resource guides, classroom materials & reproducibles, toddler-grade 8. Topics include reading, language arts, mathematics, science, the arts, social studies, English language learners, early childhood learning, Christian books & crafts.
ISBN Prefix(es): 978-0-513; 978-0-7424; 978-1-56822; 978-0-88012; 978-0-88724; 978-1-59441; 978-1-60022; 978-1-60418
Number of titles published annually: 80 Print; 80 E-Book
Total Titles: 1,200 Print; 100 E-Book
Imprints: Rainbow Bridge Publishing; Spectrum; Kelley Wingate Publications
Distributor for Key Education; Mark Twain Media

CarTech Inc
6118 Main St, North Branch, MN 55056
Tel: 651-277-1200 *Toll Free Tel:* 800-551-4754
Fax: 651-277-1203
E-mail: info@cartechbooks.com
Web Site: www.cartechbooks.com
Key Personnel
Owner & Publr: David Arnold
Founded: 1993
Automotive books.
ISBN Prefix(es): 978-1-884089; 978-1-932494; 978-1-61325
Number of titles published annually: 25 Print
Total Titles: 100 Print
Imprints: S-A Design Books
Distributor for Behemoth Publishing; Brooklands Books Ltd; California Bill's; Wolfgang Publications
Foreign Rights: Publishers Group UK (Australia, England)
Returns: Publishers Storage & Shipping, 660 S Mansfield, Ypsilanti, MI 48197 *Tel:* 734-487-9720
Warehouse: Publishers Storage & Shipping, 660 S Mansfield, Ypsilanti, MI 48197 *Tel:* 734-487-9720

Casa Bautista de Publicaciones
Affiliate of Southern Baptist Convention
130 Montoya Rd, El Paso, TX 79932
Tel: 915-566-9656 *Toll Free Tel:* 800-755-5958 (cust serv & orders)
E-mail: orders@editorialmh.org
Web Site: www.editorialmh.org
Key Personnel
CEO: Raquel Contreras
Gen Mgmt Asst: Cynthia Hernandez *Tel:* 915-566-9656 ext 113 *E-mail:* chernandez@editorialmh.org
Founded: 1905
Religious publications in Spanish. Foreign distributors also located in all Latin countries.
ISBN Prefix(es): 978-0-311
Number of titles published annually: 30 Print
Total Titles: 2,000 Print
Imprints: CBP/EMH
Distribution Center: LifeWay Christian Resources

Casemate | publishers
Division of Casemate Group
1950 Lawrence Rd, Havertown, PA 19083
Tel: 610-853-9131 *Fax:* 610-853-9146
E-mail: casemate@casematepublishers.com
Web Site: www.casematepublishers.com
Key Personnel
Pres/CEO, Casemate Group: David Farnsworth
SVP, US Dist Servs, Casemate Group: Michaela Goff
Group VP, Busn Devt: Curtis Key
VP, Sales & Mktg: Kate Stein
Publr: Ruth Sheppard
Mktg Dir, Casemate Group: Daniel Yesilonis

U.S. PUBLISHERS

Sales Dir, Casemate Group: Will Farnsworth
 E-mail: will.farnsworth@casematepublishers.com
Mktg Exec: Quinn Baumeister; Lauren Stead
Mng Ed: Tracey Mills
Commissioning Ed, Brookline Books: Jennifer Green
Ed: Lizzy Hammond; Adam Jankiewicz
Prodn Ed: Felicity Goldsack
Founded: 2001
Specialist military history publisher & book distributor. Publishing focus is on military history, including unit histories, biography & memoir, leadership titles, naval warfare & illustrated histories.
ISBN Prefix(es): 978-0-9711709; 978-1-932033; 978-1-935149; 978-1-61200
Number of titles published annually: 30 Print; 30 E-Book; 5 Audio
Total Titles: 175 Print; 175 E-Book
Imprints: Brookline Books
Foreign Office(s): Casemate UK Ltd, 47 Church St, Barnsley S70 2AS, United Kingdom, Head, Mktg & Client Rel: Louise Morgan *Tel:* (01865) 241249 *Fax:* (01865) 794449 *E-mail:* casemate-uk@casematepublishing.co.uk
Distributor for AF Editions; After the Battle; AFV Modeller; Air War Publications; Air World; Andrea Press; Arabian Publishing Ltd; Arden; Australian Scholarly Publishing; Aviation Collectables; Avonmore Books; Banovallum; Bauernfeind Press; Big Sky Publishing; Birlinn (UK); Blackman Associates; Brookline Books; Canbury Press; Carnegie Publishing; Casemate (USA); Casemate | academic; Classics Illustrated Comics; Claymore Press; Collins Books; Colourpoint; Compendium (UK); Leo Cooper; Countryside Books; Crecy Publishing Ltd; Dalrymple & Verdun; Fighting High Publishing; Fonthill Media; Formac Publishing Ltd (Canada); Fox Run Publishing; Front Street Press (USA); Frontline Books; Gallantry; Gettysburg Publishing; Gill Books; Global Collective Publishers; Greenhill Books; Griffon International; Grub Street Publishing (UK); Harpia Publishing; Heimdal; Helion & Company (UK); Helion & Company / GG Books (UK); Histoire & Collections (France); History Facts; HMH Publications; Imperial War Museum; Kagero; Karwansary Publishers; Key Publishing; Leda; Liberties Press; The Liffey Press; Lorimer; LRT Editions; Medina Publishing; Mercier Press; Messenger Publications; Military Miniature Publications; Mimesis International; MMPBooks (UK/Poland); Model Centrum Progres; Monroe Publications; Mort Homme Books; Mortons Media; Moselle River; The O'Brien Press; Origin; Oxbow Books; Pacifica Military History; Panzerwrecks; PeKo Publishing; Pen & Sword (UK); Pen & Sword Archaeology; Pen & Sword Atlas; Pen & Sword Aviation; Pen & Sword Digital; Pen & Sword Family History; Pen & Sword Fiction; Pen & Sword History; Pen & Sword Local History; Pen & Sword Maritime; Pen & Sword Military; Pen & Sword Military Classics; Pen & Sword Select; Pen & Sword Social History; Pen & Sword Transport; Pen & Sword True Crime; Penguin Random House South Africa; Polygon; Potomac Books; Praetorian Press; Protea Boekhuis; Remember When; Riebel-Roque; Rinaldi Studio Press; S I Publicaties BV; Sabrestorm Publishing; Savas Beatie (USA); Savas Publishing; Schneider Armour Research; Seaforth Publishing; Sidestone Press; Silver Link; Tattered Flag; Tempest; 30 Degrees South Publishers; George F Thompson Publishing; Timespan; Wharncliffe; Wordwell Books; Y Lolfa; Youthly; Ysec Editions
Foreign Rep(s): Casemate UK Ltd (worldwide exc Canada & USA); Login Canada (Canada)
Membership(s): The Imaging Alliance

§Catholic Book Publishing Corp
77 West End Rd, Totowa, NJ 07512
Tel: 973-890-2400 *Toll Free Tel:* 877-228-2665 *Fax:* 973-890-2410
E-mail: info@catholicbookpublishing.com
Web Site: www.catholicbookpublishing.com
Founded: 1911
For 120 years, the leading publisher of quality Catholic resources—including Bibles, Missals, Prayer books, liturgical books, spirituality books, Spanish titles & children's books. The company's trademark St Joseph Editions are distinctive for their large, easy-to-read typefaces; magnificent, full-color illustrations; & helpful & plentiful guides, summaries, notes, indices & photographs.
ISBN Prefix(es): 978-0-89942; 978-1-878718 (Resurrection Press); 978-0-529 (World Catholic Press); 978-1-933066 (Resurrection Press)
Number of titles published annually: 25 Print; 25 E-Book
Total Titles: 3,500 Print; 100 E-Book; 100 Audio
Imprints: Regina Press; Resurrection Press (spirituality & personal growth titles); World Catholic Press (complements the company's rich tradition of Bible publishing)

The Catholic Health Association of the United States
4455 Woodson Rd, St Louis, MO 63134-3797
SAN: 201-968X
Tel: 314-427-2500 *Fax:* 314-427-0029
E-mail: servicecenter@chausa.org
Web Site: www.chausa.org
Key Personnel
Dir, Communs & Mktg: Jenn Lyke
 E-mail: jlyke@chausa.org
Founded: 1915
Catholic health care resources, Catholic ministry, health, labor, medicine & nursing.
ISBN Prefix(es): 978-0-87125
Number of titles published annually: 2 Print; 9 Audio
Total Titles: 24 Print
Branch Office(s)
1625 Eye St NW, Suite 550, Washington, DC 20006 *Tel:* 202-296-3993 *Fax:* 202-296-3997

The Catholic University of America Press
Division of The Catholic University of America
240 Leahy Hall, 620 Michigan Ave NE, Washington, DC 20064
SAN: 203-6290
Tel: 202-319-5052 *Toll Free Tel:* 800-537-5487 (orders only) *Fax:* 202-319-4985
E-mail: cua-press@cua.edu
Web Site: cuapress.org
Key Personnel
Dir & Ed-in-Chief: Trevor C Lipscombe
 E-mail: lipscombe@cua.edu
Sales & Mktg Dir: Brian Roach *E-mail:* roach@cua.edu
Mng Ed: Theresa Walker *E-mail:* walkert@cua.edu
Acqs Ed, Philosophy & Theology: John B Martino *E-mail:* martinoj@cua.edu
Founded: 1939
ISBN Prefix(es): 978-0-8132
Number of titles published annually: 38 Print; 25 Online; 25 E-Book
Total Titles: 580 Print; 300 Online; 300 E-Book
Distributor for The Academy of American Franciscan History; American Maritain Association; Franciscan University Press; Humanum Academic Press; Institute for the Psychological Sciences Press (IPS); Sapientia Press
Foreign Rep(s): Brunswick Books (Canada); Eurospan University Press Group (Africa, Asia, Australia, Europe, Middle East, New Zealand, South America, UK)

Returns: HFS, c/o Maple Logistics Solutions, Lebanon Distribution Ctr, PO Box 1287, Lebanon, PA 17042-1287
Warehouse: Maple Logistics Solutions, Lebanon Distribution Ctr, 704 Legionaire Dr, Fredricksburg, PA 17042
Distribution Center: HFS (Hopkins Fulfillment Services), PO Box 50370, Baltimore, MD 21211-4370 *Tel:* 410-516-6965 *Toll Free Tel:* 800-537-5487 *Fax:* 410-516-6998 *E-mail:* hfscustserv@jh.edu *Web Site:* hfs.jhu.edu
Membership(s): Association of University Presses (AUPresses)

Cato Institute
1000 Massachusetts Ave NW, Washington, DC 20001-5403
Tel: 202-842-0200
Web Site: www.cato.org
Key Personnel
Dir, Edit Servs: Christian Schneider
 E-mail: cschneider@cato.org
Founded: 1977
Non-partisan, public-policy think tank.
ISBN Prefix(es): 978-0-932790; 978-1-882577; 978-1-930865; 978-1-933995; 978-1-935308; 978-1-939709; 978-1-94424; 978-1-948647
Number of titles published annually: 15 Print
Total Titles: 150 Print
Foreign Rights: Rights & Distribution Inc (worldwide)
Distribution Center: National Book Network (NBN), 15200 NBN Way, Blue Ridge Summit, PA 17214 *Tel:* 717-794-3800 *Toll Free Tel:* 800-462-6420 *Fax:* 717-794-3828 *Toll Free Fax:* 800-338-4550 *E-mail:* customercare@nbnbooks.com *Web Site:* www.nbnbooks.com

Frank W Cawood & Associates Inc, see FC&A Publishing

Caxton Press
Division of The Caxton Printers Ltd
312 Main St, Caldwell, ID 83605-3299
SAN: 201-9698
Tel: 208-459-7421 *Toll Free Tel:* 800-657-6465 *Fax:* 208-459-7450
E-mail: publish@caxtonpress.com
Web Site: www.caxtonpress.com
Key Personnel
Pres & Publr: Scott Gipson *E-mail:* sgipson@caxtonpress.com
Founded: 1925
Founded by J H Gipson, Caxton Press is still owned & managed by the Gipson family.
ISBN Prefix(es): 978-0-87004
Number of titles published annually: 6 Print; 5 E-Book
Total Titles: 215 Print; 75 E-Book
Distributor for Hambleton Publishing; Historic Idaho Series; Photosmith Books; Snake Country Publishing; University of Idaho Asian American Comparative Collection; University of Idaho Press
Membership(s): Association of American Publishers (AAP); Pacific Northwest Booksellers Association (PNBA); Western Writers of America (WWA)

CCAR Press, see Central Conference of American Rabbis/CCAR Press

§CCH, a Wolters Kluwer business
Subsidiary of Wolters Kluwer
2700 Lake Cook Rd, Riverwoods, IL 60015
SAN: 202-3504
Tel: 847-267-9000
Web Site: www.cch.com
Key Personnel
Dir, Communs: Leslie Bonacum *Tel:* 847-267-7153 *E-mail:* mediahelp@cch.com

Founded: 1913
Current US international tax law, business, human resources, securities & health care law, tax, small business, home office human resources & health care.
ISBN Prefix(es): 978-0-8080
Number of titles published annually: 100 Print
Total Titles: 400 Print
Subsidiaries: CCH Peterson; CCH Riverwoods; CCH St Petersburg; CCH Tax Compliance; CCH Washington DC; LIS (Legal Information Services); Washington Service Bureau
Foreign Office(s): Wolters Kluwer nv, Zuid-poolsingel 2, Postbus 1030, 2400 BA Alphen aan den Rijn, Netherlands *Tel:* (0172) 641 400 *Fax:* (0172) 474 889 *E-mail:* info@wolterskluwer.com *Web Site:* www.wolterskluwer.com
Billing Address: PO Box 4307, Carol Stream, IL 60197-4307
Returns: 7201 McKinney Circle, Frederick, MD 21704-8356
Warehouse: 4025 Peterson Ave, Chicago, IL 60646-6085

CCL - Americas, see Center for Creative Leadership LLC

Cedar Fort Inc
2373 W 700 S, Suite 100, Springville, UT 84663
Tel: 801-489-4084 *Toll Free Tel:* 800-SKY-BOOK (759-2665)
E-mail: marketinginfo@cedarfort.com
Web Site: cedarfort.com
Key Personnel
CEO: Bryce Mortimer *Tel:* 801-489-9366 *E-mail:* bmortimer@cedarfort.com
CFO: Tanya Flynn *Tel:* 801-477-9022 *E-mail:* tflynn@cedarfort.com
EVP, Sales & Mktg, Acqs & Events: Dru Huffaker *Tel:* 801-477-9025 *E-mail:* dru@cedarfort.com
VP, Digital Sales & Mktg: Clint Hunter *Tel:* 801-477-9023 *E-mail:* chunter@cedarfort.com
Dir, Logistics: Bevan Olsen *Tel:* 801-477-9038 *E-mail:* bolsen@cedarfort.com
Dir, Sourcing: Kim Clemons *Tel:* 801-477-9029 *E-mail:* kclemons@cedarfort.com
Ed-in-Chief: Kyle Lund *Tel:* 801-477-9039 *E-mail:* klund@cedarfort.com
Graphic Design Mgr: Shawnda Craig *Tel:* 801-477-9027 *E-mail:* scraig@cedarfort.com
Founded: 1986
Christian (primarily Latter-day Saints), inspirational, motivational, LDS fiction & doctrinal.
ISBN Prefix(es): 978-1-55517
Number of titles published annually: 120 Print; 50 E-Book; 5 Audio
Total Titles: 3,000 Print
Imprints: Bonneville Books; CFI; Council Press; Front Table Books; Hobble Creek Press; Horizon Publishers & Distributors Inc; King Dragon Press; Plain Sight Publishing; Sweetwater Books
See separate listing for:
Horizon Publishers & Distributors Inc

Cedar Grove Books, see Cedar Grove Publishing

§Cedar Grove Publishing
Subsidiary of WRTB Entertainment LLC
3205 Elmhurst St, Rowlett, TX 75088
SAN: 255-3732
Mailing Address: 236 W Portal Ave, No 118, San Francisco, CA 94127
Tel: 415-364-8292
E-mail: queries@cedargrovebooks.com
Web Site: www.cedargrovebooks.com
Key Personnel
Pres & Publr: Rochon Perry *E-mail:* rperry@cedargrovebooks.com
Edit Dir: J Cameron McClain *E-mail:* j.cameron.mcclain.stories@gmail.com
Dir, Soc Media: Rebecca Sims-Nichols *E-mail:* bexlnichols@gmail.com
Founded: 2010
Publish diverse & inclusive books across genres with protagonists that overcome adversity by staying true to themselves.
ISBN Prefix(es): 978-0-9835077; 978-1-941958
Number of titles published annually: 9 Print; 9 Online; 9 E-Book; 1 Audio
Total Titles: 9 Print; 9 Online; 9 E-Book; 1 Audio
Distribution Center: Independent Publishers Group (IPG), 814 N Franklin St, Chicago, IL 60610 *Web Site:* www.ipgbook.com
Membership(s): The American Library Association (ALA); Bay Area Independent Publishers Association (BAIPA); Bay Area Women in Publishing (BAWiP); Book Industry Study Group (BISG); Book Promotion Forum; California Independent Booksellers Alliance (CALIBA); The Children's Book Council (CBC); Independent Book Publishers Association (IBPA); Independent Book Publishing Professionals Group (IBPPG); Publishers Association of the West (PubWest); Publishing Professionals Network (PPN); Sisters in Crime; Southern Independent Booksellers Alliance (SIBA)

Cedar Tree Books
PO Box 4256, Wilmington, DE 19807
Tel: 302-998-4171 *Fax:* 302-998-4185
E-mail: books@ctpress.com
Web Site: www.cedartreebooks.com
Founded: 1925
This publisher has indicated that 100% of their product line is author subsidized.
ISBN Prefix(es): 978-1-892142
Number of titles published annually: 3 Print; 2 E-Book
Total Titles: 60 Print; 2 E-Book

CEF Press
Subsidiary of Child Evangelism Fellowship Inc
17482 State Hwy M, Warrenton, MO 63383-0348
Mailing Address: PO Box 348, Warrenton, MO 63383-0348
Tel: 636-456-4321 *Toll Free Tel:* 800-748-7710 (cust serv)
E-mail: info@cefonline.com
Web Site: www.cefonline.com; www.cefpress.com
Founded: 1937
Christian education curriculum.
ISBN Prefix(es): 978-1-55976
Number of titles published annually: 30 Print
Total Titles: 300 Print
Foreign Rep(s): CEFMARK (Australia)

§Cengage Learning
20 Channel Center St, Boston, MA 02210
Tel: 617-289-7700 *Toll Free Tel:* 800-354-9706 *Fax:* 617-289-7844
E-mail: esales@cengage.com
Web Site: www.cengage.com
Key Personnel
CEO: Michael Hansen
EVP & CFO: Bob Munro
CTO: George Moore
Chief Integration Offr: Rebecca McNamara
Chief Mktg Offr: Sharon Loeb
Chief People Offr & Gen Coun: Ken Carson
Chief People Offr: Gary Fortier
Chief Sales & Mktg Offr: Kevin Stone
Pres, Intl: Alexander Broich
EVP & Chief Strategy Offr: Todd Markson
SVP & Treas: Richard Veith
SVP, Brand Strategy: Daniel Sieger
SVP, Pub Aff: Susan Aspey
VP, Public & Media Rel: Lindsay Stanley
Sr Educ Advisor: George Miller
Cengage Learning delivers highly-customized learning solutions for colleges, universities, instructors, students, libraries, government agencies, corporations & professionals around the world. These solutions are delivered through specialized content, applications & services that foster academic excellence & professional development, as well as provide measurable learning outcomes to its customers.
Number of titles published annually: 150 Print
Subsidiaries: Gale (www.gale.com); Thorndike Press®
Billing Address: Cengage Learning Distribution Center, 10650 Toebben Dr, Independence, KY 41051 *Tel:* 859-525-2230
Orders to: Cengage Learning Distribution Center, 10650 Toebben Dr, Independence, KY 41051 *Tel:* 859-525-2230
Returns: Cengage Learning Distribution Center, 10650 Toebben Dr, Independence, KY 41051 *Tel:* 859-525-2230
Warehouse: Cengage Learning Distribution Center, 10650 Toebben Dr, Independence, KY 41051 *Tel:* 859-525-2230
Distribution Center: Cengage Learning Distribution Center, 10650 Toebben Dr, Independence, KY 41051 *Tel:* 859-525-2230
Membership(s): Association of American Publishers (AAP)
See separate listing for:
Charles River Media
Gale
National Geographic Learning

Center for Creative Leadership LLC
Affiliate of Smith Richardson Foundation
One Leadership Place, Greensboro, NC 27410-9427
Tel: 336-545-2810; 336-288-7210 *Fax:* 336-282-3284
E-mail: info@ccl.org
Web Site: shop.ccl.org/usa/books
Key Personnel
Pres & CEO: Martin Schneider
Chief Res & Innovation Offr: David G Altman
EVP & CFO: Bradley E Shumaker
Founded: 1970
Books on leadership & leadership development.
ISBN Prefix(es): 978-0-912879; 978-0-9638301; 978-1-882197; 978-1-64761
Number of titles published annually: 10 Print
Total Titles: 123 Print
Distributed by Jossey-Bass; John Wiley & Sons Inc
Distributor for Free Press; Harvard Business School Press; Jossey-Bass; Lominger Inc; John Wiley & Sons Inc

§Center for Futures Education Inc
345 Erie St, Grove City, PA 16127
Mailing Address: PO Box 309, Grove City, PA 16127
Tel: 724-458-5860 *Fax:* 724-458-5962
E-mail: info@thectr.com
Web Site: www.thectr.com
Founded: 1981
Print & online books on commodity futures & securities.
ISBN Prefix(es): 978-0-915513
Number of titles published annually: 12 Print
Total Titles: 50 Print; 15 E-Book

The Center for Learning
Division of Social Studies School Service
PO Box 802, Culver City, CA 90232
Tel: 310-839-2436 *Toll Free Tel:* 800-421-4246 *Fax:* 310-839-2249 *Toll Free Fax:* 800-944-5432
E-mail: access@socialstudies.com; customerservice@socialstudies.com; submissions@socialstudies.com
Web Site: www.centerforlearning.org
Key Personnel
Head, Content: Bill Walter

U.S. PUBLISHERS

Founded: 1965
Founded to publish values based curriculum materials. All materials are written by master teachers who integrate academic objectives & ethical values. Nonprofit educational publisher of value based curriculum units with reproducible handouts for teachers of English/Language Arts, social studies, novel/dramas, biographies & religion. Specialize in advanced placement, genres; American, British & World novels & literature; skills, supplementary topics, writing; economics, social & global issues, US government & history, world history; Catholic teaching, ministry, retreats, adult faith resources, marriage & parenting, divorce & blended families, abstinence education & chastity; publish lesson plans for elementary & secondary grades.
ISBN Prefix(es): 978-1-56077
Number of titles published annually: 20 Print
Total Titles: 600 Print

Center for Strategic & International Studies (CSIS)
1616 Rhode Island Ave NW, Washington, DC 20036
Tel: 202-887-0200 *Fax:* 202-775-3199
Web Site: www.csis.org
Key Personnel
Asst Dir, Pubns: Katherine Stark *Tel:* 202-775-3278 *E-mail:* kstark@csis.org
Founded: 1962
Public policy research organization.
ISBN Prefix(es): 978-0-89206; 978-1-44228; 978-1-5381
Number of titles published annually: 65 Print; 65 Online; 25 E-Book
Total Titles: 250 Print; 100 Online; 200 E-Book
Distributed by Rowman & Littlefield
Membership(s): Association of American Publishers (AAP)

Center for the Collaborative Classroom
1001 Marina Village Pkwy, Suite 110, Alameda, CA 94501-1042
Tel: 510-533-0213 *Toll Free Tel:* 800-666-7270 *Fax:* 510-464-3670
E-mail: info@collaborativeclassroom.org; clientsupport@collaborativeclassroom.org
Web Site: www.collaborativeclassroom.org
Key Personnel
Founder: Eric Schaps
Pres & CEO: Kelly Stuart *E-mail:* kstuart@collaborativeclassroom.org
SVP & CFO: Brent Welling *E-mail:* bwelling@collaborativeclassroom.org
CTO: Tim Millen
SVP, Dissemination: Isabel Sawyer
SVP, Prog Devt: Valerie Fraser
Founded: 1980
Books, teacher study packages, literature guides, in school & after school curricula in character education, reading & mathematics.
ISBN Prefix(es): 978-1-885603; 978-1-57621; 978-0-439
Number of titles published annually: 15 Print
Total Titles: 450 Print

Centering Corp
6406 Maple St, Omaha, NE 68104
SAN: 298-1815
Tel: 402-553-1200 *Toll Free Tel:* 866-218-0101 *Fax:* 402-553-0507
E-mail: orders@centeringcorp.com
Web Site: www.centering.org
Key Personnel
Founder & Pres: Joy Johnson
Exec Dir: Janet Roberts *E-mail:* centeringcorp@aol.com
Busn Dir: Marc Roberts
Dir, Devt: Ben Schroeder
Founded: 1977
Bereavement support; specializes in divorce, grief & loss. Nonprofit organization.
ISBN Prefix(es): 978-1-56123
Number of titles published annually: 10 Print
Total Titles: 150 Print

Centerstream Publishing LLC
PO Box 17878, Anaheim Hills, CA 92817-7878
SAN: 683-8022
Tel: 714-779-9390
E-mail: centerstrm@aol.com
Web Site: www.centerstream-usa.com
Key Personnel
Owner: Ron Middlebrook
Founded: 1971
Music history, bios, music instruction books, videos & DVDs: all instruments.
ISBN Prefix(es): 978-0-931759; 978-1-57467
Number of titles published annually: 20 Print; 10 CD-ROM
Total Titles: 250 Print; 30 CD-ROM
Subsidiaries: Centerbrook Publishing
Distributed by Hal Leonard Corp
Membership(s): Independent Book Publishers Association (IBPA)

Central Conference of American Rabbis/CCAR Press
355 Lexington Ave, New York, NY 10017
SAN: 204-3262
Tel: 212-972-3636
E-mail: info@ccarpress.org; info@ccarnet.org
Web Site: www.ccarpress.org
Key Personnel
Chief Exec: Hara E Person
Dir, Press: Rafael Chaiken *Tel:* 212-542-8777 *E-mail:* rchaiken@ccarnet.org
Founded: 1889
Books on liturgy & Jewish practices from a liberal point of view.
ISBN Prefix(es): 978-0-88123; 978-0-916694
Number of titles published annually: 10 Print; 10 E-Book
Total Titles: 102 Print; 59 E-Book
Imprints: Reform Judaism Publishing
Orders to: Chicago Distribution Center, 11030 S Langley Ave, Chicago, IL 60628 *Toll Free Tel:* 800-621-2736 *E-mail:* orders@press.uchicago.edu
Shipping Address: Chicago Distribution Center, 11030 S Langley Ave, Chicago, IL 60628
Warehouse: Chicago Distribution Center, 11030 S Langley Ave, Chicago, IL 60628 *Toll Free Tel:* 800-621-2736 *E-mail:* orders@press.uchicago.edu
Distribution Center: Chicago Distribution Center, 11030 S Langley Ave, Chicago, IL 60628 *Tel:* 773-702-7010 *Toll Free Fax:* 800-621-8476
Web Site: press.uchicago.edu/cdc

§Central Recovery Press (CRP)
Unit of Central Recovery LLC
3321 N Buffalo Dr, Suite 200, Las Vegas, NV 89129
Tel: 702-868-5830 *Fax:* 702-868-5831
E-mail: sales@recoverypress.com
Web Site: centralrecoverypress.com
Key Personnel
Mng Ed: Valerie Killeen *E-mail:* vkilleen@recoverypress.com
Spec Sales Mgr: John Davis *E-mail:* jdavis@recoverypress.com
Committed to building lasting & meaningful connections based on shared values & principles. Library of quality materials across the full spectrum of behavioral healthcare topics, including addiction treatment & recovery, addiction & the family, parenting, relationships, trauma, grief & loss & mindfulness. Mission is to shift the prevailing perception of addiction, co-occurring & other behavioral health issues as moral failing, character weakness, or vice, offering materials that promote a broader view of recovery & encourage a holistic approach to emotional, physical, mental & spiritual well-being.
ISBN Prefix(es): 978-1-949481; 978-1-942094; 978-1-937612; 978-1-936290; 978-0-9818482
Number of titles published annually: 12 Print; 12 E-Book; 8 Audio
Total Titles: 200 Print; 200 E-Book; 60 Audio
Distribution Center: Consortium Book Sales & Distribution, The Keg House, Suite 101, 34 13 Ave NE, Minneapolis, MN 55413-1007 *Tel:* 612-746-2600 *E-mail:* cbsdinfo@ingramcontent.com *Web Site:* www.cbsd.com

Cereals & Grains Association
3285 Northwood Circle, Suite 100, St Paul, MN 55121
Tel: 651-454-7250
E-mail: info@cerealsgrains.org
Web Site: cerealsgrains.org
Key Personnel
VP, Pubns: Greg Grahek *E-mail:* ggrahek@scisoc.org
Pubns Mktg Coord: Dawn Wuest *E-mail:* dwuest@scisoc.org
Founded: 1920 (as the American Association of Cereal Chemists)
Source for information about cereal grain science. Most books published in partnership with Elsevier.
ISBN Prefix(es): 978-1-891127 (Cereals & Grains Association/AACC); 978-0-128195 (Cereals & Grains Association/Woodhead Publishing)
Number of titles published annually: 5 Print; 5 Online; 5 E-Book
Total Titles: 100 Print

§Chain Store Guide (CSG)
3710 Corporex Park Dr, Suite 310, Tampa, FL 33619
Toll Free Tel: 800-927-9292 (orders) *Fax:* 813-627-6888
E-mail: webmaster@chainstoreguide.com
Web Site: www.chainstoreguide.com
Key Personnel
EVP: Carmen Vasquez-Perez
Founded: 1933
Directories of retail & wholesale companies.
ISBN Prefix(es): 978-0-86730
Number of titles published annually: 5 Print
Total Titles: 21 Print; 21 Online

Chalice Press
Division of Christian Board of Publication
11939 Manchester Rd, No 100, St Louis, MO 63131
SAN: 201-4408
Tel: 314-231-8500 *Toll Free Tel:* 800-366-3383
E-mail: customerservice@chalicepress.com
Web Site: www.chalicepress.com
Key Personnel
Pres & Publr: Brad Lyons *E-mail:* blyons@chalicepress.com
Assoc Publr & Opers Dir: David Woodard *E-mail:* dwoodard@chalicepress.com
Founded: 1911
Religion (Protestant) & hymnals.
ISBN Prefix(es): 978-0-8272
Number of titles published annually: 12 Print
Total Titles: 300 Print
Imprints: CBP (Christian Church (Disciples of Christ) products); Chalice Stories (fiction)
Returns: 3280 Summit Ridge Pkwy, Suite 100, Duluth, GA 30096 *Fax:* 770-280-4039
Warehouse: APG Sales & Distribution, 1501 County Hospital Rd, Nashville, TN 37218 *Tel:* 615-254-2488
Distribution Center: Baker & Taylor Publisher Services, 30 Amberwood Pkwy, Ashland, OH 44805 *Tel:* 567-215-0030 *Toll Free Tel:* 888-814-0208 *E-mail:* info@btpubservices.com *Web Site:* www.btpubservices.com

Rainbow Book Agencies, 303 Arthur St, Fairfield, Victoria 3078, Australia *Tel:* 9481-6611 *Fax:* 9481-2371 *E-mail:* rba@rainbowbooks.com.au

Chaosium Inc
3450 Wooddale Ct, Ann Arbor, MI 48104
SAN: 692-6460
Tel: 734-972-9551
E-mail: customerservice@chaosium.com
Web Site: www.chaosium.com
Key Personnel
Pres: Rick Meints *E-mail:* rick@chaosium.com
Founded: 1975
Publisher of horror anthologies & role playing games.
ISBN Prefix(es): 978-0-933635; 978-1-56882
Number of titles published annually: 15 Print; 12 E-Book
Total Titles: 241 Print; 60 E-Book
Orders to: 719 E Murray St, Rockport, TX 78382, Contact: Dustin Wright *Tel:* 361-450-0787 *E-mail:* orders@chaosium.com
Warehouse: Bang Fulfillment Service, 217 Etak Dr, Brainerd, MN 56401
Membership(s): The Game Manufacturers Association (GAMA)

Charisma Media
1150 Greenwood Blvd, Lake Mary, FL 32746
Tel: 407-333-0600 (all imprints) *Fax:* 407-333-7100 (all imprints)
E-mail: info@charismamedia.com; customerservice@charismamedia.com
Web Site: www.charismamedia.com
Key Personnel
Owner & Pres: Stephen Strang
Founded: 1975
Christianity.
ISBN Prefix(es): 978-0-88419; 978-1-63641
Number of titles published annually: 200 Print
Total Titles: 500 Print; 2 Audio
Imprints: Casa Creacion (Spanish publishing group); Charisma House (theology); Frontline (politics & current events); Siloam Press (health publishing group)
Membership(s): Evangelical Christian Publishers Association (ECPA)

§Charles Press Publishers
Subsidiary of Oxbridge Corporation
1754 Wylie St, No 4, Philadelphia, PA 19130
Tel: 215-470-5977
E-mail: mail@charlespresspub.com
Web Site: charlespresspub.com
Key Personnel
Publr: Lauren Meltzer *E-mail:* lauren@charlespresspub.com
Founded: 1974
Independent traditional publishing house specializing in social & behavioral science books for the academic, professional & trade markets.
ISBN Prefix(es): 978-0-914783
Number of titles published annually: 10 Print; 1 CD-ROM; 2 E-Book
Total Titles: 125 Print; 6 CD-ROM; 2 E-Book
Returns: c/o Self-Service Storage, 2000 Hamilton St, No 2884, Philadelphia, PA 19130 (permission must be requested in advance of returns)

Charles River Media
Imprint of Cengage Learning
20 Channel Center St, Boston, MA 02210
Tel: 617-289-7700 *Fax:* 617-289-7844
Web Site: www.cengage.com; www.delmarlearning.com/charlesriver
Founded: 1994
Publishing computer books for web development, music technology, game development, graphic design & digital video.
ISBN Prefix(es): 978-1-886801; 978-1-58450

Number of titles published annually: 50 Print; 2 CD-ROM; 150 Online; 100 E-Book
Total Titles: 200 Print; 5 CD-ROM; 150 Online; 100 E-Book
Foreign Rep(s): IPR (Middle East); Login Canada (Canada); Thomson Learning (Asia); Transatlantic (Europe); Woodslane (Australia)

Charlesbridge Publishing Inc
85 Main St, Watertown, MA 02472
Tel: 617-926-0329 *Toll Free Tel:* 800-225-3214 *Fax:* 617-926-5720 *Toll Free Fax:* 800-926-5775
E-mail: books@charlesbridge.com
Web Site: www.charlesbridge.com
Key Personnel
Pres & CEO: Brent Farmer *E-mail:* bfarmer@charlesbridge.com
Publr & COO: Mary Ann Sabia *E-mail:* masabia@charlesbridge.com
CFO: Brent Farmer, Jr *E-mail:* brent.farmer@charlesbridge.com
VP & Publr: Yolanda Scott *E-mail:* yolanda@charlesbridge.com
VP & Dir, Sales & Mktg: Megan Bencivenni Quinn
VP, Prodn: Brian Walker *E-mail:* bwalker@charlesbridge.com
Art Dir: Diane Earley *E-mail:* dearley@charlesbridge.com
Edit Dir & Exec Ed: Eileen Robinson
Retail Sales & Mktg Mgr: Jordan Standridge
Founded: 1980
Children's illustrated picture books, board books, early readers, chapter books, middle grade & young adult fiction & nonfiction. Adult imprint, Imagine Publishing: general trade, cookbooks, puzzle/game, humor & nonfiction.
ISBN Prefix(es): 978-0-88106; 978-1-57091; 978-1-56566; 978-0-934763; 978-1-890674; 978-1-879085; 978-1-58089; 978-1-936140 (Imagine)
Number of titles published annually: 60 Print; 50 E-Book
Total Titles: 750 Print; 500 E-Book
Imprints: Charlesbridge Moves; CharlesbridgeTEEN; Imagine Publishing (www.imaginebooks.net)
Orders to: Penguin Random House Publisher Services (PRHPS), 400 Hahn Rd, Westminster, MD 21157 *Toll Free Tel:* 800-733-3000 *Web Site:* prhpublisherservices.com
Returns: Penguin Random House LLC, 1019 N State Rd 47, Crawfordsville, IN 47933
Distribution Center: Penguin Random House Publisher Services (PRHPS), 400 Hahn Rd, Westminster, MD 21157 *E-mail:* distribution@randomhouse.com *Web Site:* prhpublisherservices.com
Membership(s): American Booksellers Association (ABA); The American Library Association (ALA); Association of Booksellers for Children; The Children's Book Council (CBC); Education Market Association; International Literacy Association (ILA); MSA; NCBA; New England Independent Booksellers Association (NEIBA); TLA

The Chartered Institute of Management Accountants®, see AICPA® & CIMA®

§Chelsea Green Publishing Co
Imprint of Rizzoli International Publications Inc
85 N Main St, Suite 120, White River Junction, VT 05001
SAN: 669-7631
Tel: 802-295-6300 *Toll Free Tel:* 800-639-4099 (cust serv & orders) *Fax:* 802-295-6444
E-mail: customerservice@chelseagreen.com; editorial@chelseagreen.com; publicity@chelseagreen.com; rights@chelseagreen.com
Web Site: www.chelseagreen.com

Key Personnel
Pres & CEO: Stefano Peccatori
VP, Busn Devt & Global Sales: Anne Bowman
Deputy Publr: Matthew Derr
Busn & Dist Dir: Sandi Eaton *E-mail:* seaton@chelseagreen.com
Dir, North American Sales, Mktg & Publicity: Sean Maher *E-mail:* smaher@chelseagreen.com
Prodn Dir: Patricia Stone *E-mail:* pstone@chelseagreen.com
Mng Ed: Rebecca Springer
Sr Ed: Fern Marshall Bradley *E-mail:* fbradley@chelseagreen.com; Brianne Goodspeed *E-mail:* bgoodspeed@chelseagreen.com; Michael Metivier *E-mail:* mmetivier@chelseagreen.com; Ben Watson *E-mail:* bwatson@chelseagreen.com
Author Events Mgr: Jenna Dimmick Stewart *E-mail:* jstewart@chelseagreen.com
IT Mgr: Curtis Cass
Publg Partnerships Mgr: Kirsten Drew
Spec & Corp Sales Mgr: Darrell Koerner *E-mail:* dkoerner@chelseagreen.com
Prodn Coord: Alexander Bullett *E-mail:* abullet@chelseagreen.com
Founded: 1984
Books for sustainable living including: environment, building, nature, outdoors, sustainability, organic gardening, home, renewable energy, homesteading, politics & current events.
ISBN Prefix(es): 978-0-930031; 978-1-890132; 978-1-933392; 978-1-60358
Number of titles published annually: 35 Print; 35 E-Book
Total Titles: 300 Print; 250 E-Book
Foreign Office(s): Chelsea Green Publishing UK Ltd, South Wing, Somerset House, Strand, London WC2R 1LA, United Kingdom, Mng Dir: Matt Haslum *E-mail:* mhaslum@chelseagreen.com
Distributor for AATEC Publications; American Council for an Energy Efficient Economy (ACEEE); Anomaly Press; Avalon House; Boye Knives Press; Cal-Earth; Earth Pledge; Eco Logic Books; Ecological Design Institute; Ecological Design Press; Empowerment Institute; Filaree Productions; Flower Press; Foundation for Deep Ecology; Fox Maple Press; Green Books; Green Building Press; Green Man Publishing; Groundworks; Hand Print Press; Holmgren Design Services; Jenkins Publishing; Knossus Project; Left To Write Press; Madison Area Community Supported Agriculture Coalition; Marion Institute; marketumbrella.org; Metamorphic Press; Moneta Publications; Ottographics; Peregrinzilla; Permanent Publications; Daniela Piazza Editore; Polyface; Propriometrics Press; Rainsource Press; Raven Press; Anita Roddick Publications; Rural Science Institute; Seed Savers; Service Employees International Union; Slow Food Editore; Solar Design Association; Stone Pier Press; Stonefield Publishing; Sun Plans Inc; Sustainability Press; Trailblazer Press; Trust for Public Land; Yes Books
Foreign Rep(s): Booktopia Publisher Services (Australia, New Zealand); Grantham Book Services (GBS) (UK); SG Distributors (South Africa); University of Toronto Press Distribution (Canada)
Returns: 22880 Quicksilver Dr, Dulles, VA 20166

Chelsea House
Imprint of Infobase Learning
132 W 31 St, 16th fl, New York, NY 10001
SAN: 169-7331
Toll Free Tel: 800-322-8755 *Toll Free Fax:* 800-678-3633
E-mail: custserv@infobase.com; info@infobase.com
Web Site: www.infobasepublishing.com; www.infobase.com (online resources)

Key Personnel
Pres & CEO, Infobase Learning: Paul Skordilis
Dir, Publicity, Infobase Learning: Laurie Katz
Dir, Mktg, Infobase Learning: Zina Scarpulla
 Tel: 800-322-8755 ext 4218
Edit Dir: Laurie Likoff
Dir, Book & Ebook Sales: Justyna Pawluk
 Tel: 800-322-8755 ext 4255 *E-mail:* jpawluk@infobaselearning.com
Dir, Licensing & Intl Sales: Ben Jacobs
Founded: 1966
Offers timely & engaging young adult sets & series ebooks spanning a wide variety of subject areas. Chelsea Clubhouse, its elementary imprint, presents easy-to-read, full-color books for young readers in grades 2-6.
ISBN Prefix(es): 978-0-87754; 978-0-7910; 978-1-55546; 978-1-60413; 978-1-4381; 978-1-61753
Number of titles published annually: 230 E-Book
Total Titles: 1,866 Print; 1,680 E-Book
Imprints: Chelsea Clubhouse
Returns: c/o Maple Logistics Solutions Distribution Ctr, 704 Legionaire Dr, Fredericksburg, PA 17026
Membership(s): The American Library Association (ALA); Association of American Publishers (AAP)

§Cheng & Tsui Co Inc
25 West St, 2nd fl, Boston, MA 02111-1213
Tel: 617-988-2400 *Toll Free Tel:* 800-554-1963
 Fax: 617-426-3669
E-mail: service@cheng-tsui.com; orders@cheng-tsui.com; marketing@cheng-tsui.com
Web Site: www.cheng-tsui.com
Key Personnel
Pres: Jill Cheng
Founded: 1979
Publisher, importer & exporter of Asian books in English. Publish & distribute Asia related books & Chinese, Japanese & Korean language learning textbooks.
ISBN Prefix(es): 978-0-917056; 978-0-88727
Number of titles published annually: 30 Print
Total Titles: 640 Print; 75 CD-ROM; 4 Online; 4 E-Book
Distributor for Action Language Learning; aha! Chinese; Bider Technology; Cengage Learning Australia; China International Book Trading Corp (CIBTC) (Beijing, selected titles only); China Soft; China Sprout; Crabtree Publishing Co; Curriculum Corp; Facets Video; Ilchokak Publishers; Italian School of East Asian Studies; Japan Times; JPT America Inc; Marshall Cavendish Singapore; Oxford University Press; Pan Asian Publications; Panmun Academic Services; Panpac Education; Paradigm Busters; Pearson Education Australia; Royal Asiatic Society (Korea Branch); SMC Publishing; Sogang University Institute; SUP Publishing Logistics; US International Publishing; White Rabbit Press; Zeitgeist Films
Returns: Publishers Storage & Shipping Corp, 46 Development Rd, Fitchburg, MA 01420
Warehouse: Publishers Storage & Shipping Corp, 46 Development Rd, Fitchburg, MA 01420
 Tel: 978-345-2121 ext 223 *Fax:* 978-348-1233
 Web Site: www.pssc.com

Cherry Hill Publishing LLC
24344 Del Amo Rd, Ramona, CA 92065
SAN: 255-0075
Tel: 858-868-1260 *Toll Free Tel:* 800-407-1072
 Fax: 760-203-1200
E-mail: operations@cherryhillpublishing.com; sales@cherryhillpublishing.com
Web Site: www.cherryhillpublishing.com
Key Personnel
Pres: Rick Roane *E-mail:* rick@cherryhillpublishing.com
Returns: Sharon Roane *Tel:* 858-735-5397
 E-mail: sharon@cherryhillpublishing.com

Founded: 2002
Publisher of audiobook titles.
ISBN Prefix(es): 978-0-9843759; 978-0-9723298; 978-0-9830086; 978-1-937028; 978-1-62079
Number of titles published annually: 5 CD-ROM; 20 Online; 25 Audio
Total Titles: 1 Print; 10 CD-ROM; 275 Online; 40 E-Book; 400 Audio
Distribution Center: Baker & Taylor, 2810 Coliseum Centre Dr, Suite 300, Charlotte, NC 28217-4574 *Toll Free Tel:* 800-775-1800
 Fax: 704-998-3100 *Web Site:* www.bakertaylor.com
Midwest Tapes, 1417 Timberwolf Dr, Holland, OH 43528 *Toll Free Tel:* 800-875-2785
 Toll Free Fax: 800-444-6645 *E-mail:* info@midwesttapes.com *Web Site:* www.midwesttapes.com
Membership(s): Audio Publishers Association

Chicago Review Press
814 N Franklin St, Chicago, IL 60610
Tel: 312-337-0747 *Toll Free Tel:* 800-888-4741
 Fax: 312-337-5110
E-mail: frontdesk@chicagoreviewpress.com
Web Site: www.chicagoreviewpress.com
Key Personnel
Group Publr: Cynthia Sherry
Exec Ed: Michelle Williams
Sr Ed: Jerome Pohlen
Sales Mgr: Melanie Roth
Founded: 1973
ISBN Prefix(es): 978-1-56976; 978-1-55652; 978-1-88305 (Ball Publishing)
Number of titles published annually: 65 Print; 65 E-Book
Total Titles: 1,000 Print; 1,000 E-Book
Imprints: Academy Chicago Publishers; Amberjack Publishing; Bright Ring; Council Oak Books; Duet Books; Interlude Press; Lawrence Hill Books; Parenting Press; Ripple Grove Press
Divisions: Independent Publishers Group (IPG)
Foreign Rights: The Susan Schulman Agency (worldwide)
Distribution Center: Independent Publishers Group (IPG), 814 N Franklin St, Chicago, IL 60610 *Tel:* 312-337-0747 *Fax:* 312-337-5985
 Toll Free Tel: 800-888-4741 *Fax:* 312-337-5985
 E-mail: frontdesk@ipgbook.com *Web Site:* www.ipgbook.com
See separate listing for:
Academy Chicago Publishers
Parenting Press

§Chickadee Prince Books LLC
1030 Lake Ave, Greenwich, CT 06830
Tel: 212-808-5500
E-mail: submissions@chickadeeprince.com
Web Site: chickadeeprince.com
Key Personnel
Exec Dir: Rebecca McLean *E-mail:* rebecca@chickadeeprince.com
Founded: 2013
Small press publishing acclaimed fiction & nonfiction of all genres, including memoirs, science fiction, thrillers, mysteries & contemporary fiction. Representative titles include Donna Levin's contemporary women's fiction novels & Ed Rucker's legal thrillers. Not a subsidy or hybrid press, we pay a small advance & cover all costs of publication, publicity & bookstores marketing/outreach. Recently acquired by CINN, we now are expanding our list. We accept unsol mss as well as agented mss. Distributed through Ingram, we employ our own bookstore representatives.
ISBN Prefix(es): 978-0-9913274; 978-0-9997569
Number of titles published annually: 40 Print; 43 Online; 40 E-Book
Total Titles: 26 Print; 26 Online; 27 E-Book
Imprints: Chickadee Prince Books

Child Welfare League of America (CWLA)
727 15 St NW, Suite 1200, Washington, DC 20005
SAN: 201-9876
Tel: 202-590-8748
E-mail: cwla@cwla.org
Web Site: www.cwla.org/pubs
Key Personnel
Dir, Pubns: Marlene Saulsbury
 E-mail: msaulsbury@cwla.org
Founded: 1920
Provide relevant & timely publications that enable CWLA members & the child welfare field at large to improve services to children & their families.
ISBN Prefix(es): 978-0-87868; 978-1-58760
Number of titles published annually: 12 Print
Total Titles: 200 Print
Imprints: CWLA Press

Children's Book Press
Imprint of Lee & Low Books
95 Madison Ave, Suite 1205, New York, NY 10016
Tel: 212-779-4400 *Fax:* 212-683-1894
E-mail: editorial@leeandlow.com; orders@leeandlow.com; customer.support@leeandlow.com
Web Site: www.leeandlow.com/imprints/childrens-book-press
Key Personnel
Pres: Craig Low
Mktg Mgr: Jalissa Corrie *E-mail:* jcorrie@leeandlow.com
Founded: 1975
Multicultural & bilingual picture books for children. Central American, African-American, Asian-American, Hispanic-American, Native American tales, folklore, contemporary fiction & nonfiction.
ISBN Prefix(es): 978-0-89239
Number of titles published annually: 6 Print
Total Titles: 30 Print
Returns: Whitehurst & Clark, c/o Lee & Low Books-Returns Dept, 1200 County Rd, Rte 523, Flemington, NJ 08822

Child's Play® Inc
Affiliate of Child's Play (International) Ltd
250 Minot Ave, Auburn, ME 04210
Tel: 207-784-7252 *Toll Free Tel:* 800-639-6404
 Fax: 207-784-7358 *Toll Free Fax:* 800-854-6989
E-mail: chpmaine@aol.com
Web Site: www.childs-play.com
Key Personnel
VP, Sales & Mktg: Joseph Gardner *Tel:* 800-472-0099 *E-mail:* joe@childsplayusa.com
Gen Mgr: Laurie Reynolds *E-mail:* laurie@childsplayusa.com
Founded: 1972
Children's books, games, toys & associated materials.
ISBN Prefix(es): 978-0-85953; 978-1-904550; 978-1-84643; 978-1-78628
Number of titles published annually: 30 Print
Total Titles: 450 Print; 8 Audio
Foreign Office(s): Ashworth Rd, Bridgemead, Swindon, Wilts SN5 7YD, United Kingdom
 Tel: (01793) 616286

§The Child's World Inc
21735 E Idyllwilde Dr, Parker, CO 80138-8892
SAN: 992-4981
Toll Free Tel: 800-599-READ (599-7323)
 Toll Free Fax: 888-320-2329
E-mail: info@childsworld.com
Web Site: www.childsworld.com
Key Personnel
Pres: Mike Peterson
Sales & Serv Mgr: Amy Dols
Founded: 1968

Publisher of educational fiction & nonfiction books for grades K-8. Distribute paperback, trade bound & library bound books, as well as single- and multi-user ebooks, to schools & libraries throughout the world.
ISBN Prefix(es): 978-0-89565; 978-0-913778; 978-1-56766; 978-1-59296; 978-1-60253; 978-1-60954; 978-1-60973; 978-1-61473; 978-1-62323; 978-1-62687; 978-1-63143; 978-1-63407; 978-1-5038
Number of titles published annually: 200 Print; 200 E-Book
Total Titles: 1,200 Print; 3,400 E-Book
Imprints: First Steps; Momentum; Storytime Tales; Stride; Wonder Books

§China Books
Division of Sinomedia International Group
360 Swift Ave, Suite 48, South San Francisco, CA 94080
SAN: 169-0167
Fax: 650-872-7808
E-mail: editor.sinomedia@gmail.com
Key Personnel
Edit Dir: Chris Robyn *Tel:* 650-872-7718 ext 312 *E-mail:* chris@sinomediausa.com
Sales Mgr: Kelly Feng *Tel:* 650-872-7076 ext 310 *E-mail:* kelly@chinabooks.com
Founded: 1960
Fiction, trade, nonfiction, dictionaries, encyclopedias, maps, atlases, periodicals, sidelines, foreign language, secondary textbooks, juvenile & young adult, subscription & mail order, hardcover & paperback trade books; government, language arts, travel.
ISBN Prefix(es): 978-0-8351
Number of titles published annually: 12 Print
Total Titles: 230 Print

China Books & Periodicals Inc, see China Books

Chosen Books
Division of Baker Publishing Group
7808 Creekridge Circle, Suite 250, Bloomington, MN 55439
Tel: 952-829-2500 *Toll Free Tel:* 800-877-2665 (orders only)
Web Site: www.chosenbooks.com
Key Personnel
CEO, Baker Publishing Group: Jesse Myers
Edit Dir: Kim Bangs *E-mail:* kbangs@bakerpublishinggroup.com
Founded: 1971
Christian.
ISBN Prefix(es): 978-0-8007
Number of titles published annually: 33 Print; 33 E-Book
Total Titles: 800 Print
Foreign Rep(s): Christian Art (South Africa); Koorong Books Ltd (Australia); Macmillan Distribution (MDL) (Europe, UK); Soul Distributors Ltd (New Zealand)

§Christian Liberty Press
502 W Euclid Ave, Arlington Heights, IL 60004-5402
Toll Free Tel: 800-348-0899 *Fax:* 847-259-2941
E-mail: custserv@christianlibertypress.com
Web Site: www.shopchristianliberty.com
Key Personnel
Dir: Lars Johnson
Cust Serv Coord: Deirdre Landgraf
Founded: 1984
Publisher of Christian education materials.
ISBN Prefix(es): 978-1-930092; 978-1-930367; 978-1-932971; 978-1-935796; 978-1-62982
Number of titles published annually: 4 Print; 3 CD-ROM; 5 Audio
Total Titles: 150 Print; 8 CD-ROM

Christian Light Publications Inc
1051 Mount Clinton Pike, Harrisonburg, VA 22802
Mailing Address: PO Box 1212, Harrisonburg, VA 22803-1212
Tel: 540-434-1003 *Toll Free Tel:* 800-776-0478
Fax: 540-433-8896
E-mail: info@clp.org; orders@clp.org
Web Site: www.clp.org
Key Personnel
Gen Mgr: Andrew K Crider
Founded: 1969
Books, booklets, tracts, Sunday school, vacation Bible school & Christian day school curriculum.
ISBN Prefix(es): 978-0-87813
Number of titles published annually: 17 Print
Total Titles: 160 Print

Christian Schools International (CSI)
99 Monroe Ave NW, Suite 200, Grand Rapids, MI 49503
SAN: 204-1804
Tel: 616-957-1070 *Toll Free Tel:* 800-635-8288
Web Site: www.csionline.org
Key Personnel
Dir, Mktg: Lindsay Monette *Tel:* 616-957-1070 ext 105 *E-mail:* lmonette@csionline.com
Exec Asst & HR Specialist: Cally Wade *Tel:* 616-957-1070 ext 101 *E-mail:* cwade@csionline.org
Founded: 1920
Classroom curriculum resources for students & teachers.
ISBN Prefix(es): 978-0-87463; 978-1-935876
Number of titles published annually: 18 Print; 2 CD-ROM
Total Titles: 172 Print; 11 CD-ROM
Imprints: CSI Publications

§The Christian Science Publishing Society
Division of The First Church of Christ, Scientist
210 Massachusetts Ave, Boston, MA 02115
Tel: 617-450-2000
E-mail: info@christianscience.com
Web Site: christianscience.com
Founded: 1879
Books on healing, health & spirituality; major title: *Science & Health with Key to the Scriptures* by Mary Baker Eddy, available in 16 languages & English braille.
ISBN Prefix(es): 978-0-87952
Number of titles published annually: 17 Print
Total Titles: 117 Print

Chronicle Books LLC
680 Second St, San Francisco, CA 94107
SAN: 202-165X
Tel: 415-537-4200 *Fax:* 415-537-4460 (perms)
E-mail: hello@chroniclebooks.com; subrights@chroniclebooks.com
Web Site: www.chroniclebooks.com
Key Personnel
Chmn & CEO: Nion McEvoy
Cont: Meghan Clarke
Pres: Tyrrell Hammer Mahoney
EVP & COO: Tom Fernald
SVP & Group Publr: Mikyla Bruder
VP, HR: Todd Presley
VP, Sales & Mktg: Kimberly Bolton Anderson
Group Publr: Lynn Grady
Publr, Gift: Christina Maheen Amini
Exec Dir, Mktg & Publicity: Lauren Hoffman
Exec Dir, Sales & Mktg Enablement: Rachel Geiger
Exec Dir, IT: Michael Conway
Exec Dir, Opers: John Carlson
Exec Dir, Prodn: Lindsay Sablosky
Exec Publg Design Dir: Sara Schneider
Exec Publg Dir, Children's: Jody Mosley
Sr Prodn Dir: Erin Thacker
Art Dir, Food & Lifestyle: Lizzie Vaughan
Design Dir, Brand: Liz Rico
Design Dir, Children's Publg: Jennifer Tolo Pierce
Design Dir, Entertainment: Neil Egan
Design Dir, Format Devt: Kristen Hewitt
Publg Dir, Chronicle Chroma: Steve Crist; Gloria Fowler
Publg Dir, Food & Lifestyle/Art: Sarah Billingsley
Dir, Fin: Kate Breiting Schmitz
Dir, Mng Edit: Beth Weber
Dir, Sales: Genny McAuley
Dir, Sales, Key Accts: Kate Herman
Dir, Spec Sales: Leslie Davisson
Assoc Dir, E-Commerce: Shivangi Sangwan
Assoc Dir, Intl Sales: Tessa Ingersoll
Assoc Dir, Mktg, Entertainment: Elizabeth Anderson
Assoc Dir, Publicity: Erica Gelbard; Diane Levinson
Assoc Dir, Publicity & School & Lib Mktg: Brittany Mitchell
Assoc Dir, Publicity, Chronicle Chroma, Chronicle Prism & PA Press: Michelle Bonanno Triant
Assoc Dir, Sales & Mktg Enablement: Elke Olson
Assoc Edit Dir, Entertainment: Brittany Hamblin McInerney
Assoc Prodn Dir: Wendy Thorpe
Assoc Sales Dir: Kristie Raycroft
Sr Dist Client Mgr: Graham Barry
Sr Mktg Mgr: Jessica Tackett
Sr Mktg Mgr, Food & Lifestyle: Elora Sullivan
Sr Prodn Mgr, Prodn Servs: Leslie Cohen
Sr Rts Mgr: Samantha Allen
Sr Sales Mgr: Liz Marotte; Jessica Mays
Sr Sales Mgr, Mass Mkt: Tracey Vega
Sr Sales Mgr, Spec Sales: Frankie Johnson
Food & Lifestyle Mktg Mgr: Samantha Simon
HR Mgr: Scott Haney
Inventory Planning Mgr: Mary O'Hara
Mktg & Publicity Mgr, Lifestyle: Alexandra Brown
Mgr, Prodn & Creative Systems: Timothy Wudurski
Oracle Tech Mgr: Hari Ram
Publg Data Mgr: Sam Goff
Sr Prodn Developer, Levine Querido & Chronicle Chroma: Freesia Blizard
Prodn Developer, Children's: Ashley Despain
Prodn Mgr, Specialty Publg: Madeleine Moe
Trade Sales Rep, New England: Emily Cervone
Trade Sales Rep, Pacific Northwest: Jamil Zaidi
Sr Mng Ed: Michele Posner
Sr Mng Ed, Children's: Claire Fletcher
Sr Mng Ed, Entertainment: Perry Crowe
Mng Ed: Jessica Ling
Mng Ed, Children's: Lucy Medrich
Mng Ed, Entertainment: Alison Petersen
Assoc Mng Ed: Gabby Vanacore
Exec Ed, Children's: Rebecca Frazer
Exec Ed, Lifestyle: Rachel Hiles
Sr Ed, Children's: Mary Colgan; Ariel Richardson
Sr Ed, Chronicle Prism: Allison Adler
Sr Ed, Entertainment & Lifestyle: Kim Romero
Ed: Mirabelle Korn; Olivia Roberts
Ed, Children's: Emily Daluga; Daria Harper
Ed-at-Large: Victoria Rock
Assoc Ed, Art: Natalie Butterfield
Assoc Ed, Food & Lifestyle: Claire Gilhuly; Dena Rayess
Assoc Proj Ed: Maddy Wong
Asst Ed: Juliette Capra
Sr Publicist, Entertainment: April Whitney
Publicist, Children's: Caitlin Ek
Publicist, Food & Lifestyle: Keely Thomas-Menter
Assoc Publicist: April Roberts
Sr Client Acct Mgr: Vanessa Navarrete
Sr Dist Client Mgr: Annabelle Oh
Sr Mgr, Brand Mktg: Natalie Nicolson
Sr Mgr, School & Lib Mktg/Children's Publicity: Linette Kim
Sr Sales Mgr: Melissa Grecco
Sr Sales Mgr, Instl & Trade: Anastasia Scott

U.S. PUBLISHERS

Sr Sales Mgr, Spec Sales: Sonya Harris
Acctg Mgr: AiLing Tjan
Compliance Mgr: Bebe Barrow
Design Mgr: Allison Weiner
Diversity, Learning & Devt Mgr: Nisha Barnes
Inventory Control Mgr: Deborah Kenmore
Mktg Mgr, Art: Sarah Lin Go
Sr Prodn Mgr: Michelle Clair
Prodn Design Mgr: Steve Kim
Publg Data Mgr: Saher Siddiqui
Royalty Mgr: Aysha Martinez
Sales Mgr, Independent Specialty Sales: Cydel Virtucio
Soc Media Mgr: Janice Yi
Subs Rts Mgr: Sara Boncha
Website Mgr: Eric Cromie
Assoc Acct Mgr, Amazon: Elina Schenker
Assoc Design Mgr, Children's: Ryan Hayes
Assoc Mgr, Events & Sales Enablement: Emily Malter
Assoc Mgr, Instl & Independent Trade Mktg: Alex Astras
Assoc Mgr, Sales & Mktg Enablement: Eve Brodsly
Assoc Mgr, Web & E-Commerce: Maggie Haas
Assoc Sales Mgr, Natl Specialty: Bora Kim
Sr Designer, Art: Kayla Ferriera
Sr Designer, Brand: Lauren Kiri Chin
Sr Designer, Entertainment: Maggie Edelman; Jonathan Glick
Sr Designer, Petit Collage: Nora Aoyagi
Sr Graphic & Prodn Designer: Alexandria Martinez
Sr Prod Developer, Ridley's & Petit Collage: Harriet Steeds
Sr Prodn Designer: Kevin Armstrong
Prodn Developer, Entertainment: Heather Fisk
Brand Designer: Sarah Hamilton
Brand Photog: Ryan Cunningham
Designer, Children's: Sandy Frank; Julia Marvel
Designer, Entertainment: Evelyn Furuta
Designer, Food & Lifestyle: Rachel Harrell
Prodn Designer: Aki Neumann
Jr Designer, Children's: Eugenia Yoh
Jr Prodn Designer: Gabriel Martinez
Sr Busn Analyst: Molly Krauss
Sr Sales, eCommerce & Fin Analyst: R Barrett Hooper
Budget Analyst: Sam Mariucci
Fin Analyst: Marlene Kwasnik
Jr Fin Analyst: Desirae Grier
Jr Busn Systems Analyst: Prilliana McCauley
Staff Accountant: David Villanueva
Prodn Mgr, Reprints: Terri Lancaster
Sr Prodn Coord: Rachael Marks
Dist Client Sales Coord: Carlee Boomer
Mktg Coord: Reg Lim
Mktg Coord, Children's: Emma Hill
Opers Coord: Elizabeth Hambrick; Adam Moody
Sales & Mktg Coord: Hannah Poor
Sales Coord, Specialty Prods: Jonah Thedorff
Soc Media Coord: Gabriella Frenes
Subs Rts Coord: Zora Driscoll
Independent Specialty Sales Asst: Sophia Fox
Mktg & Publicity Asst, Adult: Ailyn Pambid
Natl Specialty Sales Asst: Bridget Cooke
Trade Sales Asst: Olivia Monical
Publicity Asst: Cappy Yarbrough
Sales, Mktg & Publicity Asst: Kathryn Libertini
Specialty Sales Asst: Hannah Delgado
Copywriter: Deanna Quinones
Founded: 1967
General nonfiction & fiction, cloth & paperbound: fine arts, gift, nature, outdoors, nationwide regional guidebooks, stationery, calendars & ancillary products.
ISBN Prefix(es): 978-0-87701; 978-0-8118; 978-0-938491; 978-1-4521; 978-1-7972
Number of titles published annually: 300 Print
Total Titles: 1,500 Print
Imprints: Chronicle Bridge (Chinese-language children's books); Chronicle Chroma (visual arts & pop culture); Chronicle Prism
Divisions: PA Press
Distributor for Amicus Ink; BIS Publishers; Blackwell & Ruth; Brass Monkey; The Creative Company; Galison; Games Room; Hardie Grant Books; Laurence King Publishing Ltd; Levine Querido; Mudpuppy; PA Press; Paperblanks (CN & US); Petit Collage; Quadrille Publishing Ltd; Ridley Games; Sierra Club; Twirl Books
Foreign Rep(s): A-Z Africa Book Services (Anita Zih-De Haan) (Eastern Africa, Western Africa); Ampersand Inc (Alberta, CN, British Columbia, CN, Manitoba, CN, Saskatchewan, CN); Asia Publishers Services Ltd (Hong Kong); Jonathan Ball Publishers (South Africa); Bookreps NZ Ltd (New Zealand); Tim Burland (Japan); Isadora Garcia-Jacinto (Micronesia, Philippines); Hachette Book Group (Bermuda, Caribbean, Latin America); Hachette UK Ltd (Cambodia, Hong Kong, India, Indonesia, Malaysia, Middle East, North America, Pakistan, Singapore, Southern China, Taiwan, Thailand, Turkey, Vietnam); Hardie Grant Books (Australia); Hornblower Group Inc (New Brunswick, CN, Newfoundland and Labrador, CN, Nova Scotia, CN, Prince Edward Island, CN, Quebec, CN); Information and Culture Korea (South Korea); Dan Lain-Lain (Malaysia); Raincoast Books (Canada); Times Distribution (Singapore); Jenny Wang (Northern China)
Foreign Rights: Nibbe Literary Agency (Bettina Nibbe) (Germany); Nordin Agency AB (Netherlands, Scandinavia); Tao Media (China)
Returns: Chronicle Books Returns, c/o Hachette Book Group Inc, 322 S Enterprise Blvd, Lebanon, IN 46052
Distribution Center: Raincoast Books Distribution Ltd, 2440 Viking Way, Richmond, BC V6V 1N2, Canada (Canada)
See separate listing for:
Handprint Books Inc
PA Press

Cider Mill Press Book Publishers LLC
Imprint of HarperCollins Focus LLC
501 Nelson Place, Nashville, TN 37214
Toll Free Tel: 800-250-5308
E-mail: focuscc@harpercollins.com
Web Site: www.cidermillpress.com
Key Personnel
VP & Publr: John Whalen, III
Founded: 2005
Publish creative, innovative, inspiring & visually stunning books & gift books.
ISBN Prefix(es): 978-1-933662; 978-1-60433; 978-1-64643; 978-1-951511
Number of titles published annually: 50 Print; 4 Audio
Total Titles: 135 Print
Imprints: Applesauce Press; Cider Mill Press
Distributed by Simon & Schuster, LLC
Foreign Rights: Print Co Verlagsgesellschaft (Gabriella Scolik) (Europe)
Membership(s): American Booksellers Association (ABA)

§Circlet Press
Imprint of Riverdale Avenue Books (RAB)
5676 Riverdale Ave, Suite 101, Riverdale, NY 10471
Tel: 212-279-6418
E-mail: customerservice@riverdaleavebooks.com; rab@riverdaleavebooks.com; customerservice@riverdaleavebooks.com (orders)
Web Site: www.circlet.com; riverdaleavebooks.com (orders & edit)
Key Personnel
Publr: Lori Perkins
Founded: 1992
Anthologies of erotic science fiction/fantasy, paranormal romance, alternative sexuality & fiction with transgender themes.
ISBN Prefix(es): 978-0-9633970; 978-1-885865
Number of titles published annually: 10 Print; 2 Online; 12 E-Book; 5 Audio
Total Titles: 125 Print; 2 Online; 150 E-Book; 5 Audio
Imprints: Circlet
Foreign Rep(s): Bulldog Books (Australia); Turnaround Ltd (Europe, UK)
Foreign Rights: Lawrence Schimel (all other territories)

Cistercian Publications
Imprint of Liturgical Press
Saint John's Abbey, PO Box 7500, Collegeville, MN 56321
SAN: 202-1668
Tel: 320-363-2213 Toll Free Tel: 800-436-8431 Fax: 320-363-3299 Toll Free Fax: 800-445-5899
E-mail: sales@litpress.org
Web Site: www.cistercianpublications.org
Key Personnel
Dir: Therese Ratliff
Sales Dir: Brian Woods
Founded: 1969
Religion (Roman Catholic) & history.
ISBN Prefix(es): 978-0-87907
Number of titles published annually: 10 Print
Total Titles: 260 Print
Distributed by Liturgical Press
Returns: Liturgical Press, 2950 St John's Rd, Collegeville, MN 56321 Web Site: www.litpress.org
Shipping Address: Liturgical Press, 2950 St John's Rd, Collegeville, MN 56321 Web Site: www.litpress.org

Citadel Press, see Kensington Publishing Corp

City Lights Publishers
261 Columbus Ave, San Francisco, CA 94133
SAN: 202-1684
Tel: 415-362-8193
E-mail: staff@citylights.com
Web Site: citylights.com
Key Personnel
Exec Dir & Publr: Elaine Katzenberger
PR & Mktg Dir: Stacey Lewis
Prodn & Design Mgr: Gerilyn Attebery
Publicist & Digital Mktg Mgr: Chris Carosi
Events Coord: Peter Maravelis
Publr Asst: Emma Hager
Founded: 1955
Publisher of progressive political nonfiction, innovative literature & poetry.
ISBN Prefix(es): 978-0-87286
Number of titles published annually: 12 Print
Total Titles: 350 Print
Foreign Rights: Agencia Literaria Carmen Balcells SA (Portugal, Spain); Bardon-Chinese Media Agency (China, Taiwan); Agence Hoffman GmbH (France, Germany); International Editor's Co (Brazil); Japan UNI Agency (Japan); Agenzia Letteraria Internazionale (Italy); ONK Agency Inc (Turkey); Owls Agency Inc (Japan); Plima Agency (Bosnia and Herzegovina, Croatia, Czechia, Poland, Serbia); PubHub Literary Agency (South Korea); Shinwon Agency (South Korea)
Distribution Center: Consortium Book Sales & Distribution, 34 13 Ave NE, Suite 101, Minneapolis, MN 55413-1007 Tel: 612-746-2600 Toll Free Tel: 866-400-5351 E-mail: cbsdinfo@ingramcontent.com Web Site: www.cbsd.com
SAN: 200-6049

Clarion Books
Imprint of HarperCollins Children's Books
195 Broadway, New York, NY 10007
Tel: 212-207-7000 Toll Free Tel: 800-242-7737
E-mail: consumercare@harpercollins.com
Web Site: www.harpercollins.com/collections/books-by-clarion-books

Key Personnel
VP & Publg Dir: Nancy Inteli
VP & Publr: Erin Clarke
VP & Edit Dir, Children's Div: Anne Hoppe
Edit Dir: Kate O'Sullivan
Exec Ed: Amy Cloud
Sr Ed: Chris Krones; Lynne Polvino
Founded: 1965
Picture, chapter, middle grade & young adult books, fiction & nonfiction.
ISBN Prefix(es): 978-0-547; 978-0-544; 978-1-328
Number of titles published annually: 40 Print
Imprints: Allida Books

§Clarity Press Inc
2625 Piedmont Rd NE, Suite 56, Atlanta, GA 30324
SAN: 688-9530
Tel: 404-647-6501
E-mail: claritypress@usa.net (foreign rts & perms)
Web Site: www.claritypress.com
Key Personnel
Edit Dir: Diana G Collier
Busn Mgr: Annette Gordon
    E-mail: businessmanager@claritypress.com
Founded: 1984
Scholarly works on contemporary justice & human rights issues.
ISBN Prefix(es): 978-0-9845255; 978-0-9860362; 978-0-9972870; 978-0-9996947; 978-0-9833539; 978-1-949762; 978-1-963892
Number of titles published annually: 6 Print; 6 E-Book
Total Titles: 120 Print; 95 E-Book; 4 Audio
Imprints: Clear Day Books (print-on-demand, rare books); Streaming Clarity (online streaming library)
Foreign Rep(s): Marston Books (UK & the continent)
Foreign Rights: Chengdu Rightol Media (China)
Distribution Center: SCB Distributors, 15608 S New Century Dr, Gardena, CA 90248, Contact: Victor Duran *Tel:* 310-532-9400 *Toll Free Tel:* 800-729-6423 *Fax:* 310-532-7001 *E-mail:* victor@scbdistributors.com *Web Site:* www.scbdistributors.com
Marston Book Services Ltd, 160 Eastern Ave, Abingdon, Oxon OX14 4SB, United Kingdom (includes Europe) *Tel:* (01235) 465500 *Fax:* (01235) 465555 *E-mail:* trade.orders@marston.co.uk *Web Site:* www.marston.co.uk

Classical Academic Press
515 S 32 St, Camp Hill, PA 17011
Tel: 717-730-0711 *Toll Free Tel:* 866-730-0711 *Fax:* 717-730-0721 *Toll Free Fax:* 866-730-0721
E-mail: info@classicalsubjects.com; orders@classicalsubjects.com
Web Site: classicalacademicpress.com
Key Personnel
CEO: Christopher Perrin
Pres: Greg Lowe
VP, Prod Devt: Jesse Hake
VP, Sales, Mktg & Opers: Joelle Hodge
Mng Ed & Creative Designer: Lauraine Gustafson
Sales & Mktg Mgr: Tristin Schambach
    E-mail: tschambach@classicalsubjects.com
Founded: 2001
K-12 educational textbooks & media. Focus on classical education.
ISBN Prefix(es): 978-1-60051
Number of titles published annually: 12 Print; 2 Online; 12 E-Book; 3 Audio
Total Titles: 150 Print; 1 Online; 12 E-Book; 10 Audio
Imprints: Plum Tree Books
Foreign Rep(s): Baker & Taylor (New Zealand, UK)
Returns: Maple Distribution Center, 60 Grumbacher Rd, York, PA 17406

Shipping Address: Baker & Taylor, 2550 W Tyvola Rd, Charlotte, NC 28217 *Tel:* 704-998-3100
Membership(s): Independent Book Publishers Association (IBPA)
See separate listing for:
Plum Tree Books

Clear Light Publishers
823 Don Diego Ave, Santa Fe, NM 87505
Tel: 505-989-9590 *Toll Free Tel:* 800-253-2747 (orders)
E-mail: info@clearlightbooks.com
Web Site: www.clearlightbooks.com
Key Personnel
Publr: Harmon Houghton
Founded: 1981
ISBN Prefix(es): 978-0-940666; 978-1-57416
Number of titles published annually: 18 Print
Total Titles: 200 Print
Foreign Rights: Harmon Houghton Clear Light Books
Membership(s): American Booksellers Association (ABA); The American Library Association (ALA); Mountains & Plains Booksellers Association (MPBA); New Mexico Book Association

§Clearfield Co Inc
Subsidiary of Genealogical Publishing Co
3600 Clipper Mill Rd, Suite 229, Baltimore, MD 21211
Tel: 410-837-8271 *Toll Free Tel:* 800-296-6687 (orders & cust serv) *Fax:* 410-752-8492
E-mail: sales@genealogical.com
Web Site: www.genealogical.com
Key Personnel
Mktg Dir: Joe Garonzik *Tel:* 410-804-1558
    E-mail: jgaronzi@genealogical.com
Founded: 1989
Leading publisher of short-run genealogy how-to books, reference books & CD-ROM publications in the US.
ISBN Prefix(es): 978-0-8063
Number of titles published annually: 20 Print; 1 CD-ROM
Total Titles: 1,000 Print; 10 CD-ROM
Membership(s): American Booksellers Association (ABA); American Name Society; National Genealogical Society

Cleis Press
Imprint of Start Publishing LLC
221 River St, 9th fl, Hoboken, NJ 07030
Tel: 212-431-5455
E-mail: cleis@cleispress.com
Web Site: cleispress.com; www.vivaeditions.com
Key Personnel
Mktg & Publicity Asst: Ashley Calvano
    E-mail: calvano@cleispress.com
Founded: 1980
Outriders. Outwriters. Outliers. Cleis Press publishes works in the areas of fiction & LGBTQ+ studies, as well as romance, erotica, how-to sex guides, human rights, memoirs & women's studies. Viva Editions are books that inform, entertain & enlighten. Books contain inspiration, self-help, women's issues, lifestyle, health, parenting, reference, gift & relationship advice.
ISBN Prefix(es): 978-0-939416; 978-1-57344; 978-1-62778
Number of titles published annually: 30 Print; 30 E-Book; 150 Audio
Total Titles: 600 Print; 400 E-Book
Foreign Rep(s): Peter Hyde Associates (South Africa)
Foreign Rights: DropCap Rights Agency (Allison Olson)
Orders to: Simon & Schuster, LLC (US & intl orders) *Toll Free Tel:* 800-223-2336 *Toll Free Fax:* 800-943-9831 *E-mail:* purchaseorders@simonandschuster.com; Simon & Schuster, LLC

(CN orders) *Toll Free Tel:* 800-268-3216 *Toll Free Fax:* 888-849-8151 *E-mail:* canadian.orders@simonandschuster.com

Clerisy Press
Imprint of AdventureKEEN
306 Greenup St, Covington, KY 41011
Tel: 859-815-7204
E-mail: info@clerisypress.com
Web Site: www.clerisypress.com
Key Personnel
Pres, AdventureKEEN: Richard Hunt *Tel:* 859-815-7204 *E-mail:* richard@clerisypress.com
Founded: 2006
Trade & custom publisher.
ISBN Prefix(es): 978-1-57860
Number of titles published annually: 10 Print; 10 E-Book
Total Titles: 100 Print; 100 E-Book
Billing Address: 2204 First Ave S, Suite 102, Birmingham, AL 35233, Contact: Lisa Myers *Tel:* 205-443-7992 *Fax:* 205-326-1012 *E-mail:* lisa@adventurewithkeen.com
Distribution Center: Publishers Group West (PGW), 1700 Fourth St, Berkeley, CA 94710, Contact: Kevin Votel
Membership(s): American Booksellers Association (ABA)

§Clinical and Laboratory Standards Institute (CLSI)
1055 Westlakes Dr, Suite 300, Berwyn, PA 19312
Mailing Address: PO Box 334, Malvern, PA 19355
Tel: 610-688-0100 *Toll Free Tel:* 877-447-1888 (orders) *Fax:* 610-688-0700
E-mail: customerservice@clsi.org
Web Site: www.clsi.org
Key Personnel
Dir: Lorin Bachmann
Founded: 1968
Voluntary consensus standards & guidelines for medical testing & in vitro diagnostic products & healthcare services.
ISBN Prefix(es): 978-1-56238; 978-1-68440
Number of titles published annually: 25 Print
Total Titles: 200 Print

Close Up Publishing
Division of Close Up Foundation
671 N Glebe Rd, Suite 900, Arlington, VA 22203
Tel: 703-706-3300 *Toll Free Tel:* 800-CLOSE-UP (256-7387)
E-mail: info@closeup.org
Web Site: www.closeup.org
Key Personnel
CEO: Eric Adydan
VP, Mktg: Jodi Miteva
Sr Dir, Acct Engagement: Luke Stallings
Founded: 1971
Publish supplemental texts, videos, teachers' guides & simulation activities for secondary school & college social studies, political science, government, economics, international relations & history courses & for general readership.
ISBN Prefix(es): 978-0-932765; 978-1-930810
Number of titles published annually: 1 Print; 12 Online; 3 Audio
Total Titles: 56 Print; 20 Online; 19 Audio

Closson Press
257 Delilah St, Apollo, PA 15613-1933
Tel: 724-337-4482
E-mail: clossonpress@comcast.net
Web Site: www.clossonpress.com
Key Personnel
Founder & Owner: Marietta Closson
Founded: 1976
Printer & publisher of history, family history & genealogy books.
ISBN Prefix(es): 978-0-933227; 978-1-55856
Number of titles published annually: 40 Print

U.S. PUBLISHERS

Total Titles: 800 Print
Distributed by Janaway Publishing; Masthof Press
Distributor for Hearthside Books; Darvin Martin CDs; Retrospect Publishing
Foreign Rep(s): Brian Mitchell (Ireland); Cornelia Schrader (France, Germany)

CLSI, see Clinical and Laboratory Standards Institute (CLSI)

CMF Press, see Country Music Foundation Press

§CN Times Books
Imprint of CN Times Inc
100 Jericho Quadrangle, Suite 337, Jericho, NY 11791
Tel: 516-719-0886
E-mail: yanliu@cntimesbooks.com
Web Site: www.cntimesbooks.com
Key Personnel
Pres & Publr: George Zhu
Sales & Mktg Mgr: Paul Myatovich
Founded: 2013
ISBN Prefix(es): 978-1-62774
Number of titles published annually: 21 Print
Total Titles: 55 Print; 7 E-Book
Distributor for Bashu Publishing; Foreign Language Press; Intercontinental Press; Phoenix Publishing
Orders to: Ingram Publisher Services, 14 Ingram Blvd, Mail Stop 631, La Vergne, TN 37086 *Toll Free Tel:* 855-802-8317 *Toll Free Fax:* 800-838-1149 *Web Site:* ipage.ingramcontent.com
Returns: Ingram Publisher Services, 191 Edwards Dr, Jackson, TN 38301
Distribution Center: Ingram Publisher Services, 14 Ingram Blvd, Mail Stop 631, La Vergne, TN 37086 *Toll Free Tel:* 855-802-8317 *Toll Free Fax:* 800-838-1149 *Web Site:* www.ingrampublisherservices.com
Membership(s): American Booksellers Association (ABA)

Coaches Choice
PO Box 1828, Monterey, CA 93942
Toll Free Tel: 888-229-5745
E-mail: info@coacheschoice.com
Web Site: www.coacheschoice.com
Key Personnel
Pres: James Peterson
Edit Mgr: Kristi Huelsing *E-mail:* kristih@coacheschoice.com
Founded: 1999
Instructional books & DVDs for coaches (football, basketball, baseball, softball, volleyball, soccer, track & field, etc); health, fitness & sports medicine professionals & camp professionals.
ISBN Prefix(es): 978-1-57167; 978-1-58518; 978-1-60679
Number of titles published annually: 40 Print

§Codhill Press
420 E 23 St, Suite 3H, New York, NY 10010
E-mail: info@codhill.com
Web Site: www.codhill.com
Key Personnel
Founder: David Appelbaum *E-mail:* david@codhill.com
Publr: Susannah Appelbaum *Tel:* 845-594-9450 *E-mail:* susannah@codhill.com
Ed: David Appelbaum *E-mail:* appelbad@gmail.com
Founded: 1998
Literary small press.
ISBN Prefix(es): 978-1-930337
Number of titles published annually: 6 Print; 2 Online; 2 E-Book
Total Titles: 200 Print; 6 Online; 6 E-Book

Distributed by State University of New York Press
Orders to: State University of New York Press, PO Box 960, Herndon, VA 20172 *Tel:* 703-661-1575 *Toll Free Tel:* 877-204-6073 *Fax:* 703-996-1010 *Toll Free Fax:* 877-204-6074
Warehouse: Books International, 22883 Quicksilver Dr, Dulles, VA 20166 *Tel:* 703-661-1500
Membership(s): Community of Literary Magazines & Presses (CLMP)

Coffee House Press
79 13 Ave NE, Suite 110, Minneapolis, MN 55413
SAN: 206-3883
Tel: 612-338-0125 *Fax:* 612-338-4004
E-mail: info@coffeehousepress.org
Web Site: coffeehousepress.org
Key Personnel
Exec Dir: Linda Ewing *E-mail:* linda@coffeehousepress.org
Devt Dir: Mara Winke *E-mail:* mara@coffeehousepress.org
Dir, Mktg: Mark Haber *E-mail:* mark@coffeehousepress.org
Ed-in-Chief: Jeremy M Davies
Prodn Ed: Abbie Phelps *E-mail:* abbie@coffeehousepress.org
Devt Asst: Kristen Bledsoe *E-mail:* kristen@coffeehousepress.org
Edit & Prodn Asst: Quynh Van *E-mail:* quynh@coffeehousepress.org
Publg Asst: Daphne DiFazio *E-mail:* daphne@coffeehousepress.org
Founded: 1984
Fine editions & trade books; contemporary poetry, short fiction, novels, literary essays & memoirs.
ISBN Prefix(es): 978-0-918273; 978-1-56689
Number of titles published annually: 14 Print
Total Titles: 250 Print
Distribution Center: Consortium Book Sales & Distribution, The Keg House, 34 13 Ave NE, Suite 101, Minneapolis, MN 55413 *Tel:* 612-746-2600 *E-mail:* cbsdinfo@ingramcontent.com *Web Site:* www.cbsd.com SAN: 200-6049

Cognizant Communication Corp
PO Box 37, Putnam Valley, NY 10579-0037
Tel: 845-603-6440 *Fax:* 845-603-6442
E-mail: inquiries@cognizantcommunication.com; sales@cognizantcommunication.com
Web Site: www.cognizantcommunication.com
Key Personnel
Chmn & Publr: Robert N Miranda
Pres: Lori Miranda
Founded: 1992
STM & social science books & journals. Subjects include: tourism research & leisure studies, medical research, engineering & psychology.
ISBN Prefix(es): 978-1-882345; 978-0-971587
Number of titles published annually: 7 Print; 9 Online
Total Titles: 7 Print; 9 Online; 1 Audio
Imprints: Innovation & Tourisms (INTO); Miranda Press Trade Division; Tourism Dynamic

Cokesbury, see Abingdon Press

§Cold Spring Harbor Laboratory Press
Division of Cold Spring Harbor Laboratory
500 Sunnyside Blvd, Woodbury, NY 11797-2924
SAN: 203-6185
Tel: 516-422-4100 *Toll Free Tel:* 800-843-4388
E-mail: cshpress@cshl.edu
Web Site: www.cshlpress.com
Key Personnel
Exec Dir: John Inglis *E-mail:* inglis@cshl.edu
Dir, Prod Devt & Mktg: Wayne Manos *E-mail:* manos@cshl.edu

Fin Dir: Steve Nussbaum *E-mail:* nussbau@cshl.edu
Asst Dir: Richard Sever
Head, Ad & Sponsorship Sales: Marcie Siconolfi *E-mail:* siconolf@cshl.edu
Prodn Mgr: Denise Weiss *E-mail:* weiss@cshl.edu
Subn Fulfillment Mgr: Kathy Cirone *E-mail:* cironek@cshl.edu
Asst Mktg Mgr: Robert Redmond *E-mail:* rredmond@cshl.edu
Exec Asst to Publr: Jennifer Quereau *E-mail:* quereau@cshl.edu
Founded: 1933
Scholarly & scientific books, journals & electronic media.
ISBN Prefix(es): 978-0-87969; 978-1-62182; 978-1-936113
Number of titles published annually: 20 Print
Total Titles: 220 Print; 1 CD-ROM; 15 E-Book; 2 Audio
Foreign Rep(s): Kinokuniya Co Ltd (Japan); NBN International (Europe, UK)
Orders to: c/o Oxford University Press, 2001 Evans Rd, Cary, NC 27513 *Toll Free Tel:* 800-445-9714 *Fax:* 919-677-1303
Distribution Center: c/o Oxford University Press, 2001 Evans Rd, Cary, NC 27513 *Toll Free Tel:* 800-445-9714 *Fax:* 919-677-1303

§The College Board
250 Vesey St, New York, NY 10281
SAN: 269-0829
Tel: 212-713-8000 *Toll Free Tel:* 866-630-9305
Web Site: www.collegeboard.com
Key Personnel
CEO: David Coleman
Pres: Jeremy Singer
Founded: 1900
Educational & trade books in the fields of college admission, continuing education, guidance, curriculum, financial aid, educational research, college-level & advanced placement examinations & school reform.
ISBN Prefix(es): 978-0-87447
Number of titles published annually: 7 Print
Total Titles: 100 Print; 7 CD-ROM; 4 E-Book; 1 Audio
Branch Office(s)
1919 "M" St NW, Suite 300, Washington, DC 20036 *Tel:* 202-741-4700
11955 Democracy Dr, Reston, VA 20190-5662 *Tel:* 571-485-3000 *Fax:* 571-485-3099
Distributed by Macmillan

College Publishing
12309 Lynwood Dr, Glen Allen, VA 23059
Tel: 804-364-8410 *Fax:* 804-364-8408
E-mail: collegepub@mindspring.com
Web Site: www.collegepublishing.us
Key Personnel
Publr: Stephen R Mosberg
Founded: 2001
Publish college textbooks in engineering, literature, linguistics & scholarly journals in engineering.
ISBN Prefix(es): 978-0-9679121; 978-1-932780
Number of titles published annually: 10 Print; 10 Online; 8 E-Book
Total Titles: 30 Print; 10 Online; 8 E-Book

§Columbia Books & Information Services (CBIS)
1530 Wilson Blvd, Suite 400, Arlington, VA 22209
Tel: 202-464-1662 *Fax:* 301-664-9600
E-mail: info@columbiabooks.com
Web Site: www.columbiabooks.com; www.association-insight.com; www.ceoupdate.com; www.thealmanacofamericanpolitics.com; www.thompsongrants.com

Key Personnel
Pres & CEO: Brittany Carter *Tel:* 240-235-0270
 E-mail: bcarter@columbiabooks.com
Chief Revenue Offr: Matthew Louie
VP, Mktg: Erin Murphy *Tel:* 202-221-4996
 E-mail: emurphy@columbiabooks.com
Dir, Data Servs & Technol: Vish Bhotla
Founded: 1965
Publish print directories, reference books, newsletters & reports. Do not accept mss.
ISBN Prefix(es): 978-0-910416; 978-1-880873; 978-0-9715487; 978-0-9747322; 978-1-938939
Number of titles published annually: 10 Print; 2 Online; 1 E-Book
Total Titles: 10 Print; 2 Online; 1 E-Book

§Columbia University Press
61 W 62 St, New York, NY 10023
SAN: 212-2472
Tel: 212-459-0600 *Toll Free Tel:* 800-944-8648
 Fax: 212-459-3678
Web Site: cup.columbia.edu
Key Personnel
Assoc Provost & Dir: Jennifer Crewe
Dir, Editing, Design & Prodn: Marielle Poss
Dir, Sales & Opers: Brad Hebel
Promos Dir: Meredith Howard
Publr, Fin & Economics: Myles Thompson
Publr, Philosophy & Religion: Wendy Lochner
Sr Ed: Caelyn Cobb; Christine Dunbar; Philip Leventhal; Miranda Martin; Stephen Wesley
Sr Publicist: Caitlin Hurst; Robyn Massey
Founded: 1893
Books of scholarly value, including nonfiction, general interest, scientific & technical books, textbooks in special fields at the university level & reference books.
ISBN Prefix(es): 978-0-231
Number of titles published annually: 200 Print; 220 E-Book
Total Titles: 7 CD-ROM; 4 Online; 3,000 E-Book
Imprints: Columbia Business School Publishing (business, finance & economics titles); Wallflower Press (film titles)
Distributor for Agenda Publishing; Austrian Film Museum Books; Barbara Budrich Publishers; Chinese University Press; Columbia Books on Architecture & the City; Maria Curie-Sklodowska University Press; ERIS (worldwide); Fernwood Publishing; Floating Opera Press (Africa, Asia, Australia, Middle East, New Zealand, North America & South America); Hitchcock Annual; ibidem Press (English language titles exc China & India); Jagiellonian University Press; Lincoln Institute of Land Policy; Peterson Institute for International Economics; Social Science Research Council; Stanford University Press; Transcript Verlag; Tulika Books; University of Tokyo Press; Miriam & Ira D Wallach Art Gallery
Foreign Rep(s): Apex Knowledge Sdn Bhd (Simon Tay) (Brunei, Malaysia); Avicenna Partnership Ltd (Claire de Gruchy) (Algeria, Cyprus, Israel, Jordan, Malta, Morocco, Palestine, Tunisia, Turkey); Avicenna Partnership Ltd (Bill Kennedy) (Bahrain, Egypt, Iran, Iraq, Kuwait, Lebanon, Libya, Oman, Qatar, Saudi Arabia, Syria, United Arab Emirates); Dominique Bartshukoff (Benelux, Greece, Portugal, Spain); Booknet Co Ltd (Suphaluck Sattabuz) (Thailand); Everest International Publishing Services (Wei Zhao) (China); Helena Groeneveld (South Africa); Simon Gwynn (France, Italy); Information & Culture Korea (ICK) (Se-Yung Jun) (South Korea); Peter Jacques (Austria, Baltic States, Central Europe, Denmark, Eastern Europe, Finland, Germany, Norway, Poland, Russia, Scandinavia, Sweden, Switzerland); MegaTEXTS Phil Inc (Jean Lim) (Philippines); MHM Limited (Mark Gresham) (Japan); B K Norton Ltd (Chiafeng Peng) (Singapore, Taiwan); Penguin Random House India (Bangladesh, Bhutan, India, Nepal, Pakistan, Sri Lanka); Rockbook (Akiko Iwamoto & Gilles Fauveau) (Hong Kong, Japan); Robert Towers (Ireland, Northern Ireland); The University Press Group Ltd (Lois Edwards) (Europe, UK); Kelvin van Hasselt Publishing Services (Africa exc South Africa); Wiley Distribution Services Ltd (Africa, Europe, Middle East, South Africa, UK); John Wiley & Sons Australia (Australia, New Zealand)
Foreign Rights: Akcali Copyright Agency (Mustafa Urgen) (Turkey); Bardon-Chinese Media Agency (Complex-Luisa Yeh) (China); Bardon-Chinese Media Agency (Simplified-Ivan Zhang) (China); Bestun Korea (Ms Yumi Chun) (South Korea); Dar Cherlin (Amelie Cherlin) (Arab Middle East); Agencia Literaria Raquel de la Concha (Spain); English Agency Japan Co Ltd (Tsutomu Yawata) (Japan); Paul & Peter Fritz AG (Germany); Graal Literary Agency (Lukasz Wrobel) (Poland); Danny Hong Agency (Danny Hong) (South Korea); Korea Copyright Center Ltd (KCC) (Joeun Lee) (South Korea); Alexander Korzhenevski Agency (Alexander Korzhenevski) (Russia & former USSR); Andrew Nurnberg Associates International (Complex-Whitney Hsu & Jackie Huang) (China); Oxford Literary & Rights Agency (Hana Whitton) (Croatia, Czechia, Hungary, North Macedonia); Reiser Literary Agency (Roberto Gilodi) (Italy); Sebes & Bisseling Literary Agency (Paul Sebes) (Denmark, Finland, Netherlands, Norway, Sweden); Seibel Publishing Services (Patricia Seibel) (Brazil, Portugal); Livia Stoia Literary Agency (Antonia Girmacea) (Eastern Europe, Romania); Tuttle-Mori Agency Inc (Fumika Ogihara) (Japan); Eric Yang Agency (Jackie Yang) (South Korea)
Orders to: Ingram Academic, 210 American Dr, Jackson, TN 38301 *Toll Free Tel:* 800-343-4499 *Toll Free Fax:* 800-838-1149
 E-mail: ipsjacksonorders@ingramcontent.com
Membership(s): American Association of University Presses (AAUP); Association of American Publishers (AAP)

§Comex Systems Inc
9380 Nastrand Circle, Port Charlotte, FL 33981
Tel: 908-881-6301
E-mail: mail@comexsystems.com
Web Site: www.comexsystems.com
Founded: 1973
Publish test preparation & other educational books.
ISBN Prefix(es): 978-1-56030
Number of titles published annually: 5 Print; 10 CD-ROM; 5 E-Book
Total Titles: 30 Print; 50 CD-ROM; 5 E-Book

Commonwealth Editions
Imprint of Arcadia Publishing Inc
210 Wingo Way, Suite 200, Mount Pleasant, SC 29464
Tel: 843-853-2070
E-mail: retailers@arcadiapublishing.com; publishing@arcadiapublishing.com
Web Site: www.arcadiapublishing.com
Key Personnel
Assoc Publr: Katie Parry
Founded: 1988
Publisher of nonfiction books about New England & its historic places.
ISBN Prefix(es): 978-1-889833; 978-1-933212
Number of titles published annually: 12 Print
Total Titles: 125 Print

Concordia Publishing House
Subsidiary of The Lutheran Church, Missouri Synod
3558 S Jefferson Ave, St Louis, MO 63118-3968
SAN: 202-1781
Tel: 314-268-1000; 314-268-1268 (bookshop)
Toll Free Tel: 800-325-3040 (cust serv)
Toll Free Fax: 800-490-9889 (cust serv)
E-mail: order@cph.org
Web Site: www.cph.org
Key Personnel
Pres & CEO: Jonathan D Schultz *Tel:* 314-268-1225 *E-mail:* jonathan.schultz@cph.org
Chief Cust Impact & Growth Offr: Rick Johnson *E-mail:* rick.johnson@cph.org
VP, Edit: Rev Jacob Corzine *E-mail:* jacob.corzine@cph.org
Exec Dir, Fin: Collin Bivens *E-mail:* collin.bivens@cph.org
Exec Dir, Prodn Control & Quality Systems: Karen Capps *E-mail:* karen.capps@cph.org
Exec Dir, Sales & E-Commerce: Mr Loren D Pawlitz *E-mail:* loren.pawlitz@cph.org
Dir, Graphic Design: Alex Ha *E-mail:* alex.ha@cph.org
Dir, HR: Dana Neuhaus *E-mail:* dana.neuhaus@cph.org
Dir, Mktg: Anna Johnson *E-mail:* anna.johnson@cph.org
Dir, Opers: Charlie Black *E-mail:* charlie.black@cph.org
Dir, PR: Elizabeth Pittman *E-mail:* elizabeth.pittman@cph.org
Founded: 1869
Theological works, sacred & family, devotional music, curriculum, computer software, bulletins, envelopes.
ISBN Prefix(es): 978-0-570; 978-0-7586
Number of titles published annually: 150 Print; 2 CD-ROM
Total Titles: 1,000 Print; 10 CD-ROM
Divisions: Concordia Gospel Outreach; Concordia Technology Solutions; Editorial Concordia
Membership(s): Evangelical Christian Publishers Association (ECPA); Protestant Church-Owned Publishers Association (PCPA)

The Conference Board Inc
845 Third Ave, New York, NY 10022-6600
SAN: 202-179X
Tel: 212-759-0900; 212-339-0345 (cust serv)
E-mail: customer.service@tcb.org
Web Site: www.conference-board.org/us; www.linkedin.com/company/the-conference-board
Key Personnel
Pres & CEO: Steve Odland
Chief Exec Progs Offr: Tricia La Marca *E-mail:* tlamarca@tcb.org
Chief HR Offr: Jennifer Tarlow *E-mail:* jtarlow@tcb.org
Chief Strategy Offr: Carol Orenstein *E-mail:* corenstein@tcb.org
EVP, CFO & Treas: Jim Slamp *E-mail:* jslamp@tcb.org
Exec Dir, ESG Ctr: Paul Washington *E-mail:* pwashington@tcb.org
Mng Dir, Intl: Sara Murray *E-mail:* smurray@tcb.org
Ctr Leader, Mktg & Communs: Ivan Pollard *Tel:* 212-339-0297 *E-mail:* ipollard@tcb.org
Founded: 1916
Periodic studies in management practices, economics & public affairs.
ISBN Prefix(es): 978-0-8237
Number of titles published annually: 25 Print; 25 Online
Branch Office(s)
The Conference Board of Canada, 255 Smyth Rd, Ottawa, ON K1H 8M7, Canada (affiliate) *Toll Free Tel:* 866-711-2262 *Web Site:* www.conferenceboard.ca
Foreign Office(s): Chaussee de La Hulpe 178, 6th fl, 1170 Brussels, Belgium, Exec Dir, Exec Progs, EMEA: Sara Murray *Tel:* (02) 675 5405 *E-mail:* brussels@tcb.org
E Gongxiao Bldg, 3rd fl, No 28 Guandongdian, Chaoyang District, Beijing 100020, China

U.S. PUBLISHERS

Tel: (0185) 10281838 (cell) E-mail: service.
ap@tcb.org
21/F, 14 Taikoo Wan Rd, Taikoo Shing, Hong
Kong Tel: 2804 1000
Al Asimah, Ahmad Al Jaber St, Dar Al Awadhi,
2nd fl, Off 5411, Kuwait City, Kuwait
Tel: 22322907 E-mail: tcbgulfcenter@tcb.org
22 Cross St, Singapore 048421, Singapore
Tel: 8298 3403

§The Connecticut Law Tribune
Division of ALM Media LLC
c/o 10 Talcott Ridge Rd, Unit A3, Farmington,
CT 06032
Toll Free Tel: 877-256-2472
E-mail: editorial@alm.com
Web Site: www.law.com/ctlawtribune/
Key Personnel
Ed-in-Chief: Michael Marciano
E-mail: mmarciano@alm.com
Founded: 1974
Publisher of books, newspapers & other materials
for the legal community & the public.
ISBN Prefix(es): 978-0-910051; 978-1-62881;
978-1-57625
Number of titles published annually: 5 Print
Total Titles: 40 Print; 1 E-Book

Consumer Press
13326 SW 28 St, Suite 102, Fort Lauderdale, FL
33330-1102
SAN: 297-7888
Tel: 954-370-9153
E-mail: info@consumerpress.com
Web Site: www.consumerpress.com
Key Personnel
Pres: Diana Gonzalez
Edit Dir: Joseph J Pappas
Mktg & Publicity Dir: Linda Muzzarelli
Founded: 1989
Consumer-oriented self-help & how-to titles. Specialize in nutrition, health & homeowner issues.
ISBN Prefix(es): 978-0-9628336; 978-1-891264;
978-0-9637641
Number of titles published annually: 9 Print
Total Titles: 12 Print
Imprints: Breton Publishing & Communications;
Women's Publications
Membership(s): American Booksellers Association (ABA); American Society of Journalists & Authors (ASJA); Independent Book Publishers Association (IBPA)

Continental AfrikaPublishers
Division of Afrikamawu Miracle Mission, AMI
Inc
182 Stribling Circle, Spartanburg, SC 29301
E-mail: afrikalion@aol.com;
profafrikadzatadeku@yahoo.com;
profafrikadzatadeku@facebook.com
Web Site: www.afrikacentricity.com
Key Personnel
Publr: Prof Afrikadzata Deku, PhD
Founded: 1990
Afrikacentric books, booklets & video documentaries, calendars, films on Continental Afrikan studies, Afrika Centricity, Pan-Continental Afrikanism, Continental Afrikan Government MIRACLE Project of the Century-its what, why, how & when.
ISBN Prefix(es): 978-1-56454
Number of titles published annually: 20 Print;
260 Online; 500 E-Book; 20 Audio
Total Titles: 260 Print; 260 Online; 638 E-Book;
20 Audio
Foreign Office(s): PO Box 209, Dansoman-Accra,
Ghana, Chmn: Afrikanenyo Deku
Foreign Rep(s): Continental/Diaspora Afrikan
(worldwide)

David C Cook
4050 Lee Vance Dr, Colorado Springs, CO 80918
Tel: 719-536-0100 Toll Free Tel: 800-323-7543
(orders & cust serv) Toll Free Fax: 800-430-0726 (cust serv)
E-mail: bookstores@davidccook.org;
customercare@davidccook.org
Web Site: www.davidccook.org
Key Personnel
CEO: Bill Reeves
Chief HR Offr: David Bervig
Chief Mktg Offr: Chris Baggett
COO: Jana Zachman
Gen Coun: Karen Davis
Pres, Integrity Music: Jonathan Brown
EVP, Learning Resources Group: Chadd Miller
VP, Communs: Cathy Herholdt
Sr Dir, Curriculum Portfolio: Lindsay Black
Sr Dir, Mktg: Michele Baird
Sr Dir, Music Opers, Integrity Music: Wendi Lord
Acqs Ed & Women's Community Lead, Esther
Press: Susan McPherson
Founded: 1875
Publish & distribute leadership & discipleship
resources.
ISBN Prefix(es): 978-0-912692; 978-0-89191;
978-1-55513; 978-1-56476; 978-0-89693; 978-0-7847; 978-0-8307; 978-0-7814; 978-0-88207;
978-1-4347
Number of titles published annually: 50 Print
Total Titles: 2,500 Print
Imprints: Esther Press (biblical resources by &
for women); Standard Publishing
Divisions: Integrity Music (music publg &
recording)
Foreign Office(s): Bostel House, 3rd fl Suite, 37
West St, Brighton, Sussex BN1 2RE, United
Kingdom, Dir, Intl Sales, Rts & Subs Rts:
Paul Owen Tel: (01273) 713521 E-mail: paul.
owen@davidccook.com
Foreign Rights: Paige Walton (worldwide)
Returns: 850 N Grove, Elgin, IL 60120
Membership(s): Evangelical Christian Publishers
Association (ECPA)
See separate listing for:
Standard Publishing

§Copper Canyon Press
Fort Worden State Park, Bldg 313, Port
Townsend, WA 98368
SAN: 206-488X
Mailing Address: PO Box 271, Port Townsend,
WA 98368
Tel: 360-385-4925
E-mail: poetry@coppercanyonpress.org;
publicity@coppercanyonpress.org;
digitalcontent@coppercanyonpress.org
Web Site: www.coppercanyonpress.org
Key Personnel
Publr: Ryo Yamaguchi
Artistic Dir & Exec Ed: Michael Wiegers
E-mail: michael@coppercanyonpress.org
Dir, Fin & Opers: Julie Johnson E-mail: juliej@
coppercanyonpress.org
Ed: Ashley Wynter E-mail: ash@
coppercanyonpress.com
Digital Content Mgr: Marisa Vito
Reader Servs Mgr: Janeen Armstrong
E-mail: janeen@coppercanyonpress.com
Founded: 1972
Hardcover & paperback trade books of poetry.
ISBN Prefix(es): 978-0-914742; 978-1-55659;
978-1-61932
Number of titles published annually: 32 Print
Total Titles: 400 Print
Distributor for American Poetry Review/Honickman
Distribution Center: Consortium Book Sales &
Distribution, The Keg House, Suite 101, 34
13 Ave NE, Minneapolis, MN 55413-1007
Tel: 612-746-2600 Toll Free Tel: 866-400-5351
(cust serv, Jackson, TN) E-mail: cbsdinfo@
ingramcontent.com Web Site: www.cbsd.com
SAN: 200-6049

Cornell Maritime Press
Imprint of Schiffer Publishing Ltd
4880 Lower Valley Rd, Atglen, PA 19310
SAN: 203-5901
Tel: 610-593-1777 Fax: 610-593-2002
E-mail: info@schifferbooks.com
Web Site: www.schifferbooks.com
Key Personnel
Pres: Pete Schiffer
Founded: 1938
Professional, technical books in maritime arts &
sciences; boats & boat building; related hobbies
& crafts.
ISBN Prefix(es): 978-0-87033
Number of titles published annually: 5 Print
Total Titles: 300 Print
Imprints: Tidewater Publishers
Distributor for Chesapeake Bay Maritime Museum; Independent Seaport Museum; Literary
House Press; Maryland Historical Trust Press;
Maryland Sea Grant Program

Cornell University Press
Division of Cornell University
Sage House, 512 E State St, Ithaca, NY 14850
SAN: 202-1862
Tel: 607-253-2338
E-mail: cupressinfo@cornell.edu; cupress-sales@cornell.edu; cupress-perms@cornell.edu
(reprint/class use permissions)
Web Site: www.cornellpress.cornell.edu
Key Personnel
Press Dir: Jane Bunker E-mail: jfb324@cornell.
edu
Edit Dir: Mr Mahinder S Kingra Tel: 607-253-2339 E-mail: msk55@cornell.edu
Edit Dir, Comstock Publishing Associates: Kitty
Liu Tel: 607-253-2347 E-mail: khl8@cornell.
edu
Edit Dir, Three Hills: Meagan Levinson
E-mail: mps45@cornell.edu
Mktg & Sales Dir: Martyn Beeny Tel: 607-253-2397 E-mail: mb2545@cornell.edu
Asst Edit Dir: Bethany Wasik Tel: 607-253-2318
E-mail: bethany.wasik@cornell.edu
Mng Ed, CEAS: Alexis Siemon E-mail: kas578@
cornell.edu
Mng Ed, Southeast Asia Program Publications:
Sarah E M Grossman Tel: 607-255-4359
E-mail: sg265@cornell.edu
Sr Ed, ILR Press: James Lance Tel: 413-727-2265
E-mail: jml554@cornell.edu
Sr Acqs Ed, Northern Illinois University Press:
Amy Farranto E-mail: afarranto@niu.edu
Acqs Ed: Jackie Teoh Tel: 607-254-5824
E-mail: jt648@cornell.edu
Subs Rts Mgr: Tonya Cook Tel: 607-255-2069
E-mail: tcc6@cornell.edu
Publicist: Rebecca Brutus Tel: 607-254-5693
E-mail: rtb93@cornell.edu; Alex Vlahov
E-mail: ajv87@cornell.edu
Founded: 1869 (reconstituted in 1930)
General nonfiction, scholarly books & monographs; hardcover & paperbacks.
ISBN Prefix(es): 978-0-8014; 978-0-87546; 978-1-5017
Number of titles published annually: 175 Print;
188 E-Book
Total Titles: 5,000 Print; 2,800 E-Book
Imprints: Comstock Publishing Associates; Cornell East Asia Series; ILR Press; Northern Illinois University Press; Southeast Asia Program
Publications; Three Hills
Distributor for Leuven University Press
Foreign Rep(s): Ampersand (Canada); Combined
Academic Publishers (CAP) (Africa, Asia, Europe, Middle East, Oceania, UK); US PubRep
Inc (Craig Falk) (Latin America)
Foreign Rights: EULAMA (Alexander von Prellwitz) (Italy); Graal Literary Agency (Lukasz
Wrobel) (Eastern Europe); Maya Publishers
(Mr Surit Mitra) (India); La Nouvelle Agence
(Vanessa Kling) (France); RDC Agencia Literaria (Beatriz Coll) (Brazil, Portugal, Spain);

Thomas Schlueck GmbH (Sarah Knofius) (Germany)
Returns: Longleaf Services Inc, c/o Ingram Publisher Services, 1210 Ingram Dr, Chambersburg, PA 17202 *E-mail:* credit@longleafservices.org
Distribution Center: Longleaf Services Inc, 116 S Boundary St, Chapel Hill, NC 27514-3808 *Toll Free Tel:* 800-848-6224 *Toll Free Fax:* 800-272-6817 *E-mail:* customerservice@longleafservices.org SAN: 203-3151
University of Toronto Distribution, 5201 Dufferin St, Downsview, Toronto, ON M3H 5T8, Canada *Tel:* 416-667-7791 *Toll Free Tel:* 800-565-9523 *Fax:* 416-667-7832 *Toll Free Fax:* 800-221-9985
Combined Academic Publishers (CAP), 39 E Parade, Harrogate, N Yorks HG1 5LQ, United Kingdom *Tel:* (01423) 526350 *E-mail:* enquiries@combinedacademic.co.uk *Web Site:* www.combinedacademic.co.uk
Membership(s): Association of University Presses (AUPresses)
See separate listing for:
Northern Illinois University Press

Cornerstone Book Publishers
PO Box 8423, Hot Springs Village, AR 71910
Tel: 504-215-6258
E-mail: 1cornerstonebooks@gmail.com
Web Site: cornerstonepublishers.com
Key Personnel
Owner: Michael R Poll
Founded: 1995
Masonic, Scottish Rite, Rosicrucian, metaphysical, Louisiana themed & classic outdoor & bushcraft books.
ISBN Prefix(es): 978-1-887560; 978-1-61342; 978-1-934935
Number of titles published annually: 6 Print; 10 E-Book
Total Titles: 33 Print; 65 E-Book
Foreign Rep(s): Ingram (UK)

§Corwin
Division of SAGE Publishing
2455 Teller Rd, Thousand Oaks, CA 91320
Tel: 805-499-9734 *Toll Free Tel:* 800-233-9936 *Fax:* 805-499-5323 *Toll Free Fax:* 800-417-2466
E-mail: info@corwin.com; order@corwin.com
Web Site: www.corwin.com
Key Personnel
VP, Corwin Global Sales & Strategic Devt: Chris Devling
VP, Mktg & Opers: Elena Nikitina
Assoc VP, Global Prof Learning: Sonja Hollins-Alexander, EdD
Founded: 1990
Offers practical, research-based books, journals & multimedia resources specifically developed for principals, administrators, teachers, staff developers, curriculum developers, special & gifted educators & other PreK-12 education professionals.
ISBN Prefix(es): 978-0-7619; 978-0-8039; 978-1-4129; 978-1-8904; 978-1-57517; 978-1-5697; 978-1-879179
Number of titles published annually: 120 Print
Total Titles: 1,900 Print
Distributor for SAGE UK Resources for Educators
Foreign Rep(s): SAGE India (India); SAGE London (Europe, UK); SAGE Singapore (Asia-Pacific)

§Cosimo Inc
Old Chelsea Sta, PO Box 416, New York, NY 10011-0416
Tel: 212-989-3616 *Fax:* 212-989-3662
E-mail: info@cosimobooks.com
Web Site: www.cosimobooks.com
Founded: 2005
Specialty publisher for independent authors, not-for-profit organizations & innovative businesses, dedicated to publishing books that inspire, inform & engage readers around the world. We offer authors & organizations full publishing support, while using the newest technologies to present their works in the most timely & effective way.
ISBN Prefix(es): 978-1-931044 (Paraview print on demand titles); 978-1-4165 (Paraview Pocket Books); 978-1-59605; 978-1-60206; 978-1-60520; 978-1-61640
Number of titles published annually: 100 Print; 20 E-Book
Total Titles: 3,000 Print
Imprints: Cosimo Books; Cosimo Classics; Cosimo Reports; Paraview Pocket Books; Paraview Special Editions
Divisions: Paraview Press

Cotsen Institute of Archaeology Press
Division of University of California, Los Angeles
308 Charles E Young Dr N, Fowler A210, Box 951510, Los Angeles, CA 90095
Tel: 310-206-9384 *Fax:* 310-206-4723
E-mail: cioapress@ioa.ucla.edu
Web Site: www.ioa.ucla.edu
Key Personnel
Dir, Institute: Willeke Wendrich
Dir, Pubns: Randi Danforth
Founded: 1974
Books, monographs & occasional papers in the field of archaeology.
ISBN Prefix(es): 978-0-917956; 978-1-938770; 978-1-931745
Number of titles published annually: 5 Print
Total Titles: 100 Print; 100 E-Book
Foreign Rep(s): ISD LLC (worldwide)
Distribution Center: ISD, 70 Enterprise Dr, Suite 2, Bristol, CT 06010, Pres: Ian Stevens *Tel:* 860-584-6546 *E-mail:* ian@isdistribution.com *Web Site:* www.isdistribution.com

§Council for Exceptional Children (CEC)
3100 Clarendon Blvd, Suite 600, Arlington, VA 22201
Toll Free Tel: 888-232-7733
E-mail: service@exceptionalchildren.org
Web Site: www.exceptionalchildren.org
Key Personnel
Exec Dir: Chad Rummel *Tel:* 703-264-9404 *E-mail:* crummel@exceptionalchildren.org
Dir, Pubns: Annie Drinkard *Tel:* 703-264-9455 *E-mail:* adrinkard@exceptionalchildren.org
Founded: 1922
Mail order books & other products to improve the educational success of individuals with disabilities +/or gifts & talents.
ISBN Prefix(es): 978-0-86586
Number of titles published annually: 4 Print
Total Titles: 75 Print
Branch Office(s)
CEC Publications, PO Box 79026, Baltimore, MD 21279-0026
Distributor for Brookes (selected titles); Free Spirit (selected titles); Guilford (selected titles); National Professional Resources (selected titles)
Distribution Center: Amazon
Baker & Taylor
Barnes & Noble

Council for Research in Values & Philosophy
The Catholic University of America, Gibbons Hall, B-20, 620 Michigan Ave NE, Washington, DC 20064
Tel: 202-319-6089
E-mail: cua-rvp@cua.edu
Web Site: www.crvp.org
Key Personnel
VP: Dr Willaim Sweet
Exec Dir: Hu Yeping *E-mail:* huy@cua.edu
Comm Chair: William Barbieri *E-mail:* barbieri@cua.edu
Founded: 1983
Works on philosophy, values, education, civil society, culture.
ISBN Prefix(es): 978-1-56518
Number of titles published annually: 12 Print; 12 Online
Total Titles: 300 Print; 300 Online
Orders to: Oblate School of Theology (OST), 285 Oblate Dr, San Antonio, TX 78216, Contact: Mathew C Martin *Tel:* 210-341-1366 ext 205 *E-mail:* mmartin@ost.edu

The Council of State Governments
1776 Avenue of the States, Lexington, KY 40511
Tel: 859-244-8000 *Fax:* 859-244-8001
E-mail: membership@csg.org
Web Site: www.csg.org
Key Personnel
Exec Dir & CEO: David Adkins *E-mail:* dadkins@csg.org
Founded: 1933
Nonprofit association representing state government officials in all three branches. Publish reference guides, books, directories, journals, newsletters & conference proceedings & hold major regional & special topical conferences. Will contract or do grant-funded topic research. Specialize in corrections & public safety.
ISBN Prefix(es): 978-0-87292
Number of titles published annually: 10 Print
Total Titles: 72 Print
Branch Office(s)
1107 Ninth St, Suite 730, Sacramento, CA 95814, Exec Dir: Edgar E Ruiz *Tel:* 916-553-4423 *Fax:* 916-446-5760 *E-mail:* csgw@csg.org *Web Site:* www.csgwest.org
444 N Capitol St NW, Suite 401, Washington, DC 20001, Asst Dir, Opers: Jessica Kirby *Tel:* 202-624-5460 *E-mail:* jkirby@csg.org *Web Site:* www.csg.org
1946 Clairmont Rd, Decatur, GA 30033, Dir: Lindsey Gray *Tel:* 404-633-1866 *Fax:* 404-633-4896 *E-mail:* slc@csg.org *Web Site:* csgsouth.org
701 E 22 St, Suite 110, Lombard, IL 60148, Dir: Laura Tomaka *Tel:* 630-925-1922 *E-mail:* csgm@csg.org *Web Site:* www.csgmidwest.org
22 Cortlandt St, 22nd fl, New York, NY 10007, Dir: David Biette *Tel:* 212-482-2320 *Fax:* 212-482-2344 *E-mail:* info@csg-erc.org *Web Site:* www.csgeast.org

Council on Foreign Relations Press
Division of Council on Foreign Relations
The Harold Pratt House, 58 E 68 St, New York, NY 10065
SAN: 201-7784
Tel: 212-434-9400 *Fax:* 212-434-9800
E-mail: publications@cfr.org
Web Site: www.cfr.org
Key Personnel
Edit Dir: Patricia Dorff *Tel:* 212-434-9514 *Fax:* 212-434-9807 *E-mail:* pdorff@cfr.org
Founded: 1922
Scholarly books on foreign policy, international economics, international affairs.
ISBN Prefix(es): 978-0-87609
Number of titles published annually: 10 Print
Total Titles: 245 Print
Branch Office(s)
1777 "F" St NW, Washington, DC 20006 *Tel:* 202-509-8400 *Fax:* 202-509-8490
Membership(s): Association of American Publishers (AAP)

Council on Social Work Education (CSWE), see CSWE Press

U.S. PUBLISHERS

Counterpath Press
7935 E 14 Ave, Denver, CO 80220
E-mail: counterpath@counterpathpress.org
Web Site: www.counterpathpress.org
Key Personnel
Co-Founder & Dir: Tim Roberts
Co-Founder & Assoc Dir: Julie Carr
Founded: 2006
Independent, nonprofit, literary publisher of poetry, fiction, drama, cross-genre work, literary & cultural theory & criticism, translations, reprints & high-quality Internet material.
ISBN Prefix(es): 978-1-933996
Number of titles published annually: 6 Print
Total Titles: 60 Print
Membership(s): Community of Literary Magazines & Presses (CLMP)

Counterpoint Press LLC
2560 Ninth St, Suite 318, Berkeley, CA 94710
Tel: 510-704-0230 *Fax:* 510-704-0268
E-mail: info@counterpointpress.com
Web Site: counterpointpress.com; softskull.com
Key Personnel
CEO: Elizabeth R Koch
COO & Publr, Catapult Book Group: Alyson Forbes
SVP & Edit Dir, Catapult/Soft Skull Press: Dan Smetanka
VP/Assoc Publr, Publicity, Catapult/Counterpoint/Soft Skull Press: Megan Fishmann
Assoc Publr & Exec Dir, Mktg, Counterpoint/Catapult/Soft Skull Press: Rachel Fershleiser
VP, Company Culture/Sr Mng Ed, Books, Catapult/Counterpoint/Soft Skull Press: Wah-Ming Chang
Creative Dir, Catapult/Counterpoint/Soft Skull Press: Nicole Caputo
Asst Dir, Publicity, Catapult/Counterpoint/Soft Skull Press: Lena Moses-Schmitt
Ed-in-Chief, Catapult: Kendall Storey
Ed-in-Chief, Soft Skull Press: Mensah Demary
Ed, Catapult: Alicia Kroell
Soc Media Ed, Catapult/Counterpoint/Soft Skull Press: Dustin Kurtz
Asst Ed: Dan Lopez
Asst Prodn Ed, Catapult/Counterpoint/Soft Skull Press: Tracy Danes
Busn Mgr: Kelli Adams
Prodn Mgr, Catapult/Counterpoint/Soft Skull Press: Olenka Burgess
Sr Publicist, Catapult/Counterpoint/Soft Skull Press: Andrea Cordova
Contracts & Rts Assoc/Awards Coord, Catapult/Counterpoint/Soft Skull Press: Miriam Vance
Sales & Mktg Assoc, Catapult/Counterpoint/Soft Skull Press: Katie Qiaoling Mantele
Founded: 2007 (through acquisition of Counterpoint, Shoemaker & Hoard, & Soft Skull Press)
Publish literary work with an emphasis on fiction, natural history, philosophy & contemporary thought, history, art, poetry, narrative & nonfiction.
ISBN Prefix(es): 978-1-887178; 978-1-58243; 978-1-61902 (Counterpoint); 978-1-933368 (Soft Skull Press); 978-1-57805 (Sierra Club Books); 978-0-9796636 (Soft Skull Press); 978-1-932360 (Soft Skull Press); 978-1-887128 (Soft Skull Press)
Number of titles published annually: 60 Print
Total Titles: 60 Print
Imprints: Catapult; Counterpoint; Sierra Club Books; Soft Skull Press
Foreign Rep(s): Ingram Publisher Services International (worldwide exc Australia, Canada, Europe & USA); Ingram Publisher Services UK/Grantham Book Services (GBS) (Europe); NewSouth Books (Australia); Publishers Group Canada/Raincoast (Canada)
Foreign Rights: Kleinworks Agency (Judy Klein)
Distribution Center: Penguin Random House Publisher Services (PRHPS) (worldwide)

Country Music Foundation Press
Division of Country Music Hall of Fame® & Museum
222 Rep John Lewis Way S, Nashville, TN 37203
Tel: 615-416-2001
E-mail: info@countrymusichalloffame.org
Web Site: www.countrymusichalloffame.org
Founded: 1967
Publish books & exhibition catalogs. Also author books for trade publications & co-publish with Vanderbilt University Press.
ISBN Prefix(es): 978-0-8265; 978-0-915608
Number of titles published annually: 3 Print
Total Titles: 40 Print

§Countryman Press
Division of W W Norton & Company Inc
c/o W W Norton & Company Inc, 500 Fifth Ave, New York, NY 10110
SAN: 206-4901
Tel: 212-354-5500 *Fax:* 212-869-0856
E-mail: countrymanpress@wwnorton.com
Web Site: wwnorton.com/countryman-press
Key Personnel
Edit Dir: Ann Treistman
Sr Ed: James Jayo
Asst Ed: Emma Peters
Founded: 1973
ISBN Prefix(es): 978-0-936399; 978-1-58157; 978-0-914378; 978-0-88150; 978-0-942440
Number of titles published annually: 70 Print
Total Titles: 350 Print
Distributed by Penguin Books (CN only)
Foreign Rep(s): W W Norton & Co Inc
Foreign Rights: Casanovas & Lynch (Portugal, Spain)
Warehouse: National Book Co Inc, 800 Keystone Industrial Park, Scranton, PA 18512-4601

§Covenant Communications Inc
Division of Deseret Book Co
1226 S 630 E, Suite 4, American Fork, UT 84003
Tel: 801-756-1041
E-mail: info@covenant-lds.com; covenantorders@covenant-lds.com
Web Site: www.covenant-lds.com
Key Personnel
VP, Mktg: Robby Nichols *Tel:* 801-756-1041 ext 106
Dir, Content: Phil Reschke
Founded: 1958
Publish for the LDS (Mormon) market.
ISBN Prefix(es): 978-1-55503; 978-1-57734; 978-1-59156; 978-1-59811; 978-1-60681; 978-1-62108; 978-1-68047
Number of titles published annually: 100 Print; 100 E-Book; 50 Audio
Total Titles: 300 Print; 500 E-Book; 450 Audio

CQ Press
Imprint of SAGE Publishing
2600 Virginia Ave NW, Suite 600, Washington, DC 20037
Tel: 202-729-1900; 202-729-1800
 Toll Free Tel: 866-4CQ-PRESS (427-7737)
E-mail: customerservice@cqpress.com
Web Site: www.cqpress.com; library.cqpress.com
Founded: 1959
Publisher of reference & text books, directories, periodicals & online products on American government & politics, journalism & mass communication.
ISBN Prefix(es): 978-0-87187; 978-1-56802; 978-0-9625531; 978-1-56692; 978-0-7401; 978-1-933116; 978-1-60426; 978-0-9823537; 978-1-60871
Number of titles published annually: 50 Print
Total Titles: 300 Print; 4 CD-ROM; 1 Online; 3 E-Book
Foreign Rep(s): SAGE Publications (Amanda Fox); SAGE Publications (Sarah Broomhead); SAGE Publications Asia-Pacific Pte Ltd (Rosalia da Garcia)

§Crabtree Publishing Co
347 Fifth Ave, Suite 1402-145, New York, NY 10016
Tel: 212-496-5040 *Toll Free Tel:* 800-387-7650
 Toll Free Fax: 800-355-7166
E-mail: custserv@crabtreebooks.com
Web Site: www.crabtreebooks.com
Key Personnel
CEO: Craig Culliford *Tel:* 212-496-5040 ext 236
 E-mail: craig_c@crabtreebooks.com
Pres: Peter A Crabtree *Tel:* 212-496-5040 ext 225
 E-mail: peter_c@crabtreebooks.com
Publr: Bobbie Kalman *E-mail:* bobbiek@crabtreebooks.com
VP, Edit: Kathy Middleton *Tel:* 212-496-5040 ext 226 *E-mail:* kathy_m@crabtreebooks.com
VP, Mktg: Julie Alguire *Tel:* 212-496-5040 ext 235 *E-mail:* julie_a@crabtreebooks.com
Dir, Art & New Media: Robert MacGregor *Tel:* 212-496-5040 ext 231 *E-mail:* rob_m@crabtreebooks.com
Sales Dir: Andrea Crabtree *Tel:* 212-496-5040 ext 265 *E-mail:* andrea_c@crabtreebooks.com
Warehouse Mgr: Karl Kasper *Tel:* 212-496-5040 ext 237 *E-mail:* warehouse@crabtreebooks.com
Cust Serv: Candice Pinkerton *Tel:* 212-496-5040 ext 221 *E-mail:* candice_c@crabtreebooks.com
Founded: 1978
Publisher of children's nonfiction & fiction; library binding & paperback for school & trade.
ISBN Prefix(es): 978-0-86505; 978-0-7787; 978-1-4271; 978-1-0396; 978-1-0398
Number of titles published annually: 619 Print; 988 E-Book
Total Titles: 5,421 Print; 4,566 E-Book; 1,968 Audio
Imprints: Crabtree Blossoms; Crabtree Branches; Crabtree Classics; Crabtree Crown; Crabtree Forest; Crabtree Leaves; Crabtree Little Honey; Crabtree Roots; Crabtree Seedlings; Crabtree Sunshine; Look, Listen & Learn
Subsidiaries: Crabtree Publishing Co Ltd (CN)
Distributor for Bayard; Seahorse Publishing; Sequoia Kids Media
Foreign Rep(s): Everybody's Books (Namibia, South Africa); Macmillan Marketing Services (European Union, UK); Novella (Australia, New Zealand)
Warehouse: 2321 Kenmore Ave, Buffalo, NY 14207
Membership(s): American Booksellers Association (ABA); The American Library Association (ALA); Educational Book & Media Association (EBMA); Museum Store Association (MSA); National Science Teachers Association (NSTA)

§Craftsman Book Co
6058 Corte Del Cedro, Carlsbad, CA 92011
SAN: 159-7000
Tel: 760-438-7828 *Toll Free Tel:* 800-829-8123
 Fax: 760-438-0398
Web Site: www.craftsman-book.com
Key Personnel
Chmn & Intl Rts: Gary Moselle *E-mail:* gary@costbook.com
Publr, Data Licensing: Ben Moselle *Tel:* 760-438-7828 ext 122 *E-mail:* ben@costbook.com
Dir, Lib Sales & Mgr, Sales & Ad: Jennifer Johnson *Tel:* 760-438-7828 ext 105
 E-mail: johnson@costbook.com
Edit Mgr & Rts & Perms: Laurence Jacobs *Tel:* 760-438-7828 ext 108 *E-mail:* jacobs@costbook.com
Founded: 1952
Estimating software, trade & professional, state-specific contract-writing software, subscription, mail order & download, reference; construction industry.
ISBN Prefix(es): 978-0-934041; 978-0-910460; 978-1-57218
Number of titles published annually: 8 Print; 2 CD-ROM; 150 Online; 11 E-Book

Total Titles: 150 Print; 2 CD-ROM; 150 Online; 100 E-Book
Distributed by The Aberdeen Group; BNI Publications; Builders Book Inc
Distributor for BNI Publications; Builders Book Inc; Building News Inc; Home Builders Press
Foreign Rep(s): Gauge Publications (Canada)
Distribution Center: Quality Books Inc, 103 W Pines Rd, Oregon, IL 61061-9680 *Tel:* 815-732-4450 *Toll Free Tel:* 800-323-4241 *Fax:* 815-732-4499 *E-mail:* info@quality-books.com *Web Site:* www.quality-books.com

§CRC Press
Imprint of Routledge
2385 Executive Center Dr, Suite 320, Boca Raton, FL 33431
Toll Free Tel: 800-354-1420; 800-634-7064 (orders)
E-mail: orders@taylorandfrancis.com
Web Site: www.routledge.com/go/crc-press
Founded: 1913
Books & digital resources in science, technology, engineering, mathematics & medicine.
ISBN Prefix(es): 978-0-8493; 978-0-935184; 978-1-57491; 978-0-87762; 978-1-56676; 978-0-87819; 978-1-58488; 978-1-58716; 978-1-4200; 978-1-4398; 978-1-4665; 978-1-4822; 978-1-4987; 978-1-032
Number of titles published annually: 1,300 Print
Total Titles: 23,000 Print
Warehouse: Taylor & Francis, 7625 Empire Dr, Florence, KY 41042

§Creative Editions
Imprint of The Creative Company
2140 Howard Dr W, North Mankato, MN 56003
SAN: 990-252X
Mailing Address: PO Box 227, Mankato, MN 56002
Tel: 507-388-6273 *Toll Free Tel:* 800-445-6209 *Fax:* 507-388-2746
E-mail: info@thecreativecompany.us; orders@thecreativecompany.us
Web Site: www.thecreativecompany.us
Key Personnel
Owner & Publr: Tom Peterson *Tel:* 507-388-6273 ext 225 *E-mail:* tjpeterson@thecreativecompany.us
Publicity: Ali Bryniarski *Tel:* 507-388-6273 ext 204 *E-mail:* abryniarski@thecreativecompany.us
Sales: Anna Erickson *Tel:* 414-728-1566 *E-mail:* aerickson@thecreativecompany.us
Founded: 1932
Gift books.
ISBN Prefix(es): 978-0-87191; 978-0-88682; 978-0-89812; 978-1-56660; 978-1-56846; 978-1-60818; 978-1-62832; 978-1-58341
Number of titles published annually: 110 Print
Total Titles: 3,500 Print
Imprints: Creative Digital; Creative Education; Creative Paperbacks
Foreign Rep(s): Ampersand Inc (British Columbia, CN, Ontario, CN); Hachette Book Group Inc (Carlos Azula); Hornblower Group Inc (New Brunswick, CN, Newfoundland and Labrador, CN, Nova Scotia, CN, Prince Edward Island, CN); Raincoast Books (Canada)
Returns: c/o Hachette Book Group Inc, 322 S Enterprise Blvd, Lebanon, IN 46052

Creative Homeowner
Imprint of Fox Chapel Publishing Co Inc
903 Square St, Mount Joy, PA 17552
Tel: 717-560-4703 *Toll Free Tel:* 844-307-3677 *Toll Free Fax:* 888-369-2885
E-mail: customerservice@foxchapelpublishing.com; sales@foxchapelpublishing.com
Web Site: www.foxchapelB2B.com
Founded: 1978
Quality trade paperbacks for kitchen & bath design & decor, gardening, landscaping, outdoor hobbies & home improvement.
ISBN Prefix(es): 978-0-932944; 978-1-880029; 978-1-58011
Number of titles published annually: 25 Print
Total Titles: 220 Print

Creston Books
PO Box 9369, Berkeley, CA 94709
Web Site: www.crestonbooks.co
Key Personnel
Publr & Ed: Marissa Moss *E-mail:* marissamoss@crestonbooks.co
Founded: 2013
Children's book publisher.
ISBN Prefix(es): 978-1-939547; 978-1-954354
Number of titles published annually: 8 Print
Total Titles: 81 Print
Sales Office(s): Lerner Publisher Services, 241 First Ave N, Minneapolis, MN 55401 *Toll Free Tel:* 800-328-4929 *E-mail:* custserve@lernerbooks.com *Web Site:* lernerbooks.com
Billing Address: Lerner Publisher Services, 241 First Ave N, Minneapolis, MN 55401 *Toll Free Tel:* 800-328-4929 *E-mail:* custserve@lernerbooks.com *Web Site:* lernerbooks.com
Orders to: Lerner Publisher Services, 241 First Ave N, Minneapolis, MN 55401 *Toll Free Tel:* 800-328-4929 *E-mail:* custserve@lernerbooks.com *Web Site:* lernerbooks.com
Returns: Lerner Publisher Services, 241 First Ave N, Minneapolis, MN 55401 *Toll Free Tel:* 800-328-4929 *E-mail:* custserve@lernerbooks.com *Web Site:* lernerbooks.com
Warehouse: Lerner Publisher Services, 241 First Ave N, Minneapolis, MN 55401 *Toll Free Tel:* 800-328-4929 *E-mail:* custserve@lernerbooks.com *Web Site:* lernerbooks.com
Distribution Center: Lerner Publisher Services, 241 First Ave N, Minneapolis, MN 55401 *Toll Free Tel:* 800-328-4929 *E-mail:* custserve@lernerbooks.com *Web Site:* lernerbooks.com
Membership(s): American Booksellers Association (ABA); California Independent Booksellers Alliance (CALIBA); The Children's Book Council (CBC)

§Cricket Cottage Publishing LLC
275 Medical Dr, No 4773, Carmel, IN 46082
E-mail: thecricketpublishing@gmail.com
Web Site: thecricketpublishing.com; www.facebook.com/CricketCottagePublishing
Key Personnel
Partner: Michael Murray *E-mail:* m@thecricketpublishing.com
Founded: 2012
Micro-publisher combining the best of traditional & modern publishing. Strictly royalty-based, giving authors a new chance & making use of social media to help promote the company & its books. Basic editing/proofing, book formatting & cover design. Online distribution for paperback & ebook versions.
ISBN Prefix(es): 978-0-692; 978-0-9991224
Number of titles published annually: 15 Print; 12 Online; 15 E-Book
Total Titles: 28 Print; 24 Online; 24 E-Book

§Cross-Cultural Communications
Division of Cross-Cultural Literary Editions Inc
239 Wynsum Ave, Merrick, NY 11566-4725
SAN: 208-6122
Tel: 516-868-5635 *Fax:* 516-379-1901
E-mail: ccpoetry@aol.com
Web Site: www.facebook.com/CrossCulturalCommunications.NY
Key Personnel
Publr & Ed-in-Chief: Stanley H Barkan *Tel:* 516-849-7054 (cell)
Art Ed: Bebe Barkan *E-mail:* bebebrushes@aol.com
Asst Ed: Mia Barkan Clarke *E-mail:* miaart@aol.com
Founded: 1971
Traditionally neglected languages & cultures in bilingual format, primarily poetry, some fiction, drama, music & art. Cross-Cultural review series of world literature & art in sound, print & motion.
Membership(s): Immagine&Poesia; Korean Expatriate Literature; Legas; Voices Israel.
ISBN Prefix(es): 978-0-89304
Number of titles published annually: 20 Print; 1 CD-ROM; 100 Online; 1 Audio
Total Titles: 750 Print; 3 CD-ROM; 400 Online; 16 Audio
Imprints: Cross-Cultural Prototypes; Expressive Editions; Fact Publishers (Ukraine); Midrashic Editions; Nightingale Editions; Ostrich Editions; The Seventh Quarry (Wales, Seventh Quarry Chapbook Series); The Seventh Quarry Press (Wales)
Subsidiaries: Bulgarian-American Cultural Society ALEKO (Chicago/Sofia, Bulgaria); Varlik (Turkey)
Branch Office(s)
3131 Mott Ave, Far Rockaway, NY 11691, Contact: Roy Cravzow *Tel:* 718-327-4714
HC 67, Box 1206, Big Sur, CA 93920-9629, Contact: Patricia Holt *Tel:* 831-667-2433 *E-mail:* surph8@yahoo.com
Foreign Office(s): Antigruppo Siciliano, Via Mogia 8, 90138 Palermo, Sicily PA, Italy, Contact: Nicolo D'Alessandro *Tel:* (091) 322030 *E-mail:* nicolodalessandro@virgilio.it
Distributor for Ad Infinitum Books; Arba Sicula (Magazine, US); Center of Emigrants from Serbia (Serbia); Greenfield Review Press (US); Immagine&Poesia (Italy); Legas Publishers (CN); Lips (Magazine & Press) (US); The New Feral Press (US); Pholiota Press Inc (England); The Seventh Quarry Press (Wales); Shabdaguchha (Magazine & Press) (Bangladesh & US); Sicilia Parra (Magazine, US)
Foreign Rep(s): Hassanal Abdullah (Bangladesh, USA); Lidia Chiarelli Actis (Italy); Karen Alkalay-Gut (Israel); August Bover (Catalonia); Gaetano Cipolla (Italy, USA); Nicolo D'Alessandro (Sicily, Italy); Kristine Doll (Spain, USA); Germain Droogenbroodt (Belgium, Spain); Christopher Fauske (Norway, USA); Isaac Goldemberg (Peru, USA); Luisa A Igloria (Philippines, USA); Daleep Jhaveri (India); Dovid Katz (Wales); Naoshi Koriyama (Japan); Dariusz Thomasz Lebioda (Poland); Vladimir Levchev (Bulgaria, USA); Bijana D Obradovic (Montenegro, Serbia, USA); Mark Polyakov (Russia, USA); Ritva Poom (Estonia, Finland, USA); Kyung-Nyun "Kay" Kim Richards (South Korea, USA); Gabriel Rosenstock (Ireland); Stephen A Sadow (Argentina, USA); Marco Scalabrino (Sicily, Italy); Stoyan "Tchouki" Tchoukanov (Bulgaria); Peter Thabit Jones (Wales); Sona Van (Armenia, USA); Tino Villanueva (Mexico, USA); Dorit Weisgman (Israel); Sepideh Zamani (Iran, USA)

§The Crossroad Publishing Co
831 Chestnut Ridge Rd, Chestnut Ridge, NY 10977
SAN: 287-0118
Tel: 845-517-0180
E-mail: info@crossroadpublishing.com; office@crossroadpublishing.com
Web Site: crossroadpublishing.com
Founded: 1980
Independent book publisher in religion, spirituality, theology, personal growth, leadership & parenting.
ISBN Prefix(es): 978-0-8245
Number of titles published annually: 30 Print; 1 CD-ROM; 1 Online; 20 E-Book; 1 Audio
Total Titles: 550 Print; 1 CD-ROM; 1 Online; 20 E-Book; 4 Audio

U.S. PUBLISHERS

Imprints: Crossroad (trade secular & religious); Herder & Herder (Catholic parish & academic)
Foreign Rep(s): John Garratt (Australia); Novalis (Canada)
Billing Address: Independent Publishers Group (IPG), 814 N Franklin St, Chicago, IL 60610 Toll Free Tel: 800-888-4741 E-mail: orders@ipgbook.com Web Site: www.ipgbook.com
Membership(s): Association of Catholic Publishers Inc

Crossway
Division of Good News Publishers
1300 Crescent St, Wheaton, IL 60187
SAN: 211-7991
Tel: 630-682-4300 Toll Free Tel: 800-635-7993 (orders); 800-543-1659 (cust serv) Fax: 630-682-4785
E-mail: info@crossway.org
Web Site: www.crossway.org
Key Personnel
Pres: Josh Dennis
EVP, Book Publg: Justin Taylor
EVP, Busn Opers: Anthony Gosling
EVP, Creative: Dan Farrell
EVP, Publg: Don Jones
SVP, Fin: Paul Thomas
SVP, Ministry & Licensing: Randy Jahns
Book Publg Mgr & ISBN Contact: Jill Carter E-mail: jcarter@crossway.org
Intl Rts: Aaron Camp E-mail: acamp@crossway.org
Perms: Nicole Gosling E-mail: ngosling@crossway.org
Founded: 1969
Books with an evangelical Christian perspective aimed at the religious market.
ISBN Prefix(es): 978-0-89107; 978-1-58134; 978-1-4335; 978-8-8749
Number of titles published annually: 90 Print
Total Titles: 548 Print; 9 Audio

§Crown House Publishing Co LLC
Division of Crown House Publishing Ltd (UK Co)
81 Brook Hills Circle, White Plains, NY 10605
SAN: 013-9270
Tel: 914-946-3517 Toll Free Tel: 877-925-1213 (cust serv) Fax: 914-946-1160
E-mail: info@chpus.com
Web Site: www.crownhousepublishing.com
Key Personnel
Pres: Mark Tracten E-mail: mtracten@chpus.com
Founded: 1996
Publisher of quality books in psychology & education.
ISBN Prefix(es): 978-1-89983; 978-1-90442; 978-1-84590; 978-0-98235
Number of titles published annually: 30 Print; 1 CD-ROM; 6 Audio
Total Titles: 330 Print; 2 CD-ROM; 30 Audio
Distributor for Developing Press Co; Human Alchemy Publications; Institute Press; Transforming Press
Foreign Rights: Anglo-American Book Co Ltd (Europe, UK)
Billing Address: PO Box 2223, Williston, VT 05495
Orders to: PO Box 2223, Williston, VT 05495, Contact: Matt Drake Fax: 802-864-7626 E-mail: mdrake@aidcvt.com
Returns: American International Distribution Corp (AIDC), 82 Winter Sport Lane, Williston, VT 05495, Contact: Matt Drake E-mail: mdrake@aidcvt.com
Shipping Address: PO Box 2223, Williston, VT 05495, Contact: Laurie Kenyon Tel: 802-862-0095 ext 113 Fax: 802-864-7626
Warehouse: PO Box 2223, Williston, VT 05495
Distribution Center: American International Distribution Corp (AIDC), 82 Winter Sport Lane, Williston, VT 05495, Contact: Laurie Kenyon Tel: 802-862-0095 Toll Free Tel: 800-678-2432 Fax: 802-864-7749 E-mail: lkenyon@aidcvt.com Web Site: www.aidcvt.com

Crown Publishing Group
Division of Penguin Random House LLC
c/o Penguin Random House LLC, 1745 Broadway, New York, NY 10019
Tel: 212-782-9000 Toll Free Tel: 888-264-1745 Fax: 212-940-7408
E-mail: crownosm@penguinrandomhouse.com
Web Site: crownpublishing.com
Founded: 1933
Leading publisher of bestselling fiction & critically acclaimed narrative nonfiction in categories that include biography & memoirs, history, science, politics & current events.
Penguin Random House & its publishing entities are not accepting unsol submissions, proposals, mss, or submission queries via e-mail at this time.
Number of titles published annually: 400 Print
Imprints: Amphoto Books; Broadway Books; Andy Cohen Books; Crown Archetype; Crown Business; Crown Currency; Crown Forum; Crown Publishers; Hogarth; Image Books; Clarkson Potter; Ten Speed Press; Three Rivers Press; Watson-Guptill
See separate listing for:
Clarkson Potter
Ten Speed Press
Watson-Guptill

§Crystal Clarity Publishers
14618 Tyler Foote Rd, Nevada City, CA 95959
Mailing Address: PO Box 76, Nevada City, CA 95959
Toll Free Tel: 800-424-1055
E-mail: info@crystalclarity.com
Web Site: www.crystalclarity.com
Key Personnel
CEO: Allison Romano Tel: 310-339-4676 E-mail: dharmadevi@crystalclarity.com
Pres: Philip Romano Tel: 310-339-9270 E-mail: narayan@crystalclarity.com
Founded: 1968
Mind, body, spirit publisher. Self-help, psychology, philosophy, religion, business, books, videos, metaphysical, health/healing, spirituality.
ISBN Prefix(es): 978-0-916124; 978-1-878265; 978-1-56589
Number of titles published annually: 9 Print; 9 E-Book; 8 Audio
Total Titles: 200 Print; 50 E-Book; 20 Audio
Imprints: Clarity Sound & Light
Foreign Rep(s): Brumby Books (Australia)
Foreign Rights: Alexandra McGilloway
Warehouse: 1123 Goodrich Blvd, Commerce, CA 90022, Contact: Michael Iyob
Membership(s): Independent Book Publishers Association (IBPA)

CSHL Press, see Cold Spring Harbor Laboratory Press

The CSIS Press, see Center for Strategic & International Studies (CSIS)

§CSLI Publications
Stanford University, Cordura Hall, 220 Panama St, Stanford, CA 94305-4115
Tel: 650-723-1839 Fax: 650-725-2166
E-mail: pubs@csli.stanford.edu
Web Site: cslipublications.stanford.edu
Key Personnel
Dir: Dikran Karagueuzian Tel: 650-723-1712 E-mail: dikran@csli.stanford.edu
Founded: 1985
Subjects include computer science, computational linguistics, linguistics & philosophy.

ISBN Prefix(es): 978-0-937073; 978-1-881526; 978-1-57586; 978-0-226
Number of titles published annually: 6 Print
Total Titles: 375 Print; 7 Online
Distributed by University of Chicago Press

CSWE Press
Division of Council on Social Work Education
333 John Carlyle St, Suite 400, Alexandria, VA 22314-3457
Tel: 703-683-8080 Fax: 703-683-8493
E-mail: publications@cswe.org; info@cswe.org
Web Site: www.cswe.org
Key Personnel
Pres & CEO: Darla Spence Coffey, PhD
Pubns Mgr: Elizabeth Simon Tel: 703-519-2076 E-mail: esimon@cswe.org
Founded: 1952
Professional books.
ISBN Prefix(es): 978-0-87293
Number of titles published annually: 3 Print
Total Titles: 75 Print
Orders to: c/o Ware-Pak, 2427 Bond St, University Park, IL 60484 Toll Free Tel: 877-751-5053 E-mail: cswe@ware-pak.com
Returns: c/o Ware-Pak, 2427 Bond St, University Park, IL 60484 Toll Free Tel: 877-751-5053 E-mail: cswe@ware-pak.com
Membership(s): Copyright Clearance Center (CCC)

CUA Press, see The Catholic University of America Press

§Cypress House
Imprint of Comp-Type Inc
155 Cypress St, Suite A, Fort Bragg, CA 95437
Tel: 707-964-9520 Toll Free Tel: 800-773-7782 Fax: 707-964-7531
E-mail: office@cypresshouse.com
Web Site: www.cypresshouse.com
Key Personnel
Pres: Cynthia Frank E-mail: cynthia@cypresshouse.com
Mng Ed: Joe Shaw E-mail: joeshaw@cypresshouse.com
Founded: 1986
ISBN Prefix(es): 978-1-879384
Number of titles published annually: 4 E-Book; 1 Audio
Total Titles: 140 Print; 20 E-Book; 1 Audio
Imprints: Lost Coast Press; QED Press
Membership(s): American Booksellers Association (ABA); California Independent Booksellers Alliance (CALIBA); Independent Book Publishers Association (IBPA); Pacific Northwest Booksellers Association (PNBA)

Dafina Books, see Kensington Publishing Corp

Dalkey Archive Press
Imprint of Deep Vellum Publishing
c/o Deep Vellum Publishing, 3000 Commerce St, Dallas, TX 75226
E-mail: admin@deepvellum.org
Web Site: www.dalkeyarchive.com
Key Personnel
Exec Dir: Will Evans E-mail: will@deepvellum.org
Mktg & Sales Dir: Sara Balabanlilar E-mail: sara@deepvellum.org
Rts Dir: Sarah McEachern E-mail: sm@deepvellum.org
Ed-in-Chief: Chad Post E-mail: chad@deepvellum.org
Publicity & Programming Mgr: Walker Rutter-Bowman E-mail: walker@deepvellum.org
Founded: 1984
Literary fiction, translations & criticism. We keep works of literary value in print.

ISBN Prefix(es): 978-0-916583; 978-1-56478; 978-1-62897; 978-1-943150
Number of titles published annually: 60 Print
Total Titles: 750 Print
Foreign Rep(s): Canadian Manda Group (Canada); John Toomey (Europe, UK & Commonwealth)
Distribution Center: Consortium Books Sales & Distribution, The Keg House, 34 13 Ave NE, Suite 101, Minneapolis, MN 55413 *Tel:* 612-746-2600 *Fax:* 612-746-2606 *E-mail:* info@cbsd.com *Web Site:* www.cbsd.com
Ingram Content Group LLC (intl dist)

Dancing Dakini Press
2935 NE 77 Ave, Portland, OR 97213
Tel: 503-415-0229
E-mail: editor@dancingdakinipress.com
Web Site: www.dancingdakinipress.com
Key Personnel
CFO: Ben Long *E-mail:* ben@benllong.com
Founded: 2012
Small publisher creating well-crafted books to inspire compassionate awareness, skillful means, authentic lives & a deep respect for all.
ISBN Prefix(es): 978-0-9836333
Number of titles published annually: 3 Print; 2 E-Book
Total Titles: 7 Print; 5 E-Book
Imprints: Dancing Ants Press

Dancing Lemur Press LLC
PO Box 383, Pikeville, NC 27863-0383
E-mail: admin@dancinglemurpress.com
Web Site: www.dancinglemurpressllc.com
Founded: 2008
Dedicated to bringing outstanding & inspiring science fiction & fantasy, new adult/young adult, mystery, paranormal, middle grade, nonfiction, Christian & more to readers.
ISBN Prefix(es): 978-0-9816210; 978-0-9827139; 978-1-939844
Number of titles published annually: 5 Print; 6 E-Book; 2 Audio
Total Titles: 55 Print; 60 E-Book; 12 Audio
Imprints: Freedom Fox Press
Distribution Center: Ingram Content Group, One Ingram Blvd, La Vergne, TN 37086 (US) *Tel:* 615-793-5000 *Web Site:* www.ingramcontent.com

D&B Hoovers™
Subsidiary of Dun & Bradstreet
7700 W Parmer Lane, Bldg A, Austin, TX 78729
Tel: 512-374-4500 *Toll Free Tel:* 855-858-5974
Web Site: www.dnb.com/products/marketing-sales/dnb-hoovers.html
Founded: 1990
Business reference books & online services.
ISBN Prefix(es): 978-1-878753; 978-1-57311; 978-1-59274; 978-1-63053
Number of titles published annually: 7 Print
Total Titles: 7 Print; 3 Online
Imprints: Hoover's Business Press; Hoover's Handbooks

Dark Horse Comics
Affiliate of Dark Horse Entertainment
10956 SE Main St, Milwaukie, OR 97222
Tel: 503-652-8815 *Fax:* 503-654-9440
E-mail: dhcomics@darkhorse.com
Web Site: www.darkhorse.com
Key Personnel
Founder & CEO: Michael Richardson
VP, Mktg: Cara O'Neil
Founded: 1986
Primary area is graphic novels; pop culture; limited edition hardcovers & comics.
ISBN Prefix(es): 978-1-56971
Number of titles published annually: 200 Print
Total Titles: 600 Print
Imprints: Albatross Funnybooks; Berger Books; Dark Horse Books; Dark Horse Manga; Dogu Publishing; Flux House Books; Jinxworld; M Press
Distributed by LPC Group Inc
Distribution Center: Penguin Random House Publisher Services (PRHPS), 1745 Broadway, New York, NY 10019
E-mail: distribution@penguinrandomhouse.com
Web Site: prhpublisherservices.com

§Data Trace Publishing Co (DTP)
110 West Rd, Suite 227, Towson, MD 21204-2316
Mailing Address: PO Box 1239, Brooklandville, MD 21022-1239
Tel: 410-494-4994 *Toll Free Tel:* 800-342-0454 *Fax:* 410-494-0515
E-mail: info@datatrace.com; customerservice@datatrace.com; salesandmarketing@datatrace.com; editorial@datatrace.com
Web Site: www.datatrace.com
Key Personnel
VP, Edit & Client Servs: Kimberly Collignon
Dir, Mktg: Holly Ballard
Ad Mgr: Frank Tufariello
Founded: 1987
Full service specialty publisher with interest in science, technical, law & medicine.
ISBN Prefix(es): 978-0-9637468; 978-1-57400
Number of titles published annually: 20 Print; 25 E-Book
Total Titles: 125 Print; 15 CD-ROM; 30 Online; 15 E-Book
Foreign Rep(s): Eurospan (worldwide exc Canada & USA)

Daughters of St Paul, see Pauline Books & Media

§Davies Publishing Inc
32 S Raymond Ave, Suites 4 & 5, Pasadena, CA 91105-1961
SAN: 217-3255
Tel: 626-792-3046 *Toll Free Tel:* 877-792-0005 *Fax:* 626-792-5308
E-mail: info@daviespublishing.com
Web Site: daviespublishing.com
Key Personnel
Pres & Publr: Michael Davies *E-mail:* mikedavies@daviespublishing.com
Edit Dir: Christina Moose *E-mail:* chrismoose@daviespublishing.com
Corp Secy & Opers Mgr: Janet Heard *E-mail:* janetheard@daviespublishing.com
Prodn Mgr: Charlene Locke *E-mail:* charlenelocke@daviespublishing.com
Founded: 1981
Ultrasound education & test preparation: books, software, DVDs, mock examinations & flashcards.
ISBN Prefix(es): 978-0-941022
Number of titles published annually: 2 Print; 2 CD-ROM
Total Titles: 48 Print; 10 CD-ROM
Membership(s): Association of American Publishers (AAP); Independent Book Publishers Association (IBPA)

§F A Davis Co
1915 Arch St, Philadelphia, PA 19103
SAN: 200-2078
Tel: 215-568-2270; 215-440-3001
Toll Free Tel: 800-523-4049 *Fax:* 215-568-5065; 215-440-3016
E-mail: info@fadavis.com; orders@fadavis.com
Web Site: www.fadavis.com
Key Personnel
Pres: Robert H Craven, Jr
Founded: 1879
Publisher of educational solutions for the nursing & health science professions.
ISBN Prefix(es): 978-0-8036; 978-1-7196
Number of titles published annually: 75 Print; 1 Online; 65 E-Book; 5 Audio
Total Titles: 399 Print; 150 E-Book; 10 Audio
Foreign Rep(s): ChoiceTEXTS (Brunei, Cambodia, China, Hong Kong, Indonesia, Laos, Malaysia, Myanmar, Palau, Philippines, Saipan, Singapore, South Korea, Taiwan, Thailand, Vietnam); Eurospan (Africa, Asia-Pacific, Europe); International Publishers Representatives Ltd (Algeria, Cyprus, Egypt, Ethiopia, Iran, Iraq, Israel, Jordan, Kuwait, Lebanon, Libya, Malta, Morocco, Oman, Pakistan, Qatar, Saudi Arabia, Sudan, Syria, Tunisia, United Arab Emirates, Virgin Islands, West Bank, Yemen); Jaypee Bros Medical Publishers (Bangladesh, India, Nepal, Sri Lanka)
Distribution Center: Login Canada, 300 Saulteaux Crescent, Winnipeg, MB R3J 3T2, Canada *Tel:* 204-837-2987 *Toll Free Tel:* 800-665-1148 *Web Site:* lb.ca

§DAW Books
Imprint of Astra Publishing House Inc
19 W 21 St, No 1201, New York, NY 10010
E-mail: info@astrapublishinghouse.com
Web Site: astrapublishinghouse.com/imprints/daw-books
Key Personnel
Publr: Elizabeth R Wollheim
Exec Mng Ed: Joshua Starr *E-mail:* jstarr@astrapublishinghouse.com
Exec Ed: Navah Wolfe *E-mail:* nwolfe@astrapublishinghouse.com
Sr Ed: Katie Hoffman *E-mail:* khoffman@astrapublishinghouse.com
Edit Asst: Madeline Goldberg *E-mail:* mgoldberg@astrapublishinghouse.com
Sr Mktg Mgr: Sarah Christensen Fu *E-mail:* sfu@astrapublishinghouse.com
Sr Publicist: Alexis Nowicki *E-mail:* a.nowicki@astrapublishinghouse.com
Mktg & Publicity Mgr: Laura Fitzgerald
Founded: 1971
Science fiction; fantasy; paperbound originals & reprints; hardcover editions, trade paperbacks & ebooks.
Number of titles published annually: 60 Print; 60 E-Book
Total Titles: 325 Print
Foreign Rep(s): Books Crossing Borders (Betty Anne Crawford)
Distribution Center: Penguin Random House, 400 Hahn Rd, Westminster, MD 21157 *Toll Free Tel:* 800-733-3000 *Toll Free Fax:* 800-659-2436

The Dawn Horse Press
Division of The Adidam Holy Institution
12040 N Seigler Rd, Middletown, CA 95461
Mailing Address: PO Box 70, Lower Lake, CA 95457
Tel: 707-928-6590 *Toll Free Tel:* 877-770-0772 *Fax:* 707-928-5068
E-mail: dhp@adidam.org
Web Site: www.dawnhorsepress.com
Key Personnel
Publr: James Minkin
Founded: 1972
Produces & markets books, CDs & AV materials on every aspect of authentic spiritual life & human development based upon the wisdom & teaching of Avatar Adi Da Samraj.
ISBN Prefix(es): 978-0-913922; 978-0-918801; 978-0-918801; 978-1-57097; 978-0-929929
Number of titles published annually: 8 Print; 5 CD-ROM; 12 Online; 4 Audio
Total Titles: 100 Print; 40 CD-ROM; 65 Online; 1 E-Book; 33 Audio
Shipping Address: 12312 Hwy 175, Cobb Mountain, CA 95426, Contact: Patrick Forristal
Distribution Center: New Leaf Distributing Co, 1085 E Lotus Dr, Silver Lake, WI 53170 *Tel:* 262-889-8501 *Toll Free Tel:* 800-326-

U.S. PUBLISHERS

2665 *Fax:* 262-889-8598 *E-mail:* orders@newleafdist.com SAN: 169-1449
Membership(s): Independent Book Publishers Association (IBPA)

§DawnSignPress
6130 Nancy Ridge Dr, San Diego, CA 92121-3223
Tel: 858-625-0600 *Toll Free Tel:* 800-549-5350 *Fax:* 858-625-2336
E-mail: contactus@dawnsign.com
Web Site: www.dawnsign.com
Key Personnel
Founder & Pres: Joe Dannis
Mktg & Lib Sales Dir: Becky Ryan
Founded: 1979
Specialty publisher of instructional sign language & educational deaf studies materials for both children & adults.
ISBN Prefix(es): 978-0-915035; 978-1-58121
Number of titles published annually: 5 Print; 5 E-Book
Total Titles: 96 Print; 1 CD-ROM; 10 Online; 10 E-Book
Distributor for Gallaudet University Press; MIT Press; Penguin Random House LLC
Foreign Rep(s): Amazon UK (UK)
Foreign Rights: Gloval Interprint (Hong Kong)
Distribution Center: Amazon
Barnes & Noble
Diglo
Follett

dbS Productions
PO Box 94, Charlottesville, VA 22902
Tel: 434-293-5502 *Toll Free Tel:* 800-745-1581
E-mail: info@dbs-sar.com
Web Site: www.dbs-sar.com
Key Personnel
CEO & Sr Scientist: Robert J Koester *E-mail:* robert@dbs-sar.com
Founded: 1989
Search & rescue.
ISBN Prefix(es): 978-1-879471
Number of titles published annually: 5 Print
Total Titles: 17 Print; 2 CD-ROM
Distributed by CMC

DC Comics Inc
Unit of DC Entertainment
4000 Warner Blvd, Burbank, CA 91522
Web Site: www.dc.com
Key Personnel
EVP, Busn & Mktg Strategy, Direct to Consumer & Global Franchise Mgmt: Amit Desai
Co-Publr: Dan Didio
Co-Publr & Chief Creative Offr: Jim Lee
Founded: 1935
Innovative comics publishing in periodical & book formats. In addition to the world's most popular superheroes, Superman, Batman & Wonder Woman, DC publishes cutting edge fantasy, horror, mystery, adventure, humor, nonfiction & general interest titles & maintains a 500+ title backlist in print. *MAD* Books is based on the classic magazine featuring Alfred E Neuman, Spy vs Spy & other icons. DC/MAD properties are also licensed for various publishing formats, as well as media, promotions & consumer products. DC Comics does not accept unsol mss. For more information, visit our web site at www.dcentertainment.com.
ISBN Prefix(es): 978-0-930289; 978-1-56389; 978-1-4012
Number of titles published annually: 240 Print
Total Titles: 2,778 Print
Imprints: DC (readers 13 years & older); DC Black Label (readers 17 years & older); DC Comics; DC Kids (middle grade); MAD Books
Distribution Center: Penguin Random House Publisher Services (PRHPS),

1745 Broadway, New York, NY 10019
E-mail: distribution@randomhouse.com *Web Site:* prhpublisherservices.com

§Walter De Gruyter Inc
Division of Walter de Gruyter GmbH
121 High St, 3rd fl, Boston, MA 02110
Tel: 857-284-7073; 617-377-4392 *Fax:* 857-284-7358
E-mail: service@degruyter.com; orders@degruyter.com
Web Site: www.degruyter.com
Key Personnel
Pres: Steve Fallon
Founded: 1749
Scholarly & scientific books, journals, paperbacks & hardcover reprints.
ISBN Prefix(es): 978-0-311; 978-0-89925; 978-3-11; 978-1-56445; 978-1-934078; 978-1-61451; 978-1-5015
Number of titles published annually: 200 Print; 5 CD-ROM
Total Titles: 8,500 Print; 20 CD-ROM; 15 Online; 10 E-Book
Foreign Office(s): Walter de Gruyter GmbH, Genthinerstr 13, 10785 Berlin, Germany *Tel:* (030) 260 05 0 *Fax:* (030) 260 05 251
Foreign Rep(s): Allied Publishers Pvt Ltd (India, Nepal, Sri Lanka); Book Club International (Bangladesh); Combined Representatives Worldwide Inc (Philippines); D A Books & Journals (Australia, New Zealand); Verlags und Kommissionsbuchhandlung Dr Franz Hain (Austria); Kumi Trading (South Korea); Kweilin Bookstore (Taiwan); Maruzen Co Ltd (Japan); Pak Book Corp (Pakistan); Parry's Book Center (Sendjrjan Berhad) (Brunei, Malaysia, Singapore); Swinden Book Co Ltd (Hong Kong)
Orders to: TriLiteral, 100 Maple Ridge Dr, Cumberland, RI 02864 *Tel:* 401-531-2800 *Toll Free Tel:* 800-405-1619 *Fax:* 401-531-2801 *Toll Free Fax:* 800-406-9145 *E-mail:* orders@triliteral.org; Sigloch Distribution, Am Buchberg 8, 74572 Blaufelden, Germany (outside US)
Distribution Center: Ingram Academic & Professional (CN, Caribbean, Latin America & US)

DecisionHealth, see HCPro/DecisionHealth

§Deep River Books LLC
PO Box 310, Sisters, OR 97759
Tel: 541-549-1139
E-mail: info@deepriverbooks.com
Web Site: deepriverbooks.com
Key Personnel
Founding Publr: Bill Carmichael; Nancie Carmichael
Publr: Andy Carmichael *E-mail:* andy@deepriverbooks.com
Assoc Dir/Sr Ed: Tamara Barnet
Founded: 2001
Publisher of Christian/inspirational books.
This publisher has indicated that 70% of their product line is author subsidized.
ISBN Prefix(es): 978-1-940269; 978-1-63269; 978-1-935265
Number of titles published annually: 40 Print; 40 E-Book
Total Titles: 500 Print; 300 E-Book
Imprints: Deep River Books; FishPond
Orders to: Baker & Taylor Publisher Services, 30 Amberwood Pkwy, Ashland, OH 44805 *Tel:* 567-215-0030 *Toll Free Tel:* 888-814-0208 *E-mail:* info@btpubservices.com *Web Site:* www.btpubservices.com
Returns: Baker & Taylor Publisher Services, 30 Amberwood Pkwy, Ashland, OH 44805 *Tel:* 567-215-0030 *Toll Free Tel:* 888-814-0208 *E-mail:* info@btpubservices.com *Web Site:* www.btpubservices.com

Distribution Center: Baker & Taylor Publisher Services, 30 Amberwood Pkwy, Ashland, OH 44805 *Tel:* 567-215-0030 *Toll Free Tel:* 888-814-0208 *E-mail:* info@btpubservices.com *Web Site:* www.btpubservices.com
Membership(s): Evangelical Christian Publishers Association (ECPA)

Delphinium Books
Affiliate of HarperCollins Publishers
16350 Ventura Blvd, Suite D, Encino, CA 91436
Tel: 917-301-7496 (e-mail first)
Web Site: www.delphiniumbooks.com
Key Personnel
Edit Dir: Joseph Olshan *E-mail:* joseph@delphiniumbooks.com
Founded: 1986
ISBN Prefix(es): 978-1-953002
Number of titles published annually: 12 Print; 7 E-Book; 5 Audio
Total Titles: 120 Print; 45 E-Book; 15 Audio
Distributed by HarperCollins Publishers

Demos Medical Publishing
Imprint of Springer Publishing Co
902 Carnegie Center Dr, Princeton, NJ 08540
Tel: 212-431-4370
E-mail: info@springerpub.com; cs@springerpub.com
Web Site: www.springerpub.com/medicine
Founded: 1986
Publish professional medical & consumer health titles.
ISBN Prefix(es): 978-1-888799; 978-0-8261; 978-0-939957; 978-1-932603; 978-1-933864; 978-1-934559; 978-1-935281; 978-1-936287; 978-1-936303; 978-1-61705; 978-1-62070
Number of titles published annually: 40 Print
Total Titles: 150 Print; 100 E-Book
Imprints: Demos Health
Foreign Rep(s): Eurospan Group (Africa, Europe, Middle East, UK); Login Canada (Canada); Taylor & Francis Books Pvt Ltd (Ritesh Kumar) (Asia)
Foreign Rights: Viva Books (India)
Returns: Springer Publishing, c/o IPS Pub 5225, 1250 Ingram Dr, Chambersburg, PA 17202
Membership(s): Association of American Publishers (AAP)

§Deseret Book Co
Subsidiary of Deseret Management Corp
55 N 300 W, 3rd fl, Salt Lake City, UT 84101-3502
SAN: 201-3185
Mailing Address: PO Box 30178, Salt Lake City, UT 84130-0178
Tel: 801-517-3369; 801-534-1515 (corp)
Toll Free Tel: 800-453-4532 (orders); 888-846-7302 (orders) *Fax:* 801-517-3126
E-mail: service@deseretbook.com
Web Site: www.deseretbook.com
Key Personnel
Pres: Laurel Day
Publr: Lisa Mangum *E-mail:* lmangum@deseretbook.com
Founded: 1886
Juveniles & young adults, trade paperbacks; fiction, general nonfiction, religion (Latter-day Saint).
ISBN Prefix(es): 978-0-87747; 978-1-59038; 978-1-57345; 978-0-87579; 978-1-60908; 978-1-60641; 978-1-60907; 978-1-62972; 978-1-62973; 978-1-63993
Number of titles published annually: 150 Print
Total Titles: 1,100 Print; 1 CD-ROM; 120 Audio
Imprints: Deseret Book; Faith & Media Initiative (FAMI); Shadow Mountain
Divisions: Covenant Communications Inc
Shipping Address: 2240 W 1500 S, Salt Lake City, UT 84104-4126 *Tel:* 801-517-3285
See separate listing for:
Covenant Communications Inc

PUBLISHERS

§DEStech Publications Inc
439 N Duke St, Lancaster, PA 17602-4967
SAN: 990-6916
Tel: 717-290-1660 *Toll Free Tel:* 877-500-4DES (500-4337) *Fax:* 717-509-6100
E-mail: info@destechpub.com; orders@destechpub.com
Web Site: www.destechpub.com
Key Personnel
Pres & Owner: Anthony A Deraco *Tel:* 717-290-1660 ext 101 *E-mail:* aderaco@destechpub.com
Prodn Dir: Stephen Spangler *Tel:* 717-290-1660 ext 102 *E-mail:* sspangler@destechpub.com
Art Dir: Holly High *Tel:* 717-290-1660 ext 103 *E-mail:* hhigh@destechpub.com
Acqs Dir: Susan Farmer *Tel:* 717-290-1660 ext 104 *E-mail:* sfarmer@destechpub.com
Founded: 2001
Science, technical & medical publisher; proceedings publishing.
ISBN Prefix(es): 978-1-605950
Number of titles published annually: 15 Print; 2 Online; 15 E-Book
Total Titles: 175 Print; 15 E-Book
Foreign Rep(s): Areesh Education & Trading Sdn Bhd (Malaysia); CRW Marketing Services for Publishers Inc (American Samoa, Guam, Philippines, Virgin Islands); DKG Info Systems (China, Hong Kong, Indonesia, Japan, Malaysia, Singapore, South Korea, Taiwan, Thailand); LSR Libros Servicios y Representaciones (Caribbean, Central America, Mexico, South America); Publisher's Representatives (Pakistan); Shankars Book Agency Pvt Ltd (India); Transatlantic Publishers Group Ltd (Europe, Middle East, North Africa, UK)

§Destiny Image Inc
Subsidiary of Nori Media Group
167 Walnut Bottom Rd, Shippensburg, PA 17257
SAN: 253-4339
Mailing Address: PO Box 310, Shippensburg, PA 17257
Tel: 717-532-3040 *Toll Free Tel:* 800-722-6774 (orders only) *Fax:* 717-532-9291
Web Site: www.destinyimage.com
Key Personnel
Pres & CEO: Don Nori
Founded: 1983
Publisher of Christian books.
ISBN Prefix(es): 978-0-914903; 978-1-56043; 978-0-938612; 978-0-7684
Number of titles published annually: 60 Print
Total Titles: 1,900 Print
Foreign Rep(s): Koorong (Australia)
Membership(s): American Booksellers Association (ABA); Evangelical Christian Publishers Association (ECPA)

Development Concepts Inc, see Impact Publications/Development Concepts Inc

DeVorss & Co
1100 Flynn Rd, Unit 104, Camarillo, CA 93012
SAN: 168-9886
Mailing Address: PO Box 1389, Camarillo, CA 93011-1389
Tel: 805-322-9010 *Toll Free Tel:* 800-843-5743 *Fax:* 805-322-9011
E-mail: service@devorss.com
Web Site: www.devorss.com
Key Personnel
Pres: Gary R Peattie *Tel:* 805-322-9010 ext 14 *E-mail:* gpeattie@devorss.com
Off & Cust Serv Mgr: Debbie Krovitz *E-mail:* dkrovitz@devorss.com
Buyer: Sonia Dominguez *E-mail:* sdominguez@devorss.com
Founded: 1929
Publisher of metaphysical, spiritual, inspirational, self-help, body/mind/spirit & New Thought books.
ISBN Prefix(es): 978-0-87516
Number of titles published annually: 10 Print
Total Titles: 270 Print; 85 E-Book; 4 Audio
Imprints: DeVorss Publications
Distributor for Acropolis Books (Joel S Goldsmith titles); Touch for Health; White Eagle Publishing Trust (England)
Foreign Rep(s): Brumby Books (Australia); Deep Books (UK); Dempsey Canada (Canada); New Horizons (South Africa)
Billing Address: PO Box 1389, Camarillo, CA 93011-1389
Distribution Center: Publishers Group West (PGW), 1700 Fourth St, Berkeley, CA 94710 *Tel:* 510-809-3700 *Toll Free Tel:* 866-400-5351 *Fax:* 510-809-3777 *E-mail:* info@pgw.com *Web Site:* www.pgw.com SAN: 202-8522

§Dewey Publications Inc
1840 Wilson Blvd, Suite 203, Arlington, VA 22201
SAN: 694-1451
Tel: 703-524-1355
Web Site: deweypub.com
Founded: 1984
ISBN Prefix(es): 978-1-878810; 978-1-932612
Number of titles published annually: 9 Print; 4 CD-ROM; 4 E-Book

Dharma Publishing
35788 Hauser Bridge Rd, Cazadero, CA 95421
SAN: 201-2723
Tel: 707-847-3717 *Fax:* 707-847-3380
E-mail: contact@dharmapublishing.com
Web Site: www.dharmapublishing.com
Key Personnel
Dir: Arnaud Maitland
Sales Dir: Rima Tamar *Tel:* 707-847-3717 ext 210 *E-mail:* rimat@dharmapublishing.com
Founded: 1975
Asian art, Eastern philosophy & psychology, Tibetan meditation & yoga, scholarly, history, biography, cosmology, juveniles, Asian culture.
ISBN Prefix(es): 978-0-913546; 978-0-89800
Number of titles published annually: 10 Print; 6 E-Book; 36 Audio
Total Titles: 120 Print; 12 E-Book; 48 Audio
Sales Office(s): 2210 Harold Way, Berkeley, CA 94704 *Tel:* 510-809-1540
Foreign Rep(s): Ka-Nying (India, Nepal); Nyingma Centrum Nederland (Netherlands); Nyingma Do Brazil (Brazil); Nyingma Gemeinschaft (Germany); Windhorse (Australia); Wisdom Publications (UK)
Membership(s): Association of American Publishers (AAP)

Dial Books for Young Readers
Imprint of Penguin Young Readers Group
c/o Penguin Random House LLC, 1745 Broadway, New York, NY 10019
Tel: 212-782-9000
Web Site: www.penguin.com/dial-overview/
Key Personnel
Pres & Publr, Dial Books for Young Readers & GP Putnam's Sons Books for Young Readers: Jennifer Klonsky
SVP & Exec Art Dir, Dial Books for Young Readers, Nancy Paulsen Books, GP Putnam's Sons Books for Young Readers & Rocky Pond Books: Lily Malcom
Sr Exec Ed: Kate Harrison
Exec Ed: Jessica Dandino Garrison
Sr Ed: Ellen Cormier
Ed: Rosie Ahmed
Assoc Ed: Michelle Lee
Edit Asst: Zora Squish Pruitt
Art Dir, Dial Books for Young Readers & Rocky Pond Books: Jenny Kelly
Assoc Art Dir, Dial Books for Young Readers & Rocky Pond Books: Jason Henry
Founded: 1961

U.S. PUBLISHERS

Penguin Random House & its publishing entities are not accepting unsol submissions, proposals, mss, or submission queries via e-mail at this time.
Number of titles published annually: 70 Print
Total Titles: 383 Print

DiscoverNet Publishing
Division of DiscoverNet
1000 N Main St, Suite 102, Fuquay Varina, NC 27526
Tel: 919-301-0109 *Fax:* 919-557-2261
E-mail: info@discovernet.com
Web Site: www.discovernet.com
Founded: 2002
ISBN Prefix(es): 978-0-9728053; 978-0-9742787; 978-0-9746943; 978-1-932813
Number of titles published annually: 50 Print; 45 Online; 28 E-Book
Total Titles: 162 Print; 130 Online; 130 E-Book
Imprints: Althos; DiscoverNet; LearnQIC

Disney-Hyperion Books
Imprint of Disney Book Group
1101 Flower St, Glendale, CA 91201
Web Site: books.disney.com/imprint/disney-hyperion
Key Personnel
Art Dir: Marci Senders
Art Dir, Hyperion Avenue: Amy King
Creative Dir: Joann Hill
Edit Dir: Jennifer Levesque
Exec Ed: Sylvie Frank
Exec Ed, Hyperion Avenue: Adam Wilson
Mng Ed: Sara Liebling
Sr Ed: Brittany Rubiano; Kieran Viola
Sr Ed, Rick Riordan Presents: Rebecca Kuss
Ebook Ed & Publg Coord: Liz Usuriello
Assoc Ed: Kelsey Sullivan; Regan Winter
Founded: 1991
Publish high quality picture books, young adult fiction & nonfiction.
ISBN Prefix(es): 978-0-7868
Number of titles published annually: 250 Print
Total Titles: 2,200 Print
Imprints: Michael di Capua Books; Hyperion Avenue; Jump at the Sun; Rick Riordan Presents; Volo
Foreign Rep(s): Little, Brown Canada Ltd; Little, Brown International
Foreign Rights: ACER Agencia Literaria (Spain); Big Apple Agency Inc (China); BMSR Agencia Literaria (Brazil); English Agency Japan Co Ltd (Japan); Harris/Elon Agency (Israel); The Italian Literary Agency Srl (Italy); Jacqueline Miller (France); Sebes & Bisseling Literary Agency (Netherlands)
Membership(s): The Children's Book Council (CBC)
See separate listing for:
Jump at the Sun

Disney Press
Imprint of Disney Publishing Worldwide
1101 Flower St, Glendale, CA 91201
Web Site: books.disney.com
Key Personnel
VP & Global Publr, Franchise Content & Creative: Lynn Waggoner
Founded: 1990
Publish fiction & fantasy.
ISBN Prefix(es): 978-1-56282; 978-0-7868
Number of titles published annually: 55 Print
Total Titles: 1,000 Print
Foreign Rep(s): Little, Brown Canada Ltd; Little, Brown International
Foreign Rights: ACER Agencia Literaria (Spain); Big Apple Agency Inc (China); BMSR Agencia Literaria (Brazil); English Agency Japan Co Ltd (Japan); Harris/Elon Agency (Israel); A M Heath & Co Ltd (England); Monica Heyum Agency (Denmark, Finland, Iceland, Norway,

U.S. PUBLISHERS

Sweden); The Italian Literary Agency Srl (Italy); Agence Michelle Lapautre (France); Sebes & Bisseling Literary Agency (Netherlands)
Warehouse: 53 State St, Boston, MA 02109

Disney Publishing Worldwide
Subsidiary of The Walt Disney Co
1101 Flower St, Glendale, CA 91201
Web Site: books.disney.com
Key Personnel
SVP & Publr: Tonya Agurto
VP & Global Publr, Franchise Content & Creative: Lynn Waggoner
Publr, Freedom Fire: Kwame Mbalia
Edit Dir: Jennifer Levesque
Exec Ed, Disney Lucasfilm Press: Jennifer Heddle
Ed-in-Chief, Andscape: Raina Kelley
Founded: 1930
Publisher of children's books, comics & magazines.
ISBN Prefix(es): 978-1-56115
Number of titles published annually: 275 Print
Total Titles: 1,000 Print
Imprints: Andscape Books; Disney Editions; Disney-Hyperion; Disney Lucasfilm Press; Disney Press; Freedom Fire; Freeform; Hyperion Books for Children; Jump at the Sun; Kingswell; Marvel
Divisions: Disney Children's Book Group
Branch Office(s)
500 S Buena Vista St, Burbank, CA 91521
Tel: 914-288-4100
Foreign Rights: Sebes & Bisseling Literary Agency (Netherlands)
Distribution Center: Penguin Random House Publisher Services (worldwide)
See separate listing for:
Disney Press

Dissertation.com
Imprint of Universal-Publishers Inc
200 Spectrum Center Dr, 3rd fl, Irvine, CA 92618
SAN: 299-3635
Tel: 561-750-4344 *Toll Free Tel:* 800-636-8329
Fax: 561-750-6797
Web Site: www.dissertation.com
Key Personnel
Publr & CEO: Dr Jeffrey Young
Artistic & Edit Dir: Shereen Siddiqui
Founded: 1997
Academic books.
This publisher has indicated that 50% of their product line is author subsidized.
ISBN Prefix(es): 978-1-58112; 978-0-9658564; 978-1-59942; 978-1-61233; 978-1-62734
Number of titles published annually: 50 Print; 50 Online; 50 E-Book
Total Titles: 500 Print; 300 Online; 500 E-Book

Diversion Books
Division of Diversion Publishing Corp
11 E 44 St, Suite 1603, New York, NY 10017
SAN: 990-6304
Tel: 212-961-6390
E-mail: info@diversionbooks.com
Web Site: www.diversionbooks.com
Key Personnel
Co-Founder & CEO: Scott Waxman
Exec Ed & Ed-in-Chief: Keith Wallman
Sr Ed, Fiction: Tonia Kirkpatrick
Acqs Ed: Elizabeth Gassman
Mktg Mgr: Shannon Donnelly
Asst Mktg Mgr: Alex Sprague
Opers Mgr: Sue Mercer
Publg Coord: Evan Phail
Publg Asst: Clara Linhoff
Founded: 2010
An innovative indie publisher, combining decades of traditional experience with new, digital strategies. In publishing a mix of original titles & giving old titles a digital life, our high royalties, quick turnaround & tailored marketing plans are helping us to create a space between legacy publishing & the uneven field of self-publishing. We are taking advantage of the abundance of opportunities that new models of distribution & purchasing provide, while executing our core publishing capabilities, ultimately connecting great books with avid readers.
ISBN Prefix(es): 978-0-9845151; 978-0-9829050; 978-0-9838395; 978-0-9839885; 978-0-9833371; 978-1-938120
Number of titles published annually: 50 Print; 350 E-Book
Total Titles: 500 Print; 1,300 E-Book
Distributor for Zubaan Books
Foreign Rights: Waxman Literary Agency (Ashley Lopez) (worldwide)
Distribution Center: Ingram Publisher Services, 14 Ingram Blvd, Mail Stop 631, La Vergne, TN 37086 *Toll Free Tel:* 866-400-5351 (orders)
Web Site: www.ingrampublisherservices.com
Membership(s): Association of American Publishers (AAP); Independent Book Publishers Association (IBPA); International Thriller Writers Inc (ITW); Media Women's Association (MWA)

DK
Division of Penguin Random House LLC
c/o Penguin Random House LLC, 1745 Broadway, 20th fl, New York, NY 10019
Tel: 646-674-4000 *Toll Free Tel:* 800-733-3000
Fax: 646-674-4020
E-mail: marketing@dk.com (lib servs); publicity@dk.com; csorders@penguinrandomhouse.com; customerservice@penguinrandomhouse.com
Web Site: www.dk.com
Key Personnel
CEO: Paul Kelly
SVP & Publr (IN off): Mike Sanders
VP & Dir, Natl Accts, Penguin Publishing Group & DK: Chrissy Helaine
VP, Commercial Fin & Opers, North America: Scott Grande
VP, Mktg & Publicity: Gayley Avery
VP, Sales: Carol Stokke
Sr Dir, Opers: Sheila Phelan
Dir, Custom Publg: Meghan O'Brien Marton
Dir, Field Sales: Emily Bruce
Dir, Publicity: Jennifer Brunn
Dir, Publg Opers: Billy Fields
Asst Dir, Educ & Lib Mktg: Kristin Pozzuoli
Sr Mgr, Digital Strategy: Leila Siddiqui
Brand Mgr: Katie Schloss
Sales Mgr: Shawn Sarles
Mktg Mgr, Children's: Michael Ploetz
Publicity Mgr: Kristen Fisher
Founded: 1974 (in UK)
Illustrated reference books on a wide range of topics for adults & children, including travel, health, history, sports, pets, atlases, dictionaries, music, art, decorating, astrology, sex & cooking.
Penguin Random House & its publishing entities are not accepting unsol submissions, proposals, mss, or submission queries via e-mail at this time.
Number of titles published annually: 392 Print
Total Titles: 1,850 Print
Imprints: Dorling Kindersley
Branch Office(s)
800 E 96 St, Indianapolis, IN 46240 *Tel:* 317-728-3000
Foreign Rep(s): Dorling Kindersley Ltd (UK)
Membership(s): American Booksellers Association (ABA); The American Library Association (ALA); The Children's Book Council (CBC); International Association of Culinary Professionals (IACP); International Literacy Association (ILA); National Council of Teachers of English (NCTE); National Science Teachers Association (NSTA)

Caitlyn Dlouhy Books, see Simon & Schuster Children's Publishing

§Dogwise Publishing
Division of Direct Book Service Inc
403 S Mission St, Wenatchee, WA 98801
SAN: 132-9545
Tel: 509-663-9115 *Toll Free Tel:* 800-776-2665
E-mail: mail@dogwise.com
Web Site: www.dogwise.com
Key Personnel
Owner & Publr: Charlene Woodward
Owner: Larry Woodward
Founded: 2002
Publish how-to books on dog care, training, behavior, health & competition.
ISBN Prefix(es): 978-1-929242; 978-1-61781
Number of titles published annually: 10 Print
Total Titles: 90 Print; 260 E-Book
Membership(s): Book Publishers of the Northwest (BPNW); Independent Book Publishers Association (IBPA)

The Donning Company Publishers
Subsidiary of Walsworth
731 S Brunswick St, Brookfield, MO 64628
Toll Free Tel: 800-369-2646 (ext 3377)
Web Site: www.donning.com
Key Personnel
Gen Mgr: Lex Cavanah
Ed: Anne Burns
Prodn Supv: Nathan Stufflebean *E-mail:* nathan.stufflebean@donning.com
Founded: 1974
Specialty book publisher of limited-edition commemorative volumes, pictorial histories & contemporary portraits.
ISBN Prefix(es): 978-0-915442; 978-0-89865
Number of titles published annually: 80 Print
Imprints: Portraits of America
Foreign Rights: Writers House Inc

§Doodle and Peck Publishing
413 Cedarburg Ct, Yukon, OK 73099
Tel: 405-354-7422
E-mail: mjones@doodleandpeck.com
Web Site: www.doodleandpeck.com
Key Personnel
Publr & Sr Ed: Marla F Jones
  E-mail: iluvrocksmj@yahoo.com
Founded: 2015
Creates family-friendly books with oodles of "read-aloud-ability." Most books for young children have a literacy component for parents & caregivers to use. Also operates Marla Jones Book Design (partnership publishing arrangement in which the author pays initial production costs; imprint carries out all the same marketing, distribution & PR that the parent company does with a traditional publishing contract).
ISBN Prefix(es): 978-0-9966205; 978-0-9972351
Number of titles published annually: 7 Print; 5 E-Book
Total Titles: 60 Print; 35 E-Book
Imprints: Marla Jones, Book Design (hybrid publg prog)
Distribution Center: D&P Books
  E-mail: doodleandpeck@gmail.com
Brodart Books & Library Services (US)
Ingram (US)
Membership(s): Independent Book Publishers Association (IBPA); Society of Children's Book Writers & Illustrators (SCBWI)

Dordt Press
Affiliate of Dordt University

700 Seventh St NE, Sioux Center, IA 51250-1671
Tel: 712-722-6420 *Toll Free Tel:* 800-343-6738
 Fax: 712-722-6035
 E-mail: dordtpress@dordt.edu; bookstore@dordt.edu
Web Site: www.dordt.edu/about-dordt/publications/dordt-press-catalog
Key Personnel
Mng Ed: John H Kok *Tel:* 712-722-2254
 E-mail: jkok@dordt.edu
Founded: 1978
Publishes primarily academic books & monographs, plus a quarterly journal.
ISBN Prefix(es): 978-0-932914; 978-1-940567
Number of titles published annually: 6 Print
Total Titles: 75 Print; 1 E-Book

Dorrance Publishing Co Inc
585 Alpha Dr, Suite 103, Pittsburgh, PA 15238
Toll Free Tel: 800-695-9599; 800-788-7654 (gen cust orders) *Fax:* 412-387-1319
E-mail: dorrinfo@dorrancepublishing.com
Web Site: www.dorrancepublishing.com
Key Personnel
Pres: David Zeolla
Founded: 1920
Full service author services company.
This publisher has indicated that 100% of their product line is author subsidized.
ISBN Prefix(es): 978-0-8059; 978-1-4349; 978-1-4809; 978-1-64426; 978-1-64530; 978-1-64610
Number of titles published annually: 1,000 Print; 1,000 Online; 1,000 E-Book; 10 Audio
Total Titles: 6,000 Print; 6,000 Online; 4,000 E-Book; 5 Audio
Imprints: RoseDog Books

§Doubleday
Imprint of Knopf Doubleday Publishing Group
c/o Penguin Random House LLC, 1745 Broadway, New York, NY 10019
Tel: 212-751-2600 *Fax:* 212-940-7390 (dom rts); 212-572-2662 (foreign rts)
Web Site: knopfdoubleday.com/imprint/doubleday/; knopfdoubleday.com
Key Personnel
EVP, Publr & Ed-in-Chief: William Thomas
VP & Exec Dir, Sales Mgmt & Planning: Beth Meister
VP & Exec Dir, Strategic Insights: Laura Crisp
VP & Sr Dir, Strategy & Fin: May Choy
VP & Exec Ed: Edward Kastenmeier
VP & Dir, Creative Mktg & Ad Servs: Judy Jacoby
VP & Edit Dir, Nonfiction: Kristine Puopolo
VP & Exec Ed: Lee Boudreaux; Thomas Gebremedhin; Jason Kaufman
Sr Art Dir: Emily Mahon
Sr Dir, Mktg: Milena Brown
Sr Dir, Publicity: Michael Goldsmith
Creative Dir: Oliver Munday
Dir, Ebook Prodn: Austin O'Malley
Dir, Publicity: Elena Hershey
Mktg Dir: Jess Deitcher
Asst Dir, Foreign & Subs Rts: Sal Ruggiero
Asst Dir, Publicity: Julie Ertl
Sr Ad Mgr: Nic Ishaq
Sr Mgr: Lindsay Mandel
Sr Mktg Mgr: Anne Jaconette
Sr Publicity Mgr: Tricia Cave
Publicist: Sara Hayet
Assoc Publicist: Jillian Briglia; Emma Joss; Mark Lee
Lead Mng Ed: Vimi Santokhi
Sr Ed: Jennifer Jackson
Ed: Cara Reilly; Carolyn Williams
Assoc Ed: Khari Dawkins; Dan Meyer
Asst Ed: Ana Espinoza; Nora Grubb; Chris Howard-Woods; Maya Pasic; Johanna Zwirner
Sr Mgr: Zachary Lutz; Marisa Melendez
Sr Mktg Mgr, Audience Devt: Daniela Ayuso
Backlist Mgr: Erin Merlo
Busn Mgr: Andrew Unger

Mktg Mgr: Matthew Sciarappa
Mktg Mgr, Consumer Insights: Hannah Engler
Sr Designer: Anna Knighton
Mktg Assoc: Morgan Fenton
Founded: 1897
Penguin Random House & its publishing entities are not accepting unsol submissions, proposals, mss or submission queries via e-mail at this time.
Foreign Rights: ALS-Agenzia Letteraria Santachiara (Roberto Santachiara) (Italy); Anthea Agency (Katalina Sabeva) (Bulgaria); Bardon-Chinese Media Agency (Xu-Weiguang) (China); Bardon-Chinese Media Agency (Yu-Shiuan Chen) (Taiwan); English Agency Japan Co Ltd (Junzo Sawa) (Japan); Graal Literary Agency (Maria Strarz-Zielinska) (Poland); The Deborah Harris Agency (Ilana Kurshan) (Israel); JLM Literary Agency (Nelly Moukakos) (Greece); Katai & Bolza Literary (Peter Bolza) (Croatia, Hungary); Simona Kessler International (Simona Kessler) (Romania); Korea Copyright Center Inc (KCC) (MiSook Hong) (South Korea); Licht & Burr Literary Agency (Trine Licht) (Scandinavia); La Nouvelle Agence (Vanessa Kling) (France); Kristin Olson Literary Agency (Kristin Olson) (Czechia); Sebes & Bisseling Literary Agency (Paul Sebes) (Netherlands)

§Dover Publications Inc
Subsidiary of Lakeside Book Co
1325 Franklin Ave, Suite 250, Garden City, NY 11530
Tel: 516-294-7000 *Toll Free Tel:* 800-223-3130 (orders) *Fax:* 516-742-6953
E-mail: rights@doverpublications.com
Web Site: store.doverpublications.com; store.doverdirect.com
Key Personnel
Inside Sales Specialist: Stephanie Fidis
Founded: 1941
Trade adult & children's, crafts, art, music; higher education.
ISBN Prefix(es): 978-0-486; 978-1-60660; 978-0-88660; 978-1-306
Number of titles published annually: 600 Print; 400 E-Book
Total Titles: 10,000 Print; 36 CD-ROM; 6,500 E-Book; 22 Audio
Foreign Rep(s): Bill Baily Group (Eastern Europe); HarperCollins India (Indian subcontinent); International Publishers Representatives (Mideast); JCC Enterprises Inc (Caribbean, Central America, Mexico); Peribo (Australia); Publishers International Marketing (Asia exc Japan)
Foreign Rights: Biagi Literary Management (worldwide exc North America)
Membership(s): American Booksellers Association (ABA)

Down East Books
Imprint of The Globe Pequot Press
4501 Forbes Blvd, Suite 200, Lanham, MD 20706
Web Site: rowman.com/page/downeastbooks
Key Personnel
Edit Dir: Michael Steere *E-mail:* msteere@rowman.com
Founded: 1954
Publisher of Maine- & New England-themed books.
ISBN Prefix(es): 978-0-924357; 978-0-89272
Number of titles published annually: 30 Print; 30 E-Book; 3 Audio
Total Titles: 450 Print; 250 E-Book; 12 Audio
Editorial Office(s): PO Box 358, Lincolnville, ME 04849
Sales Office(s): National Book Network, 15200 NBN Way, Bldg C, Blue Ridge Summit, PA 17214 *Toll Free Tel:* 800-462-6420 ext 3024

Distribution Center: National Book Network, 15200 NBN Way, Bldg C, Blue Ridge Summit, PA 17214, VP, Opers: Mike Cornell *Tel:* 717-794-3800 *Toll Free Tel:* 800-462-6420 ext 3024 *Fax:* 717-794-3803 *Toll Free Fax:* 800-338-4550 *E-mail:* mcornell@nbnbooks.com

Down The Shore Publishing
Unit of Down The Shore Books LLC
106 Forge Rd, West Creek, NJ 08092
SAN: 661-082X
Mailing Address: PO Box 100, West Creek, NJ 08092
Tel: 609-812-5076 *Fax:* 609-812-5098
E-mail: downshore@gmail.com
Web Site: www.down-the-shore.com
Key Personnel
Founder & Pres: Raymond G Fisk
Founded: 1984
Regional books, history; calendars; videos; note cards.
ISBN Prefix(es): 978-0-9615208; 978-0-945582; 978-1-59322
Number of titles published annually: 6 Print
Total Titles: 95 Print
Imprints: Bufflehead Books; Cormorant Books; Cormorant Calendars; Terrapin Greetings
Billing Address: Down The Shore Books LLC, PO Box 100, West Creek, NJ 08092
Membership(s): Independent Book Publishers Association (IBPA)

§Dragon Door Publications
2999 Yorkton Blvd, Suite 2, Little Canada, MN 55117
Tel: 651-487-2180
E-mail: support@dragondoor.com
Web Site: www.dragondoor.com
Key Personnel
Publr & Ed-in-Chief: John Du Cane
ISBN Prefix(es): 978-0-938045
Number of titles published annually: 5 Print
Total Titles: 115 Print; 35 E-Book

Dramatic Publishing Co
311 Washington St, Woodstock, IL 60098-3308
SAN: 201-5676
Tel: 815-338-7170 *Toll Free Tel:* 800-448-7469 *Fax:* 815-338-8981 *Toll Free Fax:* 800-334-5302
E-mail: customerservice@dpcplays.com
Web Site: www.dramaticpublishing.com
Key Personnel
Pres: Christopher Sergel, III
SVP: Susan Sergel
VP: Gayle Sergel
Founded: 1885
Acting editions of plays & musicals & licensing productions of same.
ISBN Prefix(es): 978-0-87129; 978-1-58342; 978-1-61959
Number of titles published annually: 55 Print
Total Titles: 2,000 Print
Foreign Rep(s): DALRO Pty Ltd (Southern Africa); Origin Theatrical Pty Ltd (Australia); The Play Bureau NZ Ltd (New Zealand)

Dramatists Play Service Inc
Imprint of Broadway Licensing
440 Park Ave S, New York, NY 10016
E-mail: dpsinfo@broadwaylicensing.com; publications@broadwaylicensing.com
Web Site: www.dramatists.com
Key Personnel
CEO: Sean Cercone
SVP, Acqs & Artistic Servs: Kent Nicholson
Sr Mgr, Pubns: Leah Barker
Founded: 1936
Publisher & licensor of plays & musicals. Partner of Dramatists Guild of America Inc.
ISBN Prefix(es): 978-0-8222
Number of titles published annually: 60 Print

Total Titles: 4,000 Print
Foreign Rights: DALRO (South Africa); Hal Leonard Australia Pty Ltd (Australia, New Zealand); Josef Weinberger (UK)

Dreamscape Media LLC
Division of RBmedia
1417 Timberwolf Dr, Holland, OH 43528
Tel: 419-867-6965 *Toll Free Tel:* 877-983-7326
E-mail: info@dreamscapeab.com
Web Site: www.dreamscapepublishing.com
Key Personnel
Pres: Sean McManus
Publr: Levine Querido
Acqs Dir: Kerri Buckley
Art Dir: Karen Swenar
Dir, Prodn: Erick Black
Dir, Strategic Partnerships: Lorna Henry
Audiobook Acqs Ed: Michael Olah
  E-mail: molah@dreamscapeab.com
Edit Assoc: Emily Solomon
Sr Audio Engr: Michael Jones
Prodn Mgr: Ben Coy
Sr Staff Accountant: Raj Mavi
Sr Designer: Neil Harrington
Designer: Jessica Lakatos
Content Mktg Specialist: Anna Goolsby
Mktg Specialist: Lauren Smetzer; Megan Smith
Founded: 2010
Audio & video media publisher.
ISBN Prefix(es): 978-0-9745563; 978-0-9747118; 978-0-9760996; 978-0-9761981; 978-0-9771510; 978-0-9772338; 978-0-9774680; 978-0-9776262; 978-0-9777098; 978-1-933938; 978-1-61120; 978-1-62406; 978-1-62923; 978-1-63379
Number of titles published annually: 50 E-Book; 250 Audio
Total Titles: 600 E-Book; 1,500 Audio
Editorial Office(s): 150 N Wacker Dr, Suite 2250, Chicago, IL 60606
Distributed by Blackstone Publishing
Distributor for Berrett-Koehler Publishers; Gildan Media; Hallmark Publishing; HarperCollins; Ideal Audiobooks; Mayo Clinic Press; Penguin Random House LLC; Radio Archives
Foreign Rep(s): CVS Midwest Tape (Canada)
Membership(s): Audio Publishers Association

Duke University Press
905 W Main St, Suite 18B, Durham, NC 27701
SAN: 201-3436
Mailing Address: PO Box 90660, Durham, NC 27708-0660
Tel: 919-688-5134 *Toll Free Tel:* 888-651-0122 (US) *Fax:* 919-688-2615 *Toll Free Fax:* 888-651-0124
E-mail: orders@dukepress.edu
Web Site: www.dukeupress.edu
Key Personnel
Dir: Dean Smith
Dir, Digital Strategy & Systems: Allison Belan
  E-mail: allison.belan@dukeupress.edu
Dir, Editing, Design & Prodn: Nancy Hoagland
Dir, Edit, Design & Prodn: Amy Ruth Buchanan
Dir, Mktg & Sales: Cason Lynley
Edit Dir: Gisela Fosado *E-mail:* gisela.fosado@dukeupress.edu
Journals Dir: Rob Dilworth
  E-mail: journalsdirector@dukeupress.edu
Sr Exec Ed: Ken Wissoker *E-mail:* kwiss@duke.edu
Exec Ed: Courtney Berger *E-mail:* cberger@dukeupress.edu
Sr Ed, Journals: Erich Staib *E-mail:* erich.staib@dukeupress.edu
Ed: Elizabeth Ault *E-mail:* elizabeth.ault@dukeupress.edu
Assoc Ed: Miriam Angress *E-mail:* miriam.angress@dukeupress.edu
Asst Ed: Sandra Korn *E-mail:* sandra.korn@dukeupress.edu; Joshua Gutterman Tranen *E-mail:* joshua.tranen@dukeupress.edu

Sales Mgr: Jennifer Schaper *E-mail:* jennifer.schaper@dukeupress.edu
Founded: 1921
Scholarly, trade & textbooks.
ISBN Prefix(es): 978-0-8223
Number of titles published annually: 120 Print
Total Titles: 1,300 Print
Distributor for Forest History Society
Foreign Rep(s): Academic Marketing Services (Pty) Ltd (Mike Brightmore) (Southern Africa); AfricaConnection.co.uk (Guy Simpson) (Africa exc South Africa); Avicenna Partnership Ltd (Bill Kennedy) (Bahrain, Egypt, Iran, Iraq, Kuwait, Lebanon, Oman, Qatar, Saudi Arabia, Syria, United Arab Emirates, Yemen); Avicenna Partnership Ltd (Claire de Gruchy) (Algeria, Israel, Jordan, Malta, Morocco, Tunisia, Turkey); China Publishers Marketing (Benjamin Pan) (China, Hong Kong, Taiwan); CoInfo Ltd (Debra Triplett) (Australia, Fiji, New Zealand, Papua New Guinea); Leonidas Diamantopoulos (Cyprus, Greece); Charles Gibbs (Cyprus, Greece); Ben Greig (Denmark, Iceland, Southern Sweden); Steven Haslemere (Sweden); Wilf Jones (Finland, Norway); Jacek Lewinson (Eastern Europe, Russia); Lexa Publishers' Representatives (Mical Moser) (Canada); Mare Nostrum (Lauren Keane) (Belgium, France, Luxembourg, Netherlands); Mare Nostrum (Frauke Feldmann) (Austria, Germany, Switzerland); Mare Nostrum (Francesca Pollard) (Italy); Publishers International Marketing (Chris Ashdown) (Brunei, Cambodia, Indonesia, Japan, Laos, Malaysia, Philippines, Singapore, South Korea, Thailand, Timor-Leste, Vietnam); Quantum Publishing Solutions Ltd (James Wickham) (UK); Cristina De Lara Ruiz (Portugal, Spain); Viva Books Pvt Ltd (Bangladesh, Bhutan, India, Maldives, Nepal, Sri Lanka); World Press (Saleem A Malik) (Pakistan)
Returns: 120 Golden Dr, Durham, NC 27705
Distribution Center: Combined Academic Publishers (CAP), 39 E Parade, Harrogate, N Yorks HG1 5LQ, United Kingdom (Africa, Asia, Europe, Middle East, Pacific & UK)
Tel: (01423) 526350 *E-mail:* enquiries@combinedacademic.co.uk *Web Site:* www.combinedacademic.co.uk

Dumbarton Oaks
1703 32 St NW, Washington, DC 20007
Tel: 202-339-6400 *Fax:* 202-339-6401; 202-298-8407
E-mail: doaksbooks@doaks.org; press@doaks.org
Web Site: www.doaks.org
Key Personnel
Dir, Pubns: Kathy Sparkes
Mng Ed, Art & Archaeology: Sara Taylor
ISBN Prefix(es): 978-0-88402
Number of titles published annually: 8 Print
Total Titles: 260 Print
Distributed by Harvard University Press

§Dun & Bradstreet
103 JFK Pkwy, Short Hills, NJ 07078
Tel: 973-921-5500 *Toll Free Tel:* 844-869-8244; 800-234-3867 (cust serv)
Web Site: www.dnb.com
Key Personnel
CEO: Anthony Jabbour
Pres: Stephen C Daffron
CFO: Richard H Veldran
Chief Content & Technol Offr: Curtis Brown
Chief Data Offr: Gary Kotovets
Chief People Offr: Roslynn Williams
Business & business reference; US & international coverage, country information.
ISBN Prefix(es): 978-1-56203
Total Titles: 31 Print; 20 CD-ROM
Subsidiaries: Hoover's Inc
See separate listing for:
D&B Hoovers™

§Dutton
Imprint of Penguin Publishing Group
c/o Penguin Random House LLC, 1745 Broadway, New York, NY 10019
Tel: 212-366-2000
Web Site: www.penguin.com/dutton-overview/; www.penguin.com/plume-books-overview/; www.penguin.com/tiny-reparations-overview/
Key Personnel
Pres, Putnam/Dutton/Berkley: Ivan Held
Founder, Tiny Reparations Books: Phoebe Robinson
SVP & Exec Creative Dir, Putnam/Dutton/Berkley: Anthony Ramondo
VP & Publr: John Parsley
VP & Edit Dir: Maya Ziv
Exec Dir, Ad & Promo: Jaime Mendola-Hobbie
Exec Dir, Publicity: Amanda Walker
Edit Dir, Dutton & Plume: Jill Schwartzman
Dir, Mktg: Stephanie Cooper
Assoc Dir, Publicity, Dutton & Dir, Publicity, Plume & Tiny Reparations Books: Jamie Knapp
Asst Dir, Publicity: Emily Brock Canders
Exec Ed: Emi Ikkanda; Lindsey Rose
Sr Ed: Pilar Garcia-Brown
Ed: Rachael Kelly; Cassidy Sachs
Ed, Tiny Reparations Books: Lashanda Anakwah
Assoc Ed: David Howe; Grace Layer; Katie Zaborsky
Edit Asst: Hannah Feeney; Ella Kurki; Charlotte Peters
Sr Mgr, Subs Rts, Dutton & TarcherPerigee: Jillian Fata
Sr Mktg Mgr: Isabel DaSilva
Mktg Mgr, Dutton/Plume: Caroline Payne
Mktg Mgr, Dutton/Putnam: Katie Parry
Soc Media Mgr: Erika Semprun
Publicity Mgr: Sarah Thegeby
Sr Publicist: Lauren Morrow
Publicist: Becky Odell
Assoc Publicist, Dutton/Plume: Hannah Poole
Founded: 1864
Penguin Random House & its publishing entities are not accepting unsol submissions, proposals, mss, or submission queries via e-mail at this time.
Number of titles published annually: 50 Print
Total Titles: 130 Print
Imprints: Plume; Tiny Reparations Books

Dutton Children's Books
Imprint of Penguin Young Readers Group
c/o Penguin Random House LLC, 1745 Broadway, New York, NY 10019
Tel: 212-782-9000
Web Site: www.penguin.com/dutton-childrens-overview/
Key Personnel
Pres & Publr: Julie Strauss-Gabel
Exec Ed: Andrew Karre
Founded: 1852 (as Dutton)
Penguin Random House & its publishing entities are not accepting unsol submissions, proposals, mss, or submission queries via e-mail at this time.
Number of titles published annually: 15 Print
Total Titles: 355 Print

Eakin Press
Imprint of Wild Horse Media Group
PO Box 331779, Fort Worth, TX 76163
Tel: 817-344-7036 *Toll Free Tel:* 888-982-8270
Fax: 817-344-7036
Web Site: www.eakinpress.com
Key Personnel
CEO: Billy Huckaby
Founded: 1979
ISBN Prefix(es): 978-0-89015; 978-1-57168
Number of titles published annually: 25 Print

Total Titles: 1,000 Print; 220 E-Book; 1 Audio
Membership(s): Independent Publishers Association

East West Discovery Press
PO Box 3585, Manhattan Beach, CA 90266
Tel: 310-545-3730 *Fax:* 310-545-3731
E-mail: info@eastwestdiscovery.com
Web Site: www.eastwestdiscovery.com
Key Personnel
Publr & Ed: Icy Smith
Dir: Michael Smith
Founded: 2000
Independent publisher & distributor of multicultural & bilingual books in 50+ languages.
ISBN Prefix(es): 978-0-9701654; 978-0-9669437; 978-0-9799339; 978-0-9821675; 978-0-9856237; 978-0-9913454; 978-0-9832278; 978-0-9973947; 978-1-949567
Number of titles published annually: 3 Print
Total Titles: 72 Print
Membership(s): APALA; The Children's Book Council (CBC); Independent Book Publishers Association (IBPA)

Eastland Press
2421 29 Ave W, Seattle, WA 98199
Mailing Address: PO Box 99749, Seattle, WA 98139
Tel: 206-931-6957 (cust serv) *Fax:* 206-283-7084 (orders)
E-mail: info@eastlandpress.com; orders@eastlandpress.com
Web Site: www.eastlandpress.com
Key Personnel
Mng Ed: John O'Connor
Med Ed: Dan Bensky
Art Dir/Prodn Mgr: Patricia O'Connor
Founded: 1981
Chinese medicine, osteopathic & manual medicine, yoga.
ISBN Prefix(es): 978-0-939616
Number of titles published annually: 4 Print; 5 E-Book
Total Titles: 65 Print; 40 E-Book
Distributor for Journal of Chinese Medicine Publications
Warehouse: PSSC, 660 S Mansfield St, Ypsilanti, MI 48197
Membership(s): Publishers Association of the West (PubWest)

§Easy Money Press
Subsidiary of Wolford & Associates
82-5800 Napo'opo'o Rd, Captain Cook, HI 96704
Tel: 808-313-2808
E-mail: easymoneypress@yahoo.com
Key Personnel
Creative Dir: Henry Wolford *E-mail:* hcwolford@yahoo.com
Mktg Dir: Sheri Kephart
Prodn Dir: P J Max
Founded: 1996
ISBN Prefix(es): 978-0-9654563; 978-1-929714
Number of titles published annually: 1 Print; 2 E-Book
Total Titles: 12 Print; 20 E-Book
Imprints: Big Tree Books; EMP; Haase House

ECS, see The Electrochemical Society (ECS)

ECS Publishing Group
1727 Larkin Williams Rd, Fenton, MO 63026
Tel: 636-305-0100 *Toll Free Tel:* 800-647-2117
Web Site: ecspublishing.com; www.facebook.com/ecspublishing
Key Personnel
Pres: Mark Lawson
Dir, Mktg & Communs: Jessica Burcher
E-mail: jburcher@morningstarmusic.com
Founded: 2014 (first imprint was E C Shirmer, dating back to 1921)
Music publishing (sheet music).
ISBN Prefix(es): 978-0-911318 (E C Schirmer)
Number of titles published annually: 125 Print
Total Titles: 10,200 Print
Imprints: ARSIS Audio; Aureole Editions; Galaxy Music Corp; Highgate Press; Ione Press; MorningStar Music Publishers; E C Schirmer Music Co
Distributor for Randol Bass Music; Colla Voce; Consort Press; Edition Delrieu; Layali Music Publishing; Prime Music; Stainer & Bell Ltd; Vireo Press
Orders to: Canticle Distributing, 1727 Larkin Williams Rd, Fenton, MO 63026-2024
Tel: 636-305-0100 *Toll Free Tel:* 800-647-2117 (US & CN only) *E-mail:* customerservice@canticledistributing.com
Distribution Center: Canticle Distributing, 1727 Larkin Williams Rd, Fenton, MO 63026-2024
Tel: 636-305-0100 *Toll Free Tel:* 800-647-2117 (US & CN only) *E-mail:* customerservice@canticledistributing.com
Membership(s): Music Publishers Association (MPA); National Music Publishers' Association (NMPA)

EDC Publishing
Division of Educational Development Corp
5402 S 122 E Ave, Tulsa, OK 74146
Tel: 918-622-4522 *Toll Free Tel:* 800-475-4522 *Fax:* 918-663-2525 *Toll Free Fax:* 800-743-5660
E-mail: orders@edcpub.com
Web Site: www.edcpub.com
Key Personnel
Pres & CEO: Craig M White
Founded: 1978
Children's books (fiction & nonfiction).
ISBN Prefix(es): 978-0-88110; 978-0-7460; 978-0-86020; 978-0-7945; 978-1-58086; 978-1-60130; 978-0-4095; 978-0-4749
Number of titles published annually: 200 Print
Total Titles: 1,800 Print
Imprints: Learning Wrap-ups; Kane Miller Books; PaperPie; SmartLab

Edgewise Press Inc
24 Fifth Ave, Suite 224, New York, NY 10011
Tel: 212-387-0931
E-mail: epinc@mindspring.com
Web Site: www.edgewisepress.org
Key Personnel
Co-Publr & CEO: Howard Johnson, Jr
Co-Publr & Mng Ed: Joy L Glass
Co-Publr & Ed: Richard Milazzo
Founded: 1995
Publisher of serious art & literary books.
ISBN Prefix(es): 978-0-9646466; 978-1-893207
Number of titles published annually: 3 Print
Total Titles: 40 Print
Distributor for Editions d'Afrique du Nord; Libri Canali Bassi; Paolo Torti degli Alberti; Tsukuda Island Press

ediciones Lerner
Imprint of Lerner Publishing Group Inc
241 First Ave N, Minneapolis, MN 55401
Tel: 612-332-3344 *Toll Free Tel:* 800-328-4929 *Fax:* 612-332-7615 *Toll Free Fax:* 800-332-1132
E-mail: info@lernerbooks.com; custserve@lernerbooks.com
Web Site: www.lernerbooks.com; www.facebook.com/lernerbooks
Key Personnel
Chmn: Harry J Lerner
EVP & COO: Mark Budde
EVP & CFO: Margaret Thomas
Pres & Publr: Adam Lerner
EVP, Sales: David Wexler
VP & Ed-in-Chief: Andy Cummings
VP, Mktg: Rachel Zugschwert
Publg Dir, School & Lib: Jenny Krueger
Dir, HR: Margaret Wolfson *E-mail:* mwolfson@lernerbooks.com
Dir, Rts, Spec Sales & Intl Dist: Maria Kjoller
School & Lib Mktg Dir: Lois Wallentine
Publishes fiction & nonfiction books for PreK-4 in Spanish.
ISBN Prefix(es): 978-0-8225; 978-0-7613
Number of titles published annually: 20 Print; 20 E-Book
Total Titles: 300 Print; 300 E-Book
Foreign Rep(s): Bounce Sales & Marketing Ltd (Europe, India, Middle East, Pakistan, Scandinavia, UK); CrossCan Education (Canada); DuBois (New Zealand); Novella (Australia); Phambili Agencies (Botswana, Lesotho, Namibia, Southern Africa, Swaziland, Zimbabwe); Publishers Marketing Services (Brunei, Malaysia, Singapore); Saunders (school & lib) (Canada)
Foreign Rights: AC2 Literary (Italy); Sandra Bruna Literary Agency (Brazil, Portugal, Spain); CA-Link (Hong Kong, Macau, Mainland China, Taiwan); Japan Foreign-Rights Centre (JFC) (Japan); Korea Copyright Center Inc (KCC) (South Korea); Agence Michelle Lapautre (France); RightsMix (Eastern Europe, Greece, Israel, Netherlands, Russia, Scandinavia, UK); Literarische Agentur Silke Weniger (Germany)
Warehouse: CGC Fulfillment Warehouse, 150 Kingswood Dr, Mankato, MN 56001

Editorial Bautista Independiente
Division of Baptist Mid-Missions
3417 Kenilworth Blvd, Sebring, FL 33870-4469
Tel: 863-382-6350 *Toll Free Tel:* 800-398-7187 (US) *Fax:* 863-382-8650
E-mail: info@ebi-bmm.org
Web Site: www.ebi-bmm.org
Key Personnel
Gen Dir & Busn Mgr: Bruce Burkholder
Founded: 1950
Theology titles, Sunday school materials, extension materials, Bible study-all in Spanish.
ISBN Prefix(es): 978-1-879892
Number of titles published annually: 25 Print
Total Titles: 300 Print; 20 E-Book
Distributor for Casa Bautista; CLIE; Portavoz
Membership(s): Letra Viva; Spanish Evangelical Publishers Association (SEPA)

Editorial de la Universidad de Puerto Rico
Subsidiary of University of Puerto Rico
PO Box 23322, San Juan, PR 00931-3322
SAN: 208-1245
Tel: 787-525-7654
Web Site: www.facebook.com/editorialupr
Key Personnel
Dir: Edder Gonzalez Palacios
Founded: 1947
General fiction & nonfiction, reference books, college texts; Latin America.
ISBN Prefix(es): 978-0-8477
Number of titles published annually: 10 Print; 10 E-Book
Total Titles: 1,047 Print; 50 E-Book
Imprints: Coleccion Antologia Personal; Coleccion Aqui y Ahora; Coleccion Caribena; Coleccion Ciencias Naturales; Coleccion Clasicos No Tan Clasicos; Coleccion Cuadernos La Torre; Coleccion Cuentos de un Mundo Perdido; Coleccion Cultura Basica; Coleccion Obras Completas Eugenio Maria de Hostos (edicion critica); Coleccion Dos Lenguas; Coleccion Mujeres de Palabra; Coleccion Nueve Pececitos; Coleccion Puertorriquena; Coleccion San Pedrito
Foreign Rep(s): Baker & Taylor/Libros Sin Fronteras (USA); DESA (Latin America); Lectorum

U.S. PUBLISHERS

Publications (USA); Libreria La Trinitaria (Dominican Republic)
Membership(s): American Association of University Presses (AAUP)

Editorial Mundo Hispano, see Casa Bautista de Publicaciones

Editorial Portavoz
Division of Kregel Publications
2450 Oak Industrial Dr NE, Grand Rapids, MI 49505
SAN: 298-9115
Toll Free Tel: 877-733-2607 (ext 206)
E-mail: kregelbooks@kregel.com
Web Site: www.portavoz.com
Key Personnel
Pres: Jerold W Kregel *E-mail:* jerry@kregel.com
Publr: Tito Mantilla *E-mail:* tito@portavoz.com
Founded: 1970
Christian products.
ISBN Prefix(es): 978-0-8254
Number of titles published annually: 30 Print
Total Titles: 500 Print
Membership(s): Evangelical Christian Publishers Association (ECPA); Spanish Evangelical Publishers Association (SEPA)

§Editorial Unilit
8167 NW 84 St, Medley, FL 33166
Tel: 305-592-6136; 305-592-6135
  Toll Free Tel: 800-767-7726 *Fax:* 305-592-0087
E-mail: info@editorialunilit.com; ventas@editorialunilit.com (sales)
Web Site: www.editorialunilit.com
Key Personnel
Pres: Timothy Ecklebarger
Sales Dir: Mariana Tafura *E-mail:* mariana@editorialunilit.com
Sales: Joaquin Maldonado *E-mail:* joaquin@editorialunilit.com; Angela Peralta
  E-mail: angela@editorialunilit.com
Founded: 1973
Publishing for the Spanish family.
ISBN Prefix(es): 978-1-56063; 978-0-7899; 978-0-945792
Number of titles published annually: 40 Print
Total Titles: 900 Print

Editorial UPR, see Editorial de la Universidad de Puerto Rico

Educational Insights®
Division of Learning Resources Inc
152 W Walnut St, Suite 201, Gardena, CA 90248
SAN: 282-762X
Toll Free Tel: 800-995-4436 *Toll Free Fax:* 888-892-8731
E-mail: info@educationalinsights.com; cs@educationalinsights.com
Web Site: www.educationalinsights.com
Key Personnel
VP, Sales: Kent Brings
Sr Dir, Prod Devt: Heather Weeks
Sr Prod Mgr: Brent Geppert
Prod Mgr: Michael Sheridan
Gen Mgr: Lisa Guili
Founded: 1962
El-hi instructional materials; teacher's aids, teaching machines & games.
ISBN Prefix(es): 978-1-56767; 978-0-88679
Number of titles published annually: 4 Print; 2 Audio
Total Titles: 92 Print
Distribution Center: Learning Resources Inc, 380 N Fairway Dr, Vernon Hills, IL 60061
  Toll Free Tel: 800-222-3909 *Web Site:* www.learningresources.com

Educator's International Press Inc (EIP)
756 Linderman Ave, Kingston, NY 12401
Tel: 518-334-0276 *Toll Free Tel:* 800-758-3756
  Fax: 703-661-1547
E-mail: info@edint.com
Key Personnel
Publr: William Clockel
Founded: 1997
Educational foundations, teacher research, curriculum, special education.
ISBN Prefix(es): 978-0-9658339; 978-1-891928
Number of titles published annually: 4 Print; 4 E-Book
Total Titles: 40 Print; 4 E-Book

Edupress Inc
Division of Teacher Created Resources Inc
12621 Western Ave, Garden Grove, CA 92841
Toll Free Tel: 800-662-4321 *Toll Free Fax:* 800-525-1254
E-mail: custserv@teachercreated.com
Web Site: www.teachercreated.com
Founded: 1956
Publisher of teacher resource materials.
ISBN Prefix(es): 978-1-56472
Number of titles published annually: 20 Print
Total Titles: 220 Print

Wm B Eerdmans Publishing Co
4035 Park East Ct SE, Grand Rapids, MI 49546
SAN: 220-0058
Tel: 616-459-4591 *Toll Free Tel:* 800-253-7521
E-mail: customerservice@eerdmans.com; sales@eerdmans.com
Web Site: www.eerdmans.com
Key Personnel
Pres & Publr: Anita Eerdmans
VP & Ed-in-Chief: James Ernest
VP, Sales: Shane White *E-mail:* swhite@eerdmans.com
VP, Sales & Mktg: Will Bergkamp
Art Dir, Eerdmans Books for Young Readers: Holly Hoover
Dir, Mktg, Academic, Trade & Children's: Sarah Gombis
Edit Dir, Eerdmans Books for Young Readers: Kathleen Merz
Asst Mng Ed, Eerdmans Books for Young Readers: Courtney Zonnefeld *E-mail:* czonnefeld@eerdmans.com
Edit Assoc: Amy R Kent *E-mail:* akent@eerdmans.com
Sr Acct Mgr: Natalie Kompik *E-mail:* nkompik@eerdmans.com
Inside Sales-Cust Serv Mgr: Ingrid Wolf
  E-mail: iwolf@eerdmans.com
Mktg & Publicity Mgr: Jason Pearson
Subs Rts Mgr: Tom DeVries *E-mail:* tdevries@eerdmans.com
Acctg Specialist: Karl Eerdmans
Digital Mktg Specialist: Claire McColley
Ad & Promos Coord: Will Hearn
Publicity & Author Care Assoc: Jeff Dundas
Prodn Buyer: Karen Stange *E-mail:* kstange@eerdmans.com
Founded: 1911
Scholarly religious & religious reference, religion & social concerns, children's books.
ISBN Prefix(es): 978-0-8028; 978-1-4674
Number of titles published annually: 130 Print
Total Titles: 1,200 Print
Imprints: Eerdmans Books for Young Readers
Foreign Rep(s): Acts TCCN Bookshop (Nigeria); Asian Trading Corp (India); Bethesda Book Centre (East Asia, Singapore); Challenge Enterprises of Ghana (Ghana); Christian Art Distributors (South Africa); Christian Book Discounters (South Africa); Co Info Pty Ltd (Australia); Cru Asia Ltd (East Asia, Singapore); Culturasia (East Asia, Singapore); Evangelical Outreach (Philippines); Fitzhenry & Whiteside Limited (Canada); John Garratt Publishing (Australia); KCBS (South Korea); Kyo Bun Kwan Inc (Japan); Lion Sales Services Ltd (Andrew Wormleighton) (Europe, UK); Manna Christian Stores (New Zealand); Momentum Christian Literature (Indonesia); OM Books Foundation (India); OMF Literature (Philippines); Pustaka Sufes Sdn Bhd (Malaysia); SKS Books Warehouse (East Asia, Singapore); Tien Dao Publishing House (Hong Kong)
Warehouse: Books International Inc, 22881 Quicksilver Dr, Dulles, VA 20166 *Tel:* 703-661-1513
Distribution Center: Independent Publishers Group (IPG), 814 N Franklin St, Chicago, IL 60610 *Tel:* 312-337-0747 *Toll Free Tel:* 800-888-4741 *Fax:* 312-337-5985 *E-mail:* orders@ipgbook.com *Web Site:* www.ipgbook.com
Baker & Taylor Publisher Services, 30 Amberwood Pkwy, Ashland, OH 44805 (select intl mkts only) *Tel:* 567-215-0030 *Toll Free Tel:* 888-814-0208 *E-mail:* orders@btpubservices.com *Web Site:* www.btpubservices.com
Fitzhenry & Whiteside Limited, 195 Allstate Pkwy, Markham, ON L3R 4T8, Canada *E-mail:* bookinfo@fitzhenry.ca *Web Site:* www.fitzhenry.ca
Lion Sales Services Ltd, 74 Mill Lane, Southport, Merseyside PR9 7PE, United Kingdom, Dir: Andrew Wormleighton *E-mail:* andrew@lionsalesservices.com *Web Site:* www.lionsalesservices.com

§Eifrig Publishing LLC
PO Box 66, Lemont, PA 16851
Tel: 814-954-9445
E-mail: info@eifrigpublishing.com
Web Site: www.eifrigpublishing.com
Key Personnel
Founder & Ed-in-Chief: Penelope Eifrig
  E-mail: penny@eifrigpublishing.com
Founded: 2006
Primarily children's titles with social, ecological, community & self-esteem emphasis.
ISBN Prefix(es): 978-1-63233
Number of titles published annually: 6 Print; 6 Online; 6 E-Book; 3 Audio
Total Titles: 135 Print; 3 CD-ROM; 135 Online; 130 E-Book; 5 Audio
Imprints: Berry Street Books; Eifrig Publishing; Getting Smart; Mt Nittany Press; Pickleball Press; YACK!
Foreign Office(s): Knobelsdorffstr 44, 14059 Berlin, Germany
Foreign Rep(s): Sylvia Hayse Literary Agency (worldwide)
Foreign Rights: Sylvia Hayse Literary Agency (worldwide)
Membership(s): Independent Book Publishers Association (IBPA)

Eisenbrauns
Imprint of Penn State University Press
820 N University Dr, USB 1, Suite C, University Park, PA 16802-1003
SAN: 200-7835
Tel: 814-865-1327 *Toll Free Tel:* 800-326-9180 (orders & cust serv) *Fax:* 814-863-1408
Toll Free Fax: 877-778-2665 (orders)
E-mail: orders@psupress.org; customerservice@psupress.org
Web Site: www.eisenbrauns.org
Key Personnel
Dir, Penn State University Press: Patrick Alexander *E-mail:* pha3@psu.edu
Sales & Mktg Dir: Brendan Coyne *Tel:* 814-863-5994 *E-mail:* bcc5228@psu.edu
Assoc Dir, Penn State University Press/Design & Prodn Mgr: Jennifer Norton *Tel:* 814-863-8061 *E-mail:* jsn4@psu.edu
Mng Ed: Alex Ramos *E-mail:* ajr586@psu.edu
Acqs Ed: Maria J Metzler
Digital Mktg Mgr: Janice North *Tel:* 814-867-2831 *E-mail:* jrn61@psu.edu
Fin Mgr: Lisa Weller *Tel:* 814-867-3691
  E-mail: law479@psu.edu

IT Mgr: Ed Spicer *E-mail:* res122@psu.edu
Journals Mgr: Julie Lambert *E-mail:* jas1035@psu.edu
Journals Mktg Mgr: Christopher Miller
 E-mail: cam1051@psu.edu
Publicist: Mackenzie Brunnhuber
 E-mail: mjb6664@psu.edu
Publicity: Cate Fricke *Tel:* 814-865-1329
 E-mail: crf16@psu.edu
Founded: 1975
Educational books, books on the Ancient Near East.
ISBN Prefix(es): 978-0-931464; 978-1-57506
Number of titles published annually: 40 Print; 40 E-Book
Total Titles: 615 Print; 10 CD-ROM; 432 E-Book
Foreign Rep(s): Lexa Publishers' Representatives (Mical Moser) (Canada); MHM Ltd (Japan); The Oxford Publicity Partnership Ltd (Matthew Surzyn) (Europe, UK); Sino Publishers Services Ltd (Rance Fu) (China); US PubRep (Craig Falk) (Caribbean, Central America, Mexico, South America); The White Partnership (Andrew White) (India, Southeast Asia)
Orders to: University of Toronto Press, 5201 Dufferin St, North York, ON M3H 5T8, Canada *Tel:* 416-667-7791 *Fax:* 416-667-7832 *E-mail:* utpbooks@utpress.utoronto.ca *Web Site:* www.utpress.utoronto.ca/distribution. php; Woodslane Pty Ltd, 10 Apollo St, Warriewood, NSW 2102, Australia (Australia, Fiji, New Zealand & Papua-New Guinea) *Tel:* (02) 8445 2300 *E-mail:* info@woodslane.com.au *Web Site:* www.woodslane.com.au; MHM Ltd, 1-1-13-4F Kanda Jimbocho, Chiyoda-ku, Tokyo 101-0051, Japan *Tel:* (03) 3518-9449 *E-mail:* purchasing@mhmlimited.co.jp *Web Site:* www.mhmlimited.co.jp; John Wiley & Sons Ltd, European Dist Ctr, New Era Estate, Oldlands Way, Bognor Regis, West Sussex PO22 9NQ, United Kingdom (Europe & UK) *Tel:* (01243) 843291 *E-mail:* pennstate.csd@wiley.com

§Elderberry Press Inc
1393 Old Homestead Dr, Oakland, OR 97462-9690
Tel: 541-459-6043
E-mail: editor@elderberrypress.com
Web Site: www.elderberrypress.com
Key Personnel
Co-Owner & Exec Ed: Valerie St John
Co-Owner: Asia St John
Founded: 1997
Works closely with authors, from first reading of their ms to publishing & long after to ensure their book finds up to 50,000 or more readers. This publisher has indicated that 100% of their product line is author subsidized.
ISBN Prefix(es): 978-0-9658407; 978-1-930859; 978-1-932762; 978-1-934956
Number of titles published annually: 6 Print; 12 Online; 12 E-Book
Total Titles: 300 Print; 120 Online; 100 E-Book; 1 Audio
Foreign Rep(s): Ingram Book Co (worldwide)
Membership(s): Independent Book Publishers Association (IBPA)

§The Electrochemical Society (ECS)
65 S Main St, Bldg D, Pennington, NJ 08534-2839
Tel: 609-737-1902 *Fax:* 609-737-0629
E-mail: publications@electrochem.org; customerservice@electrochem.org; ecs@ioppublishing.com
Web Site: www.electrochem.org
Key Personnel
Exec Dir/CEO: Christopher J Jannuzzi *Tel:* 609-737-1902 ext 101
Dir, Pubns: Adrian Plummer *Tel:* 609-737-1902 ext 103
Edit Mgr: Paul Cooper

Founded: 1902
Technical journals, membership magazine, proceedings volumes, monographs, ECS Digital Library.
ISBN Prefix(es): 978-1-56677; 978-1-60768; 978-1-62332
Number of titles published annually: 4 Online
Total Titles: 4 Online
Distributed by IOP Publishing (journals & magazines); Wiley Inc (books & monographs)
Membership(s): American Society of Association Executives™ (ASAE)

Edward Elgar Publishing Inc
The William Pratt House, 9 Dewey Ct, Northampton, MA 01060-3815
SAN: 299-4615
Tel: 413-584-5551 *Toll Free Tel:* 800-390-3149 (orders) *Fax:* 413-584-9933
E-mail: elgarinfo@e-elgar.com; elgarsales@e-elgar.com; elgarsubmissions@e-elgar.com (edit)
Web Site: www.e-elgar.com; www.elgaronline.com (ebooks & journals)
Key Personnel
Sales & Mktg Mgr: Katy Wight *E-mail:* kwight@e-elgar.com
Exec Ed: Alan Sturmer *E-mail:* asturmer@e-elgar.com
Founded: 1986
Leading international publisher of academic books, ebooks & journals in economics, finance, business & management, law, environment, public & social policy.
ISBN Prefix(es): 978-1-85898; 978-1-85278; 978-1-84064; 978-1-84376; 978-1-84542; 978-1-84720; 978-1-84844; 978-1-78536; 978-1-78471; 978-1-78347; 978-1-78100; 978-1-78254; 978-1-84980
Number of titles published annually: 450 Print; 450 E-Book; 1 Audio
Total Titles: 8,100 Print; 5,000 E-Book; 1 Audio
Foreign Office(s): Edward Elgar Publishing Ltd, the Lypiatts, 15 Lansdown Rd, Cheltenham, Glos GL50 2JA, United Kingdom, Mng Dir: Tim Williams *Tel:* (01242) 226934 *Fax:* (01242) 262111 *E-mail:* info@e-elgar.co.uk *Web Site:* www.e-elgar.co.uk
Warehouse: Books International Inc, 22883 Quicksilver Dr, Dulles, VA 20166, Cust Serv: Todd Riggleman *Tel:* 703-661-1596 *Toll Free Tel:* 800-390-3149 *Fax:* 703-996-1010 *E-mail:* elgar.orders@presswarehouse.com

Elite Books
PO Box 222, Petaluma, CA 94953-0222
Tel: 707-525-9292 *Toll Free Fax:* 800-330-9798
E-mail: support@eftuniverse.com
Web Site: www.elitebooksonline.com
Key Personnel
Ed: Stephanie Marohn *E-mail:* angel@stephaniemarohn.com
ISBN Prefix(es): 978-0-9720028; 978-0-9710888; 978-1-60070
Number of titles published annually: 5 Print
Total Titles: 40 Print
Distribution Center: Baker & Taylor Publisher Services, 30 Amberwood Pkwy, Ashland, OH 44805 *Tel:* 567-215-0030 *Toll Free Tel:* 888-814-0208 *E-mail:* info@btpubservices.com *Web Site:* www.btpubservices.com
Membership(s): Independent Book Publishers Association (IBPA)

Elsevier Health Sciences
Division of RELX Group plc
1600 John F Kennedy Blvd, Suite 1800, Philadelphia, PA 19103-2899
Tel: 215-239-3900 *Toll Free Tel:* 800-523-1649 *Fax:* 215-239-3990
Web Site: www.us.elsevierhealth.com
Founded: 1906

ISBN Prefix(es): 978-0-7506; 978-0-443; 978-0-444; 978-0-932883; 978-1-56053; 978-0-8016; 978-0-8151; 978-0-7216; 978-0-7020; 978-0-7234; 978-0-323; 978-0-7236; 978-1-4160; 978-1-55664; 978-0-920513; 978-1-898507; 978-1-932141; 978-1-4377; 978-1-4557
Number of titles published annually: 2,000 Print
Imprints: Churchill Livingstone; Mosby; Saunders
Distributor for G W Medical Publisher
Foreign Rights: John Scott & Co (Jake Scott)
Shipping Address: PO Box 437, Linn, MO 65051-0437
Distribution Center: 1799 Hwy 50 E, Linn, MO 65051 *Tel:* 573-897-3694 *Fax:* 573-897-4387

§Elsevier Inc
Subsidiary of RELX Group plc
230 Park Ave, Suite 800, New York, NY 10169
Tel: 212-989-5800 *Fax:* 212-633-3990
Web Site: www.elsevier.com
Founded: 1880
Books for professionals, researchers & students in the sciences, technology, engineering, business & media. Also research monographs, major reference works & serials.
Number of titles published annually: 2,500 Print; 400 E-Book
Total Titles: 40,000 Print
Imprints: Morgan Kaufmann
Divisions: Knovel Corp
Branch Office(s)
2171 Monroe Ave, Suite 203, Rochester, NY 14618 *Tel:* 585-442-8170 *Fax:* 585-442-8171
24422 Avenida De La Carlota, Suite 235, Leguna Hills, CA 92653 *Tel:* 801-485-6500
Marquis One, 245 Peachtree Ctr Ave, Suite 1900, Atlanta, GA 30303 *Tel:* 404-669-9400 *Toll Free Tel:* 800-999-6274 *Fax:* 404-669-9339
5635 Fishers Lane, Suite 510, Rockville, MD 20852
50 Hampshire St, 5th fl, Cambridge, MA 02139 *Tel:* 617-661-7057 *Fax:* 617-661-7061
Glenwood Hills Bldg, 1890 Kraft Ave, Suite 305, Grand Rapids, MI 49512 *Tel:* 616-530-9206 *Fax:* 616-530-9245
3251 Riverport Lane, Maryland Heights, MO 63043 *Tel:* 314-447-8000 *Fax:* 314-447-8033
1600 John F Kennedy Blvd, Suite 1800, Philadelphia, PA 19103-2398 *Tel:* 215-239-3900 *Fax:* 215-239-3990
111 Center Park Dr, Suite 175, Knoxville, TN 37922 *Toll Free Tel:* 800-999-6274
11011 Richmond Ave, Suite 450, Houston, TX 77042 *Toll Free Tel:* 800-950-2728 *Fax:* 713-838-7787
Foreign Office(s): Elsevier Ltd, The Boulevard, Langford Lane, Kidlington, Oxford OX5 1GB, United Kingdom *Tel:* (01865) 843000 *Fax:* (01865) 843010
Foreign Rep(s): Elsevier Ltd (Europe)
Membership(s): Association of American Publishers (AAP)
See separate listing for:
Morgan Kaufmann

Elva Resa Publishing
8362 Tamarack Village, Suite 119-106, St Paul, MN 55125
Tel: 651-357-8770 *Fax:* 501-641-0777
E-mail: staff@elvaresa.com
Web Site: www.elvaresa.com; www.militaryfamilybooks.com
Founded: 1997
Books for & about military families.
ISBN Prefix(es): 978-1-934617; 978-0-9657483
Number of titles published annually: 4 Print
Total Titles: 34 Print; 5 E-Book
Imprints: Alma Little (children's books); Elva Resa (books for & about military families); Juloya (inspirational works that help people celebrate life)
Distribution Center: Independent Publishers Group (IPG), 814 N Franklin St, Chicago,

IL 60610 *Toll Free Tel:* 800-888-4741
E-mail: orders@ipgbook.com *Web Site:* www.ipgbook.com
Membership(s): Independent Book Publishers Association (IBPA); Midwest Independent Publishing Association (MIPA)

Emerald Books
Affiliate of YWAM Publishing
PO Box 55787, Seattle, WA 98155
Tel: 425-771-1153 *Toll Free Tel:* 800-922-2143 *Fax:* 425-775-2383
E-mail: books@ywampublishing.com
Web Site: www.ywampublishing.com
Founded: 1992
Christian theme.
ISBN Prefix(es): 978-1-883002; 978-1-932096; 978-1-62486
Number of titles published annually: 15 Print
Total Titles: 364 Print
Distributed by YWAM Publishing
Shipping Address: 7825 230 St SW, Edmonds, WA 98026 *Web Site:* ywampublishing.com

Emmaus Road Publishing Inc
Division of St Paul Center for Biblical Theology
1468 Parkview Circle, Steubenville, OH 43952
Tel: 750-264-9535 *Fax:* 740-475-0230 (orders)
E-mail: questions@emmausroad.org
Web Site: stpaulcenter.com/emmaus-road-publishing
Key Personnel
Edit Dir: Chris Erickson
Mng Ed: Melissa Girard
Acct Mgr: Michelle Olenick
 E-mail: michelleolenick@stpaulcenter.com
Founded: 1998
Bible studies, biblically based apologetics & other materials faithful to the teaching of the Catholic church. Restocking fee of 20% for returns.
ISBN Prefix(es): 978-0-9663223; 978-1-931018; 978-1-937155; 978-1-941447; 978-1-940329; 978-1-63446
Number of titles published annually: 12 Print; 12 E-Book
Total Titles: 80 Print; 1 CD-ROM; 50 E-Book; 10 Audio

Enchanted Lion Books
248 Creamer St, Studio 4, Brooklyn, NY 11231
Tel: 646-785-9272
E-mail: enchantedlion@gmail.com
Web Site: www.enchantedlion.com
Key Personnel
Publr: Claudia Zoe Bedrick
Founded: 2002
Independent children's book publisher. We publish illustrated books from around the world, convinced by the power of cultural exchange to inspire curiosity, awareness & wonder in children everywhere.
ISBN Prefix(es): 978-1-59270
Number of titles published annually: 20 Print
Total Titles: 100 Print
Foreign Rep(s): Verok Agency (Veronique Kirchhoff) (worldwide)
Orders to: Ingram, 1094 Flex Dr, Jackson, TN 38301-5070 *Toll Free Tel:* 800-283-3572 *Toll Free Fax:* 800-351-5073
Returns: Ingram, 193 Edwards Dr, Jackson, TN 38301-5070 *Toll Free Tel:* 866-400-5351
Distribution Center: Consortium Book Sales & Distribution, The Keg House, Suite 101, 34 13 Ave NE, Minneapolis, MN 55413-1007 *Tel:* 612-746-2600 *Toll Free Tel:* 866-400-5351 (cust serv, Jackson, TN) *E-mail:* cbsdinfo@ingramcontent.com *Web Site:* www.cbsd.com
SAN: 200-6049

Encounter Books
Division of Encounter for Culture & Education
900 Broadway, Suite 601, New York, NY 10003
Tel: 212-871-6310 *Toll Free Tel:* 855-203-7220
E-mail: publicity@encounterbooks.com
Web Site: www.encounterbooks.com
Key Personnel
Pres & Publr: Roger Kimball
Exec Dir, Opers: Nola Tully *E-mail:* ntully@encounterbooks.com
Dir, Mktg: Sam Schneider *E-mail:* sschneider@encounterbooks.com
Dir, Prodn: Elizabeth Bachmann
 E-mail: ebachmann@encounterbooks.com
Dir, Publicity: Lauren Miklos *E-mail:* lmiklos@encounterbooks.com
Dir, Spec Initiatives: Malcolm Salovaara
 E-mail: msalovaara@encounterbooks.com
Opers Mgr: Clare Rahner *E-mail:* crahner@encounterbooks.com
Founded: 1998
Serious nonfiction books about history, culture, current events, religion, politics, social criticism & public policy.
ISBN Prefix(es): 978-1-893554; 978-1-59403; 978-1-64177
Number of titles published annually: 30 Print; 30 E-Book
Total Titles: 400 Print; 250 E-Book
Orders to: Two Rivers Distribution, 191 Edwards Dr, Jackson, TN 38301 (Australia, CN & US) *Toll Free Tel:* 800-343-4499 *Toll Free Fax:* 800-351-5073 *E-mail:* pd_orderentry@ingramcontent.com *Web Site:* www.tworiversdistribution.com
Returns: Indiepubs Returns, 193 Edwards Dr, Jackson, TN 38301 *Fax:* (07154) 1327-13 *E-mail:* indiepubssupport@ingramcontent.com
Distribution Center: Two Rivers Distribution, 191 Edwards Dr, Jackson, TN 38301 (Australia, CN & US) *Toll Free Tel:* 800-343-4499 *Toll Free Fax:* 800-351-5073 *E-mail:* pd_orderentry@ingramcontent.com *Web Site:* www.tworiversdistribution.com
Membership(s): American Booksellers Association (ABA); The American Library Association (ALA); Independent Book Publishers Association (IBPA)

§Encyclopaedia Britannica Inc
325 N La Salle St, Suite 200, Chicago, IL 60654
Tel: 312-347-7000 (all other countries)
 Toll Free Tel: 800-323-1229 (US & CN)
 Fax: 312-294-2104
E-mail: contact@eb.com
Web Site: www.britannica.com
Key Personnel
Global CEO: Jorge Cauz
Global CFO: Steve Brodsky
EVP, Corp Secy & Gen Coun: Douglas Eveleigh
SVP & CFO: Jim Conners
SVP, Britannica Digital Learning Intl: Leah Mansoor
VP, Consumer Mkts: Chris Mayland
VP, Mktg & Channel Devt: Sal De Spirito
Founded: 1768
Reference works, print & online for consumers & institutions.
ISBN Prefix(es): 978-0-87827; 978-0-8347; 978-0-85229; 978-1-61535; 978-0-9823824; 978-1-62513; 978-1-59339; 978-1-60835; 978-0-9823823; 978-0-9823819; 978-0-7826; 978-0-9823820; 978-0-9823821; 978-0-9823822
Subsidiaries: Merriam-Webster Inc
Foreign Office(s): Encyclopaedia Britannica Australia Ltd, PO Box 5608, Chatswood, NSW 1515, Australia (Asia Pacific, Australia & New Zealand) *Tel:* 1800 801 001 (within Australia); 0800 225 044 (within New Zealand) *Fax:* (02) 9419 5247 *E-mail:* contact@britannica.com.au *Web Site:* britannica.com.au
Melingo Ltd, 16 Tozeret Ha'aretz St, Tel Aviv 67891, Israel *E-mail:* i-melingo@melingo.com
Britannica Japan Co Ltd, Sanbancho Tokyo Bldg, 8th fl, 8-1 Sanbancho, Chiyoda-ku, Tokyo, Japan *Tel:* (03) 5436 1388 *Fax:* (03) 5436 1390 *E-mail:* japansales@britannica.co.jp *Web Site:* www.britannica.co.jp
Encyclopaedia Britannica (UK) Ltd, Unity Wharf, 2nd fl, Mill St, London SE1 2BH, United Kingdom (Africa, Europe & Middle East) *Tel:* (020) 7500 7800 *Fax:* (020) 7500 7878 *E-mail:* enqbol@britannica.co.uk *Web Site:* www.britannica.co.uk
See separate listing for:
Merriam-Webster Inc

Endless Mountains Publishing Co
72 Glenmaura National Blvd, Suite 104B, Moosic, PA 18507
Tel: 862-251-2296
E-mail: info@endlessmountainspublishing.com
Web Site: kalaniotbooks.com
Key Personnel
Publr & Creative Dir: Lilian Rosenstreich
 E-mail: lili@endlessmountainspublishing.com
Publr & Busn Mgr: Mitchel Weiss
 E-mail: mitchel@endlessmountainspublishing.com
Founded: 2017
We are a niche publisher focusing on books of interest to Jewish children. We also publish books of regional interest to Northeast Pennsylvania.
ISBN Prefix(es): 978-0-9988527 (Endless Mountains Publishing Co & Kalaniot Books); 979-8-9863965 (Kalaniot Books)
Number of titles published annually: 6 Print
Total Titles: 17 Print
Imprints: Kalaniot Books (Jewish culture & history)
Distribution Center: National Book Network (NBN), 15200 NBN Way, Blue Ridge Summit, PA 17214, Natl Accts Mgr: Spencer Gale *Tel:* 717-794-3800 *Toll Free Tel:* 800-462-6420 *Toll Free Fax:* 800-338-4550 *E-mail:* sgale@nbnbooks.com *Web Site:* nbnbooks.com
See separate listing for:
Kalaniot Books

Energy Psychology Press
Division of Energy Psychology Group
PO Box 222, Petaluma, CA 94953-0222
Tel: 707-525-9292 *Toll Free Tel:* 800-330-9798
E-mail: energypsychologypress@gmail.com; support@eftuniverse.com
Web Site: www.energypsychologypress.com; www.elitebooksonline.com
Key Personnel
Publr: Dawson Church
Ed-in-Chief & Prodn Coord: Stephanie Marohn
 E-mail: angel@stephaniemarohn.com
Founded: 1994
ISBN Prefix(es): 978-1-60415
Number of titles published annually: 5 Print
Total Titles: 40 Print
Distribution Center: Baker & Taylor Publisher Services, 30 Amberwood Pkwy, Ashland, OH 44805 *Tel:* 567-215-0030 *Toll Free Tel:* 888-814-0208 *E-mail:* info@btpubservices.com *Web Site:* www.btpubservices.com
Membership(s): Independent Book Publishers Association (IBPA)

§Enslow Publishing LLC
101 W 23 St, Suite 240, New York, NY 10011
Toll Free Tel: 800-398-2504 *Fax:* 908-771-0925
Toll Free Fax: 877-980-4454
E-mail: customerservice@enslow.com
Web Site: www.enslow.com
Key Personnel
Pres: Roger Rosen
Founded: 1976
Educational nonfiction books for children & young adults.
ISBN Prefix(es): 978-0-89490; 978-0-7760; 978-1-59845; 978-1-4644; 978-1-4645; 978-1-4646;

978-1-62285; 978-1-62293; 978-1-62324; 978-1-62400
Number of titles published annually: 200 Print; 200 E-Book
Total Titles: 2,400 Print
Imprints: Enslow (middle & high school books); Enslow Elementary (PreK-5); MyReportLinks.com Books (Internet supported books); West 44 Books (hi-lo middle grade & young adult fiction)
Foreign Rep(s): CrossCan Educational Services Inc (Canada); EduCan Media (Canada); Everybody's Books (Warren Halford) (South Africa); Read Pacific (New Zealand)
Membership(s): AASL; The American Library Association (ALA); Educational Book & Media Association (EBMA); TLA

Entangled Publishing LLC
644 Shrewsbury Commons Ave, Suite 181, Shrewsbury, PA 17361
Toll Free Tel: 877-677-9451
E-mail: publisher@entangledpublishing.com
Web Site: www.entangledpublishing.com
Key Personnel
Publr & CEO: Liz Pelletier
CFO: Peter DeGiglio
VP, Opers: Stacy Cantor Abrams
Assoc Publr & Edit Dir, Adult: Jessica Turner
Edit Dir, Red Tower Books: Molly Majumder
Edit Dir, Teen: Elana Cohen
Fin Dir & Mng Ed: Katie Clapsadl
Publicity Dir: Lizzy Mason
Mktg & Publicity Mgr: Lauren Cepero
Soc Media Mgr: Meredith Johnson
ISBN Prefix(es): 978-1-937044; 978-1-62266; 978-1-62061
Number of titles published annually: 48 Print; 312 E-Book
Imprints: Amara (upmarket single title romance); Bliss (sweet romance, with small-town, family vibe); Brazen (sexy contemporary category romance); Covet (contemporary category romance with a paranormal twist); Embrace (new adult romance); Entangled Select (adult single title romance); Entangled Teen (young adult single title romance); Ignite (suspenseful category romance); Indulgence (rich & powerful alpha heroes); Little Lark (picture books); Lovestruck (romantic comedy & fun, flirty romance); Red Tower Books (adult commercial fiction focused on romantic fantasy & science fiction); Scandalous (historical category romance); Scorched (erotic romance); TEEN Crave (teen contemporary category romance with a paranormal twist); TEEN Crush (teen contemporary category romance)
Distributed by Macmillan

Entomological Society of America
170 Jennifer Rd, Suite 230, Annapolis, MD 21401
Tel: 301-731-4535 *Fax:* 301-731-4538
E-mail: esa@entsoc.org
Web Site: www.entsoc.org
Key Personnel
Exec Dir: Chris Stelzig *E-mail:* cstelzig@entsoc.org
Dir, Pubns: Matt Hudson *E-mail:* mhudson@entsoc.org
Founded: 1889
Professional scientific society for entomologists. Publish research journals on all areas of entomology.
ISBN Prefix(es): 978-0-938522; 978-0-9776209; 978-0-9966674
Number of titles published annually: 3 Print
Total Titles: 25 Print
Distributed by Oxford University Press

§Environmental Law Institute
1730 "M" St NW, Suite 700, Washington, DC 20036
Tel: 202-939-3800 *Toll Free Tel:* 800-433-5120
Fax: 202-939-3868
E-mail: law@eli.org
Web Site: www.eli.org
Key Personnel
Pres: Jordan Diamond *E-mail:* diamond@eli.org
Ed, The Environmental Forum: Stephen Dujack *E-mail:* dujack@eli.org
Ed, Environmental Law Reporter: Jay Austin *E-mail:* austin@eli.org
Founded: 1969
Environmental studies, references, online database services, monographs, policy studies.
ISBN Prefix(es): 978-0-911937; 978-1-58576
Number of titles published annually: 3 Print; 18 Online; 3 E-Book
Total Titles: 60 Print; 60 E-Book
Distributed by West Academic (ELI Press)

§Epicenter Press Inc
6524 NE 181 St, Suite 2, Kenmore, WA 98028
Tel: 425-485-6822 (edit, mktg, busn off)
Fax: 425-481-8253
E-mail: info@epicenterpress.com
Web Site: www.epicenterpress.com
Key Personnel
Pres & Acqs: Phil Garrett *E-mail:* phil@epicenterpress.com
Assoc Publr & Exec Ed: Jennifer McCord *E-mail:* jennifer@coffeetownpress.com
Founded: 1988
Regional nonfiction trade publisher. Specialize in titles about Alaska & the Pacific Northwest.
ISBN Prefix(es): 978-0-945397; 978-0-9708493; 978-0-9724944; 978-0-9800825; 978-1-935347
Number of titles published annually: 30 Print; 30 E-Book
Total Titles: 425 Print; 425 E-Book
Imprints: Camel Press (genre fiction: mystery & romance); Coffeetown Press (memoir & literary fiction); Fanny Press (erotica); Northwest Corner Books (regional)
Foreign Rights: Susan Schulman Agency (Camel Press & Coffeetown Press) (worldwide); Wales Literary Agency (worldwide)
Membership(s): Independent Book Publishers Association (IBPA); Pacific Northwest Booksellers Association (PNBA)

EPS School Specialty
Division of Cambridge Information Group Inc/Excolere Equity Partners
625 Mount Auburn St, Suite 202, Cambridge, MA 02138-3039
SAN: 201-8225
Toll Free Tel: 800-225-5750 *Toll Free Fax:* 888-440-2665
E-mail: curriculumcare@schoolspecialty.com; curriculumorders@schoolspecialty.com
Web Site: eps.schoolspecialty.com
Key Personnel
Dir, Opers & Spec Progs: Mariel Warnock
Dir, Strategic Partnerships: Carra Pappalardo
Founded: 1952
PreK-12 curriculum company providing supplemental ELA & math solutions that promote achievement & equitable education for all students. Provides solutions combining research-based curriculum & customized professional learning.
ISBN Prefix(es): 978-0-8388; 978-1-4293
Number of titles published annually: 25 Print
Total Titles: 800 Print
Imprints: Modern Learning Press
Returns: 80 Northwest Blvd, Nashua, NH 03063

Erewhon Books, see Kensington Publishing Corp

§Etruscan Press
Wilkes University, 84 W South St, Wilkes-Barre, PA 18766
Tel: 570-408-4546 *Fax:* 570-408-3333
E-mail: books@etruscanpress.org
Web Site: www.etruscanpress.org
Key Personnel
Exec Dir: Dr Philip Brady
Exec Ed: Dr Robert Mooney
Mng Ed: Bill Schneider *E-mail:* bill@etruscanpress.org
Founded: 2001
Housed at Wilkes University & partnering with Youngstown State University, Etruscan is a nonprofit literary press working to produce & promote books that nurture the dialogue across genres, cultures & voices. We publish books of poems, novels, short stories, creative nonfiction, criticism, translation & anthologies.
ISBN Prefix(es): 978-0-9832944; 978-0-9797450; 978-0-9833294; 978-0-9897532; 978-0-9886922; 978-0-9903221; 978-0-9987508; 978-0-9977455
Number of titles published annually: 6 Print
Total Titles: 83 Print
Distribution Center: Consortium Book Sales & Distribution, The Keg House, Suite 101, 34 13 Ave NE, Minneapolis, MN 55413-1007
Tel: 612-746-2600 *Toll Free Tel:* 866-400-5351 (cust serv, Jackson, TN) *E-mail:* cbsdinfo@ingramcontent.com *Web Site:* www.cbsd.com
SAN: 200-6049
Membership(s): Community of Literary Magazines & Presses (CLMP); Independent Book Publishers Association (IBPA)

Europa Editions
Subsidiary of E/O Edizioni SRL
27 Union Sq W, Suite 302, New York, NY 10003
Tel: 212-868-6844 *Fax:* 212-868-6845
E-mail: info@europaeditions.com; books@europaeditions.com; publicity@europaeditions.com
Web Site: www.europaeditions.com
Key Personnel
Publr & Co-Founder: Sandro Ferri
Publr, Pres & Co-Founder: Sandra Ozzola Ferri
Publr-at-Large: Kent Carroll
Fin Offr: Rosa Finamore
Dir, Sales, Mktg & Busn Devt: Kathy Wiess
Ed-in-Chief: Michael Reynolds
Ed: Edoardo Andreoni
Asst Ed: Autumn Toennis
Publicist: Kristi Bontrager
Founded: 2005
Publisher of international literary fiction in translation, domestic literary fiction, crime & narrative nonfiction.
ISBN Prefix(es): 978-1-933372; 978-1-60945
Number of titles published annually: 35 Print
Total Titles: 300 Print
Imprints: Europa Compass; Tonga Books; World Noir
Foreign Office(s): Via Gabriele Camozzi 1, 00195 Rome RM, Italy, Mng Ed: Gianluca Catalano *Tel:* (06) 3722829 *Fax:* (06) 37351096 *E-mail:* gianlucacatalano@europaeditions.com
Europa Editions UK, 24 Artesian Rd, Flat 1, London W2 5AR, United Kingdom, Contact: Daniela Petracco *Tel:* (020) 7792 4103 *E-mail:* danielapetracco@europaeditions.co.uk
Web Site: www.europaeditions.co.uk
Distributed by Jonathan Ball Publishers; NewSouth Books
Foreign Rights: The Ella Sher Literary Agency (Catalan, Portuguese & Spanish-speaking countries)
Distribution Center: Publishers Group West (PGW), 1700 Fourth St, Berkeley, CA 94710 *Toll Free Tel:* 866-400-5351 *Toll Free Fax:* 800-838-1149 *E-mail:* ips@ingramcontent.com SAN: 202-8522
Publishers Group Canada, c/o Raincoast Books, 2440 Viking Way, Richmond, BC V6V 1N2, Canada *Toll Free Tel:* 800-663-5714 *Toll Free*

U.S. PUBLISHERS

Fax: 800-565-3770 *E-mail:* customerservice@raincoast.com
Membership(s): Community of Literary Magazines & Presses (CLMP)

§Evan-Moor Educational Publishers
10 Harris Ct, Suite C-3, Monterey, CA 93940
Tel: 831-649-5901 *Toll Free Tel:* 800-777-4362 (orders) *Fax:* 831-649-6256 *Toll Free Fax:* 800-777-4332 (orders)
E-mail: sales@evan-moor.com; marketing@evan-moor.com
Web Site: www.evan-moor.com
Key Personnel
Pres & CEO: Judy Harris
VP, Sales: James O'Donnell, III
Dir, Fin: David Miller
Dir, Opers & Fulfillment: Anney Banales
Dir, Technol Prods: Keli Winters
Exec Ed: Lisa Vitarisi Mathews
Founded: 1979
Supplemental teaching resources for parents & teachers of children grades PreK-8 in print & ebook formats, activity books & an online learning library. Subjects include science, social studies, critical thinking, STEAM, STEM, social & emotional learning, reading, phonics, spelling, writing & art.
ISBN Prefix(es): 978-1-55799; 978-1-62938; 978-1-61367; 978-1-61366; 978-1-59673; 978-1-4409; 978-1-60792; 978-1-61368; 978-1-61365; 978-1-60793; 978-1-935353; 978-1-60823; 978-1-60963
Number of titles published annually: 25 Print; 60 Online; 25 E-Book
Total Titles: 450 Print; 450 Online; 450 E-Book
Membership(s): American Booksellers Association (ABA); The American Library Association (ALA); Association of American Publishers PreK-12 Learning Group; Education Market Association

M Evans & Company
Imprint of Rowman & Littlefield Publishing Group
c/o Rowman & Littlefield Publishing Group, 4501 Forbes Blvd, Suite 200, Lanham, MD 20706
Tel: 301-459-3366 *Fax:* 301-429-5748
Web Site: rowman.com
Key Personnel
Ed: Rick Rinehart *Tel:* 203-458-4656
 E-mail: rrinehart@rowman.com
Founded: 1963
Health, medical & business books.
ISBN Prefix(es): 978-0-87131; 978-1-59077
Number of titles published annually: 30 Print
Total Titles: 250 Print
Foreign Rights: Rights Unlimited
Shipping Address: National Book Network, 15200 NBN Way, Blue Ridge Summit, PA 17214 *Tel:* 717-794-3800 *Toll Free Tel:* 800-462-6420 *Fax:* 717-794-4801 *Toll Free Fax:* 800-338-4550
Distribution Center: National Book Network, 15200 NBN Way, Blue Ridge Summit, PA 17214 *Tel:* 717-794-3800 *Toll Free Tel:* 800-462-6420 *Fax:* 717-794-4801 *Toll Free Fax:* 800-338-4550

Evergreen Pacific Publishing Ltd
10114 19 Ave SE, Suite 8, PMB 703, Everett, WA 98208
Tel: 425-493-1451
E-mail: sales@evergreenpacific.com
Web Site: www.evergreenpacific.com
Key Personnel
Pres: Paul Hamstra
Founded: 1996
Books, charts & guides for water related recreations.
ISBN Prefix(es): 978-0-945265; 978-0-9609036; 978-1-934707
Number of titles published annually: 4 Print
Total Titles: 25 Print
Imprints: Evergreen Pacific Publishing

§Everyman's Library
Imprint of Knopf Doubleday Publishing Group
c/o Penguin Random House LLC, 1745 Broadway, New York, NY 10019
Tel: 212-751-2600 *Fax:* 212-940-7390 (dom rts); 212-572-2662 (foreign rts)
Web Site: knopfdoubleday.com/imprint/everymans-library/; knopfdoubleday.com
Founded: 1906
Penguin Random House & its publishing entities are not accepting unsol submissions, proposals, mss or submission queries via e-mail at this time.
Foreign Rights: ALS-Agenzia Letteraria Santachiara (Roberto Santachiara) (Italy); Anthea Agency (Katalina Sabeva) (Bulgaria); Bardon-Chinese Media Agency (Xu-Weiguang) (China); Bardon-Chinese Media Agency (Yu-Shiuan Chen) (Taiwan); English Agency Japan Co Ltd (Junzo Sawa) (Japan); Graal Literary Agency (Maria Strarz-Zielinska) (Poland); The Deborah Harris Agency (Ilana Kurshan) (Israel); JLM Literary Agency (Nelly Moukakos) (Greece); Katai & Bolza Literary (Peter Bolza) (Croatia, Hungary); Simona Kessler International (Simona Kessler) (Romania); Korea Copyright Center Inc (KCC) (MiSook Hong) (South Korea); Licht & Burr Literary Agency (Trine Licht) (Scandinavia); La Nouvelle Agency (Vanessa Kling) (France); Kristin Olson Literary Agency (Kristin Olson) (Czechia); Sebes & Bisseling Literary Agency (Paul Sebes) (Netherlands)

Everything Goes Media LLC
PO Box 1524, Milwaukee, WI 53201
Tel: 312-226-8400
E-mail: info@everythinggoesmedia.com
Web Site: www.everythinggoesmedia.com
Key Personnel
Owner & Publr: Sharon Woodhouse
 E-mail: sharon@everythinggoesmedia.com
Founded: 1994
"The book is the medium." Traditional publisher with unconventional approaches.
ISBN Prefix(es): 978-1-893121
Number of titles published annually: 5 Print; 4 E-Book
Total Titles: 40 Print; 12 E-Book
Imprints: Everything Goes Media (nonfiction-lifestyle, hobby, gift & business); Lake Claremont Press (nonfiction-Chicago guidebooks & histories); S Woodhouse Books (nonfiction-ideas, history, trends & current events)
Subsidiaries: Tiny Golem Press
Divisions: Conspire Creative

Excalibur Publications
6855 W Ina Rd, Tucson, AZ 85743-9633
Tel: 520-575-9057
E-mail: excaliburpublications@centurylink.net
Key Personnel
Ed-in-Chief: Alan M Petrillo
Founded: 1990
ISBN Prefix(es): 978-1-880677
Number of titles published annually: 3 Print
Total Titles: 16 Print
Distribution Center: Barnes & Noble, One Barnes & Noble Way, Suite B, Monroe, NJ 08831
Amazon.com, 1200 12 Ave S, Suite 1200, Seattle, WA 98144-2734

Excelsior Editions
Imprint of State University of New York Press
10 N Pearl St, 4th fl, Albany, NY 12207
SAN: 760-7261
Tel: 518-944-2800 *Toll Free Tel:* 866-430-7869 *Fax:* 518-320-1592
E-mail: info@sunypress.edu
Web Site: www.sunypress.edu
Key Personnel
Co-Dir: James Peltz *Tel:* 518-944-2815
 E-mail: james.peltz@sunypress.edu
Founded: 2008
Publish regional & trade books.
ISBN Prefix(es): 978-0-7914; 978-1-929373 (Hudson Valley region); 978-1-4384; 978-0-9722977 (Uncrowned Queens)
Number of titles published annually: 25 Print
Total Titles: 272 Print; 222 E-Book; 1 Audio
Distributor for Albany Institute of History & Art; Uncrowned Queens
Foreign Rep(s): Ingram Publisher Services UK (UK & the continent); Lexa Publishers' Representatives (Elise & Mical Moser) (Canada); MHM Ltd (Japan); US PubRep Inc (Craig Falk) (Caribbean, Central America, Mexico, Puerto Rico, South America)
Orders to: SUNY Press, PO Box 960, Herndon, VA 20172-0960, Cust Serv *Tel:* 703-661-1575 *Toll Free Tel:* 877-204-6073 *Fax:* 703-996-1010 *Toll Free Fax:* 877-204-6074 *E-mail:* suny@presswarehouse.com
Returns: SUNY Press, Returns Dept, 22883 Quicksilver Dr, Dulles, VA 20166, Cust Serv *Tel:* 703-661-1575 *Toll Free Tel:* 877-204-6073 *Fax:* 703-996-1010 *Toll Free Fax:* 877-204-6074 *E-mail:* suny@presswarehouse.com
Shipping Address: SUNY Press, 22835 Quicksilver Dr, Dulles, VA 20166, Cust Serv *Tel:* 703-661-1575 *Toll Free Tel:* 877-204-6073 *Fax:* 703-996-1010 *Toll Free Fax:* 877-204-6074 *E-mail:* suny@presswarehouse.com
Warehouse: SUNY Press, PO Box 960, Herndon, VA 20172-0960, Cust Serv *Tel:* 703-661-1575 *Toll Free Tel:* 877-204-6073 *Fax:* 703-996-1010 *Toll Free Fax:* 877-204-6074 *E-mail:* suny@presswarehouse.com

The Experiment
220 E 23 St, Suite 600, New York, NY 10010-4658
Tel: 212-889-1659
E-mail: info@theexperimentpublishing.com
Web Site: www.theexperimentpublishing.com
Key Personnel
Pres, Publr & CEO: Matthew Lore
COO & CFO: Peter Burri
Assoc Publr: Jennifer Hergenroeder
Exec Dir, Publg & Prodn: Pamela Schechter
Contracts & Rts Dir: Margie Guerra
 E-mail: margie@theexperimentpublishing.com
Creative Dir: Beth Bugler
Gen Dir & Roving Ed: Karen Giangreco
Mng Ed: Zachary Pace
Exec Ed: Nick Cizek
Assoc Ed: Danica Donovan
Ed: Sara Zatopek
Sr Designer: Jack Dunnington
Sr Publicist: Besse Lynch
Sales & Mktg Mgr: Will Rhino
Contracts & Rts Assoc: Madeleine Feinberg
Publg Assoc: Hannah Matuszak
Edit Asst: Michael Ripa
Founded: 2008
ISBN Prefix(es): 978-1-61519
Number of titles published annually: 50 Print; 50 E-Book
Total Titles: 410 Print; 410 E-Book
Distributed by W W Norton Company Inc
Foreign Rep(s): Affirm Press (Australia, New Zealand); Bill Bailey Publishers' Representatives (Europe); Canadian Manda Group (Canada); Michelle Morrow Curreri (Asia, Middle East); InterMediaAmericana Ltd (David Williams) (Caribbean, Latin America, South America); Melia Publishing Services Ltd (UK); Phambili (South Africa)
Foreign Rights: Agentur Brauer (Germany); Japan UNI Agency Inc (Japan); Alexander Korzhenevski Agency (Russia & former USSR);

Linwood Messina Literary Agency (Australia, France, French-speaking countries, India, New Zealand, UK); Agencia Riff (Brazil); Right Thing Agency (RTA) (Thailand, Vietnam)
Returns: Hachette Book Group, Attn: Returns Dept, 322 S Enterprise Blvd, Lebanon, IN 46052; University of Toronto Press Distribution, 5201 Dufferin St, Toronto, ON M3H 5T8, Canada *Toll Free Tel:* 800-565-9523 *Toll Free Fax:* 800-221-9985 *E-mail:* uptbooks@utpress.utoronto.ca
Distribution Center: Hachette Book Group, 1290 Avenue of the Americas, New York, NY 10104-0051 *Toll Free Tel:* 800-759-0190 *E-mail:* orders@hbgusa.com *Web Site:* hachettebookgroup.com
Membership(s): Association of American Publishers (AAP)

Facts Cures & Answers, see FC&A Publishing

§Facts On File
Imprint of Infobase Learning
1000 N West St, Suite 1281-230, Wilmington, DE 19801
SAN: 201-4696
Tel: 212-967-8800 *Toll Free Tel:* 800-322-8755 *Toll Free Fax:* 800-678-3633
E-mail: custserv@factsonfile.com
Web Site: infobasepublishing.com
Key Personnel
Pres & CEO: John Donoghue
CFO: Jim Housley
Dir, Book & Ebook Sales/Licensing & Busn Devt: Tonia Slain *E-mail:* tslain@infobase.com
Dir, Mktg & Publicity: Zina Scarpulla *E-mail:* zscarpulla@infobase.com
Dir, Sales & Opers: Mark Zielinski
Edit Dir, Print: Laurie Likoff
Founded: 1941
Award-winning publisher of authoritative curriculum-related print & online reference materials for schools & libraries.
ISBN Prefix(es): 978-0-8160; 978-0-87196; 978-1-60057; 978-1-60413; 978-1-4381; 978-1-57852; 978-1-61753
Number of titles published annually: 135 Print; 28 Online; 135 E-Book
Total Titles: 940 Print; 37 Online; 934 E-Book
Returns: Maple Logistics Solutions, Lebanon Distribution Center, 704 Legionaire Dr, Fredericksburg, PA 17026
Warehouse: Maple Logistics Solutions, Lebanon Distribution Center, 704 Legionaire Dr, Fredericksburg, PA 17026
Distribution Center: Maple Logistics Solutions, Lebanon Distribution Center, 704 Legionaire Dr, Fredericksburg, PA 17026

Fair Winds Press
Imprint of Quarto Publishing Group USA Inc
100 Cummings Ctr, Suite 265-D, Beverly, MA 01915
Tel: 978-282-9590 *Fax:* 978-282-7765
E-mail: sales@quarto.com
Web Site: www.quartoknows.com
Key Personnel
SVP & Group Publg Dir, US: Winnie Prentiss *E-mail:* winnie.prentiss@quarto.com
Group Publr: Erik Gilg *E-mail:* erik.gilg@quarto.com
Founded: 2001
Offer nonfiction books in a range of practical categories, including nutrition & cookery, fitness, parenting, beauty, treating sickness, mental health & using new medicine.
ISBN Prefix(es): 978-1-59233
Number of titles published annually: 30 Print
Total Titles: 200 Print

Fairchild Books
Division of Bloomsbury Publishing Plc
1385 Broadway, 5th fl, New York, NY 10018
SAN: 201-470X
Tel: 212-419-5300 *Toll Free Tel:* 800-932-4724; 888-330-8477 (orders)
Web Site: www.bloomsbury.com/us/discover/bloomsbury-academic/fairchild-books/
Key Personnel
Publr: Emily Samulski *E-mail:* emily.samulski@bloomsbury.com
Dir, Scholarly & Student Publg US: Haaris Naqvi
Asst Ed: Maria Nunez
Devt Mgr: Joseph Miranda *E-mail:* joseph.miranda@bloomsbury.com
Higher Educ Rep: Kirby Pendergast *E-mail:* kirby.pendergast@bloomsbury.com
Founded: 1910
Interior design, fashion, merchandising, marketing, management, retailing, careers market, research art foundation, clothing, textiles.
Membership(s): Interior Design Educators Council (IDEC); International Textiles Apparel Association (ITAA).
ISBN Prefix(es): 978-0-87005; 978-1-56367; 978-1-60901
Number of titles published annually: 40 Print; 30 CD-ROM
Total Titles: 375 Print; 60 CD-ROM
Orders to: MPS Distribution Center, 16365 James Madison Hwy, Gordonsville, VA 22942-8501
Returns: MPS Distribution Center, 16365 James Madison Hwy, Gordonsville, VA 22942-8501
Warehouse: MPS Distribution Center, 16365 James Madison Hwy, Gordonsville, VA 22942-8501
Distribution Center: MPS Distribution Center, 16365 James Madison Hwy, Gordonsville, VA 22942-8501

Faith & Fellowship Publishing
Subsidiary of Church of the Lutheran Brethren
1020 W Alcott Ave, Fergus Falls, MN 56537
Tel: 218-736-7357 *Toll Free Tel:* 800-332-9232
E-mail: ffpublishing@clba.org
Web Site: www.clba.org
Key Personnel
Dir: Tim Mathiesen
Religious books, newsletters.
ISBN Prefix(es): 978-0-943167
Number of titles published annually: 6 Print
Total Titles: 59 Print

§Faith Library Publications
Subsidiary of RHEMA Bible Church
PO Box 50126, Tulsa, OK 74150-0126
Tel: 918-258-1588 *Toll Free Tel:* 888-258-0999 (orders) *Fax:* 918-872-7710 (orders)
E-mail: flp@rhema.org
Web Site: www.rhema.org/store
Key Personnel
Dept Head, Kenneth Hagin Ministries: Brian Cumberland
Founded: 1963
ISBN Prefix(es): 978-0-89276; 978-1-60616
Number of titles published annually: 4 Print; 15 CD-ROM
Total Titles: 185 Print; 115 CD-ROM; 185 E-Book
Distributed by Harrison House; Whitaker

§Faithlife Corp
1313 Commercial St, Bellingham, WA 98225
Tel: 360-527-1700 *Toll Free Tel:* 888-563-0382
E-mail: support@faithlife.com; customerservice@logos.com
Web Site: faithlife.com
Key Personnel
CEO: Bill McCarthy
Founded: 1992
Electronic & ebook publisher & technology provider.
ISBN Prefix(es): 978-1-57799 (Lexham Press); 978-1-68359
Number of titles published annually: 30 CD-ROM; 200 E-Book
Total Titles: 200 CD-ROM; 4,000 E-Book
Imprints: Lexham Press
Membership(s): Evangelical Christian Publishers Association (ECPA); Society of Bible Literature (SBL)

§Familius
PO Box 1249, Reedley, CA 93654
Tel: 559-876-2170 *Fax:* 559-876-2180
E-mail: orders@familius.com
Web Site: www.familius.com
Key Personnel
Founder & CEO: Christopher Robbins *E-mail:* christopher@familius.com
Founder & Acqs: Michele Robbins
Edit Dir: Brooke Jorden *E-mail:* brooke@familius.com
Dir, Sales & Mktg: Ashley Mireles-Guerrero *E-mail:* ashley@familius.com
Founded: 2012
ISBN Prefix(es): 978-1-938301; 978-1-939629; 978-1-942672
Number of titles published annually: 60 Print; 50 E-Book; 40 Audio
Total Titles: 300 Print; 120 E-Book; 100 Audio
Distributed by Abrams Books (worldwide exc CN)
Foreign Rep(s): Baker & Taylor (worldwide exc Australia, Canada, New Zealand, UK & USA)
Foreign Rights: Drop Cap Agency (worldwide exc USA)
Membership(s): Independent Book Publishers Association (IBPA)

§Farcountry Press
2750 Broadwater Ave, Helena, MT 59602-9202
Mailing Address: PO Box 5630, Helena, MT 59604-5630
Tel: 406-422-1263 *Toll Free Tel:* 800-821-3874 (sales off) *Fax:* 406-443-5480
E-mail: books@farcountrypress.com; sales@farcountrypress.com
Web Site: www.farcountrypress.com
Key Personnel
Publr: Linda Netschert *E-mail:* linda.netschert@farcountrypress.com
Pubns Dir: Kathy Springmeyer *E-mail:* kathy@farcountrypress.com
Publicist: Shannon Johnston
Founded: 1980
Softcover & hardcover color photography books showcasing the nation's cities, states, national parks & wildlife. Also publish nonfiction children's series, guidebooks, cookbooks & regional history titles nationwide.
ISBN Prefix(es): 978-0-93814; 978-1-56037; 978-1-59152 (Sweetgrass Books)
Number of titles published annually: 25 Print
Membership(s): APPL; The Association of Publishers for Special Sales (APSS); Independent Book Publishers Association (IBPA); Publishers Association of the West (PubWest)

Farrar, Straus & Giroux Books for Young Readers
Imprint of Macmillan Children's Publishing Group
120 Broadway, New York, NY 10271
Tel: 212-741-6900 *Toll Free Tel:* 888-330-8477 (orders)
E-mail: childrens.publicity@macmillanusa.com; childrensrights@macmillanusa.com
Web Site: us.macmillan.com/mackids
Key Personnel
Pres, Macmillan Children's Publishing Group: Jennifer Besser
SVP & Publr: Allison Verost
VP & Assoc Publr: Bess Braswell
VP & Exec Dir, Publicity: Molly Ellis
VP & Exec Edit Dir: Joy Peskin

U.S. PUBLISHERS

VP & Sr Creative Dir: Beth Clark
VP, Mktg: Mariel Dawson
VP, Subs Rts: Kristin Dulaney
Sr Art Dir: Sharismar Rodriguez
Art Dir: Aurora Parlagreco
Creative Dir: Kirk Benshoff
Dir, Acct Mktg: Johanna Allen
Dir, Mktg: Robert Brown; Melissa Zar
Dir, Publicity: Morgan Kane; Kelsey Marrujo
Dir, School & Lib Mktg: Mary Van Akin
Assoc Art Dir: Samira Iravani
Assoc Dir, Mktg: Katie Quinn
Assoc Dir, Prodn Edit: Kat Kopit
Exec Ed: Wesley Adams; Janine O'Malley
Sr Mng Ed: Allyson Floridia
Sr Ed: Grace Kendall
Sr Prodn Ed: Mia Moran; Avia Perez; Helen Seachrist; Kathy Wielgosz; Ilana Worrell
Ed: Trisha de Guzman
Asst Ed: Asia Harden
Sr Mgr, Acct Mktg: Nicole Schaeffer
Sr Mgr, Subs Rts: Kaitlin Loss
Sr Mktg Mgr, School & Lib: Alexandra Quill
Sr Mktg Designer: Danielle Imperiale
Mktg Mgr: Teresa Ferraiolo; Jordin Streeter; Elysse Villalobos
Publicity Mgr: Morgan Rath
Assoc Mktg Mgr: Leigh Ann Higgins; Gabriella Salpeter
Asst Mgr, Subs Rts: Jordan Winch
Sr Publicist: Chantal Gersch
Publicist: Tatiana Merced-Zarou; Samantha Sacks
Mktg Coord: Carlee Maurier
Sr Designer: Cassie Gonzales; Mariam Quraishi; Lindsey Whitt
Designer: Ashley Caswell
Jr Designer: Abby Granata
Assoc Designer: Naomi Silverio
Mktg Assoc: Megan McDonald; Naheid Shahsamand
Publicity Asst: Sara Elroubi
Publisher's Asst: Hana Tzou
Founded: 1953
Preschool through young adult fiction & nonfiction, hardcover & paperback.
ISBN Prefix(es): 978-0-374
Number of titles published annually: 80 Print
Total Titles: 700 Print
Orders to: MPS-Virginia, 16365 James Madison Hwy, Gordonsville, VA 22942-8501 *Toll Free Tel:* 888-330-8477 *Toll Free Fax:* 800-672-2054 *E-mail:* orders@mpsvirginia.com SAN: 631-5011
Membership(s): The Children's Book Council (CBC)

Farrar, Straus & Giroux, LLC
Subsidiary of Macmillan
120 Broadway, New York, NY 10271
SAN: 206-782X
Tel: 212-741-6900
E-mail: fsg.publicity@fsgbooks.com; sales@fsgbooks.com
Web Site: us.macmillan.com/fsg
Key Personnel
Chmn & Exec Ed: Jonathan Galassi
Pres & Publr: Mitzi Angel
Publr, MCD/FSG: Sean McDonald
SVP & Dir, Publicity: Sarita Varma *Tel:* 917-940-2542 *E-mail:* sarita.varma@fsgbooks.com
SVP & Dir, Publicity & Mktg: Sheila O'Shea *Tel:* 917-257-8412 *E-mail:* sheila.oshea@fsgbooks.com
SVP & Edit Dir, MCD/AUWA Books: Alexis Rosenzweig
SVP & Ed-in-Chief: Jenna Johnson
VP & Contracts Dir: Erika Seidman
VP & Edit Dir, Nonfiction: Eric Chinski
VP & Exec Mng Ed: Debra Helfand
VP, Subs Rts: Devon Mazzone
Publr & Ed-in-Chief, MCD/AUWA Books: Ahmir "Questlove" Thompson
Creative Dir: Na Kim
Dir, Mktg: Hillary Tisman
Dir, Mktg, MCD/FSG & Picador: Daniel del Valle
Assoc Art Dir: Thomas Colligan
Assoc Dir, Prodn: Nina Frieman
Assoc Dir, Publicity: Brian Gittis; Steve Weil *Tel:* 610-608-8413 *E-mail:* stephen.weil@fsgbooks.com
Sr Mng Ed: Scott Auerbach
Exec Ed: Alex Star
Exec Ed, MCD/AUWA Books: Malaika Adero
Sr Ed, MCD/FSG: Jackson Howard
Sr Prodn Ed: Bri Panzica
Ed: Trish de Guzman
Ed-at-Large: Ileene Smith
Assoc Ed: Milo Walls; Ian Van Wye
Asst Ed: Ben Brooks; Lianna Culp
Sr Mgr, Subs Rts: Flora Esterly
Assoc Mktg Mgr: Caitlin Cataffo; Jonathan Woollen
Sr Publicist: Rose Sheehan
Sr Publicist/Mktg Strategist, MCD/FSG: Claire Tobin
Publicist: Jillian Briglia *Tel:* 503-577-2349 *E-mail:* jillian.briglia@fsgbooks.com; Sarah Haeckel
Mktg Assoc: Isabella Miranda
Founded: 1946
General fiction, nonfiction, poetry & juveniles.
ISBN Prefix(es): 978-0-374
Number of titles published annually: 150 Print
Total Titles: 1,400 Print
Imprints: Farrar, Straus & Giroux Books for Young Readers; FSG Originals; Hill & Wang; MCD/AUWA Books; MCD/FSG; North Point Press
Distributor for Drawn & Quarterly; Gray Wolf Books
Foreign Rep(s): Raincoast Books (Canada)
Foreign Rights: ANA Baltic (Tatjana Zoldnere) (Estonia, Latvia, Lithuania); AnatoliatLit Agency (Amy Spangler & Eda Caca) (Turkey); Anthea Agency (Katalina Sabeva) (Bulgaria); Bardon-Chinese Media (David Tsai) (China, Taiwan); Anoukh Foerg Agency (Germany); Deborah Harris Agency (Geula Geurts) (Israel); International Copyright Agency (Simon Kessler & Marina Adriana) (Romania); The Italian Literary Agency Srl (Claire Sabatie-Garat) (Italy); Anna Jarota Agency (Dominika Bojanowska) (Poland); Anna Jarota Agency Poland (Zuzanna Brzezinska) (Russia); Katai & Bolza (Peter Bolza) (Hungary); Korea Copyright Center Inc (KCC) (Joeun Lee) (South Korea); Marotte et Compagnie Agence Littéraire (Corinne Marotte) (France); Maxima Creative Agency (Santo Manurung) (Indonesia); MB Agencia Literaria (Monica Martin & Ines Planells) (Portugal, Spain); Kristin Olson Literarni Agentura (Czechia, Slovakia); Plima Literary Agency (Vuk Perisic) (Albania, Croatia, Serbia, Slovenia); Read n Right Agency (Nike Davarinou) (Greece); Riff Agency (Laura & Joao Paulo Riff) (Brazil); Sebes & Bisseling Literary Agency (Paul Sebes) (Netherlands); Tuttle-Mori Agency Inc (Asako Kawachi) (Japan)
Warehouse: MPS Distribution Center, 16365 James Madison Hwy, Gordonsville, VA 22942 *Toll Free Tel:* 888-330-8477 *E-mail:* orders@mpsvirginia.com *Web Site:* us.macmillan.com/mps
Membership(s): The Children's Book Council (CBC)
See separate listing for:
Hill & Wang
North Point Press

§Father & Son Publishing Inc
4909 N Monroe St, Tallahassee, FL 32303-7015
Tel: 850-562-2712 *Toll Free Tel:* 800-741-2712 (orders only) *Fax:* 850-562-0916
Web Site: www.fatherson.com
Key Personnel
Pres: Lance Coalson *E-mail:* lance@fatherson.com
Founded: 1982
Publishers of nonfiction, historical fiction, cookbooks, giftbooks & children's books.
ISBN Prefix(es): 978-0-942407; 978-1-935802
Number of titles published annually: 12 Print; 3 Audio
Total Titles: 212 Print; 15 Audio
Distributor for BADM Books
Membership(s): American Booksellers Association (ABA); Florida Authors & Publishers Association Inc (FAPA); National Association of Independent Publishers (NAIP)

FC&A Publishing
103 Clover Green, Peachtree City, GA 30269
Tel: 770-487-6307 *Toll Free Tel:* 800-226-8024
Web Site: www.fca.com
Key Personnel
CFO: Tim Anders
Founded: 1969
Specialize in nonfiction self-help publications.
ISBN Prefix(es): 978-0-915099; 978-1-890957; 978-1-932470; 978-1-935574
Number of titles published annually: 3 Print; 3 Online
Total Titles: 36 Print; 30 Online

Federal Street Press
Division of Merriam-Webster Inc
47 Federal St, Springfield, MA 01102
Mailing Address: PO Box 281, Springfield, MA 01102
Tel: 413-734-3134 (ext 8158) *Toll Free Tel:* 800-828-1880 *Fax:* 413-731-5979
E-mail: sales@federalstreetpress.com; customerservice@federalstreetpress.com; orders@federalstreetpress.com
Web Site: federalstreetpress.com
Founded: 1998
Offers up-to-date, quality, value-priced language reference titles created in cooperation with the editors of Merriam-Webster Inc.
ISBN Prefix(es): 978-1-892859; 978-1-59695
Number of titles published annually: 5 Print
Total Titles: 45 Print

Philipp Feldheim Inc, see Feldheim Publishers

Feldheim Publishers
208 Airport Executive Park, Nanuet, NY 10954
SAN: 207-0545
Tel: 845-356-2282 *Toll Free Tel:* 800-237-7149 (orders) *Fax:* 845-425-1908
E-mail: sales@feldheim.com
Web Site: www.feldheim.com
Key Personnel
Pres: Yitzchak Feldheim
Mng Dir: Eli M Hollander *E-mail:* eli3@feldheim.com
Sales Mgr: Suzanne Brandt *E-mail:* suzanne@feldheim.com
Founded: 1939
Translations from Hebrew of Jewish classical works & works of contemporary authors in the field of Orthodox Jewish thought & contemporary Jewish literature for ages three & up.
This publisher has indicated that 50% of their product line is author subsidized.
ISBN Prefix(es): 978-0-87306; 978-1-58330; 978-1-59826; 978-1-68025
Number of titles published annually: 80 Print
Total Titles: 800 Print
Imprints: Ayal Press; Sapir Press
Foreign Office(s): F Books Ltd, Box 43163, 91431 Jerusalem, Israel
Distributor for Adir Press; Jerusalem Publications; Mosaica Press

PUBLISHERS

The Feminist Press at The City University of New York
365 Fifth Ave, Suite 5406, New York, NY 10016
SAN: 213-6813
Tel: 212-817-7915 *Fax:* 212-817-1593
E-mail: info@feministpress.org
Web Site: www.feministpress.org
Key Personnel
Exec Dir & Publr: Margot Atwell
　E-mail: margot@feministpress.org
Art Dir: Drew Stevens *E-mail:* drew@feministpress.org
Dir, Community Engagement: Lucia Brown
　E-mail: lucia@feministpress.org
Devt Coord & Prodn Ed: Rachel Page
　E-mail: rachel@feministpress.org
Publicity & Events Coord: Nadine Santoro
　E-mail: nadine@feministpress.org
Sales & Mktg Coord: Rachel Gilman
　E-mail: rgilman@feministpress.org
Exec & Prog Asst: Alicia Lim *E-mail:* alicia@feministpress.org
Founded: 1970
Popular culture, African studies, Asian American studies, international studies, history of feminism, women's studies, working class studies, current issues & women's literature from the Middle East, Africa, Asia & Latin America & US women writers.
ISBN Prefix(es): 978-0-912670; 978-0-935312; 978-1-55861; 978-1-936932
Number of titles published annually: 18 Print; 10 E-Book
Total Titles: 400 Print; 50 E-Book
Foreign Rights: AnatoliaLit Agency (Amy Spangler) (Turkey); The Foreign Office (Teresa Vilarrubla) (Latin America, Spain); The Deborah Harris Agency (Geula Geurts) (Israel); Japan UNI Agency (Miko Yamanouchi) (Japan); Natoli, Stefan & Oliva (Roberta Oliva) (Italy); VBMLitag (Luciana Villas-Boas) (Brazil, Portugal); Literary Agent Silke Weniger (Germany)
Distribution Center: Consortium Book Sales & Distribution, The Keg House, Suite 101, 34 13 Ave NE, Minneapolis, MN 55413-1007 *Tel:* 612-746-2600 *Toll Free Tel:* 866-400-5351 (cust serv, Jackson, TN) *E-mail:* cbsdinfo@ingramcontent.com *Web Site:* www.cbsd.com
SAN: 200-6049
Baker & Taylor International, 652 E Main St, PO Box 6920, Bridgewater, NJ 08807-0920 (worldwide exc Africa, Asia, Canada, Continental Europe, Middle East, UK & US) *Tel:* 908-218-0400 *Fax:* 908-707-4387 *E-mail:* btinfo@btol.com *Web Site:* btol.com/international.cfm
Turnaround Publisher Services Ltd, Unit 3, Olympia Trading Estate, Coburg Rd, Wood Green, London, United Kingdom (Africa, Asia, Continental Europe, Middle East & UK) *Tel:* (020) 8829 3000 *Fax:* (020) 8881 5088 *E-mail:* orders@turnaround-uk.com *Web Site:* www.turnaround-uk.com
Membership(s): Association of American Publishers (AAP); Community of Literary Magazines & Presses (CLMP); National Council for Research on Women (NCRW)

Fence Books
Imprint of Fence Magazine Inc
36-09 28 Ave, Apt 3R, Astoria, NY 11103-4518
Tel: 518-567-7006
Web Site: www.fenceportal.org
Key Personnel
Co-Edit Dir: Emily Wallis Hughes *Tel:* 530-220-4373; Jason Zuzga *Tel:* 267-902-0731
Fence Digital Ed: Robbie Held
Web Ed: Menachem Kaiser
Dist: Emily Wallis Hughes
Edit & Spec Projs Asst: Amy Beth Sisson
Founded: 2001
ISBN Prefix(es): 978-1-934200; 978-0-9771064; 978-0-9713189; 978-0-9663324; 978-0-9740909; 978-0-9864373; 978-1-944380
Number of titles published annually: 6 Print
Total Titles: 90 Print
Imprints: Fence Digital; La Presse
Distribution Center: Consortium Book Sales & Distribution, The Keg House, 34 13 Ave NE, Suite 101, Minneapolis, MN 55413 *Tel:* 612-746-2600 *E-mail:* cbsdinfo@ingramcontent.com *Web Site:* www.cbsd.com

Feral House
1240 W Sims Way, Suite 124, Port Townsend, WA 98368
Tel: 323-666-3311
E-mail: info@feralhouse.com
Web Site: feralhouse.com
Key Personnel
Pres & Publr: Jessica Parfrey
Founded: 1989
Pop culture, alternative, art, nonfiction, religion, sociology & social sciences.
ISBN Prefix(es): 978-0-922915; 978-1-932595
Number of titles published annually: 12 Print
Total Titles: 120 Print
Imprints: Process Media Inc
Distribution Center: Consortium Book Sales & Distribution/Ingram, The Keg House, Suite 101, 34 13 Ave NE, Minneapolis, MN 55413-1007 *Tel:* 612-746-2600 *Toll Free Tel:* 866-400-5351 (cust serv, Jackson, TN) *E-mail:* cbsdinfo@ingramcontent.com *Web Site:* www.cbsd.com SAN: 200-6049
Turnaround Publisher Services, Olympia Trading Estate, Unit 3, Coburg Rd, London N22 6TZ, United Kingdom *Tel:* (020) 8829 3000 *Fax:* (020) 8881 5088 *E-mail:* orders@turnaround-uk.com

§Ferguson Publishing
Imprint of Infobase Learning
132 W 31 St, 16 fl, New York, NY 10001
Tel: 212-967-8800 *Toll Free Tel:* 800-322-8755
　Toll Free Fax: 800-678-3633
E-mail: custserv@infobase.com
Web Site: infobasepublishing.com
Key Personnel
CEO: John Donoghue
CFO: Neil Hamilton
Chief Revenue Offr: Tonia Slain *E-mail:* tslain@infobase.com
VP & Edit Dir: Laurie Likoff
VP, Mktg: Lesley Weller
Dir, Book & Ebook Sales: James Chambers
　E-mail: jchambers@infobase.com
Dir, Mktg: Zina Scarpulla
With its acclaimed career guidance & reference materials, Ferguson Publishing is known among librarians & guidance counselors as the premier publisher in the career education field.
ISBN Prefix(es): 978-0-8160; 978-0-87196; 978-0-89434; 978-1-60413; 978-1-4381
Number of titles published annually: 74 Print; 74 E-Book
Total Titles: 200 Print; 200 E-Book

Fiction Collective 2 (FC2)
Imprint of University of Alabama Press
c/o University of Alabama Press, Box 870380, Tuscaloosa, AL 35487-0380
Web Site: fc2.org
Founded: 1974
Publish formally innovative fiction.
ISBN Prefix(es): 978-1-57366
Number of titles published annually: 6 Print
Total Titles: 200 Print
Distributed by University of Alabama Press
Foreign Rep(s): Eurospan Group (Jessica Ennis) (Africa, Asia, Caribbean, Europe, Latin America, Middle East, The Pacific, South America, UK)

U.S. PUBLISHERS

Distribution Center: University of Alabama Press, Chicago Distribution Center, 11030 S Langley Ave, Chicago, IL 60628 *Tel:* 773-702-7000 *Toll Free Tel:* 800-621-2736 *Fax:* 773-702-7212 *Toll Free Fax:* 800-621-8476 *E-mail:* orders@press.uchicago.edu *Web Site:* www.uapress.ua.edu
University of Toronto Press Distribution, 5201 Dufferin St, Toronto, ON M3H 5T8, Canada *Tel:* 416-667-7791 *Toll Free Tel:* 800-565-9523 *Fax:* 416-667-7832 *Toll Free Fax:* 800-221-9985 *E-mail:* utpbooks@utpress.utoronto.ca
Membership(s): Community of Literary Magazines & Presses (CLMP)

1517 Media, see Augsburg Fortress Publishers, Publishing House of the Evangelical Lutheran Church in America

Fifth Estate Publishing
2795 County Hwy 57, Blountsville, AL 35031
SAN: 852-6419
Tel: 256-631-5107
E-mail: josephlumpkin@hotmail.com
Web Site: fifthestatepub.com
Founded: 2003
Publisher & distributor.
ISBN Prefix(es): 978-0-9746336; 978-0-9760992; 978-0-9768233; 978-1-933580; 978-1-936533
Number of titles published annually: 6 Print; 6 Online; 6 E-Book
Total Titles: 101 Print; 91 Online; 172 E-Book

Filter Press LLC
PO Box 95, Palmer Lake, CO 80133
SAN: 201-484X
Tel: 719-481-2420 *Toll Free Tel:* 888-570-2663
　Fax: 719-481-2420
E-mail: info@filterpressbooks.com; orders@filterpressbooks.com
Web Site: filterpressbooks.com
Key Personnel
Pres: Doris Baker *E-mail:* doris@filterpressbooks.com
Founded: 1957
Publisher of books on the American West, Western expansion, children's historical fiction, Colorado history & biography.
ISBN Prefix(es): 978-0-910584; 978-0-86541
Number of titles published annually: 3 Print; 1 Audio
Total Titles: 110 Print; 2 CD-ROM; 67 E-Book; 2 Audio
Returns: 19980 Top O'Moor W, Monument, CO 80132
Shipping Address: 19980 Top O'Moor W, Monument, CO 80132
Membership(s): Colorado Association of Libraries; Colorado Independent Publishers Association (CIPA); Women Writing the West

Financial Times Press
Imprint of Pearson Education Ltd
221 River St, Hoboken, NJ 07030
E-mail: customer-service@informit.com; community@informit.com
Web Site: www.informit.com/promotions/pearson-ft-press-141135
Publisher of business, management, investment & finance books for general consumers, professionals & students.
ISBN Prefix(es): 978-0-13; 978-1-292
Number of titles published annually: 165 Print
Total Titles: 5,143 Print; 6,580 E-Book
Imprints: FT Press
Returns: c/o Pearson Returns Facility, 5536 W 74 St, Indianapolis, IN 46268

Fine Creative Media, Inc
589 Eighth Ave, 6th fl, New York, NY 10018
Tel: 212-595-3500 *Fax:* 212-202-4195
E-mail: info@mjfbooks.com

U.S. PUBLISHERS

Key Personnel
Founder & CEO: Michael J Fine *E-mail:* mjf@mjfbooks.com
VP, Acqs, MJF Books: Antony Fine
   E-mail: afine@mjfbooks.com
Dir, Admin & HR: Steven Fine
Dir, Prodn: Benjamin Lee
Acqs Ed, MJF Books: Kaethe Fine
Founded: 1991
Leading independent publisher of hardcover & paperback promotional reprints of fiction & nonfiction under the MJF Books imprint. Subject categories include self-improvement, mind/body/spirit, business, history & reference. Also publisher of the Barnes & Noble Classics series, produced in conjunction with Barnes & Noble Inc.
ISBN Prefix(es): 978-1-56731 (MJF Books); 978-1-59308 (Barnes & Noble Classics); 978-1-60671 (MJF Books)
Number of titles published annually: 80 Print
Total Titles: 1,500 Print
Imprints: Barnes & Noble Classics; MJF Books

FineEdge.com LLC
910 25 St, Unit B, Anacortes, WA 98221
Tel: 360-299-8500 *Fax:* 360-299-0535
E-mail: orders@fineedge.com; info@waggonerguide.com
Web Site: www.waggonerguidebooks.com; waggonerguide.com
Key Personnel
Publr & Ed: Mark Bunzel
Mng Ed: Leonard Landon; Lorena Landon
Founded: 1986
Publishing, wholesaling, outdoor guidebooks & maps. Specialize in nautical books & mountain biking publications.
ISBN Prefix(es): 978-0-938665; 978-1-932310
Number of titles published annually: 3 Print
Total Titles: 50 Print; 2 Online
Distributed by Heritage House; Sunbelt Publications Inc

§Fire Engineering Books & Videos
Clarion Events LLC, 110 S Hartford, Suite 220, Tulsa, OK 74120
Tel: 918-831-9421 *Toll Free Tel:* 800-752-9764
   Fax: 918-831-9555
E-mail: info@fireengineeringbooks.com
Web Site: fireengineeringbooks.com
Key Personnel
Devt Ed: Chris Barton *E-mail:* christopher.barton@clarionevents.com
Prodn Mgr: Tony Quinn
Founded: 1877
Fire science, suppression & protection, petroleum, electric power, water, hazardous materials books & videos.
ISBN Prefix(es): 978-0-912212; 978-1-59370
Number of titles published annually: 10 Print; 5 CD-ROM
Total Titles: 120 Print; 10 CD-ROM
Distributed by David Publishing; Fire Protection Publications
Distributor for Brady; Idea Bank; IFSTA; Mosby
Foreign Rep(s): Disvan Enterprises (Ish Dawar) (India); Eurospan (Africa, Asia, Australasia, Europe, Middle East); Tony Poh (Southeast Asia); Publishers Representatives (Tahir M Lodhi) (Pakistan)

§Firefall Editions
Imprint of Firefallmedia
4905 Tunlaw St, Alexandria, VA 22312
Tel: 510-549-2461
E-mail: literary@att.net
Web Site: www.firefallmedia.com
Key Personnel
Mng Dir: Robinson Joyce
Mktg Dir: Kathryn DeLappe *E-mail:* prize@att.net
Founded: 1996
Specialize in fiction, photography, art, autobiographies, textbooks, audiobooks & documentary films.
ISBN Prefix(es): 978-0-915090; 978-1-939434
Number of titles published annually: 7 Print; 2 E-Book; 5 Audio
Total Titles: 111 Print; 10 E-Book; 32 Audio
Imprints: Firefall Originals
Foreign Office(s): Firefallmedia, 17 Shore Rd, Drummore, by Stranraer, Dumfries & Galloway DG9 9PU, United Kingdom
Distribution Center: Brodart Books & Library Services, 500 Arch St, Williamsport, PA 17701
Web Site: www.brodartbooks.com

First Avenue Editions
Imprint of Lerner Publishing Group Inc
241 First Ave N, Minneapolis, MN 55401
Tel: 612-332-3344 *Toll Free Tel:* 800-328-4929
   Fax: 612-332-7615 *Toll Free Fax:* 800-332-1132
E-mail: info@lernerbooks.com; custserve@lernerbooks.com
Web Site: www.lernerbooks.com; www.facebook.com/lernerbooks
Key Personnel
Chmn: Harry J Lerner
EVP & COO: Mark Budde
EVP & CFO: Margaret Thomas
Pres & Publr: Adam Lerner
EVP, Sales: David Wexler
VP & Ed-in-Chief: Andy Cummings
VP, Mktg: Rachel Zugschwert
Dir, HR: Margaret Wolfson *E-mail:* mwolfson@lernerbooks.com
Dir, Rts, Spec Sales & Intl Dist: Maria Kjoller
Publg Dir, School & Lib: Jenny Krueger
School & Lib Mktg Dir: Lois Wallentine
Social studies, picture storybooks, art, multicultural issues, activity books & beginning readers.
Number of titles published annually: 10 Print; 10 E-Book
Total Titles: 240 Print; 240 E-Book
Foreign Rep(s): Bounce Sales & Marketing Ltd (Europe, India, Middle East, Pakistan, Scandinavia, UK); CrossCan Education (Canada); Lerner Publishing Group (Maria Kjoller) (Australia, New Zealand); Phambili Agencies (Botswana, Lesotho, Namibia, Southern Africa, Swaziland, Zimbabwe); Publishers Marketing Services (PMS) (Brunei, Malaysia, Singapore); Saunders (school & lib) (Canada)
Foreign Rights: AC2 Literary (Italy); Sandra Bruna Literary Agency (Brazil, Portugal, Spain); CA-Link (Hong Kong, Macau, Mainland China, Taiwan); Japan Foreign-Rights Centre (JFC) (Japan); Korea Copyright Center Inc (KCC) (South Korea); Agence Michelle Lapautre (France); RightsMix (Eastern Europe, Greece, Israel, Netherlands, Russia, Scandinavia, UK); Literarische Agentur Silke Weniger (Germany)
Warehouse: CGC Fulfillment Warehouse, 150 Kingswood Dr, Mankato, MN 56001

Fitzroy Books
Imprint of Regal House Publishing
c/o Regal House Publishing, 806 Oberlin Rd, No 12094, Raleigh, NC 27605
E-mail: info@regalhousepublishing.com
Web Site: fitzroybooks.com
Key Personnel
Founder, Publr & Ed-in-Chief: Jaynie Royal
Mng Ed: Pam Van Dyk
Ed: Elizabeth Lowenstein
Founded: 2014
Fitzroy Books is dedicated to the publication & promotion of high-quality literature in the children's, young adult, & middle grade fiction categories. We provide extensive editorial support to our authors & strong pre- & post-release digital marketing campaigns to further amplify our authors' outreach efforts. We seek authors with whom we can form meaningful partnerships, working together in a collaborative fashion to best polish & promote their work. We are delighted to accept submissions directly from authors at: regalhousepublishing.submittable.com/submit.
ISBN Prefix(es): 978-0-9912612; 978-0-9988398; 978-1-947548
Number of titles published annually: 11 Print; 11 E-Book
Foreign Rights: Gotham Group (film/tv rts partner); Rightol Media (Asia)
Orders to: Independent Publishers Group (IPG), 814 N Franklin St, Chicago, IL 60610 *Toll Free Tel:* 800-888-4741 *Web Site:* www.ipgbook.com
Distribution Center: Independent Publishers Group (IPG), 814 N Franklin St, Chicago, IL 60610 *Tel:* 312-337-0747 *Fax:* 312-337-5085 *Web Site:* www.ipgbook.com
Membership(s): American Booksellers Association (ABA); The Children's Book Council (CBC); Community of Literary Magazines & Presses (CLMP); Independent Book Publishers Association (IBPA); Southern Independent Booksellers Alliance (SIBA)

FJH Music Co Inc
100 SE Third Ave, Suite 1000, Fort Lauderdale, FL 33394
Tel: 954-382-6061 *Fax:* 954-382-3073
E-mail: sales@fjhmusic.com
Web Site: www.fjhmusic.com
Key Personnel
VP: Kevin Hackinson *E-mail:* kevinh@fjhmusic.com; Kyle Hackinson
Founded: 1988
Educational music publications.
ISBN Prefix(es): 978-0-929666; 978-1-56939
Number of titles published annually: 100 Print
Distributed by Alfred Music

Flamingo Books
Imprint of Penguin Young Readers Group
c/o Penguin Random House LLC, 1745 Broadway, New York, NY 10019
Tel: 212-782-9000
Web Site: www.penguin.com/flamingo-overview/
Key Personnel
VP & Publr: Margaret Anastas
Ed: Cheryl Eissing
Asst Ed, Viking Children's Books & Flamingo Books: Claire Tattersfield
Asst Art Dir: Sophie Erb
Specializes in commercial picture books.
Penguin Random House & its publishing entities are not accepting unsol submissions, proposals, mss, or submission queries via e-mail at this time.
Number of titles published annually: 12 Print
Total Titles: 44 Print

Flashlight Press
527 Empire Blvd, Brooklyn, NY 11225
Tel: 718-288-8300 *Fax:* 718-972-6307
Web Site: www.flashlightpress.com
Key Personnel
Publr: Harry Mauer *E-mail:* publisher@flashlightpress.com
Ed: Shari Dash Greenspan *E-mail:* editor@flashlightpress.com
Founded: 2004
Children's picture books that explore & illuminate.
ISBN Prefix(es): 978-0-9729225; 978-0-9799746; 978-1-993612; 978-1-936261
Number of titles published annually: 3 Print
Total Titles: 32 Print; 33 E-Book
Returns: Independent Publishers Group (IPG), c/o Returns Dept, 814 N Franklin

St, Chicago, IL 60610 *Tel:* 312-337-0747 *Toll Free Tel:* 800-888-4741 *Fax:* 312-337-5985 *E-mail:* frontdesk@ipgbook.com *Web Site:* www.ipgbook.com
Distribution Center: Independent Publishers Group (IPG), 814 N Franklin St, Chicago, IL 60610 *Tel:* 312-337-0747 *Toll Free Tel:* 800-888-4741 *Fax:* 312-337-5985 *E-mail:* frontdesk@ipgbook.com *Web Site:* www.ipgbook.com

§Focus
Imprint of Hackett Publishing Co Inc
PO Box 390007, Cambridge, MA 02139-0001
Tel: 317-635-9250 *Fax:* 317-635-9292
E-mail: customer@hackettpublishing.com; editorial@hackettpublishing.com
Web Site: focusbookstore.com; www.hackettpublishing.com
Key Personnel
Pres, Publr & CEO: Deborah Wilkes
Edit Dir: Brian Rak
Rts Mgr: Maura Gaughan
Founded: 1985
Publisher of textbooks in modern languages, classical languages, philosophy & classics.
ISBN Prefix(es): 978-0-941051; 978-1-58510
Number of titles published annually: 30 Print; 30 E-Book
Total Titles: 900 Print; 500 E-Book
Distributor for Domus Latina Publishing
Foreign Rep(s): Accademia Vivarium Novum (Lingua Latina titles) (Continental Europe exc Portugal & Spain); Cultura Clasica SL (Lingua Latina titles) (Portugal, Spain); Gazelle Book Services Ltd (Europe, UK); NewSouth Books (Australia, New Zealand)
Orders to: PO Box 44937, Indianapolis, IN 46244-0937
Returns: 3333 Massachusetts Ave, Indianapolis, IN 46218
Shipping Address: 3333 Massachusetts Ave, Indianapolis, IN 46218

Focus on the Family
8605 Explorer Dr, Colorado Springs, CO 80920-1051
Tel: 719-531-5181 *Toll Free Tel:* 800-A-FAMILY (232-6459) *Fax:* 719-531-3424
Web Site: www.focusonthefamily.com; www.facebook.com/focusonthefamily
Key Personnel
VP, Communs: Paul Batura
Founded: 1986
Case bound & soft cover books (adult & children) dealing with family relationships & emphasizing the importance of values & Christian principles in people's lives.
ISBN Prefix(es): 978-0-929608; 978-1-56179; 978-1-58997; 978-1-60482; 978-1-62405; 978-1-62471
Number of titles published annually: 25 Print
Total Titles: 300 Print; 25 CD-ROM; 60 Audio
Imprints: Adventures in Odyssey; Heritage Builders; Life on the Edge; Radio Theatre; Ribbits; That the World May Know
Distributed by Baker Books; Moody Press; Tyndale House Publishers Inc; Zondervan

Fons Vitae
(Fountain of Life)
49 Mockingbird Valley Dr, Louisville, KY 40207-1366
Tel: 502-897-3641 *Fax:* 502-893-7373
E-mail: fonsvitaeky@aol.com
Web Site: www.fonsvitae.com
Key Personnel
Dir: Gray Henry *E-mail:* grayh101@aol.com
Proj Dir: Elena Lloyd-Sidle
Busn Mgr: Lucy Jones
Mktg & Multimedia: Mustafa Gouverneur
Founded: 1997
Fons Vitae is both an academic charity with 501(c)(3) charitable status & a peer-reviewed publishing house which ensures the highest scholarly standards for its publications. Authentic text, impeccably translated & exquisitely produced, make these volumes useful for both the university classroom & for those interested in the eternal verities with no compromise to a recent soft focus on spirituality.
ISBN Prefix(es): 978-1-887752
Number of titles published annually: 10 Print; 5 CD-ROM
Total Titles: 198 Print; 5 CD-ROM
Distributor for African American Islamic Institute; Anqa Press (UK); Aperture (NY); Archetype (UK); Broadstone Books; Dar Nun; Golganooza Press (UK); Islamic Texts Society (UK); Matheson Trust; Parabola; Paragon; Parvardigar Press; Pir Press (NY); Qiblah Books; Quilliam Press (UK); Sandala Productions; Sophia Perennis; Sri Lanka Institute of Traditional Studies; Thesaurus Islamicus Foundation; Tradigital; White Thread Press (US); Wisdom Foundation; World Wisdom (US); Zaytuna Institute Press (US)
Foreign Rep(s): American University in Cairo Press (AUC) (Middle East)
Distribution Center: Independent Publishers Group (IPG), 814 N Franklin St, Chicago 60610, IL *Tel:* 312-337-0747 *Toll Free Tel:* 800-888-4741 *Fax:* 312-337-5985 *E-mail:* frontdesk@ipgbook.com *Web Site:* www.ipgbook.com

Fordham University Press
Joseph A Martino Hall, 45 Columbus Ave, 3rd fl, New York, NY 10023
SAN: 201-6516
Fax: 347-842-3083
Web Site: www.fordhampress.com
Key Personnel
Dir: Fredric Nachbaur *Tel:* 646-868-4201
 E-mail: fnachbaur@fordham.edu
Edit Dir: Richard W Morrison *Tel:* 646-868-4208
 E-mail: rmorrison7@fordham.edu
Assoc Dir/Mktg & Sales Dir: Kathleen O'Brien-Nicholson *Tel:* 646-868-4204
 E-mail: bkaobrien@fordham.edu
Sr Acqs Ed: Tom Lay *Tel:* 646-868-4209
 E-mail: tlay@fordham.edu
Acqs Ed: John Garza *E-mail:* jgarza2@fordham.edu
Proj Ed: Kem Crimmins *E-mail:* crimmins@fordham.edu
Busn Mgr: Margaret Noonan *Tel:* 646-868-4206
 E-mail: mnoonan@fordham.edu
Asst Busn Mgr: Marie Hall *Tel:* 646-868-4207
 E-mail: mhall21@fordham.edu
Mktg Mgr: Katie Sweeney Parmiter *Tel:* 646-868-4205 *E-mail:* kasweeney@fordham.edu
Prodn & Design Mgr: Mark Lerner
 E-mail: mlerner7@fordham.edu
Rts & Perms Mgr: Will Cerbone *Tel:* 646-868-4203 *E-mail:* wcerbone@fordham.edu
Founded: 1907
Scholarly books & journals, New York regional books, general trade books & videos.
ISBN Prefix(es): 978-0-8232; 978-0-96529; 978-1-882763
Number of titles published annually: 70 Print
Total Titles: 450 Print
Imprints: American Literatures Initiative; Empire State Editions; The Modern Language Initiative
Distributed by Oxford University Press (US & CN)
Distributor for Creighton University Press; Institute for Advanced Study in the Theatre Arts (IASTA); Little Room Press; Rockhurst University Press; St Bede's Publications; University of San Francisco Press
Foreign Rep(s): Academic Marketing Services Pty Ltd (Mike Brightmore) (Southern Africa); Africa Connection (Guy Simpson) (Sub-Saharan Africa); Booktopia Publisher Services (BPS) (Australia, Fiji, New Zealand, Papua New Guinea); Canadian Manda Group (Canada); China Publishers Marketing (Benjamin Pan) (Asia, The Pacific); Combined Academic Publishers (CAP) (George Banbury) (Africa, Australia, Europe, Ireland, Middle East, New Zealand, Pacific Region, UK); Leonidas Diamantopoulos (Cyprus, Greece); Colin Flint Ltd (Ben Greig) (Denmark, Iceland); Colin Flint Ltd (Steven Haslemere) (Sweden); Colin Flint Ltd (Wilf Jones) (Finland, Norway); Ingram Publisher Services International (Tricia Remark) (Canada); International Publishers Representatives (Middle East, North Africa); Jacek Lewinson (Eastern Europe, Russia); Manohar Publishers & Distributors (Bangladesh, Bhutan, India, Maldives, Nepal, Sri Lanka); Mare Nostrum (Cristina De Lara Ruiz) (Portugal, Spain); Mare Nostrum (Lauren Keane) (Benelux, Netherlands); Mare Nostrum (Charlotte Anderson) (Austria, Central Europe, Germany, Switzerland); Mare Nostrum (Charlene Gaubert) (France); Mare Nostrum (Sara Lilliu) (Italy); Publishers International Marketing (Chris Ashdown) (Brunei, Cambodia, Indonesia, Japan, Laos, Malaysia, Philippines, Singapore, South Korea, Thailand, Timor-Leste, Vietnam); World Press (Saleem A Malik) (Pakistan)
Returns: Maple Logistics Solutions, Lebanon Distribution Ctr, 704 Legionaire Dr, Fredricksburg, PA 17026
Distribution Center: Ingram Publisher Services, 14 Ingram Blvd, Mail Stop 631, La Vergne, TN 37086 (CN & US) *Toll Free Tel:* 844-841-0258 *E-mail:* ordersupport@ingramcontent.com
Web Site: www.ingrampublisherservices.com
SAN: 631-8630
Membership(s): Association of American Publishers (AAP); Association of Jesuit University Presses; Association of University Presses (AUPresses)

Fortress Press, see Augsburg Fortress Publishers, Publishing House of the Evangelical Lutheran Church in America

§Forum Publishing Co
383 E Main St, Centerport, NY 11721
Tel: 631-754-5000 *Toll Free Tel:* 800-635-7654
 Fax: 631-754-0630
E-mail: forumpublishing@aol.com
Web Site: www.forum123.com
Key Personnel
Publr & CEO: Martin Stevens
Founded: 1981
Business magazines & books.
ISBN Prefix(es): 978-0-9626141
Number of titles published annually: 5 Print
Total Titles: 15 Print; 6 CD-ROM

Forward Movement
Affiliate of The Episcopal Church
412 Sycamore St, Cincinnati, OH 45202-4110
Tel: 513-721-6659 *Toll Free Tel:* 800-543-1813
 Fax: 513-721-0729 (orders)
E-mail: orders@forwardmovement.org (orders & cust serv)
Web Site: www.forwardmovement.org
Key Personnel
Dir, Busn Opers: Kathy Jose *E-mail:* kjose@forwardmovement.org
Dir, Mktg: Jason Merritt *E-mail:* jmerritt@forwardmovement.org
Ed: Richelle Thompson *E-mail:* rthompson@forwardmovement.org
Founded: 1935
Inspires disciples & empowers evangelists around the globe through offerings that encourage spiritual growth in individuals & congregations.
ISBN Prefix(es): 978-0-88028

U.S. PUBLISHERS

Number of titles published annually: 5 Print
Total Titles: 60 Print; 1 Audio
Imprints: FMP
Distributor for Anglican Book Centre
Warehouse: APG, 1501 County Hospital Rd, Nashville, TN 37218

Walter Foster Jr, see Walter Foster Publishing

Walter Foster Publishing
Imprint of Quarto Publishing Group USA Inc
26391 Crown Valley Pkwy, Suite 220, Mission Viejo, CA 92691
SAN: 249-051X
Tel: 949-380-7510 *Fax:* 949-380-7575
E-mail: walterfoster@quarto.com
Web Site: www.quartoknows.com/walter-foster
Key Personnel
VP & Group Publr: Anne Landa *E-mail:* anne.landa@quarto.com
Publr: Rebecca Razo *E-mail:* rebecca.razo@quarto.com
Founded: 1922
Instructional art books, specialty art & creative products.
ISBN Prefix(es): 978-0-929261; 978-1-56010; 978-1-60058; 978-1-63322
Number of titles published annually: 30 Print
Total Titles: 600 Print

Foundation Press
Imprint of West Academic
c/o West Academic, 860 Blue Gentian Rd, Eagan, MN 55121
Toll Free Tel: 877-888-1330
E-mail: support@westacademic.com
Web Site: www.westacademic.com
Key Personnel
Chief Content Offr & Publr: Pamela Siege Chandler *E-mail:* pamela.siege@westacademic.com
Dir, Mktg: Alice Hayward *E-mail:* alice.hayward@westacademic.com
Founded: 1931
Law, business, political science, criminal justice, curriculum books, graduate & undergraduate, primarily in law.
ISBN Prefix(es): 978-0-88277; 978-1-56662; 978-1-58778; 978-1-59941
Number of titles published annually: 120 Print
Total Titles: 500 Print

Fowler Museum at UCLA
PO Box 951549, Los Angeles, CA 90095-1549
Tel: 310-825-4361 *Fax:* 310-206-7007
E-mail: fowlerws@arts.ucla.edu
Web Site: www.fowler.ucla.edu
Key Personnel
Mng Ed: Marina Belozerskaya *Tel:* 310-794-9582 *E-mail:* mbelozerskaya@arts.ucla.edu
Founded: 1963
Active publisher of African, Southeast Asian & Latin American arts publications.
ISBN Prefix(es): 978-0-930741; 978-0-9748729
Number of titles published annually: 4 Print
Total Titles: 146 Print
Distributed by University of Washington Press
Shipping Address: 308 Charles E Young Dr N, Los Angeles, CA 90095

Fox Chapel Publishing Co Inc
1970 Broad St, East Petersburg, PA 17520
Tel: 717-560-4703 *Toll Free Tel:* 800-457-9112
Fax: 717-560-4702
E-mail: customerservice@foxchapelpublishing.com
Web Site: www.foxchapelpublishing.com
Key Personnel
CFO: Jeff Baughman *E-mail:* baughman@foxchapelpublishing.com
Pres: Alan Giagnocavo *E-mail:* alan@foxchapelpublishing.com
VP, Content: Chris Reggio *E-mail:* reggio@foxchapelpublishing.com
Founded: 1991
Publisher of illustrated nonfiction books, magazines, patterns & videos for craft, hobby & do-it-yourself enthusiasts, as well as children's books, journals & other stationery book products. Fox Chapel Publishing inspires & informs readers who enjoy woodworking, needlework, pyrography, home & garden, cooking, outdoor recreation, coloring, Zentangle®, kids crafts & more. Fox Chapel publishes 3 magazines, *Woodcarving Illustrated, Scroll Saw, Woodworking & Crafts & DO Magazine.*
ISBN Prefix(es): 978-1-58011 (Creative Homeowner); 978-1-56523 (Fox Chapel); 978-1-4972 (Design Originals); 978-1-5048 (IMM Lifestyle); 978-1-64178 (Quiet Fox); 978-1-64124 (Happy Fox); 978-1-62008 (CompanionHouse); 978-1-62187 (CompanionHouse); 978-1-912158 (Old Pond)
Number of titles published annually: 200 Print
Total Titles: 3,000 Print
Imprints: CompanionHouse Books; Creative Homeowner; Design Originals; Happy Fox; Heliconia Press; IMM Lifestyle Books; Landauer Publishing; Old Pond; Quiet Fox
Distributor for Reader's Digest; Taunton Sterling Dover
Membership(s): Craft Hobby Association (CHA); Publishers Association of the West (PubWest)
See separate listing for:
Creative Homeowner
Landauer Publishing

§Franciscan Media
28 W Liberty St, Cincinnati, OH 45202
SAN: 204-6237
Tel: 513-241-5615
E-mail: admin@franciscanmedia.org
Web Site: www.franciscanmedia.org
Key Personnel
Publr & CEO: Rev Dan Kroger, OFM *E-mail:* dkroger@franciscanmedia.org
Pres: Kelly McCracken *E-mail:* kmccracken@franciscanmedia.org
Dir, Design & Prodn: Mark Sullivan *E-mail:* msullivan@franciscanmedia.org
Dir, Mktg: Patty Crawford *E-mail:* pcrawford@franciscanmedia.org
Founded: 1893
Religion-Catholic. Nonprofit ministry of the Franciscan Friars of the St John the Baptist Province, publishing books, audiobooks, ebooks, *St Anthony Messenger*, monthly magazine.
ISBN Prefix(es): 978-0-912228; 978-0-86716; 978-1-61636; 978-1-63253; 978-1-63254
Number of titles published annually: 12 Print; 12 E-Book; 12 Audio
Total Titles: 165 Print; 100 E-Book; 200 Audio
Foreign Rep(s): Freedom Publishing (Australia); Redemptorist Publications Book Service (UK)
Membership(s): Association of Catholic Publishers Inc; Catholic Media Association (CMA); Society of Professional Journalists (SPJ)

§Franklin, Beedle & Associates Inc
10350 N Vancouver Way, No 5012, Portland, OR 97217
Tel: 503-284-6348 *Toll Free Tel:* 800-322-2665
Fax: 503-625-4434
Web Site: www.fbeedle.com
Key Personnel
Ed: Tom Sumner *E-mail:* tsumner@fbeedle.com
Founded: 1985
College textbooks in computer science, information systems & computers in education, educational software, computer engineering, computer information systems, information technology.
ISBN Prefix(es): 978-0-938661; 978-1-887902; 978-1-59028

Number of titles published annually: 10 Print; 5 E-Book
Total Titles: 50 Print; 5 E-Book
Imprints: William, James & Co (humanities publr); Xpat Fiction
Foreign Rep(s): Transatlantic Publishers (Europe, Middle East, UK)
Membership(s): Association for Computing Machinery (ACM)

Frederick Fell Publishers Inc
1403 Shoreline Way, Hollywood, FL 33019
SAN: 208-2365
Tel: 954-925-5242
E-mail: fellpub@aol.com (admin only)
Web Site: www.fellpub.com
Key Personnel
Pres & Publr: Donald L Lessne *E-mail:* donlessne@aol.com
Ed-in-Chief: Susan Moustaki *E-mail:* felleditor@aol.com
Founded: 1943
An award-winning publisher of general trade books. Series published include the Know-It-All Guides, Top 100 series, Heroes & Heroines series & So You Want To Be series.
ISBN Prefix(es): 978-0-88391
Number of titles published annually: 24 Print; 50 E-Book
Total Titles: 150 Print; 250 E-Book
Foreign Rep(s): Gazelle Book Services Ltd (UK & the continent); Jarir Bookstore (Tony Herold) (Saudi Arabia); Parrot Reads Publishers (Indian subcontinent); USBD Distribution (Singapore)
Foreign Rights: Akcali Copyright Agency (Turkey); Agencia Literaria Carmen Balcells SA (Latin America exc Brazil, Portugal, Spain); Lorella Belli Literary Agency (UK); Big Apple Agency Inc (Maggie Han) (China); Big Apple Agency Inc (Taiwan); Book Publishers Association of Israel (Beverley Levit) (Israel); Graal Literary Agency (Marcin Biegaj) (Poland); Imprima Korea Agency (South Korea); International Copyright Agency Ltd (Simona Kessler) (Romania); Christiane Janssen (Germany); Japan UNI Agency Inc (Japan); Jarir Bookstore (Tony Herold) (Saudi Arabia); LEX Copyright Office (Norbert Uzseka) (Hungary); Maxima Creative Agency (Santo Manurung) (Indonesia); Nova Littera S L (Konstantin Paltchikov) (Russia); Andrew Nurnberg Associates Ltd (Tatjana Zoldnere) (Latvia, Lithuania, Ukraine); Andrew Nurnberg Associates Prague (Petra Tobiskova) (Czechia); Andrew Nurnberg Associates Sofia (Anna Droumeva) (Bulgaria); OA Literary Agency (Greece); Plima Literary Agency (Mila Perisic) (Croatia, Serbia, Slovenia); Schindler's Literary Agency (Brazil); Tuttle-Mori Agency Inc (Japan, Thailand)
Distribution Center: Independent Publishers Group (IPG), 814 N Franklin St, No 100, Chicago, IL 60610, VP: Alex Kampmann *Tel:* 312-337-0747 *Fax:* 312-337-5985 *Web Site:* www.ipg.com

§Free Spirit Publishing Inc
Imprint of Teacher Created Materials
9850 51 Ave N, Suite 100, Minneapolis, MN 55442
Tel: 714-891-2273 *Toll Free Tel:* 800-858-7339
Fax: 714-230-7070 *Toll Free Fax:* 888-877-7606
E-mail: customerservice@tcmpub.com
Web Site: www.teachercreatedmaterials.com/free-spirit-publishing
Key Personnel
Founder & CEO: Rachelle Cracchiolo
Pres: Connie Burton
EVP, Strategic Devt: Deanne Mendoza
Founded: 1983

Offer books & learning materials for parents, educators, children & teens. Topics include: self-esteem, stress management, school success, creativity, relationships with friends & family, social action, special needs (i.e. children with LD/learning differences, gifted & talented & at-risk youth), bullying & conflict resolution.
ISBN Prefix(es): 978-0-915793; 978-1-57542; 978-0-9665988; 978-1-58661; 978-1-63198
Number of titles published annually: 25 Print; 1 CD-ROM
Total Titles: 170 Print; 2 CD-ROM; 3 Audio
Foreign Rep(s): Educational Distributors (New Zealand); Georgetown Publications (Canada); Incentive Plus (UK)

§W H Freeman
Imprint of Macmillan Learning
c/o Macmillan Learning, One New York Plaza, Suite 46, New York, NY 10004
Tel: 212-576-9400
Web Site: www.macmillanlearning.com/college/us
Founded: 1946
Science & mathematics texts for the higher education market & high school advanced courses.
ISBN Prefix(es): 978-1-57259; 978-1-4292; 978-0-7167; 978-0-9747077; 978-1-936221
Number of titles published annually: 25 Print; 20 Online; 20 E-Book
Total Titles: 500 Print
Warehouse: Macmillan Publisher Services (MPS), 16365 James Madison Hwy, Gordonsville, VA 22942 *Toll Free Tel:* 888-330-8477 *Fax:* 540-672-7540 (cust serv) *Toll Free Fax:* 800-672-2054 (orders) *E-mail:* orders@mpsvirginia.com

Samuel French, Inc
Imprint of Concord Theatricals
250 W 57 St, 6th fl, New York, NY 10107-0102
Toll Free Tel: 866-979-0447
E-mail: info@concordtheatricals.com
Web Site: www.concordtheatricals.com/a/4346/samuel-a-french
Key Personnel
VP, Music & Pubns: David Geer *E-mail:* david.geer@concord.com
Sr Mgr, Pubns: Ben Keiper *E-mail:* ben.keiper@concord.com
Pubns Coord: Faith Williams *E-mail:* faith.williams@concord.com
Founded: 1830
Plays.
ISBN Prefix(es): 978-0-573; 978-0-87440
Number of titles published annually: 70 Print
Foreign Office(s): Samuel French Ltd, Aldwych House, 71-91 Aldwych, London WC2B 4HN, United Kingdom *Tel:* (020) 7054 7298 *E-mail:* customerservices@concordtheatricals.co.uk *Web Site:* www.concordtheatricals.co.uk
Distributed by Baker's Plays; Samuel French Ltd (UK)
Distributor for Baker's Plays; Samuel French Ltd (UK)
Foreign Rights: DALRO Pty Ltd (Botswana, Lesotho, Namibia, South Africa, Swaziland); Drama League of Ireland (Ireland); Origin Theatrical (Australia); Play Bureau (NZ) Ltd (New Zealand)

Fresh Air Books
Imprint of Upper Room Books
1908 Grand Ave, Nashville, TN 37212
Tel: 615-340-7200 *Toll Free Tel:* 800-972-0433 (orders)
Web Site: books.upperroom.org
Key Personnel
Edit Dir: Michael Stephens *Tel:* 615-340-7220 *E-mail:* mstephens@upperroom.org
Founded: 2009
Nonprofit publisher of religious materials.
ISBN Prefix(es): 978-1-935205
Number of titles published annually: 1 Print; 2 E-Book
Total Titles: 14 Print; 10 E-Book
Warehouse: APG Books/WFS LLC, 1501 County Hospital Rd, Nashville, TN 37218

Friends United Press
Subsidiary of Friends United Meeting
101 Quaker Hill Dr, Richmond, IN 47374
SAN: 201-5803
Tel: 765-962-7573 *Fax:* 765-966-1293
E-mail: friendspress@fum.org; orders@fum.org
Web Site: www.friendsunitedmeeting.org; bookstore.friendsunitedmeeting.org
Founded: 1969
Religion; Quaker history; Quakerism; Christian Curriculum.
ISBN Prefix(es): 978-0-913408; 978-0-944350
Number of titles published annually: 3 Print; 3 Online; 2 E-Book
Total Titles: 110 Print; 70 Online; 2 E-Book
Membership(s): Christian Small Publishers Association; Independent Book Publishers Association (IBPA); Quakers Uniting in Publications

FSG, see Farrar, Straus & Giroux, LLC

FT Press, see Financial Times Press

Fulcrum Publishing Inc
3970 Youngfield St, Wheat Ridge, CO 80033
SAN: 200-2825
Tel: 303-277-1623 *Toll Free Tel:* 800-888-4741 (orders)
E-mail: info@fulcrumbooks.com
Web Site: www.fulcrumbooks.com
Key Personnel
Pres: Sam Scinta
Dir, Sales & Mktg: Kateri Kramer *Tel:* 303-277-1623 ext 216 *E-mail:* kateri@fulcrumbooks.com
Ed: Allison Auch
Founded: 1984
Nonfiction trade: Western culture & history, Native American culture & history, environment & nature, popular culture, lifestyle, outdoor recreation, public policy & gardening.
ISBN Prefix(es): 978-1-55591; 978-1-56373; 978-0-912347; 978-1-936218; 978-1-938486
Number of titles published annually: 15 Print; 15 E-Book
Total Titles: 600 Print; 250 E-Book
Orders to: Independent Publishers Group (IPG), 814 N Franklin St, Chicago, IL 60610 *E-mail:* orders@ipgbook.com *Web Site:* www.ipgbook.com
Distribution Center: Independent Publishers Group (IPG), 814 N Franklin St, Chicago, IL 60610 *E-mail:* orders@ipgbook.com *Web Site:* www.ipgbook.com
Membership(s): American Booksellers Association (ABA); Association of American Publishers (AAP); Midwest Independent Booksellers Association (MIBA); Mountains & Plains Independent Booksellers Association (MPIBA); Pacific Northwest Booksellers Association (PNBA)

§Future Horizons Inc
107 W Randol Mill Rd, Suite 100, Arlington, TX 76011
Tel: 817-277-0727 *Toll Free Tel:* 800-489-0727
E-mail: info@fhautism.com
Web Site: www.fhautism.com
Founded: 1996
Resources on Autism/Asperger's Syndrome, including books, magazines & conferences.
ISBN Prefix(es): 978-1-885477; 978-1-932565; 978-1-935274
Number of titles published annually: 7 Print
Total Titles: 500 Print

Gagosian Gallery
980 Madison Ave, New York, NY 10075
Tel: 212-744-2313 *Fax:* 212-772-7962
E-mail: newyork@gagosian.com
Web Site: www.gagosian.com
Key Personnel
Publg Dir: Alison McDonald
Founded: 1989
Publish fine editions & illustrated books on contemporary & modern art.
ISBN Prefix(es): 978-1-880154
Number of titles published annually: 30 Print
Total Titles: 600 Print
Branch Office(s)
456 N Camden Dr, Beverly Hills, CA 90210
Tel: 310-271-9400 *Fax:* 310-271-9420
E-mail: losangeles@gagosian.com

§Galaxy Press Inc
7051 Hollywood Blvd, Los Angeles, CA 90028
SAN: 254-6906
Tel: 323-466-3310 *Toll Free Tel:* 877-8GALAXY (842-5299)
E-mail: info@galaxypress.com; customers@galaxypress.com
Web Site: www.galaxypress.com
Key Personnel
SVP, Sales: Kim Catalano *E-mail:* kcatalano@galaxypress.com
VP, Sales: Juliet Wills *E-mail:* jwills@galaxypress.com
Mdse Specialist, Independent & Specialty Sales: Mitch Breuer *E-mail:* mitch@galaxypress.com
Founded: 2002
Publisher of the fiction works of L Ron Hubbard.
ISBN Prefix(es): 978-1-59212; 978-1-61986
Number of titles published annually: 10 Print; 10 E-Book; 6 Audio
Total Titles: 110 Print; 110 E-Book; 100 Audio
Imprints: Galaxy Audio

Galde Press Inc
PO Box 774, Hendersonville, NC 28793
Tel: 828-702-3032
Web Site: www.galdepress.com
Key Personnel
Founder & Pres: Phyllis Galde *E-mail:* phyllis@galdepress.com
Founded: 1991
Independent publisher of books on a variety of subjects with over 100 titles in print.
ISBN Prefix(es): 978-1-880090; 978-1-931942
Number of titles published annually: 11 Print
Total Titles: 108 Print

§Gale
Division of Cengage Learning
27555 Executive Dr, Suite 270, Farmington Hills, MI 48331
SAN: 213-4373
Toll Free Tel: 800-877-4253 *Toll Free Fax:* 877-363-4253
E-mail: gale.customerexperience@cengage.com
Web Site: www.gale.com
Key Personnel
SVP, Mng Dir, Intl: Terry Robinson
SVP & Gen Mgr: Paul Gazzolo
SVP, North American Sales: Brian McDonough
VP, Mktg & Communs: Harmony Faust
Founded: 1954
Gale, a Cengage company, partners with librarians & educators around the world to connect learners to essential content through user-friendly technology that enhances experiences & improves learning outcomes. For more than 65 years, Gale has collaborated with academic institutions, schools & public libraries around the world to empower the discovery of knowledge & insights that push the boundaries of traditional research & advance learners in all areas of life.
ISBN Prefix(es): 978-0-8103; 978-0-7876
Number of titles published annually: 50 Print

Total Titles: 4,381 Print; 38,890 Online; 38,890 E-Book
Imprints: Christian Large Print; Five Star™; Large Print Press™; Macmillan Reference USA™; Primary Source Media™; St James Press®; Schirmer Reference™; Scholarly Resources Inc; The TAFT Group®; Thorndike Press®; U X L™; Wheeler Publishing™
Distribution Center: 10650 Toebben Dr, Independence, KY 41051 *Tel:* 859-525-2230
See separate listing for:
Macmillan Reference USA™
St James Press®
Thorndike Press®

§Gallaudet University Press
800 Florida Ave NE, Washington, DC 20002-3695
SAN: 205-261X
Tel: 202-651-5488 *Fax:* 202-651-5489
E-mail: gupress@gallaudet.edu
Web Site: gupress.gallaudet.edu
Key Personnel
Exec Dir: Gary Aller
Dir: Angela Leppig
Founded: 1980
Reference books, scholarly, educational & general interest books on deaf studies, deaf culture & issues, sign language textbooks.
ISBN Prefix(es): 978-0-913580; 978-0-930323; 978-1-56368; 978-1-944838
Number of titles published annually: 16 Print
Total Titles: 250 Print; 4 CD-ROM
Imprints: Clerc Books; Kendall Green
Warehouse: Chicago Distribution Center, 11030 S Langley Ave, Chicago, IL 60628, Contact: Karen Hyzy *Tel:* 773-702-7000 *Toll Free Tel:* 800-621-2736 *Fax:* 773-702-7212 *Toll Free Fax:* 800-621-8476 *E-mail:* orders@press.uchicago.edu
Membership(s): Association of University Presses (AUPresses)

Gallery Books
Imprint of Gallery Publishing Group
1230 Avenue of the Americas, New York, NY 10020
Toll Free Tel: 800-456-6798 *Fax:* 212-698-7284
E-mail: consumer.customerservice@simonandschuster.com
Web Site: www.simonandschuster.com
Key Personnel
SVP & Publr, Gallery Books Group: Jennifer Bergstrom *Tel:* 212-698-2117 *E-mail:* jennifer.bergstrom@simonandschuster.com
VP, Deputy Publr, Gallery Books Group; Publr, Pocket Books: Jennifer Long *Tel:* 212-698-1139 *E-mail:* jennifer.long@simonandschuster.com
Publr, 13A: Charles M Suitt *E-mail:* charles.suitt@simonandschuster.com
VP, Edit Dir, Gallery Books Group: Aimee Bell *Tel:* 212-698-7234 *E-mail:* aimee.bell@simonandschuster.com
VP, Exec Ed, Scout Press: Alison Callahan *Tel:* 212-698-2442 *E-mail:* alison.callahan@simonandschuster.com
VP, Exec Ed: Pamela Cannon *E-mail:* pamela.cannon@simonandschuster.com; Carrie Feron *E-mail:* carrie.feron@simonandschuster.com
VP, Exec Ed, Gallery Books, Threshold Editions: Natasha Simons *Tel:* 212-698-7287 *E-mail:* natasha.simons@simonandschuster.com
VP, Exec Ed: Lauren Spiegel *Tel:* 212-698-7678 *E-mail:* lauren.spiegel@simonandschuster.com
Sr Publg Mgr, Gallery Books & Pocket Books: Eliza Hanson *Tel:* 212-698-1212 *E-mail:* eliza.hanson@simonandschuster.com
Exec Ed, Licensing Mgr, Gallery Books & Gallery 13: Ed Schlesinger *Tel:* 212-698-7463 *E-mail:* ed.schlesinger@simonandschuster.com
Exec Ed: Abby Zidle *Tel:* 212-698-2898 *E-mail:* abby.zidle@simonandschuster.com
com; James Melia *E-mail:* james.melia@simonandschuster.com
Sr Mng Ed: Caroline Pallotta *E-mail:* caroline.pallotta@simonandschuster.com
Asst Mng Ed: Emily Arzeno *E-mail:* emily.arzeno@simonandschuster.com
Mng Edit Asst: Angel Musyimi *Tel:* 212-698-7227 *E-mail:* angel.musyimi@simonandschuster.com
Sr Ed: Hannah Braaten *Tel:* 212-698-2729 *E-mail:* hannah.braaten@simonandschuster.com; Molly Gregory *Tel:* 212-698-2125 *E-mail:* molly.gregory@simonandschuster.com
Sr Ed, Gallery Books, Threshold Editions: Paul Choix *E-mail:* paul.choix@simonandschuster.com
Ed: Max Meltzer *Tel:* 212-698-7401 *E-mail:* max.meltzer@simonandschuster.com; Ghjulia Romiti *E-mail:* ghjulia.romiti@simonandschuster.com; Rebecca Strobel *Tel:* 212-698-2476 *E-mail:* rebecca.strobel@simonandschuster.com
Asst Ed: Kimberly Laws *Tel:* 212-698-2493 *E-mail:* kimberly.laws@simonandschuster.com; Mia Robertson *E-mail:* mia.robertson@simonandschuster.com; Taylor Rondestvedt *E-mail:* taylor.rondestvedt@simonandschuster.com; Sarah Schlick *E-mail:* sarah.schlick@simonandschuster.com
Edit Asst: Sierra Fang-Horvath *E-mail:* sierra.fang-horvath@simonandschuster.com
Publg Asst: Madeleine (Maddy) Voorhees *E-mail:* madeleine.voorhees@simonandschuster.com
VP & Dir, Subs Rts, Gallery Books Group: Paul O'Halloran *Tel:* 212-698-7367 *E-mail:* paul.o'halloran@simonandschuster.com
VP, Dir of Publicity & Mktg: Sally Marvin *Tel:* 212-698-2360 *E-mail:* sally.marvin@simonandschuster.com
VP & Exec Publicist, Gallery Books Group: Jennifer Robinson *Tel:* 212-698-2719 *E-mail:* jennifer.robinson@simonandschuster.com
Deputy Dir, Publicity: Jessica Roth *Tel:* 212-698-4665 *E-mail:* jessica.roth@simonandschuster.com
Exec Publicist: Jill Siegel *E-mail:* jill.siegel@simonandschuster.com
Sr Publicist: Lucy Nalen *E-mail:* lucy.nalen@simonandschuster.com
Sr Publicity Mgr: Lauren Carr *E-mail:* lauren.carr@simonandschuster.com
Publicity Mgr: Sydney Morris *E-mail:* sydney.morris@simonandschuster.com
Publicity Asst: Abby DeGasperis *E-mail:* abby.degasperis@simonandschuster.com
Dir, Mktg: Mackenzie Hickey *E-mail:* mackenzie.hickey@simonandschuster.com
Mktg Assoc: Tianna Kelly *E-mail:* tianna.kelly@simonandschuster.com
Sr Art Dir, Gallery Books, Pocket Books: Lisa Litwack *E-mail:* lisa.litwack@simonandschuster.com
Art Dir: Min Choi *E-mail:* min.choi@simonandschuster.com; John Vairo *E-mail:* john.vairo@simonandschuster.com
Sr Art Mgr: Pamela Grant *E-mail:* pamela.grant@simonandschuster.com
Subs Rts Assoc: Rachel Podmajersky *E-mail:* rachel.podmajersky@simonandschuster.com
Subs Rts Coord: Fiona Sharp *E-mail:* fiona.sharp@simonandschuster.com
Founded: 1939
Trade paperbacks & hardcovers; mass market, reprints & originals.
ISBN Prefix(es): 978-0-671; 978-0-7434; 978-1-4165
Imprints: Gallery 13; Jeter Publishing; Lemonada Books (in partnership with Lemonada Media); Pocket Books; Scout Press; Star Trek®; 13A
Foreign Rights: Akcali Copyright Agency (Atilla Izgi Turgut & Begum Ayfer) (Turkey); Berla & Griffini Rights Agency (Italy); Book Publishers Association of Israel (Beverley Levit) (Israel); International Editors Co (Amaiur Fernandez) (Portugal, Spain); Japan UNI Agency (Miko Yamanouchi & Ayako Sasamoto) (Japan); JLM Literary Agency (John Moukakos) (Greece); Korea Copyright Center Inc (KCC) (Sangeun Lee) (South Korea); Mohrbooks AG Literary Agency (Sebastian Ritscher) (Germany); La Nouvelle Agence (Vanessa Kling & Anne Maizeret) (France); Andrew Nurnberg Associates (Ludmilla Sushkova) (Russia); Andrew Nurnberg Associates (Whitney Hsu) (Taiwan); Andrew Nurnberg Associates (Mira Droumeva) (Bulgaria, Montenegro, Romania, Serbia); Andrew Nurnberg Associates (Jackie Huang) (China); Andrew Nurnberg Associates (Judit Hermann) (Croatia, Hungary); Andrew Nurnberg Associates (Marta Soukopova) (Czechia, Slovakia, Slovenia); Andrew Nurnberg Associates (Tatjana Zoldnere) (Estonia, Latvia, Lithuania); Andrew Nurnberg Associates (Marcin Biegaj) (Poland); Andrew Nurnberg Associates International (Helen Lin) (Taiwan); Agencia Riff (Brazil); Sebes & Bisseling Literary Agency (Paul Sebes & Willem Bisseling) (Netherlands); Ulf Toregard Agency AB (Ulf Toregard) (Denmark, Finland, Iceland, Norway, Sweden); Tuttle-Mori Agency Inc (Pumi Boonyatud) (Thailand)

Gallery 13, see Gallery Books

§Gallopade International Inc
611 Hwy 74 S, Suite 2000, Peachtree City, GA 30269
SAN: 213-8441
Mailing Address: PO Box 2779, Peachtree City, GA 30269
Tel: 770-631-4222 *Toll Free Tel:* 800-536-2438 *Fax:* 770-631-4810 *Toll Free Fax:* 800-871-2979
E-mail: customerservice@gallopade.com
Web Site: www.gallopade.com
Key Personnel
Owner & CEO: Carole Marsh *E-mail:* carole@gallopade.com
Pres & Intl Rts: Michele Yother *E-mail:* michele@gallopade.com
Pres: Michael Longmeyer *E-mail:* michael@gallopade.com
Dir, Mktg: Michael C Conley *E-mail:* michael.conley@gallopade.com
Founded: 1979
"State stuff" for all 50 states including activity books, games, maps, posters, stickies, etc. Subjects include travel, regional, school travel supply, home school, juvenile mysteries, human sex education, multicultural, preschool through adult.
ISBN Prefix(es): 978-0-935326; 978-1-55609; 978-0-7933; 978-0-635
Number of titles published annually: 500 Print; 50 CD-ROM; 200 Online; 200 E-Book
Total Titles: 15,000 Print; 200 CD-ROM; 10,050 Online; 10,050 E-Book; 13 Audio
Imprints: American Milestones; Black Heritage: Celebrating Culture; The Day That Was Different; Here & Now; Heroes & Helpers; Carole Marsh Books; Carole Marsh Mysteries; New Traditions; 1000 Readers; Smart Sex Stuff for Kids; State Experience; State Stuff
Subsidiaries: Six House; The World's Largest Publishing Co
Membership(s): Education Market Association

Gareth Stevens Publishing
Imprint of The Rosen Publishing Group Inc
29 E 21 St, New York, NY 10010
Tel: 212-777-3017 *Toll Free Tel:* 800-542-2595
Toll Free Fax: 877-542-2596
E-mail: customerservice@gspub.com
Web Site: garethstevens.com

Founded: 1983
High-interest nonfiction titles aligned to meet curriculum objectives for grades PreK-8.
ISBN Prefix(es): 978-0-918831; 978-1-55532; 978-0-8368; 978-1-4339
Number of titles published annually: 400 Print
Total Titles: 1,500 Print
Foreign Rep(s): CrossCan Educational Services Inc (Canada)
Returns: Maple Logistics Solutions, York Distribution Center, 60 Grumbacher Rd, York, PA 17406

§Gatekeeper Press
7853 Gunn Hwy, Suite 209, Tampa, FL 33626
Toll Free Tel: 866-535-0913 *Fax:* 216-803-0350
E-mail: info@gatekeeperpress.com
Web Site: www.gatekeeperpress.com
Key Personnel
CEO: Robert Price *Tel:* 866-535-0913 ext 713
 E-mail: rprice@gatekeeperpress.com
Founded: 2015
The Gold Standard in publishing service providers. Authors retain 100% of their rights, have 100% creative control & earn 100% of their royalties. Distribution networks reach readers worldwide. Services include editorial, design, formatting, illustrations, marketing & audiobooks.
This publisher has indicated that 100% of their product line is author subsidized.
ISBN Prefix(es): 978-1-61984
Number of titles published annually: 500 Print
Membership(s): Independent Book Publishers Association (IBPA)

§Gateways Books & Tapes
Division of Institute for the Development of the Harmonious Human Being Inc
PO Box 370, Nevada City, CA 95959-0370
SAN: 211-3635
Tel: 530-271-2239 *Toll Free Tel:* 800-869-0658
Web Site: www.gatewaysbooksandtapes.com
Key Personnel
Sr Ed: Mr Iven Lourie *Tel:* 530-277-5380
 E-mail: artemisbooks@gmail.com
Founded: 1971
Trade & fine art book publisher. Categories include psychology, spirituality, metaphysics, Judaica, science fiction & limited editions.
ISBN Prefix(es): 978-0-89556
Number of titles published annually: 6 Print; 4 CD-ROM; 4 E-Book; 4 Audio
Total Titles: 110 Print; 8 CD-ROM; 84 E-Book; 300 Audio
Imprints: Artemis Books; Consciousness Classics; Gateways Fine Art Series; Retro Science Fiction
Distributor for Cloister Recordings (audio & video tapes)
Distribution Center: Independent Publishers Group (IPG), 814 N Franklin St, Chicago, IL 60610 *Tel:* 312-337-5985 *Toll Free Tel:* 800-888-4741 *E-mail:* support@ipgbook.freshdesk.com *Web Site:* www.ipgbook.com

Gauthier Publications Inc
PO Box 806241, St Clair Shores, MI 48080
SAN: 857-2119
Tel: 313-458-7141 *Fax:* 586-279-1515
E-mail: info@gauthierpublications.com
Web Site: www.gauthierpublications.com
Key Personnel
CEO: Daniel J Gauthier *E-mail:* daniel@gauthierpublications.com
Creative Dir: Elizabeth Gauthier
 E-mail: elizabeth@gauthierpublications.com
Founded: 2008
Devoted to printing high quality literary work. Our mission is simple, to introduce reading early & help promote a lifetime love for the written word by putting out captivating & unique titles that are tailored to their audience. We are proud to say all of our books are printed & bound in the US & our Hungry Goat Press line is made with 100% post consumer recycled paper because we think a good book means more than an exciting plot-line. Distribution also by Amazon.
ISBN Prefix(es): 978-0-9820812; 978-0-9833593
Number of titles published annually: 15 Print
Total Titles: 65 Print
Imprints: DragonFish Comics (graphic novels); Frog Legs Ink (children's books); Hungry Goat Press (young adult books)
Distribution Center: Follett School Solutions Inc, 1340 Ridgeview Dr, McHenry, IL 60050 *Tel:* 815-759-1700 *Toll Free Tel:* 888-511-5114 (cust serv) *Fax:* 815-759-9831 *Toll Free Fax:* 800-852-5458 *E-mail:* info@follettlearning.com *Web Site:* www.follettlearning.com SAN: 169-1902
Diamond, 1966 Greenspring Dr, Suite 300, Timonium, MD 21093 *Toll Free Tel:* 800-452-6642
Membership(s): American Booksellers Association (ABA)

GemStone Press
Imprint of Turner Publishing Co LLC
4507 Charlotte Ave, Suite 100, Nashville, TN 37209
SAN: 134-5621
Tel: 615-255-BOOK (255-2665) *Fax:* 615-255-5081
E-mail: marketing@turnerpublishing.com
Web Site: gemstonepress.com; www.turnerpublishing.com
Key Personnel
Pres & Publr, Turner Publishing Co: Todd Bottorff
Founded: 1987
Books on buying, enjoying, identifying & selling jewelry & gems for the consumer, collector, hobbyist, investor & jewelry trade.
ISBN Prefix(es): 978-0-943763
Number of titles published annually: 5 Print; 1 E-Book
Total Titles: 15 Print

§Genealogical Publishing Co
Subsidiary of Genealogical.com
3600 Clipper Mill Rd, Suite 229, Baltimore, MD 21211
Tel: 410-837-8271 *Toll Free Tel:* 800-296-6687 *Fax:* 410-752-8492 *Toll Free Fax:* 800-599-9561
E-mail: info@genealogical.com; web@genealogical.com
Web Site: www.genealogical.com
Key Personnel
VP & Ed-in-Chief: Michael Tepper
 E-mail: mtepper@genealogical.com
Mktg Dir: Joe Garonzik *E-mail:* jgaronzi@genealogical.com
Data Processing Mgr: Roger Sherr
 E-mail: rsherr@genealogical.com
Founded: 1959
Genealogy, local history, immigration history & source records. Products are nonreturnable, unless mis-shipped or damaged in shipment.
ISBN Prefix(es): 978-0-8063
Number of titles published annually: 50 Print; 1 CD-ROM; 30 E-Book
Total Titles: 2,000 Print; 84 CD-ROM; 100 Online; 800 E-Book
Subsidiaries: Clearfield Co Inc
See separate listing for:
Clearfield Co Inc

The Geological Society of America Inc (GSA)
3300 Penrose Place, Boulder, CO 80301-1806
SAN: 201-5978
Mailing Address: PO Box 9140, Boulder, CO 80301-9140
Tel: 303-357-1000 *Toll Free Tel:* 800-472-1988 *Fax:* 303-357-1070
E-mail: pubs@geosociety.org (prodn); editing@geosociety.org (edit); books@geosociety.org; gsaservice@geosociety.org (sales & serv)
Web Site: www.geosociety.org
Key Personnel
Dir, Pubns: Bridgette Moore *Tel:* 303-357-1086
 E-mail: bmoore@geosociety.org
Sr Mng Ed: April Leo *Tel:* 303-357-1037
 E-mail: aleo@geosociety.org
Assoc Ed: Katelyn Turner *Tel:* 303-357-1020
 E-mail: kturner@geosociety.org
Ad Mgr: Ann H Crawford *Tel:* 303-357-1053
 E-mail: acrawford@geosociety.org
Edit Mgr: Cary Cosper *Tel:* 303-357-1022
 E-mail: ccosper@geosociety.org
Sales & Licensing Mgr: Jon Raessler *Tel:* 303-357-1051 *E-mail:* jraessler@geosociety.org
Graphic Designer & Prodn Specialist: Heather Sutphin *Tel:* 303-357-1002 *E-mail:* hsutphin@geosociety.org
Founded: 1888
General earth sciences, cover such areas as geology, economic geology, engineering geology, geochemistry, geomorphology, marine geology, mineralogy, paleontology, petrology, seismology, solid earth geophysics, structural geology, tectonics & environmental geology.
ISBN Prefix(es): 978-0-8137
Number of titles published annually: 9 Print
Total Titles: 200 Print
Branch Office(s)
1200 New York Ave NW, Suite 400, Washington, DC 20005 *Tel:* 202-669-0466
Foreign Rep(s): Geological Society of London (UK)

§GeoLytics Inc
507 Horizon Way, Branchburg, NJ 08853
Mailing Address: PO Box 5336, East Brunswick, NJ 08876
Tel: 908-707-1505 *Toll Free Tel:* 800-577-6717
E-mail: support@geolytics.com; questions@geolytics.com
Web Site: www.geolytics.com
Key Personnel
Mktg Dir: Katia Segre Cohen
Founded: 1996
Provider of census, demographic & geographic data for academic & business researchers.
ISBN Prefix(es): 978-1-892445
Number of titles published annually: 7 CD-ROM; 7 Online
Total Titles: 55 CD-ROM; 55 Online

Georgetown University Press
3520 Prospect St NW, Suite 140, Washington, DC 20007
Tel: 202-687-5889 (busn) *Fax:* 202-687-6340 (edit)
E-mail: gupress@georgetown.edu
Web Site: press.georgetown.edu
Key Personnel
Dir: Alfred Bertrand *Tel:* 202-687-5912
 E-mail: ab3463@georgetown.edu
Mktg & Sales Dir: Virginia Veiga Bryant
 Tel: 202-687-9856 *E-mail:* vvb6@georgetown.edu
Asst Dir of Press & Busn Mgr: Ioan Suciu
 Tel: 202-687-5641 *E-mail:* suciui@georgetown.edu
Sr Acqs Ed & Intl Aff, Public Policy: Donald Jacobs *Tel:* 202-687-5218 *E-mail:* dpj5@georgetown.edu
Edit Designer & Prodn Mgr: Glenn Saltzman
 Tel: 202-687-6251 *E-mail:* gls43@georgetown.edu
Founded: 1964
Bioethics; international affairs & human rights; languages & linguistics; political science, public policy & public management; religion & ethics.

ISBN Prefix(es): 978-0-87840; 978-1-58901; 978-1-62616
Number of titles published annually: 40 Print; 2 Audio
Total Titles: 500 Print; 9 Audio
Foreign Rep(s): Apex Knowledge Sdn Bhd (Simon Tay) (Brunei, Malaysia); Avicenna Partnership Ltd (Middle East); Booknet Co Ltd (Ms Suphaluck Sattabuz) (Cambodia, Laos, Myanmar, Thailand, Vietnam); ChoiceTEXTS (Asia) Pte Ltd (Philip Ang) (Indonesia, Singapore); Columbia University Sales Consortium (Catherine Hobbs) (Canada); Durnell Marketing Ltd (Andrew Durnell) (Continental Europe); iCaves Ltd (Eddy Lam) (China, Hong Kong, Macau); iGroup (Asia Pacific) Ltd (Estela Suyat) (Philippines); iGroup Korea (IDC Asia) (Mr DJ Kim) (South Korea); KW Publishers Pvt Ltd (Bangladesh, Bhutan, India, Nepal); MHM Ltd (Mark Gresham) (Japan); The Oxford Publicity Partnership Ltd (Matthew Surzyn) (UK exc Ireland); Taiwan Publisher Marketing Service Ltd (George Liu) (Taiwan)
Orders to: HFS (Hopkins Fulfillment Services), PO Box 50370, Baltimore, MD 21211-4370
Tel: 410-516-6965 Toll Free Tel: 800-537-5487 Fax: 410-516-6998 E-mail: hfscustserv@jh.edu Web Site: hfs.jhu.edu; Ingram Publisher Services UK, 10 Thornbury Rd, Plymouth PL6 7PP, United Kingdom (Africa, Europe, Middle East & UK) Tel: (01752) 202301 E-mail: IPSUK.Cservs@ingramcontent.com Web Site: www.ingrampublisherservices.co.uk
Returns: HFS, c/o Maple Logistics Solutions, Lebanon Distribution Ctr, 704 Legionaire Dr, Fredericksburg, PA 17026
Warehouse: Maple Logistics Solutions, Lebanon Distribution Ctr, 704 Legionaire Dr, Fredericksburg, PA 17026
Distribution Center: Brunswick Books, 20 Maud St, Suite 303, Toronto, ON M5V 2M5, Canada Tel: 416-703-3598 Fax: 416-703-6561 E-mail: orders@brunswickbooks.ca Web Site: www.brunswickbooks.ca

§Getty Publications
1200 Getty Center Dr, Suite 500, Los Angeles, CA 90049-1682
SAN: 208-2276
Tel: 310-440-7365 Toll Free Tel: 800-223-3431 (orders) Fax: 310-440-7758
E-mail: pubsinfo@getty.edu
Web Site: www.getty.edu/publications
Key Personnel
Publr: Kara Kirk Tel: 310-440-6066 E-mail: kkirk@getty.edu
Assoc Publr: Maureen Winter Tel: 310-440-6117 E-mail: mwinter@getty.edu
Rts Mgr: Leslie Rollins Tel: 310-440-7102 E-mail: lrollins@getty.edu
Sales & Mktg Mgr: Joanne Kenny Tel: 310-440-6119 E-mail: jkenny@getty.edu
Founded: 1982
Produces a wide variety of books in the fields of art, photography, archaeology, architecture, conservation & the humanities for both general & specialized audiences. These award-winning publications complement & often result from the work of the J Paul Getty Museum, the Getty Conservation Institute & the Getty Research Institute. Publications include illustrated exhibition catalogues, illustrated works on single artists & art history, works on cultural history, scholarly monographs, critical editions of translated works, comprehensive studies of the Getty's collections, educational books to interest children of all ages in art & gift books.
ISBN Prefix(es): 978-0-89236; 978-1-60606
Number of titles published annually: 50 Print; 2 Online; 3 E-Book
Total Titles: 500 Print; 5 Online; 5 E-Book
Distributed by Harry N Abrams Inc (CN & US, new juvenile/young adult only); University of Chicago Press (CN & US exc new juvenile/young adult)
Foreign Rep(s): Yale University Press, London (worldwide exc North America)
Distribution Center: Chicago Distribution Center, 11030 S Langley Ave, Chicago, IL 60628 Tel: 773-702-7000 Toll Free Tel: 800-621-2736 Fax: 773-702-7212 Toll Free Fax: 800-621-8476 E-mail: custserv@press.uchicago.edu Web Site: www.press.uchicago.edu
Membership(s): Association of American Publishers (AAP); Association of University Presses (AUPresses); International Association of Museum Publishers (IAMP)

GIA Publications Inc
7404 S Mason Ave, Chicago, IL 60638
Tel: 708-496-3800 Toll Free Tel: 800-GIA-1358 (442-1358)
E-mail: custserv@giamusic.com
Web Site: www.giamusic.com
Key Personnel
Pres & COO: Alec Harris E-mail: alech@giamusic.com
Founded: 1941
Publish sacred choral music, hymnals, books, recordings & music education materials.
ISBN Prefix(es): 978-0-941050; 978-1-57999
Number of titles published annually: 200 Print
Total Titles: 6,000 Print; 250 Audio

§Gibbs Smith Publisher
1877 E Gentile St, Layton, UT 84041
Mailing Address: PO Box 667, Layton, UT 84041-0667 SAN: 201-9906
Tel: 801-544-9800 Toll Free Tel: 800-748-5439; 800-835-4993 (orders) Fax: 801-544-5582 Toll Free Fax: 800-213-3023 (orders only)
E-mail: info@gibbs-smith.com; orders@gibbs-smith.com
Web Site: gibbs-smith.com
Key Personnel
CEO: Brad Farmer
Publr & Chief Creative Offr: Suzanne Gibbs Taylor
Dir, Sales: Moneka Hewlett
Founded: 1969
ISBN Prefix(es): 978-0-87905; 978-1-58685
Number of titles published annually: 80 Print; 50 Online; 80 E-Book
Total Titles: 350 Print; 200 Online; 350 E-Book
Foreign Rep(s): Jonathan Ball (South Africa); Gilles Fauveau (Japan, South Korea); Jaime Gregorio (Philippines); Penguin Books India Pvt Ltd (Sharad Mohan) (Bangladesh, India, Maldives, Nepal, Pakistan, Sri Lanka); Peribo (Australia, New Zealand); Perseus Book Group UK (Europe exc UK); Perseus International (Caribbean, Latin America, Middle East, North Africa, Singapore); Perseus International (Suk Lee) (Malaysia, Singapore); June Poonpanich (Cambodia, Indonesia, Laos, Thailand, Vietnam); Publishers Group UK (UK); Raincoast Books (Canada); Nicky Stubbs (South Africa); Wei Zhao (China, Hong Kong, Taiwan)
Returns: 570 N Sportsplex Dr, Kaysville, UT 84037
Shipping Address: 570 N Sportsplex Dr, Kaysville, UT 84037
Membership(s): Association of American Publishers (AAP)

Gifted Unlimited LLC
12340 US Hwy 42, No 453, Goshen, KY 40026
Tel: 502-715-6306
E-mail: info@giftedunlimitedllc.com; orders@giftedunlimitedllc.com
Web Site: www.giftedunlimitedllc.com
Founded: 1982
Educational guide books & books for parents & adults relating to social/emotional needs & other characteristics of gifted children & adults.
ISBN Prefix(es): 978-0-910707
Number of titles published annually: 5 Print
Total Titles: 58 Print; 4 CD-ROM; 1 Audio
Membership(s): Independent Book Publishers Association (IBPA)

Gingko Press Inc
2332 Fourth St, Suite E, Berkeley, CA 94710
Tel: 510-898-1195 Fax: 510-898-1196
E-mail: books@gingkopress.com
Web Site: www.gingkopress.com
Key Personnel
Pres: Damon Snitkin E-mail: damon@gingkopress.com
VP & Publr: David Lopes E-mail: dl@gingkopress.com
VP, Sales & Mktg: Rick Markell E-mail: rmarkell@gingkopress.com
Founded: 1991
Publisher & distributor.
ISBN Prefix(es): 978-1-58423; 978-1-934471
Number of titles published annually: 100 Print; 1 E-Book
Total Titles: 450 Print; 2 E-Book
Imprints: Rebel Arts
Distributor for Art Power; Basheer; Choi's Gallery; CYPI; Gingko Press; Rebel Arts; Sandu Publications; Sendpoints Books Co Ltd; Upper Playground; Victionary; Zero+ Publishing
Distribution Center: Ingram Publisher Services, 14 Ingram Blvd, Mail Stop 631, La Vergne, TN 37086 Tel: 615-793-5000 Toll Free Tel: 866-400-5351 (orders) Web Site: www.ingrampublisherservices.com

Glitterati Editions, see Glitterati Inc

Glitterati Inc
PO Box 3781, New York, NY 10163
Tel: 212-810-7519
E-mail: info@glitteratiincorporated.com; media@glitteratiincorporated.com; sales@glitteratiincorporated.com; trade@glitteratiincorporated.com
Web Site: glitteratiinc.com
Key Personnel
Pres & CEO: Marta Hallett E-mail: mhallett@glitteratiincorporated.com
Founded: 2002
Independent producer & publisher of distinctive illustrated books, ancillary gift products & electronic media for domestic & international markets.
ISBN Prefix(es): 978-0-9721152; 978-0-9765851; 978-0-9777531; 978-0-9793384; 978-0-9801557; 978-0-9822669; 978-0-9823412; 978-0-9823799; 978-0-9832702; 978-0-9851696; 978-0-9881745; 978-0-9891704; 978-0-9913419; 978-0-9905320; 978-0-9862500; 978-0-9962930; 978-1-943876; 978-0-9903808; 978-0-9987474; 978-0-9992430
Number of titles published annually: 9 Print
Total Titles: 58 Print; 1 Audio
Foreign Office(s): 148 Columbia Rd, London NW3 2HY, United Kingdom Tel: (020) 7267 8339
Distribution Center: National Book Network (NBN), 4501 Forbes Blvd, Suite 200, Lanham, MD 20706 Tel: 301-459-3366 Toll Free Tel: 800-462-6420 Fax: 301-429-5746 Toll Free Fax: 800-338-4550 E-mail: customercare@nbnbooks.com Web Site: www.nbnbooks.com

Global Authors Publications (GAP)
38 Bluegrass, Middleberg, FL 32068
Tel: 904-425-1608
E-mail: gapbook@yahoo.com
Web Site: www.globalauthorspublications.com
Key Personnel
Co-Owner & Publr: Kathleen Walls
Co-Owner: Kathy Barnett
Founded: 2003

Offer complete subsidy publishing services & consider any genre except pornography or textbooks. Books must be at least 48 pages & not more than 700. We have set a literary standard with all the books we have published already & we do not plan to change our reputation. We won't publish everything that is offered us. Provide an affordable alternative to traditional publishing.
This publisher has indicated that 100% of their product line is author subsidized.
ISBN Prefix(es): 978-0-9742161; 978-0-9766449; 978-0-9779680; 978-0-9798087; 978-0-9845926; 978-0-9846536; 978-0-9821223
Number of titles published annually: 6 Print
Total Titles: 30 Print

Global Publishing Solutions LLC
PO Box 2043, Matteson, IL 60443
Toll Free Tel: 888-351-2411
E-mail: info@globalpublishingsolutions.com
Web Site: globalpublishingsolutions.com
Key Personnel
Owner & Mgr: Gloria Foster *E-mail:* admin@globalpublishingsolutions.com
Founded: 2020
Publishes high quality fiction & nonfiction books in a wide range of subjects. We bring long-standing writing experience to our business for potential editing services. Our services include book editing, design, & publishing. We offer marketing with a book release. Our company creates web sites for authors with an existing novel.
This publisher has indicated that 75% of their product line is author subsidized.
ISBN Prefix(es): 978-1-7372244; 979-8-9853892
Number of titles published annually: 6 Print; 6 E-Book
Total Titles: 3 Print; 3 E-Book

Global Training Center
550 S Mesa Hills Dr, Suite E4, El Paso, TX 79912
Mailing Address: PO Box 221977, El Paso, TX 79913
Tel: 915-534-7900 *Toll Free Tel:* 800-860-5030
Fax: 915-534-7903
E-mail: contact@globaltrainingcenter.com
Web Site: www.globaltrainingcenter.com
Key Personnel
Seminar Dir: Elsa Solorzano
Founded: 1992
International trade training for US importers & exporters. Products bought & sold globally require the special trade knowledge of rules & regulations to get products to customers. GTC provides trade training to build & sharpen those skills, so shipments reach their destination avoiding factors that ultimately cost your business time & money.
ISBN Prefix(es): 978-1-891249
Number of titles published annually: 23 Print
Total Titles: 23 Print

The Globe Pequot Press
Division of Rowman & Littlefield Publishing Group
64 S Main St, Essex, CT 06426
SAN: 201-9892
Tel: 203-458-4500 *Toll Free Tel:* 800-243-0495 (orders only); 888-249-7586 (cust serv)
Fax: 203-458-4601 *Toll Free Fax:* 800-820-2329 (orders & cust serv)
E-mail: editorial@globepequot.com; info@rowman.com; orders@rowman.com
Web Site: rowman.com
Key Personnel
Dir, Mktg & Publicity: Shana Capozza
Edit Dir, TwoDot Books: Erin Turner *Tel:* 406-442-6708 *E-mail:* eturner@rowman.com
Mgr, Dist Busn: Andrea Jacobs *Tel:* 203-458-4552 *E-mail:* ajacobs@rowman.com
Founded: 1947
Travel guidebooks, regional books, sports, how-to, outdoor recreation, personal finance, self-help, sports, cooking, entertaining, military history, fishing, hunting, gift books.
ISBN Prefix(es): 978-0-937959; 978-1-56044; 978-1-57380; 978-1-57540; 978-1-882997; 978-0-87842; 978-0-87106; 978-0-7627; 978-0-89933; 978-0-934641; 978-1-56440; 978-0-912367; 978-0-933469; 978-0-934802; 978-0-934318; 978-1-57034; 978-1-58592; 978-1-901970 (Sawday)
Number of titles published annually: 500 Print; 500 E-Book
Total Titles: 2,800 Print; 1,000 E-Book
Imprints: Astragal Press; Cheap Bastards; Down East Books; Falcon®; Globe Pequot; Gooseberry Patch; GPP® Travel; The Lyons Press; North Country Books; Pineapple Press; Prometheus Books; Taylor Trade; TwoDot®; Western Horseman
Foreign Rep(s): Faradawn (South Africa); Pansing (Singapore); Les Petriw (Canada); Woodslane NZ Ltd (New Zealand); Woodslane Pty Ltd (Australia)
Returns: National Book Network (NBN), 15200 NBN Way, Blue Ridge Summit, PA 17214
Warehouse: National Book Network (NBN), 15200 NBN Way, Blue Ridge Summit, PA 17214
Distribution Center: National Book Network (NBN), 15200 NBN Way, Blue Ridge Summit, PA 17214
Membership(s): American Booksellers Association (ABA); Association of American Publishers (AAP); Book Industry Study Group (BISG); New England Independent Booksellers Association (NEIBA)
See separate listing for:
Applause Theatre & Cinema Books
Astragal Press
Backbeat Books
Down East Books
The Lyons Press
Pineapple Press
Prometheus Books

Godine
184 Belknap St, Concord, MA 01742
E-mail: info@godine.com
Web Site: www.godine.com
Key Personnel
Publr: David Allender *E-mail:* da@godine.com
Edit Dir: Joshua Bodwell *E-mail:* jbodwell@godine.com
Founded: 1970
Fiction & nonfiction, history, biography, typography, art & photography, poetry, horticulture, Americana, cooking, regional, mysteries, juveniles.
ISBN Prefix(es): 978-0-87923; 978-1-56792; 978-0-87685; 978-1-57423
Number of titles published annually: 40 Print
Total Titles: 500 Print
Imprints: Black Sparrow; Godine; Nonpareil Books; Verba Mundi
Sales Office(s): PO Box 450, Jaffrey, NH 03452
Foreign Rep(s): Big Apple Agency Inc (Kelly Chang) (Taiwan); Sandra Bruna Agency (Spain); English Agency Japan Co Ltd (Hamish Macaskill) (Japan); Paul & Peter Fritz Agency (Peter Fritz) (Switzerland); Graal Literary Agency (Magda Koceba) (Poland); Korea Copyright Center (Jae-Yeon Ryu) (South Korea); Agence Michelle Lapautre (France); Natoli Stefan & Oliva Agenzia (Roberta Oliva) (Italy); Agencia Literara SUN (Crina Chitan) (Romania)
Foreign Rights: Sandra Bruna Agency (Spain); English Agency Japan Co (Japan); Paul & Peter Fritz (Germany); Korea Copyright Center (South Korea); Agence Michelle Lapautre (Catherine Lapautre) (France); Natoli, Stefan & Oliva (Italy)
Orders to: PO Box 450, Jaffrey, NH 03452 *Toll Free Tel:* 800-344-4771 *Toll Free Fax:* 800-226-0934 *E-mail:* order@godine.com
Returns: PO Box 450, Jaffrey, NH 03452 *Toll Free Tel:* 800-344-4771 *Toll Free Fax:* 800-226-0934
Warehouse: PO Box 450, Jaffrey, NH 03452 *Tel:* 603-532-4100 *Toll Free Tel:* 800-344-4771 *Fax:* 603-532-5940 *Toll Free Fax:* 800-226-0934 *E-mail:* order@godine.com
Distribution Center: Two Rivers Distribution, an Ingram brand, Ingram Content Group LLC, One Ingram Blvd, La Vergne, TN 37086 *Toll Free Tel:* 866-400-5351 *E-mail:* ips@ingramcontent.com
Membership(s): Association of American Publishers (AAP)

Golden West Cookbooks
Division of American Traveler Press
5738 N Central Ave, Phoenix, AZ 85012-1316
Tel: 602-234-1574 *Toll Free Tel:* 800-521-9221 *Fax:* 602-234-3062
E-mail: info@americantravelerpress.com
Web Site: www.americantravelerpress.com
Key Personnel
Gen Mgr: Bill Fessler
Founded: 1973
Cookbooks & nonfiction books on the Southwest & the Rocky Mountains.
ISBN Prefix(es): 978-0-914846; 978-1-885590
Number of titles published annually: 5 Print
Total Titles: 150 Print
Membership(s): Publishers Association of the West (PubWest)

Goodheart-Willcox Publisher
18604 W Creek Dr, Tinley Park, IL 60477-6243
SAN: 203-4387
Tel: 708-687-5000 *Toll Free Tel:* 800-323-0440 *Toll Free Fax:* 888-409-3900
E-mail: custserv@g-w.com; orders@g-w.com
Web Site: www.g-w.com
Key Personnel
Pres & CEO: Shannon DeProfio
CFO: Carolyn Gomez
Chief Sales & Mktg Offr: Todd Scheffers
Sr Graphic Designer: Mary Lynn Griffin *Tel:* 708-623-1813 *E-mail:* mgriffin@g-w.com
Founded: 1921
Industrial technical; family & consumer sciences; career; health & health sciences; agriculture textbooks.
ISBN Prefix(es): 978-0-87006; 978-1-56637; 978-1-59070; 978-1-60525; 978-1-63126; 978-1-68584; 978-1-64564; 979-8-88817; 979-8-89118; 978-1-61960; 978-1-64925
Number of titles published annually: 50 Print
Total Titles: 150 Print; 100 CD-ROM; 150 Online
Foreign Rep(s): Baker & Taylor International (Europe)

Goose River Press
3400 Friendship Rd, Waldoboro, ME 04572-6337
Tel: 207-832-6665
E-mail: gooseriverpress@gmail.com
Web Site: gooseriverpress.com
Key Personnel
Owner & Ed: Deborah J Benner
Acct Exec: Meredith K Sanders *E-mail:* mksanders@roadrunner.com
Founded: 1999
Traditional publisher, but also offers self-publishing services to the authors of books that do not meet literary quality or who would prefer to self-publish.
This publisher has indicated that 25% of their product line is author subsidized.
ISBN Prefix(es): 978-1-930648; 978-1-59713

U.S. PUBLISHERS

Number of titles published annually: 15 Print; 10 E-Book
Total Titles: 100 Print; 30 E-Book
Distribution Center: Ingram Content Group, 1246 Heil Quaker Blvd, La Vergne, TN 37086, Contact: Jim Patterson *Tel:* 615-213-4475 *Fax:* 615-213-4725 *E-mail:* jim.patterson@lightningsource.com
Membership(s): Maine Writers & Publishers Alliance (MWPA); Waldoboro Business Association

Gorgias Press LLC
PO Box 6939, Piscataway, NJ 08854-6939
Tel: 732-885-8900 *Fax:* 732-885-8908
E-mail: helpdesk@gorgiaspress.com
Web Site: www.gorgiaspress.com
Key Personnel
Co-Founder & Pres: George Anton Kiraz, PhD
Co-Founder & VP: Christine Kiraz, PhD
Acqs Ed: Melonie Schmierer-Lee, PhD
Founded: 2001
Academic publishers of specialty books; provides for author/small publisher's digitization & publishing services needs.
ISBN Prefix(es): 978-1-59333; 978-0-9713097; 978-0-9715986; 978-1-931956; 978-1-60724; 978-1-4632
Number of titles published annually: 75 Print
Total Titles: 3,000 Print
Distributor for Yeshiva University Museum Press
Membership(s): Independent Book Publishers Association (IBPA)

§Gospel Publishing House
Imprint of My Healthy Church
1445 Boonville Ave, Springfield, MO 65802-1894
SAN: 206-8826
Tel: 417-866-8014 *Toll Free Tel:* 855-642-2011 *Fax:* 417-862-0414 *Toll Free Fax:* 877-840-5100
E-mail: custsrv@myhealthychurch.com
Web Site: myhealthychurch.com/store
Founded: 1914
Religion (Assemblies of God); sign language textbooks & curricular materials.
ISBN Prefix(es): 978-0-88243; 978-1-60731; 978-1-89516
Number of titles published annually: 6 Print
Total Titles: 250 Print

GPH, see Gospel Publishing House

The Graduate Group/Booksellers
86 Norwood Rd, West Hartford, CT 06117-2236
Mailing Address: PO Box 370351, West Hartford, CT 06137-0351
Tel: 860-233-2330
E-mail: graduategroup@hotmail.com
Web Site: www.graduategroup.com
Key Personnel
Partner: Mara Whitman
Lib Sales Dir: Robert Whitman *Tel:* 860-232-3100
Founded: 1964
Publish career oriented reference books & self-help books for libraries, career & placement offices in the US & abroad, law enforcement, career series, exam preparation.
ISBN Prefix(es): 978-0-938609
Number of titles published annually: 20 Print; 1 Online
Total Titles: 100 Print; 2 Online

§Grand & Archer Publishing
463 Coyote, Cathedral City, CA 92234
Tel: 323-493-2785
E-mail: grandandarcher@gmail.com
Key Personnel
Owner & CEO: Will Tom Shoaff
Chief Content Offr: Max Visconti

Founded: 2016
Boutique publishing agency.
ISBN Prefix(es): 978-1-929730
Number of titles published annually: 3 Print; 5 E-Book; 3 Audio
Total Titles: 3 Print
Membership(s): Independent Book Publishers Association (IBPA)

§Grand Central Publishing
Division of Hachette Book Group Inc
1290 Avenue of the Americas, New York, NY 10104
Tel: 212-364-1100
Web Site: www.hachettebookgroup.com/imprint/grand-central-publishing/
Key Personnel
Pres & Publr: Ben Sevier
SVP, Deputy Publr: Beth deGuzman
SVP, Ed-in-Chief: Colin Dickerman
VP & Publr, Balance: Nana Twumasi
VP & Publr, Legacy Lit: Krishan Trotman
VP, Exec Edit Dir, Fiction: Karen Kosztolnyik
VP, Exec Ed: Lyssa Keusch; Suzanne O'Neill
Publr, Forever: Leah Hultenschmidt
Exec Ed, GCP & Ed-in-Chief, Forever: Amy Pierpont
Exec Ed: Amar Deol; Alex Logan; Karyn Marcus
Exec Ed, Balance: Diana Ventimiglia
Sr Ed: Maddie Caldwell
Sr Ed, Forever: Madeleine Colavita; Junessa Viloria
Ed: Kirsiah Depp
Ed, Balance: Hannah Robinson
VP & Exec Dir, Publicity & Mktg: Matthew Ballast
Sr Publicity Dir: Jimmy Franco
Publicity & Mktg Dir, Forever: Estelle Hallick
Publicity & Mktg Dir, Twelve: Megan Perritt-Jacobson
Mktg Proj Dir, Legacy Lit: Kathryn Gordon
Publicity Dir, Fiction: Andy Dodds
Publicity Dir, Legacy Lit: Tara Kennedy
Assoc Publicity Dir: Staci Burt
Publicity Mgr: Kamrun Nesa
Sr Publicist, Balance: Alexandra Hernandez
Publicist: Stef Acquaviva; Alli Rosenthal
Dir, Mktg Opers: Andrew Duncan
Assoc Dir, Mktg & Ad: Joe Benincase
Assoc Dir, Mktg: Theresa DeLucci; Janine Perez; Tiffany Porcelli; Kimberly Lew
Mktg Mgr: Alana Spendley
Mktg Mgr, Legacy Lit: Maya Lewis
Assoc Mktg & Publicity Mgr, Forever: Dana Cuadrado
Dir, Ad & Promo: Alexis Gilbert
VP & Creative Dir: Albert Tang
Exec Art Dir: Flamur Tonuzi
Art Dir, Balance & Twelve: Jim Datz
Art Dir: Daniela Medina
Sr Designer: Sarah Congdon
Imprint Sales Dir: Elizabeth Blue Guess
Founded: 1970
Hardcover, trade paperback & mass market paperback, reprint & original, fiction & nonfiction, audiobooks. Unsol/unagented mss not accepted.
ISBN Prefix(es): 978-0-445; 978-0-446; 978-0-89296
Number of titles published annually: 360 Print
Total Titles: 3,392 Print
Imprints: Balance; Forever (includes Forever Yours); Grand Central; Legacy Lit; Twelve
Foreign Rights: Antonella Antonelli Agenzia (Italy); Bardon Far Eastern Agents (Taiwan); Graal Literary Agency (Poland); Imprima Korea Agency (South Korea); Katai & Bolza Literary Agents (Hungary); Simona Kessler International Copyright Agency Ltd (Romania); La Nouvelle Agence (France); Andrew Nurnberg Associates Ltd (Baltic States, Bulgaria, Mainland China, Russia); OA Literary Agency (Greece); Kristin Olson Literary Agency SRO (Czechia, Slovakia); Pikarski Agency (Israel); Prava i prevodi (Croatia, Slovenia); RDC Agencia Literaria (Brazil, Latin America, Spain); Thomas Schlueck GmbH (Germany)
Advertising Agency: Publishers Advertising
Shipping Address: Hachette Book Group Inc Distribution Center, 121 N Enterprise Blvd, Lebanon, IN 46052 *Tel:* 765-483-9900 *Fax:* 765-483-0706
Membership(s): Association of American Publishers (AAP); Book Industry Study Group (BISG)

Donald M Grant Publisher Inc
19 Surrey Lane, Hampton Falls, NH 03844
Mailing Address: PO Box 187, Hampton Falls, NH 03844-0187
Tel: 603-778-7191 *Fax:* 603-778-7191
Web Site: secure.grantbooks.com
Key Personnel
Pres: Robert K Wiener *E-mail:* robert@grantbooks.com
Founded: 1964
Horror, science fiction, art & fantasy illustrated books.
ISBN Prefix(es): 978-0-937986; 978-1-880418
Number of titles published annually: 6 Print
Total Titles: 50 Print
Distributor for Archival; Oswald Train

Graphic Universe™
Imprint of Lerner Publishing Group Inc
241 First Ave N, Minneapolis, MN 55401
Tel: 612-332-3344 *Toll Free Tel:* 800-328-4929 *Fax:* 612-332-7615 *Toll Free Fax:* 800-332-1132
E-mail: info@lernerbooks.com; custserve@lernerbooks.com
Web Site: www.lernerbooks.com; www.facebook.com/lernerbooks
Key Personnel
Chmn: Harry J Lerner
Pres & Publr: Adam Lerner
EVP & COO: Mark Budde
EVP & CFO: Margaret Thomas
EVP, Sales: David Wexler
VP & Ed-in-Chief: Andy Cummings
VP, Mktg: Rachel Zugschwert
Dir, HR: Margaret Wolfson *E-mail:* mwolfson@lernerbooks.com
Dir, Rts, Spec Sales & Intl Dist: Maria Kjoller
Edit Dir: Greg Hunter
Publg Dir, School & Lib: Jenny Krueger
School & Lib Mktg Dir: Lois Wallentine
Founded: 2006
Publish fiction & nonfiction graphic novels for beginning readers, middle grade readers & young adults.
Number of titles published annually: 20 Print; 20 E-Book
Total Titles: 200 Print; 200 E-Book
Foreign Rep(s): Bounce Sales & Marketing Ltd (Europe, India, Middle East, Pakistan, Scandinavia, UK); CrossCan Education (Canada); Phambili Agencies (Botswana, Lesotho, Namibia, Southern Africa, Swaziland, Zimbabwe); Publishers Marketing Services (PMS) (Brunei, Malaysia, Singapore); Saunders (school & lib) (Canada); Walker Australia (Australia, New Zealand)
Foreign Rights: AC2 Literary (Italy); Sandra Bruna Literary Agency (Brazil, Portugal, Spain); CA-Link (Hong Kong, Macau, Mainland China, Taiwan); Japan Foreign-Rights Centre (JFC) (Japan); Korea Copyright Center Inc (KCC) (South Korea); Agence Michelle Lapautre (France); RightsMix (Eastern Europe, Greece, Israel, Netherlands, Russia, Scandinavia, UK); Literarische Agentur Silke Weniger (Germany)
Warehouse: CGC Fulfillment Warehouse, 150 Kingswood Dr, Mankato, MN 56001

Gray & Company Publishers
1588 E 40 St, Suite 1B, Cleveland, OH 44103

PUBLISHERS

Tel: 216-431-2665 *Toll Free Tel:* 800-915-3609
E-mail: sales@grayco.com; editorial@grayco.com; publicity@grayco.com
Web Site: www.grayco.com
Key Personnel
Pres: David Gray
Founded: 1991
Books about Cleveland, Northeast Ohio & Ohio.
ISBN Prefix(es): 978-1-886228; 978-0-9631738; 978-1-59851; 978-1-938441
Number of titles published annually: 4 Print; 4 E-Book
Total Titles: 120 Print; 80 E-Book

Graywolf Press
212 Third Ave N, Suite 485, Minneapolis, MN 55401
Tel: 651-641-0077 *Fax:* 651-641-0036
E-mail: wolves@graywolfpress.org (no ms queries, sample chapters or proposals)
Web Site: www.graywolfpress.org
Key Personnel
Exec Dir & Publr: Carmen Gimenez
Assoc Publr: Katie Dublinski *E-mail:* dublinski@graywolfpress.org
Dir, Advancement & Opers: Rachel Fulkerson
Dir, Mktg & Engagement: Marisa Atkinson
Dir, Poetry & Exec Ed: Jeffrey Shotts
Edit Dir: Ethan Nosowsky
Publicity Dir: Claire Laine *E-mail:* laine@graywolfpress.org
Sales Dir: Casey O'Neil *E-mail:* oneil@graywolfpress.org
Sr Devt Offr: Josh Ostergaard
Exec Ed: Yuka Igarashi
Ed: Chantz Erolin
Assoc Ed: Anni Liu
Mktg Mgr: Ill Nippashi
Sales & Opers Mgr: Mattan Comay
Mktg & Events Coord: Shaina Robinson
Publicist: Claudia Acevedo Quinones; Caelan Ernest Nardone
Devt Assoc: Alana Keiser
Edit Asst: Jessica Williams-Sullivan
Founded: 1974
Graywolf Press publishes 21st century American & international literature in the form of poetry, fiction, nonfiction & work in translation. Due to the volume of submissions & the size of their list, Graywolf Press no longer accepts unsol queries, book proposals or mss.
ISBN Prefix(es): 978-1-55597; 978-1-64445
Number of titles published annually: 35 Print
Total Titles: 200 Print; 30 E-Book
Distributed by Macmillan
Foreign Rights: AnatoliaLit Agency (Amy Spangler) (Turkey); Big Apple Agency (Vincent Lin) (China, Taiwan); Casanovas & Lynch Agencia Literaria (Maria Lynch) (Latin America, Portugal, Spain); Ersilia Literary Agency (Evangelia Avloniti) (Greece); Deborah Harris Agency (Geula Geurts) (Israel); Agence Michelle Lapautre (Catherine Lapautre) (France); Clementina Liuzzi Agency (Clementina Liuzzi) (Italy); Michael Meller Agency (Niclas Schmoll) (Central Europe, Eastern Europe, Germany, Russia); Tuttle-Mori Agency (Asako Kawachi) (Japan)
Orders to: MPS Distribution Center, 16365 James Madison Hwy, Gordonsville, VA 22942 *Toll Free Tel:* 888-330-8477 *Toll Free Fax:* 800-672-2054 *E-mail:* orders@mpsvirginia.com; Raincoast Books, 2440 Viking Way, Richmond, BC V6V 1N2, Canada *Tel:* 604-448-7100 *Toll Free Tel:* 800-663-5714 *Fax:* 604-270-7161 *Toll Free Fax:* 800-565-3770 *E-mail:* customerservice@raincoast.com *Web Site:* www.raincoast.com

Green Dragon Books
2275 Ibis Isle Rd W, Palm Beach, FL 33480
Mailing Address: PO Box 1608, Lake Worth, FL 33460
Tel: 561-533-6231 *Toll Free Tel:* 800-874-8844
Fax: 561-533-6233 *Toll Free Fax:* 888-874-8844
E-mail: info@greendragonbooks.com
Web Site: greendragonbooks.com
Key Personnel
Chmn & Publr: Gary Wilson *Tel:* 404-409-1930
Mng Dir: Jennifer Wilson *E-mail:* jennifer@greendragonbooks.com
Founded: 1969
Publications include Learning Center guides, early learning activity guides, children's picture books, general trade books, Legacies memoir series & SleuthHound mystery series.
ISBN Prefix(es): 978-1-62386; 978-0-89334
Number of titles published annually: 25 Print; 25 Online; 30 E-Book; 10 Audio
Total Titles: 475 Print; 475 Online; 500 E-Book; 10 Audio
Distribution Center: Baker & Taylor
Ingram Book Co
New Leaf Distributing Co, 1085 E Lotus Dr, Silver Lake, WI 53170 *Tel:* 262-889-8501 *Toll Free Tel:* 800-326-2665 *Fax:* 262-889-8598 *E-mail:* orders@newleafdist.com SAN: 169-1449
Membership(s): American Booksellers Association (ABA); American Marketing Association; ASCD; Independent Book Publishers Association (IBPA); National Education Association (NEA); National Press Club (NPC); Southern Independent Booksellers Alliance (SIBA); Toastmasters International

Green Integer
750 S Spaulding Ave, Suite 112, Los Angeles, CA 90036
SAN: 216-3063
E-mail: info@greeninteger.com
Web Site: www.greeninteger.com
Key Personnel
Publr: Douglas Messerli *E-mail:* douglasmesserli@gmail.com
Founded: 1976
Contemporary fiction, criticism, drama & poetry.
ISBN Prefix(es): 978-0-940650; 978-1-55713; 978-1-892295; 978-1-931243; 978-1-933382
Number of titles published annually: 15 Print
Total Titles: 300 Print
Imprints: New American Fiction Series; New American Poetry Series; Sun & Moon Classics; Zerogram Press
Foreign Rights: Eliane Benesti Literary Agency (France); Bookbank SA (Spain); Copenhagen Literary Agency ApS (Scandinavia); Paul & Peter Fritz AG Literary Agency (Germany, Switzerland); Japan UNI Agency Inc (Japan); Natoli, Stefan & Oliva Literary Agency (Italy); Rogan Pikarski Literary Agency (Israel)

Greenhaven Publishing
Imprint of The Rosen Publishing Group Inc
2544 Clinton St, Buffalo, NY 14224
Toll Free Tel: 844-317-7404 *Toll Free Fax:* 844-317-7405
Web Site: greenhavenpublishing.com; www.rosenpublishing.com
Founded: 1970
Middle school, high school & college (grades 7-12+) nonfiction social studies & debate books for classrooms & libraries: social studies reference series; library & paper bound books in area studies, criminal justice, the environment, health, Literary Companion & American History series & AT Issues series.
ISBN Prefix(es): 978-0-89908; 978-1-56510; 978-0-7377
Number of titles published annually: 200 Print
Total Titles: 3,500 Print
Imprints: KidHaven Publishing (grades K-6); Lucent Press (grades 7-10+)
Distributed by Lucent Press (grades 7-10+); Perfection Learning®
See separate listing for:
Lucent Press

Greenleaf Book Group LLC
PO Box 91869, Austin, TX 78709
Tel: 512-891-6100 *Fax:* 512-891-6150
E-mail: contact@greenleafbookgroup.com; orders@greenleafbookgroup.com; foreignrights@greenleafbookgroup.com; media@greenleafbookgroup.com
Web Site: greenleafbookgroup.com
Key Personnel
Founder: Clint Greenleaf
CEO: Tanya Hall
CFO: Brian Viktorin
COO: Carrie Jones
Art Dir: Neil Gonzalez
Dir, Consulting & Sales: Justin Branch
Sr Ed: Nathan True
Founded: 1997
Publisher & distributor specializing in the development of independent authors & the growth of small presses. Our publishing model was designed to support independent authors & allow writers to retain the rights to their work & still compete with major publishing houses. We also distribute select titles from small & independent publishers to major trade outlets, including bookstores, libraries & airport retailers. We serve the small & independent publishing community by offering industry guidance, business development, production, distribution & marketing services.
ISBN Prefix(es): 978-0-9665319; 978-1-929774; 978-0-9790842; 978-1-60832; 978-1-61486; 978-1-62634
Number of titles published annually: 100 Print
Total Titles: 350 Print
Imprints: An Inc Original; Greenleaf Book Group Press; River Grove Books
Returns: Archway, 20770 Westwood Dr, Strongsville, OH 44149
Membership(s): The American Library Association (ALA); Association of American Publishers (AAP); BookSense Publisher Partner; Independent Book Publishers Association (IBPA); National Speakers Association (NSA)

Greenleaf Book Group Press, see Greenleaf Book Group LLC

§Grey House Publishing Inc™
4919 Rte 22, Amenia, NY 12501
Mailing Address: PO Box 56, Amenia, NY 12501-0056
Tel: 518-789-8700 *Toll Free Tel:* 800-562-2139
Fax: 518-789-0556
E-mail: books@greyhouse.com; customerservice@greyhouse.com
Web Site: greyhouse.com
Key Personnel
Pres: Richard Gottlieb *E-mail:* rhg@greyhouse.com
VP, Mktg: Jessica Moody *Tel:* 518-789-8700 ext 101 *E-mail:* jmoody@greyhouse.com
Publr: Leslie Mackenzie *E-mail:* lmackenzie@greyhouse.com
Edit Dir: Laura Mars *E-mail:* lmars@greyhouse.com
Founded: 1981
Directories, reference books & encyclopedias in history, business, economics, health & demographic areas.
ISBN Prefix(es): 978-1-930956; 978-1-891482; 978-0-939300; 978-1-59237; 978-1-61925; 978-1-64265; 978-1-63700; 978-1-68217
Number of titles published annually: 185 Print; 50 E-Book

U.S. PUBLISHERS

Imprints: R R Bowker's Books in Print Series; Grey House; Financial Ratings Series; Salem Press; H W Wilson
Divisions: Grey House Publishing Canada
Returns: 5979 N Elm Ave, Suite 113, Millerton, NY 12546
Warehouse: 5979 N Elm Ave, Suite 113, Millerton, NY 12546
Membership(s): The American Library Association (ALA)
See separate listing for:
Salem Press

Group Publishing Inc
1515 Cascade Ave, Loveland, CO 80538
Tel: 970-669-3836 *Toll Free Tel:* 800-447-1070
E-mail: puorgbus@group.com (submissions)
Web Site: www.group.com
Key Personnel
Founder & Chmn: Thom Schultz
Founded: 1974
ISBN Prefix(es): 978-1-55945; 978-0-7644; 978-1-4707
Number of titles published annually: 40 Print
Total Titles: 300 Print; 20 CD-ROM; 30 E-Book
Foreign Rights: Canaanland (Malaysia); CLC Wholesale (UK); Group Canada (Canada); KCBS Inc (South Korea); Koorung Books Pty Ltd (Australia); Manna Christian Stores (New Zealand); SKS (Singapore); Word Bookstores (Australia)
Returns: 1615 Cascade Ave, Loveland, CO 80538
Membership(s): Evangelical Christian Publishers Association (ECPA)

Grove Atlantic Inc
154 W 14 St, 12th fl, New York, NY 10011
SAN: 201-4890
Tel: 212-614-7850 *Toll Free Tel:* 800-521-0178
Fax: 212-614-7886
E-mail: info@groveatlantic.com; sales@groveatlantic.com; publicity@groveatlantic.com; rights@groveatlantic.com
Web Site: www.groveatlantic.com
Key Personnel
Publr & CEO: Morgan Entrekin
  E-mail: mentrekin@groveatlantic.com
Assoc Publr: Judy Hottensen *E-mail:* jhottensen@groveatlantic.com
VP & Deputy Publr: Peter Blackstock
VP & Dir, Publicity: Deb Seager
  E-mail: dseager@groveatlantic.com
VP & Edit Dir: Elisabeth Schmitz
  E-mail: eschmitz@groveatlantic.com
VP, Exec Ed & Dir, Subs Rts: Amy Hundley
  E-mail: ahundley@groveatlantic.com
Dir, Mktg: Natalie Church
Exec Ed: George Gibson
Sr Ed: Joe Brosnan
Ed: Olivia Rutigliano
Assoc Ed: Emily Burns
Sr Publicity Mgr: John Mark Boling
Publicity Mgr: Justina Batchelor
Digital Mktg Mgr: Nick Stewart
Rts Mgr: Erica Nunez *E-mail:* enunez@groveatlantic.com
Publicist: Kait Astrella
Founded: 1917
General fiction & nonfiction, hardcover & paperbound.
ISBN Prefix(es): 978-0-8021; 978-1-55584; 978-0-87113; 978-1-61185
Number of titles published annually: 120 Print; 90 E-Book
Total Titles: 2,700 Print; 3,000 E-Book
Imprints: Atlantic Monthly Press; Black Cat; Roxane Gay Books; Grove Press; Grove Press UK
Foreign Rep(s): Jonathan Ball Publishers (South Africa); Book Promotions (Nicky Stubbs) (South Africa); Gilles Fauveau (Japan, South Korea); Jaime Gregorio (Philippines); Ingram Publisher Services (Edison Garcia) (Asia); Ingram Publisher Services UK (Matthew Dickie) (Europe, Ireland, Latin America, UK); Sharad Mohan (Bangladesh, India, Maldives, Nepal, Pakistan, Sri Lanka); NewSouth Books (Australia, New Zealand); June Poonpanich (Cambodia, Indonesia, Laos, Thailand, Vietnam); Wei Zhao (China, Hong Kong, Taiwan)
Foreign Rights: AnatoliaLit Agency (Amy Spangler) (Turkey); Eliane Benisti Agency (Eliane Benisti) (France); Casanovas & Lynch Agencia Literaria (Maria Lynch) (Latin America, Portugal, Spain); Ersilia Literary Agency (Evangelia Avloniti) (Greece); Graal Literary Agency (Filip Wojciechowski) (Poland); International Copyright Agency (Simona Kessler) (Romania); The Italian Literary Agency Srl (Claire Sabatie-Garat) (Italy); Japan UNI Agency Inc (Miko Yamanouchi) (Japan); Katai & Bolza (Peter Bolza) (Hungary); Korea Copyright Center Inc (KCC) (Rockyoung Lee) (South Korea); Andrew Nurnberg Associates (Tatjana Zoldnere) (Estonia, Latvia, Lithuania); Andrew Nurnberg Associates, Beijing Representative Office (Jackie Huang) (China); Andrew Nurnberg Associates, Taiwan Representative Office (Whitney Hsu) (Taiwan); Kristin Olson Literary Agency (Kristin Olson) (Czechia); Plima Literary Agency (Vuk Perisic) (Bosnia and Herzegovina, Bulgaria, Croatia, North Macedonia, Serbia, Slovenia); The Riff Agency (Laura Riff & Joao Paulo Riff) (Brazil); Elisabeth Ruge Agentur GmbH (Elisabeth Ruge) (Germany); Synopsis Literary Agency (Natalia Sanina) (Russia); Ulf Toregard Agency AG (Ulf Toregard) (Netherlands, Scandinavia); Tuttle-Mori Agency Inc (Ken Mori) (Japan)
Orders to: Ingram Publisher Services International, 1400 Broadway, Suite 520, New York, NY 10018 *Tel:* 212-714-9000 *E-mail:* ips_internationalsales@ingramcontent.com; Ingram Content Group LLC, One Ingram Blvd, La Vergne, TN 37086 *Tel:* 615-793-5000 *E-mail:* ips@ingramcontent.com; Publishers Group Canada, c/o Raincoast Books, 2440 Viking Way, Richmond, BC V6V IN2, Canada *Toll Free Tel:* 800-663-5714 *E-mail:* customerservices@raincoast.com; Grantham Book Services (GBS), Trent Rd, Grantham. Lincs NG31 7XQ, United Kingdom *Tel:* (01476) 541000 *Fax:* (01476) 541060 *Web Site:* www.thebookservice.co.uk
Returns: Ingram Publisher Services, Returns Dept, 191 Edwards Dr, Jackson, TN 38301; Raincoast Books, 2440 Viking Way, Richmond, BC V1N 2, Canada *Toll Free Tel:* 800-663-5714 *Toll Free Fax:* 800-565-3770 *E-mail:* customerservice@raincoast.com
Distribution Center: Ingram Content Group LLC, One Ingram Blvd, La Vergne, TN 37086
Membership(s): Association of American Publishers (AAP)

Gryphon Editions
PO Box 241823, Omaha, NE 68124
Tel: 402-298-5385 (intl) *Toll Free Tel:* 888-655-0134 (US & CN)
E-mail: customerservice@gryphoneditions.com
Web Site: www.gryphoneditions.com
Founded: 1977
Reprints: medicine, law, political philosophy, science; fine editions.
Number of titles published annually: 25 Print
Total Titles: 750 Print

Gryphon House Inc
Subsidiary of Kaplan Early Learning Co
6848 Leon's Way, Lewisville, NC 27023
Mailing Address: PO Box 10, Lewisville, NC 27023
Toll Free Tel: 800-638-0928 *Toll Free Fax:* 877-638-7576
E-mail: info@ghbooks.com
Web Site: www.gryphonhouse.com

BOOK

Key Personnel
Pres: Jennifer Lewis *E-mail:* jennifer@ghbooks.com
Founded: 1971
Publishes & distributes books for teachers & parents of young children.
ISBN Prefix(es): 978-0-87659
Number of titles published annually: 12 Print; 12 E-Book
Total Titles: 310 Print; 300 E-Book
Distributor for Aha Communications; Book Peddlers; Deya Brashears; Bright Ring Publishing; Building Blocks; Center for the Child Care Workforce; Chatterbox Press; Chicago Review Press; Children's Resources International; Circle Time Publishers; Sydney Gurewitz Clemens; Conari Press; Council Oak Books; DawnSignPress; Delmar Publishers Inc; Early Educator's Press; Educators for Social Responsibility; Family Center of Nova University; Jean Feldman; Floris Books; Hawthorne Press; Kaplan Press; Miss Jackie Inc; Monjeu Press; National Center Early Childhood Workforce; New England AEYC; Nova Southeastern University; Pademelon Press; Partner Press; Pollyanna Productions; Robins Lane Press; School Renaissance; Southern Early Childhood Association; Steam Press; Syracuse University Press; Teaching Strategies LLC; Telshare Publishing
Foreign Rep(s): Pademelon Press (Australia); University of Toronto Press (Canada)

Guideposts Book & Inspirational Media
100 Reserve Rd, Suite E200, Danbury, CT 06810
Mailing Address: PO Box 5815, Harlan, IA 51593
Tel: 203-749-0200 *Toll Free Tel:* 800-932-2145 (cust serv)
E-mail: gpsprod@cdsfulfillment.com; gdpcustserv@cdsfulfillment.com
Web Site: guideposts.org
Key Personnel
Pres & CEO: John F Temple, III
Founded: 1945
Inspirational books & videos.
ISBN Prefix(es): 978-0-9661766
Number of titles published annually: 30 Print

§The Guilford Press
370 Seventh Ave, Suite 1200, New York, NY 10001-1020
SAN: 212-9442
Tel: 212-431-9800 *Toll Free Tel:* 800-365-7006
Fax: 212-966-6708
E-mail: info@guilford.com; orders@guilford.com
Web Site: www.guilford.com
Key Personnel
CEO: Tim Stookesberry
Dir, Opers: David Mitchell *E-mail:* david.mitchell@guilford.com
Mktg Dir: Andrea Lansing *E-mail:* andrea.lansing@guilford.com
Sales Dir: Anne Patota *Tel:* 212-431-9800 ext 217 *E-mail:* anne.patota@guilford.com
Subs Rts Dir: Kathy Kuehl *E-mail:* kathy.kuehl@guilford.com
Ed-in-Chief: Laurie Rosatone
Mng Ed: Elizabeth Geller
Credit Mgr: Vernita Hurston *Tel:* 212-431-9800 ext 230 *E-mail:* vernita.hurston@guilford.com
Fulfillment Mgr: Christopher Etsell *Tel:* 800-365-7006 ext 260 *E-mail:* christopher.etsell@guilford.com
Founded: 1973
Publisher of authoritative, evidence-based professional & consumer trade books & journals in psychology & the behavioral sciences, research methods & education & literacy.
ISBN Prefix(es): 978-0-89862; 978-1-57230; 978-1-59385; 978-1-60623; 978-1-60918; 978-1-4625

PUBLISHERS

U.S. PUBLISHERS

Number of titles published annually: 70 Print; 70 E-Book
Total Titles: 1,400 Print; 1,300 E-Book
Foreign Rep(s): Avicenna (Middle East); Information & Culture Korea (South Korea); itsabook (Caribbean, Central America, Mexico, South America); Taylor & Francis Asia Pacific (Asia-Pacific); Taylor & Francis Group Ltd (Europe, UK); Taylor & Francis Group Ltd/Jonathan Ball Publishers Pty Ltd (South Africa); Taylor & Francis India (India); Taylor & Francis Pakistan (Pakistan); Unifacmanu (Taiwan); Woodslane Pty Ltd (Australia, New Zealand)
Returns: Maple Logistics Solutions, York Distribution Ctr, 60 Grumbacher Rd, York, PA 17406
Warehouse: Maple Logistics Solutions, York Distribution Ctr, 60 Grumbacher Rd, York, PA 17406

Guilford Publications Inc, see The Guilford Press

§Gulf Energy Information
2 Greenway Plaza, Suite 1020, Houston, TX 77046
Mailing Address: PO Box 2608, Houston, TX 77252
Tel: 713-520-4498; 713-529-4301
E-mail: store@gulfpub.com; customerservice@gulfenergyinfo.com
Web Site: www.gulfenergyinfo.com
Key Personnel
Exec Chmn: John T Royall
CFO: Catherine Watkins
Pres: Andy McDowell
SVP, Prodn & Opers: Sheryl Stone
VP, Content: Lee Nichols
VP, Events: Jacob Adams Mireles
VP, Mktg & Audience Devt: Roger Jordan *E-mail:* roger.jordan@gulfenergyinfo.com
Founded: 1916
Communications company dedicated to the petrochemical industry & related industries.
ISBN Prefix(es): 978-1-933762; 978-0-9765113
Number of titles published annually: 10 Print; 3 CD-ROM
Total Titles: 20 Print; 30 CD-ROM
Distributor for Editions Technip; Elsevier; Pennwell; Wiley

§Hachai Publishing
527 Empire Blvd, Brooklyn, NY 11225
SAN: 251-3749
Tel: 718-633-0100 *Fax:* 718-633-0103
E-mail: info@hachai.com
Web Site: www.hachai.com
Key Personnel
Pres: Yerachmiel Binyominson
Publr & Sales: Yossi Leverton *E-mail:* yossi@hachai.com
Ed: Dina Rosenfeld *E-mail:* dlr@hachai.com
Founded: 1988
Full color children's Judaica books.
ISBN Prefix(es): 978-0-922613; 978-1-929628; 978-1-945560; 979-8-88806
Number of titles published annually: 6 Print
Total Titles: 110 Print; 1 E-Book
Distributor for Attara; Kerem; Living Lessons
Membership(s): Association of Jewish Libraries; Independent Book Publishers Association (IBPA)

Hachette Audio
Division of Hachette Book Group Inc
1290 Avenue of the Americas, New York, NY 10104
Tel: 212-364-1100
Web Site: www.hachettebookgroup.com/imprint/hachette-audio/
Key Personnel
VP & Publr: Ana Maria Allessi
VP, Assoc Publr: Kim Sayle
Exec Dir of Prodn, Exec Prodr: Michele McGonigle De Young
Assoc Dir, Social Media, Publicity & Mktg: Nita Basu
Audio Data & Opers Mgr: Mishell Velez
Audio Post-Prodn Supv: Tom Messina
Audio Ed: Laura Essex
Studio Mgr & Audio Opers Assoc: Charles McCrorey
Sr Audio Prodn Assoc: Michelle Figueroa; Ghenet Harvey
Publicity & Mktg Coord: Oriel Voegele
Number of titles published annually: 470 Audio
Total Titles: 4,421 Audio

Hachette Book Group Inc
Division of Hachette Livre
1290 Avenue of the Americas, New York, NY 10104
Tel: 212-364-1100 *Toll Free Tel:* 800-759-0190 (cust serv) *Fax:* 212-364-0933 (intl orders) *Toll Free Fax:* 800-286-9471 (cust serv)
E-mail: customer.service@hbgusa.com; orders@hbgusa.com
Web Site: www.hachettebookgroup.com
Key Personnel
CEO: David Shelley
Deputy CEO: Richard Kitson
Pres & Publr, Grand Central Publishing: Ben Sevier
Pres & Publr, Little, Brown and Company: Sally Kim
Pres & Publr, Little, Brown Books for Young Readers: Megan Tingley
Pres & Publr, Orbit: Tim Holman
EVP & Gen Coun: Min Lee
EVP & CFO: Stephen Mubarek
EVP & Dir of Sales: Lauren Monaco
SVP & CIO: Puneet Kukkal
SVP & Chief Mktg Offr: Leigh Marchant
SVP, Communs: Gabrielle Gambrell
SVP, HR: Andrea Weinzimer
SVP, Culture & DEI: Carrie Bloxson
SVP, Deputy Group Sales Dir: Chrissy Heleine
SVP, Publg Opers & Strategy: Dylan Hoke
SVP, Publr: Reagan Arthur
SVP & Publr, Basic Books Group: Lara Heimert
SVP & Publr, Running Press Group: Kristin Kiser
SVP & Publr, Workman Publishing, Artisan & Black Dog & Leventhal: Lia Ronnen
VP & Publr, Hachette Audio: Ana Maria Alessi
VP & Publr, Hachette Nashville: Daisy Hutton
VP & Exec Mng Ed, Hachette: Rena Kornbluh
VP, Corp Busn Devt & Strategy: Todd McGarity
VP, Subs Rts: Nancy Wiese
VP, Dist: Frank Casolaro
VP, Sales, Intl, Canada & Spec Mkts: Maritza Lumpris
VP & Dir, Intl & Canada Sales: Sara High
VP, Mass Mdse, Wholesale & Lib Mktg: Laura Pennock
VP, Spec Mkts: Andrea Rosen
VP, Mfg: Ruiko Tokunaga
VP, Digital Opers: Michael Gaudet
Founded: 2006 (when Time Warner Book Group was purchased by Hachette Livre)
Hachette Book Group (HBG) is a leading trade publisher based in New York & a division of Hachette Livre (a Lagardere Groupe company), the third largest trade & educational publisher in the world. HBG is made up of several publishing groups: Basic Books Group; Grand Central Publishing; Hachette Audio; Hachette Books; Hachette Nashville; Little, Brown and Company; Little, Brown Books for Young Readers; Orbit; Running Press Group & Workman Publishing.
ISBN Prefix(es): 978-1-56282; 978-0-7868; 978-0-316; 978-1-4013
Divisions: Basic Books Group; Grand Central Publishing; Hachette Audio; Hachette Books; Hachette Nashville; Little, Brown and Company; Little, Brown Books for Young Readers;
Orbit; Running Press Group; Workman Publishing
Distributor for Harry N Abrams Inc; Nicholas Brealey Publishing; Callaway Arts & Entertainment (US & CN); Chronicle Books; Gildan Media; Hachette UK Ltd; Houghton Mifflin Harcourt; Kids Can Press; Lonely Planet; Moleskine; Nosy Crow Inc; Octopus Books; Peterson's; Phaidon Press; Phoenix International Publications (PiKids); Quarto Publishing Group; Quercus Books; Sheldon Press (all print & digital); Time Inc Books; Yen Press
Orders to: Order Dept, 53 State St, Boston, MA 02109 (US orders) *Toll Free Tel:* 800-759-0190 *Toll Free Fax:* 800-286-9471
Returns: Returns Dept, 322 S Enterprise Blvd, Lebanon, IN 46052
Shipping Address: Hachette Book Group Inc Distribution Center, 121 N Enterprise Blvd, Lebanon, IN 46052 *Tel:* 765-483-9900 *Fax:* 765-483-0706
See separate listing for:
Basic Books Group
Grand Central Publishing
Hachette Audio
Hachette Nashville
Little, Brown and Company
Little, Brown Books for Young Readers (LBYR)
Orbit
Running Press
Workman Publishing

Hachette Nashville
Division of Hachette Book Group Inc
6100 Tower Circle, Room 210, Franklin, TN 37067
Tel: 615-221-0996 *Fax:* 615-221-0962
Web Site: www.hachettebookgroup.com/imprint/hachette-nashville/
Key Personnel
VP & Publr: Daisy Hutton
VP, Mktg & Publicity: Patsy S Jones
VP, Nashville & Client Opers: Billy Clark
VP & Assoc Publr: Jeana Ledbetter
Assoc Publr, WorthyKids: Peggy Schaefer
Mktg Dir: Rudy Kish
Mktg Dir, Worthy Publishing: Cat Hoort
Channel Dir, Clients & Nashville: Gina Wynn
Fin Dir: Deirdre Baule
Imprint Sales Dir: Elizabeth Blue Guess
Publicity Dir: Laini Brown
Assoc Art Dir: Edward Crawford
Exec Ed: Jenny Baumgartner
Edit Dir: Beth Adams
Sr Ed, WorthyKids: Melinda Rathjen
Asst Ed, WorthyKids: Rebekah Moredock
Founded: 2001
Publish books for the growing inspirational market. No unsol mss.
ISBN Prefix(es): 978-0-446
Number of titles published annually: 95 Print
Total Titles: 556 Print
Imprints: Center Street (nonfiction conservative political & military titles); FaithWords; Worthy Publishing (includes Elle Claire, Worthy Books & WorthyKids/Ideals)
Orders to: Hachette Book Group Inc, 53 State St, Boston, MA 02109 *Toll Free Tel:* 800-759-0190 *Toll Free Fax:* 800-286-9471
Membership(s): Evangelical Christian Publishers Association (ECPA)

Hackett Publishing Co Inc
3333 Massachusetts Ave, Indianapolis, IN 46218
SAN: 201-6044
Mailing Address: PO Box 390007, Cambridge, MA 02139
Tel: 317-635-9250 (orders & cust serv); 617-497-6303 (edit off & sales) *Fax:* 317-635-9292; 617-661-8703 (edit off) *Toll Free Fax:* 800-783-9213

U.S. PUBLISHERS

E-mail: customer@hackettpublishing.com; editorial@hackettpublishing.com
Web Site: www.hackettpublishing.com
Key Personnel
Pres, Publr & CEO: Deborah Wilkes
VP, Mktg Dir & Dir, Opers: John Pershing Tel: 617-234-0371 E-mail: johnp@hackettpublishing.com
Secy & Treas: Cheri Brown
Promos Mgr: Mr Ryan Picazio Tel: 617-497-6307 E-mail: ryanp@hackettpublishing.com
Founded: 1972
College textbooks & scholarly books; emphasis on philosophy, political theory, political science, classics, history & literature.
ISBN Prefix(es): 978-0-915144; 978-0-915145; 978-0-87220; 978-1-60384
Number of titles published annually: 30 Print; 30 E-Book
Total Titles: 840 Print; 300 E-Book
Imprints: Focus
Distributor for Bryn Mawr Commentaries
Foreign Rep(s): Gazelle Book Services Ltd (Europe, UK); UNIREPS (Australia, New Zealand)
Foreign Rights: Eulama
See separate listing for:
Focus

§Hal Leonard LLC
7777 W Bluemound Rd, Milwaukee, WI 53213
Mailing Address: PO Box 13819, Milwaukee, WI 53213-0819
Tel: 414-774-3630
E-mail: info@halleonard.com; sales@halleonard.com
Web Site: www.halleonard.com
Key Personnel
Exec Bd Memb: Larry Morton
EVP: Jeff Schroedl
Sr Sales & Mktg Mgr, Book Trade & Ebooks: Mike Hansen
Sales Mgr: David Cywinski
Founded: 1947
The world's largest music print publisher, with an incomparable selection of sheet music, songbooks, music related books, self-instruction books, CD packs & videos, music reference & special interest titles, music biographies, children's music products; CD-ROMs, DVDs, performance videos & more. Additional offices in Minnesota, New York, Nashville, Australia, Belgium, France, Germany, Holland, Italy, Switzerland & the UK.
ISBN Prefix(es): 978-1-57467; 978-0-88188; 978-0-7935; 978-0-87910; 978-0-87930; 978-0-634; 978-0-9607350; 978-1-56516; 978-1-61713; 978-1-61774; 978-1-61780; 978-1-4584; 978-1-4768; 978-1-4803; 978-0-931340; 978-1-4950
Number of titles published annually: 2,000 Print
Total Titles: 200,000 Print; 15 CD-ROM
Imprints: Berklee Press; Cherry Lane Music Co; Ashley Mark Publishing Co; Musicians Institute Press; G Shirmer; Vintage Guitar
Divisions: Hal Leonard Performing Arts Publishing Group
Distributor for Arrangers Publishing LLC; Ashley Music; Berklee Press; Leonard Bernstein; Fred Bock Music Company; Boosey & Hawkes; Boston Music; Centerstream Publishing LLC; Le Chant du Monde; Cherry Lane Music Co; Chester Music; Choudens; De Haske Publications; Dots & Lines Inc; DSCH; Editions Durand; Editions Max Eschig; Editions Salabert; EM Books; Faber Music Ltd; Fleamarket Music; Mark Foster Music; Gentry Publications; Guitar World; Wilhelm Hansen; G Henle Verlag; Hinshaw Music; Homespun Tapes; Hot Licks; Hudson Music; Lauren Keiser Music; Robert King; LeDuc; Edward B Marks Music; Modern Drummer Publications; Music Minus One; Musicians Institute Press; Novello; Pavane Publishing; Peermusic Classical; PWM Editions; The Richmond Organization; Ricordi; Lee Roberts Publications; Rock House; Rubank Publications; Schaum Publications; G Schirmer Inc/Associated Music Publishers Inc; Schott Music; Second Floor Music; Shawnee Press; Sikorski; Southern Music; String Letter Publishing; Tara Publications; Tycoon Percussion; Union Musical Ediciones; Vintage Guitar; Waltons Irish Music; Willis Music; Sylvia Woods
Foreign Rep(s): Publishers Group UK (Europe, UK)
Foreign Rights: Robert Lecker Agency Inc
Returns: 1210 Innovation Dr, Winona, MN 55987
Shipping Address: 1210 Innovation Dr, Winona, MN 55987
Warehouse: 1210 Innovation Dr, Winona, MN 55987
Distribution Center: 1210 Innovation Dr, Winona, MN 55987

Hameray Publishing Group Inc
5212 Venice Blvd, Los Angeles, CA 90019
Toll Free Tel: 866-918-6173 Fax: 858-369-5201
E-mail: info@hameraypublishing.com (cust serv); sales@hameraypublishing.com (sales)
Web Site: www.hameraypublishing.com
Founded: 2008
Hameray Publishing Group's mission is to help inspire budding readers with leveled books that make the learning process more pleasurable. We strive to help teachers foster a love of reading that will last a lifetime with fun & immersive stories from leading authors like Joy Cowley.
For US customers, our shipping & handling is $6 or 10% (whichever is greater). For international customers, shipping & handling rates will vary depending on your location. We typically process & ship orders within 2 business days of receipt. Our warehouse is in California, so packages can take 1 to 5 business days to arrive once shipped. Hameray Publishing Group is a sole-source vendor & an approved New York City vendor (# HAM736846).
ISBN Prefix(es): 978-1-60559; 978-1-62817; 978-1-64039
Number of titles published annually: 200 Print
Total Titles: 1,000 Print
Imprints: Bear & Bobcat Books
Membership(s): Reading Recovery Council of North America
See separate listing for:
Bear & Bobcat Books

Hamilton Books
Imprint of Rowman & Littlefield Publishing Group
4501 Forbes Blvd, Suite 200, Lanham, MD 20706
Tel: 301-459-3366 Toll Free Tel: 800-462-6420 (cust serv) Fax: 301-429-5748
Toll Free Fax: 800-388-4550 (cust serv)
Key Personnel
Dir, Edit: Nicolette Amstutz E-mail: namstutz@rowman.com
Acqs Ed: Brooke Bures E-mail: bbures@rowman.com
Founded: 2002
Provides authors of serious nonfiction titles, including corporate leaders, politicians, scholars, war veterans & family historians, the opportunity to sign with a top-quality publisher without the typical hassles & extreme selectivity enforced by other publishers.
ISBN Prefix(es): 978-0-7618
Number of titles published annually: 40 Print; 40 E-Book
Total Titles: 500 Print; 500 E-Book

Hamilton Stone Editions
PO Box 43, Maplewood, NJ 07040
Tel: 973-378-8361
E-mail: hstone@hamiltonstone.org
Web Site: www.hamiltonstone.org
Key Personnel
Edit Dir: Meredith Sue Willis
E-mail: meredithsuewillis@gmail.com
Artistic Dir: Lynda Schor E-mail: lynda.schor@gmail.com
Dir: Nathan Leslie E-mail: nleslie@nvcc.edu; Carole Rosenthal E-mail: crlrosenthal@gmail.com
Founded: 2003
Independent press for independent literary writing. Dedicated to vivid writing that probes the hidden realities of the everyday, valuing most highly the kind of writing that displays a multifaced vision. Interested in keeping new books in print & bringing forgotten, excellent old books back into print.
ISBN Prefix(es): 978-0-9654043; 978-0-9714873
Number of titles published annually: 4 Print; 4 E-Book
Total Titles: 50 Print; 50 E-Book
Imprints: Irene Weinberger Books (literary books in ebook & trade paperback format, often in collaboration with other presses)
Shipping Address: 447 Tremont Place, Orange, NJ 07050

Hampton Roads Publishing
Imprint of Red Wheel/Weiser
65 Parker St, Suite 7, Newburyport, MA 01950-4600
Tel: 978-465-0504 Toll Free Tel: 800-423-7087 (orders) Fax: 978-465-0243 Toll Free Fax: 877-337-3309
E-mail: orders@rwwbooks.com; rights@rwwbooks.com
Web Site: www.redwheelweiser.com
Key Personnel
Publicity Mgr: Eryn Carter Eaton
E-mail: ecarter@rwwbooks.com
Founded: 1989
Trade publishing. Specialize in metaphysics, self-help, integrative medicine, visionary fiction & paranormal phenomena.
ISBN Prefix(es): 978-1-878901; 978-1-57174; 978-1-61283
Number of titles published annually: 12 Print
Total Titles: 350 Print; 2 Audio
Distributed by Red Wheel/Weiser
Foreign Rep(s): Deep Books Ltd (Europe, UK); Firefly Books Ltd (Canada); NewSouth Books (Australia)

§Hancock House Publishers
4550 Birch Bay Lynden Rd, Suite 104, Blaine, WA 98230-9436
Tel: 604-538-1114 Toll Free Tel: 800-938-1114 Fax: 604-538-2262 Toll Free Fax: 800-983-2262
E-mail: sales@hancockhouse.com
Web Site: www.hancockhouse.com
Key Personnel
Publr & Intl Rts: Myles Lamont
Founded: 1975
Specialize in natural history (world), regional northwest history & Native art.
ISBN Prefix(es): 978-0-88839
Number of titles published annually: 15 Print
Total Titles: 600 Print
Branch Office(s)
19313 Zero Ave, Surrey, BC V3Z 9R9, Canada

Handprint Books Inc
Imprint of Chronicle Books
413 Sixth Ave, Brooklyn, NY 11215
Tel: 718-768-3696 Toll Free Tel: 800-759-0190 (orders)
E-mail: hello@chroniclebooks.com (orders); publicity@chroniclebooks.com
Web Site: www.handprintbooks.com
Key Personnel
Pres & Publr: Christopher Franceschelli
E-mail: cmf@handprintbooks.com

Founded: 2000
Publisher of high-quality books for children.
ISBN Prefix(es): 978-1-929766; 978-1-59354
Number of titles published annually: 12 Print
Distributed by Chronicle Books
Returns: Hachette Book Returns, 322 S Enterprise Blvd, Lebanon, IN 46052

Hanging Loose Press
231 Wyckoff St, Brooklyn, NY 11217
SAN: 206-4960
Tel: 347-529-4738 *Fax:* 347-227-8215
E-mail: print225@aol.com
Web Site: www.hangingloosepress.com
Key Personnel
Ed & Intl Rts: Robert Hershon
Ed: Dick Lourie; Mark Pawlak
Founded: 1966
Poetry & short fiction.
ISBN Prefix(es): 978-0-914610; 978-1-882413; 978-1-931236
Number of titles published annually: 8 Print
Total Titles: 225 Print
Membership(s): Community of Literary Magazines & Presses (CLMP)

§Hannacroix Creek Books Inc
1127 High Ridge Rd, PMB 110, Stamford, CT 06905
SAN: 299-9560
Tel: 203-968-8098
E-mail: hannacroix@aol.com
Key Personnel
Pres & CEO: Dr Jan Yager
Founded: 1996
Trade publisher of quality & innovative fiction & nonfiction books & journals that entertain, educate & inform.
ISBN Prefix(es): 978-1-889262; 978-1-938998
Number of titles published annually: 7 Print; 10 E-Book
Total Titles: 38 Print; 18 E-Book
Foreign Rep(s): International Editors' Co (Flavia Sala) (Brazil)
Foreign Rights: Guiliana Bernardi Literary Agent (Italy); DS Rights (Eastern Europe); Antonia Kerrigan Literary Agency (Spain); Eric Yang Agency (South Korea)
Membership(s): Association of American Publishers (AAP); Independent Book Publishers Association (IBPA); Women's Media Group

Hanover Publisher Services, see Steerforth Press & Services

§Hanser Publications LLC
Subsidiary of Carl Hanser Verlag GmbH & Co KG
c/o CFAS, 5667 Kyles Lane, Liberty Township, OH 45044
Toll Free Tel: 800-950-8977; 888-558-2632 (orders)
E-mail: info@hanserpublications.com
Web Site: www.hanserpublications.com
Founded: 1993
Technical & reference books & related products in manufacturing, metalworking & products finishing. Hanser Publishers: technical, engineering & science reference books, monographs, textbooks & journals in plastics technology, polymer & materials science.
ISBN Prefix(es): 978-1-56990
Number of titles published annually: 17 Print
Total Titles: 312 Print; 250 Online
Foreign Office(s): Carl Hanser Verlag, Kolbergerstr 22, 81679 Munich, Germany *Tel:* (089) 99830-0 *Fax:* (089) 99830-269 *Web Site:* www.hanser.de
Foreign Rep(s): Aalborg Centerboghandel (Denmark); about 3 Pty Ltd (Australia); Aditya Books Pvt Ltd (India); Allied Publishers Pvt Ltd (Mr R N Purwar) (India); Eurospan Ltd (Africa, Asia-Pacific, Europe, Middle East, UK); Carl Hanser Verlag GmbH & Co KG (Germany); Kuba Libri Ltd (Czechia); Prospero's Konyvei Budapest KFT (Hungary); Sci-Tech Books & Periodicals (India); Ian Taylor Associates Ltd (China)
Returns: Ingram Publisher Services, 120 Ingram Dr, Chambersburg, PA 17202 *Toll Free Tel:* 888-558-2632 *E-mail:* ips@ingramcontent.com
Distribution Center: Ingram Publisher Services, 14 Ingram Blvd, Mail Stop 631, La Vergne, TN 37086 *Toll Free Tel:* 888-558-2632 (orders) *E-mail:* ips@ingramcontent.com *Web Site:* www.ingramcontent.com

Harlequin Enterprises Ltd
Division of HarperCollins
195 Broadway, 24th fl, New York, NY 10007
SAN: 200-2450
Mailing Address: PO Box 9049, Buffalo, NY 14269-9049
Tel: 212-207-7000 *Toll Free Tel:* 888-432-4879; 800-370-5838 (ebooks)
E-mail: customerservice@harlequin.com
Web Site: www.harlequin.com/shop/index.html; corporate.harlequin.com
Key Personnel
VP, Publicity: Heather Connor *Tel:* 212-207-7978 *E-mail:* heather.connor@harpercollins.com
VP & Deputy Dir, Sales: Kelly Roberts
Exec Dir, Sales Opers & Trade Shows: Ann Dye
Dir, Subs Rts & Harlequin Audio: Reka Rubin
Edit Dir, Park Row Books: Erika Imranyi
Sr Exec Ed: Glenda Howard
Sr Ed: Gail Chasan
Sr Ed, Carina Press: Stephanie Doig
Sr Ed, Graydon House Books: Melanie Fried
Sr Ed, Harlequin Romantic Suspense: Allison Lyons
Ed, Mira: Dina Davis
Assoc Ed, Harlequin Desire: John Jacobson
Assoc Ed, Mira: Leah Mol
Asst Ed: Caroline Timmings
Asst Ed, Park Row Books: Nicole Luongo
Publicity Mgr: Leah Morse
Founded: 1980
Adult contemporary, historical romance novels & women's fiction.
ISBN Prefix(es): 978-0-373
Number of titles published annually: 1,400 Print
Total Titles: 40,000 Print
Imprints: Canary Street Press; Carina Press; Graydon House Books; Hanover Square Press; Harlequin; Harlequin Audio; Harlequin Teen; Love Inspired®; MIRA; Park Row Books; Worldwide Mystery
Divisions: Harlequin Brand Group; Harlequin Trade Publishing Group
Branch Office(s)
Harlequin Enterprises ULC, 22 Adelaide St W, 41st fl, Toronto, ON M5H 4E3, Canada (headquarters), VP, Sales & Mktg: Cory Beatty
Distributed by Simon & Schuster, LLC
Distribution Center: Harlequin Fulfillment Services, 3010 Walden Ave, Depew, NY 14043 *Tel:* 716-686-1800 *Web Site:* harlequinfulfillment.com
Membership(s): Association of American Publishers (AAP); Association of Canadian Publishers (ACP); Book Industry Study Group (BISG)
See separate listing for:
Love Inspired Books

HarperCollins Children's Books
Division of HarperCollins Publishers
195 Broadway, New York, NY 10007
SAN: 200-2086
Tel: 212-207-7000
Web Site: www.harpercollins.com/childrens
Key Personnel
Pres & Publr: Liate Stehlik
SVP & Exec Dir, Publg: Rich Thomas
VP & Publr: Virginia Duncan; Nancy Inteli; Erica Sussman; Tara Weikum
VP & Publr, HarperAlley: Andrew Arnold
VP & Assoc Publr/Head, Art Dept: Jean McGinley
VP & Creative Dir: Amy Ryan
VP & Edit Dir: Rosemary Brosnan
VP, Direct-to-Consumer: Kerry Saretsky
VP, Mktg & Publicity: Nellie Kurtzman
VP, Publicity & Integrated Mktg Strategy: Kelly Rudolph
Exec Dir, Fin: Tom Pombo
Exec Dir, Publicity & Events: Jennifer Corcoran
Exec Dir, Sales Opers & Trade Shows: Ann Dye
Sr Dir, Content Creation & Soc Media Strategy: Sam Fox
Sr Dir, Digital Mktg: Colleen O'Connell
Sr Dir, Mktg: Robert Imfeld
Sr Dir, Mktg, Teen Team: Audrey Diestelkamp
Sr Dir, Publicity: Cindy Hamilton
Sr Dir, School & Lib Mktg: Patty Rosati
Sr Dir, Subs Rts: Rachel Horowitz
Dir, Content Creation & Video Strategy: Carlos Rosario
Dir, Mktg Design: Audrey Steuerwald
Dir, Sales Forecasting & Analysis: Megan Pagano
Edit Dir: Alyson Day; Dave Linker; Bethany Vinhateiro
Edit Dir, Versify Books: Luana Kay Horry
Edit Dir, Quill Tree Books: Jennifer Ung
Assoc Art Dir: Jenna Stempel-Lobell
Assoc Creative Dir: Alison Donalty; Rick Farley
Assoc Dir, Children's Natl Accts: Jen Wygand
Assoc Dir, Children's Online Sales: Jess Abel
Assoc Dir, Mktg, Middle Grade Team: Sabrina Abballe
Assoc Dir, Prodn: Allison Brown; Kristen Eckhardt
Assoc Dir, Video: Spencer Alben
Asst Dir, Design: David Walker
Exec Ed: Maria Barbo; Megan Ilnitzki; Andrew Harwell; Mabel Hsu; Alex Preziosi
Exec Ed, Licensed Publg: Tomas Palacios
Sr Digital Prodn Ed: Kat Keating
Sr Ed: Alice Jerman
Sr Ed, HarperAlley: Rose Pleuler
Sr Ed, Quill Tree Books: Alyssa Miele
Sr Prodn Ed: Erin Hamling; Laura Harshbarger; Caitlin Lonning
Ed: Sarah Homer; Elizabeth Lynch; Carolina Ortiz; Sara Schonfeld; Alexandra West
Ed, Harper Group: Erika DiPasquale
Ed, Quill Tree Books: Courtney Stevenson
Prodn Ed: Mikayla Lawrence
Assoc Ed: Caitlin Johnson; Clare Vaughn
Assoc Ed, Balzer + Bray: Tiara Kittrell
Assoc Ed, Quill Tree Books: Allison Weintraub
Asst Ed: Ciera Burch; Louisa Currigan; Jenny Ly; Eva Lynch-Comer; Arianna Robinson
Asst Ed, HarperAlley: Sophie Schmidt
Sr Mgr, Conferences & Conventions Dept: LaToya Maitland
Sr Mgr, Prodn: Melissa Cicchitelli
Sr Mgr, School & Lib Mktg: Mimi Rankin
Sr Mktg Mgr: Michael D'Angelo; Emily Mannon; Lauren Tambini
Sr Proj Mgr, Mktg Opers: Rae Gande
Sr Publicity Mgr: Taylan Salvati
Sr Designer: Michelle Bigman; Mariner Brito; Chris Kwon; Cecilia Payseur
Designer: Kendall Klapp; Maddy Price; Marisa Rother; Julia Tyler
Asst Designer, Mktg Design: Sheila Machicado
Design Mgr: David Curtis; Jessie Gang; Celeste Knudsen
Mgr, Conferences & Conventions: Stephanie Macy
Mgr, Publg: Reid Sewell
Proj Mgr: Farah Reza
Publicity Mgr: Anna Bernard; Lauren Levite; Jenny Lu
Sr Publicist: Samantha Ruth Brown
Publicist: Katie Boni; Abby Dommert; Anna Ravenelle

U.S. PUBLISHERS

Assoc Publicist: Kelly Haberstroh; Sabrina Kenoun
Asst Mgr, School & Lib Mktg: Christina Carpino
Asst Mgr, Subs Rts: Theresia Kowara
Sr Fin Analyst, Children's: Melissa Wu
Fin Analyst: Harlow Steele
Coord, School & Lib Mktg: Elise Damasco
Mktg Coord: Benny Sisson
Mktg Coord, School & Lib Mktg: Josie Dallam
Sr Assoc, Middle Grade Mktg: Nicole Wills
Sr Mktg Assoc: Shannon Cox; Anais Villa
Sr Mktg Assoc, Teen Team: Lisa Calcasola
Mktg Assoc: Seoling Dee; Kadeen Griffiths; Emma Meyer; Emily Zhu
Mktg Assoc, Soc Media & Influencer Partnerships: Avery Coffey
Mktg & Publicity Assoc: Matt Maguda
Prodn Assoc: Sean Cavanagh
Rts Assoc: Cassidy Miller
Admin Asst, Publicity: Andrew Aguirre
Board books, novelty books, early readers, picture books, chapter books, juvenile fiction, young adult novels & nonfiction across all categories.
ISBN Prefix(es): 978-0-06; 978-0-688; 978-0-380; 978-0-694; 978-0-690
Imprints: Clarion Books; Greenwillow Books; HarperAlley; HarperAudio; HarperCollins; HarperCollins e-books; Heartdrum Books; Quill Tree Books; Versify Books; Walden Pond Press
Membership(s): The Children's Book Council (CBC)
See separate listing for:
Clarion Books

HarperCollins General Books Group, see HarperCollins Publishers LLC

§HarperCollins Publishers LLC
Subsidiary of News Corp
195 Broadway, New York, NY 10007
SAN: 200-2086
Tel: 212-207-7000
Web Site: www.harpercollins.com
Key Personnel
Pres & CEO: Brian Murray
EVP, CFO & Head, North American Opers: Dan Schwartz
Global CIO: Matt Bennett
Pres & Publr, Harper: Jonathan Burnham
Pres & Publr, Morrow Group: Liate Stehlik
Pres & Publr, HarperOne/HarperVia/Amistad/Rayo/HarperCollins Espanol: Judith Curr
Pres, Sales: Ed Spade
SVP & Chief People Offr: Zandra Magarino
SVP & Deputy CFO: John Zappola
SVP & Publr, Harper Business: Hollis Heimbouch
SVP & Deputy Publr, Harper Group/Publr, Harper Perennial: Doug Jones
SVP & Dir, Creative Devt: Lisa Sharkey
SVP & Edit Dir, William Morrow Nonfiction: Mauro DiPreta
SVP & Exec Ed, Harper: Karen Rinaldi
SVP: Sara Nelson
SVP, Dist & Logistics: Skip Fischer
SVP, Publicity: Tina Andreadis
SVP, Rts & Perms: Jean McGinley
VP & Deputy Gen Coun: Beth Silfin
VP & Publr, Broadside Books: Eric Nelson
VP & Publr, Dey Street Books: Carrie Thornton
VP & Publr, Ecco: Helen Atsma
VP & Publr, Mariner Books: Peter Hubbard
VP & Deputy Publr, Amistad, HarperCollins Espanol & HarperVia: Tara Parsons
VP & Deputy Publr, HarperOne: Laina Adler
VP & Assoc Publr, Ecco: Miriam Parker
VP & Assoc Publr, Harper/Harper Business/Harper Wave/Broadside: Leah Wasielewski
VP & Sr Art Dir, William Morrow: Jeanne Reina
VP & Exec Dir, Children's Sales: Kerry Moynagh
VP & Edit Dir: Deb Brody
VP & Edit Dir, Amistad: Abby West
VP & Edit Dir, Avon: May Chen; Tessa Woodward
VP & Edit Dir, Fiction, Mariner Books: Kate Nintzel
VP & Edit Dir, HarperOne: Nina Shield
VP & Edit Dir, William Morrow Fiction: Emily Krump; Jessica Williams
VP & Deputy Dir, Sales: Kelly Roberts
VP & Group Exec Mng Ed: Pamela Barricklow
VP & Exec Ed: Noah Eaker
VP & Exec Ed, Harper: Sean Desmond
VP & Deputy Dir, Sales: Mary Beth Thomas
VP, Assoc Publr & Edit Dir, Harper Perennial/Harper Paperbacks: Amy Baker
VP, Exec Ed, Edit Dir, William Morrow: Cassie Jones
VP, Edit Dir & Gen Mgr: Gideon Weil
VP, Central Mktg & Strategy: Jim Hanas
VP, Children's Mktg & Publicity: Nellie Kurtzman
VP, Cust Serv & Sales Opers: Jocelyn Tiller
VP, Digital Busn Devt: Adam Silverman
VP, Diversity, Equity & Inclusion: Gisselda Nunez
VP, Fin, Morrow Group: Marina Schiffman
VP, Fin, US & Intl: Mike Rohrs
VP, Fin Projs: Tara Feehan
VP, Independent Sales & Wholesale: Kathy Faber
VP, Natl Accts: Andy LeCount
VP, Prodn & Creative Opers: Tracey Menzies
VP, Prodn Opers: John Herring
VP, Publicity & Integrated Mktg Strategy, Morrow Group: Kelly Rudolph
VP, Royalty Acctg: Christine Jones
VP, Sales Fin: Megan Hodnett
VP, Sales, General Books: Stefanie Lindner
VP, Spec Mkts: James Phirman
Deputy Publr, Fiction/Branded Fiction: Jennifer Hart
Deputy Publr, Nonfiction: Benjamin Steinberg
Assoc Publr, HarperAudio: Brad Hill
Exec Dir, Mktg, Ecco: Meghan Deans
Exec Dir, Mktg, Harper/Harper Influence/Broadside Books: Katie O'Callaghan
Exec Dir, Mktg, Harper/Harper Influence/Broadside Books/Harper Business: Amanda Pritzker
Exec Dir, Mktg, HarperOne: Aly Mostel
Exec Dir, Mktg, William Morrow: Tavia Kowalchuk
Exec Dir, Publicity, HarperOne: Melinda Mullin
Exec Dir, Publicity, Morrow Group: Maureen Cole
Exec Dir, Publicity, William Morrow: Anwesha Basu; Heidi Richter
Sr Art Dir, Ecco: Allison Saltzman
Sr Dir, Content Creation & Soc Media Strategy, Morrow Group: Sam Fox
Sr Dir, Cust Serv: Elizabeth (Liz) Ball
Sr Dir, Divisional Sales & Sales Planning: Kristine Macrides
Sr Dir, Prodn: Susan Kosko; Nicole Moulaison
Sr Dir, Publicity: Maya Baran
Sr Dir, Publicity & Mktg, Avon/Harper Voyager/Morrow Fiction: Danielle Bartlett
Sr Dir, Publicity, Ecco: Sonya Cheuse
Sr Dir, Publicity, Harper/Harper Business/Harper Perennial/Harper Paperbacks Group: Heather Drucker
Sr Dir, Publg, William Morrow: Kaitlin Harri
Sr Dir, Sales, General Books, Natl Accts & Amazon: Ashley Mihlebach
Sr Dir, Video & Group Exec Prodr: David Heydt
Sr Dir, Warehouse Opers: Matt Gannon
Sr Mktg Dir, Harper Perennial/Harper Paperbacks: Lisa Erickson
Sr Mktg Dir, Harvest: Andrea DeWerd
Sr Mktg Dir, Morrow Group: Allison Carney
Sr Mktg Dir, William Morrow: Melissa Esner; Kayleigh George
Art Dir, Children's Mktg: Marisa Domenech
Art Dir, HarperVia/Amistad/HarperCollins Espanol: Stephen Brayda
Creative Dir, HarperAudio: Suzanne Mitchell
Dir, Adult Mass Mdse Sales: Rachel Levenberg
Dir, Children's Natl Accts & Brand Mgmt: Jen Wygand
Dir, Children's Prodn: Trish McGinley
Dir, Content Creation & Video Strategy, Morrow Group: Carlos Rosario
Dir, Digital Ad: Rick Garcia
Dir, Fin, Harper: Kleopatra Benyam
Dir, Fin, HarperOne: Chris Anderson
Dir, Foreign Rts: Catherine Barbosa Ross
Dir, Independent Sales & Retail Mktg: Wendy Ceballos
Dir, Mktg & Brand Strategy, Avon: DJ DeSmyter
Dir, Mktg, Hardcover Imprints: Jessica Gilo
Dir, Mktg, Harper/Harper Influence/Broadside Books: Tom Hopke; Becca Putman
Dir, Mktg, HarperOne: Julia Kent
Dir, Mktg, Morrow Group: Kelsey Manning
Dir, Prodn: Andrew DiCecco
Dir, Prodn, HarperAudio: Nathan Rosborough
Dir, Prodn Edit, Harper/Harper Business/Collins Reference: John Jusino
Dir, Publicity, Ecco: Cordelia Calvert
Dir, Publicity, HarperOne: Louise Braverman; Courtney Nobile
Dir, Publicity, Morrow Group: Sarah Falter
Dir, Publicity, William Morrow: Eliza Rosenberry
Dir, Reprint Prodn: Dion Fisco
Dir, Spec Mkts: Cheryl Dickemper
Dir, Spec Mkts Sales & Specialty Publg: Gillian Wise
Edit Dir, Harper Voyager: David Pomerico
Edit Dir, HarperVia: Juan Mila
Mktg Dir, Morrow Group: Liz Psaltis
Sales Dir: Sarah Rucker
Assoc Art Dir, Ecco: Sara Wood
Assoc Dir, Children's Online Sales: Jess Abel
Assoc Dir, Custom & Proprietary Publg: Christina Tomasulo
Assoc Dir, Mktg, Amistad/HarperVia/HarperCollins Espanol: Brieana Garcia
Assoc Dir, Mktg, Harper Wave/Harper Business: Penny Makras
Assoc Dir, Mktg, Morrow Group: Katie Tull
Assoc Dir, Publicity, Harper Group: Theresa Dooley
Assoc Dir, Publicity, HarperOne: Ashley Yepsen
Assoc Dir, Publicity, Morrow Group: Lindsey Kennedy
Assoc Dir, Publg, Harper Group: Jennifer Civiletto
Assoc Dir, Retail Mktg: Ronnie Kutys
Assoc Dir, Sales Opers: Kara Coughlin
Assoc Dir, Spec Mkts: Kim Sorrell
Asst Dir, Design, William Morrow Group/HarperCollins Children's Books: David Walker
Asst Dir, Mktg, Morrow Group: Beatrice Jason
Asst Dir, Publicity: Julie Paulauski
Exec Ed: Luke Dempsey; Adenike Olanrewaju
Exec Ed, Amistad: Patrik Bass
Exec Ed, Avon: Laura Schreiber
Exec Ed, Creative Devt: Matt Harper
Exec Ed, Dey Street Books: Stuart Roberts
Exec Ed, Ecco: Sarah Murphy
Exec Ed, Harper: Sarah Stein
Exec Ed, HarperOne: Elizabeth Mitchell; Gabriella Page-Fort; Rakesh Satyal; Juan Mila Valcarcel
Exec Ed, Harvest: Sarah Pelz
Exec Ed, Mariner Books: Rakia Clark
Exec Ed, William Morrow: Rachel Kahan; Liz Stein
Exec Ed, William Morrow/Avon: Priyanka Krishnan
Sr Ed: Sarah Haugen
Sr Ed, Dey Street Books: Matthew Daddona
Sr Ed, Ecco: Gabriella Doob; Deborah Ghim
Sr Ed, HarperElixir: Libby Edelson
Sr Ed, HarperOne: Miles Doyle; Angela Guzman; Stephanie Duncan Smith; Hilary Swanson
Sr Ed, HarperOne/HarperVia/Amistad: Daniella Wexler
Sr Ed, Harvest: Stephanie Fletcher; Sarah Kwak
Sr Ed, Mariner Books: Nicole Angeloro

PUBLISHERS

Sr Ed, William Morrow: Danielle Dieterich; Julia Elliott
Sr Ed, William Morrow/Avon: Nicole Fischer
Developmental Ed, Dey Street Books: Anna Montague
Developmental Ed, William Morrow: Andrew Yackira
Ed: Maddie Pillari
Ed, Avon: Shannon Plackis
Ed, Harper/Harper Business: Kirby Sandmeyer
Ed, Harper/Harper Perennial: Mary Gaule; Caroline Weishuhn
Ed, William Morrow: Nick Amphlett; Tessa James
Ed, William Morrow/Avon: Elle Keck; Asante Simons
Sr Ed, William Morrow/Avon: Ariana Sinclair
Assoc Ed, Ecco: Rachel Sargent
Assoc Ed, Harper: Edie Astley
Assoc Ed, Harper/Harper Perennial: Emma Kupor
Assoc Ed, HarperVia: Alexa Frank
Assoc Ed, Harper Wave: Haley Swanson
Assoc Ed, Harper Wave/Harper Business: Rachel Kambury; Rebecca Raskin
Assoc Ed, Mariner Books: Ivy Givens; Jessica Vestuto
Assoc Ed, William Morrow: Vedika Khanna; Nate Lanman
Asst Ed, Dey Street Books: Drew Henry; Rosy Tahan
Asst Ed, Harper: Alicia Tan
Asst Ed, Harper/Harper Perennial: Liz Velez
Asst Ed, Harper Perennial: Sophia Kaufman
Asst Ed, HarperVia: Alfredo Fee
Asst Ed, William Morrow: Mireya Chiriboga; Peter Kispert; Jill Zimmerman
Exec Prodr, HarperAudio: Almeda Beynon
Sr Mgr, Mktg & Publicity, Morrow Group: Lara Baez
Sr Mgr, Spec Mkts: Nicole Pingelton
Sr Mktg Mgr, HarperOne: Makenna Holford
Sr Mktg Mgr, Morrow Group: Rachel Berquist
Sr Prodn Mgr: Fametta Sawyer
Sr Publicity Mgr, Ecco: Martin Wilson
Sr Publicity Mgr, Morrow Group: Alison Coolidge
Sr Publicity Mgr, William Morrow: Erin Reback
Mgr, Consolidations: Colleen Slick
Mgr, Fin Compliance: Shannon Arnone
Mktg Mgr: Samantha Lubash
Mktg Mgr, Amistad/HarperCollins Espanol/HarperVia: Gretchen Schmid
Mktg Mgr, Harper Perennial/Harper Paperbacks: Megan Looney
Mktg Mgr, Morrow Group: Kasey Feather; Amelia Wood
Mktg & Publicity Mgr, Morrow Group: Mary Interdonati
Mktg & Publicity Opers Lead, Morrow Group: Darelyanel Medina
Natl Acct Mgr, Barnes & Noble: Hannah Neff
Proj Mgr, Spec Mkts: Michelle Ramos
Publicity Mgr: Camille Collins
Publicity Mgr, HarperOne: Sarah Schoof
Publicity Mgr, Morrow Group: Jessica Lyons
Publicity Mgr, William Morrow Group: Emily Fisher
Sr Publicist, Harper: Bel Banta; Rachel Molland
Sr Publicist, Morrow Group: Alex Casement
Sr Publicist, William Morrow: Kelly Cronin
Publicist, HarperOne: Alison Cerri
Publicist, Morrow Group: Ellie Anderson; Jessica Cozzi; Kelly Shi
Assoc Publicist, HarperOne: Ashley Candelario
Sales & Retail Mktg Mgr: Rio Cortez
Sales Mgr, Educ Sales: Emma Tomko
Asst Mktg Mgr, Harper: Chris Connolly
Events Coord, Harper: Melissa Alonzo
Mktg Coord, William Morrow: Taylor Turkington
Sales Support Coord: Raven Andrus
Sr Analyst, Pricing & Analytics: Laura Norman
Sr Data Scientist: Eduard Febregat
Sr Mktg Assoc, Amistad/HarperCollins Espanol/HarperVia: Laura Gonzalez
Sr Mktg Assoc, Morrow Group: Kelly Dasta; Lisa McAuliffe
Sr Sales Assoc, Spec Mkts: Karlee Stephney
Sales Analyst: Jeffrey Chin
Mktg Assoc, William Morrow: Deanna Bailey
Assoc Sales Rep: Patricia Day
Sr Admin Asst, HarperOne: Daphney Guillaume
Founded: 1817
Second-largest consumer book publisher in the world, with operations in 15 countries. With 200 years of history & more than 120 branded imprints around the world, HarperCollins publishes approximately 10,000 new books every year in 16 languages & has a print & digital catalog of more than 200,000 titles.
ISBN Prefix(es): 978-0-06; 978-0-688; 978-0-380; 978-0-694
Number of titles published annually: 10,000 Print
Imprints: Amistad; Avon; Avon Impulse (digital only); Betty Crocker®; Broadside Books; Dey Street Books; Ecco; Harper; Harper Business; Harper Influence; Harper Luxe (large print); Harper Perennial; Harper Voyager; Harper Wave; HarperAudio; HarperCollins Espanol; HarperLegend; HarperOne; HarperVia; Harvest; Mariner Books; Morrow Gift; William Morrow; William Morrow Paperbacks; Rayo; Witness Impulse
Divisions: HarperAudio; HarperCollins Canada Ltd; HarperCollins Children's Books; HarperCollins Christian Publishing; HarperCollins Holland; HarperCollins Hungary; HarperCollins Italia SpA; HarperCollins Japan; HarperCollins Nordic AB; HarperCollins Publishers Australia; HarperCollins Publishers New Zealand; HarperCollins UK
Membership(s): Association of American Publishers (AAP); Book Industry Study Group (BISG)
See separate listing for:
HarperCollins Children's Books

Harrington Park Press
9 E Eighth St, Box 331, New York, NY 10003
Tel: 347-882-3545 (edit & publicity) *Fax:* 646-602-1349 (edit & publicity)
Web Site: harringtonparkpress.com
Key Personnel
Publr & Ed-in-Chief: Bill Cohen
 E-mail: bcohen@harringtonparkpress.com
Founded: 2010
Privately owned small scholarly LBGTQ press. Inquiries regarding distribution, such as discounts, shipping, publication date updates, etc, should go directly to Columbia University Press.
ISBN Prefix(es): 978-1-939594
Number of titles published annually: 4 Print; 4 E-Book
Total Titles: 11 Print; 11 E-Book
Distributed by Columbia University Press
Membership(s): American Association of Law Libraries; The American Library Association (ALA); Association of American Publishers (AAP); Association of American Publishers Professional & Scholarly Publishing Division; Crossref; Medical Library Association; Society for Scholarly Publishing (SSP); Special Libraries Association (SLA)

§Harrison House
Subsidiary of Nori Media Group
167 Walnut Bottom Rd, Shippensburg, PA 17257
SAN: 253-4339
Tel: 717-532-3040
Web Site: norimediagroup.com
Founded: 1975
Charismatic/Christian publishing house.
ISBN Prefix(es): 978-1-57794; 978-0-89274
Number of titles published annually: 50 Print
Total Titles: 1,000 Online

Hartman Publishing Inc
1313 Iron Ave SW, Albuquerque, NM 87102
Tel: 505-291-1274 *Toll Free Tel:* 800-999-9534
Toll Free Fax: 800-474-6106
E-mail: info@hartmanonline.com
Web Site: www.hartmanonline.com
Key Personnel
Publr: Mark Hartman
Mng Ed: Susan Alvare Hedman
Founded: 1994
Publish a variety of textbooks for health occupations, such as nursing assistants, home health aides, medication aides, EKG technicians, phlebotomy technicians & medical assistants.
ISBN Prefix(es): 978-1-888343
Number of titles published annually: 12 Print; 1 CD-ROM; 1 Audio
Total Titles: 40 Print; 1 CD-ROM; 1 Audio
Membership(s): New Mexico Book Association

Harvard Art Museums
32 Quincy St, Cambridge, MA 02138
Tel: 617-495-9400
Web Site: www.harvardartmuseums.org
Key Personnel
Dir, Communs: Daron Manoogian *Tel:* 617-495-2397 *E-mail:* daron_manoogian@harvard.edu
Dir, Edit & Design Servs: Micah Buis *Tel:* 617-496-6529 *E-mail:* micah_buis@harvard.edu
Sr Ed: Sarah Kuschner *Tel:* 617-496-5467
 E-mail: sarah_kuschner@harvard.edu
Ed: Cheryl Pappas *Tel:* 617-495-9686
 E-mail: cheryl_pappas@harvard.edu
Founded: 1901
Art history.
ISBN Prefix(es): 978-0-916724; 978-1-891771
Number of titles published annually: 5 Print
Total Titles: 70 Print
Distributed by Yale University Press

Harvard Business Review Press
Division of Harvard Business Publishing
20 Guest St, Suite 700, Brighton, MA 02135
Tel: 617-783-7400 *Fax:* 617-783-7489
E-mail: custserv@hbsp.harvard.edu
Web Site: www.harvardbusiness.org
Key Personnel
Commercial Dir & Assoc Publr: Erika Heilman
Edit Dir & Assoc Publr: Melinda Merino
Mktg Dir: Julie Devoll
Assoc Dir, Publicity: Felicia Sinusas
Ed-in-Chief: Adi Ignatius
Exec Ed: Jeff Kehoe
Assoc Ed: Ania Wieckowski
Founded: 1984
Trade & professional books for the business management & academic audiences in the areas of strategy, leadership, innovation, organizational behavior/human resource management, finance management, marketing, production & operations management. *Harvard Business Review*, reference books & Internet.
ISBN Prefix(es): 978-0-87584; 978-1-57851; 978-1-4221; 978-1-59139
Number of titles published annually: 70 Print
Total Titles: 700 Print
Imprints: Harvard Business Reference
Foreign Rep(s): McGraw-Hill Education (Africa, Asia, Australia, Canada, Europe, Middle East, New Zealand); United Publishers Services Ltd (Japan)
Distribution Center: Two Rivers Distribution, an Ingram brand, 1400 Broadway, Suite 520, New York, NY 10018 *Toll Free Tel:* 866-400-5351
Web Site: www.tworiversdistribution.com

Harvard Common Press
Imprint of Quarto Publishing Group USA Inc
100 Cummings Ctr, Suite 265-D, Beverly, MA 01915
Tel: 978-282-9590 *Fax:* 978-282-7765
Web Site: www.quartoknows.com/harvard-common-press

U.S. PUBLISHERS

Key Personnel
SVP & Group Publg Dir, US: Winnie Prentiss
  E-mail: winnie.prentiss@quarto.com
Edit Dir: Dan Rosenberg *E-mail:* dan.rosenberg@quarto.com
Founded: 1976
General nonfiction: cookbooks, health, self-help, child care & parenting.
ISBN Prefix(es): 978-0-916782; 978-0-87645; 978-1-55832
Number of titles published annually: 24 Print
Total Titles: 150 Print

§Harvard Education Publishing Group
Division of Harvard Graduate School of Education
8 Story St, 1st fl, Cambridge, MA 02138
Tel: 617-495-3432 *Fax:* 617-496-3584
Web Site: www.hepg.org
Key Personnel
Dir: Jessica T Fiorillo *E-mail:* jessica_fiorillo@gse.harvard.edu
Ed-in-Chief: Jayne M Fargnoli
  E-mail: jayne_fargnoli@harvard.edu
Dir, Sales, Mktg & Busn Devt: Kelly Fattman
  E-mail: kelly_fattman@gse.harvard.edu
Edit & Prodn Dir: Sumita Mukherji
  E-mail: sumita_mukherji@gse.harvard.edu
Publisher of books & journals on education practice, research & policy.
ISBN Prefix(es): 978-1-891792; 978-1-883433; 978-0-916690; 978-1-934742; 978-1-61250; 978-1-68253
Number of titles published annually: 30 Print; 1 CD-ROM; 20 E-Book
Total Titles: 285 Print; 1 CD-ROM; 120 E-Book
Imprints: Harvard Education Press; Harvard Educational Review
Foreign Rep(s): Eurospan Group (worldwide exc Canada & USA)
Orders to: Publishers Shipping & Storage, 46 Development Rd, Fitchburg, MA 01420 *Tel:* 978-345-2121 *Toll Free Tel:* 888-437-1437 *Fax:* 978-348-1233 *E-mail:* orders@pssc.com *Web Site:* pssc.com
Returns: Publishers Shipping & Storage, 46 Development Rd, Fitchburg, MA 01420 *Toll Free Tel:* 888-437-1437 *Fax:* 978-348-1233 *E-mail:* orders@pssc.com *Web Site:* pssc.com
Warehouse: Publishers Shipping & Storage, 46 Development Rd, Fitchburg, MA 01420 *Tel:* 978-345-2121 *Toll Free Tel:* 888-437-1437 *Fax:* 978-348-1233 *E-mail:* orders@pssc.com *Web Site:* pssc.com

Harvard Square Editions
Beachwood Terr, Hollywood, CA 90068
Tel: 323-203-0233
E-mail: submissions@harvardsquareeditions.org
Web Site: harvardsquareeditions.org
Key Personnel
Outreach Dir: Simone Weingarten *E-mail:* sw@harvardsquareeditions.org
Founded: 2000
Run by Harvard alumni, Harvard Square Editions publishes authors of literary fiction of environmental, spiritual or social value. Harvard Square Editions books have won National Book Foundation, Nautilus & other awards. Its mission is to publish fiction that transcends national boundaries, especially mss that are international, political, literary, diverse, multicultural, science fiction, climate fiction, fantasy, utopia & dystopia. They appreciate aesthetic value & constructive social & political content, especially mss related to climate change, deforestation & conservation, but have a low tolerance for profanity & graphic violence.
ISBN Prefix(es): 978-0-9833216; 978-0-9895960; 978-1-941861
Number of titles published annually: 10 Print; 10 E-Book
Total Titles: 55 Print; 58 E-Book

Distribution Center: Gardners Books, One Whittle Dr, Eastbourne, East Sussex BN23 6QH, United Kingdom *Tel:* (01323) 521555 *Web Site:* www.gardners.com

Harvard Ukrainian Research Institute
Subsidiary of Harvard University
34 Kirkland St, Cambridge, MA 02138
SAN: 208-967X
Tel: 617-495-4053 *Fax:* 617-495-8097
E-mail: huripubs@fas.harvard.edu
Web Site: books.huri.harvard.edu
Key Personnel
Mgr, Pubns: Dr Oleh Kotsyuba
  E-mail: kotsyuba@fas.harvard.edu
Founded: 1973
ISBN Prefix(es): 978-0-916458; 978-1-932650
Number of titles published annually: 5 Print; 3 Online
Total Titles: 100 Print; 6 Online
Distributed by Harvard University Press

Harvard University Press
79 Garden St, Cambridge, MA 02138-1499
SAN: 200-2043
Tel: 617-495-2600; 401-531-2800 (intl orders) *Toll Free Tel:* 800-405-1619 (orders) *Fax:* 617-495-5898 (gen); 617-496-4677 (edit & rts); 401-531-2801 (intl orders) *Toll Free Fax:* 800-406-9145 (orders)
E-mail: contact_hup@harvard.edu
Web Site: www.hup.harvard.edu
Key Personnel
CFO: Dan Wackrow *E-mail:* dan_wackrow@harvard.edu
Dir: George Andreou
Dir, Design & Prodn: Tim Jones
  E-mail: tim_jones@harvard.edu
Dir, Intellectual Property: Stephanie Vyce
  E-mail: stephanie_vyce@harvard.edu
Dir, Intl Sales & Mktg (UK Office): Richard Howells *Tel:* (07802) 432594 (cell)
  E-mail: richard_howells@harvard.edu
Edit Dir: Sharmila Sen *E-mail:* sharmila_sen@harvard.edu
Mktg Dir: Ken Carpenter *E-mail:* ken_carpenter@harvard.edu
Sales Dir: Vanessa Vinarub
  E-mail: vanessa_vinarub@harvard.edu
Exec Ed, History: Kathleen McDermott
  E-mail: kathleen_mcdermott@harvard.edu
Exec Ed-at-Large (Europe) & Sr Exec Ed, Economics (Global): Ian Malcolm
  E-mail: imalcolm@harvardup.co.uk
Sr Ed, Economics, Law & Technol: Grigory Tovbis
Ed: Joseph Pomp *E-mail:* joseph_pomp@harvard.edu; Emily Silk *E-mail:* emily_silk@harvard.edu
Ed-at-Large: Wendy Wolf *E-mail:* wendy_wolf@harvard.edu
Founded: 1913
General scholarly, humanities, social sciences, life/physical sciences.
ISBN Prefix(es): 978-0-674
Number of titles published annually: 200 Print
Total Titles: 8,000 Print
Imprints: Belknap Press
Foreign Office(s): Harvard University Press International Office, 8 Coldbath Sq, London EC1R 5HL, United Kingdom *Tel:* (020) 3463 2350 *E-mail:* info@harvardup.co.uk *Web Site:* www.hup.harvard.edu
Distributed by W W Norton Company Inc
Distributor for Harvard Center for Middle Eastern Studies; Harvard Center for Population Studies; Harvard Center for the Study of World Religions; Harvard College Library (including Houghton Library Judaica div); Harvard Department of Sanskrit & Indian Studies; Harvard Department of the Classics; Harvard Ukrainian Research Institute; Harvard University Asia Center; Harvard University David Rockefeller Center for Latin American Studies; Harvard-Yenching Institute; Peabody Museum of Archaeology & Ethnology
Foreign Rep(s): Avicenna Ltd (Bill Kennedy) (Bahrain, Egypt, Iran, Iraq, Kuwait, Lebanon, Libya, Oman, Qatar, Saudi Arabia, Sudan, Syria, United Arab Emirates, Yemen); Avicenna Ltd (Claire de Gruchy) (Algeria, Cyprus, Jordan, Malta, Morocco, Palestine, Tunisia, Turkey); B K Agency (Taiwan); Blue Weaver (Sub-Saharan Africa); Durnell Marketing (Europe exc UK); John Eklund (Canada exc British Columbia, Midwestern States); Everest International Publishing Services (Wei Zhao) (China); HarperCollins India (Indian subcontinent); Harvard University Press International Office (UK); Information & Culture Korea (ICK) (South Korea); Patricia Nelson (British Columbia, CN, Southwest, Western USA); Rockbook Inc (Hong Kong, Japan); Wiley Australia (Australia, New Zealand); Yuha Associates (Malaysia)
Foreign Rights: Akcali Agency (Turkey); Bardon-Chinese Media Agency (China, Hong Kong, Taiwan); Dar Cherlin (Arab Middle East); English Agency Japan Co Ltd (Japan); Graal Literary Agency (Poland); The Deborah Harris Agency (Israel); International Editors' Co - Yanez Agencia Literaria (Central America, Latin America, South America, Spain); Alexander Korzhenevski Agency (Russia); Liepman Agency AG (Germany, Switzerland); Marotte et Compagnie (France); Ilidio Matos Agencia (Portugal); OA Literary Agency (Greece); Oxford Literary & Rights Agency (Bosnia and Herzegovina, Croatia, Czechia, Estonia, Latvia, Lithuania, Montenegro, Serbia, Slovakia, Slovenia, Ukraine); Seibel Publishing Services (Brazil)
Shipping Address: Triliteral LLC, 100 Maple Ridge Dr, Cumberland, RI 02864-1769
Membership(s): American Association of University Presses (AAUP); Association of American Publishers (AAP); Book Industry Study Group (BISG)

Harvest House Publishers Inc
PO Box 41210, Eugene, OR 97404-0322
SAN: 207-4745
Tel: 541-343-0123 *Toll Free Tel:* 888-501-6991 *Fax:* 541-343-9711
E-mail: admin@harvesthousepublishers.com; permissions@harvesthousepublishers.com
Web Site: harvesthousepublishers.com
Key Personnel
Pres: Bob Hawkins, Jr
Intl Rts: Sharon Shook
Founded: 1974
Evangelical Christian books; no unsol mss.
ISBN Prefix(es): 978-0-89081; 978-1-56507; 978-0-7369
Number of titles published annually: 90 Print
Total Titles: 1,750 Print
Imprints: Harvest Kids; Harvest Prophecy; Ten Peaks Press
Membership(s): Book Industry Study Group (BISG)

§Hatherleigh Press Ltd
62545 State Hwy 10, Hobart, NY 13788
Toll Free Tel: 800-528-2550
E-mail: info@hatherleighpress.com; publicity@hatherleighpress.com
Web Site: www.hatherleighpress.com
Key Personnel
Pres & CEO: Andrew Flach
Assoc Publr: Ryan Tumambing
Mng Ed: Ryan Kennedy
Founded: 1995
Motto: "Improve your life. Change your world."
Expert content in health, wellness, fitness, exercise, nutrition, inspiration, healthy living &

sustainability. Print books, ebooks, audio, digital & filmed entertainment.
ISBN Prefix(es): 978-1-886330; 978-1-57826
Number of titles published annually: 30 Print; 30 E-Book
Total Titles: 300 Print; 100 E-Book; 4 Audio
Imprints: GetFitNow.com Books; Healthy Living Books
Distributed by Penguin Random House LLC
Foreign Rights: Nigel Yorweth (worldwide)
Distribution Center: Penguin Random House Publisher Services (PRHPS) *Toll Free Tel:* 800-733-3000; 888-523-9292 (CN sales) *Toll Free Fax:* 800-659-2436; 888-562-9924 (CN sales) *E-mail:* csorders@randomhouse.com *Web Site:* prhpublisherservices.com

§Hay House LLC
PO Box 5100, Carlsbad, CA 92018-5100
Tel: 760-431-7695 (ext 1, intl) *Toll Free Tel:* 800-654-5126 (ext 1, US) *Toll Free Fax:* 800-650-5115
Web Site: www.hayhouse.com
Key Personnel
Pres & CEO: Reid Tracy
COO: Margarete Nielsen
Publr & VP: Patricia Gift
Assoc Publr: Betsy Beier
Edit Dir: Melody Guy
Assoc Dir, Publicity & Book Mktg: Lindsay McGinty
Exec Ed (NY): Anne Barthel
Exec Ed: Lisa Cheng; Marisa Vigilante
Sr Acqs Ed: Allison Janice
Sr Ed: Anna Cooperberg; Sally Mason-Swaab
Sr Prodn Mgr: Danielle Monaco
Founded: 1984
Self-help/New Age, health, philosophy, spiritual growth & awareness, mental & environmental harmony books; also self-healing; biography, producers & distributors of recordings & video pertaining to health of mind, body & spirit. Accept agented submissions only.
ISBN Prefix(es): 978-0-937611; 978-1-56170; 978-1-4019; 978-1-58825; 978-0-945923; 978-1-891751
Number of titles published annually: 50 Print; 50 Audio
Total Titles: 1,000 Print; 1,000 Audio
Branch Office(s)
665 Broadway, Suite 1200, New York, NY 10012 *Tel:* 646-484-4950 *Fax:* 646-484-4956
Foreign Office(s): Hay House Australia Pty Ltd, 18/36 Ralph St, Alexandria, NSW 2015, Australia *Tel:* (02) 9669 4299 *Fax:* (02) 9669 4144 *Web Site:* www.hayhouse.com.au
Hay House Publishers (India) Pvt Ltd, Muskaan Complex, Plot No 3, B-2, Vasant Kunj, New Delhi 110 070, India, Assoc VP: Raghav Khattar *Tel:* (011) 4176 1620 *Fax:* (011) 4176 1630 *E-mail:* contact@hayhouse.co.in *Web Site:* www.hayhouse.co.in
Hay House UK Ltd, Watson House, 6th fl, 54 Baker St, London W1U 7BU, United Kingdom, Edit Dir: Helen Rochester *Tel:* (020) 3927 7290 *Fax:* (020) 3675 2451 (cust care) *Web Site:* www.hayhouse.co.uk
Returns: Penguin Random House LLC, 1019 N State Rd 47, Crawfordsville, IN 47933
Distribution Center: Penguin Random House Publisher Services

Haynes North America Inc
Division of InfoPro Digital
2801 Townsgate Rd, Suite 340, Westlake Village, CA 91361
Tel: 805-498-6703 *Toll Free Tel:* 800-4-HAYNES (442-9637) *Fax:* 805-498-2867
E-mail: customerservice.haynes@infopro-digital.com
Web Site: www.haynes.com
Key Personnel
Pres: Harvey Wolff
Mktg Dir: Jon Louie
Founded: 1960
Publisher & importer of books on domestic & foreign autos & motorcycles & historical & technical motoring. Haynes Repair Manuals, Haynes DIY Repair Manuals, Chilton Repair Manuals, Clymer Repair Manuals & I&T Tractor Manuals.
ISBN Prefix(es): 978-0-946609; 978-1-56392
Number of titles published annually: 13 Print
Total Titles: 690 Print

Haynes Repair Manuals, see Haynes North America Inc

§Hazelden Publishing
Division of The Hazelden Betty Ford Foundation
15251 Pleasant Valley Rd, Center City, MN 55012-0011
SAN: 125-1953
Mailing Address: PO Box 176, Center City, MN 55012-0176
Tel: 651-213-4200 *Toll Free Tel:* 800-257-7810; 866-328-9000 *Fax:* 651-213-4793
Web Site: www.hazelden.org
Key Personnel
Publr: Joseph Jaksha
Founded: 1954
Adult trade hardcover & paperbacks; curriculum, workbooks, gift books, video & audio; self-help, addiction & recovery, personal & spiritual growth; computer based products, wellness products, young adult nonfiction.
ISBN Prefix(es): 978-0-89486; 978-1-56838; 978-0-89638; 978-0-942421; 978-0-935908; 978-1-56246; 978-0-934125
Number of titles published annually: 12 Print
Total Titles: 500 Print; 500 E-Book; 10 Audio
Imprints: Hazelden/Johnson Institute; Hazelden/Keep Coming Back; Hazelden-Pittman Archives Press
Distributed by Health Communications Inc (trade); Simon & Schuster, LLC
Distributor for Obsessive Anonymous
Foreign Rep(s): Eurospan (Europe, Ireland, UK); RecoverOz (Australia, New Zealand)

Hazy Dell Press
1001 SE Water Ave, Suite 132, Portland, OR 97214
Tel: 971-279-5779
E-mail: info@hazydellpress.com
Web Site: www.hazydellpress.com
Key Personnel
Edit Dir: Kyle Sullivan
Art Dir: Derek Sullivan
Mktg Dir: Renee Yama
Founded: 2015
Headquartered in the Pacific Northwest with offices in Portland & Seattle, Hazy Dell Press publishes quirky, grown-up-friendly children's books that promote empathy, diversity & imagination.
ISBN Prefix(es): 978-0-9965787; 978-1-948931
Number of titles published annually: 5 Print; 4 E-Book
Total Titles: 14 Print; 10 E-Book
Orders to: Consortium Book Sales & Distribution, 210 American Dr, Jackson, TN 38301 *Toll Free Tel:* 866-400-5351 *E-mail:* ipsjacksonorders@ingramcontent.com; Publishers Group Canada, c/o Raincoast Books, 2440 Viking Way, Richmond, BC V6V 1N2, Canada *Toll Free Tel:* 800-663-5714 *E-mail:* customerservice@raincoast.com
Distribution Center: Consortium Book Sales & Distribution, 210 American Dr, Jackson, TN 38301 *Toll Free Tel:* 866-400-5351 *E-mail:* ipsjacksonorders@ingramcontent.org
Membership(s): Publishers Association of the West (PubWest)

HCI, see Health Communications Inc

§HCPro/DecisionHealth
Division of BLR®—Business & Legal Resources
5511 Virginia Way, Suite 150, Brentwood, TN 37027
Mailing Address: PO Box 5094, Brentwood, TN 37024
Toll Free Tel: 800-650-6787 *Toll Free Fax:* 800-785-9212
E-mail: customer@hcpro.com
Web Site: www.hcpro.com
Founded: 1986
Specialize in healthcare administration & management.
ISBN Prefix(es): 978-1-885829; 978-1-55645
Number of titles published annually: 110 Print; 4 CD-ROM; 30 Online; 5 E-Book; 60 Audio
Total Titles: 125 Print; 5 CD-ROM; 40 Online; 25 E-Book; 75 Audio
Membership(s): NEPA

Health Administration Press
Division of Foundation of the American College of Healthcare Executives
300 S Riverside Plaza, Suite 1900, Chicago, IL 60606
SAN: 207-0464
Tel: 312-424-2800 *Fax:* 312-424-0014
E-mail: hapbooks@ache.org
Web Site: www.ache.org/hap (orders)
Key Personnel
Pres & CEO: Deborah J Bowen
VP, Pubns: Michael Cunningham *Tel:* 312-424-9470 *E-mail:* mcunningham@ache.org
Asst Dir/Mktg & Sales Mgr: Nancy Vitucci *Tel:* 312-424-9450 *Fax:* 312-424-0023 *E-mail:* nvitucci@ache.org
Mgr, Content Acq: La'Toya Carter *Tel:* 312-424-9426 *E-mail:* lcarter@ache.org
Founded: 1972
Health administration, health care, law & medicine, professional association.
ISBN Prefix(es): 978-0-910701; 978-1-56793
Number of titles published annually: 20 Print
Total Titles: 200 Print; 1 E-Book
Imprints: American College of Healthcare Executives Management Series; AUPHA Press/Health Administration Press; Executive Essentials; Gateway to Healthcare Management
Orders to: Independent Publishers Group (IPG), 814 N Franklin St, Suite 100, Chicago, IL 60610 *Tel:* 312-337-0747 *Toll Free Tel:* 800-888-4741 *Fax:* 312-337-5985 *E-mail:* orders@ipgbook.com *Web Site:* www.ipgbook.com
Returns: Independent Publishers Group (IPG), 814 N Franklin St, Suite 100, Chicago, IL 60610 *Tel:* 312-337-0747 *Toll Free Tel:* 800-888-4741 *Fax:* 312-337-5985
Shipping Address: Independent Publishers Group (IPG), 814 N Franklin St, Suite 100, Chicago, IL 60610 *Tel:* 312-337-0747 *Toll Free Tel:* 800-888-4741 *Fax:* 312-337-5985 *E-mail:* orders@ipgbook.com *Web Site:* www.ipgbook.com
Warehouse: Independent Publishers Group (IPG), 814 N Franklin St, Suite 100, Chicago, IL 60610 *Tel:* 312-337-0747 *Toll Free Tel:* 800-888-4741 *Fax:* 312-337-5985 *E-mail:* orders@ipgbook.com *Web Site:* www.ipgbook.com
Distribution Center: Independent Publishers Group (IPG), 814 N Franklin St, Suite 100, Chicago, IL 60610 *Tel:* 312-337-0747 *Toll Free Tel:* 800-888-4741 *Fax:* 312-337-5985 *E-mail:* orders@ipgbook.com *Web Site:* www.ipgbook.com

§Health Communications Inc
301 Crawford Blvd, Suite 200, Boca Raton, FL 33432
SAN: 212-100X
Tel: 561-453-0696 *Toll Free Tel:* 800-441-5569 (cust serv & orders) *Fax:* 561-453-1009
Toll Free Fax: 800-943-9831 (orders)

U.S. PUBLISHERS

E-mail: editorial@hcibooks.com
Web Site: hcibooks.com
Key Personnel
Founder & Pres: Peter Vegso
EVP, Fin: Craig Jarvie
EVP, Publg: Christian Blonshine
Art Dir: Larissa Henoch
Dir, Sales & Cust Support: Lori Golden
Mng Ed: Christine Belleris
Ed: Darcie Abbene
PR & Mktg Coord: Lindsey Triebel
Founded: 1977
Publisher of nonfiction paperbacks & hardcover books on self-help, personal growth, diet, fitness, inspiration, health, parenting, women's issues, teens, religion, psychology, addiction & recovery.
ISBN Prefix(es): 978-0-932194; 978-1-55874; 978-0-7573; 978-0-9910732
Number of titles published annually: 50 Print; 50 E-Book
Total Titles: 500 Print; 500 E-Book; 18 Audio
Imprints: HCI Books; HCI Teens
Distributed by Simon & Schuster, LLC

§**Health Forum Inc**
Subsidiary of American Hospital Association
155 N Wacker Dr, Suite 400, Chicago, IL 60606
SAN: 216-5872
Tel: 312-893-6800 *Toll Free Tel:* 800-242-2626
Web Site: www.ahaonlinestore.com; www.aha.org
Founded: 1986
Publisher of professional books & textbooks for health care professionals. Specialize in books that help hospital executives & department heads manage their business better & achieve improved patient satisfaction. Also provide ICD-10-CM/PCS & data information from the AHA Central Office & the American Hospital Association annual survey of hospitals.
ISBN Prefix(es): 978-1-55648; 978-0-87258
Number of titles published annually: 10 Print; 2 CD-ROM; 2 E-Book
Total Titles: 30 Print; 2 CD-ROM; 3 E-Book
Distribution Center: Rittenhouse Book Distributors, 511 Feheley Dr, King of Prussia, PA 19406, Contact: Nicole Gallo *Toll Free Tel:* 800-345-6425 *Toll Free Fax:* 800-223-7488 *E-mail:* n.gallo@rittenhouse.com *Web Site:* www.rittenhouse.com
Membership(s): Independent Book Publishers Association (IBPA)

§**Health Professions Press**
Imprint of Paul H Brookes Publishing Co Inc
409 Washington Ave, Suite 500, Towson, MD 21204
SAN: 297-7338
Mailing Address: PO Box 10624, Baltimore, MD 21285-0624
Tel: 410-337-9585 *Toll Free Tel:* 888-337-8808
Fax: 410-337-8539
Web Site: www.healthpropress.com
Key Personnel
Pres: Melissa Behm *E-mail:* mbehm@healthpropress.com
Dir, Pubns: Mary H Magnus *E-mail:* mmagnus@healthpropress.com
Mktg Mgr: Kaitlin Konecke *E-mail:* kkonecke@healthpropress.com
Founded: 1989
Hardcover, paperback & digital professional resources & textbooks in aging, Alzheimer's disease, long-term care & health administration.
ISBN Prefix(es): 978-1-878812; 978-1-932529; 978-1-938870
Number of titles published annually: 6 Print; 5 E-Book
Total Titles: 105 Print; 5 CD-ROM; 37 E-Book
Foreign Rep(s): Eurospan Ltd (Africa, Asia, Europe, Middle East, UK); Login Brothers (Canada); Woodslane Pty Ltd (Australia, Cook Islands, Fiji, New Zealand, Papua New Guinea, Solomon Islands, Tonga)
Warehouse: Maple Logistics Solutions, 60 Grumbacher Rd I-83 Industrial Park, PO Box 15100, York, PA 17406
Membership(s): Independent Book Publishers Association (IBPA)

Healthy Learning, see Coaches Choice

§**HeartMath LLC**
14700 W Park Ave, Boulder Creek, CA 95006
Tel: 831-338-8500 *Toll Free Tel:* 800-711-6221
Fax: 831-338-8504
E-mail: info@heartmath.org; service@heartmath.org
Web Site: www.heartmath.org
Key Personnel
Pres & CEO: Sara Childre
CFO & Dir, Sales: Brian Kabaker
EVP & Dir, Res: Rollin McCraty, PhD
Dir, PR: Gabriella Boehmer *E-mail:* gboehmer@heartmath.org
Founded: 1998
Publishers of The HeartMath System.
ISBN Prefix(es): 978-1-879052; 978-0-9700286
Number of titles published annually: 16 Print
Total Titles: 2 CD-ROM; 25 E-Book; 7 Audio

Hearts 'n Tummies Cookbook Co
Division of Quixote Press
3544 Blakslee St, Wever, IA 52658
Tel: 319-372-7480 *Toll Free Tel:* 800-571-2665
E-mail: quixotepress@gmail.com; heartsntummies@gmail.com
Web Site: www.heartsntummies.com
Key Personnel
Pres & Intl Rts: Bruce Carlson
Founded: 1982
Cookbooks.
ISBN Prefix(es): 978-1-878488; 978-1-57166
Number of titles published annually: 20 Print
Total Titles: 400 Print

Hebrew Union College Press
Division of Hebrew Union College
3101 Clifton Ave, Cincinnati, OH 45220
Tel: 513-221-1875 *Fax:* 513-221-0321
Web Site: press.huc.edu
Key Personnel
Co-Dir: Jordan Finkin *Tel:* 513-487-3287
  E-mail: jfinkin@huc.edu; Jason Kalman *Tel:* 513-221-1875 ext 3248 *E-mail:* jkalman@huc.edu
Mng Ed: Sonja Rethy *E-mail:* srethy@huc.edu
Founded: 1921
Scholarly Jewish books.
ISBN Prefix(es): 978-0-87820
Number of titles published annually: 11 Print
Total Titles: 100 Print
Distribution Center: ISD, 70 Enterprise Dr, Bristol, CT 06010 *Tel:* 860-584-6546 *E-mail:* orders@isdistribution.com *Web Site:* isdistribution.com

Heimburger House Publishing Co
7236 W Madison St, Forest Park, IL 60130
Tel: 708-366-1973 *Fax:* 708-366-1973
E-mail: info@heimburgerhouse.com
Web Site: www.heimburgerhouse.com
Key Personnel
Publr: Donald J Heimburger
Founded: 1962
Publish books & magazines on railroad & other transportation subjects; list includes more than 350 book titles.
ISBN Prefix(es): 978-0-911581
Number of titles published annually: 3 Print
Total Titles: 50 Print
Distributor for Child's Play International; Evergreen Press; Firefly Books Ltd; Fordham University Press; Globe Pequot Press; HarperCollins; Johns Hopkins University Press; Houghton Mifflin Harcourt; Iconografix; Indiana University Press; Kalmbach Publishing Co; Krause Publications Inc; Motorbooks; National Book Network; New York University Press; W W Norton & Company Inc; Penguin Putnam Inc; Pictorial Histories Publishing Co; Steam Passages Publishing; Sugar Cane Press; Syracuse University Press; Thunder Bay Press; Union Square & Co; University of Minnesota Press; John Wiley & Sons

§**William S Hein & Co Inc**
2350 N Forest Rd, Suite 10A, Getzville, NY 14068
Tel: 716-882-2600 *Toll Free Tel:* 800-828-7571
Fax: 716-883-8100
E-mail: mail@wshein.com; marketing@wshein.com; customerservice@wshein.com
Web Site: home.heinonline.org
Key Personnel
Chmn of the Bd: William S Hein, Jr
Pres & CEO: Shane Marmion
  E-mail: smarmion@wshein.com
VP, Sales & Mktg: Ben Boron *E-mail:* bboron@wshein.com
VP, Technol: Kyle Daving *E-mail:* kdaving@wshein.com
Sr Dir, Sales: Tim Hooge *E-mail:* thooge@wshein.com
Founded: 1961
HeinOnline is a premier online research platform by William S Hein & Co Inc, providing an extensive collection of resources. It includes over 200 million pages of legal & multidisciplinary materials used by academic institutions, government agencies, law firms & organizations globally. HeinOnline's fully searchable image-based PDFs replicate the original print materials, ensuring access to authoritative sources. Trusted for over a century, Hein continues to empower researchers & libraries with invaluable legal & academic references.
ISBN Prefix(es): 978-0-8377; 978-0-89941; 978-1-57588
Number of titles published annually: 30 Print; 1 Online
Total Titles: 5,000 Print; 200,000 Online; 20,000 E-Book
Distributor for American Bar Association; American Law Institute; Ashgate; Aspen; Brill Nijhoff; Butterworths; Cambridge University Press; Edward Elgar Publishing; Emerald Publishing; De Gruyter; Oxford University Press; SAGE Publishing; Sweet & Maxwell; Taylor & Francis Group; John Wiley & Sons Inc; Wolters Kluwer
Foreign Rep(s): Balani Infotech (India); CE-Logic (Philippines); Eastern Book Co (India); EBSCO (Italy, Turkey); Flysheet (Taiwan); Global Database Information Co Ltd (GDI) (South Korea); Maruzen (Japan); Mohan Law House (India); Publicacoes Tecnicas Internacionais (PTI) (Brazil); vLex (Brazil); Wells (China)
Membership(s): American Association of Law Libraries; American Bar Association (ABA); The American Library Association (ALA); Canadian Association of Law Libraries

§**Heinemann**
Division of Houghton Mifflin Harcourt
145 Maplewood Ave, Suite 300, Portsmouth, NH 03801
SAN: 210-5829
Mailing Address: PO Box 528, Portsmouth, NH 03801
Tel: 603-431-7894 *Toll Free Tel:* 800-225-5800 (US) *Fax:* 603-547-9917
E-mail: custserv@heinemann.com
Web Site: www.heinemann.com

Key Personnel
SVP & Gen Mgr: Maggie DeMont
 E-mail: maggie.demont@hmhco.com
Founded: 1978
Education - professional books for teachers K-12. Literacy, math, social studies & English teaching. Paperbound.
ISBN Prefix(es): 978-0-86709; 978-0-325; 978-0-435
Number of titles published annually: 25 Print; 25 E-Book
Total Titles: 2,500 Print; 300 E-Book
Distributed by Pearson (Australia, CN & New Zealand)

HeinOnline, see William S Hein & Co Inc

§Hellgate Press
Imprint of L & R Publishing LLC
PO Box 3531, Ashland, OR 97520
Tel: 541-973-5154
E-mail: sales@hellgatepress.com
Web Site: www.hellgatepress.com
Key Personnel
Owner: Harley B Patrick *E-mail:* harley@hellgatepress.com
Founded: 1997
Military history, adventure travel, veteran memoirs, historical & adventure fiction.
This publisher has indicated that 25% of their product line is author subsidized.
ISBN Prefix(es): 978-1-55571; 978-1-945163
Number of titles published annually: 25 Print
Total Titles: 175 Print; 175 E-Book

Hendrickson Publishers Inc
Imprint of Hendrickson Publishing Group
c/o Tyndale House Publishers, 351 Executive Dr, Carol Stream, IL 60188
Toll Free Tel: 855-277-9400 *Toll Free Fax:* 866-622-9474
E-mail: consumers@tyndale.com
Web Site: www.hendricksonrose.com
Founded: 1980
Religious reference, language, history & theology.
ISBN Prefix(es): 978-0-913573; 978-0-943575; 978-0-917006; 978-1-56563
Number of titles published annually: 80 Print; 3 CD-ROM
Total Titles: 450 Print
Imprints: Aspire Press; Hendrickson Academic; Hendrickson Bibles; Rose Kidz; Rose Publishing
Foreign Rep(s): Alban Books Ltd (Europe, UK)
Foreign Rights: KCBS (South Korea)

Her Own Words LLC
PO Box 5264, Madison, WI 53705-0264
Tel: 608-271-7083 *Fax:* 608-271-0209
Web Site: www.herownwords.com; www.nontraditionalcareers.com
Key Personnel
Mgr: Jocelyn Riley *E-mail:* jocelynriley@herownwords.com
Founded: 1986
Women's history, literature, arts & women in non-traditional careers.
ISBN Prefix(es): 978-1-60118
Number of titles published annually: 3 Print
Total Titles: 36 Print
Imprints: Her Own Words; Literature & Arts; Women In Nontraditional Careers; Women's History

Herald Press
Imprint of MennoMedia
PO Box 866, Harrisonburg, VA 22803
SAN: 202-2915
Toll Free Tel: 800-245-7894 (orders) *Fax:* 540-242-4476 *Toll Free Fax:* 877-271-0760
E-mail: info@mennomedia.org; customerservice@mennomedia.org
Web Site: www.heraldpress.com; store.mennomedia.org
Key Personnel
Exec Dir & Publr: Amy Gingerich
 E-mail: amyg@mennomedia.org
Mng Ed: Meghan Florian *Tel:* 540-574-4874
 E-mail: meghanf@mennomedia.org
Acqs Ed: Dayna Olson-Getty *E-mail:* daynaog@mennomedia.org
Founded: 1908
General Christian trade books, family, devotional, cookbooks, juveniles, adult fiction, Bible study, theology, peace & social concerns, missions, Amish & Mennonite history & culture, songbooks.
ISBN Prefix(es): 978-0-8361
Number of titles published annually: 20 Print
Total Titles: 500 Print
Membership(s): Evangelical Christian Publishers Association (ECPA)

§Heritage Books Inc
5810 Ruatan St, Berwyn Heights, MD 20740
Toll Free Tel: 800-876-6103 *Toll Free Fax:* 800-876-6103; 800-297-9954
E-mail: orders@heritagebooks.com; submissions@heritagebooks.com
Web Site: www.heritagebooks.com
Key Personnel
Pres & CEO: Craig R Scott *Tel:* 800-876-6103 ext 700 *E-mail:* crscott@heritagebooks.com
Founded: 1978
Books on local history, genealogy & Americana.
ISBN Prefix(es): 978-0-917890; 978-1-55613; 978-0-7884; 978-1-58549; 978-0-940907; 978-1-888265; 978-1-68034
Number of titles published annually: 200 Print; 200 E-Book
Total Titles: 10,000 Print; 1,200 CD-ROM; 5,000 E-Book
Imprints: Antient Press; Colonial Roots; Delmarva Roots; Eagle Editions; Fireside Fiction; Heritage Books; Willow Bend Books
Distributor for Fairfax Genealogical Society; National Genealogical Society; Virginia Genealogical Society

§The Heritage Foundation
214 Massachusetts Ave NE, Washington, DC 20002-4999
Tel: 202-546-4400 *Toll Free Tel:* 800-546-2843 *Fax:* 202-546-8328
E-mail: info@heritage.org
Web Site: www.heritage.org
Key Personnel
Pres: Dr Kevin Roberts
Founded: 1973
Domestic policy, foreign policy & defense.
ISBN Prefix(es): 978-0-89195
Number of titles published annually: 10 Print; 2 CD-ROM
Total Titles: 19 Print; 2 CD-ROM; 8 E-Book

Heuer Publishing LLC
PO Box 248, Cedar Rapids, IA 52406
Tel: 319-368-8008 *Toll Free Tel:* 800-950-7529 *Fax:* 319-368-8011
E-mail: orders@heuerpub.com; customerservice@heuerpub.com
Web Site: www.hitplays.com
Founded: 1928
Publishes plays, musicals, operas/operettas & guides (choreography, costume, production/staging) for amateur & professional markets including junior & senior high schools, college/university & community theatres. Focus includes comedy, drama, fantasy, mystery & holiday with special interest focus in multicultural, historic, classic literature, Shakespearian theatre, interactive, teen issues & biographies.
Pays by percentage royalty or outright purchase.
ISBN Prefix(es): 978-1-61588
Number of titles published annually: 25 Print
Total Titles: 150 Print

Hewitt Homeschooling Resources
Division of Hewitt Research Foundation
8117 N Division, Suite D, Spokane, WA 99208
Mailing Address: PO Box 28010, Spokane, WA 99228
Toll Free Tel: 800-348-1750 *Fax:* 360-835-8697
E-mail: sales@hewitthomeschooling.com
Web Site: hewitthomeschooling.com
Key Personnel
Pres: Jack Lewis
Founded: 1964
Homeschooling, curriculum.
ISBN Prefix(es): 978-0-913717; 978-1-57896
Number of titles published annually: 6 Print
Total Titles: 150 Print

Heyday
1808 San Pablo Ave, Suite A, Berkeley, CA 94702
SAN: 207-2351
Mailing Address: PO Box 9145, Berkeley, CA 94709-0145
Tel: 510-549-3564
E-mail: heyday@heydaybooks.com
Web Site: heydaybooks.com
Key Personnel
Publr & Exec Dir: Steve Wasserman
Edit Dir: Gayle Wattawa
Sr Acqs Ed: Marthine Satris
Founded: 1974
Nonprofit publisher of nonfiction in the following subject areas: history, nature, social justice & California Indians (preference for Native writers). Publishes the quarterly magazine *News from Native California*.
ISBN Prefix(es): 978-0-930588; 978-1-890771; 978-0-9666691; 978-1-59714
Number of titles published annually: 20 Print
Total Titles: 225 Print
Imprints: Sierra College Press
Returns: Ingram Publisher Services, 191 Edwards Dr, Jackson, TN 38301
Distribution Center: Publishers Group West, 1700 Fourth St, Berkeley, CA 94710 *Tel:* 510-809-3700 *Toll Free Tel:* 800-788-3123 *Fax:* 510-809-3777 *E-mail:* info@pgw.com *Web Site:* www.pgw.com

Hi Willow Research & Publishing
146 S 700 E, Provo, UT 84601
Tel: 801-755-1122
E-mail: lmcsourceutah@gmail.com
Web Site: www.lmcsource.com; www.davidvl.org
Key Personnel
Owner: David V Loertscher
Founded: 1978
Books for schools & libraries.
ISBN Prefix(es): 978-0-931510; 978-1-933170
Number of titles published annually: 4 E-Book
Total Titles: 100 E-Book

Higginson Book Company LLC
219 Mill Rd, Morgantown, PA 19543
Tel: 484-249-0378
Web Site: www.higginsonbooks.com
Key Personnel
Off Mgr: Mitchell Peiffer *E-mail:* mitch@higginsonbooks.com
Founded: 1969
Publish reprints of rare & out of print genealogies, local history & Civil War regimentals.
ISBN Prefix(es): 978-0-8328; 978-0-7404
Number of titles published annually: 400 Print
Total Titles: 15,000 Print

High Plains Press
PO Box 123, Glendo, WY 82213

Tel: 307-735-4370 *Toll Free Tel:* 800-552-7819
 Fax: 307-735-4590
E-mail: editor@highplainspress.com
Web Site: highplainspress.com
Key Personnel
Publr & Primary Ed: Nancy Curtis
Founded: 1984
Books about Wyoming & the American West.
ISBN Prefix(es): 978-0-931271
Number of titles published annually: 3 Print; 3 E-Book
Total Titles: 70 Print; 15 E-Book; 1 Audio
Membership(s): Independent Book Publishers Association (IBPA); Publishers Association of the West (PubWest)

§High Tide Press
Subsidiary of The Trinity Foundation
101 Hempstead Place, Suite 1A, Joliet, IL 60433
Tel: 779-702-5540
E-mail: orders@hightidepress.org; award@hightidepress.org
Web Site: hightidepress.org
Key Personnel
Dir, Pubns: Anne Ward
Founded: 1995
Publisher of books, training materials, interactive learning materials & other digital media products for professionals & administrators in human services, health care, nonprofit management, government agencies & the community. Specialize in the fields of developmental & intellectual disabilities, behavioral health, nonprofit management, social enterprise & leadership.
ISBN Prefix(es): 978-1-892696
Number of titles published annually: 12 Print; 4 Online; 12 E-Book; 2 Audio
Total Titles: 50 Print; 6 Online; 30 E-Book; 3 Audio
Imprints: How Do We Want To Be Together Series (short titles on organizational culture)
Membership(s): Independent Book Publishers Association (IBPA)

Highlights for Children Inc
815 Church St, Honesdale, PA 18431
Tel: 570-253-1164 *Toll Free Tel:* 800-490-5111
 Fax: 570-253-0179
E-mail: salesandmarketing@highlightspress.com
Web Site: www.highlightspress.com; www.highlights.com; www.facebook.com/HighlightsforChildren
Key Personnel
Pres, Consumer Busn: Lece Lohr
EVP, Busn Strategy & Prod Devt: Mary-Alice Moore
SVP, Retail: Dennis Hupp
VP & Publr, Highlights Book Group: Michael Eisenberg *E-mail:* michael.eisenberg@highlights.com
VP & Gen Mgr, Books & Consumer Prods: Chris Bauerle
VP, Brand Mktg: Kent Rademaker
VP, Busn Opers & Strategic Planning: Hadi Teleb
VP, Third Party E-Commerce: Jay Gaughan
Sr Dir, Creative: Saul Jimenez, Marie O'Neill
Dir, Analytics: Stephanie Lewis
Dir, Mktg & Publicity: Rachel Barry
Dir, Sales: Todd Jones
Dir, Specialty & Gift Sales, Highlights Book Group: Janine G Webb *E-mail:* janine.webb@highlights.com
Asst Ed, Highlights Press: Christy Thomas
Retail Mktg Mgr, Highlights Press: Monica Jankauskas
Founded: 1946
ISBN Prefix(es): 978-0-87534
Number of titles published annually: 150 Print
Imprints: Highlights Learning; Highlights Press
Orders to: Penguin Random House LLC, 400 Hahn Rd, Westminster, MD 21157 *Toll Free Tel:* 800-733-3000; Penguin Random House LLC International Dept, 1745 Broadway, New York, NY 10019 *Tel:* 212-572-6083 *Fax:* 212-572-6045 *E-mail:* international@penguinrandomhouse.com; Penguin Random House Canada, 320 Front St W, Suite 1400, Toronto, ON M5V 3B6, Canada *Toll Free Tel:* 888-523-9292 *Toll Free Fax:* 888-562-9924
Returns: Penguin Random House LLC, Attn: Returns Dept, 1019 N State Rd 47, Crawfordsville, IN 47933; Penguin Random House Canada, Attn: Returns Dept, 6971 Columbus Rd, Mississauga, ON L5T 1K1, Canada

Hill & Wang
Imprint of Farrar, Straus & Giroux, LLC
120 Broadway, New York, NY 10271
SAN: 201-9299
Tel: 212-741-6900
E-mail: fsg.publicity@fsgbooks.com; sales@fsgbooks.com
Web Site: us.macmillan.com/fsg
Key Personnel
SVP & Dir, Publicity, FSG: Sarita Varma *Tel:* 917-940-2542 *E-mail:* sarita.varma@fsgbooks.com
VP & Contracts Dir, FSG: Erika Seidman
Founded: 1956
General nonfiction, history & drama.
ISBN Prefix(es): 978-0-374; 978-0-8090
Number of titles published annually: 10 Print
Total Titles: 312 Print
Foreign Rep(s): Raincoast Books (Canada)
Foreign Rights: ANA Baltic (Tatjana Zoldnere) (Estonia, Latvia, Lithuania); AnatoliaLit Agency (Amy Spangler & Eda Caca) (Turkey); Anthea Agency (Katalina Sabeva) (Bulgaria); Bardon-Chinese Media (David Tsai) (China, Taiwan); Anoukh Foerg Agency (Germany); Deborah Harris Agency (Geula Geurts) (Israel); International Copyright Agency (Simon Kessler & Marina Adriana) (Romania); The Italian Literary Agency srl (Claire Sabatie-Garat) (Italy); Anna Jarota Agency (Dominika Bojanowska) (Poland); Anna Jarota Agency Poland (Zuzanna Brzezinska) (Russia); Katai & Bolza (Peter Bolza) (Hungary); Korea Copyright Center Inc (KCC) (Joeun Lee) (South Korea); Marotte et Compagnie Agence Litteraire (Corinne Marotte) (France); Maxima Creative Agency (Santo Manurung) (Indonesia); MB Agencia Literaria (Monica Martin & Ines Planells) (Portugal, Spain); Kristin Olson Literarni Agentura (Czechia, Slovakia); Plima Literary Agency (Vuk Perisic) (Albania, Croatia, Serbia, Slovenia); Read n Right Agency (Nike Davarinou) (Greece); Riff Agency (Laura & Joao Paulo Riff) (Brazil); Sebes & Bisseling Literary Agency (Paul Sebes) (Netherlands); Tuttle-Mori Agency Inc (Asako Kawachi) (Japan)
Warehouse: MPS Distribution Center, 16365 James Madison Hwy, Gordonsville, VA 22942 *Toll Free Tel:* 888-330-8477 *E-mail:* orders@mpsvirginia.com *Web Site:* us.macmillan.com/mps

Hillsdale College Press
Division of Hillsdale College
33 E College St, Hillsdale, MI 49242
Tel: 517-437-7341 *Toll Free Tel:* 800-437-2268
 Fax: 517-607-2658
E-mail: pr@hillsdale.edu
Web Site: www.hillsdale.edu
Key Personnel
Ed & VP, External Aff: Douglas A Jeffrey
Founded: 1974
Single author books & collected essays of historical, political & economic interest.
ISBN Prefix(es): 978-0-916308

§Hilton Publishing Co
Division of HPC International Inc
5261-A Fountain Dr, Crown Point, IN 46307
Tel: 219-922-4868 *Fax:* 219-924-6811
E-mail: info@hpcinternationalinc.com
Web Site: www.hpcinternationalinc.com; www.hpcinternationalinc.com/bookstore (orders)
Key Personnel
EVP: Megan Lippert *E-mail:* mlippert@hpcinternationalinc.com
Sr Dir, Fin & Acctg: Tammy Gauthier *E-mail:* tgauthier@hpcinternationalinc.com
Founded: 1996
Publish books in health & wellness, minority health, religion (health-related). Consistent themes of publications include living with & preventing various disease states, illustrating & promoting components of healthy living, embracing & illuminating cultural diversity related to health & well-being & fostering health in the Christian community. Books are peer-reviewed by experts in the appropriate fields to insure we have included the most current, accurate & relevant information. We publish informative & educational books for the general public as well as books aimed at the medical community.
ISBN Prefix(es): 978-0-9675258; 978-0-9716067; 978-0-9743144; 978-0-9764443; 978-0-9773160; 978-0-9777779; 978-0-9800649; 978-0-9815381; 978-0-9841447; 978-0-9847566
Number of titles published annually: 12 Print; 10 E-Book
Total Titles: 50 Print; 20 E-Book
Membership(s): National Minority Supplier Development Council (NMSDC)

Himalayan Institute Press
Division of Himalayan International Institute of Yoga Science & Philosophy
952 Bethany Tpke, Honesdale, PA 18431
Tel: 570-253-5551 *Toll Free Tel:* 800-822-4547
E-mail: trade@himalayaninstitute.org
Web Site: www.himalayaninstitute.org
Key Personnel
Chmn & Spiritual Head: Pandit Rajmani Tigunait, PhD
Dir: Stephen Moulton *E-mail:* smoulton@himalayaninstitute.org
Founded: 1971
Publish CDs, DVDs & books on yoga, meditation, holistic health, philosophy, psychology & stress management.
ISBN Prefix(es): 978-0-89389
Number of titles published annually: 1 Print; 40 E-Book; 2 Audio
Total Titles: 60 Print; 20 Audio
Foreign Rights: DropCap (worldwide)

§Hippocrene Books Inc
171 Madison Ave, Suite 1605, New York, NY 10016
Tel: 212-685-4373
E-mail: info@hippocrenebooks.com; orderdept@hippocrenebooks.com (orders)
Web Site: www.hippocrenebooks.com
Key Personnel
Publr & Edit Dir: Priti Chitnis Gress *E-mail:* pgress@hippocrenebooks.com
Fin Offr: Awilda Alvarez
Publicity Mgr & Ed: Colette Laroya *Tel:* 212-685-4371 ext 4
Founded: 1971
Foreign language dictionaries & self-study guides in over 120 languages; international cookbooks, history & travel.
ISBN Prefix(es): 978-0-87052; 978-0-7818
Number of titles published annually: 25 Print
Total Titles: 500 Print; 150 E-Book
Foreign Rights: A B E Marketing (Poland); Bookery Pty Ltd (Australia); Gazelle Book Services Ltd (England); Publishers Group Canada (Canada)

PUBLISHERS
U.S. PUBLISHERS

Shipping Address: Whitehurst & Clark Book Services, 1200 County Rd, Rte 523, Flemington, NJ 08822
Warehouse: Whitehurst & Clark Book Services, 1200 County Rd, Rte 523, Flemington, NJ 08822
Membership(s): Independent Book Publishers Association (IBPA)

§The Historic New Orleans Collection
533 Royal St, New Orleans, LA 70130
Tel: 504-523-4662 *Fax:* 504-598-7108
E-mail: wrc@hnoc.org
Web Site: www.hnoc.org
Key Personnel
Pres & CEO: Daniel Hammer *Tel:* 504-598-7112
  E-mail: daniel.hammer@hnoc.org
Dir, Pubns: Dr Jessica Dorman *Tel:* 504-598-7174
  E-mail: jessica.dorman@hnoc.org
Founded: 1966
Publications related to Louisiana history & to the holdings of The Historic New Orleans Collection; preservation manuals for family papers, photographs, etc.
ISBN Prefix(es): 978-0-917860
Number of titles published annually: 3 Print
Total Titles: 83 Print; 3 E-Book
Distributed by University of Virginia Press
Membership(s): Southern Independent Booksellers Alliance (SIBA)

§History Publishing Co LLC
PO Box 700, Palisades, NY 10964
SAN: 850-5942
Tel: 845-359-1765 *Fax:* 845-818-3730 (sales)
E-mail: info@historypublishingco.com
Web Site: www.historypublishingco.com
Key Personnel
Owner & Publr: Don Bracken *E-mail:* djb@historypublishingco.com
Sr Ed: Alexis Starke *E-mail:* alex@historypublishingco.com
Founded: 2007
Trade book publisher.
ISBN Prefix(es): 978-19339-09; 978-19407-73
Number of titles published annually: 12 Print; 75 Online; 100 E-Book
Total Titles: 75 Print; 75 Online; 100 E-Book
Imprints: Chronology Books (history books from a 3rd party perspective); History Publishing Company (early & recent history); History Publishing Company Global (cyber-first platform); Today's Books (current issues); Today's Titles
Warehouse: Whitehurst & Clark, 1200 County Rte 523, Flemington, NJ 08822 *Tel:* 908-782-2323 *Fax:* 908-237-2407 *Web Site:* www.wcbks.com
Distribution Center: INscribe Digital, 444 Spear St, Suite 213, San Francisco, CA 94105
Membership(s): Association of American Publishers (AAP); Independent Book Publishers Association (IBPA)

Histria Books
Division of Histria LLC
7181 N Hualapai Way, Suite 130-86, Las Vegas, NV 89166
Tel: 561-299-0802
E-mail: info@histriabooks.com; orders@histriabooks.com; rights@histriabooks.com
Web Site: histriabooks.com
Key Personnel
Dir: Kurt Brackob
Graphics Dir: Silvio Sequera
Asst Dir: Diana Livesay *E-mail:* diana@histriabooks.com
Mgr: Dana Ungureanu *E-mail:* dana@histriabooks.com
Asst Mgr: J D Mabbot
Founded: 1996
Publishes general interest books, fiction & literature, children's books, as well as scholarly books in a broad range of categories. Histria Books is an independent publishing house with offices in Las Vegas, NV & Palm Beach, FL.
ISBN Prefix(es): 978-973-9432 (Center for Romanian Studies); 978-973-98091 (Center for Romanian Studies); 978-973-98392 (Center for Romanian Studies); 978-1-59211; 978-0-9801164 (Addison & Highsmith)
Number of titles published annually: 60 Print; 40 E-Book; 20 Audio
Total Titles: 400 Print; 250 E-Book; 50 Audio
Imprints: Addison & Highsmith Publishers (high quality works of fiction); Center for Romanian Studies (history & culture of Romania); Gaudium Publishing (contemporary lifestyle, culture, sports, politics, biography & autobiography); Histria Kids (children's & young adult books that educate & entertain); Prende Publishing (arts & entertainment, graphic novels, poetry & lifestyle); Vindicta Publishing (nonfiction, politics & international affairs); Vita Histria (academic books with a focus on history, culture & the arts)
Branch Office(s)
931 Village Blvd, No 905-269, West Palm Beach, FL 33409
Foreign Rights: Susan Schulman Literary Agency (worldwide exc North America & UK)
Orders to: Independent Publishers Group (IPG), 814 N Franklin St, Chicago 60610 *Toll Free Tel:* 800-888-4741 *Fax:* 312-337-5985 *E-mail:* orders@ipgbook.com *Web Site:* ipgbook.com
Shipping Address: Independent Publishers Group (IPG), 814 N Franklin St, Chicago, IL 60610 *Toll Free Tel:* 800-888-4741 *Fax:* 312-337-5985; Books International, 22883 Quicksilver Dr, Dulles, VA 20166; POD Worldwide, 9 Culley Ct, Orton Southgate, Peterborough PE2 6XD, United Kingdom
Warehouse: IPG Distribution Center, 600 N Pulaski Rd, Chicago, IL 60624 *Tel:* 773-722-5527
Books International, 22883 Quicksilver Dr, Dulles, VA 20166 (Casemate | publishers US) *Tel:* 703-661-1500 *Fax:* 703-661-1501 *Web Site:* booksintl.presswarehouse.com
Orca Book Services Ltd, United Independent Distributors - BDC, Lancaster Way, Unit 2, Biggelswade, Beds SG18 8YL, United Kingdom *E-mail:* tradeorders@orcabookservices.co.uk *Web Site:* www.orcabookservices.co.uk
Distribution Center: Independent Publishers Group (IPG), 814 N Franklin St, Suite 100, Chicago, IL 60610 *Tel:* 312-337-0747 *Fax:* 312-337-5985 *E-mail:* orders@ipgbook.com *Web Site:* ipgbook.com
Eurospan, Gray's Inn House, 127 Clerkenwell Rd, London EC1R 5DB, United Kingdom (Europe & UK) *Tel:* (01235) 465577 *E-mail:* info@eurospanbookstore.com *Web Site:* www.eurospanbookstore.com
Membership(s): American Association for the Advancement of Slavic Studies (AAASS); Independent Book Publishers Association (IBPA); Independent Publishers Caucus (IPC); Independent Publisher's Guild (IPG); Midwest Independent Booksellers Association (MIBA); New Atlantic Independent Booksellers Association (NAIBA); Publishers Association of the West (PubWest)

HMH Assessments, see Houghton Mifflin Harcourt Assessments

W D Hoard & Sons Co
28 W Milwaukee Ave, Fort Atkinson, WI 53538
Mailing Address: PO Box 801, Fort Atkinson, WI 53538-0801
Tel: 920-563-5551
E-mail: hdbooks@hoards.com; editors@hoards.com
Web Site: www.hoards.com
Key Personnel
Assoc Ed: Abby Bauer
Founded: 1870
Dairy oriented & some agricultural, regional publications, catalogs & specialty projects.
ISBN Prefix(es): 978-0-932147
Number of titles published annually: 5 Print
Total Titles: 22 Print
Imprints: Hoard's Dairyman Magazine

Hobblebush Books
PO Box 1285, Concord, NH 03302
Tel: 603-715-9615
E-mail: info@hobblebush.com
Web Site: www.hobblebush.com
Key Personnel
Owner: Kirsty Walker
Founded: 1993
Independent publisher of both literary & non-literary titles.
ISBN Prefix(es): 978-0-9636413; 978-0-9760896; 978-0-9801672; 978-1-939449
Number of titles published annually: 3 Print; 3 E-Book
Total Titles: 45 Print; 3 E-Book
Membership(s): Community of Literary Magazines & Presses (CLMP); Independent Publishers of New England (IPNE); New Hampshire Writers' Project (NHWP)

§Hogrefe Publishing Corp
Subsidiary of Hogrefe Verlag GmbH & Co Kg
44 Merrimac St, Suite 207, Newburyport, MA 01950
SAN: 293-2792
Tel: 978-255-3700 (off)
E-mail: customersupport@hogrefe.com
Web Site: www.hogrefe.com/us
Key Personnel
Publg Mgr: Robert Dimbleby *E-mail:* robert.dimbleby@hogrefe.com
Founded: 1978
Books, journals, assessment tools & online resources in the fields of psychiatry, psychology, psychotherapy & medicine.
ISBN Prefix(es): 978-0-88937; 978-0-920887; 978-1-61676 (ebooks); 978-1-61334 (EPUB)
Number of titles published annually: 12 Print; 12 E-Book
Total Titles: 150 Print; 120 E-Book
Foreign Office(s): Hogrefe Verlag GmbH & Co Kg, Merkelstr 3, 37085 Goettingen, Germany *Tel:* (0551) 999 50-0 *Fax:* (0551) 999 50
Distributor for Hogrefe AG (Switzerland); Hogrefe Verlag (Germany)
Orders to: Baker & Taylor Publisher Services, 30 Amberwood Pkwy, Ashland, OH 44805 *Tel:* 567-215-0030 *Toll Free Tel:* 888-814-0208 *E-mail:* info@btpubservices.com *Web Site:* www.btpubservices.com
Returns: Baker & Taylor Publisher Services, 30 Amberwood Pkwy, Ashland, OH 44805 *Tel:* 567-215-0030 *Toll Free Tel:* 888-814-0208 *E-mail:* info@btpubservices.com *Web Site:* www.btpubservices.com
Distribution Center: Baker & Taylor Publisher Services, 30 Amberwood Pkwy, Ashland, OH 44805 *Tel:* 567-215-0030 *Toll Free Tel:* 888-814-0208 *E-mail:* info@btpubservices.com *Web Site:* www.btpubservices.com
Membership(s): Association of American Publishers (AAP); STM

Hohm Press
Subsidiary of HSM LLC
PO Box 4410, Chino Valley, AZ 86323
Tel: 928-636-3331 *Toll Free Tel:* 800-381-2700
  Fax: 928-636-7519
E-mail: publisher@hohmpress.com
Web Site: www.hohmpress.com

U.S. PUBLISHERS

Key Personnel
Gen Mgr & Publr: Dasya Anthony Zuccarello
Mng Ed: Regina Sara Ryan
Prodn Mgr: Joe Bala Zuccarello
Founded: 1975
Independent publisher of books on spirituality & consciousness studies.
ISBN Prefix(es): 978-0-934252; 978-1-890772
Number of titles published annually: 6 Print; 6 E-Book
Total Titles: 300 Print; 80 E-Book; 6 Audio
Imprints: Kalindi Press (books on natural health & nutrition, children's & family health)
Foreign Rep(s): Gazelle Book Services Ltd (Europe)
Foreign Rights: HBG Productions (Deanna Leah) (worldwide)
Shipping Address: 860 Staley Lane, Chino Valley, AZ 86323
Warehouse: 860 Staley Lane, Chino Valley, AZ 86323
Distribution Center: SCB Distributors, 15608 S New Century Dr, Gardena, CA 90248 (CN, UK & US) *Toll Free Tel:* 800-729-6423 *Web Site:* www.scbdistributors.com

Holiday House Publishing Inc
50 Broad St, New York, NY 10004
SAN: 202-3008
Tel: 212-688-0085 *Fax:* 212-421-6134
E-mail: info@holidayhouse.com
Web Site: www.holidayhouse.com
Key Personnel
SVP, Global Integration & Planning: Derek Stordahl
SVP, Sales, Mktg & Busn Opers, US & CN: Mary Marotta
VP & Ed-in-Chief: Mary Cash *E-mail:* mcash@holidayhouse.com
VP & Dir, Prodn: Lisa Lee *E-mail:* llee@holidayhouse.com
VP, Consumer & Brand Mktg: Karen Walsh
VP, Mktg: Terry Borzumato-Greenberg *E-mail:* tborzumato@holidayhouse.com
VP, Publicity: Tracy Miracle
VP, Rts, Perms & Digital Publg: Julia Gallagher *E-mail:* jgallagher@holidayhouse.com
VP, Trade Mktg: Michelle Montague
Publr, Margaret Ferguson Books: Margaret Ferguson *E-mail:* mferguson@holidayhouse.com
Publr, Neal Porter Books: Neal Porter *E-mail:* nporter@holidayhouse.com
Creative Dir: Kerry Martin *E-mail:* kmartin@holidayhouse.com
Creative Dir, Neal Porter Books/Sr Art Dir, Margaret Ferguson Books: Jennifer Browne
Dir, Subs Rts: Miriam Miller *E-mail:* mmiller@holidayhouse.com
Retail Dir, Sales: Jess Brigman
Sales Dir: Morgan Hillman
Assoc Art Dir, Novels & Middle Grade: Chelsea Hunter
Exec Ed: Grace Maccarone *E-mail:* gmaccarone@holidayhouse.com; Sally Morgridge
Exec Ed, Neal Porter Books: Taylor Norman
Mng Ed: Raina Putter
Assoc Mng Ed: Jamie Evans
Ed & Coord, Spanish Lang Publg: Alexandra Aceves
Ed: Mora Couch; Della Farrell; Elizabeth Law
Asst Ed: Kade Dishmon; Laura Kincaid
Sr Digital Mktg Mgr: Mary Joyce Perry
Sr Natl Acct Mgr, Amazon: Karen Menzie
Data Mgr: Hannah Finne
Mktg Mgr, Trade: Alison Tarnofsky; Elyse Vincenty
Publicity Mgr: Sara DiSalvo
Sr Publicist: Anna Gjesteby Abell
Publicist: Bree Martinez
Assoc Mktg Mgr, School & Lib: Darby Guinn
Sr Designer: Chris Russo
Sr Mktg Designer: Jim Secula

Mktg Designer: Allie Jones
Designer: Nicole Gureli
Consumer Mktg Coord: Neda Kamalhedayat
Digital Mktg Coord: Alex Howard; Melissa See
Mktg Coord, School & Lib: Tiffany Coelho
Prodn Coord: Joselin Pichardo
Publicity Coord: Kayla Phillips
Sales Coord: Adelaide Cronin
Mktg Asst, School & Lib: Saskia den Boon; Annie Rosenbladt
Mktg/Publicity Asst: Mary Wolford
Trade Mktg Asst: Caitlyn Davis
Founded: 1935
Juvenile & young adult books.
ISBN Prefix(es): 978-0-8234
Number of titles published annually: 90 Print
Total Titles: 800 Print; 300 E-Book
Imprints: Margaret Ferguson Books; Neal Porter Books
Distributed by Pengin Random House
Foreign Rights: Big Apple Agency Inc (Vincent Lin) (China); Sandra Bruna Agencia Literaria (Sandra Bruna) (Spanish-speaking countries); The Deborah Harris Agency (Efrat Lev) (Israel); The Italian Agency (Chiara Piovan) (Italy); Japan UNI Agency (Takeshi Oyama) (Japan); Korea Copyright Center Inc (KCC) (Hansol Lee) (South Korea); Agence Michelle Lapautre (Catherine Lapautre) (French-speaking countries); Seibel Publishing Services (Patricia Natalia Seibel) (Brazil, Portugal); Tuttle-Mori Agency (Thailand) Co Ltd (Nawara Hirankan) (Indonesia, Thailand, Vietnam); Watson Little Ltd (Rachel Richardson) (British Commonwealth, Eastern Europe, Greece, Hungary, Netherlands); Literarische Agentur Silke Weniger (Silke Weniger, Alexandra Legath & Sabrina Gold) (Austria, Germany, Switzerland (German-speaking))
Orders to: Penguin Random House (US) *Toll Free Tel:* 800-733-3000
Shipping Address: Penguin Random House (US)
Distribution Center: Penguin Random House Publisher Services (PRHPS)
Membership(s): The Children's Book Council (CBC)

Hollym International Corp
2647 Gateway Rd, No 105-223, Carlsbad, CA 92009
SAN: 211-0172
Tel: 760-814-9880 *Fax:* 908-353-0255
E-mail: contact@hollym.com
Web Site: www.hollym.com
Key Personnel
Pres: Gene S Rhie
Founded: 1977
Publish & distribute books in English on Korea related topics.
ISBN Prefix(es): 978-0-930878; 978-1-56591
Number of titles published annually: 10 Print
Total Titles: 155 Print
Foreign Office(s): Hollym Corp, 13-13 Gwancheol-dong, Jongno-gu, 110-111 Seoul, South Korea, Contact: Kim-Man Ham *Tel:* (02) 735-7551 *Fax:* (02) 730-5149 *E-mail:* info@hollym.co.kr *Web Site:* www.hollym.co.kr

Holmes Publishing Group LLC
PO Box 2370, Sequim, WA 98382
Tel: 360-681-2900
E-mail: holmespub@fastmail.fm
Web Site: www.jdholmes.com
Key Personnel
Pres & CEO: J D Holmes *E-mail:* jdholmes@fastmail.fm
Founded: 1971
Specialize in books, both Holmes published & distributed private press titles, in alchemy, magic & esoteric subjects.
ISBN Prefix(es): 978-1-55818; 978-0-916411
Number of titles published annually: 4 Print
Total Titles: 588 Print

Imprints: Alchemical Press; Alexandrian Press; Contra/Thought; Holmes Publishing Group; Near Eastern Press; Sure Fire Press
Distributor for Jerusalem Press (UK); Starfire Publishing (UK); Theion Publishing (Germany); Three Hands Press (US); Von Zos Publishing; Xoanon Publishing (US)
Distribution Center: New Leaf Distributing Co, 1085 E Lotus Dr, Silver Lake, WI 53170 *Tel:* 262-889-8501 *Toll Free Tel:* 800-326-2665 *Fax:* 262-889-8598 *E-mail:* orders@newleafdist.com SAN: 169-1449

Henry Holt and Company, LLC
Division of Macmillan
120 Broadway, 23rd fl, New York, NY 10271
SAN: 200-2108
Tel: 646-307-5151 *Toll Free Tel:* 888-330-8477 (orders) *Fax:* 646-307-5285
Web Site: www.henryholt.com
Key Personnel
Pres & Publr: Andrew Miller
SVP & Assoc Publr: Maggie Richards
VP & Assoc Publr: Caitlin Mulrooney-Lyski
VP & Group Creative Dir: Christopher Sergio
VP & Sr Creative Dir, Children's: Beth Clark
VP & Edit Dir, Fiction: Emily Griffin
VP & Exec Ed: Tim Duggan; Retha Powers
Publr, Godwin Books: Laura Godwin
Sr Art Dir: Sharismar Rodriguez
Sr Dir, Mktg: Laura Flavin
Sr Dir, Publicity: Marian Brown
Edit Dir, Children's: Ann Marie Wong
Deputy Dir, Publicity: Carolyn O'Keefe
Assoc Art Dir: Nicolette Seeback
Assoc Art Dir, Henry Holt Books for Younger Readers: Samira Irayani
Assoc Creative Dir, Henry Holt Books for Younger Readers: Kirk Benshoff
Asst Dir, Mktg: Allison Carney
Asst Dir, Publg Opers: Conor Mintzer
Exec Mng Ed, Adult Trade: Kenn Russell
Exec Ed: Serena Jones; Caroline Zancan
Exec Ed, Henry Holt Books for Young Readers: Kate Farrell; Brian Geffen
Sr Ed: Ruby Rose Lee
Sr Ed, Children's: Dana Chidiac
Ed, Children's: Jess Harold
Ed, Henry Holt Books for Young Readers: Mark Podesta
Assoc Ed: Micaela Carr
Assoc Ed, Henry Holt Books for Younger Readers: Rachel Murray
Asst Ed: Kerry Cullen; Natalia Ruiz; Anita Sheih
Asst Ed, Children's: Carina Licon
Ed-at-Large: Sarah Crichton; Retha Powers
Sr Mgr, Publicity: Clarissa Long
Mktg Assoc: Arriel Vinson
Studio Mgr: Ginny Dominguez
Asst Mktg Mgr: Alyssa Weinberg
Sr Publicist: Catryn Silbersack
Publicist: Sarah Fitts
Sr Designer: Emily Mahar
Sr Designer, Mktg Dept: Ashley Lau
Mktg Assoc: Sonja Flancher
Founded: 1866
ISBN Prefix(es): 978-0-8050 (Holt)
Number of titles published annually: 56 Print
Total Titles: 3,000 Print
Imprints: Godwin Books; Henry Holt; Henry Holt Books for Younger Readers; Holt Paperbacks; John Macrae Books; Times Books
Foreign Rep(s): Raincoast (Canada)
Foreign Rights: A/S Bookman Literary Agency (Denmark, Finland, Iceland, Norway, Sweden); AnatoliaLit Agency (Turkey); Anthea Agency (Bulgaria); Author Rights Agency Ltd (Russia); Bardon-Chinese Media Agency (Mainland China, Taiwan); Eliane Benisti Literary Agency (France); Copenhagen Literary Agency ApS (Scandinavia); English Agency Japan Co Ltd (Japan); Farrar, Straus and Giroux (USA); Graal Literary Agency (Maria Strarz-Zielinska) (Poland); The Deborah Harris Agency (Israel);

Internationaal Literatuur Bureau BV (Netherlands); International Copyright Agency Ltd (Simona Kessler) (Romania); The Italian Literary Agency Srl (Italy); Katai & Bolza Literary Agents (Hungary); Korea Copyright Center Inc (KCC) (South Korea); Liepman Agency (Eva Koralnik & Ronit Zafran) (Germany); Literarni Aventura sro (Czechia, Slovakia); MB Agencia Literaria (Portugal, Spain); Plima Literary Agency (Croatia, Serbia, Slovenia); RIFF (Brazil)
Advertising Agency: Verso Advertising, 50 W 17 St, New York, NY 10010 *Tel:* 212-292-2990 *Web Site:* www.versoadvertising.com
Warehouse: MPS, 16365 James Madison Hwy, Gordonsville, VA 22942 *Tel:* 540-672-7698
SAN: 631-5011
Membership(s): Association of American Publishers (AAP)

§Holy Cow! Press
PO Box 3170, Mount Royal Sta, Duluth, MN 55803
Tel: 218-606-2792
E-mail: holycow@holycowpress.org
Web Site: www.holycowpress.org
Key Personnel
Publr & Ed: Jim Perlman
Founded: 1977
ISBN Prefix(es): 978-0-930100; 978-0-9779458; 978-1-7374051
Number of titles published annually: 4 Print; 3 E-Book
Total Titles: 120 Print; 8 E-Book
Distribution Center: Consortium Book Sales & Distribution, The Keg House, Suite 101, 34 13 Ave NE, Minneapolis, MN 55413-1007 *Tel:* 612-746-2600 *Toll Free Tel:* 866-400-5351 (cust serv, Jackson, TN) *E-mail:* cbsdinfo@ingramcontent.com *Web Site:* www.cbsd.com
SAN: 200-6049

Holy Cross Orthodox Press
Division of Hellenic College Holy Cross
50 Goddard Ave, Brookline, MA 02445
Tel: 617-731-3500; 617-850-1303
E-mail: press@hchc.edu
Web Site: www.hchc.edu
Key Personnel
Contact: Rev Anton Vrame
Founded: 1974
Books on Orthodox Christian religion.
This publisher has indicated that 25% of their product line is author subsidized.
ISBN Prefix(es): 978-0-917651; 978-1-885652; 978-0-916586; 978-1-935317
Number of titles published annually: 10 Print
Total Titles: 120 Print

§Homa & Sekey Books
Mack-Cali Ctr II, N Tower, 3rd fl, 140 E Ridgewood Ave, Paramus, NJ 07652
Tel: 201-261-8810 *Fax:* 201-261-8890
E-mail: info@homabooks.com
Web Site: www.homabooks.com
Key Personnel
Publr: Shawn Xian Ye
Founded: 1997
Publisher & distributor of books on Asia.
ISBN Prefix(es): 978-1-931907; 978-0-966542; 978-1-62246
Number of titles published annually: 15 Print
Distributor for China Encyclopedia Publishing House; China Intercontinental Press; China Zhejiang Publishing United Group
Foreign Rights: Eric Yang Agency (South Korea)
Membership(s): Independent Book Publishers Association (IBPA)

§Homestead Publishing
Affiliate of Book Design Ltd
Box 193, Moose, WY 83012-0193
Tel: 307-733-6248 *Fax:* 307-733-6248
E-mail: info@homesteadpublishing.com; orders@homesteadpublishing.net
Web Site: www.homesteadpublishing.net
Key Personnel
Publr: Carl Schreier *Tel:* 760-832-7152
Contact: Diane Henderson
Founded: 1980
Publisher of guidebooks.
ISBN Prefix(es): 978-0-943972
Number of titles published annually: 12 Print; 6 E-Book
Total Titles: 268 Print; 16 E-Book
Branch Office(s)
650 N Phillips Rd, Palm Springs, CA 92262
Tel: 760-832-7152
Returns: 4030 W Lake Creek Dr, Wilson, WY 83014
Warehouse: 4030 W Lake Creek Dr, Wilson, WY 83014

Hoover Institution Press
Subsidiary of Hoover Institution on War, Revolution & Peace
Stanford University, 434 Galvez Mall, Stanford, CA 94305-6003
SAN: 202-3024
Tel: 650-723-3373 *Toll Free Tel:* 800-935-2882 (US only); 877-466-8374 (US only) *Fax:* 650-723-8626
E-mail: hooverpress@stanford.edu
Web Site: www.hoover.org/publications/hooverpress
Key Personnel
Exec Ed: Barbara Arellano
Book Prodn Mgr: Marshall Blanchard *Tel:* 650-725-3460
Founded: 1962
Studies on domestic & international policy, studies of nationalities in Central & Eastern Europe, history & political science; bibliographies & surveys of Hoover Institution's resources.
ISBN Prefix(es): 978-0-8179
Number of titles published annually: 20 Print
Total Titles: 700 Print; 100 Online; 700 E-Book
Foreign Rep(s): Eurospan (Africa, Continental Europe, Europe, Middle East)
Orders to: Independent Publishers Group (IPG), 814 N Franklin St, Chicago, IL 60610 *Tel:* 312-337-0747 *Toll Free Tel:* 800-888-4741 *Fax:* 312-337-5985 *E-mail:* orders@ipgbook.com *Web Site:* www.ipgbook.com
Returns: Independent Publishers Group (IPG), Returns Dept, 814 N Franklin St, Chicago, IL 60610 (call or write) *Tel:* 312-337-8747 *Web Site:* www.ipgbook.com
Distribution Center: Independent Publishers Group (IPG), 814 N Franklin St, Chicago, IL 60610 *Tel:* 312-337-0747 *Toll Free Tel:* 800-888-4741 *Fax:* 312-337-5985 *E-mail:* orders@ipgbook.com *Web Site:* www.ipgbook.com

Hope Publishing Co
380 S Main Place, Carol Stream, IL 60188
Tel: 630-665-3200 *Toll Free Tel:* 800-323-1049
E-mail: hope@hopepublishing.com
Web Site: www.hopepublishing.com
Key Personnel
Pres: John Shorney *E-mail:* john@hopepublishing.com
VP: Scott A Shorney *E-mail:* scott@hopepublishing.com; Steve Shorney *E-mail:* steve@hopepublishing.com
Founded: 1892
Choir music, hymnals, instrumental music books & hand bell music.
ISBN Prefix(es): 978-0-916642
Number of titles published annually: 50 Print
Divisions: Agape; Providence Press; Somerset Press; Tabernacle Publishing
Advertising Agency: Lamplighter Agency

Horizon Publishers & Distributors Inc
Imprint of Cedar Fort Inc
191 N 650 E, Bountiful, UT 84010-3628
Tel: 801-292-7102
E-mail: ldshorizonpublishers1@gmail.com
Web Site: www.ldshorizonpublishers.com
Key Personnel
Owner & CEO: Duane S Crowther; Jean D Crowther
Founded: 1971
Christian (primarily Latter-day Saints), inspirational, health foods, self-sufficient living, music, marriage & family, children's activities, needlework, nonfiction, biography paperbacks & hardbound.
ISBN Prefix(es): 978-0-88290
Number of titles published annually: 15 Print
Total Titles: 521 Print; 35 CD-ROM; 40 Audio
Distributed by Cedar Fort Inc

Hospital & Healthcare Compensation Service
Subsidiary of John R Zabka Associates Inc
3 Post Rd, Suite 3, Oakland, NJ 07436
Mailing Address: PO Box 376, Oakland, NJ 07436-0376
Tel: 201-405-0075 *Fax:* 201-405-2110
E-mail: allinfo@hhcsinc.com
Web Site: www.hhcsinc.com
Key Personnel
Dir, Reports: Rosanne Zabka *Tel:* 201-405-0075 ext 11 *E-mail:* rzabka@hhcsinc.com
Client Servs: Tracy Schilling *Tel:* 201-405-0075 ext 13 *E-mail:* tschilling@hhcsinc.com
Founded: 1971
Publisher of salary & benefits reports for hospital, nursing home, assisted living, CCRC, home care, hospice & rehabilitation employees.
ISBN Prefix(es): 978-0-939326; 978-1-934847
Number of titles published annually: 11 Print; 11 CD-ROM
Total Titles: 10 Print; 11 CD-ROM

Host Publications
3408 West Ave, Austin, TX 78705
Mailing Address: PO Box 302920, Austin, TX 78703
E-mail: editors@hostpublications.com
Web Site: www.hostpublications.com
Key Personnel
Art Dir & Mng Ed: Annar Verold
 E-mail: annar@hostpublications.com
Sr Ed: Claire Bowman
Founded: 1988
Publishes radical poetry & fiction by emerging LGBTQ+, BIPOC, intersectional feminist & immigrant voices.
ISBN Prefix(es): 978-0-924047
Number of titles published annually: 6 Print
Total Titles: 50 Print
Distribution Center: Asterism Books, 568 First Ave S, Suite 120, Seattle, WA 98104 *E-mail:* info@asterismbooks.com *Web Site:* www.asterismbooks.com
Membership(s): Independent Book Publishers Association (IBPA)

§Houghton Mifflin Harcourt
Subsidiary of Veritas Capital
125 High St, Boston, MA 02110
SAN: 200-2388
Tel: 617-351-5000 *Toll Free Tel:* 855-969-4642; 800-225-5425 (K-12 educ materials); 800-323-9540 (assessment materials); 877-219-1537 (SkillsTutor); 888-242-6747 (Innovation in Educ Group); 800-225-3362 (Trade & Ref Div)
Toll Free Fax: 800-269-5232
E-mail: myhmhco@hmhco.com
Web Site: www.hmhco.com
Key Personnel
Pres & CEO: John (Jack) J Lynch, Jr
CFO: Joseph P Abbott, Jr
Chief Revenue Offr: Mike Evans

U.S. PUBLISHERS

CTO: Peter George
EVP & Gen Coun: William Bayers
EVP & Gen Mgr, Core Solutions Div: Jim O'Neill
EVP & Gen Mgr, Heinemann: Vicki Boyd
EVP & Gen Mgr, Prof Servs: Amy Dunkin
EVP & Gen Mgr, Supplemental & Intervention Solutions: Matthew Mugo Fields
SVP & Chief People Offr: Alejandro Reyes
SVP, Corp Aff: Bianca Olson
SVP, Mktg: Matt Schweitzer
VP, Investor Rel: Chris Symanoskie
Sr Dir, Publg Opers: Cara Coggins
Dir, Field Sales & Events: Rachel Sanders
Dir, Perms & Assoc Dir, Subs Rts: Ron Hussey
Assoc Dir, Digital Mktg & Opers: Meghan Gocke
Sr Sales Opers Mgr: James Stamos
Dist Client Mgr & Natl Accts: Morgan Gould
Mktg Assoc: Lisa McAuliffe
Natl Acct Mgr: Emily Logan
Sales Mgr: Carissa Ray
Founded: 1832

With education products & services used by more than 50 million students in more than 150 countries, Houghton Mifflin Harcourt is a global education & learning company. The world's largest provider of materials for PreK-12 learning, HMH is leading the way with innovative solutions & approaches to the challenges facing education today. Through curricula excellence coupled with technology innovations & professional services, HMH collaborates with school districts, administrators, teachers, parents & students, providing interactive, results-driven learning solutions. Its Educational Consulting Services group works to increase student achievement in underperforming schools by developing, implementing & supporting education transformation through sustained district partnerships. With origins dating back to 1832, the company also publishes an extensive line of reference works & award-winning literature for adults & young readers.

ISBN Prefix(es): 978-0-395; 978-0-618; 978-0-547; 978-0-544; 978-0-9709455; 978-0-9747343; 978-1-933196; 978-1-935588
Divisions: Houghton Mifflin Harcourt K-12 Publishers; The Learning Company; SkillsTutor
Branch Office(s)
2180 S McDowell Blvd, Suite B, Petaluma, CA 94954 Tel: 707-769-2222
One Harbor Dr, Sausalito, CA 94965 Tel: 415-332-4181
5680 Greenwood Plaza Blvd, Suite 550, Greenwood Village, CO 80111 Tel: 303-504-9312
9400 Southpark Center Loop, Orlando, FL 32819 Tel: 407-345-2000
7584 Presidents Way, Orlando, FL 32809 Tel: 407-345-2000
909 Davis St, Suite 300, Evanston, IL 60201 Toll Free Tel: 800-225-5425
1900 S Batavia Ave, Geneva, IL 60134-3399 Tel: 630-232-2550
One Pierce Place, Suite 900W, Itasca, IL 60143 Toll Free Tel: 800-767-8420
761 District Dr, Itasca, IL 60143
255 38 Ave, Suite L, St Charles, IL 60174 Tel: 630-208-5876
2700 N Richardt Ave, Indianapolis, IN 46219 Tel: 317-359-5585
465 S Lincoln Dr, Troy, MO 63379 Tel: 636-528-8110
361 Hanover St, Portsmouth, NH 03801 Tel: 630-467-7000
3 Park Ave, New York, NY 10016 Tel: 212-420-5800
132 W 31 St, New York, NY 10001
1587 Rte 146, Rexford, NY 12148 Tel: 518-399-2776
2270 Spring Lake Rd, Suite 600, Farmers Branch, TX 75234 Toll Free Tel: 800-225-5425
2700 La Frontera Blvd, Round Rock, TX 78681 Tel: 512-721-7000
4200 Blvd St Laurent, Suite 1203, Montreal, QC H2W 2R2, Canada Tel: 514-598-0444
B7 Calle Tabonuco, Suite 1410, Guaynabo 00968-3003, Puerto Rico Tel: 787-520-9599; 787-520-9585
Foreign Office(s): 59 Zhongguancun St, Rm 1004, Haidian District, Beijing 100872, China Tel: (010) 62602236
152-160 Pearse St, Dublin 2, Ireland Tel: (01) 240 5900
67 Ubi Rd, No 05-08 Oxley Bizhub, Singapore 408730, Singapore Tel: 6635 6825
No 501 KGIT SangAm Ctr, 1601, SangAm-dong, Mapo-gu, Seoul 123-913, South Korea Tel: (02) 6393 5790; (02) 6393 5792
Distributor for Old Farmer's Almanac
Membership(s): American Bar Association (ABA); American Booksellers Association (ABA); The American Library Association (ALA); Association of American Publishers (AAP); Association of American Publishers PreK-12 Learning Group; Association of Booksellers for Children; Association of Catholic Publishers Inc; Association of Test Publishers; The Children's Book Council (CBC); Dictionary Society of North America; National Catholic Education Association (NCEA); Society of Printers; Software & Information Industry Association (SIIA)
See separate listing for:
Heinemann
Houghton Mifflin Harcourt Assessments
Houghton Mifflin Harcourt K-12 Publishers
Math Solutions®

Houghton Mifflin Harcourt Assessments
Subsidiary of Houghton Mifflin Harcourt
One Pierce Place, Itasca, IL 60143
Tel: 630-467-7000 Toll Free Tel: 800-323-9540
Fax: 630-467-7192 (cust serv)
E-mail: assessmentsorders@hmhco.com
Web Site: www.hmhco.com/classroom-solutions/assessment
Key Personnel
Assessment Consultant Exec: Sue Rawls
E-mail: sue.rawls@hmhco.com
Founded: 1852 (as Riverside Press)
Develops & sells print & digital assessment tools for the education market.
ISBN Prefix(es): 978-0-8292
Number of titles published annually: 20 Print

Houghton Mifflin Harcourt K-12 Publishers
Division of Houghton Mifflin Harcourt
125 High St, Boston, MA 02110
SAN: 200-2388
Tel: 617-351-5020
E-mail: corporate.communications@hmhco.com
Web Site: www.hmhco.com/classroom (solutions); www.hmhco.com
K-12 textbooks, educational materials & services.
Imprints: Rigby; Saxon
Sales Office(s): 9205 Southpark Center Loop, Orlando, FL 32819 Toll Free Tel: 800-225-5425 Toll Free Fax: 800-269-5232 E-mail: k-12orders@hmhco.com

§Houghton Mifflin Harcourt Trade & Reference Division
Division of HarperCollins
125 High St, Boston, MA 02110
SAN: 200-2388
Tel: 617-351-5000
Web Site: www.hmhco.com
Key Personnel
Pres & CEO: John (Jack) J Lynch, Jr
Chief Equity & Inclusion Offr: Benita Flucker
Pres, Trade Publg Group: Ellen Archer
SVP & Trade Assoc Publr: Becky Saikia-Wilson
SVP & Exec Dir, Publicity: Lori Glazer
SVP, Mktg: Matt Schweitzer
VP & Creative Dir: Michaela Sullivan
VP, Mktg & Communs: Adriana Rizzo
VP, Prodn: Jill Lazer
Exec Dir, Mktg & Brand Strategy, Children's: Veronica Wasserman
Art Dir, Children's: Jennifer Keenan
Edit Dir: Millicent Bennett
Edit Dir, Rux Martin Books: Rux Martin
Mktg Dir, Children's: Ann Dye
Publicity Dir, Lifestyle: Shara Alexander
Assoc Art Dir: Whitney Leader-Picone; Brian Moore
Assoc Dir, Digital Mktg & Opers: Meghan Gocke
Assoc Dir, Subs Rts: Candace Finn
Asst Dir, Mktg: Julie Yeater
Sr Exec Ed: Deanne Urmy
Sr Exec Ed, Children's: Kate O'Sullivan
Exec Ed, CliffsNotes: Greg Tubach
Mng Ed, Children's: Mary Magrisso
Mng Ed, Digital Formats: Kristin Brodeur
Mng Ed, Publg Workflow Specialist: Rebecca Springer
Sr Ed: Rakia Clark
Sr Ed, Children's: Kait Feldman; Alessandra Preziosi
Ed, Children's: Lily Kessinger; Christine Krones
Assoc Ed: Tim Mudie
Assoc Ed, Children's: Harriet Low; Nicole Sclama
Ed-at-Large: David Rosenthal
Lead Designer: Lyndsay Calusine
Sr Mktg Designer, Children's: Abigail Stahlman
Designer, Children's: Alice Wang
Sr Mktg Mgr: Zoe Del Mar
Sr Publicity Mgr, Culinary & Lifestyle Books: Sari Kamin
Culinary Publicity Mgr: Brittany Edwards
Mgr, Children's Spec Sales: Melissa Cicchitelli
Sales Mgr, Specialty Retail & Intl: Olivia Wilson
Assoc Mktg Mgr, Lifestyle: Samantha Simon
Lead Prodn Coord, General Interest/Lifestyle: Kim Kiefer
Lead Sales Coord, Natl Accts: Jackie Sassa
Prodn Coord, Children's: Jillian Crab; Emma Grant
Digital Mktg & Publicity Specialist: Tara Sonin Schlesinger
Edit Assoc: Olivia Bartz
Edit Assoc, Children's: Gabriella Abbate; Eleanor Hinkle; Allison Vroegop
Mktg Opers Assoc: Benny Sisson
Sr Publicist: Emma Gordon
Publicist: Marissa Page
Publicist, Culinary & Lifestyle Books: Bridget Nocera
Publicity Asst: Emily Moon
Publicity Assoc, Children's: Anna Ravenelle
General literature, fiction, nonfiction, biography, autobiography, history, poetry & juvenile publications, dictionary, reference books, cookbooks & guidebooks.
ISBN Prefix(es): 978-0-89919; 978-0-395; 978-1-85697; 978-0-7534; 978-0-618; 978-1-88152
Number of titles published annually: 400 Print; 1 CD-ROM; 1 Online; 14 Audio
Total Titles: 3,300 Print; 2 CD-ROM; 2 Online; 110 Audio
Imprints: The American Heritage® Dictionaries; CliffsNotes™; Graphia; Harcourt Children's Books; HMH Audio; HMH Franchise; Houghton Mifflin Harcourt; Rux Martin Books; Sandpiper; Webster's New World® College Dictionary
Editorial Office(s): 3 Park Ave, New York, NY 10016
Distributed by Hachette Book Group Inc
Distributor for Larousse; Old Farmer's Almanac
Orders to: Houghton Mifflin Harcourt Trade Customer Service, 9205 Southpark Center Loop, 3rd fl, Orlando, FL 32819 Toll Free Tel: 800-225-3362 Toll Free Fax: 800-634-7568 E-mail: tradecustomerservice@hmhpub.com
Returns: Houghton Mifflin Harcourt, Trade Returns Dept, 2700 N Richardt Ave, Indianapolis, IN 46219

Distribution Center: Raincoast Books, 2440 Viking Way, Richmond, BC V6V 1N2, Canada *Tel:* 604-448-7100 *Fax:* 604-270-7161 *E-mail:* customerservice@raincoast.com

House to House Publications
Division of DOVE International
11 Toll Gate Rd, Lititz, PA 17543
Tel: 717-627-1996 *Toll Free Tel:* 800-848-5892 *Fax:* 717-627-4004
E-mail: h2hp@dcfi.org
Web Site: www.h2hp.com
Founded: 1997
Provide resources for the body of Christ worldwide.
ISBN Prefix(es): 978-1-886973
Number of titles published annually: 4 Print; 15 E-Book; 1 Audio
Total Titles: 63 Print; 5 Audio
Imprints: Partnership Publications

Housing Assistance Council
1025 Vermont Ave NW, Suite 606, Washington, DC 20005
Tel: 202-842-8600 *Fax:* 202-347-3441
E-mail: hac@ruralhome.org
Web Site: www.ruralhome.org
Key Personnel
Sr Policy Analyst: Leslie R Strauss
E-mail: leslie@ruralhome.org
Founded: 1971
Provides technical housing services, loans, program & policy assistance, training, research & information. Specialize in research reports, technical manuals & information pieces, all exclusively about low-income rural housing in the US.
ISBN Prefix(es): 978-1-58064
Number of titles published annually: 8 Print; 8 Online
Total Titles: 80 Print; 50 Online

§HRD Press
PO Box 2600, Amherst, MA 01004
SAN: 201-9213
Tel: 413-253-3488 *Toll Free Tel:* 800-822-2801
E-mail: info@hrdpress.com; customerservice@hrdpress.com
Web Site: www.hrdpress.com
Key Personnel
Publr: Robert W Carkhuff
Cust Rel Mgr: Sam MacLeod
Founded: 1972
Textbooks & off-the-shelf workshops on human resource development, management & training. Packaged training materials & assessments.
ISBN Prefix(es): 978-0-914234; 978-0-87425
Number of titles published annually: 25 Print
Total Titles: 600 Print; 200 E-Book
Foreign Rep(s): Eurospan Ltd (Europe); Management Learning Resources (UK)

Hudson Institute
1201 Pennsylvania Ave NW, 4th fl, Washington, DC 20004
Tel: 202-974-2400 *Fax:* 202-974-2410
E-mail: info@hudson.org
Web Site: www.hudson.org
Key Personnel
Mng Ed: Mark Melton
Asst Ed: David Altman *E-mail:* daltman@hudson.org
Founded: 1961
Books, monographs, briefing papers, newsletters.
ISBN Prefix(es): 978-1-55813
Number of titles published annually: 20 Print; 500 Online
Total Titles: 60 Print; 60 E-Book

§Human Kinetics Inc
1607 N Market St, Champaign, IL 61820
Tel: 217-351-5076 *Toll Free Tel:* 800-747-4457 *Fax:* 217-351-1549 (orders/cust serv)
E-mail: info@hkusa.com
Web Site: us.humankinetics.com
Key Personnel
Founder & Pres: Rainer Martens
CEO: Skip Maier
CFO: Tina Daniel
VP & Coach Educ Dir: Ted Miller
VP & Dir, Sales & Mktg: Steve Ruhlig
VP & HR Dir: Holly Gilly
VP, Trade & Prof Div Dir: Jason Muzinic
Academic Div Dir: Ray Vallese
Journals Div Dir: Kathleen Burgener
Founded: 1974
Scholarly books, college textbooks, continuing education courses & trade books in physical education, sports medicine & science, coaching, sport technique & fitness, courses.
ISBN Prefix(es): 978-0-931250; 978-0-87322; 978-0-88011; 978-0-918438; 978-0-7360; 978-0-912781; 978-1-4504; 978-1-4925
Number of titles published annually: 200 Print
Total Titles: 1,165 Print; 804 E-Book
Branch Office(s)
Human Kinetics Canada, 475 Devonshire Rd, Unit 100, Windsor, ON N8Y 2L5, Canada *Tel:* 519-971-9500 *Toll Free Tel:* 800-465-7301 *Fax:* 519-971-9797 *E-mail:* info@hkcanada.com *Web Site:* canada.humankinetics.com
Foreign Office(s): Human Kinetics UK, Europe & Middle East, 107 Bradford Rd, Stanningley, Leeds LS28 6AT, United Kingdom *Tel:* (0113) 255 5665 *Fax:* (0113) 255 5885 *E-mail:* hk@hkeurope.com
Foreign Rep(s): Academic & Professional Book Distributors (South Africa); Alkem Co (S) Pte Ltd (Bangladesh, Brunei, Laos, Malaysia, Singapore, Vietnam); China Publishers Services Ltd (China, Hong Kong, Macau); CRW Marketing Services for Publishers Inc (Philippines, Saipan); Latinfly LLC (Argentina, The Bahamas, Barbados, Bermuda, Bolivia, Brazil, Caribbean, Chile, Colombia, Costa Rica, Ecuador, El Salvador, Guyana, Honduras, Jamaica, Mexico, Nicaragua, Panama, Paraguay, Peru, Puerto Rico, Trinidad and Tobago, Uruguay, Venezuela, Virgin Islands); Mare Nostrum Group (Albania, Andorra, Angola, Armenia, Austria, Azerbaijan, Bahrain, Belarus, Belgium, Botswana, Bulgaria, Burkina Faso, Burundi, Cameroon, Canary Islands, Cape Verde, Central Africa, Chad, Comoros, Congo (Brazzaville), Croatia, Cyprus, Czechia, Denmark, Djibouti, Egypt, Equatorial Guinea, Estonia, Ethiopia, France, Gabon, The Gambia, Georgia, Germany, Ghana, Gibraltar, Greece, Guinea, Guinea-Bissau, Hungary, Iceland, India, Iran, Iraq, Ireland, Israel, Jordan, Kazakhstan, Kenya, Kuwait, Latvia, Lebanon, Lesotho, Liberia, Libya, Liechtenstein, Lithuania, Luxembourg, Madagascar, Malawi, Mali, Malta, Mauritania, Mauritius, Moldova, Monaco, Montenegro, Morocco, Mozambique, Namibia, Netherlands, Niger, Norway, Oman, Pakistan, Poland, Portugal, Qatar, Romania, Russia, Rwanda, San Marino, Sao Tome and Principe, Saudi Arabia, Senegal, Serbia, Sierra Leone, Slovakia, Slovenia, Somalia, Spain, Sri Lanka, Sudan, Swaziland, Sweden, Switzerland, Tanzania, Tasmania, Togo, Tunisia, Turkey, Uganda, Ukraine, United Arab Emirates, UK, West Bank, Yemen, Zambia, Zimbabwe); ChongHo Ra (North Korea, South Korea); Research Periodicals & Book Services (Tanzania); Wendy Simpson (Australia, Cook Islands, Fiji, Micronesia, New Zealand, Tonga); Unifacmanu Trading Co Ltd (Taiwan); The White Partnership (Indonesia, Thailand)

§Human Rights Watch
350 Fifth Ave, 34th fl, New York, NY 10118-3299
Tel: 212-290-4700 *Fax:* 212-736-1300
E-mail: hrwpress@hrw.org
Web Site: www.hrw.org
Key Personnel
Communs Dir: Emma Daly *Tel:* 212-216-1835
Sr Media Offr: Philippa Stewart
Founded: 1978
Nonprofit human rights organization publishing books & newsletters on human rights practices in more than 80 countries worldwide; documents arbitrary imprisonment, censorship, disappearances, due process of law, murder, prison conditions, torture, violations of laws of war & other abuses of internationally recognized human rights.
ISBN Prefix(es): 978-0-938579; 978-0-929692; 978-1-56432
Number of titles published annually: 67 Print
Total Titles: 1,000 Print; 60 E-Book
Imprints: Human Rights Watch Books

Humanix Books LLC
Division of Newsmax Media
805 Third Ave, New York, NY 10022
Toll Free Tel: 855-371-7810
E-mail: info@humanixbooks.com
Web Site: www.humanixbooks.com
Key Personnel
Deputy Publr: Keith Pfeffer *E-mail:* keithp@humanixbooks.com
Founded: 2012
Specialize in books on finance, investing, health, wellness, lifestyle, business, leadership, management, politics, current events, success, motivation, history & military.
ISBN Prefix(es): 978-1-63006
Number of titles published annually: 8 Print; 8 Online; 8 E-Book
Total Titles: 15 Print; 15 Online; 15 E-Book; 1 Audio
Orders to: Two Rivers Distribution, an Ingram brand, 1400 Broadway, Suite 520, New York, NY 10018 *Toll Free Tel:* 866-400-5351 *Web Site:* www.tworiversdistribution.com
Distribution Center: Two Rivers Distribution, an Ingram brand, 1400 Broadway, Suite 520, New York, NY 10018 *Toll Free Tel:* 866-400-5351 *Web Site:* www.tworiversdistribution.com
Membership(s): Association of American Publishers (AAP)

§Huntington Press Publishing
3665 Procyon St, Las Vegas, NV 89103-1907
Tel: 702-252-0655 *Toll Free Tel:* 800-244-2224 *Fax:* 702-252-0675
E-mail: editor@huntingtonpress.com
Web Site: www.huntingtonpress.com
Key Personnel
Publr: Anthony Curtis *E-mail:* publisher@huntingtonpress.com
Founded: 1983
Books relating to gambling & Las Vegas.
ISBN Prefix(es): 978-0-929712; 978-1-935396; 978-1-944877
Number of titles published annually: 5 Print
Total Titles: 145 Print; 200 Online; 85 E-Book

§Hutton Publishing
Subsidiary of Jones Hutton Literary Associates
12 Golden Hill St, Norwalk, CT 06854
Tel: 203-558-4478
E-mail: huttonbooks@hotmail.com
Key Personnel
Ed-in-Chief: Caroline DuBois Hutton
Sr Ed: Arthur B Layton *E-mail:* arthurllayton3@gmail.com
Founded: 2004
Digital publishing for Kindle, Nook, etc; print-on-demand. All books receive personal attention & are professionally designed & listed for distribution in the Ingram catalog, available through Amazon, B&N Online & local bookstores. Pro-

motion notes available for all Huttonelectronicpublishing.com authors. All royalties are split 50-50, author & publisher. Some books paid 100% by authors, others, by special arrangement with the publisher, at varying percentages subsidized by the publisher. Please inquire by e-mail for further information. Prize-winning illustrators available as needed.
This publisher has indicated that 100% of their product line is author subsidized.
ISBN Prefix(es): 978-0-9742894; 978-0-9785171
Number of titles published annually: 10 Print; 10 E-Book
Total Titles: 40 Print; 20 E-Book
Distribution Center: Lightning Source Inc, 1246 Heil Quaker Blvd, La Vergne, TN 37086

Ibex Publishers
PO Box 30087, Bethesda, MD 20824
SAN: 696-866X
Tel: 301-718-8188 *Toll Free Tel:* 888-718-8188 *Fax:* 301-907-8707
E-mail: info@ibexpub.com
Web Site: ibexpub.com
Key Personnel
Publr: Mr Farhad Shirzad *E-mail:* fs@ibex.net
Founded: 1979
English & Persian language books about Iran.
ISBN Prefix(es): 978-0-936347; 978-1-58814
Number of titles published annually: 30 Print
Total Titles: 600 Print; 3 CD-ROM; 5 Audio
Imprints: Ibex Press; Iranbooks Press
Distributor for Farhang Moaser

IBFD North America Inc (International Bureau of Fiscal Documentation)
Division of IBFD Foundation
8300 Boone Blvd, Suite 380, Vienna, VA 22182
Tel: 703-442-7757
E-mail: info@ibfd.org
Web Site: www.ibfd.org
Key Personnel
Regl Acct Mgr: Horacio Jarquin *E-mail:* h.jarquin@ibfd.org
Founded: 1938
International taxation & investment & tax law.
Number of titles published annually: 30 Print
Total Titles: 30 Print; 1 CD-ROM; 42 Online
Foreign Office(s): Reitlandpark 301, 1019 DW Amsterdam, Netherlands (headquarters) *Tel:* (020) 554 0100

ICMA, see International City/County Management Association (ICMA)

Idyll Arbor Inc
2432 39 St, Bedford, IN 47421
Tel: 812-675-6623
E-mail: sales@idyllarbor.com
Web Site: www.idyllarbor.com
Key Personnel
Co-Pres: Lori Barnes *E-mail:* lori@idyllarbor.com
Founded: 1984
Publish health care books, information for recreational therapists & activity directors & books on social issues. The Issues Press imprint covers important social issues such as addictions & health care for returning military personnel. Titles published under the Pine Winds Press imprint relate to discussions of the life force, including spiritual reality, Bigfoot, fairies & other strange phenomena. Anne Wyld is our new imprint which publishes young adult fiction.
ISBN Prefix(es): 978-1-882883; 978-0-937663; 978-1-930461; 978-1-61158
Number of titles published annually: 8 Print; 8 E-Book
Total Titles: 100 Print; 50 E-Book; 1 Audio
Imprints: Issues Press; Pine Winds Press; Anne Wyld

Foreign Rights: Columbine Communications (worldwide exc Canada & USA)
Membership(s): Book Publishers of the Northwest (BPNW); Independent Book Publishers Association (IBPA); Pacific Northwest Booksellers Association (PNBA)

§IEEE Computer Society
2001 "L" St NW, Suite 700, Washington, DC 20036-4928
SAN: 264-620X
Tel: 202-371-0101 *Toll Free Tel:* 800-678-4333 (memb info) *Fax:* 202-728-9614
E-mail: help@computer.org
Web Site: www.computer.org
Key Personnel
Publr: Robin Baldwin *E-mail:* rbaldwin@computer.org
Mgr, Mktg & Communs: Katherine Mansfield *E-mail:* k.mansfield@computer.org
Founded: 1980
Tutorials, reports, reprint collections, conference proceedings, textbooks & CD-ROMs.
ISBN Prefix(es): 978-0-8186; 978-0-7695
Number of titles published annually: 155 Print
Total Titles: 1,000 Print; 5 CD-ROM
Branch Office(s)
10662 Los Vaqueros Circle, Los Alamitos, CA 90720-1314 *Tel:* 714-821-8380 *Fax:* 714-821-4010
Foreign Office(s): KFK Bldg, 2-14-14 Minami-Aoyama, Minato-ku, Tokyo 107-0062, Japan *Tel:* (03) 3408 3118 *Fax:* (03) 3408 3553
E-mail: tokyo.ofc@computer.org

§IEEE Press
Division of Institute of Electrical & Electronics Engineers Inc (IEEE)
445 Hoes Lane, Piscataway, NJ 08854
Tel: 732-981-0060 *Fax:* 732-867-9946
E-mail: pressbooks@ieee.org (proposals & info)
Web Site: www.ieee.org/press
Key Personnel
Mng Ed: Vaishali Damle *Tel:* 732-465-6655 *E-mail:* v.damle@ieee.org
Founded: 1971
Professional books & texts in electrical & computer engineering, computer science, electrotechnology, general engineering, applied mathematics. Tutorials in technical subjects.
ISBN Prefix(es): 978-0-87942; 978-0-7803; 978-0-471
Number of titles published annually: 40 Print
Total Titles: 900 Print; 800 E-Book
Imprints: Wiley-IEEE Press
Distributed by John Wiley & Sons Inc
Foreign Rep(s): John Wiley & Sons Inc
Foreign Rights: John Wiley & Sons Inc
Membership(s): Association of American Publishers (AAP)

IET USA Inc
379 Thornall St, Edison, NJ 08837
Tel: 732-321-5575 *Fax:* 732-321-5702
E-mail: ietusa@theiet.org
Web Site: www.theiet.org
Key Personnel
VP & Gen Mgr: Michael Ornstein
Founded: 1871
Professional books, journals, magazines & conference proceedings in many areas of electrical & electronic engineering, including telecommunications, computing, power, control, radar, circuits, materials & more.
ISBN Prefix(es): 978-0-85296; 978-0-906048; 978-0-86341
Number of titles published annually: 30 Print
Total Titles: 500 Print; 300 E-Book
Imprints: IEE; Inspec; Peter Peregrinus Ltd
Foreign Office(s): The IET, Suite G, 10F, China Merchants Tower, No 118 Jianguo Rd, Chaoyang District, Beijing 100022, China

Tel: (010) 6566 4687 *E-mail:* china@theiet.org
Web Site: www.theiet.org.cn
IET Hong Kong, 4412-4413 Cosco Tower, 183 Queen's Rd Central, Hong Kong, Hong Kong *Tel:* 2778 1611 *Fax:* 2778 1711 *E-mail:* admin@theiet.org.hk
IET India, Unit No 405 & 406, 4th fl, West Wing, Raheja Towers, MG Rd, Bangalore 560 001, India *Tel:* (080) 4089 2222 *E-mail:* india@theiet.in *Web Site:* theiet.in
The Institution of Engineering & Technology, Michael Faraday House, 6 Hills Way, Stevenage, Herts SG1 2AY, United Kingdom (journal & magazine sales), Contact: Neil Dennis *Tel:* (01438) 313 311 *E-mail:* postmaster@theiet.org
Orders to: c/o Books International Inc, PO Box 605, Herndon, VA 20172 *Tel:* 703-661-1573 *Toll Free Tel:* 800-230-7286 (US & CN) *Fax:* 703-661-1501 *E-mail:* ieemail@presswarehouse.com
Distribution Center: c/o Books International Inc, PO Box 605, Herndon, VA 20172 *Tel:* 703-661-1500 *Fax:* 703-661-1501
Membership(s): Association of Learned & Professional Society Publishers (ALPSP); STM

IFPRI, see International Food Policy Research Institute

§Ignatius Press
Division of Guadalupe Associates Inc
1348 Tenth Ave, San Francisco, CA 94122-2304
SAN: 214-3887
Toll Free Tel: 800-651-1531 (orders); 888-615-3186 (cust serv) *Fax:* 415-387-0896
E-mail: info@ignatius.com
Web Site: www.ignatius.com
Key Personnel
Pres: Mark Brumley *E-mail:* mark@ignatius.com
Art Dir: Roxanne Lum *E-mail:* roxanne@ignatius.com
Mktg Dir: Anthony J Ryan *E-mail:* tony@ignatius.com
Ed: Fr Joseph Fessio SJ
Prodn Ed: Carolyn Lemon
Mktg Mgr: Eva Mutean *E-mail:* eva@ignatius.com
Foreign Rts: Penelope Boldrick *E-mail:* penelope@ignatius.com
Founded: 1978
ISBN Prefix(es): 978-0-89870; 978-1-58617; 978-1-62164; 978-1-68149
Number of titles published annually: 60 Print
Total Titles: 750 Print; 25 Audio
Distributor for Bethlehem Books; Veritas
Foreign Rep(s): Ancoh Enterprises (Nigeria); B Broughton Co Ltd (Canada); Freedom Publishing (Australia, New Zealand); Gracewing Publishing (Europe, UK); John XXIII Fellowship Co-op Ltd (Australia, New Zealand); St Andrew's Church Supply (Canada); Sunrise Marian Distribution (Canada); Veritas Publications (Ireland)

IHS Press, see Indiana Historical Society Press

IHS Press
222 W 21 St, Suite F-122, Norfolk, VA 23517
Toll Free Tel: 877-447-7737 *Toll Free Fax:* 877-447-7737
E-mail: query@ihspress.com; tradesales@ihspress.com (wholesale sales); order@ihspress.com; pr@ihspress.com
Web Site: www.ihspress.com
Founded: 2001
Social teachings of the Catholic church.
ISBN Prefix(es): 978-0-9714894; 978-0-9718286; 978-1-932528; 978-1-60570
Number of titles published annually: 12 Print; 12 E-Book
Total Titles: 42 Print; 42 E-Book

Imprints: Gates of Vienna Books
Distribution Center: Independent Publishers Group (IPG), 814 N Franklin St, Chicago, IL 60610

§Illinois State Museum Society
Affiliate of Illinois State Museum
502 S Spring St, Springfield, IL 62706-5000
Tel: 217-782-7386 *Fax:* 217-782-1254
E-mail: subscriptions@museum.state.il.us
Web Site: www.illinoisstatemuseum.org
Key Personnel
Museum Dir: Cinnamon Catlin-Legutko
Mng Ed: Andy Hanson *Tel:* 217-782-6700
 E-mail: andrew.hanson@illinois.gov
Founded: 1877
Softcover texts, quarterly magazines, quarterly newsletters, quarterly calendars of events & activities brochures, educational posters & CD-ROM.
ISBN Prefix(es): 978-0-89792
Number of titles published annually: 4 Print
Total Titles: 1 CD-ROM

§Illuminating Engineering Society of North America (IES)
120 Wall St, 17th fl, New York, NY 10005-4001
Tel: 212-248-5000 *Fax:* 212-248-5017; 212-248-5018
E-mail: ies@ies.org
Web Site: www.ies.org
Key Personnel
Mktg Mgr: Clayton Gordon *Tel:* 212-248-5000 ext 110 *E-mail:* cgordon@ies.org
Founded: 1906
ISBN Prefix(es): 978-0-87995
Number of titles published annually: 10 Print; 1 E-Book
Total Titles: 90 Print; 2 E-Book
Distributor for Taylor & Francis; Techstreet

§ImaJinn Books
Imprint of BelleBooks
PO Box 300921, Memphis, TN 38130
E-mail: bellebooks@bellebooks.com
Web Site: www.imajinnbooks.com
Founded: 1998
Specialize in publishing & selling paranormal romance, urban fantasy, regency romance & erotica.
ISBN Prefix(es): 978-1-893896; 978-0-9759653; 978-1-933417; 978-1-61026; 978-1-61194
Number of titles published annually: 25 Print
Total Titles: 150 Print
Membership(s): The Association of Publishers for Special Sales (APSS); Independent Book Publishers Association (IBPA)

IMF Publishing Division, see International Monetary Fund (IMF), Editorial & Publications Division

Immedium
Imprint of Immedium Inc
535 Rockdale Dr, San Francisco, CA 94127
Mailing Address: PO Box 31846, San Francisco, CA 94131
Tel: 415-452-8546 *Fax:* 360-937-6272
E-mail: orders@immedium.com; sales@immedium.com
Web Site: www.immedium.com
Key Personnel
Publr: Oliver Chin *E-mail:* o.chin@comcast.net
Ed: Don Menn
Acqs Ed: Amy Ma
Founded: 2005
Publish wonderfully illustrated children's picture books, Asian American topics & contemporary arts & culture.
ISBN Prefix(es): 978-1-59702

Number of titles published annually: 3 Print; 3 Online; 3 E-Book
Total Titles: 50 Print; 50 Online; 50 E-Book; 10 Audio
Foreign Rights: DropCap (worldwide); HarperCollins UK (UK & Commonwealth)
Orders to: Consortium Book Sales & Distribution, The Keg House, Suite 101, 34 13 Ave NE, Minneapolis, MN 55413-1007 *Tel:* 612-746-2600 *Toll Free Tel:* 866-400-5351 (cust serv, Jackson, TN) *E-mail:* cbsdinfo@ingramcontent.com *Web Site:* www.cbsd.com SAN: 200-6049
Returns: Consortium Book Sales & Distribution, The Keg House, Suite 101, 34 13 Ave NE, Minneapolis, MN 55413-1007 *Tel:* 612-746-2600 *Toll Free Tel:* 866-400-5351 (cust serv, Jackson, TN) *E-mail:* cbsdinfo@ingramcontent.com *Web Site:* www.cbsd.com SAN: 200-6049
Shipping Address: Consortium Book Sales & Distribution, The Keg House, Suite 101, 34 13 Ave NE, Minneapolis, MN 55413-1007 *Tel:* 612-746-2600 *Toll Free Tel:* 866-400-5351 (cust serv, Jackson, TN) *E-mail:* cbsdinfo@ingramcontent.com *Web Site:* www.cbsd.com SAN: 200-6049
Warehouse: Consortium Book Sales & Distribution, The Keg House, Suite 101, 34 13 Ave NE, Minneapolis, MN 55413-1007 *Tel:* 612-746-2600 *Toll Free Tel:* 866-400-5351 (cust serv, Jackson, TN) *E-mail:* cbsdinfo@ingramcontent.com *Web Site:* www.cbsd.com SAN: 200-6049
Distribution Center: Consortium Book Sales & Distribution, The Keg House, Suite 101, 34 13 Ave NE, Minneapolis, MN 55413-1007 *Tel:* 612-746-2600 *Toll Free Tel:* 866-400-5351 (cust serv, Jackson, TN) *E-mail:* cbsdinfo@ingramcontent.com *Web Site:* www.cbsd.com SAN: 200-6049

§Impact Publications/Development Concepts Inc
7820 Sudley Rd, Suite 100, Manassas, VA 20109
Tel: 703-361-7300 *Toll Free Tel:* 800-361-1055 (cust serv) *Fax:* 703-335-9486
E-mail: query2@impactpublications.com
Web Site: www.impactpublications.com
Key Personnel
Pres & Admin: Ruth Sanders, PhD
Founded: 1982
Career, re-entry & education publications.
ISBN Prefix(es): 978-1-57023; 978-0-942710
Number of titles published annually: 18 Print
Total Titles: 167 Print
Distribution Center: National Book Network (NBN), 4501 Forbes Blvd, Suite 200, Lanham, MD 20706 *Tel:* 301-459-3366 *Toll Free Tel:* 800-462-6420 *Fax:* 301-429-5746 *Toll Free Fax:* 800-338-4550 *E-mail:* customercare@nbnbooks.com *Web Site:* www.nbnbooks.com

In the Garden Publishing
Division of What Would Love Do Int'l LLC
6460 E Grant Rd, No 31944, Tucson, AZ 85715
Mailing Address: PO Box 31944, Tucson, AZ 85751 SAN: 920-3389
Tel: 937-317-0859
E-mail: admin@inthegardenpublishing.com
Web Site: www.inthegardenpublishing.com
Key Personnel
Publr: Christine Horner
Founded: 2012
Discover your inner guru. Conscious community & brilliant minds unite. Together, what can we create?
ISBN Prefix(es): 978-0-9855314; 978-0-9888333
Number of titles published annually: 5 Print; 5 Online; 5 E-Book
Total Titles: 9 Print; 15 Online; 8 E-Book
Imprints: Yugen Press (fiction)

§Incentive Publications by World Book
180 N LaSalle St, Suite 900, Chicago, IL 60101
Toll Free Tel: 800-967-5325; 800-975-3250; 888-482-9764 (trade dept) *Toll Free Fax:* 888-922-3766
E-mail: tradeorders@worldbook.com
Web Site: www.incentivepublications.com
Founded: 1968 (acquired by World Book 2013)
Preschool through high school supplementary educational materials for students, parents & teachers.
ISBN Prefix(es): 978-0-913916; 978-0-86530
Number of titles published annually: 25 Print
Total Titles: 425 Print; 1 CD-ROM

§Independent Institute
100 Swan Way, Oakland, CA 94621-1428
Tel: 510-632-1366 *Fax:* 510-568-6040
Web Site: www.independent.org
Key Personnel
Chmn & CEO: Mary L G Theroux
Pres: Graham H Walker
Pubns Coun: Christopher B Briggs
 E-mail: cbriggs@independent.org
Dir, Media Rel: Robert Ade *E-mail:* rade@independent.org
Dir, Sales: Matthew Maschino
 E-mail: mmaschino@independent.org
Mng Ed: Kathleen Curran *E-mail:* kcurran@independent.org
Mktg Mgr: Shruti Kothiwal *E-mail:* skothiwal@independent.org
Founded: 1986
Nonprofit research & publication. Branch office in Washington, DC.
ISBN Prefix(es): 978-0-945999; 978-1-59813
Number of titles published annually: 6 Print; 6 E-Book
Total Titles: 110 Print; 90 E-Book
Branch Office(s)
1455 Pennsylvania Ave NW, Suite 400, Washington, DC 20004
Foreign Rights: Graal Literary Agency (Eastern Europe)
Distribution Center: Independent Publishers Group (IPG), 814 N Franklin St, Chicago, IL 60610 *Toll Free Tel:* 800-888-4741 *E-mail:* orders@ipgbook.com *Web Site:* www.ipgbook.com
Membership(s): Association of American Publishers (AAP); Independent Book Publishers Association (IBPA)

Indiana Historical Society Press
450 W Ohio St, Indianapolis, IN 46202-3269
SAN: 201-5234
Tel: 317-232-1882; 317-234-0026 (orders); 317-234-2716 (edit) *Toll Free Tel:* 800-447-1830 (orders) *Fax:* 317-234-0562 (orders); 317-233-0857 (edit)
E-mail: ihspress@indianahistory.org; orders@indianahistory.org (orders)
Web Site: www.indianahistory.org; shop.indianahistory.org (orders)
Key Personnel
Pres & CEO: Jody Blankenship
Sr Ed: Ray Boomhower *E-mail:* rboomhower@indianahistory.og
Natl Sales Coord: Becke Bolinger *Tel:* 317-234-3683 *E-mail:* bbolinger@indianahistory.org
Founded: 1886
Books, journals & newsletters on Indiana history, including an illustrated history magazine & a family history magazine. Also offers videos, recordings, prints, note cards & other gift items.
ISBN Prefix(es): 978-0-87195
Number of titles published annually: 4 Print; 1 Online; 4 E-Book
Total Titles: 100 Print; 1 Online; 3 Audio

U.S. PUBLISHERS

Indiana University African Studies Program
Indiana University, 355 N Eagleson Ave, Rm GA 3072, Bloomington, IN 47405-1105
Tel: 812-855-8284 *Fax:* 812-855-6734
E-mail: afrist@indiana.edu
Web Site: www.indiana.edu/~afrist; www.go.iu.edu/afrist
Key Personnel
Dir: Beth Samuelson *E-mail:* blsamuel@iu.edu
Assoc Dir: Tavy Aherne *E-mail:* taherne@indiana.edu
Founded: 1965
Monograph & working papers, humanities, interdisciplinary study of Africa.
ISBN Prefix(es): 978-0-941934
Number of titles published annually: 50 Print
Total Titles: 52 Print

§Indiana University Press
Off of Scholarly Publg, Herman B Wells Library 350, 1320 E Tenth St, Bloomington, IN 47405-3907
SAN: 202-5647
Tel: 812-855-8817 *Fax:* 812-855-7931; 812-855-8507
E-mail: iupress@indiana.edu
Web Site: iupress.org
Key Personnel
Dir, IU Press & Digital Publg: Gary Dunham *Tel:* 812-855-4773 *E-mail:* dunhamg@indiana.edu
Assoc Dir: Dave Hulsey *Tel:* 812-855-6553 *E-mail:* hulseyd@indiana.edu
Dir, Opers & Electronic Publg: Michael Regoli *Tel:* 812-855-3830 *E-mail:* regoli@indiana.edu
Acq Ed: Allison Chaplin *Tel:* 812-855-5261 *E-mail:* abchapli@iu.edu; Bethany Mowry *Tel:* 812-855-3194 *E-mail:* brmowry@iu.edu
Busn Mgr: Brent Starr *Tel:* 812-855-5366 *E-mail:* brstarr@indiana.edu
Exhibits & Journals, Mktg Mgr: Jesse Balzer *E-mail:* jebalzer@indiana.edu
Mgr, Accts Receivable: Kimberly Bower *Tel:* 812-855-4134 *E-mail:* kchilder@indiana.edu
Mktg Mgr: Samantha (Sami) Heffner *Tel:* 812-855-9449 *E-mail:* srheffne@iu.edu; Stephen Williams *Tel:* 812-855-6314 *E-mail:* smw9@indiana.edu
Soc Media Mgr: Alyssa Henning *Tel:* 812-855-8287 *E-mail:* anhennin@iu.edu
Founded: 1950
Trade & scholarly nonfiction; film & media studies, literature & music, African studies, backlist, classical studies, contemporary issues, cultural studies, folklore, international studies, Jewish studies, journals, Middle East studies, paleontology, philanthropy, politics/political science, railroads & transportation, Russian studies.
ISBN Prefix(es): 978-0-253; 978-1-68435 (Red Lightning Books)
Number of titles published annually: 100 Print; 2 CD-ROM; 5 Online; 100 E-Book; 15 Audio
Total Titles: 3,672 Print; 8 CD-ROM; 2,500 E-Book
Imprints: Quarry Books (regional imprint for Midwest)
Divisions: Red Lightning Books
Foreign Rights: Agencia Literaria Carmen Balcells SA (Maribel Luque) (Spain); Bookman Literary Agency (Ib H Lauritzen) (Denmark); English Agency Japan Co Ltd (Tsutomu Yawata) (Japan); The Deborah Harris Agency (Efrat Lev) (Israel); The Italian Literary Agency Srl (Maria Stefania Fietta) (Italy); Liepman AG (Marc Koralnik) (Germany); La Nouvelle Agence (Anne Maizeret) (France); O A Literary Agency (Michael Avramides) (Greece)
Distribution Center: HFS (Hopkins Fulfillment Services), 2715 N Charles St, Baltimore, MD 21218 *Tel:* 410-516-6965 Toll *Free Tel:* 800-537-5487 *Fax:* 410-516-6998
E-mail: hsfcustserv@jh.edu *Web Site:* hfs.jhu.edu

§Industrial Press Inc
One Chestnut St, South Norwalk, CT 06854
Mailing Address: PO Box 320, South Norwalk, CT 06856
Tel: 203-956-5593 *Toll Free Tel:* 888-528-7852 (ext 1, cust serv)
E-mail: info@industrialpress.com
Web Site: books.industrialpress.com; ebooks.industrialpress.com
Key Personnel
Owner & Pres: Alex Luchars *E-mail:* aluchars@industrialpress.com
Cont: Vanisse Mascia *E-mail:* vmascia@industrialpress.com
Publr: Judy Bass *E-mail:* jbass@industrialpress.com
Mng Ed & Ed, Machinery's Handbook: Laura Brengelman *E-mail:* lbrengelman@industrialpress.com
Sales Assoc: Jana Rahrig *E-mail:* jrahrig@industrialpress.com
Founded: 1883
Scientific & technical handbooks, professional & reference books for engineering, technology, manufacturing & education.
ISBN Prefix(es): 978-0-8311
Number of titles published annually: 20 Print; 20 E-Book
Total Titles: 320 Print; 30 CD-ROM; 260 E-Book
Foreign Rep(s): Accelerize Academy (India); Amazon Australia (Australia, New Zealand); Booktopia (Australia, New Zealand); Infotech Standards India (India); Ingram Publisher Services (Europe, Middle East); Login (Canada)
Membership(s): Association of American Publishers (AAP)

Information Age Publishing Inc
PO Box 79049, Charlotte, NC 28271-7047
Tel: 704-752-9125 *Fax:* 704-752-9113
E-mail: infoage@infoagepub.com
Web Site: www.infoagepub.com
Key Personnel
Pres & Publr: George F Johnson *E-mail:* george@infoagepub.com
Founded: 1999
Social science publisher of academic & scholarly book series & journals. Specialties include black studies, educational technology & leadership titles.
Information Age is a no returns publisher.
ISBN Prefix(es): 978-1-930608; 978-1-931576; 978-1-59311; 978-1-60752; 978-1-61735; 978-1-62396; 978-1-68123
Number of titles published annually: 240 Print; 120 E-Book
Total Titles: 3,500 Print; 1,500 E-Book
Foreign Rep(s): Co Info Pty Ltd (Australia); The Eurospan Group (Europe); Login Canada (Canada); Maruzen Co Ltd (Japan); Sara Books Pvt Ltd (India); Taylor & Francis Asia Pacific (Mohamed Feroz) (Indonesia, Singapore); Taylor & Francis Asia Pacific (David Yeong) (Brunei, Malaysia); Taylor & Francis Asia Pacific (Barry Clark) (South Korea); Taylor & Francis Asia Pacific (Chris Ye) (Shanghai, China); Taylor & Francis Asia Pacific (Cherry Wang) (Guangdong, China); Taylor & Francis Asia Pacific (Jeffrey Lim) (China, Hong Kong, Indochina, Philippines, Taiwan, Thailand, Vietnam)
Foreign Rights: International Publishers Representatives (IPR) (worldwide)

§Information Gatekeepers Inc (IGI)
Division of IGI Group Inc
PO Box 606, Winchester, MA 01890
Tel: 617-782-5033 *Fax:* 617-507-8338
E-mail: info@igigroup.com
Web Site: www.igigroup.com
Key Personnel
Chief Analyst & Ed-in-Chief: Dr Hui Pan *E-mail:* hpan@igigroup.com
Mng Ed: Bev Wilson *E-mail:* editor@igigroup.com
Founded: 1977
Fiber optics, optical networks, wireless, ATM, XDSL & telecommunications, trade shows, conferences, newsletters, market studies & consulting.
ISBN Prefix(es): 978-0-918435; 978-1-56851
Number of titles published annually: 35 Print; 100 CD-ROM; 20 E-Book
Total Titles: 540 Print; 100 CD-ROM; 50 E-Book
Foreign Rep(s): Children Magazine Services (England); Global Information Inc (Japan); Investment Publications Information Service (Australia); Overseas Information Center (OIC) (South Korea)
Membership(s): Institute of Electrical and Electronics Engineers Inc (IEEE); Optica; Plastic Optical Fiber Trade Organization (POFTO)

§Information Today, Inc
143 Old Marlton Pike, Medford, NJ 08055-8750
Tel: 609-654-6266 *Toll Free Tel:* 800-300-9868 (cust serv) *Fax:* 609-654-4309
E-mail: custserv@infotoday.com
Web Site: informationtodayinc.com
Key Personnel
Pres & CEO: Thomas H Hogan
VP, Mktg & Busn Devt: Thomas Hogan, Jr
VP, IT: Bill Spence *E-mail:* spence@infotoday.com
Dir of Sales, Lib & Info Div: LaShawn Fugate *E-mail:* lashawn@infotoday.com
Prodn Mgr: Tiffany Chamenko *E-mail:* tchamenko@infotoday.com
Content Mktg & Exhibits Mgr: Robert Colding *E-mail:* rcolding@infotoday.com
Founded: 1980
Publisher specializing in: Books, directories, newspapers, journals, newsletters, conferences & information services for users & producers of digital information content & technologies, including professionals in the library, publishing, online information, K-12 education, business research & IT, knowledge management, customer relationship management, speech technology & streaming media industries. ITI's reference division is the publisher of *LMP, ILMP, American Book Trade Directory, Library and Book Trade Almanac* & other professional reference titles.
ISBN Prefix(es): 978-0-938734; 978-1-57387; 978-0-910965
Number of titles published annually: 28 Print; 15 E-Book
Total Titles: 460 Print; 230 E-Book
Imprints: CyberAge Books (books for tech-savvy consumers & business information users; nationally distributed to the book trade by IPG); Information Today Books (practical books for library & information professionals)
Membership(s): Association for Independent Information Professionals; Mystery Writers of America (MWA); Special Libraries Association (SLA)

Infosources Publishing
140 Norma Rd, Teaneck, NJ 07666

Tel: 201-836-7072
Web Site: www.infosourcespub.com
Key Personnel
Publr & Ed: Arlene L Eis
Founded: 1981
Legal reference books, newsletters, online databases. Publisher of *The Informed Librarian Online*.
ISBN Prefix(es): 978-0-939486; 978-0-9842928; 978-0-9842214
Number of titles published annually: 3 Print; 1 Online
Total Titles: 6 Print

Inner Traditions International Ltd
One Park St, Rochester, VT 05767
Mailing Address: PO Box 388, Rochester, VT 05767
Tel: 802-767-3174 Toll Free Tel: 800-246-8648 Fax: 802-767-3726
E-mail: customerservice@InnerTraditions.com
Web Site: www.InnerTraditions.com
Key Personnel
Pres: Ehud C Sperling E-mail: prez@InnerTraditions.com
VP, Opers: Diane Shepard E-mail: dianes@InnerTraditions.com
Ed-in-Chief: Jeanie Levitan E-mail: jeaniel@InnerTraditions.com
Acqs Ed: Jon Graham E-mail: jong@InnerTraditions.com
Curator, Sacred Planet Books: Richard Grossinger
Audiobook Mgr: Mahar Sperling E-mail: mahars@InnerTraditions.com
Print Mgr: Jon Desautels E-mail: jond@InnerTraditions.com
Foreign Rts & Perms: Maria Loftus E-mail: marial@InnerTraditions.com
Publicity: Manzanita Carpenter E-mail: manzanitac@InnerTraditions.com
Sales & Mktg: Andrea Raymond E-mail: andyr@InnerTraditions.com
Spec Sales: Jessica Arsenault E-mail: jessa@InnerTraditions.com
Founded: 1975
Nonfiction cloth & quality trade paperbacks; audio cassettes & CDs (ethnic music & meditation aids).
ISBN Prefix(es): 978-0-89281; 978-1-899171; 978-1-84409; 978-1-59477; 978-1-62055; 978-0-905249; 978-1-64411
Number of titles published annually: 76 Print; 72 E-Book; 60 Audio
Total Titles: 1,599 Print; 1,217 E-Book; 128 Audio
Imprints: Bear & Co Inc; Bear Cub Books; Bindu Books; Destiny Books; Destiny Recordings; Earthdancer Books; Findhorn Press; Healing Arts Press; Inner Traditions; Inner Traditions Audio; Inner Traditions en Espanol; Inner Traditions India; Park Street Press
Foreign Rights: Akcali Copyright Agency (Turkey); Big Apple Agency Inc (China, Taiwan); Blackbird Literary Agency (Netherlands); The Book Publishers' Association of Israel, International Promotion & Literary Rights Dept (Israel); Graal Literary Agency (Poland); Ilidio Matos Agency (Portugal); International Editors' Co - Yanez Agencia Literaria (Spain); The Italian Literary Agency Srl (Italy); Simona Kessler International Copyright Agency Ltd (Romania); Alexander Korzhenevski Agency (Russia); George Millett Agency (Brazil); Andrew Nurnberg Associates (Baltic States, Bulgaria, Czechia, Hungary); Plima doo (Croatia); Read n Right Agency (Greece); Thomas Schlueck GmbH (Germany); Agence Schweiger (France); Tuttle-Mori Agency Inc (Indonesia, Japan, Thailand); Eric Yang Agency (South Korea)
Orders to: Inner Traditions International - Bear & Co, c/o Simon & Schuster, LLC, 100 Front St, Riverside, NJ 08075 Toll Free Tel: 800-223-2336 Toll Free Fax: 800-943-9831 E-mail: purchaseorders@simonandschuster.com
Returns: Simon & Schuster, LLC, c/o Jacobson Logistics, 4406 Industrial Park Rd, Bldg 7, Camp Hill, PA 17011 (truckload shipments must call for an appt: 800-967-3914 ext 5318)
Warehouse: Inner Traditions International - Bear & Co, c/o Simon & Schuster, LLC, 100 Front St, Riverside, NJ 08075 Toll Free Tel: 800-943-9831 E-mail: purchaseorders@simonandschuster.com
See separate listing for:
Bear & Co Inc

The Innovation Press
7511 Greenwood Ave N, No 4132, Seattle, WA 98103
Tel: 360-870-9988
E-mail: info@theinnovationpress.com
Web Site: www.theinnovationpress.com
Key Personnel
Publr: Asia Citro
Founded: 2015
We publish unique, creative books (often with a STEM-focus) for kids PreK-grade 6.
ISBN Prefix(es): 978-1-943147; 978-1-959244
Number of titles published annually: 5 Print; 3 E-Book
Total Titles: 14 Print; 7 E-Book
Foreign Rep(s): Michael Abbott (Africa, Europe, Middle East); Jason Howell (Canada); Suk Lee (Asia); Nella Soeterboek (Australia); James Wickham (UK)
Foreign Rights: Kaplan/DeFiore Rights (Linda Kaplan) (worldwide)
Warehouse: Baker & Taylor Publisher Services (BTPS), 30 Amberwood Pkwy, Ashland, OH 44805 Toll Free Tel: 888-814-0208 Web Site: www.btpubservices.com
Distribution Center: Baker & Taylor Publisher Services (BTPS), 30 Amberwood Pkwy, Ashland, OH 44805 Toll Free Tel: 888-814-0208 Web Site: www.btpubservices.com
Membership(s): The Children's Book Council (CBC); Pacific Northwest Booksellers Association (PNBA)

Insight Editions
800 "A" St, San Rafael, CA 94901
Tel: 415-526-1370 Toll Free Tel: 800-809-3792 Toll Free Fax: 866-509-0515
E-mail: info@insighteditions.com; marketing@insighteditions.com
Web Site: insighteditions.com
Key Personnel
Publr & CEO: Raoul Goff
Publr & VP: Vanessa Lopez
CFO: Simon Fraser
Edit Dir, Weldon Owen International & Mandala Earth: Katie Killebrew
Publg Dir, Gaming: Mike Degler
Publg Dir, Insight Gift, Lifestyle & Entertainment: Jamie Thompson
Head, Global Sales & Mktg: Maha Khalil
Exec Ed, Weldon Owen: Edward Ash-Milby
Mng Ed: Maria Spano
Asst Ed: Sadie Lowry
Sales Mgr: Jacqui Goff E-mail: j.goff@insighteditions.com
Trade Sales Mgr: Jeff Barton
Assoc Mgr, Mktg: Aliya Burke
Sr Sales Coord: Kristi Visser
Prodn Assoc: Tiffani Patterson
Mktg & Publicity Asst: Yasuaki Daito
Founded: 2000
Renowned for creating beautiful, innovative books that excel in the marketplace. Insight Editions brings the vision & style of high-end illustrated books to the realm of the arts & entertainment.
ISBN Prefix(es): 978-1-933784
Number of titles published annually: 200 Print
Total Titles: 3,000 Print
Imprints: Mandala Earth; Reinhart Pop-Up Studio
Subsidiaries: Weldon Owen International
Foreign Office(s): 66 Old Compton St, London W1D 4UH, United Kingdom, Subs Rts Mgr: Isabel Miller
Distributed by Simon & Schuster, LLC
Distribution Center: National Book Travelers
See separate listing for:
Mandala Earth

Institute of Continuing Legal Education
1020 Greene St, Ann Arbor, MI 48109-1444
Tel: 734-764-0533 Toll Free Tel: 877-229-4350 Fax: 734-763-2412 Toll Free Fax: 877-229-4351
E-mail: icle@umich.edu
Web Site: www.icle.org
Key Personnel
Dir: David R Watson
Educ Dir: Jeffrey E Kirkey
Founded: 1959
Michigan law books in print & online.
ISBN Prefix(es): 978-0-88288
Number of titles published annually: 23 Print
Total Titles: 58 Print; 56 Online
Imprints: ICLE

§Institute of Environmental Sciences & Technology - IEST
1827 Walden Office Sq, Suite 400, Schaumburg, IL 60173
Tel: 847-981-0100 Fax: 847-981-4130
E-mail: information@iest.org
Web Site: www.iest.org
Key Personnel
Exec Dir: Angela McKay Tel: 847-981-0100 ext 6010 E-mail: executive@iest.org
Mgr, Tech Progs: Jennifer Sklena Tel: 847-981-0100 ext 6011 E-mail: technicaldept@iest.org
Coord, Membership & Acctg: Mara Douvris Tel: 847-981-0100 ext 6109 E-mail: membershipdept@iest.org
Coord, Educ & Meetings: Heather Wooden Tel: 847-981-0100 ext 6014 E-mail: education@iest.org
Asst, Memb & Corp Rel: Susan Stamatkin Tel: 847-981-0100 ext 6015 E-mail: customerservice@iest.org
Communs & Mktg: Heather Swink E-mail: communications@iest.org
Corp Growth & Devt: Christine Davis Tel: 224-875-6112 E-mail: marketing@iest.org
Founded: 1953
A multidisciplinary, international society whose members are recognized worldwide for their contributions to the environmental sciences in the area of contamination control & cleanrooms; environmental testing; or nanotechnology facilities.
ISBN Prefix(es): 978-0-915414; 978-1-877862; 978-0-9747313; 978-0-9787868; 978-0-9841330; 978-1-937280
Number of titles published annually: 3 Print; 1 CD-ROM; 3 Online
Total Titles: 75 Print; 26 CD-ROM; 48 Online

Institute of Governmental Studies
Subsidiary of University of California, Berkeley
109 Moses Hall, No 2370, Berkeley, CA 94720-2370
Tel: 510-642-1428
E-mail: igspress@berkeley.edu
Web Site: www.igs.berkeley.edu
Key Personnel
Dir, Pubns: Ethan Rarick E-mail: erarick@berkeley.edu
Pubns Ed: Maria Wolf E-mail: mariaw@berkeley.edu
Public policy issues.
ISBN Prefix(es): 978-0-87772
Number of titles published annually: 6 Print
Total Titles: 54 Print

U.S. PUBLISHERS

§Institute of Jesuit Sources (IJS)
Boston College Institute for Advanced Jesuit Studies, 140 Commonwealth Ave, Chestnut Hill, MA 02467
Tel: 617-552-2568 *Fax:* 617-552-2575
E-mail: jesuitsources@bc.edu
Web Site: jesuitsources.bc.edu
Key Personnel
Dir: Fr Casey Beaumier
Founded: 1961
Books on history & spirituality of the society of Jesus (Jesuits) translated from non-English sources & originally in English.
ISBN Prefix(es): 978-0-912422; 978-1-880810; 978-1-947617; 978-0-9972823
Number of titles published annually: 8 Print
Total Titles: 150 Print; 1 CD-ROM

Institute of Police Technology & Management (IPTM)
Division of University of North Florida
12000 Alumni Dr, Jacksonville, FL 32224-2678
Tel: 904-620-4786 *Fax:* 904-620-2453
E-mail: info@iptm.org
Web Site: iptm.unf.edu
Key Personnel
Dir: Cameron Pucci *E-mail:* cpucci@unf.edu
Assoc Dir: Donnie Barker *E-mail:* dbarker@unf.edu
Founded: 1980
In-service training for law enforcement, civilian personnel; marketing of publications, templates & videos. Specialize in traffic crash investigation & reconstruction; law enforcement management & supervision; criminal investigation; forensic technology; DUI & drug law enforcement; radar/laser speed enforcement; gangs & other specialized subjects.
ISBN Prefix(es): 978-1-884566
Number of titles published annually: 7 Print; 2 CD-ROM
Total Titles: 65 Print; 6 CD-ROM
Foreign Rep(s): Paul Feenan (Australia, South Pacific)
Foreign Rights: Pacific Traffic Education Centre (Canada)

The Institutes™
720 Providence Rd, Suite 100, Malvern, PA 19355-3433
Tel: 610-644-2100 *Toll Free Tel:* 800-644-2101
Fax: 610-640-9576
E-mail: customerservice@theinstitutes.org
Web Site: www.theinstitutes.org
Key Personnel
Pres & CEO: Peter Miller
Property-casualty continuing insurance education.
ISBN Prefix(es): 978-0-89463; 978-0-89462
Number of titles published annually: 12 Print
Total Titles: 120 Print

The Institution of Engineering & Technology, see IET USA Inc

Inter-American Development Bank
Division of Multilateral Development Bank
1300 New York Ave NW, Washington, DC 20577
Tel: 202-623-1000 *Fax:* 202-623-3096
E-mail: pic@iadb.org
Web Site: publications.iadb.org
Key Personnel
Pres: Luis Alberto Moreno
EVP: Julie T Katzman
Founded: 1959
Economic development in Latin America & the Caribbean.
ISBN Prefix(es): 978-0-940602; 978-1-886938; 978-1-931003; 978-1-59782
Number of titles published annually: 30 Print
Total Titles: 160 Print
Distributed by Johns Hopkins University Press

§Inter-University Consortium for Political & Social Research (ICPSR)
Affiliate of University of Michigan Institute for Social Research
330 Packard St, Ann Arbor, MI 48104
Mailing Address: PO Box 1248, Ann Arbor, MI 48106-1248
Tel: 734-647-5000; 734-647-2200 *Fax:* 734-647-8200
E-mail: icpsr-help@umich.edu
Web Site: www.icpsr.umich.edu
Key Personnel
Dir: Maggie Levenstein *Tel:* 734-615-8400
  E-mail: maggiel@umich.edu
Assoc Dir: J Trent Alexander *Tel:* 734-647-7736
  E-mail: jtalex@umich.edu
Asst Dir & Ctr Admin: John Lemmer
  E-mail: jwlemmer@umich.edu
Founded: 1962
Provides access to social science data collections & documentation. Training on quantitative methods & data management, data sharing services.
ISBN Prefix(es): 978-0-89138
Number of titles published annually: 300 Online
Total Titles: 7,500 Online

Intercultural Development Research Association (IDRA)
5815 Callaghan Rd, Suite 101, San Antonio, TX 78228
Tel: 210-444-1710 *Fax:* 210-444-1714
E-mail: contact@idra.org
Web Site: www.idra.org
Key Personnel
Pres & CEO: Celina Moreno
Dir, Communs: Christie Goodman
Founded: 1973
Independent, nonprofit organization. Our mission is to achieve equal educational opportunity for every child through strong public schools that prepare all students to access & succeed in college. IDRA strengthens & transforms public education by providing dynamic training; useful research, evaluation & frameworks for action; timely policy analyses; & innovative materials & programs.
ISBN Prefix(es): 978-1-878550; 978-1-935737
Number of titles published annually: 10 Print
Total Titles: 50 Print

Interlink Publishing Group Inc
46 Crosby St, Northampton, MA 01060
SAN: 664-8908
Tel: 413-582-7054 *Toll Free Tel:* 800-238-LINK (238-5465)
E-mail: info@interlinkbooks.com; publicity@interlinkbooks.com; sales@interlinkbooks.com
Web Site: www.interlinkbooks.com
Key Personnel
Owner: Hannah Moushabeck; Leyla Moushabeck; Maha Moushabeck; Harrison Williams
Publicist: Garrett Pinder
Founded: 1987
World travel, world literature, world history/politics/current affairs, art, international cooking & illustrated children's books.
ISBN Prefix(es): 978-1-56656; 978-1-62371
Number of titles published annually: 80 Print; 40 E-Book
Total Titles: 1,000 Print; 500 E-Book
Imprints: Crocodile Books; Interlink Books; Olive Branch Press
Distributed by Simon & Schuster, LLC
Foreign Rep(s): Turnaround Books UK (Europe, UK)
Orders to: Simon & Schuster, LLC
Returns: Simon & Schuster, LLC
Shipping Address: Simon & Schuster, LLC
Warehouse: Simon & Schuster, LLC

International Book Centre Inc
2391 Auburn Rd, Shelby Township, MI 48317
SAN: 208-7022
Tel: 586-254-7230 *Fax:* 586-254-7230
E-mail: ibc@ibcbooks.com
Web Site: www.ibcbooks.com
Key Personnel
Owner: Doris Mukalla
Founded: 1974
Publisher of foreign language books. Specialize in the language & culture of the Middle East.
ISBN Prefix(es): 978-0-86685; 978-0-7189
Number of titles published annually: 2 Print; 2 Audio
Total Titles: 28 Print; 5 Audio
Distributor for Barron's; Cambridge University Press; Capstone; Cengage Learning; Compass Publications; Edenridge Press; English Discoveries; Fisher Hill Publishing; Library du Liban (Lebanon); McGraw Hill; New Readers Press; Oxford University Press; Pearson-Longman; Raven Tree Press; Stacey International Ltd (London); The University of Michigan Press; Usborne Publishing

§International City/County Management Association (ICMA)
777 N Capitol St NE, Suite 500, Washington, DC 20002-4201
Tel: 202-962-3680 *Toll Free Tel:* 800-745-8780
Fax: 202-962-3500
E-mail: customerservices@icma.org
Web Site: icma.org/about-icma-publications
Key Personnel
Exec Dir & CEO: Marc A Ott
Founded: 1914
Publisher of books, reports, survey research, study guides, case studies & other resources used by local government management professionals, municipal & county associations & colleges & universities.
ISBN Prefix(es): 978-0-87326
Number of titles published annually: 10 Print; 2 CD-ROM; 25 Online
Total Titles: 200 Print; 7 CD-ROM; 85 Online
Warehouse: PBD, 1650 Bluegrass Lakes Pkwy, Alpharetta, GA 30004 *Tel:* 770-280-4171 *Fax:* 770-280-0092 *E-mail:* icma-orders@pbd.com
Distribution Center: PBD, 1650 Bluegrass Lakes Pkwy, Alpharetta, GA 30004 *Tel:* 770-442-8633 *Fax:* 770-280-0092 *E-mail:* icma-orders@pbd.com

International Code Council Inc
3060 Saturn St, Suite 100, Brea, CA 92821
Tel: 562-699-0541 *Toll Free Tel:* 888-422-7233
Fax: 562-908-5524 *Toll Free Fax:* 866-891-1695
E-mail: order@icc-es.org
Web Site: www.iccsafe.org
Key Personnel
EVP & Dir, Busn Devt: Mark Johnson *Tel:* 562-699-0541 ext 3248 *E-mail:* mjohnson@icc-es.org
Founded: 1922
Publisher of construction codes & regulations used in US & abroad.
ISBN Prefix(es): 978-1-58001; 978-1-884590; 978-1-892395; 978-1-60983
Number of titles published annually: 60 Print; 10 CD-ROM
Total Titles: 300 Print; 20 CD-ROM

§International Council of Shopping Centers (ICSC)
1251 Avenue of the Americas, 41st fl, New York, NY 10020-1099
Web Site: www.icsc.com
Key Personnel
VP, Communs & Publg: Dana Muldrow *Tel:* 646-728-3571 *E-mail:* dmuldrow@icsc.com
Founded: 1957

ISBN Prefix(es): 978-0-927547; 978-0-913598; 978-1-58268
Number of titles published annually: 20 E-Book
Total Titles: 2 CD-ROM; 60 E-Book
Foreign Office(s): 29 Queen Anne's Gate, London SW1H 9BU, United Kingdom *Tel:* (020) 7976 3102 *Fax:* (020) 7976 3101 *E-mail:* info.europe@icsc.org
Distribution Center: BrightKey, 9050 Junction Dr, Annapolis Junction, MD 20701 *Tel:* 301-362-6900

International Food Policy Research Institute
Member of Consultative Group on International Agricultural Research (CGIAR)
1201 Eye St NW, Washington, DC 20005-3915
Tel: 202-862-5600 *Fax:* 202-862-5606
E-mail: ifpri@cgiar.org
Web Site: www.ifpri.org
Key Personnel
Dir Gen: Shenggen Fan
Dir, Communs & Pub Aff: Rajul Pandya-Lorch *Tel:* 202-862-8185 *E-mail:* r.pandya-lorch@cgiar.org
Founded: 1975
Research reports, occasional papers & newsletter series, books, briefs, abstracts.
ISBN Prefix(es): 978-0-89629
Number of titles published annually: 270 Print; 2 CD-ROM; 270 Online
Total Titles: 3,980 Print; 21 CD-ROM; 3,634 Online
Distributed by Johns Hopkins University Press

International Foundation of Employee Benefit Plans
18700 W Bluemound Rd, Brookfield, WI 53045
Mailing Address: PO Box 69, Brookfield, WI 53008-0069
Tel: 262-786-6700 *Toll Free Tel:* 888-334-3327 *Fax:* 262-786-8780
E-mail: editor@ifebp.org
Web Site: www.ifebp.org
Key Personnel
Dir, Res & Pubns: Kelli Kolsrud *E-mail:* kellik@ifebp.org
Founded: 1954
ISBN Prefix(es): 978-0-89154
Number of titles published annually: 2 Print; 5 E-Book
Total Titles: 30 Print; 20 E-Book
Membership(s): AM&P Network; Independent Book Publishers Association (IBPA)

The International Institute of Islamic Thought
500 Grove St, Suite 200, Herndon, VA 20170
Tel: 703-471-1133 *Fax:* 703-471-3922
E-mail: iiit@iiit.org
Web Site: www.iiit.org
Founded: 1981
Books, audiobooks & videos.
ISBN Prefix(es): 978-0-912463; 978-1-56564
Number of titles published annually: 40 Print
Total Titles: 500 Print

§International Linguistics Corp
12220 Blue Ridge Blvd, Suite G, Kansas City, MO 64030
Tel: 816-765-8855 *Toll Free Tel:* 800-237-1830 (orders)
E-mail: learnables@sbcglobal.net
Web Site: www.learnables.com
Key Personnel
Gen Mgr: Jennifer Elliott
Founded: 1976
Foreign & English language materials, language teaching materials.
ISBN Prefix(es): 978-0-939990; 978-1-887371; 978-0-9814540

Number of titles published annually: 3 Print; 3 CD-ROM; 1 Online; 3 Audio
Total Titles: 52 Print; 10 CD-ROM; 1 Online; 50 Audio

International Literacy Association (ILA)
PO Box 8139, Newark, DE 19714-8139
Tel: 302-731-1600 *Toll Free Tel:* 800-336-7323 (US & CN)
E-mail: customerservice@reading.org
Web Site: www.literacyworldwide.org; www.reading.org
Key Personnel
Exec Dir: Marcie Craig Post
Founded: 1956
Books & journals related to reading instruction & literary education.
ISBN Prefix(es): 978-0-87207
Number of titles published annually: 10 Print; 5 E-Book
Total Titles: 150 Print; 15 E-Book
Foreign Rights: Academics Plus (Andrea Permel) (UK); Eurospan Group (Catherine Lawn) (Trinidad and Tobago)

§International Monetary Fund (IMF), Editorial & Publications Division
700 19 St NW, HQ1-5-355, Washington, DC 20431
SAN: 203-8188
Mailing Address: IMF Publications, PO Box 92780, Washington, DC 20090
Tel: 202-623-7430
E-mail: publications@imf.org
Web Site: bookstore.imf.org; elibrary.imf.org (online collection); www.imf.org/publications
Key Personnel
Publr: Linda Kean
Assoc Publr: Jim Beardow; Joy De Vera
Founded: 1946
Publishes a variety of books, periodicals & digital products covering global economics, international finance, monetary policy, statistics, exchange rates & general macroeconomic issues.
ISBN Prefix(es): 978-0-939934; 978-1-55775; 978-1-58906; 978-1-61635
Number of titles published annually: 150 Print; 500 Online; 500 E-Book
Total Titles: 3,500 Print; 23,630 Online; 23,630 E-Book
Orders to: IMF Publications, PO Box 92780, Washington, DC 20090
Membership(s): Association of American Publishers (AAP); Association of Learned & Professional Society Publishers (ALPSP); Association of University Presses (AUPresses); Crossref

§International Press of Boston Inc
387 Somerville Ave, Somerville, MA 02143
Mailing Address: PO Box 502, Somerville, MA 02143
Tel: 617-623-3016 (orders & cust serv) *Fax:* 617-623-3101
E-mail: ipb-orders@intlpress.com
Web Site: www.intlpress.com
Founded: 1992
Publishers of scholarly mathematical & scientific peer-reviewed journals & books.
ISBN Prefix(es): 978-1-57146
Number of titles published annually: 5 Print
Total Titles: 125 Print; 3 CD-ROM
Distributed by American Mathematical Society (AMS)

International Publishers Co Inc
235 W 23 St, New York, NY 10011
SAN: 202-5655
Tel: 212-366-9816 *Fax:* 212-366-9820
E-mail: service@intpubnyc.com
Web Site: www.intpubnyc.com
Key Personnel
Pres: Garry Bono

VP: Tony Pecinovsky
Founded: 1924
Short discount titles & Marxist classics. Mostly paperback, some cloth, general nonfiction, social sciences, classic & contemporary Marxism-Leninism, literature, poetry & biography, labor, women's studies.
ISBN Prefix(es): 978-0-7178
Number of titles published annually: 12 Print; 20 Online; 10 E-Book
Total Titles: 200 Print; 40 Online; 50 E-Book
Imprints: International Publishers
Foreign Rep(s): Global Book Marketing (London, UK)
Returns: Whitehurst & Clark, 1200 County Rd, Rte 523, Flemington, NJ 08822
Warehouse: Whitehurst & Clark, 1200 County Rd, Rte 523, Flemington, NJ 08822, Contact: Brad Searles *Tel:* 908-782-2323 *Fax:* 908-237-2407
Membership(s): American Booksellers Association (ABA); The Association of Publishers for Special Sales (APSS); Independent Book Publishers Association (IBPA); National Association of College Stores (NACS)

§International Risk Management Institute Inc
12222 Merit Dr, Suite 1600, Dallas, TX 75251-2266
Tel: 972-960-7693 *Fax:* 972-371-5120
E-mail: info27@irmi.com
Web Site: www.irmi.com
Key Personnel
CFO: Ron Allen
Pres: Jack Gibson
Founded: 1978
Publish both print & online books on commercial & personal lines of insurance.
ISBN Prefix(es): 978-1-886813; 978-0-938358; 978-1-933686
Number of titles published annually: 20 Print; 36 Online
Total Titles: 35 Print

§International Society for Technology in Education
2111 Wilson Blvd, Suite 300, Arlington, VA 22201
Tel: 503-342-2848 (intl) *Toll Free Tel:* 800-336-5191 (US & CN) *Fax:* 541-302-3778
E-mail: iste@iste.org
Web Site: www.iste.org
Key Personnel
CEO: Richard Culatta
COO: Cheretta Clerkley
Chief Experience Offr: Jennifer Ragan-Fore
Chief Innovation Offr: Joseph South
Chief of Staff: Layla Allahverdi
Deputy Exec Dir: Penny Reinart
Founded: 1979
Work with experienced educators to develop & produce practical resources for classroom teachers, teacher educators & technology leaders. Home of the National Educational Technology Standards (NETS), ISTE is the trusted source for educational technology books & courseware.
ISBN Prefix(es): 978-1-56484
Number of titles published annually: 12 Print
Total Titles: 60 Print
Branch Office(s)
621 SW Morrison St, Suite 800, Portland, OR 97205

§International Society of Automation (ISA)
3252 S Miami Blvd, Suite 102, Durham, NC 27703
Mailing Address: PO Box 12277, Research Triangle Park, NC 27709-2277
Tel: 919-549-8411 *Fax:* 919-549-8288
E-mail: info@isa.org

U.S. PUBLISHERS

Web Site: www.isa.org/standards-and-publications/isa-publications
Key Personnel
Exec Dir: Claire Fallon
Founded: 1945
Technical books, references, journals, webinars, software, standards, proceedings, electronic references.
ISBN Prefix(es): 978-1-55617; 978-0-87664; 978-0-9791330; 978-1-936007; 978-1-941546; 978-0-9792343; 978-1-934394; 978-1-937560; 978-1-945541; 978-1-64331
Number of titles published annually: 20 Print
Total Titles: 139 Print; 10 CD-ROM; 20 E-Book
Foreign Office(s): Luchthavenweg 54, 5657 AB Eindhoven, Netherlands *Tel:* (06) 33 609 357 *E-mail:* info@isaeurope.org *Web Site:* isaeurope.com
Foreign Rep(s): Eurospan (Europe)

§International Wealth Success (IWS)
Imprint of Kallisti Publishing Inc
332 Center St, Wilkes-Barre, PA 18702
Tel: 570-825-3598
E-mail: admin@iwsmoney.com
Web Site: iwealthsuccess.com
Key Personnel
Publr: Anthony Raymond Michalski
Founded: 1966
Publishes a variety of business & financial titles in the fields of small business, real estate, mail order, import-export & financing as well as the highly regarded IW$ Newsletter.
ISBN Prefix(es): 978-0-934311; 978-0-914306; 978-1-56150
Number of titles published annually: 6 Print; 1 Online; 200 E-Book
Total Titles: 120 Print; 200 Online; 200 E-Book
Imprints: IW$ Press
Distributed by Kallisti Publishing Inc

InterVarsity Press
Subsidiary of InterVarsity Christian Fellowship/USA
430 Plaza Dr, Westmont, IL 60559-1234
SAN: 202-7089
Mailing Address: PO Box 1400, Downers Grove, IL 60515
Tel: 630-734-4000 *Toll Free Tel:* 800-843-9487
Fax: 630-734-4200
E-mail: email@ivpress.com
Web Site: www.ivpress.com
Key Personnel
Publr: Terumi Echols *Tel:* 630-734-4001 *E-mail:* techols@ivpress.com
Div VP & Dir, Edit: Cindy Bunch *Tel:* 630-734-4078 *E-mail:* cbunch@ivpress.com
Div VP, Go-to-Market: Justin Paul Lawrence *Tel:* 630-734-4124 *E-mail:* jplawrence@ivpress.com
Assoc Publr & Edit Dir, Academic: Jon Boyd *E-mail:* jboyd@ivpress.com
Assoc Publr & Edit Dir, Trade: Ted Olsen *E-mail:* tolsen@ivpress.com
Creative Dir: David Fassett *E-mail:* dfassett@ivpress.com
Dir, Strategic Partnerships & Prod Innovation: Helen Lee *Tel:* 630-734-4038 *E-mail:* hlee@ivpress.com
Assoc Dir, Rts & Contracts: Ellen Hsu *Tel:* 630-734-4034 *E-mail:* ehsu@ivpress.com
Trade Ed: Kelli Trujillo
Assoc Proj Ed: Rachel Freire O'Connor
Founded: 1947
Religion (interdenominational); fiction, nonfiction, textbooks.
ISBN Prefix(es): 978-0-87784; 978-0-8308
Number of titles published annually: 130 Print; 130 E-Book; 10 Audio
Total Titles: 2,000 Print; 1,200 E-Book; 50 Audio
Imprints: IVP (thoughtful books on church, leadership, culture & mission); IVP Academic (publishing to facilitate broader conversations in the academy & the church); IVP Bible Studies (resources for Bible study & small groups); IVP Formatio (books following the rich tradition of the church in the journey of spiritual formation); IVP Kids (faith-filled, formative & fun books for young readers)
Distribution Center: Longleaf Services Inc, 116 S Boundary St, Chapel Hill, NC 27514-3808 *Tel:* 919-966-7449 *Toll Free Tel:* 800-848-6224 *Fax:* 919-962-2704 *Toll Free Fax:* 800-272-6817 *E-mail:* orders@longleafservices.org *Web Site:* www.longleafservices.org SAN: 203-3151
Ingram Publisher Services UK, 10 Thornbury Rd, Plymouth, Devon PL6 7PP, United Kingdom (UK & outside North America) *Tel:* (01752) 202301 *E-mail:* ipsuk.orders@ingramcontent.com *Web Site:* www.ingrampublisherservices.co.uk
Membership(s): Evangelical Christian Publishers Association (ECPA)

§Interweave Press LLC
Imprint of Golden Peak Media
4868 Innovation Dr, Fort Collins, CO 80525
Web Site: www.interweave.com
Founded: 1975
ISBN Prefix(es): 978-0-934026; 978-1-883010; 978-1-931499; 978-0-9796073; 978-1-4402; 978-1-63250; 978-1-59668; 978-1-62033
Number of titles published annually: 9 Print
Total Titles: 350 Print

Iris Press
Imprint of The Iris Publishing Group Inc
969 Oak Ridge Tpke, No 328, Oak Ridge, TN 37830
Web Site: www.irisbooks.com
Key Personnel
Publr: Robert Cumming *E-mail:* rcumming@irisbooks.com
Ed & Designer: Beto Cumming *E-mail:* bcumming@irisbooks.com
Founded: 1975
Publisher of print editions of high quality poetry & literary prose.
ISBN Prefix(es): 978-0-916078; 978-1-60454
Number of titles published annually: 8 Print
Total Titles: 180 Print

§Iron Gate Publishing
PO Box 999, Niwot, CO 80544
Tel: 303-530-2551
E-mail: editor@irongate.com
Web Site: www.irongate.com
Key Personnel
Publr & Ed: Dina C Carson
Founded: 1990
Genealogy, family history, Colorado local history, self-publishing, reference.
ISBN Prefix(es): 978-1-879579; 978-0-9724975; 978-1-68224
Number of titles published annually: 15 Print; 25 E-Book
Total Titles: 250 Print; 100 E-Book
Membership(s): The Association of Publishers for Special Sales (APSS); Colorado Independent Publishers Association (CIPA); Independent Book Publishers Association (IBPA); Publishers Association of the West (PubWest)

Iron Stream Media
Formerly Lighthouse Publishing of the Carolinas; LPC Books
Affiliate of Christian Devotions Ministries
100 Missionary Ridge, Birmingham, AL 35242
E-mail: info@ironstreammedia.com
Web Site: ironstreammedia.com
Key Personnel
COO: Bradley Isbell *E-mail:* bradley.isbell@ironstreammedia.com
ISBN Prefix(es): 978-0-9833196; 978-0-9822065; 978-0-9847655; 978-1-938499
Number of titles published annually: 30 Print; 30 E-Book; 20 Audio
Total Titles: 550 Print; 550 Online; 550 E-Book; 120 Audio
Imprints: BLING! Romance (clean contemporary romance with an edge); Brookstone Publishing Group; Candlelight Romance (inspirational contemporary romance); Firefly Southern Fiction (Southern characters & tradition, historical & contemporary); Guiding Light Women's Fiction (contemporary & historical); Harambee Press (writers of color); Heritage Beacon Fiction (historical fiction); IlluminateYA Fiction (fiction & nonfiction that reflect today's authentic youth culture, morals & values); Iron Stream (general nonfiction); Iron Stream Fiction (Christian fiction); Iron Stream Kids; Lamplighter Mysteries & Suspense (cozy murder mysteries, thrillers & suspense); Life Bible Study (bible study materials); New Hope Publishers; Smitten Historical Romance (stories from Regency era through 1970s); Sonrise Devotionals (Christian devotionals); Straight Street Books (Christian living nonfiction); Trailblazer Western Fiction (tales of the American West)
Distribution Center: Amazon
Ingram
Spring Arbor
Membership(s): Evangelical Christian Publishers Association (ECPA); Independent Book Publishers Association (IBPA)

Island Press
2000 "M" St NW, Suite 480-B, Washington, DC 20036
SAN: 212-5129
Tel: 202-232-7933 *Toll Free Tel:* 800-621-2736
Fax: 202-234-1328
E-mail: info@islandpress.org
Web Site: www.islandpress.org
Key Personnel
Pres: David Miller
SVP & CFO: Ken Hartzell
SVP & Edit Dir: Heather Boyer
VP & Dir, Devt: Brandi Stanton
VP & Dir, Mktg & Sales: Julie Marshall
Dir, Acctg & Admin: Laura Hess
Assoc Dir, Mktg: Jason Leppig
Assoc Dir, Prodn & Mfg: Sharis Simonian
Assoc Dir, Publicity: Jaime Jennings
Sr Ed: Stacy Eisenstark; Emily Turner
Ed: Erin Johnson
Ed & Rts Mgr: Rebecca Bright *E-mail:* rbright@islandpress.org
Asst Ed: Annie Byrnes
Online Mktg Mgr: Kyler Geoffroy
Partnership Mgr: Jen Hawse
Devt Coord: Andrea Kimberling
Busn Systems Analyst: Christerpher Beaudry
Publicity & Mktg Assoc: Julie Greene
Founded: 1978
Books about the environment for professionals, students & general readers, autobiography-scientific; land use planning; environmental economics; nature essays; "green" architecture.
ISBN Prefix(es): 978-0-933280; 978-1-55963; 978-1-59726; 978-1-61091; 978-1-64283
Number of titles published annually: 40 Print; 40 E-Book
Total Titles: 1,000 Print; 800 E-Book
Imprints: Shearwater Books
Distributed by University of British Columbia Press
Foreign Rep(s): Tim Burland (Japan); Catamount Content (Ethan Atkin) (Caribbean, South America); China Publishers Marketing (Benjamin Pan) (China, Hong Kong, Taiwan); Durnell Marketing (Europe); The Oxford Publicity Partnership (UK); University of British Columbia Press (Canada); The Andrew White Partnership (East Asia, Southeast Asia); Woodslane Pty Ltd (Australia, New Zealand)
Foreign Rights: Bardon-Chinese Media Agency (Ivan Zhang, simplified) (China); Bardon-

Chinese Media Agency (Luisa Yeh, complex) (China); Duran Kim Agency (Duran Kim) (South Korea); RDC Agencia Literaria (Beatriz Coll) (Brazil, Latin America, Portugal, Spain); Tuttle Mori (Fumika Ogihara) (Japan)
Distribution Center: Chicago Distribution Center (CDC), 11030 S Langley Ave, Chicago, IL 60628 *Tel:* 773-702-7000 *Toll Free Tel:* 800-621-2736 *Fax:* 773-702-7212 *Toll Free Fax:* 800-621-8476 *E-mail:* orders@press.uchicago.edu
UTP Distribution, 5201 Dufferin St, Toronto, ON M3H 5T8, Canada *Tel:* 416-667-7791 *Toll Free Tel:* 800-565-9523 *Fax:* 416-667-7832 *Toll Free Fax:* 800-221-9985 *E-mail:* utpbooks@utpress.utoronto.ca
Marston Book Services, 160 Eastern Ave, Milton Park, Abingdon, Oxon OX14 4SB, United Kingdom *Tel:* (01235) 465521 *Fax:* (01235) 465555 *E-mail:* direct.orders@marston.co.uk

Islandport Press
247 Portland St, Bldg C, Yarmouth, ME 04096
Mailing Address: PO Box 10, Yarmouth, ME 04096
Tel: 207-846-3344
E-mail: info@islandportpress.com; orders@islandportpress.com
Web Site: www.islandportpress.com
Key Personnel
Founder & Ed-in-Chief: Dean L Lunt
VP, Opers: Shannon M Butler *E-mail:* shannon@islandportpress.com
Ed-at-Large: Genevieve Morgan
Asst Ed, Design & Prodn: Emily A Lunt
Asst Ed, Edit: Marion F Fearing *E-mail:* marion@islandportpress.com
Sales Rep: Holly K Eddy *E-mail:* holly@islandportpress.com
Founded: 1999
Islandport is a dynamic, award-winning publisher dedicated to stories rooted in the essence & sensibilities of New England.
ISBN Prefix(es): 978-0-9671662; 978-0-9763231; 978-1-934031; 978-1-939017; 978-1-944762
Number of titles published annually: 15 Print; 5 E-Book
Total Titles: 200 Print; 30 E-Book
Foreign Rights: Transatlantic Literary Agency (worldwide exc USA)
Distribution Center: Baker & Taylor Publisher Services, 30 Amberwood Pkwy, Ashland, OH 44805 *Toll Free Tel:* 800-537-6727 *E-mail:* tradesales@btpubservices.com *Web Site:* www.btpubservices.com

ISM, see Iron Stream Media

ISTE, see International Society for Technology in Education

§Italica Press
99 Wall St, Suite 650, New York, NY 10005
SAN: 695-1805
Tel: 917-371-0563
E-mail: inquiries@italicapress.com
Web Site: www.italicapress.com
Key Personnel
Pres & Publr, Electronic Publg: Eileen Gardiner *E-mail:* egardiner@italicapress.com
Secy & Publr, Electronic Publg: Ronald G Musto *E-mail:* rgmusto@italicapress.com
Founded: 1985
English translations of Latin & Italian works from the Middle Ages to the present.
ISBN Prefix(es): 978-0-934977; 978-1-59910
Number of titles published annually: 6 Print; 6 E-Book
Total Titles: 220 Print; 160 E-Book
Imprints: Pierrepont Street Press

§Italics Publishing
100 Northcliffe Dr, No 223, Gulf Breeze, FL 32561
E-mail: submissions@italicspublishing.com (submissions)
Web Site: italicspublishing.com
Founded: 2016
Italics Publishing is a traditional (non-subsidy) publisher specializing in small press, POD, & digital publishing. Combining cutting edge, best-in-class publishing practices with selective criteria for signing up new authors, Italics caters to the new generations of readers, keen on technology & with little time to spare. Our imprint welcomes submissions from young-at-heart, bright authors who deliver intriguing, mold-breaking work in adult genre fiction, contemporary fiction, commercial fiction, & short stories collections. Through the voices of our avant-garde authors, we invite readers to embark on an entertaining, yet intellectually stimulating adventure, inspired by the challenging realm of our modern social, technological, & business environment.
ISBN Prefix(es): 978-0-9843846; 978-0-945302
Number of titles published annually: 6 Print; 8 E-Book; 4 Audio
Total Titles: 12 Print; 12 E-Book; 6 Audio

iUniverse
Division of Author Solutions LLC
1663 Liberty Dr, Bloomington, IN 47403
Toll Free Tel: 800-AUTHORS (288-4677); 844-349-9409
E-mail: media@iuniverse.com
Web Site: www.iuniverse.com
Key Personnel
COO, Author Solutions: Bill Becher
Pres, Author Solutions: Bill Elliott
Founded: 1999
iUniverse is the industry's leading book marketing, editorial services & supported self-publishing company. The iUniverse management team has extensive editorial & managerial experience with traditional publishers such as Random House, Wiley, Macmillan, Chronicle Books & Addison-Wesley. iUniverse maintains a strategic alliance with Chapters Indigo in Canada & titles accepted into the iUniverse Rising Star program are featured in a special collection on www.barnesandnoble.com.
This publisher has indicated that 100% of their product line is author subsidized.
ISBN Prefix(es): 978-0-9665514; 978-1-58348; 978-0-9668591; 978-1-893652; 978-0-595
Number of titles published annually: 2,500 Print
Total Titles: 40,000 Print
Distribution Center: Baker & Taylor LLC
Ingram Book Group

§Jain Publishing Co
164 Concho Dr, Fremont, CA 94539
SAN: 213-6503
Tel: 510-659-8272
E-mail: mail@jainpub.com
Web Site: www.jainpub.com
Key Personnel
Pres & Publr: Mukesh Jain
Founded: 1989
A humanities & social sciences publisher that publishes academic & scholarly references, as well as books for the general reader in both print & electronic formats.
ISBN Prefix(es): 978-0-89581; 978-0-87573
Number of titles published annually: 6 Print; 6 E-Book
Total Titles: 200 Print; 40 E-Book
Imprints: Asian Humanities Press

Alice James Books
Division of Alice James Poetry Cooperative Inc
60 Pineland Dr, Suite 206, New Gloucester, ME 04260
SAN: 201-1158
Tel: 207-926-8283
E-mail: info@alicejamesbooks.org
Web Site: alicejamesbooks.org
Key Personnel
Exec Ed & Dir: Carey Salerno
Mng Ed: Alyssa Neptune
Sr Press Asst: Emily Marquis
Bookkeeper: Debra Norton
Founded: 1973
ISBN Prefix(es): 978-0-914086; 978-1-882295; 978-1-938584
Number of titles published annually: 8 Print
Total Titles: 266 Print; 3 Audio
Distribution Center: Consortium Book Sales & Distribution, The Keg House, Suite 101, 34 13 Ave NE, Minneapolis, MN 55413 *Tel:* 612-746-2600 *Toll Free Tel:* 866-400-5351 (cust serv, Jackson, TN) *E-mail:* cbsdinfo@ingramcontent.com *Web Site:* www.cbsd.com SAN: 200-6049

Jeter Publishing, see Gallery Books

Jewish Lights Publishing
Imprint of Turner Publishing Co LLC
4507 Charlotte Ave, Suite 100, Nashville, TN 37209
SAN: 134-5621
Tel: 615-255-BOOK (255-2665) *Fax:* 615-255-5081
E-mail: marketing@turnerpublishing.com
Web Site: jewishlights.com; www.turnerpublishing.com
Key Personnel
Pres & Publr, Turner Publishing Co: Todd Bottorff
Founded: 1990
General trade adult & children's books on spirituality, theology, philosophy, mysticism, women's studies, recovery/self-help/healing & history for people of all faiths & backgrounds.
ISBN Prefix(es): 978-1-879045; 978-1-58023
Number of titles published annually: 5 Print; 5 E-Book
Total Titles: 500 Print; 450 E-Book

The Jewish Publication Society
Imprint of University of Nebraska Press
c/o Gratz College, 7605 Old York Rd, Melrose Park, PA 19027
SAN: 201-0240
Tel: 215-832-0600
Web Site: www.jps.org; www.nebraskapress.unl.edu/jps/
Key Personnel
Dir: Dr Elias Sacks *E-mail:* esacks@jps.org
Mktg & Communs Dir: Deena Schoenfeld *E-mail:* dschoenfeld@jps.org
Mng Ed: Joy Weinberg *E-mail:* jweinberg@jps.org
Acctg Mgr: Rachna Khanna *E-mail:* rkhanna@jps.org
Founded: 1888
Books of Jewish interest.
ISBN Prefix(es): 978-0-8276
Number of titles published annually: 8 Print; 8 E-Book
Total Titles: 250 Print
Foreign Rep(s): Eurospan (Europe, Latin America, Middle East, UK & Commonwealth); Scholarly Book Service (Canada)
Orders to: Longleaf Services Inc, 116 S Boundary St, Chapel Hill, NC 27514-3808 *Tel:* 919-966-7449 *Toll Free Tel:* 800-848-6224 ext 1 *Toll Free Fax:* 800-272-6817 *E-mail:* orders@longleafservices.org *Web Site:* longleafservices.org
Membership(s): Association of University Presses (AUPresses)

U.S. PUBLISHERS

§Jhpiego
Affiliate of Johns Hopkins University
1615 Thames St, Baltimore, MD 21231-3492
Tel: 410-537-1800
E-mail: info@jhpiego.org
Web Site: www.jhpiego.org
Key Personnel
Pres & CEO: Leslie D Mancuso, PhD
Chief Operating & Fin Offr: Abhi Bhasin
Chief HR & Admin Offr: Bernadette Channer
CIO: Glenn R Strachan, MA
VP, DC Opers: Koki Agarwal
VP, Global Engagement & Communs: Naomi Giges Downey
VP, Global Progs: Debora Bossemeyer
VP, New Prog Devt: Richard Lamporte
VP, Tech Leadership & Innovation: Wendy Taylor
Founded: 1973
Reproductive health, medical texts, family planning, maternal health, HIV/AIDS & cervical cancer prevention & treatment, infection prevention.
ISBN Prefix(es): 978-0-929817; 978-1-943408
Number of titles published annually: 20 Print
Total Titles: 80 Print; 4 CD-ROM

JHU Press, see Johns Hopkins University Press

§JIST Publishing
Division of Kendall Hunt Publishing Co
4050 Westmark Dr, Dubuque, IA 52002
Tel: 563-589-1000 *Toll Free Tel:* 800-328-1452; 800-228-0810 *Fax:* 563-589-1046
Toll Free Fax: 800-772-9165
E-mail: orders@kendallhunt.com
Web Site: www.paradigmeducation.com
Key Personnel
Acct Mgr: Bob Grilliot *Tel:* 855-213-0737
Founded: 1981
Job search (resumes, cover letters, interviewing), career planning, job retention, occupational reference, assessment, self-help, career exploration, occupational information, character education, life skills, CD-ROMs & reference books, videos & software.
ISBN Prefix(es): 978-0-942784; 978-1-56370; 978-1-57112; 978-1-930780; 978-1-55864; 978-1-59357; 978-1-63332
Number of titles published annually: 50 Print; 2 CD-ROM; 20 E-Book; 1 Audio
Total Titles: 350 Print; 6 CD-ROM; 250 E-Book; 1 Audio
Imprints: JIST Career Solutions
Membership(s): Independent Book Publishers Association (IBPA)

§Johns Hopkins University Press
Affiliate of Johns Hopkins University
2715 N Charles St, Baltimore, MD 21218-4363
SAN: 202-7348
Tel: 410-516-6900; 410-516-6987
Toll Free Tel: 800-537-5487 (book orders & cust serv); 800-548-1784 (journal orders)
Fax: 410-516-6968; 410-516-6998 (orders)
E-mail: hfscustserv@press.jhu.edu (cust serv); jrnlcirc@jh.edu (journal orders)
Web Site: www.press.jhu.edu; muse.jhu.edu
Key Personnel
Exec Dir: Barbara Kline Pope *E-mail:* bkp@press.jhu.edu
Assoc Exec Dir & Sr Dir, Fin & Admin: Erik A Smist *E-mail:* eas@press.jhu.edu
Edit Dir: Gregory M Britton *E-mail:* gb@press.jhu.edu
Journals Publr: William M Breichner *E-mail:* wmb@press.jhu.edu
Co-Mktg & Sales Dir: Davida Breier *E-mail:* dgb@press.jhu.edu; Heidi M Vincent *E-mail:* hmv@press.jhu.edu
Dir, Journals Sales & Mktg: Lisa Klose *E-mail:* llk@press.jhu.edu
Dir Publg Opers, Books: Diem Bloom *E-mail:* dbloom8@jhu.edu
Publicity Dir: Kait Howard *E-mail:* kehoward@jhu.edu
Assoc Mktg Dir, Books: Claire McCabe Tamberino *E-mail:* cmt@press.jhu.edu
Sr Acqs Ed: Robin W Coleman *E-mail:* rwc@press.jhu.edu; Tiffany Gasbarrini *E-mail:* tg@press.jhu.edu; Matthew McAdam *E-mail:* mxm@press.jhu.edu; Suzanne Staszak-Silva *E-mail:* sstasza1@jhu.edu
Acqs Ed: Laura Davulis *E-mail:* lbd@press.jhu.edu
Sr Digital Mktg Mgr: Kelly Hannagan *E-mail:* khannag1@jhu.edu
Acqs Admin Mgr: Alena Jones *E-mail:* alenaj@jhu.edu
Fulfillment Systems Proj Mgr, Journals: Matt Brook *E-mail:* mb@press.jhu.edu
Journals Opers Mgr: Shannon T Fortner *E-mail:* stf@press.jhu.edu
Journals Prodn Mgr: Carol Hamblen *E-mail:* crh@press.jhu.edu
Prodn Mgr, Books: Jennifer Paulson *E-mail:* jpaulso6@jhu.edu
Publicist: Anthony Blake *E-mail:* ablake20@jhu.edu; Alison Mailloux
Assoc Publicist: Fajr Abdul-Azeez *E-mail:* fadula6@jhu.edu
Rts Mgr: Kelly Rogers *E-mail:* klr@press.jhu.edu
Sales Mgr: Rachel Miller *E-mail:* rmill157@jhu.edu
Mktg & Sales Coord: Catherine Bergeron *E-mail:* cab@press.jhu.edu
Promos Coord: Kristina Lykke *E-mail:* kkl@press.jhu.edu
Graphic Artist: Stephen Schlegel *E-mail:* schleg1@jhu.edu
Mktg Specialist: Gioia Milano *E-mail:* gmilano2@jhu.edu
Sales Asst, Hopkins Sales Partners: Thalia Barry
Founded: 1878
Scholarly books, nonfiction of general interest, paperbacks, scholarly journals.
ISBN Prefix(es): 978-0-8018; 978-1-4214
Number of titles published annually: 140 Print
Total Titles: 4,200 Print; 5 Online; 3,200 E-Book
Divisions: HFS
Sales Office(s): Southeastern Book Travelers LLC, 104 Owens Pkwy, Suite J, Birmingham, AL 35244 (AL, FL, MS, TN (west)), Rep: Chip Mercer *Tel:* 205-682-8570 *Fax:* 770-804-2013 *E-mail:* chipmercer@bellsouth.net *Web Site:* southeasternbooktravelers.com
Southeastern Book Travelers LLC, 206 Bainbridge Rd, Florence, AL 35634 (GA, NC, SC, TN (east), VA, WV), Rep: Stewart Koontz *Tel:* 256-483-7969 *Fax:* 770-804-2013 *E-mail:* cskoontz@hotmail.com
Wilcher Associates, 26652 Merienda, No 7, Laguna Hills, CA 92656 (AK, AR, CA (south), HI, NV), Rep: Tom McCorkell *Tel:* 949-362-0597 *E-mail:* tmcork@sbcglobal.net
Wilcher Associates, 2318 32 Ave, San Francisco, CA 94116 (CA (north), ID, MO, OR, WA), Rep: Bob Rosenberg *Tel:* 415-564-1248 *E-mail:* bob@bobrosenberggroup.com
Wilcher Associates, 2838 Shadowglen Dr, Colorado Springs, CO 80918 (CO, NM, UT, WY), Rep: Jim Sena *Tel:* 719-210-5222 *E-mail:* sena.wilcher@gmail.com
Miller Trade Book Marketing, 363 W Erie St, Suite 7-E, Chicago, IL 60654 (Midwest), Contact: Bruce Miller *Tel:* 773-275-8156 *E-mail:* bruce@millertrade.com *Web Site:* www.millertradebook.com
Northeast Publisher Reps, 161-5 Flower Lane, Dracut, MA 01826 (CT, MA, RI), Rep: Beth Martin *Tel:* 978-221-5758 *Fax:* 978-710-3544 *E-mail:* ee_martin@comcast.net *Web Site:* nepubreps.com
Northeast Publisher Reps, 81 Indian Ridge Rd, Contoocook, NH 03229 (New England), Rep: Bill Palizzolo *Tel:* 603-496-1352 *E-mail:* billp@nepubreps.com *Web Site:* nepubreps.com
Northeast Publisher Reps, 20 Davenport Rd, Montville, NJ 07045 (Mid-Atlantic), Rep: Lisa Sirak *Tel:* 973-299-0085 *E-mail:* lisas@nepubreps.com *Web Site:* nepubreps.com
Southeastern Book Travelers LLC, 2007 E 13 St, Austin, TX 78702 (OK (west), TX (central, north)), Rep: Larry Hollern *Tel:* 806-236-7808 *Fax:* 281-360-5215 *E-mail:* lhollern@aol.com
Southeastern Book Travelers LLC, 3415 Havenbrook Dr, Apt 602, Kingwood, TX 77339 (AL, LA, OK (east), TX (south)), Rep: Sal McLemore *Tel:* 281-772-8807 *Fax:* 770-804-2013 *E-mail:* mchoffice@suddenlink.net
Foreign Rep(s): Avicenna Partnership Ltd (Bill Kennedy) (Bahrain, Cyprus, Egypt, Greece, Iran, Iraq, Kuwait, Lebanon, Libya, Malta, Oman, Qatar, Saudi Arabia, Sudan, Syria, Turkey, United Arab Emirates, Yemen); B K Agency Ltd (Taiwan); Durnell Marketing Ltd (Albania, Armenia, Austria, Azerbaijan, Belarus, Belgium (Dutch-speaking), Belgium (French-speaking), Bosnia and Herzegovina, Bulgaria, Croatia, Czechia, Denmark, Estonia, Finland, France, Georgia, Germany, Hungary, Iceland, Ireland, Italy, Kazakhstan, Kosovo, Kyrgyzstan, Latvia, Lithuania, Luxembourg, Montenegro, Netherlands, Norway, Poland, Portugal, Romania, Serbia, Slovakia, Slovenia, Spain, Sweden, Switzerland, Tajikistan, Turkmenistan, Ukraine, Uzbekistan); Everest International Publishing Services (Wei Zhao) (China); Hornblower Books (Roberta Samec) (Canada); Mr Se-Yung Jun (North Korea, South Korea); MHM Ltd (Japan); Oxford Publicity Partnership Ltd (Matthew Surzyn) (UK); Mr PC Tham (Singapore); Kelvin van Hasselt (Africa, Caribbean); The White Partnership (Andrew White) (Hong Kong, India, Indonesia, Malaysia, Philippines, Thailand); Woodslane Pty Ltd (Andrew Guy) (Australia, Fiji, New Zealand, Papua New Guinea); World Press (Saleem Malik)
Foreign Rights: Arrowsmith Agency (Germany); English Agency Japan Co Ltd (Japan); Gending Rights Agency (China); Graal Literary Agency (Poland); The Deborah Harris Agency (Israel); IECO Agency (Spain); Japan UNI Agency (Japan); JLM Literary Agency (Greece); The Kalem Literary Agency (Turkey); Duran Kim Agency (South Korea); La Nouvelle Agence (France); Reiser Literary Agency (Italy); Sebes & Bisseling Literary Agency (Netherlands); Seibel Publishing Services (Brazil); Tuttle-Mori Agency Inc (Japan)
Orders to: HFS, PO Box 50370, Baltimore, MD 21211-4370 *Tel:* 410-516-6965 *Toll Free Tel:* 800-537-5487 *Fax:* 410-516-6998 *E-mail:* hfscustserv@jh.edu *Web Site:* hfs.jhu.edu
Returns: HFS, c/o Maple Logistic Solutions, Lebanon Distribution Ctr, 704 Legionaire Dr, Lebanon, PA 17042
Warehouse: Maple Logistics Solutions, Lebanon Distribution Center, 704 Legionaire Dr, Fredricksburg, PA 17026
Membership(s): Association of American Publishers (AAP); Book Industry Study Group (BISG)

Lyndon B Johnson School of Public Affairs
University of Texas at Austin, 2300 Red River St, Stop E2700, Austin, TX 78712-1536
Mailing Address: University of Texas at Austin, PO Box Y, E2700, Austin, TX 78713-8925
Tel: 512-471-3200
E-mail: lbjdeansoffice@austin.utexas.edu
Web Site: lbj.utexas.edu
Key Personnel
Chief Communs Offr: Victoria Yu *Tel:* 512-232-4054 *E-mail:* victoriajyu@austin.utexas.edu
Founded: 1972
Working papers; public service monographs; policy research projects; conference proceedings.

Return policy: No refunds; replace damaged books only. All sales are final. Prepayment usually required.
ISBN Prefix(es): 978-0-89940
Number of titles published annually: 8 Print
Total Titles: 300 Print

§Jones & Bartlett Learning LLC
Division of Ascend Learning
25 Mall Rd, Burlington, MA 01803
Tel: 978-443-5000 *Toll Free Tel:* 800-832-0034
Fax: 978-443-8000
E-mail: info@jblearning.com; customerservice@jblearning.com
Web Site: www.jblearning.com
Founded: 1983
Academic & professional publisher.
ISBN Prefix(es): 978-0-86720; 978-0-7637; 978-1-59822; 978-0-9778582; 978-1-4496; 978-1-284; 978-1-934015; 978-1-889458; 978-1-890369
Number of titles published annually: 300 Print
Total Titles: 2,500 Print; 100 CD-ROM
Foreign Rep(s): Advanced Marketing Associates (Kevin Fong) (Brunei, Singapore); Africa Connection (Guy Simpson) (East Africa); Booknet Co Ltd (Suphaluck Sattabuz) (Thailand, Vietnam); Merry Chang (Taiwan); China Publishers Services Ltd (Ben Bai) (China); Class Publishing (Clare McMillan) (Europe, UK); Discovery Book Store (Gary Goh) (Malaysia); IGroup (Asia Pacific) Ltd (Marivel Cornita) (Guam, Northern Mariana Islands, Philippines); IGroup (Asia Pacific) Ltd (Helwis Tjhai) (Indonesia); Impact Korea (ChongHo Ra) (South Korea); IPR (International Publishers Representatives) (David Atiyah) (Middle East); Jones & Bartlett India Pvt Ltd (Vinod Vasishta) (Bangladesh, India, Nepal, Sri Lanka); Latin Fly (Enrique Gallego) (Caribbean, Latin America); Northrose Educational Resources Inc (Jim Rozsa) (Canada); Watson Marketing (Jill Watson) (South Africa); The White Partnership (Andrew White) (Ethiopia, Japan); World Press (Saleem Malik) (Pakistan)
Returns: 905 Carlow Dr, Unit B, Bolingbrook, IL 60490
Warehouse: 905 Carlow Dr, Unit B, Bolingbrook, IL 60490

§Joshua Tree Publishing
3 Golf Ctr, Suite 201, Hoffman Estates, IL 60169
Tel: 312-893-7525
E-mail: info@joshuatreepublishing.com; info@centaurbooks.com
Web Site: www.joshuatreepublishing.com; www.centaurbooks.com
Key Personnel
Pres & Publr: John Paul Owles *E-mail:* jpo@joshuatreepublishing.com
Assoc Publr: Patricia Ploss *Tel:* 312-783-2295
Founded: 1977
Believe in authors & dedicated to making the dream of being a published author a reality. Specialize in works that uplift the human spirit, inspire people to reach for higher goals & touch the hearts of readers.
ISBN Prefix(es): 978-0-9710954; 978-0-9778311; 978-0-9768677; 978-0-9845904; 978-0-9823703; 978-0-9829803; 978-1-941049; 978-1-956823
Number of titles published annually: 30 Print; 30 E-Book
Total Titles: 250 Print; 100 E-Book
Imprints: Centaur Books; Chiral House
Membership(s): Independent Book Publishers Association (IBPA)

Judaica Press Inc
123 Ditmas Ave, Brooklyn, NY 11218
SAN: 204-9856
Tel: 718-972-6200 *Toll Free Tel:* 800-972-6201
Fax: 718-972-6204
E-mail: info@judaicapress.com; orders@judaicapress.com; submissions@judaicapress.com
Web Site: www.judaicapress.com
Key Personnel
Pres: Gloria Goldman
Mng Ed: Nachum Shapiro
Founded: 1963
Classic & contemporary Jewish literature in Hebrew & English.
ISBN Prefix(es): 978-0-910818; 978-1-880582; 978-1-932443; 978-1-60763
Number of titles published annually: 25 Print; 6 E-Book
Total Titles: 400 Print; 19 E-Book
Imprints: Zahava Publications
Foreign Rep(s): Kulmus (Israel); Lehmanns (Europe, UK)

Judson Press
Division of American Baptist Churches in the USA
1075 First Ave, King of Prussia, PA 19406
SAN: 201-0348
Toll Free Tel: 800-458-3766 *Fax:* 610-768-2107
E-mail: publisher@judsonpress.com; editor@judsonpress.com; marketing@judsonpress.com
Web Site: www.judsonpress.com
Key Personnel
Publr: Rev Cheryl L Price
Ed: Rachael Lawrence
Busn Mgr: Alma Hazboun
Founded: 1824
Religion (Baptist & nondenominational Christian), African American, women & multicultural; cloth & paperback.
ISBN Prefix(es): 978-0-8170
Number of titles published annually: 12 Print; 2 Audio
Total Titles: 350 Print; 1 CD-ROM; 2 Audio

Jump!
5357 Penn Ave, Minneapolis, MN 55419
Toll Free Tel: 888-799-1860 *Toll Free Fax:* 800-675-6679
E-mail: customercare@jumplibrary.com
Web Site: www.jumplibrary.com
Key Personnel
Pres: Gabe Kaufman *E-mail:* gabe@jumplibrary.com
Founded: 2012
Publish children's nonfiction with a focus on high-interest subjects for beginning & emergent readers. Books combine vibrant colors with captivating photography & corresponding text to draw readers into the subject & encourage reading success.
ISBN Prefix(es): 978-1-62031; 978-1-62496; 978-1-645276; 978-1-641289; 978-1-645270
Number of titles published annually: 175 Print; 175 E-Book; 30 Audio
Total Titles: 900 Print; 900 E-Book
Imprints: Blue Owl Books (social & emotional learning, health & wellness); Bullfrog Books; Pogo; Tadpole Books (preK)
Foreign Rep(s): Saunders Book Co (Canada)
Returns: 2150 Howard Dr W, North Mankato, MN 56003
Shipping Address: 2150 Howard Dr W, North Mankato, MN 56003
Warehouse: 2150 Howard Dr W, North Mankato, MN 56003
Distribution Center: 2150 Howard Dr W, North Mankato, MN 56003
Membership(s): Educational Book & Media Association (EBMA)

Jump at the Sun
Imprint of Disney-Hyperion Books
125 West End Ave, 3rd fl, New York, NY 10023
Web Site: books.disney.com
Founded: 1998
Books celebrating the African-American experience & culture.
ISBN Prefix(es): 978-0-7868
Number of titles published annually: 2 Print; 2 E-Book
Total Titles: 100 Print; 100 E-Book

§Just World Books LLC
PO Box 57075, Washington, DC 20037
Toll Free Tel: 888-506-3769
E-mail: sales@justworldbooks.com; info@justworldbooks.com; rights@justworldbooks.com
Web Site: justworldbooks.com
Key Personnel
Founder & CEO: Helena Cobban
Founded: 2010
ISBN Prefix(es): 978-0-9845056; 978-1-935982; 978-1-68257
Number of titles published annually: 8 Print
Total Titles: 41 Print; 30 E-Book
Distribution Center: Independent Publishers Group (IPG), 814 N Franklin St, Chicago, IL 60610 *Tel:* 321-337-0747 *Toll Free Tel:* 800-888-4741 *E-mail:* orders@ipgbook.com *Web Site:* www.ipgbook.com

Kaeden Publishing
24700 Center Ridge Rd, Suite 240, Westlake, OH 44145
Mailing Address: PO Box 16190, Rocky River, OH 44116-0190
Tel: 440-617-1400 *Toll Free Tel:* 800-890-7323
Fax: 440-617-1403
E-mail: sales@kaeden.com
Web Site: www.kaeden.com
Key Personnel
Pres: Craig Urmston *Tel:* 800-890-7323 ext 106 *E-mail:* curmston@kaeden.com
Founded: 1991
Educational books for emergent, early & fluent readers, grades K-4, STEM & graphic novels.
ISBN Prefix(es): 978-1-899835; 978-1-57874; 978-1-61181; 978-1-63584
Number of titles published annually: 56 Print
Total Titles: 560 Print
Imprints: Kaeden; Kaeden Books
Membership(s): Educational Book & Media Association (EBMA); International Literacy Association (ILA); Reading Recovery Council of North America

Kalaniot Books
Imprint of Endless Mountains Publishing Co
72 Glenmaura National Blvd, Suite 104B, Moosic, PA 18507
Tel: 862-251-2296; 570-451-6095
E-mail: info@kalaniotbooks.com
Web Site: www.kalaniotbooks.com
Key Personnel
Publr & Creative Dir: Lilian Rosenstreich *E-mail:* lili@kalaniotbooks.com
Publr & Busn Mgr: Mitchel Weiss *E-mail:* mitchel@kalaniotbooks.com
Founded: 2018
Our mission is to help young children & their families explore the diverse mosaic of Jewish culture & history.
ISBN Prefix(es): 978-0-9988527; 979-8-9863965
Number of titles published annually: 8 Print
Total Titles: 22 Print
Distribution Center: National Book Network (NBN), 15200 NBN Way, Blue Ridge Summit, PA 17214, Natl Accts Mgr: Jason Brockwell *Tel:* 717-794-3800 *Toll Free Tel:* 800-462-6420 *Toll Free Fax:* 800-338-4550 *E-mail:* jbrockwell@nbnbooks.com *Web Site:* nbnbooks.com

U.S. PUBLISHERS

Kallisti Publishing Inc
332 Center St, Wilkes-Barre, PA 18702
Tel: 570-825-3598
E-mail: editor@kallistipublishing.com
Web Site: www.kallistipublishing.com; arisbooks.com
Key Personnel
Publr: Anthony Raymond Michalski
 E-mail: anthony@kallistipublishing.com
Founded: 2000
Founded with a goal of publishing books you need to succeed, Kallisti publishes personal development & business books that expand the mind, generate ideas, & grow profits. We have grown to be the home to authors who are leaders & experts in their fields & write books that inform, inspire, & impel. We sell traditional books & ebooks through distributors & retailers, direct to the reader, & in bulk to companies & organizations. Kallisti comes from the Greek word 'kallos' which means beauty.
ISBN Prefix(es): 978-0-9678514; 978-0-9761111; 978-0-9848162; 978-1-7359792
Number of titles published annually: 8 Print; 8 E-Book
Total Titles: 32 Print; 32 E-Book
Imprints: ARIS Books (author-subsidized); International Wealth Success (IWS) (includes IW$ Press); Kallisti Publishing
See separate listing for:
International Wealth Success (IWS)

Kalmbach Media Co
21027 Crossroads Circle, Waukesha, WI 53186
Mailing Address: PO Box 1612, Waukesha, WI 53187-1612
Tel: 262-796-8776
Web Site: www.kalmbach.com
Key Personnel
Books Ed: Eric White *E-mail:* ewhite@kalmbach.com
Founded: 1934
Special interest books, calendars & magazines in astronomy, science, trains, toy trains & model railroading.
ISBN Prefix(es): 978-0-89024; 978-0-913135; 978-0-89778; 978-0-8238; 978-0-87116; 978-0-933168; 978-1-62700; 978-1-96120
Number of titles published annually: 12 Print
Imprints: Greenberg Books; Kalmbach Books

§Kamehameha Publishing
Division of Kamehameha Schools
567 S King St, Honolulu, HI 96813
E-mail: publishing@ksbe.edu
Web Site: kamehamehapublishing.org
Key Personnel
Dir: Ron Cox
Founded: 1933
Book, journal & poster publishing in the areas of Hawaiian history, studies, language & culture.
ISBN Prefix(es): 978-0-87336
Number of titles published annually: 12 Print
Total Titles: 100 Print; 7 E-Book
Imprints: Kamehameha Schools Press
Distribution Center: The Islander Group, 269 Palii St, Mililani, HI 96789 *Toll Free Tel:* 877-828-4852 *E-mail:* customerservice@islandergroup.com *Web Site:* www.islandergroup.com
Membership(s): Hawaii Book Publishers Association (HBPA); Independent Book Publishers Association (IBPA)

Kapp Books LLC
3602 Rocky Meadow Ct, Fairfax, VA 22033
Tel: 703-261-9171 *Fax:* 703-621-7162
E-mail: info@kappbooks.com
Web Site: www.kappbooks.com
Key Personnel
Principal: Parveen Ahuja
Founded: 2006

ISBN Prefix(es): 978-1-60346
Number of titles published annually: 100 Print
Total Titles: 350 Print; 10 CD-ROM

Kar-Ben Publishing
Imprint of Lerner Publishing Group Inc
241 First Ave N, Minneapolis, MN 55401
Tel: 612-332-3344 *Toll Free Tel:* 800-4-KARBEN (452-7236) *Fax:* 612-332-7615
Toll Free Fax: 800-332-1132
E-mail: custserve@karben.com
Web Site: www.karben.com
Key Personnel
Chmn: Harry J Lerner
Pres: Adam Lerner
Publr: Fran Greenman-Schmitz
Dir, Rts, Spec Sales & Intl Dist: Maria Kjoller
Founded: 1974
Jewish-themed picture books, calendars; preschool & primary, holiday books, folktales, bible stories.
ISBN Prefix(es): 978-1-58013
Number of titles published annually: 25 Print; 25 E-Book
Total Titles: 300 Print; 195 E-Book; 15 Audio
Foreign Rep(s): Bravo (UK)
Membership(s): Association of Jewish Libraries

Kazi Publications Inc
3023 W Belmont Ave, Chicago, IL 60618
Tel: 773-267-7001 *Fax:* 773-267-7002
E-mail: info@kazi.org
Web Site: www.kazi.org
Key Personnel
Pres: Liaquat Ali
Mktg Dir: Mary Bakhtiar
Founded: 1972
Nonprofit organization; print, publish & distribute; Islamic books in Arabic, English & Urdu.
ISBN Prefix(es): 978-0-935782; 978-1-56744; 978-0-933511; 978-1-871031; 978-1-930637
Number of titles published annually: 30 Print; 6 E-Book
Total Titles: 401 Print; 150 E-Book
Imprints: ABC International Group Inc; Abjad Books; Great Books of the Islamic World; Library of Islam

§J J Keller & Associates, Inc®
3003 Breezewood Lane, Neenah, WI 54957
Mailing Address: PO Box 368, Neenah, WI 54957-0368
Tel: 920-722-2848 *Toll Free Tel:* 877-564-2333
Toll Free Fax: 800-727-7516
E-mail: customerservice@jjkeller.com; sales@jjkeller.com
Web Site: www.jjkeller.com
Key Personnel
Chmn: Robert L Keller
VChmn & Treas: Jim Keller
Pres & CEO: Rustin Keller
CFO: Dana S Gilman
EVP, Content & Consulting Servs: Steven Murray
EVP, HR & Assoc Servs: Amy Jansen
EVP, Managed Servs: Shaun Gunderson
EVP, Mfg & Supply Chain: Timothy Little
EVP, Mktg: Lisa Karpinski
EVP, Sales: Chad Govin
EVP, Technol Solutions: Lacie Callan
Head, Corp Communs: Susan Baranczyk
 Tel: 920-727-7391 *E-mail:* sbaranczyk@jjkeller.com
Mktg & Communs Specialist: Kyle Florence *Tel:* 970-722-2848 ext 2947
 E-mail: kflorence@jjkeller.com
Founded: 1953
Publish regulatory compliance, "best practices" & training products dealing with occupational safety, job safety, environment & industry & motor-carrier (trucking) operations. On de-

mand, print, CD-ROM, intranet & Internet formats.
ISBN Prefix(es): 978-1-57943; 978-0-934674; 978-1-877798; 978-1-59042; 978-0-9789130; 978-1-60287; 978-1-61099; 978-1-68008
Number of titles published annually: 4 Print; 12 E-Book
Total Titles: 300 Print; 100 CD-ROM
Branch Office(s)
7273 State Rd 76, Neenah, WI 54956
Distributor for Chilton Book Co; International Air Transport Association; National Archives & Records Administration; National Institute of Occupational Safety & Health; Office of the Federal Register; Research & Special Programs Administration of the US Department of Transportation; John Wiley & Sons Inc

Kelsey Street Press
2824 Kelsey St, Berkeley, CA 94705
E-mail: info@kelseystreetpress.org
Web Site: www.kelseystreetpress.org
Key Personnel
Founding Ed: Patricia Dienstfrey; Rena Rosenwasser
Founded: 1974
Nonprofit press, publish experimental poetry & short fiction by women & collaborations between poets & artists.
ISBN Prefix(es): 978-0-932716
Number of titles published annually: 3 Print
Total Titles: 45 Print
Membership(s): Community of Literary Magazines & Presses (CLMP)

Kendall Hunt Publishing Co
4050 Westmark Dr, Dubuque, IA 52002-2624
SAN: 203-9184
Mailing Address: PO Box 1840, Dubuque, IA 52004-1840
Tel: 563-589-1000 *Toll Free Tel:* 800-228-0810 (orders) *Fax:* 563-589-1071 *Toll Free Fax:* 800-772-9165
E-mail: ordernow@kendallhunt.com
Web Site: www.kendallhunt.com
Key Personnel
Chmn & CEO: Mark C Falb
Pres & COO: Chad M Chandlee
VP, Higher Educ Div: David Tart
VP, K-12 Div: Charles Cook
VP, Opers: Kevin Johnson
Founded: 1969
Higher education custom publishing, K-12 math, science & TAG curriculum.
ISBN Prefix(es): 978-0-8403; 978-0-7872; 978-0-7575; 978-1-4652; 978-1-5249; 978-1-7924; 979-8-7657; 979-8-3851
Number of titles published annually: 1,500 Print; 200 Online
Total Titles: 6,500 Print; 10 CD-ROM; 5,500 Online; 6,500 E-Book
Divisions: JIST Publishing
Membership(s): National Council of Supervisors of Mathematics (NCSM); National Council of Teachers of Mathematics (NCTM); National Science Teachers Association (NSTA)
See separate listing for:
JIST Publishing

Kennedy Information LLC
Division of Bloomberg Industry Group
24 Railroad St, Keene, NH 03431
Tel: 603-357-8103 *Toll Free Tel:* 800-531-0140
Key Personnel
VP, Opers: Candace Batten
Founded: 1970
Newsletters, special reports, books, directories of management consultants, executive recruiters & outplacement consultants.
ISBN Prefix(es): 978-0-916654; 978-1-885922; 978-1-58673; 978-1-932079; 978-1-934717

Number of titles published annually: 15 Print; 1 CD-ROM; 3 Online
Total Titles: 50 Print; 1 CD-ROM

Kensington Books, see Kensington Publishing Corp

Kensington Cozies, see Kensington Publishing Corp

Kensington Publishing Corp
900 Third Ave, 26th fl, New York, NY 10022
SAN: 207-9860
Tel: 212-407-1500 Toll Free Tel: 800-221-2647
Fax: 212-935-0699
Web Site: www.kensingtonbooks.com
Key Personnel
Chmn, Pres & CEO: Steven Zacharius
 E-mail: szacharius@kensingtonbooks.com
VP & CFO: Peter Sallese E-mail: psallese@kensingtonbooks.com
VP & Dir, Busn Rel: Lynn Cully E-mail: lcully@kensingtonbooks.com
VP & Gen Mgr: Adam Zacharius
 E-mail: azacharius@kensingtonbooks.com
Gen Coun: Barbara Bennett Tel: 212-407-1558
 E-mail: bbennett@kensingtonbooks.com
Publr: Jackie Dinas Tel: 212-407-1578
 E-mail: jdinas@kensingtonbooks.com
Publr, Erewhon Books: Sarah Guan
 E-mail: sguan@kensingtonbooks.com
Creative Dir, Mktg: Jhonson Eteng Tel: 212-407-1522 E-mail: jeteng@kensingtonbooks.com
Dir, Communs: Vida Engstrand Tel: 212-407-1573 E-mail: vengstrand@kensingtonbooks.com
Dir, Opers: Angela Tucker E-mail: atucker@kensingtonbooks.com
Dir, Soc Media & Digital Sales: Alex Nicolajsen
 E-mail: anicolajsen@kensingtonboooks.com
Edit Dir: Gary Goldstein; Wendy McCurdy
 E-mail: wmccurdy@kensingtonbooks.com
Edit Dir, Dafina: Leticia Gomez
IT Dir: Jonathan Cohen
Prodn Dir: Joyce Kaplan Tel: 212-407-1515
 E-mail: jkaplan@kensingtonbooks.com
Assoc Dir, Lib & Indie Bookstore Mktg: Matt Johnson Tel: 212-407-1541
 E-mail: mjohnson@kensingtonbooks.com
Assoc Dir, Sales: Darla Freeman
 E-mail: dfreeman@kensingtonbooks.com
Assoc Dir, Subs Rts: Susanna Gruninger
 E-mail: sgruninger@kensingtonbooks.com
Asst Dir, Soc Media: Lauren Jernigan
Ed-in-Chief, Citadel Press: Michaela Hamilton
Ed-in-Chief, Kensington: John Scognamiglio
 E-mail: jscognamiglio@kensingtonbooks.com
Exec Ed, Citadel Press: Denise Silvestro
 E-mail: dsilvestro@kensingtonbooks.com
Sr Ed: Elizabeth May; Alex Hoopes Sunshine
Ed: James Abbate; Elizabeth Trout
Asst Ed, Erewhon Books: Viengsamai Fetters
Sr Communs Mgr, Diverse & Issue Driven Titles: Michelle Addo-Chazet Tel: 212-407-1571
 E-mail: maddo@kensingtonbooks.com
Sr Communs Mgr, Mysteries: Larissa Ackerman
 Tel: 212-407-1598 E-mail: lackerman@kensingtonbooks.com
Sr Communs Mgr, Nonfiction: Ann Pryor
 Tel: 212-407-1526 E-mail: apryor@kensingtonbooks.com
Sr Communs Mgr, Romance: Jane Nutter Tel: 212-407-1542 E-mail: jnutter@kensingtonbooks.com
Communs Mgr: Jesse Cruz Tel: 212-407-1528
 E-mail: jcruz@kensingtonbooks.com
Communs Mgr, SciFi & Fantasy: Martin Cahill Tel: 212-407-1577 E-mail: mcahill@kensingtonbooks.com
Copy Mgr, Mktg: Shannon Gray-Winter Tel: 212-407-1547 E-mail: sgray@kensingtonbooks.com
Digital Mktg Mgr: Kristin McLaughlin; Megan Zimlich
Asst Mgr, Mktg & Influencer Outreach: Kristen Vega Tel: 212-407-1551 E-mail: kvega@kensingtonbooks.com
Asst Soc Media Mgr: Kait Johnson
Digital Content Coord: Bre'Anna Girdy
Founded: 1974
Independent commercial publisher of popular fiction & nonfiction across all formats.
ISBN Prefix(es): 978-0-8065; 978-0-7860; 978-1-4967; 978-1-4201; 978-1-5161
Number of titles published annually: 400 Print
Imprints: Citadel Press (nonfiction); Dafina (commercial fiction & nonfiction centered on race & cultural identity); Erewhon Books (speculative fiction & sci-fi fantasy); Kensington Cozies (cozy mysteries); Kensington Hardcover (commercial fiction); Kensington Mass-Market (commercial fiction); Kensington Trade Paperback (commercial fiction); Lyrical Press (digital first); Pinnacle Books (westerns); John Scognamiglio Books (editorially driven commercial fiction); Zebra Books (mass market fiction)
Distributor for Black Odyssey Media; Urban Books
Foreign Rights: ANA Sofia (Mira Droumeva) (Bulgaria); Big Apple Agency Inc (China, Indonesia, Malaysia, Taiwan, Thailand, Vietnam); The Book Publishers' Association of Israel, International Promotion & Literary Rights Dept (Beverley Levit) (Israel); Sandra Bruna Agency (Brazil, Mexico, South America, Spain); Donzelli Fietta Agency SRLS (Stephania Fietta) (Italy); Eastern European & Asian Rights Agency (Tatjana Zoldnere) (Baltic States); English Agency Japan Co Ltd (Japan); Graal Literary Agency (Poland); Imprima Korea Agency (South Korea); Nurcihan Kesim Literary Agency Ltd (Turkey); La Nouvelle Agence (France); Andrew Nurnberg Associates (Judit Hermann) (Croatia, Hungary); Andrew Nurnberg Literary Agency (Russia); Kristin Olson Literary Agency SRO (Czechia, Slovakia); Read n Right Agency (Nike Davarinou) (Greece); Thomas Schlueck GmbH (Germany); Sebes & Bisseling Literary Agency (Finland, Iceland, Netherlands, Scandinavia); Dorie Simmonds Agency (Australia, British Commonwealth, UK & Commonwealth, UK Commonwealth); Tuttle-Mori Agency Inc (Misa Morikawa) (Japan)
Warehouse: Penguin Publishing Group, Pittston, PA
Distribution Center: Penguin Random House Publisher Services (PRHPS), 400 Hahn Rd, Westminster, MD 21157 Toll Free Tel: 800-733-3000 Toll Free Fax: 800-659-2436
 E-mail: customerservice@randomhouse.com
Web Site: prhpublisherservices.com

Kent State University Press
1118 University Library Bldg, 1125 Risman Dr, Kent, OH 44242
SAN: 201-0437
Mailing Address: PO Box 5190, Kent, OH 44242-0001
Tel: 330-672-7913 Fax: 330-672-3104
E-mail: ksupress@kent.edu
Web Site: www.kentstateuniversitypress.com
Key Personnel
Dir: Susan Wadsworth-Booth
 E-mail: swadswo2@kent.edu
Mng Ed: Mary D Young E-mail: mdyoung@kent.edu
Acqs Ed: Clara Totten E-mail: ctotten1@kent.edu
Assoc Ed: Kat Saunders E-mail: ksaunde5@kent.edu
Design & Prodn Mgr: Christine Brooks
 E-mail: cbrooks@kent.edu
Mktg & Sales Mgr: Julia Wiesenberg
 E-mail: jwiesenb@kent.edu
Mktg Assoc & Designer: Darryl Crosby
 E-mail: dcrosby@kent.edu
Founded: 1965
Scholarly nonfiction, with emphasis on Civil War history, literary studies (Tolkien, C S Lewis, Hemingway), biography & Midwest regional.
ISBN Prefix(es): 978-0-87338; 978-1-60635
Number of titles published annually: 30 Print; 35 E-Book; 5 Audio
Total Titles: 850 Print; 1,250 E-Book; 20 Audio
Imprints: Black Squirrel Books
Foreign Rep(s): Eurospan Ltd (Africa, Asia, Australia, Caribbean, Europe, Latin America, Middle East, New Zealand, UK)
Orders to: Baker & Taylor Publisher Services, 30 Amberwood Pkwy, Ashland, OH 44805 Toll Free Tel: 800-247-6553
 E-mail: orders@btpubservices.com Web Site: www.btpubservices.com
Returns: Baker & Taylor Publisher Services, 30 Amberwood Pkwy, Ashland, OH 44805 Toll Free Tel: 800-247-6553 Web Site: www.btpubservices.com
Warehouse: Baker & Taylor Publisher Services, 30 Amberwood Pkwy, Ashland, OH 44805 Toll Free Tel: 800-247-6553
 E-mail: orders@btpubservices.com Web Site: www.btpubservices.com
Distribution Center: Baker & Taylor Publisher Services, 30 Amberwood Pkwy, Ashland, OH 44805 Toll Free Tel: 800-247-6553 E-mail: orders@btpubservices.com Web Site: www.btpubservices.com
Membership(s): American Booksellers Association (ABA); Association of American Publishers (AAP); Association of University Presses (AUPresses)

Kessinger Publishing LLC
PO Box 1404, Whitefish, MT 59937
Web Site: www.kessingerpublishing.com
Key Personnel
Pres: Roger A Kessinger
Founded: 1988
On demand publisher. Specialize in rare, scarce & out of print books.
ISBN Prefix(es): 978-0-922802; 978-1-56459; 978-0-7661; 978-1-4191; 978-1-891620; 978-0-548; 978-1-104; 978-1-120; 978-1-160; 978-1-162; 978-1-163; 978-1-164; 978-1-165; 978-1-166; 978-1-167; 978-1-168; 978-1-169; 978-1-4179; 978-1-4253; 978-1-4254; 978-1-4286; 978-1-4304; 978-1-4325; 978-1-4326; 978-1-4367; 978-1-4370; 978-1-4373; 978-1-4365; 978-1-4368; 978-1-4371; 978-1-4374; 978-1-4366; 978-1-4369; 978-1-4372
Number of titles published annually: 5,000 Print; 5,000 E-Book
Imprints: Kessinger Publishing®

Kidsbooks LLC, see Kidsbooks® Publishing

Kidsbooks® Publishing
5306 Ballard Ave NW, Suite 311, Seattle, WA 98107
SAN: 666-3729
E-mail: customerservice@kidsbookspublishing.com
Web Site: www.kidsbookspublishing.com
Key Personnel
Mng Dir: Link Dyrdahl
Founded: 1987
Promotional book publishers of children, juvenile & hardcover, Search & Find®, board books, cloth books & other novelty books.
ISBN Prefix(es): 978-0-942025; 978-1-56156; 978-1-58865; 978-1-62885; 978-1-63854
Number of titles published annually: 100 Print
Total Titles: 3,000 Print
Imprints: Rainstorm Publishing

U.S. PUBLISHERS

Jessica Kingsley Publishers Inc
123 S Broad St, Suite 2750, Philadelphia, PA 19109
SAN: 256-2391
Tel: 215-922-1161 *Toll Free Tel:* 866-416-1078 (cust serv) *Fax:* 215-922-1474
E-mail: hello.usa@jkp.com
Web Site: us.jkp.com
Key Personnel
Chmn: Jessica Kingsley
VP, Sales & Mktg: David Corey
Assoc Mktg Dir: Katelynn Bartleson
 E-mail: katelynn.bartleson@jkp.com
Sales & Mktg Opers Mgr: Stephanie DeMuzio
Sales Acct Mgr: Julia Zullo
Founded: 1987 (US office opened 2004)
Publish books for the consumer on autism spectrum disorders & related developmental disorders; books for professionals in expressive arts therapies: art, music, drama & dance & social work; books on Tai Chi & Quigong.
ISBN Prefix(es): 978-1-85302; 978-1-84310; 978-1-84819; 978-1-874579; 978-1-900990; 978-0-902817; 978-1-904787; 978-1-905818; 978-1-84642; 978-1-84905; 978-1-84985; 978-0-85701; 978-0-85700; 978-1-78450
Number of titles published annually: 250 Print
Total Titles: 1,800 Print
Imprints: Singing Dragon
Foreign Office(s): 73 Collier St, London N1 9BE, United Kingdom *Tel:* (020) 7833 2307 *Fax:* (020) 7837 2917 *E-mail:* hello@jkp.com
Foreign Rep(s): APD Singapore Pte Ltd (Brunei, Cambodia, Indonesia, Laos, Malaysia, Myanmar, Philippines, Singapore, Thailand, Vietnam); Jonathan Ball Publishers (South Africa); Beijing New Knowledge Era (Wei Zhao) (China); Brookside Publishing Services (Michael Darcy) (Ireland); Hachette (Mariafrancesca Ierace) (Southern Europe); Hachette (Anna Martini) (Eastern Europe); Hachette (Kerri Logan) (France); Hachette Book Publishing India Pvt Ltd (India); Hachette UK (Zoe Rutherford) (Europe); Hachette UK (UK); Hachette UK (Anne-Katrine Buch) (Denmark, Estonia, Finland, Iceland, Latvia, Lithuania, Norway, Sweden); Hachette UK Ltd (Joan Wamae & Tilda Eid) (Middle East); Tulia Publishing Ltd (Africa exc South Africa); UBC Press (Canada); Woodslane Pty Ltd (Australia, New Zealand)
Distribution Center: Books International, PO Box 960, Herndon, VA 20172 *Toll Free Tel:* 866-416-1078 *Fax:* 703-611-1501
E-mail: jkpmail@presswarehouse.com

Kiva Publishing Inc
10 Bella Loma, Santa Fe, NM 87506
Tel: 909-896-0518
E-mail: kivapub@aol.com
Web Site: www.kivapub.com
Key Personnel
Publr: Stephen W Hill
Founded: 1993
Publish Native American & Southwest regional books & cards.
ISBN Prefix(es): 978-1-885772
Number of titles published annually: 3 Print
Total Titles: 40 Print
Membership(s): The Association of Publishers for Special Sales (APSS); Independent Book Publishers Association (IBPA); New Mexico Publishers Association; Publishers Association of the West (PubWest)

Klutz®
Imprint of Scholastic Trade Publishing
557 Broadway, New York, NY 10012
Tel: 212-343-6360 *Toll Free Tel:* 800-737-4123 (cust serv)
E-mail: scholasticmarketing@scholastic.com; scholasticstore@scholastic.com
Web Site: www.scholastic.com/parents/klutz.html; store.scholastic.com
Key Personnel
VP, Publr & Creative Dir: Netta Rabin
Art Dir: Vanessa Han
Founded: 1977
Premium brand of book-based activity kits, committed to inspiring creativity in every kid with a unique combination of crystal clear instructions, custom tools & materials & a hearty helping of humor.
ISBN Prefix(es): 978-0-932592; 978-1-57054; 978-1-878257; 978-1-59174; 978-0-545
Number of titles published annually: 30 Print
Total Titles: 140 Print
Foreign Rep(s): Scholastic Asia (Selina Lee) (Asia); Scholastic Australia Ltd (Australia); Scholastic Canada Ltd (Canada); Scholastic Ltd (UK); Scholastic New Zealand Ltd (New Zealand)
Orders to: 2931 E McCarty St, Jefferson City, MO 65101 *Toll Free Tel:* 888-724-1872 *Toll Free Fax:* 877-724-1872 *E-mail:* orders@klutz.com
Membership(s): American Specialty Toy Retailing Association (ASTRA)

Kluwer Law International (KLI), see Wolters Kluwer Law & Business

§Alfred A Knopf
Imprint of Knopf Doubleday Publishing Group
c/o Penguin Random House LLC, 1745 Broadway, New York, NY 10019
Tel: 212-751-2600 *Fax:* 212-940-7390 (dom rts); 212-572-2662 (foreign rts)
Web Site: knopfdoubleday.com/imprint/knopf/; knopfdoubleday.com
Key Personnel
EVP, Publr & Ed-in-Chief: Jordan Pavlin
SVP & Exec Ed: Jennifer Barth
VP & Exec Dir, Sales Mgmt & Planning: Beth Meister
VP & Exec Dir, Publicity: Erinn Hartman
VP & Exec Dir, Strategic Insights: Laura Crisp
VP & Sr Dir, Mktg: Laura Keefe
VP & Sr Dir, Strategy & Fin: May Choy
VP & Art Dir, Knopf/Design: Chip Kidd
VP & Creative Dir: John Gall
VP & Edit Dir, Fiction: Jennifer Jackson
VP & Exec Ed: Erroll McDonald
VP & Exec Publicist: Kathy Zuckerman
Assoc Publr: Gabrielle Brooks
Sr Art Dir, Knopf Cooks: Kelly Blair
Sr Dir, Brand Devt: Lauren Weber
Sr Dir, Publicity: Jessica Purcell; Jordan Rodman
Dir: Lisa Montebello
Dir, Ebook Prodn: Austin O'Malley
Dir, Translation Rts: Suzanne Smith
Edit Dir, Knopf Cooks & Sr Ed, Alfred A Knopf: Lexy Bloom
Rts Dir: Sean Yule
Assoc Dir, Mktg: Sara Eagle; Emily Murphy
Assoc Dir, Publicity: Sarah New
Asst Dir, Foreign & Subs Rts: Sal Ruggiero
Asst Dir, Publicity: Emily Reardon
Mng Ed: Anne Achenbaum
Exec Ed: Emily Cunningham; John Freeman; Diana Tejerina Miller
Exec Ed & Poetry Ed: Deborah Garrison
Sr Ed: Quynh Do; Tom Pold
Ed: Maris Dyer; Vanessa Haughton; Todd Portnowitz
Assoc Ed: Michael Tizzano
Asst Ed: Brian Etling; Morgan Hamilton; Marc Jaffee; Izzy Meyers; Sarah Perrin; Rob Shapiro; Tiara Sharma
Ed-at-Large: Carole Baron
Sr Publicity Mgr: Tricia Cave
Sr Publicist: Sarah Nisbet
Publicist: Penelope Belnap; Amy Hagedorn; Elizabeth Lindsay; Katie Schoder
Assoc Publicist: Elka Roderick
Sr Ad Mgr: Nic Ishaq
Sr Mgr: Zachary Lutz; Marisa Melendez; Felecia O'Connell
Busn Mgr: Andrew Unger
Mktg Mgr: Abby Endler; Matthew Sciarappa
Prodn Mgr: Hilary DiLoreto
Designer: Marisa Nakasone
Mktg Assoc: Morgan Fenton
Edit Asst: Zuleima Ugalde
Publicity Asst: Olivia Decker; Micah Kelsey
Founded: 1915
Penguin Random House & its publishing entities are not accepting unsol submissions, proposals, mss, or submission queries via e-mail at this time.
Imprints: Knopf Cooks
Foreign Rights: ALS-Agenzia Letteraria Santachiara (Roberto Santachiara) (Italy); Anthea Agency (Katalina Sabeva) (Bulgaria); Bardon-Chinese Media Agency (Xu Weiguang) (China); Bardon-Chinese Media Agency (Yu-Shiuan Chen) (Taiwan); English Agency Japan Co Ltd (Junzo Sawa) (Japan); Graal Literary Agency (Maria Strarz-Zielinska) (Poland); The Deborah Harris Agency (Ilana Kurshan) (Israel); JLM Literary Agency (Nelly Moukakos) (Greece); Katai & Bolza Literary (Peter Bolza) (Croatia, Hungary); Simona Kessler International (Simona Kessler) (Romania); Korea Copyright Center Inc (KCC) (MiSook Hong) (South Korea); Licht & Burr Literary Agency (Trine Licht) (Scandinavia); La Nouvelle Agence (Vanessa Kling) (France); Kristin Olson Literary Agency (Kristin Olson) (Czechia); Sebes & Bisseling Literary Agency (Paul Sebes) (Netherlands)

Knopf Doubleday Publishing Group
Division of Penguin Random House LLC
c/o Penguin Random House LLC, 1745 Broadway, New York, NY 10019
Tel: 212-751-2600 *Fax:* 212-940-7390 (dom rts); 212-572-2662 (foreign rts)
Web Site: knopfdoubleday.com
Key Personnel
Pres & Publr: Maya Mavjee
SVP & Group Deputy Publr, Publg & Sales Opers: Christopher Dufault
SVP & Dir, Prodn, SVP & Dir, Prodn, Knopf Doubleday Publishing Group & Penguin Publishing Group: Robert Wojciechowski
SVP, Publicity & Communs: Todd Doughty
SVP & Exec Mng Ed, Knopf Doubleday Publishing Group & Penguin Publishing Group: Meredith Dros
VP & Assoc Publr, Backlist & Vintage Books: Gabrielle Brooks
Dir, Art & Design: Kristen Bearse
Dir, Prodn Edit: Ellen Feldman
Dir, Title Mgmt: Orlene Gabrino
Sr Lib Mktg Dir: Erica Meinichok
Mktg Mgr: Sarah Engelmann
Publg & Mktg Mgr, Vintage Espanol: Michelle Dominguez
Penguin Random House & its publishing entities are not accepting unsol submissions, proposals, mss, or submission queries via e-mail at this time.
Imprints: Doubleday; Everyman's Library; Alfred A Knopf; Pantheon Books; Schocken Books; Nan A Talese; Vintage Crime/Black Lizard
See separate listing for:
Doubleday
Everyman's Library
Alfred A Knopf
Pantheon Books
Schocken Books
Nan A Talese
Vintage Books

Kodansha USA Inc
Subsidiary of Kodansha Ltd (Japan)
451 Park Ave S, 7th fl, New York, NY 10016

SAN: 201-0526
Tel: 917-322-6200 *Fax:* 212-935-6929
E-mail: info@kodansha-usa.com
Web Site: kodansha.us
Key Personnel
CEO: Alvin Lu
COO: Takashi Sakuda
Founded: 2008
Publishes hardcover & paperback books in English on Japanese cultures, history, art, architecture, design, craft, gardening, literature, material arts, language, cookbooks, travel & memoirs.
ISBN Prefix(es): 978-0-87011; 978-1-56836; 978-1-935429; 978-1-61262; 978-1-63236
Number of titles published annually: 4 Print
Total Titles: 270 Print
Imprints: Kodansha America; Kodansha Globe; Kodansha International
Distributor for Japan Publications Inc; Japan Publications Trading Co Ltd
Foreign Rep(s): Bill Bailey Publishers' Representatives (Baltic States, Hungary, Southeast Europe, Western Europe); Intermediaamericana Ltd (Eastern Europe); Turnaround Publisher Services Ltd (Ireland, UK)
Distribution Center: Penguin Random House Publisher Services (PRHPS) (worldwide exc Continental Europe, Ireland & UK)
Penguin Random House Canada, 320 Front St W, Suite 1400, Toronto, ON M5V 3B6, Canada *Toll Free Tel:* 888-523-9292 *Toll Free Fax:* 888-562-9924

§Kogan Page
8 W 38 St, Suite 902, New York, NY 10018
Tel: 212-812-4414
E-mail: info@koganpage.com
Web Site: www.koganpage.com
Founded: 1967
Books, ebooks & digital solutions.
ISBN Prefix(es): 978-0-7494
Number of titles published annually: 120 Print; 120 E-Book
Total Titles: 900 Print; 500 E-Book
Editorial Office(s): 45 Gee St, London EC1V 3RS, United Kingdom *Tel:* (020) 7278 0433 *E-mail:* kpinfo@koganpage.com
Foreign Office(s): Kogan Page Ltd, 45 Gee St, London EC1V 3RS, United Kingdom *Tel:* (020) 7278 0433
Foreign Rep(s): Kogan Page Ltd (London) (worldwide exc USA)
Foreign Rights: Kogan Page Ltd (London) (worldwide exc USA)
Orders to: Ingram Publisher Services, 14 Ingram Blvd, Mail Stop 631, La Vergne, TN 37086, *Web Site:* www.ingrampublisherservices.com
Returns: Ingram Publisher Services, 191 Edwards Dr, Jackson, TN 38301
Distribution Center: Ingram Publisher Services, 14 Ingram Blvd, Mail Stop 631, La Vergne, TN 37086 *Web Site:* www.ingrampublisherservices.com

§Koho Pono LLC
15024 SE Pinegrove Loop, Clackamas, OR 97015
Tel: 503-723-7392
E-mail: info@kohopono.com; orders@ingrambook.com
Web Site: kohopono.com
Key Personnel
Publr: Scott Burr *Tel:* 408-689-0888; Dayna Hubenthal
Founded: 2010
Multimedia publishing company that is passionate about growth & improvement for all aspects of life: business, career, relationships & personal. Specialize in innovation, awareness, process improvement, change management & strengthening relationships for business & individuals. Support the evolution of consciousness, self-exploration & the pursuit of increasing relevance in life.
ISBN Prefix(es): 978-0-984554
Number of titles published annually: 3 Print; 3 Online; 3 E-Book; 3 Audio
Total Titles: 6 Print; 6 Online; 2 E-Book; 3 Audio
Shipping Address: Lightning Source Inc, 1246 Heil Quaker Blvd, La Vergne, TN 37086, Contact: Amy Waugh *Tel:* 615-213-5815 *Fax:* 615-213-4725 *E-mail:* inquiry@lightningsource.com
Warehouse: Lightning Source Inc, 1246 Heil Quaker Blvd, La Vergne, TN 37086, Contact: Amy Waugh *Tel:* 615-213-5815 *Fax:* 615-213-4725 *E-mail:* inquiry@lightningsource.com
Distribution Center: Ingram Book Co, One Ingram Blvd, La Vergne, TN 37086 *Tel:* 615-793-5000 *Toll Free Tel:* 800-937-8200 *E-mail:* customer.service@ingrambook.com
Lightning Source Inc, 1246 Heil Quaker Blvd, La Vergne, TN 37086, Contact: Amy Waugh *Tel:* 615-213-5815 *Fax:* 615-213-4725 *E-mail:* inquiry@lightningsource.com

Kokila
Imprint of Penguin Young Readers Group
c/o Penguin Random House LLC, 1745 Broadway, New York, NY 10019
Tel: 212-782-9000
Web Site: www.penguin.com/kokila-books-overview/
Key Personnel
Pres & Publr: Namrata Tripathi
Assoc Publr: Joanna Cardenas
Art Dir: Jasmin Rubero
Exec Ed: Zareen Jaffery
Assoc Ed: Sydnee Monday
Asst Ed, Kokila & Nancy Paulsen Books: Jenny Ly
Publg Asst: Tenisha Anderson-Kenkpen
Jr Designer: Asiya Ahmed
Publishes books that inspire & entertain readers & add nuance & depth to the way children & young adults see the world & their place in it.
Penguin Random House & its publishing entities are not accepting unsol submissions, proposals, mss, or submission queries via e-mail at this time.
Number of titles published annually: 4 Print

Konecky & Konecky LLC
72 Ayers Point Rd, Old Saybrook, CT 06475
Tel: 860-388-0878
E-mail: sean.konecky@gmail.com
Web Site: www.koneckyandkonecky.com
Key Personnel
Publr: Sean Konecky *E-mail:* sean.konecky@gmail.com
Founded: 1982
Hardcover art books & Civil War history, military history, biography, religion & spirituality.
ISBN Prefix(es): 978-1-56852; 978-0-914427
Number of titles published annually: 10 Print
Total Titles: 250 Print
Imprints: Konecky & Konecky (K&K); Tabard Press
Distributor for Octavo Editions

§Krause Publications Inc
Imprint of Penguin Random House LLC
1745 Broadway, New York, NY 10019
Tel: 212-782-9000
Web Site: www.penguinrandomhouse.com
Founded: 1952
Penguin Random House & its publishing entities are not accepting unsol submissions, proposals, mss, or submission queries via e-mail at this time.
Number of titles published annually: 150 Print
Total Titles: 1,000 Print

§Kregel Publications
Division of Kregel Inc
2450 Oak Industrial Dr NE, Grand Rapids, MI 49505
SAN: 298-9115
Tel: 616-451-4775 *Toll Free Tel:* 800-733-2607 *Fax:* 616-451-9330
E-mail: kregelbooks@kregel.com
Web Site: www.kregel.com
Key Personnel
Pres: Jerold W Kregel *Tel:* 616-451-4775 ext 216 *E-mail:* jerry@kregel.com
Publr & Rts & Perms: Catherine DeVries *Tel:* 616-451-4775 ext 212 *E-mail:* catherined@kregel.com
Exec Dir, Sales & Mktg: David Hill *Tel:* 616-451-4775 ext 235 *E-mail:* dave@kregel.com
Founded: 1949
Evangelical Christian books & resource materials.
ISBN Prefix(es): 978-0-8254
Number of titles published annually: 75 Print
Total Titles: 1,500 Print
Imprints: Editorial Portavoz (Spanish lang div); Kregel Academic & Ministry; Kregel Bibles; Kregel Children's; Kregel Classics
Distributor for Muddy Pearl (Scotland)
Foreign Rep(s): Christian Art Wholesale (South Africa); Christian Literature Crusade (Japan); Omega Distribution (New Zealand); SPCK Publishing Group (UK & the continent); Word of Life Press (South Korea); WordAlive (Canada)
Membership(s): Evangelical Christian Publishers Association (ECPA)
See separate listing for:
Editorial Portavoz

Krieger Publishing Co
1725 Krieger Lane, Malabar, FL 32950
SAN: 202-6562
Tel: 321-724-9542 *Fax:* 321-951-3671
E-mail: info@krieger-publishing.com
Web Site: www.krieger-publishing.com
Key Personnel
Pres: Donald E Krieger
Cust Serv: Ann Krieger
Founded: 1969
A scientific-technical publisher serving the college textbook market. Reprints & new titles: technical, science, psychology, geology, humanities, ecology, history, social sciences, engineering, mathematics, chemistry, adult educational, herpetology, space science.
ISBN Prefix(es): 978-0-88275; 978-0-89464; 978-0-89874; 978-1-57524
Number of titles published annually: 5 Print
Total Titles: 800 Print
Imprints: Anvil Series; Orbit Series; Professional Practices
Advertising Agency: Krieger Enterprises Inc

KTAV Publishing House Inc
527 Empire Blvd, Brooklyn, NY 11225
Tel: 201-963-9524; 718-972-5449 *Fax:* 718-972-6307
E-mail: orders@ktav.com
Web Site: www.ktav.com
Key Personnel
Founder: Bernie Scharfstein *E-mail:* bernie@ktav.com
Owner & CEO: Moshe Heller *E-mail:* moshe@ktav.com
VP, Busn Devt: Raphael Freeman *E-mail:* raphael@ktav.com
Publr: Tzvi Mauer *E-mail:* tzvi@ktav.com
Publr, Targum Publishers: Akiva Atwood *E-mail:* akiva@ktav.com
Mgr: Levi Rodal *E-mail:* levi@ktav.com
Founded: 1921
Books of Jewish interest; juvenile, textbooks; scholarly Judaica & interfaith issues.
ISBN Prefix(es): 978-0-87068; 978-0-88125; 978-1-60280
Number of titles published annually: 20 Print

U.S. PUBLISHERS

Total Titles: 840 Print
Distributor for Yeshiva University Press

Kumarian Press
Imprint of Lynne Rienner Publishers Inc
1800 30 St, Suite 314, Boulder, CO 80301
Tel: 303-444-6684 *Fax:* 303-444-0824
E-mail: questions@rienner.com
Web Site: www.rienner.com
Key Personnel
CEO: Lynne Rienner
Founded: 1977
Academic, professional books, college textbooks in social sciences: international development, international relations, political science, political economy, economics, globalization, women & gender studies, conflict resolution, environment, sustainability, civil society & NGOs.
ISBN Prefix(es): 978-0-931816; 978-1-56549; 978-1-887208
Number of titles published annually: 3 Print; 3 E-Book
Total Titles: 300 Print; 300 E-Book
Foreign Rep(s): Catamount (Latin America); China Publishers Marketing (China, Hong Kong, Taiwan); Eurospan (Australia, Europe, New Zealand, UK); MHM Ltd (Japan); Taylor & Francis (Asia-Pacific, South Korea, Southeast Asia); Viva Books (India)
Membership(s): Association of American Publishers (AAP)

Kumon Publishing North America Inc (KPNA)
Subsidiary of Kumon Publishing Co Ltd
301 Rte 17 N, Suite 704, Rutherford, NJ 07070-2581
Tel: 201-836-2105; 201-836-1559; 703-661-1501 (orders) *Toll Free Tel:* 800-657-7970 (cust serv) *Fax:* 201-836-1559
E-mail: books@kumon.com; kumon@presswarehouse.com
Web Site: kumonbooks.com
Key Personnel
SVP: Brian Klingborg
Founded: 2004
Publisher of children's educational books & toys.
ISBN Prefix(es): 978-1-933241; 978-1-93500; 978-1-941082
Number of titles published annually: 30 Print
Total Titles: 160 Print
Foreign Rep(s): ABC Marketing (Raymond Wong) (China); Elm Tree Distributors Pte Ltd (Agnes Lim) (Malaysia, Singapore); Gazelle Book Services Ltd (Europe); IPR (Mark Cox) (Middle East); National Book Store (Mike Longno) (Philippines); Pearson Holdings South Africa (Pty) Ltd (Nicolet Du Randt) (South Africa); Peribo Pty Ltd (Michael Coffey) (Oceania); Popular (L S Yee) (Malaysia, Singapore); Sketch Books (Aubrey Marquez) (Philippines); SOLUSI Educational Technology (Ervida Lin) (Indonesia)

L & R Publishing, see Hellgate Press

Lake Superior Publishing LLC
109 W Superior St, Suite 200, Duluth, MN 55802
Mailing Address: PO Box 16417, Duluth, MN 55816-0417
Tel: 218-722-5002 *Toll Free Tel:* 888-BIG-LAKE (244-5253) *Fax:* 218-722-4096
E-mail: edit@lakesuperior.com
Web Site: www.lakesuperior.com
Key Personnel
Publr: Beth Bily *E-mail:* beth@lakesuperior.com; Ron Brochu *E-mail:* rb@lakesuperior.com
Ed: Konnie Le May *E-mail:* kon@lakesuperior.com
Founded: 1979
Began as regional magazine publisher & expanded services to include books, travel guides, calendars, maps & merchandise.

ISBN Prefix(es): 978-0-942235
Number of titles published annually: 2 Print
Total Titles: 32 Print
Membership(s): Content Delivery & Storage Association (CDSA); Midwest Independent Booksellers Association (MIBA); Midwest Independent Publishing Association (MIPA); Minnesota Magazine & Publications Association (MMPA)

LAMA Books
2381 Sleepy Hollow Ave, Hayward, CA 94545
Tel: 510-785-1091 *Toll Free Tel:* 888-452-6244 *Fax:* 510-785-1099
Web Site: www.lamabooks.com
Key Personnel
CEO, CFO & Secy: Steve J Meyer
Founded: 1970
Develop & publish books for heating, ventilating & air conditioning (HVAC) field; occupational trades, reading development, teacher preparation; directories-occupational programs in California community colleges.
ISBN Prefix(es): 978-0-88069
Number of titles published annually: 5 Print
Total Titles: 50 Print

Lanahan Publishers Inc
324 Hawthorne Rd, Baltimore, MD 21210-2303
SAN: 859-1288
Tel: 410-366-2434 *Toll Free Tel:* 866-345-1949 *Fax:* 410-366-8798
E-mail: lanahan@aol.com
Web Site: www.lanahanpublishers.com
Key Personnel
Pres: Donald W Fusting
Founded: 1995
College textbook publisher.
ISBN Prefix(es): 978-0-9652687; 978-1-930398
Number of titles published annually: 4 Print
Total Titles: 20 Print

Landauer Publishing
Imprint of Fox Chapel Publishing Co Inc
903 Square St, Mount Joy, PA 17552
Tel: 717-560-4703 *Toll Free Tel:* 800-457-9112 *Fax:* 717-560-4702
E-mail: customerservice@foxchapelpublishing.com
Web Site: landauerpub.com
Key Personnel
Pres & Publr: Jeramy Landauer
Founded: 1991
Publishing & licensing for the home arts working with leading designers & artists.
ISBN Prefix(es): 978-1-890621; 978-0-9646870; 978-0-9793711; 978-0-9770166; 978-1-935726; 978-0-9825586; 978-0-9818040
Number of titles published annually: 12 Print
Total Titles: 114 Print
Foreign Rep(s): A Great Notion (Canada); Alba Patchwork (Spain); N Jefferson (Canada); Quilt Source (Canada); John Reed Book Distribution (Australia); RJR Fabrics (Europe); Roundhouse Group (England); Stallion Press (Singapore); Virka (Iceland)
Membership(s): American Booksellers Association (ABA); Independent Book Publishers Association (IBPA)

Landisfarne Books, see SteinerBooks Inc

§Peter Lang Publishing Inc
Subsidiary of Peter Lang AG (Switzerland)
80 Broadway, 5th fl, New York, NY 10004
SAN: 241-5534
Tel: 703-661-1584 *Toll Free Tel:* 800-770-5264 (cust serv) *Fax:* 703-996-1010
E-mail: info@peterlang.com; newyork.editorial@peterlang.com; customerservice@plang.com
Web Site: www.peterlang.com

Key Personnel
SVP & Global Head, Edit: Dr Farideh Koohi-Kamali
Global Sales & Mktg Dir: Patricia Mulrane Clayton
Founded: 1982
Scholarly monographs & textbooks in the humanities, social sciences, media studies, Festschriften & conference proceedings.
ISBN Prefix(es): 978-0-8204; 978-1-4331; 978-1-4539 (ebooks)
Number of titles published annually: 240 Print
Total Titles: 2,500 Print
Foreign Office(s): PIE Peter Lang SA Editions Scientifiques Internationales, One Ave Maurice, 6e etage, 1050 Brussels, Belgium *Tel:* (02) 347 72 36 *Fax:* (02) 347 72 37 *E-mail:* brussels@peterlang.com
Peter Lang GmbH Internationaler Verlag der Wissenschaften, Fehlerstr 8, 12161 Berlin, Germany *Tel:* (030) 232567900 *Fax:* (030) 232567902 *E-mail:* berlin@peterlang.com
Peter Lang GmbH Wydawnictwo Naukowe, ul Zimorowica 2 m 11, 02-062 Warsaw, Poland, Contact: Lukasz Galecki *Tel:* (66) 0759467 *E-mail:* l.galecki@peterlang.com
Peter Lang AG, Wabernstr 40, 3007 Bern, Switzerland *Tel:* (031) 306 17 17 *Fax:* (031) 306 17 27 *E-mail:* bern@peterlang.com
Peter Lang GmbH Uluslararasi Bilimsel Yayinevi, 3 Cadde, Sardalya Sokak No 7, 34450 Sariyer, Istanbul, Turkey, Contact: Esra Bahsi *Tel:* (0212) 271 7755; (0541) 541 12 33 (cell) *E-mail:* e.bahsi@peterlang.com
Peter Lang Ltd International Academic Publishers, 52 St Giles, Oxford OX1 3LU, United Kingdom (Ireland & UK) *Tel:* (01865) 514160 *Fax:* (01865) 604028 *E-mail:* oxford@peterlang.com
Distribution Center: IBI, PO Box 960, Herndon, VA 20172 (US only) *Tel:* 703-661-1584 *Fax:* 703-996-1010 *E-mail:* peterlang@presswarehouse.com
University of Toronto Press, 5201 Dufferin St, Toronto, ON M3H 5T8, Canada *Tel:* 416-667-7791 *Toll Free Tel:* 800-565-9523 (North America) *Fax:* 416-667-7832 *Toll Free Fax:* 800-221-9985 (North America) *E-mail:* utpbooks@utpress.utoronto.ca
Hachette Livre, One Ave Gutenberg, 78316 Maurepas Cedex, France (French-language titles in French-speaking Europe exc Switzerland & including French CN) *Tel:* 01 30 66 20 66 *E-mail:* webmaster-saisie@hachette-livre.fr *Web Site:* www.hachette-diffusion.fr
NBN, 10 Thornbury Rd, Plymouth PL6 7PP, United Kingdom (worldwide exc CN, French-speaking Europe, Switzerland & US) *Tel:* (01752) 202301 *Fax:* (01752) 202333 *E-mail:* orders@nbninternational.com

Lantern Publishing & Media
128 Second Place, Garden Suite, Brooklyn, NY 11231
Web Site: lanternpm.org
Key Personnel
Dir, Publg: Martin Rowe *E-mail:* martin@lanternpm.org
Founded: 2020
Publishers of books on veganism, social justice, family therapy & non-violence issues.
ISBN Prefix(es): 978-1-59056; 978-1-930051
Number of titles published annually: 15 Print
Total Titles: 180 Print; 200 Online; 150 E-Book; 50 Audio
Divisions: LanternMedia
Distributed by Red Wheel/Weiser
Foreign Rep(s): Deep Books (Europe, UK)
Foreign Rights: Findhorn Press (Sabine Weeke) (worldwide exc USA)
Membership(s): American Booksellers Association (ABA)

PUBLISHERS

LARB Books
Division of Los Angeles Review of Books
6671 Sunset Blvd, Suite 1521, Los Angeles, CA 90028
Tel: 323-952-3950
E-mail: larbbooks@lareviewofbooks.org
Web Site: larbbooks.org
Key Personnel
Ed-in-Chief/Dir: Tom Lutz *E-mail:* tom@lareviewofbooks.org
Exec Ed: Boris Dralyuk *E-mail:* boris@lareviewofbooks.org
Asst Dir: Stephanie Malak *E-mail:* smalak@lareviewofbooks.org
Publicity & Mktg: Nanda Dyssou *E-mail:* nanda@lareviewofbooks.org
Mng Dir: Jessica Kubinec *E-mail:* jessica@lareviewofbooks.org
Founded: 2013
ISBN Prefix(es): 978-1-940660; 978-1-942904
Number of titles published annually: 5 Print; 5 E-Book
Total Titles: 7 Print; 5 E-Book
Imprints: Les Figues Press; Outcaste Press
Foreign Rights: Agencia Literaria Carmen Balcells SA (Anna Bofill) (Spanish-speaking countries)
Distribution Center: Publishers Group West (PGW), 1700 Fourth St, Berkeley, CA 94710 *Tel:* 510-809-3700 *Toll Free Tel:* 866-400-5351 (cust serv) *Fax:* 510-809-3777 *E-mail:* info@pgw.com *Web Site:* www.pgw.com SAN: 202-8522

Laredo Publishing Co
465 Westview Ave, Englewood, NJ 07631
Tel: 201-408-4048
E-mail: info@laredopublishing.com
Web Site: www.laredopublishing.com
Key Personnel
Pres: Sam Laredo *E-mail:* laredo@laredopublishing.com
VP & Exec Ed: Raquel Benatar *E-mail:* raquel@laredopublishing.com
Founded: 1991
ISBN Prefix(es): 978-1-56492
Number of titles published annually: 25 Print
Total Titles: 150 Print
Imprints: Renaissance House
See separate listing for:
Renaissance House

Larson Publications
4936 State Rte 414, Burdett, NY 14818
Tel: 607-546-9342 *Toll Free Tel:* 800-828-2197 *Fax:* 607-546-9344
E-mail: custserv@larsonpublications.com
Web Site: www.larsonpublications.com
Key Personnel
Mktg Dir & Publr: Amy Opperman Cash *E-mail:* amy@larsonpublications.com
Publr & Ed: Paul R Cash *E-mail:* paul@larsonpublications.com
Founded: 1982
Resources for spiritual independence & social relevance.
ISBN Prefix(es): 978-0-943914; 978-1-936012
Number of titles published annually: 6 Print; 1 CD-ROM; 1 Online; 5 E-Book
Total Titles: 99 Print; 1 CD-ROM; 25 E-Book; 3 Audio
Foreign Rep(s): Gazelle Book Services Ltd (Europe, UK); Bokforlaget Robert Larson (Scandinavia)
Foreign Rights: Literaryventuresfund (Mary Bisbee-Beek)
Distribution Center: National Book Network, 15200 NBN Way, Blue Ridge Summit, PA 17214 *Toll Free Tel:* 800-462-6420 *Toll Free Fax:* 800-338-4550 *E-mail:* custserv@nbnbooks.com *Web Site:* www.nbnbooks.com
New Leaf Distributing Co, 1085 E Lotus Dr, Silver Lake, WI 53170 *Tel:* 262-889-8501 *Toll Free Tel:* 800-326-2665 *Fax:* 262-889-8598 *E-mail:* orders@newleafdist.com SAN: 169-1449

§Lasaria Creative Publishing
4094 Majestic Lane, Suite 352, Fairfax, VA 22033
E-mail: info@lasariacreative.com
Web Site: www.lasariacreative.com
Key Personnel
Publg Analyst: Adam Lee
Founded: 2003
Author-owned independent publishing company looking for nonfiction, general fiction, short stories & juvenile fiction books. We encourage first time authors & are willing to help get your work into mainstream distribution channels. Also offer editing services for new authors.
ISBN Prefix(es): 978-0-9818367; 978-0-9836671
Number of titles published annually: 10 Print; 10 Online; 10 E-Book
Total Titles: 14 Print; 12 Online; 12 E-Book

Laughing Elephant Books
3645 Interlake N, Seattle, WA 98103
Tel: 206-447-9229 *Toll Free Tel:* 800-354-0400 *Fax:* 206-447-9189
E-mail: support@laughingelephant.com
Web Site: www.laughingelephant.com
Key Personnel
Pres: Benjamin Darling
Founded: 1986
Publish books, cards & printed gifts with an emphasis on imagery, especially from antique children's books, self-generating content.
ISBN Prefix(es): 978-1-883211; 978-0-9621131; 978-1-59583
Number of titles published annually: 5 Print
Total Titles: 80 Print

§Law School Admission Council (LSAC)
662 Penn St, Newtown, PA 18940
Tel: 215-968-1101 *Toll Free Tel:* 800-336-3982
E-mail: lsacinfo@lsac.org
Web Site: www.lsac.org
Key Personnel
SVP, Chief Mktg & Communs Offr: Melissa Harris Thirsk
Founded: 1947
Standardized testing, legal education & law school admission activities, law school admission test preparation.
ISBN Prefix(es): 978-0-9846360; 978-1-7334330
Number of titles published annually: 4 Print; 2 Online; 3 E-Book
Total Titles: 30 Print; 2 Online; 8 E-Book
Orders to: Ingram Publisher Services, 14 Ingram Blvd, Mail Stop 631, La Vergne, TN 37086 *Toll Free Tel:* 866-400-5351 *Web Site:* www.ingrampublisherservices.com SAN: 631-8630
Distribution Center: Ingram Publisher Services, 14 Ingram Blvd, Mail Stop 631, La Vergne, TN 37086 *Toll Free Tel:* 866-400-5351 *Web Site:* www.ingrampublisherservices.com SAN: 631-8630

The Lawbook Exchange, Ltd
33 Terminal Ave, Clark, NJ 07066-1321
Tel: 732-382-1800 *Toll Free Tel:* 800-422-6686 *Fax:* 732-382-1887
E-mail: law@lawbookexchange.com
Web Site: www.lawbookexchange.com
Key Personnel
Pres: Gregory F Talbot *E-mail:* greg@lawbookexchange.com
Graphic Artist: Peter Lo Ricco *E-mail:* peter@lawbookexchange.com
Founded: 1981
Publisher of books on legal history & political science. Publisher of reprints of legal classics, many with new scholarly introductions.
ISBN Prefix(es): 978-1-886363; 978-1-58477; 978-0-9630106
Number of titles published annually: 20 Print
Total Titles: 1,300 Print; 9 E-Book
Imprints: Talbot Publishing
Membership(s): Antiquarian Booksellers Association of America (ABAA); International League of Antiquarian Booksellers (ILAB)

§Lawyers & Judges Publishing Co Inc
917 N Swan Rd, Suite 300, Tucson, AZ 85711
Mailing Address: PO Box 30040, Tucson, AZ 85751-0040
Tel: 520-323-1500 *Fax:* 520-323-0055
E-mail: sales@lawyersandjudges.com
Web Site: www.lawyersandjudges.com
Key Personnel
Pres & Publr: Steve Weintraub
Founded: 1963
Professional, text & reference materials in law, accident reconstruction, legal economics & taxation, forensics, medicine.
ISBN Prefix(es): 978-0-88450; 978-0-913875; 978-1-930056
Number of titles published annually: 20 Print; 8 CD-ROM; 25 E-Book
Total Titles: 200 Print; 16 CD-ROM; 100 E-Book

Leadership Ministries Worldwide
1928 Central Ave, Chattanooga, TN 37408
Tel: 423-855-2181 *Toll Free Tel:* 800-987-8790
E-mail: info@lmw.org
Web Site: lmw.org; store.lmw.org
Key Personnel
Pres & CEO: Anthony Raffa
Sr Ed: Rick Steele
Opers Mgr: Angie Raffa
Mktg Coord: Angela Walden
Accountant: Ruth Strothers
Founded: 1992
Commentaries.
ISBN Prefix(es): 978-1-57407; 978-0-945863
Number of titles published annually: 12 Print
Total Titles: 275 Print
Membership(s): Evangelical Christian Publishers Association (ECPA)

Leaf Storm Press
PO Box 4670, Santa Fe, NM 87502-4670
Tel: 505-216-6155
E-mail: leafstormpress@gmail.com
Web Site: leafstormpress.com
Key Personnel
Publr: Andy Dudzik *E-mail:* publisher@leafstormpress.com
Founded: 2014
ISBN Prefix(es): 978-0-9914105; 978-0-9970207
Number of titles published annually: 6 Print; 2 E-Book
Total Titles: 14 Print; 4 E-Book
Distribution Center: Ingram/Publishers Group West (PGW), 1700 Fourth St, Berkeley, CA 94710 *Tel:* 510-809-3700 *Toll Free Tel:* 866-400-5351 (cust serv) *Fax:* 510-809-3777 *Web Site:* www.pgw.com
Membership(s): American Booksellers Association (ABA); Association of American Publishers (AAP); Independent Book Publishers Association (IBPA)

Learnables Foreign Language Courses, see International Linguistics Corp

§THE Learning Connection®
4100 Silverstar Rd, Suite D, Orlando, FL 32808
Toll Free Tel: 800-218-8489 *Fax:* 407-292-2123
E-mail: tlc@tlconnection.com
Web Site: www.tlconnection.com
Key Personnel
Gen Mgr: Ryan Handberg *E-mail:* ryan@tlconnection.com
Founded: 1991

U.S. PUBLISHERS

Thematic literacy centers & teacher's guides for early childhood & middle school; parent involvement & family literacy; bilingual, math, science, multicultural, manipulatives, technology.
ISBN Prefix(es): 978-1-56831
Number of titles published annually: 15 Print; 15 CD-ROM; 5 Audio
Total Titles: 1,000 Print; 15 CD-ROM; 50 Audio
Imprints: PAKS-Parents & Kids
Branch Office(s)
300 E 93 St, Suite 29C, New York, NY 10128, VP, NJ Accts: Timothy Sasman
Membership(s): International Literacy Association (ILA)

§Learning Links-USA Inc
18 Haypress Rd, Suite 414, Cranbury, NJ 08512
SAN: 175-081X
Mailing Address: PO Box 326, Cranbury, NJ 08512 SAN: 175-081X
Tel: 516-437-9071 *Toll Free Tel:* 800-724-2616 *Fax:* 732-329-6994
E-mail: info@learninglinks.com
Web Site: www.learninglinks.com
Founded: 1976
Publisher of teacher guides for K-12 literature. Distribute paperback books, audios, videos, craft kits & book-related toys.
ISBN Prefix(es): 978-0-88122; 978-1-56982; 978-0-7675
Number of titles published annually: 25 Print
Total Titles: 850 Print
Imprints: Novel-Ties Study Guides
Divisions: Swan Books
Membership(s): International Literacy Association (ILA); National Council of Teachers of English (NCTE)

LearningExpress
Unit of EBSCO Information Services
224 W 29 St, 3rd fl, New York, NY 10001
Toll Free Tel: 800-295-9556 (ext 2)
Web Site: learningexpresshub.com
Key Personnel
Chief Revenue Offr: Kheil McIntyre
CTO: Tammy Cunningham
SVP, Content: Ilsa Halpern, PhD
Dir, Cust Serv: Shana Ashwood-Viala
Dir, Mktg: Janine Y Swenson *E-mail:* jswenson@ebsco.com
Founded: 1995
Publishes print & online test-preparation resources, skill building tools, study guides & career guidance materials for the trade, library, school & consumer markets.
ISBN Prefix(es): 978-1-57685; 978-1-61103
Number of titles published annually: 32 Print; 15 E-Book
Sales Office(s): National Book Network, 4501 Forbes Blvd, Suite 200, Lanham, MD 20706 *Tel:* 301-459-3366 *Fax:* 301-429-5746
Orders to: National Book Network, 15200 NBN Way, Blue Ridge Summit, PA 17214 *Tel:* 717-794-3800 *Toll Free Tel:* 800-462-6420 *Fax:* 717-794-3828 *Toll Free Fax:* 800-338-4550 *E-mail:* customercare@nbnbooks.com
Returns: National Book Network, 15200 NBN Way, Blue Ridge Summit, PA 17214 *Tel:* 717-794-3800 *Toll Free Tel:* 800-462-6420 *Fax:* 717-794-3828 *Toll Free Fax:* 800-338-4550 *E-mail:* customercare@nbnbooks.com
Warehouse: National Book Network, 15200 NBN Way, Blue Ridge Summit, PA 17214

Lectorum Publications Inc
10 New Maple Ave, Suite 303, Pine Brook, NJ 07058
Tel: 201-559-2200 *Toll Free Tel:* 800-345-5946
E-mail: lectorum@lectorum.com
Web Site: www.lectorum.com
Key Personnel
Pres & CEO: Alex Correa *E-mail:* acorrea@lectorum.com
Opers Mgr: Fernando Febus *E-mail:* ffebus@lectorum.com
Mgr, Collection Devt & Spec Sales: Marjorie Samper *E-mail:* msamper@lectorum.com
Mgr, Educ Sales, Schools & School Libs: Hilda Viskovic *E-mail:* hviskovic@lectorum.com
Public Lib Sales: Chastery Tiburcio *E-mail:* ctiburcio@lectorum.com
Cust Serv Mgr: Gladys Ochoa *E-mail:* gochoa@lectorum.com
Founded: 1960 (as a trade bookstore)
Distribute children & adult books in Spanish, with over 25,000 titles from more than 500 domestic & foreign publishers. Serves schools & libraries, as well as the trade & various specialized markets, with children's books in Spanish, including works originally written in Spanish, translations from other languages & the Spanish language editions of many popular children's books.
ISBN Prefix(es): 978-1-880507; 978-1-930332; 978-0-9625162; 978-1-933032; 978-1-941802; 978-1-63245
Number of titles published annually: 10 Print
Total Titles: 300 Print

Lederer Books
Division of Messianic Jewish Publishers
6120 Day Long Lane, Clarksville, MD 21029
Tel: 410-531-6644 *Toll Free Tel:* 800-410-7367 (orders)
Web Site: www.messianicjewish.net
Key Personnel
Pres: Barry Rubin *E-mail:* president@messianicjewish.net
Mktg Dir & Asst to Pres: Lisa Rubin *E-mail:* lisa@messianicjewish.net
Founded: 1949
Publish & distribute Messianic Jewish books, bibles & other resources.
ISBN Prefix(es): 978-1-880226; 978-1-936716
Number of titles published annually: 6 Print
Total Titles: 155 Print; 30 E-Book
Distributor for Jewish New Testament Publications
Foreign Rights: Riggin's Rights
Membership(s): Evangelical Christian Publishers Association (ECPA)

Lee & Low Books Inc
95 Madison Ave, Suite 1205, New York, NY 10016
Tel: 212-779-4400 *Toll Free Tel:* 888-320-3190 (ext 28, orders only) *Fax:* 212-683-1894 (orders only); 212-532-6035
E-mail: general@leeandlow.com
Web Site: www.leeandlow.com
Key Personnel
Pres: Craig Low *E-mail:* clow@leeandlow.com
Publr: Jason Low
Exec Ed: Jessica Echeverria
Sr Ed: Elise McMullen-Ciotti
Asst Ed: Stephanie Frescas Macias
Ed-at-Large: Louise May
Asst Mktg Mgr: Shaughnessy Miller
Mktg Coord: Jennifer Khawam
Educ Sales Assoc: Niki Marion
Publicist: Sacha Chadwick
Founded: 1991
Publisher of high quality multicultural children's books. We provide for the school, library & bookstore market.
ISBN Prefix(es): 978-1-880000; 978-1-885008; 978-1-58430; 978-1-60060; 978-0-89239; 978-1-62014
Number of titles published annually: 15 Print; 15 E-Book
Total Titles: 650 Print; 50 E-Book; 50 Audio
Imprints: Bebop Books; Children's Book Press; Cinco Puntos Press; Dive Into Reading; Lee & Low Games; Shen's Books; Tu Books
See separate listing for:
Children's Book Press
Shen's Books

Legacy Bound
Division of Legacy Toys
5 N Central Ave, Ely, MN 55731
Tel: Legacy Bound *Toll Free Tel:* 800-909-9698
E-mail: orders@legacybound.net
Web Site: www.legacybound.net
Key Personnel
Sales & Mktg: Laura Moberly *E-mail:* laura@legacybound.net
Founded: 1999
ISBN Prefix(es): 978-0-9677057; 978-0-9677057; 978-0-9766264; 978-0-9794202; 978-0-9801045; 978-0-9819307; 978-0-9883508; 978-0-9835189
Number of titles published annually: 3 Print
Total Titles: 25 Print
Imprints: Rosebud Books
Warehouse: 7703 Commerce Way, Eden Prairie, MN 55344, Mgr: Dan Schaefer *E-mail:* dan@legacytoys.com
Distribution Center: Baker & Taylor, 501 S Gladiolus St, Momence, IL 60954-1799, Mdse Admin: Ms Robin Bright *Tel:* 908-541-7425 *Toll Free Tel:* 800-775-2300 *Fax:* 815-802-2444 *Toll Free Fax:* 800-411-8433 *E-mail:* pc@baker-taylor.com *Web Site:* www.baker-taylor.com
Membership(s): Independent Book Publishers Association (IBPA); Midwest Independent Publishing Association (MIPA)

Lehigh University Press
Affiliate of Rowman & Littlefield Publishing Group
B-040 Christmas-Saucon Hall, 14 E Packer Ave, Bethlehem, PA 18015
Tel: 610-758-3933 *Fax:* 610-758-6331
E-mail: inlup@lehigh.edu
Web Site: lupress.cas2.lehigh.edu
Key Personnel
Dir: Kate Crassons
Mng Ed: Tricia J Moore
Founded: 1985
18th century American studies, East Asian studies, literary theory & criticism, history & technology, science, sociology, biography & the arts. Submissions welcome on any topic that is intellectually substantive.
ISBN Prefix(es): 978-1-61146
Number of titles published annually: 10 Print
Total Titles: 149 Print
Distributed by Rowman & Littlefield

§Leisure Arts Inc
Division of Liberty Media
104 Champs Blvd, Suite 100, Maumelle, AR 72113
SAN: 666-9565
Tel: 501-868-8800 *Toll Free Tel:* 800-643-8030 *Toll Free Fax:* 877-710-5603 (catalog)
E-mail: customer_service@leisurearts.com
Web Site: www.leisurearts.com
Key Personnel
SVP, Sales & Mktg: Ray Wolf
VP, Publg: Peg Couch
VP, Retail Sales: Martha Adams
Founded: 1971
Hard & soft cover books featuring instructions for needlework, crafts, cooking & gardening.
ISBN Prefix(es): 978-0-942237; 978-1-57486; 978-1-60140; 978-1-60900; 978-1-4647
Number of titles published annually: 200 Print
Total Titles: 2,000 Print

Lemonada Books, see Gallery Books

PUBLISHERS

§The Lentz Leadership Institute LLC
540 Arlington Lane, Grayslake, IL 60030
SAN: 857-7994
Tel: 702-719-9214
E-mail: orders@lentzleadership.com
Web Site: www.lentzleadership.com; www.refractivethinker.com; www.pensieropress.com; www.narratorepress.com
Key Personnel
The Academic Entrepreneur: Dr Cheryl Lentz
  E-mail: drcheryllentz@gmail.com
Founded: 2008
Publishes scholarly materials as part of The Anthology Series: The Refractive Thinker Series, to include the educational seminar series for public speaking. Individual books & individual doctoral or graduate level publications by participating authors are also published. Offer APA doctoral & graduate editing services.
This publisher has indicated that 85% of their product line is author subsidized.
ISBN Prefix(es): 978-0-9823036; 978-0-9828740; 978-0-9840054
Number of titles published annually: 18 Print; 8 Online; 25 E-Book; 1 Audio
Total Titles: 31 Print; 31 Online; 200 E-Book; 2 Audio
Imprints: Narratore Press; Pensiero Press; The Refractive Thinker® Press
Distribution Center: Ingram/Lightning Source Inc, 1246 Heil Quaker Blvd, La Vergne, TN 37086 *Tel:* 615-213-5815 *Fax:* 615-213-4725 *E-mail:* inquiry@lightningsource.com *Web Site:* www.lightningsource.com
Membership(s): The Association of Publishers for Special Sales (APSS); Independent Book Publishers Association (IBPA)

Lerner Publications
Imprint of Lerner Publishing Group Inc
241 First Ave N, Minneapolis, MN 55401
SAN: 201-0828
Tel: 612-332-3344 *Toll Free Tel:* 800-328-4929
Fax: 612-332-7615 *Toll Free Fax:* 800-332-1132
E-mail: info@lernerbooks.com; custserve@lernerbooks.com
Web Site: www.lernerbooks.com; www.facebook.com/lernerbooks
Key Personnel
Chmn: Harry J Lerner
Pres & Publr: Adam Lerner
EVP & COO: Mark Budde
EVP & CFO: Margaret Thomas
EVP, Sales: David Wexler
VP, Ed-in-Chief: Andy Cummings
VP, Mktg: Rachel Zugschwert
Dir, HR: Maggie Wolfson
Dir, Rts, Spec Sales & Intl Dist: Maria Kjoller
Publg Dir, School & Lib: Jenny Krueger
School & Lib Mktg Dir: Lois Wallentine
Founded: 1959
Juveniles: science, history, sports, fiction, art, geography, aviation, environment, ethnic, multicultural issues & activity books.
Number of titles published annually: 300 Print; 300 E-Book; 100 Audio
Total Titles: 5,000 Print; 5,000 E-Book; 1,000 Audio
Foreign Rep(s): Bounce Sales & Marketing Ltd (Europe, India, Middle East, Pakistan, Scandinavia, UK); CrossCan Education (Canada); DuBois (New Zealand); Novella (Australia); Phambili Agencies (Botswana, Lesotho, Namibia, South Africa, Swaziland, Zimbabwe); Publishers Marketing Services (PMS) (Brunei, Malaysia, Singapore); Saunders (school & lib) (Canada)
Foreign Rights: AC2 Literary (Italy); Sandra Bruna Literary Agency (Brazil, Portugal, Spain); CA-Link (Hong Kong, Macau, Mainland China, Taiwan); Japan Foreign-Rights Centre (JFC) (Japan); Korea Copyright Center Inc (KCC) (South Korea); Agence Michelle Lapautre (France); RightsMix (Eastern Europe, Greece, Israel, Netherlands, Russia, Scandinavia, UK); Literarische Agentur Silke Weniger (Germany)
Warehouse: CGC Fulfillment Warehouse, 150 Kingswood Dr, Mankato, MN 56001

Lerner Publishing Group Inc
Division of Lerner Universal Corp
241 First Ave N, Minneapolis, MN 55401
SAN: 201-0828
Tel: 612-332-3344 *Toll Free Tel:* 800-328-4929
Fax: 612-332-7615 *Toll Free Fax:* 800-332-1132
E-mail: info@lernerbooks.com; custserve@lernerbooks.com
Web Site: www.lernerbooks.com; www.facebook.com/lernerbooks
Key Personnel
Chmn: Harry J Lerner
Publr & CEO: Adam Lerner
EVP & COO: Mark Budde
EVP & CFO: Margaret Thomas
EVP, Sales: David Wexler
VP, Ed-in-Chief: Andy Cummings
VP, Mktg: Rachel Zugschwert
Dir, HR: Margaret Wolfson
Dir, Rts, Spec Sales & Intl Dist: Maria Kjoller
Edit Dir, Graphic Universe: Greg Hunter
Publg Dir, School & Lib: Jenny Krueger
School & Lib Mktg Dir: Lois Wallentine
School & Lib Sales Mgr: Brad Richason
Founded: 1959
ISBN Prefix(es): 978-0-87614; 978-1-58013; 978-0-8225; 978-0-7613; 978-1-57505; 978-0-92937; 978-0-93049; 978-1-58196
Number of titles published annually: 450 Print; 100 Audio
Total Titles: 6,000 Print; 6,000 E-Book; 1,000 Audio
Imprints: Carolrhoda Books Inc; Carolrhoda Lab™; Cheriton Children's Books; Darby Creek Publishing; ediciones Lerner; First Avenue Editions; Gecko Press; Graphic Universe™; Kar-Ben Publishing; Lerner Digital; Lerner Publications; LernerClassroom; Millbrook Press; Twenty-First Century Books; Zest Books
Divisions: Lerner Publisher Services
Distributor for Andersen Press; Big & Small; Cheriton Children's Books; Creston Books; Flying Start Books; Full Tilt Press; Gecko Press; Hungry Tomato®; Intergalactic Afikoman; Knowledge Books; Lantana Publishing; Lorimer Children & Teens; Maverick Arts Publishing; New Frontier Publishing; Page Education Foundation; Planting People Growing Justice Press; Quarto Library; Red Chair Press; Ruby Tuesday Books; Soaring Kite Books; We Do Listen Foundation
Foreign Rep(s): Bravo (Kar-Ben) (UK & the continent); CrossCan Education (Canada); DuBois (New Zealand); Novella (Kar-Ben) (Australia); Phambili Agencies (Botswana, Lesotho, Namibia, South Africa, Swaziland, Zimbabwe); Publishers Marketing Services (PMS) (Brunei, Malaysia, Singapore); Saunders (school & lib) (Canada)
Foreign Rights: ACER (Zest Books) (Brazil, Portugal, Spain); AC2 Literary (Italy); Arrowsmith Agency (Zest Books) (Germany); Sandra Bruna Literary Agency (Brazil, Portugal, Spain); CA-Link (Hong Kong, Macau, Mainland China, Taiwan); EnterKorea (Zest Books) (South Korea); Japan Foreign-Rights Centre (JFC) (Japan); Korea Copyright Center Inc (KCC) (South Korea); Agence Michelle Lapautre (France); RightsMix (Eastern Europe, Greece, Israel, Netherlands, Russia, Scandinavia, UK); Literarische Agentur Silke Weniger (Germany)
Warehouse: CGC Fulfillment Warehouse, 150 Kingswood Dr, Mankato, MN 56001
See separate listing for:
Carolrhoda Books Inc
Carolrhoda Lab™
ediciones Lerner
First Avenue Editions
Graphic Universe™
Kar-Ben Publishing
Lerner Publications
LernerClassroom
Millbrook Press
Twenty-First Century Books
Zest Books

LernerClassroom
Imprint of Lerner Publishing Group Inc
241 First Ave N, Minneapolis, MN 55401
Tel: 612-332-3344 *Toll Free Tel:* 800-328-4929
Fax: 612-332-7615 *Toll Free Fax:* 800-332-1132
E-mail: info@lernerbooks.com; custserve@lernerbooks.com
Web Site: www.lernerbooks.com; www.facebook.com/lernerbooks
Key Personnel
Chmn: Harry J Lerner
Pres & Publr: Adam Lerner
EVP & COO: Mark Budde
EVP & CFO: Margaret Thomas
EVP, Sales: David Wexler
VP & Ed-in-Chief: Andy Cummings
VP, Mktg: Rachel Zugschwert
Dir, HR: Margaret Wolfson *E-mail:* mwolfson@lernerbooks.com
Dir, Rts, Spec Sales & Intl Dist: Maria Kjoller
Publg Dir, School & Lib: Jenny Krueger
School & Lib Mktg Dir: Lois Wallentine
Nonfiction children's publications.
Number of titles published annually: 50 Print; 50 E-Book
Total Titles: 860 Print; 860 E-Book
Foreign Rep(s): Bounce Sales & Marketing Ltd (Europe, India, Middle East, Pakistan, Scandinavia, UK); CrossCan Education (Canada); DuBois (New Zealand); Novella (Australia); Phambili Agencies (Botswana, Lesotho, Namibia, Southern Africa, Swaziland, Zimbabwe); Publishers Marketing Services (PMS) (Brunei, Malaysia, Singapore); Saunders (school & lib) (Canada)
Foreign Rights: AC2 Literary (Italy); Sandra Bruna Literary Agency (Brazil, Portugal, Spain); CA-Link (Hong Kong, Macau, Mainland China, Taiwan); Japan Foreign-Rights Centre (JFC) (Japan); Korea Copyright Center Inc (KCC) (South Korea); Agence Michelle Lapautre (France); RightsMix (Eastern Europe, Greece, Israel, Netherlands, Russia, Scandinavia, UK); Literarische Agentur Silke Weniger (Germany)
Warehouse: CGC Fulfillment Warehouse, 150 Kingswood Dr, Mankato, MN 55401

Lexington Books
Imprint of Rowman & Littlefield Publishing Group
4501 Forbes Blvd, Suite 200, Lanham, MD 20706
Tel: 301-459-3366
Web Site: rowman.com/page/lexington
Key Personnel
Dir, Edit: Nicolette Amstutz *Tel:* 301-459-3366 ext 5514 *E-mail:* namstutz@rowman.com
Premier publisher of scholarly monographs in the social sciences & humanities. Subjects include political science, political theory, philosophy, history, international relations, literary studies, sociology, anthropology, religion, communications, cultural studies, education, psychology, linguistics & area studies.
ISBN Prefix(es): 978-0-7391; 978-1-4985; 978-1-7936

U.S. PUBLISHERS

Number of titles published annually: 750 Print; 750 E-Book
Total Titles: 7,500 Print; 6,500 E-Book
Orders to: Rowman & Littlefield Publishing Group, 15200 NBN Way, Blue Ridge Summit, PA 17214 *Tel:* 717-794-3800 *Toll Free Tel:* 800-462-6420 *Fax:* 717-794-3803 *E-mail:* customercare@rowman.com
Membership(s): Association of American Publishers (AAP)

§LexisNexis®
Division of RELX Group plc
230 Park Ave, Suite 7, New York, NY 10169
SAN: 202-6317
Tel: 212-309-8100 *Toll Free Fax:* 800-437-8674
Web Site: www.lexisnexis.com
Key Personnel
CEO: Mike Walsh
Founded: 1897
Multivolume legal reference works, state codes & single-volume legal texts, treatises & casebooks. Most material also in online versions.
ISBN Prefix(es): 978-0-409; 978-0-87215; 978-0-672; 978-0-87473; 978-0-406; 978-0-327; 978-0-88063; 978-0-930273; 978-1-55834; 978-1-56257
Imprints: Michie
Shipping Address: Broome Corp Park, 136 Carlin Rd, Conklin, NY 13748 *Tel:* 607-772-2600 *Toll Free Fax:* 800-323-9608

§LexisNexis® Matthew Bender®
Member of The LexisNexis® Group
701 E Water St, Charlottesville, VA 22902
Tel: 434-972-7600 *Toll Free Tel:* 800-223-1940 (sales)
Web Site: www.lexisnexis.com; store.lexisnexis.com/categories/publishers/matthew-bender-850
Founded: 1887
Treatises, text & form books, newsletters, periodicals & manuals for the legal, accounting, insurance, banking & related professions, selected libraries on CD-ROM.
ISBN Prefix(es): 978-0-8205; 978-1-4224
Total Titles: 577 Print; 277 CD-ROM; 27 Online; 277 E-Book
Branch Office(s)
136 Carlin Rd, Conklin, NY 13748 *Tel:* 607-772-2600 *Toll Free Fax:* 800-323-9608

Liberty Fund Inc
11301 N Meridian St, Carmel, IN 46032-4564
Tel: 317-842-0880 *Toll Free Tel:* 800-955-8335; 800-866-3520 *Fax:* 317-579-6060 (cust serv); 708-534-7803
E-mail: books@libertyfund.org; info@libertyfund.org
Web Site: www.libertyfund.org
Key Personnel
Mng Ed: Patti Ordower
Mktg & Fulfillment Coord: Michele Roberts *Tel:* 317-842-0880 ext 4920 *E-mail:* mroberts@libertyfund.org
Founded: 1960
A publisher of print & electronic scholarly resources including new editions of classic works in American constitutional history, European history, natural law, law, modern political thought, economics & education.
ISBN Prefix(es): 978-0-913966; 978-0-86597; 978-1-61487
Number of titles published annually: 10 Print; 3 Online
Total Titles: 425 Print; 150 Online; 1 Audio
Foreign Rep(s): Academic Sales & Marketing (Andrew Jones) (Midlands, Northern England); Chris Ashdown (Asia); Mara Cheli (Italy); Leonidas Diamantopoulos (Cyprus, Greece); Everybodys Book's (Warren Halford) (Southern Africa); Export Sales Agency (Ted Dougherty) (Austria, Germany, Switzerland); Four Corners Sales Agency (Michael Darcy) (Ireland, London, Scotland, Southern England, Wales); Gazelle Academic (Mark Trotter) (London); Iberian Book Services (Peter & Charlotte Prout) (Gibraltar, Portugal, Spain); Flavio Marcello (Italy); Marketing Solutions LLP (Andrew Wallace) (Central London, UK, East Anglia, England); Maya Publishers Pvt Ltd (India); David Towle (Baltic States, Northern Europe, Scandinavia)
Returns: c/o Ware-Pak, Returns Dept, 2427 Bond St, University Park, IL 60484
Distribution Center: Ingram Publisher Services, 14 Ingram Blvd, Mail Stop 961, La Vergne, TN 37086 (US & CN) *Tel:* 615-793-5000 *Toll Free Tel:* 866-400-5351 *Web Site:* www.ingrampublisherservices.com
Scholarly Book Services Inc, 289 Ridgeland Ave, Unit 105, Toronto, ON M6A 1Z6, Canada *Toll Free Tel:* 800-847-9736 *Toll Free Fax:* 800-220-9895
Membership(s): The American Library Association (ALA); Association of American Publishers (AAP)

Libraries Unlimited
Imprint of Bloomsbury Publishing Inc
1385 Broadway, 5th fl, New York, NY 10018
Tel: 212-419-5300
Web Site: www.bloomsbury.com/us/
Founded: 1964
Library science textbooks, annotated bibliographies, reference books, professional books for school media specialists as well as resource & activity books for librarians & teachers; storytelling resources & collections.
ISBN Prefix(es): 978-0-313; 978-0-87287; 978-1-56308; 978-1-59158
Number of titles published annually: 80 Print
Total Titles: 600 Print; 5 Audio

Library of America
14 E 60 St, New York, NY 10022-1006
SAN: 286-9918
Tel: 212-308-3360 *Fax:* 212-750-8352
E-mail: info@loa.org
Web Site: www.loa.org
Key Personnel
Pres & Publr: Max Rudin
COO: Daniel W Baker
Assoc Publr: Brian McCarthy
Edit Dir: John Kulka
Dir, Mktg: David Cloyce Smith
Publicity Dir: Leslie Schwartz
Mng Ed: Trish Hoard
Cust Serv Mgr: Laura Gazlay
Founded: 1979
Collected editions of classic American authors; literature, history, philosophy, drama, poetry & journalism.
ISBN Prefix(es): 978-0-940450; 978-1-883011; 978-1-931082; 978-1-59853
Number of titles published annually: 16 Print
Total Titles: 500 Print
Distributed by Penguin Random House LLC
Foreign Rep(s): Penguin Random House Canada (Canada); United Publishers Service (Japan)
Warehouse: Penguin Random House LLC, One Grosset Dr, Kirkwood, NY 13795

Mary Ann Liebert Inc
140 Huguenot St, 3rd fl, New Rochelle, NY 10801-5215
Tel: 914-740-2100 *Toll Free Tel:* 800-654-3237 *Fax:* 914-740-2101
E-mail: info@liebertpub.com
Web Site: www.liebertonline.com
Key Personnel
Publr & CEO: Mary Ann Liebert *E-mail:* mliebert@liebertpub.com
SVP: Harriet I Matysko
Ad Prodn Mgr: Kathleen De Souza
Founded: 1980
Medical & sci-tech journals, books & newspapers. Additional subjects include: biomedical research, integrative medicine (CAM), public policy, public health/policy, gender & population studies, regenerative medicine, clinical medicine, biotechnology, environmental studies, humanities, life sciences, allied health & surgery.
ISBN Prefix(es): 978-0-913113; 978-1-934854
Number of titles published annually: 3 Print; 3 Online
Total Titles: 65 Print; 70 Online
Divisions: Genetic Engineering & Biotechnology News
Foreign Office(s): Impress Media, Carrington Kirk, Carrington, Midlothian EH23 4LR, United Kingdom, Contact: Hilary Turnbull *Tel:* (01875) 825700 *Fax:* (01875) 825701 *E-mail:* hturnbull@genengnews.com

Life Cycle Books
Division of Life Cycle Books Ltd (Canada)
PO Box 799, Fort Collins, CO 80522
SAN: 692-7173
Toll Free Tel: 800-214-5849
E-mail: orders@lifecyclebooks.com
Web Site: www.lifecyclebooks.com
Key Personnel
Founder & Pres: Paul Broughton *E-mail:* paulb@lifecyclebooks.com
Founded: 1973
Books, pamphlets, brochures & audiovisuals on human life issues.
ISBN Prefix(es): 978-0-919225
Number of titles published annually: 6 Print
Total Titles: 41 Print

Light-Beams Publishing
36 Blandings Way, Biddeford, ME 04005
Tel: 603-659-1300
E-mail: info@light-beams.com
Web Site: www.light-beams.com
Key Personnel
Mktg Mgr & Trade Contact: Barry Kane *E-mail:* bkane@light-beams.com
Founded: 2000
Specialize in & publishes award-winning children's books & videos for children ages 3 & up.
ISBN Prefix(es): 978-0-9708104; 978-0-9766289
Number of titles published annually: 8 Print

§Light Publications
306 Thayer St, Suite 2462, Providence, RI 02906
Mailing Address: PO Box 2462, Providence, RI 02906
Tel: 401-484-0228
E-mail: info@lightpublications.com; pr@lightpublications.com (media rel)
Web Site: lightpublications.com
Key Personnel
Pres: Stephen Brendan *E-mail:* stephen@lightpublications.com
Media Rel: Lou Light Pop
Founded: 1999
ISBN Prefix(es): 978-0-9702642; 978-0-9824707; 978-1-940060
Number of titles published annually: 2 Print; 3 Online; 3 E-Book; 2 Audio
Total Titles: 24 Print; 25 Online; 25 E-Book; 15 Audio
Membership(s): Independent Book Publishers Association (IBPA)

§Light Technology Publishing LLC
4030 E Huntington Dr, Flagstaff, AZ 86004
Mailing Address: PO Box 3540, Flagstaff, AZ 86003-3540
Tel: 928-526-1345 *Toll Free Tel:* 800-450-0985 *Fax:* 928-714-1132
E-mail: publishing@lighttechnology.com
Web Site: www.lighttechnology.com

Key Personnel
Owner & Publr: O'Ryin Swanson
Founded: 1991
Sedona Journal, metaphysical publications, mostly channeled - monthly Jan-Oct, Predictions double issue Nov/Dec.
ISBN Prefix(es): 978-1-891824; 978-1-929385; 978-1-62233
Number of titles published annually: 10 Print; 1 Online; 10 E-Book; 10 Audio
Total Titles: 250 Print; 1 Online; 250 E-Book; 10 Audio
Distribution Center: Afrikan World Books (US)
Amazon.com (US)
Baker & Taylor (US)
Bookazine (US)
Ingram Books
Brumby (Australia)
Membership(s): Association of American Publishers (AAP)

Lighthouse Publishing of the Carolinas, see Iron Stream Media

Liguori Publications
One Liguori Dr, Liguori, MO 63057-1000
Tel: 636-464-2500 *Toll Free Tel:* 800-325-9521
Toll Free Fax: 800-325-9526 (sales)
E-mail: liguori@liguori.org (sales & cust serv)
Web Site: www.liguori.org
Key Personnel
Pres & Publr: Fr Byron Miller
Dir, Fin & Busn Opers: Tracey Kane
Dir, Sales, Mktg & Prod Devt: Mary Wuertz von Holt
Sales & Cust Serv Mgr: Chuck Healy
Founded: 1947 (by Redemptorist priests & brothers)
Roman Catholic publisher & nonprofit ministry of the Catholic Redemptorist congregation of fathers & brothers. Our mission is to spread the Word of God & the gospel of Jesus Christ through print & electronic media. We publish inspirational books & pamphlets, parish bulletins, newsletters & other religious education materials, along with our flagship product, *Liguorian* magazine.
ISBN Prefix(es): 978-0-89243; 978-0-7648
Number of titles published annually: 20 Print
Total Titles: 2,000 Print; 40 CD-ROM; 2,000 Online; 600 E-Book
Imprints: Liguori; Libros Liguori (Spanish language titles)
Distributor for Redemptorist Publications
Foreign Rep(s): Garratt (Australia); Majellan (Australia); Redemptorist Publications (England)
Membership(s): Association of Catholic Publishers Inc; Catholic Media Association (CMA)

Limelight Editions
Imprint of Rowman & Littlefield Publishing Group
64 S Main St, Essex, CT 06426
Tel: 973-223-5039
Web Site: limelighteditions.com
Key Personnel
Acq Ed: John Cerullo *E-mail:* jcerullo@rowman.com
Full service educational & professional training publisher that produces books, book/media on the performing arts including cinema, dance & theater.
ISBN Prefix(es): 978-0-87910
Number of titles published annually: 20 Print; 10 Audio
Total Titles: 400 Print; 50 Audio
Foreign Rep(s): Publishers Group UK (UK); Rowman & Littlefield International (worldwide exc Canada, Ireland, UK & USA)

Orders to: National Book Network, 15200 NBN Way, Blue Ridge Summit, PA 17214 *Toll Free Tel:* 800-462-6420 *Toll Free Fax:* 800-338-4550
Returns: National Book Network, Returns Dept, 15200 NBN Way, Bldg B, Blue Ridge Summit, PA 17214
Warehouse: National Book Network, 15200 NBN Way, Blue Ridge Summit, PA 17214 *Tel:* 717-794-3800
Distribution Center: National Book Network, 15200 NBN Way, Blue Ridge Summit, PA 17214 *Tel:* 717-794-3800

Linden Publishing Co Inc
2006 S Mary St, Fresno, CA 93721
Tel: 559-233-6633 *Toll Free Tel:* 800-345-4447 (orders) *Fax:* 559-233-6933
Web Site: lindenpub.com; quilldriverbooks.com
Key Personnel
Pres & Publr: Richard Sorsky *E-mail:* richard@lindenpub.com
Founded: 1977
ISBN Prefix(es): 978-0-941936; 978-1-933502; 978-1-884956; 978-1-884995
Number of titles published annually: 10 Print; 8 E-Book
Total Titles: 250 Print; 130 E-Book; 3 Audio
Imprints: Craven Street Books; Pace Press; Quill Driver Books
Foreign Rights: Books Crossing Borders (worldwide)
Distribution Center: Ingram Publisher Services, 14 Ingram Blvd, La Vergne, TN 37086 *Web Site:* www.ingramdistributionservices.com
Membership(s): Independent Book Publishers Association (IBPA)

LinguaText LLC
103 Walker Way, Newark, DE 19711
SAN: 238-0307
Tel: 302-453-8695
E-mail: text@linguatextbooks.com
Web Site: www.linguatextbooks.com
Key Personnel
Owner & Publr: Michael Bolan
Founded: 1978
Publish foreign language textbooks, Hispanic monographs & classics of Spanish & French literature designed for the English-speaking college student.
ISBN Prefix(es): 978-0-936388; 978-0-942566; 978-1-58871; 978-1-58977
Number of titles published annually: 15 Print
Total Titles: 400 Print; 3 CD-ROM; 2 E-Book
Imprints: Cervantes & Co (Spanish classics series); Juan de la Cuesta Hispanic Monographs (literary criticism, monographs, critical editions); Moliere & Co (French classics series)
Distribution Center: GOBI® Library Solutions from EBSCO, 999 Maple St, Contoocook, NH 03229 *Tel:* 603-746-3102 *Toll Free Tel:* 800-258-3774 *Fax:* 603-746-5628 *Web Site:* gobi.ebsco.com
Baker & Taylor, 2550 W Tyvola Rd, Suite 300, Charlotte, NC 28217 *Toll Free Tel:* 800-775-1800 *E-mail:* btinfo@baker-taylor.com
Ingram, One Ingram Blvd, La Vergne, TN 37086 *Toll Free Tel:* 866-400-5351 *E-mail:* ips@ingramcontent.com
Membership(s): Textbook & Academic Authors Association (TAA)

§Lippincott Williams & Wilkins
Unit of Wolters Kluwer Health
333 Seventh Ave, New York, NY 10001
Toll Free Tel: 800-933-6525
E-mail: orders@lww.com
Web Site: www.lww.com
Key Personnel
Dir, Corp Commums, Health Learning, Res & Practice: Connie Hughes *Tel:* 646-674-6348 *E-mail:* connie.hughes@wolterskluwer.com

Founded: 1792
Medicine, dentistry life sciences, nursing, allied health, veterinary medicine books, journals, textbooks, looseleaf, newsletters & media.
ISBN Prefix(es): 978-0-8021; 978-0-397; 978-0-316; 978-0-683; 978-0-7817; 978-1-4698; 978-1-60929; 978-1-60831; 978-0-8067; 978-1-60547; 978-1-881063; 978-0-88167; 978-0-89004; 978-0-89313; 978-0-89640; 978-0-911216
Total Titles: 4,000 E-Book
Branch Office(s)
351 W Camden St, Baltimore, MD 21201
Tel: 410-528-4000
2 Commerce Sq, 2001 Market St, Philadelphia, PA 19103 *Tel:* 215-521-8300 *Fax:* 215-521-8902
Foreign Office(s): Lippincott Williams & Wilkins Pty Ltd, 66 Talavera Rd, Macquarie Park, NSW 2113, Australia *Tel:* (02) 9857 1313
Lippincott Williams & Wilkins Asia Ltd, 15/F, W Sq, 314-324 Hennessy Rd, Wan Chai, Hong Kong *Tel:* 2610 7000 *Fax:* 2610 7098
25 Canada Sq, Canary Wharf, 41st fl, London E14 5LQ, United Kingdom *Tel:* (020) 3197 6500 *Fax:* (020) 3197 6501
Warehouse: 16522 Hunters Green Pkwy, Hagerstown, MD 21740 *Tel:* 301-223-2300 *Fax:* 301-223-2400
Distribution Center: 16522 Hunters Green Pkwy, Hagerstown, MD 21740 *Tel:* 301-223-2300 *Fax:* 301-223-2400

Listen & Live Audio Inc
803 13 St, Union City, NJ 07087
Tel: 201-558-9000
Web Site: www.listenandlive.com
Key Personnel
Pres: Alfred C Martino *E-mail:* alfred@listenandlive.com
Publr: Alisa Weberman *E-mail:* alisa@listenandlive.com
Founded: 1995
Audiobooks: Self-help, fiction, teen/children's, outdoor adventure & mysteries.
ISBN Prefix(es): 978-1-885408; 978-1-931953; 978-1-59316
Number of titles published annually: 40 Audio
Total Titles: 1,000 Audio

little bee books
598 Broadway, 7th fl, New York, NY 10012
SAN: 992-0242
Tel: 212-321-0237 *Toll Free Tel:* 844-321-0237
E-mail: info@littlebeebooks.com; sales@littlebeebooks.com; publicity@littlebeebooks.com
Web Site: littlebeebooks.com
Key Personnel
CEO: Shimul Tolia
CFO: Thomas Morgan
Art Dir: Rob Wall
Dir, Sales: Alexis Lunsford
Edit Dir: Brett Duquette
Exec Ed, BuzzPop: Jeanine Le Ny
Mng Ed: Kristin Errico
Ed: Charlie Ilgunas
Assoc Ed: Jaime Gelman
Sr Mgr, Spec Mkts: David Sweeney
Sales Mgr: Alexis Lassiter
Mktg & Publicity Assoc: Maggie Salko
Founded: 2014
Creative & fun books for busy little bees ages 0-12 designed to entertain, inspire & educate. Agented submissions only. No unsol mss accepted.
ISBN Prefix(es): 978-1-4998
Number of titles published annually: 150 Print
Total Titles: 46 Print
Imprints: BuzzPop; Yellow Jacket (middle grade readers 8-14)
Distributed by Simon & Schuster, LLC

U.S. PUBLISHERS

Foreign Rep(s): Bonnier Publishing (James Tavendale) (worldwide)
Foreign Rights: Bonnier Publishing (Nick Franklin) (worldwide)
Orders to: Simon & Schuster, LLC, 100 Front St, Riverside, NJ 08075 *Toll Free Tel:* 800-223-2336; 800-268-3216 (CN) *Toll Free Fax:* 800-943-9831; 800-849-8151 (CN) SAN: 200-2442
Shipping Address: Simon & Schuster, LLC, 100 Front St, Riverside, NJ 08075 *Toll Free Tel:* 800-223-2336; 800-268-3216 (CN) *Toll Free Fax:* 800-943-9831; 800-849-8151 (CN) SAN: 200-2442
Warehouse: Simon & Schuster, LLC, 100 Front St, Riverside, NJ 08075 *Toll Free Tel:* 800-223-2336; 800-268-3216 (CN) *Toll Free Fax:* 800-943-9831; 800-849-8151 (CN) SAN: 200-2442
Distribution Center: Simon & Schuster, LLC, 100 Front St, Riverside, NJ 08075 *Toll Free Tel:* 800-223-2336; 800-268-3216 (CN) *Toll Free Fax:* 800-943-9831; 800-849-8151 (CN) SAN: 200-2442
Membership(s): Association of American Publishers (AAP)

§Little, Brown and Company
Division of Hachette Book Group Inc
1290 Avenue of the Americas, New York, NY 10104
Tel: 212-364-1100 *Fax:* 212-364-0952
E-mail: firstname.lastname@hbgusa.com
Web Site: www.hachettebookgroup.com/imprint/little-brown-and-company/
Key Personnel
Pres & Publr: Sally Kim
VP, Edit Dir, Little, Brown Spark: Talia Krohn
VP, Exec Ed/Edit Dir, Mulholland Books: Joshua Kendall
VP, Publr & Edit Dir, Algonquin Books: Betsy Gleick
VP, Publr (James Patterson titles): Ned Rust
VP, Publr, Voracious & Little, Brown Spark: Michael Szczerban
VP, Assoc Publr: Michael Barrs
VP, Creative Dir: Mario Pulice
VP & Exec Dir, Publicity: Sabrina Callahan
VP, Exec Ed: Asya Muchnick
Assoc Publr, Algonquin Books: Michael McKenzie
Edit Dir, Voracious: Raquel Pelzel
Edit Dir (James Patterson titles): Denise Roy
Exec Ed: Bryn Clark; Alex Littlefield; Liese Mayer
Exec Ed, Algonquin Books: Amy Gash
Exec Ed, Little, Brown & Mulholland Books: Helen O'Hare
Exec Ed, Little, Brown Spark: Cara Bedick
Sr Ed: Vivian Lee; Gabriella Mongelli
Sr Ed (James Patterson titles): Shannon Jamieson Vazquez
Assoc Ed, Voracious: Thea Diklich-Newell
Asst Ed: Morgan Wu
Asst Ed (James Patterson titles): Emily Williams
Asst Ed, Mulholland Books: Liv Ryan
Exec Dir, Mktg Opers: Brandon Kelley
Sr Mktg Dir, Little, Brown & Mulholland Books: Bryan Christian
Sr Mktg Dir, Little, Brown Spark & Voracious: Jessica Chun
Sr Mktg Mgr, Little, Brown Spark & Voracious: Katherine Akey
Sr Mktg Mgr, Little, Brown & Mulholland Books: Danielle Finnegan
Sr Dir, Soc Media: Lauren Hesse
Sr Dir, Publicity: Katharine Myers; Elizabeth Garriga
Dir, Publicity: Lena Little
Dir, Publicity, Little, Brown Spark & Voracious: Juliana (Jules) Horbachevsky
Asst Dir, Publicity, Little, Brown & Mulholland Books: Alyssa Persons
Sr Publicity Mgr: Lauren Roberts
Publicity Mgr: Lauren Ortiz
Publicty Mgr, Algonquin Books: Marisol Salaman
Publicity Assoc, Algonquin Books: Katrina Tiktinsky
Publicist: Gabrielle Leporati
Exec Art Dir: Gregg Kulick
Sr Art Dir: Julianna Lee
Sr Art Dir, Ad & Promo: Tim Harrington
Creative Dir, Algonquin Books: Christopher Moisan
Sr Designer: Kirin Diemont
Sr Ad Mgr: Charlotte Morrison
Sr Digital Ad Mgr: Kini Allen
Imprint Sales Dir: Jennifer Trzaska
Founded: 1837
Little, Brown and Company, the adult trade division of Hachette Book Group Inc, is one of the country's oldest & most distinguished publishing houses. Unsol/unagented mss not accepted.
ISBN Prefix(es): 978-0-912697 (Algonquin Books); 978-0-945575 (Algonquin Books); 978-1-56512 (Algonquin Books); 978-0-8212; 978-0-316; 978-0-7611 (Algonquin Books); 978-0-7595; 978-1-64375 (Algonquin Books); 978-1-64904 (Algonquin Books)
Number of titles published annually: 279 Print
Total Titles: 2,023 Print
Imprints: Algonquin Books; Back Bay Books; Little, Brown Spark; Mulholland Books; Voracious
Sales Office(s): Hachette Book Group Inc, 1290 Avenue of the Americas, New York, NY 10104 (spec mkts) *Toll Free Tel:* 800-222-6747 *Toll Free Fax:* 800-477-5925
Foreign Rights: Agencia Literaria Carmen Balcells SA (Portugal, Spain); Bardon-Chinese Media Agency (China, Taiwan); BMSR Ag Literaria (Brazil); The Italian Literary Agency Srl (Italy); JLM Literary Agency (Greece); Nurcihan Kesim Literary Agency Ltd (Turkey); The KM Agency (Netherlands); Agence Michelle Lapautre (France); Mohrbooks AG Literary Agency (Germany); Andrew Nurnberg Associates Ltd (Baltic States, Bulgaria, Croatia, Czechia, Hungary, Poland, Romania, Russia & former USSR); I Pitarski Ltd Literary Agency (Israel); Tuttle-Mori Agency Inc (Japan); Eric Yang Agency (South Korea)
Orders to: Hachette Book Group Inc, 53 State St, Boston, MA 02109 *Toll Free Tel:* 800-759-0190 *Toll Free Fax:* 800-286-9471
Returns: Hachette Book Group Inc, 322 S Enterprise Blvd, Lebanon, IN 46052
Shipping Address: Hachette Book Group Inc, 121 N Enterprise Blvd, Lebanon, IN 46052

Little, Brown Books for Young Readers (LBYR)
Division of Hachette Book Group Inc
1290 Avenue of the Americas, New York, NY 10104
SAN: 200-2205
Tel: 212-364-1100 *Toll Free Tel:* 800-759-0190 (cust serv)
E-mail: rights@lbchildrens.com
Web Site: www.hachettebookgroup.com/imprint/little-brown-books-for-young-readers/
Key Personnel
Pres & Publr: Megan Tingley
VP, Edit Dir, Picture Books: Andrea Spooner
VP, Deputy Publr: Jackie Engel
VP, Publr, Christy Ottaviano Books: Christy Ottaviano
VP & Ed-in-Chief: Alvina Ling
VP, Creative Dir: David Caplan
VP, Exec Dir, Mktg: Emilie Polster
VP, Publicity & Strategic Communs: Mary McCue
Edit Dir, Little, Brown Ink: Andrea Colvin
Exec Dir, School & Lib Mktg: Victoria Stapleton
Exec Edit Dir: Lisa Yoskowitz
Dir, Subs Rts: Janelle DeLuise
Dir, Fin: Tom Guerin
Dir, Creative Opers: Nisha Panchal Terhune
Assoc Creative Dir: Sasha Illingworth
Sr Graphic Designer, Mktg: Jessica Mercado
Designer: Patrick Hulse
Exec Art Dir: Saho Fujii
Exec Art Dir, JIMMY Patterson Books: Tracy Shaw
Art Dir, Mktg & Communs: Becky Munich
Assoc Art Dir: Jenny Kimura
Sr Mktg Mgr: Bill Grace
Sr Mktg Mgr (YA): Stefanie Hoffman
Sr Mgr, School & Lib Mktg: Christie Michel
Mktg Coord: Andie Divelbiss
Mktg Asst: Alice Gelber
Mktg Opers Assoc: Allison Broelis
Sr Digital Mktg Mgr: Savannah Kennelly
Digital Mktg Coord: Mara Brashem
Digital Engagement Mgr, JIMMY Patterson Books: Joshua Johns
Assoc Publicity Dir: Cheryl Lew
Publicity Mgr: Kelly Moran; Sadie Trombetta
Sr Publicist: Hannah Klein
Founded: 1926
Specializes in board books, novelty items, picture books, middle reader, young adult fiction & nonfiction & selected media tie-ins.
ISBN Prefix(es): 978-0-8212; 978-0-316; 978-0-7596; 978-0-7595; 978-1-61620 (Algonquin Young Readers)
Number of titles published annually: 135 Print
Total Titles: 1,845 Print
Imprints: Algonquin Young Readers; LB kids™; Little, Brown Ink; Christy Ottaviano Books; JIMMY Patterson Books; Poppy
Orders to: Hachette Book Group Inc, 53 State St, Boston, MA 02109 *Toll Free Tel:* 800-759-0190 *Toll Free Fax:* 800-286-9471
Shipping Address: Hachette Book Group Inc Distribution Center, 121 N Enterprise Blvd, Lebanon, IN 46052 *Tel:* 765-483-9900 *Fax:* 765-483-0706
Membership(s): The American Library Association (ALA); Association of American Publishers (AAP); The Children's Book Council (CBC); Women's National Book Association (WNBA)

The Little Entrepreneur
Imprint of Harper Arrington Publishing & Media
c/o Harper Arrington Media, 33228 W 12 Mile Rd, Suite 105, Farmington Hills, MI 48334
Toll Free Tel: 888-435-9234 *Fax:* 248-281-0373
E-mail: support@digitalfashionpro.com
Key Personnel
Co-Founder & Publr: Jay Arrington; Michael Harper
Media Rel: John Thomas
Founded: 2004
Educating aspiring & established fashion designers. Fashion books, manufacturer lists & supplies. Creates fashion design software.
ISBN Prefix(es): 978-0-9764161
Number of titles published annually: 3 Print; 1 CD-ROM
Total Titles: 5 Print; 2 CD-ROM; 1 Online
Distributed by Harper Arrington Publishing

Little Simon®, see Simon & Schuster Children's Publishing

§Liturgical Press
Division of The Order of St Benedict Inc
PO Box 7500, St John's Abbey, Collegeville, MN 56321-7500
SAN: 202-2494
Tel: 320-363-2213 *Toll Free Tel:* 800-858-5450 *Fax:* 320-363-3299 *Toll Free Fax:* 800-445-5899
E-mail: sales@litpress.org
Web Site: www.litpress.org
Key Personnel
Dir & CEO: Therese L Ratliff
Fin Dir: Sandra Eiynck *Tel:* 320-363-2225
  E-mail: seiynck@litpress.org

Sales & Mktg Mgr: Brian Woods *Tel:* 320-363-3953 *E-mail:* bwoods@litpress.org
Founded: 1926
Began publishing for the church in 1926 & continues to sustain the original mission of proclaiming the good news of Jesus Christ. Liturgical Press is a trusted publisher of liturgy, scripture, theology & spirituality evolving to serve the changing needs of the church.
ISBN Prefix(es): 978-0-87907; 978-0-8146
Number of titles published annually: 80 Print; 50 E-Book
Total Titles: 2,500 Print; 950 E-Book; 20 Audio
Imprints: Cistercian Publications; Michael Glazier Books; Liturgical Press Academic; Liturgical Press Books; Pueblo Books
Foreign Rep(s): B Broughton Co Ltd (Canada); The Catholic Bookshop (South Africa); Claretian Publications (Philippines); John Garratt Publishing (Australia); Katong Catholic Book Centre Pte Ltd (Malaysia, Singapore); Norwich Books & Music (European Union, Ireland, UK); Pleroma Christian Supplies (New Zealand); Spring Arbor/Ingram (Tennessee)
See separate listing for:
Cistercian Publications

Liturgy Training Publications
Subsidiary of Archdiocese of Chicago
3949 S Racine Ave, Chicago, IL 60609-2523
SAN: 670-9052
Tel: 773-579-4900 *Toll Free Tel:* 800-933-1800 (US & CN only orders) *Fax:* 773-579-4929
E-mail: orders@ltp.org
Web Site: www.ltp.org
Key Personnel
Dir: Deanna M Keefe *Tel:* 773-579-4900 ext 3570 *E-mail:* dkeefe@ltp.org
Mng Ed: Michael A Dodd *Tel:* 773-579-4900 ext 3586
Mktg & Sales Mgr: Melissa Budak *Tel:* 773-579-4900 ext 3591
Sales Supv & Trade Rep: Irene Sanchez *Tel:* 773-579-4900 ext 3566 *E-mail:* isanchez@ltp.org
Founded: 1964
Books & periodicals on Roman Catholic liturgy, worship & prayer in the home & church.
ISBN Prefix(es): 978-0-929650; 978-1-56854; 978-1-59525
Number of titles published annually: 30 Print; 2 CD-ROM; 20 E-Book; 2 Audio
Total Titles: 500 Print; 6 CD-ROM; 80 E-Book; 7 Audio
Imprints: Catechesis of the Good Shepherd Publications; Hillenbrand Books
Distributor for United States Catholic Conference Publications (select titles)
Foreign Rep(s): The Catholic Bookshop (South Africa); Garrett Publishing (Australia); Katong Catholic Book Centre (Malaysia, Philippines); McCrimmons Bookstore/Publisher (UK exc Ireland); Pleroma Christian Supplies (New Zealand)
Membership(s): Association of Catholic Publishers Inc

Living Language
Imprint of Penguin Random House LLC
c/o Penguin Random House LLC, 1745 Broadway, New York, NY 10019
Tel: 212-782-9000 *Toll Free Tel:* 800-733-3000 (orders)
E-mail: support@livinglanguage.com
Web Site: www.livinglanguage.com
Key Personnel
Pres & Publr: Amanda D'Acierno, Penguin Random House Audio Group
VP, Content Prodn: Dan Zitt
VP, Mktg: Heather Dalton
VP, Publicity: Katherine Fleming Punia
Assoc Dir, Digital Content: Alison Skrabek
Ed: Suzanne McQuade
Founded: 1946

Self-study foreign language & ESL. Online courses & digital content; Sign Language & dictionaries. Penguin Random House & its publishing entities are not accepting unsol submissions, proposals, mss, or submission queries via e-mail at this time.
Total Titles: 15 Print; 83 Online; 140 E-Book; 62 Audio
Returns: Penguin Random House LLC, 1019 N State Rd 47, Crawfordsville, IN 47933
Distribution Center: Penguin Random House LLC, 400 Hahn Rd, Westminster, MD 21157
Toll Free Tel: 800-940-7046

§Living Stream Ministry (LSM)
2431 W La Palma Ave, Anaheim, CA 92801
Mailing Address: PO Box 2121, Anaheim, CA 92814-0121
Tel: 714-236-6050 *Toll Free Tel:* 800-549-5164 *Fax:* 714-236-6054
E-mail: books@lsm.org
Web Site: www.lsm.org
Key Personnel
Lib Sales Dir & Intl Rts: Yorke Warden *E-mail:* yorke@lsm.org
Founded: 1963
Religious publications.
ISBN Prefix(es): 978-0-87083; 978-1-57593; 978-0-7363
Number of titles published annually: 100 Print
Total Titles: 2,000 Print

Livingston Press
Division of University of West Alabama
University of West Alabama, Sta 22, Livingston, AL 35470
SAN: 851-917X
Tel: 205-652-3470
Web Site: livingstonpress.uwa.edu
Key Personnel
Dir: Joe Taylor *E-mail:* jwt@uwa.edu
Founded: 1984
ISBN Prefix(es): 978-0-942979; 978-0-930501; 978-1-931982; 978-1-60489
Number of titles published annually: 8 Print; 8 Online; 8 E-Book; 2 Audio
Total Titles: 160 Print; 120 Online; 90 E-Book; 2 Audio
Imprints: Swallow's Tale Press
Membership(s): Community of Literary Magazines & Presses (CLMP); Independent Book Publishers Association (IBPA)

Llewellyn Publications
Division of Llewellyn Worldwide Ltd
2143 Wooddale Dr, Woodbury, MN 55125
SAN: 201-100X
Tel: 651-291-1970 *Toll Free Tel:* 800-843-6666 *Fax:* 651-291-1908
E-mail: publicity@llewellyn.com; customerservice@llewellyn.com
Web Site: www.llewellyn.com
Key Personnel
Publr: Bill Krause
Art Dir: Stephanie Ingle
Dir, Sales & Mktg: Tom Lund *E-mail:* toml@llewellyn.com
Sr Publicist: Kat Sanborn *Tel:* 651-312-8452 *E-mail:* kats@llewellyn.com
Publicist: Jake-Ryan Kent
Interior Book Designer: Colleen McLaren
Founded: 1901
Body, mind, spirit. Trade publisher.
ISBN Prefix(es): 978-0-87542; 978-1-56718; 978-0-7387
Number of titles published annually: 110 Print; 10 CD-ROM
Total Titles: 900 Print
Imprints: Llewellyn; Midnight Ink
Distributor for Blue Angel Publishing; Lo Scarabeo

Foreign Rep(s): PGUK (Ireland, UK)
Foreign Rights: Oxana Schroeder (worldwide)

The Local History Co
112 N Woodland Rd, Pittsburgh, PA 15232-2849
Tel: 412-362-2294 *Toll Free Tel:* 866-362-0789 (orders) *Fax:* 412-362-8192
E-mail: info@thelocalhistorycompany.com; sales@thelocalhistorycompany.com; editor@thelocalhistorycompany.com
Web Site: www.thelocalhistorycompany.com
Founded: 2001
Publishers of history & heritage.
ISBN Prefix(es): 978-0-9711835; 978-0-9744715; 978-0-9770429
Number of titles published annually: 10 Print
Total Titles: 25 Print
Imprints: Towers Maguire Publishing
Membership(s): Independent Book Publishers Association (IBPA)

The Lockman Foundation
900 S Euclid St, Unit A, La Habra, CA 90631
Mailing Address: PO Box 2279, La Habra, CA 90632-2279
Tel: 714-879-3055
E-mail: lockman@lockman.org
Web Site: www.lockman.org
Founded: 1942
Publisher of the New American Standard Bible.
ISBN Prefix(es): 978-0-910618; 978-1-58135; 978-1-885217
Number of titles published annually: 2 Print
Total Titles: 20 Print
Distribution Center: Anchor Distributors, 1030 Hunt Valley Circle, New Kensington, PA 15068
Toll Free Fax: 800-444-4484

Locks Art Publications/Locks Gallery
Division of Locks Gallery
600 Washington Sq S, Philadelphia, PA 19106
Tel: 215-629-1000
E-mail: info@locksgallery.com
Web Site: www.locksgallery.com
Key Personnel
Dir: Sueyun Locks
Founded: 1968
Exhibition catalogue, monographs on contemporary art.
ISBN Prefix(es): 978-1-879173; 978-0-9623799
Number of titles published annually: 8 Print
Total Titles: 45 Print

§Loft Press Inc
9293 Fort Valley Rd, Fort Valley, VA 22652
Tel: 540-933-6210 *Fax:* 540-933-6523
E-mail: Books@LoftPress.com
Web Site: www.loftpress.com
Key Personnel
Pres & Publr: Stephen R Hunter
Ed-in-Chief: Ann A Hunter
Founded: 1987
ISBN Prefix(es): 978-0-9630797; 978-1-893846
Number of titles published annually: 3 Print; 1 CD-ROM
Total Titles: 145 Print; 2 CD-ROM
Imprints: Eschat Press (religion); Far Muse Press; Merry Muse Press; Punch Press
Subsidiaries: AAH Graphics Inc
Advertising Agency: AAH Advertising *Tel:* 540-933-6211
Membership(s): Washington Publishers (WP)

Logos Press
Imprint of thinkBiotech LLC
3909 Witmer Rd, Suite 416, Niagara Falls, NY 14305
Fax: 815-346-3514
E-mail: info@logos-press.com
Web Site: www.logos-press.com
Key Personnel
Ed: Yali Friedman
Founded: 2003

Specialize in reference & textbooks addressing the use of knowledge to make intelligent strategic decisions. Target audiences include college & advanced courses, business managers, directors & C-level executives. The objective is to help advanced students & decision makers implement their ideas based on solid fundamentals.
ISBN Prefix(es): 978-0-9734676; 978-1-934899
Number of titles published annually: 4 Print; 4 Online
Total Titles: 12 Print; 4 Online

Lonely Planet Publications Inc
Subsidiary of Red Ventures
124 Linden St, Oakland, CA 94607
Tel: 510-250-6400 *Toll Free Tel:* 800-275-8555 (orders)
E-mail: info@lonelyplanet.com
Web Site: www.lonelyplanet.com
Founded: 1973
Create & deliver the most compelling & comprehensive travel content in the world, giving travellers trustworthy information, engaging opinions, powerful images & informed perspectives on destinations around the globe. While known primarily for its 600+ travel guidebooks, we also offer an award-winning web site, photographic image library, television production, distribution & digital travel content licensing.
ISBN Prefix(es): 978-0-908086; 978-0-86442
Number of titles published annually: 100 Print
Total Titles: 600 Print
Imprints: Lonely Planet Kids
Branch Office(s)
Lonely Planet USA LLC, 1101 Red Ventures Dr, Fort Mill, SC 29707
Foreign Office(s): Lonely Planet China, OB5A, Off Tower B, East Gate Plaza, No 29 Dongzhong St, Dongcheng District, Beijing 100027, China
Lonely Planet India Pvt Ltd, M-34 Saket, New Delhi 110 017, India
Lonely Planet Ireland, Digital Depot, The Digital Hub, Roe Lane, Off Thomas St, Dublin D08 TCV4, Ireland
Distributed by Hachette Book Group Inc

§Long River Press
Imprint of Sinomedia International Group
360 Swift Ave, Suite 48, South San Francisco, CA 94080
Tel: 650-872-7718 (ext 312) *Fax:* 650-872-7808
E-mail: editor@sinomediausa.com
Key Personnel
Sr Ed: Chris Robyn
Founded: 2002
Independent small press publishing trade titles in Asian history, philosophy, culture, mind-body-spirit. Unsol proposals are accepted but cannot be returned without SASE.
ISBN Prefix(es): 978-1-59265
Number of titles published annually: 10 Print; 5 E-Book
Total Titles: 120 Print; 20 E-Book

Looseleaf Law Publications Inc
Division of Warodean Corp
43-08 162 St, Flushing, NY 11358
Mailing Address: PO Box 650042, Fresh Meadows, NY 11365-0042
Tel: 718-359-5559 *Toll Free Tel:* 800-647-5547
Fax: 718-539-0941
E-mail: info@looseleaflaw.com
Web Site: www.looseleaflaw.com
Key Personnel
Owner: Michael L Loughrey
VP & Edit: Mary Loughrey
Sales Dir: Hilary McKeon
Founded: 1967
Law books; study aids for law enforcement, students, attorneys & court personnel.

ISBN Prefix(es): 978-0-930137; 978-1-889031; 978-1-932777
Number of titles published annually: 200 Print
Total Titles: 25 CD-ROM

§Lorenz Educational Press
Division of The Lorenz Corp
501 E Third St, Dayton, OH 45402
Mailing Address: PO Box 802, Dayton, OH 45401-0802
Toll Free Tel: 800-444-1144 *Fax:* 937-223-2042
E-mail: service@lorenz.com
Web Site: www.lorenzeducationalpress.com
Founded: 2008
Educational publishing division includes visual resources, instructional guides & reproducibles, elementary supplementals.
ISBN Prefix(es): 978-1-42911
Number of titles published annually: 10 Print
Total Titles: 75 Print; 75 E-Book; 7 Audio
Membership(s): Education Market Association

Lost Classics Book Company LLC
411 N Wales Dr, Lake Wales, FL 33853-3881
Tel: 863-632-1981 (edit off)
E-mail: mgeditor@lostclassicsbooks.com
Web Site: www.lostclassicsbooks.com
Key Personnel
Owner: Michael Alan Fitterling
Founded: 1996
Republish late 19th & early 20th century literature & textbooks to aid parents & teachers in educating children.
ISBN Prefix(es): 978-0-9652735; 978-1-890623
Number of titles published annually: 5 Print
Total Titles: 26 Print
Imprints: Road Dog Publications (subsidiary imprint publishing motorcycle & adventure travel books)
Distribution Center: National Book Network, 15200 NBN Way, Blue Ridge Summit, PA 17214 *Tel:* 717-794-3800 *Fax:* 717-794-3828
E-mail: customercare@nbnbooks.com *Web Site:* www.nbnbooks.com

Lost Horse Press
1025 S Garry Rd, Liberty Lake, WA 99019
Tel: 208-597-3008 *Fax:* 208-255-1560
E-mail: losthorsepress@mindspring.com
Web Site: www.losthorsepress.org
Key Personnel
Publr: Christine Holbert
Founded: 1998
Nonprofit independent press that publishes poetry titles of emerging as well as published poets & makes available fine contemporary literature through cultural, educational & publishing programs & activities.
ISBN Prefix(es): 978-0-9668612; 978-0-9717265; 978-0-9762114; 978-0-9800289
Number of titles published annually: 10 Print; 1 Audio
Total Titles: 126 Print; 2 CD-ROM; 1 Audio
Distributed by Washington State University Press
Membership(s): Community of Literary Magazines & Presses (CLMP)

Lotus Light Publications, see Lotus Press

Lotus Press
Division of Lotus Brands Inc
1100 E Lotus Dr, Silver Lake, WI 53170
Mailing Address: PO Box 325, Twin Lakes, WI 53181-0325
Tel: 262-889-8561 *Toll Free Tel:* 800-824-6396 (orders) *Fax:* 262-889-2461; 262-889-8591
E-mail: lotuspress@lotuspress.com
Web Site: www.lotuspress.com
Key Personnel
Pres: Santosh Krinsky *E-mail:* santosh@lotuspress.com

Founded: 1981
Health, yoga, Native American & New Age metaphysics, Vedic astrology.
ISBN Prefix(es): 978-0-941524; 978-0-910261; 978-0-914955; 978-0-940985; 978-0-940676; 978-1-60869
Number of titles published annually: 6 Print; 2 CD-ROM; 6 Online; 6 E-Book; 3 Audio
Total Titles: 350 Print; 5 CD-ROM; 300 Online; 300 E-Book; 42 Audio
Imprints: Arcana Publishing; Dipti; Shangri-La; Specialized Software
Distributor for Back to Eden Books; Dipti; East West Cultural Center; Les Editions ETC; Inner Worlds Music; SABDA; Sri Aurobindo Ashram; Star Sounds

Louisiana State University Press
338 Johnston Hall, Baton Rouge, LA 70803
Tel: 225-578-6294
E-mail: lsupress@lsu.edu
Web Site: lsupress.org
Key Personnel
Dir: Alisa Plant *Tel:* 225-578-6144
  E-mail: alisaplant1@lsu.edu
Ed-in-Chief: Rand Dotson *Tel:* 225-578-6412
  E-mail: pdotso1@lsu.edu
Mng Ed: Catherine Kadair *Tel:* 225-578-3349
  E-mail: clkadair@lsu.edu
Busn Mgr: Kate Barton *Tel:* 225-578-6415
  E-mail: kbarto4@lsu.edu
Design & Prodn Mgr: Barbara Bourgoyne
  Tel: 225-578-2488 *E-mail:* bnbourg@lsu.edu
Founded: 1935
Scholarly, regional, general; humanities & social sciences; southern history & literature; environmental studies; poetry; food & foodways; music; creative nonfiction.
ISBN Prefix(es): 978-0-8071
Number of titles published annually: 80 Print; 60 E-Book
Total Titles: 1,500 Print
Foreign Rep(s): Eurospan (Europe exc Russia & Turkey)
Foreign Rights: McIntosh & Otis
Orders to: Longleaf Services Inc, 116 S Boundary St, Chapel Hill, NC 27514-3808 *Tel:* 919-966-7449 *Toll Free Tel:* 800-848-6224 *Fax:* 919-962-2704 *Toll Free Fax:* 800-272-6817 *E-mail:* customerservice@longleafservices.org *Web Site:* www.longleafservices.org
Returns: Longleaf Services Inc, c/o Ingram Publisher Services, 1250 Ingram Dr, Chambersburg, PA 17202
Warehouse: Longleaf Services Inc, c/o Ingram Publisher Services, 1250 Ingram Dr, Chambersburg, PA 17202
Membership(s): American Association of University Presses (AAUP)

Love Inspired Books
Imprint of Harlequin Enterprises Ltd
233 Broadway, Suite 1001, New York, NY 10279
SAN: 200-2450
Tel: 212-553-4200 *Toll Free Tel:* 888-432-4879
Fax: 212-227-8969
E-mail: customerservice@harlequin.ca
Web Site: www.harlequin.com
Key Personnel
Publr & CEO: Craig Swinwood
Exec Ed: Tina James
Ed: Emily Rodmell
Founded: 1997
Inspirational romance novels, romantic suspense & women's fiction.
ISBN Prefix(es): 978-0-373
Number of titles published annually: 192 Print
Imprints: Love Inspired®; Love Inspired® Historical; Love Inspired® Suspense
Distribution Center: 3010 Walden Ave, Depew, NY 14043

§Loving Healing Press Inc
5145 Pontiac Trail, Ann Arbor, MI 48105
SAN: 255-7770
Tel: 734-417-4266 *Toll Free Tel:* 888-761-6268 (US & CN) *Fax:* 734-663-6861
E-mail: info@lovinghealing.com; info@lhpress.com
Web Site: www.lovinghealing.com; www.modernhistorypress.com (imprint)
Key Personnel
Pres: Prof Victor R Volkman *E-mail:* victor@lhpress.com
Founded: 2003
Dedicated to producing books about innovative & rapid therapies to empower authors in redefining what is possible for healing the mind & spirit.
ISBN Prefix(es): 978-1-932690
Number of titles published annually: 15 Print; 15 E-Book; 10 Audio
Total Titles: 250 Print; 250 E-Book; 71 Audio
Imprints: AMI Press (official press of Applied Metapsychology International); Future Psychiatry Press (rethinking psychiatry & pharmacology); Marvelous Spirit Press (dedicated to helping your spiritual transformation & growth); Modern History Press (memoirs of people who have lived through significant events); Rocky Mountain Region Disaster Mental Health Institute Press (leading the way for strategic management of crisis response, first responders & rural responders); Victorian Heritage Press (showcasing the best of 19th century contemporary histories)
Foreign Rep(s): Ingram International (Australia, Europe, UK & Commonwealth)
Foreign Rights: IPR Licensing (worldwide exc USA)
Membership(s): Independent Book Publishers Association (IBPA)

Loyola Press
8770 W Bryn Mawr Ave, Suite 1125, Chicago, IL 60631
SAN: 211-6537
Tel: 773-281-1818 *Toll Free Tel:* 800-621-1008 *Fax:* 773-281-0555 (cust serv); 773-281-4129 (edit)
E-mail: customerservice@loyolapress.com
Web Site: www.loyolapress.com
Key Personnel
Pres & Publr: Joellyn Cicciarelli
Exec Ed, Acqs: Gary Jansen
Busn Devt & Mktg Mgr: Andrew Yankech
Founded: 1912
Catholic publisher of books for elementary schools, parishes & the general trade.
ISBN Prefix(es): 978-0-8294
Number of titles published annually: 25 Print; 5 Audio
Total Titles: 350 Print
Imprints: 4U2B Books & Media
Returns: 677 Brighton Beach Rd, Menasha, WI 54952

LPC Books, see Iron Stream Media

LPD Press/Rio Grande Books
925 Salamanca NW, Los Ranchos de Albuquerque, NM 87107-5647
Tel: 505-269-8324
Web Site: nmsantos.com
Key Personnel
Publr: Paul Rhetts *E-mail:* prhetts1@gmail.com
Founded: 1984
Publisher of books on the American Southwest & a quarterly magazine on the art & culture of the American Southwest.
ISBN Prefix(es): 978-0-9641542; 978-1-890689; 978-1-943681
Number of titles published annually: 10 Print; 10 E-Book
Total Titles: 350 Print; 1 CD-ROM; 50 E-Book
Imprints: Rio Grande Books
Membership(s): Independent Book Publishers Association (IBPA); New Mexico Book Association; New Mexico Book Co-op

§LRP Publications
360 Hiatt Dr, Palm Beach Gardens, FL 33418
Mailing Address: PO Box 24668, West Palm Beach, FL 33416-4668
Tel: 561-622-6520 *Toll Free Tel:* 800-341-7874 *Fax:* 561-622-2423
E-mail: custserve@lrp.com
Web Site: www.lrp.com; www.shoplrp.com
Key Personnel
Pres: Kenneth F Kahn
Founded: 1977
Legal & general nonfiction in the areas of education, bankruptcy, employment, disability, workers compensation, personal injury & human resources.
ISBN Prefix(es): 978-0-934753
Number of titles published annually: 500 Print; 10 CD-ROM; 95 Online; 5 Audio
Total Titles: 9,000 Print; 10 CD-ROM; 95 Online; 8 Audio
Subsidiaries: LRP Magazine Group
Divisions: Jury Verdict Research
Branch Office(s)
1350 Market St, Suite 202, Tallahassee, FL 32312
Tel: 850-219-9600
747 Dresher Rd, Suite 500, Horsham, PA 19044
Tel: 215-784-0941 *Fax:* 215-784-9639

LRS
Division of Library Reproduction Service
6150 Little Willow Rd, Payette, ID 83661
Toll Free Tel: 800-255-5002
E-mail: largeprint@lrsbooks.com
Web Site: www.lrsbooks.com
Key Personnel
Pres: Melissa Rawlins
Founded: 1946
Large print books for adults & children including classics & fiction.
ISBN Prefix(es): 978-1-58118
Number of titles published annually: 10 Print
Total Titles: 150 Print

Lucent Press
Imprint of Greenhaven Publishing
2544 Clinton St, Buffalo, NY 14224
Toll Free Tel: 844-317-7404 *Toll Free Fax:* 844-317-7405
Web Site: greenhavenpublishing.com
Founded: 1988
Curriculum-related nonfiction books aimed at the junior high level that explore current issues, historical topics, health, science/technology & biography. Active series include: *Diseases & Disorders, Hot Topics, People in the News, Technology 360 & World History*.
ISBN Prefix(es): 978-1-56006; 978-1-59018
Number of titles published annually: 85 Print; 60 E-Book
Distributor for Greenhaven Publishing; KidHaven Publishing

Luna Bisonte Prods
137 Leland Ave, Columbus, OH 43214
Tel: 614-846-4126
Web Site: www.johnmbennett.net; www.lulu.com/spotlight/lunabisonteprods
Key Personnel
Head & Intl Rts: John M Bennett *E-mail:* bennettjohnm@gmail.com
Founded: 1984
Avant-garde to experimental literature & poetry.
ISBN Prefix(es): 978-0-935350; 978-1-892280; 978-1-938521
Number of titles published annually: 25 Print; 2 Audio
Total Titles: 400 Print; 53 Audio

Lutheran Braille Workers Inc
13471 California St, Yucaipa, CA 92399
Mailing Address: PO Box 5000, Yucaipa, CA 92399-1450
Tel: 909-795-8977 *Toll Free Tel:* 800-925-6092
E-mail: lbw@lbwloveworks.org
Web Site: www.lbwloveworks.org
Key Personnel
Pres: Daniel Jenkins
Founded: 1943
Produce & distribute free braille & large print biblical & Christian literature in more than 30 languages for the blind & visually impaired in over 120 countries.
Number of titles published annually: 5 Print
Total Titles: 200 Print

Lynx House Press
420 W 24 St, Spokane, WA 99203
Tel: 509-624-4894
E-mail: lynxhousepress@gmail.com
Web Site: www.lynxhousepress.org
Key Personnel
Dir & Ed-in-Chief: Christopher Howell *E-mail:* cnhowell@ewu.edu
Assoc Ed: Kristina Morgan
Intl Rts: Jodi Miller-Hunter
Founded: 1972
Fiction, nonfiction & poetry.
ISBN Prefix(es): 978-0-89924
Number of titles published annually: 6 Print
Total Titles: 201 Print
Distributed by Washington State University Press

The Lyons Press
Imprint of The Globe Pequot Press
64 S Main St, Essex, CT 06426
Tel: 203-458-4500
E-mail: info@rowman.com
Web Site: rowman.com/page/lyonspress
Key Personnel
Edit Dir: Eugene F Brissie, Jr
Subs Rts Dir: Sean McDonagh *E-mail:* smcdonagh@rowman.com
Founded: 1978
Outdoors, natural history, sports, military history, fishing, hunting, nonfiction, practical, Americana, outdoor skills, pets, nautical, survival & adventure.
ISBN Prefix(es): 978-1-55821; 978-0-8329; 978-1-58574; 978-1-59228; 978-0-936644; 978-0-941130
Number of titles published annually: 150 Print; 150 E-Book
Total Titles: 1,500 Print; 1,500 E-Book
Imprints: Eclipse Press; Muddy Boots; Sheridan House
Distribution Center: National Book Network, 4501 Forbes Blvd, Suite 200, Lantham, MD 20706 *Tel:* 301-459-3366 *Web Site:* nbnbooks.com

M U Press, see Marquette University Press

MAA Press, see The Mathematical Association of America

§Macmillan
Division of Verlagsgruppe Georg von Holtzbrinck GmbH
120 Broadway, 22nd fl, New York, NY 10271
E-mail: press.inquiries@macmillan.com
Web Site: us.macmillan.com
Key Personnel
CEO, Macmillan Publishers US: Jon Yaged
COO: Neil Strong
CFO: Clare O'Rourke

U.S. PUBLISHERS

Assoc Gen Coun: Randi Moore
Coun, Employee Rel: Heather Hili
Chmn & Exec Ed, Farrar, Straus & Giroux: Jonathan Galassi
Pres & Publr, Macmillan Audio: Mary Beth Roche
Pres & Publr, Farrar, Straus & Giroux: Mitzi Angel
Pres & Publr, Tor Publishing Group: Devi Pillai
Pres, Macmillan Children's Publishing Group: Jennifer Besser
EVP, Busn Devt & Strategy: Alyssa Awe
EVP, Edit Devt & Content Innovation: Will Schwalbe
EVP, People & Culture: Gracie Mercado
EVP, Sales: Tim Greco
SVP & Gen Coun: Paul Sleven
SVP, Diversity, Equity & Inclusion: LaToya Rose
SVP, Fin: Edward Garrett
SVP, Online & Digital Sales Opers & Analysis/Mgr, Amazon, E-Book Sales & Sales & Opers Teams: Tom Stouras
SVP, Platform Devt: Rob Guttman
SVP, Publg & Mktg Strategy: Cristina Gilbert
SVP, Publg Opers & Technol: Leslie Padgett
SVP, Technol: Kaustubh Kamat
SVP, Trade Fin & Analytics: Cameron Ackroyd
VP, Busn Systems: Hillary Scarbrough
VP, Central Mktg: Maggie Cassion
VP, Children's Sales: Shawn Foster
VP, Communs & Community: Kelly Collins
VP, Data Sci & Analytics: Jason Arvelo
VP, Digital Mktg & Technol: Cara Chirichella
VP, Field Sales, Diversified Sales & Sales Strategy: Jennifer Edwards
VP, Fin Opers: Brad Umbaugh
VP, Intl Sales & Mktg: Devin Kirk Luna
VP, Inventory Mgmt: Debbie Derevjanik
VP, Mng Edit: Kenn Russell
VP, Mdse & Dist: Christine Jaeger
VP, Prodn: Diana Gee
VP, Publr Servs & Dist: Liz Tzetzo
VP, Sales Opers: Brian McSharry
VP, Spec Mkts, Premium Retail, Retail & Wholesale: Alice Baker
VP, Strategy & Investments, Busn Devt Team: Jessica Miles
VP, Trade, Intl & CN Sales: John Edwards
Publr-at-Large: Jamie Raab; Sally Richardson
Sr Dir, Amazon: Brad Wood
Sr Dir, Author Events & Servs: Melissa Campion
Sr Dir, Busn Planning: Esther Kim
Sr Dir, Central Analytics: Grace Van Etten
Sr Dir, Client Servs: Veronica Gonzalez
Sr Dir, Communs: Catherine Marvin
Sr Dir, Data Engg: Matt Kangas
Sr Dir, Fin: Kemi Umogbai
Sr Dir, Inventory Mgmt: Alison Tromp
Sr Dir, Prod Mgmt, Platform Devt: Beter Said
Sr Dir, Spec Mkts: Talia Sherer
Sr Dir, Talent & Devt: Sonali Goel
Dir, Acctg: Yana Hosken
Dir, Adult Trade Prodn/Mfg: Carolyn Telesca
Dir, Busn Opers: Kevin Thomas
Dir, CN Trade Sales & Raincoast: Jeanette Zwart
Dir, Central Mktg: Francesca Oddo-Budinoff
Dir, Field Sales: Holly Ruck
Dir, Fin: Sameer Chaudhari
Dir, Fin Projs: Katie Kraska
Dir, Mktg Intelligence: Maya Battle
Dir, Natl Specialty Retail: Jackie Waggner
Dir, Prodn Edit: Michael Clark; Chris O'Connell
Dir, State, Local & Indirect Taxes: Lea Kim
Dir, Systems Integration, Biblio: Rachel Menth
Dir, Talent Programming: Katie Gore
Dir, Workflow Systems: Sean Ford
Assoc Dir, Children's Prodn: Allene Cassagnol; John Nora
Assoc Dir, Contracts: Amanda Schoonmaker
Assoc Dir, Custom Sales: Taylor Armstrong
Assoc Dir, Design: Donna Noetzel
Assoc Dir, Lib Mktg: Amanda Crimarco
Assoc Dir, Prodn: Vincent Stanley
Assoc Dir, Prodn Edit: Megan Kiddoo
Assoc Dir, Sales: Cristina Cushing
Assoc Dir, Sales-Specialty Retail: Elena Guzman
Assoc Dir, Sales Strategy/Analysis & Amazon, Children's: Rebecca Schmidt
Asst Dir, Busn Planning: Jennifer Didik
Asst Dir, Contracts: Katrina Washington
Asst Dir, Sales Planning & Analytics: Colin Krainin
Sr Mng Ed: Emily Walters
Mng Ed: Merilee Croft
Mng Ed, Trade: Janel Brown
Assoc Mng Ed: Elizabeth Hubbard; Heather Niver
Sr Prodn Ed: Jeff LaSala; Frances Sayers
Sr Prodn Ed, Trade Prodn Team: Cassie Gutman
Prodn Ed, Mng Edit: Susannah Noel
Prodn Ed: Sam Dauer; Gail Friedman; Morgan Mitchell
Sr Client Acct Mgr: Valerie Esposito
Sr Mgr, Busn Systems: Justin Blackman; Daniela Plunkett
Sr Mgr, DEI Strategy & Digital Innovation: Darlene Fernandes
Sr Mgr, Digital Dist: Walter Mazurak
Sr Mgr, Digital Prodn: Christopher Gonzalez
Sr Mgr, Diversified Sales Mktg: Jessica Sorentino
Sr Mgr, Global Anti-Piracy & Content Protection: Catherine Bogin
Sr Mgr, Natl Accts: Jennifer Golding
Sr Mgr, Prodn: Celeste Cass; Amanda Gutierrez; Casey Sears
Sr Mgr, Sales Opers: Joseph O'Leary
Sr Natl Acct Mgr, Ebook Team Lead: Diego Molano Rodriguez
Sr Natl Accts Mgr: Patricia Doherty; Trish Madson
Sr Prodn Mgr: Diane Dilluvio; Jocelyn Marquez O'Dowd; Jason Reigal
Sr Spec Sales Mgr, Natl Accts: Kayla Burson
Sr Talent Acq Mgr: Natasha Taylor
Sr Admin, Procurement: Tracy Eisele
Acctg Mgr: Aurelina Joran
Author Devt & Backlist Mgr: Cassidy Leyendecker
Benefits Mgr: Lisa Edgar
Client Acct Mgr: Shavon Bilis; Kaitlyn Herbert; Vanessa Martinez
Contracts Mgr: Melissa Golding; Mindy Rosenkrantz
Custom Sales Mgr: Gretchen Fredericksen
Environmental Sustainability Mgr: Ethan Tolpin
Intl Sales Mgr: Molly Kong
Inventory Mgr: Dylan Dobrenis
Mgr, Communs: Tova Rohatiner
Mgr, Data Sci: Abigail Burrus
Mgr, Digital Mktg Strategy: Emma Skeels
Mgr, Fin Opers: Amy Fodera
Mgr, Gift Sales: Amy Solov
Mgr, HR Busn Partner: Kristen Pecci
Mgr, Intl Sales: Kristin Boran
Mgr, Lib Mktg: Emily Day
Mgr, Mktg Technol Opers: Pritpaul Bains
Mgr, Metadata: Christopher Urban
Mgr, Tech Cust Support: Andrew Arens
Mgr, Tech Support: Rob Acosta
Mgr, Workflow Systems: Chris Letso
Natl Acct Mgr: Susan Carner
Natl Acct Mgr, Barnes & Noble: Meaghan Leahy
Natl Acct Mgr, Ebooks: Chris Venkatesh
Natl Acct Mgr, Children's Sales Dept: Natalia Becerra
Natl Accts Mgr: Jaime McNutt Bode
Prod Mgr, Platform Devt Team: Anna Shilova
Prod Mgr, Sales Team: Eunice Pak
Prodn Mgr: Offauna Goodman; Jacqueline Huber-Rodriguez
Prog Mgr, Talent & Devt: Gayatri Dubey
Proj Mgr: Nicholas Iannacone
Reprint Prodn Mgr, Trade Prodn Team: Katy DiRienzo
Retail Mktg Mgr, Trade Sales: Kara Warschausky
Royalty Contract Admin: Daphne Lopez
Royalties Mgr: Jared Adler; Dawn Barley
Royalty Mgr: Jordan Yehudiel
Treasury Mgr & Sr Fin Analyst: Christine Lau
Assoc Mgr, Custom Sales: Matt Mich
Assoc Mgr, Digital Opers: Caitlyn Rush
Assoc Mgr, Lib Mktg: Samantha Slavin
Assoc Mgr, Sales Strategy: Lisa Huang
Assoc Natl Acct Mgr, Children's Sales: Ansley Kent
Assoc Natl Accts Mgr: Kathleen McCutcheon
Assoc Prod Mgr: Maggie Byrd
Assoc Sales Mgr, Spec Mkts: Jazz Key
Asst Mgr, Gift Sales: Ally McNamara
Contracts Assoc: Adelynne Chang; Karen Chau
Intl Sales Assoc: Kristin Janecek
Academic Mktg Coord: Margo McCoy
Coord, Custom Sales: Lauren McNamara
Lib Mktg Coord: Michelle Timmins
Sales Coord, Children's Natl Accts: D'Kela Duncan; Isaac Loewen; Julia Metzger
Sr Accountant: Fei Zhu
Lead Busn Analyst, Platform Devt: Karen Rucker
Sr Analyst, Sales Planning: Nikita Chatoredussy
Sr Analyst, Treasury & Insurance: Michelle Suter
Sr Busn Analyst: Michelle Pohl
Sr Busn Analyst, Platform Devt: Sunanda Movva
Sr ETL Developer: Dmitriy Firer
Sr Fin Analyst: Travis Porteous; Ryan Meese; Kemdi O'koro; Sofiya Skelly; Rosana Zagaceta
Analyst, Data Systems: Ling Ling Lu
Analyst, Sales Planning: Matthew Miller
Busn Systems Analyst: Michael Benton
Inventory Analyst, Supply Chain: Macey Best
Jr Analyst, Platform Devt Team: Sierra Moon
Principal Frontend Engr: Rinat Ussenov
Lead Data Analyst, Platform Devt: Veena Vittal
Lead Data Engr: Bhaskaran Mani
Lead Frontend Engr, Platform Devt Team: Eric Chapman
Lead Platform Developer: Vasudevareddy Cheluri
Busn Devt Specialist: Madeline Winter
Tech Specialist: Jared Christopher
Designer/Front-End Developer: Sara Wentworth
Sr Compliance Assoc: Alison Macke
Sr Talent Partner: Victor Galloway
Recruiting Specialist, HR: Polina Udalova
Assoc: Emily Miiller
Author Events Assoc: Nora Afghani; Meg Collins
Contracts Assoc: Anaka Allen
HR Info System Assoc: Sarah Ramsudh
Metadata Assoc: Margaret Sweeney
Prodn Assoc: Emily Kleinburg
Prodn Assoc, Reprints Prodn Team: Sandra Moore
Sales Assoc: Jennifer Macancela; Reagan Reynolds
Supply Chain Assoc: Ghada Daoud
Field Sales Rep: Dylan Hamilton
Indie Sales Rep: Brittany Greenway
Inside Sales Rep: Sage Daugherty; Madison Dye
Academic & Lib Mktg Asst: Hallie Young
Contracts Asst: Naomi Spratley
Field Sales Asst: Gwyneth Bechunas
Lib Mktg Asst: Ellie Bate
Retail Mktg Asst: Nomaris Garcia Rivera
Sales Asst: Bryn Goldstein; Kylie Thalheimer
Sales Asst, Natl & Wholesale Accts: Rae Bowman
Sales Asst, Spec Mkts, Trade Sales: Kaitlyn Connors
Cost Accountant: Becca Ramsey
Cost Accountant, Acctg & Fin: Donna Willson
Jr Cost Accountant: Hemali Patel
Jr Royalties Accountant: Jonathan-Cheehong Chia
Founded: 1986
Macmillan is the administrative, sales, distribution & information technology arm of the Macmillan group in the US, which includes Farrar, Straus & Giroux, LLC; Henry Holt and Company, LLC; Macmillan Audio; Macmillan Children's Publishing Group; Picador; St Martin's Press; Tor Books.
Imprints: 23rd Street Books
Subsidiaries: Macmillan Learning; St Martin's Press LLC; Tor Publishing Group

Divisions: Henry Holt and Company LLC; Macmillan Audio; Macmillan Children's Publishing Group; Macmillan Speakers
Distributor for Bloomsbury USA; The College Board; Drawn & Quarterly; Entangled Publishing; Graywolf Press; Guinness World Records; Kingfisher; Macmillan Collectors Library; Media Lab Books; Page Street Publishing Co; Page Two Books; Pan Macmillan UK
Distribution Center: MPS Distribution Center, 16365 James Madison Hwy, Gordonsville, VA 22942 *Toll Free Tel:* 888-330-8477 *Fax:* 540-672-7540 (cust serv) *Toll Free Fax:* 800-672-2054 (orders) *E-mail:* orders@mpsvirginia.com SAN: 631-5011
See separate listing for:
Farrar, Straus & Giroux, LLC
Henry Holt and Company, LLC
Macmillan Audio
Macmillan Learning
St Martin's Press, LLC
Tor Publishing Group

Macmillan Audio
Division of Macmillan
120 Broadway, 22nd fl, New York, NY 10271
Tel: 646-600-7856 *Toll Free Tel:* 888-330-8477 (cust serv) *Toll Free Fax:* 800-672-7703
E-mail: macmillan.audio@macmillanusa.com
Web Site: us.macmillan.com/audio
Key Personnel
CEO, Macmillan Publishers US: Jon Yaged
Pres & Publr: Mary Beth Roche
VP & Assoc Publr: Robert Allen
VP, Mktg: Samantha Edelson
Exec Creative Dir: Margo Goody
Exec Prodr & Sr Dir: Guy Oldfield
Exec Mng Ed: Matt DeMazza
Sr Mgr, Design: Abigail Starr
Sr Mgr, Publicity: Drew Kilman
Sr Mktg Mgr: Emily Dyer
Assoc Mktg Mgr: Claire Beyette; Maria Snelling
Founded: 1987
ISBN Prefix(es): 978-1-55927; 978-0-7927; 978-0-940687; 978-1-59397; 978-1-4272
Number of titles published annually: 500 Audio
Orders to: MPS Order Dept, 16365 James Madison Hwy, Gordonsville, VA 22942-8501 *Toll Free Tel:* 888-330-8477 *Fax:* 540-672-7540 *Toll Free Fax:* 800-672-2054
Membership(s): Audio Publishers Association; Publishers' Publicity Association

§**Macmillan Learning**
Subsidiary of Macmillan
One New York Plaza, Suite 46, New York, NY 10004
Tel: 212-576-9400
E-mail: salesoperations@macmillanusa.com
Web Site: www.macmillanlearning.com/college/us
Key Personnel
CEO: Susan Winslow
Chief Strategy & Learning Offr: Adam Black, PhD
EVP & Gen Mgr: Charles Linsmeier
SVP, Fin & Opers: Simon Horrer
VP, Communs & Training: Kate Geraghty
VP, Strategy: Elizabeth Widdicombe
VP, Supply Chain: Bill Gadoury
Sr Dir, Accessibility Outreach & Commun: Rachel Comerford
Dir, Inside Sales: Charlie Fiscia
Gen Mgr, Instl Busn: Craig Bleyer
Founded: 1999
Imprints: Bedford, Freeman & Worth Publishers; Bedford/St Martin's; W H Freeman; Hayden-McNeil; Worth Publishers
Branch Office(s)
75 Arlington St, Boston, MA 02116
14903 Pilot Dr, Plymouth, MI 48170
3058 E Elm St, Springfield, MO 65802
300 American Metro Blvd, Suite 140, Hamilton, NJ 08619

Quarry Oaks II, Suite 300, 10900 Stonelake Blvd, Austin, TX 78759
Orders to: Macmillan Publisher Services (MPS), 16365 James Madison Hwy, Gordonsville, VA 22942 *Toll Free Tel:* 888-330-8477 *E-mail:* orders@mpsvirginia.com SAN: 631-5011
See separate listing for:
Bedford/St Martin's
W H Freeman
Worth Publishers

§**Macmillan Reference USA™**
Imprint of Gale
27500 Drake Rd, Farmington Hills, MI 48331-3535
Tel: 248-699-4253 *Toll Free Tel:* 800-877-4253 *Toll Free Fax:* 877-363-4253
E-mail: gale.customercare@cengage.com
Web Site: www.gale.cengage.com/macmillan
Key Personnel
SVP, Gen Mgr: Paul Gazzolo
SVP, Mng Dir, Intl: Terry Robinson
SVP, Sales North America: Brian McDonough
VP, Mktg & Communs: Harmony Faust
ISBN Prefix(es): 978-0-02
Number of titles published annually: 22 E-Book
Total Titles: 107 E-Book

Mage Publishers Inc
5600 Wisconsin Ave, No 1408, Chevy Chase, MD 20815
Web Site: www.mage.com
Key Personnel
Publr & Ed: Mohammad Batmanglij
 E-mail: mb@mage.com
Art Dir: Najmieh Batmanglij *E-mail:* nb@mage.com
Asst to Publr & Rts Contact: Amin Sepehri
 E-mail: as@mage.com
Founded: 1985
Persian literature, art & culture in English; poetry, fiction, art & history.
ISBN Prefix(es): 978-0-934211; 978-1-933823; 978-1-949445
Number of titles published annually: 4 Print
Total Titles: 75 Print
Imprints: Mage Persian Editions
Returns: Maple Logistics, 704 Legionaire Dr, Fredericksburg, PA 17026
Warehouse: Maple Logistics, 704 Legionaire Dr, Fredericksburg, PA 17026, Mgr: Jennifer Comly *Tel:* 717-865-7600 *E-mail:* fmgvideo@maplesoln.com
Membership(s): Association of American Publishers (AAP)

The Magni Co
Subsidiary of The Magni Group Inc
7106 Wellington Point Rd, McKinney, TX 75072
Tel: 972-540-2050 *Fax:* 972-540-1057
E-mail: sales@magnico.com; info@magnico.com
Web Site: www.magnico.com
Key Personnel
CEO: Evan B Reynolds *E-mail:* ereynolds@magnico.com
Founded: 1982
Health & beauty, weight loss, informative & organizer books.
ISBN Prefix(es): 978-1-882330; 978-1-937026
Number of titles published annually: 5 Print; 1 CD-ROM; 3 Online; 50 E-Book; 2 Audio
Total Titles: 65 Print; 2 CD-ROM; 50 Online; 52 E-Book; 9 Audio
Imprints: MAGNI
Membership(s): American Booksellers Association (ABA)

§**Maharishi International University Press**
Formerly Maharishi University of Management Press
Subsidiary of Maharishi International University

MIU Press Marketing, MR 785, Fairfield, IA 52557
Tel: 641-472-1101 *Toll Free Tel:* 800-831-6523
E-mail: miupress@miu.edu
Web Site: miupress.org
Founded: 1974
Specialize in books about transcendental meditation.
ISBN Prefix(es): 978-0-9616944; 978-0-923569
Number of titles published annually: 5 Print
Total Titles: 50 Print
Distributed by Penguin Publishing Group (select titles)
Orders to: 1000 N Fourth St, DB-1155, Fairfield, IA 52557-1155

Maharishi University of Management Press, see Maharishi International University Press

Management Advisory Services & Publications (MASP)
PO Box 81151, Wellesley Hills, MA 02481-0001
SAN: 203-8692
Tel: 781-235-2895 *Fax:* 781-235-5446
E-mail: info@masp.com
Web Site: www.masp.com
Key Personnel
Principal & Ed: Jay Kuong *E-mail:* jaykmasp@aol.com
Founded: 1972
A well established publications & advisory & training services company with a concentration in enterprise governance, internal controls, information technology security, auditing & contingency planning & business continuity fields. This includes reference books, journals & practitioners' manuals. Under the enterprise governance field, MASP publishes books on Sarbanes-Oxley compliance. Additionally, as part of the diversification efforts, we publish a few literary fiction books.
ISBN Prefix(es): 978-0-940706
Number of titles published annually: 3 Print
Total Titles: 75 Print
Foreign Office(s): Santa Fe Ave, Buenos Aires, Argentina, Contact: D Ramos
 E-mail: dramos@satlink.com

§**Management Sciences for Health**
200 Rivers Edge Dr, Medford, MA 02155
Tel: 617-250-9500 *Fax:* 617-250-9090
E-mail: bookstore@msh.org
Web Site: www.msh.org
Key Personnel
Deputy Dir, Pubns: Barbara K Timmons *Tel:* 617-250-9291 *E-mail:* btimmons@msh.org
Procurement Offr: Natasha Mahoney *Tel:* 617-250-9262
Founded: 1971
Established to assist, promote, evaluate, manage & perform research on the delivery of health care, establish methods & procedures leading to the improvement of health & social services & conduct education & publishing in these areas. MSH's publications unit develops & distributes books & a quarterly periodical to further MSH's mission, which is to help close the gap between knowledge about public health problems & action to solve them.
MSH currently stocks about 3 dozen products, most of which are books (including monographs, manuals & handbooks, some are available on CD-ROM). Many are available in languages other than English. Major products are The Manager continuing education quarterly; Managing Drug Supply (first published in 1981); instructional manuals (CORE, MOST, HOSPITAL, FIMAT); the Lessons from MSH & Stubbs monograph series; the series of success stories (20-page color booklets that present the highlights of successful programs) & books ranging from textbooks to syntheses of research.

MHS has offices in Afghanistan, Angola, Guinea, Haiti, Indonesia, Malawi, Philippines & Senegal.
ISBN Prefix(es): 978-0-913723
Number of titles published annually: 2 Print; 1 CD-ROM
Total Titles: 39 Print; 4 CD-ROM
Branch Office(s)
45 Broadway, Suite 320, New York, NY 10006
4301 N Fairfax Dr, Suite 400, Arlington, VA 22203-1627 *Tel:* 703-524-6575 *Fax:* 703-524-7898
Distributed by Kumarian Press
Membership(s): Independent Book Publishers Association (IBPA)

Mandala Earth
Imprint of Insight Editions
800 "A" St, San Rafael, CA 94901
Tel: 415-526-1370 *Toll Free Fax:* 866-509-0515
E-mail: info@mandalapublishing.com
Web Site: www.mandalaeartheditions.com
Key Personnel
Publr & CEO: Raoul Goff *E-mail:* raoul@insighteditions.com
Edit Dir: Katie Killebrew
Sales Dir: Julie Hamilton *E-mail:* j.hamilton@insighteditions.com
Sales Mgr: Jacqui Goff *E-mail:* j.goff@insighteditions.com
Full color coffee table books & minibooks, as well as decks, calendars, journals, greeting cards, art prints & incense. Topics include: environmental issues, women's studies, Asian art, music, philosophy, cross-cultural issues & Hinduism. Cutting-edge environmental & cultural topics that feature the unique voices & new concepts of leading thinkers, environmentalists, photojournalists, cultural commentators & artists.
ISBN Prefix(es): 978-1-886069; 978-1-932771; 978-1-60109; 978-0-945475
Number of titles published annually: 15 Print; 2 Audio
Total Titles: 300 Print; 200 Online; 10 Audio
Distributed by Simon & Schuster, LLC
Foreign Rep(s): Bill Bailey Publishers Representatives (Europe); Book Promotions (Jonathan Ball) (South Africa); Gilles Fauveau (Japan, South Korea); Jaime Gregorio (Philippines); NewSouth Books (Australia, New Zealand); Penguin Books India (Bangladesh, India, Maldives, Nepal, Pakistan, Sri Lanka); Perseus International (Suk Lee) (Malaysia, Singapore); Perseus International (Edison Garcia) (Caribbean, Latin America, Middle East, North Africa); June Poonpanich (Cambodia, Indonesia, Laos, Thailand, Vietnam); Publishers Group UK (UK); Wei Zhao (China, Hong Kong, Taiwan)

Mandel Vilar Press
Affiliate of Americas for Conservation + the Arts
19 Oxford Ct, Simsbury, CT 06070
Tel: 806-790-4731
E-mail: info@mvpress.org
Web Site: www.mvpublishers.org
Key Personnel
Co-Founder & Sr Ed: Dr Dena Mandel
Co-Publr & Press Dir: Dr Robert A Mandel *E-mail:* robert@mandelvilar.org
Co-Publr & Ed: Irene Vilar *E-mail:* irene@americasforconservation.org
Ed-in-Chief, Fig Tree Books: Fred Price
Ms & Prodn Ed: Mary Beth Hinton *E-mail:* mbhinton2@gmail.com
Prodn & Design Mgr: Barbara Werden *E-mail:* barbarawerden@gmail.com
Founded: 2014
Nonprofit publishing arm of Americas for Conservation + the Arts (a 501(c)(3) organization) dedicated to connecting the literature of the Americas by uniting the works of the best writers of Latin & Latino America with the leading ethnic & minority writers of North America.
ISBN Prefix(es): 978-1-942134; 978-1-94149 (Fig Tree Books)
Number of titles published annually: 5 Print; 5 E-Book
Total Titles: 15 Print; 12 E-Book
Imprints: Fig Tree Books
Branch Office(s)
430 W Ninth Ave, Denver, CO 80204 *Tel:* 303-330-6597
Distributor for Dryad Press
Distribution Center: Consortium Book Sales & Distribution, The Keg House, Suite 101, 34 13 Ave NE, Minneapolis, MN 55413-1007 (an Ingram brand) *Tel:* 612-746-2600 *Toll Free Tel:* 866-400-5351 (cust serv, Jackson, TN) *E-mail:* cbsdinfo@ingramcontent.com *Web Site:* www.cbsd.com SAN: 200-6049

Manic D Press Inc
250 Banks St, San Francisco, CA 94110
Mailing Address: PO Box 410804, San Francisco, CA 94141
Tel: 415-648-8288
E-mail: info@manicdpress.com
Web Site: www.manicdpress.com
Key Personnel
Publr & Intl Rts: Jennifer Joseph
Founded: 1984
Poetry & unusual fiction & nonfiction & alternative childrens books, emphasis on innovative, new & established writers & artists, paperbacks, general adult books.
ISBN Prefix(es): 978-0-916397; 978-1-933149; 978-1-945665
Number of titles published annually: 4 Print; 4 E-Book
Total Titles: 200 Print; 100 E-Book; 12 Audio
Foreign Rep(s): Ingram Group; Publishers Group Canada (Canada); Turnaround Distribution (Europe)
Distribution Center: Consortium Book Sales & Distribution, The Keg House, Suite 101, 34 13 Ave NE, Minneapolis, MN 55413-1007 *Tel:* 612-746-2600 *Toll Free Tel:* 866-400-5351 (cust serv, Jackson, TN) *E-mail:* cbsdinfo@ingramcontent.com *Web Site:* www.cbsd.com

§Manning Publications Co
20 Baldwin Rd, PO Box 761, Shelter Island, NY 11964
Tel: 203-626-1510
E-mail: sales@manning.com; support@manning.com (cust serv)
Web Site: www.manning.com
Key Personnel
Publr: Marjan Bace *E-mail:* maba@manning.com
Assoc Publr: Michael Stephens
Founded: 1990
Full-scale company whose titles are distributed in the US, Europe & Asia.
ISBN Prefix(es): 978-1-884777; 978-1-930110; 978-1-932394; 978-1-933988; 978-1-61729; 978-1-935182; 978-1-63343
Number of titles published annually: 25 Print; 10 E-Book
Total Titles: 800 Print; 20 CD-ROM; 500 E-Book
Distributed by Pearson Education; Simon & Schuster, LLC (US & CN)
Distribution Center: Institute of Electrical & Electronics Engineers, 3 Park Ave, 17th fl, New York, NY 10016-5997 (worldwide) *Tel:* 212-419-7900 *E-mail:* contactcenter@ieee.org *Web Site:* www.ieee.org
O'Reilly Media Inc, 1005 Granvenstein Hwy N, Sebastopol, CA 95472 (US & CN) *Tel:* 707-829-0515 *Toll Free Tel:* 800-998-9939 *Toll Free Fax:* 800-997-9901 *E-mail:* retailcs@oreilly.com *Web Site:* www.oreilly.com
Woodslane Pty Ltd, Unit 7/5 Vuko Place, Warriewood, NSW 2102, Australia (Australia, New Zealand, Pacific Islands) *Tel:* (02) 9970 5111 *Fax:* (02) 9970 5002 *E-mail:* info@woodslane.com.au *Web Site:* www.woodslane.com.au
Pansing Distribution Pte Ltd, 438 Ang Mo Kio Industrial Park 1, off Ang Mo Kio Ave 10, Singapore, Singapore (Hong Kong, Malaysia, Singapore, South Korea, Taiwan, Thailand) *Tel:* 6319 9939 *Fax:* 6459 4931 *E-mail:* infobooks@pansing.com
Pearson Education, Edinburgh Gate, Harlow, Essex CM20 2JE, United Kingdom (Africa, Europe, UK) *Tel:* (01279) 623928 *Fax:* (01279) 414130 *E-mail:* enq.orders@pearsoned-ema.com *Web Site:* www.pearson-books.com

MapEasy Inc
PO Box 80, Wainscott, NY 11975-0080
Tel: 631-537-6213 *Fax:* 631-537-4541
E-mail: info@mapeasy.com
Web Site: www.mapeasy.com
Founded: 1990
Guidemaps & location guides to cities in North America, Western Europe & Asia.
ISBN Prefix(es): 978-1-878979; 978-1-929038
Number of titles published annually: 4 Print
Total Titles: 72 Print

MAR*CO Products Inc
PO Box 686, Hatfield, PA 19440
Tel: 215-956-0313 *Toll Free Tel:* 800-448-2197 *Fax:* 215-956-9041
E-mail: help@marcoproducts.com; sales@marcoproducts.com
Web Site: www.marcoproducts.com
Key Personnel
Founder & Dir: Arden Martenz
Pres: Cameon Funk
VP: Warren Funk
Founded: 1977
Educational guidance materials for elementary & secondary counselors, psychologists & social workers.
ISBN Prefix(es): 978-1-884063; 978-1-57543
Number of titles published annually: 12 Print; 20 Online; 25 E-Book
Total Titles: 300 Print; 400 Online
Distributed by ASCA; Boulden Publishing; Burnell Books; Calloway House; Career Kids FYI; CFKR Career; Character Development; Community Intervention; Courage to Change; Cress Productions Co; EDU Reference; Educational Media Corp; Incentive Plus; Jist; Mental Health Resources; National Center for Youth Issues/STARS; National Professional Resources; National Resource Center for Youth Services; Paperbacks for Educators; School Speciality; SourceResource; WRS Group; YouthLight Inc
Distributor for Boulden Publishing; Educational Media Corp; HarperCollins; National Center for Youth Issues/STARS
Returns: 214 Kale Rd, New Bern, NC 28562
Distribution Center: NIMCO Bookstore

Marathon Press
1500 Square Turn Blvd, Norfolk, NE 68701
Mailing Address: PO Box 407, Norfolk, NE 68702-0407
Tel: 402-371-5040 *Toll Free Tel:* 800-228-0629 *Fax:* 402-371-9382
E-mail: info@marathonpress.net
Web Site: www.marathonpress.com
Key Personnel
Owner: Max Alewel
Pres: Bruce Price
Founded: 1974
Books on professional photography.
This publisher has indicated that 90% of their product line is author subsidized.
ISBN Prefix(es): 978-0-934420
Number of titles published annually: 5 Print
Total Titles: 650 Print

PUBLISHERS

Maren Green Publishing Inc
7900 Excelsior Blvd, Suite 105K, Hopkins, MN 55343
Tel: 651-439-4500 *Toll Free Tel:* 800-287-1512
Fax: 651-439-4532
E-mail: info@marengreen.com
Web Site: www.marengreen.com
Key Personnel
Owner & Pres: Todd Snow *E-mail:* toddsnow@marengreen.com
Founded: 2006
Fiction & nonfiction books for children newborn to age 9.
This publisher has indicated that 100% of their product line is author subsidized.
ISBN Prefix(es): 978-1-934277
Number of titles published annually: 5 Print
Total Titles: 25 Print
Imprints: Books Good For Young Children™
Foreign Rights: Sylvia Hayse Literary Agency (worldwide)

Marick Press
1342 Three Mile Dr, Grosse Pointe Park, MI 48230
Tel: 313-407-9236
E-mail: orders@marickpress.com; info@marickpress.com
Web Site: www.marickpress.com
Key Personnel
Founding Publr: Mariela Griffor *E-mail:* mgriffor@marickpress.com
Art Dir: Sean Tai
Assoc Ed: Christine Howson; Scott Minar; Brigitte Rabaut
A not-for-profit literary publisher founded to preserve the best work by poets around the world including many under published women poets. We seek out & publish the best new work from an eclectic range of aesthetics - work that is technically accomplished, distinctive in style & thematically fresh.
ISBN Prefix(es): 978-0-9779703; 978-1-934851
Number of titles published annually: 8 Print
Total Titles: 70 Print
Distribution Center: Ingram Content Group, One Ingram Blvd, La Vergne, TN 37086

Marine Education Textbooks
124 N Van Ave, Houma, LA 70363-5895
SAN: 215-9651
Tel: 985-879-3866 *Fax:* 985-879-3911
E-mail: email@marineeducationtextbooks.com
Web Site: www.marineeducationtextbooks.com
Key Personnel
Opers Mgr: Gwen M Block *E-mail:* gwen@ourmet.com
Ed: Richard A Block
Founded: 1970
Training & educational books for preparation of USCG Exams. Marine safety signs, nautical charts.
ISBN Prefix(es): 978-0-934114; 978-1-879778
Number of titles published annually: 6 Print
Total Titles: 40 Print
Imprints: Marine Survey Press

Marine Techniques Publishing
311 W River Rd, Augusta, ME 04330-3991
SAN: 298-7805
Tel: 207-622-7984
E-mail: promariner@roadrunner.com
Key Personnel
Owner & Pres: James L Pelletier
Founded: 1983
Industry specific directories; maritime/worldwide merchant marine; naval architecture; marine biology, chemistry, geology; civil, marine engineering; electrical, electronic marine engineering; energy, oil & gas offshore; mechanical marine engineering; transportation, marine. Commercial merchant marine - worldwide directories, *Mariner's Employment Guide* & maritime autobiographies (true maritime stories).
This publisher has indicated that 25% of their product line is author subsidized.
ISBN Prefix(es): 978-0-9644915; 978-0-9798008
Number of titles published annually: 5 Print; 10 Online; 2 E-Book; 2 Audio
Total Titles: 25 Print; 8 CD-ROM; 10 Online; 2 E-Book; 2 Audio
Distributed by Elsevier Inc; PennWell Business & Industrial Division
Distributor for Academic Press; Best Publishing Co; Butterworth-Heinemann; Clarkson Research Services Ltd; Elsevier Inc; Focal Press; Gulf Professional Publishers; PennWell Business & Industrial Division; Saunders; Waterfront Soundings Productions; Witherby Seamanship International Ltd
Foreign Rep(s): Chapters Inc (Canada); W H Everett & Sons Ltd (England, London, UK); Lavoisier (France)
Distribution Center: Follett School Solutions Inc, 1340 Ridgeview Dr, McHenry, IL 60050 *Tel:* 815-759-1700 *Toll Free Tel:* 888-511-5114 (cust serv) *Fax:* 815-759-9831 *Toll Free Fax:* 800-852-5458 *E-mail:* info@follettlearning.com *Web Site:* www.follettlearning.com SAN: 169-1902
Baker, Lyman & Co Inc, 5250 Veterans Memorial Blvd, Metairie, LA 70006 *Toll Free Tel:* 800-535-6956 *E-mail:* sales@bakerlyman.com *Web Site:* www.bakerlyman.com
Emery-Pratt Co, 1966 W Main St, Owosso, MI 48867 *Toll Free Tel:* 800-248-3887 *Toll Free Fax:* 800-523-6379 *Web Site:* www.emery-pratt.com
Membership(s): American Maritime Association; American Society of Naval Engineers; Association of Marine Engineers; The Association of Publishers for Special Sales (APSS); Independent Book Publishers Association (IBPA); Independent Publishers of New England (IPNE); Lloyd's Maritime Information Register; Women's Maritime Association (WMA)

Markowski International Publishers
One Oakglade Circle, Hummelstown, PA 17036-9525
Tel: 717-566-0468
E-mail: info@possibilitypress.com
Web Site: www.possibilitypress.com; www.aeronauticalpublishers.com
Key Personnel
Publr: Michael Anthony Markowski
Founded: 1981
Books on personal development, business, success, motivation, aviation & model aviation.
ISBN Prefix(es): 978-0-938716
Number of titles published annually: 3 Print
Total Titles: 75 Print
Imprints: Aeronautical Publishers; Possibility Press
Membership(s): AOPA

Marquette University Press
Division of Marquette University
1415 W Wisconsin Ave, Milwaukee, WI 53233
Mailing Address: PO Box 3141, Milwaukee, WI 53201-3141
Tel: 414-288-1564
Web Site: www.marquette.edu/mupress
Key Personnel
Dir: Dr Sarah Wadsworth *E-mail:* sarah.wadsworth@marquette.edu
Mgr: Maureen Kondrick *E-mail:* maureen.kondrick@marquette.edu
Founded: 1916
Publications in the humanities by scholars of international reputation. Specialize in philosophy, theology, humanities & history in addition to regional studies relating to the city of Milwaukee & the state of Wisconsin.
ISBN Prefix(es): 978-0-87462; 978-1-62600

U.S. PUBLISHERS

Number of titles published annually: 10 Print; 7 E-Book
Total Titles: 450 Print; 275 E-Book
Foreign Rep(s): Europspan (Africa, Europe, Middle East)
Orders to: Baker & Taylor Publisher Services, 30 Amberwood Pkwy, Ashland, OH 44805, Contact: Elaine Lattanzi *Tel:* 567-215-0030 *Toll Free Tel:* 888-814-0208 *E-mail:* info@btpubservices.com *Web Site:* www.btpubservices.com
Returns: Baker & Taylor Publisher Services, 30 Amberwood Pkwy, Ashland, OH 44805, Contact: Elaine Lattanzi *Tel:* 567-215-0030 *Toll Free Tel:* 888-814-0208 *E-mail:* info@btpubservices.com *Web Site:* www.btpubservices.com
Distribution Center: Baker & Taylor Publisher Services, 30 Amberwood Pkwy, Ashland, OH 44805, Contact: Elaine Lattanzi *Tel:* 567-215-0030 *Toll Free Tel:* 888-814-0208 *E-mail:* info@btpubservices.com *Web Site:* www.btpubservices.com
Membership(s): Association of Jesuit University Presses; Association of University Presses (AUPresses)

Marquis Who's Who
Imprint of Marquis Who's Who Ventures LLC
350 RXR Plaza, Uniondale, NY 11556
Tel: 908-673-0100; 908-279-0100
Toll Free Tel: 844-394-6946 *Fax:* 908-356-0184
E-mail: info@marquisww.com; customerservice@marquisww.com (cust serv, sales)
Web Site: marquiswhoswho.com
Founded: 1898
Publisher of comprehensive biographical references available in print, online & mailing list. Major Marquis Who's Who publications include *Who's Who in America*, *Who's Who in the World* & *Who's Who of American Women*.
ISBN Prefix(es): 978-0-8379
Number of titles published annually: 8 Print
Total Titles: 12 Print; 1 Online

Marriage Transformation LLC
PO Box 249, Harrison, TN 37341
Tel: 423-599-0153
E-mail: staff@marriagetransformation.com
Web Site: www.marriagetransformation.com; www.transformationlearningcenter.com
Key Personnel
Pres: Susanne M Alexander *E-mail:* susanne@marriagetransformation.com
Founded: 2004
Relationship & marriage education.
This publisher has indicated that 90% of their product line is author subsidized.
ISBN Prefix(es): 978-0-9726893; 978-0-9816666; 978-1-940062
Number of titles published annually: 3 Print; 3 E-Book
Total Titles: 20 Print; 20 E-Book
Foreign Rights: Columbine (worldwide)
Distribution Center: Ingram Spark, One Ingram Blvd, La Vergne, TN 37086 (worldwide) *Tel:* 615-793-5000
Membership(s): National Association for Relationship & Marriage Education (NARME)

Marshall Cavendish Education
Member of Times International Publishing Group
99 White Plains Rd, Tarrytown, NY 10591-9001
Tel: 914-332-8888 *Toll Free Tel:* 800-821-9881
Fax: 914-332-1082
E-mail: mce@marshallcavendish.com; customerservice@marshallcavendish.com
Web Site: www.mceducation.us
Key Personnel
Dir, US: Vivian Cheng
Accts Payable/Accts Receivable Assoc: Imelda Guarin
Sr Educ Consultant: Christopher Coyne

U.S. PUBLISHERS

Educ/Sales Consultant: Thomas Corbia; Ellen Lauterbach
Founded: 1970
International publisher of books, directories, magazines & digital platforms. Products reach across the globe in 13 languages & our publishing network spans Asia & the US. Dedicated to the promotion of lifelong learning & self-development.
ISBN Prefix(es): 978-1-85435; 978-0-7614
Number of titles published annually: 320 Print; 10 Online; 300 E-Book
Total Titles: 1,200 Print; 57 Online; 590 E-Book
Imprints: Marshall Cavendish Adult Trade; Marshall Cavendish Benchmark; Marshall Cavendish Digital; Marshall Cavendish Education; Marshall Cavendish Reference
Distributed by Marshall Cavendish Ltd (UK)
Foreign Rep(s): Peter Pal Library Suppliers (Australia)
Warehouse: Swan Packaging, 415 Hamburg Tpke, Wayne, NJ 07470
Distribution Center: Baker & Taylor Publisher Services, 30 Amberwood Pkwy, Ashland, OH 44805 *Tel:* 567-215-0030 *Toll Free Tel:* 888-814-0208 *E-mail:* orders@btpubservices.com *Web Site:* www.btpubservices.com
Membership(s): The American Library Association (ALA); The Children's Book Council (CBC)

Martindale-Hubbell®, see Martindale LLC

§Martindale LLC
121 Chanlon Rd, Suite 110, New Providence, NJ 07974
SAN: 205-8863
Tel: 908-464-6800; 908-771-7777 (intl)
Toll Free Tel: 800-526-4902 *Fax:* 908-771-8704
E-mail: info@martindale.com
Web Site: www.martindale.com
Founded: 1868
Publisher of the *Martindale-Hubbell Law Directory* in hard copy, on CD-ROM & available online; containing listings of over 1 million lawyers & law firms worldwide. Other publications include *Law Digest*, a summary of laws from each of the 50 states & 80 countries; *Martindale-Hubbell International Law Directory*, designed for the international legal community & *Martindale-Hubbell Bar Register of Preeminent Lawyers*, listing of over 8,900 law practices designated as outstanding by members of the legal community.
ISBN Prefix(es): 978-1-56160; 978-1-934528; 978-1-60366
Number of titles published annually: 5 Print; 1 CD-ROM; 1 Online
Total Titles: 5 Print; 1 CD-ROM; 1 Online
Imprints: Martindale-Hubbell®

Maryland Center for History & Culture (MCHC)
610 Park Ave, Baltimore, MD 21201
Tel: 410-685-3750; 410-685-3750 ext 377 (orders) *Fax:* 410-385-2105
E-mail: shop@mdhistory.org
Web Site: www.mdhistory.org; shop.mdhistory.org
Key Personnel
VP, Res: Martina Kado, PhD *Tel:* 410-685-3750 ext 335 *E-mail:* mkado@mdhistory.org
Founded: 1844
Publish historical books.
ISBN Prefix(es): 978-0-938420; 978-0-9842135; 978-0-9965944
Number of titles published annually: 5 Print
Total Titles: 45 Print
Distribution Center: HFS (Hopkins Fulfillment Services), 2715 N Charles St, Baltimore, MD 21218 *Tel:* 410-516-6965 *Toll Free Tel:* 800-537-5487 (US & CN) *Fax:* 410-516-6998
E-mail: hfscustserv@jhu.edu *Web Site:* hfs.jhu.edu

Maryland History Press
6913 Seneca Dr, Snow Hill, MD 21863
Tel: 443-397-0912
Web Site: www.marylandhistorypress.com
Key Personnel
Owner & Pres: Helen Elaine Patterson
E-mail: ehpatterson@earthlink.net
Founded: 1999
Editing, proofreading for almost any topic/web site. Publish books on diversified topics by various authors to help celebrate America's uniqueness...people, events, culture & environs. Services provided are publishing services, author-subsidy program, consignments, distribution services via national company, book searches & web site exposure through major online booksellers.
This publisher has indicated that 85% of their product line is author subsidized.
ISBN Prefix(es): 978-0-9703802
Number of titles published annually: 3 Print
Total Titles: 13 Print; 12 Online
Distributor for Tapestry Press Ltd

Mason Crest Publishers
Imprint of National Highlights
450 Parkway Dr, Suite D, Broomall, PA 19008
SAN: 990-6800
Tel: 610-543-6200 *Toll Free Tel:* 866-MCP-BOOK (627-2665) *Fax:* 610-543-3878
Web Site: www.masoncrest.com
Key Personnel
CEO: Dan Hilferty *Tel:* 610-543-6200 ext 104 *E-mail:* dhilferty@nationalhighlights.com
Pres: Louis Cohen *Tel:* 917-763-7760
E-mail: lcohen@nationalhighlights.com
Cont: Diana Daniels *Tel:* 610-543-6200 ext 109 *E-mail:* ddaniels@nationalhighlights.com
Intl Rts & Mktg Dir: Michelle Luke *Tel:* 812-604-1603 *E-mail:* mluke@nationalhighlights.com
Busn Devt: Becki Stewart *Tel:* 954-243-7180 *E-mail:* bstewart@nationalhighlights.com
Founded: 2001
Mason Crest Publishers is committed to publishing the finest nonfiction school, library & curriculum products available today. Our titles are full-color & include a glossary, index, further reading section, Internet resources & are library bound. Subjects include reality shows.
ISBN Prefix(es): 978-1-59084; 978-1-4222; 978-1-59482
Number of titles published annually: 300 Print; 1,500 E-Book
Total Titles: 2,000 Print; 2,500 E-Book
Foreign Rep(s): Mare Nostrum Distributors (Maura Brescia) (Argentina, Chile, Uruguay); Missing Link Education CC (Farida Adam & Moreblessing Ngwenya) (South Africa); PSI/Publishers' Services International Inc (James Schmelzer) (worldwide); Saunders Book Co (James Saunders) (Canada); Target Book Sales (Jonathan Brooks) (UK)
Returns: 701 Ashland Ave, Bays 1 & 2, Folcroft, PA 19032, Opers Mgr: Lee Wark *Tel:* 610-583-0211 *Fax:* 610-583-0212
Shipping Address: 701 Ashland Ave, Bays 1 & 2, Folcroft, PA 19032, Opers Mgr: Lee Wark *Tel:* 610-583-0211 *Fax:* 610-583-0212
Warehouse: 701 Ashland Ave, Bays 1 & 2, Folcroft, PA 19032, Opers Mgr: Lee Wark *Tel:* 610-583-0211 *Fax:* 610-583-0212
Distribution Center: 701 Ashland Ave, Bays 1 & 2, Folcroft, PA 19032, Opers Mgr: Lee Wark *Tel:* 610-583-0211 *Fax:* 610-583-0212
Membership(s): Friends of Libraries of USA (FOLUSA); Independent Book Publishers Association (IBPA)

The Massachusetts Historical Society
1154 Boylston St, Boston, MA 02215-3695
Tel: 617-536-1608 *Fax:* 617-859-0074
E-mail: publications@masshist.org
Web Site: www.masshist.org
Key Personnel
Chief Technol & Media Offr: Chris Coveney *Tel:* 617-646-0539 *E-mail:* ccoveney@masshist.org
Dir, Communs: Carol Knauff *Tel:* 617-646-0554 *E-mail:* cknauff@masshist.org
Dir, Pubns: Ondine E Le Blanc *Tel:* 617-646-0524 *E-mail:* oleblanc@masshist.org
Worthington C Ford Ed of Pubns: Ondine E Le Blanc *Tel:* 617-646-0524 *E-mail:* oleblanc@masshist.org
Assoc Ed: Jim Connolly *Tel:* 617-646-0513 *E-mail:* jconnolly@masshist.org
Robert Treat Paine Papers Asst Ed: Christina Carrick *Tel:* 617-646-0576 *E-mail:* ccarrick@masshist.org
Founded: 1792
Scholarly historical regional publications.
ISBN Prefix(es): 978-0-934909; 978-0-9652584; 978-1-936520
Number of titles published annually: 3 Print
Total Titles: 500 Print
Distributed by University of Virginia Press

§Master Books®
Imprint of New Leaf Publishing Group LLC
3142 Hwy 103 N, Green Forest, AR 72638
Mailing Address: PO Box 726, Green Forest, AR 72638
Tel: 870-438-5288 *Toll Free Tel:* 800-999-3777
E-mail: sales@masterbooks.com; nlp@nlpg.com; submissions@newleafpress.net
Web Site: www.masterbooks.com; www.nlpg.com
Key Personnel
Pres, New Leaf Publishing Group: Randy Pratt
Ed-in-Chief: Laura Welch
Edit Asst: Craig Froman
Founded: 1976
Publish Biblically-based, scientifically sound creation materials & curriculum.
ISBN Prefix(es): 978-0-89051
Number of titles published annually: 35 Print; 30 E-Book
Total Titles: 700 Print; 3 CD-ROM; 700 E-Book; 2 Audio

Mastery Education
Subsidiary of Peoples Educational Holdings Inc
25 Philips Pkwy, Suite 105, Montvale, NJ 07645
Tel: 201-708-2349 *Toll Free Tel:* 800-822-1080 *Fax:* 201-712-0045
E-mail: cs@masteryeducation.com
Web Site: masteryeducation.com; www.measuringuplive2.com
Founded: 1990
Publisher & marketer of print & electronic educational materials for the K-12 school market. We focus our efforts in test preparation, assessment & instruction & college preparation.
ISBN Prefix(es): 978-1-61526; 978-1-61527; 978-1-936029; 978-1-61602; 978-1-61734; 978-1-60979; 978-1-936026; 978-1-56256; 978-1-58984; 978-1-4138; 978-1-64090; 978-1-60605; 979-8-88711
Number of titles published annually: 50 Print
Total Titles: 2,000 Print
Imprints: Asante®; Measuring Up®
Membership(s): International Society for Technology in Education (ISTE®)

Materials Research Society
506 Keystone Dr, Warrendale, PA 15086-7537
SAN: 686-0125
Tel: 724-779-3003 *Fax:* 724-779-8313
E-mail: info@mrs.org
Web Site: www.mrs.org

Key Personnel
Dir, Communs: Eileen Kiley
Founded: 1973
Scientific reports on leading edge topics in materials research.
ISBN Prefix(es): 978-0-931837; 978-1-55899
Number of titles published annually: 30 Print
Total Titles: 1,100 Print

Math Solutions®
Unit of Houghton Mifflin Harcourt
One Harbor Dr, Suite 101, Sausalito, CA 94965
Toll Free Tel: 877-234-7323 *Toll Free Fax:* 800-724-4716
E-mail: info@mathsolutions.com; orders@mathsolutions.com
Web Site: www.mathsolutions.com; store.mathsolutions.com
Key Personnel
Founder: Marilyn Burns
VP & Gen Mgr: Patricio Dujan
Sr Dir, Mktg: Mary Garrison
Dir, Content Devt: Patty Clark
Dir, Prof Learning: Lisa Bush
Assoc Dir, Fin: John Fortune
Assoc Dir, Opers: Taber Auren
Assoc Dir, Opers & Busn Systems: Taeyana Kamir
Exec Ed: Jamie Cross *E-mail:* jcross@mathsolutions.com
Sr Mktg Mgr: Kelli Cook
Founded: 1994
Dedicated to improving the teaching of mathematics by providing professional development of the highest quality to teachers & administrators.
ISBN Prefix(es): 978-0-941355; 978-1-935099
Number of titles published annually: 10 Print
Total Titles: 80 Print
Returns: Houghton Mifflin Harcourt, Intervention Services Group Book Returns, 1900 S Batavia Ave, Geneva, IL 60134
Shipping Address: 1805 S McDowell Blvd, Petaluma, CA 94954, Contact: Taber Auren *Tel:* 707-769-0722
Warehouse: 1805 S McDowell Blvd, Petaluma, CA 94954, Contact: Taber Auren *Tel:* 707-769-0722
Membership(s): ASCD; National Council of Teachers of Mathematics (NCTM)

Math Teachers Press Inc
4850 Park Glen Rd, Minneapolis, MN 55416
Tel: 952-545-6535 *Toll Free Tel:* 800-852-2435 *Fax:* 952-546-7502
E-mail: info@movingwithmath.com
Web Site: www.movingwithmath.com
Key Personnel
Founder & Pres: Caryl K Pierson
 E-mail: cpierson@movingwithmath.com
Founded: 1980
PreK-12 manipulative-based math curriculum.
ISBN Prefix(es): 978-0-933383; 978-1-891192; 978-1-931106; 978-1-59167
Number of titles published annually: 3 Print
Total Titles: 70 Print

The Mathematical Association of America
1529 18 St NW, Washington, DC 20036-1358
SAN: 203-9737
Tel: 202-387-5200 *Toll Free Tel:* 800-741-9415 *Fax:* 202-265-2384
E-mail: maahq@maa.org; advertising@maa.org (pubns)
Web Site: www.maa.org
Key Personnel
Chief Busn Offr: Ben Spaisman
Exec Dir: Michael Pearson *E-mail:* mpearson@maa.org
Dir, Fin: Kimberly Rutland-Starks
Dir, Pubns Opers: Carol Baxter *E-mail:* cbaxter@maa.org

Sr Acqs Ed: Stephen Kennedy *E-mail:* kennedy@maa.org
Founded: 1915
Membership organization comprised of college mathematics educators, high school teachers & others interested in mathematics.
ISBN Prefix(es): 978-0-88385; 978-0-9835005; 978-1-939512; 978-1-61444
Number of titles published annually: 3 Online; 2 E-Book
Imprints: MAA Press
Orders to: MAA Service Center, PO Box 91112, Washington, DC 20090-1112 *Tel:* 301-617-7800 *Toll Free Tel:* 800-331-1622 *Fax:* 240-396-5647 *E-mail:* maaservice@maa.org

§Mazda Publishers Inc
PO Box 2603, Costa Mesa, CA 92628
SAN: 658-120X
Tel: 714-751-5252 *Fax:* 714-751-4805
E-mail: mazdapub@aol.com
Web Site: www.mazdapublishers.com
Key Personnel
Publr & CEO: Dr A Kamron Jabbari
VP: Fay Zamani
Ed-at-Large: Noel Silver; Ann West; Diane L Wilcox
Acqs Ed: Hilary Eastwood
Founded: 1980
Publishes scholarly books dealing with the Middle East, Central Asia & North Africa; critical reviews of poetry; Central Asia including art & architecture.
ISBN Prefix(es): 978-1-56859
Number of titles published annually: 32 Print
Total Titles: 634 Print
Imprints: Blind Owl Press

McBooks Press
Imprint of Rowman & Littlefield Publishing Group
246 Goose Lane, Guildord, CT 06357
Tel: 203-458-4500
E-mail: info@rowman.com
Web Site: www.mcbooks.com
Founded: 1979
Trade books. Specialize in historical fiction, vegetarianism, New York State regional books, period nautical, military fiction, sports including boxing.
ISBN Prefix(es): 978-1-59013
Number of titles published annually: 6 Print; 6 E-Book
Total Titles: 185 Print; 145 E-Book
Foreign Rep(s): Gazelle Book Services Ltd (Europe, UK)
Orders to: National Book Network *Toll Free Tel:* 800-462-6420 *Toll Free Fax:* 800-338-4550 *E-mail:* customercare@nbnbooks.com *Web Site:* www.nbnbooks.com
Distribution Center: National Book Network *Toll Free Tel:* 800-462-6420 *Toll Free Fax:* 800-338-4550 *E-mail:* customercare@nbnbooks.com *Web Site:* www.nbnbooks.com
Membership(s): Association of American Publishers (AAP)

The McDonald & Woodward Publishing Co
695 Tall Oaks Dr, Newark, OH 43055
Tel: 740-641-2691 *Toll Free Tel:* 800-233-8787 *Fax:* 740-641-2692
E-mail: mwpubco@mwpubco.com
Web Site: www.mwpubco.com
Key Personnel
Publr & Intl Rts Mgr: Jerry N McDonald
 E-mail: jmcd@mwpubco.com
Mktg Mgr: Trish Newcomb *E-mail:* tnewcomb@mwpubco.com
Founded: 1986
Books (primarily adult) in natural history & cultural history; co-publish with educational & governmental entities.

ISBN Prefix(es): 978-0-939923
Number of titles published annually: 8 Print
Total Titles: 80 Print

Margaret K McElderry Books, see Simon & Schuster Children's Publishing

McFarland
960 NC Hwy 88 W, Jefferson, NC 28640
Mailing Address: Box 611, Jefferson, NC 28640-0611
Tel: 336-246-4460 *Toll Free Tel:* 800-253-2187 (orders) *Fax:* 336-246-5018; 336-246-4403 (orders)
E-mail: info@mcfarlandpub.com
Web Site: mcfarlandbooks.com
Key Personnel
Founder & Ed-in-Chief: Robert Franklin
Pres: Rhonda Herman *E-mail:* rherman@mcfarlandpub.com
VP & Edit Dir: Steve Wilson *E-mail:* swilson@mcfarlandpub.com
VP, Sales & Mktg: Karl-Heinz Roseman
 E-mail: kroseman@mcfarlandpub.com
Sr Acqs Ed: Gary Mitchem *E-mail:* gmitchem@mcfarlandpub.com
Subs & Intl Rts: Adam Phillips
 E-mail: aphillips@mcfarlandpub.com
Founded: 1979
A leading independent publisher of academic & nonfiction books, known for covering popular topics in a serious fashion & for manufacturing books to meet high library standards.
ISBN Prefix(es): 978-0-89950; 978-0-7864
Number of titles published annually: 360 Print; 355 E-Book; 5 Audio
Total Titles: 6,500 Print; 5,000 E-Book; 40 Audio
Imprints: Exposit Books; Toplight Books
Subsidiaries: McFarland & Co Ltd Publishers (London, UK)
Foreign Rep(s): Eurospan (Africa, Asia-Pacific, Australia, Europe, India, Middle East)
Returns: 961 NC Hwy 88 W, Jefferson, NC 28640
Shipping Address: 961 NC Hwy 88 W, Jefferson, NC 28640

McGraw-Hill Create
Division of McGraw-Hill Higher Education
2 Penn Plaza, New York, NY 10121
Toll Free Tel: 800-962-9342
E-mail: mhhe.create@mheducation.com
Web Site: create.mheducation.com; shop.mheducation.com
Key Personnel
Dir, Content & Opers: Cat Mattura *Tel:* 201-618-2497 *E-mail:* cat.mattura@mheducation.com
Dir, Print Solutions, The McGraw Hill Cos: Beth Kundert
Custom products derived from McGraw-Hill copyrighted material; college textbook & ebook adaptations; supplemental materials.
ISBN Prefix(es): 978-1-308; 978-1-309
Number of titles published annually: 20 Print
Distribution Center: The McGraw-Hill Companies Distribution Center, 860 Taylor Station Rd, Blacklick, OH 43004-0504

§McGraw-Hill Education
2 Penn Plaza, New York, NY 10121-2298
Tel: 212-904-2000
E-mail: international_cs@mheducation.com; seg_customerservice@mheducation.com (PreK-12); hep_customerservice@mheducation.com (higher education)
Web Site: www.mheducation.com
Key Personnel
Pres & CEO: Simon Allen
Chief Communs Offr: Catherine J Mathis
Chief Digital Offr: Stephen Laster
CIO: Angelo T DeGenaro

U.S. PUBLISHERS

Pres, McGraw-Hill Education Higher Educ: William Okun
Pres, McGraw-Hill & Profl: Scott Grillo
SVP & Gen Coun: David Stafford
Pres, School Group: Heath Morrison
Founded: 1989
McGraw-Hill Education, a division of The McGraw-Hill Companies (NYSE: MHP), is a leading global provider of instructional, assessment & reference solutions that empower professionals & students of all ages. McGraw-Hill Education has offices in numerous countries & publishes in more than 40 languages.
ISBN Prefix(es): 978-1-259; 978-1-260; 978-1-264; 978-1-265; 978-1-266
Imprints: Glencoe/McGraw-Hill; The Grow Network/McGraw-Hill; Macmillan/McGraw-Hill; McGraw-Hill Contemporary; McGraw-Hill Create; McGraw-Hill Education Australia, New Zealand & South Africa; McGraw-Hill Education Europe, Middle East and Africa; McGraw-Hill Education Latin America; McGraw-Hill Education Mexico; McGraw-Hill Education Spain; McGraw-Hill Humanities, Social Sciences, Languages; McGraw-Hill/Irwin; McGraw-Hill Professional; McGraw-Hill Professional Development; McGraw-Hill Ryerson; McGraw-Hill School Education Group; McGraw-Hill Science, Engineering, Mathematics; SRA/McGraw-Hill; Tata/McGraw-Hill
Distribution Center: The McGraw-Hill Companies Distribution Center, 2460 Kerper Blvd, Dubuque, IA 52001-0545
The McGraw-Hill Companies Distribution Center, 860 Taylor Station Rd, Blacklick, OH 43004-0504
Membership(s): Association of American Publishers (AAP)
See separate listing for:
McGraw-Hill Higher Education
McGraw-Hill Professional Publishing Group
McGraw-Hill School Education Group

§McGraw-Hill Higher Education
Division of McGraw-Hill Education
1325 Avenue of the Americas, New York, NY 10019
Toll Free Tel: 800-338-3987 (cust serv)
  Toll Free Fax: 800-953-8691 (cust serv)
Web Site: www.mheducation.com/highered
Key Personnel
Pres, Higher Educ: Michael Ryan
Founded: 1996
College texts.
ISBN Prefix(es): 978-0-07; 978-0-697; 978-0-256; 978-0-87; 978-1-25
Number of titles published annually: 1,100 Print; 50 CD-ROM; 750 Online; 800 E-Book; 5 Audio
Total Titles: 12,000 Print; 1,600 CD-ROM; 6,000 Online; 6,000 E-Book; 120 Audio
Divisions: McGraw-Hill Create
See separate listing for:
McGraw-Hill Create

§McGraw-Hill Professional Publishing Group
Division of McGraw-Hill Education
2 Penn Plaza, New York, NY 10121
Tel: 646-766-2000
Web Site: www.mhprofessional.com; www.mheducation.com
Key Personnel
CFO: J Garrett Henn
Pres: Scott Grillo
VP: James Shanahan
Sr Ed, Fin, Investing, Opers & HR: Judith Newlin
ISBN Prefix(es): 978-1-260

McGraw-Hill School Education Group
Division of McGraw-Hill Education
8787 Orion Place, Columbus, OH 43240
Tel: 614-430-4000 *Toll Free Tel:* 800-848-1567

Web Site: www.mheducation.com
Key Personnel
Chief Sales Offr: Pete Silva
Pres, School: Heath Morrison
Founded: 1971
Educational materials for elementary, middle school & high school.
ISBN Prefix(es): 978-0-02; 978-0-07; 978-0-31; 978-0-39; 978-0-53; 978-0-65; 978-0-67; 978-0-80; 978-0-84; 978-0-89; 978-0-93; 978-0-96; 978-1-57; 978-1-58; 978-1-88
Branch Office(s)
303 E Wacker Dr, Chicago, IL 60601 *Tel:* 312-233-6500
2 Penn Plaza, New York, NY 10121 *Tel:* 212-904-2000
Foreign Rep(s): The McGraw-Hill Companies (worldwide); McGraw-Hill Ryerson Limited (Canada)
Orders to: 860 Taylor Station Rd, Blacklick, OH 43004-0543 *Tel:* 614-759-3825 ext 3825 *Toll Free Tel:* 800-334-7344 *Fax:* 614-759-3670
Returns: 6405 Commerce Ct, Groveport, OH 43125
Shipping Address: 6405 Commerce Ct, Groveport, OH 43125 *Tel:* 614-835-2302 *Fax:* 614-835-2303
Distribution Center: 6405 Commerce Ct, Groveport, OH 43125 *Toll Free Tel:* 800-334-7344

McPherson & Co
148 Smith Ave, Kingston, NY 12401
SAN: 203-0632
Mailing Address: PO Box 1126, Kingston, NY 12402-1126
Tel: 845-331-5807
E-mail: bmcphersonco@gmail.com
Web Site: www.mcphersonco.com
Key Personnel
Publr & Ed-in-Chief: Bruce R McPherson
Founded: 1973
ISBN Prefix(es): 978-0-914232; 978-0-929701; 978-1-878352 (Saroff Editions); 978-1-62054
Number of titles published annually: 5 Print; 5 E-Book
Total Titles: 155 Print; 21 E-Book; 2 Audio
Imprints: Documentext; Recovered Classics; Saroff Editions; Treacle Press
Subsidiaries: Waverley West
Foreign Rights: Kerigan-Moro Literary (Portugal, Spain); La Nouvelle Agence (France); Prava i prevodi (Bulgaria, Czechia, Hungary, Poland, Serbia, Slovenia); Literarische Agentur Simon (Germany); Rita Vivian Literary (Italy)
Orders to: PO Box 1126, Kingston, NY 12402-1126
Distribution Center: Central Books Ltd, 50 Freshwater Rd, Chadwell Heath RM8 1RX, United Kingdom (UK only) *Tel:* (020) 8525 8800 *Fax:* (020) 8599 2694 *E-mail:* contactus@centralbooks.com *Web Site:* www.centralbooks.com
Membership(s): Community of Literary Magazines & Presses (CLMP)

McSweeney's Publishing
849 Valencia St, San Francisco, CA 94110
E-mail: custserv@mcsweeneys.net
Web Site: www.mcsweeneys.net
Key Personnel
Publr: Amanda Uhle
Founded: 1998
ISBN Prefix(es): 978-1-936365
Number of titles published annually: 25 Print
Total Titles: 150 Print
Foreign Rights: The Wylie Agency (worldwide)
Distribution Center: Baker & Taylor Publisher Services, 30 Amberwood Pkwy, Ashland, OH 44805 *Tel:* 567-215-0030 *Toll Free Tel:* 888-814-0208 *E-mail:* orders@btpubservices.com *Web Site:* www.btpubservices.com

me+mi publishing inc
2600 Beverly Dr, Unit 113, Aurora, IL 60502
Tel: 630-588-9801 *Toll Free Tel:* 888-251-1444
Web Site: www.memima.com
Key Personnel
Principal & Publr: Gladys Rosa-Mendoza; Mark Wesley
Founded: 2002
Independent publisher dedicated to creating the highest quality books available in 2 or more languages for infants & toddlers.
ISBN Prefix(es): 978-0-9679748; 978-1-931398
Total Titles: 33 Print
Imprints: The English Spanish Foundation Series
Membership(s): Independent Book Publishers Association (IBPA)

§R S Means from The Gordian Group
1099 Hingham St, Suite 201, Rockland, MA 02370
Toll Free Tel: 800-448-8182 (cust serv); 800-334-3509 (sales) *Toll Free Fax:* 800-632-6732
Web Site: www.rsmeans.com
Founded: 1942
A leader in construction cost estimating data, analytics & life cycle cost analysis available in 4 convenient formats: online, books, ebooks +/or CDs.
ISBN Prefix(es): 978-0-911950; 978-0-87629; 978-1-936335
Number of titles published annually: 25 Print
Total Titles: 150 Print
Divisions: Cost Annuals
Distributed by John Wiley & Sons Inc
Advertising Agency: The Stancliff Agency

Medals of America Press
Division of Medals of America
114 Southchase Blvd, Fountain Inn, SC 29644
Toll Free Tel: 800-605-4001 *Toll Free Fax:* 800-407-8640
Web Site: moapress.com
Key Personnel
Publr: Frank Foster *Tel:* 864-275-1527 *Fax:* 864-601-1108 *E-mail:* ffoster@moapress.com
Wholesale Mgr: Steve Heckenthorn
  E-mail: sheck@usmedals.com
Founded: 1992
Offer complete illustrated guides to United States military medals, decorations & insignia of the Army, Navy, Marines, Air Force, Coast Guard & Merchant Marines, United Nations & Vietnam.
ISBN Prefix(es): 978-1-884452
Number of titles published annually: 6 Print; 1 CD-ROM; 18 Online; 8 E-Book
Total Titles: 16 Print; 1 CD-ROM; 18 Online; 12 E-Book
Imprints: Military Medals of America
Distributed by Medals of America

Medical Group Management Association (MGMA)
104 Inverness Terr E, Englewood, CO 80112-5306
Tel: 303-799-1111; 303-799-1111 (ext 1888, book orders) *Toll Free Tel:* 877-275-6462
E-mail: support@mgma.com; infocenter@mgma.com
Web Site: www.mgma.com
Founded: 1926
Specialize in medical practice management.
ISBN Prefix(es): 978-1-56829; 978-0-933948
Number of titles published annually: 8 Print; 4 CD-ROM; 1 E-Book
Total Titles: 150 Print; 15 CD-ROM; 1 E-Book; 2 Audio
Branch Office(s)
Government Affairs, 1717 Pennsylvania Ave NW, No 600, Washington, DC 20006, Con-

tact: Anders Gilberg *Tel:* 202-293-3450
E-mail: govaff@mgma.org
Distributor for American Medical Association; Aspen Publishers; Greenbranch; HAP (Health Adminstration Press); J Wiley & Sons

Medical Physics Publishing Corp (MPP)
4555 Helgesen Dr, Madison, WI 53718
Tel: 608-224-4508 (returns) *Toll Free Tel:* 800-442-5778 (cust serv) *Fax:* 608-224-5016
E-mail: mpp@medicalphysics.org
Web Site: www.medicalphysics.org
Key Personnel
Gen Mgr & Intl Rts: Ms Bobbett Shaub
E-mail: bobbett@medicalphysics.org
Ed: Todd Hanson *E-mail:* todd@medicalphysics.org
Founded: 1985
Publish & distribute books for medical physics & related fields.
ISBN Prefix(es): 978-0-944838; 978-1-930524; 978-1-951134
Number of titles published annually: 6 Print; 6 E-Book
Total Titles: 100 Print; 8 CD-ROM; 50 E-Book
Foreign Rights: Eurospan (worldwide exc North America)

Medieval Institute Publications (MIP)
Division of Medieval Institute of Western Michigan University
Western Michigan University, Walwood Hall, 1903 W Michigan Ave, Mail Stop 5432, Kalamazoo, MI 49008-5432
Tel: 269-387-8755
Web Site: wmich.edu/medievalpublications
Key Personnel
Dir: Robert F Berkhofer, III *Tel:* 269-387-8745
Ed-in-Chief: Theresa M Whitaker *Tel:* 269-387-8747
Founded: 1978
Academic publications on late antique & medieval studies.
ISBN Prefix(es): 978-1-918720; 978-1-879288; 978-1-58044
Number of titles published annually: 14 Print
Total Titles: 215 Print
Membership(s): Association of University Presses (AUPresses)

§MedMaster Inc
360 NE 191 St, Miami, FL 33179
Mailing Address: PO Box 640028, Miami, FL 33164-0028
Tel: 954-962-8414
E-mail: info@medmaster.net
Web Site: www.medmaster.net
Key Personnel
Founder & Ed-in-Chief: Stephen Goldberg
Pres: Michael Goldberg
Founded: 1979
Medical book & software publishers; medical subjects for education of medical students & other health professionals.
This publisher has indicated that 100% of their product line is author subsidized.
ISBN Prefix(es): 978-0-940780; 978-1-935660
Number of titles published annually: 6 Print; 1 CD-ROM; 1 E-Book
Total Titles: 31 Print; 8 CD-ROM

Mel Bay Publications Inc
16 N Gore Ave, Suite 203, Webster Groves, MO 63119-2315
Tel: 636-257-3970 *Toll Free Tel:* 800-863-5229
E-mail: email@melbay.com
Web Site: www.melbay.com
Key Personnel
Pres: Bill Bay
Acct Mgr: Julie Wakefield *E-mail:* julie@melbay.com
Info Systems Mgr: Sharon Feldmann
E-mail: sharon@melbay.com
Founded: 1947
Innovative instructional & performance material for most instruments.
ISBN Prefix(es): 978-0-7866; 978-0-87166; 978-1-56222; 978-1-60974; 978-1-61065; 978-1-61911; 978-1-5134
Number of titles published annually: 60 Print; 60 E-Book
Total Titles: 4,000 Print; 2,600 E-Book
Imprints: Mel Bay
Distributor for AMA; William Bay Music; Dancing Hands; Stefan Grossman's Guitar Workshop

The Edwin Mellen Press
450 Ridge St, Lewiston, NY 14092
Mailing Address: PO Box 450, Lewiston, NY 14092-0450 SAN: 207-110X
Tel: 716-754-2266; 716-754-2788 (order fulfillment)
E-mail: editor@mellenpress.com; librarian@mellenpress.com
Web Site: www.mellenpress.com
Key Personnel
Founder & Ed: Prof Herbert Richardson
Founded: 1974
Non-subsidy academic publisher of books in the humanities of social sciences. Publish monographs, critical editions, collections, translations, revisionist studies, constructive essays, bibliographies, dictionaries, reference guides & dissertations.
ISBN Prefix(es): 978-0-88946; 978-0-7734; 978-0-935106; 978-0-7799; 978-1-4955
Number of titles published annually: 200 Print
Total Titles: 8,000 Print

Menasha Ridge Press
Imprint of AdventureKEEN
2204 First Ave S, Suite 102, Birmingham, AL 35233
Toll Free Tel: 888-604-4537 *Fax:* 205-326-1012
E-mail: info@adventurewithkeen.com
Web Site: www.menasharidge.com; www.adventurewithkeen.com
Key Personnel
Publr & COO: Molly Merkle *Tel:* 205-443-7993
E-mail: mmerkle@menasharidge.com
Mktg & Publicity: Travis Bryant *Tel:* 205-443-7987 *E-mail:* tbryant@menasharidge.com
Founded: 1982
Outdoor recreation, travel, nature & reference guides.
ISBN Prefix(es): 978-0-89732; 978-1-63404
Number of titles published annually: 35 Print; 35 E-Book
Total Titles: 226 Print; 200 E-Book
Orders to: Publishers Group West, 1700 Fourth St, Berkeley, CA 94710 *Tel:* 510-809-3700 *Toll Free Tel:* 800-788-3123 *Fax:* 510-809-3733 *E-mail:* tom.lupoff@pgw.com *Web Site:* www.pgw.com
Membership(s): American Booksellers Association (ABA); Southern Independent Booksellers Alliance (SIBA)

MennoMedia
841 Mount Clinton Pike, Harrisonburg, VA 22802
Mailing Address: PO Box 866, Harrisonburg, VA 22803
Toll Free Tel: 800-245-7894 (orders & cust serv US) *Toll Free Fax:* 877-271-0760
E-mail: info@mennomedia.org
Web Site: www.mennomedia.org
Key Personnel
Exec Dir & Publr: Amy Gingerich
E-mail: amyg@mennomedia.org
Mng Ed: Elisabeth Ivey *E-mail:* elisabethi@mennomedia.org
Founded: 1878
An agency of Mennonite Church USA & Mennonite Church Canada. Small denominational publisher. Specialize in the production of innovative Christian education resources for children, youth, young adults, adults & intergenerational groups. Topics of interest include materials on peace & justice, evangelism, Christian service & radical Christian discipleship.
ISBN Prefix(es): 978-0-8361 (Herald Press); 978-1-5138
Number of titles published annually: 10 Print
Imprints: Herald Press
Branch Office(s)
718 N Main St, Newton, KS 67114 *Tel:* 316-281-4412 *Toll Free Tel:* 800-245-7894 *Fax:* 540-242-4476
See separate listing for:
Herald Press

Mercer University Press
368 Orange St, Macon, GA 31201
Mailing Address: 1501 Mercer University Dr, Macon, GA 31207 SAN: 220-0716
Tel: 478-301-2880 *Toll Free Tel:* 866-895-1472 *Fax:* 478-301-2585
E-mail: mupressorders@mercer.edu
Web Site: www.mupress.org
Key Personnel
Dir: Marc Jolley *Tel:* 478-301-2880
E-mail: jolley_ma@mercer.edu
Mktg Dir: Mary Beth Kosowski *Tel:* 478-301-4262 *E-mail:* kosowski_mb@mercer.edu
Pubn Specialist: Marsha Luttrell *Tel:* 478-301-4266 *E-mail:* luttrell_mm@mercer.edu
Client Servs Asst: Kelley Land *Tel:* 478-301-4261 *E-mail:* land_k@mercer.edu
Busn Office: Jenny Toole *Tel:* 478-301-4267 *E-mail:* toole_rw@mercer.edu
Founded: 1979
History, philosophy, religion, Southern studies, Southern literature, literary studies, regional interest.
ISBN Prefix(es): 978-0-86554; 978-0-88146
Number of titles published annually: 40 Print
Total Titles: 1,700 Print
Foreign Rep(s): Eurospan Ltd (Africa, Asia, Caribbean, Continental Europe, Latin America, Middle East, UK)
Warehouse: 1701 Seventh St, Macon, GA 31206
Membership(s): Association of University Presses (AUPresses)

Meriwether Publishing
Division of Pioneer Drama Service Inc
c/o Pioneer Drama Service, 109 Inverness Dr E, Suite H, Centennial, CO 80112
Mailing Address: PO Box 4267, Englewood, CO 80155-4267
Tel: 303-779-4035 *Toll Free Tel:* 800-333-7262 *Fax:* 303-779-4315
Web Site: meriwetherpublishing.com; www.pioneerdrama.com
Key Personnel
Publr & CEO: Steven Fendrich
Publr: Debra Fendrich
Book Dept Mgr: Lori Conary
Founded: 1967
Books on theater, drama, performing arts, costuming, stagecraft, theatre games, play anthologies, improvisation, plays, musicals, theatre arts DVDs, theatre/drama education.
ISBN Prefix(es): 978-0-916260; 978-1-56608
Number of titles published annually: 4 Print
Total Titles: 200 Print
Foreign Rep(s): Gazelle Book Services Ltd (Europe, UK)
Returns: 9707 E Easter Lane, Suite A, Englewood, CO 80112
Membership(s): Publishers Association of the West (PubWest)

§Merriam-Webster Inc
Subsidiary of Encyclopaedia Britannica Inc

U.S. PUBLISHERS

47 Federal St, Springfield, MA 01102
Mailing Address: PO Box 281, Springfield, MA 01102-0281
Tel: 413-734-3134 *Toll Free Tel:* 800-828-1880 (orders & cust serv) *Fax:* 413-731-5979 (sales)
E-mail: support@merriam-webster.com
Web Site: www.merriam-webster.com
Key Personnel
Pres: Greg Barlow
VP & Dir, Sales: Jed Santoro *E-mail:* jsantoro@m-w.com
VP, Busn Devt: Matthew Dube
Dir, Mktg: Meghan Lunghi *E-mail:* mlunghi@m-w.com
Founded: 1828
Dictionaries & language reference products.
ISBN Prefix(es): 978-0-87779; 978-1-68150
Number of titles published annually: 4 Print
Total Titles: 102 Print; 7 CD-ROM; 2 Online; 2 E-Book
Imprints: Merriam-Webster Kids
Divisions: Federal Street Press
See separate listing for:
Federal Street Press

Mesorah Publications Ltd
313 Regina Ave, Rahway, NJ 07065
SAN: 213-1269
Tel: 718-921-9000 *Toll Free Tel:* 800-637-6724 *Fax:* 718-680-1875
E-mail: info@artscroll.com; orders@artscroll.com
Web Site: www.artscroll.com
Key Personnel
Publr: Nosson Scherman
Contact: Jacob Brander
Founded: 1976
Judaica, Bible study, liturgical materials, juvenile, history, Holocaust, Talmud, novels.
ISBN Prefix(es): 978-0-89906; 978-1-57819; 978-1-4226
Number of titles published annually: 100 Print
Total Titles: 3,000 Print
Imprints: Art Scroll Series; Shaar Press; Tamar Books
Distributor for NCSY Publications
Foreign Rep(s): Stephen Blitz (Israel)

§Messianic Jewish Publishers
Division of Messianic Jewish Communications
6120 Day Long Lane, Clarksville, MD 21029
Tel: 410-531-6644; 616-970-2449
  Toll Free Tel: 800-410-7367 (orders)
  Fax: 410-531-9440; 717-761-7273 (orders)
  Toll Free Fax: 800-327-0048 (orders)
E-mail: editor@messianicjewish.net; customerservice@messianicjewish.net
Web Site: messianicjewish.net/publish
Key Personnel
Pres & Publr: Barry Rubin
Founded: 1949
Publish & distribute Messianic Jewish books & other products.
ISBN Prefix(es): 978-1-880226; 978-1-936716
Number of titles published annually: 12 Print; 6 E-Book
Total Titles: 82 Print; 40 E-Book
Divisions: Lederer Books
Distributor for Chosen People Ministries; First Fruits of Zion; Jewish New Testament Publications
Distribution Center: Baker & Taylor Publisher Services, 30 Amberwood Pkwy, Ashland, OH 44805 (worldwide) *Tel:* 567-215-0030 *Toll Free Tel:* 888-814-0208 *E-mail:* orders@btpubservices.com *Web Site:* www.btpubservices.com
Membership(s): Evangelical Christian Publishers Association (ECPA)
See separate listing for:
Lederer Books

Metropolitan Classics
Division of Fort Ross Inc
26 Arthur Place, Yonkers, NY 10701
Tel: 914-375-6448
Web Site: www.fortrossinc.com
Key Personnel
Pres & Exec Dir: Dr Vladimir Kartsev *E-mail:* vkartsev2000@yahoo.com
Founded: 1992
Books in Russian. Russia, Ukraine, Kazakhstan-related books in English, co-publishing.
ISBN Prefix(es): 978-1-57480
Number of titles published annually: 4 Print; 4 Online; 4 E-Book
Total Titles: 50 Print; 4 Online; 4 E-Book
Foreign Rep(s): Nova Littera (Baltic States, Belarus, Eastern Europe, Russia, Ukraine)

§The Metropolitan Museum of Art
1000 Fifth Ave, New York, NY 10028
SAN: 202-6279
Tel: 212-535-7710
E-mail: editorial@metmuseum.org
Web Site: www.metmuseum.org
Key Personnel
Pres & CEO: Daniel Weiss
Chief of Staff: Laurel Britton
Dir: Max Hollein
Publr & Ed-in-Chief: Mark Polizzotti
SVP, Secy & Gen Counsel: Sharon Cott
Deputy Dir, Exhibitions: Quincy Houghton
Assoc Publr & Gen Mgr, Pubns: Gwen Roginsky
Chief Prodn Mgr: Peter Antony
Founded: 1870
Art books, exhibition catalogs, quarterly bulletin, annual journal.
ISBN Prefix(es): 978-0-87099; 978-1-58839
Number of titles published annually: 30 Print
Total Titles: 300 Print; 5 CD-ROM
Distributed by Yale University Press
Foreign Rep(s): Yale University Press
Warehouse: Middle Village, Queens, NY 11381-0001

MFA Publications
Imprint of Museum of Fine Arts Boston
465 Huntington Ave, Boston, MA 02115
Tel: 617-369-4233
E-mail: publications@mfa.org
Web Site: www.mfa.org/publications
Key Personnel
Head, Prodn & Design: Terry McAweeney
Pubns Coord: Hope Stockton *E-mail:* hstockton@mfa.org
Founded: 1877
Exhibition & collection catalogues; general interest & trade arts publications, children's books. No returns accepted.
ISBN Prefix(es): 978-0-87846
Number of titles published annually: 12 Print
Total Titles: 80 Print
Imprints: ArtWorks
Distributed by Thames & Hudson (outside of North America)
Warehouse: c/o PSSC, 46 Development Rd, Fitchburg, MA 01420
Distribution Center: Distributed Art Publishers Inc, 75 Broad St, Suite 630, New York, NY 10004 (worldwide) *Tel:* 212-927-1999 *Fax:* 212-627-9484 *Web Site:* www.artbook.com

MH Sub I LLC, see NOLO

Michelin Maps & Guides
Division of Michelin North America Inc
One Parkway S, Greenville, SC 29615-5022
E-mail: michelin.guides@michelin.com
Web Site: guide.michelin.com; michelinmedia.com
Key Personnel
Consumer PR: Lauren McClure *Tel:* 864-458-6871 *E-mail:* lauren.mcclure@michelin.com
Founded: 1900
Specialize in travel publications; hotel & restaurant guides.
ISBN Prefix(es): 978-2-06
Number of titles published annually: 50 Print
Total Titles: 175 Print
Distributed by Editions du Renouveau Pedagogique (French titles in Canada); Langenscheidt Publishing Group; MAPART Publishing (CN only); NBN (guides for North America); Penguin Canada (English titles in Canada)
Orders to: PO Box 19001, Greenville, SC 29615 *Toll Free Tel:* 800-423-0485 *Toll Free Fax:* 800-378-7471

§Michigan State University Press (MSU Press)
Division of Michigan State University
Manly Miles Bldg, Suite 25, 1405 S Harrison Rd, East Lansing, MI 48823-5245
SAN: 202-6295
Tel: 517-355-9543 *Fax:* 517-432-2611
Web Site: msupress.org
Key Personnel
Dir: Gabriel Dotto *Tel:* 517-884-6900 *E-mail:* dotto@msu.edu
Asst Dir & Ed-in-Chief: Julie L Loehr *Tel:* 517-884-6905 *E-mail:* loehr@msu.edu
Mktg & Sales Mgr: Julie K Reaume *Tel:* 517-884-6920 *E-mail:* reaumej@msu.edu
Mng Ed: Kristine M Blakeslee *Tel:* 517-884-6912 *E-mail:* blakes17@msu.edu
Digital Prodn Specialist: Annette K Tanner *Tel:* 517-884-6910 *E-mail:* tanneran@msu.edu
Busn & Fin Offr: Julie Wrzesinski *Tel:* 517-884-6922 *E-mail:* wrzesin2@msu.edu
Founded: 1947
Scholarly works & general nonfiction trade books.
ISBN Prefix(es): 978-0-944311; 978-0-937191; 978-0-87013; 978-1-62896; 978-1-62895; 978-1-60917; 978-1-61186; 978-1-938065; 978-1-941258; 978-0-9967252
Number of titles published annually: 40 Print; 2 CD-ROM; 10 E-Book
Total Titles: 650 Print; 4 CD-ROM; 59 E-Book
Distributed by UBC Press, Canada
Distributor for Aquatic Ecosystem Health & Management Society Books; MSU Museum; University of Manitoba Press
Foreign Rep(s): Eurospan (Europe); Raincoast Books-University of British Columbia Press (Canada)
Orders to: Chicago Distribution Center, 11030 S Langley Ave, Chicago, IL 60628 *Tel:* 773-702-7000 *Toll Free Tel:* 800-621-2736 *Fax:* 773-702-7212 *Toll Free Fax:* 800-621-8476 *E-mail:* orders@press.uchicago.edu *Web Site:* www.press.uchicago.edu
Returns: Chicago Distribution Center, 11030 S Langley Ave, Chicago, IL 60628 *Tel:* 773-702-7000 *Toll Free Tel:* 800-621-2736 *Fax:* 773-702-7212 *Toll Free Fax:* 800-621-8476 *E-mail:* orders@press.uchicago.edu *Web Site:* www.press.uchicago.edu
Distribution Center: Chicago Distribution Center, 11030 S Langley Ave, Chicago, IL 60628 *Tel:* 773-702-7000 *Toll Free Tel:* 800-621-2736 *Fax:* 773-702-7212 *Toll Free Fax:* 800-621-8476 *E-mail:* orders@press.uchicago.edu *Web Site:* www.press.uchicago.edu
Membership(s): American Association of University Presses (AAUP); Society for Scholarly Publishing (SSP)

Midnight Marquee Press Inc
9721 Britinay Lane, Baltimore, MD 21234
Tel: 410-665-1198
E-mail: mmarquee@aol.com
Web Site: www.midmar.com
Key Personnel
Pres: Gary Svehla
VP & Lib Sales Dir: Susan Svehla
Founded: 1995

Publisher of books, two magazines, graphic novels with the main focus on film history, biographies & mysteries.
ISBN Prefix(es): 978-1-887664; 978-1-936168; 978-1-64430
Number of titles published annually: 4 Print
Total Titles: 150 Print

§Mighty Media Press
Division of Mighty Media Inc
1201 Currie Ave, Minneapolis, MN 55403
Tel: 612-455-0252; 612-399-1969 *Fax:* 612-338-4817
E-mail: info@mightymedia.com
Web Site: www.mightymediapress.com
Key Personnel
Publr & Creative Dir: Nancy Tuminelly
  E-mail: nancy@mightymedia.com
Mktg Dir & Publicity: Sammy Bosch
  E-mail: sammy@mightymedia.com
Publg Dir: Lauren Kukla *E-mail:* lauren@mightymedia.com
Founded: 2005
Delivers captivating books & media that ignite a child's curiosity, imagination, social awareness & sense of adventure.
ISBN Prefix(es): 978-0-9765201; 978-0-9798249; 978-0-9824584; 978-0-9830219; 978-1-938063
Number of titles published annually: 6 Print; 6 E-Book
Total Titles: 36 Print; 40 E-Book
Imprints: Mighty Media Junior Readers (middle grade literature); Mighty Media Kids (picture books & first reader/beginner books); Red Portal Press
Foreign Rights: Letter Soup Rights Agency (Allison Olson) (worldwide)
Returns: Publishers Group West, Returns Dept, 193 Edwards Dr, Jackson, TN 38301
Distribution Center: Publishers Group West, 1700 Fourth St, Berkeley, CA 94710 *Tel:* 510-809-3700 *Toll Free Tel:* 866-400-5351 *Fax:* 510-809-3777
Membership(s): American Booksellers Association (ABA); The Children's Book Council (CBC); Midwest Independent Booksellers Association (MIBA); Midwest Independent Publishing Association (MIPA); Minnesota Book Publishers Roundtable; Minnesota Bookbuilders; Society of Children's Book Writers & Illustrators (SCBWI)

Mike Murach & Associates Inc
3730 W Swift, Fresno, CA 93722
SAN: 264-2255
Tel: 559-440-9071 *Toll Free Tel:* 800-221-5528
  Fax: 559-440-0963
E-mail: murachbooks@murach.com
Web Site: www.murach.com
Key Personnel
Pres: Ben Murach
Founded: 1974
Computer books.
ISBN Prefix(es): 978-0-911625; 978-1-890774; 978-1-943872; 978-1-943873
Number of titles published annually: 5 Print
Total Titles: 50 Print
Foreign Rep(s): BPB Publications Ltd (India); Gazelle Book Services Ltd (Continental Europe, UK); Woodslane Pty Ltd (Australia, New Zealand)

§Milady
Division of Cengage Group
5191 Natorp Blvd, Mason, OH 45040
Toll Free Tel: 866-848-5143 *Fax:* 518-373-6309
E-mail: info@milady.com
Web Site: www.milady.com
Key Personnel
SVP & Gen Mgr: Sandra Bruce *E-mail:* sandra.bruce@cengage.com
VP, Prod & Cust Experience: Corina Santoro
  E-mail: corina.santoro@cengage.com
Sr Mktg Dir: Slavik Volinsky *E-mail:* slavik.volinsky@cengage.com
Founded: 1928
Textbooks, digital learning platform, workbooks, exam preps & reviews, instructional videos, newsletters, cosmetology & beauty education.
ISBN Prefix(es): 978-0-8273; 978-0-7668; 978-0-87350; 978-1-4018; 978-1-4180; 978-1-28576
Number of titles published annually: 20 Print
Total Titles: 50 Print
Foreign Office(s): Cengage Learning-Australia, 80 Dorcas St, Level 7, South Melbourne, Victoria 3205, Australia *Tel:* (03) 9685 4111 *Fax:* (03) 9685 4199 *Web Site:* cengage.com.au
Cengage Learning-Latin America, WeWork - Reforma Latino Av Paseo de la Reforma, 296, piso 24, oficina 13, Juarez, Cuauhtemoc, 06600 Mexico, CDMX, Mexico *Tel:* (0155) 1500 6000 *E-mail:* mexico.ssa@cengage.com *Web Site:* latam.cengage.com
Cengage Learning-EMEA, Cheriton House, North Way, Andover, Hants SP10 5BE, United Kingdom *Tel:* (01264) 332424 *Fax:* (01264) 342763 *E-mail:* emea.edureply@cengage.com *Web Site:* cengage.com.uk
Foreign Rep(s): Laura Salazar (Latin America)
Distribution Center: 10650 Toebben Dr, Independence, KY 41051 *Tel:* 859-525-2230
Membership(s): American Association of Cosmetology Schools (AACS); National Association of Barber Boards of America (NABBA); The National-Interstate Council of State Boards of Cosmetology Inc (NIC); Professional Beauty Association (PBA)

Milford Books™
Imprint of Milford Books LLC
243 W Lafayette St, Milford, MI 48381
Tel: 734-255-9530
E-mail: eic@milfordbooks.com
Web Site: milfordbooks.com
Key Personnel
Owner: Dan Armijo
Founded: 2024
Hybrid publisher of nonfiction & children's books. Also offers consulting services (strategy, editorial, design, & marketing) to authors wishing to self-publish. The Purpose First Press™ imprint supports independent authors whose primary purpose in publishing is to make the world a better place.
This publisher has indicated that 100% of their product line is author subsidized.
ISBN Prefix(es): 979-8-9898584
Number of titles published annually: 12 Print; 12 E-Book; 12 Audio
Imprints: Purpose First Press™
Membership(s): Independent Book Publishers Association (IBPA)

Military Info Publishing
PO Box 41211, Plymouth, MN 55442
Tel: 763-533-8627
E-mail: publisher@military-info.com
Web Site: www.military-info.com
Key Personnel
Publr: Bruce A Hanesalo
Founded: 1987
Reprint historical military technology, including 34 books, 11,000 photocopies & 400 other items.
ISBN Prefix(es): 978-1-886848
Number of titles published annually: 4 Print
Total Titles: 41 Print

Military Living Publications
Division of Military Marketing Services Inc
333 Maple Ave E, Suite 3130, Vienna, VA 22180-4717
Tel: 703-237-0203 *Fax:* 703-552-8855
E-mail: customerservice@militaryliving.com; sales@militaryliving.com; editor@militaryliving.com
Web Site: www.militaryliving.com
Key Personnel
CEO: William R Crawford, Sr
Founded: 1969
Publisher of military travel atlases, maps & directories; for military only.
ISBN Prefix(es): 978-0-914862; 978-1-931424
Number of titles published annually: 8 Print
Total Titles: 12 Print
Foreign Rep(s): US Forces Exchanges

Milkweed Editions
1011 Washington Ave S, Suite 300, Minneapolis, MN 55415-1246
Tel: 612-332-3192 *Toll Free Tel:* 800-520-6455
E-mail: orders@milkweed.org
Web Site: milkweed.org
Key Personnel
Publr & CEO: Daniel Slager
VP, Engagement & Chief Innovation Offr: Katie Hill *E-mail:* katie_hill@milkweed.org
VP, Sales & Mktg: Craig Popelars
  E-mail: craig_popelars@milkweed.org
Mng Ed: Broc Rossell *E-mail:* broc_rossell@milkweed.org
Sr Ed: Joey McGarvey
Assoc Ed: Bailey Hutchinson
  E-mail: bailey_hutchinson@milkweed.org
Sales & Opers Mgr: Shannon Blackmer
  E-mail: shannon_blackmer@milkweed.org
Warehouse Assoc: Kerri Sandve
Exec Asst: Meilina Dalit *E-mail:* meilina_dalit@milkweed.org
Founded: 1980
Literary, nonprofit, independent press.
ISBN Prefix(es): 978-0-915943; 978-1-57131
Number of titles published annually: 18 Print; 18 E-Book; 1 Audio
Total Titles: 350 Print; 10 E-Book; 5 Audio
Distribution Center: Publishers Group West, 1700 Fourth St, Berkeley, CA 94710 *Tel:* 510-809-3700 *Toll Free Tel:* 866-400-5351 *Fax:* 510-809-3777
Membership(s): American Booksellers Association (ABA); The Children's Book Council (CBC); Community of Literary Magazines & Presses (CLMP); Independent Book Publishers Association (IBPA); Midwest Independent Booksellers Association (MIBA); Southern Independent Booksellers Alliance (SIBA)

Millbrook Press
Imprint of Lerner Publishing Group Inc
241 First Ave N, Minneapolis, MN 55401
Tel: 612-332-3344 *Toll Free Tel:* 800-328-4929
  Fax: 612-332-7615 *Toll Free Fax:* 800-332-1132
E-mail: info@lernerbooks.com; custserve@lernerbooks.com
Web Site: www.lernerbooks.com; www.facebook.com/millbrookpress
Key Personnel
Chmn: Harry J Lerner
Pres & Publr: Adam Lerner
EVP & COO: Mark Budde
EVP & CFO: Margaret Thomas
EVP, Sales: David Wexler
VP & Ed-in-Chief: Andy Cummings
VP, Mktg: Rachel Zugschwert
Publg Dir, School & Lib: Jenny Krueger
Dir, HR: Cyndi Radant
Dir, Rts, Spec Sales & Intl Dist: Maria Kjoller
Edit Dir: Carol Hinz
School & Lib Mktg Dir: Lois Wallentine
Founded: 1989
ISBN Prefix(es): 978-1-56294; 978-1-878841; 978-0-7613; 978-1-878137
Total Titles: 630 Print; 775 E-Book
Foreign Rep(s): Bounce Sales & Marketing Ltd (UK); INT Books (Australia); J Appleseed,

U.S. PUBLISHERS

A Division of Saunders (Canada); Phambili Agencies (Botswana, Lesotho, Namibia, Southern Africa); Publishers Marketing Services (Brunei, Malaysia, Singapore); Saunders Book Co (educ) (Canada); South Pacific Books (New Zealand)
Foreign Rights: Japan Foreign-Rights Centre (Japan); Korea Copyright Center Inc (KCC) (South Korea); Agence Michelle Lapautre (France); Literarische Agentur Silke Weniger (Germany)
Warehouse: 1251 Washington Ave N, Minneapolis, MN 55401, Mgr: Ken Rued

Richard K Miller Associates
2413 Main St, Suite 331, Miramar, FL 33025
Tel: 404-276-3376 *Fax:* 404-581-5335
Web Site: rkma.com
Key Personnel
Pres: Richard K Miller *E-mail:* richard.miller@rkma.com
Founded: 1972
Market research reference handbooks for college & corporate libraries. Subjects include consumer behavior, marketing, retail, travel, healthcare, entertainment & restaurants.
ISBN Prefix(es): 978-1-57783
Number of titles published annually: 10 Online; 10 E-Book
Total Titles: 10 Online; 10 E-Book

§Milliken Publishing Co
Division of The Lorenz Corp
501 E Third St, Dayton, OH 45402
Mailing Address: PO Box 802, Dayton, OH 45401-0802
Toll Free Tel: 800-444-1144 *Fax:* 937-223-2042
E-mail: service@lorenz.com
Web Site: www.lorenzeducationalpress.com
Founded: 1960
Educational publishing division includes visual resources, instructional guides & reproducibles; elementary supplementals.
ISBN Prefix(es): 978-0-88335; 978-1-55863; 978-1-4291; 978-0-7877
Number of titles published annually: 20 Print
Total Titles: 400 Print; 20 CD-ROM; 400 E-Book; 6 Audio
Membership(s): Education Market Association

Denene Millner Books, see Simon & Schuster Children's Publishing

§The Minerals, Metals & Materials Society (TMS)
5700 Corporate Dr, Suite 750, Pittsburgh, PA 15237
Tel: 724-776-9000 *Toll Free Tel:* 800-759-4867 *Fax:* 724-776-3770
E-mail: publications@tms.org (orders)
Web Site: www.tms.org/bookstore (orders); www.tms.org
Key Personnel
Exec Dir: James J Robinson *E-mail:* robinson@tms.org
Dept Head, Content: Matt Baker *E-mail:* mbaker@tms.org
Founded: 1871
Leading professional society dedicated to the development & dissemination of scientific & engineering knowledge for materials-centered technology. The society is the only professional organization that encompasses the entire spectrum of materials & engineering, from minerals processing through the advanced applications of materials.
Many of the programs conducted by TMS are made possible by the generous financial support of the American Institute of Mining, Metallurgical, and Petroleum Engineers (AIME).
ISBN Prefix(es): 978-0-87339
Number of titles published annually: 20 Print

Total Titles: 200 Print; 150 E-Book
Distributed by Springer

Minnesota Historical Society Press
Division of Minnesota Historical Society
345 Kellogg Blvd W, St Paul, MN 55102-1906
SAN: 202-6384
Tel: 651-259-3205 *Fax:* 651-297-1345
E-mail: info-mnhspress@mnhs.org
Web Site: www.mnhs.org/mnhspress
Key Personnel
Ed-in-Chief: Ann Regan *Tel:* 651-259-3206 *E-mail:* ann.regan@mnhs.org
Mng Ed: Shannon M Pennefeather *Tel:* 651-259-3212 *E-mail:* shannon.pennefeather@mnhs.org
Mktg & Publicity Mgr: Jim Cihlar *Tel:* 651-259-3202 *E-mail:* jim.cihlar@mnhs.org
Sales Mgr: Riley Jay Davis *Tel:* 651-259-3204 *E-mail:* riley.davis@mnhs.org
Founded: 1849
Scholarly & trade books on Upper Midwest history & prehistory.
ISBN Prefix(es): 978-0-87351; 978-1-68134
Number of titles published annually: 20 Print; 10 E-Book
Total Titles: 430 Print; 140 E-Book; 6 Audio
Warehouse: Ingram Publisher Services, 191 Edwards Dr, Jackson, TN 38301 *Web Site:* www.ingrampublisherservices.com
Membership(s): American Association of University Presses (AAUP)

MIT List Visual Arts Center
MIT E 15-109, 20 Ames St, Cambridge, MA 02139
Tel: 617-253-4680
E-mail: listinfo@mit.edu
Web Site: listart.mit.edu
Key Personnel
Dir: Paul C Ha
Founded: 1966
Contemporary art.
ISBN Prefix(es): 978-0-938437; 978-0-262
Number of titles published annually: 6 Print
Distribution Center: Distributed Art Publishers Inc, 75 Broad St, Suite 630, New York, NY 10004 *Tel:* 212-627-1999 *Fax:* 212-627-9484
Web Site: www.artbook.com

§The MIT Press
One Broadway, 12th fl, Cambridge, MA 02142
SAN: 202-6414
Tel: 617-253-5255 *Toll Free Tel:* 800-405-1619 (orders) *Fax:* 617-258-6779; 617-577-1545 (orders)
Web Site: mitpress.mit.edu
Key Personnel
CFO: Brent Oberlin *Tel:* 617-253-5250 *E-mail:* brento@mit.edu
Cont: Charles Hale *Tel:* 617-258-0577 *E-mail:* chale@mit.edu
Dir: Amy Brand *E-mail:* amybrand@mit.edu
Dir, Journals & Open Access: Nick Lindsay *Tel:* 617-258-0594 *E-mail:* nlindsay@mit.edu
Dir, Sales: David Goldberg *Tel:* 617-253-8838 *E-mail:* davidgol@mit.edu
Dir, Sales & Mktg: William Smith *E-mail:* smithwmj@mit.edu
Edit Dir: Janice Audet
Head, Author Rel & Mgr, Global Publicity: Nicholas DiSabatino
Head, Communs: Jessica Pellien *E-mail:* pellien@mit.edu
Exec Ed: Marie Lee *Tel:* 617-253-1558 *E-mail:* marielee@mit.edu
Exec Ed-at-Large: Gita Manaktala *E-mail:* manak@mit.edu
Mng Ed: Michael Sims *Tel:* 617-253-2080 *E-mail:* msims@mit.edu
Exec Ed: Robert Prior *Tel:* 617-253-1584 *E-mail:* prior@mit.edu

Exec Ed, Economics, Fin & Busn: Catherine Woods
Sr Acqs Ed: Phil Laughlin *Tel:* 617-252-1636 *E-mail:* laughlin@mit.edu; Douglas Sery *Tel:* 617-253-5187 *E-mail:* dsery@mit.edu
Sr Acqs Ed, Art & Architecture: Thomas Weaver
Sr Acqs Ed, Physical Sci, Math & Engg: Andrew Kinney
Acqs Ed: Beth Clevenger *Tel:* 617-253-4113 *E-mail:* eclev@mit.edu
Acqs Ed, Physical Sciences, Engg & Math: Jermey Matthews
Asst Acqs Ed: Laura Keeler *Tel:* 617-253-3757 *E-mail:* lkeeler@mit.edu
Sr Mgr, Digital Prods: Gabe Harp
Design Mgr: Yasuyo Iguchi *Tel:* 617-253-8034 *E-mail:* iguchi@mit.edu
Exhibits Mgr: John Costello *Tel:* 617-258-5764 *E-mail:* jcostell@mit.edu
Prodn Mgr: Janet Rossi *Tel:* 617-253-2882 *E-mail:* janett@mit.edu
Exec Publicist: Colleen Lanick *Tel:* 617-253-2874 *E-mail:* colleenl@mit.edu
Textbook Promos Mgr: Michelle Pullano *Tel:* 617-253-3620 *E-mail:* mpullano@mit.edu
Bookstore Mgr: John Jenkins *Tel:* 617-253-5249 *E-mail:* jjenkins@mit.edu
Founded: 1962
Scholarly & professional books, advanced textbooks, nonfiction trade books & reference books; architecture & design, cognitive sciences & linguistics, computer science & artificial intelligence, economics & management sciences, environmental studies; philosophy, neuroscience; technology studies; new media; paperbacks, journals.
ISBN Prefix(es): 978-0-262; 978-0-89706
Number of titles published annually: 250 Print
Total Titles: 8,000 Print; 5 CD-ROM; 2 Online; 1 E-Book
Imprints: Bradford Books
Foreign Office(s): The MIT Press Ltd, One Duchess St, Suite 2, London W1W 6AN, United Kingdom *Tel:* (020) 7306 0603 *Fax:* (020) 7306 0604 *E-mail:* info@mitpress.org.uk
Distributor for AAAI Press; Afterall Books; Canadian Centre for Architecture; no place press; Semiotext(e)
Foreign Rep(s): APD Singapore Pte Ltd (Ian Pringle) (Brunei, Cambodia, Indonesia, Laos, Malaysia, Myanmar, Philippines, Singapore, Thailand, Vietnam); Aromix Books Company Ltd (Jane Lam & Nick Wonn) (Hong Kong); Avicenna Partnership Ltd (Claire de Gruchy) (Algeria, Cyprus, Israel, Jordan, Malta, Morocco, Palestine, Tunisia, Turkey); Avicenna Partnership Ltd (Bill Kennedy) (Bahrain, Egypt, Iran, Iraq, Kuwait, Lebanon, Libya, Oman, Qatar, Saudi Arabia, Syria, United Arab Emirates); Everest International Publishing Services (Wei Zhao) (China); Information & Culture Korea (ICK) (Se-Yung Jun & Min-Hwa Yoo) (South Korea); Itsabook (James Papworth) (Caribbean, Latin America); BK Norton (Chiafeng Peng) (Taiwan); Penguin Random House India Pvt Ltd (Bangladesh, Bhutan, India, Nepal, Pakistan, Sri Lanka); Rockbook Inc (Akiko Iwamoto & Gilles Fauveau) (Japan); University Press Group (Dominique Bartshukoff) (Austria, Croatia, Czechia, Germany, Greece, Hungary, Netherlands, Portugal, Slovenia, Spain); University Press Group (Peter Jacques) (Belgium, Europe, France, Italy, Poland, Scandinavia, Switzerland); University Press Group (Ben Mitchell) (Europe, Ireland, UK)
Foreign Rights: Agencia Literaria Carmen Balcells SA (Maribel Luque) (Spain); Bardon-Chinese Media Agency (Joanne Yang) (Taiwan); The Berlin Agency (Frauke Jung-Lindemann) (Germany); English Agency Japan Co Ltd (Tsutomu Yawata) (Japan); Graal Literary Agency (Lukasz Wrobel) (Poland); The

Deborah Harris Agency (Ilana Kurshan) (Israel); The Kayi Agency (Dilek Kayi) (Turkey); Korea Copyright Center Inc (KCC) (Sageun Lee) (South Korea); Alexander Korzheneveski Agency (Alexander Korzheneveski) (Russia); OA Literary Agency (Michael Avramides) (Greece); Reiser Literary Agency (Roberto Gilodi) (Italy); Agencia Riff (Joao Riff) (Brazil)
Distribution Center: Penguin Random House Publisher Services, 400 Hahn Rd, Westminster, MD 21157 *Tel:* 410-848-1900 *Toll Free Tel:* 800-726-0600 *Web Site:* prhpublisherservices.com
Membership(s): Association of American Publishers (AAP); Association of University Presses (AUPresses)

Mitchell Lane Publishers Inc
2001 SW 31 Ave, Hallandale, FL 33009
SAN: 858-3749
Tel: 954-985-9400 *Toll Free Tel:* 800-223-3251 *Fax:* 954-987-2200
E-mail: customerservice@mitchelllane.com
Web Site: www.mitchelllane.com
Key Personnel
Sales Mgr, Mktg Mgr & Prod Content: Rachel Collin *E-mail:* rachel@mitchelllane.com
Founded: 1993
Nonfiction for children & young adults.
ISBN Prefix(es): 978-1-883845; 978-1-58415; 978-1-61228; 978-1-68020
Number of titles published annually: 100 Print; 100 E-Book
Total Titles: 1,500 Print; 650 E-Book
Foreign Rep(s): CrossCan Educational (Canada); Edu-Reference (Canada); David Hall (Africa, Australia, Continental Europe, Ireland, Malaysia, Singapore, South Africa)
Membership(s): Educational Book & Media Association (EBMA)

MLA, see Modern Language Association (MLA)

MOA Press, see Medals of America Press

§Modern Language Association (MLA)
85 Broad St, New York, NY 10004
SAN: 202-6422
Tel: 646-576-5000
E-mail: help@mla.org
Web Site: www.mla.org; x.com/MLAnews; www.facebook.com/modernlanguageassociation; www.linkedin.com/company/modern-language-association
Key Personnel
Exec Dir: Paula Krebs
Sr Dir: Angela Gibson *E-mail:* agibson@mla.org
Dir, Outreach: Anna Chang *E-mail:* achang@mla.org
Founded: 1883
Research & teaching tools in languages & literature; professional publications for college teachers.
ISBN Prefix(es): 978-0-87352; 978-1-60329
Number of titles published annually: 15 Print
Total Titles: 400 Print
Distribution Center: HFS (Hopkins Fulfillment Services), 2715 N Charles St, Baltimore, MD 21218 *Tel:* 410-516-6965 *Toll Free Tel:* 800-537-5487 (US & CN) *Fax:* 410-516-6998 *E-mail:* hfscustserv@jh.edu *Web Site:* hfs.jhu.edu

Modern Memoirs Inc
417 West St, Suite 104, Amherst, MA 01002
Tel: 413-253-2353
Web Site: www.modernmemoirs.com
Key Personnel
Pres: Megan St Marie *E-mail:* megan@modernmemoirs.com
VP: Sean St Marie *E-mail:* sean@modernmemoirs.com
Dir, Publg: Ali de Groot *E-mail:* ali@modernmemoirs.com
Publg Assoc: Emma Solis *E-mail:* emma@modernmemoirs.com
Book Designer: Nicole Miller *E-mail:* nicole@modernmemoirs.com
Genealogist: Liz Sonnenberg *E-mail:* liz@modernmemoirs.com
Founded: 1994
Private publishing services for discerning clients. This publisher has indicated that 100% of their product line is author subsidized.
ISBN Prefix(es): 978-0-9662602; 978-0-9772337; 978-0-9856595; 978-0-9834752; 978-0-9905709
Number of titles published annually: 20 Print
Total Titles: 250 Print
Imprints: White Poppy Press

MoMA, see The Museum of Modern Art (MoMA)

The Monacelli Press
Imprint of Phaidon Press Ltd
65 Bleecker St, 8th fl, New York, NY 10012
Tel: 212-652-5400
E-mail: contact@monacellipress.com
Web Site: www.phaidon.com/monacelli
Key Personnel
Pres & Publr: Gianfranco Monacelli
Publr: Holly LaDue
VP, Prodn: Michael Vagnetti
Dir, Mktg & Publicity: Laura Mintz
Edit Dir: Alan Rapp
Sr Ed: Carla Sakamoto
Ed (design, fine art, gardening, interior design, lifestyle): Jenny Florence
Ed-at-Large: Elizabeth White
Mktg & Publicity Asst: Caroline Jones
Founded: 1994
High-quality, illustrated, hardcover & paperback books on art, architecture, decorative arts, interior design, fashion, photography, landscape, urbanism & graphic design.
ISBN Prefix(es): 978-1-58093; 978-1-885254
Number of titles published annually: 24 Print; 1 E-Book
Total Titles: 400 Print; 10 E-Book
Imprints: Monacelli Studio (applied arts)
Foreign Rep(s): Penguin Random House Canada (Canada); Publishers Group UK (Ireland, UK)
Distribution Center: Hachette Book Group, 121 Enterprise Blvd, Lebanon, IN 46052 *Toll Free Tel:* 800-759-0190 *E-mail:* customer.service@hbgusa.com *Web Site:* www.hachettebookgroup.com

§Mondial
203 W 107 St, Suite 6-C, New York, NY 10025
Tel: 646-807-8031 *Fax:* 208-361-2863
E-mail: contact@mondialbooks.com
Web Site: www.mondialbooks.com
Key Personnel
Owner: Uday K Dhar
Publr: Ulrich Becker
Founded: 2004
Specialize in fiction & nonfiction translated into English from other languages or originally written in English or German. All kinds of publications (fiction & nonfiction) in the international language Esperanto.
ISBN Prefix(es): 978-1-59569
Number of titles published annually: 15 Print; 15 E-Book
Total Titles: 510 Print; 1 CD-ROM; 250 Online; 210 E-Book
Imprints: German101; Golden Sky

The Mongolia Society Inc
Indiana University, 703 Eigenmann Hall, 1900 E Tenth St, Bloomington, IN 47406-7512
Tel: 812-855-4078 *Fax:* 812-855-4078
E-mail: monsoc@indiana.edu
Web Site: mongoliasociety.org
Key Personnel
VP & Chmn of the Bd: Dr Christopher Atwood
Pres: Dr Alicia Campi
Exec Dir: Susie Drost
Co-Mng Ed: Dr Timothy May; Dr Peter Marsh
Treas: Tserenchunt Ledges
Secy: Dr Melissa Chakars
Founded: 1961
Interests, culture & language of Mongolia.
ISBN Prefix(es): 978-0-910980
Number of titles published annually: 4 Print
Total Titles: 60 Print

Monkfish Book Publishing Co
22 E Market St, Suite 304, Rhinebeck, NY 12572
Tel: 845-876-4861
Web Site: www.monkfishpublishing.com
Key Personnel
Publr: Paul Cohen *E-mail:* paul@monkfishpublishing.com
Dir, Design, Prodn & Admin: Colin Rolfe
Literary Ed: Anne McGrath *E-mail:* anne@monkfishpublishing.com
Religion Ed: Jon M Sweeney *E-mail:* jon@monkfishpublishing.com
Founded: 2002
Publisher of spirituality & religion titles. Also operates a self-publishing company.
ISBN Prefix(es): 978-0-9823246; 978-0-9766843; 978-0-9726357; 978-0-9798828; 978-0-9749359; 978-0-9789427; 978-0-9824530; 978-0-9825255; 978-0-9826441; 978-0-9830517; 978-0-9833589; 978-1-936940; 978-1-939681; 978-1-944037
Number of titles published annually: 18 Print; 4 Online; 18 E-Book; 3 Audio
Total Titles: 135 Print; 32 Online; 130 E-Book; 15 Audio
Divisions: Epigraph Publishing Service (subsidy publishers)
Orders to: Consortium Book Sales & Distribution, The Keg House, Suite 101, 34 13 Ave NE, Minneapolis, MN 55413-1007 *Tel:* 612-746-2600 *Toll Free Tel:* 866-400-5351 (cust serv, Jackson, TN) *E-mail:* cbsdinfo@ingramcontent.com *Web Site:* www.cbsd.com
SAN: 200-6049
Distribution Center: Consortium Book Sales & Distribution, The Keg House, Suite 101, 34 13 Ave NE, Minneapolis, MN 55413-1007 *Tel:* 612-746-2600 *Toll Free Tel:* 866-400-5351 (cust serv, Jackson, TN) *E-mail:* cbsdinfo@ingramcontent.com *Web Site:* www.cbsd.com
SAN: 200-6049
Membership(s): Independent Book Publishers Association (IBPA)

Montemayor Press
663 Hyland Hill Rd, Washington, VT 05675
Mailing Address: PO Box 546, Montpelier, VT 05601
Tel: 802-552-0750
E-mail: mail@montemayorpress.com
Web Site: www.montemayorpress.com
Key Personnel
Publr: Edward Myers
Exec Ed: Edith Poor
Founded: 1999
Independent publisher whose mission is to print & distribute quality fiction & nonfiction to adult, young adult & juvenile audiences.
ISBN Prefix(es): 978-0-9674477; 978-1-932727
Number of titles published annually: 2 Print; 1 E-Book

U.S. PUBLISHERS

Total Titles: 36 Print; 4 E-Book
Membership(s): Community of Literary Magazines & Presses (CLMP); Independent Book Publishers Association (IBPA)

Monthly Review Press
Division of Monthly Review Foundation Inc
134 W 29 St, Suite 706, New York, NY 10001
SAN: 202-6481
Tel: 212-691-2555
E-mail: social@monthlyreview.org
Web Site: monthlyreview.org
Key Personnel
Mng Dir: Martin Paddio
Edit Dir: Michael D Yates
Founded: 1949
Economics, politics, history, sociology & world affairs.
ISBN Prefix(es): 978-0-85345; 978-1-58367
Number of titles published annually: 15 Print
Total Titles: 550 Print
Distributed by New York University Press
Foreign Rep(s): APD Singapore Pte Ltd (Ian Pringle) (Southeast Asia); Catamount Content LLC (Ethan Atkin) (Caribbean, Latin America); Central Books Ltd (UK); China Publishers Marketing (Benjamin Pan) (China); Combined Academic Publishers (David Pickering) (Africa, Europe, Middle East, UK); ICK (Information & Culture Korea) (Se-Yung Jun) (South Korea); MHM Ltd (Mark Gresham) (Japan); B K Norton (Chiafeng Peng) (Hong Kong, Taiwan); University of Toronto Press (Canada); Viva Books Pvt Ltd (Bangladesh, Bhutan, India, Maldives, Nepal, Sri Lanka); Woodslane Pty Ltd (Australia, New Zealand, Pacific Islands)
Billing Address: New York University Press, 411 Layfayette St, 6th fl, New York, NY 10003
Orders to: New York University Press, 411 Layfayette St, 6th fl, New York, NY 10003 *Tel:* 212-998-2575 *E-mail:* nyupressinfo@nyu.edu
Returns: Ingram Publisher Services, 191 Edwards Dr, Jackson, TN 38301 *Web Site:* www.ingrampublisherservices.com
Warehouse: Ingram Publisher Services, 191 Edwards Dr, Jackson, TN 38301 *Web Site:* www.ingrampublisherservices.com

Moody Publishers
Affiliate of The Moody Bible Institute
820 N La Salle Blvd, Chicago, IL 60610
SAN: 202-5604
Tel: 312-329-2101 *Toll Free Tel:* 800-678-8812 *Fax:* 312-329-2144 *Toll Free Fax:* 800-678-3329
E-mail: mpcustomerservice@moody.edu; mporders@moody.edu; publicity@moody.edu
Web Site: www.moodypublishers.com
Key Personnel
VP: Paul Santhouse
Assoc Publr: John Hinkley
Founded: 1894
Religion (interdenominational).
ISBN Prefix(es): 978-0-8024; 978-1-881273 (Northfield Publishing)
Number of titles published annually: 75 Print
Total Titles: 1,000 Print; 10 Audio
Imprints: Northfield Publishing; River North Fiction; WingSpread Publishers
Foreign Rep(s): Biblicum AS (Norway); Bookhouse Australia Ltd (Australia); Christian Art Wholesale (South Africa); Christian Literature Crusade (Hong Kong); David C Cook Distribution (Canada); Editeurs de Litterature Biblique (Germany); Euro-Outreach Ministries (East Africa, Kenya, Nairobi); Hong Kong Tien Dao Publishing House Ltd (Belgium); Kesho Publications (Zimbabwe); Matopo Book Room (Philippines); Overseas Missionary Fellowship (Canada); Rhema Boekimport (Singapore); S & U Book Centre (New Zealand); S-U Wholesale
Shipping Address: 215 W Locust St, Chicago, IL 60610

Moonshine Cove Publishing LLC
150 Willow Point, Abbeville, SC 29620
E-mail: publisher@moonshinecovepublishing.com
Web Site: moonshinecovepublishing.com
Key Personnel
Publr: Gene D Robinson *E-mail:* robinsgd@wctel.net
Founded: 2011
Independently owned small publisher currently accepting queries. Do not send anything by regular mail, electronic submission only. Submit your query to robinsgd@wctel.net or publisher@moonshinecovepublishing.com. Do not send anything except a query letter with the first 5 pages of your ms pasted into the body of the e-mail (pasted, not attached). We will not open attachments or click on embedded links. If we ask to see your ms, send it only if it's your final edit. If you're still thinking of making changes, make them before sending your ms. We like story lines that hold readers' attention by moving right along at a good pace. We are not looking for messages. For nonfiction, we are open to receiving well researched mss dealing with global warming & climate change.
ISBN Prefix(es): 978-1-937327; 978-1-945181; 978-1-952439
Number of titles published annually: 23 Print; 23 E-Book
Total Titles: 250 Print; 280 E-Book; 1 Audio

Morehouse Publishing
Imprint of Church Publishing Inc
19 E 34 St, New York, NY 10016
SAN: 202-6511
Tel: 212-592-1800 *Toll Free Tel:* 800-242-1918 (retail orders only)
E-mail: churchpublishingorders@pbd.com
Web Site: www.churchpublishing.org
Key Personnel
VP, Prodn: Lorraine Simonello
 E-mail: churchpublishingorders@pbd.com
Founded: 1884
Spirituality, religious, lay ministry, liturgy, church supplies, music CDs, all from an Episcopal/Anglican perspective. No illustrated children's books.
ISBN Prefix(es): 978-0-8192
Number of titles published annually: 40 Print; 35 E-Book
Total Titles: 800 Print; 650 E-Book
Foreign Rep(s): Norwich Books & Music (Europe)
Warehouse: PBD Worldwide, Alpharetta, GA

Morgan James Publishing
5 Penn Plaza, 23rd fl, New York, NY 10001
Tel: 212-655-5470 *Fax:* 516-908-4496
E-mail: support@morganjamespublishing.com
Web Site: www.morganjamespublishing.com
Key Personnel
Founder: David L Hancock *E-mail:* david@morganjamespublishing.com
Founded: 2003
An unconventional, traditional trade publisher - the nation's first hybrid publisher according to *Publishers Weekly.*
ISBN Prefix(es): 978-0-9746133; 978-0-9758570; 978-0-9760901; 978-0-9768491; 978-1-933596; 978-1-60037; 978-0-9815058; 978-0-9817906; 978-0-9820750; 978-0-9823793; 978-0-9835013; 978-0-9840316; 978-1-938467; 978-0-9846170; 978-0-9828590; 978-0-9833715; 978-1-61448; 978-0-9837125; 978-1-63047; 978-1-63195
Number of titles published annually: 200 Print; 200 E-Book; 50 Audio

Total Titles: 3,800 Print; 3,000 E-Book; 500 Audio
Imprints: Guerrilla Marketing Press; Morgan James Faith; Morgan James Fiction; Morgan James Kids
Foreign Rep(s): Kimberly Brabec (worldwide)
Returns: IPS Warehouse, 1280 Ingram Dr, Chambersburg, PA 17201
Distribution Center: Publishers Group West (PGW), 1700 Fourth St, Berkeley, CA 94710 *Toll Free Tel:* 866-400-5351 *E-mail:* info@pgw.com *Web Site:* www.pgw.com SAN: 202-8522
Membership(s): Association of American Publishers (AAP)

Morgan Kaufmann
Imprint of Elsevier Inc
50 & 60 Hampshire St, 5th fl, Cambridge, MA 02139
Web Site: www.elsevier.com/books-and-journals/morgan-kaufmann
Founded: 1984
Computer science book publishers including database, networking, architecture, engineering, graphics & artificial intelligence.
ISBN Prefix(es): 978-0-12; 978-1-55860
Number of titles published annually: 65 Print
Total Titles: 552 Print; 606 E-Book
Orders to: 3251 Riverport Lane, Maryland Heights, MO 63043
Returns: 3251 Riverport Lane, Maryland Heights, MO 63043
Warehouse: 3251 Riverport Lane, Maryland Heights, MO 63043

Moriah Books
PO Box 1094, Casper, WY 82602
Web Site: moriahbook.com
Founded: 2014
Independent publisher of Rocky Mountain regional, history, historical fiction & religious titles.
ISBN Prefix(es): 978-0-9970417
Number of titles published annually: 6 Print
Total Titles: 3 Print

§Morning Sun Books Inc
1200 County Rd 523, Flemington, NJ 08822
Tel: 908-806-6216 *Fax:* 908-237-2407
E-mail: sales@morningsunbooks.com
Web Site: morningsunbooks.com
Key Personnel
Pres: Robert J Yanosey
Founded: 1986
Vintage railroad photography.
ISBN Prefix(es): 978-1-878887; 978-1-58248
Number of titles published annually: 36 Print
Total Titles: 500 Print
Editorial Office(s): 9 Pheasant Lane, Scotch Plains, NJ 07076

Morton Publishing Co
925 W Kenyon Ave, Unit 12, Englewood, CO 80110
SAN: 210-9174
Tel: 303-761-4805 *Fax:* 303-762-9923
E-mail: contact@morton-pub.com; returns@morton-pub.com
Web Site: www.morton-pub.com
Key Personnel
Pres: David Ferguson *E-mail:* davidf@morton-pub.com
VP, Opers: Chrissy DeMier *E-mail:* chrissyd@morton-pub.com
VP, Sales & Mktg: Carter Fenton
 E-mail: carterf@morton-pub.com
Returns: Heather Herman *E-mail:* heatherh@morton-pub.com
Founded: 1977
Allied health, biology, chemistry, pharmacy, physical science.

PUBLISHERS

ISBN Prefix(es): 978-0-89582; 978-1-61731; 978-1-64043
Number of titles published annually: 10 Print
Total Titles: 50 Print
Foreign Rep(s): Northrose Associates (Canada)

Mountain Press Publishing Co
1301 S Third W, Missoula, MT 59801
SAN: 202-8832
Mailing Address: PO Box 2399, Missoula, MT 59806-2399
Tel: 406-728-1900 *Toll Free Tel:* 800-234-5308 *Fax:* 406-728-1635
E-mail: info@mtnpress.com
Web Site: www.mountain-press.com
Key Personnel
History Ed: Gwen McKenna
Natural History & Roadside Geology Series Ed: Jennifer Carey
Gen Mgr: John Rimel *E-mail:* johnargyle@aol.com
Busn Mgr: Rob Williams
Mktg Mgr: Anne Iverson *Tel:* 406-728-1900 ext 131 *E-mail:* anne@mtnpress.com
Graphic Design: Jeannie Painter
Founded: 1948
ISBN Prefix(es): 978-0-87842; 978-0-9632562; 978-0-9626999; 978-1-886370; 978-1-889921; 978-1-892784; 978-0-9676747; 978-0-9717748; 978-0-9724827
Number of titles published annually: 20 Print
Total Titles: 150 Print
Imprints: Geology Underfoot Series; Mountain Sports Press Series; Roadside Geology Series; Roadside History Series; Tumbleweed Series
Distributor for Bucking Horse Books; Clark City Press; Hops Press; Npustin Press; RainStone Press; Western Edge Press

Mountaineers Books
Division of The Mountaineers
1001 SW Klickitat Way, Suite 201, Seattle, WA 98134
Tel: 206-223-6303 *Fax:* 206-223-6306
E-mail: mbooks@mountaineersbooks.org; customerservice@mountaineersbooks.org
Web Site: www.mountaineers.org/books
Key Personnel
Publr: Tom Helleberg *Tel:* 206-521-6069 *E-mail:* tomh@mountaineersbooks.org
Exec Dir, Conservation & Advancement: Helen Cherullo *Tel:* 206-521-6058 *E-mail:* helenc@mountaineersbooks.org
Dir, Sales & Mktg: Darryl Booker *Tel:* 206-521-6054 *E-mail:* darrylb@mountaineersbooks.org
Mktg Mgr: Laura Grange *Tel:* 206-521-6063 *E-mail:* laurag@mountaineersbooks.org
Ed-in-Chief: Kate Rogers *Tel:* 206-521-6062 *E-mail:* kater@mountaineersbooks.org
Mng Ed: Janet Kimball *Tel:* 206-521-6059 *E-mail:* janetk@mountaineersbooks.org
Sr Ed: Mary Metz *Tel:* 206-521-6066 *E-mail:* marym@mountaineersbooks.org
Ed: Laura Shauger *Tel:* 206-521-6064 *E-mail:* laurash@mountaineersbooks.org
Acqs Ed: Emily White *E-mail:* emilyw@mountaineersbooks.org
Publicist: Marissa Litak *Tel:* 206-521-6065 *E-mail:* marissal@mountaineersbooks.org; Kate Jay *Tel:* 206-521-6068 *E-mail:* katej@mountaineersbooks.org
Founded: 1961
Mountaineering, backpacking, hiking, cross-country skiing, bicycling, canoeing, kayaking, trekking, nature, conservation, green living & sustainability; outdoor how-to, guidebooks & maps; nonfiction adventure-travel accounts; biographies of outdoor people; reprint editions of mountaineering classics; adventure narratives.
ISBN Prefix(es): 978-0-89886; 978-0-916890; 978-0-938567; 978-1-59485; 978-1-63374; 978-1-68051
Number of titles published annually: 30 Print
Total Titles: 550 Print
Imprints: Braided River (conservation); Skipstone (sustainable lifestyle)
Distributor for Adventure Cycling Association; The American Alpine Club Press; Appalachian Trail Conservancy (ATC); Colorado Mountain Club Press; Green Trails Maps
Foreign Rep(s): Cordee Publishing (UK)

§De Gruyter Mouton
Imprint of Walter de Gruyter GmbH
125 Pearl St, Boston, MA 02110
Mailing Address: 121 High St, 3rd fl, Boston, MA 02110
Tel: 857-284-7073 *Fax:* 857-284-7358
E-mail: service@degruyter.com
Web Site: www.degruyter.com
Founded: 1956
Scholarly books & journals.
ISBN Prefix(es): 978-0-311; 978-90-279
Number of titles published annually: 100 Print; 2 Online
Total Titles: 2,500 Print; 3 CD-ROM; 10 Online
Foreign Office(s): Walter de Gruyter GmbH, Genthinerstr 13, 10728 Berlin, Germany *Tel:* (030) 260 05-0 *Fax:* (030) 260 05-251
Distributed by Walter de Gruyter Inc
Foreign Rep(s): Allied Publishers Pvt Ltd (India, Nepal, Sri Lanka); Book Club International (Bangladesh); Combined Representatives Worldwide Inc (Philippines); D A Books & Journals (Australia, New Zealand); Walter de Gruyter Inc (Canada, Mexico); Verlags und Kommissionsbuchhandlung Dr Franz Hain (Austria); Kumi Trading (South Korea); Kweilin Bookstore (Taiwan); Maruzen Co Ltd (Japan); Pak Book Corp (Pakistan); Parry's Book Center (Sendjrjan Berhad) (Brunei, Malaysia, Singapore); Swinden Book Co Ltd (Hong Kong)
Distribution Center: PO Box 361, Birmingham, AL 35242 (journals & yearbooks) *Tel:* 205-995-1567 *Toll Free Tel:* 800-633-4931 *Fax:* 205-995-1588 *E-mail:* degruyterus@subscriptionoffice.com
TriLiteral LLC, 100 Maple Ridge Dr, Cumberland, RI 02864 (books, ebooks & bundles, databases) *Tel:* 401-531-2800 *Toll Free Tel:* 800-405-1619 *E-mail:* orders@triliteral.org
HGV Hanseatische Gesellschaft fuer Verlagsservice mbH, Holzwiesenstr 2, 72127 Kusterdingen, Germany (worldwide exc the Americas) *Tel:* (07071) 9353-55 *Fax:* (07071) 9353-93 *E-mail:* orders@degruyter.com

Moznaim Publishing Corp
4304 12 Ave, Brooklyn, NY 11219
SAN: 214-4123
Tel: 718-438-7680 *Fax:* 718-438-1305
E-mail: info@moznaim.com
Web Site: www.moznaim.com
Founded: 1977
Judaica books in Hebrew, English & Spanish.
ISBN Prefix(es): 978-0-940118; 978-1-885220
Number of titles published annually: 7 Print
Total Titles: 200 Print
Foreign Office(s): 10 Telmie Yosef St, Mishor Adumim, Israel *Tel:* (02) 5333441 *Fax:* (02) 5354345
Distributor for Avamra Institute; Breslov Research Institute; Red Wheel/Weiser/Conari

MTV Books, see Simon & Schuster Children's Publishing

§Multicultural Publications Inc
1939 Manchester Rd, Akron, OH 44314
Mailing Address: PO Box 8001, Akron, OH 44320-0001
Tel: 330-865-9578 *Fax:* 330-865-9578
E-mail: multiculturalpub@prodigy.net
Web Site: www.multiculturalpub.net
Key Personnel
Pres & CEO: Bobby L Jackson
Dir, Mktg & Promos & Intl Rts: James Lynell
Lib Sales Dir: Rae Neal
Founded: 1992
Books, greeting cards, dolls & stuffed toys, multimedia.
ISBN Prefix(es): 978-0-9634932; 978-1-884242
Number of titles published annually: 1 Print; 1 CD-ROM; 1 Online
Total Titles: 28 Print; 2 CD-ROM; 28 Online; 4 Audio

Multnomah
Imprint of Random House Publishing Group
10807 New Allegiance Dr, Suite 500, Colorado Springs, CO 80921
Tel: 719-590-4999 *Toll Free Tel:* 800-603-7051 (orders) *Fax:* 719-590-8977
E-mail: info@waterbrookmultnomah.com
Web Site: waterbrookmultnomah.com
Founded: 2006
Publishes Christian books that proclaim the Gospel & equip followers of Jesus to make disciples. Seek timeless messages from trusted Christian voices that challenge readers to approach life from a Biblical perspective.
ISBN Prefix(es): 978-1-59052; 978-1-60142
Number of titles published annually: 19 Print
Membership(s): Evangelical Christian Publishers Association (ECPA)

The Museum of Modern Art (MoMA)
Publications Dept, 11 W 53 St, New York, NY 10019
SAN: 202-5809
Tel: 212-708-9400
E-mail: moma_publications@moma.org
Web Site: www.moma.org
Key Personnel
Publr & Chief Curator-at-Large: Michelle Kuo
Assoc Publr: Curtis R Scott
Busn & Mktg Dir: Hannah Kim
Prodn Dir: Joseph Mohan
Founded: 1929
Art, architecture, design, photography, film.
ISBN Prefix(es): 978-0-87070; 978-1-63345
Number of titles published annually: 18 Print
Total Titles: 1,250 Print
Foreign Rep(s): Thames & Hudson Ltd (worldwide exc Canada & USA)
Warehouse: South River Distribution, South River, NJ 08882
Distribution Center: Distributed Art Publishers Inc, 75 Broad St, Suite 630, New York, NY 10004 (US & CN only) *Tel:* 212-627-1999 *Fax:* 212-627-9484 *Web Site:* www.artbook.com
Membership(s): American Alliance of Museums (AAM); American Association of University Presses (AAUP); College Art Association of America Inc (CAA)

§Museum of New Mexico Press
Unit of New Mexico State Department of Cultural Affairs
725 Camino Lejo, Suite C, Santa Fe, NM 87505
SAN: 202-2575
Mailing Address: PO Box 2087, Santa Fe, NM 87504-2087
Tel: 505-476-1155; 505-272-7777 (orders) *Toll Free Tel:* 800-249-7737 (orders) *Fax:* 505-476-1156 *Toll Free Fax:* 800-622-8667 (orders)
Web Site: www.mnmpress.org
Key Personnel
Dir: Anna Gallegos *Tel:* 505-476-1154 *E-mail:* anna.gallegos@state.nm.us
Art Dir & Prodn Mgr: David Skolkin *Tel:* 505-476-1159 *E-mail:* david.skolkin@state.nm.us
Edit Dir: Lisa Pachaco *Tel:* 505-476-1157 *E-mail:* lisa.pachaco@state.nm.us

U.S. PUBLISHERS

Mktg & Sales Dir: Janet L Dick *Tel:* 504-476-1158 *E-mail:* janetldick@state.nm.us
Founded: 1951
Publications related to Native America, Hispanic Southwest, 20th century art, photography, folk art & folklore, nature & gardening, architecture & the Americas.
ISBN Prefix(es): 978-0-89013
Number of titles published annually: 15 Print
Total Titles: 140 Print
Distributed by University of New Mexico Press
Foreign Rep(s): Gazelle Book Services Ltd (Europe)
Orders to: University of New Mexico Press, 1312 Basehart Rd SE, Albuquerque, NM 87106-4363 *E-mail:* custserv@upress.unm.edu
Warehouse: University of New Mexico Press, 1312 Basehart Rd SE, Albuquerque, NM 87106-4363 *E-mail:* custserv@upress.unm.edu

Mutual Publishing LLC
1215 Center St, Suite 210, Honolulu, HI 96816
Tel: 808-732-1709 *Fax:* 808-734-4094
E-mail: info@mutualpublishing.com
Web Site: www.mutualpublishing.com
Key Personnel
Publr: Bennett Hymer
Founded: 1974
Publishing, print brokering & packaging. Editorial & design services; trade, mass market paperback, coffee table & souvenir books.
ISBN Prefix(es): 978-1-56647; 978-0-935180
Number of titles published annually: 30 Print
Total Titles: 330 Print
Imprints: Scripta
Membership(s): Hawaii Book Publishers Association (HBPA)

NAB, see National Association of Broadcasters (NAB)

NACE International
15835 Park Ten Place, Houston, TX 77084
Tel: 281-228-6200; 281-228-6223
  Toll Free Tel: 800-797-NACE (797-6223)
  Fax: 281-228-6300
E-mail: firstservice@nace.org
Web Site: www.nace.org
Key Personnel
CEO: Bob Chalker *Tel:* 281-228-6250
Pubns Activities Dir: Bernardo Duran
Founded: 1943
Publishes technical books on corrosion control & prevention & materials selection, design & degradation issues. Books are developed by individual authors/editors utilizing corrosion experts to contribute text. Compilations of technical papers from NACE conferences & symposia are also issued on an annual basis.
ISBN Prefix(es): 978-1-877914; 978-0-915567; 978-1-57590
Number of titles published annually: 7 Print; 1 E-Book
Distributed by Australasian Corrosion Association Inc
Distributor for ASM International; ASTM; AWS; Butterworth-Heinemann; Cambridge University Press; CASTI Publishing; Compass Publications; CRC Press; Marcel Dekker Inc; E&FN Spon; Elsevier Science Publishers; Gulf Publishing; Industrial Press; Institute of Materials; ISO; McGraw-Hill; MTI; Prentice Hall; Professional Publications; Swedish Corrosion Institute; John Wiley & Sons Inc
Foreign Rep(s): ABI (India); ATP (Europe); BI Publications (Asia); IBS (India)

NASW Press
Division of National Association of Social Workers (NASW)
750 First St NE, Suite 800, Washington, DC 20002
SAN: 202-893X
Tel: 202-408-8600 *Fax:* 203-336-8312
E-mail: press@naswdc.org
Web Site: www.naswpress.org
Key Personnel
Publr: Cheryl Bradley *Tel:* 202-336-8214
  E-mail: cbradley.nasw@socialworkers.org
Mng Ed, Journals & Books: Julie Gutin *Tel:* 202-408-8600 ext 281 *E-mail:* jgutin.nasw@socialworkers.org
Sr Ed: Sarah Lowman *Tel:* 202-408-8600 ext 398 *E-mail:* slowman.nasw@socialworkers.org
Founded: 1955
Professional & scholarly books & journals in the social sciences.
ISBN Prefix(es): 978-0-87101
Number of titles published annually: 6 Print; 2 CD-ROM; 6 E-Book
Total Titles: 120 Print; 70 E-Book
Billing Address: PBD Worldwide Fulfillment Services, 1650 Bluegrass Lakes Pkwy, Alpharetta, GA 30004 *Tel:* 770-238-0450 *Toll Free Tel:* 800-227-3590 *Fax:* 770-442-9742 *Toll Free Fax:* 866-494-1499
Orders to: PBD Worldwide Fulfillment Services, 1650 Bluegrass Lakes Pkwy, Alpharetta, GA 30004 *Tel:* 770-238-0450 *Toll Free Tel:* 800-227-3590 *Fax:* 770-442-9742 *Toll Free Fax:* 866-494-1499
Returns: PBD Worldwide Fulfillment Services, 1650 Bluegrass Lakes Pkwy, Alpharetta, GA 30004 *Tel:* 770-238-0450 *Toll Free Tel:* 800-227-3590 *Fax:* 770-442-9742 *Toll Free Fax:* 866-494-1499
Distribution Center: PBD Worldwide Fulfillment Services, 1650 Bluegrass Lakes Pkwy, Alpharetta, GA 30004 *Tel:* 770-238-0450 *Toll Free Tel:* 800-227-3590 *Fax:* 770-442-9742 *Toll Free Fax:* 866-494-1499

Nataraj Books
7967 Twist Lane, Springfield, VA 22153
Tel: 703-455-4996
E-mail: orders@natarajbooks.com; natarajbooks@gmail.com
Web Site: www.natarajbooks.com
Key Personnel
Pres: Vinod Mahajan
Founded: 1986
Books from South Asia.
ISBN Prefix(es): 978-1-881338
Number of titles published annually: 7 Print
Total Titles: 70 Print

§National Academies Press (NAP)
Division of The National Academies of Sciences, Engineering & Medicine
500 Fifth St NW, Washington, DC 20001
SAN: 202-8891
Toll Free Tel: 800-624-6242 *Fax:* 202-334-2451 (cust serv); 202-334-2793 (mktg dept)
E-mail: customer_service@nap.edu
Web Site: www.nap.edu
Key Personnel
Publr: Alphonse MacDonald *Tel:* 202-334-3625
  E-mail: amacdonald@nas.edu
Dir, Design: Rebekah Hanover-Pettit *Tel:* 202-334-3943 *E-mail:* rhanoverpettit@nas.edu
Pubns Dir: Rachel Marcus *Tel:* 202-334-2275
  E-mail: rmarcus@nas.edu
Sales & Dist Mgr: Barbara Murphy *Tel:* 202-334-1902 *E-mail:* bmurphy@nas.edu
Founded: 1863
Science, technology & health, scholarly & trade books.
ISBN Prefix(es): 978-0-309
Number of titles published annually: 500 Print; 500 Online; 500 E-Book
Total Titles: 6,000 Print; 12,000 Online; 6,000 E-Book
Foreign Rep(s): Marston Book Services Ltd (Africa, The Balkans exc Bulgaria, Greece & Turkey, Baltic States, Eastern Europe, Europe, Middle East, Scandinavia, UK, Western Europe); Maruzen Co Ltd (Japan); World Scientific Publishing Co Pte Ltd (Brunei, China, Hong Kong, India, Indonesia, Malaysia, Philippines, Singapore, South Korea, Taiwan, Thailand)
Foreign Rights: Berla & Griffini Rights Agency SRL (Italy); Big Apple Agency Inc; Amelie Cherlin (Arab Middle East); Japan UNI Agency Inc (Japan); Andrew Nurnberg Associates (China); Rightol Media; Tuttle-Mori Agency Inc (Japan); Eric Yang Agency (South Korea, Taiwan)
Orders to: Marston Book Services Ltd, 160 Eastern Ave, Abingdon, Oxon OX14 4SB, United Kingdom (for UK & Europe) *Tel:* (01235) 465500 *Fax:* (01235) 465555 *Web Site:* www.marston.co.uk
Returns: Books International, 22883 Quicksilver Dr, Dulles, VA 20166 *Web Site:* booksintl.presswarehouse.com
Membership(s): American Association for the Advancement of Slavic Studies (AAASS); American Association of University Presses (AAUP); Association of American Publishers (AAP)

National Association of Broadcasters (NAB)
One "M" St SE, Washington, DC 20003
Tel: 202-429-5300
E-mail: nab@nab.org
Web Site: www.nab.org
Key Personnel
Pres & CEO: Curtis LeGeyt
CFO & EVP, Opers: Tea Gennaro
Chief of Staff & EVP, Pub Aff: Michelle Lehman
CTO & EVP, Technol: Sam Matheny
Chief Diversity Offr & Pres, NAB Leadership Foundation: Michelle Duke
Chief Legal Offr & EVP, Legal & Regulatory Aff: Rick Kaplan
EVP & Mng Dir, Global Connections & Events: Karen Chupka
EVP, Govt Rel: Shawn Donilon
EVP, Indus Aff: April Carty-Sipp
Founded: 1922
Trade association representing radio & television stations & companies that serve the broadcasting industry.
ISBN Prefix(es): 978-0-89324
Number of titles published annually: 15 Print
Total Titles: 71 Print
Distributed by Lawrence Erlbaum Associates; Focal Press; Macmillan; Tab Books

§National Association of Insurance Commissioners
1100 Walnut St, Suite 1500, Kansas City, MO 64106-2197
Tel: 816-842-3600 *Fax:* 816-783-8175
E-mail: prodserv@naic.org
Web Site: www.naic.org
Key Personnel
Mgr, Implementation: Renee Brownfield
  E-mail: rbrownfield@naic.org
Founded: 1871
ISBN Prefix(es): 978-0-89382; 978-1-59917
Number of titles published annually: 110 Print
Total Titles: 356 Print; 110 Online; 110 E-Book
Branch Office(s)
NAIC Government Relations, Hall of the States, Suite 700, 4444 N Capitol St NW, Washington, DC 20001, Dir: Ethan Sonnichsen *Tel:* 202-471-3990 *Fax:* 816-460-7493
Capital Markets & Investment Analysis Office, One New York Plaza, Suite 4210, New York, NY 10004, Dir: Chris Evangel *Tel:* 212-398-9000 *Fax:* 212-382-4207

National Book Co
Division of Educational Research Associates
PO Box 3428, Hillsboro, OR 97123-1943
SAN: 212-4661
Tel: 503-245-1500 *Fax:* 810-885-5811

PUBLISHERS

E-mail: info@eralearning.com
Web Site: www.eralearning.com
Key Personnel
Dir, Spec Materials: Mark Salser
Founded: 1965
Individualized mastery learning programs for elementary, secondary & college levels, consisting of multimedia materials in business education, home economics, language skills, mathematics, science, shorthand skills, social studies, general & vocational education; special trade publications, particularly in subjects relating to education. Computer software, reference books, Black/Afro-American history, ESL.
ISBN Prefix(es): 978-0-89420
Number of titles published annually: 20 Print
Total Titles: 150 Print; 100 Audio
Imprints: Halcyon House

National Braille Press
88 Saint Stephen St, Boston, MA 02115-4312
Tel: 617-266-6160 *Toll Free Tel:* 800-548-7323 (cust serv); 888-965-8965 *Fax:* 617-437-0456
E-mail: contact@nbp.org
Web Site: www.nbp.org
Key Personnel
Pres: Brian A MacDonald *E-mail:* bmacdonald@nbp.org
VP, Braille Pubns: Tony Grima *Tel:* 617-266-6160 ext 429 *E-mail:* agrima@nbp.org
VP, Devt & Major Gifts: Joseph Quintanilla
VP, Prodn: Jackie Sheridan-Witterschein
Dir, Sales: Nicole Noble
Founded: 1929
Braille books & magazines.
ISBN Prefix(es): 978-0-939173
Number of titles published annually: 40 Print; 20 E-Book
Total Titles: 65 Print; 40 E-Book

National Catholic Educational Association
200 N Glebe Rd, Suite 310, Arlington, VA 22203
Tel: 571-257-0010 *Toll Free Tel:* 800-711-6232 *Fax:* 703-243-0025
E-mail: nceaadmin@ncea.org
Web Site: www.ncea.org
Key Personnel
VP, Communs, PR & Pubns Mgr: Margaret Kaplow *E-mail:* mkaplow@ncea.org
VP, Mktg: Crystal Berry *E-mail:* cberry@ncea.org
Graphic Design & Prodn Mgr: Bea Ruiz *E-mail:* ruiz@ncea.org
Mktg Mgr: Beth Rucinski *E-mail:* brucinski@ncea.org
Founded: 1904
Professional development organization that also produces publications in the area of nonfiction: educational trends, methodology, innovative programs, teacher education & in-service, research, technology, financial & public relations programs, management systems all applicable to nonpublic education.
ISBN Prefix(es): 978-1-55833
Number of titles published annually: 25 Print; 25 E-Book
Total Titles: 450 Print; 250 E-Book

§National Center for Children in Poverty
Division of Mailman School of Public Health at Columbia University
722 W 168 St, New York, NY 10032
Tel: 646-284-9600; 212-304-6073
E-mail: info@nccp.org
Web Site: www.nccp.org
Key Personnel
Dir: Heather Koball, PhD
Founded: 1989
Nonprofit publisher of monographs, reports, statistical updates, working papers & issue briefs concerning children under 6 who live in poverty in the US. Topics cover impact of poverty on child health & development; statistical profiles of poor children & their families; research programs on the effects of poverty; research on policies that could reduce the young child poverty rate; integrated social & human services (private & public) for low-income families. Welfare reform & children, research forum on children, families & the new federalism.
ISBN Prefix(es): 978-0-926582
Number of titles published annually: 24 Print
Total Titles: 40 Print; 20 E-Book

National Center For Employee Ownership (NCEO)
440 N Barranca Ave, Suite 3554, Covina, CA 91723
Tel: 510-208-1300
E-mail: customerservice@nceo.org
Web Site: www.nceo.org
Key Personnel
Exec Dir: Loren Rodgers *Tel:* 510-208-1307 *E-mail:* lrodgers@nceo.org
Dir, Publg & Info Technol: Scott Rodrick *Tel:* 510-208-1315 *E-mail:* srodrick@nceo.org
Founded: 1981
Employee ownership books, pamphlets & newsletter.
ISBN Prefix(es): 978-0-926902; 978-1-932924; 978-1-938220
Number of titles published annually: 8 Print; 8 E-Book
Total Titles: 60 Print

National Conference of State Legislatures (NCSL)
7700 E First Place, Denver, CO 80230
Tel: 303-364-7700
E-mail: press-room@ncsl.org
Web Site: www.ncsl.org
Key Personnel
CEO: Tim Storey
Dir, Digital Communs: Lesley Kennedy *E-mail:* lesley.kennedy@ncsl.org
Founded: 1975
Books, magazines, series of papers & issue briefs on state public policy issues.
ISBN Prefix(es): 978-1-55516; 978-1-58024; 978-0-941336
Number of titles published annually: 100 Print
Total Titles: 200 Print
Branch Office(s)
444 N Capitol St NW, Suite 515, Washington, DC 20001 *Tel:* 202-624-5400

National Council of Teachers of English (NCTE)
340 N Neil St, Suite 104, Champaign, IL 61820
Tel: 217-328-3870 *Toll Free Tel:* 877-369-6283 (cust serv) *Fax:* 217-328-9645
E-mail: customerservice@ncte.org
Web Site: ncte.org
Key Personnel
Exec Dir: Emily Kirkpatrick
Dir, Pubns: Colin Murcray *Tel:* 217-278-3604 *E-mail:* cmurcray@ncte.org
Sr Books Ed: Kurt Austin *Tel:* 217-278-3619 *E-mail:* kaustin@ncte.org
Purch & Prodn Mgr: Charles Hartman *Tel:* 217-278-3664
Founded: 1911
Nonprofit professional association of educators in English studies, literacy & language arts. Specialize in the teaching of English & the language arts at all grade levels; research reports; guidelines & position statements; journals; professional development books.
ISBN Prefix(es): 978-0-8141
Number of titles published annually: 15 Print; 10 E-Book
Total Titles: 250 Print; 2 CD-ROM; 70 E-Book
Imprints: Principles in Practice

Distribution Center: Consortium Book Sales & Distribution, The Keg House, Suite 101, 34 13 Ave NE, Minneapolis, MN 55413-1007 *Tel:* 612-746-2600 *E-mail:* cbsdinfo@ingramcontent.com *Web Site:* www.cbsd.com

§National Council of Teachers of Mathematics (NCTM)
1906 Association Dr, Reston, VA 20191-1502
SAN: 202-9057
Tel: 703-620-9840 *Toll Free Tel:* 800-235-7566 *Fax:* 703-476-2970
E-mail: nctm@nctm.org
Web Site: www.nctm.org
Key Personnel
Exec Dir: Ken Krehbiel
Dir, Pubns: Scott Rodgerson
Founded: 1920
Professional publications, including books (printed & online), monographs & yearbooks. Members include individuals, institutions, students, teachers & educators. Multiyear plans available to individual & institutional members.
ISBN Prefix(es): 978-0-87353; 978-1-68054
Number of titles published annually: 10 Print; 3 Online
Total Titles: 175 Print; 15 E-Book
Distributed by Eric Armin Inc Education Ctr; Delta Education; Didax Educational Resources; Educators Outlet; ETA Cuisenaire; Lakeshore Learning Materials; NASCO; Spectrum

National Education Association (NEA)
1201 16 St NW, Washington, DC 20036-3290
Tel: 202-833-4000 *Fax:* 202-822-7974
Web Site: www.nea.org
Key Personnel
Pres: Becky Pringle
VP: Princess R Moss
Secy/Treas: Noel Candelaria
Exec Dir: Kim A Anderson
Founded: 1857
Professional development publications for K-12 & higher education & AV materials for educators. Web site with resources & general information for educators & the general public.
ISBN Prefix(es): 978-0-8106
Number of titles published annually: 7 Print; 2 CD-ROM; 2 Online
Total Titles: 189 Print; 2 CD-ROM; 9 Online
Imprints: NEA Professional Library

§National Gallery of Art
Sixth & Constitution Ave NW, Washington, DC 20565
Mailing Address: 2000 B South Club Dr, Landover, MD 20785
Tel: 202-842-6280
E-mail: thecenter@nga.gov
Web Site: www.nga.gov
Key Personnel
Exec Offr, Collections, Exhibitions & Progs: Kate Haw
Deputy Dir: Eric L Motley
Founded: 1941
Exhibition catalogues, catalogues of the collection & scholarly monographs.
ISBN Prefix(es): 978-0-89468
Number of titles published annually: 15 Print; 3 Online
Total Titles: 112 Print; 2 CD-ROM; 3 Online
Divisions: Department of Education Resources
Distributed by Abrams; DAP; Lund Humphries/Ashgate; Princeton University Press; Thames & Hudson; University of Chicago Press; Yale University Press

National Geographic Books
Division of National Geographic Partners LLC
1145 17 St NW, Washington, DC 20036-4688
SAN: 202-8956
Tel: 202-857-7000 *Toll Free Tel:* 877-866-6486

U.S. PUBLISHERS

E-mail: ngbooks@cdsfulfillment.com
Web Site: www.nationalgeographic.com/books/; ngbooks.buysub.com
Key Personnel
SVP & Gen Mgr, Books: Hector Sierra
   E-mail: hector.sierra@natgeo.com
SVP, Kids Content: Jennifer Emmett
   E-mail: jennifer.emmett@natgeo.com
VP & Edit Dir, Kids Books: Rebecca Baines
   E-mail: rebecca.baines@natgeo.com
Publr & Edit Dir, Adult Books: Lisa Thomas
   E-mail: lisa.thomas@natgeo.com
Sr Dir, Digital Book Publg: Rachel Graham
   E-mail: rachel.graham@natgeo.com
Sr Dir Mktg, Books: Daneen Goodwin
   E-mail: daneen.goodwin@natgeo.com
Dir, Kids Mktg: Ruth Chamblee *E-mail:* ruth.chamblee@natgeo.com
Deputy Ed, Adult Books: Hilary Black
   E-mail: hilary.black@natgeo.com
Edit Mgr: Bridget Hamilton *E-mail:* bridget.hamilton@natgeo.com
Founded: 1888
Nonfiction general illustrated reference, travel, photography, history, science. Children's nonfiction with emphasis on school & library markets.
ISBN Prefix(es): 978-0-7922; 978-0-87044; 978-1-4262; 978-1-4263
Number of titles published annually: 140 Print
Total Titles: 2,500 Print; 500 E-Book
Imprints: National Geographic Kids Books; National Geographic Under the Stars (kids fiction)
Distributed by HarperCollins UK (Australia, New Zealand & UK-kids books); Penguin Random House (worldwide exc UK); Simon & Schuster UK (UK-adult books)
Membership(s): Association of American Publishers (AAP); The Children's Book Council (CBC)

National Geographic Learning
Unit of Cengage Learning
20 Channel Center St, Boston, MA 02210
Tel: 617-289-7900
E-mail: schoolcustomerservice@cengage.com
Web Site: www.ngl.cengage.com/school
Key Personnel
SVP & Gen Mgr: Marty Lange
Founded: 1980
Provides quality PreK-12, academic & adult education instructional solutions for reading, science, social studies, mathematics, world languages, ESL/ELD, advanced, honors & electives, career & technical education & professional development. Catalog available online at ngl.cengage.com/assets/html/catalogs.
ISBN Prefix(es): 978-0-917837; 978-1-56334
Number of titles published annually: 10 CD-ROM; 10 Online
Membership(s): Association of American Publishers (AAP)

§National Golf Foundation
501 N Hwy A1A, Jupiter, FL 33477-4577
Tel: 561-744-6006 *Toll Free Tel:* 888-275-4643
   Fax: 561-744-9085
E-mail: general@ngf.org
Web Site: www.ngf.org
Key Personnel
Pres & CEO: Dr Joseph Beditz
Founded: 1936
Premier publisher of research & information for the business of golf. Over 200 publications are offered on golf consumer research, industry & market trends, golf facility development & operations, golf range development, instruction & player development.
ISBN Prefix(es): 978-0-9638647; 978-1-57701
Number of titles published annually: 4 Print
Total Titles: 100 Print; 1 CD-ROM; 2 Online; 1 Audio

§National Information Standards Organization (NISO)
3600 Clipper Mill Rd, Suite 302, Baltimore, MD 21211-1948
Tel: 301-654-2512 *Fax:* 410-685-5278
E-mail: nisohq@niso.org
Web Site: www.niso.org
Key Personnel
Exec Dir: Todd Carpenter
Assoc Exec Dir: Nettie Lagace
Dir, Strategic Initiatives: Jason Griffey
Dir, Busn Devt & Communs: Mary Beth Barilla
Communs & Events Coord: Sara Groveman
Educ Prog Mgr & DEIA Advocate: Kimberly Gladfelter Graham
Asst Standards Prog Mgr: Keondra Bailey
Off Mgr: Lisa Jackson
Founded: 1939 (incorporated as US 501(c)(3) in 1982)
Maintain & develop technical standards for libraries, publishers & information services.
ISBN Prefix(es): 978-1-880124; 978-1-937522
Number of titles published annually: 6 Print; 10 E-Book
Total Titles: 70 Print; 70 Online; 70 E-Book
Imprints: NISO Press
Membership(s): The American Library Association (ALA); Association for Information Science & Technology (ASIS&T); Book Industry Study Group (BISG); Coalition for Diversity & Inclusion in Scholarly Communications (C4DISC)

National Institute for Trial Advocacy (NITA)
1685 38 St, Suite 200, Boulder, CO 80301-2735
Tel: 720-890-4860 *Toll Free Tel:* 877-648-2632;
   800-225-6482 (orders & returns) *Fax:* 720-890-7069
E-mail: customerservice@nita.org; sales@nita.org
Web Site: www.nita.org
Key Personnel
Exec Dir: Wendy McCormack
   E-mail: wmccormack@nita.org
Dir, Mktg: Daniel McHugh *E-mail:* dmchugh@nita.org
Assoc Exec Dir, Opers: Jennifer Schneider
   E-mail: jschneider@nita.org
Dir, Pubns: Eric Sorensen *E-mail:* esorensen@nita.org
Founded: 1970
Legal & litigation training.
ISBN Prefix(es): 978-1-55681; 978-1-60156
Number of titles published annually: 20 Print; 1 CD-ROM
Total Titles: 350 Print; 2 CD-ROM; 12 Audio

National Learning Corp
212 Michael Dr, Syosset, NY 11791
Tel: 516-921-8888 *Toll Free Tel:* 800-632-8888
   Fax: 516-921-8743
E-mail: info@passbooks.com
Web Site: www.passbooks.com
Key Personnel
Pres & CEO: Michael P Rudman
Founded: 1967
Basic competency tests for college, high school & occupations; functional literacy; career, general, vocational & technical, adult & continuing, special, cooperative & community education; professional licensure; test preparation books for civil service, postal service, government careers, armed forces, high school & college equivalency; college, graduate & professional school enhancement; certification & licensing in engineering & technical careers, teaching, law, dentistry, medicine & allied health professions.
ISBN Prefix(es): 978-0-8373; 978-0-8293
Number of titles published annually: 7 Print
Total Titles: 6,000 Print
Imprints: Career Examination Passbooks®

Subsidiaries: Delaney Books Inc; Frank Merriwell Inc
Membership(s): Association of American Publishers (AAP)

National Notary Association (NNA)
9350 De Soto Ave, Chatsworth, CA 91311-4926
Mailing Address: PO Box 2402, Chatsworth, CA 91313-2402
Tel: 818-739-4000 *Toll Free Tel:* 800-876-6827
   Toll Free Fax: 800-833-1211
E-mail: services@nationalnotary.org
Web Site: www.nationalnotary.org
Key Personnel
Pres & CEO: Thomas A Heymann
CFO: Rob Clark
VP & CIO/CTO: Dave Stephenson
EVP: Deborah M Thaw
VP, Busn Devt: Chris Sturdivant
VP, Mktg: Thomas K Hayden
Founded: 1957
Publish books, periodical, videos, seminars.
ISBN Prefix(es): 978-0-9600158; 978-0-933134; 978-1-891133; 978-1-59767
Number of titles published annually: 15 Print
Total Titles: 40 Print

National Resource Center for Youth Services
Division of University of Oklahoma Outreach
Schusterman Ctr, Bldg 4W, 4502 E 41 St, Tulsa, OK 74135-2512
Tel: 918-660-3700 *Toll Free Tel:* 800-274-2687
E-mail: nrcys@ou.edu
Web Site: www.nrcys.ou.edu
Key Personnel
Dir: Kristi Charles *E-mail:* klcharles@ou.edu
Founded: 1985
Curricula & resource manuals for professionals & volunteers who work with foster care & at-risk teenagers.
ISBN Prefix(es): 978-1-878848
Number of titles published annually: 3 Print
Total Titles: 20 Print

§National Science Teachers Association (NSTA)
1840 Wilson Blvd, Arlington, VA 22201-3000
Tel: 703-243-7100 *Toll Free Tel:* 800-277-5300
   (orders) *Fax:* 703-243-7177 *Toll Free Fax:* 888-433-0526 (orders)
E-mail: nstapress@nsta.org (edit); orders@nsta.org; pubsales@nsta.org
Web Site: www.nsta.org/bookstore
Founded: 1944
Books, periodicals & journals.
ISBN Prefix(es): 978-0-87355; 978-1-93353; 978-1-936137; 978-1-935155; 978-1-936959; 978-1-938946; 978-1-941316
Number of titles published annually: 25 Print; 25 E-Book
Total Titles: 350 Print; 350 E-Book
Imprints: NSTA Ebooks+; NSTA Kids; NSTA Press®
Foreign Rep(s): Alkem Co (S) Pte Ltd (Brunei, Cambodia, Indonesia, Laos, Malaysia, Myanmar, Philippines, Singapore, Thailand, Vietnam); Eurospan (worldwide exc Canada & Southeast Asia); University of Toronto Press (Canada)
Orders to: PO Box 90214, Washington, DC 20090-0214
Returns: c/o NSTA Returns Dept, 46 Development Rd, Fitchburg, MA 01420
Membership(s): AM&P Network; Association of American Publishers (AAP); Association of American Publishers PreK-12 Learning Group; Independent Book Publishing Professionals Group (IBPPG)

The National Underwriter Co
Division of ALM Media LLC
4157 Olympic Blvd, Suite 225, Erlanger, KY 41018

Tel: 859-692-2100 *Toll Free Tel:* 800-543-0874
E-mail: customerservice@nuco.com
Web Site: www.nationalunderwriter.com
Founded: 1897
ISBN Prefix(es): 978-0-87218; 978-1-936362; 978-1-938130; 978-1-939829; 978-1-941627
Number of titles published annually: 11 Print
Total Titles: 216 Print; 46 E-Book

National Wildlife Federation
11100 Wildlife Center Dr, Reston, VA 20190-5362
Mailing Address: PO Box 1583, Merrifield, VA 22116-1583
Toll Free Tel: 800-477-5034
Web Site: www.zoobooks.com
Key Personnel
Sales Mgr: Kurt Von Hertsenberg *E-mail:* kurt@zoobooks.com
Founded: 1980
Books on wildlife & animals. Publisher of *Zoobooks* magazine.
ISBN Prefix(es): 978-0-937934; 978-1-888153
Number of titles published annually: 27 Print; 27 E-Book
Total Titles: 200 Print; 200 E-Book
Membership(s): Association of American Publishers PreK-12 Learning Group

§Naval Institute Press
Division of US Naval Institute
291 Wood Rd, Annapolis, MD 21402-5034
SAN: 202-9006
Tel: 410-268-6110 *Toll Free Tel:* 800-233-8764
Fax: 410-295-1084
E-mail: customer@usni.org (cust inquiries)
Web Site: www.usni.org/press/books; www.usni.org
Key Personnel
Publr & CEO: Peter H Daly
Dir, Sales & Mktg: Robin Noonan *E-mail:* rnoonan@usni.org
Press Dir: Adam Kane *E-mail:* akane@usni.org
Deputy Press Dir: Claire Noble *E-mail:* cnoble@usni.org
Mng Ed: Susan Corrado *E-mail:* scorrado@usni.org
Sr Acqs Ed, Subs Rts, Imports: Susan Todd Brook *E-mail:* sbrook@usni.org
Sr Acqs Ed: Pat Carlin *E-mail:* pcarlin@usni.org; Steve Catalano *E-mail:* scatalano@usni.org; Glenn Griffith *E-mail:* ggriffith@usni.org
Sr Prodn Ed: Ashley Baird *E-mail:* sbaird@usni.org
Prodn Ed: Brennan Knight *E-mail:* bknight@usni.org
Publicity Mgr: Sam Caggiula *E-mail:* scaggiula@usni.org
Sales & Mktg Mgr: Jack Russell *E-mail:* jrussell@usni.org
Publg Asst: Elena Pelton *E-mail:* epelton@usni.org
Founded: 1898
Naval & maritime subjects: professional, biography, science, history, ship & aviation references, US Naval Institute magazines; literature.
ISBN Prefix(es): 978-0-87021; 978-1-55750; 978-1-59114; 978-1-61251; 978-1-68247
Number of titles published annually: 70 Print; 40 E-Book
Total Titles: 1,379 Print; 794 E-Book
Foreign Rep(s): Eurospan Group (Africa, Asia, Australia, Europe, India, Middle East, Oceania, UK)
Warehouse: Books International, 22883 Quicksilver Dr, Dulles, VA 20166 *Tel:* 703-661-1500 *Fax:* 703-661-1501 *Web Site:* booksintl.presswarehouse.com
Distribution Center: Ingram CoreSource, One Ingram Blvd, La Vergne, TN 37086 (digital only) *Web Site:* www.ingramcontent.com
Membership(s): Association of University Presses (AUPresses)

NavPress Publishing Group
Division of The Navigators
3820 N 30 St, Colorado Springs, CO 80904
SAN: 211-5352
Web Site: www.navpress.com
Founded: 1975
Paperbacks, mass market & trade, hardcovers; religious (Protestant) materials.
ISBN Prefix(es): 978-0-89109; 978-1-57683; 978-1-60006; 978-1-61521; 978-1-61747; 978-1-61291; 978-1-63146; 978-1-64158
Number of titles published annually: 15 Print
Total Titles: 600 Print; 2 Audio
Imprints: NavPress
Distributed by Tyndale House Publishers Inc
Orders to: Tyndale House Publishers Inc, 351 Executive Dr, Carol Stream, IL 60188

§NBM Publishing Inc
300 E 54 St, No 12C, New York, NY 10022-5021
SAN: 210-0835
Tel: 917-628-6777
E-mail: nbmgn@nbmpub.com
Web Site: www.nbmpub.com
Key Personnel
Pres & Publr: Terry Nantier
Mktg Mgr: JT Yost *E-mail:* jtyost@nbmpub.com
Founded: 1976
Graphic novels.
ISBN Prefix(es): 978-0-918348; 978-1-56163; 978-1-68112
Number of titles published annually: 12 Print; 12 E-Book
Total Titles: 250 Print; 300 E-Book
Foreign Rep(s): IPG (Canada); Turnaround (Europe, UK)
Orders to: IPG Distribution Center, 600 N Pulaski Rd, Chicago, IL 60624 *Toll Free Tel:* 800-888-IPG1 (888-4741)
Returns: IPG Distribution Center, 600 N Pulaski Rd, Chicago, IL 60624
Warehouse: IPG Distribution Center, 600 N Pulaski Rd, Chicago, IL 60624
Distribution Center: Independent Publishers Group (IPG), 814 N Franklin St, Chicago, IL 60610 *E-mail:* sales@ipgbook.com *Web Site:* www.ipgbook.com
Membership(s): Independent Publishers Caucus (IPC)

§New City Press
Subsidiary of Focolare Media
202 Comforter Blvd, Hyde Park, NY 12538
SAN: 203-7335
Tel: 845-229-0335 *Toll Free Tel:* 800-462-5980 (orders only) *Fax:* 845-229-0351
E-mail: info@newcitypress.com; orders@newcitypress.com
Web Site: www.newcitypress.com
Key Personnel
Assoc Publr: Greg Metzger *E-mail:* greg.metzger@newcitypress.com
Accts Payable: Manuel Salazar *E-mail:* manuel.salazar@newcitypress.com
Cust Serv: Nikte Murguia *Tel:* 845-229-0335 ext 108
Founded: 1964
Publishes spiritual works of all Christian eras, including the Church Fathers, the spiritual masters of the middle-ages, as well as publications of contemporary spirituality & theology.
ISBN Prefix(es): 978-0-911782; 978-1-56548
Number of titles published annually: 15 Print
Total Titles: 300 Print
Imprints: NCP
Distributor for Ciudad Nueva (Argentina, Spain); New City (Great Britain)
Foreign Rep(s): Enderle Book Co (Japan); John Garratt Publishing (Australia); Jerome's Specialist Booksellers (New Zealand); Joseph's Inspirational (Canada); New City (China, England, Ireland, Philippines); Preca Bookshop (Malta)

§New Concepts Publishing
5265 Humphreys Rd, Lake Park, GA 31636
E-mail: newconcepts@newconceptspublishing.com
Web Site: www.newconceptspublishing.com
Key Personnel
Pres & PR: Madris De Pasture *E-mail:* madris@newconceptspublishing.com
Founded: 1996
ISBN Prefix(es): 978-1-58608; 978-1-891020; 978-1-60394
Number of titles published annually: 50 Print; 192 Online; 144 E-Book
Total Titles: 200 Print; 700 Online; 700 E-Book

New Directions Publishing Corp
80 Eighth Ave, 19th fl, New York, NY 10011
SAN: 202-9081
Tel: 212-255-0230
E-mail: editorial@ndbooks.com; publicity@ndbooks.com
Web Site: ndbooks.com
Key Personnel
Pres & Publr: Barbara Epler
EVP: Laurie Callahan
Art Dir & Prodn Mgr: Erik Rieselbach
Foreign Rts Dir: Declan Spring *E-mail:* dspring@ndbooks.com
Publicity Dir: Mieke Chew; Brittany Dennison
Founded: 1936
Modern literature, poetry, criticism & belles lettres.
ISBN Prefix(es): 978-0-8112
Number of titles published annually: 30 Print
Total Titles: 930 Print
Distributed by W W Norton & Company Inc
Foreign Rep(s): Everest International Publishing Services (Wei Zhao) (China); B K Norton Ltd (South Korea, Taiwan); W W Norton & Co Ltd (Africa, Europe, Ireland, Middle East, UK); Pansing Distribution Pte Ltd (Brunei, Malaysia, Singapore); Publishers Group Canada (Canada); Rockbook (Gilles Fauveau) (Japan); Transglobal Publishers Services Ltd (Hong Kong, Macau); US PubRep Inc (Caribbean, Central America, Mexico, South America); John Wiley & Sons Australia Ltd (Australia, New Zealand)
Foreign Rights: Agencia Literaria Carmen Balcells SA (Anna Bofill) (Spain); The Deborah Harris Agency (Deborah Harris) (Israel); Agence Hoffman GmbH (Luisa Straub) (Germany); The Italian Literary Agency Srl (Beatrice Beraldo) (Italy); Agence Michelle Lapautre (Catherine Lapoutre) (France); Orion Literary Agency (Harumi Sakai) (Japan); Peters, Fraser & Dunlop Literary Agents (Laura McNeill) (British Commonwealth); Agencia Riff (Lucia Riff) (Brazil)

§New Forums Press Inc
1018 S Lewis St, Stillwater, OK 74074
Mailing Address: PO Box 876, Stillwater, OK 74076-0876
Tel: 405-372-6158 *Toll Free Tel:* 800-606-3766
Fax: 405-377-2237
Web Site: www.newforums.com
Key Personnel
Pres: Douglas Dollar *E-mail:* ddollar@newforums.com
Founded: 1981
Practical & innovative academic journals, newsletters & books for educators in colleges & universities. Textbooks are also a primary interest.
ISBN Prefix(es): 978-0-913507; 978-1-58107
Number of titles published annually: 25 Print; 8 Online; 3 E-Book
Total Titles: 350 Print; 295 Online; 20 E-Book

U.S. PUBLISHERS

Advertising Agency: Copy & Art, 219 E Greenvale Ct, Stillwater, OK 74075 *Tel:* 405-372-6158
Membership(s): The Association of Publishers for Special Sales (APSS)

New Harbinger Publications Inc
5674 Shattuck Ave, Oakland, CA 94609
Tel: 510-652-0215 *Toll Free Tel:* 800-748-6273 (orders only) *Fax:* 510-652-5472
Toll Free Fax: 800-652-1613
E-mail: customerservice@newharbinger.com
Web Site: www.newharbinger.com
Key Personnel
Publr: Catharine A Meyers
VP, Sales & Mktg: Julie Kahn
Dir, Intl Rts: Dorothy Smyk
Prodn Mgr: Michele Waters
Publicity Mgr: Cassie Stossel *Tel:* 510-594-6142
E-mail: cassie.stossel@newharbinger.com
Founded: 1973
We offer the best in self-help psychology; real tools for real change. Now offering spirituality titles from our Non-Duality Press & Reveal Press imprints, which offer new wisdom for living consciously in our modern world.
ISBN Prefix(es): 978-1-57224; 978-0-934986; 978-1-879223; 978-1-60882; 978-1-62625
Number of titles published annually: 60 Print; 60 E-Book
Total Titles: 800 Print; 450 E-Book; 20 Audio
Imprints: Context Press; Impact Publishers; Instant Help Books; Non-Duality Press; Reveal Press
Subsidiaries: Praxis Continuing Education & Training
Foreign Rep(s): Bookreps NZ Ltd (New Zealand); Booktopia Publishers Services (Australia); Little, Brown Book Group (Europe, UK); Raincoast Books (Canada); SG Distributors (South Africa)
Returns: 660 S Mansfield St, Ypsilanti, MI 48197

New Issues Poetry & Prose
Affiliate of Western Michigan University
c/o Western Michigan University, 1903 W Michigan Ave, Kalamazoo, MI 49008-5463
Tel: 269-387-8185
E-mail: new-issues@wmich.edu
Web Site: newissuespress.com
Key Personnel
Mng Ed: Kimberly Kolbe
Founded: 1996
ISBN Prefix(es): 978-1-930974; 978-0-932826; 978-1-936970
Number of titles published annually: 12 Print
Total Titles: 180 Print
Distribution Center: Chicago Distribution Center (CDC), 11030 S Langley Ave, Chicago, IL 60628 *Tel:* 773-702-7000 *Toll Free Tel:* 800-621-2736 *Toll Free Fax:* 800-621-8476
E-mail: custserv@press.uchicago.edu

New Leaf Press
Imprint of New Leaf Publishing Group LLC
3142 Hwy 103 N, Green Forest, AR 72638-2233
Mailing Address: PO Box 726, Green Forest, AR 72638-0726
Tel: 870-438-5288 *Toll Free Tel:* 800-999-3777
Fax: 870-438-5120
E-mail: submissions@nlpg.com
Web Site: www.nlpg.com
Key Personnel
CEO, New Leaf Publishing Group: Jerrod Vaughan
Pres, New Leaf Publishing Group: Randy Pratt
Ed-in-Chief, New Leaf Publishing Group: Laura Welch
Asst Ed: Craig Froman
Founded: 1975
Christian living & creation books; evangelical, devotionals.

ISBN Prefix(es): 978-0-89221
Number of titles published annually: 30 Print; 30 E-Book
Total Titles: 556 Print; 500 E-Book

The New Press
120 Wall St, 31st fl, New York, NY 10005
Tel: 212-629-8802 *Fax:* 212-629-8617
E-mail: newpress@thenewpress.com
Web Site: thenewpress.com
Key Personnel
Chief Devt Offr: Natalie Schulmonds
Chief Fin & Admin Offr: Rosa Del Saz
Exec Dir: Diane Wachtell
Sr Dir, Prodn: Fran Forte
Dir, Edit Progs: Marc Favreau
Dir, Publicity & Book Mktg: Derek Warker
Dir, Sales & Subs Rts: Sharon Swados
Prodn Dir: Fran Forte
Sr Mng Ed: Maury Botton
Sr Ed: Zakia Henderson-Brown; Ben Woodward
Prodn Ed: Gia Gonzales
Assoc Ed: Ishan Desai-Geller; Rachel Vega-DeCesario
Acctg Mgr: Monika Thobani
HR Mgr: Aima Mahmood
Mgr, Inventory & Sales Opers: Jessamine Cheng
Mktg Mgr & Assoc Publicist: Jay Pabarue
Publicity Mgr: Josh Zajdman
Publicist: Emily Janakiram
Edit & Serial Rts Coord: Benjamin Woodward
Edit & Academic Mktg Assoc: Jay Gupta
Founded: 1990
Nonprofit publisher in the public interest; politics, education, current affairs, history, biography, economics, international fiction in translation.
ISBN Prefix(es): 978-1-56584; 978-1-59558; 978-1-62097
Number of titles published annually: 50 Print
Total Titles: 1,200 Print; 200 E-Book
Foreign Rep(s): Jonathan Ball (Elmasie Stodart) (South Africa); Canadian Manda Group (Canada); Ingram Publisher Services International (Karis Moelker) (South Africa); Ingram Publisher Services International (Tricia Remark) (Australia, Canada, New Zealand); Ingram Publisher Services International (Edison Garcia) (Asia, India, Middle East); Ingram UK (Europe, Ireland, UK); Ingram UK (Matthew Dickie) (Caribbean, Europe, Latin America); NewSouth Books (Australia); Penguin Books India Pvt Ltd (India)
Orders to: Ingram Content Group LLC, One Ingram Blvd, La Vergne, TN 37086 *Toll Free Tel:* 800-400-5351 *E-mail:* ips@ingramcontent.com

New Readers Press
Division of ProLiteracy
104 Marcellus, Syracuse, NY 13204
SAN: 202-1064
Tel: 315-422-9121 *Toll Free Tel:* 800-448-8878
Toll Free Fax: 866-894-2100
E-mail: nrp@proliteracy.org
Web Site: www.newreaderspress.com
Key Personnel
Sales & Busn Dir: Susan Willey *Tel:* 315-422-9121 ext 2470
Founded: 1965
Books & periodicals for adults & young adult reading at a 0-8 reading level, basic reading & writing materials, ESL, mathematics & GED prep.
ISBN Prefix(es): 978-0-88336; 978-1-56420; 978-1-56853; 978-0-929631; 978-1-944057
Number of titles published annually: 20 Print
Total Titles: 400 Print; 41 Audio
Foreign Rights: Laubach Literacy Ontario (Canada)

New World Library
Division of Whatever Publishing Inc

14 Pamaron Way, Novato, CA 94949
SAN: 211-8777
Tel: 415-884-2100 *Fax:* 415-884-2199
E-mail: escort@newworldlibrary.com
Web Site: www.newworldlibrary.com
Key Personnel
Pres: Marc Allen *E-mail:* marc@newworldlibrary.com
Edit Dir: Georgia Hughes *E-mail:* georgia@newworldlibrary.com
Prodn Dir: Tona Pearce Meyers *E-mail:* tona@newworldlibrary.com
Publicity Dir: Monique Muhlenkamp *E-mail:* monique@newworldlibrary.com
Exec Ed: Jason Gardner *E-mail:* jason@newworldlibrary.com
Submissions Ed: Joel Prins *E-mail:* joel@newworldlibrary.com
Soc Media Mgr & Sr Publicist: Kim Corbin *E-mail:* kim@newworldlibrary.com
Spec Sales Mgr: Ami Parkerson *E-mail:* ami@newworldlibrary.com
Founded: 1977
Publisher of books on self-improvement, personal growth & spirituality, health & wellness, pets & animals, psychology & women's interest.
ISBN Prefix(es): 978-0-915811; 978-0-931432; 978-1-880032; 978-0-945934; 978-1-57731; 978-1-882591; 978-1-930722; 978-1-932073; 978-1-60868
Number of titles published annually: 35 Print; 35 E-Book; 6 Audio
Total Titles: 600 Print; 500 E-Book; 48 Audio
Imprints: Amber-Allen Publishing; HJ Kramer Inc; Nataraj; Eckhart Tolle Editions
Foreign Rep(s): Akasha Books (New Zealand); Brumby Books (Australia); Ingram International (Continental Europe, India, Japan, Latin America, Middle East, Philippines, South America, South Korea, Southeast Asia, Taiwan); Publishers Group Canada (Canada); Publishers Group UK (UK)
Distribution Center: Publishers Group West, 193 Edwards Dr, Jackson, TN 38301-7795 *Toll Free Tel:* 800-788-3123 *Web Site:* www.pgw.com
Membership(s): Association of American Publishers (AAP); Publishers Association of the West (PubWest); Publishing Professionals Network (PPN)

New York Academy of Sciences (NYAS)
7 World Trade Center, 40th fl, 250 Greenwich St, New York, NY 10007-2157
SAN: 203-753X
Tel: 212-298-8600 *Toll Free Tel:* 800-843-6927
Fax: 212-298-3650
E-mail: nyas@nyas.org; annals@nyas.org; customerservice@nyas.org
Web Site: www.nyas.org
Key Personnel
Pres & CEO: Ellis Rubenstein *Tel:* 212-298-8686
E-mail: erubenstein@nyas.org
EVP & COO: T C Wescott *Tel:* 212-298-8695
E-mail: tcwescott@nyas.org
SVP & Chief Admin Offr: Wendy Caruso Schneider *Tel:* 212-298-8680 *E-mail:* wschneider@nyas.org
SVP, Opers: Erica Cullmann *Tel:* 212-298-8619
E-mail: ecullman@nyas.org
Exec Dir, Sci Pubns & Ed-in-Chief, Annals of the NYAS: Douglas Braaten, PhD *Tel:* 212-298-8634 *E-mail:* dbraaten@nyas.org
Founded: 1817
Annals & transactions of the New York Academy of Sciences; also publish *Update Magazine*.
ISBN Prefix(es): 978-0-89072; 978-0-89766; 978-1-57331
Number of titles published annually: 28 Print
Total Titles: 333 Print
Distributed by Wiley Blackwell Publishers

The New York Botanical Garden Press
Division of New York Botanical Garden

2900 Southern Blvd, Bronx, NY 10458-5126
Tel: 718-817-8721 *Fax:* 718-817-8842
E-mail: nybgpress@nybg.org
Web Site: www.nybgpress.org
Founded: 1896
Dissemination of information on the scientific study of plants.
ISBN Prefix(es): 978-0-89327
Number of titles published annually: 10 Print
Total Titles: 244 Print
Warehouse: Maple Logistics Solutions, York Distribution Center, PO Box 15100, York, PA 17405
Distribution Center: Maple Logistics Solutions, York Distribution Center, PO Box 15100, York, PA 17405
Membership(s): Association of American Publishers (AAP)

§**New York State Bar Association**
One Elk St, Albany, NY 12207
SAN: 226-1952
Tel: 518-463-3200 *Toll Free Tel:* 800-582-2452 *Fax:* 518-463-5993
E-mail: mrc@nysba.org
Web Site: nysba.org
Key Personnel
Pubns Coord: Naomi Pitts *E-mail:* npitts@nysba.org
Legal Ed & Content Developer: Christian Nolan
Copy Ed/Proofreader: Alexander Dickson
  E-mail: adickson@nysba.org; Reyna Eisenstark
  E-mail: reisenstark@nysba.org; Howard Healy
  E-mail: hhealy@nysba.org
Founded: 1985
Legal publications, including hardbound, looseleaf, softbound & ebooks.
ISBN Prefix(es): 978-0-942954; 978-1-57969
Number of titles published annually: 110 Print; 6 CD-ROM
Total Titles: 600 Print; 500 Online

New York University Press
838 Broadway, 3rd fl, New York, NY 10003-4812
SAN: 658-1293
Tel: 212-998-2575 (edit) *Toll Free Tel:* 800-996-6987 (orders) *Fax:* 212-995-4798 (orders)
E-mail: nyupressinfo@nyu.edu (cust care)
Web Site: www.nyupress.org
Key Personnel
Dir: Eric I Schwartz
Mktg & Sales Dir: Mary Beth Jarrad
  E-mail: mary.jarrad@nyu.edu
Assoc Dir & Ed-in-Chief: Eric Zinner
  E-mail: eric.zinner@nyu.edu
Exec Ed: Ilene Kalish *E-mail:* ilene.kalish@nyu.edu
Sr Ed: Jennifer Hammer *E-mail:* jennifer.hammer@nyu.edu
Ed: Clara Platter *E-mail:* clara.platter@nyu.edu
Design & Prodn Mgr: Charles Hames
  E-mail: charles.hames@nyu.edu
Publicity Mgr: Betsy Steve *E-mail:* betsy.steve@nyu.edu
Sr Opers Supv: Kevin Cooper *E-mail:* kevin.cooper@nyu.edu
Founded: 1916
Publish a wide array of provocative & compelling titles, as well as works of lasting scholarly & reference value.
ISBN Prefix(es): 978-0-8147; 978-1-4798
Number of titles published annually: 125 Print
Total Titles: 2,000 Print
Distributor for Monthly Review Press; New Village Press
Returns: Ingram Publisher Services, 191 Edwards Dr, Jackson, TN 38301
Membership(s): Association of American Publishers (AAP); Association of University Presses (AUPresses)

Newbury Street Press
Imprint of New England Historic Genealogical Society
99-101 Newbury St, Boston, MA 02116
Tel: 617-226-1206 *Toll Free Tel:* 888-296-3447 (NEHGS membership) *Fax:* 617-536-7307
E-mail: thebookstore@nehgs.org
Web Site: www.americanancestors.org
Key Personnel
Pres & CEO: D Brenton Simons
EVP & COO: Ryan Woods *Tel:* 617-226-1205
  E-mail: rwoods@nehgs.org
VP, Advancement: Meghan Hallock *Tel:* 617-226-1218 *E-mail:* meghan.hallock@nehgs.org
Publg Dir: Sharon Inglis *Tel:* 617-226-1210
  E-mail: sharon.inglis@nehgs.org
Ed-in-Chief: Scott C Steward *Tel:* 617-226-1208
  E-mail: scott.steward@nehgs.org
Busn Mgr: Don Reagan *Tel:* 617-226-1281
  E-mail: don.reagan@nehgs.org
Founded: 1996
A special publications division of the New England Historic Genealogical Society which publishes compiled genealogies.
ISBN Prefix(es): 978-0-88082
Number of titles published annually: 20 Print; 5 E-Book
Total Titles: 150 Print; 5 E-Book

NewSouth Books
Imprint of University of Georgia Press
105 S Court St, Montgomery, AL 36104
Tel: 334-834-3556
E-mail: info@newsouthbooks.com
Web Site: www.newsouthbooks.com
Key Personnel
Co-Founder & Publr: Suzanne La Rosa
  E-mail: suzanne@newsouthbooks.com
Co-Founder & Ed-in-Chief: Randall Williams
Founded: 2000
Premier independent publisher based in the South. Books include literary fiction & nonfiction, with a special emphasis on books about the history & culture of the South. Selective acquisitions with the goal of publishing works that help develop understanding of racial, ethnic, religious & political identities.
ISBN Prefix(es): 978-1-58838; 978-1-60306
Number of titles published annually: 20 Print; 15 Online; 15 E-Book
Total Titles: 800 Print; 450 Online; 450 E-Book
Returns: Ingram Publisher Services, 191 Edwards Dr, Jackson, TN 38301 *Web Site:* www.ingrampublisherservices.com
Shipping Address: Ingram Publisher Services, 191 Edwards Dr, Jackson, TN 38301 *Web Site:* www.ingrampublisherservices.com
Warehouse: Ingram Publisher Services, 191 Edwards Dr, Jackson, TN 38301 *Web Site:* www.ingrampublisherservices.com
Distribution Center: Ingram Publisher Services (IPS), 14 Ingram Blvd, Mail Stop 631, La Vergne, TN 37086 *Web Site:* www.ingrampublisherservices.com
Membership(s): Southern Independent Booksellers Alliance (SIBA)

NFB Publishing
119 Dorchester Rd, Buffalo, NY 14213
Tel: 716-510-0520
E-mail: submissions@nfbpublishing.com
Web Site: www.nfbpublishing.com
Key Personnel
Founder: Mark Pogodzinski
Founded: 2009
Publishing new & engaging authors. Provides editorial services, interior & cover design, publicity & a chance to succeed. Accepting submissions in all genres, fiction, nonfiction, poetry, short stories, children's books.
ISBN Prefix(es): 978-0-9978317; 978-0-9984018
Number of titles published annually: 10 Print; 10 E-Book
Total Titles: 85 Print; 75 E-Book
Imprints: Amelia Press (children's books); NFB
Membership(s): Association of American Publishers (AAP); Better Business Bureau (BBB)

§**Nilgiri Press**
Division of Blue Mountain Center of Meditation
3600 Tomales Rd, Tomales, CA 94971
Mailing Address: PO Box 256, Tomales, CA 94971
Tel: 707-878-2369
E-mail: info@easwaran.org
Web Site: www.easwaran.org
Key Personnel
Press Coord: Debbie McMurray *E-mail:* debbie.mcmurray@nilgiripress.org
Intl Rts: Jennifer Jones *E-mail:* jennifer.jones@nilgiripress.org
Founded: 1972
Timeless wisdom for daily living books, videos, audios & online courses.
ISBN Prefix(es): 978-0-915132; 978-1-888314; 978-1-58638
Number of titles published annually: 3 Print; 10 E-Book; 10 Audio
Total Titles: 28 Print
Foreign Rep(s): Publishers Group West
Foreign Rights: Publishers Group West (Canada)

NIU Press, see Northern Illinois University Press

No Frills Buffalo, see NFB Publishing

§**No Starch Press**
245 Eighth St, San Francisco, CA 94103
Tel: 415-863-9900 *Toll Free Tel:* 800-420-7240 *Fax:* 415-863-9950
E-mail: info@nostarch.com; sales@nostarch.com; editors@nostarch.com; marketing@nostarch.com
Web Site: www.nostarch.com
Key Personnel
Founder: William Pollock
Assoc Dir, Sales & Mktg: Lauren Magee
Mng Ed: Jill Franklin
Mktg Mgr: Sarah De Vos
Founded: 1994
Carefully crafts the finest in geek entertainment. The growing list of award-winning No Starch Press best sellers covers topics like hacking, computer security, STEM, programming, science, LEGO & math. Our titles have personality, our authors are passionate & our books tackle topics that people care about.
ISBN Prefix(es): 978-1-886411; 978-1-59627
Number of titles published annually: 50 Print; 350 Online; 59 E-Book; 2 Audio
Total Titles: 350 Print; 350 E-Book
Distributed by Penguin Random House
Distribution Center: Penguin Random House Publisher Services (PRHPS), 400 Hahn Rd, Westminster, MD 21157
  E-mail: distribution@penguinrandomhouse.com
  Web Site: prhpublisherservices.com
Membership(s): Association of American Publishers (AAP); Independent Book Publishers Association (IBPA)

§**NOLO**
Subsidiary of Internet Brands Inc
909 N Pacific Coast Hwy, 11th fl, El Segundo, CA 90245
SAN: 206-7935
Web Site: www.nolo.com
Founded: 1971
Leading provider of plain-English legal & business books, software, online forms & information for consumers & businesses. Founded by 2 legal aid attorneys, Nolo products help you handle many legal matters yourself. All books are written in concise, conversational English

U.S. PUBLISHERS

by Nolo's team of lawyer editors & regularly revised & updated to comply with changes in the law & technology. With over 50 web properties, the Nolo Network is one of the Web's largest libraries of free consumer-friendly legal information. Nolo also offers a Lawyer Directory for consumers & small businesses that want to find a local lawyer to handle or consult on a particular legal problem.
This publisher has indicated that 100% of their product line is author subsidized.
ISBN Prefix(es): 978-0-87337; 978-1-41330
Number of titles published annually: 43 Print; 200 Online; 103 E-Book
Total Titles: 103 Print; 200 Online; 103 E-Book
Distribution Center: Ingram Content Group LLC, One Ingram Blvd, La Vergne, TN 37086 *E-mail:* ips@ingramcontent.com *Web Site:* www.ingramcontent.com
Membership(s): The American Library Association (ALA); Independent Book Publishers Association (IBPA)

Norilana Books
PO Box 209, Highgate Center, VT 05459-0209
SAN: 851-8556
E-mail: service@norilana.com
Web Site: www.norilana.com
Key Personnel
Owner & Publr: Vera Nazarian
Founded: 2006
Beautifully produced & packaged editions, primarily classics of world literature & quality originals.
ISBN Prefix(es): 978-1-934169; 978-1-934648; 978-1-60762
Number of titles published annually: 3 Print
Total Titles: 300 Print
Imprints: Curiosities; Leda; Spirit; The Sword of Norilana; TaLeKa; YA Angst

§North Atlantic Books (NAB)
Division of Society for the Study of Native Arts & Sciences
2526 Martin Luther King Jr Way, Berkeley, CA 94704
SAN: 203-1655
Tel: 510-549-4270
Web Site: www.northatlanticbooks.com
Key Personnel
Publr: Tim McKee *E-mail:* tmckee@northatlanticbooks.com
Sr Dir, Organizational Devt: Susan Bumps *E-mail:* sbumps@northatlanticbooks.com
Sr Dir, Fin: Alla Spector *E-mail:* aspector@northatlanticbooks.com
Edit Dir: Emily Boyd *E-mail:* eboyd@northatlanticbooks.com
Art Dir: Jasmine Hromjak *E-mail:* jhromjak@northatlanticbooks.com
Commus Dir: Bevin Donahue *E-mail:* bdonahue@northatlanticbooks.com
Assoc Dir, Rights: Sarah Serafimidis *E-mail:* sserafimidis@northatlanticbooks.com
Assoc Dir, Acqs: Shayna Keyles *E-mail:* skeyles@northatlanticbooks.com
Assoc Dir, Publicity: Julia Sadowski *E-mail:* jsadowski@northatlanticbooks.com
Assoc Dir, Sales & Dist: Drew Cavanaugh *E-mail:* dcavanaugh@northatlanticbooks.com
Founded: 1974
North Atlantic Books has been located in Berkeley, California since 1977. Over this period, North Atlantic has become a leading publisher of alternative health, nutrition, bodywork, martial arts & spiritual titles.
ISBN Prefix(es): 978-1-883319; 978-0-913028; 978-0-938190; 978-1-55643; 978-1-58394 (Frog Ltd Books); 978-0-942941
Number of titles published annually: 50 Print; 50 E-Book; 10 Audio
Total Titles: 1,000 Print; 600 E-Book; 10 Audio

Imprints: Blue Snake Books; Evolver Editions; Frog Books
Distributor for DharmaCafe; Energy Arts; Ergos Institute; Heaven & Earth Publishing LLC; New Pacific Press
Foreign Rep(s): Faradawn (South Africa); Penguin Random House Canada (Canada); Penguin Random House LLC International Sales Div (worldwide); Publishers Group UK (UK)
Orders to: Penguin Random House Publisher Services (PRHPS), 400 Hahn Rd, Westminster, MD 21157 (bookstore orders) *Toll Free Tel:* 800-733-3000 *Toll Free Fax:* 800-659-2436 *E-mail:* customerservice@penguinrandomhouse.com *Web Site:* prhpublisherservices.com
Returns: Penguin Random House Returns Dept, 1019 N State Rd 47, Crawfordsville, IN 47933
Distribution Center: Penguin Random House Publisher Services (PRHPS), 400 Hahn Rd, Westminster, MD 21157 *Web Site:* prhpublisherservices.com
Membership(s): Book Promotion Forum

North Carolina Office of Archives & History
Historical Publications Branch, 4622 Mail Service Ctr, Raleigh, NC 27699-4622
Tel: 919-733-7442
E-mail: historical.publications@ncdcr.gov
Web Site: www.dncr.nc.gov/about-us/office-archives-and-history
Founded: 1903
State government agency that publishes nonfiction hardcover & trade paperback books relating to North Carolina as well as the *North Carolina Historical Review*, a quarterly scholarly journal of history.
ISBN Prefix(es): 978-0-86526
Number of titles published annually: 8 Print
Total Titles: 160 Print
Distribution Center: University of North Carolina Press, c/o Longleaf Services, 116 S Boundary St, Chapel Hill, NC 27514-3808 *Toll Free Tel:* 800-848-6224 *Toll Free Fax:* 800-272-6817 *E-mail:* orders@longleafservices.org *Web Site:* www.longleafservices.org

North Country Press
126 Main St, Unity, ME 04988
SAN: 247-9680
Tel: 207-948-2208
E-mail: info@northcountrypress.com
Web Site: www.northcountrypress.com
Key Personnel
Publr: Patricia Newell
Founded: 1977
Regional press dealing with New England subjects (specialize in Maine). Three lines: outdoor (hunting, fishing, etc); humor, lore; literature (mysteries, essays, poetry).
ISBN Prefix(es): 978-0-945980; 978-1-943424
Number of titles published annually: 9 Print
Total Titles: 75 Print

North Point Press
Imprint of Farrar, Straus & Giroux, LLC
120 Broadway, New York, NY 10271
Tel: 212-741-6900
E-mail: sales@fsgbooks.com
Web Site: us.macmillan.com/fsg
Key Personnel
SVP & Dir, Publicity, FSG: Sarita Varma *Tel:* 917-940-2542 *E-mail:* sarita.varma@fsgbooks.com
VP & Contracts Dir, FSG: Erika Seidman
Founded: 1981
Nonfiction, environment, nature, design, food, spirituality, travel, ecology, music & cultural criticism.
ISBN Prefix(es): 978-0-86547
Number of titles published annually: 10 Print
Foreign Rep(s): Raincoast Books (Canada)

Foreign Rights: ANA Baltic (Tatjana Zoldnere) (Estonia, Latvia, Lithuania); AnatoliaLit Agency (Amy Spangler & Eda Caca) (Turkey); Anthea Agency (Katalina Sabeva) (Bulgaria); Bardon-Chinese Media Agency (David Tsai) (China, Taiwan); Anoukh Foerg Agency (Germany); Deborah Harris Agency (Geula Geurts) (Israel); International Copyright Agency (Simon Kessler & Marina Adriana) (Romania); The Italian Literary Agency srl (Claire Sabatie-Garat) (Italy); Anna Jarota Agency (Dominika Bojanowska) (Poland); Anna Jarota Agency Poland (Zuzanna Brzezinska) (Russia); Katai & Bolza (Peter Bolza) (Hungary); Korea Copyright Center Inc (KCC) (Joeun Lee) (South Korea); Marotte et Compagnie Agence Litteraire (Corinne Marotte) (France); Maxima Creative Agency (Santo Manurung) (Indonesia); MB Agencia Literaria (Monica Martin & Ines Planells) (Portugal, Spain); Kristin Olson Literary Agency sro (Czechia, Slovakia); Plima Literary Agency (Vuk Perisic) (Albania, Croatia, Serbia, Slovenia); Read n Right Agency (Nike Davarinou) (Greece); Riff Agency (Laura & Joao Paulo Riff) (Brazil); Sebes & Bisseling Literary Agency (Paul Sebes) (Netherlands); Tuttle-Mori Agency Inc (Asako Kawachi) (Japan)
Warehouse: MPS Distribution Center, 16365 James Madison Hwy, Gordonsville, VA 22942 *Toll Free Tel:* 888-330-8477 *E-mail:* orders@mpsvirginia.com *Web Site:* us.macmillan.com/mps

North River Press Publishing Corp
27 Rosseter St, Great Barrington, MA 01230
SAN: 202-1048
Mailing Address: PO Box 567, Great Barrington, MA 01230-0567
Tel: 413-528-0034 *Toll Free Tel:* 800-486-2665 *Fax:* 413-528-3163 *Toll Free Fax:* 800-BOOK-FAX (266-5329)
E-mail: info@northriverpress.com
Web Site: www.northriverpress.com
Key Personnel
Pres: Amy Gallagher
Founded: 1971
General nonfiction, business books, hardcovers & paperback.
ISBN Prefix(es): 978-0-88427
Number of titles published annually: 6 Print; 6 E-Book
Total Titles: 40 Print; 40 E-Book; 20 Audio

North Star Editions Inc
2297 Waters Dr, Mendota Heights, MN 55120
SAN: 990-2325
Toll Free Tel: 888-417-0195 *Fax:* 952-582-1000
E-mail: sales@northstareditions.com; publicity@northstareditions.com
Web Site: www.northstareditions.com
Key Personnel
Sales Mgr: Sam Temple
Founded: 2016
ISBN Prefix(es): 978-0-7387; 978-0-9848801; 978-0-9886491; 978-1-939967; 978-1-63163; 978-1-63517; 978-1-63583
Number of titles published annually: 125 Print; 125 E-Book; 4 Audio
Total Titles: 222 Print; 240 E-Book; 4 Audio
Imprints: Flux; Focus Readers (juvenile nonfiction); Jolly Fish Press (middle grade fiction); Little Blue Readers (guided reading levels PreK-1); North Star Classroom (paperback K-8 titles); Press Box Books (sports)
Foreign Rights: DropCap Rights Agency (Allison Olson)
Returns: c/o Corporate Graphics, 150 Kingswood Dr, Mankato, MN 56001

North Star Press of Saint Cloud Inc
19485 Estes Rd, Clearwater, MN 55320

Tel: 320-558-9062
E-mail: info@northstarpress.com
Web Site: www.northstarpress.com
Key Personnel
Owner, Book Designer, Graphic Designer & Ed: Liz Dwyer
Ed & Busn Mgr: Curtis Weinrich
Founded: 1969
Regional, Minnesota history & fiction, general fiction, poetry.
ISBN Prefix(es): 978-0-87839; 978-1-68201
Number of titles published annually: 15 Print; 15 E-Book
Total Titles: 1,000 Print; 150 E-Book
Membership(s): Midwest Independent Publishing Association (MIPA); Minnesota Library Association (MLA)

Northern Illinois University Press
Imprint of Cornell University Press
Sage House, 512 E State St, Ithaca, NY 14850
SAN: 202-8875
Tel: 607-253-2338
Web Site: cornellpress.cornell.edu/imprints/northern-illinois-university-press
Key Personnel
Sr Acqs Ed: Amy Farranto *E-mail:* afarranto@niu.edu
Founded: 1965
Publishes scholarly & trade books on a variety of topics in the humanities & social sciences. In fulfilling its educational mission, the Press publishes books for both specialists & general readers.
ISBN Prefix(es): 978-0-87580; 978-1-60909
Number of titles published annually: 25 Print
Total Titles: 600 Print
Distribution Center: Longleaf Services Inc, 116 S Boundary St, Chapel Hill, NC 27514-3808 (US) *Tel:* 919-966-7449 *Toll Free Tel:* 800-848-6224 *Fax:* 919-962-2704 *Toll Free Fax:* 800-272-6817 *E-mail:* orders@longleafservices.org *Web Site:* longleafservices.org
Membership(s): American Association for the Advancement of Slavic Studies (AAASS); American Association of University Presses (AAUP); American Historical Association; Organization of American Historians (OAH)

Northwestern University Press
629 Noyes St, Evanston, IL 60208-4210
SAN: 202-5787
Tel: 847-491-2046 *Toll Free Tel:* 800-621-2736 (orders only) *Fax:* 847-491-8150
E-mail: nupress@northwestern.edu
Web Site: www.nupress.northwestern.edu
Key Personnel
Dir: Parneshia Jones *E-mail:* p-jones3@northwestern.edu
Mng Ed: Anne Gendler *Tel:* 847-491-3844 *E-mail:* a-gendler@northwestern.edu
Sr Acqs Ed, Scholarly: Faith Wilson Stein *E-mail:* faith.stein@northwestern.edu
Sr Acqs Ed, Trade: Marisa Siegel *E-mail:* marisa.siegel@northwestern.edu
Acqs Ed: Trevor Perri *E-mail:* trevor.perri@northwestern.edu
Prodn Mgr: Morris (Dino) Robinson *Tel:* 847-467-3392 *E-mail:* morris-robinson@northwestern.edu
Acqs Coord: Patrick Samuel *E-mail:* patrick.samuel2@northwestern.edu
Digital Content & Systems Coord: Emily Dalton *Tel:* 847-476-2434 *E-mail:* emily.dalton@northwestern.edu; Kirsten Markusic *E-mail:* kirsten.markusic@northwestern.edu
Busn Analyst: Amy Schultz *Tel:* 847-491-8310 *E-mail:* amy.schultz@northwestern.edu
Intellectual Property Specialist: Liz Hamilton *Tel:* 847-491-2458 *E-mail:* emhamilton@northwestern.edu
Founded: 1958

Part of Northwestern University, the Press publishes mostly scholarly books, with an emphasis on literature & language, philosophy, works in translation & theater, as well as trade books in the areas of fiction, poetry & play scripts.
ISBN Prefix(es): 978-0-8101
Number of titles published annually: 65 Print
Imprints: Curbstone Books; TriQuarterly Books (contemporary American fiction & poetry)
Distributor for Lake Forest College Press (Chicago area studies); Tia Chucha Press
Orders to: Chicago Distribution Center, 11030 S Langley, Chicago, IL 60628 *Toll Free Tel:* 800-621-2736 *Toll Free Fax:* 800-621-8476
Distribution Center: Chicago Distribution Center, 11030 S Langley, Chicago, IL 60628 *Toll Free Tel:* 800-621-2736 *Toll Free Fax:* 800-621-8476
Membership(s): Association of University Presses (AUPresses)
See separate listing for:
TriQuarterly Books

§W W Norton & Company Inc
500 Fifth Ave, New York, NY 10110-0017
SAN: 202-5795
Tel: 212-354-5500 *Toll Free Tel:* 800-233-4830 (orders & cust serv) *Fax:* 212-869-0856
Toll Free Fax: 800-458-6515
E-mail: orders@wwnorton.com
Web Site: wwnorton.com
Key Personnel
Chmn & Pres: Julia A Reidhead
VChmn: Roby Harrington
VChmn & Publg Dir: Jeannie Luciano
COO: Jorie Krumpfer
Chief Communs Offr: Louise Brockett
CFO: Stephen King
VP & Exec Art Dir: Ingsu Liu
VP & Sr Publicity Dir: Elizabeth Riley
VP & Sr Publicity Dir, Liveright: Peter Miller
VP & Dir, Coll Dept: Michael Wright
VP & Dir, Intl Sales: Dorothy M Cook
VP & Dir, Mktg: Meredith McGinnis
VP & Dir, Prof Books Div: Deborah A Malmud
VP & Dir, Subs Rts: Elisabeth Kerr
VP & Dir, Trade Prodn: Julia Druskin
VP & Edit Dir, Digital Media: Karl Bakeman
VP & Exec Ed: John Glusman; Alane Mason; Tom Mayer
VP & Exec Ed, Liveright: Robert Weil
VP & Exec Ed, Trade Dept: Jill Bialosky
VP & Mng Ed: Nancy K Palmquist
VP & Sr Ed: Amy Cherry; Matt Weiland
VP & Ed: Jon Durbin; Erik Fahlgren; Sheri Snavely; Betsy Twitchell
VP & Ed, Digital Media: Steve Hoge
VP & Music Ed: Maribeth Payne
VP & Sr Proj Mgr: April Lange
VP & HR Mgr: Jamie Finkelman
VP, Opers: Nomi Victor
VP, Prodn: Tim McGuire
VP, Spec Accts: Rick Raeber
Sr Publicity Dir: Erin Sinesky Lovett; Rachel Salzman
Dir, Coll Dept: Stephen P Dunn
Dir, Mktg & Publicity: Kevin Olsen
Dir, Norton Trade Group: Brendan Curry
Dir, Trade Sales: Steven Pace
Publg Dir, Norton Young Readers: Simon Boughton
Sales Dir, Client Publg: George Tattersfield
Ed-in-Chief: Dan Gerstle
Ed-in-Chief, Liveright: Peter J Simon
Exec Ed: Melanie Tortoroli
Sr Ed: Maria Goldverg
Sr Ed, Liveright: Katie Henderson Adams; Gina Iaquinta
Sr Ed, Norton Trade: Merry Sun; Jessica Yao
Ed: Marilyn Moller; Jack Repcheck
Assoc Ed: Nneoma Amadi-obi; Mo Crist
Sr Publicist: Kyle Radler
Sr Publicist, Liveright: Fanta Diallo
Publicist: Gina Savoy

Assoc Publicist: Gabrielle Nugent
Assoc Publicist, Liveright: Clio Hamilton
Founded: 1923
General nonfiction & fiction; trade paperbacks; college texts, professional books, architecture & interior design.
No unsol mss accepted.
ISBN Prefix(es): 978-0-393; 978-0-87140 (Liveright & Co); 978-1-324
Number of titles published annually: 400 Print; 110 E-Book
Total Titles: 4,800 Print; 75 CD-ROM; 600 E-Book
Imprints: Liveright; Norton Young Readers
Divisions: The Countryman Press
Foreign Office(s): W W Norton & Company Ltd, 15 Carlisle St, London W1D 3BS, United Kingdom *Tel:* (020) 7323 1579 *E-mail:* academic@wwnorton.co.uk *Web Site:* www.wwnorton.co.uk
Distributor for Abbeville Press; Akashic Books; Albatross; Blue Guides; George Braziller Inc; The Experiment; Fantagraphics Books; Harvard University Press; Kales Press; Mysterious Press; New Directions Publishing Corp; Penzler; Persea Books; Pushcart Press; Thames & Hudson; Tilbury House Publishers; Tin House Books; Well-Trained Mind Press; Yale University Press
Foreign Rep(s): Everest International Publishing Services (Wei Zhao) (China); Hardy Bigfoss International Co Ltd (Cambodia, Laos, Myanmar, Thailand, Vietnam); B K Norton Ltd (South Korea, Taiwan); W W Norton & Company Ltd (UK) (Africa, Europe, India, Ireland, Middle East, UK); Pansing Distribution Pte Ltd (Brunei, Malaysia, Singapore); Penguin Random House Canada (Canada); Rockbook (Gilles Fauveau) (Japan); Transglobal Publishers Services Ltd (Hong Kong, Macau); US PubRep Inc (Caribbean, Central America, Mexico, South America); John Wiley & Sons Australia Ltd (Australia, New Zealand)
Foreign Rights: Akcali Copyright Agency (Turkey); Bardon-Chinese Media Agency (China, Taiwan); Casanovas & Lynch (Portugal, Spain); Graal Literary Agency (Poland); The Deborah Harris Agency (Israel); International Copyright Agency (Romania); Japan UNI Agency (Japan); Katai & Bolza (Hungary); Duran Kim Agency (South Korea); Mohrbooks AG Literary Agency (Germany); Nordin Agency (Scandinavia); Andrew Nurnberg Associates (Baltic States, Bulgaria, Russia); Kristin Olson Literary Agency sro (Czechia); The Riff Agency (Brazil); Roberto Santachiara Literary Agency (Italy); Marianne Schoenbach Literary Agency BV (Netherlands)
Advertising Agency: Verso Advertising
Shipping Address: National Book Co Inc, Keystone Industrial Park, Scranton, PA 18512
See separate listing for:
Countryman Press

Norwood House Press
Imprint of The Rosen Publishing Group Inc
PO Box 1306, Fairport, NY 14450
Tel: 773-467-0837 *Toll Free Tel:* 866-565-2900 *Fax:* 773-467-9686 *Toll Free Fax:* 866-565-2901
E-mail: customerservice@norwoodhousepress.com
Web Site: www.norwoodhousepress.com
Founded: 2005
Specialize in children's books for the school & library.
ISBN Prefix(es): 978-1-59953; 978-1-60357; 978-1-68404; 978-1-68450
Number of titles published annually: 100 Print; 100 E-Book; 25 Audio
Total Titles: 1,000 Print; 500 E-Book
Warehouse: Corporate Graphics, 150 Kingswood Dr, Mankato, MN 56001

U.S. PUBLISHERS

§Nosy Crow Inc
Subsidiary of Nosy Crow Ltd (UK)
145 Lincoln Rd, Lincoln, MA 01773
E-mail: nosycrowinc@nosycrow.com; salesinfo@nosycrow.com; export@nosycrow.com (export sales); rights@nosycrow.com
Web Site: nosycrow.us
Key Personnel
Pres: John Mendelson
Ed: Jennifer B Greene; Allison Hunter Hill
Mktg Mgr: Ally Russell
Assoc Mktg Mgr: Avery Cook
Founded: 2022
Independent publisher of child-focused, parent-friendly books. Nosy Crow aims to create books that inspire children to read for pleasure, ultimately to become lifelong readers. We publish high-quality, commercial fiction & non-fiction books for children ages 0-12 by well-known authors & illustrators as well as new talent. All Nosy Crow picture & board books come with a free digital audio version using an innovation we've called Stories Aloud. Books with this amazing extra include a free audio reading, complete with sound effects & original music, accessible via a QR code on the back or inside cover.
ISBN Prefix(es): 979-8-88777
Number of titles published annually: 62 Print
Total Titles: 95 Print
Foreign Office(s): Nosy Crow Ltd, Wheat Wharf, 27a Shad Thames, London SE1 2XZ, United Kingdom *Tel:* (020) 7089 7575 *E-mail:* hello@nosycrow.com
Distribution Center: Hachette Book Group, Attn: Order Dept, 185 N Mount Zion Rd, Lebanon, IN 46052 *Toll Free Tel:* 800-759-0190 *Toll Free Fax:* 800-286-9471 *E-mail:* orders@hbgusa.com
Membership(s): The Children's Book Council (CBC); Educational Book & Media Association (EBMA); Independent Book Publishers Association (IBPA); New England Independent Booksellers Association (NEIBA)

§Nova Press
PO Box 692023, West Hollywood, CA 90069
Tel: 310-601-8551
E-mail: novapress@aol.com
Web Site: www.novapress.net
Key Personnel
Pres & Electronic Publg: Jeff Kolby
Founded: 1993
Publishes test prep books, software, phone apps & online courses for the SAT, ACT, GRE, LSAT, GMAT, MCAT & TOEFL.
ISBN Prefix(es): 978-1-889057; 978-1-944595
Number of titles published annually: 6 Print; 6 Online
Total Titles: 40 Print; 6 CD-ROM; 40 Online; 40 E-Book

Nova Science Publishers Inc
400 Oser Ave, Suite 1600, Hauppauge, NY 11788-3619
Tel: 631-231-7269 *Fax:* 631-231-8175
E-mail: nova.main@novapublishers.com
Web Site: www.novapublishers.com
Key Personnel
Pres: Nadya Columbus
Founded: 1985
Scientific, technical, medical & social sciences publishing. Trade books, hardcover & softcover.
ISBN Prefix(es): 978-0-941743; 978-1-56072; 978-1-59033; 978-1-59454; 978-1-60021; 978-1-60456; 978-1-60692; 978-1-60741; 978-1-60876; 978-1-61668; 978-1-61728; 978-1-61761; 978-1-61122; 978-1-61209; 978-1-61324; 978-1-61470; 978-1-62100; 978-1-61942; 978-1-62081; 978-1-62257; 978-1-62417; 978-1-62618; 978-1-62808; 978-1-62948; 978-1-63117; 978-1-63321; 978-1-63463; 978-1-63482; 978-1-63483; 978-1-63484; 978-1-63485; 978-1-5361
Number of titles published annually: 2,000 Print; 10 CD-ROM
Total Titles: 25,000 Print
Imprints: Kroshka Publications; Noel; Nova Biomedical Publications; Nova Business & Management Publications; Nova ESL Publications; Nova Global Affairs Publications; Nova History Publications; Nova Music Publications; Nova Publications; Nova Video Productions; Novinka Publications; Snova; Troitsa Publications

NRCYS, see National Resource Center for Youth Services

NRP Direct
220 College Ave, Suite 618, Athens, GA 30601-9801
Tel: 908-517-0780 *Toll Free Tel:* 844-592-4197
E-mail: info@nrpdirect.com
Web Site: www.nrpdirect.com
Key Personnel
Ad & Gen Sales: April Tann *Tel:* 908-517-5939 *E-mail:* atann@nrpdirect.com
Edit: Eileen Fanning *Tel:* 908-517-1057 ext 408 *E-mail:* efanning@nrpdirect.com
Founded: 1915
Publisher of business information directories available in print, online & mailing list for commercial & reference use.
ISBN Prefix(es): 978-0-87217
Number of titles published annually: 5 Print
Total Titles: 5 Print; 1 Online

Nursesbooks.org, The Publishing Program of ANA
Division of American Nurses Association
8515 Georgia Ave, Suite 400, Silver Spring, MD 20910-3492
SAN: 851-3481
Tel: 301-628-5000 *Toll Free Tel:* 800-274-4262; 800-637-0323 (orders) *Fax:* 301-628-5342
E-mail: anp@ana.org
Web Site: www.Nursesbooks.org; www.NursingWorld.org
Key Personnel
Publr: Joe Vallina *Tel:* 301-628-5118 *E-mail:* joseph.vallina@ana.org
Ed & Proj Mgr: Erin Walpole *E-mail:* erin.walpole@ana.org
Sr Mktg Specialist: Novella Green *Tel:* 301-628-5072 *E-mail:* novella.green@ana.org
Publishes books on ANA core issues & programs, including ethics, leadership, quality, specialty practice, advanced practice & the profession's enduring legacy. Best known for the foundational documents of the profession on nursing ethics, scope & standards of practice & social policy, Nursesbooks.org is the publisher for the professional, career-oriented nurse, reaching & serving nurse educators, administrators, managers & researchers as well as staff nurses in the course of their professional development.
ISBN Prefix(es): 978-1-55810
Number of titles published annually: 14 Print; 10 E-Book
Total Titles: 95 Print; 60 E-Book
Imprints: ANCC Magnet Recognition Program; Nursing Knowledge Center
Sales Office(s): American Nurses Association (ebook site license sales), Busn Opers Specialist, Publg: Tony Ward *Tel:* 301-628-5194 *E-mail:* tony.ward@ana.org
ANA Nursing Knowledge Center (pubn sales integrated with other prods & servs), Specialist, Prod Sales & Servs: Mary Louise Cobb *Tel:* 301-628-5274 *E-mail:* marylouise.cobb@ana.org
Distribution Center: PBD Worldwide Inc, 1650 Bluegrass Lakes Pkwy, Alpharetta, GA 30004, Acct Coord: Lisa Johansen *Tel:* 770-280-0105 *E-mail:* lisa.johansen@pbd.com *Web Site:* www.pbd.com
Membership(s): AM&P Network

NYBG Press, see The New York Botanical Garden Press

§Nystrom Education
Division of Social Studies School Service
PO Box 802, Culver City, CA 90232
Tel: 310-839-2436 *Toll Free Tel:* 800-421-4246 *Fax:* 310-839-2249 *Toll Free Fax:* 800-944-5432
E-mail: access@socialstudies.com; customerservice@socialstudies.com
Web Site: www.socialstudies.com
Key Personnel
Natl Sales Dir: Jennifer Carlson *E-mail:* jcarlson@socialstudies.com
Founded: 1903
Social studies, history & geography programs, maps, globes, atlases & multimedia.
ISBN Prefix(es): 978-0-7825; 978-0-88463
Number of titles published annually: 3 Print
Total Titles: 50 Print; 5 CD-ROM; 1 E-Book

NYU Press, see New York University Press

§OAG Worldwide
801 Warrenville Rd, Suite 555, Lisle, IL 60532
Tel: 630-515-5300 *Toll Free Tel:* 800-342-5624 (cust serv)
E-mail: contactus@oag.com
Web Site: www.oag.com
Key Personnel
CEO: Phil Callow
CFO: Matt Plose
Founded: 1929
Supplier of independent travel info.
ISBN Prefix(es): 978-0-9776295
Number of titles published annually: 7 Print; 5 CD-ROM; 5 Online
Total Titles: 11 Print; 5 CD-ROM; 5 Online
Branch Office(s)
9130 S Dadeland Blvd, Suite 1620, Miami, FL 33156
55 Chapel St, Suite 103, Newton, MA 02458
Foreign Office(s): No 3710B Jingguang Bldg, Hujialou, Chaoyang District, Beijing 100020, China *Tel:* 5095 5965 *Fax:* 5095 5961
701 Cross Office, 1-18-6 Nishi Shinbashi, Minato-ku, Tokyo 105-0003, Japan *Tel:* 36402 7301 *Fax:* 36402 7306 *E-mail:* acustsvcjpn@oag.com
6 Shenton Way, OUE Downtown 2, No 24-08A, Singapore 068809, Singapore *Tel:* 6395-5888 *Fax:* 6395-5866
One Capability Green, Luton, Beds LU1 3LU, United Kingdom (headquarters) *Tel:* (01582) 695050 *Fax:* (01582) 695230 *E-mail:* customers@oag.com

Oak Knoll Press
310 Delaware St, New Castle, DE 19720
Tel: 302-328-7232 *Fax:* 302-328-7274
E-mail: oakknoll@oakknoll.com; orders@oakknoll.com; publishing@oakknoll.com
Web Site: www.oakknoll.com
Key Personnel
Pres, Owner & Antiquarian Dir: Robert Fleck, III *E-mail:* rob@oakknoll.com
Generalist: Erin Evans *E-mail:* erin@oakknoll.com
Founded: 1978
Publish scholarly books (books about books), bibliographies, book arts & book history.
ISBN Prefix(es): 978-1-884718; 978-1-58456; 978-1-872116; 978-0-938768; 978-0-91661
Number of titles published annually: 25 Print
Total Titles: 1,100 Print; 1 CD-ROM
Distributor for AdVenture SA; American Antiquarian Society; Bibliographical Society of

America; Bibliographical Society of University of Virginia; The Bibliographical Society (UK); Block Museum; Boston College; John Carter Brown Library; Bryn Mawr College; Catalpa Press; Caxton Club; Center for Book Arts; Chapin Library; Club of Odd Volumes; Codex Foundation; Cotsen Children's Library (Princeton); Editions Koch; Fondation Custodia; The Grolier Club; Historic New Orleans Collection; Huntington Library; Library of Congress-Center for the Book; The Manuscript Society; New England Bibliographies; Providence Athenaeum; Rivendale Press; Scripps College Press; Tate Galleries; Texas State Historical Association; Typophiles; University of Pennsylvania Libraries; Winterthur Museum; Yushodo Press
Membership(s): Antiquarian Booksellers Association of America (ABAA); Association of American Publishers (AAP); International League of Antiquarian Booksellers (ILAB)

§The Oaklea Press Inc
41 Old Mill Rd, Richmond, VA 23226-3111
Tel: 804-218-2394
Web Site: oakleapress.com
Key Personnel
Publr: Stephen Hawley Martin
Founded: 1995
Trade book publisher. Fees charged for ghostwriting & proofing. Send message via web site.
ISBN Prefix(es): 978-1-892538; 978-1-892538; 978-1-892538
Number of titles published annually: 12 Print; 12 E-Book; 6 Audio
Total Titles: 180 Print; 12 E-Book; 6 Audio
Membership(s): Independent Book Publishers Association (IBPA)

Ocean Tree Books
1325 Cerro Gordo Rd, Santa Fe, NM 87501
Mailing Address: PO Box 1295, Santa Fe, NM 87504 SAN: 241-0478
Tel: 505-983-1412 *Fax:* 505-983-0899
E-mail: richard@oceantree.com
Web Site: www.oceantree.com
Key Personnel
Dir: Richard Polese
Publicity & Mktg: Hudson White
Off Mgr: Martin Burch
Founded: 1983
General trade with emphasis on southwestern & southern travel, faith & spirit & peacemaking.
ISBN Prefix(es): 978-0-943734; 978-0-9712548
Number of titles published annually: 4 Print
Total Titles: 30 Print
Imprints: Adventure Roads Travel; OTB Legacy Editions; Peacewatch Editions
Distributed by Treasure Chest Books
Foreign Rep(s): Blessingway Author Services (worldwide)
Foreign Rights: Blessingway Author Services
Distribution Center: Baker & Taylor
Books West LLC
New Leaf Distributing Co
Membership(s): Independent Book Publishers Association (IBPA); New Mexico Book Association; Publishers Association of the West (PubWest)

Oceanview Publishing Inc
PO Box 3168, Sarasota, FL 34230
Tel: 941-387-8500
Web Site: oceanviewpub.com
Key Personnel
Dir, Mktg & Publicity: Faith Matson
 E-mail: faithm@oceanviewpub.com
Publg Mgr: Lee Randall *E-mail:* leer@oceanviewpub.com
Founded: 2006
ISBN Prefix(es): 978-1-933515; 978-1-60809
Number of titles published annually: 13 Print

Total Titles: 52 Print
Distribution Center: Independent Publishers Group (IPG), 814 N Chicago, IL 60610 *Tel:* 312-337-0747 *Toll Free Tel:* 800-888-4741 *Fax:* 312-337-5985 *E-mail:* orders@ipgbook.com *Web Site:* www.ipgbook.com
Membership(s): International Thriller Writers Inc (ITW); Mystery Writers of America (MWA)

§OCP
340 Oswego Pointe Dr, Lake Oswego, OR 97034
Tel: 503-281-1191 *Toll Free Tel:* 800-LITURGY (548-8749) *Fax:* 503-282-3486
Toll Free Fax: 800-843-8181
E-mail: liturgy@ocp.org
Web Site: www.ocp.org
Key Personnel
Chief Prod Offr: Jim Wasko
Publr: Wade Wisler
Cust Serv Mgr: Jessie Mason
Founded: 1922
Books of music & liturgy.
ISBN Prefix(es): 978-0-915531; 978-0-9602378; 978-0-912405; 978-1-56929; 978-0-915903; 978-1-57992
Number of titles published annually: 25 Print; 25 Audio
Total Titles: 500 Print; 1 CD-ROM; 1 Online; 2,500 Audio
Imprints: Pastoral Press
Foreign Rights: Decani Music; Rainbow Book Agencies (Australia); Universal Songs Ltd (Europe, Ireland, UK)
Membership(s): Church Music Publishers Association (CMPA)

§Octane Press
1211 W Sixth St, Suite 600-144, Austin, TX 78703
Tel: 512-334-9441; 512-761-4555 (sales)
E-mail: info@octanepress.com; sales@octanepress.com
Web Site: octanepress.com/content/submissions
Key Personnel
Founder & Publr: Lee Klancher *Tel:* 512-430-1940 *E-mail:* lee@octanepress.com
Founded: 2010
Niche book publisher.
ISBN Prefix(es): 978-0-9821733; 978-0-9829131; 978-1-937747; 978-1-64234
Number of titles published annually: 10 Print; 5 E-Book; 1 Audio
Total Titles: 200 Print; 100 E-Book
Foreign Rep(s): Publishers Group UK (Continental Europe)
Returns: WarePak, Attn: Octane Press Returns, 2427 Bond St, University Park, IL 60484
Shipping Address: WarePak, 2427 Bond St, University Park, IL 60484
Warehouse: WarePak, 2427 Bond St, University Park, IL 60484
Membership(s): Independent Book Publishers Association (IBPA)

Odyssey Books
Division of The Ciletti Publishing Group Inc
2421 Redwood Ct, Longmont, CO 80503-8155
Tel: 720-494-1473 *Fax:* 720-494-1471
E-mail: books@odysseybooks.net
Key Personnel
Pres & Publr: Barbara Ciletti
Promo: Erin Jones
Founded: 1995
Provides fiction & nonfiction for the retail trade, library, education & consumer markets.
ISBN Prefix(es): 978-0-9768655
Number of titles published annually: 20 Print
Membership(s): American Booksellers Association (ABA); The American Library Association (ALA); CMN; Independent Book Publishers Association (IBPA); International Literacy Association (ILA); National Council of Teachers of English (NCTE); National Science Teachers Association (NSTA)

§OECD Washington Center
Division of Organization for Economic Cooperation & Development (France)
1776 "I" St NW, Suite 450, Washington, DC 20006
Tel: 202-785-6323 *Toll Free Tel:* 800-456-6323 (dist ctr/pubns orders) *Fax:* 202-785-0350
E-mail: washington.contact@oecd.org; oecdilibrary@oecd.org (sales)
Web Site: www.oecd-ilibrary.org
Key Personnel
Sales & Mktg Mgr: Iain Williamson *Tel:* 202-822-3870 *E-mail:* iain.williamson@oecd.org
Founded: 1961
Periodicals, books, online services & statistical data.
ISBN Prefix(es): 978-92-64; 978-92-821; 978-92-65; 978-0-9501741
Number of titles published annually: 450 Online; 450 E-Book
Total Titles: 15,600 Online; 15,600 E-Book
Foreign Office(s): 2 rue Andre-Pascal, 75775 Paris Cedex 16, France *Tel:* 01 45 24 82 00 *Fax:* 01 45 24 85 00
Distributor for International Energy Agency; International Transportation Forum; Nuclear Energy Agency

Ohio Genealogical Society
611 State Rte 97 W, Bellville, OH 44813-8813
Tel: 419-886-1903
E-mail: ogs@ogs.org
Web Site: www.ogs.org
Key Personnel
Pres: Dorothea Martin *E-mail:* president@ogs.org
Exec Dir: Noel Poirier *E-mail:* npoirier@ogs.org
Founded: 1959
Family history library & society.
ISBN Prefix(es): 978-0-935057
Number of titles published annually: 3 Print
Total Titles: 25 Print

The Ohio State University Press
180 Pressey Hall, 1070 Carmack Rd, Columbus, OH 43210-1002
Tel: 614-292-6930 *Fax:* 614-292-2065
Toll Free Fax: 800-621-8476
E-mail: OSUPInfo@osu.edu
Web Site: ohiostatepress.org
Key Personnel
Dir: Tony Sanfilippo *Tel:* 614-292-7818
 E-mail: sanfilippo.16@osu.edu
Edit Dir: Kristen Elias Rowley *Tel:* 614-292-8256
 E-mail: eliasrowley.1@osu.edu
Asst Dir, Mng Ed & Acqs Ed: Tara Cyphers
 Tel: 614-292-6198 *E-mail:* cyphers.3@osu.edu
Publicist & Mktg Mgr: Samara Rafert *Tel:* 614-292-4713 *E-mail:* rafert.1@osu.edu
Founded: 1957
General scholarly & trade nonfiction & fiction; classics.
ISBN Prefix(es): 978-0-8142
Number of titles published annually: 40 Print
Total Titles: 300 Print
Imprints: Mad Creek Books; Trillium
Distribution Center: University of Chicago Distribution Center, 11030 S Langley Ave, Chicago, IL 60628 *Tel:* 773-568-1550 *Toll Free Tel:* 800-621-2736 *Fax:* 773-702-7212 *E-mail:* custserv@press.uchicago.edu *Web Site:* press.uchicago.edu

Ohio University Press
Alden Library, Suite 101, 30 Park Place, Athens, OH 45701-2909
Tel: 740-593-1154
Web Site: www.ohioswallow.com

U.S. PUBLISHERS

Key Personnel
Dir & Prodn Mgr: Beth Pratt *Tel:* 740-593-1162
  E-mail: prattb@ohio.edu
Mng Ed: Tyler Balli *E-mail:* tylerballi@ohio.edu
Acqs Ed: Ricky S Huard *Tel:* 740-593-1157
  E-mail: huard@ohio.edu
Acqs Admin, Rts & Perms: Sally R Welch
  E-mail: welchs@ohio.edu
Sales Mgr: Jeff Kallet *Tel:* 740-593-1158
  E-mail: kallet@ohio.edu
Publicity Coord: Laura Andre *Tel:* 740-593-1153
  E-mail: andrel@ohio.edu
Founded: 1964
Publisher of scholarly & trade books.
ISBN Prefix(es): 978-0-8214; 978-0-8040; 978-0-89680; 978-0-940717
Number of titles published annually: 50 Print
Total Titles: 600 Print
Imprints: Swallow Press
Foreign Rep(s): Combined Academic Publishers (CAP) (UK); Scholarly Book Services Inc (Canada)
Orders to: Chicago Distribution Center, 11030 S Langley Ave, Chicago, IL 60628 *Tel:* 773-702-7212 *Toll Free Tel:* 800-621-2736 *Fax:* 773-702-7212 *Toll Free Fax:* 800-621-8476
Warehouse: Chicago Distribution Center, 11030 S Langley Ave, Chicago, IL 60628 *Tel:* 773-702-7212 *Toll Free Tel:* 800-621-2736 *Toll Free Fax:* 800-621-8476
Membership(s): American Association of University Presses (AAUP)
See separate listing for:
Swallow Press

§Olde & Oppenheim Publishers
3219 N Margate Place, Chandler, AZ 85224
E-mail: olde_oppenheim@hotmail.com
Key Personnel
Dir, Mktg: Mike Gratz
Business, how-to, animation, satire, slice-of-life, mystery & detective fiction.
ISBN Prefix(es): 978-0-944861
Number of titles published annually: 3 Print; 5 Online; 2 E-Book
Total Titles: 13 Print

Omnibus Press
Imprint of Music Sales Group
180 Madison Ave, 24th fl, New York, NY 10016
Tel: 212-254-2100 *Toll Free Tel:* 800-431-7187 *Fax:* 212-254-2013 *Toll Free Fax:* 800-345-6842
E-mail: info@omnibuspress.com
Web Site: www.omnibuspress.com; www.musicsales.com
Key Personnel
Off Mgr: Kari Shannon
Founded: 1976
Pop culture, music & film books.
ISBN Prefix(es): 978-0-8256; 978-0-7119; 978-0-86001; 978-1-84449
Number of titles published annually: 40 Print
Total Titles: 500 Print
Distributor for Big Meteor Publishing; Gramophone
Distribution Center: Music Sales Distribution Center, 445 Bellvale Rd, Chester, NY 10918 *Tel:* 845-469-4699 *Toll Free Tel:* 800-431-7187 *Fax:* 845-469-7544 *Toll Free Fax:* 800-345-6842 *E-mail:* info@musicsales.com *Web Site:* www.musicsales.com
Independent Publishers Group (IPG), 814 N Franklin St, Chicago, IL 60610 *Toll Free Tel:* 800-888-4741 *E-mail:* orders@ipgbook.com *Web Site:* www.ipgbook.com

Omnidawn
1632 Elm Ave, Richmond, CA 94805
SAN: 299-3236
Tel: 510-439-6285
E-mail: manager@omnidawn.com
Web Site: www.omnidawn.com
Key Personnel
Co-Founder & Co-Publr: Rusty Morrison
Co-Publr: Laura Joakimson
Founded: 2001
Publishers of poetry, fabulist & new wave fabulist fiction.
ISBN Prefix(es): 978-1-890650
Number of titles published annually: 14 Print
Total Titles: 131 Print
Distribution Center: Chicago Distribution Center (CDC), 11030 S Langley Ave, Chicago, IL 60628 *Tel:* 773-702-7010 *Toll Free Fax:* 800-621-8476

§Omnigraphics Inc
615 Griswold, Suite 520, Detroit, MI 48226
SAN: 249-2520
Tel: 610-461-3548 *Toll Free Tel:* 800-234-1340 (cust serv) *Fax:* 610-532-9001 *Toll Free Fax:* 800-875-1340 (cust serv)
E-mail: contact@omnigraphics.com; customerservice@omnigraphics.com
Web Site: omnigraphics.com
Key Personnel
Publr: Peter E Ruffner
VP: Kevin Hayes
Founded: 1985
Reference books, directories, periodicals & journals for libraries & schools.
ISBN Prefix(es): 978-1-55888; 978-0-7808
Number of titles published annually: 40 Print; 1 Online
Total Titles: 400 Print; 1 Online
Advertising Agency: Marley & Cratchit
Orders to: PO Box 8002, Aston, PA 19014-8002
Returns: 105 Commerce Dr, Aston, PA 19014

Omohundro Institute of Early American History & Culture
Swem Library, Ground fl, 400 Landrum Dr, Williamsburg, VA 23185
Mailing Address: PO Box 8781, Williamsburg, VA 23187-8781 SAN: 201-5161
Tel: 757-221-1114 *Fax:* 757-221-1047
E-mail: ieahc1@wm.edu
Web Site: oieahc.wm.edu
Key Personnel
Exec Dir: Catherine E Kelly *Tel:* 757-221-1118
  E-mail: cekelly01@wm.edu
Books Ed: Nicholas Popper *E-mail:* nspopper@wm.edu
Founded: 1943
Scholarly books on the histories & cultures of North America circa 1450-1820, including related developments in the British Isles, Europe, West Africa & the Caribbean. Founded & still sponsored by the College of William & Mary.
ISBN Prefix(es): 978-0-910776
Number of titles published annually: 6 Print
Total Titles: 247 Print
Distributed by The University of North Carolina Press

§On the Write Path Publishing
Division of Martin-McLean Literary Associates LLC
5023 W 120 Ave, Suite 228, Broomfield, CO 80020
Tel: 303-465-2056 *Fax:* 303-465-2056
Key Personnel
Publr: Lisa Ann Martin, PhD
  E-mail: martinmcleanlit@aol.com
Founded: 2010
On The Write Path Publishing specializes in simplifying self-publishing, making it a fun & painless experience for our authors. We are committed to producing superior-quality books, while offering full service support & maximum author flexibility in all phases of the publishing journey. All of our books are available worldwide through our strategic distributorships with Ingram, Amazon, & Barnes & Noble online, among many others.
This publisher has indicated that 100% of their product line is author subsidized.
ISBN Prefix(es): 978-0-9827321
Number of titles published annually: 12 Print; 12 E-Book
Total Titles: 45 Print; 45 E-Book

§One On One Book Publishing/Film-Video Publications
7944 Capistrano Ave, West Hills, CA 91304
SAN: 211-1527
Tel: 818-340-6620; 818-340-0175 *Fax:* 818-340-6620
E-mail: onebookpro@aol.com
Key Personnel
Pres & Publr: Alan Gadney
VP & Exec Ed: Carolyn Porter
Ed: Nancy Gadney
Founded: 1974
Reference books, directories & audio/video cassettes on film, video, photography, TV/radio broadcasting, writing, theater, business & finance, performing arts, publishing.
ISBN Prefix(es): 978-0-930828
Number of titles published annually: 20 Print; 4 E-Book; 10 Audio
Total Titles: 23 Print; 4 E-Book; 16 Audio
Foreign Rep(s): Australia & New Zealand Book Co (Australia); Fitzhenry & Whiteside (Canada); Reed Methuen Publishers (New Zealand)
Advertising Agency: Carolyn Chadwick Advertising
Membership(s): The Association of Publishers for Special Sales (APSS); Book Publicists of Southern California (BPSC); BookWorks; The Independent Author Network™ (IAN); Independent Book Publishers Association (IBPA); Publishing Professionals Network (PPN)

§Ooligan Press
Portland State University, PO Box 751, Portland, OR 97207
Tel: 503-725-9748 *Fax:* 503-725-3561
E-mail: ooligan@ooliganpress.pdx.edu
Web Site: www.ooliganpress.com
Key Personnel
Publr: Robin Crummer *E-mail:* publisher@ooliganpress.pdx.edu
Founded: 2001
Student run publishing house that seeks to publish regionally significant works of literary, historical & social value to the Pacific Northwest.
ISBN Prefix(es): 978-1-932010; 978-1-947845
Number of titles published annually: 4 Print; 4 E-Book; 4 Audio
Total Titles: 30 Print
Membership(s): Association of Writers & Writing Programs (AWP); Publishers Association of the West (PubWest)

§Open Books Press
Imprint of Pen & Publish LLC
4719 Holly Hills Ave, St Louis, MO 63116
Tel: 314-827-6567
E-mail: info@openbookspress.com
Web Site: openbookspress.com
Key Personnel
Owner & Publr: Jennifer Geist *E-mail:* jennifer@openbookspress.com
Founded: 2010
Publish quality trade paperbacks & ebooks worldwide, including adult nonfiction & fiction for all ages.
Number of titles published annually: 2 Print; 2 E-Book
Total Titles: 42 Print; 30 E-Book
Membership(s): Independent Book Publishers Association (IBPA); St Louis Publishers Association

PUBLISHERS

Open Court Publishing Co
Division of Cricket Media Inc
1751 Pinnacle Dr, Suite 600, McLean, VA 22102
Tel: 703-885-3400
E-mail: mediarelations@cricketmedia.com; licensing@cricketmedia.com; support@cricketmedia.com
Web Site: cricketmedia.com/open-court-publishing
Founded: 1887
Publisher of academic philosophy, popular culture & philosophy books.
ISBN Prefix(es): 978-0-87548; 978-0-912050; 978-0-89688; 978-0-8126
Number of titles published annually: 12 Print
Total Titles: 350 Print

Open Horizons Publishing Co
PO Box 271, Dolan Springs, NM 86441
Tel: 575-741-1581
E-mail: books@bookmarketingbestsellers.com
Web Site: bookmarketingbestsellers.com
Key Personnel
Owner & Publr: John Kremer
 E-mail: johnkremer@bookmarket.com
Founded: 1982
Books for publishers & direct marketers.
ISBN Prefix(es): 978-0-912411
Number of titles published annually: 3 Print; 3 CD-ROM; 3 Online; 40 E-Book; 3 Audio
Total Titles: 21 Print; 16 CD-ROM; 6 Online; 43 E-Book; 12 Audio
Distribution Center: National Book Network, 4720 Boston Way, No A, Lanham, MD 20706-4310, Pres: Jed Lyons *Tel:* 301-459-3366 *Fax:* 301-459-2118
Membership(s): The Association of Publishers for Special Sales (APSS); Independent Book Publishers Association (IBPA)

Open Letter
University of Rochester, Dewey Hall, 1-219, Box 278968, Rochester, NY 14627
Tel: 585-319-0823 *Fax:* 585-273-1097
E-mail: contact@openletterbooks.org
Web Site: www.openletterbooks.org
Key Personnel
Publr: Chad W Post *E-mail:* chad.post@rochester.edu
Edit Dir: Kaija Straumanis *E-mail:* kaija.straumanis@rochester.edu
Poetry Ed: Anastasia Nikolis *E-mail:* anikolis@ur.rochester.edu
Publish books in translation.
ISBN Prefix(es): 978-1-934824; 978-1-940953; 978-1-948830
Number of titles published annually: 10 Print
Distribution Center: Consortium Book Sales & Distribution, 34 13 Ave NE, Suite 101, Minneapolis, MN 55413 (North America) *Toll Free Tel:* 800-283-3572 *E-mail:* sales.orders@cbsd.com *Web Site:* www.cbsd.com
Turnaround Distribution, Unit 3, Olympia Trading Estate, Coburg Rd, Wood Green, London N22 6TZ, United Kingdom *Tel:* (020) 8829 3000 *Fax:* (020) 8881 5088 *E-mail:* orders@turnaround-uk.com

Optometric Extension Program Foundation (OEPF)
2300 York Rd, Suite 113, Timonium, MD 21093
Tel: 410-561-3791 *Fax:* 410-252-1719
Web Site: www.oepf.org
Key Personnel
Exec Dir: Ms Line Vreven *E-mail:* line.vreven@oepf.org
Founded: 1928
Optometric postgraduate education. Books, journals, magazines, pamphlets, catalogs & directories.
ISBN Prefix(es): 978-0-943599; 978-0-929780
Number of titles published annually: 10 Print; 1 CD-ROM
Total Titles: 150 Print; 3 CD-ROM

§OptumInsight™
11000 Optum Circle, Eden Prairie, MN 55344
Tel: 952-833-7100 *Toll Free Tel:* 888-445-8745
Web Site: www.optum.com
Key Personnel
CEO: Robert Musslewhite
Founded: 1983
Books & software for health care professionals.
ISBN Prefix(es): 978-1-56337; 978-1-56329
Number of titles published annually: 90 Print; 5 Online
Total Titles: 90 Print; 8 CD-ROM; 5 Online
Distributed by American Medical Association; Mosby
Distributor for American Medical Association; Medical Economics; Mosby

Orange Frazer Press Inc
37 1/2 W Main St, Wilmington, OH 45177
Mailing Address: PO Box 214, Wilmington, OH 45177-0214
Tel: 937-382-3196 *Fax:* 937-383-3159
E-mail: ofrazer@erinet.com
Web Site: www.orangefrazer.com
Key Personnel
Publr: Marcy Hawley
Ed: John Baskin
Proj Mgr: Sarah Hawley
Founded: 1987
Regional book publisher specializing in Ohio nonfiction (reference, sports, commentary, travel, nature, etc). Production & design is considered "high-end".
This publisher has indicated that 80% of their product line is author subsidized.
ISBN Prefix(es): 978-1-882203; 978-0-9619637; 978-1-933197
Number of titles published annually: 25 Print
Total Titles: 200 Print

Orbis Books
Division of Maryknoll Fathers & Brothers
PO Box 302, Maryknoll, NY 10545-0302
SAN: 202-828X
Tel: 914-941-7636 *Toll Free Tel:* 800-258-5838 (orders, Mon-Fri 8AM-4PM EST) *Fax:* 914-941-7005
E-mail: orbisbooks@maryknoll.org
Web Site: orbisbooks.com
Key Personnel
Publr & Ed-in-Chief: Robert Ellsberg
 E-mail: rellsberg@maryknoll.org
Assoc Publr & Mktg Mgr: Bernadette B Price
 E-mail: bprice@maryknoll.org
Busn Mgr: William Medeot *E-mail:* bmedeot@maryknoll.org
Sales Mgr: Michael Lawrence
 E-mail: mlawrence@maryknoll.org
Acqs Ed: Paul McMahon *E-mail:* pmcmahon@maryknoll.org; Jill O'Brien *E-mail:* jobrien@maryknoll.org
Rts & Perms: Doris Goodnough
 E-mail: dgoodnough@maryknoll.org
Founded: 1970
Offering a wide range of books on prayer, spirituality, Catholic life, theology, mission & current affairs.
ISBN Prefix(es): 978-0-88344; 978-1-57075; 978-1-60833; 978-1-62698
Number of titles published annually: 50 Print; 50 E-Book
Total Titles: 900 Print; 615 E-Book
Foreign Rep(s): Bayard/Novalis Distribution (Canada); Catholic Book Shop (South Africa); Garratt Publishing (Australia)
Advertising Agency: Roth Advertising, PO Box 96, Sea Cliff, NY 11579-0096, Pres: Daniel Roth *Tel:* 516-674-8603 *Fax:* 516-368-3885 *E-mail:* dan@rothadvertising.com

U.S. PUBLISHERS

Warehouse: Maryknoll Center Warehouse, 79 Ryder Rd, Ossining, NY 10562, Mgr: Al Sanders *Tel:* 914-941-7636 ext 2458
Membership(s): American Booksellers Association (ABA); Association of Catholic Publishers Inc

Orbit
Division of Hachette Book Group Inc
1290 Avenue of the Americas, New York, NY 10104
Tel: 212-364-1100 *Toll Free Tel:* 800-759-0190
Web Site: www.orbitbooks.net; www.hachettebookgroup.com/imprint/orbit
Key Personnel
Pres & Publr: Tim Holman
VP, Assoc Publr: Alex Lencicki
VP, Creative Dir: Lauren Panepinto
Exec Ed: Brit Hvide
Sr Ed: Bradley Englert
Acq Ed, Orbit Works: Stephanie Clark
Ed: Alyea Canada
Publicity Dir: Ellen Wright
Publicist: Angela Man
Assoc Publicist: Oliver Wehner
Mktg Mgr: Maggie Curley
Art Dir: Lisa Marie Pompilio
Assoc Art Dir: Stephanie Hess
Designer: Crystal Ben
Imprint Sales Dir: Elizabeth Blue Guess
Founded: 2007
Orbit is a leading publisher of science fiction & fantasy with imprints in the UK, US & Australia. We publish across the spectrum of science fiction & fantasy—from action-packed urban fantasy to widescreen space opera; from sweeping epic adventures to near-future thrillers.
Number of titles published annually: 40 Print
Total Titles: 400 Print
Imprints: Orbit Works (ebook & digital audio); Redhook; Run for It (horror)
Orders to: Hachette Book Group Inc, 53 State St, Boston, MA 02109 *Toll Free Tel:* 800-759-0190 *Toll Free Fax:* 800-286-9471
Shipping Address: Hachette Book Group Inc Distribution Center, 121 N Enterprise Blvd, Lebanon, IN 46052 *Tel:* 765-483-9900 *Fax:* 765-483-0706

Oregon Catholic Press, see OCP

Oregon State University Press
121 The Valley Library, Corvallis, OR 97331-4501
SAN: 202-8328
Tel: 541-737-3166
Key Personnel
Dir: Tom Booth *E-mail:* thomas.booth@oregonstate.edu
EDP Mgr: Micki Reaman *E-mail:* micki.reaman@oregonstate.edu
Acqs Ed: Kim Hogeland *E-mail:* kim.hogeland@oregonstate.edu
Mktg Mgr: Marty Brown *E-mail:* marty.brown@oregonstate.edu
Founded: 1961
ISBN Prefix(es): 978-0-87071
Number of titles published annually: 20 Print
Total Titles: 350 Print
Distribution Center: Chicago Distribution Center, 11030 S Langley Ave, Chicago, IL 60628 *Toll Free Tel:* 800-621-2736
Membership(s): Association of University Presses (AUPresses); Pacific Northwest Booksellers Association (PNBA); Publishers Association of the West (PubWest)

O'Reilly Media Inc
1005 Gravenstein Hwy N, Sebastopol, CA 95472

U.S. PUBLISHERS

Tel: 707-827-7000; 707-827-7019 (cust support) Toll Free Tel: 800-998-9938; 800-889-8969 Fax: 707-829-0104; 707-824-8268
E-mail: orders@oreilly.com; support@oreilly.com
Web Site: www.oreilly.com
Key Personnel
Founder & CEO: Tim O'Reilly
Founded: 1978
Technology & business learning solutions provider.
ISBN Prefix(es): 978-0-937175; 978-1-56592; 978-0-596
Number of titles published annually: 140 Print; 65 E-Book
Total Titles: 800 Print
Branch Office(s)
2 Ave de Lafayette, 6th fl, Boston, MA 02111 Tel: 617-354-5800 Fax: 617-661-1116
Foreign Office(s): O'Reilly Beijing, Cheng Ming Mansion, Bldg C, Suite 807, No 2 Xizhimen South St, Xicheng District, Beijing 100035, China, Contact: Michelle Chen Tel: (010) 88097475 Fax: (010) 88097463 E-mail: orb@oreilly.com Web Site: www.oreilly.com.cn
Intelligent Plaza, Bldg 1-F, 12-22, Yotsuyasaka-machi, Shinjuku-ku, Tokyo 160-0002, Japan, General Dept Section, Sales: Kenji Watari E-mail: japan@oreilly.co.jp Web Site: www.oreilly.co.jp
5 St George's Yard, Farnham, Surrey GU9 7LW, United Kingdom Tel: (01252) 721284 Fax: (01252) 722337 E-mail: information@oreilly.co.uk
Distributor for Packt Publishing (technol ebook prog)
Foreign Rep(s): WoodsLane (Australia, New Zealand)

Organization for Economic Cooperation & Development (OECD), see OECD Washington Center

Oriental Institute Publications
Division of University of Chicago
1155 E 58 St, Chicago, IL 60637
Tel: 773-702-5967
E-mail: oi-publications@uchicago.edu
Web Site: oi.uchicago.edu
Key Personnel
Mng Ed, Pubns: Andrew Baumann
Founded: 1919
Academic publications.
ISBN Prefix(es): 978-0-918986; 978-1-885923
Number of titles published annually: 10 Print; 10 Online
Total Titles: 250 Print; 1,000 Online
Distribution Center: ISD, 70 Enterprise Dr, Suite 2, Bristol, CT 06010 Tel: 860-584-6546

§The Original Falcon Press
1753 E Broadway Rd, No 101-277, Tempe, AZ 85282
Tel: 602-708-1409
E-mail: info@originalfalcon.com
Web Site: www.originalfalcon.com
Key Personnel
Pres: Nicholas Tharcher E-mail: nick@originalfalcon.com
Founded: 1982
Books, audios & videos.
ISBN Prefix(es): 978-1-935150; 978-1-61869
Number of titles published annually: 10 Print; 10 E-Book; 10 Audio
Total Titles: 50 Print; 40 E-Book; 30 Audio
Imprints: Falcon Press; Golden Dawn Publications; New Falcon Publications
Distribution Center: Gazelle Book Services Ltd, White Cross Mills, Hightown, Lancaster, Lancs LA1 4XS, United Kingdom Tel: (0152) 528500 Fax: (0152) 528510 E-mail: sales@gazellebookservices.co.uk Web Site: www.gazellebookservices.co.uk

ORO editions
31 Commercial Blvd, Suite F, Novato, CA 94949
Mailing Address: 1705 Clark Lane, Suite 2, Redondo Beach, CA 90278
Tel: 415-883-3300 Fax: 415-883-3309
E-mail: info@oroeditions.com
Web Site: www.oroeditions.com
Key Personnel
Contact: Gordon Goff E-mail: gordon@oroeditions.com
Founded: 2003
ISBN Prefix(es): 978-0-9746800; 978-0-9774672; 978-0-9793801; 978-0-9795395; 978-0-9814628; 978-0-9820607; 978-0-9819857; 978-0-9826226; 978-0-935935
Number of titles published annually: 100 Print; 4 E-Book
Total Titles: 1 E-Book
Imprints: Applied Research + Design Publishing; Goff Books
Foreign Rep(s): Antique Collectors Club (ACC) (Africa, Europe, Middle East); APD Singapore Pte Ltd (Singapore); Asia Publishers Services Ltd (China, Hong Kong, South Korea, Taiwan); NewSouth Books (Australia, New Zealand)
Distribution Center: Ingram Publisher Services, 14 Ingram Blvd, Mail Stop 631, La Vergne, TN 37086 Web Site: www.ingrampublisherservices.com
Membership(s): Independent Book Publishers Association (IBPA); Independent Publishers Association; Publishing Professionals Network (PPN)

Other Press
267 Fifth Ave, 6th fl, New York, NY 10016
Tel: 212-414-0054 Toll Free Tel: 877-THEOTHER (843-6843) Fax: 212-414-0939
E-mail: editor@otherpress.com; marketing@otherpress.com; publicity@otherpress.com
Web Site: otherpress.com
Key Personnel
Publr: Judith Gurewich
CFO: Bill Foo
Cont: Ed Sokolowski
Dir, Mktg: Terrie Akers
Dir, Subs Rts: Lauren Shekari
Edit Dir: Janice Goldklang
Publicity Dir: Jessica Greer
Mng Ed: Yvonne Cardenas
Sr Ed: Alexander Poreda
Opers Mgr: Iisha Stevens
Intl Publg Coord: Mona Bismuth
Digital Mktg: Shawn Nicholls
Publicist: Leah Morse
Edit Asst: Gage Desser
Founded: 1998
Publish literary fiction, literature in translation, trade nonfiction, memoirs, cultural studies, biographies & other subjects.
ISBN Prefix(es): 978-1-892746; 978-1-59051
Number of titles published annually: 25 Print; 25 E-Book
Foreign Rep(s): AnatoliaLit Agency (Amy Marie Spangler) (Turkey); English Agency Japan Co Ltd (Hamish Macaskill) (Japan); Guenter Berg Literary Agency GmbH & Co KG (Guenter Berg) (Germany); The Deborah Harris Agency (Geula Geurts) (Israel); Danny Hong Agency (Danny Hong) (South Korea); Iris Literary Agency (Catherine Fragou) (Greece); Andrew Nurnberg Associates (Charlotte Seymour) (UK); Prava i prevodi (Milena Kaplarevic) (Baltic States, Eastern Europe); Vicki Satlow Literary Agency (Vicki Satlow) (Italy)
Foreign Rights: MB Agencia Literaria (Monica Martin) (Brazil, Catalonia, Portugal, Spain); Peony Literary Agency (Marysia Juszczakiewicz & Tina Chou) (China, Taiwan)
Distribution Center: Penguin Random House LLC, International Sales, 1745 Broadway, New York, NY 10019 Fax: 212-572-6045

E-mail: international@penguinrandomhouse.com
Penguin Random House LLC, Customer Service, 400 Hahn Rd, Westminster, MD 21157 Toll Free Tel: 800-733-3000 Toll Free Fax: 800-659-2436 E-mail: csorders@penguinrandomhouse.com Web Site: www.penguinrandomhouse.biz
Penguin Random House Canada, Customer Service, 320 Front St W, Suite 1400, Toronto, ON M5V 3B6, Canada Toll Free Tel: 888-523-9292 Toll Free Fax: 888-562-9924 E-mail: csorders@penguinrandomhouse.com Web Site: www.penguinrandomhouse.biz
Membership(s): American Booksellers Association (ABA); Community of Literary Magazines & Presses (CLMP); Independent Book Publishers Association (IBPA)

§Our Daily Bread Publishing
Division of Our Daily Bread Ministries
3000 Kraft Ave SE, Grand Rapids, MI 49512
Mailing Address: PO Box 3566, Grand Rapids, MI 49501-3566
Toll Free Tel: 800-653-8333 (cust serv)
E-mail: customerservice@odb.org
Web Site: ourdailybreadpublishing.org
Key Personnel
Publr: Chriscynethia Floyd
Exec Ed: Dawn Anderson; Joyce Dinkins
Founded: 1987
Religious trade books.
ISBN Prefix(es): 978-0-929239; 978-1-57293; 978-1-64070
Number of titles published annually: 12 Print; 2 Audio
Total Titles: 150 Online; 2 Audio
Membership(s): Evangelical Christian Publishers Association (ECPA)

§Our Sunday Visitor Publishing
Division of Our Sunday Visitor Inc (OSV)
200 Noll Plaza, Huntington, IN 46750
SAN: 202-8344
Tel: 260-356-8400 Toll Free Tel: 800-348-2440 (orders) Toll Free Fax: 800-498-6709
E-mail: osvbooks@osv.com (book orders); customerservice@osv.com
Web Site: www.osv.com
Key Personnel
Publr: Scott Richert E-mail: srichert@osv.com
Founded: 1912
Religious books: trade, adult & juvenile general interest & reference, hardcover & paperback, early childhood school; newsweekly, religious magazines & newspapers, CD-ROM.
ISBN Prefix(es): 978-0-87973; 978-1-931709; 978-0-9707756; 978-1-59276; 978-1-61278; 978-1-68192
Number of titles published annually: 60 Print
Total Titles: 600 Print; 6 CD-ROM; 8 Audio
Foreign Rep(s): Broughton's (Canada); Freedom Publishing (Australia); Gracewing (UK); Veritas (Ireland)

The Overlook Press
Imprint of Harry N Abrams Inc
195 Broadway, 9th fl, New York, NY 10007
SAN: 200-2434
Tel: 212-206-7715
E-mail: abrams@abramsbooks.com; sales@abramsbooks.com (orders)
Web Site: www.abramsbooks.com/imprints/overlookpress
Key Personnel
Edit Dir: Jamison Stoltz
Exec Ed: Tina Pohlman
Founded: 1971
Publisher of adult fiction & drama.
ISBN Prefix(es): 978-0-87951; 978-1-58567; 978-1-59020; 978-1-4683; 978-1-4197

Number of titles published annually: 40 Print; 25 E-Book
Total Titles: 1,200 Print; 1,000 E-Book
Imprints: Ardis Russian Literature
Distributed by Hachette Book Group Inc
Foreign Rights: ANA International Ltd (Jackie Huang) (China); AnatoliaLit Agency (Dilek Akdemir) (Turkey); Agencia Literaria Carmen Balcells SA (Anna Bofill) (Portugal, South America, Spain); Agence Litteraire Eliane Benisti (Noemie Rollet) (France); Berla & Griffini Agency (Erica Berla) (Italy); The Deborah Harris Agency (Geula Gerts) (Israel); Japan UNI Agency (Junko Hirano) (Japan); JLM Literary Agency (John L Moukakos) (Greece); Katai & Boltza Literary Agents (Peter Bolza) (Hungary); Simona Kessler International (Simona Kessler) (Romania); Licht & Burr Literary Agency ApS (Trine Licht) (Scandinavia); Andrew Nurnberg Associates (Marta Ziolkowska) (Poland); Andrew Nurnberg Associates International Ltd (Whitney Hsu) (Taiwan, Thailand, Vietnam); Kristin Olson Literary Agency (Kristin Olson) (Czechia, Slovakia, Slovenia); Plima doo (Vuk Perisic) (Albania, Croatia, North Macedonia, Serbia); Agencia Riff (Laura Riff) (Brazil); Thomas Schlueck GmbH (Franka Zastrow) (Germany); Sebes & Bisseling Literary Agency (Paul Sebes) (Netherlands, Scandinavia); Synopsis Literary Agency (Natasha Sanina) (Baltic States, Georgia, Russia); Eric Yang Agency (Eunsu Lee) (South Korea)
Returns: Hachette Book Group Inc, Attn: Returns Dept, 322 S Enterprise Blvd, Lebanon, IN Toll Free Tel: 800-759-0190 E-mail: customer.service@hbgusa.com
Warehouse: Hachette Book Group Inc, 121 S Enterprise Blvd, Lebanon, IN 46052
Membership(s): Association of American Publishers (AAP); National Book Foundation

Richard C Owen Publishers Inc
PO Box 585, Katonah, NY 10536-0585
Tel: 914-232-3903 *Toll Free Tel:* 800-336-5588 *Fax:* 914-232-3977
Web Site: www.rcowen.com
Key Personnel
Pres & Publr: Richard C Owen
  E-mail: richardowen@rcowen.com
Founded: 1982
Education, language arts & literacy.
ISBN Prefix(es): 978-0-913461; 978-1-878450; 978-1-57274
Number of titles published annually: 5 Print
Total Titles: 378 Print
Warehouse: 247 Rte 100, Somers, NY 10589

§Oxford University Press USA
Division of University of Oxford
198 Madison Ave, New York, NY 10016
SAN: 202-5892
Toll Free Tel: 800-451-7556 (orders); 800-445-9714 (cust serv) *Fax:* 919-677-1303
E-mail: custserv.us@oup.com
Web Site: global.oup.com
Key Personnel
Pres & Academic Publr: Niko Pfund
Dir, Content Devt & Ref: Damon Zucca
Dir, Inventory & Mfg: Deborah Shor
Academic Prod Dir: Casper Grathwohl
Ed-in-Chief, Humanities: Theo Calderara
Ed-in-Chief, Medicine: Craig Panner
Ed-in-Chief, Soc & Behavioral Sciences: David McBride
Edit Dir, Higher Educ: Patrick Lynch
Sr Acqs Ed: Katie Helke
Facilities Mgr: Lorraine Betancourt
Founded: 1896
Scholarly, professional & reference books in the humanities, science, medicine & social studies; nonfiction trade, Bibles, college textbooks, music, ESL, paperbacks, children's books, journals, online reference & online scholarly. Prospective authors should consult the Oxford University Press web site for submission guidelines & proposal submission policy.
ISBN Prefix(es): 978-0-19
Number of titles published annually: 3,000 Print; 6 CD-ROM; 200 Online; 500 E-Book; 30 Audio
Total Titles: 26,000 Print; 27 CD-ROM; 400 Online; 700 E-Book; 250 Audio
Imprints: Clarendon Press; Sinauer Associates
Branch Office(s):
4000 CentreGreen Way, Suite 310, Cary, NC 27513 (cust serv)
Foreign Office(s): Great Clarendon St, Oxford OX2 6DP, United Kingdom (worldwide headquarters) *Tel:* (018165) 556767 *Fax:* (018165) 556646 *E-mail:* onlinequeries.uk@oup.com
Distributor for The American Chemical Society; American University in Cairo; Arnold Clarendon; Cold Spring Harbor Laboratory Press; Engineering Press; Getty; Greenwich Medical Media; Grove Dictionaries; Hurst; IRL; Kodansha; Roxbury Publishing; Saunders; Stamford University Press; Thomson Publishing
Foreign Rights: Gersh Agency
Distribution Center: Ingram Publisher Services, 14 Ingram Blvd, Mail Stop 631, La Vergne, TN 37086 *Tel:* 615-793-5000 *Toll Free Tel:* 866-400-5351 *Web Site:* www.ingrampublisherservices.com
Membership(s): American Association of University Presses (AAUP); Association of American Publishers (AAP); Book Industry Study Group (BISG)

Ozark Mountain Publishing Inc
PO Box 754, Huntsville, AR 72740-0754
Tel: 479-738-2348 *Toll Free Tel:* 800-935-0045 *Fax:* 479-738-2448
E-mail: info@ozarkmt.com
Web Site: www.ozarkmt.com
Key Personnel
Gen Mgr: Nancy Vernon E-mail: nancy@ozarkmt.com
Gen Mgr Asst: Grace Burgess E-mail: grace@ozarkmt.com
Founded: 1992
Publish nonfiction & fiction, new age/metaphysical & spiritual type books. No poetry, cards or daily inspirational books.
ISBN Prefix(es): 978-0-9632776; 978-1-886940; 978-1-940265; 978-1-950639 (Big Sandy Press); 978-1-950608; 978-1-962858
Number of titles published annually: 10 Print; 10 E-Book; 5 Audio
Total Titles: 126 Print; 111 E-Book; 14 Audio
Imprints: Big Sandy Press; Ozark Mountain Publishing
Distributed by Red Wheel/Weiser/Conari

P & R Publishing Co
1102 Marble Hill Rd, Phillipsburg, NJ 08865
SAN: 205-3918
Mailing Address: PO Box 817, Phillipsburg, NJ 08865
Tel: 908-454-0505 *Toll Free Tel:* 800-631-0094
E-mail: sales@prpbooks.com; info@prpbooks.com
Web Site: www.prpbooks.com
Key Personnel
Pres: Bryce H Craig E-mail: bryce@prpbooks.com
Sr Proj Mgr: Aaron Gottier E-mail: aarong@prpbooks.com
Founded: 1930
Christian books for all ages (Reformed Theology).
ISBN Prefix(es): 978-0-87552; 978-1-59638
Number of titles published annually: 40 Print; 100 E-Book
Total Titles: 750 Print; 1 CD-ROM; 200 E-Book
Foreign Rights: F J Rudy & Associates (Fred Rudy) (worldwide)
Membership(s): Evangelical Christian Publishers Association (ECPA)

PA Press
Division of Chronicle Books
202 Warren St, Hudson, NY 12534
Tel: 518-671-6100 *Toll Free Tel:* 800-722-6657 (dist); 800-759-0190 (sales)
E-mail: sales@papress.com
Web Site: www.papress.com
Key Personnel
Owner: Jack Jensen
Publr: Lynn Grady
Edit Dir: Jennifer Lippert *Tel:* 518-671-6100 ext 302 E-mail: jennifer@papress.com
Design Dir: Paul Wagner E-mail: paul@papress.com
Mktg Dir: Kim Dayman
Prodn Dir: Janet Behning E-mail: behning@papress.com
Prog Dir, Children's: Rob Shaeffer E-mail: rob@papress.com
Prog Dir, Paper & Goods: Sara McKay E-mail: mckay@papress.com
Sales & Mktg Dir: Lia Hunt E-mail: lia@papress.com
Sr Ed: Allison Serrell
Prodn Ed: Parker Menzimer
Assoc Ed: Stephanie Holstein
Sr Mktg Mgr: Jessica Tackett
Prodn Coord: Marisa Tesoro
Founded: 1981
Publisher of high quality books in architecture, graphic design & visual culture, arts & photography, children's & stationery.
ISBN Prefix(es): 978-0-910413; 978-1-878271; 978-1-56898; 978-1-61689; 978-1-7972; 978-0-9636372; 978-1-64896; 978-1-885232
Number of titles published annually: 75 Print; 50 E-Book
Total Titles: 1,000 Print
Distributed by Chronicle Books
Distributor for Moleskine Books
Foreign Rep(s): Abrams & Chronicle UK (Europe, Ireland, UK); Hachette Book Group Inc (Central America, Latin America, Middle East, South America, USA); Sonya Jeffery (Australia); Raincoast Books (Canada)

Pace University Press
Subsidiary of Pace University
Pace University, One Pace Plaza, New York, NY 10038
Tel: 212-346-1417 *Fax:* 212-346-1417
E-mail: paceupress@gmail.com
Web Site: www.pace.edu/press
Key Personnel
Dir: Manuela Soares E-mail: msoares@pace.edu
Assoc Dir: Eileen Kreit E-mail: ekreit@pace.edu
Founded: 1988
Academic books in the humanities.
ISBN Prefix(es): 978-0-944473
Number of titles published annually: 8 Print
Total Titles: 55 Print
Membership(s): EBSCO; Independent Book Publishers Association (IBPA); Independent Publishers Association; Women's Media Group

Pacific Press® Publishing Association
Division of Seventh-Day Adventist Church
1350 N Kings Rd, Nampa, ID 83687-3193
Mailing Address: PO Box 5353, Nampa, ID 83653-5353
Tel: 208-465-2500 *Fax:* 208-465-2531
E-mail: booksubmissions@pacificpress.com
Web Site: www.pacificpress.com
Key Personnel
Pres: Dale Galusha
VP, Fin: Robert Hastings

U.S. PUBLISHERS

VP, Mktg & Sales: Doug Church *E-mail:* doug.church@pacificpress.com
VP, Prod Devt: Miguel Valdivia
VP, Prodn: Eric Petersen
Dir, IT: Ed Bahr
Founded: 1874
Religion (Seventh-day Adventist).
ISBN Prefix(es): 978-0-8163; 978-1-5180
Number of titles published annually: 39 Print
Total Titles: 350 Print; 2 CD-ROM; 675 Online; 2 Audio

Pact Press
Imprint of Regal House Publishing
c/o Regal House Publishing, 806 Oberlin Rd, No 12094, Raleigh, NC 27605
E-mail: info@regalhousepublishing.com
Web Site: pactpress.com
Founded: 2016
Pact Press is dedicated to the publication & promotion of high-quality literature that speaks to topical social issues such as religious tolerance, gender equality, immigration, discrimination, racism, poverty, addiction, & LGBTQIA+ concerns. Pact Press publishes poetry, full-length fiction, memoirs & through the auspices of our nonprofit, The Regal House Initiative, an anthology series that benefits reputable nonprofits. We provide extensive editorial support to our authors & strong pre- & post-release digital marketing campaigns to further amplify our authors' outreach efforts. We seek authors with whom we can form meaningful partnerships, working together in a collaborative fashion to best polish & promote their work. We are delighted to accept submissions directly from authors at: regalhousepublishing.submittable.com/submit.
ISBN Prefix(es): 978-0-9912612; 978-0-9988398; 978-1-947548
Number of titles published annually: 15 Print; 15 E-Book
Foreign Rights: Gotham Group (film/tv rts partner); Rightol Media (Asia)
Orders to: Independent Publishers Group (IPG), 814 N Franklin St, Chicago, IL 60610 *Toll Free:* 800-888-4741 *Web Site:* www.ipgbook.com
Distribution Center: Independent Publishers Group (IPG), 814 N Franklin St, Chicago, IL 60610 *Tel:* 312-337-0747 *Fax:* 312-337-5985 *Web Site:* www.ipgbook.com
Membership(s): American Booksellers Association (ABA); The Children's Book Council (CBC); Community of Literary Magazines & Presses (CLMP); Independent Book Publishers Association (IBPA); Southern Independent Booksellers Alliance (SIBA)

Paintbox Press
275 Madison Ave, Suite 600, New York, NY 10016
Tel: 212-878-6610
E-mail: info@paintboxpress.com
Web Site: www.paintboxpress.com
Key Personnel
Owner: Pamela Pease
PR: Kelly Crawford
Founded: 1998
Pop-ups & books on art & design.
ISBN Prefix(es): 978-0-966943; 978-0-977790
Number of titles published annually: 4 Print
Total Titles: 10 Print
Membership(s): AIGA, the professional association for design; The Children's Book Council (CBC); Society of Illustrators

§Palgrave Macmillan
Imprint of Springer Nature
One New York Plaza, Suite 4500, New York, NY 10004-1562
Tel: 212-726-9200
E-mail: sales-ny@springernature.com
Web Site: www.palgrave.com; www.springernature.com
Key Personnel
Trade Sales Dir, Americas: Marit Vagstad
Founded: 1952
Scholarly & trade publisher - cross market publisher.
ISBN Prefix(es): 978-0-312; 978-0-333; 978-1-4039; 978-0-230
Number of titles published annually: 3,200 Print; 2 Online; 850 E-Book
Total Titles: 28,000 Print
Distributor for Berg Publishers; British Film Institute; Manchester University Press; Pluto Press; I B Tauris & Co Ltd; Zed Books
Membership(s): Association of American Publishers Professional & Scholarly Publishing Division

Palladium Books Inc
39074 Webb Ct, Westland, MI 48185
SAN: 294-9504
Tel: 734-721-2903 (orders)
Web Site: www.palladiumbooks.com
Key Personnel
Pres: Kevin Siembieda *E-mail:* ksiembieda@palladiumbooks.com
Sr Ed: Alex Marciniszyn *E-mail:* alex@palladiumbooks.com
Founded: 1981
Role-playing game books & supplements.
ISBN Prefix(es): 978-0-916211; 978-1-57457
Number of titles published annually: 12 Print
Total Titles: 200 Print

§Palm Island Press
2039 Geogia St, Sebring, FL 33870
SAN: 298-4024
Tel: 305-296-3102
E-mail: pipress2@gmail.com
Key Personnel
Gen Mgr: Donald Langille
Founded: 1994
ISBN Prefix(es): 978-0-9643434; 978-0-9743524
Number of titles published annually: 3 Print; 2 E-Book
Total Titles: 15 Print; 2 E-Book
Membership(s): Florida Authors & Publishers Association Inc (FAPA); Independent Book Publishers Association (IBPA)

Pangaea Publications
110183 Friendship Lane S, Chaska, MN 55318
Tel: 651-226-2032
E-mail: info@pangaea.org
Web Site: pangaea.org
Key Personnel
Publr & Ed: Bonnie Hayskar *E-mail:* bonzi@pangaea.org
Founded: 1991
Publisher for nature & peoples of the Earth.
ISBN Prefix(es): 978-0-9630180; 978-1-929165
Number of titles published annually: 4 Print
Total Titles: 32 Print

§Pantheon Books
Imprint of Knopf Doubleday Publishing Group
c/o Penguin Random House LLC, 1745 Broadway, New York, NY 10019
Tel: 212-751-2600 *Fax:* 212-940-7390 (dom rts); 212-572-2662 (foreign rts)
Web Site: knopfdoubleday.com/imprint/pantheon/; knopfdoubleday.com
Key Personnel
VP & Exec Dir, Sales Mgmt & Planning: Beth Meister
VP & Sr Dir, Publicity: Michiko Clark
VP & Edit Dir: Denise Oswald
Sr Dir, Mktg: Julianne Clancy
Art Dir: Linda Huang
Dir: Peggy Samedi
Dir, Ad: Katie Burns
Dir, Publicity: Kathy Zuckerman
Assoc Dir, Mktg: Bianca Ducasse; Sara Eagle
Exec Ed: Naomi Gibbs
Sr Mng Ed: Vimi Santokhi
Assoc Mng Ed: Elizabeth Palumbo
Sr Ed: Concepcion de Leon
Ed: Anna Kaufman; Zach Phillips
Ed-at-Large: David Treuer
Asst Ed: Lisa Kwan
Mktg Mgr: Dani Toth
Mktg Assoc: Sophie Normil
Assoc Mgr: Asharee Peters
Sr Publicist: Rose Cronin-Jackman
Publicist: Demetri Papadimitropoulos; Emily Reardon
Assoc Publicist: Ciara Tomlinson
Publicity Asst: Andreia Wardlaw
Founded: 1942
Penguin Random House & its publishing entities are not accepting proposals, mss or submission queries via e-mail at this time.
Foreign Rep(s): Century Hutchinson Group (South America); Colt Associates (Africa exc South Africa); Steve Franklin (Israel); India Book Distributors (India); International Publishers Representatives (Middle East exc Israel); Pandemic Ltd (Continental Europe exc Scandinavia); Penguin Random House Canada (Canada); Penguin Random House New Zealand (New Zealand); Penguin Random House UK (UK); Periodical Management Group Inc (Mexico); Random Century (Australia); Saga Books ApS (Scandinavia); Sonrisa Book Service (Latin America exc Mexico); Yohan (Japan)
Foreign Rights: Arts & Licensing International (China); Agencia Literaria Carmen Balcells SA (Spain); Agencia Literaria BMSR (Brazil); DRT International (South Korea); English Agency Japan Co Ltd (Japan); Graal Literary Agency (Poland); JLM Literary Agency (Greece); Katai & Bolza (Hungary); Agence Michelle Lapautre (France); Licht & Licht Agency (Scandinavia); Literarni Agentura (Czechia); Roberto Santachiara (Italy); Sebes & Bisseling Literary Agency (Netherlands)

§Pants On Fire Press
10441 Waterbird Way, Bradenton, FL 34209
Tel: 941-405-3078
E-mail: submission@pantsonfirepress.com
Web Site: www.pantsonfirepress.com
Key Personnel
Publr: David Powers *E-mail:* david@pantsonfirepress.com
Sr Ed: Becca Goldman *E-mail:* editor@pantsonfirepress.com
Founded: 2007
Award-winning book publisher of middle grade, young adult, new adult, travel & tourism books.
ISBN Prefix(es): 978-0-9827271
Number of titles published annually: 6 Print; 6 E-Book; 4 Audio
Total Titles: 97 Print; 94 E-Book; 4 Audio
Foreign Rights: The Gersh Agency (Joe Veltre) (worldwide)
Distribution Center: Independent Publishers Group (IPG), 814 N Franklin St, Chicago, IL 60610 *Tel:* 415-489-7000 *Fax:* 415-489-7049
Membership(s): Independent Book Publishers Association (IBPA)

Papercutz
Imprint of Mad Cave Studios Inc
8838 SW 129 St, Miami, FL 33176
Tel: 786-953-4195
E-mail: contact@papercutz.com; snellis@madcavestudios.com
Web Site: www.papercutz.com
Key Personnel
CEO: Mark London

Ed-in-Chief: Mike Marts
Founded: 2005
Graphic novels for ages 7-14.
ISBN Prefix(es): 978-1-59707; 978-1-62991
Number of titles published annually: 50 Print; 50 E-Book
Total Titles: 350 Print; 200 E-Book
Imprints: Children of the Phoenix; Digital Lizards of Doom
Distributed by Simon & Schuster, LLC
Distribution Center: MPS Distribution Center, 16365 James Madison Hwy, Gordonsville, VA 22942 *Toll Free Tel:* 888-330-8477 *Toll Free Fax:* 800-672-2054
Membership(s): Association of American Publishers (AAP); The Children's Book Council (CBC)

Parachute Publishing LLC
Division of Parachute Properties LLC
PO Box 320249, Fairfield, CT 06825
Tel: 203-255-1303
Key Personnel
Chmn & CEO: Joan Waricha *E-mail:* jwaricha@parachuteproperties.com
Founded: 1983
Children's & adult fiction & nonfiction: original books & series, books from licensed properties.
ISBN Prefix(es): 978-0-938753
Number of titles published annually: 100 Print
Total Titles: 1,000 Print
Distributed by Bantam; Bendon; Berkley; Dorling Kindersley; Grosset; Harcourt; HarperCollins; HarperEntertainment; Kensington; Little, Brown; Penguin Random House LLC; Pocket Books; Running Press; Scholastic; Simon & Schuster, LLC
Membership(s): American Book Producers Association (ABPA); The Children's Book Council (CBC)

Paraclete Press Inc
100 Southern Eagle Cartway, Brewster, MA 02631
SAN: 282-1508
Mailing Address: PO Box 1568, Orleans, MA 02653-1568
Tel: 508-255-4685 *Toll Free Tel:* 800-451-5006
E-mail: mail@paracletepress.com; customerservice@paracletepress.com
Web Site: www.paracletepress.com
Founded: 1981
Spirituality, Christian classics, devotionals, poetry, fiction, children's books, Gregorian chant & sacred music CDs.
ISBN Prefix(es): 978-1-55725; 978-0-941478
Number of titles published annually: 38 Print; 3 Audio
Total Titles: 145 Print; 90 Audio
Imprints: Iron Pen (poetry); Raven (literary fiction)
Distributor for Abbey of Saint Peter of Solesmes; Gloriae Dei Cantores
Distribution Center: Books International, 22883 Quicksilver Dr, Dulles, VA 20166 *Tel:* 703-661-1500 *Fax:* 703-661-1501 *Web Site:* booksintl.presswarehouse.com
Membership(s): Association of Catholic Publishers Inc; Evangelical Christian Publishers Association (ECPA)

§Paradigm Publications
Division of Redwing Book Co
202 Bendix Dr, Taos, NM 87571
Tel: 575-758-7758 *Toll Free Tel:* 800-873-3946 (US); 888-873-3947 (CN) *Fax:* 575-758-7768
E-mail: info@paradigm-pubs.com
Web Site: www.paradigm-pubs.com; www.redwingbooks.com
Key Personnel
Publr: Robert L Felt *E-mail:* bob@paradigm-pubs.com
Founded: 1980
Scholarly books on traditional Chinese medicine & acupuncture.
ISBN Prefix(es): 978-0-912111; 978-0-9908698
Number of titles published annually: 2 Print
Total Titles: 60 Print; 40 E-Book

Paradise Cay Publications Inc
120 Monda Way, Blue Lake, CA 95525
Mailing Address: PO Box 29, Arcata, CA 95518-0029
Tel: 707-822-9063 *Toll Free Tel:* 800-736-4509 *Fax:* 707-822-9163
E-mail: info@paracay.com; orders@paracay.com
Web Site: www.paracay.com
Key Personnel
Owner & Dir: Jim Morehouse *E-mail:* james@paracay.com
Founded: 1977
Nautical books, videos, art prints, cruising guides & software.
ISBN Prefix(es): 978-0-939837; 978-0-9646036; 978-1-937196; 978-1-929214
Number of titles published annually: 6 Print
Total Titles: 82 Print; 4 Audio
Imprints: Pardey Publications
Foreign Rep(s): Boat Books (Australia); Islamorado Internacional (Panama); The Nautical Mind (Canada); Transpacific Marine (New Zealand)

Paragon House
3600 Labore Rd, Suite 1, St Paul, MN 55110-4144
Tel: 651-644-3087 *Toll Free Tel:* 800-447-3709 *Fax:* 651-644-0997
E-mail: paragon@paragonhouse.com
Web Site: www.paragonhouse.com
Key Personnel
Pres: Dr Gordon L Anderson
Founded: 1963
Nonfiction; academic/scholarly monographs, trade & college paperbacks. History, philosophy, culture, governance, economy.
ISBN Prefix(es): 978-1-55778; 978-0-913729; 978-0-913757; 978-0-89226; 978-0-943852; 978-0-88702; 978-1-885118; 978-1-61083 (ebooks)
Number of titles published annually: 4 Print
Total Titles: 400 Print
Foreign Rep(s): Roundhouse Publishing (Europe, UK)
Orders to: Baker & Taylor Publisher Services, 30 Amberwood Pkwy, Ashland, OH 44805 *Tel:* 567-215-0030 *Toll Free Tel:* 888-814-0208 *E-mail:* orders@btpubservices.com *Web Site:* www.btpubservices.com
Distribution Center: Baker & Taylor Publisher Services, 30 Amberwood Pkwy, Ashland, OH 44805 *Tel:* 567-215-0030 *Toll Free Tel:* 888-814-0208 *E-mail:* orders@btpubservices.com *Web Site:* www.btpubservices.com

§Parallax Press
Division of Plum Village Community of Engaged Buddhism
2236B Sixth St, Berkeley, CA 94710
Mailing Address: PO Box 7355, Berkeley, CA 94707-0355
Tel: 510-325-2945 *Toll Free Tel:* 800-863-5290 (orders)
Web Site: www.parallax.org
Key Personnel
Publr: Hisae Matsuda *E-mail:* hisae@parallax.org
Creative Dir: Katie Eberle *E-mail:* katie@parallax.org
Dir, Sales, Mktg & New Media: Elizabeth McKellar *E-mail:* elizabeth@parallax.org
Edit Dir, Palm Leaves Press: Terry Barber *E-mail:* terry@parallax.org
Publicity Dir: Earlita K Chenault *E-mail:* earlita@parallax.org
Sr Ed: Matthew Friberg
Founded: 1986
Nonprofit organization publishing books about mindfulness, justice & joy.
ISBN Prefix(es): 978-0-938077; 978-1-888375; 978-1-935209; 978-0-9846271; 978-1-937006; 978-1-941529
Number of titles published annually: 24 Print
Total Titles: 200 Print; 7 Audio
Imprints: Palm Leaves Press (scholarly Buddhist titles); Plum Blossom Books (mindfulness books for children)
Foreign Rights: Cecile Barendsma (worldwide exc Germany, India, Thailand & Vietnam); Brother Phap Kham (Vietnam); Literaturmanufaktur (Ursula Richard) (Germany); Plum Village Foundation (Thailand); Shantum Seth (India)
Distribution Center: Penguin Random House Publisher Services (PRHPS), 400 Hahn Rd, Westminster, MD 21157 *Toll Free Tel:* 800-659-2436 *E-mail:* distribution@penguinrandomhouse.com *Web Site:* prhpublisherservices.com
Penguin Random House Publisher Services (PRHPS), 1745 Broadway, New York, NY 10019 *Fax:* 212-572-4961 *E-mail:* distribution@penguinrandomhouse.com *Web Site:* prhpublisherservices.com
Penguin Random House Canada, 320 Front St W, Suite 1400, Toronto, ON M5V 3B6, Canada *Web Site:* www.penguinrandomhouse.ca
SAN: 201-3975

Paramount Market Publishing Inc
274 N Goodman St, Suite D214, Rochester, NY 14607
Tel: 607-275-8100
E-mail: editors@paramountbooks.com
Web Site: www.paramountbooks.com
Founded: 1999
Marketing, market research, market segments & brand management.
ISBN Prefix(es): 978-0-9571439; 978-0-9725290; 978-0-9766973; 978-0-9786602; 978-0-9801745; 978-0-9819869; 978-0-9830436
Number of titles published annually: 6 Print; 6 E-Book
Total Titles: 110 Print; 80 E-Book
Imprints: PMP

Parenting Press
Imprint of Chicago Review Press
13751 Lake City Way NE, Suite 110, Seattle, WA 98125
Mailing Address: PO Box 75267, Seattle, WA 98175-0267
Tel: 206-364-2900 *Toll Free Tel:* 800-99-BOOKS (992-6657) *Fax:* 206-364-0702
E-mail: office@parentingpress.com; marketing@parentingpress.com
Web Site: www.parentingpress.com
Founded: 1979
Parenting, social skill building, personal safety for children, discipline, feelings, temperament, development, boundaries, problem solving, social relations.
ISBN Prefix(es): 978-0-943990; 978-0-9602862 (co-published with Raefield-Roberts); 978-1-884734; 978-1-936903
Number of titles published annually: 6 Print; 26 Online; 2 E-Book
Total Titles: 85 Print; 5 Online; 44 E-Book
Distribution Center: Independent Publishers Group (IPG), 814 N Franklin St, Chicago, IL 60610 *Tel:* 312-337-0747 *Toll Free Tel:* 800-888-4741 *Fax:* 312-337-5985 *Web Site:* www.ipgbook.com
Membership(s): Book Publishers of the Northwest (BPNW); Independent Book Publishers Association (IBPA); Publishers Association of the West (PubWest)

U.S. PUBLISHERS

§Park Place Publications
410 Central Ave, No 3, Pacific Grove, CA 93950-2836
SAN: 297-5238
Tel: 831-649-6640
E-mail: publishingbiz@sbcglobal.net
Web Site: www.parkplacepublications.com
Key Personnel
Owner & Publr: Patricia Hamilton
Founded: 1991 (a continuation of book publishing for the owner, Patricia Hamilton, Publisher & CEO of Hamilton Commercial Indoor Plant Books)
Provides book publishing, graphic design & prepress services. Founded on the premise that "Books make a world of difference."
This publisher has indicated that 90% of their product line is author subsidized.
ISBN Prefix(es): 978-1-935530; 978-1-943887; 978-1-953120
Number of titles published annually: 15 Print; 15 Online; 10 E-Book; 2 Audio
Total Titles: 300 Print; 40 Online; 25 E-Book; 2 Audio
Imprints: Alamos Press (American & Mexican culture & bilingual); At Home on the Road (travel); Hamilton Plant Books (professional design & care for commercial tropical indoor plants); Keepers of Our Culture (personal & historical stories, memoirs); Pacific Grove Books (city related content)
Distribution Center: Ingram Content Group, One Ingram Blvd, La Vergne, TN 37086 *Tel:* 615-793-5000 *Web Site:* www.ingramcontent.com
Membership(s): Association of Personal Historians; The Association of Publishers for Special Sales (APSS); Independent Book Publishers Association (IBPA); Writers & Publishers Network (WPN)

§Parmenides Publishing
3753 Howard Hughes Pkwy, Suite 200, Las Vegas, NV 89169
SAN: 254-4342
Tel: 702-892-3934 *Fax:* 702-892-3939
E-mail: info@parmenides.com; editor@parmenides.com
Web Site: www.parmenides.com
Key Personnel
Publr & CEO: Sara Hermann
VP & Sales Dir: Gale Carr
Founded: 2000
Independent publishing house. Specialize in literature on philosophy, especially ancient Greek philosophy for the academic & trade markets.
ISBN Prefix(es): 978-1-930972
Number of titles published annually: 4 Print; 4 Online; 4 E-Book; 4 Audio
Total Titles: 49 Print; 49 Online; 45 E-Book; 4 Audio
Divisions: ParmenidesAudio™; ParmenidesFiction™
Foreign Rep(s): APAC (Tom Cassidy) (Brunei, Cambodia, China, Hong Kong, Indonesia, Malaysia, Myanmar, Singapore, Taiwan, Thailand, Vietnam)
Orders to: The University of Chicago Press Distribution Center, 11030 S Langley Ave, Chicago, IL 60628 *Toll Free Tel:* 800-621-2736 *Fax:* 773-702-9756 *Toll Free Fax:* 800-621-8476 *E-mail:* orders@press.uchicago.edu
Returns: The University of Chicago Press Distribution Center, 11030 S Langley Ave, Chicago, IL 60628 *Tel:* 773-702-7700 *Fax:* 773-702-9756 *Toll Free Fax:* 800-621-8476 *E-mail:* orders@press.uchicago.edu
Shipping Address: The University of Chicago Press Distribution Center, 11030 S Langley Ave, Chicago, IL 60628 *Tel:* 773-702-7700 *Fax:* 773-702-9756 *Toll Free Fax:* 800-621-8476 *E-mail:* orders@press.uchicago.edu
Warehouse: The University of Chicago Press Distribution Center, 11030 S Langley Ave, Chicago, IL 60628 *Tel:* 773-702-7700 *Fax:* 773-702-9756 *Toll Free Fax:* 800-621-8476 *E-mail:* orders@press.uchicago.edu
Distribution Center: The University of Chicago Press Distribution Center, 11030 S Langley Ave, Chicago, IL 60628 *Tel:* 773-702-7700 *Toll Free Tel:* 800-621-2736 (orders) *Fax:* 773-702-9756 *Toll Free Fax:* 800-621-8476 *E-mail:* orders@press.uchicago.edu
Membership(s): Association of American Publishers (AAP)

Path Press Inc
708 Washington St, Evanston, IL 60202
SAN: 630-2041
Tel: 847-492-0177
E-mail: pathpressinc@aol.com
Key Personnel
Pres: Bennett J Johnson
Founded: 1962
Books for African-American & Third World people.
This publisher has indicated that 25% of their product line is author subsidized.
ISBN Prefix(es): 978-0-910671
Number of titles published annually: 6 Print
Total Titles: 51 Print
Subsidiaries: African-American Book Distributors Inc
Membership(s): Independent Book Publishers Association (IBPA)

Pathfinder Publishing Inc
120 S Houghton Rd, Suite 138, Tucson, AZ 85748
SAN: 694-2571
Tel: 520-647-0158
Web Site: www.pathfinderpublishing.com
Key Personnel
Pres & CEO: Bill Mosbrook
Founded: 1985
Books & audiobooks. Specialize in music, psychology, nautical & military history.
ISBN Prefix(es): 978-0-934793
Number of titles published annually: 3 Print; 1 Audio
Total Titles: 50 Print; 3 Audio
Membership(s): Independent Book Publishers Association (IBPA)

Paul Dry Books
1700 Sansom St, Suite 700, Philadelphia, PA 19103
Tel: 215-231-9939
E-mail: editor@pauldrybooks.com
Web Site: www.pauldrybooks.com
Key Personnel
Owner & Publr: Paul Dry *E-mail:* pdry@pauldrybooks.com
Mng Ed: Mara Brandsdorfer; Maude Kushto; Julia Sippel
Philosophy, fiction, history, essays, young adult fiction & nonfiction.
ISBN Prefix(es): 978-0-9664913; 978-0-9679675; 978-1-58988
Number of titles published annually: 12 Print
Total Titles: 175 Print; 75 E-Book

Pauline Books & Media
Division of Daughters of St Paul
50 Saint Paul's Ave, Boston, MA 02130
SAN: 203-8900
Tel: 617-522-8911 *Toll Free Tel:* 800-876-4463 (orders); 800-836-9723 (cust serv) *Fax:* 617-541-9805
E-mail: editorial@paulinemedia.com (ms submissions); orderentry@pauline.org (cust serv)
Web Site: www.pauline.org/pbmpublishing
Key Personnel
Publr: Sr Marie James Hunt
Digital Mgr: Sr Kathryn James Hermes
Edit Mgr: Sr Mary Leonora Wilson
Promo Mgr: Sr Maria Kim-Ngan Bui
Adult Acqs Ed: Sr Maria Grace Denato; Sr Christina Wegendt
Book Center Acqs: Anthony Ruggiero
Children's & Teen Ed: Sr Marlyn Evangelina Monge; Troy Norman
Edit Asst, Acqs: Courtney Ward
Intl Rts & Perms: Nicole Anzuoni
Founded: 1932
Spirituality, prayer books, teachers' resources for religious education, liturgical books, church documents, adult religious instruction, saints lives, faith & culture, music & music CDs.
ISBN Prefix(es): 978-0-8198
Number of titles published annually: 50 Print; 30 E-Book; 1 Audio
Total Titles: 600 Print; 72 Audio
Imprints: Catholic Approach Series; Encounter the Saints Series (children); Faith & Culture; Pauline Comics & Graphic Novels (children & teens); Pauline Teen; The Saints Series; Theology of the Body Series
Membership(s): Association of Catholic Publishers Inc; Catholic Media Association (CMA); Society of Children's Book Writers & Illustrators (SCBWI)

§Paulist Press
997 Macarthur Blvd, Mahwah, NJ 07430-9990
SAN: 202-5159
Tel: 201-825-7300 *Toll Free Tel:* 800-218-1903 *Fax:* 201-825-6921
E-mail: info@paulistpress.com; publicity@paulistpress.com
Web Site: www.paulistpress.com
Key Personnel
Pres & Publr: Rev Mark-David Janus, PhD
Founded: 1865
Resources with emphasis on biblical studies, Christian, Catholic & ecumenical formation & education, ethics & social issues, pastoral ministry, personal growth, spirituality, philosophy, theology.
ISBN Prefix(es): 978-0-8091
Number of titles published annually: 60 Print
Total Titles: 1,650 Print; 1,000 E-Book; 3 Audio
Imprints: The Newman Press; Stimulus Books
Foreign Rep(s): Bayard Novalis Distribution (Canada); Brumby Sunstate (Australia); Katong Catholic Book Center (Singapore); KCBS Inc (South Korea); Norwich Books & Music (Europe); Pleroma Christian Supplies (New Zealand); St Pauls-India (India)
Returns: 39 Ramapo Valley Rd, Mahwah, NJ 07430
Warehouse: 39 Ramapo Valley Rd, Mahwah, NJ 07430
Membership(s): Association of Catholic Publishers Inc

Nancy Paulsen Books
Imprint of Penguin Young Readers Group
c/o Penguin Random House LLC, 1745 Broadway, New York, NY 10019
Tel: 212-782-9000
Web Site: www.penguin.com/nancy-paulsen-books-overview/
Key Personnel
Pres & Publr: Nancy Paulsen
Assoc Publr: Stacey Barney
SVP & Exec Art Dir, Dial Books for Young Readers, Nancy Paulsen Books, GP Putnam's Sons Books for Young Readers & Rocky Pond Books: Lily Malcom
Art Dir, GP Putnam's Sons Books for Young Readers & Nancy Paulsen Books: Marikka Tamura
Assoc Art Dir, GP Putnam's Sons Books for Young Readers & Nancy Paulsen Books: Eileen Savage
Ed: Caitlin Tutterow

Asst Ed, Kokila & Nancy Paulsen Books: Jenny Ly
Founded: 2011
Penguin Random House & its publishing entities are not accepting unsol submissions, proposals, mss, or submission queries via e-mail at this time.
Number of titles published annually: 30 Print

Peabody Museum Press
Unit of Peabody Museum of Archaeology & Ethnology, Harvard University
11 Divinity Ave, Cambridge, MA 02138
Tel: 617-495-4255; 617-495-3938 (edit)
E-mail: peapub@fas.harvard.edu
Web Site: www.peabody.harvard.edu/publications
Key Personnel
Dir, Pubns: Joan O'Donnell
Founded: 1888
ISBN Prefix(es): 978-0-87365
Number of titles published annually: 6 Print
Total Titles: 140 Print
Distributed by Harvard University Press
Orders to: Harvard University Press, c/o TriLiteral LLC, 100 Maple Ridge Dr, Cumberland, RI 02864-1769 *Tel:* 401-531-2300 *Toll Free Tel:* 800-405-1619 *Fax:* 401-531-2801 *Toll Free Fax:* 800-406-9145 *E-mail:* customer.care@triliteral.org

§Peachpit Press
Imprint of Pearson Education Ltd
1301 Sansome St, San Francisco, CA 94111
Toll Free Tel: 800-283-9444
E-mail: info@peachpit.com; ask@peachpit.com
Web Site: www.peachpit.com
Founded: 1986
ISBN Prefix(es): 978-0-201; 978-1-56609; 978-0-321; 978-0-938151
Number of titles published annually: 180 Print
Total Titles: 400 Print
Imprints: New Riders

Peachtree Publishing Co Inc
Division of Trustbridge Global Media
1700 Chattahoochee Ave, Atlanta, GA 30318-2112
SAN: 212-1999
Tel: 404-876-8761 *Toll Free Tel:* 800-241-0113 *Fax:* 404-875-2578 *Toll Free Fax:* 800-875-8909
E-mail: hello@peachtree-online.com; orders@peachtree-online.com; sales@peachtree-online.com
Web Site: www.peachtreebooks.com; www.peachtree-online.com
Key Personnel
Publr: Margaret Quinlin
SVP, Global Integration & Planning: Derek Stordahl
SVP, Sales, Mktg & Busn Opers, US & CN: Mary Marotta
VP & Assoc Publr: Kathy Landwehr
VP, Consumer & Brand Mktg: Karen Walsh
VP, Publicity: Tracy Miracle
VP, Trade Mktg: Michelle Montague
Sr Art Dir: Jennifer Browne
Creative Dir: Kerry Martin
Retail Dir, Sales: Jess Brigman
Assoc Art Dir, Novels & Middle Grade: Chelsea Hunter
Assoc Mng Ed: Jamie Evans
Sr Ed, Peachtree/Peachtree Teen: Jonah Heller
Sr Ed, Peachtree Teen: Ashley Hearn
Sr Digital Mktg Mgr: Mary Joyce Perry
Sr Natl Acct Mgr, Amazon: Karen Menzie
Educ Sales Mgr: Laura Palermo
Mktg Mgr, Trade: Elyse Vincenty
Prodn Mgr: Courtney Hood
Publicity Mgr: Sara DiSalvo
Sr Publicist: Anna Gjesteby Abell
Consumer Mktg Coord: Neda Kamalhedayat
Digital Mktg Coord: Melissa See
Mktg Coord, School & Lib: Tiffany Coelho
Publicity Coord: Kayla Phillips
Sales Coord: Adelaide Cronin
Lead Designer: Lily Steele
Designer: Lucy Ricketts
Mktg Designer: Allie Jones
Subs Rts: Farah Gehy *E-mail:* gehy@peachtree-online.com
Mktg Asst, School & Lib: Saskia den Boon
Trade Mktg Asst: Caitlyn Davis
Founded: 1977
Children's & young adult fiction & nonfiction, self-help & health/parenting & regional guides.
ISBN Prefix(es): 978-0-931948; 978-0-934601; 978-1-56145; 978-1-68263; 978-99927-862
Number of titles published annually: 40 Print
Total Titles: 400 Print
Imprints: Freestone; Peachtree Jr; Peachtree Teen; Margaret Quinlin Books
Foreign Rep(s): Fitzhenry & Whiteside Limited (Canada)
Distribution Center: Penguin Random House Publisher Services (PRHPS) (worldwide)

§Pearson Business Publishing
Unit of Pearson Higher Education
221 River St, Hoboken, NJ 07030-4772
Tel: 201-236-7000
Web Site: www.pearsonhighered.com
Key Personnel
Mgr, Content Prodn: Melissa Feimer

Pearson Education Ltd
225 River St, Hoboken, NJ 07030-4772
Tel: 201-236-7000 *Fax:* 201-236-6549
Web Site: www.pearson.com
ISBN Prefix(es): 978-0-582
See separate listing for:
Pearson ELT
Pearson Higher Education

Pearson ELT
Division of Pearson Education Ltd
221 River St, Hoboken, NJ 07030
Tel: 815-862-4472
Web Site: www.pearson.com/languages
ISBN Prefix(es): 978-0-13; 978-1-292
Number of titles published annually: 100 Print

Pearson Higher Education
Division of Pearson Education Ltd
221 River St, Hoboken, NJ 07030
Tel: 201-236-7000
Web Site: www.pearson.com/en-us/highered-education.html
ISBN Prefix(es): 978-0-13; 978-0-205; 978-0-8428; 978-0-87618; 978-0-87619; 978-0-87628; 978-0-89303
See separate listing for:
Pearson Business Publishing
Pearson Learning Solutions

Pearson Learning Solutions
Unit of Pearson Higher Education
501 Boyleston St, Suite 900, Boston, MA 02116
SAN: 214-0225
Tel: 617-671-3300 *Toll Free Tel:* 800-428-4466 (orders); 800-635-1579
E-mail: pcp@pearson.com
Web Site: www.pearsoned.com
ISBN Prefix(es): 978-0-8087; 978-0-536; 978-1-4386; 978-0-555; 978-0-558; 978-1-256; 978-1-269; 978-1-323
Branch Office(s)
Pearson Custom Publishing, 7110 Ohms Lane, Edina, MN 55439-2143 *Tel:* 952-831-1881 *Toll Free Tel:* 800-922-2579 *Fax:* 952-831-3167

Pelican Publishing
Imprint of Arcadia Publishing Inc
990 N Corporate Dr, Suite 100, New Orleans, LA 70123
Tel: 504-684-8976 *Toll Free Tel:* 844-868-1798 (orders)
E-mail: editorial@pelicanpub.com (submissions)
Web Site: www.pelicanpub.com; www.arcadiapublishing.com/imprints/pelican-publishing
Key Personnel
Publr: Scott Campbell *E-mail:* scampbell@arcadiapublishing.com
Ed-in-Chief: Nina Kooij
Mng Ed: David Mandel
Sales Mgr: John Scheyd *E-mail:* jscheyd@arcadiapublishing.com
Founded: 1926
Specialize in publishing books with a special emphasis on life in New Orleans & surrounding regions.
ISBN Prefix(es): 978-0-911116; 978-0-88289; 978-1-56554; 978-1-58980; 978-1-4556
Number of titles published annually: 30 Print; 25 E-Book
Total Titles: 2,600 Print; 12 CD-ROM; 1,100 E-Book; 35 Audio
Membership(s): Museum Store Association (MSA); Southern Independent Booksellers Alliance (SIBA)

§Pen & Publish LLC
4719 Holly Hills Ave, St Louis, MO 63116
Tel: 314-827-6567
E-mail: info@penandpublish.com
Web Site: www.penandpublish.com
Key Personnel
Owner & Publr: Jennifer Geist *E-mail:* jennifer@penandpublish.com
Founded: 2004
Publishes books by & for schools & nonprofits. Also offers author services to help writers with self-publishing, editing, design & more. Its traditional imprints include Brick Mantel Books, Open Books Press & Transformation Media Books.
This publisher has indicated that 50% of their product line is author subsidized.
ISBN Prefix(es): 978-1-941799; 978-0-9768391; 978-0-9779530; 978-0-9790446; 978-0-9800429; 978-0-9817264; 978-0-9823850; 978-0-9842258; 978-0-9844600; 978-0-9845751; 978-0-9846359; 978-0-9852737; 978-0-9859367
Number of titles published annually: 3 Print; 3 E-Book
Total Titles: 100 Print; 14 E-Book
Imprints: Brick Mantel Books (literary fiction & poetry); Open Books Press (fiction for all ages & nonfiction for adults); Transformation Media Books (body/mind/spirit)
Membership(s): Independent Book Publishers Association (IBPA); Midwest Independent Booksellers Association (MIBA); St Louis Publishers Association
See separate listing for:
Open Books Press

Pen-L Publishing
12 W Dickson St, No 4455, Fayetteville, AR 72702
E-mail: info@pen-l.com
Web Site: www.pen-l.com
Key Personnel
Publr: Kimberly Pennell
Founded: 2012
ISBN Prefix(es): 978-1-942428; 978-1-942428; 978-1-68313
Number of titles published annually: 24 Print; 24 E-Book; 4 Audio
Total Titles: 91 Print; 91 E-Book; 6 Audio
Membership(s): Independent Book Publishers Association (IBPA); International Thriller Writers

U.S. PUBLISHERS

Inc (ITW); Society of Children's Book Writers & Illustrators (SCBWI); Western Writers of America (WWA)

Pendragon Press
Subsidiary of Camelot Publishing Co Inc
52 White Hill Rd, Hillsdale, NY 12529-5839
Mailing Address: PO Box 190, Hillsdale, NY 12529
Tel: 518-325-6100 *Toll Free Tel:* 877-656-6381 (orders)
E-mail: editor@pendragonpress.com; orders@pendragonpress.com
Web Site: www.pendragonpress.com
Key Personnel
Mng Ed: Robert J Kessler
Founded: 1972
Reference works on books & musicology including music/aesthetics, biographies, music theory, organ, harpsichord, historic brass, 20th century music, French opera, music & religion.
ISBN Prefix(es): 978-0-918728; 978-0-945193; 978-1-57647
Number of titles published annually: 10 Print
Total Titles: 400 Print
Distributed by LIM Editrice SRL (Italy); G Ricordi (Italy)
Foreign Rep(s): Eurospan Ltd (Europe)

Penfield Books
215 Brown St, Iowa City, IA 52245
SAN: 221-6671
Tel: 319-337-9998 *Toll Free Tel:* 800-728-9998 *Fax:* 319-351-6846
E-mail: penfield@penfieldbooks.com; orders@penfieldbooks.com
Web Site: www.penfieldbooks.com
Founded: 1979 (as Penfield Press)
Ethnic titles including Czech, Danish, Dutch, Finnish, French, German, Irish, Italian, Mexican, Norwegian, Polish, Scandinavian, Scottish, Slovak, Swedish & Ukrainian; cookbooks; crafts & folk art; history; ethnic cultural cookbooks, cookbooks of the states. No unsol mss.
ISBN Prefix(es): 978-0-941016; 978-1-932043; 978-1-57216
Number of titles published annually: 6 Print; 6 CD-ROM; 20 E-Book
Total Titles: 174 Print; 268 Online; 75 E-Book

Penguin Books, see Viking Penguin

Penguin Press
Imprint of Penguin Publishing Group
c/o Penguin Random House LLC, 1745 Broadway, New York, NY 10019
Tel: 212-782-9000
E-mail: penguinpress@penguinrandomhouse.com
Web Site: www.penguin.com/penguin-press-overview/
Key Personnel
Pres & Ed-in-Chief: Ann Godoff
VP & Publr: Scott Moyers
VP & Art Dir: Darren Haggar
VP & Publicity Dir: Sarah Hutson
VP, Assoc Publr & Dir, Mktg: Matt Boyd
Dir, Contracts: Robin Simon
Deputy Publicity Dir: Gail Brussel
Assoc Mktg Dir: Danielle Plafsky
Assoc Publicity Dir/Ed: Juliana Kiyan
Exec Ed: William Heyward; Virginia Smith Younce
Sr Ed: Kiara Barrow
Ed: Mia Council; Casey Denis
Ed-at-Large: Sara Bershtel; John Burnham Schwartz
Assoc Ed: Caroline Sydney
Asst Ed: Natalie Coleman; Helen Rouner
Sr Mktg Mgr: Lauren Lauzon
Publicity Mgr: Christine Johnston
Publicist: Mollie Reid
Assoc Mktg Mgr: Jessie Stratton Zhou
Founded: 2003
Publishers of literary fiction & select nonfiction.
Penguin Random House & its publishing entities are not accepting unsol submissions, proposals, mss, or submission queries via e-mail at this time.
Number of titles published annually: 38 Print
Total Titles: 127 Print

Penguin Publishing Group
Division of Penguin Random House LLC
c/o Penguin Random House LLC, 1745 Broadway, New York, NY 10019
Tel: 212-782-9000
Web Site: www.penguin.com
Key Personnel
Pres, Penguin Publishing Group: Allison Dobson
Founder, Pres & Publr, Portfolio: Adrian Zackheim
Pres & Publr, Viking/Penguin: Brian Tart
Pres & Publr, Riverhead Books: Geoffrey Kloske
Pres & Ed-in-Chief, Penguin Press: Ann Godoff
Pres, Penguin Young Readers: Jennifer Loja
Pres, Putnam/Dutton/Berkley: Ivan Held
SVP, Backlist: Benjamin Lee
SVP & Dir, Prodn, Knopf Doubleday Publishing Group & Penguin Publishing Group: Robert Wojciechowski
SVP & Exec Mng Ed, Knopf Doubleday Publishing Group & Penguin Publishing Group: Meredith Dros
VP & Art Dir of Interiors: Claire Vaccaro
VP & Group Sales Dir: Andy Dudley
VP & Dir, Subs Rts: Tom Dussel
VP, Subs Rts: Sabila Khan
Sr Exec Dir, Nonfiction Backlist: Carrie Swetonic
Exec Dir, Ad & Promo: Ashley Fisher-Tranese
Sr Dir, Title Mgmt: Colleen Kurzbach
Dir, Art & Design: Jennifer Heuer; Jess Morpheus
Dir, Publg & Mktg Opers: Liza Cassity
Dir, Subs Rts: Melanie Koch
Asst Dir, Mktg: Jordan Aaronson
Mktg Assoc: Andrew Taets
Publg Assoc: Maralee Diana
Subs Rts Assoc: Julie Lubwama
Founded: 1939 (as Penguin Books Ltd)
Publisher of consumer books in both hardcover & paperback for adults & children. Also produces maps, calendars, audiobooks & mass merchandise products.
Adult: hardcover, trade paperbacks & mass market paperbacks (originals & reprints)
Children: hardcover picture books, paperback picture books, board & novelty books
Young Adult: hardcover & trade paperback
Mass merchandise products.
Penguin Random House & its publishing entities are not accepting unsol submissions, proposals, mss, or submission queries via e-mail at this time.
Imprints: Avery; Berkley (includes Ace); Dutton (hardcover; includes Plume & Tiny Reparations Books); Family Tree Books; Impact Books; Krause Publications (includes Krause Craft); North Light Books; Penguin Press; Popular Woodworking Books; Portfolio (includes Sentinel & Thesis); GP Putnam's Sons (hardcover); Riverhead Books (hardcover & pbk); TarcherPerigee; Viking Penguin (hardcover); Writer's Digest Books
Membership(s): Association of American Publishers (AAP)
See separate listing for:
Avery
Berkley
Dutton
Penguin Press
Portfolio
GP Putnam's Sons
Riverhead Books
TarcherPerigee
Viking Penguin
Writer's Digest Books

Penguin Random House Audio Publishing Group
Division of Penguin Random House LLC
1745 Broadway, New York, NY 10019
Toll Free Tel: 800-793-2665 (cust serv)
E-mail: audio@penguinrandomhouse.com; ecustomerservice@penguinrandomhouse.com
Web Site: www.penguinrandomhouseaudio.com
Key Personnel
Pres & Publr: Amanda D'Acierno
SVP, Content & Busn Devt: Lance Fitzgerald
SVP, Content Prodn: Dan Zitt
SVP, Mktg & Publicity: Donna Passannante
VP, Audio Fin & Strategy: Leonard Wiggins
VP, Audio Prodn: Karen Dzienkonski
VP, Mktg: Heather Dalton
VP, Post-Prodn & Tech: Ok Hee Kolwitz
VP, Publicity: Katie Punia
Sr Dir, Mng Edit & Prodn: Linda Schmidt
Sr Dir, Opers: Siobhan O'Hare
Dir, Art & Design: Theresa Capan
Dir, Audio Prodn & Creative Partner Devt: Kelly Gildea
Dir, Audio Strategy & Acqs: Catherine Bucaria
Dir, Casting, Digital Prodn Platforms & Strategic Partnerships: Julie Wilson
Dir, Fin: John McGalagly
Dir, Mktg: Nicole McArdle
Dir, Pre-Prodn & Exec Prodr: Matie Argiropoulos
Dir, Publicity: Ellen Folan
Dir, Spanish & Original Content: Laura Wilson
Dir, Strategic Mktg: Taraneh DJangi
Assoc Dir, Lib Mktg, Books on Tape: Jennifer Rubins
Assoc Dir, Mng Edit: Kaitlyn Robinson
Assoc Dir, Opers: Kelly Atkinson Wenzel
Assoc Dir, Mktg: Alexis Patterson
Asst Dir, Mktg: Becca Stumpf
Asst Dir, Mktg Strategy: Robert Guzman
Sr Exec Prodr: Sarah Jaffe; Linda Korn; Nick Martorelli; Diane McKiernan; Orli Moskowitz
Exec Prodr: Brady Emerson; Iris McElroy
Prodr: Amber Beard; Lauren Klein; Denise Lee; Nithya Rajendran; Brian Ramcharan; Jorge Reyes
Assoc Prodr: Olivia Langen
Mng Ed: Benny Goldmintz
Assoc Mng Ed: Heather Palmer
Asst Mng Ed: Cady Zeng
Sr Acqs Ed: Jennifer Donovan
Sr Ed: Abby Nutter
Assoc Ed: Leah Jackson
Asst Acqs Ed: Katie Lakina
Asst Ed: Desiree Johnson
Edit Asst: Alazane Cameron
Edit Strategy & Licensing Asst: Carly Quinn
Sr Mgr, Backlist, Art Rts & Perms: Tara Hart
Sr Mgr, Licensing & Busn Devt: Lauren Diaz Morgan
Sr Publicity Mgr: Brisa Robinson
Sr Soc Media Mgr: Juliette DeSena
Mktg Mgr, Listening Library: Dakota Cohen
Assoc Mktg Mgr: Erin Murphy
Mktg Assoc: Sana Iqbal; Marissa Secreto
Sr Audio Engr: Mor Mezrich
Sr Publicist: Brittanie Black; Lizbeth Gutierrez
Publicist: Kayla Kohlmeister
Publicist, Listening Library: Alexandra Hernandez; Kate Smith
Publicity & Mktg Asst: Brian Laurito
Art Rts Assoc: Shannon Blackbriar
Soc Media & Spec Projs Assoc: Jasmin Ayala
Jr Fin Analyst: Dee Santana
Exec Asst: Chelly-Ann Aydinian
Penguin Random House & its publishing entities are not accepting unsol submissions, proposals, mss, or submission queries via e-mail at this time.
Number of titles published annually: 300 Audio
Total Titles: 20,000 Audio

PUBLISHERS

Imprints: Books on Tape™ (libraries & schools); Listening Library (children & young adults); Penguin Audio (adult); Random House Audio (adult); Random House Large Print; Random House Puzzles and Games; Random House Reference
See separate listing for:
Books on Tape™
Random House Large Print
Random House Reference/Random House Puzzles & Games

Penguin Random House Large Print, see Random House Large Print

§Penguin Random House LLC
1745 Broadway, New York, NY 10019
SAN: 202-5507
Tel: 212-782-9000 *Toll Free Tel:* 800-726-0600
Web Site: www.penguinrandomhouse.com
Key Personnel
Chmn: Philip Hoffman
CEO: Nihar Malaviya
CFO/EVP, Head Mergers & Acqs: Manuel Sansigre
COO: Jeff Abraham
Chief Revenue Offr: Jaci Updike
Deputy Chief Revenue Offr: Jeff Weber
Chief Strategy Offr: Divya Sawhney
Pres & Publr, Knopf Doubleday Publishing Group: Maya Mavjee
Pres & Publr, Random House Children's Books: Barbara Marcus
Pres, Ballantine Books: Kara Welsh
Pres, Random House Worlds/EVP, Publr & Dir, Strategy, Del Rey & Inklore: Scott Shannon
EVP & Chief Legal Offr: Anke Steinecke
EVP & Publr, One World & Roc Lit 101: Christopher Jackson
EVP & Dir, Corp Communs: Claire von Schilling
EVP & Dir, Strategy for Diversity, Equity & Inclusion: Kimberly Ayers Shariff
EVP, Busn Strategy: Bill Takes
EVP: Catharine Lynch
SVP & Deputy Gen Coun: Matthew Martin
SVP & Deputy Publr: Avideh Bashirrad
SVP & Dir, Publicity: Susan Corcoran
SVP & Group Deputy Publr, Publg & Sales Opers, Knopf Doubleday Publishing Group: Christopher Dufault
SVP & Dir, Ebook Devt & Opers: Liisa McCloy-Kelley
SVP & Dir, Prodn, Knopf Doubleday Publishing Group & Penguin Publishing Group: Robert Wojciechowski
SVP & Dir, Publg Opers: Janet Rasche
SVP & Exec Mng Ed, Knopf Doubleday Publishing Group & Penguin Publishing Group: Meredith Dros
SVP, Author Devt: Christine McNamara
SVP, Cust Solutions, Logistics & Strategy: Alison Martin
SVP, Dist & Returns Opers: Lori De Reza
SVP, Dist, Engg & Systems: Alyssa Oles
SVP, Global Transportation & Logistics: Tracey Presley
SVP, Mktg: Emily Romero
SVP, Consumer Mktg: Erica Curtis
SVP, Digital Strategy: Matt Schwartz
SVP, IT: Chris Hart
SVP, Lib Sales & Digital Strategy/SVP & Dir, Sales Opers: Skip Dye
SVP, Mass Mdse & Dist Sales: Tom Cox
SVP, Online & Digital Sales: Michael Rotondo
SVP, Publicity & Communs, Knopf Doubleday Publishing Group: Todd Doughty
SVP, Sales Devt: Randi Rosenkranz
SVP, Sales Strategic Planning: Julie Black
SVP, Strategic Busn Planning, US Digital Prod Devt, Audio & Fodor's: Susan Livingston
SVP, Subs Rts, Children's: Helen Boomer
VP & Assoc Gen Coun: Dan Novack
VP & Publr, Knopf Books for Young Readers: Melanie Nolan
VP & Publr, Random House Worlds & Inklore/Publr, Del Rey: Keith Clayton
VP & Exec Dir, Prodn Planning, Analytics & Paper Purch: Michael DeFazio
VP & Sr Dir, Strategy & Fin: May Choy
VP & Dir, Consumer Data & Mktg Automation: Suzie Sisoler
VP & Dir, Digital Video: John Clinton
VP & Dir, Lib Mktg & Digital Lib Sales Group: Jennifer Childs
VP & Dir, Online Marketplace: Emilia Pisani
VP & Dir, Prodn Edit: Mark McCauslin
VP & Dir, Proprietary & Premium Sales: Lisa Vitelli
VP & Dir, Publg Opers Systems: Matt Godzieba
VP & Imprint Sales Dir, Crown Trade, Crown Forum, Crown Currency, WaterBrook, Multnomah, Image & Convergent: Todd Berman
VP & Publr & Ed-in-Chief, Del Rey: Tricia Narwani
VP, Edit Dir (Digital) & Assoc Publr (Romance): Gina Wachtel
VP, Acct Mktg: Ruth Liebmann
VP, Acct Mktg & Event Strategy: Lara Phan
VP, Busn Opers: Bryan Bixler
VP, Consumer Strategy & Engagement: Leslie Prives
VP, Cust Opers: Thea James
VP, Cust Opers & Strategy: Jessica Wells
VP, Educ Dist Sales: Cletus Durkin
VP, Educ Sales & Mktg: Michael Gentile
VP, Field Sales: Beth Koehler
VP, Global Talent Mgmt: Jo Mallia-Barsati
VP, Mergers & Acqs: Cara Deey
VP, Mktg Devt: Matteo Costa
VP, Natl Accts: Erin Reilly; Sasha Sadikot
VP, Proprietary & Premium Sales: Christine Dillon
VP, Spec Mkts & Strategic Mkt Devt: Sarah Williams
Publr, Ballantine Books: Jennifer Hershey
Publr, John Grisham: Suzanne Herz
Internal Leadership & Talent Coach: Rebecca Smart
Exec Art Dir, Gift: Danielle Deschenes
Exec Dir, Brand Devt (John Grisham): Lauren Weber
Exec Dir, Inventory Mgmt, Adult: Larry Mallach
Exec Dir, Publg Opers Systems: Heather Peterson
Sr Dir, Licensing: Rachael Perriello
Sr Dir, Subs Rts: Tawanna Sullivan
Art Dir, Books: Stephanie Huntwork
Dir, Art & Design, Knopf Doubleday Publishing Group: Kristen Bearse
Dir, Author Devt: Stephanie Bowen
Dir, Diversity, Equity & Inclusion: Annysa Polanco
Dir, Global Strategy & Corp Devt: Iria Alvarez
Dir, Mktg Analytics: Court Clinch
Dir, Natl Accts, Walmart Adult Sales: Jessica Ko
Dir, PreK-12 Educ Mktg: Kaiulani Williams
Dir, Prodn Edit, Knopf Doubleday Publishing Group: Ellen Feldman
Dir, Proprietary Sales, Children's: Jocelyn Lange
Dir, Sales Opers: Stephen Shodin
Dir, Specialty Retail Field & Category Sales: Christine Palomino
Dir, Strategy, Diversity, Equity & Inclusion: Susette Brooks
Dir, Title Mgmt, Knopf Doubleday Publishing Group: Orlene Gabrino
Edit Dir, Convergent: Derek Reed
Edit Dir, Inklore: Rebecca "Tay" Taylor
Edit Dir, Picture Books, Knopf Books for Young Readers: Rotem Moscovich
Digital Mktg Dir: Paige Smith
Multicultural Mktg Dir: Anthony Key
Prodn Dir: Luisa Francavilla
Sales Dir, Higher Educ: Kimberly Woods
Sales Dir, K-12 School Educ: Travis Temple
Assoc Dir, Author Devt: Phil Stamper-Halpin
Assoc Dir, Consumer Shows & Conferences: Lindsey Elias
Assoc Dir, Mktg Automation & Data Sci: Jason Newman
Assoc Dir, Natl Dist Sales: Morgan Green
Assoc Dir, Sales Servs & Admin: Dorothy Auld
Assoc Dir, Subs Rts Contracts: Grace Beehler; Beth Pizio; Jeremy Wrubel
Asst Dir, Digital Cust Opers: Allison Rothstein
Asst Dir, Digital Opers: Andrea Saggau
Asst Mktg Dir, Graphic & Licensing: Paola Crespo
Asst Mktg Dir, Harmony Books/Rodale Books: Odette Fleming
Asst Prodn Dir: Jane Chinn; Phil Leung; Heather Williamson
Assoc, Global Strategy & Corp Devt: Lea Stoeger
Exec Ed, Random House: David Ebershoff
Exec Ed, Zeitgeist: Susan Randol; Kim Suarez
Mng Ed/Sr Prodn Ed, Zeitgeist: Bethany Reis
Assoc Mng Ed, The Princeton Review: Amanda Yee
Assoc Mng Ed, Random House Children's Books: Megan Williams
Sr Ed, Del Rey: Emily Archbold
Sr Ed, Inklore: Sarah Peed
Sr Prodn Ed, Zeitgeist: Shara Underweiser
Ed, Clarkson Potter: Sahara Clement
Ed, Convergent: Mathew Burdette
Ed, Del Rey: Tom Hoeler
Ed, Knopf Books for Young Readers: Esther Cajahuaringa
Prodn Ed: Ashley Pierce
Prodn Ed, Vintage Espanol: Indira Pupo
Assoc Ed, Clarkson Potter: Gabrielle Van Tassel
Assoc Ed, Convergent: Leita Williams
Assoc Ed, One World/Roc Lit 101: Sun Robinson-Smith
Asst Ed, Knopf Books for Young Readers: Karen Greenberg
Asst Ed, One World: Oma Beharry
Sr Lib Mktg Mgr, Knopf Doubleday Publishing Group: Erica Melnichok
Sr Mgr, Analytics & Metadata: Pooja Karnane
Sr Mgr, Consumer Data Servs: Megan Vinciguerra
Sr Mgr, Content Mktg, Brightly: Jennifer Clare
Sr Mgr, Digital Cust Opers: Ayisha Clarke
Sr Mgr, Mktg Analytics: Andrew Carver
Sr Mktg Mgr, Convergent Books: Jessalyn Foggy
Sr Publg Mgr, Del Rey & Random House Worlds: Alex Larned
Sr Sales Mgr, Intl Direct Comic Mkt & Caribbean: Hector Torres
Sr Sales Mgr, Lib Mktg & Digital Lib Sales Group: Hugo Bresson; Brian Nelsen
Lib Mktg Mgr, Penguin Group: Liz Camfird
Mgr, Acct Mktg: Hal Hlavinka
Mgr, Content Mktg: Kathryn Monaco
Mgr, Edit Opers & Publg, Inklore: Logan Balestrino
Mgr, E-mail Mktg Opers: Lynn Rickert
Mgr, Sales Opers: Tom Broucksou
Mktg Mgr: Sharnell Johnson
Mktg Mgr, Harmony Books/Rodale Books: Jonathan Sung
Mktg Mgr, Inklore: Steph Hocutt
Publicity Mgr, Harmony Books/Rodale Books: Ray Arjune; Kelly Doyle
Publg & Mktg Mgr, Vintage Espanol: Michelle Dominguez
Metadata Coord: Savannah Sanocki
Creative Devt Lead, Content Mktg: Abbe Wright
Jr Designer: Irene Ng
Penguin Random House & its publishing entities are not accepting unsol submissions, proposals, mss, or submission queries via e-mail at this time.
Imprints: Ballantine Wellspring; Crescent Books; Crimeline; Dell Yearling; Doubleday/Galilee; Island; Ivy Books; Living Language; Potter Craft; Potter Style; Quickie Books; Random House Digital; Schwartz & Wade Books; SJP;

U.S. PUBLISHERS

Skylark; Spectra; Sylvan Learning; Vintage Children's Classics; Wings Books; Zeitgeist
Divisions: Crown Publishing Group; DK; Knopf Doubleday Publishing Group; Penguin Publishing Group; Penguin Random House Audio Publishing Group; Penguin Young Readers Group; Random House Children's Publishing; Random House Publishing Group

Branch Office(s)
Ten Speed Press/Crown Publishing Group, 6001 Shellmound St, Suite 600, Emeryville, CA 94608 *Tel:* 510-285-3000
Books on Tape Studios, 20970-B Warner Center Lane, Woodland Hills, CA 91367 *Tel:* 818-676-0969
Penguin Random House Espanol, 8950 SW 74 Ct, Suite 2010, Miami, FL 33156, Pres: Silvia Matute *Tel:* 786-509-8730
Appetite by Random House, 55 Water St, Suite 512, Vancouver, BC V6B 1A1, Canada *Tel:* 604-566-9806
Penguin Random House Canada, 320 Front St W, Suite 1400, Toronto, ON M5V 2B6, Canada, CEO: Kristin Cochrane *Tel:* 416-364-4449 *Toll Free Tel:* 888-523-9292 (orders) *Fax:* 416-598-7764 *Web Site:* penguinrandomhouse.ca

Foreign Office(s): Penguin Random House Grupo Editorial, Humberto Primo 555, C1103ACK Buenos Aires, Argentina *Tel:* (011) 5235-4400
Penguin Random House Australia, 100 Pacific Hwy, Level 3, North Sydney, NSW 2060, Australia, CEO: Julie Burland *Tel:* (02) 9954 9966
Penguin Random House Australia, 707 Collins St, Melbourne, Victoria 3008, Australia *Tel:* (03) 9811 2400
United Book Distributors, 30 Centre Rd, Scoresby, Victoria 3179, Australia *Tel:* (03) 8537 4599
Penguin Random House Grupo Editorial/Editorial Sudamericana Chilena SA, Merced 280, Piso 6, Santiago, Chile *Tel:* (02) 27828200
Penguin Random House China, B-7 Jiaming Ctr, 27 E Third Ring Rd N, Chaoyang District, Beijing 100020, China *Tel:* (010) 8587 7777
Penguin Random House China, Suite 2001-02, 20/F Central Plaza, No 227 Huangpi Rd N, Shanghai 200003, China *Tel:* (010) 8587 7711
Penguin Random House Grupo Editorial, Carrera 5A, No 34A-09, Bogota, Cundinamarca, Colombia *Tel:* (01) 743-0700
DK Verlag GmbH, Arnulfstr 124, Munich 80636, Germany *Tel:* (089) 44 23 26 0
Penguin Random House India, Penguin Offices, 7th fl, Infinity Tower C, DLF Cyber City, Gurgaon, Haryana 122 002, India *Tel:* (0124) 478-5600
DK, DKMindmill Corporate Tower, 3rd fl, Plot No 24A, Sector 16A, Film City, Noida, Uttar Pradesh 201 301, India *Tel:* (0120) 468-9600
Penguin Random House Malaysia, Level 1, Tower 2A, Ave 5 Bangsar S, No 8 Jl Kerinchi, 59200 Kuala Lumpur, Malaysia *Tel:* (03) 2247-3800
Penguin Random House Grupo Editorial, Miguel de Cervantes Saavedra, 301, piso 1, Colonia Granada, Delegacion Miguel Hidalgo, 11520 Mexico, CDMX, Mexico *Tel:* (0155) 30678400
Penguin Random House New Zealand, 67 Apollo Dr, Rosedale, Auckland 0632, New Zealand, CEO: Julie Burland *Tel:* (09) 442-7400
Penguin Random House Grupo Editorial, Av Ricardo Palma 341, Oficina 504 Miraflores, Lima, Peru *Tel:* (01) 206 3260
Penguin Random House Grupo Editorial Portugal Lda, Rua Alfredo da Silva, 14, 2610-016 Amadora, Portugal *Tel:* 214676749 *E-mail:* correio@penguinrandomhouse.com *Web Site:* www.penguinlivros.pt
Penguin Random House Singapore, 9 N Buona Vista Dr, No 13-01, The Metropolis Tower One, Singapore 138588, Singapore *Tel:* 6715 8989
Penguin Random House South Africa, The Estuaries No 4, Oxbow Crescent, Century Way, Century City, Cape Town 7441, South Africa, CEO: Steve Connolly *Tel:* (021) 460-5400
Penguin Random House South Africa, Rose Bank Office Park, Block D, 181 Jan Smuts Ave, Parktown N, Johannesburg 2193, South Africa *Tel:* (011) 327-3550
Penguin Random House Korea, 373 Gangnamdaero, 15F, Seocho-gu, Seoul 06621, South Korea
Penguin Random House Grupo Editorial SAU, Travessera de Gracia 47-49, 08021 Barcelona, Spain *Tel:* 93 366 03 00
Penguin Random House Grupo Editorial SAU, Luchana, 23 1a Planta, 28010 Madrid, Spain *Tel:* 91 535 81 90
The Book Service Distribution Center, Colchester Rd, Frating Green, Colchester, Essex C07 7DW, United Kingdom *Tel:* (01206) 256000
Grantham Book Services (GBS), Trent Rd, Grantham, Lincs NG31 7XQ, United Kingdom *Tel:* (01476) 541000 *Fax:* (01476) 541060 *Web Site:* www.thebookservice.co.uk
Random House Children's, 61-63 Uxbridge Rd, Ealing, London W5 5SA, United Kingdom *Tel:* (020) 8231 6800
Random House UK Ltd, 20 Vauxhall Bridge Rd, London SW1V 2SA, United Kingdom, CEO: Tom Weldon *Tel:* (020) 7840 8400 *Fax:* (020) 7233 8791
Transworld Publishers, 61-63 Uxbridge Rd, Ealing, London W5 5SA, United Kingdom *Tel:* (020) 8579 2652
Penguin Random House Grupo Editorial/Editorial Sudamericana Uruguaya SA, Colonia 950 Piso 6, 11100 Montevideo, Uruguay *Tel:* 29013668

Distribution Center: Crawfordsville Distribution Center, 1021 N State Rd 47, Crawfordsville, IN 47933, SVP: Lori De Reza *Tel:* 765-362-5125
Hampstead Distribution Center, 630 Hanover Pike, Hampstead, MD 21074
Westminster Distribution Center, 400 Bennett Cerf Dr, Westminster, MD 21157, VP: Tina Ruppert *Tel:* 410-848-1900
Reno Distribution Center, 1160 Trademark Dr, Suite 111, Reno, NV 89521, SVP: Lori De Reza
Mississauga Distribution Centre, 6971 Columbus Rd, Mississauga, ON L5T 1K1, Canada *Tel:* 416-364-4449
Rugby Distribution Center, Warwicks CV23 0WB, United Kingdom *Tel:* (01788) 514300
Membership(s): Association of American Publishers (AAP); Book Industry Study Group (BISG)
See separate listing for:
Crown Publishing Group
DK
Knopf Doubleday Publishing Group
Krause Publications Inc
Living Language
Penguin Publishing Group
Penguin Random House Audio Publishing Group
Penguin Young Readers Group
Random House Children's Books
Random House Publishing Group

Penguin Workshop
Imprint of Penguin Young Readers Group
c/o Penguin Random House LLC, 1745 Broadway, New York, NY 10019
Tel: 212-782-9000
Web Site: www.penguin.com/publishers/penguinworkshop/
Key Personnel
Pres & Publr: Francesco Sedita
Assoc Publr & Edit Dir: Rob Valois
VP & Publr: Cecily Kaiser
Dir, Nonfiction Publg: Paula Manzanero
Exec Ed: Renee Kelly
Sr Ed: Elizabeth Lee; Nick Magliato
Sr Ed, Mad Libs: Brian Clark
Assoc Ed: Anu Ohioma; Alex Wolfe
Asst Ed: Tyiana Combs; Celina Sun
Founded: 2017
Penguin Random House & its publishing entities are not accepting unsol submissions, proposals, mss, or submission queries via e-mail at this time.
Number of titles published annually: 170 Print

Penguin Young Readers Group
Division of Penguin Random House LLC
c/o Penguin Random House LLC, 1745 Broadway, New York, NY 10019
Tel: 212-782-9000
Web Site: www.penguin.com/penguin-young-readers-overview
Key Personnel
Pres: Jennifer Loja
Pres & Publr, Dial Books for Young Readers & GP Putnam's Sons Books for Young Readers: Jennifer Klonsky
Pres & Publr, Dutton Children's Books: Julie Strauss-Gabel
Pres & Publr, Kokila: Namrata Tripathi
Pres & Publr, Nancy Paulsen Books: Nancy Paulsen
Pres & Publr, Penguin Workshop: Francesco Sedita
Pres & Publr, Rocky Pond Books: Lauri Hornik
EVP & Assoc Publr: Jocelyn Schmidt
SVP & Exec Dir, Publicity & Corp Communs: Shanta Newlin
SVP, Busn Opers & Strategy: Robyn Bender
SVP, Sales: Becky Green
VP & Publr, Grosset & Dunlap, Licenses & Brands: Daniel Moreton
VP & Exec Dir, Brand & Content Devt Strategy: Stephanie Sabol
VP & Exec Dir, Publicity: Elyse Marshall
VP & Dir, Mng Edit & Prodn Edit: Nico Medina
VP & Dir, Trade Sales: Debra Polansky
VP, School & Lib Mktg & Creative Servs Dir: Carmela Iaria
Sr Dir, Creative & Strategy, World of Eric Carle: Mary Mekarnom
Sr Dir, Publicity: Olivia Russo
Dir, Preschool & Young Readers Mktg: Jed Bennett
Assoc Dir, Digital Mktg: Lauren Festa
Assoc Dir, Publicity: Kaitlin Kneafsey; Elizabeth Montoya Vaughan
Assoc Dir, School & Lib Mktg: Trevor Ingerson
Asst Dir, Brand Mktg: Vaishali Nayak
Sr Mktg Mgr: Brianna Lockhart
Digital Mktg Mgr: James Akinaka
Publicity Mgr: Lizzie Goodell
Publicist: Jenna Smith
Publg Assoc: Sarah Jospitre
Mktg Coord: Danielle Presley
Publicity Asst: Jaleesa Davis
Founded: 1997
Children's hardcover picture books; fiction & nonfiction; trade paperbacks; picture book paperbacks; board & novelty books; calendars.
Penguin Random House & its publishing entities are not accepting unsol submissions, proposals, mss, or submission queries via e-mail at this time.
Imprints: Dial Books for Young Readers; Dutton Children's Books; Flamingo Books; Grosset & Dunlap; Kokila; Nancy Paulsen Books; Penguin Workshop; Penguin Young Readers; Penguin Young Readers Licenses; Philomel Books; Price Stern Sloan; Puffin Books; GP Putnam's Sons Books for Young Readers; RISE x Penguin Workshop; Rocky Pond Books; Viking Children's Books; Frederick Warne Books; Wee Sing; World of Eric Carle
See separate listing for:
Dial Books for Young Readers
Dutton Children's Books
Flamingo Books
Kokila
Nancy Paulsen Books
Penguin Workshop

PUBLISHERS / U.S. PUBLISHERS

Philomel Books
Puffin Books
GP Putnam's Sons Books for Young Readers
Rocky Pond Books
Viking Children's Books

Penn Press, see University of Pennsylvania Press

Penn State University Press
Division of Penn State University Libraries
University Support Bldg 1, Suite C, 820 N University Dr, University Park, PA 16802-1003
SAN: 213-5760
Tel: 814-865-1327 *Toll Free Tel:* 800-326-9180 (orders & cust serv) *Fax:* 814-863-1408
Toll Free Fax: 877-778-2665 (book orders)
E-mail: orders@psupress.org; customerservice@psupress.org
Web Site: www.psupress.org
Key Personnel
Art Dir: Regina Starace *E-mail:* ras35@psu.edu
Sales & Mktg Dir: Erika Valenti
  E-mail: efv5159@psu.edu
Assoc Dir, Design & Prodn Mgr: Jennifer Norton
  Tel: 814-863-8061 *E-mail:* jsn4@psu.edu
Assoc Mktg Dir: Cate Fricke *Tel:* 814-865-1329
  E-mail: crf16@psu.edu
Asst Dir & Ed-in-Chief: Kendra Boileau
  E-mail: klb60@psu.edu
Exec Ed & Mgr, Grants & Spec Projs: Eleanor Goodman *E-mail:* ehg11@psu.edu
Mng Ed: Alex Ramos *E-mail:* ajr586@psu.edu
Mng Ed, Journals: Astrid Meyer *Tel:* 814-863-3830 *E-mail:* aum38@psu.edu
Founded: 1956
Scholarly books & journals; art & architectural history; literature & literary criticism, philosophy, religion, archaeology, biblical studies, languages of the ancient Near East, social sciences, law, history, Latin American studies, regional books on Mid-Atlantic area. Special Series: Literature & Philosophy; Penn State Series in the History of the Book; Re-Reading the Canon; Keystone Books (regional); American & European Philosophy; Magic in History; Rural Studies; Refiguring Modernism; Buildings, Landscapes & Societies.
ISBN Prefix(es): 978-0-271; 978-1-575; 978-1-883 (formerly CDL); 978-0-962 (formerly CDL); 978-0-966 (formerly CDL); 978-0-873 (formerly CDL)
Number of titles published annually: 100 Print; 45 E-Book
Total Titles: 2,200 Print; 55 Online; 400 E-Book; 2 Audio
Imprints: Eisenbrauns (specialize in ancient Near East); Graphic Mundi (comics for adults & young adults); Keystone Books (regional titles); Metalmark (reprints of public domain books on Pennsylvania)
Distributor for Abo Akademi University (specialize in ancient Near East); American Oriental Society; Deo Publishing; National Gallery of Singapore; Neo-Assyrian Text Corpus (FFAR, Helsinki, Finland)
Foreign Rep(s): Lexa Publishers' Representatives (Mical Moser) (Canada); MHM Ltd (Japan); The Oxford Publicity Partnership Ltd (Europe, UK); Sino Publishers Services Ltd (Rance Fu) (China); US PubRep (Craig Falk) (Caribbean, Central America, Mexico, South America); The White Partnership (Andrew White) (India, Southeast Asia); Woodslane Pty Ltd (Australia, Fiji, New Zealand, Papua New Guinea)
Orders to: Parson Weems' Publisher Services LLC, 310 N Front St, Suite 4-10, Wilmington, NC 28401, Mgr: Causten Stehle
  Tel: 914-948-4259 *Toll Free Fax:* 866-651-0337 *E-mail:* office@parsonweems.com *Web Site:* www.parsonweems.com
Membership(s): American Academy of Religion (AAR); American Council of Learned Societies (ACLS); Art Libraries Society (ARLIS); Association of American Publishers (AAP); Association of University Presses (AUPresses); Book Industry Study Group (BISG); Modern Language Association (MLA); Organization of American Historians (OAH); Society for Scholarly Publishing (SSP); Society of Bible Literature (SBL)
See separate listing for:
Eisenbrauns

Pennsylvania Historical & Museum Commission
Subsidiary of The Commonwealth of Pennsylvania
State Museum Bldg, 300 North St, Harrisburg, PA 17120-0053
SAN: 282-1532
Tel: 717-787-3362; 717-787-5526 (orders)
E-mail: ra-shoppaheritage@pa.gov
Web Site: www.phmc.pa.gov; www.shoppaheritage.com
Key Personnel
Exec Dir: Andrea Bakewell Lowery
  E-mail: alowery@pa.gov
Founded: 1945
Books, booklets & references on Pennsylvania prehistory, history, culture & natural history, both scholarly & popular.
ISBN Prefix(es): 978-0-911124; 978-0-89271
Number of titles published annually: 5 Print
Total Titles: 145 Print

§Pennsylvania State Data Center
Subsidiary of Institute of State & Regional Affairs
Penn State Harrisburg, 777 W Harrisburg Pike, Middletown, PA 17057-4898
Tel: 717-948-6336 *Fax:* 717-948-6754
E-mail: pasdc@psu.edu
Web Site: pasdc.hbg.psu.edu
Key Personnel
Dir: Jennifer Shultz *Tel:* 717-519-9547
  E-mail: jjb131@psu.edu
Founded: 1981
Policy, demographical analytical reports, hard copy & computer discs.
ISBN Prefix(es): 978-0-939667; 978-1-58036
Number of titles published annually: 5 Print; 5 CD-ROM
Total Titles: 130 Print; 130 CD-ROM; 1 E-Book

Pennsylvania State University Press, see Penn State University Press

PennWell Books
Division of PennWell Books LLC
10050 E 52 St, Tulsa, OK 74146
SAN: 992-0161
Toll Free Tel: 866-777-1814 *Fax:* 918-550-8962
E-mail: sales@pennwellbooks.com
Web Site: www.pennwellbooks.com
Key Personnel
Publr: Matthew Dresher *E-mail:* matt@pennwellbooks.com
Founded: 1970
Publisher of technical & nontechnical books for the energy industry. Our books are written by highly sought-after industry experts who can present highly technical information in an engaging way. PennWell Books will help you broaden your skills in your current area of expertise, understand other related disciplines, provide quick-glance references as topics arise in your daily routine & make excellent classroom & training texts.
ISBN Prefix(es): 978-0-912212; 978-0-87814; 978-1-59370; 978-0-9795633; 978-1-955578
Number of titles published annually: 8 Print
Total Titles: 200 Print; 67 E-Book
Divisions: PennWell Petroleum Books; PennWell Power Books
Foreign Rep(s): Eurospan (Africa, Asia, Australasia, Europe, Middle East)

Penny-Farthing Productions
Imprint of Penny-Farthing Productions Inc
One Sugar Creek Center Blvd, Suite 820, Sugar Land, TX 77478
Tel: 713-780-0300 *Toll Free Tel:* 800-926-2669 *Fax:* 713-780-4004
E-mail: corp@pfproductions.com
Web Site: www.pfproductions.com
Key Personnel
Mktg Coord: Julia Ahadi *E-mail:* julia@pfproductions.com
Proj Dir: Courtney Huddleston
  E-mail: courtney@pfproductions.com
Graphic Designer: Andre McBride
  E-mail: design@pfproductions.com
Corp Off Mgr: Pam Johnston
Founded: 1998
Penny-Farthing Productions Inc officially opened its doors in 1998 as Penny-Farthing Press Inc with a small staff & a plan to create comic books & children's books exemplifying quality storytelling, artwork, & printing. Starting with *The Victorian*, PFP expanded its line to 10 titles, keeping output small enough to maintain the highest quality. PFP has won numerous awards including the Gutenberg D'Argent Medal & several Spectrum Awards & was also featured in the Dec 24, 2001 issue of Publisher's Weekly. PFP & President Ken White strive to work with talented & energetic individuals in order to put exquisite pieces of art into the hands of readers everywhere.
ISBN Prefix(es): 978-0-9673683; 978-0-9719012; 978-0-9842143; 978-0-9991709
Number of titles published annually: 4 Print
Total Titles: 24 Print; 3 Online; 3 E-Book
Distribution Center: Amazon
Bookazine
Brodart Books & Library Services
Children's Plus Inc
Follett School Solutions
Membership(s): American Booksellers Association (ABA); Independent Book Publishers Association (IBPA); Publishers Association of the West (PubWest)

Pentecostal Publishing House, see Pentecostal Resources Group

§Pentecostal Resources Group
Formerly Pentecostal Publishing House
Subsidiary of United Pentecostal Church International
36 Research Park Ct, Weldon Spring, MO 63304
SAN: 219-3817
Tel: 636-229-7900 *Toll Free Tel:* 866-819-7667
Web Site: www.pentecostalpublishing.com
Key Personnel
Ed-in-Chief & Publr: Mr Robin Johnston
  E-mail: rjohnston@upci.org
Assoc Ed: Lee Ann Alexander
  E-mail: lalexander@upci.org
Founded: 1945
Trade paperbacks, periodicals, bibliographies; religion (Protestant), Bibles, foreign languages, crafts, self-help.
ISBN Prefix(es): 978-0-912315; 978-0-932581; 978-1-56722; 978-0-7577
Number of titles published annually: 10 Print; 10 CD-ROM; 10 E-Book
Total Titles: 400 Print; 35 CD-ROM; 200 E-Book; 1 Audio
Imprints: WAP Academic; WAP Children; Word Aflame Press
Distributed by Christian Network International; Innovative Marketing

U.S. PUBLISHERS

Distribution Center: Anchor Distributors, 1030 Hunt Valley Circle, New Kensington, PA 15068 *Toll Free Tel:* 800-444-4484 *Toll Free Fax:* 800-765-1960 *E-mail:* anchor.customerservice@anchordistributors.com
Spring Arbor Distributors Inc, One Ingram Blvd, La Vergne, TN 37086 *Toll Free Tel:* 800-395-4340 *Toll Free Fax:* 800-876-0186 *E-mail:* customerservice@ingramcontent.com

Peradam Press
Subsidiary of The Center for Cultural & Naturalist Studies
PO Box 6, North San Juan, CA 95960-0006
Tel: 530-277-9324 *Fax:* 530-559-0754
E-mail: peradam@earthlink.net
Key Personnel
Pres & Sr Ed: Linda Birkholz
Exec Ed: Corinne Boyle
Ed: Patricia Hicks
Founded: 1993
General trade books hardcover & paperbacks.
ISBN Prefix(es): 978-1-885420
Number of titles published annually: 10 Print
Total Titles: 81 Print
Shipping Address: 19074 Oak Tree Rd, Nevada City, CA 95959

Perfection Learning®
1000 N Second Ave, Logan, IA 51546-1061
Mailing Address: PO Box 500, Logan, IA 51546-0500
Tel: 712-644-2831 *Toll Free Tel:* 800-831-4190 *Toll Free Fax:* 800-543-2745
E-mail: orders@perfectionlearning.com
Web Site: www.perfectionlearning.com
Key Personnel
Pres & CEO: Steve Keay
SVP, Publg: Robert Methven
VP, Prod Mktg & Engagement: Dori Veto
VP, Natl Sales & Prof Devt: Leah Ames
Exec Dir, Prof Devt: Barbara Quincer Coulter
Regl Dir, Educ Partnerships: Kim Vance
Edit Dir: Carol Francis
Dir, Creative Design: Matthew Pollock
Design Dir: Randy Messer *E-mail:* rmesser@perfectionlearning.com
Dir, Mktg Opers: Lance Thompson
Dir, Mktg: Kristin Hipwell
Dir, Digital Mktg: Rebecca Keay
Dir, Sales Enablement & Cust Experience: Thomas Bower
Dir of Sales, East: Mark James
Founded: 1926
Elementary & secondary product line covers such content areas as reading, literature, language arts, math, test preparation, social studies, world languages, science & more.
ISBN Prefix(es): 978-0-89598; 978-0-7807; 978-0-7891; 978-0-8124; 978-1-56312; 978-0-7569; 978-1-60686; 978-1-63419; 978-1-62974; 978-1-62766; 978-1-61563; 978-1-61383; 978-1-61384; 978-1-62299; 978-1-62359; 978-1-62765; 978-1-68064; 978-1-68065; 978-1-68240
Number of titles published annually: 30 Print
Total Titles: 500 Print
Imprints: Cover Craft; Cover-to-Cover; Literature & Thought; Passages; Retold Classics; Tale Blazers
Divisions: Turtleback Books
Distributor for Abrams; Ace Books; Airmont; Annick Press; Archway; Atheneum; Baker Books; Ballantine; Bantam; Barrons; Berkley; Blake Books; Candlewick Press; Charlesbridge Press; Chelsea House; Children's Press; Chronicle Books; Crabtree Publishing Co; Crown; Disney Press; Distri Books; DK; Doubleday; Dutton; Farrar, Straus & Giroux Inc; Fawcett; Firefly; First Avenue; Free Spirit; Fulcrum; Golden Books; Greenhaven Publishing; Hammond; Hayes; Gareth Stevens; Frederick Warne Books
Foreign Rep(s): School Book Fairs Ltd (Ron Grant) (Canada)

§The Permanent Press
4170 Noyac Rd, Sag Harbor, NY 11963
SAN: 213-1633
Tel: 631-725-1101
E-mail: info@thepermanentpress.com
Web Site: www.thepermanentpress.com
Key Personnel
Publr: Judith Shepard *E-mail:* judith@thepermanentpress.com
Mng Ed: Caleb Kercheval *E-mail:* caleb@thepermanentpress.com
Founded: 1978
Committed to publishing works of social & literary merit.
ISBN Prefix(es): 978-0-933256 (Second Chance Press); 978-1-877946; 978-0-932966; 978-1-57962
Number of titles published annually: 6 Print
Total Titles: 480 Print
Imprints: Second Chance Press
Foreign Rights: AnatoliaLit Agency (Amy Marie Spangler) (Turkey); English Agency Japan Co Ltd (Atsushi Hori) (Japan); Lora Fountain Literary Agency (Lora Fountain) (France); Jill Hughes (Eastern Europe); Andrew Nurnberg Associates International Ltd (Jackie Huang) (China); Andrew Nurnberg Associates International Ltd (Whitney Hsu) (Taiwan); Thomas Schlueck GmbH (Franka Zastrow) (Germany); R Vivian Literary Agency (Rita Vivian) (Italy); Eric Yang Agency (Sue Yang) (South Korea); Zarana Agencia Literaria (Marta Sevilla) (Brazil, Portugal, Spain)

Persea Books
90 Broad St, Suite 2100, New York, NY 10004
SAN: 212-8233
Tel: 212-260-9256
E-mail: info@perseabooks.com; poetry@perseabooks.com; publicity@perseabooks.com
Web Site: www.perseabooks.com
Key Personnel
Pres & Publr: Michael Braziller
VP & Edit Dir: Karen Braziller
Poetry Ed: Gabriel Fried
Publicity: Jonah Fried
Founded: 1975
ISBN Prefix(es): 978-0-89255
Number of titles published annually: 12 Print; 10 E-Book
Total Titles: 500 Print; 40 E-Book
Imprints: A Karen & Michael Braziller Book
Distributed by W W Norton & Company Inc (worldwide exc CN); Penguin Random House Canada (CN only)
Orders to: W W Norton & Company Inc, 500 Fifth Ave, New York, NY 10110 *Toll Free Tel:* 800-233-4830
Distribution Center: W W Norton & Company Inc c/o National Book Co, Keystone Industrial Park, Scranton, PA 18512 *Toll Free Fax:* 800-233-4830

Peter Pauper Press, Inc
202 Mamaroneck Ave, Suite 400, White Plains, NY 10601-5376
SAN: 204-9449
Tel: 914-681-0144 *Fax:* 914-681-0389
E-mail: customerservice@peterpauper.com; orders@peterpauper.com; marketing@peterpauper.com
Web Site: www.peterpauper.com
Key Personnel
CEO: Laurence Beilenson *E-mail:* lbeilenson@peterpauper.com
VP: John Hartley *E-mail:* jhartley@peterpauper.com
Creative Dir: Heather Zschock *E-mail:* hzschock@peterpauper.com
Dir, Spec Sales: Esther Beilenson
Founded: 1928
Decorated hardcover gift, inspirational; quotations, miniatures, journals, photo albums, children's picture books, children's activity books, travel guides.
ISBN Prefix(es): 978-0-88088; 978-1-59359; 978-1-44130; 978-1-44131; 978-1-44132
Number of titles published annually: 150 Print; 5 E-Book
Total Titles: 1,300 Print; 270 E-Book
Foreign Rep(s): Alejandra Garza (Mexico); Saskia Knobbe (Netherlands); Bara Kristinsdottir (Iceland); Peter Pauper Press Pty (Australia); Peter Pauper Press UK (UK); Phambili (Southern Africa); Israel Ring (Brazil)
Returns: Conri Services Inc, 5 Skyline Dr, Hawthorne, NY 10532
Shipping Address: Conri Services Inc, 5 Skyline Dr, Hawthorne, NY 10532, Contact: Connie Levene *Tel:* 914-592-2300 *Fax:* 914-592-2174
Warehouse: Conri Services Inc, 5 Skyline Dr, Hawthorne, NY 10532, Contact: Connie Levene *Tel:* 914-592-2300 *Fax:* 914-592-2174

§Peterson Institute for International Economics (PIIE)
1750 Massachusetts Ave NW, Washington, DC 20036-1903
SAN: 293-2865
Tel: 202-328-9000
E-mail: media@piie.com
Web Site: piie.com
Key Personnel
Pres: Adam S Posen *E-mail:* apoffice@piie.com
VP, Pubns: Steven R Weisman *Tel:* 202-454-1331
Founded: 1981
International economic policy publications.
ISBN Prefix(es): 978-0-88132
Number of titles published annually: 15 Print; 8 Online; 8 E-Book
Total Titles: 300 Print; 50 E-Book
Foreign Rep(s): Columbia University Press (Africa, Eastern Europe, Iran, Israel, Russia, Turkey, Western Europe)
Returns: Columbia University Press, 61 W 62 St, New York, NY 10023
Distribution Center: Columbia University Press, 61 W 62 St, New York, NY 10023
Membership(s): Association of American Publishers (AAP); Society for Scholarly Publishing (SSP); Washington Publishers (WP)

§Peterson's
8740 Lucent Blvd, Suite 400, Highlands Ranch, CO 80129
Tel: 609-896-1800 *Toll Free Tel:* 800-338-3282
E-mail: pubmarketing@petersons.com
Web Site: www.petersons.com
Key Personnel
Publg Dir: Bernadette Webster
Founded: 1966
Education, career books, software & CD-ROM, data licensing, test preparation, financial aid & adult education, online lead generation.
ISBN Prefix(es): 978-0-87866; 978-1-56079; 978-0-7689
Number of titles published annually: 50 Print; 10 E-Book
Total Titles: 120 Print; 10 E-Book
Imprints: Peterson's/Pacesetter Books
Foreign Rights: Ann-Christine Daniellsson Agency (Scandinavia); International Editors' Co - Yanez Agencia Literaria (Latin America, Spain); Frederique Parretta Agency (Canada (French-speaking), France); Pikarski (Israel); Tuttle-Mori Agency Inc (Japan, Thailand)
Orders to: Hachette Book Group Inc, 53 State St, Boston, MA 02109 (US & CN) *Toll Free Tel:* 800-759-0190 *Toll Free Fax:* 800-286-9471; Hachette Book Group Inc, 1290 Avenue

of the Americas, New York, NY 10104 (intl orders) *Tel:* 212-364-1325 *Fax:* 212-364-0933
E-mail: international@hbgusa.com
Distribution Center: Two Rivers Distribution, an Ingram brand, 1400 Broadway, Suite 520, New York, NY 10018 *Toll Free Tel:* 866-400-5351 *E-mail:* ips@ingramcontent.com *Web Site:* tworiversdistribution.com
Membership(s): Book Industry Study Group (BISG)

§Petroleum Extension Service (PETEX)
Unit of The University of Texas at Austin, Cockrell School of Engineering
JJ Pickle Research Campus, 10100 Burnet Rd, Bldg 2, Austin, TX 78758-4445
Tel: 512-471-5940 *Toll Free Tel:* 800-687-4132 *Fax:* 512-471-9410 *Toll Free Fax:* 800-687-7839
E-mail: info@petex.utexas.edu
Web Site: cee.utexas.edu/ce/petex
Key Personnel
Dir, Publg, Communs & Branding: Debby Denehy
Founded: 1944
Develops, produces & delivers technical & non-technical training courses, publications & e-product solutions for employees in various sectors of the petroleum industry.
ISBN Prefix(es): 978-0-88698
Number of titles published annually: 10 Print
Total Titles: 400 Print
Branch Office(s)
4702 N Sam Houston Pkwy W, Suite 800, Houston, TX 77086

§Pflaum Publishing Group
Division of Bayard Inc
3055 Kettering Blvd, Suite 100, Dayton, OH 45439
Toll Free Tel: 800-523-4625; 800-543-4383 (ext 1136, cust serv) *Toll Free Fax:* 800-370-4450
E-mail: service@pflaum.com
Web Site: www.pflaum.com
Key Personnel
VP & Dir, Sales: Michael Raffio
Publr & Edit Dir: David Dziena
Founded: 1885
Weekly liturgical magazines for PreK-8. Sacramental preparation for children & teens, catechetical resources for PreK-12, religious educators & youth ministers.
ISBN Prefix(es): 978-0-937997; 978-0-89837; 978-1-933178; 978-1-935042; 978-1-939105
Number of titles published annually: 20 Print
Total Titles: 75 Print
Membership(s): Association of Catholic Publishers Inc; National Catholic Education Association (NCEA); National Catholic Educational Exhibitors (NCEE)

Phaidon
65 Bleecker St, 8th fl, New York, NY 10012
Tel: 212-652-5400 *Toll Free Tel:* 800-759-0190 (cust serv) *Fax:* 212-652-5410
Toll Free Fax: 800-286-9471 (cust serv)
E-mail: enquiries@phaidon.com
Web Site: www.phaidon.com
Key Personnel
CEO: Keith Fox
COO: Philip Ruppel
VP & Group Publr: Deborah Aaronson
Assoc Publr: Emilia Terragni
Global Dir, Mktg & Publicity: Siobhan Bent
Dir, Mktg & Digital Initiatives: Ellie Levine
Dir, Spec Mkts & Retail Sales: Sarah Chester
Publicity Dir, North America: Alex Coumbis
Exec Commissioning Ed, Food: Emily Takoudes
Exec Ed: Lynne Ciccaglione
Mng Ed, Culinary: Ellie Smith
Proj Ed: Simon Hunegs
Sr Content Mktg Mgr: Sierra Cortner
Mktg Mgr: Audree Damiba
Mktg Mgr, North America: Tessa Houstoun
Natl Sales Mgr: Ruby Modell
Publicist: Eva Baron
Founded: 1923
Premier global publisher of the creative arts with over 1,500 titles in print. We work with the world's most influential artists, chefs, writers & thinkers to produce innovative books on art, photography, design, architecture, fashion, food & travel & illustrated books for children. Headquartered in London & New York City.
ISBN Prefix(es): 978-0-7148
Number of titles published annually: 80 Print
Total Titles: 1,500 Print
Imprints: Monacelli
Foreign Office(s): Phaidon Sarl, 55 rue Traversiere, 75012 Paris, France *Tel:* 01 55 28 38 38 *Fax:* 01 55 28 38 39
Phaidon Verlag, Innstr 30, 10243 Berlin, Germany *Tel:* (030) 28 04 08 35 *Fax:* (030) 28 04 48 79
Phaidon Press Ltd, 18 Regents Wharf, All Saints St, London N1 9PA, United Kingdom *Tel:* (020) 7843 1000 *Fax:* (020) 7843 1010

Philadelphia Museum of Art
PO Box 7646, Philadelphia, PA 19101-7646
Tel: 215-763-8100 *Fax:* 215-236-4465
Web Site: www.philamuseum.org
Key Personnel
Prodn Mgr: Rich Bonk
Ed: Mary Cason; Kathleen Krattenmaker; David Updike
Founded: 1901
Illustrated scholarly works on the permanent collection & exhibitions at the museum.
ISBN Prefix(es): 978-0-87633
Number of titles published annually: 5 Print
Total Titles: 114 Print
Distributed by Yale University Press

Philomel Books
Imprint of Penguin Young Readers Group
c/o Penguin Random House LLC, 1745 Broadway, New York, NY 10019
Tel: 212-782-9000
Web Site: www.penguin.com/philomel/
Key Personnel
VP & Publr, Philomel Books & Viking Children's Books: Tamar Brazis
VP & Publr: Jill Santopolo
VP & Sr Dr, Art & Design: Ellice Lee
Ed: Talia Benamy; Kelsey Murphy
Founded: 1980
Penguin Random House & its publishing entities are not accepting unsol submissions, proposals, mss, or submission queries via e-mail at this time.
Number of titles published annually: 41 Print
Total Titles: 367 Print

Philosophical Library Inc
275 Central Park W, Suite 12D, New York, NY 10024
Tel: 212-873-6070 *Fax:* 212-873-6070
E-mail: editors@philosophicallibrary.com
Web Site: philosophicallibrary.com
Key Personnel
Dir: Regeen Runes Kiernan-najar
Founded: 1941
Comprehensive collection of mid-level reference books. A consistent source for serious readers, libraries, academic institutions & booksellers worldwide. Also have a program for print on demand.
ISBN Prefix(es): 978-0-8022
Number of titles published annually: 125 Print; 170 E-Book; 75 Audio
Total Titles: 2,500 Print; 300 E-Book
Distributed by Open Road Integrated Media

Philosophy Documentation Center
PO Box 7147, Charlottesville, VA 22906-7147
Tel: 434-220-3300 *Toll Free Tel:* 800-444-2419 *Fax:* 434-220-3301
E-mail: order@pdcnet.org
Web Site: www.pdcnet.org
Key Personnel
Dir: George Leaman *E-mail:* leaman@pdcnet.org
Assoc Dir: Pamela K Swope *E-mail:* pkswope@pdcnet.org
Electronic Publg & Mktg: Susanne Mueller-Grote *E-mail:* smg@pdcnet.org
Founded: 1966
Scholarly, nonprofit publisher of peer-reviewed journals, book series, conference proceedings & specialized reference materials. Provides a range of publishing services, including online hosting of full-text content, secure access solutions, membership management, order fulfillment for print or electronic publications & rights management.
ISBN Prefix(es): 978-0-912632; 978-1-889680; 978-1-63435
Number of titles published annually: 15 Print; 30 Online; 10 E-Book
Total Titles: 150 Print; 200 Online; 30 E-Book
Distributor for Zeta Books (online access)
Membership(s): Society for Scholarly Publishing (SSP)

Piano Press
1425 Ocean Ave, Suite 5, Del Mar, CA 92014
Mailing Address: PO Box 85, Del Mar, CA 92014-0085
Tel: 619-884-1401
E-mail: pianopress@pianopress.com
Web Site: www.pianopress.com
Key Personnel
Owner & Ed: Elizabeth C Axford
E-mail: lizaxford@pianopress.com
Music Typesetter: David Murray; Mark So
Audio Engr: John Dawes; Denny Martin; Matthew Dela Pola; Peter Sprague; Kris Stone
Edit Asst: Kathy Alward; Carol Buckley; Katie Cook; Dee Crowell; Gay Salo
Exec Asst: Melanie Matthews; Brandy Montgomery
Founded: 1998
Publishes songbooks & CDs as well as music-related coloring books & poetry for the educational & family markets.
ISBN Prefix(es): 978-0-9673325; 978-1-931844; 979-8-88790
Number of titles published annually: 12 Print; 1 Audio
Total Titles: 200 Print
Membership(s): The American Society of Composers, Authors and Publishers (ASCAP); Recording Academy (NARAS); Society of Children's Book Writers & Illustrators (SCBWI)

Picador
Imprint of Pan Macmillan
120 Broadway, New York, NY 10271
Tel: 646-307-5151 *Fax:* 212-253-9627
E-mail: publicity@picadorusa.com
Web Site: us.macmillan.com/picador
Key Personnel
SVP & Dir, Publicity: Sarita Varma
E-mail: svarma@fsgbooks.com
VP & Assoc Publr: James Meader
VP, Mktg & Sales: Darin Keesler *E-mail:* darin.keesler@picadorusa.com
Sr Art Dir: Alex Merto
Dir, Mktg: Daniel del Valle
Dir, Publicity: Lottchen Shivers
Assoc Dir, Mktg: Hillary Tisman
Assoc Dir, Publicity: Brian Gittis; Steve Weil
Exec Ed: Anna deVries
Mng Ed: Rebecca Caine
Sr Mktg Mgr: Nick Stewart
Assoc Mktg Mgr: Amber Williams

U.S. PUBLISHERS

Asst Mktg Mgr: Caitlin O'Beirne
Sr Publicist: Brianna Scharfenberg
Publicist: Sarah Haeckel
Asst Publicist: Madeline Day; Jonathan Woollen
Mktg Asst: Carina Imbornone; Liat Kaplan
Founded: 1995
ISBN Prefix(es): 978-0-312; 978-0-374
Number of titles published annually: 90 Print
Total Titles: 7,000 Print
Foreign Rep(s): Macmillan General Books (Africa, Caribbean, Europe, India, Latin America, Middle East); Macmillan Publishers (New Zealand); Melia Publishing Services (Ireland, UK); Pan Macmillan (Asia, Australia); Pan Macmillan South Africa (South Africa); Publishers Group Canada (Canada)
Distribution Center: VHPS Distribution Center, 16365 James Madison Hwy, Gordonsville, VA 22942-8501 Toll Free Tel: 888-330-8477 Toll Free Fax: 800-672-2054 (orders)
Raincoast Book Distribution, 2440 Viking Way, Richmond, BC V6V 1NZ, Canada Toll Free Tel: 800-663-5714 Toll Free Fax: 800-565-3770 E-mail: orders@raincoastbooks.com

The Picasso Project
Imprint of Alan Wofsy Fine Arts
1109 Geary Blvd, San Francisco, CA 94109
Tel: 415-292-6500 Fax: 415-292-6594
E-mail: editeur@earthlink.net (edit); picasso@art-books.com (orders)
Web Site: www.art-books.com
Key Personnel
Mgr: Adios Butler
Ed: Alan Hyman
Founded: 1990
Publish & distribute comprehensive catalogues on the works of Pablo Picasso. Distribution center located in Ashland, OH.
ISBN Prefix(es): 978-0-915346; 978-1-55660
Number of titles published annually: 6 Print; 4 CD-ROM
Total Titles: 100 Print; 12 CD-ROM
Imprints: Beauxarts; Collegium Graphicum
Distributed by Alan Wofsy Fine Arts
Distributor for Cramer (Switzerland); Galerie Kornfeld Verlag AG (Bern); Ramie (France)
Billing Address: PO Box 2210, San Francisco, CA 94126-2110
Membership(s): Association of American Publishers (AAP)

Pieces of Learning Inc
1112 N Carbon St, Suite A, Marion, IL 62959-8976
SAN: 298-461X
Tel: 618-964-9426 Toll Free Tel: 800-729-5137 Toll Free Fax: 800-844-0455
E-mail: info@piecesoflearning.com
Web Site: piecesoflearning.com
Key Personnel
Pres: Tyler Young
Founded: 1989
Teacher supplementary educational books; mail order.
ISBN Prefix(es): 978-1-880505; 978-0-9623835; 978-1-931334; 978-1-934358; 978-1-937113
Number of titles published annually: 16 Print
Total Titles: 500 Print; 50 E-Book
Membership(s): Education Market Association

The Pilgrim Press/United Church Press
700 Prospect Ave, Cleveland, OH 44115-1100
Tel: 216-736-2100 Toll Free Tel: 800-537-3394 (orders)
E-mail: permissions@thepilgrimpress.com; store@ucc.org (orders)
Web Site: www.thepilgrimpress.com
Key Personnel
Publr: Rev Rachel Hackenberg
Dir, Sales & Dist: Marie Tyson E-mail: tysonm@ucc.org
Founded: 1617
Diverse spiritualities; peace & justice; world religions; contemporary ministry.
ISBN Prefix(es): 978-0-8298
Number of titles published annually: 10 Print
Total Titles: 500 Print

Pineapple Press
Imprint of The Globe Pequot Press
c/o The Globe Pequot Press, 64 S Main St, Essex, CT 06426
E-mail: pineappleedit@rowman.com
Web Site: www.pineapplepress.com
Founded: 1982
Gardening, nature, art, folklore, history, travel, children's books & fiction that features Florida & the American Southeast.
ISBN Prefix(es): 978-0-910923; 978-1-56164; 978-1-68334
Number of titles published annually: 20 Print
Total Titles: 365 Print
Distribution Center: National Book Network (NBN), 15200 NBN Way, Blue Ridge Summit, PA 17214 Tel: 717-794-3800 Toll Free Tel: 800-462-6420 Toll Free Fax: 800-338-4550 E-mail: customercare@nbnbooks.com
Web Site: www.nbnbooks.com

Pinnacle Books, see Kensington Publishing Corp

Planert Creek Press
E4843 395 Ave, Menomonie, WI 54751
SAN: 855-7454
Tel: 715-235-4110
E-mail: publisher@planertcreekpress.com
Web Site: www.planertcreekpress.com
Key Personnel
Publr: David Tank
Founded: 2008
Specialize in 3D books & topics related to West Central Wisconsin.
This publisher has indicated that 100% of their product line is author subsidized.
ISBN Prefix(es): 978-0-9815064; 978-0-9962218
Number of titles published annually: 3 Print; 3 Online
Total Titles: 13 Print; 3 Online; 1 Audio
Membership(s): National Stereoscopic Association (NSA); Society of Children's Book Writers & Illustrators (SCBWI)

Planners Press
Imprint of Routledge
205 N Michigan Ave, Suite 1200, Chicago, IL 60601
Tel: 312-431-9100 Fax: 312-786-6700
E-mail: customerservice@planning.org
Web Site: www.planning.org
Key Personnel
Sr Ed: Kate Schell E-mail: kathryn.schell@taylorandfrancis.com
Founded: 1978
Books on planning.
ISBN Prefix(es): 978-0-918286; 978-1-884829; 978-1-932364
Number of titles published annually: 5 Print
Total Titles: 120 Print; 15 E-Book
Warehouse: LSC North, 7539-7621 Zionsville Rd, Indianapolis, IN 46268 Toll Free Tel: 800-634-7064

Platypus Media LLC
725 Eighth St SE, Washington, DC 20003
Tel: 202-546-1674 Toll Free Tel: 877-PLATYPS (752-8977) Fax: 202-546-2356
E-mail: info@platypusmedia.com
Web Site: www.platypusmedia.com
Key Personnel
Pres & Dir: Dia L Michels
Founded: 2000
An independent publisher creating books for families, teachers & parenting professionals.
ISBN Prefix(es): 978-1-930775
Number of titles published annually: 7 Print
Total Titles: 32 Print; 1 Audio
Imprints: Science, Naturally
Distribution Center: National Book Network, 4501 Forbes Blvd, Suite 200, Lanham, MD 20706 Tel: 301-459-3366 Toll Free Tel: 800-464-6420 Fax: 301-459-5746 Toll Free Fax: 800-338-4550 Web Site: www.nbnbooks.com
Membership(s): The Association of Publishers for Special Sales (APSS); The Children's Book Council (CBC); Independent Book Publishers Association (IBPA); Washington Publishers (WP); Women's National Book Association (WNBA)
See separate listing for:
Science, Naturally

Pleasure Boat Studio: A Literary Press
3710 SW Barton St, Seattle, WA 98126
Tel: 206-962-0460
E-mail: pleasboatpublishing@gmail.com
Web Site: www.pleasureboatstudio.com
Key Personnel
Publr: Lauren Grosskopf
Founded: 1996
Fiction, nonfiction & poetry.
ISBN Prefix(es): 978-0-9651413; 978-1-929355; 978-0-912887
Number of titles published annually: 10 Print; 5 E-Book
Total Titles: 120 Print; 20 E-Book
Imprints: Aequitas Books (nonfiction only); Caravel Books (mysteries only)
Foreign Rights: Books Crossing Borders (worldwide)
Membership(s): Community of Literary Magazines & Presses (CLMP); Independent Book Publishers Association (IBPA)

Plexus Publishing, Inc.

§Plexus Publishing, Inc
Affiliate of Information Today, Inc
143 Old Marlton Pike, Medford, NJ 08055
Tel: 609-654-6500 Fax: 609-654-4309
E-mail: info@plexuspublishing.com
Web Site: www.plexuspublishing.com
Key Personnel
Pres & CEO: Thomas H Hogan
VP, Mktg & Busn Devt: Thomas Hogan, Jr
Content Mktg & Exhibits Mgr: Robert Colding Tel: 609-654-6500 ext 330 E-mail: rcolding@plexuspublishing.com
Sales & Admin: Deb Kranz Tel: 609-654-6500 ext 117 E-mail: dkranz@plexuspublishing.com
HR Dir: Mary S Hogan E-mail: shogan@plexuspublishing.com
Founded: 1977
Regional book publisher specializing in nature, history & fiction for readers interested in the NJ Pinelands, Atlantic City/Jersey shore, Philadelphia & surrounds. No children's books, poetry, religion, or calendars.
ISBN Prefix(es): 978-0-937548; 978-0-9666748
Number of titles published annually: 3 Print
Total Titles: 52 Print; 25 E-Book; 2 Audio

Imprints: Medford Press; Plexus Books (regional titles/NJ topics especially Southern NJ history, nature/Pinelands, fiction)
Membership(s): Independent Book Publishers Association (IBPA); Mystery Writers of America (MWA)

§Plough Publishing House
151 Bowne Dr, Walden, NY 12586-2832
SAN: 202-0092
Mailing Address: PO Box 398, Walden, NY 12586-0398
Tel: 845-572-3455 *Toll Free Tel:* 800-521-8011
E-mail: info@plough.com; editor@plough.com
Web Site: www.plough.com
Key Personnel
Mgr: Sam Hine
Founded: 1920
Religion (Anabaptist), church history, children's education, Christian communal living; music; social justice, radical Christianity; social issues.
ISBN Prefix(es): 978-0-87486
Number of titles published annually: 10 Print; 10 Online; 10 E-Book; 1 Audio
Total Titles: 150 Print; 150 Online; 150 E-Book; 5 Audio
Foreign Office(s): 4188 Gwydir Hwy, Elsmore, NSW 2360, Australia
Brightling Rd, Robertsbridge, East Sussex TN32 5DR, United Kingdom *E-mail:* contact@ploughbooks.co.uk
Distribution Center: Ingram Publisher Services, 14 Ingram Blvd, Mail Stop 631, La Vergne, TN 37086 *Toll Free Tel:* 866-400-5351 *Web Site:* www.ingrampublisherservices.com

Ploughshares
Subsidiary of Ploughshares Inc
Emerson College, 120 Boylston St, Boston, MA 02116
Tel: 617-824-3757
E-mail: pshares@pshares.org
Web Site: www.pshares.org
Key Personnel
Exec Dir & Ed-in-Chief: Ladette Randolph
Founded: 1971
Journal publishing.
ISBN Prefix(es): 978-0-933277; 978-1-933058; 978-1-62608
Number of titles published annually: 4 Print
Total Titles: 118 Print; 9 E-Book
Membership(s): Combined Book Exhibit (CBE)

§Plowshare Media
405 Vincente Way, La Jolla, CA 92037
SAN: 857-2933
Tel: 858-454-5446
E-mail: sales@plowsharemedia.com
Web Site: plowsharemedia.com
Key Personnel
Mng Partner: Maryann Callery *E-mail:* mc@plowsharemedia.com; Thomas P Tweed *E-mail:* tt@plowsharemedia.com
Founded: 2008
Handle all aspects of book publishing including acquisition, editing, typesetting, cover design, printing, marketing & promotion.
ISBN Prefix(es): 978-0-9860428; 978-0-9821145
Number of titles published annually: 2 Print; 2 E-Book
Total Titles: 14 Print; 12 E-Book
Imprints: RELS Press (nonprofit)
Membership(s): Independent Book Publishers Association (IBPA)

§Plum Tree Books
Imprint of Classical Academic Press
2151 Market St, Camp Hill, PA 17011
Tel: 717-730-0711
E-mail: info@classicalsubjects.com
Web Site: www.plumtreebooks.com
Key Personnel
Publr: Christopher Perrin *E-mail:* cperrin@classicalsubjects.com
Founded: 2012
Old Virtues, New Stories™ - children's stories presented entirely through digital formats.
ISBN Prefix(es): 978-1-60051
Number of titles published annually: 10 E-Book

Plunkett Research Ltd
PO Drawer 541737, Houston, TX 77254-1737
Tel: 713-932-0000 *Fax:* 713-932-7080
E-mail: customersupport@plunkettresearch.com
Web Site: www.plunkettresearch.com
Key Personnel
Publr & CEO: Jack W Plunkett *E-mail:* jack_plunkett@plunkettresearch.com
Founded: 1985
A leading provider of global business & industry information to corporate, library, academic & government markets. Plunkett's unique reference books & online service offer comprehensive market research, industry statistics & trends analysis covering all of the world's vital industries.
ISBN Prefix(es): 978-0-9638268; 978-1-891775; 978-1-59392; 978-1-60879; 978-1-62831
Number of titles published annually: 40 Print; 29 CD-ROM; 40 Online; 40 E-Book
Total Titles: 40 Print; 40 Online; 40 E-Book

Pocket Books, see Gallery Books

§Pocket Press Inc
PO Box 25124, Portland, OR 97298-0124
Toll Free Tel: 888-237-2110 *Toll Free Fax:* 877-643-3732
E-mail: sales@pocketpressinc.com
Web Site: www.pocketpressinc.com
Key Personnel
Pres: Bruce Coorpender
Sales & Mktg: Bob Born
Founded: 1992
Reference books for law enforcement.
ISBN Prefix(es): 978-1-884493; 978-1-61371
Number of titles published annually: 120 Print
Total Titles: 120 Print

§Pocol Press
320 Sutton St, Punxsutawney, PA 15767
SAN: 253-6021
Tel: 703-870-9611
E-mail: chrisandtom@erols.com
Web Site: www.pocolpress.com
Key Personnel
Owner & Publr: J Thomas Hetrick
Founded: 1999
Pocol Press continues to be a leader in short fiction & baseball history from first time non-agented authors. Several books used as college textbooks. All titles also ebooks available from Amazon for Kindle. Dozens of audiobook titles recently added. Also feature Eighties Baseball, a tabletop sports simulation.
ISBN Prefix(es): 978-1-929763
Number of titles published annually: 4 Print; 4 E-Book
Total Titles: 105 Print; 105 E-Book; 60 Audio
Membership(s): The Association of Publishers for Special Sales (APSS)

Pointed Leaf Press
136 Baxter St, New York, NY 10013
Tel: 212-941-1800 *Fax:* 212-941-1822
E-mail: info@pointedleafpress.com
Web Site: www.pointedleafpress.com
Key Personnel
Publr & Edit Dir: Suzanne Slesin
Founded: 2002
This publisher has indicated that 50% of their product line is author subsidized.
ISBN Prefix(es): 978-0-9727661; 978-0-9777875; 978-0-9823585; 978-0-9833889; 978-1-938461
Number of titles published annually: 9 Print

Poisoned Pen Press
Imprint of Sourcebooks Inc
4014 N Goldwater Blvd, Suite 201, Scottsdale, AZ 85251
Tel: 480-945-3375 *Toll Free Tel:* 800-421-3976
Fax: 480-949-1707
E-mail: info@poisonedpenpress.com
Web Site: www.poisonedpenpress.com
Key Personnel
Ed Dir, Sourcebooks & Poisoned Pen Press: Anna Michels *E-mail:* anna.michels@sourcebooks.com
Dir, Devt: Robert Rosenwald *E-mail:* robert@poisonedpenpress.com
Dir, Mktg: Molly Waxman *E-mail:* molly.waxman@sourcebooks.com
Mng Ed: Diane DiBiase *E-mail:* diane.dibiase@sourcebooks.com
Sr Mgr, Publicity & Mktg: Mandy Chahal
Mktg Asst: Emily Engwall
Data Entry Specialist: Kacie Blackburn *E-mail:* kacie@poisonedpenpress.com
Founded: 1997
Publishing high quality works in the field of mystery. Interested in publishing books that we think booksellers everywhere & especially independent mystery booksellers would want to have available to sell. Electronic submissions only. Visit www.poisonedpenpress.com, click on Submission for guidelines & information.
ISBN Prefix(es): 978-1-890208; 978-1-929345 (The Poisoned Pencil); 978-1-59058; 978-1-46420; 978-1-61595 (ebooks)
Number of titles published annually: 60 Print; 60 E-Book
Total Titles: 800 Print; 500 E-Book
Distribution Center: Sourcebooks Inc, 1935 Brookdale Rd, Suite 139, Naperville, IL 60563 *Tel:* 630-961-3900 *E-mail:* customerservice@sourcebooks.com *Web Site:* www.sourcebooks.com
Membership(s): Association of American Publishers (AAP); Independent Book Publishers Association (IBPA); Publishers Association of the West (PubWest)

§Polar Bear & Company
Imprint of Solon Center for Research & Publishing
8 Brook St, Solon, ME 04979
Mailing Address: PO Box 311, Solon, ME 04979-0311 SAN: 858-8902
Tel: 207-319-4727
Web Site: polarbearandco.com
Key Personnel
Exec Dir: Paul du Houx
Founded: 1998
To help build community with quality books & art.
ISBN Prefix(es): 978-1-882190
Number of titles published annually: 6 Print; 6 E-Book
Total Titles: 60 Print; 8 E-Book
Orders to: Ingram Lightning Source Inc, 1246 Heil Quaker Blvd, La Vergne, TN 37086
E-mail: inquiry@lightningsource.com *Web Site:* www.lightningsource.com
Distribution Center: Ingram Lightning Source Inc, 1246 Heil Quaker Blvd, La Vergne, TN 37086 *Toll Free Tel:* 800-509-4156
E-mail: inquiry@lightningsource.com *Web Site:* www.lightningsource.com
Membership(s): Independent Publishers of New England (IPNE); Maine Writers & Publishers Alliance (MWPA)

Polebridge Press
Imprint of Westar Institute

U.S. PUBLISHERS

Willamette University, 900 State St, Salem, OR 97301
Mailing Address: 3300 N Triumph Blvd, No 100, Lehi, UT 84043
Tel: 651-200-2372
E-mail: orders@westarinstitute.org
Web Site: www.westarinstitute.org
Key Personnel
Publr: Arthur J Dewey *E-mail:* adewey@westarinstitute.org
Founded: 1986
Publishes up-to-date reference works for biblical scholars, primarily in support of research on the historical Jesus & the origins of Christianity as well as philosophical theology; scholarly books produced by Westar seminars, research projects & by individual scholars; books & periodicals that disseminate the results of critical scholarship on religion to the public.
ISBN Prefix(es): 978-1-59815; 978-0-944344
Number of titles published annually: 10 Print; 6 E-Book; 3 Audio
Total Titles: 110 Print; 30 E-Book; 93 Audio

Police Executive Research Forum
1120 Connecticut Ave NW, Suite 930, Washington, DC 20036
Tel: 202-466-7820
Web Site: www.policeforum.org
Key Personnel
Exec Dir: Chuck Wexler *Tel:* 202-454-8326 *E-mail:* cwexler@policeforum.org
Dir, Communs: Craig Fischer *Tel:* 202-454-8332 *E-mail:* cfischer@policeforum.org
Chief of Staff: Andrea Luna *Tel:* 202-454-8346 *E-mail:* aluna@policeforum.org
Communs Coord: James McGinty *Tel:* 202-454-8310 *E-mail:* jmcginty@policeforum.org
Founded: 1977
Community policing, POP, police research & management, police & criminal justice.
ISBN Prefix(es): 978-1-878734; 978-1-934485
Number of titles published annually: 7 Print
Total Titles: 70 Print
Distribution Center: Whitehurst & Clark, 1200 Rte 523, Flemington, NJ 08822, Contact: Brad Searles *Toll Free Tel:* 888-202-4563 *Fax:* 908-237-2407 *E-mail:* wcbooks@aol.com

Polis Books
1201 Hudson St, No 211S, Hoboken, NJ 07030
E-mail: info@polisbooks.com; submissions@polisbooks.com
Web Site: www.polisbooks.com; facebook.com/PolisBooks; x.com/PolisBooks
Key Personnel
Publr: Jason Pinter *E-mail:* jpinter@polisbooks.com
Founded: 2013
Publishing primarily commercial fiction in adult, young adult & middle grade.
ISBN Prefix(es): 978-1-940610
Number of titles published annually: 30 Print; 50 E-Book; 40 Audio
Imprints: Agora
Foreign Rights: Biagi Literary Management (worldwide)
Distribution Center: Publishers Group West, 1700 Fourth St, Berkeley, CA 94710 *Toll Free Tel:* 800-788-3123 *SAN:* 202-8522
Membership(s): International Thriller Writers Inc (ITW); Mystery Writers of America (MWA); Society of Children's Book Writers & Illustrators (SCBWI)

Pomegranate Communications Inc
105 SE 18 Ave, Portland, OR 97214
Tel: 503-328-6500 *Toll Free Tel:* 800-227-1428 *Fax:* 503-328-9330 *Toll Free Fax:* 800-848-4376
E-mail: hello@pomegranate.com
Web Site: www.pomegranate.com
Key Personnel
Pres & Intl Rts: Thomas F Burke
Publr: Cory Mimms
Exec Dir: Darius Burke
Founded: 1968
Fine arts publisher of books, calendars, puzzles, stationery & children's products.
ISBN Prefix(es): 978-0-87654; 978-1-56640; 978-0-7649
Number of titles published annually: 12 Print
Total Titles: 120 Print
Imprints: PomegranateKids
Foreign Rep(s): Ashton International Marketing Services (Julian Ashton) (Far East, Middle East); Canadian Manda Group (Canada); Pen Paper Gift (Europe, UK)
Membership(s): American Specialty Toy Retailing Association (ASTRA); MSA

Portfolio
Imprint of Penguin Publishing Group
c/o Penguin Random House LLC, 1745 Broadway, New York, NY 10019
Tel: 212-782-9000
Web Site: www.penguin.com/portfolio-overview/; www.penguin.com/sentinel-overview/; www.penguin.com/thesis/
Key Personnel
Founder, Pres & Publr: Adrian Zackheim
VP & Assoc Publr: Tara Gilbride
VP & Ed-in-Chief: Niki Papadopoulos
Assoc Publr & Dir, Publicity & Mktg: Margot Stamas
Sr Dir, Subs Rts: Ritsuko Okumura
Dir, Publicity: Amanda Lang
Assoc Dir, Mktg: Mary Kate Rogers
Asst Dir, Mktg: Mary Kate Skehan
Asst Dir, Publicity: Stefanie Rosenblum Brody
Exec Ed, Portfolio & Edit Dir, Sentinel: Bria Sandford
Exec Ed: Casey Ebro; Helen Healey-Cunningham; Noah Schwartzberg
Sr Ed: Trish Daly; Leah Trouwborst; Lydia Yadi
Asst Ed: Megan McCormack
Edit Asst: Sabrey Manning; Leila Sandlin; Megan Wenerstrom
Sr Publicity Mgr: Kirstin Berndt
Mktg Mgr: Heather Faulls
Assoc Publicist: Esin Coskun; Taylor Williams
Founded: 2001
Specialize in management, leadership, marketing, business narrative, investing, personal finance, economics, technology, sales, entrepreneurship & career advice.
Penguin Random House & its publishing entities are not accepting unsol submissions, proposals, mss, or submission queries via e-mail at this time.
Number of titles published annually: 78 Print
Total Titles: 286 Print
Imprints: Optimism Press; Sentinel; Thesis

Potomac Books
Imprint of University of Nebraska Press
c/o University of Nebraska Press, 1225 "L" St, Suite 200, Lincoln, NE 68588-0630
Mailing Address: PO Box 880630, Lincoln, NE 68588-0630
Tel: 402-472-5937
Web Site: www.nebraskapress.unl.edu/potomac/
Key Personnel
Ed: Taylor Gilreath *E-mail:* tgilreath2@unl.edu
Rts & Perms Coord: Leif Milliken *Tel:* 402-472-7702 *E-mail:* lmilliken2@unl.edu
Founded: 1983 (as imprint of Brassey's)
ISBN Prefix(es): 978-1-57488; 978-1-59797; 978-1-61234
Number of titles published annually: 80 Print; 50 E-Book
Total Titles: 550 Print; 400 E-Book
Foreign Rep(s): Casemate UK Ltd (Andrew Tarring) (Europe, UK); Peribo (Australia, New Zealand)
Foreign Rights: The Asano Agency Inc (Japan); CA-LINK International LLC (China); Graal Literary Agency (Eastern Europe, Poland); International Editors' Co - Yanez Agencia Literaria (Spanish-speaking countries); Natoli, Stefan & Oliva Literary Agency (Italy); La Nouvelle Agence (France)
Orders to: Longleaf Services Inc, 116 S Boundary St, Chapel Hill, NC 27514-3808 *Tel:* 919-966-7449 *Toll Free Tel:* 800-848-6224 *Fax:* 919-962-2704 *Toll Free Fax:* 800-272-6817 *E-mail:* customerservice@longleafservices.org
Membership(s): Association of University Presses (AUPresses)

Clarkson Potter
Imprint of Crown Publishing Group
1745 Broadway, New York, NY 10019
Tel: 212-782-9000
Web Site: crownpublishing.com/archives/imprint/clarkson-potter
Founded: 1959
Dedicated lifestyle group within Penguin Random House, home to a community of award-winning & bestselling chefs, cooks, designers, arts & writers-visionaries who see to entertain, engage & teach. Commercial & literary diverse list, including cookbooks, illustrated gift books & a growing line of paper products such as journals, postcards, stationery & games.
Penguin Random House & its publishing entities are not accepting unsol submissions, proposals, mss, or submission queries via e-mail at this time.
Number of titles published annually: 145 Print
Total Titles: 1,000 Print
Foreign Rep(s): Penguin Random House LLC (worldwide)
Orders to: Penguin Random House LLC, 400 Hahn Rd, Westminster, MD 21157 *Toll Free Tel:* 800-733-3000 *E-mail:* csorders@randomhouse.com; Penguin Random House of Canada Inc, 320 Front St W, Suite 410, Toronto, ON M5V 3B6, Canada *Toll Free Tel:* 800-668-4247 *Fax:* 416-598-7764

powerHouse Books
Imprint of powerHouse Cultural Entertainment Inc
32 Adams St, Brooklyn, NY 11201
Tel: 212-604-9074
E-mail: sales@powerhousebooks.com; publicity@powerhousebooks.com
Web Site: www.powerhousebooks.com; www.powerhousebookstores.com
Founded: 1995
Contemporary art, photography & image-based cultural books.
ISBN Prefix(es): 978-1-57687
Number of titles published annually: 35 Print
Total Titles: 700 Print
Imprints: Archway Editions
Distributed by Simon & Schuster, LLC
Distributor for Antinous Press; Juno Books; MTV Press; Throckmorton Press; VH1 Press; Vice Books
Foreign Rep(s): Penguin Random House (worldwide)
Foreign Rights: Bookwise International Pty Ltd (Australia); Critiques Livres (France); Turnaround (UK)
Warehouse: Simon & Schuster, LLC, Jackson, TN
Distribution Center: Simon & Schuster, LLC, Order Processing Dept, 100 Front St, Riverside, NJ 08075 *Toll Free Tel:* 800-223-2336 *Toll Free Fax:* 800-943-9831 *E-mail:* purchaseorders@simonandschuster.com

§PPI, A Kaplan Company
332 Front St, Suite 501, La Crosse, WI 54601
SAN: 264-6315

Tel: 650-593-9119 *Fax:* 650-592-4519
E-mail: info@ppi2pass.com
Web Site: ppi2pass.com
Key Personnel
Prod Mktg Mgr: Jared Schulze
Founded: 1975
Provider of exam review books, online products & live & online classes in the fields of engineering, land surveying, LEED, architecture, interior design & landscape architecture. Specialty engineering areas include civil, structural, seismic, mechanical, electrical, environmental, chemical, nuclear, geotechnical & industrial engineering fields.
ISBN Prefix(es): 978-0-932276; 978-0-912045; 978-1-888577; 978-1-59126
Number of titles published annually: 10 Print; 1 CD-ROM; 2 Online; 5 E-Book
Total Titles: 120 Print; 20 Online; 20 E-Book
Distributor for American Association of State Highway & Transportation Officials; American Wood Council (American Forest & Paper Association) (National Design Specification for Wood Construction (NDS) & others); International Code Council; McGraw-Hill Professional (green building, design & construction titles, LEED titles); National Council of Examiners for Engineering & Surveying; SmartPros; Transportation Research Board (TRB); US Green Building Council (LEED reference guides)
Membership(s): American Society of Civil Engineers; American Society of Engineering Educators; American Society of Mechanical Engineers (ASME); National Society of Professional Engineers; US Green Building Council (USGBC)

§Practice Management Information Corp (PMIC)
4727 Wilshire Blvd, Suite 302, Los Angeles, CA 90010
SAN: 139-438X
Tel: 323-954-0224 *Fax:* 323-954-0253
E-mail: customer.service@pmiconline.com
Web Site: pmiconline.stores.yahoo.net
Key Personnel
Pres & Publr: James B Davis
Founded: 1986
Books & software for physicians, hospitals, insurance companies & other healthcare professionals on medical coding, reimbursement, practice management, financial management & medical risk management.
ISBN Prefix(es): 978-1-878487 (Health Information Press); 978-1-57066; 978-1-885987; 978-1-936977; 978-1-939852; 978-1-943009
Number of titles published annually: 35 Print
Total Titles: 35 Print
Imprints: Health Information Press (HIP)
Sales Office(s): 200 W 22 St, Suite 253, Lombard, IL 60148 *Toll Free Tel:* 800-633-4215; 800-MEDSHOP (orders) *Toll Free Fax:* 800-633-6556 (orders)

§Practising Law Institute (PLI)
1177 Avenue of the Americas, 2nd fl, New York, NY 10036
SAN: 203-0136
Tel: 212-824-5710 (cust serv) *Toll Free Tel:* 800-260-4PLI (260-4754) *Toll Free Fax:* 800-321-0093 (cust serv)
E-mail: info@pli.edu; membership@pli.edu
Web Site: www.pli.edu
Key Personnel
Treas & Chief Busn Offr: Alan G Cohen
 E-mail: acohen@pli.edu
CIO: Christopher Rousseau *E-mail:* crousseau@pli.edu
CFO: Emilia Sima *E-mail:* esima@pli.edu
Pres: Sharon L Crane *E-mail:* scrane@pli.edu
SVP, Membership & Accreditation: Craig A Miller *E-mail:* cmiller@pli.edu
SVP, HR & Facilities: Joan D Sternberg
 E-mail: jsternberg@pli.edu
Chief Mktg Offr: David M Smith
 E-mail: dsmith@pli.edu
SVP, Progs: Kara L O'Brien *E-mail:* kobrien@pli.edu
Founded: 1933
Professional books for lawyers; CDs, DVDs, CD-ROMs, programs.
ISBN Prefix(es): 978-0-87224; 978-1-4024
Number of titles published annually: 210,330 Print
Total Titles: 4 CD-ROM; 330 Online
Imprints: PLI
Branch Office(s)
455 Market St, Suite 2300, San Francisco, CA 94105 *Tel:* 415-498-2800 *Toll Free Tel:* 800-260-4754
Shipping Address: PMDS, 1780A Crossroads Dr, Odenton, MD 21113 *Tel:* 301-604-3305

PRB Productions
963 Peralta Ave, Albany, CA 94706-2144
Tel: 510-526-0722
E-mail: prbprdns@aol.com
Web Site: www.prbmusic.com
Key Personnel
Prop & Publr: Peter R Ballinger; Leslie J Gold
Founded: 1989
Specialize in publishing high-quality performing editions of instrumental & vocal music from the Baroque & Classical eras, along with original contemporary works for early & contemporary instruments & voices. Customized music typesetting services available by special arrangement.
ISBN Prefix(es): 978-1-56571
Number of titles published annually: 10 Print
Total Titles: 300 Print

Presbyterian Publishing Corp (PPC)
100 Witherspoon St, Louisville, KY 40202
Tel: 502-569-5000 *Toll Free Tel:* 800-533-4371; 800-523-1631 (US only) *Fax:* 502-569-5113
E-mail: customerservice@presbypub.com
Web Site: www.ppcbooks.com; www.wjkbooks.com
Key Personnel
Pres & Publr: David Dobson *E-mail:* ddobson@wjkbooks.com
VP & COO: Monty Anderson
 E-mail: manderson@wjkbooks.com
VP, Mktg & E-Commerce: Alicia Samuels
 E-mail: asamuels@wjkbooks.com
Edit Dir: Dr Bridgett Green *E-mail:* bgreen@wjkbooks.com
Founded: 1838
Academic & scholarly books, general trade religious books & children's picture books.
ISBN Prefix(es): 978-0-664; 978-0-8042
Number of titles published annually: 60 Print; 2 CD-ROM; 60 E-Book; 10 Audio
Total Titles: 2,100 Print; 5 CD-ROM; 1,000 E-Book
Imprints: Flyaway Books (children's picture books); Westminster John Knox Press (WJK) (adult academic & trade)
Distributor for Epworth; SCM
Foreign Rep(s): SCM Press (Europe, UK)
Foreign Rep(s): Mosaic Rights Services (worldwide exc North America & UK)
Warehouse: Ingram Publisher Services, 191 Edwards Dr, Jackson, TN 38301 *Toll Free Tel:* 866-400-5351 *Web Site:* www.ingrampublisherservices.com
Distribution Center: Spring Arbor Distributors *Toll Free Tel:* 800-395-4340 *Toll Free Fax:* 800-876-0186 *E-mail:* orders@springarbor.com
Membership(s): Association of American Publishers (AAP); The Children's Book Council (CBC); Society of Children's Book Writers & Illustrators (SCBWI)
See separate listing for:
Westminster John Knox Press (WJK)

The Press at California State University, Fresno
Unit of California State University, Fresno
2380 E Keats, M/S MB 99, Fresno, CA 93740-8024
Tel: 559-278-4103
E-mail: press@csufresno.edu
Key Personnel
Mng Ed: Brenna Barks *E-mail:* bbarks@csufresno.edu
Founded: 1982
Art, architecture, drama, music, film & the media, photography, New Age politics, business, autobiography, Armenian history, Fresno history & literary magazine. Peer-reviewed multidisciplinary victimology journal.
ISBN Prefix(es): 978-0-912201
Number of titles published annually: 4 Print; 1 Online; 1 E-Book
Total Titles: 40 Print; 1 E-Book

Prevention Products & Services Inc, see The Bureau for At-Risk Youth

Primary Research Group Inc
2585 Broadway, Suite 156, New York, NY 10025
Tel: 212-736-2316 *Fax:* 212-412-9097
E-mail: primaryresearchgroup@gmail.com
Web Site: www.primaryresearch.com
Key Personnel
Pres: James Moses
Founded: 1989
Monographs, books, surveys & research reports on library science industry, economics, publishing (book, electronic & magazine), telecommunication, entertainment & higher education.
ISBN Prefix(es): 978-0-9626749; 978-1-57440
Number of titles published annually: 65 Print
Total Titles: 425 Print
Distributed by Academic Book Center; Ambassador Books; Coutts Library Service; Croft House Books; Eastern Book Company; Ebsco; MarketResearch.com; Midwest Library Service; OPAMP Technical Books; Emory Pratt; ProQuest LLC; Research & Markets; Rittenhouse Book Distributors; Total Information; Yankee Book Peddler

Princeton Architectural Press, see PA Press

§Princeton Book Co Publishers
15 W Front St, Trenton, NJ 08608
Tel: 609-426-0602 *Toll Free Tel:* 800-220-7149 *Fax:* 609-426-1344
E-mail: pbc@dancehorizons.com
Web Site: www.dancehorizons.com
Key Personnel
Pres: Charles H Woodford
Ed-in-Chief: Connie Woodford
Founded: 1975
Specialize in dance.
ISBN Prefix(es): 978-0-916622; 978-0-87127; 978-0-903102; 978-0-85418; 978-0-932582; 978-0-7121; 978-0-8463; 978-0-340
Number of titles published annually: 1 Print; 3 E-Book
Total Titles: 50 Print; 16 E-Book
Imprints: Dance Horizons; Elysian Editions (adult nonfiction)
Distributor for Dance Notation Bureau (Labanotation books)
Foreign Rep(s): Gazelle Book Services Ltd (Europe, UK); John Reed Book Distribution (Australia, New Zealand)
Distribution Center: Independent Publishers Group (IPG), 814 N Franklin St, Chicago,

U.S. PUBLISHERS

IL 60610 *Toll Free Tel:* 800-888-4741 *E-mail:* orders@ipgbook.com *Web Site:* www.ipgbook.com

§The Princeton Review
Imprint of Random House Children's Books
110 E 42 St, 7th fl, New York, NY 10017
Toll Free Tel: 800-273-8439 (orders only)
Web Site: www.princetonreview.com
Key Personnel
CEO: Joshua Hyoung-Jun Park
CFO: Juwon Lee
VP, Instl Sales: John Calvello
VP, Cust Success: Lauren Lobdell
Ed-in-Chief: Robert Franek
Sr Dir, Content Devt: David Soto
Founded: 1981
Test preparation, college & graduate school guides, career guides & general study aids.
Penguin Random House & its publishing entities are not accepting unsol submissions, proposals, mss, or submission queries via e-mail at this time.
Number of titles published annually: 75 Print; 12 CD-ROM
Total Titles: 230 Print; 15 CD-ROM

Princeton University Press
41 William St, Princeton, NJ 08540-5237
Tel: 609-258-4900 *Fax:* 609-258-6305
E-mail: info@press.princeton.edu
Web Site: press.princeton.edu
Key Personnel
CIO: Dennis Langlois *Tel:* 609-258-3083 *E-mail:* dennis_langlois@press.princeton.edu
Chief Digital Mktg Strategist: Colleen Suljic
Chief Textbook Sales & Mktg Strategist: Ken Barton
Dir: Christie Henry *E-mail:* christie_henry@press.princeton.edu
Dir, Publg Opers: Cathy Felgar
Exec Asst to Dir: Martha Camp *Tel:* 609-258-4953 *E-mail:* martha_camp@press.princeton.edu
Assoc Dir & CFO: Scot Kuehm *Tel:* 609-258-3083 *E-mail:* scot_kuehm@press.princeton.edu
Asst Dir/Global Devt Dir/Publr (history): Brigitta van Rheinberg *Tel:* 609-258-4935 *E-mail:* brigitta_vanrheinberg@press.princeton.edu
Ad & Mktg Art Dir: Heather Hansen *E-mail:* heather_hansen@press.princeton.edu
Dir, Ad & Soc Media: Donna Liese *Tel:* 609-258-4924 *E-mail:* donna_liese@press.princeton.edu
Dir, Fin, Sales: Timothy Wilkins *Tel:* 609-258-4877 *E-mail:* timothy_wilkins@press.princeton.edu
Dir, Web Technol & Servs: Ann Ambrose *E-mail:* ann_ambrose@press.princeton.edu
Global Promos Dir: Julia Haav *Tel:* 609-258-2831 *E-mail:* julia_haav@press.princeton.edu
Intl Sales Dir: Andrew Brewer *E-mail:* andrew_brewer@press.princeton.edu
Mktg Dir: Katie Hope
UK Intl Rts Dir/Digital & Audio Publr: Kim Williams *E-mail:* kimberley_williams@press.princeton.edu
Assoc Dir, Mktg Opers: Leslie Nangle *Tel:* 609-258-5881 *E-mail:* leslie_nangle@press.princeton.edu
Assoc Dir, Sales & Mktg: Laurie Schlesinger *Tel:* 609-258-4898 *E-mail:* laurie_schlesinger@press.princeton.edu
Asst Dir & Dir, Editing, Design & Prodn: Neil Litt *Tel:* 609-258-5066 *E-mail:* neil_litt@press.princeton.edu
Asst Promos Dir: Maria Whelan
Publr (anthropology, religion): Fred Appel *Tel:* 609-258-2484 *E-mail:* fred_appel@press.princeton.edu
Publr (architecture, art): Michelle Komie *Tel:* 609-258-4569 *E-mail:* michelle_komie@press.princeton.edu
Publr (field guides) & Exec Ed (biology, natural history, ornithology): Robert Kirk *Tel:* 609-258-4884 *E-mail:* robert_kirk@press.princeton.edu
Publr (humanities) & Asst Ed-in-Chief (ancient history, archaeology, classics, philosophy, political theory): Robert Tempio *Tel:* 609-258-0843 *E-mail:* robert_tempio@press.princeton.edu
Publr (literature): Anne Savarese *Tel:* 609-258-4937 *E-mail:* anne_savarese@press.princeton.edu
Edit Dir (humanities): Eric Crahan *Tel:* 609-258-4922 *E-mail:* eric_crahan@press.princeton.edu
Edit Dir (sciences): Alison Kalett *Tel:* 609-258-9232 *E-mail:* alison_kalett@press.princeton.edu
Intl Rts Exec: Eleanor Smith
Exec Ed (mathematics): Diana Gillooly *E-mail:* diana_gillooly@press.princeton.edu; Vickie Kearn *Tel:* 609-258-2321 *E-mail:* vickie_kearn@press.princeton.edu
Exec Ed (political science & American history): Bridget Flannery-McCoy *E-mail:* bridget_flannerymccoy@press.princeton.edu
Mng Ed: Elizabeth Byrd *Tel:* 609-258-2589 *E-mail:* elizabeth_byrd@press.princeton.edu
Sr Ed (economics, finance): Joe Jackson *Tel:* 609-258-9428 *E-mail:* joe_jackson@press.princeton.edu
Sr Ed (history): Priya Nelson
Sr Ed (humanities): Ben Tate
Sr Ed (neuroscience & computer science): Hallie Stebbins
Sr Ed (sociology & anthropology): Rachael Levay
Ed (engineering, mathematics): Susannah Shoemaker
Assoc Ed (ancient world, philosophy, political theory): Matt Rohal
Assoc Ed (economics, political sci): Hannah Paul *E-mail:* hannah_paul@press.princeton.edu
Assoc Ed (history): Amanda Peery *Tel:* 609-258-4920 *E-mail:* amanda_peery@press.princeton.edu
Assoc Ed (physical sciences): Abigail Johnson
Asst Ed: James Collier; Whitney Rauenhorst
Asst Ed (history): Thalia Leaf *E-mail:* thalia_leaf@press.princeton.edu
Asst Ed (paperbacks): Jacqueline Delaney
Edit Coord: Allegra Martschenko
Edit Assoc: Charlie Allen; Lauren Bucca *E-mail:* lauren_bucca@press.princeton.edu; Chloe Coy; Kenneth Guay; Pamela Weidman *E-mail:* pamela_weidman@press.princeton.edu; Kristin Zodrow *E-mail:* kristin_zodrow@press.princeton.edu
Ed-at-Large (higher education): Peter Daugherty *Tel:* 609-258-6778 *E-mail:* peter_daugherty@press.princeton.edu
Sr Opers Analyst: Alexandria Leonard
Sr Contracts Mgr: Ceylan Akturk
Sr Mgr, Busn Systems Integration: Larissa Shurka
Sr Promos Mgr & Trade Mktg Strategist: James Schneider
Copy & Mktg Data Mgr: David Campbell
Design Mgr: Jessica Massabrook *E-mail:* jessica_massabrook@press.princeton.edu
Digital Partnerships Mgr: Paige Clunie
Intl Rts Mgr: Emma Morgan
Mgr, Indie Rel & Mktg/Midwest Rep: Lanora Jennings
Mgr, Sciences: Sara Henning-Stout
Off Mgr: Jorge Cabrera
Perms Mgr: Lisa Black
Promos Mgr: James Schneider
Publicity Mgr: Carmen Jimenez
Curator, Audio: Danielle D'Orlando
Curator, Ideas & Partnerships: Debra Liese *E-mail:* debra_liese@press.princeton.edu
Sr Publicist: Kate Hensley; Katie Lewis *E-mail:* katie_lewis@press.princeton.edu; Jodi Price; Alyssa Sanford; Kathryn Stevens; Matt Taylor *E-mail:* matt_taylor@press.princeton.edu
Publicist: Tayler Lord *E-mail:* tayler_lord@press.princeton.edu
Assoc Publicist: Charlotte Coyne
Digital Promos Specialist: Stephanie Rojas *E-mail:* stephanie_rojas@press.princeton.edu
Academic Spec Sales & Mktg Assoc: Barbara Tonetti
Awards & Spec Sales & Grassroots Mktg Assoc: Steve Stillman
Field & Spec Sales Assoc: Corrynn Johnson
Higher Educ Sales & Mktg Assoc: Nikki Anderson
Intellectual Property & Contracts Assoc: Taylor Sumereau
Prodn Assoc: Danielle Amatucci
Promos Assoc: Tyler Hubbert; Nathalie Levine
Spec Sales & Mktg Assoc: Jennifer Zuccaro
Ad Coord: Meredith McMahon *E-mail:* meredith_mcmahon@press.princeton.edu
Digital Mktg Coord: Ally Lopez
Mktg Coord: Sydney Bartlett
Textbook Coord, Edit: Sophia Zengierski
Sr Designer: Chris Ferrante *E-mail:* chris_ferrante@press.princeton.edu
Designer: Hunter Finch
Designer (Mktg): Felix Summ
Exhibits: Melissa Burton *Tel:* 609-258-4915 *E-mail:* melissa_burton@press.princeton.edu
Northeast Sales Rep, Spec Sales Accts: Karen Corvello
Founded: 1905
Scholarly, scientific & trade books on all subjects.
ISBN Prefix(es): 978-0-691
Number of titles published annually: 250 Print; 125 E-Book
Total Titles: 4,000 Print; 2,000 E-Book
Imprints: Bollingen Series; PUP Audio
Foreign Office(s): Princeton Asia (Beijing) Consulting Co Ltd, NUO Ctr, Unit 2702, Chaoyang Qu 100016, China, Mng Dir: Lingxi Li *Tel:* (010) 8457 8802 *E-mail:* pupchina@press.princeton.edu
99 Banbury Rd, Oxford OX2 6JX, United Kingdom, Co-Head: Caroline Priday *Tel:* (01993) 814500 *Fax:* (01993) 814504 *E-mail:* caroline_priday@press.princeton.edu
Distributed by Jonathan Ball Publishers (South Africa)
Distributor for Princeton University Art Museum; Zone Books
Foreign Rep(s): ADP Singapore Pte Ltd (Lilian Koe) (Malaysia); ADP Singapore Pte Ltd (Ian Pringle) (Singapore, Southeast Asia); Avicenna Partnership Ltd (Claire de Gruchy) (Algeria, Cyprus, Israel, Jordan, Libya, Malta, Morocco, Palestine, Tunisia, Turkey); Avicenna Partnership Ltd (Bill Kennedy) (Bahrain, Egypt, Iran, Iraq, Kuwait, Lebanon, Libya, Oman, Qatar, Saudi Arabia, Syria, United Arab Emirates); Dominique Bartshukoff (Europe); Book Marketing Services (S Janakiraman) (Bangladesh, India, Sri Lanka); Craig Faulk (Caribbean, Central America, South America); Information & Culture Korea (ICK) (Se-Yung Jun) (South Korea); Peter Jacques (Europe); Lexa Publishers' Representatives (Mical Moser) (Canada); MHM Ltd (Japan); B K Norton Ltd (Lillian Hsiao) (Taiwan); Princeton Asia (Beijing) Consulting Co Ltd (Lingxi Li) (China); Rockbook (Gilles Fauveau) (Japan); University Press Group (Europe, South Africa, UK); Kelvin van Hasselt Publishing Services (Africa exc North & South Africa); World Press (Saleem Malik) (Pakistan)
Foreign Rights: Akcali Copyright (Mustafa Urgen) (Turkey); ANA Sofia Ltd (Mira Droumeva) (Bulgaria, Romania); Agencia Literaria Carmen Balcells SA (Maribel Luque) (Latin America, Spain); Bardon-Chinese Media Agency (David Tsai) (China); BookLab Literary Agency (Agata Zabowska) (Poland); Bookman Literary Agency (Mr Ib H Lauritzen) (Denmark, Finland, Iceland, Norway, Sweden); Dar Cherlin (Amelie Cherlin) (Arab Middle East); English Agency Japan Co Ltd

(Tsutomu Yawata) (Japan); Paul & Peter Fritz AG (Christian Dittus) (Germany); The Deborah Harris Agency (Geula Geurts) (Israel); JLM Literary Agency (John L Moukakos) (Greece); Ilidio Matos Agencia Literaria Lda (Goncalo Gama Pinto) (Portugal); Andrew Nurnberg Associates (Judit Hermann) (Croatia, Hungary); Andrew Nurnberg Associates (Lucie Polakova) (Czechia, Slovakia, Slovenia); Andrew Nurnberg Associates Baltic (Tatjana Zoldnere) (Estonia, Latvia, Lithuania); Prava i prevodi (Nada Cipranic) (Montenegro, Serbia); Reiser Literary Agency (Roberto Gilodi) (Italy); Agencia RIFF (Joao Paulo Riff) (Brazil); Marianne Schoenbach Literary Agency (Marianne Schoenbach) (Netherlands); Synopsis Literary Agency (Olga Zasetskaya) (Russia); Eric Yang Agency (Sue & Jackie Yang) (South Korea)
Orders to: Ingram Publisher Services (Asia (exc Japan), Australia, CN, Latin America & US) *Toll Free Tel:* 866-400-5351 *E-mail:* ordersupport@ingramcontent.com; The University Press Group Ltd, New Era Estate, Oldlands Way, Bognor Regis, West Sussex PO22 9NQ, United Kingdom (Europe, South Africa & UK), Off Mgr: Lois Edwards *Tel:* (01243) 842165 *Fax:* (01243) 842167 *E-mail:* lois@upguk.com
Distribution Center: NewSouth Books, UNSW Randwick Campus, Bldg R1F, 22-32 King St, Randwick, NSW 2031, Australia (Australia & New Zealand) *Tel:* (02) 8936 1400 *Fax:* (02) 8936 1440 *Web Site:* www.newsouthbooks.com.au
Membership(s): American Association of University Presses (AAUP); Association of American Publishers (AAP); Book Industry Study Group (BISG)

§PRINTING United Alliance
10015 Main St, Fairfax, VA 22031
Tel: 703-385-1335 *Toll Free Tel:* 888-385-3588 *Fax:* 703-273-0456
E-mail: assist@printing.org; info@printing.org
Web Site: www.printing.org
Key Personnel
Mng Ed: Lauren Searson *E-mail:* lsearson@printing.org
Founded: 2020 (thru the merger of Printing Industries of America & Specialty Graphic Imaging Association)
Textbooks & reference books on graphic communications techniques & technology.
ISBN Prefix(es): 978-0-88362
Number of titles published annually: 3 Print; 2 E-Book
Total Titles: 200 Print; 10 E-Book
Branch Office(s)
1325 "G" St NW, Suite 500, Washington, DC 20005 *Tel:* 202-627-6925 ext 504
2000 Corporate Dr, Suite 205, Wexford, PA 15090, Mgr, Pubn: Samuel G Shea *Tel:* 412-741-6860 *Toll Free Tel:* 800-910-4283 *Fax:* 412-741-2311

PRO-ED Inc
8700 Shoal Creek Blvd, Austin, TX 78757-6897
SAN: 221-1349
Tel: 512-451-3246 *Toll Free Tel:* 800-897-3202 *Fax:* 512-451-8542 *Toll Free Fax:* 800-397-7633
E-mail: info@proedinc.com
Web Site: www.proedinc.com
Key Personnel
COO & Gen Coun: Robert Lum *Tel:* 512-451-3246 ext 664 *E-mail:* blum@proedinc.com
Exec Ed: Kathy Synatschk *E-mail:* ksynatschk@proedinc.com
Founded: 1977
College & professional reference books, tests, student materials, journals in education & psychology.

ISBN Prefix(es): 978-0-936104; 978-0-89079; 978-0-88744; 978-1-933014; 978-1-944480; 978-1-4164
Number of titles published annually: 50 Print
Total Titles: 1,500 Print

Pro Lingua Associates Inc
74 Cotton Mill Hill, Suite A-315, Brattleboro, VT 05301
SAN: 216-0579
Tel: 802-257-7779 *Toll Free Tel:* 800-366-4775 *Fax:* 802-257-5117
E-mail: info@prolinguaassociates.com
Web Site: www.prolinguaassociates.com
Key Personnel
Pres & Publr: Arthur A Burrows *E-mail:* andy@prolinguaassociates.com
VP & Ed: Raymond C Clark
Treas & Lib Sales Dir: Elise C Burrows
Secy: Mike Jerald
Founded: 1980
Teacher resource handbooks, language teacher training handbooks, English language & foreign language texts.
ISBN Prefix(es): 978-0-86647
Number of titles published annually: 7 Print
Total Titles: 120 Print; 44 Audio
Foreign Rep(s): English Central (Canada); English Language Bookshop (England); Foreign Language Bookshop (Australia); Foreign Language Ltd (South Korea); Independent Publishers International (Japan); Nellie's Group Ltd (Japan)
Membership(s): The Children's Book Council (CBC); TESOL International Association

§Productivity Press
Imprint of Routledge
605 Third Ave, 22nd fl, New York, NY 10158
Toll Free Tel: 800-634-7064 (orders); 800-797-3803
E-mail: orders@taylorandfrancis.com
Web Site: www.crcpress.com
Key Personnel
Publr: Michael Sinocchi *Tel:* 646-901-0024 *E-mail:* michael.sinocchi@taylorandfrancis.com
Sr Acqs Ed: Kristine Mednansky *Tel:* 630-482-9886 *E-mail:* kristine.mednansky@taylorandfrancis.com
Founded: 1983
Books & AV programs. Publishes & distributes materials on productivity, quality improvement, product development, corporate management, profit management & employee involvement for business & industry. Many products are direct source materials from Japan that have been translated into English for the first time.
ISBN Prefix(es): 978-0-915299; 978-1-56327; 978-0-527
Number of titles published annually: 85 Print
Total Titles: 200 Print; 4 CD-ROM
Imprints: Healthcare Performance Press; Productivity Press Spanish Imprint
Foreign Rep(s): Asia Pacific Research Center (Singapore); Books Aplenty (South Africa); Learning & Productivity (Australia); Prism Books Private Ltd (India); Productivity Editorial Consultores SPD CV (Mexico)

Professional Communications Inc
1223 W Main, Suite 1427, Durant, OK 74702-1427
Tel: 580-745-9838 *Toll Free Tel:* 800-337-9838 *Fax:* 580-745-9837
E-mail: info@pcibooks.com
Web Site: www.pcibooks.com
Key Personnel
Pres & Publr: J Malcolm Beasley *Tel:* 631-661-2852 *Fax:* 631-661-2167 *E-mail:* jmbpci@earthlink.net
VP: Phyllis Jones Freeny
Founded: 1992

Medical publishing & communications company.
ISBN Prefix(es): 978-1-884735; 978-0-9632400; 978-0-932610; 978-1-943236
Number of titles published annually: 5 Print
Total Titles: 55 Print
Branch Office(s)
400 Center Bay Dr, West Islip, NY 11795 (bulk sales only)

§The Professional Education Group LLC (PEG)
700 Twelve Oaks Center Dr, Suite 104, Wayzata, MN 55391
Tel: 952-933-9990 *Toll Free Tel:* 800-229-2531
E-mail: orders@proedgroup.com
Web Site: www.proedgroup.com
Key Personnel
Pres & Owner: Kristi Paulson *E-mail:* kristi@proedgroup.com
Founded: 1981
Continuing legal education materials; audio & video programs & books.
ISBN Prefix(es): 978-0-943380; 978-1-932831
Number of titles published annually: 6 Print; 1 CD-ROM; 6 Online
Total Titles: 43 Print; 40 CD-ROM; 40 Online
Distributor for American Bar Association; American Law Institute; Chicago Review Press; Penguin Random House; Wolters Kluwer
Membership(s): Association for Continuing Legal Education (ACLEA)

Professional Publications Inc, see PPI, A Kaplan Company

Professional Resource Press
Imprint of Professional Resource Exchange Inc
5864 Elegant Orchid Way, Sarasota, FL 34232
SAN: 240-1223
Mailing Address: PO Box 3197, Sarasota, FL 34230-3197
Tel: 941-343-9601 *Toll Free Tel:* 800-443-3364 (orders & cust serv) *Fax:* 941-343-9201 *Toll Free Fax:* 866-804-4843 (orders only)
E-mail: cs@prpress.com
Web Site: www.prpress.com
Key Personnel
Pres: Jeffrey D Klosterman *E-mail:* jdk@prpress.com
Mng Ed: Laurie Y Girsch *E-mail:* lyg@prpress.com
Founded: 1980
Books on clinical & forensic psychology, CD-ROMs, DVDs, continuing education programs & texts for mental health & health care professionals. Includes medicine & nursing.
ISBN Prefix(es): 978-0-943158; 978-1-56887
Number of titles published annually: 3 Print; 1 CD-ROM; 4 E-Book
Total Titles: 230 Print; 10 CD-ROM; 4 E-Book; 17 Audio
Membership(s): The Association of Publishers for Special Sales (APSS)

Progressive Press
4028 Texas St, No 7, San Diego, CA 92104
SAN: 222-5395
E-mail: info@progressivepress.com
Web Site: www.progressivepress.com
Key Personnel
Owner: John-Paul Leonard
Founded: 1973
Small publisher of political trade paperbacks. Also provides distribution for one Canadian publisher & several self-published authors. Frontlist: politics, backlist: New Age.
ISBN Prefix(es): 978-0-930852; 978-1-61577
Number of titles published annually: 6 Print
Total Titles: 60 Print
Imprints: Arthritis Research; Banned Books; Collections Livrier; Leaves of Healing; Prensa Pensar; Tree of Life Books
Distributor for Global Research

U.S. PUBLISHERS

Foreign Rep(s): Gazelle Book Services Ltd (UK); New Horizons (South Africa); Woodslane (Australia, New Zealand)
Foreign Rights: Beniamino Soressi (Italy); Thinkers Library (Malaysia); Gerhard Wisnewski (Germany)
Membership(s): The Imaging Alliance; Independent Book Publishers Association (IBPA)

Prometheus Books
Imprint of The Globe Pequot Press
59 John Glenn Dr, Amherst, NY 14228-2119
SAN: 202-0289
Fax: 716-691-0137
E-mail: marketing@prometheusbooks.com; editorial@prometheusbooks.com; rights@prometheusbooks.com
Web Site: www.prometheusbooks.com
Key Personnel
Publr: Jonathan Kurtz *E-mail:* jkurtz@prometheusbooks.com
VP, Busn & Admin Dir: Lynette Nisbet *E-mail:* lnisbet@prometheusbooks.com
VP, Mktg: Jill Maxick *E-mail:* jmaxick@prometheusbooks.com
Dir, Rts: Gretchen Kurtz *E-mail:* gkurtz@prometheusbooks.com
Edit Dir, Pyr: Rene Sears *E-mail:* rsears@prometheusbooks.com
Edit Dir, Seventh Street Books: Dan Mayer *E-mail:* dmayer@prometheusbooks.com
Ed-in-Chief: Steven L Mitchell *E-mail:* smitchell@prometheusbooks.com
Ed: Jake Bonar
Mgr, Print-on-Demand Div: Patrick Martin *E-mail:* pmartin@prometheusbooks.com
Founded: 1969
Provocative, progressive & independent nonfiction press publishing under 4 imprints, including 2 genre fiction imprints.
ISBN Prefix(es): 978-0-87975; 978-1-57392; 978-1-59102; 978-1-61614
Number of titles published annually: 85 Print; 85 E-Book
Total Titles: 2,800 Print; 1,800 E-Book
Imprints: Humanity Books (scholarly/academic)
Distribution Center: National Book Network (NBN), 4501 Forbes Blvd, Suite 200, Lanham, MD 20706 *Toll Free Tel:* 800-462-6420 *Toll Free Fax:* 800-338-4550 *E-mail:* customercare@nbnbooks.com *Web Site:* www.nbnbooks.com

§ProQuest LLC, part of Clarivate PLC
789 E Eisenhower Pkwy, Ann Arbor, MI 48108
Mailing Address: PO Box 1346, Ann Arbor, MI 48106-1346
Tel: 734-761-4700 *Toll Free Tel:* 800-521-0600; 877-779-6768 (sales)
E-mail: sales@proquest.com
Web Site: www.proquest.com
Key Personnel
SVP, Global Sales, Mktg & Cust Experience: James Holmes
Founded: 1872
Publisher, distributor & aggregator of value-added information to libraries, government, universities & schools in over 160 countries. Access to information in periodicals, newspapers, doctoral dissertations & out of print books (retrospective scholarly works). Produce & publish Dissertation Abstracts International.
ISBN Prefix(es): 978-0-912380; 978-0-88692; 978-0-89093; 978-1-55655; 978-0-8357; 978-0-608; 978-0-7837; 978-0-591; 978-0-9702937; 978-0-599; 978-1-931694; 978-1-59399; 978-0-496; 978-0-542; 978-1-4247; 978-0-9778091; 978-1-4345; 978-0-549; 978-1-60205; 978-1-109; 978-1-124; 978-1-267; 978-1-303; 978-1-321; 978-1-339
Number of titles published annually: 56 Print
Total Titles: 56 Print

Branch Office(s)
699 James L Hart Pkwy, Ypsilanti, MI 48197 *Tel:* 734-879-5300 *Fax:* 734-879-5301
6413 Congress Ave, Suite 260, Boca Raton, FL 33487
620 S Third St, Suite 500, Louisville, KY 40202 *Tel:* 502-583-4111
PO Box 8134, Bridgewater, NJ 08807
888 Seventh Ave, 17th fl, New York, NY 10019 *Tel:* 212-331-7700
3 Ingram Blvd, La Vergne, TN 37086 *Tel:* 615-793-5000
5252 N Edgewood Dr, Suite 125, Provo, UT 84604 *Tel:* 801-765-1737
99 Canal Center Plaza, Suite 200, Alexandria, VA 22314 *Tel:* 703-212-8520
1501 First Ave S, Suite 400, Seattle, WA 98134 *Tel:* 206-336-7510
Foreign Office(s): 607 St Kilda Rd, 1st fl, Melbourne, Victoria 3004, Australia *Tel:* (03) 8517 8333 *Fax:* (03) 8517 8399
Unit 804, Tower E1, Beijing Oriental Plaza, No 1 E Chang An Ave, Dong Cheng District, Beijing 100738, China *Tel:* (010) 5977 6010 *Fax:* (010) 8460 8669
Taskoepruestr 1, 22761 Hamburg, Germany *Tel:* (040) 89 809 0 *Fax:* (040) 89 809 250
16A W Sq, 318 Hennessy Rd, Wanchai, Hong Kong *Tel:* 2836 5636 *Fax:* 2834 7133
315, AKD Tower, Near HUDA Off, Sector 14, Gurgaon 122 001, India *Tel:* (0124) 4100615
Mitsubishi Juko Yokohama Bldg, 3-3-1, Minatomirai, Nishi-ku, Yokohama-shi, Kanagawa 220-8401, Japan *Tel:* (045) 342 4780 *Fax:* (045) 342 4784
B909, Phileo Damansara 1, No 9 Jl 16/11, 46350 Petaling Jaya, Selangor, Malaysia *Tel:* (03) 7954 2880 *Fax:* (03) 7958 3446
Regus Kraanspoor, Kraanspoor 50, 1033 SE Amsterdam, Netherlands *Tel:* (020) 6353190 *Fax:* (020) 6337765
Sungil Bldg, 4th fl, 584 Gangnam-daego, Gangnam-gu, Seoul 06043, South Korea *Tel:* (02) 733-5119 *Fax:* (02) 734-5120
Velazquez 100-5° D, 28006 Madrid, Spain *Tel:* 91 575 5597 *Fax:* 91 575 5585
Al-Thurayya II, Off 1304, PO Box 502568, Dubai, United Arab Emirates *Tel:* (04) 4331810 *Fax:* (04) 3697646
The Quorum, Barnwell Rd, Cambridge CB5 8SW, United Kingdom *Tel:* (01223) 215 512 *Fax:* (01223) 215 513
3 Dorset Rise, 5th fl, London EC4Y 8EN, United Kingdom *Tel:* (020) 7832 1700 *Fax:* (020) 7832 1710
Avon House, Headlands Business Park, Salisbury Rd, Ringwood, Hants BH24 3PB, United Kingdom *Tel:* (01425) 471160

ProStar Publications Inc
226 W Florence Ave, Inglewood, CA 90301
SAN: 210-525X
Toll Free Tel: 800-481-6277
E-mail: editor@prostarpublications.com
Web Site: www.prostarpublications.com
Key Personnel
Pres & Publr: Peter L Griffes *E-mail:* peter@prostarpublications.com
Founded: 1965
Books about boating: regional guides, planning, navigation data, nautical charts, marine fauna, how-to, travel, technical, general fiction & music.
ISBN Prefix(es): 978-0-930030; 978-1-57785; 978-1-942388
Number of titles published annually: 145 Print
Total Titles: 440 Print; 30 CD-ROM
Imprints: Atlantic Boating Almanac; Lighthouse Press; Pacific Boating Almanac; US Coast Pilot

§The PRS Group Inc
5800 Heritage Landing Dr, Suite E, East Syracuse, NY 13057-9358

Tel: 315-431-0511 *Fax:* 315-431-0200
E-mail: custserv@prsgroup.com
Web Site: www.prsgroup.com
Key Personnel
Pres & CEO: Christopher McKee
Exec Dir: Dianna Spinner *E-mail:* dspinner@prsgroup.com
Circ Mgr: Patti Davis
Founded: 1979
Over 100 reports, newsletters, journals & volumes per year for international business. No returns without prior approval.
ISBN Prefix(es): 978-1-933539; 978-1-931077; 978-1-941119; 978-1-936241
Number of titles published annually: 3 Print
Total Titles: 20 Print; 100 CD-ROM; 100 Online; 100 E-Book
Imprints: International Country Risk Guide; Political Risk Services

PSMJ Resources Inc
10 Midland Ave, Newton, MA 02458
Tel: 617-965-0055 *Toll Free Tel:* 800-537-PSMJ (537-7765) *Fax:* 617-965-5152
Web Site: www.psmj.com
Founded: 1980
Books, survey reports & digital toolbox programs for architects, engineers, interior designers, urban designers, planners, landscape architects on business & financial management; marketing; time & personnel management; legal topics; project management; human resources; newsletters; consulting & educational seminars.
ISBN Prefix(es): 978-1-55538
Number of titles published annually: 15 Print; 12 E-Book
Total Titles: 50 Print; 25 E-Book
Branch Office(s)
2746 Rangewood Dr, Atlanta, GA 30345 *Tel:* 770-723-9651 *Fax:* 815-461-7478
Foreign Office(s): PO Box 773, Artarmon, NSW 2064, Australia *Tel:* (02) 9411 4819 *Fax:* (02) 9419 6044
419 City Rd, South Melbourne, Victoria 3205, Australia *Tel:* (03) 9686-3846 *Fax:* (03) 9686-1958

§Psychological Assessment Resources Inc (PAR)
16204 N Florida Ave, Lutz, FL 33549
Tel: 813-449-4065 *Toll Free Tel:* 800-331-8378 *Fax:* 813-961-2196 *Toll Free Fax:* 800-727-9329
Web Site: www.parinc.com
Key Personnel
Exec Chmn & Founder: R Bob Smith, III *E-mail:* bsmith@parinc.com
CEO: Kristin Greco
Pres & COO: Travis White *E-mail:* twhite@parinc.com
Exec VP & CIO: Jim Eddy
Exec VP & CFO: Donna Drackett
VP, Mktg: Eric Jessen *E-mail:* ejessen@parinc.com
VP, Dist: Greg Presson
Dir, Sales: David Houser
Dir, Prod Devt: Melissa A Messer
Dir, Cust Support: Daniel McFadden *E-mail:* dmcfadden@parinc.com
Founded: 1978
Career, psychological, neuropsychology, educational & clinical assessments products; software.
ISBN Prefix(es): 978-0-911907
Number of titles published annually: 10 Print; 2 CD-ROM; 1 Online
Total Titles: 150 Print; 20 CD-ROM; 3 Online; 5 Audio
Distributed by ACER; Pro-Ed; Western Psychological Service
Distributor for American Guidance Service; Pro-Ed; Rorschach Workshops

Foreign Rep(s): ACER (Australia); Tea Ediciones (Spain); Testzentrale (Germany)
Returns: 16130 N Florida Ave, Lutz, FL 33549 *E-mail:* gpresson@parinc.com
Warehouse: 16130 N Florida Ave, Lutz, FL 33549 *E-mail:* gpresson@parinc.com

Public Citizen
1600 20 St NW, Washington, DC 20009
Tel: 202-588-1000
Web Site: www.citizen.org
Key Personnel
Pres: Robert Weissman
EVP: Lisa Gilbert
Founded: 1971
Books & reports; consumer advocacy organization.
ISBN Prefix(es): 978-0-937188; 978-1-58231
Number of titles published annually: 47 Print
Total Titles: 48 Print
Divisions: Congress Watch; Democracy Is For People; Energy Program; Global Trade Watch; Health Research Group; Litigation Group
Branch Office(s)
215 Pennsylvania Ave SE, Washington, DC 20003 *Tel:* 202-546-4996
309 E 11 St, Suite 2, Austin, TX 78701 *Tel:* 512-477-1155
Distributed by Addison-Wesley; Simon & Schuster, LLC
Foreign Rights: Random House-Pantheon

§Publication Consultants
8370 Eleusis Dr, Anchorage, AK 99502
Tel: 907-349-2424 *Fax:* 907-349-2426
E-mail: books@publicationconsultants.com
Web Site: www.publicationconsultants.com
Key Personnel
Owner & Publr: Evan Swensen *E-mail:* evan@publicationconsultants.com
Founded: 1978
ISBN Prefix(es): 978-0-9644809; 978-1-888125; 978-1-59433
Number of titles published annually: 50 Print; 50 E-Book
Total Titles: 460 Print; 330 E-Book
Membership(s): Alaska Writers Guild; Better Business Bureau (BBB)

Publications International Ltd (PIL)
8140 N Lehigh Ave, Morton Grove, IL 60053
Tel: 847-676-3470 *Fax:* 847-676-3671
E-mail: customer_service@pubint.com
Web Site: pilbooks.com
Key Personnel
CEO: Louis Weber
VP, Acqs & Proj Mgmt: Jenny Barney
Dir, Natl Accts: Scott Cox
Founded: 1967
ISBN Prefix(es): 978-0-88176; 978-1-56173; 978-1-68022
Number of titles published annually: 400 Print

§Puffin Books
Imprint of Penguin Young Readers Group
c/o Penguin Random House LLC, 1745 Broadway, New York, NY 10019
Tel: 212-782-9000
Web Site: www.penguin.com/puffin-overview/
Founded: 1978
Penguin Random House & its publishing entities are not accepting unsol submissions, proposals, mss, or submission queries via e-mail at this time.
Number of titles published annually: 150 Print
Membership(s): The Children's Book Council (CBC)

Purdue University Press
Stewart Ctr 190, 504 W State St, West Lafayette, IN 47907-2058
SAN: 203-4026
Tel: 765-494-2038 *Fax:* 765-496-2442
E-mail: pupress@purdue.edu
Web Site: www.thepress.purdue.edu
Key Personnel
Dir: Justin Race *Tel:* 765-494-8251 *E-mail:* racej@purdue.edu
Edit, Design & Prodn Mgr: Katherine Purple *E-mail:* kpurple@purdue.edu
Sales & Mktg Mgr: Bryan Shaffer *E-mail:* bshaffer@purdue.edu
Founded: 1960
Publisher of scholarly titles with emphasis on business, veterinary medicine, health issues & the humanities.
ISBN Prefix(es): 978-0-911198; 978-1-55753
Number of titles published annually: 25 Print; 25 E-Book
Total Titles: 350 Print; 50 E-Book
Foreign Rep(s): The Eurospan Group (Continental Europe, Israel, Middle East, UK)
Orders to: Longleaf Services Inc, 116 S Boundary St, Chapel Hill, NC 27514 *Toll Free Tel:* 800-627-7377 *E-mail:* orders@longleafservices.org *Web Site:* www.longleafservices.org
Distribution Center: Longleaf Services Inc, 116 S Boundary St, Chapel Hill, NC 27514 *Toll Free Tel:* 800-627-7377 *E-mail:* orders@longleafservices.org *Web Site:* www.longleafservices.org
UTP Distribution, 5201 Dufferin St, Toronto, ON M3H 5T8, Canada *Toll Free Tel:* 800-565-9523 *E-mail:* utpbooks@utpress.utoronto.ca *Web Site:* www.utpdistribution.com
Eurospan Group, Gray's Inn House, 127 Clerkenwell Rd, London EC1R 5DB, United Kingdom (worldwide exc CN & US) *Tel:* (01767) 604972 *E-mail:* info@eurospangroup.com *Web Site:* www.eurospanbookstore.com/purdue
Membership(s): American Association of University Presses (AAUP)

Purple House Press
Imprint of Purple House Inc
8100 US Hwy 62 E, Cynthiana, KY 41031
Mailing Address: PO Box 787, Cynthiana, KY 41031
Tel: 859-235-9970
Web Site: www.purplehousepress.com
Key Personnel
Publr: Jill Morgan *E-mail:* jill@purplehousepress.com
Dir, Cust Fulfillment, Managed Info Servs: Ray Sanders *E-mail:* ray@purplehousepress.com
Prepress & Clerical: Hayley Morgan-Sanders *E-mail:* hayley@purplehousepress.com
Founded: 2000
Reissue of children's classics from the 1920s-1990s.
ISBN Prefix(es): 978-1-930900; 978-1-984959; 979-8-88818
Number of titles published annually: 20 Print; 5 E-Book
Total Titles: 150 Print; 30 E-Book
Foreign Rights: McIntosh & Otis (worldwide)

Pushcart Press
PO Box 380, Wainscott, NY 11975-0380
SAN: 202-9871
Tel: 631-324-9300
Web Site: www.pushcartprize.com/pushcartpress
Key Personnel
Pres: Bill Henderson
Founded: 1972
Trade books, literary anthologies.
ISBN Prefix(es): 978-0-916366; 978-1-888889; 978-0-9600977; 979-8-9854697
Number of titles published annually: 6 Print
Total Titles: 65 Print
Distributed by W W Norton & Company Inc

GP Putnam's Sons
Imprint of Penguin Publishing Group
c/o Penguin Random House LLC, 1745 Broadway, New York, NY 10019
Tel: 212-782-9000
Web Site: www.penguin.com/putnam/
Key Personnel
Pres, Putnam/Dutton/Berkley: Ivan Held
SVP & Exec Creative Dir, Putnam/Dutton/Berkley: Anthony Ramondo
VP & Dir, Publicity: Alexis Welby
VP & Ed-in-Chief: Lindsay Sagnette
Assoc Publr & Mktg Dir: Ashley Pattison McClay
Exec Dir, Ad & Promo: Jaime Mendola-Hobbie
Sr Dir, Subs Rts: Ritsuko Okumura
Dir, Copy-Editing: Linda Rosenberg
Dir, Prodn: William Peabody
Assoc Dir, Mktg: Molly Pieper
Asst Dir, Mktg: Brennin Cummings
Asst Dir, Publicity: Ashley Hewlett; Katie McKee
Exec Ed: Tara Singh Carlson; Daphne Ming Durham; Michelle Howry
Sr Ed: Kate Dresser
Asst Ed: Ashley Di Dio; Aranya Jain; Tricja Okuniewska; Aranya Jain
Mktg Mgr: Regina Andreoni; Shina Patel
Sr Publicist: Kristen Bianco
Publicist: Nicole Biton
Founded: 1838
Fiction & general nonfiction.
Penguin Random House & its publishing entities are not accepting unsol submissions, proposals, mss, or submission queries via e-mail at this time.
Number of titles published annually: 65 Print
Total Titles: 208 Print
Imprints: Putnam; Marian Wood Books

GP Putnam's Sons Books for Young Readers
Imprint of Penguin Young Readers Group
c/o Penguin Random House LLC, 1745 Broadway, New York, NY 10019
Tel: 212-782-9000
Web Site: www.penguin.com/putnam-young-readers/
Key Personnel
Pres & Publr, Dial Books for Young Readers & GP Putnam's Sons Books for Young Readers: Jennifer Klonsky
SVP & Exec Art Dir, Dial Books for Young Readers, Nancy Paulsen Books, GP Putnam's Sons Books for Young Readers & Rocky Pond Books: Lily Malcom
VP & Assoc Publr: Nancy Mercado
Sr Exec Ed: Susan Kochan; Ruta Rimas
Exec Ed: Stephanie Pitts
Sr Ed: Christopher Hernandez
Ed: Polo Orozco
Assoc Ed: Gretchen Durning; Matt Phipps
Art Dir, GP Putnam's Sons Books for Young Readers & Nancy Paulsen Books: Marikka Tamura
Assoc Art Dir, GP Putnam's Sons Books for Young Readers & Nancy Paulsen Books: Eileen Savage
Founded: 1838
Penguin Random House & its publishing entities are not accepting unsol submissions, proposals, mss, or submission queries via e-mail at this time.
Number of titles published annually: 50 Print
Total Titles: 386 Print
Membership(s): The Children's Book Council (CBC)

Pyncheon House
6 University Dr, Suite 105, Amherst, MA 01002
SAN: 297-6269
Key Personnel
Ed-in-Chief: David R Rhodes
Founded: 1991

U.S. PUBLISHERS

Fine editions & trade books; contemporary poetry, short fiction, novels & essays; member of Library of Congress CIP Program.
ISBN Prefix(es): 978-1-881119
Number of titles published annually: 4 Print
Total Titles: 15 Print

Quail Ridge Press (QRP)
Imprint of Capen Publishing Co Inc
2451 Atrium Way, Nashville, TN 37214
Toll Free Tel: 800-358-0560 *Fax:* 615-391-2815
Web Site: www.swphbooks.com/quail-ridge-press.html
Key Personnel
Publr: Sheila Thomas *E-mail:* sthomas@swpublishinggroup.com
Founded: 1978
Cookbook publisher.
ISBN Prefix(es): 978-0-937552; 978-1-893062; 978-1-938879; 978-1-934193
Number of titles published annually: 4 Print
Total Titles: 150 Print

Quarto Publishing Group USA Inc
Division of Quarto Group Inc (London, UK)
100 Cummings Ctr, Suite 265D, Beverly, MA 01915
Tel: 978-282-9590 *Toll Free Tel:* 800-328-0590 (sales) *Fax:* 978-283-2742
E-mail: sales@quartous.com
Web Site: www.quartoknows.com
Key Personnel
SVP & Group Publg Dir, US: Winnie Danenbarger
SVP, Sales & Mktg: Martha Bucci
VP, Global Busn Devt & Publr, Custom, Proprietary & Value Publg: Wendy Friedman
VP & Dir, US & CN Sales: Stephanie Warner
Group Publr: Rage Kindelsperger
Publr, Children's Illustrated Nonfiction: Jo Hanks
Dir, New Busn Devt: Scott Sheppard *Tel:* 978-282-3581 *E-mail:* scott.sheppard@quarto.com
Dir, Publicity & Mktg: Giuliana Caranante
Assoc Dir, Children's Mktg: Angela Corpus
Sr Acqs Ed: Nicole James; Thom O'Hearn
Sales Opers Mgr: Deb Moreau *Tel:* 978-272-3510 *E-mail:* deb.moreau@quarto.com
Founded: 2004
Represents a dynamic group of imprints dedicated to providing quality & excellence to its readers. Each imprint embodies the breadth & scope of its specialty topics.
ISBN Prefix(es): 978-0-86573; 978-0-7603; 978-1-59253; 978-0-929261; 978-1-56010; 978-1-59233; 978-1-58923; 978-1-59186; 978-1-61673; 978-1-61058; 978-1-61059; 978-1-61060; 978-1-62788; 978-0-89738; 978-0-912612; 978-1-63159; 978-0-9640392; 978-1-888608; 978-1-930604; 978-1-936309; 978-1-60058; 978-1-937994; 978-1-939581; 978-1-63106; 978-1-63322; 978-1-942875
Number of titles published annually: 300 Print
Total Titles: 4,000 Print
Imprints: becker&mayer!; Book Sales; Burgess Lea Press; Cool Springs Press; Creative Publishing International; Fair Winds Press; Walter Foster Jr; Walter Foster Publishing; Harvard Common Press; MoonDance Press; Motorbooks; Quarry Books; QDS; Race Point Publishers; Rock Point Gift & Stationery; Rockport Publishers; Seagrass Press; SmartLab Toys; Voyager Press; Wellfleet Press
Branch Office(s)
26391 Crown Valley Pkwy, Suite 220, Mission Viejo, CA 92691 *Tel:* 949-380-7510 *Fax:* 949-380-7575 SAN: 249-051X
142 W 36 St, 4th fl, New York, NY 10018 *Tel:* 212-779-4972 *Fax:* 212-779-6058
11120 NE 33 Place, Suite 201, Bellevue, WA 98004 *Tel:* 425-827-7120 *Fax:* 425-828-9659
Distributed by Allen & Unwin (Australia & New Zealand); Hachette Book Group Inc (North America)

Distributor for Batsford (Pavillion Books Group imprint, CN & US); CLEVER Publishing
See separate listing for:
Book Sales
Fair Winds Press
Walter Foster Publishing
Harvard Common Press

Quincannon Publishing Group
PO Box 8100, Glen Ridge, NJ 07028-8100
Tel: 973-380-9942
E-mail: editors@quincannongroup.com (query first via e-mail)
Web Site: www.quincannongroup.com
Key Personnel
Ed-in-Chief: Alan Quincannon
Ed: Holly Benedict
Trade Sales/Consulting Ed: Jeanne Wilcox
Lib Sales/Admin Asst: Patricia McCauley
Publicity: Nora Dempsey
Founded: 1990
Regional mystery novels made unique by involving some element of a region's history (i.e. the story's setting & time frame or the mystery's origin). Custom tailored history books for local or regional museums, municipalities & organizations. May consider historical fiction tied to a local or regional museum.
ISBN Prefix(es): 978-1-878452
Number of titles published annually: 3 Print
Total Titles: 39 Print
Imprints: Compass Point Mysteries; Jersey Yarns; Learning & Coloring Books; Quincannon; Rune-Tales; Tory Corner Editions

§Quintessence Publishing Co Inc
411 N Raddant Rd, Batavia, IL 60510
SAN: 215-9783
Tel: 630-736-3600 *Toll Free Tel:* 800-621-0387 *Fax:* 630-736-3633
E-mail: contact@quintbook.com; service@quintbook.com
Web Site: www.quintpub.com
Key Personnel
Pres: H W Haase
EVP: William Hartman *Tel:* 630-736-3600 ext 413 *E-mail:* whartman@quintbook.com
Founded: 1950
Professional & scholarly books, journals, medicine, dentistry, health & nutrition, medical history.
ISBN Prefix(es): 978-0-931386; 978-0-86715; 978-1-85097; 978-1-883695
Number of titles published annually: 20 Print; 2 CD-ROM
Total Titles: 410 Print; 80 CD-ROM; 250 Audio
Imprints: Quintessence Books; Quintessence of Dental Technology
Foreign Office(s): 2-4 Ifenpfad, 12107 Berlin, Germany *Tel:* (030) 761-805 *Fax:* (030) 761-80693 *E-mail:* info@quintessenz.de *Web Site:* www.quintessenz.de
Quint House Bldg, 326 Hongo, Bunkyo-ku Tokyo, Japan *Tel:* (03) 5842-2270 *Fax:* (03) 5800-7598 *E-mail:* info@quint-j.co.jp *Web Site:* www.quint-j.co.jp
2 Grafton Rd, New Malden, Surrey KT3 3AB, United Kingdom *Tel:* (020) 8949-6087 *Fax:* (020) 8336-1484 *E-mail:* info@quintpub.co.uk *Web Site:* www.quintpub.co.uk
Distributor for Quintessence Publishing Co Ltd (Japan); Quintessence Publishing Ltd (London); Quintessence Verlags GmbH
Advertising Agency: QPC Advertising Inc

Quirk Books
215 Church St, Philadelphia, PA 19106
Tel: 215-627-3581 *Fax:* 215-627-5220
E-mail: general@quirkbooks.com
Web Site: www.quirkbooks.com
Key Personnel
Chmn & Founder: David Borgenicht

Pres & Publr: Jhanteigh Kupihea *E-mail:* jhanleigh@quirkbooks.com
EVP & Deputy Publr: Nicole De Jackmo *E-mail:* nicole@quirkbooks.com
VP, Fin: Megan DiPasquale
Creative Dir: Andie Reid
Edit Dir, Children's: Alex Arnold
Prodn Dir: Mandy Sampson
Asst Dir, Busn Devt & Subs Rts: Katherine McGuire *E-mail:* katherine@quirkbooks.com
Principal, Contracts & Rts: Shaquona Crews
Mng Ed: Jane Morley
Ed: Jess Zimmerman
Assoc Ed: Rebecca Gyllenhaal
Asst Ed: Jessica Yang
Sr Publicity & Mktg Mgr: Ivy Weir *E-mail:* iweir@quirkbooks.com
Sr Sales Mgr: Kate Brown *E-mail:* kbrown@quirkbooks.com
Digital Mktg Mgr: Christina Tatulli *E-mail:* christina@quirkbooks.com
Digital Mktg Design Assoc: Kim Ismael
Sr Designer: Elissa Flanigan
Founded: 2002
Publishing list focuses on irreverent pop-culture, humor, gift, self-help & "impractical" reference books. The actual subject matter of our books is quite diverse. Publish everything from childcare tips & magic tricks to advice on stain removal. All of our books have a distinct sense of style, a refreshing sense of humor & innovative production values.
ISBN Prefix(es): 978-1-931686; 978-1-59474
Number of titles published annually: 25 Print
Total Titles: 150 Print
Foreign Rights: AnatoliaLit Agency (Turkey); Big Apple Agency (Shanghai) (Maggie Han, Wendy King, Erica Zhou) (China, Vietnam); Big Apple Agency (Taipei) (Chris Lin) (China); DS Budapest Kft (Margit Gruber) (Hungary); Ersilia Literary Agency (adult) (Evangelia Avloniti) (Greece); Ersilia Literary Agency (children's) (Avgi Deferera) (Greece); ICSTI (Tatiana Vaniat) (Russia, Ukraine); Japan UNI Agency Inc (adult) (Mami Nakajima) (Japan); Japan UNI Agency Inc (children's) (Takeshi Oyama) (Japan); Ute Koerner Literary Agent SLU (Inigo Cebollada) (Portugal, Spain); Josef Kolar Foreign Rights Sales (Josef Kolar) (Czechia, Estonia, Latvia, Lithuania, Slovakia); Macadamia Literary Agency (Kamila Kanafa) (Poland); Maxima Creative Literary (Santo Manurung) (Indonesia); Michael Meller Literary Agency (adult) (Regina Seitz) (Germany); Michael Meller Literary Agency (children's) (Cristina Bernardi) (Germany); NiKa Literary Agency (Vania Kadiyska) (Bulgaria); Right Thing Agency (Winnie Waropas) (Thailand); Sea of Stories Agency (Sidonie Bancquart-Warren) (Belgium (French-speaking), France); Livia Stoia Agency (Antonia Girmacea) (The Balkans, Croatia, Romania, Slovenia); Trentin Agency (Rossano Trentin) (Italy)
Distribution Center: Penguin Random House Publisher Services (PRHPS), 1745 Broadway, New York, NY 10019 *Toll Free Tel:* 800-733-3000 *Toll Free Fax:* 800-659-2436 *E-mail:* distribution@penguinrandomhouse.com *Web Site:* prhpublisherservices.com

Quite Specific Media Group Ltd
Division of Silman-James Press Inc
7373 Pyramid Place, Hollywood, CA 90046
E-mail: info@quitespecificmedia.com
Web Site: quitespecificmedia.com
Founded: 1967
Publish original books as well as co-publish with foreign publishers. Specialize in costumes, fashion & theatre.
ISBN Prefix(es): 978-0-89676
Number of titles published annually: 8 Print
Total Titles: 380 Print

Imprints: Costume & Fashion Press; Drama Publishers
Foreign Rep(s): Nick Hern Books (UK)
Orders to: Silman-James Press Inc, 141 N Clark Dr, Unit 1, West Hollywood, CA 90048 *Tel:* 310-205-0665 *E-mail:* info@silmanjamespress.com *Web Site:* www.silmanjamespress.com
Distribution Center: Silman-James Press Inc, 141 N Clark Dr, Unit 1, West Hollywood, CA 90048 *Tel:* 310-205-0665 *E-mail:* info@silmanjamespress.com *Web Site:* www.silmanjamespress.com

Quixote Press
3544 Blakslee St, Wever, IA 52658
Tel: 319-372-4383 *Toll Free Tel:* 800-571-2665
E-mail: heartsntummies@gmail.com
Web Site: heartsntummies.com
Founded: 1985
Regional paperback books of humor or folklore & cookbooks. Consulting work for self-publishers.
ISBN Prefix(es): 978-1-878488; 978-1-57166
Number of titles published annually: 30 Print
Total Titles: 350 Print
Divisions: Black Iron Cookin' Co; Hearts 'n Tummies Cookbook Co; Kid Help Publishing Co; PYO (Publish Your Own Co); Raise the Dough in 30 Days Co
See separate listing for:
Hearts 'n Tummies Cookbook Co

§Radix Press
11715 Bandlon Dr, Houston, TX 77072
Tel: 281-879-5688
Web Site: www.vvfh.org; www.specialforcesbooks.com; vinabooks.us
Key Personnel
Dir: Stephen Sherman *E-mail:* sherman1@flash.net
Founded: 1983
Directories, reference books. All unsol mss sent will be discarded.
ISBN Prefix(es): 978-0-9624009; 978-0-9623992; 978-1-929932
Number of titles published annually: 10 Print; 1 CD-ROM; 10 E-Book
Total Titles: 100 Print; 14 CD-ROM; 100 E-Book
Imprints: Electric Strawberry Press; VVFH (Vietnam Veterans for Factual History)

§RAND Corp
1776 Main St, Santa Monica, CA 90407-2138
Mailing Address: PO Box 2138, Santa Monica, CA 90407-2138
Tel: 310-393-0411 *Fax:* 310-393-4818
Web Site: www.rand.org
Key Personnel
Mng Dir, Off External Aff: Jeremy Rawitch *E-mail:* jrawitch@rand.org
Dir, Research Edit & Prodn: Erin-Elizabeth Johnson *E-mail:* ejohnson@rand.org
Assoc Dir, Communs: Steve Kistler
Mgr, Busn: Laura Shaw *E-mail:* lshaw@rand.org
Mgr, Prodn: Todd Duft *E-mail:* duft@rand.org
Mgr, Operational Prodn & OEA Busn Advisor: Tim Erickson *Tel:* 310-393-0411 ext 6141 *E-mail:* tim@rand.org
Cust Serv Supv: Amy Majczyk *Tel:* 412-683-2300 ext 4929 *E-mail:* amajczyk@rand.org
Founded: 1948
Public policy research.
ISBN Prefix(es): 978-0-8330
Number of titles published annually: 400 Print; 100 Online; 50 E-Book
Total Titles: 30,000 Print; 24,000 Online; 1,800 E-Book
Divisions: Office of External Affairs
Foreign Rep(s): Ingram Publisher Services UK (Europe, Middle East, UK); NBN Canada (Canada); NBN/DA Trade (Australia, New Zealand)
Orders to: RAND Distribution Services, 4570 Fifth Ave, Pittsburgh, PA 15213, Cust Serv Mgr: Amy Majczyk *Tel:* 310-451-7002 *Toll Free Tel:* 877-584-8642 *Fax:* 412-683-2800 *E-mail:* order@rand.org
Distribution Center: National Book Network, 15200 NBN Way, Blue Ridge Summit, PA 17214 *Tel:* 717-794-3800 *Toll Free Tel:* 800-462-6420 *Toll Free Fax:* 800-338-4550 *E-mail:* vfunk@nbnbooks.com *Web Site:* www.nbnbooks.com
Membership(s): AIGA, the professional association for design; American Association of University Presses (AAUP); Public Relations Society of America Inc (PRSA); Society for Scholarly Publishing (SSP)

§Rand McNally
9855 Woods Dr, Skokie, IL 60077
SAN: 203-3917
Mailing Address: PO Box 7600, Chicago, IL 60680-7600
Tel: 847-329-8100 *Toll Free Tel:* 877-446-4863 *Toll Free Fax:* 877-469-1298
E-mail: mediarelations@randmcnally.com; tndsupport@randmcnally.com
Web Site: www.randmcnally.com
Key Personnel
CEO: Stephen Fletcher
CTO: Yusuf Ozturk
VP, Mktg: Kendra Ensor
Design Dir: Joerg Metzner
Prod Mgr: Mastan Holtzer
Founded: 1856
Road atlases & maps; world atlases; mileage & routing publications & software; educational maps, atlases; children's atlases, maps, books; electronic multimedia products; retail & online stores; online travel services, travel software.
Publisher of the *Thomas Guide* atlas series.
ISBN Prefix(es): 978-0-528
Number of titles published annually: 20 Print
Total Titles: 100 Print; 5 CD-ROM
Imprints: Rand McNally for Kids
Warehouse: 106 Hi-Lane, Richmond, KY 40475

Rand Smith LLC, see Rand-Smith Publishing

Rand-Smith Publishing
204 College Ave, Ashland, VA 23005
Tel: 804-874-6012
E-mail: randsmithllc@gmail.com
Web Site: www.rand-smith.com
Key Personnel
Publr: David Smitherman
Acqs: Jeff Howard
Founded: 2019
ISBN Prefix(es): 978-1-950544
Number of titles published annually: 15 Print; 15 E-Book
Total Titles: 4 Print; 4 E-Book
Distribution Center: Ingram

Peter E Randall Publisher
5 Greenleaf Woods Dr, Suite 102, Portsmouth, NH 03801
Tel: 603-431-5667 *Fax:* 603-431-3566
E-mail: media@perpublisher.com
Web Site: www.perpublisher.com
Key Personnel
Owner & CEO: Deidre C Randall
 E-mail: deidre@perpublisher.com
Founded: 1970
This publisher has indicated that 100% of their product line is author subsidized.
ISBN Prefix(es): 978-0-914339; 978-1-931807; 978-0-9817898; 978-0-9828236; 978-1-937721
Number of titles published annually: 20 Print; 5 E-Book
Imprints: Bugle Boy Press

Random House Children's Books
Division of Penguin Random House LLC
c/o Penguin Random House LLC, 1745 Broadway, New York, NY 10019
Tel: 212-782-9000
Web Site: www.rhcbooks.com
Key Personnel
Pres & Publr: Barbara Marcus
Pres & Publr, Beginner Books & Dr Seuss Publg Prog: Cathy Goldsmith
EVP & Publr, Random House Books for Young Readers: Mallory Loehr
EVP & Deputy Publr, Dr Seuss Publg: Judith Haut
EVP, Publg Opers: Rich Romano
SVP & Publr, RHCB Brands & RH Graphic: Michelle Nagler
SVP, Mktg: John Adamo
SVP, Mass Mdse Sales: Mark Santella
SVP, Publicity, Corp Communs & Author Brand Strategy: Dominique Cimina
SVP, Retail: Becky Green
VP & Publr, Anne Schwartz Books: Anne Schwartz
VP & Publr, Bright Matter Books: Tom Russell
VP & Publr, Crown Children's/Exec Dir, Little Tiger: Sonali Fry
VP & Publr, Delacorte Press: Wendy Loggia
VP & Publr, Random House Studio: Lee Wade
VP & Assoc Publr, Delacorte Press: Krista Marino
VP & Exec Creative Dir: Martha Rago
VP & Exec Dir, Prodn: Amy Bowman
VP & Exec Dir, Publicity & Media Strategy: Noreen Herits
VP & Sales Dir, Mass Mdse Natl Accts: Christina Jeffries
VP & Ed-in-Chief, Labyrinth Road: Liesa Abrams
VP & Ed-at-Large, Crown Children's: Phoebe Yeh
VP, Brand Mgmt & Busn Devt: Kerry Milliron
VP, Mktg, Licensed & Proprietary Brands: Kerri Benvenuto
VP, Online Sales: Enid Chaban
Assoc Publr: Caroline Abbey
Exec Art Dir: Nicole de las Heras; Roberta Ludlow; April Ward
Exec Dir, Copy-Editing: Alison Kolani
Exec Dir, Mktg Prodn & Opers: Beth Conte
Exec Dir, Prodn: Patty Collins
Exec Dir, Publicity & School Event Strategy: Kathy Dunn
Exec Dir, School & Lib Mktg: Adrienne Waintraub
Exec Edit Dir, Random House Brands & Graphic: Heidi Kilgras
Sr Art Dir: Sharon Burkle; Jason Zamajtuk
Sr Art Dir, Children's Mktg: Maureen McLaughlin
Sr Dir, Digital Mktg: Kate Keating
Sr Dir, Mktg, Design & Opers/Licensed Publg: Derek Elmer
Sr Dir, Publicity: Jillian Vandall
Sr Dir, Subs Rts: Kim Wrubel
Sr Dir, Trade Mktg: Kelly McGauley
Sr Publg Dir, Bright Matter Books: Alison Stoltzfus
Art Dir: Katrina Damkoehler; Sarah Hokanson; Veronique Sweet
Art Dir & Book Designer: Liz Dresner
Dir, Consumer Strategy & Analysis: Diana Blough
Dir, Copy-Editing: Melinda Ackell
Dir, Digital Mktg Strategy: Elizabeth Ward
Dir, Lib Mktg: Katie Halata
Dir, Licensing: Rachel Bader
Edit Dir, Little Golden Books/Sesame Street: Andrea Posner-Sanchez
Edit Dir, Random House Graphic: Shana Corey
Dir, Publg Opers: Hanna Glidden
Dir, Subs Rts: Hannah Babcock
Group Sales Dir: Joe English
Sales Dir: Emily Bruce

U.S. PUBLISHERS — BOOK

Assoc Art Dir: Carol Ly
Assoc Art Dir, Interiors & Pbks: Jinna Shin
Assoc Dir, Audience Engagement Strategy: Jenn Inzetta
Assoc Dir, Mng Edit: Jake Eldred
Assoc Dir, Prodn: Jennifer Moreno
Assoc Dir, Publicity & DEI Strategy: Kristopher Kam
Assoc Dir, Publicity & Media Strategy: Josh Redlich
Assoc Dir, Trade Mktg: Jules Kelly
Assoc Prod Dir: Whitney Aaronson
Assoc Publg Dir, Knopf Children's: Melanie Nolan
Asst Art Dir: Bob Bianchini; Shane Eichacker; Nicole Gastonguay; Casey Moses; Catherine Mucciardi; Marianna Smirnova; Elizabeth Tardiff
Asst Art Dir, Mktg Design: Allyssa Price
Asst Design Dir, Mktg: Michael Caiati
Asst Dir, Digital Mktg: Sarah Reck
Asst Dir, Prodn: Mary Ellen Owens
Asst Dir, School Mktg: Michelle Campbell
Sr Exec Ed: Mary Man-Kong; Sara Sargent
Sr Exec Ed, Knopf Books for Young Readers: Nancy Siscoe
Ed-in-Chief, Doubleday Books for Young Readers: Frances Gilbert
Exec Ed: Farrin Jacobs; Alice Jonaitis; Annie Kelley; Tiffany Liao
Exec Ed, Delacorte Press: Kelsey Horton
Exec Ed, Knopf Books for Young Readers: Katherine Harrison
Exec Ed, Random House Brands: Frank Berrios
Exec Ed, Random House Graphic: Whitney Leopard
Sr Mng Ed: Rebecca Vitkus
Mng Ed: Katy Miller; Tisha Paul
Mng Ed, Digital: Tom Marquet
Mng Ed, Opers: Jennifer Chung-Castillo
Assoc Mng Ed: Emily Hoffman
Asst Mng Ed: Kari Webb
Sr Copy Ed: Stephanie Bay; Debra DeFord-Minerva
Sr Ed: Tricia Lin
Sr Ed, Crown Children's: Kelly Delaney
Sr Ed, Delacorte Press: Hannah Hill; Bria Ragin
Sr Ed, Dr Seuss Publg: Cat Reynolds
Sr Ed, Random House Brands & Graphic: Jenna Lettice
Bilingual Copy Ed: Denise Morales Soto
Copy Ed: Bess Schelper Sampson; Bess Schelper
Ed: Lauren Clauss
Ed, Knopf Children's: Marisa Dinovis
Ed, Make Me a World: Lois Evans
Ed, Random House Graphic: Jordan Blanco; Alex Lu
Assoc Ed: Maria Correa; Elizabeth Stranahan
Assoc Ed, Delacorte Press: Alison Romig
Assoc Ed, Knopf Children's: Gianna Lakenauth
Assoc Ed, Licensed Publg Edit Group: Angela Song
Assoc Ed, Random House Brands & Graphic: Jasmine Hodge
Assoc Ed, Wendy Lamb Books: Dana Carey
Asst Ed: Tia Resham Cheema
Asst Ed, Anne Schwartz Books: Anne-Marie Varga
Asst Ed, Delacorte Press: Lydia Gregovic
Asst Ed, Dr Seuss Publg: Renee Cantor
Asst Ed, Labyrinth Road: Emily Harburg
Asst Ed, Random House Studio: Charlotte Roos
Sr Mgr, Ad: Tricia Ryzner; Bessa Zenebework
Sr Mgr, School Mktg: Natalie Capogrossi
Sr Mgr, Soc Media Strategy: Meredith Wagner
Sr Mktg Mgr: Megan Mitchell
Sr Prodn Mgr: Tracy Heydweiller; Jen Jie Li
Busn Mgr: Ken Kong
Content Mktg Mgr, Audience Engagement: Megan Barlog Hughes
Mgr, Communs & Analytics: Elena Meuse
Mgr, Digital Mktg: Stephania Villar
Mgr, Lib Mktg: Erica Stone
Mgr, Mktg Licenses & Proprietary Brands: Jena DeBois
Mgr, Prodn: Melissa Fariello; Claribel Vasquez
Mgr, School & Lib Digital Mktg: Katie Dutton
Mgr, Subs Rts: Claire Rivkin
Mktg Mgr: Catherine O'Mara
Prod Mgr: Nadia Vertlib
Prodn Mgr: Natalia Dextre
Publicity Mgr: Lili Feinberg
Publg Mgr: Kortney Hartz
Assoc Brand Mgr: Alyssa Prado
Assoc Mgr, Prod Devt: Kate Glider
Assoc Mgr, Prodn: Maggie Gibson
Assoc Mgr, Subs Rts: Alyssa Eatherly; Mariana Ramos
Assoc Mktg Mgr: Kristin Guy
Asst Mgr, School & Lib Mktg: Emily Petrick
Asst Mgr, Subs Rts: Dakota Reed
Asst Prodn Mgr: Alice Rahaeuser
Sr Assoc, Audience Engagement: Jordan Bishop
Sr Assoc, Soc Media: Katie Burton
Sr Mktg Assoc: David Gilmore
Admin Assoc, Creative Servs: Stacey Sundar
Assoc, Prodn: CJ Han
Assoc Marketer, School & Lib Mktg: Jasmine Ferrufino
Mktg Coord: Caite Arocho
Mktg Assoc: Natali Cavanagh
Prodn Supv: Luke McCord; Donna Rocco; Erika Schwartz
Prodn Assoc: Lizzy Indek; Vincent Perez; Liz Sutton; Lauren Taglienti
Sr Publicist: Madison Furr
Publicist: Joey Ho; Lena Reilly
Assoc Publicist: Sarah Lawrenson; Cynthia Lliguichuzhca; Kim Small
Sr Digital Artist: John Wyffels
Sr Designer: Melanie Bermudez; Michelle Cunningham; Michelle Kim; Suzanne Lee; Xiomara Nieves; Mark Patti; Mike Rich; Ray Shappel; Jen Valero
Designer: Taline Boghosian; Michelle Crowe; Juliet Goodman; Jade Hector; Monique Razzouk
Designer/Digital Artist: Jamie Yee
Jr Designer: Adam Castro; Brittany Ramirez; Megan Shortt; Isabelle Snyder
Fin Analyst: Crisandry Javier
Penguin Random House & its publishing entities are not accepting unsol submissions, proposals, mss, or submission queries via e-mail at this time.
Imprints: Bluefire; Bright Matter Books; Crown Books for Young Readers; Delacorte Press; Dragonfly Books; Ember; Golden Books; Joy Revolution (young adult romance); Alfred A Knopf Books for Young Readers; Labyrinth Road; Laurel-Leaf; Little Tiger; Make Me A World; The Princeton Review; Random House Books for Young Readers; Random House Graphic; Random House Studio; Rodale Kids; Anne Schwartz Books; Dr Seuss Beginner Books; Seuss Studios; Step Into Reading; Sylvan Learning; Underlined; Wendy Lamb Books; Yearling Books
Warehouse: Crawfordsville Distribution Center, 1021 N State Rd 47, Crawfordsville, IN 47933
Tel: 765-362-5125
Distribution Center: Crawfordsville Distribution Center, 1021 N State Rd 47, Crawfordsville, IN 47933 Tel: 765-362-5125
See separate listing for:
The Princeton Review

Random House Large Print
Imprint of Penguin Random Audio Publishing Group
1745 Broadway, New York, NY 10019
Tel: 212-782-9000
Web Site: www.penguinrandomhouse.com
Founded: 1990
Acquires & publishes general interest fiction & nonfiction in large print editions.
Penguin Random House & its publishing entities are not accepting unsol submissions, proposals, mss, or submission queries via e-mail at this time.
Number of titles published annually: 40 Print
Total Titles: 300 Print

Random House Publishing Group
Division of Penguin Random House LLC
1745 Broadway, New York, NY 10019
SAN: 202-5507
Toll Free Tel: 800-200-3552
Web Site: www.randomhousebooks.com
Key Personnel
CFO, Penguin Random House & EVP, Head Mergers & Acqs: Manuel Sansigre
Pres: Sanyu Dillon
Pres, Ballantine Books: Kara Welsh
Pres, Harmony Books/Rodale Books: Theresa Zoro
Pres, Random House Worlds/EVP, Publr & Dir, Strategy, Del Rey: Scott Shannon
EVP & Publr, One World & Roc Lit 101: Christopher Jackson
EVP, Assoc Publr & Exec Edit Dir: Kate Medina
EVP, Busn Strategy: Bill Takes
EVP, Corp Communs: Claire von Schilling
Group SVP & Creative Dir: Paolo Pepe
SVP & Deputy Publr: Alison Rich
SVP & Deputy Publr, Ballantine Bantam Dell: Kim Hovey
SVP & Deputy Publr, Harmony Books/Rodale Books: Gail Gonzales
SVP & Exec Dir, Subs Rts: Denise Cronin
SVP & Dir, Penguin Random House Intl Sales & Mktg: Cyrus Kheradi
SVP & Dir, Publicity: Susan Corcoran
SVP & Edit Dir: Linda Marrow
SVP & Group Sales Dir: Cynthia Lasky
SVP, Backlist Strategy & Devt: Hannah Rahill; Matt Schwartz
SVP, Ed-in-Chief & Publr, Harmony Books/Rodale Books: Diana Baroni
VP & Publr, Random House Worlds & Inklore/Publr, Del Rey: Keith Clayton
VP & Deputy Publr, Fiction, Random House/Hogarth: Rachel Rokicki
VP & Assoc Publr: Gina Wachtel
VP & Exec Art Dir, Christian Publishing & Harmony/Rodale: Joe Perez
VP & Exec Art Dir, Random House/One World: Greg Mollica
VP & Exec Dir, Foreign Rts: Rachel Kind
VP & Sr Dir, Publicity & Mktg, Random House Worlds: David Moench
VP & Sr Dir, Publicity, Mktg & Brand Strategy, Harmony Books/Rodale Books: Cindy Murray
VP & Dir, Publicity, Harmony Books/Rodale Books: Tammy Blake
VP & Dir, Publicity, Random House/Dial Press/Modern Library/Hogarth: Maria Braeckel
VP & Exec Ed: Mark Warren; Jamia Wilson
VP & Exec Ed, One World/Roc Lit 101: Kierna Mayo
VP & Exec Ed, Random House: Andrea Walker
VP & Exec Ed, One World: Elizabeth Mendez Berry
VP & Dir, Mktg, Random House/Hogarth: Windy Dorresteyn
VP & Dir, Media Coaching & Creative Messaging: Barbara Fillon
VP & Dir, Natl Accts: Lynn Kovach
VP & Dir, Publicity, Ballantine Bantam Dell: Jennifer Garza
VP & Dir, Sales Mktg: Stacey Witcraft
VP & Edit Dir, Ballantine Bantam Dell: Kate Miciak
VP & Edit Dir, Nonfiction: Hilary Redmon
VP & Edit Dir, Rodale Books: Marnie Cochran
VP & Ed-in-Chief: Ben Greenberg
VP & Ed-in-Chief, Ballantine Bantam Dell: Kara Cesare
VP & Ed-in-Chief, Hogarth: David Ebershoff

VP & Ed-in-Chief, The Dial Press: Whitney Frick
VP & Exec Ed, Ballantine: Susanna Porter
VP & Imprint Sales Dir: Allyson Pearl
VP, Copy: Grant Neumann
VP, Publr & Ed-in-Chief, Del Rey: Tricia Narwani
VP, Worldwide Reporting & Planning: Carlos Perez
Publr, Ballantine Books: Jennifer Hershey
Publr, Random House: Andy Ward
Deputy Publr, Random House Worlds: Julie Leung
Exec Dir, Art/Design: Robbin Schiff
Exec Dir, Dom Rts: Toby L Ernst
Sr Art Dir: Beck Stvan
Sr Art Dir, Del Rey: Regina Flath
Sr Dir, Creative Servs: Annette Melvin
Sr Dir, Online Content, Strategy & Optimization: Daniel Christensen
Sr Dir, Random House: Ayelet Durantt
Sr Prodn Dir: Jane Haas Sankner
Art Dir: Lucas Heinrich; Lynne Yeamans
Art Dir, Dial/Hogarth: Donna Cheng
Backlist Dir, Ballantine Bantam Dell: Jean Quinn
Busn Dir, Licensing & Brands: Kristin Conte
Creative Dir: Jenny Davis
Creative Dir, Del Rey: Elizabeth Schaefer
Dir, Ad & Creative Opers: Rochelle Clark
Dir, Creative & Ad Opers: Daniel Wikey
Dir, DEI Strategy: Porscha Burke
Dir, Mktg, Ballantine Bantam Dell: Quinne Rogers
Dir, Mktg, Harmony Books/Rodale Books: Christina Foxley
Dir, Publicity, One World/Roc Lit 101: Carla Bruce-Eddings
Edit Dir, Ballantine: Hilary Teeman
Edit Dir, Dell: Shauna Summers
Edit Dir, Fiction: Caitlin McKenna; Elizabeth Schaefer
Edit Dir, Nonfiction & Illustrated: Sarah Malarkey
Edit Dir, Nonfiction, Ballantine Books: Sara Weiss
Mktg Dir, One World: Lulu Martinez
Deputy Dir, Ballantine Bantam Dell: Allison Schuster
Deputy Dir, Dial Press: Michelle Jasmine
Deputy Dir, Foreign Rts: Donna Duverglas
Deputy Dir, Hogarth: Carrie Neill
Deputy Dir, Publicity: London King
Deputy Dir, Publicity, Random House: Greg Kubie
Deputy Dir, Publg: Erica Gonzalez
Deputy Dir, Random House Worlds: Ashleigh Heaton
Assoc Art Dir, WaterBrook/Multnomah: Sonia Persad
Assoc Dir, Ad Opers & Proj Mgmt: Emily Jarrett
Assoc Dir, Backlist Strategy & Analysis: Morgan Carattini
Assoc Dir, Ballantine Bantam Dell: Taylor Noel; Kathleen Quinlan
Assoc Dir, Consumer Strategy & Engagement: Aparna Rishi
Assoc Dir, Lib Mktg: Elizabeth Fabian
Assoc Dir, Mng Edit: Mark Birkey
Assoc Dir, Publicity: Melanie DeNardo; Gwyneth Stansfield
Assoc Dir, Publicity, Ballantine Bantam Dell: Emily Isayeff
Asst Copy Dir: Camille Dewing-Vallejo
Asst Dir, Publicity: Steven Boriack
Exec Mng Ed: Pam Alders
Exec Ed: Sara Birmingham; Marie Pantojan
Exec Ed, Ballantine Bantam Dell: Jenny Chen; Tracy Devine; Natalie Hallak; Andra Miller; Mary Reynics; Brendan Vaughan
Exec Ed, Convergent Books: Kathryn Renz Hamilton
Exec Ed, Hogarth: Parisa Ebrahimi
Exec Ed, One World: Nicole Counts
Exec Ed, The Dial Press: Katy Nishimoto
Exec Prodn Ed: Nancy Delia
Sr Ed: Anna Pitoniak
Sr Ed, Ballantine Books: Chelcee Johns
Sr Ed, Dial Press: Maya Millett
Sr Ed, Random House: Molly Turpin
Sr Ed, Random House Worlds: Tom Hoeler
Sr Ed, The Dial Press: Emma Caruso; Annie Chagnot
Ed: Kate Collins Curnin; Anne Groell; Sam Nicholson; Clio Seraphim
Ed, Ballantine Bantam Dell: Emily Hartley; Jesse Shuman
Ed, Dial Press: Samantha Zukergood
Ed, Hogarth/Modern Library: Helen Thomaides
Ed, One World: Victory Matsui
Ed, Random House Worlds: Alex Davis; Jacinta O'Halloran
Ed-at-Large: Susan Mercandetti
Assoc Ed, Ballantine Books: Sydney Collins; Wendy Wong
Assoc Ed, Harmony Books/Rodale Books: Katherine Leak
Assoc Ed, One World: Erica Min
Assoc Ed, One World/Roc Lit 101: Sun Robinson-Smith
Assoc Ed, Random House: Noa Shapiro
Asst Ed: Miriam Khanukaev
Asst Ed, Ballantine Bantam Dell: Mae Martinez
Asst Ed, Harmony Books/Rodale Books: Tiffany Ma
Asst Ed, Random House: Kaeli Subberwal
Asst Ed, Random House Worlds: Gabriella Munoz
Franchise Lead, Minecraft & Stranger Things Fiction: Erum Khan
Sr Events Mgr: Soriya K Chum
Sr Mgr: Jessica Cashman
Sr Mgr, Consumer Insights: Kesley Tiffey
Sr Mgr, Digital Publg: Susan Seeman
Sr Mktg Mgr: Michael Hoak
Sr Publg Mgr, Ballantine Bantam Dell: Erin Kane
Sr Publg Mgr, Del Rey & Random House Worlds: Alex Larned
Sr Soc Media Mgr: Sophie Vershbow
Mgr, Creative Content: Danielle Siess
Mgr, Digital Opers: Dannalie Diaz
Mgr, Events: Kaitlin Darcy Russolese
Mgr, Foreign Rts: Claire Posner-Greco
Mgr, Influencer Mktg: Megan Tripp
Mgr, Metadata Analytics: Heidi Lilly
Mktg & Publicity Mgr: Sarah Bode
Mktg Mgr, Ballantine/Dial Press: Corina Diez
Mktg Mgr, Del Rey: Tori Henson
Mktg Mgr, Random House/Dial Press: Madison Dettlinger
Partnerships Mgr: Stacy Horowitz
Publicity Mgr: Allyson Lord
Publicity Mgr, Random House: Vanessa DeJesus
Publg Mgr: Bridget Kearney
Publg Mgr, Christian Publg & Forum: Jennifer Reyes
Publg Mgr, One World/The Dial Press: Raaga Rajagopala
Assoc Events Mgr: Kate Trine
Assoc Mgr, Ballantine: Emma Thomasch
Assoc Mgr, Digital Opers: Ryan Kearney
Assoc Mgr, Metadata Opers: Madeleine Kenney
Assoc Mgr, Online Copy Optimization: Hannah Frank
Assoc Mktg Mgr, Ballantine: Megan Whalen
Assoc Mktg Mgr, One World/Roc Lit 101: Tiffani Ren
Sr Analyst, Busn Insights: Thomas Yuhas
Sr Publicist: Isabella Biedenharn
Sr Publicist, Ballantine Bantam Dell: Melissa Folds
Sr Publicist: Christine Johnston; Dhara Parikh; Stacey Stein
Sr Publicist, Random House/Dial Press: Erin Richards
Publicist: Jordan Pace; Andrea Pura
Assoc Publicist: Maya Franson
Assoc Publicist, Ballantine Bantam Dell: Katie Horn
Assoc Publicist: Ella Maslin; Courtney Mocklow; Melissa Sanford
Assoc, Digital Opers: Shannon Mondesir
Assoc, Mng Edit: Saige Francis
Assoc, Mng Edit/Prodn Edit: Christa Guild
Assoc, Subs Rts: Sarah Lehman
Mktg & Publicity Assoc, One World/Roc Lit 101: Maggie Salko
Assoc Marketer, Del Rey: Sabrina Shen
Prodn Supv: Sam Wetzler
Prodn Assoc: Jenna Kass; Meghan O'Leary
Soc Media Assoc: Jane Popova
Soc Media Assoc, One World/Del Rey: Maya Fenter
Sr Designer: Sarah Horgan; Ella Laytham
Sr Designer, Inklore: Bones Leopard
Analyst, Consumer Insights: Caitlin Meuser
Asst Copy Chief, Modern Library: Craig Adams
Founded: 1925
General fiction & nonfiction hardcover, trade & mass market paperbacks.
Penguin Random House & its publishing entities are not accepting unsol submissions, proposals, mss, or submission queries via e-mail at this time.
ISBN Prefix(es): 978-0-307; 978-1-101; 978-0-89141; 978-0-345; 978-0-449; 978-0-8129; 978-0-307; 978-1-4000; 978-1-58836; 978-0-8041
Number of titles published annually: 700 Print; 150 E-Book
Total Titles: 5,900 Print; 1,100 E-Book
Imprints: Alibi (mystery, thriller, suspense); Ballantine Books; Bantam Books; BOOM! Studios; Convergent Books; Crown Publishing Group; Del Rey; Delacorte Press; Dell; The Dial Press; Flirt (new adult); Harmony Books; Hogarth; Hydra (science fiction & fantasy); LENNY; Loveswept (digital only romance); Lucas Books; Modern Library; Multnomah; One World; Presidio Press; Random House; Random House Worlds (licensed book publg); Roc Lit 101; Rodale Books; Villard; WaterBrook; Zinc Ink
Warehouse: 400 Hahn Rd, Westminster, MD 21157
See separate listing for:
BOOM! Studios
Multnomah
WaterBrook

Random House Reference/Random House Puzzles & Games
Imprint of Penguin Random House Audio Publishing Group
c/o Penguin Random House LLC, 1745 Broadway, New York, NY 10019
Tel: 212-782-9000
Web Site: www.penguinrandomhouse.com
Key Personnel
Pres & Publr: Amanda D'Acierno
Publishes reference, crossword puzzle books & chess books & price guides for collectibles.
Penguin Random House & its publishing entities are not accepting unsol submissions, proposals, mss, or submission queries via e-mail at this time.
Total Titles: 215 Print
Imprints: Boston Globe Puzzle Books; Chicago Tribune Crosswords; House of Collectibles; Los Angeles Times Crosswords; New York Times Crosswords; Random House Webster's; Washington Post Crosswords

Rational Island Publishers
Division of The Re-evaluation Counseling Communities
719 Second Ave N, Seattle, WA 98109
Tel: 206-284-0311
E-mail: ircc@rc.org
Web Site: www.rc.org
Key Personnel
Ed: Lisa Kauffman

Founded: 1954
Articles about Re-evaluation Counseling (Co-Counseling) - the theory, the practice, the applications & implications.
ISBN Prefix(es): 978-0-911214; 978-0-913937; 978-1-885357; 978-1-58429; 978-1-893165
Number of titles published annually: 6 Print
Total Titles: 263 Print

§Rattapallax Press
532 La Guadia Place, Suite 353, New York, NY 10012
Web Site: www.rattapallax.com
Key Personnel
Founder & Pres: Ram Devineni
Ed-in-Chief: Flavia Rocha
Founded: 2000
ISBN Prefix(es): 978-1-892494
Number of titles published annually: 4 Print; 1 CD-ROM; 15 Online; 15 E-Book; 15 Audio
Total Titles: 15 Print; 1 CD-ROM; 15 Online; 15 E-Book; 15 Audio
Membership(s): Community of Literary Magazines & Presses (CLMP)

§Raven Publishing Inc
125 Cherry Creek Rd, Norris, MT 59745
SAN: 254-5861
Mailing Address: PO Box 2866, Norris, MT 59745
Tel: 406-685-3545 *Toll Free Tel:* 866-685-3545
E-mail: info@ravenpublishing.net
Web Site: www.ravenpublishing.net
Key Personnel
Founder & Pres: Janet Muirhead Hill
  E-mail: janet@ravenpublishing.net
Founded: 2001
ISBN Prefix(es): 978-0-9714161; 978-0-9772525; 978-0-9820893; 978-0-9827377; 978-1-937849
Number of titles published annually: 2 Print; 2 E-Book
Total Titles: 52 Print; 2 CD-ROM; 49 E-Book; 2 Audio
Billing Address: PO Box 2866, Norris, MT 59745

§Ravenhawk™ Books
Division of The 6DOF Group
311 E Drowsey Circle, Payson, AZ 85541
Tel: 520-402-9033 *Fax:* 520-402-9033
Web Site: www.facebook.com/6DOFRavenhawk
Key Personnel
Publr: Karl Lasky
Founded: 1998
Royalty publisher. Specialize in general trade, hard/softcover, fiction, nonfiction, self-help, teaching texts for professionals, crime, mystery & suspense fiction. Ebooks, CD/DVD audiobooks. Ms submissions are by invitation only through acknowledged literary agents.
ISBN Prefix(es): 978-1-893660
Number of titles published annually: 6 Print; 4 CD-ROM; 4 Online; 12 E-Book; 4 Audio
Total Titles: 44 Print; 4 Online; 4 E-Book
Distribution Center: Baker & Taylor LLC, 2550 W Tyvola Rd, Suite 300, Charlotte, NC 28217 *Tel:* 704-998-3100 *Fax:* 704-998-3319 *E-mail:* btinfo@baker-taylor.com *Web Site:* www.baker-taylor.com
Ingram Content Group Inc, One Ingram Blvd, La Vergne, TN 37086-1986 *Tel:* 615-793-5000 *Web Site:* www.ingramcontent.com
Membership(s): Interactive Creative Artists Network (ICAN); National Writers Association (NWA); Society of Southwestern Authors

Razorbill, see GP Putnam's Sons Books for Young Readers

Reader's Digest Select Editions
Division of Trusted Media Brands Inc
44 S Broadway, White Plains, NY 10601
Tel: 914-238-1000 *Toll Free Tel:* 877-732-4438 (cust serv)
Web Site: www.rd.com/article/select-editions/; www.facebook.com/selecteditions
Key Personnel
Exec Ed: Amy Reilly
Founded: 1950
Publishers of hardcover fiction anthology books in condensed form. Selections are licensed from original publisher.
ISBN Prefix(es): 978-0-89577

Reader's Digest Trade Publishing
Division of Trusted Media Brands Inc
44 S Broadway, White Plains, NY 10601
SAN: 240-9720
Tel: 914-238-1000
Web Site: rdtradepublishing.com
Founded: 1971
Illustrated trade (retail) reference books on home maintenance & repair, gardening, home decorating, crafts, art instruction, cooking, health & fitness, pet care, music, family reference, religion & inspiration, science & nature, travel & atlases, humor.
ISBN Prefix(es): 978-0-7621; 978-1-61765; 978-1-62145
Number of titles published annually: 100 Print
Total Titles: 350 Print
Distributed by Simon & Schuster, LLC
Orders to: Simon & Schuster, LLC, 100 Front St, Riverside, NJ 08075 *Toll Free Tel:* 800-223-2336 (US); 800-268-3216 (CN) *Toll Free Fax:* 800-943-9831 (US); 888-849-8151 (CN)

REBL Enterprises LLC, see Global Training Center

Recorded Books Inc, an RBmedia company
8400 Corporate Dr, Landover, MD 20785
SAN: 677-8887
Toll Free Tel: 800-305-3450
Web Site: rbmediaglobal.com/recorded-books
Key Personnel
CEO: Michael Paull
COO: Edward Longo
CFO: Mike Bauer
Chief Content Offr: Troy Juliar
Chief Prod & Mktg Offr: John Shea
CTO: Mike Pyland
Founded: 1979
Independent publisher of unabridged audiobooks & distributor of films & other media content delivered in CD & downloadable formats, to consumers, libraries & schools.
ISBN Prefix(es): 978-0-7887; 978-1-4025; 978-1-55690; 978-1-84197; 978-1-4193; 978-1-84505; 978-1-4281; 978-1-4361; 978-1-4407; 978-1-4498; 978-1-4561; 978-1-4618; 978-1-4640; 978-1-4703; 978-1-4906; 978-1-5019
Number of titles published annually: 700 Print; 250 CD-ROM; 100 Online; 50 E-Book; 787 Audio
Total Titles: 8,000 Print; 1,000 CD-ROM; 100 Online; 50 E-Book; 5,808 Audio
Imprints: Ascent Audio; BookaVivo; Classics Library; Clipper Audio (UK); Film Movement; The Great Courses; Griot Audio; Harlequin Romance Library™; ITK (In the Know) Audio; Lone Star Audio; Maple Leaf Audio; Mystery Library; RB Shorts; Recorded Books Audiolibros; Recorded Books Development; Recorded Books Inspirational; Romantic Sounds Audio; Sci-Fi Audio; Southern Voices Audio; Western Library; Your Coach in a Box
Foreign Office(s): WF Howes Ltd, Unit 4, Rearsby Business Park, Gaddesby Lane, Rearsby, Leics LE7 4YH, United Kingdom (recorded books) *Tel:* (01664) 423000 *Fax:* (01664) 423005 *E-mail:* info@wfhowes.co.uk *Web Site:* www.wfhowes.co.uk
Membership(s): Audio Publishers Association

Red Chair Press
PO Box 333, South Egremont, MA 01258-0333
Tel: 413-528-2398 (edit off) *Toll Free Tel:* 800-328-4929 (orders & cust serv)
E-mail: info@redchairpress.com
Web Site: www.redchairpress.com
Key Personnel
CFO: David P Sheehan *Tel:* 917-608-6198
  E-mail: david@redchairpress.com
Pres & Publr: Keith Garton *E-mail:* keith@redchairpress.com
Art Dir: Jeff Dinardo *Tel:* 978-371-0111 ext 1
  E-mail: jeff@redchairpress.com
Founded: 2009
Fiction & nonfiction books & ebooks; social & emotional learning with an emphasis on good decision-making for ages 3-10. No unsol mss.
ISBN Prefix(es): 978-1-936163; 978-1-937529; 978-1-63440; 978-1-947159 (One Elm Books)
Number of titles published annually: 30 Print; 24 E-Book
Total Titles: 150 Print; 32 CD-ROM; 120 E-Book
Imprints: One Elm Books (middle grade novels); Rocking Chair Kids (picture books ages 5 & under)
Foreign Rep(s): Lerner Publishing Group Inc (Maria Kjoller) (worldwide exc Canada & USA)
Distribution Center: Lerner Publisher Services, 1251 Washington Ave N, Minneapolis, MN 55401 *Toll Free Tel:* 800-328-4929 *Web Site:* www.lernerbooks.com
Membership(s): American Booksellers Association (ABA); Association of American Publishers PreK-12 Learning Group; The Children's Book Council (CBC); Independent Book Publishers Association (IBPA); Independent Publishers of New England (IPNE); Society of Children's Book Writers & Illustrators (SCBWI)

Red Hen Press
PO Box 40820, Pasadena, CA 91114
Tel: 626-356-4760 *Fax:* 626-356-9974
Web Site: www.redhen.org
Key Personnel
Publr: Mark E Cull *E-mail:* mark@redhen.org
Mng Ed: Kate Gale *E-mail:* kategale@verizon.net
Founded: 1994
Publish perfect bound collections of poetry, short stories & books of a literary nature. Also sponsor several literary awards, along with the literary journal *The Los Angeles Review*.
ISBN Prefix(es): 978-0-9890361; 978-1-888996; 978-1-59709
Number of titles published annually: 22 Print
Total Titles: 350 Print
Imprints: Arktoi Books; Boreal Books; Hybrid Nation; Pighog Books; Story Line Press; Xeno Books
Distribution Center: Chicago Distribution Center, 11030 S Langley, Chicago, IL 60628 *Toll Free Tel:* 800-621-2736 *Toll Free Fax:* 800-621-8476 *E-mail:* orders@press.uchicago.edu
Membership(s): Association of Writers & Writing Programs (AWP); Community of Literary Magazines & Presses (CLMP)

Red Moon Press
PO Box 2461, Winchester, VA 22604-1661
Tel: 540-722-2156
Web Site: www.redmoonpress.com
Key Personnel
Owner: Jim Kacian *E-mail:* jim.kacian@redmoonpress.com
Founded: 1993
Largest & most prestigious publisher of English-language haiku & related forms in the world.
ISBN Prefix(es): 978-1-9657818; 978-1-893959; 978-1-936848; 978-1-947271; 978-1-958408
Number of titles published annually: 15 Print
Total Titles: 450 Print
Imprints: Pond Frog Editions; Soffietto Editions

PUBLISHERS

The Red Sea Press Inc
Affiliate of Africa World Press Inc
541 W Ingham Ave, Suite B, Trenton, NJ 08638
Tel: 609-695-3200 *Fax:* 609-695-6466
E-mail: customerservice@africaworldpressbooks.com
Web Site: www.africaworldpressbooks.com
Key Personnel
Fin Cont: Senait Kassahun Checole
Founded: 1983
Publisher of books on the Horn of Africa, Latin America; distributor of books on the Third World.
ISBN Prefix(es): 978-0-932415; 978-1-56902
Number of titles published annually: 100 Print
Total Titles: 1,200 Print
Imprints: Karnak House
Foreign Rights: Turnaround Publisher Services (Europe, London)

Red Wheel/Weiser
65 Parker St, Suite 7, Newburyport, MA 01950
Tel: 978-465-0504 *Toll Free Tel:* 800-423-7087 (orders) *Fax:* 978-465-0243
E-mail: info@rwwbooks.com
Web Site: www.redwheelweiser.com
Key Personnel
Pres & CEO: Michael Kerber *Tel:* 978-465-0504 ext 1115 *E-mail:* mkerber@rwwbooks.com
Assoc Publr, Career Press: Michael Pye
Creative Dir: Kathryn Sky-Peck
Dir, Busn Devt & Community Engagement: John Hays
Dir, Publicity: Eryn Eaton
Prodn Dir: Michael Conlon
Sales Dir, Natl Accts: Laurie Kelly-Pye
Mng Ed: Jane Hagaman
Sr Acqs Ed: Amy Lyons
Assoc Designer: Brittany Craig
Founded: 1957
Self-help, spirituality, inspiration, women's interest & esoteric subjects from many traditions.
ISBN Prefix(es): 978-0-87728 (Weiser); 978-1-57863 (Weiser); 978-1-59003 (Red Wheel)
Number of titles published annually: 50 Print
Total Titles: 1,200 Print
Imprints: Career Press; Dharma Spring; Disinformation Books; Hampton Roads Publishing; MUFON Books; Quest Books; Red Wheel Audio
Distributor for Crossed Crow Books; Nicolas Hays Inc; Lantern Publishing & Media; Moon Dust Press; Ozark Mountain Publishing Inc; Rockpool Publishing; Womancraft Publishing
Foreign Rep(s): Brumby Books (Australia); Deep Books (UK); Georgetown Publications (Canada)
Warehouse: Books International Inc, 22883 Quicksilver Dr, Dulles, VA 20166
Membership(s): American Booksellers Association (ABA)
See separate listing for:
Hampton Roads Publishing

Redleaf Press®
Division of Think Small
10 Yorkton Ct, St Paul, MN 55117
SAN: 212-8691
Tel: 651-641-0508 *Toll Free Tel:* 800-423-8309
Fax: 651-641-0115
E-mail: customerservice@redleafpress.org; info@redleafpress.org; marketing@redleafpress.org
Web Site: www.redleafpress.org
Key Personnel
Pres & CEO: Barbara Yates *Tel:* 651-641-6645
COO: Mark Cross *Tel:* 651-641-6619
SVP, Early Childhood Progs: Cisa Keller *Tel:* 615-641-6635
VP, Devt: Jonathan May *Tel:* 651-641-6609
VP, Equity & Prog Supports: Candace Yates *Tel:* 651-641-6671
VP, Outreach & Fin Supports: Jacquiline Perez *Tel:* 651-641-6606
Admin Dir: Gail Bultman *Tel:* 651-641-6674
Dir: Nikki Darling-Kuria *Tel:* 651-641-1511
Founded: 1973
Resources for early childhood professionals including. early childhood curriculum, professional development, family child care business, record keeping & parenting.
ISBN Prefix(es): 978-0-934140; 978-1-884834; 978-1-929610; 978-1-933653; 978-1-60554
Number of titles published annually: 30 Print; 1 CD-ROM; 2 Online; 27 E-Book
Total Titles: 350 Print; 15 CD-ROM; 10 Online; 300 E-Book; 1 Audio
Distributor for New Shoots Publishing (New Zealand)
Foreign Rights: Nordlyset Literary Agency (worldwide)
Distribution Center: Consortium Book Sales & Distribution, The Keg House, Suite 101, 34 13 Ave NE, Minneapolis, MN 55413-1007 (US book trade & libs) *Tel:* 612-746-2600 *Toll Free Tel:* 866-400-5351 (cust serv, Jackson, TN) *E-mail:* cbsdinfo@ingramcontent.com *Web Site:* www.cbsd.com SAN: 200-6049
Login Canada, 300 Saulteaux Crescent, Winnipeg, MB R3J 3T2, Canada, Mktg Mgr: Melanie Lauze *Tel:* 204-837-2987 *Toll Free Tel:* 800-665-1148 *Fax:* 204-837-3116 *Toll Free Fax:* 800-665-0103 *E-mail:* orders@lb.ca *Web Site:* www.lb.ca
Pademelon Press Pty Ltd, PO Box 41, Jamberoo, NSW 2533, Australia (Australia & New Zealand) *Tel:* (02) 4236 1881 *E-mail:* enquiry@pademelonpress.com.au *Web Site:* www.pademelonpress.com.au
Eurospan Group, Gray's Inn House, 127 Clerkenwell Rd, London EC1R 5DB, United Kingdom (Africa, Asia, Continental Europe, Middle East & UK) *Tel:* (01767) 604972 *Fax:* (01767) 601640 *E-mail:* eurospan@turpin-distribution.com *Web Site:* www.eurospanbookstore.com/redleaf
Membership(s): Education Market Association

Robert D Reed Publishers
PO Box 1992, Bandon, OR 97411-1192
Tel: 541-347-9882 *Fax:* 541-347-9883
E-mail: 4bobreed@msn.com
Web Site: rdrpublishers.com
Key Personnel
Publr: Robert D Reed
Founded: 1977
All types of publications for trade, educational institutions, individuals & corporations.
ISBN Prefix(es): 978-1-889710; 978-1-885003; 978-1-931741
Number of titles published annually: 25 Print
Total Titles: 225 Print
Foreign Rep(s): Sylvia Hayse Literary Agency

Reedswain Inc
88 Wells Rd, Spring City, PA 19475
Tel: 610-495-9578 *Toll Free Tel:* 800-331-5191 *Fax:* 610-495-6632
E-mail: orders@reedswain.com
Web Site: www.reedswain.com
Key Personnel
Pres & Foreign Rts: Richard Kentwell
Founded: 1987
Soccer coaching books.
ISBN Prefix(es): 978-1-59164; 978-0-9651020; 978-1-890946
Number of titles published annually: 10 Print
Total Titles: 190 Print

Referee Books
Imprint of Referee Enterprises Inc
2017 Lathrop Ave, Racine, WI 53405
Tel: 262-632-8855 *Toll Free Tel:* 800-733-6100 *Fax:* 262-632-5460
E-mail: customerservice@referee.com
Web Site: www.referee.com

U.S. PUBLISHERS

Key Personnel
Pres: Barry Mano *E-mail:* bmano@naso.org
Dir, Admin: Corey Ludwin
Founded: 1976
Publish sports officiating publications; magazines, books, manuals & booklets on officiating, umpiring, baseball, basketball, football, soccer, softball & athletics referee books.
ISBN Prefix(es): 978-1-58208; 978-0-9660209
Number of titles published annually: 30 Print
Total Titles: 75 Print

Reference Publications Inc
5419 Fawn Lake Rd, Shelbyville, MI 49344
SAN: 208-4392
Mailing Address: PO Box 344, Algonac, MI 48001-0344
Key Personnel
Pres: Dominique Irvine
Founded: 1975
Mail order & reference books. Specialize in botanical & medicinal plants, Americana, Amerindian & African reference books & botanical works.
ISBN Prefix(es): 978-0-917256
Number of titles published annually: 2 Print
Total Titles: 24 Print

ReferencePoint Press Inc
17150 Via del Campo, Suite 205, San Diego, CA 92127
Mailing Address: PO Box 27779, San Diego, CA 92198
Tel: 858-618-1314 *Toll Free Tel:* 888-479-6436 *Fax:* 858-618-1730
E-mail: info@referencepointpress.com
Web Site: www.referencepointpress.com
Key Personnel
Pres & Publr: Dan Leone *Tel:* 858-618-1314 ext 102 *E-mail:* dan@referencepointpress.com
Founded: 2006
Publish series nonfiction for young adults: current issues, health, science & paranormal.
ISBN Prefix(es): 978-1-60152; 978-1-68282
Number of titles published annually: 100 Print; 100 E-Book
Total Titles: 700 Print; 700 E-Book
Foreign Rep(s): Saunders Book Co (Canada)
Returns: Bang Fulfillment, 217 Etak Dr, Brainerd, MN 56401
Warehouse: Bang Fulfillment, 217 Etak Dr, Brainerd, MN 56401, Contact: Perry Gienger *Toll Free Tel:* 800-328-0450 *Fax:* 218-829-7145 *E-mail:* perryg@bangprinting.com

Reformation Heritage Books
2965 Leonard St NE, Grand Rapids, MI 49525
Tel: 616-977-0889 *Fax:* 616-285-3246
E-mail: orders@heritagebooks.org
Web Site: www.heritagebooks.org
Key Personnel
Chmn: Joel R Beeke
Contact: Jonathan Engelsma
Founded: 1994
Sell new & used religious books with emphasis on experiential religion. Also republish out-of-print Puritan works.
ISBN Prefix(es): 978-1-892777; 978-1-60178
Number of titles published annually: 40 Print
Total Titles: 250 Print; 70 E-Book

Regal House Publishing
806 Oberlin Rd, No 12094, Raleigh, NC 27605
E-mail: info@regalhousepublishing.com
Web Site: regalhousepublishing.com
Key Personnel
Founder, Publr & Ed-in-Chief: Jaynie Royal
Mng Ed: Pam Van Dyk
Founded: 2014
Passionately dedicated to the furtherance of exquisitely written literary works & the writers who pen them. Traditional publishing house accepting submissions directly from writers.

U.S. PUBLISHERS

Provide extensive editorial support for writers & formulate a marketing partnership pre- & post-publication.
ISBN Prefix(es): 978-0-9912612; 978-0-9988398; 978-1-947548
Number of titles published annually: 35 Print; 35 E-Book
Imprints: Fitzroy Books (middle grade, new adult & young adult fiction); Pact Press (anthologies, poetry & short story collections, full-length & literary fiction)
Foreign Rights: Gotham Group (film/tv rts partner); Rightol Media (Asia)
Distribution Center: Independent Publishers Group (IPG), 814 N Franklin St, Chicago, IL 60610 Tel: 312-337-0747 Fax: 312-337-5985
Web Site: www.ipgbook.com
Membership(s): American Booksellers Association (ABA); The Children's Book Council (CBC); Community of Literary Magazines & Presses (CLMP); Independent Book Publishers Association (IBPA); Poets & Writers; Southern Independent Booksellers Alliance (SIBA)
See separate listing for:
Fitzroy Books
Pact Press

Regent Press Printers & Publishers
2747 Regent St, Berkeley, CA 94705
Tel: 510-845-1196
E-mail: regentpress@mindspring.com
Web Site: www.regentpress.net
Key Personnel
Owner, Publr & Mng Ed: Mark Weiman
Founded: 1978
This publisher has indicated that 50% of their product line is author subsidized.
Number of titles published annually: 20 Print; 1 CD-ROM; 15 E-Book
Total Titles: 250 Print; 30 CD-ROM; 30 E-Book

Regnery Publishing
Imprint of Skyhorse Publishing Inc
122 "C" St NW, Suite 515, Washington, DC 20001
Tel: 202-216-0600
Web Site: www.regnery.com
Founded: 1947
Trade book publisher.
ISBN Prefix(es): 978-0-89526; 978-1-59698; 978-1-62157; 978-1-68451; 978-1-61017 (ISI Books)
Number of titles published annually: 75 Print; 75 E-Book
Total Titles: 1,200 Print; 1,000 E-Book
Imprints: Gateway Editions; ISI Books; Little Patriot Press; Regnery; Regnery Faith; Regnery History; Regnery Kids; Salem Books
Distributed by Simon & Schuster, LLC
Foreign Rights: Akcali Copyright Agency (Turkey); Big Apple Agency Inc (China, Southeast Asia exc India & Japan); CA-Link (China, Taiwan); Graal Literary Agency (Central Europe, Eastern Europe); Anna Gurgui (French-speaking countries, Spanish- & Portuguese-speaking countries); Duran Kim (South Korea); Rightol (China, Indian subcontinent, Taiwan); Ulf Toregard (Scandinavia); Tuttle-Mori Agency Inc (Japan)
Membership(s): American Booksellers Association (ABA)

Regular Baptist Press
Division of General Association of Regular Baptist Churches
3715 N Ventura Dr, Arlington Heights, IL 60004
Tel: 847-843-1600 Toll Free Tel: 800-727-4440 (cust serv) Fax: 847-843-3757
E-mail: orders@rbpstore.org
Web Site: regularbaptistpress.org
Key Personnel
Dir: David Gunn
Busn Dir: Tony Randolph
Founded: 1952
Curriculum & Christian books.
ISBN Prefix(es): 978-0-87227; 978-1-59402; 978-1-60776; 978-1-62940
Number of titles published annually: 6 Print
Imprints: Regular Baptist Books (trade books)

§Remember Point Inc
PO Box 1448, Pacific Palisades, CA 90272
Tel: 310-896-8716
E-mail: info@rememberpoint.com
Web Site: www.rememberpoint.com; www.longfellowfindsahome.com
Key Personnel
Pres & Publr: Linda Sue Miller
Mktg Dir: Terry Megan
Founded: 2010
ISBN Prefix(es): 978-0-9988351
Number of titles published annually: 4 Print; 4 E-Book; 1 Audio
Total Titles: 7 Print; 1 Online; 5 E-Book

Renaissance House
Imprint of Laredo Publishing Co
465 Westview Ave, Englewood, NJ 07631
Tel: 201-408-4048
Web Site: www.renaissancehouse.net
Key Personnel
Pres: Sam Laredo E-mail: laredo@laredopublishing.com
VP & Exec Ed: Raquel Benatar E-mail: raquel@renaissancehouse.net
Founded: 1991
Bilingual Spanish-English children's books. Specialize in the creation, development & management of educational & multicultural publishing projects for the Latino market, bilingual Spanish-English. Manages editorial & art projects, works with more than 60 illustrators & offers editorial services, translations English to Spanish, illustrations & art project management. See web site & contact us for available publishing rights.
ISBN Prefix(es): 978-1-56492
Number of titles published annually: 30 Print
Total Titles: 150 Print

Research & Education Association (REA)
Subsidiary of Lakeside Book Co
258 Prospect Plains Rd, Cranbury, NJ 08512
Toll Free Tel: 833-591-2798 (cust care) Fax: 516-742-5049 (orders)
E-mail: info@rea.com
Web Site: www.rea.com
Key Personnel
Publr: Pamela Weston E-mail: pweston@rea.com
Edit Dir: Larry Kling E-mail: lkling@rea.com
Founded: 1959
Professional books, secondary & college study guides & test preparation books (including AP, GED, CLEP credit-by-exam & teacher certification), biology, business, mathematics, general science, history, social sciences, accounting & computer science.
ISBN Prefix(es): 978-0-87891; 978-0-7386
Number of titles published annually: 15 Print; 10 Online; 5 E-Book
Total Titles: 200 Print; 2 CD-ROM; 80 Online; 150 E-Book; 3 Audio
Membership(s): Independent Book Publishers Association (IBPA)

Research Press
2612 N Mattis Ave, Champaign, IL 61822
SAN: 203-381X
Mailing Address: PO Box 7886, Champaign, IL 61826
Tel: 217-352-3273 Toll Free Tel: 800-519-2707 Fax: 217-352-1221
E-mail: rp@researchpress.com; orders@researchpress.com
Web Site: www.researchpress.com
Key Personnel
Chmn of the Bd: Amanda Martin
Pres: Judy Parkinson
Fin Mgr: Dawn Dockrill
Founded: 1968
ISBN Prefix(es): 978-0-87822
Number of titles published annually: 4 Print
Total Titles: 400 Print; 400 Online
Foreign Rep(s): Eurospan (Africa, Asia-Pacific, Caribbean, Europe, Latin America, Middle East, UK)
Foreign Rights: Books Crossing Borders

§Revell
Division of Baker Publishing Group
Publishing Div, 6030 E Fulton Rd, Ada, MI 49301
Mailing Address: PO Box 6287, Grand Rapids, MI 49516-6287 SAN: 203-3801
Tel: 616-676-9185 Toll Free Tel: 800-877-2665 (orders only) Fax: 616-676-9573
Toll Free Fax: 800-398-3111 (orders only)
E-mail: media@bakerpublishinggroup.com; orders@bakerpublishinggroup.com; sales@bakerpublishinggroup.com
Web Site: www.bakerpublishinggroup.com/revell
Key Personnel
EVP, Trade Publg: Jennifer Leep
Founded: 1870
Religious publisher.
ISBN Prefix(es): 978-0-8007
Number of titles published annually: 100 Print
Total Titles: 5 Audio
Imprints: Spire Books
Foreign Rep(s): Bible Society New Zealand (New Zealand); Christian Art Distributors (South Africa); Koorong Books (Australia); Synergy Book Sale UK Ltd (Alexandra McDonald) (Europe, UK)

Lynne Rienner Publishers Inc
1800 30 St, Suite 314, Boulder, CO 80301
SAN: 683-1869
Tel: 303-444-6684 Fax: 303-444-0824
E-mail: questions@rienner.com; cservice@rienner.com
Web Site: www.rienner.com
Key Personnel
Pres & CEO: Lynne Rienner
Dir, Mktg & Sales: Sally Glover
E-mail: sglover@rienner.com
Sr Acqs Ed, Political Sci & Intl Rel: Marie-Claire Antoine
Cust Serv Mgr: Patty Troiano
Founded: 1984
Scholarly & reference books & journals, college textbooks; comparative politics, US politics, international relations, sociology, Third World literature & literary criticism.
ISBN Prefix(es): 978-1-56549; 978-0-931477; 978-1-55587; 978-0-89410; 978-1-58826; 978-1-935049 (FirstForumPress); 978-1-62637
Number of titles published annually: 70 Print
Total Titles: 1,050 Print
Imprints: FirstForumPress (scholarly monographs); Kumarian Press
Distributor for Center for US-Mexican Studies; Ayebia Clarke Publishing Ltd (African lit); St Andrews Center for Syrian Studies
Foreign Rep(s): China Publishers Marketing (China, Hong Kong, Taiwan); Co Info Pty Ltd (Australia); Far Eastern Booksellers (Japan); Kinokuniya Co Ltd (Japan); KL Book Distributors (Malaysia); Maruzen Co Ltd (Japan); PMS Publishers Services Pte Ltd (Brunei, Indonesia, Malaysia, Singapore); Viva (India)
Warehouse: c/o Books International, 22883 Quicksilver Dr, Dulles, VA 20166
Membership(s): Association of American Publishers (AAP)
See separate listing for:
Kumarian Press

PUBLISHERS

Rio Nuevo Publishers
451 N Bonita Ave, Tucson, AZ 85745
Mailing Address: PO Box 5250, Tucson, AZ 85703
Tel: 520-623-9558 *Toll Free Tel:* 800-969-9558 *Fax:* 520-624-5888 *Toll Free Fax:* 800-715-5888
E-mail: info@rionuevo.com (cust serv)
Web Site: www.rionuevo.com
Founded: 1999
Publisher of fine regional southwestern & western photographic, cooking, art, culture & historical books & quality Native American books.
ISBN Prefix(es): 978-1-887896; 978-1-933855; 978-0-918080; 978-1-940322; 978-0-9700750
Number of titles published annually: 12 Print
Total Titles: 125 Print
Imprints: Rio Chico (educ & children's books)

Rising Sun Publishing
PO Box 70906, Marietta, GA 30007-0906
Tel: 770-518-0369 *Fax:* 770-587-0862
E-mail: info@rspublishing.com
Web Site: www.rspublishing.com
Key Personnel
CFO: Mychal Wynn
Founded: 1982
Primary focus is college planning training & materials.
ISBN Prefix(es): 978-1-880463
Number of titles published annually: 5 Print
Total Titles: 32 Print; 4 Audio

River City Publishing
1719 Mulberry St, Montgomery, AL 36106
Tel: 334-265-6753
Key Personnel
Publr: Carolyn Newman
Ed: Fran Norris
Founded: 1989
Acquisition, editing, design, composition, marketing & sales of new books. Regional fiction & narrative nonfiction, especially books about the South, civil rights, folk art, contemporary fiction, regionally related travel history.
ISBN Prefix(es): 978-1-881320; 978-0-9622815; 978-1-57966; 978-0-913515; 978-1-880216
Number of titles published annually: 4 Print; 4 E-Book
Total Titles: 200 Print
Imprints: Elliott & Clark Publishing; River City Kids; Starrhill Press
Membership(s): Southern Independent Booksellers Alliance (SIBA)

§Riverdale Avenue Books (RAB)
5676 Riverdale Ave, Bronx, NY 10471
Tel: 212-279-6418
E-mail: customerservice@riverdaleavebooks.com
Web Site: www.riverdaleavebooks.com
Key Personnel
Publr: Lori Perkins *E-mail:* lori@riverdaleavebooks.com
Subs Rts Dir: David T Valetin
Founded: 2012
Hybrid publisher of fiction & nonfiction, digital & print.
ISBN Prefix(es): 978-1-936833 (Magnus); 978-1-62601 (RAB)
Number of titles published annually: 60 Print; 60 E-Book
Total Titles: 450 Print; 450 E-Book
Imprints: Binge Watcher's Guide (TV/movie pop culture); Circlet (erotic sci-fi/fantasy); Dagger (mystery/thriller); Hera (fiction & nonfiction for women of a certain age); 120 Days (reprints of LGBTQ pulp fiction); RAB Afraid (horror); RAB Desire (erotica & romance); RAB Gaming; RAB Pop (pop culture); RAB SFF (science fiction/fantasy); RAB Sports; RAB Truth (memoir & biography); RAB Verve (lifestyle); Riverdale/Magnus (LGBTQ titles)
Foreign Rights: Linda Biagli (worldwide)
Distribution Center: OverDrive, One OverDrive Way, Cleveland, OH 44125 *Tel:* 216-573-6886 *Fax:* 216-573-6888 *Web Site:* company.overdrive.com
Ingram Content Group Inc, One Ingram Blvd, La Vergne, TN 37086-1986 *Tel:* 615-793-5000
Membership(s): Association of American Publishers (AAP)
See separate listing for:
Circlet Press

§Riverhead Books
Imprint of Penguin Publishing Group
c/o Penguin Random House LLC, 1745 Broadway, New York, NY 10019
Tel: 212-782-9000
Web Site: www.penguin.com/riverhead-overview/
Key Personnel
Pres & Publr: Geoffrey Kloske
SVP & Ed-in-Chief: Sarah McGrath
VP, Designer & Art Dir: Helen Yentus
VP & Deputy Publr: Jynne Dilling Martin
VP & Edit Dir: Rebecca Saletan
Dir, Contracts: Robin Simon
Dir, Mktg: Nora Alice Demick
Publicity Dir: Ashley Garland
Assoc Dir, Publicity: Claire McGinnis
Publg Assoc: Ariel So
Exec Ed: Jake Morrissey; Courtney Young
Assoc Ed: Catalina Trigo
Ed-at-Large: Han Zhang
Mktg Mgr: Michelle Waters
Publicity Mgr: Bianca Flores
Founded: 1994
Penguin Random House & its publishing entities are not accepting unsol submissions, proposals, mss, or submission queries via e-mail at this time.
Number of titles published annually: 40 Print
Total Titles: 115 Print

Riverside Publishing, see Houghton Mifflin Harcourt Assessments

Rizzoli International Publications Inc
Subsidiary of RCS Rizzoli Corp New York
300 Park Ave S, 4th fl, New York, NY 10010-5399
Tel: 212-387-3400 *Toll Free Tel:* 800-522-6657 (orders only) *Fax:* 212-387-3535
E-mail: publicity@rizzoliusa.com
Web Site: www.rizzoliusa.com
Key Personnel
Chmn of the Bd: Marco Ausenda
Pres & CEO: Stefano Peccatori
VP & Publr: Charles Miers
VP, Fin & Admin: Randy Barlow
VP, Global Sales, Mktg & Opers: Jennifer deForest Pierson
Assoc Publr, HLLA, Universe & Welcome Books: Jim Muschett
Assoc Publr, Universe: Jessica Fuller
Dir, Publicity: Jessica Napp
Dir, Spec Sales & Fulfillment: Tracey Petitt
Assoc Dir, Prodn: Kaija Markoe
Client Publr Sales Mgr: Sarah Carstens
Foreign Sales Mgr: Jerry Hoffnagle
Mktg Mgr, Creative Servs & Soc/New Media: Linda Pricci
Sales Mgr: John Deen
Founded: 1974
Fine arts, architecture, photography, decorative arts, cookbooks, gardening & landscape design, fashion & sports.
ISBN Prefix(es): 978-0-8478; 978-0-941807; 978-1-932183; 978-1-59962
Number of titles published annually: 100 Print
Imprints: Chelsea Green; Ex Libris; Marsilio; Rizzoli Electa; Rizzoli, New York; Universe; Welcome Enterprises Inc
Distributed by Penguin Random House
Distributor for Editions Flammarion; National Trust; Pavilion Books; Pavilion Children's; Pitkin; Portico; Skira Editore; Smith Street Books
Advertising Agency: Rizzoli Graphic Studios
Orders to: Penguin Random House Publisher Services (PRHPS), 400 Hahn Rd, Westminster, MD 21157 *Toll Free Tel:* 800-733-3000 *Toll Free Fax:* 800-659-2436 *Web Site:* prhpublisherservices.com; Penguin Random House of Canada Ltd, 2775 Matheson Blvd E, Mississaugua, ON L4W 4P7, Canada *Toll Free Tel:* 800-733-3000 *Toll Free Fax:* 800-659-2436
Returns: Penguin Random House, 1019 N State Rd 47, Crawfordsville, IN 47933; Penguin Random House of Canada Ltd, 2775 Matheson Blvd E, Mississaugua, ON L4W 4P7, Canada *Toll Free Tel:* 800-733-3000 *Toll Free Fax:* 800-659-2436
See separate listing for:
Chelsea Green Publishing Co
Universe Publishing
Welcome Books

The RoadRunner Press
Subsidiary of RoadRunner Press LLC
124 NW 32 St, Oklahoma City, OK 73118
Mailing Address: PO Box 2564, Oklahoma City, OK 73101
Tel: 405-524-6205 *Fax:* 405-524-6312
E-mail: info@theroadrunnerpress.com; orders@theroadrunnerpress.com
Web Site: www.theroadrunnerpress.com
Key Personnel
Publr & Ed: Jeanne Devlin *Tel:* 405-615-8293
E-mail: jeanne@theroadrunnerpress.com
Founded: 2011
Small indie publishing house specializing in quality young adult fiction & regional nonfiction as well as select nonfiction & literary fiction with an emphasis on Native American voices from the American West.
ISBN Prefix(es): 978-1-937054
Number of titles published annually: 10 Print; 6 E-Book; 1 Audio
Total Titles: 30 Print; 8 E-Book
Foreign Rep(s): Fitzhenry & Whiteside Limited (Canada)
Billing Address: The RoadRunner Press, PO Box 2564, Oklahoma City, OK 73101
Membership(s): The Children's Book Council (CBC); Independent Book Publishers Association (IBPA); Midwest Independent Publishing Association (MIPA); Mountains & Plains Independent Publishers Association; New Mexico Book Association; New Mexico Book Co-op; Publishers Association of the West (PubWest); Western Writers of America (WWA)

Roaring Brook Press
Member of Macmillan Children's Publishing Group
120 Broadway, New York, NY 10271
Tel: 646-307-5151
Web Site: us.macmillan.com/publishers/roaring-brook-press
Key Personnel
Pres, Macmillan Children's Publg Group: Jennifer Besser
SVP & Publr: Allison Verost
VP & Assoc Publr: Bess Braswell
VP & Exec Dir, Publicity: Molly Ellis
VP & Exec Edit & Creative Dir, First Second Books/23rd Street Books: Mark Siegel
VP & Sr Creative Dir: Beth Clark
VP, Mktg: Mariel Dawson
VP, Subs Rts: Kristin Dulaney
Exec Dir, Ad & Promo: Mariel Dawson
Sr Art Dir: Sharismar Rodriguez
Art Dir: Aurora Parlagreco
Creative Dir, First Second Books/23rd Street Books: Kirk Benshoff

U.S. PUBLISHERS

Dir, Mktg: Kathryn Little; Melissa Zar
Dir, Publicity: Morgan Kane; Kelsey Marrujo; Mary Van Akin
Dir, School & Lib Mktg: Lucy Del Priore
Edit Dir: Connie Hsu
Edit Dir, First Second Books/23rd Street Books: Calista Brill
Assoc Art Dir: Samira Irayani
Assoc Art Dir, First Second Books: Sunny Lee
Assoc Dir, Mktg: Johanna Allen; Robert Brown; Katie Quinn
Assoc Dir, Prodn Edit: Kat Kopit
Sr Mng Ed: Allyson Floridia; Hayley Jozwiak
Asst Mng Ed: Arik Harden
Sr Prodn Ed: Mia Moran; Avia Perez; Taylor Pitts; Helen Seachrist; Kathy Wielgosz; Ilana Worrell
Exec Ed: Emily Feinberg
Sr Ed: Katherine Jacobs; Kate Meltzer
Sr Ed, First Second Books: Robyn Chapman
Ed: Mekisha Telfer
Ed, First Second Books: Kiara Valdez
Ed, 23rd Street Books: Tess Banta
Assoc Ed: Luisa Beguiristain
Assoc Ed, First Second Books: Samia Fakih
Asst Ed: Nicolas Ore-Giron; Emilia Sowersby
Sr Mgr, Subs Rts: Kaitlin Loss
Sr Mktg Mgr: Alexandra Quill; Nicole Schaeffer
Design Mgr, Mktg: Danielle Imperiale
Mktg Mgr: Teresa Ferraiolo; Allegra Green; Jordin Streeter
Publicity Mgr: Morgan Rath
Studio Mgr: Ginny Dominguez
Assoc Mktg Mgr: Gabriella Salpeter; Elysse Villalobos
Asst Mgr, Subs Rts: Jordan Winch
Sr Designer: Lindsey Whitt
Sr Designer, First Second Books: Molly Johanson
Designer: Ashley Caswell; Cassie Gonzales
Assoc Designer: Naomi Silverio
Jr Designer: Abby Granata
Sr Publicist: Chantal Gersch
Publicist: Tatiana Merced-Zarou; Samantha Sacks
Sr Coord: Debbie Cobb
Mktg Coord: Kathryn Deaton; Leigh Ann Higgins; Olivia Oleck; Carlee Maurier
Mktg Assoc: Megan McDonald; Naheid Shahsamand
Mktg Asst: Elinor Toler
Publicity Asst: Sara Elroubi
Publisher's Asst: Hana Tzou
Founded: 2002
ISBN Prefix(es): 978-0-7613; 978-1-59643
Number of titles published annually: 50 Print
Imprints: First Second Books; 23rd Street Books

The Rockefeller University Press
Unit of Rockefeller University
950 Third Ave, 2nd fl, New York, NY 10022
Tel: 212-327-7938
E-mail: rupress@rockefeller.edu
Web Site: www.rupress.org
Key Personnel
Fin Dir: Ray Fastiggi *Tel:* 212-327-8567 *E-mail:* fastigg@rockefeller.edu
Prodn Dir: Robert J O'Donnell *Tel:* 212-327-8545 *E-mail:* odonner@rockefeller.edu
Mktg Assoc: Laraine Karl *E-mail:* lkarl@rockefeller.edu
Founded: 1906
Currently publishes biomedical journals & books.
ISBN Prefix(es): 978-0-87470
Number of titles published annually: 3 Print
Total Titles: 36 Print; 3 Online
Foreign Rep(s): iGroup Asia Pacific Ltd (Asia-Pacific)
Membership(s): Association of American Publishers Professional & Scholarly Publishing Division; Association of Learned & Professional Society Publishers (ALPSP); Association of University Presses (AUPresses); Society for Scholarly Publishing (SSP)

RockHill Publishing LLC
PO Box 62523, Virginia Beach, VA 23466-2523
Tel: 757-692-2021
Web Site: rockhillpublishing.com
Key Personnel
Publr: James L Hill *E-mail:* jlhill@rockhillpublishing.com
Founded: 2013
Independent publishing house.
ISBN Prefix(es): 978-1-945286
Number of titles published annually: 3 Print; 3 Online; 3 E-Book
Total Titles: 19 Print; 19 Online; 19 E-Book
Membership(s): Independent Book Publishers Association (IBPA)

Rocky Mountain Mineral Law Foundation
9191 Sheridan Blvd, Suite 203, Westminster, CO 80031
Tel: 303-321-8100 *Fax:* 303-321-7657
E-mail: info@rmmlf.org
Web Site: www.rmmlf.org
Key Personnel
Exec Dir: Alex Ritchie *Tel:* 303-321-8100 ext 101
Dir, Pubns: Margo MacDonnell *Tel:* 303-321-8100 ext 116
Assoc Dir: Frances Hartogh *Tel:* 303-321-8100 ext 107; Mark Holland *Tel:* 303-321-8100 ext 106 *E-mail:* mholland@rmmlf.org
Founded: 1955
Natural resources & legal education.
ISBN Prefix(es): 978-0-929047; 978-1-882047; 978-1-943497
Number of titles published annually: 6 Print
Total Titles: 81 Print; 1 CD-ROM

Rocky Pond Books
Imprint of Penguin Young Readers Group
c/o Penguin Random House LLC, 1745 Broadway, New York, NY 10019
Tel: 212-782-9000
Web Site: www.penguin.com/rocky-pond-overview/
Key Personnel
Pres & Publr: Lauri Hornik
SVP & Exec Art Dir, Dial Books for Young Readers, Nancy Paulsen Books, GP Putnam's Sons Books for Young Readers & Rocky Pond Books: Lily Malcom
Art Dir, GP Putnam's Sons Books for Young Readers & Rocky Pond Books: Jenny Kelly
Assoc Art Dir, GP Putnam's Sons Books for Young Readers & Rocky Pond Books: Jason Henry
Founded: 2023
Books for ages 2 through teen, with a primary focus on mental health & social-emotional learning.
Penguin Random House & its publishing entities are not accepting unsol submissions, proposals, mss, or submission queries via e-mail at this time.
Number of titles published annually: 6 Print

Rod & Staff Publishers Inc
14193 Hwy 172, Crockett, KY 41413
Mailing Address: PO Box 3, Crockett, KY 41413-0003
Tel: 606-522-4348 *Fax:* 606-522-4896
Key Personnel
Mgr: John D Martin
Founded: 1958
Religious storybooks; church, Sunday & Christian school materials & tracts.
ISBN Prefix(es): 978-0-7399
Number of titles published annually: 20 Print
Total Titles: 700 Print

§Rodin Books
666 Old Country Rd, Suite 510, Garden City, NY 11530
Tel: 917-685-1064
Web Site: www.rodinbooks.com
Key Personnel
Publr: Arthur Klebanoff *E-mail:* aklebanoff@rodinbooks.com
Founded: 2022
High impact thought leadership titles.
This publisher has indicated that 100% of their product line is author subsidized.
ISBN Prefix(es): 978-1-957588
Number of titles published annually: 10 Print; 10 E-Book; 10 Audio
Total Titles: 15 Print; 15 E-Book; 15 Audio
Distributed by Simon & Schuster, LLC

Roman Catholic Books
Division of Catholic Media Apostolate Inc
PO Box 2286, Fort Collins, CO 80522-2286
Tel: 970-490-2735 *Fax:* 904-493-8781
Web Site: www.booksforcatholics.com
Key Personnel
Pres: Roger A McCaffrey *E-mail:* cxpeditor@gmail.com
Founded: 1981
Traditional Catholic books.
ISBN Prefix(es): 978-0-912141; 978-1-929291; 978-0-9793540; 978-1-934888
Number of titles published annually: 10 Print
Total Titles: 270 Print

Roncorp Music
Division of Northeastern Music Publications Inc
PO Box 1210, Coatesville, PA 19320
Tel: 610-679-5400
E-mail: info@nemusicpub.com
Web Site: www.nemusicpub.com
Key Personnel
Pres: Randy Navarre
Founded: 1978
Music & music texts.
ISBN Prefix(es): 978-0-939103
Number of titles published annually: 15 Print
Total Titles: 300 Print
Distributed by Carl Fischer/Theodore Presser

Ronin Publishing Inc
PO Box 3436, Oakland, CA 94609
Tel: 510-420-3669 *Fax:* 510-420-3672
E-mail: ronin@roninpub.com
Web Site: www.roninpub.com
Key Personnel
Publr: Dr Beverly Potter *E-mail:* beverly@roninpub.com
Founded: 1983
Small, independent publisher in San Francisco Bay Area.
ISBN Prefix(es): 978-0-914171; 978-1-57951
Number of titles published annually: 4 Print; 4 E-Book
Total Titles: 125 Print; 100 E-Book; 2 Audio
Imprints: And/Or Press; Books for Independent Minds
Foreign Rep(s): Ingram (worldwide); Ingram/PGW (worldwide)
Foreign Rights: Interlicense LLC (worldwide)
Distribution Center: Ingram/Publishers Group West, 1700 Fourth St, Berkeley, CA 94710
Tel: 510-809-3700 *Fax:* 510-809-3777
E-mail: info@pgw.com *Web Site:* www.pgw.com

§Rootstock Publishing
Imprint of Multicultural Media Inc
27 Main St, Suite 6, Montpelier, VT 05602
SAN: 299-1543
Tel: 802-839-0371
E-mail: info@rootstockpublishing.com
Web Site: www.rootstockpublishing.com
Key Personnel
Pres: Stephen McArthur *E-mail:* stephen@rootstockpublishing.com
Founded: 1994 (as Multicultural Media Inc)
Fiction & nonfiction book publisher.

This publisher has indicated that 80% of their product line is author subsidized.
ISBN Prefix(es): 978-1-57869
Number of titles published annually: 6 Print
Total Titles: 8 Print
Membership(s): Independent Book Publishers Association (IBPA); Independent Publishers of New England (IPNE); New England Independent Booksellers Association (NEIBA); New England Library Association (NELA)

The Rosen Publishing Group Inc
29 E 21 St, New York, NY 10010
SAN: 203-3720
Toll Free Tel: 800-237-9932 *Toll Free Fax:* 888-436-4643
E-mail: info@rosenpub.com
Web Site: www.rosenpublishing.com
Key Personnel
Chmn: Roger Rosen
Pres & CEO: Ken Katula
Founded: 1950
Hardcover, library editions, vocational guidance; personal guidance; music & art catalogs; drug abuse prevention, self-esteem development, values & ethics, new international writing, multicultural, African heritage, graphic nonfiction, curriculum related nonfiction. Grades PreK-12.
ISBN Prefix(es): 978-0-8239; 978-1-4042; 978-1-4358; 978-1-60851; 978-1-60852; 978-1-60853; 978-1-60854; 978-1-61511; 978-1-61512; 978-1-61513; 978-1-61514; 978-1-61530; 978-1-61531; 978-1-61532; 978-1-61533; 978-1-4488; 978-1-4777; 978-1-4824; 978-1-4994; 978-1-68048; 978-1-5081
Number of titles published annually: 200 Print
Total Titles: 2,000 Print
Imprints: Britannica Educational Publishing; Editorial Buenas Letras; Gareth Stevens Publishing; Greenhaven Publishing (includes KidHaven Publishing & Lucent Press); The New York Times Educational Publishing; Norwood House Press; PowerKids Press; Rosen Central; Rosen Digital; Rosen Young Adult; Windmill Books
Divisions: Rosen Classroom Books & Materials
Warehouse: Maple Logistics Solutions, York Distribution Ctr, 60 Grumbacher Rd, York, PA 17406
See separate listing for:
Gareth Stevens Publishing
Greenhaven Publishing
Norwood House Press

§RosettaBooks
Imprint of RB Content LLC (operates ebook catalog, print imprint operated by RosettaBooks LLC)
1035 Park Ave, No 3A, New York, NY 10028-0912
Tel: 917-685-1064
Web Site: www.rosettabooks.com; www.rosettaebooks.com
Key Personnel
Founding Publr: Arthur Klebanoff
 E-mail: aklebanoff@rosettabooks.com
Founded: 2001
ISBN Prefix(es): 978-0-7953
Number of titles published annually: 25 E-Book
Total Titles: 10 Print; 800 E-Book; 10 Audio
Distributed by Simon & Schuster, LLC

§Ross Books
PO Box 4340, Berkeley, CA 94704-0340
Tel: 510-841-2474 *Fax:* 510-295-2531
E-mail: sales@rossbooks.com
Web Site: www.rossbooks.com
Key Personnel
Owner & Pres: Franz H Ross *E-mail:* franz@rossbooks.com
Sales: Benny Juarez
Founded: 1977

General trade books & ebooks.
ISBN Prefix(es): 978-0-89496
Number of titles published annually: 4 Print; 1 CD-ROM; 3 E-Book; 1 Audio
Total Titles: 26 Print; 2 CD-ROM; 2 Online; 6 E-Book; 2 Audio
Imprints: Baldar
Membership(s): Book Promotion Forum

§Rothstein Associates Inc
4 Arapaho Rd, Brookfield, CT 06804-3104
Tel: 203-740-7400 *Toll Free Tel:* 888-768-4783
 Fax: 203-740-7401
E-mail: info@rothstein.com
Web Site: www.rothstein.com; www.rothsteinpublishing.com
Key Personnel
Pres & CEO: Philip Jan Rothstein *E-mail:* pjr@rothstein.com
Founded: 1985
Publisher of digital & print content in business continuity, risk management, crisis communications, crisis management & emergency management for professionals & students.
ISBN Prefix(es): 978-0-9641648; 978-1-931332; 978-1-944480
Number of titles published annually: 15 Print; 9 CD-ROM; 25 E-Book
Total Titles: 80 Print; 36 CD-ROM; 30 E-Book
Divisions: NDY Publishing; Rothstein Publishing
Foreign Rep(s): iGroup.net (Asia-Pacific, Australasia)

§The Rough Notes Co Inc
Subsidiary of Insurance Publishing Plus Corp
11690 Technology Dr, Carmel, IN 46032-5600
Tel: 317-582-1600 *Toll Free Tel:* 800-428-4384 (cust serv) *Fax:* 317-816-1000
 Toll Free Fax: 800-321-1909
E-mail: rnc@roughnotes.com
Web Site: www.roughnotes.com
Key Personnel
EVP & COO: Sam Berman
Ad & Natl Sales Dir: Eric Hall *E-mail:* ehall@roughnotes.com
Founded: 1878
Technical/educational reference material specific to the property/casualty insurance industry.
ISBN Prefix(es): 978-1-56461; 978-0-942326; 978-1-877723
Number of titles published annually: 13 Print
Total Titles: 38 Print; 4 Online
Advertising Agency: AdCom Group

Round Table Companies
Subsidiary of Writers of the Round Table Press Inc
PO Box 1603, Deerfield, IL 60015
Toll Free Tel: 833-750-5683
Web Site: www.roundtablecompanies.com
Key Personnel
Founder & CEO: Corey Michael Blake
 E-mail: corey@roundtablecompanies.com
Dir, Stories & Learning: Kelsey Schurer
Company Integrator: Sunny DiMartino
 E-mail: sun@roundtablecompanies.com
Fin & HR: Andrea Yahr
Exec Asst: Liz Bauman
Founded: 1996
Round Table Companies (RTC) support leaders interested in changing the world. Clients see their purpose brought to life while their thought leadership brand infrastructure is executed & their community built. Core values are brilliance, love, joy, courage, momentum, honesty, community & growth which create an atmosphere where transformation occurs through the magic of storytelling & the impact of human connection.
This publisher has indicated that 90% of their product line is author subsidized.

ISBN Prefix(es): 978-0-61066; 978-0-9814545; 978-0-9822206; 978-1-939418
Number of titles published annually: 6 Print; 6 E-Book
Total Titles: 99 Print; 66 E-Book
Imprints: Round Table Comics
Foreign Rights: Graal Literary Agency (Albania, Bulgaria, Croatia, Czechia, Estonia, Hungary, Latvia, Lithuania, Poland, Romania, Serbia, Slovakia, Slovenia); Grayhawk Agency (China, Indonesia, Taiwan, Thailand, Vietnam); Danny Hong Agency (South Korea); International Editors' Co - Yanez Agencia Literaria (Argentina, Brazil, Portugal, Spain); Tuttle-Mori Agency Inc (Japan)
Shipping Address: Lightning Source Inc, 1246 Heil Quaker Blvd, La Vergne, TN 37086, Content Acq Publr Sales Rep: Pam Dover *Tel:* 615-213-4437 *Fax:* 615-213-4735 *E-mail:* pam.dover@ingramcontent.com
Distribution Center: Lightning Source Inc, 14 Ingram Blvd, PO Box 3006, La Vergne, TN 37086-1986, Content Acq Publr Sales Rep: Pam Dover *Tel:* 615-213-4437 *Fax:* 615-213-4735 *E-mail:* pam.dover@ingramcontent.com
Membership(s): Independent Book Publishers Association (IBPA)

Routledge
Member of Taylor & Francis Group, an Informa Business
711 Third Ave, New York, NY 10017
SAN: 213-196X
Tel: 212-216-7800 *Toll Free Tel:* 800-634-7064 (order enquiries, cust serv) *Fax:* 212-564-7854
Web Site: www.routledge.com
Founded: 1836
Academic books in the humanities, social & behavioral sciences. Academic reference. Professional titles in architecture, education & the behavioral sciences.
ISBN Prefix(es): 978-0-915202; 978-1-55959; 978-0-89503; 978-0-87630; 978-1-883001; 978-1-57958; 978-0-8153; 978-0-8058; 978-0-88163; 978-1-57004; 978-1-880393; 978-0-9611800; 978-0-87332; 978-1-56324; 978-0-7656; 978-0-918286; 978-1-884829; 978-0-415; 978-0-87830; 978-1-85000; 978-0-86656; 978-0-917724; 978-0-918393; 978-1-56023; 978-1-56024; 978-0-7890; 978-0-86078; 978-0-85142; 978-0-7007; 978-1-85346; 978-1-873394; 978-0-419; 978-1-85383; 978-1-85743; 978-0-7146; 978-0-946439; 978-1-85575; 978-0-904180; 978-0-7103; 978-0-948875; 978-1-85196; 978-0-7448; 978-0-906890; 978-0-7099; 978-0-422; 978-0-901877; 978-0-900650; 978-0-7130; 978-1-85728; 978-1-58391; 978-1-84142; 978-0-7546; 978-1-930556; 978-1-932364; 978-1-891853; 978-1-902683; 978-1-84465; 978-1-84407; 978-1-933115; 978-1-884964; 978-0-7507; 978-1-905763; 978-0-9583902; 978-0-9794822; 978-1-59667; 978-1-84872; 978-0-901286; 978-1-84312; 978-0-203; 978-1-59874; 978-1-61132; 978-1-59451; 978-1-61205; 978-1-62958; 978-1-4724; 978-1-84893; 978-0-948905; 978-1-85713; 978-1-138; 978-1-134; 978-1-136; 978-0-367; 978-0-677; 978-0-7102; 978-0-85354; 978-0-85626; 978-0-913178; 978-0-914755; 978-0-931231; 978-0-947593; 978-0-947854; 978-0-9533571; 978-0-9537105; 978-0-9537262; 978-0-9537611; 978-0-9635680; 978-0-9641887; 978-0-9644313; 978-0-9675798; 978-0-9679960; 978-0-9701679; 978-0-9815769; 978-0-9834803; 978-1-135; 978-1-1315; 978-1-351; 978-1-61190; 978-1-62159; 978-1-62956; 978-1-84235; 978-1-873410; 978-1-874719; 978-1-884585; 978-1-890871; 978-1-903350; 978-1-909293; 978-1-910174; 978-1-911186; 978-1-921348; 978-1-934432; 978-1-936523; 978-1-937134; 978-1-942108
Number of titles published annually: 2,000 Print; 2,000 Online; 2,000 E-Book

U.S. PUBLISHERS

Total Titles: 33,000 Print; 21,000 Online; 21,000 E-Book
Imprints: CRC Press; Planners Press; Productivity Press
Sales Office(s): Taylor & Francis, 6000 Broken Sound Pkwy NW, Suite 300, Boca Raton, FL 33487, VP, Books (Americas): Evelyn Elias *E-mail:* evelyn.elias@taylorandfrancis.com
Foreign Office(s): 3 Park Sq, Milton Park, Abingdon, Oxon OX14 4RN, United Kingdom, Group Sales Dir: Christoph Chesher *E-mail:* christoph.chesher@tandf.co.uk
Warehouse: Taylor & Francis, 7625 Empire Dr, Florence, KY 41042 *Toll Free Tel:* 800-634-7064 *Toll Free Fax:* 800-248-4724 *E-mail:* orders@taylorandfrancis.com
See separate listing for:
CRC Press
Planners Press
Productivity Press

Rowe Publishing LLC
655 Old Lifsey Springs Rd, Molena, GA 30258
Tel: 785-302-0451
E-mail: info@rowepub.com
Web Site: www.rowepub.com
Founded: 2010
Publisher of education, fiction, nonfiction, & children books.
ISBN Prefix(es): 978-0-9833971; 978-0-9851196; 978-1-939054; 978-1-64446
Number of titles published annually: 10 Print; 5 E-Book
Total Titles: 125 Print; 41 E-Book
Imprints: Rowe Publishing; Rowe Publishing & Design

Rowman & Littlefield
4501 Forbes Blvd, Suite 200, Lanham, MD 20706
SAN: 208-5143
Tel: 301-459-3366 *Toll Free Tel:* 800-462-6420 (ext 3024, cust serv) *Fax:* 301-429-5748
Web Site: rowman.com
Key Personnel
Group CEO: Jed Lyons
COO: Robert Marsh
CFO: Michael Lippenholz
SVP & Publr: Julie Kirsch
VP & Sr Exec Acqs Ed: Jonathan Sisk *E-mail:* jsisk@rowman.com
VP, Sales & Mktg: Karen Allman *E-mail:* kallman@rowman.com
Dir, Rts & Perms: Clare Cox *E-mail:* ccox@rowman.com
Sr Exec Ed: John Cerullo
Sr Exec Ed, Religion: Richard Brown
Exec Ed: Jacqueline Flynn
Sr Acq Ed: Carol Flannery
Sr Prodn Ed: Clare Cerullo
Busn Devt Mgr: Michael Lyons
Founded: 1949
Nonfiction publishing in the humanities & social sciences.
ISBN Prefix(es): 978-0-8476; 978-1-56699; 978-0-7425; 978-1-4422; 978-0-87471; 978-0-9632978; 978-1-888051; 978-1-931890; 978-1-933494; 978-1-936283; 978-1-61281; 978-1-4616; 978-1-4617; 978-1-62093; 978-1-4758
Number of titles published annually: 600 Print; 600 E-Book; 50 Audio
Total Titles: 20,000 Print; 12,000 E-Book
Imprints: Sheed & Ward (books for Catholic readers)
Foreign Office(s): 10 Thornbury Rd, Plymouth, Devon PL6 7PP, United Kingdom, Contact: Ben Glover *Tel:* (020) 3111 1080 *Fax:* (020) 3111 1091 *E-mail:* bglover@rowman.com
Distributor for The Brookings Institution Press
Foreign Rep(s): APD Singapore Pte Ltd (Brunei, Cambodia, Indonesia, Laos, Malaysia, Singapore, Thailand, Vietnam); Aristotle House (Simons Watts) (Cameroon, Ethiopia, The Gambia, Ghana, Kenya, Malawi, Mauritius, Nigeria, Tanzania, Uganda); Asia Publishers Service Ltd (China, Hong Kong, Philippines, Taiwan); Avicenna Partnership Ltd (Middle East, North Africa); Co Info Pty Ltd (Australia, New Zealand, Papua New Guinea); Durnell Marketing Ltd (Andrew Durnell) (Europe); Juta & Co Ltd (Botswana, Lesotho, Namibia, South Africa, Swaziland, Zimbabwe); Overleaf (Bangladesh, Bhutan, India, Nepal, Sri Lanka); Publishers Representatives (Tahir Lodhi) (Pakistan); Quantum Publishing Solutions Ltd (Jim Chalmers) (UK); United Publishers Services Ltd (Japan); Wise Book Solutions (South Korea)
Warehouse: 15200 NBN Way, Warehouse C, Blue Ridge Summit, PA 17214 *Tel:* 717-794-3800 *Fax:* 717-794-3803

Royal Fireworks Press
41 First Ave, Unionville, NY 10988
Mailing Address: PO Box 399, Unionville, NY 10988
Tel: 845-726-4444
E-mail: mail@rfwp.com
Web Site: www.rfwp.com
Key Personnel
Dir, Order Dept & Cust Rel: Margaret Foley *Tel:* 845-726-3434
Founded: 1977
Educational materials for gifted children, their parents & teachers; reading materials; adult literacy/education materials; fiction series for middle school: mystery & adventure; novels of growing up; young adult science fiction; youth against violence early childhood program (K-3).
ISBN Prefix(es): 978-0-89824; 978-0-88092
Number of titles published annually: 100 Print
Total Titles: 1,000 Print; 120 E-Book
Distributor for KAV Books; Silk Label Books

Running Press
Division of Hachette Book Group Inc
1290 Avenue of the Americas, New York, NY 10104
Tel: 212-364-1100 *Toll Free Tel:* 800-759-0190 (cust serv) *Fax:* 212-364-0933 (intl orders) *Toll Free Fax:* 800-286-9471 (cust serv)
E-mail: customer.service@hbgusa.com; orders@hbgusa.com
Web Site: www.hachettebookgroup.com/imprint/running-press/; www.moon.com (Moon Travel Guides)
Key Personnel
SVP & Publr: Kristin Kiser
VP & Publr, Avalon Travel: Jaimee Callaway
VP, Ed-in-Chief, Moon Travel Guides: Grace Fujimoto
VP, Prodn, Avalon Travel: Jane Musser
VP, Deputy Publr: Betsy Hulsebosch
Publr: Shannon Fabricant
Exec Asst to the Publr: Tina Camma
Edit Dir, RP Kids: Julie Matysik
Edit Dir, RP Entertains: Cindy Sipala
Mng Ed, Moon Travel Guides: Hannah Brezack
Assoc Mng Ed, Rick Steves: Sierra Machado
Prodn Ed: Leah Gordon
Sr Ed: Shannon Kelly
Sr Ed & Licensing Mgr: Jordana Hawkins
Sr Ed, Moon Travel Guides: Kathryn Ettinger
Sr Ed, Rick Steves: Madhu Prasher
Sr Ed, RP Kids: Allison Cohen
Sr Cartography Ed, Avalon Travel: Albert Angulo
Ed: Randall Lotowycz
Ed, Rick Steves: Jamie Andrade
Assoc Ed: Britny Perilli
Assoc Ed, Avalon Travel: Kristi Mitsuda
Asst Ed: Maria Riillo; Maria Simione
Acqs Ed, Avalon Travel: Rachael Sablik
Mktg Dir, Avalon Travel: Lindsay Fradkoff
Sr Mktg Mgr, Licensing: Amy Cianfrone
Mktg & Publicity Mgr, RP Kids: Rebecca Matheson
Publicity Dir: Kara Thornton
Sr Publicity Mgr: Seta Bedrosian Zink
Publg Technologies Mgr, Avalon Travel: Darren Alessi
VP, Creative Dir: Frances Soo Ping Chow
Dir, RP Minis & Licensing: Jennifer Leczkowski
Assoc Design Dir: Susan Van Horn
Dir, Prod Devt: Frank Sipala
Sr Prodn Designer, Avalon Travel: Rue Flaherty
Sr Prodn Assoc: Kyle Moore
Dim Designer/Sampler: Mark Governa
Sr Graphic Designer: Daniel Cantada
Sr Designer: Amanda Richmond
Cartography Dir, Avalon Travel: Katherine Bennett
Imprint Sales Dir: Jennifer Trzaska
Founded: 1972
As of January 1, 2025, Running Press Group & Workman Publishing will merge to form Workman Running Press Group. Complete details were not available at the time of publication.
ISBN Prefix(es): 978-0-762; 978-1-631 (Avalon Travel)
Imprints: Avalon Travel (includes Moon Travel Guides & Rick Steves); RP Adult; RP Inspires; RP Minis; RP Studio; Running Press Kids

Russell Sage Foundation
112 E 64 St, New York, NY 10065
SAN: 201-4521
Tel: 212-750-6000 *Toll Free Tel:* 800-524-6401 *Fax:* 212-371-4761
E-mail: info@rsage.org
Web Site: www.russellsage.org
Key Personnel
Pres: Sheldon Danzinger
Dir, Communs: David Haproff *Tel:* 212-750-6037
Dir, Pubns: Suzanne Nichols
Founded: 1907
Sociology, economics, political science.
ISBN Prefix(es): 978-0-87154; 978-1-61044
Number of titles published annually: 20 Print
Total Titles: 1,000 Print
Shipping Address: Chicago Distribution Center, 11030 S Langley Ave, Chicago, IL 60628 *Tel:* 773-702-7010 *Toll Free Fax:* 800-621-8476 *Web Site:* press.uchicago.edu

Rutgers University Press
Division of Rutgers, The State University of New Jersey
106 Somerset St, 3rd fl, New Brunswick, NJ 08901
SAN: 203-364X
Tel: 848-445-7762; 848-445-7761 (sales) *Fax:* 732-745-4935
E-mail: sales@rutgersuniversitypress.org
Web Site: www.rutgersuniversitypress.org
Key Personnel
Dir: Micah Kleit *Tel:* 848-445-7784 *E-mail:* mbk82@press.rutgers.edu
Asst to the Dir & Assoc Ed: Elisabeth Maselli *Tel:* 848-445-7785 *E-mail:* esm102@press.rutgers.edu
Edit Dir: Kimberly Guinta *Tel:* 848-445-7786 *E-mail:* kimberly.guinta@rutgers.edu
Fin Dir: David Flum *Tel:* 848-445-7763 *E-mail:* dflum@press.rutgers.edu
Prodn & Art Dir: Jennifer Blanc-Tal *Tel:* 848-445-7764 *E-mail:* jfb131@press.rutgers.edu
Sales & Mktg Dir: Jeremy Grainger *Tel:* 848-445-7781 *E-mail:* jg1160@press.rutgers.edu
Exec Ed: Peter Mickulas *Tel:* 848-445-7752 *E-mail:* mickulas@press.rutgers.edu; Nicole Solano *Tel:* 848-445-7787 *E-mail:* nicole.solano@rutgers.edu
Prodn Ed: Daryl Browler *Tel:* 848-445-7761 *E-mail:* djb147@press.rutgers.edu; Vincent Nordhaus *Tel:* 848-445-7797 *E-mail:* vincent.nordhaus@press.rutgers.edu; Alissa Zarro

Tel: 848-445-7756 E-mail: ajz45@press.rutgers.edu
Ed: Lisa Banning Tel: 848-445-7791
E-mail: lmb333@press.rutgers.edu
Sr Promo Mgr: Brice Hammack Tel: 848-445-7765 E-mail: bhammack@press.rutgers.edu
IT Mgr: Penny Burke E-mail: pborden@press.rutgers.edu
Publicity Mgr: Courtney Brach Tel: 848-445-7775 E-mail: clb301@press.rutgers.edu
Founded: 1936
Since its founding as a nonprofit publisher, Rutgers University Press has been dedicated to the advancement & dissemination of knowledge to scholars, students & the general reading public. An integral part of one of the leading public research & teaching universities in the US, the Press reflects & is essential to the University's missions of research, instruction & service. To carry out these goals, books are published in electronic & print format in a broad array of disciplines across the humanities, social sciences & sciences. Fulfilling its mandate to serve the people of New Jersey, books of scholarly & popular interest on the state & surrounding region are also published. Working with authors throughout the world, the Press seeks books that meet high editorial standards, facilitate the exchange of ideas, enhance teaching & make scholarship accessible to a wide range of readers. It celebrates & affirms its role as a major cultural institution that contributes significantly to the ideas that shape the critical issues of our day.
ISBN Prefix(es): 978-0-8135; 978-1-9788
Number of titles published annually: 90 Print; 80 Online; 80 E-Book
Total Titles: 3,500 Print; 1,600 Online; 1,600 E-Book
Foreign Office(s): 99 Banbury Rd, Oxford OX2 6JX, United Kingdom
Distributed by University of British Columbia Press (CN)
Distributor for Bucknell University Press (worldwide); University of Delaware Press (worldwide)
Foreign Rep(s): Eurospan (worldwide exc Canada & USA); University of British Columbia Press (Canada)
Foreign Rights: McIntosh & Otis Inc (worldwide)
Returns: Chicago Distribution Center (CDC), 11030 S Langley Ave, Chicago, IL 60628
SAN: 202-5280
Distribution Center: Chicago Distribution Center (CDC), 11030 S Langley Ave, Chicago, IL 60628 Tel: 773-702-7000 Toll Free Tel: 800-621-2736 Fax: 773-702-7212 Toll Free Fax: 800-621-8476 E-mail: orders@press.uchicago.edu Web Site: press.uchicago.edu/cdc
SAN: 202-5280
Eurospan Ltd, Gray's Inn, 127 Clerkenwell Rd, London EC1R 5DB, United Kingdom (Europe, UK & rest of world) Tel: (020) 3286 2420 E-mail: info@eurospangroup.com Web Site: www.eurospan.com
Membership(s): American Association of University Presses (AAUP); American Booksellers Association (ABA); New Atlantic Independent Booksellers Association (NAIBA); New England Independent Booksellers Association (NEIBA)

§Saddleback Educational Publishing
151 Kalmus Dr, Suite J-1, Costa Mesa, CA 92626
SAN: 860-0902
Tel: 714-640-5200 Toll Free Tel: 888-SDLBACK (735-2225); 800-637-8715 Fax: 714-640-5297
Toll Free Fax: 888-734-4010
E-mail: contact@sdlback.com
Web Site: www.sdlback.com
Key Personnel
Pres: Arianne McHugh
Founded: 1982
Publish high-interest, low-readabilty material for middle school & high school. Solutions for struggling learners.
ISBN Prefix(es): 978-1-56254; 978-1-59905; 978-1-61651; 978-1-60291; 978-1-62250; 978-1-62670; 978-1-63078; 978-1-68021
Number of titles published annually: 200 Print; 10 CD-ROM; 20 E-Book; 10 Audio
Total Titles: 2,000 Print; 150 CD-ROM; 400 E-Book; 150 Audio
Distributed by Children's Plus
Distribution Center: Follett School Solutions Inc, 1340 Ridgeview Dr, McHenry, IL 60050 Tel: 815-759-1700 Toll Free Tel: 888-511-5114 (cust serv) Fax: 815-759-9831 Toll Free Fax: 800-852-5458 E-mail: info@follettlearning.com Web Site: www.follettlearning.com SAN: 169-1902
Saunders Book Co, PO Box 308, Collingwood, ON L9Y 3Z7, Canada Tel: 705-445-4777 Toll Free Tel: 800-461-9120 Fax: 705-445-9569 Toll Free Fax: 800-561-1763 E-mail: info@saundersbooks.ca
Membership(s): American Educational Publishers; Educational Book & Media Association (EBMA)

§William H Sadlier Inc
9 Pine St, New York, NY 10005
SAN: 204-0948
Tel: 212-227-2120 Toll Free Tel: 800-221-5175 (cust serv) Fax: 212-312-6080
E-mail: customerservice@sadlier.com
Web Site: www.sadlier.com
Key Personnel
Chmn of the Bd: Frank S Dinger
Pres & CEO: Raymond Fagan
VP & Dir, Mktg: Alexandra Rivas-Smith
VP & Natl Field Sales Mgr: Dan McElhinny
VP & Natl Sales Admin: Kevin O'Donnell
Creative Dir: Vincent Gallo
Gen Coun: Angela Dinger
Cust Serv: Melissa Gibbons
Founded: 1832
Preschool, elementary & secondary textbooks on catechetics, sacraments, reading/language arts, mathematics; adult catechetical programs.
ISBN Prefix(es): 978-0-87105; 978-0-8215; 978-1-4217
Number of titles published annually: 4 Print

§SAE (Society of Automotive Engineers International)
400 Commonwealth Dr, Warrendale, PA 15096-0001
SAN: 216-0811
Tel: 724-776-4841; 724-776-4970 (outside US & CN) Toll Free Tel: 877-606-7323 (cust serv) Fax: 724-776-0790 (cust serv)
E-mail: publications@sae.org; customerservice@sae.org
Web Site: www.sae.org
Key Personnel
CEO: David L Schutt
Founded: 1905
Scientific & technical publications.
ISBN Prefix(es): 978-0-89883; 978-1-56091; 978-0-7680; 978-1-4686
Number of titles published annually: 150 Print
Total Titles: 650 Print; 23 CD-ROM; 1 Online; 15 E-Book; 1 Audio
Branch Office(s)
1200 "G" St NW, Suite 800, Washington, DC 20005 Tel: 202-434-8943 Fax: 202-463-7319
Effective Training Inc (ETI), 14143 Farmington Rd, Livonia, MI 48154 Tel: 734-744-5940 Toll Free Tel: 800-886-0909 Fax: 734-744-5979
Automotive Headquarters, 755 W Big Beaver Rd, Suite 1600, Troy, MI 48084 Tel: 248-273-2455 Fax: 248-273-2494
Foreign Office(s): 280 Blvd du Souverain, 1160 Brussels, Belgium Tel: (02) 789-23-44 E-mail: info-sae-europe@associationhq.com
SAE International China Off, Rm 2503, Litong Plaza, No 1350 N Sichuan Rd, Hongkou District, Shanghai 200080, China Tel: (021) 6140 8900 Fax: (021) 6140 8901
SAE Aerospace Standards, One York St, London W1U 6PA, United Kingdom Tel: (020) 7034 1250 Fax: (020) 7034 1257
Distributor for Coordinating Research Council Inc
Foreign Rep(s): Aeromarine Vehicles (Singapore); Allied Publishers Pvt Ltd (India); Booknet Co Ltd (Thailand); Catarac (China); China National Publications Import & Export (Group) Corp (China); China Publishers Marketing (China); EBSCO Korea (South Korea); Eurospan (Marc Bedwell) (Asia-Pacific exc China); Eurospan Group (Africa, Asia-Pacific, Australasia, Brazil, Europe, Middle East, Oceania); Eurospan India (India); GDI Co Ltd (South Korea); IHS de Mexico (Latin America, Mexico); Kinokuniya Co Ltd (Japan); Maruzen Co Book Division (Japan); Normdocs (Russia); Pak Book Corp (Pakistan); PB for Books (Pathumthani) Co Ltd (Thailand); SAE Australasia (Australasia, Oceania); SAE Brasil (Brazil); SAE of Japan (Japan); Ta Tong Book Co Ltd (Taiwan); UBS Library Services Pte Ltd (Singapore); UBSD Distribution Sdn Bhd (Malaysia); Unifacamanu Trading Co Ltd (Taiwan); YPJ Publications & Distributors Sdn Bhd (Malaysia)

Safari Press
15621 Chemical Lane, Bldg B, Huntington Beach, CA 92649
Tel: 714-894-9080 Toll Free Tel: 800-451-4788 Fax: 714-894-4949
E-mail: info@safaripress.com
Web Site: www.safaripress.com
Key Personnel
CEO: Ludo J Wurfbain
Chief Ed: Jacque Neufeld
Founded: 1984
Specialize in big-game hunting, firearms, wingshooting, Africana & sporting; hardcover trade & limited editions.
ISBN Prefix(es): 978-0-940143; 978-1-57157
Number of titles published annually: 10 Print
Total Titles: 340 Print
Distributor for Quiller

Safer Society Press
Division of Safer Society International Inc
PO Box 340, Brandon, VT 05733-0340
Tel: 802-247-3132 Fax: 802-247-4233
E-mail: info@safersociety.org
Web Site: safersocietypress.org
Key Personnel
Exec Dir & Edit Dir: Mary Falcon
Dir: Steve Zeoli E-mail: steve@safersociety.org
Dir, Continuing Educ Ctr: David Prescott
Dir, Opers: Sarah Snow Haskell
Asst Opers Mgr: Michelle Shubert
Mktg Assoc: Natalie Zawistowska
Founded: 1985
Specialize in titles relating to the prevention & treatment of sexual abuse.
ISBN Prefix(es): 978-1-884444
Number of titles published annually: 4 Print
Total Titles: 80 Print
Foreign Rep(s): Open Leaves Books (Australia); Visions Book Store Ltd (Canada)

Sagamore Publishing LLC
3611 N Staley Rd, Suite B, Champaign, IL 61822
SAN: 292-5788
Tel: 217-359-5940 Toll Free Tel: 800-327-5557 (orders) Fax: 217-359-5975
E-mail: web@sagamorepub.com
Web Site: www.sagamorepub.com
Key Personnel
Publr: Dr Joseph J Bannon, Sr
Pres: Peter L Bannon
Dir, Prodn & Devt: Susan M Davis

U.S. PUBLISHERS

Sales & Mktg Mgr: Misti Gilles
 E-mail: mgilles@sagamorepub.com
Founded: 1974
ISBN Prefix(es): 978-0-915611; 978-1-57167; 978-1-58382
Number of titles published annually: 13 Print
Total Titles: 210 Print; 6 Online
Distributor for American Academy for Park & Recreation Administration
Foreign Rep(s): Gazelle Book Services Ltd (Continental Europe, Ireland, UK); HM Leisure Planning (Australia, New Zealand)

SAGE Publishing
2455 Teller Rd, Thousand Oaks, CA 91320
Toll Free Tel: 800-818-7243 *Toll Free Fax:* 800-583-2665
E-mail: info@sagepub.com; orders@sagepub.com
Web Site: www.sagepublishing.com
Key Personnel
Founder: Sara Miller McCune
Pres & CEO: Blaise R Simqu
Sr Acqs Ed, Psychology: Matthew Wright
Founded: 1965
SAGE Publishing is an independent company that disseminates journals, books & library products for the educational, scholarly & professional markets.
ISBN Prefix(es): 978-0-8039
Number of titles published annually: 800 Print
Imprints: CQ Press; Learning Matters; Adam Matthew
Divisions: Corwin
Branch Office(s)
2600 Virginia Ave NW, Suite 600, Washington, DC 20037
Foreign Office(s): SAGE Publishing Australia, 114 William St, Level 20, Melbourne, Victoria 3000, Australia *Web Site:* au.sagepub.com
SAGE Publications India Pvt Ltd, B1/I-1 Mohan Cooperative Industrial Area, Mathura Rd, New Delhi 110 044, India *Tel:* (011) 4053 9222 *Fax:* (011) 4053 9234 *Web Site:* in.sagepub.com
18 Cross St, No 10-10/11/12, China Sq Central, Singapore 048423, Singapore
SAGE Publications Ltd, One Oliver's Yard, 55 City Rd, London EC1Y 1SP, United Kingdom *Tel:* (020) 7324 8500 *Fax:* (020) 7324 8600 *E-mail:* market@sagepub.co.uk *Web Site:* uk.sagepub.com
Foreign Rep(s): Sage Publications India Pvt Ltd (India, South Asia); Sage Publications Ltd (Africa, Asia-Pacific, Europe, Middle East, UK); United Publishers Services Ltd (Japan, South Korea)
See separate listing for:
Corwin
CQ Press

St Augustine's Press Inc
PO Box 2285, South Bend, IN 46680-2285
Tel: 574-291-3500 *Fax:* 574-291-3700
Web Site: www.staugustine.net
Key Personnel
Pres & Publr: Bruce Fingerhut *E-mail:* bruce@staugustine.net
Acqs: Katie Godfrey *E-mail:* catherine@staugustine.net
Prodn: Benjamin Fingerhut *Tel:* 773-983-8471 *E-mail:* benjaminfingerhut@yahoo.com
Founded: 1996
Scholarly & trade publishing in humanities.
ISBN Prefix(es): 978-1-890318; 978-1-883357; 978-1-58731
Number of titles published annually: 25 Print
Total Titles: 600 Print; 75 E-Book
Imprints: Carthage Reprints
Editorial Office(s): 17917 Killington Way, South Bend, IN 46614-9773, Contact: Bruce Fingerhut *Tel:* 574-291-3500 *E-mail:* bruce@staugustine.net

Sales Office(s): University of Chicago Press, Sales Dept, 1429 E 60 St, Chicago, IL 60637-2954 *Tel:* 773-702-7248 *Fax:* 773-702-9756 *E-mail:* orders@press.uchicago.edu
Distributed by University of Chicago Press
Distributor for Dumb Ox Books (publishes the Aristotelian Commentaries of Thomas Aquinas & like works); Hardwood Press (trade books, mostly in sports & regional works)
Foreign Rights: Jeremy Beer (worldwide exc USA)
Billing Address: Chicago Distribution Center, 11030 S Langley Ave, Chicago, IL 60628-3893
Orders to: Chicago Distribution Center, 11030 S Langley Ave, Chicago, IL 60628-3893 *Tel:* 773-702-7000 *Toll Free Tel:* 800-621-2736 *Fax:* 773-702-7212 *Toll Free Fax:* 800-621-8476 *E-mail:* orders@press.uchicago.edu
Returns: Chicago Distribution Center, 11030 S Langley Ave, Chicago, IL 60628-3893
Shipping Address: Chicago Distribution Center, 11030 S Langley Ave, Chicago, IL 60628-3893 *Tel:* 773-702-7000 *Toll Free Tel:* 800-621-2736 *Fax:* 773-702-7212 *Toll Free Fax:* 800-621-8476 *E-mail:* orders@press.uchicago.edu
Warehouse: Chicago Distribution Center, 11030 S Langley Ave, Chicago, IL 60628-3893
Distribution Center: Chicago Distribution Center, 11030 S Langley Ave, Chicago, IL 60628-3893 *Toll Free Tel:* 800-621-8471 *Toll Free Fax:* 800-621-8471 *E-mail:* kh@press.uchicago.edu

St Herman Press
Subsidiary of St Herman of Alaska Brotherhood
4430 Mushroom Lane, Platina, CA 96076
SAN: 661-583X
Mailing Address: PO Box 70, Platina, CA 96076-0070
Tel: 530-352-4430 *Fax:* 530-352-4432
E-mail: stherman@stherman.com
Web Site: www.sainthermanmonastery.com
Key Personnel
CFO: Nicholas Liebmann
Pres: Abbott Damascene
Secy: Paisius Bjerke
Founded: 1965
Publisher of books about the Orthodox Christian faith & Orthodox monasticism. Special emphasis on recent saints & spirituality, curriculum & textbooks.
ISBN Prefix(es): 978-0-938635; 978-1-887904
Number of titles published annually: 3 Print
Total Titles: 77 Print
Imprints: St Herman of Alaska Brotherhood; Fr Seraphim Rose Foundation; St Xenia Skete
Distributed by Light & Life Publishing Co
Foreign Rep(s): Vladimir Ivlenkov (Australia); Orthodox Christian Books Ltd (Nicholas Chapman) (England)

§St James Press®
Imprint of Gale
27500 Drake Rd, Farmington Hills, MI 48331-3535
Tel: 248-699-4253 *Toll Free Tel:* 800-877-4253 (orders) *Toll Free Fax:* 877-363-4253
E-mail: gale.customerservice@cengage.com
Web Site: www.gale.com
Founded: 1968
ISBN Prefix(es): 978-1-55862; 978-0-912289; 978-1-4103
Number of titles published annually: 8 E-Book
Total Titles: 303 Print

St Johann Press
315 Schraalenburgh Rd, Haworth, NJ 07641
Tel: 201-387-1529 *Fax:* 201-501-0698
Web Site: www.stjohannpress.com
Key Personnel
Pres: David Biesel *E-mail:* d.biesel@verizon.net
VP: Diane Biesel

BOOK

Dir, Sales & Promos: Deborah Brugger
Founded: 1990
Started as a book packager & consultant. Began publishing in 1998.
ISBN Prefix(es): 978-1-878282; 978-1-937943
Number of titles published annually: 12 Print
Total Titles: 170 Print
Membership(s): American Academy of Religion (AAR); The American Library Association (ALA); Combined Book Exhibit (CBE); Independent Book Publishers Association (IBPA); Society for American Baseball Research; USMC Combat Correspondents Association (USMCCCA)

St Joseph's University Press
5600 City Ave, Philadelphia, PA 19131-1395
SAN: 240-8368
Tel: 610-660-3402 *Fax:* 610-660-3412
E-mail: sjupress@sju.edu
Web Site: www.sjupress.com
Key Personnel
Dir: Mr Carmen R Croce *E-mail:* ccroce@sju.edu
Edit Dir: Rev Joseph F Chorpenning *Tel:* 610-660-1214 *E-mail:* jchorpen@sju.edu
Founded: 1971
Scholarly books on early modern Catholicism & the visual arts, regional studies (Philadelphia & environs), Jesuit studies (history, visual arts).
ISBN Prefix(es): 978-0-916101
Number of titles published annually: 5 Print
Total Titles: 78 Print
Membership(s): American Association of University Presses (AAUP); Association of Jesuit University Presses

St Martin's Press, LLC
Subsidiary of Macmillan
120 Broadway, New York, NY 10271
E-mail: publicity@stmartins.com; trademarketing@stmartins.com; foreignrights@stmartins.com
Web Site: us.macmillan.com/smp
Key Personnel
Chmn: Sally Richardson
Pres & Publr: Jennifer Enderlin
EVP & COO, Macmillan Trade Publg: Steve Cohen
EVP, Mktg & Digital Media Strategy: Jeff Dodes
SVP & Exec Publg Dir/Publr, Minotaur Books: Andrew Martin
SVP & Publg Dir, St Martin's Paperbacks & Griffin/Assoc Publr, St Martin's Essentials: Anne Marie Tallberg
SVP & Ed-in-Chief: George Witte
VP & Assoc Publr: Laura Clark
VP & Assoc Publr, Wednesday Books/Saturday Books: Eileen Rothschild
VP & Exec Creative Dir: Michael Storrings
VP & Creative Dir: Stephen Snider
VP & Edit Dir: Marc Resnick
VP & Edit Dir, Acq Outreach: Monique Patterson
VP & Edit Dir, Wednesday Books/Saturday Books: Sara Goodman
VP & Edit Dir, St Martin's Essentials: Joel Fotinos
VP & Publg Dir, Minotaur Books: Kelley Ragland
VP & Exec Ed: Charles Spicer; Peter Wolverton
VP, Creative Servs & Ad: Tom Thompson
VP, Fin & Acctg: John Cusack
VP, Mktg: Paul Hochman
VP, Mktg & Sales Opers: Joe Goldschein
VP, Mktg, Communs & Audience Devt: Brant Janeway
VP, Publicity & Ed-at-Large: Dori Weintraub
VP, Rts: Kerry Nordling
Div VP, Publg Opers: Sidney Conde
Exec Art Dir: David Rotstein
Sr Art Dir: Danielle Fiorella Christopher
Sr Art Dir, Creative Servs Group: Michael Criscitelli
Sr Art Dir, Wednesday Books: Kerri Resnick

Art Dir: Jonathan Bush; Young Lim
Dir, Ad & Audience Devt: Erik Platt
Dir, Creative Services: Kim Ludlam
Dir, Intl Rts: Marta Fleming
Dir, Mktg & Bookseller Strategy: Martin Quinn
Dir, Mktg & Multicultural Initiatives: Erica Martirano
Dir, Subs Rts: Chris Scheina
Edit Dir, Minotaur Books: Catherine Richards
Assoc Dir, Mktg & Influencer Strategy: Marissa Sangiacomo
Assoc Dir, Publicity: Gabrielle Gantz; John Karle; Rebecca Lang; Jessica Zimmerman
Assoc Dir, Publicity, Minotaur Books: Sarah Melnyk
Asst Dir, Mktg: Michelle Cashman; Allison Ziegler
Asst Dir, Publicity: Katie Bassel
Asst Studio Dir: Janetta Dancer
Exec Mng Ed: John Rounds
Sr Mng Ed: Hannah Jones
Mng Ed: Ben Allen; Lizz Blaise
Exec Ed: Sarah Cantin; Elisabeth Dyssegaard; Michael Flamini; Alexandra Sehulster
Exec Ed, Minotaur Books: Kristin Sevick
Exec Ed, Wednesday Books: Vicki Lame
Exec Ed-at-Large: Leslie Gelbman
Sr Ed: Michael Homler; Courtney Littler; Sallie Lotz; Hannah O'Grady
Sr Prodn Ed: Carla Benton; Jeremy Pink
Ed & Mgr, Acqs Outreach: Tiffany Shelton
Ed: Hannah Phillips
Ed, Wednesday Books: Jennie Conway
Assoc Ed: Brigitte Dale; Cassidy Graham; Alice Pfeifer
Assoc Ed, Minotaur Books: Nettie Finn; Madeline Haupt
Assoc Ed, Wednesday Books: Mara Delgado-Sanchez
Asst Ed: Alex Brown; Claire Cheek; Lily Cronig; Grace Gay; Christina Lopez; Kelly Stone; Drue VanDuker
Asst Ed, Minotaur: Madeline Houpt
Asst Ed, Wednesday Books: Vanessa Aguirre
Sr Mgr, Media & Audience Intelligence: Hannah Nesbat
Sr Mktg Mgr: Sara Beth Haring
Sr Prodn Mgr: Janna Dokos
Sr Publicity Mgr: Kathryn Hough Boutross
Sr Publg Mgr, St Martin's Press/Castle Point Books: Nichole Argyres
Sr Rts Mgr: Witt Phillips
Mgr, Audience Devt, SMPG Creative Studio: Mac Nicholas
Mgr, Audience Experience, SMPG Creative Studio: Alexis Neuville
Mgr, Mktg & Sales Opers: Kirsi Balazs
Mktg Mgr: Stephen Erickson; Alexis Neuville
Publicity Mgr: Meghan Harrington
Assoc Mgr, Mktg & Sales Opers: Angela Hinck
Assoc Mktg Mgr: Beatrice Jason; Rivka Holler
Sr Publicist: Sophia Lauriello
Sr Publicist, Minotaur Books: Kayla Janas
Publicist: Alyssa Gammello; Zoe Miller
Assoc Publicist: Sara La Cotti; Clare Mauer
Sr Designer & Admin Lead: Lisa Shimabukuro
Sr Designer: Rowen Davis; Devan Norman
Designer & Animation Lead: Lance Ehlers
Designer & Digital Lead: Farina Jaw
Designer: Nikolaas Eickelbeck; Olya Kirilyuk
Assoc Designer: Soleil Paz
Coord, Soc Media Content: Julia Sudusky
Mktg Coord: Austin Adams
Assoc, Foreign Rts: Emily Miiller
Assoc, Mktg: Ana Couto
Founded: 1952
General nonfiction, fiction, reference, scholarly, mass market, travel, children's books.
ISBN Prefix(es): 978-0-312; 978-1-4039; 978-0-230; 978-1-4272; 978-1-250; 978-1-4299; 978-1-4668
Number of titles published annually: 1,000 Print
Imprints: Castle Point Books; Griffin; Minotaur Books; St Martin's Essentials; St Martin's Paperbacks; St Martin's Press; Saturday Books (younger adults & readers 18-30); Wednesday Books
Distribution Center: MPS Distribution Center, 16365 James Madison Hwy, Gordonsville, VA 22942 Toll Free Tel: 888-330-8477 Toll Free Fax: 800-672-2054 E-mail: orders@mpsvirginia.com
Membership(s): Association of American Publishers (AAP)

Saint Mary's Press
Subsidiary of Christian Brothers Publications
702 Terrace Heights, Winona, MN 55987-1320
SAN: 203-073X
Tel: 507-457-7900 Toll Free Tel: 800-533-8095 Toll Free Fax: 800-344-9225
E-mail: smpress@smp.org
Web Site: www.smp.org
Key Personnel
Pres & CEO: John M Vitek
Exec Dir, Delivery: Caren Yang
Libn & ISBN Contact: Connie Jensen
 E-mail: cjensen@smp.org
Founded: 1943
High school curriculum, paperbound & digital; religion (Catholic); Bibles, youth ministry resources.
ISBN Prefix(es): 978-0-88489; 978-1-59982
Number of titles published annually: 25 Print; 8 E-Book
Total Titles: 500 Print; 30 E-Book
Distributor for Group Publishing
Foreign Rep(s): The Bible Society (New Zealand); B Broughton Ltd (Canada); Catholic News, Books & Media (Singapore); John Garratt Publishing (Australia); Herald Publications Sdn Bhd (Malaysia); Pleroma Christian Supplies (New Zealand); Redemptorist Publications (UK)

St Nectarios Press
10300 Ashworth Ave N, Seattle, WA 98133-9410
SAN: 159-0170
Tel: 206-522-4471 Toll Free Tel: 800-643-4233
E-mail: orders@stnectariospress.com
Web Site: www.stnectariospress.com
Founded: 1977
Traditional Eastern Orthodox books.
ISBN Prefix(es): 978-0-913026
Number of titles published annually: 3 Print
Total Titles: 70 Print

St Pauls
Division of The Society of Saint Paul
2187 Victory Blvd, Staten Island, NY 10314-6603
SAN: 201-2405
Tel: 718-761-0047 (edit & prodn); 718-698-2759 (mktg & billing) Toll Free Tel: 800-343-2522 Fax: 718-761-0057
E-mail: sales@stpauls.us; marketing@stpauls.us
Web Site: www.stpauls.us
Key Personnel
Dir, Apostolate, Treas & Mktg: Fr Tony Bautista
 Tel: 718-698-2759 E-mail: frtonyssp@gmail.com
Art Dir & Prodn Mgr: Br Edward Donaher
 E-mail: edonaher@aol.com
Ed-in-Chief & Content, ISBN & Rts & Perms: Br Frank Sadowski E-mail: editor@stpauls.us
Founded: 1961
Religion (Catholic), bible, education, pastoral care, prayer books, biography, spirituality, psychology, philosophy, theology, Spanish titles (Roman Catholic), bereavement, church, ethics, homilies, liturgy, marriage & family life, prayer, religious education, saints' lives, scripture, cassettes & videos.
ISBN Prefix(es): 978-0-8189
Number of titles published annually: 24 Print; 10 CD-ROM; 20 Online; 20 E-Book
Total Titles: 425 Print; 85 CD-ROM; 105 Online; 105 E-Book
Foreign Office(s): Edizioni Paoline, Piazza Soncino 5, 520092 Cinisello Balsamo MI, Italy

Salaam Reads, see Simon & Schuster Children's Publishing

Salem Press
Imprint of Grey House Publishing Inc™
2 University Plaza, Suite 310, Hackensack, NJ 07601
SAN: 208-838X
Tel: 201-968-0500 Toll Free Tel: 800-221-1592 Fax: 201-968-0511
E-mail: csr@salempress.com
Web Site: salempress.com
Key Personnel
Gen Mgr: Jim Wright E-mail: jwright@salempress.com
Founded: 1949
Reference books & online products for middle school, secondary school, colleges & public libraries.
ISBN Prefix(es): 978-0-89356; 978-1-58765
Number of titles published annually: 50 Print; 50 Online; 50 E-Book
Total Titles: 750 Print; 750 Online; 750 E-Book
Imprints: Magill's Choice
Foreign Rep(s): Aditya Books Pvt Ltd (Bangladesh, India, Nepal, Pakistan, Sri Lanka); Alkem Co (S) Pte Ltd (Brunei, Hong Kong, Indonesia, Malaysia, Philippines, Singapore, South Korea, Taiwan, Thailand, Vietnam); Eurospan Ltd (Africa, Europe, Middle East, UK); Grey House Publishing Canada (Canada); Yushodo Co Ltd (Japan)

Salina Bookshelf Inc
1120 W University Ave, Suite 102, Flagstaff, AZ 86001
SAN: 253-0503
Toll Free Tel: 877-527-0070 Fax: 928-526-0386
Web Site: www.salinabookshelf.com
Key Personnel
Pres: Eric Lockard Tel: 877-527-0700 ext 425
 E-mail: elockard@salinabookshelf.com
Art Dir: Corey Begay Tel: 877-527-0700 ext 202
Founded: 1994
Publisher of multicultural books with a strong focus on the stories of the Navajo people. Our textbooks, children's picture books & electronic media in Navajo & English are resources for the home, library & classroom. We recognize the importance of portraying traditional language & culture & of making this knowledge accessible to a broad spectrum of curious minds.
ISBN Prefix(es): 978-1-893354; 978-0-9644189
Number of titles published annually: 10 Print; 3 Audio
Total Titles: 100 Print; 1 CD-ROM; 20 Audio
Membership(s): American Indian Library Association; The Children's Book Council (CBC); Independent Book Publishers Association (IBPA); Publishers Association of the West (PubWest)

SAMS Technical Publishing LLC
Division of AGS Capital Inc
9850 E 30 St, Indianapolis, IN 46229
Toll Free Tel: 800-428-7267
E-mail: customercare@samswebsite.com
Web Site: www.samswebsite.com
Key Personnel
COO: Alan McFarland
Journalist Publr: Alan Symons
Founded: 1946
Publisher of Quickfact & Photofact® service manuals.
ISBN Prefix(es): 978-0-7906
Number of titles published annually: 150 Print
Total Titles: 4,800 Print

U.S. PUBLISHERS

Imprints: Indy-Tech Publishing; Photofact®; Quickfact®
Distributor for Butterworth-Heinemann; McGraw-Hill; Prompt Publications

San Diego State University Press
Division of San Diego State University Foundation
Arts & Letters 283/MC 6020, 5500 Campanile Dr, San Diego, CA 92182-6020
Tel: 619-594-6220 (orders); 619-594-1524 (returns)
E-mail: memo@sdsu.edu
Web Site: sdsupress.sdsu.edu
Key Personnel
Dir & Ed: Dr Bill Nericcio *E-mail:* bnericci@sdsu.edu
Founded: 1959
Scholarly & trade, monographs.
ISBN Prefix(es): 978-0-916304; 978-1-879691
Number of titles published annually: 8 Print; 3 E-Book
Total Titles: 230 Print; 20 E-Book
Imprints: Amatl Comix; Binational Press; Hyperbole
Distributor for Institute for Regional Studies of the Californias

§Santa Monica Press LLC
249 S Hwy 101, No 301, Solana Beach, CA 92075
SAN: 298-1459
Mailing Address: PO Box 850, Solana Beach, CA 92075
Tel: 858-832-7906 *Toll Free Tel:* 800-784-9553
E-mail: books@santamonicapress.com; acquisitions@santamonicapress.com (edit submissions)
Web Site: www.santamonicapress.com
Key Personnel
Publr: Jeffrey Goldman *E-mail:* jgoldman@santamonicapress.com
Founded: 1994
Publishes an eclectic line of nonfiction books. List of lively & modern nonfiction titles includes books in such categories as pop culture, film, music, humor, biography, travel & sports, as well as regional titles focused on California. Young adult historical fiction & narrative nonfiction has also been added to the list.
ISBN Prefix(es): 978-0-9639946; 978-1-891661; 978-1-59580
Number of titles published annually: 12 Print; 12 E-Book
Total Titles: 250 Print; 100 E-Book
Imprints: Santa Monica Press/Teen (young adult historical fiction & narrative nonfiction)
Foreign Rep(s): Ingram Publisher Services (worldwide exc North America); Ingram Publisher Services/Publishers Group West (North America)
Foreign Rights: Kaplan/DeFiore Rights (Linda Kaplan) (worldwide)
Orders to: Ingram Publisher Services, 14 Ingram Dr, Mail Stop 631, La Vergne, TN 37086 *Toll Free Tel:* 800-400-5351 *Web Site:* www.ingrampublisherservices.com
Returns: Ingram Publisher Services, 191 Edwards Dr, Jackson, TN 38301 *Toll Free Tel:* 800-400-5351 *Web Site:* www.ingrampublisherservices.com
Warehouse: Ingram Publisher Services, 191 Edwards Dr, Jackson, TN 38301 *Web Site:* www.ingrampublisherservices.com
Distribution Center: Publishers Group West (PGW), an Ingram brand, 1700 Fourth St, Berkeley, CA 94710 *Toll Free Tel:* 800-343-4499 *Toll Free Fax:* 800-351-5073 *E-mail:* info@pgw.com *Web Site:* www.pgw.com

SAR Press, see School for Advanced Research Press

Sarabande Books Inc
822 E Market St, Louisville, KY 40206
Tel: 502-458-4028 *Fax:* 502-458-4065
E-mail: info@sarabandebooks.org
Web Site: www.sarabandebooks.org
Key Personnel
Exec Dir & Ed-in-Chief: Kristen Renee Miller *E-mail:* kmiller@sarabandebooks.org
Dir, Mktg & Publicity: Joanna Englert *E-mail:* joanna@sarabandebooks.org
Prodn Mgr: Danika Isdahl *E-mail:* danika@sarabandebooks.org
Founded: 1994
Short fiction, poetry & literary nonfiction collections.
ISBN Prefix(es): 978-1-889330; 978-1-932511; 978-0-9641151; 978-1-936747; 978-1-941411
Number of titles published annually: 10 Print; 1 E-Book
Total Titles: 220 Print; 1 E-Book
Distribution Center: Consortium Books Sales & Distribution, an Ingram brand, The Keg House, Suite 101, 34 13 Ave NE, Minneapolis, MN 55413-1007 *Tel:* 612-746-2600 *Toll Free Tel:* 866-400-5351 *E-mail:* cbsdinfo@ingramcontent.com *Web Site:* www.cbsd.com
Membership(s): Academy of American Poets; American Booksellers Association (ABA); Association of Writers & Writing Programs (AWP); Community of Literary Magazines & Presses (CLMP); PEN Center USA

§SAS Press
Imprint of SAS Institute Inc
100 SAS Campus Dr, Cary, NC 27513-2414
Tel: 919-677-8000 *Toll Free Tel:* 800-727-0025 *Fax:* 919-677-4444
E-mail: saspress@sas.com
Web Site: support.sas.com/en/books.html
Key Personnel
Publisher: Sian Roberts *Tel:* 919-531-2548 *E-mail:* sian.roberts@sas.com
Founded: 1990
Books about SAS or JMP software.
ISBN Prefix(es): 978-1-55544; 978-1-58025; 978-1-59047; 978-1-61290; 978-1-59994; 978-1-60764; 978-1-62959; 978-1-62960; 978-1-63526; 978-1-64295; 978-1-951684; 978-1-951685
Number of titles published annually: 20 Print
Total Titles: 125 Print; 120 Online; 120 E-Book
Distributor for John Wiley & Sons Inc (ebook formats only)

SAS Publishing, see SAS Press

Sasquatch Books
1904 S Third Ave, Suite 710, Seattle, WA 98101
SAN: 289-0208
Tel: 206-467-4300 *Toll Free Tel:* 800-775-0817 *Fax:* 206-467-4301
E-mail: custserv@sasquatchbooks.com
Web Site: sasquatchbooks.com
Key Personnel
VP, Sales & Strategy: Jenny Abrami *Tel:* 510-749-9838 *E-mail:* jabrami@sasquatchbooks.com
Publr: Jennifer Worick
Publr, Spruce Books: Sharyn Rosart
Dir, Mktg: Nicole Sprinkle *Tel:* 206-826-4318 *E-mail:* nsprinkle@sasquatchbooks.com
Assoc Mgr, Mktg & Publicity, Little Bigfoot: Whitney Berger *Tel:* 206-826-4321 *E-mail:* wberger@sasquatchbooks.com
Sr Ed: Hannah Elnan
Acqs Ed: Jill Saginario
Design & Prodn Mgr: Alison Keefe
Publicist: Molly Woolbright *Tel:* 206-826-4326 *E-mail:* mwoolbright@sasquatchbooks.com
Founded: 1986
Nonfiction of & from the West Coast.
ISBN Prefix(es): 978-0-934007; 978-0-912365; 978-1-57061; 978-1-63217
Number of titles published annually: 40 Print
Total Titles: 390 Print; 3 Audio
Imprints: Little Bigfoot; Spruce Books
Foreign Rep(s): Random House of Canada Inc (Canada)
Foreign Rights: Park Literary & Media
Orders to: Penguin Random House LLC, 400 Hahn Rd, Westminster, MD 21157 (Attn: order entry) *Toll Free Tel:* 800-733-3000 *Toll Free Fax:* 800-659-2436 *E-mail:* customerservices@penguinrandomhouse.com; Random House of Canada Inc, Diversified Sales, 2775 Matheson Blvd E, Mississauga, ON L4W 4P4, Canada *Toll Free Tel:* 800-668-4247 *Fax:* 905-624-6217 *E-mail:* canadaspecialmarkets@penguinrandomhouse.com

§Satya House Publications
22 Turkey St, Hardwick, MA 01037
Mailing Address: PO Box 122, Hardwick, MA 01037
Web Site: www.satyahouse.com
Key Personnel
Publr: Julie Murkette *E-mail:* julie@satyahouse.com
Founded: 2003
Independent publishing company.
This publisher has indicated that 25% of their product line is author subsidized.
ISBN Prefix(es): 978-0-9729191; 978-0-9818720; 978-1-9358740
Number of titles published annually: 4 Print; 4 E-Book
Total Titles: 30 Print; 1 CD-ROM; 9 E-Book
Imprints: Lost Valley Press (hybrid publg servs)
Foreign Rep(s): Gazelle Book Services Ltd (UK)
Foreign Rights: Sylvia Hayse Literary Agency LLC (worldwide exc USA)
Distribution Center: Independent Publishers Group (IPG), 814 N Franklin St, Chicago, IL 60610 *Tel:* 312-337-0747 *Web Site:* www.ipgbook.com
Membership(s): Independent Book Publishers Association (IBPA); Independent Publishers of New England (IPNE)

Savant Books & Publications LLC
2630 Kapiolani Blvd, Suite 1601, Honolulu, HI 96826
Tel: 808-941-3927 (9AM-noon HST)
E-mail: savantbooks@gmail.com; savantdistribution@gmail.com
Web Site: www.savantbooksandpublications.com; www.savantdistribution.com
Key Personnel
Owner: Daniel S Janik
Ed-in-Chief: David Shinsato
Founded: 2007
Publishes unpublished, post-modern works of enduring value "with a twist" for English readers throughout the world. Special interest areas include: fiction (novels - all genres), nonfiction (transformative education, memoirs, academic theses & dissertations of note, single-author textbooks & workbooks). Under the Aignos Publishing imprint publishes avant garde, experimental & innovative works that "push the leading edge" of all genres of fiction & nonfiction.
ISBN Prefix(es): 978-0-9841175; 978-0-9845552; 978-0-9829987; 978-0-9832861; 978-0-9852506; 978-0-9886640; 978-0-9915622; 978-0-9963255; 978-0-9972472; 978-0-9860233 (Aignos); 978-0-9895191 (Aignos); 978-0-9904322 (Aignos); 978-0-9970020 (Aignos)
Number of titles published annually: 15 Print; 1 CD-ROM; 15 Online; 15 E-Book; 1 Audio
Total Titles: 140 Print; 1 CD-ROM; 110 Online; 140 E-Book; 5 Audio

Imprints: Aignos Publishing (avant garde)
Membership(s): Independent Book Publishers Association (IBPA)

§Savvas Learning Co LLC
15 E Midland Ave, Suite 502, Paramus, NJ 07652
Toll Free Tel: 800-848-9500
Web Site: www.savvas.com
Key Personnel
CEO: Bethlam Forsa
SVP, Prodn & Opers: Paul Despins
SVP, Chief Admin Offr: Paul Fletcher
SVP, CTO: John Lewis
SVP, Mktg & Communs: Maureen Link
SVP, Head, Sales & Sales Opers: James Lippe
SVP, CIO: Bryan Smith
SVP, Gen Coun: Andy Yoo
VP, HR: Cindy Fleming
VP, Intl Busn Devt: Lori Beckwith
ISBN Prefix(es): 978-0-13; 978-0-328; 978-1-4183
Branch Office(s)
3075 W Ray Rd, Chandler, AZ 85226
3088 Sanders Rd, Northbrook, IL 60062
501 Boylston St, Boston, MA 02116

SBL Press
Unit of Society of Biblical Literature
The Luce Ctr, Suite 350, 825 Houston Mill Rd, Atlanta, GA 30329
Tel: 404-727-3100 *Fax:* 404-727-3101 (corp)
E-mail: sbl@sbl-site.org
Web Site: www.sbl-site.org
Key Personnel
Dir: Bob Buller *E-mail:* bob.buller@sbl-site.org
Mktg & Sales Mgr: Heather McMurray *E-mail:* heather.mcmurray@sbl-site.org
Prodn Mgr: Nicole Tilford *E-mail:* nicole.tilford@sbl-site.org
Founded: 1880
Publishing program of the Society of Biblical Literature, a learned society whose purpose is to stimulate the critical investigation of Biblical literature.
ISBN Prefix(es): 978-0-89130; 978-0-7885; 978-0-88414; 978-1-58983
Number of titles published annually: 43 Print; 43 Online; 43 E-Book
Total Titles: 850 Print; 200 Online; 200 E-Book
Distributor for Brown Judaic Studies; Sheffield Phoenix Press
Orders to: PO Box 2243, Williston, VT 05495-2243 *Tel:* 802-864-6185 *Toll Free Tel:* 877-725-3334 *Fax:* 802-864-7626
Returns: 82 Winter Sport Lane, Williston, VT 05495 *Tel:* 802-864-6185 *Toll Free Tel:* 877-725-3334 *Fax:* 802-864-7626
Warehouse: 82 Winter Sport Lane, Williston, VT 05495 *Tel:* 802-864-6185 *Toll Free Tel:* 877-725-3334 *Fax:* 802-864-7626
Membership(s): Association of University Presses (AUPresses)

SBP, see Strategic Book Publishing (SBP)

§Scarsdale Publishing Ltd
333 Mamaroneck Ave, White Plains, NY 10607
E-mail: scarsdale@scarsdalepublishing.com
Web Site: scarsdalepublishing.com
Key Personnel
Publr & CEO: Sharona Wilhelm
Mng Dir: Joseph Moore
Mng Ed: Kimberly Comeau
Founded: 2014
ISBN Prefix(es): 978-0-9972146; 978-0-9980815
Number of titles published annually: 40 Print; 10 Audio
Total Titles: 20 Print; 50 E-Book
Imprints: Blue Vista (women's fiction); Clairmont House (historical romance); Darklake (paranormal/fantasy); East Point (contemporary romance); Flame (LGBTQ); Half Hour Reads; Scarsdale Voices

Scepter Publishers
PO Box 360694, Strongsville, OH 44149
Tel: 212-354-0670 *Toll Free Tel:* 800-322-8773
  Fax: 646-417-7707
E-mail: info@scepterpublishers.org
Web Site: www.scepterpublishers.org
Key Personnel
Assoc Publr: Robert Singerline *E-mail:* robert@scepterpublishers.org
Orders & Cust Serv: Kevin Lay *E-mail:* kevin@scepterpublishers.org
Founded: 1954
Catholic book publishing including doctrinal works, theology & liturgy.
ISBN Prefix(es): 978-0-933932; 978-0-1889334; 978-1-594170
Number of titles published annually: 10 Print
Total Titles: 170 Print

Schaffner Press
PO Box 41567, Tucson, AZ 85717
Web Site: www.schaffnerpress.com
Key Personnel
Publr: Tim Schaffner *E-mail:* tim@schaffnerpress.com
Ed: Sean Murphy *Tel:* 520-869-7632
  E-mail: sean@schaffnerpress.com
Founded: 2001
Independent publisher of books of social relevance for the discerning reader.
ISBN Prefix(es): 978-0-9710598; 978-0-9801394; 978-0-9824332; 978-1-936182; 978-1-943156
Number of titles published annually: 8 Print; 8 E-Book
Total Titles: 60 Print; 60 E-Book
Foreign Rights: Susan Schulman Literary Agency LLC
Distribution Center: Baker & Taylor Publisher Services, 30 Amberwood Pkwy, Ashland, OH 44805 *Tel:* 567-215-0030 *Toll Free Tel:* 888-814-0208 *E-mail:* orders@btpubservices.com
Web Site: www.btpubservices.com

Schiffer Publishing Ltd
4880 Lower Valley Rd, Atglen, PA 19310
SAN: 208-8428
Tel: 610-593-1777 *Fax:* 610-593-2002
E-mail: info@schifferbooks.com; customercare@schifferbooks.com; sales@schifferbooks.com; marketing@schifferbooks.com
Web Site: www.schifferbooks.com
Key Personnel
Pres & Ed-in-Chief: Pete Schiffer
Founded: 1974
Collecting, art books, antiques, architecture, toys, woodcarving, hobbies, weaving, color, metaphysics, aviation, military books, automotive books, design & fashion.
ISBN Prefix(es): 978-0-87033; 978-0-916838; 978-0-88740; 978-0-7643; 978-0-89538; 978-0-978278; 978-1-5073
Number of titles published annually: 300 Print
Total Titles: 5,000 Print
Imprints: Cornell Maritime Press; Geared Up Publications; LW Books; Red Feather; Schiffer; Schiffer Craft; Schiffer Fashion Press; Schiffer Kids; Schiffer LTD; Schiffer Military History; Tidewater Publishers; Whitford Press
Distributor for The Donning Company Publishers
Foreign Rep(s): Gazelle Book Services Ltd (Europe, UK); Harper Group (Mid-Atlantic States, Midwest USA, Southern USA); Peter Hyde Associates (South Africa); JCC Enterprises Inc (Caribbean, Central America, Mexico, South America); Nationwide Book Distributors Ltd (New Zealand); Peribo Pty Ltd (Australia); Publishers International Marketing Ltd (Asia); Sara Books Pvt Ltd (India)
Foreign Rights: Bushwood Books (Europe)
See separate listing for:
Cornell Maritime Press

G Schirmer Inc/Associated Music Publishers Inc
Unit of Wise Music Group
180 Madison Ave, 24th fl, New York, NY 10016
Tel: 212-254-2100 *Fax:* 212-254-2013
E-mail: schirmer@schirmer.com
Web Site: www.musicsalesclassical.com
Key Personnel
CEO: Tomas Wise *E-mail:* tomas.wise@wisemusic.com
EVP & CFO: John Castaldo *E-mail:* john.castaldo@wisemusic.com
Pres: Robert Thompson *E-mail:* robert.thompson@wisemusic.com
Dir, Prodn: Peter Stanley Martin *E-mail:* peter.martin@schirmer.com
Dir, Publg Admin: David Flachs *E-mail:* david.flachs@schirmer.com
Committed to intelligent, educational & entertaining books about all aspects of music, especially the recording arts, music business, genre histories & musician biographies.
ISBN Prefix(es): 978-0-8256; 978-0-7119
Number of titles published annually: 25 Print
Total Titles: 300 Print
Membership(s): American Booksellers Association (ABA); American Society of Journalists & Authors (ASJA); Independent Book Publishers Association (IBPA); Women's National Book Association (WNBA)

§Schlager Group Inc
10228 E Northwest Hwy, No 1151, Dallas, TX 75238
Toll Free Tel: 888-416-5727 *Fax:* 469-325-3700
E-mail: info@schlagergroup.com; sales@schlagergroup.com
Web Site: www.schlagergroup.com
Key Personnel
Pres: Neil Schlager *Tel:* 888-416-5727 ext 801 *E-mail:* neil@schlagergroup.com
VP: Benjamin Painter *Tel:* 888-416-5727 ext 802 *E-mail:* benjamin@schlagergroup.com; Sarah Robertson *Tel:* 888-416-5727 ext 804 *E-mail:* sarah@schlagergroup.com
Founded: 1997
Publisher of books & Internet materials for libraries as well as higher education & K-12 courses in history & related subjects.
ISBN Prefix(es): 978-1-935306; 978-0-9797758
Number of titles published annually: 3 Print; 1 Online; 3 E-Book
Total Titles: 10 Print; 1 Online; 10 E-Book
Imprints: Milestone Documents; Schlager Reference

§Schocken Books
Imprint of Knopf Doubleday Publishing Group
c/o Penguin Random House LLC, 1745 Broadway, New York, NY 10019
Tel: 212-751-2600 *Fax:* 212-940-7390 (dom rts); 212-572-2662 (foreign rts)
Web Site: knopfdoubleday.com/imprint/schocken/; knopfdoubleday.com
Key Personnel
VP & Exec Dir, Sales Mgmt & Planning: Beth Meister
Edit Dir: Ben Hyman
Dir, Ad: Katie Burns
Assoc Dir, Mktg: Bianca Ducasse; Sara Eagle
Mktg Mgr: Dani Toth
Founded: 1931
Penguin Random House & its publishing entities are not accepting unsol submissions, proposals, mss, or submission queries via e-mail at this time.
Foreign Rep(s): Century Hutchinson Group (South America); Colt Associates (Africa exc

U.S. PUBLISHERS

South Africa); Steve Franklin (Israel); India Book Distributors (India); International Publishers Representatives (Middle East exc Israel); Pandemic Ltd (Continental Europe exc Scandinavia); Penguin Random House Canada (Canada); Penguin Random House New Zealand (New Zealand); Penguin Random House UK (UK); Periodical Management Group Inc (Mexico); Random Century (Australia); Saga Books ApS (Scandinavia); Sonrisa Book Service (Latin America exc Mexico); Yohan (Japan)
Foreign Rights: Arts & Licensing International (China); Agencia Literaria Carmen Balcells SA (Spain); Agencia Literaria BMSR (Brazil); DRT International (South Korea); English Agency Japan Co Ltd (Japan); Graal Literary Agency (Poland); JLM Literary Agency (Greece); Katai & Bolza (Hungary); Agence Michelle Lapautre (France); Licht & Licht Agency (Scandinavia); Literarni Agentura (Czechia); Roberto Santachiara (Italy); Sebes & Bisseling Literary Agency (Netherlands)

Scholastic Education Solutions
Division of Scholastic Inc
557 Broadway, New York, NY 10012
Tel: 212-343-6100 *Fax:* 212-343-6189
Web Site: www.scholastic.com
Key Personnel
Pres: Beth Polcari
SVP, Scholastic LitPro & Collections: Michael Haggen
SVP, Strategic Sales: Harold Edwards
SVP, Field & Inside Sales: Chris Hedrick
SVP, Prof Learning Servs: Dr Carol Chanter
SVP, Mktg & Customer Experience: Natalie Boyne
SVP, Transformation & Opers: Kelly Shaw
SVP, Curriculum: Jessica Wollman
SVP, Teacher Solutions: Tara Welty
SVP, Ed-in-Chief, Magazines: Lauren Tarshis
SVP, Literacy Initiatives/FACE: Dwaine Millard
VP, Data Analysis & Academic Planning: Karen Burke
Scholastic Education Solutions is a leading provider of literacy curriculum & a responsive partner of schools & districts. Through print & technology-based learning programs for Pre-K to grade 12, expert professional development, family & community engagement, & learning supports, Scholastic Education Solutions provides teachers, families, & communities with the tools they need to support each & every child.
ISBN Prefix(es): 978-0-516; 978-0-590; 978-0-531; 978-0-7172; 978-0-439; 978-0-926891; 978-1-55998; 978-1-57809; 978-1-59009; 978-0-545
Divisions: Assessment; Curriculum Solutions; Early Childhood Education; Professional Development; Publishing Services; Research; Sales & Marketing; Technology

Scholastic Inc
557 Broadway, New York, NY 10012
Tel: 212-343-6100 *Toll Free Tel:* 800-SCHOLASTIC (724-6527)
Web Site: www.scholastic.com
Key Personnel
Pres & CEO: Peter Warwick
EVP & Chief Strategy Offr & Pres, Scholastic Entertainment Inc: Iole Lucchese
Chief Mktg & Transformation Offr: Mary Beech
Chief People Offr: Cristina Juvier
Chief Inclusion Offr: Lindsey Cotter
Chief Impact Offr: Judy Newman
CIO: Raghushri Sankarin
Chief Supply Chain Offr: Kevin Conklin
Pres, Scholastic International: Kenneth J Cleary
EVP & Pres, Scholastic Trade Publishing: Ellie Berger
EVP & Pres, Scholastic School Reading Events: Sasha Quinton
EVP & Pres, Scholastic Education Solutions: Beth Polcari
EVP, Gen Coun & Secy: Andrew Hedden
EVP, Corp Devt & Investor Rels: Jeffrey Mathews
Founded: 1920
For more than 100 years, Scholastic Corporation (NASDAQ: SCHL) has been encouraging the personal & intellectual growth of all children, beginning with literacy. Having earned a reputation as a trusted partner to educators & families, Scholastic is the world's largest publisher & distributor of children's books, a leading provider of literacy curriculum, professional services, & classroom magazines, & a producer of educational & entertaining children's media. The company creates & distributes bestselling books & ebooks, print & technology-based learning programs for pre-K through grade 12, & other products & services that support children's learning & literacy, both in school & at home. With 15 international operations & exports to 165 countries, Scholastic makes quality, affordable books available to all children around the world through school-based book clubs & book fairs, classroom libraries, school & public libraries, retail, & online. Learn more at www.scholastic.com.
ISBN Prefix(es): 978-0-590; 978-0-439
Subsidiaries: Scholastic Canada Ltd
Divisions: Scholastic Classroom Magazines; Scholastic Education Solutions; Scholastic Entertainment Inc (media); Scholastic International; Scholastic Library Publishing; Scholastic School Reading Events; Scholastic Trade Publishing
Distribution Center: 2931 E McCarty St, Jefferson City, MO 65101
100 Plaza Drive W, Secaucus, NJ 07094
Membership(s): The American Library Association (ALA); Association of American Publishers (AAP); Association of National Advertisers Inc (ANA); The Children's Book Council (CBC); The Council of Chief State School Officers (CCSSO); Council of Great City Schools; Education Commission of the States; International Literacy Association (ILA); National Governor's Association (NGA); New York Women in Communications Inc (NYWICI); SocialMedia.org; Software & Information Industry Association (SIIA)
See separate listing for:
Scholastic Education Solutions
Scholastic International
Scholastic Trade Publishing

§Scholastic International
Division of Scholastic Inc
557 Broadway, New York, NY 10012
Tel: 212-343-6100; 646-330-5288 (intl cust serv)
Toll Free Tel: 800-SCHOLASTIC (724-6527)
Fax: 646-837-7878
E-mail: international@scholastic.com
Key Personnel
Pres: Kenneth J Cleary
SVP & Publr, Intl Educ: Duriya Aziz
VP, Intl Fin: Joe Macca
CTO: Rajit Anand
Scholastic International includes the publication & distribution of products & services outside the US by the company's international operations & its export sales business. Scholastic has operations in Canada, the UK, Australia, New Zealand & Asia, & export sales representatives in the rest of the world.
ISBN Prefix(es): 978-0-590; 978-0-439; 978-0-545
Subsidiaries: Scholastic Asia (with cos in China, India, Malaysia & Singapore & sales offs in Indonesia, Philippines, Taiwan & Thailand); Scholastic Australia Pty Ltd; Scholastic Canada Ltd; Scholastic Ltd UK; Scholastic New Zealand Ltd

Scholastic Trade Publishing
Division of Scholastic Inc
557 Broadway, New York, NY 10012
Tel: 212-343-6100; 212-343-4685 (export sales)
Fax: 212-343-4714 (export sales)
Web Site: www.scholastic.com
Key Personnel
Pres: Ellie Berger
SVP, Fin & Strategic Initiatives: David Ascher
SVP, Mktg: Erin M Berger
VP, Publr & Creative Dir, Klutz®: Netta Rabin
VP, Group Publr & Pres, Scholastic Audio: Lori Benton
VP, Publr & Edit Dir, Scholastic Press: David Levithan
VP, Publr: Liza Baker
VP, Publr-at-Large: Ken Geist
VP, Publr, Licensing: Debra Dorfman
VP, Ed-at-Large: Andrea Pinkney
VP, Creative Dir & Edit Dir, Graphix™: David Saylor
VP, Trade Sales: Elizabeth Whiting
VP, Fin: Ken Yamamoto
VP, Publg Opers: JoAnne Mojica
VP & Mng Ed: Leslie Garych
VP, Global Brand Publicity: Charisse Meloto
VP, Publicity: Seale Ballenger
Exec Ed & Mgr, Scholastic en espanol: Maria Dominguez
Exec Ed: Mallory Kass; Anna Bloom
Edit Dir, AFK & Graphix™: Michael Petranek
Edit Dir, Scholastic Press: Amanda Maciel
Sr Dir, Publicity: Lauren Donovan
Sr Dir, Mktg Opers: Vicki Tisch
Dir, Lib & Educ Mktg: Emily Heddelson
Dir, Prodn, Trade Mktg: Steve Alexandrov
Art Dir, Licensing, Brands & Media: Katie Fitch
Art Dir: Maeve Norton
Art Dir, Klutz®: Vanessa Han
Scholastic Trade Books is an award-winning publisher of original children's books. Scholastic publishes more than 600 new hardcover, paperback & novelty books each year & brings beloved stories & characters to life beyond the printed page via virtually every platform or screen kids access.
ISBN Prefix(es): 978-0-590; 978-0-439; 978-0-545
Number of titles published annually: 600 Print
Total Titles: 6,000 Print
Imprints: AFK; Cartwheel Books®; Chicken House®; Graphix™; Klutz®; Orchard Books®; Point™; PUSH; Scholastic Audio (including Weston Woods); Scholastic en espanol; Scholastic Focus; Scholastic Inc; Scholastic Press; Scholastic Reference™
Distribution Center: 2931 E McCarty St, Jefferson City, MO 65102 *Tel:* 573-635-5881
See separate listing for:
Klutz®

§Schonfeld & Associates Inc
1932 Terramar Lane, Virginia Beach, VA 23456
SAN: 255-2361
Toll Free Tel: 800-205-0030
E-mail: saiinfo@saibooks.com
Web Site: www.saibooks.com
Key Personnel
Pres: Carol Greenhut *E-mail:* cgreenhut@saibooks.com
Founded: 1977
Author statistical reference works.
ISBN Prefix(es): 978-1-878339; 978-1-932024; 978-0-989055; 978-0-996048; 978-0-996248; 978-1-945225
Number of titles published annually: 3 E-Book
Total Titles: 9 E-Book

PUBLISHERS

School for Advanced Research Press
660 Garcia St, Santa Fe, NM 87505
Mailing Address: PO Box 2188, Santa Fe, NM 87504-2188
E-mail: press@sarsf.org
Web Site: sarweb.org
Key Personnel
Acqs Ed: Sarah Soliz *E-mail:* soliz@sarsf.org
Founded: 1907
Scholarly & general-interest books on anthropology, archaeology, Native American art & the American Southwest.
ISBN Prefix(es): 978-1-930618; 978-0-933452; 978-1-934691; 978-1-938645
Number of titles published annually: 5 Print
Total Titles: 150 Print
Distributed by University of New Mexico Press
Orders to: University of New Mexico Press *Tel:* 919-966-7449 *Toll Free Tel:* 800-848-6224
Web Site: www.unmpress.com

School Guide Publications
420 Railroad Way, Mamaroneck, NY 10543
Tel: 914-632-1220 *Toll Free Tel:* 800-433-7771
E-mail: info@schoolguides.com
Web Site: www.graduateguide.com; www.schoolguides.com; www.religiousministries.com
Key Personnel
Pres & Publr: Myles Ridder *E-mail:* mridder@schoolguides.com
Founded: 1886
Directories for colleges, institutions & religious communities.
Number of titles published annually: 5 Print; 3 Online
Total Titles: 15 Print; 3 Online
Membership(s): National Association of College Admission Counseling (NACAC)

§School Zone Publishing Co
1819 Industrial Dr, Grand Haven, MI 49417
Tel: 616-846-5030 *Toll Free Tel:* 800-253-0564
Fax: 616-846-6181
Web Site: www.schoolzone.com
Key Personnel
Pres: Jonathan Hoffman
VP, Sales & Mktg: Sharon Winningham *Tel:* 616-846-5030 ext 217 *E-mail:* sharonw@schoolzone.com
Founded: 1979
Instructional materials for early childhood, PreK to 6th grade; educational workbooks, flashcards & software.
ISBN Prefix(es): 978-0-88743; 978-0-938256; 978-1-58947; 978-1-60041; 978-1-68147; 978-1-60159
Number of titles published annually: 12 Print; 12 CD-ROM
Total Titles: 350 Print; 50 CD-ROM

Schreiber Publishing
Member of Jackson Westgate Publishing Group
PO Box 858, Savage, MD 20763
SAN: 203-2465
Tel: 301-589-5831 *Toll Free Tel:* 800-296-1961 (sales)
E-mail: language@schreiberpublishing.net
Web Site: schreiberlanguage.com; shengold.com; elstreeteducational.com
Founded: 1954
Books on language & translation, Judaica history, Holocaust memoirs, juveniles, reference books, fiction, art books.
ISBN Prefix(es): 978-0-9625963 (Elstreet Educational); 978-0-88400; 978-1-887563
Number of titles published annually: 10 Print; 5 E-Book; 1 Audio
Total Titles: 105 Print; 32 E-Book; 1 Audio
Imprints: Elstreet Educational; Shengold Publishers

Foreign Rights: Gazelle Book Services Ltd (Europe, UK); Importadora Agrimen (Latin America)
Distribution Center: Independent Publishers Group (IPG), 814 N Franklin St, Chicago, IL 60610 *Tel:* 312-337-0747 *Toll Free Tel:* 800-888-4741 *Fax:* 312-337-5985 *Web Site:* www.ipgbook.com

§Science & Humanities Press
Subsidiary of Banis & Associates
63 Summit Point, St Charles, MO 63301-0571
Key Personnel
Publr & CEO: Robert (Bud) J Banis
Founded: 1994
Publish books with a mission. Titles include adapting to living with a disability, computer capabilities, education & specialized medical/wellness topics. Most interested in books that have enduring human value, promoting the kind of world we all want to live in. Prefer inquiries by e-mail. No unsol mss.
ISBN Prefix(es): 978-1-888725; 978-1-59630
Number of titles published annually: 20 Print; 20 E-Book; 1 Audio
Total Titles: 110 Print; 10 Online; 60 E-Book; 4 Audio
Imprints: BeachHouse Books; Early Editions Books; Heuristic Books; MacroPrintBooks
Membership(s): Independent Book Publishers Association (IBPA); St Louis Publishers Association

Science History Publications USA Inc
Subsidiary of Publishers' Design & Production Services Inc
349 Old Plymouth Rd, Sagamore Beach, MA 02562
Mailing Address: PO Box 1480, Sagamore Beach, MA 02562
E-mail: orders@shpusa.com
Web Site: www.shpusa.com
Key Personnel
Mgr: Laura Bergeron
Founded: 1971
Scholarly books on the history, philosophy & sociology of science, technology & medicine.
ISBN Prefix(es): 978-0-88135
Number of titles published annually: 5 Print
Total Titles: 120 Print
Imprints: Prodist; Science History Publications USA; Neale Watson Academic Publications

Science, Naturally
Imprint of Platypus Media LLC
725 Eighth St SE, Washington, DC 20003
Tel: 202-465-4798 *Fax:* 202-558-2132
E-mail: info@sciencenaturally.com
Web Site: www.sciencenaturally.com
Key Personnel
Publr: Dia L Michels *E-mail:* dia@sciencenaturally.com
Founded: 2001
Committed to creating & distributing engaging & educational STEM books for kids.
ISBN Prefix(es): 978-0-9678020; 978-0-9700106; 978-1-938492
Number of titles published annually: 8 Print; 8 E-Book; 1 Audio
Total Titles: 34 Print; 34 E-Book; 1 Audio
Distributor for Genius Games LLC
Distribution Center: National Book Network, 4501 Forbes Blvd, Suite 200, Lanham, MD 20706 *Tel:* 301-459-3366 *Fax:* 301-429-5746 *E-mail:* customercare@nbnbooks.com *Web Site:* nbnbooks.com

Scout Press, see Gallery Books

Scribner
Imprint of Scribner Publishing Group

1230 Avenue of the Americas, New York, NY 10020
Web Site: www.simonandschusterpublishing.com/scribner/
Key Personnel
SVP & Publr: Nan Graham *Tel:* 212-632-4930 *E-mail:* nan.graham@simonandschuster.com
Assoc Publr: Stu Smith *Tel:* 212-698-7414 *E-mail:* stuart.smith@simonandschuster.com
VP & Ed-in-Chief: Colin Harrison *Tel:* 212-632-4942 *E-mail:* colin.harrison@simonandschuster.com
VP, Dir of Subs Rts: Paul O'Halloran *Tel:* 212-698-7367 *E-mail:* paul.o'halloran@simonandschuster.com
VP, Dir of Publicity & Mktg: Brian Belfiglio *Tel:* 212-632-4945 *E-mail:* brian.belfiglio@simonandschuster.com
Publicity Dir: Paul Samuelson *E-mail:* paul.samuelson@simonandschuster.com
Deputy Dir of Publicity & Dir of Publicity & Mktg for Stephen King: Katie Monaghan *Tel:* 212-632-4950 *E-mail:* katie.monaghan@simonandschuster.com
Sr Art Dir: Jaya Miceli *Tel:* 212-632-4959 *E-mail:* jaya.miceli@simonandschuster.com
VP & Edit Dir: Kathryn Belden *Tel:* 212-632-4932 *E-mail:* kathryn.belden@simonandschuster.com
VP & Exec Ed: Rick Horgan *Tel:* 212-698-1129 *E-mail:* rick.horgan@simonandschuster.com
Exec Ed: Kara Watson *Tel:* 212-632-4936 *E-mail:* kara.watson@simonandschuster.com; Christopher Richards *E-mail:* chris.richards@simonandschuster.com; Katie Raissian *E-mail:* katie.raissian@simonandschuster.com
Sr Ed: Sally Howe *Tel:* 212-698-2445 *E-mail:* sally.howe@simonandschuster.com
Ed: Rebekah Jett *Tel:* 212-698-2286 *E-mail:* rebekah.jett@simonandschuster.com
Assoc Ed: Emily Polson *E-mail:* emily.polson@simonandschuster.com
Asst Ed: Sabrina Pyun *E-mail:* sabrina.pyun@simonandschuster.com
Edit Asst: Joie Asuquo *E-mail:* joie.asuquo@simonandschuster.com; Madison Than *E-mail:* madison.than@simonandschuster.com
Exec Dir, Mktg: Brianna Yamashita *Tel:* 212-698-1226 *E-mail:* brianna.yamashita@simonandschuster.com
Mktg Mgr: Lauren Dooley *E-mail:* lauren.dooley@simonandschuster.com
Assoc Dir, Mktg: Ashley Gilliam Rose *Tel:* 212-698-2889 *E-mail:* ashley.rose@simonandschuster.com
Publg & Mktg Assoc Mgr: Mark Galarrita *E-mail:* mark.galarrita@simonandschuster.com
Publg Asst: Sophie Guimaraes *E-mail:* sophie.guimaraes@simonandschuster.com
Publicity Mgr: Abigail Novak *E-mail:* abigail.novak@simonandschuster.com
Publicist: Georgia Brainard *E-mail:* georgia.brainard@simonandschuster.com
Sr Publicist: Kassandra Rhoads *E-mail:* kassandra.rhoads@simonandschuster.com
Publicity Asst: Eleanor Crowley *E-mail:* ellie.crowley@simonandschuster.com
Sub Rts Coord: Fiona Sharp *E-mail:* fiona.sharp@simonandschuster.com
Art Asst: Sydney Newman *E-mail:* sydney.newman@simonandschuster.com
Founded: 1846
ISBN Prefix(es): 978-0-684; 978-0-7432
Number of titles published annually: 70 Print
Imprints: Scribner Classics; Scribner Poetry

Scripta Humanistica Publishing International
Subsidiary of Brumar Communications
1383 Kersey Lane, Potomac, MD 20854
Tel: 301-294-7949 *Fax:* 301-424-9584
E-mail: info@scriptahumanistica.com
Web Site: www.scriptahumanistica.com

U.S. PUBLISHERS

Founded: 1984
Publish reference books in the humanities.
ISBN Prefix(es): 978-0-916379; 978-1-882528
Number of titles published annually: 5 Print
Total Titles: 175 Print; 175 Online
Editorial Office(s): Dept of Romance Languages, 512 Williams Hall, Philadelphia, PA 19104-6305, Gen Ed: Jose M Regueiro *Tel:* 215-898-5124 *Fax:* 215-898-0933 *E-mail:* jregueir@sas.upenn.edu
Foreign Rep(s): Grant & Cutler Ltd (Northern Europe, UK); Leader Books SA (Greece, Middle East); Portico (Africa, Southern Europe, Spain); Scripta Humanistica (Caribbean, Latin America); Spain Shobo Co Inc (Asia, Australia, New Zealand)
Distribution Center: Baker & Taylor, 501 S Gladiolus Ave, Momence, IL 60954-1799 *Tel:* 815-472-2444
Ingram/Lightning Source, 7315 Innovation Blvd, Fort Wayne, IN 46818-1371 *E-mail:* csacademic@ingramcontent.com *Web Site:* www.ingramcontent.com
Midwest Library Service, 11443 Saint Charles Rock Rd, Bridgeton, MO 63044-2789 *Tel:* 314-739-3100 *Fax:* 314-739-1326 *E-mail:* madden@midwestls.com *Web Site:* www.midwestls.com
Yankee Book Peddler Inc, 999 Maple St, Contoocook, NH 03229-3374 *Tel:* 603-746-3102 *Fax:* 603-746-5628
Scripta Humanistica, Calle Union 657, Miramar 00907, Puerto Rico *Tel:* 809-723-2445
Leader Books SA, 62 Koniaristr, 115 21 Ampelokipi, Greece *Tel:* 210 6452825 *Fax:* 210 6449924
Spain Shobo Co Ltd, Yamoto, PO Box 12, Miyagui 981-0503, Japan *Tel:* (0225) 84-1280 *Fax:* (0225) 84-1283 *E-mail:* info@spainshobo.co.jp
Portico Librerias SA, Calle Munoz Seca 6, 50005 Zaragoza, Spain *Tel:* 976 55 70 39 *Fax:* 976 35 32 26 *E-mail:* jalcrudo@porticolibrerias.es
Grant & Cutler Ltd, 55-57 Great Marlborough St, London W1V 1DD, United Kingdom *Tel:* (0171) 734-2012

Seedling Publications Inc
Imprint of Continental Press Inc
520 E Bainbridge St, Elizabethtown, PA 17022
Toll Free Tel: 800-233-0759 *Toll Free Fax:* 888-834-1303
E-mail: edcsr@continentalpress.com
Web Site: www.continentalpress.com
Key Personnel
CEO: Daniel Raffensperger
Pres: Eric Beck
VP & Publr: Megan Bergonzi
VP, Mktg: Robyn Matus
Founded: 1992
Books for beginning readers grades K-2, leveled readers-parental involvement materials.
ISBN Prefix(es): 978-0-8454
Number of titles published annually: 15 Print
Total Titles: 275 Print
Distributed by Kendall Hunt Publishing
Foreign Rep(s): PSI

SelectBooks Inc
325 W 38 St, Suite 306, New York, NY 10018
Tel: 212-206-1997 *Fax:* 212-206-3815
E-mail: info@selectbooks.com
Web Site: www.selectbooks.com
Key Personnel
Founder & Publr: Kenzi Sugihara *E-mail:* kenzi@selectbooks.com
Dir, Mktg: Kenichi Sugihara *E-mail:* kenichi@selectbooks.com
Founded: 2001
ISBN Prefix(es): 978-1-59079
Number of titles published annually: 21 Print; 23 E-Book; 2 Audio
Total Titles: 100 Print; 3 Audio

Foreign Rights: Waterside Productions (worldwide)
Orders to: Midpoint Trade Books, 814 N Franklin St, Suite 100, Chicago, IL 60610 *Tel:* 312-337-0747 *Toll Free Tel:* 800-888-4741 *Fax:* 312-337-5985 *E-mail:* orders@ipgbook.com *Web Site:* www.midpointtrade.com
Returns: Midpoint Trade Books, 814 N Franklin St, Suite 100, Chicago, IL 60610 *Tel:* 312-337-0747 *Toll Free Tel:* 800-888-4741 *Fax:* 312-337-5985 *E-mail:* orders@ipgbook.com *Web Site:* www.midpointtrade.com
Distribution Center: Midpoint Trade Books, 814 N Franklin St, Suite 100, Chicago, IL 60610 *Tel:* 312-337-0747 *Toll Free Tel:* 800-888-4741 *Fax:* 312-337-5985 *E-mail:* orders@ipgbook.com *Web Site:* www.midpointtrade.com
Baker & Taylor, 2550 W Tyvola Rd, Suite 300, Charlotte, NC 28217 *Tel:* 704-998-3100 *Toll Free Tel:* 800-775-1800 *Web Site:* www.bakertaylor.com
Ingram Content Group Inc, One Ingram Blvd, La Vergne, TN 37086 *Tel:* 615-793-5000 *E-mail:* inquiry@ingramcontent.com *Web Site:* www.ingramcontent.com
Membership(s): Independent Book Publishers Association (IBPA)

Self-Realization Fellowship Publishers
3208 Humboldt St, Los Angeles, CA 90031
SAN: 204-5788
Tel: 323-276-6002 *Toll Free Tel:* 888-773-8680
E-mail: sales@yogananda-srf.org
Web Site: www.yogananda-srf.org; bookstore.yogananda-srf.org (online retail orders)
Key Personnel
Mktg/Sales Mgr: Mike Baake *E-mail:* mikeb@yogananda-srf.org
Founded: 1920 (by Paramahansa Yogananda)
Publisher for the complete works of Paramahansa Yogananda.
ISBN Prefix(es): 978-0-87612; 978-1-68568
Number of titles published annually: 10 Print; 7 Audio
Returns: 3225 Lacy St, Los Angeles, CA 90031, Contact: Mark Russell *Tel:* 323-276-6000 *E-mail:* markr@yogananda-srf.org SAN: 204-5688
Membership(s): Independent Book Publishers Association (IBPA)

§Sentient Publications LLC
PO Box 1851, Boulder, CO 80306
Tel: 303-443-2188
E-mail: contact@sentientpublications.com
Web Site: www.sentientpublications.com
Key Personnel
Publr: Deborah Weisser *E-mail:* dw@sentientpublications.com
Founded: 2001
Publish quality nonfiction books with cutting edge perspectives.
ISBN Prefix(es): 978-0-9710786; 978-1-59181
Number of titles published annually: 5 E-Book
Total Titles: 115 Print; 130 E-Book; 10 Audio
Foreign Rights: ANA Sofia Ltd (Bulgaria, Romania); Asli Karasuil Telif Haklari Ajansi (Turkey); Book Publishers Association of Israel (Israel); Giro di Parole (Italy); English Agency Japan Co Ltd (Japan); International Editors' Co - Yanez Agencia Literaria (Spain); JLM Literary Agency (Greece); Agence Michelle Lapautre (France); Maxima Creative Agency (Indonesia); Andrew Nurnberg (China); Piper & Poppenhusen (Germany); H Katia Schumer (Brazil); Silkroad Publishers Agency (Thailand)
Orders to: National Book Network, 4720 Boston Way, Lanham, MD 20706 *Tel:* 301-459-3366 *Toll Free Tel:* 800-462-6420 *Fax:* 301-459-1705 *Web Site:* www.nbnbooks.com
Shipping Address: National Book Network, 4720 Boston Way, Lanham, MD 20706 *Tel:* 301-459-

3366 *Toll Free Tel:* 800-462-6420 *Fax:* 301-459-1705 *Web Site:* www.nbnbooks.com
Distribution Center: National Book Network, 4720 Boston Way, Lanham, MD 20706 *Tel:* 301-459-3366 *Toll Free Tel:* 800-462-6420 *Fax:* 301-459-1705 *Web Site:* www.nbnbooks.com

Serindia Publications
PO Box 10335, Chicago, IL 60610-0335
E-mail: info@serindia.com
Web Site: www.serindia.com
Key Personnel
Publr: Shane Suvikapakornkul
Founded: 1976 (in London)
ISBN Prefix(es): 978-1-932476; 978-1-956165
Number of titles published annually: 11 Print
Total Titles: 60 Print
Distributed by Serindia Publications Inc (CN & US)
Foreign Rep(s): Kodansha Europe (Europe, UK); Serindia Gallery Co Ltd (China, Hong Kong, Singapore, Southeast Asia, Thailand); The Variety Book Depot (Bhutan, India, Nepal, South Asia)

Seven Stories Press
140 Watts St, New York, NY 10013
Tel: 212-226-8760 *Toll Free Tel:* 800-733-3000 (orders) *Fax:* 212-226-1411
E-mail: sevenstories@sevenstories.com
Web Site: www.sevenstories.com
Key Personnel
Publr: Daniel Simon
Dir, Mktg & Publicity, Triangle Square Books for Young Readers: Ruth Weiner *E-mail:* ruth@sevenstories.com
Dir, Mktg, Seven Stories/Triangle Square Books for Young Readers: Claire Kelley
Opers Dir: Jon Gilbert *E-mail:* jon@sevenstories.com
Rts Dir: Silvia Stramenga
Sr Ed: Lauren Hooker
Founded: 1995
Publish original hardcover & paperback books for the general reader in the area of literature, literature in translation, popular culture, politics, media studies, health & nutrition & sports & children's books under our Triangle Square Books for Young Readers imprint. No unsol mss.
ISBN Prefix(es): 978-1-58322; 978-1-888363; 978-1-60980
Number of titles published annually: 50 Print; 50 E-Book; 2 Audio
Total Titles: 750 Print; 500 E-Book
Imprints: Siete Cuentos Editorial (Spanish language); Triangle Square Books for Young Readers
Foreign Rep(s): Penguin Random House (all other territories); Turnaround Distribution (UK)
Foreign Rights: AnatoliaLit Agency (Turkey); Big Apple Agency Inc (China, Taiwan); Paul & Peter Fritz Agency (Germany); Deborah Harris Literary Agency (Israel); Japan UNI Agency Inc (Japan); Katai & Bolza Agency (Hungary); Duran Kim Agency (South Korea); MB Agencia Literaria (Spain, Spanish Latin America); Piergiorgio Nicolazzini Literary Agency (Italy); Sandorf Literary Agency (Croatia, Serbia, Slovenia); Ludmilla Shuskova (Russia); Villas-Boas & Moss Agencia Literaria (Brazil, Portugal)
Distribution Center: Penguin Random House, 400 Hahn Rd, Westminster, MD 21157 *Tel:* 612-746-2600 *Toll Free Tel:* 800-283-3572 (cust serv) *Fax:* 612-746-2606 *Web Site:* www.penguinrandomhouse.com
Membership(s): American Booksellers Association (ABA)

1765 Productions
2911 Hunting Hills Ct, Oakton, VA 22124-1752

Tel: 202-813-9421
E-mail: 1765productions@gmail.com
Key Personnel
Publr & Prodr: P G Finegan
Founded: 1990
Subject specialties include finance, film scripts & screenplays.
ISBN Prefix(es): 978-1-878905
Number of titles published annually: 4 Print
Total Titles: 6 Print

§Shadow Mountain Publishing
PO Box 30178, Salt Lake City, UT 84130-0178
Tel: 801-534-1515 *Toll Free Tel:* 800-453-3876
E-mail: info@shadowmountain.com; submissions@shadowmountain.com
Web Site: shadowmountain.com
Key Personnel
Edit Mgr & Acqs Ed: Lisa Mangum
Subs Rts Mgr: Dave Brown
Founded: 1985
US-based publisher committed to providing books (print, electronic & audio) that offer value-based messages for readers of all ages. Publish quality children's fantasy & numerous bestsellers in the inspiration, fiction, history & business genres.
ISBN Prefix(es): 978-0-88494; 978-0-87747; 978-1-59038; 978-1-57345; 978-1-57008; 978-0-87579; 978-1-60908; 978-1-60641; 978-1-60907; 978-1-62972; 978-1-62973
Number of titles published annually: 25 Print; 2 Online; 25 E-Book; 10 Audio
Total Titles: 200 Print; 2 Online; 70 E-Book; 80 Audio
Imprints: Proper Romance
Distribution Center: Baker & Taylor, 2550 W Tyvola Rd, Suite 300, Charlotte, NC 28217 *Tel:* 704-998-3100 *Web Site:* btol.com
Ingram Content Group, One Ingram Blvd, La Vergne, TN 37086 *Tel:* 615-793-5000 *Web Site:* www.ingramcontent.com
Membership(s): The Children's Book Council (CBC); Independent Book Publishers Association (IBPA); Mountains & Plains Independent Publishers Association; Romance Writers of America (RWA)

§Shambhala Publications Inc
2129 13 St, Boulder, CO 80302
SAN: 203-2481
Tel: 978-829-2599 (intl callers)
  Toll Free Tel: 866-424-0030 (off); 888-424-2329 (orders & cust serv) *Fax:* 617-236-1563
E-mail: customercare@shambhala.com; royalties@shambhala.com
Web Site: www.shambhala.com
Key Personnel
Founder & Ed-in-Chief: Samuel Bercholz
Owner, EVP, Publr of Roost Books: Sara Bercholz
Owner, EVP, Publr of Bala Kids & Course Prodn Mgr: Ivan Bercholz
Pres: Nikko Odiseos
Cover Design Dir: Daniel Urban-Brown
Fin Dir: Dorothy Brow
Interior Design Dir: Lora Zorian
Exec Ed: Beth Frankl
Mng Ed: Liz Shaw *E-mail:* lshaw@shambhala.com
Ed: Peter Schumacher *E-mail:* pschumacher@shambhala.com
Contracts & Royalties Mgr: Stephan Downes
Mktg & Publicity Mgr: Katelin Ross
Prodn Mgr: Karissa Kloss
Rts Mgr: Oliver Glosband
Sales & Edit Opers Mgr: John Golebiewski
  E-mail: jgolebiewski@shambhala.com
Founded: 1969
Trade books; art, literature, comparative religion, philosophy, science, psychology & related subjects.

ISBN Prefix(es): 978-0-307; 978-0-87773; 978-1-56957; 978-1-57062; 978-1-59030; 978-1-61180
Number of titles published annually: 85 Print; 50 Online
Total Titles: 1,050 Print; 50 Online
Imprints: Bala Kids; Prajna Studios; Roost Books; Snow Lion
Distributed by Penguin Random House LLC
Foreign Rep(s): Airlift Books (UK); Penguin Random House Australia Ltd (Australia); Penguin Random House of Canada Ltd (Canada); Penguin Random House of New Zealand (New Zealand)
Foreign Rights: ACER (Elizabeth Atkins) (Brazil, Portugal, Spain); Akcali Copyright Agency (Atilla Izgi Turgut) (Turkey); Anthea Agency (Katalina Sabeva) (Bulgaria); Bardon-Chinese Media Agency (Chang-Chih Tsai) (China); English Agency Japan Co Ltd (Junzo Sawa) (Japan); Ersilia Literary Agency (Evangelia Avloniti) (Greece); Anoukh Foerg (Germany); The Deborah Harris Agency (Ms Efrat Lev) (Israel); International Copyright Agency Ltd (Simona Kessler) (Romania); Katai & Bolza Literary Agents (Peter Bolza) (Croatia, Hungary, Slovenia); Alexander Korzhenevski Agency (Alexander Korzhenevski) (Russia); Macadamia Literary Agency (Poland); Maxima Creative Agency (Santo Manurung) (Indonesia); La Nouvelle Agence (Vanessa Kling) (France); Andrew Nurnberg Associates Baltic (Tatjana Zoldnere) (Estonia, Latvia, Lithuania); Kristin Olson Literary Agency (Kristin Olson) (Czechia, Slovakia); Marianne Schonbach Literary Agency (Marianne Schoenbach) (Netherlands); Alexander Schwarz Literary Agency (Alexander Schwarz) (Denmark, Finland, Norway, Sweden); Sibylle Books Literary Agency (Ms Young-Sun Choi) (South Korea); Tuttle-Mori Agency Inc (Ms Pimolporn Yutisri) (Thailand, Vietnam); Susanna Zevi Agenzia Letteraria (Susanna Zevi) (Italy)
Advertising Agency: Vermillion Graphics, Boulder, CO 80302
Returns: Penguin Random House, Returns Dept, 400 Bennett Dr, Westminster, MD 21157
Shipping Address: Penguin Random House Distribution Center, 400 Hahn Rd, Westminster, MD 21157
See separate listing for:
Snow Lion

Shen's Books
Imprint of Lee & Low Books Inc
95 Madison Ave, Suite 1205, New York, NY 10016
Tel: 212-779-4400 *Fax:* 212-683-1894
E-mail: general@leeandlow.com
Web Site: www.leeandlow.com
Founded: 1985
Children's books.
ISBN Prefix(es): 978-1-885008
Number of titles published annually: 3 Print
Total Titles: 27 Print
Membership(s): American Booksellers Association (ABA); Independent Book Publishers Association (IBPA)

§Shepard Publications
1117 N Garden St, Apt 302, Bellingham, WA 98225
Web Site: www.shepardpub.com
Key Personnel
Owner & Pres: Aaron Shepard
ISBN Prefix(es): 978-0-938497; 978-1-62035; 978-0-9849616
Number of titles published annually: 4 Print; 6 E-Book
Total Titles: 71 Print; 64 E-Book
Imprints: Islander Images (photography); Islander Press; Next River Books; Shepard & Piper (literary fiction & nonfiction); Simple Productions (nonviolence, lifestyle alternatives, music); Skyhook Press (children's)
Membership(s): Independent Book Publishers Association (IBPA)

Sherman Asher Publishing
126 Candelario St, Santa Fe, NM 87501
Tel: 505-988-7214
E-mail: westernedge@santa-fe.net
Web Site: www.shermanasher.com; www.westernedgepress.com
Key Personnel
Owner & Publr: James Mafchir
Founded: 1995
Literary books that include Spanish, English & bilingual memoirs & Judaica.
ISBN Prefix(es): 978-0-9644196; 978-1-890932
Number of titles published annually: 3 Print
Total Titles: 35 Print
Imprints: Western Edge Press
Distribution Center: SCB Distributors, 15608 S New Century Dr, Gardena, CA 90248 *Tel:* 310-532-9400 *Toll Free Tel:* 800-729-6423 *Fax:* 310-532-7001
See separate listing for:
Western Edge Press

SIAM, see Society for Industrial & Applied Mathematics

Siglio
PO Box 111, Catskill, NY 12414
Tel: 310-857-6935
E-mail: publisher@sigliopress.com
Web Site: sigliopress.com
Key Personnel
Publr: Lisa Pearson
Founded: 2008
Dedicated to publishing uncommon books that live at the intersection of art & literature.
ISBN Prefix(es): 978-0-9799562; 978-1-938221
Number of titles published annually: 4 Print
Total Titles: 38 Print
Distribution Center: Distributed Art Publishers Inc, 75 Broad St, Suite 630, New York, NY 10004 *Tel:* 212-627-1999 *Toll Free Tel:* 800-338-2665 (trade accts) *Fax:* 212-627-9484 *Web Site:* www.artbook.com

Signalman Publishing
3700 Commerce Blvd, Kissimmee, FL 34741
Tel: 407-504-4103 *Toll Free Tel:* 888-907-4423
E-mail: info@signalmanpublishing.com
Web Site: www.signalmanpublishing.com
Key Personnel
Pres: John McClure
Founded: 2008
Specialize in bringing nonfiction works to the Kindle format. Have also branched out into trade paper with both nonfiction & fiction works.
This publisher has indicated that 45% of their product line is author subsidized.
ISBN Prefix(es): 978-0-9840614; 978-1-935991; 978-1-940145
Number of titles published annually: 12 Print; 14 E-Book
Total Titles: 56 Print; 76 E-Book
Imprints: Trinity Grace Press
Orders to: Lightning Source, 1246 Heil Quaker Blvd, La Vergne, TN 37086, Contact: Justine Bylo *Tel:* 212-714-9000 *Fax:* 615-213-4725 *E-mail:* justine.bylo@ingramcontent.com
Shipping Address: Lightning Source, 1246 Heil Quaker Blvd, La Vergne, TN 37086, Contact: Justine Bylo *Tel:* 212-714-9000 *Fax:* 615-213-4725 *E-mail:* justine.bylo@ingramcontent.com
Membership(s): The Association of Publishers for Special Sales (APSS); Christian Small Publishers Association

Signature Books Publishing LLC
564 W 400 N, Salt Lake City, UT 84116-3411

U.S. PUBLISHERS

SAN: 217-4391
Toll Free Tel: 800-356-5687
E-mail: people@signaturebooks.com
Web Site: www.signaturebooks.com; www.signaturebookslibrary.org
Key Personnel
Pres & Co-Founder: George D Smith
Dir: Gary James Bergera
Ed: John Hatch
Busn Mgr: Keiko Jones
Edit Mgr: Ronald L Priddis
Mktg Mgr: Devery S Anderson
Prodn Mgr: Jason Francis
Prodn Asst: Greg Jones
Founded: 1981
Specialize in the promotion of the study of Mormonism.
ISBN Prefix(es): 978-0-941214; 978-1-56085
Number of titles published annually: 7 Print; 4 E-Book
Distribution Center: Chicago Distribution Center, 11030 S Langley Ave, Chicago, IL 60628
Tel: 773-702-7010 *Toll Free Tel:* 800-621-2736 *Toll Free Fax:* 800-621-8476 *E-mail:* orders@press.uchicago.edu *Web Site:* www.press.uchicago.edu

§SIL International
7500 W Camp Wisdom Rd, Dallas, TX 75236-5629
E-mail: publications_intl@sil.org
Web Site: www.sil.org; www.sil.org/resources/publications; www.ethnologue.com
Founded: 1934
Academic organization.
ISBN Prefix(es): 978-0-88312; 978-1-55671
Number of titles published annually: 5 Print; 4 E-Book
Total Titles: 230 Print; 945 Online; 21 E-Book
Subsidiaries: Summer Institute of Linguistics

Silman-James Press Inc
141 N Clark Dr, Unit 1, West Hollywood, CA 90048
Tel: 310-205-0665
E-mail: info@silmanjamespress.com
Web Site: www.silmanjamespress.com
Key Personnel
Publr: Gwen Feldman; Jim Fox
Founded: 1990
Publisher of books on film, filmmaking, the motion picture industry & the performing arts.
ISBN Prefix(es): 978-1-879505; 978-1-935247
Number of titles published annually: 5 Print
Total Titles: 150 Print; 45 E-Book
Divisions: Quite Specific Media; Siles Press (chess & nonfiction titles)
Returns: 660 S Mansfield, Ypsilanti, MI 48197
Warehouse: 660 S Mansfield, Ypsilanti, MI 48197
See separate listing for:
Quite Specific Media Group Ltd

Silver Leaf Books LLC
1661 Washington St, Suite 6460, Holliston, MA 01746-6460
Mailing Address: PO Box 6460, Holliston, MA 01746
E-mail: sales@silverleafbooks.com; editor@silverleafbooks.com; customerservice@silverleafbooks.com
Web Site: www.silverleafbooks.com
Key Personnel
Mng Dir & Dir, Fin: Clifford B Bowyer
E-mail: cbbowyer@silverleafbooks.com
Founded: 2003
ISBN Prefix(es): 978-0-9744354; 978-0-9787782; 978-1-60975
Number of titles published annually: 16 Print; 25 E-Book
Total Titles: 130 Print; 129 E-Book

Simon & Schuster
Imprint of Simon & Schuster Publishing Group
1230 Avenue of the Americas, New York, NY 10020
SAN: 200-2450
Tel: 212-698-7000 *Toll Free Tel:* 800-223-2348 (cust serv); 800-223-2336 (orders)
Toll Free Fax: 800-943-9831 (orders)
Web Site: simonandschusterpublishing.com/simonandschuster/
Key Personnel
Pres & CEO, Publr: Jonathan Karp
 E-mail: jonathan.karp@simonandschuster.com
SVP & Publr, Summit Books: Judy Clain
 E-mail: judy.clain@simonandschuster.com
SVP & Publr, 37 Ink: Dawn Davis *E-mail:* dawn.davis@simonandschuster.com
VP, Assoc Publr: Irene Kheradi *E-mail:* irene.kheradi@simonandschuster.com
VP, Assoc Publr, Publicity & Mktg: Julia Prosser
 E-mail: julia.prosser@simonandschuster.com
VP, Assoc Publr & Dir of Publicity, Summit Books: Josefine Kals *E-mail:* josefine.kals@simonandschuster.com
VP & Ed-in-Chief: Priscilla Painton
 E-mail: priscilla.painton@simonandschuster.com
VP & Edit Dir: Jonathan Jao *E-mail:* jonathan.jao@simonandschuster.com
VP & Edit Dir, Fiction: Tim O'Connell
 E-mail: tim.oconnell@simonandschuster.com
VP & Exec Ed: Eamon Dolan *E-mail:* eamon.dolan@simonandschuster.com; Stephanie Frerich *E-mail:* stephanie.frerich@simonandschuster.com; Mindy Marques *E-mail:* mindy.marques@simonandschuster.com; Sean Manning *E-mail:* sean.manning@simonandschuster.com; Stephen Morrow *E-mail:* stephen.morrow@simonandschuster.com
VP & Exec Art Dir, Trade Art: Jackie Seow
 E-mail: jackie.seow@simonandschuster.com
VP & Dir, Subs Rts: Mike Nardullo
 E-mail: mike.nardullo@simonandschuster.com
Sub Rts Asst Dir: Sandy Hill *E-mail:* sandy.hill@simonandschuster.com
Sub Rts Mgr: Mabel Marte Taveras
 E-mail: mabel.marte.taveras@simonandschuster.com
Dom Rts Mgr/Film & TV Liaison: Lesley Collins
 E-mail: lesley.collins@simonandschuster.com
Exec Ed: Dawn Davis *E-mail:* dawn.davis@simonandschuster.com; Carina Guiterman *E-mail:* carina.guiterman@simonandschuster.com
Exec Ed, Summit Books: Laura Perciasepe
 E-mail: laura.perciasepe@simonandschuster.com
Edit Dir, Saga Press: Joe Monti *E-mail:* joe.monti@simonandschuster.com
Sr Mng Ed: Annie Craig *E-mail:* annie.craig@simonandschuster.com
Mng Ed: Allison Green *E-mail:* allison.green@simonandschuster.com
Assoc Mng Ed: Lauren Gomez *E-mail:* lauren.gomez@simonandschuster.com; Shelby Pumphrey *E-mail:* shelby.pumphrey@simonandschuster.com; Rafael Taveras *E-mail:* rafael.taveras@simonandschuster.com
Asst Mng Ed: Lacee Burr *E-mail:* lacee.burr@simonandschuster.com
Sr Ed: Amara Hoshijo *E-mail:* amara.hoshijo@simonandschuster.com; Yahdon Israel *E-mail:* yahdon.israel@simonandschuster.com; Robert Messenger *E-mail:* robert.messenger@simonandschuster.com; Olivia Taylor Smith *E-mail:* olivia.smith@simonandschuster.com
Ed: Megan Hogan *E-mail:* megan.hogan@simonandschuster.com; Ian Straus *E-mail:* ian.straus@simonandschuster.com; Tzipora Baitch *E-mail:* tzipora.baitch@simonandschuster.com; Hana Park *E-mail:* hana.park@simonandschuster.com; Emily Simonson *E-mail:* emily.simonson@simonandschuster.com
Assoc Ed: Johanna Li *E-mail:* johanna.li@simonandschuster.com
Asst Edit: Maria Mendez *E-mail:* maria.mendez@simonandschuster.com
Asst Ed: Brittany Adames *E-mail:* brittany.adames@simonandschuster.com
Asst Ed, Saga Press/S&S: Jela Lewter
 E-mail: jela.lewter@simonandschuster.com
Edit Asst: Sophia Benz *E-mail:* sophia.benz@simonandschuster.com; Isabel Casares *E-mail:* isabel.casares@simonandschuster.com
Deputy Dir, Publicity: Larry Hughes
 E-mail: larry.hughes@simonandschuster.com; Anne Tate Pearce *E-mail:* anne.pearce@simonandschuster.com
Assoc Dir, Spec Mkts: Lauren Castner
 E-mail: lauren.castner@simonandschuster.com
Asst Dir, Publicity: Margaret Southard
 E-mail: margaret.southard@simonandschuster.com; Elizabeth Herman *E-mail:* elizabeth.herman@simonandschuster.com; Cat Boyd *E-mail:* cat.boyd@simonandschuster.com; Brianna Scharfenberg *E-mail:* brianna.scharfenberg@simonandschuster.com
Sr Publicist: Rebecca Rozenberg *E-mail:* rebecca.rozenberg@simonandschuster.com; Christine Calella *E-mail:* christine.calella@simonandschuster.com; Hannah Bishop *E-mail:* hannah.bishop@simonandschuster.com
Publicist: Shannon Hennessey *E-mail:* shannon.hennessey@simonandschuster.com; Chonise Bass *E-mail:* chonise.bass@simonandschuster.com
Assoc Publicist: Omesha Edwards
 E-mail: omesha.edwards@simonandschuster.com; Martha Langford *E-mail:* martha.langford@simonandschuster.com
Publicity Asst: Cassandra Perez
 E-mail: cassandra.perez@simonandschuster.com
Dir, Digital Opers: Erin Kanar *E-mail:* erin.kanar@simonandschuster.com
VP, Mktg: Stephen Bedford *E-mail:* stephen.bedford@simonandschuster.com
Mktg Dir: Danielle Prielipp *E-mail:* danielle.prielipp@simonandschuster.com
Assoc Dir, Mktg: Elizabeth Venere
 E-mail: elizabeth.venere@simonandschuster.com
Assoc Dir, Mktg, Summit Books: Anna Skrabacz
 E-mail: anna.skrabacz@simonandschuster.com
Sr Mktg Mgr, Adult Lib: Melissa Croce
 E-mail: melissa.croce@simonandschuster.com
Mktg Mgr: Tyanni Niles *E-mail:* tyanni.niles@simonandschuster.com
Digital Mktg Mgr: Andie Schoenfeld
 E-mail: andie.schoenfeld@simonandschuster.com
Independent Retail Mktg Mgr: Liv Stratman
 E-mail: liv.stratman@simonandschuster.com
Mktg Assoc: Savannah Breckenridge
 E-mail: savannah.breckenridge@simonandschuster.com; Emily Farebrother *E-mail:* emily.farebrother@simonandschuster.com
Mgr, Spec Mkts: Caitlin Morrow *E-mail:* caitlin.morrow@simonandschuster.com
Asst Mgr, Spec Mkts: Vanessa Ioannidi
 E-mail: vanessa.ioannidi@simonandschuster.com
Mktg Assoc, Children's Schools & Libraries: Caleigh Flegg *E-mail:* caleigh.flegg@simonandschuster.com
Mktg Coord, Children's Schools & Libraries: Jasmine Normil *E-mail:* jasmine.normil@simonandschuster.com
Sr Art Dir: Alison Forner *E-mail:* alison.forner@simonandschuster.com
Art Dir: Math Monahan *E-mail:* math.monahan@simonandschuster.com
Assoc Art Dir: Natalia Olbinski *E-mail:* natalia.olbinski@simonandschuster.com

PUBLISHERS

Art Asst: Emma Shaw *E-mail:* emma.shaw@simonandschuster.com
Sr Designer: Clay Smith *E-mail:* clay.smith@simonandschuster.com
Founded: 1924
ISBN Prefix(es): 978-0-684
Number of titles published annually: 125 Print
Imprints: Folger Shakespeare Library; Free Press; Saga Press; Summit Books; 37 Ink
Foreign Rights: Ackali Copyright Agency (Turkey); Antonella Antonelli Agenzia (Italy); Book Publishers Association of Israel (Israel); Japan UNI Agency (Japan); JLM Literary Agency (Greece); Korea Copyright Center Inc (KCC) (South Korea); Mohrbooks AG Literary Agency (Germany); La Nouvelle Agence (France); Andrew Nurnberg Associates (Bulgaria, Croatia, Czechia, Estonia, Hungary, Latvia, Lithuania, Montenegro, Poland, Romania, Serbia, Slovakia, Slovenia); Sebes & Bisseling Literary Agency (Netherlands); Tuttle-Mori Agency Inc (Thailand)

Simon & Schuster Audio
Division of Simon & Schuster, LLC
1230 Avenue of the Americas, New York, NY 10020
Web Site: audio.simonandschuster.com
Key Personnel
Pres & Publr: Chris Lynch
VP & Exec Prodr: Elisa Shokoff
VP & Edit Dir: Tom Spain
VP, Pimsleur Language Programs: Tom McLean
VP & Assoc Publr: Sarah Lieberman
Asst Dir, Mktg & Publicity: Lauren Pires
Sr Acqs Ed, Original Audio: Lara Blackman Audiobooks & Pimsleur Language Programs.
ISBN Prefix(es): 978-0-684; 978-0-7435; 978-0-671; 978-1-4423
Number of titles published annually: 500 Audio
Imprints: Audioworks; Beyond Words; Encore; Pimsleur®; Sound Ideas
Distributor for Monostereo
Shipping Address: Total Warehouse Services, 2207 Radcliffe St, Bristol, PA 19007

Simon & Schuster Books for Young Readers,
see Simon & Schuster Children's Publishing

§Simon & Schuster Children's Publishing
Division of Simon & Schuster, LLC
1230 Avenue of the Americas, New York, NY 10020
Tel: 212-698-7000
Web Site: www.simonandschuster.com/kids; www.simonandschuster.com/teen; simonandschuster.net; simonandschuster.biz
Key Personnel
Pres & Publr: Jon Anderson
SVP & Publr, S&S Books for Young Readers, Atheneum, McElderry, Salaam Reads, Caitlyn Dlouhy Books, Denene Millner Books: Justin Chanda
SVP & Publr, Little Simon®, Simon Spotlight®, Aladdin Books, MTV Books: Valerie Garfield
VP & Publr, Beach Lane Books: Allyn Johnston
VP & Publr, Caitlyn Dlouhy Books: Caitlyn Dlouhy
VP & Publr, Denene Millner Books: Denene Millner
VP & Deputy Publr, S&S Books for Young Readers, Atheneum, McElderry, Paula Wiseman, Beach Lane, Caitlyn Dlouhy, Salaam Reads, Denene Millner: Anne Zafian
VP, Edit Dir, McElderry: Karen Wojtyla
VP, Edit Dir, Little Simon® & Ed, Boynton Bookworks: Jeffrey Salane
VP, Edit Dir, Simon Spotlight®: Siobhan Ciminera
VP, Dir, Mng Edit: Katherine Devendorf
Sr Dir, Mgr Edit, Beach Lane, Paula Wiseman, S&S Books for Young Readers, McElderry, Atheneum: Dorothy Gribbin
Assoc Dir, Mng Edit, Simon Spotlight®, Libros para ninos, Little Simon®, Boynton Bookworks, Aladdin, Simon Pulse, MTV Books: Christina Solazzo
Assoc Dir, Mng Edit, S&S Books for Young Readers, Paula Wiseman, McElderry: Jenica Nasworthy
Assoc Publr, S&S Children's Licensed, Novelty & Branded Publg: Anna Jarzab
Edit Dir, S&S Books for Young Readers: Kendra Levin
Edit Dir, Atheneum: Reka Simonsen
Edit Dir, Aladdin: Kristin Gilson
Edit Dir, Sarah Barley Books: Sarah Barley
Dir, Branded Publg & Ed, MTV Books: Kara Sargent
Brand Mgr, Simon Spotlight®: Tishana Williams
Exec Ed, Aladdin: Allyson Heller
Exec Ed, Beach Lane Books: Andrea Welch
Exec Ed, Little Simon®: Hannah Lambert
Exec Ed, S&S Books for Young Readers: Celia Lee; Krista Vitola
Exec Ed, Simon Spotlight®: Karen Nagel
Sr Mng Ed, Simon Spotlight®, Little Simon®, Libros para ninos: Christine Marshall
Sr Ed: Alexa Pastor
Sr Ed, Aladdin Books: Jessica Smith
Sr Ed, Beach Lane Books: Catherine Laudone
Sr Ed, McElderry: Sarah McCabe
Sr Ed, S&S Books for Young Readers: Nicole Ellul
Sr Ed, S&S Books for Young Readers, Salaam Reads: Deeba Zargarpur
Sr Ed, Simon Spotlight®: Beth Barton; Lisa Lauria
Ed, Atheneum: Julia McCarthy; Feather Flores; Sophia Jimenez
Ed, McElderry: Kate Prosswimmer
Ed, S&S Books for Young Readers: Alyza Liu
VP & Creative Dir: Dan Potash
Exec Art Dir, Atheneum, McElderry, Beach Lane: Sonya Chaghatzbanian
Exec Art Dir, Little Simon®, Simon Spotlight®: Laura Roode
Exec Art Dir, S&S Books for Young Readers, Paula Wiseman Books, Denene Millner Books: Lucy Cummins
Exec Art Dir, Aladdin: Karin Paprocki
Art Dir, McElderry: Greg Stadnyk
Art Dir, Little Simon®, Simon Spotlight®: Leslie Mechanic
Assoc Art Dir: Laura Eckes; Brittany Fetcho
Assoc Art Dir, Atheneum, McElderry, Beach Lane: Rebecca Syracuse
VP, Subs Rts: Stephanie Voros
Sr Dir, Subs Rts: Amy Habayeb
VP, Dir of Mktg: Chrissy Noh
VP, Dir of Educ & Lib Mktg: Michelle Leo
Sr Mktg Dir, S&S Books For Young Readers, Salaam Reads, Atheneum, Caitlyn Dlouhy Books, Paula Wiseman Books, Beach Lane Books, Denene Millner Books: Erin Toller
Sr Mktg Dir, Aladdin, Little Simon®, Simon Spotlight®, McElderry, Boynton Bookworks: Caitlin Sweeny
Dir, Digital Mktg: Ashley Mitchell
Asst Dir, Digital Mktg, Kids: Nadia Almahdi
VP, Dir of Publicity: Lisa Moraleda
Sr Dir, Publicity, Aladdin, Little Simon®, Simon Spotlight®, Paula Wiseman Books: Nicole Russo
Dir, Publicity: Tara Shanahan; Alex Kelleher
Exec Dir, Design & Emerging Tech, Little Simon®, Simon Spotlight®, McElderry: Nick Sciacca
VP, Prodn Dir: Martha Hanson
Dir, Prodn: Julie Doebler
Dir, Prodn/Creative Solutions: Elizabeth Blake-Linn
Assoc Dir, Prodn: Chava Wolin
Preschool through young adult, hardcover & paperback fiction, nonfiction, trade, library, mass market titles & novelty books.
ISBN Prefix(es): 978-0-02; 978-0-609; 978-0-689; 978-0-7434; 978-1-4169
Number of titles published annually: 750 Print
Total Titles: 4,329 Print
Imprints: Aladdin Books (includes chapter books, middle grade fiction, series, graphic novels); Atheneum Books for Young Readers (picture books, middle grade & teen fiction & nonfiction); Sarah Barley Books; Beach Lane Books (picture books; includes Paula Wiseman Books backlist); Boynton Bookworks; Caitlyn Dlouhy Books; Little Simon® (preschool & novelty); Margaret K McElderry Books (picture books, middle grade, teen & fantasy fiction); Denene Millner Books (books for all ages on the Black American experience); MTV Books (young adult, in partnership with MTV Entertainment); Salaam Reads (books for all ages on the Muslim experience); Simon & Schuster Books for Young Readers (picture books, chapter books, middle grade & teen fiction & nonfiction); Simon Spotlight® (beginning readers, licensed publishing)

§Simon & Schuster, LLC
1230 Avenue of the Americas, New York, NY 10020
SAN: 200-2450
Tel: 212-698-7000 *Toll Free Tel:* 800-223-2336 (orders) *Fax:* 212-698-7007 *Toll Free Fax:* 800-943-9831 (orders)
E-mail: firstname.lastname@simonandschuster.com; purchaseorders@simonandschuster.com (orders)
Web Site: www.simonandschuster.com
Key Personnel
Pres & CEO, Publr, S&S Trade: Jonathan Karp
 E-mail: jonathan.karp@simonandschuster.com
EVP & COO: Dennis Eulau
EVP & CFO: Allen Lindstrom
EVP & Gen Coun: Veronica Jordan
Pres & Publr, Simon & Schuster Audio: Chris Lynch
Pres & Publr, Simon & Schuster Canada: Nicole Winstanley
Pres & Publr, Simon & Schuster Children's Publishing: Jon Anderson
SVP & Publr, Atria Publishing Group: Libby McGuire
SVP & Publr, Gallery Publishing Group: Jennifer Bergstrom
SVP & Publr, Scribner: Nan Graham
SVP & Publr, Summit Books: Judy Clain
SVP & Publr, 37 Ink: Dawn Davis
VP & Publr, Adams Media: Karen Cooper
VP & Publr, Avid Reader Press: Jofie Ferrari-Adler
CEO, VBK (Veen Bosch & Keuning): Genevieve Waldmann
Chief Exec & Publr, Simon & Schuster UK Ltd: Ian Chapman
Mng Dir, Simon & Schuster (Australia) Pty Ltd: Dan Ruffino
Mng Dir, Simon & Schuster India: Rahul Srivastava
SVP, Global Chief Mktg & Communs Offr: Wibke Grutjen
SVP, Simon & Schuster Publr Servs: Michael Perlman *Tel:* 212-698-7061 *E-mail:* michael.perlman@simonandschuster.com
SVP, Corp Devt & Busn Opers: Doug Stambaugh
VP, HR: David Snow
VP, Sr Coun: Felice Javit
VP, Prodn Strategy & Opers: Samantha Cohen
VP, Busn Devt: Joe Bulger
VP, Opers & Dist Servs: Pat Kelman
VP, Warehouse Opers (Jackson): Bradley Batcher
VP, Dir of Educ & Lib Mktg: Michelle Leo
VP, Contracts: Lourdes Lopez

U.S. PUBLISHERS

VP & Exec Dir, Subs Rts, Adult Imprints: Nicole Bond
VP, Mktg: Sienna Farris
VP, Dir, Technol & Prod: Stephen Morgan
VP, Ad & Creative Servs: Rick Pascocello
SVP, Sales: Kim Shannon
VP, Independent Retail Sales: Wendy Sheanin *Tel:* 212-698-7359
VP & Dir, Children's Sales: Christina Pecorale *Tel:* 212-698-1126
VP, Digital & Online Sales: Ali Cutrone
VP, Spec Sales: Nicole Vines Verlin *Tel:* 212-698-7409
VP, Dist Client Sales: Kim Gray *Tel:* 212-698-2192
VP, Dir, Sales Opers & Client Servs: Eileen Gentillo *Tel:* 212-698-7470
VP, Email Mktg: Adam Feifer
Exec Dir, Prodn: Lisa Erwin
Dir, Workplace Culture & Diversity Initiatives: Amanda Armstrong-Frank
Dir, Ad, Promo & Creative Servs: Molly Weissman
Dir, Dist & Logistics: Lori Perino
Founded: 1924
ISBN Prefix(es): 978-1-55850; 978-0-02; 978-0-941831; 978-1-885223; 978-0-7867; 978-0-13; 978-1-878990; 978-0-07; 978-0-7318; 978-0-669; 978-0-86417; 978-1-58062; 978-1-58180; 978-0-88708; 978-0-7434; 978-1-58270; 978-1-86842; 978-0-7435; 978-1-4169; 978-1-4165; 978-1-59337; 978-0-89256; 978-0-9674601; 978-0-9711953; 978-1-58229; 978-1-59309; 978-1-60061; 978-1-84737; 978-1-84738; 978-1-84739; 978-0-684; 978-0-7432; 978-0-689; 978-0-671; 978-1-4391; 978-1-903650; 978-1-4423; 978-1-4424; 978-1-4516; 978-1-84983; 978-0-9870685; 978-0-85720; 978-0-85707; 978-1-62266; 978-1-4711; 978-1-4767; 978-1-4814; 978-1-922052; 978-1-925030; 978-0-85783; 978-0-85941; 978-0-87605; 978-1-5011; 978-1-925184; 978-1-59869; 978-1-60550; 978-1-4405; 978-1-939867; 978-1-925310; 978-1-5082; 978-1-925368; 978-1-925456; 978-1-5072; 978-1-4403; 978-1-5344; 978-1-936399; 978-1-925533; 978-1-925596; 978-1-925640; 978-1-935562; 978-1-935562; 978-81-933552; 978-81-933552; 978-1-925750; 978-1-925791; 978-1-9821; 978-93-86797; 978-93-86797; 978-1-76085; 978-1-925048; 978-1-925685; 978-1-902421; 978-1-7971; 978-0-6481008; 978-0-6482267; 978-0-9924565; 978-992-4563; 978-1-6659; 978-1-6680; 978-1-76110; 978-1-76142; 978-1-935165; 978-1-946289; 979-1-946464; 978-1-947520; 978-1-950571; 978-1-951317; 978-93-92099
Branch Office(s)
Beach Lane Books, 5666 La Jolla Blvd, No 154, La Jolla, CA 92037 *Tel:* 858-551-0860 *Fax:* 858-551-0492
Pimsleur Language Programs, Damonmill Sq, 9 Pond Lane, Suite 6B, Concord, MA 01742 *Tel:* 978-369-7525
Adams Media, 100 Technology Center Dr, Suite 501, Stoughton, MA 02072 *Tel:* 508-427-7100
1639 Rte 10 E, Parsippany, NJ 07054 (royalties, accts payable, fin) *Tel:* 973-656-6000 *Fax:* 973-656-6070
Simon & Schuster Canada, 166 King St E, Suite 300, Toronto, ON M5A 1J3, Canada *Tel:* 647-427-8882 *Fax:* 647-430-9446
Foreign Office(s): Simon & Schuster (Australia) Pty Ltd, Suite 19a, Level 1, Bldg C, 450 Miller St, Cammeray, NSW 2062, Australia *Tel:* (02) 9983 6600 *Fax:* (02) 9988 4232 (edit, sales & mktg) *E-mail:* pr@simonandschuster.com.au *Web Site:* www.simonandschuster.com.au
Simon & Schuster India, 163, Tower A, The Corenthum, A -41, Sector -62, Noida 201301, India *Tel:* (0120) 4089 389 *Fax:* (0120) 4089 301 *E-mail:* enquiries@simonandschuster.co.in *Web Site:* www.simonandschuster.co.in
Veen Bosch & Keuning Uitgeversgroep BV, Herculesplein 94, 3584 AA Utrecht, Netherlands *Tel:* (088) 700 2600 *E-mail:* info@vbku.nl *Web Site:* www.vbku.nl
Simon & Schuster UK Ltd, 222 Gray's Inn Rd, 1st fl, London WC1X 8HB, United Kingdom *Tel:* (020) 7316-1900 *Fax:* (020) 7316-0332 *E-mail:* uk.sales@simonandschuster.co.uk *Web Site:* www.simonandschuster.co.uk
Distributor for Aconyte; AHOY Comics; Alexander Lowen Foundation; American Girl Publishing; Andrews McMeel Publishing LLC; Applesauce Press; Arctis Books USA; Artists, Writers & Artisans; Authors Equity; Baen Books; Baseball America; Behemoth Entertainment; BenBella Books Inc; Black Mask Studios; Boom! Studios; Callisto Media; Canterbury Classics; Cardoza Publishing; Centennial Media; Central Avenue Publishing; Cernunnos; Chicken Soup for the Soul Publishing; City Point Press; Cold Spring Press; The Collective Book Studio; Dark Ink; David Zwirner Books; Devil's Due Comics; Diversion Books; Downtown Bookworks; ECW Press; 80/20 Publishing; Evil Eye Concepts; Fabled Films LLC; Fabled Films Press LLC; Fantoons; Flame Tree Publishing; Forefront Books; Frederator Books LLC; Gakken; Gallup Press; Galvanized Media; Games Workshop; Hallmark Publishing; Hampton Creek Press; Hazelden Publishing; Health Communications Inc; Heavy Metal Entertainment; Hooked on Phonics; Humanoids Inc; Igloo Books; Image Comics; Indigo River Publishing; Insight Editions; Interlink Publishing; Inimitable Books; Juniper Publishing; Kaplan Publishing; Katalitix; Keenspot; Keeperton; Kinfolk; Lake Press; Law & Crime; Leaders Press; Legendary Comics; Libra Press; Library Tales Publishing; little bee books; Little Genius Books; Mad Cave Studios; Manhattan Prep; Manning Publications; Mattel Press; Merck Publishing Group; NorthSouth Books; Omnific Publishing; Oneworld Publications; Oni Press; Open Road Publications; Page & Vine; Papercutz; Pegasus Books; Permuted Press LLC; Petzel Gallery; Piggyback Interactive; Pikachu Press; Pike and Powder; The Pokemon Company International; Portable Press; Post Hill Press LLC; powerHouse Books; Printers Row Publishing Group; Reader's Digest Children's Books; Rebellion; Red 5 Comics; Regan Arts; Regnery Books; Ripley; Rise Books; Rising Action Publishing Co; Rocketship Entertainment; Rockpool Publishing; Rodin Books; Row House Press; Ryland Peters & Small; Scout Comics; She Writes Press; Silver Dolphin; Skyhorse Publishing; Source Point Press; SparkPress; Start Publishing LLC; Studio Fun; Sublime; Tanglewood Books; Thunderbay Press; To The Stars; Tra Publishing; Trusted Media Brands; Ulysses Press; Uncrate LLC; Vault Comics; VeloPress Books; Viz Media LLC; Waterhouse Press; Weldon Owen; Winged Hussar Publishing; Wisdom; World Almanac (div of Facts on File); Yilin Press; YoYo Books USA; Zaffre Books; Z2 Comics; Zuiker Press
Returns: American Book Co, 10267 Kingston Pike, Knoxville, TN 37922
Warehouse: Riverside Distribution Center, 100 Front St, Riverside, NJ 08075 (trade, children's, audio, mass-market & dist clients), VP, Warehouse Opers & Logistics: Diane Lalli *Tel:* 856-461-6500 *Fax:* 856-824-2402
Jackson Distribution Facility, 55 Gerdau Rd, Jackson, TN 38305, VP, Warehouse Opers & Logistics: Bradley Bratcher *Tel:* 731-574-9182 *Fax:* 731-574-9190
Membership(s): Association of American Publishers (AAP); Book Industry Study Group (BISG)
See separate listing for:
Adams Media
Avid Reader Press
Simon & Schuster Audio
Simon & Schuster Children's Publishing

Simon Spotlight®, see Simon & Schuster Children's Publishing

§Sinauer Associates
Imprint of Oxford University Press (OUP)
Oxford University Press Higher Education, 2001 Evans Rd, Cary, NC 27513
Toll Free Tel: 800-280-0280 *Fax:* 919-678-1435
E-mail: highered.us@oup.com; custserv.us@oup.com
Web Site: sinauer.com
Founded: 1969
College textbooks & reference works in the biological & behavioral sciences.
ISBN Prefix(es): 978-0-87893; 978-1-60535
Number of titles published annually: 10 Print
Total Titles: 100 Print; 10 CD-ROM; 7 Online
Foreign Rep(s): Oxford University Press ANZ (Australia, New Zealand); Oxford University Press Canada (Canada); Oxford University Press Hong Kong (Hong Kong); Oxford University Press India (India); Oxford University Press Japan (Japan); Oxford University Press Malaysia (Malaysia, Singapore); Oxford University Press UK (Africa exc South Africa, Europe, Middle East, UK); Oxford University Press USA (worldwide exc Africa, Australia, Canada, Europe, Hong Kong, India, Japan, Malaysia, New Zealand, Singapore, South Korea & UK); Shinil Books Co Ltd (South Korea); World Science Publishing Co (South Korea)

§SkillPath Publications
Division of The Graceland University Center for Professional Development & Lifelong Learning Inc
6900 Squibb Rd, Mission, KS 66202
Mailing Address: PO Box 2768, Mission, KS 66201-2768
Tel: 913-362-3900 *Toll Free Tel:* 800-873-7545 *Fax:* 913-362-4241
E-mail: customercare@skillpath.com; products@skillpath.com
Web Site: www.skillpath.com
Founded: 1989
Books, audio programs, computer based training.
ISBN Prefix(es): 978-1-878542; 978-1-57294; 978-1-929874; 978-1-934589; 978-1-60811
Number of titles published annually: 4 Print
Total Titles: 124 Print; 26 Audio
Divisions: CompuMaster
Branch Office(s)
8300 Lawson Rd, Milton, ON L9T 0A4, Canada
Web Site: www.skillpath.ca
Distributor for Franklin Covey; Pearson Technology; Thomson Publishing; John Wiley & Sons Inc

Skinner House Books
Imprint of Unitarian Universalist Association
c/o Unitarian Universalist Assn, 24 Farnsworth St, Boston, MA 02210-1409
Tel: 617-742-2100 *Fax:* 617-948-6466
E-mail: skinnerhouse@uua.org
Web Site: www.uua.org/publications/skinnerhouse
Key Personnel
Edit Dir: Mary Benard *Tel:* 617-948-4603
 E-mail: mbenard@uua.org
Pubns Assoc Dir: Joni McDonald *Tel:* 617-948-4602 *E-mail:* jmcdonald@uua.org
Ed: Larisa Hohenboken *Tel:* 617-948-4660
 E-mail: lhohenboken@uua.org
Mktg Assoc: Pierce Alquist *Tel:* 617-948-4646
 E-mail: palquist@uua.org
Edit Asst: Kiana Nwaobia *Tel:* 617-948-4644
 E-mail: knwaobia@uua.org
Founded: 1975
Specialize in spirituality, inspirational literature, books on church resources for religious liberals.
ISBN Prefix(es): 978-0-933840; 978-1-55896

Number of titles published annually: 15 Print; 15 E-Book
Total Titles: 265 Print
Sales Office(s): inSpirit: The UU Book & Gift Shop, 24 Farnsworth St, Boston, MA 02210 *Toll Free Tel:* 800-215-9076 (orders) *E-mail:* bookstore@uua.org
Returns: inSpirit: The UU Book & Gift Shop, c/o PSSC, 46 Development Rd, Fitchburg, MA 01420
Distribution Center: Consortium Book Sales & Distribution, The Keg House, Suite 101, 34 13 Ave NE, Minneapolis, MN 55413-1007 *Tel:* 612-746-2600 *E-mail:* cbsdinfo@ingramcontent.com *Web Site:* www.cbsd.com SAN: 200-6049

Sky Pony Press
Imprint of Skyhorse Publishing Inc
307 W 36 St, 11th fl, New York, NY 10018
Tel: 212-643-6816 *Fax:* 212-643-6819
E-mail: info@skyhorsepublishing.com; skyponysubmissions@skyhorsepublishing.com
Web Site: www.skyhorsepublishing.com/sky-pony-press
Key Personnel
Pres & Publr: Tony Lyons *E-mail:* tlyons@skyhorsepublishing.com
Founded: 2011
ISBN Prefix(es): 978-1-61145; 978-1-60239; 978-1-61608; 978-1-62087; 978-1-62636; 978-1-63220; 978-1-62914; 978-1-62873; 978-1-5107; 978-1-63158; 978-1-63450
Number of titles published annually: 100 Print
Total Titles: 800 Print
Foreign Rights: Biagi Literary Management (Linda Biagi) (worldwide)
Orders to: Simon & Schuster, LLC, 1230 Avenue of the Americas, New York, NY 10020 (intl orders) *Toll Free Tel:* 800-223-2336 *Fax:* 212-698-7616 *Web Site:* www.simonandschuster.biz/c/biz-international-sales; Simon & Schuster, LLC, Order Processing Dept, 100 Front St, Riverside, NJ 08075 *Toll Free Tel:* 800-223-2336 *Toll Free Fax:* 800-943-9831 *E-mail:* orders@simonandschuster.com

SkyLight Paths® Publishing
Imprint of Turner Publishing Co LLC
4507 Charlotte Ave, Suite 100, Nashville, TN 37209
SAN: 134-5621
Tel: 615-255-BOOK (255-2665) *Fax:* 615-255-5081
E-mail: marketing@turnerpublishing.com
Web Site: www.skylightpaths.com; www.turnerpublishing.com
Key Personnel
Pres & Publr, Turner Publishing Co: Todd Bottorff
Founded: 1999
General trade books for seekers & believers of all faith traditions. Subject areas include spirituality, children's, self-help, crafts, interfaith, spiritual living, eastern & western religion.
ISBN Prefix(es): 978-1-893361; 978-1-59473
Number of titles published annually: 5 Print; 5 E-Book
Total Titles: 350 Print; 350 E-Book

§SLACK® Incorporated, A Wyanoke Group Company
6900 Grove Rd, Thorofare, NJ 08086-9447
SAN: 201-8632
Tel: 856-848-1000 *Toll Free Tel:* 800-257-8290 *Fax:* 856-848-6091
E-mail: sales@slackinc.com; editor@slackinc.com; customerservice@slackinc.com
Web Site: www.healio.com/books
Key Personnel
Chief Prod Offr: April Underwood
Chief Sales Offr: Mike Graziani
VP, Digital Innovation & Busn Devt: Christine Martynick
VP, Mktg & Audience Devt: Lee Gaymon
VP, Mktg, Health Care Books & Journals: Michelle Gatt
Edit Dir: Katrina Altersitz Wells
Edit Dir, Health Care Books & Journals: Karen G Stanwood
Head, Global Mktg: Kelly Watkins
Exec Ed: John Schoen
Mng Ed: Gina Brockenbrough
Founded: 1960
Academic textbooks & professional reference books: medicine, occupational therapy, physical therapy, ophthalmology, gastroenterology, orthopedics, athletic training, pediatrics, nursing & other areas.
ISBN Prefix(es): 978-1-55642
Number of titles published annually: 35 Print; 35 E-Book
Total Titles: 250 Print; 250 E-Book
Foreign Rep(s): Eurospan (Europe); Login Canada (Canada)
Foreign Rights: John Scott Co
Advertising Agency: Alcyon Advertising
Distribution Center: 200 Richardson Ave, Bldg B, Swedesboro, NJ 08085

Sleeping Bear Press™
Imprint of Cherry Lake Publishing Group (CLPG)
2395 S Huron Pkwy, Suite 200, Ann Arbor, MI 48104
Toll Free Tel: 800-487-2323 *Fax:* 734-794-0004
E-mail: customerservice@sleepingbearpress.com
Web Site: www.sleepingbearpress.com
Key Personnel
CEO: Ben Mondloch
Publr: Heather Hughes
Mgr, Publicity: Julia Hlavac *E-mail:* julia.hlavac@sleepingbearpress.com
Sales & Mktg: Amy Patrick *E-mail:* amy.patrick@sleepingbearpress.com
Founded: 1998
Publisher of children's books infants to young adults.
ISBN Prefix(es): 978-1-57504; 978-1-886947; 978-1-58536
Number of titles published annually: 40 Print
Total Titles: 500 Print
Membership(s): The American Library Association (ALA); Association of Children's Booksellers; International Literacy Association (ILA)

§Small Beer Press
150 Pleasant St, No 306, Easthampton, MA 01027
Tel: 413-240-4197
E-mail: info@smallbeerpress.com
Web Site: smallbeerpress.com
Key Personnel
Founder & Publr: Gavin J Grant
Founder: Kelly Link
CTO: Michael J Deluca
Founded: 2000
Closed to submissions.
ISBN Prefix(es): 978-1-931520; 978-1-61873
Number of titles published annually: 8 Print; 10 E-Book
Total Titles: 100 Print; 150 E-Book
Sales Office(s): Consortium Book Sales & Distribution, The Keg House, Suite 101, 34 13 Ave N, Minneapolis, MN 55413-1007 *Tel:* 612-746-2600 *Toll Free Tel:* 866-400-5351 (cust serv, Jackson, TN) *E-mail:* cbsdinfo@ingramcontent.com *Web Site:* www.cbsd.com SAN: 200-6049
Foreign Rights: CookeMcDermid Literary Management (Ron Eckel) (worldwide)
Billing Address: Consortium Book Sales & Distribution, The Keg House, Suite 101, 34 13 Ave N, Minneapolis, MN 55413-1007 *Tel:* 612-746-2600 *Toll Free Tel:* 866-400-5351 (cust serv, Jackson, TN) *E-mail:* cbsdinfo@ingramcontent.com *Web Site:* www.cbsd.com SAN: 200-6049
Orders to: Consortium Book Sales & Distribution, The Keg House, Suite 101, 34 13 Ave N, Minneapolis, MN 55413-1007 *Tel:* 612-746-2600 *Toll Free Tel:* 866-400-5351 (cust serv, Jackson, TN) *E-mail:* cbsdinfo@ingramcontent.com *Web Site:* www.cbsd.com SAN: 200-6049
Returns: Consortium Book Sales & Distribution, The Keg House, Suite 101, 34 13 Ave N, Minneapolis, MN 55413-1007 *Tel:* 612-746-2600 *Toll Free Tel:* 866-400-5351 (cust serv, Jackson, TN) *E-mail:* cbsdinfo@ingramcontent.com *Web Site:* www.cbsd.com SAN: 200-6049
Shipping Address: Consortium Book Sales & Distribution, The Keg House, Suite 101, 34 13 Ave N, Minneapolis, MN 55413-1007 *Tel:* 612-746-2600 *Toll Free Tel:* 866-400-5351 (cust serv, Jackson, TN) *E-mail:* cbsdinfo@ingramcontent.com *Web Site:* www.cbsd.com SAN: 200-6049
Warehouse: Consortium Book Sales & Distribution, The Keg House, Suite 101, 34 13 Ave N, Minneapolis, MN 55413-1007 *Tel:* 612-746-2600 *Toll Free Tel:* 866-400-5351 (cust serv, Jackson, TN) *E-mail:* cbsdinfo@ingramcontent.com *Web Site:* www.cbsd.com SAN: 200-6049
Distribution Center: Consortium Book Sales & Distribution, The Keg House, Suite 101, 34 13 Ave N, Minneapolis, MN 55413-1007 *Tel:* 612-746-2600 *Toll Free Tel:* 866-400-5351 (cust serv, Jackson, TN) *E-mail:* cbsdinfo@ingramcontent.com *Web Site:* www.cbsd.com SAN: 200-6049
Membership(s): PEN America; Science Fiction and Fantasy Writers of America, Inc (SFWA)

Small Business Advisors Inc
2005 Park St, Atlantic Beach, NY 11509
Tel: 516-374-1387 *Fax:* 516-374-1175
E-mail: info@smallbusinessadvice.com
Web Site: www.smallbusinessadvice.com
Key Personnel
CEO & Founder: Joe Gelb *E-mail:* joe@smallbusinessadvice.com
VP, Admin: Arthur VanDam *E-mail:* arthurvandam1@gmail.com
Contact: Barbara Goetz *E-mail:* barbara@smallbusinessadvice.com
Founded: 1991
Publisher of books, ebooks & blogs on small business, finance & marketing/copyrighting.
ISBN Prefix(es): 978-1-890158
Number of titles published annually: 4 Print
Total Titles: 20 Print; 1 Audio
Membership(s): The American Library Association (ALA); Association of Accredited Small Business Consultants (AASBC); Independent Book Publishers Association (IBPA)

§SME (Society of Manufacturing Engineers)
1000 Town Ctr, Suite 1910, Southfield, MI 48075
SAN: 203-2376
Tel: 313-425-3000 *Toll Free Tel:* 800-733-4763 (cust serv) *Fax:* 313-425-3400
E-mail: publications@sme.org
Web Site: www.sme.org
Key Personnel
Exec Dir & CEO: Robert Willig *Tel:* 313-425-3100 *E-mail:* rwillig@sme.org
Dir, Prof Devt: Jeannine Kunz
E-Libn: Carol Tower *Tel:* 313-425-3288 *E-mail:* ctower@sme.org
Books & TU Billing Serv: Maria Mukavitz *Tel:* 313-425-3028
Founded: 1932
Professional engineering association.
ISBN Prefix(es): 978-0-87263; 978-1-62104
Number of titles published annually: 3 Print
Total Titles: 150 Print; 21 CD-ROM
Branch Office(s)
7100 Woodbine Ave, Suite 312, Markham, ON L3R 5J2, Canada *Tel:* 905-752-4415 *Toll Free Tel:* 888-322-7333 *Fax:* 905-479-0113 *E-mail:* canadasales@sme.org

U.S. PUBLISHERS

Distributed by American Technical Publishers Inc; McGraw-Hill; Productivity Press
Distributor for Industrial Press; McGraw-Hill; Prentice Hall; John Wiley & Sons Inc
Foreign Rights: American Technical Publishers (UK); DA Books Pty Ltd (Australia); Elsevier Science Publishers (Netherlands)

Smith & Kraus Publishers Inc
177 Lyme Rd, Hanover, NH 03755
Mailing Address: PO Box 32, Newton, IL 62448
Tel: 618-783-0519 Toll Free Tel: 877-668-8680
Fax: 618-783-0520
E-mail: editor@smithandkraus.com; info@smithandkraus.com; customerservice@smithandkraus.com
Web Site: www.smithandkraus.com
Key Personnel
Co-Founder: Eric Kraus
Co-Founder & Publr: Marisa Smith
Founded: 1990
Drama books, monologues, books of interest to our theatrical community, play anthologies.
ISBN Prefix(es): 978-0-9622722; 978-1-880399; 978-1-57525
Number of titles published annually: 84 Print
Total Titles: 500 Print
Imprints: In an Hour Books LLC (playwrights); Smith & Kraus Books For Kids (young adult fiction)
Subsidiaries: Smith & Kraus Global (world affairs)

§M Lee Smith Publishers
Division of BLR®—Business & Legal Resources
100 Winners Circle, Suite 300, Brentwood, TN 37027
Mailing Address: PO Box 5094, Brentwood, TN 37024-5094
Tel: 615-373-7517 Toll Free Tel: 800-274-6774; 800-727-5257
E-mail: custserv@mleesmith.com; service@blr.com
Web Site: www.mleesmith.com; www.blr.com
Key Personnel
CFO: Lawton Miller
VP, Legal: Brad Forrister
Founded: 1975
Legal newsletters/legal book related titles.
ISBN Prefix(es): 978-0-925773; 978-1-60029; 978-0-9605796
Number of titles published annually: 130 Print
Total Titles: 2 CD-ROM; 60 Online

Smithsonian Institution Scholarly Press
Division of Smithsonian Institution
Aerospace Bldg, 704-A, MRC 957, Washington, DC 20013
Mailing Address: PO Box 37012, Washington DC, DC 20013-7012
Tel: 202-633-3017 Fax: 202-633-6877
E-mail: schol_press@si.edu
Web Site: scholarlypress.si.edu
Key Personnel
Prog Asst: Stephanie Summerhays
Founded: 1966
General trade & adult nonfiction.
ISBN Prefix(es): 978-0-87474; 978-1-56098; 978-0-9788460; 978-1-935623; 978-1-944466
Number of titles published annually: 8 Print
Total Titles: 800 Print
Distributed by Penguin Random House LLC

§Smyth & Helwys Publishing Inc
6316 Peake Rd, Macon, GA 31210-3960
Tel: 478-757-0564 Toll Free Tel: 800-747-3016 (orders only) Fax: 478-757-1305
E-mail: information@helwys.com
Web Site: www.helwys.com
Key Personnel
Pres & CEO: Cecil P Staton, Jr
Publr & EVP: Keith Gammons E-mail: keith@helwys.com
Ed, Adult Formations: Darrell Pursiful E-mail: darrell@helwys.com
Ed, Connection Series: Michael L Ruffin E-mail: michael@helwys.com
Ed, Reflections: Carol Younger E-mail: carol@helwys.com
Founded: 1990
Christian books, literature, Sunday school books (curriculum).
ISBN Prefix(es): 978-1-880837; 978-0-9628455; 978-1-57312
Number of titles published annually: 30 Print
Total Titles: 330 Print
Foreign Rep(s): Grace Wing Publishers (England)

Snow Lion
Imprint of Shambhala Publications Inc
4720 Walnut St, Boulder, CO 80301
E-mail: customercare@shambhala.com
Web Site: www.shambhala.com/snowlion
Key Personnel
Pres: Nikko Odiseos E-mail: nodiseos@shambhala.com
Founded: 1980
Trade & scholarly books on Tibetan Buddhism & Tibet.
ISBN Prefix(es): 978-0-937938; 978-1-55939
Number of titles published annually: 20 Print; 20 E-Book
Total Titles: 350 Print; 250 E-Book; 1 Audio

Society for Human Resource Management (SHRM)
1800 Duke St, Alexandria, VA 22314
Tel: 703-548-3440 Toll Free Tel: 800-283-7476 (orders)
E-mail: books@shrm.org
Web Site: www.shrm.org
Key Personnel
Mgr, Book Publg: Matthew Davis
Founded: 1948
Professional association with more than 275,000 members in over 160 countries.
ISBN Prefix(es): 978-1-58644
Number of titles published annually: 12 Print; 12 E-Book
Total Titles: 134 Print; 71 E-Book; 1 Audio
Foreign Rights: Russo Rights (worldwide exc USA)

§Society for Industrial & Applied Mathematics
3600 Market St, 6th fl, Philadelphia, PA 19104-2688
Tel: 215-382-9800 Toll Free Tel: 800-447-7426
E-mail: siam@siam.org
Web Site: www.siam.org
Key Personnel
Exec Dir: Suzanne L Weeks
Pubns Dir: Kivmars H Bowling
Prodn Mgr: Donna Gibbons
Pubns Mgr: Mitch Chernoff
Exec Ed: Elizabeth Greenspan
Mng Ed: Kelly Thomas
Sr Pubns Coord: Heather Blythe
Prodn Coord: Cally Shrader
Founded: 1952
Journals, books, conferences & reprints in mathematics/computer science/statistics/physical science.
ISBN Prefix(es): 978-0-89871; 978-1-61197
Number of titles published annually: 20 Print
Total Titles: 450 Print; 400 E-Book

§Society for Mining, Metallurgy & Exploration
12999 E Adam Aircraft Circle, Englewood, CO 80112
Tel: 303-948-4200 Toll Free Tel: 800-763-3132 Fax: 303-973-3845
E-mail: cs@smenet.org; books@smenet.org
Web Site: www.smenet.org
Key Personnel
Exec Dr: Dave Kanagy
Sr Ed: Bill Gleason Tel: 303-948-4234 E-mail: gleason@smenet.org; Georgene Renner Tel: 303-948-4254 E-mail: renner@smenet.org
Pubns Ed: Steve Kral Tel: 303-948-4245 E-mail: kral@smenet.org
Founded: 1871
Publish mining related monthly magazine, quarterly journal, trade books, hardbound & paperback.
ISBN Prefix(es): 978-0-87335
Number of titles published annually: 3 Print; 5 E-Book
Total Titles: 80 Print; 15 CD-ROM
Foreign Rep(s): Affiliated East-West Press Pvt Ltd (India); Australian Mineral Foundation (Australia)

Society of American Archivists
17 N State St, Suite 1425, Chicago, IL 60602-4061
SAN: 211-7614
Tel: 312-606-0722 Toll Free Tel: 866-722-7858 Fax: 312-606-0728
Web Site: www.archivists.org
Key Personnel
Edit & Prodn: Abigail Christian E-mail: achristian@archivists.org
Founded: 1936
Archival literature; preservation.
ISBN Prefix(es): 978-0-931828; 978-1-931666
Number of titles published annually: 5 Print
Total Titles: 72 Print

Society of Automotive Engineers International, see SAE (Society of Automotive Engineers International)

Society of Biblical Literature, see SBL Press

Society of Environmental Toxicology & Chemistry (SETAC)
229 S Baylen St, 2nd fl, Pensacola, FL 32502
Tel: 850-469-1500 Toll Free Fax: 888-296-4136
E-mail: setac@setac.org
Web Site: www.setac.org
Key Personnel
Pubns Mgr: Jennifer Lynch Tel: 850-469-1500 ext 109 E-mail: jen.lynch@setac.org
Founded: 1979
Supports publications of scientific value relating to environmental topics. Proceedings of technical workshops that explore current & prospective environmental issues are published as peer-reviewed technical documents. Publications are used by scientists, engineers & managers because of their technical basis & comprehensive, state-of-the-science reviews; association press; nonprofit, professional society.
Journal publications co-published with John Wiley & Sons. Some books jointly published with CRC Press or John Wiley & Sons.
ISBN Prefix(es): 978-1-880611
Number of titles published annually: 2 Print; 1 CD-ROM; 2 Online; 2 E-Book
Total Titles: 105 Print; 5 CD-ROM; 3 Online; 2 E-Book
Imprints: SETAC Press
Foreign Office(s): Av de la Toison d'Or 67 b 6, 1060 Brussels, Belgium Tel: (02) 772 72 81 Fax: (02) 770 53 86 E-mail: setaceu@setac.org

§Society of Exploration Geophysicists
8801 S Yale Ave, Suite 500, Tulsa, OK 74137
Tel: 918-497-5500 Fax: 918-497-5557
E-mail: web@seg.org
Web Site: www.seg.org
Key Personnel
Assoc Exec Dir, Knowledge Mgmt: Ted Bakamjian Tel: 918-497-5506 E-mail: tbakamjian@seg.org

Dir, Journals & Books: Jennifer Cobb *Tel:* 918-497-5537 *E-mail:* jcobb@seg.org
Founded: 1930
Textbooks, videos, technical journals, magazines & meeting papers.
ISBN Prefix(es): 978-1-56080; 978-0-931830
Number of titles published annually: 5 Print; 5 Online; 5 E-Book
Total Titles: 87 Print; 9 CD-ROM; 141 Online; 141 E-Book
Shipping Address: 8801 S Yale Ave, Suite 110, Tulsa, OK 74137
Distribution Center: Eurospan, Gray's Inn House, 127 Clerkenwell Rd, London EC1R 5DB, United Kingdom *Tel:* (020) 3286 2420

Society of Manufacturing Engineers, see SME (Society of Manufacturing Engineers)

The Society of Naval Architects & Marine Engineers (SNAME)
99 Canal Center Plaza, Suite 310, Alexandria, VA 22314
SAN: 202-0572
Tel: 703-997-6701 *Toll Free Tel:* 800-798-2188 *Fax:* 703-997-6702
Web Site: www.sname.org
Key Personnel
Exec Dir: Gene Sanders *Tel:* 703-997-6704 *E-mail:* gsanders@sname.org
Dir, Mktg & Communs: Val Hutnan *Tel:* 703-997-6709 *E-mail:* vhutnan@sname.org
Mktg & Communs Coord: Deryck White *Tel:* 703-997-6711 *E-mail:* dwhite@sname.org
Reference books, directories, periodicals, technical research reports & bulletins on naval architecture, marine engineering & ocean engineering.
ISBN Prefix(es): 978-0-9603048; 978-0-939773; 978-1-941762
Number of titles published annually: 4 Print
Total Titles: 29 Print
Foreign Office(s): c/o ELKCO Marine Consultants, 61, Poseidonos Ave, Paleo Faliro, 175 62 Attica, Greece *Tel:* 210 452 8205 *Fax:* 210 452 8202

Soho Press Inc
853 Broadway, New York, NY 10003
SAN: 202-5531
Tel: 212-260-1900
E-mail: soho@sohopress.com; publicity@sohopress.com
Web Site: sohopress.com
Key Personnel
Publr: Bronwen Hruska *E-mail:* bhruska@sohopress.com
Assoc Publr: Juliet Grames
VP & Dir, Mktg & Publicity: Paul Oliver *E-mail:* poliver@sohopress.com
VP & Exec Ed: Mark Doten *E-mail:* mdoten@sohopress.com
VP & Dir, Mktg: Rudy Martinez *E-mail:* rmartinez@sohopress.com
Art Dir: Janine Agro
Dir, Sales: Steven Tran
Mng Ed: Rachel Kowal
Ed & Publicist: Alexa Wejko
Assoc Ed: Taz Urnov; Nick Whitney
Digital Mktg Mgr: Kevin Murphy *E-mail:* kmurphy@sohopress.com
Sr Publicist: Abby Koski; Erica Loberg
Assoc Publicist: Lily Detaeye
Mktg Asst: Emma Levy
Founded: 1986 (first books published in 1987)
Hard & softcover trade books: fiction, mysteries, general nonfiction, history & social history.
ISBN Prefix(es): 978-0-939149; 978-1-56947; 978-1-61695
Number of titles published annually: 90 Print; 68 E-Book
Total Titles: 350 Print

Imprints: Hell's Hundred (horror); Soho Crime; Soho Press; Soho Teen
Foreign Rights: ACER Agencia Literaria (Elizabeth Atkins) (Spain); AnatoliaLit Agency (Amy Spangler) (Turkey); English Agency Japan Co Ltd (Corinne Shioji) (Japan); Grayhawk Agency (Gray Tan) (Taiwan); Deborah Harris Agency (Ilana Kurshan) (Israel); International Editors Co (Flavia Sala) (Brazil); Leonardt & Hoier Literary Agency (Anneli Hoier) (Denmark, Finland, Norway, Sweden); Michael Meller Literary Agency (Franka Zastrow) (Germany); Jan Michael (Belgium, Netherlands); Daniela Micura Literary Services (Italy); PLS (Publishing Language Service) (Yang Young Chul) (South Korea); Prava i prevodi (Nada Popovic) (Bulgaria, Croatia, Czechia, Estonia, Hungary, Latvia, Lithuania, Poland, Romania, Russia, Serbia, Slovakia, Slovenia); Read n Right Agency (Nike Davarinou) (Greece)
Orders to: Penguin Random House Publisher Services (PRHPS), 400 Hahn Rd, Westminster, MD 21157 *Toll Free Tel:* 800-733-3000; 800-669-1536 (electronic orders) *Toll Free Fax:* 800-659-2436 *Web Site:* prhpublisherservices.com SAN: 631-760X; Penguin Random House Canada, 2775 Matheson Blvd E, Mississauga, ON L4W 4P7, Canada *Toll Free Tel:* 888-523-9292; 800-258-4233 (electronic orders) *Toll Free Fax:* 888-562-9924
Distribution Center: Penguin Random House Publisher Services (PRHPS), 400 Hahn Rd, Westminster, MD 21157 *Toll Free Tel:* 800-733-3000; 800-669-1536 (electronic orders) *Toll Free Fax:* 800-659-2436 *Web Site:* prhpublisherservices.com SAN: 631-760X; Penguin Random House Canada, 2775 Matheson Blvd E, Mississauga, ON L4W 4P7, Canada *Toll Free Tel:* 888-523-9292; 800-258-4233 (electronic orders) *Toll Free Fax:* 888-562-9924

Soil Science Society of America (SSSA)
5585 Guilford Rd, Madison, WI 53711-5801
Tel: 608-273-8080 *Fax:* 608-273-2021
Web Site: www.soils.org
Key Personnel
CEO: Nicholas J Goeser, PhD *Tel:* 608-327-9034
CFO: Wes Meixelsperger *Tel:* 608-268-4958
Dir of Publns: Matt Wascavage *Tel:* 608-819-3916
Mng Ed, Books, Monographs, Spec Pubns, Methods of Soil Sciences: Danielle Lynch *Tel:* 608-268-4976
Founded: 1936
Technical books for professionals in soil science.
ISBN Prefix(es): 978-0-89118
Number of titles published annually: 6 E-Book
Total Titles: 90 Print

§Solano Press Books
PO Box 773, Point Arena, CA 95468
Tel: 707-884-4508 *Toll Free Tel:* 800-931-9373
E-mail: spbooks@solano.com
Web Site: www.solano.com
Key Personnel
Acqs Ed: Natalie Macris *Tel:* 415-533-1399 *E-mail:* nmacris@solano.com
Founded: 1985
Professional books: law, public administration, real estate, land use, environment, urban planning, environmental analysis & management.
ISBN Prefix(es): 978-0-9614657; 978-0-923956; 978-1-938166
Number of titles published annually: 4 Print
Total Titles: 25 Print; 8 E-Book

Solution Tree
555 N Morton St, Bloomington, IN 47404
Tel: 812-336-7700 *Toll Free Tel:* 800-733-6786 *Fax:* 812-336-7790

E-mail: pubs@solutiontree.com; orders@solutiontree.com
Web Site: www.solutiontree.com
Key Personnel
Chief Mktg Offr: Erica Dooley-Dorocke *E-mail:* erica.dooley-dorocke@solutiontree.com
VP, Sales: Joan Brooks *Tel:* 800-733-6786 ext 472 *E-mail:* joan.brooks@solutiontree.com
Founded: 1998
Works to transform education worldwide by empowering educators to raise student achievement. With more than 48,962 educators attending professional learning events & more than 5,500 professional development days in schools each year, Solution Tree helps teachers & administrators confront essential challenges. Solution Tree has a catalog of more than 500 titles, hundreds of videos & online courses & is the creator of Global PD, an online tool that facilitates the work of professional learning communities for more than 20,000 educators.
ISBN Prefix(es): 978-1-879639; 978-1-932127
Number of titles published annually: 45 Print; 45 E-Book
Total Titles: 500 Print; 420 E-Book; 4 Audio
Imprints: Solution Tree Press
Branch Office(s)
Solution Tree Education Canada, PO Box 3250, Mission, BC V2V 4J4, Canada, Exec Dir, Busn Devt & Opers: Chris Allen *Toll Free Tel:* 800-733-6786 ext 023 *E-mail:* chris.allen@solutiontree.com

Somerset Hall Press
416 Commonwealth Ave, Suite 612, Boston, MA 02215
Tel: 617-236-5126
E-mail: info@somersethallpress.com
Web Site: www.somersethallpress.com
Key Personnel
Publr: Dean Papademetriou
Founded: 2001
Independent press specializing in literary & scholarly titles with a special interest in Greek studies.
ISBN Prefix(es): 978-0-9724661; 978-0-9774610; 978-1-935244
Number of titles published annually: 3 Print
Total Titles: 40 Print

Soncino Press Ltd
123 Ditmas Ave, Brooklyn, NY 11218
Tel: 718-972-6200 *Toll Free Tel:* 800-972-6201 *Fax:* 718-972-6204
E-mail: info@soncino.com
Web Site: www.soncino.com
Key Personnel
Pres: Gloria Goldman
Mng Ed: Norman Shapiro
Bible, Talmud & Judaism.
ISBN Prefix(es): 978-1-871055; 978-0-900689
Number of titles published annually: 20 Print
Total Titles: 100 Print

Sophia Institute Press®
18 Celina Ave, Unit 1, Nashua, NH 03063
Mailing Address: PO Box 5284, Manchester, NH 03108 SAN: 657-7172
Tel: 603-641-9344 *Toll Free Tel:* 800-888-9344 *Fax:* 603-641-8108 *Toll Free Fax:* 888-288-2259
E-mail: orders@sophiainstitute.com
Web Site: www.sophiainstitute.com
Key Personnel
Pres: Charlie McKinney
VP, Mktg: Tom Allen
Dir, Prodn: Sheila M Perry
Dir, Sales: Molly Russo
Founded: 1983
Books on religion (Roman Catholicism).
ISBN Prefix(es): 978-0-918477; 978-1-928832; 978-1-933184

U.S. PUBLISHERS

Number of titles published annually: 102 Print
Total Titles: 400 Print
Foreign Rep(s): Cenacle House Ltd (UK); Family Life International (New Zealand); John XXIII Fellowship (Australia); Redemptorist Publications (UK); St Joseph's Workshops (Canada); Sunrise Marion Center (Canada)

§Soul Mate Publishing
3210 Sherwood Dr, Walworth, NY 14568
Web Site: www.soulmatepublishing.com
Key Personnel
Founder & Sr Ed: Deborah Gilbert
   E-mail: debby@soulmatepublishing.com
Founded: 2011
ISBN Prefix(es): 978-1-61935
Number of titles published annually: 100 E-Book
Total Titles: 15 Print; 120 E-Book
Membership(s): Romance Writers of America (RWA)

§Sound Feelings Publishing
18375 Ventura Blvd, No 8000, Tarzana, CA 91356
Tel: 818-757-0600
E-mail: information@soundfeelings.com
Web Site: www.soundfeelings.com
Key Personnel
Founder & Pres: Howard Richman
This publisher has indicated that 80% of their product line is author subsidized.
ISBN Prefix(es): 978-0-9615963; 978-1-882060
Number of titles published annually: 3 Print; 3 E-Book; 2 Audio
Total Titles: 15 Print; 10 E-Book; 11 Audio
Foreign Rep(s): Gazelle Book Services Ltd (Europe)

Sounds True Inc
413 S Arthur Ave, Louisville, CO 80027
Tel: 303-665-3151 Toll Free Tel: 800-333-9185 (US); 888-303-9185 (US & CN)
E-mail: customerservice@soundstrue.com; stpublicity@soundstrue.com
Web Site: www.soundstrue.com
Key Personnel
Founder & Publr: Tami Simon
Assoc Publr: Jaime Schwalb
VP, Opers: Wendy Pardo
Sr Art Dir: Rachael Murray
Edit Dir: Sarah Stanton
Exec Ed: Jennifer Brown
Acqs Ed: Melissa Valentine; Angela Wix
Children's Acq Ed: Jen Adams
Developmental Ed: Lyric Dodson
Freelance Ed-at-Large: Caroline Pincus
Asst Ed: Sahar Al-Nima
Opers Mgr: April Sargent
Prod Mktg Mgr: Jaclyn Hawkins; Chloe Prusiewicz
Publicity Mgr: Nick Small
Founded: 1985
ISBN Prefix(es): 978-1-56455; 978-1-59179; 978-1-60407; 978-1-62203
Number of titles published annually: 30 Print; 30 E-Book; 40 Audio
Total Titles: 200 Print; 150 E-Book; 800 Audio
Distributed by Macmillan

§Sourcebooks LLC
1935 Brookdale Rd, Suite 139, Naperville, IL 60563
SAN: 666-7864
Mailing Address: PO Box 4410, Naperville, IL 60567-4410
Tel: 630-961-3900 Toll Free Tel: 800-432-7444
Fax: 630-961-2168
E-mail: info@sourcebooks.com
Web Site: www.sourcebooks.com
Key Personnel
Publr & CEO: Dominique Raccah
Pres: Barbara Briel
SVP & Chief Digital Officer: Mike Zuccato
SVP & Publr, Children's Books: Jennifer Gonzalez
SVP & Edit Dir: Todd Stocke Tel: 630-536-0543 E-mail: todd.stocke@sourcebooks.com
SVP, Sales: Paula Amendolara
VP & Cont: Michael Zarley
VP & Dir, Publg Sales: Sarah Cardillo
VP, Intl Sales: Shawn Abraham
VP, Sales, Natl & Independent Retail Accts: Sean Murray
Exec Dir, Mktg, Fiction: Molly Waxman
Exec Dir, Online Mktg: Kavita Wright
Sr Art Dir: John Aardema; Angela Navarra; Heather VenHuizen
Sr Art Dir, Children's: Celeste Knudson
Sr Art Dir, Fiction: Erin Fitzsimmons
Sr Art Dir, Sourcebooks Kids: Maryn Arreguin
Sr Creative Dir, Adult & Young Adult: Kelly Lawler
Sr Dir, Content Devt, Custom & Proprietary Sales: Alexis Banyon
Sr Dir, Data & Analytics: Christy Droege
Sr Dir, HR: Rebecca Johnson
Sr Dir, Mktg, Adult Nonfiction: Kayleigh George
Sr Dir, Mktg, Retail Mktg & Creative Sales: Valerie Pierce Tel: 630-961-3900 ext 233 E-mail: valerie.pierce@sourcebooks.com
Sr Dir, Mktg, Sourcebooks Kids: Heather Moore E-mail: heather.moore@sourcebooks.com
Sr Dir, Publicity & Brand Mktg: Pamela Jaffee
Sr Dir, Sales, Schools, Lib & Indie Bookstores: Margaret Coffee
Sr Dir, Sales, Natl Accts: Tracy Nelson
Sr Edit Dir, Sourcebooks & Sourcebooks Landmark: Shana Drehs Tel: 630-536-0535 E-mail: shana.drehs@sourcebooks.com
Art Dir: Sarah Sisterson
Art Dir, Children's: Sarah Boecher; Allison Sundstrom
Art Dir, Nonfiction: Jillian Rahn
Creative Dir, Children's: Jordan Kost
Creative Dir, Retail Mktg & Creative Servs: Jenna Quatraro
Dir, Analytics: Jess Johns
Dir, E-Commerce & Performance Mktg: Katia Herrera
Dir, Independent Retail Sales: Courtney Payne
Dir, Mktg & Publicity, Sourcebooks Fire: Karen Masnica
Dir, Mktg, Nonfiction & Mystery: Liz Kelsch
Dir, Publg Opers Technol: Tina George
Dir, Spec Mkts & Gift Sales: Christina Noriega
Edit Dir: Mabel Hsu; Ben Rosenthal
Edit Dir, Bloom Books: Christa Desir
Edit Dir, duopress: Mauricio Velazquez de Leon
Edit Dir, Sourcebooks & Poisoned Pen Press: Anna Michels
Edit Dir, Sourcebooks Casablanca: Deb Werksman Tel: 203-876-9790 E-mail: deb.werksman@sourcebooks.com
Edit Dir, Sourcebooks Fire, Sourcebooks Jabberwocky & Sourcebooks Young Readers: Jenne Abramowitz
Edit Dir, Sourcebooks Jabberwocky (nonfiction) & Sourcebooks eXplore: Kelly Barrales-Saylor
Edit Opers Dir: Lynn Sikora
Intl Sales Dir: Andy Augusto
Assoc Mng Dir, duopress: Michele Suchomel-Casey
Assoc Art Dir: Sarah Brody; Michelle Mayhall; Stephanie Rocha
Assoc Art Dir, Adult Nonfiction: Heather Morris
Assoc Art Dir, Bloom Books: Nicole Lecht
Assoc Creative Dir, Calendars & Gift: Brittany Vibbert
Assoc Dir, Cust Experience: Bonnie Svoboda
Assoc Dir, Intl Mktg & Publicity: Shannon McCain
Assoc Dir, Mktg & Publicity, Children's Books: Shara Zaval
Assoc Dir, Publicity & Mktg, Sourcebooks Landmark: Cristina Arreola
Assoc Dir, Sales, Mass Mdse Adult: Raquel Latko
Assoc Dir, Sales, Mass Mdse Kids: Jess Elliott
Assoc Dir, Subs Rts: Marleen Reimer
Assoc Dir, Talent Acq: Gigi Curran
Assoc Dir, Training & Devt: Kay Birkner
Asst Edit Dir, Sourcebooks Casablanca & Poisoned Pen Press: Mary Altman
Sr Mng Ed: Bret Kehoe
Mng Ed: Heather Hall
Assoc Mng Ed: Kelsey Fenske; Eliza Smith; Jessica Thelander
Exec Ed: Annie Berger
Exec Ed, Sourcebooks Jabberwocky: Melissa Manlove
Sr Ed: MJ Johnston
Sr Ed, Bloom Books: Shaina Olmanson
Sr Ed, Nonfiction: Ariel Curry
Sr Ed, Sourcebooks Jabberwocky, Sourcebooks Young Readers & Sourcebooks Fire: Wendy McClure
Sr Ed, Simple Truths: Meg Gibbons
Sr Prodn Ed: Chelsey Moler Ford; Emily Proano; Katrina "Katy" Turner
Ed: Jenna Jankowski
Ed, Bloom Books: Gretchen Stelter
Ed, Sourcebooks eXplore: Anna Sargeant
Ed-at-Large, Children's: Steve Geck Tel: 212-414-1701 ext 2226 E-mail: steve.geck@sourcebooks.com
Prodn Ed: India Hunter; Renee Letz
Prodn Ed, Bloom Books & Sourcebooks Casablanca: Shannon Barr
Prodn Ed, Children's: Nicholas Sweeney
Assoc Ed: Rachel Gilmer; Emma Hintzen; Kate Roddy
Assoc Prodn Ed: Sarah George; Ellie Tiemens
Asst Content Ed: Rachel Gilmer
Asst Ed: Taylor Geldermann; Jocelyn Travis
Asst Ed, Adult Fiction & Nonfiction: Liv Turner
Asst Ed, Bloom Books: Letty Mundt
Asst Ed, Children's & Young Adult: Gabbi Calabrese; Jenny Lopez
Asst Proj Ed: Julia Steffy
Sr Acctg Mgr, Royalties & Accts Receivables: Jessica Ogg
Sr Mgr, Cust Experience: Margaret Kelly
Sr Mktg Mgr: BrocheAroe Fabian
Sr Mktg Mgr, Bloom Books & Casablanca: Maranda Seney
Sr Mktg Mgr, Events: Monica Palenzuela
Sr Mktg Mgr, Sourcebooks Casablanca & Sourcebooks Fire: Beth Sochacki
Sr Online Sales Mgr: Trent Harmon
Sr Publicity & Mktg Mgr: Siena Koncsol
Sr Publg Mgr, Wonderland: Karen Shapiro
Sr Purch Mgr: Deve McLemore
Acctg Mgr, Callisto: Anthony DeLuca
Communs Mktg Mgr: Audrey Barsella
Edit Mgr, Illustration & Art Servs: Kerry Finnamore
Mktg Mgr: Tiffany Schultz
Mktg & Publicity Mgr, Bloom Books & Sourcebooks Casablanca: Brittany Pearlman
Natl Accts Mgr: Teresa Devanzo
Natl Accts Mgr, Gift & Regl: Liz Otte
Natl Sales Mgr, Gift & Specialty: Stephanie Levasseur
Prodn Mgr, Backlist: Lin Miceli
Publg Opers Mgr, Sourcebooks Kids: April Wills
Sales & Mktg Mgr, Intl: Sophie Kossakowski
Assoc Digital Mktg Mgr: Allison Lewis; Morgan Vogt
Assoc Digital Mktg Mgr, Spec Projs: Alexandra Derdall
Assoc Mktg Mgr, Bloom Books: Madison Nankervis
Assoc Mktg Mgr, Bloom Books & Sourcebooks Casablanca: Katie Stutz
Assoc Mktg Mgr, Sourcebooks Casablanca: Alyssa Garcia
Assoc Natl Accts Mgr: Jackie Olmos
Asst Busn Mgr: Cari Zwolinski
Asst Design Mgr, Digital: Viridiana Contreras

Asst Mktg & Publicity Mgr: Rebecca Atkinson
Asst Sales Mgr: Keri Haddrill
Sr Sales Coord: Carrie Conlisk
Custom Sales Coord: Cecilia Petee
Ebook Prodn Coord: Ashley Holstrom; Jessica Zulli
Intl Sales Coord: Lismarie Cuevas
Mktg Coord, Bloom Books & Sourcebooks Casablanca: Tianna Kelly
Spec Mkts Sales Coord: Morgan Pfeiffer
Subs Rts Coord: Liz Logback
Asst Digital Mktg Coord: Kelsey Kulp
Asst Publg Coord, Children's Fiction & Nonfiction: Olivia Haase
Sr Data Scientist: Drew French
Sr Mktg Assoc: Madeleine Brown; Amy Jackson
Mktg Specialist, Retail & Creative Servs: Emily Luedloff
Digital Mktg Assoc: Zoya Boskovic
Mktg Assoc: Cana Clark; Anna Venckus
Mktg Assoc, Sourcebooks Fire: Jackie Douglass
Mktg & Soc Media Assoc: Delaney Heisterkamp; Michelle Lecumberry
Performance Mktg Assoc: Zaina Maswood
Sales Assoc: Timothy Foszcz; Alexa Rosenberg
Mktg Specialist: Caitlin Lawler
Metadata Strategy Specialist: Jennifer Sterkowitz
Sr Book Designer: Jessica Nordskog
Sr Designer: Hannah DiPietro; Stephanie Gafron; Antoaneta "Ant" Georgieva; Danielle McNaughton; Amanda Skolek
Designer: Hannah Strassburger
E-Commerce Digital Designer: Dave Schmitt
Graphics Designer: Charlie McGroarty
Prodn Designer III: Laura Boren
Prodn Designer II: Diane Cunningham; Rosie Gaynor; Tara Jaggers
Prodn Designer I: Milly McKinnish
Prodn Designer I, Callisto: Jeffrey Piekarz
Prodn Designer: Anna Campbell
Buyer II: Lori Bigham; Maddie Herr; Erin LaPointe
Print Buyer III: Michelle Denney
Print Buyer II: Emma Grant
Print Buyer III, Packaging, Spec Projs & Progs: Cristina Wilson
Digital Content Specialist: Katie Cooper
Tech Support Specialist II: Shane Saldana
Sr Busn Analyst: Lauren McClearn
Sr Staff Accountant: Ian Cook
Sr Systems Developer: Darren Orange
Developer: Benjamin Sherrard
Cyber Security Engr: Rafik Dayem
Data Engr: Rama Kandel
Application Developer II: Jay Farahani
Systems Analyst II: Anthony Feliciano
Sr Mktg Assoc, Callisto: Hannah Kil
Acctg Assoc: Zuha Mohammed; Nate Rapach
Accts Payable Assoc: Claudette Soriano
Subs Rts & Intl Sales Assoc: Sophia Ramos
Mktg Asst: Lucy Marcum
Mktg Asst, Bloom Books: Alexis Boni
Mktg Asst, Bloom Books & Sourcebooks Casablanca: Diana Schmidt
Publg Mktg Asst: Corrin Bronersky
Cust Experience Order Specialist: Ashley Delaney
Cust Experience Rep II: Megan O'Brien; Anthony Perez; Peter Racenis; Rachael Renner
Cust Experience Rep: Sonja Holzman; Sonja Meigs; Jordan Payne
HR Generalist: Priscilla Tellez
Founded: 1987
Nonfiction, fiction, romance, mystery, horror, children's books, young adult, gift books & calendars.
ISBN Prefix(es): 978-0-942061; 978-1-57071; 978-1-57248; 978-0-913825; 978-1-883518; 978-0-9629162; 978-1-887166; 978-1-4022; 978-1-4926; 978-1-7282
Number of titles published annually: 500 Print; 350 E-Book
Total Titles: 5,000 Print; 2,500 E-Book
Imprints: Bloom Books; Callisto; Cumberland House™ (cookbooks & bartending); duopress; Hometown World; Little Pickle Press (children's nonfiction); Poisoned Pen Press (mystery, thriller, horror); Put Me In The Story; Simple Truths (busn & personal devt); Sourcebooks (adult nonfiction & ref); Sourcebooks Casablanca (romance fiction); Sourcebooks eXplore (children's nonfiction); Sourcebooks Fire (young adult); Sourcebooks Jabberwocky (children's books); Sourcebooks Kids; Sourcebooks Landmark (adult fiction); Sourcebooks Wonderland; Sourcebooks Young Readers
Branch Office(s)
18 Cherry St, Suite 1W, Milford, CT 06460
Tel: 203-876-9790
Sourcebooks New York, 232 Madison Ave, Suite 805, New York, NY 10018 *Tel:* 212-414-1701
Distributed by Penguin Random House India (India & subcontinent)
Distributor for DK Ltd (Europe & UK)
Foreign Rights: Eliane Benisti Literary Agency (Eliane Benisti) (France); The Deborah Harris Agency (Israel); Inter-Ko (South Korea); International Editors' Co - Yanez Agencia Literaria (Spain); Nurcihan Kesim Literary Agency Ltd (Turkey); Maxima Creative Agency (Indonesia); Piergiorgio Nicolazzini (Italy); Nova Littera Ltd (Russia); Prava i prevodi (Eastern Block, Slovakia); Schindler's Literary Agency (Brazil); Tuttle-Mori Agency Inc (Japan, Thailand)
Returns: LSC Communications, Attn: Sourcebooks Returns, 677 Brighton Beach Rd, Menasha, WI 54952
Warehouse: LSC Communications, N9234 Lake Park Rd, Appleton, WI 54915 *Tel:* 920-969-6400 *Fax:* 920-969-6441
Distribution Center: Baker & Taylor Global Publishers Services (GPS), 2550 W Tyvola Rd, Chicago, IL 28217 *E-mail:* gps@baker-taylor.com
Raincoast Books, 2440 Viking Way, Richmond, BC V6V 1N2, Canada *Toll Free Tel:* 800-663-5714 *Toll Free Fax:* 800-565-3770 *E-mail:* info@raincoast.com
See separate listing for:
Poisoned Pen Press

Sourced Media Books
15 Via Picato, San Clemente, CA 92673
Tel: 949-813-0182
E-mail: editor@sourcedmediabooks.com
Web Site: sourcedmediabooks.com
Key Personnel
Publr: Amy Cook, PhD; Jennifer Durrant
Sr Ed: J'Nel Wright
Founded: 2009
ISBN Prefix(es): 978-0-9841068; 978-1-937458
Number of titles published annually: 10 Print; 15 Online; 15 E-Book
Total Titles: 45 Print; 18 Online; 18 E-Book
Distributed by Gibbs-Smith; Many Hats Media
Distribution Center: Brigham Distributing, 110 S 800 W, Brigham City, UT 84302

§South Carolina Bar
1501 Park St, Columbia, SC 29201
Mailing Address: PO Box 608, Columbia, SC 29202-0608
Tel: 803-799-6653 *Toll Free Tel:* 800-768-7787
E-mail: scbar-info@scbar.org
Web Site: www.scbar.org
Key Personnel
Continuing Legal Educ Dir: Terry Burnett
 Tel: 803-799-6653 ext 152 *E-mail:* tburnett@scbar.org
Pubns Dir: Alicia Chandler Hutto *Tel:* 803-576-3819 *E-mail:* ahutto@scbar.org
Pubns Coord: Alyssia Jay *Tel:* 803-771-0333 ext 126
Founded: 1979
Law materials, legal treatises, manuals & software.
ISBN Prefix(es): 978-0-943856
Number of titles published annually: 12 Print; 25 E-Book
Total Titles: 100 Print; 25 E-Book

South Dakota Historical Society Press
900 Governors Dr, Pierre, SD 57501
Tel: 605-773-6009 *Fax:* 605-773-6041
E-mail: info@sdhspress.com; orders@sdhspress.com
Web Site: sdhspress.com
Key Personnel
Dir & Ed-in-Chief: Dedra McDonald Birzer, PhD
 Tel: 605-773-4371 *E-mail:* Dedra.Birzer@state.sd.us
Mng Ed: Slater Sabo, MA *Tel:* 605-773-6008
 E-mail: Slater.Sabo@state.sd.us
Assoc Ed: Craig Walters *Tel:* 605-773-8380
 E-mail: Craig.Walters@state.sd.us
Founded: 1997
The South Dakota Historical Society Press is committed to producing books that reflect the rich & varied history of South Dakota & the region.
ISBN Prefix(es): 978-0-9622621; 978-0-9715171; 978-0-9749195; 978-0-9777955; 978-0-9798940; 978-0-9845041; 978-0-9846505; 978-0-9852905; 978-0-9860355; 978-1-941813; 978-0-9822749; 978-0-9852817
Number of titles published annually: 7 Print; 2 E-Book; 2 Audio
Total Titles: 100 Print; 20 E-Book; 4 Audio
Foreign Rep(s): Eurospan Group (worldwide exc North America)
Membership(s): Association of University Presses (AUPresses); Western Writers of America (WWA)

South Platte Press
PO Box 163, David City, NE 68632-0163
Tel: 402-367-3554
E-mail: railroads@windstream.net
Web Site: www.southplattepress.net
Key Personnel
Publr: James J Reisdorff
Founded: 1982
Railroad related titles.
ISBN Prefix(es): 978-0-942035
Number of titles published annually: 5 Print
Total Titles: 25 Print

Southern Historical Press Inc
375 W Broad St, Greenville, SC 29601
Mailing Address: PO Box 1267, Greenville, SC 29602-1267
Tel: 864-233-2346
E-mail: southernhistoricalpress@gmail.com
Web Site: www.southernhistoricalpress.com
Key Personnel
Pres: LaBruce M S Lucas
Founded: 1967
Historical & genealogical books.
ISBN Prefix(es): 978-0-89308
Number of titles published annually: 20 Print
Total Titles: 370 Print

Southern Illinois University Press
Division of Southern Illinois University
1915 University Press Dr, SIUC Mail Code 6806, Carbondale, IL 62901-4323
SAN: 203-3623
Tel: 618-453-2281 *Fax:* 618-453-1221
E-mail: rights@siu.edu
Web Site: www.siupress.com
Key Personnel
Dir: Amy Etcheson *Tel:* 618-453-6623
 E-mail: aetcheson@siu.edu
Acqs Ed/Rts & Perms Mgr: Kristine Priddy
 Tel: 618-453-6631 *E-mail:* mkpriddy@siu.edu
Founded: 1956
Scholarly nonfiction, educational material, rhetoric & composition, aviation, history, theatre, regional history & poetry.
ISBN Prefix(es): 978-0-8093

U.S. PUBLISHERS

Number of titles published annually: 30 Print; 30 E-Book
Total Titles: 1,400 Print; 2 CD-ROM; 400 E-Book; 17 Audio
Foreign Rep(s): Eurospan (Andrew Wong) (Europe, Middle East); Scholarly Book Services Inc (Laura Rust) (Canada)
Distribution Center: Chicago Distribution Center, 11030 S Langley Ave, Chicago, IL 60628-3830 *Toll Free Tel:* 800-621-2736 *Toll Free Fax:* 800-621-8476
Membership(s): Association of University Presses (AUPresses)

Southwestern Publishing House Inc, see Capen Publishing Co Inc

Soyinfo Center
1021 Dolores Dr, Lafayette, CA 94549-0234
SAN: 212-8411
Tel: 925-283-2991
Web Site: www.soyinfocenter.com
Key Personnel
Pres & Ed-in-Chief: William Shurtleff
Founded: 1976
Books & bibliographies on all aspects of soybeans & soyfoods; industry & marketing studies. 90 books since 2008 published in PDF format on the web free of charge.
ISBN Prefix(es): 978-0-933332; 978-1-928914; 978-1-948436
Number of titles published annually: 10 Print; 10 Online
Total Titles: 162 Print; 60 Online

Spanish House Inc, see Editorial Unilit

Sparkhouse, see Augsburg Fortress Publishers, Publishing House of the Evangelical Lutheran Church in America

Sparkhouse Family, see Augsburg Fortress Publishers, Publishing House of the Evangelical Lutheran Church in America

SPIE
1000 20 St, Bellingham, WA 98225-6705
Mailing Address: PO Box 10, Bellingham, WA 98227-0010
Tel: 360-676-3290 *Toll Free Tel:* 888-504-8171 (orders) *Fax:* 360-647-1445
E-mail: help@spie.org; customerservice@spie.org (orders)
Web Site: www.spie.org
Key Personnel
Pubns Dir: Eric Pepper *Tel:* 360-685-5473
 E-mail: eric@spie.org
Pubns Busn Devt Mgr: Mary Summerfield
 Tel: 360-685-5588 *E-mail:* marysu@spie.org
SPIE Press Mgr: Tim Lamkins *Tel:* 360-685-5475
 E-mail: timl@spie.org
Journals Mgr: Karolyn Labes *Tel:* 360-685-5421
 E-mail: karolyn@spie.org
Founded: 1955
Scientific, technical books & journals, proceedings of symposia.
ISBN Prefix(es): 978-0-8194
Number of titles published annually: 30 Print; 400 Online; 30 E-Book
Total Titles: 400 Print; 407 E-Book
Imprints: Proceedings of SPIE (spie.org/publications/conference-proceedings); SPIE Digital Library (www.spiedigitallibrary.org); SPIE Journals (spie.org/publications/spie-journals); SPIE Press (spie.org/publications/books)
Foreign Rep(s): Applied Media (India); Eurospan (Europe, Middle East, North Africa); Princeton Selling Group (Canada, USA)

Foreign Rights: Applied Media (India)
Membership(s): Copyright Clearance Center (CCC); Crossref; Society for Scholarly Publishing (SSP)

SPIE, The international society for optics and photonics, see SPIE

Spizzirri Publishing Inc
PO Box 9397, Rapid City, SD 57709-9397
Tel: 605-348-2749 *Toll Free Tel:* 800-325-9819 *Fax:* 605-348-6251 *Toll Free Fax:* 800-322-9819
E-mail: spizzpub@aol.com
Web Site: www.spizzirri.com
Key Personnel
Pres: Linda Spizzirri
Founded: 1978
Educational coloring books, book-CD packages, activity books, workbooks & how-to-draw books. PreK-5th grade featuring realistic illustrations & museum curator approved texts on topics, including everything from dinosaurs to space.
ISBN Prefix(es): 978-0-86545
Number of titles published annually: 3 Print
Total Titles: 200 Print

§Springer
Subsidiary of Springer Nature
One New York Plaza, Suite 4600, New York, NY 10004-1562
Tel: 212-460-1500 *Toll Free Tel:* 800-SPRINGER (777-4643) *Fax:* 212-460-1700
E-mail: customerservice@springernature.com
Web Site: www.springer.com
Key Personnel
Chief Commercial Offr, Springer Nature Group: Carolyn Honour
VP, HR: Eileen Purelis
VP, Journals, Devt, Policy & Strategy: Harry Blom
VP, Prodn: Henry Krell
Edit Dir, Clinical Medicine: Antoinette Cimino
 E-mail: antoinette.cimino@springernature.com; Richard Lansing *E-mail:* richard.lansing@springernature.com
Edit Dir, Journals, Computer Sci: Jennifer Evans
Founded: 1842 (1964 NY off)
Scientific, medical, technical, research, reference books & periodicals.
ISBN Prefix(es): 978-0-387
Number of titles published annually: 6,500 Print; 6,000 E-Book
Total Titles: 70,000 Print; 36,000 Online; 38,000 E-Book
Imprints: Apress; BioMed Central; Birkhauser Science; Copernicus; Springer Healthcare
Foreign Office(s): Tiergartenstr 15-17, 69121 Heidelberg, Germany
Membership(s): International Association of Scientific, Technical & Medical Publishers (ISTM)

§Springer Publishing Co
11 W 42 St, 15th fl, New York, NY 10036-8002
SAN: 203-2236
Tel: 212-431-4370 *Toll Free Tel:* 877-687-7476
E-mail: marketing@springerpub.com; cs@springerpub.com (orders); textbook@springerpub.com; specialsales@springerpub.com
Web Site: www.springerpub.com
Key Personnel
CEO: Mary E Gatsch *E-mail:* mgatsch@springerpub.com
Publr, Nursing: Elizabeth Nieginski
 E-mail: enieginski@springerpub.com
Sr Sales Dir, Higher Educ: Gary Darlington; Jill Ferguson
Dir, Behavioral Sciences: Kate Dimock
 E-mail: kdimock@springerpub.com

Dir, Digital Devt: Suzanne Toppy
 E-mail: stoppy@springerpub.com
Dir, Licensing & Busn Devt: Mindy Anderson
Dir, Nurse Educ: Adrianne Brigido
 E-mail: abrigido@springerpub.com
Sales Dir, Trade, Pharma & Rts: Reina Santana
 E-mail: rsantana@springerpub.com
Sr Acqs Ed, Healthcare Admin & Oncology: David D'Addona *E-mail:* ddaddona@springerpub.com
Sr Acqs Ed, Textbooks: Rhonda Dearborn
 E-mail: rdearborn@springerpub.com
Sr Ed, Nursing: Joe Morita *E-mail:* jmorita@springerpub.com
Assoc Acqs Ed, Nursing: Rachel Landes
 E-mail: rlandes@springerpub.com
Founded: 1950 (Feb 2004, acquired by Mannheim Holdings, LLC, subsidiary of Mannheim Trust)
Professional books, encyclopedias, college textbooks & journals; nursing, psychology, gerontology/geriatrics, medical education, public health, rehabilitation, social work & scholarly health sciences.
ISBN Prefix(es): 978-0-8261
Number of titles published annually: 100 Print
Total Titles: 700 Print
Imprints: Demos Medical Publishing
Foreign Rep(s): Avicenna Partnership Ltd (Middle East); The Eurospan Group (Africa, Europe, UK); Login Canada (Canada); Nankodo Co Ltd (Japan); Taylor & Francis Asia Pacific (Brunei, China, Hong Kong, Indonesia, Malaysia, Philippines, Singapore, South Korea, Taiwan, Thailand, Vietnam); Viva Books Pvt Ltd (Vinod Vasishtha & Pradeep Kumar) (India)
Membership(s): American Medical Publishers Association; Association of American Publishers (AAP); STM
See separate listing for:
Demos Medical Publishing

Square One Publishers Inc
115 Herricks Rd, Garden City Park, NY 11040
Tel: 516-535-2010 *Toll Free Tel:* 877-900-BOOK (900-2665) *Fax:* 516-535-2014
E-mail: sq1publish@aol.com
Web Site: www.squareonepublishers.com
Key Personnel
Pres & Publr: Rudy Shur
Art Dir: Jeannie Tudor
VP, Mktg, PR & Rts: Anthony Pomes
Sales Dir: Ken Kaiman
Mgr, Opers: Robert Love
Exec Ed: Joanne Abrams
Sr Ed: Marie Caratozzolo
Ed: Michael Weatherhead
Founded: 2000
Specialize in adult nonfiction books. Topics covered include collectibles, cooking, general interest, history, how-to, parenting, self-help & health.
ISBN Prefix(es): 978-0-7570
Number of titles published annually: 25 Print
Total Titles: 500 Print; 1 Audio
Imprints: Ocean Publishing; Upper Access
Distributor for InnoVision Health Media; Rainbow Ridge Books
Foreign Rep(s): Brumby Sunstate (Australia, New Zealand); G D Daby (Southeast Asia); Deep Books Ltd (Europe, UK); Phambili Agencies (South Africa)
Membership(s): American Booksellers Association (ABA); The American Library Association (ALA); The Association of Publishers for Special Sales (APSS); Independent Book Publishers Association (IBPA)

§Stackpole Books
Imprint of Rowman & Littlefield Publishing Group
31 E Main St, New Kingstown, PA 17072

Mailing Address: PO Box 90, New Kingstown, PA 17072
Tel: 717-590-8974
Web Site: www.stackpolebooks.com
Key Personnel
Publr: Judith Schnell *E-mail:* jschnell@rowman.com
Founded: 1933
Trade book publisher in the categories of outdoor sports, nature, crafts, history, military reference & regional. Strong in fly fishing, nature guides, military history & military reference, we publish deep in our niche areas. Presently expanding into the fast-growing world of ebooks while continuing to produce alternative, high-quality hardcovers & trade paperbacks.
ISBN Prefix(es): 978-0-8117
Number of titles published annually: 60 Print
Total Titles: 1,500 Print
Distribution Center: National Book Network, 15200 NBN Way, Blue Ridge Summit, PA 17214 *Tel:* 717-794-3800 *Fax:* 717-794-3828

§Standard Publishing
Imprint of David C Cook
4050 Lee Vance Dr, Colorado Springs, CO 80918
SAN: 110-5515
Tel: 719-536-0100 *Toll Free Tel:* 800-323-7543 (orders & cust serv) *Toll Free Fax:* 800-430-0726 (cust serv)
Founded: 1866
Religious children's books, Sunday school literature & supplies, youth & adult trade books.
ISBN Prefix(es): 978-0-87239; 978-0-87403; 978-0-7847
Number of titles published annually: 75 Print
Total Titles: 700 Print; 30 CD-ROM
Imprints: HeartShaper®; Standard Lesson Commentary®; Standard Lesson Quarterly®; Standard Lesson Resources®

§Standard Publishing Corp
10 High St, Boston, MA 02110
Tel: 617-457-0600 *Toll Free Tel:* 800-682-5759 *Fax:* 617-457-0608
Web Site: www.spcpub.com
Key Personnel
Pres & Publr: John C Cross, Esq *E-mail:* j.cross@spcpub.com
Edit: Deborah Dukeshire
Mktg Mgr: Susanne Edes Dillman *Tel:* 617-457-0611 ext 77 *E-mail:* s.dillman@spcpub.com
Founded: 1865
Information for insurance professionals.
ISBN Prefix(es): 978-0-923240
Number of titles published annually: 10 Print
Total Titles: 10 Print; 3 CD-ROM
Subsidiaries: John Liner Organization
Branch Office(s)
Insurance Record, 9601 White Rock Trail, Suite 213, Dallas, TX 75238
Distributed by LexisNexis®; Silverplume, a Vertafore Co

Stanford University Press
425 Broadway St, Redwood City, CA 94063-3126
SAN: 203-3526
Tel: 650-723-9434 *Fax:* 650-725-3457
E-mail: info@www.sup.org; publicity@www.sup.org; sales@www.sup.org
Web Site: www.sup.org
Key Personnel
Dir: Dr Alan Harvey *Tel:* 650-723-6375 *E-mail:* aharvey@stanford.edu
Publg Dir & Ed-in-Chief: Kate Wahl *Tel:* 650-498-9420 *E-mail:* kwahl@stanford.edu
Dir, Edit, Design & Prodn: David Zielonka *Tel:* 650-724-5365 *E-mail:* zielonka@stanford.edu
Dir, Fin & Opers: Amy Schultz
Art Dir: Robert Ehle *E-mail:* ehle@stanford.edu
Mktg & Sales Dir: Adam Schnitzer

Exec Ed: Richard Narramore *E-mail:* richard.narramore@stanford.edu; Erica Wetter *Tel:* 650-725-7717 *E-mail:* ewetter@stanford.edu
Sr Ed: Steve Catalano *Tel:* 650-724-7079 *E-mail:* catalan@stanford.edu; Marcela Maxfield *Tel:* 650-498-3396 *E-mail:* mmaxfiel@stanford.edu; Friederike Sundaram *Tel:* 650-736-8207 *E-mail:* fsundara@stanford.edu
Acqs Ed: Margo Irvin *Tel:* 650-498-9023 *E-mail:* mcirvin@stanford.edu
Asst Ed: Caroline McKusick *Tel:* 650-498-9420 *E-mail:* cmck@stanford.edu
Contracts & Rts Mgr: Greta Lindquist *Tel:* 650-725-0815
Mktg Mgr: Stephanie Adams *Tel:* 650-736-1782 *E-mail:* stephanie.adams@stanford.edu
Prodn Mgr: Mike Sagara *Tel:* 650-725-0839 *E-mail:* msagara@stanford.edu
Sales & Exhibits Mgr: Kate Templar *Tel:* 650-725-0820
Publicist: Bridget Kinsella Tiernan *Tel:* 510-465-3853 *E-mail:* bridgetkinsella@stanford.edu
Sales Coord: Emma Mundorff
Founded: 1925
ISBN Prefix(es): 978-0-8047; 978-1-5036
Number of titles published annually: 140 Print; 40 E-Book
Total Titles: 4,000 Print; 400 E-Book
Imprints: Redwood Press; Stanford Briefs; Stanford Business Books
Distributed by Columbia University Press
Foreign Rep(s): Canadian Manga Group (Canada); Combined Academic Publishers (CAP) (Africa, Asia-Pacific, Europe, Middle East); Ingram UK (Matthew Dickie) (Caribbean, Latin America)
Distribution Center: Ingram Content Group LLC, One Ingram Blvd, La Vergne, TN 37086 *Toll Free Tel:* 866-400-5351 *E-mail:* ordersupport@ingramcontent.com
Membership(s): Association of American Publishers (AAP); Association of University Presses (AUPresses)

Star Bright Books Inc
13 Landsdowne St, Cambridge, MA 02139
Tel: 617-354-1300 *Fax:* 617-354-1399
E-mail: info@starbrightbooks.com; orders@starbrightbooks.com
Web Site: www.starbrightbooks.org
Key Personnel
Publr: Deborah Shine
Founded: 1994
Independent children's book publisher focused on diversity & inclusion. Star Bright Books is committed to producing high quality board books, picture books & chapter books that meet the needs of all children. Books are available in 26 languages.
ISBN Prefix(es): 978-1-887734; 978-1-932065; 978-1-59572
Number of titles published annually: 16 Print
Total Titles: 400 Print; 80 E-Book
Foreign Rep(s): Fitzhenry & Whiteside Limited (Canada); Roundhouse Group (Europe, UK)
Membership(s): American Booksellers Association (ABA); The American Library Association (ALA); Association of Children's Booksellers; National Association for the Education of Young Children (NAEYC); Society of Children's Book Writers & Illustrators (SCBWI); Women's Business Enterprise National Council; Women's Business Enterprise Network (WBENC)

Star Publishing Co Inc
PO Box 5165, Belmont, CA 94002-5165
SAN: 212-6958
Tel: 650-591-3505
E-mail: starpublishing@gmail.com
Web Site: www.starpublishing.com

Key Personnel
Publr: Stuart A Hoffman
Founded: 1978
College/university textbooks, laboratory manuals; reference books; professional books; California history/local history.
ISBN Prefix(es): 978-0-89863
Number of titles published annually: 14 Print
Total Titles: 450 Print
Imprints: Encore Editions

Star Trek®, see Gallery Books

§STARbooks Press
PO Box 711612, Herndon, VA 20171
E-mail: publish@starbookspress.com; contact@starbookspress.com
Web Site: www.starbookspress.com
Key Personnel
Sr Edit Dir: Eric Summers
Founded: 1989
ISBN Prefix(es): 978-1-877978; 978-1-891855
Number of titles published annually: 8 Print
Total Titles: 30 Print; 1 Audio

§Starcrafts LLC
68A Fogg Rd, Epping, NH 03042
SAN: 208-5380
Tel: 603-734-4300 *Toll Free Tel:* 866-953-8458 (24/7 message ctr) *Fax:* 603-734-4311
E-mail: astrosales@astrocom.com
Web Site: www.astrocom.com
Key Personnel
Owner & Publr: Maria K Simms *E-mail:* maria@astrocom.com
Cust Serv: Thomas Canfield *E-mail:* tom@astrocom.com
Founded: 1973
Astrology: ephemerides, chart interpretation.
ISBN Prefix(es): 978-0-935127; 978-0-917086; 978-0-9762422; 978-1-934976
Number of titles published annually: 4 Print; 1 CD-ROM
Total Titles: 60 Print; 5 CD-ROM; 1 Audio
Imprints: ACS Publications; Starcrafts Publishing
Distribution Center: New Leaf Distributing Co, 1085 E Lotus Dr, Silver Lake, WI 53170 *Tel:* 262-889-8501 *Toll Free Tel:* 800-326-2665 *Fax:* 262-889-8598 *E-mail:* orders@newleafdist.com SAN: 169-1449

Stargazer Publishing Co
958 Stanislaus Dr, Corona, CA 92881
Mailing Address: PO Box 77002, Corona, CA 92877-0100
Tel: 951-898-4619
E-mail: stargazer@stargazerpub.com; orders@stargazerpub.com
Web Site: www.stargazerpub.com
Founded: 1995
Publisher of educational & business books.
ISBN Prefix(es): 978-0-9643853; 978-1-933277; 978-0-9713756
Number of titles published annually: 10 Print; 5 E-Book
Total Titles: 50 Print; 5 CD-ROM; 5 E-Book
Warehouse: Publishers Storage & Shipping, 660 S Mansfield, Ypsilanti, MI 48197
Membership(s): Independent Book Publishers Association (IBPA); National Association of College Stores (NACS); Publishers Association of Los Angeles

StarGroup International Inc
1194 Old Dixie Hwy, Suite 201, West Palm Beach, FL 33413
Tel: 561-547-0667 *Fax:* 561-843-8530
E-mail: info@stargroupinternational.com
Web Site: stargroupinternational.com
Key Personnel
Pres & CEO: Brenda Star *E-mail:* brenda@stargroupinternational.com
Creative Dir: Mel Abfier

U.S. PUBLISHERS

Head Writer & Film/Video Prodr: Gwen Carden; Linda Haas
Internet Mktg Coord: Butch Butler
Mktg, Media & Web Site Devt: Rusty Durham
Media Specialist: Sam Smyth
Founded: 1983
Create books to be used as marketing & media tools. For over 2 decades have maintained access to the best researchers, writers, editors, proofreaders, designers & printers in the industry, while offering public relations & marketing services. Specialize in creating books for clients to enhance their credibility & position them as experts in their field.
This publisher has indicated that 75% of their product line is author subsidized.
ISBN Prefix(es): 978-1-884886
Number of titles published annually: 25 Print
Total Titles: 150 Print
Membership(s): Florida Authors & Publishers Association Inc (FAPA); Independent Book Publishers Association (IBPA)

State University of New York Press
10 N Pearl St, 4th fl, Albany, NY 12207
SAN: 760-7261
Tel: 518-944-2800 Toll Free Tel: 877-204-6073 (orders) Fax: 518-320-1592 Toll Free Fax: 877-204-6074 (orders)
E-mail: info@sunypress.edu (edit off); suny@presswarehouse.com (orders)
Web Site: www.sunypress.edu
Key Personnel
Co-Dir & Acqs: James Peltz Tel: 518-944-2815 E-mail: james.peltz@sunypress.edu
Dir, Mktg & Publicity: Fran Keneston Tel: 518-944-2807 E-mail: fran.keneston@sunypress.edu
Rts & Perms: Sharla Clute Tel: 518-944-2803 E-mail: sharla.clute@sunypress.edu
Founded: 1966
Scholarly nonfiction, especially works in philosophy, psychology, African American studies, gender/sexuality studies, American Indian studies, museum/archival science, Asian studies & religious studies.
ISBN Prefix(es): 978-0-87395; 978-0-88706; 978-0-7914; 978-1-4384
Number of titles published annually: 150 Print; 140 Online; 140 E-Book
Total Titles: 6,140 Print; 4,000 Online; 6,040 E-Book; 2 Audio
Imprints: Excelsior Editions
Distributor for Albany Institute of History & Art; Codhill Press; Samuel Dorsky Museum of Art; Mount Ida Press; Muswell Hill Press; New Netherland Institute; Rockefeller Institute Press; Uncrowned Queens
Foreign Rep(s): Cassidy & Associates Inc (China, Hong Kong, Taiwan); Lexa Publishers' Representatives (Canada); MHM Ltd (Japan); US PubRep (Caribbean, Central America, Mexico, Puerto Rico, South America)
Billing Address: PO Box 960, Herndon, VA 20172-0960, Cust Serv Tel: 703-661-1575 Fax: 703-996-1010
Orders to: PO Box 960, Herndon, VA 20172-0960, Cust Serv Tel: 703-661-1575 Fax: 703-996-1010
Returns: 22883 Quicksilver Dr, Dulles, VA 20166, Cust Serv Tel: 703-661-1575 Fax: 703-996-1010
Shipping Address: 22835 Quicksilver Dr, Dulles, VA 20166 Tel: 703-661-1575 Fax: 703-996-1010
Warehouse: PO Box 960, Herndon, VA 20172-0960, Cust Serv Tel: 703-661-1575 Fax: 703-996-1010
Distribution Center: Ingram Publisher Services UK, 10 Thornbury Rd, Plymouth PL6 7PP, United Kingdom Tel: (01752) 202301 E-mail: IPSUK.Cservs@ingramcontent.com
Web Site: www.ingrampublisherservices.co.uk

Membership(s): American Booksellers Association (ABA); Association of University Presses (AUPresses)
See separate listing for:
Excelsior Editions

Steerforth Press, see Steerforth Press & Services

Steerforth Press & Services
Formerly Steerforth Press
Imprint of Pushkin Press
31 Hanover St, Suite 1, Lebanon, NH 03766
Tel: 603-643-4787 Fax: 603-643-4788
E-mail: info@steerforth.com
Web Site: www.steerforth.com
Key Personnel
Publg Opers Dir: Devin Wilkie E-mail: devin@steerforth.com
Sales & Mktg Dir: David Goldberg E-mail: david@steerforth.com; Helga Schmidt E-mail: helga@steerforth.com
Sr Ed: Chip Fleischer E-mail: chip@steerforth.com
Assoc Mgr, Mktg & Publicity: Zandra Rose
Founded: 1993
ISBN Prefix(es): 978-1-883642; 978-0-944072; 978-1-58195; 978-1-58642
Number of titles published annually: 10 Print
Total Titles: 300 Print
Foreign Rights: Big Apple Agency Inc (Taiwan); Agence Bookman (Scandinavia); English Agency Japan Co Ltd (Japan); Anouk H Foerg; Harris-Elon Agency (Israel); International Editors' Co - Yanez Agencia Literaria (Argentina, Brazil, Latin America, Portugal, Spain); Katai & Bolza (Hungary); David Marshall; Daniela Micura Literary Services (Italy); Onk Agency Inc (Turkey)
Distribution Center: Penguin Random House Distribution Center, 400 Hahn Rd, Westminster, MD 21157 Toll Free Tel: 800-733-3000 Toll Free Fax: 800-659-2436
Membership(s): American Booksellers Association (ABA); Independent Book Publishers Association (IBPA); New England Independent Booksellers Association (NEIBA)

§SteinerBooks Inc
Imprint of Anthroposophic Press Inc
610 Main St, Suite 1, Great Barrington, MA 01230
Tel: 413-528-8233
E-mail: service@steinerbooks.org; friends@steinerbooks.org
Web Site: steiner.presswarehouse.com
Key Personnel
Edit & Artistic Dir: Mary Giddens E-mail: mary@steinerbooks.org
Ed-in-Chief: Christopher Bamford E-mail: cbamford@cbamford.cnc.net
Sr Ed & Translator: Marsha Post E-mail: marsha@steinerbooks.org
Prodn Mgr: Stephan O'Reilly E-mail: stephan@steinerbooks.org
Founded: 1928
American & English editions of works by Rudolf Steiner & related authors.
ISBN Prefix(es): 978-0-910142; 978-0-88010; 978-0-89345; 978-0-9674562; 978-0-9779825; 978-0-9804044; 978-0-9831984; 978-0-9832261; 978-0-9853658; 978-1-62148
Number of titles published annually: 15 Print
Distributed by Rudolf Steiner Press UK
Distributor for Chiron Publications; Clairview Books; Floris Books; Hawthorn Press; Lantern Books; Rudolph Steiner Press; Temple Lodge Publishing
Foreign Rep(s): Ceres (New Zealand); Peter Hyde & Associates (South Africa); Rudolf Steiner Press (UK)
Orders to: PO Box 960, Herndon, VA 20172-0960 Tel: 703-661-1594 Fax: 703-661-1501 SAN: 201-1824

Stellar Publishing
2114 S Live Oak Pkwy, Wilmington, NC 28403
SAN: 860-2298
Tel: 910-269-7444
Web Site: www.stellar-publishing.com
Key Personnel
Publr: Jasper Williams E-mail: publisher@stellar-publishing.com
Founded: 2000
This publisher has indicated that 50% of their product line is author subsidized.
ISBN Prefix(es): 978-0-970341
Number of titles published annually: 3 Print
Total Titles: 9 Print

§Stenhouse Publishers
Division of Highlights for Children Education Group
1400 Goodale Blvd, Suite 200, Grandview Heights, OH 43212
Toll Free Tel: 800-988-9812 Toll Free Fax: 800-992-6087
E-mail: customerservice@stenhouse.com; editors@stenhouse.com
Web Site: www.stenhouse.com
Founded: 1993
Professional books for teachers.
ISBN Prefix(es): 978-1-57110; 978-1-62531
Number of titles published annually: 25 Print; 3 Online; 15 E-Book
Total Titles: 400 Print; 275 E-Book; 3 Audio
Distributor for Pembroke Publishers Ltd
Foreign Rep(s): Eurospan (Africa, Asia-Pacific, Caribbean, Europe, Latin America, Middle East); Hawker Brownlow Education (Australia, New Zealand); Pembroke Publishers Ltd (Canada); PMS Publishers Services Pte Ltd (Brunei, Malaysia, Singapore)

§Stewart, Tabori & Chang
Imprint of Harry N Abrams Inc
195 Broadway, 9th fl, New York, NY 10007
SAN: 239-0361
Tel: 212-206-7715 Fax: 212-519-1210
E-mail: abrams@abramsbooks.com
Web Site: www.abramsbooks.com/imprints/stc
Key Personnel
Pres & CEO: Michael Jacobs E-mail: mjacobs@abramsbooks.com
SVP & Publr, Adult Trade: Michael Sand E-mail: msand@abramsbooks.com
SVP, Mktg & Publicity: Melanie Chang E-mail: mchang@abramsbooks.com
Founded: 1981
Art, illustrated gift books, gardening, cookbooks, African American history, interior design, New Age, photography, popular culture, humor, weddings.
ISBN Prefix(es): 978-1-55670; 978-0-941434; 978-1-58479; 978-1-61769
Number of titles published annually: 80 Print
Total Titles: 350 Print
Foreign Rights: General Publishing (Canada); HI Marketing Ltd (Europe, UK); Korea Copyright Center Inc (KCC) (South Korea); New Holland (Australia); Onslow Books Ltd (Europe); Sigma Literary Agency (South Korea); Southern Publishers Group (New Zealand); Tuttle-Mori Agency Inc (Japan); David Williams (South America)

§Stipes Publishing LLC
204 W University Ave, Champaign, IL 61820
Mailing Address: PO Box 526, Champaign, IL 61824-0526
Tel: 217-356-8391 Fax: 217-356-5753
E-mail: stipes01@sbcglobal.net
Web Site: www.stipes.com
Key Personnel
Partner: J L Hecker
Founded: 1927
Primarily educational, some overlap trade publishing in music & horticulture.

ISBN Prefix(es): 978-0-87563; 978-1-58874
Number of titles published annually: 15 Print
Total Titles: 550 Print; 2 CD-ROM; 1 Online; 1 E-Book; 2 Audio

STM Learning Inc
1220 Paddock Dr, Florissant, MO 63033
Tel: 314-434-2424
E-mail: info@stmlearning.com; orders@stmlearning.com
Web Site: www.stmlearning.com
Key Personnel
Pres: Glenn Whaley *E-mail:* glenn@stmlearning.com
VP: Marianne Whaley *E-mail:* marianne@stmlearning.com
Founded: 1993
STM Learning is the expert in publishing leading clinical research for professionals who are in positions to serve & protect victims of abuse. Our customers consider STM Learning products to be the most trusted scientific, technical & medical resources available to aid in their efforts to identify, report, treat & prevent child maltreatment & domestic violence.
ISBN Prefix(es): 978-1-878060; 978-1-936590; 978-1-953119
Number of titles published annually: 8 Print; 8 E-Book
Total Titles: 65 Print; 70 E-Book
Foreign Rep(s): CoreSource (worldwide); Eurospan (worldwide)
Advertising Agency: GW Graphics & Publishing
Distribution Center: Amazon.com
Baker & Taylor
Barnes & Noble
ProQuest
Rittenhouse Book Distributors Inc, 511 Feheley Dr, King of Prussia, PA 19406 *Toll Free Tel:* 800-345-6425 *Toll Free Fax:* 800-223-7488
Web Site: www.rittenhouse.com

STOCKCERO Inc
3785 NW 82 Ave, Suite 314, Doral, FL 33166
Tel: 305-722-7628 *Fax:* 305-722-7628
E-mail: academicservices@stockcero.com; sales@stockcero.com
Web Site: www.stockcero.com
Key Personnel
CEO: Pablo Agrest Berge *E-mail:* pagrest@stockcero.com
Founded: 2000
Committed to building an ever expanding collection of significant books, comprising Spanish literature, both Peninsular & Latin American. Our editions are conceived with modern non-native Spanish-speaking readers & students in mind, so they include updated & sharply focused footnotes, prefaces & bibliographies written by scholarly literary editors.
ISBN Prefix(es): 978-1-934768
Number of titles published annually: 14 Print
Total Titles: 181 Print; 157 Online

§Stone Bridge Press Inc
1393 Solano Ave, Suite C, Albany, CA 94706
Mailing Address: PO Box 8208, Berkeley, CA 94706
Tel: 510-524-8732
E-mail: sbp@stonebridge.com; sbpedit@stonebridge.com
Web Site: www.stonebridge.com
Key Personnel
Founder & Publr: Peter Goodman
Founded: 1989
Books on Japan & Asia.
ISBN Prefix(es): 978-0-89346 (Heian International); 978-1-880656; 978-0-9628137; 978-1-933330; 978-1-61172
Number of titles published annually: 6 Print; 10 Online; 10 E-Book
Total Titles: 120 Print; 15 Online; 75 E-Book
Imprints: MONKEY (Japanese fiction in translation); Three L Media
Foreign Rep(s): Perseus International (Australia)
Distribution Center: Consortium Book Sales & Distribution, The Keg House, 34 13 Ave NE, Suite 101, Minneapolis, MN 55413-1007 (US & CN) *Tel:* 612-746-2600 *Toll Free Tel:* 866-400-5351 (cust serv, Jackson, TN) *E-mail:* cbsdinfo@ingramcontent.com *Web Site:* www.cbsd.com SAN: 200-6049
Membership(s): Independent Book Publishers Association (IBPA)

Stone Pier Press
PO Box 170572, San Francisco, CA 94117
Tel: 415-484-2821
E-mail: hello@stonepierpress.org
Web Site: www.stonepierpress.org
Key Personnel
Publr: Clare Ellis *E-mail:* clare@stonepierpress.org
Founded: 2017
Environmental publisher with a food focus producing books & news that highlight how to eat, grow & dispose of our food in a way that builds a cooler, kinder & healthier world. Our thinking is that by focusing on solutions, we make it easier for any one of us to act on them.
ISBN Prefix(es): 978-0-9988623
Number of titles published annually: 2 Print; 2 E-Book
Distributed by Chelsea Green Publishing Co

Stoneydale Press Publishing Co
523 Main St, Stevensville, MT 59870-2839
Mailing Address: PO Box 188, Stevensville, MT 59870-0188
Tel: 406-777-2729 *Toll Free Tel:* 800-735-7006 *Fax:* 406-777-2521
E-mail: stoneydale@stoneydale.com
Web Site: www.stoneydale.com
Key Personnel
Publr: Dale A Burk
Founded: 1976
Outdoor recreation, regional history & reminisces of Northern Rockies region.
ISBN Prefix(es): 978-0-912299; 978-1-931291; 978-1-938707
Number of titles published annually: 8 Print
Total Titles: 190 Print
Membership(s): Mountains & Plains Booksellers Association (MPBA); Pacific Northwest Booksellers Association (PNBA)

Story Monsters LLC
4696 W Tyson St, Chandler, AZ 85226-2903
Tel: 480-940-8182 *Fax:* 480-940-8787
Web Site: www.StoryMonsters.com; www.StoryMonstersBookAwards.com; www.AuthorBookings.com; www.StoryMonstersBookAwards.com/sma-details; www.StoryMonstersInk.com
Key Personnel
Pres: Linda F Radke *E-mail:* Linda@StoryMonsters.com
Founded: 1985
Dedicated to helping authors of all genres strive for excellence with book production, marketing & promotion. Publish the award-winning *Story Monsters Ink®* magazine. Provide publishers support services in areas such as editing, cover design & publicity. Sponsor of the Story Monsters® Book Awards.
ISBN Prefix(es): 978-0-9619853; 978-1-877749; 978-1-58985
Number of titles published annually: 10 Print
Total Titles: 72 Print; 12 E-Book
Imprints: Book Street Press (adult books); School Express Press (publishing plan for schools, teachers & librarians); Story Monsters Press (children's books)
Divisions: AuthorBookings.com (connecting authors, artists, schools & libraries); Story Monsters Ink (literary resource for teachers, librarians & parents)
Membership(s): Arizona Professional Writers (APW); The Children's Book Council (CBC); Independent Book Publishers Association (IBPA); National Federation of Press Women; New Mexico Publishers Association; Writers & Publishers Network (WPN)

Story Monsters Press, see Story Monsters LLC

§The Story Plant
Division of Gramarye Media Inc
1270 Caroline St, Suite D120-381, Atlanta, GA 30307
Tel: 203-722-7920
E-mail: thestoryplant@thestoryplant.com
Web Site: www.thestoryplant.com
Key Personnel
CEO: John Adcox *E-mail:* john.adcox@thestoryplant.com
Chief Literary Offr: Lou Aronica *E-mail:* lou.aronica@thestoryplant.com
Pres: Alice Neuhauser *E-mail:* alice.neuhauser@thestoryplant.com
Founded: 2008
Independent publisher of commercial & literary fiction with alignments in all other media.
ISBN Prefix(es): 978-1-61188; 978-1-945839
Number of titles published annually: 40 Print; 40 E-Book; 25 Audio
Total Titles: 225 Print; 225 E-Book; 40 Audio
Distribution Center: National Book Network, 4501 Forbes Blvd, Lanham, MD 20706 *Tel:* 301-459-3366
Membership(s): American Booksellers Association (ABA); Association of American Publishers (AAP)

§Storyworkz Inc
PO Box 567, Montpelier, VT 05601
Tel: 802-223-4955
E-mail: orders@storyworkz.com
Web Site: www.storyworkz.com
Key Personnel
Pres & Publr: Paul E Richardson *E-mail:* paulr@storyworkz.com
Founded: 1990
Publish magazines (including *Russian Life*), books, info, maps for business & independent travel to Russia.
ISBN Prefix(es): 978-1-880100
Number of titles published annually: 3 Print; 3 E-Book
Total Titles: 30 Print; 30 E-Book

§Strategic Book Publishing (SBP)
Durham, CT 06422
SAN: 853-8492
Tel: 860-331-1201; 361-244-1058
E-mail: bookorder@sbpra.net; support@sbpra.net
Web Site: sbpra.net; www.facebook.com/sbpra.us
Key Personnel
Contract Mgr: Lynn Eddy *E-mail:* lynn@sbpra.net
Founded: 2007
Provides book publishing, marketing & ebook services to writers around the world. Catalog of more than 10,000 authors. Books are available through Ingram as well as in bookstores such as Barnes & Noble & all online channels. Attends & exhibits at the major book expositions in London, New York, China & Germany each year.
This publisher has indicated that 50% of their product line is author subsidized.
ISBN Prefix(es): 978-1-60911; 978-1-61204; 978-1-62516; 978-1-62857; 978-1-68235; 978-1-952269; 978-1-63135; 978-1-68181; 978-1-948260; 978-1-948858; 978-1-949483; 978-1-950015; 978-1-950860

Number of titles published annually: 475 Print; 85 E-Book
Total Titles: 2,786 Print; 3,062 Online; 336 E-Book

§Strategic Media Books LLC
782 Wofford St, Rock Hill, SC 29730
Tel: 803-366-5440
E-mail: contact@strategicmediabooks.com
Web Site: strategicmediabooks.com
Key Personnel
Pres: Ron Chepesiuk
Partner: Barbara Casey
Founded: 2010
Publisher of crime, true crime & southern interest books.
ISBN Prefix(es): 978-0-9852440; 978-1-939521
Number of titles published annually: 8 Print; 8 Online; 8 E-Book; 3 Audio
Total Titles: 28 Print; 25 Online; 25 E-Book; 3 Audio
Foreign Rep(s): Cardinal Publishers Group (UK)
Membership(s): Independent Book Publishers Association (IBPA)

Stress Free Kids®
2561 Chimney Springs Dr, Marietta, GA 30062
Tel: 678-642-9555 *Toll Free Fax:* 866-302-2759
E-mail: media@stressfreekids.com
Web Site: www.stressfreekids.com
Key Personnel
Founder: Lori Lite; Rick Lite
Founded: 1996
Books, CDs (physical & digital formats), lesson plans to help children & teens manage stress, lower anxiety & decrease anger, while improving self-esteem.
ISBN Prefix(es): 978-0-9708633; 978-0-9787781; 978-0-9800328
Number of titles published annually: 2 Print; 5 Online; 4 E-Book; 4 Audio
Total Titles: 35 Print; 12 Audio

The Jesse Stuart Foundation (JSF)
4440 13 St, Ashland, KY 41102
SAN: 245-8837
Mailing Address: PO Box 669, Ashland, KY 41105-0669
Tel: 606-326-1667 *Fax:* 606-325-2519
E-mail: jsf@jsfbooks.com
Web Site: www.jsfbooks.com
Key Personnel
CEO & Sr Ed: James M Gifford, PhD
Founded: 1979
Publisher of Appalachia-Kentuckiana. Not accepting unsol mss at this time.
ISBN Prefix(es): 978-0-945084
Number of titles published annually: 4 Print
Total Titles: 75 Print

§Stylus Publishing LLC
22883 Quicksilver Dr, Sterling, VA 20166-2019
SAN: 299-1853
Tel: 703-661-1504 (edit & sales)
 Toll Free Tel: 800-232-0223 (orders & cust serv) *Fax:* 703-661-1547
E-mail: stylusmail@styluspub.com (orders & cust serv); stylusinfo@styluspub.com
Web Site: styluspub.com
Key Personnel
Pres & Publr: John von Knorring *E-mail:* jvk@styluspub.com
VP, Mktg & Publicity Mgr: Andrea Ciecierski *Tel:* 703-996-1036 *E-mail:* andrea@styluspub.com
Founded: 1996
Publish books for faculty & administrators in higher education. Distributes educational & scholarly titles.
ISBN Prefix(es): 978-1-57922; 978-1-62036; 978-1-64267

Number of titles published annually: 30 Print; 30 E-Book
Total Titles: 400 Print; 2 CD-ROM; 150 E-Book
Distributor for Baseball Prospectus; Cabi Books; Campus Compact; CSREA; Mercury Learning & Information; Myers Education Press; National Resource Center for The First-Year Experience & Students in Transition; Thorogood Publishing; Trentham Books Ltd; UCL IOE Press; World Health Organization (WHO)
Foreign Rep(s): Catamount International (Central America, South America); Eurospan (Asia, Australia, Europe, Middle East, UK)
Distribution Center: Books International Inc, 22883 Quicksilver Dr, Dulles, VA 20166

Summer Institute of Linguistics Inc, see SIL International

§Summertime Publications Inc
4115 E Palo Verde Dr, Phoenix, AZ 85018
E-mail: summertime.publications@gmail.com
Web Site: www.summertimepublications.com
Key Personnel
Dir, Pubns & CEO: Laurel Leffmann
Founded: 2009
Small press. Quality books about France; also memoirs, history, science fiction, short story, literary fiction & nonfiction.
ISBN Prefix(es): 978-0-9823698; 978-1-940333
Number of titles published annually: 3 Print; 4 E-Book
Total Titles: 9 Print; 14 E-Book
Imprints: PWN; Summertime
Distributor for ACHCBYZ (Paris academic press specializing in Byzantine history)
Foreign Rights: IPR License Ltd (worldwide exc China); Rightol Media (China)
Membership(s): Independent Book Publishers Association (IBPA)

§Summit University Press
63 Summit Way, Gardiner, MT 59030
Tel: 406-848-9292; 406-848-9500 (retail orders) *Fax:* 406-848-9555
E-mail: info@tsl.org; rights@summituniversitypress.com
Web Site: www.summituniversitypress.com
Key Personnel
Publg Dir: Steven Webb *E-mail:* swebb@summituniversitypress.com
Foreign Rts Dir: Phyllis Blain
Publg Mgr: Frank Sarlo *E-mail:* fsarlo@tsl.org
Founded: 1975
Global publisher of fine books, ebooks, audiobooks & DVDs on spirituality. Very active foreign rights sales. Specialize in New Age & mind, body & spirit.
ISBN Prefix(es): 978-0-916766; 978-0-922729; 978-1-932890; 978-1-60988
Number of titles published annually: 4 Print; 45 Online; 45 E-Book
Total Titles: 100 Print; 20 CD-ROM; 45 Online; 47 E-Book; 70 Audio
Distribution Center: DeVorss & Co, 553 Constitution Ave, Camarillo, CA 93012-8510 *E-mail:* orders@devorss.com *Web Site:* www.devorss.com
Ingram Content Group, One Ingram Blvd, La Vergne, TN 37086 (intl) *Tel:* 615-793-5000 *Web Site:* www.ingramcontent.com
New Leaf Distributing Co, 1085 E Lotus Dr, Silver Lake, WI 53170 *Tel:* 262-889-8501 *Toll Free Tel:* 888-326-2665 *Fax:* 262-889-8598 *E-mail:* orders@newleafdist.com
Quanta, 3015 Kennedy Rd, Unit 3B, Toronto, ON M1V 1E7, Canada *Tel:* 416-410-9411 *Toll Free Tel:* 888-436-7962 *Fax:* 416-291-8764 *E-mail:* quantamail@quanta.ca *Web Site:* www.quanta.ca
Membership(s): Independent Book Publishers Association (IBPA)

Sun Books, see Sun Publishing Company

Sun Publishing Company
Division of The Sun Companies
PO Box 5588, Santa Fe, NM 87502-5588
SAN: 206-1325
Tel: 505-471-5177; 505-660-0704
 Toll Free Tel: 877-849-0051
E-mail: info@sunbooks.com
Web Site: www.sunbooks.com; abooksource.com
Key Personnel
Pres & Rts/Perms: Skip Whitson
Founded: 1973
Motivational, success, business, recovery, inspirational, history, self-help, new thought, philosophy, western mysticism, scholarly; oriental philosophy & studies. No unsol mss. Query first by e-mail.
ISBN Prefix(es): 978-0-89540
Number of titles published annually: 10 Print
Total Titles: 400 Print
Imprints: Far West Publishing; Sun Books
Advertising Agency: Sun Agency

§Sunbelt Publications Inc
664 Marsat Ct, Suite A, Chula Vista, CA 91911
SAN: 630-0790
Tel: 619-258-4911 *Toll Free Tel:* 800-626-6579 (cust serv) *Fax:* 619-258-4916
E-mail: info@sunbeltpub.com; service@sunbeltpub.com
Web Site: sunbeltpublications.com
Key Personnel
CEO & Sales Mgr: Lisa Gulick
COO: Nichole Groschup-Black *E-mail:* nichole@sunbeltpub.com
CFO: Maria Groschup-Black *E-mail:* maria@sunbeltpub.com
Pubns Mgr: Debi Young *E-mail:* dyoung@sunbeltpub.com
Founded: 1984
Publisher & distributor of natural history, citizen science, pictorial & travel specializing in Southwest US & Baja, California.
ISBN Prefix(es): 978-0-932653; 978-0-916251
Number of titles published annually: 10 Print
Total Titles: 75 Print
Imprints: Bobolink Media
Membership(s): Association of Earth Science Editors (AESE); Independent Book Publishers Association (IBPA); Outdoor Writers Association of America (OWAA); Publishers Association of the West (PubWest)

Sundance/Newbridge Publishing
Division of Rowman & Littlefield Publishing Group
33 Boston Post Rd W, Suite 440, Marlborough, MA 01752
Toll Free Tel: 888-200-2720; 800-343-8204
 Toll Free Fax: 800-456-2419 (orders)
E-mail: info@sundancenewbridge.com; orders@sundancenewbridge.com
Web Site: www.sundancenewbridge.com
Key Personnel
Pres: Paul Konowitch *E-mail:* pkonowitch@sundancepub.com
SVP, Sales: Richard Elliott *E-mail:* relliott@sundancepub.com
Founded: 1981
Supplemental educational publisher for PreK-8 that creates standards-based classroom materials for reading in the content areas.
ISBN Prefix(es): 978-1-56784; 978-1-58273; 978-1-4007
Number of titles published annually: 150 Print; 36 Audio
Total Titles: 680 Print; 118 Audio
Imprints: Decoder Kids; Early Math; Early Science; Early Social Studies; GoFacts Guided Reading; Newbridge Discovery Links for Science & Social Studies; Ranger Rick Science Program; Thinking Like a Scientist

Membership(s): Association of American Publishers (AAP); International Literacy Association (ILA); National Science Teachers Association (NSTA)

§Sunrise River Press
Affiliate of Cartech Books/Specialty Press
838 Lake St S, Forrest Lake, MN 55025
Tel: 651-277-1400 *Toll Free Tel:* 800-895-4585
E-mail: info@sunriseriverpress.com; sales@sunriseriverpress.com
Web Site: www.sunriseriverpress.com
Key Personnel
Sales & Mktg: Bob Wilson
Publisher of consumer books & books for the professional healthcare market with an emphasis on self-help, weight loss, nutrition, diet, food & recipes with additional focus on family health, fitness & specific diseases such as cancer, anorexia, Alzheimer's, autism & depression.
ISBN Prefix(es): 978-0-9624814; 978-1-934716
Number of titles published annually: 10 Print

Sunstone Press
PO Box 2321, Santa Fe, NM 87504-2321
SAN: 214-2090
Tel: 505-988-4418
E-mail: orders@sunstonepress.com
Web Site: sunstonepress.com
Key Personnel
Pres & Treas: James Clois Smith, Jr
Dir, Opers & Sales: Carl Daniel Condit
Founded: 1971
Mainstream & Southwestern US titles, general nonfiction, fiction & how-to craft books.
ISBN Prefix(es): 978-0-913270; 978-0-86534; 978-1-61139 (ebooks); 978-1-63293
Number of titles published annually: 100 Print; 80 E-Book
Total Titles: 2,000 Print; 200 E-Book
Membership(s): Independent Book Publishers Association (IBPA); Publishers Association of the West (PubWest)

SUNY Press, see State University of New York Press

Superintendent of Documents, see US Government Publishing Office (GPO)

Surrey Books
Imprint of Agate Publishing
1328 Greenleaf St, Evanston, IL 60202
SAN: 275-8857
Tel: 847-475-4457 *Toll Free Tel:* 800-326-4430
Web Site: agatepublishing.com/surrey
Key Personnel
Pres & Publr: Doug Seibold *E-mail:* seibold@agatepublishing.com
Founded: 1982
Trade books. Specialize in nonfiction: cooking, health & lifestyle.
ISBN Prefix(es): 978-0-940625; 978-1-57284
Number of titles published annually: 20 Print
Total Titles: 120 Print
Distribution Center: Publishers Group West, 1700 Fourth St, Berkeley, CA 94710 *Tel:* 510-809-3700 *Toll Free Tel:* 800-788-3123 (cust serv) *Fax:* 510-809-3777 *E-mail:* info@pgw.com *Web Site:* www.pgw.com
Membership(s): International Association of Culinary Professionals (IACP)

§Swallow Press
Imprint of Ohio University Press
Alden Library, Suite 101, 30 Park Place, Athens, OH 45701-2909
Tel: 740-593-1154
Web Site: www.ohioswallow.com

Key Personnel
Acqs Ed: Ricky S Huard *Tel:* 740-593-1157
E-mail: huard@ohio.edu
Acqs Admin, Rts & Perms: Sally R Welch
E-mail: welchs@ohio.edu
Founded: 1940
Publisher of scholarly & trade books.
ISBN Prefix(es): 978-0-8214; 978-0-8040
Number of titles published annually: 45 Print
Foreign Rep(s): Combined Academic Publishers (CAP) (Africa, Europe, Middle East, Pacific Rim)
Orders to: Chicago Distribution Center, 11030 S Langley Ave, Chicago, IL 60628 *Toll Free Tel:* 800-621-2736 *Toll Free Fax:* 800-621-8476
Warehouse: Chicago Distribution Center, 11030 S Langley Ave, Chicago, IL 60628 *Toll Free Tel:* 800-621-2736 *Toll Free Fax:* 800-621-8476

Swan Isle Press
c/o Chicago Distribution Ctr, 11030 S Langley Ave, Chicago, IL 60628
Tel: 773-636-1818 (edit)
E-mail: info@swanislepress.com
Web Site: www.swanislepress.com
Key Personnel
Founder, Dir & Ed: David Rade
Founded: 1999
Not-for-profit, 501(c)(3) literary publisher, dedicated to publishing fiction, nonfiction & poetry in translation.
ISBN Prefix(es): 978-0-9678808; 978-0-9748881
Number of titles published annually: 4 Print; 2 E-Book
Total Titles: 30 Print; 6 E-Book
Distributed by University of Chicago Press
Foreign Rep(s): University of Chicago Press (worldwide)
Orders to: Chicago Distribution Center, 11030 S Langley Ave, Chicago, IL 60628 *Tel:* 773-702-7000 *Toll Free Tel:* 800-621-2736 *Fax:* 773-702-7212 *Toll Free Fax:* 800-621-8476 *E-mail:* orders@press.uchicago.edu *Web Site:* press.uchicago.edu/cdc.html; Baker & Taylor, 2550 W Tyvola Rd, Suite 300, Charlotte, NC 28217 *Tel:* 704-998-3100 *Toll Free Tel:* 800-775-1800 *E-mail:* btinfo@baker-taylor.com *Web Site:* www.baker-taylor.com; Ingram Book Co, One Ingram Blvd, La Vergne, TN 37086 *Tel:* 615-793-5000 *Toll Free Tel:* 800-937-8200 *E-mail:* customer.service@ingrambook.com *Web Site:* www.ingrambook.com
Membership(s): Association of American Publishers (AAP)

Swedenborg Foundation
320 N Church St, West Chester, PA 19380
SAN: 202-5280
Tel: 610-430-3222 *Toll Free Tel:* 800-355-3222 (cust serv) *Fax:* 610-430-7982
E-mail: info@swedenborg.com
Web Site: swedenborg.com
Key Personnel
Exec Dir: Morgan Beard *Tel:* 610-430-3222 ext 102 *E-mail:* mbeard@swedenborg.com
Ed: John Connolly *Tel:* 610-430-3222 ext 101 *E-mail:* jconnolly@swedenborg.com
Mktg Coord: Amy Acquarola *Tel:* 610-430-3222 ext 103 *E-mail:* aacquarola@swedenborg.com
Founded: 1849
Books & DVDs by, or relating to, the theological works & spiritual insights of Emanuel Swedenborg & related literature.
ISBN Prefix(es): 978-0-87785
Number of titles published annually: 10 Print
Total Titles: 200 Print
Orders to: Continental Sales Inc (CSI), 213 W Main St, Barrington, IL 60010 *Tel:* 847-381-6530 *Fax:* 847-382-0419 *E-mail:* bookreps@wybel.com; Wybel Marketing Group Inc, 213 W Main St, Barrington, IL 60010 *Tel:* 847-382-0384 *Fax:* 847-382-0385

E-mail: bookreps@wybel.com; Faherty & Associates, 17548 Redfern Ave, Lake Oswego, OR 97035 *Tel:* 503-639-3113 *Fax:* 503-213-6168 *E-mail:* faherty@fahertybooks.com *Web Site:* www.fahertybooks.com; Southern Territory Associates, 4508 64 St, Lubbock, TX 79414 *Tel:* 806-799-9997 *Fax:* 806-799-9777 *E-mail:* sta77@suddenlink.net; Rainbow Book Agencies, 303 Arthur St, Fairfield 3078, Australia *Tel:* (0613) 9481 6611 *Fax:* (0613) 9481 2371 *E-mail:* rba@rainbowbooks.com.au *Web Site:* www.rainbowbooks.com.au
Returns: University of Chicago Press/The Chicago Distribution Center, 11030 S Langley Ave, Chicago, IL 60628
Distribution Center: University of Chicago Press/The Chicago Distribution Center, 11030 S Langley Ave, Chicago, IL 60628

§SYBEX
Imprint of John Wiley & Sons Inc
111 River St, Suite 300, Hoboken, NJ 07030-5774
SAN: 211-1667
Tel: 201-748-6000 *Fax:* 201-748-6088
Toll Free Fax: 800-565-6802
Web Site: www.wiley.com/en-us/Sybex
Founded: 1976
For beginning, intermediate & advanced users of all types of software & hardware, including how-to books on various networking, word processing, database, graphics & spreadsheet software, certification, as well as computer games & Internet books, graphics & programming.
ISBN Prefix(es): 978-0-89588; 978-0-7821; 978-1-119; 978-0-935715; 978-1-894893; 978-1-897177
Number of titles published annually: 150 Print
Total Titles: 601 Print; 2 CD-ROM
Foreign Rep(s): Robert Blake (Central America, Mexico); Phillip Bowie (Caribbean); Lidel Edicoes Tecnicas Lda (Portugal); Ledy Martinez (Brazil, South America); John Wiley & Sons Canada Ltd (Canada); John Wiley & Sons Ltd (Natalie Lord) (Europe exc Austria, Germany & Switzerland, UK); John Wiley & Sons Singapore Pte Ltd (Singapore); Wiley-VCH Verlag GmbH (Austria, Germany, Switzerland)

Syracuse University Press
621 Skytop Rd, Suite 110, Syracuse, NY 13244-5290
SAN: 206-9776
Tel: 315-443-5534 *Toll Free Tel:* 800-365-8929 (cust serv) *Fax:* 315-443-5545
E-mail: supress@syr.edu
Web Site: press.syr.edu
Key Personnel
Dir: Alice Randal Pfeiffer *Tel:* 315-443-5535
E-mail: arpfeiff@syr.edu
Acqs Ed: Deborah Manion *Tel:* 315-443-5647
E-mail: dmmanion@syr.edu; Peggy Solic *Tel:* 315-443-5543 *E-mail:* masolic@syr.edu
Sr Busn Mgr: Karen Lockwood *Tel:* 315-443-5536 *E-mail:* kflockwo@syr.edu
Edit & Prodn Mgr: Kay Steinmetz *Tel:* 315-443-9155 *E-mail:* kasteinm@syr.edu
Sr Designer: Lynn Wilcox *Tel:* 315-443-1975
E-mail: lphoppel@syr.edu
Mktg Coord: Lisa Kuerbis *Tel:* 315-443-5546
E-mail: lkuerbis@syr.edu
Acctg Asst: Bobbi Clapps *Tel:* 315-443-5538
E-mail: baclaps@syr.edu
Founded: 1943
Scholarly, general & regional nonfiction; Middle East, Irish studies, medieval, women's studies, Iroquois studies, television, religion & politics, geography, sports & leisure, space, place & society, literature, Jewish studies (fiction & nonfiction).
ISBN Prefix(es): 978-0-8156
Number of titles published annually: 50 Print; 50 E-Book

Total Titles: 1,800 Print; 400 E-Book
Distributed by Arlen House; Dedalus Press
Distributor for Arlen House; Pucker Gallery; Sheep Meadow Press (poetry)
Foreign Rep(s): Eurospan University Press Group Ltd (Africa, Asia, Continental Europe, Middle East, UK); Rob Igoe Jr (New York State); Miller Trade Book Marketing (Midwestern States); Bob Rosenberg Group (13 Western States); UMG Publishers Representatives (David K Brown) (Eastern States); UTP Distribution (Canada)
Orders to: Longleaf Services Inc, 116 S Boundary St, Chapel Hill, NC 27514-8895 *Tel:* 919-966-7449 *Toll Free Tel:* 800-848-6224 *Fax:* 919-962-2704 *Toll Free Fax:* 800-272-6817 *E-mail:* customerservice@longleafservices.org *Web Site:* www.longleafservices.org
Returns: Longleaf Services Inc, c/o Ingram Publisher Services, 1550 Heil Quaker Blvd, Suite 200, La Vergne, TN 37086 *Tel:* 919-966-7449 *Toll Free Tel:* 866-400-5351 *Fax:* 919-962-2704 *Toll Free Fax:* 800-272-6817 *E-mail:* credit@longleafservices.org
Distribution Center: Longleaf Services Inc, 116 S Boundary St, Chapel Hill, NC 27514-8895 *Tel:* 919-966-7449 *Toll Free Tel:* 800-848-6224 *Fax:* 919-962-2704 *Toll Free Fax:* 800-272-6817 *E-mail:* customerservice@longleafservices.org *Web Site:* www.longleafservices.org
Membership(s): American Association of University Presses (AAUP)

Tachyon Publications LLC
1459 18 St, No 139, San Francisco, CA 94107
Tel: 415-285-5615
E-mail: tachyon@tachyonpublications.com; submissions@tachyonpublications.com
Web Site: www.tachyonpublications.com
Key Personnel
Publr & Ed: Jacob Weisman *E-mail:* jw@tachyonpublications.com
Mng Ed: Jill Roberts *E-mail:* jill@tachyonpublications.com
Ed: Jaymee Goh *E-mail:* jaymee.goh@tachyonpublications.com
Publicity Mgr: Rick Klaw *Tel:* 512-777-9036 *E-mail:* rick@tachyonpublications.com
Publicist: Kasey Lansdale *E-mail:* kasey@tachyonpublications.com
Lead Designer: Elizabeth Story *E-mail:* elizabeth@tachyonpublications.com
Founded: 1995
Science fiction, fantasy & genre publishing.
ISBN Prefix(es): 978-0-9648320; 978-1-892391; 978-1-61696
Number of titles published annually: 10 Print; 12 E-Book
Total Titles: 173 Print; 80 E-Book
Foreign Rep(s): Andi Richman (worldwide)
Foreign Rights: JABberwocky Literary Agency (Joshua Bilmes) (worldwide)
Orders to: Baker & Taylor Publisher Services, 30 Amberwood Pkwy, Ashland, OH 44805 *Tel:* 567-215-5030 *Toll Free Tel:* 888-814-0208 *E-mail:* info@btpubservices.com *Web Site:* www.btpubservices.com
Distribution Center: Baker & Taylor Publisher Services, 30 Amberwood Pkwy, Ashland, OH 44805 *Tel:* 567-215-5030 *Toll Free Tel:* 888-814-0208 *E-mail:* info@btpubservices.com *Web Site:* www.btpubservices.com
Membership(s): Science Fiction and Fantasy Writers of America, Inc (SFWA)

§Tahrike Tarsile Qur'an Inc
8008 51 Ave, Elmhurst, NY 11373
Tel: 718-446-6472 *Fax:* 718-446-4370
E-mail: read@koranusa.org
Web Site: www.koranusa.org

Key Personnel
Pres: Aun Ali Khalfan
Publishers & distributors of the Holy Quran & other Islamic books, videos & CDs.
ISBN Prefix(es): 978-0-940368; 978-1-879402
Number of titles published annually: 125 Print
Total Titles: 150 Print

§Nan A Talese
Imprint of Knopf Doubleday Publishing Group
c/o Penguin Random House LLC, 1745 Broadway, New York, NY 10019
Tel: 212-751-2600 *Fax:* 212-940-7390 (dom rts); 212-572-2662 (foreign rts)
Web Site: knopfdoubleday.com/imprint/nan-a-talese/; knopfdoubleday.com
Key Personnel
Assoc Ed: Dan Meyer
Founded: 1990
Penguin Random House & its publishing entities are not accepting unsol submissions, proposals, mss or submission queries via e-mail at this time.
Foreign Rights: ALS-Agenzia Letteraria Santachiara (Roberto Santachiara) (Italy); Anthea Agency (Katalina Sabeva) (Bulgaria); Bardon-Chinese Media Agency (Xu-Weiguang) (China); Bardon-Chinese Media Agency (Yu-Shiuan Chen) (Taiwan); English Agency Japan Co Ltd (Junzo Sawa) (Japan); Graal Literary Agency (Maria Strarz-Zielinska) (Poland); The Deborah Harris Agency (Ilana Kurshan) (Israel); JLM Literary Agency (Nelly Moukakos) (Greece); Katai & Bolza Literary (Peter Bolza) (Croatia, Hungary); Simona Kessler International (Simona Kessler) (Romania); Korea Copyright Center Inc (KCC) (MiSook Hong) (South Korea); Licht & Burr Literary Agency (Trine Licht) (Scandinavia); La Nouvelle Agency (Vanessa Kling) (France); Kristin Olson Literary Agency (Kristin Olson) (Czechia); Sebes & Bisseling Literary Agency (Paul Sebes) (Netherlands)

§TAN Books
Imprint of Saint Benedict Press LLC
PO Box 269, Gastonia, NC 28053
Tel: 704-731-0651 *Toll Free Tel:* 800-437-5876 *Fax:* 815-226-7770
E-mail: customerservice@tanbooks.com
Web Site: www.tanbooks.com
Founded: 1967
Publish traditional Catholic books, especially reprint classic works.
ISBN Prefix(es): 978-0-89555
Number of titles published annually: 15 Print
Total Titles: 550 Print

T&T Clark International
Imprint of Bloomsbury Publishing PLC
1385 Broadway, 5th fl, New York, NY 10018
E-mail: askacademic@bloomsbury.com
Web Site: www.bloomsbury.com/us/academic/academic-subjects/theology/t-t-clark
Founded: 1821
Biblical studies, theology & church history.
ISBN Prefix(es): 978-0-8264; 978-1-56338; 978-0-334; 978-0-7162; 978-0-567
Number of titles published annually: 100 Print
Total Titles: 2,200 Print
Orders to: Bloomsbury USA, MPS/BUSA Orders, 16365 James Madison Hwy, Gordonsville, VA 22942 *Toll Free Tel:* 888-330-8477 *Toll Free Fax:* 800-672-2054 *E-mail:* orders@mpsvirginia.com

Tanglewood Publishing
1060 N Capitol Ave, Suite E-395, Indianapolis, IN 46204
Tel: 812-877-9488 *Toll Free Tel:* 800-788-3123 (orders)

E-mail: info@tanglewoodbooks.com; orders@tanglewoodbooks.com; submission@tanglewoodbooks.com
Web Site: www.tanglewoodbooks.com
Key Personnel
Publr: Peggy Tierney *E-mail:* ptierney@tanglewoodbooks.com
Publg Mgr: Matt Buchanan *E-mail:* matt@tanglewoodbooks.com
Acqs Ed: Kairi Hamlin
Founded: 2003
ISBN Prefix(es): 978-0-9749303; 978-1-933718
Number of titles published annually: 5 Print; 1 Audio
Total Titles: 37 Print; 2 Audio
Distributed by Simon & Schuster, LLC

Tantor Media Inc
Division of Recorded Books
6 Business Park, Old Saybrook, CT 06475
Tel: 860-395-1155 *Toll Free Tel:* 877-782-6867 *Toll Free Fax:* 888-782-7821
E-mail: service@tantor.com; rights@tantor.com
Web Site: www.tantor.com
Key Personnel
Dir, Acqs: Ron Formica *Tel:* 877-782-6867 ext 31
Founded: 2000
Independent publisher & producer of audiobooks.
Number of titles published annually: 1,000 Online; 1,000 Audio
Total Titles: 7,000 Online; 7,000 Audio
Imprints: Tantor Audio; Tantor Media
Foreign Rep(s): IPS (worldwide)
Membership(s): The American Library Association (ALA); Audio Publishers Association; Public Library Association (PLA)

Tapestry Press Ltd
19 Nashoba Rd, Littleton, MA 01460
Tel: 978-486-0200 *Toll Free Tel:* 800-535-2007
E-mail: publish@tapestrypress.com
Web Site: www.tapestrypress.com
Key Personnel
Co-Owner: Michael J Miskin
Co-Owner & Publr: Elizabeth A Larsen Miskin
Pres: Sara E Hofeldt
Founded: 1988
College textbooks & journals; custom textbooks & anthologies.
ISBN Prefix(es): 978-0-924234; 978-1-56888; 978-1-59830
Number of titles published annually: 70 Print
Total Titles: 75 Print

TarcherPerigee
Imprint of Penguin Publishing Group
c/o Penguin Random House LLC, 1745 Broadway, New York, NY 10019
Tel: 212-782-9000
Web Site: www.penguin.com/tarcherperigee-overview/; www.facebook.com/TarcherPerigee
Key Personnel
SVP & Publr, Avery/TarcherPerigee: Tracy Behar
VP & Ed-in-Chief: Marian Lizzi
Assoc Publr & Dir, Mktg & Publicity, Avery/TarcherPerigee: Lindsay Gordon
Mktg Dir, Avery/TarcherPerigee: Farin Schlussel
Publicity Dir, Avery/TarcherPerigee: Anne Kosmoski; Casey Maloney
Asst Dir, Publicity, Avery/TarcherPerigee: Lillian Ball
Exec Ed: Lauren Appleton
Sr Ed: Batya Rosenblum
Ed: Lauren O'Neal
Assoc Ed, Avery/TarcherPerigee: Isabel McCarthy; Hannah Steigmeyer
Sr Mgr, Subs Rts, Dutton & TarcherPerigee: Jillian Fata
Sr Mktg Mgr, Avery/TarcherPerigee: Neda Dallal
Mktg Mgr, Avery/TarcherPerigee: Roshe Anderson; Carla Iannone

PUBLISHERS

Assoc Mktg Mgr, Avery/TarcherPerigee: Katie MacLeod-English
Publicity Mgr, Avery/TarcherPerigee: Alyssa Adler; Jamie Lescht
Founded: 2015
Core publishing areas include self-improvement, creativity, parenting, spirituality & gift/inspiration.
Penguin Random House & its publishing entities are not accepting unsol submissions, proposals, mss, or submission queries via e-mail at this time.
Number of titles published annually: 73 Print
Total Titles: 517 Print

Taschen America
NeueHouse, 6121 Sunset Blvd, Los Angeles, CA 90028
Tel: 323-463-4441 *Toll Free Tel:* 888-TASCHEN (827-2436)
E-mail: contact-us@taschen.com
Web Site: www.taschen.com
Key Personnel
Busn Mgr: Meghan Clarke *E-mail:* m.clarke@taschen.com
Founded: 1996
Publishers of high-quality, reasonably priced illustrated books on the subjects of art, architecture, design, photography, erotica, gay interest & popular culture.
ISBN Prefix(es): 978-3-8228; 978-3-8365
Number of titles published annually: 120 Print
Total Titles: 500 Print
Imprints: Taschen GmbH
Distribution Center: Ingram, One Ingram Blvd, La Vergne, TN 37086 *Toll Free Tel:* 888-558-2624

§Taunton Books
Formerly The Taunton Press Inc
Imprint of Harry N Abrams Inc
63 S Main St, Newtown, CT 06470
SAN: 210-5144
Mailing Address: PO Box 5563, Newtown, CT 06470-5563
Tel: 203-426-8171 *Toll Free Tel:* 866-505-4689 (orders) *Fax:* 203-270-9373
Key Personnel
Pres & CEO: Renee Jordan
Group Edit Dir: Tom McKenna
Dir, Book Sales: John Bacigalupi
Founded: 1975
Woodworking, home building, fiber arts, cooking & gardening books, magazines, DVDs & web sites.
ISBN Prefix(es): 978-0-918804; 978-0-942391; 978-1-56158; 978-1-60085; 978-1-63186
Number of titles published annually: 25 Print; 10 CD-ROM; 25 E-Book; 1 Audio
Total Titles: 525 Print; 100 CD-ROM; 10 Online; 300 E-Book; 1 Audio
Distributor for Guild of Master Craftsman (North America); Lucky Spool (North America & Australia)
Foreign Rep(s): Guild of Master Craftsman
Warehouse: 141 Sheridan Dr, Naugatuck, CT 06770
Distribution Center: Two Rivers Distribution, 1400 Broadway, Suite 3200, New York, NY 10018 *Toll Free Tel:* 800-937-8200; 800-343-4499 ips@ingramcontent.com *Web Site:* www.tworiversdistribution.com

The Taunton Press Inc, see Taunton Books

Taylor & Francis Inc
530 Walnut St, Suite 850, Philadelphia, PA 19106
Tel: 215-625-8900 *Toll Free Tel:* 800-354-1420
  Fax: 215-207-0050; 215-207-0046 (cust serv)
E-mail: support@tandfonline.com
Web Site: www.taylorandfrancis.com
Key Personnel
CEO: Annie Callanan
Global Publg Dir, Journals: Leon Heward-Mills
Mng Dir, Books Publg: Jeremy North
Founded: 1974
Journals in engineering, physical science, psychology, sociology, physics, chemistry, mathematics, environmental science, business, public health, marketing, arts, anthropology, political science, library science & LGBT studies.
ISBN Prefix(es): 978-1-56032; 978-0-87630; 978-0-86377; 978-0-8448; 978-0-85066; 978-0-85109; 978-0-905273; 978-1-85000
Number of titles published annually: 585 Print
Total Titles: 1,500 Print
Imprints: Cogent OA; CRC Press; Garland Science; Routledge; Taylor & Francis Asia Pacific; Taylor & Francis Books
Foreign Office(s): Taylor & Francis Group, an Informa Business, Milton Park, 2 & 4 Park Sq, Abingdon, Oxon OX14 4RN, United Kingdom *Tel:* (020) 7017 6000 *Fax:* (020) 7017 6699 *E-mail:* enquiries@taylorandfrancis.com
Orders to: 7625 Empire Dr, Florence, KY 41042-2929 *Tel:* 859-727-5000 *Toll Free Tel:* 800-634-7064 *Fax:* 859-647-4029 *Toll Free Fax:* 800-248-4724 *E-mail:* orders@taylorandfrancis.com; Bookpoint Ltd, 130 Park Dr, Abingdon, Oxon OX14 4SE, United Kingdom (Africa, Asia, Australia, Europe) *Tel:* (01235) 400 400 *Web Site:* bookpoint.wp.hachette.co.uk
Distribution Center: 7625 Empire Dr, Florence, KY 41042 *Tel:* 859-727-5000 *Toll Free Tel:* 800-634-7064 *Fax:* 859-647-4029 *Toll Free Fax:* 800-248-4724 *E-mail:* orders@taylorandfrancis.com

TCU Press
3000 Sandage Ave, Fort Worth, TX 76109
Tel: 817-257-7822
E-mail: tcupress@tcu.edu
Web Site: www.tcupress.com
Key Personnel
Dir: Dan Williams *Tel:* 817-257-5907 *E-mail:* d.e.williams@tcu.edu
Assoc Ed: Marco Roc *Tel:* 817-257-5074
  E-mail: m.roc@tcu.edu
Prodn Mgr: Abegail Jennings *Tel:* 817-257-6872
  E-mail: abby.jennings@tcu.edu
Mktg Coord: James Lehr *Tel:* 817-257-6874
  E-mail: j.e.lehr@tcu.edu
Founded: 1947
History & literature of Texas & the American West.
ISBN Prefix(es): 978-0-912646; 978-0-87565
Number of titles published annually: 15 Print; 20 Online
Total Titles: 492 Print; 20 Online; 100 E-Book; 1 Audio
Distribution Center: Independent Publishers Group (IPG), 814 N Franklin St, Chicago, IL 60610 (worldwide exc North America) *Toll Free Tel:* 800-888-4741 *E-mail:* orders@ipgbook.com *Web Site:* www.ipgbook.com; Longleaf Services Inc, 116 S Boundary St, Chapel Hill, NC 27514-3808 *Tel:* 919-966-7449 *Toll Free Tel:* 800-848-6224 *Fax:* 919-962-2704 *Toll Free Fax:* 800-272-6817 *E-mail:* orders@longleafservices.org *Web Site:* www.longleafservices.org SAN: 203-3151
Membership(s): Association of University Presses (AUPresses)

Teacher Created Resources Inc
12621 Western Ave, Garden Grove, CA 92481
Tel: 714-891-7895 *Toll Free Tel:* 800-662-4321; 888-343-4335 *Toll Free Fax:* 800-525-1254
E-mail: custserv@teachercreated.com
Web Site: www.teachercreated.com
Key Personnel
Founder & Pres: Mary Dupuy Smith
Founded: 1977
Publishes PreK-12 curriculum programs, supplemental resource materials & technology products. Also provides professional staff development for teachers.
ISBN Prefix(es): 978-1-55734; 978-1-57690; 978-1-4206; 978-1-4570
Number of titles published annually: 250 Print
Total Titles: 1,500 Print
Divisions: Edupress Inc
See separate listing for:
Edupress Inc

§Teachers College Press
Affiliate of Teachers College, Columbia University
1234 Amsterdam Ave, New York, NY 10027
SAN: 213-263X
Tel: 212-678-3929 *Fax:* 212-678-4149
E-mail: tcpress@tc.edu
Web Site: www.tcpress.com
Key Personnel
Dir: Jennifer Feldman *E-mail:* jfeldman@tc.edu
Creative Dir: Dave Strauss
Prodn Dir: Giraud Lorber *E-mail:* glorber@tc.edu
Mng Prodn Ed: Michael Olivo *E-mail:* molivo@tc.edu
Exec Acqs Ed: Brian Ellerbeck
  E-mail: ellerbeck@tc.edu
Sr Acqs Ed: Allison Scott *E-mail:* ascott@tc.edu
Acqs Ed: Emily Spangler *E-mail:* spangler@tc.edu
Prodn Ed & Electronic Publg Specialist: John Bylander
Busn Mgr: Monica Carrera
Digital Mktg Mgr: Emily Freyer
Mktg Mgr: Nancy Power
Sales & New Busn Devt Mgr: Sally Kling
  E-mail: skling@tc.edu
Subs Rts & Perms Mgr: Christina Brianik
  E-mail: cbrianik@tc.edu
Outreach Coord: Michael McGann
Founded: 1904
Scholarly & professional books in education; tests, classroom materials & reference works.
ISBN Prefix(es): 978-0-8077
Number of titles published annually: 70 Print; 1 CD-ROM
Total Titles: 1,800 Print; 1 CD-ROM
Foreign Rep(s): Eurospan Ltd (worldwide exc Canada & USA); University of Toronto Guidance Center (Canada)
Orders to: Hawker Brownlow Education, 2/47 Wangara Rd, Cheltenham, Victoria 3192, Australia (select Australia editions) *Tel:* (03) 8558 2444 *Fax:* (03) 8558 2400 *E-mail:* tdupay@hbe.com.au *Web Site:* www.hbe.com.au; University of Toronto Press-Guidance Centre, 5201 Dufferin St, Toronto, ON M3H 5T8, Canada (CN) *Toll Free Tel:* 800-565-9523 *Toll Free Fax:* 800-221-9985 *E-mail:* utpbooks@utpress.utoronto.ca *Web Site:* www.utpguidancecentre.com
Returns: Attn: Returns Dept, 30 Amberwood Pkwy, Ashland, OH 44805
Distribution Center: Baker & Taylor Publisher Services, 30 Amberwood Pkwy, Ashland, OH 44805 *Toll Free Tel:* 800-575-6566 *Toll Free Fax:* 866-406-1274 *E-mail:* tcp.orders@btpubservices.com
Membership(s): American Association of University Presses (AAUP); Association of American Publishers (AAP); Book Industry Study Group (BISG)

§Teacher's Discovery®
Division of American Eagle Co Inc
2741 Paldan Dr, Auburn Hills, MI 48326
Toll Free Tel: 800-TEACHER (832-2437)
Toll Free Fax: 800-287-4509
E-mail: help@teachersdiscovery.com; orders@teachersdiscovery.com
Web Site: www.teachersdiscovery.com

U.S. PUBLISHERS

Key Personnel
Owner: Skip McWilliams
Dir, Mktg: Steve Giroux
Founded: 1968
Sell supplemental classroom teaching materials for Spanish, French, German, English & Social Studies. See www.vocesdigital.com for prize-winning digital courseware (e-textbooks).
ISBN Prefix(es): 978-1-884473; 978-0-7560
Number of titles published annually: 200 Print

§Teaching & Learning Co
Division of The Lorenz Corp
501 E Third St, Dayton, OH 45402
Mailing Address: PO Box 802, Dayton, OH 45401-0802
Toll Free Tel: 800-444-1144 *Fax:* 937-223-2042
E-mail: service@lorenz.com
Web Site: www.lorenzeducationalpress.com
Founded: 1994
Educational publishing division includes visual resources, instructional guides & reproducibles, elementary supplementals.
ISBN Prefix(es): 978-1-57310
Number of titles published annually: 35 Print
Total Titles: 400 Print; 325 E-Book; 10 Audio
Membership(s): Education Market Association

§Teaching Strategies LLC
4500 East-West Hwy, Suite 300, Bethesda, MD 20814
Tel: 301-634-0818 *Toll Free Tel:* 800-637-3652
E-mail: info@teachingstrategies.com; support@teachingstrategies.com
Web Site: teachingstrategies.com
Key Personnel
CEO: John Olsen
CFO: Heather O'Shea
COO: Scott Balwinski
Chief Mktg Offr: Autumn Taylor
CTO: Denis Khazan
Pres, Prod: Celia Stokes
VP, Educ Content: Breeyn Mack
Founded: 1988
Curriculum, assessment & training materials for early childhood education (birth-age 8) & parent's guides; web subscription service.
ISBN Prefix(es): 978-1-879537; 978-0-9602892; 978-1-60617
Number of titles published annually: 5 Print
Total Titles: 66 Print

§Temple University Press
Division of Temple University of the Commonwealth System of Higher Education
1852 N Tenth St, Philadelphia, PA 19122-6099
SAN: 202-7666
Tel: 215-926-2140 *Toll Free Tel:* 800-621-2736
Fax: 215-926-2141
E-mail: tempress@temple.edu
Web Site: tupress.temple.edu
Key Personnel
Dir: Mary Rose Muccie *E-mail:* maryrose.muccie@temple.edu
Assoc Dir, Fin Mgr: Karen Baker *E-mail:* karen.baker@temple.edu
Ed-in-Chief: Aaron Javsicas *E-mail:* aaron.javsicas@temple.edu
Sr Prodn Ed: Ashley Petrucci *E-mail:* ashley.petrucci@temple.edu
Ed: Ryan A Mulligan *E-mail:* ryan.mulligan@temple.edu; Shaun Vigil *E-mail:* shaun.vigil@temple.edu
Rts & Contracts Coord: Will Forrest *E-mail:* wforrest@temple.edu
Publicity Mgr: Gary Kramer *E-mail:* gkramer@temple.edu
Ad & Promo Mgr: Irene Imperio Kull *E-mail:* irene.imperio@temple.edu
Founded: 1969
Scholarly books; all regional interests.
ISBN Prefix(es): 978-0-87722; 978-1-56639; 978-1-59213; 978-1-4399
Number of titles published annually: 45 Print
Total Titles: 1,450 Print
Foreign Rep(s): Baker & Taylor Ltd (Asia, The Pacific, worldwide exc Canada); Combined Academic Publishers (CAP) (Europe); Lynn McClory (Canada)
Returns: Temple University Press Chicago Distribution Center, 11030 S Langley, Chicago, IL 60628 *Tel:* 773-702-7000 *Fax:* 773-702-7000 *Toll Free Fax:* 800-621-8476
Warehouse: Temple University Press Chicago Distribution Center, 11030 S Langley, Chicago, IL 60628, Contact: Karen Hyzy *Tel:* 773-702-7000 *Fax:* 773-702-7000 *Toll Free Fax:* 800-621-8476
Membership(s): Association of University Presses (AUPresses); Society for Scholarly Publishing (SSP)

Temporal Mechanical Press
Division of Enos Mills Cabin Museum
6760 Hwy 7, Estes Park, CO 80517-6404
Tel: 970-586-4706
E-mail: info@enosmills.com
Web Site: www.enosmills.com
Key Personnel
Owner: Elizabeth M Mills; Eryn Mills
ISBN Prefix(es): 978-1-928878
Number of titles published annually: 3 Print
Total Titles: 32 Print

Ten Speed Press
Imprint of Crown Publishing Group
6001 Shellmound St, Suite 600, Emeryville, CA 94608
Tel: 510-285-3000 *Toll Free Tel:* 800-841-BOOK (841-2665)
Web Site: www.randomhousebooks.com/imprint/ten-speed-press/; crownpublishing.com/archives/imprint/ten-speed-press
Founded: 1971
Illustrated books. Actively seeks out new & established authors who are authorities & tastemakers in the world of food, drink, design, reference & humor. Create cookbooks, illustrated gift titles, popular business titles & groundbreaking self-help titles.
Penguin Random House & its publishing entities are not accepting unsol submissions, proposals, mss, or submission queries via e-mail at this time.
Number of titles published annually: 100 Print
Total Titles: 587 Print
Imprints: Food52 Works; 4 Color Books; Lorena Jones Books (cooking & lifestyle); Ten Speed Graphic
Foreign Rep(s): Penguin Random House LLC (worldwide)
Orders to: Penguin Random House LLC, 400 Hahn Rd, Westminster, MD 21157 *Toll Free Tel:* 800-733-3000 *E-mail:* csorders@randomhouse.com; Penguin Random House of Canada Inc, 320 Front St W, Suite 410, Toronto, ON M5V 3B6, Canada *Toll Free Tel:* 800-668-4247 *Fax:* 416-598-7764

Teora USA LLC
9443 Rosehill Dr, Bethesda, MD 20817
SAN: 256-1220
Tel: 301-986-6990
E-mail: teorausa@gmail.com
Web Site: www.teora.com
Key Personnel
Busn Mgr: Teodor Raducanu
Founded: 2003
ISBN Prefix(es): 978-1-59496
Number of titles published annually: 6 Print
Total Titles: 60 Print
Imprints: Teora
Membership(s): Independent Book Publishers Association (IBPA)

Terra Nova Books
33 Alondra Rd, Santa Fe, NM 87508
Tel: 505-670-9319 *Fax:* 509-461-9333
E-mail: publisher@terranovabooks.com; marketing@terranovabooks.com
Web Site: www.terranovabooks.com
Key Personnel
Co-Owner & Publr: Scott Gerber
Co-Owner & Ed: Marty Gerber *Tel:* 505-470-6797 *E-mail:* editor@terranovabooks.com
VP, Mktg: Joanna V Hill *Tel:* 267-304-8521
Founded: 2012
Innovative independent book publisher actively developing fresh new titles & authors titles across a wide range of genres.
ISBN Prefix(es): 978-1-938288; 978-1-948749
Number of titles published annually: 8 Print; 8 E-Book
Total Titles: 72 Print; 40 E-Book
Sales Office(s): SCB Distributors, 15608 S New Century Dr, Gardena, CA 90248, Sales & Mktg Mgr: Gabriel Wilmoth *Tel:* 310-532-9400 *Toll Free Tel:* 800-729-6423 *E-mail:* gabriel@scbdistributors.com *Web Site:* scbdistributors.com
Foreign Rep(s): SCB Distributors (Steve Paton) (Western Canada); SCB Distributors (Terry Fernihough) (New Brunswick, CN, Nova Scotia, CN, Ontario, CN, Prince Edward Island, CN); SCB Distributors (Karen Stacey) (Quebec, CN)
Orders to: SCB Distributors, 15608 S New Century Dr, Gardena, CA 90248, Sales & Mktg Mgr: Gabriel Wilmoth *Tel:* 310-532-9400 *Toll Free Tel:* 800-729-6423 *E-mail:* gabriel@scbdistributors.com *Web Site:* scbdistributors.com
Returns: SCB Distributors, 15608 S New Century Dr, Gardena, CA 90248, Sales & Mktg Mgr: Gabriel Wilmoth *Tel:* 310-532-9400 *Toll Free Tel:* 800-729-6423 *E-mail:* gabriel@scbdistributors.com *Web Site:* scbdistributors.com
Distribution Center: SCB Distributors, 15608 S New Century Dr, Gardena, CA 90248, Sales & Mktg Mgr: Gabriel Wilmoth *Tel:* 310-532-9400 *Toll Free Tel:* 800-729-6423 *E-mail:* gabriel@scbdistributors.com *Web Site:* scbdistributors.com

TESOL Press
Division of TESOL International Association
1925 Ballenger Ave, Suite 550, Alexandria, VA 22314-6820
Tel: 703-518-2500; 703-518-2501 (cust serv)
Toll Free Tel: 888-891-0041 (cust serv)
Fax: 703-691-5327
E-mail: publications@tesol.org; press@tesol.org; members@tesol.org
Web Site: www.tesol.org
Key Personnel
Exec Dir: Rosa Aronson, PhD *Tel:* 703-518-2500 ext 505 *E-mail:* raronson@tesol.org
Founded: 1966
Education association & publisher of professional education books & products for the ESL teaching profession.
ISBN Prefix(es): 978-0-939791; 978-1-1931; 978-1-931185; 978-1-942223; 978-1-942799; 978-1-945351
Number of titles published annually: 6 Print
Total Titles: 90 Print; 1 CD-ROM
Distributed by Alta Book Center Publishers; New Readers Press; Saddleback Educational Publishing
Foreign Rep(s): Eurospan Group (worldwide)
Returns: Independent Publishers Group (IPG), Returns Dept, 600 N Pulaski Rd, Chicago, IL 60624 *Toll Free Tel:* 800-888-4741 *E-mail:* frontdesk@ipgbook.com

Distribution Center: Eurospan Group, Gray's Inn House, 127 Clerkenwell Rd, London EC1R 5DB, United Kingdom (Africa, Asia-Pacific, Caribbean, Europe, Latin America, Middle East & UK) *Tel:* (01235) 465576 *Fax:* (01235) 465577 *Web Site:* www.eurospanbookstore.com/tesol
Independent Publishers Group (IPG) *Toll Free Tel:* 800-888-4741 *E-mail:* orders@ipgbook.com

Teton NewMedia Inc
5286 Dunewood Dr, Florence, OR 97439
Tel: 541-991-3342
E-mail: lodgepole@tetonnm.com
Web Site: www.tetonnm.com
Key Personnel
Pres & CEO: John Febiger Spahr, Jr
Prod Mgr: Mike Albiniak *Tel:* 307-883-5640 *E-mail:* mike@fiftysixforty.com
Founded: 1999 (by John Sphar & Carroll Cann)
Health science publisher that focuses on producing high quality, affordable veterinary text & reference books.
ISBN Prefix(es): 978-1-893441; 978-1-59161
Number of titles published annually: 3 Print; 3 E-Book
Total Titles: 30 Print; 30 E-Book
Distributed by Taylor & Francis/CRC Press
Distributor for LifeLearn
Foreign Rights: John Scott & Co (worldwide)

Texas A&M University Press
Division of Texas A&M University
John H Lindsey Bldg, Lewis St, 4354 TAMU, College Station, TX 77843-4354
SAN: 207-5237
Tel: 979-845-1436 *Toll Free Tel:* 800-826-8911 (orders) *Fax:* 979-847-8752 *Toll Free Fax:* 888-617-2421 (orders)
E-mail: bookorders@tamu.edu
Web Site: www.tamupress.com
Key Personnel
Dir: Dr Jay Dew *Tel:* 979-458-3980 *E-mail:* jaydew@tamu.edu
Lib Sales Dir & Mktg Mgr: Kyle Littlefield *Tel:* 979-458-3983 *E-mail:* k-littlefield@tamu.edu
Ed-in-Chief: Dr Thom Lemmons *Tel:* 979-845-0758 *E-mail:* thom.lemmons@tamu.edu
Design Mgr: Mary Ann Jacob *Tel:* 979-845-3694 *E-mail:* m-jacob@tamu.edu
Fin Mgr: Dianna Sells *Tel:* 979-845-0146 *E-mail:* d-sells@tamu.edu
Mgr, Cust Rel: Wynona McCormick *Tel:* 979-458-3994 *E-mail:* wynona@tamu.edu
Publicity & Ad Mgr: Christine Brown *Tel:* 979-458-3982 *E-mail:* christinebrown@tamu.edu
Trade Sales: Kathryn Lloyd *Tel:* 979-458-3981 *E-mail:* k-lloyd@tamu.edu
Founded: 1974
Scholarly nonfiction, regional studies, economics, history, natural history, presidential studies, anthropology, US-Mexican borderlands studies, women's studies, nautical archaeology, military studies, agriculture, Texas history & archaeology.
ISBN Prefix(es): 978-0-89096; 978-1-58544; 978-1-60344; 978-1-60344
Number of titles published annually: 60 Print; 1 CD-ROM
Total Titles: 1,500 Print; 2 CD-ROM; 1,450 E-Book; 45 Audio
Distributor for Stephen F Austin State University Press; McWhiney Foundation Press/State House Press; Texas Christian University Press; Texas Review Press; Texas State Historical Association; University of North Texas Press
Foreign Rep(s): Eurospan Group (Europe, UK); Scholarly Book Services Inc (Laura Rust) (Canada); US PubRep (Craig Falk) (Latin America)
Foreign Rights: Tamu Press
Membership(s): Association of University Presses (AUPresses)

Texas Christian University Press, see TCU Press

Texas State Historical Association
3001 Lake Austin Blvd, Suite 3.116, Austin, TX 78703
Tel: 512-471-2600 *Fax:* 512-473-8691
Web Site: www.tshaonline.org
Key Personnel
Pubns Dir: Rick McCaslin *E-mail:* rick.mccaslin@tshaonline.org
Founded: 1897
Books & articles related to Texas history.
ISBN Prefix(es): 978-0-87611; 978-1-62511
Number of titles published annually: 4 Print; 4 E-Book
Total Titles: 100 Print; 33 E-Book
Distributed by Texas A&M University Press

Texas Tech University Press
1120 Main St, 2nd fl, Lubbock, TX 79401
SAN: 218-5989
Mailing Address: PO Box 41037, Lubbock, TX 79409-1037 SAN: 218-5989
Tel: 806-742-2982 *Toll Free Tel:* 800-832-4042
E-mail: ttup@ttu.edu
Web Site: www.ttupress.org
Key Personnel
Dir: Brian L Ott
Mng Dir: Joanna Conrad *E-mail:* joanna.conrad@ttu.edu
Sr Acqs Ed: Travis Snyder *E-mail:* travis.snyder@ttu.edu
Ed: Christie Perlmutter *E-mail:* christie.perlmutter@ttu.edu
Sales & Mktg Mgr: John Brock *E-mail:* john.brock@ttu.edu
Sr Designer: Hannah Gaskamp *E-mail:* hannah.gaskamp@ttu.edu
Founded: 1971
Scholarly books & journals: History, culture & natural history of Texas, the Southwest & the Great Plains; photography; military history; sports history; American roots music; memoirs, especially of the American West; sustainability studies; gender in the American West.
ISBN Prefix(es): 978-0-89672; 978-1-68283; 978-1-945797 (Texas Tech University Libraries)
Number of titles published annually: 20 Print; 15 E-Book
Total Titles: 450 Print; 100 E-Book
Distributor for National Ranching Heritage Center
Foreign Rep(s): Eurospan Group (Africa, Asia, Europe, Middle East, The Pacific, UK)
Distribution Center: Longleaf Services Inc, 116 S Boundary St, Chapel Hill, NC 27514-3808 *Toll Free Tel:* 800-848-6224 ext 1 *Fax:* 919-962-2704 *E-mail:* orders@longleafservices.org
Membership(s): Association of University Presses (AUPresses); Publishers Association of the West (PubWest)

§University of Texas Press
Division of University of Texas
3001 Lake Austin Blvd, 2.200, Austin, TX 78703
SAN: 212-9876
Mailing Address: PO Box 7819, Austin, TX 78713-7819
Tel: 512-471-7233 *Fax:* 512-232-7178
E-mail: utpress@uts.cc.utexas.edu; info@utpress.utexas.edu
Web Site: utpress.utexas.edu
Key Personnel
CFO: Joyce Lewandoski
Dir: Robert Devens
Dir, Press: Dave Hamrick
Asst Dir, Sales & Mktg Mgr: Gianna LaMorte
Acq Ed: Jim Burr
Mgr & Intl Rts Contact: Ines ter Horst
Ad, Exhibits Mgr: Chris Farmer
Credit Mgr & Cust Serv: Brenda Jo Hoggutt
Natl Sales Mgr: Bob Barnett
Prodn Mgr: Ellen McKie
Asst Mktg Mgr: Nancy Bryan
Founded: 1950
General scholarly nonfiction, Latin America, Middle Eastern studies, Southwest regional, social sciences, humanities & science, linguistics, architecture, classics, natural history, Latin American literature in translation.
ISBN Prefix(es): 978-0-292
Number of titles published annually: 100 Print
Total Titles: 3,000 Print; 1 CD-ROM; 1 Online
Distributor for Bat Conservation International; Institute for Mesoamerican Studies; Menil Foundation; Rothko Chapel; Texas Parks & Wildlife Department
Foreign Rep(s): Codash (Canada); Combined Academic Publishers (CAP) (Australia, New Zealand); Nicholas Esson (Europe, UK); Marketing Dept, University of Texas (Caribbean)
Distribution Center: Chicago Distribution Center (CDC), 11030 S Langley Ave, Chicago, IL 60628 (North America) *Tel:* 773-702-7010 *Toll Free Tel:* 800-621-8476 *Web Site:* press.uchicago.edu/cdc
Membership(s): Association of American Publishers (AAP); Association of University Presses (AUPresses)

Texas Western Press
Affiliate of University of Texas at El Paso
c/o University of Texas at El Paso, 500 W University Ave, El Paso, TX 79968-0633
SAN: 202-7712
Tel: 915-747-5688 *Toll Free Tel:* 800-488-3798 (orders only) *Fax:* 915-747-5345
E-mail: twpress@utep.edu
Web Site: twp.utep.edu
Key Personnel
Dir: Robert Stakes
Founded: 1952
Scholarly books on the history, art, photography & culture of the American Southwest.
ISBN Prefix(es): 978-0-87404
Number of titles published annually: 2 Print
Total Titles: 63 Print; 1 Audio
Imprints: Southwestern Studies
Distributed by University of Texas Press

Thames & Hudson
500 Fifth Ave, New York, NY 10110
SAN: 202-5795
Tel: 212-354-3763 *Toll Free Tel:* 800-233-4830 *Fax:* 212-398-1252
E-mail: bookinfo@thames.wwnorton.com
Web Site: www.thamesandhudsonusa.com
Key Personnel
Publr & CEO: Sophy Thompson
Publr & Pres: Will Balliett
Assoc Edit Dir: Elizabeth Keene
Publicity: Harry Burton
Founded: 1977
Nonfiction trade, quality paperbacks & college texts on art, archaeology, architecture, crafts, history & photography.
ISBN Prefix(es): 978-0-500
Number of titles published annually: 150 Print
Total Titles: 1,000 Print
Distributed by W W Norton & Company Inc
Advertising Agency: Verso
Shipping Address: National Book Co Inc, Keystone Industrial Park, Scranton, PA 18512
Membership(s): Association of American Publishers (AAP)

Theatre Communications Group
520 Eighth Ave, 24th fl, New York, NY 10018-4156
Tel: 212-609-5900 *Fax:* 212-609-5901

U.S. PUBLISHERS

E-mail: info@tcg.org
Web Site: www.tcg.org
Key Personnel
Exec Dir & CEO: Teresa Eyring
Deputy Dir & COO: Adrian Budhu
Publr: Terence Nemeth *Tel:* 212-609-5900 ext 239
  E-mail: tnemeth@tcg.org
Dir, Ad: Carol Van Keuren *Tel:* 212-609-5900 ext 240 *E-mail:* cvankeuren@tcg.org
Edit Dir: Kathy Sova *Tel:* 212-609-5900 ext 243
  E-mail: ksova@tcg.org
Assoc Art Dir: Monet Cogbill *Tel:* 212-609-5900 ext 221 *E-mail:* mcogbill@tcg.org
Pubns Mgr: Erin Salvi *Tel:* 212-609-5900 ext 246
  E-mail: esalvi@tcg.org
Founded: 1961
Performing arts, dramatic literature.
ISBN Prefix(es): 978-0-930452; 978-1-55936
Number of titles published annually: 24 Print; 20 E-Book
Total Titles: 450 Print; 200 E-Book
Distributor for Chance Magazine; 53rd State Press; Nick Hern Books; League of Professional Theatre Women; Padua Playwrights Press; PAJ Publications; Playscripts Inc; Playwrights Canada Press; Martin E Segal Theatre Center Publications; Ubu Repertory Theatre Publications
Foreign Rep(s): Nick Hern Books (UK); Playwrights Canada Press (Canada)

§Theosophical University Press
Affiliate of Theosophical Society (Pasadena)
PO Box C, Pasadena, CA 91109-7107
SAN: 205-4299
Tel: 626-798-3378
E-mail: tupress@theosociety.org
Web Site: www.theosociety.org
Key Personnel
Dir: Randell C Grubb
Mgr & Intl Rts: Will Thackara
Cust Serv: Ina Belderis
Founded: 1886
Quality theosophical literature.
ISBN Prefix(es): 978-0-911500; 978-1-55700
Number of titles published annually: 2 Print; 5 Online; 2 E-Book
Total Titles: 86 Print; 1 CD-ROM; 115 Online; 84 E-Book; 7 Audio
Imprints: Sunrise Library
Foreign Office(s): Theosophischer Verlag GmbH, Brunnenstr 11, 56414 Hundsangen, Germany, Contact: Jochen Hannappel *Tel:* (06435) 96033 *Fax:* (06435) 96053 *E-mail:* info@theosophischer-verlag.de *Web Site:* www.theosophischer-verlag.de
Theosophical University Press Agency, Daal en Bergselaan 68, 2565 AG The Hague, Netherlands, Contact: Coen Vonk *Tel:* (070) 323 1776 *Fax:* (070) 325 7275 *E-mail:* tupa@theosofie.net *Web Site:* www.theosofie.net
Theosophical University Press South African Agency, PO Box 504, Constantia 7848, South Africa, Contact: Dewald Bester *Tel:* (021) 4342281 *E-mail:* besterdewald@gmail.com
The Theosophical Society, 43 Stephenson Grove, Rainhill, Merseyside L35 9AB, United Kingdom, Contact: Patrick Powell *E-mail:* ts-uk@talktalk.net *Web Site:* www.theosophical.org.uk
Warehouse: 2416 N Lake Ave, Altadena, CA 91001

§Thieme Medical Publishers Inc
Subsidiary of Georg Thieme Verlag KG
333 Seventh Ave, 18th fl, New York, NY 10001
SAN: 202-7399
Tel: 212-760-0888 *Toll Free Tel:* 800-782-3488
  Fax: 212-947-1112
E-mail: customerservice@thieme.com
Web Site: www.thieme.com
Key Personnel
Mng Dir: Dr Cathrin Weinstein
Founded: 1979

Electronic products, apps, books, journals, textbooks in clinical medicine, dentistry, speech & hearing, allied health, audiology, organic chemistry plus electronic products, medical education & databases.
ISBN Prefix(es): 978-0-913258; 978-0-86577; 978-1-58890; 978-1-60406; 978-1-62623
Number of titles published annually: 50 Print; 3 CD-ROM; 50 Online
Total Titles: 605 Print; 50 Online; 605 E-Book
Foreign Office(s): Thieme Publishers Rio, Argentina Bldg, 16th fl, Ala A, 228, Praia do Botafogo, 22250-040 Rio de Janeiro-RJ, Brazil, VP: Daniel Schiff *Tel:* (021) 3736-3631
Georg Thieme Verlag, PO Box 30 11 20, 70451 Stuttgart, Germany *Tel:* (0711) 89310 *Fax:* (0711) 8931410 *E-mail:* customerservice@thieme.de *Web Site:* www.thieme.de
Thieme Medical & Scientific Publishers Pvt Ltd, A-12, Sector 2, 2nd fl, Noida, Uttar Pradesh 201 301, India *Tel:* (0120) 427 4461 *Fax:* (0120) 427 4465 *E-mail:* customerservice@thieme.in
Distributor for AO Foundation
Foreign Rep(s): Login Canada (Canada); Woodslane (Australia)
Foreign Rights: Heike Schwabenthan (worldwide)
Warehouse: Mount Joy Distribution Center, 1000 Strickler Rd, Mount Joy, PA 17552
Membership(s): Association of American Publishers (AAP); Independent Publishers Association; STM

Third World Press Foundation
7822 S Dobson Ave, Chicago, IL 60619
Mailing Address: PO Box 19730, Chicago, IL 60619
Tel: 773-651-0700
E-mail: twpbooks@thirdworldpressfoundation.org
Web Site: thirdworldpressfoundation.org
Key Personnel
Publr: Haki R Madhubuti
Founded: 1967
Publishers of quality Black fiction, nonfiction, poetry, drama, young adult & children literature; primarily adult literature.
ISBN Prefix(es): 978-0-88378
Number of titles published annually: 10 Print
Total Titles: 140 Print
Distribution Center: Ingram Publisher Services, 14 Ingram Blvd, Mail Stop 631, La Vergne, TN 37086 *Toll Free Tel:* 866-400-5351 *Web Site:* www.ingrampublisherservices.com

13A, see Gallery Books

Charles C Thomas Publisher Ltd
2600 S First St, Springfield, IL 62704
SAN: 201-9485
Tel: 217-789-8980 *Toll Free Tel:* 800-258-8980
  Fax: 217-789-9130
E-mail: books@ccthomas.com
Web Site: www.ccthomas.com
Key Personnel
Pres: Michael Payne Thomas
Founded: 1927
Medicine, allied health sciences, science, technology, education, public administration, law enforcement, behavioral & social sciences, special education.
ISBN Prefix(es): 978-0-398
Number of titles published annually: 60 Print
Total Titles: 905 Print
Advertising Agency: Thomas Advertising Agency

§Thomas Nelson
Subsidiary of HarperCollins Christian Publishing
501 Nelson Place, Nashville, TN 37214
SAN: 209-3820
Mailing Address: PO Box 141000, Nashville, TN 37214-1000

Tel: 615-889-9000 *Toll Free Tel:* 800-251-4000
Web Site: www.thomasnelson.com
Key Personnel
Pres & CEO, Christian Publg Div: Mark Schoenwald
SVP & Group Publr, Bibles: John Kramp
SVP & Group Publr, Trade Books: Don Jacobson
SVP, Children's & Gift Group Publr: Laura Minchew
SVP, Sales: Dan Van Gorp
SVP, Sales & Centralized Mktg: Doug Lockhart
VP & Publr, Gift Div: Jennifer Gott
VP & Publr, Nelson Books: Timothy Paulson; Andrew Stoddard
VP & Publr, Spanish Div: Cris Garrido
VP & Publr, Thomas Nelson Bibles: Philip Nation
VP & Publr, Tommy Nelson: Shannon Marchese
VP & Publr, W Publishing: Damon Reiss
VP, Digital Prods, Harper Christian: Stephen Smith
VP, Mktg, Nelson Books: Brian Scharp; Jennifer Smith
Publr, Fiction: Amanda Bostic
Assoc Publr: Daniel Marrs; Becky Monds
Assoc Publr, Bibles: Brian Dembowczyk
Assoc Publr, Nelson Books: Jennifer Gingerich
Assoc Publr, Spanish Div (Vida/Grupo Nelson): Matthew McGhee
Assoc Publr, W Publishing: Carrie Marrs
Sr Dir, Mktg, Fiction Books: Nekasha Pratt
Dir, Corp Communs: Casey Harrell
Dir, Mktg: Stephanie Tresner
Dir, Publicity, Nelson Books: Lisa Beech
Mktg Dir, Bible Group: Clark Christian
Exec Ed, Nelson Books: Janet Hill Talbert
Sr Acqs Ed: Lisa-Jo Baker
Sr Ed: Jodi Hughes
Acqs Ed: Jocelyn Bailey; Dawn Hollomon; Laura Wheeler
Founded: 1798
Bibles & Testaments, trade, Christian & inspirational books, gift books, children's books & videos.
ISBN Prefix(es): 978-0-8407; 978-1-4047
Number of titles published annually: 600 Print
Total Titles: 3,500 Print
Imprints: Emanate Books; Magnolia Publications; Nelson Books; Grupo Nelson (Spanish-language); Tommy Nelson®; W Publishing Group
See separate listing for:
Tommy Nelson®

§Thomson West
Imprint of Thomson Reuters Legal Solutions
610 Opperman Dr, Eagan, MN 55123
Tel: 651-687-7000 *Toll Free Tel:* 888-728-7677 (cust serv)
Web Site: store.legal.thomsonreuters.com/law-products/brands/thomson-west/c/20287
Founded: 1804
Publisher of state statutes, attorney general opinions & practice manuals for the US & international.
ISBN Prefix(es): 978-0-314; 978-0-8322; 978-0-7620; 978-0-8366; 978-0-87632; 978-1-5392
Returns: 525 Wescott Rd, Bldg B, Eagan, MN 55123

Thorndike Press®
Imprint of Gale
10 Water St, Suite 310, Waterville, ME 04901
Tel: 207-861-1514 *Toll Free Tel:* 800-877-4253 (option 1) *Toll Free Fax:* 800-558-4676 (orders)
E-mail: gale.printorders@cengage.com; gale.customerservice@cengage.com
Web Site: www.gale.com/thorndike
Founded: 1980
Large print titles for the public library market.

PUBLISHERS

ISBN Prefix(es): 978-0-7862; 978-1-4104; 978-1-58724; 978-1-59414; 978-1-59413; 978-1-59415
Number of titles published annually: 1,500 Print
Total Titles: 4,000 Print
Distributor for Grand Central/Hachette Large Print; HarperLuxe; Mills & Boon Large Print; Random House Large Print

ThunderStone Books
6575 Horse Dr, Las Vegas, NV 89131
E-mail: info@thunderstonebooks.com
Web Site: www.thunderstonebooks.com
Key Personnel
Mng Dir: Robert Noorda *E-mail:* robert.noorda@thunderstonebooks.com
Edit Dir: Rachel Noorda *E-mail:* rachel.noorda@thunderstonebooks.com
Founded: 2014
Specialize in children's books that have an educational aspect. We are not looking for curriculum for learning certain subjects, but rather stories that encourage learning for children, whether that be learning about a new language/culture or learning more about science & math in a fun, fictional format. We want to help children to gain a love for other languages & subjects so that they are curious about the world around them. We are currently accepting fiction & nonfiction submissions. In the area of language, our expertise lies in stories concerning Mandarin Chinese (language, culture, setting +/or mythology), but we are open to other languages as well. For submissions concerning other subjects, we are quite open to anything which creatively teaches & inspires, particularly in areas such as math or science. Fiction submissions that have an educational element are encouraged & welcome.
ISBN Prefix(es): 978-1-63411
Number of titles published annually: 6 Print; 6 E-Book
Total Titles: 5 Print; 5 E-Book
Foreign Office(s): 3B Bow St, Stirling FK8 1BS, United Kingdom *Tel:* (07825) 483348
Orders to: Ingram Content Group LLC, One Ingram Blvd, La Vergne, TN 37086, Contact: Ron Smithson *Tel:* 615-793-5000 *Toll Free Tel:* 800-937-8222 ext 35176 *E-mail:* ron.smithson@ingramcontent.com
Returns: Ingram Content Group LLC, One Ingram Blvd, La Vergne, TN 37086, Contact: Ron Smithson *Tel:* 615-793-5000 *Toll Free Tel:* 800-937-8222 ext 35176 *E-mail:* ron.smithson@ingramcontent.com
Shipping Address: Ingram Content Group LLC, One Ingram Blvd, La Vergne, TN 37086, Contact: Ron Smithson *Tel:* 615-793-5000 *Toll Free Tel:* 800-937-8222 ext 35176 *E-mail:* ron.smithson@ingramcontent.com
Warehouse: Ingram Content Group LLC, One Ingram Blvd, La Vergne, TN 37086, Contact: Ron Smithson *Tel:* 615-793-5000 *Toll Free Tel:* 800-937-8222 ext 35176 *E-mail:* ron.smithson@ingramcontent.com
Distribution Center: Ingram Content Group LLC, One Ingram Blvd, La Vergne, TN 37086, Contact: Ron Smithson *Tel:* 615-793-5000 *Toll Free Tel:* 800-937-8222 ext 35176 *E-mail:* ron.smithson@ingramcontent.com
Membership(s): Publishers Association of the West (PubWest)

Tide-mark Press
207 Oakwood Ave, West Hartford, CT 06119
SAN: 222-1802
Tel: 860-310-3370 *Toll Free Tel:* 800-338-2508 *Fax:* 860-310-3654
E-mail: customerservice@tide-mark.com
Key Personnel
Publr: Scott Kaeser *Tel:* 860-310-3370 ext 108 *E-mail:* scott@tide-mark.com
ISBN Prefix(es): 978-1-63114
Number of titles published annually: 3 Print
Total Titles: 48 Print
Foreign Rep(s): Gazelle Book Services Ltd (Europe)
Membership(s): American Booksellers Association (ABA); Museum Store Association (MSA)

Tiger Tales
5 River Rd, Suite 128, Wilton, CT 06897-4069
SAN: 253-6382
Tel: 920-387-2333 *Fax:* 920-387-9994
Web Site: www.tigertalesbooks.com
Key Personnel
Art Dir: Michelle Martinez
Sales Dir: Barb Knight *E-mail:* barbknight@tigertalesbooks.com
Opers Mgr: Jeannie Rubsam *Tel:* 203-834-0005 *Fax:* 203-834-0004 *E-mail:* jrubsam@tigertalesbooks.com
Ed: Tammi Salzano
Founded: 2000
Publishes imaginative & entertaining hardcover picture books as well as board books for children ages 2-7. For ages 6-10, Tiger Tales publishes fiction series: *Pet Rescue Adventures & There's a Dragon...* Middle-grade nonfiction imprint *360 Degrees* is dedicated to building a broader view of our world. Tiger Tales remains steadfast in its commitment to publishing children's books that will capture the imagination of children.
ISBN Prefix(es): 978-1-58925; 978-1-68010; 978-1-944530 (360 Degrees)
Number of titles published annually: 100 Print
Total Titles: 650 Print
Imprints: 360 Degrees
Sales Office(s): PO Box 70, Iron Ridge, WI 53035
Orders to: 1263 Southwest Blvd, Kansas City, KS 66103, Contact: Vanessa Ottens *Tel:* 913-362-7400 *Fax:* 913-362-7401 *E-mail:* vanessa@midpt.com
Returns: 1263 Southwest Blvd, Kansas City, KS 66103 *Tel:* 913-362-7400 *Fax:* 913-362-7401 *E-mail:* lreeder@tigertalesbooks.com
Shipping Address: 1263 Southwest Blvd, Kansas City, KS 66103, Contact: Vanessa Ottens *Tel:* 913-362-7400 *Toll Free Tel:* 888-454-0097 *Fax:* 913-362-7401 *E-mail:* vanessa@midpt.com
Warehouse: 1263 Southwest Blvd, Kansas City, KS 66103, Contact: Vanessa Ottens *Tel:* 913-362-7400 *Toll Free Tel:* 888-454-0097 *Fax:* 913-362-7401 *E-mail:* vanessa@midpt.com
Membership(s): American Booksellers Association (ABA)

Tilbury House Publishers
Imprint of Cherry Lake Publishing Group (CLPG)
12 Starr St, Thomaston, ME 04861
Tel: 207-582-1899 *Toll Free Tel:* 800-582-1899 (orders) *Fax:* 207-582-8227
E-mail: tilbury@tilburyhouse.com
Web Site: www.tilburyhouse.com
Key Personnel
Publr: Tristram Coburn; Jonathan Eaton
Founded: 1990
ISBN Prefix(es): 978-0-88448
Number of titles published annually: 25 Print
Total Titles: 175 Print
Distributed by W W Norton & Company Inc
Distributor for Marshall Wilkes Publishing
Membership(s): American Booksellers Association (ABA); Independent Book Publishers Association (IBPA)

TLC, see THE Learning Connection®

The Toby Press LLC
Imprint of Koren Publishers Jerusalem
PO Box 8531, New Milford, CT 06776-8531

U.S. PUBLISHERS

SAN: 253-9985
Tel: 203-830-8508 *Fax:* 203-830-8512
E-mail: info@tobypress.com; orders@korenpub.com
Web Site: www.korenpub.com/collections/toby
Founded: 1999
Publish Jewish religious texts, Jewish philosophy, Holocaust memoirs.
ISBN Prefix(es): 978-1-902881; 978-1-59264
Number of titles published annually: 50 Print
Total Titles: 800 Print
Imprints: Koren Publishers (Hebrew Bibles & other Jewish religious texts); Maggid Books (contemporary Jewish thought); Menorah; Toby Press
Distributor for Ofeq Books

§Todd Publications
15494 Fiorenza Circle, Delray Beach, FL 33446
SAN: 207-0804
Tel: 561-910-0440 *Fax:* 561-910-0440
E-mail: toddpub@yahoo.com
Key Personnel
Ed/Publr: Barry Klein
Founded: 1973
Directories & reference books to the trade. Returns accepted within 30 days when in resalable condition.
This publisher has indicated that 50% of their product line is author subsidized.
ISBN Prefix(es): 978-0-87340; 978-0-915344; 978-0-873400
Number of titles published annually: 3 Print; 3 E-Book

Tommy Nelson®
Imprint of Thomas Nelson
501 Nelson Place, Nashville, TN 37214
Mailing Address: PO Box 141000, Nashville, TN 37214-1000
Tel: 615-889-9000; 615-902-1485 (cust serv)
Toll Free Tel: 800-251-4000
Web Site: www.tommynelson.com
Key Personnel
Pres & CEO: Mark Schoenwald
VP & Publr: Shannon Marchese
Publr, Harper Christian Specialty Div: MacKenzie Howard
Sr Dir, Mktg: Robin Richardson
Founded: 1984
Inspirational children's books for evangelical & secular marketplace & other products.
ISBN Prefix(es): 978-0-8499; 978-1-4003
Number of titles published annually: 75 Print; 10 Audio
Total Titles: 400 Print; 8 E-Book; 50 Audio

§Top Publications Ltd
5101 Brouette Ct, Plano, TX 75023
Tel: 972-628-6414 *Fax:* 972-233-0713
E-mail: bill@topfiction.net (sales & admin)
Web Site: toppub.com
Key Personnel
Mgr: Bill Manchee *E-mail:* wm.manchee@gmail.com
Founded: 1999
ISBN Prefix(es): 978-0-9666366; 978-1-929976; 978-1-935722; 978-1-7333283
Number of titles published annually: 2 Print; 2 E-Book
Total Titles: 61 Print; 50 E-Book; 19 Audio
Imprints: TOP
Orders to: IngramSpark, La Vergne, TN 37086-3650 *Web Site:* ingramspark.com

Tor/Forge Books, see Tor Publishing Group

Tor Publishing Group
Subsidiary of Macmillan
120 Broadway, New York, NY 10271
Toll Free Tel: 800-455-0340 (Macmillan)

E-mail: torpublicity@tor.com; forgepublicity@forgebooks.com
Web Site: us.macmillan.com/torpublishinggroup
Key Personnel
Pres & Publr: Devi Pillai
SVP & Assoc Publr: Lucille Rettino
VP & Exec Dir, Mktg: Eileen Lawrence
VP & Exec Dir, Publicity: Sarah Reidy
VP & Edit Dir, Bramble: Monique Patterson
Publr, Forge: Linda Quinton
Sr Assoc Dir, Ad & Promo: Stephanie Sirabian
Sr Assoc Dir, Publicity, Macmillan/Tor/Forge/Tor Teen: Alexis Saarela
Creative Dir: Peter Lutjen
Dir, Intl Rts: Marta Fleming
Dir, Mktg: Emily Mlynek
Dir, reactormag.com: Chris Lough
Edit Dir, Tor/Nightfire/Tor Teen/Starscape: Claire Eddy; Will Hinton
Sr Assoc Art Dir: Jamie Stafford-Hill
Sr Assoc Dir, Mktg: Michael Dudding
Sr Assoc Dir, School & Lib Mktg: Anthony Parisi
Assoc Art Dir: Katie Klimowicz; Lesley Worrell
Assoc Creative Dir, Ad & Promo: Megan Barnard
Asst Dir, Mktg: Isa Caban; Jennifer McClelland-Smith; Renata Sweeney
Exec Ed: Alison Fisher; Bob Gleason; Lindsey Hall; Kelly O'Connor Lonesome; Erika Tsang; Miriam Weinberg
Sr Ed: Carl Engle-Laird; Stephanie Stein
Ed, Forge & Busn Opers Mgr, Tor/Forge: Robert Davis
Ed-at-Large: Patrick Nielsen Hayden
Prodn Ed, Tor/Forge: Dakota Griffin
Assoc Ed: Kristin Tempe
Asst Ed: Sanaa Ali-Virani; Oliver Dougherty; Emily Goldman; Troix Jackson; Molly McGhee; Matthew Rusin; Dianna Vega
Sr Brand Mgr: Alex Cameron
Sr Mgr, Ad/Promo & Mktg: Rebecca Yeager
Sr Mgr, Publg Opers: Michelle Foytek
Sr Mktg Mgr: Julia Bergen; Jordan Hanley; Rachel Taylor
Sr Publicity Mgr: Saraciea Fennell; Caro Perny
Publicity Mgr: Desirae Friesen
Assoc Mgr, Publg Opers: Rebecca Naimon
Asst Mktg Mgr: Andrew King
Sr Publicist: Libby Collins; Laura Etzkorn
Publicist: Giselle Gonzalez
Assoc Publicist: Jocelyn Bright; Khadija Lokhandwala
Ad Promo Sr Designer: Amy Sefton
Ad/Promo Designer: Angie Rao
Assoc Designer: Jess Kiley
Ad Promo Coord: Makenna Sidle
Ad/Promo Coord: Yvonne Ye
Digital Mktg Coord: Amanda Melfi
Digital Mktg Coord, Tor/Forge: Sarah Pannenberg
Mktg Coord: Ariana Carpentieri; Natassja Haught
Mktg Assoc: Samantha Friedlander; Emily Honer
Mktg Asst: Valeria Castorena
Publg Opers Assoc: Erin Robinson
Publg Strategy Assoc: Lizzy Hosty
Founded: 1980
Mass market & trade paperbacks; trade hardcover: fiction, horror, science fiction, fantasy, mystery, suspense, techno-thrillers, western fiction, American historicals, nonfiction, paranormal romance, true crime & biography.
ISBN Prefix(es): 978-0-8125; 978-0-7653; 978-1-250
Number of titles published annually: 425 Print
Total Titles: 2,224 Print
Imprints: Bramble; Forge; Nightfire; Orb Books; Starscape; Tor; Tor Classics; Tor Teen; Tordotcom Publishing
Distributed by Macmillan
Foreign Rights: St Martin's Press
Distribution Center: MPS Distribution Center, 16365 James Madison Hwy, Gordonsville, VA 22942 *Toll Free Tel:* 888-330-8477 *Fax:* 540-672-7540 (cust serv) *Toll Free Fax:* 800-672-2054 (orders) *E-mail:* orders@mpsvirginia.com

Torah Umesorah Publications
Division of Torah Umesorah-National Society for Hebrew Day Schools
620 Foster Ave, Brooklyn, NY 11230
Tel: 718-259-1223
E-mail: publications@torahumesorah.org
Web Site: www.torahumesorah.org/publications
Key Personnel
Dir, Pubns: Shmuel Yaakov Klein
Founded: 1946
Text teaching aids & visual aids for Yeshiva day schools & Hebrew schools, students & teachers; posters & workbooks.
ISBN Prefix(es): 978-0-914131; 978-1-878895
Number of titles published annually: 5 Print
Total Titles: 82 Print

Tortuga Press
2777 Yulupa Ave, PMB 181, Santa Rosa, CA 95405
SAN: 299-1756
Tel: 707-544-4720 *Fax:* 707-595-5331
E-mail: info@tortugapress.com
Web Site: www.tortugapress.com
Key Personnel
Publr: Matthew Gollub *E-mail:* mg@tortugapress.com
Off Mgr: Simone Peters
Founded: 1997
Creator of award-winning children's literature & multimedia products to delight & open young people's minds.
ISBN Prefix(es): 978-1-889910
Number of titles published annually: 4 Print; 2 Audio
Total Titles: 28 Print; 8 Audio
Warehouse: CubeSmart, 220 Business Park Dr, Rohnert Park, CA 94928
Membership(s): California Association of Bilingual Education; California School Library Association (CSLA); Independent Book Publishers Association (IBPA); Texas Library Association

§TotalRecall Publications Inc
1103 Middlecreek, Friendswood, TX 77546
Tel: 281-992-3131
E-mail: sales@totalrecallpress.com
Web Site: www.totalrecallpress.com
Key Personnel
Pres: Bruce Moran *E-mail:* bruce@totalrecallpress.com
Founded: 1998
Publish nonfiction books in a variety of professional fields, including library science & library assistant/technician education (Learn Library Skills Series) & financial certification exam preparation, with many titles adopted as college texts. The exam preparation study guides offer free downloads of a proprietary interactive test engine that generates randomized mock exams designed to identify a candidate's strengths & weaknesses & determine where to allocate study time. These titles are also distributed electronically to libraries, corporations & government agencies via EBSCOHost, ebrary & Books24x7.com. The company has expanded into fiction, especially mystery/thrillers, along with self-help, travel & religion.
ISBN Prefix(es): 978-1-59095
Number of titles published annually: 50 Print; 10 Online; 50 E-Book
Total Titles: 400 Print; 120 Online; 250 E-Book

§Tower Publishing Co
650 Cape Rd, Standish, ME 04084
Tel: 207-642-5400 *Toll Free Tel:* 800-969-8693
E-mail: info@towerpub.com
Web Site: www.towerpub.com
Key Personnel
Publr: Michael Lyons
Mng Ed: Mary Anne Hildreth
Business & manufacturing directories, law publications, business databases.
ISBN Prefix(es): 978-0-89442
Number of titles published annually: 20 Print

TPR Education LLC, see The Princeton Review

§Tracks Publishing
458 Dorothy Ave, Ventura, CA 93003
Tel: 805-754-0248
E-mail: tracks@cox.net
Web Site: www.startupsports.com
Key Personnel
Owner: Doug Werner
Founded: 1993
ISBN Prefix(es): 978-1-884654; 978-1-935937
Number of titles published annually: 2 Print; 6 E-Book
Total Titles: 45 Print; 135 E-Book
Distribution Center: Independent Publishers Group (IPG), 814 N Franklin St, Chicago, IL 60610 *Tel:* 312-337-0747 *Fax:* 312-337-5985 *E-mail:* frontdesk@ipgbook.com *Web Site:* www.ipgbook.com
Membership(s): Independent Book Publishers Association (IBPA)

Trafalgar Square Books
388 Howe Hill Rd, North Pomfret, VT 05053
SAN: 213-8859
Mailing Address: PO Box 257, North Pomfret, VT 05053-0257
Tel: 802-457-1911 *Toll Free Tel:* 800-423-4525 *Fax:* 802-457-1913
E-mail: contact@trafalgarbooks.com
Web Site: www.trafalgarbooks.com; www.horseandriderbooks.com
Key Personnel
Pres & Publr: Caroline Robbins
Mng Dir: Martha Cook *E-mail:* mcook@trafalgarbooks.com
Dir, Opers: Amy E Wilson *E-mail:* awilson@trafalgarbooks.com
Mng Ed: Rebecca Didier *E-mail:* rdidier@trafalgarbooks.com
Founded: 1972
ISBN Prefix(es): 978-0-943955; 978-1-57076; 978-1-64601
Number of titles published annually: 25 Print
Total Titles: 400 Print
Distributor for J A Allen; Kenilworth Press; We-Horse
Distribution Center: Ingram Publisher Services, 14 Ingram Blvd, Mail Stop 631, La Vergne, TN 37086 *Tel:* 615-793-5000 *Web Site:* www.ingrampublisherservices.com

Trafford Publishing
Division of Author Solutions LLC
1663 Liberty Dr, Bloomington, IN 47403
Toll Free Tel: 844-688-6899
E-mail: customersupport@trafford.com; sales@trafford.com
Web Site: www.trafford.com
Key Personnel
COO, Author Solutions: Bill Becher
Pres, Author Solutions: Bill Elliott
Founded: 1995
The first company in the world to offer an "on-demand publishing service" & led the independent publishing revolution since its establishment. One of the earliest publishers to utilize the Internet for selling books. More than 16,000 authors from over 120 countries have utilized Trafford's experience for self-publishing their books.
This publisher has indicated that 100% of their product line is author subsidized.
ISBN Prefix(es): 978-1-55369; 978-1-55212; 978-1-55395; 978-1-4120; 978-1-4122; 978-1-4251
Number of titles published annually: 800 Print
Total Titles: 2,243 Print

Distribution Center: Baker & Taylor LLC, 2550 W Tyvola Rd, Suite 300, Charlotte, NC 28217 *Tel:* 704-998-3100 *Toll Free Tel:* 800-775-1800 *E-mail:* btinfo@baker-taylor.com *Web Site:* www.baker-taylor.com
Ingram Book Group, One Ingram Blvd, La Vergne, TN 37086 *Tel:* 615-793-5000 *Toll Free Tel:* 800-937-8200 *E-mail:* customer.service@ingrambook.com *Web Site:* www.ingrambook.com
Membership(s): American Booksellers Association (ABA)

Trans-Atlantic Publications Inc
33 Ashley Dr, Schwenksville, PA 19473
SAN: 694-0234
Tel: 215-925-2762 *Fax:* 215-925-1912
Web Site: www.transatlanticpub.com; www.businesstitles.com
Key Personnel
Pres & Intl Rts: Jeffry Goldstein *Tel:* 484-919-6486 *E-mail:* jeffgolds@comcast.net
Founded: 1984
Popular culture.
ISBN Prefix(es): 978-1-891696
Number of titles published annually: 200 Print
Total Titles: 2,500 Print
Imprints: BainBridgeBooks
Distributor for Book Guild; Financial Times Publishing; Hodder Education; IndieBooks; Longman; Arnoldo Mondadori Electa; Nexus Special Interests; Pearson Education

Transcontinental Music Publications (TMP)
Division of American Conference of Cantors (ACC)
1375 Remington Rd, Suite M, Schaumburg, IL 60173-4844
Tel: 847-781-7800 *Fax:* 847-781-7801
E-mail: tmp@accantors.org
Web Site: www.transcontinentalmusic.com
Key Personnel
Chair: Steven Weiss
Dir: Joe Eglash
Founded: 1938
Publishers of Jewish music.
ISBN Prefix(es): 978-1-8074
Number of titles published annually: 50 Print; 5 Audio
Total Titles: 1,000 Print; 75 Audio
Imprints: Hazamir; Theophilis
Membership(s): National Music Publishers' Association (NMPA); News/Media Alliance

§Transportation Research Board (TRB)
Division of The National Academies of Sciences, Engineering & Medicine
500 Fifth St NW, Washington, DC 20001
Tel: 202-334-2934; 202-334-3213 (bookshop)
E-mail: trbsales@nas.edu; mytrb@nas.edu
Web Site: www.nationalacademies.org/trb/transportation-research-board
Key Personnel
Pubns Dir: Natalie Barnes *Tel:* 202-334-2304 *E-mail:* nbarnes@nas.edu
Assoc Pubns Dir: Heather DiAngelis *Tel:* 202-334-2355 *E-mail:* hdiangelis@nas.edu
Supv, Pubns Sales: Cydni Wolfinger *Tel:* 202-334-3072 *E-mail:* cjohnson@nas.edu
Founded: 1920
Research results, TRR (online journal), bibliographies & abstracts on books pertaining to civil engineering, public transit, aviation, freight, transportation administration & economics & transportation law.
ISBN Prefix(es): 978-0-309
Number of titles published annually: 150 Print; 5 CD-ROM; 100 Online
Total Titles: 2,600 Print; 40 CD-ROM; 1,000 Online
Orders to: Lockbox 936135, 3585 Atlanta Ave, Hapeville, GA 30354

Travelers' Tales
Subsidiary of Solas House Inc
2320 Bowdoin St, Palo Alto, CA 94306
Tel: 650-462-2110
E-mail: ttales@travelerstales.com; info@travelerstales.com
Web Site: travelerstales.com
Key Personnel
Publr: James O'Reilly
Exec Ed: Larry Habegger
Ed-at-Large: Sean O'Reilly
Founded: 1993
Sponsors annual Solas Awards for Best Travel Writing. For more information see www.besttravelwriting.com.
ISBN Prefix(es): 978-1-885211; 978-1-932361
Number of titles published annually: 5 Print; 5 E-Book; 1 Audio
Total Titles: 160 Print; 1 Audio
Sales Office(s): Publishers Group West, 1700 Fourth St, Berkeley, CA 94710 *Tel:* 510-528-1444 *Fax:* 510-528-3444
Billing Address: Publishers Group West, 1700 Fourth St, Berkeley, CA 94710 *Tel:* 510-528-1444 *Fax:* 510-528-3444
Orders to: Publishers Group West, 1700 Fourth St, Berkeley, CA 94710 *Tel:* 510-528-1444 *Fax:* 510-528-3444
Shipping Address: Ingram Publisher Services, 191 Edwards Dr, Jackson, TN 38301 *Web Site:* www.ingrampublisherservices.com
Warehouse: Ingram Publisher Services, 191 Edwards Dr, Jackson, TN 38301 *Web Site:* www.ingrampublisherservices.com
Distribution Center: Publishers Group West, 1700 Fourth St, Berkeley, CA 94710 *Tel:* 510-528-1444 *Fax:* 510-528-3444

Treasure Bay Inc
PO Box 119, Novato, CA 94948
Tel: 415-884-2888 *Fax:* 415-884-2840
E-mail: customerservice@treasurebaybooks.com
Web Site: www.treasurebaybooks.com
Key Personnel
Pres: Don Panec
Founded: 1997
Publishes educational children's books, specializing in books for parent involvement in reading.
ISBN Prefix(es): 978-1-891327; 978-1-60115
Number of titles published annually: 10 Print
Total Titles: 100 Print

Treehaus Communications Inc
PO Box 249, Loveland, OH 45140-0249
Tel: 513-683-5716 *Toll Free Tel:* 800-638-4287 (orders) *Fax:* 513-683-2882 (orders)
E-mail: treehaus@treehaus1.com; treehauscommunications@gmail.com
Web Site: www.treehaus1.com
Key Personnel
Owner & Publr: Gerard A Pottebaum
Founded: 1972
Children's books, liturgical & catechetical material for children & adults.
ISBN Prefix(es): 978-0-929496; 978-1-886510
Number of titles published annually: 6 Print
Total Titles: 55 Print

§The Trinity Foundation
PO Box 68, Unicoi, TN 37692-0068
Tel: 423-743-0199
Web Site: www.trinityfoundation.org
Key Personnel
Pres & Dir: Thomas W Juodaitis *E-mail:* tjtrinityfound@aol.com
Founded: 1977
Scholarly Christian books.
ISBN Prefix(es): 978-0-940931; 978-1-891777
Number of titles published annually: 5 Print; 5 E-Book; 1 Audio
Total Titles: 85 Print; 1 CD-ROM; 32 E-Book; 2 Audio

Trinity University Press
Unit of Trinity University
One Trinity Place, San Antonio, TX 78212-7200
Tel: 210-999-8884 *Fax:* 210-999-8838
E-mail: books@trinity.edu
Web Site: www.tupress.org
Key Personnel
Publr & Dir: Thomas Payton
Asst Dir/Dir, Mktg & Sales: Ms Burgin Streetman
Mng Ed: Sarah Nawrocki
Acqs & Proj Ed: Steffanie Mortis Stevens
Ed-at-Large: Yvette Benavides
Busn Mgr: Lee Ann Sparks
Founded: 2002 (after 14 years of inoperation)
Publish titles for the general trade & academic markets.
ISBN Prefix(es): 978-1-59534; 978-0-911536
Number of titles published annually: 12 Print; 12 E-Book
Total Titles: 150 Print; 100 E-Book
Imprints: Maverick Books; Terra Firma Books; Tinta Books
Distribution Center: Publishers Group West, 1700 Fourth St, Berkeley, CA 94710 (booksellers & libraries) *Toll Free Tel:* 800-788-3123 *Fax:* 510-528-3614

TriQuarterly Books
Imprint of Northwestern University Press
629 Noyes St, Evanston, IL 60208
Tel: 847-491-7420 *Toll Free Tel:* 800-621-2736 (orders only) *Fax:* 847-491-8150
E-mail: nupress@northwestern.edu
Web Site: www.nupress.northwestern.edu
Key Personnel
Dir: Parneshia Jones
Founded: 1989
Special attention to new writing talent, the non-commercial work of established writers & writing in translation. Special emphasis on poetry.
ISBN Prefix(es): 978-0-8101
Number of titles published annually: 8 Print
Total Titles: 75 Print

TRISTAN Publishing
2355 Louisiana Ave N, Minneapolis, MN 55427
Tel: 763-545-1383 *Toll Free Tel:* 866-545-1383 *Fax:* 763-545-1387
E-mail: info@tristanpublishing.com
Web Site: www.tristanpublishing.com
Key Personnel
Owner & Publr: Brett Waldman *E-mail:* bwaldman@tristanpublishing.com
Owner & VP Sales, Mktg & Relationships: Sheila Waldman *E-mail:* swaldman@tristanpublishing.com
Founded: 2002
Exquisite gift books that inspire, uplift & touch lives.
ISBN Prefix(es): 978-0-931674
Number of titles published annually: 6 Print
Total Titles: 60 Print; 2 Audio
Imprints: Have a Little Faith; TRISTAN Outdoors; Waldman House Press

§Triumph Books LLC
814 N Franklin St, Chicago, IL 60610
Tel: 312-337-0747 *Toll Free Tel:* 800-888-4741 (cust serv) *Fax:* 312-280-5470; 312-337-7985
Web Site: www.triumphbooks.com
Key Personnel
Group Publr: Cynthia Sherry *E-mail:* csherry@chicagoreviewpress.com
Publr: Noah Amstadter *E-mail:* n.amstadter@triumphbooks.com
Dir, Author Engagement: Bill Ames *E-mail:* b.ames@triumphbooks.com
Mng Ed: Jesse Jordan *E-mail:* j.jordan@triumphbooks.com

U.S. PUBLISHERS

Exec Ed: Adam Motin *E-mail:* a.motin@triumphbooks.com
Assoc Acqs Ed: Clarissa Young *E-mail:* c.young@triumphbooks.com
Acqs Mgr: Josh Williams *E-mail:* j.williams@triumphbooks.com
Founded: 1989
Leading publisher of sports titles & official rule books of NFL, NHL, MLB, NCAA, among others.
ISBN Prefix(es): 978-0-9624436; 978-1-880141; 978-1-57243; 978-1-892049 (Benchmark Press); 978-1-60078; 978-1-62368; 978-1-61749; 978-1-62937
Number of titles published annually: 95 Print; 75 E-Book
Total Titles: 600 Print; 450 E-Book
Imprints: Benchmark Press; Triumph Entertainment
Foreign Rep(s): Monarch Books of Canada (Canada); Peribo Pty Ltd (Australia, New Zealand)
Foreign Rights: RoundHouse Publishing Ltd (Europe, UK)
Returns: Independent Publishers Group (IPG), 600 N Pulaski Rd, Chicago, IL 60624
Distribution Center: Independent Publishers Group (IPG), 600 N Pulaski Rd, Chicago, IL 60624 *E-mail:* orders@ipgbook.com *Web Site:* www.ipgbook.com
Membership(s): American Booksellers Association (ABA)

Trusted Media Brands Inc
750 Third Ave, 3rd fl, New York, NY 10017
SAN: 212-4416
Tel: 646-293-6299 *Toll Free Tel:* 877-732-4438 (cust serv) *Fax:* 646-293-6251
E-mail: customercare@trustedmediabrands.com; press@trustedmediabrands.com
Web Site: www.trustedmediabrands.com; www.rd.com
Key Personnel
Pres & CEO: Bonnie Kintzer
Chief Content Offr: Beth Tomkiw
Chief Content Offr, Reader's Digest: Bruce Kelley
Chief Digital Offr: Vincent Errico
Chief People Offr: Jen Tyrrell
CTO: Nick Contardo
CFO: Dean Durbin
Chief Mktg Offr: Alec Casey
Chief Revenue Offr: John Boland
SVP, HR: Phyllis Gebhardt
SVP, Sales: Lora Gier *E-mail:* lora.gier@trustedmediabrands.com
VP, Gen Coun & Secy: Mark Sirota
Divisions: Reader's Digest Trade Publishing
Branch Office(s)
44 S Broadway, White Plains, NY 10601
Tel: 914-238-1000
1610 N Second St, Suite 102, Milwaukee, WI 53212
Membership(s): Association of American Publishers (AAP)
See separate listing for:
Reader's Digest Trade Publishing

TSG Foundation, see TSG Publishing Foundation Inc

TSG Publishing Foundation Inc
8685 E Stagecoach Pass Rd, Scottsdale, AZ 85266
SAN: 250-6726
Mailing Address: PO Box 7068, Cave Creek, AZ 85327-7068
Tel: 480-502-1909
E-mail: info@tsgfoundation.org
Web Site: www.tsgfoundation.org
Key Personnel
Pres & Intl Rts: Gita Saraydarian

Founded: 1987
Publish & sell books by Torkom Saraydarian, spiritual training center.
ISBN Prefix(es): 978-0-929874; 978-0-911794; 978-0-9656203
Number of titles published annually: 3 Print
Total Titles: 120 Print; 1 CD-ROM

Tughra Books
Imprint of Paramus Publishing
335 Clifton Ave, Clifton, NJ 07011
Tel: 646-415-9331 *Fax:* 646-827-6228
E-mail: info@tughrabooks.com
Web Site: www.tughrabooks.com
Key Personnel
Dir, Pubns: Huseyin Senturk *E-mail:* senturk@tughrabooks.com
Dir, Mktg: Ahmet Idil *E-mail:* agi@tughrabooks.com
Sr Ed: Hakan Yesilova *E-mail:* yesilova@tughrabooks.com
Founded: 2001
Publishing, design & printing.
ISBN Prefix(es): 978-975-7388; 978-0-9704370; 978-1-59784; 978-1-68236
Number of titles published annually: 15 Print
Total Titles: 225 Print
Imprints: The Fountain; The Light
Foreign Rep(s): Gazelle Book Services Ltd (Europe, UK)
Distribution Center: National Book Network (NBN), 4501 Forbes Blvd, Suite 200, Lanham, MD 20706 *Tel:* 301-459-3366 *Fax:* 301-429-5746 *Web Site:* www.nbnbooks.com
Membership(s): American Booksellers Association (ABA); Association of American Publishers (AAP); Independent Book Publishers Association (IBPA)

Tumblehome Learning Inc
201 Newbury St, Suite 201, Boston, MA 02116
E-mail: info@tumblehomelearning.com
Web Site: www.tumblehomelearning.com
Key Personnel
Chair: Penny Noyce *E-mail:* penny@tumblehomelearning.com
Pres: Barnas Monteith *E-mail:* barnas@tumblehomelearning.com
Opers: Yuyi Ling *E-mail:* yuyi@tumblehomelearning.com
Founded: 2010
Helps kids imagine themselves as young scientists & engineers & encourages them to experience science through adventure & discovery. Publish science & adventure mystery stories, picture books & occasional nonfiction.
ISBN Prefix(es): 978-0-9850008; 978-0-9897924; 978-0-9907829; 978-1-943431
Number of titles published annually: 6 Print; 4 E-Book
Total Titles: 54 Print; 6 E-Book
Membership(s): The Children's Book Council (CBC); National Science Teachers Association (NSTA)

Tupelo Press Inc
60 Roberts Dr, Suite 308, North Adams, MA 01247
SAN: 254-3281
Tel: 413-664-9611 *Fax:* 413-664-9711
E-mail: info@tupelopress.org
Web Site: www.tupelopress.org
Key Personnel
Publr: Jeffrey Levine *E-mail:* publisher@tupelopress.org
Ed-in-Chief: Kristina Marie Darling *E-mail:* kdarling@tupelopress.org
Founded: 1999
Independent, nonprofit literary press.
ISBN Prefix(es): 978-1-932195; 978-1-936797
Number of titles published annually: 16 Print; 7 E-Book

Total Titles: 223 Print; 17 E-Book; 12 Audio
Membership(s): Association of Writers & Writing Programs (AWP); Community of Literary Magazines & Presses (CLMP)

Turner Publishing Co LLC
4507 Charlotte Ave, Suite 100, Nashville, TN 37209
Tel: 615-255-BOOK (255-2665) *Fax:* 615-255-5081
E-mail: info@turnerpublishing.com; marketing@turnerpublishing.com; submissions@turnerpublishing.com; editorial@turnerpublishing.com; admin@turnerpublishing.com; orders@turnerpublishing.com
Web Site: turnerpublishing.com; www.facebook.com/turner.publishing
Key Personnel
CFO: Melissa Schneider
Pres & Publr: Todd Bottorff
Mng Ed: Amanda Chiu Krohn
Founded: 1984
Trade publisher.
ISBN Prefix(es): 978-1-879045 (Jewish Lights); 978-1-58023 (Jewish Lights); 978-1-893361 (SkyLight Paths); 978-1-59120 (Basic Health Publications); 978-1-59473 (SkyLight Paths); 978-1-56311; 978-1-68442; 978-1-5131
Number of titles published annually: 36 Print
Total Titles: 5,000 Print
Imprints: Ancestry Publishing; Basic Health Publications Inc (health & wellness); Conari Press; Fieldstone Alliance (business books for nonprofits); GemStone Press; Gurze Books; Hunter House Publishers (health, wellness & sexuality); Iroquois Press (fiction & literature); Jewish Lights Publishing; Keylight Books (fiction titles adaptable for film, TV & streaming); LifeLights™; Ramsey & Todd (children's books); SkyLight Paths® Publishing; Tiger Van Books; Turner; West Margin Press; Westwinds Press®; Wiley; Woo! Jr Kids Activities
Warehouse: c/o IPS, 1210 Ingram Dr, Chambersburg, PA 17202
Distribution Center: Ingram Publisher Services, 14 Ingram Blvd, Mail Stop 631, La Vergne, TN 37086 *Toll Free Tel:* 800-937-8000 *E-mail:* ips@ingramcontent.com *Web Site:* www.ingrampublisherservices.com
Membership(s): American Booksellers Association (ABA); Association of American Publishers (AAP); Independent Book Publishers Association (IBPA)
See separate listing for:
Basic Health Publications Inc
GemStone Press
Jewish Lights Publishing
SkyLight Paths® Publishing
West Margin Press

Turtle Point Press
208 Java St, 5th fl, Brooklyn, NY 11222-5748
Tel: 212-741-1393
E-mail: info@turtlepointpress.com
Web Site: www.turtlepointpress.com
Key Personnel
Publr & Edit Dir: Ruth Greenstein
Publg Assoc & Proj Ed: Jeffrey Peer
Founded: 1990
Contemporary & rediscovered fiction, poetry, literary nonfiction.
ISBN Prefix(es): 978-0-9627987; 978-1-885983; 978-1-885583; 978-1-933527
Number of titles published annually: 10 Print
Total Titles: 120 Print
Imprints: Books & Co/Turtle Point; Helen Marx/Turtle Point; Turtle Point
Foreign Rep(s): Turnaround (UK)
Distribution Center: Consortium Book Sales & Distribution, The Keg House, Suite 101, 34 13 Ave NE, Minneapolis, MN 55413-1007
Tel: 612-746-2600 *Toll Free Tel:* 866-400-5351

(cust serv, Jackson, TN) *E-mail:* cbsdinfo@ingramcontent.com *Web Site:* www.cbsd.com
SAN: 200-6049

§Tuttle Publishing
Member of Periplus Publishing Group
Airport Business Park, 364 Innovation Dr, North Clarendon, VT 05759-9436
SAN: 213-2621
Tel: 802-773-8930 *Toll Free Tel:* 800-526-2778 *Fax:* 802-773-6993 *Toll Free Fax:* 800-FAX-TUTL (329-8885)
E-mail: info@tuttlepublishing.com; orders@tuttlepublishing.com
Web Site: www.tuttlepublishing.com
Key Personnel
Pres & CEO: Eric Oey
Secy: Michael Sargent
Sales & Mktg Dir: Laura J Ferguson
Founded: 1948
Founded by Charles E Tuttle in Tokyo, Tuttle Publishing publishes books to span the East & West, publisher of high quality books & book kits on a wide range of topics including Asian culture, cooking, martial arts, spirituality, philosophy, travel, language, art, architecture & design.
ISBN Prefix(es): 978-0-8048; 978-4-333 (Kosei Publishing Co); 978-1-85391 (Merehurst Ltd); 978-0-460 (Everyman Paperbacks); 978-4-07 (Shufunotomo Co); 978-4-900737; 978-962-593 (Periplus Editions); 978-0-945971 (Periplus Editions); 978-0-935621 (Healing Tao Books); 978-0-933756 (Paperweight Press); 978-0-7946 (Periplus Editions); 978-0-970171 (Kotan); 978-1-840590 (Milet); 978-4-8053
Number of titles published annually: 152 Print
Total Titles: 2,000 Print; 20 Audio
Imprints: Everyman's Classic Library in Paperback; Kosei Publishing Co; Kotan Publishing Inc; Merehurst Ltd; Milet Publishing Ltd; Periplus Editions
Foreign Office(s): Yaekari Bldg, 3rd fl, 5-4-12 Osaki, 141-0032 Shinagawa-ku, Tokyo 141-0032, Japan *Tel:* (03) 5437 0171 *Fax:* (03) 5437 0755 *E-mail:* sales@tuttle.co.jp *Web Site:* www.tuttle.co.jp
Distributor for Healing Tao Books; Kosei Publishing Co; Kotan Publishing Inc; Milet Publishing Ltd; Paperweight Press; Periplus Editions; Shanghai Press; Shufunotomo Co; Tai Chi Foundation
Foreign Rep(s): Bill Bailey Publishers Representatives (Europe); David Bateman Ltd (New Zealand); Berkeley Books Pte Ltd (Southeast Asia); Ingram (Matthew Dickie) (Caribbean, Latin America); Therese Nasr (Middle East); NewSouth Books (Australia); Penguin Books India Pvt Ltd (India); Publishers Group Canada (Canada); Publishers Group UK (UK); SG Distributors (South Africa); Tuttle Publishing (Japan); Van Ditmar Boekenimport BV (Netherlands)

Tuxedo Press
546 E Springville Rd, Carlisle, PA 17015
Tel: 717-258-9733 *Fax:* 717-243-0074
E-mail: info@tuxedo-press.com
Web Site: tuxedo-press.com
Key Personnel
Publr: Thomas R Benjey *E-mail:* tom@tuxedo-press.com
Founded: 2005
Small press of nonfiction books. Titles released to date have been historical in nature. Future releases may also include political topics. New releases are offset print; reprints are POD. Considering expansion to audiobooks. Titles are of US interest only.
ISBN Prefix(es): 978-0-9774486; 978-1-936161
Number of titles published annually: 3 Print
Total Titles: 15 Print; 3 E-Book

Advertising Agency: Anne Dozier & Associates, 313 E 84 St, Suite 1-B, New York, NY 10028, Contact: Anne Dozier *Tel:* 212-717-0276 *E-mail:* annedozier@aol.com
Orders to: Ingram Book Co, 14 Ingram Blvd, La Vergne, TN 37086 *Tel:* 615-213-5335 *Fax:* 615-213-5430
Distribution Center: Ingram Book Co, 14 Ingram Blvd, La Vergne, TN 37086 *Tel:* 615-213-5335 *Fax:* 615-213-5430
Membership(s): Independent Book Publishers Association (IBPA)

Twenty-First Century Books
Imprint of Lerner Publishing Group Inc
241 First Ave N, Minneapolis, MN 55401
Tel: 612-332-3344 *Toll Free Tel:* 800-328-4929 *Fax:* 612-332-7615 *Toll Free Fax:* 800-332-1132
E-mail: info@lernerbooks.com; custserve@lernerbooks.com
Web Site: www.lernerbooks.com; www.facebook.com/lernerbooks
Key Personnel
Chmn: Harry J Lerner
Pres & Publr: Adam Lerner
EVP & COO: Mark Budde
EVP & CFO: Margaret Thomas
EVP, Sales: David Wexler
VP & Ed-in-Chief: Andy Cummings
VP, Mktg: Rachel Zugschwert
Dir, HR: Maggie Wolfson
Dir, Rts, Spec Sales & Intl Dist: Maria Kjoller
Publg Dir, School & Lib: Jenny Krueger
School & Lib Mktg Dir: Lois Wallentine
Publisher of nonfiction books for the upper grades & young adults.
ISBN Prefix(es): 978-0-8050; 978-1-56294; 978-0-7613; 978-0-941477
Number of titles published annually: 15 Print; 15 E-Book
Total Titles: 500 Print; 500 E-Book
Foreign Rep(s): Bounce Sales & Marketing Ltd (Europe, India, Middle East, Pakistan, Scandinavia, UK); CrossCan Education (Canada); DuBois (New Zealand); Novella (Australia); Phambili Agencies (Botswana, Lesotho, Namibia, Southern Africa, Swaziland, Zimbabwe); Publishers Marketing Services (PMS) (Brunei, Malaysia, Singapore); Saunders (school & lib) (Canada)
Foreign Rights: AC2 Literary (Italy); Sandra Bruna Literary Agency (Brazil, Portugal, Spain); CA-Link (Hong Kong, Macau, Mainland China, Taiwan); Japan Foreign-Rights Centre (JFC) (Japan); Korea Copyright Center Inc (KCC) (South Korea); Agence Michelle Lapautre (France); RightsMix (Eastern Europe, Greece, Israel, Netherlands, Russia, Scandinavia, UK); Literarische Agentur Silke Weniger (Germany)
Warehouse: CGC Fulfillment Warehouse, 150 Kingswood Dr, Mankato, MN 56001

§Twenty-Third Publications
Division of Bayard Inc
One Montauk Ave, Suite 200, New London, CT 06320
Tel: 860-437-3012 *Toll Free Tel:* 800-321-0411 (orders) *Toll Free Fax:* 800-572-0788
E-mail: resources@twentythirdpublications.com
Web Site: www.twentythirdpublications.com
Key Personnel
Assoc Publr/Sales & Mktg Dir: Dan Smart *E-mail:* dsmart@twentythirdpublications.com
Art Dir: Jeff McCall *E-mail:* jeff.mccall@bayard-inc.com
Edit Dir: Dan Connors *E-mail:* dan.connors@bayard-inc.com
Assoc Dir, Sales & Mktg: Kerry Moriarty *E-mail:* kerry.moriarty@bayard-inc.com
Acqs Ed: Heidi Busse *E-mail:* heidi.busse@bayard-inc.com

Founded: 1967
ISBN Prefix(es): 978-0-89622; 978-1-58595
Number of titles published annually: 45 Print; 6 CD-ROM; 10 Online; 20 E-Book
Total Titles: 450 Print; 10 Online; 60 E-Book
Distributed by John Garrett (Australia); Novalis (Canada); Redemptorist Publications (UK); St Paul's Publications (Australia)
Distributor for Novalis (Canada)
Foreign Rights: Bayard Presse International (worldwide)
Membership(s): Association of Catholic Publishers Inc

§Twilight Times Books
PO Box 3340, Kingsport, TN 37664-0340
Tel: 423-390-1111 *Fax:* 423-390-1111
E-mail: publisher@twilighttimes.com
Web Site: www.twilighttimesbooks.com
Key Personnel
Publr: Lida E Quillen
Mng Ed: Ardy M Scott
Ed: Eric Olsen
Founded: 1999
Royalty paying small press trade publisher of speculative fiction. Our mission is to promote excellence in writing & great literature. Currently publishing limited edition hardcover, first edition trade paperback books & ebooks as downloads in various formats.
ISBN Prefix(es): 978-1-931201; 978-1-933353; 978-1-60619
Number of titles published annually: 14 Print; 14 E-Book
Total Titles: 125 Print; 175 E-Book
Imprints: Paladin Timeless Books; Twilight Visions
Distribution Center: Follett Library Resources, 1340 Ridgeview Dr, McHenry, IL 60050-7048
Brodart Books & Library Services, 50 Arch St, Williamsport, PA 17701 *Tel:* 570-326-2461 *Toll Free Tel:* 800-474-9816 *Toll Free Fax:* 800-999-6799 *E-mail:* support@brodart.com *Web Site:* www.brodartbooks.com
Membership(s): Association of American Publishers (AAP); The Association of Publishers for Special Sales (APSS); Electronically Published Internet Connection (EPIC); Independent Book Publishers Association (IBPA); Speculative Literature Foundation; Writers & Publishers Network (WPN)

§Tyndale House Publishers Inc
351 Executive Dr, Carol Stream, IL 60188
SAN: 206-7749
Tel: 630-668-8300 *Toll Free Tel:* 800-323-9400; 855-277-9400 *Toll Free Fax:* 866-622-9474
Web Site: www.tyndale.com
Key Personnel
Pres & CEO: Mark Taylor
SVP & Group Publr: Ron Beers
Sr Dir, Corp Media: Alan Huizenga
Dir, Intl Publg: James Elwell
PR Dir: Katie Dodillet
Founded: 1962
Religion: hardcover & paperback originals & reprints, ebooks, Bibles, reference, DVDs, audio CDs & software.
ISBN Prefix(es): 978-0-8423; 978-1-4143
Number of titles published annually: 125 Print; 1 CD-ROM; 73 Online; 75 E-Book; 25 Audio
Total Titles: 1,000 Print; 5 CD-ROM; 300 E-Book; 225 Audio
Imprints: BarnaBooks (George Barna titles); Living Books (mass mkt pbk); Refresh (health & wellness); Resurgence (Mars Hill Church); SaltRiver (deeper Christian thought); Tyndale Audio (adult audiobooks); Tyndale Entertainment (kids' audio/video products); Tyndale Kids (children's); Tyndale Momentum; Tyndale Ninos (Spanish children's)
Distributor for Focus on the Family; NavPress

U.S. PUBLISHERS

Advertising Agency: Design Promotion
Membership(s): Evangelical Christian Publishers Association (ECPA)

UCLA Latin American Center Publications
Unit of University of California, Los Angeles
UCLA Latin American Institute, 10343 Bunche Hall, Los Angeles, CA 90095
Mailing Address: PO Box 951447, Los Angeles, CA 90095-1447
Tel: 310-825-4571 *Fax:* 310-206-6859
E-mail: latinamctr@international.ucla.edu
Web Site: www.international.ucla.edu/lai
Key Personnel
Dir: Kevin Terraciano *E-mail:* terraciano@international.ucla.edu
Dir, Pubns: Orchid Mazurkiewicz *E-mail:* orchidm@ucla.edu
Asst Dir: Bryan Pitts *E-mail:* bpitts@international.ucla.edu
Pubns Mgr: Marcelo Jatoba *Tel:* 310-825-6634 *E-mail:* mjatoba@international.ucla.edu
Founded: 1959
Publish scholarly books & journals in Latin American studies & the *Hispanic American Periodicals Index (HAPI).*
ISBN Prefix(es): 978-0-87903
Number of titles published annually: 6 Print; 1 CD-ROM; 1 Online
Total Titles: 124 Print; 1 CD-ROM; 1 Online

UGA Press, see University of Georgia Press

Ugly Duckling Presse
The Old American Can Factory, 232 Third St, Suite E303, Brooklyn, NY 11215
Tel: 347-948-5170
E-mail: office@uglyducklingpresse.org; orders@uglyducklingpresse.org; publicity@uglyducklingpresse.org; rights@uglyducklingpresse.org
Web Site: uglyducklingpresse.org
Key Personnel
Ed: Anna Moschovakis *E-mail:* anna@uglyducklingpresse.org; Rebekah Smith *E-mail:* rebekah@uglyducklingpresse.org
Founded: 1993
A nonprofit arts & publishing collective.
ISBN Prefix(es): 978-0-9727684; 978-1-946433
Number of titles published annually: 24 Print; 2 Audio
Total Titles: 200 Print
Distributor for United Artists
Distribution Center: Distributed Art Publishers Inc, 75 Broad St, Suite 630, New York, NY 10004 (art-related titles) *Tel:* 212-627-1999 *Fax:* 212-627-9484 *Web Site:* www.artbook.com
Raincoast Books Distribution Ltd, 2440 Viking Way, Richmond, BC V6V 1N2, Canada *Tel:* 604-448-7100 *Toll Free Tel:* 800-663-5714 (cust serv) *Toll Free Fax:* 800-565-3770 (orders) *E-mail:* info@raincoast.com *Web Site:* www.raincoast.com
Antenne Books, The Sunroom, Hackney Downs Studios, 17 Amhurst Terr, London E8 2BT, United Kingdom (UK art-related titles) *Tel:* (020) 3582 8257
Inpress Books, Milburn House, Dean St, Newcastle upon Tyne NE1 1LF, United Kingdom *Tel:* (0191) 230 8104 *E-mail:* enquiries@inpressbooks.co.uk *Web Site:* inpressbooks.co.uk
Membership(s): Community of Literary Magazines & Presses (CLMP)

UL Press, see University of Louisiana at Lafayette Press

Ulysses Press
195 Montague St, 14th fl, Brooklyn, NY 11201
Mailing Address: PO Box 3440, Berkeley, CA 94703
Tel: 510-601-8301 *Toll Free Tel:* 800-377-2542 *Fax:* 510-601-8307
E-mail: ulysses@ulyssespress.com
Web Site: www.ulyssespress.com
Key Personnel
CEO: Keith Riegert *E-mail:* keithriegert@ulyssespress.com
Dir, Edit & Acqs: Casie Vogel *E-mail:* casievogel@ulyssespress.com
Dir, Mktg & Opers: Bridget Thoreson *E-mail:* bridgetthoreson@ulyssespress.com
Acqs Ed: Claire Sielaff *E-mail:* clairesielaff@ulyssespress.com
Asst Ed: Ashten Evans *E-mail:* ashtenevans@ulyssespress.com
Founded: 1983
Health & fitness books, cookbooks, pop culture & trivia, lifestyle, crafts & hobbies titles, mind, body & spirit.
ISBN Prefix(es): 978-0-915233; 978-1-56975
Number of titles published annually: 60 Print; 50 E-Book
Total Titles: 600 Print
Imprints: Amorata Press; Hidden Travel Series; Seastone; VeloPress
Distributed by Simon & Schuster, LLC
Foreign Rep(s): Hi Marketing (Central America, Continental Europe, Far East, South Africa, South America, UK); Raincoast Book Distribution Ltd (Canada)
Foreign Rights: Linda Biagi (worldwide)
Orders to: Simon & Schuster, LLC, Order Processing Dept, 100 Front St, Riverside, NJ 08075 *E-mail:* purchaseorders@simonandschuster.com
Shipping Address: 3286 Adeline St, Suite 1, Berkeley, CA 94703 *Toll Free Tel:* 800-377-2542
Membership(s): Independent Book Publishers Association (IBPA); Society of American Travel Writers (SATW)

Unarius Academy of Science Publications
Division of Unarius Educational Foundation
145 S Magnolia Ave, El Cajon, CA 92020-4522
SAN: 168-9614
Mailing Address: PO Box 731, El Cajon, CA 92022
Tel: 619-444-7062 *Toll Free Tel:* 800-475-7062
E-mail: uriel@unarius.org
Web Site: www.unarius.org
Key Personnel
Ed: Celeste Appel
Founded: 1954
Books, CDs/MP3s & DVDs/MP4s describing a new science of life, past life therapy, extraterrestrial civilizations, the prehistory of earth, the psychology of consciousness: a course in self-mastery. Unarius provides the foundation for personal growth that will lead to the development of self-mastery & the clairvoyant aptitudes of the mind. Classes in past-life therapy are webcast on Sunday & Wednesday 7pm PT.
ISBN Prefix(es): 978-0-932642; 978-0-935097
Number of titles published annually: 4 Print
Total Titles: 90 Print; 70 Audio
Divisions: Audio Books; Unarius Video Productions; Visionary Art

Union Square & Co
Subsidiary of Barnes & Noble Inc
1166 Avenue of the Americas, 17th fl, New York, NY 10036-2715
SAN: 211-6324
Mailing Address: PO Box 5078, New York, NY 10087-5078
Tel: 212-532-7160 *Toll Free Tel:* 800-367-9692 *Fax:* 212-213-2495 *Toll Free Fax:* 800-542-7567
E-mail: custservice@sterlingpublishing.com; customerservice@sterlingpublishing.com; editorial@sterlingpublishing.com; tradesales@sterlingpublishing.com
Web Site: www.sterlingpublishing.com
Key Personnel
Publr & Chief Creative Offr: Emily Meehan
VP, Fin: Thomas M Allen
VP, Sales Opers & Inventory Planning: Adria Dougherty
Dir, HR: Kerri Cuocci
Edit Dir: Amanda Englander
Exec Mng Ed: Marina Padakis Lowry
Exec Ed: Kate Zimmermann
Exec Ed, Children's: Suzy Capozzi
Exec Ed, Classics: Mika Kasuga
Sr Ed: Jessica Firger; Caitlin Leffel; Jay Sacher
Ed-at-Large: Claire Wachtel
Sr Mgr, Foreign & Subs Rts: Toula Ballas *E-mail:* tballas@sterlingpublishing.com
Founded: 1949
Publisher of quality nonfiction & fiction books for adults & children. Subject categories include art & photography, cookbooks, wine, self-improvement, mind/body/spirit, business, history, reference, science & nature, home reference, gardening, music, sports, lifestyle & design, hobbies, crafts, classics, study guides, puzzles & games, children's nonfiction, picture, board & humor books.
This publisher has indicated that 50% of their product line is author subsidized.
ISBN Prefix(es): 978-0-7607; 978-0-937274 (Lark Books); 978-1-887374 (Lark Books); 978-1-57990 (Lark Books); 978-0-8069; 978-1-895569 (Sterling/Tamos); 978-1-4027; 978-1-58816 (Hearst); 978-1-58663 (SparkNotes); 978-1-59308 (Barnes & Noble Classics); 978-1-60059 (Lark Books); 978-1-4114 (SparkNotes); 978-1-934618 (Begin Smart); 978-1-4351 (Fall River Press); 978-1-4547 (Lark Books); 978-1-4549; 978-1-60736 (Ecosystem); 978-1-61837 (Hearst)
Number of titles published annually: 800 Print
Total Titles: 5,000 Print
Imprints: Boxer Books; Flash Kids; Hearst Books; Puzzlewright Press; Sterling Ethos; Union Square Kids
Distributor for Against All Odds Productions; Amber Books Ltd; Boxer Books; Brooklyn Botanic Garden; Enchanted World; Liminal 11; Sally Milner Publishing; Salaryia; Sixth&Spring Books; White Star Publishers
Foreign Rep(s): David Bateman Ltd (New Zealand); Canadian Manda Group (Canada); GMC Distribution (Asia, Europe, Middle East, UK); NewSouth Books (Australia)
Foreign Rights: ANA Sofia Ltd (Bulgaria, Romania, Southeast Europe); Guiliana Bernardi (Italy); Agence Litteraire Lora Fountain (Lora Fountain) (France); Graal Literary Agency (Tomasz Berezinski) (Poland); Katai & Bolza Literary Agents (Peter Bolza) (Hungary); Ute Koerner Literary Agent SLU (Sandra Rodericks) (Portugal, Spain); Korea Copyright Center Inc (KCC) (Seong-ah Bak) (South Korea); Alexander Korzhenevski (Russia); Andrew Nurnberg Associates International Ltd (Whitney Hsu) (Taiwan); Andrew Nurnberg Associates International Ltd (Jackie Huang) (China); Kristin Olson Literary Agency SRO (Czechia); Literarische Agentur Silke Weniger (Silke Weniger) (Germany)
Returns: LSC Communications, Attn: Returns, 677 Brighton Beach Rd, Menasha, WI 54952
Warehouse: LSC Communications-Lake Park, N9234 Lake Park Rd, Appleton, WI 54915
Distribution Center: Pinnacle Booksales UK, Stanmore Business & Innovation Ctr, Howard Rd, Stanmore, Middx HA7 1BT, United Kingdom, Sales Admin: Karen Thomas *Tel:* (020) 8731 5209 *E-mail:* sales@pinnaclebooksales.co.uk *Web Site:* pinnaclebooksales.co.uk

PUBLISHERS

§United Nations Publications
405 E 42 St, 11th fl, New York, NY 10017
SAN: 206-6718
Tel: 703-661-1571
E-mail: publications@un.org
Web Site: shop.un.org
Key Personnel
Chief: Mary Glenn *E-mail:* mary.glenn@un.org
Acqs Offr: Nicolas Bovay *E-mail:* bovay@un.org
Sales & Mktg Offr: Irina Lumelsky
  E-mail: lumelsky@un.org
Founded: 1946
Promotes the knowledge & work of the UN to scholars, information specialists, policy-makers & influencers. We publish approximately 500 new titles per year in economic & social development, international law & justice, peacekeeping & security, human rights & refugees, natural resources & more.
ISBN Prefix(es): 978-92-1 (United Nations Publications); 978-92-807 (UNEP); 978-92-808 (United Nations University); 978-92-806 (UNICEF); 978-88-000 (UNICEF); 978-184-966 (DESA); 978-1-849 (UNEP); 978-1-618 (UNFPA); 978-92-9137 (ITC)
Number of titles published annually: 500 Print
Total Titles: 3,370 Print; 700 E-Book
Sales Office(s): Books International, PO Box 960, Herndon, VA 20172
Distributor for Food & Agriculture Organization of the United Nations (FAO); International Atomic Energy Agency (IAEA); International Criminal Tribunal for Rwanda (UNICTR); International Criminal Tribunal for the former Yugoslavia (ICTY); International Organization for Migration (IOM); International Trade Centre (ITC); Office of the United Nations High Commissioner for Human Rights (OHCHR); United Nations Children's Fund (UNICEF); United Nations Development Programme (UNDP); United Nations Economic & Social Commission for Asia & the Pacific (ESCAP); United Nations Economic & Social Commission for Western Asia (ESCWA); United Nations Economic Commission for Africa (ECA); United Nations Economic Commission for Europe (ECE); United Nations Economic Commission for Latin America & the Caribbean (ECLAC); United Nations High Commissioner for Refugees (UNHCR); United Nations Human Settlements Programme (UN-HABITAT); United Nations Industrial Development Organization (UNIDO); United Nations Institute for Disarmament Research (UNIDIR); United Nations Institute for Training & Research (UNITAR); United Nations International Research & Training Institute for the Advancement of Women (INSTRAW); United Nations Interregional Crime & Justice Research Institute (UNICRI); United Nations Office for Project Services (UNOPS); United Nations Office for the Coordination of Humanitarian Affairs (OCHA); United Nations Office on Drugs & Crime (UNODC); United Nations Population Fund (UNFPA); United Nations Research Institute for Social Development (UNRISD); United Nations University (UNU)
Foreign Rep(s): Eurospan Group (Africa, Asia, China, Europe, Hong Kong, Middle East, Taiwan)
Returns: Books International, 22883 Quicksilver Dr, Dulles, VA 20166
Shipping Address: Books International, PO Box 960, Herndon, VA 20172
Warehouse: Books International, 22883 Quicksilver Dr, Dulles, VA 20166

§United States Holocaust Memorial Museum
100 Raoul Wallenberg Place SW, Washington, DC 20024-2126
Tel: 202-488-0400; 202-488-6144 (orders)
  Toll Free Tel: 800-259-9998 (orders)
E-mail: academicpublications@ushmm.org
Web Site: www.ushmm.org
Key Personnel
Dir, Academic Pubns: Laura Foster
Pubns Offr, Academic Pubns: Mel Hecker
Prog Coord, Academic Pubns: Rosie Cain
Asst Ed, Academic Pubns: Michelle Magin
Founded: 1993
Co-publish original monographs, translations, classic reprints, testimonial materials & a scholarly journal; publish memoirs & related titles of Holocaust Publications' Holocaust Library imprint (assets acquired in 1993) as well as occasional papers, exhibition catalogues & related works.
ISBN Prefix(es): 978-0-89604
Number of titles published annually: 12 Print
Total Titles: 160 Print
Imprints: Holocaust Library
Foreign Rights: Goldfarb & Associates (selected titles)

United States Institute of Peace Press
2301 Constitution Ave NW, Washington, DC 20037
Tel: 703-661-1590 (cust serv) *Toll Free Tel:* 800-868-8064 (cust serv)
E-mail: usipmail@presswarehouse.com (orders)
Web Site: bookstore.usip.org
Key Personnel
Dir, Pubns: Jake Harris
Mng Ed: Richard Walker
Founded: 1989
Publisher of influential books, reports & briefs on the prevention, management & peaceful resolution of international conflicts. All books & reports arise from research & fieldwork sponsored by the Institute's many programs & the Press is committed to extending the reach of the Institute's work by continuing to publish significant & sustainable publications for practitioners, scholars, diplomats & students. In keeping with the best traditions of scholarly publishing, each work undergoes thorough peer review by external subject experts to ensure that the research & conclusions are balanced, relevant & sound.
This publisher has indicated that 100% of their product line is author subsidized.
ISBN Prefix(es): 978-1-878379; 978-1-929223; 978-1-601270
Number of titles published annually: 10 Print
Total Titles: 250 Print
Orders to: PO Box 605, Herndon, VA 20172-0605 (sales & returns/bookseller, wholesaler & instl) *E-mail:* usipmail@presswarehouse.com
SAN: 254-6965
Shipping Address: 22883 Quicksilver Dr, Dulles, VA 20166 (indiv returns)

United States Pharmacopeia (USP)
12601 Twinbrook Pkwy, Rockville, MD 20852-1790
Tel: 301-881-0666 *Toll Free Tel:* 800-227-8772
E-mail: marketing@usp.org
Web Site: www.usp.org
Key Personnel
Dir, Pubns: Caroline Martin *Tel:* 301-816-8521
  E-mail: cmw@usp.org
Founded: 1820
Reference books & directories; Databases in print & electronic formats.
ISBN Prefix(es): 978-0-913595
Number of titles published annually: 5 Print
Total Titles: 25 Print; 2 CD-ROM
Distributed by Consumer Reports
Foreign Rep(s): A&C American Chemicals Ltd (Canada); ABS International FZE (Ethiopia, Kenya, Uganda); AE Alchemists Inc (Philippines); Al Massat Life Sciences DMCC (United Arab Emirates); Al Massat Life Sciences Egypt (Egypt, Sudan); Al Massat Lil Tewridat Alkimawia LLC (Algeria, Gaza Strip, Gulf States, Iraq, Jordan, Lebanon, Tunisia, West Bank); Azelis Tr Kimya Endustrisi Urunleri Ithalat Ihracat Ticaret ve Sanayi Anonim Sirketi (Turkey); Bangkok Chemart Ltd (Thailand); Beijing Usand Technology & Development Co Ltd (Mainland China); BTJ Sverige AB (Sweden); C&S Specialty Inc (South Korea); Carpe Scheider y Cia SA (Argentina, Venezuela); ChemSupply Australia (Australia); Chromachemie Laboratory Pvt Ltd (Bangladesh, India, Nepal, Pakistan, Sri Lanka); Conepre SA de CV (Mexico); CSK Enpro (South Korea); CWO Chile SpA (Chile); Cymit Quimica SL (Portugal, Spain); Daejung Chemicals & Metals Co Ltd (South Korea); Delta Origin LLC (Armenia, Belarus, Kazakhstan, Kyrgyzstan, Russia); Deutscher Apotheker Verlag (Austria, Germany, Poland, Switzerland); DPB New Brands LLP (Kazakhstan, Turkmenistan, Uzbekistan); DRK Pharma Solutions (Pakistan); Eurofins PHAST GmbH (Europe); Eurolab SA (Argentina, Bolivia, Paraguay, Peru, Uruguay); Farma International (Caribbean, Central America, South America); HC LEGD Group SAC (Peru); Hechun Biotechnology (Shanghai) Co Ltd (Mainland China); Holland Moran Ltd (Israel); JMC NC Inc (Brazil, Central America); Katchey Co Ltd (Nigeria); Kimia Trading Ltda (Colombia, Venezuela); Labmix24 GmbH (Europe); LAS do Brasil Ltda (Brazil); Maruzen-Yushodo Co Ltd (Japan); PT Megasetia Agung Kimia (Indonesia); Merck KgaA (Europe exc Russia & Turkey); Merck Ltd (New Zealand); Merck Pty Ltd (Australia); Nihon Validation Technologies Corp (Japan); Pasteur Pharmatech Solutions Pte Ltd (Bangladesh); PhamNguyen Trading Co Ltd (Vietnam); Pharma Scientific (Central America); Pharmaceutical & Medical Device Regulatory Science Society of Japan (Japan); Proquifa (Mexico); Samchun Chemical Co Ltd (South Korea); Shinil Books Co (South Korea); Sinopharm Chemical Reagent Co Ltd (Mainland China); Stargate Scientific (South Africa, Sub-Saharan Africa); Tin Hang Technology Ltd (Hong Kong); Ultra International (India); Uni-Onward Corp (China, Taiwan)

Univelt Inc
Affiliate of American Astronautical Society
740 Metcalf St, No 13, Escondido, CA 92025
Mailing Address: PO Box 28130, San Diego, CA 92198-0130
Tel: 760-746-4005 *Fax:* 760-746-3139
E-mail: sales@univelt.com
Web Site: www.univelt.com; www.astronautical.org
Key Personnel
Pres & Publr: Robert H Jacobs
Founded: 1970
Publisher for American Astronautical Society, International Academy of Astronautics, Lunar & Planetary Society, National Space Society. Specialize in astronautics & aerospace engineering.
ISBN Prefix(es): 978-0-912183; 978-0-87703
Number of titles published annually: 10 Print; 6 CD-ROM
Total Titles: 363 Print
Distributor for Astronautical Society of Western Australia; US Space Foundation

Universal-Publishers Inc
200 Spectrum Center Dr, Suite 300, Irvine, CA 92618-5004
SAN: 299-3635
Tel: 561-750-4344 *Toll Free Tel:* 800-636-8329 (US only) *Fax:* 561-750-6797
Web Site: www.universal-publishers.com
Key Personnel
Publr & CEO: Jeffrey R Young
Artistic & Edit Dir: Shereen Siddiqui, PhD
Founded: 1997
Dictionaries, encyclopedias, textbooks-all, university presses. Scholarly books, reprints, profes-

sional books, paperbacks, directories & reference books.
ISBN Prefix(es): 978-1-58112; 978-1-59942; 978-1-61233; 978-1-62734
Number of titles published annually: 60 Print; 50 E-Book
Total Titles: 1,500 Print; 1,000 E-Book
Imprints: Brown Walker Press (brownwalker.com); Dissertation.com
Distribution Center: Ingram Book Group, One Ingram Blvd, La Vergne, TN 37086 *Tel:* 615-793-5000 *Web Site:* www.ingramcontent.com
See separate listing for:
Dissertation.com

Universe Publishing
Imprint of Rizzoli International Publications Inc
300 Park Ave S, 4th fl, New York, NY 10010
Tel: 212-387-3400 *Fax:* 212-387-3535
Web Site: www.rizzoliusa.com
Founded: 1990
Architecture, fine art, photography, illustrated gift books, fashion, culinary, popular culture, children's, design, style & calendars.
ISBN Prefix(es): 978-0-87663; 978-1-55550; 978-0-7893
Number of titles published annually: 60 Print
Imprints: Universe; Universe Calendars
Distributed by Random House
Foreign Rep(s): Angell Eurosales (Gill Angell & Stewart Siddall) (Scandinavia); Bill Bailey Publishers' Representatives (Austria, Benelux, France, Germany, Switzerland); David Bateman Ltd (New Zealand); Bookport Associates (Greece, Italy, Malta, Portugal, Spain); Michelle Curreri (Far East, Indian subcontinent, Southeast Asia); Hardie Grant Books (Australia); Marston Book Services Ltd (Europe, UK); Penguin Random House of Canada (Canada); Publishers Group UK (UK); Rizzoli International Publications (Jerry Hoffnagle) (Eastern Europe, Sub-Saharan Africa); SG Distributors (Giulietta Campanelli) (Botswana, Mozambique, Namibia, South Africa, Zimbabwe); Cynthia Zimpfer (Caribbean, Latin America)

University Council for Educational Administration (UCEA)
Michigan State University, College of Education, 620 Farm Lane, 432 Erickson Hall, East Lansing, MI 48824
Tel: 434-243-1041
E-mail: ucea@msu.edu
Web Site: www.ucea.org
Key Personnel
Exec Dir: Monica Byrne-Jimenez
 E-mail: mcbyrnej@iu.edu
Founded: 1947
Books, journals, monographs, newsletters.
ISBN Prefix(es): 978-1-55996
Number of titles published annually: 5 Print
Total Titles: 23 Print

University of Alabama Press
200 Hackberry Lane, 2nd fl, Tuscaloosa, AL 35487
Mailing Address: PO Box 870380, Tuscaloosa, AL 35487-0380
Tel: 205-348-5180 *Fax:* 205-348-9201
Web Site: www.uapress.ua.edu
Key Personnel
Dir: JD Wilson *Tel:* 205-348-1560
 E-mail: jdwilson7@ua.edu
Dir, Sales & Mktg: Blanche Sarratt *Tel:* 205-348-3476 *E-mail:* bsarratt@uapress.ua.edu
Ed-in-Chief: Daniel Waterman *Tel:* 205-348-5538
 E-mail: dwaterman@uapress.ua.edu
Mng Ed: Jon Berry *Tel:* 205-348-1565
 E-mail: jberry@uapress.ua.edu
Asst Mng Ed: Joanna Jacobs *Tel:* 205-348-1563
 E-mail: jjacobs@uapress.ua.edu
Sr Acqs Ed: Claire Lewis Evans *Tel:* 205-348-7108 *E-mail:* cevans@uapress.ua.edu; Wendi Schnaufer *Tel:* 205-348-1161 *E-mail:* wschnaufer@uapress.ua.edu
Asst Acqs Ed & Rts & Perms Mgr: Kristen Hop *Tel:* 205-348-1561 *E-mail:* kmhop@ua.edu
Busn Mgr: Rosalyn Carr *Tel:* 205-348-1567
 E-mail: rcarr@uapress.ua.edu
Prodn & Design Mgr: Michele Myatt Quinn *Tel:* 205-348-1570 *E-mail:* mquinn@uapress.ua.edu
Sales Mgr: Nick Shahan *Tel:* 205-348-9534
 E-mail: rnshahan@ua.edu
Mktg Coord: Samantha Huff-Roberson *Tel:* 205-348-1566 *E-mail:* sjhuffrobertson@ua.edu
Founded: 1945
American & Latin American history & culture, religious & ethnohistory, rhetoric & communications, African American & Native American studies, Judaic studies, Southern regional studies, theatre & regional trade titles.
ISBN Prefix(es): 978-0-8173; 978-0-914590; 978-0-932511; 978-1-57366
Number of titles published annually: 70 Print; 25 E-Book
Total Titles: 1,200 Print; 100 E-Book
Imprints: Deep South Books; Fiction Collective 2 (FC2); Fire Ant
Foreign Rep(s): Eurospan (Europe)
Orders to: Chicago Distribution Center, 11030 S Langley Ave, Chicago, IL 60628 *Tel:* 773-702-7000 *Toll Free Tel:* 800-621-2736 *Fax:* 773-702-7212 *Toll Free Fax:* 800-621-8476 SAN: 630-6047
Distribution Center: Chicago Distribution Center, 11030 S Langley Ave, Chicago, IL 60628 *Tel:* 773-702-7000 (orders) *Toll Free Tel:* 800-621-2736 (orders) *Fax:* 773-702-7212 *Toll Free Fax:* 800-621-8476 SAN: 630-6047
See separate listing for:
Fiction Collective 2 (FC2)

§University of Alaska Press
Imprint of University Press of Colorado
Elmer E Rasmuson Library, 1732 Tanana Loop, Suite 402, Fairbanks, AK 99775
Mailing Address: PO Box 756240, Fairbanks, AK 99775-6240 SAN: 203-3011
Tel: 907-474-5831 *Toll Free Tel:* 888-252-6657 (US only) *Fax:* 907-474-5502
Web Site: www.alaska.edu/uapress
Key Personnel
Dir & Acqs Ed: Nate Bauer *Tel:* 907-687-4453
 E-mail: nate.bauer@alaska.edu
Sales & Mktg Mgr: Laura Walker *E-mail:* laura.walker@alaska.edu
Prodn Ed: Krista West *Tel:* 907-474-6413
 E-mail: krista.west@alaska.edu
Founded: 1967
Emphasis on scholarly & nonfiction works related to Alaska, the circumpolar regions & the North Pacific rim.
ISBN Prefix(es): 978-0-912006; 978-1-889963; 978-1-60223
Number of titles published annually: 24 Print
Total Titles: 220 Print
Imprints: Alaska Literary Series; Alaska Writer Laureate Series; Classic Reprint Series; Geology & Geography of Alaska Series; Great Explorer Series; LanternLight Library; Literary Reprint Series; Oral Biography Series; Rasmuson Library Historical Translation Series; Snowy Owl Books
Distributor for Alaska Native Language Center; Alaska Quarterly Review; Alaska Sea Grant; Alutiiq Museum; Anchorage Museum Association; Anchorage Museum of Art History; Arctic Studies Center of the Smithsonian Museum; Far to the North Press; Geophysical Institute; Limestone Press; Spirit Mountain Press; UA Museum; Vanessapress
Distribution Center: Chicago Distribution Center, 11030 S Langley Ave, Chicago, IL 60628 *Toll Free Tel:* 800-621-2736 *Toll Free Fax:* 800-621-8476
Membership(s): Alaska History Association; Alaska Library Association; Association of University Presses (AUPresses); Independent Book Publishers Association (IBPA); Pacific Northwest Booksellers Association (PNBA)

The University of Arizona Press
1510 E University Blvd, Tucson, AZ 85721
SAN: 205-468X
Mailing Address: PO Box 210055, Tucson, AZ 85721-0055
Tel: 520-621-1441 *Toll Free Tel:* 800-621-2736 (orders) *Fax:* 520-621-8899 *Toll Free Fax:* 800-621-8476 (orders)
E-mail: uap@uapress.arizona.edu
Web Site: www.uapress.arizona.edu
Key Personnel
Dir: Kathryn Conrad *E-mail:* kconrad@uapress.arizona.edu
Art Dir & Book Designer: Leigh McDonald *E-mail:* lmcdonald@uapress.arizona.edu
Ed-in-Chief: Kristen Buckles *E-mail:* kbuckles@uapress.arizona.edu
Sr Ed: Dr Allyson Carter *E-mail:* acarter@uapress.arizona.edu
Asst Ed: Elizabeth Wilder *E-mail:* ewilder@uapress.arizona.edu
Edit, Design & Prodn Mgr: Amanda Krause *E-mail:* akrause@uapress.arizona.edu
Mktg Mgr: Abby Mogollon *E-mail:* amogollon@uapress.arizona.edu
Publicity Mgr: Mary Reynolds
 E-mail: mreynolds@uapress.arizona.edu
Digital Publg Specialist: Sara Thaxton
 E-mail: sthaxton@email.arizona.edu
Edit Asst: Alana Enriquez *E-mail:* aenriquez@uapress.arizona.edu
Founded: 1959
Scholarly & regional nonfiction about Arizona, the American West & Mexico, Latino studies, Latin American studies, Native American studies, anthropology & environmental studies.
ISBN Prefix(es): 978-0-8165
Number of titles published annually: 55 Print
Total Titles: 1,600 Print
Foreign Rep(s): Eurospan Group (Africa, Europe, Middle East); Craig Falk (Latin America); University of British Columbia Press (Canada)
Orders to: c/o Chicago Distribution Center, 11030 S Langley Ave, Chicago, IL 60628 *Toll Free Tel:* 800-621-2736 *Toll Free Fax:* 800-621-8476 *E-mail:* orders@press.uchicago.edu
Returns: c/o Chicago Distribution Center, 11030 S Langley Ave, Chicago, IL 60628
Membership(s): American Association of University Presses (AAUP); Arizona Book Publishing Association; Publishers Association of the West (PubWest)

The University of Arkansas Press
Division of The University of Arkansas
McIlroy House, 105 N McIlroy Ave, Fayetteville, AR 72701
Tel: 479-575-7544
E-mail: info@uapress.com
Web Site: www.uapress.com
Key Personnel
Dir & Publr: Mike Bieker *Tel:* 479-575-3859
 E-mail: mbieker@uark.edu
Editor-in-Chief: David Scott Cunningham
 Tel: 479-575-5767 *E-mail:* dscunnin@uark.edu
Mng Ed: Janet Foxman *Tel:* 479-575-5295
 E-mail: foxman@uark.edu
Ad & Communs Mgr: Charlie Shields *Tel:* 479-575-7258 *E-mail:* cmoss@uark.edu
Busn & Dist Servs Mgr: Sam Ridge *Tel:* 479-575-3858 *E-mail:* sridge@uark.edu
Mktg & Sales Mgr: Melissa King *Tel:* 479-575-7715 *E-mail:* mak001@uark.edu
Prodn Mgr: Liz Lester *Tel:* 479-575-6780
 E-mail: lizl@uark.edu

Founded: 1980
General humanities: civil rights, poetry, sports, food, regional.
ISBN Prefix(es): 978-0-938626; 978-1-55728; 978-0-912456; 978-1-68226; 978-1-61075
Number of titles published annually: 20 Print
Total Titles: 620 Print; 150 E-Book
Distributor for Butler Center for Arkansas Studies; Moon City Press; Ozark Society
Foreign Rep(s): Eurospan Group (Africa, Asia-Pacific, Continental Europe, Middle East, UK); Scholarly Book Services (Bev Calder) (Canada)
Foreign Rights: Eurospan (Africa, Europe, Middle East, UK)
Distribution Center: Chicago Distribution Center, 11030 S Langley Ave, Chicago, IL 60628 *Tel:* 773-702-7000 *Toll Free Tel:* 800-621-2736 *Fax:* 773-702-7212 *E-mail:* orders@press.uchicago.edu
Membership(s): American Association of University Presses (AAUP)

University of California, ANR Publications, see ANR Publications University of California

§University of California Institute on Global Conflict & Cooperation
Subsidiary of University of California
9500 Gilman Dr, MC 0518, La Jolla, CA 92093-0518
Tel: 858-534-6106 *Fax:* 858-534-7655
E-mail: igcc-communications@ucsd.edu
Web Site: igcc.ucsd.edu
Key Personnel
Mng Ed: Lindsay Morgan *E-mail:* l2morgan@ucsd.edu
Founded: 1983
Policy briefs & newsletters, policy papers & books authored by members of the University of California faculty & other participants in sponsored research programs.
ISBN Prefix(es): 978-0-934637
Number of titles published annually: 2 Print
Total Titles: 74 Print; 60 E-Book
Distributed by The Brookings Institution Press; Columbia International Affairs Online (CIAO); Cornell University Press; Garland Publishers; Lynn-Reinner Publishing; Penn State University Press; Princeton University Press; Transaction Publishers Inc; University of Michigan Press; Westview Press

§University of California Press
155 Grand Ave, Suite 400, Oakland, CA 94612-3758
Tel: 510-883-8232 *Fax:* 510-836-8910
E-mail: customerservice@ucpress.edu
Web Site: www.ucpress.edu
Key Personnel
Exec Dir: Tim Sullivan
Dir: Erich van Rijn
Deputy Dir: Kim Robinson
Dir, Design & Prodn: Lia Tjandra
Dir, Mktg & Sales: Elena McAnespia
Dir, Sales & Licensing: Clare Wellnitz
Assoc Dir, Sales: Chris Cook
Acqs Ed: Niels Hooper; Michelle Lipinski; Reed Malcolm; Kate Marshall; Archna Patel; Naomi Schneider
Assoc Ed: Raina Polivka; Maura Roessner
Assoc Ed, Environmental Studies & Geography: Naja Pulliam Collins
Assoc Ed, Art History & Music: LeKeisha Hughes
Founded: 1893
Trade nonfiction, scholarly & scientific nonfiction, translations & journals; paperbacks, limited fiction (reprints).
ISBN Prefix(es): 978-0-520
Number of titles published annually: 260 Print; 10 Online; 10 E-Book
Total Titles: 4,200 Print; 60 Online; 60 E-Book

Distributor for art-SITES; British Film Institute; Sierra Club Books (adult trade)
Foreign Rep(s): Avicenna Partnership Ltd (Claire De Gruchy) (Algeria, Cyprus, Israel, Jordan, Malta, Middle East, Morocco, North Africa, Palestine, Southeast Europe, Tunisia, Turkey); Avicenna Partnership Ltd (Bill Kennedy) (Bahrain, Egypt, Iran, Iraq, Kuwait, Lebanon, Libya, Oman, Qatar, Saudi Arabia, Syria, United Arab Emirates, Yemen); B K Agency Ltd (Chiafeng Peng) (Brunei, Cambodia, Indonesia, Laos, Malaysia, Myanmar, Philippines, Singapore, Taiwan, Thailand, Vietnam); Everest International Publishing Service (Wei Zhao) (China); Information & Culture Korea (ICK) (Se-Yung Jun) (South Korea); Penguin Random House India Pvt Ltd (Rajeev Das) (Bangladesh, Bhutan, India, Nepal, Pakistan, Sri Lanka); Rockbook (Gilles Fauveau & Ayako Owada) (Hong Kong, Japan); University Press Group (Simon Gwynn & Lois Edwards) (Europe, South Africa, UK); University Press Group (Ben Mitchell) (Ireland, UK); University Press Group (Peter Jacques) (Belgium, France, Italy, Poland, Scandinavia, Switzerland); University Press Group (Dominique Bartshukoff) (Austria, Croatia, Czechia, Germany, Greece, Hungary, Netherlands, Portugal, Russia, Slovenia, Spain); US PubRep (Craig Falk) (Caribbean, Central America, Mexico, South America); Kelvin Van Hasselt (Africa exc North & South Africa)
Advertising Agency: Fiat Lux
Orders to: Ingram Publisher Services, 14 Ingram Blvd, Mail Stop 631, La Vergne, TN 37086 (CN & US) *Toll Free Tel:* 866-400-5351 *Web Site:* www.ingrampublisherservices.com; Wiley Australia, PO Box 1226, Milton, Qld 4064, Australia (Australia & New Zealand) *Tel:* (07) 3859 9611 *Fax:* (07) 3859 9626 *E-mail:* custservice@wiley.com *Web Site:* www.wiley.com/en-au/contactus; John Wiley & Sons Ltd, LEC-1 New Era Estates, Oldlands Way, Bognor Regis, West Sussex PO22 9NQ (Africa, Europe, India & Middle East) *Tel:* (01243) 843291 *Fax:* (01243) 843302 *E-mail:* customer@wiley.co.uk *Web Site:* www.upguk.com
Returns: Ingram Publisher Services, Returns Center, 191 Edwards Dr, Jackson, TN 38301 *Web Site:* www.ingrampublisherservices.com
Membership(s): Association of American Publishers (AAP)

University of Chicago Press
1427 E 60 St, Chicago, IL 60637-2954
SAN: 202-5280
Tel: 773-702-7700; 773-702-7600
 Toll Free Tel: 800-621-2736 (orders) *Fax:* 773-702-9756; 773-660-2235 (orders); 773-702-2708
E-mail: custserv@press.uchicago.edu; marketing@press.uchicago.edu
Web Site: www.press.uchicago.edu
Key Personnel
Dir: Garrett P Kiely *Tel:* 773-702-8878 *E-mail:* gkiely@uchicago.edu
Deputy Dir: Christopher Heiser *Tel:* 773-702-2998 *E-mail:* cheiser@uchicago.edu
Sr Dir, IT: Wayne Willis
Dir, Intellectual Property: Laura Leichum *Tel:* 773-702-6096 *E-mail:* lleichum@uchicago.edu
Dir, IT: Patti O'Shea *Tel:* 773-702-8521 *E-mail:* poshea@uchicago.edu
Dir, Journals: Ashley Towne *Tel:* 773-753-4241 *E-mail:* atowne@uchicago.edu
Edit Dir, Humanities & Sci: Alan G Thomas *Tel:* 773-702-7644 *E-mail:* athomas2@uchicago.edu
Mktg Dir, Books Div: Levi Stahl *E-mail:* levi@uchicago.edu
Global Sales Dir: Laura Waldron

Exec Ed, American History, Urban Studies & Regl Titles: Timothy Mennel *Tel:* 773-702-0158 *E-mail:* tmennel@uchicago.edu
Exec Ed, Art & Ancient Studies: Karen Levine
Exec Ed, Economics, Busn & Public Policy: Chad Zimmerman *E-mail:* chadzimmerman@uchicago.edu
Exec Ed, Ref & Writing Guides: Mary Laur *Tel:* 773-702-7326 *E-mail:* mlaur@uchicago.edu
Exec Ed, Sci, Digital Studies & Mathematics: Joseph Calamia *E-mail:* jcalamia@uchicago.edu
Exec Ed, Sci Studies: Karen Merikangas Darling *Tel:* 773-702-7641 *E-mail:* darling@uchicago.edu
Sr Ed, Educ, Jazz & Sociology: Elizabeth Branch Dyson *Tel:* 773-702-7637 *E-mail:* ebd@uchicago.edu
Ed: Marta Tonegutti *Tel:* 773-702-0427 *E-mail:* mtonegut@uchicago.edu
Ed, Anthropology & History: Mary Al-Sayed *E-mail:* maryalsayed@uchicago.edu
Ed, Religious Studies, Philosophy, Rhetoric & Commun: Kyle Wagner *E-mail:* kwagner@uchicago.edu
Prodn Ed: Stephen Twilley
Assoc Ed, Ref: David Olsen *E-mail:* dbolsen@uchicago.edu
Asst Ed: Randolph Petilos *Tel:* 773-702-7647 *E-mail:* rpetilos@uchicago.edu
Asst Ed, Art & Ancient Studies: Dylan Montanari *E-mail:* dmontanari@uchicago.edu
UK Ed-at-Large: James Attlee
Asst to Dir: Ellen Zalewski *Tel:* 773-702-8879 *E-mail:* emz1@uchicago.edu
Intl Rts Mgr: Lucina Schell *Tel:* 773-702-7741 *E-mail:* lschell@uchicago.edu
Founded: 1891
Scholarly, nonfiction, advanced texts, monographs, clothbound & paperback, scholarly & professional journals, reference books & atlases.
ISBN Prefix(es): 978-0-226
Number of titles published annually: 250 Print
Total Titles: 5,400 Print; 1 E-Book
Foreign Rep(s): Academic Book Promotions (Benelux, France, Scandinavia); The American University Press Group (Hong Kong, Japan, South Korea, Taiwan); Thomas Cassidy (China); Ewa Ledochowicz (Eastern Europe); Uwe Ludemann (Austria, Germany, Italy, Switzerland); Mediamatics (India); Publishers Marketing & Research Associates (Caribbean, Latin America); Arie Ruitenbeek (Portugal, Spain); The University Press Group (Australia, Canada, New Zealand); University Presses Marketing (Greece, Ireland, Israel, UK); Yale Representation Ltd (UK)
Distribution Center: Chicago Distribution Center (CDC), 11030 S Langley Ave, Chicago, IL 60628 *Toll Free Fax:* 800-621-8476 (US & CN)
John Wiley & Sons Ltd, European Dist Ctr, New Era Estate, Oldlands Way, Bognor Regis, West Sussex PO22 9NQ, United Kingdom *Tel:* (01243) 779777 *Fax:* (01243) 820250 *E-mail:* cs-books@wiley.co.uk
Membership(s): American Association of University Presses (AAUP); Association of American Publishers (AAP)

University of Delaware Press
200A Morris Library, 181 S College Ave, Newark, DE 19717-5267
Tel: 302-831-1149 *Toll Free Tel:* 800-462-6420 (orders) *Fax:* 302-831-6549
E-mail: ud-press@udel.edu; orders@rowman.com
Web Site: library.udel.edu/udpress
Key Personnel
Dir: Julia Oestreich *E-mail:* joestrei@udel.edu
Founded: 1922

U.S. PUBLISHERS

Literary studies, especially Shakespeare, Renaissance & early modern literature; 18th century studies, French literature, art history & history & cultural studies of Delaware & the Eastern Shore.
Ms editorial, design & production services are provided by the University of Virginia Press.
ISBN Prefix(es): 978-0-87413; 978-1-61149
Number of titles published annually: 37 Print
Total Titles: 1,053 Print
Distributed by Rutgers University Press (worldwide)
Distribution Center: Rowman & Littlefield, 15200 NBN Way, PO Box 191, Blue Ridge Summit, PA 17214 *Tel:* 717-794-3800 *Toll Free Tel:* 800-462-6420 *Fax:* 717-794-3803 *Toll Free Fax:* 800-338-4550 *E-mail:* orders@rowman.com *Web Site:* www.rowman.com
Quantum Publishing Solutions Ltd, 2 Cheviot Rd, Paisley PA2 8AN, United Kingdom *Tel:* (07702) 831967 *E-mail:* sales@njonesbooks.co.uk
Durnell Marketing Ltd, 2 Linden Close, Tunbridge Wells TN4 8HH, United Kingdom (Europe including Ireland) *Tel:* (01892) 544272 *Fax:* (01892) 511152 *E-mail:* orders@durnell.co.uk

University of Georgia Press
Main Library, 3rd fl, 320 S Jackson St, Athens, GA 30602
Fax: 706-542-2558; 706-542-6770
Web Site: www.ugapress.org
Key Personnel
Dir: Lisa Bayer *Tel:* 706-542-0027 *E-mail:* lbayer@uga.edu
Dir, Mktg & Sales: Steven Wallace *Tel:* 706-542-4145 *E-mail:* smwallace@uga.edu
Asst Dir for Edit, Design & Prodn: Jon Davies *Tel:* 706-542-2101 *E-mail:* jdavies@uga.edu
Publr, NewSouth Books: Suzanne La Rosa
Ed-in-Chief: Nathaniel Holly *Tel:* 706-542-4728 *E-mail:* nfholly@uga.edu
Acqs Ed: Mick Gusinde-Duffy *Tel:* 706-206-0707 *E-mail:* mickgd@uga.edu
Acqs Ed/Acqs Coord: Beth Snead *Tel:* 706-542-7613 *E-mail:* bsnead@uga.edu
Ed-at-Large: Cynthia R Greenlee
Busn Mgr: Phyllis Wells *Tel:* 706-542-7250 *E-mail:* pwells@uga.edu
Asst Edit, Design & Prodn Mgr: Melissa Buchanan *Tel:* 706-542-4488 *E-mail:* melissa.buchanan@uga.edu
Digital Publg & Metadata Coord: Lana M Brand *Tel:* 706-542-9758 *E-mail:* lana.brand@uga.edu
Founded: 1938
Publisher of scholarly works, creative & literary works, regional works & digital projects.
ISBN Prefix(es): 978-0-8203
Number of titles published annually: 70 Print; 60 E-Book
Total Titles: 2,000 Print; 600 E-Book
Imprints: Milestone Press; NewSouth Books
Foreign Rep(s): Eurospan Group (worldwide exc Canada & USA)
Orders to: Longleaf Services Inc, 116 S Boundary St, Chapel Hill, NC 27514-3808 *Tel:* 919-966-7449 *Toll Free Tel:* 800-848-6224 *Fax:* 919-962-2704 *Toll Free Fax:* 800-272-6817 *E-mail:* orders@longleafservices.org *Web Site:* www.longleafservices.org
Returns: Longleaf Services Inc - Returns, c/o Ingram Publisher Services, 1250 Ingram Dr, Chambersburg, PA 17202 *E-mail:* credit@longleafservices.org
Shipping Address: Longleaf Services Inc, 116 S Boundary St, Chapel Hill, NC 27514-3808 *Tel:* 919-966-7449 *Toll Free Tel:* 800-848-6224 *Fax:* 919-962-2704 *Toll Free Fax:* 800-272-6817 *E-mail:* customerservice@longleafservices.org *Web Site:* www.longleafservices.org
Warehouse: Longleaf Services Inc, 116 S Boundary St, Chapel Hill, NC 27514-3808 *Tel:* 919-966-7449 *Toll Free Tel:* 800-848-6224 *Fax:* 919-962-2704 *Toll Free Fax:* 800-272-6817 *E-mail:* customerservice@longleafservices.org *Web Site:* www.longleafservices.org
Membership(s): Association of University Presses (AUPresses)
See separate listing for:
NewSouth Books

University of Hawaii Press
2840 Kolowalu St, Honolulu, HI 96822-1888
SAN: 202-5353
Tel: 808-956-8255 *Toll Free Tel:* 888-UHPRESS (847-7377) *Toll Free Fax:* 800-650-7811
E-mail: uhpbooks@hawaii.edu
Web Site: www.uhpress.hawaii.edu
Key Personnel
Interim Dir & Publr: Clem Guthro *E-mail:* guthroc@hawaii.edu
Exec Ed: Masako Ikedia *E-mail:* masakoi@hawaii.edu
Mng Ed: Gianna Marsella *E-mail:* gmarsell@hawaii.edu; Malia Collins *E-mail:* maliaeco@hawaii.edu
Acqs Ed: Stephanie Chun *E-mail:* chuns@hawaii.edu; Emma Ching *E-mail:* emma6@hawaii.edu
Prodn Mgr: Santos Barbasa *E-mail:* barbasa@hawaii.edu
Digital Publg Mgr: Trond Knutsen *E-mail:* tknutsen@hawaii.edu
Digital Mktg Mgr: Blaine Tolentino *E-mail:* blainemt@hawaii.edu
Promo Mgr: Carol Abe *E-mail:* abec@hawaii.edu
IT Specialist: Collin Wong *Tel:* 808-956-6209 *E-mail:* cwong808@hawaii.edu
Founded: 1947
Scholarly & general books & monographs, particularly those dealing with the Pacific & Asia; regional books; journals.
ISBN Prefix(es): 978-0-8248; 978-0-87022
Number of titles published annually: 70 Print; 100 E-Book
Total Titles: 1,500 Print; 1,500 E-Book
Imprints: Kolowalu Books; Latitude 20
Distributor for Ai Pohaku Press; Asian Civilisations Museum; Ateneo De Manila University Press; BDK America; College of Tropical Agriculture & Human Resources; Denby Fawcett; Hawaii Nikkei; Hawaiian Mission Children's Society; Hui Hanai; Huia Publishers; Institute of Buddhist Studies; iPRECIATION; Island Research & Education Initiative; Isle Botanica; Japan Playwrights Association; Kailua Historical Society; Kalamaku Press; Kanji Press; Korea Institute, Harvard University; Levesque Publications; Little Island Press; The Lontar Foundation; Manoa Heritage Center; MerwinAsia; The Mozhai Foundation; Jonathan Napela Center, Brigham Young University-Hawaii; Native Books; NIAS Press; North Beach-West Maui Benefit Fund Inc; Ocarina Books; Permanent Agriculture Resources; Punahou School; Renaissance Books; Seoul Selection; Shanghai Press & Publishing Development Co; Richard F Taitano Micronesia Area Research Center; Three Pines Press; University of the Philippines Press
Foreign Rep(s): The Eurospan Group (Africa, Continental Europe, Middle East, UK); University of British Columbia Press (Canada)
Membership(s): American Association of University Presses (AAUP); Hawaii Book Publishers Association (HBPA)

University of Illinois Press
Unit of University of Illinois
1325 S Oak St, MC-566, Champaign, IL 61820-6903
SAN: 202-5310
Tel: 217-333-0950 *Fax:* 217-244-8082
E-mail: uipress@uillinois.edu; journals@uillinois.edu
Web Site: www.press.uillinois.edu
Key Personnel
Art Dir: Dustin Hubbart *Tel:* 217-333-9227 *E-mail:* dhubbart@uillinois.edu
Ed-in-Chief: Daniel Nasset
Direct Mktg & Ad Mgr: Denise Peeler *Tel:* 217-244-4690 *E-mail:* dpeeler@uillinois.edu
Edit Design & Prodn Mgr: Jennifer Comeau *Tel:* 217-244-3279 *E-mail:* jlcomeau@uillinois.edu
Exhibits Mgr: Margo Chaney *Tel:* 217-244-6491 *E-mail:* mechaney@uillinois.edu
Journals Mgr: Clydette Wantland *Tel:* 217-244-6496 *E-mail:* cwantland@uillinois.edu
Dir: Laurie Matheson *Tel:* 217-244-4685 *E-mail:* lmatheso@uillinois.edu
Mktg & Sales Mgr: Michael Roux *Tel:* 217-244-4683 *E-mail:* mroux@uillinois.edu
Prodn Mgr: Kristine Ding *Tel:* 217-244-4701 *E-mail:* kding@uillinois.edu
Publicity Mgr: Heather Gernenz *Tel:* 217-244-4689 *E-mail:* gernenz2@illinois.edu
Founded: 1918
Working-class & ethnic studies, religion, architecture, film studies, communication & media studies, political science, folklore, Chicago, food studies, immigration studies, American history, women's history, music history, regional history, sport history, gender & sexuality studies.
ISBN Prefix(es): 978-0-252
Number of titles published annually: 90 Print
Total Titles: 2,400 Print; 10 Online; 1,100 E-Book
Imprints: 3 Fields Books
Foreign Rep(s): Combined Academic Publishers (CAP) (Africa, China, Europe, Middle East, UK); B K Norton Ltd (Hong Kong, South Korea, Taiwan); US PubRep (Caribbean, Latin America); Woodslane (Australia, New Zealand)
Orders to: Chicago Distribution Center, 11030 S Langley Ave, Chicago, IL 60628 *Tel:* 773-702-7000 *Toll Free Tel:* 800-621-2736 *Fax:* 773-702-7212 *Toll Free Fax:* 800-621-8476 *E-mail:* orders@press.uchicago.edu
Returns: Chicago Distribution Center, 11030 S Langley Ave, Chicago, IL 60628 *Tel:* 773-702-7000 *Toll Free Tel:* 800-621-2736 *Fax:* 773-702-7212 *Toll Free Fax:* 800-621-8476 *E-mail:* orders@press.uchicago.edu
Warehouse: Chicago Distribution Center, 11030 S Langley Ave, Chicago, IL 60628 *Tel:* 773-702-7000 *Toll Free Tel:* 800-621-2736 *Fax:* 773-702-7212 *Toll Free Fax:* 800-621-8476 *E-mail:* orders@press.uchicago.edu
Membership(s): Association of American Publishers (AAP); Association of University Presses (AUPresses)

University of Iowa Press
119 W Park Rd, 100 Kuhl House, Iowa City, IA 52242-1000
SAN: 282-4868
Tel: 319-335-2000 *Toll Free Tel:* 800-621-2736 (orders only) *Fax:* 319-335-2055 *Toll Free Fax:* 800-621-8476 (orders only)
E-mail: uipress@uiowa.edu
Web Site: www.uipress.uiowa.edu
Key Personnel
Dir: James McCoy *Tel:* 319-335-2013 *E-mail:* james-mccoy@uiowa.edu
Assoc Dir/Design & Prodn Mgr: Karen Copp *Tel:* 319-335-2014 *E-mail:* karen-copp@uiowa.edu
Mktg Dir: Allison T Means *Tel:* 319-335-3440 *E-mail:* allison-means@uiowa.edu
Mng Ed: Susan Hill Newton *Tel:* 319-335-2011 *E-mail:* susan-hillnewton@uiowa.edu
Acqs Ed: Meredith Stabel *Tel:* 319-335-2012 *E-mail:* meredith-stabel@uiowa.edu
Off Mgr: Angie Dickey *Tel:* 319-335-3424 *E-mail:* angela-dickey@uiowa.edu

Rts & Perms Mgr: Suzanne Glemot *Tel:* 319-335-2008
Founded: 1969
Poetry, short fiction & creative nonfiction. As the only university press in the state, Iowa is also dedicated to preserving the literature, history, culture, wildlife & natural areas of the Midwest.
ISBN Prefix(es): 978-0-87745; 978-1-58729; 978-1-60938
Number of titles published annually: 35 Print; 35 E-Book
Total Titles: 800 Print
Foreign Rep(s): Eurospan Group (Africa, Asia, Australia, Europe, Middle East, UK)
Orders to: Chicago Distribution Center, 11030 S Langley Ave, Chicago, IL 60628 *Tel:* 773-702-7010 *Toll Free Tel:* 800-621-2736 *Fax:* 773-660-2235 *Toll Free Fax:* 800-621-8476 *E-mail:* orders@press.uchicago.edu
Returns: Chicago Distribution Center, 11030 S Langley Ave, Chicago, IL 60628 *Tel:* 773-702-7010 *Toll Free Tel:* 800-621-2736 *Fax:* 773-660-2235 *Toll Free Fax:* 800-621-8476 *E-mail:* orders@press.uchicago.edu
Distribution Center: Chicago Distribution Center, 11030 S Langley Ave, Chicago, IL 60628 *Tel:* 773-702-7010 *Toll Free Tel:* 800-621-2736 *Fax:* 773-660-2235 *Toll Free Fax:* 800-621-8476 *E-mail:* orders@press.uchicago.edu
Membership(s): American Association of University Presses (AAUP)

University of Louisiana at Lafayette Press
PO Box 43558, Lafayette, LA 70504-3558
Tel: 337-482-6027
E-mail: press.submissions@louisiana.edu
Web Site: ulpress.org
Key Personnel
Publr & Dir: Dr Joshua Caffery
Mng Ed: Devon Lord
Prodn Mgr: Mary Duhe
Sales & Mktg Mgr: Somer Greer
Founded: 1973
Publish titles on Louisiana culture & history.
ISBN Prefix(es): 978-0-940984; 978-1-887366; 978-1-935754; 978-1-946160
Number of titles published annually: 12 Print; 5 E-Book
Total Titles: 200 Print; 25 E-Book
Shipping Address: 302 E Saint Mary Blvd, Lafayette, LA 70504

University of Massachusetts Press
New Africa House, 180 Infirmary Way, 4th fl, Amherst, MA 01003-9289
Web Site: www.umasspress.com
Key Personnel
Dir: Mary V Dougherty *E-mail:* mvd@umpress.umass.edu
Mktg & Sales Dir: Courtney J Andree *Tel:* 413-545-4987 *E-mail:* cjandree@umpress.umass.edu
Ed-in-Chief: Matt Becker *E-mail:* mbecker@umpress.umass.edu
Sr Ed: Brian Halley *E-mail:* brian.halley@umb.edu
Assoc Prodn Mgr & Design: Sally Nichols *E-mail:* snichols@umpress.umass.edu
Founded: 1963
Scholarly works & serious nonfiction, including African American studies, American history, American studies, architecture & landscape design, disability studies, environmental studies, gender studies, history of the book, journalism & media studies, literary & cultural studies, Native American studies, technology studies, urban studies & books of regional interest.
ISBN Prefix(es): 978-0-87023; 978-1-55849; 978-1-62534
Number of titles published annually: 45 Print; 35 E-Book
Total Titles: 1,000 Print; 400 E-Book

Imprints: Bright Leaf Books (trade titles about New England)
Distributor for Tagus Press
Foreign Rep(s): Eurospan (Africa, Europe, Middle East, UK)
Distribution Center: Chicago Distribution Center, 11030 S Langley Ave, Chicago, IL 60628 *Tel:* 773-702-7010 *Web Site:* press.uchicago.edu/cdc.html
Membership(s): Association of University Presses (AUPresses)

University of Michigan Press
Unit of University of Michigan
839 Greene St, Ann Arbor, MI 48104-3209
SAN: 202-5329
Tel: 734-764-4388 *Fax:* 734-615-1540
E-mail: um.press@umich.edu
Web Site: www.press.umich.edu
Key Personnel
Dir: Charles Watkinson
Founded: 1930
Aims for diversity in its books & in its audiences.
ISBN Prefix(es): 978-0-472
Number of titles published annually: 110 Print; 100 E-Book
Total Titles: 3,500 Print
Distributor for Center for Chinese Studies, University of Michigan; Center for Japanese Studies, University of Michigan; Center for South & Southeast Asian Studies, University of Michigan
Foreign Rep(s): Eurospan (Europe)
Foreign Rights: University of Chicago Press
Returns: Chicago Distribution Center (CDC), 11030 S Langley Ave, Chicago, IL 60628 *Toll Free Tel:* 800-621-2736 *Toll Free Fax:* 800-621-8476 *E-mail:* orders@press.uchicago.edu
Distribution Center: Chicago Distribution Center (CDC), 11030 S Langley Ave, Chicago, IL 60628 *Toll Free Tel:* 800-621-2736 *Toll Free Fax:* 800-621-8476 *E-mail:* orders@press.uchicago.edu

University of Minnesota Press
Unit of University of Minnesota
111 Third Ave S, Suite 290, Minneapolis, MN 55401-2520
SAN: 213-2648
Tel: 612-301-1990 *Fax:* 612-301-1980
E-mail: ump@umn.edu
Web Site: www.upress.umn.edu
Key Personnel
Dir: Doug Armato
Edit Dir: Jason Weidemann
Assoc Dir: Susan Doerr
Asst Dir, Book Div & Mktg Dir: Emily Hamilton
Mng Ed: Laura Westlund
Regl Ed: Erik Anderson
Prodn Mgr: Daniel Ochsner
Sales Mgr: Matt Smiley
Direct Mail: Maggie Sattler
Intl Rts & Perms: Jeff Moen
Publicist: Heather Skinner
Founded: 1925
Recognized internationally for its innovative, boundary-breaking editorial program in the humanities & social sciences & as publisher of the Minnesota Multiphasic Personality Inventory (MMPI), the most widely used objective tests of personality in the world. Minnesota also maintains as part of its mission a strong commitment to publishing books on the people, history & natural environment of Minnesota & the upper Midwest.
Among the founding members of the Association of University Presses (AUPresses).
ISBN Prefix(es): 978-0-8166; 978-1-4529
Number of titles published annually: 110 Print; 95 E-Book
Total Titles: 3,360 Print; 2,899 E-Book
Distributed by University of Toronto Press (CN)
Distributor for Univocal Publishing

Foreign Rep(s): Combined Academic Publishers (CAP) (Africa, Asia exc Japan, Europe, Middle East, UK); Lexa Publishers' Representatives (Canada); NewSouth Books (Australia, New Zealand); United Publishers Services Ltd (Japan)
Returns: Chicago Distribution Center, 11030 S Langley Ave, Chicago, IL 60628
Shipping Address: Chicago Distribution Center, 11030 S Langley Ave, Chicago, IL 60628 *Tel:* 773-568-1550 *Toll Free Tel:* 800-621-2736 (orders only) *Toll Free Fax:* 800-621-8476 (orders only)
Warehouse: Chicago Distribution Center, 11030 S Langley Ave, Chicago, IL 60628 *Tel:* 773-702-7000 *Toll Free Tel:* 800-621-2736 *Fax:* 773-702-7212 *Toll Free Fax:* 800-621-8476
Membership(s): Association of American Publishers (AAP); Association of University Presses (AUPresses); Crossref; Minnesota Book Publishers Roundtable

University of Missouri Press
113 Heinkel Bldg, 201 S Seventh St, Columbia, MO 65211
SAN: 203-3143
Tel: 573-882-7641; 573-882-9672 (publicity & sales enquiries) *Toll Free Tel:* 800-621-2736 (orders) *Fax:* 573-884-4498 *Toll Free Fax:* 800-621-8476 (orders)
E-mail: upress@missouri.edu; umpmarketing@missouri.edu (publicity & sales enquiries)
Web Site: upress.missouri.edu
Key Personnel
Dir: David M Rosenbaum *Tel:* 573-882-9478 *E-mail:* rosenbaumd@missouri.edu
Ed-in-Chief: Andrew J Davidson *Tel:* 573-882-9997 *E-mail:* davidsonaj@missouri.edu
Busn Mgr: Tracy Tritschler *Tel:* 573-882-9459 *E-mail:* tritschlert@missouri.edu
Prodn Mgr: Drew Griffith *Tel:* 573-882-3044 *E-mail:* griffithd@missouri.edu
Sales & Mktg Mgr: Ms Robin Rennison *Tel:* 573-882-9672 *E-mail:* rennisonr@missouri.edu
Mktg Coord: Deanna Davis *E-mail:* davisdea@missouri.edu
Mktg Asst: Austin Woods *E-mail:* aaw3df@mail.missouri.edu
Founded: 1958
Scholarly books, general trade, art, regional, intellectual thought, US history, literary criticism, African-American history, journalism, political science, sports & women's studies. Also publishes original works by, for & about Missourians.
ISBN Prefix(es): 978-0-8262
Number of titles published annually: 14 Print
Total Titles: 900 Print
Distributor for Missouri History Museum; Missouri Life Magazine; St Louis Mercantile Library
Foreign Rep(s): The Eurospan Group (Africa, Europe, Middle East); RTM Asia-Pacific Book Marketing (Asia, Australia, New Zealand, Pacific Islands)
Orders to: Chicago Distribution Center, 11030 S Langley Ave, Chicago, IL 60628 *E-mail:* orders@press.uchicago.edu
Membership(s): Association of University Presses (AUPresses)

University of Nebraska Press
Division of University of Nebraska-Lincoln
1225 "L" St, Suite 200, Lincoln, NE 68588-0630
Tel: 402-472-3581; 919-966-7449 (cust serv & foreign orders) *Toll Free Tel:* 800-848-6224 (cust serv & US orders) *Fax:* 402-472-6214; 919-962-2704 (cust serv & foreign orders) *Toll Free Fax:* 800-272-6817 (cust serv & US orders)
E-mail: presswebmail@unl.edu
Web Site: www.nebraskapress.unl.edu

U.S. PUBLISHERS

Key Personnel
Dir: Jane Ferreyra *Tel:* 402-472-2861
 E-mail: jferreyra@unl.edu
Ed-in-Chief: Bridget Barry *Tel:* 402-472-0645
 E-mail: bbarry2@unl.edu
Mktg & Sales Mgr: Rosemary Sekora *Tel:* 402-472-7710 *E-mail:* rsekora@unl.edu
Rts & Perms Coord: Leif Milliken *Tel:* 402-472-7702 *E-mail:* lmilliken2@unl.edu
Publicist: Tayler Lord *E-mail:* tayler.lord@unl.edu
Founded: 1941
General scholarly nonfiction, including anthropology, sports history, literature & criticism, history of the Trans-Mississippi West.
ISBN Prefix(es): 978-0-8032
Number of titles published annually: 150 Print; 150 E-Book
Total Titles: 4,000 Print; 1,000 E-Book
Imprints: The Backwaters Press; Bison Books; The Jewish Publication Society; Nebraska; Potomac Books
Distributor for Buros Center for Testing; History Nebraska; Salish Kootenai College Press; Society for American Baseball Research (SABR); Whale and Star Press
Foreign Rep(s): Ampersand (Canada); Combined Academic Publishers (CAP) (Europe)
Advertising Agency: Scholarly Press Advertising Services
Warehouse: Longleaf Services Inc, c/o Ingram Publisher Services, 1250 Ingram Dr, Chambersburg, PA 17202
Distribution Center: Longleaf Services Inc, 116 S Boundary St, Chapel Hill, NC 27514-3808 *Tel:* 919-966-7449 *Toll Free Tel:* 800-848-6224 *Fax:* 919-962-2704 *Toll Free Fax:* 800-272-6817 *E-mail:* customerservice@longleafservices.org *Web Site:* www.longleafservices.org
Membership(s): American Association of University Presses (AAUP)
See separate listing for:
The Jewish Publication Society
Potomac Books

University of Nevada Press
c/o University of Nevada, Continuing Educ Bldg, MS 0166, Reno, NV 89557-0166
SAN: 203-316X
Tel: 775-784-6573 *Fax:* 775-784-6200
Web Site: www.unpress.nevada.edu
Key Personnel
Dir: JoAnne Banducci *Tel:* 775-682-7387
 E-mail: jbanducci@unpress.nevada.edu
Edit, Design & Prodn Mgr: Virginia Fontana
 E-mail: vfontana@unpress.nevada.edu
Mktg & Sales Mgr: Sara Hendricksen *Tel:* 775-682-7395 *E-mail:* shendricksen@unpress.nevada.edu
Founded: 1961
ISBN Prefix(es): 978-0-87417; 978-1-948908; 978-1-943859
Number of titles published annually: 20 Print; 20 E-Book; 1 Audio
Total Titles: 400 Print; 400 E-Book; 3 Audio
Foreign Rep(s): Eurospan University Press Group (Africa, Central America, Europe, Middle East, South America, UK)
Orders to: Chicago Distribution Center, 11030 S Langley Ave, Chicago, IL 60628 *Toll Free Tel:* 800-621-2736 *Toll Free Fax:* 800-621-8476 *E-mail:* custserv@press.uchicago.edu
Warehouse: Chicago Distribution Center, 11030 S Langley Ave, Chicago, IL 60628 *Toll Free Tel:* 800-621-2736 *Toll Free Fax:* 800-621-8476 *E-mail:* custserv@press.uchicago.edu
Membership(s): American Association of University Presses (AAUP); Publishers Association of the West (PubWest)

University of New Mexico Press
One University of New Mexico, Albuquerque, NM 87131-0001
SAN: 213-9588
Mailing Address: MSC05 3185, One University of New Mexico, Albuquerque, NM 87131-0001
Tel: 505-272-7777 *Fax:* 505-277-3343
E-mail: custserv@unm.edu (order dept)
Web Site: unmpress.com
Key Personnel
Dir: Stephen Hull *Tel:* 505-277-3280
 E-mail: sphull@unm.edu
Sr Acqs Ed: Elise M McHugh *Tel:* 505-277-3327
 E-mail: elisemc@unm.edu; Michael Millman
 Tel: 505-277-3284 *E-mail:* mmillman@unm.edu
Sr Ed: Alexandra Hoff *Tel:* 505-277-3436
 E-mail: aewhoff@unm.edu
Edit, Design & Prodn Mgr: James Ayers
 Tel: 505-277-3324 *E-mail:* ayers@unm.edu
Mktg & Sales Mgr: Katherine White *Tel:* 505-277-3294 *E-mail:* kwhite03@unm.edu
Sr Book Designer: Felicia Cedillos *Tel:* 505-277-3322 *E-mail:* fcedillo@unm.edu; Mindy Hill *Tel:* 505-277-3333 *E-mail:* mindybasingerhill@unm.edu
Acqs Coord & Ebook Prodn Ed: Sonia Dickey *Tel:* 505-277-3297 *E-mail:* soniad@unm.edu
Founded: 1929
General, scholarly & regional books, Latin American studies & native studies.
ISBN Prefix(es): 978-0-8263
Number of titles published annually: 75 Print
Total Titles: 1,750 Print
Imprints: High Road Books
Distributor for BowArrow Publishing; Fresco-Books/SF Design LLC; La Frontera Publishing; New Mexico Magazine; School for Advanced Research; Sunbelt Editions; West End Press (not actively publishing)
Foreign Rep(s): Eurospan Ltd (Africa, Asia, Australia, Europe, Middle East, New Zealand, UK); UBC Press (Canada); US PubRep (Craig Falk) (Caribbean, Latin America, Mexico, Puerto Rico)
Foreign Rights: Jennifer Schaper (worldwide exc USA)
Distribution Center: Longleaf Services Inc, 116 S Boundary St, Chapel Hill, NC 27514-3808 *Tel:* 919-966-7449 *Toll Free Tel:* 800-848-6224 *Fax:* 919-962-2704 *Toll Free Fax:* 800-272-6817 *E-mail:* orders@longleafservices.org *Web Site:* www.longleafservices.org
Membership(s): Association of University Presses (AUPresses)

§University of New Orleans Press
Division of University of New Orleans
2000 Lakeshore Dr, New Orleans, LA 70148
Tel: 504-280-7457
E-mail: unopress@uno.edu
Web Site: www.uno.edu/unopress
Key Personnel
Ed-in-Chief: Abram Shalom Himelstein
Mng Ed: George Darby
Ed: Chelsey Shannon
Founded: 2003
ISBN Prefix(es): 978-0-9728143; 978-0-9706190; 978-1-60801
Number of titles published annually: 15 Print; 15 E-Book
Total Titles: 200 Print; 200 E-Book
Distribution Center: HFS (Hopkins Fulfillment Services), PO Box 50370, Baltimore, MD 21211-4370 *Tel:* 410-516-6965 *Toll Free Tel:* 800-537-5487 *Fax:* 410-516-6998 *E-mail:* hfscustserv@jh.edu *Web Site:* hfs.jhu.edu
Hornblower Group, 14 Afton Ave, Toronto, ON M6J 1R7, Canada, Co-Owner & Assoc Partner: Karen Stacey *Tel:* 416-461-7973 *E-mail:* kstacey@hornblowerbooks.com *Web Site:* www.hornblowerbooks.com

§The University of North Carolina Press
Affiliate of The University of North Carolina System
116 S Boundary St, Chapel Hill, NC 27514-3808
SAN: 203-3151
Tel: 919-966-3561; 919-966-7449 (orders)
 Toll Free Tel: 800-848-3224 (orders) *Fax:* 919-962-2704 (orders) *Toll Free Fax:* 800-272-6817 (orders)
E-mail: uncpress@unc.edu
Web Site: uncpress.org
Key Personnel
Dir: John Sherer *Tel:* 919-962-3748 *E-mail:* john.sherer@uncpress.org
Asst Dir/Sr Dir, Mktg & Digital Busn Devt: Dino Battista *E-mail:* dino.battista@uncpress.org
Art Dir: Lindsay Starr *Tel:* 919-843-8021
 E-mail: lindsay.starr@uncpress.org
Dir, PR & Communs: Peter L Perez
 E-mail: peter.perez@uncpress.org
Dir, Publicity: Sonya Bonczek *Tel:* 919-962-0581
 E-mail: sonya.bonczek@uncpress.org
Dir, Edit, Design & Prodn: Kim Bryant *Tel:* 919-962-0571 *E-mail:* kim.bryant@uncpress.org
Wyndham Robertson Edit Dir: Dawn Durante
Sales Dir: Susan Garrett *Tel:* 919-843-7697
 E-mail: susan.garrett@uncpress.org
Asst Edit Dir: Debbie Gershenowitz
 E-mail: debbie.gershenowitz@uncpress.org
Sr Exec Ed: Mark Simpson-Vos *E-mail:* mark.simpson-vos@uncpress.org
Exec Ed: Lucas Church *E-mail:* lucas.church@uncpress.org
Mng Ed: Mary Caviness *Tel:* 919-962-0545
 E-mail: mary.caviness@uncpress.org
Ed: Andreina Fernandez *E-mail:* andreina.fernandez@uncpress.org; Maria Isela Garcia *E-mail:* maria.garcia@uncpress.org; Cate Hodorowicz *E-mail:* catherine.hodorowicz@uncpress.org; Andrew Winters *E-mail:* andrew.winters@uncpress.org
Asst Ed: Thomas Bedenbaugh *E-mail:* thomas.bedenbaugh@uncpress.org; Carol Seigler *E-mail:* carol.seigler@uncpress.org
Founded: 1922
General, scholarly, regional.
ISBN Prefix(es): 978-1-8078
Number of titles published annually: 100 Print
Total Titles: 776 E-Book
Imprints: Ferris & Ferris Books
Distributor for Museum of Early Southern Decorative Arts; North Carolina Museum of Art; Southeastern Center for Contemporary Art; Valentine Museum
Foreign Rep(s): EDIREP (Caribbean, Central America, Mexico, South America); Eurospan University Press Group (Africa, Continental Europe, Middle East, UK); Scholarly Book Services Inc (Canada)
Advertising Agency: Brimley Agency
Orders to: Longleaf Services Inc, 116 S Boundary St, Chapel Hill, NC 27514-3808 *E-mail:* customerservice@longleafservices.org *Web Site:* www.longleafservices.org
Returns: Longleaf Returns, c/o Ingram Publisher Services, 1210 Ingram Dr, Chambersburg, PA 17202
Membership(s): Association of American Publishers (AAP); Book Industry Study Group (BISG)

§University of North Texas Press
941 Precision Dr, Denton, TX 76207
SAN: 249-4280
Mailing Address: 1155 Union Circle, No 311336, Denton, TX 76203-5017
Tel: 940-565-2142 *Fax:* 940-369-8760
Web Site: untpress.unt.edu
Key Personnel
Dir: Ronald Chrisman *E-mail:* ronald.chrisman@unt.edu
Mng Ed: Amy Maddox *E-mail:* amy.maddox@unt.edu

Mktg Mgr: Joe Alderman *E-mail:* joseph.
alderman@unt.edu
Founded: 1987
ISBN Prefix(es): 978-0-929398; 978-1-57441
Number of titles published annually: 16 Print; 5
Online; 16 E-Book
Total Titles: 600 Print; 75 Online; 100 E-Book
Foreign Rep(s): East-West Export Books (Asia,
Australia, Hawaii, New Zealand, Pacific Islands); Eurospan Group (Europe); Scholarly
Book Services Inc (Canada); US PubRep (Latin
America)
Distribution Center: Texas A&M University Press
Consortium, John H Lindsey Bldg, Lewis St,
4354 TAMU, College Station, TX 77843-
4354 *Toll Free Tel:* 800-826-8911 *Toll Free
Fax:* 888-617-2421
Membership(s): American Association of University Presses (AAUP)

University of Notre Dame Press
310 Flanner Hall, Notre Dame, IN 46556
SAN: 203-3178
Tel: 574-631-6346 *Fax:* 574-631-8148
E-mail: undpress@nd.edu
Web Site: www.undpress.nd.edu
Key Personnel
Dir: Stephen Wrinn
Sr Acqs Ed: Emily King *E-mail:* eking8@nd.edu
Assoc Acqs Ed: Rachel Kindler *Tel:* 574-631-
4913 *E-mail:* rkindler@nd.edu
Busn Mgr/IT: Paul Ashenfelter *Tel:* 574-631-7415
E-mail: pashenfe@nd.edu
Mng Ed: Matthew Dowd *Tel:* 574-631-4914
E-mail: mdowd1@nd.edu
Asst Prodn Ed: David Juarez *Tel:* 574-631-4908
E-mail: djuarez@nd.edu
Asst Dir & Dir, Mktg, Sales & Devt: Michelle
Sybert *Tel:* 574-631-4910 *E-mail:* msybert@nd.
edu
Mktg & Publicity Mgr: Laura Moran Walton
Tel: 574-631-3267 *E-mail:* lmoran@nd.edu
Digital Assets Mgr: Jennifer Bernal *Tel:* 574-631-
3266 *E-mail:* jbernal2@nd.edu
Exhibits & Digital Mktg Mgr: Stephanie Marchman *Tel:* 574-631-4905 *E-mail:* shoffma7@nd.
edu
Prodn & Design Mgr: Wendy McMillen *Tel:* 574-
631-4907 *E-mail:* wmcmille@nd.edu
Founded: 1949
Academic books, hardcover & paperback; philosophy, Irish studies, literature, theology, international relations, sociology & general interest.
ISBN Prefix(es): 978-0-268
Number of titles published annually: 50 Print
Total Titles: 1,200 Print
Foreign Rep(s): CAP (Europe)
Returns: Longleaf Services Inc, 16 S Boundary St, Chapel Hill, NC 27514 *Tel:* 919-
966-7449 *Toll Free Tel:* 800-848-6224 ext 1
Fax: 919-962-2704 *E-mail:* customerservice@
longleafservices.org *Web Site:* longleafservices.
org
Distribution Center: Longleaf Services Inc, 16 S
Boundary St, Chapel Hill, NC 27514 *Tel:* 919-
966-7449 *Toll Free Tel:* 800-848-6224 ext 1
Fax: 919-962-2704 *E-mail:* customerservice@
longleafservices.org *Web Site:* longleafservices.
org
Membership(s): Association of University Presses
(AUPresses)

University of Oklahoma Press
2800 Venture Dr, Norman, OK 73069-8216
SAN: 203-3194
Tel: 405-325-2000
Web Site: www.oupress.com
Key Personnel
Dir, Fin & Opers & Dir, Sales & Mktg: Dale
Bennie *Tel:* 405-325-3207 *E-mail:* dbennie@
ou.edu
Mng Ed: Steven Baker *Tel:* 405-325-1325
E-mail: steven.b.baker@ou.edu
EDP Mgr: Tony Roberts *Tel:* 405-325-3186
E-mail: tonyroberts@ou.edu
Publicity Mgr: Katie Baker *Tel:* 405-325-3200
E-mail: katie-baker@ou.edu
Founded: 1928
Scholarly & general interest books on Americana,
Native American studies, Western history, regional interest, natural history, anthropology,
archaeology, military history, literature, classical studies, women's studies & political science.
ISBN Prefix(es): 978-0-8061; 978-0-87062
(Arthur H Clark Co)
Number of titles published annually: 90 Print; 80
E-Book
Total Titles: 2,059 Print; 5 CD-ROM; 1,961 E-
Book
Imprints: Arthur H Clark Co
Distributor for Cherokee Heritage Press; Denver
Art Museum; Gilcrease Museum
Distribution Center: Longleaf Services Inc, 116
S Boundary St, Chapel Hill, NC 27514-3808
Toll Free Tel: 800-848-6224 ext 1 *Fax:* 919-
962-2704 *Toll Free Fax:* 800-272-6817
E-mail: customerservice@longleafservices.org
Web Site: www.longleafservices.org SAN: 203-
3151
Membership(s): Association of University Presses
(AUPresses)

**§University of Pennsylvania Museum of
Archaeology & Anthropology**
Division of University of Pennsylvania
3260 South St, Philadelphia, PA 19104-6324
Tel: 215-898-4119; 215-898-4000
E-mail: publications@pennmuseum.org
Web Site: www.penn.museum
Key Personnel
Dir, Pubns: Page Selinsky, PhD
Founded: 1887
ISBN Prefix(es): 978-0-934718; 978-0-924171;
978-1-931707; 978-1-949057; 978-1-934536
Number of titles published annually: 4 Print; 4 E-
Book
Total Titles: 210 Print; 18 CD-ROM
Distributed by University of Pennsylvania Press
Billing Address: Ingram Publisher Services,
14 Ingram Blvd, Mail Stop 631, La Vergne,
TN 37086 *Toll Free Tel:* 866-400-5351 *Web
Site:* www.ingrampublisherservices.com
Orders to: Ingram Publisher Services, 14 Ingram
Blvd, Mail Stop 631, La Vergne, TN 37086
Toll Free Tel: 866-400-5351 *Web Site:* www.
ingrampublisherservices.com
Returns: Ingram Publisher Services, 191 Edwards Dr, Jackson, TN 38301 *Web Site:* www.
ingrampublisherservices.com
Shipping Address: Ingram Publisher Services,
191 Edwards Dr, Jackson, TN 38301 *Web
Site:* www.ingrampublisherservices.com

University of Pennsylvania Press
3905 Spruce St, Philadelphia, PA 19104
SAN: 202-5345
Tel: 215-898-6261 *Fax:* 215-898-0404
E-mail: custserv@pobox.upenn.edu
Web Site: www.pennpress.org
Key Personnel
Dir: Mary C Francis
Ed-in-Chief: Walter Biggins *E-mail:* wbiggins@
upenn.edu
Mng Ed: Lily Palladino *E-mail:* lilypall@upenn.
edu
Sr Ed: Robert Lockhart *E-mail:* rlockhar@upenn.
edu; Elisabeth Maselli *E-mail:* emaselli@
upenn.edu
Assoc Ed: Jenny Tan *E-mail:* jennytan@upenn.
edu
Busn Mgr: Joseph Guttman *Tel:* 215-898-1670
E-mail: josephgg@upenn.edu
Editing & Prodn Mgr: Elizabeth Glover *Tel:* 215-
898-1675 *E-mail:* gloverel@upenn.edu
Publicity & PR Mgr: Gigi Lamm *Tel:* 215-898-
1674 *E-mail:* glamm@upenn.edu
Founded: 1890
Scholarly & semipopular nonfiction, especially in
history, literature & criticism, social sciences &
human rights.
ISBN Prefix(es): 978-0-8122; 978-1-5128
Number of titles published annually: 120 Print;
120 Online
Total Titles: 3,250 Print; 2,650 E-Book
Imprints: Wharton School Press (WSP)
Distributor for The American Philosophical Society
Foreign Rep(s): Combined Academic Publishers
(CAP) (Africa, Arab Middle East, Asia, Austria, China, UK); Durnell Marketing Ltd (Continental Europe); Scholarly Book Services Inc
(Canada)
Returns: Ingram Publisher Services, 193 Edwards
Dr, Jackson, TN 38301
Warehouse: Ingram Publisher Services, 193 Edwards Dr, Jackson, TN 38301
Marston Book Services Ltd, 160 Eastern Ave,
Milton Park, Oxon OX14 4SB, United Kingdom, Asst Cust Servs & Trade Mgr: Donna
Green *Tel:* (01235) 465630 *Fax:* (01235)
465555 *E-mail:* donna.green@marston.co.uk
Web Site: www.marston.co.uk/home.htm
Membership(s): American Association of University Presses (AAUP); Association of American
Publishers Professional & Scholarly Publishing
Division

University of Pittsburgh Press
7500 Thomas Blvd, Pittsburgh, PA 15260
Tel: 412-383-2456 *Fax:* 412-383-2466
E-mail: info@upress.pitt.edu
Web Site: www.upress.pitt.edu
Key Personnel
Dir: Peter W Kracht *E-mail:* pkracht@upress.pitt.
edu
Dir, Mktg & Sales: John Fagan *E-mail:* jfagan@
upress.pitt.edu
Dir, Opers: David Baumann *E-mail:* dbaumann@
upress.pitt.edu
Opers Admin: Eileen O'Malley
E-mail: eomalley@upress.pitt.edu
Edit Dir: Sandy Crooms *E-mail:* scrooms@
upress.pitt.edu
Edit & Prodn Dir: Alexander Wolfe
E-mail: awolfe@upress.pitt.edu
Mng Ed: Amy Sherman *E-mail:* asherman@
upress.pitt.edu
Sr Acqs Ed: Abby Collier *E-mail:* acollier@
upress.pitt.edu; Joshua Shanholtzer
E-mail: jshanholtzer@upress.pitt.edu
Prodn Ed: Melissa Dias-Mandoly
E-mail: mdiasmandoly@upress.pitt.edu
Ad & Soc Media Mgr: Kelly Thomas
E-mail: kthomas@upress.pitt.edu
Design & Prodn Mgr: Joel Coggins
E-mail: jcoggins@upress.pitt.edu
Publicity Mgr: Lesley Rains *E-mail:* lrains@
upress.pitt.edu
Mktg Coord: Caleb Gill *E-mail:* cgill@upress.pitt.
edu
Mktg Asst: Sheena Carroll *E-mail:* scarroll@
upress.pitt.edu
Publicist: Chloe Wertz *E-mail:* cwertz@upress.
pitt.edu
Founded: 1936
Scholarly nonfiction, poetry, regional books, short
fiction, Russian & East European studies, composition & rhetoric, Latin American studies,
environmental history, urban studies, philosophy of science, political science.
ISBN Prefix(es): 978-0-8229
Number of titles published annually: 65 Print
Total Titles: 1,700 Print; 1,300 E-Book
Foreign Rep(s): Casemate UK (Africa, Europe,
Middle East, UK); Oxbow Books (Africa, Europe, Middle East, UK)

U.S. PUBLISHERS

Distribution Center: Longleaf Services Inc, 116 S Boundary St, Chapel Hill, NC 27514-3808 Toll Free Tel: 800-848-6224 Toll Free Fax: 800-272-6817 E-mail: orders@longleafservices.org
Web Site: longleafservices.org
Membership(s): Association of University Presses (AUPresses)

University of Rochester Press
Affiliate of Boydell & Brewer Inc
668 Mount Hope Ave, Rochester, NY 14620-2731
Tel: 585-275-0419 Fax: 585-271-8778
E-mail: boydell@boydellusa.net
Web Site: www.urpress.com
Key Personnel
Edit Dir: Sonia Kane E-mail: sonia.kane@rochester.edu
Prodn Dir: Sue Smith E-mail: smith@boydellusa.net
Founded: 1989
ISBN Prefix(es): 978-1-878822; 978-1-58046
Number of titles published annually: 27 Print
Total Titles: 650 Print
Foreign Office(s): PO Box 9, Woodbridge, Suffolk IP12 3DF, United Kingdom
Foreign Rep(s): Boydell & Brewer (Europe, Japan)
Warehouse: Ingram Academic Services

§University of South Carolina Press
Affiliate of University of South Carolina
1600 Hampton St, Suite 544, Columbia, SC 29208
SAN: 203-3224
Tel: 803-777-5245 Toll Free Tel: 800-768-2500 (orders) Fax: 803-777-0160 Toll Free Fax: 800-868-0740 (orders)
Web Site: uscpress.com
Key Personnel
Dir: Michael J McGandy Tel: 803-777-2243 E-mail: mcgandy@mailbox.sc.edu
Edit, Design & Prodn Dir: Pat Callahan Tel: 803-777-2449 E-mail: mpcallah@mailbox.sc.edu
Mktg & Sales Dir: Cathy Esposito Tel: 803-777-2021 E-mail: ce26@mailbox.sc.edu
Assoc Edit Dir: Aurora Bell Tel: 803-777-4859 E-mail: aurorab@mailbox.sc.edu
Prodn Ed: Kerri Tolan Tel: 803-777-5075 E-mail: kerrit@mailbox.sc.edu
Acqs Ed, African American Studies, Civil Rights & Southern History: Ehren Foley Tel: 803-777-9055 E-mail: foleyk@email.sc.edu
Busn Mgr: Vicki Leach Tel: 803-777-7754 E-mail: vleach@mailbox.sc.edu
Digital Publg Coord: Ashley Mathias Tel: 803-777-2238 E-mail: samathi@mailbox.sc.edu
Mktg & Design Coord: Kemi Ogunji Tel: 803-777-5029 E-mail: ogunji@mailbox.sc.edu
Publg Asst: Lily Stephens Tel: 803-777-5245 E-mail: ls54@mailbox.sc.edu
Founded: 1944
American history/studies, Southern studies, military history, maritime history, literary studies including contemporary American & British literature & modern world literature, religious studies, speech/communication, social work.
ISBN Prefix(es): 978-0-87249; 978-1-57003; 978-1-64336
Number of titles published annually: 50 Print; 2 Audio
Total Titles: 1,500 Print; 2 CD-ROM
Distributor for McKissick Museum; South Carolina Bar Association; South Carolina Historical Society
Foreign Rep(s): Eurospan University Press Group (Europe, UK); Scholarly Book Services Inc (Canada)
Warehouse: HFS (Hopkins Fulfillment Services), PO Box 50370, Baltimore, MD 21211-4370 Tel: 410-516-6965 Toll Free Tel: 800-537-5487 Fax: 410-516-6998 E-mail: hfscustserv@jh.edu Web Site: hfs.jhu.edu

Distribution Center: HFS (Hopkins Fulfillment Services), PO Box 50370, Baltimore, MD 21211-4370 Tel: 410-516-6965 Toll Free Tel: 800-537-5487 Fax: 410-516-6998 E-mail: hfscustserv@jh.edu Web Site: hfs.jhu.edu
Membership(s): American Association of University Presses (AAUP); Southern Independent Booksellers Alliance (SIBA)

University of Tennessee Press
Division of University of Tennessee
323 Hodges Library, 1015 Volunteer Blvd, Knoxville, TN 37996
SAN: 212-9930
Tel: 865-974-3321 Toll Free Tel: 800-621-2736 (orders) Toll Free Fax: 800-621-2736 (orders)
E-mail: custserv@utpress.org
Web Site: www.utpress.org
Key Personnel
Dir: Scott Danforth E-mail: danforth@utk.edu
Assoc Dir & Acqs Ed: Thomas Wells E-mail: twells@utk.edu
Busn Mgr: Lisa Davis E-mail: ldavis49@utk.edu
Mktg Mgr: Tom Post Tel: 865-974-5466 E-mail: tpost@utk.edu
Founded: 1940
Scholarly & regional nonfiction.
ISBN Prefix(es): 978-0-87049; 978-1-57233; 978-1-62190
Number of titles published annually: 40 Print
Total Titles: 1,200 Print
Foreign Rep(s): East-West Export Books Inc (Asia, The Pacific); Eurospan Group (Africa, Central Asia, Europe, Middle East, UK)
Distribution Center: Chicago Distribution Center, 11030 S Langley Ave, Chicago, IL 60628 Toll Free Tel: 800-621-2736 Fax: 773-702-7212
Membership(s): Association of American Publishers (AAP); Association of University Presses (AUPresses)

§The University of Utah Press
Subsidiary of University of Utah
J Willard Marriott Library, Suite 5400, 295 S 1500 E, Salt Lake City, UT 84112-0860
SAN: 220-0023
Tel: 801-585-9786 Fax: 801-581-3365
E-mail: hannah.new@utah.edu
Web Site: www.uofupress.com
Key Personnel
Dir & Mng Ed: Glenda Cotter E-mail: glenda.cotter@utah.edu
Prodn Mgr: Jessica Booth E-mail: jessica.booth@utah.edu
Busn Mgr & Perms: Janalyn Guo E-mail: janalyn.guo@utah.edu
Founded: 1949
Scholarly books, regional studies, anthropology, archaeology, linguistics, Mesoamerican studies, natural history, Western history, outdoor recreation.
ISBN Prefix(es): 978-0-87480; 978-1-60781; 978-1-67469
Number of titles published annually: 32 Print; 30 E-Book
Total Titles: 600 Print
Imprints: Bonneville Books (trade); Boxelder Books
Distributor for BYU Museum of Peoples & Cultures; BYU Studies; KUED (Utah PBS affiliate); Western Epics Publications
Foreign Rep(s): Eurospan (Africa, Europe)
Orders to: The Chicago Distribution Center, 11030 S Langley Ave, Chicago, IL 60628 Tel: 773-702-7000 Toll Free Tel: 800-621-2736 Fax: 773-702-7212 Toll Free Fax: 800-621-8741 Web Site: www.uofupress.com
Returns: The Chicago Distribution Center, 11030 S Langley Ave, Chicago, IL 60628

University of Virginia Press
Affiliate of University of Virginia
PO Box 400318, Charlottesville, VA 22904-4318
Tel: 434-924-3469 (cust serv) Toll Free Tel: 800-831-3406 Fax: 434-982-2655
Toll Free Tel: 877-288-6400
E-mail: vapress@virginia.edu
Web Site: www.upress.virginia.edu
Key Personnel
Dir: Eric Brandt Tel: 434-982-3033 E-mail: eab7fb@virginia.edu
Dir, Digital Publg: Patricia Searl Tel: 434-982-2310 E-mail: pls4e@virginia.edu
Dir, Mktg & Sales: Jason Coleman Tel: 434-924-1450 E-mail: jgc3h@virginia.edu
Dir, Opers: Brenda Fitzgerald E-mail: bwf@virginia.edu
Mng Ed, Ms Edit/Design & Prodn: Ellen Satrom Tel: 434-924-6065 E-mail: esatrom@virginia.edu
Acqs Ed, Africana Studies: Beth Colon E-mail: ehz2wg@virginia.edu
Acqs Ed, Architecture & Environmental: Mark Mones Tel: 434-924-1373 E-mail: emm4t@virginia.edu
Acqs Ed, Soc Sci & History: Nadine Zimmerli Tel: 434-924-7301 E-mail: nzimmerli@virginia.edu
Database Mgr: Leah Stearns E-mail: leahsterns@virginia.edu
Publicist: Mark Kate Maco Tel: 434-982-2932 E-mail: faa6je@virginia.edu
Founded: 1963
General scholarly nonfiction with emphasis on history, literature & regional books.
UVA Press provides ms editorial, design & production services for the University of Delaware Press.
ISBN Prefix(es): 978-0-8139; 978-978-0
Number of titles published annually: 70 Print; 2 Online; 60 E-Book; 5 Audio
Total Titles: 1,600 Print; 28 Online; 800 E-Book; 10 Audio
Distributor for Colonial Society of Massachusetts; George Mason University Press; The Historic New Orleans Collection; James Madison University; Massachusetts Historical Society; Samovar Press; George F Thompson Publishing
Foreign Rep(s): Eurospan (Africa, Asia, Europe, Latin America, Oceania); University of Toronto Press (Canada)
Shipping Address: Longleaf Services Inc, 116 S Boundary St, Chapel Hill, NC 27514-3808 Toll Free Tel: 800-848-6224 Toll Free Fax: 800-272-6817 E-mail: orders@longleafservices.org
SAN: 203-3151
Membership(s): American Association of University Presses (AAUP)

§University of Washington Press
Unit of University of Washington Libraries
4333 Brooklyn Ave NE, Seattle, WA 98105-9570
SAN: 212-2502
Mailing Address: PO Box 359570, Seattle, WA 98195-9570
Toll Free Tel: 800-537-5487 (orders) Fax: 206-543-3932; 410-516-6998 (orders)
E-mail: uwapress@uw.edu
Web Site: uwapress.uw.edu
Key Personnel
Dir: Nicole F Mitchell Tel: 206-685-9373 E-mail: nfmm@uw.edu
Art Dir: Katrina Noble Tel: 206-221-7004 E-mail: krnoble@uw.edu
Dir, Mktg & Sales: Julie Fergus Tel: 206-543-4053 E-mail: jaf88@uw.edu
Exec Ed: Lorri Hagman Tel: 206-221-4989 E-mail: lhagman@uw.edu
Ed-in-Chief: Larin McLaughlin Tel: 206-221-4995 E-mail: lmclaugh@uw.edu
Sr Acqs Ed: Andrew Berzanskis
Sr Proj Ed: Julie Van Pelt Tel: 206-685-9165 E-mail: jvp@uw.edu
Acqs Ed: Mike Baccam Tel: 206-897-1738 E-mail: mbaccam@uw.edu

Editing, Design & Prodn Mgr: Margaret Sullivan *Tel:* 206-221-4987 *E-mail:* mksu@uw.edu
Mktg Mgr: Laura Fish
Publicity Mgr: Kait Heacock *Tel:* 206-221-4994 *E-mail:* kheacock@uw.edu
Founded: 1920
General scholarly nonfiction, reprints, imports.
ISBN Prefix(es): 978-0-295
Number of titles published annually: 68 Print
Total Titles: 1,500 Print; 1 CD-ROM
Distributor for Art Gallery of New South Wales; Fowler Museum at UCLA; International Sculpture Center; LM Publishers; Museum for African Art; National Gallery of Australia; Power Publications; Silkworm Books; UCLA Chicano Studies Research Center Press
Foreign Rep(s): Ampersand (Canada); Combined Academic Publishers (CAP) (worldwide exc Canada, Caribbean, Central America, Mexico, Puerto Rico & USA); University of Toronto Press Distribution (Canada); US PubRep (Craig Kalk) (Caribbean, Central America, Mexico, Puerto Rico, South America)
Distribution Center: HFS (Hopkins Fulfillment Services), PO Box 50370, Baltimore, MD 21211-4370 (US) *Tel:* 410-516-6965 *Toll Free Tel:* 800-537-5487 *Fax:* 410-516-6998 *E-mail:* hfscustserv@jh.edu *Web Site:* hfs.jhu.edu
Membership(s): Association of University Presses (AUPresses)

University of Wisconsin Press
Unit of University of Wisconsin-Madison
728 State St, Suite 443, Madison, WI 53706-1418
SAN: 501-0039
Tel: 608-263-1110; 608-263-0668 (journal orders) *Toll Free Tel:* 800-621-2736 (book orders) *Fax:* 608-263-1173 *Toll Free Fax:* 800-621-2736 (book orders)
E-mail: uwiscpress@uwpress.wisc.edu
Web Site: uwpress.wisc.edu
Key Personnel
Dir: Dennis Lloyd *E-mail:* dlloyd2@wisc.edu
Ed-in-Chief: Dan Crissman
Acqs Ed: Nathan Macbrien *E-mail:* macbrien@wisc.edu
Edit, Design & Prodn Mgr/ISBN Contact: Adam Mehring *Tel:* 608-263-0856 *E-mail:* amehring@wisc.edu
Journals Mgr: Toni Gunnison *Tel:* 608-263-0667 *E-mail:* gunnison@wisc.edu
Publicity Mgr: Alison Shay *Tel:* 608-263-0734 *E-mail:* amshay@wisc.edu
Rts & Perms Mgr: Anne McKenna *Tel:* 608-263-1131 *E-mail:* atmckenna@wisc.edu
Sales & Mktg Mgr: Casey LaVela *Tel:* 608-263-0814 *E-mail:* casey.lavela@wisc.edu
Founded: 1936
Academic press, including regional Midwest titles & trade titles.
ISBN Prefix(es): 978-0-87972; 978-0-299; 978-1-928755; 978-0-9671787; 978-8-158; 978-0-9682722; 978-0-924119; 978-0-9655464; 978-0-9718963; 978-0-9624369; 978-0-932900; 978-1-931569; 978-0-9623206; 978-0-9653519; 978-0-9700602; 978-0-9789590; 978-0-9817723
Number of titles published annually: 60 Print; 60 E-Book
Total Titles: 1,480 Print; 1,100 E-Book
Distributor for The Center for the Study of Upper Midwestern Culture; Wisconsin Veterans Museum
Foreign Rep(s): Eurospan Ltd (Africa, Asia, Australia, Continental Europe, Iceland, Ireland, Middle East, New Zealand, The Pacific, UK)
Advertising Agency: Ad Vantage *E-mail:* advertising@uwpress.wisc.edu
Orders to: Chicago Distribution Center, 11030 S Langley Ave, Chicago, IL 60628-3892 *Tel:* 773-702-7000 *Toll Free Tel:* 800-621-2736 *Fax:* 773-702-7212 *Toll Free Fax:* 800-621-8476 *E-mail:* custserv@press.uchicago.edu
SAN: 202-5280
Returns: Chicago Distribution Center, 11030 S Langley Ave, Chicago, IL 60628-3892
SAN: 202-5280
Shipping Address: Chicago Distribution Center, 11030 S Langley Ave, Chicago, IL 60628-3892 *E-mail:* custserv@press.uchicago.edu
SAN: 202-5280
Warehouse: Chicago Distribution Center, 11030 S Langley Ave, Chicago, IL 60628-3892 *E-mail:* custserv@press.uchicago.edu
SAN: 202-5280
Distribution Center: Chicago Distribution Center, 11030 S Langley Ave, Chicago, IL 60628-3892 *Tel:* 773-568-1550 *Toll Free Tel:* 800-621-2736 *Fax:* 773-660-2235 *Toll Free Fax:* 800-621-8476 SAN: 202-5280
Eurospan Group, Gray's Inn House, 127 Clerkenwell Rd, London EC1R 5DB, United Kingdom (Africa, Asia, Australia, Eurasia, Europe, Middle East, New Zealand, the Pacific, Russia & UK) *Tel:* (01235) 465576 *E-mail:* trade.orders@marston.co.uk
Membership(s): Association of University Presses (AUPresses); Great Lakes Independent Booksellers Association (GLIBA); Midwest Independent Booksellers Association (MIBA); Wisconsin Library Association

University Press of America Inc
4501 Forbes Blvd, Suite 200, Lanham, MD 20706
SAN: 200-2256
Tel: 301-459-3366 *Toll Free Tel:* 800-462-6420
Web Site: www.univpress.com
Key Personnel
Dir, Edit: Nicolette Amstutz *E-mail:* namstutz@rowman.com
Founded: 1975
Scholarly monographs, college texts, conference proceedings, professional books & reprints in the social sciences & the humanities.
ISBN Prefix(es): 978-0-8191; 978-0-7618
Number of titles published annually: 100 Print; 100 E-Book
Total Titles: 10,000 Print; 2,000 E-Book
Foreign Rep(s): NBN Plymbridge (Europe, UK); United Publishers Services (Japan)
Foreign Rights: United Publishers Service (Japan)
Shipping Address: 15200 NBN Way, Blue Ridge Summit, PA 17214-0191 *Toll Free Tel:* 800-462-6420 *Fax:* 717-794-3812 *Toll Free Fax:* 800-338-4550
Membership(s): Association of American Publishers (AAP)

University Press of Colorado
1580 N Logan St, Suite 660, PMB 39883, Denver, CO 80203-1942
SAN: 202-1749
Tel: 720-406-8849 *Toll Free Tel:* 800-621-2736 (orders) *Fax:* 720-406-3443
Web Site: www.upcolorado.com
Key Personnel
Dir: Darrin Pratt *E-mail:* darrin@upcolorado.com
Founded: 1965
Scholarly & regional nonfiction.
ISBN Prefix(es): 978-0-87081; 978-0-87421 (Utah State University Press, pre-2012); 978-1-60223 (University of Alaska Press backlist); 978-1-60732; 978-1-64642
Number of titles published annually: 50 Print; 50 E-Book
Total Titles: 1,300 Print; 3 CD-ROM; 1,200 E-Book; 1 Audio
Imprints: University of Alaska Press; University of Wyoming Press; Utah State University Press
Distributor for Center for Literary Publishing; History Colorado; Institute for Mesoamerican Studies; International Association for Society & Natural Resources; Society for American Archaeology; Western Press Books
Foreign Rep(s): Ingram Publisher Services UK (Asia, Australia, UK & the continent)
Orders to: Chicago Distribution Center, 11030 S Langley, Chicago, IL 60628 *Toll Free Tel:* 800-621-2736 *E-mail:* custserv@press.uchicago.edu
Returns: Chicago Distribution Center, Returns Processing Ctr, 11030 S Langley, Chicago, IL 60628 *Toll Free Tel:* 800-621-2736
Distribution Center: Chicago Distribution Center, 11030 S Langley, Chicago, IL 60628 *Toll Free Tel:* 800-621-2736
Membership(s): Association of University Presses (AUPresses)
See separate listing for:
University of Alaska Press
Utah State University Press

University Press of Florida
Affiliate of State University System of Florida
2046 NE Waldo Rd, Suite 2100, Gainesville, FL 32609
SAN: 207-9275
Tel: 352-392-1351 *Toll Free Tel:* 800-226-3822 (orders only) *Fax:* 352-392-0590 *Toll Free Fax:* 800-680-1955 (orders only)
E-mail: press@upress.ufl.edu; orders@upress.ufl.edu
Web Site: www.upf.com
Key Personnel
Dir & Dir, Sales & Mktg: Romi Gutierrez *E-mail:* romi@upress.ufl.edu
Assoc Dir & EDP Mgr: Michele Fiyak-Burkley *E-mail:* mf@upress.ufl.edu
Assoc Dir & IT Dir: Bryan Lutz *E-mail:* bryan@upress.ufl.edu
Asst Dir & Opers Mgr: Jackie Panetta *E-mail:* jackie@upress.ufl.edu
Mng Ed: Marthe Walters *E-mail:* marthe@upress.ufl.edu
Founded: 1945
Scholarly & regional nonfiction.
ISBN Prefix(es): 978-0-8130
Number of titles published annually: 100 Print; 100 E-Book
Total Titles: 2,830 Print; 1,850 E-Book
Foreign Rights: Codasat Canada (Canada); Eurospan Group (Africa, Asia, Europe, Middle East, The Pacific, UK)
Membership(s): American Association of University Presses (AAUP)

§University Press of Kansas
2502 Westbrooke Circle, Lawrence, KS 66045-4444
SAN: 203-3267
Tel: 785-864-4154 *Fax:* 785-864-4586
E-mail: upress@ku.edu
Web Site: www.kansaspress.ku.edu
Key Personnel
Dir: Tim Paulson *Tel:* 785-864-1984 *E-mail:* timpaulson@ku.edu
Mng Dir: Kelly Chrisman Jacques *Tel:* 785-864-9186 *E-mail:* kjchrism@ku.edu
Art Dir & Webmaster: Karl Janssen *Tel:* 785-864-9164 *E-mail:* kjanssen@ku.edu
Mktg & Publicity Dir: Derek Helms *Tel:* 785-864-9170 *E-mail:* helms@ku.edu
Asst Mktg Dir: Suzanne Galle *Tel:* 785-864-9167 *E-mail:* sgalle@ku.edu
Ed-in-Chief: Joyce Harrison *Tel:* 785-864-9162 *E-mail:* joyce@ku.edu
Sr Acqs Ed: David Congdon *Tel:* 785-864-6059 *E-mail:* dcongdon@ku.edu
Prodn Ed: Erica Nicholson *Tel:* 785-854-1036 *E-mail:* ericanicholson@ku.edu
Asst Ed: Alec Loganbill *Tel:* 785-864-1258 *E-mail:* atloganbill@ku.edu
Busn Mgr: Zach Zeigler *Tel:* 785-864-1385 *E-mail:* zzeigler@ku.edu
Mktg & Sales Asst: Andrea Laws *Tel:* 785-864-9125 *E-mail:* alaws09@ku.edu
Founded: 1946

Represents the six state universities: Emporia State University, Fort Hays State University, Kansas State University, Pittsburg State University, the University of Kansas & Wichita State University. Established as a consortium by the Board of Regents, the press is governed by a Board of Trustees, who are the chief academic officers of the six universities & who appoint faculty members from each institution to serve on the advisory Editorial Committee. The press is located on the west campus of the University of Kansas. The press publishes work on American politics (including the presidency, American political thought & public policy), military history & intelligence studies, American history (especially political, cultural, intellectual & western), environmental policy & history, American studies, film studies, law & legal history, Native American studies & books about Kansas & the Midwest. Our books have reached a wide audience both inside & outside the academy & have been recognized for their contributions to important scholarly & public debates.
ISBN Prefix(es): 978-978-07006
Number of titles published annually: 45 Print; 45 E-Book
Total Titles: 1,786 Print; 543 E-Book; 15 Audio
Foreign Rep(s): Eurospan Ltd (Africa, Europe, Middle East, UK); Scholarly Book Services Inc (Canada)
Orders to: Longleaf Services Inc, 116 S Boundary St, Chapel Hill, NC 27514-3808 Toll Free Tel: 800-848-6224 E-mail: orders@longleafservices.org Web Site: www.longleafservices.org SAN: 203-3151
Returns: Longleaf Services Inc, c/o IPS Distribution Solutions Returns, 1550 Heil Quaker Blvd, Suite 200, La Vergne, TN 37086, Credit & Collections Mgr: Terry Miles Toll Free Tel: 800-848-6224 ext 2 E-mail: credit@longleafservices.org Web Site: www.longleafservices.org SAN: 203-3151
Membership(s): Association of University Presses (AUPresses)

The University Press of Kentucky
663 S Limestone St, Lexington, KY 40508-4008
SAN: 203-3275
Tel: 859-257-8400 Fax: 859-323-1873
Web Site: www.kentuckypress.com
Key Personnel
Dir: Ashley Runyon Tel: 859-257-8432
  E-mail: ashley.runyon@uky.edu
Deputy Dir: Teresa Collins Tel: 859-257-8405
  E-mail: teresa.collins@uky.edu
Prodn Dir: Laura Hohman Tel: 859-257-8434
  E-mail: laura.hohman@uky.edu
Sales & Mktg Dir: Brooke Raby Tel: 859-257-4249 E-mail: brooke.raby@uky.edu
Mng Ed: David Cobb Tel: 859-257-4252
  E-mail: dlcobb2@email.uky.edu
Ed, Screen Door Press: Crystal Wilkinson
Founded: 1943
ISBN Prefix(es): 978-0-8131
Number of titles published annually: 60 Print; 60 E-Book
Total Titles: 2,200 Print; 2,000 E-Book
Imprints: Screen Door Press
Distributor for Kentucky Historical Society
Foreign Rep(s): Oxbow/Casemate (UK & the continent)
Orders to: HFS (Hopkins Fulfillment Services), PO Box 50370, Baltimore, MD 21211-4370 Tel: 410-516-6956 Toll Free Tel: 800-537-5487 Fax: 410-516-6998 E-mail: hfscustserv@jh.edu Web Site: hfs.jhu.edu
Returns: HFS, c/o Maple Logistics Solutions, Lebanon Distribution Ctr, 704 Legionaire Dr, Fredericksburg, PA 17026 Tel: 410-516-6965 Toll Free Tel: 800-537-5487 Fax: 410-516-6998
  E-mail: hfscustserv@jh.edu Web Site: hfs.jhu.edu
Membership(s): Association of American Publishers (AAP); Association of University Presses (AUPresses)

University Press of Mississippi
3825 Ridgewood Rd, Jackson, MS 39211-6492
SAN: 203-1914
Tel: 601-432-6205 Toll Free Tel: 800-737-7788 (orders & cust serv) Fax: 601-432-6217
E-mail: press@mississippi.edu
Web Site: www.upress.state.ms.us
Key Personnel
Dir: Craig Gill E-mail: cgill@mississippi.edu
Assoc Dir/Mktg Dir: Steve Yates E-mail: syates@mississippi.edu
Asst to the Dir: Carlton McGrone
  E-mail: cmcgrone@mississippi.edu
Sr Acqs Ed: Katie Keene E-mail: kkeene@mississippi.edu
Proj Ed: Valerie Jones E-mail: vjones@mississippi.edu
Assoc Proj Ed: Laura Strong E-mail: lstrong@mississippi.edu
Assoc Ed: Emily Snyder Bandy E-mail: ebandy@mississippi.edu; Lisa McMurtray
  E-mail: lmcmurtray@mississippi.edu
Edit Assoc: Mary Heath E-mail: mheath@mississippi.edu
Busn Mgr: Tonia Lonie E-mail: tlonie@mississippi.edu
Data Servs & Course Adoptions Mgr: Kathy Burgess E-mail: kburgess@mississippi.edu
Electronic, Exhibits & Direct-to-Consumer Sales Mgr: Kristin Kirkpatrick E-mail: kkirkpatrick@mississippi.edu
Prodn & Design Mgr: Todd Lape E-mail: tlape@mississippi.edu
Proj Mgr: Mrs Shane Gong Stewart
  E-mail: sgong@mississippi.edu
Publicity & Promos Mgr: Courtney McCreary
  E-mail: cmccreary@mississippi.edu
Rts & Contracts Mgr: Cynthia Foster
  E-mail: cfoster@mississippi.edu
Mktg Asst & Digital Publg Coord: Ms Jordan Nettles E-mail: jnettles@mississippi.edu
Cust Serv & Order Supv: Ms Sandy Alexander
  E-mail: salexander@mississippi.edu
Sr Book Designer: Pete Halverson
  E-mail: phalverson@mississippi.edu
Book Designer: Jennifer Mixon E-mail: jmixon@mississippi.edu
Founded: 1970
Publisher of trade & scholarly books, nonfiction, fiction & regional.
ISBN Prefix(es): 978-0-87805; 978-1-57806; 978-1-934110; 978-1-60473; 978-1-61703; 978-1-62103; 978-1-62846; 978-1-62674; 978-1-4968
Number of titles published annually: 80 Print; 80 E-Book
Total Titles: 2,500 Print; 2,000 E-Book
Foreign Rep(s): Eurospan (Africa, Asia-Pacific, Caribbean, Continental Europe, Indian subcontinent, Ireland, Latin America, Middle East, UK); University of British Columbia Press (Canada)
Returns: Maple Logistics Solutions, Lebanon Distribution Ctr, 704 Legionaire Dr, Fredericksburg, PA 17026 (non-USPS deliveries); Maple Logistics Solutions, Lebanon Distribution Ctr, PO Box 1287, Lebanon, PA 17042 (all USPS deliveries)
Warehouse: Maple Logistics Solutions, Lebanon Distribution Ctr, 704 Legionaire Dr, Fredericksburg, PA 17026
Membership(s): Association of University Presses (AUPresses)

University Publishing House
PO Box 1664, Mannford, OK 74044
Tel: 918-865-4726
E-mail: upub5@outlook.com
Web Site: www.universitypublishinghouse.net
Key Personnel
Owner & Pres: Randell Nyborg
Founded: 1987
Industrial & automotive, classic fiction reprints, mail order books & industrial processes.
ISBN Prefix(es): 978-1-877767; 978-1-57002
Number of titles published annually: 5 Print
Total Titles: 140 Print

University Science Books
Imprint of AIP Publishing LLC
1305 Walt Whitman Rd, Suite 110, Melville, NY 11747
SAN: 213-8085
Tel: 703-661-1572 (cust serv & orders) Fax: 703-661-1501
E-mail: usbmail@presswarehouse.com (cust serv, orders)
Web Site: uscibooks.aip.org
Key Personnel
Publr: Jane Ellis E-mail: jellis@aip.org
Dir, Mktg & Prodn: Barbara Dickson
  E-mail: bdickson@aip.org
Acqs Ed: Katerina Heidhausen
  E-mail: kheidhausen@aip.org
Opers Mgr: Felicity Henson E-mail: fhenson@aip.org
Founded: 1978
Upper level college textbooks, text references & trade titles in astronomy, chemistry, biochemistry & physics, environmental science, technical writing, biology, reference books, children's books.
ISBN Prefix(es): 978-0-935702; 978-1-891389; 978-1-938787; 978-1-940380
Number of titles published annually: 8 Print; 8 E-Book
Total Titles: 200 Print; 200 E-Book
Foreign Rep(s): Scion Publishing Ltd (Europe, Middle East)
Foreign Rights: Login (Canada); SBS Livraria Internacional (Argentina, Brazil, Colombia); Sci-Tech Publishing Co Ltd (Taiwan); Scion Publishing Ltd (Europe, Middle East); UBS Library Services Pte Ltd (Singapore); Viva Books Pvt Ltd (India)
Orders to: Books International Inc, PO Box 605, Herndon, VA 20172 Tel: 703-661-1572 Fax: 703-661-1501
Returns: Books International Inc, 22883 Quicksilver Dr, Dulles, VA 20166 Tel: 703-661-1572 Fax: 703-661-1501
Distribution Center: Books International Inc, 22883 Quicksilver Dr, Dulles, VA 20166 Tel: 703-661-1572 Fax: 703-661-1501
  E-mail: usbmail@presswarehouse.com

UnKnownTruths.com Publishing Co
8815 Conroy Windermere Rd, Suite 190, Orlando, FL 32835
SAN: 255-6375
Tel: 407-929-9207
E-mail: info@unknowntruths.com
Web Site: unknowntruths.com
Key Personnel
Pres: Walter Parks E-mail: hparks@cfl.rr.com
Founded: 2002
Formed to publish true stories of the unusual or of the previously unexplained. Stories typically provide radically different views from those that have shaped the understandings of our natural world, our religions, our science, our history & even the foundations of our civilizations. Also include stories of the very important life-extending medical breakthroughs: stem cell therapies, genetic therapies, cloning & other emerging findings that promise to change the very meaning of life.
ISBN Prefix(es): 978-0-9745393
Number of titles published annually: 12 Print; 4 Online

Advertising Agency: James Brooke & Associates, 2660 Second St, Suite 1, Santa Monica, CA 90405, PR: Cherie Carter *Tel:* 310-396-8070 *Fax:* 310-396-8071 *E-mail:* cherie@unknowntruths.com
Distribution Center: Quality Books Inc, 1003 W Pines Rd, Oregon, IL 61061 *Toll Free Tel:* 800-323-4241 *Fax:* 815-732-4499
New Leaf Distributing Co, 1085 E Lotus Dr, Silver Lake, WI 53170 *Tel:* 262-889-8501 *Toll Free Tel:* 800-326-2665 *Fax:* 262-889-8598 *E-mail:* orders@newleafdist.com SAN: 169-1449
Membership(s): The Association of Publishers for Special Sales (APSS); Independent Book Publishers Association (IBPA)

UNO Press, see University of New Orleans Press

§Upper Room Books
Division of The Upper Room
1908 Grand Ave, Nashville, TN 37212
SAN: 203-3364
Tel: 615-340-7200 *Toll Free Tel:* 800-972-0433
Web Site: books.upperroom.org
Key Personnel
Edit Dir: Michael Stephens *Tel:* 615-340-7220
 E-mail: mstephens@upperroom.org
Dir, Prodn & Scheduling: Nanci Lamar
 E-mail: nlamar@upperroom.org
Founded: 1935
Prayer & devotional life publications. No fiction or poetry accepted.
ISBN Prefix(es): 978-0-8358
Number of titles published annually: 20 Print; 20 E-Book
Imprints: Fresh Air Books
Foreign Rights: Riggins Rights Management (Cindy Riggins)
Warehouse: APG Books/WFS LLC, 1501 County Hospital Rd, Nashville, TN 37218
Membership(s): American Booksellers Association (ABA); Protestant Church-Owned Publishers Association (PCPA)
See separate listing for:
Fresh Air Books

Upstart Books™
Division of Demco Inc
PO Box 7488, Madison, WI 53707
Tel: 608-241-1201 *Toll Free Tel:* 800-356-1200 (orders); 800-962-4463 (cust serv)
 Toll Free Fax: 800-245-1329 (orders)
E-mail: custserv@demco.com; order@demco.com
Web Site: www.demco.com/upstart
Key Personnel
Prod Devt Mgr, Lib Mkts: Heidi Green
Founded: 1990
Reading activities & library skills for teachers & children's librarians; storytelling activity books & Internet resources.
ISBN Prefix(es): 978-0-917846; 978-0-913853; 978-1-57950; 978-1-932146
Number of titles published annually: 12 Print
Total Titles: 100 Print

Urim Publications
527 Empire Blvd, Brooklyn, NY 11225-3121
Tel: 718-972-5449 *Fax:* 718-972-6307
E-mail: urimpublisher@gmail.com; orders@urimpublications.com
Web Site: www.urimpublications.com
Key Personnel
Publr: Tzvi Mauer
Founded: 1997
Publisher & worldwide distributor of new & classic books with Jewish content.
ISBN Prefix(es): 978-965-7108; 978-965-524; 978-965-7047
Number of titles published annually: 8 Print
Total Titles: 35 Print

Editorial Office(s): PO Box 52287, Jerusalem 9152102, Israel *Tel:* (02) 679-7633 *Fax:* (02) 679-7634
Distribution Center: Independent Publishers Group (IPG), 814 N Franklin St, Chicago, IL 60610 *Toll Free Tel:* 800-888-4741

Urzone Inc, see Zone Books

US Conference of Catholic Bishops
USCCB Publishing, 3211 Fourth St NE, Washington, DC 20017
Toll Free Tel: 800-235-8722 *Fax:* 301-779-8596 (orders)
E-mail: css@usccb.org
Web Site: store.usccb.org
Founded: 1938
The official publisher for the US Catholic Bishop & Vatican documents; English & Spanish.
ISBN Prefix(es): 978-1-55586; 978-1-57455; 978-1-60137
Number of titles published annually: 15 Print
Total Titles: 550 Print
Returns: USCCB Returns, 3570 Bladensburg Rd, Brentwood, MD 20722
Membership(s): Association of Catholic Publishers Inc

US Games Systems Inc
179 Ludlow St, Stamford, CT 06902
SAN: 206-1368
Tel: 203-353-8400 *Toll Free Tel:* 800-54-GAMES (544-2637) *Fax:* 203-353-8431
E-mail: info@usgamesinc.com
Web Site: www.usgamesinc.com
Key Personnel
Founder & Chmn: Stuart R Kaplan *Tel:* 203-353-8400 ext 301
Pres: Ricky Cruz
VP, Export Sales: Barbara Bensaid
Creative Dir: Paula Palmer
Founded: 1968
Popular & scholarly works in the field of tarot, wellness, inspiration, spirituality, educational games & the history of symbolism of playing cards; reprints of historical tarot decks & playing cards from the past five centuries.
ISBN Prefix(es): 978-0-913866; 978-0-88079; 978-1-57281
Number of titles published annually: 20 Print
Total Titles: 400 Print; 5 E-Book
Imprints: Cove Press
Distributor for Blue Angel Publishing; KonigsFurt
Foreign Rep(s): Avvalon-Lo Scarabeo (Russia); Fonix Musik (Denmark); KonigsFurt (Germany); Publishers Group (UK); Stjarn Distribution (Sweden); Vykintasd Urniezius (Lithuania)

§US Government Publishing Office (GPO)
Division of US Government
Superintendent of Documents, 732 N Capitol St NW, Washington, DC 20401
Tel: 202-512-1800 *Toll Free Tel:* 866-512-1800 (orders) *Fax:* 202-512-1998
E-mail: contactcenter@gpo.gov
Web Site: www.gpo.gov; bookstore.gpo.gov (sales)
Key Personnel
Dir & CEO: Hugh Nathanial Halpern
CFO: William Boesch
CIO: Sam Musa
Chief PR Offr: Gary Somerset
Chief, Fed Depository Support Servs: Katherine Pitcher
Inspector Gen: Michael Leary
Superintendent, Documents: Laurie Hall
Mng Dir, Security & Intelligent Documents (SID): David Ford
Dir, Sales & Mktg: Lisa Williams
Founded: 1861
Distributor & printer of federal government publications & public documents in various formats including ebooks; military, space exploration, political science.
ISBN Prefix(es): 978-0-16
Number of titles published annually: 250 Print; 15 Online
Total Titles: 2,500 Print; 140 CD-ROM
Orders to: PO Box 979050, St Louis, MO 63197-9000

Utah Geological Survey
Division of Utah Department of Natural Resources
1594 W North Temple, Suite 3110, Salt Lake City, UT 84116-3154
Mailing Address: PO Box 146100, Salt Lake City, UT 84114-6100
Tel: 801-537-3300 *Toll Free Tel:* 888-UTAH-MAP (882-4627, bookshop) *Fax:* 801-537-3400
E-mail: geostore@utah.gov
Web Site: geology.utah.gov
Key Personnel
Pubns Mgr: Jennifer Miller *E-mail:* jlmiller@utah.gov
Founded: 1949
ISBN Prefix(es): 978-1-55791
Number of titles published annually: 30 Print; 15 CD-ROM; 5 Online
Total Titles: 702 Print

Utah State University Press
Imprint of University Press of Colorado
3078 Old Main Hill, Logan, UT 84322-3078
Tel: 435-797-1362
Web Site: www.usupress.com
Key Personnel
Dir: Darrin Pratt *E-mail:* darrin@upcolorado.com
Founded: 1972
ISBN Prefix(es): 978-0-87421; 978-1-60732
Number of titles published annually: 20 Print
Total Titles: 250 Print
Membership(s): Association of University Presses (AUPresses)

UVA Press, see University of Virginia Press

VanDam Inc
The VanDam Bldg, 121 W 27 St, New York, NY 10001
Tel: 917-297-5445
E-mail: info@vandam.com
Web Site: www.vandam.com
Key Personnel
Pres/Creative Dir: Stephan Van Dam
 E-mail: stephan@vandam.com
VP, Soc Media: Patricia Grant *E-mail:* patricia.grant@vandam.com
Dir, Opers: Jessy Cerda *E-mail:* jessy@vandam.com
R&D: Jon Tyillian *E-mail:* jontyillian@vandam.com
Founded: 1984
Publisher of UNFOLDS®, StreetSmart & Pop-Up maps; Urban@tlas city atlases. Licensor of patented folding technology used to produce UNFOLDS® products.
ISBN Prefix(es): 978-0-931141; 978-1-932527; 978-1-934395
Number of titles published annually: 50 Print
Total Titles: 250 Print
Divisions: VanDam Publishing
Foreign Rep(s): LAC (Italy); RV Verlag (Germany)

Vandamere Press
3580 Morris St N, St Petersburg, FL 33713
SAN: 657-3088
Mailing Address: PO Box 149, St Petersburg, FL 33731
Tel: 727-556-0950 *Toll Free Tel:* 800-551-7776
 Fax: 727-556-2560
E-mail: orders@vandamere.com
Web Site: www.vandamere.com

U.S. PUBLISHERS

Key Personnel
Publr & Ed-in-Chief: Arthur Brown
  E-mail: abrown@vandamere.com
Dir, Spec Sales: Stephanie Brown
Sr Book Ed & Acq Ed: Jerry Frank
Wholesale Sales: John Cabin
Founded: 1984
ISBN Prefix(es): 978-0-918339
Number of titles published annually: 8 Print
Total Titles: 70 Print
Distributor for ABI Professional Publications (non-exclusive); JMC Press (exclusive to trade); NRH Press (non-exclusive); Quodlibetal Features

Vanderbilt University Press
Division of Vanderbilt University
2301 Vanderbilt Place, PMB 401813, Nashville, TN 37240-1813
SAN: 202-9308
Tel: 615-322-3585 *Toll Free Tel:* 800-848-6224 (orders only) *Fax:* 615-343-0308
E-mail: vupress@vanderbilt.edu
Web Site: www.vanderbiltuniversitypress.com
Key Personnel
Dir: Gianna Mosser
Mng Ed: Joell Smith Borne
Busn Mgr & Rts & Perms: Cynthia Yeager
Design & Prodn Mgr: Drohan DiSanto
Sales & Mktg Mgr: Betsy Phillips *E-mail:* betsy.phillips@vanderbilt.edu
Mktg & New Media Assoc: Jenna Phillips
Founded: 1940
Scholarly nonfiction, humanities, social sciences, literary criticism, history, regional studies.
ISBN Prefix(es): 978-0-8265
Number of titles published annually: 25 Print
Total Titles: 600 Print; 400 E-Book
Distributor for Country Music Foundation Press
Foreign Rep(s): Ampersand (Canada); Eurospan (all other territories)
Distribution Center: Longleaf Services Inc, 116 S Boundary St, Chapel Hill, NC 27514-3808 *Tel:* 919-966-7449 *Toll Free Tel:* 800-848-6224 (US) *Fax:* 919-962-2704 *Toll Free Fax:* 800-272-6817 (US) *E-mail:* orders@longleafservices.org
Membership(s): Association of University Presses (AUPresses)

Vault.com Inc
132 W 31 St, 16th fl, New York, NY 10001
Tel: 212-366-4212 *Toll Free Tel:* 800-535-2074 *Fax:* 212-366-6117
E-mail: mediainquiries@vault.com; customerservice@vault.com
Web Site: www.vault.com
Key Personnel
Sr Fin Ed: Derek Loosvelt
Founded: 1996
"Insider" career development for professionals.
ISBN Prefix(es): 978-1-58131
Number of titles published annually: 4 Print; 10 Online
Total Titles: 61 Print; 124 Online

Vedanta Press
Subsidiary of Vedanta Society of Southern California
1946 Vedanta Place, Hollywood, CA 90068
Tel: 323-960-1728; 323-960-1736 (catalog) *Fax:* 323-465-9568
E-mail: vpress@vedanta.com
Web Site: www.vedanta.com
Key Personnel
Mgr: Robert Adjemian *E-mail:* bob@vedanta.com
Founded: 1945
ISBN Prefix(es): 978-81-85301 (Advaita Ashrama); 978-0-87481; 978-81-8172 (Ramakrishna Math); 978-81-7505
Number of titles published annually: 1 CD-ROM; 15 Online
Total Titles: 17 CD-ROM; 25 Online
Distributor for Advaita Ashrama; Ananda Ashrama; Ramakrishna Math; Ramakrishna-Vivekananda Center of New York
Membership(s): Independent Book Publishers Association (IBPA)

Velazquez Press
Division of Academic Learning Co LLC
9682 Telstar Ave, Suite 110, El Monte, CA 91731
Tel: 626-448-3448 *Fax:* 626-602-3817
E-mail: info@academiclearningcompany.com
Web Site: www.velazquezpress.com
Key Personnel
Publr: Arthur Chou
Dir, Busn Devt: Jonathan Ruiz *E-mail:* jruiz@academiclearningcompany.com
Founded: 2003
Publisher of bilingual dictionaries.
ISBN Prefix(es): 978-1-59495
Number of titles published annually: 4 Print
Total Titles: 10 Print

The Vendome Press
244 Fifth Ave, Suite 2043, New York, NY 10001
Tel: 212-737-1857
E-mail: info@vendomepress.com
Web Site: www.vendomepress.com
Key Personnel
Pres & Publr: Mark Magowan
Prodn Dir: Jim Spivey
Publicity Dir: Meghan Phillips
Ed: Jackuelen Decter
Founded: 1981
Illustrated art, architecture & lifestyle books.
ISBN Prefix(es): 978-0-86565
Number of titles published annually: 10 Print
Total Titles: 100 Print
Distributed by Abrams Books; Thames & Hudson
Distribution Center: Abrams & Chronicle Books Ltd, 161 Farringdon Rd, 3rd fl, London EC1R 3AL, United Kingdom (Europe, India, Middle East, South Africa & UK) *Tel:* (020) 7713 2060 *Fax:* (020) 7713 2061 *E-mail:* internationalsales@abramsandchronicle.co.uk *Web Site:* www.abramsandchronicle.co.uk

Vernon Press
Imprint of Vernon Art & Science Inc
1000 N West St, Suite 1200, Wilmington, DE 19801
Tel: 302-250-4440
E-mail: info@vernonpress.com
Web Site: www.vernonpress.com
Key Personnel
Dir: Rosario Batana
ISBN Prefix(es): 978-1-62273
Number of titles published annually: 60 Print

Verso Books
388 Atlantic Ave, Brooklyn, NY 11217
Tel: 718-246-8160 *Fax:* 718-246-8165
E-mail: verso@versobooks.com
Web Site: www.versobooks.com
Key Personnel
Mng Dir: Jacob Stevens
Mng Ed: Mark Martin
Sr Publicist: Tim Thomas
Direct Mktg Mgr: Colby Groves
Founded: 1970
Nonfiction, progressive studies on politics, history, society & culture.
ISBN Prefix(es): 978-1-84467; 978-1-78168; 978-1-78478; 978-1-78663; 978-1-83976; 978-1-78873; 978-1-80429
Number of titles published annually: 80 Print
Total Titles: 2,000 Print
Imprints: Verso Fiction
Foreign Office(s): 6 Meard St, London W1F OEG, United Kingdom *Tel:* (020) 7437 3546 *Fax:* (020) 7734 0059 *E-mail:* enquiries@verso.co.uk
Distributed by Penguin (Canada)
Foreign Rep(s): Verso (England)
Foreign Rights: Verso (worldwide)
Shipping Address: Marston Book Services Ltd, Kemp Hall Bindery, Osney Mead, Oxford, United Kingdom
Membership(s): The NewsGuild-CWA (TNG-CWA)

Vesuvian Books
Division of Vesuvian Media Group Inc
711 Dolly Parton Pkwy, No 4313, Sevierville, TN 37864
E-mail: info@vesuvianmedia.com
Web Site: www.vesuvianmedia.com
Key Personnel
Founder & CEO, Vesuvian Media Group Inc: Italia Gandolfo *Tel:* 615-447-8444 *E-mail:* italia@vesuvianmedia.com
Exec Chmn: Thomas N Ellsworth
Pres: LK Griffie *Tel:* 714-243-8723 *E-mail:* lk@vesuvianmedia.com
Art Dir: Sam Shearon
Creative Dir: Michael J Canales
Dir, Acqs: Lindy Ryan
Founded: 2015
A multimedia corporation dedicated to creating quality entertainment across literary & visual arts. Vesuvian Books does not accept unsol submissions. Prospective authors & illustrators must submit their work through an agent.
ISBN Prefix(es): 978-1-944109
Number of titles published annually: 20 Print; 20 Online; 20 E-Book
Total Titles: 115 Print; 115 E-Book; 15 Audio
Imprints: Black Spot Books; Dropship; Rosewind Romance
Foreign Rights: Books Crossing Borders (Betty Anne Crawford) (worldwide exc USA)
Distribution Center: Independent Publishers Group (IPG), 814 N Franklin St, Chicago, IL 60610, VP, Publr Devt: Richard T Williams *Tel:* 312-337-0747 *Toll Free Tel:* 800-888-4741 *Fax:* 312-337-5985 *E-mail:* rwilliams@ipgbook.com *Web Site:* www.ipgbook.com
Membership(s): American Booksellers Association (ABA); Horror Writers Association (HWA); Independent Book Publishers Association (IBPA); International Thriller Writers Inc (ITW)

Viking Books, see Viking Penguin

Viking Children's Books
Imprint of Penguin Young Readers Group
c/o Penguin Random House LLC, 1745 Broadway, New York, NY 10019
Tel: 212-782-9000
Web Site: www.penguin.com/viking-childrens-books-overview/
Key Personnel
Assoc Dir, Publg & Exec Ed: Dana Leydig
Assoc Art Dir: Kate Renner
Sr Exec Ed: Jenny Bak
Ed: Aneeka Kalia; Maggie Rosenthal
Asst Ed: Meriam Metoui
Asst Ed, Viking Children's Books & Flamingo Books: Claire Tattersfield
Edit Asst: Azriel Hackett
Founded: 1933
Penguin Random House & its publishing entities are not accepting unsol submissions, proposals, mss, or submission queries via e-mail at this time.
Number of titles published annually: 60 Print
Membership(s): The Children's Book Council (CBC)

Viking Penguin
Imprint of Penguin Publishing Group
c/o Penguin Random House LLC, 1745 Broadway, New York, NY 10019
Tel: 212-782-9000

Web Site: www.penguin.com/overview-vikingbooks/; www.penguin.com/pamela-dorman-books-overview/; www.penguin.com/penguin-classics-overview/; www.penguin.com/penguin-life-overview/
Key Personnel
Pres & Publr, Viking/Penguin: Brian Tart
SVP & Publr, Pamela Dorman Books/Viking: Pamela Dorman
SVP & Assoc Publr, Viking/Penguin: Kate Stark
VP & Ed-in-Chief, Viking Books: Andrea Schulz
VP & Publr, Penguin Books: Patrick Nolan
VP & Publr, Penguin Classics: Elda Rotor
VP & Art Dir: Jason Ramirez
Publg Assoc, Viking/Penguin: Jenn Houghton
Edit Dir, Penguin Life: Meg Leder
Exec Mng Ed, Penguin Books: Matt Giarratano
Exec Ed, Pamela Dorman Books: Jeramie Orton
Exec Ed, Viking Books, Penguin Classics & Penguin Life: John Siciliano
Exec Ed, Viking Books: Allison Lorentzen; Laura Tisdel
Exec Ed, Viking/Penguin: Ibrahim Ahmad
Sr Ed, Pamela Dorman Books: Seema Mahanian
Sr Ed, Penguin Life: Amy Sun
Sr Ed, Penguin Life/The Open Field: Nina Rodriguez-Marty
Sr Ed, Viking Books: Terezia Cicel; Lindsey Schwoeri; Emily Wunderlich
Ed, The Open Field/Penguin Life: Cassidy Graham
Ed, Pamela Dorman Books: Marie Michels
Ed, Viking/Penguin: Allie Merola; Nidhi Pugalia
Assoc Ed, Penguin Classics: Elizabeth Vogt
Assoc Ed, Viking/Penguin: Camille LeBlanc
Edit Asst, Pamela Dorman Books: Jane Glaser
Edit Asst, Penguin Life: Isabelle Alexander
Edit Asst, Viking Books: Sonia Gadre; Elizabeth Pham Janowski; Paloma Ruiz
Edit Asst, Viking Books & Penguin Classics: Emma Dollar
Dir, Mktg, Viking/Penguin & Penguin Classics: Mary Stone
Assoc Dir, Mktg, Viking Books: Molly Fessenden
Sr Mktg Mgr, Soc Media, Viking/Penguin: Rachel Wainz
Digital Mktg Mgr, Penguin Books: Ryan Murphy
Mktg Assoc, Viking/Penguin: Chantal Canales
Mktg Coord, Viking/Penguin & Penguin Classics: Alex Cruz-Jimenez
Dir, Publicity, Viking/Penguin: Rebecca Marsh
Assoc Dir, Publicity: Kristina Fazzalaro
Publicity Mgr, Viking/Penguin: Sara DeLozier
Exec Publicist, Viking/Penguin: Shelby Meizlik
Sr Publicist, Penguin Books: Shris Smith
Sr Publicist, Viking/Penguin: Sara Leonard
Sr Publicist, Viking/Penguin & Penguin Classics: Julia Rickard
Publicist, Viking/Penguin: Ivy Cheng
Assoc Publicist, Viking/Penguin: Julia Falkner
Exec Dir, Ad & Promo, Viking Books: Dennis Swaim
Exec Art Dir, Ad & Promo, Penguin Books: Lynn Rogan
Dir, Contracts, Viking/Penguin: Robin Simon
Founded: 1925
Penguin Random House & its publishing entities are not accepting unsol submissions, proposals, mss, or submission queries via e-mail at this time.
Viking Penguin editors also acquire for Penguin Life. Penguin Classics & Penguin Life editors also acquire for Viking Penguin.
ISBN Prefix(es): 978-0-14; 978-0-453; 978-0-670
Number of titles published annually: 325 Print
Total Titles: 3,750 Print
Imprints: Pamela Dorman Books; The Open Field; Penguin Books; Penguin Classics; Penguin Life (includes The Open Field); Viking Books

Vintage Books
Imprint of Knopf Doubleday Publishing Group
c/o Penguin Random House LLC, 1745 Broadway, New York, NY 10019
Tel: 212-572-2420 *Fax:* 212-940-7390 (dom rts); 212-572-2662 (foreign rts)
E-mail: vintageanchorpublicity@randomhouse.com
Web Site: knopfdoubleday.com/imprint/vintage; knopfdoubleday.com
Key Personnel
SVP & Deputy Publr: Beth Lamb
VP & Assoc Publr, Vintage Books & Knopf Doubleday Publishing Group Backlist: Gabrielle Brooks
VP & Assoc Publr, Vintage Backlist: James Meader
Dir, Publicity: Angie Venezia
Exec Mng Ed: Barbara Richard
Sr Ed: Diana Secker Tesdell
Assoc Ed: Ellie Pritchett
Sr Designer: Maddie Partner
Mktg Mgr: Annie Locke
Mktg Assoc: Sophie Normil
Sr Publicist: Kelsey Curtis
Assoc Publicist: Alexandra Dos Santos
Founded: 1954
Penguin Random House & its publishing entities are not accepting unsol submissions, proposals, mss, or submission queries via e-mail at this time.
Number of titles published annually: 175 Print; 190 E-Book
Total Titles: 2,650 Print; 1,750 E-Book
Imprints: Vintage Originals; Vintage Shorts (ebooks)
Foreign Rights: Anthea Agency (Katalina Sabeva) (Bulgaria); Bardon-Chinese Media Agency (Xu Weiguang) (China); Bardon-Chinese Media Agency (Yu Shiuan Chen & David Tsai) (Taiwan); English Agency Japan Co Ltd (Hamish Macaskill & Junzo Sawa) (Japan); Graal Literary Agency (Maria Strarz-Zielinska) (Poland); The Deborah Harris Agency (Ilana Kurshan) (Israel); JLM Literary Agency (Nelly Moukakos) (Greece); Katai & Bolza Literary (Peter Bolza) (Croatia, Hungary, Serbia); Simona Kessler Agency (Simona Kessler) (Romania); Korea Copyright Center Inc (KCC) (MiSook Hong) (South Korea); Licht & Burr Literary Agency (Trine Licht) (Scandinavia); La Nouvelle Agence (Vanessa Kling) (France); Kristin Olson Literary Agency (Kristin Olson) (Czechia); Agenzia Letteraria Santachiara (Roberto Santachiara) (Italy); Sebes & Bisseling Literary Agency (Netherlands)

Visible Ink Press®
43311 Joy Rd, Suite 414, Canton, MI 48187-2075
Tel: 734-667-3211 *Fax:* 734-667-4311
E-mail: info@visibleinkpress.com
Web Site: www.visibleinkpress.com
Key Personnel
Publr: Roger Janecke
Founded: 1989
Popular reference publisher specializing in handy answer books, spiritual phenomena & multicultural history.
ISBN Prefix(es): 978-0-8103; 978-0-7876; 978-1-57859
Number of titles published annually: 10 Print; 10 E-Book
Total Titles: 200 Print; 300 E-Book
Distribution Center: Publishers Group West, 210 America Dr, Jackson, TN 38301 *Toll Free Tel:* 800-343-4499; 866-400-5351 (cust serv)
E-mail: ipsjacksonorders@ingramcontent.com

§Visual Profile Books Inc
389 Fifth Ave, Suite 1105, New York, NY 10016
SAN: 213-1552
Tel: 516-445-0116
Web Site: www.visualprofilebooks.com
Key Personnel
Publr: Larry Fuersich *E-mail:* larry@visualprofilebooks.com
Edit Dir: Roger Yee *E-mail:* rhtyee@gmail.com
Founded: 1931
Architecture, interior & graphic design.
ISBN Prefix(es): 978-0-9825989
Number of titles published annually: 15 Print
Total Titles: 568 Print
Distribution Center: National Book Network, 15200 NBN Way, Blue Ridge Summit, PA 17214 *Tel:* 717-794-3800 *Fax:* 717-794-3828 *E-mail:* customercare@nbnbooks.com *Web Site:* nbnbooks.com

Viva Editions, see Cleis Press

Ludwig von Mises Institute
518 W Magnolia Ave, Auburn, AL 36832
Tel: 334-321-2100 *Fax:* 334-321-2119
E-mail: info@mises.org
Web Site: www.mises.org
Key Personnel
CEO: Jeff Deist
Bookstore Mgr: Brandon Hill *E-mail:* brandon@mises.org
Founded: 1982
Nonprofit educational organization devoted to the Austrian School of Economics.
ISBN Prefix(es): 978-0-945466; 978-1-933550; 978-1-61016
Number of titles published annually: 5 Print; 5 Audio
Total Titles: 60 Print

§Voyager Sopris Learning Inc
Imprint of Cambium Learning Inc
17855 Dallas Pkwy, Suite 400, Dallas, TX 75287
Tel: 303-651-2829 *Toll Free Tel:* 800-547-6747 *Fax:* 303-776-5934 *Toll Free Fax:* 888-819-7767
E-mail: customerservice@voyagersopris.com
Web Site: www.voyagersopris.com
Founded: 1978
Training, development materials for educators.
ISBN Prefix(es): 978-0-944584; 978-1-57035; 978-1-59318
Number of titles published annually: 100 Print
Total Titles: 350 Print

§Wake Forest University Press
2518 Reynolda Rd, Winston-Salem, NC 27106
Mailing Address: PO Box 7333, Winston-Salem, NC 27109-7333
Tel: 336-758-5448 *Fax:* 336-842-3853
E-mail: wfupress@wfu.edu
Web Site: wfupress.wfu.edu
Key Personnel
Founder & Advising Ed: Dillon Johnston
Dir & Ed: Jefferson Holdridge
Advising Asst Dir: Candide Jones
Mgr: Amanda Keith
Founded: 1975
Contemporary Irish poetry.
ISBN Prefix(es): 978-0-916390; 978-1-930630
Number of titles published annually: 5 Print
Total Titles: 100 Print
Distribution Center: Independent Publishers Group (IPG), 814 N Franklin St, Chicago, IL 60610 *Toll Free Tel:* 800-888-4741 *Fax:* 312-337-5985 *E-mail:* orders@ipgbook.com

Walch Education
40 Walch Dr, Portland, ME 04103-1286
SAN: 203-0268
Tel: 207-772-2846 *Toll Free Tel:* 800-558-2846; 800-341-6094 (cust serv) *Fax:* 207-772-3105
Toll Free Fax: 888-991-5755
E-mail: customerservice@walch.com
Web Site: www.walch.com

Key Personnel
Pres: Al Noyes
Founded: 1927
Educational books & supplementary materials for middle school through adult.
ISBN Prefix(es): 978-0-8251
Number of titles published annually: 100 Print; 75 Online
Total Titles: 1,700 Print; 850 Online
Membership(s): ASCD; International Literacy Association (ILA); National Council for the Social Studies (NCSS); National Council of Teachers of English (NCTE); National Council of Teachers of Mathematics (NCTM); National Science Teachers Association (NSTA)

Walch Publishing, see Walch Education

Waldorf Publishing LLC
2140 Hall Johnson Rd, No 102-345, Grapevine, TX 76051
Tel: 972-674-3131
E-mail: info@waldorfpublishing.com
Web Site: www.waldorfpublishing.com
Key Personnel
Founder & CEO: Barbara Terry
Founded: 2013
ISBN Prefix(es): 978-1-68419; 978-1-943275; 978-1-943277; 978-1-944245; 978-1-945177; 978-1-64316
Number of titles published annually: 55 Print; 55 CD-ROM; 55 Online; 55 E-Book; 55 Audio
Total Titles: 200 Print; 200 CD-ROM; 200 Online; 200 E-Book; 200 Audio
Foreign Rights: Susan Schulman Literary Agency (worldwide)

Warner Press
Affiliate of Church of God Ministries
2902 Enterprise Dr, Anderson, IN 46013
Tel: 765-644-7721 *Toll Free Tel:* 800-741-7721 (orders) *Fax:* 765-640-8005
E-mail: wporders@warnerpress.org
Web Site: www.warnerpress.org
Key Personnel
Pres: Eric King
VP, Prod Mktg: Regina Jackson
VP, Sales: Valerie Duffy
Founded: 1881
Specialize in kids & family ministry resources, teaching resources, bible studies, curriculum, faith based books for adults & children, church resources & boxed greeting cards.
ISBN Prefix(es): 978-0-87162; 978-1-59317; 978-1-68434
Number of titles published annually: 8 Print; 6 E-Book

§Washington State University Press
Division of Washington State University
Cooper Publications Bldg, 2300 Grimes Way, Pullman, WA 99164-5910
SAN: 206-6688
Mailing Address: PO Box 645910, Pullman, WA 99164-5910
Tel: 509-335-7880 *Toll Free Tel:* 800-354-7360 (orders)
E-mail: wsupress@wsu.edu
Web Site: wsupress.wsu.edu
Key Personnel
Dir: Edward Sala *E-mail:* sala@wsu.edu
Asst Dir & Ed-in-Chief: Linda Bathgate *Tel:* 509-335-7630 *E-mail:* linda.bathgate@wsu.edu
Busn Opers Mgr: Kerry Darnall *E-mail:* kdarnall@wsu.edu
Mktg Mgr: Caryn Lawton *Tel:* 509-335-7877 *E-mail:* lawton@wsu.edu
Founded: 1928
Trade & scholarly books focusing on the history, natural history, military history, culture & politics of the greater Pacific Northwest region (Washington, Idaho, Oregon, Western Montana, British Columbia & Alaska). Refer to web site for submission guidelines.
ISBN Prefix(es): 978-0-87422; 978-1-63682
Number of titles published annually: 8 Print
Total Titles: 182 Print
Distributor for Lost Horse Press; Lynx House Press; Oregon California Trails Assn; Oregon Writers Colony (single title); Pacific Institute (single title); Washington State Historical Society (single title); WSU Museum of Art
Distribution Center: Baker & Taylor Books, PO Box 8888, Momence, IL 60954 (US & CN) *Toll Free Tel:* 800-775-1100 *Toll Free Fax:* 800-775-7480
Ingram Book Co, One Ingram Blvd, La Vergne, TN 37086 (US & CN) *Toll Free Tel:* 800-937-8000
Membership(s): Association of University Presses (AUPresses)

Water Environment Federation
601 Wythe St, Alexandria, VA 22314-1994
Tel: 703-684-2400 *Toll Free Tel:* 800-666-0206 (cust serv) *Fax:* 703-684-2492
E-mail: inquiry@wef.org
Web Site: www.wef.org
Key Personnel
Pubns: Karah DeMarco *Tel:* 703-684-2400 ext 7211 *E-mail:* kdemarco@wef.org
Founded: 1928
Scientific publisher of environmental titles. Seeks authors of sound, state-of-the-art environmental material.
ISBN Prefix(es): 978-0-943244; 978-1-881369; 978-1-572783
Number of titles published annually: 15 Print
Total Titles: 220 Print

§Water Resources Publications LLC
PO Box 630026, Highlands Ranch, CO 80163-0026
SAN: 209-9136
Tel: 720-873-0171 *Toll Free Tel:* 800-736-2405 *Fax:* 720-873-0173 *Toll Free Fax:* 800-616-1971
E-mail: info@wrpllc.com
Web Site: www.wrpllc.com
Founded: 1971
Publishing & distributing books & computer software on water resources & related fields.
ISBN Prefix(es): 978-0-918334; 978-1-887201
Number of titles published annually: 10 Print
Total Titles: 220 Print; 35 CD-ROM
Distributor for ASAE
Shipping Address: 10607 Flatiron Rd, Littleton, CO 80124 *Toll Free Fax:* 844-270-6832
Warehouse: 10607 Flatiron Rd, Littleton, CO 80124 *Toll Free Fax:* 844-270-6832

WaterBrook
Imprint of Random House Publishing Group
10807 New Allegiance Dr, Suite 500, Colorado Springs, CO 80921
Tel: 719-590-4999 *Toll Free Tel:* 800-603-7051 (orders) *Fax:* 719-590-8977
E-mail: info@waterbrookmultnomah.com
Web Site: waterbrookmultnomah.com
Founded: 1996
Publishes Christian books that seek to intensify & satisfy a reader's elemental thirst for a deeper relationship with God. Seek messages that draw on the Bible, experiential learning, story, practical guidance & inspiration to help readers thrive in their faith. Penguin Random House & its publishing entities are not accepting unsol submissions, proposals, mss, or submission queries via e-mail at this time.
Number of titles published annually: 41 Print
Imprints: Shaw Books
Membership(s): Evangelical Christian Publishers Association (ECPA)

§Watermark Publishing
Member of aio Media Group
1000 Bishop St, Suite 806, Honolulu, HI 96813
Tel: 808-587-7766 *Toll Free Tel:* 866-900-BOOK (900-2665) *Fax:* 808-521-3461
E-mail: info@bookshawaii.net
Web Site: www.bookshawaii.net
Key Personnel
Publr: George Engebretson *Tel:* 808-534-7167 *E-mail:* george@bookshawaii.net
Publg Opers Mgr: Kimberlin (Kimi) Patton *Tel:* 808-534-7170 *E-mail:* kim@bookshawaii.net
ISBN Prefix(es): 978-0-9720932; 978-0-9705787; 978-0-9631154; 978-0-9753740; 978-0-9779143; 978-0-9790647; 978-0-9796769; 978-0-9815086
Number of titles published annually: 8 Print
Total Titles: 55 Print
Imprints: Legacy Isle Publishing

Watson-Guptill
Imprint of Crown Publishing Group
c/o Ten Speed Press, 6001 Shellmount St, Suite 600, Emeryville, CA 94608
Web Site: crownpublishing.com/archives/imprint/watson-guptill
Founded: 1937
Hard-working & influential illustrated art books. Seeks out respected authorities who instruct & inspire artists in a wide range of art & craft. List covers both fine art & practical art instruction in traditional disciplines such as drawing, painting, sculpture & printmaking. Also publish modern books focused on artistic pursuits such as craft, collage, mixed media, comics, sequential art, cartooning, manga & animation.
Number of titles published annually: 60 Print
Total Titles: 800 Print
Orders to: Penguin Random House LLC, 400 Hahn Rd, Westminster, MD 21157 *Toll Free Tel:* 800-733-3000 *E-mail:* csorders@randomhouse.com; Penguin Random House of Canada Inc, 320 Front St W, Suite 410, Toronto, ON M5V 3B6, Canada *Toll Free Tel:* 800-668-4247 *Fax:* 416-598-7764

Waveland Press Inc
4180 IL Rte 83, Suite 101, Long Grove, IL 60047-9580
SAN: 209-0961
Tel: 847-634-0081 *Fax:* 847-634-9501
E-mail: info@waveland.com
Web Site: www.waveland.com
Key Personnel
Pres & Publr: Neil Rowe
Ed: Carol Rowe
Ed, Prodn Mgr & Intl Rts: Don Rosso
Mktg Mgr: Jennifer Slotowski
Founded: 1975
College textbooks & supplements.
ISBN Prefix(es): 978-0-88133; 978-0-917974; 978-1-57766; 978-1-4786
Number of titles published annually: 40 Print
Total Titles: 550 Print
Subsidiaries: Sheffield Publishing Co
Warehouse: 9009 Antioch Rd, Salem, WI 53168, Gen Mgr: Steve Nelson

Wayne State University Press
Leonard N Simons Bldg, 4809 Woodward Ave, Detroit, MI 48201-1309
SAN: 202-5221
Tel: 313-577-6120 *Toll Free Tel:* 800-978-7323 *Fax:* 313-577-6131
E-mail: bookorders@wayne.edu
Web Site: www.wsupress.wayne.edu
Key Personnel
Dir: Stephanie Williams *Tel:* 313-577-4607
Ed-in-Chief: Annie Martin *Tel:* 313-577-8335 *E-mail:* annie.martin@wayne.edu

PUBLISHERS

Acqs Ed: Marie Sweetman *Tel:* 313-577-4220
  E-mail: marie.sweetman@wayne.edu
Design & Prodn Mgr: Kristin Harpster *Tel:* 313-577-4604 *E-mail:* kmharpster@wayne.edu
Mktg & Sales Mgr: Emily Nowak *Tel:* 313-577-6128 *E-mail:* enowak@wayne.edu
Order Fulfillment Mgr: Theresa Martinelli *Tel:* 313-577-6126 *E-mail:* theresa.martinelli@wayne.edu
Founded: 1941
Scholarly & trade books in African American studies, film & television, women's studies, Jewish studies, poetry, speech & language pathology, fairy tales & folklore, regional studies & urban studies.
ISBN Prefix(es): 978-0-8143
Number of titles published annually: 40 Print
Total Titles: 2,500 Print; 2 CD-ROM
Imprints: Great Lakes Books; Painted Turtle Books (general interest trade)
Foreign Rep(s): Eurospan (Africa, Europe, Middle East, UK)
Warehouse: 40 W Hancock St, Detroit, MI 48201
Distribution Center: HFS (Hopkins Fulfillment Services), 2715 N Charles St, Baltimore, MD 21218 *Tel:* 410-516-6965 *Toll Free Tel:* 800-537-5487 *E-mail:* hfcustserv@jh.edu *Web Site:* hfs.jhu.edu
Membership(s): Association of University Presses (AUPresses)

Wayside Publishing
2 Stonewood Dr, Freeport, ME 04032
Toll Free Tel: 888-302-2519
E-mail: info@waysidepublishing.com; support@waysidepublishing.com
Web Site: waysidepublishing.com
Key Personnel
Pres: Greg Greuel
Mgr, Opers: Nicole Lyons
Founded: 1988
Humanities, English & foreign language textbooks & history.
ISBN Prefix(es): 978-1-877653
Number of titles published annually: 5 Print
Total Titles: 54 Print

Welcome Books
Imprint of Rizzoli International Publications Inc
300 Park Ave S, New York, NY 10010
Tel: 212-387-3400 *Fax:* 212-387-3535
Web Site: www.rizzoliusa.com/publisher/rizzoli/imprint/wb
Key Personnel
Publicity Dir: Jessica Napp *Tel:* 212-387-3465
  E-mail: jnapp@rizzoliusa.com
Foreign Rts: Klaus Kirschbaum
  E-mail: kkirschbaum@rizzoliusa.com
Founded: 1980
Illustrated books for adult trade & gift market.
ISBN Prefix(es): 978-0-8478; 978-0-941807; 978-1-932183; 978-1-59962
Number of titles published annually: 8 Print
Total Titles: 100 Print
Distributed by Random House
Distributor for AAP; Cerf & Peterson; Music Sales; Zeke Holdings Ltd
Distribution Center: Penguin Random House Distribution Services, 400 Hahn Rd, Westminster, MD 21157 *Toll Free Tel:* 800-733-3000 *Toll Free Fax:* 800-659-2436
Membership(s): American Book Producers Association (ABPA)

Welcome Rain Publishers LLC
217 Thompson St, Suite 473, New York, NY 10012
Tel: 212-686-1909
Web Site: welcomerain.com
Key Personnel
Publr: John Weber
Founded: 1997
Progressive independent publisher of fiction, non-fiction, art & photography books, humor, drama & distinguished volumes of poetry.
ISBN Prefix(es): 978-1-56649
Number of titles published annually: 21 Print
Total Titles: 200 Print
Distribution Center: National Book Network (NBN), 15200 NBN Way, Blue Ridge Summit, PA 17214 *Tel:* 717-794-3800 *Fax:* 717-794-3828

Well-Trained Mind Press
18021 The Glebe Lane, Charles City, VA 23030
Tel: 804-593-0306 *Toll Free Tel:* 877-322-3445
  Fax: 804-829-5704
E-mail: support@welltrainedmind.com
Web Site: welltrainedmind.com
Key Personnel
Owner, Ed-in-Chief & CEO: Susan Wise Bauer
Exec Admin: Breana Clarke
Sales Dir: Paul Harrington
Founded: 2001
Publish educational books for home school families & schools & books for the well-trained mind.
ISBN Prefix(es): 978-0-9714129; 978-1-933339; 978-0-9818566; 978-0-9728603; 978-1-942968; 978-1-952469; 978-1-945841; 978-1-944481
Number of titles published annually: 8 Print; 3 CD-ROM; 4 E-Book
Total Titles: 110 Print; 75 CD-ROM; 35 E-Book
Imprints: Figures in Motion; Olive Branch Books
Distributed by W W Norton & Company Inc
Foreign Rights: Richard Henshaw (Central America, South America)

Wellington Press
Division of BooksUPrint.com Inc
3811 Long & Winding Rd, Tallahassee, FL 32309
E-mail: peacegames@aol.com
Web Site: www.peacegames.com
Key Personnel
Pres & Intl Rts: David W Felder, PhD
Founded: 1982
Publish philosophy books, including texts, & role play peacegames that examine conflicts of all types.
ISBN Prefix(es): 978-0-910959; 978-1-57501
Number of titles published annually: 10 Print; 10 E-Book
Total Titles: 85 Print; 90 Online; 100 E-Book

Eliot Werner Publications Inc
31 Willow Lane, Clinton Corners, NY 12514
Mailing Address: PO Box 268, Clinton Corners, NY 12514
Tel: 845-266-4241 *Fax:* 845-266-3317
E-mail: eliotwerner217@gmail.com
Web Site: www.eliotwerner.com
Founded: 2001
Academic & scholarly books in anthropology, archaeology, psychology, sociology & related fields; writing, editing & contract publishing.
ISBN Prefix(es): 978-0-9712427; 978-0-9719587; 978-0-9752738; 978-0-9797731; 978-0-9898249
Number of titles published annually: 4 Print
Total Titles: 56 Print
Imprints: Percheron Press
Distribution Center: Ian Stevens Distribution, 70 Enterprise Dr, No 2, Bristol, CT 06010, Fin & Off Mgr: Melanie Palleria *Tel:* 860-584-6546 *Fax:* 860-516-4873 *E-mail:* melanie@isdistribution.com *Web Site:* www.isdistribution.com

Wesleyan Publishing House
Division of The Wesleyan Church
13300 Olio Rd, Fishers, IN 46037
Mailing Address: PO Box 50434, Indianapolis, IN 46250

U.S. PUBLISHERS

Tel: 317-774-3853 *Toll Free Tel:* 800-493-7539
  Fax: 317-774-3865 *Toll Free Fax:* 800-788-3535
E-mail: wph@wesleyan.org
Web Site: www.wesleyan.org/books
Key Personnel
Proj Communs Mgr: Susan LeBaron
  E-mail: lebarons@wesleyan.org
Founded: 1968
ISBN Prefix(es): 978-0-89827
Number of titles published annually: 40 Print
Total Titles: 60 Print
Membership(s): Christian Holiness Partnership (CHP); Evangelical Christian Publishers Association (ECPA); Holiness Publisher's Association (HPA); Protestant Church-Owned Publishers Association (PCPA)

Wesleyan University Press
215 Long Lane, Middletown, CT 06459-0433
Tel: 860-685-7712 *Fax:* 860-685-7712
Web Site: www.wesleyan.edu/wespress
Key Personnel
Dir & Ed-in-Chief: Suzanna L Tamminen
  Tel: 860-685-7727 *E-mail:* stamminen@wesleyan.edu
Mktg Mgr: Jaclyn Wilson *Tel:* 860-685-7725
  E-mail: jwilson05@wesleyan.edu
Publicist & Web Mgr: Stephanie Elliott *Tel:* 860-685-7723 *E-mail:* selliott@wesleyan.edu
Founded: 1957
Editorial program which has been awarded 6 Pulitzer Prizes; distinguished history of publishing scholarly & trade books that have influenced American poetry & critical thought over the last four decades.
ISBN Prefix(es): 978-0-8195
Number of titles published annually: 25 Print
Total Titles: 425 Print
Distribution Center: HFS (Hopkins Fulfillment Services), PO Box 50370, Baltimore, MD 21211-4370 (CN & US) *Tel:* 410-516-6965 *Toll Free Tel:* 800-537-5487 *Fax:* 410-516-6998 *E-mail:* hfcustserv@jh.edu *Web Site:* hfs.jhu.edu
Oxbow Books Ltd, c/o Orca Book Services, 160 Eastern Ave, Milton Park, Abingdon, Oxon OX14 4SB, United Kingdom (Europe, Middle East & UK) *Tel:* (01235) 465500 *Fax:* (01235) 465555 *E-mail:* tradeorders@orcabookservices.co.uk
Membership(s): Association of American Publishers (AAP); Association of University Presses (AUPresses)

§West Academic
444 Cedar St, Suite 700, St Paul, MN 55101
Toll Free Tel: 877-888-1330
E-mail: customerservice@westacademic.com; support@westacademic.com; media@westacademic.com
Web Site: www.westacademic.com
Key Personnel
Sr Natl & Intl Acct Mgr: Scott Duckson
  Tel: 651-202-4764 *E-mail:* scott.duckson@westacademic.com
Founded: 1953
Law school casebook, statute, study aid & career success publisher.
ISBN Prefix(es): 978-0-1590; 978-0-3141
Number of titles published annually: 50 Print; 2 CD-ROM
Total Titles: 375 Print; 10 CD-ROM; 60 Audio
Imprints: Foundation Press; Gilbert
Returns: West Academic Distribution Center, 10650 Toebben Dr, Independence, KY 41051
See separate listing for:
Foundation Press

West Margin Press
Imprint of Turner Publishing Co LLC

U.S. PUBLISHERS

4507 Charlotte Ave, Suite 100, Nashville, TN 37209
Tel: 612-255-BOOK (255-2665)
E-mail: info@turnerpublishing.com; admin@turnerpublishing.com; marketing@turnerpublishing.com; orders@turnerpublishing.com
Web Site: turnerpublishing.com
Key Personnel
Pres & Publr, Turner Publishing Co: Todd Bottorff
Founded: 1967
ISBN Prefix(es): 978-1-55868; 978-0-88240; 978-0-8108; 978-1-94182; 978-0-78108
Number of titles published annually: 35 Print; 30 E-Book
Total Titles: 300 Print; 125 E-Book
Imprints: Alaska Northwest Books®; Graphic Arts Books®
Distribution Center: Ingram Publisher Services, 14 Ingram Blvd, Mail Stop 631, La Vergne, TN 37086 *Toll Free Tel:* 800-937-8000 *E-mail:* ips@ingramcontent.com *Web Site:* www.ingrampublisherservices.com

West Virginia University Press
West Virginia University, PO Box 6295, Morgantown, WV 26506-6295
Tel: 304-293-8400
Web Site: www.wvupress.com
Key Personnel
Dir/Acqs Ed (Nonfiction): Derek Krissoff
  E-mail: derek.krissoff@mail.wvu.edu
Acqs Ed & Mktg Opers Mgr: Sarah Munroe
  E-mail: semunroe@mail.wvu.edu
Founded: 1965
ISBN Prefix(es): 978-1-933202; 978-0-937058
Number of titles published annually: 20 Print; 20 E-Book
Total Titles: 130 Print
Orders to: Chicago Distribution Center, 11030 S Langley Ave, Chicago, IL 60628 *Toll Free Tel:* 800-621-2736 *Toll Free Fax:* 800-621-8476 *E-mail:* orders@press.chicago.edu
Distribution Center: Chicago Distribution Center, 11030 S Langley Ave, Chicago, IL 60628 *Tel:* 773-702-7000 (intl) *Toll Free Tel:* 800-621-2736 *Fax:* 773-702-7212 (intl) *Toll Free Fax:* 800-621-8476
Membership(s): Association of University Presses (AUPresses)

Western Edge Press
Imprint of Sherman Asher Publishing
126 Candelario St, Santa Fe, NM 87501
Tel: 505-988-7214
E-mail: westernedge@santa-fe.net
Web Site: www.westernedgepress.com; www.shermanasher.com
Key Personnel
Owner & Publr: James Mafchir
Founded: 1995
Western nonfiction, art, cooking, history, archaeology & Spanish/English bilingual oral history.
ISBN Prefix(es): 978-1-890932
Number of titles published annually: 3 Print
Total Titles: 35 Print
Distribution Center: Mountain Press, Missoula, MT 59806 *Toll Free Tel:* 800-234-5308 *Fax:* 310-532-7001 *E-mail:* mtnpress@montana.com *Web Site:* www.mountainpresspublish.com

Western Pennsylvania Genealogical Society
4400 Forbes Ave, Pittsburgh, PA 15213-4007
Tel: 412-687-6811 (answering machine)
E-mail: info@wpgs.org
Web Site: www.wpgs.org
Founded: 1974
ISBN Prefix(es): 978-0-9745162
Number of titles published annually: 6 Print; 50 Online
Total Titles: 6 Print; 50 Online
Membership(s): National Genealogical Society

Western Reflections Publishing Co
951B N Hwy 149, Lake City, CO 81235
Mailing Address: PO Box 1149, Lake City, CO 81235-1149
Tel: 970-944-0110
E-mail: publisher@westernreflectionspublishing.com; westernreflectionspublishing@gmail.com
Web Site: www.westernreflectionspublishing.com
Key Personnel
Pres: P David Smith
Off Mgr: Jan M Smith
Founded: 1996
History & culture of the western US with an emphasis on Colorado.
ISBN Prefix(es): 978-1-890437; 978-1-932738
Number of titles published annually: 4 Print
Total Titles: 225 Print

Westernlore Press
PO Box 35305, Tucson, AZ 85740-5305
SAN: 202-9650
Tel: 520-297-5491
Key Personnel
Pres & Ed: Lynn R Bailey
Treas & ISBN Contact: Anne G Bailey
Founded: 1941
History & biography, anthropology, historic archaeology & historic sites & ethnohistory pertaining to the greater American West.
ISBN Prefix(es): 978-0-87026
Number of titles published annually: 4 Print
Total Titles: 65 Print

§Westminster John Knox Press (WJK)
Imprint of Presbyterian Publishing Corp (PPC)
100 Witherspoon St, Louisville, KY 40202-1396
SAN: 202-9669
Tel: 502-569-5052 *Toll Free Tel:* 800-523-1631 (US & CN) *Fax:* 502-569-8308 *Toll Free Fax:* 800-541-5113 (US & CN)
E-mail: customer_service@wjkbooks.com; orders@wjkbooks.com
Web Site: www.wjkbooks.com
Key Personnel
Pres & Publr: David Dobson *E-mail:* ddobson@wjkbooks.com
VP, Treas & COO: Monty Anderson
  E-mail: manderson@wjkbooks.com
VP, Mktg: Alicia Samuels *E-mail:* asamuels@wjkbooks.com
Ed-in-Chief: Robert A Ratcliff *E-mail:* rratcliff@wjkbooks.com
Rts & Perms: Michele Blum *E-mail:* mblum@wjkbooks.com
Founded: 1838
With a publishing heritage that dates back more than 160 years, WJK Press publishes religious & theological books & resources for scholars, clergy, laity & general readers. The publisher employs the motto "Challenging the Mind, Nourishing the Soul".
ISBN Prefix(es): 978-0-664; 978-0-8042
Number of titles published annually: 150 Print
Total Titles: 1,100 Print; 2 CD-ROM; 2 Audio
Distributor for Canterbury Press; Church House Publishing; St Andrews Press; SCM Press; Woodlake Publishing Inc
Foreign Rep(s): Africa Christian Textbooks (ACT) (Nigeria); Canaanland Distributors Sdn Bhd (Malaysia); Chinese Christian Literacy Mission (Rocky C L Chen) (Taiwan); Christian Book Discounters (South Africa); Claretian Communications Foundation Inc (Philippines); Cross Communications Ltd (Alexander Y C Lee) (Hong Kong); John Garratt Publishing (Australia); Korea Christian Book Service Inc (South Korea); MediaCom Education Inc (Australia); Methodist Publishing House (South Africa); Norwich Books & Music (Europe, UK); Omega Distributors (New Zealand); Pustaka SUFES Sdn Bhd (Malaysia); St Pauls India (India); SCM Press (Europe, UK); SKS Books Warehouse (Lek Eng Khiang) (Singapore)
Returns: 3904 Produce Rd, Suite 104, Louisville, KY 40218

Wheatherstone Press
Subsidiary of Dickinson Consulting Group Inc
PO Box 257, Portland, OR 97207
Tel: 503-244-8929 *Fax:* 503-244-9795
Web Site: www.wheatherstonepress.com; www.relocationbooks.com
Key Personnel
Pres & CEO: Jan Dickinson *E-mail:* jan@wheatherstonepress.com
Founded: 1983
Publishes handbooks & step-by-step guides covering all phases of relocation, including internationally.
ISBN Prefix(es): 978-0-9613011
Number of titles published annually: 3 Print
Total Titles: 49 Print

§Whiskey Creek Press
Imprint of Start Publishing LLC
221 River St, 9th fl, Suite 9137, Hoboken, NJ 07030
Tel: 212-431-5455
E-mail: publisher@whiskeycreekpress.com
Web Site: whiskeycreekpress.com
Founded: 2003
Traditional royalty-paying small press, publishing fiction in ebook & print formats. Titles can be purchased through Amazon Kindle, Barnes & Noble Nook & Apple ITunes.
ISBN Prefix(es): 978-1-60313; 978-1-61160
Number of titles published annually: 50 Print; 200 E-Book
Total Titles: 500 Print; 1,350 E-Book
Imprints: Torrid Books (sensual & erotic romances)

Whitaker House
1030 Hunt Valley Circle, New Kensington, PA 15068
Tel: 724-334-7000 *Toll Free Tel:* 800-444-4484 (sales) *Fax:* 724-334-1200
E-mail: publisher@whitakerhouse.com; sales@whitakerhouse.com
Web Site: www.whitakerhouse.com
Key Personnel
Acqs Ed: Amy Bartlett
Founded: 1970
ISBN Prefix(es): 978-0-88368; 978-1-60374; 978-1-62911; 978-1-64123; 979-8-88769
Number of titles published annually: 76 Print; 76 E-Book; 15 Audio
Total Titles: 1,300 Print; 1,300 E-Book; 150 Audio
Imprints: Whitaker Espanol
Foreign Rights: Wen-Sheuan Sung (worldwide exc Canada & USA)
Warehouse: Anchor Distributors, 1030 Hunt Valley Circle, New Kensington, PA 15068, Mgr: Jimmy Luther
Membership(s): American Christian Fiction Writers (ACFW); Evangelical Christian Publishers Association (ECPA)

White Pine Press
PO Box 236, Buffalo, NY 14201
Tel: 716-573-8202
E-mail: wpine@whitepine.org
Web Site: www.whitepine.org
Key Personnel
Publr & Ed: Dennis Maloney
  E-mail: dennismaloney@yahoo.com
Mng Dir: Elaine La Mattina
Founded: 1973
Specialize in poetry & literature in translation.

ISBN Prefix(es): 978-0-934834; 978-1-877727; 978-1-877800; 978-1-893996
Number of titles published annually: 10 Print
Total Titles: 240 Print
Distributor for Springhouse Editions
Distribution Center: Consortium Book Sales & Distribution, The Keg House, Suite 101, 34 13 Ave NE, Minneapolis, MN 55413-1007 *Tel:* 612-746-2600 *Toll Free Tel:* 866-400-5351 (cust serv, Jackson, TN) *E-mail:* cbsdinfo@ingramcontent.com *Web Site:* www.cbsd.com SAN: 200-6049

Whitman, Albert & Company, see Albert Whitman & Company

§Whittier Publications Inc
121 Regent Dr, Lido Beach, NY 11561
Tel: 516-432-8120 *Toll Free Tel:* 800-897-TEXT (897-8398) *Fax:* 516-889-0341
E-mail: info@whitbooks.com
Web Site: www.whitbooks.com
Key Personnel
Pres: Judith Etra
Founded: 1990
Textbooks, trade, self-help.
ISBN Prefix(es): 978-1-878045; 978-1-57604
Number of titles published annually: 200 Print

§Whole Person Associates Inc
101 W Second St, Suite 203, Duluth, MN 55802
Tel: 218-727-0500 *Toll Free Tel:* 800-247-6789 *Fax:* 218-727-0505
E-mail: books@wholeperson.com
Web Site: www.wholeperson.com
Key Personnel
Owner & Publr: Jack Kosmach
Founded: 1980
Stress management & wellness promotion.
ISBN Prefix(es): 978-0-938586; 978-1-57025
Number of titles published annually: 8 Print
Total Titles: 218 Print; 29 CD-ROM; 38 Audio
Membership(s): Independent Book Publishing Professionals Group (IBPPG)

§Wide World of Maps Inc
2133 E Indian School Rd, Phoenix, AZ 85016
Tel: 602-279-2323 *Toll Free Tel:* 800-279-7654
Web Site: www.maps4u.com
Key Personnel
Pres & CEO: James L Willinger
Founded: 1975
Atlases, charts, guide books, maps, map software, map accessories & more.
ISBN Prefix(es): 978-0-938448; 978-1-887749
Number of titles published annually: 6 Print; 2 CD-ROM
Total Titles: 20 Print; 2 CD-ROM
Imprints: Yellow 1
Divisions: Desert Charts; Metro Maps; Phoenix Mapping Service
Branch Office(s)
17232 N Cave Creek Rd, Phoenix, AZ 85032
Tel: 602-279-2323 ext 3 *Fax:* 602-368-1412
2155 E University Dr, Tempe, AZ 85281
Tel: 602-279-2323 ext 4
Distributed by Rand McNally
Distributor for Benchmark Maps; Big Sky Maps; Franko Maps; MacVan Maps (Colorado Springs); Metro Maps; Rand McNally

Wide World Publishing
PO Box 476, San Carlos, CA 94070-0476
SAN: 211-1462
Tel: 650-593-2839
E-mail: wwpbl@aol.com
Web Site: wideworldpublishing.com
Key Personnel
Partner & Intl Rts: Elvira Monroe
Founded: 1976

Trade paperbacks, cookbooks, mathematics books/calendars, travel books & guides.
ISBN Prefix(es): 978-0-933174; 978-1-884550
Number of titles published annually: 4 Print
Total Titles: 148 Print; 23 E-Book
Foreign Rep(s): Ingram/Publishers Group West (Asia, Canada, Europe)
Orders to: Publishers Group West, 1700 Fourth St, Berkeley, CA 94710 *Tel:* 510-809-3700 *Toll Free Tel:* 866-400-4351 *Fax:* 510-809-3777 SAN: 202-8522; Ingram Content Group, One Ingram Blvd, La Vergne, TN 37086 *Tel:* 615-795-5000 *Web Site:* www.ingramcontent.com
Distribution Center: Publishers Group West, 1700 Fourth St, Berkeley, CA 94710 *Tel:* 510-809-3700 *Toll Free Tel:* 866-400-5351 *Fax:* 510-809-3777 *Web Site:* www.pgw.com SAN: 202-8522
Ingram Publisher Services, 12101 Ingram Dr, Chambersburg, PA 17202 *E-mail:* iqsupport@ingramcontent.com *Web Site:* www.ingrampublisherservices.com/contact
Ingram Content Group, One Ingram Blvd, La Vergne, TN 37086 *Tel:* 615-793-5000 *Web Site:* www.ingramcontent.com

Markus Wiener Publishers Inc
231 Nassau St, Princeton, NJ 08542
SAN: 282-5465
Tel: 609-921-1141
E-mail: publisher@markuswiener.com
Web Site: www.markuswiener.com
Key Personnel
Pres: M Markus Wiener
VP: Shelley Frisch
Founded: 1981
Independent publisher of academic & trade books & journals in the areas of world history, Latin American & Caribbean history, Middle Eastern & African history & culture. Its publications also include related topics in music, religion, women's history, Jewish history, western civilization & slavery.
ISBN Prefix(es): 978-0-910129; 978-0-945179; 978-1-55876
Number of titles published annually: 25 Print
Total Titles: 300 Print
Foreign Rep(s): Eurospan (Europe)

Michael Wiese Productions
12400 Ventura Blvd, No 1111, Studio City, CA 91604
Tel: 818-379-8799 *Toll Free Tel:* 800-833-5738 (orders) *Fax:* 818-986-3408
E-mail: mwpsales@earthlink.net; fulfillment@portcity.com
Web Site: www.mwp.com
Key Personnel
Founder & Publr: Michael Wiese
VP: Ken Lee *Tel:* 206-271-0287 *E-mail:* kenlee@earthlink.net
Spec Sales: Michele Chong *Tel:* 818-841-4123
Founded: 1981
Publisher of books on screenwriting & filmmaking.
ISBN Prefix(es): 978-0-941188
Number of titles published annually: 15 Print
Total Titles: 300 Print
Imprints: Divine Arts
Distribution Center: Ingram Publisher Services, 14 Ingram Blvd, Mail Stop 631, La Vergne, TN 37086 *Toll Free Tel:* 866-400-5351 *Web Site:* www.ingrampublisherservices.com

§Wilderness Adventures Press Inc
45 Buckskin Rd, Belgrade, MT 59714
Tel: 406-388-0112 *Toll Free Tel:* 866-400-2012 *Toll Free Fax:* 866-400-2013
E-mail: books@wildadvpress.com
Web Site: store.wildadvpress.com

Key Personnel
Pres & Publr: Chuck Johnson *Tel:* 406-388-0112 ext 12
Secy & Treas: Blanche Johnson
Assoc Publr: Josh Bergan
Founded: 1994
Outdoor guidebooks, sporting books & cookbooks, fly fishing, dog training & big game hunting, plus maps.
ISBN Prefix(es): 978-1-885106; 978-1-932098; 978-1-940239
Number of titles published annually: 6 Print
Total Titles: 90 Print

Wildflower Press
Affiliate of Oakbrook Press
c/o Oakbrook Press, 3301 S Valley Dr, Rapid City, SD 57703
Mailing Address: PO Box 3362, Rapid City, SD 57709
Tel: 605-381-6385
E-mail: info@wildflowerpress.org
Web Site: www.wildflowerpress.org
Key Personnel
Pres: L J Bryant *E-mail:* wildflowerpress@live.com
Publicity Dir: Robert E Fuchs *E-mail:* pr@wildflowerpress.org
Literary Agent: Charlene Caulfield
Sales: Jordan Dadah
Edit: Leisette Fox
Billing: Christina MacLachlan
Founded: 2010
Small press specializing in publishing works of fiction with a significant message. Not a vanity press; no funds required to publish.
ISBN Prefix(es): 978-0-9835332
Number of titles published annually: 5 Print; 5 E-Book
Total Titles: 12 Print; 13 E-Book
Membership(s): Independent Book Publishers Association (IBPA)

Wildside Press LLC
7945 MacArthur Blvd, Suite 215, Cabin John, MD 20818
Tel: 301-762-1305
E-mail: wildside@wildsidepress.com
Web Site: wildsidepress.com
Key Personnel
Publr: John Betancourt
Founded: 1989
Reprints of classic science fiction, fantasy, mystery, reference & mainstream.
ISBN Prefix(es): 978-1-880448; 978-1-58715; 978-1-59224
Number of titles published annually: 600 Print; 400 E-Book; 100 Audio
Total Titles: 16,000 Print; 1,400 E-Book; 800 Audio
Imprints: Borgo Press; Owlswick Press
Foreign Rights: Virginia Kidd Literary Agency (worldwide)

§Wiley-Blackwell
Imprint of John Wiley & Sons Inc
111 River St, Suite 300, Hoboken, NJ 07030-5774
Tel: 201-748-6000 *Toll Free Tel:* 800-567-4797 *Fax:* 201-748-6088 *Toll Free Fax:* 800-565-6802
E-mail: info@wiley.com
Web Site: www.wiley.com
Founded: 1984
General, scholarly, reference & college texts, with an emphasis on the humanities, social sciences & business. Also medical allied health, veterinary, earth & life sciences, environment & engineering.
ISBN Prefix(es): 978-0-631; 978-0-85520; 978-0-86216; 978-1-55786; 978-1-57718; 978-0-86542; 978-0-917678; 978-0-87993; 978-0-

U.S. PUBLISHERS

88295; 978-0-8138; 978-0-7279; 978-0-901715; 978-0-632; 978-0-85238; 978-0-85298; 978-1-86058; 978-0-86380; 978-1-881089; 978-1-4051; 978-1-931303; 978-0-7273; 978-0-901702; 978-0-948825; 978-0-9701312; 978-0-9788924; 978-1-4443; 978-1-871381; 978-1-889325; 978-1-890061; 978-1-891276; 978-1-933385
Number of titles published annually: 500 Print
Total Titles: 4,500 Print

§John Wiley & Sons Inc
111 River St, Hoboken, NJ 07030-5774
SAN: 202-5183
Tel: 201-748-6000 *Toll Free Tel:* 800-225-5945 (cust serv) *Fax:* 201-748-6088
Web Site: www.wiley.com
Key Personnel
Chmn of the Bd: Jesse C Wiley
Pres & CEO: Matthew S Kissner
EVP & CFO: Christina Van Tassell
EVP & CTO: Aref Matin
EVP & Chief People Offr: Danielle McMahan
EVP & Gen Coun: Deirdre Silver
EVP, Wiley Research: Jay Flynn
Corp Secy: Joanna Jia
EVP & Gen Mgr, Educ Publg: Matt Leavy
EVP & Gen Mgr, Educ Servs: Todd Zipper
EVP & Gen Mgr, Talent Solutions: Barry Davis
EVP, Mktg: Shari Hofer
SVP & Corp Cont: Christopher Caridi
SVP & Treas: Kevin Monaco
SVP & Gen Mgr, Intl Educ: Philip Kisray
SVP, Busn Mgmt & Opers: Andrew Weber
Sr Acqs Ed: Zachary Schisgal
Assoc Ed, Wiley Business: Victoria Savanh
Founded: 1807
Global publisher of print & electronic products specializing in professional & consumer books & subscription services; scientific, technical, medical books & journals; textbooks & educational materials for undergraduate & graduate students as well as lifelong learners. Wiley has publishing, marketing & distribution centers in the US, Canada, Europe, Asia & Australia.
ISBN Prefix(es): 978-0-470; 978-0-471; 978-0-442; 978-0-8436; 978-0-87055
Number of titles published annually: 1,500 Print
Total Titles: 15,000 Print
Imprints: American Geophysical Union; Architectural Graphic Standards; Audel; Bloomberg; Capstone; Cochrane Library; CrossKnowledge; Culinary Institute of America; Current Protocols; Ernst & Sohn; Essential Evidence Plus; Everything DiSC®; Fisher Investments Press; The Five Behaviors of a Cohesive Team™; For Dummies®; GIT Verlag; Verlag Helvetica; Jacaranda; Jossey-Bass; JK Lasser; The Leadership Challenge®; Merck; MOAC; PXT Select™; RSMeans; Spectroscopy Now; SYBEX; Teach Yourself Visually; Wiley-Blackwell; Wiley Custom Select; Wiley Digital Archives; Wiley Education Services; Wiley Efficient Learning; Wiley Health Learning; Wiley-IEEE Press; Wiley Job Network; Wiley Online Library; Wiley Open Access; Wiley Science Solutions; Wiley-VCH; Wiley Visualizing; WileyPLUS; Wrightbooks; Wrox™
Branch Office(s)
1140 US Hwy 22, East Suite, Bridgewater, NJ 08807
535 Mission St, 14th fl, San Francisco, CA 94105
Union Sta, 1550 Wewatta St, Denver, CO 80202
851 Trafalgar Ct, Suite 420, Maitland, FL 32751 *Tel:* 407-618-5400
1415 W 22 St, Suite 800, Oak Brook, IL 60523 *Tel:* 630-366-2900 *Fax:* 630-528-3101
9200 Keystone Crossing, Suite 800, Indianapolis, IN 46240 *Tel:* 317-572-3000; 317-572-3994 (consumer tech support) *Toll Free Tel:* 800-434-3422
101 Station Landing, Suite 300, Medford, MA 02155 *Tel:* 781-388-8200 *Fax:* 781-388-8210
400 Hwy 169, Suite 300, Minneapolis, MN 55426 *Tel:* 763-765-2222 *Fax:* 763-765-2276
510 N Valley Mills Dr, Suite 600, Waco, TX 76710 *Tel:* 254-751-1644
90 Eglington Ave E, Suite 300, Toronto, ON M4P 2Y3, Canada *Tel:* 416-236-4433 *Toll Free Tel:* 800-567-4797 *Fax:* 416-236-4446 *Toll Free Fax:* 800-565-6802
Distribution Center: One Wiley Dr, Somerset, NJ 08875-1272 (US cust care opers/trade & wholesale) *Fax:* 732-302-2300
E-mail: custserv@wiley.com
Membership(s): Association of American Publishers (AAP)
See separate listing for:
SYBEX
Wiley-Blackwell
John Wiley & Sons Inc Global Education
John Wiley & Sons Inc Professional Development

§John Wiley & Sons Inc Global Education
Division of John Wiley & Sons Inc
111 River St, Suite 300, Hoboken, NJ 07030-5774
Tel: 201-748-6000 *Toll Free Tel:* 800-567-4797 *Fax:* 201-748-6008 *Toll Free Fax:* 800-565-6802
E-mail: info@wiley.com
Web Site: www.wiley.com
Total Titles: 615 Print

§John Wiley & Sons Inc Professional Development
Division of John Wiley & Sons Inc
111 River St, Suite 300, Hoboken, NJ 07030-5774
Tel: 201-748-6000 *Toll Free Tel:* 800-567-4797 *Fax:* 201-748-6088 *Toll Free Fax:* 800-565-6802
E-mail: info@wiley.com
Web Site: www.wiley.com
Global brands include American Geophysical Union, Capstone, For Dummies, Jossey-Bass, Pfeiffer, J K Lasser, Publicis, Wiley, Wiley-AIChE, Wiley-Blackwell, Wiley-IEEE Press & Wiley-VCH.

John Wiley & Sons Inc Scientific, Technical, Medical & Scholarly (STMS), see Wiley-Blackwell

William Carey Publishing
Division of Frontier Ventures
10 W Dry Creek Circle, Littleton, CO 80120
Tel: 720-372-7036
E-mail: publishing@wclbooks.com
Web Site: www.missionbooks.org
Key Personnel
Dir, Publg: Denise Wynn
Founded: 1969
Christian publisher. Specialize in cross-cultural Christian mission work & experiences in frontier countries. Publishing practical, tactical, theoretical, or narrative Christian missiology.
ISBN Prefix(es): 978-0-87808
Number of titles published annually: 15 Print; 15 E-Book
Total Titles: 250 Print
Imprints: William Carey Library; William Carey Press
Orders to: Anchor Distributors, 1030 Hunt Valley Circle, New Kensington, PA 15068
Membership(s): Evangelical Christian Publishers Association (ECPA); Independent Book Publishers Association (IBPA)

§Williams & Company Book Publishers
1317 Pine Ridge Dr, Savannah, GA 31406
Tel: 912-352-0404
E-mail: bookpub@comcast.net
Key Personnel
Publr & Ed-in-Chief: Thomas A Williams, PhD
Founded: 1989
ISBN Prefix(es): 978-1-878853
Number of titles published annually: 15 Print
Total Titles: 50 Print
Imprints: Venture Press; Williams & Co Publishers
Membership(s): Independent Publishers Association

Willow Creek Press
9931 Hwy 70 W, Minocqua, WI 54548
Mailing Address: PO Box 147, Minocqua, WI 54548 SAN: 991-5117
Tel: 715-358-7010 *Toll Free Tel:* 800-850-9453 *Fax:* 715-358-2807
E-mail: info@willowcreekpress.com
Web Site: www.willowcreekpress.com; www.wcpretail.com
Key Personnel
Pres: Jeremy Petrie *E-mail:* jpetrie@willowcreekpress.com
Publr & Ed-in-Chief: Tom Petrie
Natl Sales Dir: Andrew Spicer *E-mail:* aspicer@willowcreekpress.com
Sales Mgr: Wendell White *E-mail:* wwhite@willowcreekpress.com
Specialty Sales Mgr: Jessie Dube *E-mail:* jdube@willowcreekpress.com
Founded: 1986
Publish high quality books most specifically related to nature, animals, wildlife, hunting, fishing & gardening. The company also offers a unique line of cookbooks & has established a niche in the pet book market. The company also publishes high quality nature, wild life, fishing, pet & sporting calendars.
ISBN Prefix(es): 978-1-57223
Number of titles published annually: 24 Print
Total Titles: 130 Print; 3 Audio
Membership(s): Association of American Publishers (AAP)

Wilshire Book Co
22647 Ventura Blvd, No 314, Woodland Hills, CA 91364-1416
SAN: 205-5368
Tel: 818-700-1522
E-mail: sales@mpowers.com
Web Site: www.mpowers.com
Key Personnel
Pres & Rts & Perms: Marcia Powers
Founded: 1967 (by Melvin Powers)
Psychological, self-help, motivational & inspirational books, adult fables, horses, bridge; mail order, business, advertising & marketing; originals & reprints.
ISBN Prefix(es): 978-0-87980
Number of titles published annually: 3 Print
Total Titles: 23 Print

Windsor Books
Division of Windsor Marketing Corp
260 W Main St, Suite 5, Bayshore, NY 11706
SAN: 203-2945
Mailing Address: PO Box 280, Brightwaters, NY 11718
Tel: 631-665-6688 *Toll Free Tel:* 800-321-5934
E-mail: windsor.books@att.net
Web Site: www.windsorpublishing.com
Key Personnel
Founder: Alfred Schmidt
Mng Ed: Jeff Schmidt
Founded: 1968
Business, economics & investment.
ISBN Prefix(es): 978-0-930233
Number of titles published annually: 5 Print
Advertising Agency: A Schmidt Agency

PUBLISHERS

§Wings Press
PO Box 591176, San Antonio, TX 78259
E-mail: wingspresspublishing@gmail.com
Web Site: www.wingspress.com
Key Personnel
Publr & Ed: M Milligan
Founded: 1975
Literary book publishing.
ISBN Prefix(es): 978-0-916727; 978-0-930324
Number of titles published annually: 3 Print; 3 E-Book
Total Titles: 230 Print; 4 CD-ROM; 200 E-Book; 4 Audio
Foreign Rights: Independent Publisher's Group (Susan M Sewall)
Orders to: Independent Publisher's Group (IPG), 814 N Franklin St, Chicago, IL 60624 *Tel:* 312-337-0747 *Toll Free Tel:* 800-888-0747 *Fax:* 312-337-5985 *E-mail:* orders@ipgbook.com
Returns: Independent Publisher's Group Distribution Center, 600 N Pulaski Rd, Chicago, IL 60624 *Tel:* 312-337-0747 *Fax:* 312-337-5985 *Toll Free Fax:* 800-888-0747 *E-mail:* frontdesk@ipgbook.com
Shipping Address: Independent Publisher's Group Distribution Center, 600 N Pulaski Rd, Chicago, IL 60624 *Tel:* 312-337-0747 *Fax:* 312-337-5985 *E-mail:* orders@ipgbook.com
Warehouse: Independent Publisher's Group Distribution Center, 600 N Pulaski Rd, Chicago, IL 60624 *Tel:* 312-337-0747 *Fax:* 312-337-5985 *E-mail:* orders@ipgbook.com
Distribution Center: Independent Publisher's Group Distribution Center, 600 N Pulaski Rd, Chicago, IL 60624 *Tel:* 312-337-0747 *Toll Free Tel:* 800-888-0747 *Fax:* 312-337-5985 *E-mail:* orders@ipgbook.com
Membership(s): Association of Writers & Writing Programs (AWP); Community of Literary Magazines & Presses (CLMP)

Winters Publishing
705 E Washington St, Greensburg, IN 47240
SAN: 298-1645
Mailing Address: PO Box 501, Greensburg, IN 47240
Tel: 812-663-4948 *Toll Free Tel:* 800-457-3230 *Fax:* 812-663-4948
E-mail: winterspublishing@gmail.com
Web Site: www.winterspublishing.com
Key Personnel
Owner & Publr: Mr Tracy Winters
Founded: 1988
Produces high-quality, custom books for individuals & groups. We publish community & corporate history books for cities & organizations celebrating centennials, bicentennials & other milestone events. We also work with individual authors & publish children's books, books for the Christian market, cookbooks for the bed & breakfast industry & a variety of other fiction & nonfiction books.
ISBN Prefix(es): 978-0-9625329; 978-1-883651
Number of titles published annually: 15 Print; 2 E-Book
Total Titles: 105 Print; 5 E-Book
Imprints: Faith Press
Distribution Center: Ingram Book Co, One Ingram Blvd, La Vergne, TN 37086 *Tel:* 615-793-5000

Winterthur Museum, Garden & Library
5105 Kennett Pike, Winterthur, DE 19735
Tel: 302-888-4663 *Toll Free Tel:* 800-448-3883
Fax: 302-888-4950
Web Site: www.winterthur.org
Key Personnel
Contact: Onie Rollins
ISBN Prefix(es): 978-0-912724
Number of titles published annually: 4 Print
Total Titles: 80 Print
Distributed by ACC Art Books; The Monacelli Press; W W Norton & Company Inc; University of Pennsylvania Press
Membership(s): American Alliance of Museums (AAM); American Booksellers Association (ABA); Art Libraries Society (ARLIS)

Winterwolf Press
8635 W Sahara Ave, Suite 425, Las Vegas, NV 89117
Tel: 725-222-3442
E-mail: info@winterwolfpress.com
Web Site: winterwolfpress.com
Key Personnel
Owner & Founder: Laura Cantu
Dir, Opers & Acqs: Christine Contini
Dir, Busn Devt & Submissions Liaison: Jeanette Leach
Sr Ed: Jeffrey Naylor
ISBN Prefix(es): 978-0-9885851
Number of titles published annually: 6 Print; 6 Online; 6 E-Book; 6 Audio
Imprints: Shadow Wolf Press
Distributor for Shadow Wolf Press
Membership(s): Independent Book Publishers Association (IBPA)

§Wisconsin Department of Public Instruction
125 S Webster St, Madison, WI 53703
Mailing Address: PO Box 7841, Madison, WI 53707-7841
Tel: 608-266-2188 *Toll Free Tel:* 800-441-4563 (US only); 800-243-8782 (US only)
E-mail: pubsales@dpi.wi.gov
Web Site: pubsales.dpi.wi.gov
Key Personnel
State Superintendent of Public Instruction: Carolyn Stanford Taylor *Tel:* 608-266-8687 *E-mail:* carolyn.stanford.taylor@dpi.wi.gov
Specialize in English, math, science & social studies, character education, driver education & traffic safety, career & technical education, world languages & teaching strategies.
ISBN Prefix(es): 978-1-57337
Number of titles published annually: 8 Print; 4 CD-ROM
Total Titles: 120 Print; 10 CD-ROM

Wisdom Publications Inc
199 Elm St, Somerville, MA 02144
Tel: 617-776-7416 *Toll Free Tel:* 800-272-4050 (orders) *Fax:* 617-776-7841
E-mail: submission@wisdompubs.org
Web Site: wisdomexperience.org
Key Personnel
Chmn: Timothy J McNeill
Publr & CEO: Daniel T Aitken
Exec Ed: Josh Bartok
Sr Ed: Laura Cunningham; David Kittelstrom
Prodn Ed: Ben Gleason
Brand & Mktg Mgr: Kestrel Montague
Cust Serv Mgr: Pema Tsewang
Mktg Coord: Brianna Quick
Founded: 1976
Books on Buddhism published in various series encompassing theory & practice, biography, history, art & culture.
ISBN Prefix(es): 978-0-86171
Number of titles published annually: 30 Print
Total Titles: 300 Print
Imprints: Pali Text Society
Distributed by Simon & Schuster, LLC
Foreign Rep(s): Publishers Group UK (UK); Windhorse Books (Australia, New Zealand)
Foreign Rights: ACER Agencia Literaria (Elizabeth Atkins) (Portugal, Spain); ANA Sofia Ltd (Anna Droumeva) (Albania, Bosnia and Herzegovina, Bulgaria, Montenegro, North Macedonia, Serbia); AnatoliaLit Agency (Dogan Terzi) (Turkey); Agence Eliane Benisti (Noemi Rollett) (France); Blackbird Literary Agency (Wampe de Veer) (Netherlands); BooKLab Literary Agency (Aleksandra Lapinska Piotr) (Poland); Chinese Connection Agency (Gending Fan) (China); Paul & Peter Fritz AG Literary Agency (Christian Dittus) (Germany); The Deborah Harris Agency (Ms Efrat Lev) (Israel); Agnese Incisa Agenzia Letteraria (Agnese Incisa) (Italy); Japan UNI Agency Inc (Ms Eriko Takeuchi) (Japan); Katai & Bolza Literary Agents (Peter Balza) (Hungary); Simona Kessler International Copyright Agency Ltd (Romania); Alexander Korzhenevski Agency (Alexander Korzhenevski) (Russia); Kristin Olson Literary Agency SRO (Kristin Olson) (Czechia, Slovakia); Tuttle-Mori Agency (Thailand) Co Ltd (Primol Yutisri & Youthapong Charoephan) (Indonesia, Thailand, Vietnam); Eric Yang Agency (Henry Shin) (South Korea)
Orders to: Publishers Storage & Shipping (PSSC), 46 Development Rd, Fitchburg, MA 01420 *Tel:* 978-829-2555 *Fax:* 978-348-1233

Wizards of the Coast LLC
Subsidiary of Hasbro Inc
1600 Lind Ave SW, Suite 400, Renton, WA 98057-3305
Mailing Address: PO Box 707, Renton, WA 98057-0707
Tel: 425-226-6500; 425-204-8069 *Toll Free Tel:* 800-324-6496
E-mail: press@wizards.com
Web Site: company.wizards.com
Founded: 1975 (as TSR Inc)
Publisher of fantasy, science fiction & horror novels. Young adult game material; role-playing games, trading card games, board games & books, makers of Dungeons & Dragons. Not seeking proposals for our shared world lines at this time.
ISBN Prefix(es): 978-0-88038; 978-1-56076; 978-0-7869
Number of titles published annually: 50 Print; 60 E-Book
Total Titles: 300 Print

Alan Wofsy Fine Arts
1109 Geary Blvd, San Francisco, CA 94109
SAN: 207-6438
Mailing Address: PO Box 2210, San Francisco, CA 94126-2210
Tel: 415-292-6500 *Toll Free Tel:* 800-660-6403 *Fax:* 415-292-6594 (off & cust serv); 510-251-1840 (acctg)
E-mail: order@art-books.com (orders); editeur@earthlink.net (edit); beauxarts@earthlink.net (cust serv)
Web Site: www.art-books.com
Key Personnel
Chmn of the Bd: Lord Cohen
CEO: Alan Wofsy
Art Dir: Zeke Greenberg
Ed, French Books: Charles DuPont
Ed, German Books: Willi Rahm
PR Mgr: Milton J Goldbaum
Web Site Mgr: Steven Barich
Web Site & Imaging: Matt Novack
Mktg: Andy Redkin
Libn: Adios Butler
Coun: Judith Mazia
Rts: Elizabeth Regina Snowden
Founded: 1969
Art reference books, bibliographies, art books, iconographies, prints, posters & note cards. Warehouse located in Ashland, OH.
ISBN Prefix(es): 978-0-915346; 978-1-55660; 978-0-8150; 978-0-89648
Number of titles published annually: 20 Print; 5 CD-ROM; 60 Online
Total Titles: 350 Print; 10 CD-ROM; 500 Online
Imprints: Beauxarts; Collegium Graphicum; The Picasso Project
Divisions: Wittenborn Art Books
Branch Office(s)
401 Terry Francois St, Suite 202, San Francisco,

CA 94126-2133 (sales & cust serv) *Tel:* 415-872-9711 *E-mail:* emgoodman@mindspring.com
Distributor for Bora; Brusberg (Berlin); Cramer (Geneva); Galerie Kornfeld Verlag AG (Bern); Huber; Ides et Calendes; Welz; Wittenborn Art Books
Membership(s): Association of American Publishers (AAP)
See separate listing for:
The Picasso Project

Wolfman Books
410 13 St, Oakland, CA 94612
Tel: 510-679-4650
E-mail: hello@wolfmanhomerepair.com
Web Site: wolfmanhomerepair.com
Key Personnel
Founder/Dir: Justin Carder
Founded: 2014
Wolfman Books is a bookstore, small press, artist residency program, & community arts hub in downtown Oakland. As a small press, we are dedicated to hybrid & experimental nonfiction, poetry, & artist books, as well as a quarterly magazine, New Life Quarterly, largely but not exclusively focused on Bay Area writers & artists.
ISBN Prefix(es): 978-0-9983461
Number of titles published annually: 3 Print
Total Titles: 10 Print

§Wolters Kluwer Law & Business
Subsidiary of Wolters Kluwer
76 Ninth Ave, 7th fl, New York, NY 10011-5201
SAN: 203-4999
Tel: 212-771-0600; 301-698-7100 (cust serv outside US) *Toll Free Tel:* 800-234-1660 (cust serv)
E-mail: customer.service@wolterskluwer.com; lrusmedia@wolterskluwer.com
Web Site: lrus.wolterskluwer.com
Key Personnel
VP & Chief Content Offr: Gustavo Dobles
Dir, Mktg & Communs: Linda Gharib
Founded: 1959
Publisher of legal, business & health care titles for professionals. Publishes more than 500 journals, newsletters, electronic products & loose-leaf manuals & has more than 1,000 active professional & textbook titles.
ISBN Prefix(es): 978-0-89443; 978-0-912862; 978-0-8342; 978-1-56706; 978-0-87189; 978-0-8080; 978-0-444; 978-1-56542; 978-1-878375; 978-0-9625969; 978-1-56759; 978-0-7355; 978-0-7896; 978-0-87457; 978-0-87622; 978-0-916592; 978-1-4548
Number of titles published annually: 100 Print; 16 CD-ROM; 55 Online
Total Titles: 1,500 Print; 107 CD-ROM; 55 Online; 1 Audio
Foreign Rep(s): David Bartolone
Distribution Center: 7201 McKinney Circle, Frederick, MD 21704 *Tel:* 301-698-7100 *Fax:* 301-695-7931

Wolters Kluwer US Corp
Subsidiary of Wolters Kluwer NV (The Netherlands)
2700 Lake Cook Rd, Riverwoods, IL 60015
Tel: 847-267-7000
E-mail: info@wolterskluwer.com
Web Site: www.wolterskluwer.com
Medical books & journals, law books, business & tax publications.
Total Titles: 5,000 Print
Imprints: Adis International; Aspen Publishers; CCH Incorporated; CT Corporation; Lippincott, Williams & Wilkins
Foreign Office(s): Zuidpoolsingel 2, PO Box 1030, 2400 BA Alphen aan den Rijn, Netherlands (headquarters) *Tel:* (0172) 641 400

§Woodbine House
6510 Bells Mill Rd, Bethesda, MD 20817
SAN: 692-3445
Tel: 301-897-3570 *Toll Free Tel:* 800-843-7323 *Fax:* 301-897-5838
E-mail: info@woodbinehouse.com
Web Site: www.woodbinehouse.com
Key Personnel
Publr: Fran Marinaccio
Mktg Mgr & Intl Rts: Fran M Marinaccio *E-mail:* fmarinaccio@woodbinehouse.com
Mktg & Sales Mgr: Beth Binns *E-mail:* bbinns@woodbinehouse.com
Ed, Acqs Ed & Perms: Susan S Stokes *E-mail:* sstokes@woodbinehouse.com
Founded: 1985
Trade nonfiction, hardcover & paperback.
ISBN Prefix(es): 978-0-933149; 978-1-890627; 978-1-60613
Number of titles published annually: 5 Print; 5 E-Book
Total Titles: 100 Print; 60 E-Book
Foreign Rep(s): Gazelle Book Services Ltd (Europe); Silvereye Education Publications (Australia, Pacific Rim); University of Toronto Press (Canada)
Foreign Rights: Writer's House
Returns: IFC, 3570 Bladensburg Rd, Brentwood, MD 20722 *Tel:* 301-779-4660
Warehouse: c/o IFC, 3570 Bladensburg Rd, Brentwood, MD 20722

Woodrow Wilson Center Press
Division of The Woodrow Wilson International Center for Scholars
One Woodrow Wilson Plaza, 1300 Pennsylvania Ave NW, Washington, DC 20004-3027
Tel: 202-691-4122
Web Site: wilsoncenter.org/woodrow-wilson-center-press
Founded: 1988
Humanities & social sciences; policy studies.
ISBN Prefix(es): 978-0-943875; 978-1-930365
Number of titles published annually: 8 Print; 8 E-Book
Total Titles: 200 Print
Imprints: Wilson Center Press; Woodrow Wilson Center Press/Johns Hopkins University Press; Woodrow Wilson Center Press/Stanford University Press; Woodrow Wilson Center Press/Columbia University Press
Distributed by Columbia University Press; Johns Hopkins University Press; Stanford University Press; University of California Press
Membership(s): Association of American Publishers (AAP); Association of University Presses (AUPresses)

WoodstockArts
PO Box 1342, Woodstock, NY 12498
Tel: 845-679-8111; 845-679-8555 *Fax:* 419-793-3452
E-mail: info@woodstockarts.com
Web Site: woodstockarts.com
Key Personnel
Founder: Julia Blelock *E-mail:* jblelock@woodstockarts.com; Weston Blelock *E-mail:* wblelock@woodstockarts.com
Founded: 1999
All the arts of Woodstock including the art of living.
ISBN Prefix(es): 978-0-9679268; 978-0-9977164
Number of titles published annually: 3 Print; 3 E-Book
Total Titles: 10 Print
Distributor for Bushwhack Press; Opus 40; Woodstock Artists Association & Museum; Woodstock Byrdcliffe Guild
Distribution Center: BCH Fulfillment & Distribution, 33 Oakland Ave, Harrison, NY 10528 *Tel:* 914-835-0015 *Toll Free Tel:* 800-431-1579 *Fax:* 914-835-0398 *E-mail:* orders@bookch.com
Membership(s): Independent Book Publishers Association (IBPA)

Workers Compensation Research Institute
955 Massachusetts Ave, Cambridge, MA 02139
Tel: 617-661-9274 *Fax:* 617-661-9284
E-mail: wcri@wcrinet.org
Web Site: www.wcrinet.org
Key Personnel
Pubns & Admin Specialist: Sarah Solorzano
Founded: 1983
Workers compensation public policy research.
ISBN Prefix(es): 978-0-935149
Number of titles published annually: 4 Print
Total Titles: 500 Print

§Workman Publishing
Division of Hachette Book Group Inc
1290 Avenue of the Americas, New York, NY 10104
Toll Free Tel: 800-759-0190 *Fax:* 212-364-0950
E-mail: workman-inquiry@hbgusa.com
Web Site: www.hachettebookgroup.com/imprint/workman-publishing-company/
Key Personnel
Cont & Exec Dir, Fin: William Jackson
SVP & Publr, Workman Publishing, Artisan & Black Dog & Leventhal: Lia Ronnen
SVP, Workman Kids: Stacy Lellos
VP, Mktg & Publicity, Workman Kids & Workman Publishing: Rebecca Carlisle
VP & Publr, Storey Publishing: Margaret Lennon
VP & Publr, Timber Press: Kathryn Juergens
VP & Publr, Workman Calendars: Page Edmunds
Assoc Publr, Workman Publishing & Exec Mng Ed, Artisan: Zach Greenwald
Ed-in-Chief, Timber Press: Tom Fischer
Exec Dir, Publicity, Mktg & Publg Strategy, Artisan: Allison McGeehon
Sr Dir, Mktg, Workman Calendars, Workman Kids & Workman Publishing: Moira Kerrigan
Publg Dir, Black Dog & Leventhal: Becky Koh Hicks
Art Dir, Children's: Sara Corbett
Art Dir, Storey Publishing: Jessica-Lynn Armstrong
Group Creative Dir: David Schiller
Creative Dir: Kelly Lynch
Creative Dir, Artisan & Workman Publishing: Suet Chong
Creative Dir, Storey Publishing: Alethea Morrison
Prodn Dir, Artisan: Nancy Murray
Rts Dir, Storey Publishing: Maribeth Casey
Dir, Credit: Peggy Gerak
Dir, Digital Mktg: Nicole Higman
Dir, Photo Dept: Anne Kerman
Dir, Workman Speakers Bureau: Carol Schneider
Dir, Spec Mkts & Custom Publg: Emily Krasner
Publicity Dir, Storey Publishing: Amy Greeman
Dir, Publicity & Mktg, Artisan: Theresa Collier
Assoc Dir, Publicity & Mktg: Diana Griffin
Assoc Dir, Publicity & Mktg, Storey Publishing: Alee Moncy
Assoc Dir, Publicity: Ilana Gold
Assoc Dir, Publicity, Timber Press: Katlynn Nicolls
Asst Dir, Mktg & Digital Content: Cindy Lee
Assoc Dir, Mktg, Timber Press: Brian Jones Ridder
Edit Dir, Educ Resources: Karen Edwards
Edit Dir, Food & Drink: Judy Pray
Edit Dir, Storey Publishing: Carleen Madigan
Edit Dir, Timber Press: Kevin McLain
Exec Ed, Children's: Pamela Bobowicz
Exec Ed, Novelty, Activity & Gift, Workman Kids: Megan Nicolay
Mng Ed & Dir, Contracts, Storey Publishing: Jennifer Travis
Sr Ed: Wendy Williams
Sr Ed, Children's: Alisha Zucker

Sr Ed, Artisan: Shoshana Gutmajer; Bridget Monro Itkin
Sr Ed, Black Dog & Leventhal: Lisa Tenaglia
Sr Ed, Storey Publishing: Hannah Fries
Sr Ed, Workman Kids: Karen Halpenny
Sr Prodn Ed: Hillary Leary
Ed, Children's: Gracie Elliott; Megan Logan
Ed, Storey Publishing: Sarah Guare
Ed, Workman Kids: Karen Smith
Proj Ed, Storey Publishing: Michal Lumsden
Sr Prodn Ed: Kimberly A Ehart
Prodn Ed: Samantha Gil; Catherine Weening
Sr Digital Mktg Mgr: Jacklyn Wertman Schechner
Sr Key Acct Mgr, Gift Sales: Valerie Alfred
Sr Mgr, Foreign Rts & Co-editions: Allison Huggins
Dir, Creative Servs: Terri Ruffino
Asst Mgr, Cust Serv: Zoila Pena
Asst Mgr, Online Retail, Catalogs & Specialty Wholesale: Elizabeth Drooby
Digital Mktg & Ad Mgr, Artisan, Workman, Workman Calendars & Workman Kids: Michelle Hilario-Ruiz
Mktg Mgr: Abigail Sokolsky
Mktg Coord: Kate Oksen
Publicity & Mktg Assoc, Artisan, Workman, Workman Calendars & Workman Kids: Alana Bonfiglio
Publicist, Workman Kids & Workman Publishing: Meghan O'Shaughnessy
Children's Publicist, Workman Kids: Amanda Trautmann
Assoc Publicist, Storey Publishing: Tatum Wilson
Publicity Asst: Alyssa Cuevas
Publicity Asst, Workman Calendars, Workman Kids & Workman Publishing: Karolyn Mena
Sr Designer, Workman Calendars: Eric Brown
Sr Prodn Designer, Storey Publishing: Erin Dawson
Sr Book Designer, Storey Publishing: Bredna Lago
Designer, Children's: Daniella Graner
Designer, Workman Kids: Molly Magnell
Imprint Sales Dir: Jennifer Trzaska
Sales Asst, Online & Digital: Gabriella Rubino
Founded: 1967
General nonfiction, calendars.
As of January 1, 2025, Workman Publishing & Running Press Group will merge to form Workman Running Press Group. Complete details were not available at the time of publication.
ISBN Prefix(es): 978-1-884822 (Black Dog & Leventhal); 978-1-57912 (Black Dog & Leventhal); 978-0-316 (Black Dog & Leventhal); 978-0-89480; 978-1-56305; 978-0-7611; 978-1-60376 (Black Dog & Leventhal); 978-1-63191 (Black Dog & Leventhal); 978-0-911104; 978-1-5235
Number of titles published annually: 345 Print
Imprints: Artisan; Black Dog & Leventhal; Storey Publishing; Timber Press; Workman; Workman Calendars; Workman Kids
Distributor for Erewhon Books; Familius
Foreign Rep(s): Bookreps New Zealand (New Zealand); Hardie Grant Books (Australia); Melia Publishing Services (Ireland, UK)
Foreign Rights: Big Apple Agency Inc (China, Taiwan); Graal Literary Agency (Poland); International Editors' Co (Brazil); International Editors' Co - Yanez Agencia Literaria (Latin America, Portugal, Spain); Japan UNI Agency (Japan); JLM Literary Agency (Greece); Katai & Bolza Literary Agency (Hungary); Alexander Korahenevski Agency (Russia); Korea Copyright Center Inc (KCC) (South Korea); Kristin Olson Literary Agency (Czechia); Mickey Pikarski (Israel); Sebes & Bisseling Literary Agency (Netherlands)
Returns: LSC Communications, Brighton Beach Rd, Menasha, WI 54952
Warehouse: LSC Communications, Book Fulfillment Serv, N9234 Lake Park Rd, Appleton, WI 54915
Membership(s): Association of American Publishers (AAP)

World Almanac®
Imprint of Skyhorse Publishing Inc
307 W 36 St, 11 fl, New York, NY 10018
SAN: 211-6944
Tel: 212-643-6816 *Fax:* 212-643-6819
E-mail: info@skyhorsepublishing.com
Web Site: skyhorsepublishing.com
Key Personnel
Exec Ed: Sarah Janssen
Founded: 1868
Annual juvenile & adult reference books.
ISBN Prefix(es): 978-1-60057
Number of titles published annually: 6 Print
Total Titles: 9 Print; 3 E-Book
Foreign Rep(s): Adnkronos Libri SRL (Italy)

§World Bank Publications
Member of The World Bank Group
1818 "H" St NW, Washington, DC 20433
Tel: 202-473-1000 *Toll Free Tel:* 800-645-7247 (cust serv)
E-mail: books@worldbank.org; pubrights@worldbank.org (foreign rts)
Web Site: www.worldbank.org/en/research
Founded: 1944
Publish over 200 new titles annually in support of the World Bank's mission to fight poverty & distributes them globally in both print & electronic formats; electronic online subscription database; international affairs.
ISBN Prefix(es): 978-0-8213
Number of titles published annually: 200 Print; 10 CD-ROM; 3 Online; 30 E-Book
Total Titles: 2,000 Print; 50 CD-ROM; 3 Online; 50 E-Book
Imprints: World Bank
Foreign Rep(s): Africa Connection (Guy Simpson) (South Africa, Sub-Saharan Africa); Bazaar (Nepal); Eurospan Group (Africa, Australasia, Central Asia, East Asia, Europe, Ireland, UK, Western Europe); Everest Media International Services (P) Ltd (Nepal); Far Eastern Booksellers (Japan); International Publishers Representatives (Middle East, North Africa); Korean Studies Information Co Ltd (South Korea); Jacek Lewinson (Eastern Europe); Marga Institute (Sri Lanka); Micro Industries Development Assistance & Services (MIDAS) (Bangladesh); Pak Book Corp (Pakistan); David Towle (Denmark, Finland, Iceland, Norway, Sweden); Viva Books Pvt Ltd (India)
Orders to: PO Box 960, Herndon, VA 20172-0960 *Tel:* 703-661-1580 *Fax:* 703-661-1501
Membership(s): Association of American Publishers (AAP)

§World Book Inc
Subsidiary of The Scott Fetzer Co
180 N LaSalle, Suite 900, Chicago, IL 60601
SAN: 201-4815
Tel: 312-729-5800 *Toll Free Tel:* 800-967-5325 (consumer sales, US); 800-975-3250 (school & lib sales, US); 800-837-5365 (school & lib sales, CN) *Toll Free Fax:* 888-922-3766
E-mail: customerservice@worldbook.com
Web Site: www.worldbook.com
Key Personnel
Pres: Geoff Broderick
VP, Edit: Tom Evans
VP, Intl & Mktg: Eddy Kisman
VP, Technol & Opers: Jason Dole
Regl Sales VP: Dennis McQuillan; Jeff Williamson
Dir, HR: Bev Ecker
Founded: 1917
Publisher of high-quality, award-winning, educational reference & nonfiction publications for the school & library market & home market, in print & online formats.
ISBN Prefix(es): 978-0-7166
Number of titles published annually: 40 Print
Total Titles: 350 Print; 10 Online

World Citizens
Affiliate of Cinema Investments Co Inc
PO Box 131, Mill Valley, CA 94942-0131
Tel: 415-380-8020; 415-233-2822 (direct)
Key Personnel
Ed-in-Chief: Joan Ellen
Ed: John Ballard
Assoc Ed: Jack Henry
Sales Mgr & Intl Rts: Steve Ames
Founded: 1984
Cross cultural & multicultural novels & texts. Adult, educational, trade & young adult divisions.
ISBN Prefix(es): 978-0-932279
Number of titles published annually: 6 Print; 4 CD-ROM; 6 E-Book; 4 Audio
Total Titles: 18 Print
Imprints: Classroom Classics; New Horizons Book Publishing Co; Skateman Publications
Distributed by Inland
Distribution Center: Baker & Taylor Publisher Services, 30 Amberwood Pkwy, Ashland, OH 44805 *Tel:* 567-215-0030 *Toll Free Tel:* 888-814-0208 *E-mail:* info@btpubservices.com *Web Site:* www.btpubservices.com

§World Resources Institute
10 "G" St NE, Suite 800, Washington, DC 20002
Tel: 202-729-7600 *Fax:* 202-729-7610
Web Site: www.wri.org
Key Personnel
Dir: Dan Lashof *E-mail:* dan.lashof@wri.org
Deputy Dir: Debbie Weyl *E-mail:* debbie.weyl@wri.org
Founded: 1982
Professional, scholarly & general interest publications, including energy, the environment, agriculture, forestry, natural resources, economics, geography, climate, biotechnology & development. Some titles co-published with university presses & commercial publishers.
ISBN Prefix(es): 978-0-915825; 978-1-56973
Number of titles published annually: 10 Print
Total Titles: 420 Print; 2 CD-ROM

§World Scientific Publishing Co Inc
27 Warren St, Suite 401-402, Hackensack, NJ 07601
Tel: 201-487-9655 *Fax:* 201-487-9656
E-mail: sales@wspc.com; mkt@wspc.com; editor@wspc.com; customercare@wspc.com
Web Site: www.worldscientific.com
Key Personnel
Chmn & Ed-in-Chief: K K Phuna
Group Mng Dir: Doreen Liu
Mng Dir: Max Phua
Founded: 1981
ISBN Prefix(es): 978-1-944659
Number of titles published annually: 600 Print
Total Titles: 12,000 Print
Foreign Office(s): World Scientific Publishing (Beijing), B1505, Caizhi International Bldg, No 18 Zhongguancun E Rd, Haidan District, Beijing 100083, China *Tel:* (010) 82601201 *E-mail:* wspbj@wspc.com
Global Consultancy (Shanghai) Pte Ltd, Shanghai Bund International Tower, Rm 2003, No 99, Huangpu Rd, Shanghai 200080, China *Tel:* (021) 6325-4982 *Fax:* (021) 6325-4985 *E-mail:* wspsh@wspc.com
World Scientific Publishing Co Pte Ltd, Theresienstr 66, 80333 Munich, Germany *Tel:* (089) 12414-770 *Fax:* (089) 12414-7710 *E-mail:* munich@wspc.com

World Scientific Publishing (HK) Co Ltd, PO Box 72482, Kowloon Central Post Office, Hong Kong, Hong Kong *Tel:* 2771 8791 *Fax:* 2771 8155 *E-mail:* wsphk@wspc.com

World Scientific Publishing Co Pte Ltd, No 16 SW Boag Rd, T Nagar, Chennai 600 017, India *Tel:* (044) 4207 1164 *Fax:* (044) 4206 5464

World Scientific Publishing Co, Kiriat Hatikshoret-Neve Ilan, Suite 226, Harei, 90850 Yehuda, Israel *Tel:* (054) 4403728 *Fax:* (02) 5791532; (02) 5791533 *E-mail:* rspindel@wspc.com

World Scientific Publishing Co, c/o Juritsusha, 15-20-502 Ichibancho, Chiyoda-ku, Tokyo 102-0082, Japan *Tel:* (080) 81080-6881 *E-mail:* wspc_japan@wspc.com

World Scientific Publishing Co Pte Ltd, 5 Toh Tuck Link, Singapore 596224, Singapore *Tel:* 6466 5775 *Fax:* 6467 7667 *E-mail:* wspc@wspc.com.sg

World Scientific Publishing Co Pte Ltd, 8F, No 162, Sec 4, Roosevelt Rd, Taipei 10091, Taiwan *Tel:* (02) 2369-1366 *Fax:* (02) 2366-0460 *E-mail:* wsptw@ms13.hinet.net

World Scientific Publishing (UK) Ltd, 57 Shelton St, London WC2H 9HE, United Kingdom *Tel:* (020) 7836 0888 *E-mail:* sales@wspc.co.uk

Distributor for The National Academies Press (Asia-Pacific exc Australia, Japan & New Zealand)
Warehouse: 46 Development Rd, Fitchburg, MA 01420

§World Trade Press LLC
616 E Eighth St, Suite 7, Traverse City, MI 49686
Tel: 707-778-1124 *Toll Free Tel:* 800-833-8586 *Fax:* 231-642-5300
Web Site: www.worldtradepress.com
Key Personnel
Publr & CEO: Edward G Hinkelman
 Tel: 707-778-1124 ext 204 *E-mail:* egh@worldtradepress.com
Founded: 1992
The Global Knowledge Company. Large-scale databases of country information for culture, business, travel, local living & food.
ISBN Prefix(es): 978-0-9631864; 978-1-885073
Number of titles published annually: 8 Print; 240 Online; 26 E-Book
Total Titles: 118 Print; 240 Online; 126 E-Book

World Tree Press, see Lotus Press

§Worth Publishers
Imprint of Macmillan Learning
One New York Plaza, 46th fl, New York, NY 10004
Tel: 212-576-9400; 212-375-7000
E-mail: press.inquiries@macmillan.com
Web Site: www.macmillanlearning.com/college/us
Founded: 1966
Social science texts for the higher education market & advanced high school courses.
ISBN Prefix(es): 978-1-57259; 978-1-4292; 978-0-7167
Number of titles published annually: 10 E-Book
Total Titles: 300 Print
Foreign Rep(s): Macmillan East Asia (China, Hong Kong, Indonesia, Philippines, Singapore, South Korea, Thailand, Vietnam); Macmillan Publishers (Taiwan); Palgrave Macmillan (Australia, New Zealand); Palgrave Macmillan UK (Africa, Caribbean, Europe, India, Japan, Latin America, Middle East, Pakistan, UK); USBD Distribution Sdn Bhd (Malaysia)
Orders to: MPS Distribution Center, 16365 James Madison Hwy (US Rte 15), Gordonsville, VA 22942 *Toll Free Tel:* 888-330-8477 *Toll Free Fax:* 800-672-2054 *E-mail:* orders@mpsvirginia.com

Returns: MPS Returns Center, 14301 Litchfield Dr, Orange, VA 22960
Warehouse: MPS Distribution Center, 16365 James Madison Hwy (US Rte 15), Gordonsville, VA 22942 *Toll Free Tel:* 888-330-8477 *Toll Free Fax:* 800-672-2054 (orders) *E-mail:* orders@mpsvirginia.com

§Write Stuff Enterprises LLC
1001 S Andrews Ave, Suite 200, Fort Lauderdale, FL 33316
Tel: 954-462-6657 *Fax:* 954-462-6023
E-mail: info@writestuffbooks.com
Web Site: www.writestuffbooks.com
Key Personnel
Founder, Chmn & CEO: Jeffrey L Rodengen
Pres, Publr & CFO: Marianne Roberts
Founded: 1986
Leading publisher of historical works focusing on industry & technology.
ISBN Prefix(es): 978-0-945903; 978-1-932022
Number of titles published annually: 4 Print; 4 E-Book
Imprints: Write Stuff®
Membership(s): American Booksellers Association (ABA); Independent Book Publishers Association (IBPA)

WriteLife Publishing
Imprint of Boutique of Quality Books Publishing
Wilkinson Pass Lane, Waynesville, NC 28786
E-mail: writelife@boutiqueofqualitybooks.com
Web Site: www.writelife.com; www.facebook.com/writelife
Key Personnel
Pres & Publr: Terri Leidich *E-mail:* terri@bqbpublishing.com
Acqs Ed: Allison Itterly
Soc Media/IT Mgr: John Daly
 E-mail: johndailybooks@hotmail.com
Founded: 2008
ISBN Prefix(es): 978-1-60808
Number of titles published annually: 12 Print; 12 E-Book
Total Titles: 90 Print; 90 E-Book
Membership(s): Independent Book Publishers Association (IBPA); Midwest Independent Booksellers Association (MIBA); Mountains & Plains Independent Booksellers Association (MPIBA)

Writer's AudioShop
1316 Overland Stage Rd, Dripping Springs, TX 78620
Tel: 512-476-1616
E-mail: wrtaudshop@aol.com
Web Site: www.writersaudio.com
Key Personnel
Publr: Elaine Davenport
Founded: 1985
Audio publisher.
ISBN Prefix(es): 978-1-880717
Number of titles published annually: 4 Audio
Total Titles: 35 Audio
Membership(s): Audio Publishers Association

Writer's Digest Books
Imprint of Penguin Publishing Group
1745 Broadway, New York, NY 10019
Tel: 212-782-9000
Web Site: sites.prh.com/writersdigestbooks
Top-quality instructional & reference books to help creative people find personal satisfaction & professional success. Topics covered include writing, publishing, songwriting & personal growth.
Penguin Random House & its publishing entities are not accepting unsol submissions, proposals, mss, or submission queries via e-mail at this time.
Number of titles published annually: 28 Print
Total Titles: 150 Print

Distribution Center: Two Rivers Distribution, 1400 Broadway, Suite 520, New York, NY 10018 *Toll Free Tel:* 866-400-5351 *E-mail:* ips@ingramcontent.com *Web Site:* www.tworiversdistribution.com

WRP, see Water Resources Publications LLC

§Wyndham Hall Press
10372 W Munro Lake Dr, Levering, MI 49755
SAN: 686-6743
Tel: 419-648-9124
E-mail: orders@wyndhamhallpress.com
Web Site: www.wyndhamhallpress.com
Key Personnel
Mng Ed: Mark S McCullough *E-mail:* mark@wyndhamhallpress.com
Founded: 1982
Scholarly monographs & textbooks.
ISBN Prefix(es): 978-1-55605; 978-0-932269
Number of titles published annually: 8 Print
Total Titles: 240 Print

§Xist Publishing
24200 Southwest Fwy, Suite 402, PMB 290, Rosenberg, TX 77471
Tel: 949-478-2568
E-mail: info@xistpublishing.com
Web Site: www.xistpublishing.com
Key Personnel
COO: Jacob Lee
Pres: Calee Lee
Founded: 2011
Creates books that inspire discovery & delight in toddlers through ten-year-olds.
ISBN Prefix(es): 978-1-62395; 978-1-5324
Number of titles published annually: 125 Print; 125 E-Book; 100 Audio
Total Titles: 890 Print; 1,900 E-Book; 800 Audio
Foreign Rep(s): Sylvia Hayse (worldwide)
Membership(s): Educational Book & Media Association (EBMA)

Xlibris Corp
Imprint of Author Solutions LLC
1663 Liberty Dr, Suite 200, Bloomington, IN 47403
Toll Free Tel: 844-714-8691; 888-795-4274 *Fax:* 610-915-0294
E-mail: info@xlibris.com; media@xlibris.com
Web Site: www.xlibris.com; www.authorsolutions.com/our-imprints/xlibris
Key Personnel
COO: Bill Becher
CIO: Joe Steinbach
Pres: Bill Elliott
Founded: 1997
One of the leading publishing services providers for authors, Xlibris provides authors with a broad set of publishing options including hardcover, trade paperback, custom leather bound & full-color formats. In addition, Xlibris offers its authors the widest selection of professional, marketing & bookselling services. Since its founding, Xlibris has published more than 25,000 titles.
This publisher has indicated that 100% of their product line is author subsidized.
ISBN Prefix(es): 978-0-7388; 978-0-9663501; 978-1-4010; 978-1-4134; 978-1-59926; 978-1-4257; 978-1-4363; 978-1-4415
Number of titles published annually: 5,100 Print
Total Titles: 25,000 Print
Distribution Center: Baker & Taylor LLC, 2550 W Tyvola Rd, Suite 300, Charlotte, NC 28217 *Tel:* 704-998-3100 *Toll Free Tel:* 800-775-1800 *Web Site:* www.baker-taylor.com
Ingram Book Group, One Ingram Blvd, La Vergne, TN 37086 *Tel:* 615-793-5000 *Web Site:* www.ingramcontent.com
Membership(s): American Booksellers Association (ABA)

§XML Press
Subsidiary of R L Hamilton & Associates LLC
458 Dallas St, Denver, CO 80230
SAN: 920-7481
Tel: 970-231-3624
E-mail: publisher@xmlpress.net
Web Site: xmlpress.net
Key Personnel
Publr: Richard Hamilton *E-mail:* hamilton@xmlpress.net
Founded: 2008
Specialize in publications for technical communicators, content strategists, managers & marketers, with an emphasis on XML technology, social media & management. Also provides publication services to corporations that want to make their technical documentation available in print form through retail channels.
ISBN Prefix(es): 978-0-9822191; 978-1-937434
Number of titles published annually: 12 Print; 12 E-Book
Total Titles: 35 Print; 33 E-Book
Distribution Center: Ingram, One Ingram Blvd, La Vergne, TN 37086
Membership(s): Association for Computing Machinery (ACM); Independent Book Publishers Association (IBPA); Society for Technical Communication (STC)

Yale Center for British Art
1080 Chapel St, New Haven, CT 06510-2302
Mailing Address: PO Box 208280, New Haven, CT 06520-8280
Tel: 203-432-8929 *Fax:* 203-432-1626
E-mail: ycba.publications@yale.edu
Web Site: britishart.yale.edu
Key Personnel
Dir: Courtney J Martin *E-mail:* ycba.director@yale.edu
Deputy Dir, Res, Exhibitions & Pubns: Martina Droth *Tel:* 203-432-2545 *E-mail:* martina.droth@yale.edu
Head, Exhibitions & Pubns: Nathan Flis *Tel:* 203-432-6774 *E-mail:* nathan.flis@yale.edu
Devt Ed & Pubns Mgr: Deborah Cannarella *Tel:* 203-432-2141 *E-mail:* deborah.cannarella@yale.edu
Ed: Christopher Lotis
Founded: 1977
Exhibition catalogues.
ISBN Prefix(es): 978-0-930606
Number of titles published annually: 4 Print
Total Titles: 61 Print

§Yale University Press
Division of Yale University
302 Temple St, New Haven, CT 06511-8909
SAN: 203-2740
Mailing Address: PO Box 209040, New Haven, CT 06520-9040
Tel: 203-432-0960; 203-432-0966 (sales); 401-531-2800 (cust serv) *Toll Free Tel:* 800-405-1619 (cust serv) *Fax:* 203-432-0948; 203-432-8485 (sales); 401-531-2801 (cust serv) *Toll Free Fax:* 800-406-9145 (cust serv)
E-mail: sales.press@yale.edu (sales); customer.care@triliteral.org (cust serv)
Web Site: www.yalebooks.com; yalepress.yale.edu/yupbooks
Key Personnel
COO: Kate Brown
Publr, Art & Architecture/Exec Dir, E-Portal: Patricia Fidler
Dir: John Donatich
Art Dir: Nancy Ovedovitz
Dir, Edit, Design & Prodn Opers: Jenya Weinreb
Dir, Ms Editing, Design & Prodn, Art Books: Kate Zanzucchi
Dir, Mktg & Promo: Heather D'Auria
Edit Dir: Seth Ditchik
Edit Dir, Art & Architecture: Katherine Boller
Publicity Dir: Brenda King
Sales Dir: Stephen Cebik
Deputy Dir, Fin: Timothy Haire
Sr Exec Ed, Sci & Medicine: Jean E Thomson Black
Mng Ed: Dorothea Halliday
Exec Ed: Jennifer Banks; Adina Popescu
Sr Ed, History: Adina Popescu Berk
Sr Ed: Jessie Kindig
Ed: Jaya Aninda Chatterjee
Ed, Classics & Ancient World: Heather Gold
Ed, Lang, Lit & Performing Arts: Sarah Miller
Assoc Ed, Art & Architecture: Amy Canonico
Asst Ed & Mktg Mgr: Travis Kimbel
Asst Ed: Abigail Storch
Educ Mktg Mgr: Debra Bozzi
Mgr, Ad & Exhibits: Ellen Freiler
Mktg Mgr, Art & Architecture: Jessica Holahan
Natl Accts Mgr: Marty Gosser
Sr Publicist: Jennifer Doerr; Liz Pelton; Robert Pranzatelli
Publicist: Roland Coffey; Caitlin Gallagher
Art Book Dist Partner Coord: Nick Geller
Founded: 1908
Scholarly publications.
ISBN Prefix(es): 978-0-300
Number of titles published annually: 350 Print
Total Titles: 5,000 Print
Imprints: Yale Press Audio
Foreign Office(s): 47 Bedford Sq, London WC1B 3DP, United Kingdom, Head, Rts: Olivia Willis *Tel:* (020) 7079-4900 *Fax:* (020) 7079-4901 *E-mail:* sales@yaleup.co.uk *Web Site:* www.yalebooks.co.uk
Distributed by W W Norton & Company Inc
Distributor for The Art Institute of Chicago; The Bard Graduate Center; Beinecke Rare Book & Manuscript Library; Dallas Museum of Art; Harvard University Art Museums; The Jewish Museum; Kimbell Art Museum; Paul Mellon Centre; The Menil Collection; Mercatorfonds; The Metropolitan Museum of Art; National Gallery, London; National Gallery of Art (Washington, DC); Philadelphia Museum of Art; Princeton University Art Museum; Sterling & Francine Clark Art Institute; Whitney Museum of American Art; Yale Center for British Art; Yale University Art Gallery
Foreign Rep(s): Craig Falk (Latin America); Mical Moser (Canada)
Shipping Address: TriLiteral LLC, 100 Maple Ridge Dr, Cumberland, RI 02864-1769 *Tel:* 401-658-4226
Membership(s): Association of American Publishers (AAP); Association of University Presses (AUPresses)

§Yard Dog Press
710 W Redbud Lane, Alma, AR 72921-7247
Tel: 479-632-4693 *Fax:* 479-632-4693
Web Site: www.yarddogpress.com
Key Personnel
Owner & Ed-in-Chief: Selina Rosen *E-mail:* selinarosen19@gmail.som
Tech Ed & Orders Contact: Lynn Rosen *E-mail:* lynnrosen52@gmail.com
Founded: 1995
Micro press specializing in science fiction, fantasy & horror. Closed to unsol submissions. Special pricing for bulk orders.
ISBN Prefix(es): 978-1-893687; 978-0-9824704; 978-1-937105; 978-1-945941
Number of titles published annually: 4 Print; 4 E-Book
Total Titles: 130 Print; 130 E-Book
Imprints: Double Dog (flip books - two short novels); Fantasy Writers' Asylum; Just Cause (non-genre books)

YBK Publishers Inc
39 Crosby St, New York, NY 10013
Tel: 212-219-0135
E-mail: readmybook@ybkpublishers.com; info@ybkpublishers.com
Web Site: www.ybkpublishers.com
Key Personnel
Pres: Otto Barz *E-mail:* obarz@ybkpublishers.com
Founded: 2001
General trade & nonfiction.
ISBN Prefix(es): 978-0-9703923; 978-0-9764359; 978-1-936411; 978-0-9790972; 978-0-9800508; 978-0-9824012
Number of titles published annually: 7 Print; 3 E-Book
Total Titles: 110 Print; 9 E-Book
Distribution Center: Lightning Source, 1246 Heil Quaker Blvd, La Vergne, TN 37086 *Tel:* 615-213-5815 *Fax:* 615-213-4426 *E-mail:* info@ybkpublishers.com
Membership(s): Association of American Publishers (AAP); PEN America

Yeshiva University Press
500 W 185 St, New York, NY 10033
Tel: 212-960-5400
Web Site: www.yu.edu/books
Key Personnel
Pres: Ari Berman *Tel:* 646-592-4300 *E-mail:* president@yu.edu
ISBN Prefix(es): 978-0-87068; 978-0-88125; 978-1-60280
Number of titles published annually: 10 Print
Total Titles: 71 Print

YMAA Publication Center Inc
PO Box 480, Wolfeboro, NH 03894
SAN: 665-2077
Tel: 603-569-7988 *Toll Free Tel:* 800-669-8892 *Fax:* 603-569-1889
E-mail: info@ymaa.com
Web Site: www.ymaa.com
Key Personnel
Publr: David Ripianzi
Prodn Mgr: Tim Comrie
Sales Rep: David Silver
Founded: 1984
Publisher of in-depth books, videos & DVDs on martial arts, meditation, traditional Chinese medicine & alternative health therapies.
ISBN Prefix(es): 978-0-940871; 978-1-886969; 978-1-59439
Number of titles published annually: 10 Print; 10 E-Book
Total Titles: 90 Print; 70 E-Book; 4 Audio
Distributor for Wind Records (Chinese healing music)
Foreign Rep(s): Big Apple Agency Inc (Maggie Han) (China, Taiwan); The Book Publishers Association of Israel (Shoshi Grajower) (Israel); Graal Literary Agency (Madga Cabajewska) (Poland); Imprima Korea Agency (Joseph Lee) (South Korea); International Copyright Agency (Simona Kessler) (Romania); International Editors' Co - Yanez Agencia Literaria (Mexico, Spain); Japan UNI Agency (Taeko Nagatsuka) (Japan); JS Literary & Media Agency (Somjai Raksasee) (Thailand); Nurcihan Kesim Literary Agency Ltd (Filiz Karaman) (Turkey); Maxima Creative Agency (Santo Manurung) (Indonesia); Nova Littera SL (Konstantin Paltchikov) (Russia); Andrew Nurnberg Associates (Tatjana Zoldnere) (Latvia, Lithuania, Ukraine); Andrew Nurnberg Associates (Anna Droumeva) (Bulgaria); Andrew Nurnberg Associates (Petra Tobiskova) (Czechia); OA Literary Agency (Michael Avramides) (Greece); Plima Literary Agency (Mila Perisic) (Croatia, Serbia, Slovenia); Schindler's Literary Agency (Suely Pedro Dos Santos) (Brazil); Ralph & Sheila Summers (Hong Kong, Malaysia, Philippines, Singapore, South Korea, Taiwan, Thailand); Tuttle-Mori Agency Inc (Fumi Nishijima) (Japan)
Foreign Rights: Agencia Literaria (Brazil, Portugal); Big Apple Agency Inc (China, Taiwan); Bookman (Denmark, Finland, Iceland, Norway, Sweden); Imprima Korea Agency (South Ko-

U.S. PUBLISHERS

rea); International Editors' Co - Yanez Agencia Literaria (Mexico, Spain, Spanish Latin America, Spanish-speaking countries); Jarir Bookstore (Egypt, Middle East, Saudi Arabia); JS Literary & Media Agency (Thailand); La Nouvelle Agency (Belgium, Switzerland); Nova Littera Ltd (Russia); Andrew Nurnberg Associates (Baltic States); Andrew Nurnberg Associates Sofia (Bulgaria); OA Literary Agency (Greece); Permissions & Rights (Albania, Croatia, Montenegro, Serbia, Slovenia); Tuttle-Mori Agency Inc (Japan)
Orders to: Baker & Taylor, 2550 W Tyvola Rd, Charlotte, NC *Toll Free Tel:* 800-775-1800 *Fax:* 704-998-3100 *Web Site:* www.baker-taylor.com; National Book Network, 15200 NBN Way, Blue Ridge Summit, PA 17214 *Tel:* 717-794-3800 *Toll Free Tel:* 800-462-6420 *Toll Free Fax:* 800-338-4550 *E-mail:* custserv@nbnbooks.com *Web Site:* www.nbnbooks.com; Ingram Book Co, One Ingram Blvd, La Vergne, TN *Tel:* (615) 793-5000 *Toll Free Tel:* 800-937-8200 *Web Site:* www.ingrambook.com; New Leaf Distributing Co, 1085 E Lotus Dr, Silver Lake, WI 53170 *Tel:* 262-889-8501 *Toll Free Tel:* 800-326-2665 *Fax:* 262-889-8598 *E-mail:* orders@newleafdist.com SAN: 169-1449
Distribution Center: National Book Network, 15200 NBN Way, Blue Ridge Summit, PA 07214 *Tel:* 717-794-3800 *Toll Free Tel:* 800-338-4550 *Toll Free Fax:* 800-338-4550 *E-mail:* custserv@nbnbooks.com *Web Site:* www.nbnbooks.com
Membership(s): American Booksellers Association (ABA); Independent Book Publishers Association (IBPA)

§Yotzeret Publishing
PO Box 18662, St Paul, MN 55118-0662
E-mail: info@yotzeretpublishing.com; orders@yotzeretpublishing.com
Web Site: yotzeretpublishing.com
Key Personnel
Publr: Sheyna Galyan *E-mail:* publisher@yotzeretpublishing.com
Founded: 2002
No longer open to submissions.
ISBN Prefix(es): 978-1-59287
Number of titles published annually: 2 Print; 2 E-Book; 1 Audio
Total Titles: 2 Print; 4 E-Book
Imprints: Andanyon Books; Soul Guides Books
Orders to: Itasca Books, 5120 Cedar Lake Rd, Minneapolis, MN 55416, Dist Mgr: Mark Jung *Tel:* 952-345-4488 *Toll Free Tel:* 800-901-3480 *Fax:* 952-920-0541 *E-mail:* orders@itascabooks.com *Web Site:* www.itascabooks.com
Distribution Center: Itasca Books, 5120 Cedar Lake Rd, Minneapolis, MN 55416, Dist Mgr: Mark Jung *Tel:* 952-342-4888 ext 118 *Toll Free Tel:* 800-901-3480 ext 118 *Fax:* 952-920-0541 *E-mail:* orders@itascabooks.com *Web Site:* www.itascabooks.com
Membership(s): Authors Alliance; Independent Book Publishers Association (IBPA); Midwest Independent Publishing Association (MIPA)

YWAM Publishing
Division of Youth With A Mission
PO Box 55787, Seattle, WA 98155-0787
Tel: 425-771-1153 *Toll Free Tel:* 800-922-2143
E-mail: books@ywampublishing.com; marketing@ywampublishing.com
Web Site: www.ywampublishing.com
Key Personnel
Mktg Dir: Wenche Warren
Founded: 1960
Books on missions, evangelism, discipleship & homeschooling.
ISBN Prefix(es): 978-0-927545
Number of titles published annually: 10 Print; 10 E-Book; 3 Audio
Total Titles: 370 Print; 15 CD-ROM; 85 E-Book; 85 Audio
Distributor for Emerald Books
Shipping Address: 7825 230 St SW, Edmonds, WA 98026
Warehouse: 7825 230 St SW, Edmonds, WA 98026

§Zagat Inc
Division of The Infatuation Inc
424 Broadway, 5th fl, New York, NY 10013
SAN: 289-4777
E-mail: feedback@zagat.com
Web Site: www.zagat.com
Key Personnel
Gen Mgr: Nell Potter *E-mail:* nell@theinfatuation.com
Ed, Zagat Stories: Chris Mohney *E-mail:* chris.mohney@zagat.com
Opers Coord: Katie Cohen *E-mail:* katie.cohen@theinfatuation.com
Founded: 1979
Provider of consumer survey-based information on where to eat, drink, stay & play worldwide.
ISBN Prefix(es): 978-1-57006; 978-1-60478
Number of titles published annually: 49 Online

Zaner-Bloser Inc
Subsidiary of Highlights for Children Inc
1400 Goodale Blvd, Suite 200, Grandview Heights, OH 43212
Mailing Address: PO Box 16764, Columbus, OH 43216-6764
Toll Free Tel: 800-421-3018 (cust serv) *Toll Free Fax:* 800-992-6087 (orders)
E-mail: customerexperience@zaner-bloser.com
Web Site: www.zaner-bloser.com
Key Personnel
Pres: Lisa Carmona
Founded: 1888
Elementary textbooks for critical thinking, whole language, substance abuse prevention, spelling & handwriting; modality (learning styles) kit, professional education books, storytelling kits & early childhood education.
ISBN Prefix(es): 978-0-88309; 978-0-88085
Number of titles published annually: 200 Print
Foreign Rep(s): Children's Press
Advertising Agency: EDPUB
Orders to: PO Box 16764, Columbus, OH 43216-6764
Returns: 10650 Toebben Dr, Independence, KY 41051
Warehouse: 4200 Parkway Ct, Hilliard, OH 43026

Zebra Books, see Kensington Publishing Corp

§Zeig, Tucker & Theisen Inc
2632 E Thomas Rd, Suite 201, Phoenix, AZ 85016
Tel: 480-389-4342
Web Site: www.zeigtucker.com
Key Personnel
Pres: Jeffrey K Zeig, PhD *E-mail:* jeff@erickson-foundation.org
Busn Mgr: Stacey Moore *E-mail:* stacey@erickson-foundation.org
Mng Ed: Chuck Lakin *E-mail:* chuck@zeigtucker.com
Edit: Suzi Tucker
Founded: 1998
Independent publisher in the behavioral sciences.
ISBN Prefix(es): 978-1-891944; 978-1-932462; 978-1-934442
Number of titles published annually: 10 Print
Total Titles: 45 Print; 8 Audio
Orders to: AIDCVT *Toll Free Tel:* 855-446-1222 *Fax:* 802-864-7626 *E-mail:* ztt.orders@aidcvt.com

Zest Books
Imprint of Lerner Publishing Group Inc
241 First Ave N, Minneapolis, MN 55401
Tel: 612-332-3344 *Toll Free Tel:* 800-328-4929 *Toll Free Fax:* 800-332-1132
E-mail: info@lernerbooks.com; publicity@lernerbooks.com; custserve@lernerbooks.com (orders)
Web Site: lernerbooks.com
Key Personnel
Chmn: Harry J Lerner
Pres & Publr: Adam Lerner
EVP & COO: Mark Budde
EVP & CFO: Margaret Thomas
EVP, Edit: Andy Cummings
EVP, Mktg: Rachel Zugschwert
EVP, Sales: David Wexler
Dir, Rts, Spec Sales & Intl Dist: Maria Kjoller
Edit Dir: Ashley Kuehl
Publg Dir, School & Lib: Jenny Krueger
School & Lib Mktg Dir: Lois Wallentine
Founded: 2006
ISBN Prefix(es): 978-0-9772660
Number of titles published annually: 5 Print; 20 E-Book
Total Titles: 125 Print; 275 E-Book
Foreign Rep(s): Bounce Sales & Marketing Ltd (UK); Phambili Agencies (Botswana, Lesotho, Namibia, South Africa); Publishers Marketing Services (Brunei, Malaysia, Singapore); Saunders Book Co (school & lib) (Canada)
Foreign Rights: Japan Foreign-Rights Centre (Japan); Korea Copyright Center Inc (KCC) (South Korea); Agence Michelle Lapautre (France); Literarische Agentur Silke Weniger (Germany)
Warehouse: 1251 Washington Ave N, Minneapolis, MN 55401, Mgr: Ken Rued

§Zondervan
Subsidiary of HarperCollins Christian Publishing
3900 Sparks Dr SE, Grand Rapids, MI 49546
SAN: 203-2694
Tel: 616-698-6900 *Toll Free Tel:* 800-226-1122; 800-727-1309 (retail orders) *Fax:* 616-698-3350 *Toll Free Fax:* 800-698-3256 (retail orders)
E-mail: customercare@harpercollins.com
Web Site: www.zondervan.com
Key Personnel
SVP & Publr, Zondervan Reflective & Zondervan Academic: Stanley N Gundry
SVP, Children's & Gift Group Publr: Laura Minchew
SVP, Sales: Dan Van Gorp
SVP, Sales & Centralized Mktg: Doug Lockhart
VP & Publr, Fiction: Amanda Bostic
VP & Publr, Gift Div: Jennifer Gott
VP & Publr, Zonderkidz: Megan Dobson
VP & Publr, Zondervan Academic: Katya Covrett
VP & Publr, Zondervan Bible Group: Melinda Bouma
VP & Publr, Zondervan Books & Zondervan Thrive: Webster Younce
VP & Publr, Zondervan Reflective & Study Resources: Ryan Pazdur
VP, Mktg, Zonderkidz: Sara Merritt
VP, Mktg, Zondervan Books: Mark Glesne
VP, Mktg, Zondervan Books & Zondervan Thrive: Paul Fisher
VP, Mktg, Zondervan Reflective & Zondervan Academic: Jesse Hillman
Assoc Publr: Keren Baltzer; Becky Monds
Sr Dir, Mktg: Kent Hendricks *E-mail:* kent.hendricks@harpercollins.com
Sr Dir, Mktg, Fiction Books: Nekasha Pratt
Sr Mktg Dir, ZonderKidz Bibles: Kevin Traub
PR Dir, Zondervan Books & Zondervan Thrive: Robin Barnett
Publicity Dir: Amanda Woods
Publicity Dir: Jessica Westra
Sr Acqs Ed: Andrea Palpant Dilley; Paul J Pastor
Sr Acqs Ed, Zondervan Books & Zondervan Thrive: Mick Silva

Sr Ed: Jodi Hughes
Sr Ed, Zondervan Academic & Zondervan Reflective: Matt Estel
Acqs Ed: Laura Wheeler
Acqs Ed, Fiction: Jocelyn Bailey
Acqs Ed, Nonfiction: Andy Rogers
Acqs Ed, Zonderkidz: Katherine Easter
Sr Mgr, PR, Zondervan Academic, Zondervan Reflective & Thomas Nelson & Zondervan Bibles: Amy Bigler
Sr Publicity Mgr, Zondervan Books & Zondervan Thrive: Trinity McFadden
Founded: 1931
A world leader in Christian communications & the leading Christian publishing brand. For more than 75 years, Zondervan has delivered transformational Christian experiences through general & academic resources authored by influential leaders & emerging voices & been honored with more Christian Book Awards than any other publisher. Headquartered in Grand Rapids, MI, with offices in San Diego & Miami, Zondervan conducts events & publishes its bestselling Bibles, books, audio, video, curriculum, software & digital products through its Zondervan, eZondervan, Zonderkidz, Youth Specialties, Editorial Vida & National Pastors Convention brands. Zondervan resources are sold worldwide through retail stores, online & by Zondervan ChurchSource & are translated into nearly 200 languages in more than 60 countries.
ISBN Prefix(es): 978-0-310
Number of titles published annually: 200 Print; 4 CD-ROM; 30 Online; 50 E-Book; 50 Audio
Total Titles: 5,000 Print; 30 CD-ROM; 300 Online; 300 E-Book; 400 Audio
Imprints: Zondervan Academic; Zondervan Reflective; Zondervan Thrive
Divisions: Zonderkidz
Returns: 2205 E Lincoln Way, La Porte, IN 46350
Membership(s): American Booksellers Association (ABA); Association of American Publishers (AAP); Audio Publishers Association; Better Business Bureau (BBB); Book Industry Study Group (BISG); Chamber of Commerce; Evangelical Christian Publishers Association (ECPA); Evangelical Press Association (EPA); International Christian Visual Media Association (ICVM); Society of Bible Literature (SBL); Society of Children's Book Writers & Illustrators (SCBWI); Software & Information Industry Association (SIIA)

Zone Books
633 Vanderbilt St, Brooklyn, NY 11218
Tel: 718-686-0048
E-mail: info@zonebooks.org
Web Site: www.zonebooks.org
Key Personnel
Mng Dir: Meighan Gale *E-mail:* mgale@zonebooks.org
Assoc Ed & Intl Rts Mgr: Kyra Simone
E-mail: ksimone@zonebooks.org
Founded: 1985
Publish books in the arts, humanities & social sciences.
ISBN Prefix(es): 978-0-942299; 978-1-890951
Number of titles published annually: 6 Print
Total Titles: 100 Print
Foreign Rights: Casanovas & Lynch Agencia Literaria (Maria Lynch) (Brazil, Portugal, Spain); English Agency Japan Co Ltd (Kohei Hattori) (Japan); Paul & Peter Fritz Agency (Antonia Fritz) (Germany); Graal Literary Agency (Paulina Machnik) (Eastern Europe); Imprima Korea Agency (Jehee Yun) (South Korea); Marotte et Compagnie (France); Stella Nelissen (Dutch-speaking countries); Reiser Agency (Roberto Gilodi) (Italy); Rightol Media Ltd (Alice Sun) (China, Southeast Asia)
Distribution Center: Princeton University Press, 41 William St, Princeton, NJ 08540 *Tel:* 609-258-4900 *Web Site:* www.press.princeton.edu

Zoobooks, see National Wildlife Federation

Zumaya Publications LLC
3209 S Interstate 35, Suite 1086, Austin, TX 78741
Tel: 512-333-4055 (scheduled calls only)
Fax: 512-276-6745
E-mail: publisher@zumayapublications.com; acquisitions@zumayapublications.com
Web Site: www.zumayapublications.com
Key Personnel
Publr & Exec Ed: Elizabeth K Burton
Founded: 2001
Trade paperback & ebook formats offering full-length works of fiction & nonfiction.
ISBN Prefix(es): 978-1-934135; 978-1-934841; 978-1-61271
Number of titles published annually: 20 Print; 20 E-Book
Total Titles: 200 Print; 200 E-Book
Imprints: Zumaya Arcane (true ghost stories, magic-based fiction); Zumaya Boundless (LGBTQA); Zumaya Embraces (romance, women's fiction); Zumaya Enigma (mystery, thriller); Zumaya Fabled Ink (graphic novels); Zumaya Otherworlds (science fiction, fantasy, dark fantasy/horror, paranormal mystery & suspense); Zumaya Thresholds (young adult, middle grade); Zumaya Yesterdays (historical fiction & mysteries)
Distribution Center: Ingram/Lightning Source, One Ingram Blvd, La Vergne, TN 37086 *Toll Free Tel:* 800-509-4156
Membership(s): Independent Book Publishers Association (IBPA)

U.S. Publishers — Geographic Index

ALABAMA

AdventureKEEN, pg 5
Blue Book Publications Inc, pg 32
Fiction Collective 2 (FC2), pg 71
Fifth Estate Publishing, pg 71
Iron Stream Media, pg 104
Livingston Press, pg 119
Menasha Ridge Press, pg 129
NewSouth Books, pg 141
River City Publishing, pg 175
University of Alabama Press, pg 214
Ludwig von Mises Institute, pg 225

ALASKA

Alaska Native Language Center (ANLC), pg 6
Publication Consultants, pg 167
University of Alaska Press, pg 214

ARIZONA

ACMRS Press, pg 4
African American Images Inc (AAI), pg 5
American Federation of Astrologers Inc, pg 9
Excalibur Publications, pg 68
Golden West Cookbooks, pg 79
Hohm Press, pg 93
In the Garden Publishing, pg 99
Lawyers & Judges Publishing Co Inc, pg 113
Light Technology Publishing LLC, pg 116
Olde & Oppenheim Publishers, pg 146
The Original Falcon Press, pg 148
Pathfinder Publishing Inc, pg 152
Poisoned Pen Press, pg 161
Ravenhawk™ Books, pg 172
Rio Nuevo Publishers, pg 175
Salina Bookshelf Inc, pg 181
Schaffner Press, pg 183
Story Monsters LLC, pg 199
Summertime Publications Inc, pg 200
TSG Publishing Foundation Inc, pg 210
The University of Arizona Press, pg 214
Westernlore Press, pg 228
Wide World of Maps Inc, pg 229
Zeig, Tucker & Theisen Inc, pg 236

ARKANSAS

Cornerstone Book Publishers, pg 53
Leisure Arts Inc, pg 114
Master Books®, pg 126
New Leaf Press, pg 140
Ozark Mountain Publishing Inc, pg 149
Pen-L Publishing, pg 153
The University of Arkansas Press, pg 214
Yard Dog Press, pg 235

CALIFORNIA

AAAI Press, pg 1
ABC-CLIO, pg 2
AK Press, pg 6
All About Kids Publishing, pg 7
American Carriage House Publishing (ACHP), pg 8
AMMO Books LLC, pg 13
Angel City Press, pg 14
Annual Reviews, pg 14
ANR Publications University of California, pg 14
The Apocryphile Press, pg 15
Apogee Press, pg 15
Ariadne Press, pg 16
The Arion Press, pg 16
The Astronomical Society of the Pacific, pg 20
Atlas Publishing, pg 21
Baby Tattoo Books, pg 23
Bancroft Press, pg 24
Bear & Bobcat Books, pg 26
Bellerophon Books, pg 27
BePuzzled, pg 28
Berrett-Koehler Publishers Inc, pg 29
Bhaktivedanta Book Trust (BBT), pg 29
BiG GUY BOOKS, pg 29
Bitingduck Press LLC, pg 30
Bluestocking Press, pg 33
BNi Building News, pg 33
The Book Tree, pg 34
BOOM! Studios, pg 34
Boson Books™, pg 34
Bridge Publications Inc, pg 36
C&T Publishing Inc, pg 40
Capen Publishing Co Inc, pg 40
Capitol Enquiry Inc, pg 40
The Center for Learning, pg 43
Center for the Collaborative Classroom, pg 44
Centerstream Publishing LLC, pg 44
Cherry Hill Publishing LLC, pg 46
China Books, pg 47
Chronicle Books LLC, pg 47
City Lights Publishers, pg 48
Coaches Choice, pg 50
Corwin, pg 53
Cotsen Institute of Archaeology Press, pg 53
Counterpoint Press LLC, pg 54
Craftsman Book Co, pg 54
Creston Books, pg 55
Crystal Clarity Publishers, pg 56
CSLI Publications, pg 56
Cypress House, pg 56
Davies Publishing Inc, pg 57
The Dawn Horse Press, pg 57
DawnSignPress, pg 58
DC Comics Inc, pg 58
Delphinium Books, pg 58
DeVorss & Co, pg 59
Dharma Publishing, pg 59
Disney-Hyperion Books, pg 59
Disney Press, pg 59
Disney Publishing Worldwide, pg 60
Dissertation.com, pg 60
East West Discovery Press, pg 63
Educational Insights®, pg 64
Edupress Inc, pg 64
Elite Books, pg 65
Energy Psychology Press, pg 66
Evan-Moor Educational Publishers, pg 68
Familius, pg 69
Walter Foster Publishing, pg 74
Fowler Museum at UCLA, pg 74
Galaxy Press Inc, pg 75
Gateways Books & Tapes, pg 77
Getty Publications, pg 78
Gingko Press Inc, pg 78
Grand & Archer Publishing, pg 80
Green Integer, pg 81
Hameray Publishing Group Inc, pg 84
Harvard Square Editions, pg 88
Hay House LLC, pg 89
Haynes North America Inc, pg 89
HeartMath LLC, pg 90
Heyday, pg 91
Hollym International Corp, pg 94
Hoover Institution Press, pg 95
Ignatius Press, pg 98
Immedium, pg 99
Independent Institute, pg 99
Insight Editions, pg 101
Institute of Governmental Studies, pg 101
International Code Council Inc, pg 102
Jain Publishing Co, pg 105
Kelsey Street Press, pg 108
LAMA Books, pg 112
LARB Books, pg 113
Linden Publishing Co Inc, pg 117
Living Stream Ministry (LSM), pg 119
The Lockman Foundation, pg 119
Lonely Planet Publications Inc, pg 120
Long River Press, pg 120
Lutheran Braille Workers Inc, pg 121
Mandala Earth, pg 124
Manic D Press Inc, pg 124
Math Solutions®, pg 127
Mazda Publishers Inc, pg 127
McSweeney's Publishing, pg 128
Mike Murach & Associates Inc, pg 131
National Center For Employee Ownership (NCEO), pg 137
National Notary Association (NNA), pg 138
New Harbinger Publications Inc, pg 140
New World Library, pg 140
Nilgiri Press, pg 141
No Starch Press, pg 141
NOLO, pg 141
North Atlantic Books (NAB), pg 142
Nova Press, pg 144
Nystrom Education, pg 144
Omnidawn, pg 146
One On One Book Publishing/Film-Video Publications, pg 146
O'Reilly Media Inc, pg 147
ORO editions, pg 148
Paradise Cay Publications Inc, pg 151
Parallax Press, pg 151
Park Place Publications, pg 152
Peachpit Press, pg 153
Peradam Press, pg 158
Piano Press, pg 159
The Picasso Project, pg 160
Plowshare Media, pg 161
Practice Management Information Corp (PMIC), pg 163
PRB Productions, pg 163
The Press at California State University, Fresno, pg 163
Progressive Press, pg 165
ProStar Publications Inc, pg 166
Quite Specific Media Group Ltd, pg 168
RAND Corp, pg 169
Red Hen Press, pg 172
ReferencePoint Press Inc, pg 173
Regent Press Printers & Publishers, pg 174
Remember Point Inc, pg 174
Ronin Publishing Inc, pg 176
Ross Books, pg 177
Saddleback Educational Publishing, pg 179
Safari Press, pg 179
SAGE Publishing, pg 180
St Herman Press, pg 180
San Diego State University Press, pg 182
Santa Monica Press LLC, pg 182
Self-Realization Fellowship Publishers, pg 186
Silman-James Press Inc, pg 188
Solano Press Books, pg 193
Sound Feelings Publishing, pg 194
Sourced Media Books, pg 195
Soyinfo Center, pg 196
Stanford University Press, pg 197
Star Publishing Co Inc, pg 197
Stargazer Publishing Co, pg 197
Stone Bridge Press Inc, pg 199
Stone Pier Press, pg 199
Sunbelt Publications Inc, pg 200
Tachyon Publications LLC, pg 202
Taschen America, pg 203
Teacher Created Resources Inc, pg 203
Ten Speed Press, pg 204
Theosophical University Press, pg 206
Tortuga Press, pg 208
Tracks Publishing, pg 208
Travelers' Tales, pg 209
Treasure Bay Inc, pg 209
UCLA Latin American Center Publications, pg 212
Unarius Academy of Science Publications, pg 212
Univelt Inc, pg 213
Universal-Publishers Inc, pg 213
University of California Institute on Global Conflict & Cooperation, pg 215
University of California Press, pg 215
Vedanta Press, pg 224
Velazquez Press, pg 224
Watson-Guptill, pg 226
Wide World Publishing, pg 229
Michael Wiese Productions, pg 229
Wilshire Book Co, pg 230
Alan Wofsy Fine Arts, pg 231
Wolfman Books, pg 232
World Citizens, pg 233

COLORADO

Acres USA, pg 4
Alfred Music, pg 6
American Alpine Club, pg 8
American Water Works Association (AWWA), pg 13
APC Publishing, pg 15

Blue Mountain Arts Inc, pg 32
Brewers Publications, pg 36
Bull Publishing Co, pg 38
The Child's World Inc, pg 46
David C Cook, pg 52
Counterpath Press, pg 54
Filter Press LLC, pg 71
Focus on the Family, pg 73
Fulcrum Publishing Inc, pg 75
The Geological Society of America Inc (GSA), pg 77
Group Publishing Inc, pg 82
Interweave Press LLC, pg 104
Iron Gate Publishing, pg 104
Kumarian Press, pg 112
Life Cycle Books, pg 116
Medical Group Management Association (MGMA), pg 128
Meriwether Publishing, pg 129
Morton Publishing Co, pg 134
Multnomah, pg 135
National Conference of State Legislatures (NCSL), pg 137
National Institute for Trial Advocacy (NITA), pg 138
NavPress Publishing Group, pg 139
Odyssey Books, pg 145
On the Write Path Publishing, pg 146
Peterson's, pg 158
Lynne Rienner Publishers Inc, pg 174
Rocky Mountain Mineral Law Foundation, pg 176
Roman Catholic Books, pg 176
Sentient Publications LLC, pg 186
Shambhala Publications Inc, pg 187
Snow Lion, pg 192
Society for Mining, Metallurgy & Exploration, pg 192
Sounds True Inc, pg 194
Standard Publishing, pg 197
Temporal Mechanical Press, pg 204
University Press of Colorado, pg 221
Water Resources Publications LLC, pg 226
WaterBrook, pg 226
Western Reflections Publishing Co, pg 228
William Carey Publishing, pg 230
XML Press, pg 235

CONNECTICUT

Applause Theatre & Cinema Books, pg 15
Begell House Inc Publishers, pg 27
Biographical Publishing Co, pg 29
Book Marketing Works LLC, pg 33
Chickadee Prince Books LLC, pg 46
The Connecticut Law Tribune, pg 52
The Globe Pequot Press, pg 79
The Graduate Group/Booksellers, pg 80
Guideposts Book & Inspirational Media, pg 82
Hannacroix Creek Books Inc, pg 85
Hutton Publishing, pg 97
Industrial Press Inc, pg 100
Konecky & Konecky LLC, pg 111
Limelight Editions, pg 117
The Lyons Press, pg 121
Mandel Vilar Press, pg 124
McBooks Press, pg 127
Parachute Publishing LLC, pg 151
Pineapple Press, pg 160
Rothstein Associates Inc, pg 177
Strategic Book Publishing (SBP), pg 199
Tantor Media Inc, pg 202
Taunton Books, pg 203
Tide-mark Press, pg 207
Tiger Tales, pg 207
The Toby Press LLC, pg 207
Twenty-Third Publications, pg 211
US Games Systems Inc, pg 223
Wesleyan University Press, pg 227
Yale Center for British Art, pg 235
Yale University Press, pg 235

DELAWARE

Cedar Tree Books, pg 43
Facts On File, pg 69
International Literacy Association (ILA), pg 103
LinguaText LLC, pg 117
Oak Knoll Press, pg 144
University of Delaware Press, pg 215
Vernon Press, pg 224
Winterthur Museum, Garden & Library, pg 231

DISTRICT OF COLUMBIA

Academica Press, pg 3
ACS Publications, pg 4
The AEI Press, pg 5
American Association of Collegiate Registrars & Admissions Officers (AACRAO), pg 8
American Council on Education (ACE), pg 9
American Geophysical Union (AGU), pg 10
American Historical Association (AHA), pg 10
American Psychiatric Association Publishing, pg 11
American Psychological Association, pg 11
ASM Publishing, pg 19
Association of Research Libraries (ARL), pg 20
BoardSource, pg 33
The Brookings Institution Press, pg 37
BuilderBooks, pg 38
Business Research Services Inc, pg 38
The Catholic University of America Press, pg 42
Cato Institute, pg 42
Center for Strategic & International Studies (CSIS), pg 44
Child Welfare League of America (CWLA), pg 46
Council for Research in Values & Philosophy, pg 53
CQ Press, pg 54
Dumbarton Oaks, pg 62
Environmental Law Institute, pg 67
Gallaudet University Press, pg 76
Georgetown University Press, pg 77
The Heritage Foundation, pg 91
Housing Assistance Council, pg 97
Hudson Institute, pg 97
IEEE Computer Society, pg 98
Inter-American Development Bank, pg 102
International City/County Management Association (ICMA), pg 102
International Food Policy Research Institute, pg 103
International Monetary Fund (IMF), Editorial & Publications Division, pg 103
Island Press, pg 104
Just World Books LLC, pg 107
The Mathematical Association of America, pg 127
NASW Press, pg 136
National Academies Press (NAP), pg 136
National Association of Broadcasters (NAB), pg 136
National Education Association (NEA), pg 137
National Gallery of Art, pg 137
National Geographic Books, pg 137
OECD Washington Center, pg 145
Peterson Institute for International Economics (PIIE), pg 158
Platypus Media LLC, pg 160
Police Executive Research Forum, pg 162
Public Citizen, pg 167
Regnery Publishing, pg 174
Science, Naturally, pg 185
Smithsonian Institution Scholarly Press, pg 192
Transportation Research Board (TRB), pg 209
United States Holocaust Memorial Museum, pg 213
United States Institute of Peace Press, pg 213
US Conference of Catholic Bishops, pg 223
US Government Publishing Office (GPO), pg 223
Woodrow Wilson Center Press, pg 232
World Bank Publications, pg 233
World Resources Institute, pg 233

FLORIDA

A 2 Z Press LLC, pg 1
Anhinga Press Inc, pg 14
Atlantic Publishing Group Inc, pg 21
Ballinger Publishing, pg 24
Barringer Publishing, pg 24
BearManor Media, pg 26
Bella Books, pg 27
Bisk Education, pg 29
Blue Note Publications Inc, pg 32
Bridge Logos Inc, pg 36
Chain Store Guide (CSG), pg 44
Charisma Media, pg 45
Comex Systems Inc, pg 51
Consumer Press, pg 52
CRC Press, pg 55
Editorial Bautista Independiente, pg 63
Editorial Unilit, pg 64
Father & Son Publishing Inc, pg 70
FJH Music Co Inc, pg 72
Frederick Fell Publishers Inc, pg 74
Gatekeeper Press, pg 77
Global Authors Publications (GAP), pg 78
Green Dragon Books, pg 81
Health Communications Inc, pg 89
Institute of Police Technology & Management (IPTM), pg 102
Italics Publishing, pg 105
Krieger Publishing Co, pg 111
THE Learning Connection®, pg 113
Lost Classics Book Company LLC, pg 120
LRP Publications, pg 121
MedMaster Inc, pg 129
Richard K Miller Associates, pg 132
Mitchell Lane Publishers Inc, pg 133
National Golf Foundation, pg 138
Oceanview Publishing Inc, pg 145
Palm Island Press, pg 150
Pants On Fire Press, pg 150
Papercutz, pg 150
Professional Resource Press, pg 165
Psychological Assessment Resources Inc (PAR), pg 166
Signalman Publishing, pg 187
Society of Environmental Toxicology & Chemistry (SETAC), pg 192
StarGroup International Inc, pg 197
STOCKCERO Inc, pg 199
Todd Publications, pg 207
University Press of Florida, pg 221
UnKnownTruths.com Publishing Co, pg 222
Vandamere Press, pg 223
Wellington Press, pg 227
Write Stuff Enterprises LLC, pg 234

GEORGIA

AllWrite Publishing, pg 7
Ariel Press, pg 16
August House Inc, pg 22
Frederic C Beil Publisher Inc, pg 27
BookLogix, pg 34
Brentwood Christian Press, pg 36
Clarity Press Inc, pg 49
FC&A Publishing, pg 70
Gallopade International Inc, pg 76
Mercer University Press, pg 129
New Concepts Publishing, pg 139
NRP Direct, pg 144
Peachtree Publishing Co Inc, pg 153
Rising Sun Publishing, pg 175
Rowe Publishing LLC, pg 178
SBL Press, pg 183
Smyth & Helwys Publishing Inc, pg 192
The Story Plant, pg 199
Stress Free Kids®, pg 200
University of Georgia Press, pg 216
Williams & Company Book Publishers, pg 230

HAWAII

Bess Press Inc, pg 29
Easy Money Press, pg 63
Kamehameha Publishing, pg 108
Mutual Publishing LLC, pg 136
Savant Books & Publications LLC, pg 182
University of Hawaii Press, pg 216
Watermark Publishing, pg 226

IDAHO

Caxton Press, pg 42
LRS, pg 121
Pacific Press® Publishing Association, pg 149

ILLINOIS

Academy Chicago Publishers, pg 3
Academy of Nutrition & Dietetics, pg 3
ACTA Publications, pg 4
Adventures Unlimited Press (AUP), pg 5
ALA Neal-Schuman, pg 6
Albert Whitman & Company, pg 6
American Academy of Pediatrics, pg 8
American Bar Association Publishing, pg 8
American Catholic Press (ACP), pg 9
American College of Surgeons, pg 9
The American Library Association (ALA), pg 10
American Medical Association (AMA), pg 11

American Technical Publishers, pg 13
Appraisal Institute, pg 15
The Art Institute of Chicago, pg 17
ASCP Press, pg 18
Association of College & Research Libraries (ACRL), pg 19
Baha'i Publishing Trust, pg 23
Bolchazy-Carducci Publishers Inc, pg 33
Brethren Press, pg 36
CCH, a Wolters Kluwer business, pg 42
Chicago Review Press, pg 46
Christian Liberty Press, pg 47
Crossway, pg 56
Dramatic Publishing Co, pg 61
Encyclopaedia Britannica Inc, pg 66
GIA Publications Inc, pg 78
Global Publishing Solutions LLC, pg 79
Goodheart-Willcox Publisher, pg 79
Health Administration Press, pg 89
Health Forum Inc, pg 90
Heimburger House Publishing Co, pg 90
Hendrickson Publishers Inc, pg 91
High Tide Press, pg 92
Hope Publishing Co, pg 95
Houghton Mifflin Harcourt Assessments, pg 96
Human Kinetics Inc, pg 97
Illinois State Museum Society, pg 99
Incentive Publications by World Book, pg 99
Institute of Environmental Sciences & Technology - IEST, pg 101
InterVarsity Press, pg 104
Joshua Tree Publishing, pg 107
Kazi Publications Inc, pg 108
The Lentz Leadership Institute LLC, pg 115
Liturgy Training Publications, pg 119
Loyola Press, pg 121
me+mi publishing inc, pg 128
Moody Publishers, pg 134
National Council of Teachers of English (NCTE), pg 137
Northwestern University Press, pg 143
OAG Worldwide, pg 144
Oriental Institute Publications, pg 148
Path Press Inc, pg 152
Pieces of Learning Inc, pg 160
Planners Press, pg 160
Publications International Ltd (PIL), pg 167
Quintessence Publishing Co Inc, pg 168
Rand McNally, pg 169
Regular Baptist Press, pg 174
Research Press, pg 174
Round Table Companies, pg 177
Sagamore Publishing LLC, pg 179
Serindia Publications, pg 186
Society of American Archivists, pg 192
Sourcebooks LLC, pg 194
Southern Illinois University Press, pg 195
Stipes Publishing LLC, pg 198
Surrey Books, pg 201
Swan Isle Press, pg 201
Third World Press Foundation, pg 206
Charles C Thomas Publisher Ltd, pg 206
Transcontinental Music Publications (TMP), pg 209
TriQuarterly Books, pg 209
Triumph Books LLC, pg 209
Tyndale House Publishers Inc, pg 211
University of Chicago Press, pg 215
University of Illinois Press, pg 216
Waveland Press Inc, pg 226
Wolters Kluwer US Corp, pg 232
World Book Inc, pg 233

INDIANA

Ancient Faith Publishing, pg 13
AuthorHouse, pg 22
Ave Maria Press Inc, pg 22
Cricket Cottage Publishing LLC, pg 55
Friends United Press, pg 75
Hackett Publishing Co Inc, pg 83
Hilton Publishing Co, pg 92
Idyll Arbor Inc, pg 98
Indiana Historical Society Press, pg 99
Indiana University African Studies Program, pg 100
Indiana University Press, pg 100
iUniverse, pg 105
Liberty Fund Inc, pg 116
The Mongolia Society Inc, pg 133
Our Sunday Visitor Publishing, pg 148
Purdue University Press, pg 167
The Rough Notes Co Inc, pg 177
St Augustine's Press Inc, pg 180
SAMS Technical Publishing LLC, pg 181
Solution Tree, pg 193
Tanglewood Publishing, pg 202
Trafford Publishing, pg 208
University of Notre Dame Press, pg 219
Warner Press, pg 226
Wesleyan Publishing House, pg 227
Winters Publishing, pg 231
Xlibris Corp, pg 234

IOWA

Brooklyn Publishers LLC, pg 37
Dordt Press, pg 60
Hearts 'n Tummies Cookbook Co, pg 90
Heuer Publishing LLC, pg 91
JIST Publishing, pg 106
Kendall Hunt Publishing Co, pg 108
Maharishi International University Press, pg 123
Penfield Books, pg 154
Perfection Learning®, pg 158
Quixote Press, pg 169
University of Iowa Press, pg 216

KANSAS

Angelus Press, pg 14
Ascend Books LLC, pg 18
SkillPath Publications, pg 190
University Press of Kansas, pg 221

KENTUCKY

American Quilter's Society (AQS), pg 12
APH Press, pg 15
Clerisy Press, pg 49
The Council of State Governments, pg 53
Fons Vitae, pg 73
Gifted Unlimited LLC, pg 78
The National Underwriter Co, pg 138
Presbyterian Publishing Corp (PPC), pg 163
Purple House Press, pg 167
Rod & Staff Publishers Inc, pg 176
Sarabande Books Inc, pg 182
The Jesse Stuart Foundation (JSF), pg 200
The University Press of Kentucky, pg 222
Westminster John Knox Press (WJK), pg 228

LOUISIANA

Ampersand Inc/Professional Publishing Services, pg 13
The Historic New Orleans Collection, pg 93
Louisiana State University Press, pg 120
Marine Education Textbooks, pg 125
Pelican Publishing, pg 153
University of Louisiana at Lafayette Press, pg 217
University of New Orleans Press, pg 218

MAINE

All Things That Matter Press, pg 7
John Benjamins Publishing Co, pg 28
Child's Play® Inc, pg 46
Goose River Press, pg 79
Islandport Press, pg 105
Alice James Books, pg 105
Light-Beams Publishing, pg 116
Marine Techniques Publishing, pg 125
North Country Press, pg 142
Polar Bear & Company, pg 161
Thorndike Press®, pg 206
Tilbury House Publishers, pg 207
Tower Publishing Co, pg 208
Walch Education, pg 225
Wayside Publishing, pg 227

MARYLAND

Amadeus Press, pg 7
American Academy of Environmental Engineers & Scientists®, pg 8
American Fisheries Society, pg 9
AOTA Press, pg 14
Jason Aronson Inc, pg 17
Association for the Advancement of Blood & Biotherapies, pg 19
Bartleby Press, pg 24
Bernan, pg 28
Black Classic Press, pg 30
Paul H Brookes Publishing Co Inc, pg 37
Clearfield Co Inc, pg 49
Data Trace Publishing Co (DTP), pg 57
Down East Books, pg 61
Entomological Society of America, pg 67
M Evans & Company, pg 68
Genealogical Publishing Co, pg 77
Hamilton Books, pg 84
Health Professions Press, pg 90
Heritage Books Inc, pg 91
Ibex Publishers, pg 98
Jhpiego, pg 106
Johns Hopkins University Press, pg 106
Lanahan Publishers Inc, pg 112
Lederer Books, pg 114
Lexington Books, pg 115
Mage Publishers Inc, pg 123
Maryland Center for History & Culture (MCHC), pg 126
Maryland History Press, pg 126
Messianic Jewish Publishers, pg 130
Midnight Marquee Press Inc, pg 130
National Information Standards Organization (NISO), pg 138
Naval Institute Press, pg 139
Nursesbooks.org, The Publishing Program of ANA, pg 144
Optometric Extension Program Foundation (OEPF), pg 147
Recorded Books Inc, an RBmedia company, pg 172
Rowman & Littlefield, pg 178
Schreiber Publishing, pg 185
Scripta Humanistica Publishing International, pg 185
Teaching Strategies LLC, pg 204
Teora USA LLC, pg 204
United States Pharmacopeia (USP), pg 213
University Press of America Inc, pg 221
Wildside Press LLC, pg 229
Woodbine House, pg 232

MASSACHUSETTS

Academic Press, pg 3
Adams Media, pg 4
American Institute for Economic Research (AIER), pg 10
American Press, pg 11
Appalachian Mountain Club Books, pg 15
Artech House®, pg 17
Avotaynu Books LLC, pg 23
Barefoot Books, pg 24
Beacon Press, pg 25
Bentley Publishers, pg 28
Berkshire Publishing Group LLC, pg 28
Blue Crane Books Inc, pg 32
Nicholas Brealey Publishing, pg 36
Brill Inc, pg 37
Brookline Books, pg 37
Candlewick Press, pg 39
Cengage Learning, pg 43
Charles River Media, pg 45
Charlesbridge Publishing Inc, pg 45
Cheng & Tsui Co Inc, pg 46
The Christian Science Publishing Society, pg 47
Walter De Gruyter Inc, pg 58
Edward Elgar Publishing Inc, pg 65
EPS School Specialty, pg 67
Fair Winds Press, pg 69
Federal Street Press, pg 70
Focus, pg 73
Godine, pg 79
Hampton Roads Publishing, pg 84
Harvard Art Museums, pg 87
Harvard Business Review Press, pg 87
Harvard Common Press, pg 87
Harvard Education Publishing Group, pg 88
Harvard Ukrainian Research Institute, pg 88
Harvard University Press, pg 88
Hogrefe Publishing Corp, pg 93
Holy Cross Orthodox Press, pg 95
Houghton Mifflin Harcourt, pg 95
Houghton Mifflin Harcourt K-12 Publishers, pg 96
Houghton Mifflin Harcourt Trade & Reference Division, pg 96
HRD Press, pg 97
Information Gatekeepers Inc (IGI), pg 100
Institute of Jesuit Sources (IJS), pg 102
Interlink Publishing Group Inc, pg 102

U.S. PUBLISHERS — GEOGRAPHIC INDEX

International Press of Boston Inc, pg 103
Jones & Bartlett Learning LLC, pg 107
Management Advisory Services & Publications (MASP), pg 123
Management Sciences for Health, pg 123
The Massachusetts Historical Society, pg 126
R S Means from The Gordian Group, pg 128
Merriam-Webster Inc, pg 129
MFA Publications, pg 130
MIT List Visual Arts Center, pg 132
The MIT Press, pg 132
Modern Memoirs Inc, pg 133
Morgan Kaufmann, pg 134
De Gruyter Mouton, pg 135
National Braille Press, pg 137
National Geographic Learning, pg 138
Newbury Street Press, pg 141
North River Press Publishing Corp, pg 142
Nosy Crow Inc, pg 144
Paraclete Press Inc, pg 151
Pauline Books & Media, pg 152
Peabody Museum Press, pg 153
Pearson Learning Solutions, pg 153
Ploughshares, pg 161
PSMJ Resources Inc, pg 166
Pyncheon House, pg 167
Quarto Publishing Group USA Inc, pg 168
Red Chair Press, pg 172
Red Wheel/Weiser, pg 173
Satya House Publications, pg 182
Science History Publications USA Inc, pg 185
Silver Leaf Books LLC, pg 188
Skinner House Books, pg 190
Small Beer Press, pg 191
Somerset Hall Press, pg 193
Standard Publishing Corp, pg 197
Star Bright Books Inc, pg 197
SteinerBooks Inc, pg 198
Sundance/Newbridge Publishing, pg 200
Tapestry Press Ltd, pg 202
Tumblehome Learning Inc, pg 210
Tupelo Press Inc, pg 210
University of Massachusetts Press, pg 217
Wisdom Publications Inc, pg 231
Workers Compensation Research Institute, pg 232

MICHIGAN

Alexander Street, part of Clarivate PLC, pg 6
American Society of Agricultural & Biological Engineers (ASABE), pg 12
Andrews University Press, pg 14
Avery Color Studios, pg 23
Baker Books, pg 23
Brilliance Publishing Inc, pg 37
Bywater Books Inc, pg 39
Chaosium Inc, pg 45
Christian Schools International (CSI), pg 47
Editorial Portavoz, pg 64
Wm B Eerdmans Publishing Co, pg 64
Gale, pg 75
Gauthier Publications Inc, pg 77
Hillsdale College Press, pg 92
Institute of Continuing Legal Education, pg 101

Inter-University Consortium for Political & Social Research (ICPSR), pg 102
International Book Centre Inc, pg 102
Kregel Publications, pg 111
The Little Entrepreneur, pg 118
Loving Healing Press Inc, pg 121
Macmillan Reference USA™, pg 123
Marick Press, pg 125
Medieval Institute Publications (MIP), pg 129
Michigan State University Press (MSU Press), pg 130
Milford Books™, pg 131
New Issues Poetry & Prose, pg 140
Omnigraphics Inc, pg 146
Our Daily Bread Publishing, pg 148
Palladium Books Inc, pg 150
ProQuest LLC, part of Clarivate PLC, pg 166
Reference Publications Inc, pg 173
Reformation Heritage Books, pg 173
Revell, pg 174
St James Press®, pg 180
School Zone Publishing Co, pg 185
Sleeping Bear Press™, pg 191
SME (Society of Manufacturing Engineers), pg 191
Teacher's Discovery®, pg 203
University Council for Educational Administration (UCEA), pg 214
University of Michigan Press, pg 217
Visible Ink Press®, pg 225
Wayne State University Press, pg 226
World Trade Press LLC, pg 234
Wyndham Hall Press, pg 234
Zondervan, pg 236

MINNESOTA

ABDO, pg 2
Amicus, pg 13
APS PRESS, pg 16
ArtWrite Productions, pg 18
Aspatore Books, pg 19
Augsburg Fortress Publishers, Publishing House of the Evangelical Lutheran Church in America, pg 22
Bearport Publishing, pg 26
Beaver's Pond Press Inc, pg 26
Bethany House Publishers, pg 29
Black Rabbit Books, pg 30
Capstone Publishers™, pg 40
Cardiotext Publishing, pg 40
Carolrhoda Books Inc, pg 41
Carolrhoda Lab™, pg 41
CarTech Inc, pg 41
Cereals & Grains Association, pg 44
Chosen Books, pg 47
Cistercian Publications, pg 48
Coffee House Press, pg 50
Creative Editions, pg 55
Dragon Door Publications, pg 61
ediciones Lerner, pg 63
Elva Resa Publishing, pg 65
Faith & Fellowship Publishing, pg 69
First Avenue Editions, pg 72
Foundation Press, pg 74
Free Spirit Publishing Inc, pg 74
Graphic Universe™, pg 80
Graywolf Press, pg 81
Hazelden Publishing, pg 89
Holy Cow! Press, pg 95
Jump!, pg 107
Kar-Ben Publishing, pg 108

Lake Superior Publishing LLC, pg 112
Legacy Bound, pg 114
Lerner Publications, pg 115
Lerner Publishing Group Inc, pg 115
LernerClassroom, pg 115
Liturgical Press, pg 118
Llewellyn Publications, pg 119
Maren Green Publishing Inc, pg 125
Math Teachers Press Inc, pg 127
Mighty Media Press, pg 131
Military Info Publishing, pg 131
Milkweed Editions, pg 131
Millbrook Press, pg 131
Minnesota Historical Society Press, pg 132
North Star Editions Inc, pg 142
North Star Press of Saint Cloud Inc, pg 142
OptumInsight™, pg 147
Pangaea Publications, pg 150
Paragon House, pg 151
The Professional Education Group LLC (PEG), pg 165
Redleaf Press®, pg 173
Saint Mary's Press, pg 181
Sunrise River Press, pg 201
Thomson West, pg 206
TRISTAN Publishing, pg 209
Twenty-First Century Books, pg 211
University of Minnesota Press, pg 217
West Academic, pg 227
Whole Person Associates Inc, pg 229
Yotzeret Publishing, pg 236
Zest Books, pg 236

MISSISSIPPI

University Press of Mississippi, pg 222

MISSOURI

American Public Works Association (APWA), pg 12
American Society of Plant Taxonomists, pg 13
Andrews McMeel Publishing LLC, pg 14
ASET - The Neurodiagnostic Society, pg 18
Beacon Hill Press of Kansas City, pg 25
BkMk Press Inc, pg 30
The Catholic Health Association of the United States, pg 42
CEF Press, pg 43
Chalice Press, pg 44
Concordia Publishing House, pg 51
The Donning Company Publishers, pg 60
ECS Publishing Group, pg 63
Gospel Publishing House, pg 80
International Linguistics Corp, pg 103
Liguori Publications, pg 117
Mel Bay Publications Inc, pg 129
National Association of Insurance Commissioners, pg 136
Open Books Press, pg 146
Pen & Publish LLC, pg 153
Pentecostal Resources Group, pg 157
Science & Humanities Press, pg 185
STM Learning Inc, pg 199
University of Missouri Press, pg 217

MONTANA

Farcountry Press, pg 69
Kessinger Publishing LLC, pg 109
Mountain Press Publishing Co, pg 135
Raven Publishing Inc, pg 172
Stoneydale Press Publishing Co, pg 199
Summit University Press, pg 200
Wilderness Adventures Press Inc, pg 229

NEBRASKA

Addicus Books Inc, pg 5
Boys Town Press, pg 35
Centering Corp, pg 44
Gryphon Editions, pg 82
Marathon Press, pg 124
Potomac Books, pg 162
South Platte Press, pg 195
University of Nebraska Press, pg 217

NEVADA

Cardoza Publishing, pg 40
Central Recovery Press (CRP), pg 44
Histria Books, pg 93
Huntington Press Publishing, pg 97
Parmenides Publishing, pg 152
ThunderStone Books, pg 207
University of Nevada Press, pg 218
Winterwolf Press, pg 231

NEW HAMPSHIRE

Captain Fiddle Music & Publications, pg 40
Donald M Grant Publisher Inc, pg 80
Heinemann, pg 90
Hobblebush Books, pg 93
Kennedy Information LLC, pg 108
Peter E Randall Publisher, pg 169
Smith & Kraus Publishers Inc, pg 192
Sophia Institute Press®, pg 193
Starcrafts LLC, pg 197
Steerforth Press & Services, pg 198
YMAA Publication Center Inc, pg 235

NEW JERSEY

Africa World Press Inc, pg 5
ASCSA Publications, pg 18
Backbeat Books, pg 23
Behrman House Inc, pg 27
Ben Yehuda Press, pg 27
The Blackburn Press, pg 30
R R Bowker LLC, pg 34
Catholic Book Publishing Corp, pg 42
Cleis Press, pg 49
Demos Medical Publishing, pg 58
Down The Shore Publishing, pg 61
Dun & Bradstreet, pg 62
The Electrochemical Society (ECS), pg 65
Financial Times Press, pg 71
GeoLytics Inc, pg 77
Gorgias Press LLC, pg 80
Hamilton Stone Editions, pg 84
Homa & Sekey Books, pg 95
Hospital & Healthcare Compensation Service, pg 95
IEEE Press, pg 98
IET USA Inc, pg 98
Information Today, Inc, pg 100
Infosources Publishing, pg 100

PUBLISHERS

Kumon Publishing North America Inc (KPNA), pg 112
Laredo Publishing Co, pg 113
The Lawbook Exchange, Ltd, pg 113
Learning Links-USA Inc, pg 114
Lectorum Publications Inc, pg 114
Listen & Live Audio Inc, pg 117
Martindale LLC, pg 126
Mastery Education, pg 126
Mesorah Publications Ltd, pg 130
Morning Sun Books Inc, pg 134
P & R Publishing Co, pg 149
Paulist Press, pg 152
Pearson Business Publishing, pg 153
Pearson Education Ltd, pg 153
Pearson ELT, pg 153
Pearson Higher Education, pg 153
Plexus Publishing, Inc, pg 160
Polis Books, pg 162
Princeton Book Co Publishers, pg 163
Princeton University Press, pg 164
Quincannon Publishing Group, pg 168
The Red Sea Press Inc, pg 173
Renaissance House, pg 174
Research & Education Association (REA), pg 174
Rutgers University Press, pg 178
St Johann Press, pg 180
Salem Press, pg 181
Savvas Learning Co LLC, pg 183
SLACK® Incorporated, A Wyanoke Group Company, pg 191
SYBEX, pg 201
Tughra Books, pg 210
Whiskey Creek Press, pg 228
Markus Wiener Publishers Inc, pg 229
Wiley-Blackwell, pg 229
John Wiley & Sons Inc, pg 230
John Wiley & Sons Inc Global Education, pg 230
John Wiley & Sons Inc Professional Development, pg 230
World Scientific Publishing Co Inc, pg 233

NEW MEXICO

Clear Light Publishers, pg 49
Hartman Publishing Inc, pg 87
Kiva Publishing Inc, pg 110
Leaf Storm Press, pg 113
LPD Press/Rio Grande Books, pg 121
Museum of New Mexico Press, pg 135
Ocean Tree Books, pg 145
Open Horizons Publishing Co, pg 147
Paradigm Publications, pg 151
School for Advanced Research Press, pg 185
Sherman Asher Publishing, pg 187
Sun Publishing Company, pg 200
Sunstone Press, pg 201
Terra Nova Books, pg 204
University of New Mexico Press, pg 218
Western Edge Press, pg 228

NEW YORK

Abbeville Press, pg 1
Abbeville Publishing Group, pg 2
Harry N Abrams Inc, pg 2
ACC Art Books, pg 3
ACM Books, pg 4
Adirondack Mountain Club (ADK), pg 5
AIP Publishing LLC, pg 6
Akashic Books, pg 6
Algora Publishing, pg 7
Alloy Entertainment LLC, pg 7
Allworth Press, pg 7
American Federation of Arts, pg 9
American Institute of Chemical Engineers (AIChE), pg 10
American Numismatic Society, pg 11
American Society of Mechanical Engineers (ASME), pg 12
Aperture Books, pg 15
Apress Media LLC, pg 15
Arcade Publishing Inc, pg 16
Ash Tree Publishing, pg 18
Asta Publications LLC, pg 20
Astra Books for Young Readers, pg 20
Atria Books, pg 21
Avant-Guide, pg 22
Avery, pg 23
Avid Reader Press, pg 23
Barranca Press, pg 24
Barrytown/Station Hill Press, pg 24
Basic Books Group, pg 25
Bedford/St Martin's, pg 26
Bellevue Literary Press, pg 27
Berghahn Books, pg 28
Berkley, pg 28
Black Dome Press Corp, pg 30
Blood Moon Productions Ltd, pg 31
Bloom's Literary Criticism, pg 31
Bloomsbury Academic, pg 31
Bloomsbury Publishing Inc, pg 31
BlueBridge, pg 32
BOA Editions Ltd, pg 33
Bold Strokes Books Inc, pg 33
Book Sales, pg 33
Books on Tape™, pg 34
Boydell & Brewer Inc, pg 35
George Braziller Inc, pg 35
Breakaway Books, pg 36
Brick Tower Press, pg 36
Bristol Park Books, pg 37
The Bureau for At-Risk Youth, pg 38
Burford Books, pg 38
Burns Archive Press, pg 38
Business Expert Press, pg 38
Cambridge University Press, pg 39
Candid, pg 39
Central Conference of American Rabbis/CCAR Press, pg 44
Chelsea House, pg 45
Children's Book Press, pg 46
Circlet Press, pg 48
Clarion Books, pg 48
CN Times Books, pg 50
Codhill Press, pg 50
Cognizant Communication Corp, pg 50
Cold Spring Harbor Laboratory Press, pg 50
The College Board, pg 50
Columbia University Press, pg 51
The Conference Board Inc, pg 51
Cornell University Press, pg 52
Cosimo Inc, pg 53
Council on Foreign Relations Press, pg 53
Countryman Press, pg 54
Crabtree Publishing Co, pg 54
Cross-Cultural Communications, pg 55
The Crossroad Publishing Co, pg 55
Crown House Publishing Co LLC, pg 56
Crown Publishing Group, pg 56
DAW Books, pg 57
Dial Books for Young Readers, pg 59
Diversion Books, pg 60
DK, pg 60
Doubleday, pg 61
Dover Publications Inc, pg 61
Dramatists Play Service Inc, pg 61
Dutton, pg 62
Dutton Children's Books, pg 62
Edgewise Press Inc, pg 63
Educator's International Press Inc (EIP), pg 64
Elsevier Inc, pg 65
Enchanted Lion Books, pg 66
Encounter Books, pg 66
Enslow Publishing LLC, pg 66
Europa Editions, pg 67
Everyman's Library, pg 68
Excelsior Editions, pg 68
The Experiment, pg 68
Fairchild Books, pg 69
Farrar, Straus & Giroux Books for Young Readers, pg 69
Farrar, Straus & Giroux, LLC, pg 70
Feldheim Publishers, pg 70
The Feminist Press at The City University of New York, pg 71
Fence Books, pg 71
Ferguson Publishing, pg 71
Fine Creative Media, Inc, pg 71
Flamingo Books, pg 72
Flashlight Press, pg 72
Fordham University Press, pg 73
Forum Publishing Co, pg 73
W H Freeman, pg 75
Samuel French, Inc, pg 75
Gagosian Gallery, pg 75
Gallery Books, pg 76
Gareth Stevens Publishing, pg 76
Glitterati Inc, pg 78
Grand Central Publishing, pg 80
Greenhaven Publishing, pg 81
Grey House Publishing Inc™, pg 81
Grove Atlantic Inc, pg 82
The Guilford Press, pg 82
Hachai Publishing, pg 83
Hachette Audio, pg 83
Hachette Book Group Inc, pg 83
Handprint Books Inc, pg 84
Hanging Loose Press, pg 85
Harlequin Enterprises Ltd, pg 85
HarperCollins Children's Books, pg 85
HarperCollins Publishers LLC, pg 86
Harrington Park Press, pg 87
Hatherleigh Press Ltd, pg 88
William S Hein & Co Inc, pg 90
Hill & Wang, pg 92
Hippocrene Books Inc, pg 92
History Publishing Co LLC, pg 93
Holiday House Publishing Inc, pg 94
Henry Holt and Company, LLC, pg 94
Human Rights Watch, pg 97
Humanix Books LLC, pg 97
Illuminating Engineering Society of North America (IES), pg 99
International Council of Shopping Centers (ICSC), pg 102
International Publishers Co Inc, pg 103
Italica Press, pg 105
Judaica Press Inc, pg 107
Jump at the Sun, pg 107
Kensington Publishing Corp, pg 109
Klutz®, pg 110
Alfred A Knopf, pg 110
Knopf Doubleday Publishing Group, pg 110
Kodansha USA Inc, pg 110
Kogan Page, pg 111
Kokila, pg 111
Krause Publications Inc, pg 111
KTAV Publishing House Inc, pg 111
Peter Lang Publishing Inc, pg 112
Lantern Publishing & Media, pg 112
Larson Publications, pg 113
LearningExpress, pg 114
Lee & Low Books Inc, pg 114
LexisNexis®, pg 116
Libraries Unlimited, pg 116
Library of America, pg 116
Mary Ann Liebert Inc, pg 116
Lippincott Williams & Wilkins, pg 117
little bee books, pg 117
Little, Brown and Company, pg 118
Little, Brown Books for Young Readers (LBYR), pg 118
Living Language, pg 119
Logos Press, pg 119
Looseleaf Law Publications Inc, pg 120
Love Inspired Books, pg 120
Lucent Press, pg 121
Macmillan, pg 121
Macmillan Audio, pg 123
Macmillan Learning, pg 123
Manning Publications Co, pg 124
MapEasy Inc, pg 124
Marquis Who's Who, pg 125
Marshall Cavendish Education, pg 125
McGraw-Hill Create, pg 127
McGraw-Hill Education, pg 127
McGraw-Hill Higher Education, pg 128
McGraw-Hill Professional Publishing Group, pg 128
McPherson & Co, pg 128
The Edwin Mellen Press, pg 129
Metropolitan Classics, pg 130
The Metropolitan Museum of Art, pg 130
Modern Language Association (MLA), pg 133
The Monacelli Press, pg 133
Mondial, pg 133
Monkfish Book Publishing Co, pg 133
Monthly Review Press, pg 134
Morehouse Publishing, pg 134
Morgan James Publishing, pg 134
Moznaim Publishing Corp, pg 135
The Museum of Modern Art (MoMA), pg 135
National Center for Children in Poverty, pg 137
National Learning Corp, pg 138
NBM Publishing Inc, pg 139
New City Press, pg 139
New Directions Publishing Corp, pg 139
The New Press, pg 140
New Readers Press, pg 140
New York Academy of Sciences (NYAS), pg 140
The New York Botanical Garden Press, pg 140
New York State Bar Association, pg 141
New York University Press, pg 141
NFB Publishing, pg 141
North Point Press, pg 142
Northern Illinois University Press, pg 143
W W Norton & Company Inc, pg 143
Norwood House Press, pg 143
Nova Science Publishers Inc, pg 144
Omnibus Press, pg 146
Open Letter, pg 147
Orbis Books, pg 147

Orbit, pg 147
Other Press, pg 148
The Overlook Press, pg 148
Richard C Owen Publishers Inc, pg 149
Oxford University Press USA, pg 149
PA Press, pg 149
Pace University Press, pg 149
Paintbox Press, pg 150
Palgrave Macmillan, pg 150
Pantheon Books, pg 150
Paramount Market Publishing Inc, pg 151
Nancy Paulsen Books, pg 152
Pendragon Press, pg 154
Penguin Press, pg 154
Penguin Publishing Group, pg 154
Penguin Random House Audio Publishing Group, pg 154
Penguin Random House LLC, pg 155
Penguin Workshop, pg 156
Penguin Young Readers Group, pg 156
The Permanent Press, pg 158
Persea Books, pg 158
Peter Pauper Press, Inc, pg 158
Phaidon, pg 159
Philomel Books, pg 159
Philosophical Library Inc, pg 159
Picador, pg 159
Plough Publishing House, pg 161
Pointed Leaf Press, pg 161
Portfolio, pg 162
Clarkson Potter, pg 162
powerHouse Books, pg 162
Practising Law Institute (PLI), pg 163
Primary Research Group Inc, pg 163
The Princeton Review, pg 164
Productivity Press, pg 165
Prometheus Books, pg 166
The PRS Group Inc, pg 166
Puffin Books, pg 167
Pushcart Press, pg 167
GP Putnam's Sons, pg 167
GP Putnam's Sons Books for Young Readers, pg 167
Random House Children's Books, pg 169
Random House Large Print, pg 170
Random House Publishing Group, pg 170
Random House Reference/Random House Puzzles & Games, pg 171
Rattapallax Press, pg 172
Reader's Digest Select Editions, pg 172
Reader's Digest Trade Publishing, pg 172
Riverdale Avenue Books (RAB), pg 175
Riverhead Books, pg 175
Rizzoli International Publications Inc, pg 175
Roaring Brook Press, pg 175
The Rockefeller University Press, pg 176
Rocky Pond Books, pg 176
Rodin Books, pg 176
The Rosen Publishing Group Inc, pg 177
RosettaBooks, pg 177
Routledge, pg 177
Royal Fireworks Press, pg 178
Running Press, pg 178
Russell Sage Foundation, pg 178
William H Sadlier Inc, pg 179
St Martin's Press, LLC, pg 180
St Pauls, pg 181
Scarsdale Publishing Ltd, pg 183

G Schirmer Inc/Associated Music Publishers Inc, pg 183
Schocken Books, pg 183
Scholastic Education Solutions, pg 184
Scholastic Inc, pg 184
Scholastic International, pg 184
Scholastic Trade Publishing, pg 184
School Guide Publications, pg 185
Scribner, pg 185
SelectBooks Inc, pg 186
Seven Stories Press, pg 186
Shen's Books, pg 187
Siglio, pg 187
Simon & Schuster, pg 188
Simon & Schuster Audio, pg 189
Simon & Schuster Children's Publishing, pg 189
Simon & Schuster, LLC, pg 189
Sky Pony Press, pg 191
Small Business Advisors Inc, pg 191
Soho Press Inc, pg 193
Soncino Press Ltd, pg 193
Soul Mate Publishing, pg 194
Springer, pg 196
Springer Publishing Co, pg 196
Square One Publishers Inc, pg 196
State University of New York Press, pg 198
Stewart, Tabori & Chang, pg 198
Syracuse University Press, pg 201
Tahrike Tarsile Qur'an Inc, pg 202
Nan A Talese, pg 202
T&T Clark International, pg 202
TarcherPerigee, pg 202
Teachers College Press, pg 203
Thames & Hudson, pg 205
Theatre Communications Group, pg 205
Thieme Medical Publishers Inc, pg 206
Tor Publishing Group, pg 207
Torah Umesorah Publications, pg 208
Trusted Media Brands Inc, pg 210
Turtle Point Press, pg 210
Ugly Duckling Presse, pg 212
Ulysses Press, pg 212
Union Square & Co, pg 212
United Nations Publications, pg 213
Universe Publishing, pg 214
University of Rochester Press, pg 220
University Science Books, pg 222
Urim Publications, pg 223
VanDam Inc, pg 223
Vault.com Inc, pg 224
The Vendome Press, pg 224
Verso Books, pg 224
Viking Children's Books, pg 224
Viking Penguin, pg 224
Vintage Books, pg 225
Visual Profile Books Inc, pg 225
Welcome Books, pg 227
Welcome Rain Publishers LLC, pg 227
Eliot Werner Publications Inc, pg 227
White Pine Press, pg 228
Whittier Publications Inc, pg 229
Windsor Books, pg 230
Wolters Kluwer Law & Business, pg 232
WoodstockArts, pg 232
Workman Publishing, pg 232
World Almanac®, pg 233
Worth Publishers, pg 234
Writer's Digest Books, pg 234
YBK Publishers Inc, pg 235
Yeshiva University Press, pg 235
Zagat Inc, pg 236
Zone Books, pg 237

NORTH CAROLINA
AICPA® & CIMA®, pg 5
Baen Books, pg 23
Black Mountain Press, pg 30
Blair, pg 30
Carolina Academic Press, pg 41
Carson Dellosa Publishing LLC, pg 41
Center for Creative Leadership LLC, pg 43
Dancing Lemur Press LLC, pg 57
DiscoverNet Publishing, pg 59
Duke University Press, pg 62
Fitzroy Books, pg 72
Galde Press Inc, pg 75
Gryphon House Inc, pg 82
Information Age Publishing Inc, pg 100
International Society of Automation (ISA), pg 103
McFarland, pg 127
North Carolina Office of Archives & History, pg 142
Pact Press, pg 150
Regal House Publishing, pg 173
SAS Press, pg 182
Sinauer Associates, pg 190
Stellar Publishing, pg 198
TAN Books, pg 202
The University of North Carolina Press, pg 218
Wake Forest University Press, pg 225
WriteLife Publishing, pg 234

NORTH DAKOTA
Bethlehem Books, pg 29

OHIO
The American Ceramic Society, pg 9
American Society for Nondestructive Testing, pg 12
The Ashland Poetry Press, pg 19
ASM International, pg 19
Barbour Publishing Inc, pg 24
Bottom Dog Press, pg 34
Carlisle Press - Walnut Creek, pg 40
Dreamscape Media LLC, pg 62
Emmaus Road Publishing Inc, pg 66
Forward Movement, pg 73
Franciscan Media, pg 74
Gray & Company Publishers, pg 80
Hanser Publications LLC, pg 85
Hebrew Union College Press, pg 90
Kaeden Publishing, pg 107
Kent State University Press, pg 109
Lorenz Educational Press, pg 120
Luna Bisonte Prods, pg 121
The McDonald & Woodward Publishing Co, pg 127
McGraw-Hill School Education Group, pg 128
Milady, pg 131
Milliken Publishing Co, pg 132
Multicultural Publications Inc, pg 135
Ohio Genealogical Society, pg 145
The Ohio State University Press, pg 145
Ohio University Press, pg 145
Orange Frazer Press Inc, pg 147
Pflaum Publishing Group, pg 159
The Pilgrim Press/United Church Press, pg 160
Scepter Publishers, pg 183
Stenhouse Publishers, pg 198
Swallow Press, pg 201
Teaching & Learning Co, pg 204

Treehaus Communications Inc, pg 209
Zaner-Bloser Inc, pg 236

OKLAHOMA
AAPG (American Association of Petroleum Geologists), pg 1
Doodle and Peck Publishing, pg 60
EDC Publishing, pg 63
Faith Library Publications, pg 69
Fire Engineering Books & Videos, pg 72
National Resource Center for Youth Services, pg 138
New Forums Press Inc, pg 139
PennWell Books, pg 157
Professional Communications Inc, pg 165
The RoadRunner Press, pg 175
Society of Exploration Geophysicists, pg 192
University of Oklahoma Press, pg 219
University Publishing House, pg 222

OREGON
Amber Lotus Publishing, pg 8
ArtAge Publications, pg 17
Ashland Creek Press, pg 18
Blue Poppy Press, pg 32
Dancing Dakini Press, pg 57
Dark Horse Comics, pg 57
Deep River Books LLC, pg 58
Elderberry Press Inc, pg 65
Franklin, Beedle & Associates Inc, pg 74
Harvest House Publishers Inc, pg 88
Hazy Dell Press, pg 89
Hellgate Press, pg 91
Koho Pono LLC, pg 111
National Book Co, pg 136
OCP, pg 145
Ooligan Press, pg 146
Oregon State University Press, pg 147
Pocket Press Inc, pg 161
Polebridge Press, pg 161
Pomegranate Communications Inc, pg 162
Robert D Reed Publishers, pg 173
Teton NewMedia Inc, pg 205
Wheatherstone Press, pg 228

PENNSYLVANIA
American Bible Society, pg 8
The American College of Financial Services, pg 9
American Law Institute, pg 10
American Law Institute Continuing Legal Education (ALI CLE), pg 10
American Philosophical Society Press, pg 11
Art of Living, PrimaMedia Inc, pg 17
Ascension Press, pg 18
ASTM International, pg 20
Astragal Press, pg 20
Autumn House Press, pg 22
Beehive Books, pg 26
George T Bisel Co Inc, pg 29
Bookhaven Press LLC, pg 34
Breakthrough Publications Inc, pg 36
Bucknell University Press, pg 38
Camino Books Inc, pg 39
Campfield & Campfield Publishing LLC, pg 39
Carnegie Mellon University Press, pg 41

PUBLISHERS

U.S. PUBLISHERS — GEOGRAPHIC INDEX

Casemate | publishers, pg 41
Center for Futures Education Inc, pg 43
Charles Press Publishers, pg 45
Classical Academic Press, pg 49
Clinical and Laboratory Standards Institute (CLSI), pg 49
Closson Press, pg 49
Cornell Maritime Press, pg 52
Creative Homeowner, pg 55
F A Davis Co, pg 57
DEStech Publications Inc, pg 59
Destiny Image Inc, pg 59
Dorrance Publishing Co Inc, pg 61
Eifrig Publishing LLC, pg 64
Eisenbrauns, pg 64
Elsevier Health Sciences, pg 65
Endless Mountains Publishing Co, pg 66
Entangled Publishing LLC, pg 67
Etruscan Press, pg 67
Fox Chapel Publishing Co Inc, pg 74
Harrison House, pg 87
Higginson Book Company LLC, pg 91
Highlights for Children Inc, pg 92
Himalayan Institute Press, pg 92
House to House Publications, pg 97
The Institutes™, pg 102
International Wealth Success (IWS), pg 104
The Jewish Publication Society, pg 105
Judson Press, pg 107
Kalaniot Books, pg 107
Kallisti Publishing Inc, pg 108
Jessica Kingsley Publishers Inc, pg 110
Landauer Publishing, pg 112
Law School Admission Council (LSAC), pg 113
Lehigh University Press, pg 114
The Local History Co, pg 119
Locks Art Publications/Locks Gallery, pg 119
MAR*CO Products Inc, pg 124
Markowski International Publishers, pg 125
Mason Crest Publishers, pg 126
Materials Research Society, pg 126
The Minerals, Metals & Materials Society (TMS), pg 132
Paul Dry Books, pg 152
Penn State University Press, pg 157
Pennsylvania Historical & Museum Commission, pg 157
Pennsylvania State Data Center, pg 157
Philadelphia Museum of Art, pg 159
Plum Tree Books, pg 161
Pocol Press, pg 161
Quirk Books, pg 168
Reedswain Inc, pg 173
Roncorp Music, pg 176
SAE (Society of Automotive Engineers International), pg 179
St Joseph's University Press, pg 180
Schiffer Publishing Ltd, pg 183
Seedling Publications Inc, pg 186
Society for Industrial & Applied Mathematics, pg 192
Stackpole Books, pg 196
Swedenborg Foundation, pg 201
Taylor & Francis Inc, pg 203
Temple University Press, pg 204
Trans-Atlantic Publications Inc, pg 209
Tuxedo Press, pg 211
University of Pennsylvania Museum of Archaeology & Anthropology, pg 219

University of Pennsylvania Press, pg 219
University of Pittsburgh Press, pg 219
Western Pennsylvania Genealogical Society, pg 228
Whitaker House, pg 228

RHODE ISLAND

American Mathematical Society (AMS), pg 11
Light Publications, pg 116

SOUTH CAROLINA

Ambassador International, pg 7
Applewood Books, pg 15
Arbordale Publishing, pg 16
Arcadia Publishing Inc, pg 16
BJU Press, pg 30
Commonwealth Editions, pg 51
Continental AfrikaPublishers, pg 52
Medals of America Press, pg 128
Michelin Maps & Guides, pg 130
Moonshine Cove Publishing LLC, pg 134
South Carolina Bar, pg 195
Southern Historical Press Inc, pg 195
Strategic Media Books LLC, pg 200
University of South Carolina Press, pg 220

SOUTH DAKOTA

South Dakota Historical Society Press, pg 195
Spizzirri Publishing Inc, pg 196
Wildflower Press, pg 229

TENNESSEE

Abingdon Press, pg 2
B&H Publishing Group, pg 24
Basic Health Publications Inc, pg 25
BelleBooks, pg 27
BLR®—Business & Legal Resources, pg 32
BPC, pg 35
Cider Mill Press Book Publishers LLC, pg 48
Country Music Foundation Press, pg 54
Fresh Air Books, pg 75
GemStone Press, pg 77
Hachette Nashville, pg 83
HCPro/DecisionHealth, pg 89
ImaJinn Books, pg 99
Iris Press, pg 104
Jewish Lights Publishing, pg 105
Leadership Ministries Worldwide, pg 113
Marriage Transformation LLC, pg 125
Quail Ridge Press (QRP), pg 168
SkyLight Paths® Publishing, pg 191
M Lee Smith Publishers, pg 192
Thomas Nelson, pg 206
Tommy Nelson®, pg 207
The Trinity Foundation, pg 209
Turner Publishing Co LLC, pg 210
Twilight Times Books, pg 211
University of Tennessee Press, pg 220
Upper Room Books, pg 223
Vanderbilt University Press, pg 224
Vesuvian Books, pg 224
West Margin Press, pg 227

TEXAS

ACU Press, pg 4
Advance Publishing Inc, pg 5
Anaphora Literary Press, pg 13
Arte Publico Press, pg 17
Authorlink® Press, pg 22
Barcelona Publishers LLC, pg 24
Baylor University Press, pg 25
BenBella Books Inc, pg 27
Blue Whale Press, pg 32
BRAVE Books, pg 35
Brown Books Publishing Group (BBPG), pg 38
Bureau of Economic Geology, pg 38
Casa Bautista de Publicaciones, pg 41
Cedar Grove Publishing, pg 43
Dalkey Archive Press, pg 56
D&B Hoovers™, pg 57
Eakin Press, pg 62
Future Horizons Inc, pg 75
Global Training Center, pg 79
Greenleaf Book Group LLC, pg 81
Gulf Energy Information, pg 83
Host Publications, pg 95
Intercultural Development Research Association (IDRA), pg 102
International Risk Management Institute Inc, pg 103
Lyndon B Johnson School of Public Affairs, pg 106
The Magni Co, pg 123
NACE International, pg 136
Octane Press, pg 145
Penny-Farthing Productions, pg 157
Petroleum Extension Service (PETEX), pg 159
Plunkett Research Ltd, pg 161
PRO-ED Inc, pg 165
Radix Press, pg 169
Schlager Group Inc, pg 183
SIL International, pg 188
TCU Press, pg 203
Texas A&M University Press, pg 205
Texas State Historical Association, pg 205
Texas Tech University Press, pg 205
University of Texas Press, pg 205
Texas Western Press, pg 205
Top Publications Ltd, pg 207
TotalRecall Publications Inc, pg 208
Trinity University Press, pg 209
University of North Texas Press, pg 218
Voyager Sopris Learning Inc, pg 225
Waldorf Publishing LLC, pg 226
Wings Press, pg 231
Writer's AudioShop, pg 234
Xist Publishing, pg 234
Zumaya Publications LLC, pg 237

UTAH

Cedar Fort Inc, pg 43
Covenant Communications Inc, pg 54
Deseret Book Co, pg 58
Gibbs Smith Publisher, pg 78
Hi Willow Research & Publishing, pg 91
Horizon Publishers & Distributors Inc, pg 95
Shadow Mountain Publishing, pg 187
Signature Books Publishing LLC, pg 187
The University of Utah Press, pg 220
Utah Geological Survey, pg 223
Utah State University Press, pg 223

VERMONT

Art Image Publications, pg 17
Bear & Co Inc, pg 26
Brigantine Media, pg 37
Chelsea Green Publishing Co, pg 45
Inner Traditions International Ltd, pg 101
Montemayor Press, pg 133
Norilana Books, pg 142
Pro Lingua Associates Inc, pg 165
Rootstock Publishing, pg 176
Safer Society Press, pg 179
Storyworkz Inc, pg 199
Trafalgar Square Books, pg 208
Tuttle Publishing, pg 211

VIRGINIA

AIHA (American Industrial Hygiene Association), pg 6
Amakella Publishing, pg 7
American Anthropological Association (AAA), pg 8
American Correctional Association, pg 9
American Counseling Association (ACA), pg 9
American Diabetes Association, pg 9
American Geosciences Institute (AGI), pg 10
American Institute of Aeronautics and Astronautics (AIAA), pg 10
American Society of Civil Engineers (ASCE), pg 12
APPA - Leadership in Education Facilities, pg 15
ARE Press, pg 16
ASCD, pg 18
ASIS International, pg 19
Association for Information Science & Technology (ASIS&T), pg 19
Association for Talent Development (ATD) Press, pg 19
Association of School Business Officials International, pg 20
Brandylane Publishers Inc, pg 35
Christian Light Publications Inc, pg 47
Close Up Publishing, pg 49
College Publishing, pg 50
Columbia Books & Information Services (CBIS), pg 50
Council for Exceptional Children (CEC), pg 53
CSWE Press, pg 56
dbS Productions, pg 58
Dewey Publications Inc, pg 59
Firefall Editions, pg 72
Herald Press, pg 91
IBFD North America Inc (International Bureau of Fiscal Documentation), pg 98
IHS Press, pg 98
Impact Publications/Development Concepts Inc, pg 99
The International Institute of Islamic Thought, pg 103
International Society for Technology in Education, pg 103
Kapp Books LLC, pg 108
Lasaria Creative Publishing, pg 113
LexisNexis® Matthew Bender®, pg 116
Loft Press Inc, pg 119
MennoMedia, pg 129
Military Living Publications, pg 131
Nataraj Books, pg 136
National Catholic Educational Association, pg 137
National Council of Teachers of Mathematics (NCTM), pg 137

U.S. PUBLISHERS — GEOGRAPHIC INDEX

National Science Teachers Association (NSTA), pg 138
National Wildlife Federation, pg 139
The Oaklea Press Inc, pg 145
Omohundro Institute of Early American History & Culture, pg 146
Open Court Publishing Co, pg 147
Philosophy Documentation Center, pg 159
PRINTING United Alliance, pg 165
Rand-Smith Publishing, pg 169
Red Moon Press, pg 172
RockHill Publishing LLC, pg 176
Schonfeld & Associates Inc, pg 184
1765 Productions, pg 186
Society for Human Resource Management (SHRM), pg 192
The Society of Naval Architects & Marine Engineers (SNAME), pg 193
STARbooks Press, pg 197
Stylus Publishing LLC, pg 200
TESOL Press, pg 204
University of Virginia Press, pg 220
Water Environment Federation, pg 226
Well-Trained Mind Press, pg 227

WASHINGTON

Sara Anderson Children's Books, pg 13
Black Heron Press, pg 30
Books In Motion, pg 34
Candied Plums, pg 39
Copper Canyon Press, pg 52
Dogwise Publishing, pg 60
Eastland Press, pg 63
Emerald Books, pg 66
Epicenter Press Inc, pg 67
Evergreen Pacific Publishing Ltd, pg 68
Faithlife Corp, pg 69
Feral House, pg 71
FineEdge.com LLC, pg 72
Hancock House Publishers, pg 84
Hewitt Homeschooling Resources, pg 91
Holmes Publishing Group LLC, pg 94
The Innovation Press, pg 101
Kidsbooks® Publishing, pg 109
Laughing Elephant Books, pg 113
Lost Horse Press, pg 120
Lynx House Press, pg 121
Mountaineers Books, pg 135
Parenting Press, pg 151
Pleasure Boat Studio: A Literary Press, pg 160
Rational Island Publishers, pg 171
St Nectarios Press, pg 181
Sasquatch Books, pg 182
Shepard Publications, pg 187
SPIE, pg 196
University of Washington Press, pg 220
Washington State University Press, pg 226
Wizards of the Coast LLC, pg 231
YWAM Publishing, pg 236

WEST VIRGINIA

West Virginia University Press, pg 228

WISCONSIN

A-R Editions Inc, pg 1
Adams & Ambrose Publishing, pg 4
American Girl Publishing, pg 10
American Society for Quality (ASQ), pg 12
American Society of Agronomy (ASA), pg 12
Everything Goes Media LLC, pg 68
Hal Leonard LLC, pg 84
Her Own Words LLC, pg 91
W D Hoard & Sons Co, pg 93
International Foundation of Employee Benefit Plans, pg 103
Kalmbach Media Co, pg 108
J J Keller & Associates, Inc®, pg 108
Lotus Press, pg 120
Marquette University Press, pg 125
Medical Physics Publishing Corp (MPP), pg 129
Planert Creek Press, pg 160
PPI, A Kaplan Company, pg 162
Referee Books, pg 173
Soil Science Society of America (SSSA), pg 193
University of Wisconsin Press, pg 221
Upstart Books™, pg 223
Willow Creek Press, pg 230
Wisconsin Department of Public Instruction, pg 231

WYOMING

High Plains Press, pg 91
Homestead Publishing, pg 95
Moriah Books, pg 134

PUERTO RICO

Editorial de la Universidad de Puerto Rico, pg 63

U.S. Publishers — Type of Publication Index

ASSOCIATION PRESSES

AIHA (American Industrial Hygiene Association), pg 6
American Academy of Pediatrics, pg 8
American Association of Collegiate Registrars & Admissions Officers (AACRAO), pg 8
American Bar Association Publishing, pg 8
American Correctional Association, pg 9
American Counseling Association (ACA), pg 9
American Diabetes Association, pg 9
American Institute of Aeronautics and Astronautics (AIAA), pg 10
American Institute of Chemical Engineers (AIChE), pg 10
American Psychiatric Association Publishing, pg 11
American Psychological Association, pg 11
American Society for Quality (ASQ), pg 12
American Society of Civil Engineers (ASCE), pg 12
American Society of Mechanical Engineers (ASME), pg 12
American Water Works Association (AWWA), pg 13
APPA - Leadership in Education Facilities, pg 15
APS PRESS, pg 16
ASCD, pg 18
ASCP Press, pg 18
Association for Talent Development (ATD) Press, pg 19
Association for the Advancement of Blood & Biotherapies, pg 19
Association of College & Research Libraries (ACRL), pg 19
ASTM International, pg 20
BuilderBooks, pg 38
The Catholic Health Association of the United States, pg 42
Cereals & Grains Association, pg 44
The Conference Board Inc, pg 51
Council for Exceptional Children (CEC), pg 53
The Geological Society of America Inc (GSA), pg 77
Greenleaf Book Group LLC, pg 81
Health Administration Press, pg 89
Health Forum Inc, pg 90
IEEE Computer Society, pg 98
Illuminating Engineering Society of North America (IES), pg 99
International City/County Management Association (ICMA), pg 102
International Council of Shopping Centers (ICSC), pg 102
International Foundation of Employee Benefit Plans, pg 103
International Literacy Association (ILA), pg 103
Kendall Hunt Publishing Co, pg 108
Loving Healing Press Inc, pg 121
Medical Group Management Association (MGMA), pg 128
The Minerals, Metals & Materials Society (TMS), pg 132
Modern Language Association (MLA), pg 133
NACE International, pg 136
National Association of Insurance Commissioners, pg 136
National Education Association (NEA), pg 137
National Resource Center for Youth Services, pg 138
National Science Teachers Association (NSTA), pg 138
Naval Institute Press, pg 139
New Forums Press Inc, pg 139
Planners Press, pg 160
Police Executive Research Forum, pg 162
PRINTING United Alliance, pg 165
SAE (Society of Automotive Engineers International), pg 179
SME (Society of Manufacturing Engineers), pg 191
SPIE, pg 196
TESOL Press, pg 204
Vault.com Inc, pg 224
Water Environment Federation, pg 226
Wiley-Blackwell, pg 229

AUDIOBOOKS

Abingdon Press, pg 2
ACTA Publications, pg 4
AK Press, pg 6
Alaska Native Language Center (ANLC), pg 6
All Things That Matter Press, pg 7
Ambassador International, pg 7
American Bible Society, pg 8
American Carriage House Publishing (ACHP), pg 8
American Catholic Press (ACP), pg 9
American Psychiatric Association Publishing, pg 11
Andrews McMeel Publishing LLC, pg 14
Applause Theatre & Cinema Books, pg 15
Apress Media LLC, pg 15
Arbordale Publishing, pg 16
Art of Living, PrimaMedia Inc, pg 17
Ascension Press, pg 18
Ashland Creek Press, pg 18
Augsburg Fortress Publishers, Publishing House of the Evangelical Lutheran Church in America, pg 22
August House Inc, pg 22
Backbeat Books, pg 23
Baker Books, pg 23
Bancroft Press, pg 24
B&H Publishing Group, pg 24
Barefoot Books, pg 24
Beacon Press, pg 25
BearManor Media, pg 26
BenBella Books Inc, pg 27
Berrett-Koehler Publishers Inc, pg 29
Bess Press Inc, pg 29
Bethlehem Books, pg 29
Bhaktivedanta Book Trust (BBT), pg 29
Biographical Publishing Co, pg 29
Bisk Education, pg 29
BJU Press, pg 30
Black Dome Press Corp, pg 30
Bold Strokes Books Inc, pg 33
BookLogix, pg 34
Books In Motion, pg 34
Books on Tape™, pg 34
Bottom Dog Press, pg 34
Boys Town Press, pg 35
Brandylane Publishers Inc, pg 35
Bridge Publications Inc, pg 36
Brilliance Publishing Inc, pg 37
Bull Publishing Co, pg 38
Catholic Book Publishing Corp, pg 42
Cedar Grove Publishing, pg 43
Central Recovery Press (CRP), pg 44
Chelsea Green Publishing Co, pg 45
Cherry Hill Publishing LLC, pg 46
Children's Book Press, pg 46
Child's Play® Inc, pg 46
The Christian Science Publishing Society, pg 47
Cognizant Communication Corp, pg 50
Cold Spring Harbor Laboratory Press, pg 50
Continental AfrikaPublishers, pg 52
Covenant Communications Inc, pg 54
Crabtree Publishing Co, pg 54
Crossway, pg 56
Crystal Clarity Publishers, pg 56
Cypress House, pg 56
Dancing Lemur Press LLC, pg 57
Deseret Book Co, pg 58
Destiny Image Inc, pg 59
Dewey Publications Inc, pg 59
Dharma Publishing, pg 59
Doubleday, pg 61
Dreamscape Media LLC, pg 62
Eifrig Publishing LLC, pg 64
Etruscan Press, pg 67
Familius, pg 69
Fire Engineering Books & Videos, pg 72
Firefall Editions, pg 72
Focus on the Family, pg 73
Franciscan Media, pg 74
Free Spirit Publishing Inc, pg 74
Galaxy Press Inc, pg 75
Gallery Books, pg 76
Gallopade International Inc, pg 76
Gatekeeper Press, pg 77
Grand Central Publishing, pg 80
Greenleaf Book Group LLC, pg 81
The Guilford Press, pg 82
Hachette Audio, pg 83
Hachette Book Group Inc, pg 83
Hannacroix Creek Books Inc, pg 85
HarperCollins Children's Books, pg 85
Harrison House, pg 87
Harvest House Publishers Inc, pg 88
Hatherleigh Press Ltd, pg 88
Hay House LLC, pg 89
HeartMath LLC, pg 90
Heinemann, pg 90
High Tide Press, pg 92
Highlights for Children Inc, pg 92
Hilton Publishing Co, pg 92
Himalayan Institute Press, pg 92
Horizon Publishers & Distributors Inc, pg 95
Humanix Books LLC, pg 97
Ignatius Press, pg 98
Inner Traditions International Ltd, pg 101
The International Institute of Islamic Thought, pg 103
International Linguistics Corp, pg 103
International Wealth Success (IWS), pg 104
Iron Stream Media, pg 104
Italics Publishing, pg 105
JIST Publishing, pg 106
Kallisti Publishing Inc, pg 108
Alfred A Knopf, pg 110
Koho Pono LLC, pg 111
THE Learning Connection®, pg 113
Learning Links-USA Inc, pg 114
The Lentz Leadership Institute LLC, pg 115
Light Publications, pg 116
Light Technology Publishing LLC, pg 116
Limelight Editions, pg 117
Listen & Live Audio Inc, pg 117
Little, Brown and Company, pg 118
Living Language, pg 119
Macmillan, pg 121
Macmillan Audio, pg 123
Mandala Earth, pg 124
McPherson & Co, pg 128
R S Means from The Gordian Group, pg 128
Mighty Media Press, pg 131
Milady, pg 131
The Mongolia Society Inc, pg 133
National Institute for Trial Advocacy (NITA), pg 138
Naval Institute Press, pg 139
NavPress Publishing Group, pg 139
New Harbinger Publications Inc, pg 140
New Readers Press, pg 140
New World Library, pg 140
Nilgiri Press, pg 141
North Atlantic Books (NAB), pg 142
Nosy Crow Inc, pg 144
OCP, pg 145
Octane Press, pg 145
One On One Book Publishing/Film-Video Publications, pg 146
Ooligan Press, pg 146
The Original Falcon Press, pg 148
Our Daily Bread Publishing, pg 148
Pantheon Books, pg 150
Pants On Fire Press, pg 150
Parachute Publishing LLC, pg 151
Paraclete Press Inc, pg 151
Paradigm Publications, pg 151
Park Place Publications, pg 152
Parmenides Publishing, pg 152
Paulist Press, pg 152
Pen-L Publishing, pg 153
Penguin Publishing Group, pg 154
Penguin Random House Audio Publishing Group, pg 154
Penguin Random House LLC, pg 155
Pentecostal Resources Group, pg 157
Plough Publishing House, pg 161
Plum Tree Books, pg 161
Pocol Press, pg 161
Practising Law Institute (PLI), pg 163

U.S. PUBLISHERS — TYPE OF PUBLICATION INDEX

BOOK

The Professional Education Group LLC (PEG), pg 165
Professional Resource Press, pg 165
PSMJ Resources Inc, pg 166
Publication Consultants, pg 167
GP Putnam's Sons, pg 167
Raven Publishing Inc, pg 172
Ravenhawk™ Books, pg 172
Recorded Books Inc, an RBmedia company, pg 172
Revell, pg 174
Riverhead Books, pg 175
Rodin Books, pg 176
RosettaBooks, pg 177
Ross Books, pg 177
Rowman & Littlefield, pg 178
Royal Fireworks Press, pg 178
Saddleback Educational Publishing, pg 179
Scarsdale Publishing Ltd, pg 183
Schocken Books, pg 183
Scholastic Inc, pg 184
SelectBooks Inc, pg 186
Sentient Publications LLC, pg 186
Shadow Mountain Publishing, pg 187
Shambhala Publications Inc, pg 187
Simon & Schuster Audio, pg 189
Simon & Schuster, LLC, pg 189
SkillPath Publications, pg 190
Sound Feelings Publishing, pg 194
Sounds True Inc, pg 194
Sourcebooks LLC, pg 194
Spizzirri Publishing Inc, pg 196
STARbooks Press, pg 197
The Story Plant, pg 199
Strategic Book Publishing (SBP), pg 199
Strategic Media Books LLC, pg 200
Stress Free Kids®, pg 200
Summit University Press, pg 200
Nan A Talese, pg 202
Tantor Media Inc, pg 202
Texas A&M University Press, pg 205
Theosophical University Press, pg 206
Third World Press Foundation, pg 206
Tommy Nelson®, pg 207
Torah Umesorah Publications, pg 208
Travelers' Tales, pg 209
The Trinity Foundation, pg 209
Tyndale House Publishers Inc, pg 211
Unarius Academy of Science Publications, pg 212
University Press of Kansas, pg 221
Vesuvian Books, pg 224
West Academic, pg 227
Westminster John Knox Press (WJK), pg 228
Whitaker House, pg 228
Whole Person Associates Inc, pg 229
John Wiley & Sons Inc, pg 230
Willow Creek Press, pg 230
Winterwolf Press, pg 231
Workman Publishing, pg 232
Writer's AudioShop, pg 234
Yale University Press, pg 235
Zondervan, pg 236

AV MATERIALS

American Bar Association Publishing, pg 8
American Correctional Association, pg 9
Applause Theatre & Cinema Books, pg 15
Barcelona Publishers LLC, pg 24
Books on Tape™, pg 34
Bridge Publications Inc, pg 36
The Catholic Health Association of the United States, pg 42
Cheng & Tsui Co Inc, pg 46
Child's Play® Inc, pg 46
Cold Spring Harbor Laboratory Press, pg 50
Comex Systems Inc, pg 51
Crown House Publishing Co LLC, pg 56
Data Trace Publishing Co (DTP), pg 57
The Dawn Horse Press, pg 57
Destiny Image Inc, pg 59
Educational Insights®, pg 64
Gateways Books & Tapes, pg 77
Georgetown University Press, pg 77
GIA Publications Inc, pg 78
Gospel Publishing House, pg 80
Her Own Words LLC, pg 91
Himalayan Institute Press, pg 92
International Society of Automation (ISA), pg 103
J J Keller & Associates, Inc®, pg 108
THE Learning Connection®, pg 113
Learning Links-USA Inc, pg 114
Life Cycle Books, pg 116
Lippincott Williams & Wilkins, pg 117
Milady, pg 131
Multicultural Publications Inc, pg 135
National Education Association (NEA), pg 137
Nilgiri Press, pg 141
Paulist Press, pg 152
Petroleum Extension Service (PETEX), pg 159
Piano Press, pg 159
Polebridge Press, pg 161
Practising Law Institute (PLI), pg 163
PSMJ Resources Inc, pg 166
Research Press, pg 174
Ross Books, pg 177
St Pauls, pg 181
Scholastic Inc, pg 184
Scholastic International, pg 184
Sounds True Inc, pg 194
Summit University Press, pg 200
Sundance/Newbridge Publishing, pg 200
Tortuga Press, pg 208
Vault.com Inc, pg 224
Voyager Sopris Learning Inc, pg 225
Whole Person Associates Inc, pg 229
John Wiley & Sons Inc, pg 230
Zaner-Bloser Inc, pg 236
Zondervan, pg 236

BELLES LETTRES

Anaphora Literary Press, pg 13
Anhinga Press Inc, pg 14
Ariadne Press, pg 16
BkMk Press Inc, pg 30
Copper Canyon Press, pg 52
Cypress House, pg 56
Dalkey Archive Press, pg 56
Delphinium Books, pg 58
Doubleday, pg 61
Editorial de la Universidad de Puerto Rico, pg 63
Excelsior Editions, pg 68
Godine, pg 79
Graywolf Press, pg 81
Hamilton Stone Editions, pg 84
Alfred A Knopf, pg 110
Luna Bisonte Prods, pg 121
Mandel Vilar Press, pg 124
McPherson & Co, pg 128
MFA Publications, pg 130
Montemayor Press, pg 133
New Directions Publishing Corp, pg 139
Paul Dry Books, pg 152
Persea Books, pg 158
Seven Stories Press, pg 186
Somerset Hall Press, pg 193
STOCKCERO Inc, pg 199
Trinity University Press, pg 209
Turtle Point Press, pg 210
University of North Texas Press, pg 218
University of Wisconsin Press, pg 221
University Press of Mississippi, pg 222
Wings Press, pg 231
Wolfman Books, pg 232

BIBLES

American Bible Society, pg 8
Augsburg Fortress Publishers, Publishing House of the Evangelical Lutheran Church in America, pg 22
B&H Publishing Group, pg 24
Barbour Publishing Inc, pg 24
Bridge Logos Inc, pg 36
Casa Bautista de Publicaciones, pg 41
Catholic Book Publishing Corp, pg 42
Charisma Media, pg 45
The Christian Science Publishing Society, pg 47
David C Cook, pg 52
Crossway, pg 56
Destiny Image Inc, pg 59
Dover Publications Inc, pg 61
Editorial Bautista Independiente, pg 63
Editorial Unilit, pg 64
Faith Library Publications, pg 69
Faithlife Corp, pg 69
Feldheim Publishers, pg 70
Fifth Estate Publishing, pg 71
Gospel Publishing House, pg 80
Group Publishing Inc, pg 82
Guideposts Book & Inspirational Media, pg 82
Harrison House, pg 87
Harvest House Publishers Inc, pg 88
Hendrickson Publishers Inc, pg 91
Ignatius Press, pg 98
The Jewish Publication Society, pg 105
Judaica Press Inc, pg 107
Kregel Publications, pg 111
KTAV Publishing House Inc, pg 111
Liturgical Press, pg 118
Living Stream Ministry (LSM), pg 119
The Lockman Foundation, pg 119
Lutheran Braille Workers Inc, pg 121
MennoMedia, pg 129
Mesorah Publications Ltd, pg 130
The Mongolia Society Inc, pg 133
Moody Publishers, pg 134
Moznaim Publishing Corp, pg 135
NavPress Publishing Group, pg 139
Our Sunday Visitor Publishing, pg 148
Oxford University Press USA, pg 149
Paulist Press, pg 152
Pentecostal Resources Group, pg 157
Polebridge Press, pg 161
Revell, pg 174
William H Sadlier Inc, pg 179
St Pauls, pg 181
Scepter Publishers, pg 183
SIL International, pg 188
Standard Publishing, pg 197
Tantor Media Inc, pg 202
Thomas Nelson, pg 206
Tommy Nelson®, pg 207
Tyndale House Publishers Inc, pg 211
US Conference of Catholic Bishops, pg 223
Zondervan, pg 236

BIBLIOGRAPHIES

ABC-CLIO, pg 2
AK Press, pg 6
American College of Surgeons, pg 9
American Geosciences Institute (AGI), pg 10
American Institute of Aeronautics and Astronautics (AIAA), pg 10
American Numismatic Society, pg 11
American Water Works Association (AWWA), pg 13
Anaphora Literary Press, pg 13
Ariadne Press, pg 16
John Benjamins Publishing Co, pg 28
R R Bowker LLC, pg 34
Boydell & Brewer Inc, pg 35
Brentwood Christian Press, pg 36
Bureau of Economic Geology, pg 38
Clearfield Co Inc, pg 49
Cypress House, pg 56
Walter De Gruyter Inc, pg 58
Goose River Press, pg 79
Gospel Publishing House, pg 80
Homa & Sekey Books, pg 95
The International Institute of Islamic Thought, pg 103
The Lentz Leadership Institute LLC, pg 115
Libraries Unlimited, pg 116
Management Advisory Services & Publications (MASP), pg 123
The Edwin Mellen Press, pg 129
Military Info Publishing, pg 131
Modern Language Association (MLA), pg 133
The Mongolia Society Inc, pg 133
National Center for Children in Poverty, pg 137
The New York Botanical Garden Press, pg 140
Nova Science Publishers Inc, pg 144
Oak Knoll Press, pg 144
Omnigraphics Inc, pg 146
On the Write Path Publishing, pg 146
Open Horizons Publishing Co, pg 147
Pennsylvania Historical & Museum Commission, pg 157
The Picasso Project, pg 160
Routledge, pg 177
St Johann Press, pg 180
Soyinfo Center, pg 196
Transportation Research Board (TRB), pg 209
Tuttle Publishing, pg 211
University of Wisconsin Press, pg 221
Watermark Publishing, pg 226
Markus Wiener Publishers Inc, pg 229

BRAILLE BOOKS

The Christian Science Publishing Society, pg 47
Forward Movement, pg 73
Kazi Publications Inc, pg 108
Lutheran Braille Workers Inc, pg 121
Mandel Vilar Press, pg 124
National Braille Press, pg 137

CHILDREN'S BOOKS

A 2 Z Press LLC, pg 1
Abbeville Publishing Group, pg 2
ABDO, pg 2
ACC Art Books, pg 3
ACTA Publications, pg 4
Advance Publishing Inc, pg 5
AdventureKEEN, pg 5
Akashic Books, pg 6
Albert Whitman & Company, pg 6
All About Kids Publishing, pg 7
Ambassador International, pg 7
American Bible Society, pg 8
American Carriage House Publishing (ACHP), pg 8
American Girl Publishing, pg 10
Amicus, pg 13
AMMO Books LLC, pg 13
Ampersand Inc/Professional Publishing Services, pg 13
Anaphora Literary Press, pg 13
Sara Anderson Children's Books, pg 13
Andrews McMeel Publishing LLC, pg 14
Angelus Press, pg 14
Applewood Books, pg 15
Arbordale Publishing, pg 16
Arcadia Publishing Inc, pg 16
Ascend Books LLC, pg 18
Asta Publications LLC, pg 20
Astra Books for Young Readers, pg 20
Atlas Publishing, pg 21
Augsburg Fortress Publishers, Publishing House of the Evangelical Lutheran Church in America, pg 22
August House Inc, pg 22
AuthorHouse, pg 22
Avery Color Studios, pg 23
Baby Tattoo Books, pg 23
Baha'i Publishing Trust, pg 23
B&H Publishing Group, pg 24
Barbour Publishing Inc, pg 24
Barefoot Books, pg 24
Barranca Press, pg 24
Barringer Publishing, pg 24
Basic Books Group, pg 25
Beacon Press, pg 25
Bear & Bobcat Books, pg 26
Bear & Co Inc, pg 26
Bearport Publishing, pg 26
Beaver's Pond Press Inc, pg 26
Bellerophon Books, pg 27
Ben Yehuda Press, pg 27
BePuzzled, pg 28
Bess Press Inc, pg 29
Bethlehem Books, pg 29
BiG GUY BOOKS, pg 29
Biographical Publishing Co, pg 29
BJU Press, pg 30
Black Rabbit Books, pg 30
Bloomsbury Publishing Inc, pg 31
Blue Whale Press, pg 32
BookLogix, pg 34
Boys Town Press, pg 35
Brandylane Publishers Inc, pg 35
BRAVE Books, pg 35
Bridge Publications Inc, pg 36
Brown Books Publishing Group (BBPG), pg 38
The Bureau for At-Risk Youth, pg 38
Campfield & Campfield Publishing LLC, pg 39
Candied Plums, pg 39
Candlewick Press, pg 39
Capen Publishing Co Inc, pg 40
Capstone Publishers™, pg 40
Carlisle Press - Walnut Creek, pg 40
Catholic Book Publishing Corp, pg 42
Cedar Grove Publishing, pg 43
Central Conference of American Rabbis/CCAR Press, pg 44
Central Recovery Press (CRP), pg 44
Charlesbridge Publishing Inc, pg 45
Chelsea House, pg 45
Chicago Review Press, pg 46
Chickadee Prince Books LLC, pg 46
Child Welfare League of America (CWLA), pg 46
Children's Book Press, pg 46
Child's Play® Inc, pg 46
The Child's World Inc, pg 46
China Books, pg 47
Christian Liberty Press, pg 47
Christian Light Publications Inc, pg 47
Chronicle Books LLC, pg 47
Cider Mill Press Book Publishers LLC, pg 48
Clarion Books, pg 48
Clear Light Publishers, pg 49
Cold Spring Harbor Laboratory Press, pg 50
Commonwealth Editions, pg 51
Concordia Publishing House, pg 51
Continental AfrikaPublishers, pg 52
David C Cook, pg 52
Cornell Maritime Press, pg 52
Covenant Communications Inc, pg 54
Crabtree Publishing Co, pg 54
Creative Editions, pg 55
Creston Books, pg 55
Cricket Cottage Publishing LLC, pg 55
Crossway, pg 56
Cypress House, pg 56
The Dawn Horse Press, pg 57
DawnSignPress, pg 58
DC Comics Inc, pg 58
Deep River Books LLC, pg 58
DeVorss & Co, pg 59
Dharma Publishing, pg 59
Dial Books for Young Readers, pg 59
Disney-Hyperion Books, pg 59
Disney Press, pg 59
Disney Publishing Worldwide, pg 60
DK, pg 60
Doodle and Peck Publishing, pg 60
Dorrance Publishing Co Inc, pg 61
Dover Publications Inc, pg 61
Down East Books, pg 61
Down The Shore Publishing, pg 61
Dutton Children's Books, pg 62
Eakin Press, pg 62
East West Discovery Press, pg 63
EDC Publishing, pg 63
ediciones Lerner, pg 63
Editorial Bautista Independiente, pg 63
Editorial de la Universidad de Puerto Rico, pg 63
Editorial Portavoz, pg 64
Editorial Unilit, pg 64
Educational Insights®, pg 64
Wm B Eerdmans Publishing Co, pg 64
Eifrig Publishing LLC, pg 64
Elva Resa Publishing, pg 65
Enchanted Lion Books, pg 66
Endless Mountains Publishing Co, pg 66
Enslow Publishing LLC, pg 66
The Experiment, pg 68
Familius, pg 69
Farcountry Press, pg 69
Father & Son Publishing Inc, pg 70
Filter Press LLC, pg 71
First Avenue Editions, pg 72
Fitzroy Books, pg 72
Flamingo Books, pg 72
Flashlight Press, pg 72
Focus on the Family, pg 73
Walter Foster Publishing, pg 74
Fox Chapel Publishing Co Inc, pg 74
Free Spirit Publishing Inc, pg 74
Fulcrum Publishing Inc, pg 75
Galde Press Inc, pg 75
Gale, pg 75
Gallaudet University Press, pg 76
Gallopade International Inc, pg 76
Gareth Stevens Publishing, pg 76
Gatekeeper Press, pg 77
Gauthier Publications Inc, pg 77
Getty Publications, pg 78
Gibbs Smith Publisher, pg 78
Glitterati Inc, pg 78
Godine, pg 79
Goose River Press, pg 79
Gorgias Press LLC, pg 80
Gospel Publishing House, pg 80
Grand & Archer Publishing, pg 80
Graphic Universe™, pg 80
Green Dragon Books, pg 81
Greenleaf Book Group LLC, pg 81
Hachai Publishing, pg 83
Hachette Book Group Inc, pg 83
Hal Leonard LLC, pg 84
Hameray Publishing Group Inc, pg 84
Hamilton Stone Editions, pg 84
Handprint Books Inc, pg 84
Hannacroix Creek Books Inc, pg 85
HarperCollins Children's Books, pg 85
HarperCollins Publishers LLC, pg 86
Hazy Dell Press, pg 89
Herald Press, pg 91
Hewitt Homeschooling Resources, pg 91
Highlights for Children Inc, pg 92
Hollym International Corp, pg 94
Homestead Publishing, pg 95
Houghton Mifflin Harcourt, pg 95
Houghton Mifflin Harcourt Trade & Reference Division, pg 96
Ignatius Press, pg 98
Immedium, pg 99
In the Garden Publishing, pg 99
Indiana Historical Society Press, pg 99
The Innovation Press, pg 101
Interlink Publishing Group Inc, pg 102
International Book Centre Inc, pg 102
International Linguistics Corp, pg 103
Islandport Press, pg 105
Jewish Lights Publishing, pg 105
Judaica Press Inc, pg 107
Jump!, pg 107
Jump at the Sun, pg 107
Kaeden Publishing, pg 107
Kalaniot Books, pg 107
Kamehameha Publishing, pg 108
Kapp Books LLC, pg 108
Kar-Ben Publishing, pg 108
Kazi Publications Inc, pg 108
Kidsbooks® Publishing, pg 109
Kiva Publishing Inc, pg 110
Klutz®, pg 110
Kodansha USA Inc, pg 110
Koho Pono LLC, pg 111
Kokila, pg 111
Kregel Publications, pg 111
KTAV Publishing House Inc, pg 111
Kumon Publishing North America Inc (KPNA), pg 112
Lake Superior Publishing LLC, pg 112
Landauer Publishing, pg 112
Laredo Publishing Co, pg 113
THE Learning Connection®, pg 113
Learning Links-USA Inc, pg 114
Lectorum Publications Inc, pg 114
Legacy Bound, pg 114
The Lentz Leadership Institute LLC, pg 115
Light-Beams Publishing, pg 116
Liguori Publications, pg 117
Listen & Live Audio Inc, pg 117
little bee books, pg 117
Little, Brown Books for Young Readers (LBYR), pg 118
The Little Entrepreneur, pg 118
Lost Classics Book Company LLC, pg 120
Loving Healing Press Inc, pg 121
Lutheran Braille Workers Inc, pg 121
Macmillan, pg 121
Mandala Earth, pg 124
Mandel Vilar Press, pg 124
Maren Green Publishing Inc, pg 125
Maryland History Press, pg 126
Master Books®, pg 126
Math Solutions®, pg 127
Mazda Publishers Inc, pg 127
McSweeney's Publishing, pg 128
me+mi publishing inc, pg 128
Mel Bay Publications Inc, pg 129
The Metropolitan Museum of Art, pg 130
Mighty Media Press, pg 131
Milford Books™, pg 131
Milkweed Editions, pg 131
Millbrook Press, pg 131
Montemayor Press, pg 133
Multicultural Publications Inc, pg 135
Multnomah, pg 135
Mutual Publishing LLC, pg 136
Nataraj Books, pg 136
National Geographic Books, pg 137
National Science Teachers Association (NSTA), pg 138
National Wildlife Federation, pg 139
New City Press, pg 139
NewSouth Books, pg 141
Nilgiri Press, pg 141
No Starch Press, pg 141
North Atlantic Books (NAB), pg 142
North Star Editions Inc, pg 142
Norwood House Press, pg 143
Nosy Crow Inc, pg 144
OCP, pg 145
Odyssey Books, pg 145
Open Books Press, pg 146
ORO editions, pg 148
Our Daily Bread Publishing, pg 148
Our Sunday Visitor Publishing, pg 148

U.S. PUBLISHERS — TYPE OF PUBLICATION INDEX

BOOK

Richard C Owen Publishers Inc, pg 149
P & R Publishing Co, pg 149
PA Press, pg 149
Paintbox Press, pg 150
Pangaea Publications, pg 150
Pants On Fire Press, pg 150
Papercutz, pg 150
Parachute Publishing LLC, pg 151
Paraclete Press Inc, pg 151
Parallax Press, pg 151
Parenting Press, pg 151
Park Place Publications, pg 152
Pauline Books & Media, pg 152
Paulist Press, pg 152
Nancy Paulsen Books, pg 152
Peachtree Publishing Co Inc, pg 153
Pelican Publishing, pg 153
Pen & Publish LLC, pg 153
Penfield Books, pg 154
Penguin Publishing Group, pg 154
Penguin Workshop, pg 156
Penguin Young Readers Group, pg 156
Penny-Farthing Productions, pg 157
Perfection Learning®, pg 158
Peter Pauper Press, Inc, pg 158
Pflaum Publishing Group, pg 159
Phaidon, pg 159
Philomel Books, pg 159
Piano Press, pg 159
Pineapple Press, pg 160
Planert Creek Press, pg 160
Platypus Media LLC, pg 160
Plough Publishing House, pg 161
Plowshare Media, pg 161
Plum Tree Books, pg 161
Polar Bear & Company, pg 161
Polebridge Press, pg 161
Pomegranate Communications Inc, pg 162
Presbyterian Publishing Corp (PPC), pg 163
Publication Consultants, pg 167
Puffin Books, pg 167
Purple House Press, pg 167
GP Putnam's Sons Books for Young Readers, pg 167
Quarto Publishing Group USA Inc, pg 168
Rand McNally, pg 169
Random House Children's Books, pg 169
Recorded Books Inc, an RBmedia company, pg 172
Red Chair Press, pg 172
Robert D Reed Publishers, pg 173
Remember Point Inc, pg 174
Renaissance House, pg 174
Rising Sun Publishing, pg 175
The RoadRunner Press, pg 175
Roaring Brook Press, pg 175
Rocky Pond Books, pg 176
Roman Catholic Books, pg 176
Round Table Companies, pg 177
Rowe Publishing LLC, pg 178
Running Press, pg 178
Saddleback Educational Publishing, pg 179
William H Sadlier Inc, pg 179
St Martin's Press, LLC, pg 180
St Nectarios Press, pg 181
Salina Bookshelf Inc, pg 181
Sasquatch Books, pg 182
Satya House Publications, pg 182
Savant Books & Publications LLC, pg 182
Scholastic Education Solutions, pg 184
Scholastic Inc, pg 184
Scholastic International, pg 184
Scholastic Trade Publishing, pg 184
Science, Naturally, pg 185

Seedling Publications Inc, pg 186
Seven Stories Press, pg 186
Shadow Mountain Publishing, pg 187
Shen's Books, pg 187
Shepard Publications, pg 187
Simon & Schuster Children's Publishing, pg 189
Simon & Schuster, LLC, pg 189
Sky Pony Press, pg 191
SkyLight Paths® Publishing, pg 191
Sleeping Bear Press™, pg 191
Soho Press Inc, pg 193
Sounds True Inc, pg 194
Sourcebooks LLC, pg 194
Sourced Media Books, pg 195
Spizzirri Publishing Inc, pg 196
Standard Publishing, pg 197
Star Bright Books Inc, pg 197
SteinerBooks Inc, pg 198
Stellar Publishing, pg 198
Stone Bridge Press Inc, pg 199
Story Monsters LLC, pg 199
Strategic Book Publishing (SBP), pg 199
Stress Free Kids®, pg 200
Sundance/Newbridge Publishing, pg 200
Tanglewood Publishing, pg 202
Teora USA LLC, pg 204
Third World Press Foundation, pg 206
ThunderStone Books, pg 207
Tiger Tales, pg 207
Tilbury House Publishers, pg 207
Tommy Nelson®, pg 207
Tortuga Press, pg 208
Trafford Publishing, pg 208
Treasure Bay Inc, pg 209
Treehaus Communications Inc, pg 209
TRISTAN Publishing, pg 209
Trusted Media Brands Inc, pg 210
Tughra Books, pg 210
Tumblehome Learning Inc, pg 210
Turner Publishing Co LLC, pg 210
Tuttle Publishing, pg 211
Tyndale House Publishers Inc, pg 211
Ugly Duckling Presse, pg 212
Union Square & Co, pg 212
United Nations Publications, pg 213
Universe Publishing, pg 214
University of Hawaii Press, pg 216
University of Louisiana at Lafayette Press, pg 217
University Science Books, pg 222
Urim Publications, pg 223
US Government Publishing Office (GPO), pg 223
Viking Children's Books, pg 224
Waldorf Publishing LLC, pg 226
WaterBrook, pg 226
Watermark Publishing, pg 226
Wayne State University Press, pg 226
Well-Trained Mind Press, pg 227
West Margin Press, pg 227
Westminster John Knox Press (WJK), pg 228
Wheatherstone Press, pg 228
Wide World Publishing, pg 229
Wildflower Press, pg 229
Wings Press, pg 231
Winters Publishing, pg 231
Winterwolf Press, pg 231
Wisdom Publications Inc, pg 231
Woodbine House, pg 232
Workman Publishing, pg 232
World Book Inc, pg 233
World Citizens, pg 233
Xist Publishing, pg 234
Xlibris Corp, pg 234

Yard Dog Press, pg 235
Zondervan, pg 236

COMPUTER SOFTWARE

American Water Works Association (AWWA), pg 13
Apress Media LLC, pg 15
Ariel Press, pg 16
Artech House®, pg 17
Bisk Education, pg 29
Paul H Brookes Publishing Co Inc, pg 37
CCH, a Wolters Kluwer business, pg 42
Cengage Learning, pg 43
China Books, pg 47
The College Board, pg 50
Columbia Books & Information Services (CBIS), pg 50
Council for Exceptional Children (CEC), pg 53
Craftsman Book Co, pg 54
F A Davis Co, pg 57
Elsevier Health Sciences, pg 65
Gale, pg 75
Gallopade International Inc, pg 76
HeartMath LLC, pg 90
International Society of Automation (ISA), pg 103
JIST Publishing, pg 106
Law School Admission Council (LSAC), pg 113
Lawyers & Judges Publishing Co Inc, pg 113
Lippincott Williams & Wilkins, pg 117
Milady, pg 131
Modern Language Association (MLA), pg 133
NACE International, pg 136
National Academies Press (NAP), pg 136
W W Norton & Company Inc, pg 143
Nova Press, pg 144
OptumInsight™, pg 147
Pennsylvania State Data Center, pg 157
PennWell Books, pg 157
SAS Press, pg 182
Scholastic Inc, pg 184
Scholastic International, pg 184
South Carolina Bar, pg 195
Starcrafts LLC, pg 197
TotalRecall Publications Inc, pg 208
Tyndale House Publishers Inc, pg 211
United States Pharmacopeia (USP), pg 213
Water Resources Publications LLC, pg 226
John Wiley & Sons Inc, pg 230
YBK Publishers Inc, pg 235
Zaner-Bloser Inc, pg 236

DATABASES

ABC-CLIO, pg 2
AICPA® & CIMA®, pg 5
Alexander Street, part of Clarivate PLC, pg 6
American Geosciences Institute (AGI), pg 10
American Institute of Aeronautics and Astronautics (AIAA), pg 10
American Mathematical Society (AMS), pg 11
American Society of Civil Engineers (ASCE), pg 12
American Water Works Association (AWWA), pg 13
Apress Media LLC, pg 15

ASM International, pg 19
Association of College & Research Libraries (ACRL), pg 19
Authorlink® Press, pg 22
Begell House Inc Publishers, pg 27
Blue Book Publications Inc, pg 32
R R Bowker LLC, pg 34
Paul H Brookes Publishing Co Inc, pg 37
Bureau of Economic Geology, pg 38
Business Research Services Inc, pg 38
Candid, pg 39
Capitol Enquiry Inc, pg 40
Cengage Learning, pg 43
Chain Store Guide (CSG), pg 44
China Books, pg 47
Clearfield Co Inc, pg 49
Cold Spring Harbor Laboratory Press, pg 50
Columbia Books & Information Services (CBIS), pg 50
The Council of State Governments, pg 53
CQ Press, pg 54
Craftsman Book Co, pg 54
CRC Press, pg 55
Elsevier Inc, pg 65
Facts On File, pg 69
Faithlife Corp, pg 69
Ferguson Publishing, pg 71
Gale, pg 75
GeoLytics Inc, pg 77
Grey House Publishing Inc™, pg 81
Gulf Energy Information, pg 83
Hal Leonard LLC, pg 84
Health Forum Inc, pg 90
William S Hein & Co Inc, pg 90
IBFD North America Inc (International Bureau of Fiscal Documentation), pg 98
IET USA Inc, pg 98
Illinois State Museum Society, pg 99
International City/County Management Association (ICMA), pg 102
International Monetary Fund (IMF), Editorial & Publications Division, pg 103
Joshua Tree Publishing, pg 107
J J Keller & Associates, Inc®, pg 108
Kennedy Information LLC, pg 108
Logos Press, pg 119
Long River Press, pg 120
Looseleaf Law Publications Inc, pg 120
Marquis Who's Who, pg 125
The Massachusetts Historical Society, pg 126
McGraw-Hill Education, pg 127
The Edwin Mellen Press, pg 129
Modern Language Association (MLA), pg 133
NACE International, pg 136
National Academies Press (NAP), pg 136
National Association of Broadcasters (NAB), pg 136
National Association of Insurance Commissioners, pg 136
National Center For Employee Ownership (NCEO), pg 137
National Conference of State Legislatures (NCSL), pg 137
National Golf Foundation, pg 138
NRP Direct, pg 144
OECD Washington Center, pg 145
Omnigraphics Inc, pg 146
Open Horizons Publishing Co, pg 147
OptumInsight™, pg 147

250

PUBLISHERS

U.S. PUBLISHERS — TYPE OF PUBLICATION INDEX

Pennsylvania State Data Center, pg 157
Philosophy Documentation Center, pg 159
Plunkett Research Ltd, pg 161
Primary Research Group Inc, pg 163
ProQuest LLC, part of Clarivate PLC, pg 166
The PRS Group Inc, pg 166
Rand McNally, pg 169
Random House Reference/Random House Puzzles & Games, pg 171
Ross Books, pg 177
SAE (Society of Automotive Engineers International), pg 179
SAGE Publishing, pg 180
Salem Press, pg 181
SAS Press, pg 182
Schlager Group Inc, pg 183
Schonfeld & Associates Inc, pg 184
SPIE, pg 196
Thieme Medical Publishers Inc, pg 206
Tower Publishing Co, pg 208
Transportation Research Board (TRB), pg 209
UCLA Latin American Center Publications, pg 212
United Nations Publications, pg 213
United States Pharmacopeia (USP), pg 213
John Wiley & Sons Inc, pg 230
John Wiley & Sons Inc Global Education, pg 230
John Wiley & Sons Inc Professional Development, pg 230
Wolters Kluwer Law & Business, pg 232
World Trade Press LLC, pg 234
Zagat Inc, pg 236

DICTIONARIES, ENCYCLOPEDIAS

ABC-CLIO, pg 2
Academic Press, pg 3
ALA Neal-Schuman, pg 6
Alaska Native Language Center (ANLC), pg 6
American Correctional Association, pg 9
American Geosciences Institute (AGI), pg 10
Anaphora Literary Press, pg 13
Astragal Press, pg 20
Baker Books, pg 23
John Benjamins Publishing Co, pg 28
Bloomsbury Academic, pg 31
Brewers Publications, pg 36
Captain Fiddle Music & Publications, pg 40
Catholic Book Publishing Corp, pg 42
Charles Press Publishers, pg 45
Cheng & Tsui Co Inc, pg 46
China Books, pg 47
Columbia University Press, pg 51
Country Music Foundation Press, pg 54
Crown House Publishing Co LLC, pg 56
F A Davis Co, pg 57
Walter De Gruyter Inc, pg 58
DK, pg 60
ECS Publishing Group, pg 63
EDC Publishing, pg 63
Editorial Bautista Independiente, pg 63
Elderberry Press Inc, pg 65
Edward Elgar Publishing Inc, pg 65
Elsevier Health Sciences, pg 65

Elsevier Inc, pg 65
Encyclopaedia Britannica Inc, pg 66
Facts On File, pg 69
Fairchild Books, pg 69
Faithlife Corp, pg 69
Federal Street Press, pg 70
Fifth Estate Publishing, pg 71
Gale, pg 75
Gallaudet University Press, pg 76
Hal Leonard LLC, pg 84
Hanser Publications LLC, pg 85
Hendrickson Publishers Inc, pg 91
Hippocrene Books Inc, pg 92
Hollym International Corp, pg 94
Homa & Sekey Books, pg 95
Houghton Mifflin Harcourt, pg 95
Idyll Arbor Inc, pg 98
Indiana University Press, pg 100
International Book Centre Inc, pg 102
The International Institute of Islamic Thought, pg 103
International Society of Automation (ISA), pg 103
International Wealth Success (IWS), pg 104
InterVarsity Press, pg 104
Kazi Publications Inc, pg 108
Liturgical Press, pg 118
Living Language, pg 119
Macmillan Reference USA™, pg 123
Marshall Cavendish Education, pg 125
Mazda Publishers Inc, pg 127
R S Means from The Gordian Group, pg 128
Mel Bay Publications Inc, pg 129
The Edwin Mellen Press, pg 129
Merriam-Webster Inc, pg 129
Milady, pg 131
Mondial, pg 133
The Mongolia Society Inc, pg 133
De Gruyter Mouton, pg 135
NASW Press, pg 136
Nataraj Books, pg 136
National Geographic Learning, pg 138
NOLO, pg 141
Ohio University Press, pg 145
Omnigraphics Inc, pg 146
Oriental Institute Publications, pg 148
Our Sunday Visitor Publishing, pg 148
Oxford University Press USA, pg 149
Paradigm Publications, pg 151
Penfield Books, pg 154
Perfection Learning®, pg 158
Petroleum Extension Service (PETEX), pg 158
Philosophical Library Inc, pg 159
PRINTING United Alliance, pg 165
Random House Reference/Random House Puzzles & Games, pg 171
Reference Publications Inc, pg 173
Lynne Rienner Publishers Inc, pg 174
Routledge, pg 177
Rowman & Littlefield, pg 178
SAGE Publishing, pg 180
St James Press®, pg 180
St Martin's Press, LLC, pg 180
Salina Bookshelf Inc, pg 181
Schlager Group Inc, pg 183
Scholastic Inc, pg 184
Scholastic International, pg 184
Schreiber Publishing, pg 185
Shambhala Publications Inc, pg 187
Society of Exploration Geophysicists, pg 192
Springer Publishing Co, pg 196

Starcrafts LLC, pg 197
Trans-Atlantic Publications Inc, pg 209
Tuttle Publishing, pg 211
Tyndale House Publishers Inc, pg 211
United States Pharmacopeia (USP), pg 213
Universal-Publishers Inc, pg 213
University of Chicago Press, pg 215
University of Hawaii Press, pg 216
University of Louisiana at Lafayette Press, pg 217
US Games Systems Inc, pg 223
Velazquez Press, pg 224
Visible Ink Press®, pg 225
Westminster John Knox Press (WJK), pg 228
Wiley-Blackwell, pg 229
John Wiley & Sons Inc, pg 230
World Book Inc, pg 233
World Trade Press LLC, pg 234
Yale University Press, pg 235
Zondervan, pg 236

DIRECTORIES, REFERENCE BOOKS

Abbeville Publishing Group, pg 2
ABC-CLIO, pg 2
Abingdon Press, pg 2
Academic Press, pg 3
ACC Art Books, pg 3
ACS Publications, pg 4
Adams & Ambrose Publishing, pg 4
ALA Neal-Schuman, pg 6
Alexander Street, part of Clarivate PLC, pg 6
Allworth Press, pg 7
American Academy of Environmental Engineers & Scientists®, pg 8
American Academy of Pediatrics, pg 8
American Association of Collegiate Registrars & Admissions Officers (AACRAO), pg 8
American Bar Association Publishing, pg 8
The American Ceramic Society, pg 9
American Correctional Association, pg 9
American Diabetes Association, pg 9
American Fisheries Society, pg 9
American Geosciences Institute (AGI), pg 10
American Historical Association (AHA), pg 10
American Institute of Chemical Engineers (AIChE), pg 10
American Medical Association (AMA), pg 11
American Psychiatric Association Publishing, pg 11
American Technical Publishers, pg 13
American Water Works Association (AWWA), pg 13
Anaphora Literary Press, pg 13
APS PRESS, pg 16
Jason Aronson Inc, pg 17
ArtAge Publications, pg 17
ASM International, pg 19
Association for the Advancement of Blood & Biotherapies, pg 19
ASTM International, pg 20
Astragal Press, pg 20
Avotaynu Books LLC, pg 23
Baker Books, pg 23
Begell House Inc Publishers, pg 27
Bentley Publishers, pg 28

Bernan, pg 28
Bess Press Inc, pg 29
Blood Moon Productions Ltd, pg 31
Bloomsbury Academic, pg 31
Blue Book Publications Inc, pg 32
BNi Building News, pg 33
Bookhaven Press LLC, pg 34
Breakthrough Publications Inc, pg 36
Brewers Publications, pg 36
The Bureau for At-Risk Youth, pg 38
Business Research Services Inc, pg 38
Capitol Enquiry Inc, pg 40
Captain Fiddle Music & Publications, pg 40
Carlisle Press - Walnut Creek, pg 40
Carolina Academic Press, pg 41
CarTech Inc, pg 41
Cengage Learning, pg 43
Center for Creative Leadership LLC, pg 43
Center for Futures Education Inc, pg 43
Chain Store Guide (CSG), pg 44
Charles Press Publishers, pg 45
Cheng & Tsui Co Inc, pg 46
China Books, pg 47
Clearfield Co Inc, pg 49
Cleis Press, pg 49
Clinical and Laboratory Standards Institute (CLSI), pg 49
Cold Spring Harbor Laboratory Press, pg 50
The College Board, pg 50
Columbia Books & Information Services (CBIS), pg 50
Columbia University Press, pg 51
Continental AfrikaPublishers, pg 52
David C Cook, pg 52
The Council of State Governments, pg 53
Country Music Foundation Press, pg 54
Countryman Press, pg 54
CQ Press, pg 54
Craftsman Book Co, pg 54
CRC Press, pg 55
CSWE Press, pg 56
Walter De Gruyter Inc, pg 58
Dewey Publications Inc, pg 59
DK, pg 60
Dun & Bradstreet, pg 62
ECS Publishing Group, pg 63
Editorial de la Universidad de Puerto Rico, pg 63
Edward Elgar Publishing Inc, pg 65
Elsevier Health Sciences, pg 65
Elsevier Inc, pg 65
Emmaus Road Publishing Inc, pg 66
Encyclopaedia Britannica Inc, pg 66
Facts On File, pg 69
Federal Street Press, pg 70
Ferguson Publishing, pg 71
Fifth Estate Publishing, pg 71
Gale, pg 75
Gallaudet University Press, pg 76
Gareth Stevens Publishing, pg 76
GemStone Press, pg 77
Genealogical Publishing Co, pg 77
GeoLytics Inc, pg 77
Global Training Center, pg 79
Gorgias Press LLC, pg 80
The Graduate Group/Booksellers, pg 80
Green Integer, pg 81
Grey House Publishing Inc™, pg 81
The Guilford Press, pg 82
Hal Leonard LLC, pg 84
Hannacroix Creek Books Inc, pg 85
Hanser Publications LLC, pg 85
HCPro/DecisionHealth, pg 89

251

U.S. PUBLISHERS — TYPE OF PUBLICATION INDEX   BOOK

Health Forum Inc, pg 90
William S Hein & Co Inc, pg 90
Hendrickson Publishers Inc, pg 91
Heritage Books Inc, pg 91
Hollym International Corp, pg 94
Hospital & Healthcare Compensation Service, pg 95
Houghton Mifflin Harcourt, pg 95
Houghton Mifflin Harcourt Trade & Reference Division, pg 96
Idyll Arbor Inc, pg 98
Illinois State Museum Society, pg 99
Indiana University Press, pg 100
Industrial Press Inc, pg 100
Information Gatekeepers Inc (IGI), pg 100
Information Today, Inc, pg 100
Infosources Publishing, pg 100
Institute of Environmental Sciences & Technology - IEST, pg 101
Institute of Police Technology & Management (IPTM), pg 102
Intercultural Development Research Association (IDRA), pg 102
International Book Centre Inc, pg 102
International City/County Management Association (ICMA), pg 102
The International Institute of Islamic Thought, pg 103
International Monetary Fund (IMF), Editorial & Publications Division, pg 103
International Risk Management Institute Inc, pg 103
International Society of Automation (ISA), pg 103
International Wealth Success (IWS), pg 104
InterVarsity Press, pg 104
Iron Gate Publishing, pg 104
Island Press, pg 104
Jewish Lights Publishing, pg 105
Lyndon B Johnson School of Public Affairs, pg 106
Jones & Bartlett Learning LLC, pg 107
Joshua Tree Publishing, pg 107
Judaica Press Inc, pg 107
Kalmbach Media Co, pg 108
Kamehameha Publishing, pg 108
Kennedy Information LLC, pg 108
Alfred A Knopf, pg 110
Krause Publications Inc, pg 111
Krieger Publishing Co, pg 111
LAMA Books, pg 112
Lawyers & Judges Publishing Co Inc, pg 113
LearningExpress, pg 114
Libraries Unlimited, pg 116
Limelight Editions, pg 117
Lippincott Williams & Wilkins, pg 117
Little, Brown and Company, pg 118
Liturgical Press, pg 118
Loft Press Inc, pg 119
Lonely Planet Publications Inc, pg 120
Long River Press, pg 120
LRP Publications, pg 121
Macmillan Reference USA™, pg 123
Management Sciences for Health, pg 123
Marine Techniques Publishing, pg 125
Marquis Who's Who, pg 125
Marshall Cavendish Education, pg 125
Martindale LLC, pg 126

The Massachusetts Historical Society, pg 126
Master Books®, pg 126
Mazda Publishers Inc, pg 127
R S Means from The Gordian Group, pg 128
The Edwin Mellen Press, pg 129
Menasha Ridge Press, pg 129
Michigan State University Press (MSU Press), pg 130
Midnight Marquee Press Inc, pg 130
Milady, pg 131
Military Info Publishing, pg 131
Military Living Publications, pg 131
Richard K Miller Associates, pg 132
The MIT Press, pg 132
Modern Language Association (MLA), pg 133
The Mongolia Society Inc, pg 133
Morning Sun Books Inc, pg 134
De Gruyter Mouton, pg 135
NACE International, pg 136
NASW Press, pg 136
Nataraj Books, pg 136
National Academies Press (NAP), pg 136
National Association of Broadcasters (NAB), pg 136
National Association of Insurance Commissioners, pg 136
National Book Co, pg 136
National Catholic Educational Association, pg 137
National Center for Children in Poverty, pg 137
National Conference of State Legislatures (NCSL), pg 137
National Geographic Books, pg 137
National Golf Foundation, pg 138
National Science Teachers Association (NSTA), pg 138
Naval Institute Press, pg 139
The New York Botanical Garden Press, pg 140
New York University Press, pg 141
Newbury Street Press, pg 141
NOLO, pg 141
North Atlantic Books (NAB), pg 142
North River Press Publishing Corp, pg 142
NRP Direct, pg 144
OAG Worldwide, pg 144
Oak Knoll Press, pg 144
OECD Washington Center, pg 145
Omnigraphics Inc, pg 146
One On One Book Publishing/Film-Video Publications, pg 146
OptumInsight™, pg 147
Oxford University Press USA, pg 149
Palgrave Macmillan, pg 150
Park Place Publications, pg 152
Penguin Random House LLC, pg 155
Pennsylvania Historical & Museum Commission, pg 157
Pennsylvania State Data Center, pg 157
PennWell Books, pg 157
Perfection Learning®, pg 158
Peterson's, pg 158
Petroleum Extension Service (PETEX), pg 159
Philosophical Library Inc, pg 159
Philosophy Documentation Center, pg 159
Pineapple Press, pg 160
Plunkett Research Ltd, pg 161
Pocket Press Inc, pg 161
Poisoned Pen Press, pg 161

Polar Bear & Company, pg 161
Practice Management Information Corp (PMIC), pg 163
Primary Research Group Inc, pg 163
Princeton University Press, pg 164
PRO-ED Inc, pg 165
The PRS Group Inc, pg 166
Public Citizen, pg 167
Radix Press, pg 169
Rand McNally, pg 169
Random House Reference/Random House Puzzles & Games, pg 171
Reference Publications Inc, pg 173
Ross Books, pg 177
Routledge, pg 177
Rowman & Littlefield, pg 178
Running Press, pg 178
Rutgers University Press, pg 178
SAGE Publishing, pg 180
St James Press®, pg 180
St Martin's Press, LLC, pg 180
Salem Press, pg 181
SAS Press, pg 182
Schiffer Publishing Ltd, pg 183
Schlager Group Inc, pg 183
Scholastic Inc, pg 184
Schonfeld & Associates Inc, pg 184
School Guide Publications, pg 185
Schreiber Publishing, pg 185
Scripta Humanistica Publishing International, pg 185
SIL International, pg 188
SkyLight Paths® Publishing, pg 191
SLACK® Incorporated, A Wyanoke Group Company, pg 191
Smith & Kraus Publishers Inc, pg 192
M Lee Smith Publishers, pg 192
Society for Human Resource Management (SHRM), pg 192
Society of Exploration Geophysicists, pg 192
The Society of Naval Architects & Marine Engineers (SNAME), pg 193
Sourcebooks LLC, pg 194
Soyinfo Center, pg 196
SPIE, pg 196
Star Publishing Co Inc, pg 197
Starcrafts LLC, pg 197
Story Monsters LLC, pg 199
SYBEX, pg 201
Tantor Media Inc, pg 202
Teachers College Press, pg 203
Ten Speed Press, pg 204
Theatre Communications Group, pg 205
Thieme Medical Publishers Inc, pg 206
Charles C Thomas Publisher Ltd, pg 206
Thomas Nelson, pg 206
Thomson West, pg 206
Todd Publications, pg 207
Torah Umesorah Publications, pg 208
Tower Publishing Co, pg 208
Trans-Atlantic Publications Inc, pg 209
Transportation Research Board (TRB), pg 209
Tyndale House Publishers Inc, pg 211
Union Square & Co, pg 212
United Nations Publications, pg 213
United States Holocaust Memorial Museum, pg 213
United States Institute of Peace Press, pg 213
United States Pharmacopeia (USP), pg 213
Universal-Publishers Inc, pg 213

University of Iowa Press, pg 216
The University of Utah Press, pg 220
University Press of America Inc, pg 221
University Science Books, pg 222
US Conference of Catholic Bishops, pg 223
Vault.com Inc, pg 224
Visual Profile Books Inc, pg 225
Water Resources Publications LLC, pg 226
Western Pennsylvania Genealogical Society, pg 228
Wide World of Maps Inc, pg 229
Wiley-Blackwell, pg 229
John Wiley & Sons Inc Global Education, pg 230
John Wiley & Sons Inc Professional Development, pg 230
Winters Publishing, pg 231
Wisconsin Department of Public Instruction, pg 231
Alan Wofsy Fine Arts, pg 231
Wolters Kluwer Law & Business, pg 232
Woodbine House, pg 232
World Almanac®, pg 233
World Bank Publications, pg 233
World Trade Press LLC, pg 234
Zondervan, pg 236

EBOOKS OR CD-ROMS

A-R Editions Inc, pg 1
AAPG (American Association of Petroleum Geologists), pg 1
Abbeville Press, pg 1
ABC-CLIO, pg 2
Abingdon Press, pg 2
Academic Press, pg 3
ACM Books, pg 4
ACTA Publications, pg 4
Adams Media, pg 4
Adventures Unlimited Press (AUP), pg 5
African American Images Inc (AAI), pg 5
AICPA® & CIMA®, pg 5
Akashic Books, pg 6
ALA Neal-Schuman, pg 6
Alfred Music, pg 6
All About Kids Publishing, pg 7
All Things That Matter Press, pg 7
Allworth Press, pg 7
Amakella Publishing, pg 7
Ambassador International, pg 7
American Anthropological Association (AAA), pg 8
American Bible Society, pg 8
American Carriage House Publishing (ACHP), pg 8
American Catholic Press (ACP), pg 9
The American Ceramic Society, pg 9
American Diabetes Association, pg 9
American Geosciences Institute (AGI), pg 10
American Historical Association (AHA), pg 10
American Institute for Economic Research (AIER), pg 10
American Institute of Aeronautics and Astronautics (AIAA), pg 10
American Institute of Chemical Engineers (AIChE), pg 10
American Law Institute Continuing Legal Education (ALI CLE), pg 10
The American Library Association (ALA), pg 10

PUBLISHERS

U.S. PUBLISHERS — TYPE OF PUBLICATION INDEX

American Psychiatric Association Publishing, pg 11
American Society for Nondestructive Testing, pg 12
American Society for Quality (ASQ), pg 12
American Society of Agricultural & Biological Engineers (ASABE), pg 12
American Society of Civil Engineers (ASCE), pg 12
American Society of Mechanical Engineers (ASME), pg 12
American Water Works Association (AWWA), pg 13
Ampersand Inc/Professional Publishing Services, pg 13
Andrews McMeel Publishing LLC, pg 14
Angelus Press, pg 14
ANR Publications University of California, pg 14
APH Press, pg 15
APPA - Leadership in Education Facilities, pg 15
Apress Media LLC, pg 15
APS PRESS, pg 16
Arbordale Publishing, pg 16
Ariel Press, pg 16
Art of Living, PrimaMedia Inc, pg 17
Artech House®, pg 17
ASCD, pg 18
Ascend Books LLC, pg 18
ASCP Press, pg 18
Ashland Creek Press, pg 18
ASM International, pg 19
ASM Publishing, pg 19
Aspatore Books, pg 19
Association for the Advancement of Blood & Biotherapies, pg 19
ASTM International, pg 20
Atlantic Publishing Group Inc, pg 21
Atlas Publishing, pg 21
Augsburg Fortress Publishers, Publishing House of the Evangelical Lutheran Church in America, pg 22
Avant-Guide, pg 22
Baen Books, pg 23
Baker Books, pg 23
Basic Books Group, pg 25
BearManor Media, pg 26
Bella Books, pg 27
Bellevue Literary Press, pg 27
BenBella Books Inc, pg 27
Bentley Publishers, pg 28
Berrett-Koehler Publishers Inc, pg 29
Bess Press Inc, pg 29
Bhaktivedanta Book Trust (BBT), pg 29
Biographical Publishing Co, pg 29
George T Bisel Co Inc, pg 29
Bisk Education, pg 29
Bitingduck Press LLC, pg 30
BJU Press, pg 30
Black Mountain Press, pg 30
Blair, pg 30
BLR®—Business & Legal Resources, pg 32
Blue Poppy Press, pg 32
BoardSource, pg 33
Bolchazy-Carducci Publishers Inc, pg 33
Bold Strokes Books Inc, pg 33
BookLogix, pg 34
Boson Books™, pg 34
Brandylane Publishers Inc, pg 35
George Braziller Inc, pg 35
Brill Inc, pg 37

Paul H Brookes Publishing Co Inc, pg 37
The Brookings Institution Press, pg 37
BuilderBooks, pg 38
Bull Publishing Co, pg 38
The Bureau for At-Risk Youth, pg 38
Bureau of Economic Geology, pg 38
Cambridge University Press, pg 39
Candlewick Press, pg 39
Capen Publishing Co Inc, pg 40
Carolina Academic Press, pg 41
Catholic Book Publishing Corp, pg 42
CCH, a Wolters Kluwer business, pg 42
Cedar Grove Publishing, pg 43
Cengage Learning, pg 43
Center for Futures Education Inc, pg 43
Central Recovery Press (CRP), pg 44
Chain Store Guide (CSG), pg 44
Charles Press Publishers, pg 45
Chelsea Green Publishing Co, pg 45
Cheng & Tsui Co Inc, pg 46
Chickadee Prince Books LLC, pg 46
The Child's World Inc, pg 46
China Books, pg 47
Christian Liberty Press, pg 47
The Christian Science Publishing Society, pg 47
Circlet Press, pg 48
Clarity Press Inc, pg 49
Clearfield Co Inc, pg 49
Clinical and Laboratory Standards Institute (CLSI), pg 49
CN Times Books, pg 50
Codhill Press, pg 50
Cold Spring Harbor Laboratory Press, pg 50
The College Board, pg 50
Columbia Books & Information Services (CBIS), pg 50
Columbia University Press, pg 51
Comex Systems Inc, pg 51
The Connecticut Law Tribune, pg 52
Copper Canyon Press, pg 52
Corwin, pg 53
Cosimo Inc, pg 53
Council for Exceptional Children (CEC), pg 53
Countryman Press, pg 54
Covenant Communications Inc, pg 54
Crabtree Publishing Co, pg 54
Craftsman Book Co, pg 54
CRC Press, pg 55
Creative Editions, pg 55
Cricket Cottage Publishing LLC, pg 55
Cross-Cultural Communications, pg 55
The Crossroad Publishing Co, pg 55
Crown House Publishing Co LLC, pg 56
Crystal Clarity Publishers, pg 56
CSLI Publications, pg 56
Cypress House, pg 56
Data Trace Publishing Co (DTP), pg 57
Davies Publishing Inc, pg 57
F A Davis Co, pg 57
DAW Books, pg 57
DawnSignPress, pg 58
Walter De Gruyter Inc, pg 58
Deep River Books LLC, pg 58
Deseret Book Co, pg 58
DEStech Publications Inc, pg 59

Destiny Image Inc, pg 59
Dewey Publications Inc, pg 59
Dogwise Publishing, pg 60
Doodle and Peck Publishing, pg 60
Doubleday, pg 61
Dover Publications Inc, pg 61
Dragon Door Publications, pg 61
Dun & Bradstreet, pg 62
Dutton, pg 62
Easy Money Press, pg 63
Editorial Unilit, pg 64
Eifrig Publishing LLC, pg 64
Elderberry Press Inc, pg 65
The Electrochemical Society (ECS), pg 65
Elsevier Inc, pg 65
Encyclopaedia Britannica Inc, pg 66
Enslow Publishing LLC, pg 66
Environmental Law Institute, pg 67
Epicenter Press Inc, pg 67
Etruscan Press, pg 67
Evan-Moor Educational Publishers, pg 68
Everyman's Library, pg 68
Facts On File, pg 69
Faith Library Publications, pg 69
Faithlife Corp, pg 69
Familius, pg 69
Farcountry Press, pg 69
Father & Son Publishing Inc, pg 70
Ferguson Publishing, pg 71
Fire Engineering Books & Videos, pg 72
Firefall Editions, pg 72
Focus, pg 73
Forum Publishing Co, pg 73
Franciscan Media, pg 74
Franklin, Beedle & Associates Inc, pg 74
Free Spirit Publishing Inc, pg 74
W H Freeman, pg 75
Future Horizons Inc, pg 75
Galaxy Press Inc, pg 75
Gale, pg 75
Gallaudet University Press, pg 76
Gallopade International Inc, pg 76
Gatekeeper Press, pg 77
Gateways Books & Tapes, pg 77
Genealogical Publishing Co, pg 77
GeoLytics Inc, pg 77
Getty Publications, pg 78
Gibbs Smith Publisher, pg 78
Gospel Publishing House, pg 80
Grand & Archer Publishing, pg 80
Grand Central Publishing, pg 80
Grey House Publishing Inc™, pg 81
The Guilford Press, pg 82
Gulf Energy Information, pg 83
Hachai Publishing, pg 83
Hal Leonard LLC, pg 84
Hancock House Publishers, pg 84
Hannacroix Creek Books Inc, pg 85
Hanser Publications LLC, pg 85
HarperCollins Publishers LLC, pg 86
Harrison House, pg 87
Harvard Education Publishing Group, pg 88
Hatherleigh Press Ltd, pg 88
Hay House LLC, pg 89
Hazelden Publishing, pg 89
HCPro/DecisionHealth, pg 89
Health Communications Inc, pg 89
Health Forum Inc, pg 90
Health Professions Press, pg 90
HeartMath LLC, pg 90
William S Hein & Co Inc, pg 90
Heinemann, pg 90
Hellgate Press, pg 91
Heritage Books Inc, pg 91
The Heritage Foundation, pg 91
High Tide Press, pg 92
Hilton Publishing Co, pg 92

Hippocrene Books Inc, pg 92
The Historic New Orleans Collection, pg 93
History Publishing Co LLC, pg 93
Hogrefe Publishing Corp, pg 93
Holy Cow! Press, pg 95
Homa & Sekey Books, pg 95
Homestead Publishing, pg 95
Houghton Mifflin Harcourt, pg 95
Houghton Mifflin Harcourt Trade & Reference Division, pg 96
HRD Press, pg 97
Human Kinetics Inc, pg 97
Human Rights Watch, pg 97
Huntington Press Publishing, pg 97
Hutton Publishing, pg 97
IEEE Computer Society, pg 98
IEEE Press, pg 98
Ignatius Press, pg 98
Illinois State Museum Society, pg 99
Illuminating Engineering Society of North America (IES), pg 99
ImaJinn Books, pg 99
Impact Publications/Development Concepts Inc, pg 99
Incentive Publications by World Book, pg 99
Independent Institute, pg 99
Indiana University Press, pg 100
Industrial Press Inc, pg 100
Information Gatekeepers Inc (IGI), pg 100
Information Today, Inc, pg 100
Institute of Environmental Sciences & Technology - IEST, pg 101
Institute of Jesuit Sources (IJS), pg 102
Inter-University Consortium for Political & Social Research (ICPSR), pg 102
International City/County Management Association (ICMA), pg 102
International Council of Shopping Centers (ICSC), pg 102
International Linguistics Corp, pg 103
International Monetary Fund (IMF), Editorial & Publications Division, pg 103
International Press of Boston Inc, pg 103
International Risk Management Institute Inc, pg 103
International Society for Technology in Education, pg 103
International Society of Automation (ISA), pg 103
International Wealth Success (IWS), pg 104
Interweave Press LLC, pg 104
Iron Gate Publishing, pg 104
Italica Press, pg 105
Italics Publishing, pg 105
Jain Publishing Co, pg 105
Jhpiego, pg 106
JIST Publishing, pg 106
Johns Hopkins University Press, pg 106
Jones & Bartlett Learning LLC, pg 107
Joshua Tree Publishing, pg 107
Just World Books LLC, pg 107
Kamehameha Publishing, pg 108
J J Keller & Associates, Inc®, pg 108
Alfred A Knopf, pg 110
Kogan Page, pg 111
Koho Pono LLC, pg 111
Krause Publications Inc, pg 111
Kregel Publications, pg 111
Peter Lang Publishing Inc, pg 112

U.S. PUBLISHERS — TYPE OF PUBLICATION INDEX   BOOK

Lasaria Creative Publishing, pg 113
Law School Admission Council (LSAC), pg 113
Lawyers & Judges Publishing Co Inc, pg 113
THE Learning Connection®, pg 113
Learning Links-USA Inc, pg 114
Leisure Arts Inc, pg 114
The Lentz Leadership Institute LLC, pg 115
LexisNexis®, pg 116
LexisNexis® Matthew Bender®, pg 116
Light Publications, pg 116
Light Technology Publishing LLC, pg 116
Lippincott Williams & Wilkins, pg 117
Little, Brown and Company, pg 118
Liturgical Press, pg 118
Living Stream Ministry (LSM), pg 119
Loft Press Inc, pg 119
Long River Press, pg 120
Lorenz Educational Press, pg 120
Loving Healing Press Inc, pg 121
LRP Publications, pg 121
Macmillan, pg 121
Macmillan Learning, pg 123
Macmillan Reference USA™, pg 123
Maharishi International University Press, pg 123
Management Sciences for Health, pg 123
Manning Publications Co, pg 124
Martindale LLC, pg 126
Master Books®, pg 126
Mazda Publishers Inc, pg 127
McGraw-Hill Education, pg 127
McGraw-Hill Higher Education, pg 128
McGraw-Hill Professional Publishing Group, pg 128
R S Means from The Gordian Group, pg 128
MedMaster Inc, pg 129
Merriam-Webster Inc, pg 129
Messianic Jewish Publishers, pg 130
The Metropolitan Museum of Art, pg 130
Michigan State University Press (MSU Press), pg 130
Mighty Media Press, pg 131
Milady, pg 131
Milliken Publishing Co, pg 132
The Minerals, Metals & Materials Society (TMS), pg 132
The MIT Press, pg 132
Modern Language Association (MLA), pg 133
Mondial, pg 133
Morning Sun Books Inc, pg 134
De Gruyter Mouton, pg 135
Multicultural Publications Inc, pg 135
Museum of New Mexico Press, pg 135
National Academies Press (NAP), pg 136
National Association of Insurance Commissioners, pg 136
National Center for Children in Poverty, pg 137
National Council of Teachers of Mathematics (NCTM), pg 137
National Gallery of Art, pg 137
National Golf Foundation, pg 138
National Information Standards Organization (NISO), pg 138
National Science Teachers Association (NSTA), pg 138
Naval Institute Press, pg 139

NBM Publishing Inc, pg 139
New City Press, pg 139
New Concepts Publishing, pg 139
New Forums Press Inc, pg 139
New York State Bar Association, pg 141
Nilgiri Press, pg 141
No Starch Press, pg 141
NOLO, pg 141
North Atlantic Books (NAB), pg 142
W W Norton & Company Inc, pg 143
Nosy Crow Inc, pg 144
Nova Press, pg 144
Nystrom Education, pg 144
OAG Worldwide, pg 144
The Oaklea Press Inc, pg 145
OCP, pg 145
Octane Press, pg 145
OECD Washington Center, pg 145
Olde & Oppenheim Publishers, pg 146
Omnigraphics Inc, pg 146
On the Write Path Publishing, pg 146
One On One Book Publishing/Film-Video Publications, pg 146
Ooligan Press, pg 146
Open Books Press, pg 146
OptumInsight™, pg 147
The Original Falcon Press, pg 148
Our Daily Bread Publishing, pg 148
Our Sunday Visitor Publishing, pg 148
Oxford University Press USA, pg 149
Palgrave Macmillan, pg 150
Palm Island Press, pg 150
Pantheon Books, pg 150
Pants On Fire Press, pg 150
Paradigm Publications, pg 151
Parallax Press, pg 151
Park Place Publications, pg 152
Parmenides Publishing, pg 152
Paulist Press, pg 152
Peachpit Press, pg 153
Pearson Business Publishing, pg 153
Pen & Publish LLC, pg 153
Penguin Random House LLC, pg 155
Pennsylvania State Data Center, pg 157
Pentecostal Resources Group, pg 157
The Permanent Press, pg 158
Peterson Institute for International Economics (PIIE), pg 158
Peterson's, pg 158
Petroleum Extension Service (PETEX), pg 159
Pflaum Publishing Group, pg 159
Plexus Publishing, Inc, pg 160
Plough Publishing House, pg 161
Plowshare Media, pg 161
Plum Tree Books, pg 161
Pocket Press Inc, pg 161
Pocol Press, pg 161
Polar Bear & Company, pg 161
PPI, A Kaplan Company, pg 162
Practice Management Information Corp (PMIC), pg 163
Practising Law Institute (PLI), pg 163
Princeton Book Co Publishers, pg 163
The Princeton Review, pg 164
PRINTING United Alliance, pg 165
Productivity Press, pg 165
The Professional Education Group LLC (PEG), pg 165

ProQuest LLC, part of Clarivate PLC, pg 166
The PRS Group Inc, pg 166
Psychological Assessment Resources Inc (PAR), pg 166
Publication Consultants, pg 167
Puffin Books, pg 167
Quintessence Publishing Co Inc, pg 168
Radix Press, pg 169
RAND Corp, pg 169
Rand McNally, pg 169
Rattapallax Press, pg 172
Raven Publishing Inc, pg 172
Ravenhawk™ Books, pg 172
Remember Point Inc, pg 174
Revell, pg 174
Riverdale Avenue Books (RAB), pg 175
Riverhead Books, pg 175
Rodin Books, pg 176
Rootstock Publishing, pg 176
RosettaBooks, pg 177
Ross Books, pg 177
Rothstein Associates Inc, pg 177
The Rough Notes Co Inc, pg 177
Saddleback Educational Publishing, pg 179
William H Sadlier Inc, pg 179
SAE (Society of Automotive Engineers International), pg 179
St James Press®, pg 180
Santa Monica Press LLC, pg 182
SAS Press, pg 182
Satya House Publications, pg 182
Savvas Learning Co LLC, pg 183
Scarsdale Publishing Ltd, pg 183
Schlager Group Inc, pg 183
Schocken Books, pg 183
Scholastic International, pg 184
Schonfeld & Associates Inc, pg 184
School Zone Publishing Co, pg 185
Science & Humanities Press, pg 185
Sentient Publications LLC, pg 186
Shadow Mountain Publishing, pg 187
Shambhala Publications Inc, pg 187
Shepard Publications, pg 187
SIL International, pg 188
Simon & Schuster Children's Publishing, pg 189
Simon & Schuster, LLC, pg 189
Sinauer Associates, pg 190
SkillPath Publications, pg 190
SLACK® Incorporated, A Wyanoke Group Company, pg 191
Small Beer Press, pg 191
SME (Society of Manufacturing Engineers), pg 191
M Lee Smith Publishers, pg 192
Smyth & Helwys Publishing Inc, pg 192
Society for Industrial & Applied Mathematics, pg 192
Society for Mining, Metallurgy & Exploration, pg 192
Society of Exploration Geophysicists, pg 192
Solano Press Books, pg 193
Soul Mate Publishing, pg 194
Sound Feelings Publishing, pg 194
Sourcebooks LLC, pg 194
South Carolina Bar, pg 195
Springer, pg 196
Springer Publishing Co, pg 196
Stackpole Books, pg 196
Standard Publishing, pg 197
Standard Publishing Corp, pg 197
STARbooks Press, pg 197
Starcrafts LLC, pg 197
SteinerBooks Inc, pg 198
Stenhouse Publishers, pg 198
Stewart, Tabori & Chang, pg 198

Stipes Publishing LLC, pg 198
Stone Bridge Press Inc, pg 199
The Story Plant, pg 199
Storyworkz Inc, pg 199
Strategic Book Publishing (SBP), pg 199
Strategic Media Books LLC, pg 200
Stylus Publishing LLC, pg 200
Summertime Publications Inc, pg 200
Summit University Press, pg 200
Sunbelt Publications Inc, pg 200
Sunrise River Press, pg 201
Swallow Press, pg 201
SYBEX, pg 201
Tahrike Tarsile Qur'an Inc, pg 202
Nan A Talese, pg 202
TAN Books, pg 202
Taunton Books, pg 203
Teachers College Press, pg 203
Teacher's Discovery®, pg 203
Teaching & Learning Co, pg 204
Teaching Strategies LLC, pg 204
Temple University Press, pg 204
University of Texas Press, pg 205
Theosophical University Press, pg 206
Thieme Medical Publishers Inc, pg 206
Thomas Nelson, pg 206
Thomson West, pg 206
Todd Publications, pg 207
Top Publications Ltd, pg 207
TotalRecall Publications Inc, pg 208
Tower Publishing Co, pg 208
Tracks Publishing, pg 208
Transportation Research Board (TRB), pg 209
The Trinity Foundation, pg 209
Triumph Books LLC, pg 209
Tuttle Publishing, pg 211
Twenty-Third Publications, pg 211
Twilight Times Books, pg 211
Tyndale House Publishers Inc, pg 211
United Nations Publications, pg 213
United States Holocaust Memorial Museum, pg 213
University of Alaska Press, pg 214
University of California Institute on Global Conflict & Cooperation, pg 215
University of California Press, pg 215
University of New Orleans Press, pg 218
The University of North Carolina Press, pg 218
University of North Texas Press, pg 218
University of Pennsylvania Museum of Archaeology & Anthropology, pg 219
University of South Carolina Press, pg 220
The University of Utah Press, pg 220
University of Washington Press, pg 220
University Press of Kansas, pg 221
Upper Room Books, pg 223
US Government Publishing Office (GPO), pg 223
Visual Profile Books Inc, pg 225
Voyager Sopris Learning Inc, pg 225
Wake Forest University Press, pg 225
Washington State University Press, pg 226
Water Resources Publications LLC, pg 226
Watermark Publishing, pg 226

PUBLISHERS

U.S. PUBLISHERS — TYPE OF PUBLICATION INDEX

West Academic, pg 227
Westminster John Knox Press (WJK), pg 228
Whiskey Creek Press, pg 228
Whittier Publications Inc, pg 229
Whole Person Associates Inc, pg 229
Wide World of Maps Inc, pg 229
Wilderness Adventures Press Inc, pg 229
Wiley-Blackwell, pg 229
John Wiley & Sons Inc, pg 230
John Wiley & Sons Inc Global Education, pg 230
John Wiley & Sons Inc Professional Development, pg 230
Williams & Company Book Publishers, pg 230
Wings Press, pg 231
Wisconsin Department of Public Instruction, pg 231
Wolters Kluwer Law & Business, pg 232
Woodbine House, pg 232
Workman Publishing, pg 232
World Bank Publications, pg 233
World Book Inc, pg 233
World Resources Institute, pg 233
World Scientific Publishing Co Inc, pg 233
World Trade Press LLC, pg 234
Worth Publishers, pg 234
Write Stuff Enterprises LLC, pg 234
Wyndham Hall Press, pg 234
Xist Publishing, pg 234
XML Press, pg 235
Yale University Press, pg 235
Yard Dog Press, pg 235
Yotzeret Publishing, pg 236
Zagat Inc, pg 236
Zeig, Tucker & Theisen Inc, pg 236
Zondervan, pg 236

FINE EDITIONS, ILLUSTRATED BOOKS

Abbeville Press, pg 1
Abbeville Publishing Group, pg 2
Harry N Abrams Inc, pg 2
ACC Art Books, pg 3
Advance Publishing Inc, pg 5
Amber Lotus Publishing, pg 8
The American Ceramic Society, pg 9
American Federation of Arts, pg 9
American Quilter's Society (AQS), pg 12
AMMO Books LLC, pg 13
Anaphora Literary Press, pg 13
Aperture Books, pg 15
The Arion Press, pg 16
ArtWrite Productions, pg 18
Astragal Press, pg 20
Baby Tattoo Books, pg 23
Bear & Bobcat Books, pg 26
Beaver's Pond Press Inc, pg 26
Beehive Books, pg 26
BiG GUY BOOKS, pg 29
Black Dome Press Corp, pg 30
Bloomsbury Publishing Inc, pg 31
BookLogix, pg 34
Boydell & Brewer Inc, pg 35
Brandylane Publishers Inc, pg 35
George Braziller Inc, pg 35
Brown Books Publishing Group (BBPG), pg 38
Burns Archive Press, pg 38
Candlewick Press, pg 39
Catholic Book Publishing Corp, pg 42
Clerisy Press, pg 49
Codhill Press, pg 50
David C Cook, pg 52

Country Music Foundation Press, pg 54
Countryman Press, pg 54
Cross-Cultural Communications, pg 55
Cypress House, pg 56
Dark Horse Comics, pg 57
Dharma Publishing, pg 59
Disney-Hyperion Books, pg 59
Doodle and Peck Publishing, pg 60
Doubleday, pg 61
Dover Publications Inc, pg 61
Down East Books, pg 61
Down The Shore Publishing, pg 61
Edgewise Press Inc, pg 63
Elderberry Press Inc, pg 65
Etruscan Press, pg 67
Everyman's Library, pg 68
Firefall Editions, pg 72
Fons Vitae, pg 73
Gagosian Gallery, pg 75
Gauthier Publications Inc, pg 77
Gingko Press Inc, pg 78
Glitterati Inc, pg 78
Godine, pg 79
Goose River Press, pg 79
Gorgias Press LLC, pg 80
Grand & Archer Publishing, pg 80
Donald M Grant Publisher Inc, pg 80
Harvard Art Museums, pg 87
Hay House LLC, pg 89
High Plains Press, pg 91
Hilton Publishing Co, pg 92
Histria Books, pg 93
Homestead Publishing, pg 95
In the Garden Publishing, pg 99
Insight Editions, pg 101
Interlink Publishing Group Inc, pg 102
Jewish Lights Publishing, pg 105
Kelsey Street Press, pg 108
Kent State University Press, pg 109
Alfred A Knopf, pg 110
Konecky & Konecky LLC, pg 111
Library of America, pg 116
Little, Brown and Company, pg 118
Liturgical Press, pg 118
Loft Press Inc, pg 119
Lonely Planet Publications Inc, pg 120
Long River Press, pg 120
LPD Press/Rio Grande Books, pg 121
Lynx House Press, pg 121
Mage Publishers Inc, pg 123
Mandala Earth, pg 124
Master Books®, pg 126
McPherson & Co, pg 128
MFA Publications, pg 130
Midnight Marquee Press Inc, pg 130
The MIT Press, pg 132
Modern Memoirs Inc, pg 133
The Monacelli Press, pg 133
The Museum of Modern Art (MoMA), pg 135
National Geographic Books, pg 137
New Forums Press Inc, pg 139
Norilana Books, pg 142
North Carolina Office of Archives & History, pg 142
Octane Press, pg 145
Odyssey Books, pg 145
On the Write Path Publishing, pg 146
The Original Falcon Press, pg 148
ORO editions, pg 148
Oxford University Press USA, pg 149
PA Press, pg 149
Paintbox Press, pg 150
Pangaea Publications, pg 150

Paraclete Press Inc, pg 151
Park Place Publications, pg 152
Parmenides Publishing, pg 152
Pauline Books & Media, pg 152
Penfield Books, pg 154
Peter Pauper Press, Inc, pg 158
The Picasso Project, pg 160
Polar Bear & Company, pg 161
powerHouse Books, pg 162
The Press at California State University, Fresno, pg 163
ProStar Publications Inc, pg 166
Pyncheon House, pg 167
Quarto Publishing Group USA Inc, pg 168
Regent Press Printers & Publishers, pg 174
Rio Nuevo Publishers, pg 175
Rizzoli International Publications Inc, pg 175
Running Press, pg 178
Santa Monica Press LLC, pg 182
Shambhala Publications Inc, pg 187
Spizzirri Publishing Inc, pg 196
Stewart, Tabori & Chang, pg 198
Sunstone Press, pg 201
Nan A Talese, pg 202
Taschen America, pg 203
Ten Speed Press, pg 204
Trans-Atlantic Publications Inc, pg 209
Trinity University Press, pg 209
Tumblehome Learning Inc, pg 210
Turner Publishing Co LLC, pg 210
Tuttle Publishing, pg 211
Ugly Duckling Presse, pg 212
University of Pennsylvania Museum of Archaeology & Anthropology, pg 219
University Press of Mississippi, pg 222
The Vendome Press, pg 224
Visual Profile Books Inc, pg 225
Welcome Books, pg 227
West Virginia University Press, pg 228
Wilderness Adventures Press Inc, pg 229
Winterthur Museum, Garden & Library, pg 231
Alan Wofsy Fine Arts, pg 231
Wolfman Books, pg 232
WoodstockArts, pg 232
Write Stuff Enterprises LLC, pg 234
YBK Publishers Inc, pg 235
Zondervan, pg 236
Zone Books, pg 237

FOREIGN LANGUAGE & BILINGUAL BOOKS

AK Press, pg 6
Alaska Native Language Center (ANLC), pg 6
American Bible Society, pg 8
Sara Anderson Children's Books, pg 13
AOTA Press, pg 14
Arbordale Publishing, pg 16
Ariadne Press, pg 16
ArtAge Publications, pg 17
Arte Publico Press, pg 17
AuthorHouse, pg 22
Barranca Press, pg 24
Barrytown/Station Hill Press, pg 24
Bess Press Inc, pg 29
BJU Press, pg 30
Blue Mountain Arts Inc, pg 32
Bolchazy-Carducci Publishers Inc, pg 33
Boys Town Press, pg 35
Bridge Publications Inc, pg 36
Candied Plums, pg 39

Candlewick Press, pg 39
Capstone Publishers™, pg 40
Casa Bautista de Publicaciones, pg 41
Cedar Grove Publishing, pg 43
Cengage Learning, pg 43
Center for Futures Education Inc, pg 43
Charlesbridge Publishing Inc, pg 45
Cheng & Tsui Co Inc, pg 46
Children's Book Press, pg 46
Child's Play® Inc, pg 46
The Child's World Inc, pg 46
China Books, pg 47
Continental AfrikaPublishers, pg 52
Copper Canyon Press, pg 52
Council for Research in Values & Philosophy, pg 53
Crabtree Publishing Co, pg 54
Cross-Cultural Communications, pg 55
Cypress House, pg 56
Walter De Gruyter Inc, pg 58
Dover Publications Inc, pg 61
East West Discovery Press, pg 63
EDC Publishing, pg 63
ediciones Lerner, pg 63
Editorial Bautista Independiente, pg 63
Editorial de la Universidad de Puerto Rico, pg 63
Editorial Portavoz, pg 64
Editorial Unilit, pg 64
Emmaus Road Publishing Inc, pg 66
Faithlife Corp, pg 69
Forward Movement, pg 73
Free Spirit Publishing Inc, pg 74
Gallaudet University Press, pg 76
Georgetown University Press, pg 77
Gospel Publishing House, pg 80
Green Dragon Books, pg 81
Green Integer, pg 81
Hackett Publishing Co Inc, pg 83
HarperCollins Children's Books, pg 85
HarperCollins Publishers LLC, pg 86
Hippocrene Books Inc, pg 92
Hollym International Corp, pg 94
Homa & Sekey Books, pg 95
Host Publications, pg 95
Houghton Mifflin Harcourt, pg 95
Ibex Publishers, pg 98
Inner Traditions International Ltd, pg 101
International Book Centre Inc, pg 102
The International Institute of Islamic Thought, pg 103
International Linguistics Corp, pg 103
International Monetary Fund (IMF), Editorial & Publications Division, pg 103
Kamehameha Publishing, pg 108
Kazi Publications Inc, pg 108
KTAV Publishing House Inc, pg 111
Peter Lang Publishing Inc, pg 112
Laredo Publishing Co, pg 113
THE Learning Connection®, pg 113
LearningExpress, pg 114
Lectorum Publications Inc, pg 114
Liguori Publications, pg 117
LinguaText LLC, pg 117
Liturgical Press, pg 118
Liturgy Training Publications, pg 119
Living Language, pg 119
Living Stream Ministry (LSM), pg 119
Lonely Planet Publications Inc, pg 120

U.S. PUBLISHERS — TYPE OF PUBLICATION INDEX BOOK

Long River Press, pg 120
Lutheran Braille Workers Inc, pg 121
Mage Publishers Inc, pg 123
Management Advisory Services & Publications (MASP), pg 123
Management Sciences for Health, pg 123
Marick Press, pg 125
Master Books®, pg 126
Mastery Education, pg 126
McGraw-Hill Education, pg 127
me+mi publishing inc, pg 128
Mel Bay Publications Inc, pg 129
Merriam-Webster Inc, pg 129
Milady, pg 131
Modern Language Association (MLA), pg 133
Modern Memoirs Inc, pg 133
Mondial, pg 133
The Mongolia Society Inc, pg 133
Moznaim Publishing Corp, pg 135
Nataraj Books, pg 136
New Directions Publishing Corp, pg 139
OECD Washington Center, pg 145
Omnigraphics Inc, pg 146
Our Sunday Visitor Publishing, pg 148
Oxford University Press USA, pg 149
Pants On Fire Press, pg 150
Parmenides Publishing, pg 152
Pelican Publishing, pg 153
Pentecostal Resources Group, pg 157
Petroleum Extension Service (PETEX), pg 159
Phaidon, pg 159
Philosophical Library Inc, pg 159
Platypus Media LLC, pg 160
Plough Publishing House, pg 161
Polar Bear & Company, pg 161
Pro Lingua Associates Inc, pg 165
Progressive Press, pg 165
Recorded Books Inc, an RBmedia company, pg 172
Remember Point Inc, pg 174
Renaissance House, pg 174
Royal Fireworks Press, pg 178
William H Sadlier Inc, pg 179
St Herman Press, pg 180
St Pauls, pg 181
Salina Bookshelf Inc, pg 181
San Diego State University Press, pg 182
Satya House Publications, pg 182
Scholastic Inc, pg 184
Scholastic International, pg 184
Simon & Schuster, LLC, pg 189
Spizzirri Publishing Inc, pg 196
Star Bright Books Inc, pg 197
STOCKCERO Inc, pg 199
Storyworkz Inc, pg 199
Stress Free Kids®, pg 200
Summertime Publications Inc, pg 200
Sunbelt Publications Inc, pg 200
Sundance/Newbridge Publishing, pg 200
Swan Isle Press, pg 201
Teacher's Discovery®, pg 203
ThunderStone Books, pg 207
Torah Umesorah Publications, pg 208
Tortuga Press, pg 208
Trafford Publishing, pg 208
TRISTAN Publishing, pg 209
Tughra Books, pg 210
Tuttle Publishing, pg 211
Tyndale House Publishers Inc, pg 211
United Nations Publications, pg 213
University of Louisiana at Lafayette Press, pg 217
University of Wisconsin Press, pg 221
Upper Room Books, pg 223
US Conference of Catholic Bishops, pg 223
Velazquez Press, pg 224
Wayside Publishing, pg 227
Whitaker House, pg 228
Markus Wiener Publishers Inc, pg 229
Wings Press, pg 231
Wisconsin Department of Public Instruction, pg 231
World Bank Publications, pg 233
World Book Inc, pg 233
Xlibris Corp, pg 234
Yale University Press, pg 235
YBK Publishers Inc, pg 235
Zondervan, pg 236

GENERAL TRADE BOOKS - HARDCOVER

Abbeville Publishing Group, pg 2
Harry N Abrams Inc, pg 2
Academy Chicago Publishers, pg 3
ACC Art Books, pg 3
ACTA Publications, pg 4
Adams Media, pg 4
AdventureKEEN, pg 5
The AEI Press, pg 5
AICPA® & CIMA®, pg 5
Akashic Books, pg 6
Albert Whitman & Company, pg 6
Alfred Music, pg 6
Algora Publishing, pg 7
Alloy Entertainment LLC, pg 7
Allworth Press, pg 7
AllWrite Publishing, pg 7
Amadeus Press, pg 7
Amakella Publishing, pg 7
Ambassador International, pg 7
Amber Lotus Publishing, pg 8
American Alpine Club, pg 8
American Bar Association Publishing, pg 8
American Carriage House Publishing (ACHP), pg 8
The American Ceramic Society, pg 9
American Correctional Association, pg 9
American Federation of Arts, pg 9
American Institute of Chemical Engineers (AIChE), pg 10
American Medical Association (AMA), pg 11
American Psychiatric Association Publishing, pg 11
American Quilter's Society (AQS), pg 12
Ampersand Inc/Professional Publishing Services, pg 13
Andrews McMeel Publishing LLC, pg 14
Angel City Press, pg 14
Angelus Press, pg 14
Aperture Books, pg 15
Appalachian Mountain Club Books, pg 15
Applause Theatre & Cinema Books, pg 15
Applewood Books, pg 15
APS PRESS, pg 16
Arbordale Publishing, pg 16
Arcade Publishing Inc, pg 16
ARE Press, pg 16
Ariel Press, pg 16
The Art Institute of Chicago, pg 17
Art of Living, PrimaMedia Inc, pg 17
Arte Publico Press, pg 17
ArtWrite Productions, pg 18
Ascend Books LLC, pg 18
Aspatore Books, pg 19
Asta Publications LLC, pg 20
Astragal Press, pg 20
Augsburg Fortress Publishers, Publishing House of the Evangelical Lutheran Church in America, pg 22
August House Inc, pg 22
AuthorHouse, pg 22
Authorlink® Press, pg 22
Ave Maria Press Inc, pg 22
Avery, pg 23
Avery Color Studios, pg 23
Avotaynu Books LLC, pg 23
Baby Tattoo Books, pg 23
Backbeat Books, pg 23
Baen Books, pg 23
Baker Books, pg 23
Bancroft Press, pg 24
B&H Publishing Group, pg 24
Barefoot Books, pg 24
Barringer Publishing, pg 24
Barrytown/Station Hill Press, pg 24
Bartleby Press, pg 24
Basic Books Group, pg 25
Basic Health Publications Inc, pg 25
Beacon Hill Press of Kansas City, pg 25
Beacon Press, pg 25
Bear & Co Inc, pg 26
BearManor Media, pg 26
Beaver's Pond Press Inc, pg 26
Frederic C Beil Publisher Inc, pg 27
Bellevue Literary Press, pg 27
Ben Yehuda Press, pg 27
BenBella Books Inc, pg 27
Bentley Publishers, pg 28
Berkley, pg 28
Berrett-Koehler Publishers Inc, pg 29
Bethany House Publishers, pg 29
Bethlehem Books, pg 29
Biographical Publishing Co, pg 29
Black Dome Press Corp, pg 30
Black Heron Press, pg 30
Blair, pg 30
Blood Moon Productions Ltd, pg 31
Bloomsbury Academic, pg 31
Bloomsbury Publishing Inc, pg 31
Blue Crane Books Inc, pg 32
Blue Mountain Arts Inc, pg 32
Blue Note Publications Inc, pg 32
BlueBridge, pg 32
BNi Building News, pg 33
BOA Editions Ltd, pg 33
BoardSource, pg 33
Book Sales, pg 33
BookLogix, pg 34
BOOM! Studios, pg 34
Bottom Dog Press, pg 34
Boys Town Press, pg 35
Brandylane Publishers Inc, pg 35
George Braziller Inc, pg 35
Breakaway Books, pg 36
Breakthrough Publications Inc, pg 36
Nicholas Brealey Publishing, pg 36
Brethren Press, pg 36
Brick Tower Press, pg 36
Bridge Logos Inc, pg 36
Bridge Publications Inc, pg 36
Brookline Books, pg 37
Brown Books Publishing Group (BBPG), pg 38
Burford Books, pg 38
Camino Books Inc, pg 39
Capen Publishing Co Inc, pg 40
Carolina Academic Press, pg 41
CarTech Inc, pg 41
Casa Bautista de Publicaciones, pg 41
Casemate | publishers, pg 41
Cato Institute, pg 42
Caxton Press, pg 42
CCH, a Wolters Kluwer business, pg 42
Cedar Fort Inc, pg 43
Cedar Grove Publishing, pg 43
Cedar Tree Books, pg 43
Cengage Learning, pg 43
Central Recovery Press (CRP), pg 44
Cereals & Grains Association, pg 44
Chalice Press, pg 44
Charles Press Publishers, pg 45
Charlesbridge Publishing Inc, pg 45
Chelsea Green Publishing Co, pg 45
Chicago Review Press, pg 46
China Books, pg 47
Chosen Books, pg 47
Christian Light Publications Inc, pg 47
The Christian Science Publishing Society, pg 47
Chronicle Books LLC, pg 47
Cider Mill Press Book Publishers LLC, pg 48
Circlet Press, pg 48
Clarion Books, pg 48
Clear Light Publishers, pg 49
Cleis Press, pg 49
Clerisy Press, pg 49
CN Times Books, pg 50
Coffee House Press, pg 50
Columbia University Press, pg 51
Commonwealth Editions, pg 51
Concordia Publishing House, pg 51
Copper Canyon Press, pg 52
Cornell Maritime Press, pg 52
Cornell University Press, pg 52
Council for Research in Values & Philosophy, pg 53
Counterpoint Press LLC, pg 54
Country Music Foundation Press, pg 54
Countryman Press, pg 54
Covenant Communications Inc, pg 54
Cross-Cultural Communications, pg 55
The Crossroad Publishing Co, pg 55
Crown Publishing Group, pg 56
Crystal Clarity Publishers, pg 56
Cypress House, pg 56
DAW Books, pg 57
Delphinium Books, pg 58
Deseret Book Co, pg 58
Destiny Image Inc, pg 59
Dharma Publishing, pg 59
DiscoverNet Publishing, pg 59
Diversion Books, pg 60
DK, pg 60
The Donning Company Publishers, pg 60
Doodle and Peck Publishing, pg 60
Dorrance Publishing Co Inc, pg 61
Doubleday, pg 61
Dover Publications Inc, pg 61
Down East Books, pg 61
Down The Shore Publishing, pg 61
Duke University Press, pg 62
Dutton Children's Books, pg 62
Eakin Press, pg 62
East West Discovery Press, pg 63
Editorial de la Universidad de Puerto Rico, pg 63
Editorial Portavoz, pg 64
Wm B Eerdmans Publishing Co, pg 64
Eisenbrauns, pg 64
Elderberry Press Inc, pg 65

256

PUBLISHERS

U.S. PUBLISHERS — TYPE OF PUBLICATION INDEX

Elite Books, pg 65
Elva Resa Publishing, pg 65
Emmaus Road Publishing Inc, pg 66
Encounter Books, pg 66
Energy Psychology Press, pg 66
Entangled Publishing LLC, pg 67
Environmental Law Institute, pg 67
Epicenter Press Inc, pg 67
Etruscan Press, pg 67
M Evans & Company, pg 68
Everyman's Library, pg 68
Everything Goes Media LLC, pg 68
Excelsior Editions, pg 68
The Experiment, pg 68
Fair Winds Press, pg 69
Faith Library Publications, pg 69
Familius, pg 69
Farcountry Press, pg 69
Farrar, Straus & Giroux Books for Young Readers, pg 69
Farrar, Straus & Giroux, LLC, pg 70
Father & Son Publishing Inc, pg 70
Feldheim Publishers, pg 70
The Feminist Press at The City University of New York, pg 71
Feral House, pg 71
Filter Press LLC, pg 71
Financial Times Press, pg 71
Fine Creative Media, Inc, pg 71
Firefall Editions, pg 72
Focus on the Family, pg 73
Walter Foster Publishing, pg 74
Fox Chapel Publishing Co Inc, pg 74
Frederick Fell Publishers Inc, pg 74
Friends United Press, pg 75
Fulcrum Publishing Inc, pg 75
Galaxy Press Inc, pg 75
Gale, pg 75
Gallaudet University Press, pg 76
Gallery Books, pg 76
Gatekeeper Press, pg 77
Gauthier Publications Inc, pg 77
GemStone Press, pg 77
Georgetown University Press, pg 77
Getty Publications, pg 78
Gibbs Smith Publisher, pg 78
Glitterati Inc, pg 78
The Globe Pequot Press, pg 79
Godine, pg 79
Goodheart-Willcox Publisher, pg 79
Goose River Press, pg 79
Gospel Publishing House, pg 80
Grand & Archer Publishing, pg 80
Grand Central Publishing, pg 80
Donald M Grant Publisher Inc, pg 80
Gray & Company Publishers, pg 80
Graywolf Press, pg 81
Green Dragon Books, pg 81
Green Integer, pg 81
Greenleaf Book Group LLC, pg 81
Grey House Publishing Inc™, pg 81
Grove Atlantic Inc, pg 82
The Guilford Press, pg 82
Gulf Energy Information, pg 83
Hachette Book Group Inc, pg 83
Hachette Nashville, pg 83
Hal Leonard LLC, pg 84
Hampton Roads Publishing, pg 84
Hancock House Publishers, pg 84
Hanging Loose Press, pg 85
Hannacroix Creek Books Inc, pg 85
Harlequin Enterprises Ltd, pg 85
HarperCollins Publishers LLC, pg 86
Harrison House, pg 87
Harvard Business Review Press, pg 87
Harvard Common Press, pg 87
Harvest House Publishers Inc, pg 88

Hatherleigh Press Ltd, pg 88
Hazelden Publishing, pg 89
Health Professions Press, pg 90
Heimburger House Publishing Co, pg 90
Hellgate Press, pg 91
Her Own Words LLC, pg 91
The Heritage Foundation, pg 91
Heyday, pg 91
High Plains Press, pg 91
High Tide Press, pg 92
Hill & Wang, pg 92
Hilton Publishing Co, pg 92
Hippocrene Books Inc, pg 92
History Publishing Co LLC, pg 93
Histria Books, pg 93
Hohm Press, pg 93
Hollym International Corp, pg 94
Henry Holt and Company, LLC, pg 94
Holy Cow! Press, pg 95
Homa & Sekey Books, pg 95
Homestead Publishing, pg 95
Horizon Publishers & Distributors Inc, pg 95
Houghton Mifflin Harcourt, pg 95
Houghton Mifflin Harcourt Trade & Reference Division, pg 96
Humanix Books LLC, pg 97
Huntington Press Publishing, pg 97
Hutton Publishing, pg 97
Ignatius Press, pg 98
Immedium, pg 99
Impact Publications/Development Concepts Inc, pg 99
In the Garden Publishing, pg 99
Independent Institute, pg 99
Indiana Historical Society Press, pg 99
Industrial Press Inc, pg 100
Information Today, Inc, pg 100
Inner Traditions International Ltd, pg 101
Institute of Jesuit Sources (IJS), pg 102
Institute of Police Technology & Management (IPTM), pg 102
Interlink Publishing Group Inc, pg 102
International Book Centre Inc, pg 102
The International Institute of Islamic Thought, pg 103
International Risk Management Institute, pg 103
InterVarsity Press, pg 104
Island Press, pg 104
Islandport Press, pg 105
Italics Publishing, pg 105
iUniverse, pg 105
Jewish Lights Publishing, pg 105
The Jewish Publication Society, pg 105
Judaica Press Inc, pg 107
Judson Press, pg 107
Just World Books LLC, pg 107
Kallisti Publishing, pg 108
Kalmbach Media Co, pg 108
Kazi Publications Inc, pg 108
Kensington Publishing Corp, pg 109
Kent State University Press, pg 109
Alfred A Knopf, pg 110
Kodansha USA Inc, pg 110
Koho Pono LLC, pg 111
Krause Publications Inc, pg 111
Kregel Publications, pg 111
KTAV Publishing House Inc, pg 111
Landauer Publishing, pg 112
Larson Publications, pg 113
Laughing Elephant Books, pg 113
Leaf Storm Press, pg 113
THE Learning Connection®, pg 113

Lederer Books, pg 114
Lee & Low Books Inc, pg 114
Leisure Arts Inc, pg 114
Liberty Fund Inc, pg 116
Library of America, pg 116
Liguori Publications, pg 117
Linden Publishing Co Inc, pg 117
Little, Brown and Company, pg 118
The Little Entrepreneur, pg 118
Liturgical Press, pg 118
Livingston Press, pg 119
The Local History Co, pg 119
Locks Art Publications/Locks Gallery, pg 119
Loft Press Inc, pg 119
Logos Press, pg 119
Long River Press, pg 120
Lost Horse Press, pg 120
Louisiana State University Press, pg 120
Love Inspired Books, pg 120
Loving Healing Press Inc, pg 121
Loyola Press, pg 121
LPD Press/Rio Grande Books, pg 121
LRP Publications, pg 121
Lynx House Press, pg 121
The Lyons Press, pg 121
Mage Publishers Inc, pg 123
Mandel Vilar Press, pg 124
Manic D Press Inc, pg 124
Marick Press, pg 125
Maryland Center for History & Culture (MCHC), pg 126
Maryland History Press, pg 126
Master Books®, pg 126
McBooks Press, pg 127
The McDonald & Woodward Publishing Co, pg 127
McFarland, pg 127
McGraw-Hill Education, pg 127
McPherson & Co, pg 128
McSweeney's Publishing, pg 128
R S Means from The Gordian Group, pg 128
Medals of America Press, pg 128
Menasha Ridge Press, pg 129
Mercer University Press, pg 129
Messianic Jewish Publishers, pg 130
Metropolitan Classics, pg 130
MFA Publications, pg 130
Michigan State University Press (MSU Press), pg 130
Midnight Marquee Press Inc, pg 130
Mighty Media Press, pg 131
Milford Books™, pg 131
Milkweed Editions, pg 131
Minnesota Historical Society Press, pg 132
The MIT Press, pg 132
The Monacelli Press, pg 133
Monkfish Book Publishing Co, pg 133
Monthly Review Press, pg 134
Moody Publishers, pg 134
Morgan James Publishing, pg 134
Morning Sun Books Inc, pg 134
Mountain Press Publishing Co, pg 135
Mountaineers Books, pg 135
Moznaim Publishing Corp, pg 135
Multnomah, pg 135
The Museum of Modern Art (MoMA), pg 135
Museum of New Mexico Press, pg 135
Mutual Publishing LLC, pg 136
NACE International, pg 136
Nataraj Books, pg 136
National Academies Press (NAP), pg 136

National Association of Broadcasters (NAB), pg 136
National Catholic Educational Association, pg 137
National Center for Children in Poverty, pg 137
National Geographic Books, pg 137
National Wildlife Federation, pg 139
Naval Institute Press, pg 139
NavPress Publishing Group, pg 139
NBM Publishing Inc, pg 139
New City Press, pg 139
New Directions Publishing Corp, pg 139
New Leaf Press, pg 140
The New Press, pg 140
New World Library, pg 140
New York University Press, pg 141
NewSouth Books, pg 141
Nilgiri Press, pg 141
No Starch Press, pg 141
Norilana Books, pg 142
North Atlantic Books (NAB), pg 142
North Carolina Office of Archives & History, pg 142
North Country Press, pg 142
North Point Press, pg 142
North River Press Publishing Corp, pg 142
North Star Press of Saint Cloud Inc, pg 142
W W Norton & Company Inc, pg 143
Nova Science Publishers Inc, pg 144
The Oaklea Press Inc, pg 145
Ocean Tree Books, pg 145
Oceanview Publishing Inc, pg 145
Octane Press, pg 145
Odyssey Books, pg 145
Ohio Genealogical Society, pg 145
The Ohio State University Press, pg 145
Ohio University Press, pg 145
Omnidawn, pg 146
On the Write Path Publishing, pg 146
One On One Book Publishing/Film-Video Publications, pg 146
Orange Frazer Press Inc, pg 147
Orbis Books, pg 147
Oregon State University Press, pg 147
The Original Falcon Press, pg 148
ORO editions, pg 148
Other Press, pg 148
Our Daily Bread Publishing, pg 148
Our Sunday Visitor Publishing, pg 148
The Overlook Press, pg 148
Oxford University Press USA, pg 149
P & R Publishing Co, pg 149
PA Press, pg 149
Pacific Press® Publishing Association, pg 149
Palgrave Macmillan, pg 150
Pangaea Publications, pg 150
Pantheon Books, pg 150
Pants On Fire Press, pg 150
Parachute Publishing LLC, pg 151
Paraclete Press Inc, pg 151
Paradise Cay Publications Inc, pg 151
Parallax Press, pg 151
Paramount Market Publishing Inc, pg 151
Park Place Publications, pg 152
Pathfinder Publishing Inc, pg 152
Paulist Press, pg 152
Peachtree Publishing Co Inc, pg 153

257

U.S. PUBLISHERS — TYPE OF PUBLICATION INDEX

BOOK

Pelican Publishing, pg 153
Penguin Press, pg 154
Penguin Publishing Group, pg 154
Penguin Random House LLC, pg 155
Penguin Young Readers Group, pg 156
Penn State University Press, pg 157
Pennsylvania Historical & Museum Commission, pg 157
PennWell Books, pg 157
Peradam Press, pg 158
Perfection Learning®, pg 158
Persea Books, pg 158
Peter Pauper Press, Inc, pg 158
Peterson's, pg 158
Phaidon, pg 159
Picador, pg 159
The Pilgrim Press/United Church Press, pg 160
Pineapple Press, pg 160
Plexus Publishing, Inc, pg 160
Plough Publishing House, pg 161
Pointed Leaf Press, pg 161
Poisoned Pen Press, pg 161
Polar Bear & Company, pg 161
Polis Books, pg 162
Pomegranate Communications Inc, pg 162
Portfolio, pg 162
Potomac Books, pg 162
Clarkson Potter, pg 162
powerHouse Books, pg 162
Princeton University Press, pg 164
Prometheus Books, pg 166
ProStar Publications Inc, pg 166
Publication Consultants, pg 167
Publications International Ltd (PIL), pg 167
Puffin Books, pg 167
Purple House Press, pg 167
Pushcart Press, pg 167
GP Putnam's Sons, pg 167
Pyncheon House, pg 167
Quail Ridge Press (QRP), pg 168
Quarto Publishing Group USA Inc, pg 168
Quirk Books, pg 168
Quite Specific Media Group Ltd, pg 168
Peter E Randall Publisher, pg 169
Random House Publishing Group, pg 170
Rattapallax Press, pg 172
Raven Publishing Inc, pg 172
Ravenhawk™ Books, pg 172
Reader's Digest Trade Publishing, pg 172
Red Wheel/Weiser, pg 173
Robert D Reed Publishers, pg 173
Regent Press Printers & Publishers, pg 174
Regnery Publishing, pg 174
Revell, pg 174
Rio Nuevo Publishers, pg 175
River City Publishing, pg 175
Riverhead Books, pg 175
Rizzoli International Publications Inc, pg 175
The RoadRunner Press, pg 175
RockHill Publishing LLC, pg 176
Rod & Staff Publishers Inc, pg 176
Rodin Books, pg 176
Roman Catholic Books, pg 176
The Rosen Publishing Group Inc, pg 177
RosettaBooks, pg 177
Ross Books, pg 177
Rothstein Associates Inc, pg 177
Round Table Companies, pg 177
Rowe Publishing LLC, pg 178
Rowman & Littlefield, pg 178
Rutgers University Press, pg 178

William H Sadlier Inc, pg 179
Safari Press, pg 179
Sagamore Publishing LLC, pg 179
St Herman Press, pg 180
St Johann Press, pg 180
St Martin's Press, LLC, pg 180
San Diego State University Press, pg 182
Santa Monica Press LLC, pg 182
SAS Press, pg 182
Sasquatch Books, pg 182
Schiffer Publishing Ltd, pg 183
G Schirmer Inc/Associated Music Publishers Inc, pg 183
Schocken Books, pg 183
Scholastic Inc, pg 184
Scholastic International, pg 184
Schreiber Publishing, pg 185
Scribner, pg 185
SelectBooks Inc, pg 186
Sentient Publications LLC, pg 186
Seven Stories Press, pg 186
1765 Productions, pg 186
Shadow Mountain Publishing, pg 187
Shambhala Publications Inc, pg 187
Sherman Asher Publishing, pg 187
Siglio, pg 187
Signature Books Publishing LLC, pg 187
Silver Leaf Books LLC, pg 188
Simon & Schuster, pg 188
Simon & Schuster Children's Publishing, pg 189
Simon & Schuster, LLC, pg 189
SkyLight Paths® Publishing, pg 191
Small Beer Press, pg 191
Smithsonian Institution Scholarly Press, pg 192
Smyth & Helwys Publishing Inc, pg 192
Society for Mining, Metallurgy & Exploration, pg 192
Society of Environmental Toxicology & Chemistry (SETAC), pg 192
Soho Press Inc, pg 193
Solution Tree, pg 193
Soncino Press Ltd, pg 193
Sophia Institute Press®, pg 193
Sounds True Inc, pg 194
Sourcebooks LLC, pg 194
Sourced Media Books, pg 195
South Dakota Historical Society Press, pg 195
Southern Illinois University Press, pg 195
Square One Publishers Inc, pg 196
Stackpole Books, pg 196
Star Bright Books Inc, pg 197
StarGroup International Inc, pg 197
Steerforth Press & Services, pg 198
SteinerBooks Inc, pg 198
Stewart, Tabori & Chang, pg 198
Stone Bridge Press Inc, pg 199
The Story Plant, pg 199
Strategic Book Publishing (SBP), pg 199
The Jesse Stuart Foundation (JSF), pg 200
Sunbelt Publications Inc, pg 200
Sunstone Press, pg 201
Surrey Books, pg 201
Swallow Press, pg 201
Swan Isle Press, pg 201
Syracuse University Press, pg 201
Nan A Talese, pg 202
Taschen America, pg 203
Taunton Books, pg 203
Temple University Press, pg 204
Ten Speed Press, pg 204
Texas A&M University Press, pg 205

Texas State Historical Association, pg 205
Texas Tech University Press, pg 205
Thames & Hudson, pg 205
Theosophical University Press, pg 206
Third World Press Foundation, pg 206
Thomas Nelson, pg 206
Thomson West, pg 206
Tilbury House Publishers, pg 207
The Toby Press LLC, pg 207
Tommy Nelson®, pg 207
Top Publications Ltd, pg 207
Tor Publishing Group, pg 207
Tortuga Press, pg 208
TotalRecall Publications Inc, pg 208
Trafalgar Square Books, pg 208
Trafford Publishing, pg 208
Trans-Atlantic Publications Inc, pg 209
Travelers' Tales, pg 209
The Trinity Foundation, pg 209
Trinity University Press, pg 209
TriQuarterly Books, pg 209
TRISTAN Publishing, pg 209
Triumph Books LLC, pg 209
Trusted Media Brands Inc, pg 210
Tughra Books, pg 210
Tumblehome Learning Inc, pg 210
Tupelo Press Inc, pg 210
Turner Publishing Co LLC, pg 210
Tuttle Publishing, pg 211
Tuxedo Press, pg 211
Twilight Times Books, pg 211
Tyndale House Publishers Inc, pg 211
Ulysses Press, pg 212
Unarius Academy of Science Publications, pg 212
Union Square & Co, pg 212
United States Holocaust Memorial Museum, pg 213
Universe Publishing, pg 214
University of Alabama Press, pg 214
University of Alaska Press, pg 214
The University of Arizona Press, pg 214
The University of Arkansas Press, pg 214
University of California Press, pg 215
University of Georgia Press, pg 216
University of Hawaii Press, pg 216
University of Illinois Press, pg 216
University of Iowa Press, pg 216
University of Louisiana at Lafayette Press, pg 217
University of Michigan Press, pg 217
University of Missouri Press, pg 217
University of Nevada Press, pg 218
University of New Orleans Press, pg 218
University of North Texas Press, pg 218
University of Notre Dame Press, pg 219
University of Oklahoma Press, pg 219
University of Pennsylvania Press, pg 219
University of Pittsburgh Press, pg 219
University of South Carolina Press, pg 220
The University of Utah Press, pg 220
University of Washington Press, pg 220

University of Wisconsin Press, pg 221
University Press of Florida, pg 221
University Press of Kansas, pg 221
The University Press of Kentucky, pg 222
University Press of Mississippi, pg 222
Upper Room Books, pg 223
Urim Publications, pg 223
US Conference of Catholic Bishops, pg 223
US Games Systems Inc, pg 223
Vandamere Press, pg 223
Vanderbilt University Press, pg 224
The Vendome Press, pg 224
Verso Books, pg 224
Vesuvian Books, pg 224
Visible Ink Press®, pg 225
Ludwig von Mises Institute, pg 225
Waldorf Publishing LLC, pg 226
Water Resources Publications LLC, pg 226
WaterBrook, pg 226
Watermark Publishing, pg 226
Watson-Guptill, pg 226
Wayne State University Press, pg 226
Welcome Books, pg 227
Welcome Rain Publishers LLC, pg 227
Wesleyan Publishing House, pg 227
Wesleyan University Press, pg 227
West Margin Press, pg 227
West Virginia University Press, pg 228
Western Edge Press, pg 228
Western Reflections Publishing Co, pg 228
Westminster John Knox Press (WJK), pg 228
Whitaker House, pg 228
Whole Person Associates Inc, pg 229
Markus Wiener Publishers Inc, pg 229
Wilderness Adventures Press Inc, pg 229
Wiley-Blackwell, pg 229
John Wiley & Sons Inc Global Education, pg 230
John Wiley & Sons Inc Professional Development, pg 230
Williams & Company Book Publishers, pg 230
Willow Creek Press, pg 230
Wings Press, pg 231
Winters Publishing, pg 231
Winterwolf Press, pg 231
Wisdom Publications Inc, pg 231
Wizards of the Coast LLC, pg 231
WoodstockArts, pg 232
Workman Publishing, pg 232
World Bank Publications, pg 233
World Citizens, pg 233
Writer's Digest Books, pg 234
Xlibris Corp, pg 234
Yale University Press, pg 235
YBK Publishers Inc, pg 235
YMAA Publication Center Inc, pg 235
Zondervan, pg 236

JUVENILE & YOUNG ADULT BOOKS

A 2 Z Press LLC, pg 1
Abbeville Publishing Group, pg 2
ABDO, pg 2
Advance Publishing Inc, pg 5
AdventureKEEN, pg 5
African American Images Inc (AAI), pg 5

PUBLISHERS

U.S. PUBLISHERS — TYPE OF PUBLICATION INDEX

AK Press, pg 6
Akashic Books, pg 6
Albert Whitman & Company, pg 6
All About Kids Publishing, pg 7
Alloy Entertainment LLC, pg 7
Ambassador International, pg 7
American Bible Society, pg 8
Andrews McMeel Publishing LLC, pg 14
Appalachian Mountain Club Books, pg 15
Arbordale Publishing, pg 16
Arte Publico Press, pg 17
ArtWrite Productions, pg 18
Ashland Creek Press, pg 18
Asta Publications LLC, pg 20
Atlantic Publishing Group Inc, pg 21
Atlas Publishing, pg 21
Augsburg Fortress Publishers, Publishing House of the Evangelical Lutheran Church in America, pg 22
August House Inc, pg 22
AuthorHouse, pg 22
Baby Tattoo Books, pg 23
Baha'i Publishing Trust, pg 23
Baker Books, pg 23
Bancroft Press, pg 24
B&H Publishing Group, pg 24
Barbour Publishing Inc, pg 24
Barefoot Books, pg 24
Barranca Press, pg 24
Barringer Publishing, pg 24
Bartleby Press, pg 24
Basic Books Group, pg 25
Beacon Press, pg 25
Beaver's Pond Press Inc, pg 26
Bellerophon Books, pg 27
Ben Yehuda Press, pg 27
BePuzzled, pg 28
Bethlehem Books, pg 29
Biographical Publishing Co, pg 29
BJU Press, pg 30
Black Rabbit Books, pg 30
Bloom's Literary Criticism, pg 31
Blue Mountain Arts Inc, pg 32
Bluestocking Press, pg 33
Bold Strokes Books Inc, pg 33
BookLogix, pg 34
BOOM! Studios, pg 34
Boys Town Press, pg 35
BPC, pg 35
Brandylane Publishers Inc, pg 35
Brown Books Publishing Group (BBPG), pg 38
Campfield & Campfield Publishing LLC, pg 39
Candlewick Press, pg 39
Capstone Publishers™, pg 40
Carolrhoda Books Inc, pg 41
Carolrhoda Lab™, pg 41
Caxton Press, pg 42
Cedar Fort Inc, pg 43
Cedar Grove Publishing, pg 43
Centering Corp, pg 44
Central Conference of American Rabbis/CCAR Press, pg 44
Central Recovery Press (CRP), pg 44
Charlesbridge Publishing Inc, pg 45
Chelsea House, pg 45
Chickadee Prince Books LLC, pg 46
Children's Book Press, pg 46
Child's Play® Inc, pg 46
The Child's World Inc, pg 46
China Books, pg 47
Christian Liberty Press, pg 47
Chronicle Books LLC, pg 47
Clarion Books, pg 48
Close Up Publishing, pg 49
Continental AfrikaPublishers, pg 52

Cornell Maritime Press, pg 52
Covenant Communications Inc, pg 54
Crabtree Publishing Co, pg 54
Creative Editions, pg 55
Cricket Cottage Publishing LLC, pg 55
Crossway, pg 56
Cypress House, pg 56
Dancing Dakini Press, pg 57
Dancing Lemur Press LLC, pg 57
Dark Horse Comics, pg 57
Deseret Book Co, pg 58
Dharma Publishing, pg 59
Disney-Hyperion Books, pg 59
Disney Press, pg 59
Disney Publishing Worldwide, pg 60
DK, pg 60
Doodle and Peck Publishing, pg 60
Dorrance Publishing Co Inc, pg 61
Dover Publications Inc, pg 61
Down East Books, pg 61
Down The Shore Publishing, pg 61
Dreamscape Media LLC, pg 62
Dutton Children's Books, pg 62
Eakin Press, pg 62
East West Discovery Press, pg 63
EDC Publishing, pg 63
Wm B Eerdmans Publishing Co, pg 64
Elderberry Press Inc, pg 65
Elva Resa Publishing, pg 65
Emerald Books, pg 66
Emmaus Road Publishing Inc, pg 66
Enchanted Lion Books, pg 66
Endless Mountains Publishing Co, pg 66
Enslow Publishing LLC, pg 66
Entangled Publishing LLC, pg 67
Facts On File, pg 69
Familius, pg 69
Farrar, Straus & Giroux Books for Young Readers, pg 69
Farrar, Straus & Giroux, LLC, pg 70
Father & Son Publishing Inc, pg 70
Feldheim Publishers, pg 70
Ferguson Publishing, pg 71
Filter Press LLC, pg 71
Firefall Editions, pg 72
Fitzroy Books, pg 72
Focus on the Family, pg 73
Walter Foster Publishing, pg 74
Free Spirit Publishing Inc, pg 74
Friends United Press, pg 75
Fulcrum Publishing Inc, pg 75
Galaxy Press Inc, pg 75
Gale, pg 75
Gallopade International Inc, pg 76
Gareth Stevens Publishing, pg 76
Gatekeeper Press, pg 77
Gauthier Publications Inc, pg 77
Getty Publications, pg 78
Gifted Unlimited LLC, pg 78
Gingko Press Inc, pg 78
Global Authors Publications (GAP), pg 78
Global Publishing Solutions LLC, pg 79
Godine, pg 79
Goose River Press, pg 79
Gospel Publishing House, pg 80
Graphic Universe™, pg 80
Greenhaven Publishing, pg 81
Greenleaf Book Group LLC, pg 81
Hachai Publishing, pg 83
Hachette Book Group Inc, pg 83
Hamilton Stone Editions, pg 84
Hannacroix Creek Books Inc, pg 85
HarperCollins Children's Books, pg 85

HarperCollins Publishers LLC, pg 86
Harvest House Publishers Inc, pg 88
Hazelden Publishing, pg 89
Hazy Dell Press, pg 89
Health Communications Inc, pg 89
HeartMath LLC, pg 90
Herald Press, pg 91
Highlights for Children Inc, pg 92
Histria Books, pg 93
Holiday House Publishing Inc, pg 94
Hollym International Corp, pg 94
Homa & Sekey Books, pg 95
Homestead Publishing, pg 95
Houghton Mifflin Harcourt, pg 95
Houghton Mifflin Harcourt Trade & Reference Division, pg 96
Hutton Publishing, pg 97
Immedium, pg 99
In the Garden Publishing, pg 99
Indiana Historical Society Press, pg 99
Inner Traditions International Ltd, pg 101
Iron Stream Media, pg 104
Islandport Press, pg 105
iUniverse, pg 105
Jewish Lights Publishing, pg 105
JIST Publishing, pg 106
Judaica Press Inc, pg 107
Jump at the Sun, pg 107
Kamehameha Publishing, pg 108
Kazi Publications Inc, pg 108
Kidsbooks® Publishing, pg 109
Jessica Kingsley Publishers Inc, pg 110
Klutz®, pg 110
Koho Pono LLC, pg 111
Kokila, pg 111
Kregel Publications, pg 111
KTAV Publishing House Inc, pg 111
Kumon Publishing North America Inc (KPNA), pg 112
Laredo Publishing Co, pg 113
Lasaria Creative Publishing, pg 113
Leaf Storm Press, pg 113
THE Learning Connection®, pg 113
Learning Links-USA Inc, pg 114
Lectorum Publications Inc, pg 114
Legacy Bound, pg 114
The Lentz Leadership Institute LLC, pg 115
Lerner Publications, pg 115
Lerner Publishing Group Inc, pg 115
Liguori Publications, pg 117
Listen & Live Audio Inc, pg 117
Little, Brown Books for Young Readers (LBYR), pg 118
Long River Press, pg 120
Lost Classics Book Company LLC, pg 120
Lucent Press, pg 121
Macmillan, pg 121
Mandel Vilar Press, pg 124
Maren Green Publishing Inc, pg 125
Marshall Cavendish Education, pg 125
Maryland History Press, pg 126
Mason Crest Publishers, pg 126
Master Books®, pg 126
Mazda Publishers Inc, pg 127
Mel Bay Publications Inc, pg 129
Meriwether Publishing, pg 129
Mesorah Publications Ltd, pg 130
Mighty Media Press, pg 131
Milkweed Editions, pg 131
Millbrook Press, pg 131
Mitchell Lane Publishers Inc, pg 133
Montemayor Press, pg 133

Moody Publishers, pg 134
Multicultural Publications Inc, pg 135
Multnomah, pg 135
National Geographic Books, pg 137
National Science Teachers Association (NSTA), pg 138
The New Press, pg 140
NewSouth Books, pg 141
Norilana Books, pg 142
North Star Editions Inc, pg 142
Odyssey Books, pg 145
Ohio University Press, pg 145
Omnigraphics Inc, pg 146
Open Books Press, pg 146
ORO editions, pg 148
Richard C Owen Publishers Inc, pg 149
Paintbox Press, pg 150
Pangaea Publications, pg 150
Pants On Fire Press, pg 150
Papercutz, pg 150
Parachute Publishing LLC, pg 151
Paraclete Press Inc, pg 151
Paul Dry Books, pg 152
Pauline Books & Media, pg 152
Nancy Paulsen Books, pg 152
Peachtree Publishing Co Inc, pg 153
Pelican Publishing, pg 153
Pen & Publish LLC, pg 153
Pen-L Publishing, pg 153
Penguin Publishing Group, pg 154
Penguin Random House LLC, pg 155
Penguin Workshop, pg 156
Penguin Young Readers Group, pg 156
Penny-Farthing Productions, pg 157
Perfection Learning®, pg 158
Persea Books, pg 158
Pflaum Publishing Group, pg 159
Philomel Books, pg 159
Piano Press, pg 159
Planert Creek Press, pg 160
Platypus Media LLC, pg 160
Plowshare Media, pg 161
Plum Tree Books, pg 161
Polar Bear & Company, pg 161
Polis Books, pg 162
Prometheus Books, pg 166
Publication Consultants, pg 167
Puffin Books, pg 167
Purple House Press, pg 167
GP Putnam's Sons Books for Young Readers, pg 167
Random House Children's Books, pg 169
Raven Publishing Inc, pg 172
Ravenhawk™ Books, pg 172
ReferencePoint Press Inc, pg 173
Renaissance House, pg 174
Revell, pg 174
Rising Sun Publishing, pg 175
The RoadRunner Press, pg 175
Roaring Brook Press, pg 175
Rocky Pond Books, pg 176
The Rosen Publishing Group Inc, pg 177
Rowe Publishing LLC, pg 178
Rowman & Littlefield, pg 178
Royal Fireworks Press, pg 178
Running Press, pg 178
Saddleback Educational Publishing, pg 179
William H Sadlier Inc, pg 179
St Nectarios Press, pg 181
St Pauls, pg 181
Salina Bookshelf Inc, pg 181
Savant Books & Publications LLC, pg 182
Scarsdale Publishing Ltd, pg 183
Scholastic Education Solutions, pg 184

259

U.S. PUBLISHERS — TYPE OF PUBLICATION INDEX — BOOK

Scholastic Inc, pg 184
Scholastic International, pg 184
Scholastic Trade Publishing, pg 184
Schreiber Publishing, pg 185
Science, Naturally, pg 185
Shadow Mountain Publishing, pg 187
Shen's Books, pg 187
Silver Leaf Books LLC, pg 188
Simon & Schuster Children's Publishing, pg 189
Simon & Schuster, LLC, pg 189
Sky Pony Press, pg 191
SkyLight Paths® Publishing, pg 191
Sleeping Bear Press™, pg 191
Small Beer Press, pg 191
Smith & Kraus Publishers Inc, pg 192
Soho Press Inc, pg 193
Sourcebooks LLC, pg 194
Sourced Media Books, pg 195
South Dakota Historical Society Press, pg 195
Spizzirri Publishing Inc, pg 196
Standard Publishing, pg 197
Star Bright Books Inc, pg 197
Stellar Publishing, pg 198
Story Monsters LLC, pg 199
Strategic Book Publishing (SBP), pg 199
Stress Free Kids®, pg 200
The Jesse Stuart Foundation (JSF), pg 200
Summertime Publications Inc, pg 200
Tanglewood Publishing, pg 202
Tantor Media Inc, pg 202
Teaching & Learning Co, pg 204
Third World Press Foundation, pg 206
ThunderStone Books, pg 207
Tilbury House Publishers, pg 207
Tommy Nelson®, pg 207
Top Publications Ltd, pg 207
Tortuga Press, pg 208
Trafford Publishing, pg 208
Tumblehome Learning Inc, pg 210
Turner Publishing Co LLC, pg 210
Twenty-First Century Books, pg 211
Twilight Times Books, pg 211
Tyndale House Publishers Inc, pg 211
Union Square & Co, pg 212
Vesuvian Books, pg 224
Viking Children's Books, pg 224
WaterBrook, pg 226
Wayne State University Press, pg 226
West Margin Press, pg 227
West Virginia University Press, pg 228
Wide World Publishing, pg 229
Wildflower Press, pg 229
Wings Press, pg 231
Winters Publishing, pg 231
Winterwolf Press, pg 231
Wizards of the Coast LLC, pg 231
Workman Publishing, pg 232
World Book Inc, pg 233
World Citizens, pg 233
Xist Publishing, pg 234
Xlibris Corp, pg 234
Yard Dog Press, pg 235
YWAM Publishing, pg 236
Zest Books, pg 236
Zondervan, pg 236
Zumaya Publications LLC, pg 237

LARGE PRINT BOOKS

ArtAge Publications, pg 17
Asta Publications LLC, pg 20
Baker Books, pg 23
Bethany House Publishers, pg 29
Catholic Book Publishing Corp, pg 42
Central Conference of American Rabbis/CCAR Press, pg 44
Elderberry Press Inc, pg 65
Federal Street Press, pg 70
Forward Movement, pg 73
Gale, pg 75
Gatekeeper Press, pg 77
Goose River Press, pg 79
Greenleaf Book Group LLC, pg 81
Guideposts Book & Inspirational Media, pg 82
Hachette Book Group Inc, pg 83
HarperCollins Children's Books, pg 85
HarperCollins Publishers LLC, pg 86
Health Communications Inc, pg 89
Insight Editions, pg 101
Little, Brown and Company, pg 118
LRS, pg 121
Lutheran Braille Workers Inc, pg 121
Mandala Earth, pg 124
Mel Bay Publications Inc, pg 129
Nataraj Books, pg 136
Poisoned Pen Press, pg 161
Random House Large Print, pg 170
Recorded Books Inc, an RBmedia company, pg 172
Remember Point Inc, pg 174
Science & Humanities Press, pg 185
Simon & Schuster, LLC, pg 189
Strategic Book Publishing (SBP), pg 199
Thorndike Press®, pg 206
VanDam Inc, pg 223
Velazquez Press, pg 224

MAPS, ATLASES

AAPG (American Association of Petroleum Geologists), pg 1
APC Publishing, pg 15
Appalachian Mountain Club Books, pg 15
Bess Press Inc, pg 29
Bureau of Economic Geology, pg 38
Capitol Enquiry Inc, pg 40
Casa Bautista de Publicaciones, pg 41
China Books, pg 47
Walter De Gruyter Inc, pg 58
DK, pg 60
Educational Insights®, pg 64
Evergreen Pacific Publishing Ltd, pg 68
Faithlife Corp, pg 69
Federal Street Press, pg 70
FineEdge.com LLC, pg 72
The Geological Society of America Inc (GSA), pg 77
GeoLytics Inc, pg 77
History Publishing Co LLC, pg 93
Hollym International Corp, pg 94
Homestead Publishing, pg 95
Illinois State Museum Society, pg 99
Kazi Publications Inc, pg 108
Lake Superior Publishing LLC, pg 112
THE Learning Connection®, pg 113
Lonely Planet Publications Inc, pg 120
MapEasy Inc, pg 124
Menasha Ridge Press, pg 129
Michelin Maps & Guides, pg 130
Military Living Publications, pg 131
National Geographic Books, pg 137
North Carolina Office of Archives & History, pg 142
Nystrom Education, pg 144
Oxford University Press USA, pg 149
Paradise Cay Publications Inc, pg 151
Pennsylvania Historical & Museum Commission, pg 157
Pennsylvania State Data Center, pg 157
PennWell Books, pg 157
Pflaum Publishing Group, pg 159
ProQuest LLC, part of Clarivate PLC, pg 166
Rand McNally, pg 169
Routledge, pg 177
Scholastic Inc, pg 184
Storyworkz Inc, pg 199
Sunbelt Publications Inc, pg 200
Tuttle Publishing, pg 211
United States Holocaust Memorial Museum, pg 213
University of Chicago Press, pg 215
University of Hawaii Press, pg 216
University of Wisconsin Press, pg 221
US Government Publishing Office (GPO), pg 223
Utah Geological Survey, pg 223
VanDam Inc, pg 223
Washington State University Press, pg 226
Western Pennsylvania Genealogical Society, pg 228
Wide World of Maps Inc, pg 229
Wilderness Adventures Press Inc, pg 229
World Book Inc, pg 233
World Trade Press LLC, pg 234

PAPERBACK BOOKS - MASS MARKET

All Things That Matter Press, pg 7
Alloy Entertainment LLC, pg 7
ARE Press, pg 16
Ascension Press, pg 18
Asta Publications LLC, pg 20
AuthorHouse, pg 22
Avery, pg 23
Baen Books, pg 23
Baker Books, pg 23
Bancroft Press, pg 24
Barbour Publishing Inc, pg 24
Barringer Publishing, pg 24
Berkley, pg 28
Bethany House Publishers, pg 29
Bhaktivedanta Book Trust (BBT), pg 29
Black Mountain Press, pg 30
Blood Moon Productions Ltd, pg 31
Blue Note Publications Inc, pg 32
BookLogix, pg 34
Bottom Dog Press, pg 34
Bridge Logos Inc, pg 36
Brooklyn Publishers LLC, pg 37
C&T Publishing Inc, pg 40
Centerstream Publishing LLC, pg 44
Chickadee Prince Books LLC, pg 46
China Books, pg 47
Christian Light Publications Inc, pg 47
The Christian Science Publishing Society, pg 47
Continental AfrikaPublishers, pg 52
Cricket Cottage Publishing LLC, pg 55
DAW Books, pg 57
DC Comics Inc, pg 58
Disney Publishing Worldwide, pg 60
Dover Publications Inc, pg 61
Editorial Portavoz, pg 64
Editorial Unilit, pg 64
Elderberry Press Inc, pg 65
Faith Library Publications, pg 69
FC&A Publishing, pg 70
Federal Street Press, pg 70
Fine Creative Media, Inc, pg 71
Focus on the Family, pg 73
Free Spirit Publishing Inc, pg 74
Galaxy Press Inc, pg 75
Gallery Books, pg 76
Gatekeeper Press, pg 77
Gauthier Publications Inc, pg 77
Gospel Publishing House, pg 80
Grand Central Publishing, pg 80
Greenleaf Book Group LLC, pg 81
Group Publishing Inc, pg 82
Hachette Book Group Inc, pg 83
Hal Leonard LLC, pg 84
Hamilton Stone Editions, pg 84
Harlequin Enterprises Ltd, pg 85
HarperCollins Children's Books, pg 85
HarperCollins Publishers LLC, pg 86
Harrison House, pg 87
Harvest House Publishers Inc, pg 88
Hellgate Press, pg 91
Hilton Publishing Co, pg 92
Histria Books, pg 93
Hollym International Corp, pg 94
House to House Publications, pg 97
Italics Publishing, pg 105
iUniverse, pg 105
Kensington Publishing Corp, pg 109
Kessinger Publishing LLC, pg 109
Krause Publications Inc, pg 111
THE Learning Connection®, pg 113
Liguori Publications, pg 117
Liturgy Training Publications, pg 119
Living Stream Ministry (LSM), pg 119
Love Inspired Books, pg 120
Macmillan, pg 121
Marick Press, pg 125
Marriage Transformation LLC, pg 125
MedMaster Inc, pg 129
Merriam-Webster Inc, pg 129
Multicultural Publications Inc, pg 135
NavPress Publishing Group, pg 139
New Forums Press Inc, pg 139
NFB Publishing, pg 141
Octane Press, pg 145
Omnibus Press, pg 146
On the Write Path Publishing, pg 146
P & R Publishing Co, pg 149
Pacific Press® Publishing Association, pg 149
Pangaea Publications, pg 150
Penguin Publishing Group, pg 154
Penguin Random House LLC, pg 155
Planet Creek Press, pg 160
Public Citizen, pg 167
Random House Publishing Group, pg 170
Rational Island Publishers, pg 171
Red Moon Press, pg 172
Revell, pg 174
RockHill Publishing LLC, pg 176
Rootstock Publishing, pg 176
Round Table Companies, pg 177
St Martin's Press, LLC, pg 180
St Nectarios Press, pg 181
Scholastic Inc, pg 184
Scholastic International, pg 184

PUBLISHERS
U.S. PUBLISHERS — TYPE OF PUBLICATION INDEX

Shambhala Publications Inc, pg 187
Signature Books Publishing LLC, pg 187
Simon & Schuster, LLC, pg 189
Sourcebooks LLC, pg 194
StarGroup International Inc, pg 197
Story Monsters LLC, pg 199
The Story Plant, pg 199
Summertime Publications Inc, pg 200
The Toby Press LLC, pg 207
Tor Publishing Group, pg 207
Trafford Publishing, pg 208
Tyndale House Publishers Inc, pg 211
Wheatherstone Press, pg 228
Wide World Publishing, pg 229
Wiley-Blackwell, pg 229
Wizards of the Coast LLC, pg 231
World Citizens, pg 233
Xlibris Corp, pg 234
Zondervan, pg 236

PAPERBACK BOOKS - TRADE

A 2 Z Press LLC, pg 1
Abbeville Publishing Group, pg 2
Harry N Abrams Inc, pg 2
Academy Chicago Publishers, pg 3
Academy of Nutrition & Dietetics, pg 3
ACM Books, pg 4
ACTA Publications, pg 4
Adams Media, pg 4
Addicus Books Inc, pg 5
Adirondack Mountain Club (ADK), pg 5
AdventureKEEN, pg 5
Adventures Unlimited Press (AUP), pg 5
The AEI Press, pg 5
Africa World Press Inc, pg 5
AICPA® & CIMA®, pg 5
AIP Publishing LLC, pg 6
AK Press, pg 6
Akashic Books, pg 6
Albert Whitman & Company, pg 6
Alfred Music, pg 6
Algora Publishing, pg 7
Allworth Press, pg 7
AllWrite Publishing, pg 7
Amadeus Press, pg 7
Amakella Publishing, pg 7
Ambassador International, pg 7
Amber Lotus Publishing, pg 8
American Alpine Club, pg 8
The American Ceramic Society, pg 9
American Correctional Association, pg 9
American Diabetes Association, pg 9
American Federation of Arts, pg 9
American Institute for Economic Research (AIER), pg 10
American Public Works Association (APWA), pg 12
American Quilter's Society (AQS), pg 12
Ampersand Inc/Professional Publishing Services, pg 13
Anaphora Literary Press, pg 13
Ancient Faith Publishing, pg 13
Andrews McMeel Publishing LLC, pg 14
Angel City Press, pg 14
Angelus Press, pg 14
APC Publishing, pg 15
Aperture Books, pg 15
The Apocryphile Press, pg 15
Apogee Press, pg 15
Appalachian Mountain Club Books, pg 15
Applause Theatre & Cinema Books, pg 15
Applewood Books, pg 15
APS PRESS, pg 16
Arbordale Publishing, pg 16
Arcade Publishing Inc, pg 16
Arcadia Publishing Inc, pg 16
ARE Press, pg 16
Ariadne Press, pg 16
Ariel Press, pg 16
Art of Living, PrimaMedia Inc, pg 17
ArtAge Publications, pg 17
Arte Publico Press, pg 17
ArtWrite Productions, pg 18
ASCD, pg 18
Ascend Books LLC, pg 18
Ash Tree Publishing, pg 18
Ashland Creek Press, pg 18
The Ashland Poetry Press, pg 19
Aspatore Books, pg 19
Association for Talent Development (ATD) Press, pg 19
Asta Publications LLC, pg 20
Astragal Press, pg 20
Atlantic Publishing Group Inc, pg 21
Augsburg Fortress Publishers, Publishing House of the Evangelical Lutheran Church in America, pg 22
August House Inc, pg 22
Authorlink® Press, pg 22
Autumn House Press, pg 22
Avant-Guide, pg 22
Ave Maria Press Inc, pg 22
Avery, pg 23
Avery Color Studios, pg 23
Avotaynu Books LLC, pg 23
Backbeat Books, pg 23
Baen Books, pg 23
Baha'i Publishing Trust, pg 23
Baker Books, pg 23
Bancroft Press, pg 24
B&H Publishing Group, pg 24
Barbour Publishing Inc, pg 24
Barefoot Books, pg 24
Barranca Press, pg 24
Barringer Publishing, pg 24
Barrytown/Station Hill Press, pg 24
Bartleby Press, pg 24
Basic Books Group, pg 25
Basic Health Publications Inc, pg 25
Beacon Hill Press of Kansas City, pg 25
Beacon Press, pg 25
Bear & Co Inc, pg 26
BearManor Media, pg 26
Beaver's Pond Press Inc, pg 26
Bella Books, pg 27
Bellevue Literary Press, pg 27
Ben Yehuda Press, pg 27
BenBella Books Inc, pg 27
John Benjamins Publishing Co, pg 28
Bentley Publishers, pg 28
Berkley, pg 28
Berrett-Koehler Publishers Inc, pg 29
Bethany House Publishers, pg 29
Bethlehem Books, pg 29
BiG GUY BOOKS, pg 29
Biographical Publishing Co, pg 29
Bitingduck Press LLC, pg 30
BJU Press, pg 30
BkMk Press Inc, pg 30
Black Dome Press Corp, pg 30
Black Heron Press, pg 30
Blair, pg 30
Blood Moon Productions Ltd, pg 31
Bloomsbury Academic, pg 31
Bloomsbury Publishing Inc, pg 31
Blue Crane Books Inc, pg 32
Blue Mountain Arts Inc, pg 32
Blue Note Publications Inc, pg 32
Blue Poppy Press, pg 32
BlueBridge, pg 32
Bluestocking Press, pg 33
BNi Building News, pg 33
BOA Editions Ltd, pg 33
BoardSource, pg 33
Bold Strokes Books Inc, pg 33
Book Marketing Works LLC, pg 33
Book Sales, pg 33
The Book Tree, pg 34
Bookhaven Press LLC, pg 34
BookLogix, pg 34
BOOM! Studios, pg 34
Boson Books™, pg 34
Boys Town Press, pg 35
BPC, pg 35
Brandylane Publishers Inc, pg 35
George Braziller Inc, pg 35
Breakaway Books, pg 36
Breakthrough Publications Inc, pg 36
Nicholas Brealey Publishing, pg 36
Brethren Press, pg 36
Brick Tower Press, pg 36
Bridge Logos Inc, pg 36
Bridge Publications Inc, pg 36
Brookline Books, pg 37
Brown Books Publishing Group (BBPG), pg 38
BuilderBooks, pg 38
Bull Publishing Co, pg 38
Burford Books, pg 38
Bywater Books Inc, pg 39
Camino Books Inc, pg 39
Capen Publishing Co Inc, pg 40
Cardoza Publishing, pg 40
CarTech Inc, pg 41
Casa Bautista de Publicaciones, pg 41
Casemate | publishers, pg 41
Catholic Book Publishing Corp, pg 42
The Catholic Health Association of the United States, pg 42
Cato Institute, pg 42
Caxton Press, pg 42
Cedar Fort Inc, pg 43
Cedar Grove Publishing, pg 43
Cedar Tree Books, pg 43
Cengage Learning, pg 43
Center for Creative Leadership LLC, pg 43
Center for Futures Education Inc, pg 43
Center for the Collaborative Classroom, pg 44
Central Conference of American Rabbis/CCAR Press, pg 44
Central Recovery Press (CRP), pg 44
Cereals & Grains Association, pg 44
Chalice Press, pg 44
Chaosium Inc, pg 45
Charles Press Publishers, pg 45
Charlesbridge Publishing Inc, pg 45
Chelsea Green Publishing Co, pg 45
Chicago Review Press, pg 46
Chickadee Prince Books LLC, pg 46
China Books, pg 47
Chosen Books, pg 47
Christian Light Publications Inc, pg 47
Chronicle Books LLC, pg 47
Cider Mill Press Book Publishers LLC, pg 48
Circlet Press, pg 48
City Lights Publishers, pg 48
Clarity Press Inc, pg 49
Clear Light Publishers, pg 49
Clearfield Co Inc, pg 49
Cleis Press, pg 49
Clerisy Press, pg 49
Close Up Publishing, pg 49
CN Times Books, pg 50
Codhill Press, pg 50
Coffee House Press, pg 50
The College Board, pg 50
Columbia University Press, pg 51
Commonwealth Editions, pg 51
The Conference Board Inc, pg 51
David C Cook, pg 52
Copper Canyon Press, pg 52
Cornell Maritime Press, pg 52
Cornell University Press, pg 52
Cosimo Inc, pg 53
Council for Research in Values & Philosophy, pg 53
The Council of State Governments, pg 53
Counterpath Press, pg 54
Counterpoint Press LLC, pg 54
Country Music Foundation Press, pg 54
Countryman Press, pg 54
Covenant Communications Inc, pg 54
Crabtree Publishing Co, pg 54
Craftsman Book Co, pg 54
Creative Editions, pg 55
Creative Homeowner, pg 55
Cross-Cultural Communications, pg 55
The Crossroad Publishing Co, pg 55
Crossway, pg 56
Crown House Publishing Co LLC, pg 56
Crown Publishing Group, pg 56
Crystal Clarity Publishers, pg 56
Cypress House, pg 56
Dalkey Archive Press, pg 56
Dancing Dakini Press, pg 57
Dancing Lemur Press LLC, pg 57
Dark Horse Comics, pg 57
DAW Books, pg 57
The Dawn Horse Press, pg 57
DC Comics Inc, pg 58
Deep River Books LLC, pg 58
Delphinium Books, pg 58
Demos Medical Publishing, pg 58
Deseret Book Co, pg 58
DEStech Publications Inc, pg 59
Destiny Image Inc, pg 59
DeVorss & Co, pg 59
Dharma Publishing, pg 59
DiscoverNet Publishing, pg 59
Dissertation.com, pg 60
Diversion Books, pg 60
DK, pg 60
Dogwise Publishing, pg 60
The Donning Company Publishers, pg 60
Doodle and Peck Publishing, pg 60
Dordt Press, pg 60
Dorrance Publishing Co Inc, pg 61
Doubleday, pg 61
Dover Publications Inc, pg 61
Down East Books, pg 61
Down The Shore Publishing, pg 61
Dragon Door Publications, pg 61
Dramatic Publishing Co, pg 61
Dramatists Play Service Inc, pg 61
Duke University Press, pg 62
Dutton, pg 62
Eakin Press, pg 62
East West Discovery Press, pg 63
ECS Publishing Group, pg 63
Edgewise Press Inc, pg 63
Editorial Bautista Independiente, pg 63

Editorial de la Universidad de Puerto Rico, pg 63
Editorial Portavoz, pg 64
Editorial Unilit, pg 64
Wm B Eerdmans Publishing Co, pg 64
Elderberry Press Inc, pg 65
Elite Books, pg 65
Elva Resa Publishing, pg 65
Emerald Books, pg 66
Emmaus Road Publishing Inc, pg 66
Encounter Books, pg 66
Energy Psychology Press, pg 66
Entangled Publishing LLC, pg 67
Environmental Law Institute, pg 67
Epicenter Press Inc, pg 67
Etruscan Press, pg 67
Europa Editions, pg 67
M Evans & Company, pg 68
Evergreen Pacific Publishing Ltd, pg 68
Everyman's Library, pg 68
Everything Goes Media LLC, pg 68
Excalibur Publications, pg 68
Excelsior Editions, pg 68
The Experiment, pg 68
Fair Winds Press, pg 69
Faith Library Publications, pg 69
Familius, pg 69
Farcountry Press, pg 69
Farrar, Straus & Giroux Books for Young Readers, pg 69
Farrar, Straus & Giroux, LLC, pg 70
Father & Son Publishing Inc, pg 70
FC&A Publishing, pg 70
Federal Street Press, pg 70
Feldheim Publishers, pg 70
The Feminist Press at The City University of New York, pg 71
Fence Books, pg 71
Feral House, pg 71
Fiction Collective 2 (FC2), pg 71
Fifth Estate Publishing, pg 71
Filter Press LLC, pg 71
Fine Creative Media, Inc, pg 71
FineEdge.com LLC, pg 72
Firefall Editions, pg 72
First Avenue Editions, pg 72
Focus on the Family, pg 73
Walter Foster Publishing, pg 74
Fox Chapel Publishing Co Inc, pg 74
Franciscan Media, pg 74
Frederick Fell Publishers Inc, pg 74
Free Spirit Publishing Inc, pg 74
Fresh Air Books, pg 75
Friends United Press, pg 75
Fulcrum Publishing Inc, pg 75
Future Horizons Inc, pg 75
Galaxy Press Inc, pg 75
Galde Press Inc, pg 75
Gale, pg 75
Gallaudet University Press, pg 76
Gallery Books, pg 76
Gallopade International Inc, pg 76
Gatekeeper Press, pg 77
Gateways Books & Tapes, pg 77
Gauthier Publications Inc, pg 77
GemStone Press, pg 77
Georgetown University Press, pg 77
GIA Publications Inc, pg 78
Gibbs Smith Publisher, pg 78
Gifted Unlimited LLC, pg 78
Global Authors Publications (GAP), pg 78
Global Publishing Solutions LLC, pg 79
The Globe Pequot Press, pg 79
Godine, pg 79
Golden West Cookbooks, pg 79
Goodheart-Willcox Publisher, pg 79

Goose River Press, pg 79
Gospel Publishing House, pg 80
Grand & Archer Publishing, pg 80
Grand Central Publishing, pg 80
Gray & Company Publishers, pg 80
Graywolf Press, pg 81
Green Dragon Books, pg 81
Green Integer, pg 81
Greenleaf Book Group LLC, pg 81
Grey House Publishing Inc™, pg 81
Group Publishing Inc, pg 82
Grove Atlantic Inc, pg 82
Gryphon House Inc, pg 82
The Guilford Press, pg 82
Hachette Book Group Inc, pg 83
Hachette Nashville, pg 83
Hal Leonard LLC, pg 84
Hamilton Stone Editions, pg 84
Hampton Roads Publishing, pg 84
Hancock House Publishers, pg 84
Hanging Loose Press, pg 85
Hannacroix Creek Books Inc, pg 85
Harlequin Enterprises Ltd, pg 85
HarperCollins Children's Books, pg 85
HarperCollins Publishers LLC, pg 86
Harrison House, pg 87
Harvard Business Review Press, pg 87
Harvard Common Press, pg 87
Harvard Square Editions, pg 88
Harvest House Publishers Inc, pg 88
Hatherleigh Press Ltd, pg 88
Hazelden Publishing, pg 89
Health Communications Inc, pg 89
Health Professions Press, pg 90
HeartMath LLC, pg 90
Hearts 'n Tummies Cookbook Co, pg 90
Heinemann, pg 90
Hellgate Press, pg 91
Hendrickson Publishers Inc, pg 91
Her Own Words LLC, pg 91
Herald Press, pg 91
Heritage Books Inc, pg 91
The Heritage Foundation, pg 91
Heyday, pg 91
High Plains Press, pg 91
High Tide Press, pg 92
Hill & Wang, pg 92
Hilton Publishing Co, pg 92
Himalayan Institute Press, pg 92
Hippocrene Books Inc, pg 92
History Publishing Co LLC, pg 93
Histria Books, pg 93
W D Hoard & Sons Co, pg 93
Hobblebush Books, pg 93
Hohm Press, pg 93
Hollym International Corp, pg 94
Henry Holt and Company, LLC, pg 94
Holy Cow! Press, pg 95
Homa & Sekey Books, pg 95
Homestead Publishing, pg 95
Hope Publishing Co, pg 95
Horizon Publishers & Distributors Inc, pg 95
Host Publications, pg 95
Houghton Mifflin Harcourt, pg 95
Houghton Mifflin Harcourt Trade & Reference Division, pg 96
House to House Publications, pg 97
Hudson Institute, pg 97
Human Kinetics Inc, pg 97
Humanix Books LLC, pg 97
Huntington Press Publishing, pg 97
Hutton Publishing, pg 97
Idyll Arbor Inc, pg 98
Ignatius Press, pg 98
IHS Press, pg 98
Illuminating Engineering Society of North America (IES), pg 99

ImaJinn Books, pg 99
Immedium, pg 99
Impact Publications/Development Concepts Inc, pg 99
In the Garden Publishing, pg 99
Independent Institute, pg 99
Indiana Historical Society Press, pg 99
Industrial Press Inc, pg 100
Information Age Publishing Inc, pg 100
Information Today, Inc, pg 100
Inner Traditions International Ltd, pg 101
Institute of Jesuit Sources (IJS), pg 102
Institute of Police Technology & Management (IPTM), pg 102
Interlink Publishing Group Inc, pg 102
The International Institute of Islamic Thought, pg 103
International Monetary Fund (IMF), Editorial & Publications Division, pg 103
International Publishers Co Inc, pg 103
International Risk Management Institute Inc, pg 103
International Wealth Success (IWS), pg 104
InterVarsity Press, pg 104
Iron Gate Publishing, pg 104
Iron Stream Media, pg 104
Island Press, pg 104
Islandport Press, pg 105
Italica Press, pg 105
Italics Publishing, pg 105
iUniverse, pg 105
Jain Publishing Co, pg 105
Alice James Books, pg 105
Jewish Lights Publishing, pg 105
The Jewish Publication Society, pg 105
JIST Publishing, pg 106
Johns Hopkins University Press, pg 106
Joshua Tree Publishing, pg 107
Judaica Press Inc, pg 107
Judson Press, pg 107
Jump!, pg 107
Just World Books LLC, pg 107
Kaeden Publishing, pg 107
Kallisti Publishing Inc, pg 108
Kalmbach Media Co, pg 108
Kamehameha Publishing, pg 108
Kazi Publications Inc, pg 108
Kelsey Street Press, pg 108
Kensington Publishing Corp, pg 109
Kent State University Press, pg 109
Jessica Kingsley Publishers Inc, pg 110
Kiva Publishing Inc, pg 110
Alfred A Knopf, pg 110
Kodansha USA Inc, pg 110
Kogan Page, pg 111
Koho Pono LLC, pg 111
Krause Publications Inc, pg 111
Kregel Publications, pg 111
KTAV Publishing House Inc, pg 111
Kumon Publishing North America Inc (KPNA), pg 112
Lake Superior Publishing LLC, pg 112
LAMA Books, pg 112
Landauer Publishing, pg 112
Lantern Publishing & Media, pg 112
LARB Books, pg 113
Larson Publications, pg 113

Lasaria Creative Publishing, pg 113
Laughing Elephant Books, pg 113
Lawyers & Judges Publishing Co Inc, pg 113
Leaf Storm Press, pg 113
THE Learning Connection®, pg 113
Learning Links-USA Inc, pg 114
LearningExpress, pg 114
Lederer Books, pg 114
Lee & Low Books Inc, pg 114
Legacy Bound, pg 114
Leisure Arts Inc, pg 114
The Lentz Leadership Institute LLC, pg 115
LernerClassroom, pg 115
Liberty Fund Inc, pg 116
Library of America, pg 116
Life Cycle Books, pg 116
Light Technology Publishing LLC, pg 116
Liguori Publications, pg 117
Linden Publishing Co Inc, pg 117
Little, Brown and Company, pg 118
Little, Brown Books for Young Readers (LBYR), pg 118
The Little Entrepreneur, pg 118
Liturgical Press, pg 118
Living Language, pg 119
Livingston Press, pg 119
Llewellyn Publications, pg 119
The Local History Co, pg 119
Locks Art Publications/Locks Gallery, pg 119
Loft Press Inc, pg 119
Logos Press, pg 119
Lonely Planet Publications Inc, pg 120
Long River Press, pg 120
Looseleaf Law Publications Inc, pg 120
Lost Horse Press, pg 120
Lotus Press, pg 120
Louisiana State University Press, pg 120
Love Inspired Books, pg 120
Loving Healing Press Inc, pg 121
Loyola Press, pg 121
LPD Press/Rio Grande Books, pg 121
LRP Publications, pg 121
Luna Bisonte Prods, pg 121
Lynx House Press, pg 121
The Lyons Press, pg 121
Macmillan, pg 121
Macmillan Learning, pg 123
Mage Publishers Inc, pg 123
The Magni Co, pg 123
Mandel Vilar Press, pg 124
Manic D Press Inc, pg 124
MAR*CO Products Inc, pg 124
Marathon Press, pg 124
Marine Education Textbooks, pg 125
Marine Techniques Publishing, pg 125
Maryland History Press, pg 126
The Massachusetts Historical Society, pg 126
Master Books®, pg 126
McBooks Press, pg 127
The McDonald & Woodward Publishing Co, pg 127
McFarland, pg 127
McPherson & Co, pg 128
Medals of America Press, pg 128
Mel Bay Publications Inc, pg 129
Menasha Ridge Press, pg 129
MennoMedia, pg 129
Mercer University Press, pg 129
Meriwether Publishing, pg 129
Merriam-Webster Inc, pg 129
Messianic Jewish Publishers, pg 130
Metropolitan Classics, pg 130
MFA Publications, pg 130

PUBLISHERS

U.S. PUBLISHERS — TYPE OF PUBLICATION INDEX

Michigan State University Press (MSU Press), pg 130
Midnight Marquee Press Inc, pg 130
Mighty Media Press, pg 131
Mike Murach & Associates Inc, pg 131
Milford Books™, pg 131
Milkweed Editions, pg 131
Minnesota Historical Society Press, pg 132
MIT List Visual Arts Center, pg 132
The MIT Press, pg 132
Modern Language Association (MLA), pg 133
The Monacelli Press, pg 133
Mondial, pg 133
Monkfish Book Publishing Co, pg 133
Montemayor Press, pg 133
Monthly Review Press, pg 134
Moody Publishers, pg 134
Morehouse Publishing, pg 134
Morgan James Publishing, pg 134
Morning Sun Books Inc, pg 134
Mountain Press Publishing Co, pg 135
Mountaineers Books, pg 135
Multicultural Publications Inc, pg 135
Multnomah, pg 135
The Museum of Modern Art (MoMA), pg 135
Museum of New Mexico Press, pg 135
Mutual Publishing LLC, pg 136
NACE International, pg 136
National Academies Press (NAP), pg 136
National Association of Broadcasters (NAB), pg 136
National Book Co, pg 136
National Catholic Educational Association, pg 137
National Geographic Books, pg 137
National Golf Foundation, pg 138
National Learning Corp, pg 138
National Science Teachers Association (NSTA), pg 138
The National Underwriter Co, pg 138
National Wildlife Federation, pg 139
Naval Institute Press, pg 139
NavPress Publishing Group, pg 139
NBM Publishing Inc, pg 139
New City Press, pg 139
New Concepts Publishing, pg 139
New Directions Publishing Corp, pg 139
New Harbinger Publications Inc, pg 140
New Leaf Press, pg 140
The New Press, pg 140
New World Library, pg 140
New York University Press, pg 141
NewSouth Books, pg 141
NFB Publishing, pg 141
Nilgiri Press, pg 141
No Starch Press, pg 141
NOLO, pg 141
Norilana Books, pg 142
North Atlantic Books (NAB), pg 142
North Carolina Office of Archives & History, pg 142
North Country Press, pg 142
North Point Press, pg 142
North River Press Publishing Corp, pg 142
North Star Editions Inc, pg 142

North Star Press of Saint Cloud Inc, pg 142
Northwestern University Press, pg 143
W W Norton & Company Inc, pg 143
Nova Science Publishers Inc, pg 144
The Oaklea Press Inc, pg 145
Ocean Tree Books, pg 145
Oceanview Publishing Inc, pg 145
Octane Press, pg 145
Odyssey Books, pg 145
Ohio University Press, pg 145
Omnibus Press, pg 146
Omnidawn, pg 146
One On One Book Publishing/Film-Video Publications, pg 146
Ooligan Press, pg 146
Open Books Press, pg 146
Orange Frazer Press Inc, pg 147
Orbis Books, pg 147
Oregon State University Press, pg 147
O'Reilly Media Inc, pg 147
The Original Falcon Press, pg 148
ORO editions, pg 148
Other Press, pg 148
Our Daily Bread Publishing, pg 148
Our Sunday Visitor Publishing, pg 148
The Overlook Press, pg 148
Oxford University Press USA, pg 149
Ozark Mountain Publishing Inc, pg 149
P & R Publishing Co, pg 149
PA Press, pg 149
Pacific Press® Publishing Association, pg 149
Palladium Books Inc, pg 150
Palm Island Press, pg 150
Pantheon Books, pg 150
Pants On Fire Press, pg 150
Papercutz, pg 150
Paraclete Press Inc, pg 151
Paradise Cay Publications Inc, pg 151
Paragon House, pg 151
Parallax Press, pg 151
Parenting Press, pg 151
Park Place Publications, pg 152
Parmenides Publishing, pg 152
Path Press Inc, pg 152
Pathfinder Publishing Inc, pg 152
Paul Dry Books, pg 152
Pauline Books & Media, pg 152
Paulist Press, pg 152
Peachpit Press, pg 153
Peachtree Publishing Co Inc, pg 153
Pelican Publishing, pg 153
Pen & Publish LLC, pg 153
Pen-L Publishing, pg 153
Penfield Books, pg 154
Penguin Publishing Group, pg 154
Penguin Young Readers Group, pg 156
Penn State University Press, pg 157
Pennsylvania Historical & Museum Commission, pg 157
Pennsylvania State Data Center, pg 157
PennWell Books, pg 157
Pentecostal Resources Group, pg 157
Peradam Press, pg 158
Perfection Learning®, pg 158
Persea Books, pg 158
Peterson's, pg 158
Petroleum Extension Service (PETEX), pg 159
Pflaum Publishing Group, pg 159
Phaidon, pg 159

Philosophical Library Inc, pg 159
Piano Press, pg 159
Picador, pg 159
Pieces of Learning Inc, pg 160
The Pilgrim Press/United Church Press, pg 160
Pineapple Press, pg 160
Platypus Media LLC, pg 160
Pleasure Boat Studio: A Literary Press, pg 160
Plexus Publishing, Inc, pg 160
Plough Publishing House, pg 161
Plowshare Media, pg 161
Plunkett Research Ltd, pg 161
Pocol Press, pg 161
Poisoned Pen Press, pg 161
Polar Bear & Company, pg 161
Polis Books, pg 162
Portfolio, pg 162
Potomac Books, pg 162
Clarkson Potter, pg 162
powerHouse Books, pg 162
PPI, A Kaplan Company, pg 162
Practice Management Information Corp (PMIC), pg 163
Presbyterian Publishing Corp (PPC), pg 163
The Press at California State University, Fresno, pg 163
Princeton Book Co Publishers, pg 163
The Princeton Review, pg 164
Productivity Press, pg 165
Progressive Press, pg 165
Prometheus Books, pg 166
ProStar Publications Inc, pg 166
Public Citizen, pg 167
Publication Consultants, pg 167
Publications International Ltd (PIL), pg 167
Purple House Press, pg 167
Pushcart Press, pg 167
Pyncheon House, pg 167
Quail Ridge Press (QRP), pg 168
Quarto Publishing Group USA Inc, pg 168
Quincannon Publishing Group, pg 168
Quirk Books, pg 168
Quite Specific Media Group Ltd, pg 168
Quixote Press, pg 169
Radix Press, pg 169
RAND Corp, pg 169
Peter E Randall Publisher, pg 169
Random House Publishing Group, pg 170
Random House Reference/Random House Puzzles & Games, pg 171
Rational Island Publishers, pg 171
Raven Publishing Inc, pg 172
Ravenhawk™ Books, pg 172
Red Hen Press, pg 172
Red Moon Press, pg 172
Red Wheel/Weiser, pg 173
Reedswain Inc, pg 173
Referee Books, pg 173
Regent Press Printers & Publishers, pg 174
Regnery Publishing, pg 174
Regular Baptist Press, pg 174
Remember Point Inc, pg 174
Revell, pg 174
Rio Nuevo Publishers, pg 175
Rising Sun Publishing, pg 175
River City Publishing, pg 175
Riverdale Avenue Books (RAB), pg 175
Riverhead Books, pg 175
Rizzoli International Publications Inc, pg 175
The RoadRunner Press, pg 175

Roaring Brook Press, pg 175
RockHill Publishing LLC, pg 176
Rod & Staff Publishers Inc, pg 176
Rodin Books, pg 176
Roman Catholic Books, pg 176
Ronin Publishing Inc, pg 176
Rootstock Publishing, pg 176
RosettaBooks, pg 177
Ross Books, pg 177
Rothstein Associates Inc, pg 177
Rowe Publishing LLC, pg 178
Royal Fireworks Press, pg 178
Rutgers University Press, pg 178
Sagamore Publishing LLC, pg 179
St Herman Press, pg 180
St Johann Press, pg 180
St Martin's Press, LLC, pg 180
Saint Mary's Press, pg 181
St Pauls, pg 181
SAMS Technical Publishing LLC, pg 181
San Diego State University Press, pg 182
Santa Monica Press LLC, pg 182
Sarabande Books Inc, pg 182
SAS Press, pg 182
Sasquatch Books, pg 182
Satya House Publications, pg 182
Savant Books & Publications LLC, pg 182
Scarsdale Publishing Ltd, pg 183
Scepter Publishers, pg 183
Schiffer Publishing Ltd, pg 183
G Schirmer Inc/Associated Music Publishers Inc, pg 183
Schocken Books, pg 183
Scholastic Education Solutions, pg 184
Scholastic Inc, pg 184
Scholastic International, pg 184
School for Advanced Research Press, pg 185
Science & Humanities Press, pg 185
Science, Naturally, pg 185
SelectBooks Inc, pg 186
Sentient Publications LLC, pg 186
Seven Stories Press, pg 186
1765 Productions, pg 186
Shadow Mountain Publishing, pg 187
Shambhala Publications Inc, pg 187
Shepard Publications, pg 187
Sherman Asher Publishing, pg 187
Siglio, pg 187
Signalman Publishing, pg 187
Signature Books Publishing LLC, pg 187
Silver Leaf Books LLC, pg 188
Simon & Schuster, pg 188
Simon & Schuster Children's Publishing, pg 189
Simon & Schuster, LLC, pg 189
SkillPath Publications, pg 190
Skinner House Books, pg 190
SkyLight Paths® Publishing, pg 191
Small Beer Press, pg 191
Smith & Kraus Publishers Inc, pg 192
Smithsonian Institution Scholarly Press, pg 192
Smyth & Helwys Publishing Inc, pg 192
Snow Lion, pg 192
Society for Human Resource Management (SHRM), pg 192
Society for Mining, Metallurgy & Exploration, pg 192
Soho Press Inc, pg 193
Solano Press Books, pg 193
Solution Tree, pg 193
Somerset Hall Press, pg 193
Soncino Press Ltd, pg 193
Sophia Institute Press®, pg 193

263

U.S. PUBLISHERS — TYPE OF PUBLICATION INDEX   BOOK

Soul Mate Publishing, pg 194
Sounds True Inc, pg 194
Sourcebooks LLC, pg 194
Sourced Media Books, pg 195
South Carolina Bar, pg 195
South Dakota Historical Society Press, pg 195
South Platte Press, pg 195
Southern Illinois University Press, pg 195
Soyinfo Center, pg 196
SPIE, pg 196
Spizzirri Publishing Inc, pg 196
Square One Publishers Inc, pg 196
Stackpole Books, pg 196
Standard Publishing, pg 197
Star Bright Books Inc, pg 197
STARbooks Press, pg 197
Starcrafts LLC, pg 197
StarGroup International Inc, pg 197
Steerforth Press & Services, pg 198
SteinerBooks Inc, pg 198
Stellar Publishing, pg 198
Stewart, Tabori & Chang, pg 198
STOCKCERO Inc, pg 199
Stone Bridge Press Inc, pg 199
Stone Pier Press, pg 199
The Story Plant, pg 199
Storyworkz Inc, pg 199
Strategic Book Publishing (SBP), pg 199
Strategic Media Books LLC, pg 200
Stress Free Kids®, pg 200
The Jesse Stuart Foundation (JSF), pg 200
Stylus Publishing LLC, pg 200
Summertime Publications Inc, pg 200
Summit University Press, pg 200
Sun Publishing Company, pg 200
Sunbelt Publications Inc, pg 200
Sunrise River Press, pg 201
Sunstone Press, pg 201
Surrey Books, pg 201
Swallow Press, pg 201
Swan Isle Press, pg 201
Swedenborg Foundation, pg 201
SYBEX, pg 201
Syracuse University Press, pg 201
Tachyon Publications LLC, pg 202
Nan A Talese, pg 202
T&T Clark International, pg 202
TarcherPerigee, pg 202
Taschen America, pg 203
Taunton Books, pg 203
Teaching Strategies LLC, pg 204
Temple University Press, pg 204
Ten Speed Press, pg 204
Terra Nova Books, pg 204
Texas A&M University Press, pg 205
Texas State Historical Association, pg 205
University of Texas Press, pg 205
Thames & Hudson, pg 205
Theatre Communications Group, pg 205
Theosophical University Press, pg 206
Third World Press Foundation, pg 206
Charles C Thomas Publisher Ltd, pg 206
Thomas Nelson, pg 206
Thomson West, pg 206
ThunderStone Books, pg 207
Tilbury House Publishers, pg 207
The Toby Press LLC, pg 207
Tommy Nelson®, pg 207
Top Publications Ltd, pg 207
Tor Publishing Group, pg 207
Tortuga Press, pg 208
TotalRecall Publications Inc, pg 208

Tracks Publishing, pg 208
Trafalgar Square Books, pg 208
Transcontinental Music Publications (TMP), pg 209
Transportation Research Board (TRB), pg 209
Travelers' Tales, pg 209
The Trinity Foundation, pg 209
Trinity University Press, pg 209
TriQuarterly Books, pg 209
TRISTAN Publishing, pg 209
Triumph Books LLC, pg 209
TSG Publishing Foundation Inc, pg 210
Tughra Books, pg 210
Tumblehome Learning Inc, pg 210
Tupelo Press Inc, pg 210
Turner Publishing Co LLC, pg 210
Turtle Point Press, pg 210
Tuttle Publishing, pg 211
Tuxedo Press, pg 211
Twenty-Third Publications, pg 211
Twilight Times Books, pg 211
Tyndale House Publishers Inc, pg 211
Ugly Duckling Presse, pg 212
Ulysses Press, pg 212
Unarius Academy of Science Publications, pg 212
Union Square & Co, pg 212
United States Holocaust Memorial Museum, pg 213
United States Institute of Peace Press, pg 213
Universal-Publishers Inc, pg 213
Universe Publishing, pg 214
University of Alabama Press, pg 214
University of Alaska Press, pg 214
The University of Arizona Press, pg 214
The University of Arkansas Press, pg 214
University of California Press, pg 215
University of Chicago Press, pg 215
University of Georgia Press, pg 216
University of Hawaii Press, pg 216
University of Illinois Press, pg 216
University of Iowa Press, pg 216
University of Louisiana at Lafayette Press, pg 217
University of Massachusetts Press, pg 217
University of Minnesota Press, pg 217
University of Missouri Press, pg 217
University of Nebraska Press, pg 217
University of Nevada Press, pg 218
University of New Mexico Press, pg 218
University of New Orleans Press, pg 218
University of North Texas Press, pg 218
University of Notre Dame Press, pg 219
University of Oklahoma Press, pg 219
University of Pittsburgh Press, pg 219
University of South Carolina Press, pg 220
The University of Utah Press, pg 220
University of Washington Press, pg 220
University of Wisconsin Press, pg 221
University Press of Florida, pg 221
University Press of Kansas, pg 221

The University Press of Kentucky, pg 222
University Press of Mississippi, pg 222
Upper Room Books, pg 223
Urim Publications, pg 223
US Conference of Catholic Bishops, pg 223
US Games Systems Inc, pg 223
US Government Publishing Office (GPO), pg 223
Vandamere Press, pg 223
Vanderbilt University Press, pg 224
Vault.com Inc, pg 224
Vedanta Press, pg 224
Verso Books, pg 224
Vesuvian Books, pg 224
Vintage Books, pg 225
Visible Ink Press®, pg 225
Ludwig von Mises Institute, pg 225
Waldorf Publishing LLC, pg 226
Washington State University Press, pg 226
Water Resources Publications LLC, pg 226
WaterBrook, pg 226
Watermark Publishing, pg 226
Watson-Guptill, pg 226
Wayne State University Press, pg 226
Welcome Books, pg 227
Welcome Rain Publishers LLC, pg 227
Well-Trained Mind Press, pg 227
Wellington Press, pg 227
Wesleyan Publishing House, pg 227
Wesleyan University Press, pg 227
West Academic, pg 227
West Virginia University Press, pg 228
Western Edge Press, pg 228
Western Reflections Publishing Co, pg 228
Westminster John Knox Press (WJK), pg 228
Wheatherstone Press, pg 228
Whiskey Creek Press, pg 228
Whitaker House, pg 228
White Pine Press, pg 228
Whittier Publications Inc, pg 229
Whole Person Associates Inc, pg 229
Wide World Publishing, pg 229
Markus Wiener Publishers Inc, pg 229
Michael Wiese Productions, pg 229
Wilderness Adventures Press Inc, pg 229
Wildflower Press, pg 229
Wiley-Blackwell, pg 229
William Carey Publishing, pg 230
Williams & Company Book Publishers, pg 230
Willow Creek Press, pg 230
Wilshire Book Co, pg 230
Wings Press, pg 231
Winters Publishing, pg 231
Winterwolf Press, pg 231
Wisdom Publications Inc, pg 231
Wizards of the Coast LLC, pg 231
Wolfman Books, pg 232
Woodbine House, pg 232
WoodstockArts, pg 232
Workers Compensation Research Institute, pg 232
Workman Publishing, pg 232
World Bank Publications, pg 233
World Citizens, pg 233
Writer's Digest Books, pg 234
Wyndham Hall Press, pg 234
XML Press, pg 235
Yale University Press, pg 235
Yard Dog Press, pg 235

YBK Publishers Inc, pg 235
YMAA Publication Center Inc, pg 235
Yotzeret Publishing, pg 236
YWAM Publishing, pg 236
Zagat Inc, pg 236
Zondervan, pg 236
Zumaya Publications LLC, pg 237

PERIODICALS, JOURNALS

AAPG (American Association of Petroleum Geologists), pg 1
Academic Press, pg 3
Academy of Nutrition & Dietetics, pg 3
ACM Books, pg 4
Acres USA, pg 4
ACS Publications, pg 4
Adirondack Mountain Club (ADK), pg 5
Adventures Unlimited Press (AUP), pg 5
Africa World Press Inc, pg 5
AICPA® & CIMA®, pg 5
AIP Publishing LLC, pg 6
Amber Lotus Publishing, pg 8
American Academy of Environmental Engineers & Scientists®, pg 8
American Academy of Pediatrics, pg 8
American Alpine Club, pg 8
American Anthropological Association (AAA), pg 8
American Association of Collegiate Registrars & Admissions Officers (AACRAO), pg 8
American Bar Association Publishing, pg 8
American Catholic Press (ACP), pg 9
The American Ceramic Society, pg 9
American College of Surgeons, pg 9
American Correctional Association, pg 9
American Counseling Association (ACA), pg 9
American Diabetes Association, pg 9
American Fisheries Society, pg 9
American Geophysical Union (AGU), pg 10
American Geosciences Institute (AGI), pg 10
American Institute of Aeronautics and Astronautics (AIAA), pg 10
American Institute of Chemical Engineers (AIChE), pg 10
American Law Institute Continuing Legal Education (ALI CLE), pg 10
American Mathematical Society (AMS), pg 11
American Medical Association (AMA), pg 11
American Numismatic Society, pg 11
American Psychiatric Association Publishing, pg 11
American Public Works Association (APWA), pg 12
American Society for Nondestructive Testing, pg 12
American Society of Agricultural & Biological Engineers (ASABE), pg 12
American Society of Civil Engineers (ASCE), pg 12
American Society of Mechanical Engineers (ASME), pg 12

PUBLISHERS

U.S. PUBLISHERS — TYPE OF PUBLICATION INDEX

American Water Works Association (AWWA), pg 13
Anaphora Literary Press, pg 13
Ancient Faith Publishing, pg 13
Annual Reviews, pg 14
ANR Publications University of California, pg 14
AOTA Press, pg 14
Aperture Books, pg 15
Appalachian Mountain Club Books, pg 15
Appraisal Institute, pg 15
APS PRESS, pg 16
Arte Publico Press, pg 17
ASCD, pg 18
ASCP Press, pg 18
ASCSA Publications, pg 18
ASET - The Neurodiagnostic Society, pg 18
ASM International, pg 19
ASM Publishing, pg 19
Association for Information Science & Technology (ASIS&T), pg 19
Association for Talent Development (ATD) Press, pg 19
Association for the Advancement of Blood & Biotherapies, pg 19
Association of College & Research Libraries (ACRL), pg 19
Association of School Business Officials International, pg 20
ASTM International, pg 20
Astragal Press, pg 20
The Astronomical Society of the Pacific, pg 20
Augsburg Fortress Publishers, Publishing House of the Evangelical Lutheran Church in America, pg 22
Avotaynu Books LLC, pg 23
Ballinger Publishing, pg 24
John Benjamins Publishing Co, pg 28
Berghahn Books, pg 28
BLR®—Business & Legal Resources, pg 32
Bolchazy-Carducci Publishers Inc, pg 33
Breakthrough Publications Inc, pg 36
The Brookings Institution Press, pg 37
Bucknell University Press, pg 38
Business Research Services Inc, pg 38
Cambridge University Press, pg 39
Carlisle Press - Walnut Creek, pg 40
Carolina Academic Press, pg 41
The Catholic Health Association of the United States, pg 42
The Catholic University of America Press, pg 42
Cato Institute, pg 42
Center for Strategic & International Studies (CSIS), pg 44
Central Conference of American Rabbis/CCAR Press, pg 44
Cereals & Grains Association, pg 44
Child Welfare League of America (CWLA), pg 46
China Books, pg 47
Christian Light Publications Inc, pg 47
Cognizant Communication Corp, pg 50
Cold Spring Harbor Laboratory Press, pg 50
The College Board, pg 50
College Publishing, pg 50
The Connecticut Law Tribune, pg 52
Continental AfrikaPublishers, pg 52

Corwin, pg 53
Council for Exceptional Children (CEC), pg 53
The Council of State Governments, pg 53
Counterpath Press, pg 54
Country Music Foundation Press, pg 54
Covenant Communications Inc, pg 54
CRC Press, pg 55
CSWE Press, pg 56
Dalkey Archive Press, pg 56
Data Trace Publishing Co (DTP), pg 57
Walter De Gruyter Inc, pg 58
DEStech Publications Inc, pg 59
Dharma Publishing, pg 59
Disney Publishing Worldwide, pg 60
Duke University Press, pg 62
The Electrochemical Society (ECS), pg 65
Elsevier Health Sciences, pg 65
Elsevier Inc, pg 65
Entomological Society of America, pg 67
Environmental Law Institute, pg 67
Faithlife Corp, pg 69
The Feminist Press at The City University of New York, pg 71
Fire Engineering Books & Videos, pg 72
Forward Movement, pg 73
Fox Chapel Publishing Co Inc, pg 74
Franciscan Media, pg 74
Friends United Press, pg 75
Future Horizons Inc, pg 75
Gale, pg 75
Gorgias Press LLC, pg 80
Gospel Publishing House, pg 80
The Guilford Press, pg 82
Gulf Energy Information, pg 83
Hanging Loose Press, pg 85
Hannacroix Creek Books Inc, pg 85
Harvard Art Museums, pg 87
Harvard Education Publishing Group, pg 88
HCPro/DecisionHealth, pg 89
Health Administration Press, pg 89
Health Communications Inc, pg 89
Health Forum Inc, pg 90
William S Hein & Co Inc, pg 90
Heyday, pg 91
The Historic New Orleans Collection, pg 93
W D Hoard & Sons Co, pg 93
Hogrefe Publishing Corp, pg 93
Hoover Institution Press, pg 95
Host Publications, pg 95
Housing Assistance Council, pg 97
Human Kinetics Inc, pg 97
IBFD North America Inc (International Bureau of Fiscal Documentation), pg 98
IET USA Inc, pg 98
Ignatius Press, pg 98
Illinois State Museum Society, pg 99
Illuminating Engineering Society of North America (IES), pg 99
Independent Institute, pg 99
Indiana Historical Society Press, pg 99
Indiana University Press, pg 100
Information Age Publishing Inc, pg 100
Information Gatekeepers Inc (IGI), pg 100
Information Today, Inc, pg 100
Infosources Publishing, pg 100

Institute of Environmental Sciences & Technology - IEST, pg 101
International City/County Management Association (ICMA), pg 102
International Foundation of Employee Benefit Plans, pg 103
The International Institute of Islamic Thought, pg 103
International Literacy Association (ILA), pg 103
International Monetary Fund (IMF), Editorial & Publications Division, pg 103
International Society of Automation (ISA), pg 103
International Wealth Success (IWS), pg 104
Interweave Press LLC, pg 104
Islandport Press, pg 105
Johns Hopkins University Press, pg 106
Judson Press, pg 107
Kalmbach Media Co, pg 108
Kamehameha Publishing, pg 108
J J Keller & Associates, Inc®, pg 108
Kennedy Information LLC, pg 108
Kent State University Press, pg 109
Krause Publications Inc, pg 111
Lake Superior Publishing LLC, pg 112
LexisNexis®, pg 116
Mary Ann Liebert Inc, pg 116
Liguori Publications, pg 117
Lippincott Williams & Wilkins, pg 117
Liturgical Press, pg 118
Living Stream Ministry (LSM), pg 119
LPD Press/Rio Grande Books, pg 121
LRP Publications, pg 121
Management Advisory Services & Publications (MASP), pg 123
Management Sciences for Health, pg 123
Marine Techniques Publishing, pg 125
The Massachusetts Historical Society, pg 126
Materials Research Society, pg 126
The Mathematical Association of America, pg 127
McSweeney's Publishing, pg 128
Medieval Institute Publications (MIP), pg 129
The Metropolitan Museum of Art, pg 130
Michigan State University Press (MSU Press), pg 130
Midnight Marquee Press Inc, pg 130
Milady, pg 131
The Minerals, Metals & Materials Society (TMS), pg 132
Minnesota Historical Society Press, pg 132
Modern Language Association (MLA), pg 133
The Mongolia Society Inc, pg 133
NACE International, pg 136
NASW Press, pg 136
National Catholic Educational Association, pg 137
National Center For Employee Ownership (NCEO), pg 137
National Council of Teachers of English (NCTE), pg 137
National Council of Teachers of Mathematics (NCTM), pg 137
National Science Teachers Association (NSTA), pg 138

New Forums Press Inc, pg 139
New Readers Press, pg 140
New York Academy of Sciences (NYAS), pg 140
The New York Botanical Garden Press, pg 140
Newbury Street Press, pg 141
Nilgiri Press, pg 141
North Carolina Office of Archives & History, pg 142
Nova Science Publishers Inc, pg 144
The Ohio State University Press, pg 145
Omnigraphics Inc, pg 146
Optometric Extension Program Foundation (OEPF), pg 147
O'Reilly Media Inc, pg 147
ORO editions, pg 148
Our Sunday Visitor Publishing, pg 148
Oxford University Press USA, pg 149
Pace University Press, pg 149
Peabody Museum Press, pg 153
Penn State University Press, pg 157
Pennsylvania Historical & Museum Commission, pg 157
Pentecostal Resources Group, pg 157
Pflaum Publishing Group, pg 159
Philosophy Documentation Center, pg 159
Plough Publishing House, pg 161
Ploughshares, pg 161
Polebridge Press, pg 161
Clarkson Potter, pg 162
PRINTING United Alliance, pg 165
PRO-ED Inc, pg 165
ProQuest LLC, part of Clarivate PLC, pg 166
ProStar Publications Inc, pg 166
The PRS Group Inc, pg 166
Public Citizen, pg 167
Publications International Ltd (PIL), pg 167
Quintessence Publishing Co Inc, pg 168
Rational Island Publishers, pg 171
Red Moon Press, pg 172
Referee Books, pg 173
Regular Baptist Press, pg 174
The Rockefeller University Press, pg 176
The Rosen Publishing Group Inc, pg 177
SAE (Society of Automotive Engineers International), pg 179
Sagamore Publishing LLC, pg 179
SAGE Publishing, pg 180
St Augustine's Press Inc, pg 180
St Herman Press, pg 180
San Diego State University Press, pg 182
SBL Press, pg 183
Scholastic Inc, pg 184
Scholastic International, pg 184
Science & Humanities Press, pg 185
SIL International, pg 188
SLACK® Incorporated, A Wyanoke Group Company, pg 191
SME (Society of Manufacturing Engineers), pg 191
Society for Industrial & Applied Mathematics, pg 192
Society for Mining, Metallurgy & Exploration, pg 192
Society of Environmental Toxicology & Chemistry (SETAC), pg 192
Society of Exploration Geophysicists, pg 192

The Society of Naval Architects & Marine Engineers (SNAME), pg 193
SPIE, pg 196
Springer, pg 196
Springer Publishing Co, pg 196
Standard Publishing Corp, pg 197
Story Monsters LLC, pg 199
Storyworkz Inc, pg 199
Tapestry Press Ltd, pg 202
Taunton Books, pg 203
Taylor & Francis Inc, pg 203
TESOL Press, pg 204
Texas State Historical Association, pg 205
Texas Tech University Press, pg 205
University of Texas Press, pg 205
Theatre Communications Group, pg 205
Theosophical University Press, pg 206
Thieme Medical Publishers Inc, pg 206
Third World Press Foundation, pg 206
Transportation Research Board (TRB), pg 209
The Trinity Foundation, pg 209
Tughra Books, pg 210
Tyndale House Publishers Inc, pg 211
UCLA Latin American Center Publications, pg 212
Ugly Duckling Presse, pg 212
United Nations Publications, pg 213
United States Holocaust Memorial Museum, pg 213
United States Pharmacopeia (USP), pg 213
University of California Institute on Global Conflict & Cooperation, pg 215
University of California Press, pg 215
University of Chicago Press, pg 215
University of Hawaii Press, pg 216
University of Illinois Press, pg 216
University of Louisiana at Lafayette Press, pg 217
University of Nebraska Press, pg 217
University of Pennsylvania Museum of Archaeology & Anthropology, pg 219
University of Pennsylvania Press, pg 219
University of Wisconsin Press, pg 221
US Government Publishing Office (GPO), pg 223
Ludwig von Mises Institute, pg 225
Washington State University Press, pg 226
Water Environment Federation, pg 226
Wayne State University Press, pg 226
West Virginia University Press, pg 228
Western Pennsylvania Genealogical Society, pg 228
Wheatherstone Press, pg 228
Markus Wiener Publishers Inc, pg 229
Wiley-Blackwell, pg 229
John Wiley & Sons Inc, pg 230
John Wiley & Sons Inc Global Education, pg 230
John Wiley & Sons Inc Professional Development, pg 230
Wolfman Books, pg 232
Wolters Kluwer Law & Business, pg 232

Wolters Kluwer US Corp, pg 232
Workers Compensation Research Institute, pg 232
World Scientific Publishing Co Inc, pg 233
YBK Publishers Inc, pg 235

PROFESSIONAL BOOKS

A-R Editions Inc, pg 1
AAAI Press, pg 1
AAPG (American Association of Petroleum Geologists), pg 1
Abingdon Press, pg 2
Academic Press, pg 3
Academy of Nutrition & Dietetics, pg 3
ACM Books, pg 4
ACS Publications, pg 4
Adams & Ambrose Publishing, pg 4
Advance Publishing Inc, pg 5
AICPA® & CIMA®, pg 5
AIHA (American Industrial Hygiene Association), pg 6
ALA Neal-Schuman, pg 6
Allworth Press, pg 7
Amakella Publishing, pg 7
American Academy of Environmental Engineers & Scientists®, pg 8
American Academy of Pediatrics, pg 8
American Association of Collegiate Registrars & Admissions Officers (AACRAO), pg 8
American Bar Association Publishing, pg 8
American Catholic Press (ACP), pg 9
The American Ceramic Society, pg 9
American College of Surgeons, pg 9
American Correctional Association, pg 9
American Counseling Association (ACA), pg 9
American Diabetes Association, pg 9
American Historical Association (AHA), pg 10
American Institute of Aeronautics and Astronautics (AIAA), pg 10
American Institute of Chemical Engineers (AIChE), pg 10
American Law Institute, pg 10
American Law Institute Continuing Legal Education (ALI CLE), pg 10
The American Library Association (ALA), pg 10
American Medical Association (AMA), pg 11
American Psychiatric Association Publishing, pg 11
American Public Works Association (APWA), pg 12
American Society for Nondestructive Testing, pg 12
American Society of Civil Engineers (ASCE), pg 12
American Water Works Association (AWWA), pg 13
Ampersand Inc/Professional Publishing Services, pg 13
Anaphora Literary Press, pg 13
Andrews University Press, pg 14
ANR Publications University of California, pg 14
AOTA Press, pg 14
APH Press, pg 15
Appraisal Institute, pg 15
Apress Media LLC, pg 15
APS PRESS, pg 16

Ariadne Press, pg 16
Jason Aronson Inc, pg 17
The Art Institute of Chicago, pg 17
ArtAge Publications, pg 17
Artech House®, pg 17
ASCD, pg 18
ASCP Press, pg 18
ASET - The Neurodiagnostic Society, pg 18
Ashland Creek Press, pg 18
ASIS International, pg 19
ASM Publishing, pg 19
Aspatore Books, pg 19
Association for Talent Development (ATD) Press, pg 19
Association for the Advancement of Blood & Biotherapies, pg 19
Association of College & Research Libraries (ACRL), pg 19
Association of Research Libraries (ARL), pg 20
Association of School Business Officials International, pg 20
Asta Publications LLC, pg 20
ASTM International, pg 20
The Astronomical Society of the Pacific, pg 20
Atlas Publishing, pg 21
Authorlink® Press, pg 22
Baker Books, pg 23
Barcelona Publishers LLC, pg 24
Barringer Publishing, pg 24
John Benjamins Publishing Co, pg 28
Bentley Publishers, pg 28
Berrett-Koehler Publishers Inc, pg 29
Biographical Publishing Co, pg 29
George T Bisel Co Inc, pg 29
Bisk Education, pg 29
The Blackburn Press, pg 30
BLR®—Business & Legal Resources, pg 32
Blue Note Publications Inc, pg 32
Blue Poppy Press, pg 32
BNi Building News, pg 33
BoardSource, pg 33
Bolchazy-Carducci Publishers Inc, pg 33
BookLogix, pg 34
Boys Town Press, pg 35
Brandylane Publishers Inc, pg 35
Nicholas Brealey Publishing, pg 36
Paul H Brookes Publishing Co Inc, pg 37
Brookline Books, pg 37
Brown Books Publishing Group (BBPG), pg 38
BuilderBooks, pg 38
The Bureau for At-Risk Youth, pg 38
Bureau of Economic Geology, pg 38
Business Expert Press, pg 38
Captain Fiddle Music & Publications, pg 40
Cardiotext Publishing, pg 40
Carolina Academic Press, pg 41
Carson Dellosa Publishing LLC, pg 41
The Catholic Health Association of the United States, pg 42
Cengage Learning, pg 43
Center for Creative Leadership LLC, pg 43
Center for the Collaborative Classroom, pg 44
Central Conference of American Rabbis/CCAR Press, pg 44
Central Recovery Press (CRP), pg 44
Cereals & Grains Association, pg 44

Chalice Press, pg 44
Charles Press Publishers, pg 45
Charles River Media, pg 45
Child Welfare League of America (CWLA), pg 46
Christian Schools International (CSI), pg 47
Clearfield Co Inc, pg 49
Clinical and Laboratory Standards Institute (CLSI), pg 49
The College Board, pg 50
Columbia University Press, pg 51
Continental AfrikaPublishers, pg 52
David C Cook, pg 52
Cornell Maritime Press, pg 52
Cornell University Press, pg 52
Corwin, pg 53
Council for Research in Values & Philosophy, pg 53
The Council of State Governments, pg 53
Craftsman Book Co, pg 54
CRC Press, pg 55
The Crossroad Publishing Co, pg 55
Crown House Publishing Co LLC, pg 56
CSWE Press, pg 56
Cypress House, pg 56
D&B Hoovers™, pg 57
Data Trace Publishing Co (DTP), pg 57
Davies Publishing Inc, pg 57
F A Davis Co, pg 57
DawnSignPress, pg 58
dbS Productions, pg 58
Walter De Gruyter Inc, pg 58
Demos Medical Publishing, pg 58
DEStech Publications Inc, pg 59
Dewey Publications Inc, pg 59
Dharma Publishing, pg 59
DiscoverNet Publishing, pg 59
Dogwise Publishing, pg 60
Eastland Press, pg 63
Easy Money Press, pg 63
ECS Publishing Group, pg 63
Editorial de la Universidad de Puerto Rico, pg 63
Educator's International Press Inc (EIP), pg 64
Elderberry Press Inc, pg 65
Edward Elgar Publishing Inc, pg 65
Elsevier Health Sciences, pg 65
Elsevier Inc, pg 65
Financial Times Press, pg 71
Fire Engineering Books & Videos, pg 72
Forum Publishing Co, pg 73
Free Spirit Publishing Inc, pg 74
Future Horizons Inc, pg 75
Gatekeeper Press, pg 77
GemStone Press, pg 77
Getty Publications, pg 78
Gifted Unlimited LLC, pg 78
Global Training Center, pg 79
Goose River Press, pg 79
The Graduate Group/Booksellers, pg 80
Green Dragon Books, pg 81
Greenleaf Book Group LLC, pg 81
Grey House Publishing Inc™, pg 81
Group Publishing Inc, pg 82
Gryphon House Inc, pg 82
The Guilford Press, pg 82
Hal Leonard LLC, pg 84
Hameray Publishing Group Inc, pg 84
Hartman Publishing Inc, pg 87
Harvard Business Review Press, pg 87
Harvard Education Publishing Group, pg 88
Hatherleigh Press Ltd, pg 88
Hazelden Publishing, pg 89

PUBLISHERS

U.S. PUBLISHERS — TYPE OF PUBLICATION INDEX

HCPro/DecisionHealth, pg 89
Health Administration Press, pg 89
Health Forum Inc, pg 90
Health Professions Press, pg 90
William S Hein & Co Inc, pg 90
Heinemann, pg 90
Hi Willow Research & Publishing, pg 91
High Tide Press, pg 92
Histria Books, pg 93
W D Hoard & Sons Co, pg 93
Hogrefe Publishing Corp, pg 93
Houghton Mifflin Harcourt, pg 95
Housing Assistance Council, pg 97
HRD Press, pg 97
Human Kinetics Inc, pg 97
Idyll Arbor Inc, pg 98
IEEE Computer Society, pg 98
IEEE Press, pg 98
IET USA Inc, pg 98
Ignatius Press, pg 98
Illuminating Engineering Society of North America (IES), pg 99
Incentive Publications by World Book, pg 99
Industrial Press Inc, pg 100
Information Age Publishing Inc, pg 100
Information Today, Inc, pg 100
Institute of Continuing Legal Education, pg 101
Institute of Environmental Sciences & Technology - IEST, pg 101
Institute of Police Technology & Management (IPTM), pg 102
The Institutes™, pg 102
Intercultural Development Research Association (IDRA), pg 102
International City/County Management Association (ICMA), pg 102
International Foundation of Employee Benefit Plans, pg 103
The International Institute of Islamic Thought, pg 103
International Literacy Association (ILA), pg 103
International Monetary Fund (IMF), Editorial & Publications Division, pg 103
International Risk Management Institute Inc, pg 103
International Society for Technology in Education, pg 103
International Society of Automation (ISA), pg 103
International Wealth Success (IWS), pg 104
Island Press, pg 104
Jain Publishing Co, pg 105
Jhpiego, pg 106
JIST Publishing, pg 106
Johns Hopkins University Press, pg 106
Jones & Bartlett Learning LLC, pg 107
J J Keller & Associates, Inc®, pg 108
Kendall Hunt Publishing Co, pg 108
Kennedy Information LLC, pg 108
Kessinger Publishing LLC, pg 109
Jessica Kingsley Publishers Inc, pg 110
Kogan Page, pg 111
Koho Pono LLC, pg 111
Kregel Publications, pg 111
Kumarian Press, pg 112
LAMA Books, pg 112
Peter Lang Publishing Inc, pg 112
Lawyers & Judges Publishing Co Inc, pg 113
Learning Links-USA Inc, pg 114
LearningExpress, pg 114

The Lentz Leadership Institute LLC, pg 115
LexisNexis®, pg 116
LexisNexis® Matthew Bender®, pg 116
Libraries Unlimited, pg 116
Limelight Editions, pg 117
Lippincott Williams & Wilkins, pg 117
The Little Entrepreneur, pg 118
Liturgical Press, pg 118
Loft Press Inc, pg 119
Logos Press, pg 119
Looseleaf Law Publications Inc, pg 120
Louisiana State University Press, pg 120
Loving Healing Press Inc, pg 121
LRP Publications, pg 121
Management Advisory Services & Publications (MASP), pg 123
Management Sciences for Health, pg 123
MAR*CO Products Inc, pg 124
Marathon Press, pg 124
Marine Education Textbooks, pg 125
Marine Techniques Publishing, pg 125
Math Solutions®, pg 127
McFarland, pg 127
McGraw-Hill Education, pg 127
McGraw-Hill Professional Publishing Group, pg 128
R S Means from The Gordian Group, pg 128
Medical Physics Publishing Corp (MPP), pg 129
The Edwin Mellen Press, pg 129
Meriwether Publishing, pg 129
Milady, pg 131
Milford Books™, pg 131
Military Info Publishing, pg 131
Richard K Miller Associates, pg 132
The Minerals, Metals & Materials Society (TMS), pg 132
The MIT Press, pg 132
Modern Language Association (MLA), pg 133
Mondial, pg 133
The Mongolia Society Inc, pg 133
Morgan Kaufmann, pg 134
NACE International, pg 136
NASW Press, pg 136
National Academies Press (NAP), pg 136
National Association of Insurance Commissioners, pg 136
National Catholic Educational Association, pg 137
National Center for Children in Poverty, pg 137
National Center For Employee Ownership (NCEO), pg 137
National Council of Teachers of English (NCTE), pg 137
National Council of Teachers of Mathematics (NCTM), pg 137
National Education Association (NEA), pg 137
National Institute for Trial Advocacy (NITA), pg 138
National Science Teachers Association (NSTA), pg 138
Naval Institute Press, pg 139
New Forums Press Inc, pg 139
New Harbinger Publications Inc, pg 140
New York Academy of Sciences (NYAS), pg 140
The New York Botanical Garden Press, pg 140

New York State Bar Association, pg 141
New York University Press, pg 141
No Starch Press, pg 141
North Atlantic Books (NAB), pg 142
North River Press Publishing Corp, pg 142
Nova Science Publishers Inc, pg 144
Nursesbooks.org, The Publishing Program of ANA, pg 144
Oak Knoll Press, pg 144
OECD Washington Center, pg 145
On the Write Path Publishing, pg 146
One On One Book Publishing/Film-Video Publications, pg 146
Optometric Extension Program Foundation (OEPF), pg 147
OptumInsight™, pg 147
O'Reilly Media Inc, pg 147
ORO editions, pg 148
Our Sunday Visitor Publishing, pg 148
Richard C Owen Publishers Inc, pg 149
Oxford University Press USA, pg 149
P & R Publishing Co, pg 149
PA Press, pg 149
Paradigm Publications, pg 151
Park Place Publications, pg 152
Pearson Business Publishing, pg 153
Pelican Publishing, pg 153
Penfield Books, pg 154
PennWell Books, pg 157
Petroleum Extension Service (PETEX), pg 159
Philosophy Documentation Center, pg 159
Pieces of Learning Inc, pg 160
Planners Press, pg 160
Platypus Media LLC, pg 160
Plunkett Research Ltd, pg 161
Pocket Press Inc, pg 161
Police Executive Research Forum, pg 162
PPI, A Kaplan Company, pg 162
Practice Management Information Corp (PMIC), pg 163
Practising Law Institute (PLI), pg 163
Presbyterian Publishing Corp (PPC), pg 163
Princeton Book Co Publishers, pg 163
Princeton University Press, pg 164
PRINTING United Alliance, pg 165
PRO-ED Inc, pg 165
Pro Lingua Associates Inc, pg 165
Productivity Press, pg 165
Professional Communications Inc, pg 165
The Professional Education Group LLC (PEG), pg 165
Professional Resource Press, pg 165
The PRS Group Inc, pg 166
Quintessence Publishing Co Inc, pg 168
Quite Specific Media Group Ltd, pg 168
RAND Corp, pg 169
Ravenhawk™ Books, pg 172
Red Moon Press, pg 172
Redleaf Press®, pg 173
Regent Press Printers & Publishers, pg 174
Research & Education Association (REA), pg 174
Research Press, pg 174
Rising Sun Publishing, pg 175

Rocky Mountain Mineral Law Foundation, pg 176
Roncorp Music, pg 176
Ross Books, pg 177
Rothstein Associates Inc, pg 177
The Rough Notes Co Inc, pg 177
Routledge, pg 177
Rowe Publishing LLC, pg 178
Rowman & Littlefield, pg 178
Russell Sage Foundation, pg 178
Rutgers University Press, pg 178
SAE (Society of Automotive Engineers International), pg 179
Safer Society Press, pg 179
Sagamore Publishing LLC, pg 179
SAGE Publishing, pg 180
Saint Mary's Press, pg 181
SAS Press, pg 182
Savant Books & Publications LLC, pg 182
G Schirmer Inc/Associated Music Publishers Inc, pg 183
Scholastic Education Solutions, pg 184
Scholastic Inc, pg 184
Scholastic International, pg 184
Science & Humanities Press, pg 185
Scripta Humanistica Publishing International, pg 185
1765 Productions, pg 186
Shepard Publications, pg 187
SIL International, pg 188
Sinauer Associates, pg 190
Skinner House Books, pg 190
SLACK® Incorporated, A Wyanoke Group Company, pg 191
SME (Society of Manufacturing Engineers), pg 191
M Lee Smith Publishers, pg 192
Society for Human Resource Management (SHRM), pg 192
Society for Industrial & Applied Mathematics, pg 192
Society for Mining, Metallurgy & Exploration, pg 192
Society of American Archivists, pg 192
Society of Environmental Toxicology & Chemistry (SETAC), pg 192
Society of Exploration Geophysicists, pg 192
The Society of Naval Architects & Marine Engineers (SNAME), pg 193
Solano Press Books, pg 193
Solution Tree, pg 193
Sourced Media Books, pg 195
South Carolina Bar, pg 195
Southern Illinois University Press, pg 195
SPIE, pg 196
Springer, pg 196
Springer Publishing Co, pg 196
Standard Publishing Corp, pg 197
Stanford University Press, pg 197
Star Publishing Co Inc, pg 197
StarGroup International Inc, pg 197
Stellar Publishing, pg 198
Stenhouse Publishers, pg 198
STM Learning Inc, pg 199
Storyworkz Inc, pg 199
Stylus Publishing LLC, pg 200
Sundance/Newbridge Publishing, pg 200
SYBEX, pg 201
T&T Clark International, pg 202
Teachers College Press, pg 203
Teaching Strategies LLC, pg 204
Temple University Press, pg 204
TESOL Press, pg 204
Teton NewMedia Inc, pg 205
University of Texas Press, pg 205

U.S. PUBLISHERS — TYPE OF PUBLICATION INDEX BOOK

Thieme Medical Publishers Inc, pg 206
Charles C Thomas Publisher Ltd, pg 206
Thomson West, pg 206
TotalRecall Publications Inc, pg 208
Tower Publishing Co, pg 208
Trans-Atlantic Publications Inc, pg 209
Transcontinental Music Publications (TMP), pg 209
Transportation Research Board (TRB), pg 209
Twenty-Third Publications, pg 211
United States Pharmacopeia (USP), pg 213
Universal-Publishers Inc, pg 213
University of Alaska Press, pg 214
University of Pennsylvania Press, pg 219
University of South Carolina Press, pg 220
University Press of America Inc, pg 221
University Publishing House, pg 222
Upper Room Books, pg 223
US Conference of Catholic Bishops, pg 223
US Government Publishing Office (GPO), pg 223
Utah Geological Survey, pg 223
Vault.com Inc, pg 224
Visual Profile Books Inc, pg 225
Voyager Sopris Learning Inc, pg 225
Water Environment Federation, pg 226
Water Resources Publications LLC, pg 226
West Academic, pg 227
Westminster John Knox Press (WJK), pg 228
Wheatherstone Press, pg 228
Whittier Publications Inc, pg 229
Whole Person Associates Inc, pg 229
Markus Wiener Publishers Inc, pg 229
Wiley-Blackwell, pg 229
John Wiley & Sons Inc Global Education, pg 230
John Wiley & Sons Inc Professional Development, pg 230
William Carey Publishing, pg 230
Windsor Books, pg 230
Wisconsin Department of Public Instruction, pg 231
Wolters Kluwer Law & Business, pg 232
Wolters Kluwer US Corp, pg 232
World Bank Publications, pg 233
World Resources Institute, pg 233
World Trade Press LLC, pg 234
Writer's Digest Books, pg 234
Wyndham Hall Press, pg 234
XML Press, pg 235
YBK Publishers Inc, pg 235
Zaner-Bloser Inc, pg 236
Zondervan, pg 236

REPRINTS

Abbeville Publishing Group, pg 2
Adventures Unlimited Press (AUP), pg 5
American Academy of Pediatrics, pg 8
American Carriage House Publishing (ACHP), pg 8
American Psychiatric Association Publishing, pg 11
Anaphora Literary Press, pg 13

Applause Theatre & Cinema Books, pg 15
Applewood Books, pg 15
ARE Press, pg 16
Association for the Advancement of Blood & Biotherapies, pg 19
Astragal Press, pg 20
Authorlink® Press, pg 22
Baker Books, pg 23
Barbour Publishing Inc, pg 24
Beacon Press, pg 25
Ben Yehuda Press, pg 27
John Benjamins Publishing Co, pg 28
Bentley Publishers, pg 28
Bernan, pg 28
Bethlehem Books, pg 29
Biographical Publishing Co, pg 29
BJU Press, pg 30
Black Classic Press, pg 30
The Blackburn Press, pg 30
Bolchazy-Carducci Publishers Inc, pg 33
Book Sales, pg 33
The Book Tree, pg 34
BookLogix, pg 34
Boydell & Brewer Inc, pg 35
Breakaway Books, pg 36
Bridge Publications Inc, pg 36
Bristol Park Books, pg 37
Bywater Books Inc, pg 39
Central Conference of American Rabbis/CCAR Press, pg 44
Charisma Media, pg 45
Charles Press Publishers, pg 45
Chickadee Prince Books LLC, pg 46
Clearfield Co Inc, pg 49
Cleis Press, pg 49
Codhill Press, pg 50
Columbia University Press, pg 51
The Connecticut Law Tribune, pg 52
Cosimo Inc, pg 53
Counterpath Press, pg 54
Counterpoint Press LLC, pg 54
Country Music Foundation Press, pg 54
Countryman Press, pg 54
Cypress House, pg 56
Dalkey Archive Press, pg 56
Dark Horse Comics, pg 57
DC Comics Inc, pg 58
Walter De Gruyter Inc, pg 58
Dogwise Publishing, pg 60
Dover Publications Inc, pg 61
Down East Books, pg 61
Down The Shore Publishing, pg 61
Dutton, pg 62
Educator's International Press Inc (EIP), pg 64
The Electrochemical Society (ECS), pg 65
Excelsior Editions, pg 68
Father & Son Publishing Inc, pg 70
The Feminist Press at The City University of New York, pg 71
Fine Creative Media, Inc, pg 71
Fordham University Press, pg 73
Frederick Fell Publishers Inc, pg 74
Friends United Press, pg 75
Gatekeeper Press, pg 77
Gifted Unlimited LLC, pg 78
Gingko Press Inc, pg 78
Glitterati Inc, pg 78
Godine, pg 79
Goose River Press, pg 79
Gorgias Press LLC, pg 80
Grand & Archer Publishing, pg 80
Grand Central Publishing, pg 80
Greenleaf Book Group LLC, pg 81
Gryphon Editions, pg 82

Guideposts Book & Inspirational Media, pg 82
Hamilton Stone Editions, pg 84
Harvard Education Publishing Group, pg 88
Harvest House Publishers Inc, pg 88
Hazelden Publishing, pg 89
Heimburger House Publishing Co, pg 90
William S Hein & Co Inc, pg 90
Hendrickson Publishers Inc, pg 91
Heritage Books Inc, pg 91
Heyday, pg 91
Higginson Book Company LLC, pg 91
Hilton Publishing Co, pg 92
Holy Cow! Press, pg 95
Homestead Publishing, pg 95
Hutton Publishing, pg 97
Ibex Publishers, pg 98
Illinois State Museum Society, pg 99
Illuminating Engineering Society of North America (IES), pg 99
Information Age Publishing Inc, pg 100
Institute of Environmental Sciences & Technology - IEST, pg 101
The International Institute of Islamic Thought, pg 103
International Wealth Success (IWS), pg 104
Jain Publishing Co, pg 105
Jewish Lights Publishing, pg 105
Kazi Publications Inc, pg 108
Kennedy Information LLC, pg 108
Kensington Publishing Corp, pg 109
Kent State University Press, pg 109
Kessinger Publishing LLC, pg 109
Konecky & Konecky LLC, pg 111
Kregel Publications, pg 111
Krieger Publishing Co, pg 111
KTAV Publishing House Inc, pg 111
LARB Books, pg 113
Liberty Fund Inc, pg 116
Library of America, pg 116
Linden Publishing Co Inc, pg 117
Lost Classics Book Company LLC, pg 120
Lynx House Press, pg 121
Mage Publishers Inc, pg 123
Mandel Vilar Press, pg 124
Manic D Press Inc, pg 124
Maryland Center for History & Culture (MCHC), pg 126
Maryland History Press, pg 126
The McDonald & Woodward Publishing Co, pg 127
McPherson & Co, pg 128
MFA Publications, pg 130
Michigan State University Press (MSU Press), pg 130
Military Living Publications, pg 131
Minnesota Historical Society Press, pg 132
Modern Memoirs Inc, pg 133
The Mongolia Society Inc, pg 133
Nataraj Books, pg 136
Naval Institute Press, pg 139
New Directions Publishing Corp, pg 139
New Leaf Press, pg 140
The New Press, pg 140
The New York Botanical Garden Press, pg 140
NewSouth Books, pg 141
Norilana Books, pg 142
Northwestern University Press, pg 143
Oak Knoll Press, pg 144
Octane Press, pg 145
Omnigraphics Inc, pg 146

On the Write Path Publishing, pg 146
Oregon State University Press, pg 147
The Original Falcon Press, pg 148
Other Press, pg 148
The Overlook Press, pg 148
PA Press, pg 149
Peachtree Publishing Co Inc, pg 153
Pelican Publishing, pg 153
Penguin Publishing Group, pg 154
Philosophical Library Inc, pg 159
Polar Bear & Company, pg 161
Potomac Books, pg 162
Productivity Press, pg 165
Progressive Press, pg 165
Purple House Press, pg 167
Reader's Digest Select Editions, pg 172
Red Moon Press, pg 172
Red Wheel/Weiser, pg 173
Roman Catholic Books, pg 176
Ronin Publishing Inc, pg 176
Rowe Publishing LLC, pg 178
St Augustine's Press Inc, pg 180
St Johann Press, pg 180
St Nectarios Press, pg 181
Sarabande Books Inc, pg 182
Scepter Publishers, pg 183
G Schirmer Inc/Associated Music Publishers Inc, pg 183
Science & Humanities Press, pg 185
Sentient Publications LLC, pg 186
Seven Stories Press, pg 186
Signalman Publishing, pg 187
Simon & Schuster, LLC, pg 189
Small Beer Press, pg 191
Smithsonian Institution Scholarly Press, pg 192
Society for Industrial & Applied Mathematics, pg 192
Society for Mining, Metallurgy & Exploration, pg 192
Sophia Institute Press®, pg 193
Southern Historical Press Inc, pg 195
Southern Illinois University Press, pg 195
Steerforth Press & Services, pg 198
Stone Bridge Press Inc, pg 199
Story Monsters LLC, pg 199
Sunstone Press, pg 201
Swan Isle Press, pg 201
TAN Books, pg 202
Taschen America, pg 203
Temporal Mechanical Press, pg 204
Texas State Historical Association, pg 205
Texas Tech University Press, pg 205
Third World Press Foundation, pg 206
Tortuga Press, pg 208
Trinity University Press, pg 209
Triumph Books LLC, pg 209
Tuttle Publishing, pg 211
Tuxedo Press, pg 211
United States Holocaust Memorial Museum, pg 213
Universal-Publishers Inc, pg 213
The University of Arizona Press, pg 214
The University of Arkansas Press, pg 214
University of California Press, pg 215
University of Chicago Press, pg 215
University of Illinois Press, pg 216
University of Nebraska Press, pg 217
University of North Texas Press, pg 218
University of Pennsylvania Press, pg 219

PUBLISHERS

U.S. PUBLISHERS — TYPE OF PUBLICATION INDEX

University of Wisconsin Press, pg 221
University Press of Kansas, pg 221
US Government Publishing Office (GPO), pg 223
Welcome Rain Publishers LLC, pg 227
Eliot Werner Publications Inc, pg 227
West Virginia University Press, pg 228
Markus Wiener Publishers Inc, pg 229
Wiley-Blackwell, pg 229
Alan Wofsy Fine Arts, pg 231
Wolters Kluwer Law & Business, pg 232
YBK Publishers Inc, pg 235
Zumaya Publications LLC, pg 237

SCHOLARLY BOOKS

A-R Editions Inc, pg 1
AAAI Press, pg 1
AAPG (American Association of Petroleum Geologists), pg 1
Abingdon Press, pg 2
Academic Press, pg 3
Academica Press, pg 3
ACC Art Books, pg 3
ACMRS Press, pg 4
ACS Publications, pg 4
The AEI Press, pg 5
Africa World Press Inc, pg 5
AICPA® & CIMA®, pg 5
AK Press, pg 6
ALA Neal-Schuman, pg 6
Alaska Native Language Center (ANLC), pg 6
Algora Publishing, pg 7
American Association of Collegiate Registrars & Admissions Officers (AACRAO), pg 8
American Bar Association Publishing, pg 8
American Bible Society, pg 8
American Correctional Association, pg 9
American Counseling Association (ACA), pg 9
American Fisheries Society, pg 9
American Geophysical Union (AGU), pg 10
American Geosciences Institute (AGI), pg 10
American Historical Association (AHA), pg 10
American Law Institute, pg 10
American Law Institute Continuing Legal Education (ALI CLE), pg 10
American Mathematical Society (AMS), pg 11
American Numismatic Society, pg 11
American Philosophical Society Press, pg 11
American Psychiatric Association Publishing, pg 11
American Society for Nondestructive Testing, pg 12
American Society of Plant Taxonomists, pg 13
American Water Works Association (AWWA), pg 13
Anaphora Literary Press, pg 13
Andrews University Press, pg 14
AOTA Press, pg 14
APH Press, pg 15
APS PRESS, pg 16
Ariadne Press, pg 16
Jason Aronson Inc, pg 17
The Art Institute of Chicago, pg 17
ASCSA Publications, pg 18
Association for the Advancement of Blood & Biotherapies, pg 19
Association of College & Research Libraries (ACRL), pg 19
Association of School Business Officials International, pg 20
ASTM International, pg 20
Atlas Publishing, pg 21
Augsburg Fortress Publishers, Publishing House of the Evangelical Lutheran Church in America, pg 22
Baha'i Publishing Trust, pg 23
Baker Books, pg 23
Barcelona Publishers LLC, pg 24
Barringer Publishing, pg 24
Basic Books Group, pg 25
Baylor University Press, pg 25
Beacon Press, pg 25
Begell House Inc Publishers, pg 27
Ben Yehuda Press, pg 27
John Benjamins Publishing Co, pg 28
Berghahn Books, pg 28
Bernan, pg 28
Biographical Publishing Co, pg 29
Bitingduck Press LLC, pg 30
The Blackburn Press, pg 30
Bloom's Literary Criticism, pg 31
Bloomsbury Academic, pg 31
Blue Crane Books Inc, pg 32
Bolchazy-Carducci Publishers Inc, pg 33
The Book Tree, pg 34
Boydell & Brewer Inc, pg 35
Brandylane Publishers Inc, pg 35
George Braziller Inc, pg 35
Brill Inc, pg 37
Paul H Brookes Publishing Co Inc, pg 37
The Brookings Institution Press, pg 37
Brown Books Publishing Group (BBPG), pg 38
Bucknell University Press, pg 38
Bureau of Economic Geology, pg 38
Cambridge University Press, pg 39
Captain Fiddle Music & Publications, pg 40
Carolina Academic Press, pg 41
The Catholic University of America Press, pg 42
Cato Institute, pg 42
Cedar Grove Publishing, pg 43
Center for Strategic & International Studies (CSIS), pg 44
Central Conference of American Rabbis/CCAR Press, pg 44
Chalice Press, pg 44
Charles Press Publishers, pg 45
China Books, pg 47
Cistercian Publications, pg 48
Clarity Press Inc, pg 49
Clearfield Co Inc, pg 49
Codhill Press, pg 50
Cold Spring Harbor Laboratory Press, pg 50
Columbia University Press, pg 51
Continental AfrikaPublishers, pg 52
Cornell University Press, pg 52
Cotsen Institute of Archaeology Press, pg 53
Council for Exceptional Children (CEC), pg 53
Council for Research in Values & Philosophy, pg 53
The Council of State Governments, pg 53
Council on Foreign Relations Press, pg 53
Counterpath Press, pg 54
Country Music Foundation Press, pg 54
Cross-Cultural Communications, pg 55
The Crossroad Publishing Co, pg 55
Crossway, pg 56
Crystal Clarity Publishers, pg 56
CSLI Publications, pg 56
CSWE Press, pg 56
Cypress House, pg 56
The Dawn Horse Press, pg 57
DawnSignPress, pg 58
Walter De Gruyter Inc, pg 58
DEStech Publications Inc, pg 59
Dharma Publishing, pg 59
Dissertation.com, pg 60
Dordt Press, pg 60
Dover Publications Inc, pg 61
Duke University Press, pg 62
Dumbarton Oaks, pg 62
ECS Publishing Group, pg 63
Editorial de la Universidad de Puerto Rico, pg 63
Educator's International Press Inc (EIP), pg 64
Wm B Eerdmans Publishing Co, pg 64
Eisenbrauns, pg 64
Elderberry Press Inc, pg 65
The Electrochemical Society (ECS), pg 65
Edward Elgar Publishing Inc, pg 65
Elsevier Inc, pg 65
Emmaus Road Publishing Inc, pg 66
Encounter Books, pg 66
Entomological Society of America, pg 67
Excelsior Editions, pg 68
Faithlife Corp, pg 69
The Feminist Press at The City University of New York, pg 71
Fifth Estate Publishing, pg 71
Fons Vitae, pg 73
Fordham University Press, pg 73
Fowler Museum at UCLA, pg 74
Gale, pg 75
Gallaudet University Press, pg 76
Gatekeeper Press, pg 77
The Geological Society of America Inc (GSA), pg 77
Georgetown University Press, pg 77
Getty Publications, pg 78
Gifted Unlimited LLC, pg 78
Godine, pg 79
Goose River Press, pg 79
Gorgias Press LLC, pg 80
Gospel Publishing House, pg 80
The Graduate Group/Booksellers, pg 80
Grand & Archer Publishing, pg 80
Green Integer, pg 81
The Guilford Press, pg 82
Hackett Publishing Co Inc, pg 83
Hanser Publications LLC, pg 85
HarperCollins Publishers LLC, pg 86
Harrington Park Press, pg 87
Harvard Art Museums, pg 87
Harvard Education Publishing Group, pg 88
Harvard Ukrainian Research Institute, pg 88
Harvard University Press, pg 88
Health Administration Press, pg 89
Hebrew Union College Press, pg 90
William S Hein & Co Inc, pg 90
Heinemann, pg 90
Hendrickson Publishers Inc, pg 91
Herald Press, pg 91
Hill & Wang, pg 92
Hillsdale College Press, pg 92
Hilton Publishing Co, pg 92
The Historic New Orleans Collection, pg 93
Histria Books, pg 93
W D Hoard & Sons Co, pg 93
Hogrefe Publishing Corp, pg 93
Hollym International Corp, pg 94
Holy Cross Orthodox Press, pg 95
Homa & Sekey Books, pg 95
Hoover Institution Press, pg 95
Houghton Mifflin Harcourt, pg 95
Hudson Institute, pg 97
Human Kinetics Inc, pg 97
Human Rights Watch, pg 97
Hutton Publishing, pg 97
Ibex Publishers, pg 98
IEEE Computer Society, pg 98
Ignatius Press, pg 98
IHS Press, pg 98
Illinois State Museum Society, pg 99
Illuminating Engineering Society of North America (IES), pg 99
Independent Institute, pg 99
Indiana Historical Society Press, pg 99
Information Age Publishing Inc, pg 100
Information Today, Inc, pg 100
Institute of Jesuit Sources (IJS), pg 102
Inter-American Development Bank, pg 102
Intercultural Development Research Association (IDRA), pg 102
The International Institute of Islamic Thought, pg 103
International Literacy Association (ILA), pg 103
International Monetary Fund (IMF), Editorial & Publications Division, pg 103
International Press of Boston Inc, pg 103
International Publishers Co Inc, pg 103
International Society for Technology in Education, pg 103
InterVarsity Press, pg 104
Island Press, pg 104
Italica Press, pg 105
Jain Publishing Co, pg 105
Jewish Lights Publishing, pg 105
The Jewish Publication Society, pg 105
Johns Hopkins University Press, pg 106
Lyndon B Johnson School of Public Affairs, pg 106
Jones & Bartlett Learning LLC, pg 107
Judaica Press Inc, pg 107
Kamehameha Publishing, pg 108
Kazi Publications Inc, pg 108
Kent State University Press, pg 109
Kessinger Publishing LLC, pg 109
Koho Pono LLC, pg 111
Krause Publications Inc, pg 111
Kregel Publications, pg 111
Krieger Publishing Co, pg 111
KTAV Publishing House Inc, pg 111
Kumarian Press, pg 112
Peter Lang Publishing Inc, pg 112
LARB Books, pg 113
The Lawbook Exchange, Ltd, pg 113
Lehigh University Press, pg 114
The Lentz Leadership Institute LLC, pg 115
Lexington Books, pg 115
LexisNexis®, pg 116
Liberty Fund Inc, pg 116
Libraries Unlimited, pg 116

U.S. PUBLISHERS — TYPE OF PUBLICATION INDEX BOOK

Library of America, pg 116
Limelight Editions, pg 117
LinguaText LLC, pg 117
Lippincott Williams & Wilkins, pg 117
Liturgical Press, pg 118
Locks Art Publications/Locks Gallery, pg 119
Loft Press Inc, pg 119
Logos Press, pg 119
Long River Press, pg 120
Lotus Press, pg 120
Louisiana State University Press, pg 120
LPD Press/Rio Grande Books, pg 121
Mandel Vilar Press, pg 124
Marquette University Press, pg 125
Maryland Center for History & Culture (MCHC), pg 126
The Massachusetts Historical Society, pg 126
Master Books®, pg 126
Materials Research Society, pg 126
Math Solutions®, pg 127
Mazda Publishers Inc, pg 127
The McDonald & Woodward Publishing Co, pg 127
McFarland, pg 127
Medical Physics Publishing Corp (MPP), pg 129
Medieval Institute Publications (MIP), pg 129
The Edwin Mellen Press, pg 129
Mercer University Press, pg 129
Meriwether Publishing, pg 129
Mesorah Publications Ltd, pg 130
The Metropolitan Museum of Art, pg 130
MFA Publications, pg 130
Michigan State University Press (MSU Press), pg 130
Midnight Marquee Press Inc, pg 130
Milford Books™, pg 131
The Minerals, Metals & Materials Society (TMS), pg 132
Minnesota Historical Society Press, pg 132
The MIT Press, pg 132
Modern Language Association (MLA), pg 133
The Mongolia Society Inc, pg 133
Monthly Review Press, pg 134
De Gruyter Mouton, pg 135
Moznaim Publishing Corp, pg 135
NACE International, pg 136
NASW Press, pg 136
Nataraj Books, pg 136
National Academies Press (NAP), pg 136
National Catholic Educational Association, pg 137
National Center for Children in Poverty, pg 137
National Council of Teachers of English (NCTE), pg 137
National Council of Teachers of Mathematics (NCTM), pg 137
National Gallery of Art, pg 137
National Science Teachers Association (NSTA), pg 138
Naval Institute Press, pg 139
New Forums Press Inc, pg 139
The New Press, pg 140
New York Academy of Sciences (NYAS), pg 140
The New York Botanical Garden Press, pg 140
New York University Press, pg 141
Newbury Street Press, pg 141
North Atlantic Books (NAB), pg 142

North Carolina Office of Archives & History, pg 142
Northern Illinois University Press, pg 143
Northwestern University Press, pg 143
Nova Science Publishers Inc, pg 144
Nursesbooks.org, The Publishing Program of ANA, pg 144
Oak Knoll Press, pg 144
The Ohio State University Press, pg 145
Ohio University Press, pg 145
Omnigraphics Inc, pg 146
Omohundro Institute of Early American History & Culture, pg 146
On the Write Path Publishing, pg 146
Orbis Books, pg 147
Oregon State University Press, pg 147
Oriental Institute Publications, pg 148
ORO editions, pg 148
Oxford University Press USA, pg 149
P & R Publishing Co, pg 149
PA Press, pg 149
Pace University Press, pg 149
Palgrave Macmillan, pg 150
Paragon House, pg 151
Park Place Publications, pg 152
Parmenides Publishing, pg 152
Peabody Museum Press, pg 153
Pendragon Press, pg 154
Penn State University Press, pg 157
Pennsylvania Historical & Museum Commission, pg 157
PennWell Books, pg 157
Peterson Institute for International Economics (PIIE), pg 158
Philadelphia Museum of Art, pg 159
Philosophical Library Inc, pg 159
The Picasso Project, pg 160
Pleasure Boat Studio: A Literary Press, pg 160
Plough Publishing House, pg 161
Plunkett Research Ltd, pg 161
Polar Bear & Company, pg 161
Polebridge Press, pg 161
Police Executive Research Forum, pg 162
Potomac Books, pg 162
PRB Productions, pg 163
Presbyterian Publishing Corp (PPC), pg 163
The Press at California State University, Fresno, pg 163
Princeton University Press, pg 164
PRINTING United Alliance, pg 165
PRO-ED Inc, pg 165
Productivity Press, pg 165
Professional Resource Press, pg 165
Prometheus Books, pg 166
ProQuest LLC, part of Clarivate PLC, pg 166
Purdue University Press, pg 167
Pyncheon House, pg 167
Radix Press, pg 169
RAND Corp, pg 169
Red Moon Press, pg 172
The Red Sea Press Inc, pg 173
Regent Press Printers & Publishers, pg 174
Regnery Publishing, pg 174
Regular Baptist Press, pg 174
Remember Point Inc, pg 174
Research Press, pg 174
Lynne Rienner Publishers Inc, pg 174

Rising Sun Publishing, pg 175
The Rockefeller University Press, pg 176
Rocky Mountain Mineral Law Foundation, pg 176
Roncorp Music, pg 176
Ross Books, pg 177
Routledge, pg 177
Rowe Publishing LLC, pg 178
Rowman & Littlefield, pg 178
Russell Sage Foundation, pg 178
Rutgers University Press, pg 178
SAGE Publishing, pg 180
St Augustine's Press Inc, pg 180
St James Press®, pg 180
St Johann Press, pg 180
St Joseph's University Press, pg 180
St Martin's Press, LLC, pg 180
St Nectarios Press, pg 181
San Diego State University Press, pg 182
Savant Books & Publications LLC, pg 182
SBL Press, pg 183
School for Advanced Research Press, pg 185
Science & Humanities Press, pg 185
Science History Publications USA Inc, pg 185
Scripta Humanistica Publishing International, pg 185
Shambhala Publications Inc, pg 187
Signature Books Publishing LLC, pg 187
SIL International, pg 188
Skinner House Books, pg 190
SkyLight Paths® Publishing, pg 191
Smith & Kraus Publishers Inc, pg 192
Snow Lion, pg 192
Society for Industrial & Applied Mathematics, pg 192
Society of Exploration Geophysicists, pg 192
The Society of Naval Architects & Marine Engineers (SNAME), pg 193
Solano Press Books, pg 193
Somerset Hall Press, pg 193
Sourced Media Books, pg 195
South Carolina Bar, pg 195
South Dakota Historical Society Press, pg 195
Southern Illinois University Press, pg 195
Soyinfo Center, pg 196
SPIE, pg 196
Springer, pg 196
Springer Publishing Co, pg 196
Stanford University Press, pg 197
Star Publishing Co Inc, pg 197
STARbooks Press, pg 197
StarGroup International Inc, pg 197
State University of New York Press, pg 198
Stenhouse Publishers, pg 198
Stone Bridge Press Inc, pg 199
Stylus Publishing LLC, pg 200
Swallow Press, pg 201
Swan Isle Press, pg 201
Swedenborg Foundation, pg 201
Syracuse University Press, pg 201
Tahrike Tarsile Qur'an Inc, pg 202
T&T Clark International, pg 202
Teachers College Press, pg 203
Temple University Press, pg 204
TESOL Press, pg 204
Texas A&M University Press, pg 205
Texas State Historical Association, pg 205
Texas Tech University Press, pg 205
University of Texas Press, pg 205

Texas Western Press, pg 205
Theosophical University Press, pg 206
Third World Press Foundation, pg 206
Charles C Thomas Publisher Ltd, pg 206
Transcontinental Music Publications (TMP), pg 209
Transportation Research Board (TRB), pg 209
The Trinity Foundation, pg 209
Trinity University Press, pg 209
Tuttle Publishing, pg 211
UCLA Latin American Center Publications, pg 212
United States Holocaust Memorial Museum, pg 213
United States Institute of Peace Press, pg 213
Universal-Publishers Inc, pg 213
University Council for Educational Administration (UCEA), pg 214
University of Alabama Press, pg 214
University of Alaska Press, pg 214
The University of Arizona Press, pg 214
The University of Arkansas Press, pg 214
University of California Institute on Global Conflict & Cooperation, pg 215
University of California Press, pg 215
University of Chicago Press, pg 215
University of Delaware Press, pg 215
University of Georgia Press, pg 216
University of Hawaii Press, pg 216
University of Illinois Press, pg 216
University of Iowa Press, pg 216
University of Massachusetts Press, pg 217
University of Michigan Press, pg 217
University of Minnesota Press, pg 217
University of Missouri Press, pg 217
University of Nebraska Press, pg 217
University of Nevada Press, pg 218
University of New Mexico Press, pg 218
The University of North Carolina Press, pg 218
University of North Texas Press, pg 218
University of Notre Dame Press, pg 219
University of Oklahoma Press, pg 219
University of Pennsylvania Museum of Archaeology & Anthropology, pg 219
University of Pennsylvania Press, pg 219
University of Pittsburgh Press, pg 219
University of Rochester Press, pg 220
University of South Carolina Press, pg 220
University of Tennessee Press, pg 220
The University of Utah Press, pg 220
University of Washington Press, pg 220
University of Wisconsin Press, pg 221
University Press of America Inc, pg 221

PUBLISHERS U.S. PUBLISHERS — TYPE OF PUBLICATION INDEX

University Press of Colorado, pg 221
University Press of Florida, pg 221
University Press of Kansas, pg 221
The University Press of Kentucky, pg 222
University Press of Mississippi, pg 222
US Conference of Catholic Bishops, pg 223
US Government Publishing Office (GPO), pg 223
Utah State University Press, pg 223
Vanderbilt University Press, pg 224
Vernon Press, pg 224
Verso Books, pg 224
Ludwig von Mises Institute, pg 225
Washington State University Press, pg 226
Wayne State University Press, pg 226
Eliot Werner Publications Inc, pg 227
Wesleyan University Press, pg 227
West Virginia University Press, pg 228
Westernlore Press, pg 228
Westminster John Knox Press (WJK), pg 228
Whittier Publications Inc, pg 229
Wide World Publishing, pg 229
Markus Wiener Publishers Inc, pg 229
Wiley-Blackwell, pg 229
William Carey Publishing, pg 230
Winterthur Museum, Garden & Library, pg 231
Wisdom Publications Inc, pg 231
Alan Wofsy Fine Arts, pg 231
Woodrow Wilson Center Press, pg 232
WoodstockArts, pg 232
World Bank Publications, pg 233
World Resources Institute, pg 233
World Scientific Publishing Co Inc, pg 233
Wyndham Hall Press, pg 234
XML Press, pg 235
Yale Center for British Art, pg 235
Yale University Press, pg 235
YBK Publishers Inc, pg 235
Yeshiva University Press, pg 235
Zeig, Tucker & Theisen Inc, pg 236
Zondervan, pg 236
Zone Books, pg 237

SIDELINES

Amber Lotus Publishing, pg 8
Andrews McMeel Publishing LLC, pg 14
ArtAge Publications, pg 17
Barefoot Books, pg 24
Basic Books Group, pg 25
Bellerophon Books, pg 27
BePuzzled, pg 28
Blue Mountain Arts Inc, pg 32
China Books, pg 47
Chronicle Books LLC, pg 47
Cider Mill Press Book Publishers LLC, pg 48
Crystal Clarity Publishers, pg 56
The Dawn Horse Press, pg 57
Dharma Publishing, pg 59
Down The Shore Publishing, pg 61
Educational Insights®, pg 64
Gingko Press Inc, pg 78
Hannacroix Creek Books Inc, pg 85
HarperCollins Children's Books, pg 85
Hay House LLC, pg 89
Himalayan Institute Press, pg 92
Homestead Publishing, pg 95

Kiva Publishing Inc, pg 110
Klutz®, pg 110
Lake Superior Publishing LLC, pg 112
Lawyers & Judges Publishing Co Inc, pg 113
Llewellyn Publications, pg 119
Mandala Earth, pg 124
McPherson & Co, pg 128
The Museum of Modern Art (MoMA), pg 135
PA Press, pg 149
Pangaea Publications, pg 150
Parachute Publishing LLC, pg 151
Pomegranate Communications Inc, pg 162
Rizzoli International Publications Inc, pg 175
Running Press, pg 178
Starcrafts LLC, pg 197
Stewart, Tabori & Chang, pg 198
Story Monsters LLC, pg 199
Sunstone Press, pg 201
Taschen America, pg 203
Tide-mark Press, pg 207
Unarius Academy of Science Publications, pg 212
Universe Publishing, pg 214
US Games Systems Inc, pg 223
Wolfman Books, pg 232

SUBSCRIPTION & MAIL ORDER BOOKS

AAPG (American Association of Petroleum Geologists), pg 1
Acres USA, pg 4
Adventures Unlimited Press (AUP), pg 5
AICPA® & CIMA®, pg 5
ALA Neal-Schuman, pg 6
American Academy of Pediatrics, pg 8
American Historical Association (AHA), pg 10
American Institute for Economic Research (AIER), pg 10
American Water Works Association (AWWA), pg 13
Anaphora Literary Press, pg 13
Appalachian Mountain Club Books, pg 15
APS PRESS, pg 16
ARE Press, pg 16
Ariel Press, pg 16
Art of Living, PrimaMedia Inc, pg 17
ASCD, pg 18
ASET - The Neurodiagnostic Society, pg 18
Aspatore Books, pg 19
Association for the Advancement of Blood & Biotherapies, pg 19
Astragal Press, pg 20
The Astronomical Society of the Pacific, pg 20
Atlantic Publishing Group Inc, pg 21
Barbour Publishing Inc, pg 24
Bethlehem Books, pg 29
Bisk Education, pg 29
BLR®—Business & Legal Resources, pg 32
Breakthrough Publications Inc, pg 36
Bridge Publications Inc, pg 36
The Bureau for At-Risk Youth, pg 38
Capitol Enquiry Inc, pg 40
Cardoza Publishing, pg 40
Center for Creative Leadership LLC, pg 43
China Books, pg 47

Council for Exceptional Children (CEC), pg 53
CQ Press, pg 54
Craftsman Book Co, pg 54
CRC Press, pg 55
Dark Horse Comics, pg 57
Dharma Publishing, pg 59
Eisenbrauns, pg 64
The Electrochemical Society (ECS), pg 65
Forward Movement, pg 73
Free Spirit Publishing Inc, pg 74
Gallopade International Inc, pg 76
Genealogical Publishing Co, pg 77
Georgetown University Press, pg 77
Gifted Unlimited LLC, pg 78
The Graduate Group/Booksellers, pg 80
Gryphon Editions, pg 82
Guideposts Book & Inspirational Media, pg 82
Harvard Art Museums, pg 87
Hazelden Publishing, pg 89
Health Administration Press, pg 89
Heuer Publishing LLC, pg 91
Higginson Book Company LLC, pg 91
Huntington Press Publishing, pg 97
IBFD North America Inc (International Bureau of Fiscal Documentation), pg 98
IEEE Computer Society, pg 98
Ignatius Press, pg 98
IHS Press, pg 98
Information Age Publishing Inc, pg 100
Institute of Continuing Legal Education, pg 101
International City/County Management Association (ICMA), pg 102
International Literacy Association (ILA), pg 103
International Monetary Fund (IMF), Editorial & Publications Division, pg 103
International Press of Boston Inc, pg 103
International Wealth Success (IWS), pg 104
Kennedy Information LLC, pg 108
Krause Publications Inc, pg 111
LAMA Books, pg 112
Law School Admission Council (LSAC), pg 113
Lawyers & Judges Publishing Co Inc, pg 113
Library of America, pg 116
Life Cycle Books, pg 116
LRP Publications, pg 121
MAR*CO Products Inc, pg 124
Marine Techniques Publishing, pg 125
Materials Research Society, pg 126
R S Means from The Gordian Group, pg 128
The Edwin Mellen Press, pg 129
Milady, pg 131
Monthly Review Press, pg 134
National Conference of State Legislatures (NCSL), pg 137
National Learning Corp, pg 138
New Concepts Publishing, pg 139
New Readers Press, pg 140
Nilgiri Press, pg 141
Nova Science Publishers Inc, pg 144
OCP, pg 145
O'Reilly Media Inc, pg 147
Our Daily Bread Publishing, pg 148
Peterson Institute for International Economics (PIIE), pg 158

Practice Management Information Corp (PMIC), pg 163
Productivity Press, pg 165
Professional Resource Press, pg 165
The PRS Group Inc, pg 166
Public Citizen, pg 167
Ross Books, pg 177
SAE (Society of Automotive Engineers International), pg 179
Sagamore Publishing LLC, pg 179
SAGE Publishing, pg 180
St Herman Press, pg 180
Scholastic International, pg 184
South Carolina Bar, pg 195
Southern Historical Press Inc, pg 195
Standard Publishing Corp, pg 197
STARbooks Press, pg 197
SteinerBooks Inc, pg 198
Storyworkz Inc, pg 199
Theosophical University Press, pg 206
Thieme Medical Publishers Inc, pg 206
Thomson West, pg 206
Transportation Research Board (TRB), pg 209
UCLA Latin American Center Publications, pg 212
Ugly Duckling Presse, pg 212
United Nations Publications, pg 213
Univelt Inc, pg 213
University Press of Kansas, pg 221
US Government Publishing Office (GPO), pg 223
Wolters Kluwer Law & Business, pg 232
World Book Inc, pg 233

TEXTBOOKS - ELEMENTARY

A 2 Z Press LLC, pg 1
Advance Publishing Inc, pg 5
AllWrite Publishing, pg 7
Art Image Publications, pg 17
Atlas Publishing, pg 21
Bartleby Press, pg 24
Behrman House Inc, pg 27
Bess Press Inc, pg 29
BJU Press, pg 30
Carson Dellosa Publishing LLC, pg 41
Cengage Learning, pg 43
The Center for Learning, pg 43
Cheng & Tsui Co Inc, pg 46
Christian Liberty Press, pg 47
Christian Light Publications Inc, pg 47
Christian Schools International (CSI), pg 47
Classical Academic Press, pg 49
Continental AfrikaPublishers, pg 52
Educator's International Press Inc (EIP), pg 64
Edupress Inc, pg 64
EPS School Specialty, pg 67
Evan-Moor Educational Publishers, pg 68
Gale, pg 75
Gatekeeper Press, pg 77
Gibbs Smith Publisher, pg 78
Goose River Press, pg 79
Gospel Publishing House, pg 80
Hal Leonard LLC, pg 84
Heinemann, pg 90
Hewitt Homeschooling Resources, pg 91
Houghton Mifflin Harcourt, pg 95
Houghton Mifflin Harcourt K-12 Publishers, pg 96
Human Kinetics Inc, pg 97
Ignatius Press, pg 98

U.S. PUBLISHERS — TYPE OF PUBLICATION INDEX

International Book Centre Inc, pg 102
International Society for Technology in Education, pg 103
JIST Publishing, pg 106
Kendall Hunt Publishing Co, pg 108
KTAV Publishing House Inc, pg 111
Kumon Publishing North America Inc (KPNA), pg 112
THE Learning Connection®, pg 113
Learning Links-USA Inc, pg 114
Limelight Editions, pg 117
Lorenz Educational Press, pg 120
Lost Classics Book Company LLC, pg 120
Loyola Press, pg 121
Master Books®, pg 126
Mastery Education, pg 126
Math Solutions®, pg 127
McGraw-Hill Education, pg 127
McGraw-Hill Professional Publishing Group, pg 128
McGraw-Hill School Education Group, pg 128
Meriwether Publishing, pg 129
Milliken Publishing Co, pg 132
Nataraj Books, pg 136
National Geographic Learning, pg 138
Our Sunday Visitor Publishing, pg 148
Perfection Learning®, pg 158
Piano Press, pg 159
Pro Lingua Associates Inc, pg 165
Rising Sun Publishing, pg 175
Rod & Staff Publishers Inc, pg 176
Rowe Publishing LLC, pg 178
Royal Fireworks Press, pg 178
William H Sadlier Inc, pg 179
Savvas Learning Co LLC, pg 183
Scholastic International, pg 184
Science & Humanities Press, pg 185
Sound Feelings Publishing, pg 194
Story Monsters LLC, pg 199
Sundance/Newbridge Publishing, pg 200
Teachers College Press, pg 203
Treehaus Communications Inc, pg 209
Walch Education, pg 225
Wayside Publishing, pg 227
Well-Trained Mind Press, pg 227
Wellington Press, pg 227
Zaner-Bloser Inc, pg 236

TEXTBOOKS - SECONDARY

A 2 Z Press LLC, pg 1
Advance Publishing Inc, pg 5
AllWrite Publishing, pg 7
American Geosciences Institute (AGI), pg 10
American Technical Publishers, pg 13
APH Press, pg 15
Art Image Publications, pg 17
Atlas Publishing, pg 21
Ave Maria Press Inc, pg 22
Behrman House Inc, pg 27
Ben Yehuda Press, pg 27
Bess Press Inc, pg 29
BJU Press, pg 30
Bolchazy-Carducci Publishers Inc, pg 33
Carolina Academic Press, pg 41
Cengage Learning, pg 43
The Center for Learning, pg 43
Charles Press Publishers, pg 45
Cheng & Tsui Co Inc, pg 46
China Books, pg 47
Christian Liberty Press, pg 47

Christian Light Publications Inc, pg 47
Christian Schools International (CSI), pg 47
Classical Academic Press, pg 49
Close Up Publishing, pg 49
Comex Systems Inc, pg 51
Continental AfrikaPublishers, pg 52
Cypress House, pg 56
F A Davis Co, pg 57
DawnSignPress, pg 58
Dover Publications Inc, pg 61
Dramatic Publishing Co, pg 61
Educator's International Press Inc (EIP), pg 64
Edupress Inc, pg 64
EPS School Specialty, pg 67
Fairchild Books, pg 69
W H Freeman, pg 75
Gale, pg 75
Gallaudet University Press, pg 76
Gatekeeper Press, pg 77
Gibbs Smith Publisher, pg 78
Goodheart-Willcox Publisher, pg 79
Goose River Press, pg 79
Gospel Publishing House, pg 80
Hal Leonard LLC, pg 84
Hamilton Stone Editions, pg 84
Heinemann, pg 90
Hewitt Homeschooling Resources, pg 91
Houghton Mifflin Harcourt, pg 95
Houghton Mifflin Harcourt K-12 Publishers, pg 96
Human Kinetics Inc, pg 97
Ignatius Press, pg 98
International Book Centre Inc, pg 102
International Society for Technology in Education, pg 103
JIST Publishing, pg 106
Kendall Hunt Publishing Co, pg 108
Krause Publications Inc, pg 111
Krieger Publishing Co, pg 111
Learning Links-USA Inc, pg 114
Libraries Unlimited, pg 116
Limelight Editions, pg 117
Logos Press, pg 119
Lorenz Educational Press, pg 120
Marine Education Textbooks, pg 125
Mastery Education, pg 126
Math Solutions®, pg 127
McGraw-Hill Education, pg 127
McGraw-Hill Professional Publishing Group, pg 128
McGraw-Hill School Education Group, pg 128
Meriwether Publishing, pg 129
Mesorah Publications Ltd, pg 130
Milady, pg 131
Milliken Publishing Co, pg 132
Nataraj Books, pg 136
National Book Co, pg 136
National Geographic Learning, pg 138
National Learning Corp, pg 138
New Readers Press, pg 140
W W Norton & Company Inc, pg 143
Our Sunday Visitor Publishing, pg 148
Perfection Learning®, pg 158
PRINTING United Alliance, pg 165
Pro Lingua Associates Inc, pg 165
Research & Education Association (REA), pg 174
Rising Sun Publishing, pg 175
Rowe Publishing LLC, pg 178
Royal Fireworks Press, pg 178
William H Sadlier Inc, pg 179
Saint Mary's Press, pg 181
Salina Bookshelf Inc, pg 181

Savvas Learning Co LLC, pg 183
Schlager Group Inc, pg 183
Science & Humanities Press, pg 185
Smith & Kraus Publishers Inc, pg 192
Stone Bridge Press Inc, pg 199
Story Monsters LLC, pg 199
Teachers College Press, pg 203
Trans-Atlantic Publications Inc, pg 209
Walch Education, pg 225
Wayside Publishing, pg 227
Well-Trained Mind Press, pg 227
Wellington Press, pg 227
Whittier Publications Inc, pg 229
Markus Wiener Publishers Inc, pg 229
World Citizens, pg 233
Worth Publishers, pg 234

TEXTBOOKS - COLLEGE

A-R Editions Inc, pg 1
Academic Press, pg 3
Academy of Nutrition & Dietetics, pg 3
ACM Books, pg 4
ACU Press, pg 4
Adams & Ambrose Publishing, pg 4
AICPA® & CIMA®, pg 5
AIHA (American Industrial Hygiene Association), pg 6
ALA Neal-Schuman, pg 6
Alaska Native Language Center (ANLC), pg 6
AllWrite Publishing, pg 7
American Academy of Environmental Engineers & Scientists®, pg 8
The American Ceramic Society, pg 9
The American College of Financial Services, pg 9
American Correctional Association, pg 9
American Counseling Association (ACA), pg 9
American Fisheries Society, pg 9
American Geosciences Institute (AGI), pg 10
American Institute of Aeronautics and Astronautics (AIAA), pg 10
American Press, pg 11
American Psychiatric Association Publishing, pg 11
American Society for Nondestructive Testing, pg 12
American Society for Quality (ASQ), pg 12
American Society of Agricultural & Biological Engineers (ASABE), pg 12
American Technical Publishers, pg 13
Anaphora Literary Press, pg 13
Andrews University Press, pg 14
ANR Publications University of California, pg 14
AOTA Press, pg 14
APH Press, pg 15
APS PRESS, pg 16
Artech House®, pg 17
ASCP Press, pg 18
ASCSA Publications, pg 18
ASM Publishing, pg 19
Atlas Publishing, pg 21
Augsburg Fortress Publishers, Publishing House of the Evangelical Lutheran Church in America, pg 22
Autumn House Press, pg 22
Baker Books, pg 23

B&H Publishing Group, pg 24
Barcelona Publishers LLC, pg 24
Bartleby Press, pg 24
Basic Books Group, pg 25
Bedford/St Martin's, pg 26
Behrman House Inc, pg 27
Ben Yehuda Press, pg 27
John Benjamins Publishing Co, pg 28
Berrett-Koehler Publishers Inc, pg 29
Bess Press Inc, pg 29
George T Bisel Co Inc, pg 29
Bisk Education, pg 29
The Blackburn Press, pg 30
Bloomsbury Academic, pg 31
Bolchazy-Carducci Publishers Inc, pg 33
Breakthrough Publications Inc, pg 36
Paul H Brookes Publishing Co Inc, pg 37
The Brookings Institution Press, pg 37
Business Expert Press, pg 38
Cambridge University Press, pg 39
Cardiotext Publishing, pg 40
Carolina Academic Press, pg 41
CCH, a Wolters Kluwer business, pg 42
Cengage Learning, pg 43
Center for the Collaborative Classroom, pg 44
Cereals & Grains Association, pg 44
Charles Press Publishers, pg 45
Cheng & Tsui Co Inc, pg 46
China Books, pg 47
Clarity Press Inc, pg 49
Close Up Publishing, pg 49
Cognizant Communication Corp, pg 50
College Publishing, pg 50
Columbia University Press, pg 51
Comex Systems Inc, pg 51
Continental AfrikaPublishers, pg 52
Cornell Maritime Press, pg 52
Cornell University Press, pg 52
Council for Research in Values & Philosophy, pg 53
Crossway, pg 56
CSLI Publications, pg 56
Cypress House, pg 56
Data Trace Publishing Co (DTP), pg 57
Davies Publishing Inc, pg 57
F A Davis Co, pg 57
DawnSignPress, pg 58
Walter De Gruyter Inc, pg 58
DEStech Publications Inc, pg 59
Dissertation.com, pg 60
Dramatic Publishing Co, pg 61
Duke University Press, pg 62
Eastland Press, pg 63
Editorial de la Universidad de Puerto Rico, pg 63
Educator's International Press Inc (EIP), pg 64
Wm B Eerdmans Publishing Co, pg 64
Edward Elgar Publishing Inc, pg 65
Elsevier Health Sciences, pg 65
Elsevier Inc, pg 65
Fairchild Books, pg 69
Fifth Estate Publishing, pg 71
Fire Engineering Books & Videos, pg 72
Focus, pg 73
Fons Vitae, pg 73
Foundation Press, pg 74
Franklin, Beedle & Associates Inc, pg 74
W H Freeman, pg 75
Gallaudet University Press, pg 76

PUBLISHERS

U.S. PUBLISHERS — TYPE OF PUBLICATION INDEX

Gatekeeper Press, pg 77
Georgetown University Press, pg 77
Gifted Unlimited LLC, pg 78
Gingko Press Inc, pg 78
Global Training Center, pg 79
Goodheart-Willcox Publisher, pg 79
Gorgias Press LLC, pg 80
Gospel Publishing House, pg 80
Green Dragon Books, pg 81
Gryphon House Inc, pg 82
The Guilford Press, pg 82
Hackett Publishing Co Inc, pg 83
Hal Leonard LLC, pg 84
Hamilton Stone Editions, pg 84
Hanser Publications LLC, pg 85
Harrington Park Press, pg 87
Harvard Ukrainian Research Institute, pg 88
Health Administration Press, pg 89
Health Forum Inc, pg 90
Health Professions Press, pg 90
William S Hein & Co Inc, pg 90
Hendrickson Publishers Inc, pg 91
Heyday, pg 91
W D Hoard & Sons Co, pg 93
Hogrefe Publishing Corp, pg 93
Hollym International Corp, pg 94
Human Kinetics Inc, pg 97
Ibex Publishers, pg 98
Idyll Arbor Inc, pg 98
IEEE Computer Society, pg 98
IEEE Press, pg 98
Ignatius Press, pg 98
Indiana University Press, pg 100
Industrial Press Inc, pg 100
Information Age Publishing Inc, pg 100
Information Today, Inc, pg 100
International Book Centre Inc, pg 102
International City/County Management Association (ICMA), pg 102
The International Institute of Islamic Thought, pg 103
International Literacy Association (ILA), pg 103
International Press of Boston Inc, pg 103
International Society of Automation (ISA), pg 103
InterVarsity Press, pg 104
JIST Publishing, pg 106
Johns Hopkins University Press, pg 106
Jones & Bartlett Learning LLC, pg 107
Kazi Publications Inc, pg 108
Kendall Hunt Publishing Co, pg 108
Kent State University Press, pg 109
Kogan Page, pg 111
Krause Publications Inc, pg 111
Kregel Publications, pg 111
Krieger Publishing Co, pg 111
Kumarian Press, pg 112
Lanahan Publishers Inc, pg 112
Peter Lang Publishing Inc, pg 112
Lawyers & Judges Publishing Co Inc, pg 113
The Lentz Leadership Institute LLC, pg 115
LexisNexis®, pg 116
Libraries Unlimited, pg 116
Limelight Editions, pg 117
LinguaText LLC, pg 117
Lippincott Williams & Wilkins, pg 117
Liturgical Press, pg 118
Logos Press, pg 119
Looseleaf Law Publications Inc, pg 120
LRP Publications, pg 121
Macmillan Learning, pg 123

Management Sciences for Health, pg 123
Marquette University Press, pg 125
Math Solutions®, pg 127
McFarland, pg 127
McGraw-Hill Create, pg 127
McGraw-Hill Education, pg 127
McGraw-Hill Higher Education, pg 128
McGraw-Hill Professional Publishing Group, pg 128
Medical Physics Publishing Corp (MPP), pg 129
Meriwether Publishing, pg 129
Midnight Marquee Press Inc, pg 130
Milady, pg 131
The MIT Press, pg 132
Modern Language Association (MLA), pg 133
The Mongolia Society Inc, pg 133
Monthly Review Press, pg 134
Morgan Kaufmann, pg 134
Morton Publishing Co, pg 134
De Gruyter Mouton, pg 135
NACE International, pg 136
NASW Press, pg 136
Nataraj Books, pg 136
National Academies Press (NAP), pg 136
National Book Co, pg 136
National Institute for Trial Advocacy (NITA), pg 138
National Learning Corp, pg 138
National Science Teachers Association (NSTA), pg 138
Naval Institute Press, pg 139
New Forums Press Inc, pg 139
The New York Botanical Garden Press, pg 140
New York University Press, pg 141
North River Press Publishing Corp, pg 142
W W Norton & Company Inc, pg 143
Nova Science Publishers Inc, pg 144
Nursesbooks.org, The Publishing Program of ANA, pg 144
The Ohio State University Press, pg 145
Ohio University Press, pg 145
Orbis Books, pg 147
O'Reilly Media Inc, pg 147
ORO editions, pg 148
Richard C Owen Publishers Inc, pg 149
Oxford University Press USA, pg 149
P & R Publishing Co, pg 149
PA Press, pg 149
Palgrave Macmillan, pg 150
Paulist Press, pg 152
Pearson Business Publishing, pg 153
PennWell Books, pg 157
Petroleum Extension Service (PETEX), pg 159
The Pilgrim Press/United Church Press, pg 160
Planners Press, pg 160
Polebridge Press, pg 161
Potomac Books, pg 162
PPI, A Kaplan Company, pg 162
Presbyterian Publishing Corp (PPC), pg 163
Princeton Book Co Publishers, pg 163
PRINTING United Alliance, pg 165
PRO-ED Inc, pg 165
Pro Lingua Associates Inc, pg 165
Productivity Press, pg 165
Professional Resource Press, pg 165

The PRS Group Inc, pg 166
Quite Specific Media Group Ltd, pg 168
The Red Sea Press Inc, pg 173
Research & Education Association (REA), pg 174
Research Press, pg 174
Lynne Rienner Publishers Inc, pg 174
Roncorp Music, pg 176
Rothstein Associates Inc, pg 177
Routledge, pg 177
Rowe Publishing LLC, pg 178
Rowman & Littlefield, pg 178
Sagamore Publishing LLC, pg 179
SAGE Publishing, pg 180
St Augustine's Press Inc, pg 180
St Pauls, pg 181
Salina Bookshelf Inc, pg 181
SAS Press, pg 182
G Schirmer Inc/Associated Music Publishers Inc, pg 183
Schlager Group Inc, pg 183
Science & Humanities Press, pg 185
Science History Publications USA Inc, pg 185
SIL International, pg 188
Sinauer Associates, pg 190
SLACK® Incorporated, A Wyanoke Group Company, pg 191
SME (Society of Manufacturing Engineers), pg 191
Smith & Kraus Publishers Inc, pg 192
Smyth & Helwys Publishing Inc, pg 192
Society for Industrial & Applied Mathematics, pg 192
Society for Mining, Metallurgy & Exploration, pg 192
Society of Exploration Geophysicists, pg 192
The Society of Naval Architects & Marine Engineers (SNAME), pg 193
Solano Press Books, pg 193
Solution Tree, pg 193
SPIE, pg 196
Springer Publishing Co, pg 196
Square One Publishers Inc, pg 196
Stanford University Press, pg 197
Star Publishing Co Inc, pg 197
Stenhouse Publishers, pg 198
Stipes Publishing LLC, pg 198
STM Learning Inc, pg 199
Syracuse University Press, pg 201
T&T Clark International, pg 202
Tapestry Press Ltd, pg 202
Teachers College Press, pg 203
Teaching Strategies LLC, pg 204
Temple University Press, pg 204
Teton NewMedia Inc, pg 205
Texas Tech University Press, pg 205
Thames & Hudson, pg 205
Thieme Medical Publishers Inc, pg 206
Third World Press Foundation, pg 206
Charles C Thomas Publisher Ltd, pg 206
TotalRecall Publications Inc, pg 208
Trans-Atlantic Publications Inc, pg 209
Transportation Research Board (TRB), pg 209
Tuttle Publishing, pg 211
United States Institute of Peace Press, pg 213
Universal-Publishers Inc, pg 213
University of Alaska Press, pg 214
University of Hawaii Press, pg 216
University of Michigan Press, pg 217

University of Oklahoma Press, pg 219
University of Pennsylvania Press, pg 219
University of South Carolina Press, pg 220
University of Wisconsin Press, pg 221
University Press of America Inc, pg 221
University Press of Mississippi, pg 222
University Science Books, pg 222
US Government Publishing Office (GPO), pg 223
Utah State University Press, pg 223
VanDam Inc, pg 223
Water Resources Publications LLC, pg 226
Waveland Press Inc, pg 226
Wayside Publishing, pg 227
Wellington Press, pg 227
Westminster John Knox Press (WJK), pg 228
Whittier Publications Inc, pg 229
Whole Person Associates Inc, pg 229
Markus Wiener Publishers Inc, pg 229
Michael Wiese Productions, pg 229
Wiley-Blackwell, pg 229
John Wiley & Sons Inc Global Education, pg 230
William Carey Publishing, pg 230
Wisconsin Department of Public Instruction, pg 231
Wolters Kluwer Law & Business, pg 232
Wolters Kluwer US Corp, pg 232
Worth Publishers, pg 234
Writer's Digest Books, pg 234
Wyndham Hall Press, pg 234
XML Press, pg 235
Yale University Press, pg 235
YBK Publishers Inc, pg 235
Zondervan, pg 236

TRANSLATIONS

Academica Press, pg 3
Algora Publishing, pg 7
American Geophysical Union (AGU), pg 10
American Society for Nondestructive Testing, pg 12
Ariadne Press, pg 16
ArtAge Publications, pg 17
Barrytown/Station Hill Press, pg 24
BJU Press, pg 30
Blue Mountain Arts Inc, pg 32
Blue Poppy Press, pg 32
BoardSource, pg 33
Brandylane Publishers Inc, pg 35
George Braziller Inc, pg 35
The Catholic University of America Press, pg 42
Charisma Media, pg 45
Charlesbridge Publishing Inc, pg 45
Cheng & Tsui Co Inc, pg 46
China Books, pg 47
Codhill Press, pg 50
Columbia University Press, pg 51
Continental AfrikaPublishers, pg 52
Copper Canyon Press, pg 52
Cornell University Press, pg 52
Cosimo Inc, pg 53
Council for Research in Values & Philosophy, pg 53
Counterpath Press, pg 54
Countryman Press, pg 54
Cross-Cultural Communications, pg 55
Cypress House, pg 56

Dalkey Archive Press, pg 56
Dark Horse Comics, pg 57
Walter De Gruyter Inc, pg 58
Deseret Book Co, pg 58
Dharma Publishing, pg 59
Editorial Bautista Independiente, pg 63
Editorial Unilit, pg 64
Wm B Eerdmans Publishing Co, pg 64
Elderberry Press Inc, pg 65
Elsevier Inc, pg 65
Etruscan Press, pg 67
Europa Editions, pg 67
Excelsior Editions, pg 68
The Feminist Press at The City University of New York, pg 71
Fons Vitae, pg 73
Gifted Unlimited LLC, pg 78
Gingko Press Inc, pg 78
Graywolf Press, pg 81
Hackett Publishing Co Inc, pg 83
Hameray Publishing Group Inc, pg 84
Hamilton Stone Editions, pg 84
Hilton Publishing Co, pg 92
Histria Books, pg 93
Hogrefe Publishing Corp, pg 93
Hollym International Corp, pg 94
Homa & Sekey Books, pg 95
Ibex Publishers, pg 98
Indiana University Press, pg 100
Institute of Jesuit Sources (IJS), pg 102
Interlink Publishing Group Inc, pg 102
The International Institute of Islamic Thought, pg 103
International Monetary Fund (IMF), Editorial & Publications Division, pg 103
Italica Press, pg 105
Jhpiego, pg 106
Judaica Press Inc, pg 107
Kamehameha Publishing, pg 108
Kazi Publications Inc, pg 108
LARB Books, pg 113
Liguori Publications, pg 117
Long River Press, pg 120
Lynx House Press, pg 121
Mage Publishers Inc, pg 123
Mandel Vilar Press, pg 124
Marick Press, pg 125
Marquette University Press, pg 125
McPherson & Co, pg 128
The Edwin Mellen Press, pg 129
Metropolitan Classics, pg 130
Military Info Publishing, pg 131
Modern Language Association (MLA), pg 133
Modern Memoirs Inc, pg 133
Mondial, pg 133
The Mongolia Society Inc, pg 133
Moznaim Publishing Corp, pg 135
New Directions Publishing Corp, pg 139
The New Press, pg 140
Nilgiri Press, pg 141
North Atlantic Books (NAB), pg 142
Northwestern University Press, pg 143
Octane Press, pg 145
Ohio University Press, pg 145
Open Letter, pg 147
Other Press, pg 148
P & R Publishing Co, pg 149
Pangaea Publications, pg 150
Paraclete Press Inc, pg 151
Penn State University Press, pg 157
Persea Books, pg 158
Philosophical Library Inc, pg 159

Pleasure Boat Studio: A Literary Press, pg 160
Plough Publishing House, pg 161
Polebridge Press, pg 161
The Press at California State University, Fresno, pg 163
Productivity Press, pg 165
Progressive Press, pg 165
Pyncheon House, pg 167
Rational Island Publishers, pg 171
Red Moon Press, pg 172
Regular Baptist Press, pg 174
St Augustine's Press Inc, pg 180
St Herman Press, pg 180
Scepter Publishers, pg 183
G Schirmer Inc/Associated Music Publishers Inc, pg 183
Scholastic Inc, pg 184
Schreiber Publishing, pg 185
Scripta Humanistica Publishing International, pg 185
Seven Stories Press, pg 186
Shambhala Publications Inc, pg 187
Simon & Schuster, LLC, pg 189
Somerset Hall Press, pg 193
Sophia Institute Press®, pg 193
Stanford University Press, pg 197
Stone Bridge Press Inc, pg 199
Swan Isle Press, pg 201
Swedenborg Foundation, pg 201
Trinity University Press, pg 209
Tughra Books, pg 210
Turtle Point Press, pg 210
Twilight Times Books, pg 211
Ugly Duckling Presse, pg 212
Unarius Academy of Science Publications, pg 212
United States Holocaust Memorial Museum, pg 213
United States Pharmacopeia (USP), pg 213
The University of Arkansas Press, pg 214
University of California Press, pg 215
University of Hawaii Press, pg 216
University of Nebraska Press, pg 217
University of Pennsylvania Press, pg 219
The University of Utah Press, pg 220
University of Wisconsin Press, pg 221
Upper Room Books, pg 223
US Conference of Catholic Bishops, pg 223
Velazquez Press, pg 224
Wake Forest University Press, pg 225
Wayne State University Press, pg 226
Wesleyan University Press, pg 227
Westminster John Knox Press (WJK), pg 228
White Pine Press, pg 228
Markus Wiener Publishers Inc, pg 229
Wings Press, pg 231
Wisdom Publications Inc, pg 231
Yale University Press, pg 235
Zone Books, pg 237

UNIVERSITY PRESSES

ACMRS Press, pg 4
ACU Press, pg 4
Algora Publishing, pg 7
Andrews University Press, pg 14
ANR Publications University of California, pg 14
Baylor University Press, pg 25
BookLogix, pg 34

Brentwood Christian Press, pg 36
The Brookings Institution Press, pg 37
Bucknell University Press, pg 38
Cambridge University Press, pg 39
Carnegie Mellon University Press, pg 41
The Catholic University of America Press, pg 42
Columbia University Press, pg 51
Continental AfrikaPublishers, pg 52
Cornell University Press, pg 52
Council for Research in Values & Philosophy, pg 53
CSLI Publications, pg 56
Dissertation.com, pg 60
Dordt Press, pg 60
Duke University Press, pg 62
Editorial de la Universidad de Puerto Rico, pg 63
Excelsior Editions, pg 68
Fordham University Press, pg 73
Fowler Museum at UCLA, pg 74
Gallaudet University Press, pg 76
Georgetown University Press, pg 77
Greenleaf Book Group LLC, pg 81
Harvard Education Publishing Group, pg 88
Harvard University Press, pg 88
Hillsdale College Press, pg 92
Hoover Institution Press, pg 95
Indiana University African Studies Program, pg 100
Indiana University Press, pg 100
Johns Hopkins University Press, pg 106
Kent State University Press, pg 109
Lehigh University Press, pg 114
Livingston Press, pg 119
Louisiana State University Press, pg 120
Loving Healing Press Inc, pg 121
Maharishi International University Press, pg 123
Marquette University Press, pg 125
McFarland, pg 127
Medieval Institute Publications (MIP), pg 129
Mercer University Press, pg 129
Michigan State University Press (MSU Press), pg 130
National Resource Center for Youth Services, pg 138
Naval Institute Press, pg 139
New York University Press, pg 141
Northern Illinois University Press, pg 143
Northwestern University Press, pg 143
Nova Press, pg 144
The Ohio State University Press, pg 145
Ohio University Press, pg 145
Oregon State University Press, pg 147
Oxford University Press USA, pg 149
Pace University Press, pg 149
Penn State University Press, pg 157
The Press at California State University, Fresno, pg 163
Princeton University Press, pg 164
Purdue University Press, pg 167
The Rockefeller University Press, pg 176
Russell Sage Foundation, pg 178
Rutgers University Press, pg 178
St Joseph's University Press, pg 180
San Diego State University Press, pg 182
SIL International, pg 188
Southern Illinois University Press, pg 195

Stanford University Press, pg 197
State University of New York Press, pg 198
Syracuse University Press, pg 201
TCU Press, pg 203
Teachers College Press, pg 203
Temple University Press, pg 204
Texas A&M University Press, pg 205
Texas Tech University Press, pg 205
University of Texas Press, pg 205
Texas Western Press, pg 205
Theosophical University Press, pg 206
Trinity University Press, pg 209
Tughra Books, pg 210
United States Institute of Peace Press, pg 213
Universal-Publishers Inc, pg 213
University of Alabama Press, pg 214
University of Alaska Press, pg 214
The University of Arizona Press, pg 214
University of California Institute on Global Conflict & Cooperation, pg 215
University of Delaware Press, pg 215
University of Georgia Press, pg 216
University of Hawaii Press, pg 216
University of Illinois Press, pg 216
University of Massachusetts Press, pg 217
University of Michigan Press, pg 217
University of Minnesota Press, pg 217
University of Missouri Press, pg 217
University of Nebraska Press, pg 217
University of Nevada Press, pg 218
University of New Mexico Press, pg 218
University of New Orleans Press, pg 218
The University of North Carolina Press, pg 218
University of North Texas Press, pg 218
University of Notre Dame Press, pg 219
University of Oklahoma Press, pg 219
University of Pennsylvania Press, pg 219
University of Pittsburgh Press, pg 219
University of Rochester Press, pg 220
University of South Carolina Press, pg 220
University of Tennessee Press, pg 220
The University of Utah Press, pg 220
University of Virginia Press, pg 220
University of Washington Press, pg 220
University of Wisconsin Press, pg 221
University Press of Colorado, pg 221
University Press of Florida, pg 221
University Press of Kansas, pg 221
The University Press of Kentucky, pg 222
University Press of Mississippi, pg 222
Utah State University Press, pg 223
Vanderbilt University Press, pg 224

PUBLISHERS

U.S. PUBLISHERS — TYPE OF PUBLICATION INDEX

Wake Forest University Press, pg 225
Washington State University Press, pg 226
Wayne State University Press, pg 226
Wesleyan University Press, pg 227
West Virginia University Press, pg 228
Wyndham Hall Press, pg 234
Yale University Press, pg 235
Yeshiva University Press, pg 235

VIDEOS, DVDS

AAPG (American Association of Petroleum Geologists), pg 1
Abingdon Press, pg 2
Advance Publishing Inc, pg 5
Adventures Unlimited Press (AUP), pg 5
AICPA® & CIMA®, pg 5
ALA Neal-Schuman, pg 6
Alexander Street, part of Clarivate PLC, pg 6
American Bar Association Publishing, pg 8
American Carriage House Publishing (ACHP), pg 8
American Correctional Association, pg 9
American Psychiatric Association Publishing, pg 11
APS PRESS, pg 16
ArtAge Publications, pg 17
Ascension Press, pg 18
ASET - The Neurodiagnostic Society, pg 18
Augsburg Fortress Publishers, Publishing House of the Evangelical Lutheran Church in America, pg 22
B&H Publishing Group, pg 24
Bisk Education, pg 29
BJU Press, pg 30
BLR®—Business & Legal Resources, pg 32
BoardSource, pg 33
Book Marketing Works LLC, pg 33
Bottom Dog Press, pg 34
Boys Town Press, pg 35
Bridge Publications Inc, pg 36
Paul H Brookes Publishing Co Inc, pg 37
The Bureau for At-Risk Youth, pg 38
Center for the Collaborative Classroom, pg 44
Centerstream Publishing LLC, pg 44

Central Recovery Press (CRP), pg 44
Chelsea Green Publishing Co, pg 45
Cheng & Tsui Co Inc, pg 46
China Books, pg 47
Clinical and Laboratory Standards Institute (CLSI), pg 49
Close Up Publishing, pg 49
Coaches Choice, pg 50
Cold Spring Harbor Laboratory Press, pg 50
The College Board, pg 50
Comex Systems Inc, pg 51
Continental AfrikaPublishers, pg 52
Covenant Communications Inc, pg 54
Cross-Cultural Communications, pg 55
Crown House Publishing Co LLC, pg 56
Crystal Clarity Publishers, pg 56
CSWE Press, pg 56
Data Trace Publishing Co (DTP), pg 57
Davies Publishing Inc, pg 57
F A Davis Co, pg 57
DawnSignPress, pg 58
Deseret Book Co, pg 58
Dogwise Publishing, pg 60
Down The Shore Publishing, pg 61
Dragon Door Publications, pg 61
Dreamscape Media LLC, pg 62
Encyclopaedia Britannica Inc, pg 66
Faith Library Publications, pg 69
Father & Son Publishing Inc, pg 70
Fiction Collective 2 (FC2), pg 71
Fire Engineering Books & Videos, pg 72
Firefall Editions, pg 72
Fordham University Press, pg 73
Future Horizons Inc, pg 75
Gallopade International Inc, pg 76
Gifted Unlimited LLC, pg 78
Gospel Publishing House, pg 80
Group Publishing Inc, pg 82
Gulf Energy Information, pg 83
Hal Leonard LLC, pg 84
Hanser Publications LLC, pg 85
Harvest House Publishers Inc, pg 88
Hatherleigh Press Ltd, pg 88
Hay House LLC, pg 89
Hazelden Publishing, pg 89
Health Professions Press, pg 90
HeartMath LLC, pg 90
Heinemann, pg 90
Her Own Words LLC, pg 91
High Tide Press, pg 92
Hilton Publishing Co, pg 92
Himalayan Institute Press, pg 92
Homa & Sekey Books, pg 95
Ignatius Press, pg 98

Indiana Historical Society Press, pg 99
International Literacy Association (ILA), pg 103
International Wealth Success (IWS), pg 104
Jhpiego, pg 106
JIST Publishing, pg 106
Kalmbach Media Co, pg 108
Kazi Publications Inc, pg 108
J J Keller & Associates, Inc®, pg 108
Krause Publications Inc, pg 111
KTAV Publishing House Inc, pg 111
Lawyers & Judges Publishing Co Inc, pg 113
THE Learning Connection®, pg 113
Leisure Arts Inc, pg 114
Liberty Fund Inc, pg 116
Light-Beams Publishing, pg 116
Liguori Publications, pg 117
Liturgical Press, pg 118
Liturgy Training Publications, pg 119
Management Sciences for Health, pg 123
Mandala Earth, pg 124
Mazda Publishers Inc, pg 127
McPherson & Co, pg 128
Mel Bay Publications Inc, pg 129
Meriwether Publishing, pg 129
Milady, pg 131
Multicultural Publications Inc, pg 135
NACE International, pg 136
NASW Press, pg 136
Nataraj Books, pg 136
National Council of Teachers of Mathematics (NCTM), pg 137
National Institute for Trial Advocacy (NITA), pg 138
New Harbinger Publications Inc, pg 140
Nilgiri Press, pg 141
North Atlantic Books (NAB), pg 142
OCP, pg 145
Olde & Oppenheim Publishers, pg 146
The Original Falcon Press, pg 148
Paraclete Press Inc, pg 151
Paradise Cay Publications Inc, pg 151
Peachpit Press, pg 153
Pennsylvania Historical & Museum Commission, pg 157
PennWell Books, pg 157
Petroleum Extension Service (PETEX), pg 159
PPI, A Kaplan Company, pg 162

Practising Law Institute (PLI), pg 163
PRINTING United Alliance, pg 165
Productivity Press, pg 165
The Professional Education Group LLC (PEG), pg 165
Professional Resource Press, pg 165
PSMJ Resources Inc, pg 166
Rational Island Publishers, pg 171
Regent Press Printers & Publishers, pg 174
Research Press, pg 174
Ross Books, pg 177
SAGE Publishing, pg 180
St Herman Press, pg 180
St Pauls, pg 181
Scholastic Inc, pg 184
Shadow Mountain Publishing, pg 187
Shambhala Publications Inc, pg 187
SME (Society of Manufacturing Engineers), pg 191
Society of Exploration Geophysicists, pg 192
Solution Tree, pg 193
Sounds True Inc, pg 194
South Carolina Bar, pg 195
Springer Publishing Co, pg 196
Stenhouse Publishers, pg 198
Summit University Press, pg 200
Swedenborg Foundation, pg 201
Taunton Books, pg 203
Teaching Strategies LLC, pg 204
Thieme Medical Publishers Inc, pg 206
Tommy Nelson®, pg 207
Torah Umesorah Publications, pg 208
Tortuga Press, pg 208
Trafalgar Square Books, pg 208
Treehaus Communications Inc, pg 209
Tughra Books, pg 210
Tyndale House Publishers Inc, pg 211
Unarius Academy of Science Publications, pg 212
University Publishing House, pg 222
US Conference of Catholic Bishops, pg 223
Whole Person Associates Inc, pg 229
Willow Creek Press, pg 230
Wisconsin Department of Public Instruction, pg 231
World Resources Institute, pg 233
YMAA Publication Center Inc, pg 235
Zondervan, pg 236

U.S. Publishers — Subject Index

ACCOUNTING

Academic Press, pg 3
AICPA® & CIMA®, pg 5
Association of School Business Officials International, pg 20
AuthorHouse, pg 22
Bisk Education, pg 29
BuilderBooks, pg 38
Business Expert Press, pg 38
CCH, a Wolters Kluwer business, pg 42
Cengage Learning, pg 43
Edward Elgar Publishing Inc, pg 65
Elsevier Inc, pg 65
Gale, pg 75
Kogan Page, pg 111
Lawyers & Judges Publishing Co Inc, pg 113
LexisNexis® Matthew Bender®, pg 116
Macmillan Reference USA™, pg 123
Management Advisory Services & Publications (MASP), pg 123
McGraw-Hill Create, pg 127
McGraw-Hill Higher Education, pg 128
McGraw-Hill School Education Group, pg 128
National Association of Insurance Commissioners, pg 136
National Center For Employee Ownership (NCEO), pg 137
Productivity Press, pg 165
Research & Education Association (REA), pg 174
Schonfeld & Associates Inc, pg 184
Schreiber Publishing, pg 185
Science & Humanities Press, pg 185
1765 Productions, pg 186
Star Publishing Co Inc, pg 197
Strategic Book Publishing (SBP), pg 199
TotalRecall Publications Inc, pg 208
US Government Publishing Office (GPO), pg 223
Vault.com Inc, pg 224
Wheatherstone Press, pg 228
Markus Wiener Publishers Inc, pg 229
John Wiley & Sons Inc, pg 230
John Wiley & Sons Inc Global Education, pg 230
John Wiley & Sons Inc Professional Development, pg 230

ADVERTISING

Atlantic Publishing Group Inc, pg 21
AuthorHouse, pg 22
Avant-Guide, pg 22
Barringer Publishing, pg 24
Brown Books Publishing Group (BBPG), pg 38
Cengage Learning, pg 43
DiscoverNet Publishing, pg 59
Gale, pg 75
Greenleaf Book Group LLC, pg 81
Kallisti Publishing Inc, pg 108
Kogan Page, pg 111
Macmillan Reference USA™, pg 123
Richard K Miller Associates, pg 132
National Association of Broadcasters (NAB), pg 136
Olde & Oppenheim Publishers, pg 146
Open Horizons Publishing Co, pg 147
Plunkett Research Ltd, pg 161
Prometheus Books, pg 166
Ross Books, pg 177
Routledge, pg 177
SAGE Publishing, pg 180
Schonfeld & Associates Inc, pg 184
Strategic Book Publishing (SBP), pg 199
Todd Publications, pg 207

AERONAUTICS, AVIATION

American Institute of Aeronautics and Astronautics (AIAA), pg 10
American Society for Quality (ASQ), pg 12
AuthorHouse, pg 22
Book Sales, pg 33
Cengage Learning, pg 43
Charlesbridge Publishing Inc, pg 45
Crabtree Publishing Co, pg 54
DEStech Publications Inc, pg 59
Dover Publications Inc, pg 61
EDC Publishing, pg 63
Gale, pg 75
William S Hein & Co Inc, pg 90
IEEE Press, pg 98
IET USA Inc, pg 98
Institute of Environmental Sciences & Technology - IEST, pg 101
Koho Pono LLC, pg 111
Krieger Publishing Co, pg 111
Lerner Publications, pg 115
Macmillan Learning, pg 123
Macmillan Reference USA™, pg 123
Markowski International Publishers, pg 125
McFarland, pg 127
Naval Institute Press, pg 139
OAG Worldwide, pg 144
Potomac Books, pg 162
Publication Consultants, pg 167
RAND Corp, pg 169
SAE (Society of Automotive Engineers International), pg 179
Schiffer Publishing Ltd, pg 183
Southern Illinois University Press, pg 195
SPIE, pg 196
Spizzirri Publishing Inc, pg 196
Strategic Book Publishing (SBP), pg 199
Stylus Publishing LLC, pg 200
Texas A&M University Press, pg 205
Transportation Research Board (TRB), pg 209
Tumblehome Learning Inc, pg 210
Univelt Inc, pg 213
University of North Texas Press, pg 218
US Government Publishing Office (GPO), pg 223
Write Stuff Enterprises LLC, pg 234
Xlibris Corp, pg 234

AFRICAN AMERICAN STUDIES

ABDO, pg 2
Academica Press, pg 3
Africa World Press Inc, pg 5
African American Images Inc (AAI), pg 5
Akashic Books, pg 6
Alexander Street, part of Clarivate PLC, pg 6
Asta Publications LLC, pg 20
AuthorHouse, pg 22
Barrytown/Station Hill Press, pg 24
Baylor University Press, pg 25
Beacon Press, pg 25
Bellerophon Books, pg 27
Black Classic Press, pg 30
Black Rabbit Books, pg 30
The Blackburn Press, pg 30
Blair, pg 30
Bucknell University Press, pg 38
Camino Books Inc, pg 39
Carolina Academic Press, pg 41
Cedar Grove Publishing, pg 43
Cengage Learning, pg 43
Chalice Press, pg 44
Charlesbridge Publishing Inc, pg 45
Chelsea House, pg 45
Chicago Review Press, pg 46
Clarity Press Inc, pg 49
Clearfield Co Inc, pg 49
Cleis Press, pg 49
Coffee House Press, pg 50
Continental AfrikaPublishers, pg 52
Cornell University Press, pg 52
Council for Research in Values & Philosophy, pg 53
The Donning Company Publishers, pg 60
Dorrance Publishing Co Inc, pg 61
Dover Publications Inc, pg 61
Duke University Press, pg 62
Dutton, pg 62
Eakin Press, pg 62
Edupress Inc, pg 64
Enslow Publishing LLC, pg 66
Facts On File, pg 69
Father & Son Publishing Inc, pg 70
The Feminist Press at The City University of New York, pg 71
Fordham University Press, pg 73
Fowler Museum at UCLA, pg 74
Gale, pg 75
Gallopade International Inc, pg 76
Grand Central Publishing, pg 80
Greenleaf Book Group LLC, pg 81
Grey House Publishing Inc™, pg 81
HarperCollins Publishers LLC, pg 86
Harvard Education Publishing Group, pg 88
Heyday, pg 91
Indiana Historical Society Press, pg 99
Inner Traditions International Ltd, pg 101
International Publishers Co Inc, pg 103
Judson Press, pg 107
Jump at the Sun, pg 107
Kazi Publications Inc, pg 108
THE Learning Connection®, pg 113
Lexington Books, pg 115
Louisiana State University Press, pg 120
Lucent Press, pg 121
Macmillan Reference USA™, pg 123
Mandel Vilar Press, pg 124
Manic D Press Inc, pg 124
Marshall Cavendish Education, pg 125
Maryland History Press, pg 126
McFarland, pg 127
The Edwin Mellen Press, pg 129
Mercer University Press, pg 129
Michigan State University Press (MSU Press), pg 130
Modern Language Association (MLA), pg 133
De Gruyter Mouton, pg 135
National Book Co, pg 136
Naval Institute Press, pg 139
The New Press, pg 140
New York University Press, pg 141
NewSouth Books, pg 141
Northwestern University Press, pg 143
The Ohio State University Press, pg 145
Omnigraphics Inc, pg 146
Orbis Books, pg 147
Palgrave Macmillan, pg 150
Paragon House, pg 151
Path Press Inc, pg 152
Pelican Publishing, pg 153
Penn State University Press, pg 157
Pennsylvania Historical & Museum Commission, pg 157
Peter Pauper Press, Inc, pg 158
The Pilgrim Press/United Church Press, pg 160
Polar Bear & Company, pg 161
Pomegranate Communications Inc, pg 162
Prometheus Books, pg 166
Rational Island Publishers, pg 171
The Red Sea Press Inc, pg 173
Lynne Rienner Publishers Inc, pg 174
Rising Sun Publishing, pg 175
Routledge, pg 177
Rowman & Littlefield, pg 178
Royal Fireworks Press, pg 178
Rutgers University Press, pg 178
SAGE Publishing, pg 180
St James Press®, pg 180
St Martin's Press, LLC, pg 180
Salem Press, pg 181
Seven Stories Press, pg 186
Southern Illinois University Press, pg 195
State University of New York Press, pg 198
Strategic Book Publishing (SBP), pg 199
Syracuse University Press, pg 201
Tantor Media Inc, pg 202
Tapestry Press Ltd, pg 202
Temple University Press, pg 204
Texas A&M University Press, pg 205
Third World Press Foundation, pg 206
Tide-mark Press, pg 207
The University of Arkansas Press, pg 214

University of California Press, pg 215
University of Chicago Press, pg 215
University of Georgia Press, pg 216
University of Illinois Press, pg 216
University of Iowa Press, pg 216
University of Massachusetts Press, pg 217
University of Michigan Press, pg 217
University of Minnesota Press, pg 217
University of Missouri Press, pg 217
The University of North Carolina Press, pg 218
University of North Texas Press, pg 218
University of Notre Dame Press, pg 219
University of Oklahoma Press, pg 219
University of Pennsylvania Press, pg 219
University of Pittsburgh Press, pg 219
University of Tennessee Press, pg 220
The University of Utah Press, pg 220
University of Virginia Press, pg 220
University of Washington Press, pg 220
University of Wisconsin Press, pg 221
University Press of Colorado, pg 221
University Press of Florida, pg 221
University Press of Kansas, pg 221
The University Press of Kentucky, pg 222
University Press of Mississippi, pg 222
Vernon Press, pg 224
Verso Books, pg 224
Visible Ink Press®, pg 225
Wayne State University Press, pg 226
Welcome Rain Publishers LLC, pg 227
Wesleyan University Press, pg 227
West Virginia University Press, pg 228
Markus Wiener Publishers Inc, pg 229
Wiley-Blackwell, pg 229
Wisconsin Department of Public Instruction, pg 231
Wolfman Books, pg 232
World Citizens, pg 233
Wyndham Hall Press, pg 234
Yale University Press, pg 235

AGRICULTURE

Academic Press, pg 3
Acres USA, pg 4
ACS Publications, pg 4
American Press, pg 11
American Society of Agricultural & Biological Engineers (ASABE), pg 12
American Society of Agronomy (ASA), pg 12
Annual Reviews, pg 14
ANR Publications University of California, pg 14
APS PRESS, pg 16
AuthorHouse, pg 22
Countryman Press, pg 54
EDC Publishing, pg 63
Edward Elgar Publishing Inc, pg 65
Gale, pg 75

Goodheart-Willcox Publisher, pg 79
Hatherleigh Press Ltd, pg 88
William S Hein & Co Inc, pg 90
High Plains Press, pg 91
W D Hoard & Sons Co, pg 93
Hudson Institute, pg 97
IHS Press, pg 98
Indiana Historical Society Press, pg 99
International Food Policy Research Institute, pg 103
Jump!, pg 107
Krause Publications Inc, pg 111
Macmillan Reference USA™, pg 123
McGraw-Hill Higher Education, pg 128
Nataraj Books, pg 136
National Academies Press (NAP), pg 136
The New York Botanical Garden Press, pg 140
North Atlantic Books (NAB), pg 142
OECD Washington Center, pg 145
Pennsylvania State Data Center, pg 157
Plunkett Research Ltd, pg 161
Reference Publications Inc, pg 173
Soil Science Society of America (SSSA), pg 193
Stipes Publishing LLC, pg 198
Stone Pier Press, pg 199
Strategic Book Publishing (SBP), pg 199
Texas A&M University Press, pg 205
Texas Tech University Press, pg 205
United Nations Publications, pg 213
University of Iowa Press, pg 216
University of Minnesota Press, pg 217
The University Press of Kentucky, pg 222
US Government Publishing Office (GPO), pg 223
Waveland Press Inc, pg 226
John Wiley & Sons Inc, pg 230
John Wiley & Sons Inc Global Education, pg 230
John Wiley & Sons Inc Professional Development, pg 230
Wisconsin Department of Public Instruction, pg 231
World Resources Institute, pg 233

ALTERNATIVE

AK Press, pg 6
All Things That Matter Press, pg 7
Amber Lotus Publishing, pg 8
Ash Tree Publishing, pg 18
AuthorHouse, pg 22
Avery, pg 23
Barrytown/Station Hill Press, pg 24
Bear & Co Inc, pg 26
Book Sales, pg 33
The Book Tree, pg 34
Clarity Press Inc, pg 49
Continental AfrikaPublishers, pg 52
Counterpoint Press LLC, pg 54
The Crossroad Publishing Co, pg 55
Dark Horse Comics, pg 57
Eastland Press, pg 63
Feral House, pg 71
Galde Press Inc, pg 75
Gale, pg 75
Gateways Books & Tapes, pg 77
Gingko Press Inc, pg 78
Hal Leonard LLC, pg 84
HeartMath LLC, pg 90
Himalayan Institute Press, pg 92
IHS Press, pg 98

Inner Traditions International Ltd, pg 101
Larson Publications, pg 113
Llewellyn Publications, pg 119
Macmillan Reference USA™, pg 123
Maharishi International University Press, pg 123
Manic D Press Inc, pg 124
North Atlantic Books (NAB), pg 142
Orbis Books, pg 147
Ozark Mountain Publishing Inc, pg 149
Parallax Press, pg 151
Pomegranate Communications Inc, pg 162
powerHouse Books, pg 162
Quirk Books, pg 168
Ronin Publishing Inc, pg 176
Santa Monica Press LLC, pg 182
Sentient Publications LLC, pg 186
Seven Stories Press, pg 186
SteinerBooks Inc, pg 198
Stone Bridge Press Inc, pg 199
Strategic Book Publishing (SBP), pg 199
Tantor Media Inc, pg 202
Ugly Duckling Presse, pg 212
Unarius Academy of Science Publications, pg 212
Visible Ink Press®, pg 225
Wolfman Books, pg 232

AMERICANA, REGIONAL

Abbeville Publishing Group, pg 2
ABDO, pg 2
Alexander Street, part of Clarivate PLC, pg 6
American Alpine Club, pg 8
Anaphora Literary Press, pg 13
APC Publishing, pg 15
Applewood Books, pg 15
Arcadia Publishing Inc, pg 16
Astragal Press, pg 20
August House Inc, pg 22
AuthorHouse, pg 22
Baylor University Press, pg 25
Black Dome Press Corp, pg 30
Blair, pg 30
Book Sales, pg 33
Bottom Dog Press, pg 34
Camino Books Inc, pg 39
Caxton Press, pg 42
Charlesbridge Publishing Inc, pg 45
Clear Light Publishers, pg 49
Cornell Maritime Press, pg 52
Cornell University Press, pg 52
Country Music Foundation Press, pg 54
Countryman Press, pg 54
The Donning Company Publishers, pg 60
Dover Publications Inc, pg 61
Down East Books, pg 61
Down The Shore Publishing, pg 61
Eakin Press, pg 62
Elderberry Press Inc, pg 65
Epicenter Press Inc, pg 67
Everything Goes Media LLC, pg 68
Excelsior Editions, pg 68
Filter Press LLC, pg 71
Fordham University Press, pg 73
Fowler Museum at UCLA, pg 74
Fulcrum Publishing Inc, pg 75
Gale, pg 75
Gallopade International Inc, pg 76
Gibbs Smith Publisher, pg 78
Glitterati Inc, pg 78
Goose River Press, pg 79
Gray & Company Publishers, pg 80

Greenleaf Book Group LLC, pg 81
Her Own Words LLC, pg 91
Heritage Books Inc, pg 91
Heyday, pg 91
High Plains Press, pg 91
History Publishing Co LLC, pg 93
Horizon Publishers & Distributors Inc, pg 95
Indiana Historical Society Press, pg 99
Johns Hopkins University Press, pg 106
Kalmbach Media Co, pg 108
Kamehameha Publishing, pg 108
Kent State University Press, pg 109
Kiva Publishing Inc, pg 110
Landauer Publishing, pg 112
LARB Books, pg 113
Loft Press Inc, pg 119
Louisiana State University Press, pg 120
The Lyons Press, pg 121
Macmillan Reference USA™, pg 123
Mandel Vilar Press, pg 124
Manic D Press Inc, pg 124
Mason Crest Publishers, pg 126
The Massachusetts Historical Society, pg 126
McBooks Press, pg 127
The McDonald & Woodward Publishing Co, pg 127
McFarland, pg 127
The Edwin Mellen Press, pg 129
Michigan State University Press (MSU Press), pg 130
Minnesota Historical Society Press, pg 132
Mountain Press Publishing Co, pg 135
New Forums Press Inc, pg 139
New York University Press, pg 141
NewSouth Books, pg 141
North Carolina Office of Archives & History, pg 142
North Country Press, pg 142
North Star Press of Saint Cloud Inc, pg 142
Ocean Tree Books, pg 145
Ohio University Press, pg 145
Oregon State University Press, pg 147
ORO editions, pg 148
PA Press, pg 149
Palm Island Press, pg 150
Pelican Publishing, pg 153
Pennsylvania Historical & Museum Commission, pg 157
Pineapple Press, pg 160
Plexus Publishing, Inc, pg 160
Prometheus Books, pg 166
Quail Ridge Press (QRP), pg 168
Quixote Press, pg 169
Reference Publications Inc, pg 173
Rio Nuevo Publishers, pg 175
River City Publishing, pg 175
Rizzoli International Publications Inc, pg 175
Rutgers University Press, pg 178
St Joseph's University Press, pg 180
Santa Monica Press LLC, pg 182
Sasquatch Books, pg 182
Sherman Asher Publishing, pg 187
Signature Books Publishing LLC, pg 187
Sourcebooks LLC, pg 194
South Dakota Historical Society Press, pg 195
Stanford University Press, pg 197
Strategic Book Publishing (SBP), pg 199
Sun Publishing Company, pg 200
Sunstone Press, pg 201
Swallow Press, pg 201

PUBLISHERS

U.S. PUBLISHERS — SUBJECT INDEX

Syracuse University Press, pg 201
Tantor Media Inc, pg 202
TCU Press, pg 203
Ten Speed Press, pg 204
Texas A&M University Press, pg 205
Texas State Historical Association, pg 205
Texas Tech University Press, pg 205
University of Texas Press, pg 205
University of Alabama Press, pg 214
University of Alaska Press, pg 214
The University of Arizona Press, pg 214
The University of Arkansas Press, pg 214
University of Georgia Press, pg 216
University of Illinois Press, pg 216
University of Iowa Press, pg 216
University of Minnesota Press, pg 217
University of Missouri Press, pg 217
University of Nevada Press, pg 218
University of New Mexico Press, pg 218
The University of North Carolina Press, pg 218
University of North Texas Press, pg 218
University of Oklahoma Press, pg 219
University of Pittsburgh Press, pg 219
University of South Carolina Press, pg 220
University of Tennessee Press, pg 220
The University of Utah Press, pg 220
University of Wisconsin Press, pg 221
University Press of Colorado, pg 221
University Press of Florida, pg 221
University Press of Kansas, pg 221
University Press of Mississippi, pg 222
US Government Publishing Office (GPO), pg 223
Utah State University Press, pg 223
Vandamere Press, pg 223
Vanderbilt University Press, pg 224
Washington State University Press, pg 226
Wesleyan University Press, pg 227
Western Edge Press, pg 228
Western Pennsylvania Genealogical Society, pg 228
Westernlore Press, pg 228
Wide World Publishing, pg 229
Wolfman Books, pg 232
Yale University Press, pg 235

ANIMALS, PETS

A 2 Z Press LLC, pg 1
Abbeville Press, pg 1
Abbeville Publishing Group, pg 2
ABDO, pg 2
Academic Press, pg 3
AdventureKEEN, pg 5
Akashic Books, pg 6
Amber Lotus Publishing, pg 8
American Girl Publishing, pg 10
Sara Anderson Children's Books, pg 13
ANR Publications University of California, pg 14
Arbordale Publishing, pg 16
Ashland Creek Press, pg 18
Atlantic Publishing Group Inc, pg 21
AuthorHouse, pg 22
Barringer Publishing, pg 24
Beaver's Pond Press Inc, pg 26
Biographical Publishing Co, pg 29
Black Rabbit Books, pg 30
Book Sales, pg 33
Brown Books Publishing Group (BBPG), pg 38
Burford Books, pg 38
Capstone Publishers™, pg 40
Charles Press Publishers, pg 45
Charlesbridge Publishing Inc, pg 45
Chelsea House, pg 45
Child's Play® Inc, pg 46
The Child's World Inc, pg 46
Chronicle Books LLC, pg 47
Countryman Press, pg 54
Crabtree Publishing Co, pg 54
Dogwise Publishing, pg 60
Dutton, pg 62
Eakin Press, pg 62
EDC Publishing, pg 63
Edupress Inc, pg 64
Eifrig Publishing LLC, pg 64
Enslow Publishing LLC, pg 66
Fair Winds Press, pg 69
Farcountry Press, pg 69
Fox Chapel Publishing Co Inc, pg 74
Gale, pg 75
Gareth Stevens Publishing, pg 76
Gibbs Smith Publisher, pg 78
Global Authors Publications (GAP), pg 78
Goose River Press, pg 79
Greenleaf Book Group LLC, pg 81
HarperCollins Publishers LLC, pg 86
Hay House LLC, pg 89
William S Hein & Co Inc, pg 90
Hutton Publishing, pg 97
Inner Traditions International Ltd, pg 101
Jump!, pg 107
Kensington Publishing Corp, pg 109
Krause Publications Inc, pg 111
Krieger Publishing Co, pg 111
Lantern Publishing & Media, pg 112
Laughing Elephant Books, pg 113
THE Learning Connection®, pg 113
Lerner Publications, pg 115
Little, Brown and Company, pg 118
Logos Press, pg 119
The Lyons Press, pg 121
Macmillan Reference USA™, pg 123
Mason Crest Publishers, pg 126
National Geographic Books, pg 137
National Wildlife Federation, pg 139
New World Library, pg 140
North Atlantic Books (NAB), pg 142
North Star Editions Inc, pg 142
On the Write Path Publishing, pg 146
ORO editions, pg 148
PA Press, pg 149
Platypus Media LLC, pg 160
Polar Bear & Company, pg 161
Purple House Press, pg 167
Quarto Publishing Group USA Inc, pg 168
Quixote Press, pg 169
Reader's Digest Trade Publishing, pg 172
Renaissance House, pg 174
The RoadRunner Press, pg 175
SAGE Publishing, pg 180
Schiffer Publishing Ltd, pg 183
Sounds True Inc, pg 194
Sourcebooks LLC, pg 194
Star Bright Books Inc, pg 197
SteinerBooks Inc, pg 198
Stewart, Tabori & Chang, pg 198
Story Monsters LLC, pg 199
Strategic Book Publishing (SBP), pg 199
Sunstone Press, pg 201
Tantor Media Inc, pg 202
Temple University Press, pg 204
Ten Speed Press, pg 204
Teton NewMedia Inc, pg 205
Tilbury House Publishers, pg 207
Trafalgar Square Books, pg 208
Turner Publishing Co LLC, pg 210
Twilight Times Books, pg 211
Union Square & Co, pg 212
Universe Publishing, pg 214
University of Iowa Press, pg 216
Weatherstone Press, pg 228
Wilderness Adventures Press Inc, pg 229
Willow Creek Press, pg 230
Workman Publishing, pg 232

ANTHROPOLOGY

Academic Press, pg 3
Academica Press, pg 3
Adventures Unlimited Press (AUP), pg 5
Alexander Street, part of Clarivate PLC, pg 6
Amakella Publishing, pg 7
American Anthropological Association (AAA), pg 8
Annual Reviews, pg 14
August House Inc, pg 22
AuthorHouse, pg 22
Beacon Press, pg 25
John Benjamins Publishing Co, pg 28
Berghahn Books, pg 28
Captain Fiddle Music & Publications, pg 40
Carolina Academic Press, pg 41
Cengage Learning, pg 43
The Center for Learning, pg 43
Child's Play® Inc, pg 46
Clear Light Publishers, pg 49
Cognizant Communication Corp, pg 50
Continental AfrikaPublishers, pg 52
Cornell University Press, pg 52
Council for Research in Values & Philosophy, pg 53
Dissertation.com, pg 60
DK, pg 60
Dover Publications Inc, pg 61
Duke University Press, pg 62
Dumbarton Oaks, pg 62
Fowler Museum at UCLA, pg 74
Gale, pg 75
Hamilton Books, pg 84
Harvard University Press, pg 88
Hay House LLC, pg 89
Heyday, pg 91
Illinois State Museum Society, pg 99
Indiana University Press, pg 100
Inner Traditions International Ltd, pg 101
Kumarian Press, pg 112
Lexington Books, pg 115
LPD Press/Rio Grande Books, pg 121
Macmillan Reference USA™, pg 123
Mazda Publishers Inc, pg 127
The McDonald & Woodward Publishing Co, pg 127
McGraw-Hill Higher Education, pg 128
McPherson & Co, pg 128
The Edwin Mellen Press, pg 129
Michigan State University Press (MSU Press), pg 130
Monthly Review Press, pg 134
De Gruyter Mouton, pg 135
Museum of New Mexico Press, pg 135
Nataraj Books, pg 136
The New Press, pg 140
New York Academy of Sciences (NYAS), pg 140
The New York Botanical Garden Press, pg 140
New York University Press, pg 141
North Atlantic Books (NAB), pg 142
Northern Illinois University Press, pg 143
ORO editions, pg 148
Oxford University Press USA, pg 149
Palgrave Macmillan, pg 150
Pangaea Publications, pg 150
Peabody Museum Press, pg 153
Pearson Business Publishing, pg 153
Pennsylvania Historical & Museum Commission, pg 157
Peradam Press, pg 158
Polar Bear & Company, pg 161
Princeton University Press, pg 164
Reference Publications Inc, pg 173
Routledge, pg 177
Rowman & Littlefield, pg 178
Russell Sage Foundation, pg 178
Rutgers University Press, pg 178
School for Advanced Research Press, pg 185
Shambhala Publications Inc, pg 187
SIL International, pg 188
Stanford University Press, pg 197
Strategic Book Publishing (SBP), pg 199
Tantor Media Inc, pg 202
Texas A&M University Press, pg 205
University of Texas Press, pg 205
UCLA Latin American Center Publications, pg 212
University of Alabama Press, pg 214
University of Alaska Press, pg 214
The University of Arizona Press, pg 214
University of California Press, pg 215
University of Chicago Press, pg 215
University of Georgia Press, pg 216
University of Hawaii Press, pg 216
University of Illinois Press, pg 216
University of Iowa Press, pg 216
University of Michigan Press, pg 217
University of Minnesota Press, pg 217
University of Nebraska Press, pg 217
University of Nevada Press, pg 218
University of New Mexico Press, pg 218
University of Oklahoma Press, pg 219
University of Pennsylvania Museum of Archaeology & Anthropology, pg 219
University of Pennsylvania Press, pg 219
University of Rochester Press, pg 220

The University of Utah Press, pg 220
University of Washington Press, pg 220
University of Wisconsin Press, pg 221
University Press of America Inc, pg 221
University Press of Colorado, pg 221
University Press of Florida, pg 221
Vanderbilt University Press, pg 224
Vernon Press, pg 224
Washington State University Press, pg 226
Waveland Press Inc, pg 226
Eliot Werner Publications Inc, pg 227
Westernlore Press, pg 228
Wiley-Blackwell, pg 229
World Bank Publications, pg 233
Yale University Press, pg 235
YBK Publishers Inc, pg 235
Zone Books, pg 237

ANTIQUES

Abbeville Publishing Group, pg 2
ACC Art Books, pg 3
Astragal Press, pg 20
AuthorHouse, pg 22
Blue Book Publications Inc, pg 32
Book Sales, pg 33
Dover Publications Inc, pg 61
Gale, pg 75
GemStone Press, pg 77
Greenleaf Book Group LLC, pg 81
Krause Publications Inc, pg 111
Laughing Elephant Books, pg 113
Philadelphia Museum of Art, pg 159
Rizzoli International Publications Inc, pg 175
St Johann Press, pg 180
Schiffer Publishing Ltd, pg 183
Square One Publishers Inc, pg 196
Stewart, Tabori & Chang, pg 198
Strategic Book Publishing (SBP), pg 199
Universe Publishing, pg 214
Winterthur Museum, Garden & Library, pg 231
Alan Wofsy Fine Arts, pg 231

ARCHAEOLOGY

Abbeville Press, pg 1
Academic Press, pg 3
Adventures Unlimited Press (AUP), pg 5
American Numismatic Society, pg 11
Andrews University Press, pg 14
ASCSA Publications, pg 18
AuthorHouse, pg 22
Baylor University Press, pg 25
Bear & Co Inc, pg 26
Berghahn Books, pg 28
The Blackburn Press, pg 30
Bloomsbury Academic, pg 31
Bolchazy-Carducci Publishers Inc, pg 33
The Book Tree, pg 34
George Braziller Inc, pg 35
Carolina Academic Press, pg 41
Charlesbridge Publishing Inc, pg 45
Child's Play® Inc, pg 46
China Books, pg 47
Continental AfrikaPublishers, pg 52
Cornell University Press, pg 52
Cotsen Institute of Archaeology Press, pg 53
Walter De Gruyter Inc, pg 58
Dover Publications Inc, pg 61
Dumbarton Oaks, pg 62
EDC Publishing, pg 63
Wm B Eerdmans Publishing Co, pg 64
Eisenbrauns, pg 64
Elsevier Inc, pg 65
Fowler Museum at UCLA, pg 74
Galde Press Inc, pg 75
Gale, pg 75
Getty Publications, pg 78
Gorgias Press LLC, pg 80
Hebrew Union College Press, pg 90
Hendrickson Publishers Inc, pg 91
Histria Books, pg 93
Illinois State Museum Society, pg 99
Italica Press, pg 105
Krieger Publishing Co, pg 111
LPD Press/Rio Grande Books, pg 121
Macmillan Reference USA™, pg 123
Mage Publishers Inc, pg 123
Master Books®, pg 126
Mazda Publishers Inc, pg 127
The McDonald & Woodward Publishing Co, pg 127
The Edwin Mellen Press, pg 129
The Metropolitan Museum of Art, pg 130
Nataraj Books, pg 136
National Geographic Books, pg 137
North Atlantic Books (NAB), pg 142
Ocean Tree Books, pg 145
Oriental Institute Publications, pg 148
ORO editions, pg 148
Oxford University Press USA, pg 149
Peabody Museum Press, pg 153
Penn State University Press, pg 157
Pennsylvania Historical & Museum Commission, pg 157
Polebridge Press, pg 161
Princeton University Press, pg 164
Prometheus Books, pg 166
Routledge, pg 177
School for Advanced Research Press, pg 185
Strategic Book Publishing (SBP), pg 199
Tantor Media Inc, pg 202
Texas A&M University Press, pg 205
University of Texas Press, pg 205
Thames & Hudson, pg 205
University of Alabama Press, pg 214
University of Alaska Press, pg 214
The University of Arizona Press, pg 214
University of California Press, pg 215
University of Chicago Press, pg 215
University of Iowa Press, pg 216
University of Nevada Press, pg 218
University of New Mexico Press, pg 218
University of Oklahoma Press, pg 219
University of Pennsylvania Museum of Archaeology & Anthropology, pg 219
University of Tennessee Press, pg 220
The University of Utah Press, pg 220
University Press of Colorado, pg 221
University Press of Florida, pg 221
University Press of Mississippi, pg 222
Utah Geological Survey, pg 223
Vanderbilt University Press, pg 224
Washington State University Press, pg 226
Waveland Press Inc, pg 226
Eliot Werner Publications Inc, pg 227
Western Edge Press, pg 228
Westernlore Press, pg 228
Markus Wiener Publishers Inc, pg 229
Wiley-Blackwell, pg 229
Yale University Press, pg 235
Zondervan, pg 236

ARCHITECTURE & INTERIOR DESIGN

Abbeville Press, pg 1
Abbeville Publishing Group, pg 2
Harry N Abrams Inc, pg 2
ACC Art Books, pg 3
Alexander Street, part of Clarivate PLC, pg 6
Allworth Press, pg 7
Ampersand Inc/Professional Publishing Services, pg 13
Aperture Books, pg 15
The Arion Press, pg 16
The Art Institute of Chicago, pg 17
Art of Living, PrimaMedia Inc, pg 17
Astragal Press, pg 20
Atlantic Publishing Group Inc, pg 21
AuthorHouse, pg 22
Beaver's Pond Press Inc, pg 26
Black Dome Press Corp, pg 30
BNi Building News, pg 33
Book Sales, pg 33
BookLogix, pg 34
George Braziller Inc, pg 35
BuilderBooks, pg 38
China Books, pg 47
Chronicle Books LLC, pg 47
Countryman Press, pg 54
Creative Homeowner, pg 55
Walter De Gruyter Inc, pg 58
Dover Publications Inc, pg 61
Duke University Press, pg 62
EDC Publishing, pg 63
Elsevier Inc, pg 65
Fairchild Books, pg 69
Fox Chapel Publishing Co Inc, pg 74
Gale, pg 75
Getty Publications, pg 78
Gibbs Smith Publisher, pg 78
Gingko Press Inc, pg 78
Glitterati Inc, pg 78
Goodheart-Willcox Publisher, pg 79
Greenleaf Book Group LLC, pg 81
Illuminating Engineering Society of North America (IES), pg 99
Insight Editions, pg 101
International Council of Shopping Centers (ICSC), pg 102
Island Press, pg 104
Jump!, pg 107
Kodansha USA Inc, pg 110
Krieger Publishing Co, pg 111
Long River Press, pg 120
Mage Publishers Inc, pg 123
Mazda Publishers Inc, pg 127
McFarland, pg 127
R S Means from The Gordian Group, pg 128
The Edwin Mellen Press, pg 129
The MIT Press, pg 132
The Monacelli Press, pg 133
The Museum of Modern Art (MoMA), pg 135
Museum of New Mexico Press, pg 135
Nataraj Books, pg 136
National Gallery of Art, pg 137
National Golf Foundation, pg 138
The New Press, pg 140
W W Norton & Company Inc, pg 143
Octane Press, pg 145
ORO editions, pg 148
PA Press, pg 149
Paintbox Press, pg 150
Pearson Business Publishing, pg 153
Pelican Publishing, pg 153
Penn State University Press, pg 157
Pennsylvania Historical & Museum Commission, pg 157
Phaidon, pg 159
Planners Press, pg 160
Pointed Leaf Press, pg 161
Pomegranate Communications Inc, pg 162
Clarkson Potter, pg 162
PPI, A Kaplan Company, pg 162
The Press at California State University, Fresno, pg 163
Princeton University Press, pg 164
Rizzoli International Publications Inc, pg 175
Routledge, pg 177
St James Press®, pg 180
St Joseph's University Press, pg 180
Schiffer Publishing Ltd, pg 183
Shambhala Publications Inc, pg 187
Stewart, Tabori & Chang, pg 198
Stipes Publishing LLC, pg 198
Strategic Book Publishing (SBP), pg 199
Sunstone Press, pg 201
Tantor Media Inc, pg 202
Taschen America, pg 203
Taunton Books, pg 203
Texas A&M University Press, pg 205
Texas Tech University Press, pg 205
University of Texas Press, pg 205
Thames & Hudson, pg 205
Turner Publishing Co LLC, pg 210
Tuttle Publishing, pg 211
Union Square & Co, pg 212
Universe Publishing, pg 214
University of California Press, pg 215
University of Chicago Press, pg 215
University of Delaware Press, pg 215
University of Iowa Press, pg 216
University of Massachusetts Press, pg 217
University of North Texas Press, pg 218
University of Pennsylvania Press, pg 219
University of Pittsburgh Press, pg 219
University of Tennessee Press, pg 220
University of Virginia Press, pg 220
University Press of Mississippi, pg 222
The Vendome Press, pg 224
Visual Profile Books Inc, pg 225
Wayne State University Press, pg 226
John Wiley & Sons Inc, pg 230
John Wiley & Sons Inc Global Education, pg 230
John Wiley & Sons Inc Professional Development, pg 230

PUBLISHERS

Winterthur Museum, Garden & Library, pg 231
Woodrow Wilson Center Press, pg 232
Xlibris Corp, pg 234
Yale University Press, pg 235

ART

A 2 Z Press LLC, pg 1
Abbeville Press, pg 1
Abbeville Publishing Group, pg 2
Harry N Abrams Inc, pg 2
Academy Chicago Publishers, pg 3
ACC Art Books, pg 3
AK Press, pg 6
Akashic Books, pg 6
Alexander Street, part of Clarivate PLC, pg 6
Allworth Press, pg 7
Amber Lotus Publishing, pg 8
The American Ceramic Society, pg 9
American Federation of Arts, pg 9
AMMO Books LLC, pg 13
Sara Anderson Children's Books, pg 13
Aperture Books, pg 15
The Apocryphile Press, pg 15
Ariadne Press, pg 16
The Arion Press, pg 16
Art Image Publications, pg 17
The Art Institute of Chicago, pg 17
Art of Living, PrimaMedia Inc, pg 17
AuthorHouse, pg 22
Baby Tattoo Books, pg 23
Baker Books, pg 23
Barringer Publishing, pg 24
Barrytown/Station Hill Press, pg 24
Beaver's Pond Press Inc, pg 26
Beehive Books, pg 26
Bellerophon Books, pg 27
Bellevue Literary Press, pg 27
John Benjamins Publishing Co, pg 28
Black Dome Press Corp, pg 30
Black Mountain Press, pg 30
Bloomsbury Academic, pg 31
Blue Crane Books Inc, pg 32
Book Sales, pg 33
BookLogix, pg 34
Brandylane Publishers Inc, pg 35
George Braziller Inc, pg 35
Brown Books Publishing Group (BBPG), pg 38
Cambridge University Press, pg 39
C&T Publishing Inc, pg 40
Capen Publishing Co Inc, pg 40
Carnegie Mellon University Press, pg 41
Cedar Grove Publishing, pg 43
Cengage Learning, pg 43
Charlesbridge Publishing Inc, pg 45
Chelsea House, pg 45
China Books, pg 47
Chronicle Books LLC, pg 47
Clear Light Publishers, pg 49
Cornell University Press, pg 52
Counterpath Press, pg 54
Counterpoint Press LLC, pg 54
Crabtree Publishing Co, pg 54
Cross-Cultural Communications, pg 55
Dark Horse Comics, pg 57
Walter De Gruyter Inc, pg 58
Deseret Book Co, pg 58
Dharma Publishing, pg 59
DK, pg 60
Doubleday, pg 61
Dover Publications Inc, pg 61
Duke University Press, pg 62
ECS Publishing Group, pg 63

EDC Publishing, pg 63
Edgewise Press Inc, pg 63
Editorial de la Universidad de Puerto Rico, pg 63
Enslow Publishing LLC, pg 66
Epicenter Press Inc, pg 67
Evan-Moor Educational Publishers, pg 68
Facts On File, pg 69
Fairchild Books, pg 69
Feral House, pg 71
Fine Creative Media, Inc, pg 71
Firefall Editions, pg 72
Fons Vitae, pg 73
Fordham University Press, pg 73
Walter Foster Publishing, pg 74
Fowler Museum at UCLA, pg 74
Fox Chapel Publishing Co Inc, pg 74
Gagosian Gallery, pg 75
Gale, pg 75
Gateways Books & Tapes, pg 77
Gauthier Publications Inc, pg 77
Getty Publications, pg 78
Gibbs Smith Publisher, pg 78
Gingko Press Inc, pg 78
Glitterati Inc, pg 78
Godine, pg 79
Donald M Grant Publisher Inc, pg 80
Green Integer, pg 81
Greenleaf Book Group LLC, pg 81
Hancock House Publishers, pg 84
Harvard Art Museums, pg 87
Her Own Words LLC, pg 91
Heyday, pg 91
The Historic New Orleans Collection, pg 93
Histria Books, pg 93
Hohm Press, pg 93
Hollym International Corp, pg 94
Homa & Sekey Books, pg 95
Homestead Publishing, pg 95
Ignatius Press, pg 98
Illinois State Museum Society, pg 99
Immedium, pg 99
Indiana Historical Society Press, pg 99
Indiana University African Studies Program, pg 100
Indiana University Press, pg 100
Inner Traditions International Ltd, pg 101
Insight Editions, pg 101
Interweave Press LLC, pg 104
Italica Press, pg 105
Jump!, pg 107
Just World Books LLC, pg 107
Kelsey Street Press, pg 108
Kodansha USA Inc, pg 110
Konecky & Konecky LLC, pg 111
Krause Publications Inc, pg 111
Lake Superior Publishing LLC, pg 112
Laughing Elephant Books, pg 113
THE Learning Connection®, pg 113
Lerner Publications, pg 115
Little, Brown and Company, pg 118
Liturgical Press, pg 118
Locks Art Publications/Locks Gallery, pg 119
Long River Press, pg 120
LPD Press/Rio Grande Books, pg 121
Lucent Press, pg 121
Luna Bisonte Prods, pg 121
Macmillan Reference USA™, pg 123
Mage Publishers Inc, pg 123
Mandala Earth, pg 124
Manic D Press Inc, pg 124
Mazda Publishers Inc, pg 127

U.S. PUBLISHERS — SUBJECT INDEX

McGraw-Hill Education, pg 127
McGraw-Hill Higher Education, pg 128
McGraw-Hill School Education Group, pg 128
McPherson & Co, pg 128
Medieval Institute Publications (MIP), pg 129
The Edwin Mellen Press, pg 129
The Metropolitan Museum of Art, pg 130
MFA Publications, pg 130
Minnesota Historical Society Press, pg 132
MIT List Visual Arts Center, pg 132
The MIT Press, pg 132
Mitchell Lane Publishers Inc, pg 133
Modern Memoirs Inc, pg 133
The Monacelli Press, pg 133
De Gruyter Mouton, pg 135
The Museum of Modern Art (MoMA), pg 135
Museum of New Mexico Press, pg 135
Nataraj Books, pg 136
National Gallery of Art, pg 137
The New Press, pg 140
New York University Press, pg 141
North Atlantic Books (NAB), pg 142
North Star Press of Saint Cloud Inc, pg 142
Northwestern University Press, pg 143
NRP Direct, pg 144
Oak Knoll Press, pg 144
Omnigraphics Inc, pg 146
On the Write Path Publishing, pg 146
Orbis Books, pg 147
ORO editions, pg 148
Other Press, pg 148
Oxford University Press USA, pg 149
PA Press, pg 149
Paintbox Press, pg 150
Pearson Business Publishing, pg 153
Pelican Publishing, pg 153
Pen & Publish LLC, pg 153
Penn State University Press, pg 157
Pennsylvania Historical & Museum Commission, pg 157
Phaidon, pg 159
Philadelphia Museum of Art, pg 159
Philosophical Library Inc, pg 159
The Picasso Project, pg 160
Pineapple Press, pg 160
Pointed Leaf Press, pg 161
Polar Bear & Company, pg 161
Pomegranate Communications Inc, pg 162
Clarkson Potter, pg 162
powerHouse Books, pg 162
The Press at California State University, Fresno, pg 163
Princeton University Press, pg 164
Reader's Digest Trade Publishing, pg 172
Rio Nuevo Publishers, pg 175
River City Publishing, pg 175
Rizzoli International Publications Inc, pg 175
The RoadRunner Press, pg 175
Ross Books, pg 177
Routledge, pg 177
Running Press, pg 178
Rutgers University Press, pg 178
St Joseph's University Press, pg 180

San Diego State University Press, pg 182
Santa Monica Press LLC, pg 182
Sasquatch Books, pg 182
Savvas Learning Co LLC, pg 183
Schiffer Publishing Ltd, pg 183
School for Advanced Research Press, pg 185
Schreiber Publishing, pg 185
Scripta Humanistica Publishing International, pg 185
Sentient Publications LLC, pg 186
Serindia Publications, pg 186
Shambhala Publications Inc, pg 187
Siglio, pg 187
South Dakota Historical Society Press, pg 195
Spizzirri Publishing Inc, pg 196
Star Publishing Co Inc, pg 197
StarGroup International Inc, pg 197
SteinerBooks Inc, pg 198
Stewart, Tabori & Chang, pg 198
Stone Bridge Press Inc, pg 199
Strategic Book Publishing (SBP), pg 199
Sunbelt Publications Inc, pg 200
Sunstone Press, pg 201
Swallow Press, pg 201
Syracuse University Press, pg 201
Tantor Media Inc, pg 202
Taschen America, pg 203
Taunton Books, pg 203
Teacher Created Resources Inc, pg 203
Teaching & Learning Co, pg 204
Texas A&M University Press, pg 205
Texas Tech University Press, pg 205
Thames & Hudson, pg 205
Tide-mark Press, pg 207
Trinity University Press, pg 209
Tumblehome Learning Inc, pg 210
Tuttle Publishing, pg 211
Union Square & Co, pg 212
Universe Publishing, pg 214
University of Alaska Press, pg 214
University of California Press, pg 215
University of Chicago Press, pg 215
University of Delaware Press, pg 215
University of Georgia Press, pg 216
University of Hawaii Press, pg 216
University of Iowa Press, pg 216
University of Louisiana at Lafayette Press, pg 217
University of Massachusetts Press, pg 217
University of Minnesota Press, pg 217
University of Missouri Press, pg 217
University of Nevada Press, pg 218
University of New Mexico Press, pg 218
University of North Texas Press, pg 218
University of Oklahoma Press, pg 219
University of Pennsylvania Museum of Archaeology & Anthropology, pg 219
University of Washington Press, pg 220
University of Wisconsin Press, pg 221
University Press of Mississippi, pg 222
US Games Systems Inc, pg 223
Vanderbilt University Press, pg 224
The Vendome Press, pg 224
Vernon Press, pg 224
Walch Education, pg 225

Washington State University Press, pg 226
Watson-Guptill, pg 226
Wayne State University Press, pg 226
Welcome Books, pg 227
Welcome Rain Publishers LLC, pg 227
Western Edge Press, pg 228
Markus Wiener Publishers Inc, pg 229
Wiley-Blackwell, pg 229
John Wiley & Sons Inc, pg 230
John Wiley & Sons Inc Global Education, pg 230
John Wiley & Sons Inc Professional Development, pg 230
Winterthur Museum, Garden & Library, pg 231
Wisconsin Department of Public Instruction, pg 231
Wisdom Publications Inc, pg 231
Alan Wofsy Fine Arts, pg 231
Wolfman Books, pg 232
WoodstockArts, pg 232
Xlibris Corp, pg 234
Yale Center for British Art, pg 235
Yale University Press, pg 235
YBK Publishers Inc, pg 235
Zone Books, pg 237

ASIAN STUDIES

Academica Press, pg 3
Akashic Books, pg 6
AuthorHouse, pg 22
John Benjamins Publishing Co, pg 28
Berghahn Books, pg 28
Berkshire Publishing Group LLC, pg 28
Boson Books™, pg 34
George Braziller Inc, pg 35
Brill Inc, pg 37
Carolina Academic Press, pg 41
Center for Strategic & International Studies (CSIS), pg 44
Chelsea House, pg 45
Cheng & Tsui Co Inc, pg 46
China Books, pg 47
CN Times Books, pg 50
Coffee House Press, pg 50
Columbia University Press, pg 51
Copper Canyon Press, pg 52
Cornell University Press, pg 52
Council for Research in Values & Philosophy, pg 53
Cross-Cultural Communications, pg 55
Dharma Publishing, pg 59
Dover Publications Inc, pg 61
Duke University Press, pg 62
East West Discovery Press, pg 63
Edupress Inc, pg 64
Encounter Books, pg 66
Facts On File, pg 69
The Feminist Press at The City University of New York, pg 71
Focus, pg 73
Fowler Museum at UCLA, pg 74
Gale, pg 75
Gingko Press Inc, pg 78
Grey House Publishing Inc™, pg 81
Hackett Publishing Co Inc, pg 83
Hamilton Books, pg 84
HarperCollins Publishers LLC, pg 86
Harvard University Press, pg 88
Heyday, pg 91
Hollym International Corp, pg 94
Homa & Sekey Books, pg 95
Hoover Institution Press, pg 95
Hudson Institute, pg 97
Humanix Books LLC, pg 97
Immedium, pg 99
Indiana University Press, pg 100
Information Age Publishing Inc, pg 100
Inner Traditions International Ltd, pg 101
The International Institute of Islamic Thought, pg 103
Jain Publishing Co, pg 105
Kumarian Press, pg 112
THE Learning Connection®, pg 113
Lehigh University Press, pg 114
Lexington Books, pg 115
Long River Press, pg 120
Lotus Press, pg 120
Macmillan Reference USA™, pg 123
Mandala Earth, pg 124
Manic D Press Inc, pg 124
Marshall Cavendish Education, pg 125
Mason Crest Publishers, pg 126
McFarland, pg 127
The Edwin Mellen Press, pg 129
Modern Language Association (MLA), pg 133
Monthly Review Press, pg 134
De Gruyter Mouton, pg 135
Nataraj Books, pg 136
The New Press, pg 140
Nilgiri Press, pg 141
North Atlantic Books (NAB), pg 142
W W Norton & Company Inc, pg 143
Nova Science Publishers Inc, pg 144
Ohio University Press, pg 145
Paradigm Publications, pg 151
Parallax Press, pg 151
Princeton University Press, pg 164
Radix Press, pg 169
RAND Corp, pg 169
Rational Island Publishers, pg 171
Reference Publications Inc, pg 173
Lynne Rienner Publishers Inc, pg 174
Routledge, pg 177
Rowman & Littlefield, pg 178
Rutgers University Press, pg 178
SAGE Publishing, pg 180
Schaffner Press, pg 183
Serindia Publications, pg 186
Shambhala Publications Inc, pg 187
Snow Lion, pg 192
Stanford University Press, pg 197
State University of New York Press, pg 198
Stone Bridge Press Inc, pg 199
Strategic Book Publishing (SBP), pg 199
Tantor Media Inc, pg 202
ThunderStone Books, pg 207
Tuttle Publishing, pg 211
University of California Institute on Global Conflict & Cooperation, pg 215
University of California Press, pg 215
University of Chicago Press, pg 215
University of Delaware Press, pg 215
University of Hawaii Press, pg 216
University of Illinois Press, pg 216
University of Iowa Press, pg 216
University of Michigan Press, pg 217
University of Minnesota Press, pg 217
University of Pittsburgh Press, pg 219
University of Washington Press, pg 220
University Press of America Inc, pg 221
University Press of Colorado, pg 221
University Press of Mississippi, pg 222
Vernon Press, pg 224
Wayside Publishing, pg 227
White Pine Press, pg 228
Markus Wiener Publishers Inc, pg 229
William Carey Publishing, pg 230
Wisconsin Department of Public Instruction, pg 231
Wisdom Publications Inc, pg 231
Woodrow Wilson Center Press, pg 232
World Citizens, pg 233
Yale University Press, pg 235
YMAA Publication Center Inc, pg 235

ASTROLOGY, OCCULT

Adams Media, pg 4
All Things That Matter Press, pg 7
American Federation of Astrologers Inc, pg 9
The Apocryphile Press, pg 15
ARE Press, pg 16
Ariel Press, pg 16
AuthorHouse, pg 22
Bear & Co Inc, pg 26
The Book Tree, pg 34
DK, pg 60
Dover Publications Inc, pg 61
Gale, pg 75
Hay House LLC, pg 89
Histria Books, pg 93
Holmes Publishing Group LLC, pg 94
Hutton Publishing, pg 97
Inner Traditions International Ltd, pg 101
Kessinger Publishing LLC, pg 109
Larson Publications, pg 113
Light Technology Publishing LLC, pg 116
Llewellyn Publications, pg 119
Lotus Press, pg 120
Macmillan Reference USA™, pg 123
Marshall Cavendish Education, pg 125
Nataraj Books, pg 136
North Atlantic Books (NAB), pg 142
Omnigraphics Inc, pg 146
The Original Falcon Press, pg 148
Ozark Mountain Publishing Inc, pg 149
Philosophical Library Inc, pg 159
Red Wheel/Weiser, pg 173
Ross Books, pg 177
Running Press, pg 178
Schiffer Publishing Ltd, pg 183
SteinerBooks Inc, pg 198
Strategic Book Publishing (SBP), pg 199
TSG Publishing Foundation Inc, pg 210
Union Square & Co, pg 212
US Games Systems Inc, pg 223
Visible Ink Press®, pg 225
Xlibris Corp, pg 234

ASTRONOMY

Academic Press, pg 3
AdventureKEEN, pg 5
AIP Publishing LLC, pg 6
Annual Reviews, pg 14
Arbordale Publishing, pg 16
The Astronomical Society of the Pacific, pg 20
AuthorHouse, pg 22
Blue Note Publications Inc, pg 32
Cengage Learning, pg 43
Charlesbridge Publishing Inc, pg 45
Child's Play® Inc, pg 46
Christian Liberty Press, pg 47
DK, pg 60
Dover Publications Inc, pg 61
EDC Publishing, pg 63
Educational Insights®, pg 64
Elsevier Health Sciences, pg 65
Elsevier Inc, pg 65
W H Freeman, pg 75
Gale, pg 75
Jones & Bartlett Learning LLC, pg 107
Kalmbach Media Co, pg 108
Krieger Publishing Co, pg 111
Macmillan Learning, pg 123
Macmillan Reference USA™, pg 123
Master Books®, pg 126
The McDonald & Woodward Publishing Co, pg 127
McGraw-Hill Create, pg 127
McGraw-Hill Higher Education, pg 128
Nataraj Books, pg 136
National Academies Press (NAP), pg 136
National Science Teachers Association (NSTA), pg 138
North Atlantic Books (NAB), pg 142
W W Norton & Company Inc, pg 143
Pearson Business Publishing, pg 153
Princeton University Press, pg 164
Prometheus Books, pg 166
Saddleback Educational Publishing, pg 179
Science History Publications USA Inc, pg 185
SPIE, pg 196
Strategic Book Publishing (SBP), pg 199
Tantor Media Inc, pg 202
Twenty-First Century Books, pg 211
Union Square & Co, pg 212
Univelt Inc, pg 213
University of Alaska Press, pg 214
The University of Arizona Press, pg 214
University of Chicago Press, pg 215
University Science Books, pg 222
VanDam Inc, pg 223
Visible Ink Press®, pg 225
Whittier Publications Inc, pg 229
John Wiley & Sons Inc, pg 230
John Wiley & Sons Inc Global Education, pg 230
John Wiley & Sons Inc Professional Development, pg 230

AUTOMOTIVE

Abbeville Press, pg 1
Abbeville Publishing Group, pg 2
AuthorHouse, pg 22
Bentley Publishers, pg 28
CarTech Inc, pg 41
Cengage Learning, pg 43
DK, pg 60
EDC Publishing, pg 63
Gale, pg 75
Goodheart-Willcox Publisher, pg 79
Haynes North America Inc, pg 89
Krause Publications Inc, pg 111

Lawyers & Judges Publishing Co Inc, pg 113
McFarland, pg 127
Plunkett Research Ltd, pg 161
Publications International Ltd (PIL), pg 167
Quarto Publishing Group USA Inc, pg 168
SAE (Society of Automotive Engineers International), pg 179
Schiffer Publishing Ltd, pg 183
StarGroup International Inc, pg 197
Strategic Book Publishing (SBP), pg 199
Tantor Media Inc, pg 202
Tide-mark Press, pg 207
Wayne State University Press, pg 226
Write Stuff Enterprises LLC, pg 234
Xlibris Corp, pg 234

BEHAVIORAL SCIENCES

Academic Press, pg 3
American Correctional Association, pg 9
American Counseling Association (ACA), pg 9
American Press, pg 11
American Psychiatric Association Publishing, pg 11
Andrews University Press, pg 14
Annual Reviews, pg 14
Jason Aronson Inc, pg 17
AuthorHouse, pg 22
Barringer Publishing, pg 24
Barrytown/Station Hill Press, pg 24
Biographical Publishing Co, pg 29
The Blackburn Press, pg 30
Boys Town Press, pg 35
Bridge Publications Inc, pg 36
Brilliance Publishing Inc, pg 37
Paul H Brookes Publishing Co Inc, pg 37
Brookline Books, pg 37
Brown Books Publishing Group (BBPG), pg 38
Cambridge University Press, pg 39
Cengage Learning, pg 43
Center for Creative Leadership LLC, pg 43
Central Recovery Press (CRP), pg 44
Charles Press Publishers, pg 45
Cognizant Communication Corp, pg 50
CSWE Press, pg 56
dbS Productions, pg 58
Gale, pg 75
Gifted Unlimited LLC, pg 78
Greenleaf Book Group LLC, pg 81
Gryphon Editions, pg 82
The Guilford Press, pg 82
Harvard Common Press, pg 87
Harvard University Press, pg 88
Hatherleigh Press Ltd, pg 88
Hay House LLC, pg 89
Hazelden Publishing, pg 89
Health Communications Inc, pg 89
Health Professions Press, pg 90
High Tide Press, pg 92
Hilton Publishing Co, pg 92
Histria Books, pg 93
Hogrefe Publishing Corp, pg 93
Human Kinetics Inc, pg 97
Humanix Books LLC, pg 97
Hutton Publishing, pg 97
Idyll Arbor Inc, pg 98
Information Age Publishing Inc, pg 100
Inter-University Consortium for Political & Social Research (ICPSR), pg 102

The International Institute of Islamic Thought, pg 103
Krieger Publishing Co, pg 111
Macmillan Reference USA™, pg 123
Maharishi International University Press, pg 123
McGraw-Hill Higher Education, pg 128
Milford Books™, pg 131
Richard K Miller Associates, pg 132
NASW Press, pg 136
National Academies Press (NAP), pg 136
New York University Press, pg 141
North Atlantic Books (NAB), pg 142
W W Norton & Company Inc, pg 143
Nova Science Publishers Inc, pg 144
Odyssey Books, pg 145
On the Write Path Publishing, pg 146
Optometric Extension Program Foundation (OEPF), pg 147
The Original Falcon Press, pg 148
ORO editions, pg 148
Oxford University Press USA, pg 149
Penguin Publishing Group, pg 154
Pennsylvania State Data Center, pg 157
Peradam Press, pg 158
Philosophical Library Inc, pg 159
Princeton University Press, pg 164
PRO-ED Inc, pg 165
Professional Resource Press, pg 165
Prometheus Books, pg 166
Psychological Assessment Resources Inc (PAR), pg 166
RAND Corp, pg 169
Rational Island Publishers, pg 171
Research Press, pg 174
Ronin Publishing Inc, pg 176
Routledge, pg 177
Russell Sage Foundation, pg 178
Safer Society Press, pg 179
SAGE Publishing, pg 180
St Pauls, pg 181
Science & Humanities Press, pg 185
Sentient Publications LLC, pg 186
Sinauer Associates, pg 190
Springer Publishing Co, pg 196
STM Learning Inc, pg 199
Strategic Book Publishing (SBP), pg 199
Tantor Media Inc, pg 202
Taylor & Francis Inc, pg 203
Temple University Press, pg 204
Charles C Thomas Publisher Ltd, pg 206
TSG Publishing Foundation Inc, pg 210
University of Chicago Press, pg 215
University of Louisiana at Lafayette Press, pg 217
Vernon Press, pg 224
Voyager Sopris Learning Inc, pg 225
Waveland Press Inc, pg 226
Eliot Werner Publications Inc, pg 227
Wheatherstone Press, pg 228
Whole Person Associates Inc, pg 229
Wiley-Blackwell, pg 229
John Wiley & Sons Inc Global Education, pg 230
Wisconsin Department of Public Instruction, pg 231
Woodbine House, pg 232

Wyndham Hall Press, pg 234
Yale University Press, pg 235
Zeig, Tucker & Theisen Inc, pg 236

BIBLICAL STUDIES

A 2 Z Press LLC, pg 1
Ambassador International, pg 7
American Bible Society, pg 8
Ancient Faith Publishing, pg 13
Andrews University Press, pg 14
The Apocryphile Press, pg 15
Augsburg Fortress Publishers, Publishing House of the Evangelical Lutheran Church in America, pg 22
AuthorHouse, pg 22
Baker Books, pg 23
B&H Publishing Group, pg 24
Barbour Publishing Inc, pg 24
Baylor University Press, pg 25
Beacon Hill Press of Kansas City, pg 25
Ben Yehuda Press, pg 27
Bethany House Publishers, pg 29
Biographical Publishing Co, pg 29
BJU Press, pg 30
Bloomsbury Academic, pg 31
Bolchazy-Carducci Publishers Inc, pg 33
Book Sales, pg 33
The Book Tree, pg 34
Bridge Logos Inc, pg 36
Brilliance Publishing Inc, pg 37
Brown Books Publishing Group (BBPG), pg 38
Campfield & Campfield Publishing LLC, pg 39
Casa Bautista de Publicaciones, pg 41
Chalice Press, pg 44
Charisma Media, pg 45
Charles Press Publishers, pg 45
Christian Liberty Press, pg 47
Christian Light Publications Inc, pg 47
Christian Schools International (CSI), pg 47
Concordia Publishing House, pg 51
Crossway, pg 56
Walter De Gruyter Inc, pg 58
Deep River Books LLC, pg 58
Deseret Book Co, pg 58
Destiny Image Inc, pg 59
Editorial Bautista Independiente, pg 63
Editorial Portavoz, pg 64
Editorial Unilit, pg 64
Wm B Eerdmans Publishing Co, pg 64
Eisenbrauns, pg 64
Emerald Books, pg 66
Emmaus Road Publishing Inc, pg 66
Faith Library Publications, pg 69
Faithlife Corp, pg 69
Feldheim Publishers, pg 70
Forward Movement, pg 73
Franciscan Media, pg 74
Galde Press Inc, pg 75
Gale, pg 75
Gorgias Press LLC, pg 80
Gospel Publishing House, pg 80
Greenleaf Book Group LLC, pg 81
Group Publishing Inc, pg 82
Guideposts Book & Inspirational Media, pg 82
Hamilton Books, pg 84
Harvest House Publishers Inc, pg 88
William S Hein & Co Inc, pg 90
Hendrickson Publishers Inc, pg 91
Herald Press, pg 91
Histria Books, pg 93

Horizon Publishers & Distributors Inc, pg 95
House to House Publications, pg 97
Institute of Jesuit Sources (IJS), pg 102
Jewish Lights Publishing, pg 105
The Jewish Publication Society, pg 105
Judaica Press Inc, pg 107
Judson Press, pg 107
Kar-Ben Publishing, pg 108
Kessinger Publishing LLC, pg 109
Konecky & Konecky LLC, pg 111
Kregel Publications, pg 111
KTAV Publishing House Inc, pg 111
Lexington Books, pg 115
Liguori Publications, pg 117
Liturgical Press, pg 118
Living Stream Ministry (LSM), pg 119
Macmillan Reference USA™, pg 123
Master Books®, pg 126
The Edwin Mellen Press, pg 129
Mercer University Press, pg 129
Mesorah Publications Ltd, pg 130
Moody Publishers, pg 134
Moznaim Publishing Corp, pg 135
Multnomah, pg 135
NavPress Publishing Group, pg 139
New City Press, pg 139
Northern Illinois University Press, pg 143
Orbis Books, pg 147
Our Daily Bread Publishing, pg 148
Our Sunday Visitor Publishing, pg 148
Oxford University Press USA, pg 149
P & R Publishing Co, pg 149
Paraclete Press Inc, pg 151
Paulist Press, pg 152
Pelican Publishing, pg 153
Penn State University Press, pg 157
Pentecostal Resources Group, pg 157
Pflaum Publishing Group, pg 159
Pocol Press, pg 161
Polebridge Press, pg 161
Presbyterian Publishing Corp (PPC), pg 163
Progressive Press, pg 165
Prometheus Books, pg 166
Recorded Books Inc, an RBmedia company, pg 172
Regnery Publishing, pg 174
William H Sadlier Inc, pg 179
SAGE Publishing, pg 180
St Johann Press, pg 180
St Pauls, pg 181
SBL Press, pg 183
Signature Books Publishing LLC, pg 187
SIL International, pg 188
Smyth & Helwys Publishing Inc, pg 192
Standard Publishing, pg 197
Strategic Book Publishing (SBP), pg 199
Swedenborg Foundation, pg 201
T&T Clark International, pg 202
Thomas Nelson, pg 206
Torah Umesorah Publications, pg 208
The Trinity Foundation, pg 209
Twenty-Third Publications, pg 211
Tyndale House Publishers Inc, pg 211
Upper Room Books, pg 223
Urim Publications, pg 223
US Conference of Catholic Bishops, pg 223

WaterBrook, pg 226
Wesleyan Publishing House, pg 227
Westminster John Knox Press (WJK), pg 228
Whitaker House, pg 228
Wiley-Blackwell, pg 229
William Carey Publishing, pg 230
Yale University Press, pg 235
YBK Publishers Inc, pg 235
Zondervan, pg 236

BIOGRAPHY, MEMOIRS

Abbeville Press, pg 1
Abbeville Publishing Group, pg 2
ABDO, pg 2
Advance Publishing Inc, pg 5
AK Press, pg 6
Akashic Books, pg 6
All Things That Matter Press, pg 7
Amadeus Press, pg 7
Ambassador International, pg 7
American Carriage House Publishing (ACHP), pg 8
American Correctional Association, pg 9
Ampersand Inc/Professional Publishing Services, pg 13
Anaphora Literary Press, pg 13
Angelus Press, pg 14
The Apocryphile Press, pg 15
Appalachian Mountain Club Books, pg 15
Applause Theatre & Cinema Books, pg 15
Arcade Publishing Inc, pg 16
Ariadne Press, pg 16
Ascend Books LLC, pg 18
Ashland Creek Press, pg 18
Asta Publications LLC, pg 20
AuthorHouse, pg 22
Authorlink® Press, pg 22
Baha'i Publishing Trust, pg 23
Baker Books, pg 23
Bancroft Press, pg 24
Barranca Press, pg 24
Barringer Publishing, pg 24
Barrytown/Station Hill Press, pg 24
Bartleby Press, pg 24
Beacon Press, pg 25
BearManor Media, pg 26
Beaver's Pond Press Inc, pg 26
Frederic C Beil Publisher Inc, pg 27
Bellerophon Books, pg 27
BenBella Books Inc, pg 27
Berghahn Books, pg 28
Bess Press Inc, pg 29
Bethany House Publishers, pg 29
Bethlehem Books, pg 29
Biographical Publishing Co, pg 29
BJU Press, pg 30
Black Dome Press Corp, pg 30
Blair, pg 30
Blood Moon Productions Ltd, pg 31
Bloomsbury Academic, pg 31
Blue Book Publications Inc, pg 32
Blue Note Publications Inc, pg 32
BlueBridge, pg 32
Book Sales, pg 33
Bookhaven Press LLC, pg 34
BookLogix, pg 34
Books on Tape™, pg 34
Bottom Dog Press, pg 34
Brandylane Publishers Inc, pg 35
George Braziller Inc, pg 35
Brick Tower Press, pg 36
Bridge Logos Inc, pg 36
Brilliance Publishing Inc, pg 37
Brown Books Publishing Group (BBPG), pg 38
Bywater Books Inc, pg 39
Camino Books Inc, pg 39
Capstone Publishers™, pg 40

Carnegie Mellon University Press, pg 41
Carolina Academic Press, pg 41
Casemate | publishers, pg 41
The Center for Learning, pg 43
Chalice Press, pg 44
Charlesbridge Publishing Inc, pg 45
Chelsea House, pg 45
Chicago Review Press, pg 46
Chickadee Prince Books LLC, pg 46
The Child's World Inc, pg 46
China Books, pg 47
Christian Liberty Press, pg 47
Christian Light Publications Inc, pg 47
Chronicle Books LLC, pg 47
Cleis Press, pg 49
Clerisy Press, pg 49
Cornell Maritime Press, pg 52
Cornerstone Book Publishers, pg 53
Counterpoint Press LLC, pg 54
Country Music Foundation Press, pg 54
CQ Press, pg 54
Cricket Cottage Publishing LLC, pg 55
Crown Publishing Group, pg 56
Dalkey Archive Press, pg 56
Dark Horse Comics, pg 57
Deep River Books LLC, pg 58
Dharma Publishing, pg 59
Dorrance Publishing Co Inc, pg 61
Doubleday, pg 61
Dover Publications Inc, pg 61
Duke University Press, pg 62
Eakin Press, pg 62
Wm B Eerdmans Publishing Co, pg 64
Elderberry Press Inc, pg 65
Emerald Books, pg 66
Encounter Books, pg 66
Enslow Publishing LLC, pg 66
Epicenter Press Inc, pg 67
Everyman's Library, pg 68
Everything Goes Media LLC, pg 68
Excelsior Editions, pg 68
The Experiment, pg 68
Facts On File, pg 69
Familius, pg 69
Filter Press LLC, pg 71
Fine Creative Media, Inc, pg 71
Firefall Editions, pg 72
First Avenue Editions, pg 72
Fordham University Press, pg 73
Forward Movement, pg 73
Friends United Press, pg 75
Galde Press Inc, pg 75
Gale, pg 75
Gallaudet University Press, pg 76
Gallery Books, pg 76
Gareth Stevens Publishing, pg 76
Gingko Press Inc, pg 78
Glitterati Inc, pg 78
Global Authors Publications (GAP), pg 78
Godine, pg 79
Goose River Press, pg 79
Gospel Publishing House, pg 80
Gray & Company Publishers, pg 80
Greenleaf Book Group LLC, pg 81
Grey House Publishing Inc™, pg 81
Hal Leonard LLC, pg 84
Hamilton Books, pg 84
Hamilton Stone Editions, pg 84
HarperCollins Publishers LLC, pg 86
Harvard University Press, pg 88
Hay House LLC, pg 89
Health Communications Inc, pg 89
Hellgate Press, pg 91
Herald Press, pg 91
High Plains Press, pg 91

Hilton Publishing Co, pg 92
History Publishing Co LLC, pg 93
Histria Books, pg 93
Homa & Sekey Books, pg 95
Homestead Publishing, pg 95
Horizon Publishers & Distributors Inc, pg 95
Houghton Mifflin Harcourt Trade & Reference Division, pg 96
Huntington Press Publishing, pg 97
Hutton Publishing, pg 97
IHS Press, pg 98
Indiana Historical Society Press, pg 99
Indiana University Press, pg 100
Institute of Jesuit Sources (IJS), pg 102
Interlink Publishing Group Inc, pg 102
International Publishers Co Inc, pg 103
Islandport Press, pg 105
Joshua Tree Publishing, pg 107
Just World Books LLC, pg 107
Kallisti Publishing Inc, pg 108
Kamehameha Publishing, pg 108
Kensington Publishing Corp, pg 109
Kent State University Press, pg 109
Kiva Publishing Inc, pg 110
Alfred A Knopf, pg 110
Koho Pono LLC, pg 111
Konecky & Konecky LLC, pg 111
Kregel Publications, pg 111
Landauer Publishing, pg 112
Laredo Publishing Co, pg 113
Lee & Low Books Inc, pg 114
Lehigh University Press, pg 114
Lerner Publications, pg 115
Lerner Publishing Group Inc, pg 115
Libraries Unlimited, pg 116
Limelight Editions, pg 117
Linden Publishing Co Inc, pg 117
Little, Brown and Company, pg 118
Liturgical Press, pg 118
Llewellyn Publications, pg 119
The Local History Co, pg 119
Loft Press Inc, pg 119
Long River Press, pg 120
Lost Classics Book Company LLC, pg 120
Louisiana State University Press, pg 120
Loving Healing Press Inc, pg 121
Lucent Press, pg 121
Macmillan Reference USA™, pg 123
Mandel Vilar Press, pg 124
Marine Techniques Publishing, pg 125
Maryland Center for History & Culture (MCHC), pg 126
Maryland History Press, pg 126
Mason Crest Publishers, pg 126
Mazda Publishers Inc, pg 127
The McDonald & Woodward Publishing Co, pg 127
McFarland, pg 127
McPherson & Co, pg 128
The Edwin Mellen Press, pg 129
Mesorah Publications Ltd, pg 130
Metropolitan Classics, pg 130
Michigan State University Press (MSU Press), pg 130
Midnight Marquee Press Inc, pg 130
Milford Books™, pg 131
Minnesota Historical Society Press, pg 132
Mitchell Lane Publishers Inc, pg 133
Modern Memoirs Inc, pg 133

Monkfish Book Publishing Co, pg 133
Mountain Press Publishing Co, pg 135
Multicultural Publications Inc, pg 135
Multnomah, pg 135
Nataraj Books, pg 136
National Academies Press (NAP), pg 136
National Geographic Books, pg 137
Naval Institute Press, pg 139
NBM Publishing Inc, pg 139
New Directions Publishing Corp, pg 139
The New Press, pg 140
New York University Press, pg 141
NewSouth Books, pg 141
Nilgiri Press, pg 141
North Atlantic Books (NAB), pg 142
North Star Editions Inc, pg 142
North Star Press of Saint Cloud Inc, pg 142
Northern Illinois University Press, pg 143
Northwestern University Press, pg 143
W W Norton & Company Inc, pg 143
The Oaklea Press Inc, pg 145
Omnigraphics Inc, pg 146
On the Write Path Publishing, pg 146
Open Books Press, pg 146
Orbis Books, pg 147
Oregon State University Press, pg 147
ORO editions, pg 148
Other Press, pg 148
Our Sunday Visitor Publishing, pg 148
Richard C Owen Publishers Inc, pg 149
P & R Publishing Co, pg 149
PA Press, pg 149
Pact Press, pg 150
Palgrave Macmillan, pg 150
Palm Island Press, pg 150
Pantheon Books, pg 150
Park Place Publications, pg 152
Path Press Inc, pg 152
Pathfinder Publishing Inc, pg 152
Pelican Publishing, pg 153
Penfield Books, pg 154
Penguin Publishing Group, pg 154
Penn State University Press, pg 157
Pennsylvania Historical & Museum Commission, pg 157
Pentecostal Resources Group, pg 157
Persea Books, pg 158
Philosophical Library Inc, pg 159
Pineapple Press, pg 160
Planert Creek Press, pg 160
Plough Publishing House, pg 161
Pocol Press, pg 161
Polar Bear & Company, pg 161
Potomac Books, pg 162
The Press at California State University, Fresno, pg 163
Princeton University Press, pg 164
Progressive Press, pg 165
Prometheus Books, pg 166
ProStar Publications Inc, pg 166
Publication Consultants, pg 167
Purple House Press, pg 167
Rand-Smith Publishing, pg 169
Raven Publishing Inc, pg 172
Recorded Books Inc, an RBmedia company, pg 172
Red Hen Press, pg 172
Reference Publications Inc, pg 173
Regal House Publishing, pg 173

PUBLISHERS

Regent Press Printers & Publishers, pg 174
Regnery Publishing, pg 174
Renaissance House, pg 174
Revell, pg 174
Rio Nuevo Publishers, pg 175
River City Publishing, pg 175
Riverdale Avenue Books (RAB), pg 175
The RoadRunner Press, pg 175
Round Table Companies, pg 177
Running Press, pg 178
Rutgers University Press, pg 178
Saddleback Educational Publishing, pg 179
Sagamore Publishing LLC, pg 179
St Herman Press, pg 180
St James Press®, pg 180
St Johann Press, pg 180
St Martin's Press, LLC, pg 180
St Pauls, pg 181
Santa Monica Press LLC, pg 182
Savant Books & Publications LLC, pg 182
Schaffner Press, pg 183
Schocken Books, pg 183
Scholastic Inc, pg 184
Science & Humanities Press, pg 185
SelectBooks Inc, pg 186
Seven Stories Press, pg 186
Shadow Mountain Publishing, pg 187
Shambhala Publications Inc, pg 187
Signature Books Publishing LLC, pg 187
Simon & Schuster Audio, pg 189
SkyLight Paths® Publishing, pg 191
Soho Press Inc, pg 193
Somerset Hall Press, pg 193
Sourcebooks LLC, pg 194
Sourced Media Books, pg 195
Square One Publishers Inc, pg 196
Stanford University Press, pg 197
Star Bright Books Inc, pg 197
StarGroup International Inc, pg 197
Steerforth Press & Services, pg 198
SteinerBooks Inc, pg 198
Stone Pier Press, pg 199
Story Monsters LLC, pg 199
Strategic Book Publishing (SBP), pg 199
Strategic Media Books LLC, pg 200
Summertime Publications Inc, pg 200
Sunstone Press, pg 201
Swallow Press, pg 201
Nan A Talese, pg 202
TAN Books, pg 202
Tantor Media Inc, pg 202
Terra Nova Books, pg 204
Texas Tech University Press, pg 205
Third World Press Foundation, pg 206
Thomas Nelson, pg 206
Thorndike Press®, pg 206
The Toby Press LLC, pg 207
Todd Publications, pg 207
Trans-Atlantic Publications Inc, pg 209
Travelers' Tales, pg 209
Tughra Books, pg 210
Tumblehome Learning Inc, pg 210
Turtle Point Press, pg 210
Tuttle Publishing, pg 211
Tuxedo Press, pg 211
Twenty-First Century Books, pg 211
Twilight Times Books, pg 211
Tyndale House Publishers Inc, pg 211
Union Square & Co, pg 212
United States Holocaust Memorial Museum, pg 213
University of Alaska Press, pg 214
University of Chicago Press, pg 215
University of Delaware Press, pg 215
University of Georgia Press, pg 216
University of Illinois Press, pg 216
University of Iowa Press, pg 216
University of Louisiana at Lafayette Press, pg 217
University of Massachusetts Press, pg 217
University of Missouri Press, pg 217
University of Nevada Press, pg 218
University of New Mexico Press, pg 218
University of New Orleans Press, pg 218
The University of North Carolina Press, pg 218
University of North Texas Press, pg 218
University of Notre Dame Press, pg 219
University of Oklahoma Press, pg 219
University of Pittsburgh Press, pg 219
University of Rochester Press, pg 220
University of Tennessee Press, pg 220
The University of Utah Press, pg 220
University of Wisconsin Press, pg 221
University Press of America Inc, pg 221
University Press of Florida, pg 221
University Press of Kansas, pg 221
The University Press of Kentucky, pg 222
University Press of Mississippi, pg 222
Urim Publications, pg 223
US Government Publishing Office (GPO), pg 223
Vandamere Press, pg 223
Verso Books, pg 224
Vesuvian Books, pg 224
Vintage Books, pg 225
Visible Ink Press®, pg 225
Washington State University Press, pg 226
WaterBrook, pg 226
Watermark Publishing, pg 226
Welcome Rain Publishers LLC, pg 227
West Margin Press, pg 227
Western Reflections Publishing Co, pg 228
Westminster John Knox Press (WJK), pg 228
Wide World Publishing, pg 229
Markus Wiener Publishers Inc, pg 229
Wildflower Press, pg 229
Wiley-Blackwell, pg 229
Winters Publishing, pg 231
Wisdom Publications Inc, pg 231
Wolfman Books, pg 232
Woodrow Wilson Center Press, pg 232
WoodstockArts, pg 232
Write Stuff Enterprises LLC, pg 234
WriteLife Publishing, pg 234
Xlibris Corp, pg 234
Yale University Press, pg 235
Yard Dog Press, pg 235
YBK Publishers Inc, pg 235
YMAA Publication Center Inc, pg 235
Yotzeret Publishing, pg 236
Zest Books, pg 236
Zondervan, pg 236
Zumaya Publications LLC, pg 237

U.S. PUBLISHERS — SUBJECT INDEX

BIOLOGICAL SCIENCES

A 2 Z Press LLC, pg 1
Academic Press, pg 3
AIHA (American Industrial Hygiene Association), pg 6
AIP Publishing LLC, pg 6
American Fisheries Society, pg 9
American Press, pg 11
American Psychiatric Association Publishing, pg 11
American Society of Agricultural & Biological Engineers (ASABE), pg 12
American Society of Plant Taxonomists, pg 13
Annual Reviews, pg 14
APS PRESS, pg 16
Arbordale Publishing, pg 16
Artech House®, pg 17
ArtWrite Productions, pg 18
ASCP Press, pg 18
ASM Publishing, pg 19
AuthorHouse, pg 22
Begell House Inc Publishers, pg 27
BJU Press, pg 30
The Blackburn Press, pg 30
Brewers Publications, pg 36
Brill Inc, pg 37
Cambridge University Press, pg 39
Capstone Publishers™, pg 40
Carolina Academic Press, pg 41
Chelsea House, pg 45
Clinical and Laboratory Standards Institute (CLSI), pg 49
Cold Spring Harbor Laboratory Press, pg 50
Columbia University Press, pg 51
Cornell University Press, pg 52
Walter De Gruyter Inc, pg 58
DEStech Publications Inc, pg 59
DK, pg 60
Dordt Press, pg 60
Dover Publications Inc, pg 61
Educational Insights®, pg 64
The Electrochemical Society (ECS), pg 65
Elsevier Health Sciences, pg 65
Elsevier Inc, pg 65
Entomological Society of America, pg 67
Facts On File, pg 69
W H Freeman, pg 75
Gale, pg 75
Harvard University Press, pg 88
Houghton Mifflin Harcourt, pg 95
Illinois State Museum Society, pg 99
Island Press, pg 104
Johns Hopkins University Press, pg 106
Jones & Bartlett Learning LLC, pg 107
Kalmbach Media Co, pg 108
Krieger Publishing Co, pg 111
Lippincott Williams & Wilkins, pg 117
Logos Press, pg 119
Lorenz Educational Press, pg 120
Lucent Press, pg 121
Macmillan Reference USA™, pg 123
Marshall Cavendish Education, pg 125
Master Books®, pg 126
The McDonald & Woodward Publishing Co, pg 127
McGraw-Hill Create, pg 127
McGraw-Hill Education, pg 127
McGraw-Hill Higher Education, pg 128
Medical Physics Publishing Corp (MPP), pg 129
Milliken Publishing Co, pg 132
Morton Publishing Co, pg 134
Mountain Press Publishing Co, pg 135
National Academies Press (NAP), pg 136
National Center for Children in Poverty, pg 137
National Geographic Books, pg 137
National Science Teachers Association (NSTA), pg 138
New York Academy of Sciences (NYAS), pg 140
The New York Botanical Garden Press, pg 140
W W Norton & Company Inc, pg 143
Norwood House Press, pg 143
Oregon State University Press, pg 147
Oxford University Press USA, pg 149
Pangaea Publications, pg 150
Plunkett Research Ltd, pg 161
Princeton University Press, pg 164
Prometheus Books, pg 166
Research & Education Association (REA), pg 174
The Rockefeller University Press, pg 176
Rutgers University Press, pg 178
Saddleback Educational Publishing, pg 179
SAGE Publishing, pg 180
Science & Humanities Press, pg 185
Science, Naturally, pg 185
Sinauer Associates, pg 190
Society of Environmental Toxicology & Chemistry (SETAC), pg 192
South Dakota Historical Society Press, pg 195
Springer, pg 196
Star Publishing Co Inc, pg 197
Stipes Publishing LLC, pg 198
Strategic Book Publishing (SBP), pg 199
Tapestry Press Ltd, pg 202
Thieme Medical Publishers Inc, pg 206
University of Alaska Press, pg 214
University of Chicago Press, pg 215
University Press of Colorado, pg 221
University Science Books, pg 222
Waveland Press Inc, pg 226
Whittier Publications Inc, pg 229
Wiley-Blackwell, pg 229
John Wiley & Sons Inc, pg 230
World Scientific Publishing Co Inc, pg 233
Yale University Press, pg 235

BUSINESS

Adams Media, pg 4
Addicus Books Inc, pg 5
The AEI Press, pg 5
AICPA® & CIMA®, pg 5
Allworth Press, pg 7
American Bar Association Publishing, pg 8
The American College of Financial Services, pg 9
American Society for Quality (ASQ), pg 12
Ampersand Inc/Professional Publishing Services, pg 13
Aspatore Books, pg 19

U.S. PUBLISHERS — SUBJECT INDEX

BOOK

Association for Talent Development (ATD) Press, pg 19
Association of School Business Officials International, pg 20
Asta Publications LLC, pg 20
Atlantic Publishing Group Inc, pg 21
AuthorHouse, pg 22
Avant-Guide, pg 22
Ballinger Publishing, pg 24
Bancroft Press, pg 24
Barringer Publishing, pg 24
Baylor University Press, pg 25
Beaver's Pond Press Inc, pg 26
BenBella Books Inc, pg 27
Berkshire Publishing Group LLC, pg 28
Berrett-Koehler Publishers Inc, pg 29
Bisk Education, pg 29
BLR®—Business & Legal Resources, pg 32
Bluestocking Press, pg 33
BoardSource, pg 33
Bookhaven Press LLC, pg 34
BookLogix, pg 34
Boson Books™, pg 34
Brandylane Publishers Inc, pg 35
Nicholas Brealey Publishing, pg 36
Brick Tower Press, pg 36
Bridge Publications Inc, pg 36
Brigantine Media, pg 37
Brilliance Publishing Inc, pg 37
The Brookings Institution Press, pg 37
Brown Books Publishing Group (BBPG), pg 38
BuilderBooks, pg 38
Business Expert Press, pg 38
Business Research Services Inc, pg 38
Candid, pg 39
Capen Publishing Co Inc, pg 40
CCH, a Wolters Kluwer business, pg 42
Cengage Learning, pg 43
Center for Creative Leadership LLC, pg 43
Center for Futures Education Inc, pg 43
Chain Store Guide (CSG), pg 44
Chelsea Green Publishing Co, pg 45
China Books, pg 47
Clerisy Press, pg 49
Codhill Press, pg 50
Columbia Books & Information Services (CBIS), pg 50
Columbia University Press, pg 51
The Conference Board Inc, pg 51
Cornell University Press, pg 52
Cosimo Inc, pg 53
Council for Research in Values & Philosophy, pg 53
Crown House Publishing Co LLC, pg 56
Crown Publishing Group, pg 56
Crystal Clarity Publishers, pg 56
D&B Hoovers™, pg 57
Dharma Publishing, pg 59
DiscoverNet Publishing, pg 59
Diversion Books, pg 60
Dogwise Publishing, pg 60
Dover Publications Inc, pg 61
Dun & Bradstreet, pg 62
Dutton, pg 62
Easy Money Press, pg 63
Edward Elgar Publishing Inc, pg 65
Elsevier Inc, pg 65
M Evans & Company, pg 68
Familius, pg 69
FC&A Publishing, pg 70
Financial Times Press, pg 71
Fine Creative Media, Inc, pg 71
Fordham University Press, pg 73
Forum Publishing Co, pg 73
Foundation Press, pg 74
Frederick Fell Publishers Inc, pg 74
Gale, pg 75
Gallery Books, pg 76
Gallopade International Inc, pg 76
Gibbs Smith Publisher, pg 78
Global Training Center, pg 79
Goodheart-Willcox Publisher, pg 79
The Graduate Group/Booksellers, pg 80
Grand Central Publishing, pg 80
Green Dragon Books, pg 81
Greenleaf Book Group LLC, pg 81
Grey House Publishing Inc™, pg 81
Grove Atlantic Inc, pg 82
Hal Leonard LLC, pg 84
Hannacroix Creek Books Inc, pg 85
HarperCollins Publishers LLC, pg 86
Harvard Business Review Press, pg 87
Harvard University Press, pg 88
Hay House LLC, pg 89
Health Administration Press, pg 89
HeartMath LLC, pg 90
Homa & Sekey Books, pg 95
Hoover Institution Press, pg 95
Hospital & Healthcare Compensation Service, pg 95
Houghton Mifflin Harcourt Trade & Reference Division, pg 96
HRD Press, pg 97
Humanix Books LLC, pg 97
Hutton Publishing, pg 97
Impact Publications/Development Concepts Inc, pg 99
Industrial Press Inc, pg 100
Information Age Publishing Inc, pg 100
Information Today, Inc, pg 100
The Institutes™, pg 102
International Foundation of Employee Benefit Plans, pg 103
International Monetary Fund (IMF), Editorial & Publications Division, pg 103
International Risk Management Institute Inc, pg 103
International Wealth Success (IWS), pg 104
Joshua Tree Publishing, pg 107
Kallisti Publishing Inc, pg 108
J J Keller & Associates, Inc®, pg 108
Kennedy Information LLC, pg 108
Kogan Page, pg 111
Koho Pono LLC, pg 111
Krieger Publishing Co, pg 111
Lasaria Creative Publishing, pg 113
LearningExpress, pg 114
The Lentz Leadership Institute LLC, pg 115
Listen & Live Audio Inc, pg 117
The Little Entrepreneur, pg 118
Loft Press Inc, pg 119
Logos Press, pg 119
LRP Publications, pg 121
Macmillan Reference USA™, pg 123
Maharishi International University Press, pg 123
Management Advisory Services & Publications (MASP), pg 123
Markowski International Publishers, pg 125
McFarland, pg 127
McGraw-Hill Create, pg 127
McGraw-Hill Education, pg 127
McGraw-Hill Higher Education, pg 128
McGraw-Hill Professional Publishing Group, pg 128
R S Means from The Gordian Group, pg 128
The Edwin Mellen Press, pg 129
Merriam-Webster Inc, pg 129
Michigan State University Press (MSU Press), pg 130
Milford Books™, pg 131
Richard K Miller Associates, pg 132
Morgan James Publishing, pg 134
Multnomah, pg 135
National Book Co, pg 136
National Center For Employee Ownership (NCEO), pg 137
National Golf Foundation, pg 138
New Forums Press Inc, pg 139
The New Press, pg 140
New World Library, pg 140
New York University Press, pg 141
NOLO, pg 141
North River Press Publishing Corp, pg 142
NRP Direct, pg 144
The Oaklea Press Inc, pg 145
Olde & Oppenheim Publishers, pg 146
Omnigraphics Inc, pg 146
On the Write Path Publishing, pg 146
One On One Book Publishing/Film-Video Publications, pg 146
Open Horizons Publishing Co, pg 147
Other Press, pg 148
Oxford University Press USA, pg 149
Palgrave Macmillan, pg 150
Pantheon Books, pg 150
Paramount Market Publishing Inc, pg 151
Park Place Publications, pg 152
Pearson Business Publishing, pg 153
Pelican Publishing, pg 153
Penguin Publishing Group, pg 154
Pennsylvania State Data Center, pg 157
PennWell Books, pg 157
Peterson's, pg 158
Philosophical Library Inc, pg 159
Plunkett Research Ltd, pg 161
Portfolio, pg 162
The Press at California State University, Fresno, pg 163
Primary Research Group Inc, pg 163
Princeton University Press, pg 164
PRINTING United Alliance, pg 165
Productivity Press, pg 165
Prometheus Books, pg 166
The PRS Group Inc, pg 166
Purdue University Press, pg 167
Recorded Books Inc, an RBmedia company, pg 172
Robert D Reed Publishers, pg 173
Research & Education Association (REA), pg 174
Rodin Books, pg 176
Ronin Publishing Inc, pg 176
Ross Books, pg 177
Rothstein Associates Inc, pg 177
The Rough Notes Co Inc, pg 177
Round Table Companies, pg 177
Routledge, pg 177
Rowman & Littlefield, pg 178
Rutgers University Press, pg 178
SAGE Publishing, pg 180
St James Press®, pg 180
St Martin's Press, LLC, pg 180
Salem Press, pg 181
SAS Press, pg 182
Sasquatch Books, pg 182
Savvas Learning Co LLC, pg 183
Schiffer Publishing Ltd, pg 183
Schonfeld & Associates Inc, pg 184
Schreiber Publishing, pg 185
Science & Humanities Press, pg 185
Sentient Publications LLC, pg 186
1765 Productions, pg 186
Shadow Mountain Publishing, pg 187
Shambhala Publications Inc, pg 187
Signalman Publishing, pg 187
Simon & Schuster Audio, pg 189
SkillPath Publications, pg 190
Society for Human Resource Management (SHRM), pg 192
Sourcebooks LLC, pg 194
Sourced Media Books, pg 195
South Carolina Bar, pg 195
Stanford University Press, pg 197
Star Publishing Co Inc, pg 197
Stargazer Publishing Co, pg 197
StarGroup International Inc, pg 197
Stipes Publishing LLC, pg 198
Stone Bridge Press Inc, pg 199
Story Monsters LLC, pg 199
Storyworkz Inc, pg 199
Strategic Book Publishing (SBP), pg 199
Strategic Media Books LLC, pg 200
Stylus Publishing LLC, pg 200
Sun Publishing Company, pg 200
Tantor Media Inc, pg 202
Tapestry Press Ltd, pg 202
TarcherPerigee, pg 202
Ten Speed Press, pg 204
Todd Publications, pg 207
Tower Publishing Co, pg 208
Trans-Atlantic Publications Inc, pg 209
Turner Publishing Co LLC, pg 210
Tuttle Publishing, pg 211
Union Square & Co, pg 212
University of Chicago Press, pg 215
University of Iowa Press, pg 216
University of North Texas Press, pg 218
University Press of America Inc, pg 221
University Press of Mississippi, pg 222
University Publishing House, pg 222
US Government Publishing Office (GPO), pg 223
Vault.com Inc, pg 224
Vernon Press, pg 224
WaterBrook, pg 226
Watermark Publishing, pg 226
Wheatherstone Press, pg 228
Wiley-Blackwell, pg 229
John Wiley & Sons Inc, pg 230
John Wiley & Sons Inc Global Education, pg 230
John Wiley & Sons Inc Professional Development, pg 230
William Carey Publishing, pg 230
Williams & Company Book Publishers, pg 230
Windsor Books, pg 230
Wisconsin Department of Public Instruction, pg 231
Wolters Kluwer Law & Business, pg 232
Wolters Kluwer US Corp, pg 232
Workman Publishing, pg 232
World Bank Publications, pg 233
World Trade Press LLC, pg 234
Write Stuff Enterprises LLC, pg 234
Xlibris Corp, pg 234
XML Press, pg 235
Yale University Press, pg 235
Zondervan, pg 236

CAREER DEVELOPMENT

Academic Press, pg 3
Adams Media, pg 4
ALA Neal-Schuman, pg 6
American Correctional Association, pg 9
American Counseling Association (ACA), pg 9
AOTA Press, pg 14
APH Press, pg 15
Association for Talent Development (ATD) Press, pg 19
Asta Publications LLC, pg 20
Atlantic Publishing Group Inc, pg 21
AuthorHouse, pg 22
Barringer Publishing, pg 24
Berrett-Koehler Publishers Inc, pg 29
Bisk Education, pg 29
Book Marketing Works LLC, pg 33
Bookhaven Press LLC, pg 34
BookLogix, pg 34
Breakthrough Publications Inc, pg 36
Nicholas Brealey Publishing, pg 36
Brilliance Publishing Inc, pg 37
Brown Books Publishing Group (BBPG), pg 38
The Bureau for At-Risk Youth, pg 38
Business Expert Press, pg 38
Capstone Publishers™, pg 40
Cengage Learning, pg 43
Center for Creative Leadership LLC, pg 43
Crown House Publishing Co LLC, pg 56
D&B Hoovers™, pg 57
Dogwise Publishing, pg 60
Elsevier Health Sciences, pg 65
Fairchild Books, pg 69
Ferguson Publishing, pg 71
Fire Engineering Books & Videos, pg 72
Gale, pg 75
Gifted Unlimited LLC, pg 78
Goodheart-Willcox Publisher, pg 79
The Graduate Group/Booksellers, pg 80
Greenleaf Book Group LLC, pg 81
Hal Leonard LLC, pg 84
Harvard Business Review Press, pg 87
Health Administration Press, pg 89
Her Own Words LLC, pg 91
Humanix Books LLC, pg 97
Impact Publications/Development Concepts Inc, pg 99
Interweave Press LLC, pg 104
JIST Publishing, pg 106
Kallisti Publishing Inc, pg 108
Kennedy Information LLC, pg 108
Kogan Page, pg 111
Koho Pono LLC, pg 111
LAMA Books, pg 112
Law School Admission Council (LSAC), pg 113
LearningExpress, pg 114
Limelight Editions, pg 117
Living Language, pg 119
Looseleaf Law Publications Inc, pg 120
Macmillan Reference USA™, pg 123
Marine Techniques Publishing, pg 125
Mason Crest Publishers, pg 126
McGraw-Hill Higher Education, pg 128
McGraw-Hill School Education Group, pg 128
Milady, pg 131
Milford Books™, pg 131
Morgan James Publishing, pg 134
National Braille Press, pg 137
National Geographic Learning, pg 138
National Learning Corp, pg 138
National Resource Center for Youth Services, pg 138
Naval Institute Press, pg 139
Nursesbooks.org, The Publishing Program of ANA, pg 144
On the Write Path Publishing, pg 146
Peterson's, pg 158
Plunkett Research Ltd, pg 161
Portfolio, pg 162
PPI, A Kaplan Company, pg 162
Psychological Assessment Resources Inc (PAR), pg 166
Ronin Publishing Inc, pg 176
The Rosen Publishing Group Inc, pg 177
Round Table Companies, pg 177
SAGE Publishing, pg 180
Salem Press, pg 181
Savvas Learning Co LLC, pg 183
Schreiber Publishing, pg 185
Signalman Publishing, pg 187
Society for Human Resource Management (SHRM), pg 192
Sourcebooks LLC, pg 194
Stellar Publishing, pg 198
Story Monsters LLC, pg 199
Strategic Book Publishing (SBP), pg 199
Tantor Media Inc, pg 202
TarcherPerigee, pg 202
Ten Speed Press, pg 204
US Government Publishing Office (GPO), pg 223
Vault.com Inc, pg 224
Voyager Sopris Learning Inc, pg 225
West Academic, pg 227
Whole Person Associates Inc, pg 229
Wisconsin Department of Public Instruction, pg 231
World Bank Publications, pg 233
Writer's AudioShop, pg 234
Xlibris Corp, pg 234
Zondervan, pg 236

CHEMISTRY, CHEMICAL ENGINEERING

Academic Press, pg 3
ACS Publications, pg 4
AIHA (American Industrial Hygiene Association), pg 6
AIP Publishing LLC, pg 6
The American Ceramic Society, pg 9
American Institute of Chemical Engineers (AIChE), pg 10
American Press, pg 11
American Society for Quality (ASQ), pg 12
Annual Reviews, pg 14
ASTM International, pg 20
AuthorHouse, pg 22
Begell House Inc Publishers, pg 27
BJU Press, pg 30
Cengage Learning, pg 43
Cereals & Grains Association, pg 44
Clinical and Laboratory Standards Institute (CLSI), pg 49
CRC Press, pg 55
Walter De Gruyter Inc, pg 58
DEStech Publications Inc, pg 59
Dover Publications Inc, pg 61
EDC Publishing, pg 63
The Electrochemical Society (ECS), pg 65
Elsevier Health Sciences, pg 65
Elsevier Inc, pg 65
Enslow Publishing LLC, pg 66
Fire Engineering Books & Videos, pg 72
W H Freeman, pg 75
Gale, pg 75
Hanser Publications LLC, pg 85
Houghton Mifflin Harcourt, pg 95
International Society of Automation (ISA), pg 103
Jones & Bartlett Learning LLC, pg 107
Krieger Publishing Co, pg 111
Logos Press, pg 119
Macmillan Learning, pg 123
Macmillan Reference USA™, pg 123
Master Books®, pg 126
Materials Research Society, pg 126
McGraw-Hill Create, pg 127
McGraw-Hill Education, pg 127
McGraw-Hill Higher Education, pg 128
McGraw-Hill School Education Group, pg 128
Milliken Publishing Co, pg 132
Morton Publishing Co, pg 134
NACE International, pg 136
National Academies Press (NAP), pg 136
National Science Teachers Association (NSTA), pg 138
New York Academy of Sciences (NYAS), pg 140
Nova Science Publishers Inc, pg 144
Oxford University Press USA, pg 149
PennWell Books, pg 157
Plunkett Research Ltd, pg 161
PPI, A Kaplan Company, pg 162
Prometheus Books, pg 166
Research & Education Association (REA), pg 174
SAGE Publishing, pg 180
Science History Publications USA Inc, pg 185
Society of Environmental Toxicology & Chemistry (SETAC), pg 192
Springer, pg 196
Stipes Publishing LLC, pg 198
Strategic Book Publishing (SBP), pg 199
United States Pharmacopeia (USP), pg 213
University Science Books, pg 222
US Government Publishing Office (GPO), pg 223
Waveland Press Inc, pg 226
Whittier Publications Inc, pg 229
John Wiley & Sons Inc, pg 230
John Wiley & Sons Inc Global Education, pg 230
John Wiley & Sons Inc Professional Development, pg 230

CHILD CARE & DEVELOPMENT

Adams Media, pg 4
American Academy of Pediatrics, pg 8
American Counseling Association (ACA), pg 9
American Girl Publishing, pg 10
APH Press, pg 15
Atlantic Publishing Group Inc, pg 21
AuthorHouse, pg 22
Baker Books, pg 23
Barringer Publishing, pg 24
Barrytown/Station Hill Press, pg 24
Beaver's Pond Press Inc, pg 26
Biographical Publishing Co, pg 29
Boson Books™, pg 34
Boys Town Press, pg 35
Bridge Logos Inc, pg 36
Paul H Brookes Publishing Co Inc, pg 37
Brown Books Publishing Group (BBPG), pg 38
Bull Publishing Co, pg 38
The Bureau for At-Risk Youth, pg 38
Camino Books Inc, pg 39
Cedar Grove Publishing, pg 43
Cengage Learning, pg 43
Central Recovery Press (CRP), pg 44
Charles Press Publishers, pg 45
Chicago Review Press, pg 46
Cider Mill Press Book Publishers LLC, pg 48
Cleis Press, pg 49
Consumer Press, pg 52
Cornerstone Book Publishers, pg 53
Council for Exceptional Children (CEC), pg 53
DK, pg 60
Dreamscape Media LLC, pg 62
East West Discovery Press, pg 63
EDC Publishing, pg 63
Editorial Portavoz, pg 64
Emerald Books, pg 66
M Evans & Company, pg 68
The Experiment, pg 68
Fair Winds Press, pg 69
Familius, pg 69
Fine Creative Media, Inc, pg 71
Focus on the Family, pg 73
Free Spirit Publishing Inc, pg 74
Gale, pg 75
Gallaudet University Press, pg 76
Gifted Unlimited LLC, pg 78
Goodheart-Willcox Publisher, pg 79
Green Dragon Books, pg 81
Greenleaf Book Group LLC, pg 81
Gryphon House Inc, pg 82
The Guilford Press, pg 82
HarperCollins Publishers LLC, pg 86
Harvard Common Press, pg 87
Hatherleigh Press Ltd, pg 88
Hazy Dell Press, pg 89
HeartMath LLC, pg 90
Herald Press, pg 91
Immedium, pg 99
Inner Traditions International Ltd, pg 101
Inter-University Consortium for Political & Social Research (ICPSR), pg 102
Kidsbooks® Publishing, pg 109
Jessica Kingsley Publishers Inc, pg 110
THE Learning Connection®, pg 113
Life Cycle Books, pg 116
The Little Entrepreneur, pg 118
LRP Publications, pg 121
Macmillan Reference USA™, pg 123
Maren Green Publishing Inc, pg 125
Master Books®, pg 126
McGraw-Hill Education, pg 127
McGraw-Hill School Education Group, pg 128
National Braille Press, pg 137

National Center for Children in Poverty, pg 137
National Resource Center for Youth Services, pg 138
New World Library, pg 140
North Atlantic Books (NAB), pg 142
Odyssey Books, pg 145
On the Write Path Publishing, pg 146
P & R Publishing Co, pg 149
Pace University Press, pg 149
Parenting Press, pg 151
Peachtree Publishing Co Inc, pg 153
Penguin Publishing Group, pg 154
Philosophical Library Inc, pg 159
Platypus Media LLC, pg 160
Plough Publishing House, pg 161
PRO-ED Inc, pg 165
Prometheus Books, pg 166
Psychological Assessment Resources Inc (PAR), pg 166
Quarto Publishing Group USA Inc, pg 168
Rational Island Publishers, pg 171
Redleaf Press®, pg 173
Revell, pg 174
Rising Sun Publishing, pg 175
Rocky Pond Books, pg 176
Round Table Companies, pg 177
Routledge, pg 177
SAGE Publishing, pg 180
St Pauls, pg 181
Sentient Publications LLC, pg 186
Shadow Mountain Publishing, pg 187
Solano Press Books, pg 193
Sourcebooks LLC, pg 194
Square One Publishers Inc, pg 196
SteinerBooks Inc, pg 198
STM Learning Inc, pg 199
Story Monsters LLC, pg 199
Strategic Book Publishing (SBP), pg 199
Stress Free Kids®, pg 200
Tantor Media Inc, pg 202
Teachers College Press, pg 203
Teaching Strategies LLC, pg 204
Ten Speed Press, pg 204
Third World Press Foundation, pg 206
Torah Umesorah Publications, pg 208
Tortuga Press, pg 208
Tyndale House Publishers Inc, pg 211
US Government Publishing Office (GPO), pg 223
Voyager Sopris Learning Inc, pg 225
WaterBrook, pg 226
Wheatherstone Press, pg 228
Wisconsin Department of Public Instruction, pg 231
Woodbine House, pg 232
Workman Publishing, pg 232
World Bank Publications, pg 233
Xist Publishing, pg 234
Xlibris Corp, pg 234
Yale University Press, pg 235
Zondervan, pg 236

CIVIL ENGINEERING

American Academy of Environmental Engineers & Scientists®, pg 8
American Public Works Association (APWA), pg 12
American Society of Civil Engineers (ASCE), pg 12
American Water Works Association (AWWA), pg 13
ASTM International, pg 20
AuthorHouse, pg 22
Begell House Inc Publishers, pg 27
BNi Building News, pg 33
Cengage Learning, pg 43
DEStech Publications Inc, pg 59
Gale, pg 75
Krieger Publishing Co, pg 111
Macmillan Reference USA™, pg 123
McGraw-Hill Higher Education, pg 128
R S Means from The Gordian Group, pg 128
NACE International, pg 136
Plunkett Research Ltd, pg 161
PPI, A Kaplan Company, pg 162
PSMJ Resources Inc, pg 166
Stylus Publishing LLC, pg 200
Transportation Research Board (TRB), pg 209
US Government Publishing Office (GPO), pg 223
Water Resources Publications LLC, pg 226
Waveland Press Inc, pg 226

COMMUNICATIONS

American Press, pg 11
Artech House®, pg 17
Association for Talent Development (ATD) Press, pg 19
AuthorHouse, pg 22
Avant-Guide, pg 22
Barringer Publishing, pg 24
Bedford/St Martin's, pg 26
John Benjamins Publishing Co, pg 28
Bloomsbury Academic, pg 31
BookLogix, pg 34
Brown Books Publishing Group (BBPG), pg 38
The Catholic Health Association of the United States, pg 42
Cengage Learning, pg 43
Center for Strategic & International Studies (CSIS), pg 44
Cognizant Communication Corp, pg 50
Walter De Gruyter Inc, pg 58
DiscoverNet Publishing, pg 59
Elsevier Inc, pg 65
Fire Engineering Books & Videos, pg 72
Fordham University Press, pg 73
Gale, pg 75
Gingko Press Inc, pg 78
Goodheart-Willcox Publisher, pg 79
Greenleaf Book Group LLC, pg 81
Hamilton Books, pg 84
Hannacroix Creek Books Inc, pg 85
Harvard Business Review Press, pg 87
Hudson Institute, pg 97
IEEE Press, pg 98
IET USA Inc, pg 98
The International Institute of Islamic Thought, pg 103
International Literacy Association (ILA), pg 103
Kogan Page, pg 111
Peter Lang Publishing Inc, pg 112
Lexington Books, pg 115
Libraries Unlimited, pg 116
Macmillan Learning, pg 123
Macmillan Reference USA™, pg 123
McGraw-Hill Higher Education, pg 128
The Edwin Mellen Press, pg 129
Pearson Business Publishing, pg 153
Penn State University Press, pg 157
PennWell Books, pg 157
Primary Research Group Inc, pg 163
PRINTING United Alliance, pg 165
RAND Corp, pg 169
Ross Books, pg 177
Routledge, pg 177
Rowman & Littlefield, pg 178
Rutgers University Press, pg 178
SAGE Publishing, pg 180
Southern Illinois University Press, pg 195
SPIE, pg 196
Story Monsters LLC, pg 199
Strategic Book Publishing (SBP), pg 199
Syracuse University Press, pg 201
Tantor Media Inc, pg 202
Tapestry Press Ltd, pg 202
Temple University Press, pg 204
University of Alabama Press, pg 214
University of Illinois Press, pg 216
University of Massachusetts Press, pg 217
University of South Carolina Press, pg 220
University Press of America Inc, pg 221
University Press of Mississippi, pg 222
US Government Publishing Office (GPO), pg 223
Vernon Press, pg 224
Waveland Press Inc, pg 226
Wisconsin Department of Public Instruction, pg 231
World Bank Publications, pg 233
Write Stuff Enterprises LLC, pg 234
Xlibris Corp, pg 234
Zondervan, pg 236

COMPUTER SCIENCE

A-R Editions Inc, pg 1
AAAI Press, pg 1
Academic Press, pg 3
ACM Books, pg 4
Adams & Ambrose Publishing, pg 4
Annual Reviews, pg 14
Artech House®, pg 17
Association for Information Science & Technology (ASIS&T), pg 19
AuthorHouse, pg 22
Beaver's Pond Press Inc, pg 26
Cambridge University Press, pg 39
Carolina Academic Press, pg 41
Cengage Learning, pg 43
Charles River Media, pg 45
CRC Press, pg 55
CSLI Publications, pg 56
Walter De Gruyter Inc, pg 58
DEStech Publications Inc, pg 59
DiscoverNet Publishing, pg 59
Dover Publications Inc, pg 61
Elsevier Inc, pg 65
FC&A Publishing, pg 70
Franklin, Beedle & Associates Inc, pg 74
Gale, pg 75
Goodheart-Willcox Publisher, pg 79
Greenleaf Book Group LLC, pg 81
IEEE Computer Society, pg 98
IEEE Press, pg 98
IET USA Inc, pg 98
Industrial Press Inc, pg 100
Information Today, Inc, pg 100
Jones & Bartlett Learning LLC, pg 107
Macmillan Reference USA™, pg 123
Management Advisory Services & Publications (MASP), pg 123
Manning Publications Co, pg 124
Materials Research Society, pg 126
The Mathematical Association of America, pg 127
McGraw-Hill Education, pg 127
McGraw-Hill Higher Education, pg 128
McGraw-Hill School Education Group, pg 128
Mike Murach & Associates Inc, pg 131
The MIT Press, pg 132
Morgan Kaufmann, pg 134
Morton Publishing Co, pg 134
National Academies Press (NAP), pg 136
National Braille Press, pg 137
No Starch Press, pg 141
W W Norton & Company Inc, pg 143
Nova Science Publishers Inc, pg 144
O'Reilly Media Inc, pg 147
ORO editions, pg 148
Oxford University Press USA, pg 149
Peachpit Press, pg 153
Pearson Business Publishing, pg 153
Plunkett Research Ltd, pg 161
Research & Education Association (REA), pg 174
Ross Books, pg 177
SAS Press, pg 182
SIL International, pg 188
Society for Industrial & Applied Mathematics, pg 192
Springer, pg 196
Stipes Publishing LLC, pg 198
Strategic Book Publishing (SBP), pg 199
Stylus Publishing LLC, pg 200
Taylor & Francis Inc, pg 203
Todd Publications, pg 207
TotalRecall Publications Inc, pg 208
Tumblehome Learning Inc, pg 210
US Government Publishing Office (GPO), pg 223
Wiley-Blackwell, pg 229
John Wiley & Sons Inc, pg 230
Wisconsin Department of Public Instruction, pg 231
World Scientific Publishing Co Inc, pg 233
Xlibris Corp, pg 234
XML Press, pg 235

COMPUTERS

Apress Media LLC, pg 15
ASCP Press, pg 18
AuthorHouse, pg 22
Bisk Education, pg 29
Cengage Learning, pg 43
Gale, pg 75
IEEE Press, pg 98
Industrial Press Inc, pg 100
Lawyers & Judges Publishing Co Inc, pg 113
Lectorum Publications Inc, pg 114
Little, Brown and Company, pg 118
Macmillan Reference USA™, pg 123
Management Advisory Services & Publications (MASP), pg 123
Mike Murach & Associates Inc, pg 131
Moonshine Cove Publishing LLC, pg 134
No Starch Press, pg 141

PUBLISHERS

W W Norton & Company Inc, pg 143
O'Reilly Media Inc, pg 147
Plunkett Research Ltd, pg 161
Ross Books, pg 177
Science & Humanities Press, pg 185
Strategic Book Publishing (SBP), pg 199
SYBEX, pg 201
US Government Publishing Office (GPO), pg 223
Wiley-Blackwell, pg 229
John Wiley & Sons Inc Global Education, pg 230
John Wiley & Sons Inc Professional Development, pg 230

COOKERY

Abbeville Publishing Group, pg 2
Adams Media, pg 4
AdventureKEEN, pg 5
AK Press, pg 6
American Carriage House Publishing (ACHP), pg 8
American Diabetes Association, pg 9
American Girl Publishing, pg 10
Sara Anderson Children's Books, pg 13
Andrews McMeel Publishing LLC, pg 14
Applewood Books, pg 15
Art of Living, PrimaMedia Inc, pg 17
Asta Publications LLC, pg 20
Atlantic Publishing Group Inc, pg 21
AuthorHouse, pg 22
Avery, pg 23
Avery Color Studios, pg 23
Barrytown/Station Hill Press, pg 24
Bartleby Press, pg 24
Beaver's Pond Press Inc, pg 26
Berkshire Publishing Group LLC, pg 28
Bess Press Inc, pg 29
Bhaktivedanta Book Trust (BBT), pg 29
Biographical Publishing Co, pg 29
Blair, pg 30
Book Sales, pg 33
BookLogix, pg 34
BPC, pg 35
Brewers Publications, pg 36
Brick Tower Press, pg 36
Brown Books Publishing Group (BBPG), pg 38
Burford Books, pg 38
Camino Books Inc, pg 39
Capen Publishing Co Inc, pg 40
Carlisle Press - Walnut Creek, pg 40
Caxton Press, pg 42
Cedar Fort Inc, pg 43
Cedar Tree Books, pg 43
Cereals & Grains Association, pg 44
Charlesbridge Publishing Inc, pg 45
Chelsea Green Publishing Co, pg 45
China Books, pg 47
Chronicle Books LLC, pg 47
Cider Mill Press Book Publishers LLC, pg 48
Clear Light Publishers, pg 49
Cleis Press, pg 49
Cornell Maritime Press, pg 52
Countryman Press, pg 54
Crabtree Publishing Co, pg 54
Dharma Publishing, pg 59
Diversion Books, pg 60
DK, pg 60
The Donning Company Publishers, pg 60

Dover Publications Inc, pg 61
Down East Books, pg 61
Dutton, pg 62
Eakin Press, pg 62
EDC Publishing, pg 63
Editorial de la Universidad de Puerto Rico, pg 63
Epicenter Press, pg 67
M Evans & Company, pg 68
The Experiment, pg 68
Fair Winds Press, pg 69
Familius, pg 69
Farcountry Press, pg 69
Father & Son Publishing Inc, pg 70
Fine Creative Media, Inc, pg 71
Fox Chapel Publishing Co Inc, pg 74
Frederick Fell Publishers Inc, pg 74
Gale, pg 75
Gallopade International Inc, pg 76
Gibbs Smith Publisher, pg 78
Glitterati Inc, pg 78
The Globe Pequot Press, pg 79
Godine, pg 79
Golden West Cookbooks, pg 79
Goodheart-Willcox Publisher, pg 79
Goose River Press, pg 79
Greenleaf Book Group LLC, pg 81
HarperCollins Children's Books, pg 85
HarperCollins Publishers LLC, pg 86
Harvard Common Press, pg 87
Hatherleigh Press Ltd, pg 88
Health Communications Inc, pg 89
Hearts 'n Tummies Cookbook Co, pg 90
Herald Press, pg 91
Hippocrene Books Inc, pg 92
Hollym International Corp, pg 94
Homestead Publishing, pg 95
Houghton Mifflin Harcourt, pg 95
Houghton Mifflin Harcourt Trade & Reference Division, pg 96
Hutton Publishing, pg 97
Ibex Publishers, pg 98
Inner Traditions International Ltd, pg 101
Interlink Publishing Group Inc, pg 102
International Book Centre Inc, pg 102
Islandport Press, pg 105
Just World Books LLC, pg 107
Kazi Publications Inc, pg 108
Kiva Publishing Inc, pg 110
Klutz®, pg 110
Alfred A Knopf, pg 110
Kodansha USA Inc, pg 110
Krause Publications Inc, pg 111
Lake Superior Publishing LLC, pg 112
Landauer Publishing, pg 112
Larson Publications, pg 113
Laughing Elephant Books, pg 113
Leaf Storm Press, pg 113
Lectorum Publications Inc, pg 114
Leisure Arts Inc, pg 114
Lerner Publications, pg 115
Little, Brown and Company, pg 118
Louisiana State University Press, pg 120
The Lyons Press, pg 121
Mage Publishers Inc, pg 123
The Magni Co, pg 123
Mazda Publishers Inc, pg 127
Mighty Media Press, pg 131
Modern Memoirs Inc, pg 133
Multnomah, pg 135
Museum of New Mexico Press, pg 135
Mutual Publishing LLC, pg 136
Nataraj Books, pg 136

National Braille Press, pg 137
North Atlantic Books (NAB), pg 142
North Point Press, pg 142
W W Norton & Company Inc, pg 143
Ocean Tree Books, pg 145
On the Write Path Publishing, pg 146
Other Press, pg 148
Parallax Press, pg 151
Pearson Business Publishing, pg 153
Pelican Publishing, pg 153
Penfield Books, pg 154
Penguin Publishing Group, pg 154
Peter Pauper Press, Inc, pg 158
Phaidon, pg 159
Clarkson Potter, pg 162
Publications International Ltd (PIL), pg 167
Quail Ridge Press (QRP), pg 168
Quarto Publishing Group USA Inc, pg 168
Quirk Books, pg 168
Quixote Press, pg 169
Radix Press, pg 169
Reader's Digest Trade Publishing, pg 172
Robert D Reed Publishers, pg 173
Rio Nuevo Publishers, pg 175
Rizzoli International Publications Inc, pg 175
Ross Books, pg 177
St Johann Press, pg 180
St Martin's Press, LLC, pg 180
St Nectarios Press, pg 181
Sasquatch Books, pg 182
Schiffer Publishing Ltd, pg 183
Schocken Books, pg 183
Shadow Mountain Publishing, pg 187
Shambhala Publications Inc, pg 187
Shepard Publications, pg 187
Soho Press Inc, pg 193
Sourcebooks LLC, pg 194
Square One Publishers Inc, pg 196
StarGroup International Inc, pg 197
SteinerBooks Inc, pg 198
Stewart, Tabori & Chang, pg 198
Stone Pier Press, pg 199
Story Monsters LLC, pg 199
Strategic Book Publishing (SBP), pg 199
Surrey Books, pg 201
Nan A Talese, pg 202
Tantor Media Inc, pg 202
TarcherPerigee, pg 202
Taunton Books, pg 203
Ten Speed Press, pg 204
Texas Tech University Press, pg 205
Turner Publishing Co LLC, pg 210
Tuttle Publishing, pg 211
Ulysses Press, pg 212
Union Square & Co, pg 212
Universe Publishing, pg 214
University of Iowa Press, pg 216
The University of North Carolina Press, pg 218
University of North Texas Press, pg 218
University Press of Mississippi, pg 222
Urim Publications, pg 223
Washington State University Press, pg 226
WaterBrook, pg 226
Watermark Publishing, pg 226
Welcome Books, pg 227
West Margin Press, pg 227
Wide World Publishing, pg 229
Wilderness Adventures Press Inc, pg 229

U.S. PUBLISHERS — SUBJECT INDEX

John Wiley & Sons Inc, pg 230
John Wiley & Sons Inc Global Education, pg 230
John Wiley & Sons Inc Professional Development, pg 230
Willow Creek Press, pg 230
Winters Publishing, pg 231
Wisconsin Department of Public Instruction, pg 231
Workman Publishing, pg 232
World Trade Press LLC, pg 234
Xlibris Corp, pg 234
Zest Books, pg 236

CRAFTS, GAMES, HOBBIES

A 2 Z Press LLC, pg 1
Abbeville Publishing Group, pg 2
ABDO, pg 2
ACC Art Books, pg 3
Adams Media, pg 4
Allworth Press, pg 7
The American Ceramic Society, pg 9
American Girl Publishing, pg 10
American Quilter's Society (AQS), pg 12
Asta Publications LLC, pg 20
Astragal Press, pg 20
Atlantic Publishing Group Inc, pg 21
AuthorHouse, pg 22
Baker Books, pg 23
Black Rabbit Books, pg 30
The Blackburn Press, pg 30
Book Sales, pg 33
BookLogix, pg 34
BuilderBooks, pg 38
Burford Books, pg 38
C&T Publishing Inc, pg 40
Capstone Publishers™, pg 40
Cardoza Publishing, pg 40
Charlesbridge Publishing Inc, pg 45
Child's Play® Inc, pg 46
The Child's World Inc, pg 46
China Books, pg 47
Chronicle Books LLC, pg 47
Cider Mill Press Book Publishers LLC, pg 48
Cleis Press, pg 49
Cornell Maritime Press, pg 52
Countryman Press, pg 54
Crabtree Publishing Co, pg 54
Creative Homeowner, pg 55
Dark Horse Comics, pg 57
DK, pg 60
Dover Publications Inc, pg 61
Down East Books, pg 61
EDC Publishing, pg 63
Educational Insights®, pg 64
Edupress Inc, pg 64
Enslow Publishing LLC, pg 66
Evan-Moor Educational Publishers, pg 68
M Evans & Company, pg 68
Everything Goes Media LLC, pg 68
The Experiment, pg 68
Fair Winds Press, pg 69
Familius, pg 69
Walter Foster Publishing, pg 74
Fox Chapel Publishing Co Inc, pg 74
Frederick Fell Publishers Inc, pg 74
GemStone Press, pg 77
Gingko Press Inc, pg 78
Goodheart-Willcox Publisher, pg 79
Greenleaf Book Group LLC, pg 81
Group Publishing Inc, pg 82
Highlights for Children Inc, pg 92
Horizon Publishers & Distributors Inc, pg 95
Houghton Mifflin Harcourt, pg 95

289

Huntington Press Publishing, pg 97
Idyll Arbor Inc, pg 98
Interweave Press LLC, pg 104
Kamehameha Publishing, pg 108
Kiva Publishing Inc, pg 110
Klutz®, pg 110
Kodansha USA Inc, pg 110
Krause Publications Inc, pg 111
Kumon Publishing North America Inc (KPNA), pg 112
Landauer Publishing, pg 112
Leisure Arts Inc, pg 114
Lerner Publications, pg 115
Libraries Unlimited, pg 116
Light-Beams Publishing, pg 116
Linden Publishing Co Inc, pg 117
Little, Brown and Company, pg 118
Mighty Media Press, pg 131
Mitchell Lane Publishers Inc, pg 133
National Braille Press, pg 137
Norwood House Press, pg 143
PA Press, pg 149
Palladium Books Inc, pg 150
Penfield Books, pg 154
Penguin Publishing Group, pg 154
Pentecostal Resources Group, pg 157
Peter Pauper Press, Inc, pg 158
Clarkson Potter, pg 162
Primary Research Group Inc, pg 163
Quarto Publishing Group USA Inc, pg 168
Quirk Books, pg 168
Random House Reference/Random House Puzzles & Games, pg 171
Reader's Digest Trade Publishing, pg 172
Reference Publications Inc, pg 173
Ross Books, pg 177
Running Press, pg 178
St Johann Press, pg 180
St Martin's Press, LLC, pg 180
Schiffer Publishing Ltd, pg 183
Scholastic Inc, pg 184
Shambhala Publications Inc, pg 187
Shepard Publications, pg 187
Sky Pony Press, pg 191
SkyLight Paths® Publishing, pg 191
Sourcebooks LLC, pg 194
Stackpole Books, pg 196
Stewart, Tabori & Chang, pg 198
Stone Bridge Press Inc, pg 199
Strategic Book Publishing (SBP), pg 199
Sunstone Press, pg 201
Tantor Media Inc, pg 202
Taunton Books, pg 203
Ten Speed Press, pg 204
Thames & Hudson, pg 205
Trafalgar Square Books, pg 208
Tuttle Publishing, pg 211
Ulysses Press, pg 212
Union Square & Co, pg 212
University Press of Mississippi, pg 222
University Publishing House, pg 222
US Games Systems Inc, pg 223
Vesuvian Books, pg 224
Watson-Guptill, pg 226
Wellington Press, pg 227
West Margin Press, pg 227
Workman Publishing, pg 232
Xlibris Corp, pg 234
Zest Books, pg 236

CRIMINOLOGY

Academica Press, pg 3
Akashic Books, pg 6
American Correctional Association, pg 9
Annual Reviews, pg 14
AuthorHouse, pg 22
Authorlink® Press, pg 22
Brown Books Publishing Group (BBPG), pg 38
Carolina Academic Press, pg 41
Cengage Learning, pg 43
Charles Press Publishers, pg 45
Encounter Books, pg 66
Facts On File, pg 69
Fire Engineering Books & Videos, pg 72
Gale, pg 75
Global Authors Publications (GAP), pg 78
Goose River Press, pg 79
Greenhaven Publishing, pg 81
William S Hein & Co Inc, pg 90
Institute of Police Technology & Management (IPTM), pg 102
Inter-University Consortium for Political & Social Research (ICPSR), pg 102
Lawyers & Judges Publishing Co Inc, pg 113
Lexington Books, pg 115
Looseleaf Law Publications Inc, pg 120
Lucent Press, pg 121
Macmillan Reference USA™, pg 123
Mason Crest Publishers, pg 126
McGraw-Hill Higher Education, pg 128
McGraw-Hill School Education Group, pg 128
The Edwin Mellen Press, pg 129
National Academies Press (NAP), pg 136
New York University Press, pg 141
Oxford University Press USA, pg 149
Pearson Business Publishing, pg 153
Philosophical Library Inc, pg 159
Police Executive Research Forum, pg 162
Prometheus Books, pg 166
RAND Corp, pg 169
Lynne Rienner Publishers Inc, pg 174
The RoadRunner Press, pg 175
Routledge, pg 177
Rutgers University Press, pg 178
SAGE Publishing, pg 180
Southern Illinois University Press, pg 195
Stanford University Press, pg 197
Stipes Publishing LLC, pg 198
STM Learning Inc, pg 199
Strategic Book Publishing (SBP), pg 199
Strategic Media Books LLC, pg 200
Tantor Media Inc, pg 202
Temple University Press, pg 204
Third World Press Foundation, pg 206
Charles C Thomas Publisher Ltd, pg 206
University of North Texas Press, pg 218
University Press of America Inc, pg 221
Waveland Press Inc, pg 226
Eliot Werner Publications Inc, pg 227
John Wiley & Sons Inc Global Education, pg 230
John Wiley & Sons Inc Professional Development, pg 230
Wyndham Hall Press, pg 234
Xlibris Corp, pg 234
Yale University Press, pg 235

DEVELOPING COUNTRIES

Africa World Press Inc, pg 5
Algora Publishing, pg 7
Amakella Publishing, pg 7
AuthorHouse, pg 22
Berghahn Books, pg 28
Black Rabbit Books, pg 30
Brown Books Publishing Group (BBPG), pg 38
Carolina Academic Press, pg 41
China Books, pg 47
Clarity Press Inc, pg 49
Continental AfrikaPublishers, pg 52
Cornell University Press, pg 52
Council for Research in Values & Philosophy, pg 53
Edward Elgar Publishing Inc, pg 65
Father & Son Publishing Inc, pg 70
Gale, pg 75
Hatherleigh Press Ltd, pg 88
IBFD North America Inc (International Bureau of Fiscal Documentation), pg 98
Inter-American Development Bank, pg 102
International Food Policy Research Institute, pg 103
The International Institute of Islamic Thought, pg 103
International Monetary Fund (IMF), Editorial & Publications Division, pg 103
Jhpiego, pg 106
Kumarian Press, pg 112
Lexington Books, pg 115
Macmillan Reference USA™, pg 123
Management Sciences for Health, pg 123
The Edwin Mellen Press, pg 129
The Mongolia Society Inc, pg 133
Monthly Review Press, pg 134
Ohio University Press, pg 145
Orbis Books, pg 147
ORO editions, pg 148
Palgrave Macmillan, pg 150
Pangaea Publications, pg 150
Primary Research Group Inc, pg 163
Rational Island Publishers, pg 171
The Red Sea Press Inc, pg 173
Reference Publications Inc, pg 173
Lynne Rienner Publishers Inc, pg 174
Routledge, pg 177
Rutgers University Press, pg 178
SAGE Publishing, pg 180
Strategic Book Publishing (SBP), pg 199
Temple University Press, pg 204
United States Institute of Peace Press, pg 213
University of Chicago Press, pg 215
University of Rochester Press, pg 220
University Press of Florida, pg 221
Wheatherstone Press, pg 228
Markus Wiener Publishers Inc, pg 229
William Carey Publishing, pg 230
Woodrow Wilson Center Press, pg 232
World Citizens, pg 233
Xlibris Corp, pg 234
Yale University Press, pg 235

DISABILITY, SPECIAL NEEDS

Akashic Books, pg 6
American Carriage House Publishing (ACHP), pg 8
AOTA Press, pg 14
APH Press, pg 15
AuthorHouse, pg 22
Beaver's Pond Press Inc, pg 26
Brandylane Publishers Inc, pg 35
Paul H Brookes Publishing Co Inc, pg 37
Brookline Books, pg 37
The Bureau for At-Risk Youth, pg 38
Child's Play® Inc, pg 46
Council for Exceptional Children (CEC), pg 53
DawnSignPress, pg 58
Educational Insights®, pg 64
EPS School Specialty, pg 67
Free Spirit Publishing Inc, pg 74
Future Horizons Inc, pg 75
Galde Press Inc, pg 75
Gale, pg 75
Green Dragon Books, pg 81
Grey House Publishing Inc™, pg 81
The Guilford Press, pg 82
High Tide Press, pg 92
Hilton Publishing Co, pg 92
Idyll Arbor Inc, pg 98
Jessica Kingsley Publishers Inc, pg 110
Lee & Low Books Inc, pg 114
Loving Healing Press Inc, pg 121
Macmillan Reference USA™, pg 123
MAR*CO Products Inc, pg 124
Maren Green Publishing Inc, pg 125
National Braille Press, pg 137
North Star Editions Inc, pg 142
Omnigraphics Inc, pg 146
On the Write Path Publishing, pg 146
Penn State University Press, pg 157
PRO-ED Inc, pg 165
Psychological Assessment Resources Inc (PAR), pg 166
Rational Island Publishers, pg 171
Research Press, pg 174
Round Table Companies, pg 177
Routledge, pg 177
SAGE Publishing, pg 180
Science & Humanities Press, pg 185
South Carolina Bar, pg 195
Springer Publishing Co, pg 196
Star Bright Books Inc, pg 197
SteinerBooks Inc, pg 198
Story Monsters LLC, pg 199
Strategic Book Publishing (SBP), pg 199
Stress Free Kids®, pg 200
Syracuse University Press, pg 201
Teaching Strategies LLC, pg 204
Temple University Press, pg 204
Thieme Medical Publishers Inc, pg 206
Charles C Thomas Publisher Ltd, pg 206
University of Michigan Press, pg 217
University of Minnesota Press, pg 217
University Press of Mississippi, pg 222
Vandamere Press, pg 223
Wayne State University Press, pg 226
Wisconsin Department of Public Instruction, pg 231
Wolfman Books, pg 232
Woodbine House, pg 232

PUBLISHERS   U.S. PUBLISHERS — SUBJECT INDEX

Xlibris Corp, pg 234
Zondervan, pg 236

DRAMA, THEATER

Academica Press, pg 3
ACMRS Press, pg 4
Alexander Street, part of Clarivate PLC, pg 6
Allworth Press, pg 7
Anaphora Literary Press, pg 13
Applause Theatre & Cinema Books, pg 15
Ariadne Press, pg 16
The Arion Press, pg 16
ArtAge Publications, pg 17
AuthorHouse, pg 22
Baker Books, pg 23
Barrytown/Station Hill Press, pg 24
Blood Moon Productions Ltd, pg 31
Bloomsbury Academic, pg 31
Bolchazy-Carducci Publishers Inc, pg 33
Boson Books™, pg 34
Brooklyn Publishers LLC, pg 37
Carnegie Mellon University Press, pg 41
Cengage Learning, pg 43
The Center for Learning, pg 43
Child's Play® Inc, pg 46
China Books, pg 47
Counterpath Press, pg 54
Dover Publications Inc, pg 61
Dramatic Publishing Co, pg 61
Dramatists Play Service Inc, pg 61
Duke University Press, pg 62
ECS Publishing Group, pg 63
EDC Publishing, pg 63
Editorial de la Universidad de Puerto Rico, pg 63
Elsevier Inc, pg 65
Fine Creative Media, Inc, pg 71
Focus, pg 73
Fordham University Press, pg 73
Samuel French, Inc, pg 75
Gale, pg 75
Global Authors Publications (GAP), pg 78
Grand & Archer Publishing, pg 80
Green Integer, pg 81
Greenleaf Book Group LLC, pg 81
Grey House Publishing Inc™, pg 81
Grove Atlantic Inc, pg 82
Hackett Publishing Co Inc, pg 83
Hal Leonard LLC, pg 84
Hannacroix Creek Books Inc, pg 85
Heuer Publishing LLC, pg 91
Hill & Wang, pg 92
Homa & Sekey Books, pg 95
Host Publications, pg 95
Learning Links-USA Inc, pg 114
Lectorum Publications Inc, pg 114
Limelight Editions, pg 117
LinguaText LLC, pg 117
Little, Brown and Company, pg 118
Long River Press, pg 120
Macmillan Learning, pg 123
Macmillan Reference USA™, pg 123
Mazda Publishers Inc, pg 127
McFarland, pg 127
McGraw-Hill Higher Education, pg 128
McGraw-Hill School Education Group, pg 128
Medieval Institute Publications (MIP), pg 129
The Edwin Mellen Press, pg 129
Meriwether Publishing, pg 129
Modern Language Association (MLA), pg 133
Montemayor Press, pg 133
Nataraj Books, pg 136

National Council of Teachers of English (NCTE), pg 137
New Directions Publishing Corp, pg 139
Northwestern University Press, pg 143
The Overlook Press, pg 148
Pace University Press, pg 149
Palgrave Macmillan, pg 150
Penguin Random House LLC, pg 155
The Press at California State University, Fresno, pg 163
Quite Specific Media Group Ltd, pg 168
Routledge, pg 177
Running Press, pg 178
St Johann Press, pg 180
Salem Press, pg 181
Santa Monica Press LLC, pg 182
Silman-James Press Inc, pg 188
Smith & Kraus Publishers Inc, pg 192
Southern Illinois University Press, pg 195
Star Publishing Co Inc, pg 197
Story Monsters LLC, pg 199
Syracuse University Press, pg 201
Tantor Media Inc, pg 202
Temple University Press, pg 204
Texas Tech University Press, pg 205
Theatre Communications Group, pg 205
Third World Press Foundation, pg 206
Ugly Duckling Presse, pg 212
University of Alabama Press, pg 214
University of Delaware Press, pg 215
University of Illinois Press, pg 216
University of Iowa Press, pg 216
University of Michigan Press, pg 217
University of North Texas Press, pg 218
University Press of Mississippi, pg 222
Vintage Books, pg 225
Waveland Press Inc, pg 226
Whittier Publications Inc, pg 229
Wisconsin Department of Public Instruction, pg 231
Xlibris Corp, pg 234
Yale University Press, pg 235
Zondervan, pg 236

EARTH SCIENCES

AAPG (American Association of Petroleum Geologists), pg 1
ABDO, pg 2
Academic Press, pg 3
AdventureKEEN, pg 5
AIP Publishing LLC, pg 6
American Academy of Environmental Engineers & Scientists®, pg 8
American Fisheries Society, pg 9
American Geophysical Union (AGU), pg 10
American Geosciences Institute (AGI), pg 10
American Press, pg 11
American Society of Agricultural & Biological Engineers (ASABE), pg 12
Annual Reviews, pg 14
Arbordale Publishing, pg 16
ASTM International, pg 20
The Astronomical Society of the Pacific, pg 20
Atlas Publishing, pg 21

AuthorHouse, pg 22
BJU Press, pg 30
Black Rabbit Books, pg 30
The Blackburn Press, pg 30
Bureau of Economic Geology, pg 38
Capstone Publishers™, pg 40
Carolina Academic Press, pg 41
Cengage Learning, pg 43
Charlesbridge Publishing Inc, pg 45
Chelsea House, pg 45
Child's Play® Inc, pg 46
Columbia University Press, pg 51
Crabtree Publishing Co, pg 54
Walter De Gruyter Inc, pg 58
DEStech Publications Inc, pg 59
DK, pg 60
Dover Publications Inc, pg 61
EDC Publishing, pg 63
Educational Insights®, pg 64
Edupress Inc, pg 64
Elsevier Inc, pg 65
Evan-Moor Educational Publishers, pg 68
Facts On File, pg 69
W H Freeman, pg 75
Gale, pg 75
GemStone Press, pg 77
The Geological Society of America Inc (GSA), pg 77
Harvard University Press, pg 88
Hatherleigh Press Ltd, pg 88
Homestead Publishing, pg 95
Houghton Mifflin Harcourt, pg 95
Illinois State Museum Society, pg 99
Island Press, pg 104
Jones & Bartlett Learning LLC, pg 107
Jump!, pg 107
Krieger Publishing Co, pg 111
THE Learning Connection®, pg 113
Learning Links-USA Inc, pg 114
Lerner Publications, pg 115
Little, Brown and Company, pg 118
Lorenz Educational Press, pg 120
Lucent Press, pg 121
Macmillan Reference USA™, pg 123
Master Books®, pg 126
Materials Research Society, pg 126
The McDonald & Woodward Publishing Co, pg 127
McGraw-Hill Education, pg 127
McGraw-Hill Higher Education, pg 128
McGraw-Hill School Education Group, pg 128
Milford Books™, pg 131
Milliken Publishing Co, pg 132
The Minerals, Metals & Materials Society (TMS), pg 132
Mitchell Lane Publishers Inc, pg 133
Moonshine Cove Publishing LLC, pg 134
Mountain Press Publishing Co, pg 135
National Academies Press (NAP), pg 136
National Science Teachers Association (NSTA), pg 138
W W Norton & Company Inc, pg 143
Norwood House Press, pg 143
Odyssey Books, pg 145
Oregon State University Press, pg 147
ORO editions, pg 148
Richard C Owen Publishers Inc, pg 149
Oxford University Press USA, pg 149

Petroleum Extension Service (PETEX), pg 159
Princeton University Press, pg 164
Red Chair Press, pg 172
Saddleback Educational Publishing, pg 179
Salem Press, pg 181
Scholastic Inc, pg 184
Science, Naturally, pg 185
SPIE, pg 196
Star Publishing Co Inc, pg 197
Story Monsters LLC, pg 199
Strategic Book Publishing (SBP), pg 199
Sunbelt Publications Inc, pg 200
Tantor Media Inc, pg 202
Teaching & Learning Co, pg 204
Trinity University Press, pg 209
TSG Publishing Foundation Inc, pg 210
Twenty-First Century Books, pg 211
Union Square & Co, pg 212
University of Alaska Press, pg 214
The University of Arizona Press, pg 214
University of Hawaii Press, pg 216
Utah Geological Survey, pg 223
VanDam Inc, pg 223
Visible Ink Press®, pg 225
Water Resources Publications LLC, pg 226
Waveland Press Inc, pg 226
Wiley-Blackwell, pg 229
John Wiley & Sons Inc, pg 230
John Wiley & Sons Inc Global Education, pg 230
John Wiley & Sons Inc Professional Development, pg 230
Wisconsin Department of Public Instruction, pg 231
World Resources Institute, pg 233
World Trade Press LLC, pg 234
Yale University Press, pg 235

ECONOMICS

Academic Press, pg 3
The AEI Press, pg 5
AK Press, pg 6
Algora Publishing, pg 7
American Institute for Economic Research (AIER), pg 10
American Numismatic Society, pg 11
Anaphora Literary Press, pg 13
Annual Reviews, pg 14
Atlas Publishing, pg 21
AuthorHouse, pg 22
Basic Books Group, pg 25
Berkshire Publishing Group LLC, pg 28
Bernan, pg 28
BJU Press, pg 30
Black Rabbit Books, pg 30
Bluestocking Press, pg 33
Bookhaven Press LLC, pg 34
Nicholas Brealey Publishing, pg 36
The Brookings Institution Press, pg 37
Business Expert Press, pg 38
Cambridge University Press, pg 39
Capen Publishing Co Inc, pg 40
Carolina Academic Press, pg 41
Cato Institute, pg 42
Cengage Learning, pg 43
The Center for Learning, pg 43
Center for Strategic & International Studies (CSIS), pg 44
China Books, pg 47
Clarity Press Inc, pg 49
Close Up Publishing, pg 49
CN Times Books, pg 50
Columbia University Press, pg 51

U.S. PUBLISHERS — SUBJECT INDEX

The Conference Board Inc, pg 51
Cosimo Inc, pg 53
Council on Foreign Relations Press, pg 53
Walter De Gruyter Inc, pg 58
Dissertation.com, pg 60
Duke University Press, pg 62
Edward Elgar Publishing Inc, pg 65
Elsevier Inc, pg 65
Everything Goes Media LLC, pg 68
Financial Times Press, pg 71
Fordham University Press, pg 73
Galde Press Inc, pg 75
Gale, pg 75
Grey House Publishing Inc™, pg 81
Harvard Business Review Press, pg 87
Harvard University Press, pg 88
Hillsdale College Press, pg 92
Histria Books, pg 93
Homa & Sekey Books, pg 95
Hoover Institution Press, pg 95
Houghton Mifflin Harcourt, pg 95
Houghton Mifflin Harcourt Trade & Reference Division, pg 96
Hudson Institute, pg 97
IHS Press, pg 98
Independent Institute, pg 99
Inter-American Development Bank, pg 102
Inter-University Consortium for Political & Social Research (ICPSR), pg 102
The International Institute of Islamic Thought, pg 103
International Monetary Fund (IMF), Editorial & Publications Division, pg 103
International Publishers Co Inc, pg 103
Kazi Publications Inc, pg 108
Alfred A Knopf, pg 110
Krieger Publishing Co, pg 111
Kumarian Press, pg 112
Lawyers & Judges Publishing Co Inc, pg 113
The Lentz Leadership Institute LLC, pg 115
Lerner Publications, pg 115
Lexington Books, pg 115
Liberty Fund Inc, pg 116
Mary Ann Liebert Inc, pg 116
Long River Press, pg 120
Macmillan Learning, pg 123
Macmillan Reference USA™, pg 123
McGraw-Hill Create, pg 127
McGraw-Hill Higher Education, pg 128
McGraw-Hill Professional Publishing Group, pg 128
McGraw-Hill School Education Group, pg 128
The Edwin Mellen Press, pg 129
Metropolitan Classics, pg 130
Milford Books™, pg 131
The MIT Press, pg 132
Monthly Review Press, pg 134
Moonshine Cove Publishing LLC, pg 134
Nataraj Books, pg 136
National Academies Press (NAP), pg 136
National Center for Children in Poverty, pg 137
The New Press, pg 140
New York University Press, pg 141
W W Norton & Company Inc, pg 143
Norwood House Press, pg 143
Nova Science Publishers Inc, pg 144
OECD Washington Center, pg 145

Other Press, pg 148
Oxford University Press USA, pg 149
Palgrave Macmillan, pg 150
Paragon House, pg 151
Pearson Business Publishing, pg 153
Peterson Institute for International Economics (PIIE), pg 158
Plunkett Research Ltd, pg 161
Portfolio, pg 162
Primary Research Group Inc, pg 163
Princeton University Press, pg 164
The PRS Group Inc, pg 166
RAND Corp, pg 169
Rational Island Publishers, pg 171
Reference Publications Inc, pg 173
Regnery Publishing, pg 174
Research & Education Association (REA), pg 174
Routledge, pg 177
Rowman & Littlefield, pg 178
Russell Sage Foundation, pg 178
SAGE Publishing, pg 180
Salem Press, pg 181
Science & Humanities Press, pg 185
1765 Productions, pg 186
Signalman Publishing, pg 187
Society for Mining, Metallurgy & Exploration, pg 192
Stanford University Press, pg 197
SteinerBooks Inc, pg 198
Stipes Publishing LLC, pg 198
Strategic Book Publishing (SBP), pg 199
Tantor Media Inc, pg 202
Texas A&M University Press, pg 205
TotalRecall Publications Inc, pg 208
Twenty-First Century Books, pg 211
UCLA Latin American Center Publications, pg 212
United Nations Publications, pg 213
University of California Institute on Global Conflict & Cooperation, pg 215
University of Chicago Press, pg 215
University of Louisiana at Lafayette Press, pg 217
University of North Texas Press, pg 218
University Press of America Inc, pg 221
US Government Publishing Office (GPO), pg 223
Vernon Press, pg 224
Verso Books, pg 224
Ludwig von Mises Institute, pg 225
Waveland Press Inc, pg 226
John Wiley & Sons Inc, pg 230
John Wiley & Sons Inc Global Education, pg 230
John Wiley & Sons Inc Professional Development, pg 230
Windsor Books, pg 230
Wisconsin Department of Public Instruction, pg 231
Woodrow Wilson Center Press, pg 232
Workers Compensation Research Institute, pg 232
World Resources Institute, pg 233
World Trade Press LLC, pg 234
Worth Publishers, pg 234
Yale University Press, pg 235

EDUCATION

A 2 Z Press LLC, pg 1
ABDO, pg 2
Academica Press, pg 3
Advance Publishing Inc, pg 5
The AEI Press, pg 5
African American Images Inc (AAI), pg 5
AK Press, pg 6
Algora Publishing, pg 7
AllWrite Publishing, pg 7
American Association of Collegiate Registrars & Admissions Officers (AACRAO), pg 8
The American Ceramic Society, pg 9
American Council on Education (ACE), pg 9
American Counseling Association (ACA), pg 9
American Law Institute Continuing Legal Education (ALI CLE), pg 10
American Press, pg 11
American Society for Quality (ASQ), pg 12
AMMO Books LLC, pg 13
Anaphora Literary Press, pg 13
Sara Anderson Children's Books, pg 13
Andrews University Press, pg 14
Angelus Press, pg 14
AOTA Press, pg 14
APH Press, pg 15
APPA - Leadership in Education Facilities, pg 15
Art Image Publications, pg 17
ASCD, pg 18
Association of School Business Officials International, pg 20
The Astronomical Society of the Pacific, pg 20
Atlantic Publishing Group Inc, pg 21
Atlas Publishing, pg 21
AuthorHouse, pg 22
Ave Maria Press Inc, pg 22
Baker Books, pg 23
Barrytown/Station Hill Press, pg 24
Beacon Press, pg 25
Beaver's Pond Press Inc, pg 26
Behrman House Inc, pg 27
Ben Yehuda Press, pg 27
BePuzzled, pg 28
Berghahn Books, pg 28
Bernan, pg 28
Bisk Education, pg 29
BJU Press, pg 30
Bloomsbury Academic, pg 31
BoardSource, pg 33
BookLogix, pg 34
Boys Town Press, pg 35
Brandylane Publishers Inc, pg 35
Bridge Publications Inc, pg 36
Brigantine Media, pg 37
Paul H Brookes Publishing Co Inc, pg 37
The Brookings Institution Press, pg 37
Brookline Books, pg 37
The Bureau for At-Risk Youth, pg 38
Business Expert Press, pg 38
Captain Fiddle Music & Publications, pg 40
Carolina Academic Press, pg 41
Carson Dellosa Publishing LLC, pg 41
Cengage Learning, pg 43
Center for Creative Leadership LLC, pg 43
The Center for Learning, pg 43
Center for the Collaborative Classroom, pg 44
Charles Press Publishers, pg 45
Charlesbridge Publishing Inc, pg 45
China Books, pg 47
Christian Liberty Press, pg 47

Christian Light Publications Inc, pg 47
Christian Schools International (CSI), pg 47
Classical Academic Press, pg 49
Clinical and Laboratory Standards Institute (CLSI), pg 49
Close Up Publishing, pg 49
The College Board, pg 50
Comex Systems Inc, pg 51
Cornell University Press, pg 52
Corwin, pg 53
Council for Exceptional Children (CEC), pg 53
Council for Research in Values & Philosophy, pg 53
Crown House Publishing Co LLC, pg 56
Crystal Clarity Publishers, pg 56
CSWE Press, pg 56
Dancing Dakini Press, pg 57
DawnSignPress, pg 58
Walter De Gruyter Inc, pg 58
DEStech Publications Inc, pg 59
DK, pg 60
East West Discovery Press, pg 63
Editorial de la Universidad de Puerto Rico, pg 63
Educational Insights®, pg 64
Educator's International Press Inc (EIP), pg 64
Edupress Inc, pg 64
Eifrig Publishing LLC, pg 64
Elderberry Press Inc, pg 65
Emerald Books, pg 66
Encounter Books, pg 66
Encyclopaedia Britannica Inc, pg 66
Enslow Publishing LLC, pg 66
EPS School Specialty, pg 67
Evan-Moor Educational Publishers, pg 68
The Feminist Press at The City University of New York, pg 71
Fordham University Press, pg 73
Free Spirit Publishing Inc, pg 74
Future Horizons Inc, pg 75
Gale, pg 75
Gallaudet University Press, pg 76
Gallopade International Inc, pg 76
Gauthier Publications Inc, pg 77
Getty Publications, pg 78
Gifted Unlimited LLC, pg 78
Goodheart-Willcox Publisher, pg 79
Goose River Press, pg 79
Gospel Publishing House, pg 80
The Graduate Group/Booksellers, pg 80
Green Dragon Books, pg 81
Greenleaf Book Group LLC, pg 81
Grey House Publishing Inc™, pg 81
Group Publishing Inc, pg 82
Gryphon House Inc, pg 82
The Guilford Press, pg 82
Hal Leonard LLC, pg 84
Hameray Publishing Group Inc, pg 84
Hamilton Books, pg 84
Hamilton Stone Editions, pg 84
Harvard Business Review Press, pg 87
Harvard Education Publishing Group, pg 88
Hazy Dell Press, pg 89
HeartMath LLC, pg 90
William S Hein & Co Inc, pg 90
Heinemann, pg 90
Her Own Words LLC, pg 91
Hewitt Homeschooling Resources, pg 91
Hi Willow Research & Publishing, pg 91
High Tide Press, pg 92
Hillsdale College Press, pg 92
Hoover Institution Press, pg 95

PUBLISHERS — U.S. PUBLISHERS — SUBJECT INDEX

Horizon Publishers & Distributors Inc, pg 95
Houghton Mifflin Harcourt, pg 95
Houghton Mifflin Harcourt Assessments, pg 96
Houghton Mifflin Harcourt Trade & Reference Division, pg 96
Hudson Institute, pg 97
Human Kinetics Inc, pg 97
Illinois State Museum Society, pg 99
Incentive Publications by World Book, pg 99
Independent Institute, pg 99
Information Age Publishing Inc, pg 100
Information Today, Inc, pg 100
The Institutes™, pg 102
Inter-University Consortium for Political & Social Research (ICPSR), pg 102
Intercultural Development Research Association (IDRA), pg 102
International Linguistics Corp, pg 103
International Literacy Association (ILA), pg 103
International Society for Technology in Education, pg 103
Jhpiego, pg 106
JIST Publishing, pg 106
Johns Hopkins University Press, pg 106
Judson Press, pg 107
Kaeden Publishing, pg 107
Kamehameha Publishing, pg 108
Kidsbooks® Publishing, pg 109
Jessica Kingsley Publishers Inc, pg 110
Krieger Publishing Co, pg 111
Kumon Publishing North America Inc (KPNA), pg 112
LAMA Books, pg 112
Peter Lang Publishing Inc, pg 112
Laredo Publishing Co, pg 113
Law School Admission Council (LSAC), pg 113
Lawyers & Judges Publishing Co Inc, pg 113
THE Learning Connection®, pg 113
Learning Links-USA Inc, pg 114
LearningExpress, pg 114
The Lentz Leadership Institute LLC, pg 115
Lexington Books, pg 115
Liberty Fund Inc, pg 116
Libraries Unlimited, pg 116
The Little Entrepreneur, pg 118
Loft Press Inc, pg 119
Lorenz Educational Press, pg 120
Lost Classics Book Company LLC, pg 120
LRP Publications, pg 121
Macmillan Reference USA™, pg 123
Maharishi International University Press, pg 123
Mandel Vilar Press, pg 124
MAR*CO Products Inc, pg 124
Maren Green Publishing Inc, pg 125
Marine Education Textbooks, pg 125
Master Books®, pg 126
Mastery Education, pg 126
Math Solutions®, pg 127
The Mathematical Association of America, pg 127
McFarland, pg 127
McGraw-Hill Create, pg 127
McGraw-Hill Higher Education, pg 128
McGraw-Hill Professional Publishing Group, pg 128

me+mi publishing inc, pg 128
Medical Physics Publishing Corp (MPP), pg 129
Mel Bay Publications Inc, pg 129
The Edwin Mellen Press, pg 129
MennoMedia, pg 129
Meriwether Publishing, pg 129
Mesorah Publications Ltd, pg 130
Milford Books™, pg 131
Milliken Publishing Co, pg 132
Modern Language Association (MLA), pg 133
Monthly Review Press, pg 134
Multicultural Publications Inc, pg 135
Multnomah, pg 135
Nataraj Books, pg 136
National Academies Press (NAP), pg 136
National Book Co, pg 136
National Braille Press, pg 137
National Catholic Educational Association, pg 137
National Council of Teachers of English (NCTE), pg 137
National Council of Teachers of Mathematics (NCTM), pg 137
National Education Association (NEA), pg 137
National Institute for Trial Advocacy (NITA), pg 138
National Learning Corp, pg 138
National Notary Association (NNA), pg 138
National Resource Center for Youth Services, pg 138
National Science Teachers Association (NSTA), pg 138
New Forums Press Inc, pg 139
The New Press, pg 140
New Readers Press, pg 140
North Star Editions Inc, pg 142
W W Norton & Company Inc, pg 143
Nova Press, pg 144
Odyssey Books, pg 145
OECD Washington Center, pg 145
Omnigraphics Inc, pg 146
On the Write Path Publishing, pg 146
Open Books Press, pg 146
ORO editions, pg 148
Richard C Owen Publishers Inc, pg 149
Palgrave Macmillan, pg 150
Paulist Press, pg 152
Peachtree Publishing Co Inc, pg 153
Pearson Business Publishing, pg 153
Penguin Publishing Group, pg 154
Pennsylvania State Data Center, pg 157
Perfection Learning®, pg 158
Peterson's, pg 158
Pflaum Publishing Group, pg 159
Philosophical Library Inc, pg 159
Philosophy Documentation Center, pg 159
Pieces of Learning Inc, pg 160
Platypus Media LLC, pg 160
Plough Publishing House, pg 161
Plowshare Media, pg 161
Primary Research Group Inc, pg 163
Princeton University Press, pg 164
PRO-ED Inc, pg 165
Pro Lingua Associates Inc, pg 165
Publications International Ltd (PIL), pg 167
RAND Corp, pg 169
Rational Island Publishers, pg 171
Recorded Books Inc, an RBmedia company, pg 172

Red Chair Press, pg 172
Redleaf Press®, pg 173
Renaissance House, pg 174
Research Press, pg 174
Rising Sun Publishing, pg 175
The RoadRunner Press, pg 175
The Rough Notes Co Inc, pg 177
Round Table Companies, pg 177
Routledge, pg 177
Rowman & Littlefield, pg 178
Royal Fireworks Press, pg 178
Russell Sage Foundation, pg 178
Rutgers University Press, pg 178
SAGE Publishing, pg 180
St Pauls, pg 181
Santa Monica Press LLC, pg 182
Savant Books & Publications LLC, pg 182
Scholastic Education Solutions, pg 184
Scholastic Inc, pg 184
School Guide Publications, pg 185
School Zone Publishing Co, pg 185
Science & Humanities Press, pg 185
Sentient Publications LLC, pg 186
Sleeping Bear Press™, pg 191
Solution Tree, pg 193
Sound Feelings Publishing, pg 194
Sourcebooks LLC, pg 194
Sourced Media Books, pg 195
Spizzirri Publishing Inc, pg 196
Stanford University Press, pg 197
Stargazer Publishing Co, pg 197
StarGroup International Inc, pg 197
SteinerBooks Inc, pg 198
Stellar Publishing, pg 198
Stenhouse Publishers, pg 198
STM Learning Inc, pg 199
Story Monsters LLC, pg 199
Strategic Book Publishing (SBP), pg 199
The Jesse Stuart Foundation (JSF), pg 200
Stylus Publishing LLC, pg 200
Summertime Publications Inc, pg 200
Sundance/Newbridge Publishing, pg 200
Syracuse University Press, pg 201
Tahrike Tarsile Qur'an Inc, pg 202
Tantor Media Inc, pg 202
Teacher Created Resources Inc, pg 203
Teachers College Press, pg 203
Teaching & Learning Co, pg 204
Teaching Strategies LLC, pg 204
Temple University Press, pg 204
TESOL Press, pg 204
Texas Tech University Press, pg 205
Thieme Medical Publishers Inc, pg 206
Third World Press Foundation, pg 206
Charles C Thomas Publisher Ltd, pg 206
Tilbury House Publishers, pg 207
Todd Publications, pg 207
Torah Umesorah Publications, pg 208
Treehaus Communications Inc, pg 209
The Trinity Foundation, pg 209
TSG Publishing Foundation Inc, pg 210
Tughra Books, pg 210
Tumblehome Learning Inc, pg 210
UCLA Latin American Center Publications, pg 212
Ulysses Press, pg 212
University Council for Educational Administration (UCEA), pg 214
University of Chicago Press, pg 215
University of Iowa Press, pg 216

University of Massachusetts Press, pg 217
University of Minnesota Press, pg 217
University of North Texas Press, pg 218
University Press of America Inc, pg 221
University Press of Colorado, pg 221
University Press of Mississippi, pg 222
Upstart Books™, pg 223
US Conference of Catholic Bishops, pg 223
US Games Systems Inc, pg 223
US Government Publishing Office (GPO), pg 223
Utah State University Press, pg 223
VanDam Inc, pg 223
Vandamere Press, pg 223
Vanderbilt University Press, pg 224
Velazquez Press, pg 224
Vernon Press, pg 224
Voyager Sopris Learning Inc, pg 225
WaterBrook, pg 226
Waveland Press Inc, pg 226
Well-Trained Mind Press, pg 227
West Academic, pg 227
Wide World Publishing, pg 229
Wiley-Blackwell, pg 229
John Wiley & Sons Inc, pg 230
John Wiley & Sons Inc Global Education, pg 230
John Wiley & Sons Inc Professional Development, pg 230
William Carey Publishing, pg 230
Wisconsin Department of Public Instruction, pg 231
Woodbine House, pg 232
Workman Publishing, pg 232
World Bank Publications, pg 233
Wyndham Hall Press, pg 234
Xist Publishing, pg 234
Xlibris Corp, pg 234
Yale University Press, pg 235
Zaner-Bloser Inc, pg 236

ELECTRONICS, ELECTRICAL ENGINEERING

Academic Press, pg 3
The American Ceramic Society, pg 9
American Society for Quality (ASQ), pg 12
American Society of Agricultural & Biological Engineers (ASABE), pg 12
Artech House®, pg 17
AuthorHouse, pg 22
Cengage Learning, pg 43
CRC Press, pg 55
DEStech Publications Inc, pg 59
EDC Publishing, pg 63
Educational Insights®, pg 64
The Electrochemical Society (ECS), pg 65
Gale, pg 75
Goodheart-Willcox Publisher, pg 79
IEEE Computer Society, pg 98
IEEE Press, pg 98
IET USA Inc, pg 98
Illuminating Engineering Society of North America (IES), pg 99
International Society of Automation (ISA), pg 103
LAMA Books, pg 112
Macmillan Learning, pg 123

U.S. PUBLISHERS — SUBJECT INDEX

BOOK

Macmillan Reference USA™, pg 123
Materials Research Society, pg 126
McGraw-Hill Education, pg 127
McGraw-Hill Higher Education, pg 128
R S Means from The Gordian Group, pg 128
The Minerals, Metals & Materials Society (TMS), pg 132
Morgan Kaufmann, pg 134
National Academies Press (NAP), pg 136
PPI, A Kaplan Company, pg 162
Research & Education Association (REA), pg 174
SAE (Society of Automotive Engineers International), pg 179
SAGE Publishing, pg 180
SAMS Technical Publishing LLC, pg 181
SPIE, pg 196
Strategic Book Publishing (SBP), pg 199
Stylus Publishing LLC, pg 200
US Government Publishing Office (GPO), pg 223
Waveland Press Inc, pg 226

ENERGY

ABDO, pg 2
Adventures Unlimited Press (AUP), pg 5
American Institute of Chemical Engineers (AIChE), pg 10
American Society of Agricultural & Biological Engineers (ASABE), pg 12
Annual Reviews, pg 14
AuthorHouse, pg 22
Beaver's Pond Press Inc, pg 26
Begell House Inc Publishers, pg 27
Bernan, pg 28
Black Rabbit Books, pg 30
Blue Note Publications Inc, pg 32
The Brookings Institution Press, pg 37
Bureau of Economic Geology, pg 38
Center for Strategic & International Studies (CSIS), pg 44
Chelsea Green Publishing Co, pg 45
DK, pg 60
EDC Publishing, pg 63
The Electrochemical Society (ECS), pg 65
Edward Elgar Publishing Inc, pg 65
Gale, pg 75
Goodheart-Willcox Publisher, pg 79
Gulf Energy Information, pg 83
IET USA Inc, pg 98
Illuminating Engineering Society of North America (IES), pg 99
Island Press, pg 104
Light Technology Publishing LLC, pg 116
Macmillan Reference USA™, pg 123
Mandel Vilar Press, pg 124
Marine Techniques Publishing, pg 125
Materials Research Society, pg 126
Mitchell Lane Publishers Inc, pg 133
NACE International, pg 136
Nataraj Books, pg 136
National Science Teachers Association (NSTA), pg 138
OECD Washington Center, pg 145
Richard C Owen Publishers Inc, pg 149
PennWell Books, pg 157

Petroleum Extension Service (PETEX), pg 159
Plunkett Research Ltd, pg 161
Primary Research Group Inc, pg 163
Prometheus Books, pg 166
Public Citizen, pg 167
RAND Corp, pg 169
Rocky Mountain Mineral Law Foundation, pg 176
SAGE Publishing, pg 180
SPIE, pg 196
Strategic Book Publishing (SBP), pg 199
Taylor & Francis Inc, pg 203
TSG Publishing Foundation Inc, pg 210
Unarius Academy of Science Publications, pg 212
United Nations Publications, pg 213
University of Alaska Press, pg 214
University of Louisiana at Lafayette Press, pg 217
US Government Publishing Office (GPO), pg 223
World Bank Publications, pg 233
World Resources Institute, pg 233
Write Stuff Enterprises LLC, pg 234

ENGINEERING (GENERAL)

Academic Press, pg 3
AIHA (American Industrial Hygiene Association), pg 6
AIP Publishing LLC, pg 6
Alexander Street, part of Clarivate PLC, pg 6
American Academy of Environmental Engineers & Scientists®, pg 8
The American Ceramic Society, pg 9
American Institute of Aeronautics and Astronautics (AIAA), pg 10
American Institute of Chemical Engineers (AIChE), pg 10
American Public Works Association (APWA), pg 12
American Society for Quality (ASQ), pg 12
American Society of Civil Engineers (ASCE), pg 12
American Water Works Association (AWWA), pg 13
Apress Media LLC, pg 15
Artech House®, pg 17
ASM International, pg 19
ASTM International, pg 20
AuthorHouse, pg 22
Begell House Inc Publishers, pg 27
Bentley Publishers, pg 28
The Blackburn Press, pg 30
BNi Building News, pg 33
Cengage Learning, pg 43
The Child's World Inc, pg 46
College Publishing, pg 50
Crabtree Publishing Co, pg 54
Walter De Gruyter Inc, pg 58
DEStech Publications Inc, pg 59
Dover Publications Inc, pg 61
Elsevier Inc, pg 65
Gale, pg 75
Gulf Energy Information, pg 83
Hanser Publications LLC, pg 85
IEEE Computer Society, pg 98
IEEE Press, pg 98
IET USA Inc, pg 98
Industrial Press Inc, pg 100
Institute of Environmental Sciences & Technology - IEST, pg 101
Institute of Police Technology & Management (IPTM), pg 102

International Society of Automation (ISA), pg 103
Jump!, pg 107
Koho Pono LLC, pg 111
Mary Ann Liebert Inc, pg 116
Macmillan Reference USA™, pg 123
Materials Research Society, pg 126
McGraw-Hill Higher Education, pg 128
McGraw-Hill Professional Publishing Group, pg 128
R S Means from The Gordian Group, pg 128
The Minerals, Metals & Materials Society (TMS), pg 132
De Gruyter Mouton, pg 135
NACE International, pg 136
National Academies Press (NAP), pg 136
National Association of Broadcasters (NAB), pg 136
National Science Teachers Association (NSTA), pg 138
Naval Institute Press, pg 139
New York Academy of Sciences (NYAS), pg 140
No Starch Press, pg 141
ORO editions, pg 148
Pearson Business Publishing, pg 153
Petroleum Extension Service (PETEX), pg 159
Plunkett Research Ltd, pg 161
PPI, A Kaplan Company, pg 162
Productivity Press, pg 165
Purdue University Press, pg 167
Research & Education Association (REA), pg 174
Rothstein Associates Inc, pg 177
SAE (Society of Automotive Engineers International), pg 179
SAGE Publishing, pg 180
SME (Society of Manufacturing Engineers), pg 191
Society for Mining, Metallurgy & Exploration, pg 192
SPIE, pg 196
Springer, pg 196
Star Publishing Co Inc, pg 197
Stipes Publishing LLC, pg 198
Strategic Book Publishing (SBP), pg 199
Stylus Publishing LLC, pg 200
Taylor & Francis Inc, pg 203
Transportation Research Board (TRB), pg 209
Univelt Inc, pg 213
University Science Books, pg 222
Vault.com Inc, pg 224
Water Resources Publications LLC, pg 226
Waveland Press Inc, pg 226
John Wiley & Sons Inc, pg 230
John Wiley & Sons Inc Global Education, pg 230
John Wiley & Sons Inc Professional Development, pg 230
World Scientific Publishing Co Inc, pg 233
Write Stuff Enterprises LLC, pg 234
Xlibris Corp, pg 234

ENGLISH AS A SECOND LANGUAGE

AllWrite Publishing, pg 7
American Press, pg 11
Anaphora Literary Press, pg 13
Atlas Publishing, pg 21
AuthorHouse, pg 22
John Benjamins Publishing Co, pg 28

Cambridge University Press, pg 39
Carolina Academic Press, pg 41
Cengage Learning, pg 43
Close Up Publishing, pg 49
DawnSignPress, pg 58
Dover Publications Inc, pg 61
Educational Insights®, pg 64
Enslow Publishing LLC, pg 66
Evan-Moor Educational Publishers, pg 68
Gale, pg 75
Gallaudet University Press, pg 76
Hameray Publishing Group Inc, pg 84
Heinemann, pg 90
Houghton Mifflin Harcourt, pg 95
International Literacy Association (ILA), pg 103
Laredo Publishing Co, pg 113
THE Learning Connection®, pg 113
Lectorum Publications Inc, pg 114
Living Language, pg 119
Macmillan Reference USA™, pg 123
me+mi publishing inc, pg 128
Merriam-Webster Inc, pg 129
National Academies Press (NAP), pg 136
National Book Co, pg 136
National Geographic Learning, pg 138
New Readers Press, pg 140
Norwood House Press, pg 143
Oxford University Press USA, pg 149
Pennsylvania State Data Center, pg 157
Perfection Learning®, pg 158
PRO-ED Inc, pg 165
Pro Lingua Associates Inc, pg 165
Recorded Books Inc, an RBmedia company, pg 172
Renaissance House, pg 174
Research & Education Association (REA), pg 174
Saddleback Educational Publishing, pg 179
Scholastic Inc, pg 184
Schreiber Publishing, pg 185
Summertime Publications Inc, pg 200
Teacher's Discovery®, pg 203
TESOL Press, pg 204
University of Michigan Press, pg 217
Velazquez Press, pg 224
Waveland Press Inc, pg 226
William Carey Publishing, pg 230

ENVIRONMENTAL STUDIES

ABDO, pg 2
Academic Press, pg 3
Academica Press, pg 3
ACS Publications, pg 4
AIHA (American Industrial Hygiene Association), pg 6
AK Press, pg 6
Alexander Street, part of Clarivate PLC, pg 6
Amakella Publishing, pg 7
American Academy of Environmental Engineers & Scientists®, pg 8
American Fisheries Society, pg 9
American Geophysical Union (AGU), pg 10
American Geosciences Institute (AGI), pg 10
American Institute of Chemical Engineers (AIChE), pg 10

PUBLISHERS

U.S. PUBLISHERS — SUBJECT INDEX

American Public Works Association (APWA), pg 12
American Water Works Association (AWWA), pg 13
Annual Reviews, pg 14
ANR Publications University of California, pg 14
Aperture Books, pg 15
Appalachian Mountain Club Books, pg 15
Arbordale Publishing, pg 16
Ashland Creek Press, pg 18
ASTM International, pg 20
AuthorHouse, pg 22
Barrytown/Station Hill Press, pg 24
Bear & Co Inc, pg 26
Begell House Inc Publishers, pg 27
Berghahn Books, pg 28
Berkshire Publishing Group LLC, pg 28
Black Rabbit Books, pg 30
The Blackburn Press, pg 30
BLR®—Business & Legal Resources, pg 32
Brandylane Publishers Inc, pg 35
The Brookings Institution Press, pg 37
Bureau of Economic Geology, pg 38
Carolina Academic Press, pg 41
Cato Institute, pg 42
Cengage Learning, pg 43
Center for Strategic & International Studies (CSIS), pg 44
Chelsea Green Publishing Co, pg 45
Chelsea House, pg 45
China Books, pg 47
Clear Light Publishers, pg 49
Cognizant Communication Corp, pg 50
Cold Spring Harbor Laboratory Press, pg 50
College Publishing, pg 50
Columbia University Press, pg 51
Cornell Maritime Press, pg 52
Cornell University Press, pg 52
Cosimo Inc, pg 53
The Council of State Governments, pg 53
Counterpoint Press LLC, pg 54
Crabtree Publishing Co, pg 54
CRC Press, pg 55
Walter De Gruyter Inc, pg 58
DEStech Publications Inc, pg 59
EDC Publishing, pg 63
Editorial de la Universidad de Puerto Rico, pg 63
Edward Elgar Publishing Inc, pg 65
Elsevier Inc, pg 65
Enslow Publishing LLC, pg 66
Environmental Law Institute, pg 67
Everything Goes Media LLC, pg 68
The Experiment, pg 68
Facts On File, pg 69
Fulcrum Publishing Inc, pg 75
Gale, pg 75
Gareth Stevens Publishing, pg 76
The Graduate Group/Booksellers, pg 80
Greenleaf Book Group LLC, pg 81
Grey House Publishing Inc™, pg 81
Hancock House Publishers, pg 84
Hatherleigh Press Ltd, pg 88
William S Hein & Co Inc, pg 90
Heyday, pg 91
Homestead Publishing, pg 95
Hoover Institution Press, pg 95
Hudson Institute, pg 97
Illinois State Museum Society, pg 99
Independent Institute, pg 99
Institute of Environmental Sciences & Technology - IEST, pg 101

International Food Policy Research Institute, pg 103
Island Press, pg 104
Jain Publishing Co, pg 105
Lyndon B Johnson School of Public Affairs, pg 106
Jones & Bartlett Learning LLC, pg 107
Jump!, pg 107
J J Keller & Associates, Inc®, pg 108
Krieger Publishing Co, pg 111
Lantern Publishing & Media, pg 112
THE Learning Connection®, pg 113
Lee & Low Books Inc, pg 114
Lerner Publications, pg 115
Lexington Books, pg 115
Mary Ann Liebert Inc, pg 116
Little, Brown and Company, pg 118
Lorenz Educational Press, pg 120
Louisiana State University Press, pg 120
The Lyons Press, pg 121
Macmillan Learning, pg 123
Macmillan Reference USA™, pg 123
Mandala Earth, pg 124
Mandel Vilar Press, pg 124
The McDonald & Woodward Publishing Co, pg 127
McFarland, pg 127
McGraw-Hill Higher Education, pg 128
The Edwin Mellen Press, pg 129
Michigan State University Press (MSU Press), pg 130
Milford Books™, pg 131
Milliken Publishing Co, pg 132
The Minerals, Metals & Materials Society (TMS), pg 132
The MIT Press, pg 132
Mitchell Lane Publishers Inc, pg 133
Modern Language Association (MLA), pg 133
Montemayor Press, pg 133
Monthly Review Press, pg 134
Moonshine Cove Publishing LLC, pg 134
Mountain Press Publishing Co, pg 135
Mountaineers Books, pg 135
NACE International, pg 136
Nataraj Books, pg 136
National Academies Press (NAP), pg 136
National Science Teachers Association (NSTA), pg 138
The New Press, pg 140
New York Academy of Sciences (NYAS), pg 140
The New York Botanical Garden Press, pg 140
North Atlantic Books (NAB), pg 142
North Point Press, pg 142
W W Norton & Company Inc, pg 143
Nova Science Publishers Inc, pg 144
OECD Washington Center, pg 145
Ohio University Press, pg 145
Oregon State University Press, pg 147
ORO editions, pg 148
Other Press, pg 148
Oxford University Press USA, pg 149
Palgrave Macmillan, pg 150
Penn State University Press, pg 157
Peterson Institute for International Economics (PIIE), pg 158

Petroleum Extension Service (PETEX), pg 159
Pineapple Press, pg 160
Planners Press, pg 160
Prometheus Books, pg 166
Public Citizen, pg 167
RAND Corp, pg 169
Red Chair Press, pg 172
Rocky Mountain Mineral Law Foundation, pg 176
Ross Books, pg 177
Routledge, pg 177
Rowman & Littlefield, pg 178
Rutgers University Press, pg 178
SAGE Publishing, pg 180
Salem Press, pg 181
Sentient Publications LLC, pg 186
Shambhala Publications Inc, pg 187
Society for Mining, Metallurgy & Exploration, pg 192
Society of Environmental Toxicology & Chemistry (SETAC), pg 192
Solano Press Books, pg 193
Star Publishing Co Inc, pg 197
SteinerBooks Inc, pg 198
Stipes Publishing LLC, pg 198
Stone Bridge Press Inc, pg 199
Stone Pier Press, pg 199
Strategic Book Publishing (SBP), pg 199
Temple University Press, pg 204
Texas A&M University Press, pg 205
Texas Tech University Press, pg 205
Charles C Thomas Publisher Ltd, pg 206
Trinity University Press, pg 209
Tumblehome Learning Inc, pg 210
United Nations Publications, pg 213
University of Alabama Press, pg 214
University of Alaska Press, pg 214
The University of Arizona Press, pg 214
University of California Institute on Global Conflict & Cooperation, pg 215
University of California Press, pg 215
University of Delaware Press, pg 215
University of Georgia Press, pg 216
University of Iowa Press, pg 216
University of Massachusetts Press, pg 217
University of Minnesota Press, pg 217
University of Nebraska Press, pg 217
University of Nevada Press, pg 218
University of New Mexico Press, pg 218
The University of North Carolina Press, pg 218
University of North Texas Press, pg 218
University of Oklahoma Press, pg 219
University of Pittsburgh Press, pg 219
University of Tennessee Press, pg 220
The University of Utah Press, pg 220
University of Virginia Press, pg 220
University of Washington Press, pg 220
University of Wisconsin Press, pg 221
University Press of America Inc, pg 221

University Press of Colorado, pg 221
University Press of Kansas, pg 221
The University Press of Kentucky, pg 222
University Press of Mississippi, pg 222
University Science Books, pg 222
US Government Publishing Office (GPO), pg 223
VanDam Inc, pg 223
Vernon Press, pg 224
Voyager Sopris Learning Inc, pg 225
Washington State University Press, pg 226
Water Environment Federation, pg 226
Water Resources Publications LLC, pg 226
Waveland Press Inc, pg 226
Wellington Press, pg 227
Wiley-Blackwell, pg 229
William Carey Publishing, pg 230
Wisconsin Department of Public Instruction, pg 231
Wolfman Books, pg 232
World Resources Institute, pg 233
World Scientific Publishing Co Inc, pg 233
Xlibris Corp, pg 234
Yale University Press, pg 235

EROTICA

AK Press, pg 6
Asta Publications LLC, pg 20
Blue Note Publications Inc, pg 32
Bold Strokes Books Inc, pg 33
Book Sales, pg 33
Circlet Press, pg 48
Cleis Press, pg 49
Gale, pg 75
Gingko Press Inc, pg 78
Histria Books, pg 93
ImaJinn Books, pg 99
Inner Traditions International Ltd, pg 101
Macmillan Reference USA™, pg 123
New Concepts Publishing, pg 139
Polis Books, pg 162
powerHouse Books, pg 162
Riverdale Avenue Books (RAB), pg 175
Schiffer Publishing Ltd, pg 183
STARbooks Press, pg 197
Strategic Book Publishing (SBP), pg 199
Tantor Media Inc, pg 202
Taschen America, pg 203
Whiskey Creek Press, pg 228
Xlibris Corp, pg 234

ETHNICITY

ABDO, pg 2
Alexander Street, part of Clarivate PLC, pg 6
Amakella Publishing, pg 7
American Diabetes Association, pg 9
August House Inc, pg 22
AuthorHouse, pg 22
Berghahn Books, pg 28
Bess Press Inc, pg 29
Biographical Publishing Co, pg 29
Bolchazy-Carducci Publishers Inc, pg 33
George Braziller Inc, pg 35
Business Research Services Inc, pg 38
Carolina Academic Press, pg 41

295

Cedar Grove Publishing, pg 43
Charlesbridge Publishing Inc, pg 45
Clarity Press Inc, pg 49
Coffee House Press, pg 50
Continental AfrikaPublishers, pg 52
Cornell University Press, pg 52
Council for Research in Values & Philosophy, pg 53
Cross-Cultural Communications, pg 55
Edupress Inc, pg 64
Enslow Publishing LLC, pg 66
Fowler Museum at UCLA, pg 74
Gale, pg 75
Graywolf Press, pg 81
Hamilton Stone Editions, pg 84
Hazelden Publishing, pg 89
Hebrew Union College Press, pg 90
Herald Press, pg 91
Heyday, pg 91
Hippocrene Books Inc, pg 92
Holy Cow! Press, pg 95
Indiana Historical Society Press, pg 99
Kamehameha Publishing, pg 108
Kazi Publications Inc, pg 108
Kensington Publishing Corp, pg 109
Laredo Publishing Co, pg 113
THE Learning Connection®, pg 113
Long River Press, pg 120
LPD Press/Rio Grande Books, pg 121
Macmillan Reference USA™, pg 123
Mandel Vilar Press, pg 124
Marshall Cavendish Education, pg 125
Maryland History Press, pg 126
Mason Crest Publishers, pg 126
McFarland, pg 127
The Edwin Mellen Press, pg 129
Minnesota Historical Society Press, pg 132
Modern Language Association (MLA), pg 133
Multicultural Publications Inc, pg 135
National Resource Center for Youth Services, pg 138
North Star Press of Saint Cloud Inc, pg 142
The Ohio State University Press, pg 145
Ohio University Press, pg 145
Penfield Books, pg 154
Penn State University Press, pg 157
Pennsylvania Historical & Museum Commission, pg 157
Persea Books, pg 158
Peter Pauper Press, Inc, pg 158
Polar Bear & Company, pg 161
Princeton University Press, pg 164
Rational Island Publishers, pg 171
The Red Sea Press Inc, pg 173
Reference Publications Inc, pg 173
Renaissance House, pg 174
Lynne Rienner Publishers Inc, pg 174
Round Table Companies, pg 177
Routledge, pg 177
Russell Sage Foundation, pg 178
Rutgers University Press, pg 178
SAGE Publishing, pg 180
Salem Press, pg 181
Salina Bookshelf Inc, pg 181
San Diego State University Press, pg 182
Stanford University Press, pg 197
Star Bright Books Inc, pg 197
Stone Bridge Press Inc, pg 199
Strategic Book Publishing (SBP), pg 199
Syracuse University Press, pg 201

Teachers College Press, pg 203
Temple University Press, pg 204
Texas A&M University Press, pg 205
Texas Tech University Press, pg 205
Third World Press Foundation, pg 206
Tilbury House Publishers, pg 207
Todd Publications, pg 207
United States Institute of Peace Press, pg 213
The University of Arizona Press, pg 214
University of California Institute on Global Conflict & Cooperation, pg 215
University of Chicago Press, pg 215
University of Georgia Press, pg 216
University of Hawaii Press, pg 216
University of Illinois Press, pg 216
University of Minnesota Press, pg 217
University of New Mexico Press, pg 218
University of North Texas Press, pg 218
University of Notre Dame Press, pg 219
University of Rochester Press, pg 220
University of Wisconsin Press, pg 221
University Press of Colorado, pg 221
University Press of Florida, pg 221
University Press of Mississippi, pg 222
Wellington Press, pg 227
Western Pennsylvania Genealogical Society, pg 228
Markus Wiener Publishers Inc, pg 229
Wiley-Blackwell, pg 229
William Carey Publishing, pg 230
Wisconsin Department of Public Instruction, pg 231
Wolfman Books, pg 232
Woodrow Wilson Center Press, pg 232
World Citizens, pg 233
Xlibris Corp, pg 234

FASHION

Abbeville Press, pg 1
Abbeville Publishing Group, pg 2
Alexander Street, part of Clarivate PLC, pg 6
AuthorHouse, pg 22
Book Sales, pg 33
Chronicle Books LLC, pg 47
Dover Publications Inc, pg 61
Duke University Press, pg 62
EDC Publishing, pg 63
Fairchild Books, pg 69
Gale, pg 75
GemStone Press, pg 77
Gingko Press Inc, pg 78
Glitterati Inc, pg 78
Goodheart-Willcox Publisher, pg 79
Goose River Press, pg 79
Greenleaf Book Group LLC, pg 81
Kent State University Press, pg 109
Kodansha USA Inc, pg 110
The Little Entrepreneur, pg 118
Mason Crest Publishers, pg 126
The Monacelli Press, pg 133
Nataraj Books, pg 136
ORO editions, pg 148
Paintbox Press, pg 150
Palgrave Macmillan, pg 150
Pearson Business Publishing, pg 153

Phaidon, pg 159
Pointed Leaf Press, pg 161
Clarkson Potter, pg 162
powerHouse Books, pg 162
Quite Specific Media Group Ltd, pg 168
Rizzoli International Publications Inc, pg 175
Running Press, pg 178
St James Press®, pg 180
Schiffer Publishing Ltd, pg 183
Stewart, Tabori & Chang, pg 198
Strategic Book Publishing (SBP), pg 199
Union Square & Co, pg 212
Universe Publishing, pg 214
The Vendome Press, pg 224
Watson-Guptill, pg 226
Yale University Press, pg 235
Zest Books, pg 236

FICTION

A 2 Z Press LLC, pg 1
ABDO, pg 2
Academy Chicago Publishers, pg 3
ACTA Publications, pg 4
Advance Publishing Inc, pg 5
AK Press, pg 6
Akashic Books, pg 6
All Things That Matter Press, pg 7
Alloy Entertainment LLC, pg 7
Ambassador International, pg 7
Amber Lotus Publishing, pg 8
American Carriage House Publishing (ACHP), pg 8
American Girl Publishing, pg 10
Amicus, pg 13
Ampersand Inc/Professional Publishing Services, pg 13
Anaphora Literary Press, pg 13
Angelus Press, pg 14
The Apocryphile Press, pg 15
Applewood Books, pg 15
Arcade Publishing Inc, pg 16
Ariadne Press, pg 16
Ariel Press, pg 16
The Arion Press, pg 16
Arte Publico Press, pg 17
ArtWrite Productions, pg 18
Ashland Creek Press, pg 18
Asta Publications LLC, pg 20
Astra Books for Young Readers, pg 20
Atlas Publishing, pg 21
AuthorHouse, pg 22
Authorlink® Press, pg 22
Autumn House Press, pg 22
Avid Reader Press, pg 23
Baker Books, pg 23
Bancroft Press, pg 24
B&H Publishing Group, pg 24
Barbour Publishing Inc, pg 24
Barranca Press, pg 24
Barringer Publishing, pg 24
Barrytown/Station Hill Press, pg 24
Bartleby Press, pg 24
Bear & Bobcat Books, pg 26
Bearport Publishing, pg 26
Beaver's Pond Press Inc, pg 26
Behrman House Inc, pg 27
Frederic C Beil Publisher Inc, pg 27
Bella Books, pg 27
BelleBooks, pg 27
Bellevue Literary Press, pg 27
Ben Yehuda Press, pg 27
BenBella Books Inc, pg 27
BePuzzled, pg 28
Berkley, pg 28
Bethany House Publishers, pg 29
Bethlehem Books, pg 29
BiG GUY BOOKS, pg 29
Biographical Publishing Co, pg 29

Bitingduck Press LLC, pg 30
BJU Press, pg 30
BkMk Press Inc, pg 30
Black Heron Press, pg 30
Black Mountain Press, pg 30
Blair, pg 30
Blue Crane Books Inc, pg 32
Blue Mountain Arts Inc, pg 32
Blue Note Publications Inc, pg 32
BOA Editions Ltd, pg 33
Bold Strokes Books Inc, pg 33
Book Marketing Works LLC, pg 33
Book Sales, pg 33
BookLogix, pg 34
Books on Tape™, pg 34
Boson Books™, pg 34
Bottom Dog Press, pg 34
Brandylane Publishers Inc, pg 35
George Braziller Inc, pg 35
Brentwood Christian Press, pg 36
Brick Tower Press, pg 36
Brilliance Publishing Inc, pg 37
Brown Books Publishing Group (BBPG), pg 38
Bywater Books Inc, pg 39
Campfield & Campfield Publishing LLC, pg 39
Candied Plums, pg 39
Capstone Publishers™, pg 40
Carnegie Mellon University Press, pg 41
Carolrhoda Books Inc, pg 41
Carolrhoda Lab™, pg 41
Caxton Press, pg 42
Cedar Fort Inc, pg 43
Cedar Grove Publishing, pg 43
Cherry Hill Publishing LLC, pg 46
Chickadee Prince Books LLC, pg 46
Child's Play® Inc, pg 46
The Child's World Inc, pg 46
China Books, pg 47
Chronicle Books LLC, pg 47
City Lights Publishers, pg 48
Clarion Books, pg 48
Cleis Press, pg 49
CN Times Books, pg 50
Codhill Press, pg 50
Coffee House Press, pg 50
Concordia Publishing House, pg 51
Continental AfrikaPublishers, pg 52
Cornell Maritime Press, pg 52
Cornerstone Book Publishers, pg 53
Counterpath Press, pg 54
Counterpoint Press LLC, pg 54
Covenant Communications Inc, pg 54
Crabtree Publishing Co, pg 54
Cricket Cottage Publishing LLC, pg 55
Cross-Cultural Communications, pg 55
Crown Publishing Group, pg 56
Dalkey Archive Press, pg 56
Dancing Dakini Press, pg 57
Dancing Lemur Press LLC, pg 57
Dark Horse Comics, pg 57
DC Comics Inc, pg 58
Deep River Books LLC, pg 58
Delphinium Books, pg 58
Deseret Book Co, pg 58
Dial Books for Young Readers, pg 59
Disney-Hyperion Books, pg 59
Disney Press, pg 59
Disney Publishing Worldwide, pg 60
Diversion Books, pg 60
The Donning Company Publishers, pg 60
Doodle and Peck Publishing, pg 60
Dordt Press, pg 60
Dorrance Publishing Co Inc, pg 61

Doubleday, pg 61
Dover Publications Inc, pg 61
Down East Books, pg 61
Down The Shore Publishing, pg 61
Dreamscape Media LLC, pg 62
Duke University Press, pg 62
Dutton, pg 62
Eakin Press, pg 62
Easy Money Press, pg 63
EDC Publishing, pg 63
ediciones Lerner, pg 63
Editorial Portavoz, pg 64
Eifrig Publishing LLC, pg 64
Elderberry Press Inc, pg 65
Elva Resa Publishing, pg 65
Emerald Books, pg 66
Epicenter Press Inc, pg 67
Etruscan Press, pg 67
Europa Editions, pg 67
M Evans & Company, pg 68
Everyman's Library, pg 68
Excelsior Editions, pg 68
Familius, pg 69
Farrar, Straus & Giroux Books for Young Readers, pg 69
Farrar, Straus & Giroux, LLC, pg 70
Father & Son Publishing Inc, pg 70
The Feminist Press at The City University of New York, pg 71
Fence Books, pg 71
Fiction Collective 2 (FC2), pg 71
Fine Creative Media, Inc, pg 71
Firefall Editions, pg 72
First Avenue Editions, pg 72
Fitzroy Books, pg 72
Flamingo Books, pg 72
Galaxy Press Inc, pg 75
Gale, pg 75
Gallery Books, pg 76
Gareth Stevens Publishing, pg 76
Gauthier Publications Inc, pg 77
Gibbs Smith Publisher, pg 78
Global Authors Publications (GAP), pg 78
Global Publishing Solutions LLC, pg 79
Godine, pg 79
Goose River Press, pg 79
Gorgias Press LLC, pg 80
Gospel Publishing House, pg 80
Grand & Archer Publishing, pg 80
Grand Central Publishing, pg 80
Donald M Grant Publisher Inc, pg 80
Graphic Universe™, pg 80
Graywolf Press, pg 81
Green Dragon Books, pg 81
Green Integer, pg 81
Greenleaf Book Group LLC, pg 81
Grove Atlantic Inc, pg 82
Guideposts Book & Inspirational Media, pg 82
Hachette Nashville, pg 83
Handprint Books Inc, pg 84
Hanging Loose Press, pg 85
Hannacroix Creek Books Inc, pg 85
Harlequin Enterprises Ltd, pg 85
HarperCollins Children's Books, pg 85
HarperCollins Publishers LLC, pg 86
Harvard Square Editions, pg 88
Harvest House Publishers Inc, pg 88
Health Communications Inc, pg 89
Hellgate Press, pg 91
Herald Press, pg 91
Highlights for Children Inc, pg 92
History Publishing Co LLC, pg 93
Histria Books, pg 93
Hollym International Corp, pg 94
Henry Holt and Company, LLC, pg 94

Holy Cow! Press, pg 95
Homa & Sekey Books, pg 95
Homestead Publishing, pg 95
Host Publications, pg 95
Houghton Mifflin Harcourt, pg 95
Houghton Mifflin Harcourt Trade & Reference Division, pg 96
Hutton Publishing, pg 97
Ignatius Press, pg 98
ImaJinn Books, pg 99
Immedium, pg 99
In the Garden Publishing, pg 99
The Innovation Press, pg 101
Interlink Publishing Group Inc, pg 102
Iris Press, pg 104
Iron Stream Media, pg 104
Islandport Press, pg 105
Italica Press, pg 105
Italics Publishing, pg 105
Joshua Tree Publishing, pg 107
Judaica Press Inc, pg 107
Jump at the Sun, pg 107
Kaeden Publishing, pg 107
Kar-Ben Publishing, pg 108
Kelsey Street Press, pg 108
Kensington Publishing Corp, pg 109
Alfred A Knopf, pg 110
Koho Pono LLC, pg 111
Kokila, pg 111
Kregel Publications, pg 111
LARB Books, pg 113
Laredo Publishing Co, pg 113
Lasaria Creative Publishing, pg 113
Leaf Storm Press, pg 113
Learning Links-USA Inc, pg 114
Lectorum Publications Inc, pg 114
Lerner Publications, pg 115
Lerner Publishing Group Inc, pg 115
Library of America, pg 116
Light-Beams Publishing, pg 116
Light Publications, pg 116
Listen & Live Audio Inc, pg 117
little bee books, pg 117
Little, Brown and Company, pg 118
Little, Brown Books for Young Readers (LBYR), pg 118
The Little Entrepreneur, pg 118
Livingston Press, pg 119
Llewellyn Publications, pg 119
Long River Press, pg 120
Love Inspired Books, pg 120
LPD Press/Rio Grande Books, pg 121
LRS, pg 121
Lynx House Press, pg 121
The Lyons Press, pg 121
Macmillan, pg 121
Mage Publishers Inc, pg 123
Management Advisory Services & Publications (MASP), pg 123
Mandel Vilar Press, pg 124
Manic D Press Inc, pg 124
Maren Green Publishing Inc, pg 125
Marick Press, pg 125
Maryland History Press, pg 126
McBooks Press, pg 127
McPherson & Co, pg 128
McSweeney's Publishing, pg 128
Michigan State University Press (MSU Press), pg 130
Midnight Marquee Press Inc, pg 130
Mighty Media Press, pg 131
Milkweed Editions, pg 131
Modern Language Association (MLA), pg 133
Modern Memoirs Inc, pg 133
Mondial, pg 133
Monkfish Book Publishing Co, pg 133
Montemayor Press, pg 133

Moonshine Cove Publishing LLC, pg 134
Morgan James Publishing, pg 134
Moriah Books, pg 134
Multicultural Publications Inc, pg 135
Multnomah, pg 135
Museum of New Mexico Press, pg 135
Mutual Publishing LLC, pg 136
Nataraj Books, pg 136
Naval Institute Press, pg 139
NavPress Publishing Group, pg 139
NBM Publishing Inc, pg 139
New Directions Publishing Corp, pg 139
New Issues Poetry & Prose, pg 140
The New Press, pg 140
NewSouth Books, pg 141
NFB Publishing, pg 141
Norilana Books, pg 142
North Atlantic Books (NAB), pg 142
North Star Editions Inc, pg 142
North Star Press of Saint Cloud Inc, pg 142
Northwestern University Press, pg 143
W W Norton & Company Inc, pg 143
Norwood House Press, pg 143
Nosy Crow Inc, pg 144
The Oaklea Press Inc, pg 145
Oceanview Publishing Inc, pg 145
Odyssey Books, pg 145
The Ohio State University Press, pg 145
Ohio University Press, pg 145
Olde & Oppenheim Publishers, pg 146
Omnidawn, pg 146
On the Write Path Publishing, pg 146
Ooligan Press, pg 146
Open Books Press, pg 146
Open Letter, pg 147
Orbit, pg 147
Other Press, pg 148
The Overlook Press, pg 148
Richard C Owen Publishers Inc, pg 149
Ozark Mountain Publishing Inc, pg 149
P & R Publishing Co, pg 149
Pact Press, pg 150
Pantheon Books, pg 150
Pants On Fire Press, pg 150
Papercutz, pg 150
Parachute Publishing LLC, pg 151
Paraclete Press Inc, pg 151
Paradise Cay Publications Inc, pg 151
Park Place Publications, pg 152
Parmenides Publishing, pg 152
Path Press Inc, pg 152
Paul Dry Books, pg 152
Pauline Books & Media, pg 152
Nancy Paulsen Books, pg 152
Peachtree Publishing Co Inc, pg 153
Pen & Publish LLC, pg 153
Pen-L Publishing, pg 153
Penfield Books, pg 154
Penguin Press, pg 154
Penguin Publishing Group, pg 154
Penguin Random House Audio Publishing Group, pg 154
Penguin Random House LLC, pg 155
Penguin Workshop, pg 156
Penguin Young Readers Group, pg 156
Penn State University Press, pg 157
Penny-Farthing Productions, pg 157

Pentecostal Resources Group, pg 157
Perfection Learning®, pg 158
The Permanent Press, pg 158
Persea Books, pg 158
Philomel Books, pg 159
Picador, pg 159
Pineapple Press, pg 160
Planert Creek Press, pg 160
Pleasure Boat Studio: A Literary Press, pg 160
Plough Publishing House, pg 161
Ploughshares, pg 161
Plowshare Media, pg 161
Plum Tree Books, pg 161
Pocol Press, pg 161
Poisoned Pen Press, pg 161
Polar Bear & Company, pg 161
Polis Books, pg 162
Publication Consultants, pg 167
Purple House Press, pg 167
Pushcart Press, pg 167
GP Putnam's Sons, pg 167
Pyncheon House, pg 167
Quincannon Publishing Group, pg 168
Quirk Books, pg 168
Rand-Smith Publishing, pg 169
Random House Large Print, pg 170
Random House Publishing Group, pg 170
Raven Publishing Inc, pg 172
Ravenhawk™ Books, pg 172
Reader's Digest Select Editions, pg 172
Recorded Books Inc, an RBmedia company, pg 172
Red Chair Press, pg 172
Red Hen Press, pg 172
Red Moon Press, pg 172
Robert D Reed Publishers, pg 173
Regal House Publishing, pg 173
Remember Point Inc, pg 174
Revell, pg 174
River City Publishing, pg 175
Riverdale Avenue Books (RAB), pg 175
Riverhead Books, pg 175
The RoadRunner Press, pg 175
Roaring Brook Press, pg 175
RockHill Publishing LLC, pg 176
Rocky Pond Books, pg 176
Rootstock Publishing, pg 176
Ross Books, pg 177
Running Press, pg 178
Saddleback Educational Publishing, pg 179
Saint Mary's Press, pg 181
Salina Bookshelf Inc, pg 181
San Diego State University Press, pg 182
Santa Monica Press LLC, pg 182
Sarabande Books Inc, pg 182
Savant Books & Publications LLC, pg 182
Scarsdale Publishing Ltd, pg 183
Schaffner Press, pg 183
Schocken Books, pg 183
Scholastic Inc, pg 184
Schreiber Publishing, pg 185
Science & Humanities Press, pg 185
Scripta Humanistica Publishing International, pg 185
Seven Stories Press, pg 186
1765 Productions, pg 186
Shadow Mountain Publishing, pg 187
Shambhala Publications Inc, pg 187
Shepard Publications, pg 187
Sherman Asher Publishing, pg 187
Signalman Publishing, pg 187
Signature Books Publishing LLC, pg 187

Silver Leaf Books LLC, pg 188
Simon & Schuster Audio, pg 189
Simon & Schuster Children's Publishing, pg 189
Sky Pony Press, pg 191
Sleeping Bear Press™, pg 191
Small Beer Press, pg 191
Soho Press Inc, pg 193
Sourcebooks LLC, pg 194
Sourced Media Books, pg 195
Square One Publishers Inc, pg 196
Star Bright Books Inc, pg 197
STARbooks Press, pg 197
Stargazer Publishing Co, pg 197
Stone Bridge Press Inc, pg 199
Stone Pier Press, pg 199
The Story Plant, pg 199
Strategic Book Publishing (SBP), pg 199
Strategic Media Books LLC, pg 200
Sunstone Press, pg 201
Swallow Press, pg 201
Swan Isle Press, pg 201
Tachyon Publications LLC, pg 202
Nan A Talese, pg 202
Tanglewood Publishing, pg 202
Tantor Media Inc, pg 202
Texas Tech University Press, pg 205
Third World Press Foundation, pg 206
Thorndike Press®, pg 206
ThunderStone Books, pg 207
Top Publications Ltd, pg 207
Tor Publishing Group, pg 207
Tortuga Press, pg 208
TotalRecall Publications Inc, pg 208
Trans-Atlantic Publications Inc, pg 209
TriQuarterly Books, pg 209
TRISTAN Publishing, pg 209
Tupelo Press Inc, pg 210
Turner Publishing Co LLC, pg 210
Turtle Point Press, pg 210
Tuttle Publishing, pg 211
Twilight Times Books, pg 211
Tyndale House Publishers Inc, pg 211
Union Square & Co, pg 212
University of Alabama Press, pg 214
University of Alaska Press, pg 214
The University of Arizona Press, pg 214
University of Georgia Press, pg 216
University of Hawaii Press, pg 216
University of Iowa Press, pg 216
University of Louisiana at Lafayette Press, pg 217
University of Massachusetts Press, pg 217
University of Michigan Press, pg 217
University of Minnesota Press, pg 217
University of Nevada Press, pg 218
University of New Orleans Press, pg 218
University of North Texas Press, pg 218
University of Oklahoma Press, pg 219
University of Pittsburgh Press, pg 219
University Press of Mississippi, pg 222
University Publishing House, pg 222
Urim Publications, pg 223
Verso Books, pg 224
Vesuvian Books, pg 224
Viking Children's Books, pg 224
Viking Penguin, pg 224
Vintage Books, pg 225
WaterBrook, pg 226
Watermark Publishing, pg 226
Welcome Rain Publishers LLC, pg 227
West Margin Press, pg 227
West Virginia University Press, pg 228
Western Reflections Publishing Co, pg 228
Whiskey Creek Press, pg 228
Markus Wiener Publishers Inc, pg 229
Wilderness Adventures Press Inc, pg 229
Wildflower Press, pg 229
Williams & Company Book Publishers, pg 230
Wings Press, pg 231
Winterwolf Press, pg 231
Wizards of the Coast LLC, pg 231
Wolfman Books, pg 232
WoodstockArts, pg 232
Workman Publishing, pg 232
World Citizens, pg 233
Xlibris Corp, pg 234
Yard Dog Press, pg 235
Yotzeret Publishing, pg 236
Zondervan, pg 236
Zumaya Publications LLC, pg 237

FILM, VIDEO

Abbeville Press, pg 1
Abbeville Publishing Group, pg 2
Alexander Street, part of Clarivate PLC, pg 6
Allworth Press, pg 7
Anaphora Literary Press, pg 13
Applause Theatre & Cinema Books, pg 15
AuthorHouse, pg 22
Barrytown/Station Hill Press, pg 24
BearManor Media, pg 26
BenBella Books Inc, pg 27
Berghahn Books, pg 28
Black Mountain Press, pg 30
Blood Moon Productions Ltd, pg 31
Bloomsbury Academic, pg 31
Chicago Review Press, pg 46
China Books, pg 47
Columbia University Press, pg 51
Comex Systems Inc, pg 51
Concordia Publishing House, pg 51
Counterpath Press, pg 54
DiscoverNet Publishing, pg 59
DK, pg 60
Duke University Press, pg 62
Elsevier Inc, pg 65
Gale, pg 75
Gingko Press Inc, pg 78
Green Integer, pg 81
Greenleaf Book Group LLC, pg 81
Group Publishing Inc, pg 82
Hal Leonard LLC, pg 84
Hazelden Publishing, pg 89
Her Own Words LLC, pg 91
Histria Books, pg 93
Immedium, pg 99
Indiana Historical Society Press, pg 99
Indiana University African Studies Program, pg 100
Indiana University Press, pg 100
Insight Editions, pg 101
Peter Lang Publishing Inc, pg 112
Learning Links-USA Inc, pg 114
Limelight Editions, pg 117
McFarland, pg 127
McGraw-Hill Higher Education, pg 128
McPherson & Co, pg 128
The Edwin Mellen Press, pg 129
Midnight Marquee Press Inc, pg 130
Modern Language Association (MLA), pg 133
The Museum of Modern Art (MoMA), pg 135
Nataraj Books, pg 136
National Council of Teachers of English (NCTE), pg 137
Northwestern University Press, pg 143
Olde & Oppenheim Publishers, pg 146
Omnibus Press, pg 146
One On One Book Publishing/Film-Video Publications, pg 146
Open Horizons Publishing Co, pg 147
Palgrave Macmillan, pg 150
Phaidon, pg 159
The Press at California State University, Fresno, pg 163
Primary Research Group Inc, pg 163
PSMJ Resources Inc, pg 166
Running Press, pg 178
Rutgers University Press, pg 178
SAGE Publishing, pg 180
St James Press®, pg 180
Santa Monica Press LLC, pg 182
Schaffner Press, pg 183
1765 Productions, pg 186
Silman-James Press Inc, pg 188
Stone Bridge Press Inc, pg 199
Tantor Media Inc, pg 202
Teacher's Discovery®, pg 203
Temple University Press, pg 204
Trafalgar Square Books, pg 208
University of California Press, pg 215
University of Illinois Press, pg 216
University of Minnesota Press, pg 217
The University of Utah Press, pg 220
University of Wisconsin Press, pg 221
The University Press of Kentucky, pg 222
University Press of Mississippi, pg 222
Watson-Guptill, pg 226
Wayne State University Press, pg 226
Welcome Books, pg 227
Wesleyan University Press, pg 227
Michael Wiese Productions, pg 229

FINANCE

AICPA® & CIMA®, pg 5
The American College of Financial Services, pg 9
American Institute for Economic Research (AIER), pg 10
The American Library Association (ALA), pg 10
American Numismatic Society, pg 11
Annual Reviews, pg 14
Aspatore Books, pg 19
Association of School Business Officials International, pg 20
Asta Publications LLC, pg 20
Atlantic Publishing Group Inc, pg 21
Atlas Publishing, pg 21
AuthorHouse, pg 22
Avery, pg 23
Beaver's Pond Press Inc, pg 26
Bisk Education, pg 29
Bluestocking Press, pg 33
BoardSource, pg 33
Bookhaven Press LLC, pg 34
BookLogix, pg 34
Nicholas Brealey Publishing, pg 36
Brick Tower Press, pg 36
Brown Books Publishing Group (BBPG), pg 38
BuilderBooks, pg 38
Business Expert Press, pg 38
Carolina Academic Press, pg 41
Cengage Learning, pg 43
Clarity Press Inc, pg 49
Columbia University Press, pg 51
Consumer Press, pg 52
Cornell University Press, pg 52
Edward Elgar Publishing Inc, pg 65
Elsevier Inc, pg 65
Financial Times Press, pg 71
Fordham University Press, pg 73
Frederick Fell Publishers Inc, pg 74
Gale, pg 75
The Globe Pequot Press, pg 79
Greenleaf Book Group LLC, pg 81
Grey House Publishing Inc™, pg 81
Harvard Business Review Press, pg 87
Health Administration Press, pg 89
Humanix Books LLC, pg 97
Hutton Publishing, pg 97
IBFD North America Inc (International Bureau of Fiscal Documentation), pg 98
The Institutes™, pg 102
International City/County Management Association (ICMA), pg 102
International Monetary Fund (IMF), Editorial & Publications Division, pg 103
International Wealth Success (IWS), pg 104
Iron Stream Media, pg 104
Kallisti Publishing Inc, pg 108
Kogan Page, pg 111
McGraw-Hill Higher Education, pg 128
McGraw-Hill School Education Group, pg 128
National Academies Press (NAP), pg 136
National Association of Broadcasters (NAB), pg 136
National Center For Employee Ownership (NCEO), pg 137
The National Underwriter Co, pg 138
NOLO, pg 141
W W Norton & Company Inc, pg 143
NRP Direct, pg 144
OECD Washington Center, pg 145
Omnigraphics Inc, pg 146
One On One Book Publishing/Film-Video Publications, pg 146
Palgrave Macmillan, pg 150
Pennsylvania State Data Center, pg 157
Peterson Institute for International Economics (PIIE), pg 158
Plunkett Research Ltd, pg 161
Portfolio, pg 162
Princeton University Press, pg 164
The RoadRunner Press, pg 175
Rodin Books, pg 176
SAGE Publishing, pg 180
Science & Humanities Press, pg 185
1765 Productions, pg 186
Small Business Advisors Inc, pg 191
Society for Mining, Metallurgy & Exploration, pg 192
Sourcebooks LLC, pg 194
Square One Publishers Inc, pg 196
Stanford University Press, pg 197

PUBLISHERS

Strategic Book Publishing (SBP), pg 199
Tantor Media Inc, pg 202
Todd Publications, pg 207
TotalRecall Publications Inc, pg 208
United Nations Publications, pg 213
US Government Publishing Office (GPO), pg 223
Vault.com Inc, pg 224
Vernon Press, pg 224
Wiley-Blackwell, pg 229
John Wiley & Sons Inc, pg 230
John Wiley & Sons Inc Professional Development, pg 230
Windsor Books, pg 230
Wisconsin Department of Public Instruction, pg 231
Wolters Kluwer US Corp, pg 232
World Bank Publications, pg 233
World Trade Press LLC, pg 234
Xlibris Corp, pg 234
Zondervan, pg 236

FOREIGN COUNTRIES

Abbeville Publishing Group, pg 2
ABDO, pg 2
Adventures Unlimited Press (AUP), pg 5
Algora Publishing, pg 7
Amakella Publishing, pg 7
Ariadne Press, pg 16
Art of Living, PrimaMedia Inc, pg 17
AuthorHouse, pg 22
Barranca Press, pg 24
Beaver's Pond Press Inc, pg 26
BJU Press, pg 30
Black Rabbit Books, pg 30
Brandylane Publishers Inc, pg 35
Brown Books Publishing Group (BBPG), pg 38
Capstone Publishers™, pg 40
Carolina Academic Press, pg 41
Chelsea House, pg 45
Cheng & Tsui Co Inc, pg 46
China Books, pg 47
Clarity Press Inc, pg 49
Cognizant Communication Corp, pg 50
Continental AfrikaPublishers, pg 52
Cornell University Press, pg 52
Council for Research in Values & Philosophy, pg 53
Crabtree Publishing Co, pg 54
Cross-Cultural Communications, pg 55
Walter De Gruyter Inc, pg 58
EDC Publishing, pg 63
Enslow Publishing LLC, pg 66
Evan-Moor Educational Publishers, pg 68
Fowler Museum at UCLA, pg 74
Gale, pg 75
Harvard Ukrainian Research Institute, pg 88
Hippocrene Books Inc, pg 92
Hollym International Corp, pg 94
Homa & Sekey Books, pg 95
Hudson Institute, pg 97
Human Rights Watch, pg 97
Ibex Publishers, pg 98
IBFD North America Inc (International Bureau of Fiscal Documentation), pg 98
Inter-American Development Bank, pg 102
Inter-University Consortium for Political & Social Research (ICPSR), pg 102
International Monetary Fund (IMF), Editorial & Publications Division, pg 103

Just World Books LLC, pg 107
Kumarian Press, pg 112
LARB Books, pg 113
Lorenz Educational Press, pg 120
Lucent Press, pg 121
Macmillan Reference USA™, pg 123
Mage Publishers Inc, pg 123
Marshall Cavendish Education, pg 125
Milliken Publishing Co, pg 132
Mitchell Lane Publishers Inc, pg 133
Monthly Review Press, pg 134
ORO editions, pg 148
Pangaea Publications, pg 150
Penfield Books, pg 154
The PRS Group Inc, pg 166
Rational Island Publishers, pg 171
Reference Publications Inc, pg 173
Lynne Rienner Publishers Inc, pg 174
Satya House Publications, pg 182
Schaffner Press, pg 183
Stone Bridge Press Inc, pg 199
Strategic Book Publishing (SBP), pg 199
Summertime Publications Inc, pg 200
Taschen America, pg 203
Teacher's Discovery®, pg 203
ThunderStone Books, pg 207
Travelers' Tales, pg 209
Tuttle Publishing, pg 211
Twenty-First Century Books, pg 211
United States Institute of Peace Press, pg 213
University of California Institute on Global Conflict & Cooperation, pg 215
US Government Publishing Office (GPO), pg 223
The Vendome Press, pg 224
Wheatherstone Press, pg 228
William Carey Publishing, pg 230
Woodrow Wilson Center Press, pg 232
World Bank Publications, pg 233
World Citizens, pg 233
World Trade Press LLC, pg 234

GARDENING, PLANTS

Abbeville Press, pg 1
Abbeville Publishing Group, pg 2
ACC Art Books, pg 3
Acres USA, pg 4
AdventureKEEN, pg 5
All Things That Matter Press, pg 7
Sara Anderson Children's Books, pg 13
ANR Publications University of California, pg 14
APS PRESS, pg 16
Art of Living, PrimaMedia Inc, pg 17
Ash Tree Publishing, pg 18
AuthorHouse, pg 22
The Blackburn Press, pg 30
Book Sales, pg 33
BPC, pg 35
Brandylane Publishers Inc, pg 35
Brick Tower Press, pg 36
Camino Books Inc, pg 39
Cedar Fort Inc, pg 43
Charlesbridge Publishing Inc, pg 45
Chelsea Green Publishing Co, pg 45
China Books, pg 47
Chronicle Books LLC, pg 47
Cleis Press, pg 49
Cornell University Press, pg 52
Countryman Press, pg 54
Creative Homeowner, pg 55

DK, pg 60
Dover Publications Inc, pg 61
Down East Books, pg 61
Duke University Press, pg 62
EDC Publishing, pg 63
Familius, pg 69
FC&A Publishing, pg 70
Fox Chapel Publishing Co Inc, pg 74
Fulcrum Publishing Inc, pg 75
Gale, pg 75
Gibbs Smith Publisher, pg 78
Glitterati Inc, pg 78
Godine, pg 79
Gray & Company Publishers, pg 80
Greenleaf Book Group LLC, pg 81
HarperCollins Publishers LLC, pg 86
Hatherleigh Press Ltd, pg 88
Hay House LLC, pg 89
Heyday, pg 91
Houghton Mifflin Harcourt, pg 95
Idyll Arbor Inc, pg 98
Jewish Lights Publishing, pg 105
Jump!, pg 107
Klutz®, pg 110
Kodansha USA Inc, pg 110
Leisure Arts Inc, pg 114
Llewellyn Publications, pg 119
Louisiana State University Press, pg 120
Mighty Media Press, pg 131
Mitchell Lane Publishers Inc, pg 133
The Monacelli Press, pg 133
Mountain Press Publishing Co, pg 135
Museum of New Mexico Press, pg 135
The New York Botanical Garden Press, pg 140
North Point Press, pg 142
Ohio University Press, pg 145
On the Write Path Publishing, pg 146
ORO editions, pg 148
PA Press, pg 149
Park Place Publications, pg 152
Phaidon, pg 159
Pineapple Press, pg 160
Clarkson Potter, pg 162
Quarto Publishing Group USA Inc, pg 168
Reader's Digest Trade Publishing, pg 172
Rio Nuevo Publishers, pg 175
Rizzoli International Publications Inc, pg 175
Running Press, pg 178
Sasquatch Books, pg 182
Schiffer Publishing Ltd, pg 183
Sentient Publications LLC, pg 186
Stewart, Tabori & Chang, pg 198
Stipes Publishing LLC, pg 198
Stone Bridge Press Inc, pg 199
Stone Pier Press, pg 199
Strategic Book Publishing (SBP), pg 199
Sunstone Press, pg 201
Tantor Media Inc, pg 202
Taschen America, pg 203
Taunton Books, pg 203
Tuttle Publishing, pg 211
Union Square & Co, pg 212
University of Hawaii Press, pg 216
University of Iowa Press, pg 216
University Press of Florida, pg 221
University Press of Mississippi, pg 222
The Vendome Press, pg 224
Watermark Publishing, pg 226
Willow Creek Press, pg 230

Winterthur Museum, Garden & Library, pg 231
Workman Publishing, pg 232

GENEALOGY

Alexander Street, part of Clarivate PLC, pg 6
Ampersand Inc/Professional Publishing Services, pg 13
Arcadia Publishing Inc, pg 16
AuthorHouse, pg 22
Avotaynu Books LLC, pg 23
BookLogix, pg 34
Brown Books Publishing Group (BBPG), pg 38
Clearfield Co Inc, pg 49
Closson Press, pg 49
Elderberry Press Inc, pg 65
Everything Goes Media LLC, pg 68
Father & Son Publishing Inc, pg 70
Gale, pg 75
Genealogical Publishing Co, pg 77
Goose River Press, pg 79
William S Hein & Co Inc, pg 90
Heritage Books Inc, pg 91
Higginson Book Company LLC, pg 91
Horizon Publishers & Distributors Inc, pg 95
Indiana Historical Society Press, pg 99
Iron Gate Publishing, pg 104
Macmillan Reference USA™, pg 123
Maryland History Press, pg 126
The Edwin Mellen Press, pg 129
Modern Memoirs Inc, pg 133
Newbury Street Press, pg 141
North Carolina Office of Archives & History, pg 142
Ohio Genealogical Society, pg 145
Pennsylvania Historical & Museum Commission, pg 157
South Dakota Historical Society Press, pg 195
Southern Historical Press Inc, pg 195
TotalRecall Publications Inc, pg 208
University of Louisiana at Lafayette Press, pg 217
University Press of Mississippi, pg 222
Western Pennsylvania Genealogical Society, pg 228

GEOGRAPHY, GEOLOGY

ABDO, pg 2
Academic Press, pg 3
AdventureKEEN, pg 5
Alexander Street, part of Clarivate PLC, pg 6
American Geophysical Union (AGU), pg 10
American Geosciences Institute (AGI), pg 10
American Press, pg 11
APC Publishing, pg 15
AuthorHouse, pg 22
Bess Press Inc, pg 29
Black Dome Press Corp, pg 30
Black Rabbit Books, pg 30
The Blackburn Press, pg 30
Bureau of Economic Geology, pg 38
Capstone Publishers™, pg 40
Cengage Learning, pg 43
The Center for Learning, pg 43
Chelsea House, pg 45
The Child's World Inc, pg 46
China Books, pg 47

Crabtree Publishing Co, pg 54
Walter De Gruyter Inc, pg 58
Duke University Press, pg 62
East West Discovery Press, pg 63
EDC Publishing, pg 63
Educational Insights®, pg 64
Edward Elgar Publishing Inc, pg 65
Enslow Publishing LLC, pg 66
Evan-Moor Educational Publishers, pg 68
Facts On File, pg 69
First Avenue Editions, pg 72
Gale, pg 75
Gallopade International Inc, pg 76
Gareth Stevens Publishing, pg 76
The Geological Society of America Inc (GSA), pg 77
GeoLytics Inc, pg 77
The Guilford Press, pg 82
Illinois State Museum Society, pg 99
Jones & Bartlett Learning LLC, pg 107
Jump!, pg 107
THE Learning Connection®, pg 113
Learning Links-USA Inc, pg 114
Lerner Publications, pg 115
Lerner Publishing Group Inc, pg 115
Lexington Books, pg 115
Lorenz Educational Press, pg 120
Macmillan Learning, pg 123
Macmillan Reference USA™, pg 123
Marshall Cavendish Education, pg 125
Mason Crest Publishers, pg 126
Master Books®, pg 126
Mazda Publishers Inc, pg 127
The McDonald & Woodward Publishing Co, pg 127
McGraw-Hill Education, pg 127
McGraw-Hill Higher Education, pg 128
The Edwin Mellen Press, pg 129
Merriam-Webster Inc, pg 129
Milliken Publishing Co, pg 132
Mitchell Lane Publishers Inc, pg 133
Moonshine Cove Publishing LLC, pg 134
Mountain Press Publishing Co, pg 135
Nataraj Books, pg 136
National Academies Press (NAP), pg 136
National Geographic Books, pg 137
Nystrom Education, pg 144
Omnigraphics Inc, pg 146
Oxford University Press USA, pg 149
Pearson Business Publishing, pg 153
Pennsylvania State Data Center, pg 157
Petroleum Extension Service (PETEX), pg 159
Princeton University Press, pg 164
Rand McNally, pg 169
Reference Publications Inc, pg 173
Routledge, pg 177
Rowman & Littlefield, pg 178
SAGE Publishing, pg 180
Star Publishing Co Inc, pg 197
Strategic Book Publishing (SBP), pg 199
Sunbelt Publications Inc, pg 200
Syracuse University Press, pg 201
Tantor Media Inc, pg 202
Teaching & Learning Co, pg 204
Transportation Research Board (TRB), pg 209
Trinity University Press, pg 209

Tuttle Publishing, pg 211
Twenty-First Century Books, pg 211
University of Alaska Press, pg 214
The University of Arizona Press, pg 214
University of Chicago Press, pg 215
University of Georgia Press, pg 216
University of Iowa Press, pg 216
University of Minnesota Press, pg 217
University of Nevada Press, pg 218
University of North Texas Press, pg 218
The University of Utah Press, pg 220
US Government Publishing Office (GPO), pg 223
Utah Geological Survey, pg 223
Visible Ink Press®, pg 225
Washington State University Press, pg 226
Water Resources Publications LLC, pg 226
Waveland Press Inc, pg 226
Wiley-Blackwell, pg 229
Wisconsin Department of Public Instruction, pg 231
World Trade Press LLC, pg 234
Yale University Press, pg 235

GOVERNMENT, POLITICAL SCIENCE

ABDO, pg 2
Academica Press, pg 3
ACTA Publications, pg 4
The AEI Press, pg 5
AK Press, pg 6
Akashic Books, pg 6
Algora Publishing, pg 7
American Society for Quality (ASQ), pg 12
Anaphora Literary Press, pg 13
Annual Reviews, pg 14
AOTA Press, pg 14
AuthorHouse, pg 22
Bancroft Press, pg 24
Basic Books Group, pg 25
Baylor University Press, pg 25
Beacon Press, pg 25
Beaver's Pond Press Inc, pg 26
Berghahn Books, pg 28
Bernan, pg 28
BJU Press, pg 30
Bloomsbury Academic, pg 31
Blue Crane Books Inc, pg 32
Bluestocking Press, pg 33
BookLogix, pg 34
Brilliance Publishing Inc, pg 37
The Brookings Institution Press, pg 37
Brown Books Publishing Group (BBPG), pg 38
Carolina Academic Press, pg 41
The Catholic University of America Press, pg 42
Cato Institute, pg 42
Cengage Learning, pg 43
The Center for Learning, pg 43
Center for Strategic & International Studies (CSIS), pg 44
Chelsea Green Publishing Co, pg 45
Chelsea House, pg 45
China Books, pg 47
City Lights Publishers, pg 48
Clarity Press Inc, pg 49
Close Up Publishing, pg 49
CN Times Books, pg 50
Columbia Books & Information Services (CBIS), pg 50
Columbia University Press, pg 51
Continental AfrikaPublishers, pg 52
Cornell University Press, pg 52

Cosimo Inc, pg 53
Council for Research in Values & Philosophy, pg 53
The Council of State Governments, pg 53
Council on Foreign Relations Press, pg 53
Counterpoint Press LLC, pg 54
CQ Press, pg 54
Crown Publishing Group, pg 56
Dewey Publications Inc, pg 59
Dissertation.com, pg 60
Dordt Press, pg 60
Doubleday, pg 61
Duke University Press, pg 62
Eakin Press, pg 62
EDC Publishing, pg 63
Elderberry Press Inc, pg 65
Edward Elgar Publishing Inc, pg 65
Encounter Books, pg 66
Enslow Publishing LLC, pg 66
Everyman's Library, pg 68
Everything Goes Media LLC, pg 68
Facts On File, pg 69
Focus, pg 73
Fordham University Press, pg 73
Foundation Press, pg 74
Fulcrum Publishing Inc, pg 75
Gale, pg 75
Georgetown University Press, pg 77
Global Authors Publications (GAP), pg 78
The Graduate Group/Booksellers, pg 80
Greenleaf Book Group LLC, pg 81
Grey House Publishing Inc™, pg 81
Grove Atlantic Inc, pg 82
Gryphon Editions, pg 82
Hackett Publishing Co Inc, pg 83
HarperCollins Publishers LLC, pg 86
Harvard Education Publishing Group, pg 88
Her Own Words LLC, pg 91
The Heritage Foundation, pg 91
Hillsdale College Press, pg 92
History Publishing Co LLC, pg 93
Hoover Institution Press, pg 95
Houghton Mifflin Harcourt, pg 95
Hudson Institute, pg 97
Human Rights Watch, pg 97
Humanix Books LLC, pg 97
Independent Institute, pg 99
Indiana Historical Society Press, pg 99
Institute of Governmental Studies, pg 101
Inter-University Consortium for Political & Social Research (ICPSR), pg 102
Interlink Publishing Group Inc, pg 102
International City/County Management Association (ICMA), pg 102
International Monetary Fund (IMF), Editorial & Publications Division, pg 103
Lyndon B Johnson School of Public Affairs, pg 106
Jump!, pg 107
Just World Books LLC, pg 107
J J Keller & Associates, Inc®, pg 108
Kent State University Press, pg 109
Kumarian Press, pg 112
Lanahan Publishers Inc, pg 112
LARB Books, pg 113
The Lawbook Exchange, Ltd, pg 113
THE Learning Connection®, pg 113
Lerner Publications, pg 115
Lexington Books, pg 115

Liberty Fund Inc, pg 116
Libraries Unlimited, pg 116
Long River Press, pg 120
Lucent Press, pg 121
Macmillan Learning, pg 123
Macmillan Reference USA™, pg 123
Mandel Vilar Press, pg 124
Mason Crest Publishers, pg 126
McFarland, pg 127
McGraw-Hill Create, pg 127
McGraw-Hill Higher Education, pg 128
McGraw-Hill School Education Group, pg 128
The Edwin Mellen Press, pg 129
Michigan State University Press (MSU Press), pg 130
Milford Books™, pg 131
Milliken Publishing Co, pg 132
Mitchell Lane Publishers Inc, pg 133
Monthly Review Press, pg 134
Moonshine Cove Publishing LLC, pg 134
Multnomah, pg 135
Nataraj Books, pg 136
National Academies Press (NAP), pg 136
National Center for Children in Poverty, pg 137
National Conference of State Legislatures (NCSL), pg 137
The New Press, pg 140
New York University Press, pg 141
North Atlantic Books (NAB), pg 142
W W Norton & Company Inc, pg 143
Nova Science Publishers Inc, pg 144
Ocean Tree Books, pg 145
OECD Washington Center, pg 145
Ohio University Press, pg 145
On the Write Path Publishing, pg 146
The Original Falcon Press, pg 148
ORO editions, pg 148
Other Press, pg 148
Oxford University Press USA, pg 149
Palgrave Macmillan, pg 150
Pantheon Books, pg 150
Paragon House, pg 151
Penn State University Press, pg 157
Pennsylvania Historical & Museum Commission, pg 157
Pennsylvania State Data Center, pg 157
Peterson Institute for International Economics (PIIE), pg 158
Philosophical Library Inc, pg 159
Planners Press, pg 160
Polar Bear & Company, pg 161
Potomac Books, pg 162
The Press at California State University, Fresno, pg 163
Princeton University Press, pg 164
Progressive Press, pg 165
Prometheus Books, pg 166
The PRS Group Inc, pg 166
Public Citizen, pg 167
Purdue University Press, pg 167
RAND Corp, pg 169
Rational Island Publishers, pg 171
Reference Publications Inc, pg 173
Regnery Publishing, pg 173
Research & Education Association (REA), pg 174
Lynne Rienner Publishers Inc, pg 174
Rodin Books, pg 176
Rowman & Littlefield, pg 178
Russell Sage Foundation, pg 178

SAGE Publishing, pg 180
St Augustine's Press Inc, pg 180
St Martin's Press, LLC, pg 180
Salem Press, pg 181
Sasquatch Books, pg 182
Savant Books & Publications LLC, pg 182
Schaffner Press, pg 183
Science & Humanities Press, pg 185
SelectBooks Inc, pg 186
Seven Stories Press, pg 186
M Lee Smith Publishers, pg 192
Solano Press Books, pg 193
Sourcebooks LLC, pg 194
South Carolina Bar, pg 195
South Dakota Historical Society Press, pg 195
Stanford University Press, pg 197
StarGroup International Inc, pg 197
Stipes Publishing LLC, pg 198
Strategic Book Publishing (SBP), pg 199
Syracuse University Press, pg 201
Tantor Media Inc, pg 202
Teacher's Discovery®, pg 203
Temple University Press, pg 204
Texas A&M University Press, pg 205
Texas Tech University Press, pg 205
Third World Press Foundation, pg 206
Todd Publications, pg 207
Tower Publishing Co, pg 208
Triumph Books LLC, pg 209
Twenty-First Century Books, pg 211
UCLA Latin American Center Publications, pg 212
United Nations Publications, pg 213
United States Institute of Peace Press, pg 213
University of Alabama Press, pg 214
University of Alaska Press, pg 214
University of California Institute on Global Conflict & Cooperation, pg 215
University of Chicago Press, pg 215
University of Delaware Press, pg 215
University of Georgia Press, pg 216
University of Iowa Press, pg 216
University of Louisiana at Lafayette Press, pg 217
University of Massachusetts Press, pg 217
University of Michigan Press, pg 217
University of Minnesota Press, pg 217
University of Missouri Press, pg 217
University of Nebraska Press, pg 217
University of Nevada Press, pg 218
The University of North Carolina Press, pg 218
University of North Texas Press, pg 218
University of Notre Dame Press, pg 219
University of Oklahoma Press, pg 219
University of Pennsylvania Press, pg 219
University of Pittsburgh Press, pg 219
University of Virginia Press, pg 220
University of Wisconsin Press, pg 221
University Press of America Inc, pg 221
University Press of Florida, pg 221
University Press of Kansas, pg 221
The University Press of Kentucky, pg 222
University Press of Mississippi, pg 222
US Government Publishing Office (GPO), pg 223
Vanderbilt University Press, pg 224
Vernon Press, pg 224
Verso Books, pg 224
Washington State University Press, pg 226
WaterBrook, pg 226
Watermark Publishing, pg 226
Waveland Press Inc, pg 226
Wellington Press, pg 227
Wiley-Blackwell, pg 229
Woodrow Wilson Center Press, pg 232
Workers Compensation Research Institute, pg 232
Write Stuff Enterprises LLC, pg 234
Yale University Press, pg 235

HEALTH, NUTRITION

Academic Press, pg 3
Academy of Nutrition & Dietetics, pg 3
Acres USA, pg 4
Adams Media, pg 4
Addicus Books Inc, pg 5
AIHA (American Industrial Hygiene Association), pg 6
Akashic Books, pg 6
AllWrite Publishing, pg 7
Amber Lotus Publishing, pg 8
American Academy of Pediatrics, pg 8
American Correctional Association, pg 9
American Diabetes Association, pg 9
Ampersand Inc/Professional Publishing Services, pg 13
Sara Anderson Children's Books, pg 13
Annual Reviews, pg 14
ANR Publications University of California, pg 14
AOTA Press, pg 14
ARE Press, pg 16
Ariel Press, pg 16
ArtWrite Productions, pg 18
Ash Tree Publishing, pg 18
Association for the Advancement of Blood & Biotherapies, pg 19
AuthorHouse, pg 22
Avery, pg 23
Barrytown/Station Hill Press, pg 24
Bartleby Press, pg 24
Basic Health Publications Inc, pg 25
Bear & Co Inc, pg 26
Beaver's Pond Press Inc, pg 26
BenBella Books Inc, pg 27
Berghahn Books, pg 28
Biographical Publishing Co, pg 29
Black Rabbit Books, pg 30
Blue Note Publications Inc, pg 32
Blue Poppy Press, pg 32
Book Sales, pg 33
BookLogix, pg 34
BPC, pg 35
Brandylane Publishers Inc, pg 35
Brick Tower Press, pg 36
Brown Books Publishing Group (BBPG), pg 38
Bull Publishing Co, pg 38
The Bureau for At-Risk Youth, pg 38
Capstone Publishers™, pg 40
CCH, a Wolters Kluwer business, pg 42
Cedar Fort Inc, pg 43
Cengage Learning, pg 43
Cereals & Grains Association, pg 44
Charisma Media, pg 45
Charles Press Publishers, pg 45
Charlesbridge Publishing Inc, pg 45
Chelsea Green Publishing Co, pg 45
Chelsea House, pg 45
Child's Play® Inc, pg 46
China Books, pg 47
Christian Schools International (CSI), pg 47
Cleis Press, pg 49
Clerisy Press, pg 49
Clinical and Laboratory Standards Institute (CLSI), pg 49
Coaches Choice, pg 50
Consumer Press, pg 52
The Council of State Governments, pg 53
Crabtree Publishing Co, pg 54
Crystal Clarity Publishers, pg 56
Data Trace Publishing Co (DTP), pg 57
Walter De Gruyter Inc, pg 58
Demos Medical Publishing, pg 58
DeVorss & Co, pg 59
Diversion Books, pg 60
DK, pg 60
Doubleday, pg 61
Dragon Door Publications, pg 61
Dutton, pg 62
EDC Publishing, pg 63
Elsevier Health Sciences, pg 65
Enslow Publishing LLC, pg 66
M Evans & Company, pg 68
The Experiment, pg 68
Facts On File, pg 69
Fair Winds Press, pg 69
Familius, pg 69
FC&A Publishing, pg 70
Fine Creative Media, Inc, pg 71
Frederick Fell Publishers Inc, pg 74
Gale, pg 75
Gallery Books, pg 76
Goodheart-Willcox Publisher, pg 79
Green Dragon Books, pg 81
Greenleaf Book Group LLC, pg 81
The Guilford Press, pg 82
HarperCollins Publishers LLC, pg 86
Hartman Publishing Inc, pg 87
Harvard Common Press, pg 87
Hatherleigh Press Ltd, pg 88
Hay House LLC, pg 89
Hazelden Publishing, pg 89
HCPro/DecisionHealth, pg 89
Health Administration Press, pg 89
Health Communications Inc, pg 89
Health Professions Press, pg 90
HeartMath LLC, pg 90
Hilton Publishing Co, pg 92
Himalayan Institute Press, pg 92
Histria Books, pg 93
Homa & Sekey Books, pg 95
Horizon Publishers & Distributors Inc, pg 95
Houghton Mifflin Harcourt Trade & Reference Division, pg 96
Human Kinetics Inc, pg 97
Humanix Books LLC, pg 97
Idyll Arbor Inc, pg 98
Inner Traditions International Ltd, pg 101
Inter-University Consortium for Political & Social Research (ICPSR), pg 102
Johns Hopkins University Press, pg 106
Jones & Bartlett Learning LLC, pg 107
Jump!, pg 107
Kazi Publications Inc, pg 108
Kensington Publishing Corp, pg 109
Kessinger Publishing LLC, pg 109
Alfred A Knopf, pg 110
Kodansha USA Inc, pg 110
Laredo Publishing Co, pg 113
THE Learning Connection®, pg 113
Lectorum Publications Inc, pg 114
Leisure Arts Inc, pg 114
Lerner Publications, pg 115
Mary Ann Liebert Inc, pg 116
Little, Brown and Company, pg 118
Llewellyn Publications, pg 119
Lorenz Educational Press, pg 120
Lotus Press, pg 120
Loving Healing Press Inc, pg 121
Lucent Press, pg 121
Macmillan Learning, pg 123
Macmillan Reference USA™, pg 123
The Magni Co, pg 123
Management Sciences for Health, pg 123
Marshall Cavendish Education, pg 125
Mason Crest Publishers, pg 126
McBooks Press, pg 127
McGraw-Hill Create, pg 127
McGraw-Hill Education, pg 127
McGraw-Hill Higher Education, pg 128
McGraw-Hill School Education Group, pg 128
The Edwin Mellen Press, pg 129
Menasha Ridge Press, pg 129
Milford Books™, pg 131
Milliken Publishing Co, pg 132
Mitchell Lane Publishers Inc, pg 133
Morgan James Publishing, pg 134
Multnomah, pg 135
Nataraj Books, pg 136
National Academies Press (NAP), pg 136
National Book Co, pg 136
National Center for Children in Poverty, pg 137
New World Library, pg 140
New York Academy of Sciences (NYAS), pg 140
Norilana Books, pg 142
North Atlantic Books (NAB), pg 142
Nova Science Publishers Inc, pg 144
OECD Washington Center, pg 145
Omnigraphics Inc, pg 146
On the Write Path Publishing, pg 146
Optometric Extension Program Foundation (OEPF), pg 147
Other Press, pg 148
Paradigm Publications, pg 151
Park Place Publications, pg 152
Pathfinder Publishing Inc, pg 152
Peachtree Publishing Co Inc, pg 153
Pearson Business Publishing, pg 153
Penguin Publishing Group, pg 154
Penn State University Press, pg 157
Platypus Media LLC, pg 160
Clarkson Potter, pg 162
Practice Management Information Corp (PMIC), pg 163
Progressive Press, pg 165
Prometheus Books, pg 166
Public Citizen, pg 167
Purdue University Press, pg 167
Quail Ridge Press (QRP), pg 168
Quarto Publishing Group USA Inc, pg 168
RAND Corp, pg 169
Rational Island Publishers, pg 171

U.S. PUBLISHERS — SUBJECT INDEX

Reader's Digest Trade Publishing, pg 172
Red Wheel/Weiser, pg 173
Robert D Reed Publishers, pg 173
Reference Publications Inc, pg 173
The RoadRunner Press, pg 175
Rocky Pond Books, pg 176
Ronin Publishing Inc, pg 176
The Rosen Publishing Group Inc, pg 177
Ross Books, pg 177
Round Table Companies, pg 177
Rutgers University Press, pg 178
Saddleback Educational Publishing, pg 179
Sagamore Publishing LLC, pg 179
SAGE Publishing, pg 180
St Martin's Press, LLC, pg 180
Salem Press, pg 181
Savant Books & Publications LLC, pg 182
Schaffner Press, pg 183
Schiffer Publishing Ltd, pg 183
Science & Humanities Press, pg 185
Science, Naturally, pg 185
SelectBooks Inc, pg 186
Sentient Publications LLC, pg 186
Seven Stories Press, pg 186
Shadow Mountain Publishing, pg 187
Shambhala Publications Inc, pg 187
Simon & Schuster Audio, pg 189
SLACK® Incorporated, A Wyanoke Group Company, pg 191
Snow Lion, pg 192
Sound Feelings Publishing, pg 194
Sounds True Inc, pg 194
Sourcebooks LLC, pg 194
Springer Publishing Co, pg 196
Square One Publishers Inc, pg 196
Star Bright Books Inc, pg 197
StarGroup International Inc, pg 197
SteinerBooks Inc, pg 198
Stone Pier Press, pg 199
Strategic Book Publishing (SBP), pg 199
Stress Free Kids®, pg 200
Sunrise River Press, pg 201
Sunstone Press, pg 201
Surrey Books, pg 201
Tantor Media Inc, pg 202
TarcherPerigee, pg 202
Terra Nova Books, pg 204
Thieme Medical Publishers Inc, pg 206
ThunderStone Books, pg 207
Todd Publications, pg 207
TSG Publishing Foundation Inc, pg 210
Turner Publishing Co LLC, pg 210
Tuttle Publishing, pg 211
Ulysses Press, pg 212
Union Square & Co, pg 212
United States Pharmacopeia (USP), pg 213
University of Iowa Press, pg 216
University of Rochester Press, pg 220
University Press of Mississippi, pg 222
US Government Publishing Office (GPO), pg 223
Walch Education, pg 225
WaterBrook, pg 226
Waveland Press Inc, pg 226
Whittier Publications Inc, pg 229
Whole Person Associates Inc, pg 229
Wisconsin Department of Public Instruction, pg 231
Woodbine House, pg 232
Workman Publishing, pg 232
World Bank Publications, pg 233

Write Stuff Enterprises LLC, pg 234
WriteLife Publishing, pg 234
Xlibris Corp, pg 234
Yale University Press, pg 235
YMAA Publication Center Inc, pg 235
Zest Books, pg 236
Zondervan, pg 236

HISTORY

Abbeville Press, pg 1
Abbeville Publishing Group, pg 2
ABDO, pg 2
Academica Press, pg 3
Academy Chicago Publishers, pg 3
ACMRS Press, pg 4
Adams Media, pg 4
Adirondack Mountain Club (ADK), pg 5
Adventures Unlimited Press (AUP), pg 5
Africa World Press Inc, pg 5
AK Press, pg 6
Alaska Native Language Center (ANLC), pg 6
Alexander Street, part of Clarivate PLC, pg 6
Algora Publishing, pg 7
AllWrite Publishing, pg 7
Amadeus Press, pg 7
American Alpine Club, pg 8
American Girl Publishing, pg 10
American Historical Association (AHA), pg 10
American Numismatic Society, pg 11
American Philosophical Society Press, pg 11
American Press, pg 11
Ampersand Inc/Professional Publishing Services, pg 13
Anaphora Literary Press, pg 13
Andrews University Press, pg 14
APC Publishing, pg 15
The Apocryphile Press, pg 15
Applewood Books, pg 15
Arcade Publishing Inc, pg 16
Arcadia Publishing Inc, pg 16
Ariadne Press, pg 16
ASCSA Publications, pg 18
Astra Books for Young Readers, pg 20
Astragal Press, pg 20
Atlantic Publishing Group Inc, pg 21
Atlas Publishing, pg 21
AuthorHouse, pg 22
Avery Color Studios, pg 23
Baha'i Publishing Trust, pg 23
Bancroft Press, pg 24
Bartleby Press, pg 24
Basic Books Group, pg 25
Baylor University Press, pg 25
Beacon Press, pg 25
Bear & Co Inc, pg 26
Beaver's Pond Press Inc, pg 26
Bedford/St Martin's, pg 26
Beehive Books, pg 26
Frederic C Beil Publisher Inc, pg 27
Bellerophon Books, pg 27
Berghahn Books, pg 28
Berkshire Publishing Group LLC, pg 28
Bernan, pg 28
Bess Press Inc, pg 29
Bethlehem Books, pg 29
Biographical Publishing Co, pg 29
BJU Press, pg 30
Black Classic Press, pg 30
Black Dome Press Corp, pg 30
Black Rabbit Books, pg 30
Blair, pg 30

Bloomsbury Academic, pg 31
Blue Crane Books Inc, pg 32
BlueBridge, pg 32
Bluestocking Press, pg 33
Bolchazy-Carducci Publishers Inc, pg 33
Book Sales, pg 33
The Book Tree, pg 34
BookLogix, pg 34
Books on Tape™, pg 34
Boson Books™, pg 34
Boydell & Brewer Inc, pg 35
Brandylane Publishers Inc, pg 35
George Braziller Inc, pg 35
Brentwood Christian Press, pg 36
Brick Tower Press, pg 36
Brill Inc, pg 37
Brilliance Publishing Inc, pg 37
Brown Books Publishing Group (BBPG), pg 38
Burford Books, pg 38
Burns Archive Press, pg 38
Cambridge University Press, pg 39
Camino Books Inc, pg 39
Capen Publishing Co Inc, pg 40
Capstone Publishers™, pg 40
Carolina Academic Press, pg 41
Casemate | publishers, pg 41
The Catholic University of America Press, pg 42
Caxton Press, pg 42
Cedar Tree Books, pg 43
Cengage Learning, pg 43
The Center for Learning, pg 43
Centerstream Publishing LLC, pg 44
Charlesbridge Publishing Inc, pg 45
Chelsea House, pg 45
Cherry Hill Publishing LLC, pg 46
Chicago Review Press, pg 46
The Child's World Inc, pg 46
China Books, pg 47
Christian Liberty Press, pg 47
Chronicle Books LLC, pg 47
Cider Mill Press Book Publishers LLC, pg 48
Cistercian Publications, pg 48
Clarity Press Inc, pg 49
Clear Light Publishers, pg 49
Clearfield Co Inc, pg 49
Close Up Publishing, pg 49
Closson Press, pg 49
CN Times Books, pg 50
Columbia University Press, pg 51
Commonwealth Editions, pg 51
Continental AfrikaPublishers, pg 52
Cornell University Press, pg 52
Cornerstone Book Publishers, pg 53
Cosimo Inc, pg 53
Counterpath Press, pg 54
Counterpoint Press LLC, pg 54
Country Music Foundation Press, pg 54
Countryman Press, pg 54
Covenant Communications Inc, pg 54
Crabtree Publishing Co, pg 54
Crown Publishing Group, pg 56
Walter De Gruyter Inc, pg 58
Dharma Publishing, pg 59
Dissertation.com, pg 60
DK, pg 60
The Donning Company Publishers, pg 60
Dordt Press, pg 60
Doubleday, pg 61
Dover Publications Inc, pg 61
Down East Books, pg 61
Down The Shore Publishing, pg 61
Duke University Press, pg 62
Dumbarton Oaks, pg 62
Eakin Press, pg 62
East West Discovery Press, pg 63

EDC Publishing, pg 63
ediciones Lerner, pg 63
Editorial de la Universidad de Puerto Rico, pg 63
Editorial Portavoz, pg 64
Educational Insights®, pg 64
Edupress Inc, pg 64
Wm B Eerdmans Publishing Co, pg 64
Eisenbrauns, pg 64
Elderberry Press Inc, pg 65
Elva Resa Publishing, pg 65
Encounter Books, pg 66
Enslow Publishing LLC, pg 66
Epicenter Press Inc, pg 67
Evan-Moor Educational Publishers, pg 68
M Evans & Company, pg 68
Everyman's Library, pg 68
Everything Goes Media LLC, pg 68
Excalibur Publications, pg 68
Facts On File, pg 69
Fair Winds Press, pg 69
Farcountry Press, pg 69
Father & Son Publishing Inc, pg 70
The Feminist Press at The City University of New York, pg 71
Filter Press LLC, pg 71
Fine Creative Media, Inc, pg 71
First Avenue Editions, pg 72
Focus, pg 73
Fordham University Press, pg 73
Friends United Press, pg 75
Fulcrum Publishing Inc, pg 75
Galde Press Inc, pg 75
Gale, pg 75
Gallaudet University Press, pg 76
Gallery Books, pg 76
Gallopade International Inc, pg 76
Gareth Stevens Publishing, pg 76
Genealogical Publishing Co, pg 77
Getty Publications, pg 78
The Globe Pequot Press, pg 79
Godine, pg 79
Goose River Press, pg 79
Gorgias Press LLC, pg 80
Gray & Company Publishers, pg 80
Greenhaven Publishing, pg 81
Greenleaf Book Group LLC, pg 81
Grey House Publishing Inc™, pg 81
Hackett Publishing Co Inc, pg 83
Hamilton Books, pg 84
Hamilton Stone Editions, pg 84
Hancock House Publishers, pg 84
HarperCollins Children's Books, pg 85
HarperCollins Publishers LLC, pg 86
Harvard Business Review Press, pg 87
Harvard Ukrainian Research Institute, pg 88
Harvard University Press, pg 88
Hebrew Union College Press, pg 90
William S Hein & Co Inc, pg 90
Heinemann, pg 90
Hellgate Press, pg 91
Hendrickson Publishers Inc, pg 91
Her Own Words LLC, pg 91
Herald Press, pg 91
Heritage Books Inc, pg 91
Heyday, pg 91
Higginson Book Company LLC, pg 91
High Plains Press, pg 91
Hill & Wang, pg 92
Hillsdale College Press, pg 92
The Historic New Orleans Collection, pg 93
History Publishing Co LLC, pg 93
Histria Books, pg 93
Hollym International Corp, pg 94
Homa & Sekey Books, pg 95

PUBLISHERS

Homestead Publishing, pg 95
Hoover Institution Press, pg 95
Houghton Mifflin Harcourt, pg 95
Houghton Mifflin Harcourt Trade & Reference Division, pg 96
IET USA Inc, pg 98
IHS Press, pg 98
Illinois State Museum Society, pg 99
Independent Institute, pg 99
Indiana Historical Society Press, pg 99
Indiana University African Studies Program, pg 100
Indiana University Press, pg 100
Information Age Publishing Inc, pg 100
Inner Traditions International Ltd, pg 101
Insight Editions, pg 101
Institute of Jesuit Sources (IJS), pg 102
Inter-University Consortium for Political & Social Research (ICPSR), pg 102
Interlink Publishing Group Inc, pg 102
International Publishers Co Inc, pg 103
Iron Gate Publishing, pg 104
Islandport Press, pg 105
Italica Press, pg 105
Jewish Lights Publishing, pg 105
The Jewish Publication Society, pg 105
Johns Hopkins University Press, pg 106
Just World Books LLC, pg 107
Kallisti Publishing Inc, pg 108
Kazi Publications Inc, pg 108
Kensington Publishing Corp, pg 109
Kent State University Press, pg 109
Alfred A Knopf, pg 110
Kodansha USA Inc, pg 110
Konecky & Konecky LLC, pg 111
Kregel Publications, pg 111
Krieger Publishing Co, pg 111
Lake Superior Publishing LLC, pg 112
Peter Lang Publishing Inc, pg 112
LARB Books, pg 113
The Lawbook Exchange, Ltd, pg 113
Leaf Storm Press, pg 113
Learning Links-USA Inc, pg 114
Lectorum Publications Inc, pg 114
Lee & Low Books Inc, pg 114
Lehigh University Press, pg 114
Lerner Publications, pg 115
Lerner Publishing Group Inc, pg 115
Lexington Books, pg 115
Liberty Fund Inc, pg 116
Library of America, pg 116
Life Cycle Books, pg 116
Limelight Editions, pg 117
Linden Publishing Co Inc, pg 117
Little, Brown and Company, pg 118
The Local History Co, pg 119
Loft Press Inc, pg 119
Long River Press, pg 120
Lorenz Educational Press, pg 120
Lost Classics Book Company LLC, pg 120
Louisiana State University Press, pg 120
Loving Healing Press Inc, pg 121
LPD Press/Rio Grande Books, pg 121
Lucent Press, pg 121
The Lyons Press, pg 121
Macmillan Learning, pg 123

Macmillan Reference USA™, pg 123
Mage Publishers Inc, pg 123
Mandel Vilar Press, pg 124
Marquette University Press, pg 125
Marshall Cavendish Education, pg 125
Maryland Center for History & Culture (MCHC), pg 126
Maryland History Press, pg 126
Mason Crest Publishers, pg 126
The Massachusetts Historical Society, pg 126
Master Books®, pg 126
Mazda Publishers Inc, pg 127
The McDonald & Woodward Publishing Co, pg 127
McFarland, pg 127
McGraw-Hill Create, pg 127
McGraw-Hill Higher Education, pg 128
McGraw-Hill School Education Group, pg 128
Medals of America Press, pg 128
Medieval Institute Publications (MIP), pg 129
The Edwin Mellen Press, pg 129
Menasha Ridge Press, pg 129
Mercer University Press, pg 129
Metropolitan Classics, pg 130
Michigan State University Press (MSU Press), pg 130
Milford Books™, pg 131
Military Info Publishing, pg 131
Milliken Publishing Co, pg 132
Minnesota Historical Society Press, pg 132
Modern Memoirs Inc, pg 133
The Monacelli Press, pg 133
Monthly Review Press, pg 134
Moonshine Cove Publishing LLC, pg 134
Moriah Books, pg 134
Mountain Press Publishing Co, pg 135
De Gruyter Mouton, pg 135
Multnomah, pg 135
Museum of New Mexico Press, pg 135
Mutual Publishing LLC, pg 136
Nataraj Books, pg 136
National Book Co, pg 136
National Geographic Books, pg 137
Naval Institute Press, pg 139
New City Press, pg 139
The New Press, pg 140
New York University Press, pg 141
Newbury Street Press, pg 141
NewSouth Books, pg 141
NFB Publishing, pg 141
North Carolina Office of Archives & History, pg 142
North Star Editions Inc, pg 142
North Star Press of Saint Cloud Inc, pg 142
Northern Illinois University Press, pg 143
W W Norton & Company Inc, pg 143
Nova Science Publishers Inc, pg 144
Nystrom Education, pg 144
Oak Knoll Press, pg 144
Ocean Tree Books, pg 145
Ohio Genealogical Society, pg 145
Ohio University Press, pg 145
Omnigraphics Inc, pg 146
Omohundro Institute of Early American History & Culture, pg 146
Orbis Books, pg 147
Oregon State University Press, pg 147

Oriental Institute Publications, pg 148
ORO editions, pg 148
Other Press, pg 148
Oxford University Press USA, pg 149
PA Press, pg 149
Palgrave Macmillan, pg 150
Pantheon Books, pg 150
Paragon House, pg 151
Park Place Publications, pg 152
Parmenides Publishing, pg 152
Pathfinder Publishing Inc, pg 152
Paul Dry Books, pg 152
Paulist Press, pg 152
Pearson Business Publishing, pg 153
Pelican Publishing, pg 153
Pen & Publish LLC, pg 153
Penguin Publishing Group, pg 154
Penn State University Press, pg 157
Pennsylvania Historical & Museum Commission, pg 157
Philosophical Library Inc, pg 159
Pineapple Press, pg 160
Pleasure Boat Studio: A Literary Press, pg 160
Plough Publishing House, pg 161
Pocol Press, pg 161
Polar Bear & Company, pg 161
Polebridge Press, pg 161
Potomac Books, pg 162
The Press at California State University, Fresno, pg 163
Princeton University Press, pg 164
Progressive Press, pg 165
Prometheus Books, pg 166
Publication Consultants, pg 167
Publications International Ltd (PIL), pg 167
Purdue University Press, pg 167
Quarto Publishing Group USA Inc, pg 168
Quincannon Publishing Group, pg 168
Radix Press, pg 169
Raven Publishing Inc, pg 172
Recorded Books Inc, an RBmedia company, pg 172
The Red Sea Press Inc, pg 173
Reference Publications Inc, pg 173
Regent Press Printers & Publishers, pg 174
Regnery Publishing, pg 174
Research & Education Association (REA), pg 174
Rio Nuevo Publishers, pg 175
River City Publishing, pg 175
Routledge, pg 177
Rowman & Littlefield, pg 178
Royal Fireworks Press, pg 178
Russell Sage Foundation, pg 178
Rutgers University Press, pg 178
Saddleback Educational Publishing, pg 179
St Augustine's Press Inc, pg 180
St Herman Press, pg 180
St James Press®, pg 180
St Johann Press, pg 180
St Joseph's University Press, pg 180
St Pauls, pg 181
Salem Press, pg 181
Salina Bookshelf Inc, pg 181
San Diego State University Press, pg 182
Santa Monica Press LLC, pg 182
Sasquatch Books, pg 182
Schaffner Press, pg 183
Schiffer Publishing Ltd, pg 183
Schlager Group Inc, pg 183
Schocken Books, pg 183
School for Advanced Research Press, pg 185

Schreiber Publishing, pg 185
Science & Humanities Press, pg 185
Science History Publications USA Inc, pg 185
Scripta Humanistica Publishing International, pg 185
Seven Stories Press, pg 186
1765 Productions, pg 186
Shadow Mountain Publishing, pg 187
Signalman Publishing, pg 187
Signature Books Publishing LLC, pg 187
Simon & Schuster Audio, pg 189
Somerset Hall Press, pg 193
Sourcebooks LLC, pg 194
South Dakota Historical Society Press, pg 195
Southern Historical Press Inc, pg 195
Southern Illinois University Press, pg 195
Soyinfo Center, pg 196
Square One Publishers Inc, pg 196
Stackpole Books, pg 196
Stanford University Press, pg 197
Star Bright Books Inc, pg 197
Star Publishing Co Inc, pg 197
Steerforth Press & Services, pg 198
Stewart, Tabori & Chang, pg 198
Stone Bridge Press Inc, pg 199
Stoneydale Press Publishing Co, pg 199
Strategic Book Publishing (SBP), pg 199
Strategic Media Books LLC, pg 200
The Jesse Stuart Foundation (JSF), pg 200
Summertime Publications Inc, pg 200
Sun Publishing Company, pg 200
Sunstone Press, pg 201
Syracuse University Press, pg 201
Nan A Talese, pg 202
TAN Books, pg 202
Tantor Media Inc, pg 202
Tapestry Press Ltd, pg 202
TCU Press, pg 203
Teacher's Discovery®, pg 203
Temple University Press, pg 204
Temporal Mechanical Press, pg 204
Texas A&M University Press, pg 205
Texas State Historical Association, pg 205
Texas Tech University Press, pg 205
Thames & Hudson, pg 205
Thorndike Press®, pg 206
Tilbury House Publishers, pg 207
The Toby Press LLC, pg 207
Trinity University Press, pg 209
Turner Publishing Co LLC, pg 210
Tuttle Publishing, pg 211
Twenty-First Century Books, pg 211
UCLA Latin American Center Publications, pg 212
Union Square & Co, pg 212
United States Holocaust Memorial Museum, pg 213
United States Institute of Peace Press, pg 213
Univelt Inc, pg 213
University of Alabama Press, pg 214
University of Alaska Press, pg 214
The University of Arizona Press, pg 214
The University of Arkansas Press, pg 214
University of California Press, pg 215
University of Chicago Press, pg 215

University of Delaware Press, pg 215
University of Georgia Press, pg 216
University of Hawaii Press, pg 216
University of Illinois Press, pg 216
University of Iowa Press, pg 216
University of Louisiana at Lafayette Press, pg 217
University of Massachusetts Press, pg 217
University of Michigan Press, pg 217
University of Minnesota Press, pg 217
University of Missouri Press, pg 217
University of Nebraska Press, pg 217
University of Nevada Press, pg 218
University of New Mexico Press, pg 218
The University of North Carolina Press, pg 218
University of North Texas Press, pg 218
University of Notre Dame Press, pg 219
University of Oklahoma Press, pg 219
University of Pennsylvania Museum of Archaeology & Anthropology, pg 219
University of Pennsylvania Press, pg 219
University of Pittsburgh Press, pg 219
University of Rochester Press, pg 220
University of South Carolina Press, pg 220
University of Tennessee Press, pg 220
The University of Utah Press, pg 220
University of Virginia Press, pg 220
University of Washington Press, pg 220
University of Wisconsin Press, pg 221
University Press of America Inc, pg 221
University Press of Colorado, pg 221
University Press of Florida, pg 221
University Press of Kansas, pg 221
The University Press of Kentucky, pg 222
University Press of Mississippi, pg 222
UnKnownTruths.com Publishing Co, pg 222
Urim Publications, pg 223
US Government Publishing Office (GPO), pg 223
Utah State University Press, pg 223
Vandamere Press, pg 223
Vanderbilt University Press, pg 224
The Vendome Press, pg 224
Vernon Press, pg 224
Verso Books, pg 224
Visible Ink Press®, pg 225
Ludwig von Mises Institute, pg 225
Washington State University Press, pg 226
WaterBrook, pg 226
Watermark Publishing, pg 226
Waveland Press Inc, pg 226
Wayne State University Press, pg 226
Wayside Publishing, pg 227
Welcome Rain Publishers LLC, pg 227
Well-Trained Mind Press, pg 227

Wellington Press, pg 227
Wesleyan University Press, pg 227
West Margin Press, pg 227
West Virginia University Press, pg 228
Western Edge Press, pg 228
Western Pennsylvania Genealogical Society, pg 228
Western Reflections Publishing Co, pg 228
Westernlore Press, pg 228
Westminster John Knox Press (WJK), pg 228
Whittier Publications Inc, pg 229
Markus Wiener Publishers Inc, pg 229
Wiley-Blackwell, pg 229
William Carey Publishing, pg 230
Winters Publishing, pg 231
Winterthur Museum, Garden & Library, pg 231
Wisconsin Department of Public Instruction, pg 231
Wisdom Publications Inc, pg 231
Woodrow Wilson Center Press, pg 232
WoodstockArts, pg 232
WriteLife Publishing, pg 234
Xlibris Corp, pg 234
Yale University Press, pg 235
YWAM Publishing, pg 236
Zest Books, pg 236
Zondervan, pg 236
Zone Books, pg 237
Zumaya Publications LLC, pg 237

HOUSE & HOME

ACC Art Books, pg 3
Adams Media, pg 4
AdventureKEEN, pg 5
Art of Living, PrimaMedia Inc, pg 17
Atlantic Publishing Group Inc, pg 21
AuthorHouse, pg 22
Biographical Publishing Co, pg 29
Book Sales, pg 33
BPC, pg 35
BuilderBooks, pg 38
C&T Publishing Inc, pg 40
Chelsea Green Publishing Co, pg 45
Chronicle Books LLC, pg 47
Consumer Press, pg 52
Countryman Press, pg 54
Creative Homeowner, pg 55
DK, pg 60
Down East Books, pg 61
EDC Publishing, pg 63
Fair Winds Press, pg 69
Fox Chapel Publishing Co Inc, pg 74
Gale, pg 75
Gibbs Smith Publisher, pg 78
Glitterati Inc, pg 78
The Globe Pequot Press, pg 79
Goodheart-Willcox Publisher, pg 79
Greenleaf Book Group LLC, pg 81
HarperCollins Publishers LLC, pg 86
Hay House LLC, pg 89
Interweave Press LLC, pg 104
Krause Publications Inc, pg 111
Landauer Publishing, pg 112
Laughing Elephant Books, pg 113
Leaf Storm Press, pg 113
Leisure Arts Inc, pg 114
Macmillan Reference USA™, pg 123
R S Means from The Gordian Group, pg 128
The Monacelli Press, pg 133
PA Press, pg 149

Pelican Publishing, pg 153
Pennsylvania State Data Center, pg 157
Phaidon, pg 159
Clarkson Potter, pg 162
Quarto Publishing Group USA Inc, pg 168
Reader's Digest Trade Publishing, pg 172
Rizzoli International Publications Inc, pg 175
Ross Books, pg 177
Schiffer Publishing Ltd, pg 183
Shadow Mountain Publishing, pg 187
Strategic Book Publishing (SBP), pg 199
Sunstone Press, pg 201
Surrey Books, pg 201
Taunton Press, pg 203
Tuttle Publishing, pg 211
Union Square & Co, pg 212
The Vendome Press, pg 224
Watermark Publishing, pg 226
Wheatherstone Press, pg 228
Xlibris Corp, pg 234

HOW-TO

Abbeville Publishing Group, pg 2
ABDO, pg 2
Adams & Ambrose Publishing, pg 4
Adams Media, pg 4
Addicus Books Inc, pg 5
AdventureKEEN, pg 5
ALA Neal-Schuman, pg 6
All Things That Matter Press, pg 7
Allworth Press, pg 7
AllWrite Publishing, pg 7
Amadeus Press, pg 7
American Carriage House Publishing (ACHP), pg 8
The American Ceramic Society, pg 9
American Girl Publishing, pg 10
Anaphora Literary Press, pg 13
ANR Publications University of California, pg 14
Art of Living, PrimaMedia Inc, pg 17
Astragal Press, pg 20
Atlantic Publishing Group Inc, pg 21
AuthorHouse, pg 22
Beaver's Pond Press Inc, pg 26
Bess Press Inc, pg 29
Biographical Publishing Co, pg 29
Blue Note Publications Inc, pg 32
BoardSource, pg 33
Book Sales, pg 33
BookLogix, pg 34
Boson Books™, pg 34
BPC, pg 35
Brewers Publications, pg 36
Bridge Publications Inc, pg 36
BuilderBooks, pg 38
Burford Books, pg 38
C&T Publishing Inc, pg 40
Captain Fiddle Music & Publications, pg 40
Cardoza Publishing, pg 40
CarTech Inc, pg 41
Central Recovery Press (CRP), pg 44
Charles Press Publishers, pg 45
Chicago Review Press, pg 46
Chronicle Books LLC, pg 47
Clearfield Co Inc, pg 49
Consumer Press, pg 52
Continental AfrikaPublishers, pg 52
Countryman Press, pg 54
Creative Homeowner, pg 55

Cricket Cottage Publishing LLC, pg 55
Crystal Clarity Publishers, pg 56
Eakin Press, pg 62
EDC Publishing, pg 63
Editorial Unilit, pg 64
Evan-Moor Educational Publishers, pg 68
M Evans & Company, pg 68
Evergreen Pacific Publishing Ltd, pg 68
Everything Goes Media LLC, pg 68
Fine Creative Media, Inc, pg 71
Walter Foster Publishing, pg 74
Fox Chapel Publishing Co Inc, pg 74
Frederick Fell Publishers Inc, pg 74
Gale, pg 75
GemStone Press, pg 77
Genealogical Publishing Co, pg 77
The Globe Pequot Press, pg 79
Goodheart-Willcox Publisher, pg 79
Gospel Publishing House, pg 80
Greenleaf Book Group LLC, pg 81
Guideposts Book & Inspirational Media, pg 82
Hal Leonard LLC, pg 84
HarperCollins Publishers LLC, pg 86
Hatherleigh Press Ltd, pg 88
Hay House LLC, pg 89
Heuer Publishing LLC, pg 91
Homa & Sekey Books, pg 95
Homestead Publishing, pg 95
Horizon Publishers & Distributors Inc, pg 95
Humanix Books LLC, pg 97
Huntington Press Publishing, pg 97
Hutton Publishing, pg 97
Industrial Press Inc, pg 100
International Wealth Success (IWS), pg 104
Interweave Press LLC, pg 104
JIST Publishing, pg 106
Kalmbach Media Co, pg 108
Klutz®, pg 110
Krause Publications Inc, pg 111
Landauer Publishing, pg 112
Lectorum Publications Inc, pg 114
Leisure Arts Inc, pg 114
Limelight Editions, pg 117
Linden Publishing Co Inc, pg 117
The Little Entrepreneur, pg 118
The Magni Co, pg 123
Management Advisory Services & Publications (MASP), pg 123
Marine Techniques Publishing, pg 125
R S Means from The Gordian Group, pg 128
Mel Bay Publications Inc, pg 129
Menasha Ridge Press, pg 129
Meriwether Publishing, pg 129
Mighty Media Press, pg 131
Mitchell Lane Publishers Inc, pg 133
Mutual Publishing LLC, pg 136
National Braille Press, pg 137
National Golf Foundation, pg 138
No Starch Press, pg 141
NOLO, pg 141
Norwood House Press, pg 143
The Oaklea Press Inc, pg 145
Odyssey Books, pg 145
Olde & Oppenheim Publishers, pg 146
Pants On Fire Press, pg 150
Petroleum Extension Service (PETEX), pg 159
Pineapple Press, pg 160
ProStar Publications Inc, pg 166
Quarto Publishing Group USA Inc, pg 168

PUBLISHERS

Quirk Books, pg 168
Quixote Press, pg 169
Reader's Digest Trade Publishing, pg 172
Rising Sun Publishing, pg 175
Ronin Publishing Inc, pg 176
Ross Books, pg 177
St Johann Press, pg 180
Santa Monica Press LLC, pg 182
Schiffer Publishing Ltd, pg 183
Science & Humanities Press, pg 185
SelectBooks Inc, pg 186
Sentient Publications LLC, pg 186
Shadow Mountain Publishing, pg 187
Shepard Publications, pg 187
SkillPath Publications, pg 190
Sound Feelings Publishing, pg 194
Sourcebooks LLC, pg 194
Spizzirri Publishing Inc, pg 196
Square One Publishers Inc, pg 196
Stackpole Books, pg 196
Stargazer Publishing Co, pg 197
Stone Bridge Press Inc, pg 199
Story Monsters LLC, pg 199
Strategic Book Publishing (SBP), pg 199
Sunstone Press, pg 201
Surrey Books, pg 201
SYBEX, pg 201
Tantor Media Inc, pg 202
TarcherPerigee, pg 202
Taunton Books, pg 203
Ten Speed Press, pg 204
Todd Publications, pg 207
Trafalgar Square Books, pg 208
Travelers' Tales, pg 209
Triumph Books LLC, pg 209
Twilight Times Books, pg 211
Union Square & Co, pg 212
Universal-Publishers Inc, pg 213
University Press of Mississippi, pg 222
US Government Publishing Office (GPO), pg 223
Watson-Guptill, pg 226
Wheatherstone Press, pg 228
Wilderness Adventures Press Inc, pg 229
Williams & Company Book Publishers, pg 230
Willow Creek Press, pg 230
Wilshire Book Co, pg 230
Workman Publishing, pg 232
WriteLife Publishing, pg 234
Writer's Digest Books, pg 234
Xlibris Corp, pg 234
YMAA Publication Center Inc, pg 235
Zest Books, pg 236

HUMAN RELATIONS

ACTA Publications, pg 4
Alexander Street, part of Clarivate PLC, pg 6
Algora Publishing, pg 7
All Things That Matter Press, pg 7
American Counseling Association (ACA), pg 9
Association for Talent Development (ATD) Press, pg 19
Atlas Publishing, pg 21
AuthorHouse, pg 22
Authorlink® Press, pg 22
Bancroft Press, pg 24
Barringer Publishing, pg 24
Barrytown/Station Hill Press, pg 24
Bear & Co Inc, pg 26
BLR®—Business & Legal Resources, pg 32
Blue Mountain Arts Inc, pg 32
Boys Town Press, pg 35

Bridge Publications Inc, pg 36
Brown Books Publishing Group (BBPG), pg 38
The Bureau for At-Risk Youth, pg 38
Cengage Learning, pg 43
Central Recovery Press (CRP), pg 44
Chalice Press, pg 44
Council for Research in Values & Philosophy, pg 53
Crystal Clarity Publishers, pg 56
DK, pg 60
Editorial Portavoz, pg 64
Elderberry Press Inc, pg 65
Elsevier Inc, pg 65
Everything Goes Media LLC, pg 68
Fine Creative Media, Inc, pg 71
Free Spirit Publishing Inc, pg 74
Fresh Air Books, pg 75
Gale, pg 75
Gifted Unlimited LLC, pg 78
Goodheart-Willcox Publisher, pg 79
Goose River Press, pg 79
Green Dragon Books, pg 81
Greenleaf Book Group LLC, pg 81
Guideposts Book & Inspirational Media, pg 82
The Guilford Press, pg 82
HarperCollins Publishers LLC, pg 86
Harvard Business Review Press, pg 87
Harvest House Publishers Inc, pg 88
Hazelden Publishing, pg 89
Health Communications Inc, pg 89
Health Professions Press, pg 90
HeartMath LLC, pg 90
Hohm Press, pg 93
Human Rights Watch, pg 97
Humanix Books LLC, pg 97
Idyll Arbor Inc, pg 98
Inner Traditions International Ltd, pg 101
International Foundation of Employee Benefit Plans, pg 103
JIST Publishing, pg 106
J J Keller & Associates, Inc®, pg 108
Koho Pono LLC, pg 111
Listen & Live Audio LLC, pg 117
Little, Brown and Company, pg 118
LRP Publications, pg 121
Macmillan Reference USA™, pg 123
Marriage Transformation LLC, pg 125
The Edwin Mellen Press, pg 129
Milford Books™, pg 131
Nataraj Books, pg 136
National Resource Center for Youth Services, pg 138
New World Library, pg 140
Nilgiri Press, pg 141
On the Write Path Publishing, pg 146
Other Press, pg 148
Our Sunday Visitor Publishing, pg 148
P & R Publishing Co, pg 149
Paulist Press, pg 152
Penguin Publishing Group, pg 154
Philosophical Library Inc, pg 159
Plough Publishing House, pg 161
Rational Island Publishers, pg 171
Ronin Publishing Inc, pg 176
The Rosen Publishing Group Inc, pg 177
Ross Books, pg 177
Safer Society Press, pg 179
SAGE Publishing, pg 180
Science & Humanities Press, pg 185
Sentient Publications LLC, pg 186

STM Learning Inc, pg 199
Strategic Book Publishing (SBP), pg 199
Tantor Media Inc, pg 202
TarcherPerigee, pg 202
Third World Press Foundation, pg 206
TSG Publishing Foundation Inc, pg 210
Tughra Books, pg 210
United Nations Publications, pg 213
Vernon Press, pg 224
Westminster John Knox Press (WJK), pg 228
Wheatherstone Press, pg 228
Whole Person Associates Inc, pg 229
Wiley-Blackwell, pg 229
William Carey Publishing, pg 230
Wilshire Book Co, pg 230
Wolfman Books, pg 232
World Bank Publications, pg 233
Zondervan, pg 236

HUMOR

A 2 Z Press LLC, pg 1
ABDO, pg 2
Adams Media, pg 4
AdventureKEEN, pg 5
Akashic Books, pg 6
Albert Whitman & Company, pg 6
Anaphora Literary Press, pg 13
Andrews McMeel Publishing LLC, pg 14
The Apocryphile Press, pg 15
Ariel Press, pg 16
ArtWrite Productions, pg 18
AuthorHouse, pg 22
Baby Tattoo Books, pg 23
Bancroft Press, pg 24
Barringer Publishing, pg 24
Barrytown/Station Hill Press, pg 24
Beaver's Pond Press Inc, pg 26
Bella Books, pg 27
Bess Press Inc, pg 29
Blue Mountain Arts Inc, pg 32
Book Sales, pg 33
Books on Tape™, pg 34
Boson Books™, pg 34
Brandylane Publishers Inc, pg 35
Brick Tower Press, pg 36
Brown Books Publishing Group (BBPG), pg 38
Bywater Books Inc, pg 39
Charlesbridge Publishing Inc, pg 45
Child's Play® Inc, pg 46
The Child's World Inc, pg 46
China Books, pg 47
Cider Mill Press Book Publishers LLC, pg 48
David C Cook, pg 52
Countryman Press, pg 54
Cricket Cottage Publishing LLC, pg 55
Dark Horse Comics, pg 57
DC Comics, pg 58
Walter De Gruyter Inc, pg 58
Doubleday, pg 61
Dover Publications Inc, pg 61
Down East Books, pg 61
Dutton, pg 62
Easy Money Press, pg 63
Elderberry Press Inc, pg 65
Fair Winds Press, pg 69
Familius, pg 69
Father & Son Publishing Inc, pg 70
Fine Creative Media, Inc, pg 71
Galde Press Inc, pg 75
Gale, pg 75
Gallery Books, pg 76
Gauthier Publications Inc, pg 77
Gibbs Smith Publisher, pg 78

Gifted Unlimited LLC, pg 78
Godine, pg 79
Gray & Company Publishers, pg 80
Greenleaf Book Group LLC, pg 81
Grove Atlantic Inc, pg 82
Hamilton Stone Editions, pg 84
HarperCollins Children's Books, pg 85
HarperCollins Publishers LLC, pg 86
Harvest House Publishers Inc, pg 88
Hazelden Publishing, pg 89
Hazy Dell Press, pg 89
Hobblebush Books, pg 93
Hutton Publishing, pg 97
Immedium, pg 99
Iron Stream Media, pg 104
Islandport Press, pg 105
Kensington Publishing Corp, pg 109
Kidsbooks® Publishing, pg 109
Koho Pono LLC, pg 111
Larson Publications, pg 113
Lasaria Creative Publishing, pg 113
Linden Publishing Co Inc, pg 117
little bee books, pg 117
Little, Brown and Company, pg 118
Macmillan Reference USA™, pg 123
The Magni Co, pg 123
Manic D Press Inc, pg 124
Maren Green Publishing Inc, pg 125
Master Books®, pg 126
Mazda Publishers Inc, pg 127
Menasha Ridge Press, pg 129
Meriwether Publishing, pg 129
Multnomah, pg 135
NBM Publishing Inc, pg 139
NFB Publishing, pg 141
Norilana Books, pg 142
North Atlantic Books (NAB), pg 142
North Country Press, pg 142
Norwood House Press, pg 143
Octane Press, pg 145
Olde & Oppenheim Publishers, pg 146
On the Write Path Publishing, pg 146
Palm Island Press, pg 150
Papercutz, pg 150
Parachute Publishing LLC, pg 151
Park Place Publications, pg 152
Pelican Publishing, pg 153
Pen-L Publishing, pg 153
Peter Pauper Press, Inc, pg 158
Polis Books, pg 162
Pomegranate Communications Inc, pg 162
Purple House Press, pg 167
Quirk Books, pg 168
Quixote Press, pg 169
Radix Press, pg 169
Reader's Digest Trade Publishing, pg 172
Robert D Reed Publishers, pg 173
Round Table Companies, pg 177
Running Press, pg 178
SAGE Publishing, pg 180
Santa Monica Press LLC, pg 182
Savant Books & Publications LLC, pg 182
Scholastic Inc, pg 184
Schreiber Publishing, pg 185
Science & Humanities Press, pg 185
Signature Books Publishing LLC, pg 187
Silman-James Press Inc, pg 188
Simon & Schuster Audio, pg 189
Sourcebooks LLC, pg 194
Square One Publishers Inc, pg 196
StarGroup International Inc, pg 197
Stewart, Tabori & Chang, pg 198
Story Monsters LLC, pg 199

Strategic Book Publishing (SBP), pg 199
Summertime Publications Inc, pg 200
Tachyon Publications LLC, pg 202
Tantor Media Inc, pg 202
Ten Speed Press, pg 204
Todd Publications, pg 207
Tor Publishing Group, pg 207
Travelers' Tales, pg 209
Triumph Books LLC, pg 209
Twilight Times Books, pg 211
Ulysses Press, pg 212
Union Square & Co, pg 212
Universe Publishing, pg 214
University of North Texas Press, pg 218
University Press of Mississippi, pg 222
WaterBrook, pg 226
Welcome Rain Publishers LLC, pg 227
Whole Person Associates Inc, pg 229
Wildflower Press, pg 229
Willow Creek Press, pg 230
Workman Publishing, pg 232
WriteLife Publishing, pg 234
Xlibris Corp, pg 234
Yard Dog Press, pg 235
Zumaya Publications LLC, pg 237

INSPIRATIONAL, SPIRITUALITY

Abbeville Press, pg 1
ACTA Publications, pg 4
All Things That Matter Press, pg 7
Ambassador International, pg 7
Amber Lotus Publishing, pg 8
American Carriage House Publishing (ACHP), pg 8
Ampersand Inc/Professional Publishing Services, pg 13
Atlantic Publishing Group Inc, pg 21
Augsburg Fortress Publishers, Publishing House of the Evangelical Lutheran Church in America, pg 22
Ave Maria Press Inc, pg 22
Avery, pg 23
B&H Publishing Group, pg 24
Barbour Publishing Inc, pg 24
Bear & Co Inc, pg 26
Beaver's Pond Press Inc, pg 26
Bethany House Publishers, pg 29
Biographical Publishing Co, pg 29
Blue Mountain Arts Inc, pg 32
Blue Note Publications Inc, pg 32
BlueBridge, pg 32
BookLogix, pg 34
Brandylane Publishers Inc, pg 35
Bridge Logos Inc, pg 36
Brilliance Publishing Inc, pg 37
Brown Books Publishing Group (BBPG), pg 38
Campfield & Campfield Publishing LLC, pg 39
Catholic Book Publishing Corp, pg 42
Central Recovery Press (CRP), pg 44
Chalice Press, pg 44
Charles Press Publishers, pg 45
Cider Mill Press Book Publishers LLC, pg 48
Cleis Press, pg 49
David C Cook, pg 52
Cosimo Inc, pg 53
Covenant Communications Inc, pg 54
Cricket Cottage Publishing LLC, pg 55
The Crossroad Publishing Co, pg 55
Crystal Clarity Publishers, pg 56
Dancing Dakini Press, pg 57
Dancing Lemur Press LLC, pg 57
Deep River Books LLC, pg 58
Destiny Image Inc, pg 59
DeVorss & Co, pg 59
Dorrance Publishing Co Inc, pg 61
Emmaus Road Publishing Inc, pg 66
Fair Winds Press, pg 69
Familius, pg 69
Father & Son Publishing Inc, pg 70
Fine Creative Media, Inc, pg 71
Forward Movement, pg 73
Fox Chapel Publishing Co Inc, pg 74
Franciscan Media, pg 74
Friends United Press, pg 75
Gale, pg 75
Goose River Press, pg 79
Green Dragon Books, pg 81
Group Publishing Inc, pg 82
Hachette Nashville, pg 83
Hamilton Books, pg 84
Hatherleigh Press Ltd, pg 88
Herald Press, pg 91
Hilton Publishing Co, pg 92
Histria Books, pg 93
Hohm Press, pg 93
Horizon Publishers & Distributors Inc, pg 95
Idyll Arbor Inc, pg 98
In the Garden Publishing, pg 99
Inner Traditions International Ltd, pg 101
Institute of Jesuit Sources (IJS), pg 102
Iron Stream Media, pg 104
Jain Publishing Co, pg 105
Kallisti Publishing Inc, pg 108
Koho Pono LLC, pg 111
Konecky & Konecky LLC, pg 111
Kregel Publications, pg 111
Laredo Publishing Co, pg 113
Larson Publications, pg 113
Light Technology Publishing LLC, pg 116
Liguori Publications, pg 117
Liturgical Press, pg 118
Llewellyn Publications, pg 119
Love Inspired Books, pg 120
Macmillan Reference USA™, pg 123
Master Books®, pg 126
Medieval Institute Publications (MIP), pg 129
Morehouse Publishing, pg 134
Multnomah, pg 135
Mutual Publishing LLC, pg 136
New Harbinger Publications Inc, pg 140
New World Library, pg 140
North Atlantic Books (NAB), pg 142
North Point Press, pg 142
North Star Editions Inc, pg 142
The Oaklea Press Inc, pg 145
On the Write Path Publishing, pg 146
Open Books Press, pg 146
Orbis Books, pg 147
The Original Falcon Press, pg 148
ORO editions, pg 148
Ozark Mountain Publishing Inc, pg 149
P & R Publishing Co, pg 149
Paraclete Press Inc, pg 151
Pelican Publishing, pg 153
Pflaum Publishing Group, pg 159
Planert Creek Press, pg 160
Plough Publishing House, pg 161
Pocol Press, pg 161
Publications International Ltd (PIL), pg 167
Red Wheel/Weiser, pg 173
Regnery Publishing, pg 174
Revell, pg 174
Ronin Publishing Inc, pg 176
St Pauls, pg 181
Self-Realization Fellowship Publishers, pg 186
Sentient Publications LLC, pg 186
Shadow Mountain Publishing, pg 187
Skinner House Books, pg 190
SkyLight Paths® Publishing, pg 191
Sounds True Inc, pg 194
Stone Bridge Press Inc, pg 199
Strategic Book Publishing (SBP), pg 199
Summit University Press, pg 200
Tantor Media Inc, pg 202
TarcherPerigee, pg 202
Ten Speed Press, pg 204
Terra Nova Books, pg 204
Theosophical University Press, pg 206
Thorndike Press®, pg 206
Travelers' Tales, pg 209
Tuttle Publishing, pg 211
Twenty-Third Publications, pg 211
Twilight Times Books, pg 211
Tyndale House Publishers Inc, pg 211
Ulysses Press, pg 212
Unarius Academy of Science Publications, pg 212
Urim Publications, pg 223
US Conference of Catholic Bishops, pg 223
US Games Systems Inc, pg 223
WaterBrook, pg 226
Watermark Publishing, pg 226
Whitaker House, pg 228
Wildflower Press, pg 229
William Carey Publishing, pg 230
Wilshire Book Co, pg 230
Winters Publishing, pg 231
Winterwolf Press, pg 231
WriteLife Publishing, pg 234
Yotzeret Publishing, pg 236

JOURNALISM

Anaphora Literary Press, pg 13
AuthorHouse, pg 22
Beehive Books, pg 26
Ben Yehuda Press, pg 27
City Lights Publishers, pg 48
CN Times Books, pg 50
Columbia University Press, pg 51
Continental AfrikaPublishers, pg 52
Eakin Press, pg 62
Fordham University Press, pg 73
Gale, pg 75
Gallery Books, pg 76
Hannacroix Creek Books Inc, pg 85
History Publishing Co LLC, pg 93
Kalmbach Media Co, pg 108
Leaf Storm Press, pg 113
Lexington Books, pg 115
Library of America, pg 116
Linden Publishing Co Inc, pg 117
Macmillan Reference USA™, pg 123
McFarland, pg 127
McGraw-Hill Higher Education, pg 128
The Edwin Mellen Press, pg 129
Milford Books™, pg 131
Modern Language Association (MLA), pg 133
Nataraj Books, pg 136
New Forums Press Inc, pg 139
Other Press, pg 148
Prometheus Books, pg 166
Regnery Publishing, pg 174
Riverdale Avenue Books (RAB), pg 175
The RoadRunner Press, pg 175
Routledge, pg 177
SAGE Publishing, pg 180
Schaffner Press, pg 183
Science & Humanities Press, pg 185
Seven Stories Press, pg 186
Steerforth Press & Services, pg 198
Stone Pier Press, pg 199
Strategic Book Publishing (SBP), pg 199
Trinity University Press, pg 209
University of Alabama Press, pg 214
University of Illinois Press, pg 216
University of Massachusetts Press, pg 217
University of Missouri Press, pg 217
The University of North Carolina Press, pg 218
University of North Texas Press, pg 218
University Press of America Inc, pg 221
University Press of Mississippi, pg 222
Vernon Press, pg 224
Waveland Press Inc, pg 226
Williams & Company Book Publishers, pg 230
Wolfman Books, pg 232
Writer's Digest Books, pg 234
Xlibris Corp, pg 234

LABOR, INDUSTRIAL RELATIONS

ACTA Publications, pg 4
AK Press, pg 6
Algora Publishing, pg 7
Annual Reviews, pg 14
Association for Talent Development (ATD) Press, pg 19
AuthorHouse, pg 22
BLR®—Business & Legal Resources, pg 32
Business Expert Press, pg 38
Clarity Press Inc, pg 49
Cornell University Press, pg 52
Dewey Publications Inc, pg 59
Edward Elgar Publishing Inc, pg 65
Gale, pg 75
Harvard Business Review Press, pg 87
IHS Press, pg 98
International Foundation of Employee Benefit Plans, pg 103
International Publishers Co Inc, pg 103
JIST Publishing, pg 106
Koho Pono LLC, pg 111
Kumarian Press, pg 112
LRP Publications, pg 121
Macmillan Reference USA™, pg 123
McGraw-Hill Higher Education, pg 128
Monthly Review Press, pg 134
National Academies Press (NAP), pg 136
Pennsylvania State Data Center, pg 157
Petroleum Extension Service (PETEX), pg 159
Rational Island Publishers, pg 171
Russell Sage Foundation, pg 178
SAGE Publishing, pg 180

PUBLISHERS

U.S. PUBLISHERS — SUBJECT INDEX

Seven Stories Press, pg 186
M Lee Smith Publishers, pg 192
Strategic Book Publishing (SBP), pg 199
Temple University Press, pg 204
University of Chicago Press, pg 215
University of Illinois Press, pg 216
US Government Publishing Office (GPO), pg 223
Wiley-Blackwell, pg 229
World Bank Publications, pg 233

LANGUAGE ARTS, LINGUISTICS

Academica Press, pg 3
Alaska Native Language Center (ANLC), pg 6
AllWrite Publishing, pg 7
Anaphora Literary Press, pg 13
Astra Books for Young Readers, pg 20
Atlas Publishing, pg 21
AuthorHouse, pg 22
Bedford/St Martin's, pg 26
John Benjamins Publishing Co, pg 28
BJU Press, pg 30
Black Rabbit Books, pg 30
Bloomsbury Academic, pg 31
Bolchazy-Carducci Publishers Inc, pg 33
Brill Inc, pg 37
Brookline Books, pg 37
Cengage Learning, pg 43
The Center for Learning, pg 43
Charlesbridge Publishing Inc, pg 45
Cheng & Tsui Co Inc, pg 46
Child's Play® Inc, pg 46
The Child's World Inc, pg 46
China Books, pg 47
Christian Schools International (CSI), pg 47
Classical Academic Press, pg 49
College Publishing, pg 50
Columbia University Press, pg 51
Consumer Press, pg 52
Continental AfrikaPublishers, pg 52
Counterpath Press, pg 54
Creative Editions, pg 55
Cross-Cultural Communications, pg 55
CSLI Publications, pg 56
Dalkey Archive Press, pg 56
DawnSignPress, pg 58
Walter De Gruyter Inc, pg 58
Dissertation.com, pg 60
Dover Publications Inc, pg 61
Duke University Press, pg 62
EDC Publishing, pg 63
Educational Insights®, pg 64
Edupress Inc, pg 64
Eisenbrauns, pg 64
Elderberry Press Inc, pg 65
Elsevier Inc, pg 65
Enslow Publishing LLC, pg 66
EPS School Specialty, pg 67
Evan-Moor Educational Publishers, pg 68
Facts On File, pg 69
Focus, pg 73
Gale, pg 75
Gallaudet University Press, pg 76
Gareth Stevens Publishing, pg 76
Georgetown University Press, pg 77
Green Integer, pg 81
The Guilford Press, pg 82
Hackett Publishing Co Inc, pg 83
Hameray Publishing Group Inc, pg 84
Harvard Education Publishing Group, pg 88
Heinemann, pg 90

Heyday, pg 91
Hippocrene Books Inc, pg 92
Histria Books, pg 93
Hollym International Corp, pg 94
Homa & Sekey Books, pg 95
Houghton Mifflin Harcourt, pg 95
Houghton Mifflin Harcourt K-12 Publishers, pg 96
Ibex Publishers, pg 98
Information Age Publishing Inc, pg 100
International Book Centre Inc, pg 102
International Linguistics Corp, pg 103
International Literacy Association (ILA), pg 103
Joshua Tree Publishing, pg 107
Kent State University Press, pg 109
Kodansha USA Inc, pg 110
Peter Lang Publishing Inc, pg 112
Learning Links-USA Inc, pg 114
LearningExpress, pg 114
Lectorum Publications Inc, pg 114
Lexington Books, pg 115
Libraries Unlimited, pg 116
Little, Brown and Company, pg 118
Living Language, pg 119
Long River Press, pg 120
Macmillan Reference USA™, pg 123
Mastery Education, pg 126
McFarland, pg 127
McGraw-Hill Education, pg 127
McGraw-Hill Higher Education, pg 128
McGraw-Hill School Education Group, pg 128
me+mi publishing inc, pg 128
The Edwin Mellen Press, pg 129
Meriwether Publishing, pg 129
Merriam-Webster Inc, pg 129
Milliken Publishing Co, pg 132
Modern Language Association (MLA), pg 133
Mondial, pg 133
Montemayor Press, pg 133
De Gruyter Mouton, pg 135
Nataraj Books, pg 136
National Council of Teachers of English (NCTE), pg 137
National Geographic Learning, pg 138
New Readers Press, pg 140
Nystrom Education, pg 144
Odyssey Books, pg 145
The Ohio State University Press, pg 145
Richard C Owen Publishers Inc, pg 149
Oxford University Press USA, pg 149
Penn State University Press, pg 157
Perfection Learning®, pg 158
Philosophical Library Inc, pg 159
Philosophy Documentation Center, pg 159
PRO-ED Inc, pg 165
Pro Lingua Associates Inc, pg 165
Recorded Books Inc, an RBmedia company, pg 172
Red Chair Press, pg 172
Routledge, pg 177
Royal Fireworks Press, pg 178
Saddleback Educational Publishing, pg 179
William H Sadlier Inc, pg 179
Schreiber Publishing, pg 185
Shepard Publications, pg 187
SIL International, pg 188
Snow Lion, pg 192
Star Bright Books Inc, pg 197
Stone Bridge Press Inc, pg 199

Story Monsters LLC, pg 199
Storyworkz Inc, pg 199
Strategic Book Publishing (SBP), pg 199
Summertime Publications Inc, pg 200
Sundance/Newbridge Publishing, pg 200
Syracuse University Press, pg 201
Tantor Media Inc, pg 202
Tapestry Press Ltd, pg 202
Teacher Created Resources Inc, pg 203
Teachers College Press, pg 203
Teaching & Learning Co, pg 204
TESOL Press, pg 204
University of Texas Press, pg 205
Charles C Thomas Publisher Ltd, pg 206
ThunderStone Books, pg 207
Trans-Atlantic Publications Inc, pg 209
Tuttle Publishing, pg 211
University of Chicago Press, pg 215
University of Georgia Press, pg 216
University of Hawaii Press, pg 216
University of Iowa Press, pg 216
University of Nevada Press, pg 218
University of Oklahoma Press, pg 219
The University of Utah Press, pg 220
University of Wisconsin Press, pg 221
University Press of America Inc, pg 221
University Press of Colorado, pg 221
VanDam Inc, pg 223
Velazquez Press, pg 224
Vernon Press, pg 224
Voyager Sopris Learning Inc, pg 225
Walch Education, pg 225
Waveland Press Inc, pg 226
Wayside Publishing, pg 227
Well-Trained Mind Press, pg 227
Wiley-Blackwell, pg 229
John Wiley & Sons Inc, pg 230
Wisconsin Department of Public Instruction, pg 231
Wolfman Books, pg 232
Writer's AudioShop, pg 234
Writer's Digest Books, pg 234
Yale University Press, pg 235
Zaner-Bloser Inc, pg 236

LAW

Academica Press, pg 3
Adams & Ambrose Publishing, pg 4
The AEI Press, pg 5
Allworth Press, pg 7
American Bar Association Publishing, pg 8
American Correctional Association, pg 9
American Law Institute, pg 10
American Law Institute Continuing Legal Education (ALI CLE), pg 10
Anaphora Literary Press, pg 13
Annual Reviews, pg 14
Aspatore Books, pg 19
AuthorHouse, pg 22
Baylor University Press, pg 25
Beaver's Pond Press Inc, pg 26
Bernan, pg 28
George T Bisel Co Inc, pg 29
Bisk Education, pg 29
Bluestocking Press, pg 33
BookLogix, pg 34
Cambridge University Press, pg 39

Carolina Academic Press, pg 41
Cato Institute, pg 42
CCH, a Wolters Kluwer business, pg 42
Cengage Learning, pg 43
China Books, pg 47
Clarity Press Inc, pg 49
The Connecticut Law Tribune, pg 52
Continental AfrikaPublishers, pg 52
Cornell University Press, pg 52
The Council of State Governments, pg 53
CQ Press, pg 54
Data Trace Publishing Co (DTP), pg 57
Walter De Gruyter Inc, pg 58
Dewey Publications Inc, pg 59
Duke University Press, pg 62
Elderberry Press Inc, pg 65
Edward Elgar Publishing Inc, pg 65
Environmental Law Institute, pg 67
Firefall Editions, pg 72
Foundation Press, pg 74
Gale, pg 75
Gifted Unlimited LLC, pg 78
The Graduate Group/Booksellers, pg 80
Gryphon Editions, pg 82
Health Administration Press, pg 89
William S Hein & Co Inc, pg 90
Homa & Sekey Books, pg 95
Hoover Institution Press, pg 95
Human Rights Watch, pg 97
IBFD North America Inc (International Bureau of Fiscal Documentation), pg 98
Independent Institute, pg 99
Infosources Publishing, pg 100
Institute of Continuing Legal Education, pg 101
Institute of Police Technology & Management (IPTM), pg 102
Inter-University Consortium for Political & Social Research (ICPSR), pg 102
International Council of Shopping Centers (ICSC), pg 102
International Monetary Fund (IMF), Editorial & Publications Division, pg 103
International Risk Management Institute Inc, pg 103
J J Keller & Associates, Inc®, pg 108
Peter Lang Publishing Inc, pg 112
LARB Books, pg 113
Law School Admission Council (LSAC), pg 113
The Lawbook Exchange, Ltd, pg 113
Lawyers & Judges Publishing Co Inc, pg 113
Lexington Books, pg 115
LexisNexis®, pg 116
LexisNexis® Matthew Bender®, pg 116
Liberty Fund Inc, pg 116
Mary Ann Liebert Inc, pg 116
Loft Press Inc, pg 119
Looseleaf Law Publications Inc, pg 120
LRP Publications, pg 121
Macmillan Reference USA™, pg 123
The Magni Co, pg 123
Martindale LLC, pg 126
Mazda Publishers Inc, pg 127
The Edwin Mellen Press, pg 129
Merriam-Webster Inc, pg 129
De Gruyter Mouton, pg 135
Moznaim Publishing Corp, pg 135
Nataraj Books, pg 136

307

National Academies Press (NAP), pg 136
National Association of Insurance Commissioners, pg 136
National Institute for Trial Advocacy (NITA), pg 138
National Notary Association (NNA), pg 138
New Forums Press Inc, pg 139
The New Press, pg 140
New York State Bar Association, pg 141
New York University Press, pg 141
NOLO, pg 141
W W Norton & Company Inc, pg 143
Nova Press, pg 144
Ohio University Press, pg 145
Other Press, pg 148
Oxford University Press USA, pg 149
Pearson Business Publishing, pg 153
Penn State University Press, pg 157
Planners Press, pg 160
Pocket Press Inc, pg 161
Practising Law Institute (PLI), pg 163
Princeton University Press, pg 164
The Professional Education Group LLC (PEG), pg 165
Professional Resource Press, pg 165
Public Citizen, pg 167
RAND Corp, pg 169
Regent Press Printers & Publishers, pg 174
Regnery Publishing, pg 174
Rocky Mountain Mineral Law Foundation, pg 176
Rowman & Littlefield, pg 178
Rutgers University Press, pg 178
SAGE Publishing, pg 180
Salem Press, pg 181
Schreiber Publishing, pg 185
Science & Humanities Press, pg 185
1765 Productions, pg 186
M Lee Smith Publishers, pg 192
Solano Press Books, pg 193
South Carolina Bar, pg 195
Stanford University Press, pg 197
STM Learning Inc, pg 199
Strategic Book Publishing (SBP), pg 199
Tantor Media Inc, pg 202
Temple University Press, pg 204
Thomson West, pg 206
Tower Publishing Co, pg 208
Transportation Research Board (TRB), pg 209
United Nations Publications, pg 213
United States Institute of Peace Press, pg 213
University of Chicago Press, pg 215
University of Georgia Press, pg 216
University of Iowa Press, pg 216
University of Michigan Press, pg 217
University of Nevada Press, pg 218
University of North Texas Press, pg 218
University of Pennsylvania Press, pg 219
University Press of America Inc, pg 221
University Press of Kansas, pg 221
US Government Publishing Office (GPO), pg 223
Vault.com Inc, pg 224
Vernon Press, pg 224
West Academic, pg 227
Wheatherstone Press, pg 228
Markus Wiener Publishers Inc, pg 229
John Wiley & Sons Inc, pg 230
John Wiley & Sons Inc Global Education, pg 230
John Wiley & Sons Inc Professional Development, pg 230
Wolters Kluwer Law & Business, pg 232
Wolters Kluwer US Corp, pg 232
Workers Compensation Research Institute, pg 232
World Bank Publications, pg 233
Xlibris Corp, pg 234
Yale University Press, pg 235

LGBTQ+

ACTA Publications, pg 4
AK Press, pg 6
Akashic Books, pg 6
American Counseling Association (ACA), pg 9
The Apocryphile Press, pg 15
AuthorHouse, pg 22
Beacon Press, pg 25
Bella Books, pg 27
Blood Moon Productions Ltd, pg 31
Bloomsbury Academic, pg 31
Bold Strokes Books Inc, pg 33
Boson Books™, pg 34
Brandylane Publishers Inc, pg 35
Bucknell University Press, pg 38
Bywater Books Inc, pg 39
Capstone Publishers™, pg 40
Cedar Grove Publishing, pg 43
Chalice Press, pg 44
Charlesbridge Publishing Inc, pg 45
Chicago Review Press, pg 46
Chickadee Prince Books LLC, pg 46
Circlet Press, pg 48
City Lights Publishers, pg 48
Cleis Press, pg 49
Columbia University Press, pg 51
Copper Canyon Press, pg 52
Cornell University Press, pg 52
Counterpoint Press LLC, pg 54
Dalkey Archive Press, pg 56
Dark Horse Comics, pg 57
Dover Publications Inc, pg 61
Duke University Press, pg 62
Dutton, pg 62
M Evans & Company, pg 68
The Feminist Press at The City University of New York, pg 71
Gale, pg 75
Graywolf Press, pg 81
Green Integer, pg 81
Hal Leonard LLC, pg 84
Hamilton Stone Editions, pg 84
HarperCollins Publishers LLC, pg 86
Harrington Park Press, pg 87
Hazelden Publishing, pg 89
William S Hein & Co Inc, pg 90
Kensington Publishing Corp, pg 109
Koho Pono LLC, pg 111
LARB Books, pg 113
Lexington Books, pg 115
Limelight Editions, pg 117
Macmillan Reference USA™, pg 123
Manic D Press Inc, pg 124
Milford Books™, pg 131
Modern Language Association (MLA), pg 133
National Resource Center for Youth Services, pg 138
The New Press, pg 140
New York University Press, pg 141
NOLO, pg 141
North Star Editions Inc, pg 142
The Ohio State University Press, pg 145
On the Write Path Publishing, pg 146
The Original Falcon Press, pg 148
Other Press, pg 148
Palm Island Press, pg 150
Penn State University Press, pg 157
Persea Books, pg 158
The Pilgrim Press/United Church Press, pg 160
Pleasure Boat Studio: A Literary Press, pg 160
powerHouse Books, pg 162
Rational Island Publishers, pg 171
Red Hen Press, pg 172
Regal House Publishing, pg 173
Riverdale Avenue Books (RAB), pg 175
Routledge, pg 177
Running Press, pg 178
Rutgers University Press, pg 178
St James Press®, pg 180
Savant Books & Publications LLC, pg 182
Seven Stories Press, pg 186
Sherman Asher Publishing, pg 187
Soho Press Inc, pg 193
Sourcebooks LLC, pg 194
STARbooks Press, pg 197
State University of New York Press, pg 198
The Story Plant, pg 199
Strategic Book Publishing (SBP), pg 199
Tantor Media Inc, pg 202
Taschen America, pg 203
Teachers College Press, pg 203
Temple University Press, pg 204
United Nations Publications, pg 213
Universe Publishing, pg 214
University of Alabama Press, pg 214
University of Chicago Press, pg 215
University of Illinois Press, pg 216
University of Iowa Press, pg 216
University of Massachusetts Press, pg 217
University of Michigan Press, pg 217
University of Minnesota Press, pg 217
University of Nevada Press, pg 218
University of North Texas Press, pg 218
University of Wisconsin Press, pg 221
University Press of Mississippi, pg 222
Westminster John Knox Press (WJK), pg 228
Whiskey Creek Press, pg 228
Wiley-Blackwell, pg 229
Wolfman Books, pg 232
Xlibris Corp, pg 234
Yard Dog Press, pg 235
Yotzeret Publishing, pg 236
Zumaya Publications LLC, pg 237

LIBRARY & INFORMATION SCIENCES

Academic Press, pg 3
Adams & Ambrose Publishing, pg 4
ALA Neal-Schuman, pg 6
The American Library Association (ALA), pg 10
Anaphora Literary Press, pg 13
Annual Reviews, pg 14
Association of College & Research Libraries (ACRL), pg 19
Association of Research Libraries (ARL), pg 20
AuthorHouse, pg 22
John Benjamins Publishing Co, pg 28
R R Bowker LLC, pg 34
Cengage Learning, pg 43
Walter De Gruyter Inc, pg 58
Elsevier Inc, pg 65
Gale, pg 75
GeoLytics Inc, pg 77
Hi Willow Research & Publishing, pg 91
Histria Books, pg 93
Information Today, Inc, pg 100
Infosources Publishing, pg 100
Libraries Unlimited, pg 116
Macmillan Reference USA™, pg 123
McFarland, pg 127
Michigan State University Press (MSU Press), pg 130
Nataraj Books, pg 136
National Information Standards Organization (NISO), pg 138
Nova Science Publishers Inc, pg 144
Oak Knoll Press, pg 144
Omnigraphics Inc, pg 146
Pennsylvania State Data Center, pg 157
Primary Research Group Inc, pg 163
SAGE Publishing, pg 180
St Johann Press, pg 180
Science & Humanities Press, pg 185
Society of American Archivists, pg 192
Strategic Book Publishing (SBP), pg 199
TotalRecall Publications Inc, pg 208
Western Pennsylvania Genealogical Society, pg 228
Wisconsin Department of Public Instruction, pg 231

LITERATURE, LITERARY CRITICISM, ESSAYS

Abbeville Press, pg 1
Academica Press, pg 3
ACMRS Press, pg 4
ACTA Publications, pg 4
Africa World Press Inc, pg 5
AK Press, pg 6
Akashic Books, pg 6
Alexander Street, part of Clarivate PLC, pg 6
All Things That Matter Press, pg 7
American Philosophical Society Press, pg 11
Anaphora Literary Press, pg 13
The Apocryphile Press, pg 15
Applewood Books, pg 15
Arcade Publishing Inc, pg 16
Ariadne Press, pg 16
The Arion Press, pg 16
Arte Publico Press, pg 17
Ashland Creek Press, pg 18
Atlas Publishing, pg 21
August House Inc, pg 22
AuthorHouse, pg 22
Barrytown/Station Hill Press, pg 24
Baylor University Press, pg 25
Beacon Press, pg 25
Bedford/St Martin's, pg 26
Bellevue Literary Press, pg 27
Ben Yehuda Press, pg 27
BenBella Books Inc, pg 27
John Benjamins Publishing Co, pg 28
Bethlehem Books, pg 29
Biographical Publishing Co, pg 29

BJU Press, pg 30
BkMk Press Inc, pg 30
Black Heron Press, pg 30
Black Mountain Press, pg 30
Bloom's Literary Criticism, pg 31
Bloomsbury Academic, pg 31
BlueBridge, pg 32
Bolchazy-Carducci Publishers Inc, pg 33
Book Sales, pg 33
Bottom Dog Press, pg 34
Boydell & Brewer Inc, pg 35
George Braziller Inc, pg 35
Brill Inc, pg 37
Brown Books Publishing Group (BBPG), pg 38
Bucknell University Press, pg 38
Cambridge University Press, pg 39
Carnegie Mellon University Press, pg 41
Carolina Academic Press, pg 41
The Catholic University of America Press, pg 42
The Center for Learning, pg 43
Chelsea House, pg 45
Cheng & Tsui Co Inc, pg 46
Cherry Hill Publishing LLC, pg 46
China Books, pg 47
Christian Schools International (CSI), pg 47
Chronicle Books LLC, pg 47
City Lights Publishers, pg 48
Cleis Press, pg 49
Codhill Press, pg 50
Coffee House Press, pg 50
Columbia University Press, pg 51
Continental AfrikaPublishers, pg 52
Copper Canyon Press, pg 52
Cornell University Press, pg 52
Cornerstone Book Publishers, pg 53
Council for Research in Values & Philosophy, pg 53
Counterpath Press, pg 54
Counterpoint Press LLC, pg 54
Creative Editions, pg 55
Cross-Cultural Communications, pg 55
Dalkey Archive Press, pg 56
Walter De Gruyter Inc, pg 58
Delphinium Books, pg 58
Dissertation.com, pg 60
Doubleday, pg 61
Dover Publications Inc, pg 61
Down The Shore Publishing, pg 61
Duke University Press, pg 62
Edgewise Press Inc, pg 63
Editorial de la Universidad de Puerto Rico, pg 63
Educator's International Press Inc (EIP), pg 64
Elderberry Press Inc, pg 65
Encounter Books, pg 66
Enslow Publishing LLC, pg 66
Etruscan Press, pg 67
Europa Editions, pg 67
Facts On File, pg 69
Familius, pg 69
Feldheim Publishers, pg 70
The Feminist Press at The City University of New York, pg 71
Fine Creative Media, Inc, pg 71
Fordham University Press, pg 73
Gale, pg 75
Gallaudet University Press, pg 76
Gallery Books, pg 76
Gauthier Publications Inc, pg 77
Gingko Press Inc, pg 78
Goose River Press, pg 79
Graywolf Press, pg 81
Green Integer, pg 81
Greenleaf Book Group LLC, pg 81
Grove Atlantic Inc, pg 82
Hackett Publishing Co Inc, pg 83

Hamilton Books, pg 84
Hamilton Stone Editions, pg 84
HarperCollins Publishers LLC, pg 86
Harvard Ukrainian Research Institute, pg 88
Harvard University Press, pg 88
Hebrew Union College Press, pg 90
Heyday, pg 91
The Historic New Orleans Collection, pg 93
Histria Books, pg 93
Hobblebush Books, pg 93
Hollym International Corp, pg 94
Holy Cow! Press, pg 95
Homa & Sekey Books, pg 95
Homestead Publishing, pg 95
Host Publications, pg 95
Houghton Mifflin Harcourt, pg 95
Hutton Publishing, pg 97
Islandport Press, pg 105
Italica Press, pg 105
Johns Hopkins University Press, pg 106
Judaica Press Inc, pg 107
Kent State University Press, pg 109
Alfred A Knopf, pg 110
Kodansha USA Inc, pg 110
Koho Pono LLC, pg 111
Peter Lang Publishing Inc, pg 112
LARB Books, pg 113
Lectorum Publications Inc, pg 114
Lehigh University Press, pg 114
Lexington Books, pg 115
Library of America, pg 116
LinguaText LLC, pg 117
Little, Brown and Company, pg 118
Lost Classics Book Company LLC, pg 120
Louisiana State University Press, pg 120
LRS, pg 121
Luna Bisonte Prods, pg 121
Lynx House Press, pg 121
Macmillan Reference USA™, pg 123
Mage Publishers Inc, pg 123
Mandel Vilar Press, pg 124
Manic D Press Inc, pg 124
Marshall Cavendish Education, pg 125
Mazda Publishers Inc, pg 127
McFarland, pg 127
McGraw-Hill Create, pg 127
McGraw-Hill Education, pg 127
McGraw-Hill Higher Education, pg 128
McPherson & Co, pg 128
McSweeney's Publishing, pg 128
Medieval Institute Publications (MIP), pg 129
The Edwin Mellen Press, pg 129
Mercer University Press, pg 129
Merriam-Webster Inc, pg 129
Michigan State University Press (MSU Press), pg 130
Mighty Media Press, pg 131
Modern Language Association (MLA), pg 133
Modern Memoirs Inc, pg 133
Montemayor Press, pg 133
Multnomah, pg 135
Mutual Publishing LLC, pg 136
Nataraj Books, pg 136
National Council of Teachers of English (NCTE), pg 137
New Directions Publishing Corp, pg 139
New Issues Poetry & Prose, pg 140
The New Press, pg 140
New York University Press, pg 141
NewSouth Books, pg 141
Norilana Books, pg 142

North Atlantic Books (NAB), pg 142
North Country Press, pg 142
Northwestern University Press, pg 143
W W Norton & Company Inc, pg 143
Ocean Tree Books, pg 145
The Ohio State University Press, pg 145
Ohio University Press, pg 145
Omnigraphics Inc, pg 146
On the Write Path Publishing, pg 146
Open Letter, pg 147
Oregon State University Press, pg 147
The Original Falcon Press, pg 148
Other Press, pg 148
The Overlook Press, pg 148
Oxford University Press USA, pg 149
Pace University Press, pg 149
Palgrave Macmillan, pg 150
Palm Island Press, pg 150
Pantheon Books, pg 150
Parmenides Publishing, pg 152
Paul Dry Books, pg 152
Penn State University Press, pg 157
Persea Books, pg 158
Philosophical Library Inc, pg 159
Pleasure Boat Studio: A Literary Press, pg 160
Plough Publishing House, pg 161
Ploughshares, pg 161
Polar Bear & Company, pg 161
Princeton University Press, pg 164
Prometheus Books, pg 166
Purdue University Press, pg 167
Purple House Press, pg 167
Pushcart Press, pg 167
Pyncheon House, pg 167
Random House Publishing Group, pg 170
Red Hen Press, pg 172
Red Moon Press, pg 172
The Red Sea Press Inc, pg 173
Regal House Publishing, pg 173
Regent Press Printers & Publishers, pg 174
Lynne Rienner Publishers Inc, pg 174
Rising Sun Publishing, pg 175
Routledge, pg 177
Rowman & Littlefield, pg 178
Saddleback Educational Publishing, pg 179
St James Press®, pg 180
St Joseph's University Press, pg 180
Salem Press, pg 181
San Diego State University Press, pg 182
Santa Monica Press LLC, pg 182
Sarabande Books Inc, pg 182
Sasquatch Books, pg 182
Savant Books & Publications LLC, pg 182
Schaffner Press, pg 183
Scholastic Inc, pg 184
Science & Humanities Press, pg 185
Scripta Humanistica Publishing International, pg 185
Seven Stories Press, pg 186
Shambhala Publications Inc, pg 187
Sherman Asher Publishing, pg 187
Siglio, pg 187
Signature Books Publishing LLC, pg 187
Soho Press Inc, pg 193
Somerset Hall Press, pg 193
Sourcebooks LLC, pg 194
Stanford University Press, pg 197
Steerforth Press & Services, pg 198

SteinerBooks Inc, pg 198
STOCKCERO Inc, pg 199
Stone Bridge Press Inc, pg 199
Stone Pier Press, pg 199
Strategic Book Publishing (SBP), pg 199
Sunstone Press, pg 201
Swallow Press, pg 201
Swan Isle Press, pg 201
Syracuse University Press, pg 201
Nan A Talese, pg 202
Tantor Media Inc, pg 202
TCU Press, pg 203
Teacher's Discovery®, pg 203
Terra Nova Books, pg 204
Texas Tech University Press, pg 205
Third World Press Foundation, pg 206
The Toby Press LLC, pg 207
Trans-Atlantic Publications Inc, pg 209
Trinity University Press, pg 209
TriQuarterly Books, pg 209
Tupelo Press Inc, pg 210
Tuttle Publishing, pg 211
Twilight Times Books, pg 211
Ugly Duckling Presse, pg 212
University of Alabama Press, pg 214
The University of Arizona Press, pg 214
The University of Arkansas Press, pg 214
University of California Press, pg 215
University of Chicago Press, pg 215
University of Delaware Press, pg 215
University of Georgia Press, pg 216
University of Hawaii Press, pg 216
University of Illinois Press, pg 216
University of Iowa Press, pg 216
University of Louisiana at Lafayette Press, pg 217
University of Massachusetts Press, pg 217
University of Michigan Press, pg 217
University of Minnesota Press, pg 217
University of Missouri Press, pg 217
University of Nebraska Press, pg 217
University of Nevada Press, pg 218
University of New Mexico Press, pg 218
University of New Orleans Press, pg 218
The University of North Carolina Press, pg 218
University of North Texas Press, pg 218
University of Notre Dame Press, pg 219
University of Oklahoma Press, pg 219
University of Pennsylvania Press, pg 219
University of Pittsburgh Press, pg 219
University of South Carolina Press, pg 220
University of Tennessee Press, pg 220
The University of Utah Press, pg 220
University of Virginia Press, pg 220
University of Washington Press, pg 220
University of Wisconsin Press, pg 221
University Press of America Inc, pg 221

University Press of Colorado, pg 221
University Press of Florida, pg 221
University Press of Mississippi, pg 222
Vanderbilt University Press, pg 224
Verso Books, pg 224
Vintage Books, pg 225
Wake Forest University Press, pg 225
WaterBrook, pg 226
Waveland Press Inc, pg 226
Wayside Publishing, pg 227
Welcome Rain Publishers LLC, pg 227
Wesleyan University Press, pg 227
West Virginia University Press, pg 228
White Pine Press, pg 228
Markus Wiener Publishers Inc, pg 229
Wilderness Adventures Press Inc, pg 229
Wiley-Blackwell, pg 229
Wolfman Books, pg 232
World Citizens, pg 233
Xlibris Corp, pg 234
Yale University Press, pg 235
Zone Books, pg 237

MANAGEMENT

American Academy of Pediatrics, pg 8
American Bar Association Publishing, pg 8
American Correctional Association, pg 9
The American Library Association (ALA), pg 10
American Medical Association (AMA), pg 11
American Society for Quality (ASQ), pg 12
AOTA Press, pg 14
APPA - Leadership in Education Facilities, pg 15
Apress Media LLC, pg 15
Artech House®, pg 17
ASIS International, pg 19
Aspatore Books, pg 19
Association for Talent Development (ATD) Press, pg 19
Association of School Business Officials International, pg 20
Atlantic Publishing Group Inc, pg 21
Atlas Publishing, pg 21
AuthorHouse, pg 22
Beaver's Pond Press Inc, pg 26
Berrett-Koehler Publishers Inc, pg 29
BLR®—Business & Legal Resources, pg 32
Blue Note Publications Inc, pg 32
BoardSource, pg 33
BookLogix, pg 34
Nicholas Brealey Publishing, pg 36
Bridge Publications Inc, pg 36
Brilliance Publishing Inc, pg 37
Brown Books Publishing Group (BBPG), pg 38
BuilderBooks, pg 38
Business Expert Press, pg 38
Business Research Services Inc, pg 38
Candid, pg 39
Cengage Learning, pg 43
Center for Creative Leadership LLC, pg 43
Columbia University Press, pg 51
The Conference Board Inc, pg 51
Continental AfrikaPublishers, pg 52

Cornell University Press, pg 52
The Crossroad Publishing Co, pg 55
CSWE Press, pg 56
DEStech Publications Inc, pg 59
Dharma Publishing, pg 59
Easy Money Press, pg 63
Edward Elgar Publishing Inc, pg 65
Elsevier Inc, pg 65
Financial Times Press, pg 71
Gale, pg 75
The Graduate Group/Booksellers, pg 80
Green Dragon Books, pg 81
Greenleaf Book Group LLC, pg 81
Hannacroix Creek Books Inc, pg 85
Harvard Business Review Press, pg 87
HCPro/DecisionHealth, pg 89
Health Administration Press, pg 89
Health Forum Inc, pg 90
Health Professions Press, pg 90
High Tide Press, pg 92
Homa & Sekey Books, pg 95
HRD Press, pg 97
Humanix Books LLC, pg 97
IET USA Inc, pg 98
Industrial Press Inc, pg 100
Information Age Publishing Inc, pg 100
Institute of Police Technology & Management (IPTM), pg 102
International City/County Management Association (ICMA), pg 102
International Council of Shopping Centers (ICSC), pg 102
International Wealth Success (IWS), pg 104
JIST Publishing, pg 106
Kallisti Publishing Inc, pg 108
J J Keller & Associates, Inc®, pg 108
Kennedy Information LLC, pg 108
Alfred A Knopf, pg 110
Kogan Page, pg 111
Koho Pono LLC, pg 111
Kumarian Press, pg 112
Lasaria Creative Publishing, pg 113
The Lentz Leadership Institute LLC, pg 115
Logos Press, pg 119
Macmillan Reference USA™, pg 123
Management Advisory Services & Publications (MASP), pg 123
Management Sciences for Health, pg 123
McGraw-Hill Create, pg 127
McGraw-Hill Higher Education, pg 128
R S Means from The Gordian Group, pg 128
Milford Books™, pg 131
National Association of Broadcasters (NAB), pg 136
National Center For Employee Ownership (NCEO), pg 137
National Golf Foundation, pg 138
North River Press Publishing Corp, pg 142
The Oaklea Press Inc, pg 145
Palgrave Macmillan, pg 150
Pelican Publishing, pg 153
Plunkett Research Ltd, pg 161
Portfolio, pg 162
Practice Management Information Corp (PMIC), pg 163
Productivity Press, pg 165
PSMJ Resources Inc, pg 166
Rodin Books, pg 176
Ronin Publishing Inc, pg 176
Rothstein Associates Inc, pg 177
Routledge, pg 177

Sagamore Publishing LLC, pg 179
SAGE Publishing, pg 180
Schonfeld & Associates Inc, pg 184
Science & Humanities Press, pg 185
SelectBooks Inc, pg 186
Simon & Schuster Audio, pg 189
SkillPath Publications, pg 190
SME (Society of Manufacturing Engineers), pg 191
Society for Human Resource Management (SHRM), pg 192
Society for Mining, Metallurgy & Exploration, pg 192
Solano Press Books, pg 193
Sourcebooks LLC, pg 194
Stanford University Press, pg 197
Star Publishing Co Inc, pg 197
Stipes Publishing LLC, pg 198
Strategic Book Publishing (SBP), pg 199
Tantor Media Inc, pg 202
Theatre Communications Group, pg 205
US Government Publishing Office (GPO), pg 223
Vernon Press, pg 224
Wheatherstone Press, pg 228
Wiley-Blackwell, pg 229
John Wiley & Sons Inc Global Education, pg 230
John Wiley & Sons Inc Professional Development, pg 230
Xlibris Corp, pg 234
XML Press, pg 235
Zondervan, pg 236

MARITIME

Atlantic Publishing Group Inc, pg 21
AuthorHouse, pg 22
Avery Color Studios, pg 23
Bitingduck Press LLC, pg 30
The Blackburn Press, pg 30
Book Sales, pg 33
Boson Books™, pg 34
Brick Tower Press, pg 36
Carolina Academic Press, pg 41
Charlesbridge Publishing Inc, pg 45
Cornell Maritime Press, pg 52
Dover Publications Inc, pg 61
Down The Shore Publishing, pg 61
Evergreen Pacific Publishing Ltd, pg 68
FineEdge.com LLC, pg 72
HarperCollins Publishers LLC, pg 86
Kogan Page, pg 111
Lake Superior Publishing LLC, pg 112
The Lyons Press, pg 121
Marine Education Textbooks, pg 125
Marine Techniques Publishing, pg 125
McBooks Press, pg 127
National Academies Press (NAP), pg 136
Naval Institute Press, pg 139
North Carolina Office of Archives & History, pg 142
Paradise Cay Publications Inc, pg 151
Polar Bear & Company, pg 161
Potomac Books, pg 162
ProStar Publications Inc, pg 166
Routledge, pg 177
Schiffer Publishing Ltd, pg 183
The Society of Naval Architects & Marine Engineers (SNAME), pg 193
Strategic Book Publishing (SBP), pg 199

Tide-mark Press, pg 207
Tilbury House Publishers, pg 207
Transportation Research Board (TRB), pg 209
University of South Carolina Press, pg 220
US Government Publishing Office (GPO), pg 223
Washington State University Press, pg 226
Wayne State University Press, pg 226

MARKETING

American Carriage House Publishing (ACHP), pg 8
The American Library Association (ALA), pg 10
Aspatore Books, pg 19
Atlantic Publishing Group Inc, pg 21
AuthorHouse, pg 22
Avant-Guide, pg 22
Barringer Publishing, pg 24
Beaver's Pond Press Inc, pg 26
BookLogix, pg 34
Brilliance Publishing Inc, pg 37
Brown Books Publishing Group (BBPG), pg 38
Business Expert Press, pg 38
Business Research Services Inc, pg 38
The Catholic Health Association of the United States, pg 42
Cengage Learning, pg 43
The Connecticut Law Tribune, pg 52
Cosimo Inc, pg 53
Dancing Lemur Press LLC, pg 57
DiscoverNet Publishing, pg 59
Easy Money Press, pg 63
Edward Elgar Publishing Inc, pg 65
Fairchild Books, pg 69
Financial Times Press, pg 71
Gale, pg 75
GeoLytics Inc, pg 77
Goodheart-Willcox Publisher, pg 79
The Graduate Group/Booksellers, pg 80
Greenleaf Book Group LLC, pg 81
Hal Leonard LLC, pg 84
Harvard Business Review Press, pg 87
Information Age Publishing Inc, pg 100
International Council of Shopping Centers (ICSC), pg 102
Kallisti Publishing Inc, pg 108
Kogan Page, pg 111
The Lentz Leadership Institute LLC, pg 115
Macmillan Reference USA™, pg 123
McGraw-Hill Create, pg 127
McGraw-Hill Higher Education, pg 128
McGraw-Hill School Education Group, pg 128
The Edwin Mellen Press, pg 129
Richard K Miller Associates, pg 132
Morgan James Publishing, pg 134
National Association of Broadcasters (NAB), pg 136
National Golf Foundation, pg 138
NRP Direct, pg 144
On the Write Path Publishing, pg 146
One On One Book Publishing/Film-Video Publications, pg 146
Open Horizons Publishing Co, pg 147
Palgrave Macmillan, pg 150

PUBLISHERS

U.S. PUBLISHERS — SUBJECT INDEX

Paramount Market Publishing Inc, pg 151
Pennsylvania State Data Center, pg 157
Plunkett Research Ltd, pg 161
Portfolio, pg 162
Prometheus Books, pg 166
The PRS Group Inc, pg 166
PSMJ Resources Inc, pg 166
Round Table Companies, pg 177
Routledge, pg 177
SAGE Publishing, pg 180
Schonfeld & Associates Inc, pg 184
Science & Humanities Press, pg 185
SelectBooks Inc, pg 186
Small Business Advisors Inc, pg 191
Sourcebooks LLC, pg 194
Story Monsters LLC, pg 199
Strategic Book Publishing (SBP), pg 199
Tantor Media Inc, pg 202
Todd Publications, pg 207
US Government Publishing Office (GPO), pg 223
Vault.com Inc, pg 224
Vernon Press, pg 224
Wiley-Blackwell, pg 229
Wisconsin Department of Public Instruction, pg 231
WriteLife Publishing, pg 234

MATHEMATICS

Academic Press, pg 3
Advance Publishing Inc, pg 5
American Mathematical Society (AMS), pg 11
American Press, pg 11
American Society for Quality (ASQ), pg 12
Arbordale Publishing, pg 16
Astra Books for Young Readers, pg 20
Atlas Publishing, pg 21
AuthorHouse, pg 22
Beaver's Pond Press Inc, pg 26
BJU Press, pg 30
The Blackburn Press, pg 30
Cambridge University Press, pg 39
Cengage Learning, pg 43
Charlesbridge Publishing Inc, pg 45
Chelsea House, pg 45
Child's Play® Inc, pg 46
The Child's World Inc, pg 46
Christian Liberty Press, pg 47
Comex Systems Inc, pg 51
CRC Press, pg 55
Walter De Gruyter Inc, pg 58
Dover Publications Inc, pg 61
Duke University Press, pg 62
Educational Insights®, pg 64
Edupress Inc, pg 64
Elsevier Inc, pg 65
Evan-Moor Educational Publishers, pg 68
Facts On File, pg 69
W H Freeman, pg 75
Gale, pg 75
Gareth Stevens Publishing, pg 76
Goodheart-Willcox Publisher, pg 79
Heinemann, pg 90
Houghton Mifflin Harcourt, pg 95
Houghton Mifflin Harcourt K-12 Publishers, pg 96
Huntington Press Publishing, pg 97
IEEE Press, pg 98
Industrial Press Inc, pg 100
Information Age Publishing Inc, pg 100
International Press of Boston Inc, pg 103

Johns Hopkins University Press, pg 106
Jones & Bartlett Learning LLC, pg 107
Jump!, pg 107
Kendall Hunt Publishing Co, pg 108
Koho Pono LLC, pg 111
Krieger Publishing Co, pg 111
LAMA Books, pg 112
THE Learning Connection®, pg 113
Learning Links-USA Inc, pg 114
LearningExpress, pg 114
Lorenz Educational Press, pg 120
Macmillan Learning, pg 123
Macmillan Reference USA™, pg 123
Master Books®, pg 126
Mastery Education, pg 126
Math Solutions®, pg 127
Math Teachers Press Inc, pg 127
The Mathematical Association of America, pg 127
McGraw-Hill Create, pg 127
McGraw-Hill Education, pg 127
McGraw-Hill Higher Education, pg 128
McGraw-Hill School Education Group, pg 128
Milliken Publishing Co, pg 132
De Gruyter Mouton, pg 135
National Academies Press (NAP), pg 136
National Book Co, pg 136
National Council of Teachers of Mathematics (NCTM), pg 137
National Geographic Learning, pg 138
National Science Teachers Association (NSTA), pg 138
New Readers Press, pg 140
New York Academy of Sciences (NYAS), pg 140
No Starch Press, pg 141
Norwood House Press, pg 143
Nova Science Publishers Inc, pg 144
Oxford University Press USA, pg 149
Pearson Business Publishing, pg 153
Perfection Learning®, pg 158
Petroleum Extension Service (PETEX), pg 159
Philosophical Library Inc, pg 159
Polar Bear & Company, pg 161
PPI, A Kaplan Company, pg 162
Princeton University Press, pg 164
Prometheus Books, pg 166
Research & Education Association (REA), pg 174
Royal Fireworks Press, pg 178
Running Press, pg 178
Saddleback Educational Publishing, pg 179
William H Sadlier Inc, pg 179
SAS Press, pg 182
Savvas Learning Co LLC, pg 183
Scholastic Inc, pg 184
Science & Humanities Press, pg 185
Science, Naturally, pg 185
Society for Industrial & Applied Mathematics, pg 192
Springer, pg 196
Star Bright Books Inc, pg 197
Stylus Publishing LLC, pg 200
Sundance/Newbridge Publishing, pg 200
Tantor Media Inc, pg 202
Teacher Created Resources Inc, pg 203
Teaching & Learning Co, pg 204
Tumblehome Learning Inc, pg 210
University of Chicago Press, pg 215

US Government Publishing Office (GPO), pg 223
Walch Education, pg 225
Waveland Press Inc, pg 226
Whittier Publications Inc, pg 229
Wide World Publishing, pg 229
Wiley-Blackwell, pg 229
John Wiley & Sons Inc, pg 230
John Wiley & Sons Inc Global Education, pg 230
John Wiley & Sons Inc Professional Development, pg 230
Wisconsin Department of Public Instruction, pg 231
World Scientific Publishing Co Inc, pg 233

MECHANICAL ENGINEERING

Academic Press, pg 3
AIHA (American Industrial Hygiene Association), pg 6
American Academy of Environmental Engineers & Scientists®, pg 8
American Public Works Association (APWA), pg 12
American Society of Mechanical Engineers (ASME), pg 12
ASM International, pg 19
ASTM International, pg 20
AuthorHouse, pg 22
Begell House Inc Publishers, pg 27
Cengage Learning, pg 43
Cornell Maritime Press, pg 52
DEStech Publications Inc, pg 59
Dover Publications Inc, pg 61
The Electrochemical Society (ECS), pg 65
Gale, pg 75
Goodheart-Willcox Publisher, pg 79
Hanser Publications LLC, pg 85
Industrial Press Inc, pg 100
International Society of Automation (ISA), pg 103
Koho Pono LLC, pg 111
Krieger Publishing Co, pg 111
Macmillan Reference USA™, pg 123
Marine Techniques Publishing, pg 125
Materials Research Society, pg 126
McGraw-Hill Higher Education, pg 128
R S Means from The Gordian Group, pg 128
NACE International, pg 136
National Academies Press (NAP), pg 136
Nova Science Publishers Inc, pg 144
PPI, A Kaplan Company, pg 162
Research & Education Association (REA), pg 174
SAE (Society of Automotive Engineers International), pg 179
SAGE Publishing, pg 180
SME (Society of Manufacturing Engineers), pg 191
Stylus Publishing LLC, pg 200
Taylor & Francis Inc, pg 203
US Government Publishing Office (GPO), pg 223
Waveland Press Inc, pg 226

MEDICINE, NURSING, DENTISTRY

A 2 Z Press LLC, pg 1
Academic Press, pg 3
Addicus Books Inc, pg 5

Alexander Street, part of Clarivate PLC, pg 6
American Academy of Pediatrics, pg 8
American Diabetes Association, pg 9
American Medical Association (AMA), pg 11
American Psychiatric Association Publishing, pg 11
Annual Reviews, pg 14
AOTA Press, pg 14
ASCP Press, pg 18
ASET - The Neurodiagnostic Society, pg 18
Ash Tree Publishing, pg 18
ASM Publishing, pg 19
Association for the Advancement of Blood & Biotherapies, pg 19
AuthorHouse, pg 22
Beacon Press, pg 25
Beaver's Pond Press Inc, pg 26
Begell House Inc Publishers, pg 27
Boydell & Brewer Inc, pg 35
Cambridge University Press, pg 39
Cardiotext Publishing, pg 40
Carolina Academic Press, pg 41
Cengage Learning, pg 43
Charles Press Publishers, pg 45
Clinical and Laboratory Standards Institute (CLSI), pg 49
Cognizant Communication Corp, pg 50
CRC Press, pg 55
Data Trace Publishing Co (DTP), pg 57
Davies Publishing Inc, pg 57
F A Davis Co, pg 57
dbS Productions, pg 58
Walter De Gruyter Inc, pg 58
Demos Medical Publishing, pg 58
DEStech Publications Inc, pg 59
DK, pg 60
Eastland Press, pg 63
Elsevier Health Sciences, pg 65
Elsevier Inc, pg 65
M Evans & Company, pg 68
Gale, pg 75
The Graduate Group/Booksellers, pg 80
Gryphon Editions, pg 82
Hartman Publishing Inc, pg 87
Hatherleigh Press Ltd, pg 88
Health Forum Inc, pg 90
Health Professions Press, pg 90
High Tide Press, pg 92
Hogrefe Publishing Corp, pg 93
Homa & Sekey Books, pg 95
Hospital & Healthcare Compensation Service, pg 95
Idyll Arbor Inc, pg 98
Jhpiego, pg 106
Johns Hopkins University Press, pg 106
Jones & Bartlett Learning LLC, pg 107
Lawyers & Judges Publishing Co Inc, pg 113
Mary Ann Liebert Inc, pg 116
Life Cycle Books, pg 116
Lippincott Williams & Wilkins, pg 117
Little, Brown and Company, pg 118
Macmillan Reference USA™, pg 123
Master Books®, pg 126
McGraw-Hill Professional Publishing Group, pg 128
Medical Physics Publishing Corp (MPP), pg 129
MedMaster Inc, pg 129
Merriam-Webster Inc, pg 129
Milford Books™, pg 131

311

U.S. PUBLISHERS — SUBJECT INDEX

De Gruyter Mouton, pg 135
Nataraj Books, pg 136
National Academies Press (NAP), pg 136
New York Academy of Sciences (NYAS), pg 140
Nova Science Publishers Inc, pg 144
Nursesbooks.org, The Publishing Program of ANA, pg 144
On the Write Path Publishing, pg 146
Optometric Extension Program Foundation (OEPF), pg 147
OptumInsight™, pg 147
Oxford University Press USA, pg 149
Penn State University Press, pg 157
Platypus Media LLC, pg 160
Plunkett Research Ltd, pg 161
Practice Management Information Corp (PMIC), pg 163
Professional Communications Inc, pg 165
Professional Resource Press, pg 165
Quintessence Publishing Co Inc, pg 168
Reference Publications Inc, pg 173
The Rockefeller University Press, pg 176
Rutgers University Press, pg 178
SAGE Publishing, pg 180
Salem Press, pg 181
Science History Publications USA Inc, pg 185
Sinauer Associates, pg 190
SLACK® Incorporated, A Wyanoke Group Company, pg 191
SPIE, pg 196
Springer, pg 196
Springer Publishing Co, pg 196
Star Publishing Co Inc, pg 197
STM Learning Inc, pg 199
Strategic Book Publishing (SBP), pg 199
Sunrise River Press, pg 201
Tantor Media Inc, pg 202
Teton NewMedia Inc, pg 205
Thieme Medical Publishers Inc, pg 206
Charles C Thomas Publisher Ltd, pg 206
United States Pharmacopeia (USP), pg 213
University of Iowa Press, pg 216
University of Rochester Press, pg 220
University of Wisconsin Press, pg 221
US Government Publishing Office (GPO), pg 223
Vanderbilt University Press, pg 224
Whole Person Associates Inc, pg 229
Wiley-Blackwell, pg 229
John Wiley & Sons Inc, pg 230
John Wiley & Sons Inc Global Education, pg 230
John Wiley & Sons Inc Professional Development, pg 230
Wolters Kluwer US Corp, pg 232
Write Stuff Enterprises LLC, pg 234
Xlibris Corp, pg 234
Yale University Press, pg 235

MILITARY SCIENCE

American Institute of Aeronautics and Astronautics (AIAA), pg 10
AuthorHouse, pg 22
Begell House Inc Publishers, pg 27
Blue Crane Books Inc, pg 32
Brilliance Publishing Inc, pg 37
Burford Books, pg 38
Capstone Publishers™, pg 40
Casemate | publishers, pg 41
Center for Strategic & International Studies (CSIS), pg 44
China Books, pg 47
Cornell University Press, pg 52
DEStech Publications Inc, pg 59
Dover Publications Inc, pg 61
Eakin Press, pg 62
Elderberry Press Inc, pg 65
Encounter Books, pg 66
Excalibur Publications, pg 68
Facts On File, pg 69
Fordham University Press, pg 73
Greenleaf Book Group LLC, pg 81
Hellgate Press, pg 91
History Publishing Co LLC, pg 93
Institute of Environmental Sciences & Technology - IEST, pg 101
Marshall Cavendish Education, pg 125
Mason Crest Publishers, pg 126
McFarland, pg 127
Medals of America Press, pg 128
The Edwin Mellen Press, pg 129
Military Info Publishing, pg 131
Moonshine Cove Publishing LLC, pg 134
Nataraj Books, pg 136
National Academies Press (NAP), pg 136
Naval Institute Press, pg 139
New Forums Press Inc, pg 139
Pathfinder Publishing Inc, pg 152
Potomac Books, pg 162
Radix Press, pg 169
RAND Corp, pg 169
Regnery Publishing, pg 174
SAGE Publishing, pg 180
Schiffer Publishing Ltd, pg 183
Signalman Publishing, pg 187
Stackpole Books, pg 196
Stanford University Press, pg 197
StarGroup International Inc, pg 197
Strategic Book Publishing (SBP), pg 199
Tantor Media Inc, pg 202
Texas A&M University Press, pg 205
Texas Tech University Press, pg 205
Union Square & Co, pg 212
University of California Institute on Global Conflict & Cooperation, pg 215
University of North Texas Press, pg 218
University of Oklahoma Press, pg 219
University of South Carolina Press, pg 220
University Press of Kansas, pg 221
The University Press of Kentucky, pg 222
US Government Publishing Office (GPO), pg 223
Vandamere Press, pg 223
Washington State University Press, pg 226
Xlibris Corp, pg 234
Zumaya Publications LLC, pg 237

MUSIC, DANCE

A-R Editions Inc, pg 1
A 2 Z Press LLC, pg 1
Abbeville Press, pg 1
Abbeville Publishing Group, pg 2
Academica Press, pg 3
Akashic Books, pg 6
Alexander Street, part of Clarivate PLC, pg 6
Allworth Press, pg 7
Amadeus Press, pg 7
American Catholic Press (ACP), pg 9
Sara Anderson Children's Books, pg 13
AuthorHouse, pg 22
Backbeat Books, pg 23
Barcelona Publishers LLC, pg 24
Barrytown/Station Hill Press, pg 24
BearManor Media, pg 26
Beaver's Pond Press Inc, pg 26
Bedford/St Martin's, pg 26
Bellerophon Books, pg 27
Bloomsbury Academic, pg 31
Blue Note Publications Inc, pg 32
Boydell & Brewer Inc, pg 35
Captain Fiddle Music & Publications, pg 40
Cedar Grove Publishing, pg 43
Cengage Learning, pg 43
Centerstream Publishing LLC, pg 44
Charlesbridge Publishing Inc, pg 45
Chelsea House, pg 45
Chicago Review Press, pg 46
Child's Play® Inc, pg 46
China Books, pg 47
Chronicle Books LLC, pg 47
Codhill Press, pg 50
Cornell University Press, pg 52
Counterpoint Press LLC, pg 54
Country Music Foundation Press, pg 54
Walter De Gruyter Inc, pg 58
Deseret Book Co, pg 58
Doubleday, pg 61
Dover Publications Inc, pg 61
Duke University Press, pg 62
ECS Publishing Group, pg 63
EDC Publishing, pg 63
FJH Music Co Inc, pg 72
Fowler Museum at UCLA, pg 74
Gale, pg 75
Gallery Books, pg 76
GIA Publications Inc, pg 78
Gingko Press Inc, pg 78
Greenleaf Book Group LLC, pg 81
Grey House Publishing Inc™, pg 81
Hal Leonard LLC, pg 84
Heyday, pg 91
Hope Publishing Co, pg 95
Horizon Publishers & Distributors Inc, pg 95
Indiana Historical Society Press, pg 99
Indiana University Press, pg 100
Information Age Publishing Inc, pg 100
Inner Traditions International Ltd, pg 101
Insight Editions, pg 101
Klutz®, pg 110
Alfred A Knopf, pg 110
Krause Publications Inc, pg 111
THE Learning Connection®, pg 113
Learning Links-USA Inc, pg 114
Limelight Editions, pg 117
Little, Brown and Company, pg 118
Lorenz Educational Press, pg 120
Louisiana State University Press, pg 120
Macmillan Reference USA™, pg 123
Mage Publishers Inc, pg 123
Mandala Earth, pg 124
Marshall Cavendish Education, pg 125
McFarland, pg 127
McGraw-Hill Education, pg 127
McGraw-Hill Higher Education, pg 128
McGraw-Hill School Education Group, pg 128
Medieval Institute Publications (MIP), pg 129
Mel Bay Publications Inc, pg 129
The Edwin Mellen Press, pg 129
Meriwether Publishing, pg 129
Milliken Publishing Co, pg 132
De Gruyter Mouton, pg 135
Nataraj Books, pg 136
North Point Press, pg 142
W W Norton & Company Inc, pg 143
OCP, pg 145
Omnibus Press, pg 146
Oxford University Press USA, pg 149
Pantheon Books, pg 150
Pathfinder Publishing Inc, pg 152
Pearson Business Publishing, pg 153
Pelican Publishing, pg 153
Pendragon Press, pg 154
Penguin Publishing Group, pg 154
Piano Press, pg 159
Pomegranate Communications Inc, pg 162
PRB Productions, pg 163
The Press at California State University, Fresno, pg 163
Princeton Book Co Publishers, pg 163
Quarto Publishing Group USA Inc, pg 168
Roncorp Music, pg 176
Ross Books, pg 177
Routledge, pg 177
Running Press, pg 178
Rutgers University Press, pg 178
St James Press®, pg 180
Santa Monica Press LLC, pg 182
Savvas Learning Co LLC, pg 183
G Schirmer Inc/Associated Music Publishers Inc, pg 183
Shambhala Publications Inc, pg 187
Silman-James Press Inc, pg 188
Sound Feelings Publishing, pg 194
Sounds True Inc, pg 194
SteinerBooks Inc, pg 198
Stipes Publishing LLC, pg 198
Sunstone Press, pg 201
Tantor Media Inc, pg 202
Temple University Press, pg 204
Texas Tech University Press, pg 205
Todd Publications, pg 207
Tortuga Press, pg 208
Transcontinental Music Publications (TMP), pg 209
TSG Publishing Foundation Inc, pg 210
Union Square & Co, pg 212
University of California Press, pg 215
University of Chicago Press, pg 215
University of Illinois Press, pg 216
University of Iowa Press, pg 216
University of Massachusetts Press, pg 217
University of Michigan Press, pg 217
University of Nebraska Press, pg 217
University of North Texas Press, pg 218
University of Pittsburgh Press, pg 219
University of Rochester Press, pg 220
University of Wisconsin Press, pg 221
University Press of Florida, pg 221
University Press of Mississippi, pg 222
Vanderbilt University Press, pg 224
The Vendome Press, pg 224

PUBLISHERS

Watermark Publishing, pg 226
Waveland Press Inc, pg 226
Welcome Rain Publishers LLC, pg 227
Wesleyan University Press, pg 227
Westminster John Knox Press (WJK), pg 228
Wiley-Blackwell, pg 229
Wisconsin Department of Public Instruction, pg 231
Xlibris Corp, pg 234
Yale University Press, pg 235
YBK Publishers Inc, pg 235

MYSTERIES, SUSPENSE

Academy Chicago Publishers, pg 3
ACTA Publications, pg 4
Akashic Books, pg 6
Albert Whitman & Company, pg 6
All Things That Matter Press, pg 7
American Girl Publishing, pg 10
Ampersand Inc/Professional Publishing Services, pg 13
Anaphora Literary Press, pg 13
The Arion Press, pg 16
Arte Publico Press, pg 17
Ashland Creek Press, pg 18
Asta Publications LLC, pg 20
AuthorHouse, pg 22
Authorlink® Press, pg 22
Baker Books, pg 23
Bancroft Press, pg 24
Beaver's Pond Press Inc, pg 26
Bella Books, pg 27
BePuzzled, pg 28
Berkley, pg 28
Bethany House Publishers, pg 29
Biographical Publishing Co, pg 29
Bitingduck Press LLC, pg 30
BJU Press, pg 30
Bold Strokes Books Inc, pg 33
Books on Tape™, pg 34
BOOM! Studios, pg 34
Boson Books™, pg 34
Brandylane Publishers Inc, pg 35
Brick Tower Press, pg 36
Brilliance Publishing Inc, pg 37
Brown Books Publishing Group (BBPG), pg 38
Bywater Books Inc, pg 39
Capstone Publishers™, pg 40
Cedar Grove Publishing, pg 43
Charlesbridge Publishing Inc, pg 45
Cherry Hill Publishing LLC, pg 46
Chickadee Prince Books LLC, pg 46
Cleis Press, pg 49
Cornell Maritime Press, pg 52
Counterpoint Press LLC, pg 54
Covenant Communications Inc, pg 54
Creative Editions, pg 55
Cricket Cottage Publishing LLC, pg 55
Dancing Lemur Press LLC, pg 57
Dark Horse Comics, pg 57
DC Comics Inc, pg 58
Deep River Books LLC, pg 58
Doubleday, pg 61
Dover Publications Inc, pg 61
Down East Books, pg 61
EDC Publishing, pg 63
Elderberry Press Inc, pg 65
Epicenter Press Inc, pg 67
Europa Editions, pg 67
Father & Son Publishing Inc, pg 70
Firefall Editions, pg 72
Galaxy Press Inc, pg 75
Gale, pg 75
Gallery Books, pg 76
Gallopade International Inc, pg 76
Gauthier Publications Inc, pg 77
Global Authors Publications (GAP), pg 78
Godine, pg 79
Goose River Press, pg 79
Grand & Archer Publishing, pg 80
Grand Central Publishing, pg 80
Donald M Grant Publisher Inc, pg 80
Green Dragon Books, pg 81
Greenleaf Book Group LLC, pg 81
Hamilton Stone Editions, pg 84
Hannacroix Creek Books Inc, pg 85
HarperCollins Children's Books, pg 85
HarperCollins Publishers LLC, pg 86
History Publishing Co LLC, pg 93
Histria Books, pg 93
Houghton Mifflin Harcourt Trade & Reference Division, pg 96
Hutton Publishing, pg 97
Iron Stream Media, pg 104
Islandport Press, pg 105
Italics Publishing, pg 105
Jewish Lights Publishing, pg 105
Judaica Press Inc, pg 107
Kensington Publishing Corp, pg 109
Alfred A Knopf, pg 110
Koho Pono LLC, pg 111
Kregel Publications, pg 111
LARB Books, pg 113
Learning Links-USA Inc, pg 114
Lectorum Publications Inc, pg 114
Library of America, pg 116
Listen & Live Audio Inc, pg 117
Little, Brown and Company, pg 118
Llewellyn Publications, pg 119
Mandel Vilar Press, pg 124
Manic D Press Inc, pg 124
Midnight Marquee Press Inc, pg 130
Moonshine Cove Publishing LLC, pg 134
Multnomah, pg 135
Nataraj Books, pg 136
NBM Publishing Inc, pg 139
NFB Publishing, pg 141
North Atlantic Books (NAB), pg 142
North Country Press, pg 142
North Star Editions Inc, pg 142
Oceanview Publishing Inc, pg 145
Olde & Oppenheim Publishers, pg 146
On the Write Path Publishing, pg 146
Open Books Press, pg 146
Other Press, pg 148
Pace University Press, pg 149
Pantheon Books, pg 150
Papercutz, pg 150
Parachute Publishing LLC, pg 151
Park Place Publications, pg 152
Pen-L Publishing, pg 153
Penguin Publishing Group, pg 154
The Permanent Press, pg 158
Planert Creek Press, pg 160
Pocol Press, pg 161
Poisoned Pen Press, pg 161
Polar Bear & Company, pg 161
Polis Books, pg 162
Prometheus Books, pg 166
Publication Consultants, pg 167
Purple House Press, pg 167
Quincannon Publishing Group, pg 168
Ravenhawk™ Books, pg 172
Recorded Books Inc, an RBmedia company, pg 172
Regent Press Printers & Publishers, pg 174
Revell, pg 174
The RoadRunner Press, pg 175
Saddleback Educational Publishing, pg 179
St Martin's Press, LLC, pg 180
Savant Books & Publications LLC, pg 182
Scholastic Inc, pg 184
Shadow Mountain Publishing, pg 187
Silver Leaf Books LLC, pg 188
Simon & Schuster Audio, pg 189
Small Beer Press, pg 191
Soho Press Inc, pg 193
Sourcebooks LLC, pg 194
The Story Plant, pg 199
Strategic Book Publishing (SBP), pg 199
Tachyon Publications LLC, pg 202
Tantor Media Inc, pg 202
Thorndike Press®, pg 206
Tor Publishing Group, pg 207
TotalRecall Publications Inc, pg 208
TSG Publishing Foundation Inc, pg 210
Tumblehome Learning Inc, pg 210
Turner Publishing Co LLC, pg 210
Twilight Times Books, pg 211
Vesuvian Books, pg 224
WaterBrook, pg 226
Whiskey Creek Press, pg 228
Wildflower Press, pg 229
Wildside Press LLC, pg 229
Xlibris Corp, pg 234
Yard Dog Press, pg 235
Yotzeret Publishing, pg 236
Zumaya Publications LLC, pg 237

NATIVE AMERICAN STUDIES

Abbeville Publishing Group, pg 2
Academica Press, pg 3
Alexander Street, part of Clarivate PLC, pg 6
Anaphora Literary Press, pg 13
Asta Publications LLC, pg 20
AuthorHouse, pg 22
Barrytown/Station Hill Press, pg 24
Beacon Press, pg 25
Bear & Co Inc, pg 26
Beaver's Pond Press Inc, pg 26
Black Rabbit Books, pg 30
The Blackburn Press, pg 30
The Book Tree, pg 34
BPC, pg 35
Brandylane Publishers Inc, pg 35
Capstone Publishers™, pg 40
Caxton Press, pg 42
Cedar Grove Publishing, pg 43
Charlesbridge Publishing Inc, pg 45
Chelsea House, pg 45
Clarity Press Inc, pg 49
Clear Light Publishers, pg 49
Clearfield Co Inc, pg 49
Coffee House Press, pg 50
Cornell University Press, pg 52
Crabtree Publishing Co, pg 54
Cross-Cultural Communications, pg 55
Dover Publications Inc, pg 61
Edupress Inc, pg 64
Enslow Publishing LLC, pg 66
Facts On File, pg 69
Fine Creative Media, Inc, pg 71
Fowler Museum at UCLA, pg 74
Fulcrum Publishing Inc, pg 75
Gale, pg 75
Glitterati Inc, pg 78
Hay House LLC, pg 89
William S Hein & Co Inc, pg 90
Heyday, pg 91
History Publishing Co LLC, pg 93
Homestead Publishing, pg 95
Illinois State Museum Society, pg 99
Indiana Historical Society Press, pg 99
Inner Traditions International Ltd, pg 101
Kamehameha Publishing, pg 108
Kiva Publishing Inc, pg 110
Peter Lang Publishing Inc, pg 112
THE Learning Connection®, pg 113
Learning Links-USA Inc, pg 114
Lexington Books, pg 115
Lucent Press, pg 121
Macmillan Reference USA™, pg 123
Mandel Vilar Press, pg 124
Marshall Cavendish Education, pg 125
Mason Crest Publishers, pg 126
The McDonald & Woodward Publishing Co, pg 127
McFarland, pg 127
The Edwin Mellen Press, pg 129
Michigan State University Press (MSU Press), pg 130
Minnesota Historical Society Press, pg 132
Modern Language Association (MLA), pg 133
Museum of New Mexico Press, pg 135
The New Press, pg 140
New World Library, pg 140
NewSouth Books, pg 141
North Atlantic Books (NAB), pg 142
Orbis Books, pg 147
Oregon State University Press, pg 147
Pennsylvania Historical & Museum Commission, pg 157
Polar Bear & Company, pg 161
Rational Island Publishers, pg 171
Reference Publications Inc, pg 173
Rio Nuevo Publishers, pg 175
The RoadRunner Press, pg 175
St James Press®, pg 180
Salem Press, pg 181
Salina Bookshelf Inc, pg 181
School for Advanced Research Press, pg 185
SIL International, pg 188
South Dakota Historical Society Press, pg 195
Spizzirri Publishing Inc, pg 196
State University of New York Press, pg 198
Strategic Book Publishing (SBP), pg 199
Sunbelt Publications Inc, pg 200
Sunstone Press, pg 201
Syracuse University Press, pg 201
Tantor Media Inc, pg 202
Texas A&M University Press, pg 205
Texas Tech University Press, pg 205
Tide-mark Press, pg 207
Todd Publications, pg 207
Tuxedo Press, pg 211
Union Square & Co, pg 212
University of Alaska Press, pg 214
The University of Arizona Press, pg 214
University of Georgia Press, pg 216
University of Illinois Press, pg 216
University of Massachusetts Press, pg 217
University of Minnesota Press, pg 217
University of Nebraska Press, pg 217
University of Nevada Press, pg 218
University of New Mexico Press, pg 218

The University of North Carolina Press, pg 218
University of Oklahoma Press, pg 219
University of Tennessee Press, pg 220
The University of Utah Press, pg 220
University of Washington Press, pg 220
University of Wisconsin Press, pg 221
University Press of America Inc, pg 221
University Press of Colorado, pg 221
University Press of Florida, pg 221
University Press of Kansas, pg 221
University Press of Mississippi, pg 222
US Government Publishing Office (GPO), pg 223
Vernon Press, pg 224
Visible Ink Press®, pg 225
Washington State University Press, pg 226
Waveland Press Inc, pg 226
West Margin Press, pg 227
Wiley-Blackwell, pg 229
Wisconsin Department of Public Instruction, pg 231
Wolfman Books, pg 232
YBK Publishers Inc, pg 235

NATURAL HISTORY

Harry N Abrams Inc, pg 2
Adirondack Mountain Club (ADK), pg 5
AdventureKEEN, pg 5
Appalachian Mountain Club Books, pg 15
AuthorHouse, pg 22
Bess Press Inc, pg 29
BJU Press, pg 30
Black Dome Press Corp, pg 30
Black Rabbit Books, pg 30
The Blackburn Press, pg 30
Brilliance Publishing Inc, pg 37
Burford Books, pg 38
Charlesbridge Publishing Inc, pg 45
Chelsea Green Publishing Co, pg 45
Chelsea House, pg 45
Child's Play® Inc, pg 46
Chronicle Books LLC, pg 47
Cornell University Press, pg 52
Counterpoint Press LLC, pg 54
Countryman Press, pg 54
DK, pg 60
Dover Publications Inc, pg 61
Down East Books, pg 61
Down The Shore Publishing, pg 61
East West Discovery Press, pg 63
Editorial de la Universidad de Puerto Rico, pg 63
Educational Insights®, pg 64
Excelsior Editions, pg 68
Fulcrum Publishing Inc, pg 75
Gale, pg 75
Gareth Stevens Publishing, pg 76
GemStone Press, pg 77
The Globe Pequot Press, pg 79
Gray & Company Publishers, pg 80
Hancock House Publishers, pg 84
Harvard University Press, pg 88
Heyday, pg 91
Homestead Publishing, pg 95
Illinois State Museum Society, pg 99
Indiana University Press, pg 100
Island Press, pg 104
Islandport Press, pg 105

Johns Hopkins University Press, pg 106
Kent State University Press, pg 109
Krieger Publishing Co, pg 111
Legacy Bound, pg 114
Lerner Publications, pg 115
Lucent Press, pg 121
The Lyons Press, pg 121
Macmillan Reference USA™, pg 123
Mandel Vilar Press, pg 124
The McDonald & Woodward Publishing Co, pg 127
McGraw-Hill Education, pg 127
Menasha Ridge Press, pg 129
Milliken Publishing Co, pg 132
Mountain Press Publishing Co, pg 135
Mountaineers Books, pg 135
National Geographic Books, pg 137
National Wildlife Federation, pg 139
The New York Botanical Garden Press, pg 140
North Country Press, pg 142
North Point Press, pg 142
North Star Editions Inc, pg 142
North Star Press of Saint Cloud Inc, pg 142
W W Norton & Company Inc, pg 143
Oregon State University Press, pg 147
Richard C Owen Publishers Inc, pg 149
Oxford University Press USA, pg 149
Pangaea Publications, pg 150
Pennsylvania Historical & Museum Commission, pg 157
Platypus Media LLC, pg 160
Princeton University Press, pg 164
Reference Publications Inc, pg 173
Rio Nuevo Publishers, pg 175
Rowman & Littlefield, pg 178
Rutgers University Press, pg 178
Sasquatch Books, pg 182
South Dakota Historical Society Press, pg 195
Spizzirri Publishing Inc, pg 196
Stackpole Books, pg 196
Strategic Book Publishing (SBP), pg 199
Sunbelt Publications Inc, pg 200
Tantor Media Inc, pg 202
Temporal Mechanical Press, pg 204
Texas A&M University Press, pg 205
Texas Tech University Press, pg 205
University of Texas Press, pg 205
Tilbury House Publishers, pg 207
Trafalgar Square Books, pg 208
Trinity University Press, pg 209
Twenty-First Century Books, pg 211
Union Square & Co, pg 212
University of Alabama Press, pg 214
University of Alaska Press, pg 214
The University of Arizona Press, pg 214
University of California Press, pg 215
University of Chicago Press, pg 215
University of Georgia Press, pg 216
University of Hawaii Press, pg 216
University of Iowa Press, pg 216
University of Minnesota Press, pg 217
University of Nevada Press, pg 218
University of New Mexico Press, pg 218
The University of North Carolina Press, pg 218

University of Oklahoma Press, pg 219
The University of Utah Press, pg 220
University of Washington Press, pg 220
University of Wisconsin Press, pg 221
University Press of Colorado, pg 221
University Press of Florida, pg 221
University Press of Kansas, pg 221
The University Press of Kentucky, pg 222
University Press of Mississippi, pg 222
US Government Publishing Office (GPO), pg 223
Utah State University Press, pg 223
Washington State University Press, pg 226
West Margin Press, pg 227
Wilderness Adventures Press Inc, pg 229
Willow Creek Press, pg 230
Yale University Press, pg 235

NONFICTION (GENERAL)

ABDO, pg 2
Abingdon Press, pg 2
Academy Chicago Publishers, pg 3
Adams & Ambrose Publishing, pg 4
Adams Media, pg 4
Addicus Books Inc, pg 5
Advance Publishing Inc, pg 5
African American Images Inc (AAI), pg 5
Akashic Books, pg 6
Albert Whitman & Company, pg 6
Algora Publishing, pg 7
All Things That Matter Press, pg 7
Alloy Entertainment LLC, pg 7
Amakella Publishing, pg 7
American Alpine Club, pg 8
American Carriage House Publishing (ACHP), pg 8
Amicus, pg 13
Ampersand Inc/Professional Publishing Services, pg 13
Anaphora Literary Press, pg 13
Andrews McMeel Publishing LLC, pg 14
Angel City Press, pg 14
The Apocryphile Press, pg 15
Appalachian Mountain Club Books, pg 15
Applewood Books, pg 15
Arcade Publishing Inc, pg 16
Art of Living, PrimaMedia Inc, pg 17
Ascend Books LLC, pg 18
Ashland Creek Press, pg 18
Asta Publications LLC, pg 20
Astra Books for Young Readers, pg 20
Atlantic Publishing Group Inc, pg 21
AuthorHouse, pg 22
Autumn House Press, pg 22
Avant-Guide, pg 22
Ave Maria Press Inc, pg 22
Avery, pg 23
Avid Reader Press, pg 23
Baha'i Publishing Trust, pg 23
Baker Books, pg 23
Barbour Publishing Inc, pg 24
Barranca Press, pg 24
Barrytown/Station Hill Press, pg 24
Bartleby Press, pg 24
Beacon Press, pg 25
Bear & Co Inc, pg 26

Bearport Publishing, pg 26
Beaver's Pond Press Inc, pg 26
Behrman House Inc, pg 27
Frederic C Beil Publisher Inc, pg 27
BelleBooks, pg 27
Bellevue Literary Press, pg 27
Ben Yehuda Press, pg 27
BenBella Books Inc, pg 27
Bess Press Inc, pg 29
Bethany House Publishers, pg 29
Biographical Publishing Co, pg 29
BJU Press, pg 30
Black Dome Press Corp, pg 30
Black Heron Press, pg 30
Black Mountain Press, pg 30
Blair, pg 30
Blue Crane Books Inc, pg 32
BlueBridge, pg 32
Book Sales, pg 33
The Book Tree, pg 34
BookLogix, pg 34
Books on Tape™, pg 34
Boson Books™, pg 34
Bottom Dog Press, pg 34
Boys Town Press, pg 35
Brandylane Publishers Inc, pg 35
George Braziller Inc, pg 35
Nicholas Brealey Publishing, pg 36
Brick Tower Press, pg 36
Brilliance Publishing Inc, pg 37
Brown Books Publishing Group (BBPG), pg 38
Bywater Books Inc, pg 39
Camino Books Inc, pg 39
Capstone Publishers™, pg 40
Carnegie Mellon University Press, pg 41
Carolina Academic Press, pg 41
Casemate | publishers, pg 41
Caxton Press, pg 42
Cedar Fort Inc, pg 43
Charlesbridge Publishing Inc, pg 45
Chelsea Green Publishing Co, pg 45
Chelsea House, pg 45
Cherry Hill Publishing LLC, pg 46
Chicago Review Press, pg 46
Chickadee Prince Books LLC, pg 46
The Child's World Inc, pg 46
China Books, pg 47
Chronicle Books LLC, pg 47
Circlet Press, pg 48
Clarion Books, pg 48
Cleis Press, pg 49
Clerisy Press, pg 49
Codhill Press, pg 50
Coffee House Press, pg 50
Columbia University Press, pg 51
Consumer Press, pg 52
Continental AfrikaPublishers, pg 52
Cornell University Press, pg 52
Cornerstone Book Publishers, pg 53
Cosimo Inc, pg 53
Counterpath Press, pg 54
Counterpoint Press LLC, pg 54
Countryman Press, pg 54
Covenant Communications Inc, pg 54
Crabtree Publishing Co, pg 54
Crown Publishing Group, pg 56
Dalkey Archive Press, pg 56
Dancing Dakini Press, pg 57
Dark Horse Comics, pg 57
Deep River Books LLC, pg 58
Delphinium Books, pg 58
Deseret Book Co, pg 58
Dial Books for Young Readers, pg 59
Disney-Hyperion Books, pg 59
Disney Press, pg 59
DK, pg 60
The Donning Company Publishers, pg 60

Dorrance Publishing Co Inc, pg 61
Doubleday, pg 61
Dover Publications Inc, pg 61
Down The Shore Publishing, pg 61
Dreamscape Media LLC, pg 62
Duke University Press, pg 62
Dutton, pg 62
Eakin Press, pg 62
East West Discovery Press, pg 63
Easy Money Press, pg 63
EDC Publishing, pg 63
ediciones Lerner, pg 63
Editorial de la Universidad de Puerto Rico, pg 63
Wm B Eerdmans Publishing Co, pg 64
Eifrig Publishing LLC, pg 64
Elderberry Press Inc, pg 65
Elva Resa Publishing, pg 65
Emerald Books, pg 66
Encounter Books, pg 66
Enslow Publishing LLC, pg 66
Epicenter Press Inc, pg 67
Etruscan Press, pg 67
Europa Editions, pg 67
M Evans & Company, pg 68
Everyman's Library, pg 68
Everything Goes Media LLC, pg 68
Excelsior Editions, pg 68
The Experiment, pg 68
Familius, pg 69
Farrar, Straus & Giroux Books for Young Readers, pg 69
Farrar, Straus & Giroux, LLC, pg 70
Father & Son Publishing Inc, pg 70
The Feminist Press at The City University of New York, pg 71
Feral House, pg 71
Fine Creative Media, Inc, pg 71
First Avenue Editions, pg 72
Focus on the Family, pg 73
Fox Chapel Publishing Co Inc, pg 74
Fulcrum Publishing Inc, pg 75
Gale, pg 75
Gallaudet University Press, pg 76
Gallery Books, pg 76
Gareth Stevens Publishing, pg 76
Gauthier Publications Inc, pg 77
Genealogical Publishing Co, pg 77
Gibbs Smith Publisher, pg 78
Global Authors Publications (GAP), pg 78
Global Publishing Solutions LLC, pg 79
Godine, pg 79
Goose River Press, pg 79
Grand Central Publishing, pg 80
Graphic Universe™, pg 80
Gray & Company Publishers, pg 80
Graywolf Press, pg 81
Green Dragon Books, pg 81
Greenleaf Book Group LLC, pg 81
Grove Atlantic Inc, pg 82
Hamilton Books, pg 84
Hamilton Stone Editions, pg 84
Hannacroix Creek Books Inc, pg 85
HarperCollins Children's Books, pg 85
HarperCollins Publishers LLC, pg 86
Harvest House Publishers Inc, pg 88
Hatherleigh Press Ltd, pg 88
Hay House LLC, pg 89
Health Communications Inc, pg 89
Hearts 'n Tummies Cookbook Co, pg 90
Hellgate Press, pg 91
Heyday, pg 91
High Plains Press, pg 91
Highlights for Children Inc, pg 92
Hill & Wang, pg 92
Hilton Publishing Co, pg 92
Himalayan Institute Press, pg 92
History Publishing Co LLC, pg 93
Histria Books, pg 93
Hobblebush Books, pg 93
Henry Holt and Company, LLC, pg 94
Homa & Sekey Books, pg 95
Homestead Publishing, pg 95
Hoover Institution Press, pg 95
Horizon Publishers & Distributors Inc, pg 95
Houghton Mifflin Harcourt, pg 95
Houghton Mifflin Harcourt Trade & Reference Division, pg 96
House to House Publications, pg 97
Huntington Press Publishing, pg 97
Hutton Publishing, pg 97
IHS Press, pg 98
Inner Traditions International Ltd, pg 101
The Innovation Press, pg 101
Insight Editions, pg 101
Institute of Jesuit Sources (IJS), pg 102
Intercultural Development Research Association (IDRA), pg 102
International Publishers Co Inc, pg 103
Iris Press, pg 104
Iron Stream Media, pg 104
Islandport Press, pg 105
JIST Publishing, pg 106
Johns Hopkins University Press, pg 106
Jump!, pg 107
Jump at the Sun, pg 107
Just World Books LLC, pg 107
Kaeden Publishing, pg 107
Kallisti Publishing Inc, pg 108
Kar-Ben Publishing, pg 108
Kensington Publishing Corp, pg 109
Kent State University Press, pg 109
Klutz®, pg 110
Alfred A Knopf, pg 110
Koho Pono LLC, pg 111
Kokila, pg 111
Konecky & Konecky LLC, pg 111
Kregel Publications, pg 111
Kumarian Press, pg 112
LARB Books, pg 113
Lasaria Creative Publishing, pg 113
Laughing Elephant Books, pg 113
Leaf Storm Press, pg 113
THE Learning Connection®, pg 113
Learning Links-USA Inc, pg 114
Lectorum Publications Inc, pg 114
Lerner Publications, pg 115
Lerner Publishing Group Inc, pg 115
LernerClassroom, pg 115
Library of America, pg 116
Life Cycle Books, pg 116
Light Publications, pg 116
Linden Publishing Co Inc, pg 117
Listen & Live Audio Inc, pg 117
little bee books, pg 117
Little, Brown and Company, pg 118
Little, Brown Books for Young Readers (LBYR), pg 118
The Little Entrepreneur, pg 118
Llewellyn Publications, pg 119
Louisiana State University Press, pg 120
Lucent Press, pg 121
Lynx House Press, pg 121
The Lyons Press, pg 121
Macmillan, pg 121
Mandel Vilar Press, pg 124
Manic D Press Inc, pg 124
Marick Press, pg 125
Marquis Who's Who, pg 125
Mason Crest Publishers, pg 126
Master Books®, pg 126
Mazda Publishers Inc, pg 127
McFarland, pg 127
McSweeney's Publishing, pg 128
Mesorah Publications Ltd, pg 130
Michigan State University Press (MSU Press), pg 130
Mighty Media Press, pg 131
Milford Books™, pg 131
Milkweed Editions, pg 131
Millbrook Press, pg 131
Mitchell Lane Publishers Inc, pg 133
Modern Memoirs Inc, pg 133
Mondial, pg 133
Montemayor Press, pg 133
Moonshine Cove Publishing LLC, pg 134
Morgan James Publishing, pg 134
Moriah Books, pg 134
Multnomah, pg 135
Mutual Publishing LLC, pg 136
Nataraj Books, pg 136
National Academies Press (NAP), pg 136
National Geographic Books, pg 137
Naval Institute Press, pg 139
NBM Publishing Inc, pg 139
New Directions Publishing Corp, pg 139
The New Press, pg 140
NFB Publishing, pg 141
Nilgiri Press, pg 141
NOLO, pg 141
North Atlantic Books (NAB), pg 142
North Carolina Office of Archives & History, pg 142
North Point Press, pg 142
North River Press Publishing Corp, pg 142
North Star Editions Inc, pg 142
North Star Press of Saint Cloud Inc, pg 142
Northern Illinois University Press, pg 143
W W Norton & Company Inc, pg 143
Norwood House Press, pg 143
Nosy Crow Inc, pg 144
The Oaklea Press Inc, pg 145
Ocean Tree Books, pg 145
The Ohio State University Press, pg 145
Ohio University Press, pg 145
On the Write Path Publishing, pg 146
Ooligan Press, pg 146
Open Books Press, pg 146
Open Horizons Publishing Co, pg 147
Oregon State University Press, pg 147
The Original Falcon Press, pg 148
ORO editions, pg 148
Other Press, pg 148
Richard C Owen Publishers Inc, pg 149
Oxford University Press USA, pg 149
Ozark Mountain Publishing Inc, pg 149
PA Press, pg 149
Pace University Press, pg 149
Pact Press, pg 150
Palgrave Macmillan, pg 150
Palm Island Press, pg 150
Pangaea Publications, pg 150
Pantheon Books, pg 150
Pants On Fire Press, pg 150
Parachute Publishing LLC, pg 151
Paraclete Press Inc, pg 151
Paradise Cay Publications Inc, pg 151
Paragon House, pg 151
Park Place Publications, pg 152
Path Press Inc, pg 152
Paul Dry Books, pg 152
Peachtree Publishing Co Inc, pg 153
Pelican Publishing, pg 153
Pen & Publish LLC, pg 153
Pen-L Publishing, pg 153
Penfield Books, pg 154
Penguin Press, pg 154
Penguin Random House Audio Publishing Group, pg 154
Penguin Random House LLC, pg 155
Penguin Workshop, pg 156
Penguin Young Readers Group, pg 156
Penn State University Press, pg 157
Pennsylvania State Data Center, pg 157
Perfection Learning®, pg 158
Persea Books, pg 158
Peter Pauper Press, Inc, pg 158
Peterson's, pg 158
Philomel Books, pg 159
Picador, pg 159
Pineapple Press, pg 160
Planert Creek Press, pg 160
Platypus Media LLC, pg 160
Pleasure Boat Studio: A Literary Press, pg 160
Plough Publishing House, pg 161
Plowshare Media, pg 161
Plum Tree Books, pg 161
Polar Bear & Company, pg 161
Potomac Books, pg 162
powerHouse Books, pg 162
Princeton Book Co Publishers, pg 163
Prometheus Books, pg 166
Publication Consultants, pg 167
Purple House Press, pg 167
GP Putnam's Sons, pg 167
Quixote Press, pg 169
Rand-Smith Publishing, pg 169
Random House Large Print, pg 170
Random House Publishing Group, pg 170
Rational Island Publishers, pg 171
Ravenhawk™ Books, pg 172
Reader's Digest Select Editions, pg 172
Reader's Digest Trade Publishing, pg 172
Recorded Books Inc, an RBmedia company, pg 172
Red Chair Press, pg 172
Reference Publications Inc, pg 173
ReferencePoint Press Inc, pg 173
Regent Press Printers & Publishers, pg 174
Regnery Publishing, pg 174
Remember Point Inc, pg 174
Revell, pg 174
Rising Sun Publishing, pg 175
Riverdale Avenue Books (RAB), pg 175
Riverhead Books, pg 175
The RoadRunner Press, pg 175
Roaring Brook Press, pg 175
Rocky Pond Books, pg 176
Ronin Publishing Inc, pg 176
Rootstock Publishing, pg 176
The Rosen Publishing Group Inc, pg 177
Round Table Companies, pg 177
Running Press, pg 178
Saddleback Educational Publishing, pg 179
St Johann Press, pg 180
St Pauls, pg 181

U.S. PUBLISHERS — SUBJECT INDEX

Salem Press, pg 181
Santa Monica Press LLC, pg 182
Sarabande Books Inc, pg 182
Sasquatch Books, pg 182
Satya House Publications, pg 182
Savant Books & Publications LLC, pg 182
Schaffner Press, pg 183
Scholastic Education Solutions, pg 184
Scholastic Inc, pg 184
Science & Humanities Press, pg 185
Science, Naturally, pg 185
Sentient Publications LLC, pg 186
Seven Stories Press, pg 186
Shadow Mountain Publishing, pg 187
Shambhala Publications Inc, pg 187
Shepard Publications, pg 187
Signalman Publishing, pg 187
Signature Books Publishing LLC, pg 187
Simon & Schuster Audio, pg 189
Simon & Schuster Children's Publishing, pg 189
Sky Pony Press, pg 191
SkyLight Paths® Publishing, pg 191
Soho Press Inc, pg 193
Sounds True Inc, pg 194
Sourcebooks LLC, pg 194
South Dakota Historical Society Press, pg 195
Southern Illinois University Press, pg 195
Square One Publishers Inc, pg 196
Star Bright Books Inc, pg 197
STARbooks Press, pg 197
Stargazer Publishing Co, pg 197
StarGroup International Inc, pg 197
State University of New York Press, pg 198
Steerforth Press & Services, pg 198
Stone Pier Press, pg 199
Strategic Book Publishing (SBP), pg 199
Strategic Media Books LLC, pg 200
Summertime Publications Inc, pg 200
Sundance/Newbridge Publishing, pg 200
Sunstone Press, pg 201
Swallow Press, pg 201
Swan Isle Press, pg 201
Syracuse University Press, pg 201
Nan A Talese, pg 202
Tanglewood Publishing, pg 202
Tantor Media Inc, pg 202
Temple University Press, pg 204
Temporal Mechanical Press, pg 204
Ten Speed Press, pg 204
Terra Nova Books, pg 204
Texas A&M University Press, pg 205
Texas Tech University Press, pg 205
University of Texas Press, pg 205
Third World Press Foundation, pg 206
Thorndike Press®, pg 206
Tilbury House Publishers, pg 207
Top Publications, pg 207
Tor Publishing Group, pg 207
TotalRecall Publications Inc, pg 208
Travelers' Tales, pg 209
Trinity University Press, pg 209
TRISTAN Publishing, pg 209
Triumph Books LLC, pg 209
TSG Publishing Foundation Inc, pg 210
Tupelo Press Inc, pg 210
Turner Publishing Co LLC, pg 210
Tuttle Publishing, pg 211
Tuxedo Press, pg 211
Twenty-First Century Books, pg 211

Twilight Times Books, pg 211
Ugly Duckling Presse, pg 212
Union Square & Co, pg 212
Universal-Publishers Inc, pg 213
Universe Publishing, pg 214
University of Alaska Press, pg 214
University of California Press, pg 215
University of Georgia Press, pg 216
University of Hawaii Press, pg 216
University of Illinois Press, pg 216
University of Iowa Press, pg 216
University of Louisiana at Lafayette Press, pg 217
University of Massachusetts Press, pg 217
University of Michigan Press, pg 217
University of Minnesota Press, pg 217
University of Missouri Press, pg 217
University of Nevada Press, pg 218
University of New Mexico Press, pg 218
University of North Texas Press, pg 218
University of Oklahoma Press, pg 219
University of Pennsylvania Press, pg 219
University of Pittsburgh Press, pg 219
University of Tennessee Press, pg 220
The University of Utah Press, pg 220
University of Virginia Press, pg 220
University of Washington Press, pg 220
University of Wisconsin Press, pg 221
University Press of America Inc, pg 221
The University Press of Kentucky, pg 222
University Press of Mississippi, pg 222
US Government Publishing Office (GPO), pg 223
Utah State University Press, pg 223
Vanderbilt University Press, pg 224
Verso Books, pg 224
Vesuvian Books, pg 224
Viking Children's Books, pg 224
Viking Penguin, pg 224
Vintage Books, pg 225
Washington State University Press, pg 226
WaterBrook, pg 226
Watermark Publishing, pg 226
Wayne State University Press, pg 226
Welcome Rain Publishers LLC, pg 227
Well-Trained Mind Press, pg 227
West Margin Press, pg 227
West Virginia University Press, pg 228
Western Edge Press, pg 228
Westminster John Knox Press (WJK), pg 228
Wheatherstone Press, pg 228
Wiley-Blackwell, pg 229
John Wiley & Sons Inc, pg 230
William Carey Publishing, pg 230
Williams & Company Book Publishers, pg 230
Willow Creek Press, pg 230
Wings Press, pg 231
Winterwolf Press, pg 231
Wolfman Books, pg 232
WoodstockArts, pg 232

Workman Publishing, pg 232
World Bank Publications, pg 233
World Book Inc, pg 233
World Citizens, pg 233
WriteLife Publishing, pg 234
Writer's AudioShop, pg 234
Writer's Digest Books, pg 234
Xlibris Corp, pg 234
Yale University Press, pg 235
YBK Publishers Inc, pg 235
YWAM Publishing, pg 236
Zest Books, pg 236
Zondervan, pg 236
Zumaya Publications LLC, pg 237

OUTDOOR RECREATION

Adirondack Mountain Club (ADK), pg 5
AdventureKEEN, pg 5
American Alpine Club, pg 8
American Press, pg 11
APC Publishing, pg 15
Appalachian Mountain Club Books, pg 15
AuthorHouse, pg 22
Black Dome Press Corp, pg 30
Black Rabbit Books, pg 30
Blair, pg 30
Burford Books, pg 38
Capstone Publishers™, pg 40
Carolina Academic Press, pg 41
Chicago Review Press, pg 46
Chronicle Books LLC, pg 47
Cornell Maritime Press, pg 52
Countryman Press, pg 54
Creative Homeowner, pg 55
dbS Productions, pg 58
Dover Publications Inc, pg 61
Down East Books, pg 61
Epicenter Press Inc, pg 67
Evergreen Pacific Publishing Ltd, pg 68
Farcountry Press, pg 69
FineEdge.com LLC, pg 72
Fox Chapel Publishing Co Inc, pg 74
Fulcrum Publishing Inc, pg 75
Gale, pg 75
Gibbs Smith Publisher, pg 78
The Globe Pequot Press, pg 79
Gray & Company Publishers, pg 80
Greenleaf Book Group LLC, pg 81
Hancock House Publishers, pg 84
Hatherleigh Press Ltd, pg 88
Horizon Publishers & Distributors Inc, pg 95
Human Kinetics Inc, pg 97
Huntington Press Publishing, pg 97
Islandport Press, pg 105
Klutz®, pg 110
Krause Publications Inc, pg 111
Leaf Storm Press, pg 113
Legacy Bound, pg 114
Light-Beams Publishing, pg 116
The Lyons Press, pg 121
Macmillan Reference USA™, pg 123
Mason Crest Publishers, pg 126
Menasha Ridge Press, pg 129
Mountain Press Publishing Co, pg 135
Mountaineers Books, pg 135
National Golf Foundation, pg 138
North Country Press, pg 142
Octane Press, pg 145
Oregon State University Press, pg 147
Paradise Cay Publications Inc, pg 151
Polar Bear & Company, pg 161

Quarto Publishing Group USA Inc, pg 168
Rutgers University Press, pg 178
Safari Press, pg 179
Sagamore Publishing LLC, pg 179
Santa Monica Press LLC, pg 182
Sasquatch Books, pg 182
Schiffer Publishing Ltd, pg 183
Shambhala Publications Inc, pg 187
Stackpole Books, pg 196
Stoneydale Press Publishing Co, pg 199
Strategic Book Publishing (SBP), pg 199
Sunbelt Publications Inc, pg 200
TarcherPerigee, pg 202
Tide-mark Press, pg 207
Trinity University Press, pg 209
Tuttle Publishing, pg 211
University of Alaska Press, pg 214
University of Hawaii Press, pg 216
University of Nevada Press, pg 218
University of Tennessee Press, pg 220
The University of Utah Press, pg 220
University of Wisconsin Press, pg 221
University Press of Colorado, pg 221
University Press of Florida, pg 221
University Press of Mississippi, pg 222
Waveland Press Inc, pg 226
West Margin Press, pg 227
Wide World Publishing, pg 229
Wilderness Adventures Press Inc, pg 229
Willow Creek Press, pg 230

PARAPSYCHOLOGY

ARE Press, pg 16
Ariel Press, pg 16
AuthorHouse, pg 22
Bear & Co Inc, pg 26
Blue Note Publications Inc, pg 32
The Book Tree, pg 34
Clerisy Press, pg 49
Fine Creative Media, Inc, pg 71
Frederick Fell Publishers Inc, pg 74
Gale, pg 75
Hampton Roads Publishing, pg 84
Hay House LLC, pg 89
Idyll Arbor Inc, pg 98
Inner Traditions International Ltd, pg 101
Kessinger Publishing LLC, pg 109
Lectorum Publications Inc, pg 114
Light Technology Publishing LLC, pg 116
Llewellyn Publications, pg 119
Loving Healing Press Inc, pg 121
Macmillan Reference USA™, pg 123
McFarland, pg 127
North Atlantic Books (NAB), pg 142
Olde & Oppenheim Publishers, pg 146
On the Write Path Publishing, pg 146
The Original Falcon Press, pg 148
Red Wheel/Weiser, pg 173
Ronin Publishing Inc, pg 176
Schiffer Publishing Ltd, pg 183
Square One Publishers Inc, pg 196
Tantor Media Inc, pg 202
Charles C Thomas Publisher Ltd, pg 206
TSG Publishing Foundation Inc, pg 210
US Games Systems Inc, pg 223

PUBLISHERS

U.S. PUBLISHERS — SUBJECT INDEX

Yotzeret Publishing, pg 236
Zumaya Publications LLC, pg 237

PHILOSOPHY

Academica Press, pg 3
AK Press, pg 6
Alexander Street, part of Clarivate PLC, pg 6
Algora Publishing, pg 7
All Things That Matter Press, pg 7
Amber Lotus Publishing, pg 8
Anaphora Literary Press, pg 13
Andrews University Press, pg 14
The Apocryphile Press, pg 15
Ariadne Press, pg 16
Ariel Press, pg 16
AuthorHouse, pg 22
Baha'i Publishing Trust, pg 23
Barrytown/Station Hill Press, pg 24
Baylor University Press, pg 25
Beacon Press, pg 25
Bear & Co Inc, pg 26
Beaver's Pond Press Inc, pg 26
John Benjamins Publishing Co, pg 28
Bhaktivedanta Book Trust (BBT), pg 29
Bloomsbury Academic, pg 31
Blue Note Publications Inc, pg 32
Bolchazy-Carducci Publishers Inc, pg 33
The Book Tree, pg 34
George Braziller Inc, pg 35
Brill Inc, pg 37
Brilliance Publishing Inc, pg 37
Bucknell University Press, pg 38
Cambridge University Press, pg 39
The Catholic University of America Press, pg 42
Cengage Learning, pg 43
Charles Press Publishers, pg 45
China Books, pg 47
CN Times Books, pg 50
Codhill Press, pg 50
Columbia University Press, pg 51
Continental AfrikaPublishers, pg 52
Cornell University Press, pg 52
Cosimo Inc, pg 53
Council for Research in Values & Philosophy, pg 53
Counterpath Press, pg 54
Counterpoint Press LLC, pg 54
Cross-Cultural Communications, pg 55
Crystal Clarity Publishers, pg 56
CSLI Publications, pg 56
The Dawn Horse Press, pg 57
Walter De Gruyter Inc, pg 58
DeVorss & Co, pg 59
Dharma Publishing, pg 59
Dissertation.com, pg 60
Doubleday, pg 61
Dover Publications Inc, pg 61
Duke University Press, pg 62
Edgewise Press Inc, pg 63
Editorial de la Universidad de Puerto Rico, pg 63
Educator's International Press Inc (EIP), pg 64
Wm B Eerdmans Publishing Co, pg 64
Elderberry Press Inc, pg 65
Encounter Books, pg 66
Everyman's Library, pg 68
Everything Goes Media LLC, pg 68
Fifth Estate Publishing, pg 71
Fine Creative Media, Inc, pg 71
Focus, pg 73
Fordham University Press, pg 73
Gale, pg 75
Gauthier Publications Inc, pg 77
Georgetown University Press, pg 77

Gingko Press Inc, pg 78
Goose River Press, pg 79
Green Dragon Books, pg 81
Greenhaven Publishing, pg 81
Hackett Publishing Co Inc, pg 83
Hamilton Books, pg 84
Hampton Roads Publishing, pg 84
Harvard Education Publishing Group, pg 88
Harvard University Press, pg 88
Hay House LLC, pg 89
Himalayan Institute Press, pg 92
Histria Books, pg 93
Hohm Press, pg 93
Holmes Publishing Group LLC, pg 94
Homa & Sekey Books, pg 95
Humanix Books LLC, pg 97
Ignatius Press, pg 98
Indiana University Press, pg 100
Information Age Publishing Inc, pg 100
Inner Traditions International Ltd, pg 101
International Publishers Co Inc, pg 103
InterVarsity Press, pg 104
Jewish Lights Publishing, pg 105
Kessinger Publishing LLC, pg 109
Kregel Publications, pg 111
Peter Lang Publishing Inc, pg 112
Larson Publications, pg 113
Lectorum Publications Inc, pg 114
Lexington Books, pg 115
Liberty Fund Inc, pg 116
Light Technology Publishing LLC, pg 116
Liturgical Press, pg 118
Llewellyn Publications, pg 119
Loft Press Inc, pg 119
Long River Press, pg 120
Lotus Press, pg 120
Macmillan Learning, pg 123
Macmillan Reference USA™, pg 123
Mandala Earth, pg 124
Marquette University Press, pg 125
Mazda Publishers Inc, pg 127
McGraw-Hill Higher Education, pg 128
McPherson & Co, pg 128
The Edwin Mellen Press, pg 129
Mercer University Press, pg 129
Michigan State University Press (MSU Press), pg 130
Milford Books™, pg 131
The MIT Press, pg 132
De Gruyter Mouton, pg 135
Nataraj Books, pg 136
New City Press, pg 139
New World Library, pg 140
Nilgiri Press, pg 141
North Atlantic Books (NAB), pg 142
Northwestern University Press, pg 143
W W Norton & Company Inc, pg 143
Nova Science Publishers Inc, pg 144
Ohio University Press, pg 145
On the Write Path Publishing, pg 146
Open Court Publishing Co, pg 147
The Original Falcon Press, pg 148
ORO editions, pg 148
Other Press, pg 148
Our Sunday Visitor Publishing, pg 148
Oxford University Press USA, pg 149
P & R Publishing Co, pg 149
Pace University Press, pg 149

Palgrave Macmillan, pg 150
Pantheon Books, pg 150
Paragon House, pg 151
Parallax Press, pg 151
Park Place Publications, pg 152
Parmenides Publishing, pg 152
Paul Dry Books, pg 152
Paulist Press, pg 152
Pearson Business Publishing, pg 153
Penn State University Press, pg 157
Peradam Press, pg 158
Philosophical Library Inc, pg 159
Philosophy Documentation Center, pg 159
Polar Bear & Company, pg 161
Polebridge Press, pg 161
Princeton University Press, pg 164
Prometheus Books, pg 166
Purdue University Press, pg 167
Rational Island Publishers, pg 171
Red Wheel/Weiser, pg 173
Regnery Publishing, pg 174
Routledge, pg 177
Rowman & Littlefield, pg 178
Royal Fireworks Press, pg 178
Rutgers University Press, pg 178
St Augustine's Press Inc, pg 180
St Herman Press, pg 180
St Pauls, pg 181
Science History Publications USA Inc, pg 185
Scripta Humanistica Publishing International, pg 185
Sentient Publications LLC, pg 186
Shambhala Publications Inc, pg 187
SkyLight Paths® Publishing, pg 191
Snow Lion, pg 192
Somerset Hall Press, pg 193
Sophia Institute Press®, pg 193
Stanford University Press, pg 197
State University of New York Press, pg 198
SteinerBooks Inc, pg 198
Stipes Publishing LLC, pg 198
Stone Bridge Press Inc, pg 199
Strategic Book Publishing (SBP), pg 199
Sun Publishing Company, pg 200
Swedenborg Foundation, pg 201
TAN Books, pg 202
T&T Clark International, pg 202
Tantor Media Inc, pg 202
Teachers College Press, pg 203
Theosophical University Press, pg 206
The Toby Press LLC, pg 207
The Trinity Foundation, pg 209
TSG Publishing Foundation Inc, pg 210
Tuttle Publishing, pg 211
University of California Press, pg 215
University of Chicago Press, pg 215
University of Delaware Press, pg 215
University of Hawaii Press, pg 216
University of Illinois Press, pg 216
University of Massachusetts Press, pg 217
University of Minnesota Press, pg 217
University of North Texas Press, pg 218
University of Notre Dame Press, pg 219
University of Pittsburgh Press, pg 219
University of Rochester Press, pg 220
The University of Utah Press, pg 220

University Press of America Inc, pg 221
Vernon Press, pg 224
Verso Books, pg 224
Vintage Books, pg 225
Waveland Press Inc, pg 226
Welcome Rain Publishers LLC, pg 227
Wellington Press, pg 227
Westminster John Knox Press (WJK), pg 228
Wiley-Blackwell, pg 229
William Carey Publishing, pg 230
Wisconsin Department of Public Instruction, pg 231
Wisdom Publications Inc, pg 231
Yale University Press, pg 235
YMAA Publication Center Inc, pg 235
Zondervan, pg 236
Zone Books, pg 237

PHOTOGRAPHY

Abbeville Press, pg 1
Abbeville Publishing Group, pg 2
Harry N Abrams Inc, pg 2
ACC Art Books, pg 3
Akashic Books, pg 6
Allworth Press, pg 7
Anaphora Literary Press, pg 13
Aperture Books, pg 15
Arcadia Publishing Inc, pg 16
The Art Institute of Chicago, pg 17
Atlantic Publishing Group Inc, pg 21
AuthorHouse, pg 22
Baby Tattoo Books, pg 23
Beaver's Pond Press Inc, pg 26
Bellevue Literary Press, pg 27
Black Dome Press Corp, pg 30
BookLogix, pg 34
Bottom Dog Press, pg 34
Brandylane Publishers Inc, pg 35
Brown Books Publishing Group (BBPG), pg 38
Burns Archive Press, pg 38
Camino Books Inc, pg 39
Capen Publishing Co Inc, pg 40
Cengage Learning, pg 43
Chronicle Books LLC, pg 47
Clear Light Publishers, pg 49
Commonwealth Editions, pg 51
David C Cook, pg 52
Countryman Press, pg 54
Cross-Cultural Communications, pg 55
DK, pg 60
Dover Publications Inc, pg 61
Duke University Press, pg 62
EDC Publishing, pg 63
Edgewise Press Inc, pg 63
Elsevier Inc, pg 65
Farcountry Press, pg 69
Fine Creative Media, Inc, pg 71
Firefall Editions, pg 72
Gale, pg 75
Gauthier Publications Inc, pg 77
Getty Publications, pg 78
Gingko Press Inc, pg 78
Glitterati Inc, pg 78
Godine, pg 79
Goodheart-Willcox Publisher, pg 79
Gray & Company Publishers, pg 80
Greenleaf Book Group LLC, pg 81
Heyday, pg 91
Homestead Publishing, pg 95
Immedium, pg 99
In the Garden Publishing, pg 99
Insight Editions, pg 101
Krause Publications Inc, pg 111
Little, Brown and Company, pg 118
Mazda Publishers Inc, pg 127

U.S. PUBLISHERS — SUBJECT INDEX　　　　　　　　　　　　　　　　　　　　　　　　　　　　　　　　　　　　　BOOK

McBooks Press, pg 127
MFA Publications, pg 130
Modern Memoirs Inc, pg 133
The Monacelli Press, pg 133
Moonshine Cove Publishing LLC, pg 134
Morning Sun Books Inc, pg 134
The Museum of Modern Art (MoMA), pg 135
Museum of New Mexico Press, pg 135
Mutual Publishing LLC, pg 136
National Geographic Books, pg 137
The New Press, pg 140
W W Norton & Company Inc, pg 143
On the Write Path Publishing, pg 146
ORO editions, pg 148
PA Press, pg 149
Pangaea Publications, pg 150
Peachpit Press, pg 153
Penn State University Press, pg 157
Pennsylvania Historical & Museum Commission, pg 157
Phaidon, pg 159
Planert Creek Press, pg 160
Pointed Leaf Press, pg 161
Polar Bear & Company, pg 161
powerHouse Books, pg 162
The Press at California State University, Fresno, pg 163
Princeton University Press, pg 164
Reader's Digest Trade Publishing, pg 172
Rio Nuevo Publishers, pg 175
Rizzoli International Publications Inc, pg 175
Routledge, pg 177
Running Press, pg 178
St James Press®, pg 180
Santa Monica Press LLC, pg 182
Schiffer Publishing Ltd, pg 183
Shepard Publications, pg 187
South Dakota Historical Society Press, pg 195
Stackpole Books, pg 196
Stewart, Tabori & Chang, pg 198
Tantor Media Inc, pg 202
Taschen America, pg 203
Temple University Press, pg 204
Texas A&M University Press, pg 205
Texas Tech University Press, pg 205
Thames & Hudson, pg 205
Trinity University Press, pg 209
Union Square & Co, pg 212
Universe Publishing, pg 214
University of Iowa Press, pg 216
University of Louisiana at Lafayette Press, pg 217
University of Nevada Press, pg 218
University of New Mexico Press, pg 218
University of New Orleans Press, pg 218
University of North Texas Press, pg 218
University of Oklahoma Press, pg 219
University of Pittsburgh Press, pg 219
University of Wisconsin Press, pg 221
University Press of Mississippi, pg 222
The Vendome Press, pg 224
Wake Forest University Press, pg 225
Watson-Guptill, pg 226
Welcome Books, pg 227
Welcome Rain Publishers LLC, pg 227
West Margin Press, pg 227
Western Reflections Publishing Co, pg 228
YBK Publishers Inc, pg 235

PHYSICAL SCIENCES

Academic Press, pg 3
AIHA (American Industrial Hygiene Association), pg 6
AIP Publishing LLC, pg 6
American Institute of Chemical Engineers (AIChE), pg 10
American Press, pg 11
American Society of Agricultural & Biological Engineers (ASABE), pg 12
Annual Reviews, pg 14
Arbordale Publishing, pg 16
The Astronomical Society of the Pacific, pg 20
Atlas Publishing, pg 21
AuthorHouse, pg 22
Begell House Inc Publishers, pg 27
Bitingduck Press LLC, pg 30
BJU Press, pg 30
Black Rabbit Books, pg 30
The Blackburn Press, pg 30
Brilliance Publishing Inc, pg 37
Cambridge University Press, pg 39
Capstone Publishers™, pg 40
Cengage Learning, pg 43
Chelsea House, pg 45
Crabtree Publishing Co, pg 54
CRC Press, pg 55
Walter De Gruyter Inc, pg 58
DEStech Publications Inc, pg 59
Doubleday, pg 61
Dover Publications Inc, pg 61
EDC Publishing, pg 63
Educational Insights®, pg 64
Elsevier Inc, pg 65
Evan-Moor Educational Publishers, pg 68
Facts On File, pg 69
W H Freeman, pg 75
Gale, pg 75
Harvard University Press, pg 88
Houghton Mifflin Harcourt, pg 95
Human Kinetics Inc, pg 97
Johns Hopkins University Press, pg 106
Jones & Bartlett Learning LLC, pg 107
Jump!, pg 107
Learning Links-USA Inc, pg 114
Lerner Publications, pg 115
Lorenz Educational Press, pg 120
Lucent Press, pg 121
Macmillan Reference USA™, pg 123
Marshall Cavendish Education, pg 125
Master Books®, pg 126
Mastery Education, pg 126
Materials Research Society, pg 126
McGraw-Hill Education, pg 127
McGraw-Hill Higher Education, pg 128
McGraw-Hill School Education Group, pg 128
Milliken Publishing Co, pg 132
The Minerals, Metals & Materials Society (TMS), pg 132
Mitchell Lane Publishers Inc, pg 133
Moonshine Cove Publishing LLC, pg 134
Morton Publishing Co, pg 134
National Academies Press (NAP), pg 136
National Science Teachers Association (NSTA), pg 138
New York Academy of Sciences (NYAS), pg 140
Norwood House Press, pg 143
Nova Science Publishers Inc, pg 144
Princeton University Press, pg 164
Research & Education Association (REA), pg 174
Saddleback Educational Publishing, pg 179
SAGE Publishing, pg 180
Science, Naturally, pg 185
Society for Industrial & Applied Mathematics, pg 192
Sourcebooks LLC, pg 194
SPIE, pg 196
Stylus Publishing LLC, pg 200
Tantor Media Inc, pg 202
Tapestry Press Ltd, pg 202
Taylor & Francis Inc, pg 203
Teaching & Learning Co, pg 204
TSG Publishing Foundation Inc, pg 210
Twenty-First Century Books, pg 211
University of Chicago Press, pg 215
University Press of Colorado, pg 221
US Government Publishing Office (GPO), pg 223
Water Resources Publications LLC, pg 226
John Wiley & Sons Inc, pg 230
World Scientific Publishing Co Inc, pg 233
World Trade Press LLC, pg 234
Yale University Press, pg 235

PHYSICS

Academic Press, pg 3
AIP Publishing LLC, pg 6
American Geophysical Union (AGU), pg 10
American Press, pg 11
Annual Reviews, pg 14
AuthorHouse, pg 22
Begell House Inc Publishers, pg 27
BJU Press, pg 30
Black Rabbit Books, pg 30
Cengage Learning, pg 43
Dover Publications Inc, pg 61
EDC Publishing, pg 63
The Electrochemical Society (ECS), pg 65
Elsevier Inc, pg 65
Facts On File, pg 69
Gale, pg 75
Houghton Mifflin Harcourt, pg 95
Institute of Police Technology & Management (IPTM), pg 102
International Press of Boston Inc, pg 103
Johns Hopkins University Press, pg 106
Macmillan Learning, pg 123
Macmillan Reference USA™, pg 123
Materials Research Society, pg 126
McGraw-Hill Create, pg 127
McGraw-Hill Education, pg 127
McGraw-Hill Higher Education, pg 128
McGraw-Hill School Education Group, pg 128
Medical Physics Publishing Corp (MPP), pg 129
Moonshine Cove Publishing LLC, pg 134
National Academies Press (NAP), pg 136
National Science Teachers Association (NSTA), pg 138
New York Academy of Sciences (NYAS), pg 140
Nova Science Publishers Inc, pg 144
Oxford University Press USA, pg 149
Pearson Business Publishing, pg 153
Princeton University Press, pg 164
Prometheus Books, pg 166
Research & Education Association (REA), pg 174
Ross Books, pg 177
Sentient Publications LLC, pg 186
SPIE, pg 196
Springer, pg 196
Tantor Media Inc, pg 202
Tapestry Press Ltd, pg 202
Taylor & Francis Inc, pg 203
TSG Publishing Foundation Inc, pg 210
University Science Books, pg 222
US Government Publishing Office (GPO), pg 223
Visible Ink Press®, pg 225
John Wiley & Sons Inc, pg 230
John Wiley & Sons Inc Global Education, pg 230
John Wiley & Sons Inc Professional Development, pg 230
World Scientific Publishing Co Inc, pg 233
YBK Publishers Inc, pg 235

POETRY

A 2 Z Press LLC, pg 1
Africa World Press Inc, pg 5
AK Press, pg 6
Akashic Books, pg 6
American Carriage House Publishing (ACHP), pg 8
Ampersand Inc/Professional Publishing Services, pg 13
Anaphora Literary Press, pg 13
Sara Anderson Children's Books, pg 13
Andrews McMeel Publishing LLC, pg 14
Anhinga Press Inc, pg 14
The Apocryphile Press, pg 15
Apogee Press, pg 15
Applewood Books, pg 15
The Arion Press, pg 16
Arte Publico Press, pg 17
The Ashland Poetry Press, pg 19
Astra Books for Young Readers, pg 20
AuthorHouse, pg 22
Autumn House Press, pg 22
Barrytown/Station Hill Press, pg 24
Beaver's Pond Press Inc, pg 26
Ben Yehuda Press, pg 27
Biographical Publishing Co, pg 29
BkMk Press Inc, pg 30
Black Mountain Press, pg 30
Black Rabbit Books, pg 30
Blair, pg 30
Blue Mountain Arts Inc, pg 32
BOA Editions Ltd, pg 33
Book Sales, pg 33
BookLogix, pg 34
Boson Books™, pg 34
Bottom Dog Press, pg 34
Brandylane Publishers Inc, pg 35
George Braziller Inc, pg 35
Brentwood Christian Press, pg 36
Brilliance Publishing Inc, pg 37
Carnegie Mellon University Press, pg 41
Carolina Academic Press, pg 41
Cedar Grove Publishing, pg 43
Charlesbridge Publishing Inc, pg 45

PUBLISHERS

U.S. PUBLISHERS — SUBJECT INDEX

China Books, pg 47
City Lights Publishers, pg 48
Clarion Books, pg 48
Codhill Press, pg 50
Coffee House Press, pg 50
Continental AfrikaPublishers, pg 52
Copper Canyon Press, pg 52
Cornerstone Book Publishers, pg 53
Counterpath Press, pg 54
Counterpoint Press LLC, pg 54
Cricket Cottage Publishing LLC, pg 55
Cross-Cultural Communications, pg 55
Dalkey Archive Press, pg 56
Dancing Dakini Press, pg 57
Dorrance Publishing Co Inc, pg 61
Dover Publications Inc, pg 61
Down The Shore Publishing, pg 61
Duke University Press, pg 62
East West Discovery Press, pg 63
Edgewise Press Inc, pg 63
Editorial de la Universidad de Puerto Rico, pg 63
Elderberry Press Inc, pg 65
Etruscan Press, pg 67
Everyman's Library, pg 68
Excelsior Editions, pg 68
Farrar, Straus & Giroux, LLC, pg 70
Father & Son Publishing Inc, pg 70
Fence Books, pg 71
Fordham University Press, pg 73
Gale, pg 75
Gibbs Smith Publisher, pg 78
Gingko Press Inc, pg 78
Glitterati Inc, pg 78
Godine, pg 79
Goose River Press, pg 79
Graywolf Press, pg 81
Green Integer, pg 81
Grove Atlantic Inc, pg 82
Hamilton Stone Editions, pg 84
Hanging Loose Press, pg 85
Hannacroix Creek Books Inc, pg 85
HarperCollins Children's Books, pg 85
HarperCollins Publishers LLC, pg 86
High Plains Press, pg 91
Histria Books, pg 93
Hobblebush Books, pg 93
Hollym International Corp, pg 94
Holy Cow! Press, pg 95
Homa & Sekey Books, pg 95
Host Publications, pg 95
Ignatius Press, pg 98
In the Garden Publishing, pg 99
International Publishers Co Inc, pg 103
Iris Press, pg 104
Alice James Books, pg 105
Joshua Tree Publishing, pg 107
Kelsey Street Press, pg 108
Alfred A Knopf, pg 110
LARB Books, pg 113
Laredo Publishing Co, pg 113
Larson Publications, pg 113
Laughing Elephant Books, pg 113
Learning Links-USA Inc, pg 114
Lectorum Publications Inc, pg 114
Lee & Low Books Inc, pg 114
Library of America, pg 116
Liturgical Press, pg 118
Loft Press Inc, pg 119
Long River Press, pg 120
Lorenz Educational Press, pg 120
Lost Horse Press, pg 120
Louisiana State University Press, pg 120
Luna Bisonte Prods, pg 121
Lynx House Press, pg 121

Macmillan Reference USA™, pg 123
Mage Publishers Inc, pg 123
Manic D Press Inc, pg 124
Maren Green Publishing Inc, pg 125
Marick Press, pg 125
Maryland History Press, pg 126
Mazda Publishers Inc, pg 127
McSweeney's Publishing, pg 128
The Edwin Mellen Press, pg 129
Michigan State University Press (MSU Press), pg 130
Milkweed Editions, pg 131
Milliken Publishing Co, pg 132
Modern Language Association (MLA), pg 133
Modern Memoirs Inc, pg 133
Multicultural Publications Inc, pg 135
Multnomah, pg 135
Nataraj Books, pg 136
National Council of Teachers of English (NCTE), pg 137
New Directions Publishing Corp, pg 139
New Issues Poetry & Prose, pg 140
NewSouth Books, pg 141
NFB Publishing, pg 141
North Atlantic Books (NAB), pg 142
North Star Press of Saint Cloud Inc, pg 142
Northwestern University Press, pg 143
W W Norton & Company Inc, pg 143
Norwood House Press, pg 143
Odyssey Books, pg 145
The Ohio State University Press, pg 145
Ohio University Press, pg 145
Omnidawn, pg 146
On the Write Path Publishing, pg 146
Open Letter, pg 147
ORO editions, pg 148
Pact Press, pg 150
Paraclete Press Inc, pg 151
Park Place Publications, pg 152
Path Press Inc, pg 152
Paul Dry Books, pg 152
Pen-L Publishing, pg 153
Persea Books, pg 158
Piano Press, pg 159
Pleasure Boat Studio: A Literary Press, pg 160
Plough Publishing House, pg 161
Ploughshares, pg 161
Plowshare Media, pg 161
Pocol Press, pg 161
Polar Bear & Company, pg 161
Princeton University Press, pg 164
Purple House Press, pg 167
Pyncheon House, pg 167
Rational Island Publishers, pg 171
Rattapallax Press, pg 172
Raven Publishing Inc, pg 172
Red Hen Press, pg 172
Red Moon Press, pg 172
Regal House Publishing, pg 173
Regent Press Printers & Publishers, pg 174
Rising Sun Publishing, pg 175
St James Press®, pg 180
St Johann Press, pg 180
San Diego State University Press, pg 182
Sarabande Books Inc, pg 182
Satya House Publications, pg 182
Savant Books & Publications LLC, pg 182
Scholastic Inc, pg 184

Scripta Humanistica Publishing International, pg 185
Seven Stories Press, pg 186
Shambhala Publications Inc, pg 187
Sherman Asher Publishing, pg 187
Signature Books Publishing LLC, pg 187
Somerset Hall Press, pg 193
Sourcebooks LLC, pg 194
Southern Illinois University Press, pg 195
STARbooks Press, pg 197
StarGroup International Inc, pg 197
Stellar Publishing, pg 198
Stone Bridge Press Inc, pg 199
Strategic Book Publishing (SBP), pg 199
Swallow Press, pg 201
Swan Isle Press, pg 201
Teaching & Learning Co, pg 204
Temporal Mechanical Press, pg 204
Texas Tech University Press, pg 205
Third World Press Foundation, pg 206
TotalRecall Publications Inc, pg 208
TriQuarterly Books, pg 209
TSG Publishing Foundation Inc, pg 210
Tughra Books, pg 210
Tupelo Press Inc, pg 210
Turtle Point Press, pg 210
Tuttle Publishing, pg 211
Ugly Duckling Presse, pg 212
Union Square & Co, pg 212
University of Alaska Press, pg 214
The University of Arizona Press, pg 214
The University of Arkansas Press, pg 214
University of California Press, pg 215
University of Chicago Press, pg 215
University of Georgia Press, pg 216
University of Iowa Press, pg 216
University of Louisiana at Lafayette Press, pg 217
University of Massachusetts Press, pg 217
University of Nevada Press, pg 218
University of New Mexico Press, pg 218
University of New Orleans Press, pg 218
University of North Texas Press, pg 218
University of Pittsburgh Press, pg 219
The University of Utah Press, pg 220
University of Washington Press, pg 220
University of Wisconsin Press, pg 221
Utah State University Press, pg 223
Vesuvian Books, pg 224
Viking Penguin, pg 224
Vintage Books, pg 225
Wake Forest University Press, pg 225
Wayne State University Press, pg 226
Wayside Publishing, pg 227
Welcome Books, pg 227
Welcome Rain Publishers LLC, pg 227
Wesleyan University Press, pg 227
Western Reflections Publishing Co, pg 228
White Pine Press, pg 228
Williams & Company Book Publishers, pg 230
Wings Press, pg 231
Wolfman Books, pg 232

Wyndham Hall Press, pg 234
Xlibris Corp, pg 234
Yale University Press, pg 235
YBK Publishers Inc, pg 235
Yotzeret Publishing, pg 236

POP CULTURE

Akashic Books, pg 6
AMMO Books LLC, pg 13
Anaphora Literary Press, pg 13
Atlas Publishing, pg 21
Avant-Guide, pg 22
Backbeat Books, pg 23
BenBella Books Inc, pg 27
Blood Moon Productions Ltd, pg 31
Bloomsbury Academic, pg 31
Brown Books Publishing Group (BBPG), pg 38
Chicago Review Press, pg 46
Cider Mill Press Book Publishers LLC, pg 48
Countryman Press, pg 54
Dark Horse Comics, pg 57
Dutton, pg 62
Everything Goes Media LLC, pg 68
The Feminist Press at The City University of New York, pg 71
Fulcrum Publishing Inc, pg 75
Gale, pg 75
Gallery Books, pg 76
Gingko Press Inc, pg 78
Glitterati Inc, pg 78
Histria Books, pg 93
Inner Traditions International Ltd, pg 101
Kallisti Publishing Inc, pg 108
Kensington Publishing Corp, pg 109
Kodansha USA Inc, pg 110
little bee books, pg 117
Llewellyn Publications, pg 119
Long River Press, pg 120
Macmillan Reference USA™, pg 123
Mandel Vilar Press, pg 124
Manic D Press Inc, pg 124
Mason Crest Publishers, pg 126
McFarland, pg 127
Medieval Institute Publications (MIP), pg 129
Mitchell Lane Publishers Inc, pg 133
NBM Publishing Inc, pg 139
North Atlantic Books (NAB), pg 142
Open Court Publishing Co, pg 147
ORO editions, pg 148
Other Press, pg 148
PA Press, pg 149
Pace University Press, pg 149
Penny-Farthing Productions, pg 157
Quirk Books, pg 168
Rand-Smith Publishing, pg 169
Red Wheel/Weiser, pg 173
Riverdale Avenue Books (RAB), pg 175
Ronin Publishing Inc, pg 176
Rowman & Littlefield, pg 178
Running Press, pg 178
St Martin's Press, LLC, pg 180
Santa Monica Press LLC, pg 182
Schaffner Press, pg 183
Sourcebooks LLC, pg 194
Stone Bridge Press Inc, pg 199
Tantor Media Inc, pg 202
Taschen America, pg 203
Ten Speed Press, pg 204
Trans-Atlantic Publications Inc, pg 209
Union Square & Co, pg 212
Universe Publishing, pg 214
University of Iowa Press, pg 216

U.S. PUBLISHERS — SUBJECT INDEX   BOOK

University of Minnesota Press, pg 217
University of Nevada Press, pg 218
University Press of Kansas, pg 221
University Press of Mississippi, pg 222
Vintage Books, pg 225
Watson-Guptill, pg 226
Zest Books, pg 236

PSYCHOLOGY, PSYCHIATRY

Academic Press, pg 3
Alexander Street, part of Clarivate PLC, pg 6
American Correctional Association, pg 9
American Counseling Association (ACA), pg 9
American Medical Association (AMA), pg 11
American Psychiatric Association Publishing, pg 11
American Psychological Association, pg 11
Annual Reviews, pg 14
Jason Aronson Inc, pg 17
AuthorHouse, pg 22
Authorlink® Press, pg 22
Avery, pg 23
Baker Books, pg 23
Barcelona Publishers LLC, pg 24
Barringer Publishing, pg 24
Barrytown/Station Hill Press, pg 24
Bartleby Press, pg 24
Basic Books Group, pg 25
Bear & Co Inc, pg 26
Beaver's Pond Press Inc, pg 26
John Benjamins Publishing Co, pg 28
Biographical Publishing Co, pg 29
Bloomsbury Academic, pg 31
Boys Town Press, pg 35
Nicholas Brealey Publishing, pg 36
Brilliance Publishing Inc, pg 37
Paul H Brookes Publishing Co Inc, pg 37
Bull Publishing Co, pg 38
The Bureau for At-Risk Youth, pg 38
Carolina Academic Press, pg 41
Cengage Learning, pg 43
The Center for Learning, pg 43
Central Recovery Press (CRP), pg 44
Charles Press Publishers, pg 45
Cleis Press, pg 49
Consumer Press, pg 52
Crown House Publishing Co LLC, pg 56
Crystal Clarity Publishers, pg 56
Dharma Publishing, pg 59
Dissertation.com, pg 60
Doubleday, pg 61
Dutton, pg 62
Elsevier Inc, pg 65
Everything Goes Media LLC, pg 68
The Experiment, pg 68
Fair Winds Press, pg 69
Fine Creative Media, Inc, pg 71
Free Spirit Publishing Inc, pg 74
Gale, pg 75
Gateways Books & Tapes, pg 77
Gifted Unlimited LLC, pg 78
Green Dragon Books, pg 81
Greenleaf Book Group LLC, pg 81
Gryphon Editions, pg 82
The Guilford Press, pg 82
Harvard University Press, pg 88
Hatherleigh Press Ltd, pg 88
Hay House LLC, pg 89
Hazelden Publishing, pg 89

Health Communications Inc, pg 89
Health Professions Press, pg 90
HeartMath LLC, pg 90
High Tide Press, pg 92
Himalayan Institute Press, pg 92
Histria Books, pg 93
Hogrefe Publishing Corp, pg 93
Hohm Press, pg 93
Houghton Mifflin Harcourt, pg 95
Idyll Arbor Inc, pg 98
Information Age Publishing Inc, pg 100
Inner Traditions International Ltd, pg 101
Inter-University Consortium for Political & Social Research (ICPSR), pg 102
InterVarsity Press, pg 104
Johns Hopkins University Press, pg 106
Kazi Publications Inc, pg 108
Jessica Kingsley Publishers Inc, pg 110
Krieger Publishing Co, pg 111
Lanahan Publishers Inc, pg 112
Lantern Publishing & Media, pg 112
Larson Publications, pg 113
Lexington Books, pg 115
Mary Ann Liebert Inc, pg 116
Light Technology Publishing LLC, pg 116
Lotus Press, pg 120
Loving Healing Press Inc, pg 121
Macmillan Learning, pg 123
Macmillan Reference USA™, pg 123
MAR*CO Products Inc, pg 124
McGraw-Hill Higher Education, pg 128
The Edwin Mellen Press, pg 129
Metropolitan Classics, pg 130
Moonshine Cove Publishing LLC, pg 134
NavPress Publishing Group, pg 139
New Harbinger Publications Inc, pg 140
New World Library, pg 140
New York Academy of Sciences (NYAS), pg 140
New York University Press, pg 141
North Atlantic Books (NAB), pg 142
W W Norton & Company Inc, pg 143
Nova Science Publishers Inc, pg 144
On the Write Path Publishing, pg 146
The Original Falcon Press, pg 148
ORO editions, pg 148
Oxford University Press USA, pg 149
Pace University Press, pg 149
Palgrave Macmillan, pg 150
Paragon House, pg 151
Pathfinder Publishing Inc, pg 152
Pearson Business Publishing, pg 153
Peradam Press, pg 158
Philosophical Library Inc, pg 159
PRO-ED Inc, pg 165
Professional Resource Press, pg 165
Prometheus Books, pg 166
Psychological Assessment Resources Inc (PAR), pg 166
RAND Corp, pg 169
Rational Island Publishers, pg 171
Red Wheel/Weiser, pg 173
Robert D Reed Publishers, pg 173
Regent Press Printers & Publishers, pg 174

Research & Education Association (REA), pg 174
Research Press, pg 174
Ronin Publishing Inc, pg 176
Ross Books, pg 177
Routledge, pg 177
Russell Sage Foundation, pg 178
Safer Society Press, pg 179
SAGE Publishing, pg 180
St Pauls, pg 181
Savant Books & Publications LLC, pg 182
Science & Humanities Press, pg 185
Sentient Publications LLC, pg 186
Shambhala Publications Inc, pg 187
Sinauer Associates, pg 190
Sounds True Inc, pg 194
Sourcebooks LLC, pg 194
Springer, pg 196
Springer Publishing Co, pg 196
SteinerBooks Inc, pg 198
STM Learning Inc, pg 199
Strategic Book Publishing (SBP), pg 199
Nan A Talese, pg 202
Tantor Media Inc, pg 202
Tapestry Press Ltd, pg 202
TarcherPerigee, pg 202
Taylor & Francis Inc, pg 203
Temple University Press, pg 204
Third World Press Foundation, pg 206
Charles C Thomas Publisher Ltd, pg 206
Treehaus Communications Inc, pg 209
TSG Publishing Foundation Inc, pg 210
Tyndale House Publishers Inc, pg 211
Unarius Academy of Science Publications, pg 212
Union Square & Co, pg 212
University of Chicago Press, pg 215
University of Minnesota Press, pg 217
University of North Texas Press, pg 218
University Press of America Inc, pg 221
US Government Publishing Office (GPO), pg 223
Vernon Press, pg 224
Waveland Press Inc, pg 226
Eliot Werner Publications Inc, pg 227
Westminster John Knox Press (WJK), pg 228
Wheatherstone Press, pg 228
Whole Person Associates Inc, pg 229
Wiley-Blackwell, pg 229
John Wiley & Sons Inc, pg 230
John Wiley & Sons Inc Global Education, pg 230
John Wiley & Sons Inc Professional Development, pg 230
Wilshire Book Co, pg 230
Wisdom Publications Inc, pg 231
Worth Publishers, pg 234
Wyndham Hall Press, pg 234
Xlibris Corp, pg 234
Yale University Press, pg 235
YBK Publishers Inc, pg 235
Zeig, Tucker & Theisen Inc, pg 236
Zondervan, pg 236

PUBLIC ADMINISTRATION

The AEI Press, pg 5
AuthorHouse, pg 22

The Brookings Institution Press, pg 37
Brown Books Publishing Group (BBPG), pg 38
Business Research Services Inc, pg 38
Cato Institute, pg 42
Cornell University Press, pg 52
Council for Research in Values & Philosophy, pg 53
The Council of State Governments, pg 53
CQ Press, pg 54
Edward Elgar Publishing Inc, pg 65
Encounter Books, pg 66
Gale, pg 75
Georgetown University Press, pg 77
The Graduate Group/Booksellers, pg 80
Harvard Education Publishing Group, pg 88
Independent Institute, pg 99
Institute of Police Technology & Management (IPTM), pg 102
Intercultural Development Research Association (IDRA), pg 102
International City/County Management Association (ICMA), pg 102
International Risk Management Institute Inc, pg 103
Lyndon B Johnson School of Public Affairs, pg 106
Kumarian Press, pg 112
Macmillan Reference USA™, pg 123
Management Sciences for Health, pg 123
The Edwin Mellen Press, pg 129
Michigan State University Press (MSU Press), pg 130
Milford Books™, pg 131
National Academies Press (NAP), pg 136
National Conference of State Legislatures (NCSL), pg 137
Planners Press, pg 160
Police Executive Research Forum, pg 162
RAND Corp, pg 169
Russell Sage Foundation, pg 178
Solano Press Books, pg 193
Temple University Press, pg 204
Transportation Research Board (TRB), pg 209
United Nations Publications, pg 213
University of Alabama Press, pg 214
University of Pittsburgh Press, pg 219
University Press of America Inc, pg 221
University Press of Kansas, pg 221
US Government Publishing Office (GPO), pg 223
Waveland Press Inc, pg 226
Wiley-Blackwell, pg 229
Workers Compensation Research Institute, pg 232
World Bank Publications, pg 233

PUBLISHING & BOOK TRADE REFERENCE

Allworth Press, pg 7
Anaphora Literary Press, pg 13
Asta Publications LLC, pg 20
AuthorHouse, pg 22
B&H Publishing Group, pg 24
Frederic C Beil Publisher Inc, pg 27
Black Heron Press, pg 30
Book Marketing Works LLC, pg 33
Books on Tape™, pg 34

PUBLISHERS

R R Bowker LLC, pg 34
Cengage Learning, pg 43
Charles River Media, pg 45
China Books, pg 47
Clinical and Laboratory Standards Institute (CLSI), pg 49
Columbia Books & Information Services (CBIS), pg 50
Continental AfrikaPublishers, pg 52
Dancing Lemur Press LLC, pg 57
Elderberry Press Inc, pg 65
Gale, pg 75
Greenleaf Book Group LLC, pg 81
Illuminating Engineering Society of North America (IES), pg 99
Information Today, Inc, pg 100
Joshua Tree Publishing, pg 107
Kalmbach Media Co, pg 108
Krause Publications Inc, pg 111
LAMA Books, pg 112
Libraries Unlimited, pg 116
Liturgical Press, pg 118
Macmillan Reference USA™, pg 123
Marine Education Textbooks, pg 125
Morgan James Publishing, pg 134
National Geographic Books, pg 137
Oak Knoll Press, pg 144
Ocean Tree Books, pg 145
One On One Book Publishing/Film-Video Publications, pg 146
Open Horizons Publishing Co, pg 147
Our Sunday Visitor Publishing, pg 148
Pace University Press, pg 149
Perfection Learning®, pg 158
Primary Research Group Inc, pg 163
PRINTING United Alliance, pg 165
Random House Reference/Random House Puzzles & Games, pg 171
Scholastic Education Solutions, pg 184
Sentient Publications LLC, pg 186
Silman-James Press Inc, pg 188
Society for Human Resource Management (SHRM), pg 192
Story Monsters LLC, pg 199
Todd Publications, pg 207
University of Chicago Press, pg 215
University of Iowa Press, pg 216
Writer's Digest Books, pg 234
Xlibris Corp, pg 234

RADIO, TV

Allworth Press, pg 7
Applause Theatre & Cinema Books, pg 15
AuthorHouse, pg 22
BenBella Books Inc, pg 27
Bloomsbury Academic, pg 31
Cengage Learning, pg 43
DiscoverNet Publishing, pg 59
Elsevier Inc, pg 65
Gale, pg 75
Gallery Books, pg 76
Gray & Company Publishers, pg 80
Greenleaf Book Group LLC, pg 81
Insight Editions, pg 101
Joshua Tree Publishing, pg 107
Limelight Editions, pg 117
Macmillan Reference USA™, pg 123
McFarland, pg 127
National Association of Broadcasters (NAB), pg 136
One On One Book Publishing/Film-Video Publications, pg 146
Plunkett Research Ltd, pg 161

Primary Research Group Inc, pg 163
Riverdale Avenue Books (RAB), pg 175
Rutgers University Press, pg 178
Schiffer Publishing Ltd, pg 183
Silman-James Press Inc, pg 188
Syracuse University Press, pg 201
Tantor Media Inc, pg 202
Temple University Press, pg 204
University Press of Mississippi, pg 222
Waveland Press Inc, pg 226

REAL ESTATE

Appraisal Institute, pg 15
Atlantic Publishing Group Inc, pg 21
AuthorHouse, pg 22
Beaver's Pond Press Inc, pg 26
Brown Books Publishing Group (BBPG), pg 38
Cengage Learning, pg 43
Global Authors Publications (GAP), pg 78
Greenleaf Book Group LLC, pg 81
International Risk Management Institute Inc, pg 103
International Wealth Success (IWS), pg 104
LearningExpress, pg 114
NOLO, pg 141
Plunkett Research Ltd, pg 161
Solano Press Books, pg 193
South Carolina Bar, pg 195
Strategic Book Publishing (SBP), pg 199
Tantor Media Inc, pg 202
Vault.com Inc, pg 224
Wheatherstone Press, pg 228
Xlibris Corp, pg 234

REGIONAL INTERESTS

Ampersand Inc/Professional Publishing Services, pg 13
Anaphora Literary Press, pg 13
Angel City Press, pg 14
ANR Publications University of California, pg 14
APC Publishing, pg 15
Appalachian Mountain Club Books, pg 15
Arcadia Publishing Inc, pg 16
AuthorHouse, pg 22
Barranca Press, pg 24
BelleBooks, pg 27
Black Dome Press Corp, pg 30
Book Sales, pg 33
BookLogix, pg 34
Brandylane Publishers Inc, pg 35
Bucknell University Press, pg 38
Burford Books, pg 38
Carolina Academic Press, pg 41
Clerisy Press, pg 49
Commonwealth Editions, pg 51
Continental AfrikaPublishers, pg 52
Cornell Maritime Press, pg 52
Cornell University Press, pg 52
Countryman Press, pg 54
Endless Mountains Publishing Co, pg 66
Epicenter Press Inc, pg 67
Everything Goes Media LLC, pg 68
Excelsior Editions, pg 68
Familius, pg 69
Farcountry Press, pg 69
Father & Son Publishing Inc, pg 70
Fordham University Press, pg 73
Galde Press Inc, pg 75
Gale, pg 75
Gibbs Smith Publisher, pg 78

The Globe Pequot Press, pg 79
Godine, pg 79
Greenleaf Book Group LLC, pg 81
Grey House Publishing Inc™, pg 81
Hobblebush Books, pg 93
Indiana Historical Society Press, pg 99
Indiana University Press, pg 100
Islandport Press, pg 105
Kent State University Press, pg 109
Kiva Publishing Inc, pg 110
Lake Superior Publishing LLC, pg 112
LARB Books, pg 113
Leaf Storm Press, pg 113
Legacy Bound, pg 114
Linden Publishing Co Inc, pg 117
LPD Press/Rio Grande Books, pg 121
Macmillan Reference USA™, pg 123
Marquette University Press, pg 125
Maryland History Press, pg 126
McBooks Press, pg 127
Menasha Ridge Press, pg 129
Mercer University Press, pg 129
Moriah Books, pg 134
New Forums Press Inc, pg 139
North Star Press of Saint Cloud Inc, pg 142
Northern Illinois University Press, pg 143
Northwestern University Press, pg 143
The Ohio State University Press, pg 145
Ohio University Press, pg 145
On the Write Path Publishing, pg 146
Orange Frazer Press Inc, pg 147
ORO editions, pg 148
Peachtree Publishing Co Inc, pg 153
Pelican Publishing, pg 153
Penn State University Press, pg 157
Peterson Institute for International Economics (PIIE), pg 158
Plexus Publishing, Inc, pg 160
Polar Bear & Company, pg 161
Publication Consultants, pg 167
Quail Ridge Press (QRP), pg 168
Rio Nuevo Publishers, pg 175
River City Publishing, pg 175
The RoadRunner Press, pg 175
Rutgers University Press, pg 178
St Joseph's University Press, pg 180
Santa Monica Press LLC, pg 182
Schiffer Publishing Ltd, pg 183
School for Advanced Research Press, pg 185
Southern Illinois University Press, pg 195
Stackpole Books, pg 196
Stanford University Press, pg 197
Stoneydale Press Publishing Co, pg 199
Strategic Book Publishing (SBP), pg 199
Terra Nova Books, pg 204
Texas A&M University Press, pg 205
Texas Tech University Press, pg 205
University of Texas Press, pg 205
Tilbury House Publishers, pg 207
Trinity University Press, pg 209
Tuttle Publishing, pg 211
The University of Arkansas Press, pg 214
University of Delaware Press, pg 215
University of Georgia Press, pg 216
University of Hawaii Press, pg 216
University of Illinois Press, pg 216
University of Iowa Press, pg 216

University of Louisiana at Lafayette Press, pg 217
University of Massachusetts Press, pg 217
University of Michigan Press, pg 217
University of Minnesota Press, pg 217
University of Missouri Press, pg 217
University of Nevada Press, pg 218
University of North Texas Press, pg 218
University of Oklahoma Press, pg 219
University of Pittsburgh Press, pg 219
The University of Utah Press, pg 220
University of Virginia Press, pg 220
University of Wisconsin Press, pg 221
University Press of Colorado, pg 221
University Press of Kansas, pg 221
The University Press of Kentucky, pg 222
University Press of Mississippi, pg 222
Vanderbilt University Press, pg 224
Washington State University Press, pg 226
Wayne State University Press, pg 226
Wesleyan University Press, pg 227
West Virginia University Press, pg 228
Western Reflections Publishing Co, pg 228
Wildflower Press, pg 229
Willow Creek Press, pg 230
WoodstockArts, pg 232
Writer's AudioShop, pg 234
Xlibris Corp, pg 234
YWAM Publishing, pg 236

RELIGION - BUDDHIST

Abbeville Publishing Group, pg 2
All Things That Matter Press, pg 7
The Apocryphile Press, pg 15
AuthorHouse, pg 22
Barrytown/Station Hill Press, pg 24
Black Rabbit Books, pg 30
Book Sales, pg 33
The Book Tree, pg 34
Brandylane Publishers Inc, pg 35
Chelsea House, pg 45
Clear Light Publishers, pg 49
Columbia University Press, pg 51
Copper Canyon Press, pg 52
Council for Research in Values & Philosophy, pg 53
Counterpoint Press LLC, pg 54
Crystal Clarity Publishers, pg 56
Dharma Publishing, pg 59
Dover Publications Inc, pg 61
Facts On File, pg 69
Fine Creative Media, Inc, pg 71
Gale, pg 75
Gorgias Press LLC, pg 80
Green Dragon Books, pg 81
Greenleaf Book Group LLC, pg 81
Hackett Publishing Co Inc, pg 83
Hay House LLC, pg 89
Hohm Press, pg 93
Homa & Sekey Books, pg 95
Inner Traditions International Ltd, pg 101
Jain Publishing Co, pg 105
Larson Publications, pg 113
Lexington Books, pg 115
Lotus Press, pg 120

Macmillan Reference USA™, pg 123
Mandala Earth, pg 124
The Edwin Mellen Press, pg 129
Monkfish Book Publishing Co, pg 133
Nataraj Books, pg 136
New World Library, pg 140
Nilgiri Press, pg 141
North Atlantic Books (NAB), pg 142
Orbis Books, pg 147
The Original Falcon Press, pg 148
ORO editions, pg 148
Parallax Press, pg 151
Penn State University Press, pg 157
Philosophical Library Inc, pg 159
Princeton University Press, pg 164
Red Wheel/Weiser, pg 173
Routledge, pg 177
Sentient Publications LLC, pg 186
Shambhala Publications Inc, pg 187
SkyLight Paths® Publishing, pg 191
Snow Lion, pg 192
Stanford University Press, pg 197
State University of New York Press, pg 198
Stone Bridge Press Inc, pg 199
Tantor Media Inc, pg 202
TotalRecall Publications Inc, pg 208
Tuttle Publishing, pg 211
Ulysses Press, pg 212
University of California Press, pg 215
University of Chicago Press, pg 215
University of Hawaii Press, pg 216
University Press of America Inc, pg 221
Wiley-Blackwell, pg 229
Wisdom Publications Inc, pg 231

RELIGION - CATHOLIC

Abbeville Publishing Group, pg 2
Academica Press, pg 3
American Carriage House Publishing (ACHP), pg 8
American Catholic Press (ACP), pg 9
Angelus Press, pg 14
The Apocryphile Press, pg 15
Ascension Press, pg 18
Augsburg Fortress Publishers, Publishing House of the Evangelical Lutheran Church in America, pg 22
AuthorHouse, pg 22
Ave Maria Press Inc, pg 22
Biographical Publishing Co, pg 29
Black Rabbit Books, pg 30
Bloomsbury Academic, pg 31
Book Sales, pg 33
The Book Tree, pg 34
BookLogix, pg 34
Brill Inc, pg 37
Catholic Book Publishing Corp, pg 42
The Catholic Health Association of the United States, pg 42
The Catholic University of America Press, pg 42
The Center for Learning, pg 43
Charles Press Publishers, pg 45
Chelsea House, pg 45
Cistercian Publications, pg 48
Cornell University Press, pg 52
Council for Research in Values & Philosophy, pg 53
The Crossroad Publishing Co, pg 55
Crystal Clarity Publishers, pg 56
Walter De Gruyter Inc, pg 58
Doubleday, pg 61
Dover Publications Inc, pg 61

ECS Publishing Group, pg 63
Wm B Eerdmans Publishing Co, pg 64
Emmaus Road Publishing Inc, pg 66
Facts On File, pg 69
Fine Creative Media, Inc, pg 71
Fordham University Press, pg 73
Franciscan Media, pg 74
Gale, pg 75
Georgetown University Press, pg 77
Gorgias Press LLC, pg 80
Greenleaf Book Group LLC, pg 81
Hackett Publishing Co Inc, pg 83
HarperCollins Publishers LLC, pg 86
Hendrickson Publishers Inc, pg 91
Hilton Publishing Co, pg 92
Histria Books, pg 93
Ignatius Press, pg 98
IHS Press, pg 98
Institute of Jesuit Sources (IJS), pg 102
Kendall Hunt Publishing Co, pg 108
Lexington Books, pg 115
Liguori Publications, pg 117
Liturgical Press, pg 118
Liturgy Training Publications, pg 119
Loyola Press, pg 121
LPD Press/Rio Grande Books, pg 121
Macmillan Reference USA™, pg 123
Marquette University Press, pg 125
McGraw-Hill Education, pg 127
The Edwin Mellen Press, pg 129
Mercer University Press, pg 129
Monkfish Book Publishing Co, pg 133
National Catholic Educational Association, pg 137
New City Press, pg 139
New York University Press, pg 141
Nilgiri Press, pg 141
Nova Science Publishers Inc, pg 144
NRP Direct, pg 144
OCP, pg 145
Orbis Books, pg 147
The Original Falcon Press, pg 148
Our Sunday Visitor Publishing, pg 148
Paraclete Press Inc, pg 151
Pauline Books & Media, pg 152
Paulist Press, pg 152
Pelican Publishing, pg 153
Penn State University Press, pg 157
Pflaum Publishing Group, pg 159
Philosophical Library Inc, pg 159
Plough Publishing House, pg 161
Polebridge Press, pg 161
Rational Island Publishers, pg 171
Recorded Books Inc, an RBmedia company, pg 172
Regnery Publishing, pg 174
Roman Catholic Books, pg 176
Routledge, pg 177
Rowman & Littlefield, pg 178
William H Sadlier Inc, pg 179
St Augustine's Press Inc, pg 180
St Joseph's University Press, pg 180
Saint Mary's Press, pg 181
St Pauls, pg 181
Scepter Publishers, pg 183
School Guide Publications, pg 185
SkyLight Paths® Publishing, pg 191
Sophia Institute Press®, pg 193
State University of New York Press, pg 198
Strategic Book Publishing (SBP), pg 199
TAN Books, pg 202

T&T Clark International, pg 202
Tantor Media Inc, pg 202
Treehaus Communications Inc, pg 209
Twenty-Third Publications, pg 211
University of California Press, pg 215
University of Chicago Press, pg 215
University of Notre Dame Press, pg 219
University Press of America Inc, pg 221
University Press of Mississippi, pg 222
US Conference of Catholic Bishops, pg 223
Westminster John Knox Press (WJK), pg 228
Wiley-Blackwell, pg 229
World Citizens, pg 233
Yale University Press, pg 235

RELIGION - HINDU

Abbeville Publishing Group, pg 2
The Apocryphile Press, pg 15
AuthorHouse, pg 22
Bhaktivedanta Book Trust (BBT), pg 29
Black Rabbit Books, pg 30
The Book Tree, pg 34
Chelsea House, pg 45
Council for Research in Values & Philosophy, pg 53
Crystal Clarity Publishers, pg 56
Dover Publications Inc, pg 61
Facts On File, pg 69
Fine Creative Media, Inc, pg 71
Gale, pg 75
Gorgias Press LLC, pg 80
Greenleaf Book Group LLC, pg 81
Hohm Press, pg 93
Inner Traditions International Ltd, pg 101
Jain Publishing Co, pg 105
Larson Publications, pg 113
Lexington Books, pg 115
Lotus Press, pg 120
Macmillan Reference USA™, pg 123
Mandala Earth, pg 124
The Edwin Mellen Press, pg 129
Monkfish Book Publishing Co, pg 133
Nataraj Books, pg 136
Nilgiri Press, pg 141
North Atlantic Books (NAB), pg 142
Orbis Books, pg 147
The Original Falcon Press, pg 148
Philosophical Library Inc, pg 159
Routledge, pg 177
Sentient Publications LLC, pg 186
SkyLight Paths® Publishing, pg 191
State University of New York Press, pg 198
Strategic Book Publishing (SBP), pg 199
Tantor Media Inc, pg 202
TotalRecall Publications Inc, pg 208
Tuttle Publishing, pg 211
University of California Press, pg 215
University of Chicago Press, pg 215
University Press of America Inc, pg 221
Vedanta Press, pg 224
Wiley-Blackwell, pg 229
World Citizens, pg 233

RELIGION - ISLAMIC

Abbeville Publishing Group, pg 2
All Things That Matter Press, pg 7
The Apocryphile Press, pg 15
AuthorHouse, pg 22
Black Rabbit Books, pg 30
Book Sales, pg 33
The Book Tree, pg 34
Brill Inc, pg 37
Chelsea House, pg 45
Council for Research in Values & Philosophy, pg 53
Walter De Gruyter Inc, pg 58
Dover Publications Inc, pg 61
Facts On File, pg 69
Fine Creative Media, Inc, pg 71
Gale, pg 75
Georgetown University Press, pg 77
Gorgias Press LLC, pg 80
Greenleaf Book Group LLC, pg 81
Hackett Publishing Co Inc, pg 83
Inner Traditions International Ltd, pg 101
Lexington Books, pg 115
Macmillan Reference USA™, pg 123
The Edwin Mellen Press, pg 129
Monkfish Book Publishing Co, pg 133
Nataraj Books, pg 136
Nilgiri Press, pg 141
North Atlantic Books (NAB), pg 142
Orbis Books, pg 147
The Original Falcon Press, pg 148
Penn State University Press, pg 157
Philosophical Library Inc, pg 159
Princeton University Press, pg 164
Ross Books, pg 177
Routledge, pg 177
SkyLight Paths® Publishing, pg 191
Stanford University Press, pg 197
State University of New York Press, pg 198
Strategic Book Publishing (SBP), pg 199
Syracuse University Press, pg 201
Tahrike Tarsile Qur'an Inc, pg 202
Tantor Media Inc, pg 202
Tughra Books, pg 210
University of California Press, pg 215
University of Chicago Press, pg 215
The University of Utah Press, pg 220
University Press of America Inc, pg 221
University Press of Florida, pg 221
Markus Wiener Publishers Inc, pg 229
Wiley-Blackwell, pg 229
Yale University Press, pg 235

RELIGION - JEWISH

Abbeville Publishing Group, pg 2
The Apocryphile Press, pg 15
Augsburg Fortress Publishers, Publishing House of the Evangelical Lutheran Church in America, pg 22
AuthorHouse, pg 22
Avotaynu Books LLC, pg 23
Barrytown/Station Hill Press, pg 24
Behrman House Inc, pg 27
Ben Yehuda Press, pg 27
Black Rabbit Books, pg 30
Bloomsbury Academic, pg 31
Book Sales, pg 33
The Book Tree, pg 34
BookLogix, pg 34
Brandylane Publishers Inc, pg 35

Bridge Logos Inc, pg 36
Brill Inc, pg 37
Brown Books Publishing Group (BBPG), pg 38
Central Conference of American Rabbis/CCAR Press, pg 44
Copper Canyon Press, pg 52
Cornell University Press, pg 52
Council for Research in Values & Philosophy, pg 53
Cross-Cultural Communications, pg 55
Walter De Gruyter Inc, pg 58
Dover Publications Inc, pg 61
Eisenbrauns, pg 64
Facts On File, pg 69
Feldheim Publishers, pg 70
Fine Creative Media, Inc, pg 71
Fordham University Press, pg 73
Gale, pg 75
Gateways Books & Tapes, pg 77
Gorgias Press LLC, pg 80
Greenleaf Book Group LLC, pg 81
Hachai Publishing, pg 83
Hackett Publishing Co Inc, pg 83
HarperCollins Publishers LLC, pg 86
Hebrew Union College Press, pg 90
Hendrickson Publishers Inc, pg 91
Histria Books, pg 93
Inner Traditions International Ltd, pg 101
Jewish Lights Publishing, pg 105
The Jewish Publication Society, pg 105
Judaica Press Inc, pg 107
Kar-Ben Publishing, pg 108
KTAV Publishing House Inc, pg 111
Larson Publications, pg 113
Lederer Books, pg 114
Lexington Books, pg 115
Liturgical Press, pg 118
Llewellyn Publications, pg 119
Macmillan Reference USA™, pg 123
Mandel Vilar Press, pg 124
Marquette University Press, pg 125
The Edwin Mellen Press, pg 129
Mercer University Press, pg 129
Mesorah Publications Ltd, pg 130
Messianic Jewish Publishers, pg 130
Monkfish Book Publishing Co, pg 133
Moznaim Publishing Corp, pg 135
New York University Press, pg 141
North Atlantic Books (NAB), pg 142
Orbis Books, pg 147
The Original Falcon Press, pg 148
Pants On Fire Press, pg 150
Pelican Publishing, pg 153
Penn State University Press, pg 157
Peter Pauper Press, Inc, pg 158
Philosophical Library Inc, pg 159
Platypus Media LLC, pg 160
Pocol Press, pg 161
Princeton University Press, pg 164
Rational Island Publishers, pg 171
Red Wheel/Weiser, pg 173
Regnery Publishing, pg 174
Routledge, pg 177
Rowman & Littlefield, pg 178
Rutgers University Press, pg 178
Schocken Books, pg 183
Schreiber Publishing, pg 185
Seven Stories Press, pg 186
Sherman Asher Publishing, pg 187
SkyLight Paths® Publishing, pg 191
Soncino Press Ltd, pg 193
Stanford University Press, pg 197
State University of New York Press, pg 198

Story Monsters LLC, pg 199
Strategic Book Publishing (SBP), pg 199
Syracuse University Press, pg 201
T&T Clark International, pg 202
Tantor Media Inc, pg 202
Texas Tech University Press, pg 205
The Toby Press LLC, pg 207
Transcontinental Music Publications (TMP), pg 209
United States Holocaust Memorial Museum, pg 213
University of Alabama Press, pg 214
University of California Press, pg 215
University of Chicago Press, pg 215
University of Illinois Press, pg 216
University of Pennsylvania Press, pg 219
University of Washington Press, pg 220
University of Wisconsin Press, pg 221
University Press of America Inc, pg 221
University Press of Mississippi, pg 222
Urim Publications, pg 223
Wayne State University Press, pg 226
Westminster John Knox Press (WJK), pg 228
Markus Wiener Publishers Inc, pg 229
Wiley-Blackwell, pg 229
Yale University Press, pg 235
Yeshiva University Press, pg 235
Yotzeret Publishing, pg 236

RELIGION - PROTESTANT

Abingdon Press, pg 2
ACU Press, pg 4
AllWrite Publishing, pg 7
Ambassador International, pg 7
American Carriage House Publishing (ACHP), pg 8
Andrews University Press, pg 14
The Apocryphile Press, pg 15
Augsburg Fortress Publishers, Publishing House of the Evangelical Lutheran Church in America, pg 22
AuthorHouse, pg 22
Baker Books, pg 23
B&H Publishing Group, pg 24
Barbour Publishing Inc, pg 24
Baylor University Press, pg 25
Beacon Hill Press of Kansas City, pg 25
Bethany House Publishers, pg 29
Biographical Publishing Co, pg 29
BJU Press, pg 30
Black Rabbit Books, pg 30
Bloomsbury Academic, pg 31
The Book Tree, pg 34
BookLogix, pg 34
Brentwood Christian Press, pg 36
Brethren Press, pg 36
Bridge Logos Inc, pg 36
Brill Inc, pg 37
Brown Books Publishing Group (BBPG), pg 38
Carson Dellosa Publishing LLC, pg 41
Casa Bautista de Publicaciones, pg 41
CEF Press, pg 43
Chalice Press, pg 44
Chelsea House, pg 45
Chosen Books, pg 47

Christian Liberty Press, pg 47
Christian Schools International (CSI), pg 47
Concordia Publishing House, pg 51
David C Cook, pg 52
Cornell University Press, pg 52
Council for Research in Values & Philosophy, pg 53
Crossway, pg 56
Dancing Lemur Press LLC, pg 57
Destiny Image Inc, pg 59
Dordt Press, pg 60
Dover Publications Inc, pg 61
ECS Publishing Group, pg 63
Editorial Bautista Independiente, pg 63
Editorial Portavoz, pg 64
Editorial Unilit, pg 64
Wm B Eerdmans Publishing Co, pg 64
Eisenbrauns, pg 64
Emerald Books, pg 66
Facts On File, pg 69
Faith Library Publications, pg 69
Father & Son Publishing Inc, pg 70
Fine Creative Media, Inc, pg 71
Focus on the Family, pg 73
Forward Movement, pg 73
Fresh Air Books, pg 75
Friends United Press, pg 75
Gale, pg 75
Goose River Press, pg 79
Gorgias Press LLC, pg 80
Gospel Publishing House, pg 80
Greenleaf Book Group LLC, pg 81
Harrison House, pg 87
Harvest House Publishers Inc, pg 88
Hendrickson Publishers Inc, pg 91
Herald Press, pg 91
Hilton Publishing Co, pg 92
Histria Books, pg 93
House to House Publications, pg 97
InterVarsity Press, pg 104
Iron Stream Media, pg 104
Joshua Tree Publishing, pg 107
Judson Press, pg 107
Kregel Publications, pg 111
Lexington Books, pg 115
Living Stream Ministry (LSM), pg 119
Macmillan Reference USA™, pg 123
Maryland History Press, pg 126
Master Books®, pg 126
The Edwin Mellen Press, pg 129
MennoMedia, pg 129
Mercer University Press, pg 129
Monkfish Book Publishing Co, pg 133
Moody Publishers, pg 134
Multnomah, pg 135
NavPress Publishing Group, pg 139
Orbis Books, pg 147
The Original Falcon Press, pg 148
Our Daily Bread Publishing, pg 148
P & R Publishing Co, pg 149
Pacific Press® Publishing Association, pg 149
Pants On Fire Press, pg 150
Paraclete Press Inc, pg 151
Pelican Publishing, pg 153
Penn State University Press, pg 157
Pentecostal Resources Group, pg 157
Philosophical Library Inc, pg 159
Plough Publishing House, pg 161
Polebridge Press, pg 161
Presbyterian Publishing Corp (PPC), pg 163
Rational Island Publishers, pg 171
Recorded Books Inc, an RBmedia company, pg 172
Regnery Publishing, pg 174

Revell, pg 174
Rod & Staff Publishers Inc, pg 176
St Augustine's Press Inc, pg 180
St Johann Press, pg 180
Signalman Publishing, pg 187
SIL International, pg 188
SkyLight Paths® Publishing, pg 191
Smyth & Helwys Publishing Inc, pg 192
Standard Publishing, pg 197
State University of New York Press, pg 198
Strategic Book Publishing (SBP), pg 199
T&T Clark International, pg 202
Tantor Media Inc, pg 202
Tommy Nelson®, pg 207
TotalRecall Publications Inc, pg 208
The Trinity Foundation, pg 209
Tyndale House Publishers Inc, pg 211
University of California Press, pg 215
University of Chicago Press, pg 215
University of Illinois Press, pg 216
University Press of America Inc, pg 221
University Press of Mississippi, pg 222
Upper Room Books, pg 223
WaterBrook, pg 226
Wesleyan Publishing House, pg 227
Westminster John Knox Press (WJK), pg 228
Whitaker House, pg 228
Wiley-Blackwell, pg 229
William Carey Publishing, pg 230
Winters Publishing, pg 231
Yale University Press, pg 235
YWAM Publishing, pg 236
Zondervan, pg 236

RELIGION - OTHER

A 2 Z Press LLC, pg 1
ACU Press, pg 4
Africa World Press Inc, pg 5
Alexander Street, part of Clarivate PLC, pg 6
Amber Lotus Publishing, pg 8
Ancient Faith Publishing, pg 13
The Apocryphile Press, pg 15
Asta Publications LLC, pg 20
Augsburg Fortress Publishers, Publishing House of the Evangelical Lutheran Church in America, pg 22
AuthorHouse, pg 22
Baha'i Publishing Trust, pg 23
Barrytown/Station Hill Press, pg 24
Beacon Press, pg 25
Bear & Co Inc, pg 26
Beaver's Pond Press Inc, pg 26
Bethany House Publishers, pg 29
Bethlehem Books, pg 29
Bhaktivedanta Book Trust (BBT), pg 29
Biographical Publishing Co, pg 29
Black Rabbit Books, pg 30
Bloomsbury Academic, pg 31
Bolchazy-Carducci Publishers Inc, pg 33
Book Sales, pg 33
The Book Tree, pg 34
Brandylane Publishers Inc, pg 35
Bridge Logos Inc, pg 36
Bridge Publications Inc, pg 36
Brill Inc, pg 37
Brilliance Publishing Inc, pg 37
Carolina Academic Press, pg 41
Cedar Fort Inc, pg 43
The Center for Learning, pg 43
Chalice Press, pg 44
Charisma Media, pg 45

U.S. PUBLISHERS — SUBJECT INDEX

Charles Press Publishers, pg 45
Chelsea House, pg 45
Child's Play® Inc, pg 46
China Books, pg 47
Codhill Press, pg 50
Columbia University Press, pg 51
Concordia Publishing House, pg 51
Continental AfrikaPublishers, pg 52
David C Cook, pg 52
Cornerstone Book Publishers, pg 53
Cosimo Inc, pg 53
Council for Research in Values & Philosophy, pg 53
Covenant Communications Inc, pg 54
The Crossroad Publishing Co, pg 55
Crystal Clarity Publishers, pg 56
The Dawn Horse Press, pg 57
Deseret Book Co, pg 58
DeVorss & Co, pg 59
DK, pg 60
Dover Publications Inc, pg 61
Duke University Press, pg 62
Eakin Press, pg 62
Elderberry Press Inc, pg 65
Encounter Books, pg 66
Everyman's Library, pg 68
Facts On File, pg 69
Fair Winds Press, pg 69
Faith & Fellowship Publishing, pg 69
Faith Library Publications, pg 69
Faithlife Corp, pg 69
Feral House, pg 71
Fine Creative Media, Inc, pg 71
Focus, pg 73
Focus on the Family, pg 73
Fons Vitae, pg 73
Forward Movement, pg 73
Friends United Press, pg 75
Gale, pg 75
Georgetown University Press, pg 77
Gorgias Press LLC, pg 80
Gospel Publishing House, pg 80
Green Dragon Books, pg 81
Greenleaf Book Group LLC, pg 81
Grey House Publishing Inc™, pg 81
Group Publishing Inc, pg 82
Guideposts Book & Inspirational Media, pg 82
Hamilton Books, pg 84
Harvest House Publishers Inc, pg 88
Hay House LLC, pg 89
Health Communications Inc, pg 89
Hohm Press, pg 93
Holy Cross Orthodox Press, pg 95
Horizon Publishers & Distributors Inc, pg 95
Humanix Books LLC, pg 97
Idyll Arbor Inc, pg 98
Indiana University Press, pg 100
Information Age Publishing Inc, pg 100
Inner Traditions International Ltd, pg 101
Jump!, pg 107
Kazi Publications Inc, pg 108
Kessinger Publishing LLC, pg 109
Jessica Kingsley Publishers Inc, pg 110
Larson Publications, pg 113
Leadership Ministries Worldwide, pg 113
Lexington Books, pg 115
Little, Brown and Company, pg 118
Liturgical Press, pg 118
Llewellyn Publications, pg 119
The Lockman Foundation, pg 119
Lorenz Educational Press, pg 120
Macmillan Learning, pg 123
Macmillan Reference USA™, pg 123
Marquette University Press, pg 125

Mazda Publishers Inc, pg 127
Medieval Institute Publications (MIP), pg 129
The Edwin Mellen Press, pg 129
Mercer University Press, pg 129
Michigan State University Press (MSU Press), pg 130
Milliken Publishing Co, pg 132
Monkfish Book Publishing Co, pg 133
Morehouse Publishing, pg 134
Moriah Books, pg 134
Mutual Publishing LLC, pg 136
New City Press, pg 139
New Leaf Press, pg 140
New World Library, pg 140
New York University Press, pg 141
Nilgiri Press, pg 141
North Atlantic Books (NAB), pg 142
Northern Illinois University Press, pg 143
Northwestern University Press, pg 143
Ocean Tree Books, pg 145
Omnigraphics Inc, pg 146
Orbis Books, pg 147
The Original Falcon Press, pg 148
Paragon House, pg 151
Pearson Business Publishing, pg 153
Penn State University Press, pg 157
Pentecostal Resources Group, pg 157
Peter Pauper Press, Inc, pg 158
Philosophy Documentation Center, pg 159
The Pilgrim Press/United Church Press, pg 160
Platypus Media LLC, pg 160
Plough Publishing House, pg 161
Presbyterian Publishing Corp (PPC), pg 163
Princeton University Press, pg 164
Prometheus Books, pg 166
Rational Island Publishers, pg 171
Reader's Digest Trade Publishing, pg 172
Recorded Books Inc, an RBmedia company, pg 172
Red Wheel/Weiser, pg 173
Reformation Heritage Books, pg 173
Regular Baptist Press, pg 174
Ronin Publishing Inc, pg 176
Rowman & Littlefield, pg 178
St Herman Press, pg 180
St Johann Press, pg 180
St Joseph's University Press, pg 180
Saint Mary's Press, pg 181
St Nectarios Press, pg 181
SelectBooks Inc, pg 186
Self-Realization Fellowship Publishers, pg 186
Sentient Publications LLC, pg 186
Shadow Mountain Publishing, pg 187
Shambhala Publications Inc, pg 187
Signature Books Publishing LLC, pg 187
Skinner House Books, pg 190
SkyLight Paths® Publishing, pg 191
Snow Lion, pg 192
Somerset Hall Press, pg 193
Sourced Media Books, pg 195
Square One Publishers Inc, pg 196
State University of New York Press, pg 198
SteinerBooks Inc, pg 198
Strategic Book Publishing (SBP), pg 199
Summertime Publications Inc, pg 200

Swedenborg Foundation, pg 201
Syracuse University Press, pg 201
T&T Clark International, pg 202
Tantor Media Inc, pg 202
Tapestry Press Ltd, pg 202
Theosophical University Press, pg 206
Thorndike Press®, pg 206
TSG Publishing Foundation Inc, pg 210
Tuttle Publishing, pg 211
Ulysses Press, pg 212
United States Institute of Peace Press, pg 213
University of California Press, pg 215
University of Chicago Press, pg 215
University of Hawaii Press, pg 216
University of Illinois Press, pg 216
University of Iowa Press, pg 216
University of Louisiana at Lafayette Press, pg 217
The University of North Carolina Press, pg 218
University of South Carolina Press, pg 220
University of Tennessee Press, pg 220
The University of Utah Press, pg 220
University of Virginia Press, pg 220
University Press of America Inc, pg 221
University Press of Florida, pg 221
University Press of Mississippi, pg 222
Upper Room Books, pg 223
Urim Publications, pg 223
Vedanta Press, pg 224
Visible Ink Press®, pg 225
Warner Press, pg 226
Waveland Press Inc, pg 226
Wiley-Blackwell, pg 229
John Wiley & Sons Inc, pg 230
Xlibris Corp, pg 234
Yale University Press, pg 235
Zondervan, pg 236

ROMANCE

Anaphora Literary Press, pg 13
Ashland Creek Press, pg 18
Asta Publications LLC, pg 20
AuthorHouse, pg 22
Barbour Publishing Inc, pg 24
Beaver's Pond Press Inc, pg 26
Bella Books, pg 27
Berkley, pg 28
Bethany House Publishers, pg 29
Bold Strokes Books Inc, pg 33
Book Sales, pg 33
BookLogix, pg 34
Boson Books™, pg 34
Brandylane Publishers Inc, pg 35
Brilliance Publishing Inc, pg 37
Bywater Books Inc, pg 39
Cedar Fort Inc, pg 43
Chickadee Prince Books LLC, pg 46
Cleis Press, pg 49
Covenant Communications Inc, pg 54
Dark Horse Comics, pg 57
Deep River Books LLC, pg 58
Doubleday, pg 61
Elderberry Press Inc, pg 65
Entangled Publishing LLC, pg 67
Epicenter Press Inc, pg 67
Gale, pg 75
Gallery Books, pg 76
Gauthier Publications Inc, pg 77
Global Authors Publications (GAP), pg 78

Goose River Press, pg 79
Grand Central Publishing, pg 80
Greenleaf Book Group LLC, pg 81
Harlequin Enterprises Ltd, pg 85
HarperCollins Publishers LLC, pg 86
Harvest House Publishers Inc, pg 88
Histria Books, pg 93
Hutton Publishing, pg 97
ImaJinn Books, pg 99
Iron Stream Media, pg 104
Italics Publishing, pg 105
Kensington Publishing Corp, pg 109
Kregel Publications, pg 111
Love Inspired Books, pg 120
Macmillan Reference USA™, pg 123
Metropolitan Classics, pg 130
Multnomah, pg 135
New Concepts Publishing, pg 139
Norilana Books, pg 142
North Star Editions Inc, pg 142
Pantheon Books, pg 150
Parachute Publishing LLC, pg 151
Penguin Publishing Group, pg 154
Polis Books, pg 162
Publication Consultants, pg 167
Quixote Press, pg 169
Random House Publishing Group, pg 170
Recorded Books Inc, an RBmedia company, pg 172
Revell, pg 174
Riverdale Avenue Books (RAB), pg 175
RockHill Publishing LLC, pg 176
St James Press®, pg 180
St Martin's Press, LLC, pg 180
Savant Books & Publications LLC, pg 182
Scarsdale Publishing Ltd, pg 183
Scholastic Inc, pg 184
Shadow Mountain Publishing, pg 187
Simon & Schuster Audio, pg 189
Soho Press Inc, pg 193
Soul Mate Publishing, pg 194
Sourcebooks LLC, pg 194
The Story Plant, pg 199
Strategic Book Publishing (SBP), pg 199
Tantor Media Inc, pg 202
Thorndike Press®, pg 206
Top Publications Ltd, pg 207
Turner Publishing Co LLC, pg 210
Twilight Times Books, pg 211
Tyndale House Publishers Inc, pg 211
Vesuvian Books, pg 224
WaterBrook, pg 226
Whiskey Creek Press, pg 228
Xlibris Corp, pg 234
Zumaya Publications, pg 237

SCIENCE (GENERAL)

Academic Press, pg 3
AdventureKEEN, pg 5
Adventures Unlimited Press (AUP), pg 5
AIHA (American Industrial Hygiene Association), pg 6
AIP Publishing LLC, pg 6
Alexander Street, part of Clarivate PLC, pg 6
The American Ceramic Society, pg 9
American Diabetes Association, pg 9
American Fisheries Society, pg 9
American Geosciences Institute (AGI), pg 10

American Philosophical Society Press, pg 11
Andrews University Press, pg 14
Annual Reviews, pg 14
APS PRESS, pg 16
Arbordale Publishing, pg 16
Arcade Publishing Inc, pg 16
ASM International, pg 19
ASTM International, pg 20
Astra Books for Young Readers, pg 20
The Astronomical Society of the Pacific, pg 20
Atlas Publishing, pg 21
AuthorHouse, pg 22
Avery, pg 23
Basic Books Group, pg 25
Beacon Press, pg 25
Beaver's Pond Press Inc, pg 26
Begell House Inc Publishers, pg 27
Bellevue Literary Press, pg 27
BenBella Books Inc, pg 27
BJU Press, pg 30
Black Rabbit Books, pg 30
The Blackburn Press, pg 30
BlueBridge, pg 32
George Braziller Inc, pg 35
Brewers Publications, pg 36
Brilliance Publishing Inc, pg 37
Capstone Publishers™, pg 40
Carolina Academic Press, pg 41
Cengage Learning, pg 43
Cereals & Grains Association, pg 44
Charles River Media, pg 45
Charlesbridge Publishing Inc, pg 45
Chelsea Green Publishing Co, pg 45
Chelsea House, pg 45
Chicago Review Press, pg 46
Child's Play® Inc, pg 46
The Child's World Inc, pg 46
Christian Liberty Press, pg 47
Christian Schools International (CSI), pg 47
Clinical and Laboratory Standards Institute (CLSI), pg 49
Cold Spring Harbor Laboratory Press, pg 50
Columbia University Press, pg 51
Comex Systems Inc, pg 51
Continental AfrikaPublishers, pg 52
Cornell University Press, pg 52
Crabtree Publishing Co, pg 54
Creative Editions, pg 55
Crown Publishing Group, pg 56
Data Trace Publishing Co (DTP), pg 57
Walter De Gruyter Inc, pg 58
DEStech Publications Inc, pg 59
DK, pg 60
Dover Publications Inc, pg 61
East West Discovery Press, pg 63
EDC Publishing, pg 63
ediciones Lerner, pg 63
Educational Insights®, pg 64
Edupress Inc, pg 64
Elsevier Inc, pg 65
Enslow Publishing LLC, pg 66
Evan-Moor Educational Publishers, pg 68
The Experiment, pg 68
Facts On File, pg 69
Fine Creative Media, Inc, pg 71
Fire Engineering Books & Videos, pg 72
First Avenue Editions, pg 72
Gale, pg 75
Gareth Stevens Publishing, pg 76
Gryphon Editions, pg 82
Hanser Publications LLC, pg 85
HarperCollins Publishers LLC, pg 86
Harvard University Press, pg 88

Highlights for Children Inc, pg 92
Homestead Publishing, pg 95
Houghton Mifflin Harcourt, pg 95
Houghton Mifflin Harcourt K-12 Publishers, pg 96
Illinois State Museum Society, pg 99
In the Garden Publishing, pg 99
Institute of Environmental Sciences & Technology - IEST, pg 101
Institute of Police Technology & Management (IPTM), pg 102
Johns Hopkins University Press, pg 106
Jump!, pg 107
Kalmbach Media Co, pg 108
Kendall Hunt Publishing Co, pg 108
Kidsbooks® Publishing, pg 109
Klutz®, pg 110
Alfred A Knopf, pg 110
Krieger Publishing Co, pg 111
THE Learning Connection®, pg 113
Learning Links-USA Inc, pg 114
LearningExpress, pg 114
Lehigh University Press, pg 114
Lerner Publications, pg 115
Lerner Publishing Group Inc, pg 115
Listen & Live Audio Inc, pg 117
Logos Press, pg 119
Lorenz Educational Press, pg 120
Macmillan Reference USA™, pg 123
Mandel Vilar Press, pg 124
Marshall Cavendish Education, pg 125
Mason Crest Publishers, pg 126
Master Books®, pg 126
Mastery Education, pg 126
Materials Research Society, pg 126
McGraw-Hill Education, pg 127
McGraw-Hill Higher Education, pg 128
McGraw-Hill Professional Publishing Group, pg 128
McGraw-Hill School Education Group, pg 128
Medical Physics Publishing Corp (MPP), pg 129
Metropolitan Classics, pg 130
Mighty Media Press, pg 131
Milliken Publishing Co, pg 132
The MIT Press, pg 132
Moonshine Cove Publishing LLC, pg 134
National Academies Press (NAP), pg 136
National Book Co, pg 136
National Geographic Books, pg 137
National Geographic Learning, pg 138
National Science Teachers Association (NSTA), pg 138
The New Press, pg 140
New York Academy of Sciences (NYAS), pg 140
The New York Botanical Garden Press, pg 140
No Starch Press, pg 141
W W Norton & Company Inc, pg 143
Odyssey Books, pg 145
OECD Washington Center, pg 145
Oregon State University Press, pg 147
The Original Falcon Press, pg 148
ORO editions, pg 148
Richard C Owen Publishers Inc, pg 149
Oxford University Press USA, pg 149
Pantheon Books, pg 150
Penn State University Press, pg 157

Perfection Learning®, pg 158
Plunkett Research Ltd, pg 161
Princeton University Press, pg 164
Prometheus Books, pg 166
Reader's Digest Trade Publishing, pg 172
Reference Publications Inc, pg 173
ReferencePoint Press Inc, pg 173
Research & Education Association (REA), pg 174
Ross Books, pg 177
Running Press, pg 178
Rutgers University Press, pg 178
Saddleback Educational Publishing, pg 179
SAGE Publishing, pg 180
Salem Press, pg 181
San Diego State University Press, pg 182
Savvas Learning Co LLC, pg 183
Schaffner Press, pg 183
Scholastic Education Solutions, pg 184
Science & Humanities Press, pg 185
Science History Publications USA Inc, pg 185
Science, Naturally, pg 185
Sentient Publications LLC, pg 186
Shambhala Publications Inc, pg 187
Society of Environmental Toxicology & Chemistry (SETAC), pg 192
Society of Exploration Geophysicists, pg 192
Sourcebooks LLC, pg 194
Star Bright Books Inc, pg 197
SteinerBooks Inc, pg 198
Strategic Book Publishing (SBP), pg 199
Sunbelt Publications Inc, pg 200
Sundance/Newbridge Publishing, pg 200
Tahrike Tarsile Qur'an Inc, pg 202
Tantor Media Inc, pg 202
Teacher Created Resources Inc, pg 203
Teaching & Learning Co, pg 204
Temporal Mechanical Press, pg 204
University of Texas Press, pg 205
Theosophical University Press, pg 206
ThunderStone Books, pg 207
Tilbury House Publishers, pg 207
Trans-Atlantic Publications Inc, pg 209
The Trinity Foundation, pg 209
TSG Publishing Foundation Inc, pg 210
Tughra Books, pg 210
Tumblehome Learning Inc, pg 210
Union Square & Co, pg 212
Univelt Inc, pg 213
Universal-Publishers Inc, pg 213
University of Alaska Press, pg 214
University of California Press, pg 215
University of Chicago Press, pg 215
University of Iowa Press, pg 216
University of Washington Press, pg 220
University of Wisconsin Press, pg 221
University Press of Florida, pg 221
UnKnownTruths.com Publishing Co, pg 222
US Government Publishing Office (GPO), pg 223
Visible Ink Press®, pg 225
Walch Education, pg 225
Water Resources Publications LLC, pg 226
Well-Trained Mind Press, pg 227
Whittier Publications Inc, pg 229

John Wiley & Sons Inc, pg 230
Wisconsin Department of Public Instruction, pg 231
Wolters Kluwer US Corp, pg 232
World Book Inc, pg 233
World Scientific Publishing Co Inc, pg 233
Xlibris Corp, pg 234
Yale University Press, pg 235
Zest Books, pg 236

SCIENCE FICTION, FANTASY

A 2 Z Press LLC, pg 1
AK Press, pg 6
Akashic Books, pg 6
All Things That Matter Press, pg 7
Anaphora Literary Press, pg 13
Ariadne Press, pg 16
Asta Publications LLC, pg 20
AuthorHouse, pg 22
Baen Books, pg 23
Bancroft Press, pg 24
Beaver's Pond Press Inc, pg 26
Beehive Books, pg 26
Bella Books, pg 27
Berkley, pg 28
Bethany House Publishers, pg 29
BiG GUY BOOKS, pg 29
Biographical Publishing Co, pg 29
Black Heron Press, pg 30
Bold Strokes Books Inc, pg 33
Book Sales, pg 33
BookLogix, pg 34
Books on Tape™, pg 34
BOOM! Studios, pg 34
Boson Books™, pg 34
BPC, pg 35
Brandylane Publishers Inc, pg 35
Brilliance Publishing Inc, pg 37
Bywater Books Inc, pg 39
Capstone Publishers™, pg 40
Carolrhoda Books Inc, pg 41
Cedar Fort Inc, pg 43
Cedar Grove Publishing, pg 43
Chaosium Inc, pg 45
Cherry Hill Publishing LLC, pg 46
Chickadee Prince Books LLC, pg 46
Circlet Press, pg 48
Cornerstone Book Publishers, pg 53
Cricket Cottage Publishing LLC, pg 55
Dancing Lemur Press LLC, pg 57
Dark Horse Comics, pg 57
DAW Books, pg 57
DC Comics Inc, pg 58
Disney Press, pg 59
Disney Publishing Worldwide, pg 60
Dorrance Publishing Co Inc, pg 61
Dover Publications Inc, pg 61
Elderberry Press Inc, pg 65
Entangled Publishing LLC, pg 67
Firefall Editions, pg 72
Galaxy Press Inc, pg 75
Gale, pg 75
Gallery Books, pg 76
Gateways Books & Tapes, pg 77
Global Authors Publications (GAP), pg 78
Goose River Press, pg 79
Grand Central Publishing, pg 80
Donald M Grant Publisher Inc, pg 80
Greenleaf Book Group LLC, pg 81
Hamilton Stone Editions, pg 84
HarperCollins Children's Books, pg 85
HarperCollins Publishers LLC, pg 86
Histria Books, pg 93

Houghton Mifflin Harcourt, pg 95
Hutton Publishing, pg 97
ImaJinn Books, pg 99
Italics Publishing, pg 105
Jewish Lights Publishing, pg 105
Kallisti Publishing Inc, pg 108
Kensington Publishing Corp, pg 109
Koho Pono LLC, pg 111
Lasaria Creative Publishing, pg 113
Learning Links-USA Inc, pg 114
Libraries Unlimited, pg 116
Library of America, pg 116
Listen & Live Audio Inc, pg 117
Little, Brown and Company, pg 118
Mandel Vilar Press, pg 124
Manic D Press Inc, pg 124
Metropolitan Classics, pg 130
Montemayor Press, pg 133
New Concepts Publishing, pg 139
NFB Publishing, pg 141
Norilana Books, pg 142
North Atlantic Books (NAB), pg 142
North Star Editions Inc, pg 142
On the Write Path Publishing, pg 146
Orbit, pg 147
Other Press, pg 148
P & R Publishing Co, pg 149
Palladium Books Inc, pg 150
Papercutz, pg 150
Parachute Publishing LLC, pg 151
Pen-L Publishing, pg 153
Penguin Publishing Group, pg 154
Plowshare Media, pg 161
Polar Bear & Company, pg 161
Polis Books, pg 162
Prometheus Books, pg 166
Publication Consultants, pg 167
Purple House Press, pg 167
Random House Publishing Group, pg 170
Raven Publishing Inc, pg 172
Recorded Books Inc, an RBmedia company, pg 172
Riverdale Avenue Books (RAB), pg 175
RockHill Publishing LLC, pg 176
Ross Books, pg 177
Round Table Companies, pg 177
Saddleback Educational Publishing, pg 179
St James Press®, pg 180
Salem Press, pg 181
Savant Books & Publications LLC, pg 182
Scarsdale Publishing Ltd, pg 183
Scholastic Inc, pg 184
Seven Stories Press, pg 186
Shadow Mountain Publishing, pg 187
Silver Leaf Books LLC, pg 188
Simon & Schuster Audio, pg 189
Small Beer Press, pg 191
Sourcebooks LLC, pg 194
Sourced Media Books, pg 195
The Story Plant, pg 199
Strategic Book Publishing (SBP), pg 199
Summertime Publications Inc, pg 200
Tachyon Publications LLC, pg 202
Nan A Talese, pg 202
Tantor Media Inc, pg 202
Top Publications Ltd, pg 207
Tor Publishing Group, pg 207
Tumblehome Learning Inc, pg 210
Twilight Times Books, pg 211
University Press of Mississippi, pg 222
Vesuvian Books, pg 224
Wesleyan University Press, pg 227
Whiskey Creek Press, pg 228
Wildflower Press, pg 229
Wildside Press LLC, pg 229
Winterwolf Press, pg 231
Wizards of the Coast LLC, pg 231
Writer's AudioShop, pg 234
Xlibris Corp, pg 234
Yard Dog Press, pg 235
Zondervan, pg 236
Zumaya Publications LLC, pg 237

SECURITIES

The American College of Financial Services, pg 9
AuthorHouse, pg 22
CCH, a Wolters Kluwer business, pg 42
Greenleaf Book Group LLC, pg 81
International Monetary Fund (IMF), Editorial & Publications Division, pg 103
Kallisti Publishing Inc, pg 108
Plunkett Research Ltd, pg 161
Stanford University Press, pg 197
TotalRecall Publications Inc, pg 208

SELF-HELP

A 2 Z Press LLC, pg 1
Abingdon Press, pg 2
ACTA Publications, pg 4
Adams & Ambrose Publishing, pg 4
Adams Media, pg 4
Addicus Books Inc, pg 5
African American Images Inc (AAI), pg 5
All Things That Matter Press, pg 7
Allworth Press, pg 7
AllWrite Publishing, pg 7
Amber Lotus Publishing, pg 8
American Carriage House Publishing (ACHP), pg 8
American Diabetes Association, pg 9
Ampersand Inc/Professional Publishing Services, pg 13
AOTA Press, pg 14
ARE Press, pg 16
Ariel Press, pg 16
Asta Publications LLC, pg 20
Atlantic Publishing Group Inc, pg 21
Augsburg Fortress Publishers, Publishing House of the Evangelical Lutheran Church in America, pg 22
AuthorHouse, pg 22
Authorlink® Press, pg 22
Ave Maria Press Inc, pg 22
Baha'i Publishing Trust, pg 23
Baker Books, pg 23
Bancroft Press, pg 24
Barringer Publishing, pg 24
Barrytown/Station Hill Press, pg 24
Bear & Co Inc, pg 26
Beaver's Pond Press Inc, pg 26
BenBella Books Inc, pg 27
Bethany House Publishers, pg 29
Biographical Publishing Co, pg 29
Blue Mountain Arts Inc, pg 32
Blue Note Publications Inc, pg 32
BlueBridge, pg 32
The Book Tree, pg 34
Bookhaven Press LLC, pg 34
BookLogix, pg 34
Books on Tape™, pg 34
Boson Books™, pg 34
Boys Town Press, pg 35
Brandylane Publishers Inc, pg 35
Nicholas Brealey Publishing, pg 36
Brick Tower Press, pg 36
Bridge Logos Inc, pg 36
Bridge Publications Inc, pg 36
Brilliance Publishing Inc, pg 37
Brown Books Publishing Group (BBPG), pg 38
Bull Publishing Co, pg 38
The Bureau for At-Risk Youth, pg 38
Central Recovery Press (CRP), pg 44
Chalice Press, pg 44
Charles Press Publishers, pg 45
Cleis Press, pg 49
Clerisy Press, pg 49
Consumer Press, pg 52
Continental AfrikaPublishers, pg 52
Cornerstone Book Publishers, pg 53
Cosimo Inc, pg 53
Countryman Press, pg 54
Cricket Cottage Publishing LLC, pg 55
The Crossroad Publishing Co, pg 55
Crown House Publishing Co LLC, pg 56
Crystal Clarity Publishers, pg 56
Dancing Lemur Press LLC, pg 57
Destiny Image Inc, pg 59
DeVorss & Co, pg 59
Doubleday, pg 61
Dover Publications Inc, pg 61
Dutton, pg 62
Editorial Unilit, pg 64
Eifrig Publishing LLC, pg 64
Elderberry Press Inc, pg 65
Elva Resa Publishing, pg 65
Emerald Books, pg 66
M Evans & Company, pg 68
The Experiment, pg 68
Fair Winds Press, pg 69
Faith Library Publications, pg 69
Familius, pg 69
FC&A Publishing, pg 70
Fine Creative Media, Inc, pg 71
Focus on the Family, pg 73
Frederick Fell Publishers Inc, pg 74
Free Spirit Publishing Inc, pg 74
Fresh Air Books, pg 75
Fulcrum Publishing Inc, pg 75
Galde Press Inc, pg 75
Gale, pg 75
Gallery Books, pg 76
Gauthier Publications Inc, pg 77
Gibbs Smith Publisher, pg 78
Gifted Unlimited LLC, pg 78
The Globe Pequot Press, pg 79
Goose River Press, pg 79
Gospel Publishing House, pg 80
The Graduate Group/Booksellers, pg 80
Green Dragon Books, pg 81
Greenleaf Book Group LLC, pg 81
The Guilford Press, pg 82
Hachette Nashville, pg 83
Hamilton Books, pg 84
Hampton Roads Publishing, pg 84
Hannacroix Creek Books Inc, pg 85
HarperCollins Publishers LLC, pg 86
Harvard Common Press, pg 87
Harvest House Publishers Inc, pg 88
Hatherleigh Press Ltd, pg 88
Hay House LLC, pg 89
Hazelden Publishing, pg 89
Health Communications Inc, pg 89
HeartMath LLC, pg 90
Hendrickson Publishers Inc, pg 91
Hilton Publishing Co, pg 92
Histria Books, pg 93
Hogrefe Publishing Corp, pg 93
Hohm Press, pg 93
Houghton Mifflin Harcourt, pg 95
Humanix Books LLC, pg 97
Hutton Publishing, pg 97
Idyll Arbor Inc, pg 98
In the Garden Publishing, pg 99
Inner Traditions International Ltd, pg 101
International Wealth Success (IWS), pg 104
InterVarsity Press, pg 104
Jewish Lights Publishing, pg 105
JIST Publishing, pg 106
Joshua Tree Publishing, pg 107
Kallisti Publishing Inc, pg 108
Kensington Publishing Corp, pg 109
Jessica Kingsley Publishers Inc, pg 110
Koho Pono LLC, pg 111
Kumon Publishing North America Inc (KPNA), pg 112
LAMA Books, pg 112
Larson Publications, pg 113
Listen & Live Audio Inc, pg 117
Little, Brown and Company, pg 118
The Little Entrepreneur, pg 118
Llewellyn Publications, pg 119
Long River Press, pg 120
Looseleaf Law Publications Inc, pg 120
Lotus Press, pg 120
Loving Healing Press Inc, pg 121
The Magni Co, pg 123
Markowski International Publishers, pg 125
Marriage Transformation LLC, pg 125
Menasha Ridge Press, pg 129
Milford Books™, pg 131
Moonshine Cove Publishing LLC, pg 134
Morgan James Publishing, pg 134
National Braille Press, pg 137
New Harbinger Publications Inc, pg 140
New World Library, pg 140
Nilgiri Press, pg 141
NOLO, pg 141
North Atlantic Books (NAB), pg 142
The Oaklea Press Inc, pg 145
Olde & Oppenheim Publishers, pg 146
On the Write Path Publishing, pg 146
The Original Falcon Press, pg 148
Ozark Mountain Publishing Inc, pg 149
P & R Publishing Co, pg 149
Parachute Publishing LLC, pg 151
Parallax Press, pg 151
Parenting Press, pg 151
Park Place Publications, pg 152
Pathfinder Publishing Inc, pg 152
Pauline Books & Media, pg 152
Paulist Press, pg 152
Peachtree Publishing Co Inc, pg 153
Pelican Publishing, pg 153
Pen & Publish LLC, pg 153
Penguin Publishing Group, pg 154
Pentecostal Resources Group, pg 157
Clarkson Potter, pg 162
Professional Resource Press, pg 165
Prometheus Books, pg 166
Psychological Assessment Resources Inc (PAR), pg 166
Public Citizen, pg 167
Quirk Books, pg 168
Rational Island Publishers, pg 171
Ravenhawk™ Books, pg 172
Red Wheel/Weiser, pg 173
Robert D Reed Publishers, pg 173
Revell, pg 174
Ronin Publishing Inc, pg 176
The Rosen Publishing Group Inc, pg 177
Ross Books, pg 177
Round Table Companies, pg 177

PUBLISHERS

U.S. PUBLISHERS — SUBJECT INDEX

Routledge, pg 177
Rowman & Littlefield, pg 178
Safer Society Press, pg 179
Savant Books & Publications LLC, pg 182
Schreiber Publishing, pg 185
Science & Humanities Press, pg 185
SelectBooks Inc, pg 186
Shadow Mountain Publishing, pg 187
Shambhala Publications Inc, pg 187
Simon & Schuster Audio, pg 189
SkillPath Publications, pg 190
SkyLight Paths® Publishing, pg 191
Sound Feelings Publishing, pg 194
Sounds True Inc, pg 194
Sourcebooks LLC, pg 194
Sourced Media Books, pg 195
Square One Publishers Inc, pg 196
StarGroup International Inc, pg 197
SteinerBooks Inc, pg 198
Stellar Publishing, pg 198
Stone Bridge Press Inc, pg 199
Story Monsters LLC, pg 199
Strategic Book Publishing (SBP), pg 199
Stress Free Kids®, pg 200
Sun Publishing Company, pg 200
Sunrise River Press, pg 201
Sunstone Press, pg 201
Surrey Books, pg 201
Tantor Media Inc, pg 202
TarcherPerigee, pg 202
Ten Speed Press, pg 204
Third World Press Foundation, pg 206
Thomas Nelson, pg 206
Todd Publications, pg 207
Tommy Nelson®, pg 207
TotalRecall Publications Inc, pg 208
Travelers' Tales, pg 209
TSG Publishing Foundation Inc, pg 210
Tuttle Publishing, pg 211
Twilight Times Books, pg 211
Tyndale House Publishers Inc, pg 211
Ulysses Press, pg 212
Unarius Academy of Science Publications, pg 212
Union Square & Co, pg 212
Upper Room Books, pg 223
US Government Publishing Office (GPO), pg 223
Vandamere Press, pg 223
WaterBrook, pg 226
Watermark Publishing, pg 226
Westminster John Knox Press (WJK), pg 228
Wheatherstone Press, pg 228
Whittier Publications Inc, pg 229
Whole Person Associates Inc, pg 229
Wilshire Book Co, pg 230
Wisdom Publications Inc, pg 231
Workman Publishing, pg 232
WriteLife Publishing, pg 234
Writer's AudioShop, pg 234
Yard Dog Press, pg 235
YMAA Publication Center Inc, pg 235
Yotzeret Publishing, pg 236
Zondervan, pg 236

SOCIAL SCIENCES, SOCIOLOGY

Academic Press, pg 3
Academica Press, pg 3
ACTA Publications, pg 4
The AEI Press, pg 5
Africa World Press Inc, pg 5
AK Press, pg 6
Akashic Books, pg 6
Alexander Street, part of Clarivate PLC, pg 6
Algora Publishing, pg 7
Amakella Publishing, pg 7
American Correctional Association, pg 9
American Philosophical Society Press, pg 11
American Psychiatric Association Publishing, pg 11
Annual Reviews, pg 14
Aperture Books, pg 15
ArtWrite Productions, pg 18
Atlas Publishing, pg 21
AuthorHouse, pg 22
Avant-Guide, pg 22
Baha'i Publishing Trust, pg 23
Barrytown/Station Hill Press, pg 24
Basic Books Group, pg 25
Baylor University Press, pg 25
Bear & Co Inc, pg 26
Beaver's Pond Press Inc, pg 26
John Benjamins Publishing Co, pg 28
Berghahn Books, pg 28
Bernan, pg 28
Black Rabbit Books, pg 30
The Blackburn Press, pg 30
Bloomsbury Academic, pg 31
Blue Crane Books Inc, pg 32
The Book Tree, pg 34
Brill Inc, pg 37
Brilliance Publishing Inc, pg 37
The Brookings Institution Press, pg 37
Brown Books Publishing Group (BBPG), pg 38
Bucknell University Press, pg 38
Cambridge University Press, pg 39
Capstone Publishers™, pg 40
Carolina Academic Press, pg 41
Caxton Press, pg 42
Cengage Learning, pg 43
Center for Creative Leadership LLC, pg 43
The Center for Learning, pg 43
Chalice Press, pg 44
Charles Press Publishers, pg 45
Chelsea Green Publishing Co, pg 45
Chelsea House, pg 45
Cherry Hill Publishing LLC, pg 46
Child Welfare League of America (CWLA), pg 46
Child's Play® Inc, pg 46
The Child's World Inc, pg 46
China Books, pg 47
Christian Light Publications Inc, pg 47
Christian Schools International (CSI), pg 47
Clarity Press Inc, pg 49
Clerisy Press, pg 49
Close Up Publishing, pg 49
Cognizant Communication Corp, pg 50
Columbia University Press, pg 51
Consumer Press, pg 52
Continental AfrikaPublishers, pg 52
Cornell University Press, pg 52
Cornerstone Book Publishers, pg 53
Council for Research in Values & Philosophy, pg 53
Counterpath Press, pg 54
CSWE Press, pg 56
Walter De Gruyter Inc, pg 58
Doubleday, pg 61
Dover Publications Inc, pg 61
Duke University Press, pg 62
ediciones Lerner, pg 63
Editorial de la Universidad de Puerto Rico, pg 63
Educational Insights®, pg 64
Educator's International Press Inc (EIP), pg 64
Wm B Eerdmans Publishing Co, pg 64
Elderberry Press Inc, pg 65
Edward Elgar Publishing Inc, pg 65
Elsevier Inc, pg 65
Encounter Books, pg 66
Enslow Publishing LLC, pg 66
Facts On File, pg 69
The Feminist Press at The City University of New York, pg 71
Feral House, pg 71
Fine Creative Media, Inc, pg 71
Fordham University Press, pg 73
Foundation Press, pg 74
Gale, pg 75
Gallaudet University Press, pg 76
Gareth Stevens Publishing, pg 76
GeoLytics Inc, pg 77
Gingko Press Inc, pg 78
Greenhaven Publishing, pg 81
Greenleaf Book Group LLC, pg 81
The Guilford Press, pg 82
Hamilton Books, pg 84
Hannacroix Creek Books Inc, pg 85
Harvard Education Publishing Group, pg 88
Harvard University Press, pg 88
Hay House LLC, pg 89
Health Professions Press, pg 90
William S Hein & Co Inc, pg 90
Hippocrene Books Inc, pg 92
History Publishing Co LLC, pg 93
Histria Books, pg 93
Hogrefe Publishing Corp, pg 93
Houghton Mifflin Harcourt, pg 95
Housing Assistance Council, pg 97
Human Rights Watch, pg 97
IHS Press, pg 98
In the Garden Publishing, pg 99
Independent Institute, pg 99
Indiana University Press, pg 100
Information Age Publishing Inc, pg 100
Inner Traditions International Ltd, pg 101
Inter-University Consortium for Political & Social Research (ICPSR), pg 102
The International Institute of Islamic Thought, pg 103
International Publishers Co Inc, pg 103
Jain Publishing Co, pg 105
Jump!, pg 107
Jessica Kingsley Publishers Inc, pg 110
Krieger Publishing Co, pg 111
Kumarian Press, pg 112
Peter Lang Publishing Inc, pg 112
LARB Books, pg 113
Lehigh University Press, pg 114
Lexington Books, pg 115
Liberty Fund Inc, pg 116
Mary Ann Liebert Inc, pg 116
Little, Brown and Company, pg 118
Lorenz Educational Press, pg 120
Louisiana State University Press, pg 120
Macmillan Learning, pg 123
Macmillan Reference USA™, pg 123
Mastery Education, pg 126
Mazda Publishers Inc, pg 127
McFarland, pg 127
McGraw-Hill Create, pg 127
McGraw-Hill Education, pg 127
McGraw-Hill Higher Education, pg 128
McGraw-Hill School Education Group, pg 128
The Edwin Mellen Press, pg 129
Michigan State University Press (MSU Press), pg 130
Milliken Publishing Co, pg 132
The MIT Press, pg 132
Monthly Review Press, pg 134
De Gruyter Mouton, pg 135
NASW Press, pg 136
National Academies Press (NAP), pg 136
National Catholic Educational Association, pg 137
National Center for Children in Poverty, pg 137
National Geographic Learning, pg 138
The New Press, pg 140
New York Academy of Sciences (NYAS), pg 140
New York University Press, pg 141
North Atlantic Books (NAB), pg 142
Northern Illinois University Press, pg 143
W W Norton & Company Inc, pg 143
Nova Science Publishers Inc, pg 144
Nystrom Education, pg 144
Ocean Tree Books, pg 145
Odyssey Books, pg 145
OECD Washington Center, pg 145
Ohio University Press, pg 145
Omnigraphics Inc, pg 146
On the Write Path Publishing, pg 146
The Original Falcon Press, pg 148
ORO editions, pg 148
Other Press, pg 148
Oxford University Press USA, pg 149
Palgrave Macmillan, pg 150
Pangaea Publications, pg 150
Paragon House, pg 151
Parallax Press, pg 151
Pearson Business Publishing, pg 153
Pelican Publishing, pg 153
Penguin Publishing Group, pg 154
Penn State University Press, pg 157
Pennsylvania Historical & Museum Commission, pg 157
Pennsylvania State Data Center, pg 157
Peradam Press, pg 158
Philosophical Library Inc, pg 159
Polar Bear & Company, pg 161
Police Executive Research Forum, pg 162
Princeton University Press, pg 164
Progressive Press, pg 165
Prometheus Books, pg 166
Purdue University Press, pg 167
RAND Corp, pg 169
Rational Island Publishers, pg 171
The Red Sea Press Inc, pg 173
ReferencePoint Press Inc, pg 173
Regnery Publishing, pg 174
Research & Education Association (REA), pg 174
Lynne Rienner Publishers Inc, pg 174
The Rosen Publishing Group Inc, pg 177
Routledge, pg 177
Rowman & Littlefield, pg 178
Russell Sage Foundation, pg 178
Rutgers University Press, pg 178
Safer Society Press, pg 179
SAGE Publishing, pg 180
Salem Press, pg 181
Salina Bookshelf Inc, pg 181
SAS Press, pg 182
Schlager Group Inc, pg 183

U.S. PUBLISHERS — SUBJECT INDEX

BOOK

Scholastic Education Solutions, pg 184
School for Advanced Research Press, pg 185
Schreiber Publishing, pg 185
Science & Humanities Press, pg 185
Science History Publications USA Inc, pg 185
Sentient Publications LLC, pg 186
Seven Stories Press, pg 186
Sourced Media Books, pg 195
Springer Publishing Co, pg 196
Stanford University Press, pg 197
Star Bright Books Inc, pg 197
SteinerBooks Inc, pg 198
STM Learning Inc, pg 199
Sun Publishing Company, pg 200
Sundance/Newbridge Publishing, pg 200
Syracuse University Press, pg 201
Tantor Media Inc, pg 202
Tapestry Press Ltd, pg 202
Taylor & Francis Inc, pg 203
Teacher Created Resources Inc, pg 203
Temple University Press, pg 204
Texas A&M University Press, pg 205
University of Texas Press, pg 205
Third World Press Foundation, pg 206
Charles C Thomas Publisher Ltd, pg 206
Todd Publications, pg 207
Treehaus Communications Inc, pg 209
TSG Publishing Foundation Inc, pg 210
Tughra Books, pg 210
Tuttle Publishing, pg 211
Twenty-First Century Books, pg 211
UCLA Latin American Center Publications, pg 212
United Nations Publications, pg 213
University of California Press, pg 215
University of Chicago Press, pg 215
University of Georgia Press, pg 216
University of Hawaii Press, pg 216
University of Illinois Press, pg 216
University of Massachusetts Press, pg 217
University of Minnesota Press, pg 217
University of Nevada Press, pg 218
The University of North Carolina Press, pg 218
University of North Texas Press, pg 218
University of Notre Dame Press, pg 219
University of Pennsylvania Press, pg 219
University of Rochester Press, pg 220
The University of Utah Press, pg 220
University Press of America Inc, pg 221
University Press of Colorado, pg 221
The University Press of Kentucky, pg 222
University Press of Mississippi, pg 222
US Government Publishing Office (GPO), pg 223
Vanderbilt University Press, pg 224
Vernon Press, pg 224
Verso Books, pg 224
Walch Education, pg 225
Waveland Press Inc, pg 226

Eliot Werner Publications Inc, pg 227
Whittier Publications Inc, pg 229
Wiley-Blackwell, pg 229
John Wiley & Sons Inc, pg 230
John Wiley & Sons Inc Global Education, pg 230
John Wiley & Sons Inc Professional Development, pg 230
William Carey Publishing, pg 230
Wisconsin Department of Public Instruction, pg 231
Woodrow Wilson Center Press, pg 232
World Bank Publications, pg 233
World Citizens, pg 233
Worth Publishers, pg 234
Yale University Press, pg 235
YMAA Publication Center Inc, pg 235
Zondervan, pg 236
Zone Books, pg 237

SPORTS, ATHLETICS

Abbeville Press, pg 1
Abbeville Publishing Group, pg 2
ABDO, pg 2
ACTA Publications, pg 4
Akashic Books, pg 6
American Alpine Club, pg 8
American Ridge, pg 11
Appalachian Mountain Club Books, pg 15
Ascend Books LLC, pg 18
AuthorHouse, pg 22
Bancroft Press, pg 24
Beaver's Pond Press Inc, pg 26
Black Rabbit Books, pg 30
The Blackburn Press, pg 30
Blue Note Publications Inc, pg 32
Book Sales, pg 33
BookLogix, pg 34
Breakaway Books, pg 36
Brilliance Publishing Inc, pg 37
Brown Books Publishing Group (BBPG), pg 38
Burford Books, pg 38
Capstone Publishers™, pg 40
Cardoza Publishing, pg 40
Carolina Academic Press, pg 41
Cedar Grove Publishing, pg 43
Cedar Tree Books, pg 43
Cengage Learning, pg 43
Chelsea House, pg 45
Child's Play® Inc, pg 46
The Child's World Inc, pg 46
China Books, pg 47
Christian Schools International (CSI), pg 47
Chronicle Books LLC, pg 47
Clerisy Press, pg 49
Coaches Choice, pg 50
Crabtree Publishing Co, pg 54
Creative Editions, pg 55
Walter De Gruyter Inc, pg 58
DEStech Publications Inc, pg 59
Diversion Books, pg 60
DK, pg 60
Doubleday, pg 61
Dragon Door Publications, pg 61
Eakin Press, pg 62
Eastland Press, pg 63
EDC Publishing, pg 63
Enslow Publishing LLC, pg 66
M Evans & Company, pg 68
Facts On File, pg 69
First Avenue Editions, pg 72
Fox Chapel Publishing Co Inc, pg 74
Gale, pg 75
Gallery Books, pg 76
Gingko Press Inc, pg 78

The Globe Pequot Press, pg 79
Gray & Company Publishers, pg 80
Greenleaf Book Group LLC, pg 80
Grey House Publishing Inc™, pg 81
HarperCollins Children's Books, pg 85
HarperCollins Publishers LLC, pg 86
Hatherleigh Press Ltd, pg 88
Histria Books, pg 93
Houghton Mifflin Harcourt Trade & Reference Division, pg 96
Human Kinetics Inc, pg 97
Inter-University Consortium for Political & Social Research (ICPSR), pg 102
Jump!, pg 107
Krause Publications Inc, pg 111
Lasaria Creative Publishing, pg 113
Leaf Storm Press, pg 113
Learning Links-USA Inc, pg 114
Lee & Low Books Inc, pg 114
Lerner Publications, pg 115
Listen & Live Audio Inc, pg 117
The Lyons Press, pg 121
Macmillan Reference USA™, pg 123
Mason Crest Publishers, pg 126
McBooks Press, pg 127
McFarland, pg 127
Menasha Ridge Press, pg 129
Mitchell Lane Publishers Inc, pg 133
Mountaineers Books, pg 135
De Gruyter Mouton, pg 135
National Golf Foundation, pg 138
North Star Editions Inc, pg 142
Norwood House Press, pg 143
Octane Press, pg 145
On the Write Path Publishing, pg 146
Orange Frazer Press Inc, pg 147
Pelican Publishing, pg 153
Plunkett Research Ltd, pg 161
Pocol Press, pg 161
ProStar Publications Inc, pg 166
Publications International Ltd (PIL), pg 167
Quarto Publishing Group USA Inc, pg 168
Reedswain Inc, pg 173
Referee Books, pg 173
Riverdale Avenue Books (RAB), pg 175
Rizzoli International Publications Inc, pg 175
Routledge, pg 177
Running Press, pg 178
Rutgers University Press, pg 178
Safari Press, pg 179
Sagamore Publishing LLC, pg 179
St Johann Press, pg 180
St Martin's Press, LLC, pg 180
SAMS Technical Publishing LLC, pg 181
Santa Monica Press LLC, pg 182
Schaffner Press, pg 183
Schiffer Publishing Ltd, pg 183
Scholastic Inc, pg 184
Seven Stories Press, pg 186
Sourcebooks LLC, pg 194
South Dakota Historical Society Press, pg 195
Stipes Publishing LLC, pg 198
Strategic Book Publishing (SBP), pg 199
Sunstone Press, pg 201
Syracuse University Press, pg 201
Tantor Media Inc, pg 202
Temple University Press, pg 204
Texas Tech University Press, pg 205
Tracks Publishing, pg 208
Trafalgar Square Books, pg 208

Trans-Atlantic Publications Inc, pg 209
Triumph Books LLC, pg 209
Tuttle Publishing, pg 211
Tuxedo Press, pg 211
Twenty-First Century Books, pg 211
Union Square & Co, pg 212
Universe Publishing, pg 214
The University of Arkansas Press, pg 214
University of Illinois Press, pg 216
University of Iowa Press, pg 216
University of Missouri Press, pg 217
University of Nebraska Press, pg 217
University of North Texas Press, pg 218
University of Wisconsin Press, pg 221
University Press of Mississippi, pg 222
Vintage Books, pg 225
Watermark Publishing, pg 226
West Margin Press, pg 227
Wilderness Adventures Press Inc, pg 229
Workman Publishing, pg 232
World Citizens, pg 233
Xlibris Corp, pg 234
YMAA Publication Center Inc, pg 235

TECHNOLOGY

A-R Editions Inc, pg 1
Academic Press, pg 3
Advance Publishing Inc, pg 5
Adventures Unlimited Press (AUP), pg 5
AICPA® & CIMA®, pg 5
ALA Neal-Schuman, pg 6
The American Ceramic Society, pg 9
American Institute of Aeronautics and Astronautics (AIAA), pg 10
American Institute of Chemical Engineers (AIChE), pg 10
The American Library Association (ALA), pg 10
American Society for Nondestructive Testing, pg 12
American Water Works Association (AWWA), pg 13
APH Press, pg 15
Artech House®, pg 17
ASET - The Neurodiagnostic Society, pg 18
ASTM International, pg 20
Astragal Press, pg 20
Atlantic Publishing Group Inc, pg 21
Atlas Publishing, pg 21
AuthorHouse, pg 22
Avant-Guide, pg 22
Begell House Inc Publishers, pg 27
Bisk Education, pg 29
Black Rabbit Books, pg 30
The Blackburn Press, pg 30
Brewers Publications, pg 36
Bridge Publications Inc, pg 36
Brilliance Publishing Inc, pg 37
Cato Institute, pg 42
Cengage Learning, pg 43
Center for Strategic & International Studies (CSIS), pg 44
Charles River Media, pg 45
The Child's World Inc, pg 46
Cognizant Communication Corp, pg 50
Crabtree Publishing Co, pg 54
Craftsman Book Co, pg 54
CRC Press, pg 55

Data Trace Publishing Co (DTP), pg 57
DEStech Publications Inc, pg 59
DiscoverNet Publishing, pg 59
EDC Publishing, pg 63
The Electrochemical Society (ECS), pg 65
Elsevier Inc, pg 65
Enslow Publishing LLC, pg 66
Financial Times Press, pg 71
Gale, pg 75
Goodheart-Willcox Publisher, pg 79
Greenleaf Book Group LLC, pg 81
Grey House Publishing Inc™, pg 81
Hanser Publications LLC, pg 85
Harvard Business Review Press, pg 87
Harvard University Press, pg 88
IEEE Computer Society, pg 98
IEEE Press, pg 98
IET USA Inc, pg 98
Illuminating Engineering Society of North America (IES), pg 99
Indiana University African Studies Program, pg 100
Industrial Press Inc, pg 100
Information Age Publishing Inc, pg 100
Information Gatekeepers Inc (IGI), pg 100
Information Today, Inc, pg 100
Institute of Environmental Sciences & Technology - IEST, pg 101
International Literacy Association (ILA), pg 103
International Society for Technology in Education, pg 103
International Society of Automation (ISA), pg 103
Johns Hopkins University Press, pg 106
Joshua Tree Publishing, pg 107
Jump!, pg 107
Kogan Page, pg 111
Koho Pono LLC, pg 111
Krieger Publishing Co, pg 111
LAMA Books, pg 112
Lehigh University Press, pg 114
The Lentz Leadership Institute LLC, pg 115
Lerner Publications, pg 115
Mary Ann Liebert Inc, pg 116
Macmillan Reference USA™, pg 123
Management Advisory Services & Publications (MASP), pg 123
McGraw-Hill Education, pg 127
McGraw-Hill Professional Publishing Group, pg 128
McGraw-Hill School Education Group, pg 128
Military Info Publishing, pg 131
The Minerals, Metals & Materials Society (TMS), pg 132
The MIT Press, pg 132
Moonshine Cove Publishing LLC, pg 134
NACE International, pg 136
Nataraj Books, pg 136
National Academies Press (NAP), pg 136
National Association of Broadcasters (NAB), pg 136
National Braille Press, pg 137
National Council of Teachers of Mathematics (NCTM), pg 137
National Information Standards Organization (NISO), pg 138
National Science Teachers Association (NSTA), pg 138
New York Academy of Sciences (NYAS), pg 140
No Starch Press, pg 141

North Star Editions Inc, pg 142
Norwood House Press, pg 143
OECD Washington Center, pg 145
ORO editions, pg 148
Pantheon Books, pg 150
Peachpit Press, pg 153
Pearson Business Publishing, pg 153
Penn State University Press, pg 157
Petroleum Extension Service (PETEX), pg 159
Plunkett Research Ltd, pg 161
Portfolio, pg 162
PRINTING United Alliance, pg 165
Productivity Press, pg 165
Purdue University Press, pg 167
RAND Corp, pg 169
Rodin Books, pg 176
Ross Books, pg 177
Rothstein Associates Inc, pg 177
Rutgers University Press, pg 178
SAE (Society of Automotive Engineers International), pg 179
SAGE Publishing, pg 180
SAS Press, pg 182
Savvas Learning Co LLC, pg 183
Scholastic Education Solutions, pg 184
Science & Humanities Press, pg 185
SME (Society of Manufacturing Engineers), pg 191
Society for Mining, Metallurgy & Exploration, pg 192
SPIE, pg 196
Stanford University Press, pg 197
SYBEX, pg 201
Tachyon Publications LLC, pg 202
Tantor Media Inc, pg 202
Teacher Created Resources Inc, pg 203
TotalRecall Publications Inc, pg 208
Trans-Atlantic Publications Inc, pg 209
Tumblehome Learning Inc, pg 210
Union Square & Co, pg 212
Univelt Inc, pg 213
University of Massachusetts Press, pg 217
University of North Texas Press, pg 218
University Press of Florida, pg 221
Vault.com Inc, pg 224
John Wiley & Sons Inc Professional Development, pg 230
Wisconsin Department of Public Instruction, pg 231
Wolters Kluwer US Corp, pg 232
World Bank Publications, pg 233
Write Stuff Enterprises LLC, pg 234
XML Press, pg 235

THEOLOGY

Abingdon Press, pg 2
Academica Press, pg 3
ACU Press, pg 4
Alexander Street, part of Clarivate PLC, pg 6
Ambassador International, pg 7
American Bible Society, pg 8
American Catholic Press (ACP), pg 9
Andrews University Press, pg 14
Angelus Press, pg 14
Augsburg Fortress Publishers, Publishing House of the Evangelical Lutheran Church in America, pg 22
AuthorHouse, pg 22
Baha'i Publishing Trust, pg 23
Baker Books, pg 23
Baylor University Press, pg 25

Beacon Hill Press of Kansas City, pg 25
Ben Yehuda Press, pg 27
Bethany House Publishers, pg 29
Bhaktivedanta Book Trust (BBT), pg 29
BJU Press, pg 30
Bloomsbury Academic, pg 31
The Book Tree, pg 34
Bridge Logos Inc, pg 36
Brilliance Publishing Inc, pg 37
Casa Bautista de Publicaciones, pg 41
The Catholic Health Association of the United States, pg 42
The Catholic University of America Press, pg 42
Chalice Press, pg 44
Charles Press Publishers, pg 45
Cistercian Publications, pg 48
Concordia Publishing House, pg 51
Council for Research in Values & Philosophy, pg 53
Counterpoint Press LLC, pg 54
The Crossroad Publishing Co, pg 55
Crossway, pg 56
Walter De Gruyter Inc, pg 58
Deep River Books LLC, pg 58
Destiny Image Inc, pg 59
Dordt Press, pg 60
ECS Publishing Group, pg 63
Editorial Bautista Independiente, pg 63
Editorial Portavoz, pg 64
Editorial Unilit, pg 64
Wm B Eerdmans Publishing Co, pg 64
Eisenbrauns, pg 64
Emmaus Road Publishing Inc, pg 66
Faith Library Publications, pg 69
Fifth Estate Publishing, pg 71
Fine Creative Media, Inc, pg 71
Focus, pg 73
Fordham University Press, pg 73
Forward Movement, pg 73
Franciscan Media, pg 74
Friends United Press, pg 75
Gale, pg 75
Georgetown University Press, pg 77
Hamilton Books, pg 84
HarperCollins Publishers LLC, pg 86
Hebrew Union College Press, pg 90
Hendrickson Publishers Inc, pg 91
Herald Press, pg 91
Histria Books, pg 93
Hohm Press, pg 93
Holmes Publishing Group LLC, pg 94
Humanix Books LLC, pg 97
Ignatius Press, pg 98
Institute of Jesuit Sources (IJS), pg 102
InterVarsity Press, pg 104
Jewish Lights Publishing, pg 105
The Jewish Publication Society, pg 105
Judson Press, pg 107
Kregel Publications, pg 111
Peter Lang Publishing Inc, pg 112
Lexington Books, pg 115
Liguori Publications, pg 117
Macmillan Reference USA™, pg 123
Marquette University Press, pg 125
The Edwin Mellen Press, pg 129
Mercer University Press, pg 129
De Gruyter Mouton, pg 135
Moznaim Publishing Corp, pg 135
Multnomah, pg 135
Nataraj Books, pg 136

National Catholic Educational Association, pg 137
NavPress Publishing Group, pg 139
New City Press, pg 139
North Atlantic Books (NAB), pg 142
Ocean Tree Books, pg 145
On the Write Path Publishing, pg 146
Orbis Books, pg 147
The Original Falcon Press, pg 148
Oxford University Press USA, pg 149
P & R Publishing Co, pg 149
Palgrave Macmillan, pg 150
Pauline Books & Media, pg 152
Paulist Press, pg 152
Pentecostal Resources Group, pg 157
Peradam Press, pg 158
Pflaum Publishing Group, pg 159
The Pilgrim Press/United Church Press, pg 160
Polebridge Press, pg 161
Recorded Books Inc, an RBmedia company, pg 172
Rod & Staff Publishers Inc, pg 176
Ross Books, pg 177
Rowman & Littlefield, pg 178
William H Sadlier Inc, pg 179
SAGE Publishing, pg 180
St Augustine's Press Inc, pg 180
St Herman Press, pg 180
St Johann Press, pg 180
St Nectarios Press, pg 181
St Pauls, pg 181
Signalman Publishing, pg 187
Signature Books Publishing LLC, pg 187
SIL International, pg 188
Skinner House Books, pg 190
SkyLight Paths® Publishing, pg 191
Somerset Hall Press, pg 193
Sophia Institute Press®, pg 193
SteinerBooks Inc, pg 198
Swedenborg Foundation, pg 201
TAN Books, pg 202
T&T Clark International, pg 202
Tantor Media Inc, pg 202
Theosophical University Press, pg 206
The Trinity Foundation, pg 209
TSG Publishing Foundation Inc, pg 210
Tughra Books, pg 210
Twenty-Third Publications, pg 211
Tyndale House Publishers Inc, pg 211
University of Chicago Press, pg 215
University of Notre Dame Press, pg 219
University Press of America Inc, pg 221
US Conference of Catholic Bishops, pg 223
Vernon Press, pg 224
WaterBrook, pg 226
Wesleyan Publishing House, pg 227
Westminster John Knox Press (WJK), pg 228
Whitaker House, pg 228
Wiley-Blackwell, pg 229
William Carey Publishing, pg 230
Yale University Press, pg 235
YBK Publishers Inc, pg 235
YWAM Publishing, pg 236
Zondervan, pg 236

TRANSPORTATION

American Public Works Association (APWA), pg 12
APC Publishing, pg 15

Arcadia Publishing Inc, pg 16
Artech House®, pg 17
AuthorHouse, pg 22
Bentley Publishers, pg 28
BiG GUY BOOKS, pg 29
Black Dome Press Corp, pg 30
Black Rabbit Books, pg 30
Book Sales, pg 33
Capstone Publishers™, pg 40
CarTech Inc, pg 41
Charlesbridge Publishing Inc, pg 45
Chelsea House, pg 45
Cornell Maritime Press, pg 52
DK, pg 60
Dover Publications Inc, pg 61
EDC Publishing, pg 63
Edward Elgar Publishing Inc, pg 65
Enslow Publishing LLC, pg 66
Fordham University Press, pg 73
Gale, pg 75
Goodheart-Willcox Publisher, pg 79
Grey House Publishing Inc™, pg 81
Indiana Historical Society Press, pg 99
Indiana University Press, pg 100
Institute of Police Technology & Management (IPTM), pg 102
Lyndon B Johnson School of Public Affairs, pg 106
Kalmbach Media Co, pg 108
J J Keller & Associates, Inc®, pg 108
Kogan Page, pg 111
Loft Press Inc, pg 119
Marine Education Textbooks, pg 125
Marine Techniques Publishing, pg 125
McFarland, pg 127
Morning Sun Books Inc, pg 134
National Academies Press (NAP), pg 136
North Star Editions Inc, pg 142
Northern Illinois University Press, pg 143
Norwood House Press, pg 143
OAG Worldwide, pg 144
Octane Press, pg 145
OECD Washington Center, pg 145
ORO editions, pg 148
Pennsylvania Historical & Museum Commission, pg 157
Pennsylvania State Data Center, pg 157
Quarto Publishing Group USA Inc, pg 168
RAND Corp, pg 169
Saddleback Educational Publishing, pg 179
SAMS Technical Publishing LLC, pg 181
Science & Humanities Press, pg 185
Solano Press Books, pg 193
South Platte Press, pg 195
Strategic Book Publishing (SBP), pg 199
Tantor Media Inc, pg 202
Tide-mark Press, pg 207
Transportation Research Board (TRB), pg 209
Union Square & Co, pg 212
United Nations Publications, pg 213
University of Iowa Press, pg 216
US Government Publishing Office (GPO), pg 223
Washington State University Press, pg 226
World Bank Publications, pg 233
Write Stuff Enterprises LLC, pg 234
Xlibris Corp, pg 234

TRAVEL & TOURISM

Abbeville Press, pg 1
Abbeville Publishing Group, pg 2
AdventureKEEN, pg 5
Adventures Unlimited Press (AUP), pg 5
Anaphora Literary Press, pg 13
APC Publishing, pg 15
Appalachian Mountain Club Books, pg 15
Arcade Publishing Inc, pg 16
Art of Living, PrimaMedia Inc, pg 17
Atlantic Publishing Group Inc, pg 21
AuthorHouse, pg 22
Avant-Guide, pg 22
Beaver's Pond Press Inc, pg 26
Berghahn Books, pg 28
BiG GUY BOOKS, pg 29
Blair, pg 30
Nicholas Brealey Publishing, pg 36
Burford Books, pg 38
Camino Books Inc, pg 39
Capen Publishing Co Inc, pg 40
Chelsea Green Publishing Co, pg 45
China Books, pg 47
Chronicle Books LLC, pg 47
Cognizant Communication Corp, pg 50
Continental AfrikaPublishers, pg 52
Countryman Press, pg 54
DK, pg 60
The Donning Company Publishers, pg 60
Doubleday, pg 61
Dover Publications Inc, pg 61
Down East Books, pg 61
Down The Shore Publishing, pg 61
Duke University Press, pg 62
East West Discovery Press, pg 63
EDC Publishing, pg 63
Elderberry Press Inc, pg 65
Elsevier Inc, pg 65
Epicenter Press Inc, pg 67
Everything Goes Media LLC, pg 68
FineEdge.com LLC, pg 72
Fox Chapel Publishing Co Inc, pg 74
Frederick Fell Publishers Inc, pg 74
Fulcrum Publishing Inc, pg 75
Gale, pg 75
Gibbs Smith Publisher, pg 78
Gingko Press Inc, pg 78
Glitterati Inc, pg 78
Global Authors Publications (GAP), pg 78
The Globe Pequot Press, pg 79
Golden West Cookbooks, pg 79
Gorgias Press LLC, pg 80
Gray & Company Publishers, pg 80
Greenleaf Book Group LLC, pg 81
Grove Atlantic Inc, pg 82
Hellgate Press, pg 91
Heyday, pg 91
Hippocrene Books Inc, pg 92
Histria Books, pg 93
Hollym International Corp, pg 94
Homa & Sekey Books, pg 95
Homestead Publishing, pg 95
Huntington Press Publishing, pg 97
Impact Publications/Development Concepts Inc, pg 99
Islandport Press, pg 105
Italica Press, pg 105
Jewish Lights Publishing, pg 105
Kalmbach Media Co, pg 108
Klutz®, pg 110
Alfred A Knopf, pg 110
Kodansha USA Inc, pg 110
Kogan Page, pg 111
Lake Superior Publishing LLC, pg 112
Leaf Storm Press, pg 113
Legacy Bound, pg 114
Listen & Live Audio Inc, pg 117
Little, Brown and Company, pg 118
Lonely Planet Publications Inc, pg 120
Macmillan Reference USA™, pg 123
Mage Publishers Inc, pg 123
MapEasy Inc, pg 124
Mazda Publishers Inc, pg 127
The McDonald & Woodward Publishing Co, pg 127
Menasha Ridge Press, pg 129
Michelin Maps & Guides, pg 130
Military Living Publications, pg 131
Monthly Review Press, pg 134
Mountaineers Books, pg 135
Multnomah, pg 135
Nataraj Books, pg 136
National Geographic Books, pg 137
National Golf Foundation, pg 138
North Atlantic Books (NAB), pg 142
North Point Press, pg 142
North Star Editions Inc, pg 142
W W Norton & Company Inc, pg 143
OAG Worldwide, pg 144
Ocean Tree Books, pg 145
Octane Press, pg 145
Omnigraphics Inc, pg 146
On the Write Path Publishing, pg 146
Open Horizons Publishing Co, pg 147
Orange Frazer Press Inc, pg 147
ORO editions, pg 148
PA Press, pg 149
Pangaea Publications, pg 150
Pants On Fire Press, pg 150
Park Place Publications, pg 152
Pearson Business Publishing, pg 153
Pelican Publishing, pg 153
Penguin Publishing Group, pg 154
Peter Pauper Press, Inc, pg 158
Phaidon, pg 159
Pineapple Press, pg 160
Plunkett Research Ltd, pg 161
Primary Research Group Inc, pg 163
ProStar Publications Inc, pg 166
Publication Consultants, pg 167
Publications International Ltd (PIL), pg 167
Rand McNally, pg 169
Reader's Digest Trade Publishing, pg 172
Rio Nuevo Publishers, pg 175
River City Publishing, pg 175
Running Press, pg 178
Rutgers University Press, pg 178
Safari Press, pg 179
St Martin's Press, LLC, pg 180
St Nectarios Press, pg 181
Santa Monica Press LLC, pg 182
Sasquatch Books, pg 182
Schaffner Press, pg 183
Science & Humanities Press, pg 185
Sentient Publications LLC, pg 186
Soho Press Inc, pg 193
South Dakota Historical Society Press, pg 195
Stone Bridge Press Inc, pg 199
Storyworkz Inc, pg 199
Strategic Book Publishing (SBP), pg 199
Stylus Publishing LLC, pg 200
Summertime Publications Inc, pg 200
Sunbelt Publications Inc, pg 200
Nan A Talese, pg 202
Tantor Media Inc, pg 202
Ten Speed Press, pg 204
TotalRecall Publications Inc, pg 208
Travelers' Tales, pg 209
Tuttle Publishing, pg 211
Union Square & Co, pg 212
Universe Publishing, pg 214
The University of Arizona Press, pg 214
University of Hawaii Press, pg 216
University of Iowa Press, pg 216
University of North Texas Press, pg 218
University of Tennessee Press, pg 220
University of Wisconsin Press, pg 221
University Press of Mississippi, pg 222
US Government Publishing Office (GPO), pg 223
VanDam Inc, pg 223
Vintage Books, pg 225
WaterBrook, pg 226
Watermark Publishing, pg 226
Welcome Rain Publishers LLC, pg 227
West Margin Press, pg 227
Western Reflections Publishing Co, pg 228
Wheatherstone Press, pg 228
Wide World of Maps Inc, pg 229
Wide World Publishing, pg 229
Wilderness Adventures Press Inc, pg 229
Wildflower Press, pg 229
Willow Creek Press, pg 230
Winters Publishing, pg 231
World Trade Press LLC, pg 234
Xlibris Corp, pg 234
Zagat Inc, pg 236

VETERINARY SCIENCE

A 2 Z Press LLC, pg 1
Academic Press, pg 3
AuthorHouse, pg 22
Carolina Academic Press, pg 41
Charles Press Publishers, pg 45
Clinical and Laboratory Standards Institute (CLSI), pg 49
Elsevier Health Sciences, pg 65
Gale, pg 75
W D Hoard & Sons Co, pg 93
Krieger Publishing Co, pg 111
Macmillan Reference USA™, pg 123
Purdue University Press, pg 167
SAGE Publishing, pg 180
Stylus Publishing LLC, pg 200
Teton NewMedia Inc, pg 205
Texas A&M University Press, pg 205
Charles C Thomas Publisher Ltd, pg 206
Trafalgar Square Books, pg 208
John Wiley & Sons Inc, pg 230
John Wiley & Sons Inc Global Education, pg 230
John Wiley & Sons Inc Professional Development, pg 230

WESTERN FICTION

Anaphora Literary Press, pg 13
AuthorHouse, pg 22
Berkley, pg 28
Bethany House Publishers, pg 29
Bold Strokes Books Inc, pg 33
Book Sales, pg 33
BookLogix, pg 34

Boson Books™, pg 34
Brilliance Publishing Inc, pg 37
Brown Books Publishing Group (BBPG), pg 38
Cedar Fort Inc, pg 43
Chickadee Prince Books LLC, pg 46
Clear Light Publishers, pg 49
Dover Publications Inc, pg 61
Epicenter Press Inc, pg 67
Fulcrum Publishing Inc, pg 75
Galaxy Press Inc, pg 75
Gale, pg 75
Goose River Press, pg 79
Greenleaf Book Group LLC, pg 81
History Publishing Co LLC, pg 93
Histria Books, pg 93
Homestead Publishing, pg 95
Houghton Mifflin Harcourt, pg 95
Iron Stream Media, pg 104
Kensington Publishing Corp, pg 109
Lasaria Creative Publishing, pg 113
On the Write Path Publishing, pg 146
Pen-L Publishing, pg 153
Pentecostal Resources Group, pg 157
Pocol Press, pg 161
Raven Publishing Inc, pg 172
Recorded Books Inc, an RBmedia company, pg 172
The RoadRunner Press, pg 175
Royal Fireworks Press, pg 178
Savant Books & Publications LLC, pg 182
Scarsdale Publishing Ltd, pg 183
Science & Humanities Press, pg 185
Somerset Hall Press, pg 193
Strategic Book Publishing (SBP), pg 199
Sunstone Press, pg 201
Tantor Media Inc, pg 202
Tor Publishing Group, pg 207
Tyndale House Publishers Inc, pg 211
University of Nebraska Press, pg 217
University of Nevada Press, pg 218
Washington State University Press, pg 226
Wildflower Press, pg 229
Xlibris Corp, pg 234
Zumaya Publications LLC, pg 237

WINE & SPIRITS

Abbeville Publishing Group, pg 2
ACC Art Books, pg 3
ANR Publications University of California, pg 14
Art of Living, PrimaMedia Inc, pg 17
Atlantic Publishing Group Inc, pg 21
AuthorHouse, pg 22
Berkshire Publishing Group LLC, pg 28
Book Sales, pg 33
Brewers Publications, pg 36
Brick Tower Press, pg 36
Brown Books Publishing Group (BBPG), pg 38
Burford Books, pg 38
Chronicle Books LLC, pg 47
Cider Mill Press Book Publishers LLC, pg 48
Cognizant Communication Corp, pg 50
Countryman Press, pg 54
DK, pg 60
Dutton, pg 62
Fox Chapel Publishing Co Inc, pg 74

Greenleaf Book Group LLC, pg 81
W W Norton & Company Inc, pg 143
Potomac Books, pg 162
Clarkson Potter, pg 162
Rizzoli International Publications Inc, pg 175
Sasquatch Books, pg 182
Sourcebooks LLC, pg 194
StarGroup International Inc, pg 197
Tantor Media Inc, pg 202
Ten Speed Press, pg 204
Union Square & Co, pg 212
University of California Press, pg 215
West Margin Press, pg 227
Willow Creek Press, pg 230

WOMEN'S STUDIES

Abbeville Press, pg 1
Abbeville Publishing Group, pg 2
Abingdon Press, pg 2
Academica Press, pg 3
Africa World Press Inc, pg 5
AK Press, pg 6
Akashic Books, pg 6
Alexander Street, part of Clarivate PLC, pg 6
All Things That Matter Press, pg 7
American Carriage House Publishing (ACHP), pg 8
American Correctional Association, pg 9
Ampersand Inc/Professional Publishing Services, pg 13
Anaphora Literary Press, pg 13
Ariadne Press, pg 16
Arte Publico Press, pg 17
Ash Tree Publishing, pg 18
Asta Publications LLC, pg 20
AuthorHouse, pg 22
Authorlink® Press, pg 22
Barringer Publishing, pg 24
Barrytown/Station Hill Press, pg 24
Baylor University Press, pg 25
Beacon Press, pg 25
Bear & Co Inc, pg 26
Beaver's Pond Press Inc, pg 26
Begell House Inc Publishers, pg 27
Bella Books, pg 27
Bellerophon Books, pg 27
Berghahn Books, pg 28
Berkshire Publishing Group LLC, pg 28
The Blackburn Press, pg 30
Bloomsbury Academic, pg 31
Blue Crane Books Inc, pg 32
Blue Mountain Arts Inc, pg 32
BookLogix, pg 34
Bottom Dog Press, pg 34
Brandylane Publishers Inc, pg 35
Bridge Logos Inc, pg 36
Brown Books Publishing Group (BBPG), pg 38
Bucknell University Press, pg 38
Carolina Academic Press, pg 41
Chalice Press, pg 44
Charlesbridge Publishing Inc, pg 45
Chelsea House, pg 45
Chicago Review Press, pg 46
China Books, pg 47
City Lights Publishers, pg 48
Cleis Press, pg 49
Coffee House Press, pg 50
Cognizant Communication Corp, pg 50
Consumer Press, pg 52
Cornell University Press, pg 52
Counterpoint Press LLC, pg 54
Cross-Cultural Communications, pg 55
The Crossroad Publishing Co, pg 55

Deep River Books LLC, pg 58
Dover Publications Inc, pg 61
Duke University Press, pg 62
Eakin Press, pg 62
Editorial de la Universidad de Puerto Rico, pg 63
Educator's International Press Inc (EIP), pg 64
Elderberry Press Inc, pg 65
Edward Elgar Publishing Inc, pg 65
Enslow Publishing LLC, pg 66
Facts On File, pg 69
The Feminist Press at The City University of New York, pg 71
Fine Creative Media, Inc, pg 71
Focus, pg 73
Gale, pg 75
Gallaudet University Press, pg 76
Gifted Unlimited LLC, pg 78
Gorgias Press LLC, pg 80
Green Dragon Books, pg 81
Green Integer, pg 81
Greenleaf Book Group LLC, pg 81
Grove Atlantic Inc, pg 82
Hamilton Stone Editions, pg 84
Harvest House Publishers Inc, pg 88
Hay House LLC, pg 89
Hebrew Union College Press, pg 90
William S Hein & Co Inc, pg 90
Her Own Words LLC, pg 91
Heyday, pg 91
High Plains Press, pg 91
Histria Books, pg 93
Hohm Press, pg 93
Human Rights Watch, pg 97
Indiana Historical Society Press, pg 99
Indiana University Press, pg 100
Inner Traditions International Ltd, pg 101
International Publishers Co Inc, pg 103
Alice James Books, pg 105
Jewish Lights Publishing, pg 105
Judson Press, pg 107
Kazi Publications Inc, pg 108
Kelsey Street Press, pg 108
Koho Pono LLC, pg 111
Kumarian Press, pg 112
Larson Publications, pg 113
Lexington Books, pg 115
Liturgical Press, pg 118
Llewellyn Publications, pg 119
Long River Press, pg 120
Loving Healing Press Inc, pg 121
Macmillan Reference USA™, pg 123
Mage Publishers Inc, pg 123
Mandala Earth, pg 124
Mandel Vilar Press, pg 124
Manic D Press Inc, pg 124
Marshall Cavendish Education, pg 125
Maryland History Press, pg 126
McFarland, pg 127
McGraw-Hill Higher Education, pg 128
The Edwin Mellen Press, pg 129
Michigan State University Press (MSU Press), pg 130
Milford Books™, pg 131
Minnesota Historical Society Press, pg 132
Modern Language Association (MLA), pg 133
Monthly Review Press, pg 134
Nataraj Books, pg 136
National Academies Press (NAP), pg 136
National Golf Foundation, pg 138
Naval Institute Press, pg 139
New Harbinger Publications Inc, pg 140

The New Press, pg 140
New World Library, pg 140
New York University Press, pg 141
Northwestern University Press, pg 143
W W Norton & Company Inc, pg 143
Nova Science Publishers Inc, pg 144
The Ohio State University Press, pg 145
Ohio University Press, pg 145
On the Write Path Publishing, pg 146
Orbis Books, pg 147
Oxford University Press USA, pg 149
P & R Publishing Co, pg 149
Pace University Press, pg 149
Pantheon Books, pg 150
Paulist Press, pg 152
Pen-L Publishing, pg 153
Penn State University Press, pg 157
Pennsylvania State Data Center, pg 157
Persea Books, pg 158
The Pilgrim Press/United Church Press, pg 160
Platypus Media LLC, pg 160
Pleasure Boat Studio: A Literary Press, pg 160
Pocol Press, pg 161
Polebridge Press, pg 161
Pomegranate Communications Inc, pg 162
Potomac Books, pg 162
Princeton University Press, pg 164
Prometheus Books, pg 166
Rational Island Publishers, pg 171
Red Wheel/Weiser, pg 173
Robert D Reed Publishers, pg 173
Lynne Rienner Publishers Inc, pg 174
Riverdale Avenue Books (RAB), pg 175
Routledge, pg 177
Rowman & Littlefield, pg 178
Russell Sage Foundation, pg 178
Rutgers University Press, pg 178
SAGE Publishing, pg 180
St James Press®, pg 180
Salem Press, pg 181
Schaffner Press, pg 183
Sentient Publications LLC, pg 186
Seven Stories Press, pg 186
Shambhala Publications Inc, pg 187
Sherman Asher Publishing, pg 187
Signature Books Publishing LLC, pg 187
SkyLight Paths® Publishing, pg 191
Somerset Hall Press, pg 193
Sourcebooks LLC, pg 194
Southern Illinois University Press, pg 195
Springer Publishing Co, pg 196
SteinerBooks Inc, pg 198
Strategic Book Publishing (SBP), pg 199
Stylus Publishing LLC, pg 200
Sunstone Press, pg 201
Syracuse University Press, pg 201
T&T Clark International, pg 202
Tantor Media Inc, pg 202
TCU Press, pg 203
Teachers College Press, pg 203
Temple University Press, pg 204
Texas A&M University Press, pg 205
Texas Tech University Press, pg 205
Third World Press Foundation, pg 206
Travelers' Tales, pg 209

U.S. PUBLISHERS — SUBJECT INDEX

TSG Publishing Foundation Inc, pg 210
Tumblehome Learning Inc, pg 210
Tuttle Publishing, pg 211
UCLA Latin American Center Publications, pg 212
United Nations Publications, pg 213
Universe Publishing, pg 214
University of Alabama Press, pg 214
The University of Arkansas Press, pg 214
University of California Press, pg 215
University of Chicago Press, pg 215
University of Delaware Press, pg 215
University of Georgia Press, pg 216
University of Illinois Press, pg 216
University of Iowa Press, pg 216
University of Massachusetts Press, pg 217
University of Michigan Press, pg 217
University of Minnesota Press, pg 217
University of Missouri Press, pg 217
University of Nevada Press, pg 218
University of New Mexico Press, pg 218
The University of North Carolina Press, pg 218
University of North Texas Press, pg 218
University of Oklahoma Press, pg 219
University of Pittsburgh Press, pg 219
University of Rochester Press, pg 220
University of Washington Press, pg 220
University of Wisconsin Press, pg 221
University Press of America Inc, pg 221
University Press of Colorado, pg 221
University Press of Kansas, pg 221
University Press of Mississippi, pg 222
Urim Publications, pg 223
Vanderbilt University Press, pg 224
Vernon Press, pg 224
Verso Books, pg 224
Washington State University Press, pg 226
WaterBrook, pg 226
Waveland Press Inc, pg 226
Wayne State University Press, pg 226
Wesleyan University Press, pg 227
Westminster John Knox Press (WJK), pg 228
Wheatherstone Press, pg 228
White Pine Press, pg 228
Markus Wiener Publishers Inc, pg 229
Wiley-Blackwell, pg 229
Wings Press, pg 231
Wolfman Books, pg 232
Woodrow Wilson Center Press, pg 232
World Bank Publications, pg 233
World Citizens, pg 233
Yale University Press, pg 235
Zumaya Publications LLC, pg 237

Imprints, Subsidiaries & Distributors

A-R Editions Inc, *distributor for* AIM (American Institute of Musicology)

AAAI Press, *imprint of* Association for the Advancement of Artificial Intelligence, *distributed by* The MIT Press

AAH Graphics Inc, *subsidiary of* Loft Press Inc

A&D Xtreme, *imprint of* ABDO

AAP, *distributed by* Welcome Books

AAPG (American Association of Petroleum Geologists), *distributor for* Geological Society of London, *distributed by* Affiliated East-West Press Pvt Ltd, Canadian Society of Petroleum Geologists, Geological Society of London

AATEC Publications, *distributed by* Chelsea Green Publishing Co

Abbeville Kids, *imprint of* Abbeville Publishing Group

Abbeville Press, *imprint of* Abbeville Publishing Group, *distributed by* W W Norton & Company Inc

Abbey of Saint Peter of Solesmes, *distributed by* Paraclete Press Inc

ABC-CLIO, *subsidiary of* Bloomsbury Publishing Inc

ABC International Group Inc, *imprint of* Kazi Publications Inc

ABDO, *subsidiary of* Abdo Consulting Group Inc (ACGI), Abdo Consulting Group Inc (ACGI)

Abdo & Daughters, *imprint of* ABDO

Abdo Digital, *imprint of* ABDO

Abdo Kids, *imprint of* ABDO

Abdo Kids Jumbo, *imprint of* ABDO

Abdo Kids Junior, *imprint of* ABDO

Abdo Publishing, *imprint of* ABDO

Abdo Zoom, *imprint of* ABDO

The Aberdeen Group, *distributor for* Craftsman Book Co

ABI Professional Publications, *distributed by* Vandamere Press

Abingdon Press, *imprint of* The United Methodist Publishing House

Abjad Books, *imprint of* Kazi Publications Inc

Abo Akademi University, *distributed by* Penn State University Press

Abrams, *distributor for* National Gallery of Art, *distributed by* Perfection Learning®

Abrams & Chronicle Books, *distributor for* Harry N Abrams Inc

Abrams Appleseed, *imprint of* Harry N Abrams Inc

Abrams Books, *imprint of* Harry N Abrams Inc, *distributor for* Familius, The Vendome Press

Abrams Books for Young Readers, *imprint of* Harry N Abrams Inc

Abrams ComicArts, *imprint of* Harry N Abrams Inc

Harry N Abrams Inc, *subsidiary of* Media-Participations, *distributor for* American Federation of Arts, Blackwell & Ruth, Booth-Clibborn Editions, Bungie, Cameron+Company, Cernunnos, Ducasse Edition, Enchanted Lion, Familius, Getty Publications, Lucky Spool (Australia, New Zealand & North America), Milky Way Picture Books, The Museum of Modern Art, Red Comet Press, SelfMadeHero, Skittledog, Tate Publishing, Unruly, V&A Publishing, Vendome Press, *distributed by* Abrams & Chronicle Books (Great Britain), Ducasse Edition, Hachette Book Group Inc

Abrams Image, *imprint of* Harry N Abrams Inc

Abrams Noterie, *imprint of* Harry N Abrams Inc

Abrams Plus, *imprint of* Harry N Abrams Inc

Abrams Press, *imprint of* Harry N Abrams Inc

The ABS Group, *distributed by* American Academy of Environmental Engineers & Scientists®

ACA, *imprint of* American Counseling Association (ACA)

Academic Book Center, *distributor for* Primary Research Group Inc

Academic Press, *imprint of* Elsevier BV, *distributed by* Marine Techniques Publishing

Academy Chicago Publishers, *imprint of* Chicago Review Press

The Academy of American Franciscan History, *distributed by* The Catholic University of America Press

ACC Art Books, *division of* ACC Art Books (England), ACC Art Books (England), *distributor for* George Braziller Inc, Winterthur Museum, Garden & Library

ACC Distribution, *division of* ACC Art Books

ACC Editions, *imprint of* ACC Art Books

Accord Publishing, *imprint of* Andrews McMeel Publishing LLC

Ace Books, *imprint of* Berkley, *distributed by* Perfection Learning®

ACER, *distributor for* Psychological Assessment Resources Inc (PAR)

ACHCBYZ, *distributed by* Summertime Publications Inc

ACM Books, *imprint of* Association for Computing Machinery

ACMRS Press, *imprint of* Arizona Center for Medieval & Renaissance Studies (ACMRS)

Aconyte, *distributed by* Simon & Schuster, LLC

Acres USA, *division of* Acres USA Inc, Acres USA Inc

Acropolis Books, *distributed by* DeVorss & Co

ACS Publications, *division of* The American Chemical Society (ACS), *imprint of* Starcrafts LLC, *distributor for* Royal Society of Chemistry, *distributed by* Oxford University Press USA

ACTA Sports, *imprint of* ACTA Publications

Action Language Learning, *distributed by* Cheng & Tsui Co Inc

ACU Press, *affiliate of* Abilene Christian University

Ad Infinitum Books, *distributed by* Cross-Cultural Communications

Adams Business, *imprint of* Adams Media

Adams Media, *division of* Simon & Schuster, LLC

Adapted Classics, *imprint of* ArtWrite Productions

Addison & Highsmith Publishers, *imprint of* Histria Books

Addison-Wesley, *distributor for* Public Citizen

Adir Press, *distributed by* Feldheim Publishers

Adis International, *imprint of* Wolters Kluwer US Corp

Advaita Ashrama, *distributed by* Vedanta Press

333

IMPRINTS, SUBSIDIARIES & DISTRIBUTORS

Adventure Cycling Association, *distributed by* Mountaineers Books

Adventure Publications, *imprint of* AdventureKEEN

Adventure Roads Travel, *imprint of* Ocean Tree Books

AdVenture SA, *distributed by* Oak Knoll Press

AdventureKEEN, *distributor for* Kollath-Stensaas, Lake 7 Creative, Nodin Press

Adventures in Odyssey, *imprint of* Focus on the Family

Adventures Unlimited Press (AUP), *distributor for* Eagle Wing Books, EDFU Books, Yelsraek Publishing

The AEI Press, *division of* American Enterprise Institute, *distributed by* MIT (selected titles)

Aequitas Books, *imprint of* Pleasure Boat Studio: A Literary Press

Aeronautical Publishers, *imprint of* Markowski International Publishers

AF Editions, *distributed by* Casemate | publishers

Affiliated East-West Press Pvt Ltd, *distributor for* AAPG (American Association of Petroleum Geologists)

AFK, *imprint of* Scholastic Trade Publishing

Africa World Press Inc, *affiliate of* The Red Sea Press Inc

African-American Book Distributors Inc, *subsidiary of* Path Press Inc

African American Islamic Institute, *distributed by* Fons Vitae

Editions d'Afrique du Nord, *distributed by* Edgewise Press Inc

After the Battle, *distributed by* Casemate | publishers

Afterall Books, *distributed by* The MIT Press

AFV Modeller, *distributed by* Casemate | publishers

Against All Odds Productions, *distributed by* Union Square & Co

Agape, *division of* Hope Publishing Co

Agathon Press, *imprint of* Algora Publishing

The Agency at Brown Books, *subsidiary of* Brown Books Publishing Group (BBPG)

Agenda Publishing, *distributed by* Columbia University Press

Agora, *imprint of* Polis Books

aha! Chinese, *distributed by* Cheng & Tsui Co Inc

Aha Communications, *distributed by* Gryphon House Inc

AHOY Comics, *distributed by* Simon & Schuster, LLC

Ai Pohaku Press, *distributed by* University of Hawaii Press

AICPA® & CIMA®, *subsidiary of* American Institute of Certified Public Accountants, *distributor for* Wiley, *distributed by* Practitioners Publishing Co, Thomson Reuters

Aignos Publishing, *imprint of* Savant Books & Publications LLC

AIM (American Institute of Musicology), *distributed by* A-R Editions Inc

AIP Publishing LLC, *subsidiary of* American Institute of Physics, *distributed by* Springer-Verlag

Air War Publications, *distributed by* Casemate | publishers

Air World, *distributed by* Casemate | publishers

Airmont, *distributed by* Perfection Learning®

AK Press, *subsidiary of* AK Press Inc, AK Press Inc, *distributor for* Arbeiter Ring, Autonomedia, Crimethinc, Freedom Press, Charles H Kerr, Kersplebedelo

Akashic Books, *distributed by* W W Norton & Company Inc

ALA Editions, *imprint of* The American Library Association (ALA)

ALA Neal-Schuman, *imprint of* The American Library Association (ALA)

Aladdin Books, *imprint of* Simon & Schuster Children's Publishing

Alamos Press, *imprint of* Park Place Publications

Alan Wofsy Fine Arts, *distributor for* Bora, Brusberg (Berlin), Cramer (Geneva), Galerie Kornfeld Verlag AG (Bern), Huber, Ides et Calendes, The Picasso Project, Welz, Wittenborn Art Books

Alaska Literary Series, *imprint of* University of Alaska Press

Alaska Native Language Center, *distributed by* University of Alaska Press

Alaska Native Language Center (ANLC), *division of* University of Alaska Fairbanks

Alaska Northwest Books®, *imprint of* West Margin Press

Alaska Quarterly Review, *distributed by* University of Alaska Press

Alaska Sea Grant, *distributed by* University of Alaska Press

Alaska Writer Laureate Series, *imprint of* University of Alaska Press

Albany Institute of History & Art, *distributed by* Excelsior Editions, State University of New York Press

Albatross, *distributed by* W W Norton & Company Inc

Albatross Funnybooks, *imprint of* Dark Horse Comics

Alchemical Press, *imprint of* Holmes Publishing Group LLC

Alexander Lowen Foundation, *distributed by* Simon & Schuster, LLC

Alexandrian Press, *imprint of* Holmes Publishing Group LLC

Alfred Music, *distributor for* Dover Publications Inc, Drum Channel, Faber Music Ltd, FJH, FJH Music Co Inc, LudwigMasters, MakeMusic Inc, Penguin, WEA

Algonquin Books, *imprint of* Little, Brown and Company

Algonquin Young Readers, *imprint of* Little, Brown Books for Young Readers (LBYR)

Alibi, *imprint of* Random House Publishing Group

Allen & Unwin, *distributor for* Quarto Publishing Group USA Inc

J A Allen, *distributed by* Trafalgar Square Books

Allida Books, *imprint of* Clarion Books

Alloy Entertainment LLC, *member of* Warner Bros Entertainment Group, *distributed by* Avon Books, HarperCollins, Hyperion, Little, Brown and Company, Penguin Publishing Group, Penguin Random House LLC, Scholastic Books, Simon & Schuster, LLC

Allworth Press, *imprint of* Skyhorse Publishing Inc, *distributed by* Simon & Schuster, LLC

Alma Little, *imprint of* Elva Resa Publishing

Alta Book Center Publishers, *distributor for* TESOL Press

Althos, *imprint of* DiscoverNet Publishing

Alutiiq Museum, *distributed by* University of Alaska Press

AMA, *distributed by* Mel Bay Publications Inc

Amadeus Press, *imprint of* Rowman & Littlefield Publishing Group

Amara, *imprint of* Entangled Publishing LLC

PUBLISHERS

IMPRINTS, SUBSIDIARIES & DISTRIBUTORS

Amatl Comix, *imprint of* San Diego State University Press

Ambassador Books, *distributor for* Primary Research Group Inc

Ambassador International, *division of* Emerald House Inc

Amber-Allen Publishing, *imprint of* New World Library

Amber Books Ltd, *distributed by* Union Square & Co

Amber Lotus Publishing, *imprint of* Andrews McMeel Publishing LLC

Amberjack Publishing, *imprint of* Chicago Review Press

Amble Press, *imprint of* Bywater Books Inc

Amelia Press, *imprint of* NFB Publishing

American Academy for Park & Recreation Administration, *distributed by* Sagamore Publishing LLC

American Academy of Environmental Engineers & Scientists®, *distributor for* The ABS Group, CRC Press, McGraw-Hill, Pearson Education, Prentice Hall, John Wiley & Sons Inc

American Alpine Club, *distributed by* Mountaineers Books

The American Alpine Club Press, *distributed by* Mountaineers Books

American Anthropological Association (AAA), *distributed by* Wiley-Blackwell

American Antiquarian Society, *distributed by* Oak Knoll Press

American Association of School Librarians (AASL), *division of* The American Library Association (ALA)

American Association of State Highway & Transportation Officials, *distributed by* PPI, A Kaplan Company

American Bar Association, *distributed by* William S Hein & Co Inc, The Professional Education Group LLC (PEG)

American Bar Association Publishing, *division of* American Bar Association (ABA)

American Ceramic Society (ACerS), *distributor for* American Society for Nondestructive Testing

The American Chemical Society, *distributed by* Oxford University Press USA

American College of Healthcare Executives Management Series, *imprint of* Health Administration Press

American Council for an Energy Efficient Economy (ACEEE), *distributed by* Chelsea Green Publishing Co

American Council on Education (ACE), *distributed by* Rowman & Littlefield

American Federation of Arts, *distributed by* Harry N Abrams Inc, D Giles Ltd, Hirmer Publishers, Hudson Hills Press Inc, Rizzoli Electa, Scala Publishers, University of Washington Press, Yale University Press

American Geophysical Union, *imprint of* John Wiley & Sons Inc

American Geosciences Institute (AGI), *distributed by* W H Freeman, It's About Time Inc, Prentice Hall

American Girl, *imprint of* American Girl Publishing

American Girl Publishing, *subsidiary of* Mattel Inc, *distributed by* Simon & Schuster, LLC

American Guidance Service, *distributed by* Psychological Assessment Resources Inc (PAR)

The American Heritage® Dictionaries, *imprint of* Houghton Mifflin Harcourt Trade & Reference Division

American Institute of Chemical Engineers (AIChE), *distributor for* ASM International (selected titles), Engineering Foundation, IchemE (selected titles), John Wiley & Sons Inc, *distributed by* John Wiley & Sons Inc

American Law Institute, *distributed by* William S Hein & Co Inc, The Professional Education Group LLC (PEG)

American Law Institute Continuing Legal Education (ALI CLE), *affiliate of* American Law Institute

The American Library Association (ALA), *distributed by* University of Chicago Press

American Literatures Initiative, *imprint of* Fordham University Press

American Maritain Association, *distributed by* The Catholic University of America Press

American Mathematical Society (AMS), *distributor for* Annales de la faculte des sciences de Toulouse mathematiques, Bar-Ilan University Press, Brown University, European Mathematical Society, Hindustan Book Agency, Independent University of Moscow, International Press of Boston Inc, Mathematica Josephina, Mathematical Society of Japan, Narosa Publishing House, Ramanujan Mathematical Society, Science Press USA Inc, Societe Mathematique de France, Tata Institute of Fundamental Research, Theta Foundation of Bucharest, University Press, Vieweg Verlag Publications

American Medical Association, *distributor for* OptumInsight™, *distributed by* Medical Group Management Association (MGMA), OptumInsight™

American Milestones, *imprint of* Gallopade International Inc

American Oriental Society, *distributed by* Penn State University Press

The American Philosophical Society, *distributed by* University of Pennsylvania Press

American Philosophical Society Press, *distributed by* University of Pennsylvania Press

American Poetry Review/Honickman, *distributed by* Copper Canyon Press

American Psychiatric Association Publishing, *division of* American Psychiatric Association (APA), *distributor for* Group for the Advancement of Psychiatry

American Quilter's Society (AQS), *division of* Schroeder Publishing Co Inc

American School of Classical Studies at Athens, *imprint of* ASCSA Publications

American Society for Mechanical Engineers (ASME), *distributor for* American Society for Nondestructive Testing

American Society for Metals (ASM), *distributor for* American Society for Nondestructive Testing

American Society for Nondestructive Testing, *distributed by* American Ceramic Society (ACerS), American Society for Mechanical Engineers (ASME), American Society for Metals (ASM), The American Welding Society (AWS), ASTM, Edison Welding Institute, Mean Free Path

American Technical Publishers, *division of* The ATP Group Inc, *distributor for* Craftsman Book Co

American Technical Publishers Inc, *distributor for* SME (Society of Manufacturing Engineers)

American University in Cairo, *distributed by* Oxford University Press USA

The American Welding Society (AWS), *distributor for* American Society for Nondestructive Testing

American Wood Council (American Forest & Paper Association), *distributed by* PPI, A Kaplan Company

AMI Press, *imprint of* Loving Healing Press Inc

Amicus, *distributed by* The Creative Co

Amicus Ink, *imprint of* Amicus, *distributed by* Chronicle Books LLC

Amicus Learning, *imprint of* Amicus

Amistad, *imprint of* HarperCollins Publishers LLC

Amorata Press, *imprint of* Ulysses Press

Amphoto Books, *imprint of* Crown Publishing Group

335

IMPRINTS, SUBSIDIARIES & DISTRIBUTORS

Amulet Books, *imprint of* Harry N Abrams Inc

An Inc Original, *imprint of* Greenleaf Book Group LLC

Ananda Ashrama, *distributed by* Vedanta Press

ANCC Magnet Recognition Program, *imprint of* Nursesbooks.org, The Publishing Program of ANA

Ancestry Publishing, *imprint of* Turner Publishing Co LLC

Anchorage Museum Association, *distributed by* University of Alaska Press

Anchorage Museum of Art History, *distributed by* University of Alaska Press

Ancient Faith Publishing, *division of* Ancient Faith Ministries Inc, *distributed by* St Tikhon's, St Vladimir's

And/Or Press, *imprint of* Ronin Publishing Inc

Andanyon Books, *imprint of* Yotzeret Publishing

Andersen Press, *distributed by* Lerner Publishing Group Inc

Andrea Press, *distributed by* Casemate | publishers

Andrews McMeel Publishing LLC, *division of* Andrews McMeel Universal, *distributor for* Gooseberry Patch (North America), Signatures Network, Sporting News, Universe Publishing Calendars, Vegan Heritage Press, *distributed by* Simon & Schuster, LLC

Andrews University Press, *division of* Andrews University

Andscape Books, *imprint of* Disney Publishing Worldwide

Angel City Press, *distributed by* Gibbs Smith Publisher

Angelus Press, *subsidiary of* The Society of Saint Pius X, Southwest District, *distributed by* Fatima Crusader

Anglican Book Centre, *distributed by* Forward Movement

Annales de la faculte des sciences de Toulouse mathematiques, *distributed by* American Mathematical Society (AMS)

Annick Press, *distributed by* Perfection Learning®

Anomaly Press, *distributed by* Chelsea Green Publishing Co

Another Great Achiever Series, *imprint of* Advance Publishing Inc

Anqa Press, *distributed by* Fons Vitae

ANR Publications University of California, *division of* Agriculture & Natural Resources, University of California

Antient Press, *imprint of* Heritage Books Inc

Antinous Press, *distributed by* powerHouse Books

Coleccion Antologia Personal, *imprint of* Editorial de la Universidad de Puerto Rico

Anvil Series, *imprint of* Krieger Publishing Co

AO Foundation, *distributed by* Thieme Medical Publishers Inc

AOTA Press, *imprint of* The American Occupational Therapy Association Inc (AOTA)

APA Books®, *imprint of* American Psychological Association

APA Journals, *imprint of* American Psychological Association

APA Style, *imprint of* American Psychological Association

APA Video®, *imprint of* American Psychological Association

Aperture, *imprint of* Aperture Books, *distributed by* Fons Vitae

Aperture Books, *division of* Aperture Foundation Inc

APH Press, *imprint of* American Printing House for the Blind Inc (APH)

Appalachian Mountain Club Books, *division of* Appalachian Mountain Club

Appalachian Trail Conservancy (ATC), *distributed by* Mountaineers Books

Applause Theatre & Cinema Books, *imprint of* The Globe Pequot Press, *distributor for* The Working Arts Library, Glenn Young Books

Apples & Honey Press, *imprint of* Behrman House Inc

Applesauce Press, *imprint of* Cider Mill Press Book Publishers LLC, *distributed by* Simon & Schuster, LLC

Applewood Books, *imprint of* Arcadia Publishing Inc

Applied Research + Design Publishing, *imprint of* ORO editions

Appraisal Institute, *distributed by* Dearborn Trade

Apress, *imprint of* Springer

Apress Media LLC, *division of* Springer Nature

APS Books, *imprint of* American Philosophical Society Press

APS PRESS, *imprint of* The American Phytopathological Society (APS)

Aquatic Ecosystem Health & Management Society Books, *distributed by* Michigan State University Press (MSU Press)

Coleccion Aqui y Ahora, *imprint of* Editorial de la Universidad de Puerto Rico

Arabian Publishing Ltd, *distributed by* Casemate | publishers

Arba Sicula, *distributed by* Cross-Cultural Communications

Arbeiter Ring, *distributed by* AK Press

Arcade CrimeWise, *imprint of* Arcade Publishing Inc

Arcade Publishing Inc, *imprint of* Skyhorse Publishing Inc, *distributed by* Simon & Schuster, LLC

Arcadia Children's Books, *imprint of* Arcadia Publishing Inc

Arcadia Publishing, *imprint of* Arcadia Publishing Inc

Arcana Publishing, *imprint of* Lotus Press

Archaia Entertainment LLC, *imprint of* BOOM! Studios

Archetype, *distributed by* Fons Vitae

Architectural Graphic Standards, *imprint of* John Wiley & Sons Inc

Archival, *distributed by* Donald M Grant Publisher Inc

Archway, *distributed by* Perfection Learning®

Archway Editions, *imprint of* powerHouse Books

Arctic Studies Center of the Smithsonian Museum, *distributed by* University of Alaska Press

Arctis Books USA, *distributed by* Simon & Schuster, LLC

Arden, *distributed by* Casemate | publishers

Ardis Russian Literature, *imprint of* The Overlook Press

ARE Press, *division of* The Association for Research & Enlightenment Inc (ARE), The Association for Research & Enlightenment Inc (ARE)

Ariel Press, *subsidiary of* Light, *distributor for* Enthea Press, Kudzu House

The Arion Press, *division of* Lyra Corp

ARIS Books, *imprint of* Kallisti Publishing Inc

Arktoi Books, *imprint of* Red Hen Press

PUBLISHERS

IMPRINTS, SUBSIDIARIES & DISTRIBUTORS

Arlen House, *distributor for* Syracuse University Press, *distributed by* Syracuse University Press

Eric Armin Inc Education Ctr, *distributor for* National Council of Teachers of Mathematics (NCTM)

Jason Aronson Inc, *imprint of* Rowman & Littlefield Publishing Group

Arrangers Publishing LLC, *distributed by* Hal Leonard LLC

ARSIS Audio, *imprint of* ECS Publishing Group

Art Gallery of New South Wales, *distributed by* University of Washington Press

Art Image Publications, *division of* Beauchemin International Inc

The Art Institute of Chicago, *distributed by* Yale University Press

Art Power, *distributed by* Gingko Press Inc

Art Scroll Series, *imprint of* Mesorah Publications Ltd

art-SITES, *distributed by* University of California Press

Artabras, *imprint of* Abbeville Publishing Group

Arte Publico Press, *affiliate of* University of Houston

Artech House®, *subsidiary of* Horizon House Publications Inc, Horizon House Publications Inc

Artemis Books, *imprint of* Gateways Books & Tapes

Arthritis Research, *imprint of* Progressive Press

Artisan, *imprint of* Workman Publishing

Artists, Writers & Artisans, *distributed by* Simon & Schuster, LLC

ArtWorks, *imprint of* MFA Publications

ASAE, *distributed by* Water Resources Publications LLC

Asante®, *imprint of* Mastery Education

ASCA, *distributor for* MAR*CO Products Inc

ASCE Press, *imprint of* American Society of Civil Engineers (ASCE)

Ascent Audio, *imprint of* Recorded Books Inc, an RBmedia company

ASCP Press, *subsidiary of* American Society for Clinical Pathology

Ashgate, *distributed by* William S Hein & Co Inc

The Ashland Poetry Press, *affiliate of* Ashland University

Ashley Music, *distributed by* Hal Leonard LLC

Asian Civilisations Museum, *distributed by* University of Hawaii Press

Asian Humanities Press, *imprint of* Jain Publishing Co

ASM International, *distributed by* American Institute of Chemical Engineers (AIChE), NACE International

ASM Publishing, *division of* American Society for Microbiology

ASME Press, *imprint of* American Society of Mechanical Engineers (ASME)

Aspatore Books, *division of* Thomson Reuters

Aspen, *distributed by* William S Hein & Co Inc

Aspen Publishers, *imprint of* Wolters Kluwer US Corp, *distributed by* Medical Group Management Association (MGMA)

Aspire Press, *imprint of* Hendrickson Publishers Inc

Assessment, *division of* Scholastic Education Solutions

Association for Information Science & Technology (ASIS&T), *distributed by* Information Today, Inc, John Wiley & Sons Inc

Association for Library Service to Children (ALSC), *division of* The American Library Association (ALA)

Association of College & Research Libraries (ACRL), *division of* The American Library Association (ALA)

ASTM, *distributor for* American Society for Nondestructive Testing, *distributed by* NACE International

Astra Books for Young Readers, *imprint of* Astra Publishing House Inc

Astra Young Readers, *imprint of* Astra Books for Young Readers

Astragal Press, *imprint of* The Globe Pequot Press

Astronautical Society of Western Australia, *distributed by* Univelt Inc

At Home on the Road, *imprint of* Park Place Publications

Ateneo De Manila University Press, *distributed by* University of Hawaii Press

Atheneum, *distributed by* Perfection Learning®

Atheneum Books for Young Readers, *imprint of* Simon & Schuster Children's Publishing

Atlantic Boating Almanac, *imprint of* ProStar Publications Inc

Atlantic Monthly Press, *imprint of* Grove Atlantic Inc

Atria Books, *imprint of* Atria Publishing Group

Atria Books Espanol, *imprint of* Atria Books

Atria Trade Paperbacks, *imprint of* Atria Books

Attara, *distributed by* Hachai Publishing

Audel, *imprint of* John Wiley & Sons Inc

Audio Books, *division of* Unarius Academy of Science Publications

Audioworks, *imprint of* Simon & Schuster Audio

Augsburg Fortress, *imprint of* Augsburg Fortress Publishers, Publishing House of the Evangelical Lutheran Church in America

August House Audio, *imprint of* August House Inc

August House Little Folk, *imprint of* August House Inc

August House Story Cove, *imprint of* August House Inc

AUPHA Press/Health Administration Press, *imprint of* Health Administration Press

Aureole Editions, *imprint of* ECS Publishing Group

Stephen F Austin State University Press, *distributed by* Texas A&M University Press

Australasian Corrosion Association Inc, *distributor for* NACE International

Australian Scholarly Publishing, *distributed by* Casemate | publishers

Austrian Film Museum Books, *distributed by* Columbia University Press

AuthorBookings.com, *division of* Story Monsters LLC

AuthorHouse, *division of* Author Solutions LLC

Authorlink® Press, *imprint of* Authorlink®

Authors Equity, *distributed by* Simon & Schuster, LLC

Autonomedia, *distributed by* AK Press

Avalon House, *distributed by* Chelsea Green Publishing Co

Avalon Travel, *imprint of* Running Press

Avamra Institute, *distributed by* Moznaim Publishing Corp

IMPRINTS, SUBSIDIARIES & DISTRIBUTORS

Avant-Guide, *unit of* Empire Press Media Inc

Ave Maria Press Inc, *division of* United States Province of the Congregation of Holy Cross

Avery, *imprint of* Penguin Publishing Group

Aviation Collectables, *distributed by* Casemate | publishers

Avid Reader Press, *imprint of* Simon & Schuster, LLC

Avon, *imprint of* HarperCollins Publishers LLC

Avon Books, *distributor for* Alloy Entertainment LLC

Avon Impulse, *imprint of* HarperCollins Publishers LLC

Avonmore Books, *distributed by* Casemate | publishers

AWS, *distributed by* NACE International

AWWA, *imprint of* American Water Works Association (AWWA)

Ayal Press, *imprint of* Feldheim Publishers

Artes Monte Azul, *imprint of* Blue Mountain Arts Inc

Back Bay Books, *imprint of* Little, Brown and Company

Back to Eden Books, *distributed by* Lotus Press

Backbeat Books, *imprint of* The Globe Pequot Press

The Backwaters Press, *imprint of* University of Nebraska Press

BADM Books, *distributed by* Father & Son Publishing Inc

Baen Books, *distributed by* Simon & Schuster, LLC

Baha'i Distribution Service, *division of* Baha'i Publishing Trust

Baha'i Publishing, *imprint of* Baha'i Publishing Trust

Baha'i Publishing Trust, *subsidiary of* The National Spiritual Assembly of the Baha'is of the United States, The National Spiritual Assembly of the Baha'is of the United States

BainBridgeBooks, *imprint of* Trans-Atlantic Publications Inc

Baker Books, *division of* Baker Publishing Group, *distributor for* Focus on the Family, *distributed by* Perfection Learning®

Baker's Plays, *distributor for* Samuel French, Inc, *distributed by* Samuel French, Inc

Bala Kids, *imprint of* Shambhala Publications Inc

Balance, *imprint of* Grand Central Publishing

Baldar, *imprint of* Ross Books

Jonathan Ball Publishers, *distributor for* Europa Editions, Princeton University Press

Ballantine, *distributed by* Perfection Learning®

Ballantine Books, *imprint of* Random House Publishing Group

Ballantine Wellspring, *imprint of* Penguin Random House LLC

B&H Academic, *imprint of* B&H Publishing Group

B&H Espanol, *imprint of* B&H Publishing Group

B&H kids, *imprint of* B&H Publishing Group

B&H Publishing, *imprint of* B&H Publishing Group

B&H Publishing Group, *imprint of* LifeWay Christian Resources

Banned Books, *imprint of* Progressive Press

Banovallum, *distributed by* Casemate | publishers

Bantam, *distributor for* Parachute Publishing LLC, *distributed by* Perfection Learning®

Bantam Books, *imprint of* Random House Publishing Group

Bar-Ilan University Press, *distributed by* American Mathematical Society (AMS)

Barbour Books, *imprint of* Barbour Publishing Inc

Barbour Espanol, *imprint of* Barbour Publishing Inc

Barbour Kidz, *imprint of* Barbour Publishing Inc

The Bard Graduate Center, *distributed by* Yale University Press

Sarah Barley Books, *imprint of* Simon & Schuster Children's Publishing

BarnaBooks, *imprint of* Tyndale House Publishers Inc

Barnes & Noble Classics, *imprint of* Fine Creative Media, Inc

Barringer Publishing, *division of* Schlesinger Advertising & Marketing

Barron's, *distributed by* International Book Centre Inc

Barrons, *distributed by* Perfection Learning®

Bartleby Press, *member of* Jackson Westgate Publishing Group

Baseball America, *distributed by* Simon & Schuster, LLC

Baseball Prospectus, *distributed by* Stylus Publishing LLC

Basheer, *distributed by* Gingko Press Inc

Bashu Publishing, *distributed by* CN Times Books

Basic Books, *imprint of* Basic Books Group

Basic Books Group, *division of* Hachette Book Group Inc

Basic Health Guides, *imprint of* Basic Health Publications Inc

Basic Health Publications Inc, *imprint of* Turner Publishing Co LLC

Randol Bass Music, *distributed by* ECS Publishing Group

Bat Conservation International, *distributed by* University of Texas Press

Batsford, *distributed by* Quarto Publishing Group USA Inc

Bauernfeind Press, *distributed by* Casemate | publishers

William Bay Music, *distributed by* Mel Bay Publications Inc

Bayard, *distributed by* Crabtree Publishing Co

BDK America, *distributed by* University of Hawaii Press

Beach Lane Books, *imprint of* Simon & Schuster Children's Publishing

BeachHouse Books, *imprint of* Science & Humanities Press

Beacon Hill Press of Kansas City, *subsidiary of* The Foundry Publishing

Beaming Books, *imprint of* Augsburg Fortress Publishers, Publishing House of the Evangelical Lutheran Church in America

Bear & Bobcat Books, *imprint of* Hameray Publishing Group Inc, *distributed by* Hameray Publishing Group Inc

Bear & Co Inc, *imprint of* Inner Traditions International Ltd

Bear Cub Books, *imprint of* Inner Traditions International Ltd

BearManor Bare, *imprint of* BearManor Media

BearManor Fiction, *imprint of* BearManor Media

Beauxarts, *imprint of* The Picasso Project, Alan Wofsy Fine Arts

PUBLISHERS — IMPRINTS, SUBSIDIARIES & DISTRIBUTORS

Bebop Books, *imprint of* Lee & Low Books Inc

becker&mayer!, *imprint of* Quarto Publishing Group USA Inc

Beckon Books, *imprint of* Capen Publishing Co Inc

Bedford, Freeman & Worth Publishers, *imprint of* Macmillan Learning

Bedford/St Martin's, *imprint of* Macmillan Learning

Begell-Atom LLC, *subsidiary of* Begell House Inc Publishers

Beginning Readers, *imprint of* ABDO

Behemoth Entertainment, *distributed by* Simon & Schuster, LLC

Behemoth Publishing, *distributed by* CarTech Inc

Beinecke Rare Book & Manuscript Library, *distributed by* Yale University Press

Belknap Press, *imprint of* Harvard University Press

Bell Bridge Books, *imprint of* BelleBooks

Belle Isle Books, *imprint of* Brandylane Publishers Inc

Belt Publishing, *imprint of* Arcadia Publishing Inc

Belwin, *imprint of* Alfred Music

BenBella Books Inc, *distributed by* Simon & Schuster, LLC

BenBella Vegan, *imprint of* BenBella Books Inc

Benchmark Maps, *distributed by* Wide World of Maps Inc

Benchmark Press, *imprint of* Triumph Books LLC

Bendon, *distributor for* Parachute Publishing LLC

John Benjamins North America Inc, *subsidiary of* John Benjamins Publishing Co

Bentley Publishers, *division of* Robert Bentley Inc, Robert Bentley Inc

Bentley Pubs, *imprint of* Bentley Publishers

BePuzzled, *division of* University Games

Berg Publishers, *distributed by* Palgrave Macmillan

Berger Books, *imprint of* Dark Horse Comics

Berghahn Books Ltd (UK), *division of* Berghahn Books

Berklee Press, *imprint of* Hal Leonard LLC, *distributed by* Hal Leonard LLC

Berkley, *imprint of* Penguin Publishing Group, *distributor for* Parachute Publishing LLC, *distributed by* Perfection Learning®

Berkley Books, *imprint of* Berkley

Bernan, *imprint of* Rowman & Littlefield Publishing Group

Leonard Bernstein, *distributed by* Hal Leonard LLC

Berrett-Koehler Publishers, *distributed by* Dreamscape Media LLC

Berry Street Books, *imprint of* Eifrig Publishing LLC

Bess Press Inc, *distributed by* The Islander Group

Best Publishing Co, *distributed by* Marine Techniques Publishing

Emily Bestler Books, *imprint of* Atria Books

Bethany House Publishers, *division of* Baker Publishing Group

Bethlehem Books, *affiliate of* Bethlehem Community, *distributed by* Ignatius Press

Betty Crocker®, *imprint of* HarperCollins Publishers LLC

Beyond Words, *imprint of* Atria Books, Simon & Schuster Audio

Bibliographical Society of America, *distributed by* Oak Knoll Press

Bibliographical Society of University of Virginia, *distributed by* Oak Knoll Press

The Bibliographical Society (UK), *distributed by* Oak Knoll Press

Bider Technology, *distributed by* Cheng & Tsui Co Inc

Big & Small, *distributed by* Lerner Publishing Group Inc

Big Buddy Books, *imprint of* ABDO

Big Meteor Publishing, *distributed by* Omnibus Press

Big Picture Press, *imprint of* Candlewick Press

Big Sandy Press, *imprint of* Ozark Mountain Publishing Inc

Big Sky Maps, *distributed by* Wide World of Maps Inc

Big Sky Publishing, *distributed by* Casemate | publishers

BiG STUFF™, *imprint of* BiG GUY BOOKS

Big Tree Books, *imprint of* Easy Money Press

Binational Press, *imprint of* San Diego State University Press

Bindu Books, *imprint of* Inner Traditions International Ltd

Binge Watcher's Guide, *imprint of* Riverdale Avenue Books (RAB)

Biographical Publishing Co, *distributor for* Eagles Landing Publishing, Spyglass Books LLC

BioMed Central, *imprint of* Springer

Bird Dog Publishing, *imprint of* Bottom Dog Press

Birkhauser Science, *imprint of* Springer

Birlinn, *distributed by* Casemate | publishers

BIS Publishers, *distributed by* Chronicle Books LLC

Bison Books, *imprint of* University of Nebraska Press

BJU Press, *unit of* BJU Education Group

Black Cat, *imprint of* Grove Atlantic Inc

Black Classic Press, *distributed by* Publishers Group West (PGW)

Black Dog & Leventhal, *imprint of* Workman Publishing

Black Heritage: Celebrating Culture, *imprint of* Gallopade International Inc

Black Iron Cookin' Co, *division of* Quixote Press

Black Mask Studios, *distributed by* Simon & Schuster, LLC

Black Mountain Press, *unit of* Flood Gallery Fine Arts Center

Black Odyssey Media, *distributed by* Kensington Publishing Corp

Black Privilege Publishing, *imprint of* Atria Books

Black Sheep Books for Young Readers, *imprint of* Akashic Books

Black Sparrow, *imprint of* Godine

Black Spot Books, *imprint of* Vesuvian Books

Black Squirrel Books, *imprint of* Kent State University Press

Blackman Associates, *distributed by* Casemate | publishers

Blackstone Publishing, *distributor for* Dreamscape Media LLC

Blackwell & Ruth, *distributed by* Harry N Abrams Inc, Chronicle Books LLC

IMPRINTS, SUBSIDIARIES & DISTRIBUTORS

Blake Books, *distributed by* Perfection Learning®

Blind Owl Press, *imprint of* Mazda Publishers Inc

BLING! Romance, *imprint of* Iron Stream Media

Bliss, *imprint of* Entangled Publishing LLC

Block Museum, *distributed by* Oak Knoll Press

Bloody Brits Press, *imprint of* Bywater Books Inc

Bloom Books, *imprint of* Sourcebooks LLC

Bloomberg, *imprint of* John Wiley & Sons Inc

Bloom's Literary Criticism, *imprint of* Infobase Learning

Bloomsbury, *imprint of* Bloomsbury Publishing Inc

Bloomsbury Academic, *imprint of* Bloomsbury Publishing Inc, *distributor for* Paragon House, Spring Publications

Bloomsbury Publishing Inc, *subsidiary of* Bloomsbury Publishing Plc, *distributed by* Macmillan

Bloomsbury USA, *imprint of* Bloomsbury Publishing Inc, *distributed by* Macmillan

BLR®—Business & Legal Resources, *division of* Simplify Compliance LLC

Blue & Gray, *imprint of* Book Sales

Blue Angel Publishing, *distributed by* Llewellyn Publications, US Games Systems Inc

Blue Guides, *distributed by* W W Norton & Company Inc

Blue Mountain Press®, *imprint of* Blue Mountain Arts Inc

Blue Note, *imprint of* Blue Note Publications Inc

Blue Note Books, *imprint of* Blue Note Publications Inc

Blue Owl Books, *imprint of* Jump!

Blue Poppy Press, *division of* Blue Poppy Enterprises Inc

Blue Snake Books, *imprint of* North Atlantic Books (NAB)

Blue Sneaker Press, *imprint of* Capen Publishing Co Inc

Blue Vista, *imprint of* Scarsdale Publishing Ltd

BlueBridge, *imprint of* United Tribes Media Inc

Bluefire, *imprint of* Random House Children's Books

BNI Publications, *distributor for* Craftsman Book Co, *distributed by* Craftsman Book Co

Bobolink Media, *imprint of* Sunbelt Publications Inc

Fred Bock Music Company, *distributed by* Hal Leonard LLC

Bold Type Books, *imprint of* Basic Books Group

Bollingen Series, *imprint of* Princeton University Press

Bolt, *imprint of* Black Rabbit Books

Bolt Jr, *imprint of* Black Rabbit Books

Bonneville Books, *imprint of* Cedar Fort Inc, The University of Utah Press

Book Guild, *distributed by* Trans-Atlantic Publications Inc

Book House, *imprint of* Black Rabbit Books

Book Marketing Works, *subsidiary of* Book Marketing Works LLC

Book Peddlers, *distributed by* Gryphon House Inc

Book Sales, *imprint of* Quarto Publishing Group USA Inc

Book Street Press, *imprint of* Story Monsters LLC

BookaVivo, *imprint of* Recorded Books Inc, an RBmedia company

Books Alive, *imprint of* BPC

Books & Co/Turtle Point, *imprint of* Turtle Point Press

Books for Independent Minds, *imprint of* Ronin Publishing Inc

Books Good For Young Children™, *imprint of* Maren Green Publishing Inc

Books In Motion, *division of* Classic Ventures Ltd, Classic Ventures Ltd

Books on Tape™, *imprint of* Penguin Random House Audio Publishing Group, *distributor for* Listening Library®

BOOM! Box, *imprint of* BOOM! Studios

Boom! Studios, *imprint of* Random House Publishing Group, *distributed by* Simon & Schuster, LLC

Boosey & Hawkes, *distributed by* Hal Leonard LLC

Booth-Clibborn Editions, *distributed by* Harry N Abrams Inc

Bora, *distributed by* Alan Wofsy Fine Arts

Boreal Books, *imprint of* Red Hen Press

Borgo Press, *imprint of* Wildside Press LLC

Boson Books™, *imprint of* Bitingduck Press LLC

Boston College, *distributed by* Oak Knoll Press

Boston Globe Puzzle Books, *imprint of* Random House Reference/Random House Puzzles & Games

Boston Music, *distributed by* Hal Leonard LLC

Botanica Press, *imprint of* BPC

Boulden Publishing, *distributor for* MAR*CO Products Inc, *distributed by* MAR*CO Products Inc

BowArrow Publishing, *distributed by* University of New Mexico Press

R R Bowker LLC, *subsidiary of* Cambridge Information Group, *distributed by* Grey House Publishing Inc™

R R Bowker's Books in Print Series, *imprint of* Grey House Publishing Inc™

Boxelder Books, *imprint of* The University of Utah Press

Boxer Books, *imprint of* Union Square & Co, *distributed by* Union Square & Co

Boydell & Brewer Inc, *affiliate of* Boydell & Brewer Ltd (UK), *distributed by* Ingram Academic (North & South America)

Boydell Press, *imprint of* Boydell & Brewer Inc

Boye Knives Press, *distributed by* Chelsea Green Publishing Co

Boynton Bookworks, *imprint of* Simon & Schuster Children's Publishing

Boys Town Press, *division of* Father Flanagan's Boys' Home, *distributed by* CSH Educational Resources Pte Ltd (Singapore), Deep Books Ltd (Europe & UK), Silvereye Learning Resources (NSW, Australia), University of Toronto Press (Canada)

BPC, *distributor for* Cherokee Publications, Crazy Crow, CRCS Publications, Critical Path, Gentle World, Hippocrates Publications, The Magni Co, Moon River Publishing, Second Nature, Sproutman Publications, Uproar Books

BPI Records, *imprint of* Bridge Publications Inc

Bradford Books, *imprint of* The MIT Press

Brady, *distributed by* Fire Engineering Books & Videos

Braided River, *imprint of* Mountaineers Books

Bramble, *imprint of* Tor Publishing Group

Deya Brashears, *distributed by* Gryphon House Inc

PUBLISHERS — IMPRINTS, SUBSIDIARIES & DISTRIBUTORS

Brass Monkey, *distributed by* Chronicle Books LLC

BRAVE Books, *imprint of* Brave Books LLC

Brazen, *imprint of* Entangled Publishing LLC

George Braziller Inc, *distributed by* ACC Art Books, W W Norton & Company Inc

A Karen & Michael Braziller Book, *imprint of* Persea Books

Breakthrough Publications, *imprint of* Breakthrough Publications Inc

Nicholas Brealey Publishing, *imprint of* John Murray Press (UK), John Murray Press, *distributed by* Hachette Book Group Inc

Breslov Research Institute, *distributed by* Moznaim Publishing Corp

Brethren Press, *division of* Church of the Brethren

Breton Publishing & Communications, *imprint of* Consumer Press

DS Brewer, *imprint of* Boydell & Brewer Inc

Brewers Publications, *division of* Brewers Association

Brick Mantel Books, *imprint of* Pen & Publish LLC

Brick Tower Press, *subsidiary of* J T Colby & Co Inc

Bridge, *imprint of* Bridge Logos Inc

Bridge Audio, *imprint of* Bridge Publications Inc

Bridge Logos Inc, *distributor for* Warboys LLC

Bright Leaf Books, *imprint of* University of Massachusetts Press

Bright Matter Books, *imprint of* Random House Children's Books

Bright Ring, *imprint of* Chicago Review Press

Bright Ring Publishing, *distributed by* Gryphon House Inc

Brill Inc, *subsidiary of* Koninklijke Brill NV

Brill Nijhoff, *distributed by* William S Hein & Co Inc

Brilliance Audio™, *imprint of* Brilliance Publishing Inc

Brilliance Publishing Inc, *subsidiary of* Amazon Publishing

Britannica Educational Publishing, *imprint of* The Rosen Publishing Group Inc

British Film Institute, *distributed by* Palgrave Macmillan, University of California Press

Broadleaf Books, *imprint of* Augsburg Fortress Publishers, Publishing House of the Evangelical Lutheran Church in America

Broadside Books, *imprint of* HarperCollins Publishers LLC

Broadstone Books, *distributed by* Fons Vitae

Broadway Books, *imprint of* Crown Publishing Group

The Brookings Institution Press, *division of* The Brookings Institution, *distributor for* University of California Institute on Global Conflict & Cooperation, *distributed by* Rowman & Littlefield

Brooklands Books Ltd, *distributed by* CarTech Inc

Brookline Books, *imprint of* Casemate | publishers, *distributed by* Casemate | publishers

Brooklyn Botanic Garden, *distributed by* Union Square & Co

Brookes, *distributed by* Council for Exceptional Children (CEC)

Brookstone Publishing Group, *imprint of* Iron Stream Media

Brown Bear Books, *imprint of* Black Rabbit Books

Brown Books, *imprint of* Brown Books Publishing Group (BBPG)

Brown Books Business, *division of* Brown Books Publishing Group (BBPG)

Brown Books Distribution, *subsidiary of* Brown Books Publishing Group (BBPG)

Brown Books Kids, *imprint of* Brown Books Publishing Group (BBPG)

Brown Books Young Adult, *division of* Brown Books Publishing Group (BBPG)

Brown Christian Press, *imprint of* Brown Books Publishing Group (BBPG)

John Carter Brown Library, *distributed by* Oak Knoll Press

Brown Judaic Studies, *distributed by* SBL Press

Brown University, *distributed by* American Mathematical Society (AMS)

Brown Walker Press, *imprint of* Universal-Publishers Inc

Brusberg (Berlin), *distributed by* Alan Wofsy Fine Arts

Bryn Mawr College, *distributed by* Oak Knoll Press

Bryn Mawr Commentaries, *distributed by* Hackett Publishing Co Inc

Bucking Horse Books, *distributed by* Mountain Press Publishing Co

Bucknell University Press, *distributed by* Rutgers University Press, Rutgers University Press (www.rutgersuniversitypress.org/bucknell.org)

Buddy Books, *imprint of* ABDO

Barbara Budrich Publishers, *distributed by* Columbia University Press

Editorial Buenas Letras, *imprint of* The Rosen Publishing Group Inc

Bufflehead Books, *imprint of* Down The Shore Publishing

Bugle Boy Press, *imprint of* Peter E Randall Publisher

BuilderBooks, *division of* National Association of Home Builders (NAHB)

Builders Book Inc, *distributor for* Craftsman Book Co, *distributed by* Craftsman Book Co

Building Blocks, *distributed by* Gryphon House Inc

Building News Inc, *distributed by* Craftsman Book Co

Bulgarian-American Cultural Society ALEKO, *subsidiary of* Cross-Cultural Communications

Bullfrog Books, *imprint of* Jump!

Bungie, *distributed by* Harry N Abrams Inc

Bureau of Economic Geology, *unit of* University of Texas at Austin, Jackson School of Geosciences, *distributor for* Gulf Coast Association of Geological Societies, Gulf Coast Section SEPM, Texas Memorial Museum (selected titles)

Burgess Lea Press, *imprint of* Quarto Publishing Group USA Inc

Burnell Books, *distributor for* MAR*CO Products Inc

Burns Archive Press, *imprint of* Burns Archive Photographic Distributors Ltd

Buros Center for Testing, *distributed by* University of Nebraska Press

Bushwhack Press, *distributed by* WoodstockArts

Business Research Services Inc, *distributor for* Riley & Johnson

Butler Center for Arkansas Studies, *distributed by* The University of Arkansas Press

Butterworth-Heinemann, *distributed by* Marine Techniques Publishing, NACE International, SAMS Technical Publishing LLC

Butterworths, *distributed by* William S Hein & Co Inc

BuzzPop, *imprint of* little bee books

Byte Level Books, *imprint of* Ashland Creek Press

BYU Museum of Peoples & Cultures, *distributed by* The University of Utah Press

BYU Studies, *distributed by* The University of Utah Press

Cabi Books, *distributed by* Stylus Publishing LLC

Cal-Earth, *distributed by* Chelsea Green Publishing Co

Calico, *imprint of* ABDO

Calico Kid, *imprint of* ABDO

California Bill's, *distributed by* CarTech Inc

Calkins Creek, *imprint of* Astra Books for Young Readers

Callaway Arts & Entertainment, *distributed by* Hachette Book Group Inc

Callisto, *imprint of* Sourcebooks LLC

Callisto Media, *distributed by* Simon & Schuster, LLC

Calloway House, *distributor for* MAR*CO Products Inc

Cambridge University Press, *division of* University of Cambridge, *distributed by* William S Hein & Co Inc, International Book Centre Inc, NACE International

Camden House, *imprint of* Boydell & Brewer Inc

Camel Press, *imprint of* Epicenter Press Inc

Cameron+Company, *imprint of* Harry N Abrams Inc, *distributed by* Harry N Abrams Inc

Campus Compact, *distributed by* Stylus Publishing LLC

Canadian Centre for Architecture, *distributed by* The MIT Press

Canadian Society of Petroleum Geologists, *distributor for* AAPG (American Association of Petroleum Geologists)

Canary Street Press, *imprint of* Harlequin Enterprises Ltd

Canbury Press, *distributed by* Casemate | publishers

Candied Plums, *imprint of* Paper Republic LLC

Candlelight Romance, *imprint of* Iron Stream Media

Candlewick Entertainment, *imprint of* Candlewick Press

Candlewick Press, *subsidiary of* Walker Books Ltd, *distributed by* Perfection Learning®

Candlewick Studio, *imprint of* Candlewick Press

Canterbury Classics, *distributed by* Simon & Schuster, LLC

Canterbury Press, *distributed by* Westminster John Knox Press (WJK)

Gloriae Dei Cantores, *distributed by* Paraclete Press Inc

Capitol Enquiry Inc, *distributor for* Center for Investigative Reporting

Capstone, *imprint of* John Wiley & Sons Inc, *distributed by* International Book Centre Inc

Capstone Editions, *imprint of* Capstone Publishers™

Capstone Press, *imprint of* Capstone Publishers™

Caravel Books, *imprint of* Pleasure Boat Studio: A Literary Press

Cardoza Publishing, *distributed by* Simon & Schuster, LLC

Career Examination Passbooks®, *imprint of* National Learning Corp

Career Kids FYI, *distributor for* MAR*CO Products Inc

Career Press, *imprint of* Red Wheel/Weiser

Coleccion Caribena, *imprint of* Editorial de la Universidad de Puerto Rico

Carina Press, *imprint of* Harlequin Enterprises Ltd

Carnegie Publishing, *distributed by* Casemate | publishers

Carolrhoda Books Inc, *imprint of* Lerner Publishing Group Inc

Carolrhoda Lab™, *imprint of* Lerner Publishing Group Inc

Carson Dellosa Publishing LLC, *distributor for* Key Education, Mark Twain Media

CarTech Inc, *distributor for* Behemoth Publishing, Brooklands Books Ltd, California Bill's, Wolfgang Publications

Carthage Reprints, *imprint of* St Augustine's Press Inc

Cartwheel Books®, *imprint of* Scholastic Trade Publishing

Casa Bautista, *distributed by* Editorial Bautista Independiente

Casa Bautista de Publicaciones, *affiliate of* Southern Baptist Convention

Casa Creacion, *imprint of* Charisma Media

Casemate, *distributed by* Casemate | publishers

Casemate | academic, *distributed by* Casemate | publishers

Casemate | publishers, *division of* Casemate Group, *distributor for* AF Editions, After the Battle, AFV Modeller, Air War Publications, Air World, Andrea Press, Arabian Publishing Ltd, Arden, Australian Scholarly Publishing, Aviation Collectables, Avonmore Books, Banovallum, Bauernfeind Press, Big Sky Publishing, Birlinn (UK), Blackman Associates, Brookline Books, Canbury Press, Carnegie Publishing, Casemate (USA), Casemate | academic, Classics Illustrated Comics, Claymore Press, Collins Books, Colourpoint, Compendium (UK), Leo Cooper, Countryside Books, Crecy Publishing Ltd, Dalrymple & Verdun, Fighting High Publishing, Fonthill Media, Formac Publishing Ltd (Canada), Fox Run Publishing, Front Street Press (USA), Frontline Books, Gallantry, Gettysburg Publishing, Gill Books, Global Collective Publishers, Greenhill Books, Griffon International, Grub Street Publishing (UK), Harpia Publishing, Heimdal, Helion & Company (UK), Helion & Company / GG Books (UK), Histoire & Collections (France), History Facts, HMH Publications, Imperial War Museum, Kagero, Karwansary Publishers, Key Publishing, Leda, Liberties Press, The Liffey Press, Lorimer, LRT Editions, Medina Publishing, Mercier Press, Messenger Publications, Military Miniature Press, Mimesis International, MMPBooks (UK/Poland), Model Centrum Progres, Monroe Publications, Mort Homme Books, Mortons Media, Moselle River, The O'Brien Press, Origin, Oxbow Books, Pacifica Military History, Panzerwrecks, PeKo Publishing, Pen & Sword (UK), Pen & Sword Archaeology, Pen & Sword Atlas, Pen & Sword Aviation, Pen & Sword Digital, Pen & Sword Family History, Pen & Sword Fiction, Pen & Sword History, Pen & Sword Local History, Pen & Sword Maritime, Pen & Sword Military, Pen & Sword Military Classics, Pen & Sword Select, Pen & Sword Social History, Pen & Sword Transport, Pen & Sword True Crime, Penguin Random House South Africa, Polygon, Potomac Books, Praetorian Press, Protea Boekhuis, Remember When, Riebel-Roque, Rinaldi Studio Press, S I Publicaties BV, Sabrestorm Publishing, Savas Beatie (USA), Savas Publishing, Schneider Armour Research, Seaforth Publishing, Sidestone Press, Silver Link, Tattered Flag, Tempest, 30 Degrees South Publishers, George F Thompson Publishing, Timespan, Wharncliffe, Wordwell Books, Y Lolfa, Youthly, Ysec Editions

CASTI Publishing, *distributed by* NACE International

Castle Books, *imprint of* Book Sales

Castle Point Books, *imprint of* St Martin's Press, LLC

Catalpa Press, *distributed by* Oak Knoll Press

Catapult, *imprint of* Counterpoint Press LLC

Catechesis of the Good Shepherd Publications, *imprint of* Liturgy Training Publications

PUBLISHERS

Catholic Approach Series, *imprint of* Pauline Books & Media

The Catholic University of America Press, *division of* The Catholic University of America, *distributor for* The Academy of American Franciscan History, American Maritain Association, Franciscan University Press, Humanum Academic Press, Institute for the Psychological Sciences Press (IPS), Sapientia Press

Caxton Club, *distributed by* Oak Knoll Press

Caxton Press, *division of* The Caxton Printers Ltd, The Caxton Printers Ltd, *distributor for* Hambleton Publishing, Historic Idaho Series, Photosmith Books, Snake Country Publishing, University of Idaho Asian American Comparative Collection, University of Idaho Press

CBP, *imprint of* Chalice Press

CBP/EMH, *imprint of* Casa Bautista de Publicaciones

CCH, a Wolters Kluwer business, *subsidiary of* Wolters Kluwer

CCH Incorporated, *imprint of* Wolters Kluwer US Corp

CCH Peterson, *subsidiary of* CCH, a Wolters Kluwer business

CCH Riverwoods, *subsidiary of* CCH, a Wolters Kluwer business

CCH St Petersburg, *subsidiary of* CCH, a Wolters Kluwer business

CCH Tax Compliance, *subsidiary of* CCH, a Wolters Kluwer business

CCH Washington DC, *subsidiary of* CCH, a Wolters Kluwer business

Cedar Fort Inc, *distributor for* Horizon Publishers & Distributors Inc

Cedar Grove Publishing, *subsidiary of* WRTB Entertainment LLC

CEF Press, *subsidiary of* Child Evangelism Fellowship Inc, Child Evangelism Fellowship Inc

Cengage Learning, *distributed by* International Book Centre Inc

Cengage Learning Australia, *distributed by* Cheng & Tsui Co Inc

Centaur Books, *imprint of* Joshua Tree Publishing

Centennial Media, *distributed by* Simon & Schuster, LLC

Center for Book Arts, *distributed by* Oak Knoll Press

Center for Chinese Studies, University of Michigan, *distributed by* University of Michigan Press

Center for Creative Leadership LLC, *affiliate of* Smith Richardson Foundation, *distributor for* Free Press, Harvard Business School Press, Jossey-Bass, Lominger Inc, John Wiley & Sons Inc, *distributed by* Jossey-Bass, John Wiley & Sons Inc

Center for Investigative Reporting, *distributed by* Capitol Enquiry Inc

Center for Japanese Studies, University of Michigan, *distributed by* University of Michigan Press

The Center for Learning, *division of* Social Studies School Service

Center for Literary Publishing, *distributed by* University Press of Colorado

Center for Romanian Studies, *imprint of* Histria Books

Center for South & Southeast Asian Studies, University of Michigan, *distributed by* University of Michigan Press

Center for Strategic & International Studies (CSIS), *distributed by* Rowman & Littlefield

Center for the Child Care Workforce, *distributed by* Gryphon House Inc

The Center for the Study of Upper Midwestern Culture, *distributed by* University of Wisconsin Press

Center for US-Mexican Studies, *distributed by* Lynne Rienner Publishers Inc

Center of Emigrants from Serbia, *distributed by* Cross-Cultural Communications

Center Street, *imprint of* Hachette Nashville

Centerbrook Publishing, *subsidiary of* Centerstream Publishing LLC

Centerstream Publishing LLC, *distributed by* Hal Leonard LLC, Hal Leonard Corp

Central Avenue Publishing, *distributed by* Simon & Schuster, LLC

Central Recovery Press (CRP), *unit of* Central Recovery LLC

Cerf & Peterson, *distributed by* Welcome Books

Cernunnos, *imprint of* Harry N Abrams Inc, *distributed by* Harry N Abrams Inc, Simon & Schuster, LLC

Cervantes & Co, *imprint of* LinguaText LLC

CFI, *imprint of* Cedar Fort Inc

CFKR Career, *distributor for* MAR*CO Products Inc

Chalice Press, *division of* Christian Board of Publication

IMPRINTS, SUBSIDIARIES & DISTRIBUTORS

Chalice Stories, *imprint of* Chalice Press

Chance Magazine, *distributed by* Theatre Communications Group

Le Chant du Monde, *distributed by* Hal Leonard LLC

Chapin Library, *distributed by* Oak Knoll Press

Chapter Books, *imprint of* ABDO

Character Development, *distributor for* MAR*CO Products Inc

Charisma House, *imprint of* Charisma Media

Charles Press Publishers, *subsidiary of* Oxbridge Corporation

Charles River Media, *imprint of* Cengage Learning

Charlesbridge Moves, *imprint of* Charlesbridge Publishing Inc

Charlesbridge Press, *distributed by* Perfection Learning®

CharlesbridgeTEEN, *imprint of* Charlesbridge Publishing Inc

Chartwell Books, *imprint of* Book Sales

Chatterbox Press, *distributed by* Gryphon House Inc

Cheap Bastards, *imprint of* The Globe Pequot Press

Checkerboard Library, *imprint of* ABDO

Chelsea Clubhouse, *imprint of* Chelsea House

Chelsea Green, *imprint of* Rizzoli International Publications Inc

Chelsea Green Publishing Co, *imprint of* Rizzoli International Publications Inc, *distributor for* AATEC Publications, American Council for an Energy Efficient Economy (ACEEE), Anomaly Press, Avalon House, Boye Knives Press, Cal-Earth, Earth Pledge, Eco Logic Books, Ecological Design Institute, Ecological Design Press, Empowerment Institute, Filaree Productions, Flower Press, Foundation for Deep Ecology, Fox Maple Press, Green Books, Green Building Press, Green Man Publishing, Groundworks, Hand Print Press, Holmgren Design Services, Jenkins Publishing, Knossus Project, Left To Write Press, Madison Area Community Supported Agriculture Coalition, Marion Institute, marketumbrella.org, Metamorphic Press, Moneta Publications, Ottographics, Peregrinzilla, Permanent Publications, Daniela Piazza Editore, Polyface, Propriometrics Press, Rainsource Press, Raven Press, Anita Roddick Publications, Rural Science Institute, Seed Savers, Service Employees International Union, Slow Food Editore, Solar Design Association, Stone Pier Press, Stonefield Publishing, Sun Plans Inc, Sustainability Press, Trailblazer Press, Trust for Public Land, Yes Books

Chelsea House, *imprint of* Infobase Learning, *distributed by* Perfection Learning®

IMPRINTS, SUBSIDIARIES & DISTRIBUTORS

Chelsea Publishing Co Inc, *imprint of* American Mathematical Society (AMS)

Cheng & Tsui Co Inc, *distributor for* Action Language Learning, aha! Chinese, Bider Technology, Cengage Learning Australia, China International Book Trading Corp (CIBTC) (Beijing, selected titles only), China Soft, China Sprout, Crabtree Publishing Co, Curriculum Corp, Facets Video, Ilchokak Publishers, Italian School of East Asian Studies, Japan Times, JPT America Inc, Marshall Cavendish Singapore, Oxford University Press, Pan Asian Publications, Panmun Academic Services, Panpac Education, Paradigm Busters, Pearson Education Australia, Royal Asiatic Society (Korea Branch), SMC Publishing, Sogang University Institute, SUP Publishing Logistics, US International Publishing, White Rabbit Press, Zeitgeist Films

Cheriton Children's Books, *imprint of* Lerner Publishing Group Inc

Cheriton Children's Books, *distributed by* Lerner Publishing Group Inc

Cherokee Heritage Press, *distributed by* University of Oklahoma Press

Cherokee Publications, *distributed by* BPC

Cherry Lane Music Co, *imprint of* Hal Leonard LLC, *distributed by* Hal Leonard LLC

Chesapeake Bay Maritime Museum, *distributed by* Cornell Maritime Press

Chester Music, *distributed by* Hal Leonard LLC

Chicago Review Press, *distributed by* Gryphon House Inc, The Professional Education Group LLC (PEG)

Chicago Tribune Crosswords, *imprint of* Random House Reference/Random House Puzzles & Games

Chickadee Prince Books, *imprint of* Chickadee Prince Books LLC

Chickadee Prince Books LLC, *division of* Beacon International

Chicken House®, *imprint of* Scholastic Trade Publishing

Chicken Soup for the Soul Publishing, *distributed by* Simon & Schuster, LLC

Children of the Phoenix, *imprint of* Papercutz

Children's Book Press, *imprint of* Lee & Low Books, Lee & Low Books Inc

Children's Plus, *distributor for* Saddleback Educational Publishing

Children's Press, *distributed by* Perfection Learning®

Children's Resources International, *distributed by* Gryphon House Inc

Child's Play® Inc, *affiliate of* Child's Play (International) Ltd

Child's Play International, *distributed by* Heimburger House Publishing Co

Chilton Book Co, *distributed by* J J Keller & Associates, Inc®

China Books, *division of* Sinomedia International Group

China Encyclopedia Publishing House, *distributed by* Homa & Sekey Books

China Intercontinental Press, *distributed by* Homa & Sekey Books

China International Book Trading Corp (CIBTC), *distributed by* Cheng & Tsui Co Inc

China Soft, *distributed by* Cheng & Tsui Co Inc

China Sprout, *distributed by* Cheng & Tsui Co Inc

China Zhejiang Publishing United Group, *distributed by* Homa & Sekey Books

Chinese University Press, *distributed by* Columbia University Press

Chiral House, *imprint of* Joshua Tree Publishing

Chiron Publications, *distributed by* SteinerBooks Inc

Choi's Gallery, *distributed by* Gingko Press Inc

Chosen Books, *division of* Baker Publishing Group

Chosen People Ministries, *distributed by* Messianic Jewish Publishers

Choudens, *distributed by* Hal Leonard LLC

Christian Classics, *imprint of* Ave Maria Press Inc

Christian Large Print, *imprint of* Gale

Christian Network International, *distributor for* Pentecostal Resources Group

The Christian Science Publishing Society, *division of* The First Church of Christ, Scientist

Chronicle Books, *distributor for* Handprint Books Inc, PA Press, *distributed by* Hachette Book Group Inc, Perfection Learning®

Chronicle Books LLC, *distributor for* Amicus Ink, BIS Publishers, Blackwell & Ruth, Brass Monkey, The Creative Company, Galison, Games Room, Hardie Grant Books, Laurence King Publishing Ltd, Levine Querido, Mudpuppy, PA Press, Paperblanks (CN & US), Petit Collage, Quadrille Publishing Ltd, Ridley Games, Sierra Club, Twirl Books

Chronicle Bridge, *imprint of* Chronicle Books LLC

Chronicle Chroma, *imprint of* Chronicle Books LLC

Chronicle Prism, *imprint of* Chronicle Books LLC

Chronology Books, *imprint of* History Publishing Co LLC

Church House Publishing, *distributed by* Westminster John Knox Press (WJK)

Churchill Livingstone, *imprint of* Elsevier Health Sciences

Cider Mill Press, *imprint of* Cider Mill Press Book Publishers LLC

Cider Mill Press Book Publishers LLC, *imprint of* HarperCollins Focus LLC, *distributed by* Simon & Schuster, LLC

Coleccion Ciencias Naturales, *imprint of* Editorial de la Universidad de Puerto Rico

Cinco Puntos Press, *imprint of* Lee & Low Books Inc

Circle Time Publishers, *distributed by* Gryphon House Inc

Circlet, *imprint of* Circlet Press, Riverdale Avenue Books (RAB)

Circlet Press, *imprint of* Riverdale Avenue Books (RAB)

Cistercian Publications, *imprint of* Liturgical Press, *distributed by* Liturgical Press

Citadel Press, *imprint of* Kensington Publishing Corp

City Point Press, *distributed by* Simon & Schuster, LLC

Ciudad Nueva, *distributed by* New City Press

Clairmont House, *imprint of* Scarsdale Publishing Ltd

Clairview Books, *distributed by* SteinerBooks Inc

Arnold Clarendon, *distributed by* Oxford University Press USA

Clarendon Press, *imprint of* Oxford University Press USA

Clarion Books, *imprint of* HarperCollins Children's Books

Clarity Sound & Light, *imprint of* Crystal Clarity Publishers

Arthur H Clark Co, *imprint of* University of Oklahoma Press

Clark City Press, *distributed by* Mountain Press Publishing Co

Ayebia Clarke Publishing Ltd, *distributed by* Lynne Rienner Publishers Inc

PUBLISHERS

Clarkson Research Services Ltd, *distributed by* Marine Techniques Publishing

Coleccion Clasicos No Tan Clasicos, *imprint of* Editorial de la Universidad de Puerto Rico

Classic Reprint Series, *imprint of* University of Alaska Press

Classics, *imprint of* ABDO

Classics Illustrated Comics, *distributed by* Casemate | publishers

Classics Library, *imprint of* Recorded Books Inc, an RBmedia company

Classroom Classics, *imprint of* World Citizens

Claymore Press, *distributed by* Casemate | publishers

Clear Day Books, *imprint of* Clarity Press Inc

Clearfield Co Inc, *subsidiary of* Genealogical Publishing Co

Cleis Press, *imprint of* Start Publishing LLC

Sydney Gurewitz Clemens, *distributed by* Gryphon House Inc

Clerc Books, *imprint of* Gallaudet University Press

Clerisy Press, *imprint of* AdventureKEEN

CLEVER Publishing, *distributed by* Quarto Publishing Group USA Inc

CLIE, *distributed by* Editorial Bautista Independiente

CliffsNotes™, *imprint of* Houghton Mifflin Harcourt Trade & Reference Division

Clipper Audio (UK), *imprint of* Recorded Books Inc, an RBmedia company

Cloister Recordings, *distributed by* Gateways Books & Tapes

Close Up Publishing, *division of* Close Up Foundation

Closson Press, *distributor for* Hearthside Books, Darvin Martin CDs, Retrospect Publishing, *distributed by* Janaway Publishing, Masthof Press

Club of Odd Volumes, *distributed by* Oak Knoll Press

CMC, *distributor for* dbS Productions

CN Times Books, *imprint of* CN Times Inc, *distributor for* Bashu Publishing, Foreign Language Press, Intercontinental Press, Phoenix Publishing

Cochrane Library, *imprint of* John Wiley & Sons Inc

Codex Foundation, *distributed by* Oak Knoll Press

Codhill Press, *distributed by* State University of New York Press

Coffeetown Press, *imprint of* Epicenter Press Inc

Cogent OA, *imprint of* Taylor & Francis Inc

Andy Cohen Books, *imprint of* Crown Publishing Group

Cold Spring Harbor Laboratory Press, *division of* Cold Spring Harbor Laboratory, *distributed by* Oxford University Press USA

Cold Spring Press, *distributed by* Simon & Schuster, LLC

Colla Voce, *distributed by* ECS Publishing Group

Collections Livrier, *imprint of* Progressive Press

The Collective Book Studio, *distributed by* Simon & Schuster, LLC

The College Board, *distributed by* Macmillan

College of Tropical Agriculture & Human Resources, *distributed by* University of Hawaii Press

Collegium Graphicum, *imprint of* The Picasso Project, Alan Wofsy Fine Arts

Collins Books, *distributed by* Casemate | publishers

Colonial Roots, *imprint of* Heritage Books Inc

Colonial Society of Massachusetts, *distributed by* University of Virginia Press

Colorado Mountain Club Press, *distributed by* Mountaineers Books

Colourpoint, *distributed by* Casemate | publishers

Columbia Books on Architecture & the City, *distributed by* Columbia University Press

Columbia Business School Publishing, *imprint of* Columbia University Press

Columbia International Affairs Online (CIAO), *distributor for* University of California Institute on Global Conflict & Cooperation

Columbia University Press, *distributor for* Agenda Publishing, Austrian Film Museum Books, Barbara Budrich Publishers, Chinese University Press, Columbia Books on Architecture & the City, Maria Curie-Sklodowska University Press, ERIS (worldwide), Fernwood Publishing, Floating Opera Press (Africa, Asia, Australia, Middle East, New Zealand, North America & South America), Harrington Park Press, Hitchcock Annual, ibidem Press (English language titles exc China & India), Jagiellonian University Press, Lincoln Institute of Land Policy, Peterson Institute for International Economics, Social Science Research Council, Stanford University Press, Transcript Verlag, Tulika

IMPRINTS, SUBSIDIARIES & DISTRIBUTORS

Books, University of Tokyo Press, Miriam & Ira D Wallach Art Gallery, Woodrow Wilson Center Press

Commonwealth Editions, *imprint of* Arcadia Publishing Inc

Community Intervention, *distributor for* MAR*CO Products Inc

Companion Guides, *imprint of* Boydell & Brewer Inc

CompanionHouse Books, *imprint of* Fox Chapel Publishing Co Inc

Compass, *imprint of* Brigantine Media

Compass Point Mysteries, *imprint of* Quincannon Publishing Group

Compass Publications, *distributed by* International Book Centre Inc, NACE International

Compendium, *distributed by* Casemate | publishers

CompuMaster, *division of* SkillPath Publications

Comstock Publishing Associates, *imprint of* Cornell University Press

Conari Press, *imprint of* Turner Publishing Co LLC, *distributed by* Gryphon House Inc

Concord Library, *imprint of* Beacon Press

Concordia Gospel Outreach, *division of* Concordia Publishing House

Concordia Publishing House, *subsidiary of* The Lutheran Church, Missouri Synod, The Luthern Church, Missouri Synod

Concordia Technology Solutions, *division of* Concordia Publishing House

Congress Watch, *division of* Public Citizen

The Connecticut Law Tribune, *division of* ALM Media LLC

Consciousness Classics, *imprint of* Gateways Books & Tapes

Consort Press, *distributed by* ECS Publishing Group

Conspire Creative, *division of* Everything Goes Media LLC

Consumer Reports, *distributor for* United States Pharmacopeia (USP)

Context Press, *imprint of* New Harbinger Publications Inc

Continental AfrikaPublishers, *division of* Afrikamawu Miracle Mission, AMI Inc

Contra/Thought, *imprint of* Holmes Publishing Group LLC

IMPRINTS, SUBSIDIARIES & DISTRIBUTORS

Convergent Books, *imprint of* Random House Publishing Group

Cool Springs Press, *imprint of* Quarto Publishing Group USA Inc

Leo Cooper, *distributed by* Casemate | publishers

Coordinating Research Council Inc, *distributed by* SAE (Society of Automotive Engineers International)

Copernicus, *imprint of* Springer

Copper Canyon Press, *distributor for* American Poetry Review/Honickman

Core: Leadership, Infrastructure, Futures, *division of* The American Library Association (ALA)

Core Library, *imprint of* ABDO

Cormorant Books, *imprint of* Down The Shore Publishing

Cormorant Calendars, *imprint of* Down The Shore Publishing

Cornell East Asia Series, *imprint of* Cornell University Press

Cornell Maritime Press, *imprint of* Schiffer Publishing Ltd, *distributor for* Chesapeake Bay Maritime Museum, Independent Seaport Museum, Literary House Press, Maryland Historical Trust Press, Maryland Sea Grant Program

Cornell University Press, *division of* Cornell University, *distributor for* Leuven University Press, University of California Institute on Global Conflict & Cooperation

Corwin, *division of* SAGE Publishing, *distributor for* SAGE UK Resources for Educators

Cosimo Books, *imprint of* Cosimo Inc

Cosimo Classics, *imprint of* Cosimo Inc

Cosimo Reports, *imprint of* Cosimo Inc

Cost Annuals, *division of* R S Means from The Gordian Group

Costume & Fashion Press, *imprint of* Quite Specific Media Group Ltd

Cotsen Children's Library (Princeton), *distributed by* Oak Knoll Press

Cotsen Institute of Archaeology Press, *division of* University of California, Los Angeles

Council for Exceptional Children (CEC), *distributor for* Brookes (selected titles), Free Spirit (selected titles), Guilford (selected titles), National Professional Resources (selected titles)

Council Oak Books, *imprint of* Chicago Review Press, *distributed by* Gryphon House Inc

Council on Foreign Relations Press, *division of* Council on Foreign Relations

Council Press, *imprint of* Cedar Fort Inc

Counterpoint, *imprint of* Counterpoint Press LLC

Country Music Foundation Press, *division of* Country Music Hall of Fame® & Museum, *distributed by* Vanderbilt University Press

Countryman Press, *division of* W W Norton & Company Inc, *distributed by* Penguin Books (CN only)

The Countryman Press, *division of* W W Norton & Company Inc

Countryside Books, *distributed by* Casemate | publishers

Courage to Change, *distributor for* MAR*CO Products Inc

Coutts Library Service, *distributor for* Primary Research Group Inc

Cove Press, *imprint of* US Games Systems Inc

Covenant Communications Inc, *division of* Deseret Book Co

Cover Craft, *imprint of* Perfection Learning®

Cover-to-Cover, *imprint of* Perfection Learning®

Covet, *imprint of* Entangled Publishing LLC

Franklin Covey, *distributed by* SkillPath Publications

CQ Press, *imprint of* SAGE Publishing

Crabtree Blossoms, *imprint of* Crabtree Publishing Co

Crabtree Branches, *imprint of* Crabtree Publishing Co

Crabtree Classics, *imprint of* Crabtree Publishing Co

Crabtree Crown, *imprint of* Crabtree Publishing Co

Crabtree Forest, *imprint of* Crabtree Publishing Co

Crabtree Leaves, *imprint of* Crabtree Publishing Co

Crabtree Little Honey, *imprint of* Crabtree Publishing Co

Crabtree Publishing Co, *distributor for* Bayard, Seahorse Publishing, Sequoia Kids Media, *distributed by* Cheng & Tsui Co Inc, Perfection Learning®

Crabtree Publishing Co Ltd, *subsidiary of* Crabtree Publishing Co

Crabtree Roots, *imprint of* Crabtree Publishing Co

Crabtree Seedlings, *imprint of* Crabtree Publishing Co

Crabtree Sunshine, *imprint of* Crabtree Publishing Co

Craftsman Book Co, *distributor for* BNI Publications, Builders Book Inc, Building News Inc, Home Builders Press, *distributed by* The Aberdeen Group, American Technical Publishers, BNI Publications, Builders Book Inc

Cramer (Geneva), *distributed by* Alan Wofsy Fine Arts

Cramer (Switzerland), *distributed by* The Picasso Project

Craven Street Books, *imprint of* Linden Publishing Co Inc

Crazy Crow, *distributed by* BPC

CRC Press, *imprint of* Routledge, Taylor & Francis Inc, *distributed by* American Academy of Environmental Engineers & Scientists®, NACE International

CRCS Publications, *distributed by* BPC

The Creative Co, *distributor for* Amicus

The Creative Company, *distributed by* Chronicle Books LLC

Creative Digital, *imprint of* Creative Editions

Creative Editions, *imprint of* The Creative Company

Creative Education, *imprint of* Creative Editions

Creative Homeowner, *imprint of* Fox Chapel Publishing Co Inc

Creative Paperbacks, *imprint of* Creative Editions

Creative Publishing International, *imprint of* Quarto Publishing Group USA Inc

Crecy Publishing Ltd, *distributed by* Casemate | publishers

Creighton University Press, *distributed by* Fordham University Press

Crescent Books, *imprint of* Penguin Random House LLC

Cress Productions Co, *distributor for* MAR*CO Products Inc

Crestline, *imprint of* Book Sales

Creston Books, *distributed by* Lerner Publishing Group Inc

Crimeline, *imprint of* Penguin Random House LLC

Crimethinc, *distributed by* AK Press

Critical Path, *distributed by* BPC

PUBLISHERS   IMPRINTS, SUBSIDIARIES & DISTRIBUTORS

Crocodile Books, *imprint of* Interlink Publishing Group Inc

Croft House Books, *distributor for* Primary Research Group Inc

Crosley-Griffith Publishing Co Inc, *imprint of* C&T Publishing Inc

Cross-Cultural Communications, *division of* Cross-Cultural Literary Editions Inc, *distributor for* Ad Infinitum Books, Arba Sicula (Magazine, US), Center of Emigrants from Serbia (Serbia), Greenfield Review Press (US), Immagine&Poesia (Italy), Legas Publishers (CN), Lips (Magazine & Press) (US), The New Feral Press (US), Pholiota Press Inc (England), The Seventh Quarry Press (Wales), Shabdaguchha (Magazine & Press) (Bangladesh & US), Sicilia Parra (Magazine, US)

Cross-Cultural Prototypes, *imprint of* Cross-Cultural Communications

Crossed Crow Books, *distributed by* Red Wheel/Weiser

CrossKnowledge, *imprint of* John Wiley & Sons Inc

Crossroad, *imprint of* The Crossroad Publishing Co

Crossway, *division of* Good News Publishers

Crown, *distributed by* Perfection Learning®

Crown Archetype, *imprint of* Crown Publishing Group

Crown Books for Young Readers, *imprint of* Random House Children's Books

Crown Business, *imprint of* Crown Publishing Group

Crown Currency, *imprint of* Crown Publishing Group

Crown Forum, *imprint of* Crown Publishing Group

Crown House Publishing Co LLC, *division of* Crown House Publishing Ltd, Crown House Publishing Ltd (UK Co), *distributor for* Developing Press Co, Human Alchemy Publications, Institute Press, Transforming Press

Crown Publishers, *imprint of* Crown Publishing Group

Crown Publishing Group, *division of* Penguin Random House LLC, *imprint of* Random House Publishing Group

CSH Educational Resources Pte Ltd, *distributor for* Boys Town Press

CSI Publications, *imprint of* Christian Schools International (CSI)

CSLI Publications, *distributed by* University of Chicago Press

CSREA, *distributed by* Stylus Publishing LLC

CSWE Press, *division of* Council on Social Work Education

CT Corporation, *imprint of* Wolters Kluwer US Corp

Coleccion Cuadernos La Torre, *imprint of* Editorial de la Universidad de Puerto Rico

Coleccion Cuentos de un Mundo Perdido, *imprint of* Editorial de la Universidad de Puerto Rico

Culinary Institute of America, *imprint of* John Wiley & Sons Inc

Coleccion Cultura Basica, *imprint of* Editorial de la Universidad de Puerto Rico

Cumberland House™, *imprint of* Sourcebooks LLC

Curbstone Books, *imprint of* Northwestern University Press

Maria Curie-Sklodowska University Press, *distributed by* Columbia University Press

Curiosities, *imprint of* Norilana Books

Current Protocols, *imprint of* John Wiley & Sons Inc

Curriculum Corp, *distributed by* Cheng & Tsui Co Inc

Curriculum Solutions, *division of* Scholastic Education Solutions

James Curry Ltd, *imprint of* Boydell & Brewer Inc

CWLA Press, *imprint of* Child Welfare League of America (CWLA)

CyberAge Books, *imprint of* Information Today, Inc

CYPI, *distributed by* Gingko Press Inc

Cypress House, *imprint of* Comp-Type Inc

Dafina, *imprint of* Kensington Publishing Corp

Dagger, *imprint of* Riverdale Avenue Books (RAB)

Dalkey Archive Press, *imprint of* Deep Vellum Publishing

Dallas Museum of Art, *distributed by* Yale University Press

Dalrymple & Verdun, *distributed by* Casemate | publishers

Dance Horizons, *imprint of* Princeton Book Co Publishers

Dance Notation Bureau, *distributed by* Princeton Book Co Publishers

Dancing Ants Press, *imprint of* Dancing Dakini Press

Dancing Hands, *distributed by* Mel Bay Publications Inc

D&B Hoovers™, *subsidiary of* Dun & Bradstreet

DAP, *distributor for* National Gallery of Art

Dar Nun, *distributed by* Fons Vitae

Darby Creek Publishing, *imprint of* Lerner Publishing Group Inc

Dark Horse Books, *imprint of* Dark Horse Comics

Dark Horse Comics, *affiliate of* Dark Horse Entertainment, *distributed by* LPC Group Inc

Dark Horse Manga, *imprint of* Dark Horse Comics

Dark Ink, *distributed by* Simon & Schuster, LLC

Darklake, *imprint of* Scarsdale Publishing Ltd

Dash!, *imprint of* ABDO

David Publishing, *distributor for* Fire Engineering Books & Videos

David Zwirner Books, *distributed by* Simon & Schuster, LLC

Davies-Black, *imprint of* Nicholas Brealey Publishing

DAW Books, *imprint of* Astra Publishing House Inc

The Dawn Horse Press, *division of* The Adidam Holy Institution

DawnSignPress, *distributor for* Gallaudet University Press, MIT Press, Penguin Random House LLC, *distributed by* Gryphon House Inc

The Day That Was Different, *imprint of* Gallopade International Inc

DayMaker, *imprint of* Barbour Publishing Inc

dbS Productions, *distributed by* CMC

DC, *imprint of* DC Comics Inc

DC Black Label, *imprint of* DC Comics Inc

DC Comics, *imprint of* DC Comics Inc

DC Comics Inc, *unit of* DC Entertainment

DC Kids, *imprint of* DC Comics Inc

Walter De Gruyter Inc, *division of* Walter de Gruyter GmbH, Walter de Gruyter GmbH, *distributor for* De Gruyter Mouton

347

IMPRINTS, SUBSIDIARIES & DISTRIBUTORS

De Haske Publications, *distributed by* Hal Leonard LLC

Coleccion Obras Completas Eugenio Maria de Hostos, *imprint of* Editorial de la Universidad de Puerto Rico

Juan de la Cuesta Hispanic Monographs, *imprint of* LinguaText LLC

Dearborn Trade, *distributor for* Appraisal Institute

Decoder Kids, *imprint of* Sundance/Newbridge Publishing

Dedalus Press, *distributor for* Syracuse University Press

Deep Books Ltd, *distributor for* Boys Town Press

Deep River Books, *imprint of* Deep River Books LLC

Deep South Books, *imprint of* University of Alabama Press

Marcel Dekker Inc, *distributed by* NACE International

Del Rey, *imprint of* Random House Publishing Group

Delacorte Press, *imprint of* Random House Children's Books, Random House Publishing Group

Delaney Books Inc, *subsidiary of* National Learning Corp

Dell, *imprint of* Random House Publishing Group

Dell Yearling, *imprint of* Penguin Random House LLC

Delmar Publishers Inc, *distributed by* Gryphon House Inc

Delmarva Roots, *imprint of* Heritage Books Inc

Delphinium Books, *affiliate of* HarperCollins Publishers, *distributed by* HarperCollins Publishers

Delta Education, *distributor for* National Council of Teachers of Mathematics (NCTM)

Democracy Is For People, *division of* Public Citizen

Demos Health, *imprint of* Demos Medical Publishing

Demos Medical Publishing, *imprint of* Springer Publishing Co

Denby Fawcett, *distributed by* University of Hawaii Press

Denver Art Museum, *distributed by* University of Oklahoma Press

Deo Publishing, *distributed by* Penn State University Press

Department of Education Resources, *division of* National Gallery of Art

Deseret Book, *imprint of* Deseret Book Co

Deseret Book Co, *subsidiary of* Deseret Management Corp, Deseret Management Corp

Desert Charts, *division of* Wide World of Maps Inc

Design Originals, *imprint of* Fox Chapel Publishing Co Inc

Destiny Books, *imprint of* Inner Traditions International Ltd

Destiny Image Inc, *subsidiary of* Nori Media Group

Destiny Recordings, *imprint of* Inner Traditions International Ltd

Developing Press Co, *distributed by* Crown House Publishing Co LLC

Devil's Due Comics, *distributed by* Simon & Schuster, LLC

DeVorss & Co, *distributor for* Acropolis Books (Joel S Goldsmith titles), Touch for Health, White Eagle Publishing Trust (England)

DeVorss Publications, *imprint of* DeVorss & Co

Dey Street Books, *imprint of* HarperCollins Publishers LLC

Dharma Spring, *imprint of* Red Wheel/Weiser

DharmaCafe, *distributed by* North Atlantic Books (NAB)

Michael di Capua Books, *imprint of* Disney-Hyperion Books

Dial Books for Young Readers, *imprint of* Penguin Young Readers Group

The Dial Press, *imprint of* Random House Publishing Group

Didax Educational Resources, *distributor for* National Council of Teachers of Mathematics (NCTM)

Digital Lizards of Doom, *imprint of* Papercutz

Dipti, *imprint of* Lotus Press, *distributed by* Lotus Press

DiscoverNet, *imprint of* DiscoverNet Publishing

DiscoverNet Publishing, *division of* DiscoverNet

Disinformation Books, *imprint of* Red Wheel/Weiser

Disney Children's Book Group, *division of* Disney Publishing Worldwide

Disney Editions, *imprint of* Disney Publishing Worldwide

Disney-Hyperion, *imprint of* Disney Publishing Worldwide

Disney-Hyperion Books, *imprint of* Disney Book Group

Disney Lucasfilm Press, *imprint of* Disney Publishing Worldwide

Disney Press, *imprint of* Disney Publishing Worldwide, *distributed by* Perfection Learning®

Disney Publishing Worldwide, *subsidiary of* The Walt Disney Co, The Walt Disney Co

Dissertation.com, *imprint of* Universal-Publishers Inc

Distri Books, *distributed by* Perfection Learning®

Dive Into Reading, *imprint of* Lee & Low Books Inc

Diversion Books, *division of* Diversion Publishing Corp, *distributor for* Zubaan Books, *distributed by* Simon & Schuster, LLC

Divine Arts, *imprint of* Michael Wiese Productions

DK, *division of* Penguin Random House LLC, Penguin Random House LLC, *distributed by* Perfection Learning®

DK Ltd, *distributed by* Sourcebooks LLC

Caitlyn Dlouhy Books, *imprint of* Simon & Schuster Children's Publishing

Documentext, *imprint of* McPherson & Co

Dogu Publishing, *imprint of* Dark Horse Comics

Dogwise Publishing, *division of* Direct Book Service Inc

Domus Latina Publishing, *distributed by* Focus

The Donning Company Publishers, *subsidiary of* Walsworth, *distributed by* Schiffer Publishing Ltd

Dordt Press, *affiliate of* Dordt University

Dorling Kindersley, *imprint of* DK, *distributor for* Parachute Publishing LLC

Pamela Dorman Books, *imprint of* Viking Penguin

Samuel Dorsky Museum of Art, *distributed by* State University of New York Press

Coleccion Dos Lenguas, *imprint of* Editorial de la Universidad de Puerto Rico

Dots & Lines Inc, *distributed by* Hal Leonard LLC

Double Dog, *imprint of* Yard Dog Press

PUBLISHERS

IMPRINTS, SUBSIDIARIES & DISTRIBUTORS

Doubleday, *imprint of* Knopf Doubleday Publishing Group, *distributed by* Perfection Learning®

Doubleday/Galilee, *imprint of* Penguin Random House LLC

Dover Publications Inc, *subsidiary of* Lakeside Book Co, *distributed by* Alfred Music

Down East Books, *imprint of* The Globe Pequot Press

Down The Shore Publishing, *unit of* Down The Shore Books LLC

Downtown Bookworks, *distributed by* Simon & Schuster, LLC

DragonFish Comics, *imprint of* Gauthier Publications Inc

Dragonfly Books, *imprint of* Random House Children's Books

Drama Publishers, *imprint of* Quite Specific Media Group Ltd

Dramatists Play Service Inc, *imprint of* Broadway Licensing

Drawn & Quarterly, *distributed by* Farrar, Straus & Giroux, LLC, Macmillan

Dreamscape Media LLC, *division of* RBmedia, *distributor for* Berrett-Koehler Publishers, Gildan Media, Hallmark Publishing, HarperCollins, Ideal Audiobooks, Mayo Clinic Press, Penguin Random House LLC, Radio Archives, *distributed by* Blackstone Publishing

Dropship, *imprint of* Vesuvian Books

Drum Channel, *distributed by* Alfred Music

Dryad Press, *distributed by* Mandel Vilar Press

DSCH, *distributed by* Hal Leonard LLC

Ducasse Edition, *distributor for* Harry N Abrams Inc, *distributed by* Harry N Abrams Inc

Duet Books, *imprint of* Chicago Review Press

Duke University Press, *distributor for* Forest History Society

Dumb Ox Books, *distributed by* St Augustine's Press Inc

Dumbarton Oaks, *distributed by* Harvard University Press

duopress, *imprint of* Sourcebooks LLC

Dutton, *imprint of* Penguin Publishing Group, *distributed by* Perfection Learning®

Dutton Children's Books, *imprint of* Penguin Young Readers Group

Eagle Editions, *imprint of* Heritage Books Inc

Eagle Wing Books, *distributed by* Adventures Unlimited Press (AUP)

Eagles Landing Publishing, *distributed by* Biographical Publishing Co

Eakin Press, *imprint of* Wild Horse Media Group

E&FN Spon, *distributed by* NACE International

Early Childhood Education, *division of* Scholastic Education Solutions

Early Editions Books, *imprint of* Science & Humanities Press

Early Educator's Press, *distributed by* Gryphon House Inc

Early English Text Society, *imprint of* Boydell & Brewer Inc

Early Math, *imprint of* Sundance/Newbridge Publishing

Early Science, *imprint of* Sundance/Newbridge Publishing

Early Social Studies, *imprint of* Sundance/Newbridge Publishing

Earth Pledge, *distributed by* Chelsea Green Publishing Co

Earthdancer Books, *imprint of* Inner Traditions International Ltd

East Point, *imprint of* Scarsdale Publishing Ltd

East West Cultural Center, *distributed by* Lotus Press

Eastern Book Company, *distributor for* Primary Research Group Inc

Eastland Press, *distributor for* Journal of Chinese Medicine Publications

Easy Money Press, *subsidiary of* Wolford & Associates

eatrightPress, *imprint of* Academy of Nutrition & Dietetics

Ebsco, *distributor for* Primary Research Group Inc

Ecco, *imprint of* HarperCollins Publishers LLC

Eclipse Press, *imprint of* The Lyons Press

Eco Logic Books, *distributed by* Chelsea Green Publishing Co

Ecological Design Institute, *distributed by* Chelsea Green Publishing Co

Ecological Design Press, *distributed by* Chelsea Green Publishing Co

ECS Publishing Group, *distributor for* Randol Bass Music, Colla Voce, Consort Press, Edition Delrieu, Layali Music Publishing, Prime Music, Stainer & Bell Ltd, Vireo Press

ECW Press, *distributed by* Simon & Schuster, LLC

EDC Publishing, *division of* Educational Development Corp, Educational Development Corp

Edenridge Press, *distributed by* International Book Centre Inc

EDFU Books, *distributed by* Adventures Unlimited Press (AUP)

Edge of Sports, *imprint of* Akashic Books

Edgewise Press Inc, *distributor for* Editions d'Afrique du Nord, Libri Canali Bassi, Paolo Torti degli Alberti, Tsukuda Island Press

ediciones Lerner, *imprint of* Lerner Publishing Group Inc

Edison Welding Institute, *distributor for* American Society for Nondestructive Testing

Edition Delrieu, *distributed by* ECS Publishing Group

Editions Durand, *distributed by* Hal Leonard LLC

Les Editions ETC, *distributed by* Lotus Press

Editions Flammarion, *distributed by* Rizzoli International Publications Inc

Editions Koch, *distributed by* Oak Knoll Press

Editions Max Eschig, *distributed by* Hal Leonard LLC

Editions Salabert, *distributed by* Hal Leonard LLC

Editions Technip, *distributed by* Gulf Energy Information

Editorial Bautista Independiente, *division of* Baptist Mid-Missions, *distributor for* Casa Bautista, CLIE, Portavoz

Editorial Concordia, *division of* Concordia Publishing House

Editorial de la Universidad de Puerto Rico, *subsidiary of* University of Puerto Rico

Editorial Portavoz, *division of* Kregel Publications, *imprint of* Kregel Publications

EDU Reference, *distributor for* MAR*CO Products Inc

The Education Press, *division of* Brown Books Publishing Group (BBPG)

Educational Insights®, *division of* Learning Resources Inc

Educational Media Corp, *distributor for* MAR*CO Products Inc, *distributed by* MAR*CO Products Inc

Educational Publishing Foundation (EPF), *imprint of* American Psychological Association

Educators for Social Responsibility, *distributed by* Gryphon House Inc

Educators Outlet, *distributor for* National Council of Teachers of Mathematics (NCTM)

Edupress Inc, *division of* Teacher Created Resources Inc

Eerdmans Books for Young Readers, *imprint of* Wm B Eerdmans Publishing Co

Eifrig Publishing, *imprint of* Eifrig Publishing LLC

80/20 Publishing, *distributed by* Simon & Schuster, LLC

Eisenbrauns, *imprint of* Penn State University Press

Electric Strawberry Press, *imprint of* Radix Press

The Electrochemical Society (ECS), *distributed by* IOP Publishing (journals & magazines), Wiley Inc (books & monographs)

Edward Elgar Publishing, *distributed by* William S Hein & Co Inc

Elliott & Clark Publishing, *imprint of* River City Publishing

Elsevier, *distributed by* Gulf Energy Information

Elsevier Health Sciences, *division of* RELX Group plc, *distributor for* G W Medical Publisher

Elsevier Inc, *subsidiary of* RELX Group plc, *distributor for* Marine Techniques Publishing, *distributed by* Marine Techniques Publishing

Elsevier Science Publishers, *distributed by* NACE International

Elstreet Educational, *imprint of* Schreiber Publishing

Elva Resa, *imprint of* Elva Resa Publishing

Elysian Editions, *imprint of* Princeton Book Co Publishers

EM Books, *distributed by* Hal Leonard LLC

Emanate Books, *imprint of* Thomas Nelson

Ember, *imprint of* Random House Children's Books

Embrace, *imprint of* Entangled Publishing LLC

Emerald Books, *affiliate of* YWAM Publishing, *distributed by* YWAM Publishing

Emerald Publishing, *distributed by* William S Hein & Co Inc

Emmaus Road Publishing Inc, *division of* St Paul Center for Biblical Theology

EMP, *imprint of* Easy Money Press

Empire, *imprint of* Avant-Guide

Empire State Editions, *imprint of* Fordham University Press

Empowerment Institute, *distributed by* Chelsea Green Publishing Co

Enchanted Lion, *distributed by* Harry N Abrams Inc

Enchanted World, *distributed by* Union Square & Co

Encore, *imprint of* Simon & Schuster Audio

Encore Editions, *imprint of* Star Publishing Co Inc

Encounter Books, *division of* Encounter for Culture & Education

Encounter the Saints Series, *imprint of* Pauline Books & Media

Energy Arts, *distributed by* North Atlantic Books (NAB)

Energy Program, *division of* Public Citizen

Energy Psychology Press, *division of* Energy Psychology Group

Engineering Foundation, *distributed by* American Institute of Chemical Engineers (AIChE)

Engineering Press, *distributed by* Oxford University Press USA

English Discoveries, *distributed by* International Book Centre Inc

The English Spanish Foundation Series, *imprint of* me+mi publishing inc

Enslow, *imprint of* Enslow Publishing LLC

Enslow Elementary, *imprint of* Enslow Publishing LLC

Entangled Publishing, *distributed by* Macmillan

Entangled Publishing LLC, *distributed by* Macmillan

Entangled Select, *imprint of* Entangled Publishing LLC

Entangled Teen, *imprint of* Entangled Publishing LLC

Enthea Press, *imprint of* Ariel Press, *distributed by* Ariel Press

Entomological Society of America, *distributed by* Oxford University Press

Environmental Law Institute, *distributed by* West Academic (ELI Press)

Epigraph Publishing Service, *division of* Monkfish Book Publishing Co

EPS School Specialty, *division of* Cambridge Information Group Inc/Excolere Equity Partners

Epworth, *distributed by* Presbyterian Publishing Corp (PPC)

Erewhon Books, *imprint of* Kensington Publishing Corp, *distributed by* Workman Publishing

Ergos Institute, *distributed by* North Atlantic Books (NAB)

ERIS, *distributed by* Columbia University Press

Lawrence Erlbaum Associates, *distributor for* National Association of Broadcasters (NAB)

Ernst & Sohn, *imprint of* John Wiley & Sons Inc

Eschat Press, *imprint of* Loft Press Inc

Eshel Books, *imprint of* Bartleby Press

Essential Evidence Plus, *imprint of* John Wiley & Sons Inc

Essential Library, *imprint of* ABDO

Esther Press, *imprint of* David C Cook

ETA Cuisenaire, *distributor for* National Council of Teachers of Mathematics (NCTM)

Europa Compass, *imprint of* Europa Editions

Europa Editions, *subsidiary of* E/O Edizioni SRL, E/O Edizioni SRL, *distributed by* Jonathan Ball Publishers, NewSouth Books

European Mathematical Society, *distributed by* American Mathematical Society (AMS)

M Evans & Company, *imprint of* Rowman & Littlefield Publishing Group

Evergreen Pacific Publishing, *imprint of* Evergreen Pacific Publishing Ltd

Evergreen Press, *distributed by* Heimburger House Publishing Co

Everyman's Classic Library in Paperback, *imprint of* Tuttle Publishing

Everyman's Library, *imprint of* Knopf Doubleday Publishing Group

Everything, *imprint of* Adams Media

Everything DiSC®, *imprint of* John Wiley & Sons Inc

Everything Goes Media, *imprint of* Everything Goes Media LLC

Evil Eye Concepts, *distributed by* Simon & Schuster, LLC

PUBLISHERS — IMPRINTS, SUBSIDIARIES & DISTRIBUTORS

Evolver Editions, *imprint of* North Atlantic Books (NAB)

Ex Libris, *imprint of* Rizzoli International Publications Inc

Excelsior Editions, *imprint of* State University of New York Press, *distributor for* Albany Institute of History & Art, Uncrowned Queens

Executive Essentials, *imprint of* Health Administration Press

The Experiment, *distributed by* W W Norton & Company Inc, W W Norton Company Inc

Exposit Books, *imprint of* McFarland

Expressive Editions, *imprint of* Cross-Cultural Communications

Faber Music Ltd, *distributed by* Alfred Music, Hal Leonard LLC

Fabled Films LLC, *distributed by* Simon & Schuster, LLC

Fabled Films Press LLC, *distributed by* Simon & Schuster, LLC

Facets Video, *distributed by* Cheng & Tsui Co Inc

Fact Publishers, *imprint of* Cross-Cultural Communications

Facts On File, *imprint of* Infobase Learning

Fair Winds Press, *imprint of* Quarto Publishing Group USA Inc

Fairchild Books, *division of* Bloomsbury Publishing Plc

Fairfax Genealogical Society, *distributed by* Heritage Books Inc

Faith & Culture, *imprint of* Pauline Books & Media

Faith & Fellowship Publishing, *subsidiary of* Church of the Lutheran Brethren

Faith & Media Initiative (FAMI), *imprint of* Deseret Book Co

Faith Library Publications, *subsidiary of* RHEMA Bible Church, *distributed by* Harrison House, Whitaker

Faith Press, *imprint of* Winters Publishing

faithQuest, *imprint of* Brethren Press

FaithWords, *imprint of* Hachette Nashville

Falcon®, *imprint of* The Globe Pequot Press

Falcon Press, *imprint of* The Original Falcon Press

Familius, *distributed by* Abrams Books (worldwide exc CN), Harry N Abrams Inc, Workman Publishing

Family Center of Nova University, *distributed by* Gryphon House Inc

Family Tree Books, *imprint of* Penguin Publishing Group

Fanny Press, *imprint of* Epicenter Press Inc

FanPowered Press, *imprint of* C&T Publishing Inc

Fantagraphics Books, *distributed by* W W Norton & Company Inc

Fantasy Writers' Asylum, *imprint of* Yard Dog Press

Fantoons, *distributed by* Simon & Schuster, LLC

Far Muse Press, *imprint of* Loft Press Inc

Far to the North Press, *distributed by* University of Alaska Press

Far West Publishing, *imprint of* Sun Publishing Company

Farrar, Straus & Giroux Books for Young Readers, *imprint of* Farrar, Straus & Giroux, LLC, Macmillan Children's Publishing Group

Farrar, Straus & Giroux Inc, *distributed by* Perfection Learning®

Farrar, Straus & Giroux, LLC, *subsidiary of* Macmillan, *distributor for* Drawn & Quarterly, Gray Wolf Books

Father & Son Publishing Inc, *distributor for* BADM Books

Fatima Crusader, *distributor for* Angelus Press

Favorite Recipes Press, *imprint of* Capen Publishing Co Inc

Fawcett, *distributed by* Perfection Learning®

Federal Street Press, *division of* Merriam-Webster Inc

Feldheim Publishers, *distributor for* Adir Press, Jerusalem Publications, Mosaica Press

Jean Feldman, *distributed by* Gryphon House Inc

Fence Books, *imprint of* Fence Magazine Inc

Fence Digital, *imprint of* Fence Books

Margaret Ferguson Books, *imprint of* Holiday House Publishing Inc

Ferguson Publishing, *imprint of* Infobase Learning

Fernwood Publishing, *distributed by* Columbia University Press

Ferris & Ferris Books, *imprint of* The University of North Carolina Press

Fiction Collective 2 (FC2), *imprint of* University of Alabama Press, *distributed by* University of Alabama Press

Fieldstone Alliance, *imprint of* Turner Publishing Co LLC

53rd State Press, *distributed by* Theatre Communications Group

Fig Tree Books, *imprint of* Mandel Vilar Press

Fighting High Publishing, *distributed by* Casemate | publishers

Les Figues Press, *imprint of* LARB Books

Figures in Motion, *imprint of* Well-Trained Mind Press

Filaree Productions, *distributed by* Chelsea Green Publishing Co

Film Movement, *imprint of* Recorded Books Inc, an RBmedia company

Filmakers Library, *imprint of* Alexander Street, part of Clarivate PLC

Financial Ratings Series, *imprint of* Grey House Publishing Inc™

Financial Times Press, *imprint of* Pearson Education Ltd

Financial Times Publishing, *distributed by* Trans-Atlantic Publications Inc

Findhorn Press, *imprint of* Inner Traditions International Ltd

FineEdge.com LLC, *distributed by* Heritage House, Sunbelt Publications Inc

Fire Ant, *imprint of* University of Alabama Press

Fire Engineering Books & Videos, *distributor for* Brady, Idea Bank, IFSTA, Mosby, *distributed by* David Publishing, Fire Protection Publications

Fire Protection Publications, *distributor for* Fire Engineering Books & Videos

Firefall Editions, *imprint of* Firefallmedia

Firefall Originals, *imprint of* Firefall Editions

Firefly, *distributed by* Perfection Learning®

Firefly Books Ltd, *distributed by* Heimburger House Publishing Co

Firefly Southern Fiction, *imprint of* Iron Stream Media

Fireside Fiction, *imprint of* Heritage Books Inc

First Avenue, *distributed by* Perfection Learning®

IMPRINTS, SUBSIDIARIES & DISTRIBUTORS

First Avenue Editions, *imprint of* Lerner Publishing Group Inc

First Fruits of Zion, *distributed by* Messianic Jewish Publishers

First Second Books, *imprint of* Roaring Brook Press

First Steps, *imprint of* The Child's World Inc

FirstForumPress, *imprint of* Lynne Rienner Publishers Inc

Carl Fischer/Theodore Presser, *distributor for* Roncorp Music

Fisher Hill Publishing, *distributed by* International Book Centre Inc

Fisher Investments Press, *imprint of* John Wiley & Sons Inc

FishPond, *imprint of* Deep River Books LLC

Fitzroy Books, *imprint of* Regal House Publishing

The Five Behaviors of a Cohesive Team™, *imprint of* John Wiley & Sons Inc

Five Star™, *imprint of* Gale

FJH, *distributed by* Alfred Music

FJH Music Co Inc, *distributed by* Alfred Music

Flame, *imprint of* Scarsdale Publishing Ltd

Flame Tree Publishing, *distributed by* Simon & Schuster, LLC

Flamingo Books, *imprint of* Penguin Young Readers Group

Flash Kids, *imprint of* Union Square & Co

Fleamarket Music, *distributed by* Hal Leonard LLC

Flirt, *imprint of* Random House Publishing Group

Floating Opera Press, *distributed by* Columbia University Press

Floris Books, *distributed by* Gryphon House Inc, SteinerBooks Inc

Flower Press, *distributed by* Chelsea Green Publishing Co

Flux, *imprint of* North Star Editions Inc

Flux House Books, *imprint of* Dark Horse Comics

Fly!, *imprint of* ABDO

Flyaway Books, *imprint of* Presbyterian Publishing Corp (PPC)

Flying Start Books, *distributed by* Lerner Publishing Group Inc

FMP, *imprint of* Forward Movement

Focal Press, *distributor for* National Association of Broadcasters (NAB), *distributed by* Marine Techniques Publishing

Focus, *imprint of* Hackett Publishing Co Inc, *distributor for* Domus Latina Publishing

Focus on the Family, *distributed by* Baker Books, Moody Press, Tyndale House Publishers Inc, Zondervan

Focus Readers, *imprint of* North Star Editions Inc

Folger Shakespeare Library, *imprint of* Simon & Schuster

Fondation Custodia, *distributed by* Oak Knoll Press

Fons Vitae, *distributor for* African American Islamic Institute, Anqa Press (UK), Aperture (NY), Archetype (UK), Broadstone Books, Dar Nun, Golganooza Press (UK), Islamic Texts Society (UK), Matheson Trust, Parabola, Paragon, Parvardigar Press, Sophia Perennis, Pir Press (NY), Qiblah Books, Quilliam Press (UK), Sandala Productions, Sri Lanka Institute of Traditional Studies, Thesaurus Islamicus Foundation, Tradigital, White Thread Press (US), Wisdom Foundation, World Wisdom (US), Zaytuna Institute Press (US)

Fonthill Media, *distributed by* Casemate | publishers

Food & Agriculture Organization of the United Nations (FAO), *distributed by* United Nations Publications

Food52 Works, *imprint of* Ten Speed Press

For Dummies®, *imprint of* John Wiley & Sons Inc

Fordham University Press, *distributor for* Creighton University Press, Institute for Advanced Study in the Theatre Arts (IASTA), Little Room Press, Rockhurst University Press, St Bede's Publications, University of San Francisco Press, *distributed by* Heimburger House Publishing Co, Oxford University Press (US & CN)

Forefront Books, *distributed by* Simon & Schuster, LLC

Foreign Language Press, *distributed by* CN Times Books

Forest History Society, *distributed by* Duke University Press

Forest of Peace, *imprint of* Ave Maria Press Inc

Forever, *imprint of* Grand Central Publishing

Forge, *imprint of* Tor Publishing Group

Formac Publishing Ltd, *distributed by* Casemate | publishers

Fortress Press, *imprint of* Augsburg Fortress Publishers, Publishing House of the Evangelical Lutheran Church in America

Forward Movement, *affiliate of* The Episcopal Church, *distributor for* Anglican Book Centre

Mark Foster Music, *distributed by* Hal Leonard LLC

Walter Foster Jr, *imprint of* Quarto Publishing Group USA Inc

Walter Foster Publishing, *imprint of* Quarto Publishing Group USA Inc

Foundation for Deep Ecology, *distributed by* Chelsea Green Publishing Co

Foundation Press, *imprint of* West Academic

The Fountain, *imprint of* Tughra Books

4 Color Books, *imprint of* Ten Speed Press

4th Dimension Press, *imprint of* ARE Press

4U2B Books & Media, *imprint of* Loyola Press

Fowler Museum at UCLA, *distributed by* University of Washington Press

Fox Chapel Publishing Co Inc, *distributor for* Reader's Digest, Taunton Sterling Dover

Fox Maple Press, *distributed by* Chelsea Green Publishing Co

Fox Run Publishing, *distributed by* Casemate | publishers

Franciscan University Press, *distributed by* The Catholic University of America Press

Franko Maps, *distributed by* Wide World of Maps Inc

Frederator Books LLC, *distributed by* Simon & Schuster, LLC

Free Press, *imprint of* Simon & Schuster, *distributed by* Center for Creative Leadership LLC

Free Spirit, *distributed by* Council for Exceptional Children (CEC), Perfection Learning®

Free Spirit Publishing Inc, *imprint of* Teacher Created Materials

Freedom Fire, *imprint of* Disney Publishing Worldwide

Freedom Fox Press, *imprint of* Dancing Lemur Press LLC

Freedom Press, *distributed by* AK Press

Freeform, *imprint of* Disney Publishing Worldwide

W H Freeman, *imprint of* Macmillan Learning, *distributor for* American Geosciences Institute (AGI)

PUBLISHERS

IMPRINTS, SUBSIDIARIES & DISTRIBUTORS

Freestone, *imprint of* Peachtree Publishing Co Inc

Samuel French, Inc, *imprint of* Concord Theatricals, *distributor for* Baker's Plays, Samuel French Ltd (UK), *distributed by* Baker's Plays, Samuel French Ltd (UK)

Samuel French Ltd, *distributor for* Samuel French, Inc, *distributed by* Samuel French, Inc

FrescoBooks/SF Design LLC, *distributed by* University of New Mexico Press

Fresh Air Books, *imprint of* Upper Room Books

Friends United Press, *subsidiary of* Friends United Meeting

Frog Books, *imprint of* North Atlantic Books (NAB)

Frog Legs Ink, *imprint of* Gauthier Publications Inc

Front Street Press, *distributed by* Casemate | publishers

Front Table Books, *imprint of* Cedar Fort Inc

La Frontera Publishing, *distributed by* University of New Mexico Press

Frontline, *imprint of* Charisma Media

Frontline Books, *distributed by* Casemate | publishers

FSG Originals, *imprint of* Farrar, Straus & Giroux, LLC

FT Press, *imprint of* Financial Times Press

Fulcrum, *distributed by* Perfection Learning®

Full Tilt Press, *distributed by* Lerner Publishing Group Inc

FunStitch Studio, *imprint of* C&T Publishing Inc

Future Psychiatry Press, *imprint of* Loving Healing Press Inc

G W Medical Publisher, *distributed by* Elsevier Health Sciences

Gakken, *distributed by* Simon & Schuster, LLC

Galaxy Audio, *imprint of* Galaxy Press Inc

Galaxy Music Corp, *imprint of* ECS Publishing Group

Gale, *division of* Cengage Learning, *subsidiary of* Cengage Learning

Galerie Kornfeld Verlag AG (Bern), *distributed by* The Picasso Project, Alan Wofsy Fine Arts

Galison, *distributed by* Chronicle Books LLC

Gallantry, *distributed by* Casemate | publishers

Gallaudet University Press, *distributed by* DawnSignPress

Gallery Books, *imprint of* Gallery Publishing Group

Gallery 13, *imprint of* Gallery Books

Gallup Press, *distributed by* Simon & Schuster, LLC

Galvanized Media, *distributed by* Simon & Schuster, LLC

Games Room, *distributed by* Chronicle Books LLC

Games Workshop, *distributed by* Simon & Schuster, LLC

Garden Art Press, *imprint of* ACC Art Books

Gareth Stevens Publishing, *imprint of* The Rosen Publishing Group Inc

Garland Publishers, *distributor for* University of California Institute on Global Conflict & Cooperation

Garland Science, *imprint of* Taylor & Francis Inc

John Garrett, *distributor for* Twenty-Third Publications

Gates of Vienna Books, *imprint of* IHS Press

Gateway Editions, *imprint of* Regnery Publishing

Gateway to Healthcare Management, *imprint of* Health Administration Press

Gateways Books & Tapes, *division of* Institute for the Development of the Harmonious Human Being Inc, Institute for the Development of the Harmonious Human Being Inc, *distributor for* Cloister Recordings (audio & video tapes)

Gateways Fine Art Series, *imprint of* Gateways Books & Tapes

Gaudium Publishing, *imprint of* Histria Books

Roxane Gay Books, *imprint of* Grove Atlantic Inc

Geared Up Publications, *imprint of* Schiffer Publishing Ltd

Gecko Press, *imprint of* Lerner Publishing Group Inc, *distributed by* Lerner Publishing Group Inc

GemStone Press, *imprint of* Turner Publishing Co LLC

Genealogical Publishing Co, *subsidiary of* Genealogical.com

Genetic Engineering & Biotechnology News, *division of* Mary Ann Liebert Inc

Genius Games LLC, *distributed by* Science, Naturally

Gennadeion Monographs, *imprint of* ASCSA Publications

Gentle World, *distributed by* BPC

Gentry Publications, *distributed by* Hal Leonard LLC

Geological Society of London, *distributor for* AAPG (American Association of Petroleum Geologists), *distributed by* AAPG (American Association of Petroleum Geologists)

Geology & Geography of Alaska Series, *imprint of* University of Alaska Press

Geology Underfoot Series, *imprint of* Mountain Press Publishing Co

Geophysical Institute, *distributed by* University of Alaska Press

George Mason University Press, *distributed by* University of Virginia Press

German101, *imprint of* Mondial

GetFitNow.com Books, *imprint of* Hatherleigh Press Ltd

Getting Smart, *imprint of* Eifrig Publishing LLC

Getty, *distributed by* Oxford University Press USA

Getty Publications, *distributed by* Harry N Abrams Inc, Harry N Abrams Inc (CN & US, new juvenile/young adult only), University of Chicago Press (CN & US exc new juvenile/young adult)

Gettysburg Publishing, *distributed by* Casemate | publishers

Gibbs-Smith, *distributor for* Sourced Media Books

Gilbert, *imprint of* West Academic

Gilcrease Museum, *distributed by* University of Oklahoma Press

Gildan Media, *distributed by* Dreamscape Media LLC, Hachette Book Group Inc

D Giles Ltd, *distributor for* American Federation of Arts

Gill Books, *distributed by* Casemate | publishers

Gingko Press, *distributed by* Gingko Press Inc

Gingko Press Inc, *distributor for* Art Power, Basheer, Choi's Gallery, CYPI, Gingko Press, Rebel Arts, Sandu Publications, Sendpoints Books Co Ltd, Upper Playground, Victionary, Zero+ Publishing

GIT Verlag, *imprint of* John Wiley & Sons Inc

Michael Glazier Books, *imprint of* Liturgical Press

IMPRINTS, SUBSIDIARIES & DISTRIBUTORS

Glencoe/McGraw-Hill, *imprint of* McGraw-Hill Education

Global Collective Publishers, *distributed by* Casemate | publishers

Global Research, *distributed by* Progressive Press

Global Trade Watch, *division of* Public Citizen

Globe Pequot, *imprint of* The Globe Pequot Press

Globe Pequot Press, *distributed by* Heimburger House Publishing Co

The Globe Pequot Press, *division of* Rowman & Littlefield Publishing Group

Godine, *imprint of* Godine

Godwin Books, *imprint of* Henry Holt and Company, LLC

GoFacts Guided Reading, *imprint of* Sundance/Newbridge Publishing

Goff Books, *imprint of* ORO editions

Golden Books, *imprint of* Random House Children's Books, *distributed by* Perfection Learning®

Golden Dawn Publications, *imprint of* The Original Falcon Press

Golden Sky, *imprint of* Mondial

Golden West Cookbooks, *division of* American Traveler Press

Golganooza Press, *distributed by* Fons Vitae

Gooseberry Patch, *imprint of* The Globe Pequot Press, *distributed by* Andrews McMeel Publishing LLC

Gorgias Press LLC, *distributor for* Yeshiva University Museum Press

Gospel Publishing House, *imprint of* My Healthy Church

GP Putnam's Sons, *imprint of* Penguin Publishing Group

GPP® Travel, *imprint of* The Globe Pequot Press

Gracie Belle, *imprint of* Akashic Books

Gramophone, *distributed by* Omnibus Press

Grand Central, *imprint of* Grand Central Publishing

Grand Central/Hachette Large Print, *distributed by* Thorndike Press®

Grand Central Publishing, *division of* Hachette Book Group Inc

Donald M Grant Publisher Inc, *distributor for* Archival, Oswald Train

Graphia, *imprint of* Houghton Mifflin Harcourt Trade & Reference Division

Graphic Arts Books®, *imprint of* West Margin Press

Graphic Mundi, *imprint of* Penn State University Press

Graphic Novels, *imprint of* ABDO

Graphic Planet, *imprint of* ABDO

Graphic Universe™, *imprint of* Lerner Publishing Group Inc

Graphix™, *imprint of* Scholastic Trade Publishing

Gray Wolf Books, *distributed by* Farrar, Straus & Giroux, LLC

Graydon House Books, *imprint of* Harlequin Enterprises Ltd

Graywolf Press, *distributed by* Macmillan

Great Books of the Islamic World, *imprint of* Kazi Publications Inc

The Great Courses, *imprint of* Recorded Books Inc, an RBmedia company

Great Explorer Series, *imprint of* University of Alaska Press

Great Lakes Books, *imprint of* Wayne State University Press

Green Books, *distributed by* Chelsea Green Publishing Co

Green Building Press, *distributed by* Chelsea Green Publishing Co

Green Man Publishing, *distributed by* Chelsea Green Publishing Co

Green Trails Maps, *distributed by* Mountaineers Books

Greenberg Books, *imprint of* Kalmbach Media Co

Greenbranch, *distributed by* Medical Group Management Association (MGMA)

Greenfield Review Press, *distributed by* Cross-Cultural Communications

Greenhaven Publishing, *imprint of* The Rosen Publishing Group Inc, *distributed by* Lucent Press, Lucent Press (grades 7-10+), Perfection Learning®

Greenhill Books, *distributed by* Casemate | publishers

Greenleaf Book Group Press, *imprint of* Greenleaf Book Group LLC

Greenway Music Press, *imprint of* A-R Editions Inc

Greenwich Medical Media, *distributed by* Oxford University Press USA

Greenwich Publishing, *imprint of* Capen Publishing Co Inc

Greenwillow Books, *imprint of* HarperCollins Children's Books

Greenwood, *imprint of* ABC-CLIO

Grey House, *imprint of* Grey House Publishing Inc™

Grey House Publishing Canada, *division of* Grey House Publishing Inc™

Grey House Publishing Inc™, *distributor for* R R Bowker LLC

Griffin, *imprint of* St Martin's Press, LLC

Griffon International, *distributed by* Casemate | publishers

Griot Audio, *imprint of* Recorded Books Inc, an RBmedia company

The Grolier Club, *distributed by* Oak Knoll Press

Grosset, *distributor for* Parachute Publishing LLC

Grosset & Dunlap, *imprint of* Penguin Young Readers Group

Stefan Grossman's Guitar Workshop, *distributed by* Mel Bay Publications Inc

GroundSwell, *imprint of* BPC

Groundworks, *distributed by* Chelsea Green Publishing Co

Group for the Advancement of Psychiatry, *distributed by* American Psychiatric Association Publishing

Group Publishing, *distributed by* Saint Mary's Press

Grove Dictionaries, *distributed by* Oxford University Press USA

Grove Press, *imprint of* Grove Atlantic Inc

Grove Press UK, *imprint of* Grove Atlantic Inc

The Grow Network/McGraw-Hill, *imprint of* McGraw-Hill Education

Grub Street Publishing, *distributed by* Casemate | publishers

B R Gruener Publishing Co, *imprint of* John Benjamins Publishing Co

De Gruyter, *distributed by* William S Hein & Co Inc

Gryphon House Inc, *subsidiary of* Kaplan Early Learning Co, *distributor for* Aha Communications, Book Peddlers, Deya Brashears, Bright

PUBLISHERS — IMPRINTS, SUBSIDIARIES & DISTRIBUTORS

Ring Publishing, Building Blocks, Center for the Child Care Workforce, Chatterbox Press, Chicago Review Press, Children's Resources International, Circle Time Publishers, Sydney Gurewitz Clemens, Conari Press, Council Oak Books, DawnSignPress, Delmar Publishers Inc, Early Educator's Press, Educators for Social Responsibility, Family Center of Nova University, Jean Feldman, Floris Books, Hawthorne Press, Kaplan Press, Miss Jackie Inc, Monjeu Press, National Center Early Childhood Workforce, New England AEYC, Nova Southeastern University, Pademelon Press, Partner Press, Pollyanna Productions, Robins Lane Press, School Renaissance, Southern Early Childhood Association, Steam Press, Syracuse University Press, Teaching Strategies LLC, Telshare Publishing

Guerrilla Marketing Press, *imprint of* Morgan James Publishing

Guiding Light Women's Fiction, *imprint of* Iron Stream Media

Guild of Master Craftsman, *distributed by* Taunton Books

Guilford, *distributed by* Council for Exceptional Children (CEC)

Guinness World Records, *distributed by* Macmillan

Guitar World, *distributed by* Hal Leonard LLC

Gulf Coast Association of Geological Societies, *distributed by* Bureau of Economic Geology

Gulf Coast Section SEPM, *distributed by* Bureau of Economic Geology

Gulf Energy Information, *distributor for* Editions Technip, Elsevier, Pennwell, Wiley

Gulf Professional Publishers, *distributed by* Marine Techniques Publishing

Gulf Publishing, *distributed by* NACE International

Gurze Books, *imprint of* Turner Publishing Co LLC

Haase House, *imprint of* Easy Money Press

Hachai Publishing, *distributor for* Attara, Kerem, Living Lessons

Hachette Audio, *division of* Hachette Book Group Inc

Hachette Book Group Inc, *division of* Hachette Livre, *distributor for* Harry N Abrams Inc, Nicholas Brealey Publishing, Callaway Arts & Entertainment (US & CN), Chronicle Books, Gildan Media, Hachette UK Ltd, Houghton Mifflin Harcourt, Houghton Mifflin Harcourt Trade & Reference Division, Kids Can Press, Lonely Planet, Lonely Planet Publications Inc, Moleskine, Nosy Crow Inc, Octopus Books, The Overlook Press, Peterson's, Phaidon Press, Phoenix International Publications (PiKids), Quarto Publishing Group, Quarto Publishing Group USA Inc, Quercus Books, Sheldon Press (all print & digital), Time Inc Books, Yen Press

Hachette Books, *division of* Hachette Book Group Inc

Hachette Nashville, *division of* Hachette Book Group Inc

Hachette UK Ltd, *distributed by* Hachette Book Group Inc

Hackett Publishing Co Inc, *distributor for* Bryn Mawr Commentaries

Hal Leonard LLC, *distributor for* Arrangers Publishing LLC, Ashley Music, Berklee Press, Leonard Bernstein, Fred Bock Music Company, Boosey & Hawkes, Boston Music, Centerstream Publishing LLC, Le Chant du Monde, Cherry Lane Music Co, Chester Music, Choudens, De Haske Publications, Dots & Lines Inc, DSCH, Editions Durand, Editions Max Eschig, Editions Salabert, EM Books, Faber Music Ltd, Fleamarket Music, Mark Foster Music, Gentry Publications, Guitar World, Wilhelm Hansen, G Henle Verlag, Hinshaw Music, Homespun Tapes, Hot Licks, Hudson Music, Lauren Keiser Music, Robert King, LeDuc, Edward B Marks Music, Modern Drummer Publications, Music Minus One, Musicians Institute Press, Novello, Pavane Publishing, Peermusic Classical, PWM Editions, The Richmond Organization, Ricordi, Lee Roberts Publications, Rock House, Rubank Publications, Schaum Publications, G Schirmer Inc/Associated Music Publishers Inc, Schott Music, Second Floor Music, Shawnee Press, Sikorski, Southern Music, String Letter Publishing, Tara Publications, Tycoon Percussion, Union Musical Ediciones, Vintage Guitar, Waltons Irish Music, Willis Music, Sylvia Woods

Hal Leonard Performing Arts Publishing Group, *division of* Hal Leonard LLC

Halcyon House, *imprint of* National Book Co

Half Hour Reads, *imprint of* Scarsdale Publishing Ltd

Hallmark Publishing, *distributed by* Dreamscape Media LLC, Simon & Schuster, LLC

Hambleton Publishing, *distributed by* Caxton Press

Hameray Publishing Group Inc, *distributor for* Bear & Bobcat Books

Hamewith, *imprint of* Baker Books

Hamilton Books, *imprint of* Rowman & Littlefield Publishing Group

Hamilton Plant Books, *imprint of* Park Place Publications

Hammond, *distributed by* Perfection Learning®

Hampton Creek Press, *distributed by* Simon & Schuster, LLC

Hampton Roads Publishing, *imprint of* Red Wheel/Weiser, *distributed by* Red Wheel/Weiser

Hand Print Press, *distributed by* Chelsea Green Publishing Co

Handprint Books Inc, *imprint of* Chronicle Books, Chronicle Books LLC, *distributed by* Chronicle Books

Hanover Square Press, *imprint of* Harlequin Enterprises Ltd

Wilhelm Hansen, *distributed by* Hal Leonard LLC

Hanser Publications LLC, *subsidiary of* Carl Hanser Verlag GmbH & Co KG

HAP (Health Adminstration Press), *distributed by* Medical Group Management Association (MGMA)

Happy Fox, *imprint of* Fox Chapel Publishing Co Inc

Harambee Press, *imprint of* Iron Stream Media

Harcourt, *distributor for* Parachute Publishing LLC

Harcourt Children's Books, *imprint of* Houghton Mifflin Harcourt Trade & Reference Division

Hardie Grant Books, *distributed by* Chronicle Books LLC

Hardwood Press, *distributed by* St Augustine's Press Inc

Harlequin, *imprint of* Harlequin Enterprises Ltd

Harlequin Audio, *imprint of* Harlequin Enterprises Ltd

Harlequin Brand Group, *division of* Harlequin Enterprises Ltd

Harlequin Enterprises Ltd, *division of* HarperCollins, *distributed by* Simon & Schuster, LLC

Harlequin Romance Library™, *imprint of* Recorded Books Inc, an RBmedia company

Harlequin Teen, *imprint of* Harlequin Enterprises Ltd

Harlequin Trade Publishing Group, *division of* Harlequin Enterprises Ltd

Harmony Books, *imprint of* Random House Publishing Group

Harper, *imprint of* HarperCollins Publishers LLC

Harper Arrington Publishing, *distributor for* The Little Entrepreneur

Harper Business, *imprint of* HarperCollins Publishers LLC

Harper Influence, *imprint of* HarperCollins Publishers LLC

Harper Luxe, *imprint of* HarperCollins Publishers LLC

355

IMPRINTS, SUBSIDIARIES & DISTRIBUTORS

Harper Perennial, *imprint of* HarperCollins Publishers LLC

Harper Voyager, *imprint of* HarperCollins Publishers LLC

Harper Wave, *imprint of* HarperCollins Publishers LLC

HarperAlley, *imprint of* HarperCollins Children's Books

HarperAudio, *division of* HarperCollins Publishers LLC, *imprint of* HarperCollins Children's Books, HarperCollins Publishers LLC

HarperCollins, *imprint of* HarperCollins Children's Books, *distributor for* Alloy Entertainment LLC, Parachute Publishing LLC, *distributed by* Dreamscape Media LLC, Heimburger House Publishing Co, MAR*CO Products Inc

HarperCollins Canada Ltd, *division of* HarperCollins Publishers LLC

HarperCollins Children's Books, *division of* HarperCollins Publishers, HarperCollins Publishers LLC

HarperCollins Christian Publishing, *division of* HarperCollins Publishers LLC

HarperCollins e-books, *imprint of* HarperCollins Children's Books

HarperCollins Espanol, *imprint of* HarperCollins Publishers LLC

HarperCollins Holland, *division of* HarperCollins Publishers LLC

HarperCollins Hungary, *division of* HarperCollins Publishers LLC

HarperCollins Italia SpA, *division of* HarperCollins Publishers LLC

HarperCollins Japan, *division of* HarperCollins Publishers LLC

HarperCollins Nordic AB, *division of* HarperCollins Publishers LLC

HarperCollins Publishers, *distributor for* Delphinium Books

HarperCollins Publishers Australia, *division of* HarperCollins Publishers LLC

HarperCollins Publishers LLC, *subsidiary of* News Corp, News Corp

HarperCollins Publishers New Zealand, *division of* HarperCollins Publishers LLC

HarperCollins UK, *division of* HarperCollins Publishers LLC, *distributor for* National Geographic Books

HarperEntertainment, *distributor for* Parachute Publishing LLC

HarperLegend, *imprint of* HarperCollins Publishers LLC

HarperLuxe, *distributed by* Thorndike Press®

HarperOne, *imprint of* HarperCollins Publishers LLC

HarperVia, *imprint of* HarperCollins Publishers LLC

Harpia Publishing, *distributed by* Casemate | publishers

Harrington Park Press, *distributed by* Columbia University Press

Harrison House, *subsidiary of* Nori Media Group, *distributor for* Faith Library Publications

Harvard Art Museums, *distributed by* Yale University Press

Harvard Business Reference, *imprint of* Harvard Business Review Press

Harvard Business Review Press, *division of* Harvard Business Publishing

Harvard Business School Press, *distributed by* Center for Creative Leadership LLC

Harvard Center for Middle Eastern Studies, *distributed by* Harvard University Press

Harvard Center for Population Studies, *distributed by* Harvard University Press

Harvard Center for the Study of World Religions, *distributed by* Harvard University Press

Harvard College Library, *distributed by* Harvard University Press

Harvard Common Press, *imprint of* Quarto Publishing Group USA Inc

Harvard Department of Sanskrit & Indian Studies, *distributed by* Harvard University Press

Harvard Department of the Classics, *distributed by* Harvard University Press

Harvard Education Press, *imprint of* Harvard Education Publishing Group

Harvard Education Publishing Group, *division of* Harvard Graduate School of Education

Harvard Educational Review, *imprint of* Harvard Education Publishing Group

Harvard Ukrainian Research Institute, *subsidiary of* Harvard University, *distributed by* Harvard University Press

Harvard University Art Museums, *distributed by* Yale University Press

Harvard University Asia Center, *distributed by* Harvard University Press

Harvard University David Rockefeller Center for Latin American Studies, *distributed by* Harvard University Press

Harvard University Press, *distributor for* Dumbarton Oaks, Harvard Center for Middle Eastern Studies, Harvard Center for Population Studies, Harvard Center for the Study of World Religions, Harvard College Library (including Houghton Library Judaica div), Harvard Department of Sanskrit & Indian Studies, Harvard Department of the Classics, Harvard Ukrainian Research Institute, Harvard University Asia Center, Harvard University David Rockefeller Center for Latin American Studies, Harvard-Yenching Institute, Peabody Museum of Archaeology & Ethnology, Peabody Museum Press, *distributed by* W W Norton & Company Inc, W W Norton Company Inc

Harvard-Yenching Institute, *distributed by* Harvard University Press

Harvest, *imprint of* HarperCollins Publishers LLC

Harvest Kids, *imprint of* Harvest House Publishers Inc

Harvest Prophecy, *imprint of* Harvest House Publishers Inc

Hatherleigh Press Ltd, *distributed by* Penguin Random House LLC

Have a Little Faith, *imprint of* TRISTAN Publishing

Haven, *imprint of* Bridge Logos Inc

Hawaii Nikkei, *distributed by* University of Hawaii Press

Hawaiian Mission Children's Society, *distributed by* University of Hawaii Press

Hawthorn Press, *distributed by* SteinerBooks Inc

Hawthorne Press, *distributed by* Gryphon House Inc

Hayden-McNeil, *imprint of* Macmillan Learning

Hayes, *distributed by* Perfection Learning®

Haynes North America Inc, *division of* InfoPro Digital

Nicolas Hays Inc, *distributed by* Red Wheel/Weiser

Hazamir, *imprint of* Transcontinental Music Publications (TMP)

Hazelden/Johnson Institute, *imprint of* Hazelden Publishing

Hazelden/Keep Coming Back, *imprint of* Hazelden Publishing

Hazelden-Pittman Archives Press, *imprint of* Hazelden Publishing

Hazelden Publishing, *division of* The Hazelden Betty Ford Foundation, *distributor for* Obsessive Anonymous, *distributed by* Health Communications Inc (trade), Simon & Schuster, LLC

PUBLISHERS

IMPRINTS, SUBSIDIARIES & DISTRIBUTORS

HCI Books, *imprint of* Health Communications Inc

HCI Teens, *imprint of* Health Communications Inc

HCPro, *division of* BLR®—Business & Legal Resources

HCPro/DecisionHealth, *division of* BLR®—Business & Legal Resources

Healing Arts Press, *imprint of* Inner Traditions International Ltd

Healing Tao Books, *distributed by* Tuttle Publishing

Health Administration Press, *division of* Foundation of the American College of Healthcare Executives

Health Communications Inc, *distributor for* Hazelden Publishing, *distributed by* Simon & Schuster, LLC

Health Forum Inc, *subsidiary of* American Hospital Association

Health Information Press (HIP), *imprint of* Practice Management Information Corp (PMIC)

Health Professions Press, *imprint of* Paul H Brookes Publishing Co Inc

Health Research Group, *division of* Public Citizen

Healthcare Performance Press, *imprint of* Productivity Press

HealthLeaders Media, *division of* BLR®—Business & Legal Resources

Healthy Living, *imprint of* BPC

Healthy Living Books, *imprint of* Hatherleigh Press Ltd

Hearst Books, *imprint of* Union Square & Co

Heartdrum Books, *imprint of* HarperCollins Children's Books

Hearthside Books, *distributed by* Closson Press

Hearts 'n Tummies Cookbook Co, *division of* Quixote Press

HeartShaper®, *imprint of* Standard Publishing

Heaven & Earth Publishing LLC, *distributed by* North Atlantic Books (NAB)

Heavenly Light Press, *imprint of* BookLogix

Heavy Metal Entertainment, *distributed by* Simon & Schuster, LLC

Hebrew Union College Press, *division of* Hebrew Union College

Heimburger House Publishing Co, *distributor for* Child's Play International, Evergreen Press, Firefly Books Ltd, Fordham University Press, Globe Pequot Press, HarperCollins, Johns Hopkins University Press, Houghton Mifflin Harcourt, Iconografix, Indiana University Press, Kalmbach Publishing Co, Krause Publications Inc, Motorbooks, National Book Network, New York University Press, W W Norton & Company Inc, Penguin Putnam Inc, Pictorial Histories Publishing Co, Steam Passages Publishing, Sugar Cane Press, Syracuse University Press, Thunder Bay Press, Union Square & Co, University of Minnesota Press, John Wiley & Sons

Heimdal, *distributed by* Casemate | publishers

William S Hein & Co Inc, *distributor for* American Bar Association, American Law Institute, Ashgate, Aspen, Brill Nijhoff, Butterworths, Cambridge University Press, Edward Elgar Publishing, Emerald Publishing, De Gruyter, Oxford University Press, SAGE Publishing, Sweet & Maxwell, Taylor & Francis Group, John Wiley & Sons Inc, Wolters Kluwer

Heinemann, *division of* Houghton Mifflin Harcourt, *distributed by* Pearson (Australia, CN & New Zealand)

Heliconia Press, *imprint of* Fox Chapel Publishing Co Inc

Helion & Company, *distributed by* Casemate | publishers

Helion & Company / GG Books, *distributed by* Casemate | publishers

Hellgate Press, *imprint of* L & R Publishing LLC

Hell's Hundred, *imprint of* Soho Press Inc

Verlag Helvetica, *imprint of* John Wiley & Sons Inc

Hendrickson Academic, *imprint of* Hendrickson Publishers Inc

Hendrickson Bibles, *imprint of* Hendrickson Publishers Inc

Hendrickson Publishers Inc, *imprint of* Hendrickson Publishing Group

G Henle Verlag, *distributed by* Hal Leonard LLC

Henry Holt, *imprint of* Henry Holt and Company, LLC

Henry Holt and Company LLC, *division of* Macmillan

Henry Holt Books for Younger Readers, *imprint of* Henry Holt and Company, LLC

Her Own Words, *imprint of* Her Own Words LLC

Hera, *imprint of* Riverdale Avenue Books (RAB)

Herald Press, *imprint of* MennoMedia

Herder & Herder, *imprint of* The Crossroad Publishing Co

Here & Now, *imprint of* Gallopade International Inc

Heritage Beacon Fiction, *imprint of* Iron Stream Media

Heritage Books, *imprint of* Heritage Books Inc

Heritage Books Inc, *distributor for* Fairfax Genealogical Society, National Genealogical Society, Virginia Genealogical Society

Heritage Builders, *imprint of* Focus on the Family

Heritage House, *distributor for* FineEdge.com LLC

Nick Hern Books, *distributed by* Theatre Communications Group

Heroes & Helpers, *imprint of* Gallopade International Inc

Hesperia, *imprint of* ASCSA Publications

Heuristic Books, *imprint of* Science & Humanities Press

Hewitt Homeschooling Resources, *division of* Hewitt Research Foundation

HFS, *division of* Johns Hopkins University Press

Hi Jinx, *imprint of* Black Rabbit Books

Hidden Travel Series, *imprint of* Ulysses Press

High Road Books, *imprint of* University of New Mexico Press

High Tide Press, *subsidiary of* The Trinity Foundation

Highgate Press, *imprint of* ECS Publishing Group

Highland/Etling, *imprint of* Alfred Music

Highlights Learning, *imprint of* Highlights for Children Inc

Highlights Press, *imprint of* Highlights for Children Inc

Hill & Wang, *imprint of* Farrar, Straus & Giroux, LLC

Lawrence Hill Books, *imprint of* Chicago Review Press

Hillenbrand Books, *imprint of* Liturgy Training Publications

Hillsdale College Press, *division of* Hillsdale College

Hilton Publishing Co, *division of* HPC International Inc

Himalayan Institute Press, *division of* Himalayan International Institute of Yoga Science & Philosophy

IMPRINTS, SUBSIDIARIES & DISTRIBUTORS

Hindustan Book Agency, *distributed by* American Mathematical Society (AMS)

Hinshaw Music, *distributed by* Hal Leonard LLC

Hippo Park, *imprint of* Astra Books for Young Readers

Hippocrates Publications, *distributed by* BPC

Hirmer Publishers, *distributor for* American Federation of Arts

Histoire & Collections, *distributed by* Casemate | publishers

Historic Hospitality Books, *imprint of* Capen Publishing Co Inc

Historic Idaho Series, *distributed by* Caxton Press

Historic New Orleans Collection, *distributed by* Oak Knoll Press

The Historic New Orleans Collection, *distributed by* University of Virginia Press

History Colorado, *distributed by* University Press of Colorado

History Facts, *distributed by* Casemate | publishers

History Nebraska, *distributed by* University of Nebraska Press

The History Press, *imprint of* Arcadia Publishing Inc

History Publishing Company, *imprint of* History Publishing Co LLC

History Publishing Company Global, *imprint of* History Publishing Co LLC

Histria Books, *division of* Histria LLC

Histria Kids, *imprint of* Histria Books

Hitchcock Annual, *distributed by* Columbia University Press

HMH Audio, *imprint of* Houghton Mifflin Harcourt Trade & Reference Division

HMH Franchise, *imprint of* Houghton Mifflin Harcourt Trade & Reference Division

HMH Publications, *distributed by* Casemate | publishers

Hoard's Dairyman Magazine, *imprint of* W D Hoard & Sons Co

Hobble Creek Press, *imprint of* Cedar Fort Inc

Hodder Education, *distributed by* Trans-Atlantic Publications Inc

Hogarth, *imprint of* Crown Publishing Group, Random House Publishing Group

Hogrefe AG, *distributed by* Hogrefe Publishing Corp

Hogrefe Publishing Corp, *subsidiary of* Hogrefe Verlag GmbH & Co Kg, *distributor for* Hogrefe AG (Switzerland), Hogrefe Verlag (Germany)

Hogrefe Verlag, *distributed by* Hogrefe Publishing Corp

Hohm Press, *subsidiary of* HSM LLC

Holiday House Publishing Inc, *distributed by* Pengin Random House

Holman Bibles, *imprint of* B&H Publishing Group

Holmes Publishing Group, *imprint of* Holmes Publishing Group LLC

Holmes Publishing Group LLC, *distributor for* Jerusalem Press (UK), Starfire Publishing (UK), Theion Publishing (Germany), Three Hands Press (US), Von Zos Publishing, Xoanon Publishing (US)

Holmgren Design Services, *distributed by* Chelsea Green Publishing Co

Holocaust Library, *imprint of* United States Holocaust Memorial Museum

Henry Holt and Company, LLC, *division of* Macmillan, Macmillan

Matt Holt Books, *imprint of* BenBella Books Inc

Holt Paperbacks, *imprint of* Henry Holt and Company, LLC

Holy Cross Orthodox Press, *division of* Hellenic College Holy Cross

Homa & Sekey Books, *distributor for* China Encyclopedia Publishing House, China Intercontinental Press, China Zhejiang Publishing United Group

Home Builders Press, *distributed by* Craftsman Book Co

Homespun Tapes, *distributed by* Hal Leonard LLC

Homestead Publishing, *affiliate of* Book Design Ltd

Hometown World, *imprint of* Sourcebooks LLC

Hooked on Phonics, *distributed by* Simon & Schuster, LLC

Hoover Institution Press, *subsidiary of* Hoover Institution on War, Revolution & Peace

Hoover's Business Press, *imprint of* D&B Hoovers™

Hoover's Handbooks, *imprint of* D&B Hoovers™

Hoover's Inc, *subsidiary of* Dun & Bradstreet

Johns Hopkins University Press, *affiliate of* Johns Hopkins University, *distributor for* Inter-American Development Bank, International Food Policy Research Institute, Woodrow Wilson Center Press, *distributed by* Heimburger House Publishing Co

Hops Press, *distributed by* Mountain Press Publishing Co

Horizon Publishers & Distributors Inc, *imprint of* Cedar Fort Inc, *distributed by* Cedar Fort Inc

Hospital & Healthcare Compensation Service, *subsidiary of* John R Zabka Associates Inc, John R Zabka Associates Inc

Hot Licks, *distributed by* Hal Leonard LLC

Houghton Mifflin Harcourt, *subsidiary of* Veritas Capital, *imprint of* Houghton Mifflin Harcourt Trade & Reference Division, *distributor for* Old Farmer's Almanac, *distributed by* Hachette Book Group Inc, Heimburger House Publishing Co

Houghton Mifflin Harcourt Assessments, *subsidiary of* Houghton Mifflin Harcourt

Houghton Mifflin Harcourt K-12 Publishers, *division of* Houghton Mifflin Harcourt

Houghton Mifflin Harcourt Trade & Reference Division, *division of* HarperCollins, *distributor for* Larousse, Old Farmer's Almanac, *distributed by* Hachette Book Group Inc

Hourglass, *imprint of* Baker Books

House of Collectibles, *imprint of* Random House Reference/Random House Puzzles & Games

House to House Publications, *division of* DOVE International

How Do We Want To Be Together Series, *imprint of* High Tide Press

Howard Books, *imprint of* Atria Books

Huber, *distributed by* Alan Wofsy Fine Arts

Hudson Hills Press Inc, *distributor for* American Federation of Arts

Hudson Music, *distributed by* Hal Leonard LLC

Hui Hanai, *distributed by* University of Hawaii Press

Huia Publishers, *distributed by* University of Hawaii Press

Human Alchemy Publications, *distributed by* Crown House Publishing Co LLC

Human Rights Watch Books, *imprint of* Human Rights Watch

Humanity Books, *imprint of* Prometheus Books

Humanix Books LLC, *division of* Newsmax Media

PUBLISHERS / IMPRINTS, SUBSIDIARIES & DISTRIBUTORS

Humanoids Inc, *distributed by* Simon & Schuster, LLC

Humanum Academic Press, *distributed by* The Catholic University of America Press

Hungry Goat Press, *imprint of* Gauthier Publications Inc

Hungry Tomato®, *distributed by* Lerner Publishing Group Inc

Hunter House Publishers, *imprint of* Turner Publishing Co LLC

Huntington Library, *distributed by* Oak Knoll Press

Hurst, *distributed by* Oxford University Press USA

Hutton Publishing, *subsidiary of* Jones Hutton Literary Associates, Jones Hutton Literary Associates

Hybrid Nation, *imprint of* Red Hen Press

Hydra, *imprint of* Random House Publishing Group

Hyperbole, *imprint of* San Diego State University Press

Hyperion, *distributor for* Alloy Entertainment LLC

Hyperion Avenue, *imprint of* Disney-Hyperion Books

Hyperion Books for Children, *imprint of* Disney Publishing Worldwide

Hypermedia Inc, *imprint of* Frederic C Beil Publisher Inc

Ibex Press, *imprint of* Ibex Publishers

Ibex Publishers, *distributor for* Farhang Moaser

IBFD North America Inc (International Bureau of Fiscal Documentation), *division of* IBFD Foundation

ibidem Press, *distributed by* Columbia University Press

IchemE, *distributed by* American Institute of Chemical Engineers (AIChE)

ICLE, *imprint of* Institute of Continuing Legal Education

Iconografix, *distributed by* Heimburger House Publishing Co

Idea Bank, *distributed by* Fire Engineering Books & Videos

Ideal Audiobooks, *distributed by* Dreamscape Media LLC

Ides et Calendes, *distributed by* Alan Wofsy Fine Arts

IEE, *imprint of* IET USA Inc

IEEE Press, *division of* Institute of Electrical & Electronics Engineers Inc (IEEE), Institute of Electrical and Electronics Engineers Inc (IEEE), *distributed by* John Wiley & Sons Inc

IFSTA, *distributed by* Fire Engineering Books & Videos

Igloo Books, *distributed by* Simon & Schuster, LLC

Ignatius Press, *division of* Guadalupe Associates Inc, Guadalupe Associates Inc, *distributor for* Bethlehem Books, Veritas

Ignite, *imprint of* Entangled Publishing LLC

Ilchokak Publishers, *distributed by* Cheng & Tsui Co Inc

Illinois State Museum Society, *affiliate of* Illinois State Museum

IlluminateYA Fiction, *imprint of* Iron Stream Media

Illuminating Engineering Society of North America (IES), *distributor for* Taylor & Francis, Techstreet

ILR Press, *imprint of* Cornell University Press

Image Books, *imprint of* Crown Publishing Group

Image Comics, *distributed by* Simon & Schuster, LLC

Imagine Publishing, *imprint of* Charlesbridge Publishing Inc

ImaJinn Books, *imprint of* BelleBooks

IMM Lifestyle Books, *imprint of* Fox Chapel Publishing Co Inc

Immagine&Poesia, *distributed by* Cross-Cultural Communications

Immedium, *imprint of* Immedium Inc

Impact Books, *imprint of* Penguin Publishing Group

Impact Publishers, *imprint of* New Harbinger Publications Inc

Imperial War Museum, *distributed by* Casemate | publishers

In an Hour Books LLC, *imprint of* Smith & Kraus Publishers Inc

In Extenso Press, *imprint of* ACTA Publications

In the Garden Publishing, *division of* What Would Love Do Int'l LLC

Incentive Plus, *distributor for* MAR*CO Products Inc

Independent Publishers Group (IPG), *division of* Chicago Review Press

Independent Seaport Museum, *distributed by* Cornell Maritime Press

Independent University of Moscow, *distributed by* American Mathematical Society (AMS)

Indiana University Press, *distributed by* Heimburger House Publishing Co

IndieBooks, *distributed by* Trans-Atlantic Publications Inc

Indigo River Publishing, *distributed by* Simon & Schuster, LLC

Indulgence, *imprint of* Entangled Publishing LLC

Industrial Press, *distributed by* NACE International, SME (Society of Manufacturing Engineers)

Indy-Tech Publishing, *imprint of* SAMS Technical Publishing LLC

Information Gatekeepers Inc (IGI), *division of* IGI Group Inc

Information Today Books, *imprint of* Information Today, Inc

Information Today, Inc, *distributor for* Association for Information Science & Technology (ASIS&T)

Ingram Academic, *distributor for* Boydell & Brewer Inc

Inimitable Books, *distributed by* Simon & Schuster, LLC

Inland, *distributor for* World Citizens

Inner Traditions, *imprint of* Inner Traditions International Ltd

Inner Traditions Audio, *imprint of* Inner Traditions International Ltd

Inner Traditions en Espanol, *imprint of* Inner Traditions International Ltd

Inner Traditions India, *imprint of* Inner Traditions International Ltd

Inner Worlds Music, *distributed by* Lotus Press

Innovation & Tourisms (INTO), *imprint of* Cognizant Communication Corp

Innovative Marketing, *distributor for* Pentecostal Resources Group

InnoVision Health Media, *distributed by* Square One Publishers Inc

Inprint Editions, *imprint of* Black Classic Press

Insight Editions, *distributed by* Simon & Schuster, LLC

IMPRINTS, SUBSIDIARIES & DISTRIBUTORS

Insight Media, *imprint of* Alexander Street, part of Clarivate PLC

Inspec, *imprint of* IET USA Inc

Instant Help Books, *imprint of* New Harbinger Publications Inc

Institute for Advanced Study in the Theatre Arts (IASTA), *distributed by* Fordham University Press

Institute for Mesoamerican Studies, *distributed by* University of Texas Press, University Press of Colorado

Institute for Regional Studies of the Californias, *distributed by* San Diego State University Press

Institute for the Psychological Sciences Press (IPS), *distributed by* The Catholic University of America Press

Institute of Buddhist Studies, *distributed by* University of Hawaii Press

Institute of Governmental Studies, *subsidiary of* University of California, Berkeley

Institute of Materials, *distributed by* NACE International

Institute of Police Technology & Management (IPTM), *division of* University of North Florida

Institute Press, *distributed by* Crown House Publishing Co LLC

Integrity Music, *division of* David C Cook

Inter-American Development Bank, *division of* Multilateral Development Bank, *distributed by* Johns Hopkins University Press

Inter-University Consortium for Political & Social Research (ICPSR), *affiliate of* University of Michigan Institute for Social Research

Intercontinental Press, *distributed by* CN Times Books

Intergalactic Afikoman, *distributed by* Lerner Publishing Group Inc

Interlink Books, *imprint of* Interlink Publishing Group Inc

Interlink Publishing, *distributed by* Simon & Schuster, LLC

Interlink Publishing Group Inc, *distributed by* Simon & Schuster, LLC

Interlude Press, *imprint of* Chicago Review Press

International Air Transport Association, *distributed by* J J Keller & Associates, Inc®

International Association for Society & Natural Resources, *distributed by* University Press of Colorado

International Atomic Energy Agency (IAEA), *distributed by* United Nations Publications

International Book Centre Inc, *distributor for* Barron's, Cambridge University Press, Capstone, Cengage Learning, Compass Publications, Edenridge Press, English Discoveries, Fisher Hill Publishing, Library du Liban (Lebanon), McGraw Hill, New Readers Press, Oxford University Press, Pearson-Longman, Raven Tree Press, Stacey International Ltd (London), The University of Michigan Press, Usborne Publishing

International Code Council, *distributed by* PPI, A Kaplan Company

International Country Risk Guide, *imprint of* The PRS Group Inc

International Criminal Tribunal for Rwanda (UNICTR), *distributed by* United Nations Publications

International Criminal Tribunal for the former Yugoslavia (ICTY), *distributed by* United Nations Publications

International Energy Agency, *distributed by* OECD Washington Center

International Food Policy Research Institute, *member of* Consultative Group on International Agricultural Research (CGIAR), *distributed by* Johns Hopkins University Press

International Organization for Migration (IOM), *distributed by* United Nations Publications

International Press of Boston Inc, *distributed by* American Mathematical Society (AMS)

International Publishers, *imprint of* International Publishers Co Inc

International Sculpture Center, *distributed by* University of Washington Press

International Trade Centre (ITC), *distributed by* United Nations Publications

International Transportation Forum, *distributed by* OECD Washington Center

International Wealth Success (IWS), *imprint of* Kallisti Publishing Inc, *distributed by* Kallisti Publishing Inc

InterVarsity Press, *subsidiary of* InterVarsity Christian Fellowship/USA

Interweave Press LLC, *imprint of* Golden Peak Media

Ione Press, *imprint of* ECS Publishing Group

IOP Publishing, *distributor for* The Electrochemical Society (ECS)

iPRECIATION, *distributed by* University of Hawaii Press

Iranbooks Press, *imprint of* Ibex Publishers

Iris Press, *imprint of* The Iris Publishing Group Inc

IRL, *distributed by* Oxford University Press USA

Iron Pen, *imprint of* Paraclete Press Inc

Iron Stream, *imprint of* Iron Stream Media

Iron Stream Fiction, *imprint of* Iron Stream Media

Iron Stream Kids, *imprint of* Iron Stream Media

Iron Stream Media, *affiliate of* Christian Devotions Ministries

Iroquois Press, *imprint of* Turner Publishing Co LLC

ISI Books, *imprint of* Regnery Publishing

Islamic Texts Society, *distributed by* Fons Vitae

Island, *imprint of* Penguin Random House LLC

Island Press, *distributed by* University of British Columbia Press

Island Research & Education Initiative, *distributed by* University of Hawaii Press

The Islander Group, *distributor for* Bess Press Inc

Islander Images, *imprint of* Shepard Publications

Islander Press, *imprint of* Shepard Publications

Isle Botanica, *distributed by* University of Hawaii Press

ISO, *distributed by* NACE International

Issues Press, *imprint of* Idyll Arbor Inc

Italian School of East Asian Studies, *distributed by* Cheng & Tsui Co Inc

ITK (In the Know) Audio, *imprint of* Recorded Books Inc, an RBmedia company

It's About Time Inc, *distributor for* American Geosciences Institute (AGI)

iUniverse, *division of* Author Solutions LLC

IVP, *imprint of* InterVarsity Press

IVP Academic, *imprint of* InterVarsity Press

IVP Bible Studies, *imprint of* InterVarsity Press

IVP Formatio, *imprint of* InterVarsity Press

IVP Kids, *imprint of* InterVarsity Press

Ivy Books, *imprint of* Penguin Random House LLC

IW$ Press, *imprint of* International Wealth Success (IWS)

PUBLISHERS

IMPRINTS, SUBSIDIARIES & DISTRIBUTORS

Jacaranda, *imprint of* John Wiley & Sons Inc

Jagiellonian University Press, *distributed by* Columbia University Press

Alice James Books, *division of* Alice James Poetry Cooperative Inc, Alice James Poetry Cooperative Inc

James Madison University, *distributed by* University of Virginia Press

Janaway Publishing, *distributor for* Closson Press

Japan Playwrights Association, *distributed by* University of Hawaii Press

Japan Publications Inc, *distributed by* Kodansha USA Inc

Japan Publications Trading Co Ltd, *distributed by* Kodansha USA Inc

Japan Times, *distributed by* Cheng & Tsui Co Inc

Jenkins Publishing, *distributed by* Chelsea Green Publishing Co

Jersey Yarns, *imprint of* Quincannon Publishing Group

Jerusalem Press, *distributed by* Holmes Publishing Group LLC

Jerusalem Publications, *distributed by* Feldheim Publishers

Jeter Publishing, *imprint of* Gallery Books

Jewish Lights Publishing, *imprint of* Turner Publishing Co LLC

The Jewish Museum, *distributed by* Yale University Press

Jewish New Testament Publications, *distributed by* Lederer Books, Messianic Jewish Publishers

The Jewish Publication Society, *imprint of* University of Nebraska Press

Jhpiego, *affiliate of* Johns Hopkins University

Jinxworld, *imprint of* Dark Horse Comics

Jist, *distributor for* MAR*CO Products Inc

JIST Career Solutions, *imprint of* JIST Publishing

JIST Publishing, *division of* Kendall Hunt Publishing Co, Kendall Hunt Publishing Co

JMC Press, *distributed by* Vandamere Press

John Macrae Books, *imprint of* Henry Holt and Company, LLC

Johns Hopkins University Press, *affiliate of* Johns Hopkins University, *distributor for* Inter-American Development Bank, International

Food Policy Research Institute, Woodrow Wilson Center Press, *distributed by* Heimburger House Publishing Co

Jolly Fish Press, *imprint of* North Star Editions Inc

Jones & Bartlett Learning LLC, *division of* Ascend Learning

Kaylie Jones Books, *imprint of* Akashic Books

Lorena Jones Books, *imprint of* Ten Speed Press

Jossey-Bass, *imprint of* John Wiley & Sons Inc, *distributor for* Center for Creative Leadership LLC, *distributed by* Center for Creative Leadership LLC

Journal of Chinese Medicine Publications, *distributed by* Eastland Press

JourneyForth Books, *imprint of* BJU Press

Jove, *imprint of* Berkley

Joy Revolution, *imprint of* Random House Children's Books

JPT America Inc, *distributed by* Cheng & Tsui Co Inc

Judson Press, *division of* American Baptist Churches in the USA

Juloya, *imprint of* Elva Resa Publishing

Jump at the Sun, *imprint of* Disney-Hyperion Books, Disney Publishing Worldwide

Juniper Publishing, *distributed by* Simon & Schuster, LLC

Juno Books, *distributed by* powerHouse Books

Jury Verdict Research, *division of* LRP Publications

Just Cause, *imprint of* Yard Dog Press

KaBOOM!, *imprint of* BOOM! Studios

Kaeden, *imprint of* Kaeden Publishing

Kaeden Books, *imprint of* Kaeden Publishing

Kagero, *distributed by* Casemate | publishers

Kailua Historical Society, *distributed by* University of Hawaii Press

Kalamaku Press, *distributed by* University of Hawaii Press

Kalaniot Books, *imprint of* Endless Mountains Publishing Co

Kales Press, *distributed by* W W Norton & Company Inc

Kalindi Press, *imprint of* Hohm Press

Kallisti Publishing, *imprint of* Kallisti Publishing Inc

Kallisti Publishing Inc, *distributor for* International Wealth Success (IWS)

Kalmbach Books, *imprint of* Kalmbach Media Co

Kalmbach Publishing Co, *distributed by* Heimburger House Publishing Co

Kalmus, *imprint of* Alfred Music

Kamehameha Publishing, *division of* Kamehameha Schools

Kamehameha Schools Press, *imprint of* Kamehameha Publishing

Kane Press, *imprint of* Astra Books for Young Readers

Kanji Press, *distributed by* University of Hawaii Press

Kansas City Star Quilts, *imprint of* C&T Publishing Inc

Kaplan Press, *distributed by* Gryphon House Inc

Kaplan Publishing, *distributed by* Simon & Schuster, LLC

Kar-Ben Publishing, *imprint of* Lerner Publishing Group Inc

Karnak House, *imprint of* The Red Sea Press Inc

Karwansary Publishers, *distributed by* Casemate | publishers

Katalitix, *distributed by* Simon & Schuster, LLC

KAV Books, *distributed by* Royal Fireworks Press

Keenspot, *distributed by* Simon & Schuster, LLC

Keepers of Our Culture, *imprint of* Park Place Publications

Keeperton, *distributed by* Simon & Schuster, LLC

Lauren Keiser Music, *distributed by* Hal Leonard LLC

J J Keller & Associates, Inc®, *distributor for* Chilton Book Co, International Air Transport Association, National Archives & Records Administration, National Institute of Occupational Safety & Health, Office of the Federal Register, Research & Special Programs Administration of the US Department of Transportation, John Wiley & Sons Inc

Kendall Green, *imprint of* Gallaudet University Press

Kendall Hunt Publishing, *distributor for* Seedling Publications Inc

Kenilworth Press, *distributed by* Trafalgar Square Books

Kennedy Information LLC, *division of* Bloomberg Industry Group

IMPRINTS, SUBSIDIARIES & DISTRIBUTORS

Kensington, *distributor for* Parachute Publishing LLC

Kensington Cozies, *imprint of* Kensington Publishing Corp

Kensington Hardcover, *imprint of* Kensington Publishing Corp

Kensington Mass-Market, *imprint of* Kensington Publishing Corp

Kensington Publishing Corp, *distributor for* Black Odyssey Media, Urban Books

Kensington Trade Paperback, *imprint of* Kensington Publishing Corp

Kentucky Historical Society, *distributed by* The University Press of Kentucky

Kerem, *distributed by* Hachai Publishing

Charles H Kerr, *distributed by* AK Press

Kersplebedeb, *distributed by* AK Press

Kessinger Publishing®, *imprint of* Kessinger Publishing LLC

Key Education, *distributed by* Carson Dellosa Publishing LLC

Key Publishing, *distributed by* Casemate | publishers

Keylight Books, *imprint of* Turner Publishing Co LLC

Keynote Speakers Today, *imprint of* Avant-Guide

Keystone Books, *imprint of* Penn State University Press

Keywords Press, *imprint of* Atria Books

Kid Help Publishing Co, *division of* Quixote Press

KidHaven Publishing, *imprint of* Greenhaven Publishing, *distributed by* Lucent Press

Kids Can Press, *distributed by* Hachette Book Group Inc

Kimbell Art Museum, *distributed by* Yale University Press

Kinfolk, *distributed by* Simon & Schuster, LLC

King Dragon Press, *imprint of* Cedar Fort Inc

Laurence King Publishing Ltd, *distributed by* Chronicle Books LLC

The King Legacy, *imprint of* Beacon Press

Robert King, *distributed by* Hal Leonard LLC

Kingfisher, *distributed by* Macmillan

Kingswell, *imprint of* Disney Publishing Worldwide

Klutz®, *imprint of* Scholastic Trade Publishing

Alfred A Knopf, *imprint of* Knopf Doubleday Publishing Group

Alfred A Knopf Books for Young Readers, *imprint of* Random House Children's Books

Knopf Cooks, *imprint of* Alfred A Knopf

Knopf Doubleday Publishing Group, *division of* Penguin Random House LLC

Knossus Project, *distributed by* Chelsea Green Publishing Co

Knovel Corp, *division of* Elsevier Inc

Knowledge Books, *distributed by* Lerner Publishing Group Inc

Kodansha, *distributed by* Oxford University Press USA

Kodansha America, *imprint of* Kodansha USA Inc

Kodansha Globe, *imprint of* Kodansha USA Inc

Kodansha International, *imprint of* Kodansha USA Inc

Kodansha USA Inc, *subsidiary of* Kodansha Ltd (Japan), Kodansha Ltd (Japan), *distributor for* Japan Publications Inc, Japan Publications Trading Co Ltd

Kokila, *imprint of* Penguin Young Readers Group

Kollath-Stensaas, *distributed by* AdventureKEEN

Kolowalu Books, *imprint of* University of Hawaii Press

Konecky & Konecky (K&K), *imprint of* Konecky & Konecky LLC

Konecky & Konecky LLC, *distributor for* Octavo Editions

KonigsFurt, *distributed by* US Games Systems Inc

Korea Institute, Harvard University, *distributed by* University of Hawaii Press

Koren Publishers, *imprint of* The Toby Press LLC

Kosei Publishing Co, *imprint of* Tuttle Publishing, *distributed by* Tuttle Publishing

Kotan Publishing Inc, *imprint of* Tuttle Publishing, *distributed by* Tuttle Publishing

HJ Kramer Inc, *imprint of* New World Library

Krause Publications, *imprint of* Penguin Publishing Group

Krause Publications Inc, *imprint of* Penguin Random House LLC, *distributed by* Heimburger House Publishing Co

Kregel Academic & Ministry, *imprint of* Kregel Publications

Kregel Bibles, *imprint of* Kregel Publications

Kregel Children's, *imprint of* Kregel Publications

Kregel Classics, *imprint of* Kregel Publications

Kregel Publications, *division of* Kregel Inc, Kregel Inc, *distributor for* Muddy Pearl (Scotland)

Kroshka Publications, *imprint of* Nova Science Publishers Inc

KTAV Publishing House Inc, *distributor for* Yeshiva University Press

Kudzu House, *imprint of* Ariel Press, *distributed by* Ariel Press

KUED, *distributed by* The University of Utah Press

Kumarian Press, *imprint of* Lynne Rienner Publishers Inc, *distributor for* Management Sciences for Health

Kumon Publishing North America Inc (KPNA), *subsidiary of* Kumon Publishing Co Ltd

Labyrinth Road, *imprint of* Random House Children's Books

Lake Claremont Press, *imprint of* Everything Goes Media LLC

Lake Forest College Press, *distributed by* Northwestern University Press

Lake Press, *distributed by* Simon & Schuster, LLC

Lake 7 Creative, *distributed by* AdventureKEEN

Lakeshore Learning Materials, *distributor for* National Council of Teachers of Mathematics (NCTM)

Lamplighter Mysteries & Suspense, *imprint of* Iron Stream Media

Landauer Publishing, *imprint of* Fox Chapel Publishing Co Inc

Peter Lang Publishing Inc, *subsidiary of* Peter Lang AG (Switzerland), Peter Lang AG (Switzerland)

Langenscheidt Publishing Group, *distributor for* Michelin Maps & Guides

Lanier Press, *imprint of* BookLogix

Lantana Publishing, *distributed by* Lerner Publishing Group Inc

Lantern Books, *distributed by* SteinerBooks Inc

PUBLISHERS

IMPRINTS, SUBSIDIARIES & DISTRIBUTORS

Lantern Publishing & Media, *distributed by* Red Wheel/Weiser

LanternLight Library, *imprint of* University of Alaska Press

LanternMedia, *division of* Lantern Publishing & Media

LARB Books, *division of* Los Angeles Review of Books

Large Print Press™, *imprint of* Gale

Larousse, *distributed by* Houghton Mifflin Harcourt Trade & Reference Division

JK Lasser, *imprint of* John Wiley & Sons Inc

Latitude 20, *imprint of* University of Hawaii Press

Launch!, *imprint of* ABDO

Laurel-Leaf, *imprint of* Random House Children's Books

Law & Crime, *distributed by* Simon & Schuster, LLC

Layali Music Publishing, *distributed by* ECS Publishing Group

LB kids™, *imprint of* Little, Brown Books for Young Readers (LBYR)

Leaders Press, *distributed by* Simon & Schuster, LLC

The Leadership Challenge®, *imprint of* John Wiley & Sons Inc

Leafwood Publishers, *imprint of* ACU Press

League of Professional Theatre Women, *distributed by* Theatre Communications Group

Learning & Coloring Books, *imprint of* Quincannon Publishing Group

The Learning Company, *division of* Houghton Mifflin Harcourt

Learning Matters, *imprint of* SAGE Publishing

Learning Wrap-ups, *imprint of* EDC Publishing

LearningExpress, *unit of* EBSCO Information Services

LearnQIC, *imprint of* DiscoverNet Publishing

Leaves of Healing, *imprint of* Progressive Press

Leda, *imprint of* Norilana Books, *distributed by* Casemate | publishers

Lederer Books, *division of* Messianic Jewish Publishers, *distributor for* Jewish New Testament Publications

LeDuc, *distributed by* Hal Leonard LLC

Lee & Low Games, *imprint of* Lee & Low Books Inc

Left To Write Press, *distributed by* Chelsea Green Publishing Co

Legacy Bound, *division of* Legacy Toys

Legacy Isle Publishing, *imprint of* Watermark Publishing

Legacy Lit, *imprint of* Grand Central Publishing

Legas Publishers, *distributed by* Cross-Cultural Communications

Legendary Comics, *distributed by* Simon & Schuster, LLC

Lehigh University Press, *affiliate of* Rowman & Littlefield Publishing Group, *distributed by* Rowman & Littlefield

Leisure Arts Inc, *division of* Liberty Media

Lemonada Books, *imprint of* Gallery Books

LENNY, *imprint of* Random House Publishing Group

Hal Leonard Corp, *distributor for* Centerstream Publishing LLC

Lerner Digital, *imprint of* Lerner Publishing Group Inc

Lerner Publications, *imprint of* Lerner Publishing Group Inc

Lerner Publisher Services, *division of* Lerner Publishing Group Inc

Lerner Publishing Group Inc, *division of* Lerner Universal Corp, *distributor for* Andersen Press, Big & Small, Cheriton Children's Books, Creston Books, Flying Start Books, Full Tilt Press, Gecko Press, Hungry Tomato®, Intergalactic Afikoman, Knowledge Books, Lantana Publishing, Lorimer Children & Teens, Maverick Arts Publishing, New Frontier Publishing, Page Education Foundation, Planting People Growing Justice Press, Quarto Library, Red Chair Press, Ruby Tuesday Books, Soaring Kite Books, We Do Listen Foundation

LernerClassroom, *imprint of* Lerner Publishing Group Inc

Leuven University Press, *distributed by* Cornell University Press

Leveled Readers, *imprint of* ABDO

Levesque Publications, *distributed by* University of Hawaii Press

Levine Querido, *distributed by* Chronicle Books LLC

Lexham Press, *imprint of* Faithlife Corp

Lexington Books, *imprint of* Rowman & Littlefield Publishing Group

LexisNexis®, *division of* RELX Group plc, *distributor for* Standard Publishing Corp

LexisNexis® Matthew Bender®, *member of* The LexisNexis® Group

Liberties Press, *distributed by* Casemate | publishers

Libra Press, *distributed by* Simon & Schuster, LLC

Libraries Unlimited, *imprint of* Bloomsbury Publishing Inc

Library du Liban (Lebanon), *distributed by* International Book Centre Inc

Library of America, *distributed by* Penguin Random House LLC

Library of Congress-Center for the Book, *distributed by* Oak Knoll Press

Library of Islam, *imprint of* Kazi Publications Inc

Library Tales Publishing, *distributed by* Simon & Schuster, LLC

Libri Canali Bassi, *distributed by* Edgewise Press Inc

Life Bible Study, *imprint of* Iron Stream Media

Life Cycle Books, *division of* Life Cycle Books Ltd (Canada)

Life on the Edge, *imprint of* Focus on the Family

LifeLearn, *distributed by* Teton NewMedia Inc

LifeLights™, *imprint of* Turner Publishing Co LLC

LifeTools, *imprint of* American Psychological Association

The Liffey Press, *distributed by* Casemate | publishers

The Light, *imprint of* Tughra Books

Light & Life Publishing Co, *distributor for* St Herman Press

Lighthouse Press, *imprint of* ProStar Publications Inc

Liguori, *imprint of* Liguori Publications

Libros Liguori, *imprint of* Liguori Publications

Liguori Publications, *distributor for* Redemptorist Publications

LIM Editrice SRL (Italy), *distributor for* Pendragon Press

Limelight Editions, *imprint of* Rowman & Littlefield Publishing Group

IMPRINTS, SUBSIDIARIES & DISTRIBUTORS

Limestone Press, *distributed by* University of Alaska Press

Liminal 11, *distributed by* Union Square & Co

Lincoln Institute of Land Policy, *distributed by* Columbia University Press

John Liner Organization, *subsidiary of* Standard Publishing Corp

Linnaean Press, *imprint of* Bentley Publishers

Lippincott Williams & Wilkins, *unit of* Wolters Kluwer Health

Lippincott, Williams & Wilkins, *imprint of* Wolters Kluwer US Corp

Lips (Magazine & Press), *distributed by* Cross-Cultural Communications

LIS (Legal Information Services), *subsidiary of* CCH, a Wolters Kluwer business

Listening Library, *imprint of* Penguin Random House Audio Publishing Group

Listening Library®, *imprint of* Books on Tape™, *distributed by* Books on Tape™

Literary House Press, *distributed by* Cornell Maritime Press

Literary Reprint Series, *imprint of* University of Alaska Press

Literature & Arts, *imprint of* Her Own Words LLC

Literature & Thought, *imprint of* Perfection Learning®

Litigation Group, *division of* Public Citizen

little bee books, *distributed by* Simon & Schuster, LLC

Little Bigfoot, *imprint of* Sasquatch Books

Little Blue Readers, *imprint of* North Star Editions Inc

Little, Brown, *distributor for* Parachute Publishing LLC

Little, Brown and Company, *division of* Hachette Book Group Inc, *distributor for* Alloy Entertainment LLC

Little, Brown Books for Young Readers, *division of* Hachette Book Group Inc

Little, Brown Books for Young Readers (LBYR), *division of* Hachette Book Group Inc

Little, Brown Ink, *imprint of* Little, Brown Books for Young Readers (LBYR)

Little, Brown Spark, *imprint of* Little, Brown and Company

The Little Entrepreneur, *imprint of* Harper Arrington Publishing & Media, *distributed by* Harper Arrington Publishing

Little Genius Books, *distributed by* Simon & Schuster, LLC

Little Island Press, *distributed by* University of Hawaii Press

Little Lark, *imprint of* Entangled Publishing LLC

Little Patriot Press, *imprint of* Regnery Publishing

Little Pickle Press, *imprint of* Sourcebooks LLC

Little Room Press, *distributed by* Fordham University Press

Little Simon®, *imprint of* Simon & Schuster Children's Publishing

Little Tiger, *imprint of* Random House Children's Books

Liturgical Press, *division of* The Order of St Benedict Inc, *distributor for* Cistercian Publications

Liturgical Press Academic, *imprint of* Liturgical Press

Liturgical Press Books, *imprint of* Liturgical Press

Liturgy Training Publications, *subsidiary of* Archdiocese of Chicago, *distributor for* United States Catholic Conference Publications (select titles)

Liveright, *imprint of* W W Norton & Company Inc

Living Books, *imprint of* Tyndale House Publishers Inc

Living Language, *imprint of* Penguin Random House LLC

Living Lessons, *distributed by* Hachai Publishing

Livingston Press, *division of* University of West Alabama

Llewellyn, *imprint of* Llewellyn Publications

Llewellyn Publications, *division of* Llewellyn Worldwide Ltd, *distributor for* Blue Angel Publishing, Lo Scarabeo

LM Publishers, *distributed by* University of Washington Press

Locks Art Publications/Locks Gallery, *division of* Locks Gallery

Logos, *imprint of* Bridge Logos Inc

Logos Press, *imprint of* thinkBiotech LLC

Lominger Inc, *distributed by* Center for Creative Leadership LLC

Lone Star Audio, *imprint of* Recorded Books Inc, an RBmedia company

Lonely Planet, *distributed by* Hachette Book Group Inc

Lonely Planet Kids, *imprint of* Lonely Planet Publications Inc

Lonely Planet Publications Inc, *subsidiary of* Red Ventures, *distributed by* Hachette Book Group Inc

Long River Press, *imprint of* Sinomedia International Group

Longman, *distributed by* Trans-Atlantic Publications Inc

The Lontar Foundation, *distributed by* University of Hawaii Press

Look, Listen & Learn, *imprint of* Crabtree Publishing Co

Looking Glass Library, *imprint of* ABDO

Looseleaf Law Publications Inc, *division of* Warodean Corp

Lorenz Educational Press, *division of* The Lorenz Corp

Lorimer, *distributed by* Casemate | publishers

Lorimer Children & Teens, *distributed by* Lerner Publishing Group Inc

Los Angeles Times Crosswords, *imprint of* Random House Reference/Random House Puzzles & Games

Lost Coast Press, *imprint of* Cypress House

Lost Horse Press, *distributed by* Washington State University Press

Lost Valley Press, *imprint of* Satya House Publications

Lotus Press, *division of* Lotus Brands Inc, Lotus Brands Inc, *distributor for* Back to Eden Books, Dipti, East West Cultural Center, Les Editions ETC, Inner Worlds Music, SABDA, Sri Aurobindo Ashram, Star Sounds

Love Inspired®, *imprint of* Harlequin Enterprises Ltd, Love Inspired Books

Love Inspired Books, *imprint of* Harlequin Enterprises Ltd

Love Inspired® Historical, *imprint of* Love Inspired Books

Love Inspired® Suspense, *imprint of* Love Inspired Books

Lovestruck, *imprint of* Entangled Publishing LLC

Loveswept, *imprint of* Random House Publishing Group

PUBLISHERS — IMPRINTS, SUBSIDIARIES & DISTRIBUTORS

LPC Group Inc, *distributor for* Dark Horse Comics

LRP Magazine Group, *subsidiary of* LRP Publications

LRS, *division of* Library Reproduction Service

LRT Editions, *distributed by* Casemate | publishers

Lucas Books, *imprint of* Random House Publishing Group

Lucent Press, *imprint of* Greenhaven Publishing, *distributor for* Greenhaven Publishing, KidHaven Publishing

Lucky Spool, *distributed by* Harry N Abrams Inc, Taunton Books

LudwigMasters, *distributed by* Alfred Music

Lund Humphries/Ashgate, *distributor for* National Gallery of Art

LW Books, *imprint of* Schiffer Publishing Ltd

Lynn-Reinner Publishing, *distributor for* University of California Institute on Global Conflict & Cooperation

Lynx House Press, *distributed by* Washington State University Press

The Lyons Press, *imprint of* The Globe Pequot Press

Lyrical Press, *imprint of* Kensington Publishing Corp

M & H Type, *division of* The Arion Press

M Press, *imprint of* Dark Horse Comics

MAA Press, *imprint of* The Mathematical Association of America

Macmillan, *division of* Verlagsgruppe Georg von Holtzbrinck GmbH, Verlagsgruppe Georg von Holtzbrinck GmbH, *distributor for* Bloomsbury Publishing Inc, Bloomsbury USA, The College Board, Drawn & Quarterly, Entangled Publishing, Entangled Publishing LLC, Graywolf Press, Guinness World Records, Kingfisher, Macmillan Collectors Library, Media Lab Books, National Association of Broadcasters (NAB), Page Street Publishing Co, Page Two Books, Pan Macmillan UK, Sounds True Inc, Tor Publishing Group

Macmillan Audio, *division of* Macmillan

Macmillan Children's Publishing Group, *division of* Macmillan

Macmillan Collectors Library, *distributed by* Macmillan

Macmillan Learning, *subsidiary of* Macmillan

Macmillan/McGraw-Hill, *imprint of* McGraw-Hill Education

Macmillan Reference USA™, *imprint of* Gale

Macmillan Speakers, *division of* Macmillan

MacroPrintBooks, *imprint of* Science & Humanities Press

MacVan Maps, *distributed by* Wide World of Maps Inc

MAD Books, *imprint of* DC Comics Inc

Mad Cave Studios, *distributed by* Simon & Schuster, LLC

Mad Creek Books, *imprint of* The Ohio State University Press

Madison Area Community Supported Agriculture Coalition, *distributed by* Chelsea Green Publishing Co

Mage Persian Editions, *imprint of* Mage Publishers Inc

Maggid Books, *imprint of* The Toby Press LLC

Magic Cat, *imprint of* Harry N Abrams Inc

Magic Readers, *imprint of* ABDO

Magic Wagon, *imprint of* ABDO

Magill's Choice, *imprint of* Salem Press

Magination Press®, *imprint of* American Psychological Association

MAGNI, *imprint of* The Magni Co

The Magni Co, *subsidiary of* The Magni Group Inc, *distributed by* BPC

Magnolia Publications, *imprint of* Thomas Nelson

Maharishi International University Press, *subsidiary of* Maharishi International University, *distributed by* Penguin Publishing Group (select titles)

Make Me A World, *imprint of* Random House Children's Books

MakeMusic Inc, *distributed by* Alfred Music

Management Sciences for Health, *distributed by* Kumarian Press

Manchester University Press, *distributed by* Palgrave Macmillan

Mandala Earth, *imprint of* Insight Editions, *distributed by* Simon & Schuster, LLC

Mandel Vilar Press, *affiliate of* Americas for Conservation + the Arts, *distributor for* Dryad Press

Manhattan Prep, *distributed by* Simon & Schuster, LLC

Manning Publications, *distributed by* Simon & Schuster, LLC

Manning Publications Co, *distributed by* Pearson Education, Simon & Schuster, LLC (US & CN)

Manoa Heritage Center, *distributed by* University of Hawaii Press

The Manuscript Society, *distributed by* Oak Knoll Press

Many Hats Media, *distributor for* Sourced Media Books

MAPART Publishing, *distributor for* Michelin Maps & Guides

Maple Leaf Audio, *imprint of* Recorded Books Inc, an RBmedia company

MAR*CO Products Inc, *distributor for* Boulden Publishing, Educational Media Corp, HarperCollins, National Center for Youth Issues/STARS, *distributed by* ASCA, Boulden Publishing, Burnell Books, Calloway House, Career Kids FYI, CFKR Career, Character Development, Community Intervention, Courage to Change, Cress Productions Co, EDU Reference, Educational Media Corp, Incentive Plus, Jist, Mental Health Resources, National Center for Youth Issues/STARS, National Professional Resources, National Resource Center for Youth Services, Paperbacks for Educators, School Speciality, SourceResource, WRS Group, YouthLight Inc

Marble Arch Press™, *imprint of* Atria Books

Marine Survey Press, *imprint of* Marine Education Textbooks

Marine Techniques Publishing, *distributor for* Academic Press, Best Publishing Co, Butterworth-Heinemann, Clarkson Research Services Ltd, Elsevier Inc, Focal Press, Gulf Professional Publishers, PennWell Business & Industrial Division, Saunders, Waterfront Soundings Productions, Witherby Seamanship International Ltd, *distributed by* Elsevier Inc, PennWell Business & Industrial Division

Mariner Books, *imprint of* HarperCollins Publishers LLC

Marion Institute, *distributed by* Chelsea Green Publishing Co

Ashley Mark Publishing Co, *imprint of* Hal Leonard LLC

marketumbrella.org, *distributed by* Chelsea Green Publishing Co

MarketResearch.com, *distributor for* Primary Research Group Inc

Edward B Marks Music, *distributed by* Hal Leonard LLC

Marla Jones, Book Design, *imprint of* Doodle and Peck Publishing

Marquette University Press, *division of* Marquette University

IMPRINTS, SUBSIDIARIES & DISTRIBUTORS

Marquis Who's Who, *imprint of* Marquis Who's Who Ventures LLC

Carole Marsh Books, *imprint of* Gallopade International Inc

Carole Marsh Mysteries, *imprint of* Gallopade International Inc

Marshall Cavendish Adult Trade, *imprint of* Marshall Cavendish Education

Marshall Cavendish Benchmark, *imprint of* Marshall Cavendish Education

Marshall Cavendish Digital, *imprint of* Marshall Cavendish Education

Marshall Cavendish Education, *member of* Times International Publishing Group, *imprint of* Marshall Cavendish Education, *distributed by* Marshall Cavendish Ltd (UK)

Marshall Cavendish Ltd, *distributor for* Marshall Cavendish Education

Marshall Cavendish Reference, *imprint of* Marshall Cavendish Education

Marshall Cavendish Singapore, *distributed by* Cheng & Tsui Co Inc

Marsilio, *imprint of* Rizzoli International Publications Inc

Darvin Martin CDs, *distributed by* Closson Press

Rux Martin Books, *imprint of* Houghton Mifflin Harcourt Trade & Reference Division

Martindale-Hubbell®, *imprint of* Martindale LLC

Marvel, *imprint of* Disney Publishing Worldwide

Marvel Illustrated, *imprint of* ABDO

Marvel Picture Books, *imprint of* ABDO

Marvelous Spirit Press, *imprint of* Loving Healing Press Inc

Helen Marx/Turtle Point, *imprint of* Turtle Point Press

Maryland Historical Trust Press, *distributed by* Cornell Maritime Press

Maryland History Press, *distributor for* Tapestry Press Ltd

Maryland Sea Grant Program, *distributed by* Cornell Maritime Press

Mason Crest Publishers, *imprint of* National Highlights

Massachusetts Historical Society, *distributed by* University of Virginia Press

The Massachusetts Historical Society, *distributed by* University of Virginia Press

Master Books®, *imprint of* New Leaf Publishing Group LLC

Masters of Photography, *imprint of* Aperture Books

Mastery Education, *subsidiary of* Peoples Educational Holdings Inc

Masthof Press, *distributor for* Closson Press

Math Solutions®, *unit of* Houghton Mifflin Harcourt

Mathematica Josephina, *distributed by* American Mathematical Society (AMS)

Mathematical Society of Japan, *distributed by* American Mathematical Society (AMS)

Matheson Trust, *distributed by* Fons Vitae

Mattel Press, *distributed by* Simon & Schuster, LLC

Adam Matthew, *imprint of* SAGE Publishing

Maunsel & Co Publishers, *imprint of* Academica Press

Maverick Arts Publishing, *distributed by* Lerner Publishing Group Inc

Maverick Books, *imprint of* Trinity University Press

Mayo Clinic Press, *distributed by* Dreamscape Media LLC

McBooks Press, *imprint of* Rowman & Littlefield Publishing Group

MCD/AUWA Books, *imprint of* Farrar, Straus & Giroux, LLC

MCD/FSG, *imprint of* Farrar, Straus & Giroux, LLC

Margaret K McElderry Books, *imprint of* Simon & Schuster Children's Publishing

McFarland & Co Ltd Publishers, *subsidiary of* McFarland

McGraw Hill, *distributed by* International Book Centre Inc

McGraw-Hill, *distributor for* SME (Society of Manufacturing Engineers), *distributed by* American Academy of Environmental Engineers & Scientists®, NACE International, SAMS Technical Publishing LLC, SME (Society of Manufacturing Engineers)

McGraw-Hill Contemporary, *imprint of* McGraw-Hill Education

McGraw-Hill Create, *division of* McGraw-Hill Higher Education, *imprint of* McGraw-Hill Education

McGraw-Hill Education Australia, New Zealand & South Africa, *imprint of* McGraw-Hill Education

McGraw-Hill Education Europe, Middle East and Africa, *imprint of* McGraw-Hill Education

McGraw-Hill Education Latin America, *imprint of* McGraw-Hill Education

McGraw-Hill Education Mexico, *imprint of* McGraw-Hill Education

McGraw-Hill Education Spain, *imprint of* McGraw-Hill Education

McGraw-Hill Higher Education, *division of* McGraw-Hill Education

McGraw-Hill Humanities, Social Sciences, Languages, *imprint of* McGraw-Hill Education

McGraw-Hill/Irwin, *imprint of* McGraw-Hill Education

McGraw-Hill Professional, *imprint of* McGraw-Hill Education, *distributed by* PPI, A Kaplan Company

McGraw-Hill Professional Publishing Group, *division of* McGraw-Hill Education

McGraw-Hill Ryerson, *imprint of* McGraw-Hill Education

McGraw-Hill School Education Group, *division of* McGraw-Hill Education, *imprint of* McGraw-Hill Education

McGraw-Hill Science, Engineering, Mathematics, *imprint of* McGraw-Hill Education

McGraw-Hill Professional Development, *imprint of* McGraw-Hill Education

McKissick Museum, *distributed by* University of South Carolina Press

McWhiney Foundation Press/State House Press, *distributed by* Texas A&M University Press

Mean Free Path, *distributor for* American Society for Nondestructive Testing

R S Means from The Gordian Group, *distributed by* John Wiley & Sons Inc

Measuring Up®, *imprint of* Mastery Education

Medals of America, *distributor for* Medals of America Press

Medals of America Press, *division of* Medals of America, *distributed by* Medals of America

Medford Press, *imprint of* Plexus Publishing, Inc

Media Lab Books, *distributed by* Macmillan

Medical Economics, *distributed by* OptumInsight™

PUBLISHERS

IMPRINTS, SUBSIDIARIES & DISTRIBUTORS

Medical Group Management Association (MGMA), *distributor for* American Medical Association, Aspen Publishers, Greenbranch, HAP (Health Adminstration Press), J Wiley & Sons

The Medical Press, *division of* Brown Books Publishing Group (BBPG)

Medieval Institute Publications (MIP), *division of* Medieval Institute of Western Michigan University

Medina Publishing, *distributed by* Casemate | publishers

Mel Bay, *imprint of* Mel Bay Publications Inc

Mel Bay Publications Inc, *distributor for* AMA, William Bay Music, Dancing Hands, Stefan Grossman's Guitar Workshop

Paul Mellon Centre, *distributed by* Yale University Press

Menasha Ridge Press, *imprint of* AdventureKEEN

The Menil Collection, *distributed by* Yale University Press

Menil Foundation, *distributed by* University of Texas Press

Menorah, *imprint of* The Toby Press LLC

Mental Health Resources, *distributor for* MAR*CO Products Inc

Mercatorfonds, *distributed by* Yale University Press

Mercier Press, *distributed by* Casemate | publishers

Merck, *imprint of* John Wiley & Sons Inc

Merck Publishing Group, *distributed by* Simon & Schuster, LLC

Mercury Learning & Information, *distributed by* Stylus Publishing LLC

Merehurst Ltd, *imprint of* Tuttle Publishing

Meriwether Publishing, *division of* Pioneer Drama Service Inc

Merriam-Webster Inc, *subsidiary of* Encyclopaedia Britannica Inc

Merriam-Webster Kids, *imprint of* Merriam-Webster Inc

Frank Merriwell Inc, *subsidiary of* National Learning Corp

Merry Muse Press, *imprint of* Loft Press Inc

MerwinAsia, *distributed by* University of Hawaii Press

Mesorah Publications Ltd, *distributor for* NCSY Publications

Messenger Publications, *distributed by* Casemate | publishers

Messianic Jewish Publishers, *division of* Messianic Jewish Communications, *distributor for* Chosen People Ministries, First Fruits of Zion, Jewish New Testament Publications

Metalmark, *imprint of* Penn State University Press

Metamorphic Press, *distributed by* Chelsea Green Publishing Co

Metro Maps, *division of* Wide World of Maps Inc, *distributed by* Wide World of Maps Inc

Metropolitan Classics, *division of* Fort Ross Inc

The Metropolitan Museum of Art, *distributed by* Yale University Press

MFA Publications, *imprint of* Museum of Fine Arts Boston, *distributed by* Thames & Hudson (outside of North America)

Michelin Maps & Guides, *division of* Michelin North America Inc, *distributed by* Langenscheidt Publishing Group, MAPART Publishing (CN only), NBN (guides for North America), Editions du Renouveau Pedagogique (French titles in Canada), Penguin Canada (English titles in Canada)

Michie, *imprint of* LexisNexis®

Michigan State University Press (MSU Press), *division of* Michigan State University, *distributor for* Aquatic Ecosystem Health & Management Society Books, MSU Museum, University of Manitoba Press, *distributed by* UBC Press, Canada

Microtraining Associates, *imprint of* Alexander Street, part of Clarivate PLC

Midnight Ink, *imprint of* Llewellyn Publications

Midrashic Editions, *imprint of* Cross-Cultural Communications

Midwest Library Service, *distributor for* Primary Research Group Inc

Mighty Media Junior Readers, *imprint of* Mighty Media Press

Mighty Media Kids, *imprint of* Mighty Media Press

Mighty Media Press, *division of* Mighty Media Inc

Milady, *division of* Cengage Group

Milestone Documents, *imprint of* Schlager Group Inc

Milestone Press, *imprint of* University of Georgia Press

Milet Publishing Ltd, *imprint of* Tuttle Publishing, *distributed by* Tuttle Publishing

Milford Books™, *imprint of* Milford Books LLC

Military Division, *division of* Brown Books Publishing Group (BBPG)

Military Living Publications, *division of* Military Marketing Services Inc, Military Marketing Services Inc

Military Medals of America, *imprint of* Medals of America Press

Military Miniature Press, *distributed by* Casemate | publishers

Milky Way Picture Books, *distributed by* Harry N Abrams Inc

Millbrook Press, *imprint of* Lerner Publishing Group Inc

Kane Miller Books, *imprint of* EDC Publishing

Milliken Publishing Co, *division of* The Lorenz Corp, The Lorenz Corp

Denene Millner Books, *imprint of* Simon & Schuster Children's Publishing

Mills & Boon Large Print, *distributed by* Thorndike Press®

Sally Milner Publishing, *distributed by* Union Square & Co

Mimesis International, *distributed by* Casemate | publishers

The Minerals, Metals & Materials Society (TMS), *distributed by* Springer

Minerva, *imprint of* Astra Books for Young Readers

Minnesota Historical Society Press, *division of* Minnesota Historical Society

Minotaur Books, *imprint of* St Martin's Press, LLC

MIRA, *imprint of* Harlequin Enterprises Ltd

Miranda Press Trade Division, *imprint of* Cognizant Communication Corp

Miss Jackie Inc, *distributed by* Gryphon House Inc

Missouri History Museum, *distributed by* University of Missouri Press

Missouri Life Magazine, *distributed by* University of Missouri Press

MIT, *distributor for* The AEI Press

MIT Kids Press, *imprint of* Candlewick Press

MIT Press, *distributed by* DawnSignPress

367

IMPRINTS, SUBSIDIARIES & DISTRIBUTORS

The MIT Press, *distributor for* AAAI Press, Afterall Books, Canadian Centre for Architecture, no place press, Semiotext(e)

MITeen Press, *imprint of* Candlewick Press

MJF Books, *imprint of* Fine Creative Media, Inc

MMPBooks, *distributed by* Casemate | publishers

MOAC, *imprint of* John Wiley & Sons Inc

Farhang Moaser, *distributed by* Ibex Publishers

Model Centrum Progres, *distributed by* Casemate | publishers

Modern Drummer Publications, *distributed by* Hal Leonard LLC

Modern History Press, *imprint of* Loving Healing Press Inc

The Modern Language Initiative, *imprint of* Fordham University Press

Modern Learning Press, *imprint of* EPS School Specialty

Modern Library, *imprint of* Random House Publishing Group

Moleskine, *distributed by* Hachette Book Group Inc

Moleskine Books, *distributed by* PA Press

Moliere & Co, *imprint of* LinguaText LLC

Momentum, *imprint of* The Child's World Inc

Monacelli, *imprint of* Phaidon

The Monacelli Press, *imprint of* Phaidon Press Ltd, *distributor for* Winterthur Museum, Garden & Library

Monacelli Studio, *imprint of* The Monacelli Press

Arnoldo Mondadori Electa, *distributed by* Trans-Atlantic Publications Inc

Moneta Publications, *distributed by* Chelsea Green Publishing Co

Monjeu Press, *distributed by* Gryphon House Inc

MONKEY, *imprint of* Stone Bridge Press Inc

Monostereo, *distributed by* Simon & Schuster Audio

Monroe Publications, *distributed by* Casemate | publishers

Monthly Review Press, *division of* Monthly Review Foundation Inc, Monthly Review Foundation Inc, *distributed by* New York University Press

Moody Press, *distributor for* Focus on the Family

Moody Publishers, *affiliate of* Ministry of Moody Bible Institute, The Moody Bible Institute

Moon City Press, *distributed by* The University of Arkansas Press

Moon Dust Press, *distributed by* Red Wheel/Weiser

Moon River Publishing, *distributed by* BPC

MoonDance Press, *imprint of* Quarto Publishing Group USA Inc

Morehouse Publishing, *imprint of* Church Publishing Inc

Morgan James Faith, *imprint of* Morgan James Publishing

Morgan James Fiction, *imprint of* Morgan James Publishing

Morgan James Kids, *imprint of* Morgan James Publishing

Morgan Kaufmann, *imprint of* Elsevier Inc

MorningStar Music Publishers, *imprint of* ECS Publishing Group

Morrow Gift, *imprint of* HarperCollins Publishers LLC

William Morrow, *imprint of* HarperCollins Publishers LLC

William Morrow Paperbacks, *imprint of* HarperCollins Publishers LLC

Mort Homme Books, *distributed by* Casemate | publishers

Mortons Media, *distributed by* Casemate | publishers

Mosaica Press, *distributed by* Feldheim Publishers

Mosby, *imprint of* Elsevier Health Sciences, *distributor for* OptumInsight™, *distributed by* Fire Engineering Books & Videos, OptumInsight™

Moselle River, *distributed by* Casemate | publishers

Motorbooks, *imprint of* Quarto Publishing Group USA Inc, *distributed by* Heimburger House Publishing Co

Mount Ida Press, *distributed by* State University of New York Press

Mt Nittany Press, *imprint of* Eifrig Publishing LLC

Mountain Arbor Press, *imprint of* BookLogix

Mountain Press Publishing Co, *distributor for* Bucking Horse Books, Clark City Press, Hops Press, Npustin Press, RainStone Press, Western Edge Press

Mountain Sports Press Series, *imprint of* Mountain Press Publishing Co

Mountaineers Books, *division of* The Mountaineers, *distributor for* Adventure Cycling Association, American Alpine Club, The American Alpine Club Press, Appalachian Trail Conservancy (ATC), Colorado Mountain Club Press, Green Trails Maps

De Gruyter Mouton, *imprint of* Walter de Gruyter GmbH, Walter de Gruyter GmbH, *distributed by* Walter de Gruyter Inc

The Mozhai Foundation, *distributed by* University of Hawaii Press

Moznaim Publishing Corp, *distributor for* Avamra Institute, Breslov Research Institute, Red Wheel/Weiser/Conari

MSU Museum, *distributed by* Michigan State University Press (MSU Press)

MTI, *distributed by* NACE International

MTV Books, *imprint of* Simon & Schuster Children's Publishing

MTV Press, *distributed by* powerHouse Books

Muddy Boots, *imprint of* The Lyons Press

Muddy Pearl, *distributed by* Kregel Publications

Mudpuppy, *distributed by* Chronicle Books LLC

MUFON Books, *imprint of* Red Wheel/Weiser

Coleccion Mujeres de Palabra, *imprint of* Editorial de la Universidad de Puerto Rico

Mulholland Books, *imprint of* Little, Brown and Company

Multnomah, *imprint of* Random House Publishing Group

Museum for African Art, *distributed by* University of Washington Press

Museum of Early Southern Decorative Arts, *distributed by* The University of North Carolina Press

The Museum of Modern Art, *distributed by* Harry N Abrams Inc

Museum of New Mexico Press, *unit of* New Mexico State Department of Cultural Affairs, *distributed by* University of New Mexico Press

Music Inc, *imprint of* Alfred Music

Music Minus One, *distributed by* Hal Leonard LLC

Music Sales, *distributed by* Welcome Books

Musicians Institute Press, *imprint of* Hal Leonard LLC, *distributed by* Hal Leonard LLC

Muswell Hill Press, *distributed by* State University of New York Press

PUBLISHERS

IMPRINTS, SUBSIDIARIES & DISTRIBUTORS

Myers Education Press, *distributed by* Stylus Publishing LLC

MyReportLinks.com Books, *imprint of* Enslow Publishing LLC

Mysterious Press, *distributed by* W W Norton & Company Inc

Mystery Library, *imprint of* Recorded Books Inc, an RBmedia company

NACE International, *distributor for* ASM International, ASTM, AWS, Butterworth-Heinemann, Cambridge University Press, CASTI Publishing, Compass Publications, CRC Press, Marcel Dekker Inc, E&FN Spon, Elsevier Science Publishers, Gulf Publishing, Industrial Press, Institute of Materials, ISO, McGraw-Hill, MTI, Prentice Hall, Professional Publications, Swedish Corrosion Institute, John Wiley & Sons Inc, *distributed by* Australasian Corrosion Association Inc

Jonathan Napela Center, Brigham Young University-Hawaii, *distributed by* University of Hawaii Press

Narosa Publishing House, *distributed by* American Mathematical Society (AMS)

Narratore Press, *imprint of* The Lentz Leadership Institute LLC

NASCO, *distributor for* National Council of Teachers of Mathematics (NCTM)

NASW Press, *division of* National Association of Social Workers (NASW)

Nataraj, *imprint of* New World Library

National Academies Press (NAP), *division of* The National Academies of Sciences, Engineering & Medicine

The National Academies Press, *distributed by* World Scientific Publishing Co Inc

National Archives & Records Administration, *distributed by* J J Keller & Associates, Inc®

National Association of Broadcasters (NAB), *distributed by* Lawrence Erlbaum Associates, Focal Press, Macmillan, Tab Books

National Book Co, *division of* Educational Research Associates

National Book Network, *distributed by* Heimburger House Publishing Co

National Center Early Childhood Workforce, *distributed by* Gryphon House Inc

National Center for Children in Poverty, *division of* Mailman School of Public Health at Columbia University

National Center for Youth Issues/STARS, *distributor for* MAR*CO Products Inc, *distributed by* MAR*CO Products Inc

National Council of Examiners for Engineering & Surveying, *distributed by* PPI, A Kaplan Company

National Council of Teachers of Mathematics (NCTM), *distributed by* Eric Armin Inc Education Ctr, Delta Education, Didax Educational Resources, Educators Outlet, ETA Cuisenaire, Lakeshore Learning Materials, NASCO, Spectrum

National Gallery, London, *distributed by* Yale University Press

National Gallery of Art, *distributed by* Abrams, DAP, Lund Humphries/Ashgate, Princeton University Press, Thames & Hudson, University of Chicago Press, Yale University Press

National Gallery of Australia, *distributed by* University of Washington Press

National Gallery of Singapore, *distributed by* Penn State University Press

National Genealogical Society, *distributed by* Heritage Books Inc

National Geographic Books, *division of* National Geographic Partners LLC, *distributed by* HarperCollins UK (Australia, New Zealand & UK-kids books), Penguin Random House (worldwide exc UK), Simon & Schuster UK (UK-adult books)

National Geographic Kids Books, *imprint of* National Geographic Books

National Geographic Learning, *unit of* Cengage Learning

National Geographic Under the Stars, *imprint of* National Geographic Books

National Institute of Occupational Safety & Health, *distributed by* J J Keller & Associates, Inc®

National Professional Resources, *distributor for* MAR*CO Products Inc, *distributed by* Council for Exceptional Children (CEC)

National Ranching Heritage Center, *distributed by* Texas Tech University Press

National Resource Center for The First-Year Experience & Students in Transition, *distributed by* Stylus Publishing LLC

National Resource Center for Youth Services, *division of* University of Oklahoma Outreach, *distributor for* MAR*CO Products Inc

National Trust, *distributed by* Rizzoli International Publications Inc

The National Underwriter Co, *division of* ALM Media LLC

Native Books, *distributed by* University of Hawaii Press

Native Voices, *imprint of* BPC

Nature Study Guides, *imprint of* AdventureKEEN

Naval Institute Press, *division of* US Naval Institute

NavPress, *imprint of* NavPress Publishing Group, *distributed by* Tyndale House Publishers Inc

NavPress Publishing Group, *division of* The Navigators, *distributed by* Tyndale House Publishers Inc

NBN, *distributor for* Michelin Maps & Guides

NCP, *imprint of* New City Press

NCSY Publications, *distributed by* Mesorah Publications Ltd

NDY Publishing, *division of* Rothstein Associates Inc

NEA Professional Library, *imprint of* National Education Association (NEA)

Near Eastern Press, *imprint of* Holmes Publishing Group LLC

Nebraska, *imprint of* University of Nebraska Press

Nelson Books, *imprint of* Thomas Nelson

Grupo Nelson, *imprint of* Thomas Nelson

Neo-Assyrian Text Corpus, *distributed by* Penn State University Press

New American Fiction Series, *imprint of* Green Integer

New American Poetry Series, *imprint of* Green Integer

New City, *distributed by* New City Press

New City Press, *subsidiary of* Focolare Media, *distributor for* Ciudad Nueva (Argentina, Spain), New City (Great Britain)

New Directions Publishing Corp, *distributed by* W W Norton & Company Inc

New England AEYC, *distributed by* Gryphon House Inc

New England Bibliographies, *distributed by* Oak Knoll Press

New Falcon Publications, *imprint of* The Original Falcon Press

The New Feral Press, *distributed by* Cross-Cultural Communications

New Frontier Publishing, *distributed by* Lerner Publishing Group Inc

New Hope Publishers, *imprint of* Iron Stream Media

New Horizons Book Publishing Co, *imprint of* World Citizens

New Issues Poetry & Prose, *affiliate of* Western Michigan University

IMPRINTS, SUBSIDIARIES & DISTRIBUTORS

New Leaf Press, *imprint of* New Leaf Publishing Group LLC

New Mexico Magazine, *distributed by* University of New Mexico Press

New Netherland Institute, *distributed by* State University of New York Press

New Pacific Press, *distributed by* North Atlantic Books (NAB)

New Readers Press, *division of* ProLiteracy, ProLiteracy, *distributor for* TESOL Press, *distributed by* International Book Centre Inc

New Riders, *imprint of* Peachpit Press

New Shoots Publishing, *distributed by* Redleaf Press®

New Traditions, *imprint of* Gallopade International Inc

New Village Press, *distributed by* New York University Press

New World Library, *division of* Whatever Publishing Inc, Whatever Publishing Inc

New York Academy of Sciences (NYAS), *distributed by* Wiley Blackwell Publishers

The New York Botanical Garden Press, *division of* New York Botanical Garden

New York Times Crosswords, *imprint of* Random House Reference/Random House Puzzles & Games

The New York Times Educational Publishing, *imprint of* The Rosen Publishing Group Inc

New York University Press, *distributor for* Monthly Review Press, New Village Press, *distributed by* Heimburger House Publishing Co

Newbridge Discovery Links for Science & Social Studies, *imprint of* Sundance/Newbridge Publishing

Newbury Street Press, *imprint of* New England Historic Genealogical Society

The Newman Press, *imprint of* Paulist Press

NewSouth Books, *imprint of* University of Georgia Press, *distributor for* Europa Editions

Next River Books, *imprint of* Shepard Publications

Nexus Special Interests, *distributed by* Trans-Atlantic Publications Inc

NFB, *imprint of* NFB Publishing

NIAS Press, *distributed by* University of Hawaii Press

Nightfire, *imprint of* Tor Publishing Group

Nightingale Editions, *imprint of* Cross-Cultural Communications

Nilgiri Press, *division of* Blue Mountain Center of Meditation

NISO Press, *imprint of* National Information Standards Organization (NISO)

no place press, *distributed by* The MIT Press

No Starch Press, *distributed by* Penguin Random House

Nodin Press, *distributed by* AdventureKEEN

Noel, *imprint of* Nova Science Publishers Inc

NOLO, *subsidiary of* Internet Brands Inc

Non-Duality Press, *imprint of* New Harbinger Publications Inc

Nonpareil Books, *imprint of* Godine

North Atlantic Books (NAB), *division of* Society for the Study of Native Arts & Sciences, *distributor for* DharmaCafe, Energy Arts, Ergos Institute, Heaven & Earth Publishing LLC, New Pacific Press

North Beach-West Maui Benefit Fund Inc, *distributed by* University of Hawaii Press

North Carolina Museum of Art, *distributed by* The University of North Carolina Press

North Country Books, *imprint of* The Globe Pequot Press

North Light Books, *imprint of* Penguin Publishing Group

North Point Press, *imprint of* Farrar, Straus & Giroux, LLC

North Star Classroom, *imprint of* North Star Editions Inc

Northern Illinois University Press, *imprint of* Cornell University Press

Northfield Publishing, *imprint of* Moody Publishers

NorthSouth Books, *distributed by* Simon & Schuster, LLC

Northwest Corner Books, *imprint of* Epicenter Press Inc

Northwestern University Press, *distributor for* Lake Forest College Press (Chicago area studies), Tia Chucha Press

W W Norton & Company Inc, *distributor for* Abbeville Press, Akashic Books, Albatross, Blue Guides, George Braziller Inc, The Experiment, Fantagraphics Books, Harvard University Press, Kales Press, Mysterious Press, New Directions Publishing Corp, Penzler, Persea Books, Pushcart Press, Thames & Hudson, Tilbury House Publishers, Tin House Books, Well-Trained Mind Press, Winterthur Museum, Garden & Library, Yale University Press, *distributed by* Heimburger House Publishing Co

W W Norton Company Inc, *distributor for* The Experiment, Harvard University Press

Norton Young Readers, *imprint of* W W Norton & Company Inc

Norwalk Press, *imprint of* BPC

Norwood House Press, *imprint of* The Rosen Publishing Group Inc

Nosy Crow Inc, *subsidiary of* Nosy Crow Ltd, Nosy Crow Ltd (UK), *distributed by* Hachette Book Group Inc

Nova Biomedical Publications, *imprint of* Nova Science Publishers Inc

Nova Business & Management Publications, *imprint of* Nova Science Publishers Inc

Nova ESL Publications, *imprint of* Nova Science Publishers Inc

Nova Global Affairs Publications, *imprint of* Nova Science Publishers Inc

Nova History Publications, *imprint of* Nova Science Publishers Inc

Nova Music Publications, *imprint of* Nova Science Publishers Inc

Nova Publications, *imprint of* Nova Science Publishers Inc

Nova Southeastern University, *distributed by* Gryphon House Inc

Nova Video Productions, *imprint of* Nova Science Publishers Inc

Novalis, *distributor for* Twenty-Third Publications, *distributed by* Twenty-Third Publications

Novel-Ties Study Guides, *imprint of* Learning Links-USA Inc

Novello, *distributed by* Hal Leonard LLC

Novinka Publications, *imprint of* Nova Science Publishers Inc

Npustin Press, *distributed by* Mountain Press Publishing Co

NRH Press, *distributed by* Vandamere Press

NSTA Ebooks+, *imprint of* National Science Teachers Association (NSTA)

NSTA Kids, *imprint of* National Science Teachers Association (NSTA)

NSTA Press®, *imprint of* National Science Teachers Association (NSTA)

Nuclear Energy Agency, *distributed by* OECD Washington Center

PUBLISHERS

IMPRINTS, SUBSIDIARIES & DISTRIBUTORS

Coleccion Nueve Pececitos, *imprint of* Editorial de la Universidad de Puerto Rico

Number Success, *imprint of* Advance Publishing Inc

Nursesbooks.org, The Publishing Program of ANA, *division of* American Nurses Association

Nursing Knowledge Center, *imprint of* Nursesbooks.org, The Publishing Program of ANA

Nystrom Education, *division of* Social Studies School Service

Oak Knoll Press, *distributor for* AdVenture SA, American Antiquarian Society, Bibliographical Society of America, Bibliographical Society of University of Virginia, The Bibliographical Society (UK), Block Museum, Boston College, John Carter Brown Library, Bryn Mawr College, Catalpa Press, Caxton Club, Center for Book Arts, Chapin Library, Club of Odd Volumes, Codex Foundation, Cotsen Children's Library (Princeton), Editions Koch, Fondation Custodia, The Grolier Club, Historic New Orleans Collection, Huntington Library, Library of Congress-Center for the Book, The Manuscript Society, New England Bibliographies, Providence Athenaeum, Rivendale Press, Scripps College Press, Tate Galleries, Texas State Historical Association, Typophiles, University of Pennsylvania Libraries, Winterthur Museum, Yushodo Press

The O'Brien Press, *distributed by* Casemate | publishers

Obsessive Anonymous, *distributed by* Hazelden Publishing

Ocarina Books, *distributed by* University of Hawaii Press

Ocean Publishing, *imprint of* Square One Publishers Inc

Ocean Tree Books, *distributed by* Treasure Chest Books

Octavo Editions, *distributed by* Konecky & Konecky LLC

Octopus Books, *distributed by* Hachette Book Group Inc

Odyssey Books, *division of* The Ciletti Publishing Group Inc

OECD Washington Center, *division of* Organization for Economic Cooperation & Development (France), *distributor for* International Energy Agency, International Transportation Forum, Nuclear Energy Agency

Ofeq Books, *distributed by* The Toby Press LLC

Office of External Affairs, *division of* RAND Corp

Office of the Federal Register, *distributed by* J J Keller & Associates, Inc®

Office of the United Nations High Commissioner for Human Rights (OHCHR), *distributed by* United Nations Publications

Old Farmer's Almanac, *distributed by* Houghton Mifflin Harcourt, Houghton Mifflin Harcourt Trade & Reference Division

Old Pond, *imprint of* Fox Chapel Publishing Co Inc

Olive Branch Books, *imprint of* Well-Trained Mind Press

Olive Branch Press, *imprint of* Interlink Publishing Group Inc

Omnibus Press, *imprint of* Music Sales Group, *distributor for* Big Meteor Publishing, Gramophone

Omnific Publishing, *distributed by* Simon & Schuster, LLC

Omohundro Institute of Early American History & Culture, *distributed by* The University of North Carolina Press

On the Write Path Publishing, *division of* Martin-McLean Literary Associates LLC, Martin-McLean Literary Associates LLC

One Elm Books, *imprint of* Red Chair Press

120 Days, *imprint of* Riverdale Avenue Books (RAB)

One Signal Publishers, *imprint of* Atria Books

1000 Readers, *imprint of* Gallopade International Inc

One World, *imprint of* Random House Publishing Group

Oneworld Publications, *distributed by* Simon & Schuster, LLC

Oni Press, *distributed by* Simon & Schuster, LLC

OPAMP Technical Books, *distributor for* Primary Research Group Inc

Open Books Press, *imprint of* Pen & Publish LLC

Open Court Publishing Co, *division of* Cricket Media Inc

The Open Field, *imprint of* Viking Penguin

Open Lens, *imprint of* Akashic Books

Open Road Integrated Media, *distributor for* Philosophical Library Inc

Open Road Publications, *distributed by* Simon & Schuster, LLC

Open Scroll, *imprint of* Bridge Logos Inc

Optimism Press, *imprint of* Portfolio

OptumInsight™, *distributor for* American Medical Association, Medical Economics, Mosby, *distributed by* American Medical Association, Mosby

Opus 40, *distributed by* WoodstockArts

Oral Biography Series, *imprint of* University of Alaska Press

Orb Books, *imprint of* Tor Publishing Group

Orbis Books, *division of* Maryknoll Fathers & Brothers

Orbit, *division of* Hachette Book Group Inc

Orbit Series, *imprint of* Krieger Publishing Co

Orbit Works, *imprint of* Orbit

Orchard Books®, *imprint of* Scholastic Trade Publishing

Oregon California Trails Assn, *distributed by* Washington State University Press

Oregon Writers Colony, *distributed by* Washington State University Press

O'Reilly Media Inc, *distributor for* Packt Publishing (technol ebook prog)

Oriental Institute Publications, *division of* University of Chicago

Origin, *distributed by* Casemate | publishers

Orphiflamme Press™, *imprint of* Blue Mountain Arts Inc

Osprey Publishing, *imprint of* Bloomsbury Publishing Inc

Ostrich Editions, *imprint of* Cross-Cultural Communications

OTB Legacy Editions, *imprint of* Ocean Tree Books

Christy Ottaviano Books, *imprint of* Little, Brown Books for Young Readers (LBYR)

Ottographics, *distributed by* Chelsea Green Publishing Co

Our Daily Bread Publishing, *division of* Our Daily Bread Ministries

Our Sunday Visitor Publishing, *division of* Our Sunday Visitor Inc (OSV)

Outcaste Press, *imprint of* LARB Books

Outdoor Books & Maps, *imprint of* APC Publishing

The Overlook Press, *imprint of* Harry N Abrams Inc, *distributed by* Hachette Book Group Inc

Owlswick Press, *imprint of* Wildside Press LLC

Oxbow Books, *distributed by* Casemate | publishers

Oxford University Press, *distributor for* Entomological Society of America, Fordham University Press, *distributed by* Cheng & Tsui Co Inc, William S Hein & Co Inc, International Book Centre Inc

Oxford University Press USA, *division of* University of Oxford, *distributor for* ACS Publications, The American Chemical Society, American University in Cairo, Arnold Clarendon, Cold Spring Harbor Laboratory Press, Engineering Press, Getty, Greenwich Medical Media, Grove Dictionaries, Hurst, IRL, Kodansha, Roxbury Publishing, Saunders, Stamford University Press, Thomson Publishing

Ozark Mountain Publishing, *imprint of* Ozark Mountain Publishing Inc

Ozark Mountain Publishing Inc, *distributed by* Red Wheel/Weiser, Red Wheel/Weiser/Conari

Ozark Society, *distributed by* The University of Arkansas Press

PA Press, *division of* Chronicle Books, Chronicle Books LLC, *distributor for* Moleskine Books, *distributed by* Chronicle Books, Chronicle Books LLC

Pace Press, *imprint of* Linden Publishing Co Inc

Pace University Press, *subsidiary of* Pace University

Pacific Boating Almanac, *imprint of* ProStar Publications Inc

Pacific Grove Books, *imprint of* Park Place Publications

Pacific Institute, *distributed by* Washington State University Press

Pacific Press® Publishing Association, *division of* Seventh-Day Adventist Church

Pacifica Military History, *distributed by* Casemate | publishers

Packt Publishing, *distributed by* O'Reilly Media Inc

Pact Press, *imprint of* Regal House Publishing

Pademelon Press, *distributed by* Gryphon House Inc

Padua Playwrights Press, *distributed by* Theatre Communications Group

Page & Vine, *distributed by* Simon & Schuster, LLC

Page Education Foundation, *distributed by* Lerner Publishing Group Inc

Page Street Publishing Co, *distributed by* Macmillan

Page Two Books, *distributed by* Macmillan

Painted Turtle Books, *imprint of* Wayne State University Press

PAJ Publications, *distributed by* Theatre Communications Group

PAKS-Parents & Kids, *imprint of* THE Learning Connection®

Paladin Timeless Books, *imprint of* Twilight Times Books

Palgrave Macmillan, *imprint of* Springer Nature, *distributor for* Berg Publishers, British Film Institute, Manchester University Press, Pluto Press, I B Tauris & Co Ltd, Zed Books

Pali Text Society, *imprint of* Wisdom Publications Inc

Palm Leaves Press, *imprint of* Parallax Press

Pan Asian Publications, *distributed by* Cheng & Tsui Co Inc

Pan Macmillan UK, *distributed by* Macmillan

Panmun Academic Services, *distributed by* Cheng & Tsui Co Inc

Panpac Education, *distributed by* Cheng & Tsui Co Inc

Pantheon Books, *imprint of* Knopf Doubleday Publishing Group

Panzerwrecks, *distributed by* Casemate | publishers

Paolo Torti degli Alberti, *distributed by* Edgewise Press Inc

Paperbacks for Educators, *distributor for* MAR*CO Products Inc

Paperblanks, *distributed by* Chronicle Books LLC

Papercutz, *imprint of* Mad Cave Studios Inc, *distributed by* Simon & Schuster, LLC

PaperPie, *imprint of* EDC Publishing

Paperweight Press, *distributed by* Tuttle Publishing

Parabola, *distributed by* Fons Vitae

Parachute Publishing LLC, *division of* Parachute Properties LLC, *distributed by* Bantam, Bendon, Berkley, Dorling Kindersley, Grosset, Harcourt, HarperCollins, HarperEntertainment, Kensington, Little, Brown, Penguin Random House LLC, Pocket Books, Running Press, Scholastic, Simon & Schuster, LLC

Paraclete Press Inc, *distributor for* Abbey of Saint Peter of Solesmes, Gloriae Dei Cantores

Paradigm Busters, *distributed by* Cheng & Tsui Co Inc

Paradigm Publications, *division of* Redwing Book Co

Paragon, *distributed by* Fons Vitae

Paragon House, *distributed by* Bloomsbury Academic

Parallax Press, *division of* Plum Village Community of Engaged Buddhism

Paraview Pocket Books, *imprint of* Cosimo Inc

Paraview Press, *division of* Cosimo Inc

Paraview Special Editions, *imprint of* Cosimo Inc

Pardey Publications, *imprint of* Paradise Cay Publications Inc

Parenting Press, *imprint of* Chicago Review Press

Park Row Books, *imprint of* Harlequin Enterprises Ltd

Park Street Press, *imprint of* Inner Traditions International Ltd

ParmenidesAudio™, *division of* Parmenides Publishing

ParmenidesFiction™, *division of* Parmenides Publishing

Partner Press, *distributed by* Gryphon House Inc

Partnership Publications, *imprint of* House to House Publications

Parvardigar Press, *distributed by* Fons Vitae

Passages, *imprint of* Perfection Learning®

Pastoral Press, *imprint of* OCP

JIMMY Patterson Books, *imprint of* Little, Brown Books for Young Readers (LBYR)

Pauline Books & Media, *division of* Daughters of St Paul

Pauline Comics & Graphic Novels, *imprint of* Pauline Books & Media

Pauline Teen, *imprint of* Pauline Books & Media

Nancy Paulsen Books, *imprint of* Penguin Young Readers Group

Pavane Publishing, *distributed by* Hal Leonard LLC

Pavilion Books, *distributed by* Rizzoli International Publications Inc

Pavilion Children's, *distributed by* Rizzoli International Publications Inc

Peabody Museum of Archaeology & Ethnology, *distributed by* Harvard University Press

Peabody Museum Press, *unit of* Peabody Museum of Archaeology & Ethnology, Peabody Museum of Archaeology & Ethnology, Harvard University, *distributed by* Harvard University Press

PUBLISHERS

Peacewatch Editions, *imprint of* Ocean Tree Books

Peachpit Press, *imprint of* Pearson Education Ltd

Peachtree Jr, *imprint of* Peachtree Publishing Co Inc

Peachtree Publishing Co Inc, *division of* Trustbridge Global Media

Peachtree Teen, *imprint of* Peachtree Publishing Co Inc

Pearson, *distributor for* Heinemann

Pearson Business Publishing, *unit of* Pearson Higher Education

Pearson Education, *distributor for* Manning Publications Co, *distributed by* American Academy of Environmental Engineers & Scientists®, Trans-Atlantic Publications Inc

Pearson Education Australia, *distributed by* Cheng & Tsui Co Inc

Pearson ELT, *division of* Pearson Education Ltd

Pearson Higher Education, *division of* Pearson Education Ltd

Pearson Learning Solutions, *unit of* Pearson Higher Education

Pearson-Longman, *distributed by* International Book Centre Inc

Pearson Technology, *distributed by* SkillPath Publications

Pebble, *imprint of* Capstone Publishers™

Editions du Renouveau Pedagogique, *distributor for* Michelin Maps & Guides

Peermusic Classical, *distributed by* Hal Leonard LLC

Pegasus Books, *distributed by* Simon & Schuster, LLC

PeKo Publishing, *distributed by* Casemate | publishers

Pelican Children's Publishing, *imprint of* Arcadia Publishing Inc

Pelican Publishing, *imprint of* Arcadia Publishing Inc

Pembroke Publishers Ltd, *distributed by* Stenhouse Publishers

Pen & Sword, *distributed by* Casemate | publishers

Pen & Sword Archaeology, *distributed by* Casemate | publishers

Pen & Sword Atlas, *distributed by* Casemate | publishers

IMPRINTS, SUBSIDIARIES & DISTRIBUTORS

Pen & Sword Aviation, *distributed by* Casemate | publishers

Pen & Sword Digital, *distributed by* Casemate | publishers

Pen & Sword Family History, *distributed by* Casemate | publishers

Pen & Sword Fiction, *distributed by* Casemate | publishers

Pen & Sword History, *distributed by* Casemate | publishers

Pen & Sword Local History, *distributed by* Casemate | publishers

Pen & Sword Maritime, *distributed by* Casemate | publishers

Pen & Sword Military, *distributed by* Casemate | publishers

Pen & Sword Military Classics, *distributed by* Casemate | publishers

Pen & Sword Select, *distributed by* Casemate | publishers

Pen & Sword Social History, *distributed by* Casemate | publishers

Pen & Sword Transport, *distributed by* Casemate | publishers

Pen & Sword True Crime, *distributed by* Casemate | publishers

Pendragon Press, *subsidiary of* Camelot Publishing Co Inc, Camelot Publishing Co Inc, *distributed by* LIM Editrice SRL (Italy), G Ricordi (Italy)

Pengin Random House, *distributor for* Holiday House Publishing Inc

Penguin, *distributor for* Verso Books, *distributed by* Alfred Music

Penguin Audio, *imprint of* Penguin Random House Audio Publishing Group

Penguin Books, *imprint of* Viking Penguin, *distributor for* Countryman Press

Penguin Canada, *distributor for* Michelin Maps & Guides

Penguin Classics, *imprint of* Viking Penguin

Penguin Life, *imprint of* Viking Penguin

Penguin Press, *imprint of* Penguin Publishing Group

Penguin Publishing Group, *division of* Penguin Random House LLC, *distributor for* Alloy Entertainment LLC, Maharishi International University Press

Penguin Putnam Inc, *distributed by* Heimburger House Publishing Co

Penguin Random House, *distributor for* National Geographic Books, No Starch Press, Rizzoli International Publications Inc, *distributed by* The Professional Education Group LLC (PEG)

Penguin Random House Audio Publishing Group, *division of* Penguin Random House LLC

Penguin Random House Canada, *distributor for* Persea Books

Penguin Random House India, *distributor for* Sourcebooks LLC

Penguin Random House LLC, *distributor for* Alloy Entertainment LLC, Hatherleigh Press Ltd, Library of America, Parachute Publishing LLC, Shambhala Publications Inc, Smithsonian Institution Scholarly Press, *distributed by* DawnSignPress, Dreamscape Media LLC

Penguin Random House South Africa, *distributed by* Casemate | publishers

Penguin Workshop, *imprint of* Penguin Young Readers Group

Penguin Young Readers, *imprint of* Penguin Young Readers Group

Penguin Young Readers Group, *division of* Penguin Random House LLC

Penguin Young Readers Licenses, *imprint of* Penguin Young Readers Group

Penn State University Press, *division of* Penn State University Libraries, *distributor for* Abo Akademi University (specialize in ancient Near East), American Oriental Society, Deo Publishing, National Gallery of Singapore, Neo-Assyrian Text Corpus (FFAR, Helsinki, Finland), University of California Institute on Global Conflict & Cooperation

Pennsylvania Historical & Museum Commission, *subsidiary of* The Commonwealth of Pennsylvania

Pennsylvania State Data Center, *subsidiary of* Institute of State & Regional Affairs

Pennwell, *distributed by* Gulf Energy Information

PennWell Books, *division of* PennWell Books LLC

PennWell Business & Industrial Division, *distributor for* Marine Techniques Publishing, *distributed by* Marine Techniques Publishing

PennWell Petroleum Books, *division of* PennWell Books

PennWell Power Books, *division of* PennWell Books

Penny-Farthing Productions, *imprint of* Penny-Farthing Productions Inc

Pensiero Press, *imprint of* The Lentz Leadership Institute LLC

IMPRINTS, SUBSIDIARIES & DISTRIBUTORS

Pentecostal Resources Group, *subsidiary of* United Pentecostal Church International, *distributed by* Christian Network International, Innovative Marketing

Penzler, *distributed by* W W Norton & Company Inc

Peradam Press, *subsidiary of* The Center for Cultural & Naturalist Studies

Percheron Press, *imprint of* Eliot Werner Publications Inc

Peter Peregrinus Ltd, *imprint of* IET USA Inc

Peregrinzilla, *distributed by* Chelsea Green Publishing Co

Sophia Perennis, *distributed by* Fons Vitae

Perfection Learning®, *distributor for* Abrams, Ace Books, Airmont, Annick Press, Archway, Atheneum, Baker Books, Ballantine, Bantam, Barrons, Berkley, Blake Books, Candlewick Press, Charlesbridge Press, Chelsea House, Children's Press, Chronicle Books, Crabtree Publishing Co, Crown, Disney Press, Distri Books, DK, Doubleday, Dutton, Farrar, Straus & Giroux Inc, Fawcett, Firefly, First Avenue, Free Spirit, Fulcrum, Golden Books, Greenhaven Publishing, Hammond, Hayes, Gareth Stevens, Frederick Warne Books

Periplus Editions, *imprint of* Tuttle Publishing, *distributed by* Tuttle Publishing

Permanent Agriculture Resources, *distributed by* University of Hawaii Press

Permanent Publications, *distributed by* Chelsea Green Publishing Co

Permuted Press LLC, *distributed by* Simon & Schuster, LLC

Persea Books, *distributed by* W W Norton & Company Inc, W W Norton & Company Inc (worldwide exc CN), Penguin Random House Canada (CN only)

Peterson Institute for International Economics, *distributed by* Columbia University Press

Peterson's, *distributed by* Hachette Book Group Inc

Peterson's/Pacesetter Books, *imprint of* Peterson's

Petit Collage, *distributed by* Chronicle Books LLC

Petroleum Extension Service (PETEX), *unit of* The University of Texas at Austin, Cockrell School of Engineering

Petzel Gallery, *distributed by* Simon & Schuster, LLC

Pflaum Publishing Group, *division of* Bayard Inc

Phaidon Press, *distributed by* Hachette Book Group Inc

Philadelphia Museum of Art, *distributed by* Yale University Press

Philomel Books, *imprint of* Penguin Young Readers Group

Philosophical Library Inc, *distributed by* Open Road Integrated Media

Philosophy Documentation Center, *distributor for* Zeta Books (online access)

Phoenix International Publications, *distributed by* Hachette Book Group Inc

Phoenix Mapping Service, *division of* Wide World of Maps Inc

Phoenix Publishing, *distributed by* CN Times Books

Pholiota Press Inc, *distributed by* Cross-Cultural Communications

Phonics Adventure, *imprint of* Advance Publishing Inc

Photofact®, *imprint of* SAMS Technical Publishing LLC

Photosmith Books, *distributed by* Caxton Press

Daniela Piazza Editore, *distributed by* Chelsea Green Publishing Co

Picador, *imprint of* Pan Macmillan, Pan Macmillan UK

The Picasso Project, *imprint of* Alan Wofsy Fine Arts, Alan Wofsy Fine Arts, *distributor for* Cramer (Switzerland), Galerie Kornfeld Verlag AG (Bern), Ramie (France), *distributed by* Alan Wofsy Fine Arts

Pickleball Press, *imprint of* Eifrig Publishing LLC

Pictorial Histories Publishing Co, *distributed by* Heimburger House Publishing Co

Picture Books, *imprint of* ABDO

Picture Window Books, *imprint of* Capstone Publishers™

Pierrepont Street Press, *imprint of* Italica Press

Piggyback Interactive, *distributed by* Simon & Schuster, LLC

Pighog Books, *imprint of* Red Hen Press

Pikachu Press, *distributed by* Simon & Schuster, LLC

Pike and Powder, *distributed by* Simon & Schuster, LLC

Pimsleur®, *imprint of* Simon & Schuster Audio

Pinata Books, *imprint of* Arte Publico Press

Pine Winds Press, *imprint of* Idyll Arbor Inc

Pineapple Press, *imprint of* The Globe Pequot Press

Pinnacle Books, *imprint of* Kensington Publishing Corp

Pir Press, *distributed by* Fons Vitae

Pitkin, *distributed by* Rizzoli International Publications Inc

Plain Sight Publishing, *imprint of* Cedar Fort Inc

Planners Press, *imprint of* Routledge

Planting People Growing Justice Press, *distributed by* Lerner Publishing Group Inc

Playscripts Inc, *distributed by* Theatre Communications Group

Playwrights Canada Press, *distributed by* Theatre Communications Group

Plexus Books, *imprint of* Plexus Publishing, Inc

Plexus Publishing, Inc, *affiliate of* Information Today, Inc

PLI, *imprint of* Practising Law Institute (PLI)

Ploughshares, *subsidiary of* Ploughshares Inc

Plum Blossom Books, *imprint of* Parallax Press

Plum Tree Books, *imprint of* Classical Academic Press

Plumbago Books, *imprint of* Boydell & Brewer Inc

Plume, *imprint of* Dutton

Pluto Press, *distributed by* Palgrave Macmillan

PMP, *imprint of* Paramount Market Publishing Inc

Pocket Books, *imprint of* Gallery Books, *distributor for* Parachute Publishing LLC

Pogo, *imprint of* Jump!

Point™, *imprint of* Scholastic Trade Publishing

Poisoned Pen Press, *imprint of* Sourcebooks Inc, Sourcebooks LLC

The Pokemon Company International, *distributed by* Simon & Schuster, LLC

Polar Bear & Company, *imprint of* Solon Center for Research & Publishing

Polebridge Press, *imprint of* Westar Institute

The Political Press, *division of* Brown Books Publishing Group (BBPG)

Political Risk Services, *imprint of* The PRS Group Inc

PUBLISHERS — IMPRINTS, SUBSIDIARIES & DISTRIBUTORS

Pollyanna Productions, *distributed by* Gryphon House Inc

Polyface, *distributed by* Chelsea Green Publishing Co

Polygon, *distributed by* Casemate | publishers

PomegranateKids, *imprint of* Pomegranate Communications Inc

Pond Frog Editions, *imprint of* Red Moon Press

Pop!, *imprint of* ABDO

Poplar Books, *imprint of* Book Sales

Poppy, *imprint of* Little, Brown Books for Young Readers (LBYR)

Popular Woodworking Books, *imprint of* Penguin Publishing Group

Portable Press, *distributed by* Simon & Schuster, LLC

Portavoz, *distributed by* Editorial Bautista Independiente

Neal Porter Books, *imprint of* Holiday House Publishing Inc

Portfolio, *imprint of* Penguin Publishing Group

Portico, *distributed by* Rizzoli International Publications Inc

Portraits of America, *imprint of* The Donning Company Publishers

Possibility Press, *imprint of* Markowski International Publishers

Post Hill Press LLC, *distributed by* Simon & Schuster, LLC

Potomac Books, *imprint of* University of Nebraska Press, *distributed by* Casemate | publishers

Clarkson Potter, *imprint of* Crown Publishing Group

Potter Craft, *imprint of* Penguin Random House LLC

Potter Style, *imprint of* Penguin Random House LLC

Power Publications, *distributed by* University of Washington Press

powerHouse Books, *imprint of* powerHouse Cultural Entertainment Inc, *distributor for* Antinous Press, Juno Books, MTV Press, Throckmorton Press, VH1 Press, Vice Books, *distributed by* Simon & Schuster, LLC

PowerKids Press, *imprint of* The Rosen Publishing Group Inc

PPI, A Kaplan Company, *distributor for* American Association of State Highway & Transportation Officials, American Wood Council (American Forest & Paper Association) (National Design Specification for Wood Construction (NDS) & others), International Code Council, McGraw-Hill Professional (green building, design & construction titles, LEED titles), National Council of Examiners for Engineering & Surveying, SmartPros, Transportation Research Board (TRB), US Green Building Council (LEED reference guides)

Practitioners Publishing Co, *distributor for* AICPA® & CIMA®

Praeger, *imprint of* ABC-CLIO

Praetorian Press, *distributed by* Casemate | publishers

Prajna Studios, *imprint of* Shambhala Publications Inc

Emory Pratt, *distributor for* Primary Research Group Inc

Praxis Continuing Education & Training, *subsidiary of* New Harbinger Publications Inc

Prende Publishing, *imprint of* Histria Books

Prensa Pensar, *imprint of* Progressive Press

Prentice Hall, *distributor for* American Geosciences Institute (AGI), *distributed by* American Academy of Environmental Engineers & Scientists®, NACE International, SME (Society of Manufacturing Engineers)

Presbyterian Publishing Corp (PPC), *distributor for* Epworth, SCM

Presidio Press, *imprint of* Random House Publishing Group

The Press at California State University, Fresno, *unit of* California State University, Fresno

Press Box Books, *imprint of* North Star Editions Inc

La Presse, *imprint of* Fence Books

Price Stern Sloan, *imprint of* Penguin Young Readers Group

Primary Research Group Inc, *distributed by* Academic Book Center, Ambassador Books, Coutts Library Service, Croft House Books, Eastern Book Company, Ebsco, MarketResearch.com, Midwest Library Service, OPAMP Technical Books, Emory Pratt, ProQuest LLC, Research & Markets, Rittenhouse Book Distributors, Total Information, Yankee Book Peddler

Primary Source Media™, *imprint of* Gale

Prime Crime, *imprint of* Berkley

Prime Music, *distributed by* ECS Publishing Group

Primero Sueno Press, *imprint of* Atria Books

Princeton Book Co Publishers, *distributor for* Dance Notation Bureau (Labanotation books)

The Princeton Review, *imprint of* Random House Children's Books

Princeton University Art Museum, *distributed by* Princeton University Press, Yale University Press

Princeton University Press, *distributor for* National Gallery of Art, Princeton University Art Museum, University of California Institute on Global Conflict & Cooperation, Zone Books, *distributed by* Jonathan Ball Publishers (South Africa)

Principles in Practice, *imprint of* National Council of Teachers of English (NCTE)

Printers Row Publishing Group, *distributed by* Simon & Schuster, LLC

Pro-Ed, *distributor for* Psychological Assessment Resources Inc (PAR), *distributed by* Psychological Assessment Resources Inc (PAR)

Proceedings, *imprint of* American Philosophical Society Press

Proceedings of SPIE, *imprint of* SPIE

Process Media Inc, *imprint of* Feral House

Prodist, *imprint of* Science History Publications USA Inc

Productivity Press, *imprint of* Routledge, *distributor for* SME (Society of Manufacturing Engineers)

Productivity Press Spanish Imprint, *imprint of* Productivity Press

Professional Development, *division of* Scholastic Education Solutions

The Professional Education Group LLC (PEG), *distributor for* American Bar Association, American Law Institute, Chicago Review Press, Penguin Random House, Wolters Kluwer

Professional Practices, *imprint of* Krieger Publishing Co

Professional Publications, *distributed by* NACE International

Professional Resource Press, *imprint of* Professional Resource Exchange Inc

Progressive Press, *distributor for* Global Research

Prometheus Books, *imprint of* The Globe Pequot Press

Prompt Publications, *distributed by* SAMS Technical Publishing LLC

Proper Romance, *imprint of* Shadow Mountain Publishing

Propriometrics Press, *distributed by* Chelsea Green Publishing Co

IMPRINTS, SUBSIDIARIES & DISTRIBUTORS

ProQuest LLC, *distributor for* Primary Research Group Inc

Protea Boekhuis, *distributed by* Casemate | publishers

Providence Athenaeum, *distributed by* Oak Knoll Press

Providence Press, *division of* Hope Publishing Co

Psychological Assessment Resources Inc (PAR), *distributor for* American Guidance Service, Pro-Ed, Rorschach Workshops, *distributed by* ACER, Pro-Ed, Western Psychological Service

Public Citizen, *distributed by* Addison-Wesley, Simon & Schuster, LLC

Public Library Association (PLA), *division of* The American Library Association (ALA)

PublicAffairs, *imprint of* Basic Books Group

Publishers Group West (PGW), *distributor for* Black Classic Press

Publishing Services, *division of* Scholastic Education Solutions

Pucker Gallery, *distributed by* Syracuse University Press

Pueblo Books, *imprint of* Liturgical Press

Coleccion Puertorriquena, *imprint of* Editorial de la Universidad de Puerto Rico

Puffin Books, *imprint of* Penguin Young Readers Group

Punahou School, *distributed by* University of Hawaii Press

Punch Press, *imprint of* Loft Press Inc

PUP Audio, *imprint of* Princeton University Press

Purple House Press, *imprint of* Purple House Inc

Purpose First Press™, *imprint of* Milford Books™

PUSH, *imprint of* Scholastic Trade Publishing

Pushcart Press, *distributed by* W W Norton & Company Inc

Put Me In The Story, *imprint of* Sourcebooks LLC

Putnam, *imprint of* GP Putnam's Sons

GP Putnam's Sons, *imprint of* Penguin Publishing Group

GP Putnam's Sons Books for Young Readers, *imprint of* Penguin Young Readers Group

Puzzlewright Press, *imprint of* Union Square & Co

PWM Editions, *distributed by* Hal Leonard LLC

PWN, *imprint of* Summertime Publications Inc

PXT Select™, *imprint of* John Wiley & Sons Inc

PYO (Publish Your Own Co), *division of* Quixote Press

QDS, *imprint of* Quarto Publishing Group USA Inc

QED Press, *imprint of* Cypress House

Qiblah Books, *distributed by* Fons Vitae

Quadrille Publishing Ltd, *distributed by* Chronicle Books LLC

Quail Ridge Press, *imprint of* Capen Publishing Co Inc

Quail Ridge Press (QRP), *imprint of* Capen Publishing Co Inc

Quarry Books, *imprint of* Indiana University Press, Quarto Publishing Group USA Inc

Quarto Library, *distributed by* Lerner Publishing Group Inc

Quarto Publishing Group, *distributed by* Hachette Book Group Inc

Quarto Publishing Group USA Inc, *division of* Quarto Group Inc, Quarto Group Inc (London, UK), *distributor for* Batsford (Pavillion Books Group imprint, CN & US), CLEVER Publishing, *distributed by* Allen & Unwin (Australia & New Zealand), Hachette Book Group Inc (North America)

Quercus Books, *distributed by* Hachette Book Group Inc

Quest Books, *imprint of* Red Wheel/Weiser

Quest for Success, *imprint of* Advance Publishing Inc

Quickfact®, *imprint of* SAMS Technical Publishing LLC

Quickie Books, *imprint of* Penguin Random House LLC

Quiet Fox, *imprint of* Fox Chapel Publishing Co Inc

Quill Driver Books, *imprint of* Linden Publishing Co Inc

Quill Tree Books, *imprint of* HarperCollins Children's Books

Quiller, *distributed by* Safari Press

Quilliam Press, *distributed by* Fons Vitae

Quincannon, *imprint of* Quincannon Publishing Group

Margaret Quinlin Books, *imprint of* Peachtree Publishing Co Inc

Quintessence Books, *imprint of* Quintessence Publishing Co Inc

Quintessence of Dental Technology, *imprint of* Quintessence Publishing Co Inc

Quintessence Publishing Co Inc, *distributor for* Quintessence Publishing Co Ltd (Japan), Quintessence Publishing Ltd (London), Quintessence Verlags GmbH

Quintessence Publishing Co Ltd (Japan), *distributed by* Quintessence Publishing Co Inc

Quintessence Publishing Ltd (London), *distributed by* Quintessence Publishing Co Inc

Quintessence Verlags GmbH, *distributed by* Quintessence Publishing Co Inc

Quite Specific Media, *division of* Silman-James Press Inc

Quite Specific Media Group Ltd, *division of* Silman-James Press Inc

Quodlibetal Features, *distributed by* Vandamere Press

RAB Afraid, *imprint of* Riverdale Avenue Books (RAB)

RAB Desire, *imprint of* Riverdale Avenue Books (RAB)

RAB Gaming, *imprint of* Riverdale Avenue Books (RAB)

RAB Pop, *imprint of* Riverdale Avenue Books (RAB)

RAB SFF, *imprint of* Riverdale Avenue Books (RAB)

RAB Sports, *imprint of* Riverdale Avenue Books (RAB)

RAB Truth, *imprint of* Riverdale Avenue Books (RAB)

RAB Verve, *imprint of* Riverdale Avenue Books (RAB)

Rabbit's Foot Press™, *imprint of* Blue Mountain Arts Inc

Race Point Publishing, *imprint of* Quarto Publishing Group USA Inc

Radio Archives, *distributed by* Dreamscape Media LLC

Radio Theatre, *imprint of* Focus on the Family

Rainbow Bridge Publishing, *imprint of* Carson Dellosa Publishing LLC

Rainbow Ridge Books, *distributed by* Square One Publishers Inc

PUBLISHERS — IMPRINTS, SUBSIDIARIES & DISTRIBUTORS

Rainsource Press, *distributed by* Chelsea Green Publishing Co

RainStone Press, *distributed by* Mountain Press Publishing Co

Rainstorm Publishing, *imprint of* Kidsbooks® Publishing

Raise the Dough in 30 Days Co, *division of* Quixote Press

Ramakrishna Math, *distributed by* Vedanta Press

Ramakrishna-Vivekananda Center of New York, *distributed by* Vedanta Press

Ramanujan Mathematical Society, *distributed by* American Mathematical Society (AMS)

Ramie (France), *distributed by* The Picasso Project

Ramsey & Todd, *imprint of* Turner Publishing Co LLC

Rand McNally, *distributor for* Wide World of Maps Inc, *distributed by* Wide World of Maps Inc

Rand McNally for Kids, *imprint of* Rand McNally

Random House, *imprint of* Random House Publishing Group, *distributor for* Universe Publishing, Welcome Books

Random House Audio, *imprint of* Penguin Random House Audio Publishing Group

Random House Books for Young Readers, *imprint of* Random House Children's Books

Random House Children's Books, *division of* Penguin Random House LLC

Random House Children's Publishing, *division of* Penguin Random House LLC

Random House Digital, *imprint of* Penguin Random House LLC

Random House Graphic, *imprint of* Random House Children's Books

Random House Large Print, *imprint of* Penguin Random Audio Publishing Group, Penguin Random House Audio Publishing Group, *distributed by* Thorndike Press®

Random House Publishing Group, *division of* Penguin Random House LLC

Random House Puzzles and Games, *imprint of* Penguin Random House Audio Publishing Group

Random House Reference, *imprint of* Penguin Random House Audio Publishing Group

Random House Reference/Random House Puzzles & Games, *imprint of* Penguin Random House Audio Publishing Group

Random House Studio, *imprint of* Random House Children's Books

Random House Webster's, *imprint of* Random House Reference/Random House Puzzles & Games

Random House Worlds, *imprint of* Random House Publishing Group

Ranger Rick Science Program, *imprint of* Sundance/Newbridge Publishing

Rasmuson Library Historical Translation Series, *imprint of* University of Alaska Press

Rational Island Publishers, *division of* The Re-evaluation Counseling Communities

Raven, *imprint of* Paraclete Press Inc

Raven Press, *distributed by* Chelsea Green Publishing Co

Raven Tree Press, *distributed by* International Book Centre Inc

Ravenhawk™ Books, *division of* The 6DOF Group

Rayo, *imprint of* HarperCollins Publishers LLC

RB Shorts, *imprint of* Recorded Books Inc, an RBmedia company

Reader's Digest, *distributed by* Fox Chapel Publishing Co Inc

Reader's Digest Children's Books, *distributed by* Simon & Schuster, LLC

Reader's Digest Select Editions, *division of* Trusted Media Brands Inc

Reader's Digest Trade Publishing, *division of* Trusted Media Brands Inc, *distributed by* Simon & Schuster, LLC

Reading Success, *imprint of* Advance Publishing Inc

Rebel Arts, *imprint of* Gingko Press Inc, *distributed by* Gingko Press Inc

Rebellion, *distributed by* Simon & Schuster, LLC

Recorded Books Audiolibros, *imprint of* Recorded Books Inc, an RBmedia company

Recorded Books Development, *imprint of* Recorded Books Inc, an RBmedia company

Recorded Books Inspirational, *imprint of* Recorded Books Inc, an RBmedia company

Recovered Classics, *imprint of* McPherson & Co

Red Chair Press, *distributed by* Lerner Publishing Group Inc

Red Comet Press, *distributed by* Harry N Abrams Inc

Red Feather, *imprint of* Schiffer Publishing Ltd

Red 5 Comics, *distributed by* Simon & Schuster, LLC

Red Lightning Books, *division of* Indiana University Press

Red Portal Press, *imprint of* Mighty Media Press

The Red Sea Press Inc, *affiliate of* Africa World Press Inc

Red Tower Books, *imprint of* Entangled Publishing LLC

Red Wheel Audio, *imprint of* Red Wheel/Weiser

Red Wheel/Weiser, *distributor for* Crossed Crow Books, Hampton Roads Publishing, Nicolas Hays Inc, Lantern Publishing & Media, Moon Dust Press, Ozark Mountain Publishing Inc, Rockpool Publishing, Womancraft Publishing

Red Wheel/Weiser/Conari, *distributor for* Ozark Mountain Publishing Inc, *distributed by* Moznaim Publishing Corp

Redemptorist Publications, *distributor for* Twenty-Third Publications, *distributed by* Liguori Publications

Redhook, *imprint of* Orbit

Redleaf Press®, *division of* Think Small, *distributor for* New Shoots Publishing (New Zealand)

Redwood Press, *imprint of* Stanford University Press

Referee Books, *imprint of* Referee Enterprises Inc

Reference & User Services Association (RUSA), *division of* The American Library Association (ALA)

Reform Judaism Publishing, *imprint of* Central Conference of American Rabbis/CCAR Press

The Refractive Thinker® Press, *imprint of* The Lentz Leadership Institute LLC

Refresh, *imprint of* Tyndale House Publishers Inc

Regan Arts, *distributed by* Simon & Schuster, LLC

Regina Press, *imprint of* Catholic Book Publishing Corp

Regnery, *imprint of* Regnery Publishing

Regnery Books, *distributed by* Simon & Schuster, LLC

Regnery Faith, *imprint of* Regnery Publishing

Regnery History, *imprint of* Regnery Publishing

Regnery Kids, *imprint of* Regnery Publishing

IMPRINTS, SUBSIDIARIES & DISTRIBUTORS

Regnery Publishing, *imprint of* Skyhorse Publishing Inc, *distributed by* Simon & Schuster, LLC

Regular Baptist Books, *imprint of* Regular Baptist Press

Regular Baptist Press, *division of* General Association of Regular Baptist Churches

Reinhart Pop-Up Studio, *imprint of* Insight Editions

RELS Press, *imprint of* Plowshare Media

Remember When, *distributed by* Casemate | publishers

Renaissance Books, *distributed by* University of Hawaii Press

Renaissance House, *imprint of* Laredo Publishing Co

Research, *division of* Scholastic Education Solutions

Research & Education Association (REA), *subsidiary of* Lakeside Book Co

Research & Markets, *distributor for* Primary Research Group Inc

Research & Special Programs Administration of the US Department of Transportation, *distributed by* J J Keller & Associates, Inc®

Resurgence, *imprint of* Tyndale House Publishers Inc

Resurrection Press, *imprint of* Catholic Book Publishing Corp

Retold Classics, *imprint of* Perfection Learning®

Retro Science Fiction, *imprint of* Gateways Books & Tapes

Retrospect Publishing, *distributed by* Closson Press

Reveal Press, *imprint of* New Harbinger Publications Inc

Revell, *division of* Baker Publishing Group

Ribbits, *imprint of* Focus on the Family

The Richmond Organization, *distributed by* Hal Leonard LLC

Ricordi, *distributed by* Hal Leonard LLC

G Ricordi (Italy), *distributor for* Pendragon Press

Ridley Games, *distributed by* Chronicle Books LLC

Riebel-Roque, *distributed by* Casemate | publishers

Lynne Rienner Publishers Inc, *distributor for* Center for US-Mexican Studies, Ayebia Clarke Publishing Ltd (African lit), St Andrews Center for Syrian Studies

Rigby, *imprint of* Houghton Mifflin Harcourt K-12 Publishers

Riley & Johnson, *distributed by* Business Research Services Inc

Rinaldi Studio Press, *distributed by* Casemate | publishers

Rio Chico, *imprint of* Rio Nuevo Publishers

Rio Grande Books, *imprint of* LPD Press/Rio Grande Books

Rick Riordan Presents, *imprint of* Disney-Hyperion Books

Ripley, *distributed by* Simon & Schuster, LLC

Ripple Grove Press, *imprint of* Chicago Review Press

Rise Books, *distributed by* Simon & Schuster, LLC

RISE x Penguin Workshop, *imprint of* Penguin Young Readers Group

Rising Action Publishing Co, *distributed by* Simon & Schuster, LLC

Rittenhouse Book Distributors, *distributor for* Primary Research Group Inc

Rivendale Press, *distributed by* Oak Knoll Press

River City Kids, *imprint of* River City Publishing

River Grove Books, *imprint of* Greenleaf Book Group LLC

River North Fiction, *imprint of* Moody Publishers

Riverdale/Magnus, *imprint of* Riverdale Avenue Books (RAB)

Riverhead Books, *imprint of* Penguin Publishing Group

Rizzoli Electa, *imprint of* Rizzoli International Publications Inc, *distributor for* American Federation of Arts

Rizzoli International Publications Inc, *subsidiary of* RCS Rizzoli Corp New York, RCS Rizzoli Corp New York, *distributor for* Editions Flammarion, National Trust, Pavilion Books, Pavilion Children's, Pitkin, Portico, Skira Editore, Smith Street Books, *distributed by* Penguin Random House

Rizzoli, New York, *imprint of* Rizzoli International Publications Inc

Road Dog Publications, *imprint of* Lost Classics Book Company LLC

The RoadRunner Press, *subsidiary of* RoadRunner Press LLC

Roadside Geology Series, *imprint of* Mountain Press Publishing Co

Roadside History Series, *imprint of* Mountain Press Publishing Co

Roaring Brook Press, *member of* Macmillan Children's Publishing Group

Lee Roberts Publications, *distributed by* Hal Leonard LLC

Robins Lane Press, *distributed by* Gryphon House Inc

Roc Lit 101, *imprint of* Random House Publishing Group

Rock House, *distributed by* Hal Leonard LLC

Rock Point Gift & Stationery, *imprint of* Quarto Publishing Group USA Inc

Rockefeller Institute Press, *distributed by* State University of New York Press

The Rockefeller University Press, *unit of* Rockefeller University

Rocketship Entertainment, *distributed by* Simon & Schuster, LLC

Rockhurst University Press, *distributed by* Fordham University Press

Rocking Chair Kids, *imprint of* Red Chair Press

Rockpool Publishing, *distributed by* Red Wheel/Weiser, Simon & Schuster, LLC

Rockport Publishers, *imprint of* Quarto Publishing Group USA Inc

Rocky Mountain Region Disaster Mental Health Institute Press, *imprint of* Loving Healing Press Inc

Rocky Pond Books, *imprint of* Penguin Young Readers Group

Rodale Books, *imprint of* Random House Publishing Group

Rodale Kids, *imprint of* Random House Children's Books

Anita Roddick Publications, *distributed by* Chelsea Green Publishing Co

Rodin Books, *distributed by* Simon & Schuster, LLC

Roman Catholic Books, *division of* Catholic Media Apostolate Inc

Romantic Sounds Audio, *imprint of* Recorded Books Inc, an RBmedia company

Roncorp Music, *division of* Northeastern Music Publications Inc, *distributed by* Carl Fischer/Theodore Presser

Roost Books, *imprint of* Shambhala Publications Inc

PUBLISHERS — IMPRINTS, SUBSIDIARIES & DISTRIBUTORS

Rootstock Publishing, *imprint of* Multicultural Media Inc

Rorschach Workshops, *distributed by* Psychological Assessment Resources Inc (PAR)

Fr Seraphim Rose Foundation, *imprint of* St Herman Press

Rose Kidz, *imprint of* Hendrickson Publishers Inc

Rose Publishing, *imprint of* Hendrickson Publishers Inc

Rosebud Books, *imprint of* Legacy Bound

RoseDog Books, *imprint of* Dorrance Publishing Co Inc

Rosen Central, *imprint of* The Rosen Publishing Group Inc

Rosen Classroom Books & Materials, *division of* The Rosen Publishing Group Inc

Rosen Digital, *imprint of* The Rosen Publishing Group Inc

Rosen Young Adult, *imprint of* The Rosen Publishing Group Inc

RosettaBooks, *imprint of* RB Content LLC, RB Content LLC (operates ebook catalog, print imprint operated by RosettaBooks LLC), *distributed by* Simon & Schuster, LLC

Rosewind Romance, *imprint of* Vesuvian Books

Rothko Chapel, *distributed by* University of Texas Press

Rothstein Publishing, *division of* Rothstein Associates Inc

The Rough Notes Co Inc, *subsidiary of* Insurance Publishing Plus Corp, Insurance Publishing Plus Corp

Round Table Comics, *imprint of* Round Table Companies

Round Table Companies, *subsidiary of* Writers of the Round Table Press Inc

Routledge, *member of* Taylor & Francis Group, an Informa Business, *imprint of* Taylor & Francis Inc

Row House Press, *distributed by* Simon & Schuster, LLC

Rowe Publishing, *imprint of* Rowe Publishing LLC

Rowe Publishing & Design, *imprint of* Rowe Publishing LLC

Rowman & Littlefield, *imprint of* Rowman & Littlefield Publishing Group, *distributor for* American Council on Education (ACE), The Brookings Institution Press, Center for Strategic & International Studies (CSIS), Lehigh University Press

Roxbury Publishing, *distributed by* Oxford University Press USA

Royal Asiatic Society (Korea Branch), *distributed by* Cheng & Tsui Co Inc

Royal Fireworks Press, *distributor for* KAV Books, Silk Label Books

Royal Historical Society, *imprint of* Boydell & Brewer Inc

Royal Society of Chemistry, *distributed by* ACS Publications

RP Adult, *imprint of* Running Press

RP Inspires, *imprint of* Running Press

RP Minis, *imprint of* Running Press

RP Studio, *imprint of* Running Press

RSMeans, *imprint of* John Wiley & Sons Inc

Rubank Publications, *distributed by* Hal Leonard LLC

Ruby Tuesday Books, *distributed by* Lerner Publishing Group Inc

Run for It, *imprint of* Orbit

Rune-Tales, *imprint of* Quincannon Publishing Group

Running Press, *division of* Hachette Book Group Inc, *distributor for* Parachute Publishing LLC

Running Press Group, *division of* Hachette Book Group Inc

Running Press Kids, *imprint of* Running Press

Rural Science Institute, *distributed by* Chelsea Green Publishing Co

Rutgers University Press, *division of* Rutgers, The State University of New Jersey, *distributor for* Bucknell University Press, Bucknell University Press (worldwide), University of Delaware Press, University of Delaware Press (worldwide), *distributed by* University of British Columbia Press (CN)

Ryland Peters & Small, *distributed by* Simon & Schuster, LLC

S-A Design Books, *imprint of* CarTech Inc

S I Publicaties BV, *distributed by* Casemate | publishers

SABDA, *distributed by* Lotus Press

Sabrestorm Publishing, *distributed by* Casemate | publishers

Saddleback Educational Publishing, *distributor for* TESOL Press, *distributed by* Children's Plus

SAE (Society of Automotive Engineers International), *distributor for* Coordinating Research Council Inc

Safari Press, *distributor for* Quiller

Safer Society Press, *division of* Safer Society Foundation Inc, Safer Society International Inc

Saga Press, *imprint of* Simon & Schuster

Sagamore Publishing LLC, *distributor for* American Academy for Park & Recreation Administration

SAGE Publishing, *distributed by* William S Hein & Co Inc

SAGE UK Resources for Educators, *distributed by* Corwin

St Andrews Center for Syrian Studies, *distributed by* Lynne Rienner Publishers Inc

St Andrews Press, *distributed by* Westminster John Knox Press (WJK)

St Augustine's Press Inc, *distributor for* Dumb Ox Books (publishes the Aristotelian Commentaries of Thomas Aquinas & like works), Hardwood Press (trade books, mostly in sports & regional works), *distributed by* University of Chicago Press

St Bede's Publications, *distributed by* Fordham University Press

St Herman of Alaska Brotherhood, *imprint of* St Herman Press

St Herman Press, *subsidiary of* St Herman of Alaska Brotherhood, *distributed by* Light & Life Publishing Co

St James Press®, *imprint of* Gale

St Louis Mercantile Library, *distributed by* University of Missouri Press

St Martin's Essentials, *imprint of* St Martin's Press, LLC

St Martin's Paperbacks, *imprint of* St Martin's Press, LLC

St Martin's Press, *imprint of* St Martin's Press, LLC

St Martin's Press, LLC, *subsidiary of* Macmillan

Saint Mary's Press, *subsidiary of* Christian Brothers Publications, *distributor for* Group Publishing

St Pauls, *division of* The Society of Saint Paul

St Paul's Publications, *distributor for* Twenty-Third Publications

St Tikhon's, *distributor for* Ancient Faith Publishing

IMPRINTS, SUBSIDIARIES & DISTRIBUTORS

St Vladimir's, *distributor for* Ancient Faith Publishing

St Xenia Skete, *imprint of* St Herman Press

The Saints Series, *imprint of* Pauline Books & Media

Salaam Reads, *imprint of* Simon & Schuster Children's Publishing

Salaryia, *distributed by* Union Square & Co

Salem Books, *imprint of* Regnery Publishing

Salem Press, *imprint of* Grey House Publishing Inc™

Sales & Marketing, *division of* Scholastic Education Solutions

Salish Kootenai College Press, *distributed by* University of Nebraska Press

SaltRiver, *imprint of* Tyndale House Publishers Inc

Samovar Press, *distributed by* University of Virginia Press

SAMS Technical Publishing LLC, *division of* AGS Capital Inc, *distributor for* Butterworth-Heinemann, McGraw-Hill, Prompt Publications

San Diego State University Press, *division of* San Diego State University Foundation, *distributor for* Institute for Regional Studies of the Californias

San Diego Zoo Wildlife Alliance Press, *imprint of* Capen Publishing Co Inc

Coleccion San Pedrito, *imprint of* Editorial de la Universidad de Puerto Rico

Sandala Productions, *distributed by* Fons Vitae

Sandcastle, *imprint of* ABDO

Sandpiper, *imprint of* Houghton Mifflin Harcourt Trade & Reference Division

The Sandstone Press, *imprint of* Frederic C Beil Publisher Inc

Sandu Publications, *distributed by* Gingko Press Inc

Santa Monica Press/Teen, *imprint of* Santa Monica Press LLC

Sapientia Press, *distributed by* The Catholic University of America Press

Sapir Press, *imprint of* Feldheim Publishers

Saroff Editions, *imprint of* McPherson & Co

Sarto House, *imprint of* Angelus Press

SAS Press, *imprint of* SAS Institute Inc, *distributor for* John Wiley & Sons Inc (ebook formats only)

Saturday Books, *imprint of* St Martin's Press, LLC

Saunders, *imprint of* Elsevier Health Sciences, *distributed by* Marine Techniques Publishing, Oxford University Press USA

Savas Beatie, *distributed by* Casemate | publishers

Savas Publishing, *distributed by* Casemate | publishers

Saxon, *imprint of* Houghton Mifflin Harcourt K-12 Publishers

SBL Press, *unit of* Society of Biblical Literature, *distributor for* Brown Judaic Studies, Sheffield Phoenix Press

Scala Publishers, *distributor for* American Federation of Arts

Scandalous, *imprint of* Entangled Publishing LLC

Lo Scarabeo, *distributed by* Llewellyn Publications

Scarsdale Voices, *imprint of* Scarsdale Publishing Ltd

Schaum Publications, *distributed by* Hal Leonard LLC

Schiffer, *imprint of* Schiffer Publishing Ltd

Schiffer Craft, *imprint of* Schiffer Publishing Ltd

Schiffer Fashion Press, *imprint of* Schiffer Publishing Ltd

Schiffer Kids, *imprint of* Schiffer Publishing Ltd

Schiffer LTD, *imprint of* Schiffer Publishing Ltd

Schiffer Military History, *imprint of* Schiffer Publishing Ltd

Schiffer Publishing Ltd, *distributor for* The Donning Company Publishers

E C Schirmer Music Co, *imprint of* ECS Publishing Group

G Schirmer Inc/Associated Music Publishers Inc, *unit of* Wise Music Group, *distributed by* Hal Leonard LLC

Schirmer Reference™, *imprint of* Gale

Schlager Reference, *imprint of* Schlager Group Inc

Schneider Armour Research, *distributed by* Casemate | publishers

Schocken Books, *imprint of* Knopf Doubleday Publishing Group

Scholarly Digital Editions, *imprint of* Boydell & Brewer Inc

Scholarly Resources Inc, *imprint of* Gale

Scholastic, *distributor for* Parachute Publishing LLC

Scholastic Asia, *subsidiary of* Scholastic International

Scholastic Audio, *imprint of* Scholastic Trade Publishing

Scholastic Australia Pty Ltd, *subsidiary of* Scholastic International

Scholastic Books, *distributor for* Alloy Entertainment LLC

Scholastic Canada Ltd, *subsidiary of* Scholastic Inc, Scholastic International

Scholastic Classroom Magazines, *division of* Scholastic Inc

Scholastic Education Solutions, *division of* Scholastic Inc

Scholastic en espanol, *imprint of* Scholastic Trade Publishing

Scholastic Entertainment Inc, *division of* Scholastic Inc

Scholastic Focus, *imprint of* Scholastic Trade Publishing

Scholastic Inc, *imprint of* Scholastic Trade Publishing

Scholastic International, *division of* Scholastic Inc

Scholastic Library Publishing, *division of* Scholastic Inc

Scholastic Ltd UK, *subsidiary of* Scholastic International

Scholastic New Zealand Ltd, *subsidiary of* Scholastic International

Scholastic Press, *imprint of* Scholastic Trade Publishing

Scholastic Reference™, *imprint of* Scholastic Trade Publishing

Scholastic School Reading Events, *division of* Scholastic Inc

Scholastic Trade Publishing, *division of* Scholastic Inc

School Express Press, *imprint of* Story Monsters LLC

School for Advanced Research, *distributed by* University of New Mexico Press

School for Advanced Research Press, *distributed by* University of New Mexico Press

School Renaissance, *distributed by* Gryphon House Inc

PUBLISHERS

IMPRINTS, SUBSIDIARIES & DISTRIBUTORS

School Speciality, *distributor for* MAR*CO Products Inc

Schott Music, *distributed by* Hal Leonard LLC

Schreiber Publishing, *member of* Jackson Westgate Publishing Group

Schwartz & Wade Books, *imprint of* Penguin Random House LLC

Anne Schwartz Books, *imprint of* Random House Children's Books

Sci-Fi Audio, *imprint of* Recorded Books Inc, an RBmedia company

Science & Humanities Press, *subsidiary of* Banis & Associates

Science History Publications USA, *imprint of* Science History Publications USA Inc

Science History Publications USA Inc, *subsidiary of* Publishers' Design & Production Services Inc

Science, Naturally, *imprint of* Platypus Media LLC, *distributor for* Genius Games LLC

Science Press USA Inc, *distributed by* American Mathematical Society (AMS)

SCM, *distributed by* Presbyterian Publishing Corp (PPC)

SCM Press, *distributed by* Westminster John Knox Press (WJK)

John Scognamiglio Books, *imprint of* Kensington Publishing Corp

Scorched, *imprint of* Entangled Publishing LLC

Scottish Text Society, *imprint of* Boydell & Brewer Inc

Scout Comics, *distributed by* Simon & Schuster, LLC

Scout Press, *imprint of* Gallery Books

Screen Door Press, *imprint of* The University Press of Kentucky

Scribner, *imprint of* Scribner Publishing Group

Scribner Classics, *imprint of* Scribner

Scribner Poetry, *imprint of* Scribner

Scripps College Press, *distributed by* Oak Knoll Press

Scripta, *imprint of* Mutual Publishing LLC

Scripta Humanistica Publishing International, *subsidiary of* Brumar Communications

Seaforth Publishing, *distributed by* Casemate | publishers

Seagrass Press, *imprint of* Quarto Publishing Group USA Inc

Seahorse Publishing, *distributed by* Crabtree Publishing Co

Seal Press, *imprint of* Basic Books Group

Seastone, *imprint of* Ulysses Press

Second Chance Press, *imprint of* The Permanent Press

Second Floor Music, *distributed by* Hal Leonard LLC

Second Nature, *distributed by* BPC

Seed Savers, *distributed by* Chelsea Green Publishing Co

Seedling Publications Inc, *imprint of* Continental Press Inc, *distributed by* Kendall Hunt Publishing

Martin E Segal Theatre Center Publications, *distributed by* Theatre Communications Group

SelfMadeHero, *distributed by* Harry N Abrams Inc

Semiotext(e), *distributed by* The MIT Press

Sendpoints Books Co Ltd, *distributed by* Gingko Press Inc

Sentinel, *imprint of* Portfolio

Seoul Selection, *distributed by* University of Hawaii Press

Sequoia Kids Media, *distributed by* Crabtree Publishing Co

Serindia Publications, *distributed by* Serindia Publications Inc (CN & US)

Serindia Publications Inc, *distributor for* Serindia Publications

Service Employees International Union, *distributed by* Chelsea Green Publishing Co

SETAC Press, *imprint of* Society of Environmental Toxicology & Chemistry (SETAC)

Dr Seuss Beginner Books, *imprint of* Random House Children's Books

Seuss Studios, *imprint of* Random House Children's Books

7th Generation, *imprint of* BPC

The Seventh Quarry, *imprint of* Cross-Cultural Communications

The Seventh Quarry Press, *imprint of* Cross-Cultural Communications, *distributed by* Cross-Cultural Communications

Shaar Press, *imprint of* Mesorah Publications Ltd

Shabdaguchha (Magazine & Press), *distributed by* Cross-Cultural Communications

Shadow Mountain, *imprint of* Deseret Book Co

Shadow Wolf Press, *imprint of* Winterwolf Press, *distributed by* Winterwolf Press

Shambhala Publications Inc, *distributed by* Penguin Random House LLC

Shanghai Press, *distributed by* Tuttle Publishing

Shanghai Press & Publishing Development Co, *distributed by* University of Hawaii Press

Shangri-La, *imprint of* Lotus Press

Shaw Books, *imprint of* WaterBrook

Shawnee Press, *distributed by* Hal Leonard LLC

She Writes Press, *distributed by* Simon & Schuster, LLC

Shearwater Books, *imprint of* Island Press

Sheed & Ward, *imprint of* Rowman & Littlefield

Sheep Meadow Press, *distributed by* Syracuse University Press

Sheffield Phoenix Press, *distributed by* SBL Press

Sheffield Publishing Co, *subsidiary of* Waveland Press Inc

Sheldon Press, *distributed by* Hachette Book Group Inc

Shelter Publications, *imprint of* AdventureKEEN

Shengold Publishers, *imprint of* Schreiber Publishing

Shen's Books, *imprint of* Lee & Low Books Inc

Shepard & Piper, *imprint of* Shepard Publications

Sheridan House, *imprint of* The Lyons Press

W B Sheridan, *imprint of* Academica Press

G Shirmer, *imprint of* Hal Leonard LLC

Short Tales, *imprint of* ABDO

Shufunotomo Co, *distributed by* Tuttle Publishing

Sicilia Parra, *distributed by* Cross-Cultural Communications

Sidestone Press, *distributed by* Casemate | publishers

Sierra Club, *distributed by* Chronicle Books LLC

Sierra Club Books, *imprint of* Counterpoint Press LLC, *distributed by* University of California Press

IMPRINTS, SUBSIDIARIES & DISTRIBUTORS

Sierra College Press, *imprint of* Heyday

Siete Cuentos Editorial, *imprint of* Seven Stories Press

Signature Books, *division of* Brown Books Publishing Group (BBPG)

Signatures Network, *distributed by* Andrews McMeel Publishing LLC

Signet Classics, *imprint of* Berkley

Sikorski, *distributed by* Hal Leonard LLC

Siles Press, *division of* Silman-James Press Inc

Silk Label Books, *distributed by* Royal Fireworks Press

Silkworm Books, *distributed by* University of Washington Press

Siloam Press, *imprint of* Charisma Media

Silver Dolphin, *distributed by* Simon & Schuster, LLC

Silver Link, *distributed by* Casemate | publishers

Silvereye Learning Resources, *distributor for* Boys Town Press

Silverplume, a Vertafore Co, *distributor for* Standard Publishing Corp

Simon & Schuster, *imprint of* Simon & Schuster Publishing Group

Simon & Schuster Audio, *division of* Simon & Schuster, LLC, *distributor for* Monostereo

Simon & Schuster Books for Young Readers, *imprint of* Simon & Schuster Children's Publishing

Simon & Schuster Children's Publishing, *division of* Simon & Schuster, LLC

Simon & Schuster, LLC, *distributor for* Aconyte, AHOY Comics, Alexander Lowen Foundation, Alloy Entertainment LLC, Allworth Press, American Girl Publishing, Andrews McMeel Publishing LLC, Applesauce Press, Arcade Publishing Inc, Arctis Books USA, Artists, Writers & Artisans, Authors Equity, Baen Books, Baseball America, Behemoth Entertainment, BenBella Books Inc, Black Mask Studios, Boom! Studios, Callisto Media, Canterbury Classics, Cardoza Publishing, Centennial Media, Central Avenue Publishing, Cernunnos, Chicken Soup for the Soul Publishing, Cider Mill Press Book Publishers LLC, City Point Press, Cold Spring Press, The Collective Book Studio, Dark Ink, David Zwirner Books, Devil's Due Comics, Diversion Books, Downtown Bookworks, ECW Press, 80/20 Publishing, Evil Eye Concepts, Fabled Films LLC, Fabled Films Press LLC, Fantoons, Flame Tree Publishing, Forefront Books, Frederator Books LLC, Gakken, Gallup Press, Galvanized Media, Games Workshop, Hallmark Publishing, Hampton Creek Press, Harlequin Enterprises Ltd, Hazelden Publishing, Health Communications Inc, Heavy Metal Entertainment, Hooked on Phonics, Humanoids Inc, Igloo Books, Image Comics, Indigo River Publishing, Inimitable Books, Insight Editions, Interlink Publishing, Interlink Publishing Group Inc, Juniper Publishing, Kaplan Publishing, Katalitix, Keenspot, Keeperton, Kinfolk, Lake Press, Law & Crime, Leaders Press, Legendary Comics, Libra Press, Library Tales Publishing, little bee books, Little Genius Books, Mad Cave Studios, Mandala Earth, Manhattan Prep, Manning Publications, Manning Publications Co, Mattel Press, Merck Publishing Group, NorthSouth Books, Omnific Publishing, Oneworld Publications, Oni Press, Open Road Publications, Page & Vine, Papercutz, Parachute Publishing LLC, Pegasus Books, Permuted Press LLC, Petzel Gallery, Piggyback Interactive, Pikachu Press, Pike and Powder, The Pokemon Company International, Portable Press, Post Hill Press LLC, powerHouse Books, Printers Row Publishing Group, Public Citizen, Reader's Digest Children's Books, Reader's Digest Trade Publishing, Rebellion, Red 5 Comics, Regan Arts, Regnery Books, Regnery Publishing, Ripley, Rise Books, Rising Action Publishing Co, Rocketship Entertainment, Rockpool Publishing, Rodin Books, RosettaBooks, Row House Press, Ryland Peters & Small, Scout Comics, She Writes Press, Silver Dolphin, Skyhorse Publishing, Source Point Press, SparkPress, Start Publishing LLC, Studio Fun, Sublime, Tanglewood Books, Tanglewood Publishing, Thunderbay Press, To The Stars, Tra Publishing, Trusted Media Brands, Ulysses Press, Uncrate LLC, Vault Comics, VeloPress Books, Viz Media LLC, Waterhouse Press, Weldon Owen, Winged Hussar Publishing, Wisdom, Wisdom Publications Inc, World Almanac® (div of Facts on File), Yilin Press, YoYo Books USA, Zaffre Books, Z2 Comics, Zuiker Press

Simon & Schuster UK, *distributor for* National Geographic Books

Simon Element, *imprint of* Atria Books

Simon Spotlight®, *imprint of* Simon & Schuster Children's Publishing

Simple Productions, *imprint of* Shepard Publications

Simple Truths, *imprint of* Sourcebooks LLC

Sinauer Associates, *imprint of* Oxford University Press (OUP), Oxford University Press USA

Singing Dragon, *imprint of* Jessica Kingsley Publishers Inc

Six House, *subsidiary of* Gallopade International Inc

Sixth&Spring Books, *distributed by* Union Square & Co

SJP, *imprint of* Penguin Random House LLC

Skateman Publications, *imprint of* World Citizens

SkillPath Publications, *division of* The Graceland University Center for Professional Development & Lifelong Learning Inc, *distributor for* Franklin Covey, Pearson Technology, Thomson Publishing, John Wiley & Sons Inc

SkillsTutor, *division of* Houghton Mifflin Harcourt

Skinner House Books, *imprint of* Unitarian Universalist Association

Skipstone, *imprint of* Mountaineers Books

Skira Editore, *distributed by* Rizzoli International Publications Inc

Skittledog, *distributed by* Harry N Abrams Inc

Sky Pony Press, *imprint of* Skyhorse Publishing Inc

Skyhook Press, *imprint of* Shepard Publications

Skyhorse Publishing, *distributed by* Simon & Schuster, LLC

Skylark, *imprint of* Penguin Random House LLC

SkyLight Paths® Publishing, *imprint of* Turner Publishing Co LLC

Sleeping Bear Press™, *imprint of* Cherry Lake Publishing Group (CLPG)

Slow Food Editore, *distributed by* Chelsea Green Publishing Co

Smart Apple Media, *imprint of* Black Rabbit Books

Smart Pop, *imprint of* BenBella Books Inc

Smart Sex Stuff for Kids, *imprint of* Gallopade International Inc

SmartLab, *imprint of* EDC Publishing

SmartLab Toys, *imprint of* Quarto Publishing Group USA Inc

SmartPros, *distributed by* PPI, A Kaplan Company

SMC Publishing, *distributed by* Cheng & Tsui Co Inc

SME (Society of Manufacturing Engineers), *distributor for* Industrial Press, McGraw-Hill, Prentice Hall, John Wiley & Sons Inc, *distributed by* American Technical Publishers Inc, McGraw-Hill, Productivity Press

Smith & Kraus Books For Kids, *imprint of* Smith & Kraus Publishers Inc

Smith & Kraus Global, *subsidiary of* Smith & Kraus Publishers Inc

Gibbs Smith Publisher, *distributor for* Angel City Press

M Lee Smith Publishers, *division of* BLR®—Business & Legal Resources

Smith Street Books, *distributed by* Rizzoli International Publications Inc

Smithsonian Institution Scholarly Press, *division of* Smithsonian Institution, *distributed by* Penguin Random House LLC

PUBLISHERS

IMPRINTS, SUBSIDIARIES & DISTRIBUTORS

Smitten Historical Romance, *imprint of* Iron Stream Media

Snake Country Publishing, *distributed by* Caxton Press

Snova, *imprint of* Nova Science Publishers Inc

Snow Lion, *imprint of* Shambhala Publications Inc

Snowy Owl Books, *imprint of* University of Alaska Press

Soaring Kite Books, *distributed by* Lerner Publishing Group Inc

Social Science Research Council, *distributed by* Columbia University Press

Societe Mathematique de France, *distributed by* American Mathematical Society (AMS)

Society for American Archaeology, *distributed by* University Press of Colorado

Society for American Baseball Research (SABR), *distributed by* University of Nebraska Press

Soffietto Editions, *imprint of* Red Moon Press

Soft Skull Press, *imprint of* Counterpoint Press LLC

Sogang University Institute, *distributed by* Cheng & Tsui Co Inc

Soho Crime, *imprint of* Soho Press Inc

Soho Press, *imprint of* Soho Press Inc

Soho Teen, *imprint of* Soho Press Inc

Solar Design Association, *distributed by* Chelsea Green Publishing Co

Solution Tree Press, *imprint of* Solution Tree

Somerset Press, *division of* Hope Publishing Co

Sommer-Time Story Classics Series, *imprint of* Advance Publishing Inc

Sommer-Time Story Series, *imprint of* Advance Publishing Inc

Sonrise Devotionals, *imprint of* Iron Stream Media

Sorin Books, *imprint of* Ave Maria Press Inc

Soul Guides Books, *imprint of* Yotzeret Publishing

Sound Ideas, *imprint of* Simon & Schuster Audio

Sounds True Inc, *distributed by* Macmillan

Source Point Press, *distributed by* Simon & Schuster, LLC

Sourcebooks, *imprint of* Sourcebooks LLC

Sourcebooks Casablanca, *imprint of* Sourcebooks LLC

Sourcebooks eXplore, *imprint of* Sourcebooks LLC

Sourcebooks Fire, *imprint of* Sourcebooks LLC

Sourcebooks Jabberwocky, *imprint of* Sourcebooks LLC

Sourcebooks Kids, *imprint of* Sourcebooks LLC

Sourcebooks Landmark, *imprint of* Sourcebooks LLC

Sourcebooks LLC, *distributor for* DK Ltd (Europe & UK), *distributed by* Penguin Random House India (India & subcontinent)

Sourcebooks Wonderland, *imprint of* Sourcebooks LLC

Sourcebooks Young Readers, *imprint of* Sourcebooks LLC

Sourced Media Books, *distributed by* Gibbs-Smith, Many Hats Media

SourceResource, *distributor for* MAR*CO Products Inc

South Carolina Bar Association, *distributed by* University of South Carolina Press

South Carolina Historical Society, *distributed by* University of South Carolina Press

Southeast Asia Program Publications, *imprint of* Cornell University Press

Southeastern Center for Contemporary Art, *distributed by* The University of North Carolina Press

Southern Early Childhood Association, *distributed by* Gryphon House Inc

Southern Illinois University Press, *division of* Southern Illinois University

Southern Music, *distributed by* Hal Leonard LLC

Southern Voices Audio, *imprint of* Recorded Books Inc, an RBmedia company

Southwestern Studies, *imprint of* Texas Western Press

Sparkhouse, *imprint of* Augsburg Fortress Publishers, Publishing House of the Evangelical Lutheran Church in America

SparkPress, *distributed by* Simon & Schuster, LLC

Specialized Software, *imprint of* Lotus Press

Spectra, *imprint of* Penguin Random House LLC

Spectroscopy Now, *imprint of* John Wiley & Sons Inc

Spectrum, *imprint of* Carson Dellosa Publishing LLC, *distributor for* National Council of Teachers of Mathematics (NCTM)

Spellbound, *imprint of* ABDO

SPIE Digital Library, *imprint of* SPIE

SPIE Journals, *imprint of* SPIE

SPIE Press, *imprint of* SPIE

Spire Books, *imprint of* Revell

Spirit, *imprint of* Norilana Books

Spirit Mountain Press, *distributed by* University of Alaska Press

Sporting News, *distributed by* Andrews McMeel Publishing LLC

SportsZone, *imprint of* ABDO

Spotlight, *imprint of* ABDO

Spring Publications, *distributed by* Bloomsbury Academic

Springer, *subsidiary of* Springer Nature, *distributor for* The Minerals, Metals & Materials Society (TMS)

Springer Healthcare, *imprint of* Springer

Springer-Verlag, *distributor for* AIP Publishing LLC

Springhouse Editions, *distributed by* White Pine Press

Sproutman Publications, *distributed by* BPC

Spruce Books, *imprint of* Sasquatch Books

Spyglass Books LLC, *distributed by* Biographical Publishing Co

Square One Publishers Inc, *distributor for* Inno-Vision Health Media, Rainbow Ridge Books

SRA/McGraw-Hill, *imprint of* McGraw-Hill Education

Sri Aurobindo Ashram, *distributed by* Lotus Press

Sri Lanka Institute of Traditional Studies, *distributed by* Fons Vitae

Stacey International Ltd (London), *distributed by* International Book Centre Inc

Stackpole Books, *imprint of* Rowman & Littlefield Publishing Group

Stainer & Bell Ltd, *distributed by* ECS Publishing Group

Stamford University Press, *distributed by* Oxford University Press USA

IMPRINTS, SUBSIDIARIES & DISTRIBUTORS

Standard Lesson Commentary®, *imprint of* Standard Publishing

Standard Lesson Quarterly®, *imprint of* Standard Publishing

Standard Lesson Resources®, *imprint of* Standard Publishing

Standard Publishing, *imprint of* David C Cook

Standard Publishing Corp, *distributed by* Lexis-Nexis®, Silverplume, a Vertafore Co

Stanford Briefs, *imprint of* Stanford University Press

Stanford Business Books, *imprint of* Stanford University Press

Stanford University Press, *distributor for* Woodrow Wilson Center Press, *distributed by* Columbia University Press

Star Sounds, *distributed by* Lotus Press

Star Trek®, *imprint of* Gallery Books

Starcrafts Publishing, *imprint of* Starcrafts LLC

Starfire Publishing, *distributed by* Holmes Publishing Group LLC

Starrhill Press, *imprint of* River City Publishing

Starscape, *imprint of* Tor Publishing Group

Start Publishing LLC, *distributed by* Simon & Schuster, LLC

Stash Books, *imprint of* C&T Publishing Inc

State Experience, *imprint of* Gallopade International Inc

State Stuff, *imprint of* Gallopade International Inc

State University of New York Press, *distributor for* Albany Institute of History & Art, Codhill Press, Samuel Dorsky Museum of Art, Mount Ida Press, Muswell Hill Press, New Netherland Institute, Rockefeller Institute Press, Uncrowned Queens

Steam Passages Publishing, *distributed by* Heimburger House Publishing Co

Steam Press, *distributed by* Gryphon House Inc

Steerforth Press & Services, *imprint of* Pushkin Press

Rudolf Steiner Press UK, *distributor for* SteinerBooks Inc

Rudolph Steiner Press, *distributed by* SteinerBooks Inc

SteinerBooks Inc, *imprint of* Anthroposophic Press Inc, *distributor for* Chiron Publications, Clairview Books, Floris Books, Hawthorn Press, Lantern Books, Rudolph Steiner Press, Temple Lodge Publishing, *distributed by* Rudolf Steiner Press UK

Stenhouse Publishers, *division of* Highlights for Children Education Group, *distributor for* Pembroke Publishers Ltd

Step Into Reading, *imprint of* Random House Children's Books

Sterling & Francine Clark Art Institute, *distributed by* Yale University Press

Sterling Ethos, *imprint of* Union Square & Co

Gareth Stevens, *distributed by* Perfection Learning®

Stewart, Tabori & Chang, *imprint of* Harry N Abrams Inc

Stimulus Books, *imprint of* Paulist Press

Stone Arch Books, *imprint of* Capstone Publishers™

Stone Pier Press, *distributed by* Chelsea Green Publishing Co

Stonefield Publishing, *distributed by* Chelsea Green Publishing Co

Storey Publishing, *imprint of* Workman Publishing

Story Line Press, *imprint of* Red Hen Press

Story Monsters Ink, *division of* Story Monsters LLC

Story Monsters Press, *imprint of* Story Monsters LLC

The Story Plant, *division of* Gramarye Media Inc

Storytime Tales, *imprint of* The Child's World Inc

Straight Street Books, *imprint of* Iron Stream Media

Streaming Clarity, *imprint of* Clarity Press Inc

Stride, *imprint of* The Child's World Inc

String Letter Publishing, *distributed by* Hal Leonard LLC

Strong Books, *imprint of* Book Marketing Works LLC

Studio Fun, *distributed by* Simon & Schuster, LLC

Stylus Publishing LLC, *distributor for* Baseball Prospectus, Cabi Books, Campus Compact, CSREA, Mercury Learning & Information, Myers Education Press, National Resource Center for The First-Year Experience & Students in Transition, Thorogood Publishing, Trentham Books Ltd, UCL IOE Press, World Health Organization (WHO)

Sublime, *distributed by* Simon & Schuster, LLC

Suffolk Records Society, *imprint of* Boydell & Brewer Inc

Sugar Cane Press, *distributed by* Heimburger House Publishing Co

Summer Institute of Linguistics, *subsidiary of* SIL International

Summertime, *imprint of* Summertime Publications Inc

Summertime Publications Inc, *distributor for* ACHCBYZ (Paris academic press specializing in Byzantine history)

Summit Books, *imprint of* Simon & Schuster

Sun & Moon Classics, *imprint of* Green Integer

Sun Books, *imprint of* Sun Publishing Company

Sun Plans Inc, *distributed by* Chelsea Green Publishing Co

Sun Publishing Company, *division of* The Sun Companies

Sunbelt Editions, *distributed by* University of New Mexico Press

Sunbelt Publications Inc, *distributor for* FineEdge.com LLC

Sundance/Newbridge Publishing, *division of* Rowman & Littlefield Publishing Group

Sunrise Library, *imprint of* Theosophical University Press

Sunrise River Press, *affiliate of* Cartech Books/Specialty Press

SUP Publishing Logistics, *distributed by* Cheng & Tsui Co Inc

Super Sandcastle, *imprint of* ABDO

Sure Fire Press, *imprint of* Holmes Publishing Group LLC

Surely, *imprint of* Harry N Abrams Inc

Surrey Books, *imprint of* Agate Publishing

Sustainability Press, *distributed by* Chelsea Green Publishing Co

Swallow Press, *imprint of* Ohio University Press

Swallow's Tale Press, *imprint of* Livingston Press

Swan Books, *division of* Learning Links-USA Inc

Swan Isle Press, *distributed by* University of Chicago Press

Swedish Corrosion Institute, *distributed by* NACE International

Sweet & Maxwell, *distributed by* William S Hein & Co Inc

PUBLISHERS — IMPRINTS, SUBSIDIARIES & DISTRIBUTORS

Sweetwater Books, *imprint of* Cedar Fort Inc

The Sword of Norilana, *imprint of* Norilana Books

SYBEX, *imprint of* John Wiley & Sons Inc

Sylvan Learning, *imprint of* Penguin Random House LLC, Random House Children's Books

Synergy, *imprint of* Bridge Logos Inc

Syracuse University Press, *distributor for* Arlen House, Pucker Gallery, Sheep Meadow Press (poetry), *distributed by* Arlen House, Dedalus Press, Gryphon House Inc, Heimburger House Publishing Co

Tab Books, *distributor for* National Association of Broadcasters (NAB)

Tabard Press, *imprint of* Konecky & Konecky LLC

Tabernacle Publishing, *division of* Hope Publishing Co

Tadpole Books, *imprint of* Jump!

The TAFT Group®, *imprint of* Gale

Tagus Press, *distributed by* University of Massachusetts Press

Tai Chi Foundation, *distributed by* Tuttle Publishing

Richard F Taitano Micronesia Area Research Center, *distributed by* University of Hawaii Press

Talbot Publishing, *imprint of* The Lawbook Exchange, Ltd

Tale Blazers, *imprint of* Perfection Learning®

TaLeKa, *imprint of* Norilana Books

Nan A Talese, *imprint of* Knopf Doubleday Publishing Group

Talking Donkey Press, *imprint of* All About Kids Publishing

Tamar Books, *imprint of* Mesorah Publications Ltd

Tamesis Books, *imprint of* Boydell & Brewer Inc

TAN Books, *imprint of* Saint Benedict Press LLC

T&T Clark International, *imprint of* Bloomsbury Publishing PLC

Tanglewood Books, *distributed by* Simon & Schuster, LLC

Tanglewood Publishing, *distributed by* Simon & Schuster, LLC

Tantor Audio, *imprint of* Tantor Media Inc

Tantor Media, *imprint of* Tantor Media Inc

Tantor Media Inc, *division of* Recorded Books

Tapestry Press Ltd, *distributed by* Maryland History Press

Tara Publications, *distributed by* Hal Leonard LLC

TarcherPerigee, *imprint of* Penguin Publishing Group

Taschen GmbH, *imprint of* Taschen America

Tata Institute of Fundamental Research, *distributed by* American Mathematical Society (AMS)

Tata/McGraw-Hill, *imprint of* McGraw-Hill Education

Tate Galleries, *distributed by* Oak Knoll Press

Tate Publishing, *distributed by* Harry N Abrams Inc

Tattered Flag, *distributed by* Casemate | publishers

Taunton Books, *imprint of* Harry N Abrams Inc, *distributor for* Guild of Master Craftsman (North America), Lucky Spool (North America & Australia)

Taunton Sterling Dover, *distributed by* Fox Chapel Publishing Co Inc

I B Tauris & Co Ltd, *distributed by* Palgrave Macmillan

Taylor & Francis, *distributed by* Illuminating Engineering Society of North America (IES)

Taylor & Francis Asia Pacific, *imprint of* Taylor & Francis Inc

Taylor & Francis Books, *imprint of* Taylor & Francis Inc

Taylor & Francis/CRC Press, *distributor for* Teton NewMedia Inc

Taylor & Francis Group, *distributed by* William S Hein & Co Inc

Taylor Trade, *imprint of* The Globe Pequot Press

Teach Yourself Visually, *imprint of* John Wiley & Sons Inc

Teachers College Press, *affiliate of* Teachers College, Columbia University

Teacher's Discovery®, *division of* American Eagle Co Inc

Teaching & Learning Co, *division of* The Lorenz Corp

Teaching Strategies LLC, *distributed by* Gryphon House Inc

Technology, *division of* Scholastic Education Solutions

Techstreet, *distributed by* Illuminating Engineering Society of North America (IES)

TEEN Crave, *imprint of* Entangled Publishing LLC

TEEN Crush, *imprint of* Entangled Publishing LLC

Telshare Publishing, *distributed by* Gryphon House Inc

Tempest, *distributed by* Casemate | publishers

Templar Books, *imprint of* Candlewick Press

Temple Lodge Publishing, *distributed by* SteinerBooks Inc

Temple University Press, *division of* Temple University of the Commonwealth System of Higher Education

Temporal Mechanical Press, *division of* Enos Mills Cabin Museum

Ten Peaks Press, *imprint of* Harvest House Publishers Inc

Ten Speed Graphic, *imprint of* Ten Speed Press

Ten Speed Press, *imprint of* Crown Publishing Group

Teora, *imprint of* Teora USA LLC

Terra Firma Books, *imprint of* Trinity University Press

Terrapin Greetings, *imprint of* Down The Shore Publishing

TESOL Press, *division of* TESOL International Association, *distributed by* Alta Book Center Publishers, New Readers Press, Saddleback Educational Publishing

Teton NewMedia Inc, *distributor for* LifeLearn, *distributed by* Taylor & Francis/CRC Press

Texas A&M University Press, *division of* Texas A&M University, Texas A&M University, *distributor for* Stephen F Austin State University Press, McWhiney Foundation Press/State House Press, Texas Christian University Press, Texas Review Press, Texas State Historical Association, University of North Texas Press

Texas Christian University Press, *distributed by* Texas A&M University Press

Texas Memorial Museum, *distributed by* Bureau of Economic Geology

Texas Parks & Wildlife Department, *distributed by* University of Texas Press

Texas Review Press, *distributed by* Texas A&M University Press

IMPRINTS, SUBSIDIARIES & DISTRIBUTORS

Texas State Historical Association, *distributed by* Oak Knoll Press, Texas A&M University Press

Texas Tech University Press, *distributor for* National Ranching Heritage Center

University of Texas Press, *division of* University of Texas, *distributor for* Bat Conservation International, Institute for Mesoamerican Studies, Menil Foundation, Rothko Chapel, Texas Parks & Wildlife Department, Texas Western Press

Texas Western Press, *affiliate of* University of Texas at El Paso, *distributed by* University of Texas Press

Thames & Hudson, *distributor for* MFA Publications, National Gallery of Art, The Vendome Press, *distributed by* W W Norton & Company Inc

That the World May Know, *imprint of* Focus on the Family

Theatre Communications Group, *distributor for* Chance Magazine, 53rd State Press, Nick Hern Books, League of Professional Theatre Women, Padua Playwrights Press, PAJ Publications, Playscripts Inc, Playwrights Canada Press, Martin E Segal Theatre Center Publications, Ubu Repertory Theatre Publications

Theion Publishing, *distributed by* Holmes Publishing Group LLC

Theology of the Body Series, *imprint of* Pauline Books & Media

Theophilis, *imprint of* Transcontinental Music Publications (TMP)

Theosophical University Press, *affiliate of* Theosophical Society (Pasadena)

Thesaurus Islamicus Foundation, *distributed by* Fons Vitae

Thesis, *imprint of* Portfolio

Theta Books, *imprint of* Bridge Publications Inc

Theta Foundation of Bucharest, *distributed by* American Mathematical Society (AMS)

Thieme Medical Publishers Inc, *subsidiary of* Georg Thieme Verlag KG, *distributor for* AO Foundation

Thinking Like a Scientist, *imprint of* Sundance/Newbridge Publishing

13A, *imprint of* Gallery Books

30 Degrees South Publishers, *distributed by* Casemate | publishers

37 Ink, *imprint of* Simon & Schuster

Thomas Nelson, *subsidiary of* HarperCollins Christian Publishing

George F Thompson Publishing, *distributed by* Casemate | publishers, University of Virginia Press

Thomson Publishing, *distributed by* Oxford University Press USA, SkillPath Publications

Thomson Reuters, *distributor for* AICPA® & CIMA®

Thomson West, *imprint of* Thomson Reuters Legal Solutions

Thorndike Press®, *subsidiary of* Cengage Learning, *imprint of* Gale, *distributor for* Grand Central/Hachette Large Print, HarperLuxe, Mills & Boon Large Print, Random House Large Print

Thorogood Publishing, *distributed by* Stylus Publishing LLC

3 Fields Books, *imprint of* University of Illinois Press

Three Hands Press, *distributed by* Holmes Publishing Group LLC

Three Hills, *imprint of* Cornell University Press

360 Degrees, *imprint of* Tiger Tales

Three L Media, *imprint of* Stone Bridge Press Inc

Three Pines Press, *distributed by* University of Hawaii Press

Three Rivers Press, *imprint of* Crown Publishing Group

Throckmorton Press, *distributed by* powerHouse Books

Thunder Bay Press, *distributed by* Heimburger House Publishing Co

Thunderbay Press, *distributed by* Simon & Schuster, LLC

Tia Chucha Press, *distributed by* Northwestern University Press

Tidewater Publishers, *imprint of* Cornell Maritime Press, Schiffer Publishing Ltd

Tiger Van Books, *imprint of* Turner Publishing Co LLC

Tilbury House Publishers, *imprint of* Cherry Lake Publishing Group (CLPG), *distributor for* Marshall Wilkes Publishing, *distributed by* W W Norton & Company Inc

Timber Press, *imprint of* Workman Publishing

Time Inc Books, *distributed by* Hachette Book Group Inc

Time Soldiers®, *imprint of* BiG GUY BOOKS

Times Books, *imprint of* Henry Holt and Company, LLC

Timespan, *distributed by* Casemate | publishers

Tin House Books, *distributed by* W W Norton & Company Inc

Tinta Books, *imprint of* Trinity University Press

Tiny Golem Press, *subsidiary of* Everything Goes Media LLC

Tiny Reparations Books, *imprint of* Dutton

To The Stars, *distributed by* Simon & Schuster, LLC

Toby Press, *imprint of* The Toby Press LLC

The Toby Press LLC, *imprint of* Koren Publishers Jerusalem, *distributor for* Ofeq Books

Toccata Press, *imprint of* Boydell & Brewer Inc

Today's Books, *imprint of* History Publishing Co LLC

Today's Titles, *imprint of* History Publishing Co LLC

Eckhart Tolle Editions, *imprint of* New World Library

Tommy Nelson®, *imprint of* Thomas Nelson

Tonga Books, *imprint of* Europa Editions

TOP, *imprint of* Top Publications Ltd

Top Keynote Speakers, *imprint of* Avant-Guide

Toplight Books, *imprint of* McFarland

Tor, *imprint of* Tor Publishing Group

Tor Classics, *imprint of* Tor Publishing Group

Tor Publishing Group, *subsidiary of* Macmillan, *distributed by* Macmillan

Tor Teen, *imprint of* Tor Publishing Group

Torah Umesorah Publications, *division of* Torah Umesorah-National Society for Hebrew Day Schools

Tordotcom Publishing, *imprint of* Tor Publishing Group

Torrid Books, *imprint of* Whiskey Creek Press

Tory Corner Editions, *imprint of* Quincannon Publishing Group

Total Information, *distributor for* Primary Research Group Inc

Touch for Health, *distributed by* DeVorss & Co

Tourism Dynamic, *imprint of* Cognizant Communication Corp

Towers Maguire Publishing, *imprint of* The Local History Co

PUBLISHERS — IMPRINTS, SUBSIDIARIES & DISTRIBUTORS

Tra Publishing, *distributed by* Simon & Schuster, LLC

Tradigital, *distributed by* Fons Vitae

Trafalgar Square Books, *distributor for* J A Allen, Kenilworth Press, WeHorse

Trafford Publishing, *division of* Author Solutions LLC

Trailblazer Press, *distributed by* Chelsea Green Publishing Co

Trailblazer Western Fiction, *imprint of* Iron Stream Media

Oswald Train, *distributed by* Donald M Grant Publisher Inc

Trans-Atlantic Publications Inc, *distributor for* Book Guild, Financial Times Publishing, Hodder Education, IndieBooks, Longman, Arnoldo Mondadori Electa, Nexus Special Interests, Pearson Education

Transaction Publishers Inc, *distributor for* University of California Institute on Global Conflict & Cooperation

Transactions, *imprint of* American Philosophical Society Press

Transcontinental Music Publications (TMP), *division of* American Conference of Cantors (ACC)

Transcript Verlag, *distributed by* Columbia University Press

Transformation Media Books, *imprint of* Pen & Publish LLC

Transforming Press, *distributed by* Crown House Publishing Co LLC

Transportation Research Board (TRB), *division of* The National Academies of Sciences, Engineering & Medicine, *distributed by* PPI, A Kaplan Company

Travelers' Tales, *subsidiary of* Solas House Inc

Treacle Press, *imprint of* McPherson & Co

Treasure Chest Books, *distributor for* Ocean Tree Books

Tree of Life Books, *imprint of* Progressive Press

Trends Experts, *imprint of* Avant-Guide

Trentham Books Ltd, *distributed by* Stylus Publishing LLC

Triangle Square Books for Young Readers, *imprint of* Seven Stories Press

Trillium, *imprint of* The Ohio State University Press

Trinity Grace Press, *imprint of* Signalman Publishing

Trinity University Press, *unit of* Trinity University

TriQuarterly Books, *imprint of* Northwestern University Press

TRISTAN Outdoors, *imprint of* TRISTAN Publishing

Triumph Entertainment, *imprint of* Triumph Books LLC

Troitsa Publications, *imprint of* Nova Science Publishers Inc

Trust for Public Land, *distributed by* Chelsea Green Publishing Co

Trusted Media Brands, *distributed by* Simon & Schuster, LLC

Tsukuda Island Press, *distributed by* Edgewise Press Inc

Tu Books, *imprint of* Lee & Low Books Inc

Tughra Books, *imprint of* Paramus Publishing

Tulika Books, *distributed by* Columbia University Press

Tumbleweed Series, *imprint of* Mountain Press Publishing Co

Turner, *imprint of* Turner Publishing Co LLC

Turtle Point, *imprint of* Turtle Point Press

Turtleback Books, *division of* Perfection Learning®

Tuttle Publishing, *member of* Periplus Publishing Group, *distributor for* Healing Tao Books, Kosei Publishing Co, Kotan Publishing Inc, Milet Publishing Ltd, Paperweight Press, Periplus Editions, Shanghai Press, Shufunotomo Co, Tai Chi Foundation

Mark Twain Media, *distributed by* Carson Dellosa Publishing LLC

Twelve, *imprint of* Grand Central Publishing

Twenty-First Century Books, *imprint of* Lerner Publishing Group Inc

Twenty-Third Publications, *division of* Bayard Inc, *distributor for* Novalis (Canada), *distributed by* John Garrett (Australia), Novalis (Canada), Redemptorist Publications (UK), St Paul's Publications (Australia)

23rd Street Books, *imprint of* Macmillan, Roaring Brook Press

Twilight Visions, *imprint of* Twilight Times Books

Twirl Books, *distributed by* Chronicle Books LLC

TwoDot®, *imprint of* The Globe Pequot Press

Tycoon Percussion, *distributed by* Hal Leonard LLC

Tyndale Audio, *imprint of* Tyndale House Publishers Inc

Tyndale Entertainment, *imprint of* Tyndale House Publishers Inc

Tyndale House Publishers Inc, *distributor for* Focus on the Family, NavPress, NavPress Publishing Group

Tyndale Kids, *imprint of* Tyndale House Publishers Inc

Tyndale Momentum, *imprint of* Tyndale House Publishers Inc

Tyndale Ninos, *imprint of* Tyndale House Publishers Inc

Typophiles, *distributed by* Oak Knoll Press

U X L™, *imprint of* Gale

UA Museum, *distributed by* University of Alaska Press

UBC Press, Canada, *distributor for* Michigan State University Press (MSU Press)

Ubu Repertory Theatre Publications, *distributed by* Theatre Communications Group

UCL IOE Press, *distributed by* Stylus Publishing LLC

UCLA Chicano Studies Research Center Press, *distributed by* University of Washington Press

UCLA Latin American Center Publications, *unit of* University of California, Los Angeles

Udig, *imprint of* Andrews McMeel Publishing LLC

Ugly Duckling Presse, *distributor for* United Artists

Ulysses Press, *distributed by* Simon & Schuster, LLC

Unarius Academy of Science Publications, *division of* Unarius Educational Foundation

Unarius Video Productions, *division of* Unarius Academy of Science Publications

Uncrate LLC, *distributed by* Simon & Schuster, LLC

Uncrowned Queens, *distributed by* Excelsior Editions, State University of New York Press

Underlined, *imprint of* Random House Children's Books

Union Musical Ediciones, *distributed by* Hal Leonard LLC

Union Square & Co, *subsidiary of* Barnes & Noble Inc, *distributor for* Against All Odds Productions, Amber Books Ltd, Boxer Books, Brooklyn Botanic Garden, Enchanted World,

IMPRINTS, SUBSIDIARIES & DISTRIBUTORS

Liminal 11, Sally Milner Publishing, Salaryia, Sixth&Spring Books, White Star Publishers, *distributed by* Heimburger House Publishing Co

Union Square Kids, *imprint of* Union Square & Co

United Artists, *distributed by* Ugly Duckling Presse

United for Libraries (Trustees, Friends, Foundations), *division of* The American Library Association (ALA)

United Nations Children's Fund (UNICEF), *distributed by* United Nations Publications

United Nations Development Programme (UNDP), *distributed by* United Nations Publications

United Nations Economic & Social Commission for Asia & the Pacific (ESCAP), *distributed by* United Nations Publications

United Nations Economic & Social Commission for Western Asia (ESCWA), *distributed by* United Nations Publications

United Nations Economic Commission for Africa (ECA), *distributed by* United Nations Publications

United Nations Economic Commission for Europe (ECE), *distributed by* United Nations Publications

United Nations Economic Commission for Latin America & the Caribbean (ECLAC), *distributed by* United Nations Publications

United Nations High Commissioner for Refugees (UNHCR), *distributed by* United Nations Publications

United Nations Human Settlements Programme (UN-HABITAT), *distributed by* United Nations Publications

United Nations Industrial Development Organization (UNIDO), *distributed by* United Nations Publications

United Nations Institute for Disarmament Research (UNIDIR), *distributed by* United Nations Publications

United Nations Institute for Training & Research (UNITAR), *distributed by* United Nations Publications

United Nations International Research & Training Institute for the Advancement of Women (INSTRAW), *distributed by* United Nations Publications

United Nations Interregional Crime & Justice Research Institute (UNICRI), *distributed by* United Nations Publications

United Nations Office for Project Services (UNOPS), *distributed by* United Nations Publications

United Nations Office for the Coordination of Humanitarian Affairs (OCHA), *distributed by* United Nations Publications

United Nations Office on Drugs & Crime (UNODC), *distributed by* United Nations Publications

United Nations Population Fund (UNFPA), *distributed by* United Nations Publications

United Nations Publications, *distributor for* Food & Agriculture Organization of the United Nations (FAO), International Atomic Energy Agency (IAEA), International Criminal Tribunal for Rwanda (UNICTR), International Criminal Tribunal for the former Yugoslavia (ICTY), International Organization for Migration (IOM), International Trade Centre (ITC), Office of the United Nations High Commissioner for Human Rights (OHCHR), United Nations Children's Fund (UNICEF), United Nations Development Programme (UNDP), United Nations Economic & Social Commission for Asia & the Pacific (ESCAP), United Nations Economic & Social Commission for Western Asia (ESCWA), United Nations Economic Commission for Africa (ECA), United Nations Economic Commission for Europe (ECE), United Nations Economic Commission for Latin America & the Caribbean (ECLAC), United Nations High Commissioner for Refugees (UNHCR), United Nations Human Settlements Programme (UN-HABITAT), United Nations Industrial Development Organization (UNIDO), United Nations Institute for Disarmament Research (UNIDIR), United Nations Institute for Training & Research (UNITAR), United Nations International Research & Training Institute for the Advancement of Women (INSTRAW), United Nations Interregional Crime & Justice Research Institute (UNICRI), United Nations Office for Project Services (UNOPS), United Nations Office for the Coordination of Humanitarian Affairs (OCHA), United Nations Office on Drugs & Crime (UNODC), United Nations Population Fund (UNFPA), United Nations Research Institute for Social Development (UNRISD), United Nations University (UNU)

United Nations Research Institute for Social Development (UNRISD), *distributed by* United Nations Publications

United Nations University (UNU), *distributed by* United Nations Publications

United States Catholic Conference Publications, *distributed by* Liturgy Training Publications

United States Pharmacopeia (USP), *distributed by* Consumer Reports

Univelt Inc, *affiliate of* American Astronautical Society, *distributor for* Astronautical Society of Western Australia, US Space Foundation

Universe, *imprint of* Rizzoli International Publications Inc, Universe Publishing

Universe Calendars, *imprint of* Universe Publishing

Universe Publishing, *imprint of* Rizzoli International Publications Inc, *distributed by* Random House

Universe Publishing Calendars, *distributed by* Andrews McMeel Publishing LLC

University of Alabama Press, *distributor for* Fiction Collective 2 (FC2)

University of Alaska Press, *imprint of* University Press of Colorado, *distributor for* Alaska Native Language Center, Alaska Quarterly Review, Alaska Sea Grant, Alutiiq Museum, Anchorage Museum Association, Anchorage Museum of Art History, Arctic Studies Center of the Smithsonian Museum, Far to the North Press, Geophysical Institute, Limestone Press, Spirit Mountain Press, UA Museum, Vanessapress

The University of Arkansas Press, *division of* The University of Arkansas, *distributor for* Butler Center for Arkansas Studies, Moon City Press, Ozark Society

University of British Columbia Press, *distributor for* Island Press, Rutgers University Press

University of California Institute on Global Conflict & Cooperation, *subsidiary of* University of California, *distributed by* The Brookings Institution Press, Columbia International Affairs Online (CIAO), Cornell University Press, Garland Publishers, Lynn-Reinner Publishing, Penn State University Press, Princeton University Press, Transaction Publishers Inc, University of Michigan Press, Westview Press

University of California Press, *distributor for* artSITES, British Film Institute, Sierra Club Books (adult trade), Woodrow Wilson Center Press

University of Chicago Press, *distributor for* The American Library Association (ALA), CSLI Publications, Getty Publications, National Gallery of Art, St Augustine's Press Inc, Swan Isle Press

University of Delaware Press, *distributed by* Rutgers University Press, Rutgers University Press (worldwide)

University of Hawaii Press, *distributor for* Ai Pohaku Press, Asian Civilisations Museum, Ateneo De Manila University Press, BDK America, College of Tropical Agriculture & Human Resources, Denby Fawcett, Hawaii Nikkei, Hawaiian Mission Children's Society, Hui Hanai, Huia Publishers, Institute of Buddhist Studies, iPRECIATION, Island Research & Education Initiative, Isle Botanica, Japan Playwrights Association, Kailua Historical Society, Kalamaku Press, Kanji Press, Korea Institute, Harvard University, Levesque Publications, Little Island Press, The Lontar Foundation, Manoa Heritage Center, MerwinAsia, The Mozhai Foundation, Jonathan Napela Center, Brigham Young University-Hawaii, Native Books, NIAS Press, North Beach-West Maui Benefit Fund Inc, Ocarina Books, Permanent Agriculture Resources, Punahou School, Renaissance Books, Seoul Selection, Shanghai Press & Publishing Development Co, Richard F Taitano Micronesia Area Research Center, Three Pines Press, University of the Philippines Press

University of Idaho Asian American Comparative Collection, *distributed by* Caxton Press

University of Idaho Press, *distributed by* Caxton Press

PUBLISHERS

University of Illinois Press, *unit of* University of Illinois

University of Manitoba Press, *distributed by* Michigan State University Press (MSU Press)

University of Massachusetts Press, *distributor for* Tagus Press

The University of Michigan Press, *distributed by* International Book Centre Inc

University of Michigan Press, *unit of* University of Michigan, *distributor for* Center for Chinese Studies, University of Michigan, Center for Japanese Studies, University of Michigan, Center for South & Southeast Asian Studies, University of Michigan, University of California Institute on Global Conflict & Cooperation

University of Minnesota Press, *unit of* University of Minnesota, *distributor for* Univocal Publishing, *distributed by* Heimburger House Publishing Co, University of Toronto Press (CN)

University of Missouri Press, *distributor for* Missouri History Museum, Missouri Life Magazine, St Louis Mercantile Library

University of Nebraska Press, *division of* University of Nebraska-Lincoln, *distributor for* Buros Center for Testing, History Nebraska, Salish Kootenai College Press, Society for American Baseball Research (SABR), Whale and Star Press

University of New Mexico Press, *distributor for* BowArrow Publishing, FrescoBooks/SF Design LLC, La Frontera Publishing, Museum of New Mexico Press, New Mexico Magazine, School for Advanced Research, School for Advanced Research Press, Sunbelt Editions, West End Press (not actively publishing)

University of New Orleans Press, *division of* University of New Orleans

The University of North Carolina Press, *affiliate of* The University of North Carolina System, *distributor for* Museum of Early Southern Decorative Arts, North Carolina Museum of Art, Omohundro Institute of Early American History & Culture, Southeastern Center for Contemporary Art, Valentine Museum

University of North Texas Press, *distributed by* Texas A&M University Press

University of Oklahoma Press, *distributor for* Cherokee Heritage Press, Denver Art Museum, Gilcrease Museum

University of Pennsylvania Libraries, *distributed by* Oak Knoll Press

University of Pennsylvania Museum of Archaeology & Anthropology, *division of* University of Pennsylvania, *distributed by* University of Pennsylvania Press

University of Pennsylvania Press, *distributor for* The American Philosophical Society, American Philosophical Society Press, University of Pennsylvania Museum of Archaeology & Anthropology, Winterthur Museum, Garden & Library

University of Rochester Press, *imprint of* Boydell & Brewer Inc, *affiliate of* Boydell & Brewer Inc

University of San Francisco Press, *distributed by* Fordham University Press

University of South Carolina Press, *affiliate of* University of South Carolina, *distributor for* McKissick Museum, South Carolina Bar Association, South Carolina Historical Society

University of Tennessee Press, *division of* University of Tennessee

University of Texas Press, *division of* University of Texas, *distributor for* Bat Conservation International, Institute for Mesoamerican Studies, Menil Foundation, Rothko Chapel, Texas Parks & Wildlife Department, Texas Western Press

University of the Philippines Press, *distributed by* University of Hawaii Press

University of Tokyo Press, *distributed by* Columbia University Press

University of Toronto Press, *distributor for* Boys Town Press, University of Minnesota Press

The University of Utah Press, *subsidiary of* University of Utah, *distributor for* BYU Museum of Peoples & Cultures, BYU Studies, KUED (Utah PBS affiliate), Western Epics Publications

University of Virginia Press, *affiliate of* University of Virginia, *distributor for* Colonial Society of Massachusetts, George Mason University Press, The Historic New Orleans Collection, James Madison University, Massachusetts Historical Society, The Massachusetts Historical Society, Samovar Press, George F Thompson Publishing

University of Washington Press, *unit of* University of Washington Libraries, *distributor for* American Federation of Arts, Art Gallery of New South Wales, Fowler Museum at UCLA, International Sculpture Center, LM Publishers, Museum for African Art, National Gallery of Australia, Power Publications, Silkworm Books, UCLA Chicano Studies Research Center Press

University of Wisconsin Press, *unit of* University of Wisconsin-Madison, *distributor for* The Center for the Study of Upper Midwestern Culture, Wisconsin Veterans Museum

University of Wyoming Press, *imprint of* University Press of Colorado

University Press, *distributed by* American Mathematical Society (AMS)

University Press of Colorado, *distributor for* Center for Literary Publishing, History Colorado, Institute for Mesoamerican Studies, International Association for Society & Natural Resources, Society for American Archaeology, Western Press Books

University Press of Florida, *affiliate of* State University System of Florida

The University Press of Kentucky, *distributor for* Kentucky Historical Society

IMPRINTS, SUBSIDIARIES & DISTRIBUTORS

University Science Books, *imprint of* AIP Publishing LLC

University Science Books (USB), *imprint of* AIP Publishing LLC

Univocal Publishing, *distributed by* University of Minnesota Press

Unofficial Guides, *imprint of* AdventureKEEN

Unruly, *distributed by* Harry N Abrams Inc

Upper Access, *imprint of* Square One Publishers Inc

Upper Playground, *distributed by* Gingko Press Inc

Upper Room Books, *division of* The Upper Room

Uproar Books, *distributed by* BPC

Upstart Books™, *division of* Demco Inc

Urban Books, *distributed by* Kensington Publishing Corp

US Coast Pilot, *imprint of* ProStar Publications Inc

US Games Systems Inc, *distributor for* Blue Angel Publishing, KonigsFurt

US Government Publishing Office (GPO), *division of* US Government

US Green Building Council, *distributed by* PPI, A Kaplan Company

US International Publishing, *distributed by* Cheng & Tsui Co Inc

US Space Foundation, *distributed by* Univelt Inc

Usborne Publishing, *distributed by* International Book Centre Inc

User's Guides, *imprint of* Basic Health Publications Inc

Utah Geological Survey, *division of* Utah Department of Natural Resources

Utah State University Press, *imprint of* University Press of Colorado

Valentine Museum, *distributed by* The University of North Carolina Press

V&A Publishing, *distributed by* Harry N Abrams Inc

VanDam Publishing, *division of* VanDam Inc

Vandamere Press, *distributor for* ABI Professional Publications (non-exclusive), JMC Press (exclusive to trade), NRH Press (non-exclusive), Quodlibetal Features

IMPRINTS, SUBSIDIARIES & DISTRIBUTORS

Vanderbilt University Press, *division of* Vanderbilt University, *distributor for* Country Music Foundation Press

Vanessapress, *distributed by* University of Alaska Press

Varlik, *subsidiary of* Cross-Cultural Communications

Vault Comics, *distributed by* Simon & Schuster, LLC

Vedanta Press, *subsidiary of* Vedanta Society of Southern California, *distributor for* Advaita Ashrama, Ananda Ashrama, Ramakrishna Math, Ramakrishna-Vivekananda Center of New York

Vegan Heritage Press, *distributed by* Andrews McMeel Publishing LLC

Velazquez Press, *division of* Academic Learning Co LLC

VeloPress, *imprint of* Ulysses Press

VeloPress Books, *distributed by* Simon & Schuster, LLC

The Vendome Press, *distributed by* Abrams Books, Thames & Hudson

Vendome Press, *distributed by* Harry N Abrams Inc

Venture Press, *imprint of* Williams & Company Book Publishers

Verba Mundi, *imprint of* Godine

Veritas, *distributed by* Ignatius Press

Vernon Press, *imprint of* Vernon Art & Science Inc

Versify Books, *imprint of* HarperCollins Children's Books

Verso Books, *distributed by* Penguin (Canada)

Verso Fiction, *imprint of* Verso Books

Vesuvian Books, *division of* Vesuvian Media Group Inc

VH1 Press, *distributed by* powerHouse Books

Vice Books, *distributed by* powerHouse Books

Victionary, *distributed by* Gingko Press Inc

Victorian Heritage Press, *imprint of* Loving Healing Press Inc

Victory History of the Counties of England, *imprint of* Boydell & Brewer Inc

Vieweg Verlag Publications, *distributed by* American Mathematical Society (AMS)

Viking Books, *imprint of* Viking Penguin

Viking Children's Books, *imprint of* Penguin Young Readers Group

Viking Penguin, *imprint of* Penguin Publishing Group

Villard, *imprint of* Random House Publishing Group

Vindicta Publishing, *imprint of* Histria Books

Vintage Books, *imprint of* Knopf Doubleday Publishing Group

Vintage Children's Classics, *imprint of* Penguin Random House LLC

Vintage Crime/Black Lizard, *imprint of* Knopf Doubleday Publishing Group

Vintage Guitar, *imprint of* Hal Leonard LLC, *distributed by* Hal Leonard LLC

Vintage Originals, *imprint of* Vintage Books

Vintage Shorts, *imprint of* Vintage Books

Vireo Press, *distributed by* ECS Publishing Group

Virginia Genealogical Society, *distributed by* Heritage Books Inc

Visionary Art, *division of* Unarius Academy of Science Publications

Vita Histria, *imprint of* Histria Books

Viz Media LLC, *distributed by* Simon & Schuster, LLC

Volo, *imprint of* Disney-Hyperion Books

Von Zos Publishing, *distributed by* Holmes Publishing Group LLC

Voracious, *imprint of* Little, Brown and Company

Voyage, *imprint of* Brigantine Media

Voyager Press, *imprint of* Quarto Publishing Group USA Inc

Voyager Sopris Learning Inc, *imprint of* Cambium Learning Inc

VVFH (Vietnam Veterans for Factual History), *imprint of* Radix Press

W Publishing Group, *imprint of* Thomas Nelson

Walden Pond Press, *imprint of* HarperCollins Children's Books

Waldman House Press, *imprint of* TRISTAN Publishing

Walker Books US, *division of* Candlewick Press

Miriam & Ira D Wallach Art Gallery, *distributed by* Columbia University Press

Wallflower Press, *imprint of* Columbia University Press

Waltons Irish Music, *distributed by* Hal Leonard LLC

WAP Academic, *imprint of* Pentecostal Resources Group

WAP Children, *imprint of* Pentecostal Resources Group

Warboys LLC, *distributed by* Bridge Logos Inc

Frederick Warne Books, *imprint of* Penguin Young Readers Group, *distributed by* Perfection Learning®

Warner/Chappell Music Inc, *imprint of* Alfred Music

Warner Press, *affiliate of* Church of God Ministries

Washington Post Crosswords, *imprint of* Random House Reference/Random House Puzzles & Games

Washington Service Bureau, *subsidiary of* CCH, a Wolters Kluwer business

Washington Square Press, *imprint of* Atria Books

Washington State Historical Society, *distributed by* Washington State University Press

Washington State University Press, *division of* Washington State University, *distributor for* Lost Horse Press, Lynx House Press, Oregon California Trails Assn, Oregon Writers Colony (single title), Pacific Institute (single title), Washington State Historical Society (single title), WSU Museum of Art

Water Resources Publications LLC, *distributor for* ASAE

WaterBrook, *imprint of* Random House Publishing Group

Waterfront Soundings Productions, *distributed by* Marine Techniques Publishing

Waterhouse Press, *distributed by* Simon & Schuster, LLC

Watermark Publishing, *member of* aio Media Group

Watson-Guptill, *imprint of* Crown Publishing Group

Neale Watson Academic Publications, *imprint of* Science History Publications USA Inc

Waverley West, *subsidiary of* McPherson & Co

We Do Listen Foundation, *distributed by* Lerner Publishing Group Inc

WEA, *distributed by* Alfred Music

PUBLISHERS — IMPRINTS, SUBSIDIARIES & DISTRIBUTORS

Webster's New World® College Dictionary, *imprint of* Houghton Mifflin Harcourt Trade & Reference Division

Wednesday Books, *imprint of* St Martin's Press, LLC

Wee Sing, *imprint of* Penguin Young Readers Group

WeHorse, *distributed by* Trafalgar Square Books

Irene Weinberger Books, *imprint of* Hamilton Stone Editions

Welcome Books, *imprint of* Rizzoli International Publications Inc, *distributor for* AAP, Cerf & Peterson, Music Sales, Zeke Holdings Ltd, *distributed by* Random House

Welcome Enterprises Inc, *imprint of* Rizzoli International Publications Inc

Weldon Owen, *distributed by* Simon & Schuster, LLC

Weldon Owen International, *subsidiary of* Insight Editions

Well-Trained Mind Press, *distributed by* W W Norton & Company Inc

Wellfleet Press, *imprint of* Quarto Publishing Group USA Inc

Wellington Press, *division of* BooksUPrint.com Inc

Welz, *distributed by* Alan Wofsy Fine Arts

Wendy Lamb Books, *imprint of* Random House Children's Books

Wesleyan Publishing House, *division of* The Wesleyan Church

West Academic (ELI Press), *distributor for* Environmental Law Institute

West End Press, *distributed by* University of New Mexico Press

West 44 Books, *imprint of* Enslow Publishing LLC

West Margin Press, *imprint of* Turner Publishing Co LLC

Western Edge Press, *imprint of* Sherman Asher Publishing, Sherman Asher Publishing, *distributed by* Mountain Press Publishing Co

Western Epics Publications, *distributed by* The University of Utah Press

Western Horseman, *imprint of* The Globe Pequot Press

Western Library, *imprint of* Recorded Books Inc, an RBmedia company

Western Press Books, *distributed by* University Press of Colorado

Western Psychological Service, *distributor for* Psychological Assessment Resources Inc (PAR)

Westminster John Knox Press (WJK), *imprint of* Presbyterian Publishing Corp (PPC), *distributor for* Canterbury Press, Church House Publishing, St Andrews Press, SCM Press, Woodlake Publishing Inc

Westview Press, *distributor for* University of California Institute on Global Conflict & Cooperation

Westwinds Press®, *imprint of* Turner Publishing Co LLC

Whale and Star Press, *distributed by* University of Nebraska Press

Wharncliffe, *distributed by* Casemate | publishers

Wharton School Press (WSP), *imprint of* University of Pennsylvania Press

Wheatherstone Press, *subsidiary of* Dickinson Consulting Group Inc

Wheeler Publishing™, *imprint of* Gale

Whiskey Creek Press, *imprint of* Start Publishing LLC

Whitaker, *distributor for* Faith Library Publications

Whitaker Espanol, *imprint of* Whitaker House

White Eagle Publishing Trust (England), *distributed by* DeVorss & Co

White Pine Press, *distributor for* Springhouse Editions

White Poppy Press, *imprint of* Modern Memoirs Inc

White Rabbit Press, *distributed by* Cheng & Tsui Co Inc

White Star Publishers, *distributed by* Union Square & Co

White Thread Press, *distributed by* Fons Vitae

Whitford Press, *imprint of* Schiffer Publishing Ltd

Whitney Museum of American Art, *distributed by* Yale University Press

Wide World of Maps Inc, *distributor for* Benchmark Maps, Big Sky Maps, Franko Maps, MacVan Maps (Colorado Springs), Metro Maps, Rand McNally, *distributed by* Rand McNally

Wilderness Press, *imprint of* AdventureKEEN

Wildflower Press, *affiliate of* Oakbrook Press

Wiley, *imprint of* Turner Publishing Co LLC, *distributed by* AICPA® & CIMA®, Gulf Energy Information

Wiley-Blackwell, *imprint of* John Wiley & Sons Inc, *distributor for* American Anthropological Association (AAA)

Wiley Blackwell Publishers, *distributor for* New York Academy of Sciences (NYAS)

Wiley Custom Select, *imprint of* John Wiley & Sons Inc

Wiley Digital Archives, *imprint of* John Wiley & Sons Inc

Wiley Education Services, *imprint of* John Wiley & Sons Inc

Wiley Efficient Learning, *imprint of* John Wiley & Sons Inc

Wiley Health Learning, *imprint of* John Wiley & Sons Inc

Wiley-IEEE Press, *imprint of* IEEE Press, John Wiley & Sons Inc

Wiley Inc, *distributor for* The Electrochemical Society (ECS)

J Wiley & Sons, *distributed by* Medical Group Management Association (MGMA)

Wiley Job Network, *imprint of* John Wiley & Sons Inc

John Wiley & Sons, *distributed by* Heimburger House Publishing Co

John Wiley & Sons Inc, *distributor for* American Institute of Chemical Engineers (AIChE), Association for Information Science & Technology (ASIS&T), Center for Creative Leadership LLC, IEEE Press, R S Means from The Gordian Group, *distributed by* American Academy of Environmental Engineers & Scientists®, American Institute of Chemical Engineers (AIChE), Center for Creative Leadership LLC, William S Hein & Co Inc, J J Keller & Associates, Inc®, NACE International, SAS Press, SkillPath Publications, SME (Society of Manufacturing Engineers)

John Wiley & Sons Inc Global Education, *division of* John Wiley & Sons Inc, John Wiley & Sons Inc

John Wiley & Sons Inc Professional Development, *division of* John Wiley & Sons Inc

Wiley Online Library, *imprint of* John Wiley & Sons Inc

Wiley Open Access, *imprint of* John Wiley & Sons Inc

Wiley Science Solutions, *imprint of* John Wiley & Sons Inc

Wiley-VCH, *imprint of* John Wiley & Sons Inc

Wiley Visualizing, *imprint of* John Wiley & Sons Inc

WileyPLUS, *imprint of* John Wiley & Sons Inc

IMPRINTS, SUBSIDIARIES & DISTRIBUTORS

Marshall Wilkes Publishing, *distributed by* Tilbury House Publishers

William Carey Library, *imprint of* William Carey Publishing

William Carey Press, *imprint of* William Carey Publishing

William Carey Publishing, *division of* Frontier Ventures

William, James & Co, *imprint of* Franklin, Beedle & Associates Inc

Williams & Co Publishers, *imprint of* Williams & Company Book Publishers

Willis Music, *distributed by* Hal Leonard LLC

Willow Bend Books, *imprint of* Heritage Books Inc

Wilson Center Press, *imprint of* Woodrow Wilson Center Press

H W Wilson, *imprint of* Grey House Publishing Inc™

Wind Records, *distributed by* YMAA Publication Center Inc

Windmill Books, *imprint of* The Rosen Publishing Group Inc

Windsor Books, *division of* Windsor Marketing Corp, Windsor Marketing Corp

Kelley Wingate Publications, *imprint of* Carson Dellosa Publishing LLC

Winged Hussar Publishing, *distributed by* Simon & Schuster, LLC

Wings Books, *imprint of* Penguin Random House LLC

WingSpread Publishers, *imprint of* Moody Publishers

Winterthur Museum, *distributed by* Oak Knoll Press

Winterthur Museum, Garden & Library, *distributed by* ACC Art Books, The Monacelli Press, W W Norton & Company Inc, University of Pennsylvania Press

Winterwolf Press, *distributor for* Shadow Wolf Press

Wisconsin Veterans Museum, *distributed by* University of Wisconsin Press

Wisdom, *distributed by* Simon & Schuster, LLC

Wisdom Foundation, *distributed by* Fons Vitae

Wisdom Publications Inc, *distributed by* Simon & Schuster, LLC

Witherby Seamanship International Ltd, *distributed by* Marine Techniques Publishing

Witness Impulse, *imprint of* HarperCollins Publishers LLC

Wittenborn Art Books, *division of* Alan Wofsy Fine Arts, *distributed by* Alan Wofsy Fine Arts

Wizards of the Coast LLC, *subsidiary of* Hasbro Inc

Alan Wofsy Fine Arts, *distributor for* Bora, Brusberg (Berlin), Cramer (Geneva), Galerie Kornfeld Verlag AG (Bern), Huber, Ides et Calendes, The Picasso Project, Welz, Wittenborn Art Books

Wolfgang Publications, *distributed by* CarTech Inc

Wolters Kluwer, *distributed by* William S Hein & Co Inc, The Professional Education Group LLC (PEG)

Wolters Kluwer Law & Business, *subsidiary of* Wolters Kluwer, Wolters Kluwer

Wolters Kluwer US Corp, *subsidiary of* Wolters Kluwer NV (The Netherlands)

Womancraft Publishing, *distributed by* Red Wheel/Weiser

Women In Nontraditional Careers, *imprint of* Her Own Words LLC

Women's History, *imprint of* Her Own Words LLC

Women's Publications, *imprint of* Consumer Press

Wonder Books, *imprint of* The Child's World Inc

Woo! Jr Kids Activities, *imprint of* Turner Publishing Co LLC

Marian Wood Books, *imprint of* GP Putnam's Sons

S Woodhouse Books, *imprint of* Everything Goes Media LLC

Woodlake Publishing Inc, *distributed by* Westminster John Knox Press (WJK)

Woodrow Wilson Center Press, *division of* The Woodrow Wilson International Center for Scholars, Woodrow Wilson International Center for Scholars, *distributed by* Columbia University Press, Johns Hopkins University Press, Stanford University Press, University of California Press

Woodrow Wilson Center Press/Columbia University Press, *imprint of* Woodrow Wilson Center Press

Woodrow Wilson Center Press/Johns Hopkins University Press, *imprint of* Woodrow Wilson Center Press

Woodrow Wilson Center Press/Stanford University Press, *imprint of* Woodrow Wilson Center Press

Sylvia Woods, *distributed by* Hal Leonard LLC

Woodstock Artists Association & Museum, *distributed by* WoodstockArts

Woodstock Byrdcliffe Guild, *distributed by* WoodstockArts

WoodstockArts, *distributor for* Bushwhack Press, Opus 40, Woodstock Artists Association & Museum, Woodstock Byrdcliffe Guild

Word Aflame Press, *imprint of* Pentecostal Resources Group

WordSong, *imprint of* Astra Books for Young Readers

Wordwell Books, *distributed by* Casemate | publishers

The Working Arts Library, *distributed by* Applause Theatre & Cinema Books

Workman, *imprint of* Workman Publishing

Workman Calendars, *imprint of* Workman Publishing

Workman Kids, *imprint of* Workman Publishing

Workman Publishing, *division of* Hachette Book Group Inc, *distributor for* Erewhon Books, Familius

World Almanac®, *imprint of* Skyhorse Publishing Inc, *distributed by* Simon & Schuster, LLC

World Bank, *imprint of* World Bank Publications

World Bank Publications, *member of* The World Bank Group

World Book Inc, *subsidiary of* The Scott Fetzer Co

World Catholic Press, *imprint of* Catholic Book Publishing Corp

World Citizens, *affiliate of* Cinema Investments Co Inc, *distributed by* Inland

World Health Organization (WHO), *distributed by* Stylus Publishing LLC

World Noir, *imprint of* Europa Editions

World of Eric Carle, *imprint of* Penguin Young Readers Group

World Scientific Publishing Co Inc, *distributor for* The National Academies Press (Asia-Pacific exc Australia, Japan & New Zealand)

World Wisdom, *distributed by* Fons Vitae

The World's Largest Publishing Co, *subsidiary of* Gallopade International Inc

Worldwide Mystery, *imprint of* Harlequin Enterprises Ltd

Worth Publishers, *imprint of* Macmillan Learning

PUBLISHERS — IMPRINTS, SUBSIDIARIES & DISTRIBUTORS

Worthy Publishing, *imprint of* Hachette Nashville

Wrightbooks, *imprint of* John Wiley & Sons Inc

Write Stuff®, *imprint of* Write Stuff Enterprises LLC

WriteLife Publishing, *imprint of* Boutique of Quality Books Publishing

Writers & Artists on Photography Series, *imprint of* Aperture Books

Writer's Digest Books, *imprint of* Penguin Publishing Group

Wrox™, *imprint of* John Wiley & Sons Inc

WRS Group, *distributor for* MAR*CO Products Inc

WSU Museum of Art, *distributed by* Washington State University Press

Anne Wyld, *imprint of* Idyll Arbor Inc

Xeno Books, *imprint of* Red Hen Press

Xlibris Corp, *imprint of* Author Solutions LLC

XML Press, *subsidiary of* R L Hamilton & Associates LLC

Xoanon Publishing, *distributed by* Holmes Publishing Group LLC

Xpat Fiction, *imprint of* Franklin, Beedle & Associates Inc

Y Lolfa, *distributed by* Casemate | publishers

YA Angst, *imprint of* Norilana Books

YACK!, *imprint of* Eifrig Publishing LLC

Yale Center for British Art, *distributed by* Yale University Press

Yale Press Audio, *imprint of* Yale University Press

Yale University Art Gallery, *distributed by* Yale University Press

Yale University Press, *division of* Yale University, *distributor for* American Federation of Arts, The Art Institute of Chicago, The Bard Graduate Center, Beinecke Rare Book & Manuscript Library, Dallas Museum of Art, Harvard Art Museums, Harvard University Art Museums, The Jewish Museum, Kimbell Art Museum, Paul Mellon Centre, The Menil Collection, Mercatorfonds, The Metropolitan Museum of Art, National Gallery, London, National Gallery of Art, National Gallery of Art (Washington, DC), Philadelphia Museum of Art, Princeton University Art Museum, Sterling & Francine Clark Art Institute, Whitney Museum of American Art, Yale Center for British Art, Yale University Art Gallery, *distributed by* W W Norton & Company Inc

Yankee Book Peddler, *distributor for* Primary Research Group Inc

Yearling Books, *imprint of* Random House Children's Books

Yellow Jacket, *imprint of* little bee books

Yellow 1, *imprint of* Wide World of Maps Inc

Yelsraek Publishing, *distributed by* Adventures Unlimited Press (AUP)

Yen Press, *distributed by* Hachette Book Group Inc

Yes Books, *distributed by* Chelsea Green Publishing Co

Yeshiva University Museum Press, *distributed by* Gorgias Press LLC

Yeshiva University Press, *distributed by* KTAV Publishing House Inc

Yilin Press, *distributed by* Simon & Schuster, LLC

YMAA Publication Center Inc, *distributor for* Wind Records (Chinese healing music)

York Medieval Press, *imprint of* Boydell & Brewer Inc

Young Adult Library Services Association (YALSA), *division of* The American Library Association (ALA)

Glenn Young Books, *distributed by* Applause Theatre & Cinema Books

Your Coach in a Box, *imprint of* Recorded Books Inc, an RBmedia company

YouthLight Inc, *distributor for* MAR*CO Products Inc

Youthly, *distributed by* Casemate | publishers

YoYo Books USA, *distributed by* Simon & Schuster, LLC

Ysec Editions, *distributed by* Casemate | publishers

Yugen Press, *imprint of* In the Garden Publishing

Yushodo Press, *distributed by* Oak Knoll Press

YWAM Publishing, *division of* Youth With A Mission, *distributor for* Emerald Books

Zaffre Books, *distributed by* Simon & Schuster, LLC

Zagat Inc, *division of* The Infatuation Inc

Zahava Publications, *imprint of* Judaica Press Inc

Zaner-Bloser Inc, *subsidiary of* Highlights for Children Inc

Zaytuna Institute Press, *distributed by* Fons Vitae

Zebra Books, *imprint of* Kensington Publishing Corp

Zed Books, *distributed by* Palgrave Macmillan

Zeitgeist, *imprint of* Penguin Random House LLC

Zeitgeist Films, *distributed by* Cheng & Tsui Co Inc

Zeke Holdings Ltd, *distributed by* Welcome Books

Zerogram Press, *imprint of* Green Integer

Zero+ Publishing, *distributed by* Gingko Press Inc

Zest Books, *imprint of* Lerner Publishing Group Inc

Zeta Books, *distributed by* Philosophy Documentation Center

Zinc Ink, *imprint of* Random House Publishing Group

Zonderkidz, *division of* Zondervan

Zondervan, *subsidiary of* HarperCollins Christian Publishing, *distributor for* Focus on the Family

Zondervan Academic, *imprint of* Zondervan

Zondervan Reflective, *imprint of* Zondervan

Zondervan Thrive, *imprint of* Zondervan

Zone Books, *distributed by* Princeton University Press

Z2 Comics, *distributed by* Simon & Schuster, LLC

Zubaan Books, *distributed by* Diversion Books

Zuiker Press, *distributed by* Simon & Schuster, LLC

Zumaya Arcane, *imprint of* Zumaya Publications LLC

Zumaya Boundless, *imprint of* Zumaya Publications LLC

Zumaya Embraces, *imprint of* Zumaya Publications LLC

Zumaya Enigma, *imprint of* Zumaya Publications LLC

Zumaya Fabled Ink, *imprint of* Zumaya Publications LLC

Zumaya Otherworlds, *imprint of* Zumaya Publications LLC

Zumaya Thresholds, *imprint of* Zumaya Publications LLC

Zumaya Yesterdays, *imprint of* Zumaya Publications LLC

Canadian Publishers

Listed in alphabetical order are those Canadian publishers that have reported to *LMP* that they produce an average of three or more books annually. Publishers that have appeared in a previous edition of *LMP*, but whose output currently does not meet our defined rate of activity, will be reinstated when their annual production reaches the required level. It should be noted that this rule of publishing activity does not apply to publishers of dictionaries, encyclopedias, atlases or Braille books or to university presses.

The definition of a book excludes charts, pamphlets, folding maps, sheet music and material with stapled bindings. Publishers that make their titles available only in electronic or audio format are included if they meet the stated criteria. In the case of packages, the book must be of equal or greater importance than the accompanying piece. With few exceptions, new publishers are not listed prior to having published at least three titles within a year.

§ before the company name indicates those publishers involved in electronic publishing.

ACTA Press
200-4040 Bowness Rd NW, Calgary, AB T3B 3R7
Tel: 403-288-1195 *Fax:* 403-247-6851
E-mail: journals@actapress.com; publish@actapress.com; sales@actapress.com
Web Site: www.actapress.com
Key Personnel
Owner & Mng Dir: Dr Mohamed H Hamza
Founded: 1972
Scientific & technical conference proceedings & journals; computers, control & power systems, information technology, robotics, signal & image processing. Publishes the proceedings from all of the IASTED conferences & the 12 journals that IASTED generates.
Publishes in English.
ISBN Prefix(es): 978-0-88986
Number of titles published annually: 5 Print; 5 Online
Total Titles: 900 Print

Annick Press Ltd
388 Carlaw Ave, Suite 200, Toronto, ON M4M 2T4
SAN: 115-0065
Tel: 416-221-4802 *Fax:* 416-221-8400
E-mail: annickpress@annickpress.com
Web Site: www.annickpress.com
Key Personnel
Dir: Rick Wilks
Edit Dir: Katie Hearn *E-mail:* katieh@annickpress.com
Rights & Sales Dir/Acquiring Ed: Gayna Theophilus *E-mail:* gaynat@annickpress.com
Assoc Ed: Claire Caldwell
Mktg Mgr: Amanda Olson
Founded: 1975
Fiction & nonfiction for children & young adults.
Publishes in English, French.
ISBN Prefix(es): 978-0-920236; 978-0-920303; 978-1-55037; 978-1-55451
Number of titles published annually: 24 Print
Total Titles: 425 Print
Foreign Rep(s): Publishers Group West (PGW) (worldwide exc Canada & USA)
Foreign Rights: Anatolialit Agency (Turkey); Bardon-Chinese Media Agency (Jian-Mei Wang) (China); Bardon-Chinese Media Agency (Cynthia Chang) (Hong Kong, Taiwan); Gaia Cangioli (Italy); Corto Literary (Eastern Europe); International Editors' Co - Yanez Agencia Literaria (Jennifer Brooke Hoge) (Portugal, Spain); Japan UNI Agency Inc (May Fujinaga) (Japan); Simona Kessler Agency (Romania); Agence Michelle Lapautre (Catherine Lapautre) (France); Dr Paula Peretti Literarische-Agentur (Germany)
Distribution Center: University of Toronto Press, 5201 Dufferin St, Toronto, ON M3H 5T8 *Tel:* 416-667-7791 *Toll Free Tel:* 800-565-9523 *Fax:* 416-667-7832 *Toll Free Fax:* 800-221-9885 *E-mail:* utpbooks@utpress.utoronto.ca
Web Site: www.utpress.utoronto.ca

Publishers Group West (PGW), an Ingram brand, 1700 Fourth St, Berkeley, CA 94710, United States *Toll Free Tel:* 866-400-5351 *Toll Free Fax:* 800-838-1149 *E-mail:* ips@ingramcontent.com
Membership(s): Association of Canadian Publishers (ACP); Ontario Arts Council; Organization of Book Publishers of Ontario (OBPO)

Anvil Press Publishers
PO Box 3008, MPO, Vancouver, BC V6B 3X5
Tel: 604-876-8710
E-mail: info@anvilpress.com
Web Site: www.anvilpress.com
Key Personnel
Publr: Brian Kaufman
Asst Publr & Mktg Coord: Karen Green
Sr Ed: Jessica Key
Founded: 1988
Literary, all genres; theatre & modern contemporary literature. Mostly Canadian authored titles only.
Publishes in English.
ISBN Prefix(es): 978-1-895636; 978-1-897535; 978-1-927380
Number of titles published annually: 12 Print
Total Titles: 90 Print
Distribution Center: Raincoast Books, 2440 Viking Way, Richmond, BC V6V 1N3 *Toll Free Tel:* 800-663-5714 *Toll Free Fax:* 800-565-3770 *E-mail:* orders@raincoastbooks.com

§Aquila Communications Inc
176 Beacon Hill, Montreal, QC H9W 1T6
Toll Free Tel: 800-667-7071
Web Site: www.aquilacommunications.com
Key Personnel
Founder & Pres: Sami Kelada
Contact: Mike Kelada *E-mail:* mike@aquilacommunications.com
Founded: 1970
High-interest/low-vocabulary readers for learners of French as a second language, grades 4 through college. Also, short humorous situational dialogues in comic book format for kids & teens. Funny episodes of daily life of North American kids & teens (home & school).
Publishes in French.
ISBN Prefix(es): 978-0-88510; 978-2-89054
Number of titles published annually: 15 Print
Total Titles: 500 Print; 100 Audio
Imprints: Scaramouche
Distributed by Aquila Communications Ltd

Arsenal Pulp Press
211 E Georgia St, No 202, Vancouver, BC V6A 1Z6
Tel: 604-687-4233 *Toll Free Tel:* 888-600-PULP (600-7857) *Fax:* 604-687-4283
E-mail: info@arsenalpulp.com
Web Site: www.arsenalpulp.com
Key Personnel
Publr: Brian Lam
Assoc Publr: Robert Ballantyne *E-mail:* robert@arsenalpulp.com
Dir, Mktg & Publicity: Cynara Geissler *E-mail:* cynara@arsenalpulp.com
Ed: Catharine Chen
Asst Ed: Jesmine Cham
Designer & Prodn Mgr: Jazmin Welch
Mktg & Publicity Asst: Erin Chan
Founded: 1982 (as Pulp Press Book Publishers)
Literary press.
Publishes in English.
ISBN Prefix(es): 978-0-88978; 978-1-55152
Number of titles published annually: 20 Print; 20 E-Book
Total Titles: 420 Print
Imprints: Little Sister's Classics; Pulp Press; Robin's Egg Books; Tillacum Library; VS Books
U.S. Rep(s): Consortium Book Sales & Distribution
Foreign Rep(s): NewSouth Books (Australia, New Zealand); Turnaround Publisher Services (Europe, UK)
Distribution Center: University of Toronto Press Distribution, 5201 Dufferin St, Toronto, ON M3H 5T8 *Toll Free Tel:* 800-565-9523 *Toll Free Fax:* 800-221-9985 *E-mail:* utpbooks@utpress.utoronto.ca *Web Site:* www.utpress.utoronto.ca
Consortium Book Sales & Distribution, The Keg House, Suite 101, 34 13 Ave NE, Minneapolis, MN 55413-1007, United States *Tel:* 612-746-2600 *Toll Free Tel:* 866-400-5351 (cust serv, Jackson, TN) *E-mail:* cbsdinfo@ingramcontent.com *Web Site:* www.cbsd.com
Membership(s): The Association of Book Publishers of British Columbia (ABPBC); Association of Canadian Publishers (ACP); Literary Press Group

Athabasca University Press
Edmonton Learning Ctr, Peace Hills Trust Tower, 1200, 10011-109 St, Edmonton, AB T5J 3S8
Tel: 780-497-3412 *Fax:* 780-421-3298
E-mail: aupress@athabascau.ca
Web Site: www.aupress.ca
Key Personnel
Dir & Mktg/Prodn Coord: Megan Hall *Tel:* 780-428-2067 *E-mail:* director.aupress@athabascau.ca
Sr Aqs Ed: Pamela Holway *Tel:* 780-428-7278 *E-mail:* editor.aupress@athabascau.ca
Founded: 2008
This publisher has indicated that 25% of their product line is author subsidized.
Publishes in English, French.
ISBN Prefix(es): 978-0-919737; 978-0-920982; 978-1-897425; 978-1-926836; 978-1-927356
Number of titles published annually: 20 Print
Distribution Center: UBC Press, c/o UTP Distribution, 5201 Dufferin St, Toronto, ON M3H 5T8 *Tel:* 416-667-7791 *Toll Free Tel:* 800-565-9523 *Fax:* 416-667-7832 *Toll Free Fax:* 800-

221-9985 *E-mail:* utpbooks@utpress.utoronto.ca
Chicago Distribution Center, 11030 S Langley Ave, Chicago, IL 60628, United States *Tel:* 773-702-7000 *Toll Free Tel:* 800-621-2736 *E-mail:* orders@press.uchicago.edu *Web Site:* press.uchicago.edu/cdc
Combined Academic Publishers (CAP), 39 E Parade, Harrogate, N Yorks HG1 5LQ, United Kingdom (UK, Africa, China, Europe, Hong Kong, Middle East & Taiwan) *Tel:* (01423) 526350 *E-mail:* enquiries@combinedacademic.co.uk *Web Site:* www.combinedacademic.co.uk

§Bayeux Arts Inc
2403, 510-Sixth Ave SE, Calgary, AB T2G 1L7
E-mail: mail@bayeux.com
Web Site: bayeux.com
Key Personnel
Co-Publr & Dir: Dr Swapna Gupta
 E-mail: swapnagupta443@gmail.com
Co-Publr: Ashis Gupta *E-mail:* ashis.bayeux@gmail.com
Ed, Poetry/Fiction/Nonfiction: Mercedes Batiz-Benet
Founded: 1994
Committed to producing books of beauty that build bridges across cultures.
Publishes in English.
ISBN Prefix(es): 978-1-896209; 978-1-897411; 978-1-988440
Number of titles published annually: 10 Print
Imprints: Gondolier; Odd Little Books
Distribution Center: LitDistCo, 8300 Lawson Rd, Milton, ON L9T 0A4 *Toll Free Tel:* 800-591-6250 *Toll Free Fax:* 800-591-6251 *E-mail:* ordering@litdistco.ca *Web Site:* www.litdistco.ca
Chicago Distribution Center, 11030 S Langley Ave, Chicago, IL 60628, United States *Tel:* 773-702-7010 *Toll Free Fax:* 800-621-8476
Membership(s): Literary Press Group of Canada

Beliveau Editeur
567 rue Bienville, Boucherville, QC J4B 2Z5
Tel: 450-679-1933
Web Site: www.beliveauediteur.com
Key Personnel
Pres & CEO: Mathieu Beliveau
 E-mail: mbeliveau@beliveauediteur.com
Asst Ed: Diane Perreault *E-mail:* dperreault@beliveauediteur.com
Founded: 1975
Specialize in self-help, recovery, motivation, psychoeducation & yoga for children.
Publishes in English, French.
ISBN Prefix(es): 978-2-89092; 978-2-89793
Number of titles published annually: 30 Print; 30 E-Book
Total Titles: 400 Print; 200 E-Book
Foreign Rep(s): DG Diffusion (France); Servidis SA (Switzerland)
Distribution Center: Prologue Inc, 3785, Rue La Fayette Ouest, Boisbriand, QC J7H 1N5 *Tel:* 450-434-0306 *Toll Free Tel:* 800-363-2864 *Toll Free Fax:* 800-361-8088 *E-mail:* prologue@prologue.ca *Web Site:* www.prologue.ca
Membership(s): Association nationale des editeurs de livres (ANEL)

Between the Lines
401 Richmond St W, No 281, Toronto, ON M5V 3A8
SAN: 115-0189
Tel: 416-535-9914 *Toll Free Tel:* 800-718-7201
E-mail: info@btlbooks.com
Web Site: btlbooks.com
Key Personnel
Mng Ed: Amanda Crocker *E-mail:* editor@btlbooks.com
Design & Prodn Mgr: Devin Clancy
 E-mail: production@btlbooks.com
Publicity & Promos Mgr: David Gray-Donald
 E-mail: publicity@btlbooks.com
Sales, Dist & Mktg Mgr: Karina Palmitesta
 E-mail: marketing@btlbooks.com
Founded: 1977
Social movement press publishing nonfiction books that expose & challenge oppression in our society.
Publishes in English, French.
ISBN Prefix(es): 978-0-919946; 978-0-921284; 978-1-896357; 978-1-897071; 978-1-926662; 978-1-77113
Number of titles published annually: 16 Print
Total Titles: 263 Print
U.S. Rep(s): AK Press
Foreign Rep(s): Brunswick Books (Canada); Literary Press Group (Canada)
Orders to: Brunswick Books, 14 Afton Ave, Toronto, ON M6J 1R7 *Tel:* 416-703-3598; AK Press Distribution, 370 Ryan Ave, No 100, Chico, CA 95973, United States, Contact: Suzanne Shaffer *E-mail:* suzanne@akpress.org; Central Books Ltd, 50 Freshwater Rd, Chadwell Heath RM8 1RX, United Kingdom *Tel:* (020) 8525 8800 *Fax:* (020) 8599 2694 *E-mail:* contactus@centralbooks.com *Web Site:* www.centralbooks.com
Membership(s): Canada Council for the Arts; Ontario Arts Council

Black Rose Books Ltd
CP 35788, succursale Leo-Pariseau, Montreal, QC H2X 0A4
SAN: 115-2653
Tel: 514-844-4076
E-mail: info@blackrosebooks.com
Web Site: blackrosebooks.com
Key Personnel
Coord: Dimitrios Roussopoulos *E-mail:* mavros@blackrosebooks.com
Admin: Clara-Swan Kennedy *Tel:* 514-969-2589 *E-mail:* swan@blackrosebooks.com
Founded: 1969
Publishing in the social sciences & humanities.
Publishes in English.
ISBN Prefix(es): 978-0-919618; 978-0-919619; 978-0-920057; 978-0-921689; 978-1-55164; 978-1-895431
Number of titles published annually: 15 Print; 15 E-Book
Total Titles: 600 Print; 75 E-Book
Sales Office(s): University of Chicago Press/Chicago Distribution Center, 11030 S Langley Ave, Chicago, IL 60628, United States *Tel:* 773-702-7000 *Toll Free Tel:* 800-621-2736 (USA) *E-mail:* orders@press.uchicago.edu
Global Book Marketing, 50 Freshwater Rd, Chadwell Heath RM8 1RX, United Kingdom *Tel:* (020) 8590 9700 *E-mail:* tz@globalbookmarketing.co.uk *Web Site:* www.globalbookmarketing.co.uk/default.php
Distributed by University of Chicago Press (USA & International); University of Toronto Press (Canada)
Foreign Rep(s): Rightol (China)
Orders to: University of Toronto Press, 5201 Dufferin St, Toronto, ON M3H 5T8 *Toll Free Tel:* 800-565-9523 *E-mail:* utpbooks@utpress.utoronto.ca; University of Chicago Press/Chicago Distribution Center, 11030 S Langley Ave, Chicago, IL 60628, United States *Tel:* 773-702-7000 *Toll Free Tel:* 800-621-2736 (USA) *E-mail:* orders@press.uchicago.edu *Web Site:* press.uchicago.edu/index.html; Central Books Ltd, 50 Freshwater Rd, Chadwell Heath RM8 1RX, United Kingdom *Tel:* (020) 8525 8800 *E-mail:* contactus@centralbooks.com *Web Site:* www.centralbooks.com
Returns: University of Toronto Press, 5201 Dufferin St, Toronto, ON M3H 5T8; University of Chicago Press/Chicago Distribution Center, 11030 S Langley Ave, Chicago, IL 60628, United States; Central Books Ltd, 50 Freshwater Rd, Chadwell Heath RM8 1RX, United Kingdom
Membership(s): Association of Canadian Publishers (ACP); Association of English-language Publishers of Quebec (AELAQ)

Blue Bike Books
317 Fairway Dr, Stony Plain, AB T7Z 2X2
Mailing Address: 7735 Wagner Rd NW, Edmonton, AB T6E 5B1
Tel: 780-435-2376
Web Site: www.bluebikebooks.com
Key Personnel
Publr: Peter J Boer *E-mail:* peterb@bluebikebooks.com
Founded: 2005
Publish humor, trivia books & children's nonfiction. Large number of regional trivia titles as well as national ones.
Publishes in English.
ISBN Prefix(es): 978-1-897278; 978-0-9739116; 978-1-926700
Number of titles published annually: 5 Print; 5 E-Book
Total Titles: 120 Print; 70 E-Book; 40 Audio
Imprints: Mega Machines; Super Explorers
U.S. Rep(s): Lone Pine Publishing
Foreign Rep(s): Gazelle Book Services Ltd (Africa, Asia-Pacific exc China, Central Southern England, Continental Europe, Eastern Europe, UK, UK & the continent)
Orders to: Canada Book Distributors Ltd, 7735 Wagner Rd NW, Edmonton, AB T6E 5B1 *Tel:* 780-433-9333 *Toll Free Tel:* 800-661-9017 *Fax:* 780-433-9646 *Toll Free Fax:* 800-424-7173 *E-mail:* info@booklogic.ca *Web Site:* www.canadabookdistributors.com
Shipping Address: Canada Book Distributors Ltd, 7735 Wagner Rd NW, Edmonton, AB T6E 5B1 *Tel:* 780-433-9333 *Toll Free Tel:* 800-661-9017 *Fax:* 780-433-9646 *Toll Free Fax:* 800-424-7173 *E-mail:* info@booklogic.ca *Web Site:* www.canadabookdistributors.com
Distribution Center: Canada Book Distributors Ltd, 7735 Wagner Rd NW, Edmonton, AB T6E 5B1 *Toll Free Tel:* 800-661-9017 *Fax:* 780-433-9646 *Toll Free Fax:* 800-424-7173 *E-mail:* info@booklogic.ca *Web Site:* www.canadabookdistributors.com
Membership(s): Book Publishers Association of Alberta

Editions du Bois-de-Coulonge
1142 Ave de Montigny, Quebec, QC G1S 3T7
Web Site: www.ebc.qc.ca
Key Personnel
Owner & Pres: Dr Richard Leclerc, PhD
 E-mail: rleclerc@ebc.qc.ca
Founded: 1995
Publish & distribute books about music, multimedia, television & movies.
Publishes in French.
ISBN Prefix(es): 978-2-9801397
Number of titles published annually: 1 Print
Total Titles: 7 Print

§Borealis Press Ltd
8 Mohawk Crescent, Nepean, ON K2H 7G6
Tel: 613-829-0150 *Toll Free Tel:* 877-696-2585 *Fax:* 613-829-7783
E-mail: drt@borealispress.com
Web Site: www.borealispress.com
Founded: 1972
Canadian-oriented general titles of most types. No unsol mss, query first. Include synopsis +/or outline & sample chapter with SASE.
Publishes in English, French.
ISBN Prefix(es): 978-0-88887; 978-1-896133 (Tecumseh Press); 978-0-919594; 978-0-919662 (Tecumseh Press)
Number of titles published annually: 24 Print

Subsidiaries: Tecumseh Press
Distributed by Blackwell; EBSCO; Ex Libris; Hein

The Boston Mills Press
Division of Firefly Books Ltd
50 Staples Ave, Unit 1, Richmond Hill, ON L4B 0A7
Tel: 416-499-8412 *Toll Free Tel:* 800-387-6192
 Fax: 416-499-8313 *Toll Free Fax:* 800-450-0391
E-mail: service@fireflybooks.com
Web Site: www.fireflybooks.com
Founded: 1974
Canadian & American history, guide books, large format colour photograph books.
Publishes in English.
ISBN Prefix(es): 978-0-919822; 978-0-919783; 978-1-55046
Number of titles published annually: 5 Print
Total Titles: 200 Print
Distributed by Firefly Books Ltd

BPS Books
Division of Bastian Publishing Services Ltd
47 Anderson Ave, Toronto, ON M5P 1H6
Tel: 416-609-2004
Web Site: www.bpsbooks.com
Key Personnel
Publr & Ed-in-Chief: Donald G Bastian
Founded: 2007
Print-on-demand publisher of original & reprint trade paperbacks for the US, Canadian & UK markets via bookstore web sites such as the Amazon sites in all 3 countries. No unsol mss, query first using online form.
This publisher has indicated that 90% of their product is author subsidized.
Publishes in English, French.
ISBN Prefix(es): 978-1-926645; 978-0-9784402; 978-0-9809231; 978-1-927483; 978-0-9783286
Number of titles published annually: 5 Print; 5 E-Book
Total Titles: 75 Print; 26 E-Book
Membership(s): Word Guild

Brault & Bouthillier
Division of B & B School Supplies
700 ave Beaumont, Montreal, QC H3N 1V5
Tel: 514-273-9186 *Toll Free Tel:* 800-361-0378
 Fax: 514-273-8627 *Toll Free Fax:* 800-361-0378
E-mail: communicationbb@bb.ca
Web Site: bb.ca
Key Personnel
Pres & CEO: Paul Le Brun
SVP, Servs & COO: Pierre Brault
SVP, Fin & Admin/CFO: Caroline Laurin
VP, Mktg & Cust Experience: Lucie Boivin
VP, Sales: Claude Vaillancourt *Tel:* 514-273-9186 ext 227 *E-mail:* cvaillancourt@bb.ca
Sr Dir, Opers: Isaac Rojas
Founded: 1944
Pedagogical & scientific.
Publishes in English, French.
ISBN Prefix(es): 978-0-88537; 978-2-7615
Number of titles published annually: 100 Print
Branch Office(s)
2676 blvd Jacques-Cartier E, Longueuil, QC J4N 1P8 *Tel:* 450-677-5654 *Toll Free Tel:* 833-311-5654
Distributed by DPLU Inc (Montreal); B B Jocus (Toronto)

Editions Brault & Bouthillier Inc, see Kinesis Education Inc

Breakwater Books Ltd
One Stamp's Lane, St John's, NL A1C 6E6
Mailing Address: PO Box 2188, St John's, NL A1C 6E6
Tel: 709-722-6680 *Toll Free Tel:* 800-563-3333 (orders) *Fax:* 709-753-0708
E-mail: info@breakwaterbooks.com; orders@breakwaterbooks.com
Web Site: www.breakwaterbooks.com
Key Personnel
Owner & Pres: Rebecca Rose
Founded: 1973
Books primarily about education & trade books.
Publishes in English, French.
ISBN Prefix(es): 978-0-919519; 978-0-919948; 978-0-920911; 978-1-55081
Number of titles published annually: 16 Print
Total Titles: 600 Print

Brick Books
22 Spencer Ave, Toronto, ON M6K 2J6
Tel: 416-455-8385
Web Site: www.brickbooks.ca
Key Personnel
CFO: Brenda Leifso *E-mail:* brenda@brickbooks.ca
Publr: Alayna Munce
Founded: 1975
Publish poetry collections by Canadian authors.
Publishes in English.
ISBN Prefix(es): 978-0-919626; 978-1-894078; 978-1-77131
Number of titles published annually: 8 Print
Total Titles: 250 Print; 250 E-Book
Distribution Center: University of Toronto Press, 5201 Dufferin St, Toronto, ON M3H 5T8
Membership(s): Association of Canadian Publishers (ACP); Literary Press Group of Canada; Organization of Book Publishers of Ontario (OBPO)

Brindle & Glass Publishing Ltd
Imprint of TouchWood Editions
103-1075 Pendergast St, Victoria, BC V8V 0A1
Tel: 250-360-0829 *Fax:* 250-386-0829
E-mail: info@touchwoodeditions.com
Web Site: www.touchwoodeditions.com
Key Personnel
Publr: Taryn Boyd
Founded: 2001
Literary press.
Publishes in English.
ISBN Prefix(es): 978-1-897142; 978-0-9732481; 978-1-926972; 978-1-927366
Number of titles published annually: 4 Print
Total Titles: 110 Print
Foreign Rep(s): Heritage Group (Canada); Publishers Group West (PGW) (USA)
Distribution Center: Heritage Group Distribution, 19272 96 Ave, Suite 8, Surrey, BC V4N 4C1 *Tel:* 604-881-7067 *Toll Free Tel:* 800-665-3302 *Fax:* 604-881-7068 *Toll Free Fax:* 800-566-3336 *E-mail:* orders@hgdistribution.com *Web Site:* www.hgdistribution.com
Membership(s): Canada Council for the Arts

§Broadview Press
280 Perry St, Unit 5, Peterborough, ON K9J 2J4
SAN: 115-6772
Mailing Address: PO Box 1243, Peterborough, ON K9J 7H5
Tel: 705-482-5915 *Fax:* 705-743-8353
E-mail: customerservice@broadviewpress.com
Web Site: www.broadviewpress.com
Key Personnel
Founder & CEO: Don Le Pan *Tel:* 250-591-9291 *E-mail:* don.lepan@broadviewpress.com
Pres: Leslie Dema *E-mail:* dema@broadviewpress.com
Mng Ed: Tara Lowes
Accts Mgr: LeeAnna Dykstra *E-mail:* ldykstra@broadviewpress.com
Exam Copies Coord: Leighe Lacombe *E-mail:* examcopies@broadviewpress.com
Founded: 1985
The word "broadview" expresses a great deal about the approach that guides our publishing program. Our focus is very much on English studies & philosophy, but within those fields, we are open to a broad range of academic approaches & political viewpoints. We are proud to publish pedagogically valuable books that make a real contribution to scholarship. We welcome feminist perspectives & we have a strong commitment to the environment. Our publishing program is internationally oriented & our individual titles often appeal to a broad readership; we publish many titles that are of as much interest to the general reader as they are to academics & students.
Publishes in English.
ISBN Prefix(es): 978-0-921149; 978-1-55111; 978-1-55481
Number of titles published annually: 45 Print; 40 E-Book
Total Titles: 600 Print; 425 E-Book
Branch Office(s)
10 Douglas St, Suite B, Guelph, ON N1H 2S9
515-815 First St SW, Calgary, AB T2P 1N3 *Tel:* 403-232-6863 *Fax:* 403-452-0960
427G Fitzwilliam St, Unit 200, Nanaimo, BC V9R 3A9 *Tel:* 250-591-9291
213-112 Front St, Wolfville, NS B49 1A4 *Tel:* 902-697-3069
Distributor for Press Forward; Pyxis Press
U.S. Rep(s): Brad DeVetten
Returns: 555 Riverwalk Pkwy, Tonawanda, NY 14150, United States
Distribution Center: Eurospan, Gray's Inn House, 127 Clerkenwell Rd, London EC1R 5DB, United Kingdom (worldwide exc North America) *Web Site:* www.eurospanbookstore.com/broadview

Broquet Inc
97-B, Montee des Bouleaux, St-Constant, QC J5A 1A9
Tel: 450-638-3338 *Fax:* 450-638-4338
E-mail: info@broquet.qc.ca
Web Site: www.broquet.qc.ca
Key Personnel
Pres & Ed: Antoine Broquet
Artistic Dir: Brigit Levesque
Prodn Dir: Ms Josee Fortin
Founded: 1979
Nature books & astronomy.
Publishes in French.
ISBN Prefix(es): 978-2-89000; 978-2-89654
Number of titles published annually: 100 Print; 12 E-Book
Total Titles: 800 Print; 40 E-Book
Foreign Rep(s): Dilisco (Benelux, France); Servidis SA (Switzerland)
Distribution Center: Prologue Inc, 3785, Rue La Fayette Ouest, Boisbriand, QC J7H 1N5 *Tel:* 450-434-0306 *Toll Free Tel:* 800-363-2864 *Toll Free Fax:* 800-361-8088 *E-mail:* prologue@prologue.ca *Web Site:* www.prologue.ca

Brush Education Inc
6531-111 St NW, Edmonton, AB T6H 4R5
Tel: 780-989-0910 *Toll Free Tel:* 855-283-0900 *Fax:* 780-989-0930 *Toll Free Fax:* 855-283-6947
E-mail: contact@brusheducation.ca
Web Site: www.brusheducation.ca
Key Personnel
Publr & Pres: Glenn Rollans *E-mail:* glenn.rollans@brusheducation.ca
Mng Ed: Lauri Seidlitz *E-mail:* lauri.seidlitz@brusheducation.ca
Sales & Mktg Mgr: Tom Lore *E-mail:* tom.lore@brusheducation.ca
Founded: 1975
Independent publisher of books for college, university & professional audiences. Our publish-

CANADIAN PUBLISHERS

ing program includes medial & health sciences, education & K9 training.
Publishes in English.
ISBN Prefix(es): 978-1-55059
Number of titles published annually: 10 Print; 10 E-Book
Total Titles: 120 Print; 80 E-Book; 3 Audio
Distributed by University of Toronto Press
Orders to: University of Toronto Press, 5201 Dufferin St, Toronto, ON M3H 5T8 (CN & US) *Tel:* 416-667-7791 *Toll Free Tel:* 800-565-9523 *Fax:* 416-667-7832 *Toll Free Fax:* 800-221-9985 *E-mail:* utpbooks@utpress.utoronto.ca
Membership(s): Association of Canadian Publishers (ACP); Book Publishers Association of Alberta

§BWL Publishing Inc
5030 44 St, Drayton Valley, AB T7A 1B9
Tel: 780-833-1215
E-mail: bookswelove@telus.net
Web Site: bookswelove.net; bwlpublishing.ca
Key Personnel
VP: Judith (Jude) Pittman; Justin (JD) Shipton
Founded: 2010
Canadian publisher open to all genres. Primary focus is on Canadian settings & content written by Canadian authors. However, we are a full service publisher & have a great mix of authors from the US, UK & Australia. We favor popular genre fiction (no erotica). We love all forms of mysteries & thrillers, romance, sci-fi/fantasy, horror, westerns, young adult (especially adventure). Large collection of Canadian historical fiction (like our Canadian Historical Brides & Canadian Historical Mysteries). Stories like this will always get our attention as long as you are writing where you know. We are a traditional royalty-paying full service publisher.
Publishes in English.
ISBN Prefix(es): 978-1-927476; 978-1-927476; 978-1-927111; 978-0-9867433; 978-1-77145; 978-0-9867514; 978-1-926965; 978-1-77362; 978-1-77299
Number of titles published annually: 72 Print; 72 Online; 144 E-Book; 12 Audio
Total Titles: 800 Print; 800 Online; 800 E-Book; 36 Audio
Membership(s): Association of Canadian Publishers (ACP); Independent Book Publishers Association (IBPA)

Callawind Publications Inc
3551 St Charles Blvd, Suite 179, Kirkland, QC H9H 3C4
Tel: 514-685-9109
E-mail: info@callawind.com
Web Site: www.callawind.com
Key Personnel
Mktg: Marcy Claman *E-mail:* marcy@callawind.com
Founded: 1995
Custom book publisher. Specialize in children's picture books, board books, coffee table books & cookbooks.
This publisher has indicated that 100% of their product line is author subsidized.
Publishes in English.
ISBN Prefix(es): 978-1-896511
Number of titles published annually: 25 Print
Total Titles: 350 Print
Membership(s): The Association of Publishers for Special Sales (APSS); Independent Book Publishers Association (IBPA)

Canadian Bible Society
10 Carnforth Rd, Toronto, ON M4A 2S4
SAN: 112-5559
Tel: 416-757-4171 *Toll Free Tel:* 800-465-2425 *Fax:* 416-757-3376
E-mail: customerservice@biblesociety.ca
Web Site: www.biblescanada.com; www.biblesociety.ca
Founded: 1904
Bibles, new testaments, scripture portions, selections; scriptures in foreign languages.
Publishes in English, French.
ISBN Prefix(es): 978-0-88834; 978-1-77124
Number of titles published annually: 20 Print; 5 Audio
Total Titles: 2,500 Print; 50 Audio
U.S. Publishers Represented: American Bible Society
Foreign Rep(s): United Bible Societies (worldwide)
Membership(s): United Bible Societies

Canadian Circumpolar Institute (CCI) Press
Imprint of University of Alberta Press
1-16 Rutherford Library South, 11204 89 Ave NW, Edmonton, AB T6G 2J4
Tel: 780-492-3662
Web Site: www.uap.ualberta.ca
Founded: 1960 (as Boreal Institute for Northern Studies; reconfigured & renamed 1990 as CCI; acquired 2013 by University of Alberta Press)
Publishes in English.
ISBN Prefix(es): 978-1-896445; 978-0-919058
Total Titles: 140 Print
Sales Office(s): Ampersand Canada's Book & Gift Agency Inc, 321 Carlaw Ave, Suite 213, Toronto, ON M4M 2S1, Contact: Saffron Beckwith *Tel:* 416-703-0666 ext 124 *Fax:* 416-703-4745 *E-mail:* saffronb@ampersandinc.ca *Web Site:* www.ampersandinc.ca
U.S. Rep(s): Johns Hopkins University Press
Billing Address: University of Toronto Press, 5201 Dufferin St, Toronto, ON M3H 5T8 *Tel:* 416-667-7841 *Toll Free Tel:* 800-565-9523 *Fax:* 416-667-7832 *Toll Free Fax:* 800-221-9985 *E-mail:* utpbooks@utpress.utoronto.ca *Web Site:* www.utpress.utoronto.ca
Orders to: University of Toronto Press, 5201 Dufferin St, Toronto, ON M3H 5T8 *Tel:* 416-667-7841 *Toll Free Tel:* 800-565-9523 *Fax:* 416-667-7832 *Toll Free Fax:* 800-221-9985 *E-mail:* utpbooks@utpress.utoronto.ca *Web Site:* www.utpress.utoronto.ca
Returns: University of Toronto Press, 5201 Dufferin St, Toronto, ON M3H 5T8 *Tel:* 416-667-7841 *Toll Free Tel:* 800-565-9523 *Fax:* 416-667-7832 *Toll Free Fax:* 800-221-9985 *E-mail:* utpbooks@utpress.utoronto.ca *Web Site:* www.utpress.utoronto.ca
Shipping Address: University of Toronto Press, 5201 Dufferin St, Toronto, ON M3H 5T8 *Tel:* 416-667-7841 *Toll Free Tel:* 800-565-9523 *Fax:* 416-667-7832 *Toll Free Fax:* 800-221-9985 *E-mail:* utpbooks@utpress.utoronto.ca *Web Site:* www.utpress.utoronto.ca
Distribution Center: University of Toronto Press, 5201 Dufferin St, Toronto, ON M3H 5T8, Client Serv Rep: Jackie Courtney *Tel:* 416-667-7841 *Toll Free Tel:* 800-565-9523 *Fax:* 416-667-7832 *Toll Free Fax:* 800-221-9985 *E-mail:* utpbooks@utpress.utoronto.ca *Web Site:* www.utpress.utoronto.ca
Johns Hopkins University Press, 2715 N Charles St, Baltimore, MD 21218, United States (does not carry all CCI Press titles), Dir, HFS/Co-Dir, Mktg & Sales: Davida Breier *Tel:* 410-516-6961 *Fax:* 410-516-6998 *E-mail:* dgb@press.jhu.edu *Web Site:* www.press.jhu.edu
Gazelle Book Services Ltd, White Cross Mills, Hightown, Lancaster, Lancs LA1 4XS, United Kingdom *Tel:* (01524) 528500 *Fax:* (01524) 528510 *E-mail:* sales@gazellebookservices.co.uk *Web Site:* www.gazellebookservices.co.uk

Canadian Institute of Resources Law (L'Institut canadien du droit des ressources)
Faculty of Law, University of Calgary, 2500 University Dr NW, MFH 3353, Calgary, AB T2N 1N4
Tel: 403-220-3200 *Fax:* 403-282-6182
E-mail: cirl@ucalgary.ca
Web Site: www.cirl.ca
Founded: 1979
Leading national centre of expertise on legal & policy issues relating to Canada's natural resources.
Publishes in English.
ISBN Prefix(es): 978-0-919269
Number of titles published annually: 4 Print; 3 Online
Total Titles: 96 Print; 64 Online

Canadian Institute of Ukrainian Studies Press
Division of Canadian Institute of Ukrainian Studies
University of Toronto, 47 Queen's Park Crescent E, Suite B-12, Toronto, ON M5S 2C3
Tel: 416-946-7326
E-mail: cius@ualberta.ca
Web Site: www.ciuspress.com
Key Personnel
Dir: Marko R Stech *E-mail:* m.stech@utoronto.ca
Founded: 1976
Publisher of scholarly works in Ukranian studies & Ukranian Canadian studies.
Publishes in English.
ISBN Prefix(es): 978-0-920862; 978-1-895571; 978-1-894865; 978-1-894301
Number of titles published annually: 5 Print
Total Titles: 215 Print
Orders to: University of Alberta, 4-30 Pembina Hall, Edmonton, AB T6G 2H8 *Tel:* 780-492-2972 *E-mail:* cius@ualberta.ca
Returns: University of Alberta, 4-30 Pembina Hall, Edmonton, AB T6G 2H8 *Tel:* 780-492-2972 *E-mail:* cius@ualberta.ca

Canadian Museum of History (Musee canadien de l'histoire)
100 Laurier St, Gatineau, QC K1A 0M8
Tel: 819-776-7000 *Toll Free Tel:* 800-555-5621 (North American orders only) *Fax:* 819-776-7187
Web Site: www.historymuseum.ca
Key Personnel
Mgr, Publg & Corp Prods: Robyn Jeffrey *E-mail:* robyn.jeffrey@historymuseum.ca
Coord, Corp Prods & Eng Lang Ed: Lee Wyndham *Tel:* 819-776-8385 *E-mail:* lee.wyndham@historymuseum.ca
Founded: 1968 (as the National Museum of Man)
Publications in the subject areas of museology, anthropology, archaeology, ethnology, folk culture, history, Indigenous art & cultures.
Publishes in English, French.
ISBN Prefix(es): 978-1-988282
Number of titles published annually: 6 Print
Total Titles: 400 Print
Distribution Center: University of Toronto Press, 5201 Dufferin St, Toronto, ON M3H 5T8 *Toll Free Tel:* 800-565-9523 *E-mail:* utpbooks@utpress.utoronto.ca SAN: 115-1134
Membership(s): Association for the Export of Canadian Books; Association of Canadian Publishers (ACP)

§Canadian Scholars
425 Adelaide St W, Suite 200, Toronto, ON M5V 3C1
SAN: 118-9484
Tel: 416-929-2774 *Toll Free Tel:* 800-463-1998
E-mail: info@canadianscholars.ca; editorial@canadianscholars.ca
Web Site: www.canadianscholars.ca; www.womenspress.ca
Key Personnel
Pres: Andrew Wayne *Tel:* 416-929-2774 ext 220 *E-mail:* awayne@canadianscholars.ca
VP & Publr: Lily Bergh *Tel:* 416-929-2774 ext 218 *E-mail:* lily.bergh@canadianscholars.ca

PUBLISHERS

Sr Edit/Prodn Mgr: Natalie Garriga *Tel:* 416-929-2774 ext 223 *E-mail:* natalie.garriga@canadianscholars.ca
Mktg Mgr: Krista Mitchell *Tel:* 416-929-2774 ext 240 *E-mail:* krista.mitchell@canadianscholars.ca
Founded: 1986
Scholarly books & texts for post-secondary education. Trade books-feminist orientation.
Publishes in English, French.
ISBN Prefix(es): 978-0-921627; 978-1-55130; 978-0-921881; 978-0-88961 (Women's Press); 978-1-89418; 978-1-77338
Number of titles published annually: 24 Print; 20 E-Book
Total Titles: 400 Print; 300 E-Book
Divisions: Women's Press
Distribution Center: Eurospan Group, Gray's Inn House, 127 Clerkenwell Rd, London EC1R 5DB, United Kingdom (Africa, Asia Pacific, Caribbean, Europe, Latin America, Middle East & UK) *Tel:* (01235) 465576 *Fax:* (01235) 465577 *E-mail:* trade.orders@marston.co.uk *Web Site:* www.eurospanbookstore.com/page/publisher-detail/canadian-scholars
Membership(s): Association of Canadian Publishers (ACP); Canada Council for the Arts; Ontario Arts Council; Organization of Book Publishers of Ontario (OBPO)

§Captus Press Inc
1600 Steeles Ave W, Units 14 & 15, Concord, ON L4K 4M2
Tel: 905-760-2723 *Fax:* 905-760-7523
E-mail: info@captus.com
Web Site: www.captus.com
Key Personnel
Pres: Randy Hoffman *E-mail:* randy@captus.com
Mgr: Pauline Lai *E-mail:* pauline@captus.com
Accts Admin & Intl Rts: Lily Chu *E-mail:* lily@captus.com
Founded: 1987
Publication of textbooks, scholarly books, professional books, nonfiction trade books & multimedia Internet courses. Publishes in Spanish also.
Publishes in English, French.
ISBN Prefix(es): 978-0-921801; 978-1-896691; 978-1-895712; 978-1-55322
Number of titles published annually: 28 Print; 20 Online; 20 E-Book
Total Titles: 163 Print; 27 Online; 27 E-Book
Imprints: Captus Press; Captus University Publications; University Press of Canada

§Carswell
Imprint of Thomson Reuters Canada Ltd
One Corporate Plaza, 2075 Kennedy Rd, Toronto, ON M1T 3V4
Tel: 416-609-5811 (sales); 416-609-3800
 Toll Free Tel: 800-387-5164 (CN & US)
 Fax: 416-298-5094 (sales); 416-298-5082
 Toll Free Fax: 877-750-9041 (CN only)
E-mail: customersupport.legaltaxcanada@tr.com
Web Site: store.thomsonreuters.ca
Founded: 1864
Canada's leading provider of specialized information & electronic research solutions to the legal, tax, accounting & human resources markets. Carswell provides integrated information in a range of formats, including books, looseleaf services, journals, newsletters, CD-ROMs & online.
Publishes in English, French.
ISBN Prefix(es): 978-0-459; 978-0-88820; 978-0-7798
Number of titles published annually: 100 Print
Total Titles: 1,113 Print; 10 Online
Returns: 245 Bartley Dr, Toronto, ON M4A 2V8
Distribution Center: 245 Bartley Dr, Toronto, ON M4A 2V8

CCI Press, see Canadian Circumpolar Institute (CCI) Press

Centre for Reformation & Renaissance Studies (CRRS)
Division of Victoria College University of Toronto
71 Queen's Park Crescent E, Toronto, ON M5S 1K7
Tel: 416-585-4465 *Fax:* 416-585-4430 (attn: CRRS)
E-mail: crrs.publications@utoronto.ca
Web Site: crrs.ca
Key Personnel
Dir: Ethan Matt Kavaler *Tel:* 416-585-4461
Asst to Dir: Dr Natalie Oeltjen *Tel:* 416-525-4484
Fin & Pubns Coord: Noam Tzvi Lior
Founded: 1965
Specialty library & academic publisher.
Publishes in English, French.
ISBN Prefix(es): 978-0-7727; 978-0-9697512
Number of titles published annually: 10 Print
Total Titles: 102 Print
Imprints: Dovehouse Press

Centre Franco-Ontarien de Ressources en Alphabetisation (Centre FORA)
4800 rue Notre-Dame, Hanmer, ON P3P 1X5
Mailing Address: PO Box 56, Hanmer, ON P3P 1S9
Tel: 705-524-3672 *Toll Free Tel:* 888-814-4422 (orders, CN only) *Fax:* 705-524-8535
E-mail: info@centrefora.on.ca
Web Site: centrefora.com
Founded: 1989
Nonprofit organization that publishes learning materials for adult literacy & distribute education materials for all ages.
Publishes in French.
ISBN Prefix(es): 978-2-921706; 978-1-895336; 978-2-89567
Number of titles published annually: 20 Print
Total Titles: 150 Print

Charlton International Inc, see The Charlton Press Corp

The Charlton Press Corp
645 Ave Lepine, Dorval, QC H9P 2R2
Tel: 416-962-2665 *Toll Free Tel:* 866-663-8827
 Fax: 514-954-3618
E-mail: chpress@charltonpress.com; info@charltonpress.com
Web Site: www.charltonpress.com
Key Personnel
Publr: Mark Drake
Founded: 1952
Specialize in 20th century numismatics.
Publishes in English.
ISBN Prefix(es): 978-0-88968; 978-2-9800475
Number of titles published annually: 4 Print
Total Titles: 12 Print

Chartered Professional Accountants of Canada (CPA Canada)
277 Wellington St W, Toronto, ON M5V 3H2
Tel: 416-977-3222 *Toll Free Tel:* 800-268-3793
 Fax: 416-977-8585
E-mail: member.services@cpacanada.ca; customerservice@cpacanada.ca
Web Site: www.cpacanada.ca; www.facebook.com/cpacanada; cpastore.ca
Key Personnel
Pres & CEO: Pamela Steer
Founded: 1917
Taxation, accounting, auditing, financial.
Publishes in English, French.
ISBN Prefix(es): 978-0-88800; 978-1-55385
Number of titles published annually: 15 Print
Total Titles: 200 Print

CANADIAN PUBLISHERS

Branch Office(s)
205-99 Bank St, Ottawa, ON K1P 6B9 *Tel:* 613-789-7771 *Fax:* 613-789-7772
100-4200 N Fraser Way, Burnaby, BC V5J 5K7 *Tel:* 604-669-3555 *Toll Free Tel:* 800-663-1529 *Fax:* 604-689-5845
2020, blvd Robert-Bourassa, bureau 1900, Montreal, QC H3A 2A5

§ChemTec Publishing
38 Earswick Dr, Toronto, ON M1E 1C6
Tel: 416-265-2603
E-mail: orderdesk@chemtec.org
Web Site: www.chemtec.org
Key Personnel
CEO: Anna Wypych
Circ Mgr: Anna Fox
Founded: 1988
Additives, blends, polymers, recycling & rheology.
Publishes in English.
ISBN Prefix(es): 978-1-895198; 978-1-77467; 978-1-927885
Number of titles published annually: 10 Print; 10 E-Book
Total Titles: 100 Print; 10 CD-ROM; 40 E-Book
Membership(s): Copyright Clearance Center (CCC)

Cheneliere Education Inc
Division of TC Media Books Inc
5800, rue St Denis, bureau 900, Montreal, QC H2S 3L5
Tel: 514-273-1066 *Toll Free Tel:* 800-565-5531
 Fax: 514-276-0324 *Toll Free Fax:* 800-814-0324
E-mail: info@cheneliere.ca
Web Site: www.cheneliere.ca
Key Personnel
Pres & Gen Mgr: Patrick Lutzy
Founded: 1971
School, college & university textbooks; vocational; French Immersion; teaching skills & book packaging (French & English languages).
Publishes in French.
ISBN Prefix(es): 978-2-89310; 978-2-89461; 978-2-7650; 978-2-7651; 978-2-89470; 978-2-921793
Number of titles published annually: 250 Print
Total Titles: 5,700 Print
Imprints: Beauchemin; Editions de la Cheneliere; Cheneliere Education; Cheneliere/McGraw-Hill; Gaetan Morin Editeur; Graficor
U.S. Publishers Represented: McGraw-Hill Inc
Warehouse: McGraw-Hill Ryerson Limited, 300 Water St, Whitby, ON L1N 9B6
Distribution Center: Diffusion Humensis, 170 bis, blvd du Montparnasse, 75014 Paris, France (college & university) *Tel:* 01 55 42 72 43
Pirouette Editions, 7B rue des Artisans, 67920 Sundhouse, France (school-primary & secondary) *Tel:* 03 88 57 09 04 *Fax:* 03 88 57 19 65 *E-mail:* contact@pirouette-editions.fr *Web Site:* www.pirouette-editions.fr
Servidis SA, Chemin des Chalets, 7, 1279 Chavannes-de-Bogis, Switzerland, Rep: Aline Ledard *Tel:* (022) 960 95 10 *Fax:* (022) 776 35 44 *E-mail:* aledard@servidis.ch *Web Site:* www.servidis.ch
See separate listing for:
Gaetan Morin Editeur

CIUS Press, see Canadian Institute of Ukrainian Studies Press

Coach House Books
80 bpNichol Lane, Toronto, ON M5S 3J4
Tel: 416-979-2217 *Toll Free Tel:* 800-367-6360 (outside Toronto) *Fax:* 416-977-1158
E-mail: mail@chbooks.com
Web Site: www.chbooks.com

Key Personnel
Founder & Publr: Stan Bevington *E-mail:* stan@chbooks.com
Edit Dir: Alana Wilcox *E-mail:* alana@chbooks.com
Mng Ed: Crystal Sikma *E-mail:* crystal@chbooks.com
Publicist: James Lindsay *E-mail:* james@chbooks.com
Founded: 1965
Literary small press specializing in experimental fiction & poetry.
Publishes in English.
ISBN Prefix(es): 978-1-55245
Number of titles published annually: 16 Print; 16 E-Book; 7 Audio
Total Titles: 374 Print; 120 E-Book; 16 Audio
Imprints: zaagigin (Indigenous nonfiction)
Foreign Rights: AnatoliaLit Agency (Amy Spangler) (Turkey); Asterisc Agents (Natalia Berenguer Gamell) (Portugal, South America, Spain); The Grayhawk Agency (Gray Tan) (China, Taiwan); Icarias Agency (Ines Yoo) (South Korea); Mo Literary Services (Monique Oosterhof) (Netherlands); Mohr Books Literary Agency (Annelie Geissler) (Germany); Piergiorgio Nicolazzini Literary Agency (Maura Solinas) (Italy)
Distribution Center: Publishers Group Canada, 76 Stafford St, Suite 300, Toronto, ON M6J 2S1 (CN orders), Sales Dir: Lori Richardson *Tel:* 416-934-9900 *Fax:* 416-934-1410 *E-mail:* info@pgcbooks.ca *Web Site:* www.pgcbooks.ca
Consortium Book Sales & Distribution, The Keg House, Suite 101, 34 13 Ave NE, Minneapolis, MN 55413-1007, United States (US orders) *Tel:* 612-746-2600 *Toll Free Tel:* 866-400-5351 (cust serv, Jackson, TN) *E-mail:* cbsdinfo@ingramcontent.com *Web Site:* www.cbsd.com
SAN: 200-6049
Membership(s): Association of Canadian Publishers (ACP); Community of Literary Magazines & Presses (CLMP); Literary Press Group

Company's Coming Publishing Ltd
7735 Wagner Rd, Edmonton, AB T6E 5B1
Toll Free Tel: 800-661-9017 (CN) *Fax:* 780-450-1857 *Toll Free Fax:* 800-424-7133
E-mail: accounts@companyscoming.com
Web Site: companyscoming.com
Founded: 1981
Publish cookbooks, craft books & stationery products.
Publishes in English.
ISBN Prefix(es): 978-0-9690695; 978-0-9693322; 978-1-895455; 978-1-896891; 978-1-897069; 978-1-897477; 978-1-927126; 978-1-77069
Number of titles published annually: 25 Print
Total Titles: 200 Print
Distribution Center: Canada Book Distributors Ltd

Comptables professionnels agrees du Canada, see Chartered Professional Accountants of Canada (CPA Canada)

The Continuing Legal Education Society of British Columbia (CLEBC)
500-1155 W Pender St, Vancouver, BC V6E 2P4
Tel: 604-669-3544; 604-893-2121 (cust serv)
Toll Free Tel: 800-663-0437 (CN) *Fax:* 604-669-9260
E-mail: custserv@cle.bc.ca
Web Site: www.cle.bc.ca
Key Personnel
CEO: Linda Russell *Tel:* 604-893-2114
 E-mail: lindar@cle.bc.ca
Dir, Pubns: Laura Selby *Tel:* 604-893-2106
 E-mail: lselby@cle.bc.ca
Mktg Mgr: Adam Simpkins *Tel:* 604-893-2168
 E-mail: adams@cle.bc.ca

Founded: 1976
Publish course materials, practice manuals & case digests.
Publishes in English.
ISBN Prefix(es): 978-0-86504; 978-1-55258
Number of titles published annually: 35 Print; 35 Online
Total Titles: 50 Print; 1 CD-ROM; 48 Online
Imprints: CLEBC

§Cormorant Books Inc
260 Spadina Ave, Suite 502, Toronto, ON M5T 1E5
Tel: 416-925-8887
E-mail: info@cormorantbooks.com
Web Site: www.cormorantbooks.com
Key Personnel
Pres & Publr, Cormorant Books: Marc Cote
 E-mail: m.cote@cormorantbooks.com
Mng Dir: Sarah Cooper *E-mail:* s.cooper@cormorantbooks.com
Founded: 1986
Independent literary publisher of Canadian authors.
Publishes in English.
ISBN Prefix(es): 978-0-920953; 978-1-896951; 978-1-896332; 978-1-897151; 978-1-77086
Number of titles published annually: 20 Print; 16 E-Book
Total Titles: 150 Print; 100 E-Book
Imprints: DCB
Distribution Center: University of Toronto Press, 5201 Dufferin St, Toronto, ON M3H 5T8 *Tel:* 416-667-7791 *Toll Free Tel:* 800-565-9523 *Fax:* 416-667-7832 *Toll Free Fax:* 800-221-9985 *E-mail:* utpbooks@utpress.utoronto.ca *Web Site:* www.utpress.utoronto.ca
Membership(s): Literary Press Group of Canada

La Courte Echelle
4388, rue Saint-Denis, Suite 315, Montreal, QC H2J 2L1
Tel: 514-312-6950
E-mail: info@courteechelle.com
Web Site: www.groupecourteechelle.com/la-courte-echelle
Key Personnel
Gen Dir: Marieve Talbot
Artistic Dir: Julie Massy
Literary Dir & Children's Ed: Carole Tremblay
Edit Asst: Melanie Boilard
Communs Coord: Marion Feneux
Sales Coord: Marianne Dalpe
Graphic Designer: Catherine Charbonneau
Founded: 1978
Children's, young adult & adult fiction. No unsol mss accepted.
Publishes in French.
ISBN Prefix(es): 978-2-89021; 978-1-894731; 978-2-89651; 978-2-89695; 978-2-89774
Number of titles published annually: 50 Print
Total Titles: 545 Print
Distribution Center: Hachette Canada, 9001 de l'Acadie, bureau 1002, Montreal, QC H4N 3H5 *Tel:* 514-382-3034 *Toll Free Tel:* 888-422-4388 *Fax:* 514-381-5088 *E-mail:* info@hachette.qc.ca *Web Site:* www.hachette.qc.ca
Librairie du Quebec a Paris, Diffusion du Nouveau Monde (DNM), 30, rue Gay-Lussac, 75005 Paris, France (France & Europe) *Tel:* 01 43 54 49 02 *Fax:* 01 43 54 39 15 *E-mail:* dnm@librairieduquebec.fr *Web Site:* www.librairieduquebec.fr

§Crabtree Publishing Co Ltd
Subsidiary of Crabtree Publishing Co (USA)
616 Welland Ave, St Catharines, ON L2M 5V6
SAN: 115-1436
Tel: 905-682-5221 *Toll Free Tel:* 800-387-7650 *Fax:* 905-682-7166 *Toll Free Fax:* 800-355-7166

E-mail: custserv@crabtreebooks.com; sales@crabtreebooks.com; orders@crabtreebooks.com
Web Site: www.crabtreebooks.ca
Key Personnel
CEO: Craig Culliford *E-mail:* craig_c@crabtreebooks.com
Pres: Peter A Crabtree *E-mail:* peter_c@crabtreebooks.com
Publr: Bobbie Kalman *E-mail:* bobbiek@crabtreebooks.com
VP, Edit: Kathy Middleton *E-mail:* kathy_m@crabtreebooks.com
VP, Mktg: Julie Alguire *E-mail:* julie_a@crabtreebooks.com
Dir, New Media: Robert MacGregor
 E-mail: rob_m@crabtreebooks.com
Dir, Sales: Andrea Crabtree *E-mail:* andrea_c@crabtreebooks.com
Warehouse Mgr: Karl Kasper
 E-mail: warehouse@crabtreebooks.com
Cust Serv: Candice Pinkerton
 E-mail: candice_c@crabtreebooks.com
Founded: 1978
Children's nonfiction & fiction, library binding & paperback for school & trade.
Publishes in English, French.
ISBN Prefix(es): 978-0-86505; 978-0-7787; 978-1-4271; 978-1-0396; 978-1-0398
Number of titles published annually: 619 Print; 988 E-Book
Total Titles: 5,421 Print; 4,566 E-Book; 1,968 Audio
Imprints: Crabtree Blossoms; Crabtree Branches; Crabtree Classics; Crabtree Crown; Crabtree Forest; Crabtree Leaves; Crabtree Little Honey; Crabtree Roots; Crabtree Seedlings; Crabtree Sunshine; Look, Listen & Learn Audio Books
Distributor for Bayard; Seahorse Publishing; Sequoia Kids Media
Foreign Rep(s): Everybody's Books (Namibia, South Africa); Macmillan Marketing Services (European Union, UK); Novella (Australia, New Zealand)
Membership(s): American Booksellers Association (ABA); The American Library Association (ALA); Educational Book & Media Association (EBMA); Museum Store Association (MSA); National Science Teachers Association (NSTA); Ontario Library Association; Organization of Book Publishers of Ontario (OBPO)

CRRS, see Centre for Reformation & Renaissance Studies (CRRS)

CSP Books Inc, see Canadian Scholars

§Database Directories Inc
96-320 Westminster Ave, London, ON N6C 5H5
Tel: 519-433-1666
E-mail: mail@databasedirectory.com
Web Site: www.databasedirectory.com
Key Personnel
CEO: Lesley Classic *E-mail:* lclassic@databasedirectory.com
Asst Dir: Matthew Taylor *E-mail:* matt@databasedirectory.com
Founded: 1995
Directories & e-files on libraries, schools, colleges, universities, academic retailers & municipalities.
Publishes in English.
ISBN Prefix(es): 978-1-896537
Number of titles published annually: 3 Print; 4 CD-ROM; 4 Online
Total Titles: 10 Print; 10 CD-ROM; 4 Online

§DC Canada Education Publishing (DCCED)
170 Laurier Ave W, Unit 603, Ottawa, ON K1P 5V5
Tel: 613-565-8885 *Toll Free Tel:* 888-565-0262 *Fax:* 613-565-8881
E-mail: info@dc-canada.ca

Web Site: www.dc-canada.ca
Key Personnel
Owner & Publg Dir: Mei Dang
Founded: 1995
Publishes in English.
ISBN Prefix(es): 978-0-9738439; 978-0-9738440; 978-0-9808816; 978-0-9810549; 978-1-926776; 978-1-77205
Number of titles published annually: 6 Print

Doubleday Canada
Imprint of Penguin Random House Canada
320 Front St W, Suite 1400, Toronto, ON M5V 3B6
SAN: 115-0340
Tel: 416-364-4449 *Fax:* 416-598-7764
Web Site: www.penguinrandomhouse.ca
Key Personnel
CEO, PRHC: Kristin Cochrane
CFO, PRHC: Barry Gallant
Chief Strategy & Opers Offr, PRHC: Robert Wheaton
SVP & Dir, Prodn: Janine Laporte
Publr: Amy Black
Dir, Mktg & Publicity: Kaitlin Smith
Edit Dir, Bond Street Books: Janie Yoon
Edit Dir, Commercial Publg: Bhavna Chauhan
Sr Mng Ed: Susan Burns; Maria Golikova
Ed-in-Chief: Martha Kanya-Forstner
Sr Ed: Melanie Tutino
Ed: Zoe Maslow
Publg Mgr: Anna MacDiarmid
Mktg Assoc: Malaika Eyoh
Founded: 1937
General trade nonfiction (current affairs, politics, business, sports); fiction, children's illustrated.
Penguin Random House Canada & its publishing entities are not accepting unsol submissions, proposals, mss, or submission queries via e-mail at this time.
Publishes in English.
Number of titles published annually: 60 Print; 5 E-Book
Total Titles: 1,172 Print; 41 E-Book
Imprints: Anchor Canada; Bond Street Books; Seal Books
Membership(s): Canadian Publishers' Council

Douglas & McIntyre (2013) Ltd
Affiliate of Harbour Publishing Co Ltd
4437 Rondeview Rd, Madeira Park, BC V0N 2H1
E-mail: info@douglas-mcintyre.com
Web Site: www.douglas-mcintyre.com
Founded: 1970
Focus on biographies, Indigenous art & history, architecture, literary fiction & cookbooks.
Publishes in English.
ISBN Prefix(es): 978-0-88894; 978-1-55054; 978-1-55365; 978-1-77100; 978-0-920841; 978-1-55051; 978-1-926812; 978-1-926685; 978-1-926706
Number of titles published annually: 20 Print
Total Titles: 600 Print
Distributed by University of Toronto Press
Membership(s): The Association of Book Publishers of British Columbia (ABPBC); Association of Canadian Publishers (ACP)

Dundurn Press Ltd
PO Box 19510, RPO Manulife, Toronto, ON M4W 3T9
SAN: 115-0359
Tel: 416-214-5544
E-mail: info@dundurn.com; publicity@dundurn.com; sales@dundurn.com
Web Site: www.dundurn.com
Key Personnel
COO: Chris Houston
CFO: Graham Matthews
Assoc Publr: Kathryn Lane
Mng Ed: Elena Ranic
Mgr, Publg Opers: Meghan Macdonald

Sales & Mktg Mgr: Kendra Martin
Founded: 1972
Specialize in Canadian history, social sciences, some biography & art, fiction & mysteries.
Publishes in English.
ISBN Prefix(es): 978-0-919670; 978-0-9690454; 978-0-88924; 978-0-88882; 978-1-55488; 978-1-4597
Number of titles published annually: 100 Print
Total Titles: 2,500 Print; 1,800 E-Book
Imprints: Rare Machines
Distribution Center: University of Toronto Press Distribution, 5201 Dufferin St, Toronto, ON M3H 5T8 *Tel:* 416-667-7791 *Toll Free Tel:* 800-565-9523 *Fax:* 416-667-7832 *Toll Free Fax:* 800-221-9985 *Web Site:* www.utpress.utoronto.ca
Ingram Publisher Services, 14 Ingram Blvd, Mail Stop 631, La Vergne, TN 37086, United States
Web Site: www.ingrampublisherservices.com
Ingram Publisher Services (UK) *Tel:* 0800 136-0600 *E-mail:* ipsuksupport@ingramcontent.com
Membership(s): Association of Canadian Publishers (ACP)

Ecrits des Forges
992-A rue Royale, Trois-Rivieres, QC G9A 4H9
Tel: 819-840-8492
E-mail: ecritsdesforges@gmail.com
Web Site: www.ecritsdesforges.com
Key Personnel
Admin Dir: Etienne Poirier
Literary Dir: Bernard Pozier
Founded: 1971
Publish poetry.
Publishes in French.
ISBN Prefix(es): 978-2-89046; 978-2-920228; 978-2-89645
Number of titles published annually: 50 Print
Total Titles: 1,125 Print
Distributed by DCR
Distribution Center: Prologue Inc, 3785, Rue La Fayette Ouest, Boisbriand, QC J7H 1N5 *Tel:* 450-434-0306 *Toll Free Tel:* 800-363-2864 *Toll Free Fax:* 800-361-8088 *E-mail:* prologue@prologue.ca *Web Site:* www.prologue.ca
Membership(s): Association nationale des editeurs de livres (ANEL)

ECW Press
665 Gerrard St E, Toronto, ON M4M 1Y2
SAN: 115-1274
Tel: 416-694-3348
E-mail: info@ecwpress.com
Web Site: www.ecwpress.com
Key Personnel
Pres & Co-Publr: David Caron *E-mail:* david@ecwpress.com
Co-Publr: Jack David *E-mail:* jack@ecwpress.com
Sales & Rts Dir: Emily Ferko *E-mail:* emily@ecwpress.com
Founded: 1974
Publishes in English.
ISBN Prefix(es): 978-0-920763; 978-1-55022; 978-0-920802; 978-1-77041
Number of titles published annually: 50 Print
Total Titles: 1,200 Print; 400 E-Book; 300 Audio
Imprints: misFit
Distributed by Simon & Schuster, LLC
Distribution Center: Baker & Taylor Publisher Services, 30 Amberwood Pkwy, Ashland, OH 44805, United States *Tel:* 567-215-0030 *Toll Free Tel:* 888-814-0208 *E-mail:* info@btpubservices.com *Web Site:* www.btpubservices.com
Membership(s): Association of Canadian Publishers (ACP); Literary Press Group

EDGE Science Fiction & Fantasy Publishing Inc
Imprint of Hades Publications Inc

PO Box 1714, Calgary, AB T2P 2L7
Tel: 403-254-0160 *Fax:* 403-254-0456
E-mail: admin@hadespublications.com
Web Site: www.edgewebsite.com
Key Personnel
Pres & Publr: Brian Hades *E-mail:* publisher@hadespublications.com
Mktg: Janice Shoults
Founded: 1996
Encourage, produce & promote thought-provoking science fiction & fantasy & horror literature by "bringing the magic alive-one world at a time" with each new book released. Independent publisher of science fiction & fantasy novels in hardcover or trade paperback format. Produce high-quality books with lots of attention to detail & lots of marketing effort.
Publishes in English.
ISBN Prefix(es): 978-1-894063; 978-1-896944; 978-1-77053
Number of titles published annually: 8 Print
Total Titles: 87 Print; 1 Audio
Imprints: Absolute XPress; Tesseract Books
U.S. Rep(s): Baker & Taylor; Ingram Book Co
Distribution Center: Fitzhenry & Whiteside Limited, 209 Wicksteed Ave, Unit 51, Toronto, ON M4G 0B1 (CN & US) *Toll Free Tel:* 800-387-9776 *Toll Free Fax:* 800-260-9777 *E-mail:* bookinfo@fitzhenry.ca
Membership(s): Book Publishers Association of Alberta; The Imaging Alliance; Independent Book Publishers Association (IBPA); IPAC

Les Editions Alire
120 cote du Passage, Levis, QC G6V 5S9
Tel: 418-835-4441 *Fax:* 418-838-4443
E-mail: info@alire.com
Web Site: www.alire.com
Key Personnel
Admin Dir: Melanie Bissonnette *E-mail:* melanie.bissonnette@alire.com
Dir, Sales & Mktg: Louise Alain *E-mail:* louise.alain@alire.com
Edit Dir: Jean Pettigrew *E-mail:* jean.pettigrew@alire.com
Founded: 1996
Publish French Canadian popular genre fiction.
Publishes in French.
ISBN Prefix(es): 978-2-922145; 978-2-89615; 978-2-9801068
Number of titles published annually: 10 Print
Total Titles: 131 Print
Distribution Center: Messageries ADP, 2315, rue de la Province, Longueuil, QC J4G 1G4 (CN & US) *Tel:* 450-640-1237 *Fax:* 450-674-6237
Interforum Editis, Immeuble Paryseine, 3, allee de la Seine, 94854 Ivry Cedex, France (worldwide exc CN & US) *Tel:* 02 38 32 71 00 *Fax:* 02 28 32 71 28 *E-mail:* cdes-export@interforum.fr *Web Site:* www.interforum.fr
Membership(s): Association nationale des editeurs de livres (ANEL)

Les Editions ASTED
2065 rue Parthenais, Bureau 387, Montreal, QC H2K 3T1
Tel: 514-281-5012 *Fax:* 514-281-8219
E-mail: editions@asted.org; info@asted.org
Web Site: www.asted.org
Key Personnel
Exec Dir: Micheline Brule *E-mail:* mbrule@fmdoc.org
Founded: 1973
Publishes in French.
ISBN Prefix(es): 978-2-921548; 978-2-89055; 978-2-923563; 978-2-89123; 978-2-89224
Number of titles published annually: 1 Print

Les Editions Caractere
Division of TC Media Books Inc
5800, rue St-Denis, bureau 900, Montreal, QC H2S 3L5
Tel: 450-461-2782 *Toll Free Tel:* 855-861-2782

E-mail: caractere@tc.tc
Web Site: www.tcmedialivres.com
Founded: 2004
Publishes in French.
ISBN Prefix(es): 978-2-923351; 978-2-89642; 978-2-89643
Number of titles published annually: 130 Print
Distribution Center: Prologue Inc, 3785, Rue La Fayette Ouest, Boisbriand, QC J7H 1N5 *Tel:* 450-434-0306 *Toll Free Tel:* 800-363-2864 *Toll Free Fax:* 800-361-8088 *E-mail:* prologue@prologue.ca *Web Site:* www.prologue.ca

Les Editions Chouette
2515, avenue de la Renaissance, Boisbriand, QC J7H 1T9
Tel: 514-925-3325
E-mail: info@editions-chouette.com; serviceclient@editions-chouette.com; foreignrights@editions-chouette.com
Web Site: www.editions-chouette.com
Key Personnel
Publr & Ed: Anne Paradis
Founded: 1987
Produce children's books adapted to each age group from birth to age six, with the well-known Caillou character.
Publishes in English, French.
ISBN Prefix(es): 978-2-9800909; 978-2-921198; 978-2-89450; 978-2-89718
Number of titles published annually: 30 Print
Total Titles: 200 Print
Foreign Rep(s): Jonathan Ball Publishers (South Africa); Grantham Book Services (GBS) (UK); Ingram Publisher Services International (Denise Lourenco) (Caribbean, Latin America, Middle East, North Africa); Interforum Editis (France, Switzerland); Interforum SA Benelux (Belgium, Luxembourg); NewSouth Books (Australia); Ralph & Sheila Summers (Asia)
Distribution Center: Canadian Manda Group, 664 Annette St, Toronto, ON M6S 2C8 (CN exc Quebec) *Tel:* 416-516-0911 *Fax:* 416-516-0917 *E-mail:* info@mandagroup.com *Web Site:* www.mandagroup.com
Ingram Publisher Services, 14 Ingram Dr, Mail Stop 631, La Vergne, TN 37086, United States *Toll Free Tel:* 866-400-5351 *Web Site:* www.ingrampublisherservices.com SAN: 631-8630

Editions de la Pleine Lune
223 34 Ave, Lachine, QC H8T 1Z4
Tel: 514-634-7954
E-mail: editpllune@videotron.ca
Web Site: www.pleinelune.qc.ca
Key Personnel
Literary Dir: Marie-Madeleine Raoult
Founded: 1975
Publishes in French.
ISBN Prefix(es): 978-2-89024
Number of titles published annually: 8 Print
Total Titles: 250 Print
Distribution Center: Diffusion Dimedia, 539, Lebau Blvd, St-Laurent, QC H4N 1S2 *Tel:* 514-336-3941 *Fax:* 514-331-3916 *E-mail:* general@dimedia.qc.ca *Web Site:* www.dimedia.com
La Librairie du Quebec a Paris et DNM, 30, rue Gay Lussac, 75005 Paris, France *Tel:* 01 43 54 49 02 *Fax:* 01 43 54 39 15 *Web Site:* www.librairieduquebec.fr
Membership(s): Association nationale des editeurs de livres (ANEL)

Les Editions de l'Hexagone
Imprint of Groupe Ville-Marie Litterature
4545, rue Frontenac, 3rd fl, Montreal, QC H2H 2R7
Tel: 514-523-1182 *Fax:* 514-521-4434
Web Site: editionshexagone.groupelivre.com

Key Personnel
VP, Edit: Martin Balthazar
Dir, Publg: Alain-Nicolas Renaud
Head, Prodn: Sophie Deschenes
Ed: Melikah Abdelmoumen; Ariane Caron-Lacoste
Founded: 1953
Publishes in French.
ISBN Prefix(es): 978-2-89006; 978-2-89295; 978-2-89648; 978-0-88508
Number of titles published annually: 30 Print
Total Titles: 900 Print
Foreign Office(s): Immeuble Paryseine, 3, Allee de la Seine, 94854 Ivry Cedex, France *Tel:* 01 49 59 12 40 *Fax:* 06 16 94 14 38
Orders to: Messageries ADP, 2315 rue de la Province, Longueuil, QC J4G 1G4 *Tel:* 450-640-1234 *Toll Free Tel:* 800-771-3022 *Fax:* 450-640-1251 *Toll Free Fax:* 800-603-0433 *E-mail:* adpcommandes@messageries-adp.com *Web Site:* www.messageries-adp.com
Warehouse: Messageries ADP, 2315 rue de la Province, Longueuil, QC J4G 1G4 *Tel:* 450-640-1234 *Toll Free Tel:* 800-771-3022 *Fax:* 450-640-1251 *Toll Free Fax:* 800-603-0433 *Web Site:* www.messageries-adp.com

Les Editions de Mortagne
CP 116, Boucherville, QC J4B 5E6
Tel: 450-641-2387
E-mail: info@editionsdemortagne.com
Web Site: editionsdemortagne.com
Key Personnel
Pres: Sandy Pellerin
Admin & Acctg Dir: Melanie Giguere
Ed: Chloe Poitras
Proj Mgr: Aimee Verrat
Admin & Acctg Asst: Katerine Salois
Founded: 1978
Biographies, fantasy novels, thrillers, historical novels & a variety of practical guides on health, psychology, personal & spiritual development, astrology & parapsychology.
Publishes in French.
ISBN Prefix(es): 978-2-89074
Number of titles published annually: 15 Print
Total Titles: 15 Print
Distribution Center: Prologue Inc, 3785, Rue La Fayette Ouest, Broisbriand, QC J7N 1N5 *Tel:* 450-434-0306 *Toll Free Tel:* 800-363-2864 *Toll Free Fax:* 800-361-8088 *E-mail:* prologue@prologue.ca *Web Site:* www.prologue.ca
DG Diffusion, Zl de Bogues, 31750 Escalquens, France *Tel:* 05 61 00 09 99 *Fax:* 05 61 00 23 12 *Web Site:* www.dgdiffusion.com
Servidis SA, Chemin des Chalets, 7, 1279 Chavannes-de-Bogis, Switzerland *Tel:* (022) 960 95 10 *Fax:* (022) 776 35 44 *Web Site:* www.servidis.ch
Membership(s): Association nationale des editeurs de livres (ANEL)

Editions de Renouveau Pedagogique Inc, see ERPI

Les Editions du Ble
340, blvd Provencher, St Boniface, MB R2H 0G7
Tel: 204-237-8200
E-mail: direction@editionsduble.ca
Web Site: ble.avoslivres.ca
Key Personnel
Dir Gen: Emmanuelle Rigaud
Founded: 1974
Publish books in French (novels, essays, poetry) pertaining mainly to the Canadian West (but not exclusively).
Publishes in French.
ISBN Prefix(es): 978-2-921347; 978-2-923673
Number of titles published annually: 6 Print

Total Titles: 100 Print
Distribution Center: Diffusion Dimedia Inc, 539 Blvd Lebeau, Saint-Laurent, QC H4N 1S2 *Tel:* 514-336-3941 *Web Site:* www.dimedia.com

Les Editions du Boreal
4447, rue St-Denis, Montreal, QC H2J 2L2
Tel: 514-287-7401 *Fax:* 514-287-7664
E-mail: info@editionsboreal.qc.ca; boreal@editionsboreal.qc.ca; communications@editionsboreal.qc.ca
Web Site: www.editionsboreal.qc.ca
Key Personnel
Mng Dir: Pascal Assathiany
Publg Dir: Jean Bernier
Deputy Gen Dir: Philippe Gendreau
    E-mail: pgendreau@editionsboreal.qc.ca
Deputy Edit Dir: Renaud Roussel
    E-mail: rroussel@editionsboreal.qc.ca
Head, Communs: Marianne Thornton
Prodn Mgr: Stephanie Mallette
    E-mail: smallette@editionsboreal.qc.ca
Foreign Rts: Sebastian Lefebvre
    E-mail: slefebvre@editionsboreal.qc.ca
Founded: 1963
General literature, essays, history, translations, children's & philosophy.
Publishes in French.
ISBN Prefix(es): 978-2-89052; 978-2-7646; 978-0-88503
Number of titles published annually: 70 Print
Total Titles: 2,000 Print
Distributed by Editions Du Seuil (Europe)
Foreign Rights: AMV Agencia Literaria (Eduardo Melon Vallat) (Portugal, Spain); AnatoliaLit Literary & Copyright Agency (Cansu Canseven) (Turkey); Balla & Co Literary Agents (Catherine Balla) (Hungary); Bureau des Copyrights Francais (Corinne Quentin) (Japan); The Grayhawk Agency (Nicolas Wu) (Taiwan); Lester Agency (Anastasia Lester) (Belarus, Bosnia and Herzegovina, Bulgaria, Croatia, Czechia, Estonia, Kosovo, Latvia, Lithuania, Montenegro, North Macedonia, Poland, Russia, Serbia, Slovakia, Slovenia, Ukraine); Liepman AG Literary Agency (Marc Koralnik) (Germany); Rightol Media Ltd (Haley Shi) (China); Anna Spadolini Agency (Anna Spadolini) (Italy); Villas-Boas & Moss Literary Agency (Luciana Villas-Boas) (Brazil)
Distribution Center: Diffusion Dimedia, 539, blvd Lebeau, Ville St-Laurent, QC H4N 1S2 *Tel:* 514-336-3941 *Fax:* 514-331-3916 *E-mail:* info@dimedia.qc.ca *Web Site:* www.dimedia.com
Exportlivre Inc, 289, blvd Desaulniers, St-Lambert, QC J4P 1M8 (US) *Tel:* 450-671-3888 *Fax:* 450-671-2121 *E-mail:* order@exportlivre.com *Web Site:* www.exportlivre.com
Volumen, 25, blvd Romain Rolland, CS 21418, 75993 Paris Cedex 14, France (Europe) *Tel:* 01 41 48 84 60 *Fax:* 01 64 48 49 63 *E-mail:* volumen@volumen.fr

Editions du CHU Sainte-Justine
Unit of Direction de l'enseignement de l'hopital
3175, chemin de la Cote-Sainte-Catherine, Montreal, QC H3T 1C5
Tel: 514-345-4671 *Fax:* 514-345-4631
E-mail: edition.hsj@ssss.gouv.qc.ca
Web Site: www.editions-chu-sainte-justine.org
Key Personnel
Publg Dir: Marise Labrecque *Tel:* 514-345-7743
    E-mail: marise.labrecque.hsj@ssss.gouv.qc.ca
Sales Dir: Jean-Francois Hebert *Tel:* 514-345-4931 ext 5541 *E-mail:* jean-francois.hebert.hsj@ssss.gouv.qc.ca
Ed: Marie-Eve Lefebvre *Tel:* 514-345-2350
    E-mail: marie-eve.lefebvre.hsj@ssss.gouv.qc.ca
Founded: 1993
ISBN Prefix(es): 978-2-921215; 978-2-921858; 978-2-922770; 978-2-89619
Number of titles published annually: 15 Print

PUBLISHERS

Total Titles: 250 Print
Foreign Office(s): One, rue de la Lizonne, 16700 Bioussac, France, Contact: Pascale Patte-Wilbert *Tel:* 01 45 85 79 00 *E-mail:* pascale.pattewilbert@gmail.com
Distribution Center: Prologue Inc, 3785, Rue La Fayette Ouest, Boisbriand, QC J7H 1N5 *Tel:* 450-434-0306 *Toll Free Tel:* 800-363-2864 *Toll Free Fax:* 800-361-8088 *E-mail:* prologue@prologue.ca *Web Site:* www.prologue.ca
CEDIF, 73, quai, Auguste Deshaies, 94200 Ivry-sur-Seine, France (Belgium, France & Luxembourg) *Tel:* 01 46 58 38 40 *Fax:* 01 46 71 25 59 *E-mail:* secretariat@ced-cedif.fr
Daudin Distribution, One, rue Guynemer, 78114 Magny-les Hameaux, France (Belgium, France & Luxembourg) *Tel:* 01 30 48 74 74 *Fax:* 01 34 98 02 44 *E-mail:* orders@daudin.fr
Servidis SA, Chemin des Chalets, 7, 1279 Chavannes-de-Bogis, Switzerland, Contact: Sophie Sandoz *Tel:* (022) 960 95 32 *Fax:* (022) 960 95 77 *E-mail:* ssandoz@servidislogistique.ch *Web Site:* www.servidis.ch

§Les Editions du Noroit
4609, rue D'Iberville, espace 202, Montreal, QC H2H 2L9
Tel: 514-727-0005
E-mail: poesie@lenoroit.com
Web Site: lenoroit.com
Key Personnel
Literary Dir: Charlotte Francoeur
    E-mail: charlotte@lenoroit.com; Melissa Labonte *E-mail:* melissa@lenoroit.com
Founded: 1971
Poetry.
Publishes in French.
ISBN Prefix(es): 978-2-89018; 978-0-88524
Number of titles published annually: 25 Print
Total Titles: 730 Print; 1 CD-ROM; 10 Audio
Distribution Center: Diffusion Dimedia Inc, 539 blvd Lebeau, Montreal, QC H4N 1S2 *Tel:* 514-336-3941 *E-mail:* general@dimedia.qc.ca *Web Site:* www.dimedia.com

Les Editions du Remue-Menage
469, Jean-Talon Ouest, bureau 401, Montreal, QC H3N 1R4
Mailing Address: CP 65057, Mozart, Montreal, QC H2S 2S0
Tel: 514-876-0097
E-mail: info@editions-rm.ca
Web Site: www.editions-rm.ca
Key Personnel
Gen & Literary Dir: Rachel Bedard
    E-mail: rbedard@editions-rm.ca
Artistic & Commercial Dir: Anne Migner-Laurin
    E-mail: amlaurin@editions-rm.ca
Founded: 1976
Specialize in feminist books.
Publishes in English, French.
ISBN Prefix(es): 978-2-89091
Number of titles published annually: 15 Print
Total Titles: 170 Print
Foreign Rep(s): Library Plaisir (Egypt); S A Vander (Belgium)
Distribution Center: Diffusion Dimedia, 539 blvd Lebeau, St-Laurent, QC H4N 1S2 *Tel:* 514-336-3941 *E-mail:* general@dimedia.qc.ca
Exportlivre, 289 Blvd Desaulniers, St-Lambert, QC J4P 1M8 (worldwide exc CN & Europe)
Hobo Diffusion, 23 rue Pradier, 75019 Paris, France (Europe) *Tel:* 06 46 79 40 71 *E-mail:* contact@hobo-diffusion.com *Web Site:* www.hobo-diffusion.com
Membership(s): Association nationale des editeurs de livres (ANEL)

Les Editions du Septentrion
86, Cote de la Montagne, bureau 200, Quebec, QC G1K 4E3
Tel: 418-688-3556 *Fax:* 418-527-4978
E-mail: info@septentrion.qc.ca
Web Site: www.septentrion.qc.ca
Key Personnel
Pres & Ed: Denis Vaugeois
Mng Dir & Ed: Gilles Herman
Communs Mgr: Alex Tremblay-Lamarche
Edit Coord: Marie-Michele Rheault
Founded: 1988
Full service publisher.
Publishes in English, French.
ISBN Prefix(es): 978-2-89448; 978-2-921114
Number of titles published annually: 30 Print
Total Titles: 700 Print
Divisions: Hamac
Distributed by Baraka Books
Distribution Center: Dimedia, 539 blvd Lebeau, St-Laurent, QC H4N 1S2

Les Editions Fides
Subsidiary of Coopsco
7333 place des Roseraies, bureau 501, Anjou, QC H1M 2X6
Tel: 514-745-4290 *Fax:* 514-745-4299
E-mail: editions@groupefides.com
Web Site: www.editionsfides.com
Key Personnel
Artistic Dir: Bruno Lamoureux
Dir, Mktg & Opers: Nancy Lauzon
Edit Dir: David Senechal
Fin Dir: Michel Perreault
Mng Ed: Valerie De Marchi
Gen Mgr: Jean-Francois Bouchard
Press Offr: Diane Therrien *Tel:* 514-745-4290 ext 351
Prodn & Contract Coord: Veronique Beaudry
Commercial Asst: Pascale Desrochers *Tel:* 514-745-4290 ext 365
Founded: 1937
Publishes in French.
ISBN Prefix(es): 978-0-7755; 978-2-7612; 978-2-87374; 978-2-89007; 978-2-923989; 978-1-897092; 978-1-931363
Number of titles published annually: 40 Print
Total Titles: 2,000 Print
Distribution Center: Socadis Inc, 420 rue Stinson, Ville St-Laurent, QC H4N 3L7 *Tel:* 514-331-3300 *Toll Free Tel:* 800-361-2847 *Fax:* 514-745-3282 *Toll Free Fax:* 866-803-5422 *E-mail:* socinfo@socadis.com *Web Site:* www.socadis.com
Sofedis, 11, rue Soufflot, 75005 Paris, France (Europe) *Tel:* 01 53 10 25 25 *Fax:* 01 53 10 25 26 *E-mail:* info@sofedis.fr

Editions FouLire
4339, rue des Becassines, Quebec, QC G1G 1V5
Tel: 418-628-4029 *Toll Free Tel:* 877-628-4029 (CN & US) *Fax:* 418-628-4801
E-mail: edition@foulire.com
Web Site: www.foulire.com
Key Personnel
Dir, Prodn & Mktg: Danielle Lajeunesse
Ed: Yvon Brochu
Founded: 2002
Publishers of books for children.
Publishes in French.
ISBN Prefix(es): 978-2-89591
Number of titles published annually: 30 Print
Total Titles: 3,500 Print
Foreign Rights: Ambre Communication (Pascale Patte-Wilbert) (France)
Distribution Center: Prologue Inc, 3785, Rue La Fayette Ouest, Boisbriand, QC J7H 1N5 *Tel:* 450-434-0306 *Toll Free Tel:* 800-363-2864 *Toll Free Fax:* 800-361-8088 *E-mail:* prologue@prologue.ca *Web Site:* www.prologue.ca
Librairie du Quebec, 30, rue Gay-Lussac, 75005 Paris, France *Tel:* 01 43 54 49 02 *Fax:* 01 43 54 39 15 *E-mail:* liquebec@noos.frbec

Les Editions Ganesha Inc
CP 484, Succursale Chabanel, Montreal, QC H2N 0A7
E-mail: courriel@editions-ganesha.qc.ca; email@editions-ganesha.qc.ca
Web Site: www.editions-ganesha.qc.ca
Key Personnel
Publr: Andre Beaudoin
Founded: 1978
Publishes in French.
ISBN Prefix(es): 978-2-89145
Number of titles published annually: 3 Print
Total Titles: 68 Print

Les Editions Goelette et Coup d-oeil Inc
1350, rue Marie-Victorin, St-Bruno-de-Montarville, QC J3V 6B9
Tel: 450-653-1337 *Toll Free Tel:* 800-463-4961 *Fax:* 450-653-9924
E-mail: info@boutiquegoelette.com; rights@goelette.ca
Web Site: boutiquegoelette.com
Key Personnel
Pres: Alain Delorme
Founded: 1997
Publishes in English, French.
ISBN Prefix(es): 978-2-9804941; 978-2-9806291; 978-2-922983; 978-2-89638; 978-2-89690; 978-2-89800
Number of titles published annually: 200 Print
Total Titles: 2,000 Print
Distribution Center: Les Messageries ADP, 2315, rue de la Province, Longueuil, QC J4G 1G4 *Tel:* 450-640-1234 *Toll Free Tel:* 800-771-3022 *Fax:* 450-640-1251 *Toll Free Fax:* 800-603-0433

Les Editions Heritage Inc
1101, ave Victoria, St-Lambert, QC J4R 1P8
Tel: 514-875-0327
E-mail: dominiqueetcie@editionsheritage.com; info@editionsheritage.com
Web Site: www.dominiqueetcompagnie.com
Key Personnel
Exec Dir: Sylvie Payette
Founded: 1968
Juvenile, adult & French language.
Publishes in French.
ISBN Prefix(es): 978-0-7773; 978-2-7625
Number of titles published annually: 250 Print
Total Titles: 2,000 Print
Distribution Center: Socadis Inc, 420 rue Stinson, Ville St-Laurent, QC H4N 3L7 *Tel:* 514-331-3300 *Toll Free Tel:* 800-361-2847 *Fax:* 514-745-3282 *Toll Free Fax:* 866-803-5422 *E-mail:* socinfo@socadis.com *Web Site:* www.socadis.com
Pollen, 81 rue Romain Rolland, 93260 Les Lilas, France (Belgium & France) *Tel:* 01 43 62 08 07
Servidis SA, Chemin des Chalets, 7, 1279 Chavannes-de-Bogis, Switzerland *Tel:* (022) 960 95 10 *Fax:* (022) 776 35 27 *Web Site:* www.servidis.ch
Membership(s): Association for Canadian Publishers in the US

Editions Hurtubise
Division of Groupe HMH
1815, ave de Lorimier, Montreal, QC H2K 3W6
Tel: 514-523-1523 *Toll Free Tel:* 800-361-1664
Web Site: editionshurtubise.com
Key Personnel
Pres: Herve Foulon
VP, Publg & Opers: Arnaud Foulon
    E-mail: arnaud.foulon@groupehmh.com
VP, Sales & Mktg: Alexandrine Foulon
Dir, Prodn: Dominique Lemay
Literary Dir: Andre Gagnon *E-mail:* andre.gagnon@editionshurtubise.com
Head, Communs & Ad: Amelie Tremblay
    E-mail: amelie.tremblay@groupehmh.com

CANADIAN PUBLISHERS

Ed: Estelle Denoncourt *E-mail:* estelle.denoncourt@editionshurtubise.com;
Jacinthe Moffet *E-mail:* jacinthe.moffet@editionshurtubise.com; Pascale Morin *E-mail:* pascale.morin@editionshurtubise.com; Catherine Ouellet *E-mail:* catherine.ouellet@editionshurtubise.com
Foreign Rts Mgr: Genevieve Lagace
  E-mail: genevieve.lagace@groupehmh.com
Founded: 1960
French Canadian publishing house. Fiction & nonfiction, adult & young adult.
Publishes in French.
ISBN Prefix(es): 978-2-89045; 978-2-89428; 978-2-89647; 978-0-7758; 978-2-89723; 978-2-89781
Number of titles published annually: 80 Print; 60 E-Book; 10 Audio
Total Titles: 1,200 Print; 850 E-Book; 50 Audio
Imprints: Bibliotheque Quebecoise (BQ)
Distributor for Bibliotheque Quebecoise; Marcel Didier; Editions MultiMondes; Editions XYZ
Foreign Rights: AC2 Literary Agency (Anna Mioni) (Italy); Editio Dialog Literary Agency (Michael Wenzel, selected titles) (France); Kalem Agency (Kardelen Genc & Nazlican Kabatas) (Turkey); Lester Literary Agency (Anastasia Lester & Laura Karayotov) (Baltic States, Central Europe, Eastern Europe); Livre Chine (Shengyue Tian, middle-grade & young adult) (China, Hong Kong, Macau, Taiwan); Tilly-Ink Rights (Mathilde Pineau-Valencienne, middle-grade & young adult) (English-speaking countries)
Warehouse: Distribution HMH (Canada) *Web Site:* distributionhmh.com
Distribution Center: Distribution HMH (Canada) *Web Site:* distributionhmh.com
Librairie du Quebec/DNM, 30, rue Gay-Lussac, 75005 Paris, France *Tel:* 01 43 54 49 02
Servidis SA, Chemin des Chalets, 7, 1279 Chavannes-de-Bogis, Switzerland *Tel:* (022) 960 95 10 *Fax:* (022) 776 35 44 *Web Site:* www.servidis.ch

Les Editions JCL
Affiliate of Groupe Bertrand Editeur
348, 9e Ave, St-Jean-sur-Richelieu, QC J2X 1K3
Tel: 450-515-4438
E-mail: info@jcl.qc.ca
Web Site: www.jcl.qc.ca
Key Personnel
Pres & Intl Rts: Daniel Bertrand
Founded: 1977
Novels, nonfiction & youth literature.
Publishes in French.
ISBN Prefix(es): 978-2-920176; 978-2-89431; 978-2-89432
Number of titles published annually: 26 Print
Total Titles: 521 Print
Foreign Rights: Gregory Messina (European Union exc France)
Distribution Center: Messageries ADP, 2315, rue de la Province, Longueuil, QC J4G 1G4 *Tel:* 450-640-1234 *Toll Free Tel:* 800-771-3022 *Fax:* 450-640-1251 *Toll Free Fax:* 800-603-0433 *Web Site:* www.messageries-adp.com
Distribution du Nouveau Monde (DNM), 30, rue Gay Lussac, 75005 Paris, France (France & other French-speaking European countries) *E-mail:* dnm@librairieduquebec.fr *Web Site:* www.librairieduquebec.fr/distribution.html
Servidis SA, Chemin des Chalets, 7, 1279 Chavannes-de-Bogis, Switzerland *Tel:* (022) 960 95 10 *Fax:* (022) 776 35 44 *Web Site:* www.servidis.ch

Editions Le Dauphin Blanc Inc
825, blvd Lebourgneuf, Suite 125, Quebec, QC G2J 0B9
Tel: 418-845-4045 *Fax:* 418-845-1933
E-mail: info@dauphinblanc.com
Web Site: dauphinblanc.com

Key Personnel
Pres & CEO: Alain Williamson
  E-mail: alainwilliamson@dauphinblanc.com
Prodn: Annie Sauvgeau *E-mail:* anniesauvgeau@dauphinblanc.com
Founded: 1991
Publishes in French.
ISBN Prefix(es): 978-2-89436
Number of titles published annually: 50 Print
Distribution Center: Prologue Inc, 3785, Rue La Fayette Ouest, Boisbriand, QC J7H 1N5 *Tel:* 450-434-0306 *Toll Free Tel:* 800-363-2864 *Toll Free Fax:* 800-361-8088 *E-mail:* prologue@prologue.ca *Web Site:* www.prologue.ca
DG Diffusion, ZI de Bogues, 31750 Escalquens, France (Belgium & France) *Tel:* 05 61 00 09 99 *Fax:* 05 61 00 23 12 *E-mail:* adv@dgdiffusion.com *Web Site:* www.dgdiffusion.com
Servidis SA, Chemin des Chalets, 7, 1279 Chavannes-de-Bogis, Switzerland *Tel:* (022) 960 95 10 *Fax:* (022) 776 35 44 *Web Site:* www.servidis.ch

Editions Marie-France
CP 32263 BP Waverly, Montreal, QC H3L 3X1
Tel: 514-329-3700 *Toll Free Tel:* 800-563-6644 (CN) *Fax:* 514-329-0630
E-mail: editions@marie-france.qc.ca
Web Site: www.marie-france.qc.ca
Key Personnel
VP: Joanne Lacombe
Founded: 1977
School, kindergarten, elementary & secondary adult & university in French, natural sciences, human sciences, music, economic education & physics. Some titles in both French & English.
Publishes in English, French.
ISBN Prefix(es): 978-2-89168
Number of titles published annually: 25 Print
Total Titles: 1,001 Print
Membership(s): Association nationale des editeurs de livres (ANEL)

§Editions Mediaspaul
3965, blvd Henri-Bourassa E, Montreal, QC H1H 1L1
Tel: 514-322-7341 *Fax:* 514-322-4281
E-mail: mediaspaul@mediaspaul.ca
Web Site: mediaspaul.ca
Key Personnel
Exec Dir: Joseph Sciortino *E-mail:* jsciortino@mediaspaul.ca
Ed: Gilles Collicelli *E-mail:* editeur@mediaspaul.ca
Edit & Prod Mgr: Pierre Catalano *E-mail:* pc.catalano@mediaspaul.ca
Founded: 1975
Religious & photographic books.
Publishes in French.
ISBN Prefix(es): 978-2-7122; 978-0-88840; 978-2-89039; 978-2-89420
Number of titles published annually: 20 Print
Total Titles: 300 Print
Distribution Center: Novalis, 4475, rue Frontenac, Montreal, QC H2H 2S5 *Tel:* 514-278-3020 *Fax:* 514-278-3087 *E-mail:* booksellers@bayardcanada.com *Web Site:* novalis.ca
Sodis, 128 Ave du Marechal de Lattre de Tassigny, 77400 Lagny-sur-Marne, France *Web Site:* www.sodis.fr

Editions Michel Quintin
2259 Papineau Ave, Suite 104, Montreal, QC H2K 4J5
SAN: 116-5356
Tel: 514-379-3774 *Fax:* 450-539-4905
E-mail: info@editionsmichelquintin.ca; commande@editionsmichelquintin.ca (orders)
Web Site: www.editionsmichelquintin.ca

Key Personnel
Pres & CEO: Michel Quintin
VP & Ed: Collette Dufresne
Rts & Mktg Dir: Charlotte Delwaide
  E-mail: cdelwaide@editionsmichelquintin.ca
Sales Dir: Sophane Beaudin-Quintin
  E-mail: squintin@editionsmichelquintin.ca
Founded: 1982
Nonfiction on fauna, nature, environment.
Publishes in French.
ISBN Prefix(es): 978-2-920438; 978-2-89435; 978-2-89762
Number of titles published annually: 50 Print
Total Titles: 700 Print; 300 E-Book
Branch Office(s)
4770 rue Foster, Waterloo, QC J0E 2N0 *Tel:* 450-539-3774
Foreign Rep(s): Bacon & Hughes (Canada); Interforum Editis

Editions MultiMondes
Affiliate of Groupe HMH
1815, Avenue de Lorimier, Montreal, QC H2K 3W6
Tel: 514-523-1523 *Toll Free Tel:* 800-361-1664
Web Site: editionsmultimondes.com
Key Personnel
Exec Dir: Dominique Lemay *E-mail:* dominique.lemay@editionsmultimondes.com
Literary Dir & Ed: Raymond Lemieux
  E-mail: raymond.lemieux@editionsmultimondes.com
Founded: 1988
Books on science & the environment.
Publishes in English, French.
ISBN Prefix(es): 978-2-921146; 978-2-89544
Number of titles published annually: 20 Print
Total Titles: 400 Print
Distribution Center: Librairie du Quebec/DNM, 30, rue Gay-Lussac, Paris 75005, France (Europe) *Tel:* 01 43 54 49 02

Les Editions Phidal Inc
5740 Ferrier St, Montreal, QC H4P 1M7
Tel: 514-738-0202 *Toll Free Tel:* 800-738-7349 *Fax:* 514-738-5102
E-mail: info@phidal.com; orders@phidal.com (sales & export)
Web Site: phidal.com
Key Personnel
Prodn Mgr: Lionel Soussan
Founded: 1979
Full service publisher.
Publishes in English, French.
ISBN Prefix(es): 978-2-89393; 978-2-7643; 978-2-920129
Number of titles published annually: 55 Print
Branch Office(s)
Phidal Inc, 20900 NE 30 Ave, Suite 407, Aventura, FL 33180, United States *Tel:* 286-288-0339
230 Fifth Ave, Suite 405, New York, NY 10001, United States

Les Editions Pierre Tisseyre
155, rue Maurice, Rosemere, QC J7A 2S8
Tel: 514-335-0777 *Fax:* 514-335-6723
E-mail: info@edtisseyre.ca
Web Site: www.tisseyre.ca
Key Personnel
Pres: Charles Tisseyre
Mng Ed: Michelle Tisseyre *E-mail:* mtisseyre@edtisseyre.ca
Sr Ed: Genevieve Mativat
Founded: 1947
Primarily publish novels, novellas, essays, memoirs, novels for young people & children's literature.
Publishes in French.
ISBN Prefix(es): 978-2-89051; 978-2-89633; 978-0-7753

PUBLISHERS

Number of titles published annually: 10 Print; 3 E-Book
Total Titles: 900 Print; 30 E-Book
Foreign Rep(s): Marc Pinelli (France)
Distribution Center: Prologue Inc, 3785, Rue La Fayette Ouest, Boisbriand, QC J7H 1N5 *Tel:* 450-434-0306 *Toll Free Tel:* 800-363-2864 *Toll Free Fax:* 800-361-8088 *E-mail:* prologue@prologue.ca *Web Site:* www.prologue.ca
Membership(s): Association nationale des editeurs de livres (ANEL)

Editions Prise de parole
359-27 rue Larch, Sudbury, ON P3E 1B7
Tel: 705-675-6491
E-mail: info@prisedeparole.ca
Web Site: www.prisedeparole.ca
Key Personnel
Co-Exec Dir & Dir, Publg: Denise Truax
 E-mail: dtruax@prisedeparole.ca
Co-Exec Dir & Dir, Mktg: Stephane Cormier
 E-mail: scormier@prisedeparole.ca
Cont: Alain Mayotte *E-mail:* amayotte@prisedeparole.ca
Founded: 1973
Poetry, novels, drama, textbooks, essays.
Publishes in French.
ISBN Prefix(es): 978-2-89423; 978-2-89744; 978-2-921573; 978-2-920814
Number of titles published annually: 18 Print; 18 Online; 16 E-Book; 3 Audio
Total Titles: 481 Print; 438 Online; 318 E-Book; 15 Audio
Distribution Center: Diffusion Dimedia, 1650, blvd Lionel-Bertrand, Boisbriand, QC J7H 1N7 *Tel:* 450-434-0306
Membership(s): Association nationale des editeurs de livres (ANEL); Regroupement des Editeurs Canadiens-Francais (RECF)

Editions Trecarre
Imprint of Groupe Librex
4545, rue Frontenac, 3rd fl, Montreal, QC H2H 2R7
Tel: 514-849-5259 *Fax:* 514-849-1388
Web Site: www.editions-trecarre.com
Key Personnel
Dir, Rts: Carole Boutin *Tel:* 514-373-2743
 E-mail: carol.boutin@groupelibrex.com
Founded: 1982
How-to books, cookbooks, practical books, health & lifestyle.
Publishes in French.
ISBN Prefix(es): 978-2-89249; 978-2-89568
Number of titles published annually: 15 Print
Total Titles: 700 Print; 100 E-Book
Foreign Rights: Berla & Griffini Rights Agency (Erica Berla) (Italy); Bureau des Copyrights Francais (Corinne Quentin, selected titles) (Japan); Dakai Agency (Solene Demigneux) (China, Taiwan); Divas International (Denise Lu) (China, Taiwan); The Grayhawk Agency (Wu Chung-Sen & Nicolas Wu) (China, Taiwan); Iris Literary Agency (Catherine Fragou) (Greece); Simona Kessler Agency (Marina Adriana) (Romania); Anastasia Lester (Belarus, Russia, Ukraine); Liepman Literary Agency (Eva Koralnik & Sandra Laederach) (Germany)
Warehouse: Les Messageries ADP, 2315, rue de la province, Longueuil, QC J4G 1G4 *Tel:* 450-640-1234 *Toll Free Tel:* 800-771-3022 *Fax:* 450-640-1251 *Toll Free Fax:* 800-603-0433 *Web Site:* www.messageries-adp.com

§Les Editions Un Monde Different
3905 Isabelle, bureau 101, Brossard, QC J4Y 2R2
Mailing Address: CP 51546, Greenfield Park, QC J4V 3N8
Tel: 450-656-2660 *Toll Free Tel:* 800-443-2582 *Fax:* 450-659-9328
E-mail: info@umd.ca
Web Site: umd.ca
Key Personnel
Ed: Michel Ferron; Lise Labbe
Asst to Ed/Press Rel: Manon Martel
Cust Serv: Monique Duchesneau
Founded: 1977
Motivational & inspirational books.
Publishes in French.
ISBN Prefix(es): 978-2-89225; 978-2-920000
Number of titles published annually: 25 Print
Total Titles: 750 Print
Distribution Center: Messageries ADP, 2315, rue de la Province, Longueuil, QC J4G 1G4 *Tel:* 450-640-1234 *Fax:* 450-640-1251
Interforum Editis, Immeuble Paryseine, 3, alle de la Seine, 94854 Ivry Cedex, France (Europe), Press Offr: Celia Barosso *Tel:* 01 49 59 12 40; 01 49 59 11 89

Les Editions XYZ inc
Affiliate of Groupe HMH
1815, ave De Lorimier, Montreal, QC H2K 3W6
Tel: 514-525-2170 *Fax:* 514-525-7537
E-mail: info@editionsxyz.com
Web Site: editionsxyz.com
Key Personnel
Ed: Guylaine Girard *Tel:* 514-525-2170 ext 270
 E-mail: guylaine.girard@editionsxyz.com
Prodn Mgr: Nathalie Tasse *Tel:* 514-525-2170 ext 255 *E-mail:* nathalie.tasse@editionsxyz.com
Founded: 1985
Novels, short stories & literary essays.
Publishes in French.
ISBN Prefix(es): 978-2-89261; 978-2-89772
Number of titles published annually: 20 Print; 20 E-Book
Total Titles: 457 Print; 175 Online; 145 E-Book
Distribution Center: Distribution HMH, 1815, Ave de Lorimier, Montreal, QC H2K 3W6 *Tel:* 514-523-1523 *Toll Free Tel:* 800-361-1664 *Fax:* 514-523-9969 *Web Site:* www.distributionhmh.com
Distribution du Nouveau Monde (DNM), 30, rue Gay Lussac, 75005 Paris, France *Tel:* 01 43 54 50 24 *Fax:* 01 43 54 39 15
Membership(s): Association nationale des editeurs de livres (ANEL)

§Editions Yvon Blais
Imprint of Thomson Reuters Canada Ltd
75 rue Queen, bureau 4700, Montreal, QC H3C 2N6
Toll Free Tel: 800-363-3047
E-mail: editionsyvonblais.commandes@tr.com (cust serv)
Web Site: store.thomsonreuters.ca/fr-ca/nouveautes
Key Personnel
Dir, Pubns: Marie-Noelle Guay
Founded: 1978
Legal publishing.
Publishes in French.
ISBN Prefix(es): 978-2-89073; 978-2-89451; 978-2-89635; 978-2-89730
Number of titles published annually: 30 Print
Total Titles: 800 Print
Returns: 245 Bartley Dr, Toronto, ON M4A 2V8

Emond Montgomery Publications Ltd
One Eglinton Ave E, Toronto, ON M4P 3A1
Tel: 416-975-3925 *Toll Free Tel:* 888-837-0815 *Fax:* 416-975-3924
E-mail: orders@emond.ca
Web Site: www.emond.ca
Founded: 1978
Academic publisher.
Publishes in English.
ISBN Prefix(es): 978-0-920722; 978-1-55239; 978-1-77462
Number of titles published annually: 30 Print; 40 E-Book
Total Titles: 200 Print; 40 E-Book
Returns: Newmarket, ON L3Y 9C3, Contact: Emond Returns *E-mail:* returns@emond.ca
Warehouse: Newmarket, ON L3Y 9C3, Contact: Andy Leitch *E-mail:* emondshipping@emond.ca

ERPI
Division of TC Media Books Inc
1611 Cremazie Blvd E, 10th fl, Montreal, QC H2M 2P2
Tel: 514-334-2690 *Toll Free Tel:* 800-263-3678 *Fax:* 514-334-4720 *Toll Free Fax:* 800-643-4720
E-mail: bienvenue@pearsonerpi.com
Web Site: pearsonerpi.com; pearsonplc.ca
Founded: 1965
Textbooks.
Publishes in English, French.
ISBN Prefix(es): 978-2-7613
Number of titles published annually: 50 Print; 12 CD-ROM; 50 Online
Total Titles: 950 Print; 15 CD-ROM; 50 Online
Membership(s): Association nationale des editeurs de livres (ANEL)

§Fairleigh Dickinson University Press
Affiliate of Rowman & Littlefield
842 Cambie St, Vancouver, BC V6B 2P6
Tel: 604-648-4476 *Fax:* 604-648-4489
E-mail: fdupress@fdu.edu
Web Site: www.fdupress.org
Key Personnel
Dir: James Gifford
Founded: 1967 (in Madison, NJ)
Publishes books in the humanities & social sciences, with special strengths in history & literature. FDU Press relocated to the Vancouver, BC campus in 2017.
Publishes in English.
ISBN Prefix(es): 978-0-8386; 978-1-61147
Number of titles published annually: 30 Print; 30 E-Book
Total Titles: 1,500 Print; 280 E-Book
Distributed by Rowman & Littlefield
Foreign Rep(s): Eurospan (Europe, UK); Scholarly Book Services (Canada); United Publishers Services (Japan)

Fernwood Publishing
2970 Oxford St, Halifax, NS B3L 2W4
Tel: 902-857-1388
E-mail: info@fernpub.ca
Web Site: fernwoodpublishing.ca
Founded: 1991
Social sciences & humanities, emphasizing labour studies, women's studies, gender studies, critical theory & research, political economy, cultural studies & social work for use in undergraduate courses in colleges & universities.
Publishes in English.
ISBN Prefix(es): 978-1-895686; 978-1-55266
Number of titles published annually: 30 Print
Total Titles: 700 Print
Imprints: Roseway Publishing
Branch Office(s)
748 Broadway Ave, Winnipeg, MB R3G 0X3 *Tel:* 204-474-2958 *Fax:* 204-475-2813
U.S. Rep(s): Columbia University Press
Foreign Rep(s): Central Books Ltd (UK)
Orders to: University of Toronto Press Distribution, 5201 Dufferin St, Toronto, ON M3H 5T8 *Tel:* 416-667-7791 *Toll Free Tel:* 800-565-9523 *Fax:* 416-667-7832 *Toll Free Fax:* 800-221-9985 *E-mail:* utpbooks@utpress.utoronto.ca *Web Site:* utpdistribution.ca; Central Books Ltd, 50 Freshwater Rd, Chadwell Heath RM8 1RX, United Kingdom *Tel:* (020) 8525 8800 *Fax:* (020) 8599 2694 *E-mail:* contactus@centralbooks.com *Web Site:* www.centralbooks.com
Returns: University of Toronto Press Distribution, 5201 Dufferin St, Toronto, ON M3H 5T8 *Tel:* 416-667-7791 *Toll Free Tel:* 800-565-9523

Fax: 416-667-7832 *Toll Free Fax:* 800-221-9985 *E-mail:* utpbooks@utpress.utoronto.ca
Web Site: utpdistribution.com

Fifth House Publishers
Division of Fitzhenry & Whiteside Limited
209 Wicksteed Ave, Unit 51, Toronto, ON M4G 0B1
Tel: 905-477-9700 *Toll Free Tel:* 800-387-9776
E-mail: godwit@fitzhenry.ca; bookinfo@fitzhenry.ca (cust serv)
Web Site: www.fifthhousepublishers.ca
Key Personnel
Publr: Tracey Dettman *E-mail:* tdettman@fitzhenry.ca
Founded: 1982
Trade publisher focusing on Western Canadian interest books & First Nations titles.
Publishes in English, French.
ISBN Prefix(es): 978-0-920079; 978-1-895618; 978-1-894004; 978-1-894856; 978-1-897252; 978-1-927083
Number of titles published annually: 18 Print
Total Titles: 211 Print; 1 CD-ROM; 5 E-Book; 1 Audio
Distributed by Fitzhenry & Whiteside Limited
Orders to: Firefly Books, 50 Staples Ave, Unit 1, Richmond Hill, ON L4B 0A7 (US only) *E-mail:* service@fireflybooks.com
Returns: Firefly Books, c/o Frontier Distributing, 145 Gruner Rd, Cheektowaga, NY 14227, United States (US only)
Membership(s): Book Publishers Association of Alberta

Firefly Books Ltd
50 Staples Ave, Unit 1, Richmond Hill, ON L4B 0A7
Tel: 416-499-8412 *Toll Free Tel:* 800-387-6192 (CN); 800-387-5085 (US) *Fax:* 416-499-8313
Toll Free Fax: 800-450-0391 (CN); 800-565-6034 (US)
E-mail: service@fireflybooks.com
Web Site: www.fireflybooks.com
Key Personnel
Pres: Lionel Koffler
Dir, Foreign Rts, Licensing & Contracts: Parisa Michailidis *Tel:* 416-499-8412 ext 157 *E-mail:* parisa@fireflybooks.com
Founded: 1977
North American publisher & distributor of nonfiction adult & children's books.
Publishes in English.
ISBN Prefix(es): 978-0-920668; 978-1-895565; 978-1-896284; 978-1-55209; 978-1-55297; 978-1-55407; 978-1-77085
Number of titles published annually: 220 Print
Total Titles: 2,000 Print; 25 Online
Divisions: The Boston Mills Press
Distributor for The Boston Mills Press; Cottage Life; Firefly Books; Fitzhenry & Whiteside Limited; Kiddy Chronicles Publishing; Mikaya Press; Robert Rose Inc; Ryland, Peters & Small
Foreign Rep(s): Angell Eurosales (Gill Angell & Stewart Siddall) (Denmark, Finland, Iceland, Norway, Scandinavia, Sweden); Ashton International Marketing Services (Julian Ashton) (Asia); Baccus Books (Owen Early) (South Africa, Sub-Saharan Africa); Bookport Associates (Joe Portelli) (Greece, Italy, Malta, Portugal, Southern Europe, Spain); European Marketing Services (Anselm Robinson) (Austria, Belgium, France, Germany, Switzerland, Western Europe); Chris Lloyd Sales & Marketing Services (Northern Europe, UK); Peribo Pty Ltd (Australia); Butler Sims Ltd (Ireland)
Returns: c/o Frontier Distributing, 145 Gruner Rd, Cheektowaga, NY 14227, United States
Membership(s): American Booksellers Association (ABA); Association of Canadian Publishers (ACP)
See separate listing for:
The Boston Mills Press

Fitzhenry & Whiteside Limited
209 Wicksteed Ave, Unit 51, Markham, ON M4G 0B1
SAN: 115-1444
Tel: 905-477-9700 *Toll Free Tel:* 800-387-9776 *Fax:* 905-477-2834
E-mail: bookinfo@fitzhenry.ca
Web Site: www.fitzhenry.ca
Key Personnel
COO: Holly Doll *E-mail:* hdoll@fitzhenry.ca
Mgr, Cust Serv: Judy Ghoura *E-mail:* jghoura@fitzhenry.ca
Founded: 1966
Trade, reference & children's books, educational material for elementary, high school & college.
Publishes in English.
ISBN Prefix(es): 978-0-88902; 978-1-55005; 978-1-55041; 978-1-55285; 978-1-894004 (Fifth House); 978-1-894856 (Fifth House); 978-0-88995; 978-1-55455; 978-1-77050
Number of titles published annually: 70 Print
Total Titles: 1,100 Print
Divisions: Fifth House Publishers; Red Deer Press Inc; Whitecap Books
Distributor for Arbordale Publishing; ArtScroll; Black Moss Press; Boulder Publications; ChiZine Publications; Crossfield Publishing; DC Books; Wm B Eerdmans Publishing Co; Epicenter Press Inc; French Battlefields; fRI Research; Front Matter Press; The Glenbow Museum; Green Jellybean Press; Grub Street Publishing; Icon Empire Press; Inhabit Media Inc; Klorofil Publishing; Kong & Park Inc; Lee & Low Books; McCarney & Associates; McDonald & Woodward Publishing; North Campus Partners; Nunavut Arctic College; Annika Parance Publishing; Peachtree Publishers; Pemmican Publications; Red Fences; The Roadrunner Press; Sands Press; Star Bright Books; teNeues; Tidewater Press; Tilbury House Publishers; Tradewind Books; Tree House Press Inc
U.S. Publishers Represented: Arbordale Publishing; ArtScroll Mesorah; Epicenter Press; Lee & Low Books; McDonald & Woodward; Peachtree Publishers; Road Runner Press; Star Bright Books; teNeues; Tilbury House Publishers
U.S. Rep(s): Firefly Books
See separate listing for:
Fifth House Publishers
Red Deer Press Inc
Whitecap Books

Flammarion Quebec
3700A, Blvd Saint-Laurent, Montreal, QC H2X 2V4
Tel: 514-499-1002 *Fax:* 514-499-1002
E-mail: info@flammarion.qc.ca
Web Site: flammarionquebec.com
Key Personnel
Publr: Erwan Leseul *E-mail:* erwan@edito-flammarionqc.com
Gen Dir, Dist: Guy Gougeon
Founded: 1998
Best sellers, translations, Quebec literature, novels.
Publishes in French.
ISBN Prefix(es): 978-2-89077; 978-2-89811
Number of titles published annually: 25 Print
Total Titles: 400 Print
Distribution Center: Socadis Inc, 420 rue Stinson, Ville St-Laurent, QC H4N 2E9 *Tel:* 514-331-3300 *Toll Free Tel:* 800-361-2847 *Fax:* 514-745-3282 *Toll Free Fax:* 866-803-5422 *E-mail:* socinfo@socadis.com *Web Site:* www.socadis.com

Flanker Press Ltd
1243 Kenmount Rd, Unit 1, Paradise, NL A1L 0V8
Mailing Address: PO Box 2522, Sta C, St John's, NL A1C 6K1
Tel: 709-739-4477 *Toll Free Tel:* 866-739-4420 *Fax:* 709-739-4420
E-mail: info@flankerpress.com; sales@flankerpress.com
Web Site: www.flankerpress.com
Key Personnel
Pres: Garry Cranford *Tel:* 709-739-4477 ext 23
Mgr: Bob Woodworth *Tel:* 709-739-4477 ext 21
Prodn Mgr: Jerry Cranford *Tel:* 709-739-4477 ext 30
Digital Coord: Peter Hanes *Tel:* 709-739-4477 ext 29
Mktg & Publicity Coord: Cassandra Aucoin *Tel:* 709-739-4477 ext 24
Sales Rep: Ed Oldford *Tel:* 709-739-4477 ext 22
Founded: 1994
Wholly Canadian-owned trade book publisher.
Publishes in English.
ISBN Prefix(es): 978-0-9698767; 978-1-894463; 978-1-897317; 978-1-926881; 978-1-77117
Number of titles published annually: 20 Print; 20 E-Book
Imprints: Brazen Books; Flanker Press; Pennywell Books
Membership(s): Association of Canadian Publishers (ACP); Atlantic Publishers Marketing Association

Flowerpot Press
2160 S Service Rd W, Oakville, ON L6L 5N1
Tel: 416-479-0695 *Toll Free Tel:* 866-927-5001
E-mail: info@flowerpotpress.com; order@flowerpotpress.com
Web Site: www.flowerpotpress.com
Founded: 2005
Publish titles for young readers ages 4-12.
Publishes in English.
ISBN Prefix(es): 978-1-77093; 978-1-4867; 978-1-926988
Number of titles published annually: 60 Print; 60 E-Book
Total Titles: 200 Print; 350 E-Book
Editorial Office(s): 142 Second Ave N, Franklin, TN 37064, United States
Distribution Center: Baker & Taylor Publisher Services, 30 Amberwood Pkwy, Ashland, OH 44805, United States (US only) *Tel:* 567-215-0030 *Toll Free Tel:* 888-814-0208 *E-mail:* info@btpubservices.com *Web Site:* www.btpubservices.com

Folklore Publishing
11717-9B Ave NW, Unit 2, Edmonton, AB T6J 7B7
Tel: 780-435-2376
Web Site: www.folklorepublishing.com
Key Personnel
Pres & Publr: Faye Boer *E-mail:* fboer@folklorepublishing.com
Founded: 2001
Publisher of popular history of North America, humor & children's nonfiction.
Publishes in English.
ISBN Prefix(es): 978-1-894864; 978-1-897206 (iThink Books); 978-1-926677; 978-1-77311
Number of titles published annually: 5 Print; 5 E-Book; 10 Audio
Total Titles: 113 Print; 55 E-Book; 11 Audio
Imprints: Full Court Press (sports history); ICON Press (celebrity bios); iThink Books (children's educ titles)
Sales Office(s): Canada Book Distributors/BookLogic, 7735 Wagner Rd NW, Edmonton, AB T6E 5B1 *Tel:* 780-433-9333 *Toll Free Tel:* 800-661-9017 *Fax:* 780-433-9646 *Toll Free Fax:* 800-424-7173 *E-mail:* info@lonepinepublishing.com *Web Site:* www.lonepinepublishing.com

PUBLISHERS

U.S. Rep(s): Lone Pine Publishing
Foreign Rep(s): Canada Book Distributors/Book-Logic (Canada (English-speaking)); Gazelle Book Services Ltd (UK & the continent)
Billing Address: Canada Book Distributors/Book-Logic, 7735 Wagner Rd NW, Edmonton, AB T6E 5B1 *Tel:* 780-433-9333 *Toll Free Tel:* 800-661-9017 *Fax:* 780-433-9646 *Toll Free Fax:* 800-424-7173 *E-mail:* accounts@lonepinepublishing.com *Web Site:* www.lonepinepublishing.com
Orders to: Canada Book Distributors/BookLogic, 7735 Wagner Rd NW, Edmonton, AB T6E 5B1 *Tel:* 780-433-9333 *Toll Free Tel:* 800-661-9017 *Fax:* 780-433-9646 *Toll Free Fax:* 800-424-7173 *E-mail:* accounts@lonepinepublishing.com *Web Site:* www.lonepinepublishing.com
Returns: Canada Book Distributors/BookLogic, 7735 Wagner Rd NW, Edmonton, AB T6E 5B1 *Tel:* 780-433-9333 *Toll Free Tel:* 800-661-9017 *Fax:* 780-433-9646 *Toll Free Fax:* 800-424-7173 *E-mail:* info@lonepinepublishing.com *Web Site:* www.lonepinepublishing.com
Distribution Center: Canada Book Distributors/BookLogic, 7735 Wagner Rd NW, Edmonton, AB T6E 5B1 *Tel:* 780-433-9333 *Toll Free Tel:* 800-661-9017 *Fax:* 780-433-9646 *Toll Free Fax:* 800-424-7173 *E-mail:* accounts@lonepinepublishing.com *Web Site:* www.lonepinepublishing.com
Lone Pine Publishing, 4471 S 134 Place, Tukwila, WA 98168, United States, Sales Mgr: Michael Campbell *Tel:* 253-394-0400 *Toll Free Tel:* 800-518-3541 *Fax:* 253-394-0405 *Toll Free Fax:* 800-548-1169 *E-mail:* order@lonepinepublishing.com *Web Site:* www.lonepinepublishing.com
Membership(s): Book Publishers Association of Alberta

Gaetan Morin Editeur
Imprint of Cheneliere Education Inc
5800, rue St-Denis, bureau 900, Montreal, QC H2S 3L5
Tel: 514-273-1066 *Toll Free Tel:* 800-565-5531 *Fax:* 514-276-0324 *Toll Free Fax:* 800-814-0324
E-mail: info@cheneliere.ca
Web Site: www.cheneliere.ca
Key Personnel
Pres & Gen Mgr: Patrick Lutzy *E-mail:* patrick.lutzy@tc.tc
Founded: 1977
Textbooks, college, university & professional books.
Publishes in French.
ISBN Prefix(es): 978-2-89105; 978-0-88612; 978-2-910749; 978-2-89632
Number of titles published annually: 20 Print; 1 CD-ROM
Total Titles: 300 Print; 2 CD-ROM

Golden Meteorite Press
11919 82 St NW, Suite 103, Edmonton, AB T5B 2W4
Tel: 587-783-0059
Web Site: goldenmeteoritepress.com
Key Personnel
Contact: Austin Mardon *E-mail:* aamardon@yahoo.ca
Founded: 1989
Preferred submission is outline. Canadian SASE or IRC is required or else material is recycled. Accept fiction & nonfiction mss in all categories & genres. Submit to editor. Response in 12 weeks on all complete ms submissions. No phone calls please.
Publishes in English, French.
ISBN Prefix(es): 978-1-895385; 978-1-897472; 978-1-894573; 978-0-929024; 978-1-897480; 978-1-77369
Number of titles published annually: 11 Print
Total Titles: 85 Print

§Goose Lane Editions
500 Beaverbrook Ct, Suite 330, Fredericton, NB E3B 5X4
SAN: 115-3420
Tel: 506-450-4251 *Toll Free Tel:* 888-926-8377 *Fax:* 506-459-4991
E-mail: orders@gooselane.com
Web Site: www.gooselane.com
Key Personnel
Publr: Susanne Alexander *Tel:* 506-450-4251 ext 222 *E-mail:* s.alexander@gooselane.com
Mng Ed: Alan Sheppard *Tel:* 506-450-4251 ext 226 *E-mail:* editor@gooselane.com
Fiction Acqs Ed: Bethany Gibson *E-mail:* fiction@gooselane.com
Nonfiction Acqs Ed: Simon Thibault *E-mail:* nonfiction@gooselane.com
Poetry Ed: Ross Leckie *E-mail:* poetry@gooselane.com
Publg Asst: Angela Williams *Tel:* 506-450-4251 ext 225 *E-mail:* awilliams@gooselane.com
Founded: 1954
Accepts submissions from Canadian citizens & permanent residents.
Publishes in English.
ISBN Prefix(es): 978-0-920110; 978-0-919197; 978-0-86492; 978-1-77310
Number of titles published annually: 30 Print; 15 E-Book; 7 Audio
Total Titles: 518 Print; 258 E-Book; 39 Audio
Distributed by University of Toronto Press
Distributor for Anchorage Press; Art Gallery of Hamilton; Art Gallery of Nova Scotia; Art Gallery of Ontario; Beaverbrook Art Gallery
Foreign Rep(s): Gazelle Book Services (European Union, UK)
Distribution Center: University of Toronto Press Distribution, 5201 Dufferin St, Toronto, ON M3H 5T8 *Toll Free Tel:* 800-565-9523 *Toll Free Fax:* 800-221-9985 *E-mail:* utpbooks@utpress.utoronto.ca
University of Toronto Press Distribution, 2250 Military Rd, Tonawanda, NY 14150, United States *Toll Free Tel:* 800-221-9523 *Toll Free Fax:* 800-221-9985
Membership(s): American Audiobook Publishers Association; Association of Canadian Publishers (ACP); Atlantic Publishers Marketing Association; Literary Press Group of Canada

Greystone Books Ltd
Affiliate of The Heritage Group
343 Railway St, Suite 302, Vancouver, BC V6A 1A4
Tel: 604-875-1550 *Fax:* 604-875-1556
E-mail: info@greystonebooks.com; rights@greystonebooks.com
Web Site: www.greystonebooks.com
Key Personnel
Publr & CEO: Rob Sanders
Publr: Jen Gauthier
Creative Dir: Jessica Sullivan
Consulting Creative Dir, Greystone Kids: Sara Gillingham
Edit Dir: Jennifer Croll
Mktg Dir: Megan Jones *Tel:* 604-875-1550 ext 207 *E-mail:* megan.jones@greystonebooks.com
Rts Dir & Prodn Mgr: Andrea Damiani *Tel:* 604-875-1550 ext 201
Ed: Paula Ayer
Ed, Aldana Libros, Greystone Kids: Patsy Aldana
Ed, Middle Reader, Greystone Kids: Linda Prussen
Ed, Picture Books, Greystone Kids: Kallie George
Edit Assoc: Lucy Kenward
Edit Asst: James Penco
Publg Mgr & Contract Mgr, Greystone Kids: Lara LeMoal
Publg Assoc: Toni Banyard
Publg Asst: Kathy Nguyen
Mktg Coord: Makenzie Pratt
Opers Coord & Asst to Publr: Alex Cooper
Sales & Mktg Coord: Hanna Nicholls

CANADIAN PUBLISHERS

Designer: Belle Wuthrich
Jr Designer: Fiona Siu
Natl Publicist: Corina Eberle
Founded: 1993
Publishes in English.
ISBN Prefix(es): 978-0-88894; 978-1-55054; 978-1-55365; 978-0-88833; 978-1-77100; 978-1-927435; 978-1-77164
Number of titles published annually: 30 Print
Total Titles: 400 Print
Imprints: Aldana Libros; Greystone Kids
Distributed by University of Toronto Press
U.S. Rep(s): Publishers Group West
Foreign Rights: AC2 Literary Agency (kids list) (Italy); Eliane Benisti Agency (France); ChoiceMaker Korea Co (kids list) (South Korea); Iniciativas Empresariales Ilustrata (Portugal, Spain); Japan UNI Agency (Japan); Libris Agency (Turkey); Andrew Nurnberg Associates Warwaw (Poland); Peony Literary Agency (China); Susanne Rolf (Germany); Livia Stoia Literary Agency (Eastern Europe)
Orders to: University of Toronto Press Distribution, 5201 Dufferin St, Toronto, ON M3H 5T8 (through Pubnet) *Tel:* 416-667-7791 *Toll Free Tel:* 800-565-9523 *Fax:* 416-667-7832 *Toll Free Fax:* 800-221-9985 *E-mail:* utpbooks@utpress.utoronto.ca SAN: 115-1134; NBNi/Ingram, One Deltic Ave, Rooksley, Milton Keynes MK13 8LD, United Kingdom *Tel:* (01752) 202301 *E-mail:* nbni.cservs@ingramcontent.com; Ingram Publisher Services International, 1400 Broadway, Suite 520, New York, NY 10018, United States *Tel:* 212-340-8153 *E-mail:* ips_intlsales@ingramcontent.com; Publishers Group West/Ingram Publisher Services, 210 American Dr, Jackson, TN 38301, United States (submit orders to sales rep via IPS Cart on iPage) *Toll Free Tel:* 866-400-5351 *Toll Free Fax:* 800-838-1149 *E-mail:* ips@ingramcontent.com *Web Site:* www.ingramcontent.com SAN: 631-8630
Membership(s): Association for the Export of Canadian Books; Association of American Publishers (AAP); The Association of Book Publishers of British Columbia (ABPBC); Association of Canadian Publishers (ACP)

Groundwood Books
Subsidiary of House of Anansi Press Inc
128 Sterling Rd, Lower Level, Toronto, ON M6R 2B7
Tel: 416-363-4343 *Fax:* 416-363-1017
E-mail: customerservice@houseofanansi.com
Web Site: www.houseofanansi.com
Key Personnel
Owner & Chmn of the Bd: Scott Griffin
Pres: Semareh Al-Hillal
VP, Fin: Allan Ibarra
VP, Sales & Mktg: Karen Brochu *Tel:* 416-363-4343 ext 243 *E-mail:* kbrochu@groundwoodbooks.com
Publr: Karen Li
Instl Mktg Dir: Fred Horler *Tel:* 416-363-4343 ext 228 *E-mail:* fhorler@groundwoodbooks.com
Trade Mktg Dir: Laura Chapnick *Tel:* 416-363-4343 ext 242 *E-mail:* lchapnick@groundwoodbooks.com
Sr Mng Ed: Maria Golikova
Natl Accts Mgr: Jessey Glibbery *Tel:* 416-363-4343 ext 233 *E-mail:* jglibbery@groundwoodbooks.com
Rts Mgr: Sonya Lalli *Tel:* 416-363-4343 ext 251 *E-mail:* slalli@groundwoodbooks.com
Founded: 1978
Publish children's books, picture books, novels, nonfiction & folktales; publishes in Spanish also.
Publishes in English.
ISBN Prefix(es): 978-0-88899; 978-1-55498; 978-1-77306
Number of titles published annually: 25 Print

CANADIAN PUBLISHERS

Total Titles: 500 Print
Sales Office(s): Martin & Associates Sales Agency, 594 Windermere Ave, Toronto, ON M6S 3L8 (ON & QC), Contact: Michael Martin *Tel:* 416-460-7115 *Fax:* 647-372-5308 *E-mail:* michael@martinsalesagency.ca
Foreign Rights: AnatoliaLit Agency (Cansu Akkoyun) (Turkey); Bardon Chinese Media Agency (Cynthia Chang & Shirley Vivi) (China); Casanovas & Lynch Literary Agency (Marina Penalva Halpin) (Latin America, Portugal, Spain); Choicemaker Korea (John Choi & Ha Young Choi) (South Korea); Paul & Peter Fritz Agency (Antonia Fritz) (Germany); Japan UNI Agency Inc (Takeshi Oyama & Maiko Fujinaga) (Japan); Sebes & Bisseling Literary Agency (Lester Hekking) (Netherlands, Scandinavia)
Returns: Ingram Publisher Services, 191 Edwards Dr, Jackson, TN 38301, United States
Distribution Center: University of Toronto Press Distribution Division, 5201 Dufferin St, Toronto, ON M3H 5T8 *Tel:* 416-667-7791 *Toll Free Tel:* 800-565-9523 *Fax:* 416-667-7832 *Toll Free Fax:* 800-221-9985 *E-mail:* utpbooks@utpress.utoronto.ca SAN: 115-1134
Publishers Group West, an Ingram brand, 1700 Fourth St, Berkeley, CA 94710, United States *Toll Free Tel:* 800-343-4499; 866-400-5351 *Toll Free Fax:* 800-351-5073 *E-mail:* ips@ingramcontent.com
Membership(s): Association of Canadian Publishers (ACP); International Board on Books for Young People (IBBY); Organization of Book Publishers of Ontario (OBPO)

§Groupe Educalivres Inc
1699, blvd le Corbusier, bureau 350, Laval, QC H7S 1Z3
Tel: 514-334-8466 *Toll Free Tel:* 800-567-3671 (info serv) *Fax:* 514-334-8387 *Toll Free Fax:* 800-267-4387
E-mail: infoservice@grandduc.com
Web Site: www.educalivres.com
Key Personnel
VP, Fin & Admin: Joe Cristofaro
School & professional textbooks.
Publishes in English, French.
ISBN Prefix(es): 978-2-7607; 978-0-03; 978-2-7655
Number of titles published annually: 12 Print
Divisions: Editions Grand Duc; Grand Duc en ligne

Groupe Modulo Inc
Imprint of TC Media Books Inc
c/o TC Media Books Inc, 5800 St Denis St, Suite 900, Montreal, QC H2S 3L5
Tel: 514-273-1066 *Toll Free Tel:* 800-565-5531 *Fax:* 514-276-0234 *Toll Free Fax:* 800-814-0324
E-mail: clientele@tc.tc
Web Site: www.groupemodulo.com
Founded: 1975
School books, dictionaries, professional & technical textbooks.
Publishes in English, French.
ISBN Prefix(es): 978-2-920922; 978-2-89443; 978-2-89113; 978-2-920210; 978-2-89593; 978-0-88560
Number of titles published annually: 100 Print
Total Titles: 2,000 Print

Groupe Sogides Inc
Division of Groupe Livre Quebecor Media Inc
955 rue Amherst, Montreal, QC H2L 3K4
Tel: 514-523-1182 *Fax:* 514-597-0370
Web Site: sogides.com
Key Personnel
Pres, Sogides: Celine Massicotte
Rts Dir, Groupe Homme: Florence Bisch
Founded: 1967

Practical books, cookbooks, biographies, general interest books, popular psychology, art books, poetry, diaries, art calendars & stationery, novels, drama.
Publishes in French.
ISBN Prefix(es): 978-2-7619; 978-0-7760; 978-2-89026; 978-2-89194; 978-2-89044; 978-2-89043; 978-2-89347
Number of titles published annually: 150 Print
Total Titles: 2,000 Print
Imprints: Les Editions de l'Homme; La Griffe; Le Jour Editeur; Juniper Publishing; Petit Homme; Utilis
Subsidiaries: Le Groupe Ville-Marie Litterature
Branch Office(s)
Les Editions de l'Homme, Immeuble Paryseine, 3 Allee de la Seine, 94854 Ivry Cedex, France, Contact: Anne Da Cunha-Guillegault *Tel:* 01 49 59 11 56 *Fax:* 01 49 59 11 33
Distributed by Vivendi Universal Publishing
Distributor for Actif; Atlas; Berlitz Fixot; Chouette; Le Cri; Edimag; Fleuve Noir; Gault & Millau; Heritage; De L'Homme; Hors Collection; JCL; Albin Michel Jeunesse; Julliard; Robert Laffont; Langues pour tous; Albin Michel; Albin Michel Education; Editions Modus Vivendi; Nathan; Nathan Education; Option Sante; Olivier Orban; Perrin; Plon; Pocket; La Presse; Presses de la Cite (Poche); Presses de la Cite Litterature; Presses Libres; Michel Quintin; Quinze; Du Rocher; Rouge & Or; Seghers; Selection du Reader's Digest; Solar; Time-Life; Trapeze; Usborne; Claire Vigne; VLB; XYZ (Typo Seulement)
U.S. Publishers Represented: Reader's Digest
Distribution Center: Messageries ADP, 2315, rue de la Province, Longueuil, QC J4G 1G4 *Tel:* 450-640-1237 *Web Site:* www.messageries-adp.com

Guerin Editeur Ltee
800, Blvd Industriel, bureau 200, St-Jean-sur-Richelieu, QC J3B 8G4
Tel: 514-842-3481 *Toll Free Tel:* 800-398-8337 *Fax:* 514-842-4923
E-mail: info@guerin-editeur.qc.ca
Web Site: www.guerin-editeur.qc.ca
Key Personnel
Pres: France Larochelle *E-mail:* france.larochelle@guerin-editeur.qc.ca
Founded: 1970
Publisher of books for schools from kindergarten to university.
Publishes in English, French.
ISBN Prefix(es): 978-2-7601
Number of titles published annually: 80 Print; 2 Audio
Total Titles: 1,500 Print; 43 Audio
Foreign Rep(s): Librairie du Quebec (France); Librairie Pelagie (Eastern Canada); Patrimoine SPRL (Belgium); Servidis SA (Switzerland); Sopodriff SARL (Africa); Pierre Carme Yves Levy (Haiti)

§Guernica Editions Inc
287 Templemead Dr, Hamilton, ON L8W 2W4
Tel: 905-599-5304
E-mail: info@guernicaeditions.com
Web Site: www.guernicaeditions.com; www.facebook.com/guernicaed
Key Personnel
Publr & Chief Admin Offr: Connie McParland *E-mail:* conniemcparland@guernicaeditions.com
Publr & Ed-in-Chief: Michael Mirolla *E-mail:* michaelmirolla@guernicaeditions.com
Assoc Publr: Anna van Valkenburg *E-mail:* annavanvalkenburg@guernicaeditions.com
Founded: 1978
Literary press specializing in Canadian writing (prose, poetry, literary criticism, drama & social studies), translation into English, some foreign publications in the English language.
Publishes in English.
ISBN Prefix(es): 978-0-919349; 978-0-920717; 978-2-89135; 978-1-55071; 978-1-77183
Number of titles published annually: 50 Print; 25 E-Book; 6 Audio
Total Titles: 550 Print
Imprints: Guernica World Editions (non-Canadian authors); MiroLand (sci-fi, mystery, memoir); 1366 Books (experimental fiction)
Sales Office(s): Literary Press Group, 425 Adelaide St W, Suite 700, Toronto, ON M5V 3C1, Sales Mgr & US Rep: Tan Light *Tel:* 416-483-1321 *Fax:* 416-483-2510 *E-mail:* sales@lpg.ca *Web Site:* www.lpg.ca
Distribution Center: University of Toronto Press, 5201 Dufferin St, Toronto, ON M3H 5T8 *Toll Free Tel:* 800-565-9523 *Toll Free Fax:* 800-221-9985
Independent Publishers Group (IPG), 814 N Franklin St, Suite 100, Chicago, IL 60610, United States *Tel:* 312-337-0747 *Toll Free Tel:* 800-888-4741 *Fax:* 312-337-5985 *E-mail:* orders@ipgbook.com *Web Site:* www.ipgbook.com
Membership(s): Association of Canadian Publishers (ACP); Association of English-language Publishers of Quebec (AELAQ); BookNet-Canada; Canada Council for the Arts; Literary Press Group of Canada; Ontario Arts Council; Organization of Book Publishers of Ontario (OBPO)

Hancock House Publishers Ltd
19313 Zero Ave, Surrey, BC V3S 9R9
Tel: 604-538-1114 *Toll Free Tel:* 800-938-1114 *Fax:* 604-538-2262 *Toll Free Fax:* 800-983-2262
E-mail: sales@hancockhouse.com; info@hancockhouse.com
Web Site: www.hancockhouse.com
Key Personnel
Pres: David Hancock
Founded: 1975
Biographical nature guide books.
Publishes in English.
ISBN Prefix(es): 978-0-88839; 978-0-919654; 978-1-55205
Number of titles published annually: 20 Print
Total Titles: 450 Print
Branch Office(s)
4550 Birch Bay-Lynden Rd, Unit 104, Blaine, WA 98230-9436, United States
Foreign Rep(s): Gazelle Book Services Ltd (UK)

§Harbour Publishing Co Ltd
4437 Rondeview Rd, Madeira Park, BC V0N 2H0
Mailing Address: PO Box 219, Madeira Park, BC V0N 2H0
Tel: 604-883-2730 *Toll Free Tel:* 800-667-2988 *Fax:* 604-883-9451 *Toll Free Fax:* 877-604-9449
E-mail: info@harbourpublishing.com; orders@harbourpublishing.com
Web Site: harbourpublishing.com
Key Personnel
Publr: Howard White
Mktg Mgr: Marisa Alps
Founded: 1974
History & culture of British Columbia & West Coast, including fiction, nonfiction & poetry by Canadian authors.
Publishes in English.
ISBN Prefix(es): 978-0-920080; 978-1-55017; 978-0-9738058
Number of titles published annually: 20 Print; 1 CD-ROM; 1 Audio
Total Titles: 600 Print; 1 CD-ROM; 5 Audio
Imprints: Lost Moose Books
Distributor for Nightwood Editions
Foreign Rep(s): Ampersand Inc (Canada)

Returns: 12672 Lagoon Rd, Madeira Park, BC V0N 2H0 *Tel:* 604-883-2460
Warehouse: 12672 Lagoon Rd, Madeira Park, BC V0N 2H0 *Tel:* 604-883-2460
Distribution Center: Ingram Book Co (print on demand titles) *Toll Free Tel:* 800-234-6737 (electronic ordering); 800-937-8000 *Toll Free Fax:* 800-876-0186 *E-mail:* orders@ingrambook.com
Publishers Group West (Europe & US) *Toll Free Tel:* 866-400-5351 *Toll Free Fax:* 800-838-1149 *E-mail:* ips@ingramcontent.com

§Harlequin Enterprises Ltd
Division of HarperCollins
Bay Adelaide Centre, East Tower, 22 Adelaide St W, 41st fl, Toronto, ON M5H 4E3
SAN: 115-3749
Tel: 416-445-5860 *Toll Free Tel:* 888-432-4879; 800-370-5838 (ebook inquiries)
E-mail: customerservice@harlequin.com
Web Site: www.harlequin.com
Key Personnel
CEO, Harlequin & HarperCollins Canada: Craig Swinwood
CFO, HarperCollins Canada & Harlequin: Kirk Marshall
EVP & Publr, Harlequin Brand Group: Brent Lewis
EVP & Publr, Harlequin Trade Publishing: Loriana Sacilotto *E-mail:* loriana.sacilotto@harpercollins.com
EVP, Direct to Consumer: Christina Clifford
VP, Edit, Harlequin Brand Group: Dianne Moggy *E-mail:* diane.moggy@harpercollins.com
VP, Sales: Alex Osuszek
VP & Assoc Publr: Farah Mullick
VP & Assoc Publr, Harlequin Trade Publishing Books: Amy Jones
Sr Dir, Intl Publg: Emily Martin
Dir, Channel Mktg: Randy Chan
Dir, Creative Opers: Roxanne Finkelstein
Edit Dir, Canary Press & Graydon House Books: Susan Swinwood
Edit Dir, MIRA: Nicole Brebner
Mktg Dir: Lindsey Reeder
Global Mng Ed: Punam Patel
Exec Ed: Kathleen Scheibling
Sr Ed: Stephanie Doig
Ed: Dana Grimaldi; Adrienne Macintosh
Ed, Harlequin Intrigue: Emma Cole
Ed, Love Inspired: Katie Gowrie
Assoc Ed, Graydon House Books: Sara Rodgers
Specialist, Brand Edit: Deirdre McCluskey
Sr Channel Mktg Mgr: Pamela Osti
Sr Mktg Mgr: Rachel Haller; Diane Lavoie
Mgr, Author Engagement: Miranda Indrigo
Natl Acct Mgr: Marianna Ricciuto
Founded: 1949 (in Winnipeg, MB, CN)
Publishes in more than 30 languages in 150 international markets on 6 continents.
Publishes in English, French.
ISBN Prefix(es): 978-0-373; 978-1-55166; 978-0-7783; 978-1-58314; 978-1-55254; 978-1-4268; 978-1-4603; 978-1-4592
Number of titles published annually: 1,320 Print; 30 Online; 1,530 E-Book; 75 Audio
Total Titles: 30 Online; 1,850 E-Book; 95 Audio
Imprints: Avon; Canary Street Press; Carina Press (digital-first); Graydon House Books (commercial women's fiction); Hanover Square Press; Harlequin Dare; Harlequin Desire; Harlequin Heartwarming; Harlequin Historical; Harlequin Intrigue; Harlequin Kimani Arabesque; Harlequin Kimani Press (African-American); Harlequin Kimani Romance; Harlequin Kimani TRU; Harlequin LUNA (fantasy/paranormal); Harlequin Medical Romance; Harlequin MIRA; Harlequin Nocturne; Harlequin Presents; Harlequin Romance; Harlequin Romantic Suspense; Harlequin Special Edition; Love Inspired® (inspirational romance); Love Inspired® Suspense; Park Row Books; Silhouette Intimate Moments (series romance); Spice (erotic fiction); Worldwide Mystery
Divisions: Harlequin Brand Group; Harlequin Trade Publishing Group
Branch Office(s)
195 Broadway, 24th fl, New York, NY 10007, United States *Tel:* 212-207-7000 SAN: 200-2450
Foreign Office(s): Harlequin Mills & Boon, Westerhill Rd, Bishopbriggs, Glasgow G64 2QT, United Kingdom *E-mail:* csmillsandboon@harpercollins.co.uk *Web Site:* www.millsandboon.co.uk
Advertising Agency: Vickers & Benson-Direct
Distribution Center: Harlequin Fulfillment Services, 3010 Walden Ave, Depew, NY 14043, United States *Tel:* 716-686-1800 *Web Site:* harlequinfulfillmentservices.com
Membership(s): Association of American Publishers (AAP); Association of Canadian Publishers (ACP); Book Industry Study Group (BISG)
See separate listing for:
Worldwide Library

§HarperCollins Canada Ltd
Division of HarperCollins Publishers
22 Adelaide St W, 41st fl, Toronto, ON M5H 4E3
Tel: 416-975-9334
E-mail: hcorder@harpercollins.com
Web Site: www.harpercollins.ca
Key Personnel
CEO, Harlequin & HarperCollins Canada: Craig Swinwood
CFO, HarperCollins Canada & Harlequin: Kirk Marshall
SVP & Exec Publr: Iris Tupholme
SVP, Sales & Mktg: Leo MacDonald
Publr, Patrick Crean Editions: Patrick Crean
Sr Coun & Dir, Legal Aff: Jeremy Rawlings
Sr Dir, Mktg & Publicity: Cory Beatty
Dir, Subs Rts & Publg Opers: Lisa Rundle
Founded: 1989
Literary & commercial fiction, nonfiction, children's books, cookbooks, reference & spiritual books. Distribute for all HarperCollins companies in the US, UK & Australia.
Publishes in English.
ISBN Prefix(es): 978-1-4434
Number of titles published annually: 100 Print
Total Titles: 1,500 Print
Imprints: Collins; Patrick Crean Editions; Harper Avenue; HarperCollins Canada; Harper Perennial; HarperWeekend

Heritage House Publishing Co Ltd
Member of The Heritage Group
1075 Pendergast St, No 103, Victoria, BC V8V 0A1
Tel: 250-360-0829 *Fax:* 250-386-0829
E-mail: heritage@heritagehouse.ca; info@heritagehouse.ca; orders@heritagehouse.ca
Web Site: www.heritagehouse.ca
Key Personnel
Publr: Rodger Touchie
Edit Dir: Lara Kordic
Edit Coord: Nandini Thaker
Mktg & Publicity Coord: Monica Miller *E-mail:* monica@heritagehouse.ca
Founded: 1969
Publishes in English.
ISBN Prefix(es): 978-1-895811; 978-1-894384; 978-1-894974; 978-0-919214; 978-0-9690546; 978-1-926613; 978-1-926936; 978-1-927051; 978-1-927527
Number of titles published annually: 30 Print
Total Titles: 175 Print
Orders to: Heritage Group Distribution, 19272 96 Ave, Suite 8, Surrey, BC V4N 4C1 *Tel:* 604-881-7067 *Toll Free Tel:* 800-665-3302 *Fax:* 604-881-7068 *Toll Free Fax:* 800-566-3336 *E-mail:* orders@hgdistribution.com *Web Site:* hgdistribution.com
Distribution Center: Heritage Group Distribution, 19272 96 Ave, Suite 8, Surrey, BC V4N 4C1 *Tel:* 604-881-7067 *Toll Free Tel:* 800-665-3302 *Fax:* 604-881-7068 *Toll Free Fax:* 800-566-3336 *E-mail:* orders@hgdistribution.com *Web Site:* hgdistribution.com
Membership(s): The Association of Book Publishers of British Columbia (ABPBC); Association of Canadian Publishers (ACP)

Les Heures bleues
4455 Coolbrook Ave, No 2, Montreal, QC H4A 3G1
Tel: 438-399-2077 *Fax:* 450-671-7718
E-mail: editions.lesheuresbleues@gmail.com
Web Site: www.heuresbleues.com
Founded: 1996
Publishes in French.
ISBN Prefix(es): 978-2-922265
Number of titles published annually: 8 Print
Total Titles: 90 Print; 40 E-Book
Distribution Center: Diffusion Dimedia, 539, blvd Lebeau, Montreal, QC H4N 1S2 *Tel:* 515-336-3941 *E-mail:* info@dimedia.qc.ca *Web Site:* www.dimedia.ca
La Librarie du Quebec a Paris, 30, rue Gay-Lussac, 75005 Paris, France *Tel:* 01 43 54 49 02 *E-mail:* libraires@librairieduquebec.fr *Web Site:* www.librairieduquebec.fr
Membership(s): Association nationale des editeurs de livres (ANEL)

§House of Anansi Press Inc
128 Sterling Rd, Lower Level, Toronto, ON M6R 2B7
Tel: 416-363-4343 *Fax:* 416-363-1017
E-mail: customerservice@houseofanansi.com
Web Site: houseofanansi.com
Key Personnel
Owner & Chmn of the Bd: Scott Griffin
Pres: Semareh Al-Hillal
VP, Fin: Allan Ibarra
VP, Publg Opers: Matt Williams
Publr: Karen Brochu
Assoc Publr: Janie Yoon
Dir, Cross-Media Dept: Laura Brady
Edit Dir: Douglas Richmond
Instl Mktg Dir: Fred Horler
Trade Mktg Dir: Laura Chapnick
Sr Mng Ed: Michelle MacAleese
Mng Ed: Maria Golikova
Poetry Ed: Kevin Connolly
Prodn Ed: Grace Shaw
Asst Ed: Joshua Greenspon
Acct Mgr, Western CN: Natassja Barry
Rts Mgr: Erica Mojzes
Sales Mgr: Jessey Glibbery
Print Prodn Coord: Ricky Lima
Sr Designer: Alysia Shewchuk
Publicist: Kirsten Brassard; Curtis Samual
Assoc Publicist: Jamin Mike
Intl Sales & Rts Assoc: Mariana Linares
Mktg Assoc: Zoe Kelsey
Sales Assoc: Katherine Kakoutis
Rts Specialist-at-Large: Sonya Lalli
Founded: 1967
Literary publishing; fiction, poetry, criticism & belles lettres.
Publishes in English.
ISBN Prefix(es): 978-0-88784; 978-1-77089; 978-1-48700
Number of titles published annually: 30 Print
Total Titles: 200 Print
Imprints: Ambrosia; Anansi International; Arachnide Editions; Astoria; Spiderline (crime fiction)
Subsidiaries: Groundwood Books
Foreign Rights: AnatoliaLit Agency (Amy Marie Spangler) (Turkey); Bestun Agency (Yumi Chun) (South Korea); Big Apple Agency Inc (Claire Feng) (Mainland China); Big Apple Agency Inc (Chris Lin) (Taiwan); BookLab Literary Agnecy (Piotr Wawrzenczyk) (Poland);

CANADIAN PUBLISHERS

Casanovas & Lynch Literary Agency (Marina Penalna Halpin) (Brazil, Latin America, Portugal, Spain); Paul & Peter Fritz Agency (Antonia Fritz) (Germany); Japan UNI Agency Inc (Miko Yamanouchi & Megumi Sakai) (Japan); Simona Kessler Agency (Simona Kessler) (Romania); Kristen Olson Literary Agency (Tereza Dubova & Martina Knapkova) (Czechia)
Distribution Center: University of Toronto Press Distribution Division, 5201 Dufferin St, Toronto, ON M3H 5T8 *Tel:* 416-667-7791 *Toll Free Tel:* 800-565-9523 *Fax:* 416-667-7832 *Toll Free Fax:* 800-221-9985 *E-mail:* utpbooks@utpress.utoronto.ca SAN: 115-1134
Publishers Group West, 1700 Fourth St, Berkeley, CA 94710, United States (US orders) *Toll Free Tel:* 866-400-5351 *Toll Free Fax:* 800-838-1149 *E-mail:* ips@ingramcontent.com *Web Site:* www.ingramcontent.com SAN: 631-8630
See separate listing for:
Groundwood Books

C D Howe Institute
67 Yonge St, Suite 300, Toronto, ON M5E 1J8
Tel: 416-865-1904 *Fax:* 416-865-1866
E-mail: cdhowe@cdhowe.org
Web Site: www.cdhowe.org
Key Personnel
CEO: William B P Robson *E-mail:* bill_robson@cdhowe.org
Pres: Duncan Munn *E-mail:* dmunn@cdhowe.org
VP & Ed: James Fleming *E-mail:* jfleming@cdhowe.org
Founded: 1958
Economics & social policy studies.
Publishes in English, French.
ISBN Prefix(es): 978-0-88806
Number of titles published annually: 50 Print
Total Titles: 150 Print

Inclusion Press International
47 Indian Trail, Toronto, ON M6R 1Z8
Tel: 416-658-5363 *Fax:* 416-658-5067
E-mail: inclusionpress@inclusion.com
Web Site: inclusion.com
Key Personnel
Co-Dir: Lynda Kuhn; Jack Pearpoint *E-mail:* jack@inclusion.com
Founded: 1989
Inclusion, change, diversity & community.
Publishes in English.
ISBN Prefix(es): 978-1-895418
Number of titles published annually: 5 Print; 2 CD-ROM; 2 E-Book
Total Titles: 100 Print; 10 CD-ROM; 4 E-Book

L'Institut canadien du droit des ressources, see Canadian Institute of Resources Law (L'Institut canadien du droit des ressources)

Institute for Research on Public Policy (IRPP)
1470 Peel St, No 200, Montreal, QC H3A 1T1
Tel: 514-985-2461 *Fax:* 514-985-2559
E-mail: irpp@irpp.org
Web Site: irpp.org
Key Personnel
Pres & CEO: Jennifer Ditchburn *E-mail:* jditchburn@irpp.org
VP, Opers: Suzanne Ostiguy McIntyre *Tel:* 514-787-0740 *E-mail:* smcintyre@irpp.org
VP, Res: France St-Hilaire *E-mail:* fsthilaire@irpp.org
Exec Dir, Centre of Excellence on the Canadian Federation: Charles Breton *E-mail:* cbreton@irpp.org
Res Dir: Colin Busby *E-mail:* cbusby@irpp.org; Natalia Mishagina *E-mail:* nmishagina@irpp.org
Founded: 1972
Research on public policy.
Publishes in English, French.
ISBN Prefix(es): 978-0-88645; 978-0-920380

Number of titles published annually: 1,000 Online
Total Titles: 500 Print

§Institute of Intergovernmental Relations
Queen's University, Robert Sutherland Hall, Rm 412, Kingston, ON K7L 3N6
Tel: 613-533-2080
E-mail: iigr@queensu.ca
Web Site: www.queensu.ca/iigr
Key Personnel
Dir: Dr Christian Leurpecht
Pubns Coord & Admin Secy: Mary Kennedy
Founded: 1965
Publish research & other scholarly work on Canadian federalism & intergovernmental relations; ethnicity, government & political science.
Publishes in English, French.
ISBN Prefix(es): 978-1-55339
Number of titles published annually: 2 Print; 69 E-Book
Total Titles: 108 Print; 85 Online; 69 E-Book
Distributed by McGill-Queen's University Press (CN)

Institute of Psychological Research, Inc, see IRP editeur

Institute of Public Administration of Canada
1075 Bay St, Suite 401, Toronto, ON M5S 2B1
Tel: 416-924-8787 *Fax:* 416-924-4992
E-mail: ntl@ipac.ca
Web Site: www.ipac.ca
Key Personnel
CEO: David Fulford *E-mail:* dfulford@ipac.ca
Mng Ed: Christy Paddick *Tel:* 905-447-6351 (cell) *E-mail:* cpaddick@ipac.ca
Ed: Evert A Lindquist
Founded: 1947
National bilingual English/French nonprofit organization, concerned with the theory & practice of public management, with 20 regional groups across Canada. Provide networks & forums regionally, nationally & internationally. Specialize in political science, Canadian history & Canadian law.
Publishes in English, French.
ISBN Prefix(es): 978-0-919400; 978-0-920715; 978-0-919696; 978-1-55061
Number of titles published annually: 10 Print; 5 E-Book
Total Titles: 600 Print; 50 Online; 10 E-Book; 5 Audio

§International Self-Counsel Press Ltd
1481 Charlotte Rd, North Vancouver, BC V7J 1H1
SAN: 115-0545
Tel: 604-986-3366 *Toll Free Tel:* 800-663-3007
E-mail: orders@self-counsel.com; sales@self-counsel.com
Web Site: www.self-counsel.com
Founded: 1971
Legal, business & reference books.
Publishes in English, French.
ISBN Prefix(es): 978-1-55180; 978-1-77040
Number of titles published annually: 24 Print; 5 CD-ROM
Total Titles: 230 Print
Branch Office(s)
Self Counsel Press Inc, 4152 Meridian St, Suite 105-471, Bellingham, WA 98226, United States
Foreign Rights: Atmarr Agency Services (China, France, Germany, Japan, Philippines, South Korea, Taiwan, Thailand)
Distribution Center: University of Toronto Press, 10 St Mary St, Suite 700, Toronto, ON M4Y 2W8 *Tel:* 416-978-2239 *Toll Free Tel:* 800-565-9523 (orders) *Fax:* 416-978-4738 *E-mail:* utpbooks@utpress.utoronto.ca
Independent Publishers Group (IPG), 814 N Franklin St, Chicago, IL 60610, United States *Toll Free Tel:* 800-888-4741 *Fax:* 312-337-5985

E-mail: orders@ipgbook.com *Web Site:* www.ipgbook.com
Membership(s): The American Library Association (ALA)

International Travel Maps & Books, see ITMB Publishing Ltd

IRP editeur
CP 68, succursale St-Dominique, Montreal, QC H2S 3K6
Tel: 514-382-3000
E-mail: info@irpcanada.com
Web Site: www.irpcanada.com
Key Personnel
Dir & Pres: Patricia Bergeron
Head, Communs & Soc Networks: Lea Goldman
Ed: Paul Goldman
Founded: 1958 (incorporated in 1964)
Psychological tests & materials.
Publishes in English, French.
ISBN Prefix(es): 978-0-88509; 978-2-89109
Number of titles published annually: 10 Print
Imprints: IPR; IRP
Distributed by Editions Editest (Belgium); Librairie du Quebec a Paris (France)
Distributor for Aseba (CN); Hogrefe France (CN); Hans Huber (Rorschach only)
U.S. Publishers Represented: Academic Therapy Publications; American Orthopsychiatric; Behavior Sciences Systems; Martin M Bruce; Cardall Associates; Center for Psychological Services; Clinical Psychology Publishing; Nigel Cox; Editions Behaviora; Educational & Clinical Publications; Educational Industrial Testing Service; Educators Publishing Services; Granada Learning; Guidance Associates of Delaware; Harvard University Press; Hogrefe UK; Industrial Psychology; Institute for Personality & Ability Testing; International Tests; Lafayette Instrument; Language Research Associates; Multi Health Systems; National Foundation for Educational Research; Pacific Book; Pro Ed; Psychological Assessment Resources; Psychological Test Specialists; Psychologists & Educators; Research Psychologist Press; Sheridan Psychological Services; Stoelting; Western Psychological Services

Irwin Law Inc
14 Duncan St, Suite 206, Toronto, ON M5H 3G8
SAN: 810-0144
Tel: 416-862-7690 *Toll Free Tel:* 888-314-9014 *Fax:* 416-862-9236
E-mail: info@irwinlaw.com; contact@irwinlaw.com
Web Site: www.irwinlaw.com
Key Personnel
Pres & Publr: Jeffrey Miller *Tel:* 416-862-7690 ext 223 *E-mail:* jmiller@irwinlaw.com
VP & Ed-in-Chief: Lesley Steeve *Tel:* 416-862-7690 ext 229 *E-mail:* lsteeve@irwinlaw.com
Founded: 1996
Publisher of books & other material for lawyers & law students.
Publishes in English.
ISBN Prefix(es): 978-1-55221
Number of titles published annually: 20 Print; 20 E-Book
Total Titles: 200 Print; 100 E-Book
Distributor for The Federation Press (North America only)
Foreign Rep(s): The Federation Press (Australia, New Zealand)
Returns: Login Brothers, 6255 Cantay Rd, Unit 1, Mississauga, ON L5R 3Z4 *Toll Free Tel:* 800-665-1148 *Fax:* 204-837-2987 *Web Site:* lb.ca
Membership(s): Association of Canadian Publishers (ACP); Organization of Book Publishers of Ontario (OBPO)

ITMB Publishing Ltd
12300 Bridgeport Rd, Richmond, BC V6V 1J5

Tel: 604-273-1400 *Fax:* 604-273-1488
E-mail: itmb@itmb.com
Web Site: www.itmb.com
Key Personnel
Pres: Jack Joyce
Founded: 1983
Publisher/distributor of international travel maps & atlases.
Publishes in English.
ISBN Prefix(es): 978-1-55341; 978-0-921463; 978-1-895907
Number of titles published annually: 30 Print
Total Titles: 425 Print
Distributor for Borch; Freytag & Bernot; Gizi; National Geographic; Nelles; Rand McNally
Membership(s): International Map Industry Association (IMIA)

Ivey Publishing
Ivey Business School Foundation, Western University, 1255 Western Rd, London, ON N6G 0N1
Tel: 519-661-3206; 519-661-3208
Toll Free Tel: 800-649-6355 *Fax:* 519-661-3485; 519-661-3882
E-mail: cases@ivey.ca
Web Site: www.iveypublishing.ca
Key Personnel
Dir: Matt Quin
Assoc Dir, Mktg & Sales: Candis McInnes
Mgr, Prod & Acq: Violetta Gallagher
Founded: 1923
Publish business case studies for university business courses.
Publishes in English, French.
ISBN Prefix(es): 978-0-919534
Number of titles published annually: 200 Print
Total Titles: 3,500 Print
Distributed by Caseplace (The Aspen Institute's Centre for Business Education); Cengage Learning (USA); Centrale de Cas et de Medias Pedagogiques (CCMP) (Paris, France); College of Commerce (National Chengchi University, Taiwan); European Case Clearing House (ECCH) (UK); IESE Publishing (Spain); Institute for International Studies & Training (IIST) (Japan); LAD Publishing (USA); McGraw-Hill (USA); National Archive Publishing (USA); Pearson Custom Publishing (USA); Study.Net (USA); University Readers Inc (USA)
Distributor for Asian Business Case Center/Nanyang Business School at Nanyang Technological University; China-Europe International Business School (CEIBS); China Management Case Sharing Centre; China University of Hong Kong; College of Commerce (National Chengchi University, Taiwan); Darden Business School; Gordon Institute of Business Science (University of Pretoria, South Africa); Harvard Business Review; Harvard Business School Publishing; Indian Institute of Management Bangalore; Indian School of Business (India); Ivey Business Journal (reprints); National University of Singapore; Northeastern University; Peking University (China); Thunderbird School of Global Management; Tsinghua University (China); University of Regina-Paul J Hill School of Business; University of West Indies; Yonsei University (Korea; Harvard Business School cases & Harvard Business Review reprints)
U.S. Rep(s): Harvard Business School Publishing (case studies & HBR reprints)
Foreign Rep(s): European Case Clearing House (Europe)

Richard Ivey School of Business, see Ivey Publishing

Kids Can Press Ltd
Division of Corus Entertainment Inc
25 Dockside Dr, Toronto, ON M5A 0B5
Tel: 416-479-7000 *Toll Free Tel:* 800-265-0884 *Fax:* 416-960-5437
E-mail: info@kidscan.com; customerservice@kidscan.com
Web Site: www.kidscanpress.com; www.kidscanpress.ca
Key Personnel
Cont, Corus Entertainment: June Samms
Publr: Naseem Hrab
Assoc Publr, Opers: Amelie Roberge
Art Dir: Marie Bartholomew
Edit Devt Dir: Yasemin Ucar
Edit Dir: Yvette Ghione
Sales & Mktg Dir: Sarah Labrie
Mng Ed: Jennifer Grimbleby
Sr Ed: Patricia Ocampo; Katie Scott
Sr Prodn Ed: Olga Kidisevic
Ed: Kathleen Keenan
Global Mgr, Educ Sales & Rts: Allison King
Mktg Mgr: Michaela Cornell
Rts & Digital Accts Mgr: Alison Lapp
US & Intl Accts Mgr: Alison Van Ginkel
Edit Coord: Anna Bendiy
Opers & Digital Assets Coord: Vanessa Giovino
Sales, Mktg & Publicity Coord: Bianca Rodrigues
Sr Designer: Barb Kelly
Book Designer: Andrew Dupuis
Digital Mktg Assoc: Emma Hunter
Mktg Assoc: Kate Patrick
Sales Assoc: Patricia Esteves
Founded: 1973
Books for children exclusively.
Publishes in English.
ISBN Prefix(es): 978-0-919964; 978-1-55074; 978-1-55337; 978-0-921103; 978-1-55453; 978-1-77138
Number of titles published annually: 75 Print
Total Titles: 500 Print
Imprints: CitizenKid™; Franklin the Turtle; KCP Loft; Kids Can Do It; Scaredy Squirrel
Distributed by Hachette Book Group Inc
Orders to: Hachette Book Group Inc, Order Dept, 53 State St, 9th fl, Boston, MA 02109, United States *Toll Free Tel:* 800-759-0190 *Toll Free Fax:* 800-286-9471 *E-mail:* order.desk@hbgusa.com *Web Site:* www.hachettebookgroup.com

Kindred Productions
Division of Mennonite Brethren Church
1310 Taylor Ave, Winnipeg, MB R3M 3Z6
Tel: 204-669-6575 *Toll Free Tel:* 800-545-7322
E-mail: kindred@mbchurches.ca
Web Site: www.kindredproductions.com
Founded: 1982
Denominational material, Low German Bible, trade books & church resources.
Publishes in English, French.
ISBN Prefix(es): 978-0-919797; 978-0-921788; 978-1-894791; 978-1-926599
Number of titles published annually: 15 Print
Total Titles: 250 Print

Kinesis Education Inc
4823 Sherbrooke St W, Suite 275, Westmount, QC H3Z 1G7
Tel: 514-932-9466 *Toll Free Tel:* 866-750-9466
E-mail: editions@ebbp.ca
Web Site: ebbp.ca
Founded: 1996
Publisher of educational textbooks, pedagogical thematic mapping, resources & educational kits.
Publishes in English, French.
ISBN Prefix(es): 978-0-88537; 978-2-7615
Number of titles published annually: 10 Print
Total Titles: 500 Print

§Knopf Canada
Imprint of Penguin Random House Canada
320 Front St W, Suite 1400, Toronto, ON M5V 3B6
SAN: 201-3975
Tel: 416-364-4449 *Toll Free Tel:* 888-523-9292 *Fax:* 416-598-7764
Web Site: www.penguinrandomhouse.ca
Key Personnel
CEO, PRHC: Kristin Cochrane
CFO, PRHC: Barry Gallant
Chief Strategy & Opers Offr, PRHC: Robert Wheaton
SVP & Dir, Prodn: Janine Laporte
Publr: Martha Kanya-Forstner
Publr, KRC: Anne Collins
Imprint Sales Dir: Matthew Sibiga
Ed-in-Chief: Lynn Henry
Exec Ed: Kiara Kent
Sr Ed: Amanda Betts
Prodn Ed: Emma Lockhart
Publg Mgr: Rick Meier
Soc Media Coord, Young Readers: Julia Wigdor
Mktg Assoc: Malaika Eyoh
Mktg Designer: Sebastian Frye
Founded: 1991
Penguin Random House Canada & its publishing entities are not accepting unsol submissions, proposals, mss, or submission queries via e-mail at this time.
Publishes in English.
Number of titles published annually: 40 Print
Imprints: Alchemy; Vintage Canada
Distributed by Penguin Random House Canada
Shipping Address: Penguin Random House Canada, 6971 Columbus Rd, Mississauga, ON L5T 1K1
Membership(s): Canadian Publishers' Council

§LexisNexis® Canada Inc
Member of The LexisNexis® Group
111 Gordon Baker Rd, Suite 900, Toronto, ON M2H 3R1
Tel: 905-479-2665 *Toll Free Tel:* 800-668-6481; 800-387-0899 (cust care); 800-255-5174 (sales)
E-mail: service@lexisnexis.ca (cust serv); sales@lexisnexis.ca
Web Site: www.lexisnexis.ca
Key Personnel
CEO: Eric Wright
Cust Serv Mgr, Print & CD-ROM Div: Barbara Brumwell *Tel:* 905-415-5816 *E-mail:* barbara.brumwell@lexisnexis.ca
Mgr, Prod Adoption & Learning: Lina Stolf
Founded: 1912
Books, looseleaf services, newsletters, journals, legal publishing & online services.
Publishes in English, French.
ISBN Prefix(es): 978-0-409; 978-0-433
Number of titles published annually: 80 Print; 20 CD-ROM
Branch Office(s)
3 Place Ville Marie, Suite 400, Montreal, QC H3B 2E3 *Tel:* 514-287-0339

Lidec Inc
800, blvd Industriel, bureau 202, St-Jean-sur-Richlieu, QC J3B 8G4
Tel: 514-843-5991 *Toll Free Tel:* 800-350-5991 (CN only) *Fax:* 514-843-5252
E-mail: lidec@lidec.qc.ca
Web Site: www.lidec.qc.ca
Founded: 1965
Publisher of school books.
Publishes in English, French.
ISBN Prefix(es): 978-2-7608
Number of titles published annually: 30 Print
Total Titles: 1,500 Print
Distribution Center: Librairie Pelagie, 221, blvd J D Gauthier, Shippagan, NB E8S 1N2 (NB, NS & PEI) *Tel:* 506-336-9777 *Fax:* 506-336-9778
Pierre Carme Yves Levy, 38, Bis rue Geffard, Petion-Ville, Port-au-Prince, Haiti *Tel:* 2-514-4181; 3-551-8554 (cell) *E-mail:* yves_levy@hotmail.com

CANADIAN PUBLISHERS

Servidis SA, Chemin des Chalets, 7, 1279 Chavannes-de-Bogis, Switzerland *Tel:* (022) 960 95 10 *Fax:* (022) 776 35 44 *Web Site:* www.servidis.ch

Life Cycle Books Ltd
11 Progress Ave, Unit 6, Toronto, ON M1P 4S7
SAN: 110-8417
E-mail: orders@lifecyclebooks.ca; billing@lifecyclebooks.ca; support@lifecyclebooks.ca
Web Site: www.lifecyclebooks.com
Key Personnel
Pres: Paul Broughton *E-mail:* paulb@lifecyclebooks.com
Founded: 1973
Human life issues.
Publishes in English, French.
ISBN Prefix(es): 978-0-919225
Number of titles published annually: 3 Print
Total Titles: 41 Print

Lone Pine Publishing
87 E Pender, Vancouver, BC V6A 1S9
SAN: 115-4125
Mailing Address: 7735 Wagner Rd NW, Edmonton, AB T6E 5B1
Tel: 780-433-9333 *Toll Free Tel:* 800-661-9017 *Fax:* 780-433-9646 *Toll Free Fax:* 800-424-7173
E-mail: info@lonepinepublishing.com
Web Site: www.lonepinepublishing.com
Key Personnel
Pres: Shane Kennedy
Founded: 1980
Natural history, travel, recreation, popular history, bird guides & gardening.
Publishes in English.
ISBN Prefix(es): 978-1-55105; 978-1-894877 (Ghost House Books); 978-0-919433
Number of titles published annually: 5 Print
Total Titles: 800 Print; 50 E-Book
Imprints: Ghost House Books
Branch Office(s)
4471 S 134 Pl, Tukwila, WA 98168, United States, Sales Mgr: Mike Campbell *Tel:* 206-453-5717 *Toll Free Tel:* 800-518-3541 *Fax:* 253-394-0405 *Toll Free Fax:* 800-548-1169 *E-mail:* order@lonepinepublishing.com
Distributor for Blue Bike Books; Dragon Hill Publishing; Eschia Books; Folklore Publishing; Editions de la Montagne Verte; Partners Publishing; Quagmire Press; Red Deer College Press
U.S. Rep(s): Baker & Taylor; Benjamin News; Book People; Ingram Book Co; Sunbelt

§James Lorimer & Co Ltd, Publishers
117 Peter St, Suite 304, Toronto, ON M5V 0M3
Tel: 416-362-4762 *Fax:* 416-362-3939
E-mail: sales@lorimer.ca; promotion@lorimer.ca; rights@lorimer.ca
Web Site: www.lorimer.ca
Key Personnel
Publr: Carrie Gleason *E-mail:* carrie.gleason@lorimer.ca; James Lorimer *E-mail:* jlorimer@lorimer.ca
Promos & Publicity: William Brown
Rts & Perms: Nancy Sewell
Sales: Daniel Campbell
Founded: 1970
Hardcover & paperback trade; business, economics, finance, history, politics; children's books; social sciences & sociology; cookbooks; illustrated history.
Publishes in English.
ISBN Prefix(es): 978-1-55028; 978-0-88862; 978-1-55277; 978-1-4594
Number of titles published annually: 12 Print
Total Titles: 600 Print
Orders to: Formac Lorimer Books, 5502 Atlantic St, Halifax, NS B3H 1G4 *Tel:* 902-421-7022 *Toll Free Tel:* 800-565-1975 *Fax:* 902-425-0166 *E-mail:* orderdesk@formac.ca *Web Site:* www.formac.ca
Warehouse: Formac Lorimer Books, 5502 Atlantic St, Halifax, NS B3H 1G4 *Tel:* 902-421-7022 *Toll Free Tel:* 800-565-1975 *Fax:* 902-425-0166 *E-mail:* orderdesk@formac.ca *Web Site:* www.formac.ca

§Madonna House Publications
2888 Dafoe Rd, Combermere, ON K0J 1L0
Tel: 613-756-3728 *Toll Free Tel:* 888-703-7110 *Fax:* 613-756-0103
E-mail: publications@madonnahouse.org
Web Site: publications.madonnahouse.org; www.madonnahouse.org/publications
Founded: 1988
Publishes in English, French.
ISBN Prefix(es): 978-0-921440; 978-1-897145
Number of titles published annually: 4 Print; 2 Audio
Total Titles: 68 Print; 68 Online; 15 Audio
Membership(s): Catholic Publishers Association; CMN

§Master Point Press
Subsidiary of 52Entertainment
214 Merton St, Suite 205, Toronto, ON M4S 1A6
Tel: 647-956-4933
E-mail: info@masterpointpress.com
Web Site: www.masterpointpress.com; www.ebooksbridge.com (ebook sales)
Key Personnel
Pres: Ray Lee
Founded: 1994
Books on contract bridge.
Publishes in English.
ISBN Prefix(es): 978-0-9698461; 978-1-894154; 978-1-897106; 978-1-55494; 978-1-77140
Number of titles published annually: 20 Print; 20 E-Book
Total Titles: 300 Print; 10 CD-ROM; 300 E-Book
Distributor for Better Bridge Now
Foreign Rep(s): The Bridge Shop (Australia); Orca Book Services (UK)
Orders to: Georgetown Terminal Warehouses Ltd, 34 Armstrong Ave, Georgetown, ON L7G 4R9 *Tel:* 905-873-2750 *Fax:* 905-873-6170 *E-mail:* orders@gtwcanada.com *Web Site:* www.gtwcanada.com; Baker & Taylor, 2550 W Tyvola Rd, Suite 300, Charlotte, NC 28217, United States *Tel:* 704-998-3100 *Toll Free Tel:* 800-775-1800 *E-mail:* btinfo@btol.com *Web Site:* www.baker-taylor.com; Ingram Book Group, One Ingram Blvd, La Vergne, TN 37086, United States *Tel:* 615-793-5000 *Toll Free Tel:* 800-937-8200 *E-mail:* customer.service@ingramcontent.com; Orca Book Services, 160 Eastern Ave, Milton Park, Abingdon, Oxon OX14 4SB, United Kingdom *Tel:* (01235) 465500 *E-mail:* tradeorders@orcabookservices.co.uk *Web Site:* www.orcabookservices.co.uk
Shipping Address: Georgetown Terminal Warehouses Ltd, 34 Armstrong Ave, Georgetown, ON L7G 4R9

§Mawenzi House Publishers Ltd
39 Woburn Ave (B), Toronto, ON M5W 1K5
Tel: 416-483-7191
E-mail: info@mawenzihouse.com
Web Site: www.mawenzihouse.com
Key Personnel
Publr: Ms Nurjehan Aziz
Founded: 1985 (as TSAR Publications)
Canadian literature, multicultural & international literature. No unsol mss, query first.
Publishes in English.
ISBN Prefix(es): 978-0-920661; 978-1-894770
Number of titles published annually: 11 Print
Total Titles: 101 Print
Distribution Center: University of Toronto Press Inc, 5201 Dufferin St, Toronto, ON M3H 5T8 (CN & US) *Tel:* 416-667-7791 *Toll Free Tel:* 800-565-9523 *Fax:* 416-667-7832 *Toll Free Fax:* 800-221-9985 *E-mail:* utpbooks@utpress.utoronto.ca
Membership(s): Literary Press Group

McClelland & Stewart Ltd
Imprint of Penguin Random House Canada
320 Front St W, Suite 1400, Toronto, ON M5V 3B6
Tel: 416-364-4449 *Toll Free Tel:* 888-523-9292
E-mail: customerservicescanada@penguinrandomhouse.com; mcclellandsubmissions@prh.com
Web Site: penguinrandomhouse.ca/imprints/mcclelland-stewart
Key Personnel
Publr: Stephanie Sinclair
Edit Dir, Fiction: Anita Chong
Sr Ed: Haley Cullingham; Kelly Joseph
Publg Mgr: Joe Lee
Founded: 1906
Publishes in English.
Number of titles published annually: 70 Print
Total Titles: 2,000 Print
Imprints: Signal (nonfiction)

McGill-Queen's University Press
1010 Sherbrooke W, Suite 1720, Montreal, QC H3A 2R7
Tel: 514-398-3750 *Fax:* 514-398-4333
E-mail: mqup@mcgill.ca
Web Site: www.mqup.ca
Key Personnel
Exec Dir: Philip Cercone *Tel:* 514-398-2910 *E-mail:* philip.cercone@mcgill.ca
Mktg Dir: Kate Fraser
Ed-in-Chief: Jonathan Crago *Tel:* 514-398-7480 *E-mail:* jonathan.crago@mcgill.ca
Mng Ed: Kathleen Fraser *Tel:* 514-398-3922 *E-mail:* kathleen.fraser@mcgill.ca
Assoc Mng Ed: Lisa Aitken
Sr Ed: Kyla Madden *Tel:* 514-398-2056 *E-mail:* kyla.madden@mcgill.ca
Acqs Ed: Khadija Coxon *Tel:* 613-533-2155 *E-mail:* khadija.coxon@queensu.ca
Fin & Busn Mgr: Lara de Beaupre *Tel:* 514-398-5336 *E-mail:* lara.debeaupre@mcgill.ca
Prodn Mgr: Elena Goranescu *Tel:* 514-398-7395 *E-mail:* elena.goranescu@mcgill.ca
Rts & Projs Mgr: Carol Bonnett *Tel:* 514-552-3757 *E-mail:* carol.bonnett@mcgill.ca
Founded: 1970
Original peer-reviewed, high-quality books in all areas of social sciences & humanities. Our emphasis is on providing an outlet for Canadian authors & scholarship. Publish authors from around the world.
Publishes in English, French.
ISBN Prefix(es): 978-0-88629; 978-0-88911; 978-0-7735; 978-0-7709; 978-1-55240; 978-0-9690334; 978-0228-0
Number of titles published annually: 130 Print
Total Titles: 3,600 Print; 5 CD-ROM
Branch Office(s)
Douglas Library Bldg, 93 University Ave, Kingston, ON K7L 5C4 *Tel:* 613-533-2155 *Fax:* 613-533-6822 *E-mail:* mqup@queensu.ca
Distributor for CIGI Press; John Deutsch Institute for the Study of Economic Policy; Fontanus Monograph Series; Institute for Research on Public Policy; McCord Museum; Queen's Policy Studies Series; Les Editions du Septentrion (English titles)
Foreign Rep(s): The African Moon Press (Chris Reinders) (South Africa); Avicenna Partnership Ltd (Bill Kennedy) (Middle East); Claire De Gruchy (Middle East); Colin Flint Ltd (Ben Greig, Steven Haslemere & Wilf Jones) (Denmark, Finland, Iceland, Norway, Sweden); Charles Gibbes (Cyprus, Greece); Mare Nostrum (Katie Machin) (Belgium, France, Luxembourg, Netherlands); Mare Nostrum (Frauke

Feldmann) (Austria, Germany, Switzerland); Mare Nostrum (Francesca Pollard & David Pickering) (Italy); Mare Nostrum (Cristina De Lara Ruiz) (Portugal, Spain); Quantum Publishing Solutions Ltd (Jim Chalmers) (England, Ireland, Scotland, Wales); Research Press (India, Indian subcontinent)
Distribution Center: UTP Distribution, 5201 Dufferin St, ON M3H 5T8 *Tel:* 416-667-7791 *Toll Free Tel:* 800-565-9523 *E-mail:* utpbooks@utpress.utoronto.ca
Chicago Distribution Center, 11030 S Langley Ave, Chicago, IL 60628, United States *Tel:* 773-702-7000 *Toll Free Tel:* 800-621-2736 *Fax:* 773-702-7212 *Toll Free Fax:* 800-621-8476 *E-mail:* orders@press.uchicago.edu SAN: 202-5280
Research Press, 302-A ABW Tower, M G Rd IFFCO Crossing, Gurgaon, Haryana 122 001, India *Tel:* (0124) 4040017 *Fax:* (011) 23281819 *E-mail:* marketing@researchpress.co.in
Marston Book Services Ltd, 160 Eastern Ave, Milton Park, Abingdon, Oxon OX14 4SB, United Kingdom *Tel:* (01235) 465500 *Fax:* (01235) 465555 *E-mail:* trade.orders@marston.co.uk *Web Site:* www.marston.co.uk
Membership(s): American Association of University Presses (AAUP); Association of Canadian Publishers (ACP); Association of Canadian University Presses (ACUP)

§McGraw-Hill Ryerson
Division of McGraw-Hill Education
300 Water St, Whitby, ON L1N 9B6
SAN: 115-060X
Tel: 905-430-5000 *Toll Free Tel:* 800-565-5758 (cust serv) *Fax:* 905-430-5020
Toll Free Fax: 800-463-5885
Web Site: www.mheducation.ca
Publishes & distributes higher educational & professional products in both print & non-print media.
Publishes in English.
ISBN Prefix(es): 978-0-07; 978-0-7700
Number of titles published annually: 70 Print; 40 CD-ROM; 30 Online
Total Titles: 1,300 Print; 150 CD-ROM; 200 Online; 50 E-Book
Distributed by McGraw-Hill Publishing Cos
Distributor for Glencoe/McGraw-Hill; Jamestown Education; McGraw-Hill; McGraw-Hill/Irwin; MedMaster Inc; Open Court; Osborne; Schaum's; SRA; Wright Group
U.S. Publishers Represented: The McGraw-Hill Cos
Membership(s): Canadian Educational Resources Council; Canadian Publishers' Council

Modus Vivendi Publishing Inc
55, rue Jean-Talon Ouest, Montreal, QC H2R 2W8
Tel: 514-272-0433 *Fax:* 514-272-7234
E-mail: info@groupemodus.com
Web Site: www.groupemodus.com
Key Personnel
Founder & CEO: Marc Alain
VP, Publg & Opers: Isabelle Jodoin
Founded: 1992
General trade publishing.
Publishes in French.
ISBN Prefix(es): 978-2-921556; 978-2-89523; 978-2-89543 (Presses Aventure); 978-2-923720 (Editions Bravo!); 978-2-89670 (Editions Bravo!)
Number of titles published annually: 200 Print
Divisions: Editions Bravo!; Presses Aventure
Distribution Center: Les Messageries ADP, 2315, rue de la Province, Longueuil, QC J4G 1G4 (French) *Tel:* 450-640-1237 *Toll Free Tel:* 866-874-1237 *Fax:* 450-674-6237 *Toll Free Fax:* 866-874-6237 *E-mail:* adpcommandes@sogides.com
Georgetown Publications, 34 Armstrong Ave, Georgetown, ON L7G 4R9 (English) *Tel:* 905-702-7093

Moose Hide Books
Imprint of Moose Enterprise Book & Theatre Play Publishing
684 Walls Rd, Prince Township, ON P6A 6K4
Tel: 705-779-3331 *Fax:* 705-779-3331
E-mail: mooseenterprises@on.aibn.com
Web Site: www.moosehidebooks.com
Key Personnel
Owner & Publr: Richard Mousseau
  E-mail: rmousseau@moosehidebooks.com
Ed: Edmond Alcid *E-mail:* ealcid@moosehidebooks.com
Book & theatre play publishing. Full author royalties paid. 90% of authors are new. House assists new first time authors.
This publisher has indicated that 50% of their product line is author subsidized.
Publishes in English.
ISBN Prefix(es): 978-1-894650; 978-1-927393
Number of titles published annually: 7 Print; 7 E-Book; 1 Audio
Total Titles: 200 Print; 100 Online; 25 E-Book; 1 Audio

§Mosaic Press
1252 Speers Rd, Units 1 & 2, Oakville, ON L6L 5N9
Tel: 905-825-2130 *Fax:* 905-825-2130
E-mail: info@mosaic-press.com
Web Site: www.mosaic-press.com
Key Personnel
Publr: Howard Aster
Founded: 1975
Literary scholarly books. No unsol mss.
ISBN Prefix(es): 978-0-88962; 978-1-77161
Number of titles published annually: 20 Print
Total Titles: 502 Print
Distribution Center: Independent Publishers Group (IPG), 814 N Franklin St, Chicago, IL 60610, United States (US, CN, Australia & New Zealand) *Tel:* 312-337-0747 *Toll Free Tel:* 800-888-4741 *Fax:* 312-337-5985 *E-mail:* orders@ipgbook.com *Web Site:* www.ipgbook.com
Orca Book Services, 160 Eastern Ave, Milton Park, Abingdon, Oxon OX14 4SB, United Kingdom *Tel:* (01235) 465 521 *Fax:* (01235) 465 521 *E-mail:* tradeorders@orcabookservices.co.uk *Web Site:* www.orcabookservices.co.uk

Musee canadien de l'histoire, see Canadian Museum of History (Musee canadien de l'histoire)

Narada Press
591 Leighland Dr, Waterloo, ON N2T 2J9
Tel: 519-886-1969
Founded: 1993
General books on economics, development studies, Asian studies, Vietnamese studies. Directories, reference books, foreign language, scholarly books, college textbooks.
Publishes in English.
ISBN Prefix(es): 978-1-895938
Number of titles published annually: 5 Print

National Gallery of Canada Boutique
380 Sussex Dr, Ottawa, ON K1N 9N4
Tel: 613-990-0962 (mail order sales)
E-mail: ngcbook@gallery.ca
Web Site: www.gallery.ca
Founded: 1980
Exhibition catalogues, monographs, permanent collection series, books on photography, posters.
Publishes in English, French.
ISBN Prefix(es): 978-0-88884
Number of titles published annually: 4 Print

Nelson Education Ltd
Affiliate of Cengage Learning
1120 Birchmount Rd, Scarborough, ON M1K 5G4
Tel: 416-752-9448 *Toll Free Tel:* 800-268-2222 (cust serv) *Fax:* 416-752-9646
E-mail: peopleandengagement@nelson.com
Web Site: www.nelson.com
Key Personnel
Pres & CEO: Steven Brown
CFO: John Bell
EVP & Mng Dir: Jessica Mosher
EVP, Opers: David Ashton
SVP, Digital Strategy & Technol: Ben Higgins
SVP, People & Engagement: Jessica Phinn
Founded: 1914
School, college, test, professional & reference.
Publishes in English.
ISBN Prefix(es): 978-0-919913; 978-1-896081; 978-0-7705; 978-0-17; 978-0-7725; 978-1-85032
Number of titles published annually: 700 Print
Total Titles: 11,864 Print; 30 CD-ROM; 30 E-Book; 100 Audio
U.S. Publishers Represented: American Technical Publishers Inc (ATP); Aseba; Brooks-Cole Publishing; Canada Housing & Mortgage Corp (CMHC); Centennial Press; Course Technology Inc; Craftsman; DC Heath Canada Ltd (school & coll); Delmar Publishers Inc; Douglas & McIntyre; Duxbury Press; Exclusive; Goodheart Willcox; Great Source Educational; Groupe Beauchemin; HarperCollins; Heinemann; Heinle & Heinle Publishers Inc; Houghton Mifflin Harcourt Publishing Company (school, coll & trade); Indigo Instrument; Industrial Press; International Thomson Publishing Services; Irwin Publishing; Learning Media Co; McDougall Littell & Co; Mondo; Nelson Thomson Learning; Nelson Thomson Learning Australia; Norbry; Peterson's; Phoenix Learning Resources; PWS Publishing; Reidmore Publishing; The Riverside Publishing Co; William H Sadlier; Scott Jones; South Western Education & College Publishing; Texere; Thomas Learning Asia; VideoActive Production; Wadsworth Publishers; West Publishing (educ prods only); West Virginia University (FIT)
Membership(s): Canadian Educational Resources Council; Canadian Publishers' Council

§New Author Publishing
4 E Fulford Place, Brockville, ON K6V 2Z8
Tel: 613-865-7471
Web Site: www.newauthorpublishing.com
Key Personnel
Owner: Gary Wolfe *E-mail:* gary@newauthorpublishing.com
Founded: 2013
Print on demand & ebook publishing.
Publishes in English.
ISBN Prefix(es): 978-1-928045
Number of titles published annually: 8 Print; 8 Online; 8 E-Book
Total Titles: 30 Print; 30 Online; 30 E-Book

New Star Books Ltd
107-3477 Commercial St, Vancouver, BC V5N 4E8
SAN: 115-1908
Tel: 604-738-9429
E-mail: info@newstarbooks.com
Web Site: www.newstarbooks.com
Key Personnel
Pres & Publr: Rolf Maurer
Founded: 1970
Publishers of contemporary prose literature including fiction, criticism & memoir, poetry,

CANADIAN PUBLISHERS

nonfiction on social issues & current affairs, politics, labor, feminism, sexuality/gender. Emphasis on British Columbia & Western Canada. Publishes in English.
ISBN Prefix(es): 978-0-919888; 978-0-919573; 978-0-921586; 978-1-55420
Number of titles published annually: 10 Print
Total Titles: 110 Print
Branch Office(s)
1574 Gulf Rd, No 1517, Point Roberts, WA 98281, United States
Foreign Rights: Acacia House Publishing (worldwide exc Canada)
Distribution Center: Brunswick Books, 14 Afton Ave, Toronto, ON M6J 1R7 *Tel:* 416-703-3598 *Fax:* 416-703-6561 *E-mail:* info@brunswickbooks.ca
Membership(s): Literary Press Group

§New World Publishing (Canada)
PO Box 36075, Halifax, NS B3J 3S9
Tel: 902-576-2055 (inquiries) *Toll Free Tel:* 877-211-3334 (orders) *Fax:* 902-576-2095
Web Site: www.newworldpublishing.com
Key Personnel
Owner & Mng Ed: Dr Francis Mitchell
 E-mail: fgm2020@icloud.com
Founded: 1995
Publishes in English.
ISBN Prefix(es): 978-1-895814; 978-1-989564
Number of titles published annually: 8 Print; 5 E-Book
Total Titles: 92 Print; 7 CD-ROM; 5 Online; 22 E-Book; 5 Audio
Returns: 19 Frenchman's Rd, Oakfield, NS B2T 1A9 *E-mail:* nwp1@eastlink.ca
Warehouse: JEM Enterprises, 79 Jackson Rd, Apt 3, Dartmouth, NS B3A 4A7, Shipper: Ms Jacqui E Mitchell *Tel:* 902-449-7552 *E-mail:* nwp1@eastlink.ca
Membership(s): Atlantic Publishers Marketing Association

NeWest Press
8540 109 St, No 201, Edmonton, AB T6G 1E6
Tel: 780-432-9427 *Fax:* 780-433-3179
E-mail: info@newestpress.com; orders@newestpress.com
Web Site: www.newestpress.com
Key Personnel
Gen Mgr: Matt Bowes
Mktg & Prodn Coord: Claire Kelly
Founded: 1977
Publishes literary fiction, literary nonfiction, poetry, drama & mystery novels with a particular interest in books by Western Canadian authors. Publishes in English.
ISBN Prefix(es): 978-0-920316; 978-0-920897; 978-1-896300; 978-1-897126; 978-1-927063
Number of titles published annually: 12 Print
Total Titles: 140 Print
Imprints: Nunatak
Sales Office(s): Literary Press Group, 425 Adelaide St W, Suite 700, Toronto, ON M5V 3C1, Sales Mgr: Tan Light *Tel:* 416-483-1321 *Fax:* 416-483-2510 *E-mail:* sales@lpg.ca
Foreign Rep(s): Gazelle Book Services Ltd (Europe, UK)
Distribution Center: LitDistCo, 8300 Lawson Rd, Milton, ON L9T 0A4 *Toll Free Tel:* 800-591-6250 *Toll Free Fax:* 800-591-6251 *E-mail:* ordering@litdistco.ca *Web Site:* www.litdistco.ca
Membership(s): Association of Canadian Publishers (ACP); Book Publishers Association of Alberta; Crime Writers of Canada; Literary Press Group of Canada

Nimbus Publishing Ltd
3660 Strawberry Hill, Halifax, NS B3K 5A9
SAN: 115-0685
Mailing Address: PO Box 9166, Halifax, NS B3K 5M8
Tel: 902-455-4286 *Toll Free Tel:* 800-NIMBUS9 (646-2879) *Fax:* 902-455-5440
Toll Free Fax: 888-253-3133
E-mail: customerservice@nimbus.ca
Web Site: www.nimbus.ca
Key Personnel
Co-Owner, Art Dir & Prodn Mgr: Heather Bryan
Mng Ed: Whitney Moran
Gen Mgr: Terrilee Bulger *Tel:* 902-455-4286 ext 223 *E-mail:* tbulger@nimbus.ca
Publicist: Kate Watson *Tel:* 902-455-4286 ext 226 *E-mail:* kwatson@nimbus.ca
Founded: 1978
Regional nonfiction books, relevant to the Atlantic-Canadian experience, social & natural history, children's books, cookbooks, travel, biography, photography & nautical.
Publishes in English, French.
ISBN Prefix(es): 978-0-920852; 978-0-919380; 978-0-921054; 978-0-921128; 978-1-55109; 978-1-77108
Number of titles published annually: 45 Print
Total Titles: 1,000 Print
Imprints: Nimbus; Vagrant Press (fiction)
Distributor for Acadiensis Press; Acorn Press; Bouton D'or Acadie; Breton Books; Bunim & Bannigan; Cape Breton University Press; Chocolate River Publishing; Down East; Earth, Sky & Water; Glen Margaret Publishing; Island Studies Press; Islandport Press; Macintyre Purcell Publishing; Mountain Press; Pottersfield Press; Running the Goat; SSP Publications; Wooden Boat Books
U.S. Publishers Represented: Down East; Flat Hammock Press; Mystic Seaport Museum Inc; Sheridan House; Wooden Boat
U.S. Rep(s): Downeast Books
Distribution Center: Baker & Taylor Distribution Services, 30 Amberwood Pkwy, Ashland, OH 44805, United States (US only) *Tel:* 567-215-0030 *Toll Free Tel:* 888-814-0208 *E-mail:* info@btpubservices.com *Web Site:* www.btpubservices.com
Membership(s): Association for the Export of Canadian Books; Association of Canadian Publishers (ACP); Atlantic Publishers Marketing Association

§Novalis Publishing
Division of Bayard Canada
One Eglinton Ave E, Suite 800, Toronto, ON M4P 3A1
Tel: 416-363-3303 *Toll Free Tel:* 877-702-7773 *Fax:* 416-363-9409 *Toll Free Fax:* 877-702-7775
E-mail: books@novalis.ca
Web Site: www.novalis.ca
Key Personnel
Publg Dir: Joseph Sinasac *E-mail:* joseph.sinasac@novalis.ca
Assoc Publg Dir: Simon Appolloni *E-mail:* simon.appolloni@novalis.ca
Mktg Mgr: Patricia Bedard *E-mail:* patricia.bedard@bayardcanada.ca
Sales Mgr: Maria Medeiros *E-mail:* maria.medeiros@novalis.ca
Founded: 1936
Religious children's & adult books, periodicals & religious books (Catholic/Christian).
Publishes in English, French.
ISBN Prefix(es): 978-2-89088; 978-2-89507; 978-2-89646; 978-0-88587; 978-1-895195; 978-2-89830; 978-2-89688
Number of titles published annually: 30 Print; 20 E-Book
Total Titles: 360 Print; 5 CD-ROM; 20 E-Book
Distributed by Garratt Publishing (Australia); Redemptorist Publications (Continental Europe, Ireland & UK); Twenty-Third Publications (US)
Distributor for Ave Maria; Catholic Health Alliance of Canada (CHAC); Creative Communications for the Parish; Crossroad Publishing; Franciscan Media; Loyola Press; Orbis Books; Paulist Press; Pflaum Publishing Group; Random House/Doubleday (religous titles only); Saint Mary's Press; St Vladimir Seminary Press; Editions du Signe; Twenty Third Publications
U.S. Publishers Represented: Creative Communications for the Parish; Orbis Books; Paulist Press; Pflaum Gospel Weeklies; Saint Mary's Press
Billing Address: BND Distribution, 4475 Frontenac St, Montreal, QC H2H 2S2 *Tel:* 514-278-3020 *Toll Free Tel:* 800-387-7164 *Fax:* 514-278-3030 *Toll Free Fax:* 800-204-4140 *Web Site:* www.novalis.com
Orders to: BND Distribution, 4475 Frontenac St, Montreal, QC H2H 2S2 *Tel:* 514-278-3020 *Toll Free Tel:* 800-387-7164 *Fax:* 514-278-3030 *Toll Free Fax:* 800-204-4140 *Web Site:* www.novalis.com
Returns: BND Distribution, 4475 Frontenac St, Montreal, QC H2H 2S2 *Tel:* 514-278-3020 *Toll Free Tel:* 800-387-7164 *Fax:* 514-278-3030 *Toll Free Fax:* 800-204-4140 *Web Site:* www.novalis.com
Shipping Address: BND Distribution, 4475 Frontenac St, Montreal, QC H2H 2S2 *Tel:* 514-278-3020 *Toll Free Tel:* 800-387-7164 *Fax:* 514-278-3030 *Toll Free Fax:* 800-204-4140 *Web Site:* www.novalis.com
Warehouse: BND Distribution, 4475 Frontenac St, Montreal, QC H2H 2S2 *Tel:* 514-278-3020 *Toll Free Tel:* 800-387-7164 *Fax:* 514-278-3030 *Toll Free Fax:* 800-204-4140 *Web Site:* www.novalis.com

§One Act Play Depot
Box 335, Spiritwood, SK S0J 2M0
E-mail: plays@oneactplays.net; orders@oneactplays.net
Web Site: oneactplays.net
Key Personnel
Mng Ed: Fraser MacFarlane
Ed: K Balvenie
Founded: 2002
Publication, sale & distribution of one-act plays. Orders ship within 24 hours. Accept submissions only in February of each year.
Publishes in English.
ISBN Prefix(es): 978-1-894910; 978-1-926849
Number of titles published annually: 10 Print; 10 E-Book
Total Titles: 170 Print; 110 E-Book

Oolichan Books
PO Box 2278, Fernie, BC V0B 1M0
SAN: 115-4680
Tel: 250-423-6113
E-mail: info@oolichan.com
Web Site: www.oolichan.com
Key Personnel
Founder & Ed: Ronald Smith
Publr: Randal Macnair
Consulting Ed: Pat Smith
Founded: 1974
Publishers of literary fiction, poetry & literary nonfiction. Publish only Canadian authors.
Publishes in English.
ISBN Prefix(es): 978-0-88982
Number of titles published annually: 3 Print
Total Titles: 160 Print
Shipping Address: 542 B Second Ave, Fernie, BC V0B 1M0
Distribution Center: University of Toronto Press, 5201 Dufferin St, Toronto, ON M3H 5T8 *Toll Free Tel:* 800-565-9523 *E-mail:* utpbooks@utorontopress.com *Web Site:* utorontopress.com

Membership(s): The Association of Book Publishers of British Columbia (ABPBC); Association of Canadian Publishers (ACP); Literary Press Group

Orca Book Publishers
1016 Balmoral Rd, Victoria, BC V8T 1A8
Toll Free Tel: 800-210-5277 *Toll Free Fax:* 877-408-1551
E-mail: orca@orcabook.com
Web Site: www.orcabook.com
Key Personnel
Founder & Pres: Bob Tyrrell
Publr: Andrew Wooldridge *E-mail:* andrew@orcabook.com
Founded: 1984
Children & young adult literature.
Publishes in English, French.
ISBN Prefix(es): 978-1-55143; 978-0-920501; 978-1-4598; 978-1-55469
Number of titles published annually: 80 Print
Total Titles: 1,000 Print
Branch Office(s)
PO Box 468, Custer, WA 98240-0468, United States
Distributor for The Book Publishing Co; Creative Book Publishing; Formac Publishing; Lobster Press; James Lorimer & Co; Nimbus Publishing; Polestar Calendars; Second Story Press; 7th Generation; Sono Nis Press; Sumach Press; Tradewind Books; Tuckamore Books; Tudor House
Foreign Rights: Transatlantic Literary Agency (Amy Tompkins)
Returns: 7056 Portal Way, Suite 110, Ferndale, WA 98248, United States (US returns via courier)
Membership(s): American Booksellers Association (ABA); The American Library Association (ALA); The Association of Book Publishers of British Columbia (ABPBC); Association of Canadian Publishers (ACP); Educational Book & Media Association (EBMA)

Owlkids Books Inc
Division of Bayard Canada
10 Lower Spadina Ave, Suite 400, Toronto, ON M5V 2Z2
Tel: 416-340-2700 *Fax:* 416-340-9769
E-mail: owlkids@owlkids.com
Web Site: www.owlkidsbooks.com
Key Personnel
Publr: Karen Boersma
Dir, Sales & Mktg: Judy Brunsek
Edit Dir: Jennifer Stokes
Founded: 1976
Award-winning publisher of books for children ages 3-13.
Publishes in English.
ISBN Prefix(es): 978-0-920775; 978-1-895688; 978-1-894379; 978-1-897066; 978-1-897349; 978-1-926973; 978-0-919872; 978-1-926818
Number of titles published annually: 25 Print
Total Titles: 150 Print; 50 E-Book
Orders to: University of Toronto Press, 5201 Dufferin St, Toronto, ON M3H 5T8 *Tel:* 416-667-7791 *Toll Free Tel:* 800-565-9523 *Fax:* 416-667-7832 *Toll Free Fax:* 800-221-9985 *E-mail:* utpbooks@utpress.utoronto.ca *Web Site:* www.utpress.utoronto.ca; Publishers Group West, 1700 Fourth St, Berkeley, CA 94710, United States *Toll Free Tel:* 866-400-5351 *Toll Free Fax:* 800-838-1149 *E-mail:* ips@ingramcontent.com *Web Site:* www.pgw.com
Membership(s): Association of Canadian Publishers (ACP); Educational Book & Media Association (EBMA); Organization of Book Publishers of Ontario (OBPO)

Pacific Educational Press
Imprint of University of British Columbia Press
c/o UBC Press, 2029 West Mall, Vancouver, BC V6T 1Z2
Tel: 604-822-5959 *Toll Free Tel:* 877-377-9378
E-mail: pep.admin@ubc.ca; pep.sales@ubc.ca
Web Site: pacificedpress.ca
Founded: 1971
Textbooks for teacher education programs, education materials, materials which are generally used in classrooms or educational institutes, books on education topics & issues for a general readership.
Publishes in English.
ISBN Prefix(es): 978-0-88865; 978-1-895766
Number of titles published annually: 6 Print
Total Titles: 104 Print; 16 E-Book
Distributor for Critical Thinking Consortium (TC2)
Distribution Center: Georgetown Terminal Warehouse, 34 Armstrong Ave, Georgetown, ON L7G 4R9 *Tel:* 905-873-9781 *Toll Free Tel:* 877-864-8477 (CN only) *Fax:* 905-873-6170 *Toll Free Fax:* 877-864-4272 (CN only) *E-mail:* orders@gtwcanada.com
Membership(s): The Association of Book Publishers of British Columbia (ABPBC); Association of Canadian Publishers (ACP)

Palimpsest Press
1171 Eastlawn Ave, Windsor, ON N8S 3J1
Tel: 519-259-2112
E-mail: publicity@palimpsestpress.ca
Web Site: www.palimpsestpress.ca
Key Personnel
Publr: Aimee Parent Dunn *E-mail:* aimee@palimpsestpress.ca
Mgr: Shaun Dunn
Fiction Ed/Copy-Ed: Ginger Pharand
Poetry Ed: Jim Johnstone; Dawn Kresan *E-mail:* dawnkresan@palimpsestpress.ca
Publicity Mgr: Abigail Roelens
Founded: 2000
Publish poetry collections, nonfiction, essays, literary fiction.
Publishes in English.
ISBN Prefix(es): 978-0-9733952; 978-1-926794; 978-0-9784917
Number of titles published annually: 6 Print
Total Titles: 30 Print
Imprints: Anstruther Books
Sales Office(s): The Literary Press Group of Canada, 234 Eglinton Ave E, Suite 401, Toronto, ON M4P 1K5 *Tel:* 416-483-1321 *Fax:* 416-483-2510 *E-mail:* sales@lpg.ca *Web Site:* lpg.ca
Orders to: LitDistCo, 8300 Lawson Rd, Milton, ON L9T 0A4 *Toll Free Tel:* 800-591-6250 *Toll Free Fax:* 800-591-6251 *E-mail:* ordering@litdistco.ca *Web Site:* www.litdistco.ca
Shipping Address: LitDistCo, 8300 Lawson Rd, Milton, ON L9T 0A4 *Toll Free Tel:* 800-581-6250 *Toll Free Fax:* 800-581-6251 *Web Site:* www.litdistco.ca
Warehouse: LitDistCo, 8300 Lawson Rd, Milton, ON L9T 0A4 *Toll Free Tel:* 800-581-6250 *Toll Free Fax:* 800-581-6251 *Web Site:* www.litdistco.ca
Distribution Center: LitDistCo, 8300 Lawson Rd, Milton, ON L9T 0A4 *Toll Free Tel:* 800-591-6250 *Toll Free Fax:* 800-591-6251 *E-mail:* ordering@litdistco.ca *Web Site:* www.litdistco.ca
Membership(s): Association of Canadian Publishers (ACP); Literary Press Group of Canada

§Paulines Editions
5610 rue Beaubien est, Montreal, QC H1T 1X5
Tel: 514-253-5610 *Fax:* 514-253-1907
E-mail: editions@paulines.qc.ca; fsp-paulines@videotron.ca
Web Site: www.editions.paulines.qc.ca
Founded: 1956
Religious books.
Publishes in English, French.
ISBN Prefix(es): 978-2-920912
Number of titles published annually: 4 Print
Total Titles: 60 Print
Distributed by Mediaspaul (Montreal)

§Pearson Education Canada
Division of Pearson Canada Inc
26 Prince Andrew Place, North York, ON M3C 2H4
SAN: 115-0022
Toll Free Tel: 800-567-3800 *Fax:* 416-447-7755 *Toll Free Fax:* 800-263-7733
E-mail: cdn.ordr@pearsoned.com
Web Site: www.pearson.com/ca; www.mypearsonstore.ca
Founded: 1966
Educational textbooks, trade, reference.
Publishes in English, French.
ISBN Prefix(es): 978-0-201
Total Titles: 5,700 Print
Imprints: Addison Wesley; Longman; Prentice Hall
Orders to: Pearson Canada Operations Centre, 195 Harry Walker Pkwy N, Newmarket, ON L3Y 7B4
Returns: Pearson Canada Operations Centre, Consumer Returns Dept, 195 Harry Walker Pkwy N, Ontario L3Y 7B4
Distribution Center: Pearson Canada Operations Centre, 195 Harry Walker Pkwy N, Newmarket, ON L3Y 7B4 *Tel:* 905-853-7888 *Fax:* 905-853-7865

§Pembroke Publishers Ltd
538 Hood Rd, Markham, ON L3R 3K9
Tel: 905-477-0650 *Toll Free Tel:* 800-997-9807 *Fax:* 905-477-3691 *Toll Free Fax:* 800-339-5568
Web Site: www.pembrokepublishers.com
Key Personnel
Mng Dir: Claudia Connolly
Founded: 1985
Educational books.
Publishes in English.
ISBN Prefix(es): 978-0-921217; 978-1-55138
Number of titles published annually: 10 Print
Total Titles: 300 Print; 100 E-Book
Distributor for Stenhouse Publishers
U.S. Publishers Represented: Stenhouse Publishers
U.S. Rep(s): Stenhouse Publishers
Foreign Rep(s): Eurospan (Africa, Asia, Europe, Middle East, UK); Hawker Brownlow Education (Australia, New Zealand)
Membership(s): Organization of Book Publishers of Ontario (OBPO)

Penguin Random House Canada, a Penguin Random House company
320 Front St W, Suite 1400, Toronto, ON M5V 3B6
SAN: 201-3975
Tel: 416-364-4449 *Toll Free Tel:* 888-523-9292 (cust serv)
E-mail: canadaweb@penguinrandomhouse.com; customerservicescanada@penguinrandomhouse.com
Web Site: www.penguinrandomhouse.ca
Key Personnel
CEO: Kristin Cochrane
CFO: Barry Gallant
Chief Strategy & Opers Offr: Robert Wheaton
Cont: Kwangi Mashumba
Chief of Staff & Head, Opers: Athmika Punja
VP & Publr, Appetite by Random House: Robert McCullough
VP, Mktg & Communs: Beth Lockley
VP, Sales: Charidy Johnston
VP, Subs Rts: Adrienne Tang
Head, Insights & Strategic Busn Devt: Sarah Tutty
Head, Prodn: Carla Kean

CANADIAN PUBLISHERS

Sr Dir, Young Readers Group Sales: Kelly Glover
Group Dir, Publicity & Mktg: Erin Kelly
Group Sales Dir: Val Gow
Dir, Data Sci (Global): Andrew Myrden
Dir, Lifestyle Mktg & Publicity: Michelle Arbus
Dir, Mktg & Publicity, Cookbooks & Lifestyle: Adria Iwasutiak
Dir, Mng Edit & Sr Mng Ed, Appetite by Random House/Knopf Canada: Susan Burns
Dir, Mktg & Publicity: Tonia Addison
Dir, Online & Digital Sales: Taylor Berry
Dir, Sales Mgmt: Brent Richard
Dir, Wholesale & Spec Mkts Sales Strategy: Lavanya Narasimhan
Edit Dir, Appetite by Random House: Lindsay Paterson
Edit Dir, Tundra Books Group: Anne Shone
Assoc Dir, Mktg: Beth Cockeram
Assoc Dir, Mktg & Publicity, Young Readers: Sylvia Chan
Assoc Dir, Typesetting & Ebook Prodn: Terra Page
Sr Mng Ed, McClelland & Stewart/Signal/Strange Light: Kimberlee Kemp
Mng Ed, Canadian Pbks: Cheryl Chen
Assoc Mng Ed, Canadian Pbks: Danielle Gerritse
Exec Ed: Deborah Sun de la Cruz
Sr Ed: Sarah St Pierre
Sr Ed, McClelland & Stewart: Kelly Joseph
Sr Ed, Strange Light: Haley Cullingham
Ed: Sarah Jackson
Prodn Ed, Tundra Books: Katelyn Chan
Asst Ed, Doubleday Canada: Megan Kwan
Asst Ed, Knopf Canada: Hilary Lo
Sr Contracts Mgr: Naomi Pinn
Sr Imprint Sales Mgr, Young Readers: Kathryn Rennie
Sr Mgr, Ad Servs: Dulce Rosales
Sr Mgr, Amazon Sales: Kelly Rankin
Sr Mgr, Children's Imprint Sales: Julie Forrest
Academic Sales Mgr: Melody Tacit
Busn Mgr: Anya Oberdorf
Opers Mgr: Juan Aguilar
District Sales Mgr: Hala Kamaliddin
District Sales Mgr, Children's Independent & School Sales: Kyrell Grant
District Sales Mgr, Eastern CN: Linda Iarrera
Lib Sales Mgr, Children's Books, Manga & Graphic Novels: Krisztina Riez
Mgr, Busn Intelligence & Reporting: Jill Smith
Mgr, Comics & Specialty Category Sales: Nicole Alfaro
Mgr, Consumer Insights: Kirby Best
Mgr, Ebook & Digital Audiobook Sales & Mdsg: Sarah Seto
Mgr, Mktg & Publicity: Anais Loewen-Young
Mgr, Mktg & Publicity Opers: Emily Sheppard
Mgr, Publicity & Mktg: Danielle LeSage
Mgr, Spec Projs: Julia Hartland
Opers Mgr: Francesca Conte
Publicity Mgr: Evan Munday
Publg Mgr, McClelland & Stewart: Joe Lee
Royalty Accountant Mgr: Cheryl Nurse
Sales Mgr: Patrick Georges
Sales Mgr, Natl Accts: Karen Ma
Prodr, Audiobooks: Jaclyn Gruenberger
Sr Publicist: Erin Bonner; Natasha Tsakiris
Sr Publicist, Lifestyle: Kelly Albert
Publicist: Chalista Andadari; Kristin Cipolla; Cameron Waller
Publicist, Lifestyle: Megan Konzelman; Aakanksha Malhotra
Publicist, Young Readers: Graciela Patron Colin
Mktg Specialist: Charlotte Nip; Dara Sheere
Mktg Analyst: Kirti Henry
Comics & Graphic Novels Specialist: Aleks Wrobel
Online & Digital Sales Coord: Ellen Zhang
Ad Coord: John Castillanes; Paola Gonzalez
Audiobooks Coord: Ankanee Lagunarajan
Awards Coord: Sofia Ramirez
Communs Coord: Trudy Fegan
Events Coord: Farishteh Pavri
Spec Mkts Coord: Dilara Kurtaran
HR Coord: Ayomikun Taiwo
Imprint Sales Coord: Jaclyn Mistry
Intl Sales Coord: Alicia Edwards
Mktg & Publicity Coord: Megan Costa; Sabrina Papas; Taylor Rice
Group Asst, Mktg, Publicity & Communs: Supipi Weerasooriya
Mktg & Publicity Coord, Young Readers: Stephanie Ehmann
Off Servs Coord: Joey Arredondo
Opers Coord: Gautham Raja
Proj Coord, Mktg Design: Hailey LeBlanc
Publg Coord, Audiobooks: Geffen Semach
Sales Coord, Online Retail Ad & SEO: Zahra Abdi
Sales Coord, SEO & Ad: Kirsten Armstrong
Studio Coord: Noah Kahansky
Royalty Accountant: Sharon Ramsahai
Contracts Assoc: Jamie Steep
Mktg Assoc: Danya Elsayed
Prodn Assoc: Melanie Cheng; Rachel Guglielmelli
Rts Assoc: Catherine Ryoo
Sr Designer: Emma Dolan; Andrew Roberts
Designer: Matthew Flute
Mktg Designer, Young Readers: Anthony de Ridder
Jr Designer: Talia Abramson; Dylan Browne
Jr Mktg Designer: Megan MacKenzie
Data Scientist: Georgia Henry; Cecilia Yang
Help Desk Analyst: Ricky Utomo
Serv Desk Analyst: Emma Clerk
Jr Fin Analyst: Farnaz Lilian
Founded: 1944
Penguin Random House Canada & its publishing entities are not accepting unsol submissions, proposals, mss, or submission queries via e-mail at this time.
Publishes in English.
Imprints: Anchor Canada; Appetite by Random House; Berkley; Bond Street Books; Doubleday Canada; Emblem Editions; Fenn-M&S; Douglas Gibson Books; Hamish Hamilton Canada; Knopf Canada; Allen Lane Canada; McClelland & Stewart; Penguin Canada; Penguin Teen; Portfolio Canada; Puffin Canada; Random House Canada; Razorbill Canada; Seal Books; Signal; Strange Light; Tundra Books; Viking Canada; Vintage Canada
Divisions: Tundra Book Group
Warehouse: 6971 Columbus Rd, Mississauga, ON L5T 1K1
Membership(s): Canadian Publishers' Council
See separate listing for:
Doubleday Canada
Knopf Canada
McClelland & Stewart Ltd
Seal Books
Tundra Book Group

Pontifical Institute of Mediaeval Studies, Department of Publications
59 Queen's Park Crescent E, Toronto, ON M5S 2C4
SAN: 115-0804
Tel: 416-926-7142 *Fax:* 416-926-7292
Web Site: www.pims.ca
Key Personnel
Ed-in-Chief: Fred R Unwalla *Tel:* 416-926-7280
E-mail: unwalla@chass.utoronto.ca
Founded: 1936
Scholarly publishing on the Middle Ages.
Publishes in English, French.
ISBN Prefix(es): 978-0-88844
Number of titles published annually: 10 Print
Total Titles: 350 Print
Distributed by Brepols Publishers (outside North America)
Orders to: University of Toronto Press, 5201 Dufferin St, Toronto, ON M3H 5T8 *Tel:* 416-667-7791 *Toll Free Tel:* 800-565-9523 *Fax:* 416-667-7832 *Toll Free Fax:* 800-221-9985 *E-mail:* utpbooks@utpress.utoronto.ca *Web Site:* www.utpress.utoronto.ca
Distribution Center: University of Toronto Press, 5201 Dufferin St, Toronto, ON M3H 5T8 *Tel:* 416-667-7791 *Toll Free Tel:* 800-565-9523 *Fax:* 416-667-7832 *Toll Free Fax:* 800-221-9985 *E-mail:* utpbooks@utpress.utoronto.ca *Web Site:* www.utpress.utoronto.ca

§Porcupine's Quill Inc
68 Main St, Erin, ON N0B 1T0
Mailing Address: PO Box 160, Erin, ON N0B 1T0
Tel: 519-833-9158
E-mail: pql@sentex.net
Web Site: porcupinesquill.ca; www.facebook.com/theporcupinesquill
Key Personnel
Publr: Tim Inkster
Founded: 1974
Modern Canadian literature, poetry & art.
Publishes in English.
ISBN Prefix(es): 978-0-88984
Number of titles published annually: 8 Print
Total Titles: 100 Print
Membership(s): Association of Canadian Publishers (ACP); Canada Council for the Arts; Literary Press Group; Ontario Arts Council

Portage & Main Press
318 McDermot Ave, Suite 100, Winnipeg, MB R3A 0A2
Tel: 204-987-3500 *Toll Free Tel:* 800-667-9673 *Fax:* 204-947-0080 *Toll Free Fax:* 866-734-8477
E-mail: customerservice@portageandmainpress.com
Web Site: www.portageandmainpress.com
Key Personnel
Owner, Publr, Rts & Perms: Catherine Gerbasi
Dir, Mktg: Kirsten Phillips
Mng Ed: Laura McKay-Keizer *E-mail:* lmckay@portageandmainpress.com
Founded: 1967 (as Peguis Publishers)
Publisher of practical K–12 educational materials & Indigenous literature.
Publishes in English.
ISBN Prefix(es): 978-0-919566; 978-0-920541; 978-1-895411; 978-1-894110; 978-1-55379; 978-0-9699032; 978-0-9694264
Number of titles published annually: 14 Print; 14 E-Book
Total Titles: 200 Print; 200 E-Book
Imprints: HighWater Press
Distribution Center: Consortium Book Sales & Distribution, The Keg House, Suite 101, 34 13 Ave NE, Minneapolis, MN 55413-1007, United States *Tel:* 612-746-2600 *Toll Free Tel:* 866-400-5351 *E-mail:* cbsdinfo@ingramcontent.com *Web Site:* www.cbsd.com SAN: 200-6049

Pottersfield Press
248 Leslie Rd, East Lawrencetown, NS B2Z 1T4
SAN: 115-0790
Toll Free Tel: 800-646-2879 (orders only)
E-mail: pottersfieldcreative@gmail.com
Web Site: www.pottersfieldpress.com
Key Personnel
Pres & Publr: Lesley Choyce
Founded: 1979
Fiction, books about the sea, books of Atlantic & Canada; nonfiction, books of literary travel.
Publishes in English.
ISBN Prefix(es): 978-0-919001; 978-1-895900; 978-1-897426; 978-1-988286
Number of titles published annually: 16 Print; 16 E-Book
Total Titles: 170 Print; 2 CD-ROM; 16 E-Book; 4 Audio
Imprints: Atlantic Classics Series
Distributed by Nimbus Publishing
U.S. Rep(s): Nimbus Publishing

Orders to: c/o Nimbus Publishing, 3660 Strawberry Hill St, Halifax, NS B3K 5A9 *Toll Free Tel:* 800-646-2879 *Toll Free Fax:* 888-253-3133 *E-mail:* customerservice@nimbus.ca *Web Site:* www.nimbus.ca
Shipping Address: c/o Nimbus Publishing, 3731 MacIntosh St, Halifax, NS B3K 5A5 *Tel:* 904-455-4286-orders only *Toll Free Tel:* 800-646-2879 *Toll Free Fax:* 888-253-3133 *E-mail:* customerservice@nimbus.ca *Web Site:* www.nimbus.ca
Membership(s): Atlantic Publishers Marketing Association

PrairieView Press
625 Seventh St, Gretna, MB R0G 0V0
Mailing Address: PO Box 460, Gretna, MB R0G 0V0
Tel: 204-327-6543 *Toll Free Tel:* 800-477-7377 *Toll Free Fax:* 866-480-0253
Web Site: prairieviewpress.com
Key Personnel
Owner & Pres: Chester Goossen
Secy: Darleen Loewen
Contact: Trevor Hrappstead
Founded: 1968
Quality reading material for children & adults; songbooks. Over 2,000 titles in distribution, listed in catalog.
Publishes in English.
ISBN Prefix(es): 978-0-920035; 978-1-896199; 978-1-897080
Number of titles published annually: 36 Print
Total Titles: 1,450 Print
Branch Office(s)
PO Box 88, Neche, ND 58265-0088, United States

Les Presses de l'Université d'Ottawa, see University of Ottawa Press (Presses de l'Université d'Ottawa)

§Les Presses de l'Universite de Montreal
5450, chemin de la Cote-des-Neiges, bureau 100, Montreal, QC H3T 1Y6
Mailing Address: CP 6128, Centre-ville, Montreal, QC H3C 3J7
Tel: 514-343-6933 *Fax:* 514-343-2232
E-mail: pum@umontreal.ca
Web Site: www.pum.umontreal.ca
Key Personnel
Dir Gen: Patrick Poirier *E-mail:* poirierp@editionspum.ca
Founded: 1962
ISBN Prefix(es): 978-2-7606
Number of titles published annually: 40 Print; 80 E-Book
Foreign Rep(s): Patrimoine SPRL (Belgium, Luxembourg); Servidis SA (Switzerland); SODIS (France)
Distribution Center: Socadis Inc, 420 rue Stinson, Ville St-Laurent, QC H4N 3L7 *Tel:* 514-331-3300 *Toll Free Tel:* 800-361-2847 *Fax:* 514-745-3282 *Toll Free Fax:* 866-803-5422 *E-mail:* socinfo@socadis.com *Web Site:* www.socadis.com

Les Presses de l'Universite du Quebec
Division of Universite du Quebec
2875 blvd Laurier, Suite 450, Quebec, QC G1V 2M2
Tel: 418-657-4399 *Fax:* 418-657-2096
E-mail: puq@puq.ca
Web Site: www.puq.ca
Founded: 1969
University press publishing in the main disciplines of management science, political science, applied science, educational science, social science, psychology, communications, ethics, geography & tourism.
Publishes in English, French.
ISBN Prefix(es): 978-2-7605; 978-0-7770; 978-2-920073
Number of titles published annually: 80 Print
Total Titles: 1,600 Print
Distributor for Figura; Imaginaire du Nord; Tele-Universite
Distribution Center: Prologue Inc, 3785, Rue La Fayette Ouest, Boisbriand, QC J7H 1N5 *Tel:* 450-434-0306 *Toll Free Tel:* 800-363-2864 *Toll Free Fax:* 800-361-8088 *E-mail:* prologue@prologue.ca *Web Site:* www.prologue.ca
Sodis SARL, 128 Ave du Marechal de Lattre de Tassigny, BP 142, 77403 Lagny Cedex, France *Tel:* 01 60 07 82 99 *Fax:* 01 64 30 32 27 *E-mail:* portal@sodis.fr *Web Site:* www.sodis.fr
Sofedis, 11 Rue Soufflot, 75005 Paris, France (Belgium, France & Luxembourg) *Tel:* 01 53 10 25 25 *Fax:* 01 53 10 25 26 *E-mail:* info@sofedis.fr *Web Site:* www.sofedis.fr
Servidis SA, Chemin des Chalets, 7, 1279 Chavannes-de-Bogis, Switzerland *Tel:* (022) 940 95 10 *Fax:* (022) 776 35 44 *Web Site:* www.servidis.ch
Membership(s): Association des Libraires du Quebec (ALQ); Association nationale des editeurs de livres (ANEL); Association of Canadian University Presses (ACUP)

§Les Presses de l'Universite Laval
Division of Universite du Quebec
2180, Chemin Sainte-Foy, 1st fl, Quebec, QC G1V 0A6
Tel: 418-656-2803 *Fax:* 418-656-3305
E-mail: presses@pul.ulaval.ca
Web Site: www.pulaval.com
Key Personnel
Publr: Helene Cormier *E-mail:* helene.cormier@pul.ulaval.ca
Exec Dir: Dominique Gingras *E-mail:* dominique.gingras@pul.ulaval.ca
Ed & Asst to Exec Dir: Marie-Helene Boucher *E-mail:* marie-helene.boucher@pul.ulaval.ca
Ed: Maximilien Nolet *E-mail:* maximilien.nolet@pul.ulaval.ca
Mktg Mgr: Melissa Cote *E-mail:* melissa.cote@pul.ulaval.ca
Accountant: Kathleen Allen *E-mail:* kathleen.allen@pul.ulaval.ca
Acctg Asst & Shipping: Josyann Allen *E-mail:* josyann.allen@pul.ulaval.ca
Founded: 1950
Books in the humanities & social sciences with an emphasis on subjects of interest in Quebec & Canada, administration, economy.
Publishes in French.
ISBN Prefix(es): 978-2-7637
Number of titles published annually: 120 Print
Foreign Rep(s): Librairie du Quebec (France); Patrimoine SPRL (Belgium); Servidis SA (Switzerland)
Distribution Center: Prologue Inc, 3785, Rue La Fayette Ouest, Boisbriand, QC J7H 1N5 (CN & US) *Tel:* 450-434-0306 *Toll Free Tel:* 800-363-2864 *Toll Free Fax:* 800-361-8088 *E-mail:* prologue@prologue.ca *Web Site:* www.prologue.ca

Productive Publications
380 Brooke Ave, Lower Level, North York, ON M5M 2L6
SAN: 117-1712
Tel: 416-483-0634 *Toll Free Tel:* 877-879-2669 (orders) *Fax:* 416-322-7434
E-mail: productivepublications@rogers.com
Web Site: www.productivepublications.ca
Key Personnel
Owner & Pres: Iain Williamson
Founded: 1985
Trade paperback books; business, finance, communications, finance, computers, management, marketing, taxation, personal finance, entrepreneurship, self-help.
Publishes in English.
ISBN Prefix(es): 978-0-920847; 978-1-896210; 978-1-55270
Number of titles published annually: 28 Print
Total Titles: 180 Print

§Les Publications du Quebec
425, rue Jacques-Parizeau, 5e etage, Quebec, QC G1R 4Z1
Tel: 418-643-5150 *Toll Free Tel:* 800-463-2100 (Quebec province only) *Fax:* 418-643-6177 *Toll Free Fax:* 800-561-3479
E-mail: publicationsduquebec@cspq.gouv.qc.ca
Web Site: www.publicationsduquebec.gouv.qc.ca
Founded: 1982
Government publications.
Publishes in English, French.
ISBN Prefix(es): 978-2-550; 978-2-551; 978-0-7754
Number of titles published annually: 200 Print; 20 Online
Total Titles: 4,000 Print; 100 Online

§QA International (QAI)
Division of Groupe Quebec Amerique
7240 Rue Saint-Hubert, Montreal, QC H2R 2N1
Tel: 514-499-3000 *Fax:* 514-499-3010
Web Site: www.qa-international.com
Key Personnel
Founder & CEO: Jacques Fortin
Dir, Busn Devt: Amelie Charbonneau
Founded: 1989
Create, develop & produce editorial content built around state-of-the-art computer images for publication in print & electronic media throughout the world.
Publishes in French.
ISBN Prefix(es): 978-2-7644
Number of titles published annually: 60 Print
Total Titles: 770 Print

Quattro Books Inc
12 Concord Ave, 2nd fl, Toronto, ON M6H 2P1
Tel: 416-893-7979
E-mail: info@quattrobooks.ca
Web Site: www.quattrobooks.ca
Key Personnel
Exec Dir & Publr: Bilal Hashmi
Assoc Publr: Sonia D'Agostino
Founded: 2006
Publishes in English.
ISBN Prefix(es): 978-0-9782806; 978-0-9810186; 978-1-926802
Number of titles published annually: 16 Print; 16 E-Book
Imprints: Fourfront Editions
Distribution Center: Canadian Manda Group, 165 Dufferin St, Toronto, ON M6K 3H6 (CN trade accts) *Web Site:* www.mandagroup.com
The Literary Press Group of Canada, 425 Adelaide St W, Suite 700, Toronto, ON M5V 3C1 (US trade accts), Contact: Tan Light *Tel:* 416-483-1321 ext 4 *Fax:* 416-483-2510 *E-mail:* sales@lpg.ca *Web Site:* lpg.ca
LitDistCo, 83 Lawson Rd, Milton, ON L0T 0A4 (US trade accts) *Toll Free Tel:* 800-591-6250 *E-mail:* orders@litdistco.ca *Web Site:* www.litdistco.ca
Membership(s): Literary Press Group of Canada

Red Deer Press Inc
Division of Fitzhenry & Whiteside Limited
209 Wicksteed Ave, Unit 51, Toronto, ON M4G 0B1
Tel: 905-477-9700 *Toll Free Tel:* 800-387-9776
E-mail: bookinfo@fitzhenry.ca
Web Site: www.reddeerpress.com
Key Personnel
Publr: Holly Doll *Tel:* 905-477-9700 ext 207 *E-mail:* hdoll@fitzhenry.ca
Children's Ed: Beverley Brenna

CANADIAN PUBLISHERS

Mgr, Cust Serv: Judy Ghoura *Tel:* 800-387-9776 ext 225
Founded: 1975
Publishes in English.
ISBN Prefix(es): 978-0-88995
Number of titles published annually: 15 Print
Total Titles: 400 Print
Distribution Center: Firefly Books Ltd, 50 Staples Ave, Unit 1, Richmond Hill, ON L4B 0A7 *Tel:* 416-499-8412 *Toll Free Tel:* 800-387-6192 *Fax:* 416-499-8313 *Toll Free Fax:* 800-450-0391 *E-mail:* service@fireflybooks.com *Web Site:* www.fireflybooks.com

Rocky Mountain Books Ltd (RMB)
Member of The Heritage Group
103-1075 Pendergast St, Victoria, BC V8V 0A1
Tel: 250-360-0829 *Fax:* 250-386-0829
Web Site: rmbooks.com
Key Personnel
Publr & Acqs: Don Gorman *E-mail:* don@rmbooks.com
Art Dir: Chyla Cardinal *E-mail:* chyla@rmbooks.com
Sr Ed: Joe Wilderson *E-mail:* joe@rmbooks.com
Mktg & Publicity Mgr: Jillian van der Geest *E-mail:* jillian@rmbooks.com
Publr Asst, Soc Media, Digital Mktg & Foreign Rts: Grace Gorman *E-mail:* grace@rmbooks.com
Founded: 1979
Regional publisher of books on outdoor activities, mountain literature & mountain biographies.
Publishes in English.
ISBN Prefix(es): 978-0-9690038; 978-0-921102; 978-1-894765; 978-1-897522; 978-1-926855; 978-1-927330; 978-1-77160; 978-1-92655
Number of titles published annually: 30 Print
Total Titles: 188 Print
Orders to: Heritage Group Distribution, 19272 96 Ave, Suite 8, Surrey, BC V4N 4C1 *Tel:* 604-881-7067 *Toll Free Tel:* 800-665-3302 *Fax:* 604-881-7068 *Toll Free Fax:* 800-566-3336 *E-mail:* orders@hgdistribution.com *Web Site:* www.hgdistribution.com
Distribution Center: Heritage Group Distribution, 19272 96 Ave, Suite 8, Surrey, BC V4N 4C1 *Tel:* 604-881-7067 *Toll Free Tel:* 800-665-3302 *Fax:* 604-881-7068 *Toll Free Fax:* 800-566-3336 *E-mail:* orders@hgdistribution.com *Web Site:* www.hgdistribution.com
Membership(s): Book Publishers Association of Alberta

Ronsdale Press Ltd
125A-1030 Denman St, Vancouver, BC V6G 2M6
SAN: 116-2454
Tel: 604-738-4688
E-mail: ronsdalepress@gmail.com
Web Site: ronsdalepress.com
Key Personnel
Publr: Wendy Atkinson
Founded: 1988
Literary press, fiction, nonfiction, young adult.
Publishes in English.
ISBN Prefix(es): 978-0-921870; 978-1-55380
Number of titles published annually: 12 Print; 12 E-Book
Total Titles: 270 Print
Sales Office(s): Publishers Group Canada, 201-128A Sterling Rd, Toronto, ON M6R 2B7
Distribution Center: LitDistCo, 8300 Lawson Rd, Milton, ON L9T 0A4 (US only) *Toll Free Tel:* 800-591-6250 *Toll Free Fax:* 800-591-6251 *E-mail:* orders@litdistco.ca *Web Site:* www.litdistco.ca
Raincoast Books, 2440 Viking Way, Richmond, BC V6V 1N2 *Toll Free Tel:* 800-663-5714 *Toll Free Fax:* 800-565-3770 *E-mail:* customerservice@raincoast.com *Web Site:* www.raincoast.com
Gazelle Book Services Ltd, White Cross Mills, Hightown, Lancaster, Lancs LA1 4XS, United Kingdom (UK & Europe) *Tel:* (01524) 528500 *E-mail:* sales@gazellebookservices.co.uk *Web Site:* www.gazellebookservices.co.uk
Independent Publishers Group (IPG), 814 N Franklin St, Chicago, IL 60610, United States *Toll Free Tel:* 800-888-4741 *E-mail:* orders@ipgbook.com *Web Site:* www.ipgbook.com
Membership(s): The Association of Book Publishers of British Columbia (ABPBC); Association of Canadian Publishers (ACP); Literary Press Group of Canada

Robert Rose Inc
120 Eglinton Ave E, Suite 800, Toronto, ON M4P 1E2
Tel: 416-322-6552 *Fax:* 416-322-6936
Web Site: www.robertrose.ca
Founded: 1995
Publishes in English.
ISBN Prefix(es): 978-1-896503; 978-0-7788
Number of titles published annually: 25 Print
Total Titles: 285 Print
Distributed by Firefly Books Ltd (CN & US)

§Royal Ontario Museum Press
100 Queen's Park, Toronto, ON M5S 2C6
Tel: 416-586-8000
E-mail: info@rom.on.ca
Web Site: www.rom.on.ca
Key Personnel
Dir & CEO: John Basseches
Founded: 1912
Scholarly & general books on art, archaeology & sciences.
Publishes in English, French.
ISBN Prefix(es): 978-0-88854
Number of titles published annually: 8 Print
Total Titles: 100 Print
U.S. Rep(s): University of Toronto Press (NY)
Warehouse: University of Toronto Press, 5201 Dufferin St, Toronto, ON M3H 5T8 *Tel:* 416-667-7791 *Toll Free Tel:* 800-565-9523 *Fax:* 416-667-7832 *Toll Free Fax:* 800-221-9985 *E-mail:* utpbooks@utpress.utoronto.ca *Web Site:* www.utpress.utoronto.ca
Distribution Center: University of Toronto Press, 5201 Dufferin St, Toronto, ON M3H 5T8 *Tel:* 416-667-7791 *Toll Free Tel:* 800-565-9523 *Fax:* 416-667-7832 *Toll Free Fax:* 800-221-9985 *E-mail:* utpbooks@utpress.utoronto.ca *Web Site:* www.utpress.utoronto.ca

Saint-Jean Editeur Inc
4490, rue Garand, Laval, QC H7L 5Z6
Tel: 450-663-1777
E-mail: info@saint-jeanediteur.com
Web Site: saint-jeanediteur.com
Key Personnel
Pres: Nicole Saint-Jean *E-mail:* nicole@saint-jeanediteur.com
VP, Publg: Marie-Claire Saint-Jean *E-mail:* mclaire@saint-jeanediteur.com
Prodn/Opers Dir: Jacques Frechette *E-mail:* jacques@saint-jeanediteur.com
Gen Mgr: Jean Pare *E-mail:* jean.pare@saint-jeanediteur.com
Founded: 1981
Publishes in French.
ISBN Prefix(es): 978-2-920340; 978-2-89455; 978-2-89827
Number of titles published annually: 80 Print; 40 E-Book; 10 Audio
Total Titles: 700 Print; 40 Audio
Distribution Center: Prologue Inc, 3785, Rue La Fayette Ouest, Boisbriand, QC J7H 1N5 *Tel:* 450-434-0306 *Toll Free Tel:* 800-363-2864 *Toll Free Fax:* 800-361-8088 *E-mail:* prologue@prologue.ca *Web Site:* www.prologue.ca
Librairie du Quebec, 30, rue Gay Lussac, 75005 Paris, France *Tel:* 01 43 54 49 02 *Fax:* 01 43 54 39 15 *E-mail:* libraires@librairieduquebec.fr
Membership(s): Association nationale des editeurs de livres (ANEL)

§Sara Jordan Publishing
Division of Jordan Music Productions Inc
RPO Lakeport Box 28105, St Catharines, ON L2N 7P8
Tel: 905-938-5050 *Toll Free Tel:* 800-567-7733 *Fax:* 905-938-9970 *Toll Free Fax:* 800-229-3855
Web Site: www.sara-jordan.com; www.songsthatteach.com
Key Personnel
Pres: Sara Jordan
Founded: 1990
Publish educational resources.
Publishes in English, French.
ISBN Prefix(es): 978-1-895523; 978-1-894262; 978-1-55386
Number of titles published annually: 6 Print; 2 Audio
Total Titles: 100 Print; 60 Audio
Distribution Center: Gazelle Book Services Ltd, White Cross Mills, Hightown, Lancaster, Lancs LA1 4XS, United Kingdom *Tel:* (01524) 528500 *Fax:* (01524) 528510 *E-mail:* sales@gazellebookservices.co.uk *Web Site:* www.gazellebookservices.co.uk
Membership(s): Association of Canadian Publishers (ACP)

Scholastic Canada Ltd
Subsidiary of Scholastic Inc
175 Hillmount Rd, Markham, ON L6C 1Z7
Tel: 905-887-7323 *Toll Free Tel:* 800-268-3860 (CN) *Toll Free Fax:* 800-387-4944
E-mail: custserve@scholastic.ca
Web Site: www.scholastic.ca
Key Personnel
Pres, Fin, Opers & Admin: Anne Browne *Tel:* 905-887-7323 ext 4396 *E-mail:* abrowne@scholastic.ca
Pres, Mktg & Publg: Nancy Pearson *Tel:* 416-915-3515 *E-mail:* npearson@scholastic.ca
VP, French Div: Chantale Gravel Lalonde *Tel:* 416-915-3510 *E-mail:* clalonde@scholastic.ca
VP, Publg: Diane Kerner *Tel:* 416-915-3523 *E-mail:* dkerner@scholastic.ca
VP, Reading Club: Vicki Pasternak *Tel:* 416-915-3516 *E-mail:* vpasternak@scholastic.ca
VP, Trade: Kathy Goncharenko *Tel:* 416-915-3517 *E-mail:* kgoncharenko@scholastic.ca
Rts & Contracts Mgr: Maral Maclagan *Tel:* 416-915-3524 *E-mail:* mmaclagan@scholastic.ca
Founded: 1957
Publish & distribute children's books & educational materials in both official languages.
Publishes in English, French.
ISBN Prefix(es): 978-0-590; 978-0-439; 978-0-7791; 978-1-55268; 978-0-545; 978-1-4431; 978-1-338
Imprints: Les Editions Scholastic; North Winds Press; Scholastic Canada
Divisions: Scholastic Book Fairs Canada Inc
Branch Office(s)
604 King St W, Toronto, ON M5V 1E1
Distributor for Cartwheel Books® (exclusive in CN); Chicken House® (exclusive in CN); Children's Press (exclusive in CN); Franklin Watts (US) (exclusive in CN); Graphix™ (exclusive in CN); Grolier (exclusive in CN); Klutz® (exclusive in CN); Arthur A Levine Books (exclusive in CN); Orchard Books® (exclusive in CN); Scholastic en espanol® (exclusive in CN); Scholastic Nonfiction (exclusive in CN); Scholastic Paperbacks (exclusive in CN); Scholastic Press (exclusive in CN); Scholastic Reference (exclusive in CN)
U.S. Publishers Represented: Scholastic Inc

U.S. Rep(s): Scholastic Inc
Foreign Rights: Akcali Copyright Agency (Begum Ayfer) (Turkey); Bardon-Chinese Media Agency (Electra Chang & Shirley Vivi Chang) (Mainland China); Bardon-Chinese Media Agency (Cynthia Chang) (Taiwan); Sandra Bruna Agencia Literaria (Sandra Bruna) (Spain); Graal Literary Agency (Tomasz Berezinski) (Poland); JLM Literary Agency (Nelly, Tatiana & John Moukakos) (Greece); Simona Kessler Agency (Adriana Marina) (Romania); Maxima Creative Agency (Santo Manurung) (Indonesia); Andrew Nurnberg Agency (Olga Lutova) (Russia); Seibel Publishing Services Ltd (Patricia Seibel) (Brazil); Shinwon Agency Co (Jihyun Hwang) (South Korea); Tuttle-Mori Agency Inc (Solan Natsume) (Japan); Twinkle Books Agency (Tereza Parizkova) (Czechia)

§Seal Books
Imprint of Penguin Random House Canada
320 Front St W, Suite 1400, Toronto, ON M5V 3B6
SAN: 201-3975
Tel: 416-364-4449 *Toll Free Tel:* 888-523-9292 (order desk) *Fax:* 416-598-7764
Web Site: www.penguinrandomhouse.ca
Key Personnel
CEO, PRHC: Kristin Cochrane
CFO, PRHC: Barry Gallant
Chief Strategy & Opers Offr, PRHC: Robert Wheaton
VP & Dir, Mktg Strategy & Assoc Publr, PRHC: Scott Sellers
SVP & Dir, Prodn: Janine Laporte
Deputy Dir, Prodn: Carla Kean
Founded: 1977
No unsol mss; prefer queries in advance from potential authors.
Publishes in English.
Number of titles published annually: 18 Print
Membership(s): Canadian Publishers' Council

§Second Story Press
20 Maud St, Suite 401, Toronto, ON M5V 2M5
Tel: 416-537-7850 *Fax:* 416-537-0588
E-mail: info@secondstorypress.ca
Web Site: secondstorypress.ca
Key Personnel
Publr, Owner & Pres: Margie Wolfe
Mng Ed: Gillian Rodgerson
Assoc Ed: Jordan Ryder
Gen Mgr: Phuong Truong
Mktg & Promos Mgr: Emma Rodgers
Prodn Mgr: Melissa Kaita
Mktg Coord: Michaela Stephen
Sales Coord: Bronte Germain
Founded: 1988
Feminist-inspired books for adults & young readers.
Publishes in English.
ISBN Prefix(es): 978-0-929005; 978-1-896764; 978-1-897187; 978-0-921299; 978-1-77260; 978-1-926920
Number of titles published annually: 14 Print; 8 E-Book; 8 Audio
Total Titles: 330 Print; 240 E-Book; 35 Audio
Distributor for The Azrieli Foundation; The Book Publishing Co
U.S. Rep(s): Orca Books
Orders to: University of Toronto Press, 5201 Dufferin St, Toronto, ON M3H 5T8 *Tel:* 416-667-7791 *Toll Free Tel:* 800-565-9523 *Fax:* 416-667-7832 *Toll Free Fax:* 800-221-9985 *E-mail:* utpbooks@utpress.utoronto.ca *Web Site:* utpdistribution.com; Orca Book Publishers, PO Box 468, Custer, WA 98240-0468, United States *Toll Free Tel:* 800-210-5277 *Fax:* 250-380-1892 *Web Site:* www.us.orcabook.com
Shipping Address: University of Toronto Press, 5201 Dufferin St, Toronto, ON M3H 5T8
Tel: 416-667-7791 *Toll Free Tel:* 800-565-9523 *Fax:* 416-667-7832 *Toll Free Fax:* 800-221-9985
Distribution Center: University of Toronto Press, 5201 Dufferin St, Toronto, ON M3H 5T8
Tel: 416-667-7791 *Toll Free Tel:* 800-565-9523 *Fax:* 416-667-7832 *Toll Free Fax:* 800-221-9985 *E-mail:* utpbooks@utpress.utoronto.ca
Web Site: utpdistribution.com

Self-Counsel Press, see International Self-Counsel Press Ltd

J Gordon Shillingford Publishing Inc
PO Box 86, RPO Corydon Ave, Winnipeg, MB R3M 3S3
Tel: 204-779-6967
E-mail: jgshill2@mymts.net
Web Site: www.jgshillingford.com
Key Personnel
Pres & Publr: Gordon Shillingford
Founded: 1992
Primarily a literary publisher of nonfiction, theater, poetry & social history. Publish works of Canadian citizens only.
Publishes in English.
ISBN Prefix(es): 978-0-9689709; 978-0-920486; 978-1-896239; 978-0-9697261; 978-1-897289; 978-1-927922
Number of titles published annually: 14 Print
Total Titles: 272 Print
Imprints: The Muses' Co; Scirocco Drama; Watson & Dwyer
Distribution Center: University of Toronto Press, 5210 Dufferin St, North York, ON M3H 5T8 *Tel:* 416-667-7791 *Toll Free Tel:* 800-565-9523 *Fax:* 416-667-7856 *Toll Free Fax:* 800-221-9985 *E-mail:* utpbooks@utpress.utoronto.ca
University of Toronto Press, 2250 Military Rd, Tonowanda, NY 14150, United States *Tel:* 416-667-7791 *Toll Free Tel:* 800-565-9523 *Fax:* 416-667-7832 *Toll Free Fax:* 800-221-9985 *E-mail:* utpbooks@utpress.utoronto.ca
Membership(s): Association of Canadian Publishers (ACP); Association of Manitoba Book Publishers (AMBP); Literary Press Group

Signature Editions
PO Box 206, RPO Corydon, Winnipeg, MB R3M 3S7
Tel: 204-779-7803
E-mail: signature@allstream.net; orders@signature-editions.com
Web Site: www.signature-editions.com
Key Personnel
Publr: Karen Haughian *E-mail:* publisher@signature-editions.com
Mystery Ed: Doug Whiteway
Mktg Asst: Ashley Brekelmans
Founded: 1986 (as Nuage Editions)
Literary publisher which publishes Canadian authors in the genres of fiction, nonfiction, poetry & drama.
Publishes in English.
ISBN Prefix(es): 978-0-921833; 978-1-897109; 978-1-927426; 978-1-773240
Number of titles published annually: 10 Print; 5 E-Book
Total Titles: 170 Print; 65 E-Book; 10 Audio
Distributor for Cyclops Press
Foreign Rep(s): The Literary Press Group of Canada (Tan Light) (USA)
Orders to: University of Toronto Press (UTP), 5201 Dufferin St, North York, ON M3H 5T8 *Tel:* 416-667-7791 *Toll Free Tel:* 800-565-9523 *Fax:* 416-667-7832 *Toll Free Fax:* 800-221-9985 *E-mail:* utpbooks@utpress.utoronto.ca; University of Toronto Press (UTP), 2250 Military Rd, Tonowanda, NY 14150, United States *Tel:* 416-667-7791 *Toll Free Tel:* 800-565-9523 *Fax:* 416-667-7832 *Toll Free Fax:* 800-221-9985 *E-mail:* utpbooks@utpress.utoronto.ca
Returns: University of Toronto Press (UTP), 5201 Dufferin St, North York, ON M3H 5T8 *Tel:* 416-667-7791 *Toll Free Tel:* 800-565-9523 *Fax:* 416-667-7832 *Toll Free Fax:* 800-221-9985 *E-mail:* utpbooks@utpress.utoronto.ca
Shipping Address: University of Toronto Press (UTP), 5201 Dufferin St, North York, ON M3H 5T8 *Tel:* 416-667-7791 *Toll Free Tel:* 800-565-9523 *Fax:* 416-667-7832 *Toll Free Fax:* 800-221-9985 *E-mail:* utpbooks@utpress.utoronto.ca
Distribution Center: University of Toronto Press (UTP), 5201 Dufferin St, North York, ON M3H 5T8 *Tel:* 416-667-7791 *Toll Free Tel:* 800-565-9523 *Fax:* 416-667-7832 *Toll Free Fax:* 800-221-9985 *E-mail:* utpbooks@utpress.utoronto.ca
University of Toronto Press (UTP), 2250 Military Rd, Tonowanda, NY 14150, United States *Tel:* 416-667-7791 *Toll Free Tel:* 800-565-9523 *Fax:* 416-667-7832 *Toll Free Fax:* 800-221-9985 *E-mail:* utpbooks@utpress.utoronto.ca
Membership(s): Association of Canadian Publishers (ACP); Association of Manitoba Book Publishers (AMBP); Literary Press Group of Canada

Simon & Schuster Canada
Subsidiary of Simon & Schuster, LLC
166 King St E, Suite 300, Toronto, ON M5A 1J3
Tel: 647-427-8882 *Toll Free Tel:* 800-387-0446; 800-268-3216 (orders) *Fax:* 647-430-9446 *Toll Free Fax:* 888-849-8151 (orders)
E-mail: info@simonandschuster.ca
Web Site: www.simonandschuster.ca
Key Personnel
Pres & Publr: Nicole Winstanley
VP, Mktg & Communs: Dan French
VP, Opers: Sarah Gibson
VP, Sales: Michael Guy-Haddock
Sr Dir, Publicity: Rita Silva
Exec Ed: Jim Gifford
Mng Ed: Jasmine Elliott
Sr Ed: Adrienne Kerr; Brittany Lavery; Katherena Vermette
Publishes in English.
Imprints: Scribner Canada
Distributor for Andrews McMeel Publishing LLC; Baen Books; Baseball America; Black Library; Blue Heeler Books; BOOM! Studios; Cardoza Publishing; Cernunnos Publishing; Chicken Soup for the Soul; Cider Mill Press Book Publishers LLC; Downtown Books; Gallup Press; Galvanized Media; Games Workshop; Good Books; Hazelden Publishing; Hooked on Phonics; Insight Editions; Juniper Press; Kaplan Publishing; KinFolk; John Locke Publishing; Merck; NorthSouth Books; Oni Press; Open Road Press; Permuted Press; Piggyback Press; Pikachu Press; Post Hill Press; Printer's Row Publishing Group; Reader's Digest; Rebellion; Regnery Publishing; Restless Books; Ripley's Publishing; Simon & Schuster; SimonUK; Skyhorse Publishing; Studio Fun International; To the Stars; Ubisoft Entertainment; Uncrate; Victory Belt Publishing; Viz; Weldon Owen Publishing; Wisdom Publications; World Almanac; Zaffre Books

Simply Read Books
501-5525 West Blvd, Vancouver, BC V6M 3W6
E-mail: go@simplyreadbooks.com; orders@simplyreadbooks.com; rights@simplyreadbooks.com
Web Site: www.simplyreadbooks.com
Founded: 2001
Our approach to illustrated children's books follows the finest publishing tradition & spirit with inspired content, extraordinary artwork, outstanding graphic design form & quality production. We introduce contemporary books with a modern appeal & fresh outlook & offer a careful selection of timeless stories that

CANADIAN PUBLISHERS

link the past with the present. We specialize in high-quality, unique picture books & fiction. Before submitting, please browse our web site, bookstores & libraries to look at & read what we publish. This will give you an idea of whether or not your story or illustrations would fit with our list.
Publishes in English, French.
ISBN Prefix(es): 978-1-894965; 978-0-9688768; 978-1-897476; 978-1-927018; 978-1-77229
Number of titles published annually: 20 Print
Total Titles: 200 Print
Foreign Rep(s): Consortium Book Sales & Distribution (Canada (English-speaking), Europe, UK & Commonwealth, USA); NewSouth Books (Australia, New Zealand)
Orders to: Ingram Publisher Services, 14 Ingram Blvd, Mail Stop 631, La Vergne, TN 37086, United States (CN & US) Web Site: www.ingrampublisherservices.com; NewSouth Books, c/o Alliance Distribution Services (ADS), 9 Pioneer Ave, Tuggerah, NSW 2259, Australia (Australia & New Zealand) Tel: (02) 4390-1300 E-mail: adscs@alliancedist.com.au Web Site: www.newsouthbooks.com.au; Turnaroud Publisher Services Ltd, Olympia Trading Estate, Unit 3, Coburg Rd, Wood Green, London N22 6TZ, United Kingdom Tel: (020) 8829 3000 Fax: (020) 8881 5088 E-mail: orders@turnaround-uk.com Web Site: www.turnaround-uk.com
Returns: Ingram Publisher Services Returns Center, c/o Purolator USA Logistics Ctr, 1151 Martin Grove Rd, Rexdale, ON M9W 4W7; Ingram Publisher Services, 191 Edwards Dr, Jackson, TN 38301, United States Web Site: www.ingrampublisherservices.com
Membership(s): Association for Canadian Publishers in the US; Independent Book Publishers Association (IBPA)

§Summerthought Publishing
PO Box 2309, Banff, AB T1L 1C1
Tel: 403-762-0535
E-mail: info@summerthought.com
Web Site: summerthought.com
Key Personnel
Co-Owner & Publr: Andrew Hempstead
Sales, Mktg & Opers: Dianne Melton
  E-mail: dianne@summerthought.com
Founded: 1971
Publisher of Canadian Rockies nonfiction books.
Publishes in English.
ISBN Prefix(es): 978-0-9782375; 978-0-9699732; 978-0-9811491; 978-0-919934; 978-1-926983
Number of titles published annually: 3 Print; 3 E-Book
Total Titles: 30 Print; 9 E-Book
Imprints: EJH Literary Enterprises
Foreign Rep(s): Cordee (UK); Freytag & Berndt (Europe)

TCP Press
Imprint of The Legacy Project
20200 Marsh Hill Rd, Uxbridge, ON L9P 1R3
Tel: 905-852-3777 Toll Free Tel: 800-772-7765
E-mail: tcp@tcpnow.com
Web Site: www.tcppress.com
Key Personnel
Dir, Publg: Brian Puppa
Founded: 1984
Trade & educational books for both children & adults.
Publishes in English, French.
ISBN Prefix(es): 978-1-896232
Number of titles published annually: 4 Print; 1 CD-ROM; 5 E-Book; 1 Audio
Total Titles: 26 Print; 3 CD-ROM; 6 E-Book; 3 Audio
Membership(s): Independent Publishers Association

Tecumseh Press, see Borealis Press Ltd

Theytus Books Ltd
Subsidiary of Okanagan Indian Educational Resources Society
154 Enowkin Trail, RR 2, Site 50, Comp 8, Penticton, BC V2A 6J7
SAN: 115-1517
Tel: 250-493-7181 Fax: 250-493-5302
E-mail: order@theytus.com; marketing@theytus.com
Web Site: www.theytus.com
Key Personnel
Publr: Greg Younging Tel: 250-493-7181 ext 201
Sales & Mktg: Ann Doyon
Founded: 1980
Native history, culture, politics, education & literature.
Publishes in English, French.
ISBN Prefix(es): 978-0-919441; 978-1-894778
Number of titles published annually: 4 Print
Total Titles: 83 Print; 4 CD-ROM
Distribution Center: Sandhill Book Marketing, Mill Crook Industrial Park, Unit 4, 3308 Appaloosa Rd, Kelowna, BC V1V 2G9 (AB & BC), Contact: Nancy Wise Tel: 250-491-1446 Toll Free Tel: 800-667-3848 Fax: 250-491-4066 E-mail: info@sandhillbooks.com
University of Toronto Press, 5201 Dufferin St, North York, ON M3H 5T8 (CN exc AB & BC) Tel: 416-667-7791 Toll Free Tel: 800-565-9523 Fax: 416-667-7832 Web Site: www.utpress.utoronto.ca
Membership(s): Association of Canadian Publishers (ACP)

Thistledown Press
220 20 St W, Unit 222, Saskatoon, SK S7M 0W9
SAN: 115-1061
Tel: 306-244-1722
E-mail: tdpress@thistledownpress.com
Web Site: www.thistledownpress.com
Key Personnel
Owner: JoAnn McCaig
Edit Dir: Elizabeth Philips
Mng Ed: Rilla Friesen
Founded: 1975
Fiction, poetry, creative nonfiction & fiction for children & young adults by Canadian authors.
Publishes in English.
ISBN Prefix(es): 978-0-920066; 978-0-920633; 978-1-895449; 978-1-894345; 978-1-897235; 978-1-77187
Number of titles published annually: 10 Print
Total Titles: 250 Print
U.S. Rep(s): University of Toronto Press
Distribution Center: University of Toronto Press, 5201 Dufferin St, Toronto, ON M3H 5T8 Tel: 416-667-7791 Toll Free Tel: 800-565-9523 (CN & US) Fax: 416-667-7832 Toll Free Fax: 800-221-9985 (CN & US) E-mail: utpbooks@utpress.utoronto.ca Web Site: www.utpress.utoronto.ca

Thompson Educational Publishing Inc
20 Ripley Ave, Toronto, ON M6S 3N9
Tel: 416-766-2763 (admin & orders)
  Toll Free Tel: 877-366-2763 Fax: 416-766-0398 (admin & orders)
E-mail: info@thompsonbooks.com; support@thompsonbooks.com
Web Site: www.thompsonbooks.com
Key Personnel
CEO: Rowan Thompson
VP: Faye Thompson
Publr: Keith Thompson
Founded: 1989
High school, college & university textbooks.
Publishes in English.
ISBN Prefix(es): 978-1-55077; 978-0-921332
Number of titles published annually: 6 Print
Total Titles: 180 Print
Distribution Center: University of Toronto Press Distribution, 5201 Dufferin St, Toronto, ON M3H 5T8 (CN orders, higher educ) Toll Free Tel: 800-565-9523 Toll Free Fax: 800-221-9985 E-mail: utpbooks@utpress.utoronto.ca
Web Site: utpress.utoronto.ca
University of Toronto Press Distribution, 2250 Military Rd, Tonawanda, NY 14150, United States (US orders, higher educ) Toll Free Tel: 800-565-9523 Toll Free Fax: 800-221-9985 E-mail: utpbooks@utpress.utoronto.ca
Web Site: utpress.utoronto.ca
Membership(s): Association of Canadian Publishers (ACP); Ontario Business Educator's Association (OBEA); Organization of Book Publishers of Ontario (OBPO)

TouchWood Editions
Member of The Heritage Group
103-1075 Pendergast St, Victoria, BC V8V 0A1
Tel: 250-360-0829 Fax: 250-386-0829
E-mail: info@touchwoodeditions.com
Web Site: www.touchwoodeditions.com
Key Personnel
Publr: Taryn Boyd E-mail: taryn@touchwoodeditions.com
Founded: 1985
Publishes in English.
ISBN Prefix(es): 978-1-894898; 978-1-926741; 978-1-926971; 978-0-920663; 978-1-927129; 978-1-77151
Number of titles published annually: 12 Print; 18 E-Book
Total Titles: 224 Print; 170 E-Book
Imprints: Brindle & Glass
Orders to: Heritage Group Distribution, 19272-96 Ave, Suite 8, Surrey, BC V4N 4C1 Tel: 604-881-7067 Toll Free Tel: 800-665-3302 Fax: 604-881-7068 Toll Free Fax: 800-566-3336 E-mail: orders@hgdistribution.com Web Site: www.hgdistribution.com
Returns: Heritage Group Distribution, 19272-96 Ave, Suite 8, Surrey, BC V4N 4C1 Tel: 604-881-7067 Toll Free Tel: 800-665-3302 Fax: 604-881-7068 Toll Free Fax: 800-566-3336 E-mail: orders@hgdistribution.com Web Site: www.hgdistribution.com
Shipping Address: Heritage Group Distribution, 19272-96 Ave, Suite 8, Surrey, BC V4N 4C1 Tel: 604-881-7067 Toll Free Tel: 800-665-3302 Fax: 604-881-7068 Toll Free Fax: 800-566-3336 E-mail: orders@hgdistribution.com Web Site: www.hgdistribution.com
Warehouse: Heritage Group Distribution, 19272-96 Ave, Suite 8, Surrey, BC V4N 4C1 Tel: 604-881-7067 Toll Free Tel: 800-665-3302 Fax: 604-881-7068 Toll Free Fax: 800-566-3336 E-mail: orders@hgdistribution.com Web Site: www.hgdistribution.com
Distribution Center: Heritage Group Distribution, 19272-96 Ave, Suite 8, Surrey, BC V4N 4C1 Tel: 604-881-7067 Toll Free Tel: 800-665-3302 Fax: 604-881-7068 Toll Free Fax: 800-566-3336 E-mail: orders@hgdistribution.com Web Site: www.hgdistribution.com
Membership(s): The Association of Book Publishers of British Columbia (ABPBC); Association of Canadian Publishers (ACP)
See separate listing for:
Brindle & Glass Publishing Ltd

§Townson Publishing Co Ltd
PO Box 1404, Sta A, Vancouver, BC V6C 2P7
Tel: 604-886-0594
E-mail: gpubinc@gmail.com; translationrights@gmail.com
Web Site: generalpublishing.com
Key Personnel
Chmn: W Townson
Ed & Rts: J House
Founded: 1977
Publisher of general trade books.
Publishes in English, French.
ISBN Prefix(es): 978-0-920822; 978-1-7388280 (General Publishing Group)

Number of titles published annually: 6 Print; 6 E-Book
Total Titles: 16 Print; 6 E-Book; 4 Audio
Imprints: Townson Publishing
Subsidiaries: Associated Merchandisers Inc (USA)
Branch Office(s)
700 Harrison Ave, Unit 129, Blaine, WA 98231-0129, United States
U.S. Rep(s): K E Russell
Foreign Rep(s): Associated Merchandisers Inc (UK, USA); Wah K Lee (China, Singapore)

Tradewind Books
202-1807 Maritime Mews, Vancouver, BC V6H 3W7
Tel: 604-662-4405
E-mail: tradewindbooks@yahoo.com; tradewindbooks@gmail.com
Web Site: www.tradewindbooks.com
Key Personnel
Owner & Publr: Michael Katz
Art Dir & Co-Publr: Carol Frank
Ed: Kim Aippersbach
Copy-Ed: Viktoria Cseh
Founded: 1996
Children's picture books, chapter books & young adults novels.
Publishes in English.
ISBN Prefix(es): 978-1-896580; 978-1-926890
Number of titles published annually: 8 Print
Total Titles: 112 Print
Distributed by Fitzhenry & Whiteside Limited (CN); Orca Book Publishers (US)
U.S. Rep(s): Orca Books
Foreign Rep(s): Turnaround Publisher Services Ltd (UK)
Distribution Center: Turnaround Publisher Services Ltd, Olympia Trading Estate, Unit 3, Coburg Rd, Wood Green, London N22 6TZ, United Kingdom *Tel:* (020) 8829 3000 *Fax:* (020) 8881 5088 *E-mail:* enquirie@turnaround-uk.com
Membership(s): The Association of Book Publishers of British Columbia (ABPBC); Association of Canadian Publishers (ACP)

Tundra Book Group
Division of Penguin Random House Canada
320 Front St W, Suite 1400, Toronto, ON M5V 3B6
SAN: 115-5415
Tel: 416-364-4449 *Toll Free Tel:* 888-523-9292 (orders); 800-588-1074
E-mail: youngreaders@penguinrandomhouse.com
Web Site: www.tundrabooks.com
Key Personnel
Publr: Tara Walker
Art Dir: Gigi Lau
Edit Dir: Anne Shone
Edit Dir, Children's: David A Robertson
Sr Mng Ed: Kate Doyle
Prodn Ed: Bharti Bedi
Asst Ed: Ashley Rhamey
Founded: 1967
Canada's oldest English children's book publisher renowned for its beautifully illustrated, award-winning books. See web site for submission information.
Publishes in English.
Number of titles published annually: 50 Print
Imprints: Penguin Teen Canada; Puffin Canada; Tundra Books
Branch Office(s)
Tundra Books of Northern New York, PO Box 1030, Plattsburgh, NY 12901, United States
Distributed by Everybody's Books CC (South Africa); Forrester Books NZ Ltd (New Zealand); El Hombre de la Mancha (Costa Rica & Panama); El Hormiguero (Guatemala)
U.S. Publishers Represented: Tundra Books of Northern New York
U.S. Rep(s): Jack Eichkorn & Associates Inc; R&R Book Co; Southern Territory Associates Inc
Orders to: Penguin Random House Canada, 6971 Columbus Rd, Mississauga, ON L5T 1K1; Penguin Random House LLC - Distribution Center, 400 Hahn Rd, Westminster, MD 21157, United States *Toll Free Tel:* 800-726-0600; 800-733-3000 *Toll Free Fax:* 800-659-2436
Returns: Penguin Random House LLC, 1019 N State Rd 47, Crawfordsville, IN 47933, United States
Warehouse: Penguin Random House LLC - Distribution Center, 400 Hahn Rd, Westminster, MD 21157, United States *Toll Free Tel:* 800-726-0600 *Toll Free Fax:* 800-659-2436
Membership(s): American Booksellers Association (ABA); The American Library Association (ALA); Association of Booksellers for Children; International Board on Books for Young People (IBBY)

Turnstone Press
Artspace Bldg, 206-100 Arthur St, Winnipeg, MB R3B 1H3
SAN: 115-1096
Tel: 204-947-1555 *Toll Free Tel:* 888-363-7718 *Fax:* 204-942-1555
E-mail: info@turnstonepress.com
Web Site: www.turnstonepress.com
Key Personnel
Assoc Publr & Intl Rts: Jamis Paulson
Founded: 1976
Literary press including fiction, nonfiction, poetry, literary criticism, biography, travel fiction & adventure all with a strong Canadian focus.
Publishes in English.
ISBN Prefix(es): 978-0-88801
Number of titles published annually: 10 Print
Total Titles: 300 Print
Imprints: Ravenstone Books
Returns: LitDistCo, c/o 100 Armstrong Ave, Georgetown, ON L7G 5S4 *Toll Free Tel:* 800-591-6250 *Toll Free Fax:* 800-591-6251 *E-mail:* orders@litdistco.ca *Web Site:* www.litdistco.ca
Distribution Center: LitDistCo, c/o 100 Armstrong Ave, Georgetown, ON L7G 5S4 *Toll Free Tel:* 800-591-6250 *Toll Free Fax:* 800-591-6251 *E-mail:* orders@litdistco.ca *Web Site:* www.litdistco.ca
Membership(s): Literary Press Group of Canada

UBC Press, see University of British Columbia Press

Ulysses Travel Guides
4176, rue Saint-Denis, Montreal, QC H2W 2M5
Tel: 514-843-9882 (ext 2232); 514-843-9447 (bookstore) *Fax:* 514-843-9448
E-mail: info@ulysse.ca; st-denis@ulysse.ca
Web Site: www.guidesulysse.com
Founded: 1980
Travel books.
Publishes in English, French.
ISBN Prefix(es): 978-2-921444; 978-2-89464; 978-2-9801872; 978-1-894676
Number of titles published annually: 25 Print; 25 E-Book; 2 Audio
Total Titles: 175 Print; 175 E-Book; 2 Audio
Imprints: Guides de Voyage Ulysses
Foreign Office(s): Travel Guides Ulysse Sarl, 127, rue Amelot, 75011 Paris, France *E-mail:* travel@ulysse.ca
Distributor for A A Publications; Dakota; Footprint Handbooks; Editions Sylvain Harvey; ITMB Publishing Ltd; Odyssey Publications; PassPorter Travel Press; Rother Walking Guides; Trans Canada Trail Foundation; Vacation Works Publications

University of Alberta Press
Ring House 2, Edmonton, AB T6G 2E1
SAN: 118-9794
Tel: 780-492-3662 *Fax:* 780-492-0719
Web Site: www.uap.ualberta.ca
Key Personnel
Dir & Publr: Douglas Hildebrand *Tel:* 780-492-0717 *E-mail:* dhildebr@ualberta.ca
Assoc Dir: Cathie Crooks *Tel:* 780-492-5820 *E-mail:* ccrooks@ualberta.ca
Mng Ed: Mary Lou Roy *Tel:* 780-492-9488 *E-mail:* marylou.roy@ualberta.ca
Acq Ed: Peter Midgley *Tel:* 780-492-7714 *E-mail:* pmidgley@ualberta.ca
Busn Admin: Basia Kowal *E-mail:* bkowal@ualberta.ca
Prodn & Designer: Alan Brownoff *Tel:* 780-492-8285 *E-mail:* abrownof@ualberta.ca
Founded: 1969
Contemporary publisher of scholarly & creative books distinguished by their editorial care, exceptional design & global reach.
Publishes in English.
ISBN Prefix(es): 978-0-88864; 978-1-77212
Number of titles published annually: 22 Print; 15 E-Book
Total Titles: 400 Print; 450 E-Book; 2 Audio
Imprints: CCI Press; Gutteridge Books; Pica Pica Books; Polynya Press
Sales Office(s): Ampersand Canada's Book & Gift Agency Inc, 321 Carlaw Ave, Suite 213, Toronto, ON M4M 2S1, Contact: Saffron Beckwith *Tel:* 416-703-0666 ext 124 *Fax:* 416-703-4745 *E-mail:* saffronb@ampersandinc.ca *Web Site:* www.ampersand.ca
U.S. Rep(s): Wayne State University Press
Foreign Rep(s): Gazelle Academic (Albania, Andorra, Armenia, Austria, Bahrain, Belarus, Belgium, Bosnia and Herzegovina, Botswana, Bulgaria, Cambodia, China, Continental Europe, Croatia, Cyprus, Czechia, Denmark, Egypt, Ethiopia, Europe, Finland, France, Georgia, Germany, Gibraltar, Greece, Hungary, Iceland, India, Indonesia, Iran, Iraq, Ireland, Israel, Italy, Japan, Jordan, Kenya, Laos, Latvia, Liechtenstein, Lithuania, Luxembourg, Malaysia, Malta, Moldova, Monaco, Montenegro, Mozambique, Myanmar, Namibia, Netherlands, North Macedonia, Norway, Oman, Poland, Portugal, Qatar, Romania, Russia, Serbia, Slovakia, Slovenia, South Africa, Spain, Sweden, Switzerland, Taiwan, Turkey, Uganda, Ukraine, United Arab Emirates, UK & the continent)
Orders to: University of Toronto Press, 5201 Dufferin St, Toronto, ON M3H 5T8 *Tel:* 416-667-7841 *Toll Free Tel:* 800-565-9523 *Fax:* 416-667-7832 *Toll Free Fax:* 800-221-9985 *E-mail:* utpbooks@utpress.utoronto.ca *Web Site:* www.utpress.utoronto.ca
Returns: University of Toronto Press, 5201 Dufferin St, Toronto, ON M3H 5T8 *Tel:* 416-667-7841 *Toll Free Tel:* 800-565-9523 *Fax:* 416-667-7832 *Toll Free Fax:* 800-221-9985 *E-mail:* utpbooks@utpress.utoronto.ca *Web Site:* www.utpress.utoronto.ca
Shipping Address: University of Toronto Press, 5201 Dufferin St, Toronto, ON M3H 5T8 *Tel:* 416-667-7841 *Toll Free Tel:* 800-565-9523 *Fax:* 416-667-7832 *Toll Free Fax:* 800-221-9985 *E-mail:* utpbooks@utpress.utoronto.ca *Web Site:* www.utpress.utoronto.ca
Warehouse: University of Toronto Press, 5201 Dufferin St, Toronto, ON M3H 5T8 *Tel:* 416-667-7841 *Toll Free Tel:* 800-565-9523 *Fax:* 416-667-7832 *Toll Free Fax:* 800-221-9985 *E-mail:* utpbooks@utpress.utoronto.ca *Web Site:* www.utpress.utoronto.ca
Distribution Center: University of Toronto Press, 5201 Dufferin St, Toronto, ON M3H 5T8 *Tel:* 416-667-7841 *Toll Free Tel:* 800-565-9523 *Fax:* 416-667-7832 *Toll Free Fax:* 800-221-9985 *E-mail:* utpbooks@utpress.utoronto.ca *Web Site:* www.utpress.utoronto.ca

CANADIAN PUBLISHERS

HFS (Hopkins Fulfillment Services), 2715 N Charles St, Baltimore, MD 21218, United States *Tel:* 410-516-6965 *Toll Free Tel:* 800-537-5487 *Fax:* 410-516-6998 *E-mail:* hfscustserv@jh.edu *Web Site:* hfs.jhu.edu

Gazelle Book Services Ltd, White Cross Mills, Hightown, Lancaster, Lancs LA1 4XS, United Kingdom *Tel:* (01524) 528500 *Fax:* (01524) 528510 *E-mail:* sales@gazellebookservices.co.uk *Web Site:* www.gazellebookservices.co.uk

Membership(s): Association of Canadian Publishers (ACP); Association of Canadian University Presses (ACUP); Association of University Presses (AUPresses); Book Publishers Association of Alberta

See separate listing for:
Canadian Circumpolar Institute (CCI) Press

University of British Columbia Press
2029 West Mall, Vancouver, BC V6T 1Z2
SAN: 115-1118
Tel: 604-822-5959 *Toll Free Tel:* 877-377-9378 *Fax:* 604-822-6083 *Toll Free Fax:* 800-668-0821
E-mail: frontdesk@ubcpress.ca
Web Site: www.ubcpress.ca
Key Personnel
Dir: Melissa Pitts *Tel:* 604-822-6376
 E-mail: pitts@ubcpress.ca
Asst Dir, Acqs (Vancouver): Darcy Cullen
 Tel: 604-822-5744 *E-mail:* cullen@ubcpress.ca
Asst Dir, Prodn & Edit Servs: Michelle van der Merwe *Tel:* 604-822-4548
 E-mail: vandermerwe@ubcpress.ca
Sr Ed (Kelowna): Randy Schmidt *Tel:* 250-764-4761 *Fax:* 250-764-4709 *E-mail:* schmidt@ubcpress.ca
Sr Ed (Toronto): James MacNevin *Tel:* 289-779-2414 *E-mail:* macnevin@ubcpress.ca
Ed: Megan Brand *Tel:* 604-822-5885
 E-mail: brand@ubcpress.ca; Meagan Dyer *Tel:* 604-822-6436 *E-mail:* dyer@ubcpress.ca; Ann Macklem *Tel:* 604-822-0093
 E-mail: macklem@ubcpress.ca; Nadine Pedersen *Tel:* 604-827-1795 *E-mail:* pedersen@ubcpress.ca; Katrina Petrik *Tel:* 604-822-6436
 E-mail: petrik@ubcpress.ca
Asst Ed, Edit & Prodn: Carmen Tiampo *Tel:* 604-822-6705 *E-mail:* tiampo@ubcpress.ca
Academic Mktg Mgr: Harmony Johnson *Tel:* 604-822-1978 *E-mail:* johnson@ubcpress.ca
Ad & Promo Mgr: Gerilee McBride *Tel:* 604-822-4546 *E-mail:* mcbride@ubcpress.ca
Mktg Mgr: Laraine Coates *Tel:* 604-822-6486
 E-mail: coates@ubcpress.ca
Publicity & Events Mgr: Kerry Kilmartin
 Tel: 604-822-8244 *E-mail:* kilmartin@ubcpress.ca
Sales Mgr: Liz Hudson *Tel:* 604-328-8923
 E-mail: hudson@ubcpress.ca
Agency & Digital Mktg Coord: Megan Malashewsky *Tel:* 604-822-8226
 E-mail: malashewsky@ubcpress.ca
Digital Publg Coord: Krista Bergstrom *Tel:* 604-827-5790 *E-mail:* bergstrom@ubcpress.ca
Publg Clerk: Hailey Peterson *E-mail:* peterson@ubcpress.ca
Founded: 1971
Academic & scholarly publications; native studies, law & society, military history, northern studies, sexuality, political science & forestry.
Publishes in English.
ISBN Prefix(es): 978-0-88865; 978-0-7748
Number of titles published annually: 70 Print
Total Titles: 900 Print; 2 CD-ROM; 1 E-Book
Imprints: On Campus; On Point Press; Pacific Education Press; Purich Books; UBC Press
Branch *Office(s)*
587 Markham St, 2nd fl, Toronto, ON M6G 2L7 *Fax:* 416-535-9677
Distributor for Art Gallery of New South Wales; Athabasca University Press (worldwide); Canadian Forest Service (worldwide); Editors Canada (worldwide); Fowler Museum at UCLA; International Sculpture Center; Island Press; Jessica Kingsley Publishers; Laval University Press (worldwide, English language books); Lost Horse Press; Lynx House Press; Museum for African Art; National Gallery of Australia; Oregon State University Press; Power Publications; Rutgers University Press; Silkworm Books; UCLA Chicano Studies Research Center Press; University of Arizona Press; University of Washington Press; Western Geographical Press (worldwide)
U.S. Publishers Represented: Island Press; Oregon State University Press; Rutgers University Press; University of Alabama Press; University of Arizona Press; University of Hawaii Press; University of Massachusetts Press; University of New Mexico Press; University of Texas Press; University of Washington Press; University Press of Colorado; University Press of Florida; University Press of Mississippi; West Virginia University Press; Western Geographical Press (worldwide)
U.S. Rep(s): University of Washington Press
Foreign Rep(s): Combined Academic Publishers (CAP) (Africa, Europe, Middle East, UK); Special Book Services Ltd (South America)
Orders to: University of Toronto Press Distribution, 5201 Dufferin St, Toronto, ON M3H 5T8 *Tel:* 416-667-7791 *Toll Free Tel:* 800-565-9523 *Fax:* 416-667-7832 *Toll Free Fax:* 800-221-9985 *E-mail:* utpbooks@utpress.utoronto.ca; Chicago Distribution Center, 11030 S Langley Ave, Chicago, IL 60628, United States *Tel:* 773-702-7000 *Toll Free Tel:* 800-621-2736 *Fax:* 773-702-7212 *E-mail:* custserv@press.uchicago.edu
Distribution Center: University of Toronto Press Distribution, 5201 Dufferin St, Toronto, ON M3H 5T8 *Tel:* 416-667-7791 *Toll Free Tel:* 800-565-9523 *Fax:* 416-667-7832 *Toll Free Fax:* 800-221-9985 *E-mail:* utpbooks@utpress.utoronto.ca
Chicago Distribution Center (CDC), 11030 S Langley Ave, Chicago, IL 60628, United States *Tel:* 773-702-7010 *Toll Free Fax:* 800-621-8476 *Web Site:* press.uchicago.edu/cdc
Membership(s): The Association of Book Publishers of British Columbia (ABPBC); Association of Canadian Publishers (ACP); Association of Canadian University Presses (ACUP); Association of University Presses (AUPresses); International Association of Scholarly Publishers (IASP)

See separate listing for:
Pacific Educational Press

University of Calgary Press
2500 University Dr NW, Calgary, AB T2N 1N4
Tel: 403-220-7578
E-mail: ucpbooks@ucalgary.ca
Web Site: press.ucalgary.ca
Key Personnel
Dir: Brian Scivener *Tel:* 403-220-3511
 E-mail: brian.scivener@ucalgary.ca
Graphic Design & Print Mgmt: Melina Cusano
 Tel: 403-220-8719 *E-mail:* macusano@calgary.ca
Edit & Mktg Coord: Helen Hajnoczky *Tel:* 403-220-4208 *E-mail:* helen.hajnoczky@ucalgary.ca
Mktg Specialist: Alison Cobra *Tel:* 403-220-3979
 E-mail: alison.cobra@ucalgary.ca
Founded: 1981
Specialize in scholarly books that make a difference. Series subjects include history, parks & protected areas, regional history, Northern studies, Africa, cinema studies, cultural studies, Canadian military & military history & communications studies.
Publishes in English, French.
ISBN Prefix(es): 978-0-919813; 978-1-895176; 978-1-55238
Number of titles published annually: 20 Print; 2 CD-ROM; 10 Online; 20 E-Book
Total Titles: 400 Print; 5 CD-ROM; 25 Online; 150 E-Book
Distribution Center: University of Toronto Press, 5201 Dufferin St, Toronto, ON M3H 5T8 *Toll Free Tel:* 800-565-9523 *Toll Free Fax:* 800-221-9985 *E-mail:* utpbooks@utpress.toronto.ca *Web Site:* www.utpdistribution.com
Longleaf Services Inc, 116 S Boundary St, Chapel Hill, NC 27514-3808, United States *Tel:* 919-966-7449 *Toll Free Tel:* 800-848-6224 *Fax:* 919-962-2704 *Toll Free Fax:* 800-272-6817 *E-mail:* customerservice@longleafservices.org *Web Site:* www.longleafservices.org
Eurospan, Gray's Inn House, 127 Clerkenwell Rd, London EC1R 5DB, United Kingdom (Africa, Europe, Latin America, Middle East & Oceania) *Tel:* (020) 7250 0856 *E-mail:* info@eurospan.co.uk *Web Site:* eurospangroup.com
Membership(s): Association for Canadian Publishers in the US; Association of Canadian Publishers (ACP); Book Publishers Association of Alberta

University of Manitoba Press
University of Manitoba, 301 St Johns College, 92 Dysart Rd, Winnipeg, MB R3T 2M5
SAN: 115-5474
Tel: 204-474-9495 *Fax:* 204-474-7566
E-mail: uofmpress@umanitoba.ca
Web Site: uofmpress.ca
Key Personnel
Dir: David Carr *Tel:* 204-474-9242 *E-mail:* david.carr@cc.umanitoba.ca
Mng Ed: Glenn Bergen *Tel:* 204-474-7338
 E-mail: glenn_bergen@umanitoba.ca
Acqs Ed: Jill McConkey *Tel:* 204-474-8804
 E-mail: jill.mcconkey@umanitoba.ca
Sales & Mktg Supv: David Larsen *Tel:* 204-474-9998 *E-mail:* david.larsen@umanitoba.ca
Promos & Publicity Coord: Sarah Ens
 E-mail: sarah.ens@umanitoba.ca
Edit Asst: Barbara Romanik *Tel:* 204-474-6568
 E-mail: barbara.romanik@manitoba.ca
Founded: 1967
Scholarly & general titles in humanities & social sciences; western Canadian history & native studies.
Publishes in English.
ISBN Prefix(es): 978-0-88755
Number of titles published annually: 14 Print
Total Titles: 120 Print
Distributed by University of Toronto Press (Canadian sales); Michigan State University Press (US sales)
Distribution Center: University of Toronto Press, 5201 Dufferin St, Toronto, ON M3H 5T8 *Tel:* 416-667-7791 *Toll Free Tel:* 800-565-9523 *Fax:* 416-667-7856 *Toll Free Fax:* 800-221-9985 *E-mail:* utpbooks@utpress.utoronto.ca
Longleaf Services, 116 S Boundary St, Chapel Hill, NC 27514-3808, United States *Toll Free Tel:* 800-848-6224 *Toll Free Fax:* 800-272-6817 *E-mail:* orders@longleafservices.org

University of Ottawa Press (Presses de l'Université d'Ottawa)
Affiliate of University of Ottawa
542 King Edward Ave, Ottawa, ON K1N 6N5
Tel: 613-562-5246 *Fax:* 613-562-5247
E-mail: puo-uop@uottawa.ca; acquisitions@uottawa.ca
Web Site: press.uottawa.ca
Key Personnel
Dir: Lara Mainville, MA *Tel:* 613-562-5663
 E-mail: lara.mainville@uottawa.ca
Acqs Ed: Veronica Omana *Tel:* 613-562-5800 ext 3065
Prodn Mgr: Suzanne Cloutier *Tel:* 613-562-5800 ext 2853 *E-mail:* scloutier@uottawa.ca; Eliz-

abeth Schwaiger *Tel:* 613-562-5800 ext 3064 *E-mail:* eschwaig@uottawa.ca
Digital Prodn & Mktg Coord: Mireille Piche *Tel:* 613-562-5800 ext 2853 *E-mail:* mireille.piche@uottawa.ca
Prodn Coord: Annie-Pier Charbonneau *Tel:* 613-562-5800 ext 4922 *E-mail:* annie-pier.charbonneau@uottawa.ca
Admin Asst: Sonia Rheault
Founded: 1936
Scholarly & trade books. The oldest francophone university press & only fully bilingual university press in North America.
Publishes in English, French.
ISBN Prefix(es): 978-0-7766; 978-2-7603
Number of titles published annually: 22 Print; 22 E-Book
Total Titles: 450 Print; 400 E-Book
Foreign Rep(s): Ampersand Inc (Canada (English-speaking)); CEDIF (France); Durnell Marketing (Europe exc UK); The Oxford Publicity Partnership Ltd (UK); Patrimoine Diffusion SPRL (Belgium, Luxembourg, Netherlands); Prologue Inc (Canada (French-speaking)); Servidis SA (Switzerland)
Distribution Center: University of Toronto Press (UTP), 5201 Dufferin St, North York, ON M3H 5T8 (English titles to CN) *Tel:* 416-667-7791 *Toll Free Tel:* 800-565-9523 *Fax:* 416-667-7832 *Toll Free Fax:* 800-221-9985 *E-mail:* utpbooks@utpress.utoronto.ca *Web Site:* www.utpress.utoronto.ca
Prologue Inc, 3785, Rue La Fayette Ouest, Boisbriand, QC J7H 1N5 (French titles to CN) *Tel:* 450-434-0306 *Toll Free Tel:* 800-363-2864 *Toll Free Fax:* 800-361-8088 *E-mail:* prologue@prologue.ca *Web Site:* www.prologue.ca
Patrimoine Diffusion SPRL, 119 Milcamps Ave, 1030 Brussels, Belgium, Contact: Eric Durigneux *Tel:* (02) 736 68 47 *Fax:* (02) 736 68 47 *E-mail:* patrimoine@telenet.be
Distribution du Nouveau Monde, 30 rue Guy Lussac, 75005 Paris, France (French titles to France) *Tel:* 01 43 54 49 02 *Fax:* 01 43 54 39 15 *E-mail:* dnm@librairieduquebec.fr *Web Site:* www.librairieduquebec.fr
Servidis SA, Chemin des Chalets, 7, 1279 Chavannes-de-Bogis, Switzerland (French titles to Switzerland), Contact: Eric Filliastre *Tel:* (022) 960 95 25 *Fax:* (022) 776 35 44 *E-mail:* commande@servidis.ch *Web Site:* www.servidis.ch
Marston Book Services Ltd, 160 Eastern Ave, Abingdon, Oxon OX14 4SB, United Kingdom (English titles to Europe & UK) *Tel:* (01235) 465500 *Fax:* (01235) 465555 *E-mail:* direct.orders@marston.co.uk *Web Site:* www.marston.co.uk
Membership(s): American Association of University Presses (AAUP); Association nationale des editeurs de livres (ANEL); Association of Canadian Publishers (ACP); Association of Canadian University Presses (ACUP)

University of Regina Press
2 Research Dr, Suite 160, Regina, SK S4S 7H9
SAN: 115-0278
Mailing Address: University of Regina, 3737 Wascana Pkwy, Regina, SK S4S 0A2
Tel: 306-585-4758 *Fax:* 306-585-4699
E-mail: uofrpress@uregina.ca
Web Site: uofrpress.ca
Key Personnel
Mng Ed: Kelly Laycock *Tel:* 306-585-4787 *E-mail:* kelly.laycock@uregina.ca
Art Dir: Duncan Campbell *Tel:* 306-585-4326 *E-mail:* duncan.campbell@uregina.ca
Sr Acqs Ed: Karen Clark *Tel:* 306-585-4664 *E-mail:* karen.clark@uregina.ca
Sales & Dist Mgr: Curran Faris *E-mail:* curran.faris@uregina.ca

Admin Asst: Rita Racette *E-mail:* rita.racette@uregina.ca
Edit Asst: David McLennan *Tel:* 306-585-5488 *E-mail:* david.mclennan@uregina.ca
Founded: 1973
Scholarly paperbacks & hardcovers on cultural & economic development & history of Canadian Plains & western Canada.
Publishes in English, French.
ISBN Prefix(es): 978-0-88977
Number of titles published annually: 15 Print
Total Titles: 90 Print; 1 CD-ROM
Distribution Center: University of Toronto Press Distribution, 5201 Dufferin St, Toronto, ON M3H 5T8 *Tel:* 416-667-7791 *Toll Free Tel:* 800-565-9523 (CN & US) *Fax:* 416-667-7832 *Toll Free Fax:* 800-221-9985 (CN & US) *E-mail:* utpbooks@utpress.utoronto.ca *Web Site:* www.utpress.utoronto.ca
Ingram Publisher Services, 14 Ingram Blvd, Mail Stop 631, La Vergne, TN 37086, United States *Web Site:* www.ingrampublisherservices.com
Gazelle Book Services Ltd, White Cross Mills, Hightown, Lancaster, Lancs LA1 4XS, United Kingdom *Tel:* (01524) 528500 *Fax:* (01524) 528510 *E-mail:* sales@gazellebookservices.co.uk *Web Site:* www.gazellebookservices.co.uk
Membership(s): Association of Canadian Publishers (ACP); Association of Canadian University Presses (ACUP); Saskatchewan Publishers Group

§University of Toronto Press
Division of Multicultural History Society of Canada
Book Publishing Div, 800 Bay St, Mezzanine, Toronto, ON M5S 3A9
Tel: 416-978-2239 *Fax:* 416-978-4736
E-mail: utpbooks@utorontopress.com (orders)
Web Site: utorontopress.com
Key Personnel
Pres, Publr & CEO: Jessica Mosher
VP, Publg: Antonia Pop
Dir, Sales & Mktg: Jane Kelly *Tel:* 416-978-2239 ext 2268 *E-mail:* jkelly@utorontopress.com
Mng Ed: Lisa Jemison *Tel:* 416-978-2239 ext 2226 *E-mail:* ljemison@utorontopress.com
Assoc Mng Ed: Leah Connor *Tel:* 416-978-2239 ext 2264 *E-mail:* lconnor@utorontopress.com; Janice Evans *Tel:* 416-978-2239 ext 2236; Barb Porter *Tel:* 416-978-2239 ext 2234 *E-mail:* bporter@utorontopress.com; Christine Robertson *Tel:* 416-978-2239 ext 2246 *E-mail:* crobertson@utorontopress.com
Mktg Mgr, Humanities: Anna Maria Del Col *Tel:* 416-978-2239 ext 4224 *E-mail:* adelcol@utorontopress.com
Assoc Mktg Mgr, Soc Sciences: Breanna Muir *Tel:* 416-978-2239 ext 2257 *E-mail:* bmuir@utorontopress.com
Prodn Mgr: Ani Deyirmenjian *Tel:* 416-978-2239 ext 2227 *E-mail:* adeyirmenjian@utorontopress.com
Sales Mgr, Higher Educ: Mike Byer *Tel:* 416-978-2239 ext 4226 *E-mail:* mbyer@utorontopress.com
Publicist: Chris Reed *Tel:* 416-978-2239 ext 2248 *E-mail:* creed@utorontopress.com
Founded: 1901
Publisher, distributor & university bookstore.
Publishes in English.
ISBN Prefix(es): 978-0-8020; 978-0-7727; 978-1-4426
Number of titles published annually: 200 Print; 100 E-Book
Total Titles: 3,500 Print; 500 E-Book
Imprints: Aevo UTP; New Jewish Press; Rotman-UTP Publishing
Divisions: Pippin Publishing; University of Toronto Press Guidance Centre; University of Toronto Press Journals Division

Branch Office(s)
2250 Military Rd, Tonawanda, NY 14150, United States *Tel:* 716-693-2768 *Fax:* 716-693-2167
Distributor for Alberta Environment Protection; Annick Press; Anteism Press; ARP Books; Arsenal Pulp Press; Art Canada Institute; Aspasia Books; Associated Medical Services; Athabasca University; Baha'i Distribution Services; Biblioasis; Black Dog Press; Black Rose Books; Book*hug Press; Breakwater Books; Brush Education; Caitlin Press; Calgary Institute; Canadian Forest Services; Canadian Forestry-Ottawa; Canadian Museum of History; Canadian Museum of Nature; Canadian War Museum; Caslon Inc; CCSR; Central European University Press KFT; Centre for Studies Religion/Society; Chair of Ukranian Studies; Child's Play Publishing; Cigi; Cinematheque; Cork University Press; Cormorant Books; Cornell University Press; Cree Board of Health & Social Services of James Bay; Crowsnest Books; Crwth Press; Dingbats Notebooks; Douglas & McIntyre Publishers; Dundurn Press; Durvile Publications; The Experiment Publishing; Eyewear Publishing; Fernwood Publishing; Flying Books; Freehand Books; Friends of Joseph Schneider Haus; Goose Lane Editions; Chelsea Green Publishing; Greystone Books; Groundwood Books; Gryphon House; Guernica Editions; Guidance Centre; Hatje Cantz; Nick Hearn; Heritage Group Distribution; Heritage House Publishing; HighWater Press; House of Anansi Press; Inhabit Education Books; Integrative Leadership International Ltd; Institute Communications Agencies; International Self-Counsel Press Ltd; Island Press; ISSI; Jump Math; Jessica Kingsley Publishers; Knowledge Bureau; Laberinto Press; Peter Lang Publishing Group; Robert Langen Art Gallery; Wilfrid Laurier University Press; LCMSDS; Legas Publishing; Louisiana State University Press; Mage Publishers; Magenta Publishing; Mawenzi House; McGill Queen's University Press; McGilligan Books; Me to We Books; Microcosm Press; Museum of Modern Art; National Centre for Youth Issues (NCYI); National Museum of Science & Technology; New Society Publishers; Oolichan Books; Oregon State University; Owlkids Books; Pajama Press; Paragon Publishing; Penn State University Press; Pippin Publishing; Playwrights Canada; Plumleaf Press; Political Animal Press; Pontifical Institute of Medieval Studies; Porcupine's Quill; Portage & Main Press; Pratico-pratique; Les Presses de L'Universite Laval; Princess Margaret Hospital Foundation; Purdue University Press; Editorial RM; R K Publishing Inc; Rocky Mountain Books; Royal BC Museum; Royal Ontario Museum; Rutgers University Press; Second Story Press; Seraphim Editions; J Gordon Shillingford Publishing Inc; Sick Kids; Signature Editions; Sister Vision Press; Steidl Verlag; Subway Books; Sutherland House; Syracuse University Press; Talon Books; Teachers College Press; Texas Tech University Press; Theatre Communication Group; Theatre Museum; Theytus Books Ltd; Thistledown Press; Thompson Educational Publishing Inc; Thornapple Press; Toronto Alliance; Toronto International Film Festival; TouchWood Editions; Transaction Publishers; Twin Guinep Ltd; Universitas Press; University of Alberta Press; University of Arizona Press; University of British Columbia Press; University of Calgary Press; University of Georgia Press; University of Hawaii Press; University of Manitoba Press; University of Minnesota Press; University of Nebraska Press; University of North Carolina Press; University of Notre Dame Press; University of Oklahoma Press; University of Ottawa Press; University of Regina, Canadian Plains Research Centre; University of the West Indies Press; University of Toronto Centre for Urban & Community

CANADIAN PUBLISHERS

Studies; University of Toronto Public Management; University of Virginia Press; University of Washington Press; UTP Journals - Canadian Theatre Review; Vanderbilt University Press; Wall & Emerson Inc; Washington State University; West Indies Press; Western Geographical Press; Wolsak & Wynn Publishers; Woodbine House; Word of Mouth Production; David Zwirner Books
U.S. Rep(s): Terry & Read LLC (Southwest coast); Ben Schrager (Northeast); Trim Associates (Gary Trim) (Midwest)
Foreign Rep(s): Durnell Marketing Ltd (Andrew Durnell) (Europe, Iceland, Ireland, Israel, Northern Ireland, Russia); Everest International Publishing Services (Wei Zhao) (China); Oxford Publicity Partnership Ltd (Gary Hall) (UK); Viva Books Pvt Ltd (Pradeep Kumar) (India)
Returns: 5201 Dufferin St, North York, ON M3H 5T8 (worldwide exc CN, India, Japan, UK/Europe & US)
Warehouse: 2250 Military Rd, Tonawanda, NY 14150, United States *Tel:* 716-693-2768
5201 Dufferin St, North York, ON M3H 5T8 (worldwide exc CN, India, Japan, UK/Europe & US)
Distribution Center: 5201 Dufferin St, North York, ON M3H 5T8 (worldwide exc CN, India, Japan, UK/Europe & US) *Tel:* 416-667-7791 *Toll Free Tel:* 800-565-9523 *Fax:* 416-667-7832 *Toll Free Fax:* 800-221-9985 *E-mail:* utpbooks@utpress.utoronto.ca
HFS (Hopkins Fulfillment Services), PO Box 50370, Baltimore, MD 21211-4370, United States *Toll Free Tel:* 800-537-5487 *E-mail:* hfscustserv@jh.edu *Web Site:* hfsbooks.com SAN: 202-7348
2250 Military Rd, Tonawanda, NY 14150, United States *Tel:* 716-693-2768
Viva Books Pvt Ltd, 4737/23 Ansari Rd, Darya Ganj, New Delhi 110 002, India, Contact: Pradeep Kumar *Tel:* (011) 42242200 *Fax:* (011) 42242240 *E-mail:* pradeep.kumar@vivagroupindia.in
MHM Ltd, 1-1-13-4F Kanda Jimbocho, Chiyoda-ku, Tokyo 101-0051, Japan *Tel:* (03) 3518-9181 *Fax:* (03) 3518-9523 *E-mail:* sales@mhmlimited.co.jp
Ingram Publisher Services UK, Airport Business Centre, 10 Thornbury Rd, Plymouth, Devon PL6 7PP, United Kingdom (UK & Europe) *Tel:* (01752) 202301 *Fax:* (01752) 202333
Membership(s): American Association of University Presses (AAUP); Association of Canadian Publishers (ACP); Association of Canadian University Presses (ACUP); Organization of Book Publishers of Ontario (OBPO)

Vehicule Press
PO Box 42094, CP Roy, Montreal, QC H2W 2T3
Tel: 514-844-6073
E-mail: vp@vehiculepress.com; admin@vehiculepress.com
Web Site: www.vehiculepress.com
Key Personnel
Publr & Gen Ed: Simon Dardick; Nancy Marrelli
Mng Ed: Vicki Marcok
Ed, Esplanade Books: Dimitri Nasrallah
Ed, Signal Editions: Carmine Starnino
Mktg & Promos Mgr: Maya Assouad
Founded: 1973
Paperback trade; fiction, jazz, biography, literature, poetry, translation.
Publishes in English.
ISBN Prefix(es): 978-0-919890; 978-1-55065
Number of titles published annually: 14 Print
Total Titles: 530 Print
Imprints: Esplanade Books (fiction); Signal Editions (poetry)
U.S. Rep(s): Independent Publishers Group (IPG)
Returns: LitDistCo, 8300 Lawson Rd, Milton, ON L9T 0A4 *Tel:* 905-877-4411 *Toll Free Tel:* 800-591-6250 *Fax:* 905-877-4410 *Toll Free Fax:* 800-591-6251
Shipping Address: LitDistCo, 8300 Lawson Rd, Milton, ON L9T 0A4 *Tel:* 905-877-4411 *Toll Free Tel:* 800-591-6250 *Fax:* 905-877-4410 *Toll Free Fax:* 800-591-6251
Distribution Center: LitDistCo, 8300 Lawson Rd, Milton, ON L9T 0A4 *Tel:* 905-877-4411 *Toll Free Tel:* 800-591-6250 *Fax:* 905-877-4410 *Toll Free Fax:* 800-591-6251
Membership(s): Association of Canadian Publishers (ACP); Literary Press Group

VLB editeur
Division of Groupe Ville-Marie Litterature
4545, rue Frontenac, 3rd fl, Montreal, QC H2H 2R7
Tel: 514-849-5259
Web Site: www.edvlb.com
Key Personnel
VP, Edit: Martin Balthazar
Edit Dir: Alain-Nicolas Renaud
Ed: Ariane Caron-Lacoste; Miruna Craciunescu
Founded: 1976
Publishes in French.
ISBN Prefix(es): 978-2-89005
Number of titles published annually: 20 Print; 18 E-Book
Total Titles: 600 Print; 250 E-Book
Foreign Office(s): Immeuble Paryseine, 3, Allee de la Seine, 94854 Ivry Cedex, France *Tel:* 01 49 59 12 40 *Fax:* 06 16 94 14 38
Distribution Center: Messageries ADP, 2315 Rue de la Province, Longueuil, QC J4G 1G4 *Web Site:* www.messageries-adp.com

Weigl Educational Publishers Ltd
6325 Tenth St SE, Calgary, AB T2H 2Z9
SAN: 115-1312
Tel: 403-233-7747 *Toll Free Tel:* 800-668-0766 *Fax:* 403-233-7769
E-mail: orders@weigl.com
Web Site: www.weigl.ca
Key Personnel
Pres & Publr: Linda Weigl
Founded: 1979
School library resources & textbooks for grades K-12 in English & French. Emphasis on: Canadian history, social studies & public affairs; science; multiculturalism; career/vocational/life management; distance education; books & guides for teachers.
Publishes in English.
ISBN Prefix(es): 978-0-919879; 978-1-896990; 978-1-55388; 978-1-4872; 978-1-4896; 978-1-77071; 978-1-7911; 978-1-894705
Number of titles published annually: 40 Print
Total Titles: 200 Print
Branch Office(s)
276 Fifth Ave, Suite 704, No 917, New York, NY 10001, United States *Toll Free Tel:* 866-649-3445 *Toll Free Fax:* 866-449-3445 *E-mail:* orders@av2books.com *Web Site:* www.av2books.com
Distributed by The Creative Co (US); Rourke Publishing; Saunders Book Co (CN); Smart Apple Media (US)

Whitecap Books
Division of Fitzhenry & Whiteside Limited
314 W Cordova St, Suite 209, Vancouver, BC V6B 1E8
Tel: 604-681-6181
Web Site: www.whitecap.ca
Key Personnel
Pres & Publr: Holly Doll *Tel:* 905-477-9700 ext 207 *E-mail:* hdoll@fitzhenry.ca
Designer: Andrew Bagatella *E-mail:* andrewb@whitecap.ca
Founded: 1977
Trade books, photography, cookery, regional, gardening, outdoor guide books, natural history, juvenile nonfiction & illustrated children's books, juvenile fiction.
Publishes in English.
ISBN Prefix(es): 978-1-55110; 978-1-55285; 978-1-77050
Number of titles published annually: 85 Print
Total Titles: 480 Print
U.S. Rep(s): Firefly Books Ltd
Returns: Firefly Books Ltd, 50 Staples Ave, Richmond Hill, ON L4B 0A7

John Wiley & Sons Canada Ltd
Subsidiary of John Wiley & Sons Inc
90 Eglinton Ave E, Suite 300, Toronto, ON M4P 2Y3
Tel: 416-236-4433 *Toll Free Tel:* 800-567-4797 *Fax:* 416-236-4446 *Toll Free Fax:* 800-565-6802 (orders)
E-mail: canada@wiley.com
Web Site: www.wiley.com
Founded: 1968
Textbooks for colleges & universities; trade, professional & reference.
Publishes in English, French.
ISBN Prefix(es): 978-0-470; 978-0-471
Number of titles published annually: 50 Print
Total Titles: 600 Print
Distributor for John Wiley & Sons Inc

Wilfrid Laurier University Press
75 University Ave W, Waterloo, ON N2L 3C5
Tel: 519-884-0710 *Toll Free Tel:* 866-836-5551 (CN & US) *Fax:* 519-725-1399
E-mail: press@wlu.ca
Web Site: www.wlupress.wlu.ca
Key Personnel
Dir: Lisa Quinn *Tel:* 519-884-0710 ext 2843 *E-mail:* lquinn@wlu.ca
Mng Ed: Murray Tong *Tel:* 519-884-0710 ext 6119 *E-mail:* mtong@wlu.ca
Sr Ed: Siobhan McMenemy *Tel:* 519-884-0710 ext 3782 *E-mail:* smcmenemy@wlu.ca
Digital Projs Coord: Maia Desjardins *Tel:* 519-884-0710 ext 3029 *E-mail:* madesjardins@wlu.ca
Prodn Coord: Lindsey Hunnewell *Tel:* 519-884-0710 ext 6122 *E-mail:* lhunnewell@wlu.ca
Sales & Mktg Coord: Clare Hitchens *Tel:* 519-884-0710 ext 2665 *E-mail:* chitchens@wlu.ca
Founded: 1974
Publish scholarly & general interest books in the social sciences & humanities.
Publishes in English.
ISBN Prefix(es): 978-0-88920; 978-1-55458; 978-1-77112
Number of titles published annually: 15 Print; 15 Online; 15 E-Book; 20 Audio
Total Titles: 800 Print; 800 Online; 800 E-Book; 30 Audio
Distributed by University of Toronto Press (CN)
Distributor for The Cree Board of Health & Social Services of James Bay; Laurier Centre for Military Strategic & Disarmament Studies; Toronto International Film Festival
Foreign Rep(s): Ampersand Inc (Canada); Eurospan (worldwide exc North America); Ingram Academic (USA)
Orders to: University of Toronto Press Distribution, 5201 Dufferin St, Toronto, ON M3H 5T8 *Toll Free Tel:* 800-565-9523 *Toll Free Fax:* 800-221-9985 *E-mail:* utpbooks@utpress.utoronto.ca; Ingram Publisher Services, 14 Ingram Blvd, Mail Stop 631, La Vergne, TN 37086, United States *Toll Free Tel:* 866-400-5351 *Web Site:* www.ingrampublisherservices.com; Eurospan Ltd, Gray's Inn House, 127 Clerkenwell Rd, London EC1R 5DB, United Kingdom (outside North America) *Web Site:* eurospan.co.uk
Membership(s): Association of Canadian Publishers (ACP); Association of Canadian Univer-

sity Presses (ACUP); Association of University Presses (AUPresses); Organization of Book Publishers of Ontario (OBPO)

WLU Press, see Wilfrid Laurier University Press

Wood Lake Publishing Inc
485 Beaver Lake Rd, Kelowna, BC V4V 1S5
Tel: 250-766-2778 *Toll Free Tel:* 800-663-2775 (orders & cust serv) *Fax:* 250-766-2736
Toll Free Fax: 888-841-9991 (orders & cust serv)
E-mail: info@woodlake.com; customerservice@woodlake.com
Web Site: www.woodlake.com
Key Personnel
Pres & Publr: Patty Berube
Assoc Publr: Deb MacDonald
Mktg & Publicity: Paige Dobson
  E-mail: paiged@woodlake.com
Founded: 1980
Books, church curriculum & periodicals.
Publishes in English.
ISBN Prefix(es): 978-1-55145; 978-0-919599; 978-0-929032; 978-1-77343
Number of titles published annually: 8 Print
Total Titles: 135 Print
Imprints: CopperHouse; Seasons of the Spirit; Whole People of God Online; Wood Lake
Distributed by Augsburg Canada; Presbyterian Church of Canada; United Church of Canada
Distributor for Northstone

§Worldwide Library
Imprint of Harlequin Enterprises Ltd
Bay Adelaide Centre, East Tower, 22 Adelaide St W, 41st fl, Toronto, ON M5H 4E3
Mailing Address: PO Box 603, Fort Erie, ON L2A 5X3
Tel: 416-445-5860 *Toll Free Tel:* 888-432-4879
E-mail: customerservice@harlequin.com
Web Site: www.harlequin.com
Founded: 1982
Mass market fiction.
Publishes in English.
ISBN Prefix(es): 978-0-373
Number of titles published annually: 5 Print; 9 E-Book
Total Titles: 202 Print
Imprints: Worldwide Mystery
Branch Office(s)
PO Box 9049, Buffalo, NY 14269-9049, United States
Foreign Rights: Booklink (Europe)
Warehouse: 3010 Walden Ave, Depew, NY 14043, United States

Essential Resources

for the library, publishing, research, and business professional

www.infotoday.com

For pricing and information, contact:
The ITI Subscription Service Team
Phone: 609-654-6266 x128
Email: jwelsh@infotoday.com

143 Old Marlton Pike, Medford, NJ 08055

InformationToday

American Library Directory™
The Literary Map to U.S. and Canadian Libraries

This is only guide that gives you fast, fingertip access to comparative data, additional resources, and sales prospects for the entire U.S. and Canada. Find full profiles on public, academic, government, and special libraries organized by state and city. Each profile includes everything from official library name and address to key personnel, holdings, collections, budget, expenditures, and special services. Two extensive volumes cover more than 31,000 libraries. Also available online.

American Book Trade Directory™
Your Complete Guide to the Book Trade Industry

This comprehensive directory brings together nearly 18,000 retail and antiquarian book dealers; 1,000 software, paperback, and remainder wholesalers; 100 national and regional book trade associations; and hundreds of book trade service providers and resources from across the U.S. and Canada. No public or academic library should be without this thorough and well-organized research tool. It's simply the most comprehensive and definitive guide available. No other resource does more to keep tabs on the enormous bookselling and distribution industry.

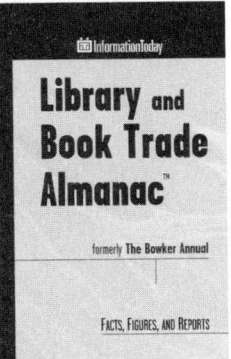

Library and Book Trade Almanac™
The Preeminent Handbook for Librarians and the Book Trade

Get the latest facts and insights into developments and trends within the library and book trade worlds, including the annual best-sellers lists, literary award winners, salary, materials acquisition, and other cost figures. This almanac contains contact information for state, regional, national, and international library associations. Put a wealth of industry data and insight at your immediate disposal. (Formerly published as *The Bowker Annual*.)

ALSO AVAILABLE

Annual Register of Grant Support™

Corporate Giving Directory

Literary Market Place™

Fulltext Sources Online

Editorial Services & Agents

Editorial Services — Activity Index

ABSTRACTING
Jeanette Almada, pg 435
Aptara Inc, pg 435
Kathleen Barnes, pg 436
Diana Barth, pg 436
Clear Concepts, pg 437
Cohesion®, pg 437
diacriTech Inc, pg 438
Fred Gebhart, pg 439
GGP Publishing Inc, pg 440
Sherry Gottlieb, pg 440
Joan K Griffitts Indexing, pg 440
L Anne Hirschel DDS, pg 440
Indexing by the Book, pg 440
JL Communications, pg 441
Barry R Koffler, pg 441
Peter Mayeux, pg 442
Mary Mueller, pg 443

ADAPTATIONS, NOVELIZATIONS
Kathleen Barnes, pg 436
Diana Barth, pg 436
Anita Bartholomew, pg 436
The Bookmill, pg 436
Jeanne Cavelos Editorial Services, pg 437
Clear Concepts, pg 437
Cypress House, pg 437
Christina Di Martino Literary Services, pg 438
The Editorial Department LLC, pg 438
Diane Gallo, pg 439
The Gary-Paul Agency (GPA), pg 439
Gelles-Cole Literary Enterprises, pg 439
GGP Publishing Inc, pg 440
JFE Editorial, pg 441
Sondra Mochson, pg 443
Schoolhouse Network, pg 444
SDP Publishing Solutions LLC, pg 444
The Writers Lifeline Inc, a Story Merchant company, pg 446

ADVERTISING & PROMOTION COPYWRITING
Accurate Writing & More, pg 435
J Adel Art & Design, pg 435
Ampersand Group, pg 435
ASJA Freelance Writer Search, pg 435
Diana Barth, pg 436
Mark E Battersby, pg 436
Bloom Ink, pg 436
Blue & Ude Writers' Services, pg 436
The Bookmill, pg 436
R E Carsch, MS-Consultant, pg 436
CeciBooks Editorial & Publishing Consultation, pg 437
Cohesion®, pg 437
Cultural Studies & Analysis, pg 437
Cypress House, pg 437
Christina Di Martino Literary Services, pg 438
Edit Etc, pg 438
Edit Resource LLC, pg 438
Editcetera, pg 438
Fine Wordworking, pg 439
Diane Gallo, pg 439
GGP Publishing Inc, pg 440
Robert M Goodman, pg 440
Jenkins Group Inc, pg 441
JFE Editorial, pg 441
Peter Mayeux, pg 442
Diane Patrick, pg 443
Proofed to Perfection Editing Services, pg 443
Vivian Sudhalter, pg 445
Windhaven®, pg 445

BIBLIOGRAPHIES
Ampersand Group, pg 435
The Bookmill, pg 436
CeciBooks Editorial & Publishing Consultation, pg 437
Cohesion®, pg 437
Cypress House, pg 437
Edit Etc, pg 438
EditAmerica, pg 438
Editcetera, pg 438
GGP Publishing Inc, pg 440
Joan K Griffitts Indexing, pg 440
Jenkins Group Inc, pg 441
JFE Editorial, pg 441
Keim Publishing, pg 441
Barry R Koffler, pg 441
Lynn C Kronzek, Richard A Flom & Robert Flom, pg 441
Polly Kummel LLC, pg 441
Peter Mayeux, pg 442
Nina Neimark Editorial Services, pg 443
Sue Newton, pg 443
Proofed to Perfection Editing Services, pg 443
Research Research, pg 444
C J Scheiner Books, pg 444
Scribendi Inc, pg 444
Roger W Smith, pg 445
Fraser Sutherland, pg 445

BROKER FOR MANUFACTURING
AAH Graphics Inc, pg 435
Aptara Inc, pg 435
Cypress House, pg 437
GGP Publishing Inc, pg 440
P M Gordon Associates Inc, pg 440
Jenkins Group Inc, pg 441
Lumina Datamatics Inc, pg 442

CONDENSATIONS
Accurate Writing & More, pg 435
Kathleen Barnes, pg 436
Diana Barth, pg 436
Bloom Ink, pg 436
Blue & Ude Writers' Services, pg 436
The Bookmill, pg 436
Hilary R Burke, pg 436
Carpe Indexum, pg 436
Clear Concepts, pg 437
Cultural Studies & Analysis, pg 437
Cypress House, pg 437
EditAmerica, pg 438
Diane Gallo, pg 439
The Gary-Paul Agency (GPA), pg 439
GGP Publishing Inc, pg 440
Sherry Gottlieb, pg 440
Paul Greenland Communications Inc, pg 440
Helm Editorial Services, pg 440
L Anne Hirschel DDS, pg 440
JFE Editorial, pg 441
Peter Mayeux, pg 442
Pat McNees, pg 442
Sue Newton, pg 443
Brooke C Stoddard, pg 445

COPY-EDITING
AAH Graphics Inc, pg 435
Aaron-Spear, pg 435
J Adel Art & Design, pg 435
AEIOU Inc, pg 435
Rodelinde Albrecht, pg 435
Ampersand Group, pg 435
Barbara S Anderson, pg 435
Angel Editing Services, pg 435
Angels Editorial Services, pg 435
Aptara Inc, pg 435
ASJA Freelance Writer Search, pg 435
Associated Editors, pg 435
Audrey Owen, pg 436
Kathleen Barnes, pg 436
Diana Barth, pg 436
BiblioGenesis, pg 436
Bloom Ink, pg 436
Blue & Ude Writers' Services, pg 436
BookBaby, pg 436
The Bookmill, pg 436
Hilary R Burke, pg 436
Carpe Indexum, pg 436
R E Carsch, MS-Consultant, pg 436
Carol Cartaino, pg 437
Claudia Caruana, pg 437
Jeanne Cavelos Editorial Services, pg 437
CeciBooks Editorial & Publishing Consultation, pg 437
Ruth Chernia, pg 437
Clear Concepts, pg 437
Clotilde's Secretarial & Management Services, pg 437
Dwight Clough, pg 437
Coastside Editorial, pg 437
Robert L Cohen, pg 437
Cohesion®, pg 437
Cypress House, pg 437
John M Daniel Literary Services, pg 438
Christina Di Martino Literary Services, pg 438
diacriTech Inc, pg 438
Double Play, pg 438
Earth Edit, pg 438
Edit Etc, pg 438
Edit Resource LLC, pg 438
EditAmerica, pg 438
Editcetera, pg 438
EditCraft Editorial Services, pg 438
The Editorial Department LLC, pg 438
Catherine C Elverston ELS, pg 439
Enough Said: Editing, Writing, Research, Project Management, pg 439
Linda Fairchild & Company LLC, pg 439
Farrar Writing & Editing, pg 439
Betsy Feist Resources, pg 439
Fine Wordworking, pg 439
Focus Strategic Communications Inc, pg 439
Sandi Frank, pg 439
The Gary-Paul Agency (GPA), pg 439
Nancy C Gerth PhD, pg 440
GGP Publishing Inc, pg 440
Robert M Goodman, pg 440
P M Gordon Associates Inc, pg 440
Paul Greenland Communications Inc, pg 440
Joan K Griffitts Indexing, pg 440
GW Inc, pg 440
Anne Hebenstreit, pg 440
Helm Editorial Services, pg 440
L Anne Hirschel DDS, pg 440
Burnham Holmes, pg 440
Integra Software Services Inc, pg 441
Jenkins Group Inc, pg 441
JFE Editorial, pg 441
JL Communications, pg 441
Just Creative Writing & Indexing Services (JCR), pg 441
Keim Publishing, pg 441
KOK Edit, pg 441
Eileen Kramer, pg 441
Lynn C Kronzek, Richard A Flom & Robert Flom, pg 441
Polly Kummel LLC, pg 441
Lachina Creative Inc, pg 441

EDITORIAL SERVICES — ACTIVITY INDEX

Land on Demand, pg 441
The Learning Source Ltd, pg 441
Little Chicago Editorial Services, pg 442
Lumina Datamatics Inc, pg 442
Phyllis Manner, pg 442
ManuscriptCritique.com, pg 442
Peter Mayeux, pg 442
Susan T Middleton, pg 442
Stephen M Miller Inc, pg 442
Kathleen Mills Editorial Services, pg 442
Sondra Mochson, pg 443
Mary Mueller, pg 443
Nina Neimark Editorial Services, pg 443
Newgen North America Inc, pg 443
Sue Newton, pg 443
Donald Nicholson-Smith, pg 443
Diane Patrick, pg 443
PeopleSpeak, pg 443
Rebecca Pepper, pg 443
Meredith Phillips, pg 443
Pictures & Words Editorial Services, pg 443
Wendy Polhemus-Annibell, pg 443
Proofed to Perfection Editing Services, pg 443
Jerry Ralya, pg 444
Research Research, pg 444
Schoolhouse Network, pg 444
Sherri Schultz/Words with Grace, pg 444
Scribendi Inc, pg 444
SDP Publishing Solutions LLC, pg 444
Alexa Selph, pg 444
Barry Sheinkopf, pg 444
Roger W Smith, pg 445
Brooke C Stoddard, pg 445
Jeri L Stolk, pg 445
Vivian Sudhalter, pg 445
Fraser Sutherland, pg 445
Thodestool Fiction Editing, pg 445
Barbara Mlotek Whelehan, pg 445
Windhaven®, pg 445
Working With Words, pg 445
Write for Success Editing Services, pg 445
The Writers Lifeline Inc, a Story Merchant company, pg 446
Zebra Communications, pg 446

FACT CHECKING

AAH Graphics Inc, pg 435
Accurate Writing & More, pg 435
AEIOU Inc, pg 435
Jeanette Almada, pg 435
Aptara Inc, pg 435
Associated Editors, pg 435
Kathleen Barnes, pg 436
BiblioGenesis, pg 436
The Bookmill, pg 436
Hilary R Burke, pg 436
Carpe Indexum, pg 436
R E Carsch, MS-Consultant, pg 436
Carol Cartaino, pg 437
Claudia Caruana, pg 437
CeciBooks Editorial & Publishing Consultation, pg 437
Ruth Chernia, pg 437
Clear Concepts, pg 437
Robert L Cohen, pg 437
Cohesion®, pg 437
Cypress House, pg 437
Christina Di Martino Literary Services, pg 438
diacriTech Inc, pg 438
DK Research Inc, pg 438
Double Play, pg 438
Edit Etc, pg 438
EditAmerica, pg 438
Editcetera, pg 438
The Editorial Department LLC, pg 438
Catherine C Elverston ELS, pg 439
Enough Said: Editing, Writing, Research, Project Management, pg 439
Fine Wordworking, pg 439
Focus Strategic Communications Inc, pg 439
Nancy C Gerth PhD, pg 440
GGP Publishing Inc, pg 440
Robert M Goodman, pg 440
Joan K Griffitts Indexing, pg 440
Helm Editorial Services, pg 440
Jenkins Group Inc, pg 441
JFE Editorial, pg 441
Just Creative Writing & Indexing Services (JCR), pg 441
Keim Publishing, pg 441
Barry R Koffler, pg 441
Lynn C Kronzek, Richard A Flom & Robert Flom, pg 441
Polly Kummel LLC, pg 441
The Learning Source Ltd, pg 441
Lumina Datamatics Inc, pg 442
Peter Mayeux, pg 442
Kathleen Mills Editorial Services, pg 442
Nina Neimark Editorial Services, pg 443
Sue Newton, pg 443
Diane Patrick, pg 443
Meredith Phillips, pg 443
Proofed to Perfection Editing Services, pg 443
Research Research, pg 444
C J Scheiner Books, pg 444
SDP Publishing Solutions LLC, pg 444
Roger W Smith, pg 445
Windhaven®, pg 445
The Writers Lifeline Inc, a Story Merchant company, pg 446

GHOSTWRITING

Accurate Writing & More, pg 435
Rodelinde Albrecht, pg 435
ASJA Freelance Writer Search, pg 435
Associated Editors, pg 435
Audrey Owen, pg 436
Kathleen Barnes, pg 436
Diana Barth, pg 436
Anita Bartholomew, pg 436
Mark E Battersby, pg 436
Bloom Ink, pg 436
Blue & Ude Writers' Services, pg 436
BookCrafters LLC Editing, pg 436
The Bookmill, pg 436
Brady Literary Management, pg 436
Hilary R Burke, pg 436
Carpe Indexum, pg 436
Carol Cartaino, pg 437
Jeanne Cavelos Editorial Services, pg 437
Clear Concepts, pg 437
Dwight Clough, pg 437
Cypress House, pg 437
John M Daniel Literary Services, pg 438
Christina Di Martino Literary Services, pg 438
Edit Etc, pg 438
Edit Resource LLC, pg 438
Editcetera, pg 438
EditCraft Editorial Services, pg 438
The Editorial Department LLC, pg 438
The Editors Circle, pg 438
Jerry Felsen, pg 439
Fine Wordworking, pg 439
Focus Strategic Communications Inc, pg 439
Diane Gallo, pg 439
The Gary-Paul Agency (GPA), pg 439
Fred Gebhart, pg 439
Gelles-Cole Literary Enterprises, pg 439
GGP Publishing Inc, pg 440
Robert M Goodman, pg 440
Paul Greenland Communications Inc, pg 440
L Anne Hirschel DDS, pg 440
Integra Software Services Inc, pg 441
Jenkins Group Inc, pg 441
JFE Editorial, pg 441
Just Creative Writing & Indexing Services (JCR), pg 441
Little Chicago Editorial Services, pg 442
Lumina Datamatics Inc, pg 442
Pat McNees, pg 442
Mary Mueller, pg 443
Elsa Peterson Ltd, pg 443
Proofed to Perfection Editing Services, pg 443
SDP Publishing Solutions LLC, pg 444
Barry Sheinkopf, pg 444
Brooke C Stoddard, pg 445
Vivian Sudhalter, pg 445
Thodestool Fiction Editing, pg 445
Wambtac Communications LLC, pg 445
Barbara Mlotek Whelehan, pg 445
Windhaven®, pg 445
Words into Print, pg 445
Write for Success Editing Services, pg 445
The Writers Lifeline Inc, a Story Merchant company, pg 446

INDEXING

AEIOU Inc, pg 435
Ampersand Group, pg 435
Aptara Inc, pg 435
Astor Indexers, pg 435
Heidi Blough, Book Indexer, pg 436
Carpe Indexum, pg 436
CeciBooks Editorial & Publishing Consultation, pg 437
Ruth Chernia, pg 437
Cohesion®, pg 437
Cypress House, pg 437
diacriTech Inc, pg 438
East Mountain Editing Services, pg 438
Editcetera, pg 438
The Editorial Department LLC, pg 438
R Elwell Indexing, pg 439
Focus Strategic Communications Inc, pg 439
Sandi Frank, pg 439
Nancy C Gerth PhD, pg 440
GGP Publishing Inc, pg 440
Joan K Griffitts Indexing, pg 440
GW Inc, pg 440
Herr's Indexing Service, pg 440
Indexing by the Book, pg 440
Integra Software Services Inc, pg 441
Jenkins Group Inc, pg 441
Just Creative Writing & Indexing Services (JCR), pg 441
Keim Publishing, pg 441
Barry R Koffler, pg 441
Lachina Creative Inc, pg 441
The Learning Source Ltd, pg 441
Elliot Linzer, pg 442
Little Chicago Editorial Services, pg 442
Lumina Datamatics Inc, pg 442
Phyllis Manner, pg 442
Peter Mayeux, pg 442
Mary Mueller, pg 443
Nina Neimark Editorial Services, pg 443
Newgen North America Inc, pg 443
Sue Newton, pg 443
Donald Nicholson-Smith, pg 443
Jerry Ralya, pg 444
Peter Rooney, pg 444
Salmon Bay Indexing, pg 444
Schoolhouse Indexing, pg 444
Schroeder Indexing Services, pg 444
Sciendex, pg 444
Alexa Selph, pg 444
Monika Shoffman-Graves, pg 445
Twin Oaks Indexing, pg 445
WordCo Indexing Services Inc, pg 445
Wright Information Indexing Services, pg 445
Wyman Indexing, pg 446

INTERVIEWING

Accurate Writing & More, pg 435
Jeanette Almada, pg 435
ASJA Freelance Writer Search, pg 435
Kathleen Barnes, pg 436
Diana Barth, pg 436
Anita Bartholomew, pg 436
Mark E Battersby, pg 436
Blue & Ude Writers' Services, pg 436
The Bookmill, pg 436
R E Carsch, MS-Consultant, pg 436
Clear Concepts, pg 437
Robert L Cohen, pg 437
Cohesion®, pg 437
Cultural Studies & Analysis, pg 437
Cypress House, pg 437
Christina Di Martino Literary Services, pg 438
Edit Etc, pg 438
Editcetera, pg 438
Enough Said: Editing, Writing, Research, Project Management, pg 439
Linda Fairchild & Company LLC, pg 439
Farrar Writing & Editing, pg 439
Fine Wordworking, pg 439
Diane Gallo, pg 439
Fred Gebhart, pg 439
GGP Publishing Inc, pg 440
Robert M Goodman, pg 440
Paul Greenland Communications Inc, pg 440
L Anne Hirschel DDS, pg 440
Jenkins Group Inc, pg 441
JFE Editorial, pg 441
JL Communications, pg 441
Keim Publishing, pg 441
Lynn C Kronzek, Richard A Flom & Robert Flom, pg 441
Lumina Datamatics Inc, pg 442
Peter Mayeux, pg 442
Pamela Dittmer McKuen, pg 442
Pat McNees, pg 442
Stephen M Miller Inc, pg 442
Diane Patrick, pg 443
Roger W Smith, pg 445
Brooke C Stoddard, pg 445
Barbara Mlotek Whelehan, pg 445
Words into Print, pg 445
Write for Success Editing Services, pg 445

& AGENTS   EDITORIAL SERVICES — ACTIVITY INDEX

LINE EDITING

Aaron-Spear, pg 435
Rodelinde Albrecht, pg 435
Ampersand Group, pg 435
Barbara S Anderson, pg 435
Angel Editing Services, pg 435
Aptara Inc, pg 435
ASJA Freelance Writer Search, pg 435
Associated Editors, pg 435
Audrey Owen, pg 436
Kathleen Barnes, pg 436
Diana Barth, pg 436
Anita Bartholomew, pg 436
BiblioGenesis, pg 436
Bloom Ink, pg 436
Blue & Ude Writers' Services, pg 436
BookBaby, pg 436
BookCrafters LLC Editing, pg 436
Brady Literary Management, pg 436
Carpe Indexum, pg 436
Carol Cartaino, pg 437
Claudia Caruana, pg 437
Jeanne Cavelos Editorial Services, pg 437
CeciBooks Editorial & Publishing Consultation, pg 437
Ruth Chernia, pg 437
Robert L Cohen, pg 437
Cohesion®, pg 437
Cultural Studies & Analysis, pg 437
Cypress House, pg 437
Christina Di Martino Literary Services, pg 438
diacriTech Inc, pg 438
Edit Etc, pg 438
Edit Resource LLC, pg 438
EditAmerica, pg 438
Editcetera, pg 438
EditCraft Editorial Services, pg 438
The Editorial Department LLC, pg 438
The Editors Circle, pg 438
Enough Said: Editing, Writing, Research, Project Management, pg 439
Linda Fairchild & Company LLC, pg 439
Farrar Writing & Editing, pg 439
Betsy Feist Resources, pg 439
Fine Wordworking, pg 439
Focus Strategic Communications Inc, pg 439
Sandi Frank, pg 439
The Gary-Paul Agency (GPA), pg 439
Gelles-Cole Literary Enterprises, pg 439
Nancy C Gerth PhD, pg 440
GGP Publishing Inc, pg 440
Robert M Goodman, pg 440
Sherry Gottlieb, pg 440
Paul Greenland Communications Inc, pg 440
Joan K Griffitts Indexing, pg 440
GW Inc, pg 440
Anne Hebenstreit, pg 440
Helm Editorial Services, pg 440
Burnham Holmes, pg 440
Integra Software Services Inc, pg 441
Jenkins Group Inc, pg 441
JFE Editorial, pg 441
JL Communications, pg 441
Just Creative Writing & Indexing Services (JCR), pg 441
Keim Publishing, pg 441
Barry R Koffler, pg 441
KOK Edit, pg 441
Eileen Kramer, pg 441

Lynn C Kronzek, Richard A Flom & Robert Flom, pg 441
Polly Kummel LLC, pg 441
Lachina Creative Inc, pg 441
Land on Demand, pg 441
The Learning Source Ltd, pg 441
Little Chicago Editorial Services, pg 442
Lumina Datamatics Inc, pg 442
ManuscriptCritique.com, pg 442
Pat McNees, pg 442
Susan T Middleton, pg 442
Stephen M Miller Inc, pg 442
Kathleen Mills Editorial Services, pg 442
Sondra Mochson, pg 443
Nina Neimark Editorial Services, pg 443
Sue Newton, pg 443
Diane Patrick, pg 443
Rebecca Pepper, pg 443
Elsa Peterson Ltd, pg 443
Meredith Phillips, pg 443
Pictures & Words Editorial Services, pg 443
Caroline Pincus Book Midwife, pg 443
Wendy Polhemus-Annibell, pg 443
Proofed to Perfection Editing Services, pg 443
Judith Riven Literary Agent LLC, pg 444
Sachem Publishing Associates Inc, pg 444
Sherri Schultz/Words with Grace, pg 444
Scribendi Inc, pg 444
SDP Publishing Solutions LLC, pg 444
Alexa Selph, pg 444
Barry Sheinkopf, pg 444
Roger W Smith, pg 445
Stackler Editorial, pg 445
Brooke C Stoddard, pg 445
Vivian Sudhalter, pg 445
Fraser Sutherland, pg 445
Thodestool Fiction Editing, pg 445
Wambtac Communications LLC, pg 445
Windhaven®, pg 445
Words into Print, pg 445
Working With Words, pg 445
Write for Success Editing Services, pg 445
The Writers Lifeline Inc, a Story Merchant company, pg 446
Zebra Communications, pg 446

MANUSCRIPT ANALYSIS

Accurate Writing & More, pg 435
Barbara S Anderson, pg 435
Angel Editing Services, pg 435
Angels Editorial Services, pg 435
Aptara Inc, pg 435
ASJA Freelance Writer Search, pg 435
Associated Editors, pg 435
Audrey Owen, pg 436
Diana Barth, pg 436
Anita Bartholomew, pg 436
BiblioGenesis, pg 436
Bloom Ink, pg 436
Blue & Ude Writers' Services, pg 436
BookCrafters LLC Editing, pg 436
The Bookmill, pg 436
Brady Literary Management, pg 436
Hilary R Burke, pg 436
R E Carsch, MS-Consultant, pg 436
Carol Cartaino, pg 437
Claudia Caruana, pg 437

Jeanne Cavelos Editorial Services, pg 437
CeciBooks Editorial & Publishing Consultation, pg 437
Ruth Chernia, pg 437
Clear Concepts, pg 437
Robert L Cohen, pg 437
Cohesion®, pg 437
Cypress House, pg 437
John M Daniel Literary Services, pg 438
Christina Di Martino Literary Services, pg 438
diacriTech Inc, pg 438
Double Play, pg 438
Editcetera, pg 438
EditCraft Editorial Services, pg 438
The Editorial Department LLC, pg 438
The Editors Circle, pg 438
Enough Said: Editing, Writing, Research, Project Management, pg 439
Linda Fairchild & Company LLC, pg 439
Farrar Writing & Editing, pg 439
Betsy Feist Resources, pg 439
Fine Wordworking, pg 439
Focus Strategic Communications Inc, pg 439
Fromer, pg 439
Diane Gallo, pg 439
The Gary-Paul Agency (GPA), pg 439
Gelles-Cole Literary Enterprises, pg 439
GGP Publishing Inc, pg 440
Sherry Gottlieb, pg 440
GW Inc, pg 440
Helm Editorial Services, pg 440
Integra Software Services Inc, pg 441
Jenkins Group Inc, pg 441
JFE Editorial, pg 441
JL Communications, pg 441
Just Creative Writing & Indexing Services (JCR), pg 441
Polly Kummel LLC, pg 441
Lachina Creative Inc, pg 441
Lumina Datamatics Inc, pg 442
Elizabeth Lyon, pg 442
Phyllis Manner, pg 442
ManuscriptCritique.com, pg 442
Peter Mayeux, pg 442
Pat McNees, pg 442
Sondra Mochson, pg 443
Nina Neimark Editorial Services, pg 443
Veronica Oliva, pg 443
PeopleSpeak, pg 443
Elsa Peterson Ltd, pg 443
Pictures & Words Editorial Services, pg 443
Caroline Pincus Book Midwife, pg 443
Proofed to Perfection Editing Services, pg 443
Judith Riven Literary Agent LLC, pg 444
Sachem Publishing Associates Inc, pg 444
Scribendi Inc, pg 444
SDP Publishing Solutions LLC, pg 444
Barry Sheinkopf, pg 444
Monika Shoffman-Graves, pg 445
Stackler Editorial, pg 445
Brooke C Stoddard, pg 445
Vivian Sudhalter, pg 445
Thodestool Fiction Editing, pg 445
Wambtac Communications LLC, pg 445
Windhaven®, pg 445

Words into Print, pg 445
Write for Success Editing Services, pg 445
The Writers Lifeline Inc, a Story Merchant company, pg 446
Writer's Relief, Inc, pg 446
Zebra Communications, pg 446

PERMISSIONS

Ampersand Group, pg 435
Aptara Inc, pg 435
BZ/Rights & Permissions Inc, pg 436
CeciBooks Editorial & Publishing Consultation, pg 437
Ruth Chernia, pg 437
Clear Concepts, pg 437
Cohesion®, pg 437
Cypress House, pg 437
diacriTech Inc, pg 438
DK Research Inc, pg 438
Edit Etc, pg 438
Editcetera, pg 438
Catherine C Elverston ELS, pg 439
Linda Fairchild & Company LLC, pg 439
Fine Wordworking, pg 439
Focus Strategic Communications Inc, pg 439
GGP Publishing Inc, pg 440
Sheri Gilbert, pg 440
Robert M Goodman, pg 440
GW Inc, pg 440
Integra Software Services Inc, pg 441
Jenkins Group Inc, pg 441
JFE Editorial, pg 441
Keim Publishing, pg 441
Lachina Creative Inc, pg 441
The Learning Source Ltd, pg 441
Lumina Datamatics Inc, pg 442
Veronica Oliva, pg 443
Elsa Peterson Ltd, pg 443
Pronk Media Inc, pg 443
Barbara S Salz LLC Photo Research, pg 444

PHOTO RESEARCH

J Adel Art & Design, pg 435
Aptara Inc, pg 435
BZ/Rights & Permissions Inc, pg 436
R E Carsch, MS-Consultant, pg 436
Ruth Chernia, pg 437
Clear Concepts, pg 437
Cohesion®, pg 437
Cypress House, pg 437
diacriTech Inc, pg 438
DK Research Inc, pg 438
Edit Etc, pg 438
Focus Strategic Communications Inc, pg 439
Foster Travel Publishing, pg 439
GGP Publishing Inc, pg 440
GW Inc, pg 440
Integra Software Services Inc, pg 441
Jenkins Group Inc, pg 441
Keim Publishing, pg 441
Lynn C Kronzek, Richard A Flom & Robert Flom, pg 441
Lachina Creative Inc, pg 441
The Learning Source Ltd, pg 441
Debra Lemonds, pg 442
Lumina Datamatics Inc, pg 442
Nina Neimark Editorial Services, pg 443
Elsa Peterson Ltd, pg 443
Pronk Media Inc, pg 443
Barbara S Salz LLC Photo Research, pg 444
C J Scheiner Books, pg 444

EDITORIAL SERVICES — ACTIVITY INDEX

Schoolhouse Network, pg 444
Toby Wertheim, pg 445

PROOFREADING

AAH Graphics Inc, pg 435
Aaron-Spear, pg 435
J Adel Art & Design, pg 435
Rodelinde Albrecht, pg 435
Ampersand Group, pg 435
Barbara S Anderson, pg 435
Angels Editorial Services, pg 435
Aptara Inc, pg 435
Associated Editors, pg 435
Kathleen Barnes, pg 436
Diana Barth, pg 436
BiblioGenesis, pg 436
Bloom Ink, pg 436
Blue & Ude Writers' Services, pg 436
BookBaby, pg 436
BookCrafters LLC Editing, pg 436
Carpe Indexum, pg 436
R E Carsch, MS-Consultant, pg 436
Carol Cartaino, pg 437
Jeanne Cavelos Editorial Services, pg 437
CeciBooks Editorial & Publishing Consultation, pg 437
Clerical Plus, pg 437
Clotilde's Secretarial & Management Services, pg 437
Coastside Editorial, pg 437
Robert L Cohen, pg 437
Cohesion®, pg 437
Cypress House, pg 437
Christina Di Martino Literary Services, pg 438
diacriTech Inc, pg 438
Double Play, pg 438
Earth Edit, pg 438
EditAmerica, pg 438
Editcetera, pg 438
The Editorial Department LLC, pg 438
Catherine C Elverston ELS, pg 439
Enough Said: Editing, Writing, Research, Project Management, pg 439
Linda Fairchild & Company LLC, pg 439
Farrar Writing & Editing, pg 439
Betsy Feist Resources, pg 439
Fine Wordworking, pg 439
Focus Strategic Communications Inc, pg 439
Sandi Frank, pg 439
The Gary-Paul Agency (GPA), pg 439
Nancy C Gerth PhD, pg 440
GGP Publishing Inc, pg 440
Robert M Goodman, pg 440
Paul Greenland Communications Inc, pg 440
Joan K Griffitts Indexing, pg 440
GW Inc, pg 440
Anne Hebenstreit, pg 440
Helm Editorial Services, pg 440
Burnham Holmes, pg 440
Indexing by the Book, pg 440
Integra Software Services Inc, pg 441
Jenkins Group Inc, pg 441
JFE Editorial, pg 441
Just Creative Writing & Indexing Services (JCR), pg 441
Keim Publishing, pg 441
Barry R Koffler, pg 441
Eileen Kramer, pg 441
Lynn C Kronzek, Richard A Flom & Robert Flom, pg 441
Lachina Creative Inc, pg 441
Land on Demand, pg 441

The Learning Source Ltd, pg 441
Lumina Datamatics Inc, pg 442
ManuscriptCritique.com, pg 442
Danny Marcus Word Worker, pg 442
Peter Mayeux, pg 442
MC2 Solutions LLC, pg 442
Kathleen Mills Editorial Services, pg 442
Sondra Mochson, pg 443
Mary Mueller, pg 443
Nina Neimark Editorial Services, pg 443
Newgen North America Inc, pg 443
Sue Newton, pg 443
Donald Nicholson-Smith, pg 443
Diane Patrick, pg 443
PeopleSpeak, pg 443
Meredith Phillips, pg 443
Pictures & Words Editorial Services, pg 443
Wendy Polhemus-Annibell, pg 443
Proofed to Perfection Editing Services, pg 443
Research Research, pg 444
Schoolhouse Network, pg 444
Sherri Schultz/Words with Grace, pg 444
Scribendi Inc, pg 444
SDP Publishing Solutions LLC, pg 444
Alexa Selph, pg 444
Monika Shoffman-Graves, pg 445
Roger W Smith, pg 445
Vivian Sudhalter, pg 445
Toby Wertheim, pg 445
Barbara Mlotek Whelehan, pg 445
Windhaven®, pg 445
Working With Words, pg 445
Write for Success Editing Services, pg 445
The Writers Lifeline Inc, a Story Merchant company, pg 446
Writer's Relief, Inc, pg 446
Zebra Communications, pg 446

RESEARCH

Accurate Writing & More, pg 435
Jeanette Almada, pg 435
Ampersand Group, pg 435
Aptara Inc, pg 435
Associated Editors, pg 435
Kathleen Barnes, pg 436
BiblioGenesis, pg 436
The Bookmill, pg 436
Hilary R Burke, pg 436
Carpe Indexum, pg 436
R E Carsch, MS-Consultant, pg 436
Claudia Caruana, pg 437
CeciBooks Editorial & Publishing Consultation, pg 437
Ruth Chernia, pg 437
Clear Concepts, pg 437
Clotilde's Secretarial & Management Services, pg 437
Robert L Cohen, pg 437
Cohesion®, pg 437
Cultural Studies & Analysis, pg 437
Cypress House, pg 437
Christina Di Martino Literary Services, pg 438
diacriTech Inc, pg 438
Double Play, pg 438
Edit Etc, pg 438
EditAmerica, pg 438
Catherine C Elverston ELS, pg 439
Enough Said: Editing, Writing, Research, Project Management, pg 439
Farrar Writing & Editing, pg 439
Jerry Felsen, pg 439
Fine Wordworking, pg 439

Focus Strategic Communications Inc, pg 439
Diane Gallo, pg 439
The Gary-Paul Agency (GPA), pg 439
Fred Gebhart, pg 439
Nancy C Gerth PhD, pg 440
GGP Publishing Inc, pg 440
Robert M Goodman, pg 440
Paul Greenland Communications Inc, pg 440
Joan K Griffitts Indexing, pg 440
L Anne Hirschel DDS, pg 440
Jenkins Group Inc, pg 441
JFE Editorial, pg 441
Keim Publishing, pg 441
Barry R Koffler, pg 441
Lynn C Kronzek, Richard A Flom & Robert Flom, pg 441
Polly Kummel LLC, pg 441
The Learning Source Ltd, pg 441
Debra Lemonds, pg 442
Lumina Datamatics Inc, pg 442
Phyllis Manner, pg 442
Peter Mayeux, pg 442
Pat McNees, pg 442
Sondra Mochson, pg 443
Nina Neimark Editorial Services, pg 443
Sue Newton, pg 443
Diane Patrick, pg 443
Elsa Peterson Ltd, pg 443
Research Research, pg 444
Sachem Publishing Associates Inc, pg 444
C J Scheiner Books, pg 444
Schoolhouse Network, pg 444
Monika Shoffman-Graves, pg 445
Roger W Smith, pg 445
Brooke C Stoddard, pg 445
Fraser Sutherland, pg 445
Toby Wertheim, pg 445
Windhaven®, pg 445
Words into Print, pg 445
The Writers Lifeline Inc, a Story Merchant company, pg 446
Writer's Relief, Inc, pg 446

REWRITING

AAH Graphics Inc, pg 435
Aaron-Spear, pg 435
Accurate Writing & More, pg 435
J Adel Art & Design, pg 435
Rodelinde Albrecht, pg 435
Jeanette Almada, pg 435
Ampersand Group, pg 435
Barbara S Anderson, pg 435
Angels Editorial Services, pg 435
Aptara Inc, pg 435
ASJA Freelance Writer Search, pg 435
Associated Editors, pg 435
Audrey Owen, pg 436
Kathleen Barnes, pg 436
Diana Barth, pg 436
Anita Bartholomew, pg 436
BiblioGenesis, pg 436
Bloom Ink, pg 436
Blue & Ude Writers' Services, pg 436
BookCrafters LLC Editing, pg 436
The Bookmill, pg 436
Brady Literary Management, pg 436
Hilary R Burke, pg 436
Carpe Indexum, pg 436
Carol Cartaino, pg 437
Claudia Caruana, pg 437
Jeanne Cavelos Editorial Services, pg 437
CeciBooks Editorial & Publishing Consultation, pg 437
Clear Concepts, pg 437

Dwight Clough, pg 437
Robert L Cohen, pg 437
Cohesion®, pg 437
Cultural Studies & Analysis, pg 437
Cypress House, pg 437
Christina Di Martino Literary Services, pg 438
diacriTech Inc, pg 438
Edit Etc, pg 438
Edit Resource LLC, pg 438
EditAmerica, pg 438
Editcetera, pg 438
EditCraft Editorial Services, pg 438
The Editorial Department LLC, pg 438
The Editors Circle, pg 438
Catherine C Elverston ELS, pg 439
Enough Said: Editing, Writing, Research, Project Management, pg 439
Linda Fairchild & Company LLC, pg 439
Farrar Writing & Editing, pg 439
Betsy Feist Resources, pg 439
Fine Wordworking, pg 439
Focus Strategic Communications Inc, pg 439
Fromer, pg 439
Diane Gallo, pg 439
The Gary-Paul Agency (GPA), pg 439
Fred Gebhart, pg 439
Gelles-Cole Literary Enterprises, pg 439
Nancy C Gerth PhD, pg 440
GGP Publishing Inc, pg 440
Robert M Goodman, pg 440
Sherry Gottlieb, pg 440
Paul Greenland Communications Inc, pg 440
GW Inc, pg 440
L Anne Hirschel DDS, pg 440
Burnham Holmes, pg 440
Integra Software Services Inc, pg 441
Jenkins Group Inc, pg 441
JFE Editorial, pg 441
Just Creative Writing & Indexing Services (JCR), pg 441
Keim Publishing, pg 441
Barry R Koffler, pg 441
Lynn C Kronzek, Richard A Flom & Robert Flom, pg 441
Polly Kummel LLC, pg 441
Land on Demand, pg 441
The Learning Source Ltd, pg 441
Little Chicago Editorial Services, pg 442
Lumina Datamatics Inc, pg 442
Phyllis Manner, pg 442
Peter Mayeux, pg 442
Pat McNees, pg 442
Susan T Middleton, pg 442
Stephen M Miller Inc, pg 442
Kathleen Mills Editorial Services, pg 442
Sondra Mochson, pg 443
Mary Mueller, pg 443
Nina Neimark Editorial Services, pg 443
Sue Newton, pg 443
Diane Patrick, pg 443
Elsa Peterson Ltd, pg 443
Pictures & Words Editorial Services, pg 443
Caroline Pincus Book Midwife, pg 443
Wendy Polhemus-Annibell, pg 443
Proofed to Perfection Editing Services, pg 443
Sachem Publishing Associates Inc, pg 444
Schoolhouse Network, pg 444

EDITORIAL SERVICES — ACTIVITY INDEX

& AGENTS

SDP Publishing Solutions LLC, pg 444
Alexa Selph, pg 444
Barry Sheinkopf, pg 444
Roger W Smith, pg 445
Brooke C Stoddard, pg 445
Vivian Sudhalter, pg 445
Fraser Sutherland, pg 445
Wambtac Communications LLC, pg 445
Barbara Mlotek Whelehan, pg 445
Windhaven®, pg 445
Words into Print, pg 445
Write for Success Editing Services, pg 445
Zebra Communications, pg 446

SPECIAL ASSIGNMENT WRITING

Accurate Writing & More, pg 435
J Adel Art & Design, pg 435
Rodelinde Albrecht, pg 435
Jeanette Almada, pg 435
Ampersand Group, pg 435
Aptara Inc, pg 435
ASJA Freelance Writer Search, pg 435
Associated Editors, pg 435
Kathleen Barnes, pg 436
Diana Barth, pg 436
Anita Bartholomew, pg 436
Mark E Battersby, pg 436
BiblioGenesis, pg 436
Bloom Ink, pg 436
Blue & Ude Writers' Services, pg 436
BookCrafters LLC Editing, pg 436
The Bookmill, pg 436
Hilary R Burke, pg 436
Carpe Indexum, pg 436
R E Carsch, MS-Consultant, pg 436
Claudia Caruana, pg 437
Jeanne Cavelos Editorial Services, pg 437
Margaret Cheasebro PhD, pg 437
Clear Concepts, pg 437
Dwight Clough, pg 437
Robert L Cohen, pg 437
Cohesion®, pg 437
Cultural Studies & Analysis, pg 437
Cypress House, pg 437
Christina Di Martino Literary Services, pg 438
diacriTech Inc, pg 438
Edit Etc, pg 438

Edit Resource LLC, pg 438
Editcetera, pg 438
The Editors Circle, pg 438
Catherine C Elverston ELS, pg 439
Enough Said: Editing, Writing, Research, Project Management, pg 439
Linda Fairchild & Company LLC, pg 439
Farrar Writing & Editing, pg 439
Betsy Feist Resources, pg 439
Jerry Felsen, pg 439
Fine Wordworking, pg 439
Foster Travel Publishing, pg 439
Fromer, pg 439
Diane Gallo, pg 439
The Gary-Paul Agency (GPA), pg 439
Fred Gebhart, pg 439
Gelles-Cole Literary Enterprises, pg 439
Nancy C Gerth PhD, pg 440
GGP Publishing Inc, pg 440
Robert M Goodman, pg 440
Sherry Gottlieb, pg 440
Paul Greenland Communications Inc, pg 440
GW Inc, pg 440
Helm Editorial Services, pg 440
L Anne Hirschel DDS, pg 440
Burnham Holmes, pg 440
Integra Software Services Inc, pg 441
Jenkins Group Inc, pg 441
JFE Editorial, pg 441
Just Creative Writing & Indexing Services (JCR), pg 441
Keim Publishing, pg 441
Barry R Koffler, pg 441
Eileen Kramer, pg 441
Lynn C Kronzek, Richard A Flom & Robert Flom, pg 441
The Learning Source Ltd, pg 441
Little Chicago Editorial Services, pg 442
Lumina Datamatics Inc, pg 442
Phyllis Manner, pg 442
Peter Mayeux, pg 442
Pamela Dittmer McKuen, pg 442
Pat McNees, pg 442
Stephen M Miller Inc, pg 442
Mary Mueller, pg 443
Nina Neimark Editorial Services, pg 443
Diane Patrick, pg 443
Proofed to Perfection Editing Services, pg 443

C J Scheiner Books, pg 444
Schoolhouse Network, pg 444
Franklin L Schulaner, pg 444
SDP Publishing Solutions LLC, pg 444
Roger W Smith, pg 445
Brooke C Stoddard, pg 445
Fraser Sutherland, pg 445
Barbara Mlotek Whelehan, pg 445
Windhaven®, pg 445
Words into Print, pg 445
Write for Success Editing Services, pg 445
Zebra Communications, pg 446

STATISTICS

Cohesion®, pg 437
Cypress House, pg 437
diacriTech Inc, pg 438
Lynn C Kronzek, Richard A Flom & Robert Flom, pg 441

TECHNICAL WRITING

Angels Editorial Services, pg 435
ASJA Freelance Writer Search, pg 435
Carpe Indexum, pg 436
Clear Concepts, pg 437
Cohesion®, pg 437
Cypress House, pg 437
diacriTech Inc, pg 438
Editcetera, pg 438
Farrar Writing & Editing, pg 439
Betsy Feist Resources, pg 439
Jerry Felsen, pg 439
Joan K Griffitts Indexing, pg 440
JFE Editorial, pg 441
Lynn C Kronzek, Richard A Flom & Robert Flom, pg 441
Lumina Datamatics Inc, pg 442
Proofed to Perfection Editing Services, pg 443
Brooke C Stoddard, pg 445
Vivian Sudhalter, pg 445
Windhaven®, pg 445
Wyman Indexing, pg 446

TRANSCRIPTION EDITING

Associated Editors, pg 435
The Bookmill, pg 436
Hilary R Burke, pg 436
Clear Concepts, pg 437

Clerical Plus, pg 437
Clotilde's Secretarial & Management Services, pg 437
Cohesion®, pg 437
Cypress House, pg 437
diacriTech Inc, pg 438
Edit Etc, pg 438
EditAmerica, pg 438
Catherine C Elverston ELS, pg 439
Enough Said: Editing, Writing, Research, Project Management, pg 439
The Gary-Paul Agency (GPA), pg 439
Sherry Gottlieb, pg 440
Joan K Griffitts Indexing, pg 440
Helm Editorial Services, pg 440
Jenkins Group Inc, pg 441
Sue Newton, pg 443
Sherri Schultz/Words with Grace, pg 444

TYPEMARKING

J Adel Art & Design, pg 435
Rodelinde Albrecht, pg 435
Angels Editorial Services, pg 435
Aptara Inc, pg 435
Associated Editors, pg 435
Ruth Chernia, pg 437
Cohesion®, pg 437
diacriTech Inc, pg 438
Earth Edit, pg 438
EditAmerica, pg 438
Enough Said: Editing, Writing, Research, Project Management, pg 439
Sandi Frank, pg 439
GGP Publishing Inc, pg 440
GW Inc, pg 440
Integra Software Services Inc, pg 441
Jenkins Group Inc, pg 441
Keim Publishing, pg 441
Eileen Kramer, pg 441
Polly Kummel LLC, pg 441
Lachina Creative Inc, pg 441
Land on Demand, pg 441
Lumina Datamatics Inc, pg 442
Susan T Middleton, pg 442
Newgen North America Inc, pg 443
Pictures & Words Editorial Services, pg 443
Wendy Polhemus-Annibell, pg 443
SDP Publishing Solutions LLC, pg 444
Windhaven®, pg 445

Editorial Services

For information on other companies who provide services to the book industry, see **Consultants, Book Producers, Typing & Word Processing Services** and **Artists & Art Services**.

AAH Graphics Inc
Subsidiary of Loft Press Inc
9293 Fort Valley Rd, Fort Valley, VA 22652
Tel: 540-933-6210 *Fax:* 540-933-6523
E-mail: aah@aahgraphics.com
Web Site: www.aahgraphics.com
Key Personnel
Pres: Ann A Hunter
Founded: 1973
Complete editorial through production serving publishers & individuals. Design of text, jackets & covers, composition & production management through manufacturing.
Membership(s): National Press Club (NPC)

Aaron-Spear
PO Box 42, Brooksville, ME 04617
Tel: 207-326-8764
Key Personnel
Prop: Jody Spear
Developmental editing & copy-editing of scholarly mss in the humanities. Rewriting for style & sensibility as well as clarity, consistency & accuracy. Specialize in art history & environmental studies.

Accurate Writing & More
16 Barstow Lane, Hadley, MA 01035
Tel: 413-586-2388
Web Site: www.accuratewriting.com; frugalmarketing.com
Key Personnel
Owner & Dir: Shel Horowitz *E-mail:* shel@principledprofit.com
Dir: Dina Friedman
Founded: 1981
Advertising & promotion copywriting, ghostwriting, editing, publishing consulting, interviewing, ms analysis, research, rewriting, special assignment writing & publishing consulting for authors, publishers & green/social change businesses.

J Adel Art & Design
586 Ramapo Rd, Teaneck, NJ 07666
Tel: 201-836-2606
E-mail: jadelnj@aol.com
Key Personnel
Creative Dir: Judith Adel
Founded: 1985
Freelance copy, illustration & design services for publishers.
Membership(s): Middletown Art Group; New Jersey Water Color Society

AEIOU Inc
894 Piermont Ave, Piermont, NY 10968
Tel: 845-359-1911
Key Personnel
Pres: Cynthia Crippen *E-mail:* ccrippen@verizon.net
Founded: 1976

Rodelinde Albrecht
274 Bradley St, Lee, MA 01238
Tel: 413-243-4350
E-mail: rodelinde@gmail.com
Founded: 1979

Editorial services (all available online & in hard copy): copy-editing; line editing; rewriting; proofreading; consulting; translation (fiction & nonfiction, German to English).

Jeanette Almada
452 W Aldine, Unit 215, Chicago, IL 60657
Tel: 773-404-9350
E-mail: jmalmada@sbcglobal.net
Founded: 1981
Writer/reporter/editor covers wide range of topics. Areas of interest include politics of food & water & some urban lifestyle topics such as gardening & food security, including food security & safety issues. Very interested in Great Lakes history, issues & developments & in small farm & organic topics.

Ampersand Group
1136 Maritime Way, Suite 717, Kanata, ON K2K 0M1, Canada
Tel: 613-435-5066
Key Personnel
Pres: Ed Matheson *E-mail:* ematheson@bell.net
Founded: 2002
Book publishing consultants for publishers, business, government & individuals with publishing problems. Specialize in project management, general book design & production.

Barbara S Anderson
706 W Davis Ave, Ann Arbor, MI 48103-4855
Tel: 734-995-0125
E-mail: bsa@watercolorbarbara.com
Rewriting, proofreading, ms analysis & line editing. For related services, see listing in Artists & Art Services.

Angel Editing Services
PO Box 752, Mountain Ranch, CA 95246
Tel: 209-728-8364
E-mail: info@stephaniemarohn.com
Web Site: www.stephaniemarohn.com
Key Personnel
Owner & Ed: Stephanie Marohn
Founded: 1993
Full range of editorial services, from developmental editing through copy-editing. Specialize in nonfiction trade books, particularly psychospiritual topics, metaphysics, natural medicine & other alternative thought.

Angels Editorial Services
1630 Main St, No 41, Coventry, CT 06238
Tel: 860-742-5279
E-mail: angelsus@aol.com
Key Personnel
Pres: Prof Claire Connelly, PhD
Founded: 1969
Ms or disk: counseling & psychotherapy, science & computers, textbooks, GLBT, fiction & non-fiction, animals.
Membership(s): American Copy Editors Society (ACES); Society for Technical Communication (STC)

Aptara Inc
Subsidiary of iEnergizer
2901 Telestar Ct, Suite 522, Falls Church, VA 22042
Tel: 703-352-0001
E-mail: moreinfo@aptaracorp.com
Web Site: www.aptaracorp.com
Key Personnel
Pres: Samir Kakar
EVP, Fin & Cont: Prashant Kapoor
SVP, Busn & Contact Ctr Opers: Ashish Madan
Busn Devt: Michael Scott *E-mail:* michael.scott@aptaracorp.com
Founded: 1988
Liaison for complete or any combination of production services, ranging from simple 1-color to complex 4-color projects & copy-editing. Offer ebook conversions & end-to-end solutions publishing services in print & digital.
Branch Office(s)
150 California St, Suite 301, Newton, MA 02458
Tel: 617-423-7755
11009 Metric Blvd, Bldg J, Suite 150, Austin, TX 78758 *Tel:* 512-876-5997
299 Elizabeth St, Level 1, Sydney 2000, Australia *Tel:* (02) 8251 0070
Tower 1 & 2, 8/100, Acharya Thulasi Rd (Shandy Rd), Pallavaram, Chennai 600 043, India *Tel:* (044) 22640676
No 2310, Doon Express Business Park, Saharanpur Rd, Bldg 2000, Dehradun 248 002, India *Tel:* (0135) 2644055
7B, Leela Infopark, Technopark, Trivandrum, Kerala 695 581, India *Tel:* (047) 14063370
A-37, Sector-60, Noida 201 301, India *Tel:* (0120) 7182424
D-10, Sector-2, Noida 201 301, India *Tel:* (0120) 24423678
SEZ Bldg 4A, 1st fl, S P Infocity, Pune Saswad Rd, Phursungi, Pune 412 308, India *Tel:* (020) 66728000

ASJA Freelance Writer Search
Affiliate of American Society of Journalists & Authors Inc
355 Lexington Ave, 15th fl, New York, NY 10017-6603
Tel: 212-997-0947
E-mail: asjaoffice@asja.org
Web Site: www.asja.org/finder
Key Personnel
Exec Dir: Kari Stringfellow
Assoc Dir: Jennifer Stone
Founded: 1948
Vital resource for anyone seeking the services of professional writers for articles, books, book proposals, brochures, annual reports, speeches, TV & film scripts, advertising copy, publicity campaigns, corporate communications & more. Free, private listing service goes only to the professional members of ASJA.

Associated Editors
27 W 96 St, New York, NY 10025
Tel: 917-744-3481; 212-662-9703
Key Personnel
Contact: Lynne Glasner *E-mail:* lyngla1@gmail.com
Copy-editing, rewriting, proofreading, research, developmental editing. Specialize in elementary & secondary textbooks; nonfiction trade books.
Membership(s): Editorial Freelancers Association (EFA)

Astor Indexers
22 S Commons, Kent, CT 06757

EDITORIAL SERVICES

Tel: 860-592-0225; 570-534-8951 (cell)
Key Personnel
Owner: Jane Farnol *E-mail:* bjfarnol@snet.net
Founded: 1970
Indexing is our only business. Staff handles all subjects; hard copy, e-mail or disk. Quality, speed & accuracy are our trademarks.

Audrey Owen
494 Eaglecrest Dr, Gibsons, BC V0N 1V8, Canada
E-mail: editor@writershelper.com
Web Site: www.writershelper.com
Founded: 2002
Besides the editing services offered by other agencies (including substantive editing), I also specialize in educative editing that becomes a mini tutorial designed for, but is not restricted to, self-publishing writers.
Membership(s): Editors' Association of Canada/Association canadienne des reviseurs (EAC); Federation of British Columbia Writers

Kathleen Barnes
238 W Fourth St, Suite 3-C, New York, NY 10014
Tel: 212-924-8084
E-mail: kbarnes@compasscommunications.org
Writing, rewriting, line editing, copy-editing & proofreading.

Diana Barth
535 W 51 St, Suite 3-A, New York, NY 10019
Tel: 212-307-5465
E-mail: diabarth99@gmail.com
Founded: 1970
All subjects; specialize in performing arts, health, psychology, education & travel. Feature, ghostwriter, reviews.

Anita Bartholomew
16650 SE Sunridge Lane, Portland, OR 97267
Tel: 774-264-8205
E-mail: anita@anitabartholomew.com
Web Site: www.anitabartholomew.com
Founded: 1993
Developmental editor. Specialize in fiction & narrative nonfiction. Have ghosted fiction & nonfiction. Co-authored a leading OB-GYN's award-winning memoir. Clients include authors (typically referred by their literary agents), publishers & nonprofits. Endorsements/testimonials available on web site & LinkedIn profile.

Mark E Battersby
PO Box 527, Ardmore, PA 19003-0527
Tel: 610-924-9157 *Fax:* 610-924-9159
E-mail: mebatt12@earthlink.net
Web Site: www.thetaxscribe.com
Founded: 1971
Freelance writer. Specialize in tax & financial features, columns, web content & white papers.

BiblioGenesis
152 Coddington Rd, Ithaca, NY 14850
Tel: 607-277-9660
Web Site: www.bibliogenesis.com
Key Personnel
Owner: Marian Hartman Rogers
 E-mail: mrogers@lightlink.com
Founded: 1987
Full editorial services encompassing all aspects of ms development: analysis, writing, rewriting, content editing, copy-editing, line editing, proofreading, fact checking, research & special assignment writing. Specialize in scholarly works (classical & medieval studies, European history & literature, anthropology & gender studies, Middle Eastern studies, geography & travel); languages (French, German, Greek, Latin).

Bloom Ink
6437 Maple Hills Dr, Bloomfield Hills, MI 48301
E-mail: info@bloomwriting.com
Web Site: www.bloomwriting.com
Key Personnel
Founder & Principal: Barbara Bloom
Founded: 2008
Provides a range of editing & publishing services including copy-editing, developmental editing, audio abridgements (fiction, nonfiction), book proposals, query letters & ghostwriting as well as assistance with self-publishing, book layout & design.
Membership(s): Editorial Freelancers Association (EFA)

Heidi Blough, Book Indexer
732 Violet Ave, Copley, OH 44321
Tel: 904-806-3923
E-mail: indexing@heidiblough.com
Web Site: www.heidiblough.com
Key Personnel
Owner: Heidi Blough
Founded: 2001
Indexing diverse topics that include: aerospace; biography; business, cooking, food & nutrition; engineering; general trade subjects; health & hospital administration; history, government & politics; how-to; maritime & transportation subjects.
Membership(s): American Society for Indexing (ASI)

Blue & Ude Writers' Services
Affiliate of Sunbreak Press (publishing & book sales)
4249 Nuthatch Way, Clinton, WA 98236
Mailing Address: PO Box 145, Clinton, WA 98236-0145
Tel: 360-341-1630
E-mail: blue@whidbey.com
Web Site: www.sunbreakpress.com
Key Personnel
Partner: Marian Blue; Wayne Ude
Founded: 1991
Provides all aspects of creative & technical writing & editing, including critiques, revisions & promotional copy.

BookBaby
Division of DIY Media Inc
7905 N Crescent Blvd, Pennsauken, NJ 08110
Tel: 856-554-2316 *Toll Free Tel:* 877-961-6878
E-mail: info@bookbaby.com
Web Site: www.bookbaby.com/book-editing-services
Founded: 2011
Full service book printing & publishing partner. Editing, design, marketing & sales for self-publishers; book printing; global book distribution.

BookCrafters LLC Editing
24 Old Glen Rd, Morristown, NJ 07960
Tel: 973-984-3868
Web Site: bookcraftersllc.com
Key Personnel
Founder, Pres & Ed: Elizabeth Zack
 E-mail: ezack@bookcraftersllc.com
Founded: 2003
Specialize in ms editing & development. Former NYC publishing industry editor with over 25 years of experience provides editorial assessments, developmental editing & line editing.

The Bookmill
501 Palisades Dr, No 315, Pacific Palisades, CA 90272-2848
Tel: 310-459-0190
E-mail: thebookmill1@verizon.net
Web Site: www.thebookmill.us
Key Personnel
Dir & Ed: Barbara Marinacci
Founded: 1982
Ms critiques; developmental editing for books, articles; preparing queries & proposals; word processing; contacts with agents, editors & publishers; blurb writing, book doctoring, proposals, restructuring & revising, transcribing.

Brady Literary Management
PO Box 64, Hartland Four Corners, VT 05049
Tel: 802-436-2455
Key Personnel
Owner: Sally R Brady *E-mail:* bradylit@vermontel.net
Founded: 1988
Ms analysis, conceptual, developmental & line editing, book doctoring, rewriting; trade fiction & nonfiction. Work on a fee basis.

Hilary R Burke
59 Sparks St, Ottawa, ON K1P 6C3, Canada
Mailing Address: Box 133, Sta B, Ottawa, ON K1P 6C3, Canada
Tel: 613-237-4658
E-mail: hburke99@yahoo.com
Promotional writing of fiction & nonfiction.

BZ/Rights & Permissions Inc
145 W 86 St, New York, NY 10024
Tel: 212-924-3000 *Fax:* 212-924-2525
E-mail: info@bzrights.com
Web Site: www.bzrights.com
Key Personnel
Pres: Barbara Zimmerman *E-mail:* bz@bzrights.com
Founded: 1980
Clears rights for literary materials, music, film & TV clips, photos, art, celebrities for educational projects - printed textbooks, spoken word recordings, new electronic media, DVDs/videocassettes. Work with film & TV producers & ad agencies. Publisher of *The Mini-Encyclopedia of Public Domain Songs* & *They Never Renewed: Songs You Never Dreamed Were in the Public Domain.*
Membership(s): Association of Independent Music Publishers (AIMP); The Copyright Society of the USA (CSUSA); Independent Book Publishers Association (IBPA)

Carpe Indexum
1960 Deer Run Rd, LaFayette, NY 13084
Tel: 315-677-3030
E-mail: info@carpeindexum.com
Web Site: www.carpeindexum.com
Key Personnel
Owner: Michele Combs *E-mail:* mrothen2@twcny.rr.com
Founded: 2004
Services include back-of-book & XML indexing services; research & fact checking; editing at various levels; copywriting & work-for-hire; XML/XSLT consulting.
Membership(s): American Society for Indexing (ASI); Editorial Freelancers Association (EFA); Society of American Archivists (SAA)

R E Carsch, MS-Consultant
1453 Rhode Island St, San Francisco, CA 94107-3248
Tel: 415-533-8356 (cell)
E-mail: recarsch@mzinfo.com
Founded: 1973

Full-range, custom information editorial services including, fact checking, interviewing, ms analysis, proofreading, research & industry overviews.

Carol Cartaino
2000 Flat Run Rd, Seaman, OH 45679
Tel: 937-764-1303 *Fax:* 937-764-1303
E-mail: cartaino@aol.com
Founded: 1986
Content, developmental & line editing; ms analysis; rewriting & collaboration. Nonfiction & fiction. Also expert assistance of all kinds for self-publishers & solutions for problem mss.

Claudia Caruana
1333 Union Ave, New York, NY 11003
E-mail: ccaruana29@hotmail.com
Copy-editing, ms analysis, rights & permissions, picture search, proofreading, research, rewriting, special assignment writing, magazine photography.

Jeanne Cavelos Editorial Services
PO Box 75, Mont Vernon, NH 03057
Tel: 603-673-6234
Web Site: jeannecavelos.com
Key Personnel
Owner: Jeanne Cavelos *E-mail:* jcavelos@comcast.net
Founded: 1994
Published, best-selling writer & former senior editor at major publishing house. Full editorial services for publishers, book packagers, businesses, agents & authors. From line edit to thorough edit, to heavy edit. Detailed reader's reports. Book proposal doctoring. Editorial consulting, creative development. Newsletters, magazine articles, novelizations. Handle the full range of fiction & nonfiction. Specialize in thrillers, literary fiction, fantasy, science fiction, horror, popular culture, self-help, health & science.
Membership(s): Horror Writers Association (HWA); Science Fiction and Fantasy Writers of America, Inc (SFWA)

CeciBooks Editorial & Publishing Consultation
7057 26 Ave NW, Seattle, WA 98117
Mailing Address: PO Box 17229, Seattle, WA 98127
E-mail: info@cecibooks.com
Web Site: www.cecibooks.com
Key Personnel
Owner: Ceci Miller *E-mail:* ceci@cecibooks.com
Founded: 1988
Provides complete content/book development from concept to publication. Innovative in assembling teams of experts to develop, write, edit, design & produce print & digital publications. Specialize in nonfiction for adults & children (both trade & curriculum). Develops adult nonfiction in the areas of health & wellness, spirituality & organizational leadership, including educational content (textbooks, teacher resources, reference) with a focus on social sciences. Produces publisher-initiated titles as well as original books. Will work with other packagers to co-produce books.
Membership(s): The Authors Guild; Independent Book Publishers Association (IBPA); Northwest Editors Guild; Society of Children's Book Writers & Illustrators (SCBWI)

Margaret Cheasebro PhD
5709 Holmes Dr, Farmington, NM 87402
Tel: 505-325-1557
E-mail: mwriter4571@yahoo.com
Web Site: www.margaretcheasebro.com; www.ifiwereatreewhatwouldibe.com
Founded: 1986
Author. Writes both nonfiction & fiction books. Some are about trees & their benefits. Others are about alternative healing methods such as Reiki. Currently working on a romance suspense novel with archaeology theme & locations in both New Mexico & Sudan, East Africa.
Membership(s): The Authors Guild; National Federation of Press Women; New Mexico Press Women

Ruth Chernia
198 Victor Ave, Toronto, ON M4K 1B2, Canada
Tel: 416-466-0164
E-mail: rchernia@editors.ca; rchernia@sympatico.ca
Web Site: www.editors.ca/profile/444/ruth-chernia
Founded: 1983
Provides professional editorial & publishing consultation to companies & individuals.
Membership(s): Editors' Association of Canada/Association canadienne des reviseurs (EAC)

Clear Concepts
1329 Federal Ave, Suite 6, Los Angeles, CA 90025
Tel: 323-285-0325
Key Personnel
Owner: Karen Kleiner
Founded: 1986
Provides writing, substantive editing & research. Specializes in holistic health, fiction, children's books, technology & business. Owner holds BA from UCLA in Communications.
Membership(s): Society for Technical Communication (STC)

Clerical Plus
97 Blueberry Lane, Shelton, CT 06484
Tel: 203-225-0879 *Fax:* 203-225-0879
E-mail: clericalplus@aol.com
Key Personnel
Pres: Rose Brown
Founded: 1990
Transcription/office support service company.

Clotilde's Secretarial & Management Services
PO Box 871926, New Orleans, LA 70187
Tel: 504-242-2912
E-mail: elcsy58@att.net
Key Personnel
Pres & Admin Mgr: Elvira C Sylve
Asst: Lillian Gail Tillman
Founded: 1989
Proofread & edit journals, newsletters, mss, research papers & medical documents. Specialize in preparing & typing research papers, grant proposals, medical & legal documents. Legal course work—Louisiana laws: briefs, business law, computer research & software, family law, interviewing, legal writing, litigation & researching in Westlaw.
Membership(s): National Association of Legal Assistants

Dwight Clough
PO Box 670, Wyocena, WI 53969
E-mail: lmp@dwightclough.com
Web Site: dwightclough.com
Founded: 1983
Serving authors & publishers, helping them to write & self-publish their books on Amazon.

Coastside Editorial
PO Box 181, Moss Beach, CA 94038
E-mail: bevjoe@pacific.net
Key Personnel
Contact: Beverly McGuire
Membership(s): Editcetera

Robert L Cohen
182-12 Horace Harding Expwy, Suite 2M, Fresh Meadows, NY 11365
Tel: 718-762-1195 *Toll Free Tel:* 866-EDITING (334-8464) *Fax:* 917-781-0703
E-mail: wordsmith@sterlingmp.com
Web Site: www.rlcwordsandmusic.com; www.linkedin.com/in/robertcohen17
Editing & rewriting of books/policy briefs/working papers for think tanks & nonprofits; copy, substantive (line) & developmental editing of scholarly, general interest & reference books; lexicography; radio & AV scriptwriting; speechwriting & other contract writing. Specialize in international relations (particularly Middle East & related regions), urban affairs & public policy, politics & government, history & military history, social sciences, psychology & education, media & communications, Judaica & religion, music, sports, biographies, memoirs. Writing teacher for businesses/nonprofits/individuals.
Membership(s): American Copy Editors Society (ACES); American Society for Jewish Music; Cambridge Academic Editors Network; Editorial Freelancers Association (EFA)

Cohesion®
511 W Bay St, Suite 480, Tampa, FL 33606
Tel: 813-999-3111 *Toll Free Tel:* 866-727-6800
Web Site: www.cohesion.com
Key Personnel
CEO: John Owens
Chief Strategy Offr: John Larson
Founded: 1982
Complete book & journal content development & production services: writing, copy-editing, developmental editing, indexing, proofreading; project management; abstracting, advertising & promotion copywriting, bibliographies, fact checking, interviewing, developmental editing, ms analysis, rewriting, special assignment writing, transcription editing; design, art rendering, photo research, covers & jackets; permissions; in-house composition as well as development of electronic publishing products, including HTML & XML coding & supervising printing. Online editing experts (visit EditExpress.com). Specialize in technical subject areas: college, medical & allied health, computer science, law, physical & life sciences & engineering.
Branch Office(s)
6760 Alexander Bell Dr, Suite 120, Columbia, MD 21046 *Toll Free Tel:* 800-560-0630
5151 Pfeiffer Rd, Suite 105, Cincinnati, OH 45242 *Tel:* 513-587-7700

Cultural Studies & Analysis
1123 Montrose St, Philadelphia, PA 19147-3721
Tel: 215-592-8544
E-mail: info@culturalanalysis.com
Web Site: www.culturalanalysis.com
Key Personnel
Dir: Margaret J King, PhD *E-mail:* mjking9@comcast.net
Sr Analyst: Jamie O'Boyle
Founded: 1994
Specialize in cultural analysis; identify consumer values & decision making. We do not provide novel writing.

Cypress House
155 Cypress St, Suite A, Fort Bragg, CA 95437
Tel: 707-964-9520 *Toll Free Tel:* 800-773-7782 *Fax:* 707-964-7531
E-mail: office@cypresshouse.com
Web Site: www.cypresshouse.com
Key Personnel
Pres: Cynthia Frank *E-mail:* cynthia@cypresshouse.com
Mng Ed: Joe Shaw *E-mail:* joeshaw@cypresshouse.com
Founded: 1986

EDITORIAL SERVICES

Complete editorial, design, production, marketing & promotion services to independent publishers. Editorial services include ms evaluation, editing, rewriting, copymarking & proofing. Production services include book, cover & page design & make-up to camera-ready. Marketing & promotion services for selected titles.
Membership(s): American Booksellers Association (ABA); Bay Area Independent Publishers Association (BAIPA); California Independent Booksellers Alliance (CALIBA); Independent Book Publishers Association (IBPA); Pacific Northwest Booksellers Association (PNBA)

John M Daniel Literary Services
PO Box 2790, McKinleyville, CA 95519
Tel: 707-839-3495
E-mail: jmd@danielpublishing.com
Web Site: www.danielpublishing.com/litserv.htm
Key Personnel
Ed: John M Daniel
Specialize in fiction & memoir.

Mari Lynch Dehmler, see Fine Wordworking

Christina Di Martino Literary Services
87 Hamilton Place, No 7G, New York, NY 10031
Tel: 212-996-9086; 561-283-1549
E-mail: writealotmail@gmail.com
Key Personnel
Owner: Christina Di Martino
Full book line services, collaboration of book projects, freelance writing for national magazines & teaching of writing.

diacriTech Inc
4 S Market St, 4th fl, Boston, MA 02109
Tel: 617-600-3366 *Fax:* 617-848-2938
Web Site: www.diacritech.com
Key Personnel
EVP: Madhu Rajamani *E-mail:* madhu@diacritech.com
Dir, Prodn & Edit Servs: Maureen Ross *E-mail:* m.ross@diacritech.com
Founded: 1997
Specialize in meeting educational publishing needs. Full service development includes project management, editorial & content development services, print & digital production, art & prepress services. In-house staff of over 800 are experienced with all phases & disciplines of K-12, college & STM. Facilities in Boston, MA, Manchester, NH & in Chennai, Madurai & Kottayam, India.

DK Research Inc
9 Wicks Dr, Commack, NY 11725-3921
Tel: 631-543-5537 *Fax:* 631-543-5549
E-mail: dkresearch@optimum.net
Web Site: www.dkresearchinc.com
Key Personnel
Owner & Pres: Diane Kraut
Founded: 1993
All phases of text & photo permission clearance. Fact checking.
Membership(s): Editorial Freelancers Association (EFA)

Double Play
303 Hillcrest Rd, Belton, MO 64012-1852
Tel: 816-651-7118
Key Personnel
Pres: Lloyd Johnson *E-mail:* wlloydj@yahoo.com
VP: Connie Johnson
Writing & research about baseball; sports, baseball museum consultant, exhibits; working on database of professional baseball.
Membership(s): Society for American Baseball Research

Earth Edit
PO Box 114, Maiden Rock, WI 54750
Tel: 715-448-3009
Key Personnel
Contact: George Dyke *E-mail:* gmdyke@gmail.com
Copy-editing & proofreading of college-level texts in geography, environmental science, oceanography, astronomy & cosmology, computer science.

East Mountain Editing Services
PO Box 1895, Tijeras, NM 87059-1895
Tel: 505-281-8422
Web Site: www.spanishindexing.com
Key Personnel
Mgr: Francine Cronshaw *E-mail:* cronshaw@nmia.com
Founded: 1992
Indexing (back-of-the-book) in Spanish or English. Also French, Italian & Portuguese. Special attention to Canadian editions. Consulting on bilingual or Spanish language editions. For experience, see web site.
Membership(s): American Society for Indexing (ASI)

Edit Etc
26 Country Lane, Brunswick, ME 04011
Tel: 914-715-5849
E-mail: atkedit@cs.com
Web Site: www.anntkeene.com
Key Personnel
Pres: Ann T Keene
Founded: 1985
Editing, writing, copywriting, research, photo research.
Membership(s): The Authors Guild

Edit Resource LLC
Division of Stanford Creative Services LLC
19265 Lincoln Green Lane, Monument, CO 80132
Tel: 719-290-0757
E-mail: info@editresource.com
Web Site: www.editresource.com
Key Personnel
Owner: Elisa Stanford *E-mail:* elisa@editresource.com; Eric Stanford *E-mail:* eric@editresource.com
Founded: 1998
A writing & editing services provider.

EditAmerica
115 Jacobs Creek Rd, Ewing, NJ 08628-1014
Tel: 609-882-5852
Web Site: www.EditAmerica.com; www.linkedin.com/in/PaulaPlantier
Key Personnel
Founder/Owner/Editor/Proofer/Fact Checker: Paula Plantier *E-mail:* paulaplantier@gmail.com
Founded: 1990
Expert copy-editing, line editing, ms editing, rewriting/revising/repurposing, fact checking & proofreading of written communications in the areas of accounting, advertising, business, college application essays, company annual reports, cover letters, curricula vitae, dissertations, education, executive biographies, fiction, finance, Forms 10-K & 10-Q, marketing, medicine, newsletters, news releases, nonfiction, peer-reviewed & refereed medical & scientific journal articles, medical & pharmaceutical advertising & marketing, pharmaceutics, pharmacology, press releases, religious treatises, resumes, theses, user's manuals & web site content. Strict adherence to client-set deadlines. Satisfaction guaranteed for editorial services performed.
Membership(s): American Copy Editors Society (ACES); Editorial Freelancers Association (EFA); Society for Advancing Business Editing and Writing (SABEW)

Editcetera
2034 Blake St, Suite 5, Berkeley, CA 94704
Tel: 510-849-1110
E-mail: info@editcetera.com
Web Site: www.editcetera.com
Key Personnel
CEO: Barbara Fuller *E-mail:* barbara@editcetera.com
Memb Servs Coord: Jen Arter *Tel:* 510-849-1229
Founded: 1971
Association of freelance publishing professionals. Clients include trade publishers, el-hi & college textbook publishers, self-publishers, authors, scholars, packagers, computer companies (software & hardware), universities & corporations. Services available include production management from mss through bound books as well as writing, rewriting, developmental editing, copy-editing, coaching of writers, proofreading, indexing & web editing. Rigorous testing & review of all members. Educational programs available to the public include live workshops, webinars, flex training & customized training.

EditCraft Editorial Services
422 Pine St, Grass Valley, CA 95945
Tel: 530-273-3934
Web Site: www.editcraft.com
Key Personnel
Prop: Eric W Engles, PhD *E-mail:* eric@editcraft.com
Founded: 1986
Editorial services for publishers, independent authors, scholars & technology companies.
Membership(s): Bay Area Editors' Forum

The Editorial Department LLC
8476 E Speedway Blvd, Suite 202, Tucson, AZ 85710
Tel: 520-546-9992
E-mail: admin@editorialdepartment.com
Web Site: www.editorialdepartment.com
Key Personnel
Founder: Renni Browne
Pres & Dir, Edit Servs: Ross Browne *E-mail:* rsb@editorialdepartment.com
Founded: 1980
Ms critique & evaluation, line & copy-editing, novelizations & adaptations, ghostwriting, book proposals, publishing consultation, screenplay critique & consultation.

The Editors Circle
24 Holly Circle, Easthampton, MA 01027
Tel: 862-596-9709
E-mail: query@theeditorscircle.com
Web Site: www.theeditorscircle.com
Key Personnel
Ed: Bonny Fetterman *Tel:* 718-739-1057 *E-mail:* bvfetterman@aol.com; Beth Lieberman *Tel:* 310-403-1602 *E-mail:* liebermanedit@socal.rr.com; John Paine *E-mail:* jpaine@johnpaine.com; Susan Schwartz *Tel:* 212-877-3211 *E-mail:* susan.sas22@gmail.com
Founded: 2005
A group of independent editors & publishing consultants with many years of in-house & freelance experience providing a wide range of editorial services for both fiction & nonfiction books, including: evaluating & critiquing book proposals & partial or complete mss; developing & editing book proposals, query letters & mss; ghostwriting, rewriting, or collaborating on book proposals & mss; consulting on self-publishing & digital publishing opportunities; providing referrals to suitable agents & publishers.

Catherine C Elverston ELS
3242 NW Fifth St, Gainesville, FL 32609
Tel: 352-222-0625 (cell)
E-mail: celverston@gmail.com
Web Site: www.celverston.com/CatherineElverstonEditingService.html
All aspects of editing, preparing mss for publication, information research & retrieval.
Membership(s): American Medical Writers Association (AMWA); Board of Editors in the Life Sciences

R Elwell Indexing
193 Main St, Cold Spring, NY 10516
Tel: 845-667-1036
E-mail: r.elwell.indexing@gmail.com
Founded: 1975
Indexing.

Enough Said: Editing, Writing, Research, Project Management
3959 NW 29 Lane, Gainesville, FL 32606
Tel: 352-262-2971
E-mail: enoughsaid@cox.net
Key Personnel
Owner/Ed: Ms Heath Lynn Silberfeld
Founded: 1984
Full range of hard copy & electronic editorial services for nonfiction trade, mass market, textbook & self-publishing projects. Skilled in editing a wide range of nonfiction & fiction subject matter: cookbooks to textbooks.

Linda Fairchild & Company LLC
101 Lucas Valley Rd, Suite 363, San Rafael, CA 94903
Tel: 415-336-6407
Web Site: www.lindafairchild.com
Key Personnel
Mng Partner & Sr Ed: Linda Fairchild
  E-mail: linda@lindafairchild.com
Partner & Chief Creative Offr: Jeffrey Keith
  Tel: 303-257-0492 *E-mail:* jeffrey@jeffreykeith.com
Founded: 2002
Unique, proprietary system for copy-editing & extensive line editing, working directly with authors to prepare mss for publication, refining their technique while maintaining their unique voices. This includes mss analysis to help the writer develop the arc of the story, tempo, pacing, structure, & overall power & punch of a successful writing style for fiction, nonfiction, & special assignment writing, including proofreading & rewrites. The Chicago Manual of Style is followed. We preserve the voice of the author, so the character & tone of the writing is not contaminated by over-editing. We follow the rules & then break the rules judiciously & artistically.

Farrar Writing & Editing
4638 Manchester Rd, Mound, MN 55364
Tel: 952-451-5982
Web Site: www.writeandedit.net
Key Personnel
Freelance Writer & Ed: Amy E Farrar
  E-mail: amyfarrar@mchsi.com
Founded: 1999
Published book author & book editor. Clients include book publishers, individuals, nonprofits, magazines, newspapers & general businesses. Subjects include fiction & nonfiction, New Age, environmental, educational, travel & health/medical.
Membership(s): Professional Editors Network (PEN)

Betsy Feist Resources
140 E 81 St, Unit 7-E, New York, NY 10028-1875
Tel: 212-861-2014
E-mail: betsyfeist@gmail.com
Key Personnel
Pres: Betsy Feist
Complete editorial services, including development, writing, project management & editorial/production coordination. Specialize in instructional & informational materials.

Jerry Felsen
3960 NW 196 St, Miami Gardens, FL 33055-1869
Tel: 305-625-5012
E-mail: jf0@mail.com
Computer science, artificial intelligence, information systems & computer applications in business & investing; professional papers & business reports.

Fine Wordworking
PO Box 3041, Monterey, CA 93942-3041
Tel: 831-375-6278
E-mail: info@finewordworking.com
Web Site: marilynch.com
Key Personnel
Owner: Mari Lynch Dehmler
Founded: 1981
Writing, editing & proofreading of literary, business, personal & other material. Ghostwriting, collaborative writing & editing of adult, young adult & children's nonfiction books. Editing & proofreading of fiction. Well versed in Chicago style. Web content development & design collaboration. Interviewing, research & other support. Phone calls welcome.

Richard A Flom, see Lynn C Kronzek, Richard A Flom & Robert Flom

Robert Flom, see Lynn C Kronzek, Richard A Flom & Robert Flom

Focus Strategic Communications Inc
15 Hunter Way, Brantford, ON N3T 6S3, Canada
Tel: 519-756-3265
E-mail: info@focussc.com
Web Site: www.focussc.com
Key Personnel
Dir: Adrianna Edwards *E-mail:* aedwards@focussc.com; Ron Edwards *E-mail:* redwards@focussc.com
Founded: 1988
Provide complete book development & production from concept & content to finished book. Innovative in assembling teams of experts to develop, write, edit, design & produce superior products. Specialty is children's nonfiction (both trade & curriculum) but also do adult books on topics such as history, biography, science, how-to & business. Also education (textbooks, teacher resources, reference), focusing on social sciences, literacy & soft science. Produce publisher-initiated titles as well as original books. Will work with other packagers to co-produce books.

Foster Travel Publishing
1623 Martin Luther King Jr Way, Berkeley, CA 94709
Tel: 510-549-2202
Web Site: www.fostertravel.com
Key Personnel
Owner & Pres: Lee Foster *E-mail:* lee@fostertravel.com
Founded: 1972
Picture search, research, writing; travel (emphasizing locations, history, wine, nature). Specialize in Northern California, the West, Mexico-Baja, Europe, the Orient. Writing & photography available on web site. Provides travel writing/photography services for print & web editorial markets.
Membership(s): American Society of Media Photographers (ASMP); Bay Area Independent Publishers Association (BAIPA); Bay Area Travel Writers; Society of American Travel Writers (SATW)

Sandi Frank
8 Fieldcrest Ct, Cortlandt Manor, NY 10567
Tel: 914-739-7088
E-mail: sfrankmail@aol.com
Specialize in nonfiction in many disciplines, including textbooks, bibliographies, medical texts & journals, social sciences, scholarly material & cookbooks.
Membership(s): American Society for Indexing (ASI)

Fromer
1606 Noyes Dr, Silver Spring, MD 20910-2224
Tel: 301-585-8827
Key Personnel
Pres: Margot J Fromer *E-mail:* margotfromer@erols.com
Founded: 1980
Writing, rewriting & consultation in all aspects of health care & medicine; ms analysis, special assignment writing.
Membership(s): American Medical Writers Association (AMWA); Science Writers' Association

Diane Gallo
49 Hilton St, Gilbertsville, NY 13776
Mailing Address: PO Box 106, Gilbertsville, NY 13776
Tel: 607-783-2386 *Fax:* 607-783-2386
E-mail: dgallo@stny.rr.com
Web Site: www.dianegallo.com
Interviewing & video scripts.

Michael Garrett, see ManuscriptCritique.com

The Gary-Paul Agency (GPA)
1549 Main St, Stratford, CT 06615
Tel: 203-345-6167
Web Site: www.thegarypaulagency.com
Key Personnel
Owner: Gary Maynard *E-mail:* garret@thegarypaulagency.com
Founded: 1994
Literary agency that represents & promotes screenplays. Specialize in script editing & development. WGAe Signatory.
Branch Office(s)
127 Horseshoe Rd, Fayston, VT 05660 *Tel:* 203-556-8671
Membership(s): Writers Guild of America, East (WGAE)

Fred Gebhart
PO Box 111, Gold Hill, OR 97525
Tel: 415-596-5819
E-mail: fgebhart@pobox.com
Web Site: www.fredgebhart.com
Founded: 1981
Editorial, whitepaper & advertorial writing in medical, pharmaceutical, medical device & healthcare topics.
Membership(s): American Medical Writers Association (AMWA); American Society of Journalists & Authors (ASJA); International Society of Travel Medicine; National Association of Science Writers

Gelles-Cole Literary Enterprises
2163 Lima Loop, PMB 01-408, Laredo, TX 78045-9452
Tel: 845-810-0029
Web Site: www.literaryenterprises.com

EDITORIAL SERVICES

Key Personnel
Founder & Pres: Sandi Gelles-Cole
  E-mail: sandigc@gmail.com
Founded: 1983
Editorial consultant (book doctor). Specialize in commercial fiction & nonfiction serving authors, publishers & literary agents; writing coach; consultant for self-publishing authors, collaboration. Editorial specialty is development of concept & character development. Provide an intense word by word tutorial focusing on concept, style, voice, pace & characterization & for nonfiction, structure. Offers help to experts & other authors developing their material for the general public. Also have small publishing arm. Soft spot for first novels.

Nancy C Gerth PhD
1431 Harlan's Trail, Sagle, ID 83860
Tel: 208-304-9066
E-mail: docnangee@nancygerth.com
Web Site: www.nancygerth.com
Founded: 2005
Freelance indexing & related services. Index focus: Scholarly, specialize in American history, indigenous studies, postmodernism. PhD in philosophy (Cornell University). Providing information services since 1988.
Membership(s): American Society for Indexing (ASI); Pacific Northwest Chapter of American Society for Indexing

GGP Publishing Inc
Larchmont, NY 10538
Tel: 914-834-8896 *Fax:* 914-834-7566
Web Site: www.GGPPublishing.com
Key Personnel
Founder, Owner & Dir: Generosa Gina Protano
  E-mail: GGProtano@GGPPublishing.com
Founded: 1991
Full service development house & packaging firm offering services from concept to finished electronic files/bound books to online distribution or for any one step of this publishing process. Specialize in educational publishing from K-12 to college/university to adult education. Have a niche in the writing, development, editing & production to finished electronic files/bound books of textbooks & trade books for the study of foreign languages such as French, German, Italian, Latin, Portuguese & Spanish. Also translates complete/partial programs or cluster of books from English into any of these languages or from any of these languages into English, edit the translation for publication & set the edited translation into book form up to finished electronic files/bound books. Develop, edit, do art/design & production of different genres both for publishing houses as well as individuals who wish to self-publish. Has produced novels, memoirs & books in the fields of religion, psychology & culinary arts among others. Special interest in memoirs. Acts as literary agents & foreign publisher representatives.
Membership(s): American Book Producers Association (ABPA)

Cathe Giffuni, see Research Research

Sheri Gilbert
123 Van Voorhis Ave, Rochester, NY 14617
Tel: 585-342-0331
E-mail: shergilb@aol.com
Web Site: www.permissionseditor.com
Reviews mss for permissions identification; preparing permissions reports; obtaining permissions for text, art, photographs & song lyrics. Creating credit lines & source notes.

Robert M Goodman
140 West End Ave, Unit 11-J, New York, NY 10023
Tel: 917-439-1097
E-mail: bobbybgood@gmail.com
Membership(s): Editorial Freelancers Association (EFA)

P M Gordon Associates Inc
Affiliate of New Door Books
2115 Wallace St, Philadelphia, PA 19130
Tel: 215-769-2525
Web Site: www.pmgordonassociates.com
Key Personnel
Pres: Peggy M Gordon
VP: Douglas C Gordon *E-mail:* doug@newdoorbooks.com
Founded: 1982
Complete design & production services.

Sherry Gottlieb
Unit of wordservices.com
300 W Ninth St, No 126, Oxnard, CA 93030-7098
Tel: 805-382-3425
E-mail: writer@wordservices.com
Web Site: www.wordservices.com
Founded: 1991
Private editorial service specializing in fiction & screenplays. Edited over 450 book mss, mostly fiction. Several clients have sold their books to major publishers.

Graphic World Inc, see GW Inc

Paul Greenland Communications Inc
5062 Rockrose Ct, Suite 209, Roscoe, IL 61073
Tel: 815-240-4108
Web Site: www.paulgreenland.com
Key Personnel
Owner: Paul R Greenland
Services include writing, ghostwriting & collaboration, research, editing & proofreading. Published nonfiction author, marketing/communications professional & former senior editor of national business magazine. Contributor to many leading reference books (Cengage Learning, University of Chicago Press, Facts on File). Interview subjects include celebrities, athletes & leading business executives. Specialize in reference, business, biography & history. References available upon request.
Membership(s): Independent Book Publishers Association (IBPA)

Joan K Griffitts Indexing
3909 W 71 St, Indianapolis, IN 46268-2257
Tel: 317-297-7312
E-mail: jkgriffitts@gmail.com
Web Site: www.joankgriffittsindexing.com
Founded: 1989
Indexing & proofreading of textbooks, trade books, reference books, technical documentation, catalogs & newspapers by former librarian. Most subjects; specialize in business, science, sports, gardening, computer science, library science, education, taxation & social science. Various computer formats & e-mail delivery. Technical editing of various types of books & magazines including crochet, knit, weaving, etc.
Membership(s): American Society for Indexing (ASI)

GW Inc
2290 Ball Dr, St Louis, MO 63146
Tel: 314-567-9854
E-mail: media@gwinc.com
Web Site: www.gwinc.com

Key Personnel
CEO: Kevin Arrow
EVP: Andy Vosburgh
VP, Content Opers: Suzanne Kastner
Complete editorial & project management services from ms through final files, including interior & cover design, composition services, electronic publishing services & art rendering.
Branch Office(s)
GW Tech Pvt Ltd, D-152, Mohali Bypass Rd, Phase 8, Sector 73, Chandigarh 140 308, India
Tel: (0172) 415 1335

Anne Hebenstreit
20 Tip Top Way, Berkeley Heights, NJ 07922
Tel: 908-665-0536
Copy-editing & proofreading of el-hi & college texts & trade books.

Helm Editorial Services
300 Canopy Walk Lane, Unit 325, Palm Coast, FL 32137
Tel: 954-525-5626
E-mail: lynnehelm12@aol.com
Freelance writing, line editing & publishing for executives & authors.

Herr's Indexing Service
76-340 Kealoha St, Kailua Kona, HI 96740-2915
Tel: 808-365-4348
Web Site: www.herrsindexing.com
Key Personnel
Owner: Linda Herr Hallinger
  E-mail: lindahallinger@gmail.com
Founded: 1944
Providing quality & affordable indexes for a variety of topics. Specialize in medical books.
Membership(s): American Society for Indexing (ASI); Editorial Freelancers Association (EFA)

L Anne Hirschel DDS
5990 Highgate Ave, East Lansing, MI 48823
Tel: 517-333-1748
E-mail: alicerichard@comcast.net
Medicine & dentistry, consumer/patient information, continuing education & editing for foreign speaking scientists.
Membership(s): American Dental Association; Medical Writers Association

Burnham Holmes
182 Lakeview Hill Rd, Poultney, VT 05764-9179
Tel: 802-287-9707 *Fax:* 802-287-9707 (computer fax/modem)
E-mail: burnham.holmes@castleton.edu
Founded: 1990
Write textbooks, fiction & general nonfiction, juvenile, young adult, plays & children's books.
Membership(s): The Authors Guild; League of Vermont Writers Inc

Indexing by the Book
5912 E Eastland St, Tucson, AZ 85711-4636
Tel: 520-405-8083
E-mail: indextran@cox.net
Web Site: www.indexingbythebook.com
Key Personnel
Indexer: Cynthia J Coan
Founded: 2003
Index books & serials. Specialize in health/medicine, history (especially Arizona/Southwest), education, language studies, library science, social sciences & psychology. Index adult, children's & Spanish language titles. Also translate print materials from Spanish & Swedish into English. Specialties in the translation field include medicine & law/patents.
Membership(s): American Literary Translators Association (ALTA); American Society for Indexing (ASI); American Translators Association (ATA)

Integra Software Services Inc
Division of Integra Software Services Pvt Ltd
2021 Midwest Rd, Suite 200, Oak Brook, IL 60523
Web Site: www.integranxt.com
Founded: 1991
Project management, development & production support for book publishers. Full range of publishing services, including developmental editing, design, rights & permissions, photo research, copy-editing & indexing, proofreading, language polishing, typesetting, XML & conversion, illustrations & artwork, ebooks & digital services. Specialty areas are business & economics, computer science, mathematics, science, history, English, medical & education texts.

Iridescent Orange Press, see Wambtac Communications LLC

Jenkins Group Inc
1129 Woodmere Ave, Suite B, Traverse City, MI 49686
Tel: 231-933-0445; 213-883-5365
E-mail: info@jenkinsgroupinc.com
Web Site: www.jenkinsgroupinc.com
Key Personnel
CEO: Jerrold R Jenkins Tel: 231-933-0445 ext 1008 E-mail: jrj@jenkinsgroupinc.com
Pres & COO: James Kalajian Tel: 231-933-0445 ext 1006 E-mail: jjk@jenkinsgroupinc.com
Ed, Independent Publisher Online: Jim Barnes E-mail: editor@independentpublisher.com
Book Prodn Mgr: Leah Nicholson Tel: 231-933-0445 ext 1015 E-mail: lnicholson@jenkinsgroupinc.com
Founded: 1990
Full service custom book publishing services for corporations, independent authors, organizations & small press publishers. Services include registrations, typesetting, cover design, color separations, ghostwriting, illustration & photo placement, galley preparation & print management.

JFE Editorial
190 Ocean Dr, Gun Barrel City, TX 75156
Tel: 817-560-7018
E-mail: jford@jfe-editorial.com
Key Personnel
Founder & Pres: June Ford E-mail: juneford1@gmail.com
Founded: 1987
Founded by Ms Ford, a nationally published author, ghostwriter, project manager, editor & proofreader. Developmental editor of children's & juvenile mss. Focus includes: writing, ghostwriting, rewriting, special assignment writing; developmental, copy, line, style & content editing; proofreading; ms analysis; permissions, interviewing; fact checking; database management, research & input, coding, editing. Published in genres ranging from children's, trade & true crime to scholastic, self-help & sports books; also a variety of magazine articles. Coordinator of many high-dollar projects & extremely successful at transforming complex material into easily understood information. Ms Ford is a speaker for grades 3-12, universities & conferences.

JL Communications
10205 Green Holly Terr, Silver Spring, MD 20902
Tel: 301-593-0640
Key Personnel
Writer, Ed & Poet: Joyce Eileen Latham
Founded: 1996

Just Creative Writing & Indexing Services (JCR)
301 Wood Duck Dr, Greensboro, MD 21639
Tel: 443-262-2136
E-mail: judy@justcreativewriting.com
Web Site: www.justcreativewriting.com
Key Personnel
Sole Prop: Judith Reveal E-mail: 19editor45@gmail.com
Founded: 2005
Provides editorial services for fiction & nonfiction; professional back-of-the-book indexing; autoethnographic dissertation editing; book reviews.
Membership(s): Eastern Shore Writers' Association (ESWA); Editorial Freelancers Association (EFA); Maryland Writers' Association

Ann T Keene, see Edit Etc

Keim Publishing
66 Main St, Suite 807, Yonkers, NY 10701
Tel: 917-655-7190
Key Personnel
Owner & Pres: Betty Keim E-mail: mieklb@gmail.com
Founded: 1985
Editorial, permissions, production, photo editing, research; fact checking; writing, rewriting. Editorial, production & development of promotional materials, corporate reports, newsletters, brochures & pamphlets; development of web sites & other electronic materials. Development & production of program books & other materials for conferences & conventions.

Barry R Koffler
Featherside, 14 Ginger Rd, High Falls, NY 12440
Tel: 845-687-9851
E-mail: barkof@feathersite.com
Founded: 1979
Indexing, proofreading, editing. Writing most subjects (including encyclopedic). Specialize in popular & scientific works on animals & natural history.

KOK Edit
15 Hare Lane, East Setauket, NY 11733-3606
Tel: 631-997-8191
E-mail: editor@kokedit.com
Web Site: www.kokedit.com; x.com/kokedit; www.facebook.com/K.OmooreKlopf; www.linkedin.com/in/kokedit; www.editor-mom.blogspot.com
Key Personnel
Owner: Katharine O'Moore-Klopf
Founded: 1995
Medical editor providing copy-editing & substantive editing to publishers of medical textbooks, professional books & journal articles & providing English language editing to researcher-authors who are non-native English speakers. Certified by the Board of Editors in the Life Sciences.
Membership(s): American Medical Writers Association (AMWA); Board of Editors in the Life Sciences; Council of Science Editors (CSE); Editorial Freelancers Association (EFA); World Association of Medical Editors (WAME)

Eileen Kramer
336 Great Rd, Stow, MA 01775
Tel: 978-897-4121
E-mail: kramer@tiac.net
Copy-editor/proofreader/ESL teacher/curriculum developer. Specialize in academic journals & textbooks for STEM.

Lynn C Kronzek, Richard A Flom & Robert Flom
Affiliate of Lynn C Kronzek & Associates

145 S Glenoaks Blvd, Suite 240, Burbank, CA 91502
Tel: 818-768-7688
Key Personnel
Principal: Lynn C Kronzek E-mail: lckronzek@sbcglobal.net
Founded: 1989
Nonfiction writing & editorial services, with particular expertise in history, multicultural & Judaic studies, government/public affairs & religion. Also, sports writing & analysis, with a focus on basketball. Additionally, expertise in career services writing & advice, particularly resumes. Professional associations include: Editorial Board; The Public Historian; National Council on Public History; American Association for State & Local History; Immigration & Ethnic History Society; The Rabbinical Assembly.

Polly Kummel LLC
624 Boardman Rd, Aiken, SC 29803
Tel: 803-641-6831
E-mail: editor@amazinphrasin.com; pollyk1@msn.com
Web Site: www.amazinphrasin.com
Founded: 1990
Nonfiction (all subjects within the humanities; trade & academic): copy-editing; substantive/developmental editing; line editing; coaching. Specialties: journalism, history, political science, memoir, equestrian subjects. Dissertation/thesis help for humanities grad students. More than 30 years of experience.
Membership(s): Editorial Freelancers Association (EFA); Professional Editors Network (PEN)

Lachina Creative Inc
3791 S Green Rd, Cleveland, OH 44122
Tel: 216-292-7959
E-mail: info@lachina.com
Web Site: www.lachina.com
Key Personnel
Founder & Pres: Jeffrey A Lachina
Founded: 1989
Project management, editorial development, copy-editing, biomedical illustration, indexing, page composition, book & jacket design, proofreading, technical illustration.

Bob Land, see Land on Demand

Land on Demand
1003 Lakeview Pkwy, Locust Grove, VA 22508
Tel: 423-366-0513
E-mail: landondemand@gmail.com
Web Site: boblandedits.blogspot.com
Key Personnel
Prop & Ed: Bob Land
Founded: 1994
Editing, proofreading. Full-time freelancer since 1994; freelancer since 1986; full-time editor, writer, proofreader 1981-1994.

The Learning Source Ltd
644 Tenth St, Brooklyn, NY 11215
E-mail: info@learningsourceltd.com
Web Site: www.learningsourceltd.com
Key Personnel
Dir: Gary Davis; Wendy Davis
Mng Ed: Brian Ableman
Provides a full range of editorial & book-producing services from concept through ms & design to film & bound book. Specialty areas include children's fiction & nonfiction, adult reference & nonfiction series & classroom materials. Sister company to Ivy Gate Books.
Membership(s): ASCD; International Literacy Association (ILA); National Council for the Social Studies (NCSS); National Council of Teachers of English (NCTE); National Council of Teachers of Mathematics (NCTM)

EDITORIAL SERVICES

Debra Lemonds
PO Box 5516, Pasadena, CA 91117-0516
Tel: 626-844-9363
E-mail: dlemonds@zoho.com
Founded: 1984
Photo editing. Graphic design.
Membership(s): American Society of Picture Professionals (ASPP)

Elliot Linzer
126-10 Powells Cove Blvd, College Point, NY 11356
Tel: 718-353-1261
E-mail: elinzer@juno.com
Founded: 1971
Indexing of trade books, textbooks, reference books & scholarly books. Over fifty years experience.
Membership(s): Editorial Freelancers Association (EFA)

Little Chicago Editorial Services
154 Natural Tpke, Ripton, VT 05766
Mailing Address: PO Box 185, Ripton, VT 05766
Tel: 802-388-9782
Web Site: andreachesman.com
Key Personnel
Writer & Ed: Andrea Chesman
  E-mail: andreachesman@gmail.com
Membership(s): International Association of Culinary Professionals (IACP)

Lumina Datamatics Inc
600 Cordwainer Dr, Unit 103, Norwell, MA 02061
Tel: 508-746-0300 *Fax:* 508-746-3233
E-mail: marketing@luminad.com
Web Site: luminadatamatics.com
Key Personnel
EVP, Busn Devt: Jack Mitchell
EVP, Solutions, Transitions & US Opers: Sandeep Dhawan
Founded: 1974
Content & solutions provider that specializes in partnering with publishers, learning companies, assessment providers & others to automate & produce results-driven learning solutions. Offers a full service solution, or can partner with you & your most valued resources to help you achieve game-changing advantages over your closest competitors. Beyond the traditional production & delivery services that include everything from authoring & development to the complete production process, specializes in assessment authoring, AIG (automatic item generation), adaptive assessment, analytics, instructional design, simulation-based learning (with reporting engine), print & digital permissions (enterprise platform & service), audio/video & more. Employs over 1,800 US & offshore resources. Areas of specialization include K-12, higher education, professional & scholarly publishing, as well as accessibility & ADA compliance. All disciplines served including, but not limited to, mathematics, history, social studies, reading, social sciences, political science, humanities, hard sciences, computer science, business, engineering, world languages, English language teaching, ESL & technical trades & workforce readiness.
Branch Office(s)
c/o Arnecke Sibeth Distribution, Rechtsanwaelte Steuerberater Partnerschaftsgesellschaft mdB, Gueterplatz 1, 60327 Frankfurt am Main, Germany, Contact: Arnecke Sibeth Dabelstein
  Tel: (06155) 862 99-0 *Fax:* (06155) 862 99-19
Ascendas International Tech Park, 12th fl, Phase II (Crest), CSIR Rd, Taramani, Chennai 600 113, India *Tel:* (044) 4017 6000; (044) 4017 6001
Santosh Raj Plaza, 1st fl, Subburaman St, Gandhi Nagar, 12/9, St, Shenoy Nagar, Madurai 625 020, India
Andheri (E), Unit 117-120, SDF - IV, SEEPZ - SEZ, Mumbai 400 096, India *Tel:* (022) 4034 0515; (022) 4034 0508 *Fax:* (022) 2829 1673
Off No 47/1, 7th fl, Tower-B, A-41, Correnthum Tower, Sector-62, Noida 201 301, India
Plot No 29-34, East Coast Rd, Saram Revenue Village, Oulgaret Municipality, Lawspet Post, Puducherry 605 008, India *Tel:* (0413) 226 4500
No 10, Vazhudavoor Rd, Pettaiyanchathiram, Thattanchavadi, Puducherry 605 009, India *Tel:* (0413) 401 1635
Apple One Equicom Tower, 11th fl, Mindanao Ave Corner Biliran St, Central (pob), Cebu Business Park, 6000 Cebu City, Cebu, Philippines
c/o SOPHI Outsourcing Inc, G/F DBPI IT Plaza, Calindagan, 6200 Dumaguete City, Negros Oriental, Philippines
Brixham Laboratory, Brixham, Devon TQ5 8BA, United Kingdom
Lumina Datamatics UK Ltd, 153 Milton Keynes Business Ctr, Linford Wood, Milton Keynes MK14 6GD, United Kingdom

Mari Lynch, see Fine Wordworking

Elizabeth Lyon
1980 Cleveland St, Eugene, OR 97405
Tel: 541-357-4181
E-mail: elyon123@comcast.net
Web Site: www.elizabethlyon.com
Founded: 1988
Full-time independent book editor. Specialize in novels, memoirs, nonfiction books & proposals. Advises writers how to write & connect with literary agents. Coaches how to self-publish. Over 60 writers have found publication with large publishers & small presses, while dozens have "gone indie," some to great success & acclaim. Elizabeth has written 6 books on writing & 2 booklets, including best-selling *Nonfiction Book Proposals Anybody Can Write* & *Manuscript Makeover* on revising novels.
Membership(s): Northwest Editors Guild; Oregon Writers Colony; Willamette Writers Association

Phyllis Manner
17 Springdale Rd, New Rochelle, NY 10804
Tel: 914-834-4707 *Fax:* 914-834-4707
E-mail: pmanner@aol.com; manneredit@gmail.com
Specialize in medicine, biochemistry & archeology.
Membership(s): American Society for Indexing (ASI); Archeological Institute of America (AIA)

ManuscriptCritique.com
PO Box 362, Clay, AL 35048
Web Site: manuscriptcritique.com
Key Personnel
Pres: Michael Garrett *E-mail:* mike@manuscriptcritique.com
Founded: 1995
Editorial services for aspiring authors, including line edit & content evaluation.

Danny Marcus Word Worker
Division of D M Enterprises
201 Captains Row, Apt 220, Chelsea, MA 02150
Tel: 781-290-9174
E-mail: emildanelle@yahoo.com
Founded: 1984
Proofreading. Specialize in politics, government, history, current events, all kinds of fiction & general nonfiction.

Peter Mayeux
8148 Regent Dr, Lincoln, NE 68507-3366
Tel: 402-466-8547
E-mail: pm41923@windstream.net
Resumes, original research, writing papers & projects, Power Point presentations, broadcast commercial writing, textbooks & media scripts.

Pamela Dittmer McKuen
87 Tanglewood Dr, Glen Ellyn, IL 60137
Tel: 630-730-1340
E-mail: pmckuen@gmail.com
Web Site: www.pamelamckuen.com; www.allthewriteplaces.com
Special assignment writing, editorial & corporate projects, periodicals, interviewing & research.

Pat McNees
10643 Weymouth St, Suite 204, Bethesda, MD 20814
Tel: 301-897-8557
E-mail: patmcnees@gmail.com
Web Site: www.patmcnees.com; www.writersandeditors.com
Founded: 1971
Articles, books, photohistories. Specialize in memoirs, personal histories, biographies & organizational histories. Teach memoir writing & do substantial editing, rewriting & book doctoring. Theme anthologies & stories about food, dancing & travel.
Membership(s): American Society of Journalists & Authors (ASJA); Association of Health Care Journalists; The Authors Guild; Biographers International Organization (BIO); Editorial Freelancers Association (EFA); Independent Book Publishers Association (IBPA); National Association of Science Writers; PEN America

MC2 Solutions LLC
5101 Violet Lane, Madison, WI 53714
Key Personnel
Writer/Ed: Mark Crawford
Founded: 1995
Servicing all audiences including academic, technical, science, corporate & public relations. Additional services include: substantive editing, promotional writing & writing of corporate histories, business writing, marketing & communications, feature writing, editing & proofreading.

Susan T Middleton
366A Norton Hill Rd, Ashfield, MA 01330-9601
Tel: 413-628-4039
E-mail: smiddle23@icloud.com
Founded: 1985
Book revision & collaboration; substantive editing, line editing & copy-editing for individuals (all subjects & genres) & for trade & college markets (especially sciences & engineering).

Stephen M Miller Inc
15727 S Madison Dr, Olathe, KS 66062
Tel: 913-945-0200
Web Site: www.stephenmillerbooks.com
Key Personnel
Pres: Stephen M Miller *E-mail:* steve@stephenmillerbooks.com
Founded: 1994
Writing, editing; bible specialty & health subspecialty. Full-time freelance writer & former editor, books, magazines & newspaper. Seminary & journalism school graduate, Kansas City area. Clientele of top national book publishers & magazines.
Membership(s): Evangelical Christian Publishers Association (ECPA); Society of Bible Literature (SBL); Wesleyan Theological Society

Kathleen Mills Editorial Services
327 E King St, Chardon, OH 44024

Tel: 440-285-4347
E-mail: mills_edit@yahoo.com
Key Personnel
Edit Dir: Kathleen Mills
Founded: 1990
More than 30 years of publishing experience. Editing, writing, author liaison & project management. Arts & humanities, social sciences, reference, medical, college, business, general nonfiction & web sites. Clients include the Cleveland Museum of Art, Akron Art Museum, Western Reserve Historical Society, Case Western Reserve University, UCLA & many others.

Sondra Mochson
18 Overlook Dr, Port Washington, NY 11050
Tel: 516-883-0961
All subjects, text & trade.

Mary Mueller
516 Bartram Rd, Moorestown, NJ 08057
Tel: 856-778-4769
E-mail: mamam49@aol.com
Abstracting, copy-editing, ghostwriting, indexing, proofreading, rewriting & book reviewing-publicity. Specialize in consumer education, gardening, health, nutrition, house & home organizing, science & technology, hobby art & craft books & how-to-books.

Nina Neimark Editorial Services
543 Third St, Brooklyn, NY 11215
Tel: 718-499-6804
E-mail: pneimark@hotmail.com
Key Personnel
Pres: Nina Neimark
Founded: 1965
Specialize in scholarly books & college texts on environmental issues, history, art, music, social sciences; also general nonfiction. Mss analysis & development, content & photo research, rewriting, copy-editing, proofreading, production editing & complete book packaging services.

Newgen North America Inc
Subsidiary of Newgen KnowledgeWorks
2714 Bee Cave Rd, Suite 201, Austin, TX 78746
Tel: 512-478-5341 Fax: 512-476-4756
E-mail: sales@newgen.co
Web Site: www.newgen.co
Key Personnel
Pres: Maran Elancheran E-mail: maran@newgen.co
EVP: Tej PS Sood E-mail: tej@newgen.co
Founded: 1955
Prepares project material for copy-editor, supervises the copy-editing, serves as liaison with the author, reviews the final ms & makes sure that all elements of the project are complete & ready to be turned over to a designer. Ensures that file conversions, coding & cleanup properly prepare book material for each stage in the process. Convert files to ebook formats. Scan printed books to prepare new print file & ebook files.

Sue Newton
1397 Cypress Point Lane, Apt 106, Ventura, CA 93003
Tel: 805-765-4412; 805-864-3065
E-mail: sue.edit@gmail.com
Ms & line editing services including the correction of spelling errors, grammar, punctuation, syntax & consistency. Minor rewrites. 20 years experience in the publishing industry including fiction, nonfiction, autobiographies, textbooks, medical records & advertising.
Membership(s): Ventura County Writers Club; Writers & Publishers Network (WPN)

Donald Nicholson-Smith
50 Plaza St E, Apt 1D, Brooklyn, NY 11238
Tel: 718-636-4732
E-mail: mnr.dns@verizon.net
French-English literary translation.
Membership(s): Translators Association (London)

Veronica Oliva
304 Lily St, San Francisco, CA 94102-5608
Tel: 415-337-7707
E-mail: veronicaoliva@sbcglobal.net
Founded: 1994
Permissions editor: Trade & educational publishers. Specialty: French, Spanish & Italian college level textbooks.
Membership(s): Bay Area Editors' Forum

Diane Patrick
140 Carver Loop, No 21A, Bronx, NY 10475-2954
E-mail: dpatrickediting@aol.com
Web Site: dianepatrick.wordpress.com
Expert who both creates & polishes written materials for publishers, editors, agents, academics, legal professionals, entertainers & business owners.
Membership(s): Editorial Freelancers Association (EFA); New York Association of Black Journalists; Society of Professional Journalists (SPJ)

PeopleSpeak
24338 El Toro Rd, No E227, Laguna Woods, CA 92637
Tel: 949-581-6190 Fax: 949-581-4958
E-mail: pplspeak@att.net
Web Site: www.peoplespeakservices.com
Key Personnel
Sr Ed: Sharon Goldinger
Founded: 1985
An eye for details. Copy-editing; specialize in nonfiction mss, marketing materials, newsletters, directories.
Membership(s): Independent Book Publishers Association (IBPA); Publishers Association of Los Angeles; San Diego Professional Editors Network

Rebecca Pepper
434 NE Floral Place, Portland, OR 97232
Tel: 503-236-5802
E-mail: rpepper@rpepper.net
Founded: 1986
Membership(s): Editcetera; Editorial Freelancers Association (EFA); Northwest Editors Guild

Elsa Peterson Ltd
41 East Ave, Norwalk, CT 06851-3919
Tel: 203-846-8331
E-mail: elsa@epltd.com
Founded: 1984
Offer a full range of editorial services personalized to your project: developmental editing, substantive editing, writing, rights clearance, picture research, translation (Spanish to English).
Membership(s): Association for Psychological Science (APS); Editorial Freelancers Association (EFA); Textbook & Academic Authors Association (TAA)

Meredith Phillips
4127 Old Adobe Rd, Palo Alto, CA 94306
Tel: 650-857-9555
E-mail: mphillips0743@comcast.net
Former author & award-nominated mystery publisher (Perseverance Press). Editing (developmental, line, copy), researching, fact checking, proofreading of trade books (fiction or nonfiction).

Pictures & Words Editorial Services
3100 "B" Ave, Anacortes, WA 98221
Tel: 360-293-8476
Web Site: www.picturesandwords.com/words
Key Personnel
Owner: Kristi Hein E-mail: kristi.editor@gmail.com
Founded: 1995
Versatile generalist serving trade publishers & authors. Cookbooks, health & well-being, gardening (including New York Times best seller *A Year in Flowers*), nature & environment, education, consumer interest & activism, business & fiction.
Membership(s): American Copy Editors Society (ACES); Bay Area Editors' Forum; Northwest Editors Guild

Caroline Pincus Book Midwife
101 Wool St, San Francisco, CA 94110
Tel: 415-516-6206
E-mail: cpincus1958@gmail.com
Web Site: www.carolinepincus.com
Key Personnel
Book Midwife: Caroline Pincus
Founded: 1998
Nonfiction proposal & ms development & book doctoring for the general trade. Specialize in natural health, personal growth, social justice, women's issues.

Wendy Polhemus-Annibell
PO Box 464, Peconic, NY 11958
Tel: 631-833-6942
E-mail: wannibell@gmail.com
Founded: 1987
Freelance copy-editing, line editing, developmental editing, proofreading, project management. Specialize in college textbooks (particularly English/grammar/writing/rhetoric texts) & fiction/nonfiction trade books, with an emphasis on editorial excellence.

Pronk Media Inc
16 Glen Davis Crescent, Toronto, ON M4E 1X5, Canada
Tel: 416-716-9660 (cell)
E-mail: info@pronk.com; hello@pronk.com
Web Site: www.pronk.com; www.h5engines.com; www.html5alive.com
Key Personnel
Pres: Gord Pronk E-mail: gord@pronk.com
Founded: 1981 (as Pronk & Associates Inc)
Print design & production, including product conceptualization & prototypes, design & art direction, photo research & licensing, infographics, charts, graphs, technical art, page design, layout & production. Interactive content development, digital games, activities, animations & complete lessons for the classroom.

Proofed to Perfection Editing Services
6519 Sherrill Baggett Rd, Godwin, NC 28344
Tel: 910-980-0832
E-mail: inquiries@proofedtoperfection.com
Web Site: www.proofedtoperfection.com
Key Personnel
Sr Ed & Proj Coord: Pamela Cangioli
 E-mail: pam@proofedtoperfection.com
Founded: 2006
Full service editing company. Specializes in comprehensive, professional book editing. Offers proofreading, copy-editing, developmental editing & book evaluations at competitive rates. Editors have traditional publishing experience & offer personal, quality service. Request a free sample edit & book critique.
Membership(s): American Christian Fiction Writers (ACFW); Editorial Freelancers Association (EFA); Evangelical Christian Publishers Association (ECPA)

EDITORIAL SERVICES

Generosa Gina Protano Publishing, see GGP Publishing Inc

Jerry Ralya
7909 Vt Rte 14, Craftsbury Common, VT 05827
Tel: 802-586-7514
E-mail: jerryralya@gmail.com
Founded: 1980
Editing, indexing & preparing online test materials for college textbooks in medicine, science, nursing & the behavioral sciences.
Membership(s): Editorial Freelancers Association (EFA)

Research Research
240 E 27 St, Suite 20-K, New York, NY 10016-9238
Tel: 212-779-9540 *Fax:* 212-779-9540
E-mail: ehtac@msn.com
Key Personnel
Pres: Cathe Giffuni
Founded: 1987

Judith Riven Literary Agent LLC
250 W 16 St, Suite 4F, New York, NY 10011
Key Personnel
Owner & Pres: Judith Riven
Founded: 1993
Editorial consultation, developmental & structural editing, line editing, ms analysis.

Peter Rooney
135 Hudson St, New York, NY 10013
Tel: 917-376-1792 *Fax:* 212-226-8047
E-mail: magneticreports@gmail.com
Web Site: www.magneticreports.xyz
Indexer, programmer/consultant for indexes, databases, directories, catalogues raisonnes. Large & small projects.
Membership(s): American Society for Indexing (ASI)

Sachem Publishing Associates Inc
402 W Lyon Farm Dr, Greenwich, CT 06831
Tel: 203-813-3077
E-mail: sachempub@optonline.net
Key Personnel
Pres & Ed: Stephen P Elliott
Founded: 1974
Complete trade & mail order book preparation & packaging; editorial services, from concept to finished books. Specialize in consumer & educational reference books, including encyclopedias & dictionaries.

Salmon Bay Indexing
26026 Wax Orchard Rd SW, Vashon, WA 98070
Tel: 206-612-3993
Web Site: salmonbayindexing.com
Key Personnel
Indexer: Beth Nauman-Montana *E-mail:* beth@salmonbayindexing.com
Founded: 2002
Professional indexer. Provides indexes for books & ebooks in all subject areas. Every project is delivered on time & according to client guidelines.

Barbara S Salz LLC Photo Research
127 Prospect Place, South Orange, NJ 07079
Tel: 646-734-5949
E-mail: bsalz.photo@gmail.com
Image research & permissions for books, magazines, exhibitions & advertising.
Membership(s): American Society of Picture Professionals (ASPP)

C J Scheiner Books
275 Linden Blvd, Unit B2, Brooklyn, NY 11226
Tel: 718-469-1089

Key Personnel
Owner: C J Scheiner
Literature searches, special assignment writing, fact checking, research, photo research illustrations provided, bibliographies & source lists, text & introduction writing. Specialize in erotica, curiosa & sexology.

Schoolhouse Indexing
10-B Parade Ground Rd, Etna, NH 03750
Tel: 603-359-5826
Web Site: schoolhouseindexing.com
Key Personnel
Owner & Indexer: Christine Hoskin
E-mail: christine@schoolhousefarm.net
Freelance indexing business. Professional indexing services offered include the fields of law & legal issues, education (in both English & French), business & economics, children's elementary education/nonfiction, travel, hospitality & tourism, social sciences & culture, health & psychology, history & biography, environmental sciences, geology, engineering, construction & architecture. Indexing queries regarding general indexing information, rates & availability are welcome.
Membership(s): American Society for Indexing (ASI)

Schoolhouse Network
PO Box 1518, Northampton, MA 01061
Tel: 480-427-4836
E-mail: schoolhousenetwork@gmail.com
Key Personnel
Pres: Marilyn Greco
Dir, Curriculum: Mary K Messick
Founded: 1998
Provides a comprehensive range of editorial service & products to educational publishers, development groups, schools & other educational institutions for PreK, K-12 & college in both print & electronic media in the areas of reading/language arts, ESL, literature, social studies, health & science. Develop student & teacher editions, leveled readers, children's books, graphic novels, fiction & nonfiction, trade book publications which include memoir, poetry, travel with accompanying art & photography.
Membership(s): Editorial Freelancers Association (EFA); International Literacy Association (ILA); National Association for the Education of Young Children (NAEYC); TESOL International Association

Schroeder Indexing Services
23 Camilla Pink Ct, Bluffton, SC 29909
Tel: 843-415-3900
E-mail: sanindex@schroederindexing.com
Web Site: www.schroederindexing.com
Key Personnel
Owner & CEO: Sandi Schroeder
Produce custom indexes using CINDEX, a dedicated indexing software. Company web site includes current information on clients & titles indexed, information on planning an index, downloadable Project Information Sheet & request for an estimate.
Membership(s): American Society for Indexing (ASI)

Franklin L Schulaner
PO Box 507, Kealakekua, HI 96750-0507
Tel: 808-322-3785
E-mail: fschulaner@hawaii.rr.com

Sherri Schultz/Words with Grace
1810 Alder St, No 105, Eugene, OR 97401
Tel: 206-928-2015
E-mail: WordsWithGraceEditorial@gmail.com
Founded: 1992
Experienced copy-editor & proofreader of fiction & nonfiction books, web content & more. Works with clients around the country. Special expertise in politics, environment, travel, literary nonfiction & art.
Membership(s): Northwest Editors Guild; Springfield/Eugene-area Editors (SEE)

Sciendex
1388 Leisure Dr, Summerville, SC 29486
Tel: 843-693-6689
Web Site: www.sciendex.com
Key Personnel
Owner/Indexer: Samantha Miller
E-mail: samanthamiller@mindspring.com
Founded: 2004
Index preparation for topics including the sciences (environmental science, biology, chemistry, geology, medicine), biographies, cooking, nutrition, & general trade subjects.

Scribendi Inc
405 Riverview Dr, Chatham, ON N7M 0N3, Canada
Tel: 519-351-1626 (cust serv) *Fax:* 519-354-0192
E-mail: customerservice@scribendi.com
Web Site: www.scribendi.com
Key Personnel
CEO: Enrico Magnani, MA *E-mail:* enrico.magnani@scribendi.com
Pres: Patrica Riopel *E-mail:* patricia.riopel@scribendi.com
Founded: 1997
On demand proofreading & editing services available 24/7. Web site offers instant quotes on all standard services; call or e-mail for special project quotes or long-term arrangements.

SDP Publishing Solutions LLC
36 Captain's Way, East Bridgewater, MA 02333
Tel: 617-775-0656
Web Site: www.sdppublishingsolutions.com
Key Personnel
Publr: Lisa Akoury-Ross *E-mail:* lross@sdppublishing.com
Developmental Ed & Copy-Ed: Robert Astle; Taylor Morris; Beth Raps; Susan Strecker
Ghostwriter, Developmental Ed & Copy-Ed: Kathleen A Tracy
Prof Proofreader/Proofchecker: Karen Grennan
Artist: Randy Jennings; Samela St Pierre
Cover & Interior Designer: Howard Johnson
Assoc: Kristen Harrigan
Admin Asst: Kim Sexton
Founded: 2009
Provides full service independent publishing services focusing on editorial services for fiction, nonfiction, medical fiction & nonfiction, memoirs, business books, children's books & more! We review each ms closely to determine the best editorial approach for each author. We help our authors become better writers! We also provide full publishing services for indie authors, including marketing & global distribution.
Membership(s): Independent Book Publishers Association (IBPA)

Alexa Selph
4300 McClatchey Circle, Atlanta, GA 30342
Tel: 404-256-3717
E-mail: lexa101@aol.com

Barry Sheinkopf
c/o The Writing Ctr, 601 Palisade Ave, Englewood Cliffs, NJ 07632
Tel: 201-567-4017 *Fax:* 201-567-7202
E-mail: bsheinkopf@optonline.net
Founded: 1977

Trade, scholarly & professional publications, book design & self-publishing since 1999 as Full Court Press (fullcourtpress.com).
Membership(s): The Authors Guild; Mystery Writers of America (MWA)

Monika Shoffman-Graves
70 Transylvania Ave, Key Largo, FL 33037
Tel: 305-451-1462
E-mail: mograv@gmail.com
Indexing, ms analysis, proofreading & research.

Roger W Smith
59-67 58 Rd, Maspeth, NY 11378-3211
Tel: 718-416-1334
E-mail: brandeis106@gmail.com
Founded: 1982
Membership(s): Editorial Freelancers Association (EFA)

Stackler Editorial
200 Woodland Ave, Summit, NJ 07901
Tel: 510-912-9187
E-mail: ed.stackler@gmail.com
Web Site: www.fictioneditor.com
Key Personnel
Owner: Ed Stackler
Founded: 1996
Editorial services for novelists of crime, thriller & suspense fiction.

Sterling Media Productions LLC, see Robert L Cohen

Brooke C Stoddard
111 S Columbus St, Alexandria, VA 22314
E-mail: stoddardbc@gmail.com
Web Site: brookecstoddard.com
Founded: 1983
Magazine & book writing & editing. Can handle design & production.
Membership(s): American Society of Journalists & Authors (ASJA); The Authors Guild; Editorial Freelancers Association (EFA); National Press Club (NPC)

Jeri L Stolk
8 Rush Vine Ct, Owings Mills, MD 21117
Tel: 410-864-8109
E-mail: jeristolk@gmail.com
Edit journals & books, especially academic.

Vivian Sudhalter
1202 Loma Dr, No 117, Ojai, CA 93023
Tel: 805-640-9737
E-mail: vivians09@att.net
Freelance editor. Specialize in fiction & nonfiction books on women's studies, holistic health, memoirs & other genres. I improve finished mss by copy-editing for good grammar, flow, punctuation, usage & consistency, while maintaining the author's authentic voice. I also help shape books from inception by working with authors to create the structure that will best serve their vision. Having been in the book publishing industry for more than 4 decades, I provide insights into the publication process, whether conventional or POD. Contact by e-mail preferred.

Fraser Sutherland
39 Helena Ave, Toronto, ON M6G 2H3, Canada
Tel: 416-652-5735
E-mail: rodfrasers@gmail.com
Founded: 1970
General editorial services. Specialize in dictionaries & reference books (lexicography), ms analysis & rewriting.
Membership(s): Dictionary Society of North America; Editors' Association of Canada/Association canadienne des reviseurs (EAC); PEN Canada

Thodestool Fiction Editing
40 McDougall Rd, Waterloo, ON N2L 2W5, Canada
Web Site: www.thodestool.ca
Key Personnel
Owner: Vanessa Ricci-Thode
E-mail: vanessariccithode@gmail.com
Founded: 2010
Focus on providing editing services for speculative fiction (science fiction, fantasy, horror) of varying lengths, with a focus on structural/developmental editing & ms evaluations.
Membership(s): Science Fiction and Fantasy Writers of America, Inc (SFWA); The Writers' Union of Canada

Twin Oaks Indexing
Division of Twin Oaks Community
138 Twin Oaks Rd, Suite W, Louisa, VA 23093
Tel: 540-894-5126
E-mail: twinoaksindexing@gmail.com
Web Site: www.twinoakscommunity.org
Key Personnel
Mgr: Rachel Nishan
Founded: 1981

Wambtac Communications LLC
1512 E Santa Clara Ave, Santa Ana, CA 92705
Tel: 714-954-0580 *Toll Free Tel:* 800-641-3936
E-mail: wambtac@wambtac.com
Web Site: www.wambtac.com; claudiasuzanne.com (prof servs)
Key Personnel
Owner, Founder & Mng Partner: Claudia Suzanne
Tel: 714-493-9105 *E-mail:* claudiasuzanne@gmail.com
Founded: 1995
Ghostwriter training, apprentice program & team-led ghostwriting services.
Membership(s): Independent Book Publishers Association (IBPA)

Toby Wertheim
240 E 76 St, New York, NY 10021
Tel: 212-472-8587
E-mail: tobywertheim@yahoo.com
Research/editor.

WFS, see Write for Success Editing Services

Barbara Mlotek Whelehan
7064 SE Cricket Ct, Stuart, FL 34997
Tel: 954-554-0765 (cell); 772-463-0818 (home)
E-mail: barbarawhelehan@bellsouth.net
More than 30 years of publishing experience. All subjects; specialize in personal finance, investments, mutual funds, business & consumer topics. Also copy-edit fiction.

White Oak Editions, see Carol Cartaino

Windhaven®
466 Rte 10, Orford, NH 03777
Tel: 603-512-9251 (cell)
Web Site: www.windhavenpress.com
Key Personnel
Dir & Ed: Nancy C Hanger *E-mail:* nhanger@windhavenpress.com
Ed & Consultant: Andrew V Phillips
E-mail: andrew@windhavenpress.com
Founded: 1985
Consulting & developmental editing, line editing, copy-editing, proofreading.
Membership(s): Editorial Freelancers Association (EFA); National Writers Union (NWU)

WordCo Indexing Services Inc
66 Franklin St, Norwich, CT 06360
E-mail: office@wordco.com
Web Site: www.wordco.com
Key Personnel
Founder & CEO: Stephen Ingle *E-mail:* sringle@wordco.com
Proj Coord: Amy Moriarty *E-mail:* amoriarty@wordco.com
Founded: 1988
Since 1988, WordCo has completed thousands of thorough & accurate indexes in hundreds of subject areas for many major publishers. WordCo's in-house team of professionally trained indexers has the experience & capability to complete your indexing projects professionally & on time. Rush service & ebook indexing available.
Membership(s): American Society for Indexing (ASI)

Words into Print
208 Java St, 5th fl, Brooklyn, NY 11222
E-mail: query@wordsintoprint.org
Web Site: wordsintoprint.org
Key Personnel
Ed: Jeff Alexander *E-mail:* jeffale73@gmail.com; Becky Cabaza *E-mail:* rtcbooks@gmail.com; Jane Fleming Fransson *E-mail:* janef13@gmail.com; Ruth Greenstein *E-mail:* rg@greenlinepublishing.com; Emily Loose *E-mail:* emilylooselit@gmail.com; Julie Miesionczek *E-mail:* julie@writewithjulie.com; Anne Cole Norman *E-mail:* acole157@gmail.com
Founded: 1998
An alliance of top New York publishing professionals who offer a broad range of editorial services to authors, publishers, literary agents, book packagers & content providers.

Words with Grace, see Sherri Schultz/Words with Grace

Working With Words
5320 SW Mayfair Ct, Beaverton, OR 97005
Tel: 503-626-4998
E-mail: editor@zzz.com
Key Personnel
Owner: Sue Mann
Founded: 1985
Freelance editorial services. General trade, nonfiction. Subjects include children's, cookbooks, creativity, historical, inspirational, memoirs, self-help, spiritual, training. Substantive editing. Online & hard copy.
Membership(s): Northwest Editors Guild

Wright Information Indexing Services
Sandia Park, NM 87047
Web Site: www.wrightinformation.com
Key Personnel
Owner & Pres: Jan C Wright *E-mail:* jancw@wrightinformation.com
Founded: 1991
Book, ebook & online indexing services. Specialize in single-source publications.
Membership(s): American Society for Indexing (ASI)

Write for Success Editing Services
PO Box 292153, Los Angeles, CA 90029-8653
Tel: 323-356-8833
E-mail: writeforsuccessediting@gmail.com
Web Site: www.writeforsuccessediting.com
Key Personnel
Owner & Ed: Christine Van Zandt
E-mail: christine@writeforsuccessediting.com
Founded: 2009
Specialize in developmental editing, critique & author coaching (mentorship). Guide writers from idea to publication via experience & insightful feedback. Accept both fiction & non-

EDITORIAL SERVICES

fiction, adult & children's, traditional & self-publishers & query letters. Also writing teacher & 3-time writing mentor for the Carnegie's 9 month Author Academy. Education includes a Master's in English literature with a specialization in children's literature. Traditionally published author (2 nonfiction picture books).
Membership(s): The Authors Guild; Editorial Freelancers Association (EFA); Independent Book Publishers Association (IBPA); San Diego Professional Editors Network; Society of Children's Book Writers & Illustrators (SCBWI)

The Writers Lifeline Inc, a Story Merchant company
Subsidiary of Story Merchant
400 S Burnside Ave, Suite 11B, Los Angeles, CA 90036
Tel: 310-968-1607
Web Site: www.thewriterslifeline.com
Key Personnel
CEO: Kenneth Atchity, PhD *E-mail:* kja@thewriterslifeline.com
Mgr: Samantha Skelton *E-mail:* sam@storymerchant.com
Founded: 1996
Helping writers bring their discipline & skills to the level of their vision & ambition. Full service editorial company providing nonfiction book writers, business, professional, technical & screenwriters with assistance in storytelling, mentoring, perfecting their style & craft, style-structure-concept-line editing, ghostwriting, publishing, consulting, development, translation, advertising & promotion, printing & self-publishing, distribution & research. Branch office in New York.
Sister companies: Atchity Productions; Story Merchant; Story Merchant Books.
Membership(s): The Authors Guild; National Academy of Television Arts & Sciences (NATAS); PEN America; Women in Film (WIF); Writers Guild of America (WGA)

Writer's Relief, Inc
18766 John J Williams Hwy, Unit 4, Box 335, Rehoboth Beach, DE 19971
Toll Free Tel: 866-405-3003 *Fax:* 201-641-1253
E-mail: info@writersrelief.com
Web Site: www.WritersRelief.com
Key Personnel
Pres: Ronnie L Smith *E-mail:* ronnie@wrelief.com
Founded: 1994
Don't have time to submit your writing? We can help. Submission leads & cover/query letter guidelines. Join the 60,000+ writers who subscribe to *Submit Write Now!*, our free e-publication. We also offer web site design & self-publishing services.

Wyman Indexing
1311 Delaware Ave SW, Suite S332, Washington, DC 20024
Tel: 443-336-5497
Web Site: www.wymanindexing.com
Key Personnel
Chief Indexer & Consultant: Pilar Wyman *E-mail:* pilarw@wymanindexing.com
Founded: 1990
Freelance indexing & consulting. Specialize in medicine, technology & current events, for print & electronic media indexes, in French, Spanish & English.
Membership(s): American Medical Writers Association (AMWA); American Society for Indexing (ASI)

Zebra Communications
13682 Hwy 92, No 3005, Woodstock, GA 30188-4734
Tel: 404-433-7507
E-mail: bobbie@zebraeditor.com
Web Site: www.zebraeditor.com
Key Personnel
Owner: Bobbie Christmas *E-mail:* bzebra@aol.com
Founded: 1992
Editorial services that specialize in fiction & nonfiction books as well as magazines.
Membership(s): Atlanta Writers Club; Florida Writers Association; Georgia Writers Association; International Guild of Professional Business Consultants; Society for the Preservation of English Language Literature (SPELL); South Carolina Writers Workshop; Southeastern Writers Association; The Writers' Network

Literary Agents

The agents listed here are among the most active in the field. Letters in parentheses following the agency name indicate fields of activity:

(L)–Literary Agent (D)–Dramatic Agent (L-D)–Literary & Dramatic Agent

Those individuals who are members of the Association of American Literary Agents Inc are identified by the presence of (AALA) after their name.

Authors seeking literary representation are advised that some agents request a nominal reading fee that may be applied to the agent's commission upon representation. Other agencies may charge substantially higher fees which may not be applicable to a future commission and which are not refundable. The recommended course is to first send a query letter with an outline, sample chapter, and a self-addressed stamped envelope (SASE). Should an agent express interest in handling the manuscript, full details of fees and commissions should be obtained in writing before the complete manuscript is sent. Should an agency require significant advance payment from an author, the author is cautioned to make a careful investigation to determine the agency's standing in the industry before entering an agreement. The author should always retain a copy of the manuscript in his or her possession.

AAA Books Unlimited (L)
3060 Blackthorn Rd, Riverwoods, IL 60015
Tel: 847-444-1220 *Fax:* 847-607-8335
Web Site: www.aaabooksunlimited.com
Key Personnel
Principal: Nancy Rosenfeld *E-mail:* nancy@aaabooksunlimited.com
Founded: 1993
Full service literary agency to provide clients with first class service "over & above" what normally is handled by a literary agency. We offer content-copy-line editing services. No unsol mss, query first.
Titles recently placed: *A is for Aries*, Micah T Dank, Priscilla Rosado-Cruz; *A Mother's Grace: Healing the World, One Woman at a Time*, Michelle Moore; *A Parent's Guide to Your Child's Mental Health Diagnosis and Treatment*, Jacqueline Corcoran, PhD, LCSW; *Aftermath*, Annette Libeskind Berkovits; *America. Underwater and Sinking: "Time to Surface with Lessons Learned Running Major Government Agencies"*, James B Lockhart III; *An Afghan Remembers: "No Matter Where I Go, I Belong to My Ancestors"*, Abdul Qayum Safi; *An End to Arguing: "101 Valuable Lessons for All Relationships"*, Linda Bloom, Charlie Bloom; *AR2 Squared: "A Global Conspiracy, A Nation at Risk, A Fallen President, A Rising Hero: The Second American Revolution"*, Lawrence Paul Hebron; *Baikonur Man: "Space, Science, American Ambition, and Russian Chaos at the Cold War's End"*, Barry Stoddard, PhD; *Bernie Weber: Math Genius (3-book series)*, Matthew Flynn; *Blue Baby and the Spokane Experience*, Tracy Berg, MD; *Breaking the Cycle: Free Yourself from Sex Addiction, Porn Obsession, and Shame*, George N Collins, MA, Andrew Adleman, MA; *Burn Out, The Rise of a Villain (2nd in the Ashes Over Avalon trilogy)*, Jordan Keller; *Champagne at Seven! (1st in the Bitches of Fifth Avenue trilogy)*, Toni Glickman; *China Code (2nd in The Bernie Weber series)*, Matthew Flynn; *Combustion, The Fall of a Kingdom (3rd in the Ashes Over Avalon trilogy)*, Jordan Keller; *Demystifying Hospice: Stories of Caregivers and Patients Partnering with Hospice*, Karen J Clayton; *Drunk Log (1st in the Day in the Life series)*, Mark E Scott; *Experience Is the Angled Road: Memoir of an Academic*, R Barbara Gitenstein; *Farewell to South Shore (2-book series)*, Charlene Wexler; *Finding Ivy Land: "Probing America's Higher Education System"*, Justin Harmon; *First Date (2nd in the Day in the Life series)*, Mark E Scott; *Forget Dieting: "It's All About Data Fueling"*, Candice P Rosen, RN, MSW; *Four Laws for the Artificially Intelligent*, Ian Domowitz; *Friend of the Devil (4th in The Joth Proctor Fixer series)*, James V Irving; *Hidden: The Mysteries of Nature and Secrets of Cheats*, Loren Pankratz, PhD; *How Concerned Should I Be?: "Questions Pertaining to the Developing Mind"*, Anandhi Narasimhan, MD; *How Surviving the Second World War Taught Me How to Live*, Sgt Daniel Altman, Fawn Zwickel; *I Love My Kids But I Don't Always Like Them*, Franki Bagdade; *In Due Time (2nd in the Filthy Rich Lawyers series)*, Brian M Felgoise, David Tabatsky; *In Search of a Theory of Everything: The Philosophy Behind Physics*, Demetris Nicolaides, PhD; *Interpersonal Psychoanalytic Theory for the 21st Century: Evolving Self*, Sue Harris, PhD, Janet R Mayes, PhD, Marilyn Miller, RN, MA, David Singer; *Into the Rabbit Hole (8-book series)*, Micah T Dank, PhD; *Jacob's Courage: "A Holocaust Love Story"*, Charles S Weinblatt; *Joth Proctor Fixer Mystery (3-book series)*, James V Irving; *Keep Your Fork: Something Sweet is Coming*, Bill Kavanagh, MA, LMFT; *KSAN! The Hippie Radio Revolution that Rocked America*, Hank Rosenfeld; *Laughing at Myself: My Education in Congress, on the Farm, and at the Movies*, Dan Glickman; *Love in the Time of Crises: "Tools for Relationships in Changing Times"*, Linda Bloom, Charlie Bloom; *Mindfulness for Borderline Personality Disorder*, Blaise Aguirre, MD, Dr Gillian Galen; *Nail in the Coffin (8th in the Into the Rabbit Hole series)*, Micah T Dank; *Nothing But the Tooth: "An Insider's Guide to Dentistry"*, Teresa Yang, DDS; *Outside the Wire: "A Tale of Murder, Love and War"*, Gary Edgington; *Outside Voices: A Memoir of the Berkeley Revolution*, Joan Gelfand; *Overcoming Destructive Anger*, Bernard Golden, PhD; *Paradise Lake (2nd in The Bill Duncan series)*, Stephen H Moriarty; *Parenting Your Child with Autism: Practical Solutions, Strategies, and Advice for Helping Your Family*, M Anjali Sastry, PhD, Blaise Aguirre, MD; *Pitchfork Populism: The Trump Effect on Ten American Dynamics*, Brad Kane; *Quantum Leaps in the Wrong Direction*, Arthur W Wiggins, Charles M Wynn, PhD, Sidney Harris; *Reimagining Men's Cancers*, Mark Boguski, MD, Michelle Berman, MD, David Tabatsky; *Reimagining Women's Cancers*, Mark Boguski, MD, Michelle Berman, MD, David Tabatsky; *Restitution (1st in The Bill Duncan series)*, Stephen H Moriarty; *Rx for Hope: A Cancer Care Model to Optimize the Immune System Integrating Low Dose Chemotherapy and Complementary Medicine*, Nick Chen, MD, PhD, David Tabatsky; *Surviving the Lion's Den (3-book series)*, Matt Scott; *The Academic Mom (5-book series)*, Jacqueline Corcoran; *The Ayatollah Takedown (3rd in the Surviving the Lion's Den series)*, Matt Scott; *The Battle of Zig Zag Pass*, C H Boyer; *The Bill Duncan Series*, Stephen H Moriarty; *The Boy Behind the Door: How Alex Winter Escaped the Nazis*, David Tabatsky; *The Corset Maker*, Annette Libeskind Berkovits; *The Education of Ryan Coleman (1st in the Filthy Rich Lawyers series)*, Brian M Felgoise, David Tabatsky; *The Fusion Factor (3rd in The Trouble with Miracles series)*, Stephen Steele; *The Hat Diaries (3-book series)*, Nadine Haruni; *The Human Side of Science*, Arthur W Wiggins, Charles M Wynn, PhD, Sidney Harris; *The Last Stand (1st in The Prohibition series)*, Brien A Roche; *The Lincoln Zoo Riot*, Larry Belling, Art Twain; *The Mysterious Secret Guardians in the London Underground (1st in The Mysterious Secret Guardians series)*, Dorothy McCoy; *The Overparenting Solution: Raising Positive, Resourceful Children to Meet Today's Challenges*, George S Glass, MD, David Tabatsky; *The Owl Mountain Doomsday Solution (2nd in The Mysterious Secret Guardians series)*, Dorothy McCoy; *The Parkinson's Blues*, John J Clayton; *The Precious Few: Holocaust Survivors Who Fought Back and Survived*, David Twain, Art Twain; *The Revenge (3-book series)*, Matthew J Flynn, David Tabatsky; *The Rise of a Hero (1st in the Ashes Over Avalon trilogy)*, Jordan Keller; *The Sacrifices of Superwomen: "It's More Than Enough¡"*, Andrea Sullivan; *The Three Stages of Elderhood*, Howard Englander; *The Trouble with Miracles (3-book series)*, Stephen Steele; *The Truth About Cardiovascular Health*, Jay N Cohn, MD; *The Unlikeliest of Places: How Nachman Libeskind Survived the Nazis, the Gulags and Soviet Communism*, Annette Libeskind Berkovits; *The Vice Chairman's Doctrine: A Guide to Rocking the Top in Industry Version 4.0*, Ian Domowitz; *Treasure Islands (6-book series)*, Stephen Steele; *Under a Dark Eye: A Family Story*, Sharon Dunn; *Unfinished Business: "News Reporter Tom Williams Hunts for Truth" (4-book series)*, Ray Dan Parker; *What's in Your Sandbox? "A Back to Basic Toolkit for Raising Happy, Healthy Families"*, Kathryn Smerling, PhD, LCSW; *You Belong to Me (2nd in The Forget-Me-Not series)*, Lisa Sherman; *You Finished Treatment, Now What? "Natural Medicine Approaches for Cancer Survivors/Thrivers"*, Amy Rothenberg, ND; *Your Money Mentor: A Financial Expert's Sage Advice to Help Millennials Make Money Work*, Russell Robb

The Aaland Agency (L)
PO Box 849, Inyokern, CA 93527-0849
Tel: 760-384-3910
E-mail: anniejo41@gmail.com
Web Site: www.the-aaland-agency.com
Key Personnel
Dir & Fiction/Nonfiction: Jo Ann Krueger
Foreign Rep, CN & Europe: Richard Allan
Romance/Adventure: Mitzi Rhone
Founded: 1991

LITERARY AGENTS

Adult fiction & nonfiction. One-inch margins & space & a half. Any format, e-mail file attachment, hard copy or CD is acceptable (e-mail file preferred). Crime drama, romance/adventure, children's stories, biographies & textbooks gladly accepted. No fees for ms review/evaluation. Complete ms or first 3 chapters. No unsol mss, query first.
Titles recently placed: *Cypher*, T R Dawson; *The Hydra Brief*, William Davison; *USS Kitty Hawk: The Last Warrior*, Marty S Bourdon

Dominick Abel Literary Agency Inc (L)
146 W 82 St, Suite 1-A, New York, NY 10024
Tel: 212-877-0710 *Fax:* 212-595-3133
E-mail: agency@dalainc.com
Web Site: www.dalainc.com
Key Personnel
Pres: Dominick Abel (AALA)
    E-mail: dominick@dalainc.com
Founded: 1975
Adult fiction & nonfiction. Handle film & TV rights. Representatives in Hollywood & all major foreign countries. Query by e-mail. Seldom open to new clients.
Foreign Rep(s): Akcali Agency (Turkey); Big Apple Agency Inc (China, Indonesia, Malaysia, Taiwan, Vietnam); The Buckman Agency (Germany, Israel, Netherlands, Portugal, Scandinavia, Spain, Spanish- & Portuguese-speaking countries); English Agency Japan Co Ltd (Japan); David Grossman Literary Agency (UK & Commonwealth); The Italian Literary Agency Srl (Italy); Korea Copyright Center Inc (KCC) (South Korea); La Nouvelle Agence (France); Prava i prevodi (Central Europe, Eastern Europe, Greece, Russia, Ukraine); Tuttle-Mori Agency Inc (Thailand)
Membership(s): Authors Registry; Copyright Clearance Center (CCC)

Acacia House Publishing Services Ltd (L)
687 Oliver St, Oak Bay, BC V8S 4W2, Canada
Tel: 226-387-4757
Key Personnel
Mng Dir: Bill Hanna *E-mail:* bhanna.acacia@rogers.com
Founded: 1985
Adult fiction; no science fiction, occult, horror; most nonfiction. Handle film & TV rights for authors. Handle foreign rights for 3 client publishers. Territories handled directly by Acacia include Australia, Bulgaria, Canada (English-speaking), Czechia, Denmark, Estonia, Finland, Iceland, Latvia, Lithuania, Norway, Slovakia, Sweden, UK, USA. No unsol mss, query first by e-mail; submit outline & first 50 pages. No reading fee. Fee charged for photocopying & postage or courier.
Foreign Rights: Akcali (Turkey); Agencia Literaria Carmen Balcells SA (Portugal, Spain); Big Apple Agency Inc (China, Hong Kong, Malaysia, Taiwan, Vietnam); Agence Deborah Druba (French-speaking countries); Paul & Peter Fritz AG (Austria, Germany); Graal Literary Agency (Poland); Harris-Elon Agency (Ilana Kurshan) (Israel); International Press Agency (South Africa); Japan UNI Agency Inc (Japan); Katai & Bolza (Bosnia and Herzegovina, Croatia, Hungary, Montenegro, Serbia, Slovenia); Simona Kessler (Romania); Duran Kim Agency (South Korea); Alexander Korzhenevski (Russia); Maxima Creative Agency (Santo Manarung) (Indonesia); Daniela Micura Literary Services (nonfiction only) (Italy); Read n Right Agency (Greece); Marianne Schoenbach Agency (Netherlands); Silk Road Agency (Thailand)

Aevitas Creative Management LLC (L-D)
19 W 21 St, Suite 501, New York, NY 10010
Tel: 212-765-6900
Web Site: www.aevitascreative.com
Key Personnel
Co-CEO: David Kuhn (AALA); Todd Shuster
Pres (Boston): Esmond Harmsworth
VP, Opers & Personnel: Kate Mack
Head of Devt & Media Rts: Allison Warren
Dir, Devt & Media Rts: Kayla Grogan
Dir, Foreign Rts: Erin Files (AALA)
    E-mail: efiles@aevitascreative.com
Sr Partner: Jennifer Gates; Laura Nolan (AALA); Rick Richter
Sr Partner (Boston): Janet Silver
Sr Partner: Wendy Strothman (AALA); Jane von Mehren
Partner: Adriana Dominguez (AALA)
Partner (DC): Bridget Wagner Matzie
Sr Agent (LA): Sarah Bowlin
Sr Agent: Chris Bucci
Sr Agent (Detroit): Jon Michael Darga
Sr Agent: Amy Thrall Flynn (AALA)
Sr Agent (Boston): Lori Galvin
Sr Agent: David Granger; Sarah Lazin (AALA); Sarah Levitt (AALA)
Sr Agent (LA): Will Lippincott
Sr Agent (Nashville): Lauren MacLeod (AALA)
Sr Agent: Jen Marshall; Andy McNicol; Penny Moore
Sr Agent (DC): Lauren Sharp
Sr Agent: Becky Sweren
Agent: Erica Bauman
Agent (LA): Karen Brailsford
Agent (Detroit): Justin Brouckaert
Agent (Boston): Maggie Cooper (AALA)
Agent (CA): Mary C Moore (AALA)
Agent: Donya Dickerson; Valerie Frankel; Caroline Marsiglia
Agent: Karen Murgolo; Nate Muscato; Anna Petkovich; Michael Signorelli
Founded: 2016 (through the merger of Kuhn Projects & Zachary Shuster Harmsworth)
Full service literary agency representing authors of the highest quality books in categories such as science & technology, religion & spirituality, memoir, history & narrative nonfiction, health & psychology, food & cookbooks, fashion & design, children's, middle grade, & young adult business & politics, humor, music, & pop culture, fiction, & arts & culture. Aevitas is home to more than 30 agents in New York; Boston, MA; Washington, DC; Los Angeles, CA; Detroit, MI; Nashville, TN; London, UK & Barcelona, Spain, representing many award-winning authors, performers, thinkers, artists, & public figures. No unsol mss, email only query letters, full plot; synopsis or detailed chapters summary plus 3 sample chapters up to 50 pages. No mss returned without SASE. No reading fee.
Foreign Office(s): Aevitas Creative Management UK, 43 Great Ormond St, London WC1N 3HZ, United Kingdom, CEO: Toby Mundy
Foreign Rights: Agencia Riff (Laura & Joao Paulo Riff) (Brazil); AnatoliaLit Agency (Turkey); BookLab Literary Agency (Poland); English Agency Japan Co Ltd (Hamish Macaskill, nonfiction) (Japan); Ersilia Literary Agency (Greece); The Foreign Office (Portugal, Spain); The Grayhawk Agency (China, Southeast Asia, Taiwan); The Deborah Harris Agency (Israel); Agence Hoffman GmbH (Andrea Wildgruber) (Germany); Danny Hong Agency (South Korea); The Italian Literary Agency SRL (Italy); Simona Kessler International Copyright Agency Ltd (Romania); Agence Michelle Lapautre (France); Nova Littera Ltd (Konstantin Palchikov) (Russia); Prava i prevodi (Eastern Europe); Sebes & Bisseling Literary Agency (Netherlands, Scandinavia); Kalina Stefanova (Bulgaria); Tuttle-Mori Agency Co Ltd (Ken Mori, fiction) (Japan)

Agency Chicago (L-D)
7000 Phoenix Ave NE, Suite 202, Albuquerque, NM 87110

EDITORIAL SERVICES

E-mail: agency.chicago@usa.com
Key Personnel
Owner: Ernest Santucci
Assoc: Shelly Chou
Founded: 1988
Professional & cross-over writers. No unsol mss, query letter first; handle film, stage & TV rights; no reading fee. True crime & police procedural, historical fiction, humor, politics, Southwest & general wellness.

Agency for the Performing Arts Inc, see APA Talent & Literary Agency

AKA Literary Management (L-D)
11445 Dallas Rd, Peyton, CO 80831
Tel: 646-846-2478
E-mail: hello@akaliterary.com
Web Site: akalm.net
Key Personnel
Literary & Foreign Rts Agent: Terrie Wolf (AALA)
Full service agency representing works of nonfiction & fiction. Seeking traditional print & ebook formats, television & film rights. No unsol mss, query first. See web site submissions page for specifics on how & when to query.
Titles recently placed: *Rez Ball*, Byron Graves; *Standing Dead (8th in The Timber Creek K-9 Mysteries series)*, Margaret Mizushima
Membership(s): American Christian Fiction Writers (ACFW); International Thriller Writers Inc (ITW); Romance Writers of America (RWA); Sisters in Crime; Society of Children's Book Writers & Illustrators (SCBWI)

AKALM, see AKA Literary Management

Betsy Amster Literary Enterprises (L-D)
607 Foothill Blvd, No 1061, La Canada Flintridge, CA 91012
E-mail: rights@amsterlit.com; b.amster.assistant@gmail.com (book queries)
Web Site: amsterlit.com
Key Personnel
Pres: Betsy Amster (AALA)
Founded: 1992
Adult areas of interest: literary fiction, upscale commercial women's fiction, voice-driven mysteries & thrillers, narrative nonfiction (especially by journalists), travelogues, memoirs (including graphic memoirs), social issues & trends, psychology, self-help, popular culture, women's issues, history & biography, lifestyle, careers, health & medicine, parenting, cooking & nutrition, gardening & quirky gift books. Does not represent children's books, romances, screenplays, poetry, westerns, fantasy, horror, science fiction, techno thrillers, spy capers, apocalyptic scenarios, self-published books, or political or religious arguments. No unsol mss, query first to b.amster.assistant@gmail.com. For fiction or narrative nonfiction, embed first 3 pages of ms in body of e-mail. For other kinds of nonfiction, embed overview of proposal.
Foreign Rights: Big Apple Agency Inc (China); Donatella d'Ormesson (France); English Agency Japan Co Ltd (Japan); Japan UNI Agency Inc (Japan); Korea Copyright Center Inc (KCC) (MiSook Hong) (South Korea); Mohrbooks AG Literary Agency (Germany); Prava i prevodi (Baltic States, Bulgaria, Croatia, Czechia, Estonia, Greece, Hungary, Latvia, Lithuania, North Macedonia, Poland, Romania, Russia, Serbia, Slovakia, Slovenia, Turkey); Lennart Sane Agency AB (Philip Sane) (Brazil, Holland, Latin America, Portugal, Scandinavia, Spain); Vicki Satlow Literary Agency (Vicki Satlow) (Italy); Abner Stein Ltd (UK)
Membership(s): PEN Center USA

Anderson Literary Management LLC (L)
244 Fifth Ave, 2nd fl, Suite F166, New York, NY 10001
Tel: 212-645-6045 *Fax:* 212-741-1936
E-mail: info@andersonliterary.com
Web Site: www.andersonliterary.com
Key Personnel
Pres: Kathleen Anderson (AALA)
　E-mail: kathleen@andersonliterary.com
Represents quality fiction & nonfiction (adult, young adult & middle grade) for print, electronic, film & television.
Membership(s): PEN America

Andy Ross Literary Agency (L)
767 Santa Ray Ave, Oakland, CA 94610
Tel: 510-238-8965
E-mail: andyrossagency@hotmail.com
Web Site: www.andyrossagency.com
Key Personnel
Agent: Andy Ross
Founded: 2008
Specialize in narrative nonfiction, journalism, history, current events, literary, commercial & young adult fiction.
Queries: send by e-mail only including "query" in the title header. Letters should be kept to a half page. State the project category in the first sentence & provide a very brief description. Proposals: submit by e-mail only. See web site for additional query & proposal guidelines. No fees.
Titles recently placed: *Empire of Resentment: Populism's Toxic Embrace of Nationalism*, Lawrence Rosenthal; *Monopolized: Life in the Age of Corporate Power*, David Dayen; *The Drone Age: How Drone Technology Will Change War and Peace*, Michael Boyle; *The Woman in Black*, Erik Tarloff

APA Talent & Literary Agency (L-D)
405 S Beverly Dr, Beverly Hills, CA 90212
Tel: 310-888-4200
Web Site: www.apa-agency.com
Key Personnel
Owner: Lee Dinstman
SVP (Nashville): Steve Lassiter
Founded: 1962
Handle film & TV rights. No unsol mss; query first. Submit outline & sample chapters & SASE. No reading fee; 10% commission. Represent writers & producers.
Branch Office(s)
3060 Peachtree Rd NW, Suite 1480, Atlanta, GA 30305 *Tel:* 404-254-5876
135 W 50 St, 17th fl, New York, NY 10020 *Tel:* 212-205-4320
150 Fourth Ave N, Penthouse, Nashville, TN 37219 *Tel:* 615-297-0100
151 Yonge St, Suite 1100, Toronto, ON M5C 2W7, Canada *Tel:* 416-646-7373
Foreign Office(s): 222 Soho Sq, London W1D 4NS, United Kingdom *Tel:* (020) 3871 0520

Arcadia (L)
159 Lake Place S, Danbury, CT 06810-7261
Tel: 203-797-0993
E-mail: arcadialit@gmail.com
Key Personnel
Pres: Victoria Gould Pryor (AALA)
Founded: 1986
Not seeking new clients.
Foreign Rights: Bardon-Chinese Media Agency (China); Japan UNI Agency Inc (Japan); Barbara Levy Agency (UK); The Marsh Agency (translation)
Membership(s): The Authors Guild

Aurous Inc (L)
PO Box 20490, New York, NY 10017
Tel: 212-628-9729 *Fax:* 212-535-7861
Key Personnel
Pres: Kay McCauley *E-mail:* kaymcc25@aol.com
Busn Mgr: Christopher Shepard
Agent: Kirby McCauley
Founded: 1974
Adult fiction & nonfiction. Motion picture & TV rights from book properties only. No unsol mss. Projects by referral only. No reading fee. Agents in all principal foreign countries.
Foreign Rights: ZENO Agency

The Axelrod Agency (L)
55 Main St, Chatham, NY 12037
Mailing Address: PO Box 357, Chatham, NY 12037
Tel: 518-392-2100
Key Personnel
Pres: Steven Axelrod (AALA) *E-mail:* steve@axelrodagency.com
Foreign Rts Dir: Lori Antonson *E-mail:* lori@axelrodagency.com
Founded: 1983
Fiction & nonfiction, film & TV rights. No unsol mss, query first. No reading fee. E-mail queries receive attention first.

Elizabeth H Backman (L)
86 Johnnycake Hollow Rd, Pine Plains, NY 12567
Mailing Address: PO Box 762, Pine Plains, NY 12567-0762
Tel: 518-398-9344
E-mail: bethcountry@gmail.com
Key Personnel
Ad Serv: Donn King Potter
Founded: 1981
Literary & commercial fiction; nonfiction; current events, politics, business, biography, the arts, cooking, diet, health, sports, gardening, history, science, self-help & psychology; audio & video cassettes. Author representatives, consulting editors, advertising & promotion copywriters. No unsol mss, query first with SASE; submit introduction, cover letter, chapter by chapter outline or table of contents, 3 sample chapters & author's bio or complete ms with cover letter & author's bio. Reading fees: $100 for proposals, $500 for complete mss; 15% agency fee plus expenses (phone, mail, photocopying, etc). Handle film & TV rights.
Foreign Rights: Lennart Sane Agency AB (Netherlands, Portugal, Scandinavia, Spain); Thomas Schlueck GmbH (Germany); Tuttle-Mori Agency Inc (Japan)

Malaga Baldi Literary Agency (L-D)
233 W 99, Suite 19C, New York, NY 10025
Tel: 212-222-3213
E-mail: baldibooks@gmail.com
Web Site: www.baldibooks.com
Key Personnel
Pres: Malaga Baldi
Founded: 1986
The agency considers cultural history, hybrid nonfiction, narrative, biography, memoir & literary-edgy-voicey fiction. Query via e-mail.
Titles recently placed: *Adult Human Male*, Oliver Radclyffe; *Audrey Hepburn: 63 Scenes in 63 dresses*, Tom Santopietro; *Bing & Billie & Frank & Ella & Judy & Barbra: The Great American Songbook*, Dan Callahan; *Frighten the Horses*, Oliver Radclyffe; *Furry Planet: A World Gone Wild*, Joe Strike; *Liberty Street: A Savannah Family, Its Golden Boy & the Civil War*, Jason Friedman; *Messy Real: Field Notes from the Anthropocene, A Lyrical Collection of Essays on the Wilderness of Climate Science, Politics & Motherhood*, Anna Henderson; *Shelter from the Storm: How Climate Change is Creating a New Era of Migration*, Julian Hatten; *The Black Woods: The Lost History, Embattled Memory, and Stubborn Legacy of Black Farmers in the Adirondacks Before the Civil War*, Amy Godine; *Yes I Can Say That: When They Come for the Comedians We're All in Trouble*, Judy Gold
Foreign Rep(s): Abner Stein (UK)
Foreign Rights: Eliane Benisti (France); Marsh Agency (Europe); Owls Agency Inc (Japan)

A Richard Barber & Associates (L)
80 N Main St, Kent, CT 06757
Mailing Address: PO Box 887, Kent, CT 06757-0887
Tel: 860-927-4911; 212-737-7266 (cell) *Fax:* 860-927-3942
E-mail: barberrich@aol.com
Key Personnel
Pres: A Richard Barber
Handle software, film & TV rights. Specialize in fiction & nonfiction. No fees. No unsol mss, query first by mail (include SASE). No fax or e-mail submissions.

Baror International Inc (L)
PO Box 868, Armonk, NY 10504-0868
Tel: 914-273-9199 *Fax:* 914-273-5058
Web Site: www.barorint.com
Key Personnel
Pres: Danny Baror *E-mail:* danny@barorint.com
Literary Agent: Heather Baror-Shapiro
　E-mail: heather@barorint.com
Specialize in international & domestic representation of literary works in both fiction & nonfiction ranging in genre including commercial fiction, literary titles, science fiction, fantasy, young adult & more. No unsol mss.

Loretta Barrett Books, Inc (L)
Brooklyn, NY 11231
Tel: 212-242-3420
E-mail: lbbagencymail@gmail.com
Web Site: www.lorettabarrettbooks.com
Key Personnel
Mng Partner: Nick Mullendore
Founded: 1990
Agency no longer accepts queries or submissions.
Foreign Rights: Akcali Copyright Agency (Turkey); Eliane Benisti Agency (France); Berla & Griffini Rights Agency (Italy); Capel & Land Ltd (Australia, UK); Andrew Nurnberg Associates International Ltd (Mainland China, Taiwan); Prava i prevodi (Baltic States, Czechia, Eastern Europe, Slovakia, Ukraine); Lennart Sane Agency AB (Scandinavia); Thomas Schlueck GmbH (Germany); Synopsis Literary Agency (Russia); Tuttle-Mori Agency Inc (Japan); Eric Yang Agency (South Korea)

Meredith Bernstein Literary Agency Inc (L)
2095 Broadway, Suite 505, New York, NY 10023
Tel: 212-799-1007 *Fax:* 212-799-1145
E-mail: MGoodBern@aol.com
Web Site: www.meredithbernsteinliteraryagency.com
Key Personnel
Agent: Meredith Bernstein (AALA)
Adult fiction (commercial & literary) & nonfiction; memoirs, current events, biography, health & fitness, women's issues, mysteries & special projects; crafts & creative endeavors. No poetry or screenplays. No unsol mss, query first online (no attachments) or by mail (include SASE). For fiction, submit a 1-page query letter; nonfiction send 1-page query letter, table of contents & information on why you are an expert in this field. Handle film & TV rights only for books represented. Representatives in foreign countries & on the West Coast. No reading fee.
Membership(s): The Authors Guild; Sisters in Crime; Women's Media Group

Vicky Bijur Literary Agency (L)
333 West End Ave, No 5B, New York, NY 10023

LITERARY AGENTS

Tel: 212-580-4108
E-mail: queries@vickybijuragency.com
Web Site: www.vickybijuragency.com
Key Personnel
Agent: Vicky Bijur (AALA)
Founded: 1988
Adult fiction & nonfiction. No poetry, science fiction, fantasy or horror. No unsol mss. Fiction: query first; paste first chapter in body of e-mail. Nonfiction: query first. No phone queries. We respond only to queries sent via e-mail. No reading fee. Agents in all principal foreign countries. Handle film & TV rights.
Titles recently placed: *Difficult Lives, Hitching Rides*, James Sallis; *Every Cocktail Has a Twist*, Carey Jones, John McCarthy; *Prom Mom*, Laura Lippman; *The Cartoon Guide to Geometry*, Larry Gonick; *The Mistress of Bhatia House*, Sujata Massey; *The Wok*, Kenji Lopez-Alt; *What Harms You*, Lisa Black
Foreign Rights: AnatoliaLit Agency (Turkey); Casanovas & Lynch (Central America, Latin America, Portugal, Portuguese-speaking countries, South America, Spain); English Agency Japan Co Ltd (Japan); The Grayhawk Agency (China, Taiwan); The Deborah Harris Agency (Israel); The Italian Literary Agency Srl (Italy); Agence Michelle Lapautre (France); Liepman Agency AG (Germany); Maxima Creative Agency (Indonesia); Prava i prevodi (Bulgaria, Czechia, Estonia, Greece, Hungary, Poland, Russia, Serbia, Slovakia); Sebes & Bisseling Literary Agency (Denmark, Finland, Holland, Netherlands, Norway, Scandinavia, Sweden); Abner Stein Agency (Australia, England); Tuttle-Mori Agency Inc (Thailand); Eric Yang Agency (South Korea)
Membership(s): The Authors Guild; Mystery Writers of America (MWA)

David Black Agency (L-D)
Subsidiary of Black Inc
335 Adams St, 27th fl, Suite 2707, Brooklyn, NY 11201
Tel: 718-852-5500 Fax: 718-852-5539
Web Site: www.davidblackagency.com
Key Personnel
Pres: David Black (AALA) E-mail: dblack@dblackagency.com
Agent: Rica Allannic E-mail: rallannic@dblackagency.com; Jennifer Herrera E-mail: jherrera@dblackagency.com; Deborah Hofmann; Gary Morris Tel: 718-852-5518 E-mail: gmorris@dblackagency.com; Susan Raihofer Tel: 718-852-5542 E-mail: sraihofer@dblackagency.com; Sarah Smith E-mail: ssmith@dblackagency.com; Mark Tavani E-mail: mtavani@dblackagency.com; Joy Tutela (AALA) Tel: 718-852-5533 E-mail: jtutela@dblackagency.com
Founded: 1990
Literary & commercial fiction & nonfiction, especially sports, politics, business, health, fitness, romance, parenting, psychology & social issues. No poetry. No unsol mss, query first with SASE. No reading fee. Agents in all principal foreign countries. Handle film & TV rights. No mysteries or thrillers.
Foreign Rights: Bardon-Chinese Media Agency (Ming-Ming Liu) (China); Eliane Benisti Agent Litteraire (Eliane Benisti & Noemi Rollet) (France); The Deborah Harris Agency (Efrat Lev) (Israel); International Editors' Co - Yanez Agencia Literaria (Latin America, Spain); The Italian Literary Agency Srl (Italy); Katai & Bolza Literary Agents (Peter Bolza) (Hungary); Maxima Creative Agency (Santo Manurung) (Indonesia); Mohrbooks AG Literary Agency (Sabine Ibach, Bettina Kaufmann, Sebastian Ritscher & Cristina Uytiepo) (Germany); Prava i prevodi (Milena Lukic, Ana Milenkovic & Jelena Todosijevic) (Bulgaria, Croatia, Czechia, Estonia, Greece, Latvia, Lithuania, Poland, Russia, Serbia, Slovenia); Agencia Riff (JP, Laura & Lucia Riff) (Brazil, Portugal); Sebes & Bisseling Literary Agency (Paul Sebes) (Netherlands); Abner Stein Agency (Caspian Dennis) (Australia, UK); Tuttle-Mori Agency Inc (Japan, Thailand); Eric Yang Agency (Sue Yang) (South Korea)

Reid Boates Literary Agency (L-D)
69 Cooks Crossroad, Pittstown, NJ 08867-0328
Mailing Address: PO Box 328, Pittstown, NJ 08867-0328
Tel: 908-797-8087
E-mail: reid.boates@gmail.com
Key Personnel
Sole Prop: Reid Boates
Founded: 1985
Narrative +/or how-to nonfiction, health, spirituality, wellness, business & sports. Handle film & TV rights. No fiction. Most new clients by referral. No reading fee. Agents in all major foreign markets. No unsol mss, submit written query with SASE.
Titles recently placed: *A Year Without Mary*, Coleman Barks; *Mindfulness*, Joseph Goldstein; *The Illuminated Hafiz*, Michael Green
Foreign Rep(s): Eliane Benisti (France); Raquel de la Concha (Spain); EYA (South Korea); Michael Meller (Eastern Europe, Germany, UK); Owl's Agency (Japan) Ltd (Japan)

Bond Literary Agency (L)
201 Milwaukee St, Suite 200, Denver, CO 80206
Tel: 303-781-9305
Web Site: bondliteraryagency.com
Key Personnel
Owner & Agent: Sandra Bond E-mail: sandra@bondliteraryagency.com
Agent: Becky LeJeune E-mail: becky@bondliteraryagency.com
Founded: 1998
Sandra represents adult literary & commercial fiction including mystery/crime fiction & women's fiction (not romance); young adult fiction; narrative nonfiction, science for a general audience, business. Nonfiction authors must have excellent credentials & a strong platform. No memoir, children's picture books, poetry, or screenplays. Becky represents adult & young adult horror, fantasy, science fiction, general fiction & cookbooks. Send query to the appropriate agent using querymanager.com, not agents' e-mails. Please check the web site to learn more about the agents, as they are sometimes closed to queries. Please do not send queries by snail mail. No phone calls, please. Full mss submissions by request only. BLA sells foreign & film/TV rights through sub-agents. No fees charged.
Titles recently placed: *ASTROLIT*, Rachel Feder, McCormick Templeman; *BORED NO MORE!: The ABCs of What to Do When There's Nothing to Do*, Julie Reiters; *DAISY: Poems*, Rachel Feder; *DRACULA: Introduction and Annotations*, Rachel Feder; *GO AS A RIVER, a Novel*, Shelley Read; *LOST IN A PLACE SO SMALL, a Novel*, Rick Collignan; *OF STARLIGHT AND BONE (1st in The Lost Colony Trilogy)*, Emily Layne; *THE DARCY MYTH: How Love Became a Scary Story, and What to Do About It*, Rachel Feder; *THE KNAVE OF SECRETS*, Alex Livingston; *TRUST THE HOURS*, Shelley Read; *UNSOLVED MYSTERIES OF TEXAS*, W C Jameson
Foreign Rights: Kleinworks Agency (Judy Klein) (worldwide exc USA)

The Book Group (TBG) (L)
20 W 20 St, Suite 601, New York, NY 10011
E-mail: info@thebookgroup.com; submissions@thebookgroup.com
Web Site: www.thebookgroup.com

EDITORIAL SERVICES

Key Personnel
Partner & Agent: Julie Barer; Faye Bender; Brettne Bloom; Elisabeth Weed
Sr Agent: Brenda Bowen; Jamie Carr
Agent & Dir, Strategy & Busn Devt: Caitlin O'Shaughnessy
Agent: Nicole Cunningham
Assoc Agent: Sophie Cudd
Founded: 2015
No unsol mss, query first via e-mail to submissions@thebookgroup.com. Send query & 10 sample pages (no attachments). Represents a broad range of fiction & nonfiction. No theatrical work or screenplays.
Titles recently placed: *All the World Beside*, Garrard Conley; *Goodnight Night Sweats: A Parody for the Menopausal (and Their Perimenopausal Friends)*, Haut Flasch, Mina Pauze (illus); *Listen for the Lie*, Amy Tintera; *Take Two, Birdie Maxwell*, Allison Winn Scotch; *The Great Divide*, Christina Henriquez; *The Werewolf at Dusk and Other Stories*, David Small
Foreign Rights: Ia Atterholm (Scandinavia); The English Agency (Japan); Lora Fountain Agency (Brazil, France, Holland, Italy, Portugal, Spain, UK); Grayhawk Agency (China, Southeast Asia); Danny Hong Agency (South Korea); KCC (South Korea); Jenny Meyer Literary Agency (worldwide exc Asia); Mohrbooks (Germany); Prava i prevodi (Eastern Europe); Abner Stein Ltd (Caspian Dennis) (UK); TBP Agency (Israel)

Bookcase Literary Agency (L-D)
5062 Lankershim Blvd, PMB 3046, North Hollywood, CA 91601
Web Site: www.bookcaseagency.com
Key Personnel
Founder, CEO & Agent: Flavia Viotti E-mail: flavia@bookcaseagency.com
Dir, Subs Rts: Meire Dias E-mail: meire@bookcaseagency.com
Client Rel Mgr: Luci Scolari
Represents authors in many areas of publishing, including traditional domestic literary representation as well as foreign rights, audio, film & television. No unsol mss currently; see web site for updated submission acceptance status.
Titles recently placed: *Weatherstone College Series*, Jaymin Eve
Foreign Rights: Bears Factor Agency (Gana Galal) (Arab Middle East); The Book Publishers Association of Israel (Israel); Book/lab (Piotr Wawrzenczyk) (Poland); Corto Literary (Andrea Spuzevic Golemac) (Bosnia and Herzegovina, Bulgaria, Croatia, Czechia, Montenegro, North Macedonia, Serbia, Slovakia, Slovenia); Eastern European & Asian Rights Agency (Tatjana Zoldnere) (Armenia, Azerbaijan, Estonia, Georgia, Latvia, Lithuania, Ukraine); The Grayhawk Agency (Clare Chi) (China, Taiwan); The Grayhawk Agency (Sherri Cheng) (Indonesia, Thailand, Vietnam); Japan UNI Agency (Miko Yamanouchi) (Japan); Nurciham Kesim Literary Agency (Filiz Karaman) (Turkey); Andrew Nurnberg Russia (Anastasia Falcon) (Russia); Read n Right Agency (Nike Davarinou) (Greece); Marianne Schoenbach Agency (Diana Gvozden) (Denmark, Finland, Iceland, Netherlands, Norway, Sweden); Shinwon Agency (Tae Eun Kim) (South Korea)

BookEnds Literary Agency (L)
136 Long Hill Rd, Gillette, NJ 07933
Web Site: www.bookendsliterary.com
Key Personnel
Pres & Literary Agent: Jessica H Faust (AALA) E-mail: jfaust@bookendsliterary.com
Sr Literary Agent: Rachel Brooks E-mail: rbrooks@bookendsliterary.com; Naomi Davis E-mail: ndavis@bookendsliterary.com;

Kim Lionetti (AALA) *E-mail:* klsubmissions@bookendsliterary.com; Moe Ferrara *E-mail:* mferrara@bookendsliterary.com
Sr Literary Agent & Foreign Rts Dir: Jessica Alvarez (AALA) *E-mail:* jalvarez@bookendsliterary.com
Sr Literary Agent, Book Ends Jr: Tracy Marchini *E-mail:* tmsubmissions@bookendsliterary.com
Literary Agent: Emily Forney *E-mail:* eforney@bookendsliterary.com; Amanda Jain *E-mail:* ajain@bookendsliterary.com; James McGowan *E-mail:* jmcgowan@bookendsliterary.com
Assoc Agent & Subs Rts Mgr: Jenissa Graham
Assoc Literary Agent: Ramona Pina
Founded: 1999
Represents fiction & nonfiction in all genres for adults & children alike. Mission is to advocate for authors while helping them achieve their dreams.
All queries should be made through Query Manager.
Titles recently placed: *A Game of Cones*, Abby Collette; *Accidentally Engaged*, Farah Heron; *Fox and the Box*, Yvonne Ivinson; *Goodbye, Mr Spalding*, Jennifer Robin Barr; *Killer Content*, Olivia Blacke; *Line of Sight*, James Queally; *Only Mostly Devastated*, Sophie Gonzales; *People You Follow*, Hayley Gene Penner; *Refraction*, Naomi Hughes; *Relative Fortunes*, Marlowe Benn; *Sealand: The Astonishing True Story of the World's Foremost Micronation and the Family Who Founded It*, Dylan Taylor-Lehman; *Take It Back*, Kia Abdullah; *The Boy Toy*, Nicola Marsh; *The Bride Test*, Helen Hoang; *The Creator Mindset*, Nir Bashan; *The Key to Happily Ever After*, Tif Marcelo; *The Obsidian Tower*, Melissa Caruso; *The October Girl*, Matthew Dow Smith; *The Secret, Book & Scone Society (4th & 5th in series)*, Ellery Adams; *The Shadows Between Us*, Tricia Levenseller; *The Sky Blues*, Robbie Couch; *Three Dads and a Baby*, Ian Jenkins, MD; *Too Sticky*, Jen Malia; *Truth Be Told*, Kia Abdullah
Foreign Rep(s): Gabriella Ambrosioni Literary Agency (Italy); BookLab Literary Agency (Poland); Corto Literary (Bosnia and Herzegovina, Bulgaria, Croatia, Hungary, Montenegro, North Macedonia, Romania, Serbia); English Agency Japan Co Ltd (Japan); Deborah Harris Agency (Israel); International Editors' Co - Yanez Agencia Literaria (Latin America, Portugal, Spain); Agence Michelle Lapautre (France); Literary Sapiens (Arabic language); Michael Meller Agency (Germany); Nova Littera Literary Agency (Russia); Andrew Nurnberg (Indonesia, Mongolia, Slovakia, Slovenia, Thailand); Andrew Nurnberg Beijing (China); ONK Agency (Turkey); Read n Right Agency (Greece); Agencia Riff (Brazil); Marianne Schonbach Literary (Finland, Netherlands, Norway, Sweden); Tuttle-Mori Agency (Japan)
Membership(s): International Thriller Writers Inc (ITW); Mystery Writers of America (MWA); Science Fiction and Fantasy Writers of America, Inc (SFWA); Society of Children's Book Writers & Illustrators (SCBWI)

Bookmark Literary (L)
189 Berdan Ave, No 101, Wayne, NJ 07470
E-mail: bookmarkliterary@gmail.com
Web Site: bookmarkliterary.com
Key Personnel
Agent: Teresa Kietlinski *E-mail:* teresa@bookmarkliterary.com
Founded: 2016
Specialize in illustrated books for children ages 12 & under. No unsol mss; submissions by referral only. Open to submissions from illustrators (email link to portfolio). No sci-fi/fantasy, romance or self-published projects.
Titles recently placed: *Building Block Books: My First Town*, Merrill Rainey; *Goodbye, Hello*, Angela H Dale, Daniel Wiseman (illus); *The Dark Is For*, Jane Kohuth, Cindy Derby (illus); *Why Did the Chicken Cross the Road*, Brianna Caplan Sayres, Mark Fearing (illus)

Books & Such (L)
2222 Cleveland Ave, No 1005, Santa Rosa, CA 95403
Tel: 707-538-4184
Web Site: booksandsuch.com
Key Personnel
Founder & Pres: Janet Kobobel Grant *E-mail:* janet@booksandsuch.com
VP: Wendy Lawton *E-mail:* wendy@booksandsuch.com
Sr Literary Agent: Cynthia Ruchti *E-mail:* cynthia@booksandsuch.com
Literary Agent: Barb Roose *E-mail:* barb@booksandsuch.com
Literary Agent, Nonfiction: Debbie Alsdorf *E-mail:* debbie@booksandsuch.com
Literary Agent, Teens, Twenties & Thirties: Rachel Kent *E-mail:* rachel@booksandsuch.com
Assoc Literary Agent: Jen Babakhan
Founded: 1996
Handles fiction & nonfiction. Submission by e-mail (no attachments). No phone calls. No unsol mss, query first. No fees.
Titles recently placed: *A Pocketful of Wonder*, Amanda Dykes; *Boy Mom on a Mission*, Molly DeFrank; *Rutabaga Series*, Lauraine Snelling, Kiersti Gieron; *Spirit of Christmas*, Cynthia Ruchti; *Tea with Elephants*, Robin Jones Gunn; *Torn and Dog-Eared*, Robin W Pearson; *Two-Minute Timeouts for Moms*, Andrea Fortenberry; *Untriggered*, Amber Lia
Branch Office(s)
PO Box 1227, Hilmar, CA 95324-1227 *Tel:* 209-634-1913
Membership(s): Advanced Writers & Speakers Association (AWSA); American Christian Fiction Writers (ACFW); The Authors Guild; Romance Writers of America (RWA)

BookStop Literary Agency LLC (L)
67 Meadow View Rd, Orinda, CA 94563
E-mail: info@bookstopliterary.com
Web Site: www.bookstopliterary.com
Key Personnel
Pres & CEO: Kendra Marcus
Literary Agent: Ms Minju Chang
Founded: 1984
Represents authors & illustrators of fiction & nonfiction for children & young adults. Please look at agent bios on the web site before submitting via Query Manager. No reading fee.
Titles recently placed: *A House for Every Bird*, Megan Maynor; *Field Trip to the Moon*, John Hare; *Go With the Flow*, Lily Williams, Karen Schneemann; *Mananaland*, Pam Munoz Ryan; *Soaked!*, Abi Cushman; *Vial of Tears*, Cristin Bishara

Georges Borchardt Inc (L-D)
136 E 57 St, New York, NY 10022
Tel: 212-753-5785
E-mail: georges@gbagency.com
Web Site: www.gbagency.com
Key Personnel
Founder: Georges Borchardt (AALA); Anne Borchardt (AALA)
Pres & Foreign Rts Dir: Valerie Borchardt (AALA) *E-mail:* valerie@gbagency.com
Agent: Samantha Shea (AALA) *E-mail:* samantha@gbagency.com
Asst: Cora Markowitz *E-mail:* cora@gbagency.com
Foreign Rts Asst: Cassie Gross *E-mail:* cassie@gbagency.com
Founded: 1967
Fiction & nonfiction. No unsol mss; handle film & TV rights & software. No fees charged.
Titles recently placed: *A Friendship in Twilight*, Jack Miles; *Animal Truth*, Sharona Muir; *Big Red*, Jerome Charyn; *Gone Like Yesterday*, Janelle Williams; *Hedge*, Jane Delury; *I Dream America*, Novuyo Tshuma; *Justine Champine*; *La Vengeance M'Appartient*, Marie Ndiaye; *Lessons*, Ian McEwan; *Moby Dyke*, Krista Burton; *Moving Water*, Dylan Tomine; *Nervous*, Jen Soriano; *Principles and Practices of Yoga*, Timothy McCall; *Six Minute Memoir*, Mary Helen Stefaniak; *Soil*, Camille Dungy; *Superhumanities*, Jeffrey Kripal; *The Bandit Queen*, Parini Shroff; *Thirst for Salt*, Madelaine Lucas; *Weimar in Princeton*, Stanley Corngold; *Woolfs in the World*, Donna Rifkind
Foreign Rights: Agencia Literaria Carmen Balcells (Maribel Luque) (Spain); Bardon-Chinese Media Agency (Ming-Ming Lui) (Chinese); Tassy Barham Associates (Brazil); English Agency Japan Co Ltd (Junzo Sawa) (Japanese); Graal Literary Agency (Marcin Biegaj) (Polish); Deborah Harris Agency (Efrat Lev) (Israel); The Italian Literary Agency Srl; Japan UNI Agency (Miko Yamanouchi) (Japanese); JLM Literary Agency (Nelly & John Moukakos) (Greek); Asli Karasuil Literary Agency (Turkish); Katai & Bolza (Peter Bolza) (Hungarian); Korea Copyright Center Inc (KCC) (Misook Hong) (Korean); Agence Michelle Lapautre (Catherine Lapautre) (France); Mohrbooks AG Literary Agency (Sebastian Ritscher) (German); Andrew Nurnberg Associates (Kristine Shatrovska) (Baltic States); Andrew Nurnberg Associates (Anna Droumeva) (Bulgarian & Romanian); Andrew Nurnberg Associates (Ludmilla Sushkova) (Russian); Kristin Olson Literary Agency sro (Kristin Olson) (Czech); RDC Agencia Literaria (Raquel de la Concha) (Portuguese) (Portugal); Marianne Schoenbach Literary Agency BV (Marianne Schoenbach) (Dutch); Sheil Land Associates (Vivien Green) (British); Abner Stein (Caspian Dennis) (UK); Ulf Toregard Agency AB (Ulf Toregard) (Scandinavia); Tuttle-Mori Agency Inc (Asako Kawachi) (Japanese)

Bradford Literary Agency (L)
5694 Mission Center Rd, Suite 347, San Diego, CA 92108
Tel: 619-521-1201
E-mail: hillary@bradfordlit.com
Web Site: www.bradfordlit.com
Key Personnel
Agent: Laura Bradford (AALA) *E-mail:* laura@bradfordlit.com; Hannah Andrade *E-mail:* hannah@bradfordlit.com; Rebecca Matte *E-mail:* rebecca@bradfordlit.com; Kaitlyn Sanchez
Founded: 2001
A boutique agency offering a full range of representation services to authors, both published & pre-published. We are an editorial-focused agency & prefer to work closely with our authors in helping to build strong, sustainable careers. We believe the best author-agent relationships extend beyond making sales. In order to best serve our client's needs, we must also be a partner, advisor, careful listener, troubleshooter & advocate.
We are currently acquiring fiction: romance (historical, romantic suspense, paranormal, category, contemporary, erotic), urban fantasy, women's fiction (contemporary, upmarket, literary), mystery, thrillers, young adult, middle grade, chapter books & graphic novels. Also nonfiction: business, relationships, biography/memoir, self-help, parenting, narrative humor, pop culture, illustrated/graphic design, food & cooking, history & social issues. We are not currently acquiring: poetry, screenplays, short stories, westerns, horror, New Age, religion, crafts.

LITERARY AGENTS

We accept unsol mss. Queries are accepted by QueryManager only (links provided on our web site). No fees.
Titles recently placed: *6 Minute Meals*, Karen Nochimowski; *Circling Back to You*, Julie Tieu; *Cruzita and the Mariacheros*, Ashley Granillo; *Grumbones*, Jenn Bennett; *Hola, Lola*, Keke Novales; *How You Grow Wings*, Rimma Onoseta; *Jasmine Zumideh Needs a Win*, Susan Azim Boyer; *Love in a Time of Serial Killers*, Alicia Thompson; *Marlowe Banks, Redesigned*, Jacqueline Firkins; *Marya Khan and the Henna Party*, Saadia Faruqi; *Maybe a Whale*, Kristin Pendreigh; *Modern Caravan*, Kate Oliver; *Moorewood Family Rules*, HelenKay Dimon; *No One Knows Us Here*, Rebecca Kelley; *Radiant Sin*, Katee Robert; *Secret Midwife*, Soraya Lane; *Secretly Yours*, Tessa Bailey; *Sleepy Happy Capy Cuddles*, Mike Allegra; *Taste of Magic*, J Elle; *The Duke Gets Even*, Joanna Shupe; *The Loophole*, Naz Kutub; *This Is Not a Personal Statement*, Tracy Badua; *To Have and to Heist*, Sara Desai; *Turning Red*, Lily Quan; *Vampires of El Norte*, Isabel Canas; *Weight of Blood*, Tiffany Jackson; *Wicked Remain*, Laura Pohl; *Yusuf Azeem is Not a Hero*, Saadia Faruqi
Foreign Rights: Taryn Fagerness Agency (Taryn Fagerness) (Albania, Argentina, Australia, Brazil, Bulgaria, Canada, China, Croatia, Czechia, Denmark, Estonia, Finland, France, Germany, Greece, Hungary, Iceland, India, Indonesia, Israel, Italy, Japan, Latvia, Lithuania, Mexico, Netherlands, Norway, Poland, Portugal, Romania, Russia, Serbia, Slovakia, South Korea, Spain, Sweden, Taiwan, Thailand, Turkey, Ukraine, UK, Vietnam)
Membership(s): The American Library Association (ALA); Romance Writers of America (RWA); Society of Children's Book Writers & Illustrators (SCBWI)

Brandt & Hochman Literary Agents Inc (L)
1501 Broadway, Suite 2310, New York, NY 10036
Tel: 212-840-5760 *Fax:* 212-840-5776
Web Site: brandthochman.com
Key Personnel
Pres: Gail Hochman (AALA)
 E-mail: ghochman@bromasite.com
Sr Agent: Mitchell Waters (AALA)
Agent & Foreign Rts: Marianne Merola (AALA)
 E-mail: mmerola@bromasite.com
Agent: Emily Forland (AALA)
 E-mail: eforland@bromasite.com; Emma Patterson (AALA) *E-mail:* epatterson@bromasite.com; Jody Kahn (AALA) *E-mail:* jkahn@bromasite.com; Henry Thayer (AALA)
 E-mail: hthayer@bromasite.com
Audio Rts & Perms Contact: Lina Granada (AALA) *E-mail:* lgranada@bromasite.com
Represents fiction & nonfiction, including literary, mystery/thriller, memoir, narrative nonfiction, journalism, history, current affairs, health, science, pop culture, lifestyle, art history & children's books. No screenplays or textbooks. No unsol mss, query first by e-mail or regular mail. Responses to e-mailed queries not guaranteed. Queries limited to 2 pages. Include SASE if sending by regular mail. See web site for specific submission preferences for each agent. No reading fee. Fee charged for making copies & book/galley purchases. Co-agents in most foreign countries.

Barbara Braun Associates Inc (L)
7 E 14 St, Suite 19F, New York, NY 10003
Tel: 917-414-3022
Web Site: www.barbarabraunagency.com
Key Personnel
Pres: Barbara Braun (AALA) *E-mail:* barbara@barbarabraunagency.com
Assoc: John F Baker

Founded: 1994
Represents both literary & commercial fiction as well as serious nonfiction, including memoir, biography, cultural history, women's issues, pop culture, art & architecture. Fiction is strong on stories for women, art-related fiction, historical & multicultural stories & mysteries & thrillers. Interested in narrative nonfiction & current affairs. No unsol mss, query by referral only, by e-mail to bbasubmissions@gmail.com. Include brief summary of book, word count, genre, any relevant publishing experience & first 5 pages of ms pasted into the body of the e-mail. No reading or other fees.
Foreign Rights: Jean V Naggar Literary Agency (Jennifer Weltz) (worldwide)
Membership(s): The Authors Guild; PEN America

Brockman Inc (L)
260 Fifth Ave, 10th fl, New York, NY 10001
Tel: 212-935-8900
E-mail: rights@brockman.com
Web Site: www.brockman.com
Key Personnel
Chmn: John Brockman
CEO: Max Brockman
Pres: Katinka Matson
VP: Russell Weinberger
Proj Coord: Anna Llewellyn
Literary & software agency. No unsol mss. Deal direct in all foreign markets. No fees charged.

Brower Literary & Management Inc (L)
13720 Old St Augustine Rd, Suite 8-512, Jacksonville, FL 32258
Tel: 646-854-6073
E-mail: admin@browerliterary.com; foreign@browerliterary.com (foreign publr inquiries); queries@browerliterary.com; subrights@browerliterary.com (busn inquiries)
Web Site: browerliterary.com
Key Personnel
Pres & Sr Literary Agent: Kimberly Brower
 E-mail: kimberly@browerliterary.com
Edit Dir & Agency Opers Mgr: Aimee Ashcraft
 E-mail: aimee@browerliterary.com
Client Rel & Royalties Mgr: Joy Kozu
 E-mail: joy@browerliterary.com
Foreign Rts Agent & Royalties Mgr: Anna Atoria
 E-mail: anna@browerliterary.com
Foreign Rts Agent: Victoria Hendersen
 E-mail: victoria@browerliterary.com
Fully-remote full-scale literary & management agency. Two separate divisions - Literary Representation & Subrights Management. No queries accepted via mail, phone or social media. Send via e-mail only, including query letter, full synopsis & first chapter (no attachments). No nonfiction, political/military/legal thrillers, children's/middle grade, picture books/graphic novels, westerns, or spiritual/religious.
Titles recently placed: *Archer's Voice*, Mia Sheridan; *From the Embers*, Ally Martinez; *The Graham Effect*, Elle Kennedy
Foreign Rights: Anthea Agency (Albania, Bulgaria, North Macedonia); Book/Lab (Poland); Corto Literary Agency (Bosnia and Herzegovina, Czechia, Montenegro, North Macedonia, Romania, Serbia, Slovakia, Slovenia); Donzelli Fietta Agency (Italy); The Israeli Association of Book Publishers (Israel); Japan UNI Agency (Japan); Nurcihan Kesim Agency (Turkey); Andrew Nurnberg Agency Baltic (Baltic States); Andrew Nurnberg Associates (Croatia, Hungary, Russia); Sebes & Bisseling Literary Agency (Netherlands, Scandinavia); Eric Yang Literary Agency (South Korea)

Curtis Brown, Ltd (L-D)
228 E 45 St, Suite 310, New York, NY 10017

EDITORIAL SERVICES

Tel: 212-473-5400 *Fax:* 212-598-0917
E-mail: info@cbltd.com
Web Site: www.curtisbrown.com
Key Personnel
CEO: Timothy F Knowlton (AALA)
Pres: Peter L Ginsberg (AALA)
EVP & Book Agent: Ginger Knowlton (AALA)
VP & Book Agent: Katherine Fausset (AALA); Elizabeth Harding (AALA); Jonathan Lyons (AALA); Laura Blake Peterson (AALA)
VP & Film/TV Rts: Holly Frederick (AALA)
Dir, Foreign Rts: Karin Schulze (AALA)
Book Agent: Kerry D'Agostino (AALA); Katie Grimm (AALA)
Assoc Agent: James Farrell (AALA); Alexandra Franklin (AALA); Jazmia Young (AALA)
Founded: 1914
Handle general trade fiction & nonfiction, adult & juvenile. No unsol mss, query first with SASE. Submit outline or sample chapters. Please refer to Agents page on web site for specific submission policies per agent. Agents do not reply to queries unless interested. No reading fee. Other fees charged (for photocopies, express mail, etc). Handle film & TV rights & merchandising & multimedia. No playwrights. Representatives in all major foreign countries.

Marie Brown Associates (L)
412 W 154 St, New York, NY 10032
Tel: 212-939-9725
E-mail: mbrownlit@gmail.com
Key Personnel
Owner & Pres: Marie D Brown
Founded: 1984
Adult & juvenile fiction & nonfiction. Handle film & TV rights through representatives. No unsol mss, query first; submit outline & sample chapters or full ms on request, 12 point, double-spaced, 1-sided only, typed, white paper & unbound. Include SASE. E-mail queries accepted. No reading fee.

Browne & Miller Literary Associates (L)
52 Village Place, Hinsdale, IL 60521
Tel: 312-922-3063
E-mail: mail@browneandmiller.com
Web Site: www.browneandmiller.com
Key Personnel
Pres: Danielle Egan-Miller (AALA)
 E-mail: danielle@browneandmiller.com
Founded: 1971
General adult trade fiction & nonfiction. No horror, sci-fi, young adult or children's books. No unsol mss, query first by e-mail. No reading fee.
Foreign Rep(s): Big Apple Agency Inc (China, Taiwan); Book Publishers Association of Israel (Israel); English Agency Japan Co Ltd (Japan); International Copyright Agency Ltd (Simona Kessler) (Romania); International Editors' Co - Yanez Agencia Literaria (Latin America, Portugal, Spain); Japan UNI Agency Inc (Japan); JLM Literary Agency (Greece); Nurcihan Kesim Literary Agency Ltd (Turkey); Macadamia Agency (Poland); Natoli, Stefan & Oliva (Roberta Oliva) (Italy); La Nouvelle Agence (France); Andrew Nurnberg Associates Baltic (Tatjana Zoldnere) (Estonia, Latvia, Lithuania); Andrew Nurnberg Associates Budapest (Croatia, Hungary); Andrew Nurnberg Associates Prague (Czechia, Slovakia, Slovenia); Andrew Nurnberg Associates Sofia (Albania, Bulgaria, North Macedonia, Serbia); Riff Agency (Brazil); rMaeng2 (Mr Hosung Maeng, Christian titles only) (South Korea); Thomas Schluck Agency (Germany); Sebes & Bisseling Literary Agency (Netherlands, Scandinavia); Synopsis Agency (Russia); Tuttle-Mori Agency Inc (Japan); Eric Yang Agency (South Korea)
Membership(s): The Authors Guild; Mystery Writers of America (MWA)

Buchwald (L)
10 E 44 St, New York, NY 10017
Tel: 212-867-1200
E-mail: info@buchwald.com
Web Site: www.buchwald.com
Key Personnel
Pres & CEO: Don Buchwald
EVP: Stephen Fisher
Agent: David Lewis; Jonathan Mason
 E-mail: jmason@buchwald.com; Joanne Nici
 E-mail: jonici@buchwald.com
Founded: 1977
Talent representatives & literary agency: TV, film, commercial, theatre & broadcasting. No unsol mss, query first. No reading fee.
Branch Office(s)
5900 Wilshire Blvd, 31st fl, Los Angeles, CA 90036 *Tel:* 323-665-7400

Don Buchwald & Associates Inc, see Buchwald

The Bukowski Agency Ltd (L)
20 Prince Arthur Ave, Suite 12-I, Toronto, ON M5R 1B1, Canada
Tel: 416-928-6728 *Fax:* 416-963-9978
E-mail: info@bukowskiagency.com
Web Site: www.bukowskiagency.com
Key Personnel
Owner & Founder: Denise Bukowski
Founded: 1986
Specialize in international literary fiction & upmarket nonfiction for adults. No children's literature, plays, poetry, or screenplays. Accepting submissions by referral only.
Titles recently placed: *Moon of the Turning Leaves*, Waubgeshig Rice; *Toddlers Made Easy: Become the Parent Every Child Wants*, Dr Cathryn Tobin; *What Time the Sexton's Spade Doth Rust*, Alan Bradley
Foreign Rights: AJA Literary Agency (Anna Jarota) (France); Berla & Griffini Rights Agency (Erica Berla) (Italy); Big Apple Agency Inc (Vincent Lin & Maggie Han) (Mainland China, Taiwan); The Foreign Office (Teresa Vilarrubla) (Brazil, Latin America, Portugal, Spain); Graal Literary Agency (Paulina Machnik) (Eastern Europe, Poland); The Deborah Harris Agency (Guela Geurts) (Israel); A M Heath & Co Ltd (Bill Hamilton) (UK); Japan UNI Agency Inc (Megumi Sakai) (Japan); JLM Literary Agency (John Moukakos) (Greece); Katai & Bolza Literary Agents (Orsolya Meszaros) (Hungary); Duran Kim Agency (Duran Kim) (South Korea); Licht & Burr (Trine Licht) (Scandinavia); Mohrbooks AG Literary Agency (Annelie Geissler) (Germany); Marianne Schoenbach Literary Agency (Marianne Schoenbach) (Netherlands); The Van Lear Agency (Katya Ilina) (Russia)

Sheree Bykofsky Associates Inc (L)
PO Box 706, Brigantine, NJ 08203
E-mail: shereebee@aol.com
Web Site: www.shereebee.com
Key Personnel
Pres & Agent: Sheree Bykofsky (AALA)
Founded: 1991
Adult trade & mass market nonfiction. No unsol mss, send query in body of e-mail. We only respond to queries we wish to pursue.
Foreign Rights: Bardon-Chinese Media Agency (China, Taiwan); Eliane Benisti Agency (France); BookLab Literary Agency (Poland); Dalia Ever Hadani (Israel); Japan UNI Agency Inc (Japan); Alexander Korzhenevski (Russia); Piergiorgio Nicolazzini (Italy); OA Literary Agency (Greece); Kristin Olson Literary Agency (Czechia, Slovakia); ONK Agency Inc (Eastern Europe, Greece, Turkey); Plima Literary Agency (Croatia, Serbia, Slovenia); RDC Agencia Literaria SL (Latin America, Portugal, Spain); Thomas Schlueck Literarische Agentur (Germany); Abner Stein Agency (UK); Eric Yang (South Korea); Pimolporn Yutsiri (Indonesia, Thailand, Vietnam)
Membership(s): Atlantic City Chamber of Commerce; PR Council

Calligraph LLC (L-D)
45 Main St, No 850, Brooklyn, NY 11201
Tel: 212-253-1074
E-mail: mail@calligraphlit.com; rights@calligraphlit.com; submissions@calligraphlit.com
Web Site: www.calligraphlit.com
Key Personnel
Founder & Agent: John Taylor "Ike" Williams
Mng Partner & Agent: Katherine Flynn (AALA); Zoe Pagnamenta (AALA)
Partner & Agent: Alison MacKeen
Principal Agent: Lucy Cleland (AALA); Eve MacSweeney; Carolyn Savarese
Agent & Edit Mgr: Sarah Khalil
Agent & Foreign Rts Mgr: Jess Hoare (AALA)
Founded: 2023 (merger of Kneerim & William Agency with Zoe Pagnamenta Agency)
Offers representation for new & established authors & sells rights for clients worldwide in print, audio, electronic, film & television. Represents literary & commercial fiction & nonfiction. Submit query letter with brief synopsis of your work & short bio, along with 25 pages of sample material in the body of the e-mail (no attachments). Include the name of the agent your are querying in the subject line of the e-mail, along with the title of your project & its genre.
Branch Office(s)
88 Broad St, No 503, Boston, MA 02110
Foreign Rights: AnatoliaLit Agency (Ozlem Oztemel) (Turkey); Amelie & Dar Cherlin (Middle East, North Africa); English Agency Japan Co Ltd (Hamish Macaskill & Kohei Hattori) (Japan); Ersilia Literary Agency (Evangelia Avloniti) (Greece); The Foreign Office (Teresa Vilarrubla) (Brazil, Portugal, Spain); Literarische Agentur Gaeb & Eggers (Franziska Hippe) (Germany); The Grayhawk Agency (Yichan Peng, Yijhen Lee & Mia Lee) (China, Taiwan); The Grayhawk Agency (Sherri Cheng) (Indonesia, Thailand, Vietnam); The Deborah Harris Agency (Geula Geurts) (Israel); The Italian Literary Agency Srl (Beatrice Beraldo) (Italy); Korean Copyright Center (Jae-Yeon Ryu) (South Korea); Marotte et Compagnie (Corinne Marotte) (France); Andrew Nurnberg Associates Baltic (Tatjana Zoldnere) (Estonia, Latvia, Lithuania, Ukraine); Andrew Nurnberg Associates International Ltd Hungary (Judit Hermann) (Croatia, Hungary); Andrew Nurnberg Associates Prague (Lucie Polakova) (Czechia, Slovakia, Slovenia); Andrew Nurnberg Associates Sofia (Anna & Mira Droumeva) (Bulgaria, Romania, Serbia); Andrew Nurnberg Associates Warsaw (Marcin Biegaj) (Poland); Andrew Nurnberg Literary Agency (Ludmilla Sushkova & Vladimir Chernyshov) (Russia); Marianne Schoenbach Literary Agency (Marianne Schoenbach) (Netherlands, Scandinavia)

Kimberley Cameron & Associates LLC (L)
1550 Tiburon Blvd, Suite 704, Tiburon, CA 94920
E-mail: info@kimberleycameron.com
Web Site: www.kimberleycameron.com
Key Personnel
Pres & Literary Agent: Kimberley Cameron (AALA) *E-mail:* kimberley@kimberleycameron.com
Literary Agent: Lisa Abellera (AALA)
 E-mail: lisa@kimberleycameron.com; Amy Cloughly (AALA) *E-mail:* amy@kimberleycameron.com; Camille Kantor (AALA) *E-mail:* camille@kimberleycameron.com; Elizabeth Kracht *E-mail:* elizabeth@kimberleycameron.com; Dorian Maffei (AALA) *E-mail:* dorian@kimberleycameron.com
Founded: 1957 (as Reece Halsey Agency)
The agency became Kimberley Cameron & Associates in 2009, with active film & foreign subrights partnerships & remote offices in Paris & New York. In 2012, Kimberley re-centered on the Bay Area location, mentoring new & upcoming local literary agents, bringing them on & expanding the agency. The agency is now a northern California-based team of collaborative & committed agents that take pride in upholding its reputation. No unsol mss, query first. Please follow submission guidelines on the web site: www.kimberleycameron.com/submissions.
Titles recently placed: *A Palace Near the Wind*, Ai Jiang; *Bat Eater*, Kylie Lee Baker; *Beyond All Doubt*, Hilton Reed; *House of Monstrous Women*, Daphne Fama; *Mistress of Bones*, Maria Z Medina; *Nesting After Divorce*, Beth Behrendt; *Saving Emma*, Allen Eskens; *The Nature of Disappearing*, Kimi Cunningham Grant; *The Payback Girls*, Alex Travis; *The Stardust Grail*, Yume Kitasei; *The White Redwood*, Maria Kelson; *Worst in Show*, Anna Collins
Foreign Rights: The Fielding Agency (Whitney Lee) (worldwide)
Membership(s): Sisters in Crime

Maria Carvainis Agency Inc (L)
Rockefeller Center, 1270 Avenue of the Americas, Suite 2915, New York, NY 10020
Tel: 212-245-6365 *Fax:* 212-245-7196
E-mail: mca@mariacarvainisagency.com
Web Site: mariacarvainisagency.com
Key Personnel
Pres: Maria Carvainis (AALA)
Contract & Subs Rts Mgr: Martha Guzman
Assoc Agent: Elizabeth Copps (AALA)
Literary Asst: Rose Friel (AALA)
Founded: 1977
Represents a wide range of fiction & nonfiction with special interest in literary & mainstream fiction, mystery & suspense, thrillers, historicals, contemporary women's fiction, young adult & middle grade, memoir, biography, history, business, psychology, pop culture & popular science. We do not represent screenplays, children's picture books, science fiction, or poetry. If you would like to query the agency, please send a query letter, a synopsis of the work, first 5-10 pages & note of any writing credentials. The agency prefers e-mailed queries.
Titles recently placed: *Always the Last to Know*, Kristan Higgins; *Confessions of a Curious Bookseller*, Elizabeth Green; *More Than Marmalade*, Rosanne Tolin; *Officer Clemmons*, Dr Francois S Clemmons; *Promises of the Heart*, Nan Rossiter; *Someone to Romance*, Mary Balogh; *Stories We Never Told*, Sonja Yoerg; *The Boatman's Daughter*, Andy Davidson; *The Girl They Left Behind*, Roxanne Veletzos; *Thick As Thieves*, Sandra Brown
Membership(s): American Booksellers Association (ABA); The Authors Guild; International Thriller Writers Inc (ITW); Mystery Writers of America (MWA); Romance Writers of America (RWA); Society of Children's Book Writers & Illustrators (SCBWI)

Linda Chester Literary Agency (L-D)
630 Fifth Ave, Suite 2000, New York, NY 10111
Tel: 212-218-3350
E-mail: submissions@lindachester.com
Web Site: www.lindachester.com
Key Personnel
Head of Agency: Laurie Fox *Tel:* 510-435-3635
 E-mail: laurie@lindachester.com
Exec Mgr: Michelle Conway *E-mail:* michelle@lindachester.com

LITERARY AGENTS

Agent: Darlene Chan *E-mail:* darlene@lindachester.com
Assoc Agent: D Patrick Miller
Quality adult fiction & nonfiction. Handle film & TV rights. No reading fes; no unsol mss, query first.
Branch office in California.
Foreign Rights: The Fielding Agency LLC (Whitney Lee)

Faith Childs Literary Agency Inc (L)
915 Broadway, Suite 1009, New York, NY 10010
Tel: 212-995-9600
Web Site: faithchildsliteraryagency.com
Key Personnel
Pres: Faith Hampton Childs (AALA)
  E-mail: faith@faithchildsliteraryagency.com
Subs Rts Assoc: Diana Lachatanere
  E-mail: dianalachatanere@faithchildsliteraryagency.com
Founded: 1990
Specialize in fiction & nonfiction film & TV rights. No unsol mss, queries or unreferred clients accepted. Agents in all principal countries.
Foreign Rep(s): English Agency Japan Co Ltd (Japan)

Cine/Lit Representation (L-D)
PO Box 802918, Santa Clarita, CA 91380-2918
E-mail: cinelit@att.net
Founded: 1991
Not accepting submissions at this time. No reading fee. Now only handling film & TV rights for books.
Membership(s): British Academy of Film and Television Arts (BAFTA) Los Angeles; Film Independent

Wm Clark Associates (L)
54 W 21 St, Suite 809, New York, NY 10010
Tel: 212-675-2784
E-mail: general@wmclark.com
Web Site: www.wmclark.com
Key Personnel
Pres: William Clark (AALA) *E-mail:* wmclark@wmclark.com
Founded: 1999
Represents mainstream & literary fiction & quality nonfiction to the book publishing, motion picture, television & new media fields. No reading fees; handle film & TV rights for books written by clients only; does not represent screenplays. In addition to selling directly in the global English language markets, translation rights are sold directly in the German, Italian, Spanish, Portuguese, Latin American, French, Dutch & Scandinavian territories; through corresponding agents in China, Bulgaria, Czechia, Latvia, Poland & Hungary, Russia, Ukraine, Japan, Greece, Israel, Turkey, Korea, Taiwan & Thailand. Other network partners provide services including editorial consultation, media training, lecture booking, marketing support & public relations. Queries sent by any method other than through web site query page will be discarded unread.
Titles recently placed: *Anni Albers: A Biography*, Nicholas Fox Weber; *Cent'anni: Caffe Dante and the Aperitivo Way of Life*, Linden Pride, Nathalie Hudson, Reggie Nadelson; *Cooler than Cool: A Biography of Elmore Leonard*, Chad Kushins; *Facing Suicide*, James Barrat; *Other Rivers: Two Generations, One Pandemic, and Four Semesters in Sichuan Province*, Peter Hessler
Foreign Rights: BookLab Literary Agency (Poland); Kalem Agency (Turkey); Andrew Nurnberg Associates Ltd (China, Taiwan); Synopsis Literary Agency (Russia & former USSR); Tuttle-Mori Agency Inc (Japan); Eric Yang Agency (Taiwan)
Membership(s): The Authors Guild; PEN International

Collier Associates (L)
309 Kelsey Park Circle, Palm Beach Gardens, FL 33410
Mailing Address: PO Box 15759, West Palm Beach, FL 33416
Tel: 561-514-6548
E-mail: dmccabooks@gmail.com
Key Personnel
Pres & Agent: Dianna Collier
Agent: Charles Todd *E-mail:* charles@charlestodd.com
Founded: 1976
Fiction & nonfiction adult books. Fiction: war novels, mysteries, true crime, romance, contemporary & historical. Nonfiction: biographies & autobiographies of well-known people, popular works of political subjects & history, exposes, popular works on medical & scientific subjects, finance, popular reference & how-to books, health, beauty & motherhood. Also handle film & TV rights for adult books only with co-agents. No unsol mss, query first with SASE; submit outline, sample chapters & bio; no reading fee for published authors of trade books, may charge fee for full-length book mss for unpublished authors; charge cost of copying ms; submission postage; books ordered for subsidiary rights. When ms is submitted it should meet the Chicago Manual of Style Guidelines, along with a sample chapter by chapter outline & SASE. Submissions must be in Microsoft Word format, 1 sided pages, all pages numbered at bottom center, header with author & title right justified, double spaced, Courier font, 12 point. All others submissions may be discarded. Include cover proposal letter & chapter-by-chapter outline. Co-agents on West Coast & in many foreign countries.
Foreign Rep(s): Big Apple Agency Inc (China, Japan, Taiwan); International Editors' Co - Yanez Agencia Literaria (Portugal, South America, Spain); International Literature Bureau BV (Netherlands); Johnson & Alcock Ltd (British Commonwealth); Mohrbooks AG Literary Agency (Austria, Germany, Switzerland); Tuttle-Mori Agency Inc (Japan)
Foreign Rights: Agence Michelle Lapautre (France); Light & Burr (Denmark, Finland, Iceland, Norway, Sweden)
Membership(s): Mystery Writers of America (MWA)

Don Congdon Associates Inc (L)
110 William St, Suite 2202, New York, NY 10038-3914
Tel: 212-645-1229 *Fax:* 212-727-2688
E-mail: dca@doncongdon.com
Web Site: www.doncongdon.com
Key Personnel
Agent: Cristina Concepcion (AALA); Michael Congdon (AALA); Katie Kotchman (AALA); Maura Kye-Casella (AALA); Susan Ramer (AALA)
Founded: 1983
Handle any & all trade books. Handle film & TV rights for regular clients. No unsol mss, query first with a 1-page synopsis of your work & relevant background & SASE or e-mail without attachments. In heading include "Query" & agent's full name. Include a sample chapter in body of e-mail. Now accepting new & professional authors. No reading fee.
Foreign Rep(s): AnatoliaLit Agency (Amy Spangler) (Turkey); Big Apple Agency Inc (Chris Lin) (Taiwan); Big Apple Agency Inc (Lily Chen, Luc Kwanten, Erica Zhou & Wendy King) (China, Thailand, Vietnam); Casanovas & Lynch Agencia Literaria (Marina Penalva) (Portugal, South America, Spain); Nurcihan Kesim Literary Agency Ltd (Filiz Karaman) (Turkey); Agence Michelle Lapautre (Catherine Lapautre) (France); Maxima Creative Agency (Santo Manurung) (Indonesia); Andrew Nurnberg Associates Baltic (Tatjana Zoldnere) (Estonia, Latvia, Lithuania); Andrew Nurnberg Associates Budapest (Judit Hermann) (Croatia, Hungary); Andrew Nurnberg Associates International (Marei Pittner) (Denmark, Finland, Iceland, Netherlands, Norway, Sweden); Andrew Nurnberg Associates International (Andrew Nurnberg & Sabine Pfannenstiel) (Germany); Andrew Nurnberg Associates Prague (Petra Tobiskova) (Czechia, Slovakia, Slovenia); Andrew Nurnberg Associates Sofia (Anna Droumeva) (Bulgaria, Romania, Serbia); Andrew Nurnberg Associates Warsaw (Marcin Biegaj) (Poland); Andrew Nurnberg Literary Agency Moscow (Ludmilla Sushkova) (Russia); Owls Agency (Monika Taga) (Japan); Read n Right Agency (Nike Davarinou) (Greece); Vicki Satlow Literary Agency (Vicki Satlow) (Italy); Abner Stein Agency (Caspian Dennis & Anna Carmichael) (UK); Tuttle-Mori Agency Inc (Asako Kawachi, Ken Mori & Misa Morikawa) (Japan); Eric Yang Agency (Henry Shin) (South Korea)

EDITORIAL SERVICES

The Doe Coover Agency (L)
PO Box 668, Winchester, MA 01890
Tel: 781-721-6000 *Fax:* 781-721-6727
E-mail: info@doecooveragency.com
Web Site: www.doecooveragency.com
Key Personnel
Pres: Doe Coover
Agent: Colleen Mohyde
Founded: 1986
Nonfiction & fiction. Specialize in literary fiction, business, history & biography, psychology, science & health, cooking & food writing, gardening, humor, sports & music. No poetry, fantasy, science fiction or screenplays. E-mail queries only; see web site for submission guidelines.
Handle film & TV rights on agency projects only. 15% commission.
Titles recently placed: *All About Dinner: Simple Meals, Expert Advice*, Molly Stevens; *Canal House Cook Something*, Christopher Hirsheimer, Melissa Hamilton; *Perini Ranch Steakhouse: Stories and Recipes for Real Texas Food*, Lisa Perini, Tom Perini, Cheryl Atlers Jamison; *The Getting This Done Workbook: 10 Moves to Stress-Free Productivity*, David Allen, Brandon Hall; *The Life She Wished to Live: Biography of Marjorie Kinnan Rawlings*, Ann McCutchan
Foreign Rights: English Agency Japan Co Ltd (Japan); The Marsh Agency (Europe); Abner Stein Agency (UK)

CreativeWell Inc (L)
PO Box 3130, Memorial Sta, Upper Montclair, NJ 07043
Tel: 973-783-7575
E-mail: info@creativewell.com
Web Site: www.creativewell.com
Key Personnel
Pres: George M Greenfield
Founded: 2003
Primarily nonfiction, film & TV rights. No unsol mss, query first. No reading fee; other fees charged (for photocopies, express mail, etc). Representatives in principal foreign countries. Also offers full service lecture representation.
Titles recently placed: *Against A Tide of Evil*, Dr Mukesha Kapila; *To Hell and Back: The Last Train from Hiroshima*, Charles Pellegrino; *We Protest: Fighting for What We Believe In*, Tish Lampert
Foreign Rights: Akcali Copyright (Atilla Turgut) (Turkey); Agentura Gramma (Tatjana Zoldnere) (Baltic States); The Deborah Harris Agency

(Ms Efrat Lev) (Israel); International Editors Co (Isabel Monteagudo) (Portugal); JLM Literary Agency (John Moukakos) (Greece); Agence Michelle Lapautre (Catherine Lapautre) (France); Michael Meller Literary Agency (Michael Meller) (Germany); Andrew Nurnberg Associates Budapest (Judith Hermann) (Hungary); Andrew Nurnberg Associates Prague (Petra Tobiskova) (Czechia, Slovakia); Andrew Nurnberg Associates Sofia (Anna & Mira Droumeva) (Bulgaria); Andrew Nurnberg Literary Agency (Russia); Agencia Riff (Joao Paulo Riff) (Brazil); Abner Stein Ltd (Sandy Violette) (UK); Tuttle-Mori Agency (Thailand) Co Ltd (Pimolporn Yutisri) (Thailand)

Crichton & Associates Inc (L)
6940 Carroll Ave, Takoma, MD 20912
Tel: 301-495-9663
E-mail: cricht1@aol.com
Key Personnel
Pres: Sha-Shana Crichton
Founded: 2002
For fiction, submit first 3 chapters with synopsis & bio. For nonfiction, submit proposal with bio. No fees charged. E-mail queries only to query@crichton-associates.com.
Membership(s): Romance Writers of America (RWA)

Richard Curtis Associates Inc (L)
Subsidiary of Harold Ober Associates
286 Madison Ave, Suite 1002, New York, NY 10017
Tel: 212-772-7363
E-mail: curtisagency@haroldober.com
Web Site: ilpliterary.com
Key Personnel
Pres: Richard Curtis (AALA)
 E-mail: rcurtisagency@gmail.com
Founded: 1979
Not accepting mss at this time.
Foreign Rights: Baror International Inc (worldwide exc USA)

Darhansoff & Verrill (L)
529 11 St, 3rd fl, Brooklyn, NY 11215
Tel: 917-305-1300
E-mail: permissions@dvagency.com
Web Site: www.dvagency.com
Key Personnel
Founder & Agent: Liz Darhansoff (AALA)
Agency Assoc: Eric Amling; Michele Mortimer
Founded: 1975
Fiction & nonfiction, literary fiction, young adult, memoirs, sophisticated suspense, history, science, biography, pop culture & current affairs. No theatrical plays or film scripts. No unsol mss, query first with SASE or by e-mail via submissions@dvagency.com. Film & TV rights handled by Los Angeles associates, Lynn Pleshette, Richard Green & UTA. Agents in many foreign countries. No fees charged.
Foreign Rights: Akcali Copyright Agency (Ozgur Emir) (Turkey); Bardon-Chinese Media Agency (Joanne Yang) (China); Eliane Benisti Agency (France); The Book Publishers Association of Israel (Dalia Ever Hadani) (Israel); English Agency Japan Co Ltd (Hamish Macaskill) (Japan); Graal Literary Agency (Maria Strarz-Zielinska) (Poland); International Copyrights Agency (Simona Kessler) (Romania); International Editors' Co - Yanez Agencia Literaria (Spain); Interrights (Svetlana Stefanova) (Bulgaria); The Italian Literary Agency Srl (Italy); JLM Literary Agency (John Moukakos) (Greece); Katai & Bolza (Peter Bolza) (Hungary); Licht & Burr (Trine Licht) (Scandinavia); Zvonimir Majdak (Croatia); Mohrbooks (Sebastian Ritscher) (Germany); Andrew Nurnberg Agency (Lumilla Shushkova) (Russia); Andrew Nurnberg Association Baltic (Tatjana Zoldnere) (Latvia); Kristin Olson Literary Agency (Kristin Olson) (Czechia); Agencia Riff (Laura Riff & Joao Paulo Riff) (Brazil, Portugal); The Sayle Agency (Rachel Calder) (UK); Sebes & Bisseling Literary Agency (Paul Sebes) (Netherlands); Shin Won Agency (Tae Kim) (South Korea)

Liza Dawson Associates (L)
121 W 27 St, Suite 1201, New York, NY 10001
Tel: 212-465-9071
Web Site: www.lizadawsonassociates.com
Key Personnel
CFO & Foreign Rts Mgr: Havis Dawson
 E-mail: hdawson@lizadawson.com
Pres: Liza Dawson (AALA)
Sr Literary Agent: Tom Miller
 E-mail: querytom@lizadawsonassociates.com
Literary Agent: Rachel Beck
 E-mail: queryrachel@lizadawson.com; Caitlin Blasdell *E-mail:* querycaitlin@lizadawson.com; Hannah Bowman *E-mail:* queryhannah@lizadawsonassociates.com
Literary Agent & Agent Asst: Caitie Flum
 E-mail: querycaitie@lizadawsonassociates.com
Assoc Agent & Agent Asst: Lauren Bajek
 E-mail: querylauren@lizadawson.com
Contracts & Payment Mgr: Joanne Fallert
 E-mail: jfallert@lizadawson.com
Founded: 1996
Agents are supported by a strong team that sells audio, foreign, licensing & television & film rights. Represent commercial fiction & literary fiction. In nonfiction, we are drawn to narratives that explore life's complexities. We represent books for most ages, some of which are award-winners & New York Times bestsellers. We work with both debut novelists as well as published writers, helping them craft their proposals.
Foreign Rights: ACER Agencia Literaria (Elizabeth Atkins) (Portugal, Spain); Akcali Copyright Agency (Atilla Izgi Turgut) (Turkey); Bears Factor (Bassem El-Kheshen) (Arabic language); Eliane Benisti Agency (Eliane Benisti & Noemie Rollet) (France); Graal Literary Agency (Marcin Biegaj) (Albania, Baltic States, Bulgaria, Greece, Hungary, Iceland, North Macedonia, Poland, Romania, Serbia, Slovenia); The Grayhawk Agency (Gray Tan) (China, Taiwan, Thailand, Vietnam); Deborah Harris Agency (Geula Geurts) (Israel); David Higham Associates (Laura West) (UK); Danny Hong Agency (Danny Hong) (South Korea); International Editors' Co (Flavia Sala & Cristina Puchio) (Brazil); Alexander Korzhenevski Agency (Alexander Korzhenevski) (Russia); Piergiorgio Nicollazzini Agency (Maura Solinas, sci-fi/fantasy only) (Italy); Kristin Olson Literary Agency (Kristin Olson) (Czechia); Lennart Sane Agency (Philip Sane) (Netherlands, Scandinavia); Thomas Schlueck GmbH (Bastian Schlueck, sci-fi/fantasy only) (Germany); Tuttle-Mori Agency Inc (Misa Morikawa, fiction; Manami Tamaoki, nonfiction) (Japan)
Membership(s): Women's Media Group

J de S Associates Inc (L)
9 Shagbark Rd, South Norwalk, CT 06854
Tel: 203-838-7571 *Fax:* 203-866-2713
Web Site: www.jdesassociates.com
Key Personnel
Pres: Jacques de Spoelberch *E-mail:* jdespoel@aol.com
Founded: 1975
Fiction & nonfiction. No unsol mss, query first. Send outline & 2 sample chapters; no reading fee. Agents & film representatives in major foreign countries.

The Jennifer DeChiara Literary Agency (L)
245 Park Ave, 39th fl, New York, NY 10167
Tel: 212-372-8989
Web Site: www.jdlit.com
Key Personnel
Owner, Pres & Agent: Jennifer DeChiara
 E-mail: jenndec@aol.com
Sr Agent: Stephen Fraser
 E-mail: fraserstephena@gmail.com
Agent: Marlo Berliner; Marie Lamba
 E-mail: marie.jdlit@gmail.com
Assoc Agent: Whitley Abell *E-mail:* whitley.jdlit@gmail.com; Alex Barba *E-mail:* alex.jdlit@gmail.com; Megan Barnard; Amy Giuffrida; Cari Lamba *E-mail:* cari.jdlit@gmail.com; David Laurell *E-mail:* dlaurell@aol.com; Damian McNicholl *E-mail:* damianmcnichollvarney@gmail.com; Stefanie Molina; Tori Sharp; Bre Stephens
Film/TV Mgr: Kimberly Guidone
Founded: 2001
Accepting queries in the following areas: children's books for every age (picture books, middle grade & young adult), adult fiction & nonfiction in a wide range of genres. Accept e-mail queries only, with "Query" in the subject line; no attachments. Co-agents in every country. No fees.
Titles recently placed: *Bees In The Trees*, Ruth Horowitz; *Daughter of Australia*, Harmony Verna; *Eliza Bing Is (Not) A Big, Fat Quitter*, Carmella Van Vleet; *Fannie Never Flinches*, Mary Cronk Farrell; *Girl*, M-E Girard; *Guts For Glory*, JoAnna Lapati; *Hazy Bloom*, Jennifer Hamburg; *Honestly, Ben*, Bill Konigsberg; *I Only Know Who I Am When I Am Somebody Else*, Danny Aiello; *I'll Be Damned*, Eric Braeden; *Irena's Children*, Mary Cronk Farrell; *Izzy Barr, Running Star*, Claudia Mills; *Luke Veracruz Saves The Day*, Jeff Anderson; *My Days...Happy and Otherwise*, Marion Ross; *My Girls: A Lifetime with Carrie and Debbie*, Todd Fisher; *Not Young, Still Restless: My Life So Far*, Jeanne Cooper; *Omega Days*, John L Campbell; *Openly Straight*, Bill Konigsberg; *Peanut Butter and Brains*, Joe McGee; *Quack*, Jennifer Hamburg; *Sitting Next to Jesus*, Carol Lynch Williams; *Skynned Alive: Keeping the Best in Lynyrd Skynyrd, America's Greatest Rock 'n' Roll Band*, Artimus Pyle; *Stuck In My Sister's Fat*, Carol Lynch Williams; *The Ed Lucas Story*, Ed Lucas, Christopher Lucas; *The Hole Story of the Doughnut*, Pat Miller; *The Jumbie Seed*, Tracey Baptiste; *The Jumbies*, Tracey Baptiste; *The Nora Notebooks*, Claudia Mills; *The One-Way Bridge*, Cathie Pelletier; *The Porcupine of Truth*, Bill Konigsberg; *The Quantum League*, Matthew Kirby; *The Summer Experiment*, Cathie Pelletier; *The Write-Brain Workbook (10th anniversary ed)*, Bonnie Neubauer; *The Year After Henry*, Cathie Pelletier; *Three Truths and a Lie*, Brent Hartinger; *Tippi*, Tippi Hedren; *To The Stars! The Story of Kathy Sullivan, First American Woman to Walk in Space*, Carmella Van Vleet, Kathy Sullivan; *Toni Tennille, A Memoir*, Toni Tennille; *Waggers*, Stacy A Nyikos; *Whistle Root*, Christopher Pennell
Foreign Rights: Books Crossing Borders (Betty Anne Crawford) (USA)

DeFiore and Company Literary Management Inc (L)
47 E 19 St, 3rd fl, New York, NY 10003
Tel: 212-925-7744 *Fax:* 212-925-9803
E-mail: info@defliterary.com; submissions@defliterary.com
Web Site: www.defliterary.com
Key Personnel
Founder & Pres: Brian DeFiore (AALA)
 E-mail: querybrian@defliterary.com
Dir, Busn Aff: Adam Schear (AALA)
 E-mail: adam@defliterary.com
Dir, Foreign Rts: Linda Kaplan
Literary Agent: Laurie Abkemeier (AALA)
 E-mail: laurie@defliterary.com; Miriam

LITERARY AGENTS

Altschuler (AALA) *E-mail:* querymiriam@defliterary.com; Reiko Davis *E-mail:* reiko@defliterary.com; Matthew Elblonk *E-mail:* matthew@defliterary.com; Lisa Gallagher *E-mail:* lgsubmissions@defliterary.com; Elise Howard; Tamara Kawar; Chris Park; Tanusri Prasanna *E-mail:* tpsubmissions@defliterary.com; Caryn Karmatz Rudy (AALA) *E-mail:* caryn@defliterary.com; Rebecca Strauss (AALA) *E-mail:* rebecca@defliterary.com
Founded: 1999
Handles mainstream fiction, literary fiction, suspense fiction, children's, business, self-help, narrative nonfiction, cookbooks & memoirs.
Titles recently placed: *Amina's Song*, Hena Kahn; *Beaverland*, Leile Philip; *Do Hard Things*, Steve Magness; *Humans*, Brandon Stanton; *Just Because*, Matthew McConaughey; *Slow Productivity*, Cal Newport; *Stars in an Italian Sky*, Jill Santopolo; *With My Little Eye*, Joshilyn Jackson
Foreign Rights: The Book Publishers Association of Israel (Delia Ever Hadani) (Israel); JLM Literary Agency (John Moukakos) (Greece); Kayi Agency (Dilek Kayi) (Turkey); Andrew Nurnberg Associates (Sabine Pfannenstiel, London) (Germany); Andrew Nurnberg Associates (Claire Anouchian, London) (France, Quebec, CN); Andrew Nurnberg Associates (Lucy Flynn) (Latin America exc Brazil, Portugal, Spain); Andrew Nurnberg Associates (Barbara Barbieri) (Brazil, Italy); Andrew Nurnberg Associates (Marei Pittner, London) (Netherlands, Scandinavia); Andrew Nurnberg Associates (Anna & Mira Droumeva, Sofia) (Bulgaria, Romania, Serbia); Andrew Nurnberg Associates (Petra Tobiskova & Jana Borovanova, Prague) (Czechia, Slovakia, Slovenia); Andrew Nurnberg Associates (Aleksandra Lapinska & Renata Paczewska, Warsaw) (Poland); Andrew Nurnberg Associates (Judit Hermann, Budapest) (Croatia, Hungary); Andrew Nurnberg Associates (Ludmilla Sushkova, Moscow) (Russia); Andrew Nurnberg Associates (Tatjana Zoldnere, Latvia) (Estonia, Latvia, Lithuania, Ukraine); Andrew Nurnberg Associates (Jackie Huang, Beijing) (China); Andrew Nurnberg Associates (Whitney Hsu, Taipei) (Taiwan); Tuttle-Mori Agency Inc (Ken Mori & Manami Tamaoki) (Japan); Tuttle-Mori Agency (Thailand) Co Ltd (Thananchai Pandey, Bangkok) (Thailand); Eric Yang Agency (Henry Shin) (South Korea)

Joelle Delbourgo Associates Inc (L)
101 Park St, Montclair, NJ 07042
Tel: 973-773-0836 (call only during standard business hours)
Web Site: www.delbourgo.com
Key Personnel
Founder, Pres, Agent & Consultant: Joelle Delbourgo (AALA) *E-mail:* joelle@delbourgo.com
Edit Consultant: Carrie Cantor *Tel:* 973-783-1005 *E-mail:* cantor.carrie@gmail.com
Founded: 2000
Boutique firm handling a wide range of adult fiction (literary & commercial) & nonfiction (narrative, prescriptive, reference). Young adult & middle grade fiction. E-mail queries only (do not mail material or self-published books). Check submission guidelines on web site. Materials will not be returned.
Titles recently placed: *Banish Bedtime Battles*, Ellen Flannery-Schroeder, PhD, Chelsea Tucker, PhD; *Childhood Narcissism*, Mary Ann Little, PhD; *Crazy to Leave You*, Marilyn Simon Rothstein; *How to Endure Hardship: An Ancient Guide to Consolation*, Philip Freeman; *Nature's Lead*, M D Usher; *Podcast Guesting Made Simple*, Michelle Glogovac; *Power: The Rise of Black Women in America*, Charity C Elder; *Scout Camp*, James Renner; *Size Wise: How Parents Can Build Healthy Habits in Kids of Every Size*, Jill Castle; *The Child Who Never Spoke: 23 1/2 Lessons in Fragility*, Cristina Nehring; *The Cocktail Parlor*, Nicola Nice; *The Counterfeit Countess*, Joanna Sliwa, PhD, Elizabeth B White, PhD; *The Liberals*, Joseph Kelly, PhD
Foreign Rights: Duran Kim Agency (South Korea); Maxima Agency (Indonesia); Jenny Meyer Literary Agency (worldwide exc Asia); Andrew Nurnberg Associates Inc (China); Tuttle-Mori Agency Inc (Japan)
Membership(s): Women's Media Group

D4EO Literary Agency (L-D)
13206 Treviso Dr, Lakewood Ranch, FL 34211
Tel: 203-545-7180 (cell)
Web Site: www.d4eoliteraryagency.com; www.publishersmarketplace.com/members/d4eo/; x.com/d4eo
Key Personnel
Principal: Robert (Bob) G Diforio *E-mail:* bob@d4eo.com
Agent: Ritu Anand *E-mail:* ritu@d4eo.com; Vanessa Campos *E-mail:* vanessa@d4eo.com; Jana Hanson *E-mail:* jana@d4eo.com; Mariah Nichols *E-mail:* mariah@d4eo.com
Founded: 1991
Full service, multi-agent literary agency representing authors of a very broad range of commercial fiction & nonfiction for children, young adults & adults. Over 5,000 published books under contract. No unsol mss, query first to only one agent. See submission guidelines for each agent on the web site.
Foreign Rights: Anthea Agency (Katalena Sabeva) (Bulgaria); Bardon-Chinese Media Agency (China); Agence Litteraire Eliane Benisti (Eliane Benisti) (France); Sandra Bruna Agency (Sandra Bruna) (Spain); Graal Literary Agency (Poland); Michael Meller Literary Agency GmbH (Michael Meller) (Germany); Nabu International Literary & Film Agency (Silvia Brunelli) (Italy); Andrew Nurnberg Associates Moscow (Russia); Torus-Books Agency (Gynn Kalman) (Hungary); Tuttle-Mori Agency Inc (Ken Mori) (Japan)

Sandra Dijkstra Literary Agency (L)
1155 Camino del Mar, PMB 515, Del Mar, CA 92014-2605
Web Site: dijkstraagency.com
Key Personnel
Pres & Agent: Sandra Dijkstra
Agency Mgr & Agent: Elise Capron *Tel:* 858-755-3115 ext 100 *E-mail:* elise@dijkstraagency.com
Agent: Thao Le *Tel:* 858-755-3115 ext 105 *E-mail:* thao@dijkstraagency.com; Jill Marr *Tel:* 858-755-3115 ext 108 *E-mail:* jill@dijkstraagency.com; Jessica Watterson *E-mail:* jessica@dijkstraagency.com
Fin Mgr: Jennifer Kim *Tel:* 858-755-3115 ext 106 *E-mail:* jennifer@dijkstraagency.com
Subrights Mgr: Andrea Cavallaro *E-mail:* andrea@dijkstraagency.com
Off Asst: Jake Lovell *Tel:* 858-755-3115 ext 101 *E-mail:* jake@dijkstraagency.com; Nick Van Orden *Tel:* 858-755-3115 ext 103 *E-mail:* nick@dijkstraagency.com
Founded: 1981
Fiction: contemporary, women's, literary, suspense, thrillers, science fiction & fantasy. Nonfiction: narrative, history, business, psychology, self-help, science & memoir/biography. Works in conjunction with foreign & film agents. E-mail submissions only. See web site for most up-to-date guidelines. No reading fee.
Foreign Rights: Bardon-Chinese Media Agency (China, Taiwan); Sandra Bruna Agencia Literaria (Portugal, Spain); English Agency Japan Co Ltd (Japan); Graal Literary Agency (Poland); The Italian Literary Agency Srl (Italy); Katai & Bolza (Hungary); Licht & Burr (Scandinavia); Maxima Creative Agency (Indonesia); La Nouvelle Agence (France); Onk Agency Inc (Turkey); Prava i prevodi (Eastern Europe); Sebes & Bisseling Literary Agency (Netherlands); Abner Stein Agency (UK); Synopsis Agency (Baltic States, Russia); TBPAI (Israel); Tuttle-Mori Agency (Thailand) Co Ltd (Thailand); Eric Yang Agency (South Korea)
Membership(s): The Authors Guild

EDITORIAL SERVICES

Janis A Donnaud & Associates Inc (L)
77 Bleecker St, No C1-25, New York, NY 10012
Tel: 212-431-2663 *Fax:* 212-431-2667
E-mail: jdonnaud@aol.com
Key Personnel
Pres: Janis A Donnaud (AALA)
Founded: 1993
Nonfiction by experts in their fields with a substantial following: cooking/food writing, memoir, health, lifestyle, mind/body/spirit, African-American, popular science, narrative nonfiction, cultural subjects, animal books, women's issues. Does NOT handle fiction, children's books, poetry, plays or screenplays. Query letter by e-mail - sample material only on request. Handle film, TV & international rights. No phone calls.
Titles recently placed: *Finding Freedom*, Erin French; *Kitchen Rules*, Melissa Clark; *Metabolical*, Robert Lustig, MD; *Natasha's Kitchen*, Natasha Kravchuk; *The Mediterranean Dish*, Suzy Karadsheh; *The Wishbone Kitchen Cookbook*, Meredith Hayden
Foreign Rights: Agence Litteraire Eliane Benisti (France); Berla & Griffini (Italy); Big Apple Agency Inc (China, Taiwan); Graal Literary Agency (Eastern Europe); Kalem Agency (Turkey); Liepman Agency (Germany); Sebes & Bisseling Literary Agency (Netherlands, Scandinavia); Shinwon Agency (South Korea); Abner Stein Agency (UK & Commonwealth); Tuttle-Mori Agency Inc (Japan)
Membership(s): The Authors Guild

Jim Donovan Literary (L)
5635 SMU Blvd, Suite 201, Dallas, TX 75206
Tel: 214-696-9411
E-mail: jdlqueries@sbcglobal.net
Key Personnel
Owner & Pres: Jim Donovan
Agent: Melissa Shultz
Founded: 1993
Literary & commercial fiction & nonfiction, especially biography, history, popular culture & sports. No poetry, short stories, science fiction/fantasy or children's. Accept unsol mss only with SASE. For nonfiction, query first with letter & SASE. For fiction, submit first 30-40 pages & synopsis with SASE. May query with e-mail, no attachments, response only if interested. No online submissions accepted. Handle film & TV rights for clients only. Agents in Hollywood & major foreign countries. No fees, 15% commission on monies earned.
Titles recently placed: *Crossing the Bloody Line*, Jeff Guinn; *Devils on Their Trail*, W K Stratton; *Four Days in Gettysburg*, Tim McGrath; *Merry Christmas from the Fam-O-Lee*, Robert Earl Keen; *Only the Brave*, Don Keith; *Perfectly Hidden Depression*, Dr Margaret Rutherford; *Rogues' Gallery*, John Oller; *The Earth Is All That Lasts*, Mark Gardner; *The Hamilton Affair*, Elizabeth Cobbs

Dunham Literary Inc (L)
487 Hardscrabble Rd, North Salem, NY 10560
Tel: 914-669-5535
E-mail: dunhamlit@gmail.com
Web Site: dunhamlit.com

Key Personnel
Founder, Pres & Agent: Jennie Dunham (AALA)
Assoc Agent: Anjanette Barr
Founded: 2000
Literary fiction & nonfiction, children's book writers & illustrators. No original plays or screenplays. Handle film & TV rights for books represented. No unsol mss, query first by e-mail only. No reading fee.
Foreign Rights: Taryn Fagerness Agency (worldwide exc USA)
Membership(s): Society of Children's Book Writers & Illustrators (SCBWI)

Dunow, Carlson & Lerner Literary Agency Inc (L)
27 W 20 St, Suite 1107, New York, NY 10011
Tel: 212-645-7606
E-mail: mail@dclagency.com
Web Site: www.dclagency.com
Key Personnel
Literary Agent: Jennifer Carlson (AALA); Arielle Datz (AALA); Stacia Decker (AALA); Henry Dunow (AALA); Erin Hosier; Eleanor Jackson; Julia Kenny (AALA); Betsy Lerner; Edward Necarsulmer, IV (AALA); Nicki Richesin; Chris Rogers; Rachel Vogel
Founded: 2005
Represents literary & commercial fiction, nonfiction & children's literature. Handle film & TV rights. Agents in all foreign territories. Query letters preferred via e-mail with first 10 pages of ms pasted in the e-mail (no attachments). Query letters send by mail must include SASE. No reading fee.
Foreign Rights: Akcali Copyright Agency (Turkey); Grayhawk Agency (China, Taiwan); The Deborah Harris Agency (Israel); David Higham Associates (UK); JLM Literary Agency (Greece); Andrew Nurnberg Associates (Eastern Europe, Europe, Russia, South America); Abner Stein Agency (UK); Tuttle-Mori Agency Inc (Japan); Eric Yang Agency (South Korea)

Dupree, Miller & Associates Inc (L)
4311 Oak Lawn Ave, Suite 650, Dallas, TX 75219
Tel: 214-559-2665
E-mail: editorial@dupreemiller.com
Web Site: www.dupreemiller.com
Key Personnel
Founder & CEO: Jan Miller *E-mail:* jmr@dupreemiller.com
Pres: Shannon Marven
Agent: Austin Miller
Fiction & nonfiction. No children's, science fiction, fantasy, horror, short stories, poetry or screenplays. No unsol mss; accept query letter only, with SASE enclosed for reply. No fees. Market & promote own books both regionally & nationally.

Dystel, Goderich & Bourret LLC (L)
One Union Sq W, Suite 904, New York, NY 10003
Tel: 212-627-9100 *Fax:* 212-627-9313
Web Site: www.dystel.com
Key Personnel
Pres & Partner: Jane Dystel (AALA)
Agent & Partner: Michael Bourret (AALA)
  E-mail: mbourret@dystel.com; Miriam Goderich *Tel:* 212-627-9100 ext 702
  E-mail: miriam@dystel.com
VP, Subs Rts Dir & Agent: Lauren E Abramo
  Tel: 212-627-9100 ext 704 *E-mail:* labramo@dystel.com
VP & Sr Agent: Jim McCarthy (AALA) *Tel:* 212-627-9100 ext 707 *E-mail:* jmccarthy@dystel.com
VP & Agent: Stacey Kendall Glick
  E-mail: sglick@dystel.com; Jessica Papin
  E-mail: jpapin@dystel.com
Sr Agent: Sharon Pelletier *Tel:* 212-627-9100 ext 711 *E-mail:* spelletier@dystel.com
Agent: Leslie Meredith *E-mail:* lmeredith@dystel.com; John Rudolph *E-mail:* jrudolph@dystel.com; Ann Leslie Tuttle
Fin Dir: Nataly Gruender *E-mail:* ngruender@dystel.com
Fin Assoc: Masie Ibrahim
Asst & Jr Agent: Kendall Berdinsky
  E-mail: kberdinsky@dystel.com
Film Rts Coord: Michaela Whatnall
  E-mail: mwhatnall@dystel.com
Subs Rts Assoc: Gracie Freeman Lifschutz
  E-mail: gfreemanlifschutz@dystel.com
Founded: 1994 (as Jane Dystel Literary Management)
General fiction & nonfiction, also cookbooks & children's books. No unsol mss, query letter or e-mail query with outline & first 50 pages. No reading fee. Handle film & TV rights. Firm also has a West Coast office staffed by Michael Bourret & Erin Young (e-mail queries only).
Titles recently placed: *100 Morning Treats*, Sarah Kieffer; *13 Things Mentally Strong People Don't Do Workbook*, Amy Morin; *A Cosmic Kind of Love*, Samantha Young; *All That's Left in the World*, Erik J Brown; *An Arrow to the Moon*, Emily X R Pan; *Attack of the Black Rectangles*, A S King; *Behind the Scenes*, Karelia Stetz-Waters; *Between Perfect and Real*, Ray Stoeve; *Blue Hour*, Tiffany Clarke Harrison; *Clarice the Brave*, Lisa McMann; *Daughter of Sparta*, Claire M Andrews; *Do You Take This Man?*, Denise Williams; *Don't Cry For Me*, Daniel Black; *Enter the Body*, Joy McCullough; *Everyday Dinners*, Jessica Merchant; *Fatty Fatty Boom Boom*, Rabia Chaudry; *Heard It in A Love Song*, Tracey Garvis Graves; *Hotel of Secrets*, Diana Biller; *I'm So Not Over You*, Kosoko Jackson; *If God Is Love, Don't Be a Jerk*, John Pavlovitz; *In the Key of Us*, Mariama Lockington; *It Starts With Us*, Colleen Hoover; *Last Night at the Telegraph Club*, Malinda Lo; *Let the Record Show*, Sarah Schulman; *Liar, Dreamer, Thief*, Maria Dong; *Lincoln's Mentors*, Michael Gerhardt; *Love By Design*, Elizabeth Everett; *Lucha and the Night Forest*, Tehlor Kay Mejia; *Lunar Love*, Lauren Kung Jessen; *Lying in the Deep*, Diana Urban; *Miseducated*, Brandon Fleming; *Mothercoin*, Elizabeth Cummins Munoz; *My Good Man*, Eric Gansworth; *My Government Means to Kill Me*, Rasheed Newson; *Nice Racism*, Robin DiAngelo; *Nobody's Princess*, Erica Ridley; *Once There Were Wolves*, Charlotte McConaghy; *One Great Lie*, Deb Caletti; *Paradise on Fire*, Jewell Parker Rhodes; *Pedro's Theory*, Marcos Gonsalez; *Pomegranate*, Helen Elaine Lee; *Robert E Lee: A Life*, Allen C Guelzo; *Sister Novelists*, Devoney Looser; *Super Fly*, Jonathan Balcombe; *Tell It Like It Is*, Roy Peter Clark; *The Arbornaut*, Meg Lowman; *The Confidante*, Christopher C Gorham; *The Disordered Cosmos*, Chanda Prescod-Weinstein; *The Doomsday Mother*, John Glatt; *The Family Plot*, Megan Collins; *The Male Gazed*, Manuel Betancourt; *The Red Palace*, June Hur; *Unprotected*, Billy Porter; *West With Giraffes*, Lynda Rutledge; *What We Kept to Ourselves*, Nancy Jooyoun Kim; *When You Wonder, You're Learning*, Gregg Behr, Ryan Rydzewski; *You Are Radically Loved*, Rosie Acosta; *You Should Be Grateful*, Angela Tucker
Foreign Rep(s): Ali (Italy); ANAW (Poland); Agence Litteraire Eliane Benisti (France); Big Apple Agency Inc (China); EAJ (Japan); International Editors' Co - Yanez Agencia Literaria (Latin America, Spain); Kayi Literary (Turkey); Mohrbooks AG Literary Agency (Germany); Andrew Nurnberg (Eastern Europe); Read n Right Agency (Greece); Agencia Riff (Brazil); Sebes & Bisseling Literary Agency (Netherlands); Abner Stein Agency (UK); TBPAI (Israel); Ulf Toregard Agency AB (Scandinavia); Tuttle-Mori Agency (Thailand) Co Ltd (Thailand); Eric Yang Agency (South Korea)

Anne Edelstein Literary Agency LLC (L)
Affiliate of Aevitas Creative Management
258 Riverside Dr, No 8D, New York, NY 10025
Tel: 212-414-4923
E-mail: info@aeliterary.com
Web Site: www.aeliterary.com
Key Personnel
Pres: Anne Edelstein (AALA)
Founded: 1990
Literary fiction & narrative nonfiction (including memoir, history, psychology, religion & culinary); handle film & TV rights; agents in all principal foreign countries.
No unsol mss.
Foreign Rights: AnatoliaLit Agency (Turkey); Silvia Bastos Agencia Literaria SL (Pau Centellas) (Spain); English Agency Japan Co Ltd (Japan); Literarische Agentur Gaeb & Eggers (Petra Eggers) (Germany); The Grayhawk Agency (China, Taiwan); The Harris Agency (Geula Geurts) (Israel); Danny Hong Agency (Danny Hong) (South Korea); The Italian Agency srl (Italy); Prava i prevodi (Eastern Europe); Sebes & Bisseling Literary Agency (Netherlands, Scandinavia); Abner Stein Ltd (Caspian Dennis) (UK); The Van Lear Agency (Russia); Villas-Boas & Moss Literary Agency (Brazil)
Membership(s): The Authors Guild

Ekus Group LLC (L)
57 North St, Hatfield, MA 01038
Tel: 413-247-9325
E-mail: info@ekusgroup.com
Web Site: ekusgroup.com
Key Personnel
Pres & Lead Agent: Sally Ekus (AALA)
  E-mail: sally@ekusgroup.com
Founded: 1982
Since inception, we have been helping both new & established authors & chefs make their mark on the culinary landscape. All of our nationally recognized culinary promotions are built on the same foundation: to create innovative strategies, pay meticulous attention to client needs & effectively & productively network across the culinary, media & publishing industries. In 2000, we expanded our award-winning expertise to include author representation & literary agent services. We have since negotiated over 500 book deals, representing over 90 authors & numerous leading publishers internationally. In 2022, we launched the first *How to Write a Cookbook* publishing course, available through our web site. We offer comprehensive media training programs designed for authors, chefs, spokespeople, show hosts & food professionals & orchestrate creative partnerships between individuals & corporations in the culinary industry. Specialty areas include: food, nutrition, health, parenting, wine & spirits. Submissions should be in the form of a complete proposal. Detailed guidelines are available on our web site. No fees, clients are billed for expenses.
Titles recently placed: *Coastal South Cookbook*, Samuel Monsour, Kassady Wiggins; *Gursha*, Beejhy Barhany, Elisa Ung; *Hot For Food All Day: Easy Recipes to Level Up Your Vegan Meals*, Lauren Toyota; *Latinisimo: Home Recipes from the Twenty-One Countries of Latin America*, Sandra Gutierrez; *Spanglish*, Monti Carlo; *The Global Pantry Cookbook: Transform Your Everyday Cooking with Tahini, Gochujang, Miso, and Other Irresistible Ingredients*, Scott Mowbray, Ann Pittman; *Tiny Humans, Big Emotions*, Alyssa Blask Campbell, Lauren Stauble

LITERARY AGENTS

Foreign Rights: The Jean V Naggar Literary Agency
Membership(s): International Association of Culinary Professionals (IACP); Women Presidents' Organization

Ethan Ellenberg Literary Agency (L)
548 Broadway, Apt 5C, New York, NY 10012
Tel: 212-431-4554
E-mail: agent@ethanellenberg.com
Web Site: www.ethanellenberg.com
Key Personnel
Pres & Agent: Ethan Ellenberg (AALA)
Agent & Head, Subs Rts: Ezra Ellenberg
 E-mail: ezra@royaltyreminder.com
Agent: Evan Gregory (AALA)
Assoc Agent & Off Mgr: BiBi Lewis
Founded: 1984
Commercial & literary fiction & nonfiction. Fiction: specialize in science fiction, fantasy, romance & all women's fiction. Suspense, thriller, mystery, first novels, all children's books including new adult & middle grade. Nonfiction: narrative nonfiction, history, adventure, science. Accepting new clients, both published & unpublished. No reading fees; accept unsol submissions with SASE. E-mail submissions without attachments accepted, but prefer submissions by mail. For fiction: first 3 chapters, synopsis & SASE. For nonfiction: proposal, including outline & author bio, sample chapters, if available. Co-agents in Hollywood & all principal foreign countries.
Titles recently placed: *Adrift*, Tony Peak; *Arkads World*, James Cambias; *Ben Franklin's in My Kitchen*, Candace Fleming; *Best Friend's Forever*, Margot Hunt; *Bulldozer 3*, Candace Fleming, Eric Rohmann; *Echo in Onyx (3 book series)*, Sharon Shinn; *Flames of Rebellion (3 books)*, Jay Allan; *Frontlines (series)*, Marko Kloos; *Hot and Badgered (3 book series)*, Shelly Laurenston; *Java Jive (series)*, Caroline Fardig; *Nest of the Monarch*, Kay Kenyon; *Persistence*, Marc Costanzo; *Shadow Hunt*, Melissa F Olson; *Solar Warden (3 book series)*, Ian Douglas; *The Body Under the Piano*, Marthe Jocelyn; *The Farmer's Daughter*, Shelly Laurenston; *The Singularity Trap*, Dennis E Taylor; *Twelve Book Deal with Tor*, John Scalzi; *Twilight's Desires*, Amanda Ashley; *We Are Legion (Bobiverse Series)*, Dennis E Taylor
Foreign Rights: Eliane Benisti (France); Berla & Griffini (Italy); Big Apple Agency Inc (China); Book Publishers Association of Israel (Israel); BookCosmos Agency (South Korea); English Agency Japan Co Ltd (Japan); Alexander Korzhenevski Agency (Russia); Mo Literary Agency (Holland); Prava i prevodi (Eastern Europe); RDC Agencia Literaria SL (Spain); Thomas Schlueck Agency (Germany)
Membership(s): The Authors Guild; Authors Registry; Mystery Writers of America (MWA); Romance Writers of America (RWA); Science Fiction and Fantasy Writers of America, Inc (SFWA); Society of Children's Book Writers & Illustrators (SCBWI)

Embolden Literary (L)
Division of Embolden Media Group
PO Box 953607, Lake Mary, FL 32795-3607
E-mail: info@emboldenmediagroup.com; submissions@emboldenmediagroup.com
Web Site: emboldenmediagroup.com/literary-representation
Key Personnel
Founder, CEO & Agent: Jevon Bolden (AALA)
Agent: Deidra Riggs; Rebekah Von Lintel
Assoc Agent: Kathy Green; Joylanda Jamison; Mytecia Myles
Founded: 2017
Boutique literary agency advocating for the works of inspirational women writers, authors of color & diverse creators of faith. No unsol mss, query first by e-mail only.
Titles recently placed: *Everyday Enneagram*, Dayo Ajanaku; *In God's Good Image: How Jesus Dignifies, Shapes, and Confronts Our Cultural Identities*, J W Buck; *When Your World Ends: God's Creative Process for Rebuilding a Life*, Dawn Mann Sanders

Felicia Eth Literary Representation (L)
555 Bryant St, Suite 350, Palo Alto, CA 94301
Mailing Address: 201 Fair Oaks St, San Francisco, CA 94110
Tel: 415-970-9717
E-mail: feliciaeth.literary@gmail.com
Web Site: www.ethliterary.com
Key Personnel
Pres: Felicia Eth (AALA)
Founded: 1989
Diverse nonfiction including narrative, psychology, health & popular science; including women's issues, investigative journalism & biography. Selective mainstream literary fiction. No unsol mss, query first for fiction, proposal for nonfiction. Prefer e-mail or written query, no phone calls please. No discs, no files by e-mail. Handle film & TV rights for clients, books only through sub-agents in Los Angeles. No reading fee. Xeroxing costs & overseas mail, FedEx charged to client, $75 for full-length ms to cover mailing. Commission is 15% domestic & 20% foreign. Foreign rights agents in all major territories.
Titles recently placed: *Boutwell: Radical Republican and Champion of Democracy*, Jeffrey Boutwell; *Elephants in the Hourglass*, Kim Frank; *The Man with Eight Pairs of Legs*, Leslie Kirk Campbell; *The Tao of Equus (revised)*, Linda Kohanov; *Water Finds a Way*, Meghan Perry

Mary Evans Inc (L)
242 E Fifth St, New York, NY 10003-8501
Fax: 212-979-5344
E-mail: info@maryevansinc.com
Web Site: maryevansinc.com
Key Personnel
Pres: Mary Evans (AALA)
Founded: 1994
Literary fiction, narrative nonfiction, commercial fiction, self-help, science & history, graphic novels & memoirs. Nonfiction should be submitted in proposal form & fiction with a query letter, a synopsis & 3 sample chapters, SASE required. Accept unsol mss. Handle film & TV rights, no reading fee.
Foreign Rights: Akcali Copyright Agency (Atilla Izgi Turgut) (Turkey); Berla & Griffini Rights Agency (Erica Berla) (Italy); English Agency Japan Co Ltd (Hamish Macaskill) (Japan); The Grayhawk Agency (Gray Tan) (China, Taiwan); International Editors' Co - Yanez Agencia Literaria (Maru De Montserrat) (Portugal, Spain); The Israeli Association of Book Publishers Ltd (Beverley Levit) (Israel); LEX Copyright Office (Norbert Uzseki) (Hungary); Licht & Burr (Trine Licht) (Scandinavia); La Nouvelle Agence (Michele Kanonidis) (France); Andrew Nurnberg Associates (Ludmila Sushkova) (Russia); Peters, Fraser & Dunlop (Caroline Michel) (UK); Prava i prevodi (Ana Milenkovic) (Eastern Europe, Greece); Riff Agency (Laura Riff) (Brazil); Elisabeth Ruge Agentur (Elisabeth Ruge) (Germany); Marianne Schonbach Agency (Marianne Schonbach) (Belgium, Netherlands); Eric Yang Agency (Henry Shin) (South Korea)

Feigenbaum Publishing Consultants Inc (L)
61 Bounty Lane, Jericho, NY 11753
Tel: 516-647-8314 (cell)

EDITORIAL SERVICES

Key Personnel
Pres: Laurie Feigenbaum
 E-mail: lauriefeigenbaum@gmail.com
Founded: 1991
Contract negotiations & review, agenting, trademark & copyright registration, permissions clearance & general publishing advice. Expertise in book publishing, magazines & digital publishing. Resume, cover letter & LinkedIn specialist in all areas of media, including print, digital, video & social media. No unsol mss, query first. Contracts negotiation, resume, cover letter & LinkedIn consulting, $95 per hour.

FinePrint Literary Management (L-D)
207 W 106 St, Suite 1D, New York, NY 10025
Tel: 212-279-6214
E-mail: info@fineprintlit.com; submissions@fineprint.com
Web Site: www.fineprintlit.com
Key Personnel
Pres & CEO: Peter Rubie (AALA)
VP & Agent: Lauren Bieker (AALA)
In-House Subs Rts Dir: Jacqueline Murphy
Agent: Christine Goss (AALA); Bonnie Swanson (AALA); Laura Wood
Assoc Agent: Mara Hollander; Zach Honey; Morgan Hughes
Online Admin: June Clark
Founded: 2007 (formed by the merger of the Peter Rubie Agency & the Imprint Agency)
Representation & management for new & established writers of fiction & nonfiction for both adults & children. Handles subsidiary rights for foreign translation, audio, TV & film. No screenplays, stage plays, or TV scripts. For fiction, submit query letter, synopsis, your bio & opening 3-4 pages in the body of your e-mail. For nonfiction, send query letter & your bio via e-mail (no attachments).
Titles recently placed: *Building Boys: Raising Great Guys in a World that Misunderstands Males*, Jennifer L W Fink; *Painting the Cosmos: How Art & Science Intersect to Reveal the Secrets of the Universe*, Nia Imara; *The Ghosts of Beatrice Bird*, Louisa Morgan
Foreign Rep(s): Lorella Belli (UK); Book/lab (Poland); The Book Publishers' Association of Israel (Israel); Donatella d'Ormesson (France); English Agency Japan Co Ltd (Japan); Grayhawk Agency (China, Taiwan); International Editors' Co - Yanez Agencia Literaria (Latin America, Spain); Japan UNI Agency Inc (Japan); JML Literary Agency (Greece); Nurcihan Kesim Literary Agency Ltd (Turkey); Lex Copywright Agency (Hungary); Maxima Creative Agency (Indonesia); PNLA (Italy); Agencia Literaria Riff (Brazil); Thomas Schlueck GmbH (Germany); Sebes & Bisseling Literary Agency (Netherlands, Scandinavia); Tuttle-Mori Agency Inc (Malaysia, Thailand, Vietnam); Eric Yang Agency (South Korea)

The Fischer-Harbage Agency Inc (L)
237 36 St, Brooklyn, NY 11232
Tel: 212-695-7105
E-mail: submissions@fischerharbage.com
Web Site: www.fischerharbage.com
Key Personnel
Pres & Agent: Ryan Fischer-Harbage
Founded: 2007
Full service boutique literary agency specializing in fiction, memoir, narrative nonfiction & current events. No unsol mss, query first with a short description, bio & first chapter of your book in the body of the e-mail.
Titles recently placed: *Eat the World: A Collection of Poems*, Marina Diamandis; *Inevitable: Inside the Messy, Unstoppable Transition to Electric Vehicles*, Mike Colias; *Saturday Night at the Lakeside Supper Club*, J Ryan Stradal
Foreign Rights: The Marsh Agency UK (worldwide)

Flannery Literary (L)
1140 Wickfield Ct, Naperville, IL 60563
E-mail: jennifer@flanneryliterary.com
Web Site: flanneryliterary.com
Key Personnel
Owner: Jennifer Flannery
Founded: 1992
Represents authors of books written for middle grade & young adult readers. Actively looking for novels. No picture books or graphic novels at this time, please. No unsol mss, query first by e-mail. No attachments unless/until requested.

Sheldon Fogelman Agency Inc (L)
420 E 72 St, New York, NY 10021
Tel: 212-532-7250 *Fax:* 212-685-8939
E-mail: info@sheldonfogelmanagency.com; submissions@sheldonfogelmanagency.com
Web Site: sheldonfogelmanagency.com
Key Personnel
Pres & Literary Agent: Sheldon Fogelman
Asst Agent: Amy Stern
Founded: 1975
Specialize in children's books of all genres, from picture books through young adult literature. Query by e-mail only with single page cover letter with brief synopsis & publication history. Novelists may include first 3 chapters. Picture book writers may include 2 mss. Illustrators should include web site portfolio links or a limited sampling of examples of their work. No reading fee.

Folio Literary Management (L)
The Film Center Bldg, 630 Ninth Ave, Suite 1101, New York, NY 10036
Tel: 212-400-1494 *Fax:* 212-967-0977
Web Site: www.foliolit.com
Key Personnel
Founding Partner: Jeff Kleinman (AALA)
Partner: Claudia Cross (AALA); Steve Troha (AALA); Emily van Beek (AALA)
E-mail: emily@foliolitmanagement.com
SVP, Dir, Opers & Agent: Frank Weimann
SVP & Agent: Erin Niumata; Marcy Posner (AALA)
VP: Erin Harris
Dir, Intl Rts & Agent: Melissa White
Contracts Mgr & Agent: Michael Harriot
Agent: Jan Baumer; Sharon Bowers (AALA); Jamie Chambliss; Rachel Ekstrom Courage; John Cusick; Dado Derviskadic; Lauren Hall; Katherine Latshaw; Don Laventhall; Angela Miller; Quressa Robinson; Jeff Silberman (AALA); Lauren Spieller (AALA)
Agent & Sr Content Devt Ed: Estelle Laure
Affiliated Agent: Jenna Land Free
Intl Rts Agent: Chiara Panzeri
Literary & Dramatic Rts Agent: Ruth Pomerance
Literary & Opers Assoc: Elissa Alves
Literary Asst: Maggie Auffartth
Founded: 2006
A full service literary agency with co-agents around the world. No unsol mss, query first via e-mail. No fees.
Titles recently placed: *10-Day Green Smoothie Cleanse*, J J Smith; *Anchor & Sophia*, Tommy Wallach; *But Enough About Me*, Burt Reynolds; *Deep Nutrition*, Dr Cate Shanahan; *Ginny Moon*, Benjamin Ludwig; *Girls on the Verge*, Sharon Biggs Waller; *Hustle*, Neal Patel, Patrick Vlaskovits, Jonas Koffler; *I Killed Zoe Spanos*, Kit Frick; *I'm Judging You*, Luvvie Ajay; *Jackie's Girl*, Kathy McKeon; *Maybe a Mermaid*, Josephine Cameron; *Only Child*, Rhiannon Navin; *Saints and Misfits*, S K Ali; *Seven Deadly Shadows*, Courtney Alameda, Valynne Maetani; *The Ballerina Body*, Misty Copeland; *The Better Liar*, Tanen Jones; *The Grown-Up's Guide to Teenage Humans*, Josh Shipp; *The Marsh King's Daughter*, Karen Dionne; *The Pieces of Piper Perish*, Kayla Cagan; *The Reminders*, Val Emmich; *The Seven Torments of Amy and Craig*, Don Zolidis; *The Wellness Mama Cookbook*, Katie Spears; *Tia and Tamera Mowry*, Twintuition; *Wallis in Love*, Andrew Morton; *Warren Buffett's Ground Rules*, Jeremy Miller; *Where the Light Gets In*, Kimberly Williams-Paisley
Foreign Rights: Berla & Griffini (Italy); The Book Publishers Association of Israel (Israel); Catherine Fragou (Greece); Graal Literary Agency (Poland); The Grayhawk Agency (China, Taiwan); Danny Hong Agency (South Korea); International Editors' Co - Yanez Agencia Literaria (Portugal); Asli Karasuil Telif Haklari (Turkey); Agence Michelle Lapautre (France); Maxima Creative Agency (Indonesia); Prava i prevodi (Czechia, Russia, Serbia); Riff Agency (Brazil); Thomas Schlueck GmbH (Germany); Marianne Schoenbach Literary Agency (Netherlands); Livia Stoia Literary Agency (Romania); Ulf Toregard Agency AB (Scandinavia); Tuttle-Mori Agency Inc (Japan, Thailand, Vietnam); Susanna Zevi Agenzia Letteraria (Italy)

Fort Ross Inc - International Representation for Artists (L)
Division of Fort Ross Inc
26 Arthur Place, Yonkers, NY 10701
Tel: 914-375-6448
Key Personnel
Pres & Exec Dir: Dr Vladimir P Kartsev
E-mail: vkartsev2000@gmail.com
Founded: 1992
Fiction: American, Kazakh & Russian classics, romance, mysteries, science fiction, fantasy, adventure. Provide publishers with texts & illustrations. Publishing books in English & Russian ("Metropolitan Classics").
Titles recently placed: *End of the Legend*, Abish Kekilbaev; *Lonely Yurt*, Smagul Yelubay; *The Code of the Word*, Olzhas Suleimenov
Foreign Rep(s): Nova Littera (Baltic States, Belarus, Russia, Ukraine)

Robert A Freedman Dramatic Agency Inc (D)
PO Box 3544, New York, NY 10163
Tel: 718-897-0950
Key Personnel
Pres: Robert A Freedman (AALA)
E-mail: rfreedmanagent@aol.com
SVP: Marta Praeger (AALA)
Founded: 1928 (as Harold Freedman Brandt & Brandt Dramatic Department Inc, until 1981)
Dramatic scripts for stage, motion picture & TV. No unsol mss, query first. No reading fee. Material placed for production/publication is subject to 10% commission. Agents in all European countries. Will co-agent with literary agents to handle film rights & books.

Sarah Jane Freymann Literary Agency LLC (L)
59 W 71 St, Suite 9-B, New York, NY 10023
Tel: 212-362-9277
E-mail: submissions@sarahjanefreymann.com
Web Site: www.sarahjanefreymann.com
Key Personnel
Owner & Agent: Sarah Jane Freymann
E-mail: sarah@sarahjanefreymann.com
Assoc: Katharine Sands *Tel:* 212-751-8892; Steven Schwartz *Tel:* 212-362-1998
E-mail: steve@sarahjanefreymann.com
Founded: 1974
Represents book-length fiction & general nonfiction. Fiction: popular fiction plus quality mainstream, literary fiction & young adult. Nonfiction: spiritual/inspirational, psychology, self-help; women's/men's issues; health (conventional & alternative); cookbooks; narrative nonfiction, natural science, nature, memoirs, biography; current events, multicultural issues, popular culture; illustrated books, lifestyle, garden, design, architecture, humor, sports, travel & business. No unsol mss, query first with SASE. Handle film & TV rights with sub-agents. Representation in all foreign markets. No reading fee.

Fredrica S Friedman & Co Inc (L)
857 Fifth Ave, New York, NY 10065
Tel: 212-639-9455
E-mail: info@fredricafriedman.com
Web Site: www.fredricafriedman.com
Key Personnel
Pres: Fredrica S Friedman
Founded: 2000
Literary management firm that represents best selling & award-winning authors. General nonfiction & fiction. No poetry, plays, screenplays, children's picture books, science fiction/fantasy or horror. No unsol mss-query first. Send all queries by e-mail, no attachments. See web site for detailed submission information. Hard copy materials will not be returned; no fees.

Candice Fuhrman Literary Agency (L)
10 Cypress Hollow Dr, Tiburon, CA 94920
Tel: 415-383-1014
E-mail: fuhrmancandice@gmail.com
Key Personnel
Pres & Owner: Candice Fuhrman
Nonfiction: health, memoir, psychology, women's issues, how-to & self-help; literary & commercial fiction. No unsol mss.
Currently not accepting new clients.
Foreign Rights: Jenny Meyer Literary Agency

The Garamond Agency Inc (L)
12 Horton St, Newburyport, MA 01950
E-mail: query@garamondagency.com
Web Site: www.garamondagency.com
Key Personnel
Dir: Lisa Adams; David Miller
Adult nonfiction, no memoir or self-help. Handle TV & movie rights. No unsol mss, query first by e-mail only.
Foreign Rights: AnatoliaLit Agency (Turkey); Bardon-Chinese Media Agency (China, Taiwan); Berla & Griffini Rights Agency (Italy); Raquel de la Concha Agencia Literaria (Portugal, Spain); Corto Literary (Croatia, Montenegro, North Macedonia, Romania, Serbia, Slovenia); Anna Jarota Agency (France, Poland); Katai & Bolza Literary Agents (Hungary); Duran Kim Agency (South Korea); Mo Literary Services (Netherlands, Scandinavia); Mohrbooks AG Literary Agency (Germany); Andrew Nurnberg Literary Agency (Russia & former USSR); The Riff Agency (Brazil); Tuttle-Mori Agency Inc (Japan)
Membership(s): The Authors Guild

Max Gartenberg Literary Agency (L)
912 N Pennsylvania Ave, Yardley, PA 19067
Tel: 215-295-9230
Web Site: www.maxgartenberg.com
Key Personnel
Agent: Anne G Devlin *E-mail:* agdevlin@aol.com
Founded: 1954
Nonfiction books of all types. No unsol mss, query first. Submit complete book proposal & sample chapters as requested. No reading fee. Handle film & TV rights. Agents in all principal foreign markets.
Titles recently placed: *Charles Addams: A Cartoonist's Life*, Linda H Davis; *Colleges Worth Your Money: A Guide to What America's Top Schools Can Do For You*, Andrew Belasco, Dave Bergman, Michael Trivette; *Epidemics: The Impact of Germs and Their Power over Humanity*, Joshua Loomis; *Not Your Average Joe*, Marc Bona, Dan Murphy; *Snow: A History of the World's Most Fascinating Flake*, Anthony R Wood; *The Dealer*, Jim Ciardella;

LITERARY AGENTS

The Edge of Malice, David Miraldi; *The Total FilmMaker*, Jerry Lewis, Leonard Maltin
Foreign Rights: International Editors' Co (Argentina); Mohrbooks AG Literary Agency (Switzerland); La Nouvelle Agence (France); Lennart Sane Agency AB (Sweden); Tuttle-Mori Agency Inc (Japan)

Gelfman Schneider Literary Agents Inc (L)
850 Seventh Ave, Suite 903, New York, NY 10019
Tel: 212-245-1993
E-mail: mail@gelfmanschneider.com
Web Site: gelfmanschneider.com
Key Personnel
Literary Agent: Jane Gelfman (AALA); Deborah Schneider (AALA); Penelope Burns (AALA)
Busn Aff: Cathy Gleason
General trade fiction & nonfiction. Queries by mail only, no e-mail queries will be considered. No unsol mss, query first with SASE. Submit sample chapters & outline. Handle film & TV rights. No reading fee.
Foreign Rights: Curtis Brown, Ltd (translation, UK)
Membership(s): The Authors Guild; Authors Registry

The Gersh Agency (TGA) (L-D)
41 Madison Ave, 29th fl, New York, NY 10010
Tel: 212-997-1818
Web Site: gersh.com/books
Key Personnel
Partner & Talent/Literary Agent: J Joseph Veltre, III
Literary/Film Agent: Alice Lawson
Literary Agent: Hannah Vaughn
Founded: 2007 (1949 as talent agency)
Fiction, nonfiction, adult & juvenile, film & TV rights & plays. No unsol mss. Unsol materials will not be accepted or considered.
Branch Office(s)
9465 Wilshire Blvd, Suite 600, Beverly Hills, CA 90212 (talent div) *Tel:* 310-274-6611

GGP Publishing Inc (L)
Larchmont, NY 10538
Tel: 914-834-8896 *Fax:* 914-834-7566
Web Site: www.GGPPublishing.com
Key Personnel
Founder, Owner & Dir: Generosa Gina Protano *E-mail:* GGProtano@GGPPublishing.com
Founded: 1991
Fiction & nonfiction; educational materials, English & foreign languages. Handle film & TV rights. No unsol mss, query first. Reading fees on all submissions, refundable from commission; fee charged for photocopying & postage or courier. Editorial & translation services also available.
Membership(s): American Book Producers Association (ABPA)

Susan Gleason (L)
325 Riverside Dr, Suite 41, New York, NY 10025
Tel: 212-662-3876
E-mail: sgleasonliteraryagent@gmail.com
Founded: 1992
Adult trade & mass market, fiction & nonfiction. No unsol mss, query first with SASE.
Handle film & TV rights, foreign rights. No reading fees.

Global Lion Intellectual Property Management Inc (L-D)
Affiliate of Millennium Lion Inc
PO Box 669238, Pompano Beach, FL 33066
Tel: 754-222-6948 *Fax:* 754-222-6948
E-mail: queriesgloballionmgt@gmail.com
Web Site: www.globallionmanagement.com

Key Personnel
Pres: Peter Miller *E-mail:* peter@globallionmgt.com
Assoc: Charlie Serabian *E-mail:* charlie@globallionmgt.com
Represents transformational & spiritual nonfiction, young adult, commercial fiction, nonfiction, true crime & celebrity books. Also handles film & TV rights for original properties. Represents literary & film properties internationally. See web site for additional submission guidelines. Works with co-agents in select foreign territories & deals directly with foreign publishers. No fees charged.
Titles recently placed: *Helter Skelter*, Vincent Bugliosi, Curt Gentry; *History of the World*, Jean-Pierre Isbouts; *Manifesto*, Sir Ken Robinson
Foreign Rep(s): Big Apple Agency Inc (China); Peter Bolza (Hungary); Tuttle-Mori Agency Inc (Japan)

Globo Libros Literary Management (L)
450 E 63 St, New York, NY 10065
Web Site: www.globo-libros.com; www.publishersmarketplace.com/members/dstockwell
Key Personnel
Literary Agent: Diane Stockwell *E-mail:* diane.stockwell@gmail.com
Founded: 2006
Specialize in nonfiction authors from the US & abroad. Looking for compelling narrative nonfiction, current events, history, cookbooks, memoir, biography, parenting & self-help by authors of any background. We also offer book length & short translations from Spanish into English. Query by e-mail only with a detailed summary of the project & author bio in the body of the message. No attachments. No fees charged.
Titles recently placed: *Cocina Ligera*, Johana Clavel; *Democracy Under Threat*, Jake Braun; *Hipster Death Rattle*, Richie Narvaez; *Killing the Story: The War on Journalists in Mexico*, Temoris Grecko; *Why Don't They Want Us Here? Stories of Resistance and Resilience from Mexicans Living in the United States*, Eileen Truax
Membership(s): The Authors Guild

Goldfarb & Associates (L-D)
721 Gibbon St, Alexandria, VA 22314
Tel: 202-466-3030
E-mail: rlglawlit@gmail.com
Web Site: www.ronaldgoldfarb.com
Key Personnel
Founder & Owner: Ronald L Goldfarb
Literary Agent: Ms Gerrie Lipson Sturman; Robbie Anna Hare
Off Mgr: Steven Seigart
Founded: 1966
Only select new clients accepted. Fiction & serious nonfiction; no romance or science fiction. No unsol mss, query first with e-mail/letter, outline or synopsis, sample of best chapter, bio & SASE. No reading fee.
Titles recently placed: *Letter to America: Our Last & Only Chance*, Faris Cassell; *The Private Equity Industry: A Startling Look at Wall Street's Magical Elixir*, Jeffrey C Hooke; *Truth From Power: Dwight D Eisenhower*, Susan Eisenhower
Branch Office(s)
177 Ocean Lane Dr, Suite 1101, Key Biscayne, FL 33149

Frances Goldin Literary Agency, Inc (L-D)
214 W 29 St, Suite 410, New York, NY 10001
Tel: 212-777-0047 *Fax:* 212-228-1660
E-mail: agency@goldinlit.com
Web Site: www.goldinlit.com

EDITORIAL SERVICES

Key Personnel
VP & Sr Agent: Ellen Geiger (AALA); Matt McGowan (AALA) *E-mail:* mm@goldinlit.com; Sam Stoloff (AALA)
Sr Agent: Caroline Eisenmann (AALA); Roz Foster
Agent & Rts Dir: Sulamita Garbuz; Tess Weitzner
Agent: Ria Julien; Alison Lewis; Jade Wong-Baxter; Ayla Zuraw-Friedland
Founded: 1977
No unsol mss or work previously submitted to publishers, query first with letter & SASE. No racist, sexist, agist, homophobic or pornographic material considered. Adult literary fiction & serious progressive nonfiction. Agents in Hollywood & all major foreign countries. No software. Handle film & TV rights. No reading fee.
Foreign Rights: Anthea Agency (Bulgaria); Eliane Benisti Agency (France); Berla & Griffini Rights Agency (Italy); Corto Literary Agency (Bosnia and Herzegovina, Croatia, Montenegro, North Macedonia, Serbia, Slovenia); Graal Literary Agency (Poland); The Grayhawk Agency (China, Taiwan); The Deborah Harris Agency (Israel); International Editors' Co - Yanez Agencia Literaria (Argentina, Brazil, Portugal, Spain); Japan UNI Agency Inc (Japan); JLM Literary Agency (Greece); Asli Karasuil (Turkey); Simona Kessler International (Romania); Liepman AG (Germany); Maxima Creative Agency (Indonesia, Malaysia, Thailand, Vietnam); Kristin Olson Literary Agency (Czechia); Lennart Sane Agency (Holland, Iceland, Scandinavia); Synopsis Literary Agency (Russia); Norbert Uzseka (Hungary); The Eric Yang Agency (South Korea)

Irene Goodman Literary Agency (L)
27 W 24 St, Suite 700B, New York, NY 10010
Tel: 212-604-0330
E-mail: queries@irenegoodman.com
Web Site: www.irenegoodman.com
Key Personnel
Pres: Irene Goodman (AALA) *E-mail:* irene.queries@irenegoodman.com
VP: Miriam Kriss *E-mail:* miriam.queries@irenegoodman.com; Barbara Poelle *E-mail:* barbara.queries@irenegoodman.com
Agent: Pam Gruber; Victoria Marini (AALA) *E-mail:* victoria.queries@irenegoodman.com; Kim Perel *E-mail:* kim.queries@irenegoodman.com; Whitney Ross *E-mail:* whitney.queries@irenegoodman.com
Founded: 1978
Commercial & literary fiction & nonfiction including mysteries, romance, women's fiction, thrillers & suspense. No poetry, inspirational fiction, screenplays or children's picture books. Handle film & TV rights through Steven Fisher in Los Angeles. No unsol mss, query first with first 10 pages & synopsis via e-mail. No snail mail. See web site under submission guidelines for each agent's preferences. No reading fee.
Foreign Rep(s): Danny Baror
Foreign Rights: Baror International Agency

Doug Grad Literary Agency Inc (L)
156 Prospect Park W, No 3L, Brooklyn, NY 11215
Tel: 718-788-6067
E-mail: query@dgliterary.com
Web Site: www.dgliterary.com
Key Personnel
Pres: Doug Grad *E-mail:* doug.grad@dgliterary.com
Founded: 2008
Commercial fiction & nonfiction in a wide variety of genres & subjects. See web site for additional information. Send cover letter only with brief description of book. Will ask to see more material if interested, via e-mail only to

query@dgliterary.com. Do not send hard copies of proposals or mss. No fees.
Titles recently placed: *American Time Bomb: The Assassination of Samuel Melville*, Joshua Melville; *Blood on the Trail*, Terrence McCauley; *First Victim*, Debbie Babitt; *Ghost Rifle*, Max McCoy; *Here Comes the Body*, Maria DiRico; *Isaac's Beacon*, David L Robbins; *Long Island Iced Tina*, Maria DiRico; *Lord High Executioner: The Legendary Mafia Boss Albert Anastasia*, Frank Dimatteo, Michael Benson; *Net Force: Attack Protocol*, Jerome Preisler; *Net Force: Dark Web*, Jerome Preisler; *Net Force: Eye of the Drone*, Jerome Preisler; *Payton and Brees: The Men Who Built the Greatest Offense in NFL History*, Jeff Duncan; *Sandbox Rules: The Wrongful Conviction of Lt Michael Behenna and Why the Army Sacrificed One of Its Own*, Michael Behenna, Vicki Behenna, Scott Behenna; *Saving Grace*, Debbie Babitt; *Sonny Pinto: The Life and Crimes of Mafia Killer Carmine DiBiase*, Frank Dimatteo, Michael Benson; *Sunday Mourning*, Terrence McCauley; *The Dog Who Took Me Up A Mountain: How Emme the Australian Terrier Changed My Life When I Needed It Most*, Rick Crandall, Joseph Cosgriff; *The Lives They Saved: The Untold Story of Medics, Mariners and the Incredible Boatlift That Evacuated 300,000 People on 9/11*, L Douglas Keeney; *They Were Soldiers: The Sacrifices and Contributions of Our Vietnam Veterans*, Joseph Galloway, Marvin J Wolf

Sanford J Greenburger Associates Inc (L)
55 Fifth Ave, New York, NY 10003
Tel: 212-206-5600
Web Site: greenburger.com
Key Personnel
Pres: Heide Lange (AALA) *E-mail:* queryhl@sjga.com
Dir, Foreign Rts: Dorothy Vincent
Sr Agent: Matt Bialer *E-mail:* querymb@sjga.com; Faith Hamlin (AALA); Dan Mandel *E-mail:* querydm@sjga.com
Agent: Stephanie Delman (AALA)
 E-mail: sdelman@sjga.com; Rachel Dillon Fried *E-mail:* rfried@sjga.com; Wendi Gu *E-mail:* wgu@sjga.com; Clare Mao *E-mail:* cmao@sjga.com; Sarah Phair *E-mail:* sphair@sjga.com; Zoe Sandler *E-mail:* zsandler@sjga.com
Assoc Agent: Abigail Frank *E-mail:* afrank@sjga.com; Sami Isman *E-mail:* sisman@sjga.com
Assoc Agent & Asst: Hannah Strouth (AALA) *E-mail:* hstrouth@sjga.com
Sr Scout: John Bowers *E-mail:* jbowers@sjga.com
Scout: Kirsten Kim *E-mail:* kkim@sjga.com
Founded: 1932
Fiction, nonfiction, young adult & children's. No unsol mss, physical or phone queries. Query via e-mail first. Submit outline or synopsis & sample chapter. No reading fee. Copying fee. Agents in all principal foreign countries.
Titles recently placed: *Low Country: A Southern Memoir*, J Nicole Jones; *Near Dark*, Brad Thor; *The Academy*, Katie Sise; *Wild Symphony*, Dan Brown
Foreign Rights: Berla & Griffini (Italy); Graal Literary Agency (Poland); Deborah Harris Agency (Israel); Licht & Burr (Scandinavia); MB Agencia Literaria (Brazil, Catalonia, Galicia, Portugal, Spain); Mohrbooks AG Literary Agency (Germany); La Nouvelle Agence (France, Quebec, CN); Andrew Nurnberg Associates Baltic (Estonia, Latvia, Lithuania, Ukraine); Andrew Nurnberg Associates Beijing (China); Andrew Nurnberg Associates Budapest (Croatia, Hungary); Andrew Nurnberg Associates Prague (Czechia, Slovakia, Slovenia); Andrew Nurnberg Associates Sofia (Albania, Bulgaria, North Macedonia, Romania, Serbia); Andrew Nurnberg Associates Taipei (Taiwan); Andrew Nurnberg Literary Agency Moscow (Russia); Read n Right Agency (Greece); Abner Stein Agency (UK); Tuttle-Mori Agency Inc (Japan); Eric Yang Agency (South Korea)

Jill Grinberg Literary Management LLC (L)
392 Vanderbilt Ave, Brooklyn, NY 11238
Tel: 212-620-5883
E-mail: info@jillgrinbergliterary.com
Web Site: www.jillgrinbergliterary.com
Key Personnel
Pres & Literary Agent: Jill Grinberg (AALA)
 E-mail: jill@jillgrinbergliterary.com
Head, Rts, Contracts & Legal/Literary Agent: Sophia Seidner (AALA) *E-mail:* sophia@jillgrinbergliterary.com
Literary Agent: Katelyn Detweiler (AALA)
 E-mail: katelyn@jillgrinbergliterary.com
Literary Agent & Foreign Rts Assoc: Sam Farkas (AALA) *E-mail:* sam@jillgrinbergliterary.com
Literary Agent: Larissa Melo Pienkowski
 E-mail: larissa@jillgrinbergliterary.com
Agent: Jessica Saint Jean *E-mail:* jessica@jillgrinbergliterary.com
Founded: 2007
Hands-on full service agency whose mission is helping authors to launch, develop & sustain successful careers. Accepting submissions in all categories for adult & children's fiction & nonfiction, as well as art portfolios from illustrators. Queries accepted via e-mail only. Send query letter & first 50 pages of ms as a docx. attachment. See web site for complete submission instructions.

Jill Grosjean Literary Agency (L)
1390 Millstone Rd, Sag Harbor, NY 11963
Tel: 631-725-7419 *Fax:* 631-725-8632
E-mail: JillLit310@aol.com
Key Personnel
Owner & Literary Agent: Jill Grosjean
Founded: 1999
Literary fiction, mystery/suspense, women's fiction. No unsol mss, query first; e-mail queries preferred, no downloads or attachments. No fees charged. Foreign rights in UK, France, Italy, Spain, Netherlands, South America.
Titles recently placed: *A Spark of Death*, Bernadette Pajer; *A Thread So Thin*, Marie Bostwick; *Beating the Babushka*, Tim Maleeny; *Betrayal in Time*, Julie McElwain; *Caught in Time*, Julie McElwain; *Comfort and Joy*, Marie Bostwick; *Emma and the Vampires*, Wayne Josephson; *Fatal Induction*, Bernadette Pajer; *House of Ashes*, Loretta Marion; *Jump*, Tim Maleeny; *Murder in Old Bombay*, Nev March; *Murder in Time*, Julie McElwain; *Nectar*, David Fickett; *Shadows in Time*, Julie McElwain; *Snow Angels*, Marie Bostwick; *Spectres in the Smoke*, Tony Broadbent; *Stealing the Dragon*, Tim Maleeny; *Storm of Secrets*, Loretta Marion; *The Black Widow Agency*, Felicia Donovan; *The Edison Effect*, Bernadette Pajer; *The Gold Pawn*, L A Chandlar; *The Lighterman's Curse*, Loretta Marion; *The Pearl Dagger*, L A Chandlar; *The Silver Gun*, L A Chandlar; *The Smoke*, Tony Broadbent; *Thread of Truth*, Marie Bostwick; *Threading the Needle*, Marie Bostwick; *Tim Cratchit's Christmas Carol*, Jim Piecuch; *Twist in Time*, Julie McElwain

Laura Gross Literary Agency (L)
PO Box 610326, Newton Highlands, MA 02461
Tel: 617-964-2977
E-mail: query@lg-la.com; rights@lg-la.com
Web Site: www.lg-la.com
Key Personnel
Pres & Agent: Laura Gross (AALA)
 E-mail: laura@lg-la.com
Agent: Lauren Scovel (AALA) *E-mail:* lauren@lg-la.com
Rights Dir: Amelia Brown
Founded: 1988
Submission guidelines are found on the web site www.lg-la.com/submissions. No reading fee.
Titles recently placed: *A Blood Red Morning*, Mark Pryor; *By Any Other Name*, Jodi Picoult; *Held Together*, Rebecca Thompson; *Just Lizzie*, Karen Wilfrid; *Longing for Connection*, Andrew Burstein; *The Alien Zoo*, Samantha van Leer; *The Domestic Detective*, Uzma Jalaluddin; *War Made Invisible*, Norman Solomon
Foreign Rights: Berla & Griffini Rights Agency (Italy); The English Agency (Japan); Paul & Peter Fritz Agency (Germany, Switzerland); Deborah Harris Agency (Israel); Anna Jarota Agency France (France); Anna Jarota Agency Poland (The Balkans, Eastern Europe); Kalem Agency (Turkey); Lutyens & Rubinstein (UK & Commonwealth); Maxima Creative Agency (Indonesia, Thailand, Vietnam); Andrew Nurnberg Literary Agency China (China); Andrew Nurnberg Literary Agency Taiwan (Taiwan); Shinwon Agency (South Korea); Livia Stoia Literary Agency (Latin America, Portugal, Romania, Spain)

The Charlotte Gusay Literary Agency (L-D)
10532 Blythe Ave, Los Angeles, CA 90064
Tel: 310-559-0831
E-mail: gusayagency1@gmail.com
Web Site: www.gusay.com
Founded: 1988
Fiction & nonfiction, screenplay, children & adult, humor, parenting; crossover literary/commercial fiction; gardening, women's & men's issues, feminism, psychology, memoir, biography, travel. Handle film & TV rights. Represent selected illustrators, especially children's. No unsol mss, query first with SASE by snail mail or by e-mail (send one paragraph describing book or film); ONLY when agency requests, submit one-page synopsis & first 3 chapters or first 50 pages (for fiction); proposal (for nonfiction). Include SASE. No reading fee. For borderline queries we sometimes give prospective clients the benefit of the doubt & impose a nominal processing fee allowing the prospective clients to decide whether to submit their material or not. Once client is signed, client is responsible for providing agency hard copies of mss (as necessary) & shipping expenses (as necessary).
Titles recently placed: *Afropessimism*, Frank B Wilderson III; *Along Comes the Association*, Russ Giguere, Ashley Wren Collins; *Everything I Need to Know I Learned in the Twilight Zone*, Mark Dawidziak (ed); *Leonard, Mariane, & Me: Magical Summers on Hydra*, Judy Scott; *Osawatomie*, Randy Michael Signor; *Outrageous Fortune: Growing Up at Leeds Castle*, Anthony Russell; *Rod Serling: His Life, Work and Imagination*, Nicholas Parisi; *Saolomea! Saolomea!: Screenplay as Poetry As Prose*, Anisia Uzeyman; *Sensing the Rhythm: Finding My Voice in a World Without Sound*, Mandy Harvey, Mark Atteberry; *The Burma Spring: Aung San Suu Kyi and the Struggle for the Soul of Burma*, Rena Pederson; *The Reputation Economy*, Michael Fertik, David Thompson; *The Shawshank Redemption Revealed: How One Story Keeps Hope Alive*, Mark Dawidziak; *Theodore Roosevelt for Nature Lovers*, Mark Dawidziak; *Waco: A Survivor's Story*, David Thibodeau, Leon Whiteson, Aviva Layton; *Working Actor: Breaking in, Making a Living and Making a Life in the Fabulous Trenches of Show Business*, David Bottrell
Foreign Rep(s): The Fielding Agency (Whitney Lee) (worldwide)
Membership(s): The Authors Guild; PEN America; PEN Center USA West

LITERARY AGENTS

Lisa Hagan Literary (L)
110 Martin Dr, Bracey, VA 23919
Tel: 434-636-4138
E-mail: Lisa@lisahaganbooks.com
Web Site: www.publishersmarketplace.com/members/LisaHagan
Key Personnel
Owner, Pres & Agent: Lisa Hagan
Founded: 1995
Health, mind/body/spirit & self-help. No unsol mss, query first with e-mail. Handles film & TV rights for books only. No fee charged.
Titles recently placed: *Aura Alchemy: Learn to Sense Energy Fields, Interpret the Color Spectrum and Manifest Success*, Amy Leigh Mercree; *Becoming Baba Yaga: Trickster, Feminist, and Witch of the Woods*, Kris Spisak; *Becoming Psychic: Lessons from the Minds of Mediums, Healers, and Psychics*, Jeff Tarrant, PhD, BCN; *Channeled Messages of Hope Conversations with History's Most Prominent Souls on the Other Side Global Warming and Climate Change*, Carolyn Thomas, John Thomas, Sam Larkin; *Cold: Three Winters at the South Pole*, Wayne L White; *Everyday Magic: How to Live a Mindful, Meaningful, Magical Life*, Marie D Jones, Denise Agnew; *Healing Through Storytelling*, Leah Lamb; *Heavenly Alliance: Call on Your Spirit Guides, Ancestors, and Angels to Manifest the Life You Want*, Samantha Fey; *Meaningful Coincidences: How and Why Synchronicity and Serendipity Happen (The Sacred Planet Books)*, Bernard Beitman, MD; *Our Journey to Sustainability: How Everyday Heroes Make a Difference*, Jon R Biemer; *Oxalate Overload: Skip Toxic Superfoods and Reclaim a Vibrant Life*, Sally K Norton; *Psychedelics Dreams and Rituals: A Guidebook for Explorers, Therapists, and Facilitators*, Gay Lynn Grigas, LMHC; *Releasing Toxic Anger for Women: Somatic Practices and CBT Skills to Transform Negative Thoughts, Soothe Stress, and Stay True to Yourself*, Karyne B Wilner, PsyD; *Secrets of Greek Mysticism: A Modern Guide to Daily Practice with the Greek Gods and Goddesses*, George Lizos; *Sober Mom: Rebuilding Relationships in Recovery from Alcoholism and Addiction*, Janice Dowd; *The Awake Dreamer: A Guide to Lucid Dreaming, Astral Travel, and Mastering the Dreamscape*, Samantha Fey; *The Element Healing Oracle Deck*, Amy Leigh Mercree; *The Green Witch's Guide to Magical Plants & Flowers: 26 Love Spells from Apples to Zinnias*, Chris Young, Susan Ottaviano; *The Intuitive Nudge*, Eboni Banks; *The Lagoon: Encounters with the Whales of San Ignacio*, James Michael Dorsey; *The Mindful Photographer: Awake in the World with a Camera*, David Ulrich; *The Rainbow Witch: Enhance Your Magic with the Secret Powers of Color (The Modern-Day Witch)*, Kac Young; *The Science of the Paranormal: The Truth Behind Telepathy, Spirits, and More Mysterious Phenomena*, JM DeBord; *The View from My Foxhole: A Marine Private's Firsthand World War II Combat Experience from Guadalcanal to Iwo Jima*, William Swanson; *The Way of the Empath*, Elaine Clayton; *Toxic Superfoods Cookbook*, Sally K Norton; *Up the Down Escalator: Medicine, Motherhood, and Multiple Sclerosis*, Lisa Doggett, MD; *Yoga of Sound: The Life and Teachings of the Celestial Songman*, Swami Nada Brahmananda, Michael Grosso

Hannigan Getzler Literary, see HG Literary

The Joy Harris Literary Agency Inc (L)
1501 Broadway, Suite 2310, New York, NY 10036
Tel: 212-924-6269 *Fax:* 212-840-5776
E-mail: contact@joyharrisliterary.com
Web Site: www.joyharrisliterary.com
Key Personnel
Pres: Joy Harris (AALA) *E-mail:* joy@joyharrisliterary.com
Agent & Subs Rts: Adam Reed (AALA) *E-mail:* adam@joyharrisliterary.com
Assoc Agent: Alice Fugate
No unsol mss, query first. No poetry, screenplays or self-help.

Hartline Literary Agency LLC (L)
123 Queenston Dr, Pittsburgh, PA 15235
Tel: 412-829-2483 *Toll Free Fax:* 888-279-6007
Web Site: www.hartlineliterary.com
Key Personnel
Founder: Joyce Hart *E-mail:* joyce@hartlineliterary.com
Pres: Jim Hart *E-mail:* jim@hartlineliterary.com
Agent: Diana Flegal *E-mail:* diana@hartlineliterary.com; Linda Glaz *E-mail:* linda@hartlineliterary.com; Cyle Young *E-mail:* cyle@hartlineliterary.com
Founded: 1992
Advise clients on how to prepare proposals & advise them concerning what various publishers are looking for. Also help clients plan their literary careers. Our expertise is in the Christian market & we also work in the general market. Looking for clean, wholesome fiction for adults & inspiring nonfiction. Mss reflecting a Christian worldview preferred, even for the general market. Fiction: romance, romantic suspense, women's fiction, mystery/suspense, humor, chick/mom lit & general fiction. Nonfiction: self-help, Christian living, prayer, health, humor & business.
Accepts unsol mss. Submit cover letter, author bio, marketing analysis, summary & 3 sample chapters. If submitting via e-mail, send as an attachment & send the entire submission in one file. We do not accept submissions in multiple files. We accept e-mail, US mail, UPS & FedEx submissions. See web site for complete submission details. No fees.
Titles recently placed: *21 Days of Grace*, Kathy Ide; *A Pair of Miracles: A Story of Autism, Faith, and Determined Parenting*, Karla Akins; *A Secret to Die For*, Lisa Harris; *All She Left Behind*, Jane Kirkpatrick; *Among the Poppies*, J'nell Ciesielski; *Anchored*, Deborah Bailey; *Anna's Crossing*, Suzanne Woods Fisher; *Assassination Generation*, Adam Davis; *At First Glance*, Susan Tuttle; *Barefoot Revolution: Biblical Spirituality for Finding God*, Paul Marshall; *Behind the Badge*, Adam Davis; *Beneath a Michigan Moon*, Candice Patterson; *Blow Out the Candles and Say Goodbye*, Linda Glaz; *C is for Christmas*, Michelle Medlock Adams; *Coffee Shop Devotions*, Tessa Emily Hall; *Confessions of an Adoptive Parent*, Mike Berry; *Coral*, Sara Ella; *Cowboys and Angels*, David Stearman; *Deadly Exchange*, Lisa Harris; *Desert Secrets*, Lisa Harris; *Everything She Didn't Say*, Jane Kirkpatrick; *Fabulous & Focused*, Michelle Medlock Adams, Gena Maselli; *Fallen Leaves*, Tessa Emily Hall; *Fatal Cover-Up*, Lisa Harris; *Finding Jesus in Israel: Through the Holy Land on the Road Less Traveled*, Buck Storm; *Fire Paste, Fast Freeze*, Tim Shoemaker; *God Needed a Puppy*, John Gray, Shanna Brickell; *Her Deadly Reunion*, Beth Ann Ziarnik; *Hidden Treasures: Finding Hope at the End of Life's Journey*, Robin Bertram; *High as the Heavens*, Kate Breslin; *In the Grip of God*, George Cargil; *Jeremy Winters (series)*, Tom Threadgill; *Jessie's Hope*, Jennifer Hallmark; *Journey Into Silence*, Chaim Bentorah; *Learning God's Love Language: A Guide to Personal Hebrew Word Study*, Chaim Bentorah; *Liar's Winter*, Cindy Sproles; *Like Me or Not*, Dawn Owens; *Lydia*, Diana Wallis Taylor; *Making God Smile*, Kim Henry; *Mary, Mother of God*, Diana Wallis Taylor; *Minding the Light*, Suzanne Woods Fisher; *Missing*, Lisa Harris; *Mountain Hideaway*, Christy Barritt; *Multiple Choice: Finding the Best Answer for Your Child's Education*, Martha Singleton; *My Heart Belongs on Mackinac Island*, Carrie Fancett Pagels; *On Command*, Adam Davis; *Operation Moonbeam*, Michelle Medlock Adams; *Overcoming Shame*, Dr Mark W Baker; *Phoebe's Light*, Suzanne Woods Fisher; *Police Marriage Devotion*, Adam Davis; *Reclaiming Sanity*, Dr Laurel Shaler; *Relational Reset*, Dr Laurel Shaler; *Renewed: A 40-Day Devotional for Healing from Church Hurt and for Loving Well in Ministry*, Leigh Powers; *Rescued Hearts*, Hope Toler Dougherty; *Resenting God*, John Snyder; *Ruffling Society*, Kay Moser; *Secrets and Wishes*, Kathleen Rouser; *Shadow of Suspicion*, Christy Barritt; *She Who Went First*, Jane Kirkpatrick; *Silent Noisy Night*, Jill Roman Lord; *Skirting Convention*, Kay Moser; *Spiritual Prepper*, Jake McCandless; *Spiritual Wisdom for a Happier Life*, Dr Mark W Baker; *Stand In Brides (No 1)*, Dorothy Clark; *That Grand Easter Day*, Jill Roman Lord; *The Baby Assignment*, Christy Barritt; *The Bravest You*, Adam Smith; *The Children of Main Street*, Merilyn Howton; *The Devil's Daughter*, Cindy Sproles; *The Light Before Day*, Suzanne Woods Fisher; *The Nanny's Secret Child*, Lorraine Beatty; *The Newcomer*, Suzanne Woods Fisher; *The Quieting*, Suzanne Woods Fisher; *The Return*, Suzanne Woods Fisher; *The Very Best Story Ever Told*, Robin Currie; *The View Through Your Window*, Greg Singleton, Martha Singleton; *Though This Be Madness (Lilly Long Mysteries)*, Penny Richards; *To Claim Her Heart*, Jodie Wolfe; *Touched by God*, Andrew Gabriel; *Unbreakable (Unblemished Trilogy)*, Sara Ella; *Unearthed: Discover Life as God's Masterpiece*, Raj Pillai; *Unraveling (Unblemished Trilogy)*, Sara Ella; *Vanishing Point*, Lisa Harris; *What Ever Happened to Happily Ever After?*, David Clarke; *What Is a Family?*, Annette Griffin; *What the Moon Saw*, D L Koontz; *Whiskey Burning*, John Turney; *Winning the Heart of Your Child*, Mike Berry; *With This Peace*, Karen Campbell Prough; *Working Women Devotionals*, Gena Maselli
Membership(s): American Christian Fiction Writers (ACFW)

EDITORIAL SERVICES

John Hawkins and Associates Inc (L)
80 Maiden Lane, Suite 1503, New York, NY 10038
Tel: 212-807-7040
E-mail: jha@jhalit.com
Web Site: jhalit.com
Key Personnel
Pres & Foreign Rts Dir: Moses Cardona (AALA) *E-mail:* moses@jhalit.com
Agent: Warren Frazier (AALA) *E-mail:* frazier@jhalit.com; Anne Hawkins (AALA) *E-mail:* ahawkins@jhalit.com; William Reiss (AALA) *E-mail:* reiss@jhalit.com
Founded: 1893 (by Paul R Reynolds)
No unsol mss, query first. Submit 1-page bio & 1- to 3-page outline with SASE. No reading fee. Photocopy charges & fees for other services. Handle film & TV rights, software.
Titles recently placed: *A Wild Winter Swan*, Gregory Maguire; *Breathe*, Joyce Carol Oates; *Hell Fire*, John Gilstrap; *JFK: Coming of Age in the American Century*, Fredrik Logevall; *Old Lovegood Girls*, Gail Godwin; *The Charmed Wife*, Olga Grushin; *The Long Call*, Ann Cleeves
Foreign Rep(s): Sara Menguc Inc (UK)
Membership(s): The Authors Guild

The Jeff Herman Agency LLC (L)
29 Park St, Stockbridge, MA 01262
Mailing Address: PO Box 1522, Stockbridge, MA 01262
Tel: 413-298-0077

Web Site: www.jeffherman.com
Key Personnel
Pres: Jeffrey H Herman (AALA) *E-mail:* jeff@jeffherman.com
VP: Deborah Levine *E-mail:* debherman3@gmail.com
Founded: 1985
Nonfiction, reference, health, self-help, how-to, business, technology, spirituality & textbooks. No unsol mss, query first with letter & SASE. No reading fee. Handle software, film & TV rights. Agents in all principal foreign countries.

HG Literary (L-D)
6 W 18 St, Suite 7R, New York, NY 10011
E-mail: foreign@hgliterary.com; rights@hgliterary.com
Web Site: www.hgliterary.com
Key Personnel
Partner & Agent: Carrie Hannigan (AALA) *E-mail:* carrie@hgliterary.com; Josh Getzler (AALA) *E-mail:* josh@hgliterary.com
VP & Agent: Soumeya Bendimerad Roberts (AALA) *E-mail:* soumeya@hgliterary.com
Agent & Intl Rts Mgr, Adult: Alex Reubert
Agent & Intl Rts Mgr, Children's & Young Adult: Ellen Goff *E-mail:* ellen@hgliterary.com
Agent: Jon Cobb *E-mail:* jon@hgliterary.com; Bri Johnson *E-mail:* brianne@hgliterary.com; Julia Kardon *E-mail:* julia@hgliterary.com; Victoria Wells-Arms (AALA) *E-mail:* victoria@hgliterary.com
Founded: 2011 (as HSG)
Full service boutique literary agency representing both fiction & nonfiction for adults & children. Sells subsidiary rights, including film, audio & UK/translation. No unsol mss, query first. Electronic submissions only. Send query letter & first 5 pages of ms (no attachments). Does not represent screenplays, romance fiction, or religious fiction.
Titles recently placed: *Carmen and Grace*, Melissa Coss Aquino; *The Laughter*, Sonora Jha
Foreign Rights: AnatoliaLit Agency (Turkey); Book/lab Literary Agency (Poland); Eastern European & Asian Rights Agency (Armenia, Azerbaijan, Estonia, Georgia, Kazakhstan, Kyrgyzstan, Latvia, Lithuania, Tajikistan, Turkmenistan, Ukraine, Uzbekistan); The Grayhawk Agency (China, Taiwan); The Italian Literary Agency (Italy); Licht & Burr Agency (Scandinavia); MB Agencia Literaria (Portugal, Spain); La Nouvelle Agence (France); Andrew Nurnberg Associates (Albania, Bosnia and Herzegovina, Bulgaria, Montenegro, North Macedonia, Romania, Serbia); Andrew Nurnberg Associates Budapest (Croatia, Hungary); Andrew Nurnberg Associates Prague (Czechia, Slovakia, Slovenia); Read n' Right Agency (Greece); Agencia Riff (Brazil); Right Thing Agency (Thailand, Vietnam); The Schlueck Agency (Germany); Marianne Schoenbach Literary Agency (Netherlands); Shinwon Agency (South Korea); Abner Stein Agency (UK); Tuttle-Mori Agency (Japan); The Van Lear Agency (Georgia, Russia)

Hill Nadell Literary Agency (L)
6442 Santa Monica Blvd, Suite 200A, Los Angeles, CA 90038
Tel: 310-860-9605
E-mail: queries@hillnadell.com; rights@hillnadell.com (rts & perms)
Web Site: www.hillnadell.com
Key Personnel
Pres: Bonnie Nadell
Sr Agent: Dara Hyde
Founded: 1979
Literary & commercial fiction, narrative nonfiction, current affairs, memoirs & pop culture; film & TV rights only if handling the book. No unsol mss, query first with SASE. No reading fee. Co-agents in all foreign countries.
Titles recently placed: *Age of Danger*, Andrew Hoehn, Thom Shanker; *Brown Boy*, Omer Aziz; *Buzzing*, Samuel Sattin, Rye Hickman; *How Not to Drown in a Glass of Water*, Angie Cruz; *Take No Names*, Daniel Nieh; *The Bodies Keep Coming*, Brian H Williams; *The Broke Hearts*, Matt Mendez
Foreign Rights: ANA Baltic (Azerbaijan, Baltic States, Eastern Armenia, Georgia, Kazakhstan, Kyrgyzstan, Tajikistan, Turkmenistan, Uzbekistan); ANA Hungary (Hungary); ANA Prague (Czechia, Slovakia, Slovenia); ANA Sofia (Albania, Bulgaria, North Macedonia, Romania, Serbia); AnatoliaLit (Turkey); Berla & Griffini Rights Agency (Italy); Big Apple Agency Inc Shanghai (China); Big Apple Agency Inc Taiwan (Taiwan); Ersilia Literary (Greece); Anoukh Foerg Literary Agency (Germany); The Foreign Office (Brazil, Latin America, Portugal, Spain); Anna Jarota Agency (France, Poland, Russia); Korea Copyright Center Inc (KCC) (South Korea); Schoenbach Literary Agency (Netherlands)

The Barbara Hogenson Agency Inc (L-D)
165 West End Ave, Suite 19-C, New York, NY 10023
Tel: 212-874-8084
E-mail: barbarahogenson@gmail.com
Key Personnel
Pres: Barbara Hogenson (AALA)
Contract Mgr: Lori Styler
Founded: 1994
Recommendation by clients only. Literary fiction, nonfiction, full-length plays, consider some illustrated books. No screenplays or teleplays. No fees.
Membership(s): The Authors Guild; Authors Registry; Dramatists Guild of America Inc; Society of Stage Directors & Choreographers (SSDC); Writers Guild of America (WGA)

Hornfischer Literary Management LP (L)
PO Box 50544, Austin, TX 78763
Tel: 512-472-0011
E-mail: queries@hornfischerlit.com
Web Site: www.hornfischerlit.com
Key Personnel
Pres: Jim Hornfischer
Founded: 2001
Quality narrative nonfiction, biography & autobiography, current events, US history, military history & world history, political & cultural subjects science, medicine/health, business/management/finance, academic writing & research that has a general-interest audience. No unsol mss; query first through e-mail, no longer accept queries through mail. No fees.
Titles recently placed: *A Darker Sea*, James L Haley; *Army of None: Autonomous Weapons and the Future of War*, Paul Scharre; *Beirut Rules: The Murder of a CIA Station Chief and Hezbollah's War Against America*, Fred Burton, Samuel M Katz; *Bringing Columbia Home: The Untold Story of a Lost Space Shuttle and Her Crew*, Michael D Leinbach, Jonathan H Ward; *Captive Paradise: A History of Hawaii*, James L Haley; *Crashback: The Power Clash Between the US and China in the Pacific*, Michael Fabey; *Destination Casablanca: Exile, Espionage, and the Battle for North Africa in World War II*, Meredith Hindley; *Giant: Elizabeth Taylor, Rock Hudson, James Dean, Edna Ferber, and the Making of a Legendary American Film*, Don Graham; *Harpoon: Inside the Covert War Against Terrorism's Money Masters*, Nitsana Darshan-Leitner, Samuel M Katz; *Harvey Penick: The Life and Wisdom of the Man Who Wrote the Book on Golf*, Kevin Robbins; *Hurricane Season: The Unforgettable Story of the 2017 Houston Astros and the Resilience of a City*, Joe Holley; *In the Arena: Good Citizens, a Great Republic, and How One Speech Can Reinvigorate America*, Pete Hegseth; *Indestructible: One Man's Rescue Mission That Changed the Course of WWII*, John R Bruning; *Necessary Evil: How to Fix Finance by Saving Human Rights*, David Kinley; *Never Call Me a Hero*, N Jack "Dusty" Kleiss, Timothy Orr, Laura Orr; *No One Cares About Crazy People: My Family and the Heartbreak of Mental Illness in America*, Ron Powers; *Phenomena: The Secret History of the US Government's Investigations Into Extrasensory Perception and Psychokinesis*, Annie Jacobsen; *Reviving America: How Repealing Obamacare, Replacing the Tax Code and Reforming The Fed will Restore Hope and Prosperity*, Steve Forbes, Elizabeth Ames; *The Cloudbuster Nine: The Untold Story of Ted Williams and the Baseball Team That Helped Win World War II*, Anne R Keene; *The Last Republicans: Inside the Extraordinary Relationship Between George H W Bush and George W Bush*, Mark K Updegrove; *The Possibility Dogs: What I Learned from Second-Chance Rescues About Service, Hope, and Healing*, Susannah Charleson

InkWell Management (L)
521 Fifth Ave, Suite 2600, New York, NY 10175
Tel: 212-922-3500 *Fax:* 212-922-0535
E-mail: info@inkwellmanagement.com; submissions@inkwellmanagement.com; permissions@inkwellmanagement.com
Web Site: inkwellmanagement.com
Key Personnel
Founder & Pres: Michael V Carlisle; Richard S Pine; Kimberly Witherspoon *E-mail:* kim@inkwellmanagement.com
Co-Dir, Foreign Rts: Lyndsey Blessing *E-mail:* lyndsey@inkwellmanagement.com; Alexis Hurley *E-mail:* alexis@inkwellmanagement.com
Agent & Ed: William Callahan
Agent: Stephen Barbara; Sharon Chudnow; Catherine Drayton; Naomi Eisenbeiss; David Forrer; Claire Friedman; Nathaniel Jacks; George Lucas; Jessica Mileo; Jacqueline Murphy; Charlie Olsen; Eliza Rothstein; David Hale Smith; Kristin van Ogtrop
Asst Agent: Michael Mungiello
Royalty & Acctg Assoc: Jessie Thorsted
Founded: 2004 (created through the merger of Arthur Pine Associates Inc, Carlisle & Co LLC & Witherspoon Associates Inc)
General nonfiction & fiction books. No screenplays, plays, poetry. Motion picture, TV & foreign rights. No unsol mss, query first by e-mail; submissions must be on an exclusive basis. No fees.
Titles recently placed: *Alone Together: Love, Grief, and Comfort in the Time of Covid-19*, Faith Adiele et al; *World Travel*, Anthony Bourdain, Laurie Woolever
Foreign Rights: Anthea (Bulgaria); Graal Literary Agency (Poland); The Deborah Harris Agency (Israel); Jlm (Greece); Katai & Bolza (Hungary); Simona Kessler (Romania); Michelle Lapautre (France); Maxima (Indonesia, Thailand, Vietnam); Mb Agency (Latin America, Portugal, Spain); Mohrbooks (Germany); Andrew Nurnberg Associates (China, Estonia, Latvia, Lithuania, Taiwan); Kristin Olson (Czechia, Slovakia); Onk Agency Inc (Turkey); Prava i prevodi (Albania, Croatia, Serbia, Slovenia); Riff (Brazil); Roberto Santachiara (Italy); Sebes & Bisseling Literary Agency (Netherlands); Synopsis (Russia); Ulf Toregard (Scandinavia); Tuttle-Mori Agency Inc (Japan); Eric Yang (South Korea)

InterLicense Ltd (L)
110 Country Club Dr, Suite A, Mill Valley, CA 94941

Tel: 415-381-9780 *Fax:* 415-381-6485
E-mail: foreignrights@interlicense.net
Web Site: interlicense.net
Key Personnel
Pres: Juliette Mroczkowski
Exec Dir: Manfred Mroczkowski
Founded: 1981
Foreign & subsidiary rights agency. No unsol mss, query first.

International Titles (L)
931 E 56 St, Austin, TX 78751-1724
Tel: 512-909-2447
Web Site: www.internationaltitles.com
Key Personnel
Dir: Loris Essary *E-mail:* loris@internationaltitles.com
Represent all genres; primary emphasis on sales of foreign rights. No fees charged, no submission policy.

International Transactions Inc (L)
28 Alope Way, Gila, NM 88038
Mailing Address: PO Box 97, Gila, NM 88038
Tel: 845-373-9696 *Fax:* 520-300-7248
E-mail: info@internationaltransactions.us
Web Site: www.intltrans.com
Key Personnel
Pres: Peter Riva *E-mail:* priva@intltrans.com
Founded: 1975
International literary & licensing agency. Specialize in nonfiction (including large projects), fiction, illustrated & children's. We cannot help every prospective author nor can we review every ms. Send a submission query (only) via e-mail. If, within 3 weeks, we are interested, we will call for more material. Also handles film & TV rights only based on books represented. No fees.
Titles recently placed: *Absinthe*, Guido Eekhaut; *An Independent Empire*, Michael Kochin, Michael Taylor; *Angelina Ballerina (series)*, Katharine Holabird, Helen Craig; *Because the Sky is a Thousand Soft Hurts*, Elizabeth Kirschner; *Freedom Trail*, Robert Wheeler; *Hemingway's Cuba*, Robert Wheeler; *Marlene Dietrich*, Maria Riva; *Normandy*, Niklas Zetterling; *Purgatory*, Guido Eekhaut; *Radical Virus*, Azeem Ibrahim; *Rising From Rape*, Pamela Braswell; *Santini's Hero*, Bernie Schein; *Splinter on the Tide*, Phillip Parotti; *The Little Vampire (series)*, Angela Sommer-Bodenburg; *The Preserve*, Steve Anderson; *The Wine Table*, Vickie Reh; *This Is Cuba*, David Ariosto; *Twinkle (series)*, Katharine Holabird, Sarah Warburton; *Within Our Grasp*, Sharman Apt Russell; *You Were There Before My Eyes*, Maria Riva
Foreign Office(s): Rechtsanwalt Roth, Gewurzmuhlstr 5, 80538 Munich, Germany *Tel:* (089) 55 26 26 55

JABberwocky Literary Agency Inc (L)
49 W 45 St, 5th fl, New York, NY 10036
Tel: 917-388-3010 *Fax:* 917-388-2998
Web Site: www.awfulagent.com
Founded: 1994
Full line of fiction & nonfiction trade books, particularly genre fiction (science fiction, fantasy, mystery, horror), literary fiction, young adult & middle grade & serious nonfiction (biography, science, history). Please be sure to look at the page of the agent you're querying on our web site for their specific submission instructions & to see which agents are currently accepting e-mail queries. No unsol mss, query first with biographical information & SASE. Will request mss after reviewing query if interested. Handle film & TV rights for regular clients. No reading fee. No fax or phone queries.
Titles recently placed: *Ghostdrift*, Suzanne Palmer; *Hate to Fake It to You*, Amanda Sellet; *How to Sell a Haunted House*, Grady Hendrix;

Silver Nitrate, Silvia Moreno-Garcia; *Slaying the Dragon: A Secret History of Dungeons & Dragons*, Ben Riggs; *The Iron Children*, Rebecca Fraimow; *The Rise and Fall of Winged Zemolai*, Samantha Mills; *These Burning Stars*, Bethany Jacobs; *Tiny Threads*, Lilliam Rivera
Foreign Rep(s): Anthea Agency (Albania); Tassy Barham Associates (Brazil); Bears Factor (Egypt); Agence Litteraire Eliane Benisti (France); The Book Publishers Association of Israel (Israel); BookLab Literary Agency (Poland); English Agency Japan Co Ltd (Japan); Paul & Peter Fritz Agency (Germany); The Grayhawk Agency (China, Indonesia, Taiwan, Thailand, Vietnam); The Danny Hong Agency (South Korea); International Copyright Agency Ltd (Romania); International Editors' Co - Yanez Agencia Literaria (Portugal, Spain); Katai & Bolza (Croatia, Hungary, Serbia); Alexander Korzhenevski Agency (Russia, Ukraine); Nurnberg Associates (Baltic States); Kristin Olson Literary Agency (Czechia, Slovenia); Read n Right Agency (Greece); Sebes & Bisseling (Netherlands, Scandinavia); Zeno Agency Ltd (UK)
Membership(s): Science Fiction and Fantasy Writers of America, Inc (SFWA)

Melanie Jackson Agency LLC (L)
41 W 72 St, Suite 3F, New York, NY 10023
Web Site: www.mjalit.com
Key Personnel
Owner & Agent: Melanie Jackson *E-mail:* m.jackson@mjalit.com
Rts Mgr: Matthew Dissen *E-mail:* m.dissen@mjalit.com
No unsol mss, query first.
Foreign Rep(s): Liepman Agency (Germany); Rogers, Coleridge & White (UK); Roberto Santachiara (Italy)

Janklow & Nesbit Associates (L-D)
285 Madison Ave, 21st fl, New York, NY 10017
Tel: 212-421-1700 *Fax:* 212-355-1403
E-mail: info@janklow.com; submissions@janklow.com; filmtvrights@janklow.com
Web Site: www.janklowandnesbit.com
Key Personnel
Co-Founder & Agent: Lynn Nesbit
Sr Coun & Sr Agent: Stefanie Lieberman
Gen Coun, Mng Dir & Head, Legal & Busn Aff: Bennett Ashley
Pres, Mng Dir & Agent: Luke Janklow
Mng Dir & Agent: Anne Sibbald
Sr Agent: Melissa Flashman; Kirby Kim; Paul Lucas; Emma Parry; Marya Spence
Agent: Ian Bonaparte; Chris Clemans; Hafizah Geter; Chad Luibl; P J Mark; Richard Morris; Jessica Spitz
Assoc Agent: Mina Hamedi (AALA)
Founded: 1989 (successor to Morton L Janklow Assoc Inc founded in 1975)
General fiction & nonfiction. Handle film & TV rights for book represented. No unsol mss, query first by e-mail only. No reading fee.
Titles recently placed: *Resurrection*, Danielle Steel; *The Absolutes: A Novel*, Molly Dektar
Foreign Office(s): Janklow & Nesbit (UK), 66-67 Newmann St, Fitrovia, London W1T 3EQ, United Kingdom, Contact: Rachel Balcombe *Tel:* (020) 7243 2975 *E-mail:* queries@janklow.co.uk *Web Site:* janklowandnesbit.co.uk
Foreign Rights: Bardon-Chinese Media Agency (Annie Chen & David Tsai) (China, Taiwan); Imprima Korea Agency (Mr Terry Kim) (South Korea); Japan UNI Agency Inc (Ms Miko Yamanouchi) (Japan); Prava i prevodi Literary Agency (Ana Milenkovic) (Eastern Europe, Russia)

Janus Literary Agency (L)
PO Box 837, Methuen, MA 01844

Tel: 978-273-4227
E-mail: janusliteraryagency@gmail.com
Web Site: janusliteraryagency.blogspot.com
Key Personnel
Owner: Lenny Cavallaro
Founded: 1980
We do NOT handle nonfiction. We restrict fiction to the more "unusual"—mostly esoteric or paranormal material. E-mail submissions only; no hard copy. If we have not responded within 2 weeks, it means we do not feel we are able to help the author.

Jellinek & Murray Literary Agency (L-D)
47-231 Kamakoi Rd, Kaneohe, HI 96744
Tel: 808-239-8451
Key Personnel
Pres: Roger Jellinek *E-mail:* rgr.jellinek@gmail.com
Founded: 1995
General adult fiction & nonfiction. No genre fiction. No unsol mss, query first with an e-mail. Submit proposal, outline, 2 sample chapters, author bio & credentials & platform, by e-mail. No reading fees. Handle film & TV rights.

Carolyn Jenks Agency (L-D)
30 Cambridge Park Dr, Suite 5115, Cambridge, MA 02140
Tel: 617-233-9130
Web Site: www.carolynjenksagency.com
Key Personnel
Owner & Dir: Carolyn Jenks *E-mail:* carolyn@carolynjenksagency.com
Founded: 1979
Literary & commercial fiction & nonfiction. All genres. Theatre, film & screenwriters represented. Signatory to Writers Guild of America. Contact by e-mail or via web site. Electronic submissions only; prefer query via web site. No fees charged. Now also developing podcast & publicity platforms for clients.
Titles recently placed: *A Tale of Two Maidens*, Anne Echols; *Capture My Heart*, Pamela Bynum River; *Sun Eye Moon Eye*, Vincent Czyz; *The Ostermann House*, John Klein; *The Secret Adventures of Order*, Vincent Czyz
Membership(s): Writers Guild of America (WGA)

JET Literary Associates Inc (L)
941 Calle Mejia, Suite 507, Santa Fe, NM 87501
Tel: 505-780-0721
E-mail: jetliterary@gmail.com
Web Site: www.jetliterary.wordpress.com
Key Personnel
Pres (Austria off): Jim Trupin
E-mail: jetliterary@gmail.com
VP: Elizabeth Trupin-Pulli *E-mail:* etpjetliterary@gmail.com
Founded: 1975
General book-length fiction & nonfiction. Specialize in adult fiction & commercial nonfiction; no memoirs, plays, poetry, how-to, business/finance, science fiction/fantasy, young adult or books for young children. No unsol mss, e-mail query first. No reading fees. Full representation in all foreign markets.
Foreign Office(s): Esterhazygasse 9A/26, 1060 Vienna, Austria *Tel:* (01) 587 0077 *Fax:* (01) 587 0077
Foreign Rep(s): Eliane Benisti (France); Big Apple Agency Inc (China); Educational Materials Enterprises (Greece); Fritz Agency (Germany); International Editors' Co - Yanez Agencia Literaria (Brazil, Spain); Nurcihan Kesim Literary Agency Ltd (Turkey); Kohn (Netherlands); Living Literary Agency (Italy); Lennart Sane Agency AB (Sweden); Tuttle-Mori Agency Inc (Japan)
Foreign Rights: Abner Stein Agency (UK)

JMW Group Inc (L)
346 Rte 6, No 867, Mahopac, NY 10541
Tel: 914-841-7105 *Fax:* 914-248-8861
E-mail: jmwgroup@jmwgroup.net
Web Site: jmwforlife.com
Key Personnel
Pres & CEO: Patti DeMatteo
VP, Rts: Pete Allen
Dir, Licensing: Sara Castle
Founded: 1949
Publisher, rights agency; no fees charged.

Jones Hutton Literary Associates (L)
140D Heritage Village, Southbury, CT 06488
Tel: 203-558-4478
E-mail: huttonbooks@hotmail.com
Key Personnel
Mng Ed: Caroline DuBois Hutton
Sr Ed: Arthur B Layton
Founded: 1994
We welcome both new & established writers & work closely with our authors to put all material in the best possible shape for submission to publishing houses. We handle both fiction & nonfiction but no sci-fi, juvenile or short story collections. We take only a few authors at a time & give to each the utmost personal attention.
To access our web site, giving editor bios & submission requirements, please send an e-mail to the address above for a link. We look forward to seeing your work &, hopefully, working with you.

The Karpfinger Agency (L)
357 W 20 St, New York, NY 10011-3379
Tel: 212-691-2690 *Fax:* 212-691-7129
E-mail: info@karpfinger.com (no queries or submissions)
Web Site: karpfinger.com
Key Personnel
Owner: Barney M Karpfinger
Foreign Rts Mgr: Cathy Jaque
Contact: Sam Chidley
Founded: 1985
Quality fiction & nonfiction. No unsol mss. See web site for specific instructions for queries. No reading fee. Direct representation in foreign markets.

Keller Media Inc (L)
578 Washington Blvd, No 745, Marina del Rey, CA 90292
Toll Free Tel: 800-278-8706
E-mail: query@kellermedia.com
Web Site: kellermedia.com/submission-guidelines
Key Personnel
Sr Agent & CEO: Wendy Keller
Founded: 1989
Represent nonfiction in the following categories: business (sales, management, marketing); finance; self-help (parenting, women's issues, relationships, pop psychology, etc); health (alternative & allopathic); metaphysical/spiritual/inspirational (never religious); nature, science, archaeology, reference, how-to (do anything). Do not send poetry, scripts, your memoir unless you are a celebrity, religious or juvenile books or first person accounts of overcoming some medical or mental condition. Most of agency's authors are either experts in their field, successful professional speakers, have their own radio, infomercial or television program, or are a household name. For best results, fill in the simple form on the web site. Please do not mail your self-published book unless requested.
Titles recently placed: *Blue Mind: Tenth Anniversary Edition*, Dr Wallace J Nichols; *Chocolate Covered Money*, Brad Yater; *Co-operative Co-parenting for Secure Kids*, Dr Aurisha Smolarski; *Flight of the Bon Monks*, Harvey Rice; Jackie Cole, HH Dalai Lama; *Illumination Code*, Kim Chestney; *Lies About Black People*, Omekongo Dibinga; *Post Traumatic Parenting*, Dr Robyn Koslowitz; *Stop the Shift Show*, Scott Greenberg; *The Energy of Success*, Rebecca Ahmed; *The Leader's Guide to Managing Risk*, K Scott Griffith; *The Suicidal Person*, Konrad Michel; *The Unspoken Truths for Career Success*, Tessa White; *The Year Science Changed Everything*, Mark O'Connell

Natasha Kern Literary Agency Inc (L)
PO Box 1069, White Salmon, WA 98672
Tel: 509-493-3803
Web Site: www.natashakernliterary.com
Key Personnel
Pres: Natasha Kern
Founded: 1986
Currently closed to all queries.
Represent commercial adult fiction, inspirational fiction & young adult fiction. Actively represent all women's fiction; multicultural fiction; mainstream fiction; inspirational, historical & contemporary romance; romantic suspense, thrillers, & all subgenres of mysteries from cozies to PIs. DO NOT represent children's, horror, science fiction, short stories, poetry, sports, scholarly or coffee-table books. Handle film & TV rights only on represented books. Represented in all principal foreign countries as well as in Hollywood.
Titles recently placed: *Castles in the Clouds*, Myra Johnson; *Keeper of the Stars*, Robin Lee Hatcher
Foreign Rep(s): Agencia Literaria Carmen Balcells SA (Spain); Agence Eliane Benisti (France); Phillip Chen (China, Taiwan); English Agency of Japan Co Ltd (Junzo Sawa) (Japan); The Italian Literary Agency Srl (Italy); Prava i prevodi (Eastern Europe); Agencia Riff (Lucia Riff) (Brazil); Lennart Sane Agency AB (Scandinavia); Thomas Schlueck GmbH (Germany); Lorna Soifer (Israel)

Louise B Ketz Agency (L)
414 E 78 St, Suite 1B, New York, NY 10075
Tel: 212-249-0668
E-mail: ketzagency@aol.com
Key Personnel
Pres: Louise B Ketz
Founded: 1986
Nonfiction only: science, business, sports, reference, history. No unsol mss, query letter, chapter outline, table of contents, sample chapter, author biography. No reading fee.
Titles recently placed: *The Traveler's Guide to Space: For One-Way Settlers and Round-Trip Tourists*, Neil F Comins
Membership(s): Editorial Freelancers Association (EFA); National Association of Professional & Executive Women (NAPEW); United States Commission on Military History

Virginia Kidd Agency Inc (L)
538 E Harford St, PO Box 278, Milford, PA 18337
Tel: 570-296-6205
Web Site: vk-agency.com
Key Personnel
Literary Agent, Ebooks, Contracts & Royalties: Vaughne L Hansen *E-mail:* vaughne@ptd.net
Literary Agent, Foreign & Translation Rts, Film Queries: Christine M Cohen *E-mail:* chrisco@ptd.net
Literary Agent, Queries, Foreign Rts: William D Reeve *E-mail:* wmreeve@ptd.net
Founded: 1965
We are seeking quality, marketable fiction with an eye toward strong character development, world-building & fresh storytelling. While our focus remains on speculative fiction, we will consider works beyond that if the story is compelling. We represent science fiction/fantasy, dark fantasy, horror, historical fiction & popular fiction. Overall, the characters & their story are more important than the genre.
Titles recently placed: *A Slice of the Dark*, Karen Heuler; *Doctor Alien*, Rajnar Vajra; *Drowned Horse Chronicle (vol 1)*, David Boop; *Maelstrom and Other Martial Tales (reprint)*, Kage Baker; *Opening Wonders*, Rajnar Vajra; *So Here's Our Leo*, D G Compton; *The Book of the Beast (The Orphan, The Captive, and The Beast)*, Robert Stallman; *The Dead Man and Other Horror Stories by Gene Wolfe*, Gene Wolfe; *The Director Should've Shot You*, Alan Dean Foster; *The Serial Killer's Son Takes A Wife*, Michael Libling; *The Splendid City*, Karen Heuler; *The Voice That Murmurs in the Darkness (short story collection)*, James Tiptree Jr; *The Wolfe At The Door*, Gene Wolfe; *Under the Hollywood Sign: The Complete Stories of Tom Reamy*, Tom Reamy
Foreign Rep(s): Bardon Chinese Media Agency (China); Paul & Peter Fritz AG (Germany); International Editors' Co - Yanez Agencia Literaria (Portugal, South America, Spain); Alexander Korzhenevski (Estonia, Finland, Latvia, Lithuania, Norway, Russia, Sweden); Maxima Creative Agency (Indonesia, Thailand, Vietnam); PNLA (France, Italy); Prava i Prevodi (Central Europe, Eastern Europe, Greece, Turkey); Tuttle-Mori Agency Inc (Japan); Eric Yang Agency Inc (South Korea)

Kirchoff/Wohlberg Inc (L)
897 Boston Post Rd, Madison, CT 06443
Tel: 203-245-7308 *Fax:* 203-245-3218
E-mail: info@kirchoffwohlberg.com
Web Site: www.kirchoffwohlberg.com
Key Personnel
Pres: Morris A Kirchoff
VP: Ronald P Zollshan
Founded: 1974
Children & young adult fiction & nonfiction trade books only. Representing author & author/illustrators. Agency does not handle adult titles. No fees.
Membership(s): AIGA, the professional association for design; The American Library Association (ALA); International Literacy Association (ILA); Society of Children's Book Writers & Illustrators (SCBWI); Society of Illustrators

Harvey Klinger Inc (L)
300 W 55 St, Suite 11V, New York, NY 10019
Tel: 212-581-7068 *Fax:* 212-315-3823
E-mail: queries@harveyklinger.com
Web Site: www.harveyklinger.com
Key Personnel
Pres: Harvey Klinger (AALA) *E-mail:* harvey@harveyklinger.com
Agent: David Dunton *E-mail:* david@harveyklinger.com; Andrea Somberg *E-mail:* andrea@harveyklinger.com; Wendy Levinson *E-mail:* wendy@harveyklinger.com; Rachel Ridout *E-mail:* rachel@harveyklinger.com; Cate Hart *E-mail:* cate@harveyklinger.com
Assoc Agent: Analieze Cervantes *E-mail:* analieze@harveyklinger.com; Jennifer Herrington *E-mail:* jennifer@harveyklinger.com
Founded: 1977
Mainstream adult & children's fiction & nonfiction. Handle film & TV rights. No unsol full mss or faxes; do not phone or fax; no reading fee. E-mail query with brief synopsis. First 5 pages ms pasted into body of e-mail also allowed. Representatives in Hollywood & all principal foreign countries.
Foreign Rights: Eliane Benisti (France); Big Apple Agency Inc (Wendy King) (China, Indonesia, Vietnam); Sandra Bruna (Latin America, Spanish- & Portuguese-speaking countries); David Grossman Literary Agency Ltd (David

LITERARY AGENTS

Grossman) (UK); Daniela Micura Literary Services (Daniela Micura) (Italy); Prava i prevodi (Ana Milenkovic) (Eastern Europe, Russia); Thomas Schlueck GmbH (Thomas Schlueck) (Germany); Sebes & Bisseling Literary Agency (Paul Sebes) (Netherlands, Scandinavia); Tuttle-Mori Agency Inc (Ken Mori) (Japan); Eric Yang Agency (Sue Yang) (South Korea)
Membership(s): PEN Center USA

The Knight Agency Inc (L)
232 W Washington St, Madison, GA 30650
E-mail: admin@knightagency.net
Web Site: www.knightagency.net
Key Personnel
Owner & Pres: Deidre Knight
VP: Judson Knight
VP, Sales & Agent: Pamela Harty
VP, Opers & Agent: Elaine Spencer (AALA)
Agent: Kristy Hunter; Melissa Jeglinski
Agent, FL Office: Lucienne Diver
Agent, CA Office: Nephele Tempest
Assoc Agent: Janna Bonikowski; Travis Pennington; Jackie Williams
Bookkeeper, Off Admin: Jamie Pritchett
Founded: 1996
Fiction: commercial fiction, women's fiction, literary & multicultural fiction, historical fiction, young adult, middle grade, romance, LGBQT, science fiction & fantasy. In nonfiction: business, self-help, finance, true crime, memoir, music/entertainment, media-related, pop culture, how-to, psychology, travel, health, inspirational/religious, reference & holiday books. No anthology collections, short stories or poetry. No unsol mss, query first by sending a brief summary or proposal, author info & first 5 pages by e-mail (no attachments). Allow a 2- to 4-week response time for queries. Upon request only submit the following:
For fiction: first 3 chapters, synopsis or outline & copy of original query.
Nonfiction: proposal or outline, first 1-3 chapters, summary of author's qualifications, unique marketing opportunities & copy of original query.
Allow 8-12 weeks for ms review. No reading fee. 15% commission on domestic sales, 15-25% on foreign. May use sub-agent for sale or film & foreign rights. Screenplays not accepted. See web site for submission details. All queries managed through querymanager.net.
Titles recently placed: *A Man to Hold on To*, Marilyn Pappano; *Archangel's Legion*, Nalini Singh; *Burning Dawn*, Gena Showalter; *Cal Leandros (series)*, Rob Thurman; *Chicagoland Vampire*, Chloe Neill; *Eversea*, Natasha Boyd; *Ghost Seer*, Robin Owens; *Ink*, Amanda Sun; *Linger*, Lauren Hawkeye; *Nexus*, Ramez Naam; *Risky Game*, Tracy Solheim; *Sanctuary Island*, Lily Everett; *Stupid Girl*, Cindy Miles; *Talk Dirty to Me*, Dakota Cassidy; *Teach Me a Lesson*, Jasmine Haynes; *The Deamon Prism*, Carol Berg; *The Duke Can Go to the Devil*, Erin Knightley; *The Golden City*, J Kathleen Cheney; *The Great Library*, Rachel Caine; *The Last Monster*, Ginger Garrett; *The Memory Child*, Steena Holmes; *Wickedly Powerful*, Deborah Blake
Branch Office(s)
14622 Ventura Blvd, No 785, Sherman Oaks, CA 91403

PO Box 2659, Land O Lakes, FL 34639
Foreign Rights: ANA Sofia Ltd (Bulgaria); The Fielding Agency (Whitney Lee) (Brazil, Bulgaria, China, Croatia, Czechia, Estonia, Greece, Hungary, Israel, Latvia, Lithuania, Poland, Portugal, Romania, Russia, Serbia, Slovakia, Slovenia, South Korea, Taiwan, UK); Graal Literary Agency (Poland); International Editors' Co - Yanez Agencia Literaria (Brazil, Portugal, Spain); Katai & Bolza Literary Agents (Hungary); Kayi Literary Agency Ltd (Turkey);

Agence Litteraire Lenclud (France); Nova Littera (Russia); Kristin Olson Literary Agency (Czechia); PNLA / Piergiorgio Nicolazzini Literary Agency (Maura Solinas) (Italy); Read n Right Agency (Greece); Lennart Sane Agency AB (Scandinavia); Thomas Schlueck GmbH (Germany)
Membership(s): The Authors Guild; Mystery Writers of America (MWA); Romance Writers of America (RWA); Science Fiction and Fantasy Writers of America, Inc (SFWA); Society of Children's Book Writers & Illustrators (SCBWI); Women's Fiction Writers Association (WFWA)

KO Media Management (L-D)
2817 Wetmore Ave, Everett, WA 98201
E-mail: info@komediamanagement.com; query@komediamanagement.com
Web Site: komediamanagement.com
Key Personnel
Founder & Agent: Kathleen Ortiz (AALA)
Licensing Agent: Shena Wolf
Literary Agent: Stephanie Winter
Assoc Agent & Licensing Coord: Kate Rogers
Founded: 2022
Full service boutique literary & media representation agency. Queries accepted from authors, illustrators & content creators. No queries via postal mail & no screenplays. Query only one agent with no attachments. Authors: Send first 5 pages of text (if picture book, paste entire text); Illustrators & content creators: Send link to portfolio.
Titles recently placed: *Good as Goldie (8th in The Breaking Cat News Adventure series)*, Georgia Dunn; *Lead With Faith, Play With Purpose: A 100-Day Devotional for Athletes*, Andy Dooley; *The Midnight Roar! (2nd in The Dragons of Ember City series)*, Shane Richardson, Sarah Marino; *The Mystery of the Intelligents (2nd in The Peculiar Woods series)*, Andres J Colmenares

The Kohner Agency (L-D)
9300 Wilshire Blvd, Suite 300, Beverly Hills, CA 90212
Tel: 310-550-1060
Web Site: kohneragency.com
Key Personnel
Pres & Owner: Pearl Wexler
Founded: 1938
Representation of 24 major publishing houses. No unsol mss.
Membership(s): Association of Talent Agents (ATA)

Linda Konner Literary Agency (LKLA) (L)
10 W 15 St, Suite 1918, New York, NY 10011
Web Site: www.lindakonnerliteraryagency.com
Key Personnel
Pres: Linda Konner (AALA) *E-mail:* ldkonner@cs.com
Founded: 1996
Health, nutrition, diet, relationships, pop psychology, pop science, self-help, parenting, cookbooks, business & career/personal finance, celebrity/pop culture. No fiction, children's or memoir. No unsol mss, query first with one-page query & one-paragraph author bio via e-mail. If told to do so, then submit book proposal & 1-2 sample chapters. No reading fee. Commission: 15% US, up to 25% foreign.
Titles recently placed: *Brain Energy: A Revolutionary Breakthrough in Understanding Mental Health*, Christopher Palmer, PhD; *From Scrappy to Self-Made: What Entrepreneurs Can Learn from an Ethiopian Refugee*, Yonas Hagos, Gary M Stern; *The Guilded Age Cookbook: Recipes & Stories from America's Golden Era*, Becky Libourel Diamond; *The Other Talent: The Curiously Complex Role*

EDITORIAL SERVICES

of Mental Health in Athletic Greatness, Matt Fitzgerald
Foreign Rights: Books Crossing Borders (Betty Anne Crawford) (worldwide exc USA)
Membership(s): American Society of Journalists & Authors (ASJA); The Authors Guild

Stuart Krichevsky Literary Agency Inc (L)
118 E 28 St, Suite 908, New York, NY 10016
Tel: 212-725-5288 *Fax:* 212-725-5275
E-mail: query@skagency.com
Web Site: skagency.com
Key Personnel
Pres: Stuart Krichevsky (AALA)
Literary Agent & Busn Mgr: Hannah Schwartz (AALA)
Literary Agent: Melissa Danaczko
E-mail: mdquery@skagency.com; Barbara Jones; David Patterson *E-mail:* dpquery@skagency.com; Aemilia Phillips
E-mail: apquery@skagency.com; Laura Usselman (AALA) *E-mail:* luquery@skagency.com; Mackenzie Brady Watson (AALA)
E-mail: mbwquery@skagency.com; Chandler Wickers
Founded: 1995
Fiction & nonfiction. No reading fee. No unsol mss, query first; prefer e-mail queries & first few (up to 10) pages of ms or proposal in the body of the e-mail (no attachments).
Titles recently placed: *A Really Strange and Wonderful Time: The Chapel Hill Music Scene 1989-1999*, Tom Maxwell; *In My Time of Dying: How I Came Face to Face with the Idea of an Afterlife*, Sebastian Junger; *Summers at the Saint*, Mary Kay Andrews
Foreign Rights: Akcali Copyright Trade & Tourism Co Ltd (Turkey); The Deborah Harris Agency (Israel); Andrew Nurnberg Associates (China, Europe, South America); Tuttle-Mori Agency Inc (Japan); Eric Yang Agency (South Korea)

The LA Literary Agency (L)
1264 N Hayworth Ave, Los Angeles, CA 90046
Tel: 323-654-5288
E-mail: laliteraryagency@mac.com
Web Site: www.laliteraryagency.com
Key Personnel
Literary Agent: Ann Cashman *E-mail:* ann@laliteraryagency.com; Eric Lasher *E-mail:* eric.laliteraryagency@mac.com; Maureen Lasher *E-mail:* maureen.laliterary@mac.com
Founded: 1980
Specialize in narrative nonfiction, commercial & literary fiction. Nonfiction: query, qualifications & proposal; Fiction: query & ms. See web site for books, clients & submission information.

Ladderbird Literary Agency (L)
460 Yellow Brick Rd, Orange, CT 06477
Mailing Address: PO Box 270, Milford, CT 06460
Tel: 203-290-1703
Web Site: www.ladderbird.com
Key Personnel
Agent/Owner: Beth Marshea (AALA) *Tel:* 617-276-2406 *E-mail:* bethmarshea@ladderbird.com
Sr Agent: Leah Pierre (AALA)
E-mail: leahpierre@ladderbird.com
Agent: Regina Carreno-Bernard
E-mail: reginabernard@ladderbird.com; Allegra Martschenko *E-mail:* allegramartschenko@ladderbird.com; Stefanie Molina
E-mail: stefaniemolina@ladderbird.com; Natalie Obando *E-mail:* natalieobando@ladderbird.com
Foreign Rts Agent: Katelin Spector
Asst Agent: Annalise Errico
E-mail: annaliseerrico@ladderbird.com
Founded: 2017

Full service literary agency offering editorial services, rights & subsidiary rights sales & royalty management. Sales commission only. No fees.
Titles recently placed: *Aliens: Vasquez*, V Castro; *Becoming Sara King*, Catherine Adel West; *Eva's Sweet Recipe*, Harshita Jerath; *Private Matters*, Martin Padgett; *Skeleanor the Decomposer*, Emily Ettlinger; *Something Like Right*, H D Hunter; *Strictly No Heroics*, B L Radley; *The Haunting of Alejandra*, V Castro; *The Leaping Laddoo*, Harshita Jerath

Peter Lampack Agency Inc (L)
350 Fifth Ave, Suite 5300, New York, NY 10118
Tel: 212-687-9106 *Fax:* 212-687-9109
Web Site: www.peterlampackagency.com
Key Personnel
Pres: Peter A Lampack
Agent & Foreign Rts: Rema Dilanyan
 E-mail: rema@peterlampackagency.com
Agent: Andrew Lampack *E-mail:* andrew@peterlampackagency.com
Off Mgr: Anna Kuznetcova
 E-mail: bookkeeping@peterlampackagency.com
Founded: 1977
Commercial & literary fiction; nonfiction by recognized experts in a given field (especially autobiography, biography, law, finance, politics, history). Handle motion picture & TV rights from book properties only. No stageplays, teleplays or screenplays. No unsol mss. Query with letter which describes the nature of the ms plus author's credentials if any, sample chapter & synopsis by e-mail only.
Titles recently placed: *Clive Cussler's Dark Vector*, Graham Brown; *Clive Cussler's Hellburner*, Mike Maden; *Clive Cussler's The Sea Wolves*, Jack Du Brul; *The Pole and Other Stories*, J M Coetzee
Foreign Rep(s): Big Apple Agency Inc (China, Taiwan); Prava i prevodi (Eastern Europe, Greece); Tuttle-Mori Agency Inc (Japan, Thailand); Eric Yang Agency (South Korea)

The Ned Leavitt Agency (L)
752 Creeklocks Rd, Rosendale, NY 12472
Tel: 845-658-3333
Web Site: www.nedleavittagency.com
Key Personnel
Pres: Ned Leavitt (AALA) *E-mail:* nedleavitt@aol.com
Agent: Jillian Sweeney *E-mail:* jsweeney@nedleavittgency.com
Literary & commercial fiction & nonfiction, books on spirituality & psychology. No unsol mss. Submissions by recommendation only. Rejections not returned, no reading fee.

Levine|Greenberg|Rostan Literary Agency (L-D)
307 Seventh Ave, Suite 2407, New York, NY 10001
Tel: 212-337-0934 *Fax:* 212-337-0948
E-mail: submit@lgrliterary.com
Web Site: lgrliterary.com
Key Personnel
Principal: Daniel Greenberg *E-mail:* dgreenberg@lgrliterary.com; James Levine *E-mail:* jlevine@lgrliterary.com; Stephanie Rostan (AALA) *E-mail:* srostan@lgrliterary.com
VP & Agent: Lindsay Edgecombe *E-mail:* ledgecombe@lgrliterary.com; Kerry Sparks *E-mail:* ksparks@lgrliterary.com; Danielle Svetcov (AALA) *E-mail:* dsvetcov@lgrliterary.com; Monika Verma (AALA) *E-mail:* mverma@lgrliterary.com
Rts Dir: Tim Wojcik *E-mail:* twojcik@lgrliterary.com
Agent: Sarah Bedingfield *E-mail:* sbedingfield@lgrliterary.com; Courtney Paganelli *E-mail:* cpaganelli@lgrliterary.com; Victoria Skurnick (AALA) *E-mail:* vskurnick@lgrliterary.com
Assoc Agent: Rebecca Rodd *E-mail:* rrodd@lgrliterary.com
Agent-at-Large: Arielle Eckstut; Greg Shaw
Busn Mgr: Melissa Rowland *E-mail:* mrowland@lgrliterary.com
Royalties Mgr: Miek Coccia *E-mail:* mcoccia@lgrliterary.com
Foreign Rts & Busn Assoc: Cristela Henriquez *E-mail:* chenriquez@lgrliterary.com
Founded: 1989
Online queries via the How To Submit page on web site or e-mail queries to submit@lgrliterary.com. Attachments limited to 50 pages. Handle film & TV rights. No reading fee.
Titles recently placed: *Come Together: The Science (and Art!) of Creating Lasting Sexual Connections*, Emily Nagoski, PhD; *Finlay Donovan Rolls the Dice: A Novel*, Elle Cosimano; *The Wharton Plot: A Novel*, Mariah Fredericks
Foreign Rights: AnatoliaLit Copyright & Translation Agency (Turkey); Bardon-Chinese Media Agency (China, Taiwan); Eliane Benisti Agence Litteraire (France); The Book Publishers Association of Israel (Israel); Bridge Communications (Thailand, Vietnam); Eastern European & Asian Rights Agency Ltd (Baltic States, Ukraine); English Agency Japan Co Ltd (Japan); Ersilia Literary Agency (Greece); The Foreign Office (Latin America, Portugal, Spain); Graal Literary Agency (Czechia, Eastern Europe, Poland); Agence Hoffman (Germany); Korea Copyright Center Inc (KCC) (South Korea); Maxima Creative Agency (Indonesia, Malaysia); Agencia Riff (Brazil); Vicki Satlow Agency (Italy); Sebes & Bisseling Literary Agency (Netherlands, Scandinavia); Abner Stein Literary Agency (UK); Synopsis Literary Agency (Russia)

Robert Lieberman Agency (L)
Subsidiary of Ithaca Film & Writing Works
475 Nelson Rd, Ithaca, NY 14850
Tel: 607-273-8801
Web Site: roberthlieberman.com
Key Personnel
Pres: Robert H Lieberman *E-mail:* RHL10@cornell.edu
Founded: 1994
ABSOLUTELY NONFICTION ONLY! WILL NOT RESPOND TO FICTION QUERIES. Specialize in college level textbooks by established & recognized academics in all fields, as well as trade books in science, math, economics, engineering, medicine, psychology, computers & other academic areas that would be of general or popular interest. Represent producers of CD-ROM/multimedia/software, film & videos that fall into these categories. Submissions can be proposals +/or sample chapters, resume & table of contents. No unsol mss, query first (prefer brief e-mail query, no calls); will give quick response by e-mail but will accept mail query with SASE; handle software; no reading fee.

Literary & Creative Artists Inc (L)
3543 Albemarle St NW, Washington, DC 20008-4213
Tel: 202-362-4688 *Fax:* 202-362-8875
E-mail: lca9643@lcadc.com (queries, no attachments)
Web Site: www.lcadc.com
Key Personnel
Founder & Pres: Muriel G Nellis
Founded: 1981
Specialize in adult trade fiction & nonfiction credentialed authors only. No poetry or academic/technical work. No unsol mss, query first by mail addressed to Muriel Nellis with SASE or by e-mail (no attachments). Require exclusive review period of 2-3 weeks. No reading fee. Visit the submission page on our web site for more information.
Membership(s): American Bar Association (ABA); American Booksellers Association (ABA); The Authors Guild

Literary Artists Representatives (L)
575 West End Ave, Suite GRC, New York, NY 10024-2711
Tel: 212-679-7788
E-mail: litartists@aol.com
Key Personnel
Pres: Sam Fleishman
Founded: 1993
Emphasizes adult trade, nonfiction (narrative, biography, memoir, current affairs, business, culture, history, how-to, film/TV, personal finance, sciences, sports, motivational). Handle film, TV electronic rights. Co-agents in Hollywood & other selected cities. No unsol mss, query first via e-mail. No fiction or poetry. No fees.
Titles recently placed: *Alley-Oop to Aliyah: African American Hoopsters in the Holy Land*, David A Goldstein; *Disney U: How Disney University Develops the World's Most Engaged, Loyal, and Customer-Centric Employees*, Doug Lipp; *Forty-Eight Seconds: The Human Account of One of America's Greatest Disasters: The San Francisco Earthquake and Fire, April 18-21, 1906*, Matthew James Davenport; *Golf's Holy War: The Battle for the Soul of a Game in an Age of Science*, Brett Cyrgalis; *Investment Mistakes Even Smart Investors Make and How to Avoid Them*, Larry E Swedroe, RC Balaban; *JFK in the Senate: Pathway to the Presidency*, John T Shaw; *John Bell Hatcher: King of the Dinosaur Hunters: A Biography*, Lowell Dingus, PhD; *Kathleen Turner on Acting: Conversations About Film, Television, and Theater*, Kathleen Turner, Dustin Morrow; *Lady in the Dark: Iris Barry and the Art of Film*, Robert Sitton; *Millionaire Expat: How to Build Wealth Living Overseas*, Andrew Hallam; *Political Mercenaries: How Fundraisers Allowed Billionaires to Take Over Politics*, Lindsay Mark Lewis, Jim Arkedis; *The $1,000 Challenge: How One Family Slashed Its Budget Without Moving Under a Bridge or Living on Government Cheese*, Brian J O'Connor; *The Intelligent Option Investor: Applying Value Investing to the World of Options*, Erik Kobayashi-Solomon; *The Women's Guide to Successful Investing: Achieving Financial Security and Realizing Your Goals*, Nancy Tengler; *Think, Act, and Invest Like Warren Buffett: The Winning Strategy to Help You Achieve Your Financial and Life Goals*, Larry Swedroe

Literary Management Group LLC (L)
1020 San Antonio Lane, Lady Lake, FL 32159
Tel: 615-812-4445
Web Site: www.literarymanagementgroup.com
Key Personnel
Founder & CEO: Bruce R Barbour *E-mail:* brb@brucebarbour.com
VP: Karen Moore *Tel:* 614-266-2876
 E-mail: karenmoorebarbour@gmail.com
Founded: 1997
Nonfiction: Christian, motivational & inspirational. No unsol mss, query first with letter prior to submission of ms for review. E-mail proposal, outline, sample chapters. We do not represent fiction, screenplays, children's, poetry, text or reference.

Lowenstein Associates Inc (L-D)
115 E 23 St, 4th fl, New York, NY 10010
Tel: 212-206-1630
E-mail: assistant@bookhaven.com (queries, no attachments)

LITERARY AGENTS

Web Site: www.lowensteinassociates.com
Key Personnel
Pres: Barbara Lowenstein (AALA)
Founded: 1976
Electronic queries (no attachments). No westerns, textbooks, children's picture books or books needing translation. Fiction: submit via authors.me or send a one-page query with first 10 pages in the body of the e-mail; nonfiction: submit via authors.me or send a one-page query, table of contents & a proposal (if available) in the body of the e-mail to assistant@bookhaven.com. Include the word QUERY & the project name in the subject line. Address the e-mail to the agent you want to consider your work. Visit our web site to find more information about each agent's interests. No reading fee.
Membership(s): Romance Writers of America (RWA)

Donald Maass Literary Agency (L)
1000 Dean St, Suite 331, Brooklyn, NY 11238
Tel: 212-727-8383
E-mail: info@maassagency.com
Web Site: www.maassagency.com
Key Personnel
Pres: Donald Maass (AALA) *E-mail:* dmaass@maassagency.com
EVP: Jennifer Jackson (AALA) *E-mail:* jjackson@maassagency.com
VP & Rts Dir: Katie Shea Boutillier (AALA) *E-mail:* ksboutillier@maassagency.com
Agent: Michael Curry (AALA) *E-mail:* mcurry@maassagency.com; Cameron McClure (AALA) *E-mail:* cmcclure@maassagency.com; Caitlin McDonald (AALA); Jennifer Goloboy (AALA); Kat Kerr
Founded: 1980
Literary agency for professional novelists, representing more than 100 authors & selling more than 150 novels every year to major publishers in the US & overseas. Also handles book-to-film & TV rights. Leading clients include Anne Bishop, Jim Butcher, Diane Duane, Kim Harrison, Darcie Little Badger, Anne Perry, Tamsyn Muir, Martha Wells & Brent Weeks. See web site for submission guidelines. Query via e-mail with 1-page letter, first 5 pages of novel & 1- to 2-page synopsis, pasted into e-mail; no attachments.
Titles recently placed: *Asunder*, Kerstin Hall; *Cinder Spires: The Olympian Affair*, Jim Butcher; *Exordia*, Seth Dickinson; *Lady in Glass and Other Stories*, Anne Bishop; *Nona the Ninth*, Tamsyn Muir; *Remember You Will Die*, Eden Robins; *The Bone Crown*, C L Polk; *The Butcher of the Forest*, Premee Mohamed; *The Saint of Bright Doors*, Vajra Chandrasekera; *The Salt Grows Heavy*, Cassandra Khaw; *The Swarm*, Andy Marino; *The Tapestry of Time*, Kate Heartfield; *Witch King*, Martha Wells
Foreign Rights: AnatoliaLit Agency (Turkey); Book Publishers Association of Israel (Israel); Donzelli Fietta Agency (Italy); English Agency Japan Co Ltd (Japan); Grayhawk Agency (China, Indonesia, Taiwan, Thailand, Vietnam); International Editors' Co - Yanez Agencia Literaria (Brazil, South America, Spain); Anna Jarota Agency (France); A Korzhenevski Agency (Russia); MBA Literary Agents Ltd (UK); Prava i prevodi (Bulgaria, Czechia, Montenegro, Poland, Romania, Serbia); Thomas Schlueck GmbH (Germany); Sebes & Bisseling Literary Agency (Denmark, Finland, Netherlands, Norway, Sweden); Eric Yang Agency (South Korea)
Membership(s): Mystery Writers of America (MWA); Science Fiction and Fantasy Writers of America, Inc (SFWA)

Gina Maccoby Literary Agency (L)
PO Box 60, Chappaqua, NY 10514-0060
Tel: 914-238-5630
E-mail: query@maccobylit.com
Web Site: www.publishersmarketplace.com/members/GinaMaccoby
Key Personnel
Principal: Gina Maccoby (AALA)
Founded: 1986
High quality fiction & nonficton for adults & children. Handle film & TV rights for clients' work only. No screenplays. No unsol mss; query first. E-mail queries only. Owing to the volume of queries received, we will only respond if interested. No reading fee. May recover the cost of books purchased for submissions; airmail shipping of books overseas; overnight shipping domestically if requested by client; bank fees incurred related to transfers of payments; legal fees incurred with prior client approval. Co-agents in Hollywood & overseas.
Titles recently placed: *A Sea of Gold*, Patricia Polacco; *Animal Poems: A Collection*, Mary Ann Hoberman; *When You Wish Upon a Star: A Twisted Tale*, Elizabeth Lim
Foreign Rights: Ginger Clark Literary
Membership(s): The Authors Guild; Society of Children's Book Writers & Illustrators (SCBWI)

Ricia Mainhardt Agency, see RMA

Carol Mann Agency (L)
55 Fifth Ave, 18th fl, New York, NY 10003
Tel: 212-206-5635 *Fax:* 212-675-4809
E-mail: submissions@carolmannagency.com
Web Site: www.carolmannagency.com
Key Personnel
Pres: Carol Mann (AALA)
Agent: Gareth Esersky; Joanne Wyckoff
Founded: 1977
Literary & commercial fiction, no genre fiction, general nonfiction & memoir. Subs-agents in Los Angeles & for all foreign languages. No unsol mss, query first. E-mail queries only (no attachments). Mailed queries no longer accepted. For fiction & memoir, send a synopsis, brief bio & first 25 pages of ms. All other nonfiction, submit synopsis & brief bio. No reading fee. Handle film & TV rights for book clients only.
Foreign Rights: Akcali Copyright Agency (Turkey); Am Oved (Dalia Ever-Hadani) (Israel); Anthea Agency (Bulgaria); Eliane Benisti Agency (France); Big Apple Agency Inc (China, Indonesia, Taiwan); Graal Literary Agency (Poland); The Italian Literary Agency Srl (Italy); JLM Literary Agency (Greece); Katai & Bolza Literary Agents (Hungary); Simona Kessler International Copyright Agency (Romania); Licht & Burr Literary Agency (Trine Licht) (Denmark, Iceland, Norway, Sweden); Mohrbooks AG Literary Agency (Germany); Andrew Nurnberg Associates Baltic (Kristine Supe) (Latvia); Andrew Nurnberg Literary Agency (Ludmilla Sushkova) (Russia); Kristin Olson Literary Agency (Czechia); Prava i prevodi (Ana Milenkovic) (Serbia); Schavelzon Graham Agencia Literaria (Jacoba Casier) (Spain); Schindler's Literary Agency (Brazil); Sebes & Bisseling Literary Agency (Paul Sebes) (Netherlands); Abner Stein Associates (Arabella Stein) (England); Tuttle-Mori Agency Inc (Manami Tamaoki) (Japan); Tuttle-Mori Agency (Thailand) Co Ltd (Pimolporn Yutisri) (Thailand); Shin Won Agency (Tae Eun Kim) (South Korea)

Denise Marcil Literary Agency LLC (L)
Affiliate of Marcil-O'Farrell Literary LLC
483 Westover Rd, Stamford, CT 06902
Tel: 203-327-9970 *Fax:* 203-327-9970
Web Site: www.marcilofarrellagency.com

EDITORIAL SERVICES

Key Personnel
Mgr & Agent: Denise Marcil (AALA)
E-mail: denise@marcilofarrellagency.com
Agent: Anne Marie O'Farrell (AALA)
Tel: 516-365-6029 *E-mail:* annemarie@marcilofarrellagency.com
Founded: 1977
Denise Marcil no longer accepts new authors. Do not query. Send nonfiction e-mail queries to Anne Marie O'Farrell at annemarie@marcilofarrellagency.com, who represents personal growth, self-help including mind, body, spirit, alternative health, spirituality, business, careers, sports, travel, cookbooks, gift books & quirky books. No unsol mss, query first via e-mail. Sub-agents in all major countries.
Titles recently placed: *Dr Knox*, Peter Spiegelman; *For Every Little Thing*, June Cotner, Nancy Tupper-Ling; *Glad to Be Human*, Irene O'Garden; *Healing the Thyroid with Ayurveda*, Dr Marianne Teitelbaum; *Herons Landing*, *Snowfall on Lighthouse Lane*, *Summer on Mirror Lake*, JoAnn Ross; *Lilac Lane*, Sherryl Woods; *Magic Lantern*, Peter Spiegelman; *The Healthy Brain Book*, Dr William Sears, Dr Vincent Fortanasce; *The Healthy Motherhood Journal*, Martha Sears, RN, Hayden Livesday Sears; *The Warrior Heart Practice*, HeatherAsh Amara; *Titanic Sisters*, Patricia Falvey; *Willow Brook Road*, Sherryl Woods
Membership(s): The Authors Guild; Women's Media Group

Mildred Marmur Associates Ltd (L)
2005 Palmer Ave, PMB 127, Larchmont, NY 10538
Tel: 914-843-5582 *Fax:* 914-833-1175
E-mail: marmur@westnet.com
Key Personnel
Pres: Mildred Marmur (AALA)
Founded: 1987
Nonfiction only. No unsol mss; referrals only. Represented in Hollywood & foreign markets. Does not charge fees.
Membership(s): The Authors Guild

Marsal Lyon Literary Agency LLC (L)
665 San Rodolfo Dr, Suite 124, PMB 121, Solana Beach, CA 92075
Tel: 760-814-8507
Web Site: www.marsallyonliteraryagency.com
Key Personnel
Owner & Literary Agent: Kevan Lyon
E-mail: kevan@marsallyonliteraryagency.com; Jill Marsal *E-mail:* jill@marsallyonliteraryagency.com
Literary Agent: Shannon Hassan
E-mail: shannon@marsallyonliteraryagency.com; Cathie Hedrick-Armstrong; Patricia Nelson *E-mail:* patricia@marsallyonliteraryagency.com; Deborah Ritchken *E-mail:* deborah@marsallyonliteraryagency.com
Founded: 2009
Dedicated to helping authors successfully place their work. Members have many years of experience in the publishing industry & possess a diverse & unique skill set. Have worked with many bestselling & award-winning authors, as well as first-time authors.
Fiction genres & categories represented: commercial, mainstream, multicultural, mystery, suspense, thriller, women's fiction, romance (all genres), young adult & middle grade. Nonfiction represented: biography, business/economics/investing/finance, diet, fitness & health, history/politics/current events, investigative journalism, lifestyle, memoirs, narrative nonfiction, parenting, pets/animals, pop culture & music, psychology, relationships/advice, science & nature, self-help, sports, women's issues. No unsol ms, query first. Writers are encouraged to visit the web site to determine who might be

the best fit for your work. For electronic submissions (preferred), send query letter & write QUERY in the subject line of the e-mail. Hard copy submissions: for fiction, send cover letter, one-page synopsis of work & first 10 pages of ms; for nonfiction, include either cover letter or cover letter & complete proposal. No fees.
The Taryn Fagerness Agency represents foreign, audio & film subsidiary rights.
Titles recently placed: *A Game Most Foul*, Alison Gervais; *All the Good Parts*, Loretta Nyhan; *Arsenic & Adobo*, Mia P Manansala; *Beach House Brunch: 100 Delicious Ways to Start Your Long Summer Days*, Lei Shishak; *Brain Health Puzzles*, Phil Fraas; *Burnout Immunity*, Kandi Wiens; *Camp So and So*, Mary McCoy; *Catch Her Death*, Melinda Leigh; *Dare to be Unstoppable*, Jill Stoddard; *Dead and Gone*, Joanna Schaffhausen; *Embedded Finance: When Payments Become An Experience (1st ed)*, Scarlett Sieber, Sophie Guibaud; *Ernesto: Hemingway's Years in Cuba*, Andrew Feldman; *Exam Empire*, Hongbin Li, Ruixue Jia, Claire Cousineau; *Gifted and Distractible*, Julie Skolnick; *Gone Again*, Minka Kent; *Hacking Darwin*, Jamie Metzl; *Holding on for Dear Life*, Dusti Bowling; *Horses of Fire*, A D Rhine; *Inflection Points: How to Work and Live with Purpose*, Matt Spielman; *It's Watching*, Lindsay Currie; *Karma Khullar's Mustache*, Kristi Wientge; *Le French Oven*, Hillary Davis; *Les Desserts*, Hillary Davis; *Mathematical Diversity*, Jo Boaler; *Medical Gaslighting*, Ilana Goldberg; *Middle School Superpowers*, Phyllis Fagell; *My Paris Market Cookbook: A Culinary Tour of Flavors and Seasonal Recipes*, Emily Dilling; *Operation: Happy*, Jenni L Walsh; *ReCulturing: Design Your Company Culture to Connect with Strategy and Purpose for Lasting Success*, Melissa Daimler; *Sir Edmund and the Wild West*, Dusti Bowling; *Situationship*, Marina Adair; *Surviving Cancer*, David Palma; *The Age of Insurrection*, David Neiwert; *The Beauty of Rain*, Jamie Beck; *The Creativity Decision*, Zorana Pringle; *The Jolt Effect: How High Performers Overcome Customer Indecision*, Matthew Dixon, Ted McKenna; *The Kiss on Castle Road*, Lauren Christopher; *The Last Library*, Frank L Cole; *The Last Place You Look*, Kristen Lepionka; *The Lava Witch*, Debra Bokur; *The Line*, Martin Limon; *The Memory Diet*, Judi Zucker, Shari Zucker; *The Mesmerist*, Caroline Woods; *The Mystery of Locked Rooms*, Lindsay Currie; *The Pain Solution*, Saloni Sharma; *The Portable Feast: Creative Meals for Work and Play*, Jeanne Kelley; *The Puppy Proposal*, Katie Meyer; *The Raven Thief*, Gigi Pandian; *The Red Car to Hollywood*, Jennie Liu; *The Rescue Effect: The Key to Saving Life on Earth*, Michael Mehta Webster; *The Rule of Three*, Heather Murphy Capps; *The Taken Ones*, Jessica Lourey; *The Tao of Running*, Gary Dudney; *The Work Happiness Method*, Stella Grizont; *This Victorian Life*, Sarah Chrisman; *To Steal a Heart*, K C Bateman; *Unsinkable*, Jenni L Walsh; *Until We Meet*, Camille Di Maio; *Visibility Marketing*, David Avrin; *What Never Happened*, Rachel Howzell Hall
Foreign Rights: Taryn Fagerness Agency (Albania, Argentina, Australia, Brazil, Bulgaria, Canada, China, Croatia, Czechia, Denmark, Estonia, Finland, France, Germany, Greece, Hungary, Iceland, India, Indonesia, Israel, Italy, Japan, Latvia, Lithuania, Mexico, Netherlands, Norway, Poland, Portugal, Romania, Russia, Serbia, Slovakia, Slovenia, South Korea, Spain, Sweden, Taiwan, Thailand, Turkey, Ukraine, UK, Vietnam)
Membership(s): Romance Writers of America (RWA)

The Evan Marshall Agency (L)
One Pacio Ct, Roseland, NJ 07068-1121
Tel: 973-287-6216
Web Site: www.evanmarshallagency.com
Key Personnel
Pres: Evan S Marshall (AALA) *E-mail:* evan@evanmarshallagency.com
Founded: 1987
Not accepting new clients. Represents all genres of adult & young adult full-length fiction.
Titles recently placed: *Bad Choices*, Joseph Souza; *Beyond the Wire*, James D Shipman; *Go Find Daddy*, Steve Goble; *Hide*, Tracy Clark; *How Snowball Stole Christmas*, Kristen McKanagh; *Murder at an Irish Castle*, Ellie Brannigan; *No Strangers Here*, Carlene O'Connor; *The Chamber*, Christopher Hawke; *The Hookup Plan*, Farrah Rochon; *The Knight's Pledge*, Heather Grothaus; *The War Girls*, V S Alexander

The Martell Agency (L)
1350 Avenue of the Americas, Suite 1205, New York, NY 10019
Tel: 212-317-2672
Web Site: www.themartellagency.com
Key Personnel
Owner: Alice Fried Martell
Contact: Stephanie Finman
Founded: 1985
Fiction & nonfiction. Handle film & TV rights. No unsol mss, query first. Submit query letters by e-mail, sample material only on request. Include market analysis for nonfiction & author biography. No reading fee. Does NOT represent children's books, young adult, romance, science fiction/fantasy, poetry, screenplays, plays. Represented in foreign markets.
Titles recently placed: *Flight Risk*, Kevin Hazzard; *Sleep Across the Animal Kingdom*, Barrett Klein; Niels Rattenborg, John Lesku; *Strength & Power: The Untold, Ignored, and Belittled Science of Women's Bodies*, Starre Vartan; *The Boundaries We Cross*, Brad Parks; *The Expert*, Ann Burgess, Steven Constantine
Foreign Rep(s): Eliane Benisti (France); Graal Literary Agency (Eastern Europe); Deborah Harris Agency (Efrat Lev) (Israel); International Editors' Co - Yanez Agencia Literaria (Sandra Biel Piera) (Brazil, Portugal, Spain, Spanish Latin America); Nurchian Kesim Literary Agency Ltd (Filiz Karaman) (Turkey); Liepman Agency (Germany, Switzerland); Maxima Creative Agency (Indonesia, Malaysia); Natoli Stefan & Oliva SA (Italy); Andrew Nurnberg Associates International (Whitney Hsu) (Taiwan); Andrew Nurnberg Associates International (Jackie Huang) (China); Read n Right Agency (Greece); Sebes & Bisseling Literary Agency (Netherlands, Scandinavia); Abner Stein (Australia, UK & Commonwealth); Tuttle-Mori Agency Inc (Japan); Tuttle-Mori Agency (Thailand) Co Ltd (Thananchai Pandey) (Thailand); Eric Yang Agency (Henry Shin) (South Korea)

Martin Literary Management (L)
914 164 St SE, Suite B12, Box 307, Mill Creek, WA 98012
Tel: 206-466-1773 (no phone queries)
Web Site: www.martinliterarymanagement.com
Key Personnel
Pres & Literary Mgr/Prodr: Sharlene Levin Martin *E-mail:* sharlene@martinliterarymanagement.com
Sr Literary Mgr: Delia Berrigan *E-mail:* delia@martinlit.com; Lindsay Guzzardo *E-mail:* lindsay@martinlit.com; Jen Newens *E-mail:* jen@martinliterarymanagement.com
Literary Mgr: Rick Lewis *E-mail:* rick@martinlit.com; Kristen Terrette *E-mail:* kristen@martinlit.com
Jr Literary Mgr: Mara Cobb *E-mail:* mara@martinlit.com
Founded: 2003
Nonfiction, picture books, middle grade, young adult, graphic novels, adult nonfiction, adult fiction, lifestyle, gift books. Query in accordance with submission guidelines & agents' preferences on web site. Now a "green agency," only e-mail queries will be accepted. No fees charged.
Titles recently placed: *Chasing Cosby*, Michelle McPhee; *Chasing Portraits*, Elizabeth Rynecki; *Dear Jacob*, Patty Wetterling, Joy Baker; *Finding My Shine*, Nastia Liukin; *Impossible Odds*, Anthony Flacco, Jessica Buchanan; *Secrets of a Marine's Wife*, Shanna Hogan; *Sole Survivor*, Holly Dunn; *The Next Everest*, Jim Davidson; *The Woman Who Stole Vermeer*, Anthony Amore; *Too Pretty to Live*, Dennis Brooks
Foreign Rights: Taryn Fagerness Agency (worldwide exc Canada & US Territories)
Membership(s): The Authors Guild

Massie & McQuilkin (L)
27 W 20 St, Suite 305, New York, NY 10011
Tel: 212-352-2055
E-mail: info@mmqlit.com
Web Site: www.mmqlit.com
Key Personnel
Agent: Maria Massie; Rob McQuilkin; Jason Anthony
No unsol mss, query first by e-mail only. Send query letter briefly describing project & personal/professional information that may be relevant, along with first 5-10 pages (no attachments). Marie Massie seeks literary fiction, memoir & narrative nonfiction. Rob McQuilkin focuses on literary fiction as well as narrative nonfiction & nonfiction in the areas of memoir, history, biography, art history & cultural criticism. Jason Anthony is interested in commercial fiction of all types. Query only one agent at a time.
Titles recently placed: *Homeland of My Body: New and Selected Poems*, Richard Blanco; *If We Burn: The Mass Protest Decade and the Missing Revolution*, Vincent Bevins; *Let Us Descend*, Jesmyn Ward; *Songs on Endless Repeat: Essays and Outtakes*, Anthony Veasna So; *The Book of James: The Power, Politics, and Passion of LeBron*, Valerie Babb

Margret McBride Literary Agency (L)
PO Box 9128, La Jolla, CA 92038
Tel: 858-454-1550
E-mail: staff@mcbridelit.com
Web Site: www.mcbrideliterary.com
Key Personnel
Owner & Pres: Margret McBride (AALA)
Agent: Faye Atchison (AALA)
Founded: 1981
Specialize in fiction, nonfiction & business. No unsol mss; submissions accepted online only via Query Manager: querymanager.com/query/1873. No poetry, romance, children's or screenplays. Foreign rights sub-agents in all major countries.
Titles recently placed: *Fanocracy*, David Meerman Scott, Reiko Scott; *Financial Freedom*, Grant Sabatier; *Keep Your Brain Young*, Dr Marc Milstein; *The Gold Standard*, Colin Cowie; *Why We Get Sick*, Dr Benjamin Bikman
Foreign Rights: Akcali Copyright (Azerbaijan, Turkey); The Asano Agency (Kiyoshi Asano) (Japan); Bardon Chinese Media Agency (David Tsai) (China); Eliane Benisti Agency (France); Raquel De La Concha Agencia Literaria (Central America, Mexico, Portugal, Spain, Spanish- & Portuguese-speaking countries, Spanish Latin America); Caroline van Gelderen Literary Agency (Netherlands); Korea Copyright Center Inc (KCC) (South Korea); Licht & Burr (Scandinavia); Maxima Creative Agency (Santo Manarung) (Indonesia); I Pikarski (Israel); Pravi i prevodi (Albania, Bosnia and Herzegov-

ina, Bulgaria, Croatia, Czechia, Eastern Block, Eastern Europe, Estonia, Georgia, Greece, Hungary, Latvia, Lithuania, Montenegro, Poland, Romania, Russia & former USSR, Serbia, Slovakia, Slovenia, Ukraine)
Membership(s): The Authors Guild; Society of Children's Book Writers & Illustrators (SCBWI); Writers Guild of America (WGA)

E J McCarthy Agency (L)
405 Maple St, Suite H, Mill Valley, CA 94941
Tel: 415-383-6639
E-mail: ejmagency@gmail.com
Web Site: www.publishersmarketplace.com/members/ejmccarthy
Key Personnel
Owner: E J McCarthy
Founded: 2003
Independent literary agency from former executive editor (Bantam Doubleday Dell, Ballentine/Random House). Subject specialties: history, military history, politics, sports, biography, media, memoir, thrillers & other nonfiction. No reading fee. Query first by e-mail.
Titles recently placed: *8 Seconds of Courage*, Flo Groberg, Tom Sileo; *Air Apaches*, Jay A Stout; *Fire and Forget: Short Stories from the Long War*, Roy Scranton (ed), Matt Gallagher (ed); *Fire in My Eyes*, Brad Snyder, Tom Sileo; *Hell's Angels*, Jay A Stout; *One Bullet Away*, Nathaniel Fick; *Our Year of War*, Daniel P Bolger; *The Sling & the Stone*, Thomas X Hammes; *The Unforgiving Minute*, Craig M Mullaney; *Wanted Dead or Alive*, Benjamin Runkle; *War Play*, Corey Mead; *When Books Went to War*, Molly Guptill Manning; *Why We Lost*, Daniel P Bolger

Gerard McCauley Agency Inc (L)
PO Box 844, Katonah, NY 10536-0844
Tel: 914-232-5700
Key Personnel
Pres: Gerard McCauley
E-mail: gerrymccauley44@gmail.com
Founded: 1970
Nonfiction; educational materials. No unsol mss. Representatives in all major foreign countries. Not currently considering new mss. Does not charge fees.

McIntosh and Otis Inc (L)
235 Main St, Suite 318, White Plains, NY 10601
Tel: 212-687-7400 *Fax:* 212-687-6894
E-mail: info@mcintoshandotis.com
Web Site: www.mcintoshandotis.com
Key Personnel
Pres & Sr Adult Agent: Elizabeth Winick Rubinstein (AALA)
Agent, Children's Dept: Christa Heschke (AALA)
Agent: Adam Muhlig
Jr Agent: Daniele Hunter
Founded: 1928
Represent adult & juvenile fiction & nonfiction books. No unsol mss, query first via e-mail. See web site for instructions. No reading fees. Handle film & TV rights for represented clients only. Agents in most major foreign countries.
Foreign Rep(s): AnatoliaLit Agency (adult) (Turkey); Bardon-Chinese Media Agency (Mainland China, Taiwan); BookLab Literary Agency (Poland); The Deborah Harris Agency (Israel); International Editors' Co - Yanez Agencia Literaria (Latin America, Portugal, Spain); The Italian Literary Agency Srl (Italy); Japan UNI Agency Inc (Japan); Simona Kessler International Copyright Agency Ltd (Romania); Korea Copyright Center Inc (KCC) (South Korea); Agence Michelle Lapautre (juvenile) (France); Mohrbooks AG Literary Agency (Germany); La Nouvelle Agence (adult) (France); Andrew Nurnberg Associates (Bulgaria, Czechia, Hungary, Latvia, Lithuania, Russia); Prava i prevodi (Croatia, Georgia, Serbia, Slovakia, Slovenia, Ukraine); Read n Right Agency (Greece); Sebes & Bisseling Literary Agency (Denmark, Finland, Netherlands, Norway, Scandinavia, Sweden); Abner Stein Agency (UK)

Mendel Media Group LLC (L)
PO Box 5032, East Hampton, NY 11937
Tel: 646-239-9896
Web Site: www.mendelmedia.com
Key Personnel
Mng Partner: Scott Mendel (AALA)
E-mail: scott@mendelmedia.com
Founded: 2002
Represent nonfiction writers in most subject areas, from biography & serious history to health & relationships. Nonfiction clientele includes individual authors & institutions whose works, collections, archives, researchers +/or policy experts contribute to important public discussions & debates. Also represent more lighthearted nonfiction projects, when they suit the market particularly well. The agency's fiction writers principally write historical & contemporary multicultural fiction, contemporary thrillers & mainstream women's fiction. E-mail submissions only to query@mendelmedia.com (do not use attachments). No longer accept or read submissions sent by mail. No fees. If we want to read more or discuss your work, we will respond to you by e-mail or phone within a few weeks. In any case, do not call or e-mail to inquire about your query.
Fiction queries: If you have a novel you would like to submit, please paste a synopsis & first 20 pages into the body of your e-mail, below a detailed letter about your publication history & the history of the project, if it has been submitted previously to publishers or other agents.
Nonfiction queries: If you have a completed nonfiction book proposal & sample chapters, you should paste those into the body of an e-mail, below a detailed letter about your publication history & the history of the project, if it has been submitted previously to any publishers or other agents.
Membership(s): American Association of University Professors; The Authors Guild; Modern Language Association (MLA); Mystery Writers of America (MWA); Romance Writers of America (RWA); Society of Children's Book Writers & Illustrators (SCBWI)

Scott Meredith Literary Agency LP (L)
1035 Park Ave, Apt 3-A, New York, NY 10028
Tel: 917-685-1064
E-mail: info@scottmeredith.com
Web Site: www.scottmeredith.com
Key Personnel
Pres: Arthur M Klebanoff *E-mail:* aklebanoff@scottmeredith.com
VP, Fin: Maxine Schweitzer
E-mail: mschweitzer@scottmeredith.com
Dir, Subs Rts: Mary Jo Anne Valko-Warner
E-mail: mjaz@ptd.net
Founded: 1946
Management of long term publishing relationships.

Metamorphosis Literary Agency (L)
12410 S Acuff Ct, Olathe, KS 66062
Tel: 646-397-1640
E-mail: info@metamorphosisliteraryagency.com
Web Site: www.metamorphosisliteraryagency.com
Key Personnel
Owner, Sr Agent & Subs Rts Mgr: Stephanie Hansen
Sr Agent & Subs Rts Asst Mgr: Amy Brewer *E-mail:* abrewer@metamorphosisliteraryagency.com; Erica Christensen *E-mail:* echristensen@metamorphosisliteraryagency.com
Sr Agent & Subs Rts Asst: Jessica Reino *E-mail:* jreino@metamorphosisliteraryagency.com
Sr Agent: Katie Salvo *E-mail:* ksalvo@metamorphosisliteraryagency.com
Jr Agent: Caroline Trussell
Asst Agent: Shania Soler
Founded: 2016
Our mission is to help authors become traditionally published. We represent commercial fiction that is well-crafted, including fantasy, mystery, romance, science fiction & young adult. The agency works closely with authors to ensure their book is in the best presentable form. Our publishing connections come from numerous conferences, luck & genuine care. We do not charge reading fees.
No unsol mss, query first. Please only query unpublished projects. Format the ms in a word document to size 12 either Times Roman or Arial font, justified align, no manual tabs, header top left (title & your name), page numbers beginning on page 2 bottom right & a cover page with just the title & your name.
Titles recently placed: *Do You See Me?*, LaRonda Gardner Middlemiss; *If You Knew My Name*, Lisa Roberts Carter; *Love Inspired Cold Case (series)*, Laurie Winter; *Mara Hears in Style*, Terri Clemmons; *Miss Matched*, Wendy Million; *Out of the Mouth of Babe*, Kelly Bennett, Brent Stevens, Stu Dressler; *Rebecca Reznik Reboots the Universe*, Samara Shanker; *Starlin*, Anitra Rowe Schulte; *The Bull in the Darkness and the One-Eyed Dog*, Robert Sharp, DVM; *The House That Babe Ruth Built*, Kelly Bennett; *The Noisy Classroom Goes to the Museum*, Angela Shante; *The Unboxing of a Black Girl*, Angela Shante
Foreign Rep(s): AnatoliaLit Agency (Amy Marie Spangler) (Turkey); Big Apple Agency (China, Hong Kong, Indonesia, Taiwan, Thailand, Vietnam); BookLab Literary Agency (Poland); Sandra Bruna Agencia Literaria (Brazil, Portugal, Spain); Corto Literary Agency (Bosnia and Herzegovina, Bulgaria, Croatia, Czechia, Hungary, Montenegro, North Macedonia, Romania, Serbia, Slovakia, Slovenia); Japan UNI Agency (Japan)

Howard Morhaim Literary Agency Inc (L)
30 Pierrepont St, Brooklyn, NY 11201-3371
Tel: 718-222-8400
E-mail: info@morhaimliterary.com
Web Site: www.morhaimliterary.com
Key Personnel
Pres: Howard Morhaim (AALA)
E-mail: howard@morhaimliterary.com
VP & Agent: Kate McKean (AALA)
E-mail: kate@morhaimliterary.com
Agent: Kim-Mei Kirtland *E-mail:* kimmei@morhaimliterary.com; Eric Showers *E-mail:* eric@morhaimliterary.com; DongWon Song *E-mail:* dongwon@morhaimliterary.com
Founded: 1979
General adult & young adult fiction & nonfiction. Howard Morhaim is not accepting unsol mss. Kate McKean is open to submissions. E-mail your query letter along with 3 sample chapters (for fiction) or full proposal (for nonfiction). No reading fee. Handle film & TV rights. Representatives in all principal foreign markets.
Foreign Rep(s): Baror International (worldwide exc Portugal, Spain & UK); Circle of Confusion (Michael Prevett, film & TV); RDC Agencia Literaria (Portugal, Spain); Abner Stein Agency (UK)

Movable Type Management (L)
244 Madison Ave, Suite 334, New York, NY 10016
Web Site: www.movabletm.com

Key Personnel
Pres & Agent: Adam Chromy *E-mail:* achromy@movabletm.com
Agent: Ginger Hutchinson *E-mail:* ghutchinson@moveabletm.com
Founded: 2002
Provides inventive literary representation & development in a wide range of fiction & nonfiction genres for the rapidly changing world. Moving stories are our specialty, but we also help create stories that move people. Our value-based storytelling methodology helps authors build narratives that people care about, thus maximizing emotional impact & audience reach. Clients include Edgar & James Beard nominees; Agatha winners; many New York Times, USA Today & international bestsellers: Tom Acitelli, Alicia Bessette, Donia Bijan, Jamie Brenner, Jane Cleland, JD Dickey, Phillip Greene, Dr Nicholas Kardaras, Zygmunt Miloszewski, Trent Preszler, Jakub Szamalek & Annelise Ryan.
Titles recently placed: *A Novel Summer*, Jamie Brenner; *Beat the Bots!*, Jane Cleland; *Change Your Money, Change Your Life*, Liz Davidson; *Epoxy Resin*, Jess Crow; *Evergreen*, Trent Preszler; *Inner Space*, Jakub Szamalek; *It Happened!*, Jim Lampley; *My Vintage Estate*, Richard Moran; *The Circle Broken*, Dorothy Carvello; *The Devil's Daughter*, Gordon Greisman; *The Last Line*, Scott Lyerly; *The Last Word*, Gerri Lewis

Bonnie Nadell Literary Agency, see Hill Nadell Literary Agency

Jean V Naggar Literary Agency Inc (JVNLA) (L)
216 E 75 St, Suite 1-E, New York, NY 10021
Tel: 212-794-1082
E-mail: jvnla@jvnla.com
Web Site: www.jvnla.com
Key Personnel
Pres & Agent: Jennifer Weltz (AALA)
  E-mail: jweltz@jvnla.com
Partner & Agent: Ariana Philips (AALA)
  E-mail: aphilips@jvnla.com; Alice Tasman
  E-mail: atasman@jvnla.com
Agent: Alicia Brooks *E-mail:* abrooks@jvnla.com
Jr Agent: Cole Hildebrand
Founded: 1978
Represents a wide range of fiction, nonfiction & children's books. International rights, film & TV rights for the books represented. No unsol mss, query first (see web site for complete, up-to-date submission guidelines). No reading fee. Commissions: 15% domestic, 20% foreign translation & film.
Titles recently placed: *Carolina Moonset*, Matt Goldman; *Children of the Catastrophe*, Sarah Shoemaker; *Everything, Beautiful*, Ella Frances Sanders; *Hither and Nigh*, Ellen Potter; *Luscious, Tender, Juicy*, Kathy Hunt; *New to Liberty*, DeMisty D Bellinger; *The Cage*, Bonnie Kistler; *The Witch and the Tsar*, Olesya Salnikova Gilmore
Foreign Rep(s): Akcali Copyright Agency (Turkey); Big Apple Agency Inc (Mainland China, Taiwan); Graal Literary Agency (Poland); Greene & Heaton (UK); Deborah Harris Agency (Israel); Danny Hong Agency (South Korea); International Editors' Co - Yanez Agencia Literaria (Brazil, Latin America, Portugal, Spain); The Italian Literary Agency Srl (Italy); JLM Literary Agency (Greece); Katai & Bolza Literary Agency (Hungary); Simona Kessler International Copyright Agency (Romania); Agence Michelle Lapautre (France); Licht & Burr Literary Agency (Scandinavia); Liepman Agency (Germany); Maxima Creative Agency (Indonesia); Mo Literary Services (Netherlands); Andrew Nurnberg Literary Agency (Baltic States, Bulgaria, Czechia, Russia); PLIMA (Montenegro, Serbia); Silkroad Publishers Agency (Thailand); Tuttle-Mori Agency Inc (Japan)

Nelson Literary Agency LLC (L)
700 Colorado Blvd, No 352, Denver, CO 80206
Tel: 303-292-2805
E-mail: info@nelsonagency.com
Web Site: www.nelsonagency.com
Key Personnel
COO/CFO: Brian Nelson
Pres & Founding Agent: Kristin Nelson (AALA)
Sr Literary Agent: Joanna MacKenzie (AALA)
Dir, Literary Devt: Angie Hodapp
Contracts Mgr & Royalty Auditor: Sam Cronin
Literary Asst: Maria Heater
Founded: 2002
In business for two decades, NLA is a full service literary & media representation agency with a proven track record & a reputation of advocating for authors above all else. Our mission is for every NLA author to make a living solely by writing. We build authors from debut to bestseller. We enjoy storytellers & love what we do.
Titles recently placed: *Across the Sand*, Hugh Howey; *And Yet*, Kate Baer; *From Hell Hollow*, John Galligan; *Gwendy's Final Task*, Richard Chizmar, Stephen King; *Minor Catastrophes*, Kathleen West; *Overtime*, Kathleen West; *Stars and Smoke*, Marie Lu; *The Blonde Identity*, Ally Carter; *The Problem with Prophesies*, Scott Reintgen; *You & Me & Us*, Alison Hammer
Foreign Rights: Jenny Meyer Literary Agency (worldwide exc Asia)
Membership(s): Romance Writers of America (RWA); Science Fiction and Fantasy Writers of America, Inc (SFWA); Society of Children's Book Writers & Illustrators (SCBWI)

The Betsy Nolan Literary Agency (L)
Division of The Nolan/Lehr Group Inc
112 E 17 St, Suite 1W, New York, NY 10003
Tel: 212-967-8200
Web Site: www.nolanlehrgroup.com
Key Personnel
Founding Partner: Betsy Nolan
Pres: Donald Lehr *E-mail:* donald@nolanlehrgroup.com
Agent: Carla Glasser *E-mail:* cmglasser25@gmail.com
Busn Mgr: Jenny Alperen *E-mail:* jenny.alperen@gmail.com
Founded: 1980
Nonfiction, popular culture, child care, psychology, cookbooks, how-to, biography, African-American & Judaica. No poetry. No unsol mss, query first; submit outline, no more than three sample chapters & author background; no reading fee; SASE.
Titles recently placed: *A House in Maine*, Maura McEvoy, Basha Burwell, Kathleen Hackett; *Field, Flower, Vase*, Chelsea Fuss; *Life in the Studio*, Frances Palmer; *Milk Jar Cookies Cookbook*, Courtney Cowan; *The Women's Heritage Sourcebook*, Emma Rollin Moore, Lauren Malloy, Ashley Moore; *Upstate Interiors*, Lisa Przystup; *When the World Feels Like a Scary Place*, Abigail Gewirtz, PhD

Objective Entertainment (L-D)
609 Greenwich St, 6th fl, New York, NY 10014
Tel: 212-431-5454
Web Site: www.objectiveent.com
Key Personnel
COO: Jarred Weisfeld *E-mail:* Jarred@objectiveent.com
Founded: 2007
Full service management company specializing in book publishing, dramatic writing, talent & television packaging. Handles literary, dramatic & film rights, all commercial & adult trade publishing. No unsol mss. Submit query letter. No fees charged.

Open Book Literary (L)
1500 Chestnut St, Suite 2, No 1436, Philadelphia, PA 19102
E-mail: info@openbooklit.com
Web Site: www.openbooklit.com
Key Personnel
Founder & Agent: Leslie Zampetti (AALA)
Bringing under-represented voices to publishing, especially those voices centering disability, poverty, women, neurodivergence, Judaism, Islam & non-western religions. No unsol mss, query first via Query Manager. Include query letter, short bio & first 5 pages of ms (or complete picture book text or dummy).
Titles recently placed: *A Few Beautiful Minutes: Experiencing a Solar Eclipse*, Kate Ellen Fox, Khoa Le (illus); *Hart & Souls*, Lisa Schmid, Carolina Vazquez (illus); *How to Dance*, Jason B Dutton
Foreign Rights: Rights People
Membership(s): Society of Children's Book Writers & Illustrators (SCBWI)

Fifi Oscard Agency Inc (L-D)
1140 Avenue of the Americas, 9th fl, New York, NY 10036
Tel: 212-764-1100
E-mail: agency@fifioscard.com
Web Site: fifioscard.com
Key Personnel
Pres & Literary Agent: Peter Sawyer *Tel:* 212-764-1100 ext 2 *E-mail:* psawyer@fifioscard.com
Founded: 1955
General fiction & nonfiction, all areas; film & TV rights; scripts for stage, motion picture & TV. Have always represented talent as well. No fees charged. No unsol mss, query first; submit outline & sample chapter if requested. See web site for more instruction.
Foreign Rep(s): Bardon-Chinese Media Agency (China); Caroline Van Gelderan (Netherlands); Imprima Korea (South Korea); International Editors' Co - Yanez Agencia Literaria (Spain); The Italian Literary Agency Srl (Italy); Agence Michelle Lapautre (France); Thomas Schlueck GmbH (Germany); Abner Stein Agency (England)

Mel Parker Books LLC (L)
215 E 68 St, 10-O, New York, NY 10065
Tel: 917-696-6105
E-mail: info@melparkerbooks.com
Web Site: melparkerbooks.com
Key Personnel
Pres: Mel Parker *Tel:* 212-982-8215
  E-mail: mel@melparkerbooks.com
Founded: 2004
Literary agent for a full range of trade books: business, health, psychology, spirituality, reference, memoir/biography, narrative, nonfiction, pop culture & fiction. No unsol mss, query first via web site. Send brief query of no more than 250 words describing your book project.
Titles recently placed: *A Call to Farms*, Jennifer Grayson; *Belonging*, Jill Fordyce; *Exhale*, David Weill, MD; *Mirror Meditation*, Tara Well, PhD; *Retribution*, Robert McCaw; *Striving for Justice*, Nathaniel Glover; *The New City*, Dickson D Despommier

Kathi J Paton Literary Agency (L)
Box 2044, Radio City Sta, New York, NY 10101-2044
Tel: 212-265-6586
E-mail: kjplitbiz@optonline.net
Web Site: www.patonliterary.com
Key Personnel
Owner: Kathi J Paton

LITERARY AGENTS

Founded: 1987
Interested in biography, technology, business/investing/finance, history, health, sports, science, literary fiction, parenting, Christian life & issues, popular culture, humor, investigative journalism & progressive politics/current affairs. No unsol mss; e-mail queries only with a brief description. No attachments. Sorry, no science fiction, horror, fantasy, poetry, juvenile, young adult or self-published books. Sub-agents in all major foreign markets & Hollywood.
Titles recently placed: *Bureau of Spies: The Secret Connections between Espionage and Journalism in Washington*, Steven T Usdin; *Catholic Women Confront Their Church: Stories of Hurt and Hope*, Celia V Wexler
Membership(s): The Authors Guild

PearlCo Literary Agency, LLC (L)
6596 Heronswood Cove, Memphis, TN 38119
Tel: 901-754-5276
Web Site: www.pearlcoliteraryagency.com
Key Personnel
Owner & Agent: Susan Perlman Cohen
 E-mail: susanperlmancohen@gmail.com
Founded: 2015
No unsol mss. Query first by mail or e-mail. No fees.

Dan Peragine Literary Agency (L)
PO Box 5032, South Hackensack, NJ 07606
Tel: 201-390-0468
E-mail: dannyperagine@aol.com
Key Personnel
Mng Dir: Dan Peragine
Founded: 1991
Specialize in behavioral sciences, biography, environment, history, Christian, inspirational, nonfiction, self-help, computers, sports, photography, all high school & college textbooks, advanced placement & testing, musical groups, World War I, World War II. Handle software, film & TV rights. Represent photographic archives & books of all types. No unsol mss, query first with a complete proposal; if sending fiction, include any type of readers report or outside review with the submission; submit sample chapters single page, double-spaced, or on disk (do not send by e-mail if it needs to be downloaded). No reading fees, fees charged for editorial development, re-writes, ghostwriters, publishing consulting, full book packaging & book marketing.
Membership(s): American Booksellers Association (ABA); American Society of Picture Professionals (ASPP); National Press Photographers Association (NPPA); Professional Photographers of America (PPA)

Alison Picard Literary Agent (L-D)
PO Box 2000, Cotuit, MA 02635
Tel: 508-477-7192 *Fax:* 508-477-7192 (call first)
E-mail: ajpicard@aol.com
Founded: 1985
Representing adult & juvenile/young adult fiction & nonfiction. Beginners welcome. No unsol mss, query first with letter & SASE; no phone or fax queries. Upon positive response, submit double-spaced complete ms. No fees charged.
Titles recently placed: *365 Days of Slow Cooker Recipes*, Stephanie O'Dea; *Curse of the Jade Lily*, David Housewright; *Decided on the Battlefield*, David Johnson; *Fear of Beauty*, Susan Froetschel; *Not Your Mother's Freezer Cookbook*, Jessica Fisher; *Seconds (new ed)*, David Ely; *The Efficiency Trap: Finding a Better Way to Achieve a Sustainable Energy Future*, Steve Hallett; *The Finest Hours (middle grade ed)*, Michael Tougias, Casey Sherman; *Three Cheers for Girls*, Sara Hunt; *Torn*, Stephanie Guerra; *Totally Together: Shortcuts to an Organized Life*, Stephanie O'Dea
Foreign Rights: John Pawsey (Europe)

Pimlico Agency, see Aurous Inc

Pinder Lane & Garon-Brooke Associates Ltd (L)
2136 NE 58 Ct, Fort Lauderdale, FL 33308
Tel: 212-489-0880 *Fax:* 212-489-7104
Web Site: www.pinderlaneandgaronbrooke.com
Key Personnel
Owner & Agent: Robert Thixton (AALA)
 E-mail: bob@pinderlane.com
Off Mgr: Peter Jones
Founded: 1996
Fiction & nonfiction, film & TV rights. No unsol mss, query first. No reading fee. Submit short synopsis, double-spaced & unbound. Representatives in Hollywood & all foreign markets.

Pippin Properties Inc (L)
110 W 40 St, Suite 1704, New York, NY 10018
Tel: 212-338-9310
E-mail: info@pippinproperties.com
Web Site: www.pippinproperties.com; www.facebook.com/pippinproperties
Key Personnel
Founder, Pres & Creative Dir: Holly M McGhee
 E-mail: hmcghee@pippinproperties.com
VP & Sr Agent: Elena Giovinazzo
Art Mgr: Ashley Valentine
Agency Assoc: Marissa Brown
Agency Asst: Morgan Hughes
Founded: 1998
Represent authors & artists for children's picture books, middle grade novels, chapter books & young adult novels. To submit, e-mail query & first chapter. Handle film, TV & foreign rights.
Foreign Rep(s): Rights People (worldwide exc USA)

Pom Inc (L-D)
18-15 215 St, Bayside, NY 11360
Key Personnel
Pres: Dan Green *E-mail:* dangreen@pomlit.com
VP: Simon Green
Founded: 1990
General nonfiction & select fiction. No unsol mss, by referral only. Handle publishing, film & TV rights. Standard industry commission.
Titles recently placed: *Inventing Equality*, Michael Bellesile; *Juice*, Robert Bryce; *Married...With Children vs. the World*, Richard Gurman; *Napoleonic Wars*, Alex Mikaberidze; *Thaddeus Stevens*, Bruce Levine; *The Republic in Peril*, Carol Berkin; *Thunder at the Gates*, Douglas Egerton

The Aaron M Priest Literary Agency Inc (L)
370 Lexington Ave, Suite 1202, New York, NY 10017
Tel: 212-818-0344 *Fax:* 212-573-9417
E-mail: info@aaronpriest.com
Web Site: www.aaronpriest.com
Key Personnel
Pres & Agent: Aaron M Priest (AALA)
 E-mail: querypriest@aaronpriest.com
Agent: Lucy Childs Baker (AALA)
 E-mail: querychilds@aaronpriest.com; Mitch Hoffman *E-mail:* queryhoffman@aaronpriest.com; Lisa Erbach Vance (AALA)
 E-mail: queryvance@aaronpriest.com
Founded: 1974
Our agents are interested in the following:
Aaron Priest: thrillers, general fiction
Lisa Erbach Vance: general fiction, mystery, thrillers, upmarket women's fiction, historical fiction, narrative nonfiction, memoir
Lucy Childs Baker: literary & commercial fiction, historical fiction, memoir, edgy women's fiction

EDITORIAL SERVICES

Mitch Hoffman: thrillers, suspense, crime fiction, literary fiction, narrative nonfiction, politics, popular science, history, memoir, current events, pop culture
For all agents: no poetry, no screenplays. The best way to query all agents is to submit a query letter via e-mail. The query should be about one page long describing your work as well as your background. No attachments, however a first chapter pasted into the body of an e-mail query is acceptable. Do not submit to more than one agent at a time at this agency (we urge you to consider each agent's emphasis before submitting). We will get back to you within 4 weeks, but only if interested. No fees are charged.

Prospect Agency (L)
551 Valley Rd, PMB 337, Upper Montclair, NJ 07043
Tel: 718-788-3217
Web Site: www.prospectagency.com
Key Personnel
Founder, Pres & Literary Agent: Emily Sylvan Kim (AALA) *E-mail:* esk@prospectagency.com
Literary Agent: Rachel Orr *E-mail:* rko@prospectagency.com; Charlotte Wenger
 E-mail: charlotte@prospectagency.com
Foreign Rts: Tina Shen
Founded: 2005
Full service literary agency representing a range of fiction, nonfiction, illustrators, romance, literary fiction, middle grade & picture books, adult commercial fiction, women's fiction & young adult titles. No unsol mss (with the exception of picture books), query first via web. Only queries submitted through our web site are accepted. Queries sent by e-mail or regular mail not accepted. Send query letter, 3 chapters & a brief synopsis via submission form on web site. No fees charged. Full guidelines on web site.
Titles recently placed: *Betrayal at Blackthorne Park*, Julia Kelly; *Bright Birds According to L. Ness Monster*, Anne Appert; *Cats in Construction Hats*, Sudipta Bardhan-Quallen, Leeza Hernandez (illus); *Cowboys at the Ballet*, Claire Bobrow; *Dino Books 1-4*, Emily L Hay Hinsdale; *Faithful Feet*, Laura Sassi; *Gingerbread Bones*, Lindsay Lovise; *In the Deep*, Hayley Krischer; *Leonard Builds a Haunted House*, Mike Ciccotello; *Lost Kites and Other Treasures*, Cathy Carr; *Pride Is Love*, Dano Moreno; *Ready to Soar*, Cori Doerrfeld; *Sweet Nightmare*, Tracy Wolff; *The Art Thieves*, Andrea L Rogers; *The Filling Station*, Vanessa Miller; *There's a Pony in My Apartment*, Jenn Harney; *Wonder and Awe*, Annie Herzig

Generosa Gina Protano Publishing, see GGP Publishing Inc

Puddingstone Literary, Authors' Agents (L-D)
Subsidiary of Cohen Group LLC
11 Mabro Dr, Denville, NJ 07834-9607
Tel: 973-366-3622
Key Personnel
Dir: Alec Bernard
Memb: Michael R Cohen
Founded: 1972
General trade & mass market fiction & nonfiction; motion picture scripts & teleplays. Handle film & TV rights. No unsol mss, query first with SASE. Submit outline & sample chapters. No reading fee. Representatives in Hollywood & foreign countries. Fee for ms copies, galleys & bound books for foreign & domestic submissions.

R&W, see Rogers & Weil Literary

Rees Literary Agency (L)
One Westinghouse Plaza, Suite A203, Boston, MA 02136
Tel: 617-227-9014
Web Site: www.reesagency.com
Key Personnel
Pres & Agent: Mr Lorin Rees (AALA)
  E-mail: lorin@reesagency.com
Sr Agent: Rebecca Podos *E-mail:* rebecca@reesagency.com
Agent: Analieze Cervantes *E-mail:* analieze@reesagency.com; Taj McCoy (AALA); Kelly Peterson *E-mail:* kelly@reesagency.com
Founded: 1983
Literary & commercial fiction, memoirs, history, biography, business, young adult & middle grade, self-help, psychology & science. For fiction, include query letter +/or synopsis & the first 3 chapters. For nonfiction, enclose a complete book proposal or substantial treatment. See web site for complete book list.
Titles recently placed: *Court of Wanderers*, Rin Chupeco; *Here's for the Weekend*, Helena Greer; *If I Dig You*, Colby Wilkens; *If I Stopped Haunting You*, Colby Wilkens; *Make the Season Bright*, Ashley Herring Blake; *The 7-10 Split*, Karmen Lee; *The Last to Pie*, Misha Popp; *Wake Me Most Wickedly*, Felicia Grossman
Foreign Rights: Taryn Fagerness Agency (Taryn Fagerness) (Albania, Argentina, Australia, Brazil, Bulgaria, Canada, China, Croatia, Czechia, Denmark, Estonia, Finland, France, Germany, Greece, Hungary, Iceland, India, Indonesia, Israel, Italy, Japan, Latvia, Lithuania, Mexico, Netherlands, Norway, Poland, Portugal, Romania, Russia, Serbia, Slovakia, Slovenia, South Korea, Spain, Sweden, Taiwan, Thailand, Turkey, Ukraine, UK, Vietnam)
Membership(s): PEN America

Regal Hoffmann & Associates LLC (L-D)
157 13 St, Brooklyn, NY 11215
Tel: 212-684-7900
E-mail: info@rhaliterary.com; submissions@rhaliterary.com
Web Site: www.rhaliterary.com
Key Personnel
Partner & Agent: Markus Hoffmann (AALA)
  E-mail: markus@rhaliterary.com; Joseph Regal *E-mail:* joe@rhaliterary.com
Agent: Elianna Kan *E-mail:* elianna@rhaliterary.com; Priscilla Posada *E-mail:* priscilla@rhaliterary.com; Stephanie Steiker *E-mail:* stephanie@rhaliterary.com
Founded: 2002 (as Regal Literary)
No unsol mss, query first via electronic submission. For fiction, include synopsis & first 10 pages of a novel or one short story from a collection in the body of the e-mail. For nonfiction, include synopsis in the body of the e-mail. Do not represent romance, poetry or screenplays. Commission: 15% domestic, 20% foreign. No reading fees.
Titles recently placed: *American Bloods: The Untamed Dynasty That Shaped a Nation*, John Kaag; *I Love You So Much It's Killing Us Both*, Mariah Stovall; *The Mysterious Case of the Alperton Angels: A Novel*, Janice Hallett
Foreign Rights: AnatoliaLit Agency (Turkey); Book/lab (Poland); Corto Literary Agency (Albania, Bulgaria, Croatia, North Macedonia, Serbia); EAJ (Japan); Gaeb & Eggers (Germany); Grayhawk Agency (China, Indonesia, Taiwan, Thailand); Greyhound Literary (Baltic States, Greece, Holland, Israel, Italy, Scandinavia); Simona Kessler (Romania); MB Agencia Literaria (Latin America, Portugal, Spain); Milkwood (South Korea); La Nouvelle Agence (France); Andrew Nurnberg Budapest (Hungary); Kristin Olson (Czechia, Slovakia, Slovenia); Tuttle-Mori Agency (Japan)

Renaissance Literary & Talent (L-D)
PO Box 17379, Beverly Hills, CA 90209
Tel: 323-848-8305
E-mail: query@renaissancemgmt.net
Web Site: renaissancemgmt.net
Key Personnel
Pres: Alan Nevins *E-mail:* alan@renaissancemgmt.net
Agent: Jacklyn Saferstein-Hansen
  E-mail: jacklyn@renaissancemgmt.net; Berta Treitl *E-mail:* berta@renaissancemgmt.net
Founded: 1993
Commercial fiction & nonfiction. Handle film & TV rights; novels. No unsol mss. Query first. Handle highly recommended mss. Submit outlines & sample chapters. No reading fee, 15% commission.

The Amy Rennert Agency Inc (L)
1880 Century Park E, No 1600, Los Angeles, CA 90067
Tel: 415-789-8955
E-mail: queries@amyrennert.com (no unsol queries)
Key Personnel
Pres: Amy Rennert
Founded: 1999
Specialize in books that matter. The agency represents a select group of quality fiction & nonfiction writers - many of them award-winners & dozens of agency books have been New York Times & national bestsellers. We provide career management for established & first time authors & our breadth of experience in many genres enables us to meet the needs of a diverse clientele. The agency has developed a reputation since its inception for a passionate commitment to agency writers. We are purposely a small organization to facilitate hands-on personalized service & attention to our authors & their books.
We are not currently accepting unsol submissions.
Foreign Rights: Taryn Fagerness Agency (Taryn Fagerness) (worldwide)
Membership(s): The Authors Guild

Ann Rittenberg Literary Agency Inc (L)
15 Maiden Lane, Suite 206, New York, NY 10038
Tel: 212-684-6936 *Fax:* 212-684-6929
E-mail: info@rittlit.com
Web Site: www.rittlit.com
Key Personnel
Pres: Ann Rittenberg (AALA)
Assoc Agent: Rosie Jonker *E-mail:* rosie@rittlit.com
Founded: 1992
Literary fiction & nonfiction; no genre fiction, no screenplays. Co-agents in all principal foreign countries as well as Hollywood. Query letter & first 3 chapters of double-spaced ms with SASE; no queries by fax.
Titles recently placed: *Safe Houses*, Dan Fesperman; *The Blue Kingfisher*, Erica Wright; *The Coronation*, Boris Akunin; *The Disappeared*, Paul Doiron; *The Doctor and the Dreamer*, Jack Nisbet; *The Field Guide to Dumb Birds of North America*, Matt Kracht; *When You Can't Stop*, James W Hall; *Wolf Pack*, C J Box; *Your First Novel (revised & expanded ed)*, Laura Whitcomb, Ann Rittenberg, Camille Goldin
Foreign Rights: Akcali Copyright Agency (Turkey); The Grayhawk Agency (China, Indonesia, Taiwan, Thailand); The Deborah Harris Agency (Israel); Japan UNI Agency Inc (Japan); JLM Literary Agency (Greece); Korea Copyright Center Inc (KCC) (South Korea); La Nouvelle Agence (France); Andrew Nurnberg Associates (Brazil, Bulgaria, Croatia, Czechia, Germany, Hungary, Italy, Netherlands, Poland, Portugal, Romania, Russia, Serbia, Slovakia, Slovenia, Spain, UK); Ulf Toregard Agency AB (Denmark, Finland, Norway, Sweden)
Membership(s): The Authors Guild

Judith Riven Literary Agent LLC (L)
250 W 16 St, Suite 4F, New York, NY 10011
Key Personnel
Owner & Pres: Judith Riven
Founded: 1993
Fiction & nonfiction. Handle film & TV rights for book clients only. One page query letter describing material with SASE. Unless requested, no mss accepted. E-mail queries are accepted but no attachments. We are not currently accepting science fiction, fantasy, or horror submissions.
Titles recently placed: *Over There: America in The Great War, 1917-1918*, Lisa Davis

Riverside Literary Agency (L)
41 Simon Keets Rd, Leyden, MA 01337
Tel: 413-772-0067 *Fax:* 413-772-0969
E-mail: rivlit@sover.net
Web Site: www.riversideliteraryagency.com
Key Personnel
Pres: Susan Lee Cohen
Founded: 1990
Adult fiction & nonfiction. No unsol mss, query first with SASE. No reading fees. Handle film & TV rights & foreign rights with co-agents.

RMA (L)
47 Tiffany Way, Plattsburgh, NY 12901
Tel: 718-434-1893 *Fax:* 518-310-0668
Web Site: ricia.com
Key Personnel
Owner: Ricia Mainhardt *E-mail:* ricia@duck.com
Founded: 1987
Popular fiction, especially science fiction, fantasy, mystery, thriller, romance; nonfiction, especially pop culture, history & science. Do not accept poetry. Online submissions preferred. For fiction, submit first 3 chapters, brief one paragraph pitch & 1-2 page synopsis in body of the e-mail. For nonfiction, in the body of the e-mail with the cover letter, include a high concept pitch & a detailed table of contents. Include first 2 chapters & final chapter. Handle audio & drama rights for client's books only. Affiliates handle translation, film & TV rights for client's books. No reading fee. Branch office in Hollywood, CA.
Membership(s): Mystery Writers of America (MWA); Romance Writers of America (RWA); Science Fiction and Fantasy Writers of America, Inc (SFWA)

Roam Agency (L)
45 Main St, Suite 727, Brooklyn, NY 11201-1076
E-mail: roam@roamagency.com
Web Site: www.roamagency.com
Key Personnel
Founder, Agent & Dir: Anthony Arnove
Founded: 2002
Adult nonfiction & fiction, handles all subsidiary rights. Not taking on new projects or clients at this time. No unsol mss. No reading fees.
Titles recently placed: *A Livable Future Is Possible*, Noam Chomsky; *Abolish Rent*, Tracy Rosenthal, Leonardo Vilchis; *Apocalypse Chow*, Arun Gupta; *Black and Asian Feminist Solidarities: An Antholog*, Rachel Kuo (ed), Jaimee Swift (ed), Tiffany Tso (ed); *Corridors of Contagion: How the Pandemic Exposed the Cruelties of Incarceration*, Victoria Law; *Dead Cities: And Other Tales*, Mike Davis; *Mastering the Universe*, Rob Larson; *Palestine in a World on Fire*, Katherine Natanel (ed), Ilan Pappe (ed)
Foreign Rights: AnatoliaLit Agency (Amy Spangler) (Turkey); BC Agency (South Korea); Berla & Griffini Rights Agency (Erica Berla)

LITERARY AGENTS

(Italy); Big Apple Agency Inc (Lily Chen & Dr Luc Kwanten) (China, Indonesia, Malaysia, Taiwan, Vietnam); Agence Deborah Druba (Deborah Druba) (France); English Agency Japan Co Ltd (Tsutomu Yawata) (Japan); Paul & Peter Fritz AG Literatur Agentur (Christian Dittus) (Germany, Switzerland); David Grossman Literary Agency (David Grossman) (English-speaking countries outside North America); Korea Copyright Center Inc (KCC) (Suyeon Jeong) (South Korea); MB Agencia Literaria SL (Monica Martin) (Spanish-speaking countries); Prava i prevodi (Nada Popovic) (Albania, Bosnia and Herzegovina, Bulgaria, Croatia, Czechia, Estonia, Hungary, Latvia, Lithuania, North Macedonia, Poland, Romania, Russia, Serbia, Slovakia, Slovenia, Ukraine); Read n Right Agency (Nike Davarinou) (Greece); Riff Agency (Laura & Joao Paulo Riff) (Brazil, Portugal); Sebes & Bisseling Literary Agency (Paul Sebes & Rik Kleuver) (Denmark, Finland, Iceland, Netherlands, Norway, Sweden).

B J Robbins Literary Agency (L)
5130 Bellaire Ave, North Hollywood, CA 91607
E-mail: robbinsliterary@gmail.com
Key Personnel
Owner & Pres: B J Robbins (AALA)
Founded: 1992
Literary & commercial fiction, general nonfiction. Handle film & TV rights for agency clients only. E-mail queries only. No unsol attachments; query can include first 10 pages in body of e-mail.
Titles recently placed: *If You Lived Here You'd be Famous by Now*, Via Bleidner; *My Heart is a Chainsaw*, Stephen Graham Jones; *Night of the Mannequins*, Stephen Graham Jones; *Pont Neuf*, Max Byrd; *The Bridge at La Fiere*, James Donovan; *The Only Good Indians*, Stephen Graham Jones; *The Sweetest Days*, John Hough Jr
Foreign Rights: The Marsh Agency (worldwide exc UK); Abner Stein Agency (UK)
Membership(s): PEN America

Rogers & Weil Literary (L-D)
530 Divisadero St, No 169, San Francisco, CA 94117
Web Site: www.rwliterary.com
Key Personnel
Principal: Sydney Rogers *E-mail:* sydney.rogers@rwliterary.com; Gideon Weil *E-mail:* gideon.weil@rwliterary.com
Full service agency representing sophisticated scientific nonfiction, narrative nonfiction & cutting-edge investigative journalism in print, digital, audio, film & television, around the world. No unsol mss, query first via online form or send query letter via e-mail. Response in 3-5 business days.
Titles recently placed: *Nowhere for Very Long: The Unexpected Road to an Unconventional Life*, Brianna Madia; *Peaceful Kitchen: More than 100 Cozy Plant-Based Recipes to Comfort the Body and Nourish the Soul*, Catherine Perez; *The Plant-Based Athlete: A Game-Changing Approach to Peak Performance*, Matt Frazier, Robert Cheeke; *This Is How Your Marriage Ends: A Hopeful Approach to Saving Relationships*, Matthew Fray

Linda Roghaar Literary Agency LLC (L)
133 High Point Dr, Amherst, MA 01002
Tel: 413-256-1921
Web Site: www.lindaroghaar.com
Key Personnel
Owner & Pres: Linda L Roghaar (AALA)
E-mail: linda@lindaroghaar.com
Founded: 1996

Full service agency handling nonfiction; lifestyle, crafts, religion & spirituality. No fiction, romance, horror or science fiction. No unsol mss, query with SASE or e-mail first. No reading fee. Domestic sales commission: 15%.
Titles recently placed: *BORO*, Shannon Mullet-Bowlsby; *Cat vs Cat (revised)*, Pam Johnson-Bennett; *Eternal Heart*, Carl McColman; *Sewing School Fashion Design*, Amy Petronis Plumley, Andria Lisle; *Simply Shetland Lacee*, Brooke Nico; *The Unplugged Family Activity Book*, Rachel Jepson Wolf; *Unteachable Lessons*, Carl McColman; *Yarn Substitution Made Easy*, Carol J Sulcoski

The Roistacher Literary Agency (L)
545 W 111 St, Suite 7J, New York, NY 10025-1965
Tel: 212-222-1405
Key Personnel
Pres: Robert E Roistacher *E-mail:* rer41@columbia.edu
Founded: 1978
General nonfiction, especially journalism, social science & public policy. Literary fiction only from published writers. No unsol mss, query first. For nonfiction, submit prospectus, curriculum vitae, 2 sample chapters, chapter outline & table of contents. No reading fee.
Titles recently placed: *Climate, Clothing, and Agriculture in Prehistory*, Ian Gilligan, Cambridge University Press

The Rosenberg Group (L)
23 Lincoln Ave, Marblehead, MA 01945
E-mail: rosenberglitsubmit@icloud.com
Web Site: www.rosenberggroup.com
Key Personnel
Agent: Barbara Collins Rosenberg (AALA)
Founded: 1998
Representing romance & women's fiction, trade nonfiction & college level textbooks for the first & second year courses. No unsol mss, query first.
Membership(s): Romance Writers of America (RWA)

Rita Rosenkranz Literary Agency (L)
440 West End Ave, Suite 15D, New York, NY 10024-5358
Tel: 212-873-6333 *Fax:* 212-873-5225
Web Site: www.ritarosenkranzliteraryagency.com
Key Personnel
Agent: Rita Rosenkranz (AALA)
 E-mail: rrosenkranz@mindspring.com
Founded: 1990
Nonfiction, adult; no unsol mss, query first with SASE or via e-mail; no fees.
Membership(s): The Authors Guild; Women's Media Group

Jane Rotrosen Agency LLC (L)
318 E 51 St, New York, NY 10022-7803
Tel: 212-593-4330
E-mail: info@janerotrosen.com
Web Site: janerotrosen.com
Key Personnel
Founder: Jane Rotrosen Berkey (AALA)
Mng Partner: Chris Prestia
Assoc Dir, Busn Aff: Julianne Tinari
Agent: Andrea Cirillo; Meg Ruley; Annelise Robey; Amy Tannenbaum; Christina Hogrebe; Rebecca Scherer (AALA); Kathy Schneider; Jessica Errera; Logan Harper *E-mail:* lharper@janerotrosen.com
Agent Liason: Casey Conniff *E-mail:* cconniff@janerotrosen.com
Dir, Data Mgmt: Kristen Comeaux
Subs Rts Sales Agent: Allison Hufford
Subs Rts Coord: Jack McIntyre
Off Mgr, Busn Aff: Maria Burfield
Founded: 1974

EDITORIAL SERVICES

Fiction & nonfiction. Query via web site only (please do not query multiple agents within the organization). Handle film & TV rights. No reading fee. 15% commission in US & CN co-represented abroad & on the West Coast.
Membership(s): The Authors Guild

Regina Ryan Books (L)
251 Central Park W, Suite 7-D, New York, NY 10024
Tel: 212-787-5589
E-mail: queries@reginaryanbooks.com
Web Site: www.reginaryanbooks.com
Key Personnel
Pres: Regina Ryan (AALA) *E-mail:* reginaryan@reginaryanbooks.com
Founded: 1976
Book-length works of nonfiction for adult & juvenile markets. Specialize in narrative nonfiction, journalism, natural history, science (especially the brain), psychology, history, business, popular culture, cooking & food (especially in relation to travel), non-religious contemporary spirituality, wellness, diet & fitness, self-help, parenting, nature, gardening, pets, architecture, biography, women's issues. No poetry, screenplays or software. To send a proposal, please read the guidelines on the web site & submit via e-mail to queries@reginaryanbooks.com. Please no queries or follow-up by fax or phone. No reading fee. Handle film, TV & foreign rights. Representation in all foreign countries.
Titles recently placed: *Birding New England*, Randi Minetor; *Birdsong for the Curious Naturalist*, Don Kroodsma; *Coves of Departure: Field Notes from the Sea of Cortez*, John S Farnsworth; *Dear Libby: Will You Answer My Questions About Friendship?*, Libby Kiszner; *Death in Acadia National Park*, Randi Minetor; *Death in Rocky Mountain National Park*, Randi Minetor; *Death on Mount Katahdin*, Randi Minetor; *Enemy Child: A Boy in the Japanese American Internment Camps of World War II*, Andrea Warren; *Historic Rocky Mountain National Park*, Randi Minetor; *Modern Manners for Moms & Dads*, Sarah Davis, Evie Granville; *New on Earth: Baby Animals in the Wild*, Suzi Eszterhas; *Rise of the Cajun Mariners: The Race for Big Oil*, Woody Falgoux; *Rotten! Vultures, Beetles and Slime: Nature's Decomposers*, Anita Sanchez; *Smart Ass: How a Donkey Challenged Me to Accept His True Nature and Rediscover My Own*, Margie Winslow; *So You Think You Know Rock and Roll? An In-Depth Q&A Tour of the Revolutionary Dacade 1965-1975*, Peter E Meltzer; *The Appalachian Trail: A Biography*, Philip D'Anieri; *The Complete Career Guide for Introverts*, Jane Finkle; *The Feminine Sixth: Women for the Defense*, Andrea D Lyon; *The Friendly Orange Glow: The Untold Story of the PLATO System and the Dawn of Cyberculture*, Brian Dear; *Wait Till It Gets Dark: A Kid's Guide to Exploring the Night*, Anita Sanchez, George Steele; *What's Wrong With My Marijuana Plant? A Cannabis Grower's Visual Guide to Easy Diagnosis and Organic Remedies*, David Deardorff, Kathryn Wadsworth; *Wild Wine Making: Easy & Adventurous Recipes Going Beyond Grapes*, Richard Bender
Foreign Rights: Books Crossing Borders (worldwide exc UK); Abner Stein Agency (UK & Commonwealth)
Membership(s): The Authors Guild; The Linnaean Society of New York; PEN America; Women's Media Group

Victoria Sanders & Associates LLC (L)
440 Buck Rd, Stone Ridge, NY 12484
Tel: 212-633-8811
Web Site: www.victoriasanders.com

Key Personnel
Agent: Victoria Sanders; Bernadette Baker-Baughman
Founded: 1992
No unsol mss.
Titles recently placed: *A Likeable Woman*, May Cobb; *Boldly Go*, William Shatner, Joshua Brandon; *Eli and the Uncles*, Jehan Madhani; *Hockey Girl Loves Drama Boy*, Faith Erin Hicks; *Karura*, Soma Mei Sheng Frazier; *One Blood*, Denene Millner; *Redwood Court*, DeLana Dameron; *The Force of Such Beauty*, Barbara Bourland; *The Last Applicant*, Rebecca Hanover; *Water, Mirror, Echo*, Jeff Chang; *You Never Know*, Connie Briscoe

Harold Schmidt Literary Agency (L-D)
415 W 23 St, Suite 6-F, New York, NY 10011
Tel: 212-727-7473
Key Personnel
Pres: Harold D Schmidt (AALA)
 E-mail: hslanyc@aol.com
Specialize in book-length fiction & nonfiction. No unsol mss, query first by e-mail & include up to the first 5 pages of your book embedded in the e-mail; do not send as an attachment. Do not handle young adult, children's or fantasy. Telephone queries not accepted. Do not send material through the mail unless requested. Representatives in Hollywood & in all principal foreign countries.

Susan Schulman Literary Agency LLC (L-D)
454 W 44 St, New York, NY 10036
Tel: 212-713-1633; 917-488-0906 (direct line)
E-mail: queries@schulmanagency.com
Web Site: www.schulmanagency.com
Key Personnel
Owner: Susan Schulman (AALA) *Tel:* 917-504-7212 *E-mail:* susan@schulmanagency.com
Rts Dir: Linda Migalti (AALA) *E-mail:* linda@schulmanagency.com
Assoc Agent: Emelie Burl *E-mail:* emelie@schulmanagency.com
Founded: 1980
Adult book-length genre & literary fiction & nonfiction especially women's studies, biography, psychology & the social sciences. No unsol mss. Query first with SASE or by e-mail. Submit outline & 3 sample chapters. No reading fee. Co-agent in all principal foreign countries. Handles film & TV rights for other agencies & individual titles.
Foreign Rep(s): ACER Agencia Literaria (Spanish Latin America, Spanish-speaking countries); Big Apple Agency Inc (China); English Agency Japan Co Ltd (Japan); EntersKorea (South Korea); Danny Hong Agency (South Korea); Japan UNI Agency Inc (Japan); Kalem Agency (Turkey); Nurcihan Kesim Literary Agency Ltd (Turkey); Duran Kim Agency (South Korea); Korea Copyright Center Inc (KCC) (South Korea); Agence Michelle Lapautre (France); Leipman AG (Germany); Macadamia Literary Agency (Poland); Piergiorgio Nicolazzini Literary Agency (Italy); Prava i prevodi (Eastern Europe); Sebes & Bisseling Literary Agency (Netherlands, Scandinavia); Shinwon Agency (South Korea); Tuttle-Mori Agency Inc (Japan); Silke Weniger Literary Agency (Germany); Eric Yang Agency (South Korea); Susanna Zevi Agenzia Letteraria (Italy)
Membership(s): The Authors Guild; Dramatists Guild of America Inc; Society of Children's Book Writers & Illustrators (SCBWI); Women in Film (WIF); Women's Media Group; Writers Guild of America, East (WGAE)

Laurens R Schwartz, Esquire (L-D)
5 E 22 St, Suite 15-D, New York, NY 10010-5325
Tel: 212-228-2614
E-mail: lschwartz@nyc.rr.com
Founded: 1981
Full service agency handling all media for all ages worldwide. No fees; standard commissions; WGA Signatory. No unsol mss, CDs, etc. Query first with synopsis of one project & resume. Also provide information relating to the project having been with other agents or shopped around. Enclose SASE. Require 4-week right of first refusal if request submission of entire project. Handle film, TV & licensing & merchandising rights.
Membership(s): Writers Guild of America (WGA)

S©ott Treimel NY (L)
434 Lafayette St, New York, NY 10003-6943
Tel: 212-505-8353
E-mail: general@scotttreimelny.com
Web Site: scotttreimelny.com; www.linkedin.com/in/scott-treimel-46658727/
Key Personnel
Owner & Pres: Scott Treimel (AALA)
Founded: 1995
Sells & administers intellectual property rights - foreign, dramatic, electronic, broadcast, merchandise, promotion - for children's book creators. Will only consider unsol mss upon recommendations from published authors & editors.
Titles recently placed: **Not* a Ghost Story*, Gail Giles; *Bat, Cat, and Rat: Three and a Half Stories*, Ame Dyckman; *Campingland*, Ame Dyckman; *Don't Blow Your Top*, Ame Dyckman; *The Passover Rat Pack*, Barbara Diamond Goldlin; *What Coco Can Do*, Maribeth Boelts
Foreign Rep(s): Akcali Copyright (Turkey); Bardon Chinese Media (China); Donatalla d'Ormesson Agent Litteraire (France); Japan UNI Agency Inc (Japan); Korea Copyright Center Inc (KCC) (South Korea); Barbara Kuper Literarische Agentur + Medienservice (Germany)
Membership(s): The Authors Guild; PEN America; Society of Children's Book Writers & Illustrators (SCBWI)

Scovil Galen Ghosh Literary Agency Inc (L)
348 W 57 St, New York, NY 10019
Tel: 212-679-8686
E-mail: info@sgglit.com
Web Site: www.sgglit.com
Key Personnel
Pres: Russell Galen (AALA)
 E-mail: russellgalen@sgglit.com
Agent: Ann Behar (AALA) *E-mail:* annbehar@sgglit.com
Founded: 1993
All types fiction & nonfiction, adult & juvenile. Handle film & TV rights. No unsol mss, query first by e-mail only (no attachments). Does not charge fees.
Foreign Rep(s): Baror International Inc (worldwide exc USA)

Lynn Seligman (L)
400 Highland Ave, Upper Montclair, NJ 07043
Tel: 973-783-3631 *Fax:* 973-783-3691
E-mail: seliglit@aol.com
Founded: 1986
Adult & young adult fiction; adult nonfiction. Handle film & TV rights through agents in Hollywood. Submit letter or e-mail describing project with short sample pasted to e-mail if desired. No attachments or unsol mss; query first with SASE if snail mail.
Titles recently placed: *Maggie Finds Her Muse*, Dee Ernst
Foreign Rights: Books Crossing Borders (Betty Anne Crawford) (worldwide)
Membership(s): Women's Media Group

Seventh Avenue Literary Agency (L)
6318 Rimrock Rd, Sechelt, BC V7Z 0L1, Canada
Tel: 604-538-7252
E-mail: info@seventhavenuelit.com
Web Site: www.seventhavenuelit.com
Key Personnel
Dir & Principal Agent: Robert Mackwood
 E-mail: rmackwood@seventhavenuelit.com
Founded: 1974
Nonfiction agency representing international authors from a wide range of subjects & interests. Taking on few new clients. No unsol mss, query first by e-mail before any physical mailings. No fees charged.
Titles recently placed: *Dancing with Robots: The 29 Strategies for Success in the Age of AI and Automation*, Bill Bishop; *Headhunting for Ghosts: A Trek to Cross Papua New Guinea*, Rick Antonson; *How to Figure Out What to Do With Your Life*, Jennifer Turliuk; *Nerve: Lessons in Leadership From Two Women Who Went First*, Martha Piper, Indira Samarasekera; *So Called Normal: A Memoir of Family, Depression, and Resilience*, Mark Henick
Foreign Rights: Big Apple Agency Inc (Luc Kwantlen & Wendy King) (China, Indonesia, Taiwan); BookLab Literary Agency (Piotr Wawrzenczyk) (Poland); Paul & Peter Fritz Literary Agency (Christan Dittus) (Germany); Deborah Harris Agency (Ilana Kurshan) (Israel); Nurcihan Kesim Literary Agency Ltd (Dilek Kaya) (Turkey); Simona Kessler Agency (Adriana Marinara) (Romania); Korea Copyright Center Inc (KCC) (Ms MiSook Hong) (South Korea); Piergiorgio Nicolazzini Agency (Maura Solinas) (Italy); Nova Littera Ltd (Russia); Kristin Olson Literary Agency (Czechia); Owl's Agency (Japan); Read n Right Agency (Nike Davarinou) (Greece); The Riff Agency (Lucia Riff) (Brazil, Portugal); Tuttle-Mori Agency Inc (Japan)

The Seymour Agency (L-D)
475 Miner Street Rd, Canton, NY 13617
Tel: 239-398-8209
Web Site: www.theseymouragency.com
Key Personnel
Pres: Nicole Resciniti *E-mail:* nicole@theseymouragency.com
VP & Agent: Julie Gwinn
Exec Dir & Agent: Marisa Cleveland
 E-mail: marisa@theseymouragency.com
Admin Dir: Tiffany Bullard *E-mail:* tiffany@theseymouragency.com
Media Rts Mgr, Communs Mgr & Agent: Lesley Sabga *E-mail:* lesley@theseymouragency.com
Agent: Georgana (Nina) Grinstead
 E-mail: georgana@theseymouragency.com; Elisa Houot; Michael L Joy *E-mail:* michaeljoy@theseymouragency.com; Cole Lanahan (AALA); Lynnette Novak *E-mail:* lynnette@theseymouragency.com; Jonathan Rosen *E-mail:* jonathan@theseymouragency.com; Joyce Sweeney (AALA) *E-mail:* joyce@theseymouragency.com; Tina Wainscott; Jennifer Wills
Founded: 1992
Christian romance & women's fiction, nonfiction & secular romance.
Membership(s): The Authors Guild; Romance Writers of America (RWA); Writers Guild of America (WGA); Writers Guild of America, East (WGAE)

Denise Shannon Literary Agency Inc (L-D)
280 Madison Ave, Suite 308, New York, NY 10016
E-mail: info@deniseshannonagency.com; submissions@deniseshannonagency.com
Web Site: deniseshannonagency.com
Key Personnel
Owner & Agent: Denise Shannon (AALA)
Founded: 2002
Specialize in literary fiction, narrative nonfiction, biography, journalism, politics, social history,

health & business. No unsol mss, query first by post, accompanied by SASE or by email to submissions@deniseshannonagency.com. Include book description & brief bio. Do not send queries regarding fiction projects until a complete ms is available for review. No reading fees.

Titles recently placed: *1974*, Francine Prose; *No One Else Is Coming*, Brandon del Pozo; *On Being Short: Men, Masculinity, and Other Disasters*, Jess Row; *Our Strangers*, Lydia Davis; *Schoenberg: Why He Matters*, Harvey Sachs; *The Antidote*, Karen Russell; *You Only Call When You're in Trouble*, Stephen McCauley

Charlotte Sheedy Literary Agency Inc (L)
Affiliate of Salky Literary Management
928 Broadway, Suite 901, New York, NY 10010
Tel: 212-780-9800
Web Site: www.sheedylit.com
Key Personnel
Owner: Charlotte Sheedy *E-mail:* charlotte@sheedylit.com
Partner, Salky Literary Management: Jesseca Salky *Tel:* 646-584-4932 *E-mail:* jsalky@salkylitmgmt.com
Fiction & nonfiction film & TV rights. No unsol mss, query first (no screenplays); submit outline & sample chapters; no reading fee. Agents in all principal countries.
Partnership with Salky Literary Management.
Titles recently placed: *A Century for Caroline*, Kaija Langley; *No Way, Wash Day*, Adrienne Thurman, Kaylani Juanita; *Pandemic of Punishment*, Amanda Klonsky; *Separation of Church and Hate*, John Fugelsang; *The Cook and the Rabbi*, Susan Simon, Zoe Zak; *The Order of Things*, Kaija Langley; *Wade in the Water*, Nyani Nkrumah; *You Know, Drugs*, Cory Silverberg, Fiona Smyth
Foreign Rights: Claire Roberts (Australia, Brazil, Denmark, Finland, France, Germany, Iceland, India, Italy, Netherlands, Norway, Poland, Portugal, Spain, Sweden, UK)

Ken Sherman & Associates (L-D)
8530 Holloway Dr, Suite 220, West Hollywood, CA 90069
Tel: 310-273-8840
E-mail: kenshermanassociates@gmail.com
Web Site: www.kenshermanassociates.com
Key Personnel
Owner & Pres: Ken Sherman
Founded: 1989
Represents international fiction & nonfiction books, screenplays, teleplays, plus film, TV & stage rights to books. No unsolicited material. Consideration by referral only. If requested, please send in bio, first 3 chapters & 1-page outline. No reading fee.
Titles recently placed: *Elena Standish series (film/tv rights)*, Anne Perry; *Shadows on the Rock (film/tv rights)*, Willa Cather; *The Final Case (film rights)*, David Guterson; *Thomas Pitt series (film/tv rights)*, Anne Perry; *William Monk series (film/tv rights)*, Anne Perry
Membership(s): American Film Institute Third Decade Council; British Academy of Film and Television Arts (BAFTA) Los Angeles; PEN International

Wendy Sherman Associates Inc (L)
138 W 25 St, Suite 1018, New York, NY 10001
Tel: 212-279-9027
E-mail: submissions@wsherman.com
Web Site: www.wsherman.com
Key Personnel
Founder, Owner & Pres: Wendy Sherman (AALA) *E-mail:* wendy@wsherman.com
Agent: Cherise Fisher *E-mail:* cherise@wsherman.com; Kelli Martin *E-mail:* kelli@wsherman.com; Laura Mazer *E-mail:* laura@wsherman.com
Agency Asst: Callie Deitrick *E-mail:* callie@wsherman.com
Founded: 1999
Represents a wide range of fiction & nonfiction. Literary & commercial fiction, including upmarket women's fiction; Nonfiction includes, memoir, narrative nonfiction, health & wellness, gender issues, practical, self-help, popular psychology, lifestyle, home & design, fashion. No unsol mss, query first with SASE. For fiction, a letter & synopsis. Paste first 10 pages, No attachments. For nonfiction, send proposal & 2 sample chapters. See web site for submission guidelines: No paper submissions. No poetry, screenplays, mysteries, romance, westerns, science fiction, fantasy or children's books.
Titles recently placed: *50 Years of Ms.*, Katherine Spillar, Eleanor Smeal; *A Brush with Love*, Mazey Eddings; *A Novel Obsession*, Caitlin Barasch; *Accidental Sisters*, Kimberly Meyer; *America, Goddam: Violence, Black Women, and the Struggle for Justice*, Treva B Lindsey; *At Sea*, Emma Fedor; *Euphoric*, Karolina Rzadkowolska; *Fashion Dystopia*, Alyssa Hardy; *Finding Grace*, Janis Thomas; *Forgotten Women*, Alena Dillon; *Frog and Toad are Doing Their Best*, Jennie Egerdie; *Greedy*, Jen Winston; *It All Comes Down to This*, Therese Anne Folwer; *Justice of the Pies*, Maya-Camille Broussard; *Love, Lists, and Fancy Ships*, Sarah Grunder Ruiz; *Miss May Does Not Exist*, Carrie Courogen; *MKW*, Michael K Williams; *Painting Can Save Your Life*, Sara Woster; *Rituals of the Soul*, Kori Hahn; *Sustain Your Game*, Alan Stein Jr; *Taming the Potted Beast*, Molly Williams; *Thieves, Beasts & Men*, Shan Leah; *This is the Way You Rebuild a World*, Jason Hernandez; *When Good Things Happen to High People*, Larry Smith, Melanie Abrams; *Wise Words*, Korey Wise; *Women Filmmakers on Making Movies and Making It Happen*, Kevin Smokler; *Yoga for Emotional Balance*, Dr Bo Forbes
Foreign Rights: Duran Kim Agency (Duran Kim) (South Korea); Jenny Meyer Literary Agency (Jenny Meyer) (worldwide exc Asia); Andrew Nurnberg Associates Inc (Whitney Hsu) (Taiwan); Andrew Nurnberg Associates Inc (Jackie Huang) (China); Tuttle-Mori Agency Inc (Japan)
Membership(s): Women's Media Group

Side by Side Literary Productions Inc (L)
145 E 35 St, Suite 7FE, New York, NY 10016
Tel: 212-685-6831
Web Site: sidebysidelit.com
Key Personnel
Founder & Pres: Laurie Bernstein *E-mail:* laurie@sidebysidelit.com
Founded: 2004
Handles general trade fiction & nonfiction as well as select juvenile titles. Specialize in popular health, medicine, self-help, parenting, popular culture, diet & narrative nonfiction. No unsol mss, query first. Will review hard copy & digital submissions. Handles film & TV rights.

Beverley Slopen Literary Agency (L)
131 Bloor St W, Suite 711, Toronto, ON M5S 1S3, Canada
Tel: 416-964-9598 *Fax:* 416-964-9598
Web Site: www.slopenagency.com
Key Personnel
Owner: Beverley Slopen *E-mail:* beverley@slopenagency.ca
Founded: 1973
Serious fiction & nonfiction. No children's books, illustrated books, science fiction or fantasy. No software, no film or TV rights handled. Query letter & brief proposal sent by e-mail. Not taking on many new clients.

Titles recently placed: *A Trial in Venice*, Roberta Rich; *Albatross a Novel*, Terry Fallis; *City of Fallen Angels*, Howard Engel; *Daughters of the Occupation*, Shelly Sanders; *Dead Reckoning*, Ken McGoogan; *Is Work Killing You?: A Doctor's Prescription for Treating Workplace Stress*, David Posen, MD; *Mr Selden's Map of China: Decoding the Secrets of a Vanished Cartographer*, Tim Brook; *Music for Love or War*, Martyn Burke; *No Relation*, Terry Fallis; *Perdita*, Hilary Scharper; *Pluck*, Donna Morrissey; *The Forgotten Daughter*, Joanna Goodman; *The Great State*, Tim Brook; *The Home for Unwanted Girls*, Joanna Goodman; *The Memory Clinic*, Tiffany Chow
Foreign Rep(s): Paul & Peter Fritz AG (Germany); The Grayhawk Agency (Gray Tan) (China); David Grossman Literary Agency Ltd (David Grossman) (UK); The Deborah Harris Agency (Israel); International Editors' Co - Yanez Agencia Literaria (Spain); International Literatuur Bureau (Netherlands); The Italian Literary Agency Srl (Italy); JLM Literary Agency (Greece); Kalem (Turkey); Katai & Bolza Literary Agency (Hungary); Alexander Korzhenevski (Russia); Agence Michelle Lapautre (France); Licht & Burr Literary Agency (Scandinavia); Agencia Riff (Lucia Riff) (Brazil); Tuttle-Mori Agency Inc (Japan); Eric Yang Agency (South Korea)

Michael Snell Literary Agency (L)
PO Box 1206, Truro, MA 02666-1206
Tel: 508-349-3718
Web Site: www.michaelsnellagency.com
Key Personnel
Chmn & CEO: Michael Snell
EVP: Patricia Snell *E-mail:* patricia@michaelsnellagency.com
Founded: 1978
Adult nonfiction; all levels of business & management from popular trade to professional reference; legal, medical, health, psychology, self-help & how-to books; animals & pets; women's issues in business, family & society; popular science & business; technical & scientific; professional & general computer books; parenting & relationships; project development & rewrite services. Welcome new authors. No unsol mss, query first. Submit outline, synopsis & up to 50 sample pages with SASE. Publication *How to Write a Book Proposal* available upon request with SASE, or consult Michael Snell's book *From Book Idea to Bestseller* (Prima Publishing). Write for information on purchasing a model book proposal. Consider new clients on an exclusive basis. No reading fee, but do arrange for developmental editors & ghostwriters who do charge a fee.
Titles recently placed: *Career Courage*, Katie C Kelley; *Don't Pay for Your MBA*, Laurie Pickard; *Excuse Me: A Guide to Business Etiquette*, Rosanne Thomas; *Finding Peace in Your Heart When Your Heart is in Pieces*, Paul Coleman; *Lead Right for Your Company Type*, William Schneider; *Springboard: Launching Your Personal Search for Success*, G Richard Shell; *Sun House*, David James Duncan; *The Long Weeping*, Jessie van Eerden; *What Keeps Leaders Up at Night: Recognizing and Resolving Your Most Troubling Management Issues*, Nicole Lipkin

Sobel Weber Associates Inc (L)
146 E 19 St, New York, NY 10003-2404
Tel: 212-420-8585
E-mail: info@sobelweber.com
Web Site: www.sobelweber.com
Key Personnel
Principal: Nat Sobel; Judith Weber
Founded: 1970
General fiction & nonfiction. No unsol mss, query first with SASE, no electronic submissions. No

reading fee. Handle film, TV & foreign rights; serialization & audio rights. Representatives on the West Coast & in all major foreign countries. Consult web site for submission guidelines & client list.
Titles recently placed: *Blood Like Mine*, Stuart Neville; *Nothing But the Bones*, Brian Panowich; *The Last Kilo*, TJ English
Foreign Rights: Akcali Copyright Agency (Turkey); Agencia Literaria Carmen Balcells SA (Maribel Luque) (Spain); Tassy Barham Associates (Brazil, Portugal); Paul & Peter Fritz Agency (Germany); The Deborah Harris Agency (Israel); Agence Michelle Lapautre (France); Andrew Nurnberg Associates International Ltd (China, Taiwan); Kristin Olson Agency (Czechia, Slovakia); Prava i prevodi (Eastern Europe exc Czechia, Hungary & Slovenia, Greece, Russia); Santachiara Literary Agency (Italy); Marianne Schoenbach Literary Agency (Netherlands); Sobel Weber Associates Inc NY (Denmark, Finland, Norway, Sweden); The Abner Stein Agency (UK); Tuttle-Mori Agency Inc (Japan); Eric Yang Agency (Indonesia, South Korea, Thailand, Vietnam)

Spectrum Literary Agency (L)
320 Central Park W, Suite 1-D, New York, NY 10025
Tel: 212-362-4323 *Fax:* 212-362-4562
Web Site: www.spectrumliteraryagency.com
Key Personnel
Pres & Agent: Eleanor Wood
Agent: Justin Bell
Founded: 1976
Science fiction, mysteries, thrillers, horror & fantasy. No unsol mss, query first with letter, synopsis, first 10 pages & SASE. No reading fee. Agents in all principal foreign countries.
Titles recently placed: *Penric's Demon*, Lois McMaster Bujold; *Spear of Light*, Brenda Cooper; *The Genius Plague*, David Walton
Foreign Rights: Big Apple Agency Inc (Mr Luc Kwanten) (China); Book Cosmos Agency (Mihai Taru) (South Korea); The Book Publishers Association of Israel (Dalia Ever-Hadani) (Israel); Graal Literary Agency (Lukasz Wrobel) (Poland); International Editors' Co - Yanez Agencia Literaria (Portugal, Spain); Japan UNI Agency Inc (Miko Yamanouchi) (Japan); Katai & Bolza Literary Agents (Peter Bolza) (Hungary); Katai & Bolza Literary Agents (Reka Bartha) (Croatia, Serbia, Slovenia); Nurcihan Kesim Literary Agency Ltd (Dilek Kayi) (Turkey); Agence Litteraire Lenclud (Anne & Pierre Lenclud) (France); Piergiorgio Nicolazzini Literary Agency (Maura Solinas) (Italy); Nova Littera Ltd (Konstantin Palchikov & Sergei Cheredov) (Russia); Andrew Nurnberg Associates Sofia (Anna Droumeva & Mira Droumeva) (Romania); Andrew Nurnberg Associates Sofia (Mira Droumeva) (Bulgaria); Kristin Olson Literary Agency SRO (Kristin Olson & Tereza Dubova) (Czechia); Prava i prevodi (Russia); Read n Right Agency (Nike Davarinou) (Greece); Thomas Schlueck GmbH (Thomas Schlueck & Franka Zastrow) (Germany); Sebes & Bisseling Literary Agency (Lester George Hekking & Jeanine Langenberg) (Netherlands)
Membership(s): Mystery Writers of America (MWA); Science Fiction and Fantasy Writers of America, Inc (SFWA)

The Spieler Agency (L)
75 Broad St, Suite 304, New York, NY 10004
Tel: 212-757-4439
E-mail: thespieleragency@gmail.com
Web Site: thespieleragency.com
Key Personnel
Agent: Joseph Spieler
Nonfiction & literary fiction; children's books including middle grade, young adult & new adult. Areas of interest include: environmental issues, business; women's issues; natural history & science for religious studies, psychology; health; history; biography. No unsol mss, query first with letter (prefer e-mail), first chapter/contents or detailed proposal. No phone queries. Submit author background, description of work & sample chapter with SASE. Handle film & TV rights only for book clients. No reading fee, only commissions.
Titles recently placed: *City at the Edge of Forever: Los Angeles Reimagined*, Peter Lunenfeld; *The People, No: A Brief History of Anti-Populism*, Thomas Frank
Foreign Rights: The Marsh Agency (Continental Europe); Abner Stein Agency (England)

Philip G Spitzer Literary Agency Inc (L)
50 Talmage Farm Lane, East Hampton, NY 11937
Tel: 631-329-3650 *Fax:* 631-329-3651
Web Site: www.spitzeragency.com
Key Personnel
Pres & Lead Agent: Anne-Lise Spitzer (AALA)
 E-mail: annelise.spitzer@spitzeragency.com
Agent & Foreign Rts: Lukas Ortiz (AALA)
 E-mail: lukas.ortiz@spitzeragency.com
Agent & Off Mgr: Kim Lombardini (AALA)
 E-mail: kim.lombardini@spitzeragency.com
Founded: 1969
Literary fiction, suspense/thriller, general nonfiction, politics, social issues, biography. No unsol mss, query first by e-mail only, submit outline & sample chapters. No reading fee, photocopying fee. Foreign rights agents in all major markets.
Titles recently placed: *Deer Creek Drive*, Beverly Lowry; *Flags on the Bayou*, James Lee Burke; *Hamlet's Children*, Richard Kluger; *Such Kindness*, Andre Dubus III; *The Deal Goes Down*, Larry Beinhart; *Wordhunter*, Stella Sands
Foreign Rights: Big Apple Agency Inc (Luc Kwanten & Lily Chen) (China, Malaysia, Taiwan, Vietnam); Big Apple Agency Inc (Erica Zhou) (Indonesia); The Deborah Harris Agency (Efrat Lev) (Israel); International Editors' Co - Yanez Agencia Literaria (Jennifer Brooke Hoge) (Latin America exc Brazil, Portugal, Spain); The Italian Literary Agency Srl (Italy); KALEM (Sedef Ilgic) (Turkey); Agence Michelle Lapautre (Catherine Lapautre) (France); Mohrbooks AG Literary Agency (Sebastian Ritcsher & Annelie Geissler) (Austria, Germany, Switzerland); Prava i prevodi (Anna Milenkovic) (Russia); Prava i prevodi (Milena Kaplarevic) (Eastern Europe exc Russia); Agencia Literaria Riff (Laura Riff & Joao Paulo Riff) (Brazil); Marianne Schoenbach Literary Agency (Netherlands); Alexander Schwarz Literary Agency (Scandinavia); Kalina Stefanova (Bulgaria); Abner Stein Agency (Caspian Dennis) (UK); Tuttle-Mori Agency Inc (Misa Morikawa) (Japan); Eric Yang Agency (Sue Yang) (South Korea)
Membership(s): The Authors Guild

Nancy Stauffer Associates (L)
PO Box 1203, Darien, CT 06820
Tel: 203-202-2500
Web Site: www.publishersmarketplace.com/members/nstauffer/
Key Personnel
Owner: Nancy Stauffer Cahoon *E-mail:* nancy@staufferliterary.com
Founded: 1989
Literary fiction & narrative nonfiction. No mysteries, science fiction, fantasy, romance novels, screenplays or children's picture books. Query by e-mail only, with first 10 pages of your work. No attachments. Agents in all foreign markets.
Titles recently placed: *Exposure*, Ramona Emerson; *Our Souls at Night*, Kent Haruf
Membership(s): The Authors Guild

Michael Steinberg Literary Agent (L)
PO Box 274, Glencoe, IL 60022-0274
Tel: 847-626-1000
E-mail: michael14steinberg@comcast.net
Key Personnel
Principal: Michael Steinberg
Founded: 1980
Book-length fiction (mystery, science fiction) & nonfiction (business topics). No unsol mss, query first. Submit outline & first 3 chapters (hard copy). Will read only by personal reference from represented author or editor.
Titles recently placed: *All About Day Trading*, Jake Bernstein

Sterling Lord Literistic Inc (L)
594 Broadway, Suite 205, New York, NY 10012
Tel: 212-780-6050 *Fax:* 212-780-6095
E-mail: info@sll.com
Web Site: www.sll.com
Key Personnel
Chmn: Peter Matson
COO: Nadyne Pike
Pres: Philippa Brophy (AALA)
EVP & Mng Partner: Laurie Liss (AALA)
SVP: Douglas Stewart
VP: Robert Guinsler; Jim Rutman (AALA)
Sr Agent: Sarah Landis; Neeti Madan
Agent: Elizabeth Bewley; Danielle Bukowski; Jessica Friedman; Mary Krienke; Jenny Stephens
Assoc Agent: Chris Combemale; Tyler Monson
Foreign Rts Mgr: Szilvia Molnar
Founded: 1952
Fiction & nonfiction; film & TV rights. No unsol mss, query first; submit outline & sample chapters with SASE. No reading fee.
Foreign Rep(s): AnatoliaLit Agency (Amy Spangler) (Turkey); Agence Eliane Benisti (Eliane Benisti) (France); Book/Lab Ltd (Agata Zabowska) (Poland); Paul & Peter Fritz Literary Agency (Antonia Fritz) (Austria, Germany); The Grayhawk Agency (Gray Tan) (China, Taiwan); The Grayhawk Agency (Itzel Hsu) (Indonesia, Thailand, Vietnam); The Deborah Harris Agency (Geula Geurts) (Israel); Danny Hong Agency (Danny Hong) (South Korea); The Italian Literary Agency (Mariavittoria Puccetti) (Italy); JLM Literary Agency (John Moukakos) (Greece); MB Agencia Literaria (Monica Martin) (Andorra, Catalonia, Portugal, Spain); Andrew Nurnberg Associates Baltic (Tatjana Zoldnere) (Estonia, Latvia, Lithuania, Ukraine); Andrew Nurnberg Associates Budapest (Blanka Enyi) (Croatia, Hungary); Andrew Nurnberg Associates Prague (Marta Soukopova) (Czechia, Slovakia, Slovenia); Andrew Nurnberg Associates Sofia (Mira Droumeva) (Albania, Bulgaria, North Macedonia, Romania, Serbia); Riff Agency (Laura Riff) (Brazil); Marianne Schoenbach Literary Agency (Marianne Schoenbach) (Netherlands); Tuttle-Mori Agency Inc (Ken Mori) (Japan); The Van Lear Agency (Liz Van Lear) (Russia)

Stimola Literary Studio Inc (L)
11 Briarwood Lane, West Tisbury, MA 02575
Mailing Address: PO Box 1066, West Tisbury, MA 02575
Tel: 945-9353 *Fax:* 201-490-5920
E-mail: info@stimolaliterarystudio.com
Web Site: www.stimolaliterarystudio.com
Key Personnel
Pres: Rosemary B Stimola (AALA) *Tel:* 508-696-9351 *E-mail:* rosemary@stimolaliterarystudio.com
VP/Agent: Peter K Ryan *Tel:* 201-362-9091
 E-mail: pete@stimolaliterarystudio.com

LITERARY AGENTS

Dir, Opers: Nicholas Croce *Tel:* 201-248-3175 *E-mail:* nick@stimolaliterarystudio.com
Sr Agent: Erica Rand Silverman *Tel:* 917-734-3943 *E-mail:* erica@stimolaliterarystudio.com
Agent & Rts Dir: Allison Hellegers *Tel:* 917-916-6768; *E-mail:* alli@stimolaliterarystudio.com
Agent: Adriana Stimola *Tel:* 617-784-8770 *E-mail:* adriana@stimolaliterarystudio.com
Assoc Agent: Allison Remcheck *Tel:* 216-704-5521 *E-mail:* allison@stimolaliterarystudio.com
Founded: 1997
Specialize in fiction & nonfiction, preschool through young adult in all formats, including graphic. Also representing cookbooks, farm to table, lifestyle & select adult fiction. See web site for submission guidelines. Respond only to those queries we wish to pursue further. No fees.
Titles recently placed: *A Very Gay Book*, Nic Scheppard, Jenson Titus; *Alebrijes*, Donna Barba Higuera; *Blue, Barry and Pancakes*, Dan Abdo, Jason Patterson; *Call Me Athena*, Cedar Colby Smith; *Can You See It?*, Susan Verde, Juliana Perdomo; *City Spies (series)*, James Ponti; *Dim Sum Palace*, X Fang; *Evergreen*, Matthew Cordell; *Fly By Night*, Tara O'Connor; *For Lamb*, Lesa Cline-Ransome; *Go Go Guys*, Rowboat Watkins; *Healing the Liminal*, Marcella Kroll; *Hoops*, Matt Tavares; *Hot Dog*, Doug Salati; *I Made It Out of Clay*, Beth Kander; *In the Kusina*, Woldy Reyes; *Little Santa's Workshop*, Lala Watkins; *Love, Nature, Magic*, Maria Rodale; *Meet Me In Another Life*, Catriona Silvey; *Monsterstreet (series)*, J H Reynolds; *Motherhood, Facing and Finding Yourself*, Lisa Marchiano; *One of Us is Back*, Katherine M McManus; *Pizza My Heart*, Mika Song; *skin & bones*, Renee Watson; *Something Good*, Kenneth Kraegel; *Spin*, Rebecca Caprara; *Survival Scout: Lost in the Mountains*, Maxwell Eaton III; *The Ballad of Songbirds and Snakes*, Suzanne Collins; *The City of Jasmine*, Nadine Presley; *The Corgi and the Queen*, Caroline L Perry; *The Liars' Society*, Alyson Gerber; *The Magic of Mindset*, Johanna Wright; *The Red Tin Box*, Matthew Burgess, Evan Turk; *The Remarkable Rescue at Milkweed Meadow*, Elaine Dimopoulis, Doug Salati; *The Tanglewood Papers*, Kalela Williams; *The Torch Trilogy*, Moira Buffini; *The Truth About Max*, Alice Provensen, Martin Provensen; *Warrior*, Shannon Stocker
Foreign Rep(s): Intercontinental Literary Agency (translation); Schleuck Agency (Germany)
Foreign Rights: Rights People (UK)
Membership(s): The American Library Association (ALA); The Authors Guild; PEN America; Society of Children's Book Writers & Illustrators (SCBWI)

Stonesong (L)
270 W 39 St, Suite 201, New York, NY 10018
Tel: 212-929-4600
E-mail: editors@stonesong.com
Web Site: www.stonesong.com
Key Personnel
Partner & Literary Agent: Alison Fargis
Partner & Prodn Servs: Ellen Scordato
EVP & Literary Agent: Judy Linden
Literary Agent & Contracts Mgr: Madelyn Burt
Literary Agent: Leila Campoli; Melissa Edwards; Alyssa Jennette
Literary Agent & Soc Media Coord: Kim Lindman
Literary Agent: Emmanuelle Morgan; Maria Ribas; Adrienne Rosado
Founded: 1979
Representing nonfiction & fiction, including middle grade, young adult & adult titles. Create & develop commercial nonfiction & popular reference books on many subjects: cooking, business, how-to, self-help, memoir, beauty & fashion. Complete trade hardcover, paperback & ebook development, from concept to delivery. Consultants on backlist exploitation, acquisitions, publicity planning & editorial systems. Custom publishing for professional associations & magazines.
No unsol mss, query first. Welcome electronic queries for fiction & nonfiction. Please review agent biographies & submit query addressed to one agent to submissions@stonesong.com. Include the word "query" in the subject line. Include first chapter or first 10 pages of your work, pasted into the body of the e-mail. No attachments. Request for more material within 12 weeks if interested.
Titles recently placed: *Amy Wu and the Warm Welcome*, Kat Zhang; *As Seen on TV*, Meredith Schorr; *Ay Mija*, Christine Suggs; *Black America Rising*, Anna Gifty Opoku-Agyeman; *Bright*, Brigit Young; *Cannelle et Vanille Bakes Simple*, Aran Goyoaga; *Carlos Alejos Has to Lose His Chichos*, Mathew Rodriguez; *Champions of Breakfast*, Reed Black; *Cocktail Dive Bar*, T Cole Newton; *Doug the Pug Picture Book*, Leslie Mosier; *Doug the Pug: Peace, Love, & Doug*, Leslie Mosier; *Embracing And*, Dr Wendy Smith, Dr Marianne Lewis; *F*ck Anxiety*, Lauren Douglas; *Feel Good Food*, Jeanine Donofrio; *Garden Roses*, Gracielinda Poulson; *Goat is the GOAT*, Bea Birdsong; *Her Name is Knight*, Yasmin Angoe; *Homestead Recipes*, Amanda Rettke; *How to Spot a Best Friend*, Bea Birdsong; *How to Talk to Your Boss About Race*, Y-Vonne Hutchinson; *How to Talk to Your Kids About Anything*, Dr Robyn Silverman; *I Rise*, Marie Arnold; *Islas*, Von Diaz; *Knock Those Doors Down*, Anna Gifty Opoku-Agyeman; *Lets Find Momo Outdoors*, Andrew Knapp; *Louisiana Table*, George Graham; *Mariana in Mexico*, Monica Mancillas; *Murder Maps US*, Adam Selzer; *Never Again Will I Visit Auschwitz*, Ari Richter; *Not So Shy*, Noa Nimrodi; *Nothing But the Truth*, Holly James; *Plant Hunter*, Terrain; *Play Your Way Sane*, Dr Clay Drinko; *Practically Vegan*, Nisha Melvani; *Prep + Rally*, Dini Klein; *Sacred Spaces*, Carley Summers; *Sigrid Schultz of the Chicago Tribune*, Dr Pamela Toler; *Smitten Kitchen Three*, Deb Perelman; *Snacks for Dinner*, Lukas Volger; *Spon Con*, Stephanie McNeal; *Stoner*, Ashley Winstead; *Sweetheart Lake*, Jaime Pope; *The Art of Bob Mackie*, Frank Vlastnik, Laura Ross; *The Bludso Family Cookbook*, Kevin Bludso, Noah Galuten; *The Don't Panic Pantry*, Noah Galuten; *The End of Ambition*, Steven Cook; *The Essential Air Fryer Oven Cookbook*, Coco Morante; *The Gingerbread Kama Sutra*, Patti Paige; *The Grow & Thrive Cookbook*, Agatha Achindu; *The Inheritance of Orquidea Divina*, Zoraida Cordova; *The Kitchen Healer*, Jules Blaine Davis; *The Little Book of Big Corgi Butts*, Zoey Acoff; *The New Jewish Essentials*, Shannon Sarna; *The New Native Kitchen*, Freddie Bitsoie, James Fraioli; *The White Allies Handbook*, Lecia Michelle; *The Woks of Life Cookbook*, Bill Leung, Judy Leung, Sarah Leung, Kaitlin Leung; *The Yowlers*, Stacy Lynn Carroll; *Things We Create*, Axel Brechensbauer; *This Could Have Been a Love Story*, Brandon Hoang; *To Asia with Love*, Hetty McKinnon
Foreign Rep(s): Baror International (Danny Baror); The Fielding Agency (Whitney Lee); Hodgman Literary (Sandy Hodgman)
Membership(s): American Book Producers Association (ABPA)

Straus Literary (L)
77 Van Ness Ave, Suite 101, San Francisco, CA 94102
Tel: 646-843-9950
Web Site: www.strausliterary.com

EDITORIAL SERVICES

Key Personnel
Agent: Jonah Straus *E-mail:* jonah@strausliterary.com
Founded: 2003
Focus on literary fiction, historical fiction, international literature, literary mystery & thriller, cookbooks, food & travel narratives, social issues, popular science, history, international affairs, biography, memoir.
Straus Literary acts as English sub-agent for: Mertin Agency (Nicole Witt), Germany.
Operates in San Francisco & New York.
Titles recently placed: *American Oasis: Finding the Future in the Cities of the Southwest*, Kyle Paoletta; *Art as a Weapon: Tina Modotti and the Mexican Cultural Renaissance*, Mark Eisner; *Blue Food: Hope in the Water, Sustainable Eating from Oceans, Lakes, and Rivers*, Andrew Zimmern, Barton Seaver; *Doctors and Distillers: The Remarkable Medicinal History of Beer, Wine, Spirits, and Cocktails*, Camper English; *Grass People: Stories from Savanna, Steppe, and Prairie*, Michael Parks; *One Thousand Vines: A New Way to Understand Wine*, Pascaline Lepeltier; *Punks: New & Selected Poems (Song Cave)*, John Keene; *Taking Care: The Story of Nursing and Its Power to Change Our World*, Sarah DiGregorio; *The Lowering Days: A Novel*, Gregory Brown; *Zion (3 novellas)*, Djaimilia Pereira de Almeida
Foreign Rights: AMO Agency (Amo Noh) (South Korea); Silvia Bastos Agency (Pau Centellas) (Latin America exc Brazil, Portugal, Spain); Big Apple Agency Inc (Luc Kwanten) (China, Southeast Asia, Thailand); DS Budapest (Szabolcs Torok) (Hungary); English Agency Japan Co Ltd (Tsutomu Yawata) (Japan); Graal Literary Agency (Paulina Machnik) (Poland); Deborah Harris Agency (Guela Geurts) (Israel); Iris Literary (Catherine Fragou) (Greece); Kalem Agency (Kardelen Genc) (Turkey); Simona Kessler International Copyright Agency (Adriana Marina) (Romania); Alexander Korzhenevski Agency (Alex Korzhenevski) (Baltic States, Russia, Ukraine); Agence Michelle Lapautre (Catherine Lapautre) (France, Quebec, CN, Switzerland (French-speaking)); Clementina Liuzzi Agency (Italy); Michael Meller Agency (Leonie Schoebel) (Austria, Germany, Switzerland (German-speaking)); Andrew Nurnberg Associates Prague (Lucie Polakova) (Czechia, Slovakia); Plima Literary (Vuk Perisic) (Albania, Bosnia and Herzegovina, Croatia, Montenegro, North Macedonia, Serbia); Riff Agency (Joao Paulo Riff) (Brazil); Lennart Sane Agency AB (Philip Sane) (Netherlands, Scandinavia); Marianne Schoenbach Literary Agency (Diana Gvozden) (Netherlands); Kalina Stefanova (Bulgaria)

Robin Straus Agency, Inc (L)
Affiliate of The Wallace Literary Agency
229 E 79 St, Suite 5A, New York, NY 10075
Tel: 212-472-3282 *Fax:* 212-472-3833
E-mail: info@robinstrausagency.com
Web Site: www.robinstrausagency.com
Key Personnel
Pres: Robin Straus (AALA) *E-mail:* robin@robinstrausagency.com
Jr Agent: Danielle Matta
Founded: 1983
High quality fiction & nonfiction. Handle film & TV rights for represented clients' books. Foreign agents in all major countries. No screenplays, plays, romance, westerns, horror, children's or poetry. E-mail query with outline or synopsis, short author biography & sample chapters; or send brief e-mail letter describing book project (no downloads).
Foreign Rights: AnatoliaLit Agency (Turkey); Deborah Harris (Israel); JLM Literary Agency (Greece); Andrew Nurnberg Associates (world-

wide exc Greece, Israel, Japan, South Korea & Turkey); Tuttle-Mori Agency Inc (Japan); Eric Yang Agency (South Korea)

The Stuart Agency (L-D)
450 North End Ave, 25C, New York, NY 10282
Tel: 917-842-7589
Web Site: www.stuartagency.com
Key Personnel
Owner & Agent: Andrew Stuart
  E-mail: andrew@stuartagency.com
Founded: 2002
Focus on titles in the area of history, science, narrative nonfiction, business, current events, memoir, psychology, sports & literary fiction. No unsol mss, query first via online form, including short project description & brief bio.
Titles recently placed: *The Internet Is Not What You Think It Is*, Justin EH Smith
Foreign Rights: Berla & Griffini (Erica Berla) (Italy); The English Agency (Hamish Macaskill) (Japan); The Foreign Office (Teresa Vilarrubia) (Brazil, Spain); The Grayhawk Agency (Yichan Peng) (China); The Deborah Harris Agency (Jessica Kasmer-Jacobs) (Israel); Anna Jarota Agency (Anna Jarota) (France); Duran Kim Agency (Duran Kim) (South Korea); Libris Agency (Mustafa Urgen) (Turkey); Maxima Creative Agency (Santo Manurung) (Indonesia, Thailand, Vietnam); Mohrbooks (Sebastian Ritscher) (Germany); Prava i prevodi (Ana Milenkovic) (Eastern Europe, Greece, Russia); Sebes & Van Gelderen Literary Agency (Paul Sebes) (Netherlands, Scandinavia)

Talcott Notch Literary (L)
127 Broad St, 2P, Milford, CT 06460
Tel: 203-876-4959
Web Site: talcottnotch.net
Key Personnel
Agent: Amy Collins (AALA) *E-mail:* acollins@talcottnotch.net; Paula Munier; Gina Panettieri; Saba Sulaiman
Jr Agent: Nadia Lynch
Founded: 2002
Represents both adult & juvenile fiction & nonfiction. No unsol mss, query first. Strongly prefer Agent Query submissions, but will respond to e-mails. Send 1- to 2-page query letter accompanied by first 10 pages of ms. For fiction, include genre, whether project is for adults or children & length of complete project in number of words. Provide brief overview of book's plot & main characters. For nonfiction, include subject area, main concept of book, word count of completed projects, your credentials to write the work & sample chapter.
Titles recently placed: *Dear Zoe*, Kyle Lukoff; *In This Family*, Shelly Anand; *The Golem of Refuse*, Kyle Lukoff; *There's No Such Thing As Vegetables*, Kyle Lukoff

Tanenbaum International Literary Agency Ltd (TILA) (L)
1035 Fifth Ave, Suite 15D, New York, NY 10028
Tel: 212-371-4120 *Fax:* 212-988-0457
E-mail: hello@tanenbauminternational.com
Web Site: tanenbauminternational.com
Key Personnel
Owner & Pres: Ann Tanenbaum (AALA)
Ed/Assoc Agent: Kate Ellsworth (AALA)
Agency Asst: Mary Noorlander
Founded: 1980
Boutique literary agency providing in-depth, personalized service to its authors, supporting them throughout the publishing process. For nonfiction, we are looking for submissions in the areas of current issues, cultural criticism, history & general narrative (see agent bios for more details). For children's, we are looking for illustrated children's books for early readers. No memoirs, self-help, romance, fantasy, mysteries, middle-grade books, young adult books or adult fiction. No unsol mss, query first by e-mail (no attachments). See web site for query guidelines by genre.
Titles recently placed: *Only the Light Moves: Flying Covert Reconnaissance Missions in the Vietnam War*, Francis A Doherty

TBG, see The Book Group (TBG)

Tessler Literary Agency LLC (L)
155 W 68 St, No 27F, New York, NY 10023
Tel: 212-242-0466
Web Site: www.tessleragency.com
Key Personnel
Pres: Michelle Tessler (AALA)
Founded: 2004
Full service boutique agency dedicated to writers of high quality fiction & nonfiction. Nonfiction list includes narrative, popular science, memoir, history, psychology, business, biography, food & travel. In fiction, represents literary, women's & commercial. No unsol mss, query first via web form. No fees charged.
Titles recently placed: *Covert City: The Cold War and the Making of Miami*, Vincent Houghton, Eric Driggs; *Cowpuppy: An Unexpected Friendship and a Scientist's Journey into the Secret World of Cows*, Gregory Berns, PhD; *Franchise: The Golden Arches in Black America*, Marcia Chatelain; *Half American: The Epic Story of African Americans Fighting at Home and Abroad*, Matthew F Delmont; *How Iceland Changed the World*, Egill Bjarnason; *I'll Come To You*, Rebecca Kauffman; *Lovers and Liars*, Amanda Eyre Ward; *Mind Over Grind: How To Break Free When Work Hijacks Your Life*, Guy Winch, PhD; *Minds I've Met: How We Went From Denying to Embracing the Inner Lives of Animals*, Frans de Waal; *The Arrogant Ape: Unlearning the Myth of Human Exceptionalism and Why it Matters*, Christine E Webb; *The Arsonists' City*, Hala Alyan; *The Tree Collectors*, Amy Stewart; *We Killed Anji Alexander*, Mira Jacob; *Wicked Problems: How to Engineer a Better World*, Guru Madhavan
Foreign Rights: The Deborah Harris Agency (Israel); Andrew Nurnberg & Associates (China, Europe, Latin America); Tuttle-Mori Agency Inc (Japan); Eric Yang Agency (South Korea)
Membership(s): Women's Media Group

3 Seas Literary Agency (L)
PO Box 444, Sun Prairie, WI 53590
Tel: 608-834-9317
E-mail: threeseaslit@aol.com
Web Site: threeseasagency.com
Key Personnel
Literary Agent: Stacey Graham; Michelle Grajkowski (AALA); Cori Deyoe *E-mail:* cori@threeseaslit.com; Linda Scalissi
Founded: 2000
E-mail queries only. For fiction titles, query with first chapter & synopsis embedded in the e-mail. For nonfiction, query with complete proposal attached. For picture books, query with complete text. Illustrations are not necessary. Considers simultaneous submissions. Responds within one month to e-mail submissions. No snail mail queries. 3 Seas will not respond to queries that are sent to e-mail addresses other than queries@threeseaslit.com. Obtains most new clients through recommendations from others & conferences. No fees charged.
Titles recently placed: *A Navy SEAL'S Surprise Baby*, Laura Marie Altom; *A Time for Home*, Alexis Morgan; *Captive*, KM Fawcett; *Changed by His Son*, Robin Gianakopoulus; *Do or Diner: A Comfort Food Mystery*, Christine Wenger; *Every Breath She Takes*, Norah Wilson; *Forever Friday*, Timothy Lewis; *Haley's Mountain Man*, Tracy Madison; *Her Perfect Cowboy*, Trish Milburn; *His Uptown Girl*, Liz Talley; *How to Write a Book in 30 Days*, Karen Wiesner; *Jimmie Joe Johnson: Manwhore*, Lindsey Brookes; *Just Perfect*, JoMarie DeGioia; *Must Love Dukes*, Elizabeth Michaels; *One Night with the Sheikh*, Kristi Gold; *Passion and Pretense*, Susan Gee Heino; *Queen of Song and Souls*, C L Wilson; *Queen of the Sylphs*, L J McDonald; *Say It With Roses*, Devon Vaughn Archer; *Six Months Later*, Natalie D Richards; *The Art of Stealing Time*, Katie MacAlister; *The Bride Next Door*, Winnie Griggs; *The Casanova Code*, Donna MacMeans; *The Champion*, Carla Capshaw; *The Rancher's Homecoming*, Cathy McDavid; *The Sister Season*, Jennifer Brown; *The Vampire With a Dragon Tattoo*, Kerrelyn Sparks; *The Winter King*, C L Wilson; *Thousand Words*, Jennifer Brown; *Three Days on Mimosa Lane*, Anna DeStefano
Foreign Rights: Marleen Seegers (China, France, Holland, Scandinavia); Ingo Stein (Germany)
Membership(s): Romance Writers of America (RWA)

Transatlantic Agency (L)
2 Bloor St E, Suite 3500, Toronto, ON M4W 1A8, Canada
Tel: 416-488-9214
E-mail: info@transatlanticagency.com; royalties@transatlanticagency.com
Web Site: www.transatlanticagency.com
Key Personnel
Pres: Samantha Haywood *E-mail:* samantha@transatlanticagency.com
Partner & Dir, Speakers Div: Rob Firing
  E-mail: rob@transatlanticagency.com
Partner & Sr Agent: Elizabeth Bennett
  E-mail: elizabeth@transatlanticagency.com; Marilyn Biderman *E-mail:* marilyn@transatlanticagency.com; Chandler Crawford *E-mail:* chandler@transatlanticagency.com; Carolyn Forde *E-mail:* carolyn@transatlanticagency.com; Amy Tompkins *E-mail:* amy@transatlanticagency.com
Sr Agent: Andrea Cascardi *E-mail:* andrea@transatlanticagency.com; Fiona Kenshole *E-mail:* fiona@transatlanticagency.com; Timothy Travaglini *E-mail:* tim@transatlanticagency.com
Agent & Dir, Opers: Pieter Swinkels
  E-mail: pieter@transatlanticagency.com
Agent: Sandra Bishop *E-mail:* sandra@transatlanticagency.com; Evan Brown *E-mail:* evan@transatlanticagency.com; Laura Cameron *E-mail:* lcameron@transatlanticagency.com; Jane Chun (AALA); Brenna English-Loeb *E-mail:* brenna@transatlanticagency.com; Ed Maxwell *E-mail:* ed@transatlanticagency.com; Amanda Orozco *E-mail:* amanda@transatlanticagency.com; Jo Ramsay *E-mail:* queryjo@transatlanticagency.com; Leonicka Valcius *E-mail:* leonicka@transatlanticagency.com
Assoc Agent & Literary Asst: Alexandra D'Amico *E-mail:* alexandra@transatlanticagency.com
Assoc Agent: Noelle Falcis Math
  E-mail: noelle@transatlanticagency.com; Lisa Rambert-Valaskova
Mgr: Barbara Miller *E-mail:* barbara@transatlanticagency.com
Contracts Admin: Laura Cook *E-mail:* laura@transatlanticagency.com; Megan Philipp *E-mail:* megan@transatlanticagency.com
Mktg Assoc: Eden Boudreau *E-mail:* eden@transatlanticagency.com
Contract Asst: Stuti Shah *E-mail:* stuti@transatlanticagency.com
Literary Asst: Eva Oakes *E-mail:* eva@transatlanticagency.com
Rts Proj Asst: Giovanna Petta *E-mail:* giovanna@transatlanticagency.com

LITERARY AGENTS

Royalties Clerk: Elsa Bornhoft *E-mail:* elsa@transatlanticagency.com
Founded: 1993
Children's, adult literary fiction & literary nonfiction. Markets Canadian & American literary properties to English language publishers in the UK, US & CN & through sub-agents to publishers around the world. Handles film & TV rights for literary properties only: no film scripts or teleplays. No unsol mss; initial letter of inquiry essential. No reading fees. See web site for individual agents' submission details.
Titles recently placed: *A Death at the Party*, Amy Stuart; *Almost Brown*, Charlotte Gill; *Foul Days*, Genoveva Dimova; *In the Upper Country*, Kai Thomas; *Kokoro*, Christine Mari; *Love Can't Feed You*, Cherry Lou Sy; *Resist: The State of Women*, Elizabeth Renzetti; *Sisters of the Lost Nation*, Nick Medina; *Soul Shift*, Rachel Macy Stafford; *The Berry Pickers*, Amanda Peters; *The Christmas Countdown*, Holly Cassidy; *The Holiday Swap*, Maggie Knox; *The Very Sound of You*, Chantal Guertin; *Toufah*, Toufah Jallow, Kim Pittaway; *Trent & Sawyer*, Kayla Miller; *Trip Wire*, Dan Kalla; *We Spread*, Iain Reid; *What Wild Women Do*, Karma Brown
Foreign Rights: ANA Sofia Ltd (Anna Droumeva & Mira Droumeva, adult list) (Albania, Bulgaria, Serbia); Berla & Griffini Rights Agency (Erica Berla) (Italy); BookLab Literary Agency (Aleksandra Lapinska) (Poland); English Agency Japan Co Ltd (Hamish Macaskill) (Japan); EntersKorea Co Ltd (Ian Im) (South Korea); The Foreign Office (Teresa Vilarrubla, adult list) (Brazil, Portugal, Spain); Agence Litteraire Lora Fountain (Lora Fountain, children's list) (France); The Grayhawk Agency (Gray Tan) (China, Indonesia, Malaysia, Taiwan, Thailand, Vietnam); Greenbook Agency (Jinhee Park) (South Korea); Danny Hong Agency (South Korea); Imprima Korea Agency (Jehee Yun) (South Korea); International Editors' Co - Yanez Agencia Literaria (Amaiur Fernandez & Jennifer Brooke Hoge, children's list) (Spain); The Israeli Association of Book Publishers Ltd (Beverly Levit) (Israel); Japan UNI Agency (Megumi Sakai) (Japan); The Anna Jarota Agency (Anna Jarota, adult list) (France); JLM Literary Agency (John Moukakos) (Greece); Kalem Literary Agency (Nazli Gurkas) (Turkey); Katai & Bolza Literary Agents (Peter Bolza, adult list) (Hungary); Katai & Bolza Literary Agents (Eszter Rozs, children's list) (Hungary); Simona Kessler Agency (Andrea Focsaneanu) (Romania); Duran Kim Agency (Duran Kim) (South Korea); Koleen Agency (Koleen Cho) (South Korea); Korea Copyright Center Inc (KCC) (Yuna Choi) (South Korea); Liepman AG Literary Agency (Hannah Fosh, adult list) (Germany); Andrew Nurnberg Associates International Ltd (Jackie Huang, children's list) (China, Taiwan); Andrew Nurnberg Associates International Ltd (Whitney Hsu) (Taiwan); Kristin Olson Literary Agency sro (Teresa Dubova) (Czechia); Orange Agency (Claire Moon, children's list) (South Korea); Peretti Literarische Agentur (Paula Peretti, children's list) (Germany); Marianne Schonbach Literary Agency (Marianne Schonbach) (Denmark, Finland, Iceland, Netherlands, Norway, Sweden); Seibel Publishing Services (Patricia Seibel) (Brazil, Portugal); Shin Won Agency Co (Jihyun Hwang, children's & young adult list) (South Korea); Shin Won Agency Co (Joe Moon, adult list) (South Korea); The Agency Sosa (Seyoung Chon) (South Korea); Kalina Stefanova (children's list) (Bulgaria); Tuttle-Mori Agency Inc (Solan Natsume) (Japan); The Van Lear Agency LLC (Olga Baykova & Elizabeth Van Lear) (Russia); Eric Yang Agency (Jully Lee) (South Korea); Young Agency (Kevin Bae, children's list) (South Korea)

Treimel, S©ott, NY, see S©ott Treimel NY

TriadaUS Literary Agency (L)
PO Box 561, Sewickley, PA 15143
Tel: 412-401-3376
Web Site: www.triadaus.com
Key Personnel
Founder & Sr Agent: Dr Uwe Stender (AALA) *E-mail:* uwe@triadaus.com
Sr Agent & Foreign Rts Mgr: Laura Crockett *E-mail:* laura@triadaus.com
Sr Agent: Brent Taylor *E-mail:* brent@triadaus.com
Agent: Amelia Appel *E-mail:* amelia@triadaus.com
Asst Agent: Ashley Reisinger *E-mail:* ashley@triadaus.com
Founded: 2004
Full service literary agency including fiction & nonfiction. Also international sales, film & TV options. No unsol mss, query first.
Titles recently placed: *A Multitude of Dreams*, Mara Rutherford; *Am I Lying to Myself*, Jane Greer; *Assistant to the Villain*, Hannah Nicole Maehrer; *Caught in a Bad Fauxmance*, Elle Gonzalez Rose; *Deathly Fates*, Tesia Tsai; *I Have Seven Dogs*, Molly Horan; *Immortal Longings*, Chloe Gong; *Last Laugh*, KR Alexander; *Masters of Death*, Olivie Blake; *My Throat an Open Grave*, Tori Bovalino; *Red*, Annie Cardi; *Road Home*, Rex Ogle; *Sona and the Golden Beasts*, Rajani LaRocca; *The Crimson Crown*, Heather Walter; *The Dos and Donuts of Love*, Adiba Jaigirdar; *The Jasmine Throne*, Tasha Suri; *The Lost Letters of Aisling*, Cynthia Ellingsen; *The School for Wicked Witches*, Will Taylor; *The Second Death of Locke*, VL Bovalino; *The Summer She Went Missing*, Chelsea Ichaso; *Wild About You*, Kaitlyn Hill
Foreign Rights: Bears Factor Literary Agency (Arab Middle East, Arabic language, United Arab Emirates); Big Apple Agency Inc (China); BookLab Literary Agency (Poland); Corto Literary (Bulgaria, Croatia, Czechia, Hungary, Romania, Slovakia, Slovenia); Donatella d'Ormesson Agent Litteraire (France); The Deborah Harris Agency (Israel); IMC Literary Agency (Mexico, Portugal, Spain); Kalem Literary Agency (Turkey); Alexander Korzhenevski Agency (Baltic States, Russia); Piergiorgio Nicolazzini Literary Agency (Italy); Plima Literary (Serbia); Riff Agency (Brazil); RTA Rights Agency (Indonesia, Thailand, Vietnam); Thomas Schlueck Agency (Germany); Sebes & Bisseling Literary Agency (Netherlands, Scandinavia); Eric Yang Agency (South Korea)
Membership(s): Association of American Publishers (AAP)

Trident Media Group LLC (L-D)
355 Lexington Ave, 12th fl, New York, NY 10017
Tel: 212-333-1511
E-mail: info@tridentmediagroup.com; press@tridentmediagroup.com; foreignrights@tridentmediagroup.com; office.assistant@tridentmediagroup.com
Web Site: www.tridentmediagroup.com
Key Personnel
Chmn: Robert Gottlieb
CEO: Daniel Strone
EVP: Ellen Levine; Scott Miller
SVP: Don Fehr
SVP, Literary Agent & Motion Picture/Television Agent: Erica Spellman-Silverman
VP: Amanda Annis; Mark Owen Gottlieb
Dir, Foreign Rts: Ana Ban
Foreign Rts Agent: Emma Fingleton
Assoc Foreign Rts Agent: Alice Berndt
Literary Agent: Audrey Crooks; Martha Wydysh

EDITORIAL SERVICES

Assoc Literary Agent: Aurora Fernandez; Claire Romine
Digital Media & Mktg Mgr: Michael Pintauro
Contracts Assoc: Julia Maziarz; Mahaylie Spain
Foreign Rts Asst: Angela Seowon Lee; Melissa Tomczak
Founded: 2000
General fiction & nonfiction. No unsol mss, query first on web site. Include only a paragraph about yourself, brief plot synopsis & your contact information. Query one literary agent only. Commission: 15% domestic (& film/TV), 20% foreign.
Titles recently placed: *Flashpoint: An FBI Thriller*, Catherine Coulter; *Indulge: Delicious and Decadent Dishes to Enjoy & Share*, Valerie Bertinelli; *Late Admissions: Confessions of a Black Conservative*, Glenn Loury; *The Devil's Fortress*, Dale Brown

2M Communications Ltd (L)
263 West End Ave, Suite 21A, New York, NY 10023
Tel: 212-741-1509 *Fax:* 212-691-4460
Web Site: www.2mcommunications.com
Key Personnel
Pres: Madeleine Morel (AALA) *E-mail:* morel@2mcommunications.com
Founded: 1982
Only represent previously published ghostwriters & collaborators who work with platformed authors already represented by recognized literary agents or acquired by the major publishing houses. Behind over 60 New York Times bestsellers but all confidential. No unsol mss, query first. Submit CV or resume. Commission: 15%.
Membership(s): PEN America; Women's Media Group

Union Literary (L-D)
30 Vandam St, Suite 5A, New York, NY 10013
Tel: 212-255-2112
Web Site: www.unionliterary.com
Key Personnel
Agent: Christina Clifford *E-mail:* christina@unionliterary.com; Trena Keating *E-mail:* tk@unionliterary.com; Sally Wofford-Girand *E-mail:* swg@unionliterary.com
Specialize in literary fiction, popular fiction, narrative nonfiction, memoir, social history, business & general big idea books, popular science, cookbooks & food writing. No unsol mss, query first. Submissions preferred by e-mail with sample pages attached in .doc or .docx format. Do not send .pdf files. Nonfiction submissions should include query letter, proposal & sample chapter. Fiction submissions should include query letter, synopsis & sample pages. No calls regarding submissions.
Titles recently placed: *Artificial: A Love Story*, Amy Kurzweil; *Safe and Sound*, Laura McHugh; *The Prospectors: A Novel*, Ariel Djanikian; *Untraceable*, Aya de Leon
Foreign Rights: AnatoliaLit Agency (Turkey); Berla & Griffini (Italy); Greene & Heaton (UK); The Deborah Harris Agency (Israel); Imprima (South Korea); KCC (South Korea); Liepman Agency (Germany); MB Agencia Literaria (Brazil, Portugal, Spain); La Nouvelle Agence (France); Andrew Nurnberg Associates International Ltd (China, Taiwan); Kristin Olson Literary Agency (Czechia); Rogers, Coleridge & White (UK); Vicki Satlow Literary Agency (Italy); Sebes & Bisseling Literary Agency (Netherlands, Scandinavia); Abner Stein (UK); UNI Agency (Japan); Elizabeth Van Lear (Russia)

United Talent Agency LLC (L-D)
9336 Civic Center Dr, Beverly Hills, CA 90210
Tel: 310-273-6700
Web Site: www.unitedtalent.com

Key Personnel
VChmn: Jay Sures
CEO: Jeremy Zimmer
COO: Bob Roback
Chief Communs Offr: Richard Siklos
Pres: David Kramer
Founded: 1991
Fiction, nonfiction. Handle film & TV rights. No unsol mss, query first; reading fee.
Titles recently placed: *Lucky Me: A Memoir of Changing the Odds*, Rich Paul; *North Woods: A Novel*, Daniel Mason; *Our Place on the Island*, Erika Montgomery; *Pageboy: A Memoir*, Elliot Page
Branch Office(s)
888 Seventh Ave, 9th fl, New York, NY 10106, Partner: Byrd Leavell *Tel:* 212-659-2600

Vigliano Associates Ltd (L-D)
575 Madison Ave, Suite 1006, New York, NY 10022
Tel: 212-888-8525
E-mail: info@viglianoassociates.com
Web Site: viglianoassociates.com
Key Personnel
Owner, CEO & Head Agent: David Vigliano
Founded: 1986
Boutique literary agency in publishing, representing everything from culinary books to commercial fiction & celebrity memoirs. No unsol mss.
Titles recently placed: *Everyday Dharma: 8 Essential Practices for Finding Success & Joy in Everything You Do*, Suneel Gupta; *Gambler: Secrets from a Life at Risk*, Billy Walters; *Magnolia Table: A Collection of Recipes for Gathering (vol 3)*, Joanna Gaines
Foreign Rights: The Amo Agency (Sona Seo) (South Korea); AnatoliaLit Agency (Amy Marie Spangler & Ozlem Oztemel) (Turkey); Arrowsmith Agency (Nina Arrowsmith & Sophie Schmale) (Germany); Graal Literary Agency (Justyna Pelaska) (Poland); Japan UNI Agency (Takeshi Oyama) (Japan); Katai & Bolza Literary Agents (Peter Bolza) (Hungary); Maxima Creative Agency (Santo Manurung) (Indonesia, Thailand, Vietnam); MB Agencia Literaria (Monica Martin) (Brazil, Latin America, Portugal, Spain); La Nouvelle Agence (Vanessa Kling) (France); Andrew Nurnberg Associates Beijing (Susan Xia) (China); Andrew Nurnberg Associates Taiwan (Whitney Hsu & Joanne Chan) (Taiwan); Prava i prevodi (Milena Kaplarevic & Ana Milenkovic) (Eastern Europe, Greece, Russia); Sebes & Bisseling Literary Agency (Rik Kleuver) (Belgium, Holland, Iceland, Netherlands, Scandinavia)

Wales Literary Agency Inc (L)
1508 Tenth Ave E, No 401, Seattle, WA 98102
Tel: 206-553-9684
E-mail: waleslit@waleslit.com
Web Site: www.waleslit.com
Key Personnel
Owner & Literary Agent: Elizabeth Wales (AALA)
Asst Agent: Karen Maeda Allman
Asst Agent & Foreign Rts: Adrienne Reed
Founded: 1990
Specialize in quality fiction & nonfiction. Does not handle screenplays, children's books, genre fiction or most category nonfiction. By referral only. No phone queries. Accept electronic submissions only. Simultaneous submissions accepted. Response provided within 3 weeks to queries, 3 months to mss.
Titles recently placed: *We Are Not Strangers*, Josh Tuininga; *Wild Chorus*, Brenda Peterson; *Wolf Odyssey*, Amaroq Weiss
Foreign Rights: Big Apple Agency Inc (China, Taiwan); Nurcihan Kesim Literary Agency Ltd (Turkey); Agence Michelle Lapautre (France); Mohrbooks AG Literary Agency (Austria, Germany, Switzerland); Andrew Nurnberg Associates (Croatia, Hungary); Reiser Agency (Italy); Sebes & Bisseling Literary Agency (Netherlands, Scandinavia); Shinwon Agency (South Korea); Silk Road Agency (Thailand); Abner Stein Agency (UK); Tuttle-Mori Agency Inc (Japan)

Warwick Associates (L)
18340 Sonoma Hwy, Sonoma, CA 95476
Tel: 707-939-9212 *Fax:* 707-938-3515
E-mail: warwick@vom.com
Web Site: www.warwickassociates.com
Key Personnel
Pres: Simon Warwick-Smith
Founded: 1985
A "one-stop" agency handling any or all parts of literary agenting through publicity & sales, etc. Specialize in spirituality, metaphysics, religion & psychology, celebrity memoirs, business & self-help, pop culture. Literary agent for a number of celebrity spiritual authors. No reading fee. Accept unsol mss, but query first with 2 chapters & SASE. No fiction or poetry.

Waterside Productions Inc (L)
2055 Oxford Ave, Cardiff, CA 92007
Tel: 760-632-9190 *Fax:* 760-632-9295
E-mail: admin@waterside.com
Web Site: www.waterside.com
Key Personnel
VP & Agent: Carole Jelen *Tel:* 925-968-9066 *E-mail:* carole@jelenpub.com
Sr Agent: Margot Maley Hutchison *Tel:* 858-483-0426 *E-mail:* mmaley@waterside.com
Foreign Rts Dir & Agent: Kimberly Brabec *E-mail:* kimberly@waterside.com
Agent: Jill Kramer *Tel:* 760-201-5737 *E-mail:* jkcats210@gmail.com; Johanna Maaghul *E-mail:* johanna@waterside.com; Kristen Moeller *E-mail:* kristen.moeller@gmail.com
Founded: 1982
Specialize in nonfiction. Professional how-to: technology, business, software, test prep. World leader in non-fungible token auctions for authors. General: self-help, spiritual, health, human interest, etc. No phone calls. No unsol mss. Submit a full book proposal per guidelines found at, or query through, the web site form. No reading fee. Handles software, film & TV rights with co-agents. In-house international division. Affiliations with PR agencies. Waterside now has its own print on demand & ebook publishing division at end of description of services.

Watkins/Loomis Agency Inc (L)
PO Box 20925, New York, NY 10025
Tel: 212-532-0080 *Fax:* 646-383-2449
E-mail: assistant@watkinsloomis.com; permissions@watkinsloomis.com
Web Site: watkins-loomis.squarespace.com
Key Personnel
Owner & Pres: Gloria Loomis
VP & Agent: Julia Masnik
Founded: 1908
Literary fiction, memoir, political nonfiction, biography. No unsol material.
Foreign Rights: The Marsh Agency (translation); Abner Stein Agency (UK)

Waxman Literary Agency (L)
Affiliate of Diversion Publishing Corp
443 Park Ave S, No 1004, New York, NY 10016
Tel: 212-675-5556
Web Site: www.waxmanliteraryagency.com
Key Personnel
Founder & Agent: Scott Waxman
Sr Agent: Larry Kirshbaum
Agent: Susan Canavan; Fleetwood Robbins

Founded: 1997
Fiction & nonfiction. No unsol mss, query first via e-mail. No reading fee, charge for reproductions.

Cherry Weiner Literary Agency (L)
925 Oak Bluff Ct, Dacula, GA 30019-6660
Tel: 732-446-2096
E-mail: cwliteraryagency@gmail.com
Key Personnel
Owner: Cherry Weiner
Founded: 1977
Science fiction, general fiction. No nonfiction. No unsol mss. Referred authors submit letter saying who referred. Submissions or recommendations only. Query letter where applicable, no downloads. No reading fee. Handle film & TV rights. Foreign representatives in England, Germany, Italy, Japan, Netherlands, Scandinavia, Russia, Spain, Eastern Europe & France.
Titles recently placed: *Calculations*, Bebe Bayless; *House of Secrets*, Lowell Caufiel; *Old Monsters Never Die*, Tim Waggoner; *Plush Life*, Gini Koch; *Sagan's Gate*, Weston Ochse; *Summer's Lease*, John D Nesbitt; *SunSpear*, Keith J Taylor; *Terrifier 2*, Tim Waggoner

The Weingel-Fidel Agency (L)
310 E 46 St, Suite 21-E, New York, NY 10017
Tel: 212-599-2959
Key Personnel
Owner: Loretta Weingel-Fidel *E-mail:* lwf@theweingel-fidelagency.com
Founded: 1989
Fiction & nonfiction. No unsol ms. Referral only.
Foreign Rep(s): Mary Clemmey (UK); Fritz Agency (Germany); Japan UNI Agency Inc (Japan); Agence Michelle Lapautre (France); Lennart Sane Agency AB (Netherlands, Scandinavia, Spain)
Foreign Rights: Jill Hughes (Albania, Bulgaria, Croatia, Estonia, Hungary, Latvia, Lithuania, Montenegro, North Macedonia, Romania, Serbia, Slovakia, Slovenia)

Westwood Creative Artists Ltd (L-D)
386 Huron St, Toronto, ON M5S 2G6, Canada
Tel: 416-964-3302 *Fax:* 416-964-3302
E-mail: wca_office@wcaltd.com
Web Site: www.wcaltd.com
Key Personnel
Chmn: Michael Levine
Pres & COO: Jackie Kaiser
EVP: Hilary McMahon
VP, Fin & Co-Head, Media Rts: Jake Babad
Intl Rts Dir & Agent: Meg Wheeler
Agent: Sara Harowitz; Emmy Nordstrom Higdon; John Pearce
Assoc Agent: Bridgette Kam
Intl Rts Assoc & Film/TV Assoc: Caroline Vassallo
Off Mgr: Briar Heckman
Founded: 1995
General trade fiction & nonfiction for international marketplace. No unsol mss, query first. Handle film & TV rights, stage adaption rights as well as podcasting & multimedia rights. No reading fee. For submission guidelines, please visit us at www.wcaltd.com/submission-guidelines.
Foreign Rights: Akcali Copyright (Kezban Akcali & Atilla Izgi Turgut) (Turkey); Sandra Bruna Literary Agency (Sandra Bruna & Natalia Berenguer) (Latin America, Portugal, Spain); The English Agency (Hamish Macaskill) (Japan); Graal Literary Agency (Tomasz Berezinksi) (Poland); The Deborah Harris Agency (Efrat Lev) (Israel); International Copyright Agency (Simona Kessler) (Romania); The Italian Literary Agency SRL (Elisa Beretta) (Italy); Japan UNI Agency Inc (Miko Suga Yamanouchi) (Japan); Anna

LITERARY AGENTS

Jarota Agency (Sandrine Bilan & Anna Jarota) (France); JLM Literary Agency (John Moukakos) (Greece); Katai & Bolza (Peter Bolza) (Hungary); Liepman Agency (Hannah Fosh) (Germany); Maxima Creative Agency (Santo Manurung) (Indonesia); Mo Literary Services (Monique Oosterhof) (Scandinavia); NiKa (Vania Kadiyska) (Bulgaria); Andrew Nurnberg Associates Beijing (Jackie Huang) (China); Andrew Nurnberg Associates Taipei (Whitney Hsu) (China, Hong Kong, Taiwan); Kristin Olson (Czechia); PLIMA (Vuk Perisic) (Croatia, North Macedonia, Serbia, Slovenia); Riff Agency (Laura Riff) (Brazil); Marianne Schoenbach Literary Agency (Stella Nelissen) (Netherlands); Shin Won Agency (Tae Eun Kim) (South Korea); Synopsis (Natalia Sanina) (Russia); Tuttle-Mori Agency (Thailand) Co Ltd (Pimolporn Yutisri) (Thailand)
Membership(s): Professional Association of Canadian Literary Agents (PACLA)

Rhoda Weyr Agency, see Dunham Literary Inc

Roger Williams Agency (L-D)
Division of New England Publishing Associates Inc
17 Paddock Dr, Lawrence Twp, NJ 08648
Mailing Address: PO Box 66066, Lawrenceville, NJ 08648-6066
Tel: 860-973-2439
E-mail: roger@rogerwilliamsagency.com
Web Site: www.rogerwilliamsagency.com
Key Personnel
Agent & Mng Dir: Roger S Williams (AALA)
Founded: 1983
No unsol mss.
Foreign Rights: Books Crossing Borders (worldwide)
Membership(s): American Booksellers Association (ABA); Organization of American Historians (OAH)

Lydia Wills LLC (L-D)
5344 N Paulina, 3F, Chicago, IL 60660
Tel: 917-292-8314
E-mail: lydiawills@gmail.com
Web Site: www.lydiawills.com
Key Personnel
Principal & Agent: Lydia Wills
Literary & management agency representing fiction & nonfiction, particularly nonfiction storytelling that sparks social change. No unsol mss, query first via e-mail.
Titles recently placed: *Articulate*, Rachel Kolb
Foreign Rights: AnatoliaLit Agency (Amy Spangler) (Turkey); Berla & Griffini Rights Agency (Erica Berla) (Italy); Big Apple Agency (Vincent Lin) (Mainland China, Taiwan); Internationaal Literatuur Bureau BV (Linda Kohn) (Netherlands); Japan UNI Agency (Miko Yamanouchi) (Japan); Milkwood Agency (Alex Lee) (South Korea); Mohrbooks AG Literary Agency (Sebastian Ritscher) (Germany); La Nouvelle Agence (Michele Kanonidis) (France); Agencia Riff (Joao Paulo Riff & Laura Riff) (Brazil); Lennart Sane Agency AB (Philip Sane) (Denmark, Finland, Iceland, Norway, Sweden); Lennart Sane Agency AB (Latin America, Portugal, Spain)

WME (L-D)
11 Madison Ave, New York, NY 10010
Tel: 212-586-5100
Web Site: www.wmeagency.com
Key Personnel
Partner & Agent: Laura Bonner; Dorian Karchmar (AALA); Margaret Riley King *E-mail:* mrk@wmeagency.com
Partner: Eve Attermann; Gail Ross; Howard Yoon
Agent: Jay Mandel; Angeline Rodriguez; Eric Simonoff

Founded: 1898
All subjects; handle software, film & TV rights. No unsol mss, query first; no reading fee.
Branch Office(s)
9560 Wilshire Blvd, Beverly Hills, CA 90210
Tel: 310-285-9000
9601 Wilshire Blvd, Beverly Hills, CA 90210
Tel: 310-285-9000
131 S Rodeo, 2nd fl, Beverly Hills, CA 90212
Tel: 310-285-9000
1666 Connecticut Ave NW, Suite 550, Washington, DC 20009
1201 Demonbreun, Nashville, TN 37203
Tel: 615-963-3000
Foreign Office(s): MLC Ctr, 19 Martin Place, Level 25, Sydney, NSW 2000, Australia
Tel: (02) 9285 8000
Center Point, 100 New Oxford St, London WC1A 1HB, United Kingdom *Tel:* (020) 8929 8400

Writers House (L)
21 W 26 St, New York, NY 10010
Tel: 212-685-2400
Web Site: www.writershouse.com
Key Personnel
Chair: Amy Berkower (AALA)
  E-mail: aberkower@writershouse.com
Pres: Simon Lipskar (AALA) *E-mail:* slipskar@writershouse.com
EVP, Fin: Maria Aughavin
EVP, Global Media & Licensing: Cecilia de la Campa
Sr Agent: Stephen Barr *E-mail:* sbarr@writershouse.com; Johanna V Castillo *E-mail:* jcastillo@writershouse.com; Susan Cohen (AALA) *E-mail:* scohensubmissions@writershouse.com; Dan Conaway (AALA) *E-mail:* conawaysubmissions@writershouse.com; Lisa DiMona *E-mail:* ldimonasubmissions@writershouse.com; Susan Ginsburg (AALA) *E-mail:* sginsburgsubmissions@writershouse.com; Susan Golomb (AALA) *E-mail:* sgolombsubmissions@writershouse.com; Merrilee Heifetz (AALA) *E-mail:* mheifetzsubmissions@writershouse.com; Dan Lazar (AALA) *E-mail:* dlazar@writershouse.com; Alexandra Levick (AALA) *E-mail:* alevicksubmissions@writershouse.com; Steven Malk *E-mail:* smalk@writershouse.com; Jodi Reamer, Esq (AALA) *E-mail:* jreamer@writershouse.com; Robin Rue (AALA) *E-mail:* rrue@writershouse.com; John Schline; Alexa Stark *E-mail:* astark@writershouse.com
Sr Agent, Juv & Young Adult: Rebecca Sherman *E-mail:* rebeccasubmissions@writershouse.com
Mng Dir, Global Licensing: Maja Nikolic
Dir, Busn Aff: Matt Fulton
Dir, Global Licensing & Audio Rts: Kate Boggs
Dir, Global Licensing & UK Rts: Alessandra Birch
UK Rts Dir: Peggy Boulos Smith
Media Rts Mgr: Tom Ishizuka
Rights Mgr: Kathryn Stuart
Founded: 1973
Represents writers of fiction & nonfiction, for both adult & juvenile books as wells as illustrators. Agents work with literary & commercial fiction, women's fiction, science fiction/fantasy, narrative nonfiction, history, memoirs, biographies, psychology, science, parenting, cookbooks, how-to, self-help, business, finance, young adult & juvenile fiction/nonfiction & picture books. Interested in & work with authors at all stages of their career. Please e-mail query letter, which includes your credentials, an explanation of what makes your book unique & special, & a synopsis. Some agents within the agency have different requirements. Please contact their individual Publisher's Marketplace (PM) profile for details. Respond to all queries, generally within 6-8 weeks. Do not represent original screenplays.

EDITORIAL SERVICES

Branch Office(s)
7660 Fay Ave, No 338H, La Jolla, CA 92037, Sr Agent: Steven Malk *E-mail:* smalk@writershouse.com
Foreign Rights: Akcali Copyright (Turkey); ANA (Judit Hermann) (Hungary); ANA (Petra Tobiskova) (Czechia, Slovakia); ANA Baltics (Baltic States); Anthea Agency (Katalina Sabeva) (Bulgaria); Ia Atterholm (Scandinavia); Bardon-Chinese Media Agency (China, Taiwan); Agence Eliane Benisti (France); Book Publishers Association of Israel (Israel); Book-Lab Literary Agency (Poland); The Deborah Harris Agency (children's) (Israel); The Italian Literary Agency Srl (Italy); Japan UNI Agency Inc (Japan); JLM Literary Agency (Greece); Simona Kessler Copyright Agency (Romania); Korea Copyright Center Inc (KCC) (South Korea); Maxima Creative Agency (Indonesia); Mo Literary Services (children's) (Netherlands); Plima Literary Agency (Croatia, Serbia, Slovenia); RDC Agencia Literaria (Portugal, Spain); Agencia Riff (Brazil); Thomas Schlueck Literary Agency (Germany); Sebes & Bisseling Literary Agency (Netherlands); Synopsis Agency (Natalia Sanina) (Russia); Tuttle-Mori Agency (Thailand) Co Ltd (Thailand)

Writers' Productions (L-D)
PO Box 630, Westport, CT 06881-0630
Tel: 203-227-8199
Key Personnel
Owner & Pres: David L Meth *E-mail:* dlm67@mac.com
Founded: 1977
Literary quality fiction & nonfiction. Handle film, TV & licensing rights. Foreign reps available as & where needed. No fees. No unsol mss; not accepting new clients. No mss or samples by e-mail. No phone calls.
Membership(s): Academy of American Poets; Dramatists Guild of America Inc; PEN America

Writers' Representatives LLC (L)
116 W 14 St, 11th fl, New York, NY 10011-7305
Tel: 212-620-9009
E-mail: transom@writersreps.com
Web Site: www.writersreps.com
Key Personnel
Principal: Lynn Chu; Glen Hartley *E-mail:* glen@writersreps.com
Founded: 1985
Represents authors of book-length works of nonfiction & literary fiction for adults. Once WR agrees to represent an author, we give advice on how best to structure or edit proposals, discuss ideas for book projects & comment on finished ms material, with the goal of placing a book with the right publisher on the best possible terms for our author. We also discuss our authors' backgrounds & interests with publishers to promote upcoming projects or to find new ones. We sell to major publishers in the US & abroad. Prefer to see ms material rather than synopses. Background about an author's professional experience, particularly that which is relevant to the book, as well as a list of previously published works. We respond within 4-6 weeks on average. We require that all authors fully advise us as to whether any project has been previously submitted to a publisher & what the response was & if the project has been submitted to another agent. Postal submissions should be accompanied by SASE. No reading fees.
Titles recently placed: *Anatomy of 55 More Songs*, Marc Myers; *Blood Money*, Peter Schweizer; *The End of Everything*, Victor Davis Hanson; *The Ghost at the Feast*, Robert Kagan; *These Are the Plunderers*, Gretchen Morgenson, Joshua Rosner

The Wylie Agency LLC (L)
250 W 57 St, Suite 2114, New York, NY 10107
Tel: 212-246-0069
E-mail: mail@wylieagency.com
Web Site: www.wylieagency.com
Key Personnel
Founder & Pres: Andrew Wylie
Literary Agent: Jin Auh; Sarah Chalfant; Jeffrey Posternak
Founded: 1980
Literary fiction & nonfiction; no unsol mss; query first with SASE. Handle film & TV rights. Contact for fee information.
Foreign Office(s): The Wylie Agency (UK) Ltd, 17 Bedford Sq, London WC1B 3JA, United Kingdom *Tel:* (020) 7908 5900 *Fax:* (020) 7908 5901 *E-mail:* mail@wylieagency.co.uk
Foreign Rights: The Wylie Agency (UK) Ltd (UK)

The Yao Enterprises (Literary Agents) LLC (L-D)
Division of The Yao Enterprises LLC
67 Banksville Rd, Armonk, NY 10504
Tel: 914-765-0296
E-mail: yaollc@gmail.com
Key Personnel
Pres: Mei C Yao
Founded: 1995
Specialize in original literary creations & subsequent world language translation of books on the art of living & practical spirituality. No unsol mss, query first (e-mail queries welcome). No reading fee. Handle software & film & TV rights.
Member of Souami School of Ikebana (Japan) & Aesthetic Pruning Association (US).
Titles recently placed: *Cancer Is Not a Disease: It's a Healing Mechanism*, Andreas Moritz
Foreign Rights: SinoStar/Chinese Connection Agency (China, Hong Kong, Taiwan)

The Young Agency (L)
213 Bennett Ave, No 3H, New York, NY 10040
Tel: 212-229-2612
Key Personnel
Prop: Marian Young
Founded: 1986
Fiction & nonfiction. No unsol mss; no reading fees. Handle film & TV rights after book is sold.

Barbara J Zitwer Agency (L-D)
525 West End Ave, Unit 11-H, New York, NY 10024
Tel: 212-501-8423
E-mail: zitwer@gmail.com
Web Site: www.barbarajzitweragency.com
Key Personnel
Pres: Barbara J Zitwer
Founded: 1991
Specialize in fiction & narrative nonfiction by writers from all around the world & selling film rights to Korean books & others. Specialize in Korean literature & global fiction & nonfiction. Represents the best writers from Korea including Booker shortlisted author Han Kang & Man Asian Prize winner, Kyouing sook Shin. We look for new, exciting literary voices from every country on the globe.
Titles recently placed: *Between Good and Evil*, Marina Ovsyannikova; *Broken Summer*, JM Lee; *Counterattack at Thirty*, Won Pyung Sohn; *I Went to See My Father*, Kyoung sook Shin; *If I'm Going to Live to One Hundred, I May as Well Be Happy*, Rhee Kun Hoo; *Second Chance Convenience Store*, Hoyeon Kim; *The Korean Book of Happiness*, Barbara J Zitwer; *The Sister*, Sung-Yoon Lee; *Walking Practice*, Dolki Min
Foreign Rights: Gabriella Ambrosioni (Italy); Donatalla D'Ormesson (France); Anoukh Foerg Litteraire Agent (Germany); Deborah Harris Agency (Israel); Imprima Korea Agency (Japan, South Korea); MO Literary Agency (Scandinavia); Andrew Nurnberg Agency (Whitney Hsu) (Taiwan); Prava i prevodi (Eastern Europe, Russia); SalmaiaLit (Portugal, Spanish-speaking countries)

Illustration Agents

Carol Bancroft & Friends
PO Box 2030, Danbury, CT 06813
Tel: 203-730-8270 *Fax:* 203-730-8275
E-mail: cbfriends@sbcglobal.net; artists@carolbancroft.com
Web Site: www.carolbancroft.com
Key Personnel
Owner: Joy Elton Tricarico
Founded: 1972
Represents many fine illustrators specializing in art for children of all ages. Servicing the publishing industry including, but not limited to, picture/mass market books & educational materials. We work with packagers, studios, toy companies & corporations in addition to licensing art to related products. Promotional packets sent upon request.
Unsol artwork & mss are not accepted.
Membership(s): Graphic Artists Guild; Society of Children's Book Writers & Illustrators (SCBWI); Society of Illustrators

B&A
Division of Great Bowery Inc
433 Broadway, Suite 420, New York, NY 10013
Tel: 212-682-1490
E-mail: info@ba-reps.com
Web Site: www.ba-reps.com
Key Personnel
Global Mng Dir: Gregg Lhotsky *E-mail:* greggl@ba-reps.com
Commercial illustration & photography.
Branch Office(s)
2-8 Elizabeth St, Suite 2.04, Paddington, NSW 2031, Australia
1029 S Zhong Shan Rd, 3F, East, Block 1, Huangpu District, Shanghai 200031, China, Exec Prodr: Jaslyn Loh *E-mail:* jaslyn.loh@amanacliq.com
B&A Germany, Mainburger Str 40, 81369 Munich, Germany
49 Borough High St, London SE1 1NB, United Kingdom, Dir, Art, Animation & Photog: Sam Summerskill *Tel:* (020) 7645 3337 *E-mail:* sam@ba-reps.com

Bernstein & Andriulli, see B&A

Byer-Sprinzeles Agency
5800 Arlington Ave, Suite 16-C, Riverdale, NY 10471
Tel: 718-543-9399
Web Site: www.maggiebyersprinzeles.com
Key Personnel
Agent: Maggie Byer-Sprinzeles *E-mail:* maggie@maggiebyersprinzeles.com
Founded: 1991
Represents children's book illustrators.
Represents 27 artists.

The CAT Agency Inc
345 Old Oaks Rd, Fairfield, CT 06825
Tel: 917-434-3141
Web Site: catagencyinc.com
Key Personnel
Owner & Agent: Christy Ewers *E-mail:* christy@catagencyinc.com
Agent: Chad W Beckerman *E-mail:* chad@catagencyinc.com
Assoc Agent: Aliza R Hoover; Christie Megill
Founded: 1994
Strictly represents illustrators, authors +/or authors/illustrators for children's literature. Illustrators: Send 4-6 jpegs of samples, live link to web site & short letter of introduction. Author/illustrators: E-mail brief synopsis of ms & several accompanying illustrations or samples of artwork. Authors: Send query letter & ms.
Represents 110 artists.
Membership(s): Society of Children's Book Writers & Illustrators (SCBWI)

Cornell & Company, LLC
44 Jog Hill Rd, Trumbull, CT 06611
Tel: 203-454-4210
Web Site: www.cornellandco.com
Key Personnel
Owner: Merial Cornell *E-mail:* merial@cornellandco.com
Founded: 1989
Professional illustrators, specializing in the children's book markets; educational, trade & mass market. Representing over 25 artists with a variety of styles & techniques.
Represents 25 artists.
Membership(s): Graphic Artists Guild; Society of Children's Book Writers & Illustrators (SCBWI)

Craven Design Inc
229 E 85 St, New York, NY 10028
Mailing Address: PO Box 282, New York, NY 10028-9998
Tel: 212-288-1022 *Fax:* 212-249-9910
E-mail: cravendesign@mac.com
Web Site: www.cravendesignstudios.com
Key Personnel
Artist Rep: Meryl Jones
Founded: 1981
Artist's representative: book illustration (text & trade), juvenile through adult; humorous, realistic, decorative & technical; maps, charts, graphs.
Represents 20 artists.

Fort Ross Inc - International Representation for Artists
Division of Fort Ross Inc
26 Arthur Place, Yonkers, NY 10701
Tel: 914-375-6448
Key Personnel
Pres & Exec Dir: Dr Vladimir P Kartsev *E-mail:* vkartsev2000@gmail.com
Founded: 1992
Foreign sales of secondary rights for illustrations, photographs & covers made by American & Canadian artists. Representation of Russian & East European artists & photographers in the US & CN.
Represents 50 artists.

Carol Guenzi Agents Inc
Subsidiary of Artagent.com
865 Delaware St, Denver, CO 80204
Tel: 303-820-2599 *Toll Free Tel:* 800-417-5120
E-mail: art@artagent.com
Web Site: artagent.com
Key Personnel
Pres: Carol Guenzi
Founded: 1984
A wide selection of talent in all areas of visual communications. Also represents 2 content developers, 4 photographers & 2 copywriters.
Represents 5 artists.
Membership(s): AIGA, the professional association for design

Herman Agency
350 Central Park W, Apt 4I, New York, NY 10025
Tel: 212-749-4907
Web Site: www.hermanagencyinc.com
Key Personnel
Owner & Pres: Ronnie Ann Herman *E-mail:* ronnie@hermanagencyinc.com
Founded: 1999
Represent illustrators, authors & author/illustrators of children's books, trade & educational.
Represents 19 artists.
Membership(s): The Authors Guild; Graphic Artists Guild; Society of Children's Book Writers & Illustrators (SCBWI)

Illustration Online LLC
13 Wingstone Lane, Devon, PA 19333
Tel: 215-232-6666
Web Site: www.illustrationonline.com
Key Personnel
Agent: Lisa Pomerantz *Tel:* 215-688-3962 (cell) *E-mail:* lisa@illustrationonline.com
Founded: 2021
Commercial illustrators & animators representative.
Represents 50 artists.

Levy Creative Management LLC
425 E 58 St, Suite 37F, New York, NY 10022
Tel: 212-687-6463
E-mail: info@levycreative.com
Web Site: www.levycreative.com
Key Personnel
Founder & Pres: Sari Schorr *E-mail:* sari@levycreative.com
Founded: 1996
Boutique agency representing only award-winning international artists.

Lindgren & Smith
888C Eighth Ave, No 329, New York, NY 10019
Tel: 212-397-7330
E-mail: info@lindgrensmith.com; hello@lindgrensmith.com
Web Site: lindgrensmith.com
Key Personnel
Owner: Pat Lindgren *E-mail:* pat@lindgrensmith.com; Piper Smith *E-mail:* piper@lindgrensmith.com
Founded: 1987
Do not accept mss. Send e-mail to info@lindgrensmith.com with "representation" in the subject line & include one small jpg of your best work.
Represents 28 artists.

Lott Representatives Ltd
PO Box 3607, New York, NY 10163
Tel: 212-755-5737
Web Site: www.lottreps.com
Key Personnel
Pres: Peter Lott *E-mail:* peter@lottreps.com
Represent commercial illustrators.

MB Artists
775 Sixth Ave, Suite 6, New York, NY 10001
Tel: 212-689-7830
Web Site: www.mbartists.com
Key Personnel
Pres & Agent: Mela Bolinao *E-mail:* mela@mbartists.com
Founded: 1986

ILLUSTRATION AGENTS

Represents illustrators whose work is primarily intended for the juvenile market.
Represents 62 artists.
Membership(s): Graphic Artists Guild; Society of Illustrators

Melissa Turk & the Artist Network
9 Babbling Brook Lane, Suffern, NY 10901
Tel: 845-368-8606
E-mail: melissa@melissaturk.com
Web Site: www.melissaturk.com
Key Personnel
Owner & Pres: Melissa Turk
Contact: Dorothy Ziff
Founded: 1986
Represents professional artists supplying quality illustration, calligraphy & cartography. Specialize in children's trade & educational illustration as well as natural science illustration (wildlife, botanical, medical, etc), publishing & interpretive signage.
Represents 12 artists.
Membership(s): Graphic Artists Guild; Society of Children's Book Writers & Illustrators (SCBWI)

Morgan Gaynin
41 N Main St, Norwalk, CT 06854
Tel: 212-475-0440
E-mail: info@morgangaynin.com
Web Site: www.morgangaynin.com
Key Personnel
Owner, Principal & Rep: Tim Mendola
Rep: Kelly Pelsue
Founded: 1974
Illustrator's representative.
Represents 25 artists.
Membership(s): Graphic Artists Guild; Society of Children's Book Writers & Illustrators (SCBWI); Society of Illustrators

Wanda Nowak Creative Illustrators Agency
231 E 76 St, Suite 5-D, New York, NY 10021
Tel: 212-535-0438
E-mail: wanda@wandanow.com
Web Site: www.wandanow.com
Key Personnel
Pres: Wanda Nowak
Founded: 1995
Children's trade books, elementary & secondary textbook illustration & book cover illustration.
Represents 16 artists.

Painted-Words Inc
310 W 97 St, Suite 24, New York, NY 10025
Tel: 212-663-2311
E-mail: info@painted-words.com
Web Site: painted-words.com
Key Personnel
Agent: Claire Easton Morance; Lori Nowicki
Founded: 1992 (as Lori Nowicki & Associates)
Artist & literary agent.
Represents 61 artists.
Membership(s): Society of Children's Book Writers & Illustrators (SCBWI)

Gerald & Cullen Rapp
41 N Main St, Suite 103, South Norwalk, CT 06854
Tel: 212-889-3337
E-mail: info@rappart.com
Web Site: www.rappart.com
Key Personnel
Rep: Nancy Moore *Tel:* 212-889-3337 ext 103
  E-mail: nancy@rappart.com
Founded: 1944
Represent leading commercial & editorial illustrators on an exclusive basis. Sell to magazine & book publishers, ad agencies, design firms & major corporations.
Represents 60 artists.
Membership(s): Graphic Artists Guild; Society of Illustrators

Kerry Reilly: Representatives
1826 Asheville Place, Charlotte, NC 28203
Tel: 704-372-6007; 704-281-5007 (cell)
E-mail: kerry@reillyreps.com
Web Site: www.reillyreps.com
Animation, illustration & photography.
Represents 25 artists.

Renaissance House
Imprint of Laredo Publishing Co
465 Westview Ave, Englewood, NJ 07631
Tel: 201-408-4048
Web Site: www.renaissancehouse.net
Key Personnel
Pres: Sam Laredo *E-mail:* laredo@laredopublishing.com
VP & Exec Ed: Raquel Benatar *E-mail:* raquel@renaissancehouse.net
Founded: 1991
Book developer that specializes in children's books & educational materials for the Latino market. Represents award-winning illustrators with a wide variety of styles & techniques. Services the advertising & publishing industries.
Represents 80 artists.

Salzman International
1751 Charles Ave, Arcata, CA 95521
Tel: 707-822-5500 *Fax:* 707-825-6600
Web Site: salzmanart.com
Key Personnel
Owner: Richard Salzman *E-mail:* richard@salzmanart.com
Founded: 1982
Agents for visual artists for educational & trade books specializing in art illustrators. Feature art for magazines & periodicals. Editorial services available.
Represents 25 artists.

Richard W Salzman Artists' Representative, see Salzman International

Storybook Arts Inc
414 Poplar Hill Rd, Dover Plains, NY 12522
Tel: 845-877-3305
Web Site: www.storybookartsinc.com
Key Personnel
Owner & Pres: Janet De Carlo *E-mail:* janet@storybookartsinc.com
Founded: 2005
Artist representative agency.
Represents 25 artists.
Membership(s): Society of Children's Book Writers & Illustrators (SCBWI)

Tugeau 2 Inc
2231 Grandview Ave, Cleveland Heights, OH 44106
Tel: 216-513-4047
Web Site: www.tugeau2.com
Key Personnel
Owner: Nicole Tugeau *E-mail:* nicole@tugeau2.com
Founded: 2003
Agency for artist representation in the children's publishing industry.
Represents 85 artists.
Membership(s): Society of Children's Book Writers & Illustrators (SCBWI)

WendyLynn & Co
2705 Willow Hill Rd, Annapolis, MD 21403
Tel: 410-533-5766
Web Site: wendylynn.com
Key Personnel
Owner & Agent: Kyle Williams *E-mail:* kyle@wendylynn.com
Founded: 2002
Specialize in the children's publishing market. Represent & promote our illustrators to publishing companies which produce work for children & young adults.
Represents 35 artists.
Membership(s): Society of Children's Book Writers & Illustrators (SCBWI)

Lecture Agents

Listed below are some of the most active lecture agents who handle tours and single engagements for writers.

American Program Bureau Inc
One Gateway Center, Suite 751, Newton, MA 02458
Tel: 617-614-1600
E-mail: apb@apbspeakers.com
Web Site: www.apbspeakers.com
Key Personnel
Founder, Chmn & CEO: Robert P Walker
SVP: Brenda Kane *E-mail:* bkane@apbspeakers.com; Drew Sullivan *E-mail:* dsullivan@apbspeakers.com
Founded: 1965
Global speaker, celebrity & entertainment agency. Branch locations in: San Diego, CA; Atlanta, GA; Chicago, IL.
Membership(s): International Association of Speakers Bureaus (IASB); National Association for Campus Activities (NACA®)

APB, see American Program Bureau Inc

Burns Entertainment
3637 Westfield Lane, Glenview, IL 60026
Tel: 847-866-9400
Web Site: burnsent.com
Key Personnel
CEO: Doug Shabelman *E-mail:* doug.shabelman@burnsent.com
Pres: Marc Ippolito *E-mail:* marc.ippolito@burnsent.com
Founded: 1970
Celebrities, influencers, music & sports entertainment marketing. Match corporations with talent for appearances, speeches & endorsements.
Branch Office(s)
379 W Broadway, Suite 430, New York, NY 10012

CAA Speakers
Subsidiary of Creative Artists Agency LLC
2000 Avenue of the Stars, Los Angeles, CA 90067
Tel: 424-288-2000 *Fax:* 424-288-2900
E-mail: speakers@caa.com
Web Site: www.caa.com/caaspeakers
Key Personnel
Agent: Andy Roth; Lindsay Samakow
Founded: 1975
Exclusively represents top talent for keynote speeches, engaging conversations & appearances. Source for celebrity, motivational, corporate, college & inspirational speakers.
Branch Office(s)
10250 Constellation Blvd, Los Angeles, CA 90067 *Tel:* 310-550-4000
CAA ICON, 5075 S Syracuse St, Suite 700, Denver, CO 80237 *Tel:* 303-557-3700
1500 "K" St NW, Washington, DC 20005 *Tel:* 202-919-2100
3652 S Third St, Suite 200, Jacksonville Beach, FL 32250 *Tel:* 904-339-0435 *Fax:* 904-758-0562
420 Lincoln Rd, Suite 340, Miami Beach, FL 33139 *Tel:* 305-538-7535
3560 Lenox Rd, Suite 1525, Atlanta, GA 30326 *Tel:* 404-816-2722
444 N Michigan Ave, Suite 3540, Chicago, IL 60611 *Tel:* 312-242-2700
405 Lexington Ave, 19th fl, New York, NY 10174 *Tel:* 212-277-9000 *Fax:* 212-277-9099
65 E 55 St, New York, NY 10022 *Tel:* 212-556-5600
6075 Poplar Ave, Suite 410, Memphis, TN 38119 *Tel:* 901-763-4900
401 Commerce St, Penthouse, Nashville, TN 37219 *Tel:* 615-383-8787 *Fax:* 615-383-4937

CreativeWell Inc
PO Box 3130, Memorial Sta, Upper Montclair, NJ 07043
Tel: 973-783-7575
E-mail: info@creativewell.com
Web Site: www.creativewell.com
Key Personnel
Pres: George M Greenfield
Founded: 2003
Literary, lecture & arts management.

The Fischer Ross Group Inc
2 Greenwich Off Park, Suite 300, Greenwich, CT 06831
Tel: 203-622-4950 *Fax:* 203-531-4132
E-mail: frgstaff@earthlink.net
Web Site: frg-speakers.com
Key Personnel
Pres: Grada Fischer
Exclusive lecture agents for authors (fiction, non-fiction, trade) & journalists (print & broadcast), as well as nationally known celebrities & personalities. Arrange lecture tours, individual speaking engagements, product endorsements, public openings & appearances for the university, association & corporate markets.

International Entertainment Bureau
3618 N Washington Blvd, Indianapolis, IN 46205
Tel: 317-926-7566
E-mail: ieb@prodigy.net
Key Personnel
Founder: David Leonards
Founded: 1972
Information on speakers, celebrities & entertainers available in the marketplace. Planning, consulting & booking.
Membership(s): Indiana Association of Fairs and Festivals (INAF)

Penguin Random House Speakers Bureau, a Penguin Random House company
1745 Broadway, Mail Drop 13-1, New York, NY 10019
Tel: 212-572-2013
E-mail: speakers@penguinrandomhouse.com
Web Site: www.prhspeakers.com
Key Personnel
VP & Exec Dir: Tiffany Tomlin
Dir: Anastasia Whalen
Exec Agent Dir: Kate Berner; Kim Thornton Ingenito; Christine Labov
Agent Dir: Kaley Baron; Madeleine Denman
Sr Agent: Alysyn Reinhardt
Agent: Hayley Shear
Sr Mgr, Contracts: Lisa Considine
Sr Mgr, Mktg: Heather Brown
Sr Analyst, Fin: Claire Seavey
Assoc Mgr, Sales: Eric Bliss
Contracts Admin: Alicia Dercole
Acct Exec: Steve Myers; Lauren Verge
Assoc: Kwabena Dinizulu
Fin Assoc: Reginald Jean-Francois
Mktg Assoc: Eva Lau
Founded: 2006
Full service lecture agency that represents best-selling authors, literary legends, cutting-edge thinkers & current tastemakers.
Membership(s): International Association of Speakers Bureaus (IASB)

Random House Speakers Bureau, see Penguin Random House Speakers Bureau, a Penguin Random House company

Jodi F Solomon Speakers Bureau Inc
PO Box 302123, Boston, MA 02130
Tel: 617-266-3450 *Fax:* 617-266-5660
E-mail: inquiries@jodisolomonspeakers.com
Web Site: www.jodisolomonspeakers.com
Key Personnel
Pres: Jodi F Solomon
Founded: 1990
Lecture & performing arts management.

Speakers Unlimited
7532 Courtyard Place, Cary, NC 27519
Tel: 919-466-7676
E-mail: prospeak@aol.com
Web Site: www.speakersunlimited.com
Key Personnel
Owner: Mike Frank
Founded: 1971
Full service speakers bureau.
Membership(s): National Speakers Association (NSA)

The Tuesday Agency
404 E College St, Suite 408, Iowa City, IA 52240
Tel: 319-338-7080; 319-400-9031 (cell)
E-mail: info@tuesdayagency.com
Web Site: tuesdayagency.com
Key Personnel
Pres: Trinity Ray
VP: Kevin Mills
Sr Agent: Ryan Barker
Jr Agent: Alexa Starry
Founded: 2011
Exclusive speaker representation.

UTA Speakers
Division of United Talent Agency LLC
888 Seventh Ave, Suite 922, New York, NY 10106
Tel: 212-659-2600; 212-645-4200
E-mail: utaspeakers@unitedtalent.com
Web Site: www.utaspeakers.com
Key Personnel
CEO: Jeremy Zimmer
Founded: 1981 (as Greater Talent Network)
Exclusive lecture & entertainment management. Represent authors, journalists & nationally & internationally known individuals. Arrange speaking engagements & tours for corporations, associations, colleges & universities, town halls, hospitals & other organizations, as well as literary, motion picture, television & radio representation.
Membership(s): International Association of Speakers Bureaus (IASB)

World Class Speakers & Entertainers
5158 Clareton Dr, Suite 1034, Agoura Hills, CA 91376
Tel: 818-991-5400
E-mail: wcse@wcspeakers.com

LECTURE AGENTS

Web Site: www.wcspeakers.com
Key Personnel
Pres: Joseph I Kessler *E-mail:* jkessler@wcspeakers.com
Founded: 1970
Represents world class speakers & entertainers. Database of 25,000 speakers & entertainers; directory/guide available.

Writers' League of Texas (WLT)
611 S Congress Ave, Suite 200 A-3, Austin, TX 78704
Mailing Address: PO Box 41355, Austin, TX 78704
Tel: 512-499-8914
E-mail: wlt@writersleague.org
Web Site: www.writersleague.org

Key Personnel
Exec Dir: Becka Oliver *E-mail:* becka@writersleague.org
Prog Dir: Samantha Babiak *E-mail:* sam@writersleague.org
Memb Servs Mgr/Digital Media Mgr: J Evan Parks
Office Coord: Lore Arnold
Founded: 1981

Associations, Events, Courses & Awards

Book Trade & Allied Associations — Index

ADVERTISING - PROMOTIONAL

Advertising Research Foundation (ARF), pg 493
American Association for the Advancement of Science (AAAS), pg 494
American Photographic Artists (APA), pg 496
American Political Science Association (APSA), pg 496
American Sociological Association (ASA), pg 497
American Speech-Language-Hearing Association (ASHA), pg 497
Association for Intelligent Information Management (AIIM), pg 498
Association of National Advertisers Inc (ANA), pg 499
Association of Publishers for Special Sales (APSS), pg 500
BMI®, pg 501
Book Publicists of Southern California, pg 501
The Center for Exhibition Industry Research (CEIR), pg 503
Florida Graphics Alliance (FGA), pg 506
4A's (American Association of Advertising Agencies), pg 506
Great Lakes Graphics Association (GLGA), pg 507
The International Women's Writing Guild (IWWG), pg 508
Library of American Broadcasting (LAB), pg 509
Linguistic Society of America (LSA), pg 509
National Coalition Against Censorship (NCAC), pg 512
National Newspaper Publishers Association (NNPA), pg 513
New Atlantic Independent Booksellers Association (NAIBA), pg 514
North Carolina Writers' Network, pg 515
Ordre des traducteurs, terminologues et interpretes agrees du quebec (OTTIAQ), pg 515
Print Industries Market Information and Research Organization (PRIMIR), pg 517
Writers' Guild of Alberta, pg 522

BOOK MANUFACTURING

American Christian Writers, pg 494
American Printing History Association, pg 496
Association for PRINT Technologies (APTech), pg 498
Association of College & University Printers, pg 499
Book Manufacturers' Institute Inc (BMI), pg 501
Guild of Book Workers, pg 507
The International Women's Writing Guild (IWWG), pg 508
New Mexico Book Association (NMBA), pg 514
Printing & Graphics Association MidAtlantic (PGAMA), pg 517
PRINTING United Alliance, pg 517
Publishers Association of the West Inc (PubWest), pg 518
Publishing Professionals Network, pg 518
Society of Illustrators (SI), pg 520
Visual Media Alliance (VMA), pg 521

BOOK TRADE SUPPLIERS

American Forest & Paper Association (AF&PA), pg 495
The International Women's Writing Guild (IWWG), pg 508
National Association of Printing Ink Manufacturers (NAPIM), pg 512
National Association of Real Estate Editors (NAREE), pg 512
National Paper Trade Association (NPTA), pg 513
Society for Technical Communication (STC), pg 519

BOOKSELLING

ABAC/ALAC, pg 493
American Booksellers Association, pg 494
American Christian Writers, pg 494
American Political Science Association (APSA), pg 496
Antiquarian Booksellers' Association of America (ABAA), pg 497
Association des Libraires du Quebec (ALQ), pg 498
Association of American Editorial Cartoonists (AAEC), pg 498
California Independent Booksellers Alliance (CALIBA), pg 502
Christian Retail Association Inc (CRA), pg 503
Connecticut Authors & Publishers Association (CAPA), pg 504
Council for Advancement & Support of Education (CASE), pg 504
Educational Book & Media Association (EBMA), pg 505
The International Women's Writing Guild (IWWG), pg 508
Livres Canada Books, pg 510
Midwest Independent Booksellers Association (MIBA), pg 510
National Association of Book Entrepreneurs (NABE), pg 511
National Association of College Stores (NACS), pg 511
New Atlantic Independent Booksellers Association (NAIBA), pg 514
New England Independent Booksellers Association Inc (NEIBA), pg 514
New Mexico Book Association (NMBA), pg 514
Ontario Library Association (OLA), pg 515
Pacific Northwest Booksellers Association (PNBA), pg 516
Playwrights Guild of Canada, pg 516
Printing Industries Association Inc of Southern California (PIASC), pg 517
Southern Independent Booksellers Alliance (SIBA), pg 520
Technical Association of the Pulp & Paper Industry (TAPPI), pg 521
The Word, A Storytelling Sanctuary Inc, pg 522
Writers' Guild of Alberta, pg 522

EDITORIAL

American Book Producers Association (ABPA), pg 494
American Christian Writers, pg 494
Editorial Freelancers Association (EFA), pg 505
Editors Canada (Reviseurs Canada), pg 505
International Association of Crime Writers Inc, North American Branch, pg 508
The International Women's Writing Guild (IWWG), pg 508
National Association of Real Estate Editors (NAREE), pg 512
New Mexico Book Association (NMBA), pg 514
Writers' Guild of Alberta, pg 522

LIBRARY

American Antiquarian Society (AAS), pg 494
The American Library Association (ALA), pg 495
Association for Information Science & Technology (ASIS&T), pg 498
Association of Jewish Libraries Inc (AJL), pg 499
Bibliographical Society of America (BSA), pg 500
Canadian Cataloguing in Publication Program, pg 502
The Center for Fiction, pg 503
Corporation of Professional Librarians of Quebec, pg 504
Federation des Milieux Documentaires, pg 505
The International Women's Writing Guild (IWWG), pg 508
Library Association of Alberta (LAA), pg 509
Library of American Broadcasting (LAB), pg 509
The Library of Congress Center for the Book, pg 509
National Freedom of Information Coalition (NFOIC), pg 513
National Information Standards Organization (NISO), pg 513
New Mexico Book Association (NMBA), pg 514
Northwest Territories Public Library Services, pg 515
Ontario Library Association (OLA), pg 515
Public Library Association (PLA), pg 518
Special Libraries Association (SLA), pg 520
Texas Library Association (TLA), pg 521
Theatre Library Association (TLA), pg 521
United for Libraries, pg 521
United States Board on Books for Young People (USBBY), pg 521
Writers' Alliance of Newfoundland & Labrador, pg 522
Writers' Guild of Alberta, pg 522

BOOK TRADE & ALLIED ASSOCIATIONS — INDEX

LITERACY

Alcuin Society, pg 493
American Literacy Council, pg 495
Association of Writers & Writing Programs (AWP), pg 500
Corporation of Professional Librarians of Quebec, pg 504
Florida Writers Association Inc, pg 506
IBBY Canada, pg 507
Institut de cooperation pour l'education des adultes-ICEA (The Institute for Cooperation on Adult Education), pg 508
International Literacy Association (ILA), pg 508
International Society of Latino Authors (ISLA), pg 508
The International Women's Writing Guild (IWWG), pg 508
Literacy Texas, pg 509
Manitoba Arts Council (MAC), pg 510
National Coalition for Literacy (NCL), pg 512
National Council of Teachers of English (NCTE), pg 512
National Writers Association, pg 514
New Mexico Book Association (NMBA), pg 514
North Carolina Writers' Network, pg 515
Ontario Library Association (OLA), pg 521
PNWA - a writer's resource, pg 517
Teachers & Writers Collaborative (T&W), pg 520
Writers' Guild of Alberta, pg 522

LITERARY

The Academy of American Poets Inc, pg 493
Alcuin Society, pg 493
American Literary Translators Association (ALTA), pg 495
Aspen Words, pg 497
Association of Publishers for Special Sales (APSS), pg 500
Association of Writers & Writing Programs (AWP), pg 500
The Authors Guild®, pg 500
Authors League Fund, pg 500
The Baker Street Irregulars (BSI), pg 500
Boston Authors Club Inc, pg 501
Canada Council for the Arts (Conseil des arts du Canada), pg 502
The Canadian Children's Book Centre, pg 502
The Center for Book Arts, pg 503
The Center for Fiction, pg 503
Community of Literary Magazines & Presses (CLMP), pg 504
Florida Writers Association Inc, pg 506
The Ibsen Society of America (ISA), pg 507
The International Women's Writing Guild (IWWG), pg 508
Jewish Book Council, pg 509
The League of Canadian Poets, pg 509
The Literary Press Group of Canada, pg 509
Literary Translators' Association of Canada, pg 509
Maine Writers & Publishers Alliance (MWPA), pg 510
The Manitoba Writers' Guild Inc (MWG), pg 510
The Melville Society, pg 510
Miniature Book Society Inc, pg 511
Modern Language Association (MLA), pg 511
National Book Critics Circle (NBCC), pg 512
New England Poetry Club, pg 514
New Hampshire Writers' Project (NHWP), pg 514
New Mexico Book Association (NMBA), pg 514
North Carolina Writers' Network, pg 515
Northern California Translators Association, pg 515
Ontario Library Association (OLA), pg 515
Palm Springs Writers Guild, pg 516
PEN America, pg 516
PEN America Los Angeles, pg 516
PEN America Washington, DC, pg 516
Playwrights Guild of Canada, pg 516
PNWA - a writer's resource, pg 517
Poetry Society of America (PSA), pg 517
Poets & Writers Inc, pg 517
Quebec Writers' Federation (QWF), pg 518
SK Arts, pg 519
The Society of Midland Authors (SMA), pg 520
Texas Institute of Letters (TIL), pg 521
United States Board on Books for Young People (USBBY), pg 521
Women Who Write Inc, pg 522
Women's National Book Association Inc, pg 522
Writers' Guild of Alberta, pg 522
The Writers' Union of Canada (TWUC), pg 523

MAGAZINE & PRESS

American Christian Writers, pg 494
American Society of Magazine Editors (ASME), pg 496
American Society of Media Photographers Inc, pg 496
Association of Writers & Writing Programs (AWP), pg 500
Canadian Bookbinders and Book Artists Guild (CBBAG), pg 502
The Canadian Circulations Audit Board (CCAB), pg 502
Catholic Media Association (CMA), pg 503
City & Regional Magazine Association (CRMA), pg 504
Community of Literary Magazines & Presses (CLMP), pg 504
Deadline Club, pg 504
EdCan Network, pg 505
Education Writers Association (EWA), pg 505
Evangelical Press Association (EPA), pg 505
Foil & Specialty Effects Association (FSEA), pg 506
International Society of Weekly Newspaper Editors (ISWNE), pg 508
The International Women's Writing Guild (IWWG), pg 508
Livestock Publications Council (LPC), pg 510
Magazines Canada (MC), pg 510
National Association of Real Estate Editors (NAREE), pg 512
National Cartoonists Society (NCS), pg 512
National Education Association (NEA), pg 513
National Newspaper Association (NNA), pg 513
National Press Club (NPC), pg 513
National Society of Newspaper Columnists (NSNC), pg 514
News/Media Alliance, pg 514
News Media Canada, pg 515
The NewsGuild - CWA, pg 515
North American Snowsports Journalists Association (NASJA), pg 515
Northern California Translators Association, pg 515
Ontario Library Association (OLA), pg 515
Poets & Writers Inc, pg 517
Printing & Graphics Association MidAtlantic (PGAMA), pg 517
Reporters Committee for Freedom of the Press, pg 518
Technical Association of the Pulp & Paper Industry (TAPPI), pg 521
Writers' Guild of Alberta, pg 522

MEDIA - COMMUNICATIONS

Academy of Motion Picture Arts & Sciences (AMPAS), pg 493
Alliance for Women in Media (AWM), pg 494
AM&P Network, pg 494
American Academy of Arts & Sciences (AAAS), pg 494
American Auto Racing Writers & Broadcasters (AARWBA), pg 494
American Civil Liberties Union (ACLU), pg 495
American Jewish Committee (AJC), pg 495
American Public Human Services Association (APHSA), pg 496
American Society of Composers, Authors & Publishers (ASCAP), pg 496
Association for Intelligent Information Management (AIIM), pg 498
The Association of Medical Illustrators (AMI), pg 499
Bibliographical Society of the University of Virginia, pg 501
BMI®, pg 501
Business Forms Management Association (BFMA), pg 502
Business Marketing NYC, pg 502
Corporation for Public Broadcasting (CPB), pg 504
Council for the Advancement of Science Writing (CASW), pg 504
CWA/SCA Canada, pg 504
Education Writers Association (EWA), pg 505
The Graphic Artists Guild Inc, pg 506
Inter American Press Association (IAPA), pg 508
International Association of Business Communicators (IABC), pg 508
The International Women's Writing Guild (IWWG), pg 508
Investigative Reporters & Editors, pg 509
Library of American Broadcasting (LAB), pg 509
Media Alliance, pg 510
Media Coalition Inc, pg 510
National Association of Black Journalists (NABJ), pg 511
National Association of Broadcasters (NAB), pg 511
National Association of Real Estate Editors (NAREE), pg 512
National Association of Science Writers Inc (NASW), pg 512
National Communication Association, pg 512
National Federation of Press Women Inc (NFPW), pg 513
National Newspaper Publishers Association (NNPA), pg 513
National Press Photographers Association Inc (NPPA), pg 514
New Mexico Book Association (NMBA), pg 514
North American Agricultural Journalists (NAAJ), pg 515
North American Snowsports Journalists Association (NASJA), pg 515
Overseas Press Club of America (OPC), pg 516
Photographic Society of America® (PSA®), pg 516
Print Industries Market Information and Research Organization (PRIMIR), pg 517
Printing & Graphics Association MidAtlantic (PGAMA), pg 517
Printing Brokerage/Buyers Association International (PBBA), pg 517
Public Relations Society of America Inc, pg 518
Publishers' Publicity Association (PPA), pg 518
Society for Technical Communication (STC), pg 519
Society of Motion Picture and Television Engineers® (SMPTE®), pg 520
Society of Professional Journalists (SPJ), pg 520
Television Academy, pg 521
Writers' Guild of Alberta, pg 522

PUBLISHING

Alcuin Society, pg 493
AM&P Network, pg 494
American Academy of Political & Social Science (AAPSS), pg 494
American Christian Writers, pg 494
American Council on Education (ACE), pg 495
American Marketing Association, pg 495
American Photographic Artists (APA), pg 496
American Political Science Association (APSA), pg 496
American Speech-Language-Hearing Association (ASHA), pg 497
Asian American Writers' Workshop (AAWW), pg 497
Association nationale des editeurs de livres-ANEL (The National Association of Book Publishers), pg 498
Association of American Publishers (AAP), pg 498
The Association of Book Publishers of British Columbia (ABPBC), pg 499
Association of Canadian Publishers (ACP), pg 499
Association of Canadian University Presses, pg 499
Association of Catholic Publishers Inc, pg 499
Association of Community Publishers Inc (ACP), pg 499

The Association of English-
 Language Publishers of Quebec-
 AELAQ (Association des Editeurs
 de Langue Anglaise du Quebec),
 pg 499
Association of Publishers for
 Special Sales (APSS), pg 500
Association of University Presses
 (AUPresses), pg 500
The Baker Street Irregulars (BSI),
 pg 500
Bay Area Women in Publishing
 (BAWiP), pg 500
Book Industry Study Group Inc
 (BISG), pg 501
The Book Publishers Association of
 Alberta (BPAA), pg 501
Business Marketing NYC, pg 502
Canada Council for the Arts
 (Conseil des arts du Canada),
 pg 502
Canadian Institute for Studies in
 Publishing (CISP), pg 502
Canadian Publishers' Council
 (CPC), pg 502
Catholic Library Association,
 pg 503
The Center for Book Arts, pg 503
Chicago Women in Publishing
 (CWIP), pg 503
The Children's Book Council
 (CBC), pg 503
Council for Advancement &
 Support of Education (CASE),
 pg 504
Educational Book & Media
 Association (EBMA), pg 505
Evangelical Christian Publishers
 Association (ECPA), pg 505
Florida Authors and Publishers
 Association Inc (FAPA), pg 506
4A's (American Association of
 Advertising Agencies), pg 506
IBBY Canada, pg 507
The Independent Book Publishers
 Association (IBPA), pg 507
Independent Publishers of New
 England (IPNE), pg 508
International Society of Latino
 Authors (ISLA), pg 508
The International Women's Writing
 Guild (IWWG), pg 508
Linguistic Society of America
 (LSA), pg 509
The Literary Press Group of
 Canada, pg 509
Magazines Canada (MC), pg 510
Manitoba Arts Council (MAC),
 pg 510
Music Publishers Association
 (MPA), pg 511
National Association of Book
 Entrepreneurs (NABE), pg 511
National Association of Hispanic
 Publications Inc (NAHP), pg 511
National Education Association
 (NEA), pg 513
National Information Standards
 Organization (NISO), pg 513
National Music Publishers'
 Association (NMPA), pg 513
New Atlantic Independent
 Booksellers Association
 (NAIBA), pg 514
New Mexico Book Association
 (NMBA), pg 514
North American Snowsports
 Journalists Association (NASJA),
 pg 515
Ontario Book Publishers
 Organization (OBPO), pg 515

Ordre des traducteurs,
 terminologues et interpretes
 agrees du quebec (OTTIAQ),
 pg 515
Print Industries Market Information
 and Research Organization
 (PRIMIR), pg 517
Printing & Graphics Association
 MidAtlantic (PGAMA), pg 517
Printing Industries Association Inc
 of Southern California (PIASC),
 pg 517
Protestant Church-Owned Publishers
 Association, pg 518
Publishers Association of the West
 Inc (PubWest), pg 518
Social Sciences & Humanities
 Research Council (SSHRC),
 pg 519
Society for Features Journalism
 (SFJ), pg 519
Society for Scholarly Publishing
 (SSP), pg 519
Society for the History of
 Authorship, Reading &
 Publishing Inc (SHARP), pg 519
Software & Information Industry
 Association (SIIA), pg 520
Technical Association of the Pulp &
 Paper Industry (TAPPI), pg 521
The Word, A Storytelling Sanctuary
 Inc, pg 522
Writers' Alliance of Newfoundland
 & Labrador, pg 522
Writers & Publishers Network
 (WPN), pg 522
Writers' Guild of Alberta, pg 522

PUBLISHING SERVICES

Access Copyright, The Canadian
 Copyright Licensing Agency,
 pg 493
AIGA, the professional association
 for design, pg 493
Alliance for Audited Media (AAM),
 pg 493
American Book Producers
 Association (ABPA), pg 494
American Christian Writers, pg 494
American Society for Indexing Inc
 (ASI), pg 496
American Translators Association
 (ATA), pg 497
Association for PRINT
 Technologies (APTech), pg 498
Association nationale des editeurs
 de livres-ANEL (The National
 Association of Book Publishers),
 pg 498
Association of American Literary
 Agents Inc (AALA), pg 498
Association of Catholic Publishers
 Inc, pg 499
Association of Manitoba Book
 Publishers (AMBP), pg 499
Association of Publishers for
 Special Sales (APSS), pg 500
Book & Periodical Council (BPC),
 pg 501
BPA Worldwide, pg 501
Committee on Scholarly Editions,
 pg 504
Editorial Freelancers Association
 (EFA), pg 505
The Graphic Artists Guild Inc,
 pg 506
Gravure AIMCAL Alliance (GAA),
 pg 507
In-Plant Printing & Mailing
 Association (IPMA), pg 507

International Standard Book
 Numbering (ISBN) US Agency,
 A Cambridge Information Group
 Co, pg 508
The International Women's Writing
 Guild (IWWG), pg 508
ISBN Canada, pg 509
National Association of Book
 Entrepreneurs (NABE), pg 511
New Mexico Book Association
 (NMBA), pg 514
Northwest Independent Editors
 Guild, pg 515
Printing Industry Association of the
 South (PIAS), pg 517
Publishers Association of the West
 Inc (PubWest), pg 518

WRITERS

American Christian Writers, pg 494
American Medical Writers
 Association (AMWA), pg 495
American Society of Journalists and
 Authors (ASJA), pg 496
Asian American Writers' Workshop
 (AAWW), pg 497
Aspen Words, pg 497
Association of Writers & Writing
 Programs (AWP), pg 500
Authors Alliance, pg 500
The Authors Guild®, pg 500
Authors League Fund, pg 500
The Authors Registry Inc, pg 500
BMI®, pg 501
Boston Authors Club Inc, pg 501
Canada Council for the Arts
 (Conseil des arts du Canada),
 pg 502
Canadian Authors Association
 (CAA), pg 502
Canadian Society of Children's
 Authors, Illustrators & Performers
 (CANSCAIP), pg 503
Cascade Christian Writers (CCW),
 pg 503
The Center for Fiction, pg 503
Chicago Women in Publishing
 (CWIP), pg 503
Colorado Authors' League, pg 504
Connecticut Authors & Publishers
 Association (CAPA), pg 504
Council for the Advancement of
 Science Writing (CASW), pg 504
Dog Writers Association of America
 Inc (DWAA), pg 505
Education Writers Association
 (EWA), pg 505
Federation of BC Writers, pg 505
Florida Freelance Writers
 Association, pg 506
Florida Outdoor Writers Association
 Inc (FOWA), pg 506
Florida Writers Association Inc,
 pg 506
La Fondation Emile Nelligan,
 pg 506
GardenComm: Garden
 Communicators International,
 pg 506
Horror Writers Association (HWA),
 pg 507
IBBY Canada, pg 507
Independent Writers of Chicago
 (IWOC), pg 508
InScribe Christian Writers'
 Fellowship (ICWF), pg 508
International Association of Crime
 Writers Inc, North American
 Branch, pg 508
International Society of Latino
 Authors (ISLA), pg 508

The International Women's Writing
 Guild (IWWG), pg 508
The League of Canadian Poets,
 pg 509
League of Vermont Writers Inc,
 pg 509
Maine Writers & Publishers
 Alliance (MWPA), pg 510
Manitoba Arts Council (MAC),
 pg 510
Midwest Travel Journalists
 Association Inc (MTJA), pg 511
Mystery Writers of America
 (MWA), pg 511
National Association of Real Estate
 Editors (NAREE), pg 512
National Association of Science
 Writers Inc (NASW), pg 512
National League of American Pen
 Women Inc, pg 513
National Writers Association,
 pg 514
National Writers Union (NWU),
 pg 514
New Hampshire Writers' Project
 (NHWP), pg 514
New Mexico Book Association
 (NMBA), pg 514
News Leaders Association (NLA),
 pg 514
North American Snowsports
 Journalists Association (NASJA),
 pg 515
North Carolina Writers' Network,
 pg 515
Outdoor Writers Association of
 America (OWAA), pg 516
Palm Springs Writers Guild, pg 516
PEN America Los Angeles, pg 516
PEN America Washington, DC,
 pg 516
PEN Canada, pg 516
Playwrights Guild of Canada,
 pg 516
PNWA - a writer's resource, pg 517
Poets & Writers Inc, pg 517
Quebec Writers' Federation (QWF),
 pg 518
Romance Writers of America®,
 pg 518
Science Fiction and Fantasy Writers
 Association, Inc (SFWA), pg 518
SF Canada, pg 519
SK Arts, pg 519
Society for Advancing Business
 Editing and Writing (SABEW),
 pg 519
Society of American Travel Writers
 (SATW), pg 519
Society of Children's Book Writers
 & Illustrators (SCBWI), pg 520
The Society of Southwestern
 Authors (SSA), pg 520
Teachers & Writers Collaborative
 (T&W), pg 520
Texas Institute of Letters (TIL),
 pg 521
Western Writers of America Inc
 (WWA), pg 521
Willamette Writers, pg 521
Women Who Write Inc, pg 522
The Word, A Storytelling Sanctuary
 Inc, pg 522
Writers' Alliance of Newfoundland
 & Labrador, pg 522
Writers & Publishers Network
 (WPN), pg 522
Writers' Federation of Nova Scotia
 (WFNS), pg 522
Writers' Guild of Alberta, pg 522
Writers Guild of America, East
 (WGAE), pg 522

Writers Guild of America West (WGAW), pg 522
Writers' League of Texas (WLT), pg 523
The Writers' Union of Canada (TWUC), pg 523

Book Trade & Allied Associations

Listed here are associations and organizations that are concerned with books, literacy, language and speech, media and communications as well as groups who provide services to the publishing community.

AAAS, see American Association for the Advancement of Science (AAAS)

AAEC, see Association of American Editorial Cartoonists (AAEC)

AALA, see Association of American Literary Agents Inc (AALA)

AAM, see Alliance for Audited Media (AAM)

AAP, see Association of American Publishers (AAP)

AARWBA, see American Auto Racing Writers & Broadcasters (AARWBA)

AATIA, see Austin Area Translators & Interpreters Association (AATIA)

ABA, see American Booksellers Association

ABAC/ALAC
c/o 1938 Bloor St W, Toronto, ON M6P 3K8, Canada
Mailing Address: PO Box 30009, Toronto, ON M6P 4J2, Canada
E-mail: info@abac.org
Web Site: www.abac.org
Key Personnel
Pres: Robert Wright
Treas: Marvin Post
Secy: Karol Krysik
Founded: 1966
The association's aim is to foster an interest in rare books & mss & to maintain high standards in the antiquarian book trade.
Number of Members: 70
Membership(s): International League of Antiquarian Booksellers (ILAB)

The Academy of American Poets Inc
75 Maiden Lane, Suite 901, New York, NY 10038
Tel: 212-274-0343
E-mail: academy@poets.org
Web Site: poets.org
Key Personnel
Pres & Exec Dir: Ricardo Alberto Maldonado
VP, Digital Engagement & Content: Jeff Gleaves
Ad & Mktg Dir: Michelle Campagna
Dir, Donor Rel: Molly Walsh
Dir, Progs: Nikay Paredes
Founded: 1934
The nation's leading champion of poets & poetry with supporters in all 50 states. The organization annually awards more funds to individual poets than any other organization through its prize program, giving a total of $1.25 million to more than 200 poets at various stages of their careers. The organization also produces Poets.org, the world's largest publicly funded web site for poets & poetry; established & organizes National Poetry Month each April; publishes the popular Poem-a-Day series & *American Poets* magazine; provides award-winning resources to K-12 educators, including the Teach This Poem series; hosts an annual series of poetry readings & special events; co-ordinates a national Poetry Coalition working to promote the value poets bring to our culture.
Number of Members: 10,000
Publication(s): *American Poets* (2 issues/yr, magazine)

Academy of Motion Picture Arts & Sciences (AMPAS)
8949 Wilshire Blvd, Beverly Hills, CA 90211
Tel: 310-247-3000 *Fax:* 310-859-9619
E-mail: ampas@oscars.org
Web Site: www.oscars.org
Key Personnel
CEO: Dawn Hudson
Founded: 1927
To advance the arts & sciences of motion pictures & to foster cooperation among the creative leadership of the motion picture industry for cultural, educational & technological progress. Confer annual awards of merit, serving as a constant incentive within the industry & focusing public attention upon the best in motion pictures.
Number of Members: 5,024

Academy of Television Arts & Sciences (ATAS), see Television Academy

Access Copyright, The Canadian Copyright Licensing Agency
69 Younge St, Suite 1100, Toronto, ON M5E 1K3, Canada
Tel: 416-868-1620 *Toll Free Tel:* 800-893-5777
Fax: 416-868-1621
E-mail: info@accesscopyright.ca
Web Site: www.accesscopyright.ca
Key Personnel
Pres & CEO: Roanie Levy
Chief Busn Aff Offr: Claire Gillis
COO: Michael Andrews
Chief Revenue Offr: JD Methot
Gen Coun: Asma Faizi
Founded: 1988
Number of Members: 34
Membership(s): Book & Periodical Council; International Federation of Reproduction Rights Organizations (IFRRO)

ACUP/APUC, see Association of Canadian University Presses

ACUP+, see Association of College & University Printers

Advertising Research Foundation (ARF)
432 Park Ave S, 4th fl, New York, NY 10016
Tel: 212-751-5656 *Fax:* 212-689-1859
E-mail: membership@thearf.org; new-member-info@thearf.org
Web Site: thearf.org
Key Personnel
Pres & CEO: Scott McDonald, PhD
CFO: Elyssa Rubin
Chief Growth Offr: Michael Heitner
Chief Res Offr: Paul Donato
SVP, Events: Rachael Feigenbaum
Founded: 1936
Advertising research service trade association.
Number of Members: 400
Publication(s): *Journal of Advertising Research (JAR)* (quarterly, print & online, free to membs, $375/yr nonmembs)

AIGA, the professional association for design
228 Park Ave S, Suite 58603, New York, NY 10003
Tel: 212-807-1990
E-mail: general@aiga.org
Web Site: www.aiga.org
Key Personnel
COO: Amy Chapman *Tel:* 212-710-3137
Exec Dir: Bennie F Johnson *Tel:* 212-710-3100
Sr Dir, Membership: Karen Kiell *Tel:* 212-710-3123
Dir, Digital Opers: Tiia Schurig *Tel:* 212-710-3134
Dir, Mktg: Michelle Koenigsknecht *Tel:* 212-710-3138
Founded: 1914
National nonprofit organization for graphic design profession. Organizes competitions, exhibitions, publications, educational activities & projects in the public interest to promote excellence in the graphic design industry.
Number of Members: 15,000
New Election: Annually in June
2025 Meeting(s): AIGA Design Conference, Los Angeles, CA, Oct 9-11, 2025

AIIM International, see Association for Intelligent Information Management (AIIM)

ALA, see The American Library Association (ALA)

Alcuin Society
PO Box 3216, Sta Terminal, Vancouver, BC V6B 3X8, Canada
Tel: 604-732-5403
E-mail: info@alcuinsociety.com; awards@alcuinsociety.com
Web Site: alcuinsociety.com
Key Personnel
Chair, Book Design Competition: Spencer Stuart
Founded: 1965
Judges book design; publishes articles on book arts, collecting, typography, private presses, book collections, book binding.
Number of Members: 325
Publication(s): *Amphora* (3 issues/yr, journal, $50/yr membs, $75 instns)

Alliance for Audited Media (AAM)
4513 Lincoln Ave, Suite 105B, Lisle, IL 60532
Tel: 224-366-6939 *Toll Free Tel:* 800-285-2220
E-mail: corpcomm@auditedmedia.com
Web Site: auditedmedia.com
Key Personnel
Pres, CEO & Mng Dir: Tom Drouillard
EVP, Audit Servs: Scott Hanson
EVP, Busn Innovation: Mark Wachowicz
EVP, Commercial Devt: Brian Condon
Founded: 1914 (as Audit Bureau of Circulations)
Cooperative association of advertisers, advertising agencies & publishers of newspapers, magazines, farm & business publications. Audit & report circulation, web site & additional digital

BOOK TRADE & ALLIED ASSOCIATIONS

edition analytics, including mobile application activity for publisher brands in North America.
Number of Members: 4,500
Branch Office(s)
20 Bloor St E, PO Box 75066, Toronto, ON M4W 3T3, Canada *Tel:* 647-793-7341

Alliance for Women in Media (AWM)
2365 Harrodsburg Rd, A325, Lexington, KY 40504
Tel: 202-750-3664 *Fax:* 202-750-3664
E-mail: info@allwomeninmedia.org
Web Site: allwomeninmedia.org
Key Personnel
Pres: Becky Brooks *E-mail:* becky.brooks@allwomeninmedia.org
Events Dir: Lisa Stephenson *E-mail:* lisa.stephenson@allwomeninmedia.org
Awards & Proj Mgr: LaTonya Jackson *E-mail:* latonya.jackson@allwomeninmedia.org
Mktg & Memb Engagement Mgr: Amy Burton *E-mail:* amy.burton@allwomeninmedia.org
Founded: 1951
For members of the electronic & media industries.
Number of Members: 3,000
Publication(s): *FastForward* (2 issues/mo, enewsletter)

AM&P Network
Division of Software & Information Industry Network (SIIA)
1620 "I" St NW, Suite 501, Washington, DC 20005
Tel: 202-289-7442 *Fax:* 202-289-7097
Web Site: www.siia.net/amp-network
Key Personnel
Edit Dir: Ronn Levine *Tel:* 202-789-4491 *E-mail:* rlevine@siia.net
Founded: 1963 (as Society of National Association Publications)
Members are subscription-based publishers representing small & large companies. Activities include e-mail, marketing, technical developments, copyright, business practices & editorial development.
Number of Members: 200
Meeting(s): AMPLIFY Content & Marketing Summit, annually in June

American Academy of Arts & Sciences (AAAS)
136 Irving St, Cambridge, MA 02138
Tel: 617-576-5000 *Fax:* 617-576-5050
E-mail: aaas@amacad.org
Web Site: www.amacad.org
Key Personnel
Chief Communs Offr: Alison Franklin *Tel:* 617-576-5043 *E-mail:* afranklin@amacad.org
COO: Mark Robinson *Tel:* 617-576-5023 *E-mail:* mrobinson@amacad.org
Chief Prog Offr: Tania Munz *Tel:* 617-576-5031 *E-mail:* tmunz@amacad.org
Pres: David W Oxtoby *Tel:* 617-576-5010 *E-mail:* president@amacad.org
Founded: 1780
Promote interchange of ideas through seminars & publications.
Number of Members: 6,068
Publication(s): *Daedalus*

American Academy of Political & Social Science (AAPSS)
220 S 40 St, Suite 201-E, Philadelphia, PA 19104-3543
Tel: 215-746-6500 *Fax:* 215-573-2667
Web Site: www.aapss.org
Key Personnel
Exec Dir: Tom Kecskemethy *Tel:* 215-746-7321 *E-mail:* thomask@asc.upenn.edu
Prog Mgr: Jessica Erfer *E-mail:* jessica.erfer@asc.upenn.edu

Digital Coord: Hannah Fields
Founded: 1889
Promotes the use of social science in the public domain & in policymaking.
Publication(s): *The Annals of the American Academy of Political and Social Science* (6 issues/yr, $138/yr indiv print, $1,275/yr instn print)

American Antiquarian Society (AAS)
185 Salisbury St, Worcester, MA 01609-1634
Tel: 508-755-5221 *Fax:* 508-754-9069
E-mail: library@mwa.org
Web Site: www.americanantiquarian.org
Key Personnel
Pres: Scott E Casper *Tel:* 508-471-2161 *E-mail:* scasper@mwa.org
VP, Advancement: Beth Kopley *Tel:* 508-471-2162 *E-mail:* bkopley@mwa.org
VP, Collections: Lauren B Hewes *Tel:* 508-471-2124 *E-mail:* lhewes@mwa.org
VP, Fin & Admin: Kristen Balash *Tel:* 508-471-2167 *E-mail:* kbalash@mwa.org
VP, Progs & Dir, Fellowships: Nan Wolverton *Tel:* 508-471-2119 *E-mail:* nwolverton@mwa.org
Founded: 1812
National research library of American history & culture through 1876.
Number of Members: 1,028
Publication(s): *Almanac* (2 issues/yr, newsletter)

American Association for the Advancement of Science (AAAS)
1200 New York Ave NW, Washington, DC 20005
Tel: 202-326-6400
E-mail: membership@aaas.org
Web Site: www.aaas.org
Key Personnel
CEO: Sudip Parikh
Chief Communs Offr: Tal Woliner
CFO: Tanisha Lewis
Chief Prog Offr: Julia MacKenzie
Sr Dir, Membership: Marietta Damond
Founded: 1848
Mission is to further the work of scientists, to facilitate cooperation among them, foster scientific freedom & responsibility, improve effectiveness of science in the promotion of human welfare & to increase public understanding & appreciation of the importance & promise of the methods of science in human progress. There are many membership organizations & professional societies which have similar aims or have interest in supporting these objectives. US regional divisions: Arctic; Caribbean; Pacific; Southwest & Rocky Mountains.
New Election: Annually in the Fall
2025 Meeting(s): Annual Meeting, Hynes Convention Center, 900 Boylston St, Boston, MA, Feb 13-15, 2025
Publication(s): *Science* (weekly, journal, $15/issue); *Science Advances* (journal); *Science Immunology* (journal); *Science Robotics* (journal); *Science Signaling* (journal); *Science Translational Medicine* (journal)

American Auto Racing Writers & Broadcasters (AARWBA)
922 N Pass Ave, Burbank, CA 91505-2703
Tel: 818-842-7005 *Fax:* 818-842-7020
E-mail: aarwba.pres@gmail.com
Web Site: aarwba.org
Key Personnel
Pres: Ms Dusty Brandel
Organization of media members devoted to auto racing coverage.
Number of Members: 300

American Book Producers Association (ABPA)
7 Peter Cooper Rd, No 7G, New York, NY 10010
E-mail: office@abpaonline.org

ASSOCIATIONS, EVENTS

Web Site: www.abpaonline.org
Key Personnel
Pres: Susan Knopf *E-mail:* president@abpaonline.org
VP & Treas: Nancy Hall
Bd of Dirs: Kelli Chipponeri; Dinah Dunn; Jan Hartman; Chris Navratil; Tim Palin; Diane Lindsey Reeves; Richard Rothschild
Founded: 1980
An organization of independent book producing companies in the US & CN.
Number of Members: 60
Publication(s): *Booknews* (membs only)

American Booksellers Association
600 Mamaroneck Ave, Suite 400, Harrison, NY 10528
Tel: 914-406-7500 *Toll Free Tel:* 800-637-0037 *Fax:* 914-417-4013
E-mail: info@bookweb.org
Web Site: www.bookweb.org
Key Personnel
CEO: Allison Hill
COO: Joy Dallanegra-Sanger *E-mail:* joy@bookweb.org
CFO: PK Sindwani
Chief Communs Offr: Ray Daniels *E-mail:* ray@bookweb.org
Meetings & Planning Offr: Jill Perlstein *E-mail:* jill@bookweb.org
Dir, Devt & Publr Rel: Matthew Zoni *E-mail:* matthew@bookweb.org
Dir, Educ: Kim Hooyboer *E-mail:* kim@bookweb.org
Dir, Membership: Ryan Quinn *E-mail:* ryan@bookweb.org
Dir, Public Policy & Advocacy: David Grogan *E-mail:* dave@bookweb.org
Technol Dir: Greg Galloway *E-mail:* greg@bookweb.org
Sr Mgr, IndieCommerce: Geetha Nathan *E-mail:* geetha@bookweb.org
ABC Group Mgr: Gen de Botton *E-mail:* gen@bookweb.org
DEIA Memb Rel Mgr: Elisa Thomas *E-mail:* elisa@bookweb.org
Memb Rel & DEIA Mgr: Mariana Calderon
Memb Rel Mgr & Data Coord: Sara Lacey Graham
Educ Mgr: Lisa Winn
Mktg Mgr: Courtney Wallace *E-mail:* courtneywallace@bookweb.org
Memb Rel & Engagement Mgr: Kamilah Clarke
Prodn Mgr: Kate Brennan
Prog Mgr: Peter Reynolds *E-mail:* peter@bookweb.org; Jessica Stauffer
Advocacy Assoc Mgr: Philomena Polefrone
Content Coord: Zoe Perzo
Educ Proj Coord: Cassie Youngstrom
Meetings & Off Coord: Maria Rodriguez
Memb Rel & Registration Coord: Cedar Fields
Lead Instrl Designer: Preethi Kannath
Educ Specialist: Emily Nason
Founded: 1900
Trade organization representing independent booksellers.
Number of Members: 3,500
Publication(s): *Book Buyers Handbook* (electronic); *Bookselling This Week* (electronic)

American Christian Writers
4854 Aster Dr, Nashville, TN 37211
Tel: 615-331-8668; 615-498-8630
E-mail: acwriters@aol.com
Web Site: acwriters.com
Key Personnel
Pres: Reg A Forder
Founded: 1988
Membership(s): Evangelical Christian Publishers Association (ECPA); Evangelical Press Association (EPA); Global Network of Christian Ministries

American Civil Liberties Union (ACLU)
125 Broad St, 18th fl, New York, NY 10004
Tel: 212-549-2500
E-mail: media@aclu.org
Web Site: www.aclu.org
Key Personnel
Pres: Deborah Archer
Chief Communs Offr: Rebecca Lowell Edwards
Chief Devt Offr: Mark Wier
Exec Dir: Anthony D Romero
Deputy Exec Dir: Dorothy M Ehrlich
Deputy Exec Dir, Opers & Gen Coun: Terence Dougherty
Protection of constitutional rights & civil liberties through litigation, legislative lobbying & public education; 54 local offices across the US.
Number of Members: 1,700,000
Publication(s): *ACLU Magazine* (free to membs)

American Council on Education (ACE)
One Dupont Circle NW, Washington, DC 20036
Tel: 202-939-9300
Web Site: www.acenet.edu
Key Personnel
Chief Learning & Innovation Offr: Louis Soares
Pres: Ted Mitchell
SVP, Educ Futures: Derrick Anderson
    E-mail: danderson@acenet.edu
VP & Chief of Staff: Jessie Brown
    E-mail: jbrown@acenet.edu
VP & Gen Coun: Peter McDonough
Asst VP & Exec Dir, ACE Connect: Gailda Pitre Davis
Founded: 1918
Membership organization that mobilizes the higher education community to shape effective public policy & foster innovative, high-quality practice.
Number of Members: 1,700
Meeting(s): ACE Experience, Washington, DC

American Forest & Paper Association (AF&PA)
1101 "K" St NW, Suite 700, Washington, DC 20005
Tel: 202-463-2700
E-mail: info@afandpa.org; comm@afandpa.org
Web Site: www.afandpa.org
Key Personnel
Pres & CEO: Heidi Brock
VP, Gen Coun & Corp Secy: Jan A Poling
VP, Govt Aff: Eric Steiner
VP, Indus Aff: Terry Webber
VP, Public Policy: Paul Noe
VP, Strategic Communs: Lindsay Murphy
VP, Strategy & Opers: Elizabeth Vandersarl
Dir, Communs & Press Secy: Tim Ebner
Founded: 1993
National trade association of the paper & wood products industry.
Number of Members: 119

American Institute of Graphic Arts, see AIGA, the professional association for design

American Jewish Committee (AJC)
Affiliate of Institute of Human Relations
Mail Code 6760, PO Box 7247, Philadelphia, PA 19170-0001
Tel: 212-751-4000 *Fax:* 212-891-1450
E-mail: social@ajc.org
Web Site: www.ajc.org
Key Personnel
CEO: David A Harris
CFO: Richard Hyne
Chief Devt Offr: Julie Schair
Chief HR & Strategy Offr: Janet Besso Becker
Pres: Michael L Tichnor
Mng Dir, Leadership: Nadine Greenfield-Binstock
Mng Dir, Mktg & Communs: Jon Schweitzer
Sr Dir, Admin & Global Aff: Melissa Weinberg Spence
Dir, Media Rel: Kenneth Bandler
Founded: 1906
Civic & religious rights of Jews in the US & abroad; intergroup relations & human rights.
Number of Members: 43,000

The American Library Association (ALA)
225 N Michigan Ave, Suite 1300, Chicago, IL 60601
SAN: 201-0062
Tel: 312-944-6780; 312-280-4299 (memb & cust serv) *Toll Free Tel:* 800-545-2433 *Fax:* 312-440-9374
E-mail: ala@ala.org; customerservice@ala.org
Web Site: www.ala.org
Key Personnel
Chief IT Offr: Rebecca Headrick
Founded: 1876
The foremost national organization providing resources to inspire library & information professionals to transform their communities through essential programs & services. Form more than 140 years, the ALA has been the trusted voice for academic, public, school, government & special libraries, advocating for the profession & the library's role in enhancing learning & ensuring access to information for all.
Number of Members: 51,000
2025 Meeting(s): LibLearnX: The Library Learning Experience, Phoenix Convention Center, 100 N Third St, Phoenix, AZ, Jan 24-27, 2025; National Library Week, Nationwide throughout the USA, April 6-12, 2025; Annual Conference & Exhibition, Philadelphia, PA, June 26-July 1, 2025
2026 Meeting(s): National Library Week, Nationwide throughout the USA, April 19-25, 2026; Annual Conference & Exhibition, Chicago, IL, June 25-30, 2026
2027 Meeting(s): Annual Conference & Exhibition, New Orleans, LA, June 24-29, 2027
2028 Meeting(s): Annual Conference & Exhibition, Denver, CO, June 22-27, 2028
Publication(s): *American Libraries* (6 issues/yr, magazine, free to membs, $70/yr instns US & CN, $80/yr instns foreign)
Branch Office(s)
1615 New Hampshire Ave NW, 1st fl, Washington, DC 20009-2520, Assoc Exec Dir: Kathi Kromer *Tel:* 202-628-8410 *Toll Free Tel:* 800-941-8478 *Fax:* 202-628-8419
E-mail: kkromer@alawash.org

American Literacy Council
c/o Los Alamos National Laboratory, Los Alamos, NM 87545
E-mail: questions@americanliteracy.com
Web Site: www.americanliteracy.com
Key Personnel
Pres: Mark Petersen
VP: Robert J McGehee
Secy/Treas: Jim Campbell
Founded: 1876
To convey information on new solutions, innovative technologies & tools for engaging more boldly in the battle for literacy.

American Literary Translators Association (ALTA)
University of Arizona, Esquire Bldg, No 205, 1230 N Park Ave, Tucson, AZ 85721
Tel: 520-621-1757
E-mail: info@literarytranslators.org
Web Site: www.literarytranslators.org
Key Personnel
Communs & Awards Mgr: Rachael Daum
    Tel: 413-200-0459 *E-mail:* rachaeldaum@literarytranslators.org
Prog Dir: Kelsi Vanada *E-mail:* kelsi@literarytranslators.org
Founded: 1978
Literary translation & translators. ALTA's programs are supported in part by a grant from the National Endowment for the Arts.
Number of Members: 800

American Marketing Association
130 E Randolph St, 22nd fl, Chicago, IL 60601
Tel: 312-542-9000 *Toll Free Tel:* 800-AMA-1150 (262-1150)
Web Site: www.ama.org
Key Personnel
CEO: Russ Klein *E-mail:* rklein@ama.org
COO: Jeremy Van Ek *E-mail:* jvanek@ama.org
Chief Alliances Offr: Barbara Grobicki
    E-mail: bgrobicki@ama.org
Chief Content Offr: Andy Friedman
    E-mail: afriedman@ama.org
Chief Experience Offr: Jennifer Severns
    E-mail: jseverns@ama.org
Dir, Integrated Academic Content: Matt Weingarden *Tel:* 312-542-9012 *E-mail:* mweingarden@ama.org
Founded: 1937
A nonprofit, educational institution. Offers online marketing info. Sponsors seminars, conferences & student marketing clubs & doctoral consortium. Publish books, journals, magazines & proceedings of conferences.
Number of Members: 30,000
Publication(s): *Journal of International Marketing* (quarterly); *Journal of Marketing* (6 issues/yr); *Journal of Marketing Research* (6 issues/yr); *Journal of Public Policy & Marketing* (2 issues/yr); *Marketing News* (monthly)

American Medical Association (AMA)
AMA Plaza, 330 N Wabash, Suite 39300, Chicago, IL 60611-5885
Tel: 312-464-5000 *Toll Free Tel:* 800-621-8335
E-mail: media@ama-assn.org (media & edit)
Web Site: www.ama-assn.org; www.jamanetwork.org
Key Personnel
EVP & CEO: James L Madara, MD
Chief Strategy Offr & Chair, Operating Comm: Kenneth J Sharigian
SVP & Chief Communs Offr: Rodrigo A Sierra
SVP & CFO: Denise M Hagerty
SVP & Chief Experience Offr: Todd Unger
SVP & Chief Health Equity Offr: Aletha Maybank, MD
SVP & CIO: Susan Malisch
SVP & Chief Mission Offr, Publg: Thomas J Easley
SVP & Gen Coun: Andra Heller
SVP & Ed-in-Chief, Scientific Pubns: Kirsten Bibbins-Domingo, PhD
SVP, HR & Corp Servs: Toni Canada
Group VP & Publr: Brian Shields
Founded: 1847
Promotes the science & art of medicine & betterment of public health. Association of physicians.
Publication(s): *JAMA Cardiology* (monthly); *JAMA Dermatology* (monthly); *JAMA Health Forum* (weekly, online, open access); *JAMA Internal Medicine* (monthly); *JAMA Neurology* (monthly); *JAMA Oncology* (monthly); *JAMA Ophthalmology* (monthly); *JAMA Otolaryngology-Head & Neck Surgery* (monthly); *JAMA Pediatrics* (monthly); *JAMA Psychiatry* (monthly); *JAMA Surgery* (monthly); *JAMA: The Journal of the American Medical Association* (48 issues/yr)
Branch Office(s)
119 Cherry Hill Rd, Parsippany, NJ 07054

American Medical Writers Association (AMWA)
9841 Washingtonian Blvd, Suite 500-26, Gaithersburg, MD 20878
Tel: 240-238-0940 *Fax:* 301-294-9006

E-mail: amwa@amwa.org
Web Site: www.amwa.org
Key Personnel
Exec Dir: Susan Krug *Tel:* 240-238-0940 ext 109
  E-mail: skrug@amwa.org
Deputy Dir: Shari Rager *Tel:* 240-238-0940 ext 107 *E-mail:* srager@amwa.org
Dir, Membership & Systems: Sharon L Ruckdeschel *Tel:* 240-238-0940 ext 111
  E-mail: sharon@amwa.org
Educ & Events Coord: Angelique Mize *Tel:* 240-238-0940 ext 112 *E-mail:* angelique@amwa.org
Mktg & Communs Coord: Mary Rosenbaum *Tel:* 240-238-0940 ext 103 *E-mail:* mary@amwa.org
Founded: 1940
Professional organization for writers, editors & other communicators of medical information.
Number of Members: 4,500
2025 Meeting(s): Medical Writing & Communication Conference, Sheraton Phoenix Downtown Hotel, 340 N Third St, Phoenix, AZ, Nov 5-8, 2025
Publication(s): *AMWA Journal* (quarterly, journal, free to membs, $75/yr nonmembs); *Freelance Directory* (online, directory, free); *Jobs Online* (monthly, classified listing)

American Photographic Artists (APA)
5042 Wilshire Blvd, No 321, Los Angeles, CA 90036
E-mail: membershiprep@apanational.org
Web Site: apanational.org
Key Personnel
Natl Exec Dir: Juliette Wolf-Robin
  E-mail: executivedirector@apanational.com
Communs Specialist: Polly Gaillard
  E-mail: polly@apanational.com
Founded: 1981 (as Advertising Photographers of America)
Not-for-profit association for professional photographers. Members include professional photographers, photo assistants, educators & students as well as professionals engaged in fields associated with photography, advertising, or visual arts. Chapters in Atlanta, Charlotte, Chicago, Los Angeles, New York, San Diego, San Francisco & Washington, DC.

American Political Science Association (APSA)
1527 New Hampshire Ave NW, Washington, DC 20036-1203
Tel: 202-483-2512 *Fax:* 202-483-2657
E-mail: apsa@apsanet.org; membership@apsanet.org; press@apsanet.org
Web Site: www.apsanet.org
Key Personnel
Exec Dir: Steven Rathgeb Smith
  E-mail: smithsr@apsanet.org
Sr Dir, Communs, Info & Opers: Dan Gibson
  E-mail: dgibson@apsanet.org
Sr Dir, Mktg & Communs: Karima D Scott
  E-mail: kscott@apsanet.org
Dir, Meetings & Events: Kristin Kessler
  E-mail: kkessler@apsanet.org
Dir, Memb Servs: Casey Harrigan
  E-mail: charrigan@apsanet.org
Founded: 1903
Provide services to facilitate research, teaching & professional development in political science, including publications & services to assist college faculty, graduate students & researchers.
Number of Members: 15,000
2025 Meeting(s): Annual Meeting & Exhibition, Vancouver, BC, CN, Sept 11-14, 2025
Publication(s): *American Political Science Review* (quarterly); *The Journal of Political Science Education* (quarterly); *Perspectives on Politics* (quarterly); *PS: Political Science & Politics* (quarterly)

American Printing History Association
PO Box 4519, Grand Central Sta, New York, NY 10163
E-mail: secretary@printinghistory.org
Web Site: printinghistory.org
Key Personnel
Pres: J Fernando Pena
VP, Membership: Harold Kyle
VP, Progs: Danelle Moon
VP, Pubns: Josef Beery
Secy: Meghan Constantinou
Treas: David Goodrich
Exec Secy: Lyndsi Barnes
Local chapters in New York City, Upstate New York, New England, Chicago, IL, Chesapeake, VA, Ohio River Valley, Southern & Northern California.
Number of Members: 700
New Election: Annually in Jan
Meeting(s): Annual Conference
Publication(s): *Printing History* (2 issues/yr, journal)

American Public Human Services Association (APHSA)
1300 17 St N, Suite 340, Arlington, VA 22209-3801
Tel: 202-682-0100 *Fax:* 202-289-6555
E-mail: memberservice@aphsa.org
Web Site: www.aphsa.org
Key Personnel
COO: Ray Davidson *Tel:* 202-866-0572
  E-mail: rdavidson@aphsa.org
Pres & CEO: Tracy Wareing Evans
  E-mail: twareing@aphsa.org
Dir, Communs: Jessica Garon *Tel:* 202-866-0535
  E-mail: jgaron@aphsa.org
Dir, Engagement Opers & Mktg: Guy DeSilva
  Tel: 202-866-0557 *E-mail:* gdesilva@aphsa.org
Dir, Membership & Events: Donna Jarvis-Miller
  Tel: 202-866-0569 *E-mail:* djarvis-miller@aphsa.org
Founded: 1930
Membership organization representing state & local health & human services agencies through top-level leadership.
Number of Members: 5,000
New Election: Annually in Dec
Publication(s): *The Connection* (2 issues/mo, enewsletter, free); *Policy & Practice* (6 issues/yr, magazine, free to membs); *This Week in Washington* (weekly when Congress is in session, enewsletter, free)

American Society for Indexing Inc (ASI)
1628 E Southern Ave, Suite 9-223, Tempe, AZ 85282
Tel: 480-245-6750
E-mail: info@asindexing.org
Web Site: www.asindexing.org
Key Personnel
Exec Dir: Gwen Henson *E-mail:* gwen@asindexing.org
Founded: 1968
Educational programs for indexing field.
Number of Members: 450
New Election: Annually in May
Publication(s): *KeyWords* (electronic, monthly, journal, free to membs, $40 nonmembs)

American Society of Composers, Authors & Publishers (ASCAP)
250 W 57 St, New York, NY 10107
Tel: 212-621-6000 *Toll Free Tel:* 800-952-7227 (cust serv) *Fax:* 212-621-6595
Web Site: www.ascap.com
Key Personnel
Chmn of the Bd & Pres: Paul Williams
CEO: Elizabeth Matthews
EVP & COO: Brian Roberts
EVP & Chief Mktg Offr: Lauren Iossa
  E-mail: liossa@ascap.com
EVP & CTO: Tristan Boutros
EVP, Membership & Chief Creative Officer: John Titta
Founded: 1914
License nondramatic right of public performance of members' copyrighted musical compositions & distribute royalties to members on basis of performances. Members are composers, songwriters, lyricists & music publishers.
Number of Members: 850,000
Branch Office(s)
7920 W Sunset Blvd, 3rd fl, Los Angeles, CA 90046 *Tel:* 323-883-1000 *Fax:* 323-883-1049
420 Lincoln Rd, Miami Beach, FL 33139 *Tel:* 305-673-3446
950 Joseph E Lowery Blvd NW, Suite 23, Atlanta, GA 30318 *Tel:* 404-685-8699 *Fax:* 404-685-8701
623 Calle Hillside, San Juan, PR 00920 *Tel:* 787-707-0782 *Fax:* 787-707-0783
Two Music Sq W, Nashville, TN 37203 *Tel:* 615-742-5000 *Fax:* 615-742-5020
4 Millbank, 2nd fl, London SW1P 3JA, United Kingdom *Tel:* (020) 7439 0909 *Fax:* (020) 7434 0073

American Society of Journalists and Authors (ASJA)
355 Lexington Ave, 15th fl, New York, NY 10017-6603
Tel: 212-997-0947
E-mail: asjaoffice@asja.org
Web Site: asja.org
Key Personnel
Exec Dir: James Brannigan
Founded: 1948
Service organization providing exchange of ideas & market information. Regular meetings with speakers from the industry, annual writers conference; medical plans available. Professional referral service, annual membership directory; first amendment advocacy group.
Number of Members: 1,400
Meeting(s): American Society of Journalists and Authors Annual Writers Conference
Publication(s): *ASJA Magazine* (quarterly, print & online, membs only); *ASJA Weekly* (enewsletter, membs only)

American Society of Magazine Editors (ASME)
23 Barnabas Rd, Suite 34, Hawleyville, CT 06440-0034
Tel: 212-872-3737
E-mail: asme@asme.media
Web Site: www.asme.media
Key Personnel
Exec Dir: Sidney Holt *Tel:* 212-872-3723
  E-mail: sholt@asme.media
Dir, Opers: Nina Fortuna *E-mail:* nfortuna@asme.media
Founded: 1963
The principal organization for the editorial leaders of magazines & web sites published in the US. ASME strives to safeguard the First Amendment, support the development of journalism & defend the editorial integrity of print & digital publications. ASME sponsors the National Magazine Awards in association with the Columbia Journalism School, conducts training programs for reporters & editors & publishes the ASME Guidelines for Editors & Publishers. Members include digital-media editors as well as print-magazine editors.
Number of Members: 400
New Election: Annually in April

American Society of Media Photographers Inc
Four Embarcadero Ctr, Suite 1400, San Francisco, CA 94111
Toll Free Tel: 844-762-3386
Web Site: asmp.org

Key Personnel
CEO: James Edmund Datri *E-mail:* jdatri@asmp.org
Gen Coun & Head, Natl Content & Educ: Thomas Maddrey *E-mail:* maddrey@asmp.org
Founded: 1944
Maintain & promote high professional standards & ethics in photography; cultivate mutual understanding among professional photographers; protect & promote interests of photographers whose work is for publication.
Number of Members: 5,785
Publication(s): *The ASMP Guide to New Markets in Photography* ($29.70); *ASMP Professional Business Practices in Photography, 7th ed* ($33.95); *Digital Photography Best Practices & Workflow Handbook*
Branch Office(s)
1629 "K" St NW, Suite 300, Washington, DC 20006
539 W Commerce St, Suite 6350, Dallas, TX 75208

American Sociological Association (ASA)
1430 "K" St NW, Suite 600, Washington, DC 20005-4701
Tel: 202-383-9005
E-mail: asa@asanet.org; communications@asanet.org; membership@asanet.org
Web Site: www.asanet.org
Key Personnel
Exec Dir: Nancy Kidd *Tel:* 202-247-9855 *E-mail:* nkidd@asanet.org
Deputy Dir: Margaret Weigers Vitullo *Tel:* 202-247-9862 *E-mail:* mvitullo@asanet.org
Dir, Communs: Preeti Vasishtha *Tel:* 202-247-9872 *E-mail:* pvasishtha@asanet.org
Dir, Governance & Admin: Mark Fernando *Tel:* 202-247-9866 *E-mail:* mfernando@asanet.org
Dir, Membership: Hedy Ross *Tel:* 202-247-9865 *E-mail:* hross@asanet.org
Dir, Pubns: Karen Gray Edwards *Tel:* 202-247-9858 *E-mail:* edwards@asanet.org
Dir, Res, Prof Devt & Academic Aff: Erynn Masi de Casanova *Tel:* 202-247-9840 *E-mail:* ecasanova@asanet.org
Founded: 1905
Nonprofit membership association dedicated to advancing sociology as a scientific discipline & profession serving the public good. Encompass sociologists who are faculty members at colleges & universities, researchers, practitioners & students.
Number of Members: 13,000
New Election: Annually, April-May
2025 Meeting(s): Annual Meeting, Hilton San Francisco Union Square & Parc 55, San Francisco, CA, Aug 8-12, 2025
2026 Meeting(s): Annual Meeting, Hilton New York Midtown & Sheraton New York Times Square, New York, NY, Aug 7-11, 2026
2027 Meeting(s): Annual Meeting, Hyatt Regency Chicago & Swissotel, Chicago, IL, Aug 6-10, 2027
Publication(s): *American Sociological Review* (6 issues/yr, journal, free online to membs, $836 instns (print & online), $752 instns (online only), $819 instns (print only); *Contemporary Sociology* (6 issues/yr, journal, free online to membs, $666 instns (print & online), $599 instns (online only), $653 instns (print only); *Contexts* (quarterly, magazine, free online to membs, $390 instns (print & online), $352 instns (online only), $382 instns (print only); *Footnotes* (quarterly, magazine, free online to membs); *Journal of Health and Social Behavior* (quarterly, free online to membs, $592 instns (print & online), $533 instns (online only), $580 instns (print only); *Social Psychology Quarterly* (quarterly, journal, free online to membs, $592 instns (print & online), $533 instns (online only), $580 instns (print only); *Sociological Methodology* (2 issues/yr, journal, free online to membs, $592 instns (print & online), $533 instns (online only), $580 instns (print only); *Sociological Theory* (quarterly, journal, free online to membs, $592 instns (print & online), $533 instns (online only), $580 instns (print only); *Sociology of Education* (quarterly, journal, free online to membs, $592 instns (print & online), $533 instns (online only), $580 instns (print only); *Socius* (journal, online only, open access); *Teaching Sociology* (quarterly, journal, free online to membs, $592 instns (print & online), $533 instns (online only), $580 instns (print only)

American Speech-Language-Hearing Association (ASHA)
2200 Research Blvd, Rockville, MD 20850-3289
Tel: 301-296-5700 *Toll Free Tel:* 800-638-8255 (nonmembs); 800-498-2071 (membs)
Fax: 301-296-5777; 301-296-8580
E-mail: actioncenter@asha.org
Web Site: www.asha.org
Founded: 1925
Membership organization for speech-language pathologists & audiologists. Provide consumers with information & referral on speech, language & hearing. Publish information brochures & packets.
Number of Members: 223,000
New Election: Annually in Sept
Publication(s): *American Journal of Audiology (AJA)* (quarterly, journal, $15/single article for 24 hours, $30 for entire site for 24 hours, $118/yr online nonmembs, $292/yr online instns, $163/yr online archive nonmembs & instns); *American Journal of Speech-Language Pathology (AJSLP)* (6 issues/yr, journal, $15/single article for 24 hours, $30 for entire site for 24 hours, $124/yr online nonmembs, $350/yr online instns, $201/yr online archive nonmembs & instns); *The ASHA Leader* (6 issues/yr, magazine, $76/yr membs, $101/yr foreign nonmembs, $114/yr instns, $143/yr foreign instns); *Journal of Speech, Language & Hearing Research (JSLHR)* (monthly, journal, $15/single article for 24 hours, $30 for entire site for 24 hours, $249/yr online nonmembs, $701/yr online instns, $470/yr online archive nonmembs & instns); *Language, Speech & Hearing Services In Schools (LSHSS)* (quarterly, journal, $15/single article for 24 hours, $30 for entire site for 24 hours, $118/yr online nonmembs, $292/yr online instns, $201/yr online archive nonmembs & instns); *Perspectives of the ASHA Special Interest Groups* (electronic, journal, $325/yr online nonmembs, $489/yr online insts, $408/yr online archive nonmembs, $816/yr online archive instns)
Branch Office(s)
444 N Capitol St NW, Suite 715, Washington, DC 20001 *Tel:* 202-624-5884

American Translators Association (ATA)
211 N Union St, Suite 100, Alexandria, VA 22314
Tel: 703-683-6100 *Fax:* 703-778-7222
E-mail: ata@atanet.org
Web Site: www.atanet.org
Key Personnel
Exec Dir: Kelli C Baxter *Tel:* 703-683-6100 ext 3010 *E-mail:* kelli@atanet.org
Founded: 1959
Members include translators, interpreters, teachers, project managers, web & software developers, language company owners, hospitals, universities & government agencies. Membership: $190/yr indivs, $350/yr corps, $235/yr instl, $80/yr students.
Number of Members: 11,000
New Election: Oct
2025 Meeting(s): Annual Conference, Boston, MA, Oct 22-25, 2025
Publication(s): *The ATA Chronicle* (6 issues/yr, free to membs); *Language Services Directory* (online only); *Newsbriefs* (2 issues/mo, enewsletter, free to membs)
Membership(s): International Federation of Translators (FIT)

Antiquarian Booksellers' Association of America (ABAA)
155 Water St, 6th fl, Suite 7, Brooklyn, NY 11201
Tel: 212-944-8291 *Fax:* 212-944-8293
E-mail: hq@abaa.org
Web Site: www.abaa.org
Key Personnel
Exec Dir: Susan Benne *E-mail:* sbenne@abaa.org
Founded: 1949
Chapters: Northern California, Southern California, Midwest, Middle Atlantic, New England, Southeast, Southwest & Pacific Northwest. Membership open to antiquarian booksellers only.
Number of Members: 450
2025 Meeting(s): California International Antiquarian Book Fair, Pasadena Convention Center, 300 E Green St, Pasadena, CA, Feb 7-9, 2025; New York International Antiquarian Book Fair, Park Avenue Armory, 643 Park Ave at 67 St, New York, NY, April 3-6, 2025; Boston International Antiquarian Book Fair, Hynes Convention Center, 900 Boylston St, Boston, MA, Nov 7-9, 2025
Publication(s): *eNewsletter* (quarterly, free)

Antiquarian Booksellers' Association of Canada/Association de la Librairie Ancienne du Canada, see ABAC/ALAC

APSA, see American Political Science Association (APSA)

ASHA, see American Speech-Language-Hearing Association (ASHA)

Asian American Writers' Workshop (AAWW)
112 W 27 St, Suite 600, New York, NY 10001
Tel: 212-494-0061
E-mail: desk@aaww.org
Web Site: aaww.org; facebook.com/AsianAmericanWritersWorkshop
Key Personnel
Exec Dir: Jafreen Uddin
Public Events & Workshops Coord: Tiffany Tran Lee
Edit Coord: Yasmin Adele Majeed
Ed-in-Chief: Jyothi Natarajan
Sr Ed: Noel T Pangilinan
Founded: 1991
Not-for-profit arts organization devoted to the creating, publishing, developing & disseminating of creative writing by Asian Americans.

ASIS&T, see Association for Information Science & Technology (ASIS&T)

ASLE, see Association for the Study of Literature and Environment (ASLE)

ASMP, see American Society of Media Photographers Inc

Aspen Words
110 E Hallam St, Suite 116, Aspen, CO 81611
Tel: 970-925-3122 *Fax:* 970-920-5700
E-mail: aspenwords@aspeninstitute.org
Web Site: www.aspenwords.org
Key Personnel
Exec Dir: Adrienne Brodeur *Tel:* 646-263-6800 *E-mail:* adrienne.brodeur@aspeninstitute.org
Mng Dir: Caroline Tory *Tel:* 970-925-3122 ext 3 *E-mail:* caroline.tory@aspeninstitute.org

BOOK TRADE & ALLIED ASSOCIATIONS

Founded: 1976
Program of the Aspen Institute. Encourages writers, inspires readers & connects people through the exchange of words, stories & ideas.
Number of Members: 6
Meeting(s): Aspen Summer Words Writing Conference & Literary Festival, Aspen, CO, June; Aspen Winter Words Author Series, Aspen, CO, Jan-April

Association des Editeurs de Langue Anglaise du Quebec, see The Association of English-Language Publishers of Quebec-AELAQ (Association des Editeurs de Langue Anglaise du Quebec)

Association des Libraires du Quebec (ALQ)
483, blvd St Joseph E, Montreal, QC H2J 1J8, Canada
Tel: 514-526-3349 *Fax:* 514-526-3340
E-mail: info@alq.qc.ca
Web Site: www.alq.qc.ca
Key Personnel
Gen Mgr: Katherine Fafard *Tel:* 514-526-3349 ext 21 *E-mail:* kfafard@alq.qc.ca
Founded: 1969
Quebec association of booksellers.
Number of Members: 125

Association des Presses Universitaires Canadiennes, see Association of Canadian University Presses

Association for Information Science & Technology (ASIS&T)
673 Potomac Station Dr, Suite 155, Leesburg, VA 20176
Tel: 301-495-0900 *Fax:* 301-495-0810
E-mail: asist@asist.org; membership@asist.org
Web Site: www.asist.org
Key Personnel
Exec Dir: Lydia Middleton *Tel:* 301-495-0900 ext 1200
Dir, Meetings & Events: Cathy L Nash *Tel:* 301-495-0900 ext 1500
Dir, Membership: Pamela A Yonker *Tel:* 301-495-0900 ext 1600 *E-mail:* pyonker@asist.org
Mng Ed: Garrett Doherty *Tel:* 301-495-0900 ext 1400
Founded: 1937
To foster & lead the advancement of information science & technology.
Number of Members: 4,000
2025 Meeting(s): ASIS&T Annual Meeting, Hyatt Regency Crystal City at Reagan National Airport, 2799 Richmond Hwy, Arlington, VA, Nov 14-18, 2025
Publication(s): *Annual Review of information Science and Technology (ARIST)* (journal); *Inside ASIS&T Newsletter*; *Journal of the Association for Information Science and Technology (JASIS&T)* (monthly)

Association for Intelligent Information Management (AIIM)
8403 Colesville Rd, No 1100, Silver Spring, MD 20910
Tel: 301-587-8202 *Toll Free Tel:* 800-477-2446 *Fax:* 301-587-2711
E-mail: hello@aiim.org
Web Site: www.aiim.org
Key Personnel
COO: Georgina Clelland *E-mail:* gclelland@aiim.org
Chief Mktg Offr: Anthony Paille *E-mail:* apaille@aiim.org
VP, Mkt Intelligence: Theresa Resek *E-mail:* tresek@aiim.org
Sales Dir: Katie Mulqueen *E-mail:* kmulqueen@aiim.org
Cust Experience Mgr: Taylor Stephenson *E-mail:* tstephenson@aiim.org
Mgr, Admin Servs: Dawn Dove *E-mail:* ddove@aiim.org
Mgr, Design: Mark Leonard *E-mail:* mleonard@aiim.org
Mktg Mgr: Jessica Bell *E-mail:* jbell@aiim.org
Membership Experience Mgr: Ally Norat *E-mail:* anorat@aiim.org
Membership Mgr: Boshia Smith *E-mail:* bsmith@aiim.org
Membership Mktg Mgr: Shelly Strickland *E-mail:* sstrickland@aiim.org
Prodn Mgr: Nina Ngobidi *E-mail:* nngobidi@aiim.org
Founded: 1943
Global association bringing together the users of document technologies with the providers of that technology.
Number of Members: 73,000
2025 Meeting(s): AIIM Conference, Hyatt Regency, Atlanta, GA, March 31-April 2, 2025

Association for PRINT Technologies (APTech)
113 Seaboard Lane, Suite C-250, Franklin, TN 37067
Tel: 703-264-7200
E-mail: aptech@aptech.org
Web Site: printtechnologies.org
Key Personnel
Pres: Thayer Long *E-mail:* tlong@aptech.org
VP, Prog Devt: Julie Shaffer *E-mail:* jshaffer@aptech.org
Sr Dir, Communs: Jane Pratt *E-mail:* jpratt@aptech.org
Founded: 1933 (as the National Printing Equipment Association)
US trade association representing more than 650 companies that manufacture & distribute equipment, software & supplies used across the workflow of printing, publishing & converting processes. Owns & produces the global PRINT® exhibition, the most comprehensive exhibition in the Americas for the printing & digital imaging industries.
Number of Members: 650
Publication(s): *LeadingPRINT* (quarterly, magazine)
Membership(s): American Society of Association Executives™ (ASAE); Council of Manufacturing Associations; International Association of Exhibitions and Events® (IAEE); National Association of Manufacturers (NAM)

Association for the Study of Literature and Environment (ASLE)
PO Box 502, Keene, NH 03431-0502
Tel: 603-357-7411 *Fax:* 603-357-7411
E-mail: info@asle.org
Web Site: www.asle.org
Key Personnel
Mng Dir: Amy McIntyre
Founded: 1992
Organization is committed to environmental justice & ecological sustainability as well as environmental research, education, literature, art & service.
Meeting(s): Biennial Conference, July, odd-numbered years
Publication(s): *ISLE: Interdisciplinary Studies in Literature and Environment* (quarterly, journal)

Association nationale des editeurs de livres-ANEL (The National Association of Book Publishers)
2514, blvd Rosemont, Montreal, QC H1Y 1K4, Canada
Tel: 514-273-8130 *Toll Free Tel:* 866-900-ANEL (900-2635)
E-mail: info@anel.qc.ca
Web Site: www.anel.qc.ca

ASSOCIATIONS, EVENTS

Key Personnel
Dir Gen: Karine Vachon *Tel:* 514-273-8130 ext 221 *E-mail:* vachon@anel.qc.ca
Head, Communs, Promo & Memb Servs: Audrey Perreault *Tel:* 514-273-8130 ext 233 *E-mail:* aperreault@anel.qc.ca
Founded: 1992
Professional association of French publishers in Canada.
Number of Members: 110

Association of American Editorial Cartoonists (AAEC)
PO Box 160314, Sacramento, CA 95816
Tel: 954-356-4945
E-mail: editorialcartoonists@gmail.com
Web Site: www.editorialcartoonists.com
Key Personnel
Pres: Jack Ohman
Gen Mgr: Kelsey Maher
Founded: 1957
Professional association of cartoonists concerned with promoting the interests of staff, freelance & student editorial cartoonists in North America.
Number of Members: 260
Publication(s): *Notebook* (annual, magazine, free to membs, $40/yr nonmembs)

Association of American Literary Agents Inc (AALA)
302A W 12 St, No 122, New York, NY 10014
Tel: 212-840-5770
E-mail: info@aalitagents.org
Web Site: aalitagents.org
Key Personnel
Pres: Regina Brooks
VP: Soumeya Bendimerad Roberts; Kelly Sonnack
Treas: Sam Stoloff
Secy: Leslie Zampetti
Founded: 1991
Voluntary & elective professional association of literary & play agents whose individual members subscribe to certain ethical practices. Members meet to discuss industry developments & problems of mutual interest.
Number of Members: 386
New Election: Annually in June

Association of American Publishers (AAP)
455 Massachusetts Ave NW, Suite 700, Washington, DC 20001-2777
Tel: 202-347-3375 *Fax:* 202-347-3690
E-mail: info@publishers.org
Web Site: publishers.org
Key Personnel
Chair: Youngsuk "YS" Chi
Vice Chair: Brian Murray
Pres & CEO: Maria Pallante
COO: Syreeta N Swann *E-mail:* sswann@publishers.org
CFO: Karen McInnis
Gen Coun: Terrence Hart
Deputy Gen Coun: Matthew Stratton
Treas: Jeremy North
EVP, Global Policy: M Lui Simpson
EVP, Govt Aff: Shelley Husband
SVP, Communs: John McKay *Tel:* 202-220-4552 *E-mail:* jmckay@publishers.org
SVP, Educ Policy & Progs: Kelly L Denson
VP, Diversity, Equity & Inclusion: Jonathan M Walker
VP, Public Policy: J Carl Maxwell
Chief of Staff: Bridget Lafferty
Founded: 1970
Monitor & promote the US publishing industry. Members are those actively engaged in the creation, publication & production of books, journals, electronic media, testing materials & a range of educational materials.
Number of Members: 450

Meeting(s): PSP Annual Conference
Publication(s): *AAP Higher Education Books and Materials* (annual, report); *AAP PreK-12 Books and Materials* (monthly, report); *AAP StatShot* (monthly, report)
Membership(s): Book Industry Study Group (BISG)

The Association of Book Publishers of British Columbia (ABPBC)
Affiliate of Association of Canadian Publishers
600-402 W Pender St, Vancouver, BC V6B 1T6, Canada
Tel: 604-684-0228
E-mail: admin@books.bc.ca
Web Site: www.books.bc.ca
Key Personnel
Exec Dir: Matea Kulic *E-mail:* matea@books.bc.ca
Prog Mgr: Kate Balfour *E-mail:* kate@books.bc.ca
Founded: 1974
Trade association representing the interests of Canadian-owned & operated book publishing companies based in British Columbia.
Number of Members: 24
New Election: Annually in April

Association of Canadian Publishers (ACP)
401 Richmond St W, Studio 257A, Toronto, ON M5V 3A8, Canada
Tel: 416-487-6116
E-mail: admin@canbook.org
Web Site: publishers.ca
Key Personnel
Exec Dir: Jack Illingworth *Tel:* 416-487-6116 ext 2340 *E-mail:* jack_illingworth@canbook.org
Membership Servs Mgr: Jazz Cook *Tel:* 416-487-6116 ext 2310 *E-mail:* jazz_cook@canbook.org
Prog Mgr: Jessica Riches *Tel:* 416-487-6116 ext 2220 *E-mail:* jessica_riches@canbook.org
Res & Communs Mgr: Dani MacDonald *Tel:* 416-487-6116 ext 2370 *E-mail:* dani_macdonald@canbook.org
Founded: 1976
Association of English language Canadian-owned book publishing companies. Sponsor professional development seminars for book publishers. Publish membership directories, studies & reports.
Number of Members: 115

Association of Canadian University Presses
542 King Edward, Ottawa, ON K1N 6N5, Canada
Tel: 780-288-2697
Web Site: acup-apuc.ca
Key Personnel
VP: Megan Hall *E-mail:* mhall@athabascau.ca
Founded: 1972
Number of Members: 16
New Election: Annually in Autumn
Membership(s): Association of University Presses (AUPresses)

Association of Catholic Publishers Inc
4725 Dorsey Hall Dr, Suite A, PMB 709, Ellicott City, MD 21042
Tel: 410-988-2926 *Fax:* 410-571-4946
E-mail: info@catholicpublishers.org
Web Site: www.catholicsread.org; www.catholicpublishers.org; www.midatlanticcongress.org
Key Personnel
Exec Dir: Therese Brown
Facilitates the sharing of professional information, networking, cooperation & friendship among those involved in Catholic book publishing in the US & abroad. Offers trade co-op catalog, mailing list, Catholic bestsellers, advertising insert program & professional skills workshops.
Number of Members: 100

New Election: Annually in Dec
Publication(s): *Promotional Brochure* (annual)

Association of College & University Printers
2006 E Marlboro Ave, Suite 104, Hyattsville, MD 20785
Tel: 571-409-3533
Web Site: www.acup-edu.org
Key Personnel
Admin Dir: Courtney Watson *E-mail:* courtney.watson@acup-edu.org
Founded: 1964
Number of Members: 300
2025 Meeting(s): Annual Conference, Hilton Orange County/Costa Mesa, 3050 Bristol St, Costa Mesa, CA, March 30-April 3, 2025

Association of Community Publishers Inc (ACP)
Formerly Association of Free Community Papers (AFCP)
8119 Circuit Rider Path, Cicero, NY 13039
Toll Free Tel: 877-203-2327 *Fax:* 315-670-3121 (memb registration)
E-mail: info@communitypublishers.com
Web Site: www.communitypublishers.com
Key Personnel
Exec Dir: Douglas Fry *E-mail:* douglas@communitypublishers.com
Exec Dir Emeritus (Liverpool, NY off): Loren Colburn *E-mail:* loren@communitypublishers.com
Assoc Exec Dir: Cassey Recore *E-mail:* cassey@communitypublishers.com
Founded: 1950
ACP members are owners, publishers, general managers & sales managers of community publications throughout North America. Our members come from all walks of the community publishing world, from small independent publications to major companies. We represent community publications from coast to coast, reaching millions of homes on a weekly, bi-weekly or monthly basis. These publications are united in providing the best advertising coverage to their clients & valuable advertising information to their strong & loyal readership base.
Number of Members: 140
Meeting(s): Annual Leadership Retreat
2025 Meeting(s): Annual Conference & Trade Show, Mobile, AL, Sept 11-12, 2025
Publication(s): *Publish Magazine* (monthly, free; digital +/or print)
Branch Office(s)
7445 Morgan Rd, Suite 3, Liverpool, NY 13090
104 Westland Dr, Columbia, TN 38401

The Association of English-Language Publishers of Quebec-AELAQ (Association des Editeurs de Langue Anglaise du Quebec)
Atwater Library, 1200 Atwater Ave, Suite 3, Westmount, QC H3Z 1X4, Canada
Tel: 514-932-5633
E-mail: admin@aelaq.org
Web Site: aelaq.org
Key Personnel
Pres: Kathleen Fraser
Exec Dir: Rebecca West
Advance the publication, distribution & promotion of English language books from Quebec.
Number of Members: 26
Publication(s): *Montreal Review of Books* (3 times/yr, report, free)

Association of Free Community Papers (AFCP), see Association of Community Publishers Inc (ACP)

Association of Jewish Libraries Inc (AJL)
Affiliate of The American Library Association (ALA)

PO Box 1118, Teaneck, NJ 07666
Tel: 201-371-3255
E-mail: info@jewishlibraries.org
Web Site: jewishlibraries.org
Key Personnel
Pres: Michelle Margolis
Member libraries in two divisions: RAS (Research Libraries, Archives & Special Collections) & SCC (Schools, Synagogues & Centers). Promote librarianship, services & standards in the field of Judaica. Also affiliate of the American Theological Library Association.
Number of Members: 600
2025 Meeting(s): AJL Conference, Digital
2026 Meeting(s): AJL Conference, Chicago, IL area
Publication(s): *AJL Conference Proceedings* (annual); *AJL News* (quarterly); *AJL Reviews* (quarterly); *Judaica Librarianship* (2 issues/yr, journal)

Association of Manitoba Book Publishers (AMBP)
100 Arthur St, Suite 404, Winnipeg, MB R3B 1H3, Canada
Tel: 204-947-3335
E-mail: ambp@mymts.net
Web Site: ambp.ca
Key Personnel
Exec Dir: Michelle Peters
Projs Coord: Chelsey Young
Founded: 1979
Publishing industry association.
Number of Members: 15
Publication(s): *Prairie books NOW* (2 issues/yr, magazine)
Membership(s): Association of Canadian Publishers (ACP)

The Association of Medical Illustrators (AMI)
201 E Main St, Suite 810, Lexington, KY 40507
Toll Free Tel: 866-393-4AMI (393-4264)
E-mail: hq@ami.org
Web Site: www.ami.org
Key Personnel
Exec Dir: Jennifer Duckworth *E-mail:* jduckworth@amrms.com
Prog Mgr: Kaitlyn Mathews *E-mail:* kmathews@amrms.com
Founded: 1945
Promote the use of high-quality artwork in medical publications to advance medical education.
Number of Members: 850

Association of National Advertisers Inc (ANA)
155 E 44 St, New York, NY 10017
Tel: 212-697-5950 *Fax:* 212-687-7310
E-mail: info@ana.net
Web Site: www.ana.net
Key Personnel
CEO: Bob Liodice *Tel:* 212-455-8050 *E-mail:* bliodice@ana.net
Pres & COO: Christine Manna *Tel:* 212-455-8060 *E-mail:* cmanna@ana.net
EVP & Chief Mktg Offr: Stephanie Fierman *Tel:* 212-455-8016 *E-mail:* sfierman@ana.net
EVP, Membership: Brian Davidson *Tel:* 212-455-8012 *E-mail:* bdavidson@ana.net
SVP, Membership: Barbara Markfield *Tel:* 212-455-8077 *E-mail:* bmarkfield@ana.net
Dir, PR: John Wolfe *Tel:* 212-455-8011 *E-mail:* jwolfe@ana.net
Founded: 1910
A member organization representing the direct marketing business to legislators, regulators & the media, also offering educational & networking experiences for members.
Number of Members: 1,500
Meeting(s): ANA Masters of Data & Technology
Branch Office(s)
2020 "K" St NW, Suite 660, Washington, DC 20006 *Tel:* 202-296-1883 *Fax:* 202-296-1430

Association of Publishers for Special Sales (APSS)
PO Box 715, Avon, CT 06001-0715
Tel: 860-675-1344
Web Site: www.bookapss.org
Key Personnel
Exec Dir: Brian Jud *E-mail:* brianjud@bookapss.org
Busn Mgr: Kaye Krassner *E-mail:* kaye@bookapss.org
A trade association for independent presses, self-publishers & pro-active authors who want to sell more books.
Publication(s): *The Sales Informer* (monthly, newsletter)

Association of University Presses (AUPresses)
1412 Broadway, Suite 2135, New York, NY 10018
Tel: 212-989-1010 *Fax:* 212-989-0275
E-mail: info@aupresses.org
Web Site: www.aupresses.org
Key Personnel
Exec Dir: Peter Berkery *Tel:* 917-288-5594 *E-mail:* pberkery@aupresses.org
Res & Communs Dir: Brenna McLaughlin *Tel:* 917-244-2051 *E-mail:* bmclaughlin@aupresses.org
Dir, Opers: Kim Miller *Tel:* 917-244-1264 *E-mail:* kmiller@aupresses.org
External Communs Mgr: Annette Windhorn *E-mail:* awindhorn@aupresses.org
Membership & Prog Communs Mgr: Kate Kolendo *Tel:* 917-244-3859 *E-mail:* kkolendo@aupresses.org
Admin Coord: Darshna Patel *Tel:* 917-244-2665 *E-mail:* dpatel@aupresses.org
Events Mgr: Alexis Fagan *Tel:* 917-244-1915 *E-mail:* afagan@aupresses.org
Membership & affiliation consists of university presses in North America & abroad that function as the publishing arms of their respective universities, issuing some 11,000 titles & more than 600 journals annually. AUPresses helps these presses do their work more economically, creatively & effectively through its own activities in professional development; fund raising; statistical research & analysis; promoting the value of university presses; community & institutional relations & through its marketing programs.
Number of Members: 157
Meeting(s): AUPresses Book, Jacket & Journal Show, annually in June
2025 Meeting(s): AUPresses Annual Meeting, Online, June 2025
2026 Meeting(s): AUPresses Annual Meeting, Westin Seattle, 1900 Fifth Ave, Seattle, WA, June 13-15, 2026
Publication(s): *Association of University Presses Directory* (annual, $30); *AUPresses Book, Jacket & Journal Show* (catalog, $20 current yr, $15 past yrs); *The Exchange* (quarterly, newsletter, free); *University Press Books for Public & Secondary School Libraries* (annual, free)
Branch Office(s)
1775 Massachusetts Ave NW, Washington, DC 20036
Membership(s): Book Industry Study Group (BISG)

Association of Writers & Writing Programs (AWP)
440 Monticello Ave, Suite 1802, PMB 73708, Norfolk, VA 23510-2670
Tel: 240-696-7700
E-mail: awp@awpwriter.org; press@awpwriter.org
Web Site: www.awpwriter.org
Key Personnel
Dir, Conferences: Colleen Cable
Dir, Pubns: Supriya Bhatnagar
Assoc Ed: Jason Gray
Founded: 1967
Magazine, publications, directory, competitions for awards (including publication), advocacy for literature & education, annual meeting, job placement.
Number of Members: 34,000
2025 Meeting(s): Annual Conference & Bookfair, Los Angeles, CA, March 26-29, 2025
Publication(s): *The Writer's Chronicle* (quarterly, free to membs)

The Associations, Media & Publishing Network, see AM&P Network

Atlantic Provinces Library Association (APLA)
Dalhouse University, Kenneth C Rowe Management Bldg, 6100 University Ave, Suite 4010, Halifax, NS B3H 4R2, Canada
Mailing Address: PO Box 15000, Halifax, NS B3H 4R2, Canada
Web Site: www.apla.ca
Key Personnel
Pres: Trecia Schell *E-mail:* president@apla.ca
Secy: Amy Lorencz *Tel:* 902-420-5174 *E-mail:* secretary@apla.ca
Founded: 1934
Promotes the interests of libraries in the Atlantic provinces while fostering the development of librarians, library technicians & information professionals through cooperative efforts & the promotion of library interests.
Meeting(s): Annual Conference
Publication(s): *APLA Bulletin* (quarterly)

AUPresses, see Association of University Presses (AUPresses)

Austin Area Translators & Interpreters Association (AATIA)
Affiliate of American Translators Association (ATA)
PO Box 92334, Austin, TX 78709-2334
E-mail: info@aatia.org; communications@aatia.org; membership@aatia.org; finance@aatia.org; profdev@aatia.org
Web Site: aatia.org
Key Personnel
Pres: Robin Bonthrone *E-mail:* president@aatia.org
Secy: Renee Koenig *E-mail:* secretary@aatia.org
Dir, Communs: Marion Lemari
Dir, Fin: Michael Meigs
Dir, Membership: Tiffany Annette Hopkins
Dir, Prof Devt: Waleska Bonthrone
Founded: 1985
Provides support, guidance & encouragement for anyone interested in translating or interpreting in central Texas. Bimonthly meeting with programs.
Publication(s): *Member Directory* (online)

Authors Alliance
2705 Webster St, No 5805, Berkeley, CA 94705
E-mail: info@authorsalliance.org
Web Site: www.authorsalliance.org
Further public interest in facilitating widespread access to works of authorship by assisting & representing authors who want to disseminate knowledge & products of the imagination broadly.

The Authors Guild®
31 E 32 St, Suite 901, New York, NY 10016
Tel: 212-563-5904 *Fax:* 212-564-5363
E-mail: staff@authorsguild.org
Web Site: www.authorsguild.org
Key Personnel
CEO: Mary Rasenberger
COO: Sandy Long
Gen Coun: Cheryl L Davis
VP, Progs: Andrea Bronson
Dir, Membership & Regl Chapters: Nicole Vazquez
Founded: 1912
National membership organization for nonfiction & fiction book authors & freelance journalists. Deals with the business & professional interests of authors in such fields as book contracts, copyright, subsidiary rights, free expression, taxes & others. Offer free contract reviews, web site development & hosting.
Number of Members: 9,000
Publication(s): *The Bulletin* (quarterly, free to membs)

Authors League Fund
155 Water St, Brooklyn, NY 11201
Tel: 212-268-1208
E-mail: staff@authorsleaguefund.org
Web Site: www.authorsleaguefund.org
Founded: 1917
Provides emergency assistance to professional writers facing financial hardship.

The Authors League of America Inc, see The Authors Guild®

The Authors Registry Inc
31 E 32 St, 7th fl, New York, NY 10016
Tel: 212-563-6920
E-mail: staff@authorsregistry.org
Web Site: www.authorsregistry.org
Key Personnel
Pres: Letty Cottin Pogrebin
Mng Dir: Mary Rasenberger
Opers Dir: Terry King
Founded: 1995
A nonprofit corporation that provides a royalty collection & distribution service.
Number of Members: 40,000

The Baker Street Irregulars (BSI)
3040 Sloat Rd, Pebble Beach, CA 93953
Tel: 831-372-8852
E-mail: service@bakerstreetirregulars.com
Web Site: bakerstreetirregulars.com
Key Personnel
Wiggins, Chmn: Michael Kean
Founded: 1934
Literary society with a small press operation including a quarterly journal with a Christmas annual & 3-4 published books annually.
Number of Members: 300
Publication(s): *The Baker Street Journal* (quarterly & Christmas annual, $41.95/yr, $55/yr foreign)

Bay Area Women in Publishing (BAWiP)
680 Second St, San Francisco, CA 94107
E-mail: bayareawomeninpublishing@gmail.com
Web Site: www.bayareawomeninpublishing.com
Key Personnel
Pres: Anne Kubek
VP: Katy Beehler
Secy: Alex Henderson
Treas: Guillian Hetzler
Membership Dir: Charlotte Abbott
Founded: 2012
Connects & supports current & aspiring colleagues who identify as women or non-binary, helping them to build professional networks in & beyond the Bay Area & advance their career goals while building community & a more equitable environment in publishing.

BFMA, see Business Forms Management Association (BFMA)

Bibliographical Society of America (BSA)
67 West St, Suite 401, Unit C17, Brooklyn, NY 11222
E-mail: bsa@bibsocamer.org

Web Site: bibsocamer.org
Key Personnel
Pres: Caroline Duroselle-Melish
VP: Megan Peiser
Secy: John T McQuillen
Treas: G Scott Clemons
Exec Dir: Erin McGuirl *E-mail:* erin.mcguirl@bibsocamer.org
Founded: 1904
Learned society. Sponsors short-term fellowships for bibliographic projects. Membership open to anyone interested in bibliographic projects & process.
Number of Members: 1,000
New Election: Annually in Jan
Meeting(s): Annual Meeting, New York, NY, Jan (Friday following the 4th Thursday)
Publication(s): *The Papers of the Bibliographical Society of America (PBSA)* (quarterly, journal, free to membs)

Bibliographical Society of the University of Virginia
2014 Hessian Rd, Charlottesville, VA 22903
Tel: 434-996-8663
E-mail: bibsoc@virginia.edu
Web Site: bsuva.org
Key Personnel
Pres: G Thomas Tanselle
Exec Secy-Treas: Anne G Ribble *E-mail:* ar3g@virginia.edu
Founded: 1947
Scholarly society promoting the study of books as physical objects, the history of the book & of printing & publishing.
Number of Members: 400
Publication(s): *Studies in Bibliography* (annual, $55)

BISG, see Book Industry Study Group Inc (BISG)

BlackPressUSA, see National Newspaper Publishers Association (NNPA)

BMI®
7 World Trade Center, 250 Greenwich St, New York, NY 10007-0030
Tel: 212-220-3000 *Toll Free Tel:* 888-689-5264 (sales)
E-mail: newyork@bmi.com
Web Site: www.bmi.com
Key Personnel
Pres & CEO: Michael O'Neill
EVP, Dist, Publr Rel & Admin Servs: Alison Smith
SVP, Dist, Publr Rel & Admin Servs: Shouvik Das
SVP, Corp Communs & Mktg: Liz Fischer
Founded: 1939
Secure & license the performing rights of music on behalf of its creators.
Number of Members: 600,000
Publication(s): *BMI MusicWorld Online* (monthly)
Branch Office(s)
8730 Sunset Blvd, 3rd fl W, West Hollywood, CA 90069-2211 *Tel:* 310-659-9109 *E-mail:* losangeles@bmi.com
3340 Peachtree Rd NE, Suite 570, Atlanta, GA 30326 *Tel:* 404-261-5151 *E-mail:* atlanta@bmi.com
10 Music Sq E, Nashville, TN 37203-4399 *Tel:* 615-401-2000 *E-mail:* nashville@bmi.com
1400 S Congress Ave, Suite B200, Austin, TX 78704 *Tel:* 512-350-2033 *E-mail:* austin@bmi.com
84 Harley House, Marylebone Rd, London NW1 5HN, United Kingdom *Tel:* (020) 7486 2036 *E-mail:* london@bmi.com

Book & Periodical Council (BPC)
36 Springhurst Ave, Toronto, ON M6K 1B6, Canada
Tel: 416-975-9366
E-mail: info@thebpc.ca
Web Site: www.thebpc.ca
Key Personnel
Exec Dir: Anne McClelland
Founded: 1975
Umbrella organization for Canadian associations that are, or whose members are, primarily involved with the writing, editing, translating, publishing, producing, distributing, lending, marketing, reading & selling of written words.
Number of Members: 30
Publication(s): *Dividends: The Value of Public Libraries in Canada* (free); *Freedom to Read Kit* (annual); *When the Censor Comes* (free online)

Book Industry Study Group Inc (BISG)
232 Madison Ave, Suite 1200, New York, NY 10016
Tel: 646-336-7141
E-mail: info@bisg.org
Web Site: www.bisg.org
Key Personnel
Bd Chair: Joshua Tallent
Exec Dir: Brian O'Leary
Opers Mgr: Jonathan Fiedler
Founded: 1975
Trade association for policy, standards & research. The member-driven organization uniquely represents all segments of our industry, from publishers & e-publishers to paper manufacturers, libraries, authors, printers, wholesalers, retailers & e-tailers, as well as organizations concerned with the book industry as a whole. BISG has provided a forum for all industry professionals to come together & efficiently address issues & concerns to advance the book community.
Number of Members: 185
New Election: Annually in Sept
Meeting(s): BISG Annual Meeting of Members
Membership(s): The American Library Association (ALA); Association of American Publishers (AAP); Book Industry Communication (BIC); BookNetCanada; EDItEUR; Independent Book Publishers Association (IBPA); National Information Standards Organization (NISO)

Book Manufacturers' Institute Inc (BMI)
7282 55 Ave E, No 147, Bradenton, FL 34203
Mailing Address: PO Box 731388, Ormond Beach, FL 32173
Tel: 386-986-4552
Web Site: bmibook.com
Key Personnel
Exec Dir: Matt Baehr *Tel:* 703-939-0679
Founded: 1933
BMI is the leading nationally recognized trade association of the book manufacturing industry.
Number of Members: 80
Meeting(s): BMI Spring Management Conference; BMI Annual Conference
Membership(s): National Association of Manufacturers (NAM)

Book Publicists of Southern California
357 S Fairfax, No 232, Los Angeles, CA 90036
Web Site: www.bookpublicists.org
Key Personnel
Pres: Bruce Braunstein *E-mail:* bruceb@bookpublicists.org
Founded: 1976
Literary club. Varied topics-anything pertinent to promotion of books & authors.

The Book Publishers Association of Alberta (BPAA)
Affiliate of Association of Canadian Publishers (ACP)
11759 Groat Rd NW, 2nd fl, Edmonton, AB T5M 3K6, Canada
Tel: 780-424-5060
E-mail: info@bookpublishers.ab.ca
Web Site: bookpublishers.ab.ca; www.readalberta.ca
Key Personnel
Exec Dir: Kieran Leblanc *E-mail:* kleblanc@bookpublishers.ab.ca
Proj Coord: Patricia Veldstra *E-mail:* pveldstra@bookpublishers.ab.ca
Proj Asst: Megan Bishop *E-mail:* mbishop@bookpublishers.ab.ca
Founded: 1975
Industry association that supports the Alberta book industry through advocacy, collective marketing projects, professional development sessions & business development initiatives.
Number of Members: 33
Publication(s): *Alberta Books for Schools Catalog*; *Alberta Weekly Bestseller List*; *Books* (2 issues/mo, newsletter); *Edmonton Weekly Bestseller List*; *Read Alberta* (monthly, newsletter); *Read Alberta Publisher Catalog*

Boston Authors Club Inc
c/o Prof Julie Dobrow, 103 Conant Rd, Lincoln, MA 01773
Tel: 781-259-1220
E-mail: bostonauthorsclub2@gmail.com
Web Site: bostonauthorsclub.org
Key Personnel
Pres: Julie Dobrow *E-mail:* jdobrow111@gmail.com
VP: Tracy Geary *Tel:* 781-334-2025 *E-mail:* geary321@hotmail.com
Membership Dir: Nancy Tupper Ling *E-mail:* ntupper@finelinepoets.com
Founded: 1899
Nonprofit organization promoting discussion & community among Boston area authors. Honors outstanding authors at the annual Julia Ward Howe Book Awards program.
Number of Members: 100
New Election: Annually in May

BPA Worldwide
100 Beard Sawmill Rd, 6th fl, Shelton, CT 06484
Tel: 203-447-2800 *Fax:* 203-447-2900
E-mail: info@bpaww.com
Web Site: www.bpaww.com
Key Personnel
Pres & CEO: Glenn J Hansen *Tel:* 203-447-2801 *E-mail:* ghansen@bpaww.com
EVP: Richard J Murphy *Tel:* 203-447-2804 *E-mail:* rmurphy@bpaww.com
VP, Busn Devt: Dan Schneider *Tel:* 203-447-2820 *E-mail:* dschneider@bpaww.com
Dir, Info Servs: Mike Miller *Tel:* 203-447-2832 *E-mail:* mmiller@bpaww.com
Mgr, Communs: Glenn Schutz *Tel:* 203-447-2873 *E-mail:* gschutz@bpaww.com
Founded: 1931
International, independent, not-for-profit organization whose membership consists of advertiser companies, advertising agencies & publications. Audit all-paid, all-controlled or any combination of paid & controlled circulation for more than 2,600 media properties including business, technical, professional publications, consumer magazines, newspapers, web sites, e-mail, newsletters & face-to-face events-expos & shows as well as more than 2,700 advertising & agency members.
Number of Members: 4,100
Branch Office(s)
CCAB (div of BPA Worldwide Inc), 111 Queen St E, No 450, Toronto, ON M5C 1S2, Canada, VP: Tim Peel *Toll Free Tel:* 877-30-AUDIT (302-8348) ext 1 *E-mail:* mpeel@bpaww.com
Sino Ocean International Ctr, Suite 2408-09, 24/F, Tower A, 56 E Fourth Ring Middle Rd, Chaoyang District, Beijing 100025, China,

BOOK TRADE & ALLIED ASSOCIATIONS

Gen Mgr: Doreen Chan *Tel:* (010) 8516 4690
Fax: (010) 8516 4644 *E-mail:* dchan@bpaww.com
Waverly House, 9 Noel St, London W1F 8GQ, United Kingdom *Tel:* (020) 3447 2804

Broadcast Music Inc, see BMI®

BSA, see Bibliographical Society of America (BSA)

Business Forms Management Association (BFMA)
1147 Fleetwood Ave, Madison, WI 53716-1417
E-mail: bfma@bfma.org
Web Site: www.bfma.org
Founded: 1958
Sponsor professional training in all aspects of information resource management; classes are conducted in major cities in the US & CN. Bestow the association's highest award, the Jo Warner Award, to professionals in the information resources industry. Recipients do not have to be BFMA members.
Number of Members: 600

Business Marketing NYC
Division of Association of National Advertisers (ANA)
155 E 44 St, New York, NY 10017
Tel: 212-697-5950 *Fax:* 212-687-7310
E-mail: info@ana.net
Web Site: www.anab2b.nyc; www.marketing.org
Founded: 1922 (as National Industrial Advertising Association)
Provides information & resources to business-to-business marketers & marketing communicators.
Number of Members: 2,300

California Independent Booksellers Alliance (CALIBA)
100 Black Diamond Rd, Stonyford, CA 95979
Tel: 415-561-7686
E-mail: info@caliballiance.org
Web Site: caliballiance.org
Key Personnel
Pres: Melinda Powers
Exec Dir: Hannah Walcher
Opers Mgr: Valentina Moberg *E-mail:* valentina@caliballiance.org
Mgr, Mktg & Promos: Emma Marie *E-mail:* emma@caliballiance.org
Founded: 1981
Support, nurture & promote independent retail bookselling in California.
Publication(s): *California Rep Directory* (free online); *Holiday Catalog*
Membership(s): American Booksellers Association (ABA)

California Writers Club (CWC)
PO Box 201, Danville, CA 94526
E-mail: membership@calwriters.org; advertising-promotion@calwriters.org
Web Site: calwriters.org
Key Personnel
Pres: Roger Lubeck *E-mail:* president@calwriters.org
VP: Bob Isbill *E-mail:* vp@calwriters.org
Secy: Elisabeth Tuck *E-mail:* secretary@calwriters.org
Treas: Constance Hanstedt *E-mail:* treasurer@calwriters.org
Dir, Publicity, PR, Ad & Promos: Bob Isbill
Membership Chair: Sandy Moffett
Founded: 1909
Professional writers club with 22 branches across the state of California. Educates writers of all levels & disciplines in the craft of writing & in the marketing of their work.

Number of Members: 1,900
Publication(s): *The Bulletin* (quarterly, newsletter); *The Literary Review* (annual)

Canada Council for the Arts (Conseil des arts du Canada)
150 Elgin St, 2nd fl, Ottawa, ON K2P 1L4, Canada
Mailing Address: PO Box 1047, Ottawa, ON K1P 5A0, Canada
Tel: 613-566-4414 *Toll Free Tel:* 800-263-5588 (CN only) *Fax:* 613-566-4390
E-mail: info@canadacouncil.ca; media@canadacouncil.ca
Web Site: canadacouncil.ca
Key Personnel
Dir & CEO: Michelle Chawla
CFO & Chief Security Offr: Tania Kingsberry
Chief of Staff & Corp Secy: Joanne Larocque-Poirier
CIO: Ian Lovsin
Dir Gen, Arts Granting Progs: Carolyn Warren
Federal cultural granting agency for Canadian literature. See web site for various awards, prize contests, fellowships & grants.

Canadian Authors Association (CAA)
45 Penetang St, Orillia, ON L3V 3N3, Canada
Tel: 705-955-0716
E-mail: office@canadianauthors.org
Web Site: www.canadianauthors.org
Key Personnel
Exec Dir: Anita Purcell *E-mail:* apurcell@canadianauthors.org
Founded: 1921
Encourage & develop a climate favorable to the literary arts in Canada. Assistance to professional & emerging writers. Represent the concerns & interests of members.
Number of Members: 600

Canadian Bookbinders and Book Artists Guild (CBBAG)
82809-467 Parliament St, Toronto, ON M5A 3Y2, Canada
E-mail: cbbag@cbbag.ca
Web Site: www.cbbag.ca
Key Personnel
Pres: Christine McNair *E-mail:* president@cbbag.ca
VP: Arielle VanderSchans
Secy: Suzan Lee
Treas: Hannah McKendry
Founded: 1983
Presents workshops & courses on a wide variety of topics, including bookbinding, box making, paper making & decorating, letterpress printing, paper conservation & more. Also maintains a reference library & DVD catalogue.
Number of Members: 380
Publication(s): *Book Arts arts du livre Canada* (2 issues/yr, online & print, magazine)

Canadian Cataloguing in Publication Program
Library & Archives Canada, 395 Wellington St, Ottawa, ON K1A 0N4, Canada
Tel: 819-994-6881 *Toll Free Tel:* 866-578-7777 (CN) *Fax:* 819-934-6777
E-mail: bac.cip.lac@canada.ca
Web Site: www.bac-lac.gc.ca/eng/services/cip/pages/cip.aspx
Voluntary program of cooperation between publishers & libraries. Its purpose is to produce standardized bibliographic descriptions for forthcoming Canadian publications.

The Canadian Children's Book Centre
425 Adelaide St W, Suite 200, Toronto, ON M5V 3C1, Canada
Tel: 416-975-0010
E-mail: info@bookcentre.ca

ASSOCIATIONS, EVENTS

Web Site: www.bookcentre.ca
Key Personnel
Exec Dir: Sarah Sahagian
Lib Coord: Meghan Howe *E-mail:* meghan@bookcentre.ca
Founded: 1976
National not-for-profit organization to promote the reading, writing & illustrating of Canadian books for young readers. We provide programs, publications & resources for teachers, librarians, authors, illustrators, publishers, booksellers & parents.
Number of Members: 472
Publication(s): *Best Books for Kids & Teens* (2 issues/yr, catalog, $5.95/issue); *Canadian Children's Book News* (quarterly, magazine, $4.95/issue, $26.95/single subn includes copies of Best Books for Kids & Teens)

The Canadian Circulations Audit Board (CCAB)
Division of BPA Worldwide
111 Queen St E, Suite 450, Toronto, ON M5C 1S2, Canada
Toll Free Tel: 877-302-8348
Web Site: www.bpaww.com
Key Personnel
VP: Tim Peel *Tel:* 877-302-8348 ext 1 *E-mail:* mpeel@bpaww.com
Founded: 1931
Number of Members: 550
Branch Office(s)
8-211, blvd Brien, Suite 433, Repentigny, QC J6A 0A4, Canada

Canadian Independent Booksellers Association (CIBA)
188 Dublin St N, Guelph, ON N1H 4P2, Canada
E-mail: info@cibabooks.ca
Web Site: cibabooks.ca
Key Personnel
Exec Dir: Laura Carter *E-mail:* laura.carter@cibabooks.ca
Admin & Proj Lead: Danielle LeBlanc *E-mail:* danielle.leblanc@cibabooks.ca
Mktg & Commus Lead: Kayla Calder *E-mail:* kayla.calder@cibabooks.ca
Prof Devt & Educ Lead: Nicola Dufficy *E-mail:* nicola.dufficy@cibabooks.ca
Founded: 2020
Offers programs & services & promotes policies that support the strengthening of Canadian independent booksellers (CIBs).
Number of Members: 200

Canadian Institute for Studies in Publishing (CISP)
Simon Fraser University at Harbour Centre, 515 W Hastings St, Suite 3576, Vancouver, BC V6B 5K3, Canada
Tel: 778-782-5242
E-mail: pub-info@sfu.ca
Web Site: publishing.sfu.ca/research-2
Key Personnel
Prog Mgr: Jo-Anne Ray
Founded: 1987
Research on print & digital publishing.

Canadian Publishers' Council (CPC)
3080 Yonge St, Suite 6060, Toronto, ON M4N 3N1, Canada
Tel: 647-255-8880
Web Site: pubcouncil.ca
Key Personnel
Exec Dir, External Rel: David Swail *E-mail:* dswail@pubcouncil.ca
Acctg Offr: Joanna Ames *Tel:* 647-255-8879 *E-mail:* james@pubcouncil.ca
Founded: 1910
Represents the interests of Canadian publishing companies that publish books & other media for elementary & secondary schools, colleges

& universities, professional & reference markets, the retail & library markets.
Number of Members: 20
New Election: Annually in Feb
Membership(s): International Federation of Reproduction Rights Organizations (IFRRO); International Publishers Association (IPA)

Canadian Society of Children's Authors, Illustrators & Performers (CANSCAIP)
720 Bathurst St, Suite 503, Toronto, ON M5S 2R4, Canada
Tel: 416-515-1559
E-mail: office@canscaip.org
Web Site: www.canscaip.org
Key Personnel
Pres: Sharon Jennings
VP: Lana Button
Treas: Paul Coccia
Admin Dir: Helena Aalto
Founded: 1977
Dedicated to the celebration & promotion of Canadian children's authors, illustrators & performers & their work. Provide promotional & networking opportunities.
Number of Members: 1,000
New Election: April, even-numbered yrs
Meeting(s): Packaging Your Imagination, Toronto, ON, CN, annually in Nov; CANSCAIP Prairie Horizons Conference, SK, CN, biennially in odd-numbered years
Publication(s): *CANSCAIP News* (quarterly, enewsletter, free to membs)

Cascade Christian Writers (CCW)
Formerly Oregon Christian Writers (OCW)
PO Box 22, Gladstone, OR 97027
Tel: 503-393-3356
E-mail: contact@oregonchristianwriters.org
Web Site: oregonchristianwriters.org
Key Personnel
Pres: Julie Bonn Blank
Prog Chmn: Dawn Shipman
Summer Conference Dir: Christina Suzann Nelson *E-mail:* summerconf@oregonchristianwriters.org
Registrar & Busn Mgr: Sue Miholer
Founded: 1963
Workshops & seminars for beginning & advanced writers; guest speakers & critiques by professional writers.
Number of Members: 400
New Election: Annually in Oct
Meeting(s): Fall One-Day Conference, annually in Oct; Cascade Christian Writers Conference, annually in June
2025 Meeting(s): Winter One-Day Conference, Peoples Church, 4500 Lancaster Dr NE, Salem, OR, March 8, 2025
Publication(s): *Enewsletter* (monthly, membs only)

CASW, see Council for the Advancement of Science Writing (CASW)

Catholic Library Association
8550 United Plaza Blvd, Suite 1001, Baton Rouge, LA 70809
Tel: 225-408-4417
E-mail: cla2@cathla.org
Web Site: cathla.org
Key Personnel
Exec Dir: Melanie Talley
Association Coord: Mary Coll
Founded: 1921
Initiate, foster & encourage activities & library programs that promote literature & libraries of a Catholic nature & of an ecumenical spirit.
Number of Members: 500
Publication(s): *Catholic Library World* (3 issues/yr, $100 nonmembs US; $140/yr foreign & $25 S&H)

Catholic Media Association (CMA)
10 S Riverside Plaza, Suite 875, Chicago, IL 60606
Tel: 312-380-6789
Web Site: www.catholicmediaassociation.org
Key Personnel
Exec Dir: Rob DeFrancesco
 E-mail: rdefrancesco@CatholicMediaAssociation.org
Proj Coord, Awards: Kathleen Holloway
 E-mail: kholloway@CatholicMediaAssociation.org; Eucarol Juarez *E-mail:* ejuarez@CatholicMediaAssociation.org
Proj Coord, Membership: Carol Arnold
 E-mail: carnold@CatholicMediaAssociation.org
Founded: 1911
Organization of Catholic publishers & media professionals facilitating the professional development & spiritual growth of its members to engage & support Catholic media.
Number of Members: 835
2025 Meeting(s): Catholic Media Conference, Phoenix, AZ, June 24-27, 2025
Publication(s): *The Catholic Journalist* (monthly (exc Aug), $29); *Catholic Press Directory* (annual)

CCAB, see The Canadian Circulations Audit Board (CCAB)

The Center for Book Arts
28 W 27 St, 3rd fl, New York, NY 10001
Tel: 212-481-0295
E-mail: info@centerforbookarts.org
Web Site: www.centerforbookarts.org
Key Personnel
Exec Dir: Corina Reynolds
Founded: 1974
Nonprofit, provides workspace, education, exhibitions & slide registry for book artists, hand papermakers & letter press printers; publication of fine art editions, lectures, outreach program.
Number of Members: 6,500
Publication(s): *Exhibition Catalogs* (quarterly, $15 membs, $20 nonmembs)

The Center for Exhibition Industry Research (CEIR)
12700 Park Central Dr, Suite 308, Dallas, TX 75251
Tel: 972-687-9242 *Fax:* 972-692-6020
E-mail: info@ceir.org
Web Site: www.ceir.org
Key Personnel
CEO: Cathy Breden *Tel:* 972-687-9201
 E-mail: cbreden@ceir.org
Promote the exhibition industry by promoting the value & benefits of exhibitions in an integrated marketing program through research, information & communication.
Number of Members: 600

The Center for Fiction
15 Lafayette Ave, Brooklyn, NY 11217
Tel: 212-755-6710
E-mail: info@centerforfiction.org
Web Site: centerforfiction.org
Key Personnel
Chmn of the Bd: Erroll McDonald
Exec Dir: Lydah Pyles DeBin
Mng Dir: Kristin Henley
Sr Dir, Public Programming: Melanie McNair
Art Dir: Matt Kafoury
Devt Dir: Linda Cicely Morgan
Head Libn & Educ Dir: Allison Escoto
PR & Mktg Mgr: Celeste Kaufman
Writing Progs Mgr: Randy Winston
Founded: 1820 (as the Mercantile Library)
Devoted to the vital art of fiction & to encourage people to read & value fiction. Circulating library of mainly fiction titles. Monthly programs, literary lectures & readings. Writers' studio. Inquiries invited.
Number of Members: 500

Center for the Book, see The Library of Congress Center for the Book

Chicago Women in Publishing (CWIP)
PO Box 60363, Chicago, IL 60660
Tel: 773-508-0351 *Fax:* 303-942-7164
E-mail: info@cwip.org
Web Site: www.cwip.org
Founded: 1972
Jobline employment listing service, monthly newsletter, monthly program meetings, freelance directory, membership directory.
Number of Members: 300
New Election: Annually in May

The Children's Book Council (CBC)
54 W 39 St, 14th fl, New York, NY 10018
E-mail: cbc.info@cbcbooks.org
Web Site: www.cbcbooks.org
Key Personnel
Exec Dir: Carl Lennertz *E-mail:* carl.lennertz@cbcbooks.org
Assoc Exec Dir: Shaina Birkhead *E-mail:* shaina.birkhead@cbcbooks.org
Founded: 1945
Nonprofit trade association of children's book publishers. Professional education; online new title features; author Q&As; Diverse Book Lists; STEM, Children's Favorites, Social Justice book prize & other awards; manages the work of Every Child a Reader, the affiliated 501(c)(3) & home of Children's Book Week, Get Caught Reading, the National Ambassador for Young People's Literature & new Kids' Book Choice Awards.
Number of Members: 105
New Election: Annually in Sept
Meeting(s): Annual Meeting
2025 Meeting(s): Children's Book Week, Nationwide across the USA, May 5-11, 2025; Children's Book Week, Nationwide across the USA, Nov 3-9, 2025
Publication(s): *Children's Favorites List* (annual); *Teacher Favorites List* (annual); *Young Adult Favorites List* (annual)

Christian Retail Association Inc (CRA)
200 West Bay Dr, Largo, FL 33770
Tel: 727-596-7625 *Toll Free Tel:* 800-868-4388 *Fax:* 727-593-3523 *Toll Free Fax:* 855-815-9277
E-mail: service@munce.com
Web Site: www.christianretailassociation.org
Key Personnel
Pres: Bob Munce
VP: Marti Munce
Ad: Christy Dollins *E-mail:* christy.dollins@munce.com
Founded: 2018
Created to help build community within the Christian retail industry & to bring beneficial assets to store owners & vendors. Offers services, trade shows, networking, training & educational materials.
Number of Members: 110
Meeting(s): Christian Product Expo™ (CPE);
Publication(s): *CRA Today* (quarterly, ezine, free to membs)

CIBA, see Canadian Independent Booksellers Association (CIBA)

CIP Program, see Canadian Cataloguing in Publication Program

CISP, see Canadian Institute for Studies in Publishing (CISP)

City & Regional Magazine Association (CRMA)
287 Richards Ave, Norwalk, CT 06850
Tel: 203-515-9294
Web Site: citymag.org
Key Personnel
Pres: Ray Paprocki
VP, Events: Mike Martinelli
VP, Membership: Scott Schumaker
Secy/Treas: Susan Farkas
Exec Dir: Cate Sanderson *E-mail:* cate@sandersonmgt.com
The purpose of the association is to facilitate professional development & training opportunities for member magazines & provide opportunities to exchange information & ideas. Sponsor of the National City & Regional Magazine Award Program at the University of Missouri School of Journalism.
Number of Members: 78
Meeting(s): Winter Publishers Retreat
2025 Meeting(s): Annual Conference, Denver, CO, June 4-7, 2025
Publication(s): *CRMA Newsletter* (free to membs, electronic)

Colorado Authors' League
700 Colorado Blvd, Denver, CO 80206
Tel: 913-369-5040
Web Site: coloradoauthors.org
Key Personnel
Pres: Jodi Bowersox *E-mail:* jodi.bowersox@gmail.com
Membership Dir: Laurie Marr Wasmund *E-mail:* lauriemarrwasmund@gmail.com
Awards Chair: Daniel Ginsberg
Founded: 1931
Organization of independent, professional writers united to further members' success.
Number of Members: 150

Committee on Scholarly Editions
Subsidiary of Modern Language Association (MLA)
c/o Modern Language Association of America, 85 Broad St, Suite 500, New York, NY 10004-2434
Tel: 646-646-5000
E-mail: cse@mla.org
Web Site: www.mla.org
Key Personnel
Staff Liaison: Anne Donlon; Laura Kiernan
Founded: 1979
Assists editors & publishers in preparing reliable scholarly editions.
Number of Members: 9

Community of Literary Magazines & Presses (CLMP)
154 Christopher St, Suite 3C, New York, NY 10014-9110
Tel: 212-741-9110
E-mail: info@clmp.org
Web Site: www.clmp.org
Key Personnel
Exec Dir: Mary Gannon *E-mail:* mgannon@clmp.org
Dir, Membership: Montana Agte-Studier *E-mail:* magte-studier@clmp.org
Communs Mgr: Emma Hine *E-mail:* ehine@clmp.org
Firecracker Awards Mgr: David Gibbs *E-mail:* dgibbs@clmp.org
Founded: 1967
A national nonprofit organization that provides services to small independent literary magazine & book publishers, including technical assistance, various publications, marketing workshops, an online directory of literary magazines & grant programs for literary magazines & presses.
Number of Members: 500
Publication(s): *The Indie Lit Update* (enewsletter, free)

Connecticut Authors & Publishers Association (CAPA)
PO Box 715, Avon, CT 06001-0715
Tel: 860-675-1344
Web Site: ctauthorsandpublishers.com
Key Personnel
Founder: Brian Jud *E-mail:* brianjud@comcast.net
Founded: 1994
Number of Members: 150
Meeting(s): Monthly Meeting, Sycamore Hills Park Community Center, Avon, CT, 3rd Saturday of the month
Publication(s): *The Authority* (monthly, newsletter, free to membs)

Conseil des arts du Canada, see Canada Council for the Arts (Conseil des arts du Canada)

Corporation for Public Broadcasting (CPB)
401 Ninth St NW, Washington, DC 20004-2129
Tel: 202-879-9600
E-mail: press@cpb.org
Web Site: cpb.org
Key Personnel
Pres & CEO: Patricia de Stacy Harrison
EVP & COO: Michael Levy
Treas & CFO: William P Tayman, Jr
SVP & Gen Coun: Westwood Smithers, Jr
SVP, Corp Secy & Chief of Staff: Teresa Safon
VP, Communs: Brendan Daly
Steward of the federal government's investment in public broadcasting & the largest single source of funding for public radio, television & related online & mobile services.

Corporation of Professional Librarians of Quebec
2065, rue Parthenais, Bureau 387, Montreal, QC H2K 3T1, Canada
Tel: 514-845-3327
E-mail: info@cbpq.qc.ca
Web Site: www.cbpq.qc.ca
Key Personnel
Exec Dir: Guy Gosselin
Founded: 1969
Publications, continuing education for information professionals.
Number of Members: 700
Publication(s): *Argus* (annual)

Council for Advancement & Support of Education (CASE)
1201 Eye St NW, Suite 300, Washington, DC 20005
Tel: 202-328-CASE (328-2273) *Fax:* 202-387-4973
E-mail: membersupportcenter@case.org
Web Site: www.case.org
Key Personnel
Pres & CEO: Sue Cunningham *E-mail:* president@case.org
VP, Data, Res & Technol: Cara Giacomini *E-mail:* cgiacomini@case.org
VP, Educ: Emily DeYoung
VP, Strategic Partnerships: Brian Flahaven *E-mail:* flahaven@case.org
VP, Volunteers Engagement & Leadership: Brett Chambers *E-mail:* chambers@case.org
Founded: 1974
International association of educational institutions. Helps its members build stronger relationships with their alumni & donors, raise funds for campus projects, produce recruitment materials, market their institutions to prospective students, diversify the profession & foster public support of education.
Number of Members: 81,000
Publication(s): *Currents* (6 issues/yr, magazine)
Branch Office(s)
Berlin 18 4to piso, Colonia Juarez, Delegacion Cuauhtemoc, 06600 Mexico, CDMX, Mexico *Tel:* (0155) 5546 3531 *E-mail:* americalatina@case.org
Shaw Foundation Alumni House, Unit 05-03, 11 Kent Ridge Dr, Singapore, Singapore *Tel:* 2478 5558 *E-mail:* asia-pacific@case.org
Paxton House, 3rd fl, 30 Artillery Lane, London E1 7LS, United Kingdom *Tel:* (020) 7448 9940 *Fax:* (020) 7377 5944 *E-mail:* europe@case.org

Council for the Advancement of Science Writing (CASW)
PO Box 17337, Seattle, WA 98127
Tel: 206-880-0177
E-mail: info@casw.org
Web Site: casw.org
Key Personnel
Exec Dir: Rosalind Reid *E-mail:* ros_reid@casw.org
Admin & Communs Mgr: Sylvia Kantor *E-mail:* sylviakantor@casw.org
Founded: 1960
To advance science writing.
Meeting(s): New Horizons in Science, annually in Sept/Oct

Crime Writers of Canada (CWC)
4C-240 Westwood Rd, Guelph, ON N1H 7W9, Canada
E-mail: info@crimewriterscanada.com
Web Site: www.crimewriterscanada.com
Key Personnel
Exec Dir: Alison Bruce *E-mail:* ed@crimewriterscanada.com
Asst Exec Dir & Awards Mgr: Ludvica Boota *E-mail:* aed@crimewriterscanada.com
Founded: 1982
National nonprofit organization for Canadian mystery & crime writers, associated professionals & others with a serious interest in Canadian crime writing.
Publication(s): *Cool Canadian Crime* (quarterly); *Crime Beat* (newsletter)

CRMA, see City & Regional Magazine Association (CRMA)

CWA/SCA Canada
2200 Prince of Wales Dr, Suite 301, Ottawa, ON K2E 6Z9, Canada
Tel: 613-820-9777 *Toll Free Tel:* 877-486-4292 *Fax:* 613-820-8188
E-mail: info@cwacanada.ca
Web Site: www.cwacanada.ca
Key Personnel
Pres: Martin O'Hanlon *Tel:* 613-820-8460 *E-mail:* mohanlon@cwacanada.ca
Contracts Coord: Marj Botsford *E-mail:* mbotsford@cwacanada.ca
Fin Coord: Joanne Scheel *E-mail:* jscheel@cwacanada.ca
Founded: 1995 (as TNG Canada)
Media union representing members in Canada.
Affiliate of: The Newspaper Guild, Communication Workers of America (CWA) & Canadian Labour Congress.
Number of Members: 7,000

CWIP, see Chicago Women in Publishing (CWIP)

Deadline Club
Division of The Society of Professional Journalists (SPJ)
c/o Salmagundi Club, 47 Fifth Ave, New York, NY 10003

Tel: 646-481-7584
E-mail: info@deadlineclub.org
Web Site: www.deadlineclub.org
Key Personnel
Chair, Exec Council: Claire Regan
Founded: 1925
Members include professionals working in print, broadcast, online & journalism education.
Number of Members: 300
Meeting(s): Annual Awards Dinner, May
Publication(s): *Deadliner Express* (newsletter)

Dog Writers Association of America Inc (DWAA)
PO Box 787, Hughesville, MD 20637
Web Site: dogwriters.org
Key Personnel
Pres: Therese Backowski
 E-mail: theresebackowski1@gmail.com
VP: Susan Willett
Secy: Emelise Baughman E-mail: emeliseb@yahoo.com
Treas: Marsha Pugh E-mail: marsha_pugh01@comcast.com
Founded: 1935
Provide information about dogs (sport, breeding & ownership) & assist writers in gaining access to exhibitions. Annual writing competition.
Number of Members: 545
Publication(s): *Ruff Drafts* (quarterly, newsletter, free to membs)

ECPA, see Evangelical Christian Publishers Association (ECPA)

EdCan Network
60 St Clair Ave E, Suite 703, Toronto, ON M4T 1N5, Canada
Tel: 416-591-6300 Toll Free Tel: 866-803-9549
Fax: 416-591-5345 Toll Free Fax: 866-803-9549
E-mail: info@edcan.ca
Web Site: www.edcan.ca
Key Personnel
CEO: Max Cooke
Founded: 1891
A national bilingual, charitable organization that promotes transformation in education.
Number of Members: 304
New Election: Annually in Sept or Oct
Publication(s): *Education Canada* (quarterly, magazine, free to membs; available for purchase through subn servs)

Editorial Freelancers Association (EFA)
266 W 37 St, 20th fl, New York, NY 10018
Tel: 212-920-4816 Toll Free Tel: 866-929-5425
E-mail: info@the-efa.org; membership@the-efa.org
Web Site: www.the-efa.org
Key Personnel
Co-Exec: Katy Grenfell E-mail: co-executives@the-efa.org; Cody Sisco E-mail: co-executives@the-efa.org
Secy: Ronane Lloyd E-mail: secretary@the-efa.org
Treas: Marcina Zaccaria E-mail: treasurer@the-efa.org
Founded: 1970
A not-for-profit 501(c)(6), volunteer-based professional association of freelance editors, writers, copy editors, proofreaders, indexers, production specialists, researchers & translators. Provides job listing service, courses, member directory & related professional services. More than 30 chapters nationwide.
Number of Members: 3,000
Publication(s): *EFA Member Directory* (online, free); *The Freelancer* (quarterly, newsletter, free to membs)

Editors Canada (Reviseurs Canada)
1507-180 Dundas St W, Toronto, ON M5G 1Z8, Canada
Tel: 416-975-1379
E-mail: info@editors.ca; info@reviseurs.ca; communications@editors.ca
Web Site: www.editors.ca; www.reviseurs.ca
Key Personnel
Exec Dir: Natasha Bood
 E-mail: executivedirector@editors.ca
Sr Communs Mgr: Michelle Ou
Training & Devt Mgr: Caitlin Stewart
Founded: 1979
Promotes professional editing as key in producing effective communication. Our members work with individuals in the corporate, technical, government, not-for-profit & publishing sectors. Sponsor professional development seminars, promotes & maintains high standards of editing & publishing in Canada, establishes guidelines to help editors secure fair pay & good working conditions, helps both in-house & freelance editors to network & cooperates with other publishing associations in areas of common concern. The association is incorporated federally as a not-for-profit organization & is governed at the national level by an executive council.
Number of Members: 1,500
New Election: Annually in June
Publication(s): *Active Voice (La Voix Active)* (2 issues/yr, newsletter, free to membs); *Editors Canada - Online Directory of Editors* (free to membs)
Membership(s): Book & Periodical Council; Cultural Human Resources Council (CHRC)

Education Writers Association (EWA)
1825 "K" St NW, Suite 200, Washington, DC 20006
Tel: 202-452-9830
Web Site: ewa.org
Key Personnel
COO: George Dieter E-mail: gdieter@ewa.org
Exec Dir: Kathy Chow E-mail: kchow@ewa.org
Asst Dir: Lori Crouch E-mail: lcrouch@ewa.org
Content Dir: Steph Smith E-mail: ssmith@ewa.org
Devt Dir: Rachel Wolin E-mail: rwolin@ewa.org
Content Mgr: Casey Fabris E-mail: cfabris@ewa.org; Naomi Harris E-mail: nharris@ewa.org
Opers Mgr: Tracee Eason E-mail: teason@ewa.org
Mng Ed, Digital Content: Kristan Obeng
 E-mail: kobeng@ewa.org
Founded: 1947
Professional organization of members of the media who cover education at all levels with a mission to increase the quality & quantity of education coverage to better inform the public. Conferences, seminars, newsletters, publications, employment services, freelance referral, workshops & national awards.
Number of Members: 3,000
Meeting(s): EWA National Seminar

Educational Book & Media Association (EBMA)
11 Main St, Suite D, Warrenton, VA 20186
Mailing Address: PO Box 3363, Warrenton, VA 20188
Tel: 540-318-7770 Fax: 202-962-3939
E-mail: info@edupaperback.org; admin@edupaperback.org
Web Site: www.edupaperback.org
Key Personnel
Exec Dir: Brian Gorg
Founded: 1975
To develop better techniques & procedures for the sales, marketing & distribution of paperback books, prebound books & related media in the school & library markets. Regular membership consists of educational paperback & prebound book wholesalers; associate members are paperback publishers.
Number of Members: 125
2025 Meeting(s): EBMA Annual Meeting, JW Marriott Las Vegas, 221 N Rampart Blvd, Las Vegas, NV, Jan 27-30, 2025

Evangelical Christian Publishers Association (ECPA)
5801 S McClintock Dr, Suite 104, Tempe, AZ 85283
Tel: 480-966-3998 Fax: 480-966-1944
E-mail: info@ecpa.org
Web Site: www.ecpa.org
Key Personnel
Pres & CEO: Jeff Crosby
Founded: 1974
Trade association supporting Christian publishers worldwide. Provides professional seminars, compiles statistical studies & presents religious book awards.
Number of Members: 280
2025 Meeting(s): ECPA Leadership Summit, Nashville, TN, April 29-30, 2025
Membership(s): Book Industry Study Group (BISG)

Evangelical Press Association (EPA)
PO Box 1787, Queen Creek, AZ 85142
Toll Free Tel: 888-311-1731
E-mail: info@evangelicalpress.com
Web Site: www.evangelicalpress.com
Key Personnel
Exec Dir: Lamar Keener
Founded: 1948
Professional association of Christian freelancers, associates, magazines, newsletters, newspapers & content-driven web sites.
Number of Members: 324
2025 Meeting(s): Annual Convention, The Branson Hilton & Convention Center, Branson, MO, May 4-6, 2025
Publication(s): *Liaison* (quarterly, newsletter)
Membership(s): RCMA, Inc

FAPA, see Florida Authors and Publishers Association Inc (FAPA)

Federation des Milieux Documentaires
2065 rue Parthenais, Bureau 387, Montreal, QC H2K 3T1, Canada
Tel: 514-281-5012
E-mail: info@fmdoc.org
Web Site: fmdoc.org
Key Personnel
Exec Dir: Micheline Brule E-mail: mbrule@fmdoc.org
Secretariat: Sylvie Langlois
Communs & Projs Coord: Patrick Carpentier
 E-mail: pcarpentier@fmdoc.org
Objective is the promotion of standards of excellence in the services & personnel of libraries, documentation & information centers.
Number of Members: 550
New Election: Annually during congress
Publication(s): *Documentation et Bibliotheques* (quarterly, journal)

Federation of BC Writers
PO Box 3503, Courtenay, BC V9N 6Z9, Canada
E-mail: hello@bcwriters.ca
Web Site: bcwriters.ca
Key Personnel
Exec Dir: Bryan Mortensen E-mail: bryan@bcwriters.ca
Founded: 1976
Not-for-profit organization established to contribute to a supportive environment for writing in the province. Writers of all levels working in all genres & specialties welcome. We publish a magazine & hold readings, workshops & literary competitions.
Number of Members: 400

BOOK TRADE & ALLIED ASSOCIATIONS

New Election: Annually in May
Publication(s): *WordWorks*

Florida Antiquarian Booksellers Association (FABA)
c/o Lighthouse Books, ABAA, 14046 Fifth St, Dade City, FL 33525
Tel: 727-234-7759
E-mail: floridabooksellers@gmail.com
Web Site: floridabooksellers.com
Key Personnel
Pres: William Chrisant
VP: Madlyn Blom
Secy: Richard Oates
Treas: Robert A Hittel
Dedicated to enhancing the business of buying & selling rare & unusual books, vintage photographs, antique maps & ephemera by promoting high standards of excellence in the industry. FABA is a membership organization & does not purchase books or provide evaluations.
2025 Meeting(s): Florida Antiquarian Book Fair, The Coliseum, 535 Fourth Ave N, St Petersburg, FL, March 1-2, 2025

Florida Authors and Publishers Association Inc (FAPA)
6237 Presidential Ct, Suite 140, Fort Myers, FL 33919
E-mail: admin@myfapa.org
Web Site: myfapa.org
Key Personnel
Pres: Robert Jacob *E-mail:* robert.jacob@myfapa.org
Founded: 1983
Networking seminars, newsletter, publishing, book shows, workshops, small presses, independents & self-publishers; annual President's Book Award competition. Affiliate of The Independent Book Publishers Association (IBPA), Association of Publishers for Special Sales (APSS) & Florida Library Association.
Number of Members: 250
Publication(s): *FAPA REaD* (monthly, electronic, newsletter, free to membs, media, booksellers, libraries & reviewers)

Florida Freelance Writers Association
Affiliate of Writers-Editors Network
45 Main St, North Stratford, NH 03590
Mailing Address: PO Box A, North Stratford, NH 03590
Tel: 603-922-8338 *Fax:* 603-922-8339
E-mail: ffwa@writers-editors.com; info@writers-editors.com
Web Site: www.writers-editors.com; writerseditorsnetwork.com
Key Personnel
Exec Dir: Dana K Cassell *E-mail:* dana@writers-editors.com
Founded: 1982
Network of freelance writers & editors, offering a job bank, Florida Markets directory, newsletter, etc.
Number of Members: 200
Publication(s): *Directory of Florida Markets for Writers* (newsletter & electronic formats, $35, free to membs); *Freelance Writer's Report* (monthly, free to membs); *Guide to WEN/FFWA Writers* (continuously updated, free to qualified publishing companies & businesses)

Florida Graphics Alliance (FGA)
Affiliate of PRINTING United Alliance
10524 Mosspark Rd, Suite 204, PMB 334, Orlando, FL 32832
Tel: 407-240-8009
E-mail: info@floridagraphics.org
Web Site: www.floridagraphics.org
Key Personnel
Pres & CEO: Gabriel Hernandez *E-mail:* gabe@floridagraphics.org
Founded: 1939
Trade association for the graphic arts industry.
Number of Members: 380
Publication(s): *Graphics Update* (monthly, free to membs)

Florida Outdoor Writers Association Inc (FOWA)
235 Apollo Beach Blvd, Unit 271, Apollo Beach, FL 33572
Tel: 813-579-0990
E-mail: info@fowa.org
Web Site: www.fowa.org
Key Personnel
Chmn of the Bd: Jennifer Huber
Pres: Desiree Harbster
Second VP: Cefus McRae
Secy: Kathy Barker
Treas: Mike Globenfelt
Exec Dir: Butch Newell
Founded: 1946
Not-for-profit 501(c)(3) statewide paid professional communicators organization made up of outdoor communicators who report & reflect upon Florida's diverse interests in the outdoors to educate & encourage the public in ways that protect & conserve our natural heritage.
Number of Members: 200
New Election: Annually in Sept
Publication(s): *The Market Edge* (6 issues/yr, enewsletter, free to membs, electronic)

Florida Writers Association Inc
127 W Fairbanks Ave, No 407, Winter Park, FL 32789
E-mail: contactus@floridawriters.org
Web Site: www.floridawriters.org
Key Personnel
Pres: Mary Ann de Stefano
EVP: Suzy Hart
VP, Admin & Membership/Secy: Michael Farrell
Founded: 2001
Association of "writers helping writers" to improve writing skills, produce good work in all genres & successfully publish.
Number of Members: 1,500
Meeting(s): Florida WritersCon, Oct
Publication(s): *The Florida Writer* (6 issues/yr, magazine, free to membs)

FMD, see Federation des Milieux Documentaires

Foil & Specialty Effects Association (FSEA)
2150 SW Westport Dr, Suite 101, Topeka, KS 66614
Tel: 785-271-5816 *Fax:* 785-271-6404
Web Site: fsea.com
Key Personnel
Exec Dir: Jeff Peterson *E-mail:* jeff@fsea.com
Asst Dir: Dianna Brodine *E-mail:* dianna@fsea.com
Sales Dir: Gayla Peterson *E-mail:* gayla@fsea.com
Founded: 1992
Trade association for graphics finishing industry.
Number of Members: 325
Publication(s): *PostPress* (quarterly, magazine)

La Fondation Emile Nelligan
100, rue Sherbrooke, Suite 202, Montreal, QC H2X 1C3, Canada
Tel: 514-278-4657
E-mail: info@fondation-nelligan.org
Web Site: www.fondation-nelligan.org
Key Personnel
Pres: Michel Dallaire
VP: Marie-Andree Beaudet
Secy/Treas: Michel Gonneville

ASSOCIATIONS, EVENTS

Exec Dir: Manon Gagnon
Founded: 1979
Sponsoring organization.

4A's (American Association of Advertising Agencies)
25 W 45 St, 16th fl, New York, NY 10036
Tel: 212-682-2500
E-mail: media@4as.org; membership@4as.org
Web Site: www.aaaa.org
Key Personnel
Pres & CEO: Marla Kaplowitz *E-mail:* mkaplowitz@4as.org
COO: Adam Cotumaccio *E-mail:* acotumaccio@4as.org
EVP, Govt Rel: Alison Pepper *E-mail:* apepper@4as.org
EVP, Strategy, Insight & Innovation: Mollie Rosen *E-mail:* mrosen@4as.org
SVP, Mktg & Communs: Tamiko Evans *E-mail:* tevans@4as.org
SVP, Memb Engagement & Devt, Central Region: David-Anthony Powell *E-mail:* dpowell@4as.org
SVP, Memb Engagement & Devt, Eastern Region: Harley Griffiths *E-mail:* hgriffiths@4as.org
SVP, Memb Engagement & Devt, Southern Region: Andy Goldsmith *E-mail:* agoldsmith@4as.org
SVP, Memb Engagement & Devt, Western Region: Juan Carlos Suarez *E-mail:* jsuarez@4as.org
Founded: 1917
National trade association for the advertising agency business.
Number of Members: 600
Branch Office(s)
11020 David Taylor Dr, Suite 305, Charlotte, NC 28262-1103 (4A's benefits) *Tel:* 704-594-6270

Friends of American Writers (FAW)
c/o 506 Rose Ave, Des Plaines, IL 60016
E-mail: info@fawchicago.org
Web Site: www.fawchicago.org
Key Personnel
Pres: Tammie Bob *E-mail:* bobtam410@gmail.com
VP: Christine Spatara
Secy: Dale Davison
Treas: Vivian Mortensen *E-mail:* vmortens@comcast.net
Membership Chair: Karen Burnett
Progs Chair: Joan Gordon
Founded: 1922
To encourage new, talented writers associated with the Midwest & to promote the arts, especially literature, among members.

GardenComm: Garden Communicators International
9825 Magnolia Ave, Suite B-415, Riverside, CA 92503
Tel: 951-899-5015
E-mail: info@gardencomm.org
Web Site: gardencomm.org
Founded: 1948
Provides opportunities for education, recognition, career development & a forum for wide-ranging interactions & collaborations for professionals in the field of gardening communication. Sponsors annual writer's contest & annual Garden Media award program for published articles or books.
Number of Members: 2,500
Publication(s): *On the QT* (quarterly, newsletter)

The Graphic Artists Guild Inc
2248 Broadway, Suite 1341, New York, NY 10024
Tel: 212-791-3400

E-mail: admin@graphicartistsguild.org; membership@graphicartistsguild.org
Web Site: www.graphicartistsguild.org
Key Personnel
Pres: Yanique DeCosta *E-mail:* president@graphicartistsguild.org
Admin Dir: Paula Hinkle
Founded: 1967
Labor organization which advocates the advancement of artists' rights. Members are illustrators, graphic & interactive designers, animators, web programmers & developers.
Number of Members: 1,100
Publication(s): *Graphic Arts Guild Handbook: Pricing & Ethical Guidelines* ($39.72 paper, 16th ed)

Gravure AIMCAL Alliance (GAA)
150 Executive Center Dr, Suite 201, Greenville, SC 29615
Tel: 803-948-9470 *Fax:* 803-948-9471
E-mail: aimcal@aimcal.org
Web Site: gaa.org
Key Personnel
Dir, Opers: Tony Donato *E-mail:* tdonato@gaa.org
Promotes the gravure printing process for publication printing, package printing & product printing. Sponsor of the Golden Cylinder Awards.
Number of Members: 270

Great Lakes Graphics Association (GLGA)
N27 W23960 Paul Rd, Suite 200, Pewaukee, WI 53072
Tel: 262-522-2210 *Toll Free Tel:* 855-522-2210 *Fax:* 262-522-2211
E-mail: info@glga.info
Web Site: glga.info
Key Personnel
Pres: Joe Lyman *E-mail:* jlyman@glga.info
Communs Dir: Sharon Flick *Tel:* 262-201-4730 *E-mail:* sflick@glga.info
Membership & Mktg Dir: Debra Warner *Tel:* 262-439-8992 *E-mail:* dwarner@glga.info
Sales & Memb Engagement Dir: Julie Lopezlena *Tel:* 773-954-6949 *E-mail:* jlopezlena@glga.info
Founded: 1886
Advocate for & provide services to printers & graphics companies in a 3-state area (Illinois, Indiana, Wisconsin).
Number of Members: 410

Great Lakes Independent Booksellers Association (GLIBA)
3123 Andrea Ct, Woodridge, IL 60517
Tel: 630-841-8129
Web Site: www.gliba.org
Key Personnel
Exec Dir: Larry Law *E-mail:* larry@gliba.org
Exec Coord: February Spikener *E-mail:* february@gliba.org
Founded: 1989
Promotes independent bookselling; strengthens partnerships among members in all aspects of the bookselling industry; promotes the Great Lakes region as a vital marketplace. The Great Lakes states are Illinois, Indiana, Kentucky, Michigan, Ohio & Wisconsin.
Meeting(s): Heartland Fall Forum, annually in Oct

Guild of Book Workers
521 Fifth Ave, New York, NY 10175
E-mail: communications@guildofbookworkers.org; membership@guildofbookworkers.org
Web Site: www.guildofbookworkers.org
Key Personnel
Pres: Bexx Caswell *E-mail:* president@guildofbookworkers.org
VP: Henry Hebert *E-mail:* vicepresident@guildofbookworkers.org
Secy: Lindsey Jackson *E-mail:* secretary@guildofbookworkers.org
Treas: Lawrence Houston *E-mail:* treasurer@guildofbookworkers.org
Founded: 1906
A national nonprofit educational organization which fosters the hand book arts: binding, calligraphy, illumination, paper decorating. Sponsor exhibits, lectures, workshops. See web site for membership fee information.
Number of Members: 850
Publication(s): *Journal* (annual, free to membs); *Newsletter* (6 issues/yr, free to membs)

Horror Writers Association (HWA)
PO Box 56687, Sherman Oaks, CA 91413
Tel: 818-220-3965
E-mail: admin@horror.org; membership@horror.org
Web Site: horror.org
Key Personnel
Pres: John Palisano *E-mail:* president@horror.org
VP: Meghan Arcuri *E-mail:* vp@horror.org
Treas: Maxwell Gold *E-mail:* treasurer@horror.org
Admin: Brad Hodson
Founded: 1985
To encourage public interest in & foster an appreciation of good horror & dark fantasy literature. Publishes monthly newsletter, provides online information & resources, Hardship Fund, Grievance Committee, scholarships. Sponsors Bram Stoker Awards® & presents an annual Lifetime Achievement Award.
Membership fees: $69 indiv, $48 supporting, $115 corp, $89 family.
Number of Members: 1,500
2025 Meeting(s): StokerCon™, Stamford, CT, June 12-15, 2025
Publication(s): *Horror Writers Association Newsletter* (monthly, electronic, free)

IABC, see International Association of Business Communicators (IABC)

IBBY Canada
Unit of International Board on Books for Young People (IBBY)
c/o The Canadian Children's Book Ctr, 425 Adelaide St W, Suite 200, Toronto, ON M5V 3C1, Canada
Fax: 416-975-8970
E-mail: info@ibby-canada.org
Web Site: www.ibby-canada.org
Key Personnel
Pres: Patti McIntosh *E-mail:* president@ibby-canada.org
First VP: Dina Thelertis *E-mail:* vicepresident@ibby-canada.org
Second VP: Josiane Polidori *E-mail:* vicepresident2@ibby-canada.org
Treas: Yvette Ghione *E-mail:* treasurer@ibby-canada.org
Founded: 1980
Helps children around the world through access to books & literacy programs & supports Canadian authors, artists, storytellers, organizations & scholars who have all contributed to producing quality children's books.
Number of Members: 200

IBPA, see The Independent Book Publishers Association (IBPA)

The Ibsen Society of America (ISA)
c/o Indiana University, Global & Intl Studies Bldg 3111, 355 N Jordan Ave, Bloomington, IN 47405-1105
Web Site: www.ibsensociety.org
Key Personnel
Pres: Olivia Noble Gunn *E-mail:* ogunn@uw.edu
VP: Dean Krouk *E-mail:* krouk@wisc.edu
Secy: Maren Anderson Johnson *E-mail:* johnma29@luther.edu
Treas: Gergana May *E-mail:* ggmay@indiana.edu
Founded: 1978
Nonprofit corporation which fosters an understanding of Ibsen's works through lectures, readings, performances, conferences & publications.
Number of Members: 250
Publication(s): *Ibsen News & Comment* (annual, free to membs)

ICEA, see Institut de cooperation pour l'education des adultes-ICEA (The Institute for Cooperation on Adult Education)

In-Plant Printing & Mailing Association (IPMA)
103 N Jefferson St, Kearney, MO 64060
Tel: 816-919-1691
E-mail: ipmainfo@ipma.org
Web Site: www.ipma.org
Key Personnel
Exec Dir: Mike Loyd *Tel:* 816-919-1691 ext 103 *E-mail:* mloyd@ipma.org
Asst to Dir: Jennifer Chambers *E-mail:* jchambers@ipma.org
Founded: 1964
Professional association dedicated to the specific needs of all industry segments of in-house professionals who provide graphic design, copy, print, mail & distribution services to their organizations. Annual Educational Conference & Vendor Fair.
Number of Members: 500

The Independent Book Publishers Association (IBPA)
1020 Manhattan Beach Blvd, Suite 204, Manhattan Beach, CA 90266
Tel: 310-546-1818
E-mail: info@ibpa-online.org
Web Site: www.ibpa-online.org
Key Personnel
Chair: Tieshena Davis
CEO: Andrea Fleck-Nisbet *E-mail:* andrea@ibpa-online.org
COO: Terry Nathan *E-mail:* terry@ibpa-online.org
Chief Content Offr: Lee Wind *E-mail:* lee@ibpa-online.org
Dir, Mktg & Communs: Adeline Lui *E-mail:* adeline@ibpa-online.org
Dir, Membership & Memb Servs: Christopher Locke *E-mail:* christopher@ibpa-online.org
Founded: 1983 (as Publishers Association of Southern California)
Not-for-profit trade association for independent publishers & self-published authors. Assists members through educational programs, vendor discounts, cooperative marketing & informational resources.
Number of Members: 4,100
Publication(s): *IBPA Independent* (6 issues/yr, magazine, free to membs, $60/yr nonmembs); *Membership & Service Directory* (free to membs)

Independent Publishers Caucus (IPC)
c/o Seven Stories Press, 140 Watts St, New York, NY 10013
E-mail: info@indiepubs.org
Web Site: www.indiepubs.org
Key Personnel
Co-Founder: Tom Hallock; Dan Simon
Dir: Anna Thorn
Founded: 2016
Founded to provide resources & education to its members; advocate for heightened awareness of independent publishers within the industry, in the media & with readers; function as "keepers of the torch" of American culture in partner-

ship with writers, translators, booksellers, book reviewers & book review editors & producers; become a bridge for its members to organizations such as ABA, AAP, AAUP, ALA & CLMP; strengthen its common cause in creating a more tolerant & inclusive industry by advocating for bringing in more people of color & diverse origins onto its staffs together with a commitment to bringing a more diverse range of writers to the reading public; find common ground & a spirit of partnership with independent booksellers.
Number of Members: 65
Publication(s): *IPC newsletter*

Independent Publishers of New England (IPNE)
c/o Eddie Vincent, Encircle Publications, Farmington, ME 04955
Tel: 339-368-8229
E-mail: talktous@ipne.org
Web Site: www.ipne.org
Key Personnel
Pres: Eddie Vincent
VP: Charlotte R Pierce
Organization of professionals, authors & companies who collaborate to help each other learn & succeed in the independent book publishing field. Serves as an advocate for the regional independent publishing community. Offers educational programs, networking, marketing opportunities, advocacy & information about publishing.
Number of Members: 200

Independent Writers of Chicago (IWOC)
332 S Michigan Ave, Suite 121-W686, Chicago, IL 60604-4434
E-mail: info@iwoc.org; membership@iwoc.org
Web Site: www.iwoc.org
Nonprofit professional association of freelance writers located primarily in the Chicago metropolitan area. Meetings, online resources, social events, Writers' Line job board & blog with topics related to the craft & business of writing.
Number of Members: 85

InScribe Christian Writers' Fellowship (ICWF)
PO Box 68025, Edmonton, AB T6C 4N6, Canada
Tel: 780-646-3068
E-mail: inscribe.mail@gmail.com
Web Site: inscribe.org
Key Personnel
Pres: Sheila Webster *E-mail:* president@inscribe.org
Treas: Marmie Pohlmann
Admin: Ruth Snyder *E-mail:* admin@inscribe.org
Founded: 1980 (as Alberta Christian Writers' Fellowship)
Stimulate, encourage & support Christians who write anywhere across Canada, to advance effective Christian writing & to promote the influence of all Christians who write.
Number of Members: 180
Meeting(s): Fall Conference, annually, last weekend in Sept
Publication(s): *FellowScript* (quarterly, magazine, $50/yr PDF, $70/yr hardcover; free to membs)

Institut de cooperation pour l'education des adultes-ICEA (The Institute for Cooperation on Adult Education)
5000 D'Iberville, Suite 304, Montreal, QC H2H 2S6, Canada
Tel: 514-948-2044
E-mail: icae@icea.qc.ca
Web Site: www.icea.qc.ca
Key Personnel
Exec Dir: Daniel Baril *Tel:* 514-948-2039
E-mail: dbaril@icea.qc.ca

R&D Offr: Herve Dignard *Tel:* 514-270-9779
E-mail: hdignard@icea.qc.ca
Adult Educ Researcher: Emilie Tremblay
E-mail: etremblay@icea.qc.ca
Founded: 1946
Promote & exercise the right of adults to lifelong learning & to adopt & develop a democratic model of continuing education.
Number of Members: 152
Publication(s): *Enewsletter* (free to membs)

The Institute for Cooperation on Adult Education, see Institut de cooperation pour l'education des adultes-ICEA (The Institute for Cooperation on Adult Education)

Inter American Press Association (IAPA)
PO Box 226606, Doral, FL 33222
Tel: 305-987-3363 *Fax:* 305-860-4264
E-mail: info@sipiapa.org
Web Site: www.sipiapa.org
Key Personnel
Exec Dir: Ricardo Trotti *E-mail:* rtrotti@sipiapa.org
Founded: 1942
To guard freedom of speech & freedom of the press; to foster & protect the general & specific interests of the daily & periodical press of the Americas; to promote & maintain the dignity, rights & responsibilities of journalism; to encourage uniform standards of professional & business conduct; to exchange ideas & information which contribute to the cultural, material & technical development of the press; to foster a wider knowledge & greater interchange in support of the basic principles of a free society & individual liberty.
Number of Members: 900
Meeting(s): General Assembly, annually in Oct; SipConnect, annually in July
Publication(s): *Hora de Cierre* (quarterly); *IAPA Annual Report*; *IAPA News* (quarterly); *IAPA Semiannual Report*; *Notisip* (quarterly)

International Association of Business Communicators (IABC)
330 N Wabash Ave, Suite 2000, Chicago, IL 60611
Tel: 312-321-6868 *Toll Free Tel:* 800-218-8097
Fax: 312-673-6708
E-mail: member_relations@iabc.com
Web Site: www.iabc.com
Key Personnel
Chief Communs Offr: Tilden Katz *Tel:* 312-673-5936 *E-mail:* tkatz@iabc.com
Exec Dir: Peter Finn *Tel:* 312-673-5448
E-mail: pfinn@iabc.com
Membership & Opers Mgr: Marlee Honcoop
Tel: 312-673-5423 *E-mail:* mhoncoop@iabc.com
Founded: 1970
Communication association.
Number of Members: 14,000
2025 Meeting(s): IABC World Conference, Vancouver, BC, CN, June 8-11, 2025
Publication(s): *Catalyst* (magazine); *Communication World* (electronic, journal)

International Association of Crime Writers Inc, North American Branch
PO Box 863, Norman, OK 73071
E-mail: crimewritersna@gmail.com
Web Site: www.crimewritersna.org
Key Personnel
Pres: Wendy Hornsby
Secy-Treas: Jim Weikart
Secy: Steven Steinbock
Exec Dir: J Madison Davis
Founded: 1987
Promote communication & free speech among crime writers worldwide & enhance awareness & encourage translations of the genre in the US & abroad.
Number of Members: 244
Publication(s): *Enewsletter* (weekly, free to membs)

International Literacy Association (ILA)
PO Box 8139, Newark, DE 19714-8139
Tel: 302-731-1600 *Toll Free Tel:* 800-336-7323 (US & CN)
E-mail: customerservice@reading.org
Web Site: www.literacyworldwide.org; www.reading.org
Key Personnel
Exec Dir: Marcie Craig Post
Founded: 1956
Conferences; publications, research, membership services; publications on reading & related topics; professional journals.
Number of Members: 60,000
Meeting(s): Annual Conference

International Society of Latino Authors (ISLA)
c/o Empowering Latino Futures, 624 Hillcrest Lane, Fallbrook, CA 92084
Tel: 760-689-2317 *Fax:* 760-434-7476
Web Site: isla.news
Key Personnel
Pres: Kirk Whisler *E-mail:* kirk@whisler.com
Founded: 2015
Open to published & unpublished Latino authors or any author writing about the Latino experience/issues, all publishers & related service providers who support Latino literacy, nationally or internationally.

International Society of Weekly Newspaper Editors (ISWNE)
Missouri Southern State University, 3950 E Newman Rd, Joplin, MO 64801-1595
Web Site: www.iswne.org
Key Personnel
Exec Dir: Dr Chad Stebbins *Tel:* 417-625-9736
E-mail: stebbins-c@mssu.edu
Founded: 1955
Help those involved in the weekly press to improve standards of editorial writing & news reporting. Encourages strong, independent editorial voices.
Number of Members: 300
Meeting(s): Annual Conference, Toronto Metropolitan University, Toronto, ON, CN
Publication(s): *Grassroots Editor* (quarterly, journal, free to membs); *ISWNE Newsletter* (8 issues/yr, membs only)

International Standard Book Numbering (ISBN) US Agency, A Cambridge Information Group Co
Affiliate of R R Bowker LLC
PO Box 8134, Bridgewater, NJ 08807
Toll Free Tel: 877-310-7333 *Fax:* 908-219-0188
E-mail: isbn-san@bowker.com
Web Site: www.isbn.org
Coordinate implementation of the ISBN & SAN standards.
Number of Members: 400,000

The International Women's Writing Guild (IWWG)
888 Eighth Ave, No 537, New York, NY 10019
Tel: 917-720-6959
E-mail: iwwgquestions@iwwg.org
Web Site: www.iwwg.org
Key Personnel
Exec Dir: Michelle Miller *E-mail:* michelle@iwwg.org
Founded: 1976
Network for the empowerment of women through writing. Services include updated list of close to 35 literary agents, independent small presses & other writing services. Writing conferences & events annually, subscriptionn to the

newsletter *Network*, regional clusters & opportunities for publications. IWWG is a supportive network open to any woman regardless of portfolio. As such, it has established a remarkable record of achievement in the publishing world as well as in circles where lifelong learning & personal information are valued for their own sake.
Number of Members: 5,000
Meeting(s): IWWG Annual Summer Conference, July; IWWG Annual Writing Conference, July
Publication(s): *Network* (quarterly, free to membs)

Investigative Reporters & Editors
Missouri School of Journalism, Lee Hills Hall, 221 S Eighth St, Columbia, MO 65201
Tel: 573-882-2042
E-mail: info@ire.org
Web Site: www.ire.org
Founded: 1975
Nonprofit organization to improve the quality of investigative journalism.
Number of Members: 5,000
Publication(s): *The IRE Journal* (quarterly, free with membership, $70/yr nonmembs, $125/yr instns, $85/yr libs, $90/yr foreign nonmembs, $150/yr foreign instns)

ISBN Canada
Unit of Library & Archives Canada
Library & Archives Canada, 550, blvd de la Cit, Gatineau, QC J8T 0A7, Canada
Tel: 819-994-6872 *Toll Free Tel:* 866-578-7777 (CN & US) *Fax:* 819-934-7535
E-mail: isbn@bac-lac.gc.ca
Web Site: www.bac-lac.gc.ca/eng/services/isbn-canada/pages/isbn-canada.aspx
Key Personnel
ISBN/ISMN Technician: Heidi Poapst

ISLA, see International Society of Latino Authors (ISLA)

Jewish Book Council
520 Eighth Ave, 4th fl, New York, NY 10018
Tel: 212-201-2920 *Fax:* 212-532-4952
E-mail: info@jewishbooks.org
Web Site: www.jewishbookcouncil.org
Key Personnel
Exec Dir: Carol Kaufman
Assoc Dir: Miri Pomerantz Dauber
Prog Dir: Evie Saphire-Bernstein *E-mail:* evie@jewishbooks.org
Founded: 1944
Sponsors programs based on its conviction that books of Jewish interest are an invaluable contribution to the welfare of the Jewish people. Works to promote the reading, writing, publishing & distribution of worthy books of Jewish content. Honors excellence in all fields of Jewish literary endeavor with awards to writers & citations to publishers. Serves as a resource providing guidance, program tools & publications; acts as a clearinghouse for information on all aspects of Jewish literature & publishing in North America.
2025 Meeting(s): Jewish Book Month, Nationwide throughout the USA, Nov 14-Dec 14, 2025
2026 Meeting(s): Jewish Book Month, Nationwide throughout the USA, Nov 4-Dec 4, 2026
2027 Meeting(s): Jewish Book Month, Nationwide throughout the USA, Nov 24-Dec 24, 2027
2028 Meeting(s): Jewish Book Month, Nationwide throughout the USA, Nov 12-Dec 12, 2028
2029 Meeting(s): Jewish Book Month, Nationwide throughout the USA, Nov 1-Dec 1, 2029
Publication(s): *Paper Brigade* (annual, journal, $25 US, $46 foreign)

The League of Canadian Poets
2 Carlton St, Suite 1519, Toronto, ON M5B 1J3, Canada
Tel: 416-504-1657
E-mail: info@poets.ca
Web Site: poets.ca
Key Personnel
Exec Dir: Lesley Fletcher *E-mail:* lesley@poets.ca
Artistic Programming Dir: Nic Brewer *E-mail:* nicole@poets.ca
Admin & Communs Coord: Caitlin Lapena *E-mail:* caitlin@poets.ca
Founded: 1966
Promote Canadian poetry & poets.
Number of Members: 700
New Election: Annually in June
Publication(s): *Between the Lines* (monthly, newsletter); *Fresh Voices* (quarterly, online); *LCP Chapbook Series*

League of Vermont Writers Inc
PO Box 5046, Burlington, VT 05402
E-mail: lvw@leagueofvermontwriters.org
Web Site: leagueofvermontwriters.org
Founded: 1929
Reader & promotional services; occasional instructional seminars & workshops, publication of anthologies of members' work, writer's service.
Number of Members: 275
New Election: Annually in Jan

Library Association of Alberta (LAA)
c/o The Alberta Library, 7 Sir Winston Churchill Sq NW, No 623, Edmonton, AB T5J 2V5, Canada
E-mail: info@laa.ca
Web Site: www.laa.ca
Key Personnel
Communs Offr: Lorisia MacLeod
Founded: 1930
Nonprofit organization whose members include librarians, library personnel, library trustees, institutions & other interested individuals & companies.
Number of Members: 700

Library of American Broadcasting (LAB)
Unit of University of Maryland Libraries
University of Maryland, Hornbake Library, College Park, MD 20742
Web Site: exhibitions.lib.umd.edu/libraryofamericanbroadcasting
Key Personnel
Devt Offr, LAB Foundation: Sally Brown *Tel:* 574-229-5833 *E-mail:* sallybrownlabf@gmail.com
Founded: 1972
National information resource serving radio & television industries & academic communities. Extensive collection of broadcast history, policy & tradition, including historic documents, professional papers, oral & video histories, books, scripts & photographs.
Number of Members: 21
New Election: Annually in Nov

The Library of Congress Center for the Book
The Library of Congress, 101 Independence Ave SE, Washington, DC 20540-4920
Tel: 202-707-5221 *Fax:* 202-707-0269
E-mail: cfbook@loc.gov
Web Site: www.read.gov/cfb
Key Personnel
Head: Guy Lamolinara *E-mail:* glam@loc.gov
Founded: 1977 (by public law)
Uses the influence & resources of the Library of Congress to promote books & libraries, literacy & reading. Its program of symposia, projects, lectures, exhibitions & publications is supported by tax-deductible contributions from corporations & individuals. National reading promotion network includes affiliate centers in the 50 states, the District of Columbia, Puerto Rico, US Virgin Islands, Northern Marianas, Guam & American Samoa.

Linguistic Society of America (LSA)
522 21 St NW, Suite 120, Washington, DC 20006-5012
Tel: 202-835-1714 *Fax:* 202-835-1717
E-mail: lsa@lsadc.org; membership@lsadc.org
Web Site: www.linguisticsociety.org
Key Personnel
Exec Dir: Alyson Reed *E-mail:* areed@lsadc.org
Meetings Mgr: Krystal Bushell
Membership Coord: Mark Schaefer
Founded: 1924
Advancing the scientific study of language & its applications.
Number of Members: 4,500
New Election: Annually in Sept
2025 Meeting(s): LSA Annual Meeting, Philadelphia Marriott Downtown, 1200 Filbert St, Philadelphia, PA, Jan 9-12, 2025
Publication(s): *Language* (quarterly, journal, free to membs, $200-$250/yr organizations); *LSA Meeting Handbook* (annual, electronic, free); *Phonological Data and Analysis (PDA)* (annual, online, open access, journal); *Semantics & Pragmatics* (annual, online, open access, journal)

Literacy Texas
PO Box 111, Texarkana, TX 75504-0111
Tel: 903-392-9802
E-mail: info@literacytexas.org
Web Site: literacytexas.org; www.facebook.com/LiteracyTX
Key Personnel
Exec Dir: Dr Jenny McCormack Walker
Statewide literacy coalition connecting & equipping literacy programs through resources, training, networking & advocacy.
2025 Meeting(s): Literacy Texas Annual Conference, Embassy Suites by Hilton San Marcos, 1001 E McCarty Lane, San Marcos, TX, Aug 5-6, 2025

The Literary Press Group of Canada
234 Eglinton Ave E, Suite 401, Toronto, ON M4P 1K5, Canada
Tel: 416-483-1321 *Fax:* 416-483-2510
E-mail: sales@lpg.ca
Web Site: www.lpg.ca
Key Personnel
Exec Dir: Laura Rock Gaughan *Tel:* 416-483-1321 ext 1 *E-mail:* laurag@lpg.ca
Busn Mgr: Barb Phillips *Tel:* 416-483-1321 ext 2 *E-mail:* barb@lpg.ca
Engagement Mgr: Lauren Perruzza *Tel:* 416-483-1321 ext 6 *E-mail:* lauren@lpg.ca
Mktg Mgr: Mandy Bayrami *Tel:* 416-483-1321 ext 3 *E-mail:* mandy@lpg.ca
Sales Mgr: Tan Light *Tel:* 416-483-1321 ext 4
Founded: 1975
National trade association providing cooperative sales, marketing, advertising & publicity services to members.
Number of Members: 63
New Election: Annually in May

Literary Translators' Association of Canada
Concordia University, LB 601, 1455 De Maisonneuve W, Montreal, QC H3G 1M8, Canada
Tel: 514-848-2424 (ext 8702)
E-mail: info@attlc-ltac.org
Web Site: www.attlc-ltac.org
Key Personnel
Pres: Bilal Hashmi
Founded: 1975
As the only organization representing literary translators in Canada, LTAC highlights the

importance of literary translation by providing access to Canada's culture, nationally & internationally & by actively participating in Canada's literary life. It does this in part by organizing public readings, lectures & panel discussions, usually in partnership with literary festivals, universities & other organizations.
Number of Members: 230
New Election: Annually in June

Livestock Publications Council (LPC)
301 Main St, Courtland, KS 66939
Mailing Address: PO Box 323, Courtland, KS 66939-0323
Tel: 785-614-5371
Web Site: livestockpublications.com
Key Personnel
Exec Dir: Lindsay Graber Runft
　E-mail: lindsay@livestockpublications.com
Founded: 1974
A nonprofit organization designed to serve the livestock communications industry.
Number of Members: 195
New Election: Annually in July
Publication(s): *Actiongram* (6 issues/yr, newsletter)

Livres Canada Books
One Nicholas, Suite 504, Ottawa, ON K1N 7B7, Canada
Tel: 613-562-2324 *Fax:* 613-562-2329
E-mail: info@livrescanadabooks.com
Web Site: www.livrescanadabooks.com
Key Personnel
Exec Dir: Francois Charette *Tel:* 613-562-2324 ext 223 *E-mail:* fcharette@livrescanadabooks.com
Deputy Exec Dir: Gabrielle Etcheverry *Tel:* 613-562-2324 ext 229 *E-mail:* getcheverry@livrescanadabooks.com
Sr Progs Mgr: Christy Doucet *Tel:* 613-562-2324 ext 225 *E-mail:* cdoucet@livrescanadabooks.com
Founded: 1972
Not-for-profit organization based in Ottawa. Its mandate is to support Canadian-owned & controlled book publishers' export sales activities in order to help publishers improve their overall export results. As the only national industry association for English & French language book publishers, Livres Canada Books connects all publishers across Canada, providing services in both official languages.
Publication(s): *Canadian Studies Collection* (annual, free); *Rights Canada Catalogue* (annual, free)

Magazines Canada (MC)
555 Richmond St W, Suite 604, Mailbox 201, Toronto, ON M5V 3B1, Canada
Tel: 416-994-6471 *Toll Free Tel:* 877-238-8354
Fax: 416-504-0437
E-mail: info@magazinescanada.ca
Web Site: magazinescanada.ca
Key Personnel
Exec Dir: Kim Coles
Dir, Dist: Chris Chambers *Tel:* 877-238-8354 ext 233 *E-mail:* cchambers@magazinescanada.ca
Accountant: Rabeet Sarfraz *Tel:* 877-238-8354 ext 240 *E-mail:* msarfraz@magazinescanada.ca
Founded: 1973
Government affairs, distribution, promotion, professional development & research for Canadian magazines.
Number of Members: 350
Publication(s): *Cover Lines* (2 issues/mo, newsletter); *Member Bulletin*

Maine Writers & Publishers Alliance (MWPA)
Glickman Family Library, 314 Forest Ave, Rm 318, Portland, ME 04101
Tel: 207-228-8263
E-mail: info@mainewriters.org
Web Site: www.mainewriters.org
Key Personnel
Exec Dir: Gibson Fay-LeBlanc *Tel:* 207-228-8264
　E-mail: director@mainewriters.org
Assoc Dir: Taryn Bowe *Tel:* 207-780-4671
　E-mail: taryn@mainewriters.org
Prog Dir: Meghan Sterling *Tel:* 207-228-8257
　E-mail: meghan@mainewriters.org
Founded: 1975
Support & promote Maine writers, publishers & literary professionals; writing retreats; writing workshops; information services.
Number of Members: 1,400
Publication(s): *Ex Libris Maine* (monthly, enewsletter, membs, supporters & parenting organizations)

Manitoba Arts Council (MAC)
525-93 Lombard Ave, Winnipeg, MB R3B 3B1, Canada
Tel: 204-945-2237 *Toll Free Tel:* 866-994-2787
Fax: 204-945-5925
Web Site: artscouncil.mb.ca
Key Personnel
Exec Dir: Randy Joynt *Tel:* 204-945-2239
　E-mail: rjoynt@artscouncil.mb.ca
Exec Coord: Christie Fischer *Tel:* 204-945-0644
　E-mail: cfischer@artscouncil.mb.ca
Communs Coord: Elyse Saurette *Tel:* 204-945-0646 *E-mail:* esaurette@artscouncil.mb.ca
Founded: 1965
Provincial arts council that funds professional Manitoban artists & arts organizations.

The Manitoba Writers' Guild Inc (MWG)
218-100 Arthur St, Winnipeg, MB R3B 1H3, Canada
Tel: 204-944-8013
E-mail: manitobawritersguild3@gmail.com
Web Site: www.mbwriter.mb.ca
Founded: 1981
Provides professional & personal support to Manitoba writers throughout their writing lives.
Membership: $60/yr regular, $30/yr students & low income, $10/yr youth under 18.
Number of Members: 300

Media Alliance
2830 20 St, Suite 102, San Francisco, CA 94110
Tel: 415-746-9475
E-mail: information@media-alliance.org; info@media-alliance.org
Web Site: www.media-alliance.org
Key Personnel
Exec Dir: Tracy Rosenberg *Tel:* 510-684-6853 (cell) *E-mail:* tracy@media-alliance.org
Info Coord: Phavia Kujichagulia
Founded: 1976
Northern California democratic communications advocate. Members include professional & citizen journalists & community-based media & communications professionals who work with the media. Members are concerned with communications rights, especially at the intersections of class, race & marginalized communities.
Membership fees: $35/yr low-income, $60/yr standard, $100/yr supporting.
Number of Members: 2,000
Publication(s): *Media How-to Guide* (book, $15 membs, $20 nonmembs)

Media Coalition Inc
19 Fulton St, Suite 407, New York, NY 10038
Tel: 212-587-4025
E-mail: info@mediacoalition.org
Web Site: mediacoalition.org
Key Personnel
Exec Dir: David Horowitz *Tel:* 212-587-4025 ext 3 *E-mail:* horowitz@mediacoalition.org
Founded: 1973
Trade association, defends first amendment rights to produce & distribute constitutionally-protected books, magazines, recordings, home video & video games.
Number of Members: 8
Publication(s): *Sense and Censorship: The Vanity of Bonfires* (free online); *Shooting the Messenger: Why Censorship Won't Stop Violence* (free online)

The Melville Society
Johns Hopkins University Press, 2715 N Charles St, Baltimore, MD 21218-4363
Web Site: melvillesociety.org
Founded: 1948
Annual & special meetings & publications. Conferences in association with the Modern Language Association annual convention & American Literature Association annual convention.
Number of Members: 450
New Election: Annually in Spring
Meeting(s): Melville Society International Conference, annually in June
Publication(s): *Leviathan: A Journal of Melville Studies* (3 issues/yr, free to membs)

Michigan Library Association (MLA)
3410 Belle Chase Way, Lansing, MI 48911
Tel: 517-394-2774
E-mail: mla@milibraries.org
Web Site: www.milibraries.org
Key Personnel
Exec Dir: Deborah E Mikula *Tel:* 517-394-2774 ext 224 *E-mail:* dmikula@milibraries.org
Membership & Communs Dir: Rachel Ash *Tel:* 517-394-2774 ext 225 *E-mail:* rfash@milibraries.org
Prog & Event Dir: Amber Sheerin *Tel:* 517-394-2774 ext 223 *E-mail:* asheerin@milibraries.org
Founded: 1891
Leads the advancement of all Michigan libraries through advocacy, education & engagement. Membership includes more than 325 libraries & 1,400 individuals throughout Michigan from public, academic, school & special libraries & organizations supportive of libraries.
Meeting(s): Annual Conference
2025 Meeting(s): Spring Institute for Youth Services, Bavarian Inn Lodge, One Covered Bridge Lane, Frankenmuth, MI, April 10-11, 2025

The Midland Authors, see The Society of Midland Authors (SMA)

Midwest Independent Booksellers Association (MIBA)
939 W Seventh St, St Paul, MN 55102
Tel: 612-208-6279
Web Site: www.midwestbooksellers.org
Key Personnel
Exec Dir: Carrie Obry *E-mail:* carrie@midwestbooksellers.org
Opers Mgr: Kate Scott
Prog Coord: Melissa Peterson
Founded: 1981
Association of independent bookstores in Midwest: Illinois, Iowa, Kansas, Minnesota, Missouri, Nebraska, North Dakota, South Dakota & Wisconsin. Annual trade show & meeting. Book catalog for member stores to use with consumers. Sponsors educational programs for booksellers, Spring meeting, Midwest Booksellers' Choice Awards & "Midwest Connections" regional marketing program.
Number of Members: 225
Publication(s): *Membership Directory* (online); *MIBA Trade Show Program* (annual); *Midwest Booksellers Association Winter Catalog* (annual)

Midwest Travel Journalists Association Inc (MTJA)
PO Box 185, Jessup, IA 50648
Tel: 319-529-1109
E-mail: admin@mtja.us
Web Site: www.mtja.us
Key Personnel
Pres: Todd Wessell
VP: Wendy Pramik
Assoc VP: Jon Jarosh
Secy: Jody Halsted
Treas: Damaine Vonada
Admin: Erin Schmitz
Founded: 2017
Not-for-profit organization for professional travel journalists & destination marketing representatives.
Number of Members: 100
Meeting(s): MTJA Spring Conference; MTJA Fall Conference

Miniature Book Society Inc
518 High St, Fall River, MA 02720
Web Site: www.mbs.org
Key Personnel
Pres: Tony Firman
Secy: Cynthia Cosgrove
Membership Coord: Donna LaVallee
  E-mail: donnambsmembership@gmail.com
Founded: 1983
Number of Members: 302
Publication(s): *Miniature Book Society Newsletter* (3 issues/yr, free to membs)
Membership(s): Fellowship of American Bibliophilic Societies (FABS)

MLA, see Modern Language Association (MLA)

Modern Language Association (MLA)
85 Broad St, New York, NY 10004
SAN: 202-6422
Tel: 646-576-5000
E-mail: help@mla.org; membership@mla.org
Web Site: www.mla.org; x.com/MLAnews; www.facebook.com/modernlanguageassociation; www.linkedin.com/company/modern-language-association
Key Personnel
Exec Dir: Paula Krebs
Sr Dir: Angela Gibson *E-mail:* agibson@mla.org
Dir, Outreach: Anna Chang *E-mail:* achang@mla.org
Founded: 1883
Convention; employment information, professional organization, scholarly publications.
Number of Members: 22,000
2025 Meeting(s): Annual Convention, New Orleans, LA, Jan 9-12, 2025
2026 Meeting(s): Annual Convention, Toronto, ON, CN, Jan 8-11, 2026
Publication(s): *MLA International Bibliography* (annual, inquire); *MLA Newsletter* (quarterly, free to membs); *PMLA* (5 issues/yr, $12/issue); *Profession* (annual, journal, free, online)

MTJA, see Midwest Travel Journalists Association Inc (MTJA)

Music Publishers Association (MPA)
442 Fifth Ave, Suite 1137, New York, NY 10018
E-mail: admin@mpa.org
Web Site: www.mpa.org
Key Personnel
Exec Dir: Brittain Ashford *E-mail:* b.ashford@mpa.org
Founded: 1895
Foster trade & commerce in the interest of those in the music publishing business & encourage understanding of & compliance with the copyright law to protect musical works against piracies & infringements.
Number of Members: 65
New Election: Annually, first week of June
Meeting(s): Annual Meeting & Awards Luncheon, June

MWPA, see Maine Writers & Publishers Alliance (MWPA)

Mystery Writers of America (MWA)
1140 Broadway, Suite 1507, New York, NY 10001
Tel: 212-888-8171
E-mail: mwa@mysterywriters.org
Web Site: mysterywriters.org
Key Personnel
EVP: Donna Andrews
Exec Dir: Margery Flax
Founded: 1945
The premier organization for mystery writers & other professionals in the mystery field. MWA watches developments in legislation & tax laws, sponsors symposia & mystery conferences, presents the Edgar Awards® & provides information for mystery writers. Membership open to published authors, editors, screenwriters & other professionals in the field.
Number of Members: 3,000
Publication(s): *Mystery Writers of American Anthology*; *The Third Degree* (10 issues/yr, free to membs)

NAB, see National Association of Broadcasters (NAB)

NAHP, see National Association of Hispanic Publications Inc (NAHP)

NASW, see National Association of Science Writers Inc (NASW)

National Association of Black Journalists (NABJ)
1100 Knight Hall, Suite 3101, College Park, MD 20742
Tel: 301-405-0248
E-mail: contact@nabj.org; press@nabj.org
Web Site: nabjonline.org
Key Personnel
Exec Dir: Drew Berry
Dir, Communs: Kanya Stewart *E-mail:* kstewart@nabj.org
Dir, Devt: Faye Sigers *E-mail:* fsigers@nabj.org
Dir, Fin: Nathaniel Chambers
  E-mail: nchambers@nabj.org
Dir, Membership: Veronique Dodson
  E-mail: vdodson@nabj.org
Dir, Opers: Angela Y Robinson
  E-mail: arobinson@nabj.org
Founded: 1975
Organization of journalists, students & media-related professionals that provides quality programs & services to & advocates on behalf of black journalists worldwide.
Number of Members: 4,000
New Election: Biennially, odd-numbered yrs
2025 Meeting(s): NABJ Convention & Career Fair, Cleveland, OH, Aug 6-10, 2025
2026 Meeting(s): NABJ Convention & Career Fair, Atlanta, GA, Aug 12-16, 2026
Publication(s): *NABJ Journal* (quarterly, journal); *NABJ Roundup* (monthly, newsletter)

National Association of Book Entrepreneurs (NABE)
PO Box 606, Cottage Grove, OR 97424
Tel: 541-942-7455 *Fax:* 541-942-7455
E-mail: nabe@bookmarketingprofits.com
Web Site: www.bookmarketingprofits.com
Key Personnel
Exec Dir: Al Galasso
Promo Dir: Russ Von Hoelscher
Assoc Dir: Ingrid Crawford
Founded: 1980
International book marketing organization of independent publishers & mail order entrepreneurs. Activities include NABE Combined Book Exhibits at national & regional conventions serving the book, educational, gift & business trade. Publishers Preview Mail Order Program, National Press Release, Electronic Marketing plus complete publisher consultation services for printing, promoting & marketing books.
Number of Members: 1,000
Publication(s): *Book Dealers World* (3 issues/yr, free to membs; nonmembs $50/yr US, $55/yr CN, $70/yr foreign)

The National Association of Book Publishers, see Association nationale des editeurs de livres-ANEL (The National Association of Book Publishers)

National Association of Broadcasters (NAB)
One "M" St SE, Washington, DC 20003
Tel: 202-429-5300
E-mail: nab@nab.org
Web Site: www.nab.org
Key Personnel
Pres & CEO: Curtis LeGeyt
CFO & EVP, Opers: Tea Gennaro
Chief of Staff & EVP, Pub Aff: Michelle Lehman
CTO & EVP, Technol: Sam Matheny
Chief Diversity Offr & Pres, NAB Leadership Foundation: Michelle Duke
Chief Legal Offr & EVP, Legal & Regulatory Aff: Rick Kaplan
EVP & Mng Dir, Global Connections & Events: Karen Chupka
EVP, Govt Rel: Shawn Donilon
EVP, Indus Aff: April Carty-Sipp
Founded: 1922
Trade association for radio & television stations. Provide products, publications (over 130) & other services related to broadcasting.
Number of Members: 9,000
Meeting(s): NAB Show® New York
2025 Meeting(s): NAB Show®, Las Vegas Convention Center, 3150 Paradise Rd, Las Vegas, NV, April 6-9, 2025

National Association of College Stores (NACS)
528 E Lorain St, Oberlin, OH 44074
Toll Free Tel: 800-622-7498 *Fax:* 440-775-4769
E-mail: info@nacs.org
Web Site: www.nacs.org
Key Personnel
CEO: Ed Schlichenmayer *Tel:* 800-622-7498 ext 2250 *E-mail:* eschlichenmayer@nacs.org
Sr Dir, Meetings & Expositions: Mary Adler-Kozak *Tel:* 800-622-7498 ext 2265
Trade association for college store industry.
Number of Members: 4,000
2025 Meeting(s): CAMEX, Forth Worth, TX, Feb 19-23, 2025
Publication(s): *Campus Marketplace* (weekly, online, newsletter); *The College Store* (6 issues/yr, magazine)

National Association of Hispanic Publications Inc (NAHP)
National Press Bldg, 529 14 St NW, Suite 923, Washington, DC 20045
Web Site: nahp.org
Key Personnel
Pres: Alvaro Gurdian
VP: Ivan Adame
VP, Mktg: Marcos Marin
VP, Membership: Pedro De Armas
VP, Sales: Ricardo Hurtado
Secy: Evelyn Castro
Treas: John Heaston
Founded: 1982
Hispanic print & digital media organization.

Number of Members: 100
Publication(s): *NAHP Newsletter* (quarterly)
Membership(s): Hispanic Association on Corporate Responsibility (HACR); National Hispanic Leadership Agenda (NHLA); United States Hispanic Chamber of Commerce (USHCC)

National Association of Printing Ink Manufacturers (NAPIM)
National Press Bldg, 529 14 St NW, Suite 1280, Washington, DC 20045
Tel: 410-940-6589
E-mail: info@napim.org
Web Site: www.napim.org
Key Personnel
Exec Dir: Molly Alton Mullins
 E-mail: mmullins@napim.org
Dir, Regulatory Aff & Technol: George Fuchs
 Tel: 864-884-8095 *E-mail:* gfuchs@napim.org
Founded: 1916
Trade association representing the printing ink industry & providing information & assistance to members to better manage their business.
Number of Members: 83
Meeting(s): Annual Convention; Technical Conference
Publication(s): *Introduction to Printing Ink* (booklet, $6 membs, $10 nonmembs); *Printing Ink Handbook, 7th ed* ($110 membs, $160 nonmembs); *Raw Materials Data Handbook, 3rd ed* ($275 membs, $475 nonmembs)

National Association of Real Estate Editors (NAREE)
1003 NW Sixth Terr, Boca Raton, FL 33486-3455
Tel: 561-391-3599
Web Site: www.naree.org
Key Personnel
Pres: Eileen McEleney Woods
Exec Dir: Mary Doyle-Kimball *Tel:* 561-391-1983 (cell) *E-mail:* mdkimball@naree.org
Founded: 1929
Nonprofit professional association of writers offering Journalism Competition, Bruss Real Estate Book Awards, & Bivins Fellowship. Active memberships available for full-time working journalists with a principal occupation (more than 50% of their time) of independent reporting, transmitting or editing of news, features & columns about real estate +/or housing. Digital, print & broadcast journalists are eligible. Associate memberships available to writers for special interest publications & communications professionals who do not qualify as full-time journalists.
Number of Members: 600
Meeting(s): Annual Real Estate Journalism Conference
Publication(s): *Annual Conference Book* (free to membs); *NAREE E-News* (free to membs); *NAREE Network Directory* (annual, free to membs); *NAREE News* (free to membs)

National Association of Science Writers Inc (NASW)
PO Box 7905, Berkeley, CA 94707
Tel: 510-859-7229
Web Site: www.nasw.org
Key Personnel
Exec Dir: Tinsley Davis *E-mail:* director@nasw.org
Founded: 1934
Professional development organization for science writers.
Number of Members: 2,460
New Election: Biennially, even-numbered yrs
2025 Meeting(s): ScienceWriters2025, Fall 2025
Publication(s): *Desk Notes* (monthly, newsletter, free to membs); *ScienceWriters* (2 issues/yr, magazine, free to membs)
Membership(s): World Federation of Science Journalists

National Book Critics Circle (NBCC)
c/o Jacob M Appel, Icahn School of Medicine at Mount Sinai, One Gustave L Levy Place, New York, NY 10029
E-mail: info@bookcritics.org; membership@bookcritics.org
Web Site: www.bookcritics.org
Key Personnel
Pres: Heather Scott Partington *E-mail:* hsp@bookcritics.org
Secy: Colette Bancroft *E-mail:* bancroft.colette72@gmail.com
Treas: Jacob M Appel *E-mail:* jacobmappel@gmail.com
VP, Awards: Keetje Kuipers *E-mail:* keetje@poetrynw.org
VP, Events: Jane Ciabattari *E-mail:* janeciab@gmail.com
VP, Fundraising: Anita Felicelli
 E-mail: anitafelicelli@gmail.com
VP, Membership & Technol: Chelsea Leu
 E-mail: leu.chelsea@gmail.com
Chair, Fiction: David Varno *E-mail:* davidvarno@bookcritics.org
Founded: 1974
Supports & encourages the art & craft of literary criticism.
Number of Members: 800

National Cartoonists Society (NCS)
PO Box 592927, Orlando, FL 32859-2927
Tel: 407-994-6703
E-mail: info@nationalcartoonists.com; membership@nationalcartoonists.com
Web Site: www.nationalcartoonists.com
Key Personnel
Pres: Jason Chatfield *E-mail:* president@nationalcartoonists.com
First VP: Ed Steckley *E-mail:* vp@nationalcartoonists.com
Second VP: John Hambrock *E-mail:* vp2@nationalcartoonists.com
Third VP: Ellen Liebenthal *E-mail:* vp3@nationalcartoonists.com
Secy: Joe Wos *E-mail:* secretary@nationalcartoonists.com
Treas: Drew Aquilina *E-mail:* treasurer@nationalcartoonists.com
Membership Chair: Greg Cravens
Founded: 1946
Organization of established professional cartoonists.
Number of Members: 500
Publication(s): *The Cartoonist*

National Coalition Against Censorship (NCAC)
19 Fulton St, Suite 407, New York, NY 10038
Tel: 212-807-6222 *Fax:* 212-807-6245
E-mail: ncac@ncac.org
Web Site: www.ncac.org
Key Personnel
CFO: Barbara Pyles *E-mail:* barbara@ncac.org
Chief Strategy & Devt Offr: Josh Corday
 E-mail: josh@ncac.org
Exec Dir: Lee Rowland
Dir, Communs: Macey Morales *E-mail:* macey@ncac.org
Dir, Youth Free Expression Prog: Christine Emeran
Founded: 1974
Promote & defend free speech, inquiry & expression; monitor & publicize censorship incidents; sponsor public programs; assist in censorship controversies through advice, materials, contacts with local organizations & individuals. Membership is comprised of 50 national participating organizations. Reprints & informational materials available upon request.
Publication(s): *Censorship News* (2 issues/yr, newsletter, online)

National Coalition for Literacy (NCL)
PO Box 2932, Washington, DC 20013-2932
E-mail: ncl@ncladvocacy.org
Web Site: www.national-coalition-literacy.org
Key Personnel
Exec Dir: Deborah Kennedy *Tel:* 202-364-1964
Founded: 1981
A member organization made up of major service, research & policy organizations in adult education, family literacy & English language acquisition. NCL's mission is to advance adult education, family literacy & English language acquisition in the US - from the most basic skills proficiency level across a continuum of services including the transition into postsecondary education & job training.
Number of Members: 30

National Communication Association
1765 "N" St NW, Washington, DC 20036
Tel: 202-464-4622 *Fax:* 202-464-4600
E-mail: inbox@natcom.org
Web Site: www.natcom.org
Key Personnel
Exec Dir: Shari Miles-Cohen, PhD *Tel:* 202-534-1116 *E-mail:* smiles-cohen@natcom.org
Founded: 1914
Advances communication as the discipline that studies all forms, modes, media & consequences of communication through humanistic, social scientific & aesthetic inquiry.
Number of Members: 6,500
2025 Meeting(s): Annual Convention, Gaylord Rockies Resort & Convention Center, Aurora, CO, Nov 20-23, 2025
2026 Meeting(s): Annual Convention, New Orleans Marriott/Sheraton New Orleans, New Orleans, LA, Nov 19-22, 2026
Publication(s): *Communication and Critical/Cultural Studies* (quarterly, journal); *Communication and Democracy* (3 times/yr, journal); *Communication Education* (quarterly, journal); *Communication Monographs* (quarterly, journal); *Communication Teacher* (quarterly, journal); *Critical Studies in Media Communication* (5 issues/yr, journal); *Journal of Applied Communication Research* (6 times/yr); *Journal of International & Intercultural Communication* (quarterly); *The Quarterly Journal of Speech*; *Review of Communication*; *Text & Performance Quarterly* (quarterly, journal)

National Council of Teachers of English (NCTE)
340 N Neil St, Suite 104, Champaign, IL 61820
Tel: 217-328-3870 *Toll Free Tel:* 877-369-6283 (cust serv) *Fax:* 217-328-9645
E-mail: customerservice@ncte.org
Web Site: ncte.org
Key Personnel
Exec Dir: Emily Kirkpatrick
Sr Books Ed: Kurt Austin *Tel:* 217-278-3619
 E-mail: kaustin@ncte.org
Prog Coord: Sarah Miller
Founded: 1911
Focus on the major concerns of teachers of English & the language arts; offer teaching aids, advice, direction & guidance for members. Publish educational books, journals, pamphlets, research reports & position papers for all levels of the English teaching profession. Hold annual convention for members in November; sponsor conferences & workshops.
Number of Members: 25,000
2025 Meeting(s): NCTE Annual Convention, Colorado Convention Center, 700 14 St, Denver, CO, Nov 20-23, 2025
Publication(s): *College Composition & Communication* (quarterly, journal, $75/yr, includes NCTE & CCCC membership); *College English* (6 issues/yr, journal, $75/yr, includes NCTE membership); *English Education* (quarterly, journal, $75/yr, includes NCTE & CEE membership); *English Journal* (6 issues/yr, $75/yr,

includes NCTE membership); *English Leadership Quarterly* (journal, $75/yr, includes NCTE & CEL membership); *Language Arts* (6 issues/yr, journal, $75/yr, includes NCTE membership); *Research in the Teaching of English* (quarterly, journal, $75/yr, includes NCTE membership); *Talking Points* (2 issues/yr, journal, $75/yr, includes NCTE & WLU membership); *Teaching English in the Two-Year College* (quarterly, journal, $75/yr, includes NCTE & TYCA membership); *Voices from the Middle* (quarterly, journal, $75/yr, includes NCTE membership)

National Education Association (NEA)
1201 16 St NW, Washington, DC 20036-3290
Tel: 202-833-4000 *Fax:* 202-822-7974
E-mail: media-relations-team@nea.org
Web Site: www.nea.org
Key Personnel
Pres: Becky Pringle
VP: Princess R Moss
Secy/Treas: Noel Candelaria
Exec Dir: Kim A Anderson
Founded: 1857
Professional employee organization for over 3 million educators, with affiliates in every state & in more than 14,000 communities committed to advancing the cause of public education.
Number of Members: 3,200,000
Publication(s): *Higher Education Advocate* (6 issues/yr, newsletter); *The NEA Almanac of Higher Education* (annual); *NEA Today* (quarterly, magazine); *NEA Today for Future Educators* (annual, magazine); *NEA Today for NEA-Retired Members* (quarterly, magazine); *Thought & Action* (annual, journal)

National Federation of Press Women Inc (NFPW)
140B Purcellville Gateway Dr, Suite 120, Purcellville, VA 20132
Tel: 571-295-5900
E-mail: info@nfpw.org
Web Site: www.nfpw.org
Key Personnel
Exec Dir: Catherine E Langley
Founded: 1936
Organization of professional women & men pursuing careers across the communications spectrum.
Number of Members: 1,000
New Election: Sept, odd-numbered yrs
2025 Meeting(s): Communications Conference, Denver Marriott West, 1717 Denver West Blvd, Golden, CO, Sept 11-13, 2025
Publication(s): *Agenda* (quarterly)

National Freedom of Information Coalition (NFOIC)
Affiliate of University of Florida-College of Journalism & Communication
PO Box 405, Williamsburg, VA 23187
Tel: 757-276-1413
E-mail: nfoic@nfoic.org
Web Site: www.nfoic.org
Key Personnel
Admin Mgr: Megan Rhyne *E-mail:* mrhyne@nfoic.org
Founded: 1989 (as National Freedom of Information Assembly)
Nonpartisan alliance of state & regional affiliates promoting collaboration, education & advocacy for open government; transparency & freedom of information.
Number of Members: 43

National Information Standards Organization (NISO)
3600 Clipper Mill Rd, Suite 302, Baltimore, MD 21211-1948
Tel: 301-654-2512 *Fax:* 410-685-5278
E-mail: nisohq@niso.org
Web Site: www.niso.org
Key Personnel
Exec Dir: Todd Carpenter
Assoc Exec Dir: Nettie Lagace
Dir, Strategic Initiatives: Jason Griffey
Dir, Busn Devt & Communs: Mary Beth Barilla
Communs & Events Coord: Sara Groveman
Educ Prog Mgr & DEIA Advocate: Kimberly Gladfelter Graham
Asst Standards Prog Mgr: Keondra Bailey
Off Mgr: Lisa Jackson
Founded: 1939 (incorporated as US 501(c)(3) in 1982)
Developing, maintaining & publishing technical standards used by libraries, information services & publishers. Accredited by the American National Standards Institute.
Number of Members: 310
Meeting(s): NISO Plus
Publication(s): *Information Organized* (online)
Membership(s): The American Library Association (ALA); Association for Information Science & Technology (ASIS&T); Book Industry Study Group (BISG); Coalition for Diversity & Inclusion in Scholarly Communications (C4DISC)

National Latino Press Association (NLPA)
1841 Columbia Rd NW, Suite 614, Washington, DC 20009
Mailing Address: PO Box 1023, Pasco, WA 99301
Tel: 202-489-9516; 509-545-3055 (off of the Pres)
E-mail: info@nationallatinopressassoc.org
Web Site: nationallatinopressassoc.org
Key Personnel
Pres: David G Cortinas *Tel:* 509-539-2753 (cell) *E-mail:* president@nationallatinopressassoc.org
VP, Corp Sales: Miguel Blanco *Tel:* 678-977-4580 (cell) *E-mail:* miguel@blancobusinesssolutions.com
VP, Trade Magazines: Ed Avis *Tel:* 709-218-7755 (cell) *E-mail:* edavis@restmex.com
Treas: Maria del Carmen Amado *Tel:* 914-473-2567 (cell) *E-mail:* westchesterhispano1@gmail.com
Furthers the excellence, recognition & use of the Latino press in the US & provides its members with access to professional development opportunities to better serve & empower their communities.

National League of American Pen Women Inc
The Pen Arts Bldg & Arts Museum, 1300 17 St NW, Washington, DC 20036-1973
Tel: 202-785-1997 *Fax:* 202-452-6868
E-mail: contact@nlapw.org
Web Site: www.nlapw.org
Key Personnel
Pres: Evelyn B Wofford
Founded: 1897
Scholarships, letters, art & music workshops, awards & prizes.
Number of Members: 3,500
Publication(s): *The Pen Woman* (quarterly, magazine, $25/yr, free to membs)

National Music Publishers' Association (NMPA)
1900 "N" St NW, Suite 500, Washington, DC 20036
Tel: 202-393-6672
E-mail: members@nmpa.org
Web Site: nmpa.org
Key Personnel
Pres & CEO: David M Israelite
EVP & Gen Coun: Danielle Aguirre
SVP, External Aff: Charlotte Sellmyer
SVP, Govt Aff: Amelia Binder
SVP, Legal & Busn Aff: Chris Bates; Ashley Joyce; Kerry Mustico
VP, External Aff & Events: Kartraice Hooper *E-mail:* khooper@nmpa.org
VP, Legal & Busn Aff: Shannon Sorenson
VP, Membership & Partnerships: Stephanie Li
Exec Asst & Dir, Opers: Bri Berkley
Mgr, External Aff: Ashley Jones; Danielle Suber
Founded: 1917
Trade association representing all American music publishers & their songwriting partners.
Number of Members: 3,000

National Newspaper Association (NNA)
PO Box 13323, Pensacola, FL 32591
Tel: 850-542-7087
Web Site: www.nna.org; nnaweb.org
Key Personnel
Exec Dir: Lynne Lance *E-mail:* lynne@nna.org
Assoc Dir: Kate Decker *Tel:* 217-820-0212 *E-mail:* kate@nna.org
Founded: 1885
Trade association with a mission to protect, promote & enhance America's community newspapers.
Number of Members: 2,500
Meeting(s): Annual Convention & Trade Show
Publication(s): *Publishers Auxiliary* (monthly, online)

National Newspaper Publishers Association (NNPA)
1816 12 St NW, Washington, DC 20009
Tel: 202-588-8764
E-mail: info@nnpa.org
Web Site: nnpa.org; blackpressusa.com
Key Personnel
Chmn of the Bd: Karen Carter Richards
Pres & CEO: Dr Benjamin F Chavis, Jr
Founded: 1941 (as the National Negro Publishers Association)
Trade association of African American-owned community newspapers from across the US.
Number of Members: 200

National Paper Trade Association (NPTA)
330 N Wabash Ave, Suite 2000, Chicago, IL 60611
Tel: 312-321-4092 *Toll Free Tel:* 800-355-NPTA (355-6782) *Fax:* 312-673-6736
Web Site: www.gonpta.com
Key Personnel
EVP: Matthew Bruno *E-mail:* mbruno@gonpta.com
Event Servs Sr Mgr: Sara Haukap *E-mail:* shaukap@gonpta.com
Membership & Opers Coord: Tori Clucas *E-mail:* tclucas@gonpta.com
Mktg & Communs Coord: Priscilla Gil *E-mail:* pgil@gonpta.com
Founded: 1903
Trade association serving the printing, publishing, catalog, direct mail, imaging, retail & corporate markets.
Number of Members: 68
New Election: Annually in Autumn
Publication(s): *Paper Merchant Insider* (newsletter, free to membs, electronic)
Membership(s): National Association of Wholesaler-Distributors (NAW)

National Press Club (NPC)
529 14 St NW, 13th fl, Washington, DC 20045
Tel: 202-662-7500
Web Site: www.press.org
Key Personnel
Pres: Jen Judson
VP: Eileen O'Reilly
Secy: Mike Basalmo
Membership Secy: Gillian Rich
Exec Dir: William McCarren *E-mail:* wmccarren@press.org
Founded: 1908

BOOK TRADE & ALLIED ASSOCIATIONS

Private professional organization for journalists. Sponsors workshops, rap sessions with authors, press forums, morning newsmakers, famous speaker luncheons; awards prizes for consumer journalism, environmental reporting; freedom of the press; diplomatic writing, Washington coverage & newsletters; book & art exhibits; computerized reference library; annual Book Fair & Authors' Night.
Number of Members: 4,000
Publication(s): *The Record* (weekly)

National Press Photographers Association Inc (NPPA)
120 Hooper St, Athens, GA 30602-3018
Tel: 706-542-2506
E-mail: info@nppa.org; director@nppa.org
Web Site: nppa.org
Key Personnel
Exec Dir: Akili Ramsess *E-mail:* aramsess@nppa.org
Prof Servs Dir: Thomas Kenniff *Tel:* 919-237-1782 *E-mail:* tkenniff@nppa.org
Founded: 1946
To promote & protect integrity & excellence in visual journalism.
Number of Members: 5,500
Publication(s): *News Photographer Magazine* (monthly, electronic, free to membs)

National Society of Newspaper Columnists (NSNC)
205 Gun Hill St, Milton, MA 02186
Tel: 617-697-6854
Web Site: www.columnists.com
Key Personnel
Exec Dir: Ginny McCabe *E-mail:* nsncdirector@gmail.com
Founded: 1977
Promotes professionalism & camaraderie among columnists & other writers of the serial essay, including bloggers. Advocates for columnists & free-press issues. Membership dues: $75/yr.
Number of Members: 400
Meeting(s): National Society of Newspaper Columnists Annual Conference, July
Publication(s): *Newsletter* (6 issues/yr, free)

National Writers Association
10940 S Parker Rd, Suite 508, Parker, CO 80134
Tel: 303-656-7235
E-mail: natlwritersassn@hotmail.com
Web Site: www.nationalwriters.com
Key Personnel
Exec Dir & Ed: Sandy Whelchel
Founded: 1937
Nonprofit representative organization of new & established writers, serving freelance writers throughout the world.
Number of Members: 2,000
Publication(s): *Authorship* (quarterly, $20/yr); *NWA Newsletter* (monthly by e-mail only)

National Writers Union (NWU)
61 Broadway, Suite 1630, New York, NY 10006
Tel: 315-545-5034
E-mail: nwu@nwu.org
Web Site: nwu.org
Key Personnel
Pres: Larry Goldbetter *E-mail:* lgoldbetter@nwu.org
Founded: 1981
Organizing for better treatment of freelance writers by publishers; negotiate union contracts with publishers; conferences. Direct services include the Technical Writers Job Hotline & the Publication Rights Clearinghouse, a groundbreaking license fee collection system. National health insurance programs around the country; national grievance officers & contract advisors; agents database online for members.

Number of Members: 1,300
Publication(s): *National Membership News* (monthly, newsletter, free to membs)

NCTA, see Northern California Translators Association

New Atlantic Independent Booksellers Association (NAIBA)
2667 Hyacinth St, Westbury, NY 11590
Tel: 516-333-0681
E-mail: kit@naiba.com
Web Site: www.naiba.com
Key Personnel
Exec Dir: Eileen Dengler *E-mail:* eileen@naiba.com
To promote cooperation & mutual interest among booksellers & to foster & advance their trade & commerce.
Meeting(s): NAIBA Fall Conference, annually in Oct

New England Independent Booksellers Association Inc (NEIBA)
One Beacon St, 15th fl, Boston, MA 02108
Tel: 617-547-3642
Web Site: www.newenglandbooks.org
Key Personnel
Pres & Exec Dir: Beth Ineson *E-mail:* beth@neba.org
Mktg Mgr: Alexandra Schmelzle *E-mail:* ali@neba.org
Mktg Coord: Rachael Conrad; Evelyn Maguire
Nonprofit trade association for the retail book industry in Connecticut, Maine, Massachusetts, New Hampshire, Rhode Island & Vermont. Educational workshops; holiday gift catalog; book awards.
Number of Members: 300
Meeting(s): The Fall Conference, Rhode Island Convention Center, Providence, RI, annually in Sept/Oct
Publication(s): *NEIBA News* (weekly, membs only)

New England Poetry Club
c/o Linda Haviland Conte, 18 Hall Ave, Apt 2, Somerville, MA 02144
E-mail: info@nepoetryclub.org; president@nepoetryclub.org
Web Site: nepoetryclub.org
Key Personnel
Co-Pres: Doug Holder; Denise Provost
VP: Hilary Sallick
Treas: Linda Haviland Conte
 E-mail: nepctreasurer@gmail.com
Commun Co-Chair: Becca Connors; Lynne Viti
Programming Chair: Wendy Drexler; David P Miller
Founded: 1915
Society for poets, publishers, readers & translators of poetry, who live in New England or have strong ties to the region. Sponsor poetry readings contests & workshops.
Number of Members: 250
Publication(s): *NEPC eNewsletter* (monthly)

New Hampshire Writers' Project (NHWP)
2500 N River Rd, Manchester, NH 03106
Tel: 603-270-5466
E-mail: info@nhwritersproject.org
Web Site: www.nhwritersproject.org
Key Personnel
Chair: Masheri Chappelle
Vice Chair: Dan Pouliot
Secy & Literary Awards Comm Chair: Claudia Decker
Treas: Kathy McKenna
Mktg Dir: Beth D'Ovidio
Founded: 1988

ASSOCIATIONS, EVENTS

Supports the development of individual writers & encourages an audience for literature in the state.
Number of Members: 780
Publication(s): *NH Writer* (6 issues/yr, newsletter)

New Jersey Business & Industry Association (NJBIA)
10 W Lafayette St, Trenton, NJ 08608-2002
Tel: 609-393-7707
Web Site: njbia.org
Key Personnel
Pres & CEO: Michele Siekerka
 E-mail: msiekerka@njbia.org
COO/CFO: Alice Gens *E-mail:* agens@njbia.org
Chief Busn Rel Offr: Wayne Staub
 E-mail: wstaub@njbia.org
Chief Communs Offr: Bob Considine
 E-mail: bconsidine@njbia.org
Chief Govt Aff Offr: Christine Buteas
 E-mail: cbuteas@njbia.org
Chief Mktg Offr & Publr: Vincent Schweikert
 E-mail: v.schweikert@njbia.org
Chief Memb Strategy Offr: Betty Boros
 E-mail: bboros@njbia.org
Founded: 1910
Statewide employer association providing information, services & advocacy for member companies.

New Mexico Book Association (NMBA)
PO Box 1285, Santa Fe, NM 87504
E-mail: libroentry@gmail.com
Web Site: www.nmbookassociation.org
Key Personnel
Pres: Jordan Jones
VP: Miguel de la Cruz
Secy: Connie Nelson
Treas: Paula Lozar
Mgr: Mari Angulo
Founded: 1994
Nonprofit association serving the interests of publishing, writing, designing, editing, selling & marketing for book professionals throughout New Mexico. Open to all involved in books or publishing. Need not be a resident of New Mexico.
Number of Members: 180
Publication(s): *LIBRO Book News* (6 issues/yr, newsletter, $50/yr membs)
Membership(s): The Association of Publishers for Special Sales (APSS); Independent Book Publishers Association (IBPA); New Mexico Library Association; Publishers Association of the West (PubWest)

News Leaders Association (NLA)
209 Reynolds Journalism Institute, Missouri School of Journalism, Columbia, MO 65211
Tel: 202-964-0912
E-mail: contact@newsleaders.org
Web Site: www.newsleaders.org
Key Personnel
Dir, Mktg & Membership: Belinda Williams
 E-mail: bwilliams@newsleaders.org
Nonprofit professional organization focused on leadership development & journalism-related issues.
Publication(s): *Newsletter* (weekly)

News/Media Alliance
4401 N Fairfax Dr, Suite 300, Arlington, VA 22203
Tel: 571-366-1000
E-mail: info@newsmediaalliance.org
Web Site: www.newsmediaalliance.org
Key Personnel
Pres & CEO: David Chavern *E-mail:* david@newsmediaalliance.org
CFO: Robert Walden *Tel:* 571-366-1140
 E-mail: robert@newsmediaalliance.org

Dir, Communs: Lindsey Loving *Tel:* 571-366-1009 *E-mail:* lindsey@newsmediaalliance.org
Dir, HR: Jen Murphy *E-mail:* jennette@newsmediaalliance.org
Dedicated to working with its members, as well as other partner organizations, to advance the industry through advocacy, critical research & resources & events that connect & inspire. Members represent nearly 2,000 diverse publishers in the US, from the largest groups & international outlets to hyperlocal sources, from digital-only & digital-first to print. Our work focuses on the key challenges & opportunities of today's media environment: Freedom of the press, public policy & legal matters, advertising growth, new revenue streams & audience development across all platforms.
Number of Members: 2,000
Publication(s): *newsXchange* (weekly)

News Media Canada
37 Front St E, Suite 200, Toronto, ON M5E 1B3, Canada
Tel: 416-923-3567 *Toll Free Tel:* 877-305-2262 *Fax:* 416-923-7206
E-mail: info@newsmediacanada.ca
Web Site: nmc-mic.ca
Key Personnel
Pres & CEO: Paul Deegan *Tel:* 647-992-5522 *E-mail:* pdeegan@newsmediacanada.ca
Founded: 2016
Advocate in public policy for daily & community media outlets & contributes to the ongoing evolution of the news media industry by raising awareness & promoting the benefits of news media across all platforms.
Number of Members: 800
Publication(s): *Enewsletter* (weekly); *The Scoop* (enewsletter); *Vendors Directory* (online)

The NewsGuild - CWA
501 Third St NW, 6th fl, Washington, DC 20001-2797
Tel: 202-434-7177 *Fax:* 202-434-1472
E-mail: guild@cwa-union.org
Web Site: www.newsguild.org
Key Personnel
Pres: Jon Schleuss
Founded: 1934
Labor union; AFL-CIO, CLC.
Number of Members: 26,000
Publication(s): *The Guild Reporter* (quarterly, free to membs, $20 subn rate nonmembs)

NFOIC, see National Freedom of Information Coalition (NFOIC)

NLA, see News Leaders Association (NLA)

NNA, see National Newspaper Association (NNA)

North American Agricultural Journalists (NAAJ)
c/o Jacqui Fatka, 6866 County Rd, 183, Fredericktown, OH 43019
Tel: 979-324-4302
E-mail: naajnews@yahoo.com
Web Site: www.naaj.net
Key Personnel
Exec Secy-Treas: Jacqui Fatka
Founded: 1952
Self-improvement seminars; annual writing contest for members & nonmembers.
Number of Members: 120
2025 Meeting(s): Annual Meeting, Washington, DC, April 2025
2026 Meeting(s): Annual Meeting, Washington, DC, April 2026
2027 Meeting(s): Annual Meeting, Washington, DC, April 2027
2028 Meeting(s): Annual Meeting, Washington, DC, April 2028
2029 Meeting(s): Annual Meeting, Washington, DC, April 2029

North American Snowsports Journalists Association (NASJA)
290 Laramie Blvd, Boulder, CO 80304
E-mail: execsec@nasja.org
Web Site: nasja.org
Key Personnel
Pres: Jeff Blumenfeld
VP: Marie-Piere Belisle-Kennedy
Founded: 1963 (founded as the US Ski Writers Association)
Professional group of writers, photographers, broadcasters, filmmakers, authors & editors who report ski & snowboard related news, info & features throughout the US & Canada.
Number of Members: 200
New Election: Annually in March
Publication(s): *SnowScoops* (10 issues/yr, newsletter)

North Carolina Writers' Network
PO Box 21591, Winston-Salem, NC 27120-1591
Tel: 336-293-8844
E-mail: mail@ncwriters.org
Web Site: www.ncwriters.org
Key Personnel
Exec Dir: Ed Southern *E-mail:* ed@ncwriters.org
Founded: 1985
Nonprofit, statewide.
Number of Members: 1,400
Publication(s): *Writers' Network News* (2 issues/yr, newspaper, free to membs)

Northern California Translators Association
2261 Market St, Suite 160, San Francisco, CA 94114-1600
Tel: 510-845-8712
E-mail: ncta@ncta.org
Web Site: ncta.org
Key Personnel
Pres: Michael Schubert
Secy: Christina Davis
Treas: Rob Nielsen
Outreach & Membership Dir: Ana Salotti
Admin: Diana Alarid Lockwood *E-mail:* administrator@ncta.org
Founded: 1978
Professional translators & interpreters association. Chapter of the American Translators Association. Online referral service.
Number of Members: 500
New Election: Annually in Feb
Publication(s): *Translorial* (2 issues/yr, online, journal, free to all at www.translorial.com; free PDF access for *Translorial Reader* registrants at www.ncta.org)

Northwest Independent Editors Guild
7511 Greenwood Ave N, No 307, Seattle, WA 98103
E-mail: info@edsguild.org
Web Site: www.edsguild.org
Key Personnel
Pres: MariLou Harveland *E-mail:* president@edsguild.org
VP, Memb Servs: Kris Ashley
Secy: Sarah M Peterson
Treas: Laura Shaw
Founded: 1997
Professional association of editors of the written word in the Pacific Northwest & beyond. The Editors Guild connects clients with professional editors, fosters community among its members & provides resources for their career development.
Number of Members: 400
Meeting(s): Red Pencil Conference

Northwest Territories Public Library Services
Unit of Department of Education, Culture & Employment
75 Woodland Dr, Hay River, NT X0E 1G1, Canada
Tel: 867-874-6531 *Toll Free Tel:* 866-297-0232 (CN) *Fax:* 867-874-3321
Web Site: ece.gov.nt.ca/en/services/nwt-public-libraries
Key Personnel
Territorial Libn: Brian Dawson *E-mail:* brian_dawson@gov.nt.ca
Community Lib Literacy Coord: Janine Hoff *E-mail:* janine_hoff@gov.nt.ca
Provide leadership in coordinating public library services throughout the Northwest Territories.
Number of Members: 21

NPPA, see National Press Photographers Association Inc (NPPA)

NPTA, see National Paper Trade Association (NPTA)

NWT Public Library Services, see Northwest Territories Public Library Services

OLA, see Ontario Library Association (OLA)

Ontario Book Publishers Organization (OBPO)
2 Amelia St, Picton, ON K0K 2T0, Canada
Tel: 416-536-7584
Web Site: obpo.ca
Key Personnel
Exec Dir: Holly Kent *E-mail:* holly@obpo.ca
Founded: 1990
Represent the needs, interests, concerns & issues of Ontario book publishers; facilitate information sharing & educational opportunities; facilitate group marketing projects.
Number of Members: 48

Ontario Library Association (OLA)
2080 Danforth Ave, Toronto, ON M4C 1J9, Canada
Toll Free Tel: 877-340-1730
E-mail: info@accessola.com
Web Site: accessola.com
Key Personnel
Exec Dir: Shelagh Paterson *E-mail:* spaterson@accessola.com
Dir, Memb Engagement & Educ: Michelle Arbuckle *E-mail:* marbuckle@accessola.com
Dir, Opers: Stephanie Pimentel *E-mail:* spimentel@accessola.com
Founded: 1900
Number of Members: 5,000
New Election: Annually in Dec
Publication(s): *The Teaching Librarian* (monthly, ezine, free to membs)

Ordre des traducteurs, terminologues et interpretes agrees du quebec (OTTIAQ)
Affiliate of Federation Internationale de Traducteurs
1108-2021 Ave Union, Montreal, QC H3A 2S9, Canada
Tel: 514-845-4411 *Toll Free Tel:* 800-265-4815 *Fax:* 514-845-9903
E-mail: info@ottiaq.org; direction@ottiaq.org; reception@ottiaq.org; communications@ottiaq.org
Web Site: www.ottiaq.org
Key Personnel
Exec Dir & Access to Info Offr/OTTIAQ Secy: Helene Gauthier *Tel:* 514-845-4411 ext 1224 *E-mail:* hgauthier@ottiaq.com
Certification Offr: Marsida Nurka *Tel:* 514-845-4411 ext 1225
Communs Offr: Nora Azouz *Tel:* 514-845-4411 ext 1222

BOOK TRADE & ALLIED ASSOCIATIONS

Mgr, Prof Aff: Benedicte Assogba *Tel:* 514-845-4411 ext 1231 *E-mail:* bassogba@ottiaq.org
Mentorship & Cust Serv: Lynda Godin *Tel:* 514-845-4411 ext 1223 *E-mail:* lgodin@ottiaq.org
Admin Asst: Joanne Trudel *Tel:* 514-845-4411 ext 1226 *E-mail:* jtrudel@ottiaq.org
Prof Aff Asst & Communs: Anne-Christel Delices *Tel:* 514-845-4411 ext 1221 *E-mail:* acdelices@ottiaq.org
Bring translators together to exchange information, send out offers of employment to members. Promote profession & protect public interest. Conferences, annual meeting, social activities, seminars, continuing education.
Number of Members: 2,671
Publication(s): *L'antenne express* (newsletter, free to membs); *Circuit* (quarterly, ezine, free)

Oregon Christian Writers (OCW), see Cascade Christian Writers (CCW)

Outdoor Writers Association of America (OWAA)
2814 Brooks St, Box 442, Missoula, MT 59801
Tel: 406-728-7434
E-mail: info@owaa.org
Web Site: owaa.org
Key Personnel
Exec Dir: Chez Chesak
Founded: 1927
A nonprofit, international organization representing professional communicators dedicated to sharing the outdoor experience.
2025 Meeting(s): Annual Conference, Chattanooga, TN, Aug 18-20, 2025

Overseas Press Club of America (OPC)
40 W 45 St, New York, NY 10036
Tel: 212-626-9220
E-mail: info@opcofamerica.org
Web Site: opcofamerica.org
Key Personnel
Exec Dir: Patricia Kranz *E-mail:* patricia@opcofamerica.org
Founded: 1939
Uphold the highest standards in news reporting, advance press freedom & promote good fellowship among colleagues while educating a new generation of journalists.
Number of Members: 500
New Election: Annually in Aug
Publication(s): *Bulletin* (monthly, newsletter, free to membs); *Dateline* (annual, magazine, free to membs)

Pacific Northwest Booksellers Association (PNBA)
520 W 13 Ave, Eugene, OR 97401-3461
Tel: 541-683-4363 *Toll Free Tel:* 800-353-6764
Fax: 541-683-3910
E-mail: info@pnba.org
Web Site: www.pnba.org
Key Personnel
Exec Dir: Brian Juenemann *E-mail:* brian@pnba.org
Founded: 1965
Nonprofit trade association that exists to promote the success of independent bookstores & support a vibrant, sustainable, innovative & inclusive independent bookselling community in our northwest region—Alaska, Idaho, Montana, Oregon, Washington & British Columbia.
Number of Members: 300
Meeting(s): Annual Tradeshow, Autumn
Publication(s): *Footnotes* (monthly e-mail, newsletter, free to membs); *nmbooklovers.org* (blog); *PNBA Member Handbook* (annual, free to membs, electronic)

Pacific Northwest Writers Association, see PNWA - a writer's resource

Palm Springs Writers Guild
44489 Town Center Way, Suite D, 369, Palm Desert, CA 92260
E-mail: pswg@geographilia.com
Web Site: palmspringswritersguild.org
Founded: 1977
Encourage, develop & support aspiring & established Coachella Valley writers.
Number of Members: 280

PEN America
Affiliate of PEN International
120 Broadway, 26th fl N, New York, NY 10271
Tel: 212-334-1660 *Fax:* 212-334-2181
E-mail: info@pen.org; membership@pen.org; education@pen.org
Web Site: pen.org
Key Personnel
CEO: Suzanne Nossel
COO: Dru Menaker *Tel:* 646-779-4828 *E-mail:* dmenaker@pen.org
Chief Communs Offr: Geraldine Baum *E-mail:* gbaum@pen.org
Chief Fin & Admin Offr: Praise Apampa *E-mail:* papampa@pen.org
Pres: Jennifer Finney Boylan
Literary Programming Chief Offr: Clarisse Rosaz Shariyf *Tel:* 646-779-4831 *E-mail:* clarisse@pen.org
Sr Dir, Free Expression Progs: Summer Lopez *E-mail:* slopez@pen.org
Dir, Eurasia & Advocacy: Polina Sadovskaya *E-mail:* psadovskaya@pen.org
Dir, Free Expression & Educ: Jonathan Friedman
Dir, Membership & Natl Engagement: Rebecca Werner *Tel:* 646-779-4824 *E-mail:* rwerner@pen.org
Prog Dir, Literary Awards: Donica Bettanin *E-mail:* dbettanin@pen.org
Sy Syms Dir, US Free Expression Progs: Kate Ruane *E-mail:* kruane@pen.org
Founded: 1922
An association of writers working to advance literature, defend free expression & foster international literary fellowship. Additional branch location in Miami, FL (PEN America Florida).
Number of Members: 7,500
Branch Office(s)
PEN America Los Angeles, 1370 N St Andrews Place, Los Angeles, CA 90028, Mng Dir: Allison Lee *Tel:* 323-607-1867
PEN America Washington, DC, 1100 13 St NW, Suite 800, Washington, DC 20005, Mng Dir: Hadar Harris

PEN America Los Angeles
Unit of PEN America
1370 N St Andrews Place, Los Angeles, CA 90028
Tel: 323-607-1867
E-mail: info@pen.org
Web Site: pen.org
Key Personnel
Mng Dir: Allison Lee
Progs Dir: Jenn Dees *E-mail:* jdees@pen.org
Founded: 1981
PEN America stands at the intersection of literature & human rights to protect free expression in the US & worldwide. We champion the freedom to write, recognizing the power of the word to transform the world. Our mission is to unite writers & their allies to celebrate creative expression & defend the liberties that make it possible.
Number of Members: 1,000
Publication(s): *Membership Directory* (annual, free to membs); *The Sentences That Create Us* (book)

PEN America Washington, DC
Unit of PEN America

ASSOCIATIONS, EVENTS

1100 13 St NW, Suite 800, Washington, DC 20005
E-mail: info@pen.org
Web Site: pen.org/region/washington-dc
Key Personnel
Mng Dir: Hadar Harris
Govt Aff Liaison: Christian Omoruyi
Lead, Congressional Aff: Laura Schroeder
Founded: 2017
Spearheads the organization's government relations efforts on key domestic & international free expression issues.

PEN Canada
401 Richmond St W, Suite 244, Toronto, ON M5V 3A8, Canada
Tel: 416-703-8448
E-mail: queries@pencanada.ca
Web Site: www.pencanada.ca
Key Personnel
Exec Dir: Brendan de Caires *Tel:* 416-703-8448 ext 2223 *E-mail:* bdecaires@pencanada.ca
Off Mgr: Theresa Johnson *Tel:* 416-703-8448 ext 2221 *E-mail:* tjohnson@pencanada.ca
Founded: 1926
Literary & human rights association of writers & supporters formed to defend freedom of expression & raise awareness to that right. It is one of 145 centres of International PEN in 102 countries & uses the power of the word to assist writers around the world persecuted or exiled for the expression of their thoughts.
PEN Canada is the Canadian chapter of PEN International, founded in England in 1921 to represent poets, essayists & novelists. PEN Canada is a non-partisan non-governmental charitable organization. Its Writers in Peril committee advocate on behalf of writers who are threatened, persecuted or imprisoned for their work; its Writers in Exile Network helps writers who have fled their homelands to make new lives in Canada; its Legal Affairs committee defends freedom of expression in Canada.
Number of Members: 300

PGAMA, see Printing & Graphics Association MidAtlantic (PGAMA)

Photographic Society of America® (PSA®)
8241 S Walker Ave, Suite 104, Oklahoma City, OK 73139
Tel: 405-843-1437 *Toll Free Tel:* 855-PSA-INFO (772-4636)
E-mail: hq@psa-photo.org
Web Site: psa-photo.org
Key Personnel
Membership Mgr: John R Key *E-mail:* membership@psa-photo.org
Founded: 1934
Sponsor workshops & awards for members.
Number of Members: 5,000
2025 Meeting(s): PSA® Photo Festival, Portland, OR, Sept 24-27, 2025
Publication(s): *PSA Journal* (monthly, free to membs)

PIASC, see Printing Industries Association Inc of Southern California (PIASC)

Playwrights Guild of Canada
401 Richmond St W, Suite 350, Toronto, ON M5V 3A8, Canada
Tel: 416-703-0201
E-mail: info@playwrightsguild.ca; marketing@playwrightsguild.ca; orders@playwrightsguild.ca; membership@playwrightsguild.ca
Web Site: playwrightsguild.ca
Key Personnel
Exec Dir: Nancy Morgan *E-mail:* execdir@playwrightsguild.ca
Prog Dir: Monique Renaud
Membership & Contracts Mgr: Rebecca Burton
Prog Mgr: Sarah Duncan

Founded: 1972
To advance the creative rights & interests of professional Canadian playwrights, promote Canadian plays nationally & internationally & foster an active, evolving community of writers for the stage.
Number of Members: 850

PNWA - a writer's resource
1420 NW Gilman Blvd, Suite 29, PMB 2717, Issaquah, WA 98027
Tel: 425-673-2665
E-mail: pnwa@pnwa.org
Web Site: www.pnwa.org
Key Personnel
Pres: Pam Binder *E-mail:* pambinder@pnwa.org
VP: Sandy McCormack
  E-mail: sandymccormack@pnwa.org
Secy: Robert Dugoni
Treas: Brian Mercer *E-mail:* brianmercer@pnwa.org
Founded: 1955
Nonprofit association. Develops writing talent through education, accessibility to publishing industry & participation in a vital writer community.
Number of Members: 1,400

Poetry Society of America (PSA)
119 Smith St, Brooklyn, NY 11201
Tel: 212-254-9628
E-mail: info@poetrysociety.org
Web Site: poetrysociety.org
Key Personnel
Exec Dir: Matt Brogan *E-mail:* matt@poetrysociety.org
Deputy Dir: Brett Fletcher Lauer *E-mail:* brett@poetrysociety.org
Devt Dir: Madeline Weinfield *E-mail:* madeline@poetrysociety.org
Founded: 1910
Contests, readings, lectures, symposia, seminars & public art.
Number of Members: 2,900

Poets & Writers Inc
90 Broad St, Suite 2100, New York, NY 10004
Tel: 212-226-3586 *Fax:* 212-226-3963
E-mail: admin@pw.org
Web Site: www.pw.org
Key Personnel
Exec Dir: Melissa Ford Gradel *Tel:* 212-226-3586 ext 223 *E-mail:* mgradel@pw.org
Dir, Fin & Admin: Tia Williams
  E-mail: twilliams@pw.org
Dir, Progs & Partnerships: Jared Jackson
Founded: 1970
Nonprofit organization which offers information, support & exposure to writers at all stages in their careers. Founded to foster the development of poets & fiction writers & to promote communication throughout the literary community. It publishes the bimonthly *Poets & Writers Magazine*, which delivers to its readers profiles of noted authors & publishing professionals, practical how-to articles, a comprehensive listing of grants & awards for writers & special sections on subjects ranging from small presses to writers conferences. The Readings/Workshops Program makes mini-grants to writers to support literary events in communities nationwide. Other programs include Mapping the Maze & Get the Word Out to help writers navigate the publishing marketplace & promote their work. Poets & Writers sponsors the $80,000 Jackson Poetry Prize, one of the largest awards for an American poet.
Publication(s): *Poets & Writers Magazine* (6 issues/yr, $15.95/yr, $25.95/2 yrs, $6.95 single copy)
Branch Office(s)
PO Box 352110, Los Angeles, CA 90035, Dir: Jamie FitzGerald *Tel:* 310-481-7195

PRIMIR, see Print Industries Market Information and Research Organization (PRIMIR)

Print Industries Market Information and Research Organization (PRIMIR)
Unit of Association for PRINT Technologies (APTech)
1899 Preston White Dr, Reston, VA 20191
Tel: 703-264-7200
E-mail: aptech@aptech.org
Web Site: www.printtechnologies.org; www.npes.org/primirresearch/primir.aspx
Key Personnel
Chair: Richard Mullen *Tel:* 803-802-8283
  E-mail: richard.mullen@domtar.com
Co-Chair: Deanna Klemesrud *Tel:* 763-398-2716
  E-mail: deanna.klemesrud@flintgrp.com
Secy: Rekha Ratnam *E-mail:* rratnam@npes.org
Founded: 2005
Global source of data, analysis & trend information about print & related communications industries through research, initiated by the industry, for the industry. Membership is open to manufacturers & distributors of equipment & supplies, printers, trade shops, publishers & paper companies.
Number of Members: 56
New Election: Annually in Dec

Printing & Graphics Association MidAtlantic (PGAMA)
9160 Red Branch Rd, Suite E-9, Columbia, MD 21045
Tel: 410-319-0900 *Toll Free Tel:* 877-319-0906 *Fax:* 410-319-0905
E-mail: info@pgama.com
Web Site: www.pgama.com
Founded: 1894
Number of Members: 200
Publication(s): *Print Matters* (quarterly)

Printing Brokerage/Buyers Association International (PBBA)
74-5576 Pawai Place, No 599, Kailua Kona, HI 96740
Tel: 808-339-0880
E-mail: contactus@pbba.org
Web Site: pbba.org
Key Personnel
Chmn: Vincent Mallardi *E-mail:* vince@pbba.org
Founded: 1985
Trade association for printing, sales brokerage & purchasing.
Number of Members: 540
Publication(s): *Brokerage* (6 issues/yr, newsletter, free to membs); *Hot Markets for Print Demand Annual Rankings of Buyers, Print Products & Geographies* (annual, $995); *Hot Markets for Print Supply Annual Rankings of Providers, Intermediaries & Geographies* (annual, $995); *Law v. Print: Avoid Problems & Protect Opportunities Buying & Selling Prints* ($395); *Printing Brokerage in North America: The Survey* ($195); *Why Use a Printing Independent? Outsourcing is In* ($95)

Printing Industries Alliance
Affiliate of PRINTING United Alliance
636 N French Rd, Suite 1, Amherst, NY 14228
Tel: 716-691-3211 *Toll Free Tel:* 800-777-4742 *Fax:* 716-691-4249
E-mail: info@pialliance.org
Web Site: pialliance.org
Key Personnel
Pres: Timothy Freeman *E-mail:* tfreeman@pialliance.org
Mktg/Progs Dir: Kimberly Tuzzo
  E-mail: ktuzzo@pialliance.org
Mgr, Membership Servs: Jerry Banks
  E-mail: jerry@pialliance.org
Off Support Mgr: Caroline Wawrzyniec
  E-mail: cwawrzyniec@pialliance.org
Trade association serving the graphic communications industry in New York State, Northern New Jersey & Northwestern Pennsylvania.
Branch Office(s)
195 Prospect Park W, Suite 1A, Brooklyn, NY 11215, EVP: Martin J Maloney *Tel:* 203-912-0804 *E-mail:* mmaloney@pialliance.org

Printing Industries Association Inc of Southern California (PIASC)
5800 S Eastern Ave, Suite 400, Los Angeles, CA 90040
Mailing Address: PO Box 910936, Los Angeles, CA 90091-0936
Tel: 323-728-9500
E-mail: info@piasc.org
Web Site: www.piasc.org
Key Personnel
Pres: Lou Caron *Tel:* 323-728-9500 ext 274
  E-mail: lou@piasc.org
Memb Servs: Kristy Villanueva *Tel:* 323-728-9500 ext 215 *E-mail:* kristy@piasc.org
Founded: 1935 (incorporated 1944)
Trade association for the graphic arts community. Branch locations in Phoenix, AZ & Portland, OR.
Number of Members: 750

Printing Industry Association of the South (PIAS)
305 Plus Park Blvd, Nashville, TN 37217
Tel: 615-366-1094 *Fax:* 615-366-4192
Web Site: www.pias.org
Key Personnel
Pres: Ed Chalifoux *Tel:* 615-366-1094 ext 214
  E-mail: echalifoux@pias.org
Dir, PR: Whitney Presley *Tel:* 615-366-1094 ext 217 *E-mail:* wpardue@pias.org
Provide services & support to the graphic arts industry in 7 states: Alabama, Arkansas, Kentucky, Louisiana, Mississippi, Tennessee & West Virginia.
Number of Members: 400

PRINTING United Alliance
10015 Main St, Fairfax, VA 22031
Tel: 703-385-1335 *Toll Free Tel:* 888-385-3588 *Fax:* 703-273-0456; 703-691-7492 (membership)
E-mail: assist@printing.org; info@printing.org
Web Site: www.printing.org
Key Personnel
CEO: Ford Bowers *E-mail:* fbowers@printing.org
EVP: James Martin *E-mail:* jmartin@printing.org
SVP, Educ & Training (PA Off): Joe Marin
  E-mail: jmarin@printing.org
VP, HR Consulting (PA Off): Adriane Harrison
  E-mail: aharrison@printing.org
VP, Govt Aff (DC Off): Lisbeth A Lyons
  E-mail: llyons@printing.org
VP, PR: Amanda Kliegl *E-mail:* akliegl@printing.org
VP, Fin & Acctg: Casey McAllister
  E-mail: cmcallister@printing.org
VP, Expositions: Lexy Olisko *E-mail:* lolisko@printing.org
Founded: 2020 (thru the merger of Printing Industries of America & Specialty Graphic Imaging Association)
Member organization providing research, educational & technical services to printing industry worldwide.
Number of Members: 14,000
2025 Meeting(s): PRINTING United Expo, Orange County Convention Center, Orlando, FL, Oct 22-24, 2025
2026 Meeting(s): PRINTING United Expo, Las Vegas Convention Center, 3150 Paradise Rd, Las Vegas, NV, Sept 23-25, 2026

BOOK TRADE & ALLIED ASSOCIATIONS

2027 Meeting(s): PRINTING United Expo, Las Vegas Convention Center, 3150 Paradise Rd, Las Vegas, NV, Sept 14-16, 2027
2028 Meeting(s): PRINTING United Expo, Georgia World Congress Center, 285 Andrew Young International Blvd NW, Atlanta, GA, Oct 18-20, 2028
2029 Meeting(s): PRINTING United Expo, Orange County Convention Center, Orlando, FL, Oct 24-26, 2029
Publication(s): *Industry Ink* (monthly, enewsletter); *PRINTING United Journal* (quarterly)
Branch Office(s)
1325 "G" St NW, Suite 500, Washington, DC 20005 *Tel:* 202-627-6925 ext 504
2000 Corporate Dr, Suite 205, Wexford, PA 15090 *Tel:* 412-741-6860 *Toll Free Tel:* 800-910-4283 *Fax:* 412-741-2311

The Private Eye Writers of America (PWA)
3665 S Needles Hwy, 7G, Laughlin, NV 89029
Web Site: www.privateeyewriters.com
Key Personnel
Exec Dir: Robert J Randisi *E-mail:* rrandisi@sbcglobal.net
Founded: 1981
Organization devoted to Private Eye fiction. Membership is open to fans, writers & publishing professionals. Sponsor of the annual Shamus Awards for private eye novels & short stories.

Protestant Church-Owned Publishers Association
841 Mount Clinton Pike, Suite D, Harrisonburg, VA 22802
Web Site: www.pcpaonline.org
Key Personnel
Exec Dir: Beth Lewis *Tel:* 763-234-4353 (cell) *E-mail:* beth.lewis@pcpaonline.org
Founded: 1951
International association of nonprofit, Protestant denominational publishers & other nonprofit Christian publishers who serve one or more Protestant denominations through the content created, published or distributed. In addition, PCPA is supported by adjunct members, companies that provide products & services that support the work of PCPA's publishing members. PCPA also has freelance, individual & student members interested in Christian publishing.
Number of Members: 60
2025 Meeting(s): ACP/PCPA Joint Conference, Chicago Marriott Naperville, 1801 N Naper Blvd, Naperville, IL, May 1-5, 2025

Public Library Association (PLA)
Division of The American Library Association (ALA)
225 N Michigan Ave, Suite 1300, Chicago, IL 60601
Toll Free Tel: 800-545-2433 (ext 5752) *Fax:* 312-280-5029
E-mail: pla@ala.org
Web Site: www.ala.org/pla/
Key Personnel
Exec Dir: Mary Davis Fournier *Tel:* 312-280-5056 *E-mail:* mfournier@ala.org
Mgr, Mktg & Membership: Samantha Lopez *Tel:* 312-280-5857 *E-mail:* slopez@ala.org
Founded: 1944
Association dedicated to supporting the needs of public library professionals across the U.S. & Canada by offering continuing education opportunities, unique public library initiatives & a conference for public library staff. PLA strives to help its members shape the essential institution of public libraries by serving as an ally for public library workers.
Number of Members: 9,000
Meeting(s): PLA Conference

Public Relations Society of America Inc
120 Wall St, 21st fl, New York, NY 10005
Tel: 212-460-1400
E-mail: membership@prsa.org
Web Site: www.prsa.org
Key Personnel
CEO: Linda Thomas Brooks *E-mail:* linda.thomasbrooks@prsa.org
Chief Communs Offr: Karen Mateo *E-mail:* karen.mateo@prsa.org
Chief Mktg & Sales Offr: Maureen Walsh *E-mail:* maureen.walsh@prsa.org
CFO: Philip T Bonaventura *E-mail:* philip.bonaventura@prsa.org
SVP, Memb Servs: Jay Starr *E-mail:* jay.starr@prsa.org
SVP, Progs: Jeneen Garcia *E-mail:* jeneen.garcia@prsa.org
VP, Busn Devt: John Robinson *E-mail:* john.robinson@prsa.org
VP, HR: Stefanie Scire *E-mail:* stefanie.scire@prsa.org
VP, IT: Alex Ortiz *E-mail:* alex.ortiz@prsa.org
VP, Meetings & Events: John Bomier *E-mail:* john.bomier@prsa.org
Founded: 1947
Empowers its members to succeed at every stage of their careers though a wide breadth of professional development, networking & leadership opportunities. Guided by its Code of Ethics, PRSA is collectively represented by more than 100 chapters & 14 Professional Interest Sections, as well as on nearly 375 college & university campuses in the US, Puerto Rico, Argentina, Colombia & Peru through its student organization, the Public Relations Student Society of America (PRSSA). PRSA's signature events include the Anvil Awards & ICON, the premier annual gathering for communications professionals & students.
Publication(s): *PRsay* (blog); *Strategies & Tactics* (10 issues/yr, online, newspaper, $125/yr US, $135/yr CN, $150/yr elsewhere; free to membs)

Publishers Association of the West Inc (PubWest)
12727 Highland Ct, Auburn, CA 95603-3634
Tel: 720-443-3637
E-mail: executivedirector@pubwest.org
Web Site: pubwest.org
Key Personnel
Pres: Miriam Warren
Founded: 1977
Members are small & medium-sized book publishers located throughout North America. Supply marketing & technical information to members; conduct annual educational seminars; promote sales in the region. Participates in MPBA & PNBA trade shows. Publisher of the *PubWest Industry Operations and Salary Report*.
Number of Members: 360

Publishers' Publicity Association (PPA)
PO Box 2437, New York, NY 10017
Tel: 212-790-7259
E-mail: publisherspublicity@gmail.com
Web Site: publisherspublicityassociation.square.site
Key Personnel
Pres: Tanya Farrell
Founded: 1963
Nonprofit professional group open to publicists of book publishing houses as well as public relations personnel in related media.

Publishing Professionals Network
c/o Postal Annex, 274 Redwood Shores Pkwy, Redwood City, CA 94065-1173
Mailing Address: PO Box 129, Redwood City, CA 94064-0129
E-mail: operations@pubpronetwork.org

ASSOCIATIONS, EVENTS

Web Site: pubpronetwork.org
Key Personnel
Pres: Dave Peattie
Founded: 1969 (as Bookbuilders West)
Specialize in supporting the book publishing industry. Offers educational programs, seminars & scholarships. Produces an annual book show & has monthly dinner meetings.
Number of Members: 400
New Election: Annually in Jan
Meeting(s): Annual Conference, Spring; Annual Book Show, Autumn
Publication(s): *PPN Post* (monthly, enewsletter)

PubWest, see Publishers Association of the West Inc (PubWest)

Quebec Writers' Federation (QWF)
1200 Atwater Ave, Suite 3, Westmount, QC H3Z 1X4, Canada
Tel: 514-933-0878
E-mail: info@qwf.org
Web Site: www.qwf.org; www.hireawriter.ca; quebecbooks.qwf.org
Key Personnel
Exec Dir: Lori Schubert *E-mail:* lori@qwf.org
Association of Quebec writers to promote English language writing in Quebec through literary awards, writing workshops, mentorship program & literary events.
Number of Members: 800

Reporters Committee for Freedom of the Press
1156 15 St NW, Suite 1020, Washington, DC 20005-1779
Tel: 202-795-9300 *Toll Free Tel:* 800-336-4243 (legal hotline for journalists)
E-mail: info@rcfp.org
Web Site: www.rcfp.org
Key Personnel
Exec Dir: Bruce Brown
Deputy Exec Dir & Legal Dir: Katie Townsend
Communs Dir: Jenn Topper
Opers Dir: Kirsten Poole
Founded: 1970
Provides pro bono legal services for journalists & news media organizations.
Publication(s): *Anti-SLAPP Legal Guide*; *Election Legal Guide*; *Open Courts Compendium* (handbook); *Open Government Guide* (handbook); *Police, Protesters and the Press* (handbook); *Press Freedom on Tribal Lands*; *A Reporter's Guide to Pre-Publication Review* (handbook); *Reporter's Privilege Compendium* (handbook); *Reporter's Recording Guide* (handbook)

Le Reseau EdCan, see EdCan Network

Romance Writers of America®
2455 E Sunrise Blvd, Suite 816, Fort Lauderdale, FL 33304
Tel: 832-717-5200
E-mail: info@rwa.org
Web Site: www.rwa.org
Founded: 1980
Romance Writers of America is dedicated to advancing the professional interests of career-focused romance writers through networking & advocacy.
Membership: $99/yr, $25 processing fee (new & reinstating).
Number of Members: 2,000

SABEW, see Society for Advancing Business Editing and Writing (SABEW)

Science Fiction and Fantasy Writers Association, Inc (SFWA)
PO Box 215, San Lorenzo, CA 94580
Tel: 860-698-0536
E-mail: office@sfwa.org; operations@sfwa.org

Web Site: www.sfwa.org
Key Personnel
CFO: Nathan Lowell *E-mail:* cfo@sfwa.org
Pres: Jeffe Kennedy *E-mail:* president@sfwa.org
VP: Tobias S Buckell *E-mail:* vp@sfwa.org
Secy: Adam Rakunas *E-mail:* secretary@sfwa.org
Exec Dir: Kate Baker
Founded: 1965
An organization of professional writers, editors, artists, agents & others in the science fiction & fantasy field.
Number of Members: 2,300
New Election: Annually in May
Publication(s): *Annual Membership Directory*; *Nebula Awards Showcase* (annual); *SFWA Bulletin* (quarterly)

SF Canada
c/o Jane Glatt, 35 Southshore Crescent, No 103, Hamilton, ON L8E 0J2, Canada
Web Site: www.sfcanada.org
Key Personnel
Pres: Margaret Curelas
VP: Robert Dawson
Secy-Treas: Jane Glatt
Founded: 1989
Exists to foster a sense of community among Canadian writers of speculative fiction, to improve communication between Canadian writers of speculative fiction, to foster the growth of quality writing in Canadian speculative fiction, to lobby on behalf of Canadian writers of speculative fiction & to encourage the translation of Canadian speculative fiction. Supports positive social action.
Number of Members: 77

SHARP, see Society for the History of Authorship, Reading & Publishing Inc (SHARP)

SIBA, see Southern Independent Booksellers Alliance (SIBA)

SK Arts
1355 Broad St, Regina, SK S4R 7V1, Canada
Tel: 306-787-4056 *Toll Free Tel:* 800-667-7526 (CN)
E-mail: info@sk-arts.ca
Web Site: sk-arts.ca
Key Personnel
CEO: Michael Jones
Dir, Admin: Gail Paul Armstrong
Founded: 1948
Provide consultation, advice, grants, programs +/or services to individual artists, arts groups & organizations & members of the public. Programs support & encourage the development of artists, arts groups & organizations in the literary, performing, visual, media & multidisciplinary arts. Also develop & maintain a permanent collection of original works by Saskatchewan artists.
Branch Office(s)
201 Avenue "B" S, Saskatoon, SK S7M 1M3, Canada *Tel:* 306-964-1155

SMPTE, see Society of Motion Picture and Television Engineers® (SMPTE®)

Social Sciences & Humanities Research Council (SSHRC)
350 Albert St, Ottawa, ON K1P 6G4, Canada
Mailing Address: PO Box 1610, Ottawa, ON K1P 6G4, Canada
Tel: 613-995-4273 *Toll Free Tel:* 855-275-2861
E-mail: research@sshrc-crsh.gc.ca
Web Site: www.sshrc-crsh.gc.ca
Key Personnel
CFO & VP, Common Admin Servs Directorate: Dominique Osterrath
Pres: Ted Hewitt
VP, Corp Aff: Valerie La Traverse
VP, Res: Dominique Berube
VP, Stakeholder Engagement & Advancement of Society: Ursula Gobel
Federal research funding agency that promotes & supports research & research training in the humanities & social sciences. Awards to Scholarly Publications (ASP) is funded by the SSHRC & supports the dissemination of Canadian social sciences & humanities research by funding the publication of high-quality scholarly monographs, books & other long-form publications.
Number of Members: 22
Publication(s): *Dialogue* (enewsletter)

Sociedad Interamericana de Prensa (SIP), see Inter American Press Association (IAPA)

Society for Advancing Business Editing and Writing (SABEW)
Walter Cronkite School of Journalism & Mass Communication, Arizona State University, 555 N Central Ave, Suite 406E, Phoenix, AZ 85004-1248
Mailing Address: PO Box 4, Fountainville, PA 18923
Tel: 602-496-7862
E-mail: sabew@sabew.org
Web Site: sabew.org
Key Personnel
Exec Dir: Kathleen Graham *Tel:* 202-549-0158 *E-mail:* kgraham@sabew.org
Prog & Content Dir: Tobin Ernst *Tel:* 480-322-3938 *E-mail:* ternst@sabew.org
Membership Coord: Tess McLaughlin *E-mail:* tmclaughlin@sabew.org
Founded: 1964
Promotes ethics & excellence in business journalism. Annual contests & awards, conferences & training programs.
Number of Members: 2,500
Meeting(s): Spring Conference

Society for Features Journalism (SFJ)
Eugene S Pulliam National Journalism Ctr, 3909 N Meridian St, Indianapolis, IN 46208
E-mail: wearesfj@gmail.com
Web Site: featuresjournalism.org
Key Personnel
Pres: Sharon Chapman *E-mail:* schapman@statesman.com
First VP: Emily Spicer *E-mail:* espicer@express-news.net
Second VP: Laura Coffey
Secy/Treas: Mesfin Fekadu
Founded: 1947 (as AASFE - American Association of Sunday & Feature Editors)
Nonprofit trade association promoting the craft of writing & innovation in lifestyle, arts & entertainment journalism.
Number of Members: 250

Society for Scholarly Publishing (SSP)
1120 Rte 73, Suite 200, Mount Laurel, NJ 08054
Tel: 856-439-1385 *Fax:* 856-439-0525
E-mail: info@sspnet.org
Web Site: www.sspnet.org
Key Personnel
Exec Dir: Melanie Dolechek *E-mail:* mdolechek@sspnet.org
Prog Dir: Susan Patton *E-mail:* spatton@sspnet.org
Mktg & Opers Mgr: Jacklyn Lord *E-mail:* jlord@sspnet.org
Membership Admin: Madelyn Stone *E-mail:* mstone@sspnet.org
Founded: 1978
Nonprofit organization to promote & advance communication among all sectors of the scholarly publication community through networking, information dissemination & facilitation of new developments in the field.
Number of Members: 1,000
2025 Meeting(s): Annual Meeting, Hilton Baltimore Inner Harbor, 401 W Pratt St, Baltimore, MD, May 28-30, 2025
2026 Meeting(s): Annual Meeting, Gaylord Pacific Resort & Convention Center, 1000 "H" St, Chula Vista, CA, May 27-29, 2026
Publication(s): *Directory* (annual, membs only)

Society for Technical Communication (STC)
3251 Blenheim Blvd, Suite 406, Fairfax, VA 22030
Tel: 703-522-4114 *Fax:* 703-522-2075
E-mail: stc@stc.org
Web Site: www.stc.org
Key Personnel
CEO: Liz Pohland *Tel:* 571-366-1901 *E-mail:* liz.pohland@stc.org
Dir, Opers, Membership & Community Rel: Erin Gallalee *Tel:* 571-366-1914 *E-mail:* erin.gallalee@stc.org
Indus Rel Mgr: Christina DeRose *Tel:* 856-437-4742 *E-mail:* cderose@stc.org
Mktg Mgr: Jessica Farrell *Tel:* 856-380-6883 *E-mail:* jfarrell@stc.org
Pubns Mgr: Krista Cornew *Tel:* 856-380-6868 *E-mail:* kcornew@stc.org
Founded: 1960 (as Society of Technical Writers & Publishers)
Professional society dedicated to the advancement of the theory & practice of technical communication in all media.
Number of Members: 5,000
Meeting(s): STC Technical Communication Summit
Publication(s): *Intercom* (8 issues/yr, magazine, free to membs, $215/yr nonmembs, $240/yr nonmembs CN, $270/yr nonmembs elsewhere); *Technical Communication* (quarterly, journal, free to membs, $275/yr nonmembs, electronic)

Society for the History of Authorship, Reading & Publishing Inc (SHARP)
c/o Johns Hopkins University Press, Journals Publishing Div, PO Box 19966, Baltimore, MD 21211-0966
Tel: 410-516-6987 *Toll Free Tel:* 800-548-1784
Fax: 410-516-3866
E-mail: members@sharpweb.org
Web Site: www.sharpweb.org
Key Personnel
Membership Secy: Lisa Maruca
Communs Coord: Anna Muenchrath *E-mail:* coordinator@sharpweb.org
Founded: 1992
Promotes the study of book history among academics & nonacademics. Publishing & scholarly attention to its history.
Number of Members: 1,175
Meeting(s): SHARP Annual Conference, July
Publication(s): *Book History* (2 issues/yr, journal, included with indiv membership, $73/yr instns); *SHARP News* (quarterly, enewsletter); *SHARP Online Membership & Periodicals Directory* (annual, access to online included with membership)
Membership(s): American Council of Learned Societies (ACLS)

Society of American Travel Writers (SATW)
355 Lexington Ave, 15th fl, New York, NY 10017
E-mail: info@satw.org
Web Site: www.satw.org
Key Personnel
Exec Dir: Marla Schrager *E-mail:* mschrager@satw.org
Founded: 1955
Promote responsible journalism, provide professional support & development for our mem-

BOOK TRADE & ALLIED ASSOCIATIONS

bers, encourage the conservation & preservation of travel resources worldwide.
Number of Members: 908
Publication(s): *Membership Directory* (annual, $250 print (+ $7.50 S&H) or as online PDF)

Society of Children's Book Writers & Illustrators (SCBWI)
6363 Wilshire Blvd, Suite 425, Los Angeles, CA 90048
Tel: 323-782-1010
E-mail: membership@scbwi.org
Web Site: www.scbwi.org
Key Personnel
Exec Dir: Sarah Baker
Dir, Mktg & Commun Strategy: Tammy Brown
Dir, Programming & Content: Kim Turrisi
Dir, Regl Team Mgmt: Patricia Wiles
Dir, Web Devt & Database Mgr: Joshua Smith
Assoc Dir, Digital Content & Awards: Sarah Diamond
Mgr, Design & Illustration: TeMika Grooms
Mgr, Events & Spec Projs: Laurie Miller
Assoc Mgr, Awards & Pubns: Danielle Monique
Logistics Coord: Brandon Clarke
Admin Asst: Chelsea Hall
Founded: 1971
An organization of children's writers & illustrators & others devoted to the interests of children's literature; annual workshops & conferences throughout the world.
Number of Members: 22,000
Meeting(s): Summer Conference, Virtual, annually in July/Aug
2025 Meeting(s): Winter Conference, New York Hilton Midtown, 1335 Avenue of the Americas, New York, NY, Jan 31-Feb 2, 2025
Publication(s): *La Cometa* (6 issues/yr, online in Spanish, bulletin); *The Essential Guide to Publishing for Children* (book); *The Essential Guide to Self-Publishing Books for Children* (book); *SCBWI Bulletin* (quarterly, free to membs); *SCBWI INSIGHT* (monthly, enewsletter, free to membs)

Society of Illustrators (SI)
128 E 63 St, New York, NY 10065
Tel: 212-838-2560 *Fax:* 212-838-2561
E-mail: info@societyillustrators.org
Web Site: www.societyillustrators.org
Key Personnel
Exec Dir: Anelle Miller *E-mail:* anelle@societyillustrators.org
Founded: 1901
Formed to promote the art of illustration. The society houses the Museum of American Illustration.
Number of Members: 1,100
New Election: Annually in June
Publication(s): *American Illustration* (annual, $50)

The Society of Midland Authors (SMA)
PO Box 10419, Chicago, IL 60610
Web Site: midlandauthors.org
Founded: 1915
Nonprofit writer's association that seeks to stimulate creative efforts & closer association among Midwest writers; maintain collections of writer's works & encourage interest in reading, literature & writing in cooperation with other educational & cultural institutions. Members are qualified authors & co-authors of works from recognized publishers or associates (non-voting) who live in Illinois, Indiana, Kansas, Michigan, Minnesota, Missouri, Nebraska, North Dakota, Ohio, South Dakota or Wisconsin. Monthly literary & professional programs.
Number of Members: 400
Publication(s): *Literary License* (monthly, newsletter)

Society of Motion Picture and Television Engineers® (SMPTE®)
White Plains Plaza, 445 Hamilton Ave, Suite 601, White Plains, NY 10601-1827
Tel: 914-761-1100
E-mail: hello@smpte.org (mktg)
Web Site: www.smpte.org
Key Personnel
Exec Dir: David Grindle *Tel:* 914-205-2370 *E-mail:* dgrindle@smpte.org
Dir, Educ: Maja Davidovic *Tel:* 914-600-2320 *E-mail:* mdavidovic@smpte.org
Dir, Events & Governance Liaison: Sally-Ann D'Amato *Tel:* 914-205-2375 *E-mail:* sdamato@smpte.org
Dir, Membership: Roberta Gorman *Tel:* 914-205-2376 *E-mail:* rgorman@smpte.org
Dir, Standards Devt: Thomas Bause Mason *Tel:* 914-205-2378 *E-mail:* tbausemason@smpte.org
Founded: 1916
To advance theory & practice of engineering in film, TV, motion imaging & allied arts & sciences; establishment of standards & practices. Annual membership dues: $165.
Number of Members: 7,000
Meeting(s): SMPTE® Media Technology Summit, annually
Publication(s): *Motion Imaging Journal* (10 issues/yr, 3 print & online, 7 online only, free to membs, $1,000/yr nonmembs)

Society of Professional Journalists (SPJ)
PO Box 441748, Indianapolis, IN 46244
Tel: 317-927-8000 *Fax:* 317-920-4789
E-mail: communications@spj.org
Web Site: www.spj.org
Key Personnel
Exec Dir: Caroline Hendrie *Tel:* 317-927-8000 ext 200 *E-mail:* chendrie@hq.spj.org
Natl Pres: Ashanti Blaize-Hopkins *E-mail:* ahsanti-blaize@gmail.com
Membership Strategist: Chrystal O'Keefe *E-mail:* cokeefe@hq.spj.org
Quill Ed/Mgr, Pubns & Awards: Lou Harry *Tel:* 317-927-8000 ext 202 *E-mail:* lharry@spj.org
Dir, Ethics & Diversity: Rod Hicks *Tel:* 317-927-8000 ext 203 *E-mail:* rhicks@spj.org
Communs Specialist: Kimberly Tsuyuki *E-mail:* ktsuyuki@spj.org
Communs Coord: Nadia Gordon *E-mail:* ngordon@spj.com
Founded: 1909 (as Sigma Delta Chi)
Professional organization that includes broadcast, print & online journalists, journalism educators & students interested in journalism as a career.
Number of Members: 6,000
Publication(s): *Quill* (quarterly, magazine, $75/yr, free to membs)

The Society of Southwestern Authors (SSA)
PO Box 30355, Tucson, AZ 85751-0355
Web Site: www.ssa-az.org
Key Personnel
Pres: Mary Ann Carman *E-mail:* macarman6@gmail.com
VP: Sharon Lashinger *E-mail:* srlashinger@hotmail.com
Treas: David Gilmore *E-mail:* lacroixpublishing@gmail.com
Recording Secy: Solomon Cantanio *E-mail:* scantanio@gmail.com
Founded: 1972
Nonprofit association of writers & other publishing professionals.
Number of Members: 400
Publication(s): *The Write Word* (6 issues/yr, newsletter, free to membs)

ASSOCIATIONS, EVENTS

Software & Information Industry Association (SIIA)
1620 Eye St NW, Washington, DC 20005
Mailing Address: PO Box 34340, Washington, DC 20043
Tel: 202-289-7442 *Fax:* 202-289-7097
E-mail: info@siia.net
Web Site: www.siia.net
Key Personnel
CFO: Carl Walker *E-mail:* cwalker@siia.net
Pres, SIIA: Jeff Joseph *E-mail:* jjoseph@siia.net
VP, Membership & Mktg: Renee Harris-Etheridge *E-mail:* rhetheridge@siia.net
Off Mgr: Rozana Abraham *E-mail:* rabraham@siia.net
Principal trade association of the software & information industry.
Number of Members: 500
Publication(s): *Signature* (6 issues/yr, magazine, free to membs)

Southern Independent Booksellers Alliance (SIBA)
51 Pleasant Ridge Dr, Asheville, NC 28805
Tel: 803-994-9530 *Fax:* 309-410-0211
E-mail: siba@sibaweb.com
Web Site: www.sibaweb.com
Key Personnel
Exec Dir: Linda-Marie Barrett *E-mail:* lindamarie@sibaweb.com
Trade association representing independent bookstores & booksellers in Alabama, Arkansas, Florida, Georgia, Kentucky, Louisiana, Mississippi, North Carolina, South Carolina, Tennessee & Virginia.
Number of Members: 250
Publication(s): *SIBA Holiday Catalog*; *The Southern Bookseller Review* (newsletter)

Special Libraries Association (SLA)
7918 Jones Branch Dr, Suite 300, McLean, VA 22102
Tel: 703-647-4900 *Fax:* 703-506-3266
E-mail: info@sla.org
Web Site: www.sla.org
Key Personnel
Mng Dir/VP, Communities & Programming: Monica Evans-Lombe *E-mail:* mevans-lombe@sla.org
Dir, Content: Stuart Hales *E-mail:* shales@sla.org
Dir, Fin: Cecilia Mason
Dir, Memb Engagement: Jordan Burghardt *E-mail:* jburghardt@sla.org
Founded: 1909
International professional association for library & information professionals. SLA offers members many opportunities for professional development. Participate in online learning programs, certificate programs, the leadership symposium & the annual conference to stay competitive, expand your knowledge & learn skills that are critical to job satisfaction & career success.
Number of Members: 8,000
Meeting(s): Annual Conference & INFO-EXPO
Publication(s): *Information Insights* (weekly, enewsletter, free to membs)

SSHRC, see Social Sciences & Humanities Research Council (SSHRC)

STC, see Society for Technical Communication (STC)

Teachers & Writers Collaborative (T&W)
20 W 20 St, Suite 801, New York, NY 10011
Mailing Address: PO Box 1208, New York, NY 10113
Tel: 212-691-6590
E-mail: info@twc.org
Web Site: www.twc.org
Key Personnel
Exec Dir: Asari Beale *E-mail:* abeale@twc.org

Educ Dir: Nancy L Weber *E-mail:* nweber@twc.org
Prog Coord: Alice Pencavel
Founded: 1967
Information source for those interested in teaching writing & literary arts; publish books & magazines about creative writing; sponsor workshops.
Publication(s): *Teachers & Writers* (monthly, ezine, free)

Technical Association of the Pulp & Paper Industry (TAPPI)
15 Technology Pkwy S, Suite 115, Peachtree Corners, GA 30092
Tel: 770-446-1400 *Toll Free Tel:* 800-332-8686 (US); 800-446-9431 (CN) *Fax:* 770-446-6947
E-mail: memberconnection@tappi.org
Web Site: www.tappi.org
Key Personnel
Pres & CEO: Larry N Montague *Tel:* 770-209-7227 *E-mail:* lmontague@tappi.org
Press Mgr: Jana Jensen *Tel:* 770-209-7242
  E-mail: jjensen@tappi.org
Founded: 1915
Technical association/nonprofit professional society of executives, operating managers, engineers, scientists & technologists serving the pulp, paper & allied industries.
Number of Members: 7,000
Meeting(s): SuperCorrExpo®
2025 Meeting(s): TAPPICon, Minneapolis Convention Center, 1301 Second Ave S, Minneapolis, MN, May 4-7, 2025
Publication(s): *Ahead of the Curve* (weekly, enewsletter); *Over the Wire* (weekly, enewsletter, membs only); *Paper360°* (6 issues/yr, free to membs, print & electronic); *TAPPI JOURNAL* (free to membs, electronic); *TAPPI STAR* (enewsletter); *Tissue360°* (2 issues/yr, free to membs, print & electronic); *Tissue360° Newsletter* (monthly, newsletter, free to membs)

Television Academy
5220 Lankershim Blvd, North Hollywood, CA 91601-3109
Tel: 818-754-2800
Web Site: www.emmys.com
Key Personnel
CEO & Chmn of the Bd: Frank Scherma
CFO & EVP, Busn Opers: Heather Cochran
Pres & COO: Maury McIntyre
SVP, Media & Brand Mgmt/Chief Mktg Offr: Susan Spencer
VP, Awards & Memb Servs: Julie Shore
VP, Content: Juan Morales
VP, Event Prodn: Barb Held
VP, Mktg: Laurel Whitcomb *E-mail:* whitcomb@televisionacademy.com
VP, Membership & Outreach: Linda Swain
Founded: 1977
Organization for those involved in national television; bestows Emmy awards for excellence in television; college television awards & college internship program; inducts deserving individuals in "Television Academy Hall of Fame".
Number of Members: 20,000
Publication(s): *EMMY Magazine*

Texas Institute of Letters (TIL)
PO Box 130294, Spring, TX 77393
Web Site: texasinstituteofletters.org
Key Personnel
Pres: David Bowles *E-mail:* president@texasinstituteofletters.org
VP: Chris Barton
Secy: Kathryn Jones *E-mail:* secretary@texasinstituteofletters.org
Treas: Cliff Hudder
Recording Secy: Marcia Hatfield Daudistel
Founded: 1936
Nonprofit honor society to celebrate Texas literature & to recognize distinctive literary achievement. The TIL awards over $20,000 annually to recognize outstanding literary works in several categories & supports the Dobie Paisano Fellowship for writers.
Number of Members: 250
Publication(s): *Newsletter* (2 issues/yr, membs only)

Texas Library Association (TLA)
3420 Executive Center Dr, Suite 301, Austin, TX 78731
Tel: 512-328-1518 *Fax:* 512-328-8852
E-mail: tla@txla.org
Web Site: txla.org
Key Personnel
Exec Dir: Shirley Robinson *Tel:* 512-328-1518 ext 151 *E-mail:* shirleyr@txla.org
Dir, Advocacy & Commun: Wendy Woodland *Tel:* 512-328-1518 ext 146 *E-mail:* wendyw@txla.org
Coord, Membership & Spec Servs: Christy Reynolds *Tel:* 512-328-1518 ext 153
  E-mail: christyr@txla.org
Founded: 1902
TLA is the largest state library association in the country promoting librarianship & library service in Texas.
Number of Members: 6,000
2025 Meeting(s): Annual Conference, Dallas, TX, April 1-4, 2025
2026 Meeting(s): Annual Conference, Houston, TX, March 30-April 2, 2026
2027 Meeting(s): Annual Conference, San Antonio, TX, March 30-April 2, 2027
2028 Meeting(s): Annual Conference, San Antonio, TX, April 24-27, 2028
Publication(s): *Texas Library Journal* (quarterly); *Texline* (irregular, enewsletter); *TLA Weekly Brief* (enewsletter); *TLACast Newsletter* (6-8 issues/yr)

Theatre Library Association (TLA)
c/o The New York Public Library for the Performing Arts, 40 Lincoln Center Plaza, New York, NY 10023
E-mail: theatrelibraryassociation@gmail.com
Web Site: www.tla-online.org
Key Personnel
Exec Secy: Dale Stinchcomb
  E-mail: dstinchcomb@fas.harvard.edu
Treas: Sophie Glidden-Lyon *E-mail:* sophie.gliddenlyon@gmail.com
Founded: 1937
Supports librarians & archivists affiliated with theatre, dance, popular entertainment, performance studies, motion picture & broadcasting collections.
Publication(s): *Performing Arts Resources* (irregularly, series)

United for Libraries
Division of The American Library Association (ALA)
225 N Michigan Ave, Suite 1300, Chicago, IL 60601
Tel: 312-280-2161 *Toll Free Tel:* 800-545-2433 (ext 2161)
E-mail: united@ala.org
Web Site: www.ala.org/united
Key Personnel
Exec Dir: Beth Nawalinski *E-mail:* bnawalinski@ala.org
Mgr, Mktg & Membership: Jillian Wentworth *E-mail:* jwentworth@ala.org
Founded: 2009
Supports those who govern, promote, advocate & fundraise for libraries & brings together library trustees, advocates, friends & foundations into a partnership that creates a powerful force for libraries in the 21st century.
Number of Members: 5,000

United States Board on Books for Young People (USBBY)
Unit of International Board on Books for Young People (IBBY)
National Luis University, Ctr for Teaching through Children's Books, 1000 Capitol Dr, Wheeling, IL 60090
Tel: 224-233-2798
E-mail: secretariat@usbby.org
Web Site: www.usbby.org
Key Personnel
Pres: Evelyn B Freeman
Exec Dir & Liaison Offr: Ellis Vance
  E-mail: executive.director@usbby.org
Secretariat: Ms Junko Yokota
Founded: 1953
Nonprofit organization devoted to building bridges of international understanding through children's & young adult books.
Number of Members: 500
Publication(s): *USBBY Newsletter* (2 issues/yr)
Membership(s): The American Library Association (ALA); The Children's Book Council (CBC); International Literacy Association (ILA); National Council of Teachers of English (NCTE)

Visual Media Alliance (VMA)
Affiliate of PRINTING United Alliance
665 Third St, Suite 500, San Francisco, CA 94107-1926
Tel: 415-495-8242 *Toll Free Tel:* 800-659-3363 *Fax:* 415-520-1126
E-mail: info@vma.bz
Web Site: main.vma.bz
Key Personnel
Pres: Ian Flynn *Tel:* 415-495-8242 ext 701
  E-mail: ian@vma.bz
EVP: David Katz *Tel:* 415-495-8242 ext 703
  E-mail: david@vma.bz
Dir, Sales & Membership: Shannon Wolford *Tel:* 415-495-8242 ext 711 *E-mail:* shannon@vma.bz
Mktg & Communs Dir: Sonali Shah *Tel:* 415-495-8242 ext 712 *E-mail:* sonali@vma.bz
Trade association offering support for creative, web media, marketing & print businesses.
Number of Members: 950
Publication(s): *Connected* (quarterly, magazine, free to membs); *Cross-Media Chronicles* (monthly, enewsletter); *eDigest* (monthly, enewsletter); *RiskReport* (quarterly)

VMA, see Visual Media Alliance (VMA)

Western Writers of America Inc (WWA)
271 CR 219, Encampment, WY 82325
Tel: 307-329-8942
Web Site: westernwriters.org
Key Personnel
Pres: Chris Enss *E-mail:* gvcenss@aol.com
Exec Dir & Secy-Treas: Candy Moulton
  E-mail: wwa.moulton@gmail.com
Founded: 1953
Nonprofit confederation of professional writers of fiction & nonfiction pertaining to, or inspired by, tradition, legends, development & history of the American West.
Number of Members: 725
Meeting(s): Annual Convention, June
Publication(s): *Roundup Magazine* (6 issues/yr, $40/yr)

Willamette Writers
5331 SW Macadam Ave, Suite 258, PMB 215, Portland, OR 97239
Tel: 971-200-5385

E-mail: wilwrite@willamettewriters.org
Web Site: willamettewriters.org
Key Personnel
Pres: Gail Pasternack
Exec Dir: Kate Ristau
Founded: 1965
Pacific Northwest writers organization committed to helping writers connect with their communities, develop their craft & expand their career.
Number of Members: 1,450
Meeting(s): Willamette Writers Annual Conference
Publication(s): *The Timberline Review* (annual, journal, free to membs)

Women Who Write Inc
PO Box 652, Madison, NJ 07940-0652
Web Site: www.womenwhowrite.org
Key Personnel
Pres: Ginger Pate *E-mail:* president@womenwhowrite.org
Secy: Kate Cutts *E-mail:* secretary@womenwhowrite.org
Treas: Pat Weissner *E-mail:* treasurer@womenwhowrite.org
VP, Membership: Megha Malhotra
 E-mail: membership@womenwhowrite.org
VP, Progs: Prachi Jain *E-mail:* programs@womenwhowrite.org; Dana Faulkner Punzo *E-mail:* programs@womenwhowrite.org
Founded: 1988
Writing groups, writers' conference, workshops, readings, literary events, newsletter & literary magazine.
Number of Members: 120
Publication(s): *Goldfinch* (annual, journal)

Women's Fiction Writers Association (WFWA)
PO Box 190, Jefferson, OR 97352
E-mail: communications@womensfictionwriters.org; membership@womensfictionwriters.org; programs@womensfictionwriters.org
Web Site: www.womensfictionwriters.org
Key Personnel
Pres: Jacki Kelly *E-mail:* president@womensfictionwriters.org
VP, Communs: Sharon Ritchey
VP, Fin & Treas: Kathy Dodson
 E-mail: treasurer@womensfictionwriters.org
VP, Progs: Kristi Leonard
Secy: Michele Montgomery *E-mail:* secretary@womensfictionwriters.org
Events Dir: Jami Sheets
Membership Dir: Wendy Rossi
Founded: 2013
Community of career-focused women's fiction writers providing networking, education & continuing support in their career growth.
Number of Members: 1,000
Meeting(s): Annual Retreat, Sept
Publication(s): *Inside WFWA* (weekly, newsletter); *Read ON!* (monthly, newsletter); *Write ON!* (quarterly, ezine)

Women's National Book Association Inc
PO Box 237, FDR Sta, New York, NY 10150-0231
Toll Free Tel: 866-610-WNBA (610-9622)
E-mail: info@wnba-books.org
Web Site: wnba-books.org
Key Personnel
Pres: Natalie Obando-Desai *E-mail:* president@wnba-books.org
Co-VP: Elise Marie Collins; NC Weil
Treas: Karen Holly
Chair, Membership Comm: Beth Frerking
Founded: 1917
Increase opportunities for women & recognition of women in the world of books. Sponsor WNBA Award since 1940, WNBA Pannell Award & WNBA Eastman Grant. Its initiative, National Reading Group Month, promotes the value of book discussion groups, organized chapter author events in October & created the annual Great Group Reads list of top 20 books for discussion groups. Twelve chapters: Metro Atlanta, Boston, Charlotte, South Florida, Los Angeles, Nashville, New Orleans, New York City, Greater Philadelphia, San Francisco & Washington, DC.
Number of Members: 1,000
New Election: Biennially in May, odd-numbered yrs
Publication(s): *The Bookwoman* (6 issues/yr, Sept-June, free to membs)

The Word, A Storytelling Sanctuary Inc
757 E 20 Ave, Suite 370-335, Denver, CO 80205
E-mail: info@thewordfordiversity.org
Web Site: www.thewordfordiversity.org
Key Personnel
Founder & Exec Dir: Viniyanka Prasad
Head, Opers: Michelle Malonzo
Opers Coord: Blaire Bridges
Prog Coord: Aida Lilly
Nonprofit public charity organization to promote voices from underserved communities & diverse backgrounds.

Writers' Alliance of Newfoundland & Labrador
Haymarket Sq, 223 Duckworth St, Suite 202, St John's, NL A1C 6N1, Canada
Tel: 709-739-5215 *Toll Free Tel:* 866-739-5215
E-mail: info@wanl.ca; membership@wanl.ca
Web Site: wanl.ca
Key Personnel
Exec Dir: Jen Winsor *E-mail:* director@wanl.ca
Memb Servs Coord: Wendy Rose
Founded: 1987
Not-for-profit, member-based organization established to contribute to a supportive environment for writing & serve the needs & protect the rights of writers in the province.
Number of Members: 250
New Election: Annually in Fall
Publication(s): *WANL Newsletter* (2 issues/mo, electronic, free to membs); *WORD Magazine* (annual, free to membs)

Writers & Publishers Network (WPN)
1129 Maricopa Hwy, No 142, Ojai, CA 93023
Web Site: writersandpublishersnetwork.com
Key Personnel
CTO: Lisa Angle
Pres: Kathleen Kaiser
Membership Dir: Adanna Moriarty
Newsletter Ed: Sandra Murphy
Founded: 1996
Provides information, resources & opportunities for anyone involved in or interested in publishing, whether they are an author, freelance writer, artist or own a publishing company. WPN encourages the exchange of ideas, information & other mutual benefits & provides a web site for the purpose of sharing information on writing, marketing & publishing. It also offers links to research sources, publishers, printers, the media & other sources that might be important to writers & authors.
Number of Members: 200
Publication(s): *W&PNews* (monthly, newsletter)

Writers' Federation of Nova Scotia (WFNS)
1113 Marginal Rd, Halifax, NS B3H 4P7, Canada
Tel: 902-423-8116 *Fax:* 902-422-0881
E-mail: contact@writers.ns.ca; wits@writers.ns.ca (awards); programs@writers.ns.ca; communications@writers.ns.ca
Web Site: writers.ns.ca
Key Personnel
Exec Dir: Marilyn Smulders *E-mail:* director@writers.ns.ca
Prog Mgr, Arts Educ: Linda Hudson
Prog Mgr, Membership Servs: Andy Verboom
Founded: 1976
Foster creative writing & the profession of writing in the province of Nova Scotia; provide advice & assistance to writers at all stages of their careers; encourage greater public recognition of Nova Scotian writers & their achievements; enhance the literary arts in our regional & national culture.
Number of Members: 600
New Election: Annually in June
Publication(s): *Subtext* (weekly, enewsletter, free to membs)

Writers' Guild of Alberta
11759 Groat Rd NW, Edmonton, AB T5M 3K6, Canada
Tel: 780-422-8174 *Toll Free Tel:* 800-665-5354 (AB only)
E-mail: mail@writersguild.ab.ca
Web Site: writersguild.ca
Key Personnel
Exec Dir: Giorgia Severini *E-mail:* gseverini@writersguild.ab.ca
Communs & Partnerships Coord: Ellen Kartz
 E-mail: ellen.kartz@writersguild.ab.ca
Memb Servs Coord: Mike Maguire
Prog & Opers Coord: Ashley Mann
 E-mail: ashley.mann@writersguild.ab.ca
Progs & Events Coord: Jason Norman
 E-mail: jason.norman@writersguild.ab.ca
Proj Asst: Sadie MacGillivray *E-mail:* sadie.macgillivray@writersguild.ab.ca
Founded: 1980
Our mission is to support, encourage & promote writers & writing, to safeguard the freedom to write & to read & to advocate for the well-being of writers.
Number of Members: 1,000
Meeting(s): Annual Conference
Publication(s): *WestWord* (quarterly, magazine)
Branch Office(s)
223 12 Ave SW, No 204, Calgary, AB T2R 0G9, Canada, Prog & Conference Coord: Dorothy Bentley *Tel:* 403-875-8058 *E-mail:* dorothy.bentley@writersguild.ab.ca

Writers Guild of America, East (WGAE)
250 Hudson St, Suite 700, New York, NY 10013
Tel: 212-767-7800 *Fax:* 212-582-1909
Web Site: www.wgaeast.org
Key Personnel
Exec Dir: Lowell Peterson *Tel:* 212-767-7828
 E-mail: lpeterson@wgaeast.org
Asst Exec Dir: Marsha Seeman *Tel:* 212-767-7820 *E-mail:* mseeman@wgaeast.org
Dir, Communs: Jason Gordon *Tel:* 212-767-7809
 E-mail: jgordon@wgaeast.org
Dir, Organizing: Justin Molito *Tel:* 212-767-7808
 E-mail: jmolito@wgaeast.org
Dir, Programming & Communs: Chiara Montalto-Giannini *E-mail:* cmontaltogiannini@wgaeast.org
Dir, Progs: Dana Weissman *Tel:* 212-767-7835
 E-mail: dweissman@wgaeast.org
Awards & Events Admin: Nancy Hathorne
 Tel: 212-767-7812 *E-mail:* nhathorne@wgaeast.org
Communs Admin: Molly Beer *Tel:* 212-767-7886
 E-mail: mbeer@wgaeast.org
Membership Admin: Kelly O'Brien *Tel:* 212-767-7821 *E-mail:* kobrien@wgaeast.org
Labor union representing professional writers in motion pictures, TV, radio, as well as digital media content. Membership available only through the sale of literary material or employment for writing services in one of these areas.
Number of Members: 4,200
New Election: Annually in Sept
Publication(s): *On Writing* (online web series)

Writers Guild of America West (WGAW)
7000 W Third St, Los Angeles, CA 90048

Tel: 323-951-4000 Toll Free Tel: 800-548-4532
Fax: 323-782-4801
Web Site: www.wga.org
Key Personnel
Pres: Meredith Stiehm
VP: Michele Mulroney
Secy-Treas: Betsy Thomas
Labor union: Collective bargaining representation for film, TV broadcast, interactive & new media writers. Awards dinner & seminars (sometimes for public).
Number of Members: 12,000

Writers' League of Texas (WLT)
611 S Congress Ave, Suite 200 A-3, Austin, TX 78704
Mailing Address: PO Box 41355, Austin, TX 78704
Tel: 512-499-8914
E-mail: wlt@writersleague.org
Web Site: www.writersleague.org
Key Personnel
Exec Dir: Becka Oliver E-mail: becka@writersleague.org
Prog Dir: Samantha Babiak E-mail: sam@writersleague.org
Memb Servs Mgr/Digital Media Mgr: J Evan Parks
Office Coord: Lore Arnold
Founded: 1981
Workshops, seminars, classes, library resource center, technical assistance, newsletter, monthly programs, educational programs for young people. Memberships: $50 (indiv/family), $100 & up (premium), $250 & up (businesses & organizations).
Number of Members: 1,200
Publication(s): *Footnotes* (26 issues/yr, enewsletter, free); *Scribe* (blog)

The Writers' Union of Canada (TWUC)
600-460 Richmond St W, Toronto, ON M5V 1Y1, Canada
Tel: 416-703-8982
E-mail: info@writersunion.ca
Web Site: www.writersunion.ca
Key Personnel
Exec Dir: John Degen Tel: 416-703-8982 ext 221 E-mail: jdegen@writersunion.ca
Assoc Dir: Siobhan O'Connor Tel: 416-703-8982 ext 222 E-mail: soconnor@writersunion.ca
Service for members & nonmembers. Programs include public readings, school visits, professional development, ms evaluation service & contracts with ghostwriters. Writers' resources as well as awards & competitions are available.
Number of Members: 2,000
Publication(s): *Write* (quarterly, magazine)

Foundations

Listed below are foundations that are closely affiliated with the book trade.

Advertising Research Foundation (ARF)
432 Park Ave S, 4th fl, New York, NY 10016
Tel: 212-751-5656 *Fax:* 212-689-1859
E-mail: membership@thearf.org; new-member-info@thearf.org
Web Site: thearf.org
Key Personnel
Pres & CEO: Scott McDonald, PhD
CFO: Elyssa Rubin
Chief Growth Offr: Michael Heitner
Chief Res Offr: Paul Donato
SVP, Events: Rachael Feigenbaum
Founded: 1936
Advertising research service trade association. Publisher of the *Journal of Advertising Research*.

The Authors Guild® Foundation
Unit of The Authors Guild®
31 E 32 St, Suite 901, New York, NY 10016
Tel: 212-563-5904 *Fax:* 212-564-5363
E-mail: staff@authorsguild.org
Web Site: authorsguild.org/foundation
Key Personnel
Exec Dir: Deborah Wilson
Exec Prodr, Literary Progs: Bernard Schwartz
Advocates for authors' rights, educates authors across the country in the business of writing & promotes an understanding of the value of writers.

Baton Rouge Area Foundation
100 North St, Suite 900, Baton Rouge, LA 70802
Tel: 225-387-6126
Web Site: www.braf.org
Key Personnel
Pres & CEO: John G Davies
EVP: John Spain
Dir, Communs: Mukul Verma *Tel:* 225-362-9260
 E-mail: mverma@braf.org
Founded: 1964
The foundation helps philanthropists pursue their causes for bettering the lives of the people of South Louisiana. Projects include the Ernest J Gaines Award for Literary Excellence.

Before Columbus Foundation
The Raymond House, 655 13 St, Suite 302, Oakland, CA 94612
SAN: 159-2955
Tel: 916-425-7916
E-mail: beforecolumbusfoundation@gmail.com
Web Site: www.beforecolumbusfoundation.com
Key Personnel
Founder: Ishmael Reed
Founded: 1976
Provide information, research, consultation & promotional services for contemporary American multicultural writers & publishers. A nonprofit service organization that also sponsors classes, workshops, readings, public events & the annual American Book Awards.

Binc Foundation, see Book Industry Charitable Foundation (BINC)

Book Industry Charitable Foundation (BINC)
3135 S State St, Suite 203, Ann Arbor, MI 48108
Toll Free Tel: 866-733-9064
E-mail: info@bincfoundation.org
Web Site: www.bincfoundation.org
Key Personnel
Exec Dir: Pamela French *E-mail:* pam@bincfoundation.org
Dir, Devt: Kathy Bartson *E-mail:* kathy@bincfoundation.org
Prog Mgr: Judey Kalchik *E-mail:* judey@bincfoundation.org; Ken White *E-mail:* ken@bincfoundation.org
Commun Coord: Erika Mantz *E-mail:* erika@bincfoundation.org
Devt Coord: Jennifer Rojas *E-mail:* jennifer@bincfoundation.org
Off Coord: Jane Regenstreif *E-mail:* jane@bincfoundation.org
Spec Projs Coord: Kate Weiss *E-mail:* kate@bincfoundation.org
Founded: 1996
Coordinates charitable programs to strengthen the bookselling community. Provides assistance to employees & shop owners who have demonstrated financial need arising from severe hardship +/or emergency circumstances.

Bridge to Asia
1505 Juanita Way, Berkeley, CA 94702
Key Personnel
Principal: Newton Liu; Jeffrey Smith
Founded: 1987
Supports higher education in developing countries in Asia, principally China. Provides books & other materials critical for higher education but too costly for most schools or scholars to afford.

The Canadian Writers' Foundation Inc (La Fondation des Ecrivains Canadiens)
PO Box 13281, Kanata Sta, Ottawa, ON K2K 1X4, Canada
Tel: 613-978-2723 *Fax:* 613-900-6393
E-mail: info@canadianwritersfoundation.org
Web Site: www.canadianwritersfoundation.org
Key Personnel
Pres: Marianne Scott *Tel:* 613-733-4223
 Fax: 613-733-8752
Exec Secy: Shelley Weber *E-mail:* sweber.cwf@gmail.com
Founded: 1931
Benevolent trust. Provides financial assistance to distinguished senior Canadian writers in need.

Cave Canem Foundation Inc
20 Jay St, Suite 310-A, Brooklyn, NY 11201-8301
Tel: 718-858-0000 *Fax:* 718-858-0002
E-mail: info@ccpoets.org
Web Site: cavecanempoets.org
Key Personnel
Exec Dir: Lisa Willis *E-mail:* lwillis@ccpoets.org
Founded: 1996
Nonprofit literary service organization committed to cultivating the artistic & professional growth of African American poets.
Number of Members: 400

Donner Canadian Foundation
8 Prince Arthur Ave, 3rd fl, Toronto, ON M5R 1A9, Canada
Tel: 416-920-6400 *Fax:* 416-920-5577
Web Site: www.donnerfoundation.org
Key Personnel
Exec Dir: Helen McLean *E-mail:* mclean@donner.ca
Sr Prog Offr: Amy Buskirk *E-mail:* buskirk@donner.ca
Founded: 1950
Ongoing funding of public policy research & support of environmental, international development & social services projects. Every year, the Donner Book Prize honors the best book on Canadian public policy. The foundation's lecture series features some of the world's most influential speakers.

La Foundation des Ecrivains Canadiens, see The Canadian Writers' Foundation Inc (La Fondation des Ecrivains Canadiens)

Graphic Arts Education & Research Foundation (GAERF)
1899 Preston White Dr, Reston, VA 20191
Tel: 703-264-7200
E-mail: gaerf@npes.org
Web Site: www.gaerf.org
Key Personnel
Pres: Thayer Long
EVP: Judith B Durham *E-mail:* jdurham@npes.org
Founded: 1983
A major source of financial support for projects & programs designed to provide a graphic communications work force for the future.

John Simon Guggenheim Memorial Foundation
90 Park Ave, New York, NY 10016
Tel: 212-687-4470 *Fax:* 212-697-3248
Web Site: www.gf.org
Key Personnel
Chmn: William P Kelly
Pres: Edward Hirsch
Founded: 1925
Provide fellowships to further the development of scholars & artists by assisting them to engage in research in any field of knowledge & creation in any of the arts; awarded to persons who have already demonstrated exceptional capacity for productive scholarship or exceptional creative ability in the arts.

The Zora Neale Hurston/Richard Wright Foundation
10 "G" St NE, Suite 600, Washington, DC 20002
E-mail: info@hurstonwright.org
Web Site: www.hurstonwright.org
Key Personnel
Exec Dir: Khadijah Z Ali-Coleman
 E-mail: khadijah@hurstonwright.org
Writing Progs Mgr: DeAndrea L Johnson
Events & Programming Coord: Molly Rufus
Founded: 1990
Dedicated to discovering, mentoring & honoring Black writers. Through workshops, master classes & readings, the organization preserves the voices of Black writers in the world literary canon, serves as a community for writers & continues a tradition of literary excellence in storytelling established by its namesakes. 501(c)(3) nonprofit.

Lannan Foundation
313 Read St, Santa Fe, NM 87501-2628
Tel: 505-986-8160
E-mail: info@lannan.org

FOUNDATIONS

Web Site: lannan.org
Key Personnel
Pres & Treas: Lawrence P Lannan, Jr
EVP, Secy & Dir, Admin: Frank C Lawler
Prog Dir, Literary & Residency Progs: Martha Jessup
Founded: 1960
Family foundation dedicated to cultural freedom, diversity & creativity through projects supporting contemporary artists & writers. Grants given to nonprofit organizations in the areas of contemporary visual art, literature, indigenous communities & cultural freedom. Awards & fellowships also given.

National Book Foundation
90 Broad St, Suite 604, New York, NY 10004
Tel: 212-685-0261 *Fax:* 212-213-6570
E-mail: nationalbook@nationalbook.org
Web Site: www.nationalbook.org
Key Personnel
Chmn & CEO: David Steinberger
Exec Dir: Ruth Dickey *E-mail:* rdickey@nationalbook.org
Dir, Progs & Partnerships: Natalie Green *E-mail:* ngreen@nationalbook.org
Dir, Technol & Spec Projs: Meredith Andrews *E-mail:* mandrews@nationalbook.org
Dir of Devt: Meg Tansey *E-mail:* mtansey@nationalbook.org
Devt Mgr: Megan Reynolds *E-mail:* mreynolds@nationalbook.org
Sr Mgr, Awards & Honors: Madeleine Shelton *E-mail:* mshelton@nationalbook.org
Sr Mgr, Mktg & Communs: Ale Romero *E-mail:* aromero@nationalbook.org
Educ Progs Mgr: Julianna Lee Marino *E-mail:* jleemarino@nationalbook.org
Awards & Communs Coord: Lilly Santiago *E-mail:* lsantiago@nationalbook.org
Progs Coord: Emily Lovett *E-mail:* elovett@nationalbook.org
Presenter of the National Book Awards. The Foundation's mission is to celebrate the best literature in America, expand its audience & ensure that books have a prominent place in American culture.

National Endowment for the Arts
400 Seventh St SW, Washington, DC 20506-0001
Tel: 202-682-5400
Web Site: www.arts.gov
Key Personnel
Dir, Admin Servs: Greg Gendron *Tel:* 202-682-5561 *E-mail:* gendrong@arts.gov
Dir, Lit: Amy Stolls *Tel:* 202-682-5771 *E-mail:* stollsa@arts.gov
Dir, Strategic Communs & Pub Aff: Helen Aguirre Ferre *Tel:* 202-682-5759 *E-mail:* ferreh@arts.gov
Asst Dir, Press: Victoria Hutter *Tel:* 202-682-5692 *E-mail:* hutterv@arts.gov
Asst Dir, Pubns: Don Ball *Tel:* 202-682-5750 *E-mail:* balld@arts.gov
Founded: 1965
Independent federal agency. Grants to organizations & individuals.

National Press Foundation
1211 Connecticut Ave NW, Suite 310, Washington, DC 20036
Tel: 202-663-7286
Web Site: nationalpress.org
Key Personnel
Pres & COO: Sonni Efron *E-mail:* sefron@nationalpress.org
Dir, Digital Strategy: Jeff Hertrick
Dir, Journalism Initiatives: Rachel Jones
Dir, Journalism Training: Anne Godlasky *E-mail:* anne@nationalpress.org
Dir, Opers: Jason Zaragoza *E-mail:* jason@nationalpress.org
Founded: 1976
Educates journalists in the US & around the world through fellowships & other programs.

Poetry Foundation
61 W Superior St, Chicago, IL 60654
Tel: 312-787-7070
E-mail: info@poetryfoundation.org
Web Site: www.poetryfoundation.org
Key Personnel
CFO & VP, Fin & Admin: Kathleen Coughlin
CTO & Dir, Digital Progs: Harlan Wallach
Asst to Pres & Secy of the Bd: Maris Maeve O'Tierney
Media & Mktg Dir: Sarah Whitcher *Tel:* 312-799-8016 *E-mail:* swhitcher@poetryfoundation.org
Prog Dir: Stephen Young
Deputy Dir, Admin: Krystal Languell
Founded: 2003
Independent 501(c)(3) literary organization committed to a vigorous presence for poetry in our culture.

WESTAF, see Western States Arts Federation (WESTAF)

Western States Arts Federation (WESTAF)
1536 Wynkoop St, Suite 522, Denver, CO 80202
Tel: 303-629-1166
E-mail: staff@westaf.org
Web Site: www.westaf.org
Key Personnel
Exec Dir: Christian Gaines *E-mail:* christian.gaines@westaf.org
Deputy Dir: David Holland *E-mail:* david.holland@westaf.org
Dir, Fin & Admin: Amy Hollrah *E-mail:* amy.hollrah@westaf.org
Dir, Mktg & Communs: Leah Horn *E-mail:* leah.horn@westaf.org
Performing, visual & folk arts programs.

The H W Wilson Foundation
750 Third Ave, 13th fl, New York, NY 10017
Tel: 212-418-8473
Web Site: www.thwwf.org
Key Personnel
Exec Dir: William Stanton
Pres: Harold Regan
VP & Treas: William Hayden
VP & Secy: Michael Regan
Founded: 1952
Scholarship grants to ALA accredited library & information science programs.

Calendar of Book Trade & Promotional Events— Alphabetical Index of Sponsors

Adelaide Festival Corp
Adelaide Festival
   February 2025, pg 535
   February 2026, pg 545

AIGA, the professional association for design
AIGA Design Conference
   October 2025, pg 543

ALA, see The American Library Association (ALA)

Alaska Center for the Book
Alaska Book Week
   October 2025, pg 543
   October 2026, pg 547
   October 2027, pg 549
   October 2028, pg 550
   October 2029, pg 552

Amelia Island Book Festival
Amelia Island Book Festival
   February 2025, pg 536

American Institute of Graphic Arts, see AIGA, the professional association for design

The American Library Association (ALA)
ALA Annual Conference & Exhibition
   June 2025, pg 540
   June 2026, pg 546
   June 2027, pg 548
   June 2028, pg 550
LibLearnX: The Library Learning Experience
   January 2025, pg 535
National Library Week
   April 2025, pg 538
   April 2026, pg 546

American Medical Writers Association (AMWA)
Medical Writing & Communication Conference
   November 2025, pg 545

American Society for Quality (ASQ)
ASQ World Conference on Quality & Improvement
   May 2025, pg 539

American Translators Association (ATA)
American Translators Association Annual Conference
   October 2025, pg 543

Antiquarian Booksellers' Association of America (ABAA)
ABAA New York International Antiquarian Book Fair
   April 2025, pg 538
Boston International Antiquarian Book Fair
   November 2025, pg 544
California International Antiquarian Book Fair
   February 2025, pg 536

Ariel Municipal Co Ltd
The Jerusalem International Book Forum (JIBF)
   May 2025, pg 540

Arizona Professional Writers (APW), Rim Country Chapter
Payson Book Festival
   Summer 2025, pg 540

ASIS&T, see Association for Information Science & Technology (ASIS&T)

Associated Collegiate Press (ACP)
ACP/CMA Fall National College Media Convention
   Autumn 2025, pg 542

Association for Information Science & Technology (ASIS&T)
ASIS&T Annual Meeting
   November 2025, pg 544

Association of University Presses (AUPresses)
AUPresses Annual Meeting
   June 2025, pg 540
   June 2026, pg 546

Association of Writers & Writing Programs (AWP)
AWP Conference & Bookfair
   March 2025, pg 537

AUPresses, see Association of University Presses (AUPresses)

Bay Area Book Festival
Bay Area Book Festival
   Spring 2025, pg 536

Beaverdale Books
DSM Book Festival
   March 2025, pg 537

Berlin Institute for Scholarly Publishing (BISP)
Academic Publishing in Europe (APE) Conference
   January 2025, pg 535

BNP Media | Packaging Group
Converters Expo
   May 2025, pg 539
Converters Expo South
   February 2025, pg 536

Boersenverein des Deutschen Buchhandels, Landesverband Baden-Wuerttemberg eV (Association of Publishers & Booksellers in Baden-Wuerttemberg eV)
Stuttgarter Buchwochen (Stuttgart Book Weeks)
   November 2025, pg 545

Bok & Bibliotek i Norden AB
Gothenburg Book Fair
   September 2025, pg 543
   September 2026, pg 547
   September 2027, pg 549
   September 2028, pg 550
   September 2029, pg 552

BolognaFiere SpA
Bologna Children's Book Fair
   March 2025, pg 537

Book Manufacturers' Institute Inc (BMI)
BMI Annual Conference
   Autumn 2025, pg 542
BMI Spring Management Conference
   Spring 2025, pg 536

Boston Book Festival
Boston Book Festival
   October 2025, pg 543

Bulgarian Book Association (BBA)
Sofia International Book Fair
   December 2024, pg 535

Catholic Media Association (CMA)
Catholic Media Conference
   June 2025, pg 541

Central Arkansas Library System (CALS)
Six Bridges Book Festival
   Autumn 2025, pg 542

Centre de Promotion du Livre de Jeunesse (CPLJ)
Salon du Livre et de la Presse Jeunesse (SLPJ)
   Autumn 2025, pg 542

Chelsea District Library
Midwest Literary Walk
   April 2025, pg 538

The Children's Book Council (CBC)
Children's Book Week
   May 2025, pg 539
   November 2025, pg 544

China National Publications Import & Export (Group) Co Ltd (CNPIEC)
Beijing International Book Fair (BIBF)
   June 2025, pg 541

Christian Retail Association Inc (CRA)
Christian Product Expo™ (CPE)
   February 2025, pg 536
   Summer 2025, pg 540

Dahlonega Literary Festival
Dahlonega Literary Festival
   March 2025, pg 537

Desert Foothills Library
Desert Foothills Book Festival
   October 2025, pg 543

The Dorothy L Sayers Society
The Dorothy L Sayers Society Annual Convention
   August 2025, pg 541

Edinburgh International Book Festival
Edinburgh International Book Festival
   August 2025, pg 541
   August 2026, pg 546
   August 2027, pg 548
   August 2028, pg 550
   August 2029, pg 551

ALPHABETICAL INDEX OF SPONSORS

Evangelical Press Association (EPA)
EPA Annual Convention
May 2025, pg 539

F R E S H Book Festival
F R E S H Book Festival
February 2025, pg 536

Federacion de Gremios de Editores de Espana (FGEE) (Spanish Association of Publishers Guilds)
LIBER Feria Internacional del Libro
October 2025, pg 544

The Federation of Children's Book Groups (FCBG)
The Federation of Children's Book Groups Annual Conference
April 2025, pg 538

Feria Internacional del Libro de Guadalajara
Feria Internacional del Libro de Guadalajara
Autumn 2025, pg 542

FGEE, see Federacion de Gremios de Editores de Espana (FGEE) (Spanish Association of Publishers Guilds)

Florida Antiquarian Booksellers Association (FABA)
Florida Antiquarian Book Fair
March 2025, pg 537

Florida Center for the Literary Arts
Miami Book Fair
November 2025, pg 545

Football Writers Association of America (FWAA)
Football Writers Association of America Annual Meeting
January 2025, pg 535

Frankfurter Buchmesse GmbH
Frankfurter Buchmesse
October 2025, pg 543
October 2026, pg 547
October 2027, pg 549

Gaithersburg Book Festival
Gaithersburg Book Festival
May 2025, pg 539

Hellenic Foundation for Culture (HFC)
Thessaloniki International Book Fair (TIBF)
May 2025, pg 540

Hong Kong Trade Development Council
Hong Kong Book Fair
July 2025, pg 541
July 2026, pg 546
July 2027, pg 548
July 2028, pg 550
July 2029, pg 551

Hudson Area Library
Hudson Children's Book Festival
May 2025, pg 540

IABC, see International Association of Business Communicators (IABC)

IBBY, see International Board on Books for Young People (IBBY)

IFLA, see International Federation of Library Associations & Institutions (IFLA) (Federation internationale des associations de bibliothecaires et des bibliotheques)

Informa Markets
EastPack®
June 2025, pg 541
WestPack®
February 2025, pg 536

International Association of Business Communicators (IABC)
IABC World Conference
June 2025, pg 541

International Association of Music Libraries, Archives & Documentation Centres Inc (IAML)
IAML Annual Congress
July 2025, pg 541
June 2026, pg 546

International Board on Books for Young People (IBBY)
IBBY World Congress
August 2026, pg 546
International Children's Book Day
April 2025, pg 538
April 2026, pg 546
April 2027, pg 548
April 2028, pg 549
April 2029, pg 551

International Federation of Library Associations & Institutions (IFLA) (Federation internationale des associations de bibliothecaires et des bibliotheques)
IFLA World Library and Information Congress (WLIC)
August 2025, pg 541

International Publishers Association (IPA)
International Publishers Congress
December 2024, pg 535

IPA, see International Publishers Association (IPA)

Jax Urban Book Festival (JUBF)
Jax Urban Book Festival (JUBF)
January 2025, pg 535

Jewish Book Council
Jewish Book Month
November 2025, pg 544
November 2026, pg 547
November 2027, pg 549
November 2028, pg 551
November 2029, pg 552

Kentucky Humanities
Kentucky Book Festival
Autumn 2025, pg 542

Key School
Annapolis Book Festival
May 2025, pg 539

Kraft Event Management Inc
Morristown Festival of Books
October 2025, pg 544

Lee County Library System
Southwest Florida Reading Festival
March 2025, pg 537

Leipziger Messe GmbH
Leipzig Book Fair (Leipziger Buchmesse)
March 2025, pg 537
March 2026, pg 545

Literacy Texas
Literacy Texas Annual Conference
August 2025, pg 542

Literary Women of Long Beach
Literary Women Long Beach Festival of Authors
April 2025, pg 538

Little Shop of Stories
Decatur Children's Book Festival
May 2025, pg 539

Los Angeles Times
Los Angeles Times Festival of Books
April 2025, pg 538

Louisiana Center for the Book
Louisiana Book Festival
Autumn 2025, pg 542

Messe Stuttgart India Pvt Ltd
Didac India
Autumn 2025, pg 542

Mississippi Book Festival
Mississippi Book Festival
Summer 2025, pg 540

MLA, see Modern Language Association (MLA)

Modern Language Association (MLA)
MLA Annual Convention
January 2025, pg 535
January 2026, pg 545

Nantucket Book Foundation
Nantucket Book Festival
June 2025, pg 541
June 2026, pg 546
June 2027, pg 548
June 2028, pg 550
June 2029, pg 551

NASW, see National Association of Science Writers Inc (NASW)

National Association of College Stores (NACS)
CAMEX
February 2025, pg 536

National Association of Science Writers Inc (NASW)
ScienceWriters2025
Autumn 2025, pg 542

National Book Council
Malta Book Festival
November 2025, pg 544

National Book Foundation
National Book Month
October 2025, pg 544
October 2026, pg 547
October 2027, pg 549
October 2028, pg 551
October 2029, pg 552

National Federation of Press Women Inc (NFPW)
NFPW Communications Conference
September 2025, pg 543

National Institute of Standards and Technology (NIST)
The Quest for Excellence® Conference
March 2025, pg 537

National Newspaper Association Foundation (NNAF)
NNAF Annual Convention and Trade Show
October 2025, pg 544

COURSES & AWARDS
ALPHABETICAL INDEX OF SPONSORS

New Hampshire Book and Literary Festival Inc
New Hampshire Book Festival
  Autumn 2025, pg 542

New Orleans Book Festival
New Orleans Book Festival
  March 2025, pg 537

New South Planning Board
Printers Row Lit Fest
  September 2025, pg 543

North American Agricultural Journalists (NAAJ)
NAAJ Annual Meeting
  April 2025, pg 538
  April 2026, pg 546
  April 2027, pg 548
  April 2028, pg 550
  April 2029, pg 551

Ohioana Library Association
Ohioana Book Festival
  Spring 2025, pg 536

Ontario Library Association
Forest of Reading Festival®
  May 2025, pg 539

Outdoor Writers Association of America (OWAA)
Outdoor Writers Association of America Annual Conference
  August 2025, pg 542

Photographic Society of America® (PSA®)
PSA® Photo Festival
  September 2025, pg 543

PMMI: The Association for Packaging and Processing Technologies
EXPO PACK Guadalajara
  June 2025, pg 541
EXPO PACK Mexico
  June 2026, pg 546
PACK EXPO East
  February 2026, pg 545
PACK EXPO International
  October 2026, pg 547
PACK EXPO Las Vegas
  September 2025, pg 543

Poudre Libraries
Fort Collins Book Fest
  February 2025, pg 536

PRINTING United Alliance
PRINTING United Expo
  October 2025, pg 544
  September 2026, pg 547
  September 2027, pg 549
  October 2028, pg 551
  October 2029, pg 552

Rain Taxi
Twin Cities Book Festival
  October 2025, pg 544

Rockport Fulton Book Festival
Rockport Fulton Book Festival
  April 2025, pg 538

RX UK
The London Book Fair
  March 2025, pg 537
  March 2026, pg 545
  Spring 2027, pg 548
  Spring 2028, pg 549
  Spring 2029, pg 551

SA Paris Livres Events
Festival du Livre de Paris (Paris Book Festival)
  April 2025, pg 538

Salon du Livre de Montreal
Salon du Livre de Montreal (Montreal Book Fair)
  November 2025, pg 545

San Antonio Book Festival LLC
San Antonio Book Festival
  April 2025, pg 538

Santa Fe International Literary Festival
Santa Fe International Literary Festival
  May 2025, pg 540

Savannah Book Festival
Savannah Book Festival
  February 2025, pg 536

Seattle Antiquarian Book Fair
Seattle Antiquarian Book Fair
  October 2025, pg 544

Sharjah Book Authority
Sharjah International Book Fair (SIBF)
  Autumn 2025, pg 542

Society for Imaging Science and Technology (IS&T)
IS&T Electronic Imaging Conference
  February 2025, pg 536

Society for Scholarly Publishing (SSP)
SSP Annual Meeting
  May 2025, pg 540
  May 2026, pg 546

Society of Children's Book Writers & Illustrators (SCBWI)
SCBWI Winter Conference
  January 2025, pg 535

Technical Association of the Pulp & Paper Industry (TAPPI)
TAPPICon
  May 2025, pg 540

Tennessee Williams & New Orleans Literary Festival
Tennessee Williams & New Orleans Literary Festival
  March 2025, pg 537

Texas Book Festival
Texas Book Festival
  Autumn 2025, pg 543
  Autumn 2026, pg 547
  Autumn 2027, pg 548
  Autumn 2028, pg 550
  Autumn 2029, pg 552

Texas Library Association (TLA)
Texas Library Association Annual Conference
  April 2025, pg 539
  March 2026, pg 545
  March 2027, pg 548
  April 2028, pg 550

Tucson Festival of Books
Tucson Festival of Books
  March 2025, pg 537

Tuyap Fairs and Exhibitions Organization Inc (Tuyap Tum Fuarlar Uretim A S)
International Istanbul Book Fair
  November 2025, pg 544

UKSG (United Kingdom Serials Group)
UKSG Annual Conference & Exhibition
  March 2025, pg 538

Unbound Book Festival
Unbound Book Festival
  April 2025, pg 539

University of Central Missouri
Children's Literature Festival
  March 2025, pg 537

University of Southern Mississippi
Fay B Kaigler Children's Book Festival
  April 2025, pg 538
  April 2026, pg 545
  April 2027, pg 548
  April 2028, pg 549

University of the District of Columbia
Imaginarium Book Festival
  June 2025, pg 541

Utah Humanities
Utah Humanities Book Festival
  October 2025, pg 544
  October 2026, pg 547
  October 2027, pg 549
  October 2028, pg 551
  October 2029, pg 552

Virginia Humanities
Virginia Festival of the Book
  March 2025, pg 538

Visual Connections Australia Ltd
PacPrint 2025
  May 2025, pg 540

Williamsburg Book Festival
Williamsburg Book Festival
  February 2025, pg 536

Woodstock Bookfest
Woodstock Bookfest
  April 2025, pg 539

Writers Alliance of Gainesville (WAG)
Sunshine State Book Festival
  January 2025, pg 535

Writers' Summer School
Swanwick: The Writers' Summer School
  August 2025, pg 542
  August 2026, pg 547
  August 2027, pg 548
  August 2028, pg 550
  August 2029, pg 551

YA by the Bay, Inc
YA by the Bay©
  April 2025, pg 539

Calendar of Book Trade & Promotional Events— Alphabetical Index of Events

ABAA New York International Antiquarian Book Fair
April 2025, pg 538

Academic Publishing in Europe (APE) Conference
January 2025, pg 535

ACP/CMA Fall National College Media Convention
Autumn 2025, pg 542

Adelaide Festival
February 2025, pg 535
February 2026, pg 545

AIGA Design Conference
October 2025, pg 543

ALA Annual Conference & Exhibition
June 2025, pg 540
June 2026, pg 546
June 2027, pg 548
June 2028, pg 550

Alaska Book Week
October 2025, pg 543
October 2026, pg 547
October 2027, pg 549
October 2028, pg 550
October 2029, pg 552

Amelia Island Book Festival
February 2025, pg 536

American Translators Association Annual Conference
October 2025, pg 543

Annapolis Book Festival
May 2025, pg 539

ASIS&T Annual Meeting
November 2025, pg 544

ASQ World Conference on Quality & Improvement
May 2025, pg 539

AUPresses Annual Meeting
June 2025, pg 540
June 2026, pg 546

AWP Conference & Bookfair
March 2025, pg 537

Bay Area Book Festival
Spring 2025, pg 536

Beijing International Book Fair (BIBF)
June 2025, pg 541

BMI Annual Conference
Autumn 2025, pg 542

BMI Spring Management Conference
Spring 2025, pg 536

Bologna Children's Book Fair
March 2025, pg 537

Boston Book Festival
October 2025, pg 543

Boston International Antiquarian Book Fair
November 2025, pg 544

California International Antiquarian Book Fair
February 2025, pg 536

CAMEX
February 2025, pg 536

Campus Market Expo, see CAMEX

Catholic Media Conference
June 2025, pg 541

Children's Literature Festival
March 2025, pg 537

Children's Book Week
May 2025, pg 539
November 2025, pg 544

Christian Product Expo™ (CPE)
February 2025, pg 536
Summer 2025, pg 540

Converters Expo
May 2025, pg 539

Converters Expo South
February 2025, pg 536

CPE, see Christian Product Expo™ (CPE)

Dahlonega Literary Festival
March 2025, pg 537

Decatur Children's Book Festival
May 2025, pg 539

Des Moines Book Festival, see DSM Book Festival

Desert Foothills Book Festival
October 2025, pg 543

Didac India
Autumn 2025, pg 542

The Dorothy L Sayers Society Annual Convention
August 2025, pg 541

DSM Book Festival
March 2025, pg 537

EastPack®
June 2025, pg 541

Edinburgh International Book Festival
August 2025, pg 541
August 2026, pg 546
August 2027, pg 548
August 2028, pg 550
August 2029, pg 551

EPA Annual Convention
May 2025, pg 539

EXPO PACK Guadalajara
June 2025, pg 541

EXPO PACK Mexico
June 2026, pg 546

F R E S H Book Festival
February 2025, pg 536

Fay B Kaigler Children's Book Festival
April 2025, pg 538
April 2026, pg 545
April 2027, pg 548
April 2028, pg 549

The Federation of Children's Book Groups Annual Conference
April 2025, pg 538

Feria Internacional del Libro de Guadalajara
Autumn 2025, pg 542

Festival du Livre de Paris (Paris Book Festival)
April 2025, pg 538

Fiera del Libro per Ragazzi, see Bologna Children's Book Fair

Florida Antiquarian Book Fair
March 2025, pg 537

FoCo Book Fest, see Fort Collins Book Fest

Football Writers Association of America Annual Meeting
January 2025, pg 535

Forest of Reading Festival®
May 2025, pg 539

Fort Collins Book Fest
February 2025, pg 536

Frankfurter Buchmesse
October 2025, pg 543
October 2026, pg 547
October 2027, pg 549

Gaithersburg Book Festival
May 2025, pg 539

Gothenburg Book Fair
September 2025, pg 543
September 2026, pg 547
September 2027, pg 549
September 2028, pg 550
September 2029, pg 552

Guadalajara International Book Fair, see Feria Internacional del Libro de Guadalajara

ALPHABETICAL INDEX OF EVENTS

Hong Kong Book Fair
July 2025, pg 541
July 2026, pg 546
July 2027, pg 548
July 2028, pg 550
July 2029, pg 551

Hudson Children's Book Festival
May 2025, pg 540

IABC World Conference
June 2025, pg 541

IAML Annual Congress
July 2025, pg 541
June 2026, pg 546

IBBY World Congress
August 2026, pg 546

IFLA World Library and Information Congress (WLIC)
August 2025, pg 541

Imaginarium Book Festival
June 2025, pg 541

International Board on Books for Young People Biennial Congress, see IBBY World Congress

International Children's Book Day
April 2025, pg 538
April 2026, pg 546
April 2027, pg 548
April 2028, pg 549
April 2029, pg 551

International Istanbul Book Fair
November 2025, pg 544

International Publishers Congress
December 2024, pg 535

IPA Congress, see International Publishers Congress

IS&T Electronic Imaging Conference
February 2025, pg 536

Jax Urban Book Festival (JUBF)
January 2025, pg 535

The Jerusalem International Book Forum (JIBF)
May 2025, pg 540

Jewish Book Month
November 2025, pg 544
November 2026, pg 547
November 2027, pg 549
November 2028, pg 551
November 2029, pg 552

Kentucky Book Festival
Autumn 2025, pg 542

Leipzig Antiquarian Book Fair, see Leipzig Book Fair (Leipziger Buchmesse)

Leipzig Book Fair (Leipziger Buchmesse)
March 2025, pg 537
March 2026, pg 545

LIBER Feria Internacional del Libro
October 2025, pg 544

LibLearnX: The Library Learning Experience
January 2025, pg 535

Literacy Texas Annual Conference
August 2025, pg 542

Literary Women Long Beach Festival of Authors
April 2025, pg 538

LIX™, see LibLearnX: The Library Learning Experience

The London Book Fair
March 2025, pg 537
March 2026, pg 545
Spring 2027, pg 548
Spring 2028, pg 549
Spring 2029, pg 551

Los Angeles Times Festival of Books
April 2025, pg 538

Louisiana Book Festival
Autumn 2025, pg 542

Malta Book Festival
November 2025, pg 544

Medical Writing & Communication Conference
November 2025, pg 545

Miami Book Fair
November 2025, pg 545

Midwest Literary Walk
April 2025, pg 538

Mississippi Book Festival
Summer 2025, pg 540

MLA Annual Convention
January 2025, pg 535
January 2026, pg 545

Montreal Book Fair, see Salon du Livre de Montreal (Montreal Book Fair)

Morristown Festival of Books
October 2025, pg 544

NAAJ Annual Meeting
April 2025, pg 538
April 2026, pg 546
April 2027, pg 548
April 2028, pg 550
April 2029, pg 551

Nantucket Book Festival
June 2025, pg 541
June 2026, pg 546
June 2027, pg 548
June 2028, pg 550
June 2029, pg 551

National Association of Science Writers Annual Meeting, see ScienceWriters2025

National Book Month
October 2025, pg 544
October 2026, pg 547
October 2027, pg 549
October 2028, pg 551
October 2029, pg 552

National Library Week
April 2025, pg 538
April 2026, pg 546

New Hampshire Book Festival
Autumn 2025, pg 542

ASSOCIATIONS, EVENTS

New Orleans Book Festival
March 2025, pg 537

New York International Antiquarian Book Fair (NYIABF), see ABAA New York International Antiquarian Book Fair

NFPW Communications Conference
September 2025, pg 543

NNAF Annual Convention and Trade Show
October 2025, pg 544

Ohioana Book Festival
Spring 2025, pg 536

Outdoor Writers Association of America Annual Conference
August 2025, pg 542

OWAA Annual Conference, see Outdoor Writers Association of America Annual Conference

PACK EXPO East
February 2026, pg 545

PACK EXPO International
October 2026, pg 547

PACK EXPO Las Vegas
September 2025, pg 543

PacPrint 2025
May 2025, pg 540

Payson Book Festival
Summer 2025, pg 540

PEERS Conference, see TAPPICon

Printers Row Lit Fest
September 2025, pg 543

PRINTING United Expo
October 2025, pg 544
September 2026, pg 547
September 2027, pg 549
October 2028, pg 551
October 2029, pg 552

PSA® Photo Festival
September 2025, pg 543

The Quest for Excellence® Conference
March 2025, pg 537

Rockport Fulton Book Festival
April 2025, pg 538

Salon du Livre de Montreal (Montreal Book Fair)
November 2025, pg 545

Salon du Livre et de la Presse Jeunesse (SLPJ)
Autumn 2025, pg 542

San Antonio Book Festival
April 2025, pg 538

Santa Fe International Literary Festival
May 2025, pg 540

Savannah Book Festival
February 2025, pg 536

COURSES & AWARDS

SCBWI Winter Conference
January 2025, pg 535

ScienceWriters2025
Autumn 2025, pg 542

Seattle Antiquarian Book Fair
October 2025, pg 544

Sharjah International Book Fair (SIBF)
Autumn 2025, pg 542

Six Bridges Book Festival
Autumn 2025, pg 542

Sofia International Book Fair
December 2024, pg 535

Southwest Florida Reading Festival
March 2025, pg 537

SSP Annual Meeting
May 2025, pg 540
May 2026, pg 546

Stuttgarter Buchwochen (Stuttgart Book Weeks)
November 2025, pg 545

Sunshine State Book Festival
January 2025, pg 535

Swanwick: The Writers' Summer School
August 2025, pg 542
August 2026, pg 547
August 2027, pg 548
August 2028, pg 550
August 2029, pg 551

TAPPICon
May 2025, pg 540

Tennessee Williams & New Orleans Literary Festival
March 2025, pg 537

Texas Book Festival
Autumn 2025, pg 543
Autumn 2026, pg 547
Autumn 2027, pg 548
Autumn 2028, pg 550
Autumn 2029, pg 552

Texas Library Association Annual Conference
April 2025, pg 539
March 2026, pg 545
March 2027, pg 548
April 2028, pg 550

Thessaloniki International Book Fair (TIBF)
May 2025, pg 540

Tucson Festival of Books
March 2025, pg 537

Twin Cities Book Festival
October 2025, pg 544

ALPHABETICAL INDEX OF EVENTS

UKSG Annual Conference & Exhibition
March 2025, pg 538

Unbound Book Festival
April 2025, pg 539

Utah Humanities Book Festival
October 2025, pg 544
October 2026, pg 547
October 2027, pg 549
October 2028, pg 551
October 2029, pg 552

VABook!, see Virginia Festival of the Book

Virginia Festival of the Book
March 2025, pg 538

WestPack®
February 2025, pg 536

Williamsburg Book Festival
February 2025, pg 536

Woodstock Bookfest
April 2025, pg 539

YA by the Bay©
April 2025, pg 539

Young Adult Reading & Leadership Festival, see YA by the Bay©

Calendar of Book Trade & Promotional Events

Arranged chronologically by year and month, this section lists book trade events worldwide. Preceding this section are two indexes: the Sponsor Index is an alphabetical list of event sponsors and includes the names and dates of the events they sponsor; the Event Index is an alphabetical list of events along with the dates on which they are held.

2024

DECEMBER

International Publishers Congress
Sponsored by International Publishers Association (IPA)
23, ave de France, 1202 Geneva, Switzerland
Tel: (022) 704 18 20
E-mail: info@internationalpublishers.org
Web Site: www.internationalpublishers.org
Key Personnel
Secretary General: Jose Borghino
 E-mail: borghino@internationalpublishers.org
Dir, Communs: James Taylor *E-mail:* taylor@internationalpublishers.org
Biennial congress, held in even-numbered years, offers an unrivalled platform for networking & discussion among the world's publishers on industry challenges & opportunities. Organized in collaboration with the Association of American Publishers (AAP) & in coordination with the Guadalajara International Book Fair.
Location: Guadalajara, Mexico
Dec 3-6, 2024

Sofia International Book Fair
Sponsored by Bulgarian Book Association (BBA)
blvd Vitosha 64, 2nd fl, ap 4, 1463 Sofia, Bulgaria
Tel: (02) 958 15 25
E-mail: office@abk.bg
Web Site: www.abk.bg
Key Personnel
Event Mgr: Vitleema Tasheva
The first Sofia International Book fair was organized in 1968. Since then it brings thousands of visitors yearly to meet with exhibiting companies from Bulgaria & abroad, & offers unrivaled access to the national & international book publishing & bookseller communities. The Sofia International Literary Festival is part of the Sofia International Book Fair.
Location: National Palace of Culture, One Bulgaria Blvd, Sofia, Bulgaria
Dec 10-15, 2024

2025

JANUARY

Academic Publishing in Europe (APE) Conference
Sponsored by Berlin Institute for Scholarly Publishing (BISP)
Lutzowstr 33, 10785 Berlin, Germany
Tel: (030) 26 00 53 14
E-mail: info@berlinstitute.org
Web Site: berlinstitute.org/ape-conference; berlinstitute.org
Annual event for exchange of information between publishers, researchers, institutions, libraries, universities, & decision-makers at local, national & EU level.
Location: ESMT Berlin, Schlossplatz 1, Berlin, Germany
Jan 14-15, 2025

Football Writers Association of America Annual Meeting
Sponsored by Football Writers Association of America (FWAA)
18652 Vista del Sol, Dallas, TX 75287
Tel: 214-870-6516
Web Site: www.sportswriters.net/fwaa; x.com/thefwaa
Key Personnel
Exec Dir: Steve Richardson *E-mail:* tiger@fwaa.com
Annual FWAA Meeting (in conjunction with the College Football Playoff National Championship Game).
Location: Westin Peachtree Plaza, 210 Peachtree St NW, Atlanta, GA, USA
Jan 17-20, 2025

Jax Urban Book Festival (JUBF)
1225 W Beaver St, Unit 117, Jacksonville, FL 32204
Tel: 904-479-6611
E-mail: info@jaxurbanbookfest.com
Web Site: jaxurbanbookfest.com
Key Personnel
Founder/Author: Dr V Brooks Dunbar
Features author showcase of various genres & book signings, & virtual masterclass sessions for aspiring authors. Sponsored exhibitors to include book industry professionals & local community resources.
Location: Jacksonville, FL, USA
Jan 25, 2025

LibLearnX: The Library Learning Experience
Sponsored by The American Library Association (ALA)
225 N Michigan Ave, Suite 1300, Chicago, IL 60601
SAN: 201-0062
Tel: 312-944-6780 *Toll Free Tel:* 800-545-2433
 Fax: 312-440-9374
E-mail: ala@ala.org
Web Site: alaliblearnx.org; www.ala.org
Key Personnel
Registration Servs Mgr: Alicia Hamann *Tel:* 800-545-2433 ext 3229 *E-mail:* ahamann@ala.org
Dir, Conference Servs: Earla Jones *Tel:* 800-545-2433 ext 3226 *E-mail:* ejones@ala.org
Mktg Specialist, Conference Servs: Donna Hunter *Tel:* 800-545-2433 ext 3218 *E-mail:* dhunter@ala.org
Conference Mgr: Kara Stachowiak
 E-mail: kstachowiak@ala.org
Conference Planner: Yvonne McLean *Tel:* 800-545-2433 ext 3222 *E-mail:* ymclean@ala.org
Emphasizes active & applied learning, networking opportunities for library professionals.
Location: Phoenix Convention Center, 100 N Third St, Phoenix, AZ, USA
Jan 24-27, 2025

MLA Annual Convention
Sponsored by Modern Language Association (MLA)
85 Broad St, New York, NY 10004
SAN: 202-6422
Tel: 646-576-5266 (convention); 646-576-5133 (registration); 646-576-5000
E-mail: convention@mla.org; registration@mla.org; help@mla.org
Web Site: www.mla.org/convention
Key Personnel
Dir of Convention & Events: Karin L Bagnall
 E-mail: kbagnall@mla.org
Members connect with one another to share research, participate in professional development & build their professional networks.
Location: New Orleans, LA, USA
Jan 9-12, 2025

SCBWI Winter Conference
Sponsored by Society of Children's Book Writers & Illustrators (SCBWI)
6363 Wilshire Blvd, Suite 425, Los Angeles, CA 90048
Tel: 323-782-1010
E-mail: support@scbwi.zendesk.com
Web Site: www.scbwi.org
Key Personnel
Exec Dir: Sarah Baker
Mgr, Events & Spec Projs: Laurie Miller
Brings together top professionals in the children's publishing world. Features renowned authors & illustrators as well as top editors, art directors & agents in the field of children's publishing.
Location: New York Hilton Midtown, 1335 Avenue of the Americas, New York, NY, USA
Jan 31-Feb 2, 2025

Sunshine State Book Festival
Sponsored by Writers Alliance of Gainesville (WAG)
P.O Box 358396, Gainesville, FL 32635-8396
E-mail: SunshineStateBookFestival@writersalliance.org
Web Site: www.sunshinestatebookfestival.com; www.facebook.com/SSBF.FL
Key Personnel
Festival Chairman: Pat Caren
Presents various authors representing diverse genres, from established literary figures to emerging talents each year. Whether you're drawn to fiction, nonfiction, poetry, or children's literature, the festival promises to captivate every literary palate.
Location: Best Western Gateway Grand Hotel, 4200 NW 97 Blvd, Gainesville, FL, USA
Jan 31-Feb 1, 2025

FEBRUARY

Adelaide Festival
Sponsored by Adelaide Festival Corp
Level 9, 33 King William St, Adelaide, SA 5000, Australia
Mailing Address: PO Box 8221, Adelaide, SA 5000, Australia
Tel: (08) 8216 4444
E-mail: info@adelaidefestival.com.au
Web Site: www.adelaidefestival.com.au; facebook.com/adelaidefestival

CALENDAR OF BOOK TRADE & PROMOTIONAL EVENTS

Key Personnel
Artistic Dir: Brett Sheehy
Chief Exec: Kath M Mainland
Assoc Dir: Wouter Van Ransbeek
Exec Asst: Emma Bargery
Dir, Adelaide Writers' Week: Louise Adler
Annual event highlighting the arts, including literature. Adelaide Writers' Week is one of the high-profile events held during the festival.
Location: Adelaide's Central Business District, Adelaide, SA, Australia
Feb 28-March 16, 2025

Amelia Island Book Festival
PO Box 15286, Fernandina Beach, FL 32035
Tel: 904-624-1665
E-mail: info@ameliaislandbookfestival.org
Web Site: www.ameliaislandbookfestival.org; facebook.com/ameliaislandbookfestival
Festival engages adults & young people in the joy of reading & writing through a series of public events featuring New York Times bestselling authors, independent publishers & authors, awards programs & workshops.
Location: Fernandina Beach Middle School, 315 Citrona Dr, Fernandina Beach, FL, USA
Feb 22, 2025

California International Antiquarian Book Fair
Sponsored by Antiquarian Booksellers' Association of America (ABAA)
155 Water St, 6th fl, Suite 7, Brooklyn, NY 11201
Tel: 212-944-8291 *Fax:* 212-944-8293
E-mail: hq@abaa.org
Web Site: www.abaa.org/cabookfair; www.abaa.org
Key Personnel
Exec Dir: Susan Benne *E-mail:* sbenne@abaa.org
Co-sponsored by International League of Antiquarian Booksellers (ILAB), produced & managed by Sanford L Smith + Associates Ltd.
Location: Pasadena Convention Center, 300 E Green St, Pasadena, CA, USA
Feb 7-9, 2025

CAMEX
Sponsored by National Association of College Stores (NACS)
528 E Lorain St, Oberlin, OH 44074
Toll Free Tel: 800-622-7498
E-mail: camex@nacs.org; expositions@nacs.org; info@nacs.org
Web Site: www.camex.org; www.facebook.com/campusmarketexpo; www.nacs.org
Key Personnel
Sr Dir, Meetings & Expositions: Mary Adler-Kozak *Tel:* 800-622-7498 ext 2265
Exhibit Mgr: Lynn Mangol *Tel:* 800-622-7498 ext 2612
Educational conference & buying expo.
Location: Forth Worth, TX, USA
Feb 19-23, 2025

Christian Product Expo™ (CPE)
Sponsored by Christian Retail Association Inc (CRA)
200 West Bay Dr, Largo, FL 33770
Tel: 727-596-7625 *Toll Free Tel:* 800-868-4388
Toll Free Fax: 855-815-9277
Web Site: cpeshow.com; www.facebook.com/CPESHOW; www.christianretailassociation.org
CPE, held twice a year, provides an opportunity for stores to be encouraged, receive training & keep informed of trends happening in retail & in our industry. CPE also provides retailers with information about new products so they can be in-stock on upcoming promotions.
Feb 2025

Converters Expo South
Sponsored by BNP Media | Packaging Group
Division of BNP Media Inc
550 W Merrill St, Suite 200, Birmingham, MI 48009
Tel: 248-362-3700
E-mail: bnp@executivevents.com (registration)
Web Site: www.packagingstrategies.com/converters-expo-south; www.bnpmedia.com
Key Personnel
Event Specialist: Ceci Guzzarde *Tel:* 847-405-4018 *E-mail:* guzzardec@bnpmedia.com
Event Sales Mgr: Tony Stein *Tel:* 484-467-7236 *E-mail:* steint@bnpmedia.com
Unites manufacturers of paper, film, plastics, foil & nonwovens. Attendees can expect to see the latest converting technology, meet with vendors, network with industry peers & find solutions to daily challenges.
Location: Greenville Convention Center, One Exposition Dr, Greenville, SC, USA
Feb 18, 2025

F R E S H Book Festival
Daytona Beach, FL 32120
Tel: 386-627-4353
E-mail: freshbookfestivals@gmail.com
Web Site: www.freshbookfestivals.net
Key Personnel
Founder & Dir: Donna Gray-Banks
Authors, editors & filmmakers convene to discuss their books, upcoming projects, share insight & wisdom related to their crafts.
Location: Julia T & Charles W Cherry Sr Cultural & Educational Center, 925 George W Engram Blvd, Daytona Beach, FL, USA
Feb 21-22, 2025

Fort Collins Book Fest
Sponsored by Poudre Libraries
301 E Olive St, Fort Collins, CO 80524
Tel: 970-221-6740
E-mail: focobookfest@poudrelibraries.org
Web Site: www.focobookfest.org
Combines the community's passion for the literary arts & our unique cultural heritage in a celebration of literature, literacy & social conversation.
Location: Various venues throughout Fort Collins, CO, USA
Feb 7-17, 2025

IS&T Electronic Imaging Conference
Sponsored by Society for Imaging Science and Technology (IS&T)
7003 Kilworth Lane, Springfield, VA 22151
Tel: 703-642-9090 *Fax:* 703-642-9094
E-mail: ei@imaging.org; registration@imaging.org; info@imaging.org
Web Site: www.imaging.org
Key Personnel
Exec Dir: Suzanne E Grinnan *E-mail:* sgrinnan@imaging.org
Conference Prog Mgr: Marion S Zoretich *E-mail:* mzoretich@imaging.org
Exec Asst: Donna Smith *E-mail:* dsmith@imaging.org
Learn about & share the latest imaging developments from industry & academia.
Location: Hyatt Regency San Francisco Airport, 1333 Old Bayshore Hwy, Burlingame, CA, USA
Feb 2-6, 2025

Savannah Book Festival
37 W Fairmont Ave, Suite 216, Savannah, GA 31406
Tel: 912-598-4040
E-mail: info@savannahbookfestival.org
Web Site: www.savannahbookfestival.org
Key Personnel
Exec Dir: Tara Setter *E-mail:* tara@savannahbookfestival.org
Promote reading, writing & civil conversation.

ASSOCIATIONS, EVENTS

Location: Lucas Theatre & various locations around Telfair, Chippewa & Wright Squares in downtown Savannah, GA, USA
Feb 6-9, 2025

WestPack®
Sponsored by Informa Markets
2901 28 St, Suite 100, Santa Monica, CA 90405
Tel: 310-445-4200; 310-445-4273 (cust serv)
Toll Free Tel: 866-267-7339 (client servs)
E-mail: registration.ime@informa.com (cust serv); clientservices.ime@informa.com
Web Site: www.imengineeringwest.com/en/show/show-brands/westpack.html; www.imengineeringwest.com/en/home.html; www.informamarkets.com
Showcasing the latest innovation & excellence in packaging solutions.
Location: Anaheim Convention Center, 800 W Katella Ave, Anaheim, CA, USA
Feb 4-6, 2025

Williamsburg Book Festival
PO Box 114, Williamsburg, VA 23187
E-mail: info@williamsburgbookfestival.org
Web Site: williamsburgbookfestival.org
Key Personnel
Pres: Peter Stipe
Treas: Tim Holland
Secy: Kathleen DesOrmeaux
The festival's mission is to promote & support the art of literary composition in the Williamsburg area & expose writers to the reading public. This free event includes authors from various genres, speakers, illustrators & publishers from Virginia & beyond.
Location: Stryker Center & Community Bldg at City Square, 412 N Boundary St, Williamsburg, VA, USA
Feb 22, 2025

SPRING

Bay Area Book Festival
1569 Solano Ave, No 635, Berkeley, CA 94707
E-mail: info@baybookfest.org
Web Site: www.baybookfest.org
Key Personnel
Founder & Advisor: Cherilyn Parsons
Mng Dir: Samee Roberts
Celebrating books, reading & community. In partnership with the San Francisco Chronicle.
Location: Various locations in downtown Berkeley, CA, USA
Spring 2025

BMI Spring Management Conference
Sponsored by Book Manufacturers' Institute Inc (BMI)
7282 55 Ave E, No 147, Bradenton, FL 34203
Tel: 386-986-4552
Web Site: bmibook.com
Key Personnel
Exec Dir: Matt Baehr *Tel:* 703-939-0679
Open to members & special invited guests only.
Spring 2025

Ohioana Book Festival
Sponsored by Ohioana Library Association
274 E First Ave, Suite 300, Columbus, OH 43201
Tel: 614-466-3831
E-mail: ohioana@ohioana.org; bookfestival@ohioana.org
Web Site: www.ohioana.org
Key Personnel
Exec Dir: Kimberlee Kiehl
Asst Dir: Kathryn Powers
Librarian: Courtney Brown

Prog Coord: Miriam Nordine
Event held each spring to celebrate Ohio writers & their books.
Location: Columbus Metropolitan Library, 96 S Grant Ave, Columbus, OH, USA
Spring 2025

MARCH

AWP Conference & Bookfair
Sponsored by Association of Writers & Writing Programs (AWP)
440 Monticello Ave, Suite 1802, PMB 73708, Norfolk, VA 23510-2670
Tel: 240-696-8250 (conference); 240-696-7700
E-mail: conference@awpwriter.org; events@awpwriter.org; awp@awpwriter.org
Web Site: www.awpwriter.org/awp_conference; www.awpwriter.org
Key Personnel
Dir, Conferences: Colleen Cable
Mgr, Conference Events: Aubrey Kamppila
Destination for writers, teachers, students, editors & publishers of contemporary creative writing. Event includes thousands of attendees, hundreds of events & exhibitors, & 4 days of essential literary conversation & celebration.
Location: Los Angeles, CA, USA
March 26-29, 2025

Bologna Children's Book Fair
Sponsored by BolognaFiere SpA
Viale della Fiera, 20, 40128 Bologna, Italy
Tel: (051) 282 111
E-mail: bookfair@bolognafiere.it
Web Site: www.bolognachildrensbookfair.com; www.facebook.com/BolognaChildrensBookFair
Key Personnel
Event Mgr: Daniela Marmocchi Tel: (051) 282 856 E-mail: daniela.marmocchi@bolognafiere.it
Publishers, illustrators, graphic designers, literary agents, authors, translators, mobile developers, licensors & licensees, packagers, printers, distributors, audiobook professionals, booksellers, brands, librarians & teachers all flock to the event each year to experience the world of books & multimedia products.
Location: Bologna Fair Centre, Piazza Costituzione, 6, Bologna, Italy
March 31-April 3, 2025

Children's Literature Festival
Sponsored by University of Central Missouri
James C Kirkpatrick Library, PO Box 800, Warrensburg, MO 64093
Tel: 660-543-4306
E-mail: clfreg@ucmo.edu
Web Site: clf.ucmo.edu
Key Personnel
Festival Dir: Maya Kucij
Budget Coord & Book Sales: Kim Anthes
Registration Coord: Patty Cary
Book Sales: Chad Marnholtz
Volunteer Coord: Kirsten Shaw
Festival allows children & adults to meet & interact with authors & illustrators whose books they have read or hope to read.
Location: University of Central Missouri, Warrensburg, MO, USA
March 9-11, 2025

Dahlonega Literary Festival
PO Box 1401, Dahlonega, GA 30533
Web Site: literaryfestival.org
Key Personnel
Contact: Sharon Thomason E-mail: set1@windstream.net
Annual celebration of books & authors held in historic downtown Dahlonega, Georgia. Events are open to everyone & most are free, unless otherwise noted, & include individual presentations, panel discussions, workshops, a festival bookstore, book signings & more.
Location: Dahlonega Baptist Church, 234 Hawkins St, Dahlonega, GA, USA
March 1, 2025

DSM Book Festival
Sponsored by Beaverdale Books
2629 Beaver Ave, Des Moines, IA 50310
Tel: 515-279-5400
E-mail: beaverdalebooksevents@gmail.com
Web Site: www.beaverdalebooks.com/dsmbookfestival
Key Personnel
Events & Mktg Coord: Jan Danielson Kaiser
Features nationally acclaimed authors, book club-style discussions led by featured commentators, lively panel discussions, hands-on activities, children's programming & more.
Location: Franklin Junior High Event Center, 4801 Franklin Ave, Des Moines, IA, USA
March 22, 2025

Florida Antiquarian Book Fair
Sponsored by Florida Antiquarian Booksellers Association (FABA)
c/o Lighthouse Books, ABAA, 14046 Fifth St, Dade City, FL 33525
Tel: 727-234-7759
E-mail: floridabookfair@gmail.com
Web Site: floridaantiquarianbookfair.com; www.facebook.com/FloridaAntiquarianBookFair
Key Personnel
Book Fair Mgr: Sarah Smith
Booksellers from all over the country bring volumes of every description from very rare to reading copies on every conceivable subject.
Location: The Coliseum, 535 Fourth Ave N, St Petersburg, FL, USA
March 1-2, 2025

Leipzig Book Fair (Leipziger Buchmesse)
Sponsored by Leipziger Messe GmbH
Messe-Allee 1, 04356 Leipzig, Germany
Tel: (0341) 678-0 Fax: (0341) 678-8762
E-mail: info@leipziger-buchmesse.de
Web Site: www.leipziger-buchmesse.de
Key Personnel
Dir: Aastrid Bohmisch
Supported by Boersenverein des Deutschen Buchhandels, the book fair covers a diverse range of topics & trends in fiction, nonfiction & specialist literature.
Held annually in conjunction with the Leipzig Antiquarian Book Fair & The Manga Comic-Con (MCC).
Location: Leipzig Exhibition Centre, Messe-Allee 1, Leipzig, Germany
March 27-30, 2025

The London Book Fair
Sponsored by RX UK
Division of RELX Group plc
Gateway House, 28 The Quadrant, Richmond, Surrey TW9 1DN, United Kingdom
Tel: (020) 8271 2124
Web Site: www.londonbookfair.co.uk
Key Personnel
Dir: Adam Ridgway
Mktg Mgr: Sophie Gilligan
Conference Mgr: Mariana Barrios
Global marketplace for rights negotiation & the sale & distribution of content across print, audio, TV, film & digital channels. Taking place each spring in the world's premier publishing & cultural capital, it is a unique opportunity to hear from authors, enjoy the vibrant atmosphere & explore innovations shaping the publishing world of the future. The London Book Fair brings you 3 days of focused access to customers, content & emerging markets.
Location: Olympia London, Hammersmith Rd, Kensington, London, UK
March 11-13, 2025

New Orleans Book Festival
200 Broadway St, Suite 126, New Orleans, LA 70118
Tel: 504-865-5000
E-mail: bookfest@tulane.edu
Web Site: bookfest.tulane.edu; facebook.com/nolabookfest
Key Personnel
Founder & Co-Chair: Cheryl Landrieu
Co-Chair: Walter Isaacson
Asst Dir, PR: Roger Dunaway Tel: 504-862-8240 E-mail: roger@tulane.edu
This event features both fiction & nonfiction, convene readings, panel discussions, symposia & keynote speeches. It also provides an opportunity for outlets, authors & readers to interact with each other in one of the most vibrant & culturally diverse cities in the world.
Location: Various Tulane University campus venues, New Orleans, LA, USA
March 27-29, 2025

The Quest for Excellence® Conference
Sponsored by National Institute of Standards and Technology (NIST)
100 Bureau Dr, Gaithersburg, MD 20899
Tel: 301-975-2000
E-mail: baldrige@nist.gov
Web Site: www.nist.gov/baldrige/qe; www.nist.gov/baldrige
Official conference of the Malcolm Baldrige National Quality Award.
Location: Baltimore Marriott Waterfront, 700 Aliceanna St, Baltimore, MD, USA
March 30-April 2, 2025

Southwest Florida Reading Festival
Sponsored by Lee County Library System
2450 First St, Fort Myers, FL 33901
Tel: 239-533-4800
E-mail: readingfestival@leegov.org
Web Site: readfest.org; facebook.com/SWFLReadingFestival
Key Personnel
Festival Coord: Melissa Baker E-mail: mbaker@leegov.com
The festival celebrates the importance of reading & brings the finest literary talent to southwest Florida.
Location: Fort Myers Regional Library Campus, 2450 First St, Fort Myers, FL, USA
March 1, 2025

Tennessee Williams & New Orleans Literary Festival
938 Lafayette St, Suite 514, New Orleans, LA 70113
Tel: 504-581-1144
E-mail: info@tennesseewilliams.net
Web Site: tennesseewilliams.net
Key Personnel
Exec Dir: Paul J Willis
Mng Dir: Tracy Cunningham
The festival serves the community through educational, theatrical, literary & musical programs as well as nurtures, supports & showcases regional, national & international writers, actors, musicians & other artists. The festival also honors Tennessee Williams.
Location: New Orleans French Quarter, New Orleans, LA, USA
March 26-30, 2025

Tucson Festival of Books
1201 E Helen St, Tucson, AZ 85721

CALENDAR OF BOOK TRADE & PROMOTIONAL EVENTS

Mailing Address: PO Box 42466, Tucson, AZ 85733
Tel: 520-621-0302
E-mail: marketing@tucsonfestivalofbooks.org
Web Site: tucsonfestivalofbooks.org; x.com/tfob
Celebrates books, authors, illustrators & readers.
Location: University of Tucson Mall, University of Arizona, Tucson, AZ, USA
March 15-16, 2025

UKSG Annual Conference & Exhibition
Sponsored by UKSG (United Kingdom Serials Group)
Witney Business & Innovation Centre, Windrush House, Windrush Industrial Park, Burford Rd, Witney, Oxon OX29 7DX, United Kingdom
Tel: (01993) 848235
E-mail: info@uksg.org
Web Site: www.uksg.org
Key Personnel
Events Exec: Vicky Drew *Tel:* (07864) 158960
E-mail: events@uksg.org
The conference attracts over 900 delegates from around the world including librarians, publishers, content providers, consultants & intermediaries. The 3-day event is open to all. UKSG members benefit from a significant discount on fees.
Location: Brighton, UK
March 31-April 2, 2025

Virginia Festival of the Book
Sponsored by Virginia Humanities
946 Grady Ave, Suite 100, Charlottesville, VA 22903
Tel: 434-924-3296
E-mail: vabook@virginia.edu
Web Site: www.vabook.org
Key Personnel
Dir: Kalela Williams
Public festival for children & adults featuring authors, illustrators, publishers, publicists, agents & other book professionals in panel discussions & readings. Most events are free. Hundreds of authors invited annually.
Location: Charlottesville, VA, USA
March 19-23, 2025

APRIL

ABAA New York International Antiquarian Book Fair
Sponsored by Antiquarian Booksellers' Association of America (ABAA)
447 W 24 St, New York, NY 10011
Tel: 212-777-5218
E-mail: info@sanfordsmith.com
Web Site: www.nyantiquarianbookfair.com; www.abaa.org
Key Personnel
Exec Dir: Susan Benne *E-mail:* sbenne@abaa.org
Co-sponsored by International League of Antiquarian Booksellers (ILAB), produced & managed by Sanford L Smith + Associates Ltd.
Location: Park Avenue Armory, 643 Park Ave at 67 St, New York, NY, USA
April 3-6, 2025

Fay B Kaigler Children's Book Festival
Sponsored by University of Southern Mississippi
University of Southern Mississippi, 118 College Dr, Suite 5146, Hattiesburg, MS 30406
Tel: 601-266-1000
Web Site: www.usm.edu/childrens-book-festival; www.facebook.com/SouthernMissCBF
Key Personnel
Events Coord: Stacy Creel *Tel:* 601-266-4228
E-mail: stacy.creel@usm.edu
Promotes children's literature, as well as writers, illustrators, publishers, librarians & educators.
Location: University of Southern Mississippi, 118 College Dr, Hattiesburg, MS, USA
April 9-11, 2025

The Federation of Children's Book Groups Annual Conference
Sponsored by The Federation of Children's Book Groups (FCBG)
Wakananai Firs Rd, Mardy, Abergavenny NP7 6NA, United Kingdom
Tel: (0789) 495 6170
E-mail: conference@fcbg.org.uk; info@fcbg.org.uk
Web Site: fcbg.org.uk/conference; x.com/fcbgnews?lang=en; www.facebook.com/fcbgnews
Organized by one of our local children's book groups in collaboration with the national executive, this conference is an opportunity for authors, illustrators, parents, teachers, librarians & all interested children's book lovers to come together to promote their mission of bringing children & books together.
Location: Monmouth, UK
April 11-13, 2025

Festival du Livre de Paris (Paris Book Festival)
Sponsored by SA Paris Livres Events
115, Blvd Saint-Germain, 75006 Paris, France
E-mail: contact@plevenements.fr
Web Site: festivaldulivredeparis.fr
Key Personnel
Mng Dir: Jean-Baptiste Passe
Celebration for all those involved in the book chain, authors, publishers, booksellers, etc to celebrate books.
Location: Grand Palais Ephemere, Place Joffre, Paris, France
April 11-13, 2025

International Children's Book Day
Sponsored by International Board on Books for Young People (IBBY)
Nonnenweg 12, 4055 Basel, Switzerland
Tel: (061) 272 29 17 *Fax:* (061) 272 27 57
E-mail: ibby@ibby.org
Web Site: www.ibby.org
Key Personnel
Exec Dir: Carolina Ballester *E-mail:* carolina.ballester@ibby.org
Admin & Communs Mgr: Catia dos Santos
E-mail: ibby.secretariat@ibby.org
On Hans Christian Andersen's birthday, April 2nd, International Children's Book Day (ICBD) is celebrated to inspire a love of reading & to call attention to children's books. Each year a different national section has the opportunity to be the international sponsor. It decides upon a theme & invites a prominent author to write a message to the children of the world & a well-known illustrator to design a poster. These materials are used in different ways to promote books & reading around the world.
Location: Worldwide
April 2, 2025

Literary Women Long Beach Festival of Authors
Sponsored by Literary Women of Long Beach
PO Box 3014, Long Beach, CA 90803
Tel: 562-546-3816
E-mail: contact@literarywomen.org
Web Site: www.literarywomen.org
Makes accessible to a wide-ranging audience of avid readers the work of outstanding contemporary women authors, encourages new writers of talent & promise & celebrates the value of literature in the lives of future readers.
Location: Long Beach Convention Center, 300 E Ocean Blvd, Long Beach, CA, USA
April 5, 2025

Los Angeles Times Festival of Books
Sponsored by Los Angeles Times
2300 E Imperial Hwy, El Segundo, CA 90245
Tel: 213-237-5000
E-mail: eventinfo@latimes.com
Web Site: events.latimes.com/festivalofbooks; www.facebook.com/latimesfob
The festival features one-on-one conversations, exciting panels, readings by authors, musical performances, TV & movie screenings, & so much more.
Location: The University of Southern California (USC), Los Angeles, CA, USA
April 26-27, 2025

Midwest Literary Walk
Sponsored by Chelsea District Library
221 S Main St, Chelsea, MI 48118
Tel: 734-475-8732 *Fax:* 734-475-6190
Web Site: www.midwestliterarywalk.org
Key Personnel
Lib Dir: Lori Coryell
Head of Mktg & Communs: Virginia Krueger
Tel: 734-475-8732 ext 229 *E-mail:* vkrueger@chelseadistrictlibrary.org
Highlights the power of literature & poetry in everyday life.
Location: Various venues in downtown Chelsea, MI, USA
April 19, 2025

NAAJ Annual Meeting
Sponsored by North American Agricultural Journalists (NAAJ)
c/o Jacqui Fatka, 6866 County Rd, 183, Fredericktown, OH 43019
E-mail: naajnews@yahoo.com
Web Site: www.naaj.net
Key Personnel
Exec Secy-Treas: Jacqui Fatka
Meeting, writing awards & scholarship benefit dance.
Location: Washington, DC, USA
April 2025

National Library Week
Sponsored by The American Library Association (ALA)
225 N Michigan Ave, Suite 1300, Chicago, IL 60601
SAN: 201-0062
Tel: 312-944-6780 *Toll Free Tel:* 800-545-2433
Fax: 312-440-9374
E-mail: campaign@ala.org; ala@ala.org
Web Site: www.ala.org/nlw
Annual celebration highlighting the valuable role libraries, librarians & library workers play in transforming lives & strengthening communities.
Location: Nationwide throughout the USA
April 6-12, 2025

Rockport Fulton Book Festival
PO Box 511, Fulton, TX 78358
E-mail: rfbookfest@gmail.com
Web Site: www.rfbookfestival.com
Key Personnel
Author: Katharine E Hamilton
Brings together authors & readers to celebrate books & reading in this free family-friendly event.
Location: Fulton Convention Center, 402 N Fulton Beach Rd, Fulton, TX, USA
April 26-27, 2025

San Antonio Book Festival
Sponsored by San Antonio Book Festival LLC

1201 Avenue "B", Unit 1011, San Antonio, TX 78215
Tel: 210-750-8951
E-mail: sabf@sabookfest.org
Web Site: sabookfestival.org
Key Personnel
Exec Dir: Lilly Gonzalez
Literary Dir: Anna Dobben
Mng Dir: Maritza Cirlos
Through active partnerships with school districts & community organizations focused on literary, education & culture, this free literary event connects with educators, parents & students, PreK through college.
Location: Central Library, 600 Soledad St & UTSA Southwest Campus, San Antonio, TX, USA
April 12, 2025

Texas Library Association Annual Conference
Sponsored by Texas Library Association (TLA)
3420 Executive Center Dr, Suite 301, Austin, TX 78731
Tel: 512-328-1518 Fax: 512-328-8852
E-mail: tlaconference@txla.org; exhibits@txla.org; tla@txla.org
Web Site: txla.org/annual-conference/; txla.org
Special author events & outstanding educational programming for all library types taught by leaders in the field & opportunities to network & connect with fellow attendees.
Location: Dallas, TX, USA
April 1-4, 2025

Unbound Book Festival
Columbia, MO 65201
E-mail: mail@unboundbookfestival.com
Web Site: www.unboundbookfestival.com; www.facebook.com/unboundbookfestival
Key Personnel
Pres: Katie Doherty
Treas: Keri Gilbert
Secy: Sadie Thibodeaux
Brings together readers & writers to create diverse communities, & to expose participants to new ideas & authors in order to inspire a life-long love of books & reading.
Location: Various venues in downtown Columbia, MO, USA
April 18-20, 2025

Woodstock Bookfest
Box 444, Boiceville, NY 12412
E-mail: info@woodstockbookfest.com
Web Site: woodstockbookfest.com; www.facebook.com/woodstockbookfest
Key Personnel
Exec Dir: Martha Frankel
E-mail: marthafrankel@me.com
Features authors, aspiring writers, readers, students & teachers.
Location: Woodstock, NY, USA
April 4-6, 2025

YA by the Bay©
Sponsored by YA by the Bay, Inc
Wesley Chapel, FL 33543
E-mail: info@yabythebay.org
Web Site: www.yabythebay.org
Key Personnel
Pres: Julie Tingley
Co-Founder & VP, Fin & Impact: Dominique Richardson
Co-Founder & VP, Devt & Philanthropy: Sorboni Banerjee
VP, Festival Planning: Libby Cope
VP, Educ Outreach: Kimberly DeFusco
VP, Author & Publr Engagement: Amanda Koji
A 2-day festival created to celebrate teen literature. The 1st day is closed to the public. YA authors will teach Tampa Bay area teens the ins & outs of writing in a series of author panels & workshops. The 2nd day is open to the public. The community is invited to come celebrate a love of reading with author signings, book panels, vendors, & more. YA by the Bay is dedicated to getting books in hands, especially in underfunded schools, & proud to offer entrance to the festival free for teens.
Location: Tampa Convention Center, 333 S Franklin St, Tampa, FL, USA
April 11-12, 2025

MAY

Annapolis Book Festival
Sponsored by Key School
534 Hillsmere Dr, Annapolis, MD 21403
Tel: 410-263-9231
Web Site: www.keyschool.org/community/annapolis-book-festival
Key Personnel
Dir, Parent Progs & Spec Events: Trish Gallant Tel: 443-321-7820 E-mail: tgallant@keyschool.org
Offers a full day of author panels, family & children's activities & live entertainment.
Location: Key School, 534 Hillsmere Dr, Annapolis, MD, USA
May 3, 2025

ASQ World Conference on Quality & Improvement
Sponsored by American Society for Quality (ASQ)
600 N Plankinton Ave, Milwaukee, WI 53203
Mailing Address: PO Box 3005, Milwaukee, WI 53201-3005
Tel: 414-272-8575 Toll Free Tel: 800-248-1946 (US & CN)
E-mail: help@asq.org
Web Site: www.asq.org
Connects quality professionals to the processes, technologies experts that can deliver curated results for their organization. With the new ability to customize schedules based on experience level, attendees will learn how to fortify essential quality methodologies within their teams while preparing to meet future challenges with sustainable quality solutions.
Location: Denver, CO, USA
May 4-7, 2025

Children's Book Week
Sponsored by The Children's Book Council (CBC)
54 W 39 St, 14th fl, New York, NY 10018
Tel: 212-966-1990
E-mail: cbc.info@cbcbooks.org
Web Site: www.cbcbooks.org; facebook.com/CBCBook; everychildareader.net/cbw/
Key Personnel
Exec Dir: Carl Lennertz E-mail: carl.lennertz@cbcbooks.org
Assoc Exec Dir: Shaina Birkhead E-mail: shaina.birkhead@cbcbooks.org
Celebration of children's books & reading administered by Every Child a Reader. Takes place twice a year.
Location: Nationwide throughout the USA
May 5-11, 2025

Converters Expo
Sponsored by BNP Media | Packaging Group Division of BNP Media Inc
550 W Merrill St, Suite 200, Birmingham, MI 48009
Tel: 248-362-3700
E-mail: bnp@executivevents.com (registration)
Web Site: www.packagingstrategies.com/converters-expo; www.bnpmedia.com
Key Personnel
Event Specialist: Ceci Guzzarde Tel: 847-405-4018 E-mail: guzzardec@bnpmedia.com
Event Sales Mgr: Tony Stein Tel: 484-467-7236 E-mail: steint@bnpmedia.com
Two-day expo in the heart of the nation's largest converting corridor bringing converters of paper, film, plastics & nonwovens together with industry buyers, specialists & suppliers. Converters Expo attracts hundreds of converters looking to find manufacturing partners, discover the latest testing & prototyping equipment, network with producers of disposables, & learn the latest in printing & packaging. A welcome reception is held the day before the expo.
Location: Lambeau Field Atrium, 1265 Lombardi Ave, Green Bay, WI, USA
May 20-21, 2025

Decatur Children's Book Festival
Sponsored by Little Shop of Stories
133A E Court Sq, Decatur, GA 30030
Tel: 404-373-6300
E-mail: info@littleshopofstories.com
Web Site: www.decaturchildrensbookfest.org
Key Personnel
Event Coord: Sydney Wilson
Celebration of children's & young adult literature, held in conjunction with the Decatur Arts Festival.
Location: Various venues in downtown Decatur, GA, USA
May 2-4, 2025

EPA Annual Convention
Sponsored by Evangelical Press Association (EPA)
PO Box 1787, Queen Creek, AZ 85142
Toll Free Tel: 888-311-1731
Web Site: epaconvention.com; www.evangelicalpress.com
Key Personnel
Exec Dir: Lamar Keener
Event for editors, publishers, writers & other staff (print & online publications). Workshop tracks & plenary sessions, opportunities for networking & fellowship.
Location: Hilton Branson Convention Center, 200 E Main St, Branson, MO, USA
May 4-6, 2025

Forest of Reading Festival®
Sponsored by Ontario Library Association
c/o Centre for Social Innovation, 192 Spadina Ave, Suite 205, Toronto, ON M5T 2C2, Canada
Toll Free Tel: 877-340-1730
E-mail: forest@accessola.com
Web Site: www.forestofreading.com/festival
Key Personnel
Dir: Meredith Tutching E-mail: mtutching@accessola.com
Canada's largest literary event for young readers. In-person & digital experience both offered.
Location: Harbourfront Centre, 235 Queens Quay W, Toronto, ON, CN
May 13-14, 2025

Gaithersburg Book Festival
506 S Frederick Ave, Gaithersburg, MD 20877
E-mail: gbf@gathersburgmd.gov
Web Site: www.gaithersburgbookfestival.org
Key Personnel
Founder & Chair: Jud Ashman E-mail: jud.ashman@gaithersburgmd.gov
Annual all-day celebration of books, writers & literary excellence. Sponsored by The Carnegie at Washingtonian Center.

CALENDAR OF BOOK TRADE & PROMOTIONAL EVENTS

Location: Bohrer Park at Summit Hill Farm, 506 S Frederick Ave, Gaithersburg, MD, USA
May 17, 2025

Hudson Children's Book Festival
Sponsored by Hudson Area Library
215 Harry Howard Ave, Hudson, NY 12534
Tel: 518-828-4360
E-mail: hudsonchildrensbookfestival@gmail.com
Web Site: www.hudsonchildrensbookfestival.com
Key Personnel
Co-Dir: Jennifer Clark; Melissa Brown
Strives to create, sustain & nurture a culture of literacy in partnership with our community & schools. This free, public event fosters a love of reading as families meet & greet world-class creators of books for children of all ages.
Location: 215 Harry Howard Ave, Hudson, NY, USA
May 3, 2025

The Jerusalem International Book Forum (JIBF)
Sponsored by Ariel Municipal Co Ltd
PO Box 26280, Jerusalem 9126201, Israel
Tel: (02) 543 5440; (02) 632 0057
Web Site: www.jbookforum.com
Key Personnel
Dir: Sharon Katz *E-mail:* ktsharon@jerusalem.muni.il
Chairman: Yoel Makov
Artistic Dir: Hadar Makov-Hasson
Program of events including panels, discussion groups, interviews, presentations & informal gatherings. Includes cultural & literary events in collaboration with the International Writers Festival.
Location: Jerusalem International YMCA, 26 King David St, Jerusalem, Israel
May 2025

PacPrint 2025
Sponsored by Visual Connections Australia Ltd
Shop 4, 123 Midson Rd, Epping, NSW 2121, Australia
Tel: (02) 9868 1577
E-mail: exhibitions@visualconnections.org.au
Web Site: www.visualconnections.org.au
Key Personnel
Gen Mgr: Peter Harper *E-mail:* peterh@visualconnections.org.au
Event Mgr: Charly Blades *E-mail:* charlyb@visualconnections.org.au
Biennial trade event, held in odd-numbered years, for the printing & graphic communications industry. Co-located with Visual Impact Expo.
Location: Sydney Showground, Sydney Olympic Park, Sydney, NSW, Australia
May 20-23, 2025

Santa Fe International Literary Festival
3775 Old Santa Fe Trail, Santa Fe, NM 87505
E-mail: info@sfinternationallitfest.org
Web Site: www.sfinternationallitfest.org
Key Personnel
Co-Founder & Exec Dir: Clare Hertel
Co-Founder: Carmella Padilla; Mark Bryant Bryant
Connecting writers, readers, & thinkers, from around the world & close to home, in the celebration of words & story. The festival is a way to celebrate our city's deep literary history & diverse community of writers. This is an opportunity to foster a love of storytelling among young writers & readers at the festival & beyond.
Location: Santa Fe Community Convention Center, 201 W Marcy St, Santa Fe, NM, USA
May 16-18, 2025

SSP Annual Meeting
Sponsored by Society for Scholarly Publishing (SSP)
1120 Rte 73, Suite 200, Mount Laurel, NJ 08054
Tel: 856-439-1385 *Fax:* 856-439-0525
E-mail: info@sspnet.org
Web Site: www.sspnet.org
Brings together academics, funders, librarians, publishers, service providers, technologists, & countless others with a communal interest & stake in the dissemination of scholarly information.
Location: Hilton Baltimore Inner Harbor, 401 W Pratt St, Baltimore, MD, USA
May 28-30, 2025

TAPPICon
Sponsored by Technical Association of the Pulp & Paper Industry (TAPPI)
15 Technology Pkwy S, Suite 115, Peachtree Corners, GA 30092
Tel: 770-446-1400 *Toll Free Tel:* 800-332-8686 (US); 800-446-9431 (CN) *Fax:* 770-446-6947
E-mail: memberconnection@tappi.org
Web Site: tappicon.org; www.tappi.org
Key Personnel
Div Mgr: Tyler Mast *Tel:* 770-209-7345 *E-mail:* tmast@tappi.org
Expanded technical program, increased & diverse networking events.
Location: Minneapolis Convention Center, 1301 Second Ave S, Minneapolis, MN, USA
May 4-7, 2025

Thessaloniki International Book Fair (TIBF)
Sponsored by Hellenic Foundation for Culture (HFC)
50 Stratigou Kallari, 154 52 Athens, Greece
Tel: 210-677-6540
Web Site: hfc-worldwide.org
Key Personnel
Pres: Nikos A Koukis
Co-organized by TIF-HELEXPO, the Municipality of Thessaloniki, associations of Greek publishers as well as independent publishers, with the support & cooperation of the Ministry of Culture.
Location: International Exhibition & Congress Centre of Thessaloniki (TIF-Helexpo), 154 Egnatia St, Thessaloniki, Greece
May 2025

SUMMER

Christian Product Expo™ (CPE)
Sponsored by Christian Retail Association Inc (CRA)
200 West Bay Dr, Largo, FL 33770
Tel: 727-596-7625 *Toll Free Tel:* 800-868-4388 *Toll Free Fax:* 855-815-9277
Web Site: cpeshow.com; www.facebook.com/CPESHOW; www.christianretailassociation.org
CPE, held twice a year, provides an opportunity for stores to be encouraged, receive training & keep informed of trends happening in retail & in our industry. CPE also provides retailers with information about new products so they can be in-stock on upcoming promotions.
Summer 2025

Mississippi Book Festival
PO Box 1185, Jackson, MS 39215
E-mail: info@msbookfestival.com
Web Site: msbookfestival.com
Key Personnel
Exec Dir: Ellen Daniels *Tel:* 662-907-9079 *E-mail:* ellen@msbookfestival.com
This annual event draws thousands to its "literary lawn party" & book lovers' celebration.
Location: Mississippi State Capitol Bldg & Grounds, 400 High St, Jackson, MS, USA
Summer 2025

Payson Book Festival
Sponsored by Arizona Professional Writers (APW), Rim Country Chapter
PO Box 1495, Payson, AZ 85547
E-mail: info@paysonbookfestival.org
Web Site: www.paysonbookfestival.org; www.facebook.com/PaysonBookFestival
Key Personnel
Media Mgr: Carol Baxter *E-mail:* media@paysonbookfestival.org
Jointly presented by the Rim Country Chapter of Arizona Professional Writers (APW) & Rim Country Artists, the festival is held to promote literacy & art, & showcase Arizona authors & artists. Our mission is to enhance the love of reading by providing a friendly environment that encourages personal interaction between Arizona authors & readers of all ages. Proceeds will benefit the scholarship funds of both Payson High School & Gila Community College. Over 80 Arizona authors participate by signing books & visiting with readers of all ages. Some will speak about their books & the craft of writing. There will be a full schedule of speakers & several workshops throughout the day.
Location: Mazatzal Hotel & Casino, Hwy 87, Mile Marker 251, Payson, AZ, USA
Summer 2025

JUNE

ALA Annual Conference & Exhibition
Sponsored by The American Library Association (ALA)
225 N Michigan Ave, Suite 1300, Chicago, IL 60601
SAN: 201-0062
Tel: 312-944-6780 *Toll Free Tel:* 800-545-2433 *Fax:* 312-440-9374
E-mail: ala@ala.org
Web Site: www.ala.org
Key Personnel
Registration Servs Mgr: Alicia Hamann *Tel:* 800-545-2433 ext 3229 *E-mail:* ahamann@ala.org
Dir, Conference Servs: Earla Jones *Tel:* 800-545-2433 ext 3226 *E-mail:* ejones@ala.org
Mktg Specialist, Conference Servs: Donna Hunter *Tel:* 800-545-2433 ext 3218 *E-mail:* dhunter@ala.org
Conference Mgr: Kara Stachowiak *E-mail:* kstachowiak@ala.org
Conference Planner: Yvonne McLean *Tel:* 800-545-2433 ext 3222 *E-mail:* ymclean@ala.org
Brings together thousands of librarians & library staff, educators, authors, publishers, friends of libraries, trustees, special guests & exhibitors.
Location: Philadelphia, PA, USA
June 26-July 1, 2025

AUPresses Annual Meeting
Sponsored by Association of University Presses (AUPresses)
1412 Broadway, Suite 2135, New York, NY 10018
Tel: 212-989-1010 *Fax:* 212-989-0275
E-mail: info@aupresses.org
Web Site: www.aupresses.org
Key Personnel
Exec Dir: Peter Berkery *Tel:* 917-288-5594 *E-mail:* pberkery@aupresses.org

Res & Communs Dir: Brenna McLaughlin
Tel: 917-244-2051 *E-mail:* bmclaughlin@aupresses.org
Dir, Opers: Kim Miller *Tel:* 917-244-1264
E-mail: kmiller@aupresses.org
Events Mgr: Alexis Fagan *Tel:* 917-244-1915
E-mail: afagan@aupresses.org
Professional development & networking event for university press & nonprofit scholarly publishers.
Location: Online
June 2025

Beijing International Book Fair (BIBF)
Sponsored by China National Publications Import & Export (Group) Co Ltd (CNPIEC) Member of China Publishing Group Co Ltd (CPG)
16 Gongti E Rd, Beijing 100020, China
Tel: (010) 6506 9507
E-mail: sales@bibf.net
Web Site: www.bibf.net/en
For industry professionals including publishers, distributors, literary agents, consumers, digital media companies, film & production companies, bookstores & distribution companies.
Location: China National Convention Center (CNCC), 7 Tianchen East Rd, Chaoyang District, Beijing, China
June 18-22, 2025

Catholic Media Conference
Sponsored by Catholic Media Association (CMA)
10 S Riverside Plaza, Suite 875, Chicago, IL 60606
Tel: 312-380-6789
Web Site: www.catholicmediaconference.org; www.catholicmediaassociation.org
Key Personnel
Exec Dir, Rob DeFrancesco
E-mail: rdefrancesco@CatholicMediaAssociation.org
Conference attended by Catholic journalists, media professionals & communicators. Sessions cover issues relevant to many aspects of developing, managing & producing all forms of communications, & the business side. Celebrate the positive impact of individuals & publications for their contributions to the Catholic press. The Catholic Press Awards Banquet is the culmination of the conference.
Location: Phoenix, AZ, USA
June 24-27, 2025

EastPack®
Sponsored by Informa Markets
2901 28 St, Suite 100, Santa Monica, CA 90405
Tel: 310-445-4200; 310-445-4273 (cust serv)
Toll Free Tel: 866-267-7339 (client servs)
E-mail: registration.ime@informa.com (cust serv); clientservices.ime@informa.com
Web Site: www.imengineeringeast.com/en/show-brands/epack.html; www.informamarkets.com
From packaging design & materials, to automation & turnkey packaging lines, EastPack is the largest regional packaging event for suppliers & buyers to discover innovation, engineer new technology & build a better tomorrow.
Location: Jacob K Javits Convention Center of New York, 429 11 Ave, New York, NY, USA
June 10-12, 2025

EXPO PACK Guadalajara
Sponsored by PMMI: The Association for Packaging and Processing Technologies
12930 Worldgate Dr, Suite 200, Herndon, VA 20170-6037
Tel: 571-612-3200 *Toll Free Tel:* 888-ASK-PMMI (275-7664)
E-mail: info@expopack.com.mx; info@pmmi.org
Web Site: www.expopackguadalajara.com.mx; www.packexpo.com; www.pmmi.org
Represents Western Mexico showcasing the latest solutions in processing & packaging. Biennial event held in odd-numbered years.
Location: Expo Guadalajara, Av Mariano Otero 1499, Colonia Verde Valle, Guadalajara, Mexico
June 10-12, 2025

IABC World Conference
Sponsored by International Association of Business Communicators (IABC)
330 N Wabash Ave, Suite 2000, Chicago, IL 60611
Tel: 312-321-6868 *Toll Free Tel:* 800-218-8097
Fax: 312-673-6708
E-mail: registration@iabc.com
Web Site: wc.iabc.com; www.iabc.com
Key Personnel
Sr Event Mgr: Laura Penning *Tel:* 312-673-5645
E-mail: LPenning@iabc.com
Event Mgr: Sara Gornik *Tel:* 312-673-5366
E-mail: SGornik@iabc.com
Tradeshow Coord: Kelsey Kwasniak *Tel:* 312-673-5387 *E-mail:* KKwasniak@iabc.com
Conference designed for today's communication professionals to connect with peers from around the globe & hear from industry experts.
Location: Vancouver, BC, CN
June 8-11, 2025

Imaginarium Book Festival
Sponsored by University of the District of Columbia
University of the District of Columbia, 4200 Connecticut Ave NW, Washington, DC 20008
E-mail: info@imaginariumbookfestival.com
Web Site: www.imaginariumbookfestival.com
Key Personnel
Event Coord & Co-Founder: Diantha Jones
E-mail: diantha@imaginariumbookfestival.com
Creative Dir & Co-Founder: Nadege Richards
E-mail: nadege@imaginariumbookfestival.com
Festival brings together people who share a love for fantastical storytelling.
Location: 4200 Connecticut Ave NW, Washington, DC, USA
June 6-7, 2025

Nantucket Book Festival
Sponsored by Nantucket Book Foundation
PO Box 5267, Nantucket, MA 02554
Tel: 508-919-6230
E-mail: info@nantucketbookfestival.org
Web Site: nantucketbookfestival.org; www.facebook.com/NantucketBookFestival
Key Personnel
Exec Dir: Kaley Kokomoor *E-mail:* director@nantucketbookfestival.org
Annual celebration of the literary arts bringing together authors, book lovers, & storytellers. For one exciting weekend each June, the island of Nantucket transforms into a book lover's paradise, featuring a lineup of author readings, panel discussions, writing workshops, & book signings. Almost all festival events are free & open to the public, ensuring that literary enjoyment is accessible to all.
Location: Various locations in Nantucket, MA, USA
June 2025

JULY

Hong Kong Book Fair
Sponsored by Hong Kong Trade Development Council
c/o Exhibition Dept, Unit 13, Expo Galleria, Hong Kong Convention & Exhibition Centre, Wan Chai, Hong Kong
Tel: 1830 668 (cust serv) *Fax:* 2824 0026; 2824 0249
Web Site: hkbookfair.hktdc.com; hkbookfair.hktdc.com/en/index.html (English)
Exhibits & sells new books & media products, reading & writing workshops, seminars & autograph sessions for book lovers.
Location: Hong Kong Convention & Exhibition Center, One Harbour Rd, Wan Chai, Hong Kong
July 2025

IAML Annual Congress
Sponsored by International Association of Music Libraries, Archives & Documentation Centres Inc (IAML)
c/o Gothenburg University Library, Music & Drama Library, Box 222, 405 30 Gothenburg, Sweden
Tel: (031) 786 40 60
E-mail: contact@iaml.info
Web Site: www.iaml.info
Key Personnel
Secy Gen: Anders Cato *E-mail:* secretary@iaml.info
Held in conjunction with The General Assembly.
Location: Salzburg, Austria
July 6-11, 2025

AUGUST

The Dorothy L Sayers Society Annual Convention
Sponsored by The Dorothy L Sayers Society
Witham Library, 18 Newland St, Witham, Essex CM8 2AQ, United Kingdom
Tel: (01376) 519625
E-mail: info@sayers.org.uk
Web Site: www.sayers.org.uk
Key Personnel
Membership Secy: Margaret Hunt
E-mail: membership@sayers.org.uk
Members only event.
Aug 2025

Edinburgh International Book Festival
121 George St, Edinburgh EH2 4YN, United Kingdom
Tel: (0131) 718 5666
E-mail: admin@edbookfest.co.uk
Web Site: www.edbookfest.co.uk
Key Personnel
Book Festival Dir: Jenny Niven
Each year we welcome over 900 international authors & over 250,000 visitors to one of the biggest book festivals in the world, hosting audiences & authors in a literary village for 18 days every August.
Location: Edinburgh Futures Institute, 56 George Sq, Edinburgh, UK
Aug 2025

IFLA World Library and Information Congress (WLIC)
Sponsored by International Federation of Library Associations & Institutions (IFLA) (Federation internationale des associations de bibliothecaires et des bibliotheques)
Prins Willem-Alexanderhof 5, 2595 BE The Hague, Netherlands
Tel: (70) 314 08 84
E-mail: conferences@ifla.org; ifla@ifla.org
Web Site: www.ifla.org/congress/; www.ifla.org

CALENDAR OF BOOK TRADE & PROMOTIONAL EVENTS

Key Personnel
Conference Mgr: Marie-Emmanuelle Marande
  E-mail: marie-emmanuelle.marande@ifla.org
International flagship professional & trade event for the library & information services sector.
Held simultaneously with IFLA General Conference and Assembly.
Aug 2025

Literacy Texas Annual Conference
Sponsored by Literacy Texas
PO Box 111, Texarkana, TX 75504-0111
Tel: 903-392-9802
E-mail: info@literacytexas.org
Web Site: www.literacytexas.org/calendar/2025-conference/; literacytexas.org; www.facebook.com/LiteracyTX
Key Personnel
Exec Dir: Dr Jenny McCormack Walker
For educators, nonprofit administrators & organizations working with literacy in Texas.
Location: Embassy Suites by Hilton San Marcos, 1001 E McCarty Lane, San Marcos, TX, USA
Aug 5-6, 2025

Outdoor Writers Association of America Annual Conference
Sponsored by Outdoor Writers Association of America (OWAA)
2814 Brooks St, Box 442, Missoula, MT 59801
Tel: 406-728-7434
E-mail: info@owaa.org
Web Site: owaa.org
Key Personnel
Exec Dir: Chez Chesak
This event is an opportunity for outdoor communicators & outdoor groups, businesses & agencies that are involved in the world of outdoor communication to learn & connect with others in the industry. It will give attendees a chance to network with other professionals, allow them to build crucial business outlets & help improve their skills. Attend sessions geared toward general business & newsmaker sessions, plus craft improvement in multiple genres of outdoor communication.
Location: Chattanooga, TN, USA
Aug 18-20, 2025

Swanwick: The Writers' Summer School
Sponsored by Writers' Summer School
The Hayes Conference Centre, Hayes Lane, Swanwick, Alfreton DE55 1AU, United Kingdom
Tel: (01290) 552248
E-mail: secretary@swanwickwritersschool.co.uk
Web Site: www.swanwickwritersschool.org.uk
A weeklong residential writing school with top name speakers & tutors, plus informative panels, talks & discussion groups. Comfortable rooms with all meals & tuition included in the price. Open to everyone, from absolute beginners to published authors. Beautiful setting, licensed bar & evening entertainment. Believed to be the longest established residential writers' school in the world, Swanwick, held annually in August, is a must attend event in every writer's diary.
Location: The Hayes Conference Centre, Swanwick, Alfreton, Derbyshire, UK
Aug 2025

AUTUMN

ACP/CMA Fall National College Media Convention
Sponsored by Associated Collegiate Press (ACP) Division of National Scholastic Press Association
2829 University Ave SE, Suite 720, Minneapolis, MN 55414
Tel: 612-200-9254 (ACP); 212-297-2195 (CMA)
E-mail: info@studentpress.org (ACP); info@collegemedia.org (CMA)
Web Site: collegemediaconvention.org
Key Personnel
Exec Dir, ACP/NSPA: Laura Widmer *Tel:* 612-200-9265
Convention & Membership Mgr: Karli Keith
  E-mail: karli@studentpress.org
Covers all aspects of college media, from rapidly changing multimedia platforms to newspaper, broadcast, yearbook & magazine journalism.
Co-sponsored by College Media Association.
Fall 2025

BMI Annual Conference
Sponsored by Book Manufacturers' Institute Inc (BMI)
7282 55 Ave E, No 147, Bradenton, FL 34203
Tel: 386-986-4552
Web Site: bmibook.com
Key Personnel
Exec Dir: Matt Baehr *Tel:* 703-939-0679
Open to members & special invited guests only.
Fall 2025

Didac India
Sponsored by Messe Stuttgart India Pvt Ltd
Soverign Corporate Tower, 11th fl, No 1118, Plot No A - 143, Sector 136, Noida 201 304, India
Tel: (0120) 6991703
E-mail: info@messe-stuttgart.in
Web Site: didacindia.com; www.facebook.com/DidacIndia/; messe-stuttgart.in
Educational resources & technology-based products & solutions for all levels & segments of the education & skill sector.
Fall 2025

Feria Internacional del Libro de Guadalajara
Av Alemania 1370, Colonia Moderna, 44190 Guadalajara, Jalisco, Mexico
Tel: (033) 3810 0331; (033) 3268 0900
E-mail: fil@fil.com.mx
Web Site: www.fil.com.mx
Key Personnel
Pres: Raul Padilla Lopez
Gen Dir: Marisol Schulz Manaut *E-mail:* marisol.schulz@fil.com.mx
Content Mgmt: Laura Niembro Diaz
  E-mail: laura.niembro@fil.com.mx
Prog Coord: Carolina Tapia Luna
  E-mail: carolina.tapia@fil.com.mx
Exhibitors Coord: Armando Montes de Santiago
  E-mail: armando.desantiago@fil.com.mx
Brings together publishers, literary agents, reading promoters, translators, distributors & librarians.
Location: Expo Guadalajara, Av Mariano Otero 1499, Colonia Verde Valle, Guadalajara, Mexico
Fall 2025

Kentucky Book Festival
Sponsored by Kentucky Humanities
206 E Maxwell St, Lexington, KY 40508
Tel: 859-257-4317 *Fax:* 859-257-5933
Web Site: kybookfestival.org
Key Personnel
Dir, Book Festival: Katerina Stoykova
  E-mail: kyhumanities@gmail.com
A celebration of reading, writing & publishing. Various weekday events culminating in a day-long celebration.
Location: Joseph-Beth Booksellers, The Mall at Lexington Green, 161 Lexington Green Circle, Lexington, KY, USA
Fall 2025

Louisiana Book Festival
Sponsored by Louisiana Center for the Book Subsidiary of State Library of Louisiana
701 N Fourth St, Baton Rouge, LA 70802
Tel: 225-219-9503 *Fax:* 225-219-9840
Web Site: louisianabookfestival.org; www.facebook.com/LABookFestival/
Key Personnel
Dir: Jim Davis *Tel:* 225-342-9714
  E-mail: jdavis@slol.lib.la.us
Asst Dir: Robert Wilson *E-mail:* lbf@state.lib.la.us
A free event celebrating readers, writers & books representing a variety of genres & related events for all ages, food demos, book sales & signings, exhibitors.
Location: State Library of Louisiana, Louisiana State Capitol, Capitol Park Event Center & nearby locations, Baton Rouge, LA, USA
Fall 2025

New Hampshire Book Festival
Sponsored by New Hampshire Book and Literary Festival Inc
PO Box 283, Contoocock, NH 03229
E-mail: nhbookfest@gmail.com
Web Site: nhbookfestival.org
Key Personnel
Co-Founder & Pres: Emilie Christie Burack
Co-Founder & Board Chair: Sarah McCraw Crow
Statewide book festival with the mission to bring authors together with readers to celebrate literacy, conversation & community.
Location: Various downtown locations, Concord, NH, USA
Fall 2025

Salon du Livre et de la Presse Jeunesse (SLPJ)
Sponsored by Centre de Promotion du Livre de Jeunesse (CPLJ)
3, rue Francois Debergue, 93100 Montreuil, France
Tel: 01 55 86 86 55 *Fax:* 01 48 57 04 62
E-mail: contact@slpj.fr
Web Site: www.slpjplus.fr
Key Personnel
Dir: Sylvie Vassallo
Leading publishing event dedicated to children's books.
Location: Montreuil, France
Fall

ScienceWriters2025
Sponsored by National Association of Science Writers Inc (NASW)
PO Box 7905, Berkeley, CA 94707
Tel: 510-859-7229
E-mail: workshops@nasw.org
Web Site: www.nasw.org
Key Personnel
Exec Dir: Tinsley Davis *E-mail:* director@nasw.org
Science communications gathering held in conjunction with the Council for the Advancement of Science Writing (CASW).
Fall 2025

Sharjah International Book Fair (SIBF)
Sponsored by Sharjah Book Authority
PO Box 73111, Sharjah, United Arab Emirates
Toll Free Tel: 800-BOOKS (26657) *Fax:* (06) 5140111
E-mail: info@sibf.com
Web Site: www.sibf.com
Includes literary events, daily writing workshops, poetry readings & book signings.
Location: Expo Center Sharjah, Al Taawun St, Sharjah, United Arab Emirates
Fall 2025

Six Bridges Book Festival
Sponsored by Central Arkansas Library System (CALS)
100 Rock St, Little Rock, AR 72201

Tel: 501-918-3000
E-mail: sixbridgesbookfest@cals.org
Web Site: cals.org/six-bridges-book-festival
Key Personnel
Festival Coord: Brad Mooy
Celebrates reading, literacy, stories & wordsmithing.
Location: Various locations in downtown Little Rock, AR, USA
Fall 2025

Texas Book Festival
1023 Springdale Rd, Bldg 14, Unit B, Austin, TX 78721
Tel: 512-477-4055
E-mail: bookfest@texasbookfestival.org
Web Site: www.texasbookfestival.org
Key Personnel
COO: Dalia Azim *E-mail:* dalia@texasbookfestival.org
CEO: Marianne DeLeon *E-mail:* marianne@texasbookfestival.org
Devt Dir: Susannah Auby *E-mail:* susannah@texasbookfestival.org
Literary Dir: Hannah Gabel *E-mail:* hannah@texasbookfestival.org
Event Prodn & Logistics Coord: Olivia Hesse *E-mail:* oliviahesse@texasbookfestival.org
Opers & Literary Coord: Anna Dolliver *E-mail:* anna@texasbookfestival.org
Communs & PR Coord: Jose Rodriguez *E-mail:* jose@texasbookfestival.org
Statewide program that promotes reading & literacy highlighted by a 2-day festival, held annually in the fall, featuring authors from Texas & across the USA. Money raised is distributed as grants to public libraries throughout the state. Includes events for Texas teens & YA programming.
Location: State Capitol Bldg, 1100 Congress Ave, Austin, TX, USA
Fall 2025

SEPTEMBER

Gothenburg Book Fair
Sponsored by Bok & Bibliotek i Norden AB
Maessans Gata 10, 412 94 Gothenburg, Sweden
Tel: (031) 708 84 00
E-mail: info@goteborg-bookfair.com; hej@bokmassan.se
Web Site: goteborg-bookfair.com; www.bokmassan.se
Key Personnel
Fair Mgr: Frida Edman *Tel:* (031) 708 84 10 *E-mail:* fe@bokmassan.se
Prog Mgr: Oskar Ekstroem *Tel:* (031) 708 84 73 *E-mail:* oe@bokmassan.se
A manifestation of arts & culture, a 4-day literary festival, a tribute to freedom of expression & a place for readers & writers to meet & celebrate the power of stories.
Location: The Swedish Exhibition & Congress Centre, Gothenburg, Sweden
Sept 25-28, 2025

NFPW Communications Conference
Sponsored by National Federation of Press Women Inc (NFPW)
140B Purcellville Gateway Dr, Suite 120, Purcellville, VA 20132
Tel: 571-295-5900
E-mail: info@nfpw.org
Web Site: www.nfpw.org
Key Personnel
Exec Dir: Catherine E Langley
For professional women & men pursuing careers across the communications spectrum.
Location: Denver Marriott West, 1717 Denver West Blvd, Golden, CO, USA
Sept 11-13, 2025

PACK EXPO Las Vegas
Sponsored by PMMI: The Association for Packaging and Processing Technologies
12930 Worldgate Dr, Suite 200, Herndon, VA 20170-6037
Tel: 571-612-3200 *Toll Free Tel:* 888-ASK-PMMI (275-7664)
E-mail: expo@pmmi.org; info@pmmi.org
Web Site: www.packexpolasvegas.com; www.packexpo.com; www.pmmi.org
Biennial event, held in odd-numbered years, features cutting-edge packaging & processing solutions from thousands of suppliers. Attendees have access to opportunities to move projects forward, develop relationships & gain valuable perspective on industry trends.
Location: Las Vegas Convention Center, 3150 Paradise Rd, Las Vegas, NV, USA
Sept 29-Oct 1, 2025

Printers Row Lit Fest
Sponsored by New South Planning Board
2600 S Michigan Ave, Suite LL-C, Chicago, IL 60616
Tel: 312-987-1980
E-mail: info@thenspb.org
Web Site: printersrowlitfest.org
Key Personnel
Exhibitors Dir: Ashley Taylor
Dir, Programming: Amy Danzer
Prog Mgr: Haley Carlson
Book fair & literary festival.
Location: On & around the area of Dearborn St, Chicago, IL, USA
Sept 6-7, 2025

PSA® Photo Festival
Sponsored by Photographic Society of America® (PSA®)
8241 S Walker Ave, Suite 104, Oklahoma City, OK 73139
Tel: 405-843-1437 *Toll Free Tel:* 855-PSA-INFO (772-4636)
E-mail: hq@psa-photo.org
Web Site: psa-photo.org
Exhibition of accepted & awarded images & prints.
Location: Holiday Inn Portland-Columbia Riverfront, 909 N Hayden Island Dr, Portland, OR, USA
Sept 24-27, 2025

OCTOBER

AIGA Design Conference
Sponsored by AIGA, the professional association for design
228 Park Ave S, Suite 58603, New York, NY 10003
Tel: 212-807-1990
Web Site: www.aiga.org; facebook.com/AIGAdesign
Key Personnel
Dir, Mktg: Michelle Koenigsknecht *Tel:* 212-710-3138
The premier conference for the design community.
Location: Los Angeles, CA, USA
Oct 9-11, 2025

Alaska Book Week
Sponsored by Alaska Center for the Book
PO Box 242074, Anchorage, AK 99524
Tel: 907-786-4379
E-mail: akbookweek@gmail.com
Web Site: alaskabookweek.org; facebook.com/alaskabookweek
Key Personnel
Chair: Trish Jenkins
The annual statewide event, usually held around the first week of October, celebrates the appreciation of books, from readings, to panels, lectures, discussions & youth activities.
Location: Statewide, AK, USA
Oct 2025

American Translators Association Annual Conference
Sponsored by American Translators Association (ATA)
211 N Union St, Suite 100, Alexandria, VA 22314
Tel: 703-683-6100 *Fax:* 703-778-7222
E-mail: ata@atanet.org
Web Site: www.atanet.org
Key Personnel
Exec Dir: Kelli C Baxter *Tel:* 703-683-6100 ext 3010 *E-mail:* kelli@atanet.org
Dir, Prof Devt & Events: Adrian Aleckna *Tel:* 703-683-6100 ext 3019 *E-mail:* adrian@atanet.org
Prof Devt & Events Coord: Cat Kenol *Tel:* 703-683-6100 ext 3009 *E-mail:* cat@atanet.org
Advance the translation & interpreting professions & foster the professional development of its members. Members include translators, interpreters, teachers, project managers, web & software developers, language company owners, hospitals, universities & government agencies.
Location: Boston, MA, USA
Oct 22-25, 2025

Boston Book Festival
720 Massachusetts Ave, Suite B, Cambridge, MA 02139
Tel: 857-259-6999 *Fax:* 617-249-2053
E-mail: info@bostonbookfest.org
Web Site: bostonbookfest.org
Key Personnel
Exec Dir: Jenny Dworkin
Founder & Bd Chair: Deborah Z Porter
Celebrating the power of words to stimulate, agitate, unite, delight & inspire.
Location: Copley Square, Boston, MA, USA
Oct 2025

Desert Foothills Book Festival
Sponsored by Desert Foothills Library
38443 N Schoolhouse Rd, Cave Creek, AZ 85331
Tel: 480-488-2286 *Fax:* 480-595-8353
Web Site: www.desertfoothillsbookfestival.com
Key Personnel
Comm Chair: Caren Cantrell *E-mail:* caren.cantrell@gmail.com
Promotes an appreciation of reading & the literary arts. Presented also by The Holland Center.
Location: The Holland Center, 34250 N 60 St, Scottsdale, AZ, USA
Oct 18, 2025

Frankfurter Buchmesse
(Frankfurt Book Fair)
Sponsored by Frankfurter Buchmesse GmbH
Braubachstr 16, 60311 Frankfurt am Main, Germany
Tel: (069) 21020 *Fax:* (069) 2102 277
E-mail: servicecenter@buchmesse.de
Web Site: www.buchmesse.de/en
Key Personnel
Pres & CEO: Juergen Boos
Major international book & media fair attracting 7,300 exhibitors & over 286,000 visitors from more than 100 countries.
Location: Frankfurt Fairgrounds, Ludwig-Erhard-Anlage One, Frankfurt, Germany
Oct 15-19, 2025

CALENDAR OF BOOK TRADE & PROMOTIONAL EVENTS

LIBER Feria Internacional del Libro
Sponsored by Federacion de Gremios de Editores de Espana (FGEE) (Spanish Association of Publishers Guilds)
Cea Bermudez, 44-2° Dcha, 28003 Madrid, Spain
Tel: 91 534 51 95
E-mail: fgee@fge.es
Web Site: www.federacioneditores.org
Key Personnel
Exec Dir: Antonio Maria Avila
Dedicated to publishing in Spanish & open to all book sectors, with special attention to digital content, new publishers, self-publishing & intellectual property.
Location: Madrid, Spain
Oct 2025

Morristown Festival of Books
Sponsored by Kraft Event Management Inc
131 Woods End Dr, Basking Ridge, NJ 07920
Tel: 908-221-0448 *Fax:* 908-221-1466
E-mail: info@morristownbooks.org
Web Site: morristownbooks.org
Destination event for authors & readers.
Location: Various downtown locations, Morristown, NJ, USA
Oct 10-11, 2025

National Book Month
Sponsored by National Book Foundation
90 Broad St, Suite 604, New York, NY 10004
Tel: 212-685-0261
E-mail: nationalbook@nationalbook.org
Web Site: www.nationalbook.org
Key Personnel
Exec Dir: Ruth Dickey *E-mail:* rdickey@nationalbook.org
Dir, Progs & Partnerships: Natalie Green *E-mail:* ngreen@nationalbook.org
Sr Mgr, Mktg & Communs: Ale Romero *E-mail:* aromero@nationalbook.org
Month-long celebration focusing on the importance of reading, writing & literature.
Location: Nationwide throughout the USA
Oct 2025

NNAF Annual Convention and Trade Show
Sponsored by National Newspaper Association Foundation (NNAF)
PO Box 13323, Pensacola, FL 32591
Tel: 850-542-7087
Web Site: www.nnafoundation.org/convention
Key Personnel
Exec Dir: Lynne Lance *E-mail:* lynne@nnafoundation.org
Exhibitors get the opportunity to meet with members on the trade show floor for one-on-one interaction conducive to making qualified contacts. Participation in the convention allows engagement with key decision makers at community newspapers across the country.
Location: Hilton Minneapolis, 1001 S Marquette Ave, Minneapolis, MN, USA
Oct 9-10, 2025

PRINTING United Expo
Sponsored by PRINTING United Alliance
10015 Main St, Fairfax, VA 22031
Tel: 703-385-1335 *Toll Free Tel:* 888-385-3588 *Fax:* 703-273-0456
E-mail: register@printingunited.com (general show inquiries); exhibit@printingunited.com (exhibitor Inquiries)
Web Site: printingunited.com; www.printing.org
Bringing together the entire print industry to see the latest trends, technology & solutions in one place.
Location: Orange County Convention Center, Orlando, FL, USA
Oct 22-24, 2025

Seattle Antiquarian Book Fair
c/o Collins Books, 13005 Third Ave NE, Seattle, WA 98125
Tel: 206-323-3999
E-mail: collinsbooks@collinsbooks.com
Web Site: www.seattlebookfair.com
Key Personnel
Prodr: Bill Wolfe
Dealers from across North America & beyond offering for sale thousands of collectible books, prints, maps, autographs, photographs, posters, postcards, ephemera, manuscripts, broadsides, fine bindings & more.
Location: Seattle Center Exhibition Hall, 301 Mercer St, Seattle, WA, USA
Oct 2025

Twin Cities Book Festival
Sponsored by Rain Taxi
PO Box 3840, Minneapolis, MN 55403
E-mail: bookfest@raintaxi.com; info@raintaxi.com
Web Site: twincitiesbookfestival.com
Key Personnel
Dir: Eric Lorberer
Gala celebration of books, featuring large book fair, author readings & signings, activities, panels, used book sale & children's events.
Location: Minnesota State Fairgrounds, 1265 Snelling Ave N, St Paul, MN, USA
Oct 2025

Utah Humanities Book Festival
Sponsored by Utah Humanities
Affiliate of Utah Center for the Book
202 W 300 N, Salt Lake City, UT 84103
Tel: 801-359-9670
Web Site: utahhumanities.org
Key Personnel
Exec Dir: Jodi Graham *Tel:* 801-359-9670 ext 101 *E-mail:* graham@utahhumanities.org
Prog Mgr: Kase Johnstun *Tel:* 801-359-9670 *E-mail:* johnstun@utahhumanities.org
Dir, Communs: Deena Pyle *Tel:* 801-359-9670 ext 111 *E-mail:* pyle@utahhumanities.org
Free literary event featuring national, regional & local authors held annually the month of October (National Book Month).
Location: Statewide, UT, USA
Oct 1-31, 2025

NOVEMBER

ASIS&T Annual Meeting
Sponsored by Association for Information Science & Technology (ASIS&T)
673 Potomac Station Dr, Suite 155, Leesburg, VA 20176
Tel: 301-495-0900
E-mail: asist@asist.org
Web Site: www.asist.org
Key Personnel
Exec Dir: Lydia Middleton *Tel:* 301-495-0900 ext 1200
Dir, Meetings & Events: Cathy L Nash *Tel:* 301-495-0900 ext 1500
International conference dedicated to the study of information, people & technology in contemporary society.
Location: Hyatt Regency Crystal City at Reagan National Airport, 2799 Richmond Hwy, Arlington, VA, USA
Nov 14-18, 2025

Boston International Antiquarian Book Fair
Sponsored by Antiquarian Booksellers' Association of America (ABAA)
447 W 24 St, New York, NY 10011
Tel: 212-777-5218
Web Site: www.abaa.org/bostonbookfair; www.abaa.org
Fall 3-day gathering for book lovers & collectors, featuring the top selection of items available on the international literary market. This event is sanctioned by the Antiquarian Booksellers' Association of America & the International League of Antiquarian Booksellers. Organized by Capricorn Event Management LLC.
Location: Hynes Convention Center, 900 Boylston St, Boston, MA, USA
Nov 7-9, 2025

Children's Book Week
Sponsored by The Children's Book Council (CBC)
54 W 39 St, 14th fl, New York, NY 10018
Tel: 212-966-1990
E-mail: cbc.info@cbcbooks.org
Web Site: www.cbcbooks.org; facebook.com/CBCBook; everychildareader.net/cbw/
Key Personnel
Exec Dir: Carl Lennertz *E-mail:* carl.lennertz@cbcbooks.org
Assoc Exec Dir: Shaina Birkhead *E-mail:* shaina.birkhead@cbcbooks.org
Celebration of children's books & reading administered by Every Child a Reader. Takes place twice a year.
Location: Nationwide throughout the USA
Nov 3-9, 2025

International Istanbul Book Fair
Sponsored by Tuyap Fairs and Exhibitions Organization Inc (Tuyap Tum Fuarlar Uretim A S)
E-5 Karayolu Uezeri, Guerpinar Kavsagi, Bueyuekcekmece, 34500 Istanbul, Turkey
Tel: (0212) 867 11 00 *Fax:* (0212) 886 66 98
E-mail: info@tuyap.com.tr
Web Site: istanbulkitapfuari.com/en/; tuyap.com.tr/en/
Annual international event organized in cooperation with the Turkish Publishers Association.
Location: TUYAP Fair Convention & Congress Center, Buyukcekmece/Istanbul, Turkey
Nov 2025

Jewish Book Month
Sponsored by Jewish Book Council
520 Eighth Ave, 4th fl, New York, NY 10018
Tel: 212-201-2920 *Fax:* 212-532-4952
E-mail: info@jewishbooks.org
Web Site: www.jewishbookcouncil.org; www.facebook.com/JewishBookCouncil; x.com/jewishbook
Key Personnel
Exec Dir: Carol Kaufman
Prog Dir: Evie Saphire-Bernstein *E-mail:* evie@jewishbooks.org
Dedicated to the celebration of Jewish books held annually during the month leading up to Hanukkah.
Location: Nationwide throughout the USA
Nov 14-Dec 14, 2025

Malta Book Festival
Sponsored by National Book Council
Bice Mizzi Vassallo Complex, Arnheim Rd, Pembroke PBK 1776, Malta
Tel: 27131574
E-mail: nationalbookcouncil@gov.mt
Web Site: ktieb.org.mt; ktieb.org.mt/en
Key Personnel
Sr Mgr: Matthew Borg *E-mail:* matthew.borg@ktieb.org.mt
50,000 visitors & more than 50 exhibitors attend annually & offers extensive networking opportunities for industry professionals.
Location: Malta Fairs & Conventions Centre, Ta' Qali, Attard, Malta
Nov 2025

COURSES & AWARDS

Medical Writing & Communication Conference
Sponsored by American Medical Writers Association (AMWA)
9841 Washingtonian Blvd, Suite 500-26, Gaithersburg, MD 20878
Tel: 240-238-0940 *Fax:* 301-294-9006
E-mail: conference@amwa.org; amwa@amwa.org
Web Site: www.amwa.org
Key Personnel
Educ & Events Coord: Angelique Mize *Tel:* 240-238-0940 ext 112 *E-mail:* angelique@amwa.org
Elevates health & well-being through medical communication.
Location: Sheraton Phoenix Downtown Hotel, 340 N Third St, Phoenix, AZ, USA
Nov 5-8, 2025

Miami Book Fair
Sponsored by Florida Center for the Literary Arts
c/o Miami Dade College, 300 NE Second Ave, Miami, FL 33132
Tel: 305-237-3258
E-mail: wbookfair@mdc.edu
Web Site: www.miamibookfair.com; www.facebook.com/MiamiBookFair
Key Personnel
Dir of Opers: Delia Lopez
Dir, Progs: Lissette Mendez
Prog Coord: Marci Cancio-Bello
Opers Mgr: Stephanie Farokhnia
Prog Coord: Paola Fernandez Rana
Annual 8-day festival held in November featuring national & international book exhibitors & a robust schedule of literary, cultural & educational events.
Location: Miami Dade College, Wolfson Campus, Miami, FL, USA
Nov 2025

Salon du Livre de Montreal (Montreal Book Fair)
Sponsored by Salon du Livre de Montreal
1264, rue Sherbrooke E, Montreal, QC H2L 1M1, Canada
Tel: 514-845-2365
E-mail: bonjour@salondulivredemontreal.com
Web Site: www.salondulivredemontreal.com; www.facebook.com/salondulivredemontreal
Key Personnel
Mng Dir: Olivier Gougeon
Promotes books & the pleasure of reading as cultural assets in Quebec society & promotes the essential role of authors, creators & artisans in the book industry & contributes to promoting the diversity of regional & national & international publishing production.
Location: Montreal, QC, CN
Nov 2025

Stuttgarter Buchwochen (Stuttgart Book Weeks)
Sponsored by Boersenverein des Deutschen Buchhandels, Landesverband Baden-Wuerttemberg eV (Association of Publishers & Booksellers in Baden-Wuerttemberg eV)
Paulinenstr 53, 70178 Stuttgart, Germany
Tel: (0711) 61 94 10 *Fax:* (0711) 61 94 14 4
E-mail: post@buchhandelsverband.de
Web Site: www.buchwochen.de; www.boersenverein-baden-wuerttemberg.de
Key Personnel
Contact: Andrea Baumann *Tel:* (0711) 61941-28 *E-mail:* baumann@buchhandelsverband.de
Since its first exhibition in 1949, the Stuttgart Book Weeks has grown from a dedicated showcase for publishers & trade members only to a cultural event open to everyone in the region of Stuttgart & beyond.
Location: Haus de Wirtschaft, Willi-Bleicher-Str 19, Stuttgart, Germany
Nov 2025

2026

JANUARY

MLA Annual Convention
Sponsored by Modern Language Association (MLA)
85 Broad St, New York, NY 10004
SAN: 202-6422
Tel: 646-576-5266 (convention); 646-576-5133 (registration); 646-576-5000
E-mail: convention@mla.org; registration@mla.org; help@mla.org
Web Site: www.mla.org/convention
Key Personnel
Dir of Convention & Events: Karin L Bagnall *E-mail:* kbagnall@mla.org
Members connect with one another to share research, participate in professional development & build their professional networks.
Location: Toronto, ON, CN
Jan 8-11, 2026

FEBRUARY

Adelaide Festival
Sponsored by Adelaide Festival Corp
Level 9, 33 King William St, Adelaide, SA 5000, Australia
Mailing Address: PO Box 8221, Adelaide, SA 5000, Australia
Tel: (08) 8216 4444
E-mail: info@adelaidefestival.com.au
Web Site: www.adelaidefestival.com.au; facebook.com/adelaidefestival
Key Personnel
Artistic Dir: Brett Sheehy
Chief Exec: Kath M Mainland
Assoc Dir: Wouter Van Ransbeek
Exec Asst: Emma Bargery
Dir, Adelaide Writers' Week: Louise Adler
Annual event highlighting the arts, including literature. Adelaide Writers' Week is one of the high-profile events held during the festival.
Location: Adelaide's Central Business District, Adelaide, SA, Australia
Feb 27-March 15, 2026

PACK EXPO East
Sponsored by PMMI: The Association for Packaging and Processing Technologies
12930 Worldgate Dr, Suite 200, Herndon, VA 20170-6037
Tel: 571-612-3200 *Toll Free Tel:* 888-ASK-PMMI (275-7664)
E-mail: expo@pmmi.org; info@pmmi.org
Web Site: www.packexpoeast.com; www.packexpo.com; www.pmmi.org
Biennial event, held in even-numbered years, focusing on packaging solutions for the East coast.
Location: Pennsylvania Convention Center, 1101 Arch St, Philadelphia, PA, USA
Feb 17-19, 2026

CALENDAR OF BOOK TRADE & PROMOTIONAL EVENTS

MARCH

Leipzig Book Fair (Leipziger Buchmesse)
Sponsored by Leipziger Messe GmbH
Messe-Allee 1, 04356 Leipzig, Germany
Tel: (0341) 678-0 *Fax:* (0341) 678-8762
E-mail: info@leipziger-buchmesse.de
Web Site: www.leipziger-buchmesse.de
Key Personnel
Dir: Aastrid Bohmisch
Supported by Boersenverein des Deutschen Buchhandels, the book fair covers a diverse range of topics & trends in fiction, nonfiction & specialist literature.
Held annually in conjunction with the Leipzig Antiquarian Book Fair & The Manga Comic-Con (MCC).
Location: Leipzig Exhibition Centre, Messe-Allee 1, Leipzig, Germany
March 19-22, 2026

The London Book Fair
Sponsored by RX UK
Division of RELX Group plc
Gateway House, 28 The Quadrant, Richmond, Surrey TW9 1DN, United Kingdom
Tel: (020) 8271 2124
Web Site: www.londonbookfair.co.uk
Key Personnel
Dir: Adam Ridgway
Mktg Mgr: Sophie Gilligan
Conference Mgr: Mariana Barrios
Global marketplace for rights negotiation & the sale & distribution of content across print, audio, TV, film & digital channels. Taking place each spring in the world's premier publishing & cultural capital, it is a unique opportunity to hear from authors, enjoy the vibrant atmosphere & explore innovations shaping the publishing world of the future. The London Book Fair brings you 3 days of focused access to customers, content & emerging markets.
Location: Olympia London, Hammersmith Rd, Kensington, London, UK
March 10-12, 2026

Texas Library Association Annual Conference
Sponsored by Texas Library Association (TLA)
3420 Executive Center Dr, Suite 301, Austin, TX 78731
Tel: 512-328-1518 *Fax:* 512-328-8852
E-mail: tlaconference@txla.org; exhibits@txla.org; tla@txla.org
Web Site: txla.org/annual-conference/; txla.org
Special author events & outstanding educational programming for all library types taught by leaders in the field & opportunities to network & connect with fellow attendees.
Location: Houston, TX, USA
March 30-April 2, 2026

APRIL

Fay B Kaigler Children's Book Festival
Sponsored by University of Southern Mississippi
University of Southern Mississippi, 118 College Dr, Suite 5146, Hattiesburg, MS 30406
Tel: 601-266-1000
Web Site: www.usm.edu/childrens-book-festival; www.facebook.com/SouthernMissCBF
Key Personnel
Events Coord: Stacy Creel *Tel:* 601-266-4228 *E-mail:* stacy.creel@usm.edu
Promotes children's literature, as well as writers, illustrators, publishers, librarians & educators.
Location: University of Southern Mississippi, 118 College Dr, Hattiesburg, MS, USA
April 8-10, 2026

CALENDAR OF BOOK TRADE & PROMOTIONAL EVENTS

International Children's Book Day
Sponsored by International Board on Books for Young People (IBBY)
Nonnenweg 12, 4055 Basel, Switzerland
Tel: (061) 272 29 17 *Fax:* (061) 272 27 57
E-mail: ibby@ibby.org
Web Site: www.ibby.org
Key Personnel
Exec Dir: Carolina Ballester *E-mail:* carolina.ballester@ibby.org
Admin & Communs Mgr: Catia dos Santos *E-mail:* ibby.secretariat@ibby.org
On Hans Christian Andersen's birthday, April 2nd, International Children's Book Day (ICBD) is celebrated to inspire a love of reading & to call attention to children's books. Each year a different national section has the opportunity to be the international sponsor. It decides upon a theme & invites a prominent author to write a message to the children of the world & a well-known illustrator to design a poster. These materials are used in different ways to promote books & reading around the world.
Location: Worldwide
April 2, 2026

NAAJ Annual Meeting
Sponsored by North American Agricultural Journalists (NAAJ)
c/o Jacqui Fatka, 6866 County Rd, 183, Fredericktown, OH 43019
E-mail: naajnews@yahoo.com
Web Site: www.naaj.net
Key Personnel
Exec Secy-Treas: Jacqui Fatka
Meeting, writing awards & scholarship benefit dance.
Location: Washington, DC, USA
April 2026

National Library Week
Sponsored by The American Library Association (ALA)
225 N Michigan Ave, Suite 1300, Chicago, IL 60601
SAN: 201-0062
Tel: 312-944-6780 *Toll Free Tel:* 800-545-2433 *Fax:* 312-440-9374
E-mail: campaign@ala.org; ala@ala.org
Web Site: www.ala.org/nlw
Annual celebration highlighting the valuable role libraries, librarians & library workers play in transforming lives & strengthening communities.
Location: Nationwide throughout the USA
April 19-25, 2026

MAY

SSP Annual Meeting
Sponsored by Society for Scholarly Publishing (SSP)
1120 Rte 73, Suite 200, Mount Laurel, NJ 08054
Tel: 856-439-1385 *Fax:* 856-439-0525
E-mail: info@sspnet.org
Web Site: www.sspnet.org
Brings together academics, funders, librarians, publishers, service providers, technologists, & countless others with a communal interest & stake in the dissemination of scholarly information.
Location: Gaylord Pacific Resort & Convention Center, 1000 "H" St, Chula Vista, CA, USA
May 27-29, 2026

JUNE

ALA Annual Conference & Exhibition
Sponsored by The American Library Association (ALA)
225 N Michigan Ave, Suite 1300, Chicago, IL 60601
SAN: 201-0062
Tel: 312-944-6780 *Toll Free Tel:* 800-545-2433 *Fax:* 312-440-9374
E-mail: ala@ala.org
Web Site: www.ala.org
Key Personnel
Registration Servs Mgr: Alicia Hamann *Tel:* 800-545-2433 ext 3229 *E-mail:* ahamann@ala.org
Dir, Conference Servs: Earla Jones *Tel:* 800-545-2433 ext 3226 *E-mail:* ejones@ala.org
Mktg Specialist, Conference Servs: Donna Hunter *Tel:* 800-545-2433 ext 3218 *E-mail:* dhunter@ala.org
Conference Mgr: Kara Stachowiak *E-mail:* kstachowiak@ala.org
Conference Planner: Yvonne McLean *Tel:* 800-545-2433 ext 3222 *E-mail:* ymclean@ala.org
Brings together thousands of librarians & library staff, educators, authors, publishers, friends of libraries, trustees, special guests & exhibitors.
Location: Chicago, IL, USA
June 25-30, 2026

AUPresses Annual Meeting
Sponsored by Association of University Presses (AUPresses)
1412 Broadway, Suite 2135, New York, NY 10018
Tel: 212-989-1010 *Fax:* 212-989-0275
E-mail: info@aupresses.org
Web Site: www.aupresses.org
Key Personnel
Exec Dir: Peter Berkery *Tel:* 917-288-5594 *E-mail:* pberkery@aupresses.org
Res & Communs Dir: Brenna McLaughlin *Tel:* 917-244-2051 *E-mail:* bmclaughlin@aupresses.org
Dir, Opers: Kim Miller *Tel:* 917-244-1264 *E-mail:* kmiller@aupresses.org
Events Mgr: Alexis Fagan *Tel:* 917-244-1915 *E-mail:* afagan@aupresses.org
Professional development & networking event for university press & nonprofit scholarly publishers.
Location: Westin Seattle, 1900 Fifth Ave, Seattle, WA, USA
June 13-15, 2026

EXPO PACK Mexico
Sponsored by PMMI: The Association for Packaging and Processing Technologies
12930 Worldgate Dr, Suite 200, Herndon, VA 20170-6037
Tel: 571-612-3200 *Toll Free Tel:* 888-ASK-PMMI (275-7664)
E-mail: expo@pmmi.org; info@pmmi.org
Web Site: www.expopackmexico.com.mx; www.pmmi.org
Latest technologies in action, sustainable solutions & a cutting-edge educational program for the packaging & processing industry. Event is held biennially in even-numbered years.
Location: EXPO Santa Fe® Mexico, Av Santa Fe 270, Santa Fe, Mexico City, Mexico
June 9-12, 2026

IAML Annual Congress
Sponsored by International Association of Music Libraries, Archives & Documentation Centres Inc (IAML)
c/o Gothenburg University Library, Music & Drama Library, Box 222, 405 30 Gothenburg, Sweden
Tel: (031) 786 40 60
E-mail: contact@iaml.info
Web Site: www.iaml.info
Key Personnel
Secy Gen: Anders Cato *E-mail:* secretary@iaml.info
Held in conjunction with The General Assembly.
Location: Thessaloniki, Greece
June 28-July 3, 2026

Nantucket Book Festival
Sponsored by Nantucket Book Foundation
PO Box 5267, Nantucket, MA 02554
Tel: 508-919-6230
E-mail: info@nantucketbookfestival.org
Web Site: nantucketbookfestival.org; www.facebook.com/NantucketBookFestival
Key Personnel
Exec Dir: Kaley Kokomoor *E-mail:* director@nantucketbookfestival.org
Annual celebration of the literary arts bringing together authors, book lovers, & storytellers. For one exciting weekend each June, the island of Nantucket transforms into a book lover's paradise, featuring a lineup of author readings, panel discussions, writing workshops, & book signings. Almost all festival events are free & open to the public, ensuring that literary enjoyment is accessible to all.
Location: Various locations in Nantucket, MA, USA
June 2026

JULY

Hong Kong Book Fair
Sponsored by Hong Kong Trade Development Council
c/o Exhibition Dept, Unit 13, Expo Galleria, Hong Kong Convention & Exhibition Centre, Wan Chai, Hong Kong
Tel: 1830 668 (cust serv) *Fax:* 2824 0026; 2824 0249
Web Site: hkbookfair.hktdc.com; hkbookfair.hktdc.com/en/index.html (English)
Exhibits & sells new books & media products, reading & writing workshops, seminars & autograph sessions for book lovers.
Location: Hong Kong Convention & Exhibition Center, One Harbour Rd, Wan Chai, Hong Kong
July 2026

AUGUST

Edinburgh International Book Festival
121 George St, Edinburgh EH2 4YN, United Kingdom
Tel: (0131) 718 5666
E-mail: admin@edbookfest.co.uk
Web Site: www.edbookfest.co.uk
Key Personnel
Book Festival Dir: Jenny Niven
Each year we welcome over 900 international authors & over 250,000 visitors to one of the biggest book festivals in the world, hosting audiences & authors in a literary village for 18 days every August.
Location: Edinburgh Futures Institute, 56 George Sq, Edinburgh, UK
Aug 2026

IBBY World Congress
Sponsored by International Board on Books for Young People (IBBY)
Nonnenweg 12, 4055 Basel, Switzerland

Tel: (061) 272 29 17 *Fax:* (061) 272 27 57
E-mail: ibby@ibby.org
Web Site: www.ibby.org
Key Personnel
Exec Dir: Carolina Ballester *E-mail:* carolina.ballester@ibby.org
Admin & Communs Mgr: Catia dos Santos *E-mail:* ibby.secretariat@ibby.org
IBBY's biennial congresses, held in even-numbered years, hosted by different countries, are the most important meeting points for IBBY members & other people involved in children's books & reading development. They are wonderful opportunities to make contacts, exchange ideas & open horizons.
Location: Ottawa, ON, CN
Aug 6-9, 2026

Swanwick: The Writers' Summer School
Sponsored by Writers' Summer School
The Hayes Conference Centre, Hayes Lane, Swanwick, Alfreton DE55 1AU, United Kingdom
Tel: (01290) 552248
E-mail: secretary@swanwickwritersschool.co.uk
Web Site: www.swanwickwritersschool.org.uk
A weeklong residential writing school with top name speakers & tutors, plus informative panels, talks & discussion groups. Comfortable rooms with all meals & tuition included in the price. Open to everyone, from absolute beginners to published authors. Beautiful setting, licensed bar & evening entertainment. Believed to be the longest established residential writers' school in the world, Swanwick, held annually in August, is a must attend event in every writer's diary.
Location: The Hayes Conference Centre, Swanwick, Alfreton, Derbyshire, UK
Aug 2026

AUTUMN

Texas Book Festival
1023 Springdale Rd, Bldg 14, Unit B, Austin, TX 78721
Tel: 512-477-4055
E-mail: bookfest@texasbookfestival.org
Web Site: www.texasbookfestival.org
Key Personnel
COO: Dalia Azim *E-mail:* dalia@texasbookfestival.org
CEO: Marianne DeLeon *E-mail:* marianne@texasbookfestival.org
Devt Dir: Susannah Auby *E-mail:* susannah@texasbookfestival.org
Literary Dir: Hannah Gabel *E-mail:* hannah@texasbookfestival.org
Event Prodn & Logistics Coord: Olivia Hesse *E-mail:* oliviahesse@texasbookfestival.org
Opers & Literary Coord: Anna Dolliver *E-mail:* anna@texasbookfestival.org
Communs & PR Coord: Jose Rodriguez *E-mail:* jose@texasbookfestival.org
Statewide program that promotes reading & literacy highlighted by a 2-day festival, held annually in the fall, featuring authors from Texas & across the USA. Money raised is distributed as grants to public libraries throughout the state. Includes events for Texas teens & YA programming.
Location: State Capitol Bldg, 1100 Congress Ave, Austin, TX, USA
Fall 2026

SEPTEMBER

Gothenburg Book Fair
Sponsored by Bok & Bibliotek i Norden AB
Maessans Gata 10, 412 94 Gothenburg, Sweden
Tel: (031) 708 84 00
E-mail: info@goteborg-bookfair.com; hej@bokmassan.se
Web Site: goteborg-bookfair.com; www.bokmassan.se
Key Personnel
Fair Mgr: Frida Edman *Tel:* (031) 708 84 10 *E-mail:* fe@bokmassan.se
Prog Mgr: Oskar Ekstroem *Tel:* (031) 708 84 73 *E-mail:* oe@bokmassan.se
A manifestation of arts & culture, a 4-day literary festival, a tribute to freedom of expression & a place for readers & writers to meet & celebrate the power of stories.
Location: The Swedish Exhibition & Congress Centre, Gothenburg, Sweden
Sept 26-27, 2026

PRINTING United Expo
Sponsored by PRINTING United Alliance
10015 Main St, Fairfax, VA 22031
Tel: 703-385-1335 *Toll Free Tel:* 888-385-3588 *Fax:* 703-273-0456
E-mail: register@printingunited.com (general show inquiries); exhibit@printingunited.com (exhibitor Inquiries)
Web Site: printingunited.com; www.printing.org
Bringing together the entire print industry to see the latest trends, technology & solutions in one place.
Location: Las Vegas Convention Center, 3150 Paradise Rd, Las Vegas, NV, USA
Sept 23-25, 2026

OCTOBER

Alaska Book Week
Sponsored by Alaska Center for the Book
PO Box 242074, Anchorage, AK 99524
Tel: 907-786-4379
E-mail: akbookweek@gmail.com
Web Site: alaskabookweek.org; facebook.com/alaskabookweek
Key Personnel
Chair: Trish Jenkins
The annual statewide event, usually held around the first week of October, celebrates the appreciation of books, from readings, to panels, lectures, discussions & youth activities.
Location: Statewide, AK, USA
Oct 2026

Frankfurter Buchmesse
(Frankfurt Book Fair)
Sponsored by Frankfurter Buchmesse GmbH
Braubachstr 16, 60311 Frankfurt am Main, Germany
Tel: (069) 21020 *Fax:* (069) 2102 277
E-mail: servicecenter@buchmesse.de
Web Site: www.buchmesse.de/en
Key Personnel
Pres & CEO: Juergen Boos
Major international book & media fair attracting 7,300 exhibitors & over 286,000 visitors from more than 100 countries.
Location: Frankfurt Fairgrounds, Ludwig-Erhard-Anlage One, Frankfurt, Germany
Oct 7-11, 2026

National Book Month
Sponsored by National Book Foundation
90 Broad St, Suite 604, New York, NY 10004
Tel: 212-685-0261
E-mail: nationalbook@nationalbook.org
Web Site: www.nationalbook.org
Key Personnel
Exec Dir: Ruth Dickey *E-mail:* rdickey@nationalbook.org
Dir, Progs & Partnerships: Natalie Green *E-mail:* ngreen@nationalbook.org
Sr Mgr, Mktg & Communs: Ale Romero *E-mail:* aromero@nationalbook.org
Month-long celebration focusing on the importance of reading, writing & literature.
Location: Nationwide throughout the USA
Oct 2026

PACK EXPO International
Sponsored by PMMI: The Association for Packaging and Processing Technologies
12930 Worldgate Dr, Suite 200, Herndon, VA 20170-6037
Tel: 571-612-3200 *Toll Free Tel:* 888-ASK-PMMI (275-7664)
E-mail: expo@pmmi.org; info@pmmi.org
Web Site: www.packexpointernational.com; www.pmmi.org
This biennial event, held in even-numbered years, offers the chance to see all the latest packaging technology & processing solutions for every vertical industry as well as educational sessions & networking opportunities.
Location: McCormick Place, 2301 S King Dr, Chicago, IL, USA
Oct 18-21, 2026

Utah Humanities Book Festival
Sponsored by Utah Humanities
Affiliate of Utah Center for the Book
202 W 300 N, Salt Lake City, UT 84103
Tel: 801-359-9670
Web Site: utahhumanities.org
Key Personnel
Exec Dir: Jodi Graham *Tel:* 801-359-9670 ext 101 *E-mail:* graham@utahhumanities.org
Prog Mgr: Kase Johnstun *Tel:* 801-359-9670 *E-mail:* johnstun@utahhumanities.org
Dir, Communs: Deena Pyle *Tel:* 801-359-9670 ext 111 *E-mail:* pyle@utahhumanities.org
Free literary event featuring national, regional & local authors held annually the month of October (National Book Month).
Location: Statewide, UT, USA
Oct 1-31, 2026

NOVEMBER

Jewish Book Month
Sponsored by Jewish Book Council
520 Eighth Ave, 4th fl, New York, NY 10018
Tel: 212-201-2920 *Fax:* 212-532-4952
E-mail: info@jewishbooks.org
Web Site: www.jewishbookcouncil.org; www.facebook.com/JewishBookCouncil; x.com/jewishbook
Key Personnel
Exec Dir: Carol Kaufman
Prog Dir: Evie Saphire-Bernstein *E-mail:* evie@jewishbooks.org
Dedicated to the celebration of Jewish books held annually during the month leading up to Hanukkah.
Location: Nationwide throughout the USA
Nov 4-Dec 4, 2026

CALENDAR OF BOOK TRADE & PROMOTIONAL EVENTS

2027

SPRING

The London Book Fair
Sponsored by RX UK
Division of RELX Group plc
Gateway House, 28 The Quadrant, Richmond, Surrey TW9 1DN, United Kingdom
Tel: (020) 8271 2124
Web Site: www.londonbookfair.co.uk
Key Personnel
Dir: Adam Ridgway
Mktg Mgr: Sophie Gilligan
Conference Mgr: Mariana Barrios
Global marketplace for rights negotiation & the sale & distribution of content across print, audio, TV, film & digital channels. Taking place each spring in the world's premier publishing & cultural capital, it is a unique opportunity to hear from authors, enjoy the vibrant atmosphere & explore innovations shaping the publishing world of the future. The London Book Fair brings you 3 days of focused access to customers, content & emerging markets.
Location: Olympia London, Hammersmith Rd, Kensington, London, UK
Spring 2027

MARCH

Texas Library Association Annual Conference
Sponsored by Texas Library Association (TLA)
3420 Executive Center Dr, Suite 301, Austin, TX 78731
Tel: 512-328-1518 *Fax:* 512-328-8852
E-mail: tlaconference@txla.org; exhibits@txla.org; tla@txla.org
Web Site: txla.org/annual-conference/; txla.org
Special author events & outstanding educational programming for all library types taught by leaders in the field & opportunities to network & connect with fellow attendees.
Location: San Antonio, TX, USA
March 30-April 2, 2027

APRIL

Fay B Kaigler Children's Book Festival
Sponsored by University of Southern Mississippi
University of Southern Mississippi, 118 College Dr, Suite 5146, Hattiesburg, MS 30406
Tel: 601-266-1000
Web Site: www.usm.edu/childrens-book-festival; www.facebook.com/SouthernMissCBF
Key Personnel
Events Coord: Stacy Creel *Tel:* 601-266-4228 *E-mail:* stacy.creel@usm.edu
Promotes children's literature, as well as writers, illustrators, publishers, librarians & educators.
Location: University of Southern Mississippi, 118 College Dr, Hattiesburg, MS, USA
April 7-9, 2027

International Children's Book Day
Sponsored by International Board on Books for Young People (IBBY)
Nonnenweg 12, 4055 Basel, Switzerland
Tel: (061) 272 29 17 *Fax:* (061) 272 27 57
E-mail: ibby@ibby.org
Web Site: www.ibby.org
Key Personnel
Exec Dir: Carolina Ballester *E-mail:* carolina.ballester@ibby.org
Admin & Communs Mgr: Catia dos Santos *E-mail:* ibby.secretariat@ibby.org
On Hans Christian Andersen's birthday, April 2nd, International Children's Book Day (ICBD) is celebrated to inspire a love of reading & to call attention to children's books. Each year a different national section has the opportunity to be the international sponsor. It decides upon a theme & invites a prominent author to write a message to the children of the world & a well-known illustrator to design a poster. These materials are used in different ways to promote books & reading around the world.
Location: Worldwide
April 2, 2027

NAAJ Annual Meeting
Sponsored by North American Agricultural Journalists (NAAJ)
c/o Jacqui Fatka, 6866 County Rd, 183, Fredericktown, OH 43019
E-mail: naajnews@yahoo.com
Web Site: www.naaj.net
Key Personnel
Exec Secy-Treas: Jacqui Fatka
Meeting, writing awards & scholarship benefit dance.
Location: Washington, DC, USA
April 2027

JUNE

ALA Annual Conference & Exhibition
Sponsored by The American Library Association (ALA)
225 N Michigan Ave, Suite 1300, Chicago, IL 60601
SAN: 201-0062
Tel: 312-944-6780 *Toll Free Tel:* 800-545-2433 *Fax:* 312-440-9374
E-mail: ala@ala.org
Web Site: www.ala.org
Key Personnel
Registration Servs Mgr: Alicia Hamann *Tel:* 800-545-2433 ext 3229 *E-mail:* ahamann@ala.org
Dir, Conference Servs: Earla Jones *Tel:* 800-545-2433 ext 3226 *E-mail:* ejones@ala.org
Mktg Specialist, Conference Servs: Donna Hunter *Tel:* 800-545-2433 ext 3218 *E-mail:* dhunter@ala.org
Conference Mgr: Kara Stachowiak *E-mail:* kstachowiak@ala.org
Conference Planner: Yvonne McLean *Tel:* 800-545-2433 ext 3222 *E-mail:* ymclean@ala.org
Brings together thousands of librarians & library staff, educators, authors, publishers, friends of libraries, trustees, special guests & exhibitors.
Location: New Orleans, LA, USA
June 24-29, 2027

Nantucket Book Festival
Sponsored by Nantucket Book Foundation
PO Box 5267, Nantucket, MA 02554
Tel: 508-919-6230
E-mail: info@nantucketbookfestival.org
Web Site: nantucketbookfestival.org; www.facebook.com/NantucketBookFestival
Key Personnel
Exec Dir: Kaley Kokomoor *E-mail:* director@nantucketbookfestival.org
Annual celebration of the literary arts bringing together authors, book lovers, & storytellers. For one exciting weekend each June, the island of Nantucket transforms into a book lover's paradise, featuring a lineup of author readings, panel discussions, writing workshops, & book signings. Almost all festival events are free & open to the public, ensuring that literary enjoyment is accessible to all.
Location: Various locations in Nantucket, MA, USA
June 2027

JULY

Hong Kong Book Fair
Sponsored by Hong Kong Trade Development Council
c/o Exhibition Dept, Unit 13, Expo Galleria, Hong Kong Convention & Exhibition Centre, Wan Chai, Hong Kong
Tel: 1830 668 (cust serv) *Fax:* 2824 0026; 2824 0249
Web Site: hkbookfair.hktdc.com; hkbookfair.hktdc.com/en/index.html (English)
Exhibits & sells new books & media products, reading & writing workshops, seminars & autograph sessions for book lovers.
Location: Hong Kong Convention & Exhibition Center, One Harbour Rd, Wan Chai, Hong Kong
July 2027

AUGUST

Edinburgh International Book Festival
121 George St, Edinburgh EH2 4YN, United Kingdom
Tel: (0131) 718 5666
E-mail: admin@edbookfest.co.uk
Web Site: www.edbookfest.co.uk
Key Personnel
Book Festival Dir: Jenny Niven
Each year we welcome over 900 international authors & over 250,000 visitors to one of the biggest book festivals in the world, hosting audiences & authors in a literary village for 18 days every August.
Location: Edinburgh Futures Institute, 56 George Sq, Edinburgh, UK
Aug 2027

Swanwick: The Writers' Summer School
Sponsored by Writers' Summer School
The Hayes Conference Centre, Hayes Lane, Swanwick, Alfreton DE55 1AU, United Kingdom
Tel: (01290) 552248
E-mail: secretary@swanwickwritersschool.co.uk
Web Site: www.swanwickwritersschool.org.uk
A weeklong residential writing school with top name speakers & tutors, plus informative panels, talks & discussion groups. Comfortable rooms with all meals & tuition included in the price. Open to everyone, from absolute beginners to published authors. Beautiful setting, licensed bar & evening entertainment. Believed to be the longest established residential writers' school in the world, Swanwick, held annually in August, is a must attend event in every writer's diary.
Location: The Hayes Conference Centre, Swanwick, Alfreton, Derbyshire, UK
Aug 2027

AUTUMN

Texas Book Festival
1023 Springdale Rd, Bldg 14, Unit B, Austin, TX 78721
Tel: 512-477-4055

E-mail: bookfest@texasbookfestival.org
Web Site: www.texasbookfestival.org
Key Personnel
COO: Dalia Azim *E-mail:* dalia@texasbookfestival.org
CEO: Marianne DeLeon *E-mail:* marianne@texasbookfestival.org
Devt Dir: Susannah Auby *E-mail:* susannah@texasbookfestival.org
Literary Dir: Hannah Gabel *E-mail:* hannah@texasbookfestival.org
Event Prodn & Logistics Coord: Olivia Hesse *E-mail:* oliviahesse@texasbookfestival.org
Opers & Literary Coord: Anna Dolliver *E-mail:* anna@texasbookfestival.org
Commuus & PR Coord: Jose Rodriguez *E-mail:* jose@texasbookfestival.org
Statewide program that promotes reading & literacy highlighted by a 2-day festival, held annually in the fall, featuring authors from Texas & across the USA. Money raised is distributed as grants to public libraries throughout the state. Includes events for Texas teens & YA programming.
Location: State Capitol Bldg, 1100 Congress Ave, Austin, TX, USA
Fall 2027

SEPTEMBER

Gothenburg Book Fair
Sponsored by Bok & Bibliotek i Norden AB
Maessans Gata 10, 412 94 Gothenburg, Sweden
Tel: (031) 708 84 00
E-mail: info@goteborg-bookfair.com; hej@bokmassan.se
Web Site: goteborg-bookfair.com; www.bokmassan.se
Key Personnel
Fair Mgr: Frida Edman *Tel:* (031) 708 84 10 *E-mail:* fe@bokmassan.se
Prog Mgr: Oskar Ekstroem *Tel:* (031) 708 84 73 *E-mail:* oe@bokmassan.se
A manifestation of arts & culture, a 4-day literary festival, a tribute to freedom of expression & a place for readers & writers to meet & celebrate the power of stories.
Location: The Swedish Exhibition & Congress Centre, Gothenburg, Sweden
Sept 23-26, 2027

PRINTING United Expo
Sponsored by PRINTING United Alliance
10015 Main St, Fairfax, VA 22031
Tel: 703-385-1335 *Toll Free Tel:* 888-385-3588 *Fax:* 703-273-0456
E-mail: register@printingunited.com (general show inquiries); exhibit@printingunited.com (exhibitor Inquiries)
Web Site: printingunited.com; www.printing.org
Bringing together the entire print industry to see the latest trends, technology & solutions in one place.
Location: Las Vegas Convention Center, 3150 Paradise Rd, Las Vegas, NV, USA
Sept 14-16, 2027

OCTOBER

Alaska Book Week
Sponsored by Alaska Center for the Book
PO Box 242074, Anchorage, AK 99524
Tel: 907-786-4379
E-mail: akbookweek@gmail.com
Web Site: alaskabookweek.org; facebook.com/alaskabookweek
Key Personnel
Chair: Trish Jenkins
The annual statewide event, usually held around the first week of October, celebrates the appreciation of books, from readings, to panels, lectures, discussions & youth activities.
Location: Statewide, AK, USA
Oct 2027

Frankfurter Buchmesse
(Frankfurt Book Fair)
Sponsored by Frankfurter Buchmesse GmbH
Braubachstr 16, 60311 Frankfurt am Main, Germany
Tel: (069) 21020 *Fax:* (069) 2102 277
E-mail: servicecenter@buchmesse.de
Web Site: www.buchmesse.de/en
Key Personnel
Pres & CEO: Juergen Boos
Major international book & media fair attracting 7,300 exhibitors & over 286,000 visitors from more than 100 countries.
Location: Frankfurt Fairgrounds, Ludwig-Erhard-Anlage One, Frankfurt, Germany
Oct 6-10, 2027

National Book Month
Sponsored by National Book Foundation
90 Broad St, Suite 604, New York, NY 10004
Tel: 212-685-0261
E-mail: nationalbook@nationalbook.org
Web Site: www.nationalbook.org
Key Personnel
Exec Dir: Ruth Dickey *E-mail:* rdickey@nationalbook.org
Dir, Progs & Partnerships: Natalie Green *E-mail:* ngreen@nationalbook.org
Sr Mgr, Mktg & Communs: Ale Romero *E-mail:* aromero@nationalbook.org
Month-long celebration focusing on the importance of reading, writing & literature.
Location: Nationwide throughout the USA
Oct 2027

Utah Humanities Book Festival
Sponsored by Utah Humanities
Affiliate of Utah Center for the Book
202 W 300 N, Salt Lake City, UT 84103
Tel: 801-359-9670
Web Site: utahhumanities.org
Key Personnel
Exec Dir: Jodi Graham *Tel:* 801-359-9670 ext 101 *E-mail:* graham@utahhumanities.org
Prog Mgr: Kase Johnstun *Tel:* 801-359-9670 *E-mail:* johnstun@utahhumanities.org
Dir, Communs: Deena Pyle *Tel:* 801-359-9670 ext 111 *E-mail:* pyle@utahhumanities.org
Free literary event featuring national, regional & local authors held annually the month of October (National Book Month).
Location: Statewide, UT, USA
Oct 1-31, 2027

NOVEMBER

Jewish Book Month
Sponsored by Jewish Book Council
520 Eighth Ave, 4th fl, New York, NY 10018
Tel: 212-201-2920 *Fax:* 212-532-4952
E-mail: info@jewishbooks.org
Web Site: www.jewishbookcouncil.org; www.facebook.com/JewishBookCouncil; x.com/jewishbook
Key Personnel
Exec Dir: Carol Kaufman
Prog Dir: Evie Saphire-Bernstein *E-mail:* evie@jewishbooks.org
Dedicated to the celebration of Jewish books held annually during the month leading up to Hanukkah.
Location: Nationwide throughout the USA
Nov 24-Dec 24, 2027

2028

SPRING

The London Book Fair
Sponsored by RX UK
Division of RELX Group plc
Gateway House, 28 The Quadrant, Richmond, Surrey TW9 1DN, United Kingdom
Tel: (020) 8271 2124
Web Site: www.londonbookfair.co.uk
Key Personnel
Dir: Adam Ridgway
Mktg Mgr: Sophie Gilligan
Conference Mgr: Mariana Barrios
Global marketplace for rights negotiation & the sale & distribution of content across print, audio, TV, film & digital channels. Taking place each spring in the world's premier publishing & cultural capital, it is a unique opportunity to hear from authors, enjoy the vibrant atmosphere & explore innovations shaping the publishing world of the future. The London Book Fair brings you 3 days of focused access to customers, content & emerging markets.
Location: Olympia London, Hammersmith Rd, Kensington, London, UK
Spring 2028

APRIL

Fay B Kaigler Children's Book Festival
Sponsored by University of Southern Mississippi
University of Southern Mississippi, 118 College Dr, Suite 5146, Hattiesburg, MS 30406
Tel: 601-266-1000
Web Site: www.usm.edu/childrens-book-festival; www.facebook.com/SouthernMissCBF
Key Personnel
Events Coord: Stacy Creel *Tel:* 601-266-4228 *E-mail:* stacy.creel@usm.edu
Promotes children's literature, as well as writers, illustrators, publishers, librarians & educators.
Location: University of Southern Mississippi, 118 College Dr, Hattiesburg, MS, USA
April 19-21, 2028

International Children's Book Day
Sponsored by International Board on Books for Young People (IBBY)
Nonnenweg 12, 4055 Basel, Switzerland
Tel: (061) 272 29 17 *Fax:* (061) 272 27 57
E-mail: ibby@ibby.org
Web Site: www.ibby.org
Key Personnel
Exec Dir: Carolina Ballester *E-mail:* carolina.ballester@ibby.org
Admin & Communs Mgr: Catia dos Santos *E-mail:* ibby.secretariat@ibby.org
On Hans Christian Andersen's birthday, April 2nd, International Children's Book Day (ICBD) is celebrated to inspire a love of reading & to call attention to children's books. Each year a different national section has the opportunity to be the international sponsor. It decides upon a theme & invites a prominent author to write a message to the children of the world & a

well-known illustrator to design a poster. These materials are used in different ways to promote books & reading around the world.
Location: Worldwide
April 2, 2028

NAAJ Annual Meeting
Sponsored by North American Agricultural Journalists (NAAJ)
c/o Jacqui Fatka, 6866 County Rd, 183, Fredericktown, OH 43019
E-mail: naajnews@yahoo.com
Web Site: www.naaj.net
Key Personnel
Exec Secy-Treas: Jacqui Fatka
Meeting, writing awards & scholarship benefit dance.
Location: Washington, DC, USA
April 2028

Texas Library Association Annual Conference
Sponsored by Texas Library Association (TLA)
3420 Executive Center Dr, Suite 301, Austin, TX 78731
Tel: 512-328-1518 *Fax:* 512-328-8852
E-mail: tlaconference@txla.org; exhibits@txla.org; tla@txla.org
Web Site: txla.org/annual-conference/; txla.org
Special author events & outstanding educational programming for all library types taught by leaders in the field & opportunities to network & connect with fellow attendees.
Location: San Antonio, TX, USA
April 24-27, 2028

JUNE

ALA Annual Conference & Exhibition
Sponsored by The American Library Association (ALA)
225 N Michigan Ave, Suite 1300, Chicago, IL 60601
SAN: 201-0062
Tel: 312-944-6780 *Toll Free Tel:* 800-545-2433 *Fax:* 312-440-9374
E-mail: ala@ala.org
Web Site: www.ala.org
Key Personnel
Registration Servs Mgr: Alicia Hamann *Tel:* 800-545-2433 ext 3229 *E-mail:* ahamann@ala.org
Dir, Conference Servs: Earla Jones *Tel:* 800-545-2433 ext 3226 *E-mail:* ejones@ala.org
Mktg Specialist, Conference Servs: Donna Hunter *Tel:* 800-545-2433 ext 3218 *E-mail:* dhunter@ala.org
Conference Mgr: Kara Stachowiak
  E-mail: kstachowiak@ala.org
Conference Planner: Yvonne McLean *Tel:* 800-545-2433 ext 3222 *E-mail:* ymclean@ala.org
Brings together thousands of librarians & library staff, educators, authors, publishers, friends of libraries, trustees, special guests & exhibitors.
Location: Denver, CO, USA
June 22-27, 2028

Nantucket Book Festival
Sponsored by Nantucket Book Foundation
PO Box 5267, Nantucket, MA 02554
Tel: 508-919-6230
E-mail: info@nantucketbookfestival.org
Web Site: nantucketbookfestival.org; www.facebook.com/NantucketBookFestival
Key Personnel
Exec Dir: Kaley Kokomoor *E-mail:* director@nantucketbookfestival.org
Annual celebration of the literary arts bringing together authors, book lovers, & storytellers. For one exciting weekend each June, the island of Nantucket transforms into a book lover's paradise, featuring a lineup of author readings, panel discussions, writing workshops, & book signings. Almost all festival events are free & open to the public, ensuring that literary enjoyment is accessible to all.
Location: Various locations in Nantucket, MA, USA
June 2028

JULY

Hong Kong Book Fair
Sponsored by Hong Kong Trade Development Council
c/o Exhibition Dept, Unit 13, Expo Galleria, Hong Kong Convention & Exhibition Centre, Wan Chai, Hong Kong
Tel: 1830 668 (cust serv) *Fax:* 2824 0026; 2824 0249
Web Site: hkbookfair.hktdc.com; hkbookfair.hktdc.com/en/index.html (English)
Exhibits & sells new books & media products, reading & writing workshops, seminars & autograph sessions for book lovers.
Location: Hong Kong Convention & Exhibition Center, One Harbour Rd, Wan Chai, Hong Kong
July 2028

AUGUST

Edinburgh International Book Festival
121 George St, Edinburgh EH2 4YN, United Kingdom
Tel: (0131) 718 5666
E-mail: admin@edbookfest.co.uk
Web Site: www.edbookfest.co.uk
Key Personnel
Book Festival Dir: Jenny Niven
Each year we welcome over 900 international authors & over 250,000 visitors to one of the biggest book festivals in the world, hosting audiences & authors in a literary village for 18 days every August.
Location: Edinburgh Futures Institute, 56 George Sq, Edinburgh, UK
Aug 2028

Swanwick: The Writers' Summer School
Sponsored by Writers' Summer School
The Hayes Conference Centre, Hayes Lane, Swanwick, Alfreton DE55 1AU, United Kingdom
Tel: (01290) 552248
E-mail: secretary@swanwickwritersschool.co.uk
Web Site: www.swanwickwritersschool.org.uk
A weeklong residential writing school with top name speakers & tutors, plus informative panels, talks & discussion groups. Comfortable rooms with all meals & tuition included in the price. Open to everyone, from absolute beginners to published authors. Beautiful setting, licensed bar & evening entertainment. Believed to be the longest established residential writers' school in the world, Swanwick, held annually in August, is a must attend event in every writer's diary.
Location: The Hayes Conference Centre, Swanwick, Alfreton, Derbyshire, UK
Aug 2028

AUTUMN

Texas Book Festival
1023 Springdale Rd, Bldg 14, Unit B, Austin, TX 78721
Tel: 512-477-4055
E-mail: bookfest@texasbookfestival.org
Web Site: www.texasbookfestival.org
Key Personnel
COO: Dalia Azim *E-mail:* dalia@texasbookfestival.org
CEO: Marianne DeLeon *E-mail:* marianne@texasbookfestival.org
Devt Dir: Susannah Auby *E-mail:* susannah@texasbookfestival.org
Literary Dir: Hannah Gabel *E-mail:* hannah@texasbookfestival.org
Event Prodn & Logistics Coord: Olivia Hesse
  E-mail: oliviahesse@texasbookfestival.org
Opers & Literary Coord: Anna Dolliver
  E-mail: anna@texasbookfestival.org
Communs & PR Coord: Jose Rodriguez
  E-mail: jose@texasbookfestival.org
Statewide program that promotes reading & literacy highlighted by a 2-day festival, held annually in the fall, featuring authors from Texas & across the USA. Money raised is distributed as grants to public libraries throughout the state. Includes events for Texas teens & YA programming.
Location: State Capitol Bldg, 1100 Congress Ave, Austin, TX, USA
Fall 2028

SEPTEMBER

Gothenburg Book Fair
Sponsored by Bok & Bibliotek i Norden AB
Maessans Gata 10, 412 94 Gothenburg, Sweden
Tel: (031) 708 84 00
E-mail: info@goteborg-bookfair.com; hej@bokmassan.se
Web Site: goteborg-bookfair.com; www.bokmassan.se
Key Personnel
Fair Mgr: Frida Edman *Tel:* (031) 708 84 10
  E-mail: fe@bokmassan.se
Prog Mgr: Oskar Ekstroem *Tel:* (031) 708 84 73
  E-mail: oe@bokmassan.se
A manifestation of arts & culture, a 4-day literary festival, a tribute to freedom of expression & a place for readers & writers to meet & celebrate the power of stories.
Location: The Swedish Exhibition & Congress Centre, Gothenburg, Sweden
Sept 28-Oct 1, 2028

OCTOBER

Alaska Book Week
Sponsored by Alaska Center for the Book
PO Box 242074, Anchorage, AK 99524
Tel: 907-786-4379
E-mail: akbookweek@gmail.com
Web Site: alaskabookweek.org; facebook.com/alaskabookweek
Key Personnel
Chair: Trish Jenkins
The annual statewide event, usually held around the first week of October, celebrates the appreciation of books, from readings, to panels, lectures, discussions & youth activities.
Location: Statewide, AK, USA
Oct 2028

COURSES & AWARDS

National Book Month
Sponsored by National Book Foundation
90 Broad St, Suite 604, New York, NY 10004
Tel: 212-685-0261
E-mail: nationalbook@nationalbook.org
Web Site: www.nationalbook.org
Key Personnel
Exec Dir: Ruth Dickey *E-mail:* rdickey@nationalbook.org
Dir, Progs & Partnerships: Natalie Green *E-mail:* ngreen@nationalbook.org
Sr Mgr, Mktg & Communs: Ale Romero *E-mail:* aromero@nationalbook.org
Month-long celebration focusing on the importance of reading, writing & literature.
Location: Nationwide throughout the USA
Oct 2028

PRINTING United Expo
Sponsored by PRINTING United Alliance
10015 Main St, Fairfax, VA 22031
Tel: 703-385-1335 *Toll Free Tel:* 888-385-3588 *Fax:* 703-273-0456
E-mail: register@printingunited.com (general show inquiries); exhibit@printingunited.com (exhibitor Inquiries)
Web Site: printingunited.com; www.printing.org
Bringing together the entire print industry to see the latest trends, technology & solutions in one place.
Location: Georgia World Congress Center, 285 Andrew Young International Blvd NW, Atlanta, GA, USA
Oct 18-20, 2028

Utah Humanities Book Festival
Sponsored by Utah Humanities
Affiliate of Utah Center for the Book
202 W 300 N, Salt Lake City, UT 84103
Tel: 801-359-9670
Web Site: utahhumanities.org
Key Personnel
Exec Dir: Jodi Graham *Tel:* 801-359-9670 ext 101 *E-mail:* graham@utahhumanities.org
Prog Mgr: Kase Johnstun *Tel:* 801-359-9670 *E-mail:* johnstun@utahhumanities.org
Dir, Communs: Deena Pyle *Tel:* 801-359-9670 ext 111 *E-mail:* pyle@utahhumanities.org
Free literary event featuring national, regional & local authors held annually the month of October (National Book Month).
Location: Statewide, UT, USA
Oct 1-31, 2028

NOVEMBER

Jewish Book Month
Sponsored by Jewish Book Council
520 Eighth Ave, 4th fl, New York, NY 10018
Tel: 212-201-2920 *Fax:* 212-532-4952
E-mail: info@jewishbooks.org
Web Site: www.jewishbookcouncil.org; www.facebook.com/JewishBookCouncil; x.com/jewishbook
Key Personnel
Exec Dir: Carol Kaufman
Prog Dir: Evie Saphire-Bernstein *E-mail:* evie@jewishbooks.org
Dedicated to the celebration of Jewish books held annually during the month leading up to Hanukkah.
Location: Nationwide throughout the USA
Nov 12-Dec 12, 2028

2029

SPRING

The London Book Fair
Sponsored by RX UK
Division of RELX Group plc
Gateway House, 28 The Quadrant, Richmond, Surrey TW9 1DN, United Kingdom
Tel: (020) 8271 2124
Web Site: www.londonbookfair.co.uk
Key Personnel
Dir: Adam Ridgway
Mktg Mgr: Sophie Gilligan
Conference Mgr: Mariana Barrios
Global marketplace for rights negotiation & the sale & distribution of content across print, audio, TV, film & digital channels. Taking place each spring in the world's premier publishing & cultural capital, it is a unique opportunity to hear from authors, enjoy the vibrant atmosphere & explore innovations shaping the publishing world of the future. The London Book Fair brings you 3 days of focused access to customers, content & emerging markets.
Location: Olympia London, Hammersmith Rd, Kensington, London, UK
Spring 2029

APRIL

International Children's Book Day
Sponsored by International Board on Books for Young People (IBBY)
Nonnenweg 12, 4055 Basel, Switzerland
Tel: (061) 272 29 17 *Fax:* (061) 272 27 57
E-mail: ibby@ibby.org
Web Site: www.ibby.org
Key Personnel
Exec Dir: Carolina Ballester *E-mail:* carolina.ballester@ibby.org
Admin & Communs Mgr: Catia dos Santos *E-mail:* ibby.secretariat@ibby.org
On Hans Christian Andersen's birthday, April 2nd, International Children's Book Day (ICBD) is celebrated to inspire a love of reading & to call attention to children's books. Each year a different national section has the opportunity to be the international sponsor. It decides upon a theme & invites a prominent author to write a message to the children of the world & a well-known illustrator to design a poster. These materials are used in different ways to promote books & reading around the world.
Location: Worldwide
April 2, 2029

NAAJ Annual Meeting
Sponsored by North American Agricultural Journalists (NAAJ)
c/o Jacqui Fatka, 6866 County Rd, 183, Fredericktown, OH 43019
E-mail: naajnews@yahoo.com
Web Site: www.naaj.net
Key Personnel
Exec Secy-Treas: Jacqui Fatka
Meeting, writing awards & scholarship benefit dance.
Location: Washington, DC, USA
April 2029

JUNE

Nantucket Book Festival
Sponsored by Nantucket Book Foundation
PO Box 5267, Nantucket, MA 02554
Tel: 508-919-6230
E-mail: info@nantucketbookfestival.org
Web Site: nantucketbookfestival.org; www.facebook.com/NantucketBookFestival
Key Personnel
Exec Dir: Kaley Kokomoor *E-mail:* director@nantucketbookfestival.org
Annual celebration of the literary arts bringing together authors, book lovers, & storytellers. For one exciting weekend each June, the island of Nantucket transforms into a book lover's paradise, featuring a lineup of author readings, panel discussions, writing workshops, & book signings. Almost all festival events are free & open to the public, ensuring that literary enjoyment is accessible to all.
Location: Various locations in Nantucket, MA, USA
June 2029

JULY

Hong Kong Book Fair
Sponsored by Hong Kong Trade Development Council
c/o Exhibition Dept, Unit 13, Expo Galleria, Hong Kong Convention & Exhibition Centre, Wan Chai, Hong Kong
Tel: 1830 668 (cust serv) *Fax:* 2824 0026; 2824 0249
Web Site: hkbookfair.hktdc.com; hkbookfair.hktdc.com/en/index.html (English)
Exhibits & sells new books & media products, reading & writing workshops, seminars & autograph sessions for book lovers.
Location: Hong Kong Convention & Exhibition Center, One Harbour Rd, Wan Chai, Hong Kong
July 2029

AUGUST

Edinburgh International Book Festival
121 George St, Edinburgh EH2 4YN, United Kingdom
Tel: (0131) 718 5666
E-mail: admin@edbookfest.co.uk
Web Site: www.edbookfest.co.uk
Key Personnel
Book Festival Dir: Jenny Niven
Each year we welcome over 900 international authors & over 250,000 visitors to one of the biggest book festivals in the world, hosting audiences & authors in a literary village for 18 days every August.
Location: Edinburgh Futures Institute, 56 George Sq, Edinburgh, UK
Aug 2029

Swanwick: The Writers' Summer School
Sponsored by Writers' Summer School
The Hayes Conference Centre, Hayes Lane, Swanwick, Alfreton DE55 1AU, United Kingdom
Tel: (01290) 552248
E-mail: secretary@swanwickwritersschool.co.uk
Web Site: www.swanwickwritersschool.org.uk
A weeklong residential writing school with top name speakers & tutors, plus informative panels, talks & discussion groups. Comfortable rooms with all meals & tuition included in the price. Open to everyone, from absolute beginners to published authors. Beautiful setting, licensed bar & evening entertainment. Believed

CALENDAR OF BOOK TRADE & PROMOTIONAL EVENTS

to be the longest established residential writers' school in the world, Swanwick, held annually in August, is a must attend event in every writer's diary.
Location: The Hayes Conference Centre, Swanwick, Alfreton, Derbyshire, UK
Aug 2029

AUTUMN

Texas Book Festival
1023 Springdale Rd, Bldg 14, Unit B, Austin, TX 78721
Tel: 512-477-4055
E-mail: bookfest@texasbookfestival.org
Web Site: www.texasbookfestival.org
Key Personnel
COO: Dalia Azim *E-mail:* dalia@texasbookfestival.org
CEO: Marianne DeLeon *E-mail:* marianne@texasbookfestival.org
Devt Dir: Susannah Auby *E-mail:* susannah@texasbookfestival.org
Literary Dir: Hannah Gabel *E-mail:* hannah@texasbookfestival.org
Event Prodn & Logistics Coord: Olivia Hesse *E-mail:* oliviahesse@texasbookfestival.org
Opers & Literary Coord: Anna Dolliver *E-mail:* anna@texasbookfestival.org
Communs & PR Coord: Jose Rodriguez *E-mail:* jose@texasbookfestival.org
Statewide program that promotes reading & literacy highlighted by a 2-day festival, held annually in the fall, featuring authors from Texas & across the USA. Money raised is distributed as grants to public libraries throughout the state. Includes events for Texas teens & YA programming.
Location: State Capitol Bldg, 1100 Congress Ave, Austin, TX, USA
Fall 2029

SEPTEMBER

Gothenburg Book Fair
Sponsored by Bok & Bibliotek i Norden AB
Maessans Gata 10, 412 94 Gothenburg, Sweden
Tel: (031) 708 84 00
E-mail: info@goteborg-bookfair.com; hej@bokmassan.se
Web Site: goteborg-bookfair.com; www.bokmassan.se
Key Personnel
Fair Mgr: Frida Edman *Tel:* (031) 708 84 10
 E-mail: fe@bokmassan.se
Prog Mgr: Oskar Ekstroem *Tel:* (031) 708 84 73
 E-mail: oe@bokmassan.se
A manifestation of arts & culture, a 4-day literary festival, a tribute to freedom of expression & a place for readers & writers to meet & celebrate the power of stories.
Location: The Swedish Exhibition & Congress Centre, Gothenburg, Sweden
Sept 27-30, 2029

OCTOBER

Alaska Book Week
Sponsored by Alaska Center for the Book
PO Box 242074, Anchorage, AK 99524
Tel: 907-786-4379
E-mail: akbookweek@gmail.com
Web Site: alaskabookweek.org; facebook.com/alaskabookweek
Key Personnel
Chair: Trish Jenkins
The annual statewide event, usually held around the first week of October, celebrates the appreciation of books, from readings, to panels, lectures, discussions & youth activities.
Location: Statewide, AK, USA
Oct 2029

National Book Month
Sponsored by National Book Foundation
90 Broad St, Suite 604, New York, NY 10004
Tel: 212-685-0261
E-mail: nationalbook@nationalbook.org
Web Site: www.nationalbook.org
Key Personnel
Exec Dir: Ruth Dickey *E-mail:* rdickey@nationalbook.org
Dir, Progs & Partnerships: Natalie Green *E-mail:* ngreen@nationalbook.org
Sr Mgr, Mktg & Communs: Ale Romero *E-mail:* aromero@nationalbook.org
Month-long celebration focusing on the importance of reading, writing & literature.
Location: Nationwide throughout the USA
Oct 2029

PRINTING United Expo
Sponsored by PRINTING United Alliance
10015 Main St, Fairfax, VA 22031
Tel: 703-385-1335 *Toll Free Tel:* 888-385-3588 *Fax:* 703-273-0456
E-mail: register@printingunited.com (general show inquiries); exhibit@printingunited.com (exhibitor Inquiries)
Web Site: printingunited.com; www.printing.org
Bringing together the entire print industry to see the latest trends, technology & solutions in one place.
Location: Orange County Convention Center, Orlando, FL, USA
Oct 24-26, 2029

Utah Humanities Book Festival
Sponsored by Utah Humanities
Affiliate of Utah Center for the Book
202 W 300 N, Salt Lake City, UT 84103
Tel: 801-359-9670
Web Site: utahhumanities.org
Key Personnel
Exec Dir: Jodi Graham *Tel:* 801-359-9670 ext 101 *E-mail:* graham@utahhumanities.org
Prog Mgr: Kase Johnstun *Tel:* 801-359-9670 *E-mail:* johnstun@utahhumanities.org
Dir, Communs: Deena Pyle *Tel:* 801-359-9670 ext 111 *E-mail:* pyle@utahhumanities.org
Free literary event featuring national, regional & local authors held annually the month of October (National Book Month).
Location: Statewide, UT, USA
Oct 1-31, 2029

NOVEMBER

Jewish Book Month
Sponsored by Jewish Book Council
520 Eighth Ave, 4th fl, New York, NY 10018
Tel: 212-201-2920 *Fax:* 212-532-4952
E-mail: info@jewishbooks.org
Web Site: www.jewishbookcouncil.org; www.facebook.com/JewishBookCouncil; x.com/jewishbook
Key Personnel
Exec Dir: Carol Kaufman
Prog Dir: Evie Saphire-Bernstein *E-mail:* evie@jewishbooks.org
Dedicated to the celebration of Jewish books held annually during the month leading up to Hanukkah.
Location: Nationwide throughout the USA
Nov 1-Dec 1, 2029

Writers' Conferences & Workshops

The following lists workshops and seminars dealing with various aspects of the book trade. See **Courses for the Book Trade** for a list of college level programs and courses.

Adult Writers Workshops
The Kenyon Review
Finn House, 102 W Wiggin St, Gambier, OH 43022-9623
Tel: 740-427-5196 *Fax:* 740-427-5417
E-mail: writers@kenyonreview.org
Web Site: kenyonreview.org/adult-writers
Key Personnel
Dir, Opers & Mktg: Alicia Misarti
Assoc Dir, Progs: Elizabeth Dark
Adult writers week-long summer residential writing workshops in fiction, nonfiction & poetry. Summer & winter online workshops also available.
Date: June & July

American Society of Journalists and Authors Annual Writers Conference
American Society of Journalists and Authors (ASJA)
355 Lexington Ave, 15th fl, New York, NY 10017-6603
Tel: 212-997-0947
E-mail: asjaoffice@asja.org
Web Site: asja.org
Key Personnel
Exec Dir: James Brannigan
Inside information from editors, agents & publishers, find inspiration & gain income-boosting ideas. Open to all, the conference features topics for newer & more experienced pros. New panels & workshops will enrich you no matter where you are in your writing career.

Appalachian Writers' Workshop
Hindman Settlement School
51 Center St, Hindman, KY 41822
Mailing Address: PO Box 844, Hindman, KY 41822-0844
Tel: 606-785-5475
E-mail: info@hindman.org
Web Site: www.hindman.org
Key Personnel
Sr Dir, Prog Devt & Implementation: Josh Mullins *E-mail:* josh@hindman.org
Poetry, nonfiction, short story, novel, dramatic writing & children's writing.
Date: July

Artists & Writers Summer Fellowships
The Constance Saltonstall Foundation for the Arts
435 Ellis Hollow Creek Rd, Ithaca, NY 14850
Tel: 607-539-3146
E-mail: artscolony@saltonstall.org
Web Site: www.saltonstall.org
Key Personnel
Exec Dir: Lesley Williamson
Provide 1- to 4-week stipend supported fellowships for New York State artists & writers June-October. Flexible, subsidized retreat space November-April.

Atlantic Center for the Arts Mentoring Artist-in-Residence Program
Atlantic Center for the Arts (ACA)
1414 Art Center Ave, New Smyrna Beach, FL 32168
Tel: 386-427-6975
E-mail: program@atlanticcenterforthearts.org
Web Site: atlanticcenterforthearts.org
Key Personnel
Exec Dir: Nancy Lowden Norman
 E-mail: nlowden@atlanticcenterforthearts.org
Communs & Foundation Rel Dir: Kelle Groom
 E-mail: kgroom@atlanticcenterforthearts.org
Curatorial & Residency Dir: Sadie Woods
 E-mail: swoods@atlanticcenterforthearts.org
Devt Dir: Heather Paternoster
 E-mail: hpaternoster@atlanticcenterforthearts.org
Membership & Data Coord: Kelly Timmons
 E-mail: ktimmons@atlanticcenterforthearts.org
Residency Coord: Jessica Green *E-mail:* jgreen@atlanticcenterforthearts.org
Since 1982, Atlantic Center's residency program has provided artists from all artistic disciplines with spaces to live, work & collaborate during 3-week residencies. Each residency session includes 3 master artists of different disciplines. The master artists each personally select a group of associates - talented, emerging artists - through an application process administered by ACA. During the residency, artists participate in informal sessions with their group, collaborate on projects & work independently on their own projects. The relaxed atmosphere & unstructured program provide considerable time for artistic regeneration & creation.

Bread Loaf Writers' Conference
Middlebury College
204 College St, Middlebury, VT 05753
Tel: 802-443-5286 *Fax:* 802-443-2087
E-mail: blwc@middlebury.edu
Web Site: www.middlebury.edu/blwc
Key Personnel
Dir: Jennifer Grotz
Admin Dir: Noreen Cargill
Coord: Jason Lamb
Ten-day conference for writers of poetry, fiction & nonfiction. Fellowship covers tuition, room & board. Bread Loaf scholarship covers tuition.
Date: Aug

Cape Cod Writers Center Conference
Cape Cod Writers Center
919 Main St, Osterville, MA 02655
Mailing Address: PO Box 408, Osterville, MA 02655
Tel: 508-420-0200
E-mail: writers@capecodwriterscenter.org
Web Site: capecodwriterscenter.org
Key Personnel
Pres: Barbara Struna
Exec Dir: Nancy Rubin Stuart
Annual conference to improve your literary skills as you learn from top professionals. Open to beginning & published authors. In addition to classes in fiction, nonfiction, mystery, poetry, children's, young adult, screenwriting, social media & promotion & other genres, the conference offers agent query & ms mentoring sessions for students. Faculty & student readings. Keynote luncheon with prominent author.
Date: Aug

Cascade Christian Writers Conference
Formerly Oregon Christian Writers One-Day Conferences
Cascade Christian Writers (CCW)
PO Box 22, Gladstone, OR 97027
Tel: 503-393-3356
E-mail: business@cascadechristianwriters.org
Web Site: cascadechristianwriters.org
Key Personnel
Prog Chmn: Dawn Shipman
Registrar & Busn Mgr: Sue Miholer
Writers' workshops.
Location: Peoples Church, 4500 Lancaster Dr NE, Salem, OR
Date: March 8, 2025

Chautauqua Writers' Workshop
The Writers' Center at Chautauqua
One Ames Ave, Chautauqua, NY 14722
Mailing Address: PO Box 28, Chautauqua, NY 14722-0408
Tel: 716-357-6255
Web Site: www.chq.org
Key Personnel
Michael I Rudell Dir of Literary Arts: Sony Ton-Aime *E-mail:* stonaime@chq.org
Dept Coord: Emily Carpenter
Writing workshop in poetry & prose at 148 year-old Chautauqua Institution.
Location: Chautauqua Institution, Chautauqua, NY
Date: Last week in June through the end of Aug

Chocorua Writing Workshop
World Fellowship Center
PO Box 2280, Conway, NH 03818-2280
Tel: 603-447-2280
E-mail: office@worldfellowship.org
Web Site: www.worldfellowship.org; www.facebook.com/World.Fellowship.Center
Key Personnel
Dir: Ellen Meeropol; Ekere Tallie
Can a letter be as powerful as a poem? Engage like good fiction? Persuade like an essay? Help the writer process like journaling? Yes! Five sessions of exploring letters & epistolary texts & writing our own.
Date: July

The Clarion Science Fiction & Fantasy Writers' Workshop
The Clarion Foundation
Arthur C Clarke Ctr for Human Imagination, UC San Diego, 9500 Gilman Dr, MC0445, La Jolla, CA 92093-0445
Tel: 858-534-6875
E-mail: clarion@ucsd.edu
Web Site: clarion.ucsd.edu; imagination.ucsd.edu
Key Personnel
Pres: Karen Joy Fowler
Asst Dir: Patrick Coleman
Science fiction & fantasy writing workshop held for 6 weeks each summer. It is mandatory that students reside in Clarion housing.

Community of Writers Summer Workshops
Community of Writers
PO Box 1416, Nevada City, CA 95959
Tel: 530-470-8440
E-mail: info@communityofwriters.org
Web Site: www.communityofwriters.org
Key Personnel
Exec Dir: Ms Brett Hall Jones
Dir, Fiction: Lisa Alvarez; Louis B Jones
Dir, Poetry Workshop: Brenda Hillman

Annual summer week-long writing workshops held in the California Sierras near Lake Tahoe. The poetry workshop is held in June. Fiction, narrative nonfiction & memoir workshops are held in July. Online short courses available year-round through The Writers Annex.
Date: June & July

Conference on Poetry & Teaching
The Frost Place
158 Ridge Rd, Franconia, NH 03580
Mailing Address: PO Box 74, Franconia, NH 03580-0074
Tel: 603-823-5510
E-mail: frost@frostplace.org
Web Site: frostplace.org
Key Personnel
Exec Dir: Maudelle Driskell
Conference Dir: Dawn Potter
Offers lectures, talks & craft panels by faculty in a 4 1/2-day program sharing hands-on techniques for teaching poetry. See web site for details.
Date: June

Djerassi Resident Artists Program
2325 Bear Gulch Rd, Woodside, CA 94062
Tel: 650-747-0691
E-mail: info@djerassi.org
Web Site: www.djerassi.org
Key Personnel
Exec Dir: Martin Rauchbauer
 E-mail: mrauchbauer@djerassi.org
One month residencies for writers & other artists.

Education Writers Association Workshops
Education Writers Association (EWA)
1825 "K" St NW, Suite 200, Washington, DC 20006
Tel: 202-452-9830
Web Site: ewa.org
Key Personnel
Exec Dir: Kathy Chow *E-mail:* kchow@ewa.org
Seminars, webinars & other events throughout the year for education reporters.

Florida WritersCon
Florida Writers Association Inc
127 W Fairbanks Ave, No 407, Winter Park, FL 32789
E-mail: contactus@floridawriters.org
Web Site: www.floridawriters.org
Key Personnel
Pres: Mary Ann de Stefano
EVP: Suzy Hart
VP, Admin & Membership/Secy: Michael Farrell
Assortment of workshops, networking, panel discussions, keynote speech, literary contest & banquet.
Date: Oct

Gell: A Finger Lakes Creative Retreat
Writers & Books
740 University Ave, Rochester, NY 14607-1259
Tel: 585-473-2590 *Fax:* 585-442-9333
Web Site: www.wab.org
Key Personnel
Dir, Communs, Opers & Spec Events: Chris Fanning *E-mail:* chrisf@wab.org
Meeting center that hosts classes, workshops, conferences, etc for groups of up to 50 people.

The Glen Workshop
Image Journal
3307 Third Ave W, Seattle, WA 98119
Tel: 206-281-2988
E-mail: image@imagejournal.org
Web Site: www.imagejournal.org

A 5-day art workshop for writers & visual artists that combines an intensive learning experience with a lively festival of the arts.
Date: July

Gotham Writers' Workshop
555 Eighth Ave, Suite 1402, New York, NY 10018-4358
Tel: 212-974-8377
E-mail: contact@gothamwriters.com
Web Site: www.gothamwriters.com
Key Personnel
Pres: Alex Steele *E-mail:* alex@gothamwriters.com
Professional writers teach acclaimed creative writing classes online & in New York City throughout the year.

Harvard Summer School Writing Center
Harvard University, Division of Continuing Education
51 Brattle St, Cambridge, MA 02138
Tel: 617-495-4024
E-mail: dcewriting@gmail.com; inquiry@summerharvard.edu
Web Site: summer.harvard.edu
Key Personnel
Dean: Sandra Naddaff
Open to all summer school students, both on campus & online. Staffed by trained tutors who provide individual conferences to students working on any writing assignment.

Hedgebrook Radical Craft Retreats
Hedgebrook
PO Box 1231, Freeland, WA 98249
Tel: 360-321-4786
E-mail: hedgebrook@hedgebrook.org
Web Site: www.hedgebrook.org/radical-craft-retreats; www.facebook.com/hedgebrook
Key Personnel
Prog Dir: Amber Flame
Prog Mgr: Jen Will-Thapa
Retreat experience with the opportunity to be in residence & study with an experienced & celebrated instructor on Whidbey Island. Participation in each class is limited to 6 writers. Fee is $3,500 with 2 partial scholarships ($1,750) available for writers who would not otherwise be able to attend the retreat. Writers at all levels of experience are accepted. Each writer attends the 5-day retreat & is housed in their own handcrafted cottage in the woods. Meals are prepared daily by Hedgebrook's chefs, featuring produce harvested from our organic garden.

Hedgebrook VorTEXT Intensives Writing Retreat
Hedgebrook
PO Box 1231, Freeland, WA 98249
Tel: 360-321-4786
E-mail: hedgebrook@hedgebrook.org; programs@hedgebrook.org
Web Site: www.hedgebrook.org/vortext; www.facebook.com/hedgebrook
Key Personnel
Prog Dir: Amber Flame
Prog Mgr: Jen Will-Thapa
Suits writers at different levels of experience & phases in the writing process. Includes a 2-hour Zoom group workshop led by an alumna instructor, virtual community gathering & group sharing & feedback sessions.

Hedgebrook Writers in Residence Program
Hedgebrook
PO Box 1231, Freeland, WA 98249
Tel: 360-321-4786
E-mail: hedgebrook@hedgebrook.org; programs@hedgebrook.org
Web Site: www.hedgebrook.org/writers-in-residence; www.facebook.com/hedgebrook
Key Personnel
Prog Dir: Amber Flame
Prog Mgr: Jen Will-Thapa
Program supporting fully funded residencies for selected women-identified writers (up to 6 at a time) at a retreat each year on Whidbey Island, WA. Writers must be women, inclusive of transgender women & female-identified individuals. Each writer is housed in a handcrafted cottage. Residents share a home-cooked evening meal prepared by Hedgebrook's chefs. Two application cycles each year. Cycle One opens in mid-February & closes by mid-March with residency February-June of the following year. Cycle Two opens mid-August & closes by mid-Sept with residency July-October of the following year.

Highland Summer Writers' Conference
The Appalachian Regional & Rural Studies Center (ARRSC)
Division of Radford University
Radford University, Cook Hall 229, Radford, VA 24142
Mailing Address: PO Box 7014, Radford, VA 24142
Tel: 540-831-5366
Web Site: www.radford.edu/content/cehd/home/appalachian-studies.html
Key Personnel
Dir, ARRSC: Dr Theresa Burriss *Tel:* 540-831-6857 *E-mail:* tburriss@radford.edu
Annual program based on Appalachian culture & writing; 3 credit hours for 1-week intensive workshop.
Location: Radford University, Radford, VA

Historical Novel Society North American Conference
Historical Novel Society
PO Box 1146, Jacksonville, AL 36265
E-mail: hnsnorthamerica@gmail.com
Web Site: hns-conference.com; historicalnovelsociety.org/event/hns-north-american-conference; historicalnovelsociety.org
Key Personnel
Conference Prog Chair: Vanitha Sankaran
Held biennially, in odd-numbered years.
Location: Caesars Palace, 3570 Las Vegas Blvd S, Las Vegas, NV
Date: June 26-28, 2025

Hub City Writing in Place Conference
Hub City Writers Project
186 W Main St, Spartanburg, SC 29306
Tel: 864-577-9349
E-mail: info@hubcity.org
Web Site: www.hubcity.org/annual-writing-in-place-conference
Key Personnel
Exec Dir & Publr: Meg Reid *E-mail:* meg@hubcity.org
Three-day series of workshops led by published novelists, poets, essayists & literary critics. Registrants must sign up for 1 genre: Poetry, fiction or creative nonfiction. Conference has openings for 48 adult writers. Ms critiques available for $50 fee (30-minute private session).
Location: Michael S Brown Village Center, Wofford College, Spartanburg, SC
Date: July

Hurston/Wright Writers Week Workshops
The Zora Neale Hurston/Richard Wright Foundation
10 "G" St NE, Suite 600, Washington, DC 20002
E-mail: info@hurstonwright.org
Web Site: www.hurstonwright.org/workshops/writers-week-workshops

Key Personnel
Exec Dir: Khadijah Z Ali-Coleman
E-mail: khadijah@hurstonwright.org
Writing Progs Mgr: DeAndrea L Johnson
Events & Programming Coord: Molly Rufus
Both in-person & virtual competitive Writers Week workshops offer selected participants: 10+ hours of writing seminars & discussions; one-on-one time with an award-winning instructor; constructive guided feedback on writing from peers & workshop leader; access to virtual & in-person panel presentations from publishing industry insiders & veteran authors.

Idyllwild Arts Summer Program
52500 Temecula Rd, No 38, Idyllwild, CA 92549
Tel: 951-659-2171
E-mail: summer@idyllwildarts.org; adultprograms@idyllwildarts.org
Web Site: idyllwildarts.org/summer
Key Personnel
Prog Registrar: Marlene Pineda *Tel:* 951-659-2171 ext 2368
Creative Nonfiction: Angela Morales
Fiction: Keenan Norris
Memoir: Vanessa Martir
Poetry: Allison Hedge Coke; Willie Perdomo
Five-day writing workshops for adults in creative nonfiction, fiction, poetry & more. Two-week writing workshops for high school students in fiction, poetry & much more.

iLEARNING+ - Orientation to the Graphic Arts
PRINTING United Alliance
10015 Main St, Fairfax, VA 22031
Tel: 703-385-1335 *Toll Free Tel:* 888-385-3588 *Fax:* 703-273-0456
E-mail: info@printing.org; assist@printing.org
Web Site: www.printing.org; www.ilearningplus.org
Key Personnel
CEO: Ford Bowers *E-mail:* fbowers@printing.org
Ongoing online workshops & courses.

Indiana University Writers' Conference
Indiana University
Ballantine Hall 440, 1020 E Kirkwood Ave, Bloomington, IN 47405-7103
E-mail: writecon@indiana.edu
Web Site: www.iuwc.indiana.edu
Key Personnel
Dir: Bob Bledsoe
Assoc Dir: Kat Carlton
Four-day annual conference for writers of fiction, poetry & creative nonfiction. Craft-based workshops & classes.
Date: June

Intensive Novel Architects Writing Workshop
Ad Astra Institute for Science Fiction & the Speculative Imagination
1809 Indiana St, Lawrence, KS 66044
Tel: 785-766-7039
Web Site: adastra-sf.com/Workshop-stuff/Johnson-Webb-Workshops.htm
Key Personnel
Assoc Dir: Kij Johnson *E-mail:* kijjohnson@gmail.com
Co-Instructor: Barbara Webb *E-mail:* bjwebb@gmail.com
Focuses on the craft of writing a speculative novel, especially structure & the perils & pitfalls unique to novel-length projects. Three offerings: 2-week residential workshop in July ($2,000 tuition); 2-week online master class in September ($1,000 tuition); 2-week advanced workshop for alumni in June ($1,000 tuition). Scholarships available.

Intimate & Inspiring Workshops for Children's Authors & Illustrators
Highlights Foundation
814 Court St, Honesdale, PA 18431
Tel: 570-253-1192
E-mail: support@highlightsfoundation.zendesk.com
Web Site: www.highlightsfoundation.org
Key Personnel
Exec Dir: George Brown *E-mail:* george.brown@highlightsfoundation.org
For children's writers & illustrators seeking to sharpen their focus. Helps to improve your craft with the help of a master, finding the time & space in which to work & marketing yourself & your books. Cost of workshops range from $695 & up which includes tuition, meals, conference supplies & housing.

Iowa Summer Writing Festival
The University of Iowa
24E Phillips Hall, University of Iowa, Iowa City, IA 52242
Tel: 319-335-4160
E-mail: iswfestival@uiowa.edu
Web Site: iowasummerwritingfestival.uiowa.edu
Key Personnel
Dir: Amy Margolis *E-mail:* amy-margolis@uiowa.edu
Annual weeklong & weekend non-credit, intensive writing workshops; online writing workshops throughout the year; in all genres, all levels (for adults).

Iowa Writers' Workshop
The University of Iowa
Graduate Program in Creative Writing, 102 Dey House, Iowa City, IA 52242-1000
Tel: 319-335-0416
Web Site: writersworkshop.uiowa.edu
Key Personnel
Prog Dir: Lan Samantha Chang
Contact: Deb West *E-mail:* deb-west@uiowa.edu
Two-year residency program culminating in the submission of a creative thesis (a novel, collection of stories, or book of poetry) & the awarding of a Master of Fine Arts degree.

IWWG Annual Summer Conference
The International Women's Writing Guild (IWWG)
888 Eighth Ave, No 537, New York, NY 10019
Tel: 917-720-6959
E-mail: iwwgquestions@iwwg.org
Web Site: www.iwwg.org
Key Personnel
Exec Dir: Michelle Miller *E-mail:* michelle@iwwg.org
Each summer, the Guild brings together women for 7 full days of writing, crafting & connecting. Offer over 30 workshops to explore the spiritual, emotional, creative & technical side of writing.
Location: New York, NY
Date: July

IWWG Annual Writing Conference
The International Women's Writing Guild (IWWG)
888 Eighth Ave, No 537, New York, NY 10019
Tel: 617-792-7272
E-mail: iwwgquestions@iwwg.org
Web Site: www.iwwg.org
Key Personnel
Exec Dir: Michelle Miller *E-mail:* michelle@iwwg.org
Location: New York, NY
Date: July

Jentel Artist Residency
Jentel Foundation
130 Lower Piney Rd, Banner, WY 82832
Tel: 307-737-2311 *Fax:* 307-737-2305
E-mail: jentel@jentelarts.org
Web Site: www.jentelarts.org
Key Personnel
Exec Dir: Mary Jane Edwards
Prog Mgr: Lynn Reeves
Offers one-month residencies throughout the year to visual artists in all media & writers in fiction, creative nonfiction & poetry. Located on a working cattle ranch in the foothills of the Big Horn Mountains, 20 miles from Sheridan, WY. The award includes comfortable accommodations, a separate private studio & a stipend. Residents are invited to share their work through various outreach opportunities in the community. For more info or an application, see web site. Deadline is September 15 & January 15 each year.

Juniper Summer Writing Institute
Juniper Institute
Affiliate of UMass Amherst MFA for Poets & Writers
c/o University Conference Services, 810 Campus Center, One Campus Center Way, Amherst, MA 01003
Tel: 413-545-5503
E-mail: juniperinstitute@hfa.umass.edu
Web Site: www.umass.edu/juniperinstitute
Key Personnel
Dir: Betsy Wheeler
Seven days of intensive writing workshops, craft sessions, readings & ms consultation in the beautiful Pioneer Valley. Scholarships available.

Kentucky Writers Conference
Southern Kentucky Book Fest (SOKY Book Fest)
c/o Warren Public Library, 1225 State St, Bowling Green, KY 42101
E-mail: sokybookfest@warrenpl.org
Web Site: sokybookfest.org/programs/ky-writers-conference
Teaching craft workshops about everything from plotting techniques to employing poetic language to getting published. Free to the public. Limited seating.

Key West Literary Seminar
717 Love Lane, Key West, FL 33040
Tel: 305-293-9291
E-mail: mail@kwls.org
Web Site: www.kwls.org/seminar
Key Personnel
Exec Dir: Arlo Haskell
Prog Coord: Katrin Schumann
A 4-day readers' event that explores a unique literary theme each January. The 2025 theme is "Family," to bring together writers who can help us understand how the ties that bind shape the stories we tell, the worlds we move through & all the imagination's possibilities for human connection.
Location: Coffee Butler Ampitheater, 21 Quay Rd, Key West, FL
Date: Jan 9-12, 2025

Key West Literary Seminar's Writers' Workshop Program
Key West Literary Seminar
717 Love Lane, Key West, FL 33040
Tel: 305-293-9291
E-mail: mail@kwls.org
Web Site: www.kwls.org
Key Personnel
Exec Dir: Arlo Haskell
Prog Coord: Katrin Schumann
Provides writers at any stage of development with opportunities to explore the craft of writing. Multiple workshops each with their own focus & application requirements. Enrollment for each workshop is limited to 12 participants.

Location: Key West, FL (various sites)
Date: Jan 5-9, 2025

Kundiman Retreat
Kundiman
Fordham University, English Dept, 113 W 60 St, Rm 924, New York, NY 10023
E-mail: info@kundiman.org
Web Site: www.kundiman.org
Key Personnel
Exec Dir: Cathy Linh Che
Deputy Dir: Kyle Lucia Wu
Fin & Opers Dir: Nereida Trujillo
Communs Mgr: Shirley Cai
Devt Mgr: Shan Rao
Progs Mgr: Gina Chung
Creative writing 5-day retreat to support emerging Asian American writers. During each retreat, 6 nationally renowned Asian American poets & fiction writers conduct craft classes & mentorship meetings. Applications are accepted December 1-January 15. Genres accepted are poetry & fiction. Submit cover letter & brief writing sample: 5-7 pages of poetry or 5 pages of prose (1,250 words maximum). Application fee: $25; Tuition fee: $375. Needs-based tuition scholarships available. Notification of application status is given by mid-March.
Location: Fordham University, Rose Hill, New York, NY

LARB/USC Publishing Workshop
Los Angeles Review of Books
6671 Sunset Blvd, Suite 1521, Los Angeles, CA 90028
E-mail: publishingworkshop@lareviewofbooks.org
Web Site: thepublishingworkshop.com
Key Personnel
Publr & Ed-in-Chief: Tom Lutz *E-mail:* tom@lareviewofbooks.org
Dir: Irene Yoon
Asst Dir: Sarah LaBrie
Mng Dir, LARB: Jessica Kubinec *E-mail:* jessica@lareviewofbooks.org
Prog Mgr: Sonia Ali
Three-week summer program on USC campus. Open to graduating college seniors, those who have already graduated (alumni of any college/university), current graduate students, or people with significant relevant experience. Optional 5-week nonresidential guided Project Incubator. Tuition: Workshop: $3,000, Incubator: $3,000, Workshop & Incubator: $5,500. Optional USC housing & scholarships available.
Location: University of Southern California (USC), Los Angeles, CA
Date: July

Lost Lake Writers Retreat
Springfed Arts
627 Lloyd Ave, Royal Oak, MI 48073
Tel: 248-589-3913
E-mail: info@springfed.org
Web Site: www.springfed.org
Key Personnel
Dir: John D Lamb *E-mail:* johndlamb@ameritech.net
Poets & writers conference, good writers, food & accommodations.
Other Sponsors: Inspiration Alcona.

Maine Writers Conference at Ocean Park
Affiliate of Ocean Park Association
14 Temple Ave, Ocean Park, ME 04063
Mailing Address: PO Box 7206, Ocean Park, ME 04063
Tel: 401-598-1424
E-mail: www.opa@oceanpark.org
Web Site: oceanpark.org

Key Personnel
Dir: Dr Jim Brosnan *E-mail:* opmewriter@gmail.com
An eclectic, economical & intensive summer conference for writers of both poetry & prose of varying abilities & accomplishments.

Medical Writing & Communication Conference
American Medical Writers Association (AMWA)
9841 Washingtonian Blvd, Suite 500-26, Gaithersburg, MD 20878
Tel: 240-238-0940 *Fax:* 301-294-9006
E-mail: amwa@amwa.org; conference@amwa.org
Web Site: www.amwa.org
Key Personnel
Educ & Events Coord: Angelique Mize *Tel:* 240-238-0940 ext 112 *E-mail:* angelique@amwa.org
Annual conference, held in the fall, includes workshops, open sessions & networking opportunities.
Location: Sheraton Phoenix Downtown Hotel, 340 N Third St, Phoenix, AZ
Date: Nov 5-8, 2025

Mountain Writers Series
2804 SE 27 Ave, Suite 2, Portland, OR 97202
E-mail: pdxmws@mountainwriters.org
Web Site: www.mountainwriters.org
Work with nationally recognized poets, fiction writers, nonfiction writers, screenwriters & agents.

Napa Valley Writers' Conference
Napa Valley College
2277 Napa-Vallejo Hwy, Off 1753, Napa, CA 94558
Tel: 707-256-7113
E-mail: info@napawritersconference.org; fiction@napawritersconference.org; poetry@napawritersconference.org
Web Site: www.napawritersconference.org
Key Personnel
Exec Dir: Angela Pneuman
Mng Dir: Andrea Bewick
Fiction Dir & Admissions Dir: Charlotte Wyatt
Poetry Dir: Iris Dunkle
Poetry Prog Dir: Nan Cohen
Poetry, fiction & translation workshops which meet for 2 hours daily over 5 days.

National Society of Newspaper Columnists Annual Conference
National Society of Newspaper Columnists (NSNC)
205 Gun Hill St, Milton, MA 02186
Tel: 617-697-6854
Web Site: www.columnists.com
Key Personnel
Exec Dir: Ginny McCabe *E-mail:* nsncdirector@gmail.com
Contest Chair: Adam Earnheardt
Conference & column writing contest; monthly newsletter; networking with staff, training webinars & more. The NSNC promotes professionalism & camaraderie among columnists & other writers of the serial essay, including bloggers.
Date: July

New York State Writers Institute
State University of New York
Division of University at Albany
University at Albany, Science Library 320, 1400 Washington Ave, Albany, NY 12222
Tel: 518-442-5620 *Fax:* 518-442-5621
E-mail: writers@albany.edu
Web Site: www.nyswritersinstitute.org
Key Personnel
Exec Dir: William Kennedy

Dir: Paul Grondahl
Literary program organization featuring year-round visiting writers, classic film, special literary events & conferences, writing courses & workshops. Write or see web site for event dates & e-mail newsletter signup.

North Carolina Writers' Network Annual Fall Conference
North Carolina Writers' Network
PO Box 21591, Winston-Salem, NC 27120-1591
Tel: 336-293-8844
E-mail: mail@ncwriters.org
Web Site: www.ncwriters.org
Key Personnel
Exec Dir: Ed Southern *E-mail:* ed@ncwriters.org
Workshops, readings, conferences, critiquing service & round table discussions, panels & meetings with agents, publishing workshops.

Oregon Christian Writers One-Day Conferences, see Cascade Christian Writers Conference

Outdoor Writers Association of America Annual Conference
Outdoor Writers Association of America (OWAA)
2814 Brooks St, Box 442, Missoula, MT 59801
Tel: 406-728-7434
E-mail: info@owaa.org
Web Site: owaa.org
Key Personnel
Exec Dir: Chez Chesak
Membership & Conference Dir: Jessica (Pollett) Seitz *E-mail:* jseitz@owaa.org
Seminars & writing workshops; photography & outdoor news & conversation.
Location: Chattanooga, TN
Date: Aug 18-20, 2025

Ozark Creative Writers Inc Annual Conference
Ozark Creative Writers Inc
c/o 900 W Dixson St, Rogers, AR 72758
E-mail: ozarkcreativewriters@ozarkcreativewriters.com
Web Site: www.ozarkcreativewriters.com
Key Personnel
Pres: Clarissa Willis *E-mail:* clarissa@clarissawillis.com
Writers' conference for beginners & professionals. Contest information on web site.
Location: Inn of the Ozarks, 207 W Van Buren St, Eureka Springs, AR
Date: 2nd full weekend in Oct

Pennwriters Conference
Pennwriters Inc
PO Box 685, Dalton, PA 18414
E-mail: conferencecoordinator@pennwriters.org; info@pennwriters.org
Web Site: pennwriters.org
Key Personnel
Pres: Leslie Tobin Smeltz *E-mail:* president@pennwriters.org
Conference Coord: Vickie Fisher; Demi Stevens
Multi-genre conference with 40+ hours of workshops, panels & sessions with authors, agents & editors. Read & critique sessions. Agent/editor appointments.

Poetry Flash Reading Series
Poetry Flash
1450 Fourth St, Suite 4, Berkeley, CA 94710
Tel: 510-525-5476
E-mail: editor@poetryflash.org
Web Site: poetryflash.org
Key Personnel
Ed & Exec Dir: Joyce Jenkins
Assoc Ed: Richard Silberg

Publication; book review & literary calendar for California, conducts a poetry reading series at various venues in Berkeley, CA. Hosts poets from all around the US.

Port Townsend Writers Conference
Centrum Foundation
223 Battery Way, Port Townsend, WA 98368
Mailing Address: PO Box 1158, Port Townsend, WA 98368
Tel: 360-385-3102 *Fax:* 360-385-2470
E-mail: info@centrum.org
Web Site: centrum.org
Key Personnel
Artistic Curator: Gary Copeland Lilley
Workshops, lectures & readings.
Location: Port Townsend, WA
Date: July

PNWA Writers Conference
PNWA - a writer's resource
1420 NW Gilman Blvd, Suite 29, PMB 2717, Issaquah, WA 98027
Tel: 425-673-2665
E-mail: pnwa@pnwa.org
Web Site: www.pnwa.org
Key Personnel
Pres: Pam Binder *E-mail:* pambinder@pnwa.org
VP: Sandy McCormack
 E-mail: sandymccormack@pnwa.org
Secy: Robert Dugoni
Treas: Brian Mercer *E-mail:* brianmercer@pnwa.org

Red Pencil Conference
Northwest Independent Editors Guild
7511 Greenwood Ave N, No 307, Seattle, WA 98103
E-mail: conference@edsguild.org
Web Site: www.edsguild.org/red-pencil-conferences
Key Personnel
Pres: MariLou Harveland *E-mail:* president@edsguild.org
VP, Memb Servs: Kris Ashley
Secy: Sarah M Peterson
Treas: Laura Shaw
Biennial conference, in odd-numbered years, with a focus on providing engaging, useful content for editors at all stages of their professional journeys. The 2023 conference theme is "Seasons of an Editing Career".

San Francisco Writers Conference
1901 Cleveland Ave, Suite D, Santa Rosa, CA 94501
Tel: 415-689-6301
E-mail: registrations@sfwriters.org; director@sfwriters.org; bizdev@sfwriters.org
Web Site: www.sfwriters.org
Key Personnel
Conference Co-Dir & Busn Devt Dir: Laurie McLean
Conference Co-Dir & Opers/Programming Dir: Lissa Provost
Dir, Mktg: Elisabeth Kauffman
Dir, Registrations/Cust Support: Praveena Raman
Dir, Volunteers: Amanda Clay Traylor
Four-day craft, commerce & community oriented writers' conference. Participants include best-selling authors, literary agents, publishers, editors & both traditional & self-publishing industry professionals.
Location: Hyatt Regency San Francisco, 5 Embarcadero Center, San Francisco, CA
Date: Feb 6-9, 2025

"Science into Fiction" Speculative Fiction Writing Workshop Series
Ad Astra Institute for Science Fiction & the Speculative Imagination
1809 Indiana St, Lawrence, KS 66044
Tel: 785-766-7039
Web Site: adastra-sf.com/Workshop-stuff/AdAstranauts-workshop.htm
Key Personnel
Dir: Christopher McKitterick *E-mail:* cmckit.sf@gmail.com
Offered 4 times annually, twice in Autumn & twice in Spring. Both in-person & online. Begins with an expert talk, then a weekend story development workshop & wraps up 6 weeks later with a weekend story critique workshop. Tuition: $300 each. Scholarships available.
Location: Kansas University, Lawrence, KS
Date: Spring & Autumn

See-More's Workshop Arts & Education Workshops
The Shadow Box Theatre Inc
325 West End Ave, New York, NY 10023
Tel: 212-724-0677
E-mail: sbt@shadowboxtheatre.org
Web Site: shadowboxtheatre.org/workshops
Key Personnel
Founding Exec & Artistic Dir: Sandra Robbins *Tel:* 212-877-7356
 E-mail: sandyartrobbins325@gmail.com
Opers Mgr: Raymond Todd
Creative theatre arts workshops for students, parents & teachers.

Sewanee Writers' Conference
735 University Ave, Sewanee, TN 37383
Tel: 931-598-1654
E-mail: swc@sewanee.edu
Web Site: www.sewaneewriters.org
Key Personnel
Dir: Leah Stewart
Assoc Dir, Mktg & Admissions: Adam Latham
 E-mail: allatham@sewanee.edu
Assoc Dir, Progs & Fin: Gwen E Kirby
 E-mail: gekirby@sewanee.edu
Workshops in poetry, fiction, nonfiction & playwriting.
Location: The University of the South, Sewanee, TN
Date: Last 2 weeks in July

Southampton Writers' Conference
Stony Brook Southampton
239 Montauk Hwy, Southampton, NY 11968
Tel: 631-632-5007
Web Site: www.stonybrook.edu/writers
Key Personnel
Conference Coord: Christian McLean
 E-mail: christian.mclean@stonybrook.edu
Five-day workshops including novel, short story, poetry, memoir & creative nonfiction, playwriting & screenwriting; also evening readings, performances & panels.

Southern California Writers' Conference (SCWC)
Division of Random Cove, ie
PO Box 433, Redmond, OR 97756
Tel: 619-303-8185 *Fax:* 619-906-7462
E-mail: msg@writersconference.com
Web Site: www.writersconference.com; www.facebook.com/SouthernCaliforniaWritersConference/
Key Personnel
Exec Dir: Michael Steven Gregory
Dir: Wes Albers *E-mail:* wes@writersconference.com
Assoc Dir: Janis Thomas
Fiction, nonfiction & scriptwriting mss eligible for advance critique submission before the conference, followed by one-on-one consultation; awards given. Major speakers; banquet; workshops in fiction, nonfiction, legacy & indie publishing; conference emphasis on fiction & nonfiction; one agent panel, multiple read & critique, craft & troubleshooting workshops.
Location: San Diego, CA
Date: Feb 14-16, 2025

SouthWest Writers Conference Series
SouthWest Writers
3200 Carlisle Blvd NE, Suite 114, Albuquerque, NM 87110-1663
Tel: 505-830-6034
E-mail: info@swwriters.com
Web Site: www.southwestwriters.com
Key Personnel
Pres: Rose Kern
Series of one-day conferences, twice-monthly programs, workshops & writing classes.

Speculative Fiction Writing Workshop
Ad Astra Institute for Science Fiction & the Speculative Imagination
1809 Indiana St, Lawrence, KS 66044
Tel: 785-766-7039
Web Site: adastra-sf.com/Workshop-stuff/Spec-Fic-Workshop.htm
Key Personnel
Dir: Christopher McKitterick *E-mail:* cmckit.sf@gmail.com
Assoc Dir: Kij Johnson *E-mail:* kijjohnson@gmail.com
Residential 2-week workshop on speculative fiction storytelling.
Location: Kansas University, Lawrence, KS
Date: June

STC Technical Communication Summit
Society for Technical Communication (STC)
3251 Blenheim Blvd, Suite 406, Fairfax, VA 22030
Tel: 703-522-4114 *Fax:* 703-522-2075
E-mail: stc@stc.org; summit@stc.org
Web Site: summit.stc.org; www.stc.org
Key Personnel
Conference Comm Co-Chair: Liz Herman
Prog Mgr: Pam Noreault
Educational conference for technical communicators. Preconference workshops.

Summer Words Writing Conference & Literary Festival
Aspen Words
110 E Hallam St, Suite 116, Aspen, CO 81611
Tel: 970-925-3122 *Fax:* 970-920-5700
E-mail: aspenwords@aspeninstitute.org
Web Site: www.aspenwords.org
Key Personnel
Exec Dir: Adrienne Brodeur *Tel:* 646-263-6800
 E-mail: adrienne.brodeur@aspeninstitute.org
Mng Dir: Caroline Tory *Tel:* 970-925-3122 ext 3
 E-mail: caroline.tory@aspeninstitute.org
A 5-day writing retreat with morning workshops in fiction, poetry, memoir, essay & more complimented by a 5-day literary festival in the afternoons & evenings, featuring events for readers & writers.
Location: Aspen, CO
Date: June

Summer Writing Courses
Sage Hill Writing Experience Inc
1831 College Ave, Suite 324, Regina, SK S4P 4V5, Canada
Tel: 306-537-7243
E-mail: sage.hill@sasktel.net; info.sagehill@sasktel.net
Web Site: www.sagehillwriting.ca
Key Personnel
Exec Dir: Tara Dawn Solheim
Prog Mgr: Caitlin Terfloth
Writing retreats offer challenging but supportive environments where you can take your literary projects to the next level, mentored by dis-

WRITERS' CONFERENCES & WORKSHOPS

tinguished faculty & as part of a welcoming community of writers. Summer courses in nonfiction, poetry, playwriting & emerging writers.

Summer Writing Seminar
Martha's Vineyard Institute of Creative Writing
7 E Pasture Rd, Aquinnah, MA 02535
Tel: 954-242-2903
Web Site: mvicw.com
Key Personnel
Dir/Prog Coord: Alexander Weinstein
  E-mail: mvicwdirector@gmail.com
Annual comprehensive weeklong writing program, providing writers with the necessary time to devote to their art, on the island of Martha's Vineyard. Program fee is $975, which covers participation in all workshops, evening readings, editing/ms consultation with one of the visiting poets or authors & Friday night dinner with visiting writers. Fee does not include travel or accommodations.

Sun Valley Writers' Conference (SVWC)
Galleria Bldg, 2nd fl, 351 Leadville Ave N, Ketchum, ID 83340
Mailing Address: PO Box 957, Ketchum, ID 83340
Tel: 208-726-5454
E-mail: info@svwc.com
Web Site: svwc.com
Key Personnel
Exec Dir: Robin Eidsmo
Literary Dir: John Burnham Schwartz
Assoc Dir, Donor Liaison: Marcia Mode-Stavros
Assoc Dir, Opers: Carrie Lightner
Assoc Dir, Writer Rel: Margaret Mitchell
Prodn Event Mgr: Cara Stone
Writer Rel Mgr: Heidi Ottley Sinnott
Four-day annual conference consisting of a number of talks & lectures by recognized writers of nonfiction & fiction.

Tin House Summer Workshop
Tin House Books
2617 NW Thurman St, Portland, OR 97210
Tel: 503-473-8663
Web Site: tinhouse.com/workshop/summer-workshop
Key Personnel
Workshop Dir: Lance Cleland
Asst Workshop Dir: India Downes-Le Guin
  E-mail: india@tinhouse.com
Weeklong workshops, seminars, panels & readings led by prominent contemporary writers. Fees: $30 application; $1,600 tuition; $400 room & board; $800-$1,000 mentorships; $500 audit.
Location: Reed College, Portland, OR
Date: July

Tin House Winter Workshop
Tin House Books
2617 NW Thurman St, Portland, OR 97210
Tel: 503-473-8663
Web Site: tinhouse.com/winter-workshop
Key Personnel
Workshop Dir: Lance Cleland
Asst Workshop Dir: India Downes-Le Guin
  E-mail: india@tinhouse.com
Weekend literary workshops - 4 sessions. Fees: $30 application; $1,600 program, room & board; $800-$1,000 mentorships.
Location: Sylvia Beach Hotel, Newport, OR
Date: Jan-Feb

VONA Voices Summer Writing Workshops
Voices of Our Nations Arts Foundation Inc (VONA)
2820 SW 20 St, Miami, FL 33145
E-mail: info@vonavoices.org
Web Site: www.vonavoices.org
Key Personnel
Pres: M Evelina Galang
VP & Treas: Stacie Evans
Secy: David Mura
Premier multi-genre workshops for BIPOC writers. VONA is a home where writers of color come to hone their craft & be in community. Offers 2 sessions of week-long workshops, both in-person & virtual.
Date: June-July

Willamette Writers' Conference
Willamette Writers
5331 SW Macadam Ave, Suite 258, PMB 215, Portland, OR 97239
Tel: 971-200-5385
E-mail: wilwrite@willamettewriters.org
Web Site: willamettewriters.org
Key Personnel
Pres: Gail Pasternack
Exec Dir: Kate Ristau
Annual summer 3-day conference: consultations with over 50 national agents, editors, film agents & producers; workshops (fiction, nonfiction, children's, screen/TV, genres, craft of writing); editing room available. Year-round: monthly meetings, writing contest, workshops, newsletter.

Winter Words Author Series
Aspen Words
110 E Hallam St, Suite 116, Aspen, CO 81611
Tel: 970-925-3122 *Fax:* 970-920-5700
E-mail: aspenwords@aspeninstitute.org
Web Site: www.aspenwords.org
Key Personnel
Exec Dir: Adrienne Brodeur *Tel:* 646-263-6800
  E-mail: adrienne.brodeur@aspeninstitute.org
Mng Dir: Caroline Tory *Tel:* 970-925-3122 ext 3
  E-mail: caroline.tory@aspeninstitute.org
Series of author talks featuring an extraordinary lineup of award-winning literary talent, including book signings.
Location: Aspen, CO
Date: Jan-April

Wordsmith
The Loft Literary Center
Open Book Bldg, Suite 200, 1011 Washington Ave S, Minneapolis, MN 55415
Tel: 612-215-2575 *Fax:* 612-215-2576
E-mail: loft@loft.org
Web Site: loft.org/conference/about-wordsmith
Key Personnel
Devt Dir: Kaitlyn Bohlin *Tel:* 612-215-2597
  E-mail: kbohlin@loft.org
Prog Dir, Spec Events: Shahenda Helmy *Tel:* 612-215-2586 *E-mail:* shelmy@loft.org
Weekend-long, in-person annual conference for writers focused on craft, career & connection. Workshops, pitch sessions, craft seminars & networking opportunities. Admission: $425, pitch add-on $60, consult add-on $125.

Write on the Sound Writers' Conference
City of Edmonds Art Commission
Frances Anderson Center, 700 Main St, Edmonds, WA 98020
Tel: 425-771-0228 *Fax:* 425-771-0253
E-mail: wots@edmondswa.gov
Web Site: www.writeonthesound.com
Key Personnel
City of Edmonds Arts & Culture Mgr: Ms Frances Chapin
Annual event, presented the 1st weekend in October, with over 30 workshops by noted authors, educators & trade professionals. Features a keynote address, on-site book shop, ms critique appointments & a themed writing contest.

Writers & Readers Days
Virginia Highlands Festival

ASSOCIATIONS, EVENTS

PO Box 801, Abingdon, VA 24212
Tel: 276-623-5266
E-mail: info@vahighlandsfestival.org
Web Site: www.vahighlandsfestival.com
Key Personnel
Co-Chair: Greg Lilly; Jo Ann Stone
Exec Prodr: Deirdre Cole
Lectures, readings & workshops in creative writing with noteworthy authors held each summer.

The Writers' Colony at Dairy Hollow
515 Spring St, Eureka Springs, AR 72632
Tel: 479-253-7444
E-mail: director@writerscolony.org
Web Site: www.writerscolony.org
Key Personnel
Mng Dir: Jeanne Glass
See web site for upcoming events & fellowships.

Writers' League of Texas (WLT)
611 S Congress Ave, Suite 200 A-3, Austin, TX 78704
Mailing Address: PO Box 41355, Austin, TX 78704
Tel: 512-499-8914
E-mail: wlt@writersleague.org
Web Site: www.writersleague.org
Key Personnel
Exec Dir: Becka Oliver *E-mail:* becka@writersleague.org
Prog Dir: Samantha Babiak *E-mail:* sam@writersleague.org
Memb Servs Mgr/Digital Media Mgr: J Evan Parks
Office Coord: Lore Arnold
Conferences, workshops, webinars, online classes, summer writing retreat.
Location: Writer's League of Texas Resource Center/Library & other locations, ongoing programs throughout Texas
Date: Year-round

Writer's Workshop at Balticon
Baltimore Science Fiction Society Inc
PO Box 686, Baltimore, MD 21203-0686
Tel: 410-563-2737
E-mail: writersworkshop@bsfs.org
Web Site: bsfs.org/bsfswriterwork.htm
Key Personnel
Balticon Chair: Eric Gasior *E-mail:* chair@bsfs.org
Balticon Vice Chair: Yakira Heistand
PR Coord: Morgan Hazelwood
  E-mail: socialmedia@bsfs.org
Workshop to improve your writing skills in the areas of science fiction & fantasy. The following aspects of writing are discussed & debated: Opening lines, outlines, themes, character development, story structure, dialogue.

Writer's Workshop at BSFS
Baltimore Science Fiction Society Inc
PO Box 686, Baltimore, MD 21203-0686
Tel: 410-563-2737
E-mail: bsfsevents@bsfs.org
Web Site: bsfs.org/bsfswriterwork.htm
Key Personnel
PR Coord: Morgan Hazelwood
  E-mail: socialmedia@bsfs.org
Day long writing workshops every 3-4 months run by active & acclaimed professional writers in the genre of science fiction & fantasy. Workshops are dedicated to improving the writing techniques of participants. The topics covered include openings & endings, plot & tension, character development, writing dialogue, the novel vs the short story & other vital aspects of writing. Fee: Typically $25 per person, with lunch included.

The Writing Center
601 E Palisade Ave, Suite 4, Englewood Cliffs, NJ 07632
Tel: 201-567-4017 *Fax:* 201-567-7202
E-mail: writingcenter@optonline.net
Web Site: www.writingcenternj.com
Key Personnel
Dir: Barry Sheinkopf *E-mail:* bsheinkopf@optonline.net
Writing seminars, editorial services, book design & publishing services.
Location: 601 Palisade Ave, Englewood Cliffs, NJ
Date: Year-round, 12-week writing seminars; Fall seminars begin Sept; Winter seminars begin Jan; Spring seminars begin April. Five-week Summer session

YA Fiction Workshop
Tin House Books
2617 NW Thurman St, Portland, OR 97210
Tel: 503-473-8663
Web Site: tinhouse.com/ya-workshop
Key Personnel
Workshop Dir: Lance Cleland
Asst Workshop Dir: India Downes-Le Guin *E-mail:* india@tinhouse.com
Weekend workshop for crafting young adult fiction. Fees: $30 application; $1,500 program, room, board & transportation; $800-$1,000 mentorships.
Location: Sylvia Beach Hotel, Newport, OR
Date: Oct/Nov

Yaddo Artists Residency
Yaddo
312 Union Ave, Saratoga Springs, NY 12866
Tel: 518-584-0746 *Fax:* 518-584-1312
Web Site: www.yaddo.org
Key Personnel
Cont: Marci Persons
Pres: Elaina Richardson
VP: Michele Hannah
Dir, Devt: Lisa Dierbeck *E-mail:* ldierbeck@yaddo.org
Prog Dir: Christin Williams *E-mail:* cwilliams@yaddo.org
Prog Asst: Kathryn Starczewski
Off Mgr: Anne-Marie Pratt
An artists' community established in Saratoga Springs, NY in 1900 by the financier Spencer Trask & his poet wife, Katrina, to offer creative artists the rare gift of a supportive environment with uninterrupted time to think, experiment & create. Over the years, Yaddo has welcomed more than 6,500 artists working in one or more of the following media: Choreography, film, literature, musical composition, painting, performance art, photography, printmaking, sculpture & video. Residencies vary from 2 weeks to 2 months. Application deadlines are January 5 & August 1.

Young Writers' Workshop
Cape Cod Writers Center
919 Main St, Osterville, MA 02655
Mailing Address: PO Box 408, Osterville, MA 02655
Tel: 508-420-0200
E-mail: writers@capecodwriterscenter.org
Web Site: capecodwriterscenter.org
Key Personnel
Pres: Barbara Struna
Exec Dir: Nancy Rubin Stuart
This program offers unique learning opportunities to young writers ages 12-18.

Young Writers Workshops
The Kenyon Review
Finn House, 102 W Wiggin St, Gambier, OH 43022-9623
Tel: 740-427-5391 *Fax:* 740-427-5417
E-mail: youngwriters@kenyonreview.org
Web Site: kenyonreview.org/high-school-workshops
Key Personnel
Dir, Opers & Mktg: Alicia Misarti
Dir, Youth Progs: Tory Weber
Assoc Dir, Progs: Elizabeth Dark
Young writers summer workshops are multi-genre & meet for 2 weeks. Summer & winter online workshops also available.
Date: June & July

Your Personal Odyssey Writing Workshop
PO Box 75, Mont Vernon, NH 03057
Tel: 603-673-6234 *Fax:* 603-673-6234
Web Site: www.odysseyworkshop.org
Key Personnel
Dir: Jeanne Cavelos *E-mail:* jcavelos@comcast.net
Intensive one-on-one online workshop for writers of fantasy, science fiction & horror. Workshop is customized for each participant. Six-week, 12-week & 18-week sessions available. Dir Jeanne Cavelos is a former Sr Ed at Bantam Doubleday Dell Publishing & winner of the World Fantasy Award. Guest lecturers include some of the top writers in the field.

Courses for the Book Trade

Various courses covering different phases of the book trade are given each year. Detailed information on any of these courses can be obtained by writing directly to the sponsoring organization. For related information see **Writers' Conferences & Workshops**.

Agate Publishing Academy
Unit of Agate Publishing Inc
1328 Greenleaf St, Evanston, IL 60202
Tel: 847-475-4457
E-mail: help@agatepublishingacademy.com
Web Site: agatepublishingacademy.com
Key Personnel
Pres: Doug Seibold
Publg Dir: David Schlesinger
Edit Mgr: Amanda Gibson
Digital Media Coord: Henry Begler
Courses & certifications for professionals seeking to begin & advance their careers in publishing.
Courses include DEI for Publishing Professionals
Introduction to Instructional Design
Publishing Basics

Arizona State University Creative Writing Program
1102 S McAllister Ave, Rm 170, Tempe, AZ 85281
Mailing Address: Dept of English, Box 871401, Tempe, AZ 85287-1401
Tel: 480-965-3168 *Fax:* 480-965-3451
Web Site: www.asu.edu/clas/english/creativewriting
Key Personnel
Prog Dir, Creative Writing: Jenny Irish
  E-mail: jennifer.irish@asu.edu
Undergraduate & graduate courses in creative writing: workshops, theory & special topics.

Arkansas State University Graphic Communications Program
Dept of Media, PO Box 1930, State University, AR 72467-1930
Tel: 870-972-3114 *Fax:* 870-972-3321
Web Site: www.astate.edu
Key Personnel
Dept Chair: Dr Brad Rawlins *E-mail:* brawlins@astate.edu
Instructor, Graphic Commun: Pradeep C Mishra
  E-mail: pmishra@astate.edu
Courses include Desktop Publishing
Digital Prepress Workflow & File Creation
Graphic Communications - Estimating & Schedules
Graphic Production Systems
Internet Communications
Internship
Intro to Digital Publishing
Intro to Visual Communication
Mass Communication in Modern Society
Multimedia Production Techniques
News Design Publication
Photography

Baylor University, Professional Writing & Rhetoric
Dept of English, One Bear Place, Unit 97404, Waco, TX 76798-7404
Tel: 254-710-1768
Web Site: english.artsandsciences.baylor.edu/undergraduate/professional-writing-rhetoric
Key Personnel
Undergraduate Prog Dir: Michael-John DePalma
  E-mail: michael-john_depalma@baylor.edu
Comprehensive writing program.
Courses include Advanced Creative Nonfiction
Argumentative & Persuasive Writing
Creative Nonfiction
Editing & Publishing
Introduction to Professional Writing & Rhetoric
Literacy Studies
New Media Writing & Rhetoric
Professional & Workplace Writing
Religious Rhetoric & Spiritual Writing
Rhetoric of Race
Special Topics in Writing Workshop
Special Topics Lecture in Writing & Rhetoric
Studies in Public & Civic Writing
Technical Writing
Tutoring Writing
Women's Writing & Rhetoric
Writing for Social Change
Writing Internship

Binghamton University Creative Writing Program
Division of State University of New York at Binghamton
c/o Dept of English, General Literature & Rhetoric, PO Box 6000, Binghamton, NY 13902-6000
Tel: 607-777-2168 *Fax:* 607-777-2408
E-mail: cwpro@binghamton.edu
Web Site: www.binghamton.edu/english/creative-writing/index.html
Key Personnel
Dir, Prog & Assoc Professor: Tina Chang
Professor: Jaimee Wriston Colbert; Thomas Glave; Leslie Heywood; Liz Rosenberg
Assoc Professor: Joe Weil; Alexi Zentner
Asst Professor: Amir Ahmadi Arian; Clair Luchette
Asst to Chmn, Eng: Colleen Burke
Undergraduate & graduate courses.
Courses include Advanced Workshops in Creative Writing
Beginning, Intermediate & Advanced Poetry Workshops
Fiction Workshop
Fundamentals of Creative Writing
Independent Study in Creative Writing
Intermediate Creative Writing
Studies for Writers

Boston University Creative Writing Program
236 Bay State Rd, Boston, MA 02215
Tel: 617-353-2510
E-mail: crwr@bu.edu
Web Site: www.bu.edu/creativewriting
Key Personnel
Prog Dir: Ha Jin *E-mail:* xjin@bu.edu
Prog Coord: Annaka Saari
Workshops. Offer one-year Master's degree MFA in creative writing.
Courses include Fiction
Poetry

Bowling Green State University Creative Writing Program
Dept of English, 212 East Hall, Bowling Green, OH 43403-0001
Tel: 419-372-6864; 419-372-2576 *Fax:* 419-372-0333
E-mail: english@bgsu.edu
Web Site: www.bgsu.edu/academics/creative-writing
Key Personnel
Prog Dir & Professor: Lawrence Coates *Tel:* 419-372-2111 *E-mail:* coatesl@bgsu.edu
Professor: Sharona Muir *Tel:* 419-372-5893
  E-mail: smuir@bgsu.edu
Assoc Professor: Larissa Szporluk *Tel:* 419-372-7539 *E-mail:* slariss@bgsu.edu
Asst Professor: Dr Reema Rajbanshi *Tel:* 419-372-9306 *E-mail:* rrajban@bgsu.edu
Providers of comprehensive & rigorous education in professional writing, editing & marketing of poetry & fiction, since 1967.
Courses include Contemporary Fiction
Contemporary Poetry
Cooperative Internship or Academic Internship
Craft of Fiction
Craft of Poetry
Creative Nonfiction Workshop
Creative Writing Workshop
Fiction Workshop
Fiction Writers' Workshop
Graphic Novel Workshop
Imaginative Writing
Internships in English Studies
Literary Editing & Publishing
Literature for Adolescents
Modern Fiction
Modern Poetry
Poetry Workshop
Poetry Writers' Workshop
Senior BFA Thesis Workshop
Special Topics in Creative Writing
World Literature Ancient Times to 1700
World Literature from 1700 to present

The Center for Book Arts
28 W 27 St, 3rd fl, New York, NY 10001
Tel: 212-481-0295
E-mail: info@centerforbookarts.org
Web Site: www.centerforbookarts.org
Key Personnel
Exec Dir: Corina Reynolds
Offers classes & workshops year-round.
Courses include Bookbinding
Letterpress Printing
Papermaking

College of Liberal & Professional Studies, University of Pennsylvania
3440 Market St, Suite 100, Philadelphia, PA 19104-3335
Tel: 215-898-7326 *Fax:* 215-573-2053
E-mail: lps@sas.upenn.edu
Web Site: www.upenn.edu/lps
Key Personnel
Vice Dean: Nora Lewis *E-mail:* nlewis@sas.upenn.edu
Writing courses, beginner through advanced, taught by published authors; non-residential; fully online available; fees vary. Program catalog available for writing courses September-July.

Columbia Publishing Course at Columbia University
Affiliate of Columbia University School of Journalism
2950 Broadway, MC 3801, New York, NY 10027
Tel: 212-854-1898; 212-854-9775
E-mail: publishing-jrn@columbia.edu
Web Site: journalism.columbia.edu/columbia-publishing-course
Key Personnel
Dir: Shaye Areheart *E-mail:* shayepc@gmail.com

Provides an intensive introduction to book, magazine, & digital publishing. Students learn the entire publishing process from established publishing professionals & gain hands-on experience in all aspects of the business, from evaluation of original mss to the sales & marketing of finished products. CPC offers 2 programs: one in New York City, held over the course of 6 weeks during June & July, & one in Oxford, England, held over the course of 4 weeks in September. In New York, the first 3 weeks are devoted to book publishing, & the following 2 weeks are devoted to magazine & digital publishing. The sixth & last week is a combination of all the interests presented by the course. In Oxford, the focus is entirely on book publishing. In both places, lectures from industry leaders in every specialty, including CEOs & legendary graduates of the course, bookend a unique workshop experience, in which students form hypothetical publishing companies—complete with prospectuses, marketing pitches, financial documents, editorial content, & jacket & cover designs. Throughout, extensive career guidance, including a resume & cover-letter critique, is offered, along with job placement assistance. Application deadline is early March.

Courses include Academic Publishing
The Author's Perspective
Children's Publishing
Design
Diversity in Publishing
How to Generate Book Ideas
Independent Publishing
Innovations in Publishing
Literary Agencies & Scouts
Managing Editorial & Production
Marketing
Online Magazines
Podcasting
Profit & Loss
Publicity & Public Relations
Publishing Contracts
Sales
Subsidiary Rights

Columbia University School of the Arts Creative Writing Program
Division of Columbia University
609 Kent Hall, New York, NY 10027
Tel: 212-854-3774
E-mail: writingprogram@columbia.edu
Web Site: arts.columbia.edu/writing
Key Personnel
Chair, MFA Writing Prog: Lis Harris
Dir, Undergraduate Creative Writing & Assoc Professor: Heidi Julavits
Courses include Fiction
Nonfiction
Poetry

Ekus Group LLC
57 North St, Hatfield, MA 01038
Tel: 413-247-9325
E-mail: info@ekusgroup.com
Web Site: ekusgroup.com
Key Personnel
Pres & Lead Agent: Sally Ekus *E-mail:* sally@ekusgroup.com
Comprehensive 1- or 2-day media training programs designed for cookbook authors, chefs, product spokespeople, show hosts & food professionals. Participants will spend their day(s) under the lights & in front of the camera, taping & critiquing actual television demonstrations of varying lengths. Courses are typically held in the professional kitchen of our Hatfield, MA, offices but off-site training is available. Visit culinarymediatraining.com to learn more.
Courses include Cookbook Publishing 101
Honing Your Edge: Media Training for Culinary Professionals
One-On-One Media Training

Emerson College Department of Writing, Literature & Publishing
180 Tremont St, 10th fl, Boston, MA 02116-4624
Mailing Address: 120 Boylston St, Boston, MA 02116-4624
Tel: 617-824-8750
Web Site: www.emerson.edu; www.emerson.edu/writing-literature-publishing
Key Personnel
Chair: Maria Koundoura
Graduate Prog Dir, MA in Publg & Writing: John Rodzvilla *E-mail:* john_rodzvilla@emerson.edu
Offers BA, MA, BFA & MFA degrees in publishing & writing.
Courses include Advanced Seminar Workshop in Nonfiction
Advanced Topics in Writing: Experimental Fiction
Advanced Topics in Writing: The Short Short
African-American Literature
After the Disaster: Post-War European Literature
American Novel 1
American Novel 2
American Women Writers
Applications for Print Publishing
Black Revolutionary Thought
Book Design & Production
Book Editing
Book Publishing Overview
Column Writing
Copyediting
Cultural Criticism
Elementary French 1
Elementary French 2
Elementary Spanish 1
Elementary Spanish 2
Fiction Workshop
Imagining the Caribbean
Intermediate Creative Writing: Comedy
Intermediate Creative Writing: Drama
Intermediate Creative Writing: Fiction
Intermediate Creative Writing: Nonfiction
Intermediate Creative Writing: Poetry
Intermediate Creative Writing: Sketch Troupe
Intermediate Magazine Writing
International Women Writers
Intro College Writing Applications
Introduction to Book Publishing
Introduction to Creative Writing: Fiction
Introduction to Creative Writing: Nonfiction
Introduction to Creative Writing: Poetry
Introduction to Electronic Publishing
Introduction to Literary Studies
Introduction to Magazine Writing
Latin American Literature & Cinema
Latin American Short Fiction
Literary Foundations
Literature, Culture & the Environment
Literature of the Gothic
Literatures in English
Magazine Design & Production
Magazine Publishing Overview
Magazine Writing
MFA Thesis
Native American Literature
Nonfiction Workshop
Novel Workshop
Poetry Workshop
Profile Writing
Publishing Management & Innovation
Research Writing-Int'l
Seminar in Short Fiction
Seminar in the Novel
Shakespearean Tragedy
Slavery & Freedom
Special Topics in Fiction Writing: Short Short Fiction
Sr Creative Thesis-all genres
Teaching College Composition
The Art of Fiction
The Art of Nonfiction
The Art of Poetry
The Editor/Writer Relationship
The Forms of Poetry: Theory and Practice
Topics in African American Literature: Afrofuturism
Topics in Community Publishing: Partnered Studio: Projections on a Large Scale
Topics in Fiction: The Literature of Extremes
Topics in Global Literature: Latin American Women Writers
Topics in Global Literature: Place, Displacement, Memory in Exile Literature
Topics in Global Literature: Utopian, Dystopian & Apocalyptic Fictions
Topics in Global Studies: Global Indigenous Literatures
Topics in Literature: Black English & its Influence on American Literature and Culture
Topics in Literature: Comic Prose
Topics in Literature: Decolonizing Literature & Anti-Colonial Theories
Topics in Literature: Democracy & American Literature
Topics in Literature: Literature of the Gothic II
Topics in Literature: Post Modern Fairy Tales
Topics in Literature: Reading & Writing Dangerous Poems
Topics in Literature: Resistance & Revolution
Topics in Literature: Shakespearean Journeys
Topics in Literature: Women Nobel-Laureates in Literature
Topics in Multiple Genres & Hybrid Forms: Literature of Evil
Topics in Multiple Genres & Hybrid Forms: Literature of Transcendence
Topics in Multiple Genres & Hybrid Forms: Translation Seminar
Topics in Multiple Genres & Hybrid: Native Northeast
Topics in Multiple Genres & Hybrid: The Writer, The Daemon, and the Craftsman
Topics in Poetry: Forms in Poetry
Topics in Poetry: The Poetic Sequence
Topics in Publishing: Writing for The Boston Globe Magazine
Topics in U.S. Multicultural Literature: Harlem Renaissance
Topics in Writing & Publishing: Introduction to Book Design
Topics in Writing & Publishing: Introduction to Book Design for Writers
Travel Literature
U.S. American Literatures
U.S. Latinx Literature
U.S. Multicultural Literatures
Web Development: Creating & Managing Content for the Web

Gabelli School of Business Communications & Media Management Program
Unit of Fordham University
140 W 62 St, Rm 440, New York, NY 10023
Tel: 212-636-6150 *Fax:* 718-817-4999
Web Site: www.fordham.edu/gabelli-school-of-business
Key Personnel
Professor: John A Fortunato *E-mail:* jfortunato@fordham.edu
Assoc Professor: Bozena I Mierzejewska *Tel:* 347-842-3049 *E-mail:* bmierzejewska@fordham.edu; Travis Russ *Tel:* 212-636-6354 *Fax:* 212-586-0575 *E-mail:* russ@fordham.edu
Asst Clinical Professor: Janet L Gallent *Tel:* 212-636-6678 *E-mail:* jgallent@fordham.edu
Courses include Applied Business Communications
Business of Entertainment Media
Business of New Media
Business of Sports Media
Personal Leadership
Persuasive Communication
Public Relations

Gaylord College of Journalism & Mass Communication, Professional Writing Program
Division of University of Oklahoma
c/o University of Oklahoma, 395 W Lindsey St, Rm 3000, Norman, OK 73019-0270
Tel: 405-325-2721
Web Site: www.ou.edu/gaylord; www.ou.edu/gaylord/undergraduate/professional-writing
Key Personnel
Prof Writing Academic Adviser: Chandler Lindsey *Tel:* 405-325-3686
  E-mail: chandlerlindsey@ou.edu
Coursework on writing for commercial publication.
Courses include Business of Professional Writing
Category Fiction
Introduction to Professional Writing
Theories of Professional Writing
Writing the Novel
Writing the Short Story

The Graphic Artists Guild Inc
2248 Broadway, Suite 1341, New York, NY 10024
Tel: 212-791-3400
E-mail: admin@graphicartistsguild.org; membership@graphicartistsguild.org
Web Site: www.graphicartistsguild.org
Key Personnel
Pres: Yanique DeCosta *E-mail:* president@graphicartistsguild.org
Admin Dir: Paula Hinkle
Business workshops & seminars for professional graphic artists.
East, Midwest, New England, South & West regions.

Hamilton College, Literature & Creative Writing
Literature & Creative Writing Dept, 198 College Hill Rd, Clinton, NY 13323
Tel: 315-859-4370 *Fax:* 315-859-4390
Web Site: www.hamilton.edu
Key Personnel
Chair: Margaret Thickstun *E-mail:* mthickst@hamilton.edu
Dir, Creative Writing Prog & Assoc Professor, Lit & Creative Writing: Anne Valente *Tel:* 315-859-4378 *E-mail:* avalente@hamilton.edu
Professor, Lit & Creative Writing: Naomi Guttman *E-mail:* nguttman@hamilton.edu; Jane Springer *E-mail:* jspringer@hamilton.edu
Academic program; students may concentrate on creative writing.

Hofstra University, Department of English
204 Mason Hall, Hempstead, NY 11549
Tel: 516-463-5454
E-mail: english@hofstra.edu
Web Site: www.hofstra.edu/english
Key Personnel
Dept Chair & Assoc Professor, Eng: Dr Karyn M Valerius *Tel:* 516-463-5455 *E-mail:* karyn.m.valerius@hofstra.edu
Assoc Chair: Dr Adam Sills *Tel:* 516-463-0272 *E-mail:* adam.g.sills@hofstra.edu
Asst Chair, Advisement & Professor, Eng: Joseph Fichtelberg, PhD *Tel:* 516-463-5465 *E-mail:* joseph.fichtelberg@hofstra.edu
Undergraduate courses in all phases of publishing & creative writing, leading to a BA in English. MA in English Literature & an MFA in creative writing.

Hollins University-Jackson Center for Creative Writing
7916 Williamson Rd, Roanoke, VA 24020
Tel: 540-362-6317
E-mail: creative.writing@hollins.edu
Web Site: www.hollins.edu; www.hollins.edu/jacksoncenter/index.shtml
Key Personnel
Dir: Prof Thorpe Moeckel
BA degree in English with concentration in creative writing - 4 academic years; MFA in creative writing - 2-year program in residency.

Louisiana State University Creative Writing Program MFA
English Dept, 260 Allen Hall, Baton Rouge, LA 70803
Tel: 225-578-4086 *Fax:* 225-578-4129
E-mail: lsucrwriting@lsu.edu
Web Site: www.lsu.edu; www.lsu.edu/hss/english/creative_writing
Key Personnel
Prof, Poetry: Laura Mullen *E-mail:* lmullen@lsu.edu
Asst Dir: Randolph Thomas *E-mail:* rdthomas@lsu.edu
A graduate program leading to a MFA degree in creative writing.
Courses include Drama Workshop, ENGL 7008
Fiction Workshop, ENGL 7006
Literary Nonfiction Workshop, ENGL 7001
Poetry Workshop, ENGL 7007
Screenwriting Workshop, ENGL 7009

Manhattanville College Master of Fine Arts in Creative Writing Program
2900 Purchase St, Purchase, NY 10577
Web Site: www.mville.edu/programs/masters-creative-writing.php
Key Personnel
Dir, MFA Prog: Iain Haley Pollock, MFA *Tel:* 914-323-7211 *E-mail:* iain.pollock@mville.edu
Offers courses with faculty who are well-known published writers & poets, all of whom are dedicated to helping writers explore their craft, sharpen their skills & take their writing to the next level, all within a thriving literary community. In addition, students can build on the skills gained in the editing & production course through work on our award-winning journal *Inkwell*, which gives them the editorial & production experience to succeed in publishing.
Courses include Advanced Seminar in Graduate Creative Writing
Fiction Workshop
Foundations in Creative Writing
Nonfiction Workshop
Poetry Workshop
Screenwriting Workshop
Thesis Project

McNeese State University MFA in Creative Writing Program
PO Box 92655, Lake Charles, LA 70609-0001
Tel: 337-475-5325; 337-475-5327
Web Site: www.mcneese.edu/academics/graduate/creative-writing
Key Personnel
Asst Professor & Dir, MFA Prog: Michael Horner *E-mail:* mhorner@mcneese.edu
Asst Professor, Dir of Composition & Poetry Instructor: Kevin Thomason
Three-year MFA program - 60 hours. Features degree tracts in both fiction & poetry. An MA in Literature can be obtained simultaneously with the MFA.
Courses include Contemporary Novel
Contemporary Poetry
Creative Writing Workshop-Fiction
Creative Writing Workshop-Poetry
Form & Theory of Fiction I
Form & Theory of Fiction II
Form & Theory of Poetry I
Form & Theory of Poetry II

Mississippi Review/University of Southern Mississippi, Center for Writers
Affiliate of University of Southern Mississippi, Dept of English
118 College Dr 5144, Hattiesburg, MS 39406-0001
Tel: 601-266-1000
Web Site: www.usm.edu/humanities/center-writers.php; sites.usm.edu/mississippi-review/index.html
Key Personnel
Ed-in-Chief: Adam Clay
Graduate & undergraduate courses in poetry, fiction & nonfiction writing.
Department is also home to the *Mississippi Review*, a nationally recognized literary magazine.

New York City College of Technology Professional & Technical Writing Program
Division of City University of New York
Namm Hall 512, 300 Jay St, Brooklyn, NY 11201
Tel: 718-260-5392
E-mail: english@citytech.cuny.edu
Web Site: www.citytech.cuny.edu/english/technical-writing-bs.aspx
Key Personnel
Eng Dept Chair & Writing Ctr Dir: Suzanne Miller *Tel:* 718-260-5393 *E-mail:* smmiller@citytech.cuny.edu
Dir, First-Year Writing Prog: Carrie Hall *E-mail:* chall@citytech.cuny.edu
Eng Dept Off Mgr: Lily Lam *E-mail:* llam@citytech.cuny.edu
Bachelor of Science program. Students gain competencies that include writing, editing, problem solving, document design, rhetoric, interpersonal communication, collaboration, specialized experience & fluency in modern communication technologies.
Courses include Advanced Professional Writing
Advanced Technical Writing
Business & Professional Communication
Digital Storytelling
History of Technology
Information Architecture
Introduction to Language & Technology
Introduction to Professional & Technical Writing
Planning & Testing User Documents
Professional & Technical Writing Internship
Professional Editing & Revising
Research & Documentation in the Information Age
Special Topics in Professional & Technical Writing
Specialized Communications for Technology Students
Technical Documentation
Writing with New Media

New York University, Center for Publishing & Applied Liberal Arts
Affiliate of NYU School of Professional Studies Continuing Education
7 E 12 St, New York, NY 10003
Tel: 212-998-7200
E-mail: sps.info@nyu.edu
Web Site: www.scps.nyu.edu/professional-pathways/topics.html
Key Personnel
Dean: Angie Kamath
Assoc Dean: Andrea Chambers
Academic Dir, Continuing Educ Progs & Clinical Asst Professor: Jenny McPhee
Academic Dir, Prof Writing & Clinical Assoc Professor: Kristine Rodriguez Kerr
Academic Dir, Publg: Paul Amodeo; Sharyn Rosart
Academic Dir, Translation & Interpreting & Clinical Asst Professor: Annelise Finegan
Assoc Dir, Admin: Afua Preston
Assoc Dir, Progs: Alicia Kubes; Miguel Ortiz-Crane

Asst Dir, Publg: Judson Simmons
Asst Dir, Progs: Anne Wolff
Prog Admin: Kenneth French
Certificates offered. The Summer Publishing Institute is an intensive residential program for recent college graduates, rising college seniors & early professionals in the publishing industry. The Advanced Publishing Institute (5-day program) is an executive education course designed for mid- to senior-level publishing professionals interested in the latest strategies & business practices in book publishing. Application deadline April 1 for MS in Publishing. Programs consist of 36 graduate credits chosen from a required core of courses. Application deadline for MS in Professional Writing is March 1 (Summer), June 1 (Fall) & September 15 (Spring).
Courses include A Career in Freelance Copyediting
Advanced Multimedia Storytelling Workshop
Advanced Podcast Workshop
Advanced Writing Workshop
Business & Organizational Writing
ChatGPT Journalism
Copyediting & Proofreading Books
Copyediting for Digital & Print Media
Creating a Narrative Podcast
Creative Nonfiction
Creative Writing for Beginners Workshop
Digital Communication in a Changing Workplace
Digital Storytelling for Fundraising: Leveraging Emerging Technology for Impact
Document Design & Media Presentation
Editing Articles & Essays to Submit for Publication
Effective Business Writing
Entertainment Journalism
Executive Business English & Global Communication
Fact-Checking for Accuracy
Feature Writing for Print & Digital Media
Fiction Writing
Freelance Journalism: How to Pitch & Sell Stories
Fundamentals of Storytelling
Grammar Review
How to Write Op-Eds & Personal Essays
Interviews & Profiles
Introduction to Podcasting & Radio Reporting
Introduction to the Media Industry
Journalism
Master Class: Guidance & Strategies for Publishing Your Book
Mastering English Grammar
Media Literacy: An Overview
Multimedia & Podcasting
Multimedia Storytelling
Newswriting & Reporting
Novel Writing
Post-Production Overview: Telling Stories with Sound or Visuals
Principles of Information Architecture
Principles of Professional Writing
Professional Copyediting, Proofreading & Fact-Checking
Professional Writing
Professional Writing & Communications
Professional Writing: Content, Purpose & Audience
Short Story Writing
Storytelling
Strategic Communications & Corporate Storytelling
Style & Rhetoric
Writing About Health & Beauty
Writing & Leadership
Writing for Digital Media
Writing for Fundraiser: Grantwriting & Case Statements
Writing for Self-Promotion & Performance Coaching
Writing Midlife & Beyond
Writing Skills: The Basics

NYU Advanced Publishing Institute
NYU SPS Center for Publishing & Applied Liberal Arts, 7 E 12 St, Suite 921, New York, NY 10003
E-mail: nyu.api@nyu.edu
Web Site: www.sps.nyu.edu
Key Personnel
Assoc Dean, Ctr for Publg & Applied Liberal Arts: Andrea Chambers *E-mail:* ac130@nyu.edu
Offered by the NYU School of Professional Studies, this is a five-day premier executive education course designed for mid- to senior-level publishing professionals. Lectures & workshops are conducted by leading publishing executives. Program is held on campus at NYU in January. Program fee: $4,500 (early), $5,000 (regular).

Ohio University, English Department, Creative Writing Program
Ohio University, English Dept, Ellis Hall, Athens, OH 45701
E-mail: english.department@ohio.edu
Web Site: www.ohio.edu/cas/english
Key Personnel
Dir: Mark Halliday *E-mail:* hallidam@ohio.edu
Offer PhD & MA degrees with creative writing emphasis.
Courses include Fiction
Form & Theory
Nonfiction
Novels
Poetry
Short Stories

Pace University, Master of Science in Publishing
163 William St, 18th fl, New York, NY 10038
Tel: 212-346-1431
E-mail: puboffice@pace.edu
Web Site: www.pace.edu/program/publishing-ms
Key Personnel
Prog Dir: Manuela Soares *Tel:* 212-346-1513
E-mail: msoares@pace.edu
Staff Assoc: Carla Strickland-Bargh
E-mail: castricklandbargh@pace.edu
Program educates its students in all pertinent aspects of the publishing business: books, magazines, print & digital publishing. Our graduates are equipped for the challenges facing the industry today.
Courses include Academic Publishing
Advanced Communication Skills: Research/Report Writing
Book Production & Design
Book Sales & Distribution Methods
Children's Book Marketing
Children's Book Publishing
Critical Financial Issues in Publishing
Digital Image Creation, Manipulation & Management
Digital Issues in Publishing
Ebooks: Technology, Workflow & Business Model
Editorial Principles & Practices
Ethics in Publishing
Financial Aspects of Publishing
Fundamentals of Trade Book Publishing
The Future of Publishing: Transmedia
Graduate Seminar: Publishing Strategies I
Graduate Seminar: Publishing Strategies II
Information Systems in Publishing
Internship I
Internship II
Introduction to Publication Design
Introduction to Supply Chain Management
Legal Aspects of Publishing
Magazine Circulation: Print & Digital
Magazine Production & Design
Marketing Principles & Practices in Publishing
Media Ad Sales
Practical Applications of Product Management in Digital Media
Principles of Publishing: Copyediting & Proofreading
Professional Editing: Rewriting & Line Editing
Publishing Business Communication Skills
Publishing Comics & Graphic Novels
Seminar in Books: Entrepreneurship in Publishing
Seminar on Books & Magazines: Creating a Magazine
Specialized Publications
Technology in Publishing
Topics: Digital Audience Development
Topics: Metadata for Books
Topics: Social Media Marketing
Topics: Writing & Editing Comics & Graphic Novels
Web Development for Publishing
Writing & Editing for Magazines & Digital Publications

Parsons School of Design, Continuing & Professional Education
Division of New School University
66 W 12 St, New York, NY 10011
Tel: 212-229-8933 ext 4076
E-mail: continuinged@newschool.edu
Web Site: www.newschool.edu/parsons
Key Personnel
Vice Provost & Academic Dean for Continuing & Prof Educ: Mariana Amatullo *E-mail:* mariana.amatullo@newschool.edu
Adult courses & programs in creative writing & journalism.
Courses include Accidental Realities: Fiction
Beginning Fiction
Books for Writers
Children's Book Illustration & Writing
Citizen Journalist
Design Explorations: Comics & Graphic Novels
Design Process & Skills
Emotional Machine: Advanced Poetry
Experiments with Poetic Forms
Finding Your Voice in Nonfiction
Form & Function: Stylish Prose
Fundamentals of Illustrated Journalism & Memoir
How to Kickstart Your Writing Routine
Illustrated Journalism & Memoir Authors Group
Intro to Printmaking
Introduction to Creative Nonfiction
Introduction to Fiction
Literary Translation Lab
Middlemarch for the 21st Century
Online Immersion: Fiction
Online Immersion: Nonfiction
Online Immersion: Poetry
Personal Essay & Memoir
Poetry & the Creative Process
Poetry The Language of Music
Product Design
Reporting the Visible World: Documentary Illustrated Storytelling
Spanish Women: Writers/Artists
Telling Your Story: First-Person Illustrated Journalism & Memoir
The Great American Short Story
The Literature of Forgiveness
The Open Space of Silence
Walking in New York
Writers Gym
Writing for Artists
Writing for NYC Newspapers, Magazines & Webzines
Writing Memoirs

PBS, see Professional Booksellers School Inc

Professional Booksellers School Inc
2667 Hyacinth St, Westbury, NY 11590
Tel: 516-333-0681
E-mail: hello@professionalbooksellers.com
Web Site: www.professionalbooksellers.com
Certification program. Students of the school must be an individual member or be employed

at an independent bookstore that has current membership in their regional booksellers' association +/or The American Booksellers Association (ABA). Each course runs from 10-16 sessions. Costs range from $125-$400.
Courses include Basic Bookselling
Bookstore Finances
Bookstore Year One
Events Management
Inventory Management
Marketing, Display & Storytelling Excellence
Store & Operations Management

Publishing Certificate Program at City College of New York
Division of Humanities NAC 5225, City College of New York, New York, NY 10031
Tel: 212-650-7925 *Fax:* 212-650-7912
E-mail: ccnypub@aol.com
Web Site: english.ccny.cuny.edu/publishing-program
Key Personnel
Dir: David Unger
Asst Dir: Christina Castro *E-mail:* ccastro2@ccny.cuny.edu
Program for undergraduates. Take 4 of 20 courses offered & then qualify for a paid internship in a publishing house of your interest.
Courses include Books for Young Readers
Copyediting & Proofreading, etc
Ebooks & Digital Publishing
The Editorial Process
Introduction to Publishing I & II
Legal Issues in Publishing
Publishing Practicum

Radcliffe Publishing Course, see Columbia Publishing Course at Columbia University

Rochester Institute of Technology, Department of Packaging & Graphic Media Science
69 Lomb Memorial Dr, Rochester, NY 14623-5603
Tel: 585-475-2728; 585-475-5336 *Fax:* 585-475-5336
E-mail: spmofc@rit.edu
Web Site: rit.edu/engineeringtechnology/department-packaging-and-graphic-media-science
Key Personnel
Dir, Indus Rel & Academic Progs: William Pope *E-mail:* wwpast@rit.edu
Classes in books & magazine production, typography, computer use, desktop prepress production, management, manufacturing, quality control, print technologies, production workflow & automation.
Courses include Computer Use
Management
Prepress Production
Print Production
Product Workflow & Automation
Quality Control
Typography

Rosemont College
Graduate Publg Prog, 1400 Montgomery Ave, Rosemont, PA 19010
Tel: 610-527-0200 (ext 2431)
Web Site: www.rosemont.edu
Key Personnel
Prog Dir, Graduate Publg: Marshall Warfield
Offers MA degree in publishing.
Courses include Business of Publishing
Children's & Young Adult
Design
Editorial

School of Visual Arts Continuing Education Programs
209 E 23 St, New York, NY 10010-3994
Tel: 212-592-2000
E-mail: registrar@sva.edu
Web Site: www.sva.edu
Courses include Advertising
Animation
Art & Activism
Artist Residency Programs
Design
Film
Filmmakers Dialogue
Fine Arts
Illustration & Comics
Interior Design
Performance
Photography & Video
Professional Development
Visible Futures Lab
Visual & Critical Studies
Visual Narrative
Writing

Susquehanna University, Department of English & Creative Writing
514 University Ave, Selinsgrove, PA 17870
Tel: 570-372-4196
Web Site: www.susqu.edu
Key Personnel
Professor, Creative Writing & Co-Dept Head: Karla Anne Kelsey, PhD *E-mail:* kelseykarla@susqu.edu
Professor, Eng & Co-Dept Head: Laurence D Roth, PhD *E-mail:* roth@susqu.edu
Assoc Professor, Creating Writing: Catherine Zobal Dent, PhD *E-mail:* dent@susqu.edu
Assoc Professor, Creative Writing: Glen Retief, PhD *E-mail:* retief@susqu.edu; Hasanthika Sirisena, MFA *E-mail:* sirisena@susqu.edu; Silas Dent Zobal *E-mail:* zobal@susqu.edu
Assoc Professor, Eng: Drew Hubbell, PhD *E-mail:* hubbell@susqu.edu; Randy Robertson, PhD *E-mail:* robertson@susqu.edu; Rachana Sachdev, PhD *E-mail:* rsachdev@susqu.edu; Betsy Verhoeven, PhD *E-mail:* verhoeven@susqu.edu
Asst Professor, Creative Writing: Matthew Neill Null, MFA *E-mail:* nullm@susqu.edu; Monica Prince, MFA *E-mail:* prince@susqu.edu
Asst Professor, Eng: Heather Lang, PhD *E-mail:* langh@susqu.edu
Majors include: English-Literature; English-Secondary Education; English-Publishing & Editing; Creative Writing; Creative Writing-Secondary Education.
Courses include Advanced Composition: Rhetoric & the Environment
Advanced Creative Nonfiction
Advanced Creative Writing
Advanced Fiction
Advanced Poetry
Aesthetics & Interpretation
Applied Knowledge in the Discipline
Black, Brown & Boisterous
Book Reviewing
The Choreopoem
College Writing
Departmental Honors
Directed Reading & Research
English Grammar & the Writing Process
Environmental Writing
Experimental Writing
Forms of Writing
History of the Book
History of the English Language (Early Period)
Independent Study
Intermediate Creative Nonfiction
Intermediate Creative Writing
Intermediate Fiction
Intermediate Poetry
Internship
Introduction to Creative Nonfiction
Introduction to Creative Writing
Introduction to Fiction
Introduction to Genre Writing
Introduction to Modern Publishing
Introduction to Poetry
Jewish Literature (Multicultural/Non-Western)
Literary Themes
Literature Studies
Making Democracy Work
Practicum
Professional & Civic Writing: Practice & Theory
Publishing: Ethics, Entertainment, Art, Politics
Reading/Writing/Teaching Difference
Senior Seminar
Small Press Publishing & Editing
Special Themes & Topics
Studies in Anglophone Literature (Multicultural/Non-Western)
Studies in Comparative Literatures of the Americas (Multicultural/Non-Western)
Studies in Literary Forms
Studies in Literature & Gender
Studies in Major Authors
Themes in Early American Literature (Early Period)
Themes in Early British Literature (Early Period)
Themes in Early Modern British Literature (Early Period)
Themes in Modern American Literature
Themes in Modern British Literature
Topics in Creative Writing
Voice & Audience
World Literature (Multicultural/Non-Western)
Writing & Editing Podcasts
Writing & Thinking

Syracuse University Creative Writing Program
401 Hall of Languages, Syracuse, NY 13244-1170
Tel: 315-443-2173 *Fax:* 315-443-3660
Web Site: artsandsciences.syracuse.edu/english-department/creative-writing-mf-program; artsandsciences.syracuse.edu/english-department/cw-undergraduate-program
Key Personnel
Dir: Jonathan Dee *E-mail:* jrdee100@syr.edu
Assoc Dir: Sarah C Harwell *E-mail:* scharwel@syr.edu
Courses include Eastern European Poetry/Translation
The Essay/Art of the Fairy Tale
Fiction Workshop
The Forms of Fiction
The Forms of Poetry
Open Workshop - Fiction
Open Workshop - Poetry
Poetry Workshop
Prose Writing
Writing of Fiction
Writing of Poetry
Writing the Novella

Syracuse University, SI Newhouse School of Public Communications
215 University Place, Syracuse, NY 13244
Tel: 315-443-3627
E-mail: newhouse@syr.edu
Web Site: newhouse.syr.edu/academics/programs
Key Personnel
Dean: Mark J Lodato *E-mail:* mlodato@syr.edu
Assoc Dean, Graduate Progs: Joel Kaplan *Tel:* 315-443-1429 *E-mail:* jkkaplan@syr.edu
Undergraduate degrees in advertising; broadcast & digital journalism, magazine, news & digital journalism; public relations; television; radio; film; graphic design; photography.
Master's degrees in advertising; public relations; television; radio & film.
PhD degree in mass communications.
Courses include Advertising
Audio Arts
Beauty & Diversity in Fashion Media
Broadcast & Digital Journalism
Broadcast & Digital Newswriting
Business & Ethics of Journalism in a Changing World

Communications & Society
Communications Law for Journalists
Cross-Media News Writing
Foundations of Data & Digital Journalism
Goldring Arts Journalism & Communications
Magazine, News & Digital Journalism
Media Studies
Multimedia, Photography & Design
Multimedia Storytelling
New Media Management
Public Diplomacy & Global Communications
Public Relations
Race, Gender & the Media
Radio
Radio & Digital Audio News Reporting
Still Photography for Broadcast Journalism
Television & Digital News Reporting
Television, Radio & Film
Videography for Broadcast Journalism

University of Alabama Program in Creative Writing
Affiliate of University of Alabama, Department of English
PO Box 870244, Tuscaloosa, AL 35487-0244
Tel: 205-348-5065 *Fax:* 205-348-1388
E-mail: english@ua.edu
Web Site: www.as.ua.edu/english
Key Personnel
Poet & Assoc Professor: Joel Brouwer *Tel:* 205-348-9524 *E-mail:* joel.brouwer@ua.edu
Fiction Writer & Assoc Professor: Wendy Rawlings *Tel:* 205-348-4507 *E-mail:* wendy.rawlings@ua.edu
Graduate Prog Coord: Jennifer Fuqua *Tel:* 205-348-0766 *E-mail:* jfuqua@ua.edu
Three-year MFA degree program & creative writing course for undergraduates, minor in creative writing. See web site for details.

University of Baltimore - Yale Gordon College of Arts & Sciences
Division of Klein Family School of Communications Design
Liberal Arts & Policy Bldg, 10 W Preston St, Rm 107, Baltimore, MD 21201
Web Site: www.ubalt.edu/cas/about-the-college/schools-and-divisions/school-of-communications-design
Key Personnel
Div Chair: Deborah Kohl *Tel:* 410-837-4698 *E-mail:* dkohl@ubalt.edu
Dir, MFA Creative Writing & Publg Arts: Betsy Boyd *Tel:* 410-837-6272 *E-mail:* bboyd@ubalt.edu
Admin Asst II: Gary Sieck *Tel:* 410-837-6038 *E-mail:* gsieck@ubalt.edu
Also supports through the School of Communications Design, an MA program in Integrated Design, an MFA in Integrated Design & an MFA in Creative Writing & Publishing Arts.
Courses include Advanced Writing Workshop
Art of the Interview
Book Arts
Copyright & Publishing
Creating the Journal
Creative Concepts
Creative Methodologies
Creativity: Ways of Seeing
Design-Business Link
Editorial Style
Electronic Publishing
Experimental Forms
Fiction Workshop
Integrated Design Studio I: Principles
Integrated Design Studio II: Typography
Integrated Design Thesis
International Writing
Introduction to Digital Video
Introduction to Graphic Design Principles
Introduction to Web Development
Literary Nonfiction Workshop
Memoir Workshop
Poetry Workshop
Portfolio
Practicum in Integrated Design
Print Publishing
Proseminar in Integrated Design
Public & Private Languages
Screenwriting
Seminar in Literature & Writing
Seminar in Publications Design
The Craft of Popularization
Theory of Visual Communication
Thesis I
Thesis III: Design
Thesis II: Writing
Type & Design for Creative Writers
Typography I
Visual & Verbal Rhetoric
Web Development
Workshop in Written Communication
Writing for Digital Environments
Writing for the Marketplace

University of British Columbia Creative Writing Program
Buchanan Rm E-462, 1866 Main Mall, Vancouver, BC V6T 1Z1, Canada
Tel: 604-822-0699
Web Site: creativewriting.ubc.ca
Key Personnel
Chair: Alix Ohlin
Graduate Advisor: Andrew Gray *E-mail:* andrew.gray@ubc.ca
Undergraduate Advisor: Heather Miller *E-mail:* crwr.undergrad@ubc.ca
Admin: Tania Chen *Tel:* 604-822-3024 *E-mail:* crwr.admin@ubc.ca
Undergraduate & graduate programs in creative writing as well as a non-credit novel writing course several times per year.

University of California Extension - Writing, Editing & Humanities
1995 University Ave, Suite 110, Berkeley, CA 94720-7000
Tel: 510-643-8916 *Fax:* 510-643-0216
E-mail: extension-letters@berkeley.edu
Web Site: www.extension.berkeley.edu
Key Personnel
Prog Dir: Jeff Metcho *Tel:* 510-643-6462
Certificate programs in editing, technical communication & writing; evening/weekend courses & asynchronous online.
Courses include Editing
Screenwriting
Technical Communication
Writing (fiction, poetry, nonfiction)

University of Chicago, Graham School Writer's Studio
1427 E 60 St, Chicago, IL 60637
Tel: 773-702-1731
Web Site: graham.uchicago.edu/programs-courses/writers-studio
Key Personnel
Prog Mgr: JM Conway *Tel:* 773-834-7120 *E-mail:* jmconway@uchicago.edu
Open enrollment courses.
Courses include Advanced Characterization
Craft Across Genres
Creative Writing Capstone
Flash Nonfiction
I Am Not a Robot: Human-Centric Business Writing in the Age of AI
Intermediate Creative Nonfiction
Introduction to Creative Nonfiction
Introduction to Playwriting
Storytelling for Business
Tension, Drama & Stakes in Writing
Writing & Walking in Essay & Memoir
Writing Compelling Content for Presentations
Writing Effectively for Business
Writing for a Digital World
Writing the One Play Act

University of Denver Publishing Institute
2000 E Asbury Ave, Denver, CO 80208
Tel: 303-871-2570 *Fax:* 303-871-2501
E-mail: pi-info@du.edu
Web Site: liberalarts.du.edu/publishing
Key Personnel
Dir: Jill Smith *E-mail:* jill.smith@du.edu
Four-week graduate program in book publishing held July-August each year. Provides hands on workshops, lecture-teaching sessions on every phase of book publishing. Faculty consists of leading executives from publishing houses across the country. Emphasis on career counseling & job placement. Offers 6 quarter hours of graduate credit.
Courses include Children's Books
College Textbooks
E-Books
Economics of Publishing
Editing Workshop
Foreign Rights
Independent Presses
International Publishing
Marketing on the Internet
Marketing Workshop
Production & Design
Publicity & Promotion
Publishing & the Law
Scholarly Books
Trade & Scholarly Books
University Presses

University of Houston Creative Writing Program
Dept of English/College of Liberal Arts & Social Science, 3687 Cullen Blvd, Rm 229, Houston, TX 77204-5008
Tel: 713-743-3015
E-mail: cwp@uh.edu
Web Site: uh.edu/class/english/programs/graduate-studies/index
Key Personnel
Dir & Professor: Kevin Prufer *Tel:* 713-743-3907 *E-mail:* kdprufer@uh.edu
Assoc Dir: Giuseppe Taurino *Tel:* 713-743-3014 *E-mail:* gtaurino@uh.edu
Offers MA, MFA & PhD in creative writing.

University of Illinois at Chicago, Program for Writers
Affiliate of University of Illinois, Department of English
College of Liberal Arts & Sciences, 601 S Morgan St, Chicago, IL 60607
Tel: 312-413-2200 (Eng dept)
E-mail: english@uic.edu
Web Site: engl.uic.edu/graduate-studies/program-for-writers
Key Personnel
Professor & Dir, Prog for Writers: Cris Mazza *Tel:* 312-413-2795 *E-mail:* cmazza@uic.edu
Professor, Fiction/Nonfiction: Luis Urrea *E-mail:* lurrea@uic.edu
Professor, Poetry: Christina Pugh *E-mail:* capugh@uic.edu
Assoc Professor, Fiction: Christopher Grimes *E-mail:* cgrimes@uic.edu
Asst Professor, Poetry: Daniel Borzutzky *E-mail:* dborz2@uic.edu
Graduate program for writers. Students in this program take literature classes as well as writing workshops. Offers MA & PhD in writing. Undergraduates seeking a BA in English may also specialize in writing.
Courses include Fiction Workshop
Nonfiction Workshop
Novel Workshop
Poetry Workshop
Publication Workshop
Translation Workshop

COURSES & AWARDS

University of Illinois, Department of Journalism
Unit of College of Media, University of Illinois
119 Gregory Hall, 810 S Wright St, Urbana, IL 61801
Tel: 217-333-0709
E-mail: journ@illinois.edu
Web Site: catalog.illinois.edu/graduate/media/journalism-ms; media.illinois.edu/journalism/degrees-programs/masters
Key Personnel
Head, Dept: Mira Sotirovic
Dir, Graduate Studies: Brant Houston
Master's degree program.
Courses include Advanced Public Affairs Reporting
Advanced Reporting Topics
Advanced Topics in Journalism
Audio Journalism
Broadcast Meteorology
Content Producing for UI7
Data Storytelling for Journalists
History of American Journalism
Immersion Journalism
Interactive Media & You
Internship Seminar
Introduction to Documentary Storytelling & Production
Introduction to Journalism
Introduction to Sports Journalism
Investigative Journalism
Journalism Ethics & Diversity
Journalism Proseminar
Master's Project
Media Law
Multimedia Reporting
Multimedia Storytelling
Navigating the Job Market
News Editing
Newsgathering Across Platforms
On-Camera Performance for UI7
Producing for UI7 Programming
Research Methods in Journalism
Science Journalism
Special Topics
Surviving Social Media
Video Reporting & Storytelling

University of Iowa, Writers' Workshop, Graduate Creative Writing Program
102 Dey House, 507 N Clinton St, Iowa City, IA 52242-1000
Tel: 319-335-0416 *Fax:* 319-335-0420
Web Site: writersworkshop.uiowa.edu
Key Personnel
Dir: Lan Samantha Chang
Graduate: fiction & poetry workshops & seminars. Undergraduate: creative, fiction & poetry writing.

University of Texas at Austin, New Writers Project
Dept of English, 204 W 21 St, B-5000, Austin, TX 78712-1164
Tel: 512-471-4991 *Fax:* 512-471-4909
E-mail: newwritersproject@utexas.edu
Web Site: liberalarts.utexas.edu/nwp
Key Personnel
Dir: Elizabeth McCracken *E-mail:* elizmccrack@utexas.edu; Lisa Olstein *E-mail:* lisaolstein@gmail.com
Asst Dir: Nina Gary *E-mail:* nina.gary@utexas.edu
Professor: Edward Carey *E-mail:* edcarey256@aol.com; Oscar Casares *E-mail:* ohcasares@utexas.edu; Bret Anthony Johnston *E-mail:* baj@austin.utexas.edu; Deb Olin Unferth *E-mail:* debou@utexas.edu
Susan Taylor McDaniel Regents Professor in Creative Writing: Peter La Salle *E-mail:* pnl315@yahoo.com

Assoc Professor: Jennifer Chang *E-mail:* twignoise@utexas.edu; Roger Reeves *E-mail:* poexeries@yahoo.com
Comprised of experienced teachers committed to advising young writers. Students work with established writers, gain editorial & teaching experience & develop the range of their work. Students graduate with an MFA in Creative Writing.

University of Texas at El Paso, Department of Creative Writing, MFA/Department of Creative Writing
M520, University Towers, Oregon St, El Paso, TX 79968
E-mail: creativewriting@utep.edu
Web Site: www.utep.edu/liberalarts/creative-writing
Key Personnel
Chair: Rosa Alcala *E-mail:* ralcala1@utep.edu
Dir, Online MFA & Assoc Professor: Daniel Chacon *E-mail:* danchacon@utep.edu
Graduate Dir & Assoc Professor: Jose de Pierola *E-mail:* jdepierola@utep.edu
Assoc Professor: Andrea Cote-Botero *E-mail:* acbotero@utep.edu; Tim Z Hernandez *E-mail:* tzhernandez@utep.edu; Sasha Pimentel *E-mail:* srpimentel@utep.edu; Jeff Sirkin *E-mail:* jsirkin@utep.edu; Lex Williford *Tel:* 915-433-1931 (cell) *E-mail:* lex@utep.edu
Monolingual & bilingual workshops in fiction, poetry, playwriting, screenwriting, nonfiction & literary translation.

Vermont College of Fine Arts MFA in Writing for Children & Young Adults Program
36 College St, Montpelier, VT 05602
Toll Free Tel: 866-934-VCFA (934-8232)
Web Site: vcfa.edu/mfa-writing-for-children-and-young-adults
Key Personnel
Faculty Co-Chair: Liz Garton Scanlon *E-mail:* liz.scanlon@vcfa.edu; Jennifer Ziegler *E-mail:* jennifer.ziegler@vcfa.edu
Prog Dir: Katie Rasmussen *E-mail:* katie.rasmussen@vcfa.edu
Asst Dir: Aidan Sammis *E-mail:* aidan.sammis@vcfa.edu
Intensive 10-day residencies & nonresident 6-month writing projects.

Vermont College of Fine Arts, MFA in Writing Program
36 College St, Montpelier, VT 05602
Tel: 802-828-8840; 802-828-8839
Toll Free Tel: 866-934-VCFA (934-8232)
Fax: 802-828-8649
Web Site: www.vcfa.edu
Key Personnel
Prog Dir: Mike Rivas *E-mail:* mike.rivas@vcfa.edu
Assoc Prog Dir: Stephanie Reich *E-mail:* stephanie.reich@vcfa.edu
Degree work in poetry, fiction, creative nonfiction.

Warren Wilson College, MFA Program for Writers
701 Warren Wilson Rd, Swannanoa, NC 28778
Mailing Address: PO Box 9000, Asheville, NC 28815-9000
Tel: 828-771-3717
E-mail: mfa@warren-wilson.edu
Web Site: www.warren-wilson.edu/programs/mfa-in-creative-writing
Key Personnel
Dir, MFA Prog: Rita Banerjee *E-mail:* rbanerjee@warren-wilson.edu
Full-time 2-year program with winter & summer semesters. Ten-day residency of classes, workshops & lectures on campus. The 6-month project that follows is supervised through correspondence, with detailed ms criticism by faculty who are both accomplished writers & committed teachers.
Courses include Fiction
Poetry

COURSES FOR THE BOOK TRADE

Writer's Digest University
Division of Active Interest Media (AIM)
5720 Flatiron Pkwy, Boulder, CO 80301
Toll Free Tel: 800-759-0963; 800-333-5441
E-mail: writersdigestuniversity@aimmedia.com
Web Site: www.writersonlineworkshops.com
Course workshops are taught by active, published writers in the appropriate area, such as fiction & nonfiction. Students participate online, via the Internet. Workshops range in length from 4 to 28 weeks. Correspondence; student has up to 2 years to complete; tuition installment plans available for most courses.
Courses include Advanced Blogging
Advanced Horror Workshop
Advanced Novel Writing
Advanced Poetry Writing
Agent One-on-One: First Ten Pages Boot Camp
Agent One-on-One: How to Craft Query Letters & Other Submission Materials That Get Noticed Boot Camp
The Art of Storytelling 101: Story Mapping & Pacing
The Art of Storytelling 102: Showing vs Telling
Blogging 101
Breaking into Copywriting 101
Build Your Novel Scene by Scene
Business Writing
Character Development: Creating Memorable Characters
Comedy Writing Workshop
Copyediting Certification Course
Creative Writing 101
Creativity & Expression
Description & Setting
Fantasy Writers
Fearless Writing
1st Person Point of View
Fitting Writing Into Your Life
Focus on the Short Story
Form & Composition
Freelance Writing
Freelance Writing for Stay at Home Moms (and Dads)
Fundamentals of Fiction
Fundamentals of Poetry Writing
Getting Started in Writing
Ghostwriting 101
Grammar & Mechanics
Horror Writing Intensive: Analyzing the Work of Genre Master Stephen King
How to Blog a Book
How to Catch an Agent's Interest with Your First Pages
How to Craft a Book that Will Sell
How to Find & Keep a Literary Agent Boot Camp
How to Hook an Agent: Queries & Beyond!-Recording
How to Plot & Structure Your Novel
How to Write an Article
Introduction to Copyediting
Literary Agent Boot Camp: Perfecting Submission Materials
Marketing Your Magazine Articles
Master in Fine Arts (Creative Writing) Application Preparation Course
Mastering Amazon for Authors
Outlining Your Novel
Picture eBook Mastery: The Unofficial Guide to Publishing & Selling Kindle Children's Books
Pitch an Article: Write for Today's Marketplace
Plot Perfect Boot Camp
Professional Copyediting: Tools of the Trade
Publishing Your Children's Book: How to Write & Pitch Young Adult, Middle Grade & Picture Book Manuscripts

COURSES FOR THE BOOK TRADE

Pulp Fiction
Query Letter in 14 Days
Read Like a Writer: Learn from the Masters
Revision & Self Editing
Sell Books on a Shoestring Budget
Short Story Fundamentals
Social Media 101
Successful Self-Publishing
Travel Writing
12 Weeks to a First Draft
Voice & Viewpoint
Wordbuilding in Science Fiction & Fantasy Writing
Write a Plot
Write Great Dialogue
Writing a Religious Book
Writing Historical Fiction
Writing Nonfiction for Children
Writing Nonfiction 101: Fundamentals
Writing Online Content
Writing the Memoir 101
Writing the Middle Grade Book
Writing the Mystery Novel
Writing the Nonfiction Book Proposal
Writing the Novel Proposal
Writing the Paranormal Novel
Writing the Personal Essay 101: Fundamentals
Writing the Picture Book
Writing the Romance Novel
Writing the Science Fiction & Fantasy Novel
Writing the Thriller Novel
Writing the Young Adult Novel
Writing Tips-Short Story Fundamentals
Writing Women's Fiction
Your Submission Tools: How to Write Excellent Queries, Opening Pages & Synopses Boot Camp

Awards, Prize Contests, Fellowships & Grants

Major awards given to books, authors and publishers by various organizations are, for the most part, not open for application. However, many prize contests may be applied for by writing to the sponsor (for prompt response, always include a self-addressed, stamped envelope). Also included in this section is information relating to fellowships and grants that are primarily available to authors and students who are pursuing publishing related studies. All are offered annually unless otherwise noted.

For more complete information about scholarships, fellowships and grants-in-aid, see *The Annual Register of Grant Support* (Information Today, Inc., 121 Chanlon Road, Suite G-20, New Providence, NJ 07974-2195).

A Public Space Fellowships
A Public Space
323 Dean St, Brooklyn, NY 11217
Tel: 718-858-8067
E-mail: general@apublicspace.org
Web Site: apublicspace.org
Key Personnel
Founding Ed: Brigid Hughes
Mktg & Devt Dir: Lauren Cerand *Tel:* 917-533-0103 *E-mail:* lauren@apublicspace.org
Writers who have not yet published or been contracted to write a book-length work are eligible. International applicants are encouraged to apply, but only submissions in English are considered. One submission per person is allowed. Submittable opens for Fellowship submissions September 15. Submit cover letter & one previously unpublished prose piece. See web site for detailed submission guidelines.
Award: $1,000 honorarium & 6 months editorial support to prepare a piece of prose for the magazine
Closing Date: Oct 15
Presented: Successful applicants informed no later than Feb 15 for Fellowship period March 1-Sept 1

A Sense of Place: The Elizabeth J Urquhart Memorial
The Poetry Society of Virginia (PSV)
PO Box 36128, North Chesterfield, VA 23235-3533
E-mail: contest@poetrysocietyofvirginia.org; info@poetryvirginia.org
Web Site: www.poetrysocietyofvirginia.org
Key Personnel
Pres: Cherryl T Cooley
  E-mail: poetrysocietypresident@gmail.com
Places—manmade, natural, personal or historical—inform poetry with the power to evoke the past & transcend the present. Any form, any subject, 48 line limit. Submit 1 copy of the poem with no identifying information but put the category in the upper right-hand-side, along with a notation as to whether you are a member of PSV (does not matter if you are a lifetime member or just joined for the contest). Submit a cover letter/page that contains the category, the name of the poem, your name & address, phone number & e-mail address. Entries will not be returned. Entry fee: Free to membs, $5 nonmembs.
Other Sponsor(s): Williamsburg Poetry Guild
Award: $50 (1st prize), $30 (2nd prize), $20 (3rd prize)

AAAS/Subaru Prize for Excellence in Science Books
American Association for the Advancement of Science (AAAS)
1200 New York Ave NW, Washington, DC 20005
Tel: 202-326-6400
E-mail: sbf@aaas.org
Web Site: www.sbfprize.org
Key Personnel
Educ Progs Sr Proj Dir: Suzanne Thurston
  E-mail: sthursto@aaas.org
Prize Mgr: Sarah Ingraffea
Proj Coord: Abigail Hils
Established: 2005
Celebrates outstanding science writing & illustration for children & young adults. Awarded in 4 categories: Children's science picture book, middle grade science book, young adult science book, hands-on science book. Only nonfiction science books are eligible & must be in the English language. See web site for rules & full eligibility criteria.
Other Sponsor(s): Subaru of America Inc
Award: $1,500 each & commemorative plaque; both author & illustrator are awarded for the children's science picture book category
Closing Date: July
Presented: AAAS Annual Meeting, Feb

J M Abraham Poetry Award
Writers' Federation of Nova Scotia (WFNS)
1113 Marginal Rd, Halifax, NS B3H 4P7, Canada
Tel: 902-423-8116 *Fax:* 902-422-0881
E-mail: wfts@writers.ns.ca (awards)
Web Site: writers.ns.ca
Key Personnel
Prog Mgr, Arts Educ: Linda Hudson
Established: 1998
Presented to the best full-length book of poetry by an Atlantic Canadian writer who has lived in one or a combination of these provinces for at least 2 concurrent years immediately prior to the submission deadline date. Non-refundable $35 administrative fee per entry.
Award: $2,000
Closing Date: Nov 1
Presented: Halifax, NS, CN, Spring

Abrams Amplify Award
Harry N Abrams Inc
195 Broadway, 9th fl, New York, NY 10007
SAN: 200-2434
E-mail: childrenspublicity@abramsbooks.com
Web Site: www.abramsbooks.com/abramsamplifyaward
Key Personnel
SVP & Publr, Children's Books: Andrew Smith
Established: 2023
To honor & uplift the voices of children's book creators from marginalized communities (Black, Asian/Pacific Islander, Latinx, Middle Eastern or Native American/Indigenous). Submissions should be middle-grade fiction or nonfiction for readers ages 8-14. Submit online entry form, first 50 pages of each ms, brief synopsis (up to 200 words) & 1-page full plot summary (up to 700 words).
Award: 1st prize: $5,000, editorial notes & one-on-one video conference meeting with Abrams editor to discuss creator's submission; 2nd prize: $2,500 & editorial notes on creator's submission from Abrams editor; 3rd prize: $1,000 & editorial notes on creator's submission from Abrams editor
Presented: Feb

Academy of American Poets Fellowship
The Academy of American Poets Inc
75 Maiden Lane, Suite 901, New York, NY 10038
Tel: 212-274-0343
E-mail: awards@poets.org
Web Site: poets.org/academy-american-poets/prizes/academy-american-poets-fellowship
Key Personnel
Pres & Exec Dir: Ricardo Alberto Maldonado
VP, Digital Engagement & Content: Jeff Gleaves
Ad & Mktg Dir: Michelle Campagna
Dir, Donor Rel: Molly Walsh
Dir, Progs: Nikay Paredes
Established: 1946
Awarded to recognize distinguished poetic achievement. No applications are accepted. Fellows are selected by majority vote of the Academy's Board of Chancellors.
Other Sponsor(s): T S Eliot Foundation
Award: $25,000 & residency at T S Eliot House, Gloucester, MA

Academy of American Poets First Book Award
The Academy of American Poets Inc
75 Maiden Lane, Suite 901, New York, NY 10038
Tel: 212-274-0343
E-mail: awards@poets.org
Web Site: poets.org/academy-american-poets/prizes/first-book-award
Key Personnel
Pres & Exec Dir: Ricardo Alberto Maldonado
VP, Digital Engagement & Content: Jeff Gleaves
Ad & Mktg Dir: Michelle Campagna
Dir, Donor Rel: Molly Walsh
Dir, Progs: Nikay Paredes
Established: 1975
Annual award for a book-length ms of poetry by a living American poet who has not published a book of poetry. Entry fee: $35. See web site for entry form & guidelines.
Award: First book publication $5,000, publication by Graywolf Press, an all-expenses-paid 6-week residency at the Civitella Ranieri Center in Italy & distribution of the winning book to thousands of Academy of American Poet members
Closing Date: Nov 1
Presented: April

The Academy of American Poets Harold Taylor Prize
Poetry Center & American Poetry Archives at San Francisco State University
511-512 Humanities Bldg, 1600 Holloway Ave, San Francisco, CA 94132
Tel: 415-338-2227 *Fax:* 415-338-0966
E-mail: poetry@sfsu.edu
Web Site: poetry.sfsu.edu
Key Personnel
Dir: Steve Dickison *E-mail:* steved@sfsu.edu
Assoc Dir: Elise Ficarra *E-mail:* eficarra@sfsu.edu
Established: 1955
SF State students may submit to the Poetry Center up to 10 pages of poetry, constituted by any

number of poems. Mss must be clearly typed & legible. Mss will not be returned. Names should appear on ms pages. The writer's name, address, telephone number & social security number should be included in a cover letter accompanying the ms.
Award: $100 check from the Academy of American Poets
Closing Date: Check postings on campus for deadlines
Presented: Late April

The Accolades, see Cordon d' Or - Gold Ribbon International Culinary Academy Awards

The Acheven Book Prize for Young Adult Fiction
Fitzroy Books
Imprint of Regal House Publishing
c/o Regal House Publishing, 806 Oberlin Rd, No 12094, Raleigh, NC 27605
E-mail: info@regalhousepublishing.com
Web Site: regalhousepublishing.com/the-acheven-book-prize-for-young-adult-fiction/
Key Personnel
Founder, Publr & Ed-in-Chief: Jaynie Royal
Mng Ed: Pam Van Dyk
Ed: Elizabeth Lowenstein
Established: 2019
Recognizing finely crafted works written for the Young Adult market. Submissions through Submittable or by post. Entry fee: $25. Fax or e-mail submissions not accepted. See web site for submission guidelines.
Award: Publication & $750 honorarium
Closing Date: Sept 30 (postmark)
Presented: Jan 10

ACP Best of the Best Awards
Formerly AFCP's Awards
Association of Community Publishers Inc (ACP)
104 Westland Dr, Columbia, TN 38401
Toll Free Tel: 877-203-2327
E-mail: info@communitypublishers.com
Web Site: www.communitypublishers.com/awards
Key Personnel
Exec Dir: Douglas Fry E-mail: douglas@communitypublishers.com
Established: 1970
Member publication only awards recognizing excellence in design, advertising, editorial, & publishing. ACP Best of the Best Awards serve as a beacon for excellence in design aesthetics, impactful advertising campaigns, compelling editorial content, & note-worthy initiatives. Material must have been published in the previous calendar year. Up to 10 total entries per membership for free; fee for each additional entry is $5 for network participants, $10 for non-network participants. Complete category & submission information available on web site.
Award: Plaques
Closing Date: Feb 28
Presented: Virtual cermeony, Spring
Branch Office(s)
8119 Circuit Rider Path, Cicero, NY 13039
7445 Morgan Rd, Suite 3, Liverpool, NY 13090

Herbert Baxter Adams Prize in European History
American Historical Association (AHA)
400 "A" St SE, Washington, DC 20003
Tel: 202-544-2422
E-mail: awards@historians.org
Web Site: www.historians.org/award-grant/herbert-baxter-adams-prize/
Established: 1905
For a distinguished book in English in the field of European history, from ancient times to 1815 (even years), 1815 through the 20th century (odd years). Entry must be the author's first substantial book & have a 2023 or 2024 copyright. Submission of an entry may be made by an author or a publisher. Publishers may submit as many entries as they wish. Along with an application form, applicants must mail a copy of their book to each prize committee member posted on our web site as the prize deadline approaches. All updated info on web site.
Award: $1,000
Closing Date: May 15, 2025
Presented: AHA Annual Meeting, Chicago, IL, Jan 2026

Willi Paul Adams Award
The Organization of American Historians (OAH)
112 N Bryan Ave, Bloomington, IN 47408-4141
Tel: 812-855-7311
E-mail: oah@oah.org
Web Site: www.oah.org/awards
Key Personnel
Exec Dir: Beth English Tel: 812-855-9836 E-mail: benglish@oah.org
Dir, Communs & Mktg: Kym Robinson Tel: 812-855-5430 E-mail: kymarobi@oah.org
Awarded biennially, in odd-numbered years, to the author of the best book on American history published in a foreign language. To be eligible, a book should be concerned with the past (recent or distant) or with issues of continuity & change. It should also be substantially concerned with events or processes that began, developed, or ended in the American colonies +/or the US. This award is not open to books whose mss were originally submitted for publication in English or by people for whom English is their first language. Each entry must have been published during the 2-year calendar period preceding that in which the award is given. Four copies of the essay & book must be mailed to the Willi Paul Adams Award Committee. See web site for full submission procedures.
Closing Date: May 1, 2026
Presented: OAH Conference on American History, Sheraton Grand Chicago, Chicago, IL, April 3-6, 2027

Jane Addams Children's Book Award
Jane Addams Peace Association
276 Fifth Ave, Suite 704, PMB 45, New York, NY 10001
Tel: 212-682-8830
E-mail: info@janeaddamspeace.org
Web Site: www.janeaddamspeace.org
Key Personnel
Award Comm Chair: Jenice Mateo Toledo
Bd Pres: Susan Freiss E-mail: president@janeaddamspeace.org
Established: 1953
Awarded to children's books published in the US the previous year with themes stressing peace, social justice, world community & the equality of the sexes & all races. Those applying must submit 1 copy to each committee member. Inquire at info@janeaddamspeace.org for the address list.
Award: Certificate & cash
Closing Date: Dec 31
Presented: Winners announced Jan 15; ceremony held 4th Wednesday in April

AFCP's Awards, see ACP Best of the Best Awards

Agatha Awards
Malice Domestic Ltd
PO Box 8007, Gaithersburg, MD 20898
Tel: 301-730-1675
E-mail: mdregservices@gmail.com
Web Site: malicedomestic.org
Key Personnel
Malice Chair: Verena Rose E-mail: malicechair@comcast.net
Chair, Agatha Awards: Cindy Silberblatt E-mail: csilberblatt@att.net
Established: 1989
Annual awards for best traditional mysteries of the previous calendar year. Awards given for best novel, best first novel, best nonfiction work, best short story, best children's/young adult novel. Those registered for Malice by December 31 each year receive a ballot to nominate.
Closing Date: Dec 31
Presented: Malice Domestic Convention, Agatha Awards Banquet, May

Aggiornamento Award
Catholic Library Association
8550 United Plaza Blvd, Suite 1001, Baton Rouge, LA 70809
Tel: 225-408-4417
E-mail: cla2@cathla.org
Web Site: cathla.org
Key Personnel
Exec Dir: Melanie Talley
Association Coord: Mary Coll
Established: 1980
Presented by the Parish and Community Library Services Section of the CLA through the Aggiornamento Award Committee to recognize contributions made by an individual or an organization for the renewal of parish & community life in the spirit of Saint John XXIII (1881-1963).
Award: Plaque
Closing Date: None; in-house votes
Presented: CLA Annual Convention, Thursday of Easter week

AHA Prize in American History
Formerly AHA Prize in United States History
American Historical Association (AHA)
400 "A" St SE, Washington, DC 20003
Tel: 202-544-2422
E-mail: awards@historians.org
Web Site: www.historians.org/award-grant/aha-prize-in-american-history/
Established: 1929
Awarded biennially, in odd-numbered years, for an outstanding monograph on any subject relating to US history that is the author's 1st or 2nd book. To be eligible for consideration for the 2025 prize, an entry must be of a scholarly historical nature with a 2023 or 2024 copyright. Research accuracy, originality & literary merit are important factors. Along with an application form, applicants must mail a copy of their book to each prize committee member posted on our web site as the prize deadline approaches. All updated info on web site.
Award: $1,000
Closing Date: May 15, 2025
Presented: AHA Annual Meeting, Chicago, IL, Jan 2026

AHA Prize in European International History
Formerly George Louis Beer Prize
American Historical Association (AHA)
400 "A" St SE, Washington, DC 20003
Tel: 202-544-2422
E-mail: awards@historians.org
Web Site: www.historians.org/award-grant/aha-prize-in-european-international-history/
Established: 1923
Awarded in recognition of outstanding historical writing in European international history since 1895 that is submitted by a scholar who is a US citizen or permanent resident. Books with a copyright of 2024 are eligible for the 2025 prize. Only books of a high scholarly historical nature should be submitted. Along with an application form, applicants must mail a copy of their book to each prize committee member posted on our web site as the prize deadline approaches. All updated info on web site.

Award: $1,000
Closing Date: May 15, 2025
Presented: AHA Annual Meeting, Chicago, IL, Jan 2026

AHA Prize in History prior to CE 1000
Formerly James Henry Breasted Prize
American Historical Association (AHA)
400 "A" St SE, Washington, DC 20003
Tel: 202-544-2422
E-mail: awards@historians.org
Web Site: www.historians.org/award-grant/aha-prize-in-history-prior-to-ce-1000/
Established: 1985
Best book in English in any field of history prior to 1000 AD. Different geographic area will be eligible each year. Entries with a 2024 copyright are eligible for the 2025 prize. Along with an application form, applicants must mail a copy of their book to each prize committee member posted on our web site as the prize deadline approaches. All updated info on web site.
Award: $1,000
Closing Date: May 15, 2025
Presented: AHA Annual Meeting, New York, NY, Jan 2026

AHA Prize in United States History, see AHA Prize in American History

AIGA 50 Books | 50 Covers
AIGA, the professional association for design
228 Park Ave S, Suite 58603, New York, NY 10003
Tel: 212-807-1990
E-mail: competitions@aiga.org
Web Site: www.aiga.org
Key Personnel
COO: Amy Chapman *Tel:* 212-710-3137
Exec Dir: Bennie F Johnson *Tel:* 212-710-3100
Dir, Devt: Heather Strelecki
Dir, Mktg: Michelle Koenigsknecht *Tel:* 212-710-3138
Established: 1923
This competition aims to identify the 50 best-designed books & book covers. The selections from the 50 Books | 50 Covers competition exemplify the best current work in book & book cover design. See web site for complete rules & eligibility.
Past selections from AIGA's book design competitions have been added to the online AIGA Design Archives as well as the physical archives at the Denver Art Museum & the Rare Book & Manuscript Library at Columbia University's Butler Library in New York City.
Closing Date: Feb
Presented: Summer

AJL Jewish Fiction Award
Association of Jewish Libraries Inc (AJL)
PO Box 1118, Teaneck, NJ 07666
Tel: 201-371-3255
E-mail: info@jewishlibraries.org
Web Site: jewishlibraries.org/AJL_Jewish_Fiction_Award
Key Personnel
Pres: Michelle Margolis
Comm Memb: Rachel Kamin *E-mail:* rachelkamin@gmail.com; Rosalind Reisner *E-mail:* roz@thereisners.net
Established: 2017
All works of fiction with significant Jewish thematic content written in English—novels, short story & flash fiction collections—by a single author published & available for purchase in the US during the award year are eligible for the award. Jewish thematic content means an extended grappling with Jewish themes throughout the book, including Judaism, Jewish history & culture, Jewish identity, etc.
Other Sponsor(s): Dan Wyman Books
Award: $1,000 cash prize & support to attend AJL conference
Presented: Association of Jewish Libraries Conference, June

AJL Judaica Bibliography Award
Association of Jewish Libraries Inc (AJL)
Affiliate of The American Library Association (ALA)
PO Box 1118, Teaneck, NJ 07666
Tel: 201-371-3255
E-mail: info@jewishlibraries.org
Web Site: jewishlibraries.org
Key Personnel
Pres: Michelle Margolis
Ref & Bibliography Awards Comm Chair: Anna Levia *E-mail:* rasawards@jewishlibraries.org
Established: 1984
Presented for best Judaica bibliography book published in previous calendar year.
Award: The seal of the Association
Closing Date: March
Presented: AJL Annual Convention, June

AJL Judaica Reference Award
Association of Jewish Libraries Inc (AJL)
Affiliate of The American Library Association (ALA)
PO Box 1118, Teaneck, NJ 07666
Tel: 201-371-3255
E-mail: info@jewishlibraries.org
Web Site: jewishlibraries.org
Key Personnel
Pres: Michelle Margolis
Ref & Bibliography Awards Comm Chair: Anna Levia *E-mail:* rasawards@jewishlibraries.org
Established: 1984
Awarded for outstanding Judaica reference book published during previous calendar year.
Award: The seal of the Association
Closing Date: March
Presented: AJL Annual Convention, June

AJL Scholarship
Association of Jewish Libraries Inc (AJL)
Affiliate of The American Library Association (ALA)
PO Box 1118, Teaneck, NJ 07666
Tel: 201-371-3255
E-mail: scholarship@jewishlibraries.org; info@jewishlibraries.org
Web Site: jewishlibraries.org/student-scholarship-award
Key Personnel
Pres: Michelle Margolis
In order to encourage students to train for & enter the field of Judaica librarianship, the Association of Jewish Libraries awards a scholarship to a student enrolled or accepted in a graduate school of library & information science. Prospective candidates should have an interest in & demonstrate a potential for pursuing a career in Judaica librarianship. In addition, applicants must provide documentation showing participation in Jewish studies at an academic or less formal level +/or experience working in Judaica libraries.
Award: $1,000 per academic year
Presented: AJL Annual Convention, June

Akron Poetry Prize
University of Akron Press
120 E Mill St, Suite 415, Akron, OH 44308
Tel: 330-972-2795
E-mail: uapress@uakron.edu
Web Site: www.uakron.edu/uapress/akron-poetry-prize
Key Personnel
Poetry Ed: Mary Biddinger *E-mail:* marybid@uakron.edu
Established: 1995
Open to all poets writing in English. Mss must be at least 48 pages. Entry fee: $25. Submissions accepted via Submittable beginning April 15.
Award: $1,500 & publication
Closing Date: June 15
Presented: Winner announced online by Sept 30

Alabama Artists Fellowship Awards
Alabama State Council on the Arts
201 Monroe St, Suite 110, Montgomery, AL 36130-1800
Tel: 334-242-4076 *Fax:* 334-240-3269
Web Site: arts.alabama.gov/programs/literary_arts/literary_fellowships.aspx
Key Personnel
Exec Dir: Elliot A Knight, PhD
Lit Prog Mgr: Anne Kimzey *Tel:* 334-242-5136 *E-mail:* anne.kimzey@arts.alabama.gov
Awarded based on quality of work +/or career status, achievement & potential; two-year residency required & service to the state.
Award: $5,000 fellowships
Closing Date: March 1
Presented: Oct 1

Alberta Book Publishing Awards
The Book Publishers Association of Alberta (BPAA)
11759 Groat Rd NW, 2nd fl, Edmonton, AB T5M 3K6, Canada
Tel: 780-424-5060
E-mail: info@bookpublishers.ab.ca
Web Site: bookpublishers.ab.ca; www.readalberta.ca
Key Personnel
Exec Dir: Kieran Leblanc *E-mail:* kleblanc@bookpublishers.ab.ca
Proj Coord: Patricia Veldstra *E-mail:* pveldstra@bookpublishers.ab.ca
Proj Asst: Megan Bishop *E-mail:* mbishop@bookpublishers.ab.ca
Established: 1989
Awarded for excellence in publishing within the province of Alberta. Publishers are selected through a peer jury process in up to 14 award categories.
Award: Certificate
Closing Date: Feb
Presented: Sept

The Albertine Youth Prize
Cultural Services of the French Embassy
972 Fifth Ave, New York, NY 10075
Tel: 332-228-2238
E-mail: info@albertine.com
Web Site: www.albertine.com/prix-albertine-jeunesse-2024/; www.albertine.com
A reader's choice award based on the vote of young readers aged 3 to 14 years old, who cast their votes for their favorite book from a collection of Francophone youth literature available in English translation. The selected books are divided into 4 categories according to age groups: 3-5 years; 6-8 years; 9-14 years. The prize seeks to reinforce the practice & love of reading in both French & English.

Alcuin Society Awards for Excellence in Book Design in Canada
Alcuin Society
PO Box 3216, Sta Terminal, Vancouver, BC V6B 3X8, Canada
Tel: 604-732-5403
E-mail: awards@alcuinsociety.com
Web Site: alcuinsociety.com
Key Personnel
Chair, Book Design Competition: Spencer Stuart
Established: 1981
Awards recognizing the work of Canadian book designers & publishers through the Alcuin Citations awarded for excellence in book design & production. Must fulfill the following criteria: titles published in Canada or titles co-

published with a publisher in another country but representing a book by a Canadian book designer. Categories are: children, limited editions, pictorial, poetry, prose fiction, prose nonfiction, prose nonfiction illustrated, reference & comics.
Award: Certificate
Closing Date: March 1
Presented: Awards ceremonies in Toronto & Vancouver, Oct

A Owen Aldridge Prize
American Comparative Literature Association (ACLA)
323 E Wacker Dr, No 642, Chicago, IL 60601
Tel: 312-600-8072
E-mail: info@acla.org
Web Site: www.acla.org/prize-awards/owen-aldridge-prize
Competition to encourage & recognize excellence in scholarship among graduate students & to reward the highest achievement by publication. Submissions must be sent to the Editor-in-Chief of CLS in University Park, PA. See web site for specific guidelines.
Other Sponsor(s): Comparative Literature Studies (CLS)
Award: Prize paper published in *Comparative Literature Studies*, monetary prize including honorarium & help with travel expenses to attend the ACLA annual meeting
Closing Date: Mid-Nov

Alex Awards
Young Adult Library Services Association (YALSA)
Division of The American Library Association (ALA)
225 N Michigan Ave, Suite 1300, Chicago, IL 60601
Tel: 312-280-4390 *Toll Free Tel:* 800-545-2433
E-mail: yalsa@ala.org
Web Site: www.ala.org/yalsa/alex-awards
Key Personnel
Exec Dir: Tammy Dillard-Steels *Tel:* 800-545-2433 ext 4391 *E-mail:* tdillard@ala.org
Prog Offr, Events & Conferences: Nichole O'Connor *Tel:* 800-545-2433 ext 4387 *E-mail:* noconnor@ala.org
Communs Specialist: Anna Lam *Tel:* 800-545-2433 ext 5849 *E-mail:* alam@ala.org
Established: 1998
Awarded to 10 books written for adults that have special appeal to young adults, ages 12-18. The winning titles are selected from the previous year's publishing.
Other Sponsor(s): Margaret A Edwards Trust
Closing Date: Dec 31

Nelson Algren Literary Awards
Chicago Tribune
160 N Stetson Ave, Chicago, IL 60601
Tel: 312-222-3001
E-mail: ctc-arts@chicagotribune.com
Web Site: www.chicagotribune.com/entertainment/books/literary-awards; algren.submittable.com
Established: 1981
Given for an outstanding unpublished short fiction, double-spaced & no more than 8,000 words in length, by an American writer. No entry form or fee required. Entry online via Submittable.
Award: One winner ($3,500), 5 finalists ($750); Grand Prize winning story will be considered for publication in a print or digital edition of the *Chicago Tribune*
Closing Date: Jan 31
Presented: Chicago, IL, July

Alice Award
Furthermore
518 Warren St, Hudson, NY 12534
Mailing Address: PO Box 667, Hudson, NY 12534
Tel: 518-828-8900
Web Site: www.furthermore.org
Key Personnel
Admin: Ann Birckmayer
Established: 2013
Awarded to a richly illustrated book that makes a valuable contribution to its field & demonstrates high standards of production. The organization submitting the book must be a 501(c)(3) & have acted as a partner in the book's production. Organizations may submit up to 2 books annually. Books published in the calendar year prior & up to submission deadline will be considered.
Other Sponsor(s): J M Kaplan Fund Program
Award: $25,000; Alice Short List selected titles each receive $5,000
Closing Date: April 1
Presented: Oct

Samuel Washington Allen Prize
New England Poetry Club
c/o Linda Haviland Conte, 18 Hall Ave, Apt 2, Somerville, MA 02144
E-mail: info@nepoetryclub.org
Web Site: nepoetryclub.org
Key Personnel
Co-Pres: Doug Holder; Denise Provost
VP: Hilary Sallick
Treas: Linda Haviland Conte
 E-mail: nepctreasurer@gmail.com
Awarded for a long poem or poem sequence of 3-10 pages, single-spaced. Only one poem per contest. Entries must be original unpublished (neither print nor online) poems in English. Submissions must be made by post or by Submittable link. See web site for full guidelines. Entry fee: Free to membs, nonmembs $5.
Award: $250, publication of winning poems on NEPC web site & opportunity to read at the NEPC (travel expenses not included)
Closing Date: May 31
Presented: Announced online Aug/Sept

ALSC Baker & Taylor Summer Reading Grant
Association for Library Service to Children (ALSC)
Division of The American Library Association (ALA)
225 N Michigan Ave, Suite 1300, Chicago, IL 60601
Tel: 312-280-2163 *Toll Free Tel:* 800-545-2433
Fax: 312-280-5271
E-mail: alsc@ala.org
Web Site: www.ala.org/alsc/awardsgrants/profawards/bakertaylor
Key Personnel
Exec Dir: Alena Rivers *Tel:* 800-545-2433 ext 5866 *E-mail:* arivers@ala.org
Awards Coord: Jordan Dubin *Tel:* 800-545-2433 ext 5839 *E-mail:* jdubin@ala.org
Prog Coord: Ann Michaud *Tel:* 800-545-2433 ext 2166 *E-mail:* amichaud@ala.org
Membership/Mktg Specialist: Elizabeth Serrano *Tel:* 800-545-2433 ext 2164 *E-mail:* eserrano@ala.org
Encourages reading programs for children (birth-14 years) in a public library. Applicant must plan & present an outline for a theme-based summer reading program in a public library.
Award: $3,000
Closing Date: Nov 15
Presented: Announced in Dec press release

Prix Alvine-Belisle
Federation des Milieux Documentaires
2065 rue Parthenais, Bureau 387, Montreal, QC H2K 3T1, Canada
Tel: 514-281-5012
E-mail: info@fmdoc.org
Web Site: www.fmdoc.org/activities/prix-alvine-belisle
Key Personnel
Exec Dir: Micheline Brule *E-mail:* mbrule@fmdoc.org
Established: 1974
Awarded to the best books for young people published in French in Canada during the previous year.
Closing Date: End of March
Presented: Mount Royale Centre, Montreal, QC, CN, Nov

Amateur Writing Contest
Baltimore Science Fiction Society Inc
PO Box 686, Baltimore, MD 21203-0686
Tel: 410-563-2737
E-mail: bsfs-amc@bsfs.org
Web Site: www.bsfs.org/bsfsssc.htm
Key Personnel
Balticon Chair: Eric Gasior *E-mail:* chair@bsfs.org
Balticon Vice Chair: Yakira Heistand
PR Coord: Morgan Hazelwood
 E-mail: socialmedia@bsfs.org
Annual contest to promote the creation of quality genre literature in the state of Maryland. Any short story that falls into the "speculative fiction" genre is eligible. Writers must be age 18 or older, a Maryland resident, or currently enrolled in a Maryland 2- or 4-year college. Members of the Science Fiction Writers of America (SFWA) are not eligible. Story must be a minimum of 1,000 words to a maximum of 5,500 words. See web site for full submission guidelines.
Award: $250 (1st prize), $100 (2nd prize), $50 (3rd prize)
Closing Date: June 15
Presented: Capclave Convention, Oct

The Ambassador Richard C Holbrooke Distinguished Achievement Award
Dayton Literary Peace Prize Foundation
PO Box 461, Wright Brothers Branch, Dayton, OH 45409-0461
Tel: 937-298-5072
E-mail: sharon.rab@daytonliterarypeaceprize.org
Web Site: www.daytonliterarypeaceprize.org
Key Personnel
Founder & Pres: Sharon Rab *E-mail:* sharon.rab@daytonliterarypeaceprize.org
Exec Dir: Nicholas A Raines
Literary award for a body of work that focuses on a central message of peace. Nominated works must have significant & enduring literary value, appeal to a variety of audiences & be in English or translated into English.
Award: $10,000 & sculpture

Ambroggio Prize
The Academy of American Poets Inc
75 Maiden Lane, Suite 901, New York, NY 10038
Tel: 212-274-0343
E-mail: awards@poets.org
Web Site: poets.org/academy-american-poets/prizes/ambroggio-prize
Key Personnel
Pres & Exec Dir: Ricardo Alberto Maldonado
VP, Digital Engagement & Content: Jeff Gleaves
Ad & Mktg Dir: Michelle Campagna
Dir, Donor Rel: Molly Walsh
Dir, Progs: Nikay Paredes
Established: 2017
Annual publication prize for a book-length poetry ms originally written in Spanish & with an English translation. If poet collaborates with a translator, both must share the prize. Online submissions only through Submittable.
Award: $1,000 & publication by University of Arizona Press

Closing Date: Feb 15
Presented: Applicants notified of prize results via e-mail by Sept 30

American Association of University Women of NC Young People's Literature Award
AAUW, North Carolina Division
Affiliate of North Carolina Literary & Historical Association
4610 Mail Service Ctr, Raleigh, NC 27699-4610
Tel: 919-814-6623
Web Site: www.ncdcr.gov/about/history/lit-and-hist/awards; www.aauw.org
Key Personnel
Awards Coord: Joseph Beatty *E-mail:* joseph.beatty@ncdcr.gov
Established: 1953
Awarded in recognition of the most significant work of original literature for young readers published over the course of the last year by a North Carolina author. Author must be a legal or physical resident of North Carolina for at least 3 years prior to the end of the contest period.
Award: Cup
Closing Date: July 15
Presented: Raleigh, NC, Fall

American Book Awards
Before Columbus Foundation
The Raymond House, 655 13 St, Suite 302, Oakland, CA 94612
SAN: 159-2955
Tel: 916-425-7916
E-mail: beforecolumbusfoundation@gmail.com
Web Site: www.beforecolumbusfoundation.com
Key Personnel
Founder: Ishmael Reed
Established: 1978
Awarded to acknowledge the excellence & multicultural diversity of American writing. The awards are nonprofit. There are no categories & all winners are accorded equal status. Award is given for books published in the previous calendar year. No application forms or fees. Must submit 2 copies of each entry.
Award: Plaque
Closing Date: Dec 31
Presented: San Francisco, CA, Oct

American Illustration/American Photography
Amilus Inc
Subsidiary of Fadner Media
225 W 36 St, Suite 602, New York, NY 10018
Tel: 646-669-8111
E-mail: info@ai-ap.com
Web Site: www.ai-ap.com
Key Personnel
Dir: Mark Heflin *E-mail:* mark@ai-ap.com
Established: 1985
Awarded for the finest illustrative work by students & professionals. Categories include: editorial, advertising & books, as well as unpublished work. Work will be published in the American Illustration annual & will include the artist's name, address & telephone. Also, similar competition & annual for photography called American Photography. Both books are published in November.
Closing Date: Feb (photography), March (illustration)
Presented: The Party, New York, NY, Nov

American Indian Youth Literature Award
American Indian Library Association
Affiliate of The American Library Association (ALA)
PO Box 41296, San Jose, CA 95160
E-mail: ailawebsite@gmail.com
Web Site: ailanet.org/activities/american-indian-youth-literature-award
Key Personnel
Exec Dir: Heather Devine-Hardy *E-mail:* hhdevine@gmail.com
Established: 2006
Awarded biennially, in even-numbered years, to identify & honor the very best writing & illustrations by & about American Indians. See web site for specific criteria.

American Printing History Association Award
American Printing History Association
PO Box 4519, Grand Central Sta, New York, NY 10163
E-mail: secretary@printinghistory.org
Web Site: printinghistory.org/programs/awards
Key Personnel
Pres: J Fernando Pena
VP, Membership: Harold Kyle
VP, Progs: Danelle Moon
VP, Pubns: Josef Beery
Treas: David Goodrich
Secy: Meghan Constantinou
Exec Secy: Lyndsi Barnes
Established: 1976
For a distinguished contribution to the study, recording, preservation or dissemination of printing history, in any specific area or in general terms.
Award: 2 framed award certificates, one for an individual & one for an institution
Presented: APHA Conference, Jan

The Amy Award
Poets & Writers Inc
90 Broad St, Suite 2100, New York, NY 10004
Tel: 212-226-3586 *Fax:* 212-226-3963
E-mail: admin@pw.org
Web Site: www.pw.org
Key Personnel
Exec Dir: Melissa Ford Gradel *Tel:* 212-226-3586 ext 223 *E-mail:* mgradel@pw.org
Presented to women poets age 30 & under living in the New York City metropolitan area or on Long Island.
Award: Honorarium & reading in New York City

Anhinga Prize for Poetry
Anhinga Press Inc
PO Box 3665, Tallahassee, FL 32315
E-mail: info@anhinga.org
Web Site: www.anhingapress.org
Key Personnel
Co-Dir: Carol Lynne Knight; Kristine Snodgrass *E-mail:* kristine.snodgrass@gmail.com
Established: 1983
Open to all poets for a ms of original poetry in English. Reading fee: $25 (by post), $28 (Submittable).
Award: $2,000 & publication
Closing Date: May 31
Presented: Tallahassee, FL

The Anisfield-Wolf Book Awards
The Cleveland Foundation
1422 Euclid Ave, Suite 1300, Cleveland, OH 44115
Tel: 216-861-3810 *Fax:* 216-861-1729
E-mail: awinfo@clevefdn.org
Web Site: www.anisfield-wolf.org; www.clevelandfoundation.org
Key Personnel
Pres & CEO, Cleveland Foundation: Ronald B Richard
Jury Chmn: Henry Louis Gates, Jr
Mgr: Karen R Long
Established: 1935
Recognizes books that have made important contributions to our understanding of racism or our appreciation of the diversity of human cultures.
Award: $10,000 each (fiction, nonfiction, poetry & Lifetime Achievement)
Closing Date: Dec 31
Presented: Playhouse Square, Cleveland, OH, Sept

R Ross Annett Award for Children's Literature
Writers' Guild of Alberta
11759 Groat Rd NW, Edmonton, AB T5M 3K6, Canada
Tel: 780-422-8174 *Toll Free Tel:* 800-665-5354 (AB only)
E-mail: mail@writersguild.ab.ca
Web Site: writersguild.ca
Key Personnel
Exec Dir: Giorgia Severini *E-mail:* gseverini@writersguild.ab.ca
Communs & Partnerships Coord: Ellen Kartz *E-mail:* ellen.kartz@writersguild.ab.ca
Memb Servs Coord: Mike Maguire
Prog & Opers Coord: Ashley Mann *E-mail:* ashley.mann@writersguild.ab.ca
Progs & Events Coord: Jason Norman *E-mail:* jason.norman@writersguild.ab.ca
Proj Asst: Sadie MacGillivray *E-mail:* sadie.macgillivray@writersguild.ab.ca
Established: 1982
Alternates yearly between picture & chapter books.
Award: $1,500
Closing Date: Dec 31
Presented: Alberta Book Awards Gala, AB, CN
Branch Office(s)
223 12 Ave SW, No 204, Calgary, AB T2R 0G9, Canada, Prog & Conference Coord: Dorothy Bentley *Tel:* 403-875-8058 *E-mail:* dorothy.bentley@writersguild.ab.ca

Annual & Rolling Grants for Artists
Vermont Arts Council
136 State St, Montpelier, VT 05633
Tel: 802-828-3291
E-mail: info@vermontartscouncil.org
Web Site: www.vermontartscouncil.org
Key Personnel
Artist Servs Mgr: Dominique Gustin *Tel:* 802-404-4602 *E-mail:* dgustin@vermontartscouncil.org
Established: 1965
Individual grants are given to Vermont residents. Artist Development Grants open in July & November. Creation Grants open in January.
Award: $250-$2,000 Artist Development Grant; $4,000 Creation Grants
Closing Date: Artist Development Grant: Sept & Feb
Presented: Award notifications for Artist Development Grants approximately 6 weeks from application deadline, Creation Grant notifications in Sept

The Arab American Book Awards
Arab American National Museum
13624 Michigan Ave, Dearborn, MI 48126
Tel: 313-429-2535 *Fax:* 313-582-1086
E-mail: librarian@accesscommunity.org
Web Site: arabamericanmuseum.org/book-awards
Key Personnel
Dir: Diana Abouali *E-mail:* dabouali@accesscommunity.org
Established: 2006
Honors outstanding books written by or about Arab Americans. Winners are chosen from 4 categories: Adult fiction, adult nonfiction (The Evelyn Shakir Nonfiction Award), poetry (The George Ellenbogen Poetry Award), children's/young adult literature. Book must be published in English with a copyright date during the preceding calendar year.
Closing Date: March 1
Presented: Autumn

AWARDS, PRIZE CONTESTS, FELLOWSHIPS & GRANTS

Arkansas Diamond Primary Book Award
Arkansas State Library
Arkansas State Library, Suite 100, 900 W Capitol Ave, Little Rock, AR 72201-3108
Tel: 501-682-2860
Web Site: www.library.arkansas.gov/programs/book-awards
Key Personnel
Lib Coord, Youth Servs: Ruth Hyatt *E-mail:* ruth.hyatt@arkansas.gov
Established: 1998
To encourage reading for students in grades K-3. The Arkansas Department of Education & the Arkansas State Library support selected books that students all over Arkansas read or have read to them. The students vote for the one book they most enjoyed & the winning title receives the award.
Other Sponsor(s): Arkansas Reading Association
Award: Medallion for 1st place, plaque for Honor Book
Closing Date: Voting takes place in May
Presented: Little Rock, AR

Art In Literature: The Mary Lynn Kotz Award
Library of Virginia
800 E Broad St, Richmond, VA 23219
Tel: 804-692-3535
Web Site: www.lva.virginia.gov/public/litawards/kotz.htm; lvafoundation.org/home/literaryawards/
Key Personnel
Exec Asst: Taylor Melton *E-mail:* taylor.melton@lva.virginia.gov
Established: 2013
Recognizes an outstanding book that is written primarily in response to a work (or works) of art while also showing the highest literary quality as a creative or scholarly work on its own merit. Works eligible for submission must be published for the first time in English in the US in the calendar year before the award is presented. New editions of previously published works are eligible for consideration if the new edition contains a substantial amount of new material. The topic of the book submitted must be the visual arts, excluding dramatic & performance arts, music, literature & interactive or computer art. Categories of acceptable work include: Fiction, journalism, poetry, history, biography, art history, social history of art, catalogs of qualified museum exhibitions & young adult books. Winner notified in August.
Other Sponsor(s): Virginia Museum of Fine Arts
Closing Date: March 15
Presented: Oct

Artist Fellowships
Rhode Island State Council on the Arts
Affiliate of Department of Rhode Island State Government
One Capital Hill, 3rd fl, Providence, RI 02908
Tel: 401-222-3880 *Fax:* 401-222-3018
Web Site: risca.online/grants/artist-fellowships
Key Personnel
Indiv Artists Progs Dir: Mollie Flanagan *E-mail:* mollie.flanagan@arts.ri.gov
Established: 1967
Awarded in each of 13 disciplines to encourage the creative development of artists by enabling them to set aside time to pursue their work & achieve specific creative & career goals. Applicants must be Rhode Island residents who are 18 years of age or older & not students in an arts discipline. Fellowship recipients are selected by a regional panel of writers. Guidelines & applications on web site.
Award: $5,000 recipient, $1,000 merit award
Closing Date: April & Oct

Artist Grants
South Dakota Arts Council
Affiliate of Department of Tourism
711 E Wells Ave, Pierre, SD 57501-3369
Tel: 605-773-3301 *Fax:* 605-773-5977
E-mail: sdac@state.sd.us
Web Site: www.artscouncil.sd.gov/grants
Key Personnel
Dir: Patrick Baker
Award presented to residents of South Dakota based on the quality of art work.
Award: $1,000-$5,000
Closing Date: March 1

Artist-in-Residence Program
New Brunswick Arts Board (Conseil des arts du Nouveau-Brunswick)
225 King St, Suite 201, Fredericton, NB E3B 1E1, Canada
Tel: 506-444-4444 *Toll Free Tel:* 866-460-ARTS (460-2787) *Fax:* 506-444-5543
E-mail: prog@artsnb.ca
Web Site: www.artsnb.ca
Key Personnel
Exec Dir: Joss Richer *Tel:* 506-478-4610 *E-mail:* direct@artsnb.ca
Prog Offr: Sarah Jonathan Parker *Tel:* 506-440-0037
Opers Mgr: Tilly Jackson *Tel:* 506-478-4422 *E-mail:* tjackson@artsnb.ca
Intended for New Brunswick public or private institutions & organizations that wish to host professional artists in order to enable them to pursue specific projects relating to their creative work. This program is also open to individual professionals who seek to advance their creative work through participation in residency opportunities at home or outside the province. The artists in residence are to contribute to the promotion & understanding of the arts by means of the artists' contact with the clientele of the establishments. Eligible artistic disciplines include the literary arts (spoken word, storytelling, literary performance & literary translation).
Award: Individuals & nonprofit organizations: 100% funding - $5,000 (up to 6 months), $10,000 (6-12 months); Institutions & for-profit organizations: 50% funding - $5,000 (up to 6 months), $10,000 (6-12 months)
Closing Date: Feb 1

Artist Research & Development Grants
Arizona Commission on the Arts
417 W Roosevelt St, Phoenix, AZ 85003-1326
Tel: 602-771-6501 *Fax:* 602-256-0282
E-mail: info@azarts.gov
Web Site: azarts.gov/grant/artist-research-and-development
Key Personnel
Artist Progs Mgr: Kesha Bruce *Tel:* 602-771-6530 *E-mail:* kbruce@azarts.gov
Designed to support individual artists from all disciplines. The purpose of this grant is to aid in the development of artistic work, support the advancement of artistic research & recognize the contributions individual artists make to Arizona's communities.
The Bill Desmond Writing Award provides support to excelling nonfiction writers for specific project-related costs. This award offers funding support in the amount of $1,000 to one nonfiction writer applying for the R&D grant & can be offered independent of, or in addition to, the R&D award. Funding for the Bill Desmond Writing Award is generously provided by the Bill & Kathy Desmond Endowment.
Award: $3,000-$5,000
Closing Date: Oct
Presented: April

Arts & Letters Awards in Literature
American Academy of Arts & Letters
633 W 155 St, New York, NY 10032
Tel: 212-368-5900
E-mail: academy@artsandletters.org
Web Site: artsandletters.org/awards
Key Personnel
Exec Dir: Cody Upton
Established: 1941
Given to fiction & nonfiction writers, poets, dramatists & translators. Candidates must be nominated by an Academy member.
Award: $10,000 each (8 awards to writers)

Arts Scholarships
New Brunswick Arts Board (Conseil des arts du Nouveau-Brunswick)
225 King St, Suite 201, Fredericton, NB E3B 1E1, Canada
Tel: 506-444-4444 *Toll Free Tel:* 866-460-ARTS (460-2787) *Fax:* 506-444-5543
E-mail: prog@artsnb.ca
Web Site: www.artsnb.ca
Key Personnel
Exec Dir: Joss Richer *Tel:* 506-478-4610 *E-mail:* direct@artsnb.ca
Prog Offr: Sarah Jonathan Parker *Tel:* 506-440-0037
Opers Mgr: Tilly Jackson *Tel:* 506-478-4422 *E-mail:* tjackson@artsnb.ca
Designed to recognize & encourage New Brunswick students who have demonstrated exceptional artistic talent & potential & who are pursuing a career in the arts. This program awards scholarships for full-time, part-time or short-term studies. Eligible artistic disciplines include the literary arts (spoken word, storytelling, literary performance & literary translation).
Award: Up to $2,500 (full-time studies) or $1,000 (part-time/short-term studies)
Closing Date: Feb 1

ASF Translation Awards
American-Scandinavian Foundation (ASF)
Scandinavia House, 58 Park Ave, New York, NY 10016
Tel: 212-779-3587
E-mail: grants@amscan.org
Web Site: www.amscan.org
Key Personnel
Prog Assoc: Monica Hidalgo
Established: 1980
Awards 3 prizes for outstanding translations of poetry, fiction, drama or literary prose written by a Nordic author born after 1900. See web site to review guidelines & begin an application.
Award: $2,500 Nadia Christensen Prize (for the best entry), $2,000 Leif & Inger Sjoberg Prize (given to an individual whose translations have not been previously published), $2,000 Wigeland Prize (for the best translation by a Norwegian). All prizes include publication of an excerpt in *Scandinavian Review* & a commemorative bronze medallion
Closing Date: Sept 1
Presented: Varies

ASI Excellence in Indexing Award
American Society for Indexing Inc (ASI)
1628 E Southern Ave, Suite 9-223, Tempe, AZ 85282
Tel: 480-245-6750
E-mail: info@asindexing.org
Web Site: www.asindexing.org/about/awards/asi-indexing-award
Key Personnel
Exec Dir: Gwen Henson *E-mail:* gwen@asindexing.org
Award Comm Chair: Connie Binder *E-mail:* connie@conniebinder.com
Established: 1978
Awarded to the indexer & the publisher of year's best index.

Award: $1,000 & certificate (indexer), certificate (publisher)
Closing Date: Feb
Presented: Annual Conference

Asian/Pacific American Award for Literature
Asian/Pacific American Librarians Association
Affiliate of The American Library Association (ALA)
PO Box 677593, Orlando, FL 32867-7593
Web Site: www.apalaweb.org/awards/literature-awards
Key Personnel
Exec Dir: Buenaventura "Ven" Basco
Awarded to honor & recognize individual work about Asian/Pacific Americans & their heritage, based on literary & artistic merit. Five award categories: Adult fiction, adult nonfiction, children's literature, young adult literature, picture books. See web site for specific guidelines & nomination form.
Award: Plaque & press release to various national publications
Closing Date: Sept 30
Presented: ALA Annual Conference & Exhibition, June

ASLE Book Awards
Association for the Study of Literature and Environment (ASLE)
PO Box 502, Keene, NH 03431-0502
Tel: 603-357-7411 *Fax:* 603-357-7411
E-mail: info@asle.org
Web Site: www.asle.org/research-write/asle-book-paper-awards
Key Personnel
Mng Dir: Amy McIntyre
Ecocriticism Book Award Coord: Nicole Seymour *E-mail:* nseymour@fullerton.edu
Environmental Creative Writing Book Award Coord: Laura-Gray Street *E-mail:* lstreet@randolphcollege.edu
Established: 2007
Presented in 2 categories: Best book-length work of scholarly ecocriticism; Best book-length work of creative writing (any genre) with an environmental theme. Works must be in English. Nominees must be current members of ASLE or an international affiliate as of January of the award year. Three copies of the nominated book should be sent to the appropriate Award Coordinator (see web site for addresses).
Award: $500 each
Closing Date: Jan of the year awards are presented
Presented: ASLE Biennial Conference, July, odd-numbered years

ASLE Graduate Student Paper Awards
Association for the Study of Literature and Environment (ASLE)
PO Box 502, Keene, NH 03431-0502
Tel: 603-357-7411 *Fax:* 603-357-7411
Web Site: www.asle.org/research-write/asle-book-paper-awards
Key Personnel
Mng Dir: Amy McIntyre
Award Coord: Sylvan Goldberg *E-mail:* aslegradawards@gmail.com
Papers can be in any aspect of the environmental humanities or any genre of environmental creative writing by a graduate student presenting at the conference. Student must be a member of ASLE or an international affiliate & should be or have been enrolled as a graduate student at some time within 7 months of the conference dates.
Award: $100 & publication in *ISLE: Interdisciplinary Studies in Literature and Environment*; up to 2 honorable mention recipients receive $100
Closing Date: June of the year awards are presented
Presented: ASLE Biennial Conference, July, odd-numbered years

ASME Award for Fiction
American Society of Magazine Editors (ASME)
23 Barnabas Rd, Suite 34, Hawleyville, CT 06440-0034
Tel: 212-872-3737
E-mail: asme@asme.media
Web Site: www.asme.media
Key Personnel
Exec Dir: Sidney Holt *Tel:* 212-872-3723 *E-mail:* sholt@asme.media
Dir, Opers: Nina Fortuna *E-mail:* nfortuna@asme.media
Established: 1966
Award honors print magazines & magazine web sites for overall excellence in fiction. An entry consists of 3 examples of short fiction written by one or more authors, published together or separately. Any consumer magazine or literary publication edited & distributed in print or online in the US is eligible for entry. Publications may submit only 1 entry. Entries may be submitted as print or digital content or as a combination of print & digital content. Content must be dated the year prior to the award, except that one story may be dated January of the award year. Entries must be submitted online at ellieawards.org. Entry fee: $40.
Other Sponsor(s): Columbia University Graduate School of Journalism
Award: Winner receives medal; finalists receive certificates of recognition
Closing Date: Nov 29
Presented: Ellie Awards, March

Aspen Words Literary Prize
Aspen Words
110 E Hallam St, Suite 116, Aspen, CO 81611
Tel: 970-925-3122 *Fax:* 970-920-5700
E-mail: literary.prize@aspeninstitute.org
Web Site: www.aspenwords.org/programs/literary-prize/; www.aspenwords.org
Key Personnel
Exec Dir: Adrienne Brodeur *Tel:* 646-263-6800 *E-mail:* adrienne.brodeur@aspeninstitute.org
Mng Dir: Caroline Tory *Tel:* 970-925-3122 ext 3 *E-mail:* caroline.tory@aspeninstitute.org
Prog Coord: Ellie Scott *Tel:* 970-925-3122 ext 5 *E-mail:* ellie.scott@aspeninstitute.org
Established: 2017
Awarded for an influential work of fiction that focuses on vital issues - social, political, economic, environmental or otherwise - thus demonstrating the transformative power that literature has on thought & culture. Submissions accepted from publishers only. Book must be work of fiction published by a US trade publisher in the prior calendar year. Submission process opens February 1. Entry fee: $65 for each title submitted; submission fees are waived for small presses. See web site for online submission form & full details.
Award: $35,000
Closing Date: Aug
Presented: Spring

Astounding Award for Best New Writer
The World Science Fiction Society
PO Box 61363, Sunnyvale, CA 94088
Web Site: astoundingaward.info; www.wsfs.org/awards
Established: 1973
Awarded to the best new science fiction or fantasy writer whose first work of science fiction or fantasy was published in a professional publication in the previous 2 calendar years.
Other Sponsor(s): Dell Magazines
Award: Plaque
Closing Date: March
Presented: Hugo Award Ceremony, Worldcon

Astra International Picture Book Writing Contest
Astra Publishing House Inc
19 W 21 St, No 1201, New York, NY 10010
E-mail: astrawritingcontest@readinglife.com
Web Site: www.readinglife.com/writingcontest
Key Personnel
Jury Pres: Leonard S Marcus
Open to writers for children, both published & unpublished. Ms must be text written for children ages 3-8, may be fiction, nonfiction or poetry & must be no longer than 1,000 words. See web site for full submission criteria.
Other Sponsor(s): minedition AG; minedition France; Thinkingdom Media Group Ltd
Award: $10,000 (Gold prize), $5,000 (Silver prize), $1,000 finalist
Closing Date: April 30
Presented: Oct/Nov

The Athenaeum Literary Award
The Athenaeum of Philadelphia
219 S Sixth St, Philadelphia, PA 19106-3794
Tel: 215-925-2688
Web Site: www.philaathenaeum.org/literary.html
Key Personnel
Exec Dir: Beth Hessel, PhD *E-mail:* bhessel@philaathenaeum.org
Libn: Jill LeMin Lee *E-mail:* jilly@philaathenaeum.org
Established: 1950
Awarded in recognition & encouragement of outstanding literary achievement among authors who are residents of Philadelphia or Pennsylvania living within a radius of 30 miles of City Hall.
Award: Citation
Closing Date: Dec 1
Presented: Spring

Atwood Gibson Writers' Trust Fiction Prize
The Writers' Trust of Canada
600-460 Richmond St W, Toronto, ON M5V 1Y1, Canada
Tel: 416-504-8222 *Toll Free Tel:* 877-906-6548 *Fax:* 416-504-9090
E-mail: info@writerstrust.com
Web Site: www.writerstrust.com
Key Personnel
Exec Dir: Charlie Foran *Tel:* 416-504-8222 ext 244 *E-mail:* cforan@writerstrust.com
Mgr, Author Progs: Devon Jackson *Tel:* 416-504-8222 ext 248 *E-mail:* djackson@writerstrust.com
Established: 1997
Awarded to the year's best novel or collection of short stories.
Other Sponsor(s): Jim Balsillie
Award: $60,000 (winner), $5,000 (finalists)
Presented: The Writers' Trust Awards, Toronto, ON, CN, Nov

Claude Aubry Award
IBBY Canada
Unit of International Board on Books for Young People (IBBY)
c/o The Canadian Children's Book Ctr, 425 Adelaide St W, Suite 200, Toronto, ON M5V 3C1, Canada
Fax: 416-975-8970
E-mail: aubry@ibby-canada.org
Web Site: www.ibby-canada.org/awards/claude-aubry-award/
Key Personnel
Award Co-Chair: Susane Duchesne; Catherine Mitchell
Established: 1981
Two awards presented biennially, in even-numbered years, from nominations of individ-

AWARDS, PRIZE CONTESTS, FELLOWSHIPS & GRANTS

uals who have made a significant contribution to Canadian children's literature in English & French.

The Audies®
Audio Publishers Association (APA)
333 Hudson St, Suite 503, New York, NY 10013
E-mail: audies@audiopub.org
Web Site: www.audiopub.org/members/audies
Key Personnel
Exec Dir: Michele Cobb *E-mail:* mcobb@audiopub.org
Established: 1996
Premier awards program in the US recognizing distinction in audiobooks & spoken word entertainment. Publishers & rights holders enter titles in various categories for recognition of achievement. Finalists are selected & announced in February. From that group of finalists, one winner is awarded. Qualifying audiobooks contain at least 51% spoken word content & are available for sale in the US as CDs +/or in digital format. Entry fee: $110 membs, $210 nonmembs.
Award: Medallions
Closing Date: Oct 15
Presented: Audies Awards Gala, March

AUPresses Book, Jacket & Journal Show
Association of University Presses (AUPresses)
1412 Broadway, Suite 2135, New York, NY 10018
Tel: 212-989-1010 *Fax:* 212-989-0275
E-mail: info@aupresses.org
Web Site: www.aupresses.org
Key Personnel
Exec Dir: Peter Berkery *Tel:* 917-288-5594
 E-mail: pberkery@aupresses.org
Dir, Opers: Kim Miller *Tel:* 917-244-1264
 E-mail: kmiller@aupresses.org
Membership & Prog Communs Mgr: Kate Kolendo *Tel:* 917-244-3859 *E-mail:* kkolendo@aupresses.org
Established: 1965
Juried design competition, open only to AUPresses publishers. Recognizes meritorious achievement in design, production & manufacture of books, jackets, covers & journals. Entry fee: $45 per book/journal, $35 per jacket/cover.
Award: Certificate, winning entries are displayed in a traveling exhibit
Closing Date: Jan
Presented: AUPresses Annual Meeting, June

Autumn House Poetry, Fiction & Nonfiction Prizes
Autumn House Press
5530 Penn Ave, Pittsburgh, PA 15206
Mailing Address: PO Box 5486, Pittsburgh, PA 15206
Tel: 412-362-2665
E-mail: info@autumnhouse.org
Web Site: www.autumnhouse.org; autumnhousepress.submittable.com/submit
Key Personnel
Ed-in-Chief: Christine Stroud *E-mail:* cstroud@autumnhouse.org
Poetry Prize: All full-length collections of poetry 50-80 pages in length are eligible.
Fiction Prize: Submissions should be approximately 200-300 double-spaced pages (50,000-75,000 words). All fiction sub-genres (short stories, short-shorts, novellas, or novels) or any combination of sub-genres are eligible.
Nonfiction Prize: Submissions should be approximately 200-300 double-spaced pages (50,000-75,000 words). All nonfiction subjects (including personal essays, memoirs, travel writing, historical narratives, nature writing) or any combination of subjects are eligible.
There is a $30 reading fee for each prize. Mss are only accepted through Submittable. Please do not mail or e-mail submissions. See web site for complete guidelines.
Award: $1,000 honorarium, book publication & $1,500 travel grant
Closing Date: June 15

Award for Excellence in Poetry for Children
National Council of Teachers of English (NCTE)
340 N Neil St, Suite 104, Champaign, IL 61820
Tel: 217-328-3870 *Toll Free Tel:* 877-369-6283 (cust serv) *Fax:* 217-328-9645
Web Site: ncte.org/awards/ncte-childrens-book-awards
Key Personnel
Prog Coord: Sarah Miller
Established: 1977
Awarded biennially, in odd-numbered years, to honor a living American poet for their aggregate work for children ages 3-13. Members of the NCTE Children's Poetry Awards Committee determine the award recipient every other year & select notable poetry books each year.
Award: Plaque, featured speaker at luncheon & invitation to present at poetry session during annual convention
Presented: Children's Book Awards Luncheon, NCTE Annual Convention

Award of Merit Medal
American Academy of Arts & Letters
633 W 155 St, New York, NY 10032
Tel: 212-368-5900
E-mail: academy@artsandletters.org
Web Site: artsandletters.org/awards
Key Personnel
Exec Dir: Cody Upton
Established: 1942
Given, in rotation, to an outstanding person in America representing one of the following arts: Painting, the short story, sculpture, the novel, poetry & drama. Candidates must be nominated by an Academy member.
Award: $25,000 & medal

AWP Award Series
Association of Writers & Writing Programs (AWP)
440 Monticello Ave, Suite 1802, PMB 73708, Norfolk, VA 23510-2670
Tel: 240-696-7700
E-mail: awp@awpwriter.org; press@awpwriter.org
Web Site: www.awpwriter.org
Key Personnel
Dir, Conferences: Colleen Cable
Dir, Pubns: Supriya Bhatnagar
Assoc Ed: Jason Gray
Established: 1967
An open competition for book-length mss in 4 categories: poetry, short fiction, novel & creative (nonfiction). Online submissions only.
Award: Publication by a major university press & an honorarium of $2,500 for nonfiction & novel. Donald Hall Prize in poetry-honorarium $5,500. Grace Paley Prize for short fiction-honorarium $5,500. One winner in each category
Closing Date: Feb 28

Axiom Business Book Awards
Independent Publisher Online
Division of Jenkins Group Inc
1129 Woodmere Ave, Suite B, Traverse City, MI 49686
Tel: 231-933-0445 *Toll Free Tel:* 800-706-4636 *Fax:* 231-933-0448
E-mail: info@axiomawards.com
Web Site: www.axiomawards.com
Key Personnel
Awards Dir: Amy Shamroe *Tel:* 800-644-0133 ext 1000 *E-mail:* amys@jenkinsgroupinc.com
Established: 2007

ASSOCIATIONS, EVENTS

US based annual award contest focused solely on business books. The goal of the awards is to celebrate the innovative, intelligent & creative aspects of the books that make us think, see & work differently every day. The awards offer no global boundaries, giving participants from every continent the opportunity to earn further recognition for their English language titles. All publishers are eligible, ranging from large multi-title publishing houses to small one title publishers. Publishers can be throughout North America & overseas publishers who publish English language books intended for the American market. Print-on-demand & other independent authors are welcome to enter their books themselves. Entry fee: $75-$95 per category.
Other Sponsor(s): Books Are Marketing Tools; Jenkins Group Inc
Award: Gold medal (1st place), silver medal (2nd place) & bronze medal (3rd place)
Closing Date: Jan
Presented: May

Marilyn Baillie Picture Book Award
The Canadian Children's Book Centre
425 Adelaide St W, Suite 200, Toronto, ON M5V 3C1, Canada
Tel: 416-975-0010
E-mail: info@bookcentre.ca
Web Site: www.bookcentre.ca
Key Personnel
Exec Dir: Sarah Sahagian
Lib Coord: Meghan Howe *E-mail:* meghan@bookcentre.ca
Established: 2006
Awarded to a Canadian author & illustrator for excellence in the illustrated picture book format for children ages 3-8.
Other Sponsor(s): Charles Baillie
Award: $20,000 cash
Closing Date: Mid-Dec

Nona Balakian Citation for Excellence in Reviewing
National Book Critics Circle (NBCC)
c/o Jacob M Appel, Icahn School of Medicine at Mount Sinai, One Gustave L Levy Place, New York, NY 10029
E-mail: info@bookcritics.org
Web Site: www.bookcritics.org/awards/balakian/
Key Personnel
Pres: Heather Scott Partington *E-mail:* hsp@bookcritics.org
Secy: Colette Bancroft *E-mail:* bancroft.colette72@gmail.com
Treas: Jacob M Appel *E-mail:* jacobmappel@gmail.com
VP, Awards: Keetje Kuipers *E-mail:* keetje@poetrynw.org
VP, Events: Jane Ciabattari *E-mail:* janeciab@gmail.com
Awarded to recognize outstanding work by a member of NBCC. All submitted reviews must have been published between December 1 of the year prior & November 30 of the award year. Send up to 5 book reviews of no more than 5,000 words collectively. Note the venue, title & word count of each piece submitted. See web site for full details & Submittable link.
Other Sponsor(s): Gregg Barrios
Award: $1,000
Closing Date: Dec 7
Presented: NBCC Awards Ceremony, March

The Balcones Fiction Prize
The Balcones Center for Creative Writing
Subsidiary of Austin Community College
Dept of Creative Writing, 6101 Highland Campus Dr, Austin, TX 78752
Tel: 512-223-7196; 512-223-3255
E-mail: balcones@austincc.edu

Web Site: sites.austincc.edu/crw/balcones-prizes
Established: 2009
Recognizes an outstanding book of fiction published during the previous calendar year. Books of prose may be submitted by author or publisher. Send 3 copies (see web site for mailing address).
Reading fee: $30.
Award: $1,500
Closing Date: Jan 31

The Balcones Poetry Prize
The Balcones Center for Creative Writing
Subsidiary of Austin Community College
Dept of Creative Writing, 6101 Highland Campus Dr, Austin, TX 78752
Tel: 512-223-7196; 512-223-3255
E-mail: balcones@austincc.edu
Web Site: sites.austincc.edu/crw/balcones-prizes
Established: 1994
Recognizes an outstanding book of poetry published during the previous calendar year. Books of poetry of 42 pages or more may be submitted by author or publisher. Send 3 copies (see web site for mailing address).
Reading fee: $25.
Award: $1,500
Closing Date: Jan 31

Ballard Spahr Prize for Poetry
Milkweed Editions
1011 Washington Ave S, Suite 300, Minneapolis, MN 55415-1246
Tel: 612-332-3192 *Toll Free Tel:* 800-520-6455
Web Site: milkweed.org/ballard-spahr-prize-for-poetry
Key Personnel
Assoc Ed: Bailey Hutchinson
 E-mail: bailey_hutchinson@milkweed.org
Established: 2011
Regional prize to support outstanding poets & bring their work to a national stage. Submissions accepted from poets currently residing in Minnesota, Iowa, North Dakota, South Dakota, Wisconsin or Michigan. No entry fee. Submissions open January 1.
Other Sponsor(s): Ballard Spahr Foundation
Award: $10,000 & publication contract
Closing Date: Feb 15
Presented: April

Balsillie Prize for Public Policy
The Writers' Trust of Canada
600-460 Richmond St W, Toronto, ON M5V 1Y1, Canada
Tel: 416-504-8222 *Toll Free Tel:* 877-906-6548
 Fax: 416-504-9090
E-mail: info@writerstrust.com
Web Site: www.writerstrust.com
Key Personnel
Exec Dir: Charlie Foran *Tel:* 416-504-8222 ext 244 *E-mail:* cforan@writerstrust.com
Mgr, Author Progs: Devon Jackson *Tel:* 416-504-8222 ext 248 *E-mail:* djackson@writerstrust.com
Established: 2021
Awarded for a book of nonfiction that advances & influences policy debates.
Other Sponsor(s): Jim Balsillie
Award: $60,000 (winner); $5,000 (finalists)
Presented: Nov

Bancroft Prizes
Columbia University
517 Butler Library, Mail Code 1101, 535 W 114 St, New York, NY 10027
Tel: 212-854-3051
E-mail: bancroft-prize@library.columbia.edu
Web Site: library.columbia.edu/about/awards/bancroft.html
Key Personnel
Asst to Vice Provost & Univ Libn: Anne Mesquita
Established: 1948
Two awards presented for distinguished books in the fields of American history (including biography) & diplomacy. Award confined to books originally published in English or those with a published English translation. Books published in the year preceding that in which the award is made are eligible. Submit 4 hard copies, 1 PDF copy & nominating letter.
Award: $10,000 each
Closing Date: Nov 1, page-proof copy may be submitted after Nov 1, provided the work will be published after that date & before Dec 31
Presented: Columbia University, New York, NY, Spring

Barbey Freedom to Write Award, see PEN/Barbey Freedom to Write Award

Bard Fiction Prize
Bard College
Campus Rd, PO Box 5000, Annandale-on-Hudson, NY 12504-5000
Tel: 845-758-7087
E-mail: bfp@bard.edu
Web Site: www.bard.edu/bfp
Established: 2001
Awarded to a promising emerging writer who is an American citizen age 39 years or younger at time of application. To apply, candidates should write a cover letter explaining the project they plan to work on while at Bard & submit CV along with 3 copies of the published book they feel best represents their work. No mss accepted.
Award: $30,000 & writer-in-residence at Bard College for 1 semester
Closing Date: June 15
Presented: Oct

Barnes & Noble Writers for Writers Award
Poets & Writers Inc
90 Broad St, Suite 2100, New York, NY 10004
Tel: 212-226-3586 *Fax:* 212-226-3963
E-mail: admin@pw.org
Web Site: www.pw.org
Key Personnel
Exec Dir: Melissa Ford Gradel *Tel:* 212-226-3586 ext 223 *E-mail:* mgradel@pw.org
Established: 1996
Celebrates authors who have given generously to other writers or to the broader literary community.

Gregg Barrios Book in Translation Prize
National Book Critics Circle (NBCC)
c/o Jacob M Appel, Icahn School of Medicine at Mount Sinai, One Gustave L Levy Place, New York, NY 10029
E-mail: info@bookcritics.org
Web Site: www.bookcritics.org/gregg-barrios-book-in-translation-prize/
Key Personnel
Pres: Heather Scott Partington *E-mail:* hsp@bookcritics.org
Secy: Colette Bancroft *E-mail:* bancroft.colette72@gmail.com
Treas: Jacob M Appel *E-mail:* jacobmappel@gmail.com
VP, Awards: Keetje Kuipers *E-mail:* keetje@poetrynw.org
VP, Barrios Prize: Mandana Chaffa
 E-mail: mandanachaffa@bookcritics.org
VP, Events: Jane Ciabattari *E-mail:* janeciab@gmail.com
Established: 2022
Honors the best book of any genre translated into English & published in the US. The prize recognizes books for their excellence & artistry & is open to translations of books authored by living or deceased writers. New translations of previously translated books are also considered.
Presented: NBCC Awards Ceremony, March

Baskerville Publishers Poetry Award
Texas Christian University
Dept of English, TCU Box 297270, Fort Worth, TX 76129
E-mail: descant@tcu.edu
Web Site: www.descant.tcu.edu
Established: 2003
Awarded for an outstanding poem or poems by a single author in an issue. All published submissions are eligible for prize consideration. There is no application process.
Other Sponsor(s): descant (publication), Dept of English, TCU
Award: $250
Presented: Winner announced in the Summer in *descant*

The Mildred L Batchelder Award
Association for Library Service to Children (ALSC)
Division of The American Library Association (ALA)
225 N Michigan Ave, Suite 1300, Chicago, IL 60601
Tel: 312-280-2163 *Toll Free Tel:* 800-545-2433
Fax: 312-280-5271
E-mail: alsc@ala.org
Web Site: www.ala.org/alsc/awardsgrants/bookmedia/batchelder
Key Personnel
Exec Dir: Alena Rivers *Tel:* 800-545-2433 ext 5866 *E-mail:* arivers@ala.org
Awards Coord: Jordan Dubin *Tel:* 800-545-2433 ext 5839 *E-mail:* jdubin@ala.org
Prog Coord: Ann Michaud *Tel:* 800-545-2433 ext 2166 *E-mail:* amichaud@ala.org
Membership/Mktg Specialist: Elizabeth Serrano *Tel:* 800-545-2433 ext 2164 *E-mail:* eserrano@ala.org
Established: 1966
Awarded to a US publisher for an outstanding children's book originally published in a foreign language in a foreign country & subsequently translated to English & published in the US during the previous year.
Award: Citation & plaque
Closing Date: Dec 31
Presented: ALA Youth Media Awards, Late Jan

The BC & Yukon Book Prizes
West Coast Book Prize Society
201-145 Keefer St, Vancouver, BC V6B 1H7, Canada
E-mail: info@bcyukonbookprizes.com
Web Site: www.bcyukonbookprizes.com
Key Personnel
Exec Dir: Sharon Bradley
Established: 1985
Prizes are awarded to a resident of BC/Yukon or one who has lived in BC/Yukon for 3 of the past 5 years: to the author of the best work of fiction; best book written for children 16 years & younger; best original nonfiction literary work; author of the best work of poetry; best book judged in terms of public appeal, initiative, design, production & content; author & illustrator of the best picture book written for children; best book that challenges or provokes the ideas & forces that shape what writing, art +/or society can become; author of the book which contributes most to the appreciation & understanding of BC (published anywhere & the author may reside outside BC).
Award: $3,000 & certificate

AWARDS, PRIZE CONTESTS, FELLOWSHIPS & GRANTS

Closing Date: Dec 1, with exceptions made for books published in Dec
Presented: The British Columbia Book Prizes Banquet, Shortlist announced in Spring, winners announced in Fall

BCHF Historial Writing Competition
British Columbia Historical Federation
PO Box 448, Fort Langley, BC V1M 2R7, Canada
E-mail: info@bchistory.ca
Web Site: www.bchistory.ca/awards/historical-writing
Key Personnel
Chair: Maurice Guibord Tel: 604-771-3047
  E-mail: maurice@bchistory.ca
Top prize is presented to the author whose book makes the most significant contribution to the historical literature of British Columbia. The book must be published within the competition year. Additional prizes also given.
Award: $2,500 & The BC Lieutenant-Governor's Medal for Historical Writing (1st place), $1,500 (2nd place), $500 (3rd place), Certificates of Honourable Mention, $500 Community History Award
Closing Date: Dec 31
Presented: BCHF Annual Conference Awards Banquet, May/June

James Beard Foundation Book Awards
James Beard Foundation
167 W 12 St, New York, NY 10011
Tel: 212-627-2308
E-mail: awards@jamesbeard.org
Web Site: www.jamesbeard.org/awards
Key Personnel
VP, Awards: Dawn Padmore
Awards Dir: Moira Sedgwick
Assoc Dir, Awards Opers: Kate Dobday
Awards Mgr: Katrina Leung
Established: 1991
Awards for cookbooks & other nonfiction food- or beverage-related books that were published in the US in the previous calendar year.
Award: Medallion (inscribed with award category) & certificate

George Louis Beer Prize, see AHA Prize in European International History

Hannah Beiter Graduate Student Research Grants
Children's Literature Association (ChLA)
140B Purcellville Gateway Dr, Suite 1200, Purcellville, VA 20132
Tel: 630-571-4520
E-mail: info@childlitassn.org
Web Site: www.childlitassn.org
Key Personnel
Association Mgr: Cate Langley
Awarded for proposals of original scholarship with the expectation that the undertaking will lead to publication or a conference presentation & contribute to the field of children's literature criticism. Winners must either be members of the Children's Literature Association or join the association before they receive any funds. Proposals should be submitted electronically as an attachment. Applications & supporting materials should be written in or translated into English.
Award: $500-$1,500 per award; $5,000 combined maximum fund per year
Closing Date: Feb 1
Presented: ChLA Annual Conference, June

The Pura Belpre Award
Association for Library Service to Children (ALSC)
Division of The American Library Association (ALA)
225 N Michigan Ave, Suite 1300, Chicago, IL 60601
Tel: 312-280-2163 Toll Free Tel: 800-545-2433
  Fax: 312-280-5271
E-mail: alsc@ala.org
Web Site: www.ala.org/alsc/awardsgrants/bookmedia/belpre
Key Personnel
Exec Dir: Alena Rivers Tel: 800-545-2433 ext 5866 E-mail: arivers@ala.org
Awards Coord: Jordan Dubin Tel: 800-545-2433 ext 5839 E-mail: jdubin@ala.org
Prog Coord: Ann Michaud Tel: 800-545-2433 ext 2166 E-mail: amichaud@ala.org
Membership/Mktg Specialist: Elizabeth Serrano Tel: 800-545-2433 ext 2164 E-mail: eserrano@ala.org
Established: 1996
Presented to a Latino/Latina writer & illustrator whose work best portrays, affirms & celebrates the Latino cultural experience in an outstanding work of literature for children & youth.
Other Sponsor(s): National Association to Promote Library & Information Services to Latinos & the Spanish Speaking (REFORMA); Young Adult Library Services Association (YALSA)
Award: Medal
Closing Date: Dec 31
Presented: ALA Youth Media Awards, Late Jan

Don Belton Fiction Reading Period
Indiana Review
Indiana University English Dept, Ballantine Hall 554, 1020 E Kirkwood Ave, Bloomington, IN 47405
Tel: 812-855-3439
E-mail: inreview@indiana.edu
Web Site: indianareview.org
Key Personnel
Ed-in-Chief: Shreya Fadia
Assoc Ed: Bernardo Wade
Fiction mss of up to 80,000 words. Submissions accepted beginning May 1. Reading fee: $25 (includes 1-year subscription to *Indiana Review*). See web site for full submission guidelines.
Award: $1,000 against future royalties & standard publication contract with Indiana University Press
Closing Date: June 30

Benjamin Franklin Awards™, see IBPA Book Awards

George Bennett Fellowship
Phillips Exeter Academy
Phillips Exeter Academy, Off of the Dean of Faculty, 20 Main St, Exeter, NH 03833-2460
Tel: 603-777-3714
E-mail: lhearon@exeter.edu
Web Site: www.exeter.edu/about-us/career-opportunities/fellowships/george-bennett-fellowship
Established: 1968
Established to provide support for one academic year for an individual contemplating or pursuing a career as a professional writer. Selection is based on the literary promise of the ms submitted. The committee favors applicants who have not yet published a book-length work with a major publisher. See web site for online application. Application fee: $15. Applications accepted beginning September 1.
Award: $15,570, housing & meals at the Academy for the academic year, medical/dental insurance & long-term disability
Closing Date: Sept 30

ASSOCIATIONS, EVENTS

Jessie Bernard Award
American Sociological Association (ASA)
c/o Governance Off, 1430 "K" St NW, Suite 600, Washington, DC 20005
Tel: 202-383-9005
E-mail: asa@asanet.org; nominations@asanet.org
Web Site: www.asanet.org/about/awards
Key Personnel
Dir, Governance & Admin: Mark Fernando
  Tel: 202-247-9866 E-mail: mfernando@asanet.org
For scholarly contributions that enlarge the horizons of sociology to encompass fully the role of women in society. Winner announced in *Footnotes* newsletter, an ASA publication. See web site for future awards.
Award: Plaque
Closing Date: Jan 1
Presented: ASA Annual Meeting, Montreal, QC, CN, Aug

The Charles Bernheimer Prize
American Comparative Literature Association (ACLA)
323 E Wacker Dr, No 642, Chicago, IL 60601
Tel: 312-600-8072
E-mail: info@acla.org
Web Site: www.acla.org/prize-awards/charles-bernheimer-prize
An outstanding dissertation in comparative literature defended in the year prior to July 1. See web site for nomination requirements.
Award: $1,000 & a certificate, complimentary registration, airfare & hotel accommodations (not including food), to facilitate the recipient attending the ACLA annual meeting
Closing Date: Nov 1
Presented: ACLA Annual Meeting

The Betty Berzon Emerging Writer Award
The Publishing Triangle
511 Avenue of the Americas, No D36, New York, NY 10011
E-mail: awards@publishingtriangle.org; info@publishingtriangle.org; publishingtriangle@gmail.com
Web Site: publishingtriangle.org/awards/betty-berzon-award
Established: 2017
Presented to an LGBTQ+ writer who has shown exceptional talent & the potential for continued literary success & significance in the future. Applicants must have published at least 1 but no more than 2 books, written in the discipline of fiction, nonfiction or poetry. Works must be in the English language. Applicants must identify as a member of the LGBTQ+ community. See web site for information & application.
Other Sponsor(s): Teresa DeCrescenzo
Award: $1,500

Best in Business Book Award
Society for Advancing Business Editing and Writing (SABEW)
Walter Cronkite School of Journalism & Mass Communication, Arizona State University, 555 N Central Ave, Suite 406E, Phoenix, AZ 85004-1248
Mailing Address: PO Box 4, Fountainville, PA 18923
Tel: 602-496-7862
E-mail: sabew@sabew.org
Web Site: sabew.org/best-in-business-book-awards
Key Personnel
Membership Coord: Tess McLaughlin
  E-mail: tmclaughlin@sabew.org
Recognizes the best business book published in each of 2 categories: Business reporting & investing/personal finance. Books must be published between August 1 of the previous year & July 31 of the award year. Entrants should upload book excerpts with 5,000 words or less.

If your book is selected for the final round of judging, you will need to send 14 hard copies or electronic mss to the judging committee. Entry fee: $100. See web site for full eligibility & submission requirements.
Other Sponsor(s): Investopedia

The Best Spiritual Literature Awards
Orison Books
PO Box 8385, Asheville, NC 28814
Tel: 828-713-1755
E-mail: editor@orisonbooks.com
Web Site: www.orisonbooks.com/submissions
Key Personnel
Founder & Ed: Luke Hankins
For unpublished single works in 3 genres: Fiction, nonfiction & poetry. Submit up to 3 poems (10 page maximum), 1 story (up to 8,000 words) or 1 work of nonfiction (up to 8,000 words). Submission period begins May 1 (electronic only via Duosuma). Original English work only. Submissions in multiple genres or multiple entries in each genre are accepted. Entry fee: $12.
Award: $500 & publication in *Best Spiritual Literature*
Closing Date: Aug 1

Best Translated Book Award
Three Percent
c/o Open Letter, University of Rochester, Dewey Hall 1-219, Box 278968, Rochester, NY 14627
Tel: 585-319-0823
E-mail: contact@openletterbooks.org
Web Site: besttranslatedbook.org
Key Personnel
Founder & Publr: Chad Post *E-mail:* chad.post@rochester.edu
Established: 2007
Recognizes the previous year's best original translation of a work of fiction & a work of poetry into English. Long & short lists announced leading up to the award. Original translations must have been published in the previous calendar year. Reprints & retranslation are ineligible. No entry fee. See web site for list of judges or contact Chad Post.
Other Sponsor(s): Amazon Literary Partnership
Award: $5,000 to both author(s) & translator(s)
Presented: May

Best Workplace in the Americas (MWA)
PRINTING United Alliance
10015 Main St, Fairfax, VA 22031
Tel: 703-385-1335 *Toll Free Tel:* 888-385-3588 *Fax:* 703-273-0456
E-mail: assist@printing.org; info@printing.org
Web Site: www.printing.org/programs/awards/best-workplace-in-the-americas
Key Personnel
CEO: Ford Bowers *E-mail:* fbowers@printing.org
Honors distinguished printing industry leaders by human resources standards.
Branch Office(s)
1325 "G" St NW, Suite 500, Washington, DC 20005 *Tel:* 202-627-6925 ext 504
2000 Corporate Dr, Suite 205, Wexford, PA 15090 *Tel:* 412-741-6860 *Toll Free Tel:* 800-910-4283 *Fax:* 412-741-2311

Doris Betts Fiction Prize
North Carolina Writers' Network
PO Box 21591, Winston-Salem, NC 27120-1591
Tel: 336-293-8844
E-mail: mail@ncwriters.org; nclrsubmissions@ecu.edu
Web Site: www.ncwriters.org
Key Personnel
Exec Dir: Ed Southern *E-mail:* ed@ncwriters.org
Ed, NCLR: Margaret Bauer *E-mail:* bauer@ecu.edu

Open to any writer who is a legal resident of North Carolina or a member of the NCWN. *North Carolina Literary Review* subscribers with North Carolina connections (lives or has lived in NC) are also eligible. The competition is for previously unpublished short stories up to 6,000 words. Multiple entries ok, but each requires a separate entry fee. No novel excerpts. Submit previously unpublished stories online at nclr.submittable.com/submit. Entry fee: $10 NCWN members or NCLR subscribers, $20 nonmembs/non-subscribers. Documents must be Microsoft Word or .rtf files. Stories should be double-spaced. Author's name should not appear on mss.
If submitting by mail, send story ms with cover sheet providing name, address, e-mail address, word count & ms title to: NCLR, ECU Mailstop, 555 English, Greenville, NC 27858-4353 (but mail payment per instructions on web site).
Award: $250 1st prize & publication in the *North Carolina Literary Review*. Finalists also considered for publication
Closing Date: Oct 31
Presented: May 1

Beullah Rose Poetry Prize
Smartish Pace
2221 Lake Ave, Baltimore, MD 21213
E-mail: smartishpace@gmail.com
Web Site: www.smartishpace.com/poetry-prizes
Key Personnel
Ed: Stephen Reichert *E-mail:* sreichert@smartishpace.com
Assoc Ed: Clare Banks *E-mail:* cbsmartishpace@gmail.com
Established: 2005
Prize for exceptional poetry by women. All poems submitted for the prize will be considered for publication in *Smartish Pace*. Online submissions: See web site for Submittable link. Simultaneous submissions are allowed. You may enter more than once. Postal submissions: Submit 3 poems, bio & $10 entry fee. Include name, address & e-mail.
Award: $200 (1st prize); Top 3 poets & all finalists are published in *Smartish Pace*
Closing Date: Jan 1
Presented: Baltimore, MD

Albert J Beveridge Award in American History, see Beveridge Family Prize in American History

Albert J Beveridge Grant for Research in the History of the Western Hemisphere, see Beveridge Family Research Grants in Western Hemisphere History

Beveridge Family Prize in American History
Formerly Albert J Beveridge Award in American History
American Historical Association (AHA)
400 "A" St SE, Washington, DC 20003
Tel: 202-544-2422
E-mail: awards@historians.org
Web Site: www.historians.org/award-grant/beveridge-family-prize-in-american-history/
Established: 1939
To promote & honor outstanding historical writing. The award is given for a distinguished book in English on the history of the US, Latin America, or Canada, from 1492 to the present. Books that employ new methodological or conceptual tools or that constitute significant re-examinations of important interpretive problems will be given preference. Literary merit is also an important criterion. Biographies, monographs & works of synthesis & interpretation are eligible; translations, anthologies & collections of documents are not. Books with a copyright of 2024 are eligible for the 2025 award; limited to 5 titles from any one publisher & must be submitted by sending a copy to each committee member, along with an application form. All updated info on web site.
Award: $1,000
Closing Date: May 15, 2025
Presented: AHA Annual Meeting, Chicago, IL, Jan 2026

Beveridge Family Research Grants in Western Hemisphere History
Formerly Albert J Beveridge Grant for Research in the History of the Western Hemisphere
American Historical Association (AHA)
400 "A" St SE, Washington, DC 20003
Tel: 202-544-2422
E-mail: awards@historians.org
Web Site: www.historians.org/award-grant/beveridge-family-research-grants-in-western-hemisphere-history/
Established: 1939
Awarded to support research in the history of the Western hemisphere (US, CN & Latin America). Only members of the association are eligible. The grants are intended to further research in progress & may be used for travel to a library or archive, for microfilms, photographs or photocopying - a list of purposes that is meant to be merely illustrative not exhaustive. Preference will be given to advanced doctoral students, non-tenured faculty & unaffiliated scholars, & to those with specific research needs, such as the completion of a project or a discrete segment thereof. Application forms available on web site. Applications must include application form with estimated budget, curriculum vitae & statement of no more than 750 words. A one-page bibliography of the most recent relevant, secondary works on the topic. Mailed & faxed submissions are not accepted. Applicants will be notified of the committee's decision by e-mail in mid-May.
Award: Individual grants up to $1,000
Closing Date: Feb 15
Presented: June

BFMA Award of Excellence
Business Forms Management Association (BFMA)
1147 Fleetwood Ave, Madison, WI 53716-1417
E-mail: bfma@bfma.org
Web Site: www.bfma.org/page/awardsexcellence
Honors a BFMA member who has made significant contributions to the association, either at a local, regional or international level. Members are encouraged to nominate an individual who they feel has exhibited outstanding service & accomplishments within the association. See web site for criteria & contact information to submit nominations & supporting documentation.
Closing Date: March 1

BFMA Professional Awards Program
Business Forms Management Association (BFMA)
1147 Fleetwood Ave, Madison, WI 53716-1417
E-mail: bfma@bfma.org
Web Site: www.bfma.org/page/awardsprofessional
Honors members & their teams in recognition of innovation & well-honed form systems analysis skills for their companies or organizations. Submission are limited to projects undertaken within the last 3 years. See web site for necessary project report components & contact information for submissions. Judging panel selects the top 3 entries for recognition. The submission with the highest point total receives the International Form Systems Professional (Team) of the Year award.
Closing Date: March 17
Presented: BFMA Annual Conference

AWARDS, PRIZE CONTESTS, FELLOWSHIPS & GRANTS

BHTG - Julie Harris Playwright Award Competition
The Beverly Hills Theatre Guild
PO Box 148, Beverly Hills, CA 90213
Tel: 310-765-1605
E-mail: submissions@beverlyhillstheatreguild.com
Web Site: www.beverlyhillstheatreguild.com
Key Personnel
Pres: Mary Levin Cutler
Competition Coord: Donna King
Established: 1978
Competition for playwrights. See web site for application & guidelines. Application fee: $25.
Award: $3,500, $2,500 & $1,500
Closing Date: Last day of Feb (postmark)
Presented: Los Angeles, CA, June 30 (announcement)

BHTG - Michael J Libow Youth Theatre Award
The Beverly Hills Theatre Guild
PO Box 148, Beverly Hills, CA 90213
Tel: 310-765-1605
E-mail: submissions@beverlyhillstheatreguild.com
Web Site: www.beverlyhillstheatreguild.com
Key Personnel
Pres: Mary Levin Cutler
Competition Coord: Donna King
Established: 1999
Award for playwrights. Children's theatre grade 6th-8th, 9th-12th grade. See web site for application & guidelines. Application fee: $25.
Award: $1,200 & $600
Closing Date: Last day of Feb (postmark)
Presented: Los Angeles, CA, June 30 (announcement)

Biblio Award
Biographers International Organization (BIO)
PO Box 33020, Santa Fe, NM 87594
Web Site: biographersinternational.org/award/biblio-award
Key Personnel
Exec Dir: Michael Gately *E-mail:* execdirector@biographersinternational.org
Established: 2012
Presented in recognition of a librarian or archivist who has made an exceptional contribution to the craft of biography. Based on nominations by BIO members.
Award: Statuette
Presented: BIO Annual Conference, May

Ray Allen Billington Prize
The Organization of American Historians (OAH)
112 N Bryan Ave, Bloomington, IN 47408-4141
Tel: 812-855-7311
E-mail: oah@oah.org
Web Site: www.oah.org/awards
Key Personnel
Exec Dir: Beth English *Tel:* 812-855-9836
E-mail: benglish@oah.org
Dir, Communs & Mktg: Kym Robinson *Tel:* 812-855-5430 *E-mail:* kymarobi@oah.org
Awarded biennially, in odd-numbered years, to the author of the best book on the history of native +/or settler peoples in frontier, border & borderland zones of intercultural contact in any century to the present & to include works that address the legacies of those zones. Each entry must be published during the 2-year calendar period preceding that in which the award is given. One copy of each entry must be mailed directly to the committee members listed on the web site.
Closing Date: Oct 1, 2026 (postmarked)
Presented: OAH Conference on American History, Sheraton Grand Chicago, Chicago, IL, April 3-6, 2027

The Geoffrey Bilson Award for Historical Fiction for Young People
The Canadian Children's Book Centre
425 Adelaide St W, Suite 200, Toronto, ON M5V 3C1, Canada
Tel: 416-975-0010
E-mail: info@bookcentre.ca
Web Site: www.bookcentre.ca
Key Personnel
Exec Dir: Sarah Sahagian
Lib Coord: Meghan Howe *E-mail:* meghan@bookcentre.ca
Established: 1988
Awarded to a Canadian author for an outstanding work of historical fiction for young people.
Award: $5,000 cash
Closing Date: Mid-Dec

Robert W Bingham Prize for Debut Short Story Collection, see PEN/Robert W Bingham Prize for Debut Short Story Collection

Binghamton University John Gardner Fiction Book Award
The Binghamton Center for Writers-State University of New York
Dept of English, General Literature & Rhetoric, Bartle Library N, Rm 1149, Vestal Pkwy E, Binghamton, NY 13902
Mailing Address: PO Box 6000, Binghamton, NY 13902-6000
Tel: 607-777-2713
Web Site: www2.binghamton.edu/english/creative-writing
Key Personnel
Dir, Creative Writing: Tina Chang *Tel:* 607-777-2327 *E-mail:* tchang@binghamton.edu
Established: 2002
Selected by judges as the strongest novel or collection of fiction published in the previous year. Each book submitted must be accompanied by an application form. Publishers may submit more than one book for prize consideration. Submit 2 copies of each book. Winners will be announced in *Poets & Writers* & the AWP *Writer's Chronicle*.
Award: $1,000
Closing Date: Feb 1

Binghamton University Milt Kessler Poetry Book Award
The Binghamton Center for Writers-State University of New York
Dept of English, General Literature & Rhetoric, Bartle Library N, Rm 1149, Vestal Pkwy E, Binghamton, NY 13902
Mailing Address: PO Box 6000, Binghamton, NY 13902-6000
Tel: 607-777-2713
Web Site: www2.binghamton.edu/english/creative-writing
Key Personnel
Dir, Creative Writing: Tina Chang *Tel:* 607-777-2327 *E-mail:* tchang@binghamton.edu
Established: 2002
For a book of poems, 48 pages or more in length, selected by our judges as the strongest collection of poems published in the previous year. Each book submitted must be accompanied by an application form. Publishers may submit more than one book for prize consideration. Submit 2 copies of each book. Winner announced in *Poets & Writers* & the AWP *Writer's Chronicle*.
Award: $1,000
Closing Date: Feb 1

Binkley-Stephenson Award
The Organization of American Historians (OAH)
112 N Bryan Ave, Bloomington, IN 47408-4141
Tel: 812-855-7311
E-mail: oah@oah.org

ASSOCIATIONS, EVENTS

Web Site: www.oah.org/awards
Key Personnel
Exec Dir: Beth English *Tel:* 812-855-9836
E-mail: benglish@oah.org
Dir, Communs & Mktg: Kym Robinson *Tel:* 812-855-5430 *E-mail:* kymarobi@oah.org
Presented for the best article that appeared in the *Journal of American History* during the preceding calendar year (March, June, September, December issues).
Presented: OAH Conference on American History, Spring

BIO Award
Biographers International Organization (BIO)
PO Box 33020, Santa Fe, NM 87594
Web Site: biographersinternational.org/award/the-bio-award
Key Personnel
Exec Dir: Michael Gately *E-mail:* execdirector@biographersinternational.org
Established: 2010
Awarded to an individual for contributions to advancing the art & craft of biography. Based on nominations by BIO members.
Award: Bronze plaque & honorarium
Presented: BIO Annual Conference, May

Biography Fellowships
The Leon Levy Center for Biography
365 Fifth Ave, Rm 6200, New York, NY 10016
Tel: 212-817-2025
E-mail: biography@gc.cuny.edu
Web Site: llcb.ws.gc.cuny.edu/fellowships
Key Personnel
Exec Dir: Kai Bird
Assoc Dir: Thad Ziolkowski
E-mail: tziolkowski@gc.cuny.edu
Four resident fellowships offered at the Graduate Center for the academic year beginning each September. Fellows devote their time to their projects & participate in monthly seminars & public events of the Leon Levy Center for Biography, including the annual lecture & annual conference & are encouraged to join in the dynamic intellectual community of the Graduate Center. Preference in the award of fellowships is given to those who have not yet published a biography or received fellowships for the writing of a biography. Applications are also welcome from published & accomplished writers who are undertaking their first biography. The Center does not award fellowships for memoirs, essays, plays, film or fiction. Applications require brief CV or resume (3 page maximum), narrative account of applicant's career (250 words), project description (750 words), sample of proposed biography (2,500 word maximum) & 2 letters of reference. Digital/online applications only.
Award: Awards include writing space, full access to research facilities, research assistance & stipend of $72,000
Closing Date: Jan 4

BIPOC Bookseller Award, see Duende-Word BIPOC Bookseller Award

Paul Birdsall Prize in European Military & Strategic History
American Historical Association (AHA)
400 "A" St SE, Washington, DC 20003
Tel: 202-544-2422
E-mail: awards@historians.org
Web Site: www.historians.org/award-grant/paul-birdsall-prize
Established: 1985
Awarded biennially, in even-numbered years, for the most important work published in English on European military or strategic history since 1870. Preference will be given to early-career academics, but established scholars & nonaca-

demic candidates will not be excluded. Books published in English & bearing a copyright date of 2024 or 2025 are eligible for the 2026 prize. Nominators must complete an online prize submission form for each book submitted. One copy of each entry must be sent to each prize committee member & clearly labeled "Birdsall Prize Entry." Electronic copies may be sent only to committee members who have indicated they will accept them.
Award: $1,000
Closing Date: May 15, 2026
Presented: AHA Annual Meeting, New Orleans, LA, Jan 2027

BISG Industry Awards
Book Industry Study Group Inc (BISG)
232 Madison Ave, Suite 1200, New York, NY 10016
Tel: 646-336-7141
E-mail: info@bisg.org
Web Site: www.bisg.org
Key Personnel
Exec Dir: Brian O'Leary
Opers Mgr: Jonathan Fiedler
Established: 2014
Categories: Sally Dedecker Award for Lifetime Service, Industry Champion Award, Industry Innovator Award. Applications are typically not accepted; a committee considers candidates & selects honorees.
Presented: BISG Annual Meeting of Members, April

Chip Bishop Fellowship
Biographers International Organization (BIO)
PO Box 33020, Santa Fe, NM 87594
Web Site: biographersinternational.org/award/chip-bishop-fellowship
Key Personnel
Exec Dir: Michael Gately *E-mail:* execdirector@biographersinternational.org
Established: 2018
Fellowship open to both members & nonmembers to help biographers in financial need to attend the BIO Annual Conference. See web site for full details.
Award: Fee waived for BIO Annual Conference & $500 to help defray travel & lodging expenses
Closing Date: April 1

Prix Harry Black
(Harry Black Prize)
The Canadian Children's Book Centre
425 Adelaide St W, Suite 200, Toronto, ON M5V 3C1, Canada
Tel: 416-975-0010
E-mail: info@bookcentre.ca
Web Site: www.bookcentre.ca
Key Personnel
Exec Dir: Sarah Sahagian
Lib Coord: Meghan Howe *E-mail:* meghan@bookcentre.ca
Established: 2017
Awarded to a Canadian author & illustrator for excellence in the illustrated French language picture book format for children ages 3-8.
Award: $5,000 cash
Closing Date: Mid-Dec

Irma Simonton & James H Black Award
Bank Street College of Education
610 W 112 St, New York, NY 10025
Tel: 212-875-4458
E-mail: bookcom@bankstreet.edu
Web Site: www.bankstreet.edu/library/center-for-childrens-literature/irma-black-award
Key Personnel
Dir, Lib Servs: Kristin Freda *E-mail:* kfreda@bankstreet.edu
Established: 1972
Award for unified excellence of story line, language & illustration in a work for young children published during the previous year. Children from the US, Canada, Europe, Asia & the United Arab Emirates participate in the voting process.
Award: Silver & gold seals
Closing Date: Dec
Presented: Bank Street College of Education, May

Black Literary Publishing Award
Community of Literary Magazines & Presses (CLMP)
154 Christopher St, Suite 3C, New York, NY 10014-9110
Tel: 212-741-9110
E-mail: info@clmp.org
Web Site: www.clmp.org
Key Personnel
Exec Dir: Mary Gannon *E-mail:* mgannon@clmp.org
Communs Mgr: Emma Hine *E-mail:* ehine@clmp.org
Established: 2020
Honors & supports Black-led presses & presses that champion the work of BIPOC authors.
Other Sponsor(s): Penguin Random House
Award: $10,000
Presented: Spring

Black Orchid Novella Award
The Wolfe Pack
PO Box 230822, Ansonia Sta, New York, NY 10023
E-mail: blackorchidaward@nerowolfe.org
Web Site: nerowolfe.org/htm/literary_awards/black_orchid_award/Black_Orchid_award_intro.htm
Key Personnel
Chair: Jane K Cleland *E-mail:* jane@janecleland.com
Established: 2006
Each entry must be an original, unpublished work of fiction in the traditional deductive style exemplified by the Nero Wolfe series. Entries must be 15,000-20,000 words in length. No electronic submissions are accepted. Submissions should be sent to Jane K Cleland, Chair, BONA, PO Box 3233, New York, NY 10163-3233. See web site for full submission criteria & eligibility requirements.
Other Sponsor(s): Alfred Hitchcock's Mystery Magazine
Award: $1,000 & publication
Closing Date: May 31
Presented: Black Orchid Banquet, New York, NY, 1st Saturday in Dec

Black Warrior Review Fiction, Nonfiction & Poetry Contest
Black Warrior Review
University of Alabama, Off of Student Media, 414 Campus Dr E, Tuscaloosa, AL 35487
Mailing Address: PO Box 870170, Tuscaloosa, AL 35487-0170
Tel: 205-348-4518 *Fax:* 205-348-8036
E-mail: blackwarriorreview@gmail.com; bwr@ua.edu
Web Site: www.bwr.ua.edu
Key Personnel
Mng Ed: Kelsey Nuttall *E-mail:* managingeditor.bwr@gmail.com
Ed: Josh Brandon
Fiction Ed: Kaushika Suresh *E-mail:* fiction.bwr@gmail.com
Nonfiction Ed: August Kelly *E-mail:* nonfiction.bwr@gmail.com
Poetry Ed: James McKenna *E-mail:* poetry.bwr@gmail.com
Established: 2005
Awards given to best nonfiction piece, short story & best poem entered. Submit 1 story (up to 7,000 words) or up to 3 poems. Submit online at bwr.submittable.com/submit. Entry fee: Free for up to 600 Black & Indigenous writers; Fiction, nonfiction & poetry: $15 ($25 intl); Flash: $6.
Award: $1,000 & publication (one for each category - poetry, nonfiction & fiction); $500 & publications in Flash category. Finalists noted & considered for publication
Closing Date: Sept 1
Presented: Oct

Blake-Dodd Prize
American Academy of Arts & Letters
633 W 155 St, New York, NY 10032
Tel: 212-368-5900
E-mail: academy@artsandletters.org
Web Site: artsandletters.org/awards
Key Personnel
Exec Dir: Cody Upton
Established: 2014
Triennial award for a nonfiction writer. Candidates must be nominated by an Academy member.
Other Sponsor(s): Anna Bowman Blake-Dodd Estate Fund
Award: $25,000

Neltje Blanchan Memorial Award
Wyoming Arts Council
Division of Wyoming Department of Parks & Cultural Resources
Barrett Bldg, 2nd fl, 2301 Central Ave, Cheyenne, WY 82002
Tel: 307-777-7742
Web Site: wyoarts.state.wy.us
Key Personnel
Creative Arts Specialist: Taylor Craig *E-mail:* taylor.craig@wyo.gov
Established: 1988
Best writing in any genre inspired by a relationship with nature. Open to Wyoming residents only. Blind judges, single juror. Submissions open in January.
Award: $1,000
Closing Date: March
Presented: Announced in Spring

Eleanor Taylor Bland Crime Fiction Writers of Color Award
Sisters in Crime (SinC)
PO Box 442124, Lawrence, KS 66044
Tel: 785-842-1325 *Fax:* 785-856-6314
E-mail: admin@sistersincrime.org
Web Site: www.sistersincrime.org
Key Personnel
Exec Dir: Beth Wasson
Awards Coord: Stephanie Gayle *E-mail:* stephgayle@gmail.com
Established: 2014
Grant is to support the recipient in such developmental & research activities as workshops, seminars, conferences & retreats, online courses & other opportunities required for completion of their debut crime fiction work. Application requirements: An unpublished work of crime fiction, written with an adult audience in mind. This may be a short story or first chapter(s) of a ms in progress, 2,500-5,000 words; resume or biographical statement; cover letter that gives a sense of the applicant as an emerging writer in the genre & briefly states how the grant money would be used. No prior writing or publishing experience is required, but the applicant should include any relevant studies or experience.
Award: $2,000 grant
Closing Date: June

AWARDS, PRIZE CONTESTS, FELLOWSHIPS & GRANTS

Theodore C Blegen Award
The Forest History Society Inc
2925 Academy Rd, Durham, NC 27705
Tel: 919-682-9319 *Fax:* 919-682-2349
Web Site: foresthistory.org/awards-fellowships/blegen-award
Key Personnel
Admin Asst: Andrea Anderson *E-mail:* andrea.anderson@foresthistory.org
Established: 1972
Presented in recognition of the best scholarship in forest & conservation history published in a journal other than *Environmental History*.
Award: $500 & plaque
Closing Date: March 15 (postmarked)

Norbert Blei/August Derleth Nonfiction Book Award
Council for Wisconsin Writers (CWW)
c/o 4414 W Fillmore Dr, Milwaukee, WI 53219
E-mail: wiswriters@gmail.com
Web Site: wiswriters.org/awards
Key Personnel
Contest Chair: Daniel Kentowski *E-mail:* dkento@milwaukee.gov
Established: 1966
Award for the best nonfiction book published by a Wisconsin-based author in the contest year. Entry fee: $25 nonmembs.
Award: $500 & 1-week residency at Shake Rag Alley Center for the Arts
Closing Date: Jan 31
Presented: CWW Annual Award Ceremony & Banquet, May

Blue Light Books Prize
Indiana Review
Indiana University English Dept, Ballantine Hall 554, 1020 E Kirkwood Ave, Bloomington, IN 47405
Tel: 812-855-3439
E-mail: inreview@indiana.edu
Web Site: indianareview.org
Key Personnel
Ed-in-Chief: Shreya Fadia
Assoc Ed: Bernardo Wade
Accept full-length poetry & fiction mss in alternating years. Mss should be 48-75 pages. Submission fee: $20. See web site for full submission guidelines.
Award: $1,000 & publishing contract, including $1,000 against future royalties from Indiana University Press
Closing Date: Oct 31
Presented: Blue Light Reading, Bloomington, IN

The Blue Mountain Novel Award
Hidden River™ Arts
PO Box 63927, Philadelphia, PA 19147
Tel: 610-764-0813
E-mail: hiddenriverarts@gmail.com
Web Site: hiddenriverarts.wordpress.com
Key Personnel
Founding Dir: Debra Leigh Scott
Established: 2020
Award for an original, unpublished novel of any length. Open to international submissions from writers in English. Each ms must be submitted separately online. Entry fee: $20. See web site for full submission guidelines.
Award: $1,000 & publication by Hidden River Press
Closing Date: March

BMO Winterset Award
ArtsNL
Newman Bldg, 2nd fl, One Springdale St, St John's, NL A1C 5H5, Canada
Mailing Address: PO Box 98, St John's, NL A1C 1C0, Canada
Tel: 709-726-2212 *Toll Free Tel:* 866-726-2212 (NL only) *Fax:* 709-726-0619
Web Site: www.nlac.ca/awards/winterset.htm
Key Personnel
Exec Dir: Reg Winsor *E-mail:* rwinsor@nlac.ca
Published literary works, written either by a native-born Newfoundlander & Labradorian, or by a current resident of the province, are eligible. Residency is defined as having lived in Newfoundland & Labrador for a minimum of 12 consecutive months immediately prior to the time of submission of works. Both emerging or established writers may be considered. Submissions must be made by the publisher & must include 4 non-returnable copies of all works submitted. Works must have been published between January & December of the current calendar year. Awarded to an outstanding literary work in any writing genre (fiction, nonfiction, poetry, published drama, etc) regardless of the subject matter. The overriding consideration will be excellence in writing by Newfoundlanders & Labradorians, as determined by the jury.
Other Sponsor(s): BMO Financial Group; Sandra Fraser Gwyn Foundation
Award: $12,500; 2 finalists each receive $3,000
Closing Date: Dec 31

BOA Short Fiction Prize
BOA Editions Ltd
250 N Goodman St, Suite 306, Rochester, NY 14607
Tel: 585-546-3410
E-mail: contact@boaeditions.org
Web Site: www.boaeditions.org/pages/boa-short-fiction-prize
Key Personnel
Publr: Peter Conners *E-mail:* conners@boaeditions.org
Established: 2010
Awarded to 10 of the most exciting & unique voices in American fiction. Submissions are invited only through Submittable or by post mail. See web site for full eligibility & guidelines. Submission fee: $25.
Award: $1,000 honorarium & book publication
Closing Date: May 31

Rebekah Johnson Bobbitt National Prize for Poetry
The Poetry & Literature Center, Library of Congress
101 Independence Ave SE, Washington, DC 20540-4861
Tel: 202-707-5000
Web Site: www.loc.gov/programs/poetry-and-literature/prizes/bobbitt-prize
Established: 1988
Awarded biennially, in even-numbered years, to recognize the most distinguished book of poetry written by an American & published during the preceding 2 years, or for lifetime achievement in poetry.
Other Sponsor(s): Family of Rebekah Johnson Bobbitt
Award: $10,000

Frederick Bock Prize
Poetry Magazine
61 W Superior St, Chicago, IL 60654
Tel: 312-787-7070
Web Site: www.poetryfoundation.org/poetrymagazine/prizes
Key Personnel
Assoc Ed: Holly Amos *E-mail:* hamos@poetrymagazine.org
Established: 1981
For poetry published during the preceding year in *Poetry* magazine. No application necessary.
Award: $500
Presented: Announced in Nov issue

George Bogin Memorial Award
Poetry Society of America (PSA)

ASSOCIATIONS, EVENTS

119 Smith St, Brooklyn, NY 11201
Tel: 212-254-9628
E-mail: info@poetrysociety.org
Web Site: poetrysociety.org/awards
Key Personnel
Exec Dir: Matt Brogan *E-mail:* matt@poetrysociety.org
Deputy Dir: Brett Fletcher Lauer *E-mail:* brett@poetrysociety.org
Devt Dir: Madeline Weinfield *E-mail:* madeline@poetrysociety.org
Established by the family & friends of George Bogin. Awarded for a selection of 4 or 5 poems that reflects the encounter of the ordinary & the extraordinary, uses language in an original way & takes a stand against oppression in any of its forms. All submissions must be through Submittable. Entry fee: Free to membs, $15 nonmembs. See web site for detailed submission guidelines.
Award: $500
Closing Date: Dec 31
Presented: Annual Awards Ceremony, New York, NY, Spring

Bogle Pratt International Library Travel Fund
International Relations Committee
Unit of The American Library Association (ALA)
c/o The American Library Association, 225 N Michigan Ave, Suite 1300, Chicago, IL 60601-7757
Tel: 312-280-3201 *Toll Free Tel:* 800-545-2433 (ext 3201) *Fax:* 312-280-4392
E-mail: intl@ala.org
Web Site: www.ala.org
Key Personnel
Dir, Off of Chapter & Intl Rel: Michael Dowling
Prog Offr: Delin Guerra *E-mail:* dguerra@ala.org
Awarded to enable librarians to travel abroad to study +/or attend first international conferences. Submit all applications via e-mail to intl@ala.org.
Other Sponsor(s): Bogle Memorial Fund; Pratt Institute School of Information & Library Science
Award: $1,000
Closing Date: Feb 15
Presented: ALA Annual Conference & Exhibition, June

Laura Day Boggs Bolling Memorial
The Poetry Society of Virginia (PSV)
PO Box 36128, North Chesterfield, VA 23235-3533
E-mail: contest@poetrysocietyofvirginia.org; info@poetryvirginia.org
Web Site: www.poetrysocietyofvirginia.org
Key Personnel
Pres: Cherryl T Cooley
E-mail: poetrysocietypresident@gmail.com
All entries must be in English, original & unpublished. Poem must be written by an adult for older school-age children (10-12 years), any rhymed or unrhymed form, 20 line limit. Submit 1 copy of the poem with no identifying information but put the category in the upper right-hand-side, along with a notation as to whether you are a member of PSV (does not matter if you are a lifetime member or just joined for the contest). Submit a cover letter/page that contains the category, the name of the poem, your name & address, phone number & e-mail address. Entries will not be returned. Entry fee: Free for membs, $5 nonmembs.
Other Sponsor(s): Children of Laura Day Boggs Bolling: Alma, Flora & Glade
Award: $50 (1st prize), $30 (2nd prize), $20 (3rd prize)
Closing Date: Feb
Presented: PSV Awards Ceremony, April

Bollingen Prize for American Poetry
Beinecke Rare Book & Manuscript Library

121 Wall St, New Haven, CT 06511
Tel: 203-432-2977 *Fax:* 203-432-4047
E-mail: beinecke.library@yale.edu
Web Site: beinecke.library.yale.edu
Established: 1949
Awarded biennially, in odd-numbered years, to an American poet to recognize a recent book or a lifetime body of work.
Award: $165,000

Book of the Year Award
American Farm Bureau Foundation for Agriculture®
600 Maryland Ave SW, Suite 1000W, Washington, DC 20024
Toll Free Tel: 800-443-8456 *Fax:* 202-314-5121
E-mail: foundation@fb.org
Web Site: www.agfoundation.org/projects/book-of-the-year-award
Key Personnel
Prog Coord: Sydney Andrews *Tel:* 202-406-3739 *E-mail:* sydneya@fb.org
Award to honor an exceptional accurate book that helps to educate & create positive public perception about agriculture & producers. Classroom curriculum is developed to add value to the book. Any publication date is accepted. Judging begins in June for the following year's award.
Presented: Flapjack Fundraiser

Book of the Year Award
Mississippi Historical Society
Affiliate of Mississippi Department of Archives & History
William F Winter Archives & History Bldg, 200 North St, Jackson, MS 39201
Mailing Address: PO Box 571, Jackson, MS 39205-0571
Tel: 601-576-6936 *Fax:* 601-576-6975
E-mail: mhs@mdah.ms.gov
Web Site: www.mdah.ms.gov
Key Personnel
Pres: Stephanie Rolph
VP: Daphne Chamberlain
Secy-Treas, Historical Society: Brother Rogers
Public Info: Emma McRaney *E-mail:* emcraney@mdah.ms.gov
Established: 1980
For distinguished scholarly book published during the previous year on a subject related to Mississippi history or biography. Prize recipient is invited to be the Thursday evening banquet speaker at the Society's annual meeting. To nominate a book, mail 4 copies to the street address above.
Award: $700 cash award plus $300 honorarium & reimbursement of travel expenses as banquet speaker
Closing Date: Nov 1
Presented: Annual Meeting, Early March

Book of the Year Awards
New Atlantic Independent Booksellers Association (NAIBA)
2667 Hyacinth St, Westbury, NY 11590
Tel: 516-333-0681
E-mail: kit@naiba.com
Web Site: www.naiba.com/page/BooksoftheYear
Key Personnel
Exec Dir: Eileen Dengler *E-mail:* eileen@naiba.com
To recognize an author who was born or lived in the region +/or a book whose story takes place in the region. The book must have been published between June 1 & May 31 (of the award year). There are 5 categories: Fiction; Nonfiction; Picture Book; Children's Literature; Special Interest.
Closing Date: June 30
Presented: NAIBA Fall Conference, Oct

Books Like Us First Novel Contest
Atria Books
Imprint of Atria Publishing Group
1230 Avenue of the Americas, New York, NY 10020
Tel: 212-698-7000
Web Site: www.simonandschuster.com/p/simon-and-schuster-books-like-us
Key Personnel
SVP & Publr: Libby McGuire *Tel:* 212-698-7675 *E-mail:* libby.mcguire@simonandschuster.com
VP & Dir, Publicity: Lisa Sciambra *Tel:* 212-698-7086 *E-mail:* lisa.sciambra@simonandschuster.com
Established: 2021
The contest facilitates accessibility to underrepresented writers & celebrates the diversity of readers across the US. Writers are invited to submit 25 pages of an original adult fiction ms. Submission must be made online & ms uploaded as a PDF or Word document (limit 10MB), along with a 250- to 500-word personal response describing your ms & its relevance to today's publishing climate. See web site for full document specifications. The contest rotates among Simon & Schuster adult imprints.
Award: $50,000 book deal
Presented: May

Boston Globe-Horn Book Award
The Boston Globe & The Horn Book Inc
c/o Book Reviews, The Horn Book Inc, Palace Road Bldg, 300 The Fenway, Suite P-311, Boston, MA 02115-5820
Tel: 617-278-0225 *Toll Free Tel:* 888-628-0225
E-mail: bghb@hbook.com
Web Site: www.hbook.com
Key Personnel
Exec Ed: Elissa Gershowitz
Established: 1967
Award honoring excellence in children's & young adult literature in 3 categories: Fiction & Poetry, Nonfiction & Picture Books. Published books only.
Award: $500 each
Closing Date: May

Boulevard Magazine Short Fiction Contest for Emerging Writers
Boulevard Magazine
3829 Hartford St, St Louis, MO 63116
E-mail: editors@boulevardmagazine.org
Web Site: www.boulevardmagazine.org
Key Personnel
Mng Ed: Dusty Freund
Asst Mng Ed: Griffin Reed
Ed: Jessica Rogen *E-mail:* jessicarogen@boulevardmagazine.org
Open to writers who have not yet published a book of fiction, poetry or creative nonfiction with a nationally distributed press. Simultaneous submissions are allowed but previously accepted or published work is ineligible. Send typed, double-spaced mss & SAS postcard for acknowledgment of receipt. No mss will be returned. 8,000 word maximum length; cover sheets not necessary. Entry fee: $16 per story with no limit per author. Includes 1-year subscription.
Award: $1,500 & publication in the Spring or the Fall issue of *Boulevard*
Closing Date: Dec

Bound to Stay Bound Books Scholarship
Association for Library Service to Children (ALSC)
Division of The American Library Association (ALA)
225 N Michigan Ave, Suite 1300, Chicago, IL 60601
Tel: 312-280-2163 *Toll Free Tel:* 800-545-2433 *Fax:* 312-280-5271
E-mail: alsc@ala.org
Web Site: www.ala.org/alsc/awardsgrants/scholarships; www.btsb.com/about-us/scholarships
Key Personnel
Exec Dir: Alena Rivers *Tel:* 800-545-2433 ext 5866 *E-mail:* arivers@ala.org
Awards Coord: Jordan Dubin *Tel:* 800-545-2433 ext 5839 *E-mail:* jdubin@ala.org
Prog Coord: Ann Michaud *Tel:* 800-545-2433 ext 2166 *E-mail:* amichaud@ala.org
Membership/Mktg Specialist: Elizabeth Serrano *Tel:* 800-545-2433 ext 2164 *E-mail:* eserrano@ala.org
Four awards for study in field of library service to children toward the MLS or beyond in an ALA-accredited program.
Other Sponsor(s): Bound-to-Stay Bound Books Inc
Award: $8,000 each
Closing Date: March 1
Presented: ALA Annual Conference & Exhibition, June

BrainStorm Poetry Contest for Mental Health Consumers
Northern Initiative for Social Action (NISA)
36 Elgin St, 2nd fl, Sudbury, ON P3C 5B4, Canada
Tel: 705-222-6472 (ext 303)
E-mail: openminds@nisa.on.ca
Web Site: www.openmindsquarterly.com/poetry-contest
Key Personnel
Publr & Ed: Sabine Gorecki
Established: 2003
Contest open internationally to people with lived experience of madness/mental health challenges/mental illness/neurodivergence. It aims to eliminate the stigma associated with these by showcasing the talents & creativity of individuals who have lived through them & provide a platform for folks to share their experiences.
Award: $250 (1st prize), $150 (2nd prize), $75 (3rd prize), plus publication in *Open Minds Quarterly*
Closing Date: Feb 14

Michael Braude Award
American Academy of Arts & Letters
633 W 155 St, New York, NY 10032
Tel: 212-368-5900
E-mail: academy@artsandletters.org
Web Site: artsandletters.org/awards
Key Personnel
Exec Dir: Cody Upton
Triennial award given for light verse written in English regardless of the writer's country of origin. Candidates must be nominated by an Academy member.
Award: $5,000

Lilian Jackson Braun Award
Mystery Writers of America (MWA)
1140 Broadway, Suite 1507, New York, NY 10001
Tel: 212-888-8171
E-mail: mwa@mysterywriters.org
Web Site: mysterywriters.org/edgars/lilian-jackson-braun-award
Key Personnel
EVP: Donna Andrews
Exec Dir: Margery Flax
Awarded for the best full-length, contemporary cozy mystery as submitted to & selected by a special MWA committee. Submitted books must be published by an MWA-approved publisher. Works may be submitted by the publisher or the author. Qualifying books must be published during the calendar year prior to the

award year. Reprints are not eligible. See web site for full eligibility requirements & submission form.
Award: $2,000
Presented: Edgar Award Banquet, Spring

Bread Loaf Fellowships & Scholarships
Bread Loaf Writers' Conference
Middlebury College, 204 College St, Middlebury, VT 05753
Tel: 802-443-5286 *Fax:* 802-443-2087
E-mail: blwc@middlebury.edu
Web Site: www.middlebury.edu/blwc
Key Personnel
Dir: Jennifer Grotz
Admin Dir: Noreen Cargill *Tel:* 802-443-5062
   E-mail: ncargill@middlebury.edu
Asst Dir: Lauren Francis-Sharma
   E-mail: lfrancissharma@middlebury.edu
Coord: Jason Lamb *E-mail:* jlamb@middlebury.edu
Categories: Fiction, nonfiction & poetry.
Award: Tuition, room & board during 10-day conference
Closing Date: Feb 15
Presented: Ripton, VT, Aug

James Henry Breasted Prize, see AHA Prize in History prior to CE 1000

The Briar Cliff Review Fiction, Poetry & Creative Nonfiction Contest
The Briar Cliff Review-Briar Cliff University
3303 Rebecca St, Sioux City, IA 51104-2100
Tel: 712-279-1651 *Fax:* 712-279-5486
Web Site: www.bcreview.org
Key Personnel
Mktg Dir: Judy Thompson
Ed: Tricia Currans-Sheehan
Poetry, creative nonfiction & fiction contest. Submit unpublished story, essay or 3 poems with $20. Entrants receive no mss. No name on mss. Include cover page with title(s), name, address, e-mail, phone. Send SASE for results only. Can also use Submittable.
Award: $1,000 each category & publication in Spring
Closing Date: Nov 1

Brick Road Poetry Book Contest
Brick Road Poetry Press
341 Lee Rd 553, Phenix City, AL 36867
Web Site: www.brickroadpoetrypress.com/poetry-book-contest
Key Personnel
Ed: Keith Badowski; Ron Self
Book-length poetry mss only, original collection of 50-100 pages of poetry, excluding cover page, contents, acknowledgments, etc. Entry fee: $30. Submissions accepted starting August 1 (electronic is preferred).
Award: $1,000, publication contract with Brick Road Poetry Press in both print & ebook formats & 25 copies of the printed book
Closing Date: Nov 1
Presented: Winners notified by end of Feb

Ann Conner Brimer Award for Atlantic Canadian Children's Literature
Writers' Federation of Nova Scotia (WFNS)
1113 Marginal Rd, Halifax, NS B3H 4P7, Canada
Tel: 902-423-8116 *Fax:* 902-422-0881
E-mail: wits@writers.ns.ca (awards)
Web Site: writers.ns.ca
Key Personnel
Prog Mgr, Arts Educ: Linda Hudson
Established: 1991
Celebrates outstanding contributions to writing for Atlantic Canadian young people. Alternates between children's literature (for readers up to age 11, submissions in odd-numbered years) & young adult literature (for readers ages 12-17, submissions in even-numbered years).
Other Sponsor(s): Brimer Family
Award: $5,000
Closing Date: Nov 1
Presented: Atlantic Book Awards Gala, Spring

Brittingham & Pollak Prizes in Poetry
University of Wisconsin Press
Dept of English, 600 N Park St, Madison, WI 53706
Web Site: creativewriting.wisc.edu/submit.html
Key Personnel
Ed: Sean Bishop; Ronald Wallace
Established: 1985
Pollak & Brittingham are two prizes from one competition for the best book-length mss of original poetry. Submissions are accepted beginning in July via Submittable. Entry fee: $28. See web site for detailed entry requirements.
Other Sponsor(s): University of Wisconsin Creative Writing Program
Award: $1,500 & publication in University of Wisconsin Press Poetry Series for each book
Closing Date: Sept 15

Sophie Brody Medal
Reference & User Services Association (RUSA)
Division of The American Library Association (ALA)
225 N Michigan Ave, Suite 1300, Chicago, IL 60601
SAN: 201-0062
Web Site: rusaupdate.org/awards/sophie-brody-medal
Key Personnel
Exec Dir: Bill Ladewski *E-mail:* bladewski@ala.org
Membership & Progs Specialist: Shuntai Sykes
   E-mail: ssykes@ala.org
Mktg Communs & Web Servs Coord: Melissa Vanyek *E-mail:* mvanyek@ala.org
Established: 2006
Awarded to encourage, recognize & commend outstanding achievement in Jewish literature. Works for adults published in the US in the preceding year are eligible. In the context of this award, Jewish literature is defined as fiction, nonfiction, or poetry that has as its central purpose the exploration of the Jewish experience.
Other Sponsor(s): Sophie & Arthur Brody Foundation
Award: Medal

Brooklyn Public Library Literary Prize
Brooklyn Public Library
10 Grand Army Plaza, Brooklyn, NY 11238
Tel: 718-230-2100
E-mail: brooklyneagles@bklynlibrary.org
Web Site: www.bklynlibrary.org/support/bpl-literary-prize
Key Personnel
Co-Chair, Eagles Leadership Comm: Emily Ashton; Divya Sashti
Established: 2015
Prize to recognize outstanding works of nonfiction & fiction. Nominations are made by librarians throughout BPL's 59 branches.
Other Sponsor(s): Brooklyn Eagles
Award: $5,000 each
Presented: Autumn

John Nicholas Brown Prize
Medieval Academy of America (MAA)
6 Beacon St, Suite 500, Boston, MA 02108
Tel: 617-491-1622 *Fax:* 617-492-3303
E-mail: info@themedievalacademy.org
Web Site: www.medievalacademy.org/page/brown_prize
Key Personnel
Exec Dir: Lisa Fagin Davis *E-mail:* lfd@themedievalacademy.org
Established: 1978
Award for a first book or monograph published in the field of medieval studies judged by the selection committee to be of outstanding quality. Author must reside in North America.
Award: $1,000 & certificate
Closing Date: Oct 15
Presented: Spring

Kurt Brown Prizes
Association of Writers & Writing Programs (AWP)
440 Monticello Ave, Suite 1802, PMB 73708, Norfolk, VA 23510-2670
Tel: 240-696-7700
E-mail: awp@awpwriter.org
Web Site: www.awpwriter.org/contests/kurt_brown_prizes_overview
Key Personnel
Dir, Membership Servs: Miranda Gonzalez
   E-mail: miranda@awpwriter.org
Three scholarships awarded to 3 first-place winners in the genre of creative nonfiction, fiction & poetry. Work must be unpublished. Prize amounts are applied to the event or workshop fees of the winners' chosen program. Apply via Submittable only. Reading fee: $10 per submission.
Award: $500 each; winners & 6 finalists also receive a 1-year AWP individual membership
Closing Date: April 15

John Brubaker Award
Catholic Library Association
8550 United Plaza Blvd, Suite 1001, Baton Rouge, LA 70809
Tel: 225-408-4417
E-mail: cla2@cathla.org
Web Site: cathla.org
Key Personnel
Exec Dir: Melanie Talley
Association Coord: Mary Coll
Established: 1978
To recognize an outstanding work of literary merit, considered on the basis of its significant interest to the library profession which was published in *Catholic Library World*. The winning article must be precise in its writing, free of ambiguity, orderly in its presentation of ideas, economical in expression, smooth in its presentation, considerate of its readers, original & stimulating. Any author is eligible for consideration.
Award: Plaque & citation

Robert Bruss Real Estate Book Awards
National Association of Real Estate Editors (NAREE)
1003 NW Sixth Terr, Boca Raton, FL 33486-3455
Tel: 561-391-3599
E-mail: nareeprograms@gmail.com
Web Site: www.naree.org/bookcontest
Key Personnel
Exec Dir: Mary Doyle-Kimball *Tel:* 561-391-1983 (cell) *E-mail:* mdkimball@naree.org
Awards for books focusing on broad field of real estate, including home building, architecture & interior design, green building, community design & sustainability, home buying & selling. Books must have been published, either in print or digitally, in the preceding calendar year. Entry fee: $100 membs, $125 nonmembs.
Award: $1,000 (gold), $500 (silver), $250 (bronze), $250 (Leigh Robinson First-Time Author)
Closing Date: May 15 (postmark)
Presented: NAREE Annual Real Estate Journalism Conference, Autumn

BSFS Poetry Contest
Baltimore Science Fiction Society Inc
PO Box 686, Baltimore, MD 21203-0686
Tel: 410-563-2737
E-mail: poetry@bsfs.org
Web Site: www.bsfs.org/bsfspoetry.htm
Key Personnel
Balticon Chair: Eric Gasior *E-mail:* chair@bsfs.org
Balticon Vice Chair: Yakira Heistand
PR Coord: Morgan Hazelwood *E-mail:* socialmedia@bsfs.org
Entries should address the themes of science fiction/fantasy/horror/science. Limit of 3 poems per person, maximum 60 lines each. No entry fee. Please, no previously published submissions.
Award: $100 (1st prize), $75 (2nd prize), $50 (3rd prize); all receive convention membership & are invited to read their winning entries at Balticon
Closing Date: March 1

Sally Buckner Emerging Writers' Fellowship
North Carolina Writers' Network
PO Box 21591, Winston-Salem, NC 27120-1591
Tel: 336-293-8844
E-mail: mail@ncwriters.org; nclrsubmissions@ecu.edu
Web Site: www.ncwriters.org
Key Personnel
Exec Dir: Ed Southern *E-mail:* ed@ncwriters.org
Fellowship Prog Coord: June Guralnick *E-mail:* juneguralnick@gmail.com
Awarded to an emerging North Carolina writer whose work shows promise of excellence & a commitment to a literary career. Applicants must be in the early stages of their careers & will not have had yet the support needed to achieve major recognition for their work. No specific academic background is required or preferred. Each year, the program will accept applications from writers working primarily in 1 of 4 specific genres: poetry/fiction/creative nonfiction/drama (stage & screen), rotated over a 4-year cycle. Applications will be accepted only via Submittable at ncwriters.submittable.com/submit. Writers must have established legal residence in North Carolina for at least 1 year prior to applying & plan on residing in North Carolina through the fellowship year. Writers must be between the ages of 21 & 35, as of December 31 of the year in which they apply. Students enrolled in degree-granting programs are not eligible to apply. Entry fee: Free to membs, $10 nonmembs.
Award: $500 fellowship, 1-year membership to North Carolina Writer's Network & scholarship aid to attend the Network's annual fall & spring conferences
Closing Date: June 30

Georges Bugnet Award for Fiction
Writers' Guild of Alberta
11759 Groat Rd NW, Edmonton, AB T5M 3K6, Canada
Tel: 780-422-8174 *Toll Free Tel:* 800-665-5354 (AB only)
E-mail: mail@writersguild.ab.ca
Web Site: writersguild.ca
Key Personnel
Exec Dir: Giorgia Severini *E-mail:* gseverini@writersguild.ab.ca
Communs & Partnerships Coord: Ellen Kartz *E-mail:* ellen.kartz@writersguild.ab.ca
Memb Servs Coord: Mike Maguire
Prog & Opers Coord: Ashley Mann *E-mail:* ashley.mann@writersguild.ab.ca
Progs & Events Coord: Jason Norman *E-mail:* jason.norman@writersguild.ab.ca
Proj Asst: Sadie MacGillivray *E-mail:* sadie.macgillivray@writersguild.ab.ca
Established: 1982
Literary award for an author that is a resident of Alberta.
Award: $1,500
Closing Date: Dec 31
Presented: Alberta Book Awards Gala, AB, CN
Branch Office(s)
223 12 Ave SW, No 204, Calgary, AB T2R 0G9, Canada, Prog & Conference Coord: Dorothy Bentley *Tel:* 403-875-8058 *E-mail:* dorothy.bentley@writersguild.ab.ca

John Burroughs Medal
John Burroughs Association Inc
500 Burroughs Dr, at Floyd Ackert, New York, NY 12493
Mailing Address: PO Box 439, West Park, NY 12493
Tel: 845-384-6556
E-mail: info@johnburroughsassociation.org
Web Site: www.johnburroughsassociation.org
Key Personnel
Pres: Joan Burroughs *E-mail:* joan@johnburroughsassociation.org
Established: 1926
Presented to the author of a distinguished nature book that combines accurate scientific information with firsthand fieldwork & creative natural history writing.
Award: Medal, cash prize & certificate of recognition to author & publisher
Closing Date: Oct
Presented: Celebratory Awards Luncheon, Yale Club, New York, NY, 1st Monday in April

John Burroughs Nature Essay Award
John Burroughs Association Inc
500 Burroughs Dr, at Floyd Ackert, New York, NY 12493
Mailing Address: PO Box 439, West Park, NY 12493
Tel: 845-384-6556
E-mail: info@johnburroughsassociation.org
Web Site: www.johnburroughsassociation.org
Key Personnel
Pres: Joan Burroughs *E-mail:* joan@johnburroughsassociation.org
Established: 1993
Awarded to an outstanding published natural history essay that presents scientifically accurate first-hand accounts, yet does more by using personal point of view in vivid writing.
Award: Certificate of recognition to author & publisher
Closing Date: Dec
Presented: Celebratory Awards Luncheon, Yale Club, New York, NY, 1st Monday in April

Cabell First Novelist Award
Virginia Commonwealth University (VCU)
901 Park Ave, Richmond, VA 23284
Mailing Address: PO Box 842033, Richmond, VA 23284
Tel: 804-828-0593
E-mail: cabellfn@vcu.edu
Web Site: firstnovelist.vcu.edu
Established: 2002
Honors an outstanding debut novel published in the preceding calendar year in the US. Self-published novels & books available in e-format only are not eligible. Winning author visits VCU in November for a celebratory reading & to offer their perspective on the writing & publishing process to the VCU & Richmond communities. To submit a novel, send one PDF file & 5 hard copies. See web site for mailing & shipping addresses.
Other Sponsor(s): Barnes & Noble @ VCU; VCU Department of English; VCU Libraries; VCU MFA Program in Creative Writing
Closing Date: Dec 30
Presented: June/July

Gerald Cable Book Award
Silverfish Review Press
PO Box 3541, Eugene, OR 97403
Tel: 541-228-0422
E-mail: sfrpress@gmail.com
Web Site: www.silverfishreviewpress.com
Key Personnel
Ed & Publr: Rodger Moody
Established: 1995
Poetry Book; for author who has not yet published a collection; selection by May. $25 reading fee.
Award: $1,000 & publication by Silverfish Review Press & 25 copies of the book
Closing Date: Oct 15

The Randolph Caldecott Medal
Association for Library Service to Children (ALSC)
Division of The American Library Association (ALA)
225 N Michigan Ave, Suite 1300, Chicago, IL 60601
Tel: 312-280-2163 *Toll Free Tel:* 800-545-2433 *Fax:* 312-280-5271
E-mail: alsc@ala.org
Web Site: www.ala.org/alsc/awardsgrants/bookmedia/caldecott
Key Personnel
Exec Dir: Alena Rivers *Tel:* 800-545-2433 ext 5866 *E-mail:* arivers@ala.org
Awards Coord: Jordan Dubin *Tel:* 800-545-2433 ext 5839 *E-mail:* jdubin@ala.org
Prog Coord: Ann Michaud *Tel:* 800-545-2433 ext 2166 *E-mail:* amichaud@ala.org
Membership/Mktg Specialist: Elizabeth Serrano *Tel:* 800-545-2433 ext 2164 *E-mail:* eserrano@ala.org
Established: 1937
Presented to the artist of the most distinguished American picture book for children published in the US during the previous year. The artist must be a citizen or resident of the US.
Award: Medal
Closing Date: Dec 31
Presented: ALA Youth Media Awards, Late Jan

CALIBA Golden Poppy Awards
California Independent Booksellers Alliance (CALIBA)
100 Black Diamond Rd, Stonyford, CA 95979
Tel: 415-561-7686
E-mail: info@caliballiance.org
Web Site: caliballiance.org/golden-poppy-awards.html
Key Personnel
Pres: Melinda Powers
Exec Dir: Hannah Walcher
Opers Mgr: Valentina Moberg *E-mail:* valentina@caliballiance.org
Mgr, Mktg & Promos: Emma Marie *E-mail:* emma@caliballiance.org
Awards to recognize the most distinguished books published by California writers & artists during the publishing year November 1-October 31. Categories: Fiction, nonfiction, cooking & food, mystery, poetry, young adult, middle grade, children's picture book, mirrors & windows, regional interest.
Closing Date: June (for books published first half of year), Oct (nominations from 2nd half of year)
Presented: March

California Book Awards
Commonwealth Club of California
110 The Embarcadero, San Francisco, CA 94105
Tel: 415-597-6700 *Fax:* 415-597-6729
E-mail: bookawards@commonwealthclub.org
Web Site: www.commonwealthclub.org/bookawards
Established: 1931

Honors the exceptional literary merit of California writers & publishers. Annual awards are presented in the categories of fiction, nonfiction, poetry, first work of fiction, juvenile literature (up to age 10), adult literature (ages 11-16), Californiana, works in translation & notable contribution to publishing. To be eligible, author must be resident in California at the time of publication & books must be published under the year in consideration.
Award: Plaques with medallions for gold & silver awardees
Closing Date: Dec
Presented: 1st Monday in June

California Young Playwrights Contest
Playwrights Project
3675 Ruffin Rd, Suite 330, San Diego, CA 92123
Tel: 858-384-2970 *Fax:* 858-384-2974
E-mail: write@playwrightsproject.org
Web Site: www.playwrightsproject.org
Key Personnel
Exec Dir: Cecelia Kouma
Established: 1985
Playwriting contest for Californians under 19 years of age.
Award: Professional production (location to be announced), royalty
Closing Date: June 1
Presented: Jan-Feb following application

Matei Calinescu Prize
Modern Language Association (MLA)
85 Broad St, New York, NY 10004
SAN: 202-6422
Tel: 646-576-5141; 646-576-5000
E-mail: awards@mla.org
Web Site: www.mla.org
Key Personnel
Coord, Book Prizes: Annie M Reiser
  E-mail: areiser@mla.org
Awarded for a distinguished work of scholarship in 20th or 21st century literature & thought in any geographical context. Preference is given to a first or second work published by an entrant. Authors need not be members of the MLA. Awarded for works published in 2024. For consideration, submit 6 print copies, PDF & letter of identification.
Award: Cash award & certificate
Closing Date: April 1, 2025
Presented: MLA Convention, Toronto, ON, CN, Jan 2026

Joe Pendleton Campbell Narrative Contest
The Poetry Society of Virginia (PSV)
PO Box 36128, North Chesterfield, VA 23235-3533
E-mail: contest@poetrysocietyofvirginia.org; info@poetryvirginia.org
Web Site: www.poetrysocietyofvirginia.org
Key Personnel
Pres: Cherryl T Cooley
  E-mail: poetrysocietypresident@gmail.com
All entries must be in English, original & unpublished. Any form, any subject, narrative poem, 64 line limit. Submit 1 copy of the poem with no identifying information but put the category in the upper right-hand-side, along with a notation as to whether you are a member of PSV (does not matter if you are a lifetime member or just joined for the contest). Submit a cover letter/page that contains the category, the name of the poem, your name & address, phone number & e-mail address. Entries will not be returned. Entry fee: Free to membs, $5 nonmembs.
Other Sponsor(s): Paula Savoy
Award: $50 (1st prize), $30 (2nd prize), $20 (3rd prize)
Closing Date: Feb
Presented: PSV Awards Ceremony, April

Canada-Japan Literary Awards
Canada Council for the Arts (Conseil des arts du Canada)
150 Elgin St, 2nd fl, Ottawa, ON K2P 1L4, Canada
Mailing Address: PO Box 1047, Ottawa, ON K1P 5A0, Canada
Tel: 613-566-4414 *Toll Free Tel:* 800-263-5588 (CN only) *Fax:* 613-566-4390
E-mail: canadajapan-prizes@canadacouncil.ca
Web Site: canadacouncil.ca/funding/prizes/canada-japan-literary-awards
Key Personnel
Prog Offr, Prizes: Lori Knoll *Tel:* 613-566-4414 ext 5573
Biennial awards to recognize literary excellence by Canadian writers & translators who write, or translate from Japanese into English or French, a work on Japan, on Japanese themes or on themes that promote mutual understanding between Japan & Canada. Nominations must be submitted by a professional book publisher.
Award: $10,000 each (1 English language work & 1 French language work)
Closing Date: April 30, even-numbered years

Canadian First Book Prize
The Griffin Trust for Excellence in Poetry
363 Parkridge Crescent, Oakville, ON L6M 1A8, Canada
Tel: 905-618-0420
E-mail: info@griffinpoetryprize.com; publicity@griffinpoetryprize.com
Web Site: griffinpoetryprize.com
Key Personnel
Founder & Chmn: Scott Griffin
  E-mail: scottgriffin@griffinpoetryprize.com
Exec Dir: Ruth Smith
Communs Dir: Melissa Shirley *Tel:* 647-389-9510
Prize is awarded to a first edition collection of poetry written in English by a Canadian citizen or permanent resident of Canada. Translations are not eligible. No shortlist or longlist for this prize.
Other Sponsor(s): Civitella Ranieri Foundation
Award: $10,000 & 6-week affiliated fellowship with Civitella Ranieri Foundation, Perugia, Italy
Presented: May

The Canadian Jewish Literary Awards
Koschitzy Centre for Jewish Studies, 763 Kaneff Tower, York University, 4700 Keele St, Toronto, ON M3J 1P3, Canada
E-mail: info@cjlawards.ca; cjs@yorku.ca (digital submissions)
Web Site: www.cjlawards.ca
Key Personnel
Chair: Edward Trapunski
Celebrates excellence in Canadian writing on Jewish themes & subjects. Authors must be Canadian by birth, by education or by residency but need not be Jewish. Books can be in English, French or Yiddish & published between June 1 of the preceding year & May 31 of the award year. Award categories: Fiction; scholarship; biography/memoir; history; youth literature; poetry; Holocaust literature; Jewish thought & culture; Yiddish. Entry fee: $50 per title.
Closing Date: May 2 (books published June 1-April 30); May 31 (books published May 1-May 31)
Presented: Gala Ceremony, York University, Toronto, ON, CN, Oct

Truman Capote Award for Literary Criticism in Honor of Newton Arvin
University of Iowa, Writers' Workshop, Graduate Creative Writing Program
102 Dey House, 507 N Clinton St, Iowa City, IA 52242-1000
Tel: 319-335-0416
Web Site: writersworkshop.uiowa.edu
Key Personnel
Dir: Lan Samantha Chang
Awarded to reward & encourage excellence in the field of literary criticism. The award was established in memory of Newton Arvin, one of the critics Capote admired.
Other Sponsor(s): Truman Capote Literary Trust
Award: $30,000
Presented: Oct

Career Development Program
New Brunswick Arts Board (Conseil des arts du Nouveau-Brunswick)
225 King St, Suite 201, Fredericton, NB E3B 1E1, Canada
Tel: 506-444-4444 *Toll Free Tel:* 866-460-ARTS (460-2787) *Fax:* 506-444-5543
E-mail: prog@artsnb.ca
Web Site: www.artsnb.ca
Key Personnel
Exec Dir: Joss Richer *Tel:* 506-478-4610
  E-mail: direct@artsnb.ca
Prog Offr: Sarah Jonathan Parker *Tel:* 506-440-0037
Opers Mgr: Tilly Jackson *Tel:* 506-478-4422
  E-mail: tjackson@artsnb.ca
Program is designed to recognize & encourage arts professionals who have demonstrated exceptional artistic talent & potential & who are pursuing a career in the arts. The program is divided in 4 components:
Arts by Innovation is for assistance to present work by invitation in established arts events.
Artist in Residence is for assistance for participation in residency opportunities of 3 months & less. The artists in residence are to contribute to the promotion & understanding of the arts by means of the artists' contact with the clientele of the establishments.
Professional Development is for assistance for professional development scholarships for studies & mentorships.
Professionalization & Promotion is designed to assist artists to produce tools related to the promotion of the artist's work & career with a view to broadening the dissemination network for their work & diversifying their sources for funding. Eligible artistic disciplines include the literary arts (spoken word, storytelling, literary performance & literary translation).
Award: Up to $2,000 including transportation & accommodation costs
Closing Date: Jan 1, March 1, May 1, July 1, Sept 1, Nov 1

The Carle Honors
The Eric Carle Museum of Picture Book Art
125 W Bay Rd, Amherst, MA 01002
Tel: 413-559-6300
E-mail: info@carlemuseum.org
Web Site: www.carlemuseum.org/content/carle-honors
Key Personnel
Founder & Comm Chair: Leonard S Marcus
Exec Dir: Jennifer Schantz
Dir, Devt: Rebecca Miller Goggins *Tel:* 413-559-6308 *E-mail:* rebeccag@carlemuseum.org
Museum's annual benefit gala, including 4 awards recognizing individuals in the picture book field for their dedication & creative vision. The awards recognize individuals in 4 distinct forms: Artist, for an individual who has shown lifelong innovation in the field; Mentor, for an editor, designer, or educator who has championed the art form; Angel, for an individual whose generous resources are crucial to making picture book art exhibitions, education programs, & related projects a reality; Bridge, for an individual who has found inspired ways

to bring the art of the picture book to larger audiences through work in other fields.
Presented: Sept

Andrew Carnegie Medals for Excellence in Fiction & Nonfiction
The American Library Association (ALA)
225 N Michigan Ave, Suite 1300, Chicago, IL 60601
SAN: 201-0062
Tel: 312-944-6780 *Toll Free Tel:* 800-545-2433
Fax: 312-440-9374
E-mail: ala@ala.org
Web Site: www.ala.org/awardsgrants/carnegieadult
Key Personnel
Exec Dir, RUSA: Jessica Hughes
    E-mail: jhughes@ala.org
Sr Prog Offr, RUSA: Leighann Wood
    E-mail: lwood@ala.org
Established: 2012
To recognize the best fiction & nonfiction books for adult readers published in the US in the previous year, chosen by selection committee.
Other Sponsor(s): Booklist; Carnegie Corporation of New York Grant; Reference & User Services Association (RUSA)
Award: $5,000 (winning authors, 1 in each category), $1,500 (2 finalists in each category)
Presented: ALA Annual Conference & Exhibition, June

Carnegie-Whitney Award
ALA Publishing Committee
Unit of The American Library Association (ALA)
225 N Michigan Ave, Suite 1300, Chicago, IL 60601
Tel: 312-280-5416 *Toll Free Tel:* 800-545-2433
Web Site: www.ala.org
Key Personnel
Grant Admin: Mary Jo Bolduc
    E-mail: mbolduc@ala.org
Established: 1902
For the preparation of bibliographic aids for research with scholarly intent & general applicability. Decisions made at the Publishing Committee Meeting each January. Completed proposals should be sent to the Grant Administrator.
Award: Up to $5,000 annually
Closing Date: Nov

The Robert & Ina Caro Research/Travel Fellowship
Biographers International Organization (BIO)
PO Box 33020, Santa Fe, NM 87594
Web Site: biographersinternational.org/award/the-robert-and-ina-caro-research-travel-fellowship
Key Personnel
Exec Dir: Michael Gately *E-mail:* execdirector@biographersinternational.org
Established: 2018
BIO members with a work in progress can apply to receive funding for research trips to archives or to important settings in their subject's lives. Fellowship is restricted to support of works of biography (not of history, autobiography or memoir). See web site for full details.
Award: One $5,000 fellowship or two $2,500 fellowships
Closing Date: Feb 1
Presented: BIO Annual Conference, May

Catholic Book Awards
Catholic Media Association (CMA)
10 S Riverside Plaza, Suite 875, Chicago, IL 60606
Tel: 312-380-6789
E-mail: awards@catholicmediaassociation.org
Web Site: www.catholicmediaassociation.org
Key Personnel
Exec Dir: Rob DeFrancesco
    E-mail: rdefrancesco@CatholicMediaAssociation.org
Proj Coord, Awards: Kathleen Holloway
    E-mail: kholloway@CatholicMediaAssociation.org; Eucarol Juarez *E-mail:* ejuarez@CatholicMediaAssociation.org
Recognizes the outstanding work of publishers, authors, & book editors. Awards are given for books promoting exceptional Catholic materials to the general public. Book submissions must have a copyright date from the year prior to the award year. Publishers may submit works published by their company. Authors may submit works of which they are they are the primary or co-author. Editors may submit their compilations or reference books. Submissions open November 15.
Award: Certificate
Closing Date: Feb
Presented: Winners announced at Catholic Media Conference, June

Catholic Media Awards
Catholic Media Association (CMA)
10 S Riverside Plaza, Suite 875, Chicago, IL 60606
Tel: 312-380-6789
E-mail: awards@catholicmediaassociation.org
Web Site: www.catholicmediaassociation.org
Key Personnel
Exec Dir: Rob DeFrancesco
    E-mail: rdefrancesco@CatholicMediaAssociation.org
Proj Coord, Awards: Kathleen Holloway
    E-mail: kholloway@CatholicMediaAssociation.org; Eucarol Juarez *E-mail:* ejuarez@CatholicMediaAssociation.org
Acknowledges the outstanding work of CLA publisher & communication members. Participants choose categories by various media that feature writing, design, production & editing skills, then by sub-categories such as news, feature stories, etc. Works completed by CMA members the year prior to the award year are accepted. Submissions open November 15.
Award: Certificate
Closing Date: Feb
Presented: Winners announced at Catholic Media Conference, June

Kay Cattarulla Award for Best Short Story
Texas Institute of Letters (TIL)
PO Box 130294, Spring, TX 77393
Web Site: texasinstituteofletters.org
Key Personnel
Pres: David Bowles *E-mail:* president@texasinstituteofletters.org
VP: Chris Barton
Secy: Kathryn Jones *E-mail:* secretary@texasinstituteofletters.org
Treas: Cliff Hudder
Award for the best short story by a Texan or about Texas. The author must have been born in Texas or have lived in Texas for at least 5 consecutive years at some time. See web site for guidelines.
Award: $1,000
Closing Date: Jan
Presented: TIL Annual Meeting & Awards Ceremony, April

Cave Canem Northwestern University Press Poetry Prize
Cave Canem Foundation Inc
20 Jay St, Suite 310-A, Brooklyn, NY 11201-8301
Tel: 718-858-0000 *Fax:* 718-858-0002
E-mail: info@ccpoets.org
Web Site: cavecanempoets.org/prizes/cave-canem-northwestern-university-press-poetry-prize/
Key Personnel
Exec Dir: Lisa Willis *E-mail:* lwillis@ccpoets.org
Awarded biennially, in even-numbered years, to an unpublished, original collection of poems written in English by a Black poet of African descent who has had no more than one full-length book of poetry published by a professional press. Submit mss online via Submittable. Hard copy submissions are not considered. One ms per poet. See web site for full submission guidelines.
Other Sponsor(s): Northwestern University Press
Award: $1,000, publication by Northwestern University Press, 15 copies of the book & feature reading in New York City
Closing Date: June 12
Presented: Aug

Cave Canem Poetry Prize
Cave Canem Foundation Inc
20 Jay St, Suite 310-A, Brooklyn, NY 11201-8301
Tel: 718-858-0000 *Fax:* 718-858-0002
E-mail: info@ccpoets.org
Web Site: cavecanempoets.org/prizes/cave-canem-poetry-prize/
Key Personnel
Exec Dir: Lisa Willis *E-mail:* lwillis@ccpoets.org
To be eligible, work must be unpublished, original collections of poems written in English by Black writers of African descent who have not had a full-length book of poetry published by a professional press. Submit mss online via Submittable. Hard copy submissions are not considered. One ms per poet. See web site for full submission guidelines.
Other Sponsor(s): University of Georgia Press
Award: $1,000, publication by University of Georgia Press, 15 copies of the book & feature reading; both the winner & runner-up are invited to individual critique sessions with the final judge
Closing Date: Jan 31
Presented: Oct

CBC Diversity Outstanding Achievement Awards
The Children's Book Council (CBC)
54 W 39 St, 14th fl, New York, NY 10018
E-mail: cbc.info@cbcbooks.org
Web Site: www.cbcbooks.org
Key Personnel
Exec Dir: Carl Lennertz *E-mail:* carl.lennertz@cbcbooks.org
Assoc Exec Dir: Shaina Birkhead *E-mail:* shaina.birkhead@cbcbooks.org
Awarded to professionals or organizations in the children's publishing industry who have made a significant impact on the publishing & marketing of diverse books, diversity in hiring & mentoring & efforts that create greater awareness with the public about the importance of diverse voices.
Presented: CBC Forum, Oct

The Center for Fiction First Novel Prize
The Center for Fiction
15 Lafayette Ave, Brooklyn, NY 11217
Tel: 212-755-6710
E-mail: info@centerforfiction.org
Web Site: www.centerforfiction.org/awards/the-first-novel-prize
Key Personnel
Writing Progs Mgr: Randy Winston
Established: 2006
Presented for the best debut novel published between January 1 & December 31 of the award year.
Award: $15,000 (1st prize), $1,000 (shortlist award)
Closing Date: March 15
Presented: The Center for Fiction's Annual Benefit & Awards Dinner, Dec

AWARDS, PRIZE CONTESTS, FELLOWSHIPS & GRANTS

Center for Publishing Departmental Scholarships
New York University, School of Continuing & Professional Studies
Midtown Ctr, Rm 429, 11 W 42 St, New York, NY 10036
Tel: 212-992-3232 *Fax:* 212-992-3233
E-mail: pub.center@nyu.edu
Web Site: www.scps.nyu.edu
Key Personnel
Asst Dir, MS in Publg: Judson Simmons
  E-mail: judson.simmons@nyu.edu
Presented to students enrolled in at least 6 credits in Master of Science in Publishing: Digital & Print Media Program. Need excellent academic record. Based on merit & number of credits taken.
Award: $1,000 & up
Presented: Fall

Cercador Prize
c/o Third Place Books, 6504 20 Ave NE, Seattle, WA 98115
E-mail: info@cercadorprize.com
Web Site: www.cercadorprize.com
Key Personnel
Chair, Prize Comm: Spencer Ruchti
Established: 2023
No formal submissions process. A committee of independent booksellers from across the US convenes in an effort to recognize works of literature in translation. Translations are published & distributed in the US in the current calendar year. Primary focus is English-language translation.
Award: $1,000 to winning translator(s)
Presented: Nov

Eugene Cervi Award
International Society of Weekly Newspaper Editors (ISWNE)
Missouri Southern State University, 3950 E Newman Rd, Joplin, MO 64801-1595
Web Site: www.iswne.org/contests
Key Personnel
Exec Dir: Dr Chad Stebbins *Tel:* 417-625-9736
  E-mail: stebbins-c@mssu.edu
Established: 1976
Awarded to recognize a career of outstanding public service through community journalism.

The CHA Best Scholarly Book in Canadian History Prize
Canadian Historical Association
130 Albert St, Suite 1201, Ottawa, ON K1P 5G4, Canada
Tel: 613-233-7885 *Fax:* 613-565-5445
E-mail: cha-shc@cha-shc.ca
Web Site: cha-shc.ca
Key Personnel
Exec Dir: Michel Duquet *E-mail:* mduquet@cha-shc.ca
Established: 1976
Awarded for the best book on Canadian history. See web site for application details.
Award: $5,000
Closing Date: Dec 1
Presented: Canadian Historical Association Annual Meeting, May

Jack L Chalker Young Writers' Contest
Baltimore Science Fiction Society Inc
PO Box 686, Baltimore, MD 21203-0686
Tel: 410-563-2737
E-mail: ywc@balticon.org
Web Site: www.bsfs.org/bsfsywc.htm
Key Personnel
Balticon Chair: Eric Gasior *E-mail:* chair@bsfs.org
Balticon Vice Chair: Yakira Heistand
PR Coord: Morgan Hazelwood
  E-mail: socialmedia@bsfs.org
Contestants shall be no younger than 14 & no older than 18 years of age as of May 29 in the contest year & shall reside in, or attend school in Maryland. Winners will be required to provide their proof of age. Submissions must be in the field of science fiction or fantasy & shall be no more than 2,500 words in length. One contestant may submit multiple entries, but only one prize may be won by any one entrant. See web site for full submission guidelines.
Award: $150 (1st prize), $100 (2nd prize), $50 (3rd prize); all receive complimentary registration for Balticon for themselves & their parents or one guest each along with a free Balticon T-shirt
Closing Date: March 31

Jane Chambers Playwriting Award
Women & Theatre Program, Association for Theatre in Higher Education
Georgetown University, 108 David Performing Arts Ctr, Box 571063, 37 & "O" St, NW, Washington, DC 20057-1063
Web Site: www.athe.org/page/jane_chambers; www.womenandtheatreprogram.com/jane-chambers
Key Personnel
Contact: Jen-Scott Mobley *E-mail:* jenscottmob@gmail.com; Maya E Roth *E-mail:* mer46@georgetown.edu
Established: 1984
Award for play or performance text by a woman or genderqueer writer which reflects a feminist perspective & contains a majority of roles for women performers. Scripts may be produced or unproduced; encourage experimentation with dramatic form. See web site for FAQ & past winners. Electronic submissions preferred. One play per playwright annually. Separate contest for student playwrights.
Award: $1,000 for reading of the winning piece at the ATHE Conference plus free registration, 2 nights lodging & up to $500 travel for the Awards Ceremony, plus one-year membership in the Dramatist Guild. Student winner, submitted separately via the WTP web site, is also recognized with $250 & selected reading of scenes
Closing Date: Feb 1
Presented: ATHE Annual Conference

The Alfred & Fay Chandler Book Award
Business History Review
c/o Harvard Business School, Connell House 301A, Boston, MA 02163
Tel: 617-495-1003 *Fax:* 617-495-2705
E-mail: bhr@hbs.edu
Web Site: www.hbs.edu/businesshistory/fellowships
Key Personnel
Ed: Walter Friedman *E-mail:* wfriedman@hbs.edu
Established: 1964
Award given every 3 years for best book published in the US on the history of business. Selection by the editorial board of the Business History Review.
Award: A scroll

G S Sharat Chandra Prize for Short Fiction
BkMk Press Inc
5 W Third St, Parkville, MO 64152
Tel: 816-200-7895
E-mail: info@bkmkpress.org
Web Site: www.bkmkpress.org
Key Personnel
Ed: Ben Furnish *E-mail:* ben@bkmkpress.org
Established: 2001
Awarded for the best book-length ms of short fiction in English by a living author. Ms must be typed on standard-sized paper in English & should be 125-300 pages double-spaced. Entries must include two title pages: one with author name, address & phone number & one with no author information. Any acknowledgments should appear on a separate piece of paper. Entries must include a table of contents. Author's name must not appear anywhere on the ms. Do not submit your ms by fax or e-mail. A SASE should be included, for notification only. Note: No mss will be returned. A reading fee of $25 in US funds (check payable to BkMk Press) must accompany each ms. Processing fee for online submissions is an additional $5. Entrants will receive a copy of the winning book when published. Entrants may also now submit online.
Award: $1,000 plus book publication of winning ms by BkMk Press
Closing Date: Jan 15
Presented: Summer

The Chautauqua Prize
Chautauqua Institution
One Ames Ave, Chautauqua, NY 14722
Mailing Address: PO Box 28, Chautauqua, NY 14722
Toll Free Tel: 800-836-ARTS (836-2787)
Web Site: www.chq.org/prize
Key Personnel
Contact, Educ Dept: Sara Toth *Tel:* 716-357-6376
  E-mail: stoth@chq.org
Established: 2012
National prize for a book of fiction or literary/narrative nonfiction that provides a richly rewarding reading experience & honors the author for a significant contribution to the literary arts. Book must be written in English & published in the calendar year prior to the year of the award. Entries must include official entry form, 8 copies of each title entered & entry fee of $75. Each nominated eligible book is evaluated by 3 Chautauquan reviewers, after which the shortlist & winner are chosen by a 3-member independent, anonymous jury.
Award: $7,500
Closing Date: Dec 15

Children's History Book Prize
New-York Historical Society
170 Central Park W, New York, NY 10024
Tel: 212-873-3400 *Fax:* 212-595-5707
E-mail: info@nyhistory.org
Web Site: www.nyhistory.org/childrens-museum/connect/book-prize
Key Personnel
Pres & CEO: Louise Mirrer
VP & Dir, DiMenna Children's History Museum: Alice Stevenson
Awarded to honor the best children's historical literature in the US for middle readers ages 9-12, fiction or nonfiction.
Award: $10,000
Closing Date: Oct

Children's Literature Association Article Award
Children's Literature Association (ChLA)
140B Purcellville Gateway Dr, Suite 1200, Purcellville, VA 20132
Tel: 630-571-4520
E-mail: info@childlitassn.org
Web Site: www.childlitassn.org
Key Personnel
Association Mgr: Cate Langley
Awarded in recognition of outstanding articles of literary criticism published in English within a given year on the topic of children's literature. Nominations should be submitted online through the web site. Eligible articles must be written in English exclusively by the author(s) or translator(s) whose name(s) appear(s) on the article & must have been published 2 years prior. Articles should provide new insights into the field, making a distinct or significant scholarly contribution to the understanding of chil-

dren's literature. Reprints of previously published articles are not eligible.
Award: Cash prize, award certificate, complimentary conference registration & banquet ticket
Closing Date: Nov 1
Presented: ChLA Annual Conference, June

Children's Literature Association Book Award
Children's Literature Association (ChLA)
140B Purcellville Gateway Dr, Suite 1200, Purcellville, VA 20132
Tel: 630-571-4520
E-mail: info@childlitassn.org
Web Site: www.childlitassn.org
Key Personnel
Association Mgr: Cate Langley
Awarded in recognition of outstanding book-length contributions to children's literature scholarship & criticism published in a given year. Nominations should be submitted online through the web site. Eligible titles must be published, book-length works that make a distinct or significant contribution to the scholarly +/or theoretical understanding of children's literature from a literary, cultural, historical, or theoretical perspective. Titles must be written in English exclusively by the author(s) or translator(s) whose names(s) appear on the title page & must bear a copyright date of the year under consideration. Translations published in the year under review may be considered regardless of what year the book was published in its first language. Reprints or new editions of previously published books are not eligible.
Award: Cash prize, award certificate, complimentary conference registration & banquet ticket
Presented: ChLA Annual Conference, June

Children's Literature Association Edited Book Award
Children's Literature Association (ChLA)
140B Purcellville Gateway Dr, Suite 1200, Purcellville, VA 20132
Tel: 630-571-4520
E-mail: info@childlitassn.org
Web Site: www.childlitassn.org
Key Personnel
Association Mgr: Cate Langley
Awarded in recognition of the contribution of outstanding collections of essays to children's literature scholarship & criticism. Nominations should be submitted online through the web site. Eligible titles must be published, book-length edited collections that make a distinct or significant contribution to our understanding of children's literature from a literary, cultural, historical, or theoretical perspective. Must be written in English exclusively by the authors whose names appear in the list of contributors & the editor(s) whose name(s) appear on the title page. Books must bear a copyright date of the year under consideration. Biographical studies & studies of children's films & other media are eligible for nomination. New editions of previously published books & books containing reprints of previously published essays are not eligible. Volumes with a primarily pedagogical focus & reference works are not eligible.
Presented: ChLA Annual Conference, June

Children's Literature Association Graduate Student Essay Award
Children's Literature Association (ChLA)
140B Purcellville Gateway Dr, Suite 1200, Purcellville, VA 20132
Tel: 630-571-4520
E-mail: info@childlitassn.org
Web Site: www.childlitassn.org
Key Personnel
Association Mgr: Cate Langley
Established: 2005

Awards to recognize outstanding papers written on the graduate level in the field of children's literature. They are considered annually & awarded as warranted. Two separate awards are given, one for an essay written at the master's level & one for an essay written at the doctoral level. Submissions should demonstrate familiarity with previous scholarship & should contain original, distinctive ideas. They should be at least 3,000 words in length & should not exceed 7,500 words, including notes & works cited. They should conform to MLA style. Work should not have been published at time of submission. Nominations should be submitted electronically on behalf of the graduate student by a faculty member & must be accompanied by a cover letter from that faculty member. Only 2 submissions per year per faculty member will be accepted. The graduate level of the nominee should be noted in the cover letter so that the essay can be evaluated with the proper peer group. This award may only be won once by an individual student at each level (Master's, PhD); previous winners will not be eligible.
Closing Date: Feb 1
Presented: ChLA Annual Conference, June

Children's Literature Lecture Award
Association for Library Service to Children (ALSC)
Division of The American Library Association (ALA)
225 N Michigan Ave, Suite 1300, Chicago, IL 60601
Tel: 312-280-2163 *Toll Free Tel:* 800-545-2433
Fax: 312-280-5271
E-mail: alsc@ala.org
Web Site: www.ala.org/alsc/awardsgrants/profawards/chll
Key Personnel
Exec Dir: Alena Rivers *Tel:* 800-545-2433 ext 5866 *E-mail:* arivers@ala.org
Awards Coord: Jordan Dubin *Tel:* 800-545-2433 ext 5839 *E-mail:* jdubin@ala.org
Prog Coord: Ann Michaud *Tel:* 800-545-2433 ext 2166 *E-mail:* amichaud@ala.org
Membership/Mktg Specialist: Elizabeth Serrano *Tel:* 800-545-2433 ext 2164 *E-mail:* eserrano@ala.org
Established: 1969
Person appointed prepares a paper of significant contribution to the field of children's literature & delivers a lecture based on the paper in April. Libraries & other institutions apply to host the lecture.
Award: Publication in the ALSC journal *Children & Libraries*
Presented: Late Jan

Children's Literature Legacy Award
Association for Library Service to Children (ALSC)
Division of The American Library Association (ALA)
225 N Michigan Ave, Suite 1300, Chicago, IL 60601
Tel: 312-280-2163 *Toll Free Tel:* 800-545-2433
Fax: 312-280-5271
E-mail: alsc@ala.org
Web Site: www.ala.org/awardsgrants/childrens-literature-legacy-award; www.ala.org/alsc/awardsgrants/bookmedia/clla
Key Personnel
Exec Dir: Alena Rivers *Tel:* 800-545-2433 ext 5866 *E-mail:* arivers@ala.org
Awards Coord: Jordan Dubin *Tel:* 800-545-2433 ext 5839 *E-mail:* jdubin@ala.org
Prog Coord: Ann Michaud *Tel:* 800-545-2433 ext 2166 *E-mail:* amichaud@ala.org
Membership/Mktg Specialist: Elizabeth Serrano *Tel:* 800-545-2433 ext 2164 *E-mail:* eserrano@ala.org
Established: 1954
Presented to an author or illustrator whose books have made a substantial & lasting contribution to children's literature. The books must have been published in the US.
Award: Citation
Closing Date: Dec 31
Presented: ALA Youth Media Awards, Late Jan

Children's Sequoyah Book Award
Oklahoma Library Association
119 Meramec Station Rd, Suite 207, Ballwin, MO 63021-6902
Toll Free Tel: 800-969-6562 (ext 5) *Fax:* 636-529-1396
E-mail: sequoyah@oklibs.org; ola@amigos.org
Web Site: www.oklibs.org
Established: 1959
School children's choice of a book published by a living US author from a selected list. Students grades 3-5 who have read/listened to at least 3 books from the Children's Masterlist are eligible to vote. Books are considered for Masterlist 2 years prior to the award being given. Voting takes place February 1-March 15 with winner announced by March 31.
Award: Medal
Presented: OLA Annual Conference, March/April

Christian Book Award®
Evangelical Christian Publishers Association (ECPA)
5801 S McClintock Dr, Suite 104, Tempe, AZ 85283
Tel: 480-966-3998 *Fax:* 480-966-1944
E-mail: info@ecpa.org
Web Site: christianbookawards.com
Key Personnel
Pres & CEO: Jeff Crosby
Program recognizes the highest quality in Christian books & Bibles. There are 11 categories: Bibles; Bible Reference Works; Bible Study; Ministry Resources; Biography & Memoir; Christian Living; Faith & Culture; Devotion & Gift; Children (0-8); Young People's Literature (ages 9-16 nonfiction); New Author. See web site for detailed submission process.
Closing Date: Sept 30
Presented: May 1

The Christopher Awards
The Christophers
5 Hanover Sq, 22nd fl, New York, NY 10004-2751
Tel: 212-759-4050 *Toll Free Tel:* 888-298-4050 (orders) *Fax:* 212-838-5073
E-mail: mail@christophers.org
Web Site: www.christophers.org
Key Personnel
Prog Mgr & Event Prodr: Tony Rossi *E-mail:* t.rossi@christophers.org
Established: 1945
For adult (nonfiction only) & juvenile fiction & nonfiction published during the current calendar year. Themes must reflect "highest values of the human spirit" criteria.
Award: Bronze medallion
Closing Date: June 1 & Nov 1; books evaluated throughout the calendar year
Presented: New York, NY, May

John Ciardi Prize for Poetry
BkMk Press Inc
5 W Third St, Parkville, MO 64152
Tel: 816-200-7895
E-mail: info@bkmkpress.org
Web Site: www.bkmkpress.org
Key Personnel
Ed: Ben Furnish *E-mail:* ben@bkmkpress.org
Established: 1998
Presented for the best full-length ms of poetry in English by a living author. Ms must be typed on standard-sized paper & should be approx-

imately 50 pages minimum, 110 pages maximum, single-spaced. Entries must include two title pages: one with author name, address & phone & one with no author information. Any acknowledgements should appear on a separate piece of paper. Entries must include a table of contents. Author's name must not appear anywhere on the ms. Do not submit your ms by fax or e-mail. A SASE should be included, for notification only. Note: No mss will be returned. A reading fee of $25 in US funds (check made payable to BkMk Press) must accompany each ms. Processing fee for online submissions is an additional $5. Entrants will receive a copy of the winning book when it is published. Entrants may also now submit online.
Award: $1,000 plus publication by BkMk Press
Closing Date: Jan 15
Presented: Summer

The City of Calgary W O Mitchell Book Prize
Writers' Guild of Alberta
11759 Groat Rd NW, Edmonton, AB T5M 3K6, Canada
Tel: 780-422-8174 *Toll Free Tel:* 800-665-5354 (AB only)
E-mail: mail@writersguild.ab.ca
Web Site: writersguild.ca
Key Personnel
Exec Dir: Giorgia Severini *E-mail:* gseverini@writersguild.ab.ca
Communs & Partnerships Coord: Ellen Kartz *E-mail:* ellen.kartz@writersguild.ab.ca
Memb Servs Coord: Mike Maguire
Prog & Opers Coord: Ashley Mann *E-mail:* ashley.mann@writersguild.ab.ca
Progs & Events Coord: Jason Norman *E-mail:* jason.norman@writersguild.ab.ca
Proj Asst: Sadie MacGillivray *E-mail:* sadie.macgillivray@writersguild.ab.ca
Established: 1996
Given in recognition of literary achievement by Calgary authors. Types may be fiction, poetry, nonfiction, children's literature & drama.
Award: $5,000
Closing Date: Dec 31
Presented: Calgary Awards, Spring
Branch Office(s)
223 12 Ave SW, No 204, Calgary, AB T2R 0G9, Canada, Prog & Conference Coord: Dorothy Bentley *Tel:* 403-875-8058 *E-mail:* dorothy.bentley@writersguild.ab.ca

City of Vancouver Book Award
City of Vancouver, Cultural Services Department
Woodward's Heritage Bldg, Suite 501, 111 W Hastings St, Vancouver, BC V6B 1H4, Canada
Tel: 604-871-6634 *Fax:* 604-871-6005
E-mail: culture@vancouver.ca
Web Site: vancouver.ca/bookaward
Key Personnel
Cultural Planner: Marnie Rice *E-mail:* marnie.rice@vancouver.ca
Established: 1989
Award for authors of books - any genre - that contribute to the appreciation & understanding of Vancouver's history, unique character or achievements of its residents.
Award: $3,000
Closing Date: May
Presented: The Mayor's Arts Awards, Sept/Oct

Civil War and Reconstruction Book Award
The Organization of American Historians (OAH)
112 N Bryan Ave, Bloomington, IN 47408-4141
Tel: 812-855-7311
E-mail: oah@oah.org
Web Site: www.oah.org/awards
Key Personnel
Exec Dir: Beth English *Tel:* 812-855-9836 *E-mail:* benglish@oah.org
Dir, Communs & Mktg: Kym Robinson *Tel:* 812-855-5430 *E-mail:* kymarobi@oah.org
Recognizes the most original book on the coming of the Civil War, the Civil War years, or the Era of Reconstruction, with the exception of works of purely military history. Each entry must be published during the calendar year preceding that in which the award is given. One copy of each entry must be mailed directly to the committee members listed on the web site.
Closing Date: Oct 1 (postmarked)
Presented: OAH Conference on American History, Spring

Ev Clark/Seth Payne Award for Young Science Journalists
Council for the Advancement of Science Writing (CASW)
PO Box 17337, Seattle, WA 98127
Tel: 206-880-0177
E-mail: info@casw.org
Web Site: casw.org/casw/evert-clarkseth-payne-award-young-science-journalists; casw.submittable.com/submit
Key Personnel
Exec Dir: Rosalind Reid *E-mail:* ros_reid@casw.org
Admin & Communs Mgr: Sylvia Kantor *E-mail:* sylviakantor@casw.org
Established: 1989
Awarded for outstanding reporting & writing in any field of science by science journalists under 30. Online submissions.
Award: $1,000
Closing Date: June 30
Presented: ScienceWriters Meeting, Oct

Page Davidson Clayton Prize for Emerging Poets
Michigan Quarterly Review
University of Michigan, 3277 Angell Hall, 435 S State St, Ann Arbor, MI 48109-1003
Tel: 734-764-9265
E-mail: mqr@umich.edu
Web Site: sites.lsa.umich.edu/mqr/about-us/prizes
Established: 2009
Awarded to the best poet appearing in MQR who has not yet published a book. See web site for submission guidelines.
Award: $500

David H Clift Scholarship
ALA Scholarship Clearinghouse
Unit of The American Library Association (ALA)
225 N Michigan Ave, Suite 1300, Chicago, IL 60601
Toll Free Tel: 800-545-2433 (ext 4279) *Fax:* 312-280-4279
E-mail: scholarships@ala.org
Web Site: www.ala.org/scholarships
Key Personnel
Prog Mgr: Kimberly L Redd *E-mail:* klredd@ala.org
Established: 1969
Awarded to worthy US or Canadian citizen or permanent resident to begin an MLS degree in an ALA-accredited program. Applications available in September.
Award: $3,000
Closing Date: March 1

CODiE Awards
Software & Information Industry Association (SIIA)
PO Box 34340, Washington, DC 20043
Tel: 202-789-4446 *Fax:* 202-289-7097
Web Site: www.siia.net
Key Personnel
Pres, SIIA: Jeff Joseph *E-mail:* jjoseph@siia.net
Mng Dir, CODiE Awards: Jennifer Baranowski *Tel:* 949-448-0545 *E-mail:* jbaranowski@siia.net
Established: 1986
Honors excellence in the education & business technology industries. Nomination period begins in November.
Award: Trophy & digital assets
Closing Date: Feb
Presented: June

Coe College Playwriting Festival
Coe College
1220 First Ave NE, Cedar Rapids, IA 52402
Tel: 319-399-8624 *Fax:* 319-399-8557
Web Site: www.theatre.coe.edu; www.coe.edu/academics/theatrearts/theatrearts_playwritingfestival
Key Personnel
Chair, Dept of Theatre Arts: Susan Wolverton *E-mail:* swolvert@coe.edu
Established: 1992
Biennial playwriting award for new, full-length, original, unproduced & unpublished play. No musicals, adaptations, translations or collaborations. Only 1 entry/individual.
Award: Publicly staged reading by students, faculty +/or individuals from the community, $500 & room, board, travel for 1 week residency
Closing Date: Nov 1, even-numbered years
Presented: Coe College, Cedar Rapids, IA, April

Carla Cohen Free Speech Award
New Atlantic Independent Booksellers Association (NAIBA)
2667 Hyacinth St, Westbury, NY 11590
Tel: 516-333-0681
E-mail: kit@naiba.com
Web Site: www.naiba.com/page/cohenfreespeechaward
Key Personnel
Exec Dir: Eileen Dengler *E-mail:* eileen@naiba.com
Established: 2010
Presented for a children's book that best exemplifies the ideals of the First Amendment.

Morton N Cohen Award for a Distinguished Edition of Letters
Modern Language Association (MLA)
85 Broad St, New York, NY 10004
SAN: 202-6422
Tel: 646-576-5141; 646-576-5000
E-mail: awards@mla.org
Web Site: www.mla.org
Key Personnel
Coord, Book Prizes: Annie M Reiser *E-mail:* areiser@mla.org
Established: 1989
Awarded biennially, in even-numbered years, for an outstanding edition of letters published in 2023, 2024 or 2025. Editions may be in single or multiple volumes. For consideration, submit 4 print copies & electronic access. Editors need not be members of the MLA.
Award: Cash award & certificate
Closing Date: May 1, 2025
Presented: MLA Annual Convention, Los Angeles, CA, Jan 2027 (winner announced Dec 2026)

The Victor Cohn Prize for Excellence in Medical Science Reporting
Council for the Advancement of Science Writing (CASW)
PO Box 17337, Seattle, WA 98127
Tel: 206-880-0177
E-mail: info@casw.org
Web Site: casw.org/casw/victor-cohn-prize-excellence-medical-science-reporting-0
Key Personnel
Exec Dir: Rosalind Reid *E-mail:* ros_reid@casw.org
Admin & Communs Mgr: Sylvia Kantor *E-mail:* sylviakantor@casw.org
Established: 2000

Awarded for medical science writing for the mass media within the last 5 years. Online submissions.
Award: $3,000
Closing Date: June 30
Presented: ScienceWriters Meeting, Oct

J R Colbeck Award for Playwriting Excellence, see Robert J Pickering/J R Colbeck Award for Playwriting Excellence

William E Colby Award
William E Colby Military Writer's Symposium, Norwich University
158 Harmon Dr, Box 60, Northfield, VT 05663
Tel: 802-485-2965
Web Site: colby.norwich.edu/award
Key Personnel
Colby Symposium Dir: W Travis Morris
Recognizes a first work of fiction or nonfiction that has made a major contribution to the understanding of military history, intelligence operations, or international affairs. The book must have been published during the previous calendar year. $60 fee per submission.
Other Sponsor(s): Pritzker Military Foundation; Pritzker Military Museum & Library
Award: $5,000 author honorarium & invitation to an appearance at the Pritzker Military Museum & Library, Chicago, IL
Closing Date: Nov 30
Presented: Norwich University, Northfield, VT

John M Collier Award for Forest History Journalism
The Forest History Society Inc
2925 Academy Rd, Durham, NC 27705
Tel: 919-682-9319 *Fax:* 919-682-2349
Web Site: foresthistory.org/awards-fellowships/collier-award
Key Personnel
Admin Asst: Andrea Anderson *E-mail:* andrea.anderson@foresthistory.org
Established: 1987
Awarded in recognition of contributions to forest or conservation history in an article or series of articles published in North America that relate to environmental issues. Open to any newspaper, or general circulation magazine (including online-only publications), or professional or freelance journalists in North America.
Award: $1,000 & option to either visit the Forest History Society Library & Archives or arrange for the presentation of award plaque at a mutually agreed upon meeting or convention
Closing Date: March 15 (postmarked)

Carr P Collins Award
Texas Institute of Letters (TIL)
PO Box 130294, Spring, TX 77393
Web Site: texasinstituteofletters.org
Key Personnel
Pres: David Bowles *E-mail:* president@texasinstituteofletters.org
VP: Chris Barton
Secy: Kathryn Jones *E-mail:* secretary@texasinstituteofletters.org
Treas: Cliff Hudder
Award for the best nonfiction book by a Texan or about Texas. The author must have been born in Texas or have lived in Texas for at least 5 consecutive years at some time. See web site for guidelines.
Award: $5,000
Closing Date: Jan
Presented: TIL Annual Meeting & Awards Ceremony, Spring

Colorado Book Awards
Colorado Humanities & Center for the Book
7935 E Prentice Ave, Suite 450, Greenwood Village, CO 80111
Tel: 303-894-7951 (ext 19) *Fax:* 303-864-9361
E-mail: info@coloradohumanities.org
Web Site: coloradohumanities.org
Key Personnel
Dir, Progs: Josephine Jones *E-mail:* jones@coloradohumanities.org
Prog Coord: Abby Kerstetter *E-mail:* abby@coloradohumanities.org
Established: 1991
Available to Colorado authors in fiction, nonfiction, young adult, children's, poetry, romance & additional categories vary from year to year.
Other Sponsor(s): The Colorado Sun; National Endowment for the Humanities; Outskirts Press
Award: $250 cash prize
Closing Date: Jan
Presented: Colorado Book Awards Event, Spring

Colorado Prize for Poetry
The Center for Literary Publishing
9105 Campus Delivery, Colorado State University, Fort Collins, CO 80523-9105
Tel: 970-491-5449
E-mail: creview@colostate.edu
Web Site: coloradoreview.colostate.edu/colorado-prize-for-poetry
Key Personnel
Dir: Stephanie G'Schwind *E-mail:* stephanie.gschwind@colostate.edu
Established: 1995
International poetry book ms contest. Ms must be at least 48 pages but no more than 100 pages & may consist of poems that have been published, but ms as a whole must be unpublished. Theme & style are both open. Translations are not eligible. Entry fee: $25 by mail, $28 online (per ms).
Award: $2,500 honorarium & publication
Closing Date: Jan
Presented: May

Betsy Colquitt Award for Poetry
Texas Christian University
Dept of English, TCU Box 297270, Fort Worth, TX 76129
E-mail: descant@tcu.edu
Web Site: www.descant.tcu.edu
Established: 1996
Awarded for best poem or series of poems by a single author in a volume. All published submissions are eligible for prize consideration. There is no application process.
Other Sponsor(s): descant (publication), Dept of English, TCU
Award: $500
Presented: Winner announced in the Summer in *descant*

Beasley Conger Jr Award for Nonfiction
New Letters
UMKC, University House, 5101 Rockhill Rd, Kansas City, MO 64110-2499
Tel: 816-235-1169
E-mail: newletters@umkc.edu
Web Site: www.newletters.org
Established: 1986
Annual literary contest. Online submission only through Submittable. See web site for submission guidelines. Entry fee: $24 (non-refundable), includes one-year subscription or renewal to *New Letters* in price of first entry. Multiple entries accepted with appropriate fees. Essay entries not to exceed 8,000 words. All entries will be considered for publication in *New Letters*. Finalists are notified in mid-August.
Award: $2,500 & publication
Closing Date: May 18
Presented: Winner & runner-up in each category announced the third week of Sept

Miles Conrad Award
National Information Standards Organization (NISO)
3600 Clipper Mill Rd, Suite 302, Baltimore, MD 21211-1948
Tel: 301-654-2512 *Fax:* 410-685-5278
E-mail: nisohq@niso.org
Web Site: www.niso.org
Key Personnel
Exec Dir: Todd Carpenter
Assoc Exec Dir: Nettie Lagace
Dir, Strategic Initiatives: Jason Griffey
Dir, Busn Devt & Communs: Mary Beth Barilla
Communs & Events Coord: Sara Groveman
Educ Prog Mgr & DEIA Advocate: Kimberly Gladfelter Graham
Asst Standards Prog Mgr: Keondra Bailey
Off Mgr: Lisa Jackson
Established: 1968
The award is presented to an individual who, like Conrad, has made a truly significant contribution to furthering information dissemination & its role in the advancement of science & scholarship.
Award: Statue

The Pat Conroy Southern Book Prize, see The Southern Book Prize

Constance Rooke Creative Nonfiction Prize
The Malahat Review
University of Victoria, PO Box 1700, Sta CSC, Victoria, BC V8W 2Y2, Canada
Tel: 250-721-8524
E-mail: malahat@uvic.ca
Web Site: www.malahatreview.ca/contests/creative_non-fiction_prize/info.html; www.malahatreview.ca
Key Personnel
Mng Ed: L'Amour Lisik
Ed: Iain Higgins *E-mail:* malahateditor@uvic.ca
Established: 2007
Open to writers worldwide. Entry must be no longer than 4,000 words (include word count on first page). No restrictions on subject matter or aesthetic approach. Submissions must be made online through Submittable. See web site for details & entry fees.
Award: $1,250 & publication in the Winter issue of *The Malahat Review*
Closing Date: Aug 1
Presented: Shortlist & winner announced online in Oct

The Cook Prize
Bank Street College of Education
610 W 112 St, New York, NY 10025
Web Site: www.bankstreet.edu/library/center-for-childrens-literature/the-cook-prize
Key Personnel
Dir, Center for Children's Lit: Cynthia Weill
Tel: 212-875-4652 *E-mail:* cweill@bankstreet.edu
Established: 2012
National children's choice award honoring the best science, technology, engineering & math (STEM) picture book for children ages 8-10. Third & fourth grade teachers & librarians are invited to read aloud, discuss & encourage students to vote for their favorite STEM book of the finalists.
Other Sponsor(s): School Library Journal
Closing Date: April
Presented: May

Cordon d' Or - Gold Ribbon International Culinary Academy Awards
Cordon d' Or - Gold Ribbon Inc
7312 Sixth Ave N, St Petersburg, FL 33710
Tel: 727-347-2437
E-mail: cordondor@aol.com

AWARDS, PRIZE CONTESTS, FELLOWSHIPS & GRANTS

Web Site: www.cordondorcuisine.com; www.florida-americasculinaryparadise.com; www.culinaryambassadorofireland.com
Key Personnel
Pres & CEO: Noreen Kinney
  E-mail: ambassadornoreen@tampabay.rr.com
Established: 2003
Literary Cookbook, Illustrated Cookbook & 'Potluck' Book (any genre) & 'Culinary Arts' Awards. Categories include cookbooks, photographers, food stylists, magazines, articles, web sites, recipes & menus. Full details about these annual awards available on the web site. Entry forms can be downloaded.
Award: $1,000 (overall winner), Crystal Globe Trophies (presented to winners in all categories)
Closing Date: Dec 31
Presented: St Petersburg, FL, May

Jeanne Cordova Prize for Lesbian/Queer Nonfiction
Lambda Literary
PO Box 20186, New York, NY 10014
Tel: 213-277-5755
E-mail: awards@lambdaliterary.org; admin@lambdaliterary.org
Web Site: www.lambdaliterary.org/awards/special-awards
Key Personnel
Awards Mgr: Brian Gentes
Established: 2018
Awarded to a writer committed to nonfiction work that captures the depth & complexity of lesbian/queer life, culture +/or history. The applicant must have published at least 1 book & show promise in continuing to produce groundbreaking & challenging work. Applicants must submit a sample from an already published work of no more than 20 pages as well as a sample form (or outline of) ongoing work (maximum 10 pages).
Award: $2,500
Closing Date: Feb 15
Presented: June

Core/Christian Larew Memorial Scholarship in Library & Information Technology
Core: Leadership, Infrastructure, Futures Division of The American Library Association (ALA)
c/o The American Library Association, 225 N Michigan Ave, Suite 1300, Chicago, IL 60601
Tel: 312-944-6780 *Toll Free Tel:* 800-545-2433 *Fax:* 312-440-9374
E-mail: scholarships@ala.org
Web Site: www.ala.org/core
Key Personnel
Exec Dir: Julie Reese *Tel:* 312-280-5030
  E-mail: jreese@ala.org
Established: 1999
Awarded jointly, the scholarship is designed to encourage the entry of qualified persons into the library & information technology field, who plan to follow a career in that field & who demonstrate academic excellence, leadership & a vision in pursuit of library & information technology. This scholarship is for study in an ALA Accredited Master of Library Science (MLS) program.
Other Sponsor(s): Baker & Taylor
Award: $3,000
Closing Date: March 1
Presented: ALA Annual Conference & Exhibition, June

Core/OCLC Spectrum Scholarship in Library & Information Technology
Core: Leadership, Infrastructure, Futures Division of The American Library Association (ALA)
c/o The American Library Association, 225 N Michigan Ave, Suite 1300, Chicago, IL 60601
Tel: 312-944-6780 *Toll Free Tel:* 800-545-2433 *Fax:* 312-440-9374
E-mail: scholarships@ala.org
Web Site: www.ala.org/core
Key Personnel
Exec Dir: Julie Reese *Tel:* 312-280-5030
  E-mail: jreese@ala.org
Established: 1991
Scholarship for qualified members of a minority group. Must be US or Canadian citizen. For applicants who plan to enter a career in the library & automation field.
Other Sponsor(s): OCLC Inc
Award: $3,000
Closing Date: March 1
Presented: ALA Annual Conference & Exhibition, June

Albert B Corey Prize
American Historical Association (AHA) & Canadian Historical Association (CHA)
c/o American Historical Association, 400 "A" St SE, Washington, DC 20003-3889
Tel: 202-544-2422
E-mail: awards@historians.org; cha-shc@cha-shc.ca
Web Site: www.historians.org/awards-and-grants/awards-and-prizes/albert-b-corey-prize; www.cha-shc.ca
Established: 1967
Awarded biennially (even-numbered years) for the best book on Canadian-American relations or on the history of both countries; awarded jointly with the Canadian Historical Association. Books bearing an imprint of 2024 or 2025 are eligible for the 2026 prize. No application form, applicants must simply mail a copy of their book to each prize committee member posted on our web site as the prize deadline approaches. All updated info on web site. The prize winner will be announced online October 2026.
Award: $1,000 cash prize
Closing Date: May 15, 2026
Presented: AHA Annual Meeting, Jan 2027

COVR Visionary Awards
The Coalition of Visionary Resources (COVR)
PO Box 1397, Palmer Lake, CO 80133
Tel: 719-487-0424
E-mail: info@covr.org
Web Site: covr.org/awards
Key Personnel
Awards Mgmt: Sue Wilhite
Awarded to entries selected from among the best new products in the Mind/Body/Spirit marketplace from the previous 3 years. Creators, vendors & publishers can submit entry form online, high-resolution graphic file of the product, along with entry fee of $75 per product per category. See web site for full guidelines & categories, including 22 book categories. Entries open February 1.
Other Sponsor(s): New Leaf Distributing Co
Closing Date: April 1
Presented: INATS®, June

The Terry J Cox Poetry Award
Regal House Publishing
806 Oberlin Rd, No 12094, Raleigh, NC 27605
E-mail: info@regalhousepublishing.com
Web Site: regalhousepublishing.com/the-terry-j-cox-poetry-award/
Key Personnel
Founder, Publr & Ed-in-Chief: Jaynie Royal
Mng Ed: Pam Van Dyk
Established: 2018
Recognizes excellence in a debut poetry collection. Submissions through Submittable or by post. Entry fee: $25. Fax or e-mail submissions not accepted. See web site for submission guidelines.
Award: Publication & $500 honorarium
Closing Date: Jan 31 (postmark)
Presented: March 30

ASSOCIATIONS, EVENTS

Marie Coyoteblanc Award for Indigenous Writing
Prince Edward Island Writers' Guild
81 Prince St, Charlottetown, PE C1A 4R3, Canada
E-mail: peiliteraryawards@gmail.com
Web Site: www.peiwritersguild.com
Acknowledges the contribution made to the Prince Edward Island literary culture by indigenous writers. Indigenous stories are an important part of our culture & ultimately this category is intended to encourage more Indigenous people to write. This prize is open to Prince Edward Island residents who identify as Indigenous. This prize is designed to recognize literary merit & promote works in all categories including fiction, nonfiction, poetry, writing for children & young adults, plays & scriptwriting. Work must be original & unpublished. Entry fee: $25 per submission. See web site for complete entry requirements.
Award: Cash prize for 1st place
Closing Date: Changes annually (see web site)
Presented: Island Literary Awards Gala, Spring

CPSA Prize in Comparative Politics
Canadian Political Science Association (CPSA)
260 Dalhousie St, Suite 204, Ottawa, ON K1N 7E4, Canada
Tel: 613-562-1202 *Fax:* 613-241-0019
E-mail: cpsaprizes@cpsa-acsp.ca; cpsa-acsp@cpsa-acsp.ca
Web Site: www.cpsa-acsp.ca
Key Personnel
Exec Dir: Silvina Danesi
Admin: C Ngako Woktcheu
Biennial prize, awarded in even-numbered years, to the author(s) of the best book published in English or in French in the field of comparative politics. To be eligible, a book may be single or multi-authored. Single-authored: author must be a member of the CPSA in the year the book is considered for the prize. Multi-authored: at least one of the authors must be a member of the CPSA in the year the book is considered for the prize. For the 2026 award, a book must have a copyright date of 2024 or 2025.
Award: Commemorative plaque & receive/share the set of books submitted to the CPSA office
Closing Date: Dec
Presented: CPSA Annual Conference

CPSA Prize in International Relations
Canadian Political Science Association (CPSA)
260 Dalhousie St, Suite 204, Ottawa, ON K1N 7E4, Canada
Tel: 613-562-1202 *Fax:* 613-241-0019
E-mail: cpsaprizes@cpsa-acsp.ca; cpsa-acsp@cpsa-acsp.ca
Web Site: www.cpsa-acsp.ca
Key Personnel
Exec Dir: Silvina Danesi
Admin: C Ngako Woktcheu
This is a biennial competition. The prize, given in odd-numbered years, was established to recognize the contribution of Canadian political scientists to the study of international relations & to encourage the best Canadian scholarship in this field. Awarded to the author of the best book published in English or in French in the field of international relations. Book may be single-authored or multi-authored. Single-authored: author must be a member of the CPSA in the year the book is considered for the prize. Multi-authored: at least one of the authors must be a member of the CPSA in the

year the book is considered for the prize. For the 2025 award, the book must have a copyright date of 2023 or 2024.
Award: Commemorative plaque & receive/share the set of books submitted to the CPSA
Closing Date: Dec
Presented: CPSA Annual Conference

The Crazyhorse Fiction Prize
Crazyhorse
College of Charleston, Dept of English, 66 George St, Charleston, SC 29424
Tel: 843-953-4470
E-mail: crazyhorse@cofc.edu
Web Site: crazyhorse.cofc.edu/prizes
Key Personnel
Mng Ed: Jonathan Heinen
Awarded for best short story. Enter up to 25 pages fiction with $20 entry fee, which includes one-year subscription. Submissions accepted during the month of January. Nationally prominent writer judges. See web site for complete instructions.
Award: $2,000 & publication in *Crazyhorse*
Closing Date: Jan 31
Presented: June 1

Creation Grant Program
New Brunswick Arts Board (Conseil des arts du Nouveau-Brunswick)
225 King St, Suite 201, Fredericton, NB E3B 1E1, Canada
Tel: 506-444-4444 *Toll Free Tel:* 866-460-ARTS (460-2787) *Fax:* 506-444-5543
E-mail: prog@artsnb.ca
Web Site: www.artsnb.ca
Key Personnel
Exec Dir: Joss Richer *Tel:* 506-478-4610
   E-mail: direct@artsnb.ca
Prog Offr: Sarah Jonathan Parker *Tel:* 506-440-0037
Opers Mgr: Tilly Jackson *Tel:* 506-478-4422
   E-mail: tjackson@artsnb.ca
Designed to provide assistance to professional New Brunswick artists for the research, development & execution of original projects in the arts. Creation Grants are intended to allow artists to devote some or most of their time to research & creative production. Eligible artistic disciplines include the literary arts (spoken word, storytelling, literary performance & literary translation).
Award: Up to $5,500 (emerging artists), up to $11,000 (mid-career artists), up to $16,500 (senior artists); includes expenses for living allowance, execution costs, transportation & accommodation costs
Closing Date: April 1, Oct 1

Creative Non-Fiction Awards
Prince Edward Island Writers' Guild
81 Prince St, Charlottetown, PE C1A 4R3, Canada
E-mail: peiliteraryawards@gmail.com
Web Site: www.peiwritersguild.com
This category includes humor writing, memoir, biography, personal essay, travel writing & feature articles. It involves writing about real events, people, or ideas, conveying a message through the use of literary techniques. The work should be accessible to a general reading audience (not written for a specialized or academic audience). Maximum length: 2,500 words. Work must be original & unpublished. Entry fee: $25 per submission. Prince Edward Island residents only. See web site for complete entry requirements.
Award: Cash prizes for 1st, 2nd & 3rd place
Closing Date: Changes annually (see web site)
Presented: Island Literary Awards Gala, Spring

Creative Residencies-Quebec
New Brunswick Arts Board (Conseil des arts du Nouveau-Brunswick)
225 King St, Suite 201, Fredericton, NB E3B 1E1, Canada
Tel: 506-444-4444 *Toll Free Tel:* 866-460-ARTS (460-2787) *Fax:* 506-444-5543
E-mail: prog@artsnb.ca
Web Site: www.artsnb.ca
Key Personnel
Exec Dir: Joss Richer *Tel:* 506-478-4610
   E-mail: direct@artsnb.ca
Prog Offr: Sarah Jonathan Parker *Tel:* 506-440-0037
Opers Mgr: Tilly Jackson *Tel:* 506-478-4422
   E-mail: tjackson@artsnb.ca
Provides professional artists with the opportunity to pursue a 1- to 3-month creation-based or professional development residency in the province of Quebec. Artists participating in this program enjoy complete autonomy & define the objectives of their period of residence & elaborate the parameters & conditions governing its realization in collaboration with an arts or community organization located in Quebec. Eligible artists are Canadian citizens or permanent residents & have resided in New Brunswick for at least one year (12 months) prior to the application deadline. Eligible artistic disciplines include the literary arts (spoken word, storytelling, literary performance & literary translation).
Other Sponsor(s): CALQ (Conseil des Arts et des Lettres du Quebec)
Award: Up to $10,000 including living allowance, project expenses & transportation/accommodation during travel to & from the residency location
Closing Date: Feb 1

Creative Writing Awards for Young People
Prince Edward Island Writers' Guild
81 Prince St, Charlottetown, PE C1A 4R3, Canada
E-mail: peiliteraryawards@gmail.com
Web Site: www.peiwritersguild.com
Students (K-12) may write on the topic of their choice & submit in 1 of 4 sub-categories: Early Elementary (grades 1-3), Late Elementary (grades 4-6), Junior High (grades 7-9), Senior High (grades 10-12). No entry fee. A maximum of 5 pages of poetry or a 10-page short story will constitute an entry. Longer submissions will not be accepted. Work must be original & unpublished. Prince Edward Island residents only. See web site for complete entry requirements.
Award: Cash prizes for 1st, 2nd & 3rd place
Closing Date: Changes annually (see web site)
Presented: Island Literary Awards Gala, Spring

Crime Writers of Canada Awards of Excellence
Crime Writers of Canada (CWC)
716 Thicket Way, Ottawa, ON K4A 3B5, Canada
E-mail: awards@crimewriterscanada.com
Web Site: www.crimewriterscanada.com/awards
Key Personnel
Exec Dir: Alison Bruce *E-mail:* ed@crimewriterscanada.com
Asst Exec Dir & Awards Mgr: Ludvica Boota
   E-mail: aed@crimewriterscanada.com
Established: 1984
Awards to acknowledge distinction in Canadian crime writing. Open to permanent residents of Canada or Canadian citizens living abroad. Nine categories: Best crime novel, best crime first novel, best traditional mystery, best crime novel set in Canada, best crime novella, best crime short story, best French crime book (fiction & nonfiction), best juvenile or young adult crime book (fiction & nonfiction), best nonfiction crime book. A 10th category, The Award for Best Unpublished Manuscript, is open to writers who are not published novelists.
Other Sponsor(s): Melodie Campbell; Jane Doe; ECW Press; Charlotte Engel; Mystery Magazine; Rakuten Kobo; Simpson & Wellenreiter LLP
Closing Date: Dec 15
Presented: CWC Awards of Excellence Gala, Last Thursday in May

Compton Crook Award
Baltimore Science Fiction Society Inc
PO Box 686, Baltimore, MD 21203-0686
Tel: 410-563-2737
E-mail: webmeister@bsfs.org
Web Site: www.bsfs.org/CCA/bsfsccnu2014.htm
Key Personnel
Balticon Chair: Eric Gasior *E-mail:* chair@bsfs.org
Balticon Vice Chair: Yakira Heistand
PR Coord: Morgan Hazelwood
   E-mail: socialmedia@bsfs.org
Established: 1983
Presented to the best English language first novel by an author in the field of science fiction, fantasy, or horror.
Award: $1,000, plaque & 2-year attendance at Balticon (including transportation & lodging)
Presented: Balticon Annual Convention

Compton Crook/Stephen Tall Award, see Compton Crook Award

Crook's Corner Book Prize
Crook's Corner Book Prize Foundation
313 Country Club Rd, Chapel Hill, NC 27514
E-mail: info@crookscornerbookprize.com
Web Site: crookscornerbookprize.com
Awarded for the best debut novel set in the American South, which includes the states Alabama, Arkansas, Florida, Georgia, Kentucky, Louisiana, Maryland, Mississippi, North Carolina, Oklahoma, South Carolina, Tennessee, Texas, Virginia, West Virginia, & the District of Columbia. Books may be self-published if they have an ISBN number. However, self-published books must be available through one of the major distributors, Baker & Taylor or Ingram, under regular reseller terms. Self-published authors can arrange for such distribution for a small fee. Books that are available only as e-books are not eligible. Submissions are welcome from authors or publishers. Entry fee: $35.
Award: $5,000 & free glass of wine at Crook's Corner restaurant every day for a year
Closing Date: May 15
Presented: Jan

Crystal Kite Awards
Society of Children's Book Writers & Illustrators (SCBWI)
6363 Wilshire Blvd, Suite 425, Los Angeles, CA 90048
Tel: 323-782-1010
E-mail: info@scbwi.org
Web Site: www.scbwi.org/awards/crystal-kite-member-choice-award
Key Personnel
Exec Dir: Sarah Baker
Assoc Dir, Digital Content & Awards: Sarah Diamond
Assoc Mgr, Awards & Pubns: Danielle Monique
Award Coord: Christopher Cheng
   E-mail: christophercheng@scbwi.org
Peer-given award to recognize excellence in the field of children's literature in 15 SCBWI regional divisions around the world. Nominated books must be a PAL book first published within the previous calendar year. Self-published books are not eligible.
Award: Crystal, engraved kite award, opportunity to present at a regional conference, silver

sticker for winning book; one winner is chosen to present at the LA Summer Conference
Closing Date: March 21
Presented: May

Cullman Center Fellowships
The Dorothy & Lewis B Cullman Center for Scholars & Writers
New York Public Library, Stephen A Schwarzman Bldg, Fifth Ave & 42 St, Rm 225, New York, NY 10018-2788
Tel: 917-275-6975
E-mail: csw@nypl.org
Web Site: www.nypl.org/help/about-nypl/fellowships-institutes
Key Personnel
Deputy Dir: Lauren Goldenberg
Fifteen fellowships awarded to outstanding scholars & writers—academics, independent scholars, journalists, creative writers (novelists, playwrights, poets), translators & visual artists. Foreign nationals conversant in English are welcome to apply. Candidates for the fellowship will need to work primarily at the Stephen A Schwarzman Bldg rather than at other divisions of the Library. People seeking funding for research leading directly to a degree are not eligible. Fellowship term runs September to May.
Award: $75,000 stipend, use of an office with a computer & full access to the library's physical & electronic resources

E E Cummings Prize
New England Poetry Club
c/o Linda Haviland Conte, 18 Hall Ave, Apt 2, Somerville, MA 02144
E-mail: info@nepoetryclub.org
Web Site: nepoetryclub.org
Key Personnel
Co-Pres: Doug Holder; Denise Provost
VP: Hilary Sallick
Treas: Linda Haviland Conte
  E-mail: nepctreasurer@gmail.com
Awarded for a compelling, lyrical, or experimental poem no more than 21 lines. Only one poem per contest. Entries must be original unpublished (neither print nor online) poems in English. Submissions must be made by post or by Submittable link. See web site for full guidelines. Entry fee: Free to membs, non-membs $5.
Award: $250, publication of winning poems on NEPC web site & opportunity to read at the NEPC (travel expenses not included)
Closing Date: May 31
Presented: Announced online Aug/Sept

Cundill History Prize
McGill University
840 Dr Penfield Ave, Rm 233, Montreal, QC H3A 1A4, Canada
Tel: 514-398-4400 (ext 00468)
E-mail: cundill.prize@mcgill.ca
Web Site: www.cundillprize.com
Established: 2008
Awarded to the book that embodies historical scholarship, originality, literary quality & broad appeal. Open to books first published in English between June 1 of the previous year & May 31 of the year of the award. Translations welcome. Publishers may not submit more than 4 titles per imprint. Longlist & shortlist announced in September, finalists in October.
Other Sponsor(s): The Peter Cundill Foundation
Award: $75,000; $10,000 each to 2 runners-up
Closing Date: May
Presented: Cundhill History Prize Gala, Montreal, QC, CN, Dec

Cunningham Commission for Youth Theatre
The Theatre School, DePaul University
Lincoln Park Campus, 2350 N Racine Ave, Chicago, IL 60614-4100
Tel: 773-325-7999
E-mail: cunninghamcommission@depaul.edu
Web Site: theatre.depaul.edu
Key Personnel
Assoc Dean, Theatre Studies: Dean Corrin
  Tel: 773-325-7932 *E-mail:* dcorrin@depaul.edu
Dir, Mktg & PR: Anna Ables *Tel:* 773-325-7938
  E-mail: aables@depaul.edu
Established: 1991
Playwriting commission limited to writers whose primary residence is within 100 miles of Chicago's Loop & alumni of The Theatre School. Please send all entries & questions to cunninghamcommission@depaul.edu.
Award: $6,000 with an additional fee provided if the play is produced as part of the Chicago Playworks series
Closing Date: April
Presented: June

Merle Curti Intellectual History Award
The Organization of American Historians (OAH)
112 N Bryan Ave, Bloomington, IN 47408-4141
Tel: 812-855-7311
E-mail: oah@oah.org
Web Site: www.oah.org/awards
Key Personnel
Exec Dir: Beth English *Tel:* 812-855-9836
  E-mail: benglish@oah.org
Dir, Communs & Mktg: Kym Robinson *Tel:* 812-855-5430 *E-mail:* kymarobi@oah.org
Awarded to the author of the best book in American intellectual history. Each entry must be published during the calendar year preceding that in which the award is given. One copy of each entry must be mailed directly to the committee members listed on the web site.
Closing Date: Oct 1 (postmarked)
Presented: OAH Conference on American History, Spring

Merle Curti Social History Award
The Organization of American Historians (OAH)
112 N Bryan Ave, Bloomington, IN 47408-4141
Tel: 812-855-7311
E-mail: oah@oah.org
Web Site: www.oah.org/awards
Key Personnel
Exec Dir: Beth English *Tel:* 812-855-9836
  E-mail: benglish@oah.org
Dir, Communs & Mktg: Kym Robinson *Tel:* 812-855-5430 *E-mail:* kymarobi@oah.org
Awarded to the author of the best book in American social history. Each entry must be published during the calendar year preceding that in which the award is given. One copy of each entry must be mailed directly to the committee members listed on the web site.
Closing Date: Oct 1 (postmarked)
Presented: OAH Conference on American History, Spring

C Michael Curtis Short Story Book Prize
Hub City Press
186 W Main St, Spartanburg, SC 29306
Tel: 864-577-9349 *Fax:* 864-577-0188
E-mail: info@hubcity.org; submit@hubcity.org
Web Site: hubcity.org/press/c-michael-curtis-short-story-book-prize
Key Personnel
Dir: Meg Reid *E-mail:* meg@hubcity.org
Mng Ed: Kate McMullen *E-mail:* kate@hubcity.org
Open to emerging writers in 13 Southern states: Alabama, Arkansas, Florida, Georgia, Kentucky, Louisiana, Mississippi, North Carolina, South Carolina, Tennessee, Texas, Virginia & West Virginia. $25 submission fee. Online submissions only beginning August 1.
Award: $10,000 & book publication
Closing Date: Jan 1

Karen & Philip Cushman Late Bloomer Award
Society of Children's Book Writers & Illustrators (SCBWI)
6363 Wilshire Blvd, Suite 425, Los Angeles, CA 90048
Tel: 323-782-1010
E-mail: info@scbwi.org
Web Site: www.scbwi.org/awards-and-grants-new
Key Personnel
Exec Dir: Sarah Baker
Assoc Dir, Digital Content & Awards: Sarah Diamond
Assoc Mgr, Awards & Pubns: Danielle Monique
Honors unpublished children's book authors or author/illustrators over the age of 50. One winner is chosen from the pool of those who have submitted material for the SCBWI Work-in-Progress Awards.
Award: $500 & free tuition to any SCBWI conference anywhere in the world
Closing Date: April 15
Presented: Announced in early Oct

The Danahy Fiction Prize
Tampa Review
University of Tampa Press, 401 W Kennedy Blvd, Tampa, FL 33606
Tel: 813-253-6266
E-mail: utpress@ut.edu
Web Site: tampareview.org/the-danahy-fiction-prize
Key Personnel
Ed: Richard Mathews
Edit Asst: Sean Donnelly
Established: 2006
Awarded for an original, previously unpublished work of short fiction. Preferred length of mss is 500-5,000 words. Handling fee: $20 per ms. See web site for full submission guidelines.
Award: $1,000 & publication in *Tampa Review*; all entrants receive 1-year subn to the journal
Closing Date: Dec 31

Benjamin H Danks Award
American Academy of Arts & Letters
633 W 155 St, New York, NY 10032
Tel: 212-368-5900
E-mail: academy@artsandletters.org
Web Site: artsandletters.org/awards
Key Personnel
Exec Dir: Cody Upton
Established: 2003
Prize, in rotation, awarded to a composer of ensemble works, a playwright & a writer. Candidates must be nominated by an Academy member.
Award: $20,000

Robert J Dau Short Story Prize for Emerging Writers, see PEN/Robert J Dau Short Story Prize for Emerging Writers

Watson Davis & Helen Miles Davis Prize
History of Science Society
Affiliate of American Council of Learned Societies
440 Geddes Hall, Notre Dame, IN 46556
Tel: 574-631-1194 *Fax:* 574-631-1533
E-mail: info@hssonline.org
Web Site: www.hssonline.org
Established: 1985
For the best book on the history of science directed to a broad public published during the preceding 3 years.
Award: $1,000 & certificate
Closing Date: April 1
Presented: Awards Banquet, Oct/Nov

COURSES & AWARDS — AWARDS, PRIZE CONTESTS, FELLOWSHIPS & GRANTS

Robert Day Award for Fiction
New Letters
UMKC, University House, 5101 Rockhill Rd, Kansas City, MO 64110-2499
Tel: 816-235-1169
E-mail: newletters@umkc.edu
Web Site: www.newletters.org
Established: 1986
Annual literary contest. All entries considered for publication.
Award: $2,500 & publication
Closing Date: May 18

Dayton Literary Peace Prize
Dayton Literary Peace Prize Foundation
PO Box 461, Wright Brothers Branch, Dayton, OH 45409-0461
Tel: 937-298-5072
Web Site: www.daytonliterarypeaceprize.org
Key Personnel
Founder & Pres: Sharon Rab *E-mail:* sharon.rab@daytonliterarypeaceprize.org
Exec Dir: Nicholas A Raines
Established: 2006
First & only annual international literary award in the US recognizing the power of the written word to promote peace. This project is the recognition of adult fiction & nonfiction books that have led readers to a better understanding of other cultures, peoples, religions & political points of view. $100 nomination fee.
Award: $10,000 each genre (fiction & nonfiction) plus $2,500 each 1st runner-up
Closing Date: March
Presented: Benjamin & Marian Schuster Performing Arts Center, Dayton, OH, Nov

Dayton Playhouse FutureFest
The Dayton Playhouse
PO Box 3017, Dayton, OH 45401-3017
Tel: 937-424-8477 *Fax:* 937-424-0062
E-mail: futurefest@daytonplayhouse.com
Web Site: wordpress.thedaytonplayhouse.com/future-fest-2
Key Personnel
Chmn of the Bd: Matthew Lindsay
FutureFest Prog Dir: Fran Pesch
Established: 1991
National playwriting competition. Entry must be an original work (no musicals or plays for children) that has not been published or produced where admission was charged prior to FutureFest. Send SASE or see web site for submission guidelines.
Award: $1,000 (1st place), $100 (5 runners up) - all 6 finalists are provided travel to & housing for the FutureFest weekend
Closing Date: Aug 1-Oct 31 (postmark)
Presented: The Dayton Playhouse, Dayton, OH, July

Delaware Division of the Arts Individual Artist Fellowships
Delaware Division of the Arts
Carvel State Off Bldg, 4th fl, 820 N French St, Wilmington, DE 19801
Tel: 302-577-8278 *Fax:* 302-577-6561
E-mail: delarts@delaware.gov
Web Site: arts.delaware.gov/grants-for-artists
Key Personnel
Prog Offr, Artist Progs & Servs: Roxanne Stanulis *Tel:* 302-577-8283 *E-mail:* roxanne.stanulis@delaware.gov
Individual artist fellowships (Established & Emerging) awarded to Delaware creative artists working in the visual, performing, media, folk, & literary arts. Applicants must be Delaware residents for at least 1 year at the time of application & remain a resident during the grant period (January 1-December 31). Masters awarded every 3 years in select disciplines on a rotating basis. Next Masters fellowship to be awarded in 2025.
Other Sponsor(s): Mid Atlantic Arts
Award: $12,000 Masters, $8,000 Established, $5,000 Emerging
Closing Date: Aug 1
Branch Office(s)
99 Kings Hwy SW, Dover, DE 19901

Rick DeMarinis Short Story Award
CUTTHROAT, A Journal of the Arts
PO Box 2414, Durango, CO 81302
Tel: 970-903-7914
E-mail: cutthroatmag@gmail.com
Web Site: www.cutthroatmag.com
Key Personnel
Ed-in-Chief: Pamela Uschuk
Mng Ed: Andrew Allport
Fiction Ed: William Luvaas
Submit 1 unpublished short story (5,000 word limit), any subject, any style. Mss must be 12 point font & double-spaced. Stories previously published or that have won contests are not eligible. Reading fee: $23.
Award: $1,200 & publication (1st prize), $250 & publication (2nd prize), publication only (honorable mention)
Closing Date: Nov
Presented: Dec

Denver Publishing Institute Scholarship
Book Industry Charitable Foundation (BINC)
3135 S State St, Suite 203, Ann Arbor, MI 48108
Toll Free Tel: 866-733-9064
E-mail: info@bincfoundation.org
Web Site: www.bincfoundation.org/denver-publishing-institute/
Key Personnel
Exec Dir: Pamela French *E-mail:* pam@bincfoundation.org
Dir, Devt: Kathy Bartson *E-mail:* kathy@bincfoundation.org
Prog Mgr: Judey Kalchik *E-mail:* judey@bincfoundation.org; Ken White *E-mail:* ken@bincfoundation.org
Commun Coord: Erika Mantz *E-mail:* erika@bincfoundation.org
Devt Coord: Jennifer Rojas *E-mail:* jennifer@bincfoundation.org
Off Coord: Jane Regenstreif *E-mail:* jane@bincfoundation.org
Spec Projs Coord: Kate Weiss *E-mail:* kate@bincfoundation.org
Established: 2019
Scholarship opportunity for current booksellers interested in exploring a career in the publishing side of the industry. Presented in collaboration with Sourcebooks & the Denver Publishing Institute.
Award: Up to $7,000 to attend the Denver Publishing Institute, including tuition, meal plan, housing & up to $2,000 to cover travel & lost wages
Closing Date: Feb 27

Der Hovanessian Prize
New England Poetry Club
c/o Linda Haviland Conte, 18 Hall Ave, Apt 2, Somerville, MA 02144
E-mail: info@nepoetryclub.org
Web Site: nepoetryclub.org
Key Personnel
Co-Pres: Doug Holder; Denise Provost
VP: Hilary Sallick
Treas: Linda Haviland Conte
 E-mail: nepctreasurer@gmail.com
Awarded for a translation from any language; the original poem should be authored by someone other than the translator. Include the poem in the original language along with the translation. Only one poem per contest. See web site for additional guidelines. Entry fee: Free to membs, nonmembs $5.
Award: $250, publication of winning poems on NEPC web site & opportunity to read at the NEPC (travel expenses not included)
Closing Date: May 31
Presented: Announced online Aug/Sept

Anne Devereaux Jordan Award
Children's Literature Association (ChLA)
140B Purcellville Gateway Dr, Suite 1200, Purcellville, VA 20132
Tel: 630-571-4520
E-mail: info@childlitassn.org
Web Site: www.childlitassn.org
Key Personnel
Association Mgr: Cate Langley
Awarded for significant contribution in scholarship +/or service to the field of children's literature. Nominations are welcome from any current ChLA member.
Award: Framed citation, complimentary conference registration, hotel for up to 4 nights during conference, banquet tickets & 1-year ChLA membership
Closing Date: Oct 1
Presented: ChLA Annual Conference, June

Anna Dewdney Read Together Award
The Children's Book Council (CBC)
54 W 39 St, 14th fl, New York, NY 10018
Web Site: everychildareader.net/anna
Key Personnel
Exec Dir: Carl Lennertz *E-mail:* carl.lennertz@cbcbooks.org
Assoc Exec Dir: Shaina Birkhead *E-mail:* shaina.birkhead@cbcbooks.org
Presented for a picture book that is both a superb read aloud & also sparks compassion, empathy & connection. Librarians, teachers, booksellers, parents/caregivers & children's book bloggers are encouraged to nominate up to 5 beloved read-together picture book favorites. Nominators must be 18 years of age or older.
Other Sponsor(s): Every Child A Reader; Penguin Young Readers Group
Award: $1,000
Closing Date: Feb 14
Presented: Children's Book Week

Alice Fay Di Castagnola Award
Poetry Society of America (PSA)
119 Smith St, Brooklyn, NY 11201
Tel: 212-254-9628
E-mail: info@poetrysociety.org
Web Site: poetrysociety.org/awards
Key Personnel
Exec Dir: Matt Brogan *E-mail:* matt@poetrysociety.org
Deputy Dir: Brett Fletcher Lauer *E-mail:* brett@poetrysociety.org
Devt Dir: Madeline Weinfield *E-mail:* madeline@poetrysociety.org
Established: 1965
Offered in memory of a benefactor & friend of the society. For 10 pages of poetry from a ms in progress. Previously published poems are acceptable. All submissions must be through Submittable. Entry fee: Free to membs, $10 nonmembs.
Award: $1,000
Closing Date: Dec 31
Presented: Annual Awards Ceremony, New York, NY, Spring

Diamonstein-Spielvogel Award for the Art of the Essay, see PEN/Diamonstein-Spielvogel Award for the Art of the Essay

Philip K Dick Award
Philadelphia Science Fiction Society

AWARDS, PRIZE CONTESTS, FELLOWSHIPS & GRANTS

PO Box 3447, Hoboken, NJ 07030
Tel: 201-876-2551
Web Site: www.philipkdickaward.org
Key Personnel
Admin: Patrick Lo Brutto; John Silbersack; Gordon Van Gelder
Established: 1983
Presented for a distinguished original science fiction paperback published for the first time in the US during the year prior to the award year.
Other Sponsor(s): Philip K Dick Trust; NorthWest Science Fiction Society
Award: $1,000
Closing Date: Dec 1
Presented: Norwescon, SeaTac, WA, Easter weekend

Emily Dickinson Award, see The Writer Magazine/Emily Dickinson Award

Annie Dillard Award for Creative Nonfiction
The Bellingham Review
Mail Stop 9053, Western Washington University, Bellingham, WA 98225
Tel: 360-650-4863
E-mail: bellingham.review@wwu.edu
Web Site: bhreview.org; bhreview.submittable.com
Key Personnel
Ed-in-Chief: Susanne Paola Antonetta
Mng Ed: Stephen Haines
Asst Mng Ed: Keegan Lawler
Established: 1993
Entry consists of one essay, one story, up to 3 pieces of flash, or up to 3 poems. Please limit prose to 4,000 words. For prose that is 1,500 words or fewer, submit up to 3 in one entry. Upload entries via Submittable beginning December 1. Paper submissions are not accepted. All submissions must be previously unpublished in North America. Entry fee: $20, $30 international.
Award: $1,000 & publication in the *Bellingham Review* (1st prize), considered for publication (2nd, 3rd & finalists)
Closing Date: March 15
Presented: June

Gordon W Dillon/Richard C Peterson Memorial Essay Contest
American Orchid Society Inc
PO Box 565477, Miami, FL 33156-5477
Tel: 305-740-2010 *Fax:* 305-747-7154
E-mail: theaos@aos.org
Web Site: www.aos.org
Key Personnel
Chief Educ & Sci Offr: Ron McHatton, PhD
   Tel: 305-740-2010 ext 106 *E-mail:* rmchatton@aos.org
Established: 1985
Essay contest (orchid topics only; new theme announced each year). Essay must be an original, unpublished article (no more than 5,000 words). Contest is open to all persons except employees of AOS & their immediate family. Mss must be submitted in English & sent electronically in MS Word or compatible file format.
Award: Cash award & certificate
Closing Date: Sept 30

Discovery Poetry Contest
Unterberg Poetry Center
Subsidiary of 92nd Street Y/Tisch Center for the Arts
1395 Lexington Ave, New York, NY 10128
Tel: 212-415-5760
E-mail: unterberg@92y.org
Web Site: www.92y.org/discovery
Key Personnel
Exec Dir: Lucas Wittmann
Established: 1951
For poets who have not published a full-length poetry collection; for guidelines visit web site. $15 entry fee must accompany the submission.
Award: Publication in *Paris Review Daily*, a reading at The Poetry Center & $500 each to the 4 winning authors
Closing Date: Jan 11 at 5PM ET
Presented: 92nd Street Y, New York, NY, Winner will be announced in the Summer

Distinguished Scholarly Book Award
American Sociological Association (ASA)
c/o Governance Off, 1430 "K" St NW, Suite 600, Washington, DC 20005
Tel: 202-383-9005
E-mail: asa@asanet.org; nominations@asanet.org
Web Site: www.asanet.org/about/awards
Key Personnel
Dir, Governance & Admin: Mark Fernando
   Tel: 202-247-9866 *E-mail:* mfernando@asanet.org
Awarded for a single book published in the 2 calendar years preceding the award year. Any member of the ASA may nominate books for consideration for this award. Nominations should include name of author, title of book, date of publication, publisher & brief statements (of no more than 300 words) as to why the book should be considered. Nominations sent from publishers who are not active members of ASA will not be accepted. Send nominations to ASA office at above address.
Award: Plaque
Closing Date: Jan 1
Presented: ASA Annual Meeting, Aug

Catherine Doctorow Innovative Fiction Prize, see The FC2 Catherine Doctorow Innovative Fiction Prize

Documentation Grant Program
New Brunswick Arts Board (Conseil des arts du Nouveau-Brunswick)
225 King St, Suite 201, Fredericton, NB E3B 1E1, Canada
Tel: 506-444-4444 *Toll Free Tel:* 866-460-ARTS (460-2787) *Fax:* 506-444-5543
E-mail: prog@artsnb.ca
Web Site: www.artsnb.ca
Key Personnel
Exec Dir: Joss Richer *Tel:* 506-478-4610
   E-mail: direct@artsnb.ca
Prog Offr: Sarah Jonathan Parker *Tel:* 506-440-0037
Opers Mgr: Tilly Jackson *Tel:* 506-478-4422
   E-mail: tjackson@artsnb.ca
Designed to provide assistance to New Brunswick arts professionals & professional artists for the research, development & execution of original documentation & contextualization (written, film, video, multimedia) of arts activities, arts products or art history. Documentation grants are intended to foster theoretical & critical discourse in the arts. Preference will be given to proposals concerning New Brunswick art or artists. Eligible artistic disciplines include the literary arts (spoken word, storytelling, literary performance & literary translation).
Award: Up to $8,500 including living allowance, execution costs, transportation & accommodation costs
Closing Date: April 1, Oct 1

Dog Writers Association of America Inc (DWAA) Annual Writing Competition
Dog Writers Association of America Inc (DWAA)
PO Box 787, Hughesville, MD 20637
Web Site: dogwriters.org
Key Personnel
Pres: Therese Backowski
   E-mail: theresebackowski1@gmail.com
VP: Susan Willett

ASSOCIATIONS, EVENTS

Treas: Marsha Pugh *E-mail:* marsha_pugh01@comcast.com
Secy: Emelise Baughman *E-mail:* emeliseb@yahoo.com
Contest Chair: Su Ewing *E-mail:* dogwriter@windstream.net
Established: 1935
To recognize an individual, club or group which has done an outstanding job in the dog writing field in numerous categories. Only original work published between September 1 & August 31 of the competition year. Submissions (online only) open September 1. See web site for details.
Other Sponsor(s): ACK Reunite; American Kennel Club; American Legion Post No 348; Canine Scribbles; Ceva Animal Health; James Colasanti Jr; Dogwise Publishing; Fear Free LLC; GNFP Digital; Babette Haggerty; International Association of Pet Fashion Professionals; Morris Animal Foundation; Pet Sitters International; Westminster Kennel Club
Award: Approximately $14,000 in cash prizes; plaques, Maxwell Medallions & certificates
Closing Date: Oct 31
Presented: Annual Awards Banquet, May

Donner Prize
Donner Canadian Foundation
c/o Naylor and Associates, 23 Empire Ave, Toronto, ON M4M 2L3, Canada
Tel: 416-368-8253
E-mail: donnerprize@naylorandassociates.com
Web Site: donnerbookprize.com
Key Personnel
Prize Mgr: Sherry Naylor *E-mail:* sherry@naylorandassociates.com
Prize to recognize & reward the best public policy thinking, writing & research by a Canadian & the role it plays in determining the well-being of Canadians & the success of Canada as a whole. All entries must be published in English or French between January 1 & December 31 of the prize year. Entries must be submitted by the publisher. Six copies of each title must be delivered to the Prize Manager by the deadline. If an electronic version is available, please e-mail a copy in addition to sending printed versions. For titles published between November 3 & December 31, the publisher may submit bound galleys or mss. See web site for full eligibility & submission guidelines.
Closing Date: Nov 30

Dorset Prize
Tupelo Press Inc
60 Roberts Dr, Suite 308, North Adams, MA 01247
SAN: 254-3281
Tel: 413-664-9611 *Fax:* 413-664-9711
E-mail: info@tupelopress.org
Web Site: www.tupelopress.org
Key Personnel
Publr: Jeffrey Levine *E-mail:* publisher@tupelopress.org
Ed-in-Chief: Kristina Marie Darling
   E-mail: kdarling@tupelopress.org
Established: 2003
Open book competition for poetry. Full guidelines on the web site. Entries accepted beginning September 1.
Award: $3,000, publication & national distribution
Closing Date: Dec 31
Presented: Spring

John Dos Passos Prize for Literature
Longwood University
Dept of English & Modern Languages, 201 High St, Farmville, VA 23909
Tel: 434-395-2155
Web Site: www.longwood.edu/english/dos-passos-prize

COURSES & AWARDS

AWARDS, PRIZE CONTESTS, FELLOWSHIPS & GRANTS

Key Personnel
Chpn, Dos Passos Prize Comm: Brandon Haffner
Established: 1980
To honor American creative writers who have produced a substantial body of significant publication that displays characteristics of John Dos Passos's writing: an intense & original exploration of specifically American themes, an experimental approach to form & an interest in a wide range of human experiences. Winners are nominated & selected by a jury. Applications not accepted.
Presented: Longwood University, Farmville, VA, Generally during fall semester

Frank Nelson Doubleday Memorial Award
Wyoming Arts Council
Division of Wyoming Department of Parks & Cultural Resources
Barrett Bldg, 2nd fl, 2301 Central Ave, Cheyenne, WY 82002
Tel: 307-777-7742
Web Site: wyoarts.state.wy.us
Key Personnel
Creative Arts Specialist: Taylor Craig
  E-mail: taylor.craig@wyo.gov
Established: 1988
Best poetry, fiction, nonfiction or drama written by a woman author. Wyoming residents only. Blind judges & single juror. Submissions open in January.
Award: $1,000
Closing Date: March
Presented: Spring

Carleton Drewry Memorial
The Poetry Society of Virginia (PSV)
PO Box 36128, North Chesterfield, VA 23235-3533
E-mail: contest@poetrysocietyofvirginia.org; info@poetryvirginia.org
Web Site: www.poetrysocietyofvirginia.org
Key Personnel
Pres: Cherryl T Cooley
  E-mail: poetrysocietypresident@gmail.com
Lyric or sonnet. Must be in English, original & unpublished. Subject: Farm life or working the Earth, 48 line limit. Submit 1 copy of the poem with no identifying information but put the category in the upper right-hand-side, along with a notation as to whether you are a member of PSV (does not matter if you are a lifetime member or just joined for the contest). Submit a cover letter/page that contains the category, the name of the poem, your name & address, phone number & e-mail address. Entries will not be returned. Entry fee: Free to membs, $5 nonmembs.
Award: $50 (1st prize), $30 (2nd prize), $20 (3rd prize)
Closing Date: Feb
Presented: PSV Awards Ceremony, April

Saint Katharine Drexel Award
Catholic Library Association
8550 United Plaza Blvd, Suite 1001, Baton Rouge, LA 70809
Tel: 225-408-4417
E-mail: cla2@cathla.org
Web Site: cathla.org
Key Personnel
Exec Dir: Melanie Talley
Association Coord: Mary Coll
Established: 1966
Recognizes an outstanding contribution to the growth of high school librarianship.
Award: Plaque
Closing Date: None; in-house votes
Presented: CLA Annual Convention, April

Drury University One-Act Play Competition
Drury University
900 N Benton Ave, Springfield, MO 65802-3344
Tel: 417-873-6821
Web Site: www.drury.edu
Key Personnel
Professor, Theatre: Dr Mick Sokol
  E-mail: msokol@drury.edu
Established: 1986
Biennial award for one-act plays. Open to all playwrights. Scripts are to be original, unpublished & unproduced; staged readings or workshop productions will not disqualify a script; musicals, monologues, children's plays & adaptations will not be considered; only stage plays will be judged; preference will be given to small cast, one-set shows with running times of no less than 20 & no more than 45 minutes; no more than one script per author; all scripts are to be typewritten & firmly bound; scripts cannot be acknowledged or returned unless accompanied by a SASE.
Award: $300 plus consideration for production by Drury University (1st prize); 2 honorable mentions $150 each
Closing Date: Dec 1, even-numbered years
Presented: By mail no later than April 1, odd-numbered years

Dubuque Fine Arts Players Annual One Act Play Festival
Dubuque Fine Arts Players
Subsidiary of Dubuque County Fine Arts Society
PO Box 1160, Dubuque, IA 52004-1160
Tel: 563-581-6521
E-mail: contact_dbqoneacts@iowa706.com
Web Site: www.dbqoneacts.org
Key Personnel
Pres: Art Roche
Contest Coord: Thomas Boxleiter
  E-mail: tomb1954@gmail.com
Established: 1977
National one-act playwriting contest. Entry form & guidelines are available at the web site. Submit the entry form, two copies of the script, a synopsis of the play & entry fee. Plays may be submitted by US mail with a $15 entry fee. SASE should be enclosed if return of the reader evaluation forms +/or the scripts is desired. Plays may be submitted online for an entry fee of $20. The higher fee pays cost of printing & binding the play. Previously published or produced works, musicals & children's plays are not accepted.
Award: $600 (1st prize), $300 (2nd prize), $200 (3rd prize), production of first 3 winning plays unless production is beyond our capacity
Closing Date: Jan 31
Presented: Loras College, Dubuque, IA, Fall

The Grace Dudley Prize for Arts Writing
The Robert B Silvers Foundation
c/o The New York Review of Books, 435 Hudson St, Suite 300, New York, NY 10014
Tel: 212-757-8070
E-mail: admin@silversfoundation.org
Web Site: silversfoundation.org/about-the-silvers-dudley-prizes
Key Personnel
Admin: Alex Beatty
Recognizes achievement in critical writing on the fine & performing arts or on cultural history. There is no application process.
Award: $135,000

Duende-Word BIPOC Bookseller Award
The Word, A Storytelling Sanctuary Inc
757 E 20 Ave, Suite 370-335, Denver, CO 80205
E-mail: info@thewordfordiversity.org
Web Site: www.thewordfordiversity.org/booksellereward
Key Personnel
Founder & Exec Dir: Viniyanka Prasad
Head, Opers: Michelle Malonzo
Prog Coord: Aida Lilly
Established: 2020
Awards to celebrate & uplift the Black & Brown independent booksellers, whose dedication to Indie bookstores & their Black, Indigenous & People of Color colleagues & communities have touched & influenced countless lives. Three categories: Activism, Innovation & Leadership.
Other Sponsor(s): Duende District
Award: $1,000 & plaque
Closing Date: July
Presented: Oct during Margins Bookstore Month

Jim Duggins PhD Outstanding Mid-Career Novelist Prize
Lambda Literary
PO Box 20186, New York, NY 10014
Tel: 213-277-5755
E-mail: awards@lambdaliterary.org; admin@lambdaliterary.org
Web Site: www.lambdaliterary.org/awards/special-awards
Key Personnel
Awards Mgr: Brian Gentes
Prize to honor LGBTQ-identified authors who have published multiple novels, built a strong reputation & following & show promise to continue publishing high quality work for years to come. Applicants must submit a sample from an already published book, no more than 20 pages, as well as a sample from (or outline of) ongoing work (maximum 10 pages).
Other Sponsor(s): James Duggins PhD Fund for Outstanding Mid-Career LGBTQ Novelists (a fund of the Horizons Foundation)
Award: $5,000
Closing Date: Feb 15
Presented: June

The Joseph R Dunlap Memorial Fellowship
William Morris Society in the United States
PO Box 53263, Washington, DC 20009
E-mail: us@morrissociety.org
Web Site: www.morrissociety.org
Key Personnel
Contact: Michael Robertson *E-mail:* mroberts@tcnj.edu
Established: 1996
For scholarly or creative projects dealing with any subject relating to William Morris (1834-1896).
Award: $1,000 or more
Closing Date: Dec 1

Eaton Literary Associates Literary Awards
Eaton Literary Agency Inc
PO Box 49795, Sarasota, FL 34230-6795
Tel: 941-366-6589
E-mail: eatonlit@aol.com
Web Site: www.eatonliterary.com
Key Personnel
Pres: Richard Lawrence
Established: 1984
Two awards are presented, one for a book-length ms & one for a short story or article. These entries should not have been previously published.
Award: $2,500 (book-length program), $500 (short story or article program)
Closing Date: March 31 (short story or article program), Aug 31 (book-length program)
Presented: April (short story or article program), Sept (book-length program)

EBSCO Information Services Library Staff Development Award
The American Library Association (ALA)
225 N Michigan Ave, Suite 1300, Chicago, IL 60601
SAN: 201-0062
Tel: 312-280-3247 *Toll Free Tel:* 800-545-2433 (ext 3247) *Fax:* 312-944-3897
E-mail: awards@ala.org

Web Site: www.ala.org/awardsgrants
Key Personnel
Prog Offr: Cheryl M Malden *E-mail:* cmalden@ala.org
Awarded to a library organization for a program of staff development designed to further the goals & objectives of the library organization.
Award: $3,500 & 24 karat gold-framed citation
Closing Date: Dec 1
Presented: ALA Annual Conference & Exhibition, June

Edgar Allan Poe Awards®, see The Edgar Awards®

The Edgar Awards®
Mystery Writers of America (MWA)
1140 Broadway, Suite 1507, New York, NY 10001
Tel: 212-888-8171
E-mail: mwa@mysterywriters.org
Web Site: theedgars.com; mysterywriters.org
Key Personnel
EVP: Donna Andrews
Exec Dir: Margery Flax
Established: 1945
For the best mystery novel & best first novel by an American author. Also awards for best juvenile novel & young adult, fact-crime writing, TV episode, short story, paperback original, critical/biographical work. The work must be published for the first time in the US in the calendar year prior to the award.
Award: Ceramic bust of Poe
Closing Date: Nov 30
Presented: New York, NY, Late Spring

Editorial Excellence Award
Biographers International Organization (BIO)
PO Box 33020, Santa Fe, NM 87594
Web Site: biographersinternational.org/award/editorial-excellence
Key Personnel
Exec Dir: Michael Gately *E-mail:* execdirector@biographersinternational.org
Established: 2014
Awarded to an outstanding editor from nominations submitted by BIO members.
Award: Statuette & reception
Presented: Reception in New York, NY, Mid-Nov

Editor's Award
Poets & Writers Inc
90 Broad St, Suite 2100, New York, NY 10004
Tel: 212-226-3586 *Fax:* 212-226-3963
E-mail: admin@pw.org
Web Site: www.pw.org/about-us/sponsored-prizes
Key Personnel
Exec Dir: Melissa Ford Gradel *Tel:* 212-226-3586 ext 223 *E-mail:* mgradel@pw.org
Established: 2009
Awarded in recognition of a book editor who has made an outstanding contribution to the publication of poetry or literary prose over a sustained period of time.
Presented: Poets & Writers Annual Dinner

Editor's Choice Award
New Letters
UMKC, University House, 5101 Rockhill Rd, Kansas City, MO 64110-2499
Tel: 816-235-1169
E-mail: newletters@umkc.edu
Web Site: www.newletters.org
Max word count is 8,000. Entry must be previously unpublished & must cross the traditional boundaries of genre & form. Entry fee: $20 per ms (includes 1-year subscription to *New Letters*). Simultaneous submissions of unpublished entries are accepted with proper notification upon acceptance elsewhere. Multiple entries are welcome with appropriate fees. All entries are considered for publication, even if not the winner. Online entries via Submittable only.
Award: $1,000 & publication
Closing Date: Oct 18
Presented: Early March (announcement)

Editors Prize for Feature Article
Poetry Magazine
61 W Superior St, Chicago, IL 60654
Tel: 312-787-7070
Web Site: www.poetryfoundation.org/poetrymagazine/prizes
Key Personnel
Assoc Ed: Holly Amos *E-mail:* hamos@poetrymagazine.org
Established: 2005
For poetry published during the preceding year in *Poetry* magazine. No application necessary.
Award: $1,000
Presented: Announced in Nov issue

Editors Prize for Reviewing
Poetry Magazine
61 W Superior St, Chicago, IL 60654
Tel: 312-787-7070
Web Site: www.poetryfoundation.org/poetrymagazine/prizes
Key Personnel
Assoc Ed: Holly Amos *E-mail:* hamos@poetrymagazine.org
Established: 2004
For poetry published during the preceding year in *Poetry* magazine. No application necessary.
Award: $1,000
Presented: Announced in Nov issue

Editors Prize for Visual Poetry
Poetry Magazine
61 W Superior St, Chicago, IL 60654
Tel: 312-787-7070
Web Site: www.poetryfoundation.org/poetrymagazine/prizes
Key Personnel
Assoc Ed: Holly Amos *E-mail:* hamos@poetrymagazine.org
Established: 2019
For poetry published during the preceding year in *Poetry* magazine. No application necessary.
Award: $1,000
Presented: Announced in Nov issue

Educators Book Award
The Delta Kappa Gamma Society International
1801 E 51 St, Suite 365-163, Austin, TX 78701
Tel: 512-478-5748 *Toll Free Tel:* 888-762-4685
Fax: 512-478-3961
Web Site: www.dkg.org
Key Personnel
Chair, Award Comm: Dr Angie Quinn *E-mail:* aquinn@pontotoc.k12.ms.us
Membership Dir/Liaison & Consultant, Award Comm: Trish Woodley *Tel:* 512-478-5478 ext 113 *E-mail:* trishw@dkg.org
Award to recognize educational research & writing by a woman author. The book must have the potential to influence the thought & action necessary to meet the needs of today's complex & global society. The content must be of more than local interest with relationship, direct or implied, to education. The book must be written by 1 or 2 women who are citizens of any country in which the Delta Kappa Gamma Society International is organized: Canada, Costa Rica, El Salvador, Estonia, Finland, Germany, Great Britain, Guatemala, Iceland, Japan, Mexico, Netherlands, Norway, Panama, Puerto Rico, Sweden or the US. The book must be copyrighted, in its first edition, or the first English translation, during the previous calendar year. All nominations are made by publishers or authors.
Award: $2,500
Closing Date: Feb 1 (postmark), in the year after copyright
Presented: DKG International Convention, New Orleans, LA, Summer

Margaret A Edwards Award
Young Adult Library Services Association (YALSA)
Division of The American Library Association (ALA)
225 N Michigan Ave, Suite 1300, Chicago, IL 60601
Tel: 312-280-4390 *Toll Free Tel:* 800-545-2433
E-mail: yalsa@ala.org
Web Site: www.ala.org/yalsa/edwards-award
Key Personnel
Exec Dir: Tammy Dillard-Steels *Tel:* 800-545-2433 ext 4391 *E-mail:* tdillard@ala.org
Prog Offr, Events & Conferences: Nichole O'Connor *Tel:* 800-545-2433 ext 4387 *E-mail:* noconnor@ala.org
Communs Specialist: Anna Lam *Tel:* 800-545-2433 ext 5849 *E-mail:* alam@ala.org
Established: 1988
Given to an author for lifetime achievement in helping adolescents become aware of themselves & addressing questions about their role & importance in relationships, society & in the world.
Other Sponsor(s): School Library Journal
Award: $2,000 & citation
Closing Date: June

Edwin Markham Prize for Poetry
Reed Magazine
San Jose State University, English Dept, One Washington Sq, San Jose, CA 95192-0090
Tel: 408-924-4441
E-mail: mail@reedmag.org
Web Site: www.reedmag.org; reedmagazine.submittable.com
All submissions must be through the online system. Writers may submit up to 5 poems per entry. Submit all poems as a single document. Reading fee: $15.
Award: $1,000 & publication in *Reed Magazine*
Closing Date: Nov 1 (submissions accepted beginning June 1)

The Maureen Egen Writers Exchange Award
Poets & Writers Inc
90 Broad St, Suite 2100, New York, NY 10004
Tel: 212-226-3586 *Fax:* 212-226-3963
E-mail: wex@pw.org; admin@pw.org
Web Site: www.pw.org
Key Personnel
Dir, Writers Exchange: Bonnie Marcus *E-mail:* bmarcus@pw.org
Prog Coord, Writers Exchange: Ricardo Hernandez
Established: 1984
Introduces emerging writers to the New York literary community & provides them with a network for professional advancement. One poet & one nonfiction writer from Nebraska will be selected as winners.
Other Sponsor(s): Maureen Mahon Egen
Award: $500 honorarium, all expenses-paid trip to New York City to meet with top literary professionals & give a public reading, 1-month residency at the Jentel Artist Residency Program in Wyoming
Closing Date: March 1
Presented: Summer

Wilfrid Eggleston Award for Nonfiction
Writers' Guild of Alberta
11759 Groat Rd NW, Edmonton, AB T5M 3K6, Canada
Tel: 780-422-8174 *Toll Free Tel:* 800-665-5354 (AB only)
E-mail: mail@writersguild.ab.ca

Web Site: writersguild.ca
Key Personnel
Exec Dir: Giorgia Severini *E-mail:* gseverini@writersguild.ab.ca
Communs & Partnerships Coord: Ellen Kartz *E-mail:* ellen.kartz@writersguild.ab.ca
Memb Servs Coord: Mike Maguire
Prog & Opers Coord: Ashley Mann *E-mail:* ashley.mann@writersguild.ab.ca
Progs & Events Coord: Jason Norman *E-mail:* jason.norman@writersguild.ab.ca
Proj Asst: Sadie MacGillivray *E-mail:* sadie.macgillivray@writersguild.ab.ca
Established: 1982
Literary award for an author that is a resident of Alberta.
Award: $1,500 plus leather-bound copy of book
Closing Date: Dec 31
Presented: Alberta Book Awards Gala, AB, CN
Branch Office(s)
223 12 Ave SW, No 204, Calgary, AB T2R 0G9, Canada, Prog & Conference Coord: Dorothy Bentley *Tel:* 403-875-8058 *E-mail:* dorothy.bentley@writersguild.ab.ca

EJK Book Award, see Ezra Jack Keats Book Award

Ekphrastic Poetry Award
The Poetry Society of Virginia (PSV)
PO Box 36128, North Chesterfield, VA 23235-3533
E-mail: contest@poetrysocietyofvirginia.org; info@poetryvirginia.org
Web Site: www.poetrysocietyofvirginia.org
Key Personnel
Pres: Cherryl T Cooley *E-mail:* poetrysocietypresident@gmail.com
Awarded in memory of Carl Edward Young Jr, Judy Fletcher & Clark Rubendall. Subject: A poem based on a work of art other than poetry (either send a copy of the work or include a link to it). Any form, 48 line limit. Submit 1 copy of the poem with no identifying information but put the category in the upper right-hand side, along with a notation as to whether you are a member of PSV (does not matter if you are a lifetime member or just joined for the contest). Submit a cover letter/page that contains the category, the name of the poem, your name & address, phone number & e-mail address. Entries will not be returned. Entry fee: Free to membs, $5 nonmembs.
Other Sponsor(s): Lynn Young
Award: $50 (1st prize), $30 (2nd prize), $20 (3rd prize)

eLit Awards
Independent Publisher Online
Division of Jenkins Group Inc
1129 Woodmere Ave, Suite B, Traverse City, MI 49686
Tel: 231-933-0445 *Toll Free Tel:* 800-706-4636 *Fax:* 231-933-0448
E-mail: info@elitawards.com
Web Site: elitawards.com
Key Personnel
Awards Dir: Andrew Paryel *Tel:* 800-706-4636 ext 1004
Established: 2009
Given in celebration of the ever growing market of electronic publishing in the wide variety of reader formats. Publishers & authors worldwide creating electronic books written in English & created for the global marketplace are eligible for entry in 65 different categories. Entry fee: $70-$90 per category.
Other Sponsor(s): Jenkins Group Inc
Award: Digital seal, certificate, winners featured online
Closing Date: Jan 31
Presented: April

Van Courtlandt Elliott Prize
Medieval Academy of America (MAA)
6 Beacon St, Suite 500, Boston, MA 02108
Tel: 617-491-1622 *Fax:* 617-492-3303
E-mail: info@themedievalacademy.org
Web Site: www.medievalacademy.org/page/elliott_prize
Key Personnel
Exec Dir: Lisa Fagin Davis *E-mail:* lfd@themedievalacademy.org
Established: 1971
Presented for a first article published in the field of medieval studies. Author must be a resident in North America.
Award: $500 & certificate
Closing Date: Oct 15
Presented: Spring

Ralph Ellison Award
Oklahoma Center for the Book (OCB)
200 NE 18 St, Oklahoma City, OK 73105-3205
Tel: 405-522-3383
Web Site: libraries.ok.gov/ocb/oklahoma-book-awards
Established: 1995
Irregular award honoring deceased individuals who have made outstanding contributions to Oklahoma's literary heritage.

Emerging Critics Fellowship
National Book Critics Circle (NBCC)
c/o Jacob M Appel, Icahn School of Medicine at Mount Sinai, One Gustave L Levy Place, New York, NY 10029
E-mail: info@bookcritics.org
Web Site: www.bookcritics.org/awards
Key Personnel
Pres: Heather Scott Partington *E-mail:* hsp@bookcritics.org
Secy: Colette Bancroft *E-mail:* bancroft.colette72@gmail.com
Treas: Jacob M Appel *E-mail:* jacobmappel@gmail.com
VP, Awards: Keetje Kuipers *E-mail:* keetje@poetrynw.org
VP, Events: Jane Ciabattari *E-mail:* janeciab@gmail.com
One-year fellowship for critics who have demonstrated a genuine interest & commitment to engaging in critical conversation about books. Each writer must submit a resume, 3 writing examples, 300- to 500-word statement of purpose & names/contact information for 2 references. To apply, see nbcc.submittable.com/submit.
Closing Date: May
Presented: Announcement in July

Emerging Playwright Award
Urban Stages
555 Eighth Ave, Suite 1800, New York, NY 10018
Tel: 212-421-1380 *Fax:* 212-421-1387
E-mail: urbanstage@aol.com
Web Site: urbanstages.org
Key Personnel
Artistic Dir & Founder: Frances Hill
Literary Dir: Antoinette Mullins
Scripts not previously produced; scripts should have no more than 5 actors; well-written, imaginative situations & dialog; multicultural scripts are given special attention. Playwrights in & around NYC are given special attention. No processing fee & SASE with all submissions. Selected scripts are first given a staged reading. A select number of staged readings are given intensive workshops. A select number of workshopped plays are given full off-Broadway productions. Award given to playwrights of full productions at Urban Stages. Submission accepted year-round.

Award: $500
Presented: New York, NY

Emerging Voices Fellowship
PEN America Los Angeles
Unit of PEN America
1370 N St Andrews Place, Los Angeles, CA 90028
Tel: 323-424-4939
E-mail: ev@pen.org; awards@pen.org; info@pen.org
Web Site: pen.org/emerging-voices-fellowship
Key Personnel
Progs Dir: Jenn Dees *E-mail:* jdees@pen.org
Established: 1996
Literary mentorship that aims to provide new writers who are isolated from the literary establishment with the tools, skills & knowledge they need to launch a professional writing career. Fellowship is directed toward poets & writers of fiction & creative nonfiction with clear ideas of what they hope to accomplish through their writing. Application period begins June 1.
Award: Five-month fellowship & $1,500 stipend
Closing Date: Aug 1

The Ralph Waldo Emerson Award
The Phi Beta Kappa Society
1606 New Hampshire Ave NW, Washington, DC 20009
Tel: 202-265-3808 *Fax:* 202-986-1601
E-mail: awards@pbk.org
Web Site: www.pbk.org/bookawards
Key Personnel
Exec Asst to the Secy: Aurora Sherman *Tel:* 202-745-3287 *E-mail:* asherman@pbk.org
Established: 1954
Awarded for scholarly studies that contribute to interpretations of the intellectual & cultural condition of humanity. To be eligible, must have been published in US by American author. Works in history, philosophy, religion & related fields such as social sciences & anthropology are eligible. Nomination must come from publisher & be submitted online.
Award: $10,000
Closing Date: Jan
Presented: Washington, DC, Dec

Empire State Award for Excellence in Literature for Young People
New York Library Association
6021 State Farm Rd, Guilderland, NY 12084
Tel: 518-432-6952 *Toll Free Tel:* 800-252-6952 *Fax:* 518-427-1697
E-mail: info@nyla.org; marketing@nyla.org
Web Site: www.nyla.org
Key Personnel
Exec Dir: Jeremy Johannesen *Tel:* 518-432-6952 ext 101 *E-mail:* director@nyla.org
Communs & Mktg Mgr: Christina Romeo *Tel:* 518-432-6952 ext 105
Established: 1990
One-time award (per author) presented to a living author or illustrator currently residing in New York State. The award honors excellence in children's or young adult literature & a body of work that has made a significant contribution to literature for young people.
Award: Engraved medallion
Closing Date: Dec 1
Presented: Annual Conference, Oct/Nov

Engel Findley Award, see Writers' Trust Engel Findley Award

Paul Engle Prize
Iowa City UNESCO City of Literature
123 S Linn St, Iowa City, IA 52240
E-mail: info@iowacityofliterature.org
Web Site: www.iowacityofliterature.org/paul-engle-prize

AWARDS, PRIZE CONTESTS, FELLOWSHIPS & GRANTS

Key Personnel
Exec Dir: John Kenyon *Tel:* 319-356-5245
 E-mail: john-kenyon@iowacityofliterature.org
Dir, Opers: Rachael Carlson *Tel:* 319-887-6100
 E-mail: rachael-carlson@iowacityofliterature.org
Mktg Asst: Sarah Nelson *E-mail:* sarah-nelson@iowacityofliterature.org
Established: 2011
Presented in honor of an individual who represents a pioneering spirit in the world of literature through writing, editing, publishing, or teaching & whose active participation in the larger issues of the day has contributed to the betterment of the world through the literary arts. Nominations open November 1.
Award: 10,000 & one-of-a-kind work of art
Presented: Iowa City Book Festival, Iowa City, IA, Oct

The Gerald Ensley Developing Writer Award
Florida State University Libraries
116 Honors Way, Suite 314, Tallahassee, FL 32306
Tel: 850-644-5211
E-mail: floridabookawards@gmail.com
Web Site: www.floridabookawards.org/index.php/ensley-award
Key Personnel
Exec Dir: Nikki Morse *Tel:* 850-645-6670
 E-mail: nmorse@fsu.edu
Established: 2019
Awarded as part of the Florida Book Awards, to honor a developing Florida author. The nominee must be a Florida resident who has written & published at least 1 but no more than 2 books of fiction, nonfiction, poetry or any of the other Florida Book Award categories. The nominee must be of demonstrated ability & show promise for continued growth. Nomination packet includes: Cover letter, short biography or CV, 3 letters of support & complete list of nominee's publishing credits.
Award: $1,000 & copy of Gerald Ensley's 2 books: *We Found Paradise* & *Write the Way You Would Talk*
Closing Date: Dec 31
Presented: April

Norma Epstein Foundation Awards in Creative Writing
University of Toronto - University College
15 King's College Circle, UC 165, Toronto, ON M5S 3H7, Canada
Tel: 416-946-0271
E-mail: uc.programs@utoronto.ca
Web Site: www.uc.utoronto.ca/norma-epstein
Key Personnel
Dir, Writing Centre: Jerry Plotnick *Tel:* 416-946-3836 *E-mail:* jerry.plotnick@utoronto.ca
Established: 1946
Biennial literary competition. Five categories: Poetry, drama, novel, short story & other prose.
Award: Up to a total of $8,000
Closing Date: May 1, odd-numbered years
Presented: Nov, odd-numbered years

Equity Fellowship
Editors Canada (Reviseurs Canada)
1507-180 Dundas St W, Toronto, ON M5G 1Z8, Canada
Tel: 416-975-1379
E-mail: info@editors.ca; info@reviseurs.ca; communications@editors.ca
Web Site: www.editors.ca/about/awards/equity-fellowship
Key Personnel
Exec Dir: Natasha Bood
 E-mail: executivedirector@editors.ca
Sr Communs Mgr: Michelle Ou
Training & Devt Mgr: Caitlin Stewart

Awarded to up to 3 successful applicants each year. Designed to support editors who have traditionally been excluded by the publishing & editing industries, including editors who are BIPOC (Black, Indigenous & people of color), 2SLGBTQIA+, neurodivergent & disabled. Editors Canada members, student affiliates & non-members can apply.
Award: $1,250 value per fellowship, including annual conference registration; 3 Editors Canada webinars; 1 copy of *Editing Canadian English*, 1 copy of ebook *From Contact to Contract*, 1 copy each of 4 Certification Test Preparation Guides; 1-yr membership in Editors Canada; 1-yr listing in Editors Canada Online Directory

Ernest Sandeen Prize in Poetry & Richard Sullivan Prize in Short Fiction
University of Notre Dame Press/Notre Dame Creative Writing Program, Dept of English
310 Flanner Hall, Notre Dame, IN 46556
Tel: 574-631-6346 *Fax:* 574-631-8148
E-mail: undpress@nd.edu; creativewriting@nd.edu
Web Site: english.nd.edu/creative-writing/awards-and-prizes/; undpress.nd.edu
Key Personnel
Dir: Stephen Wrinn
Awarded to authors who have published at least 1 volume of short fiction or 1 volume of poetry. Include a photocopy of the copyright & the title page of your previous volume. Vanity press publications do not fulfill this requirement. Please include a vita +/or a biographical statement which includes your publishing history. We will be glad to see a selection of reviews of the earlier collection. Submit 2 copies of your ms & inform us if the ms is available electronically. Include a SASE for acknowledgment of receipt of your submission. If you would like your ms returned, send a SASE. A $15 administrative fee should accompany submissions.
Both prizes are awarded biennially, Ernest Sandeen Prize in even-numbered years (applications open March 1) & Richard Sullivan Prize in odd-numbered years (applications open May 1).
Award: $1,000 prize, $500 award & $500 advance against royalties from the Notre Dame Press
Closing Date: Sept 1 (Richard Sullivan Prize); June 1 (Ernest Sandeen Prize)
Presented: Spring following submission period

Erskine J Poetry Prize
Smartish Pace
2221 Lake Ave, Baltimore, MD 21213
E-mail: smartishpace@gmail.com
Web Site: www.smartishpace.com/poetry-prizes
Key Personnel
Ed: Stephen Reichert *E-mail:* sreichert@smartishpace.com
Assoc Ed: Clare Banks *E-mail:* cbsmartishpace@gmail.com
Established: 2001
All poems submitted for the prize will be considered for publication in *Smartish Pace*. Online submissions: See web site for Submittable link. Simultaneous submissions are allowed. You may enter more than once. Postal submissions: Submit 3 poems, bio & $10 entry fee. Include name, address & e-mail.
Award: $200 (1st prize); Top 3 poets & all finalists are published in *Smartish Pace*
Closing Date: Jan 1
Presented: Baltimore, MD

David W & Beatrice C Evans Biography & Handcart Awards
Mountain West Center for Regional Studies

ASSOCIATIONS, EVENTS

Division of College of Humanities & Social Sciences-Utah State University
0735 Old Main Hill, Logan, UT 84322-0735
Tel: 435-797-0299 *Fax:* 435-797-1092
E-mail: mwc@usu.edu
Web Site: mountainwest.usu.edu
Key Personnel
Prog Dir: Molly B Cannon
Established: 1983
Awarded biennially, in even-numbered years, for the best published biography, autobiography or memoir of a person who lived a significant portion of his or her life in the Interior West, or "Mormon Country" (a region historically influenced by Mormon institutions & social practices). The Evans Handcart Award broadens the criteria to include family histories & encourages first-time & emerging authors to submit their books published during the previous 2 years.
Award: $10,000 (Evans Biography Award); $2,500 (Evans Handcart Award)
Closing Date: Feb 15
Presented: Utah State University, Logan, UT, Fall

EWA Reporting Fellowships
Education Writers Association (EWA)
1825 "K" St NW, Suite 200, Washington, DC 20006
Tel: 202-452-9830
Web Site: ewa.org
Key Personnel
Exec Dir: Kathy Chow *E-mail:* kchow@ewa.org
Competitive fellowships to support enterprise journalism that informs the public about consequential issues in education. The fellows represent diverse mix of news organizations & projects.
Other Sponsor(s): Ascendium Education Group; Wallace Foundation
Award: Up to $8,000 to help cover reporting costs, plus other assistance

EXCEL Awards
AM&P Network
Division of Software & Information Industry Network (SIIA)
1620 "I" St NW, Suite 501, Washington, DC 20005
Tel: 202-289-7442 *Fax:* 202-289-7097
E-mail: excelawards@siia.net
Web Site: siia.net/excel
Key Personnel
VP, Awards & Recognition Progs, SIIA: Amanda McMaster *Tel:* 202-789-4469
 E-mail: amcmaster@siia.net
To recognize the integration of various print, digital +/or live platforms in association media, publishing, marketing & communications. No mail-in entries are accepted. All entries (print & digital) must have been published in the previous calendar year & be in English. Entry fee: Early-$160 membs, $325 nonmembs; regular-$210 membs, $350 nonmembs; extended-$260 membs, $395 nonmembs.
Closing Date: Dec (early bird), Feb (regular), March (extended)
Presented: Excel Awards Ceremony, June

Excellence in Graphic Literature Awards
Pop Culture Classroom (PCC)
2760 W Fifth Ave, Denver, CO 80204
Tel: 303-325-1236
E-mail: egl@popcultureclassroom.org
Web Site: www.popcultureclassroom.org/events
Key Personnel
Exec Educ Prog Dir: Adam Kullberg
Established: 2018
Awards to create a greater awareness of the value the comics medium & the graphic novel format bring to the world of reading. Submissions accepted for any book-length works pub-

lished during the previous calendar year. Categories: Best in Children's Books; Best in Middle Grade Books; Best in Young Books; Best in Adult Books; Mosaic Award; Book of the Year.
Award: Trophy & medallion for book promotion

Excellence in Nonfiction for Young Adults
Young Adult Library Services Association (YALSA)
Division of The American Library Association (ALA)
225 N Michigan Ave, Suite 1300, Chicago, IL 60601
Toll Free Tel: 800-545-2433 (ext 4390)
E-mail: yalsa@ala.org
Web Site: www.ala.org/yalsa/nonfiction-award
Key Personnel
Exec Dir: Tammy Dillard-Steels *Tel:* 800-545-2433 ext 4391 *E-mail:* tdillard@ala.org
Prog Offr, Events & Conferences: Nichole O'Connor *Tel:* 800-545-2433 ext 4387 *E-mail:* noconnor@ala.org
Communs Specialist: Anna Lam *Tel:* 800-545-2433 ext 5849 *E-mail:* alam@ala.org
To honor the best nonfiction book published for young adults (ages 12-18) during a November 1-October 31 publishing year.
Presented: ALA Youth Media Awards, Late Jan

Excellence in Teaching Fellowships
The Loft Literary Center
Open Book Bldg, Suite 200, 1011 Washington Ave S, Minneapolis, MN 55415
Tel: 612-215-2575 *Fax:* 612-215-2576
E-mail: loft@loft.org
Web Site: loft.org/awards/excellence-teaching-fellowships
Key Personnel
Exec & Artistic Dir: Arleta M Little *Tel:* 612-215-2584 *E-mail:* alittle@loft.org
Mktg & Communs Dir: Chris Mackenzie Jones *Tel:* 612-215-2589 *E-mail:* cjones@loft.org
Three fellows are awarded one week at Madeline Island School for the Arts (MISA) to work on a writing project of their choice. Anyone who has taught in the year of the award & in the 2 years prior is eligible. Residency terms in July & September. Nominations are accepted from students & Loft teaching artists. Self-nominations are allowed.
Other Sponsor(s): Madeline Island School for the Arts (MISA)
Award: Week-long residency at MISA including single-occupancy lodging, on-site meals & $25 per diem for off-site dinners
Closing Date: April
Presented: May

John K Fairbank Prize in East Asian History
American Historical Association (AHA)
400 "A" St SE, Washington, DC 20003
Tel: 202-544-2422
E-mail: awards@historians.org
Web Site: www.historians.org/award-grant/john-k-fairbank-prize/
Established: 1968
Prize for an outstanding book on the history of China proper, Vietnam, Chinese Central Asia, Mongolia, Manchuria, Korea or Japan substantially after 1800. Books with a 2024 copyright are eligible for the 2025 prize. Anthologies, edited works & pamphlets are ineligible. Along with an application form, applicants must mail a copy of their book to each prize committee member posted on our web site as the prize deadline approaches. All updated info on web site.
Award: $1,000
Closing Date: May 15, 2025
Presented: AHA Annual Meeting, Chicago, IL, Jan 2026

Tom Fairley Award for Editorial Excellence
Editors Canada (Reviseurs Canada)
1507-180 Dundas St W, Toronto, ON M5G 1Z8, Canada
Tel: 416-975-1379
E-mail: fairley_award@editors.ca; info@editors.ca; communications@editors.ca
Web Site: www.editors.ca/about/awards/tom-fairley-award
Key Personnel
Exec Dir: Natasha Bood
E-mail: executivedirector@editors.ca
Sr Communs Mgr: Michelle Ou
Training & Devt Mgr: Caitlin Stewart
Established: 1983
Presented to an exceptional editor who played an important role in the success of a project completed in English or French. The work must have been published during the previous calendar year. Nominations are open to all editors, both freelance & in-house. Members & non-members of Editors Canada may be nominated. All submissions must be electronic & consist of a nomination form & supporting documents. Administrative fee: $100.
Award: $2,000 cash
Closing Date: Jan of the year after the work took place for letter of nomination & supporting material must be received by the second week in Feb
Presented: National Annual Conference, June of the year after the work took place

Far Horizons Award for Poetry
The Malahat Review
University of Victoria, PO Box 1700, Sta CSC, Victoria, BC V8W 2Y2, Canada
Tel: 250-721-8524
E-mail: malahat@uvic.ca
Web Site: www.malahatreview.ca/contests/far_horizons_poetry/info.html; www.malahatreview.ca
Key Personnel
Mng Ed: L'Amour Lisik
Ed: Iain Higgins *E-mail:* malahateditor@uvic.ca
Established: 2006
Open to writers worldwide whose poetry has yet to be published in book form. Awarded biennially in even-numbered years. Submissions must be made online through Submittable. See web site for details & entry fees.
Award: $1,000 & publication in the Fall issue of *The Malahat Review*
Closing Date: May 1, even-numbered years

Far Horizons Award for Short Fiction
The Malahat Review
University of Victoria, PO Box 1700, Sta CSC, Victoria, BC V8W 2Y2, Canada
Tel: 250-721-8524
E-mail: malahat@uvic.ca
Web Site: www.malahatreview.ca/contests/far_horizons_fiction/info.html; www.malahatreview.ca
Key Personnel
Mng Ed: L'Amour Lisik
Ed: Iain Higgins *E-mail:* malahateditor@uvic.ca
Established: 2005
Awarded biennially in odd-numbered years. Open to writers whose fiction has yet to be published in book form. Story must not exceed 3,500 words. One short story per entry, multiple entries allowed. Submissions must be made online through Submittable.
Award: $1,250 & publication in the Fall issue of *The Malahat Review*
Closing Date: May 1, odd-numbered years

Norma Farber First Book Award
Poetry Society of America (PSA)
119 Smith St, Brooklyn, NY 11201
Tel: 212-254-9628
E-mail: info@poetrysociety.org
Web Site: poetrysociety.org/awards
Key Personnel
Exec Dir: Matt Brogan *E-mail:* matt@poetrysociety.org
Deputy Dir: Brett Fletcher Lauer *E-mail:* brett@poetrysociety.org
Devt Dir: Madeline Weinfield *E-mail:* madeline@poetrysociety.org
Awarded for a first book of original poetry written by a living author who lives in the US or is a US citizen. The book must be published in either a hard or soft cover in a standard edition. Translations & chapbooks are ineligible. Books must be submitted directly by publishers. Entry forms required. Entry fee: $20 per book.
Award: $500
Closing Date: Dec 31 (postmark)
Presented: Annual Awards Ceremony, New York, NY, Spring

The FC2 Catherine Doctorow Innovative Fiction Prize
Fiction Collective 2 (FC2)
c/o University of Alabama Press, Box 870380, Tuscaloosa, AL 35487-0380
E-mail: fc2@gmail.com
Web Site: fc2.org
Open to any US writer in English with at least 3 books of fiction published. Submissions may include a collection of short stories, one or more novellas, or a novel of any length. Works that have previously appeared in magazines or in anthologies may be included. Electronic submissions only. Submission fee: $25 for each ms submitted separately.
Award: $15,000 & publication by FC2
Closing Date: Nov 1
Presented: May

The FC2 Ronald Sukenick Innovative Fiction Contest
Fiction Collective 2 (FC2)
c/o University of Alabama Press, Box 870380, Tuscaloosa, AL 35487-0380
E-mail: fc2@gmail.com
Web Site: fc2.org
Open to any US writer in English who has not previously published with Fiction Collective Two. Submissions may include a collection of short stories, one or more novellas, or a novel of any length. Works that have previously appeared in magazines or in anthologies may be included. Electronic submissions only. Submission fee: $25 for each ms submitted separately.
Award: $1,500 & publication by FC2
Closing Date: Nov 1
Presented: May

The Leslie Feinberg Award for Trans & Gender-Variant Literature
Formerly The Publishing Triangle Award for Trans & Gender-Variant Literature
The Publishing Triangle
511 Avenue of the Americas, No D36, New York, NY 10011
E-mail: awards@publishingtriangle.org; info@publishingtriangle.org; publishingtriangle@gmail.com
Web Site: publishingtriangle.org/awards/trans-gender-variant-literature
Established: 2016
Recognizes outstanding work from the gender-nonconforming community. Poetry, fiction (including for children) & nonfiction by trans or gender-variant (T/GV) authors is eligible. Nonfiction authored or co-authored by cisgender authors that is primarily about the T/GV experience or community is also eligible. Works must have been published in the preceding year. A call for submissions is posted on the web site in early Autumn. Finalists & winners

are determined by a panel of judges appointed by the awards committee.
Award: $1,000

Fellowships for Creative & Performing Artists & Writers
American Antiquarian Society (AAS)
185 Salisbury St, Worcester, MA 01609-1634
Tel: 508-755-5221 *Fax:* 508-754-9069
E-mail: library@mwa.org
Web Site: www.americanantiquarian.org
Key Personnel
Pres: Scott E Casper *Tel:* 508-471-2161
 E-mail: scasper@mwa.org
VP, Advancement: Beth Kopley *Tel:* 508-471-2162 *E-mail:* bkopley@mwa.org
VP, Collections: Lauren B Hewes *Tel:* 508-471-2124 *E-mail:* lhewes@mwa.org
VP, Fin & Admin: Kristen Balash *Tel:* 508-471-2167 *E-mail:* kbalash@mwa.org
VP, Progs & Dir, Fellowships: Nan Wolverton *Tel:* 508-471-2119 *E-mail:* nwolverton@mwa.org
Established: 1994
Award: $1,350 stipend for fellows residing on campus (rent-free) in the Society's Scholars' housing; $1,850 stipend for fellows residing off campus (no travel allowance)
Closing Date: Oct

Fellowships for Historical Research
American Antiquarian Society (AAS)
185 Salisbury St, Worcester, MA 01609-1634
Tel: 508-755-5221 *Fax:* 508-754-9069
Web Site: www.americanantiquarian.org
Key Personnel
Pres: Scott E Casper *Tel:* 508-471-2161
 E-mail: scasper@mwa.org
VP, Advancement: Beth Kopley *Tel:* 508-471-2162 *E-mail:* bkopley@mwa.org
VP, Collections: Lauren B Hewes *Tel:* 508-471-2124 *E-mail:* lhewes@mwa.org
VP, Fin & Admin: Kristen Balash *Tel:* 508-471-2167 *E-mail:* kbalash@mwa.org
VP, Progs & Dir, Fellowships: Nan Wolverton *Tel:* 508-471-2119 *E-mail:* nwolverton@mwa.org
Given to poets, fiction writers & creative nonfiction writers for month long residencies at the American Antiquarian Society in Worcester, MA, to research pre-20th century American history & culture. Submit 10 copies of up to 25 pages of poetry, fiction or creative nonfiction, a resume, 2 letters of recommendation & a 5 page project proposal.
Award: $1,350 stipend & on-campus housing provided; fellows residing off-campus receive $1,850
Closing Date: Oct

Fence Modern Poets Series
Fence Books
Imprint of Fence Magazine Inc
36-09 28 Ave, Apt 3R, Astoria, NY 11103-4518
Tel: 518-567-7006
Web Site: www.fenceportal.org
Key Personnel
Co-Edit Dir: Emily Wallis Hughes *Tel:* 530-220-4373; Jason Zuzga *Tel:* 267-902-0731
Established: 2001
For a poet of any gender or gender identity writing in English at any stage of their publishing career. Using the online submission system, submit ms 48-80 pages & $29 entry fee.
Award: $1,000 & publication
Closing Date: April 30

Shubert Fendrich Memorial Playwriting Contest
Pioneer Drama Service Inc
PO Box 4267, Englewood, CO 80155-4267
Tel: 303-779-4035 *Toll Free Tel:* 800-333-7262
 Fax: 303-779-4315
Web Site: www.pioneerdrama.com/playwrights/contest.asp
Key Personnel
Acqs Ed: Brian Taylor
Established: 1990
Presented for plays suitable for publication by Pioneer Drama Service Inc. Submission must include 100-200 word synopsis, cast list, running time, CD +/or score, set design(s), proof of production or staged reading, age of intended audience, SASE for returned materials, cover letter +/or resume. See web site for detailed guidelines.
Award: $1,000 royalty advance & publication
Closing Date: Dec 31
Presented: June 1

Edna Ferber Fiction Book Award
Council for Wisconsin Writers (CWW)
c/o 210 N Main St, No 204, Cedar Grove, WI 53013
E-mail: wiswriters@gmail.com
Web Site: wiswriters.org/awards
Key Personnel
Contest Chair: Sylvia Cavanaugh
 E-mail: bgirl4shadow@gmail.com
Established: 1965
Awarded for the best fiction book published by a Wisconsin-based author in the contest year.
Entry fee: $25 nonmembs.
Award: $500 & 1-week residency at Shake Rag Alley Center for the Arts
Closing Date: Jan 31
Presented: CWW Annual Award Ceremony & Banquet, May

The Ferro-Grumley Award for LGBTQ Fiction
The Publishing Triangle
511 Avenue of the Americas, No D36, New York, NY 10011
E-mail: awards@publishingtriangle.org; info@publishingtriangle.org; publishingtriangle@gmail.com
Web Site: publishingtriangle.org/awards/ferro-grumley-awards
Established: 1990
Honors culture-driving fiction from LGBTQ points of view. Books must have been published in the preceding year in the US or Canada. A call for submissions is posted on the web site in early Autumn. Finalists & winners are determined by a panel of judges appointed by Ferro-Grumley Literary Awards.
Other Sponsor(s): Ferro-Grumley Foundation
Award: $1,000 & residency at Art Workshop International in Assisi, Italy

Fine Arts Work Center in Provincetown
24 Pearl St, Provincetown, MA 02657
Tel: 508-487-9960
E-mail: fellowship@fawc.org
Web Site: www.fawc.org
Established: 1968
Offer 7-month fellowships to 10 artists & 10 writers, October 1-May 1. The Center aims to aid emerging artists & writers at a critical stage of their careers. See web site for application & information.
Award: Monthly stipends of up to $650 plus free rent for writers living at the Center; same for artists. Families welcome; no pets
Closing Date: Visual Arts: Feb 1; Writers: Dec 1

Firecracker Awards
Community of Literary Magazines & Presses (CLMP)
154 Christopher St, Suite 3C, New York, NY 10014-9110
Tel: 212-741-9110
E-mail: info@clmp.org
Web Site: www.clmp.org/firecracker
Key Personnel
Exec Dir: Mary Gannon *E-mail:* mgannon@clmp.org
Communs Mgr: Emma Hine *E-mail:* ehine@clmp.org
Firecracker Awards Mgr: David Gibbs
 E-mail: dgibbs@clmp.org
Celebrate & promote great literary works from independent literary publishers & self-published authors. Categories: Fiction, Creative Nonfiction & Poetry. Awards also in 3 magazine/periodical categories: Poetry, Best Debut & General Excellence.
Other Sponsor(s): American Booksellers Association
Presented: June

5 Under 35
National Book Foundation
90 Broad St, Suite 604, New York, NY 10004
Tel: 212-685-0261 *Fax:* 212-213-6570
E-mail: nationalbook@nationalbook.org
Web Site: www.nationalbook.org
Key Personnel
Exec Dir: Ruth Dickey *E-mail:* rdickey@nationalbook.org
Sr Mgr, Awards & Honors: Madeleine Shelton
 E-mail: mshelton@nationalbook.org
Sr Mgr, Mktg & Communs: Ale Romero
 E-mail: aromero@nationalbook.org
Awards & Communs Coord: Lilly Santiago
 E-mail: lsantiago@nationalbook.org
Established: 2006
Prize to honor 5 writers from around the world, under the age of 35, who published their first & only book of fiction (short story collection or novel), within the last 5 years. Honorees are selected by authors previously recognized by the National Book Foundation, either by National Book Awards (winners or finalists) or previous 5 Under 35 honorees.
Other Sponsor(s): Amazon.com
Award: $1,000 prize
Presented: Awards Ceremony

Norma Fleck Award for Canadian Children's Non-Fiction
The Canadian Children's Book Centre
425 Adelaide St W, Suite 200, Toronto, ON M5V 3C1, Canada
Tel: 416-975-0010
E-mail: info@bookcentre.ca
Web Site: www.bookcentre.ca
Key Personnel
Exec Dir: Sarah Sahagian
Lib Coord: Meghan Howe *E-mail:* meghan@bookcentre.ca
Established: 1999
Awarded to a Canadian author/illustrator for an outstanding work of nonfiction for young people.
Other Sponsor(s): Fleck Family Foundation
Award: $10,000 cash
Closing Date: Mid-Dec

The Florida Book Awards
Florida State University Libraries
116 Honors Way, Suite 314, Tallahassee, FL 32306
Tel: 850-644-5211
E-mail: floridabookawards@gmail.com
Web Site: www.floridabookawards.org
Key Personnel
Exec Dir: Nikki Morse *Tel:* 850-645-6670
 E-mail: nmorse@fsu.edu
Established: 2006
Competition for the best Florida literature. Books may be submitted by authors, publishers, literary agents, or members of the public in any of 11 categories: Cooking, Florida nonfiction, general fiction, general nonfiction, older children's

literature, poetry, popular fiction, Spanish language, visual arts, young adult literature, young children's literature. Within the poetry category, there is a chapbooks subcategory which awards a gold medal. Nominated books must have an ISBN number & a copyright date in the calendar year preceding the award year. Authors must be full-time Florida residents, except in the Florida nonfiction, visual arts & cooking categories, where the subject matter must focus on Florida. Entry fee: $60 per title, per category.
Other Sponsor(s): Florida Center for the Book; Florida Humanities; Florida Library Association; Midtown Reader; State Library & Archives of Florida; Word of South Festival
Award: Gold, silver & bronze medals in each category
Closing Date: Early Jan
Presented: April

Brigid Erin Flynn Award for Best Picture Book
Texas Institute of Letters (TIL)
PO Box 130294, Spring, TX 77393
Web Site: texasinstituteofletters.org
Key Personnel
Pres: David Bowles *E-mail:* president@texasinstituteofletters.org
VP: Chris Barton
Secy: Kathryn Jones *E-mail:* secretary@texasinstituteofletters.org
Treas: Cliff Hudder
Award for the best picture book by a Texan or about Texas. The author must have been born in Texas or have lived in Texas for at least 5 consecutive years at some time. See web site for guidelines.
Award: $1,000
Closing Date: Jan
Presented: TIL Annual Meeting & Awards Ceremony, April

Jean Flynn Award for Best Young Adult Book
Texas Institute of Letters (TIL)
PO Box 130294, Spring, TX 77393
Web Site: texasinstituteofletters.org
Key Personnel
Pres: David Bowles *E-mail:* president@texasinstituteofletters.org
VP: Chris Barton
Secy: Kathryn Jones *E-mail:* secretary@texasinstituteofletters.org
Treas: Cliff Hudder
Award for the best young adult book by a Texan or about Texas. The author must have been born in Texas or have lived in Texas for at least 5 consecutive years at some time. See web site for guidelines.
Award: $1,000
Closing Date: Jan
Presented: TIL Annual Meeting & Awards Ceremony, April

Deirdre Siobhan FlynnBass Award for Best Middle Grade Book
Texas Institute of Letters (TIL)
PO Box 130294, Spring, TX 77393
Web Site: texasinstituteofletters.org
Key Personnel
Pres: David Bowles *E-mail:* president@texasinstituteofletters.org
VP: Chris Barton
Secy: Kathryn Jones *E-mail:* secretary@texasinstituteofletters.org
Treas: Cliff Hudder
Award for the best middle grade book by a Texan or about Texas. The author must have been born in Texas or have lived in Texas for at least 5 consecutive years at some time. See web site for guidelines.
Award: $1,000
Closing Date: Jan
Presented: TIL Annual Meeting & Awards Ceremony, April

Fordham University, Gabelli School of Business
140 W 62 St, Rm 440, New York, NY 10023
Web Site: www.fordham.edu
Key Personnel
Professor & Area Chair: John A Fortunato *E-mail:* jfortunato@fordham.edu
Established: 1969
Offers MBA degree with a major in Communications & Media Management & Master of Science (MS) in Communications & Media Management for media & entertainment industries. Its mission is to educate business professionals who can manage effectively in a range of leadership roles & who are equipped for continuous growth in a changing global environment. A variety of assistantships, fellowships & scholarships are available to highly qualified MBA candidates.
Closing Date: Ongoing
Presented: Each trimester

Foreword's INDIES Awards
Foreword Reviews
Division of Foreword Magazine Inc
12935 W Bay Shore Rd, Suite 380, Traverse City, MI 49684
Tel: 231-933-3699
Web Site: www.forewordreviews.com
Key Personnel
Publr: Victoria Sutherland *E-mail:* victoria@forewordreviews.com
Established: 1998
Any independently published book, including those from self-published authors & university presses, published in the current year & available for purchase in print or ebook formats. Revised editions of previously issued books are eligible for entry only with newly issued ISBNs. Reissued editions are not eligible for entry.
Award: $1,500 each to Editor's Choice in fiction & nonfiction
Closing Date: Jan 15 for books published in previous calendar year

Morris D Forkosch Prize in British History
American Historical Association (AHA)
400 "A" St SE, Washington, DC 20003
Tel: 202-544-2422
E-mail: awards@historians.org
Web Site: www.historians.org/awards-and-grants/awards-and-prizes/morris-d-forkosch-prize
Established: 1993
Awarded in recognition of the best book in English in the field of British, British Imperial or British Commonwealth history since 1485. Submissions of books relating to the shared common law heritage of the English-speaking world are particularly encouraged. Books with a 2024 copyright are eligible for the 2025 prize. Along with an application form, applicants must mail a copy of their book to each prize committee member posted on our web site as the prize deadline approaches. All updated info on web site.
Award: $1,000
Closing Date: May 15, 2025
Presented: AHA Annual Meeting, Chicago, IL, Jan 2026

E M Forster Award
American Academy of Arts & Letters
633 W 155 St, New York, NY 10032
Tel: 212-368-5900
E-mail: academy@artsandletters.org
Web Site: artsandletters.org/awards
Key Personnel
Exec Dir: Cody Upton
Given to a young English writer toward a stay in the US. Candidates must be nominated by an Academy member.
Award: $20,000

49th Parallel Poetry Award
The Bellingham Review
Mail Stop 9053, Western Washington University, Bellingham, WA 98225
Tel: 360-650-4863
E-mail: bellingham.review@wwu.edu
Web Site: bhreview.org; bhreview.submittable.com
Key Personnel
Ed-in-Chief: Susanne Paola Antonetta
Mng Ed: Stephen Haines
Asst Mng Ed: Keegan Lawler
Established: 1983
Entry consists of one essay, one story, up to 3 pieces of flash, or up to 3 poems. Please limit prose to 4,000 words. For prose that is 1,500 words or fewer, submit up to 3 in one entry. Upload entries via Submittable beginning December 1. Paper submissions are not accepted. All submissions must be previously unpublished in North America. Entry fee: $20, $30 international.
Award: $1,000 & publication in the *Bellingham Review* (1st prize), considered for publication (2nd, 3rd & finalists)
Closing Date: March 15
Presented: June

Foster City International Writers Contest
Foster City International Writers Contest Committee
650 Shell Blvd, Foster City, CA 94404
Tel: 650-286-3380
E-mail: fostercity_writers@yahoo.com
Web Site: www.fostercity.org
Key Personnel
Comm Chair: Ilene Shaine
Recreation Mgr: Tiffany Oren
Established: 1974
For fiction, humor, poetry & personal essay, rhymed verse, blank verse. Entries must be original, previously unpublished & in English. Fiction must be no more than 3,000 words; poetry not to exceed 2 double-spaced typed pages in length. Open to all writers, no age or geographic limit. Send SASE for contest flyer. Non-refundable entry fee: $20.
Award: $250 in each category (1st prize); $100 (2nd prize): nonfiction, fiction, humor, poetry

Four Quartets Prize
Poetry Society of America (PSA)
119 Smith St, Brooklyn, NY 11201
Tel: 212-254-9628
E-mail: info@poetrysociety.org
Web Site: poetrysociety.org/awards
Key Personnel
Exec Dir: Matt Brogan *E-mail:* matt@poetrysociety.org
Deputy Dir: Brett Fletcher Lauer *E-mail:* brett@poetrysociety.org
Devt Dir: Madeline Weinfield *E-mail:* madeline@poetrysociety.org
Prize for a unified & complete sequence of poems published in America in a print or online journal, chapbook, or book in the year prior to the award year. Only 1 submission per author will be considered. Submissions accepted from authors, publishers & literary agents. Self-published work, multi-author work & translations are ineligible. See web site for detailed submission requirements.
Other Sponsor(s): T S Eliot Foundation
Award: $1,000 to each of 3 finalists, additional $20,000 to winner
Closing Date: Dec
Presented: Spring

AWARDS, PRIZE CONTESTS, FELLOWSHIPS & GRANTS

Frances Henne/YALSA Research Grant
Young Adult Library Services Association (YALSA)
Division of The American Library Association (ALA)
225 N Michigan Ave, Suite 1300, Chicago, IL 60601
Tel: 312-280-4390 *Toll Free Tel:* 800-545-2433
E-mail: yalsa@ala.org
Web Site: www.ala.org/yalsa/awardsandgrants/franceshenne
Key Personnel
Exec Dir: Tammy Dillard-Steels *Tel:* 800-545-2433 ext 4391 *E-mail:* tdillard@ala.org
Prog Offr, Events & Conferences: Nichole O'Connor *Tel:* 800-545-2433 ext 4387
 E-mail: noconnor@ala.org
Communs Specialist: Anna Lam *Tel:* 800-545-2433 ext 5849 *E-mail:* alam@ala.org
Established: 1986
Provides seed money for small scale research or action research projects that respond to the YALSA Research Agenda. Applicants must be personal members of YALSA, although the research project may be undertaken by an individual, an institution, or by a group. Student members are eligible to apply. Proposals must be submitted online. See web site for full submission requirements.
Award: $1,000
Closing Date: Dec 1
Presented: Feb

Prix Francophone de l'ACSP
Canadian Political Science Association (CPSA)
260 Dalhousie St, Suite 204, Ottawa, ON K1N 7E4, Canada
Tel: 613-562-1202 *Fax:* 613-241-0019
E-mail: cpsaprizes@cpsa-acsp.ca; cpsa-acsp@cpsa-acsp.ca
Web Site: www.cpsa-acsp.ca
Key Personnel
Exec Dir: Silvina Danesi
Admin: C Ngako Woktcheu
Established: 2014
Biennial prize, awarded in even-numbered years, to the author(s) of the best book published in French in the field of political science. To be eligible, a book may be single-authored or multi-authored. Single-authored: author must be a member of the CPSA in the year the book is considered for the award. Multi-authored: at least one of the authors must be a member of the CPSA in the year the book is considered for the award. For the 2026 award, a book must have a copyright date of 2024 or 2025.
Award: Commemorative plaque & receive/share the set of books submitted to the CPSA office
Closing Date: Dec
Presented: CPSA Annual Conference

Soeurette Diehl Fraser Translation Award
Texas Institute of Letters (TIL)
PO Box 130294, Spring, TX 77393
Web Site: texasinstituteofletters.org
Key Personnel
Pres: David Bowles *E-mail:* president@texasinstituteofletters.org
VP: Chris Barton
Secy: Kathryn Jones *E-mail:* secretary@texasinstituteofletters.org
Treas: Cliff Hudder
Established: 1990
Awarded biennially, in odd-numbered years, for the best book of translation by a Texan. The author must have been born in Texas or have lived in Texas for at least 5 consecutive years at some time. See web site for guidelines.
Award: $1,000
Closing Date: Jan
Presented: TIL Awards Ceremony, Spring

George Freedley Memorial Award
Theatre Library Association (TLA)
c/o The New York Public Library for the Performing Arts, 111 Amsterdam Ave, New York, NY 10023
E-mail: tlabookawards@gmail.com; theatrelibraryassociation@gmail.com
Web Site: www.tla-online.org/awards/bookawards
Key Personnel
Co-Chair, Book Awards Comm: Suzanne Lipkin; Annemarie van Roessel
Established: 1968
Honors English language books of scholarship in the field of live performance (including theatre, dance, vaudeville, puppetry, mime, performance arts, the circus, etc) published or distributed in the US during the previous calendar year that demonstrate exemplary use & interpretation of library & archival collections.
Award: $500 (1st prize), $250 (Special Jury Prize)
Closing Date: Feb 28
Presented: New York, NY, Oct

The Don Freeman Work-in-Progress Grant
Society of Children's Book Writers & Illustrators (SCBWI)
6363 Wilshire Blvd, Suite 425, Los Angeles, CA 90048
Tel: 323-782-1010
E-mail: info@scbwi.org
Web Site: www.scbwi.org
Key Personnel
Exec Dir: Sarah Baker
Established: 1977
Two grants awarded, one to a published illustrator & one to a pre-published illustrator. Available to all SCBWI members working on a picture book or their portfolio. All submissions must be digital.
Award: $1,000 each
Closing Date: April 15

The French-American Foundation & Florence Gould Foundation Annual Translation Prize
The French-American Foundation
28 W 44 St, Suite 812, New York, NY 10036
Web Site: www.frenchamerican.org
Key Personnel
Dir, Progs & Opers: Katie Demallie
 E-mail: kdemallie@frenchamerican.org
Prog Coord: Elizabeth McGehee
Established: 1986
Award for outstanding translations of fiction & nonfiction from French into English which have been published in the US. Translations must be submitted by the US publisher or the translator. Technical, poetry, scientific, reference works & children's literature are not accepted. Works must have been published in the previous calendar year.
Other Sponsor(s): Florence Gould Foundation
Award: 2 awards of $10,000 (1 each for fiction & nonfiction)
Closing Date: Jan 15
Presented: New York, NY, Spring

Horst Frenz Prize
American Comparative Literature Association (ACLA)
323 E Wacker Dr, No 642, Chicago, IL 60601
Tel: 312-600-8072
E-mail: info@acla.org
Web Site: www.acla.org/prize-awards/horst-frenz-prize
Awarded to the best paper presented by a graduate student at the ACLA annual meeting.
Award: $500 cash, complimentary registration to annual meeting, travel reimbursement grant up to $500 to attend the following year's meeting

ASSOCIATIONS, EVENTS

& publication of the paper in the *Yearbook of Comparative Literature*
Closing Date: July 31

Friends of American Writers Literature Awards
Friends of American Writers (FAW)
c/o 506 Rose Ave, Des Plaines, IL 60016
Tel: 847-827-8339
E-mail: info@fawchicago.org
Web Site: www.fawchicago.org
Key Personnel
Pres: Tammie Bob *E-mail:* bobtam410@gmail.com
Adult Lit Award Chair: Karen Pulver
 E-mail: lit_chair@fawchicago.org
Established: 1922
Awarded in recognition of new emerging Midwestern authors or those whose novels or non-fiction writing are set in the Midwest. Author must be a resident (or previously have been a resident for approximately 5 years) of Illinois, Indiana, Iowa, Kansas, Michigan, Minnesota, Missouri, North Dakota, Nebraska, Ohio, South Dakota or Wisconsin; or the locale of the book must be in a region identified above. Books can be fiction or creative nonfiction. Self-published (vanity press) & ebooks are not eligible. The book must be published in the calendar year prior to the awards year. The author must not have published more than 3 books under his/her own pen name, with up to & including the third book being eligible for consideration. If an author has more than one book published during that year, all of them will be considered. No applications are necessary. Forward nominations to one of the designated Literary Chairs by sending 2 copies of each book along with a short biographical material regarding the author.
Award: Two cash prizes totaling $4,000
Closing Date: Dec
Presented: The Fortnightly, Chicago, IL, May

Friends of American Writers Young People's Literature Awards
Friends of American Writers (FAW)
c/o 506 Rose Ave, Des Plaines, IL 60016
Tel: 847-827-8339
E-mail: info@fawchicago.org
Web Site: www.fawchicago.org
Key Personnel
Pres: Tammie Bob *E-mail:* bobtam410@gmail.com
Young People's Lit Chair: Angela Gall
 E-mail: younglit_chair@fawchicago.org
Established: 1960
Awarded in recognition of new emerging Midwestern authors or those whose novels or non-fiction writing are set in the Midwest. Author must be a resident (or previously have been a resident for approximately 5 years) of Illinois, Indiana, Iowa, Kansas, Michigan, Minnesota, Missouri, North Dakota, Nebraska, Ohio, South Dakota or Wisconsin; or the locale of the book must be in a region identified above. Books can be fiction or creative nonfiction. Self-published (vanity press) & ebooks are not eligible. The book must be published in the calendar year prior to the awards year. The author must not have published more than 3 books under his/her own pen name, with up to & including the third book being eligible for consideration. If an author has more than one book published during that year, all of them will be considered. No applications are necessary. Forward nominations to one of the designated Literary Chairs by sending 2 copies of each book along with a short biographical material regarding the author.
Award: Two cash prizes totaling $4,000
Closing Date: Dec
Presented: The Fortnightly, Chicago, IL, May

Friends of Literature Prize
Poetry Magazine
61 W Superior St, Chicago, IL 60654
Tel: 312-787-7070
Web Site: www.poetryfoundation.org/
poetrymagazine/prizes
Key Personnel
Assoc Ed: Holly Amos *E-mail:* hamos@
poetrymagazine.org
Established: 2002
For poetry published during the preceding year in *Poetry* magazine. No application necessary.
Award: $500
Presented: Announced in Nov issue

Frost Medal
Poetry Society of America (PSA)
119 Smith St, Brooklyn, NY 11201
Tel: 212-254-9628
E-mail: info@poetrysociety.org
Web Site: poetrysociety.org/awards
Key Personnel
Exec Dir: Matt Brogan *E-mail:* matt@
poetrysociety.org
Deputy Dir: Brett Fletcher Lauer *E-mail:* brett@
poetrysociety.org
Devt Dir: Madeline Weinfield *E-mail:* madeline@
poetrysociety.org
For distinguished lifetime achievement in American poetry. By nomination only.
Other Sponsor(s): Ironwood Foundation; Klass Family Foundation
Award: $5,000

FSG Writer's Fellowship
Farrar, Straus & Giroux, LLC
120 Broadway, New York, NY 10271
SAN: 206-782X
Tel: 212-741-6900
E-mail: fsg.publicity@fsgbooks.com
Web Site: fsgfellowship.com
Key Personnel
Pres & Publr: Mitzi Angel
SVP & Dir, Publicity & Mktg: Sheila O'Shea
Tel: 917-257-8412 *E-mail:* sheila.oshea@
fsgbooks.com
Assoc Dir, Publicity: Steve Weil *Tel:* 610-608-8413 *E-mail:* stephen.weil@fsgbooks.com
Year-long program (September-August) to give an emerging writer from an underrepresented community additional resources to build a life around writing: funding, editorial guidance & advice on how to forge a writing career. Three categories: Fiction, nonfiction & poetry. One submission in one category only. Applicants must be US permanent resident or US citizen & over the age of 18. See web site for application & eligibility requirements.
Award: $15,000 paid over 2 installments, year-long mentorship, public reading & a collection of FSG classics
Closing Date: April 15
Presented: Aug

Fulbright Scholar Program
Council for International Exchange of Scholars
Division of The Institute of International Education
1400 "K" St NW, Washington, DC 20005
Tel: 202-686-4000
E-mail: scholars@iie.org
Web Site: www.cies.org; www.iie.org
Key Personnel
Dir, Outreach: Peter Van Derwater
Dir, US Scholar Progs: Jordanna Enrich
Established: 1946
CIES cooperates with the US Department of State, Bureau of Educational & Cultural Affairs, in the administration of the Fulbright scholar program, which offers approximately 8,000 fellowships annually to US faculty & professionals for university teaching +/or advanced research in more than 160 countries.
Award: Grant benefits, which vary by country, generally include a stipend & round-trip travel for the grantee
Closing Date: Sept 15

Gabriele Rico Challenge for Nonfiction
Reed Magazine
San Jose State University, English Dept, One Washington Sq, San Jose, CA 95192-0090
Tel: 408-924-4441
E-mail: mail@reedmag.org
Web Site: www.reedmag.org; reedmagazine.submittable.com
All submissions must be through the online system. Keep submissions under 5,000 words. Reading fee: $15.
Award: $1,333 & publication in *Reed Magazine*
Closing Date: Nov 1 (submissions accepted beginning June 1)

Ernest J Gaines Award for Literary Excellence
Baton Rouge Area Foundation
100 North St, Suite 900, Baton Rouge, LA 70802
Tel: 225-387-6126
E-mail: gainesaward@braf.org
Web Site: www.ernestjgainesaward.org
Key Personnel
Dir, Communs: Mukul Verma *Tel:* 225-362-9260
E-mail: mverma@braf.org
Awarded in recognition of outstanding work from promising African-American fiction writers. Nominees must not yet be widely recognized for their work & must be an African-American US citizen. Works of fiction (novel or collection of short stories) published in the award year are eligible. Self-published books & e-mailed entries are not accepted.
Award: $15,000
Closing Date: Aug 15
Presented: Jan 30

Lewis Galantiere Translation Award
American Translators Association (ATA)
211 N Union St, Suite 100, Alexandria, VA 22314
Tel: 703-683-6100 *Fax:* 703-778-7222
E-mail: honors_awards@atanet.org
Web Site: www.atanet.org
Key Personnel
Chair, ATA Honors & Awards Comm: Karen Tkaczyk
Established: 1984
Awarded biennially, in even-numbered years, for a distinguished book-length literary translation from any language, except German into English, published in the US.
Award: $1,000, certificate of recognition & up to $500 toward expenses to attend the ATA Annual Conference
Closing Date: March 31 (even-numbered years)
Presented: ATA Annual Conference

John Kenneth Galbraith Award for Nonfiction,
see PEN/John Kenneth Galbraith Award for Nonfiction

Zona Gale Award for Short Fiction
Council for Wisconsin Writers (CWW)
c/o 4414 W Fillmore Dr, Milwaukee, WI 53219
E-mail: wiswriters@gmail.com
Web Site: wiswriters.org/awards
Key Personnel
Contest Chair: Daniel Kentowski
E-mail: dkento@milwaukee.gov
Established: 1966
Award for the best piece of short fiction published by a Wisconsin-based author in the contest year. Entry fee: $25 nonmembs.
Award: $500 & 1-week residency at Shake Rag Alley Center for the Arts
Closing Date: Jan 31
Presented: CWW Annual Award Ceremony & Banquet, May

Gannon University's High School Poetry Contest
Gannon University English Dept
Gannon University, 109 University Sq, Erie, PA 16541
Tel: 814-871-5583
Web Site: www.gannon.edu/poetrycontest
Key Personnel
Asst Professor, Eng: Dr Shreelina Ghosh
E-mail: ghosh002@gannon.edu
Established: 1985
High school students in grades 9-12 are invited to participate; must be original poetry.
Award: $100 (1st place), $75 (2nd place), $50 (3rd place), certificate (honorable mention)
Closing Date: Feb 1 (postmark)
Presented: Gannon University, Waldron Campus Center, Erie, PA, April

Francois-Xavier Garneau Medal
Canadian Historical Association
130 Albert St, Suite 1201, Ottawa, ON K1P 5G4, Canada
Tel: 613-233-7885 *Fax:* 613-565-5445
E-mail: cha-shc@cha-shc.ca
Web Site: cha-shc.ca
Key Personnel
Exec Dir: Michel Duquet *E-mail:* mduquet@cha-shc.ca
Established: 1980
Awarded every 5 years; commemorates the first Canadian Historian. Applicant should be a Canadian citizen or a legal immigrant. Given for the most outstanding scholarly book in the field of Canadian history within the previous 5 years.
Award: Minted medal & $2,000
Presented: 2025

John Gassner Memorial Playwriting Award
The New England Theatre Conference Inc
167 Cherry St, No 331, Milford, CT 06460
E-mail: gassner-award@netconline.org; mail@netconline.org
Web Site: www.netconline.org
Established: 1967
Playwriting contest for new full-length plays.
Closing Date: April 15
Presented: NETC Annual Convention, Nov

The Christian Gauss Award
The Phi Beta Kappa Society
1606 New Hampshire Ave NW, Washington, DC 20009
Tel: 202-265-3808 *Fax:* 202-986-1601
E-mail: awards@pbk.org
Web Site: www.pbk.org/bookawards
Key Personnel
Exec Asst to the Secy: Aurora Sherman *Tel:* 202-745-3287 *E-mail:* asherman@pbk.org
Established: 1954
For outstanding books in the field of literary scholarship or criticism published in the US. Nominations must come from publisher & be submitted online.
Award: $10,000
Closing Date: Jan
Presented: Washington, DC, Dec

Carol Gay Award
Children's Literature Association (ChLA)
140B Purcellville Gateway Dr, Suite 1200, Purcellville, VA 20132
Tel: 630-571-4520
E-mail: info@childlitassn.org

AWARDS, PRIZE CONTESTS, FELLOWSHIPS & GRANTS

Web Site: www.childlitassn.org
Key Personnel
Association Mgr: Cate Langley
Established: 1997
Presented to a college undergraduate for an outstanding paper which contributes to the field of children's literature. Award is considered annually & awarded as warranted. Paper should be original & at least 2,500 words, but not more than 4,000 words in length, including notes & works cited. See web site for complete guidelines. A student may only be the recipient of the Carol Gay Award once during their time as an undergraduate student. All nominated papers must be accompanied by a cover letter & submitted electronically on behalf of the student by a faculty member. Only 2 submissions per faculty member will be accepted.
Closing Date: Feb 1
Presented: ChLA Annual Conference, June

The Gaylactic Spectrum Awards
Gaylactic Spectrum Awards Foundation
1425 "S" St NW, Washington, DC 20009
E-mail: nominations@spectrumawards.org
Web Site: www.spectrumawards.org
Key Personnel
Exec Dir: Rob Gates
Established: 1998
Presented for outstanding works of science fiction, fantasy or horror which include positive explorations of gay, lesbian, bisexual or transgendered characters, themes, or issues. Awards are juried with an open nomination process & are presented in a variety of categories each year, for works released in the previous calendar year in North America in English.
Award: Statuette
Closing Date: May 31
Presented: Fall

Theodor Seuss Geisel Award
Association for Library Service to Children (ALSC)
Division of The American Library Association (ALA)
225 N Michigan Ave, Suite 1300, Chicago, IL 60601
Toll Free Tel: 800-545-2433
E-mail: alsc@ala.org
Web Site: www.ala.org/alsc/awardsgrants/bookmedia/geisel
Key Personnel
Exec Dir: Alena Rivers *Tel:* 800-545-2433 ext 5866 *E-mail:* arivers@ala.org
Awards Coord: Jordan Dubin *Tel:* 800-545-2433 ext 5839 *E-mail:* jdubin@ala.org
Established: 2004
Awarded to the author & illustrator of the most distinguished contribution to the body of American children's literature that encourages & supports the beginning reader published in English in the US during the preceding year. There are no limitations as to the character of the book considered except that it will be original & function successfully as a book for beginning readers. The award is restricted to author(s) & illustrator(s) who are citizens or residents of the US.
Award: Bronze medal
Closing Date: Dec 31

Lionel Gelber Prize
Lionel Gelber Foundation
University of Toronto, Munk School of Global Affairs & Public Policy, One Devonshire Place, Toronto, ON M5S 3K7, Canada
Tel: 416-946-5670 *Fax:* 416-946-8915
E-mail: gelberprize.munk@utoronto.ca
Web Site: munkschool.utoronto.ca/gelber; www.facebook.com/GelberPrize

Key Personnel
Prize Mgr: Stacie Bellemare *E-mail:* stacie.bellemare@utoronto.ca
Established: 1989
Given to the author of the year's most outstanding work of nonfiction in the field of international relations. Designed to encourage authors who write about international relations & to stimulate the audience for these books to grow. Open to authors of all nationalities. Six copies of each title must be submitted by the publisher. Books must be published between January 1 & December 31 in English or English translation.
Other Sponsor(s): Munk School of Global Affairs & Public Policy
Award: $15,000
Closing Date: Oct 31
Presented: Shortlist announced Jan; prize awarded in Spring

Leo Gershoy Award in Western European History
American Historical Association (AHA)
400 "A" St SE, Washington, DC 20003
Tel: 202-544-2422
E-mail: awards@historians.org
Web Site: www.historians.org/awards-and-grants/awards-and-prizes/leo-gershoy-award
Established: 1975
Awarded in recognition of outstanding work published in English on any aspect of the fields of 17th & 18th century western European history. Books with a 2024 copyright are eligible for the 2025 award. Along with an application form, applicants must mail a copy of their book (limited to 3 titles from any one publisher) to each prize committee member posted on our web site as the prize deadline approaches. All updated info on web site.
Award: $1,000
Closing Date: May 15, 2025
Presented: AHA Annual Meeting, Chicago, IL, Jan 2026

Charles M Getchell New Play Contest
Southeastern Theatre Conference (SETC)
5710 W Gate City Blvd, Suite K, Box 186, Greensboro, NC 27407
Tel: 336-265-6148
E-mail: info@setc.org
Web Site: www.setc.org
Submission begins March 1. Submitting playwright must be a current member of SETC, reside in the SETC region, or attend a college or university within the SETC region. See web site for regions, submission requirements & guidelines.
Award: $1,000, travel & expenses to annual convention; winning play is also considered for online publication & a feature in *Southern Theatre* magazine
Closing Date: June 1
Presented: Southeastern Theatre Conference Convention, March of the year following the closing date

Arrell Gibson Lifetime Achievement Award
Oklahoma Center for the Book (OCB)
200 NE 18 St, Oklahoma City, OK 73105-3205
Tel: 405-522-3383
Web Site: libraries.ok.gov/ocb/arrell-gibson/
Award that honors an Oklahoman who has contributed to the state's literary heritage.
Closing Date: Jan
Presented: April

Gilder Lehrman Lincoln Prize
The Gilder Lehrman Institute of American History
300 N Washington St, Campus Box 435, Gettysburg, PA 17325

ASSOCIATIONS, EVENTS

Tel: 717-337-8255
E-mail: lincolnprize@gettysburg.edu
Web Site: www.gilderlehrman.org
Established: 1990
Awarded for the finest scholarly work in English on Abraham Lincoln, the American Civil War soldier, or the American Civil War era. Publishers, critics & authors may submit books published in the current year. No entry fee or form. Send 6 copies of the nominated work.
Other Sponsor(s): Gettysburg College
Award: $50,000
Closing Date: Nov 1

Gilder Lehrman Prize for Military History
The Gilder Lehrman Institute of American History
49 W 45 St, 2nd fl, New York, NY 10036
Tel: 646-366-9666
E-mail: info@gilderlehrman.org
Web Site: www.gilderlehrman.org
Key Personnel
Book Prize Mgr: Daniela Muhling
Established: 2016
Award to recognize the best book on military history in the English-speaking world distinguished by its scholarship, its contribution to the literature & its appeal to both a general & an academic audience. Publishers may submit as many titles as they wish, but must send at least 5 copies to the Book Prize Manager.
Other Sponsor(s): New-York Historical Society
Award: $50,000
Closing Date: Dec 1

Giller Prize, see Scotiabank Giller Prize

Allen Ginsberg Poetry Award
The Poetry Center at Passaic County Community College
One College Blvd, Paterson, NJ 07505-1179
Tel: 973-684-6555 *Fax:* 973-523-6085
Web Site: www.poetrycenterpccc.com
Key Personnel
Exec Dir: Maria Mazziotti Gillan *E-mail:* mgillan@pccc.edu
Mgr: Susan Balik *E-mail:* sbalik@pccc.edu
Poem should not be more than 2 ms pages. Sheets which contain the poems should not contain the poet's name. Do not submit poems that imitate Allen Ginsberg's work. Entry fee: $18.
Award: $1,000 (1st prize), $600 (2nd prize), $400 (3rd prize)
Closing Date: Feb 1

Gival Press Oscar Wilde Award
Gival Press
PO Box 3812, Arlington, VA 22203
SAN: 852-9787
Tel: 703-351-0079 *Fax:* 703-351-0079 (call first)
E-mail: givalpress@yahoo.com
Web Site: www.givalpress.com; givalpress.submittable.com
Key Personnel
Publr & Ed: Robert L Giron
Established: 2002
For best LBGTQ poem.
Award: $500 & online publication
Closing Date: June 27
Presented: Sept 1

Gival Press Short Story Award
Gival Press
PO Box 3812, Arlington, VA 22203
SAN: 852-9787
Tel: 703-351-0079 *Fax:* 703-351-0079 (call first)
E-mail: givalpress@yahoo.com
Web Site: www.givalpress.com; givalpress.submittable.com

Key Personnel
Publr & Ed: Robert L Giron
Established: 2004
For best literary short story.
Award: $1,000 & online publication
Closing Date: Aug 8
Presented: Dec 1

John Glassco Translation Prize
Literary Translators' Association of Canada
Concordia University, LB 601, 1455 De Maisonneuve W, Montreal, QC H3G 1M8, Canada
Tel: 514-848-2424 (ext 8702)
E-mail: info@attlc-ltac.org
Web Site: www.attlc-ltac.org
Key Personnel
Pres: Bilal Hashmi
Established: 1982
For a first book-length literary translation from any language into French or English published in Canada during the previous year. Must be a Canadian citizen or permanent resident.
Award: $1,000 & one-year membership to LTAC
Closing Date: Typically in July
Presented: Sept 30

GLCA New Writers Awards
Great Lakes Colleges Association (GLCA)
535 W William St, Suite 301, Ann Arbor, MI 48103
Tel: 734-661-2350 *Fax:* 734-661-2349
Web Site: www.glca.org
Key Personnel
Dir, Prog Devt: Gregory R Wegner
Exec Asst: Colleen M Smith *E-mail:* smith@glca.org
Established: 1969
For a first published work of fiction or creative nonfiction or a first book of poetry. Submissions may be made only by publishers; one entry each, poetry, fiction or creative nonfiction. Submit 4 copies of the work & an author's statement agreeing to the terms. See web site for details.
Award: Reading engagements at up to 13 colleges & universities of the GLCA; each engagement includes $500 honorarium; all travel expenses are paid
Closing Date: July 25
Presented: Announcement in mid-Jan

The Danuta Gleed Literary Award
The Writers' Union of Canada (TWUC)
600-460 Richmond St W, Toronto, ON M5V 1Y1, Canada
Tel: 416-703-8982
E-mail: info@writersunion.ca
Web Site: www.writersunion.ca
Key Personnel
Exec Dir: John Degen *Tel:* 416-703-8982 ext 221
  E-mail: jdegen@writersunion.ca
Assoc Dir: Siobhan O'Connor *Tel:* 416-703-8982 ext 222 *E-mail:* soconnor@writersunion.ca
Established: 1997
Award for best first collection of short fiction by a Canadian published in the calendar year prior to the closing date & available through bookstores & libraries.
Award: $10,000 (1st prize), $500 (2nd & 3rd prizes)
Closing Date: Jan 31

Eugene & Marilyn Glick Indiana Authors Awards
Indiana Humanities
1500 N Delaware St, Indianapolis, IN 46202
Tel: 317-638-1500 *Toll Free Tel:* 800-675-8897
E-mail: info@indianaauthorsawards.org
Web Site: www.indianaauthorsawards.org
Key Personnel
Prog Mgr: Megan Telligman *Tel:* 317-616-9409
  E-mail: mtelligman@indianahumanities.org
Biennial awards, presented in even-numbered years, to recognize & celebrate the best books published by Indiana writers in the previous 2 years. Awards are given in 8 categories: Fiction, Nonfiction, Poetry, Children's, Young Adult, Drama, Genre & Emerging. Two additional awards, Literary Champion & Lifetime Achievement, will be given to authors for their legacy & contributions to Indiana's literary community. Submission fee: $30.
Other Sponsor(s): Glick Philanthropies
Award: $5,000, invitation to speak in statewide speakers program & opportunity to designate $500 award to Indiana library of their choice; Literary Champion awardee receives $2,500
Closing Date: Jan
Presented: Sept

Goddard Riverside CBC Youth Book Prize for Social Justice
Goddard Riverside Community Center
593 Columbus Ave, New York, NY 10024
Tel: 212-873-6600
E-mail: cbcprize@goddard.org
Web Site: goddard.org/bookprizes
Key Personnel
Dir, PR: Trish Anderton *Tel:* 929-249-1449 (cell)
  E-mail: tanderton@goddard.org
Established: 2017
Celebrates the power of the written word to create change in the name of justice for all. Eligible works are nonfiction books related to urban life & issues & supporting values such as community, equality, opportunity, mutual understanding, respect, caring & justice. Books must be written in English & have been published in the US between October 1 of the previous year & September 30 of the award year.
Application fee: $50 per submission (fee is waived for CBC members in good standing).
Other Sponsor(s): Children's Book Council
Closing Date: June
Presented: Goddard Riverside Book Fair Gala, Autumn

Goddard Riverside Stephan Russo Book Prize for Social Justice
Goddard Riverside Community Center
593 Columbus Ave, New York, NY 10024
E-mail: russoprize@goddard.org
Web Site: goddard.org/bookprizes
Key Personnel
Dir, PR: Trish Anderton *Tel:* 929-249-1449 (cell)
  E-mail: tanderton@goddard.org
Literary award to recognize books that focus on housing, early childhood & secondary education, older adult life, city arts, social policy & other important aspects of community life that support & promote Goddard Riverside's mission. Books must be written in English & published in the US between October 1 of the previous year & September 30 of the award year. Eight copies of each title should be submitted, along with prize entry form. Application fee: $75.
Closing Date: May 22
Presented: Goddard Riverside Book Fair Gala, Fall

Gold Medal
American Academy of Arts & Letters
633 W 155 St, New York, NY 10032
Tel: 212-368-5900
E-mail: academy@artsandletters.org
Web Site: artsandletters.org/awards
Key Personnel
Exec Dir: Cody Upton
Awarded for distinguished achievement in several different categories of the arts. Rotating categories: Belles lettres & criticism & painting; biography & music; fiction & sculpture; history & architecture (including landscape architecture); poetry & music; drama & graphic art. Candidates must be nominated by an Academy member.
Award: 2 medals

Golden Cylinder Awards
Gravure AIMCAL Alliance (GAA)
150 Executive Center Dr, Suite 201, Greenville, SC 29615
Tel: 803-948-9470 *Fax:* 803-948-9471
E-mail: aimcal@aimcal.org
Web Site: gaa.org/awards/golden-cylinder-awards
Key Personnel
Dir, Opers: Tony Donato *E-mail:* tdonato@gaa.org
Established: 2013
Given in recognition of the most creative & highest quality gravure print projects produced by various gravure operators throughout the Americas. The awards are given across multiple categories: Packaging & label, product, publication & technical innovation. Entry fees: Membs $155 each (1-4 entries), $135 each (5 or more entries); Nonmembs $305 each (1-4 entries), $265 each (5 or more entries).
Award: Golden Cylinders on pedestals
Closing Date: May
Presented: Gravure Technical Forum, Fall

Golden Kite Awards
Society of Children's Book Writers & Illustrators (SCBWI)
6363 Wilshire Blvd, Suite 425, Los Angeles, CA 90048
Tel: 323-782-1010
E-mail: info@scbwi.org
Web Site: www.scbwi.org/awards/golden-kite-award
Key Personnel
Exec Dir: Sarah Baker
Assoc Dir, Digital Content & Awards: Sarah Diamond
Assoc Mgr, Awards & Pubns: Danielle Monique
Award Coord: Bonnie Bader
  E-mail: bonniebader@scbwi.org
Established: 1973
Awarded in recognition of excellence in children's literature in 7 categories: Young reader/middle grade fiction, young adult fiction, nonfiction text for younger readers, nonfiction text for older readers, picture book text, picture book illustration & illustration for older readers. One Golden Kite winner & one Honor Book chosen per category. Authors/illustrators must be a current member through December of the previous year. Only books written or translated into English are accepted. Books must be published by PAL publishers.
Award: $2,500 plus $1,000 to donate to nonprofit organization of choice; Honor winners receive $500 plus $250 to donate
Closing Date: July 15 (books published Jan-June), Dec 15 (books published July-Dec)
Presented: Feb

The Golden Poppy Book Awards (The Poppies), see CALIBA Golden Poppy Awards

Golden Quill Award
International Society of Weekly Newspaper Editors (ISWNE)
Missouri Southern State University, 3950 E Newman Rd, Joplin, MO 64801-1595
Web Site: www.iswne.org/contests
Key Personnel
Exec Dir: Dr Chad Stebbins *Tel:* 417-625-9736
  E-mail: stebbins-c@mssu.edu
Established: 1961
All newspapers of less than daily frequency (published less than 5 days per week) are qualified to enter. Entries must have been published in the preceding calendar year. Entry fee: $10

membs, $15 nonmembs, $5 students. Two entries allowed per person.
Closing Date: Feb 1

Golden Rose Award
New England Poetry Club
c/o Linda Haviland Conte, 18 Hall Ave, Apt 2, Somerville, MA 02144
E-mail: info@nepoetryclub.org
Web Site: nepoetryclub.org
Key Personnel
Co-Pres: Doug Holder; Denise Provost
VP: Hilary Sallick
Treas: Linda Haviland Conte
 E-mail: nepctreasurer@gmail.com
Established: 1919
The oldest literary award given to a poet who has done the most for poetry in the previous year or during a lifetime. Chosen by NEPC officers.
Award: Rose sculpture
Closing Date: May 31
Presented: Announced online Aug/Sept

Laurence Goldstein Poetry Prize
Michigan Quarterly Review
University of Michigan, 3277 Angell Hall, 435 S State St, Ann Arbor, MI 48109-1003
Tel: 734-764-9265
E-mail: mqr@umich.edu
Web Site: sites.lsa.umich.edu/mqr/about-us/prizes
Established: 2002
Awarded to the author of one poem of exemplary quality. Winner is selected by an outside judge. Submissions open November 1. Entry fee: $20. See web site for submission guidelines.
Award: $1,000
Closing Date: Dec 31

Goodreads Choice Awards
Goodreads Inc
188 Spear St, 3rd fl, San Francisco, CA 94105
E-mail: press@goodreads.com
Web Site: www.goodreads.com/award
Key Personnel
CEO: Veronica Moss
VP, Communs: Suzanne Skyvara
15 nominees in each category. Books must be published in the US in English, including works in translation & other significant rereleases. Three rounds of voting open to all registered Goodreads members.

Amanda Gorman Award for Poetry
Penguin Random House LLC
1745 Broadway, New York, NY 10019
SAN: 202-5507
Tel: 212-782-9348 *Fax:* 212-782-5157
E-mail: creativewriting@penguinrandomhouse.com
Web Site: social-impact.penguinrandomhouse.com/creativewriting
Established: 2021
Award for poetry by public high school students. Entry must be an original literary composition in English. Open to all current high school students attending public schools in the US, including the District of Columbia & all US territories, planning to attend college, either a 2- or 4-year institution.
Other Sponsor(s): We Need Diverse Books (WNDB)
Award: $10,000
Closing Date: Feb 1
Presented: Winners announced in June

Gotham Book Prize
251 Park Ave S, New York, NY 10010
Web Site: www.gothambookprize.org
Key Personnel
Founder: Bradley Tusk; Howard Wolfson
Established: 2020
Award for the best book (works of fiction & nonfiction are eligible) published that calendar year that either is about New York City or takes place in New York City. Nominations open in the fall.
Award: $50,000
Closing Date: Nov 1
Presented: Spring

Karen Gould Prize in Art History
Medieval Academy of America (MAA)
6 Beacon St, Suite 500, Boston, MA 02108
Tel: 617-491-1622 *Fax:* 617-492-3303
E-mail: info@themedievalacademy.org
Web Site: www.medievalacademy.org/page/gouldprize
Key Personnel
Exec Dir: Lisa Fagin Davis *E-mail:* lfd@themedievalacademy.org
Established: 2018
Award for a book or monograph (conference proceedings & collected essays are not eligible) in medieval art history judged by the selection committee to be of outstanding quality. To be eligible, the author must be a member in good standing of the Medieval Academy of America. See web site for submission guidelines.
Award: $1,000 & certificate

Governor General's Literary Awards
Canada Council for the Arts (Conseil des arts du Canada)
150 Elgin St, 2nd fl, Ottawa, ON K2P 1L4, Canada
Mailing Address: PO Box 1047, Ottawa, ON K1P 5A0, Canada
Tel: 613-566-4414 *Toll Free Tel:* 800-263-5588 (CN only) *Fax:* 613-566-4390
E-mail: ggbooks@canadacouncil.ca
Web Site: ggbooks.ca
Key Personnel
Prog Offr, Prizes: Lori Knoll *Tel:* 613-566-4414 ext 5573
Established: 1936
Awards for the best English language & French language book in each of 7 categories: fiction, poetry, drama, nonfiction, children's literature-text, children's literature-illustration & translation (from French to English & English to French).
Award: $25,000 each; non-winning finalists receive $1,000; publisher of each winning book receives $3,000 to promote the book
Closing Date: July 31

The Gracies®
Alliance for Women in Media (AWM)
2365 Harrodsburg Rd, Suite A325, Lexington, KY 40504
Tel: 202-750-3664 *Fax:* 202-750-3664
E-mail: info@allwomeninmedia.org
Web Site: allwomeninmedia.org
Key Personnel
Pres: Becky Brooks *E-mail:* becky.brooks@allwomeninmedia.org
Events Dir: Lisa Stephenson *E-mail:* lisa.stephenson@allwomeninmedia.org
Awards & Proj Mgr: LaTonya Jackson
 E-mail: latonya.jackson@allwomeninmedia.org
Awarded for programming in all mediums which contributes to positive & realistic portrayals of women, addresses interests of concern to women, enhances women's image, position & welfare.
Award: Statue
Presented: May

Graduate & Undergraduate Hopwood Contest
University of Michigan, College of Literature, Science & Arts
1176 Angell Hall, 435 S State St, Ann Arbor, MI 48109-1003
Tel: 734-764-6296 *Fax:* 734-764-3128
E-mail: abeauch@umich.edu
Web Site: lsa.umich.edu/hopwood
Graduate or undergraduate awards in nonfiction, short fiction & poetry divisions. Novel, drama & screenplay divisions are combined categories in which graduates & undergraduates compete together. A qualifying writing course is mandatory. See web site for submission guidelines & list of courses.
Closing Date: Feb 7, by 12 noon

The Judy Grahn Award for Lesbian Nonfiction
The Publishing Triangle
511 Avenue of the Americas, No D36, New York, NY 10011
E-mail: awards@publishingtriangle.org; info@publishingtriangle.org; publishingtriangle@gmail.com
Web Site: publishingtriangle.org/awards/judy-grahn-lesbian-nonfiction
Established: 1997
Recognizes works that are by or about lesbians, bisexual women +/or trans women, or that have a significant influence upon the lives of queer women. A call for submissions is posted on the web site in early Autumn. Finalists & winners are determined by a panel of judges appointed by the awards committee.
Award: $1,000

Grand Master Award
Crime Writers of Canada (CWC)
716 Thicket Way, Ottawa, ON K4A 3B5, Canada
E-mail: info@crimewriterscanada.com
Web Site: www.crimewriterscanada.com/awards
Key Personnel
Exec Dir: Alison Bruce *E-mail:* ed@crimewriterscanada.com
Asst Exec Dir & Awards Mgr: Ludvica Boota
 E-mail: aed@crimewriterscanada.com
Established: 2014
Biennial award (alternating with the Derrick Murdoch Award) to recognize a Canadian crime writer with a substantial body of work who has garnered national & international recognition. Awarded in even-numbered years.

Grant Program for Diverse Voices
The MIT Press
One Broadway, 12th fl, Cambridge, MA 02142
SAN: 202-6414
Web Site: mitpress.mit.edu/grant-program-diverse-voices
Key Personnel
Community & Resource Devt Assoc: Kate Silverman Wilson *E-mail:* kswilson@mit.edu
Grants will be awarded to authors who are underrepresented in their field worldwide. Both current & prospective authors with strong proposals for a book-length work who have significant personal experience or engagement with communities that are underrepresented in scholarly publishing are encouraged to apply. Grants may support a variety of needs, including research travel, copyright permission fees, parental/family care, developmental editing & any other costs associated with the research & writing process. Authors must first submit a query directly to the MIT Press acquisitions editor in the field in which the author publishes. See mitpress.mit.edu/acquisitions-staff. Grant applications are accepted on a rolling basis & will be evaluated twice a year, in the spring & the fall.
Other Sponsor(s): MIT Press Fund for Diverse Voices
Award: Typically $1,000-$5,000 (2-4 grants per calendar yr)

The Hillary Gravendyk Prize
Inlandia Institute
4178 Chestnut St, Riverside, CA 92501

SAN: 992-6380
E-mail: inlandia@inlandiainstitute.org
Web Site: inlandiainstitute.org/books/the-hillary-gravendyk-prize
Key Personnel
Exec Dir: Cati Porter
Progs & Mktg Coord: Janine Pourroy Gamblin
Open poetry book competition for all writers. Ms page limit 48-100, all styles & forms of poetry. Electronic submissions only via Submittable. Reading fee: $20.
Award: Two prizes of $1,000 & book publication
Closing Date: April 30
Presented: Late Summer/Fall for publication in the next year

Carla Gray Memorial Scholarship
Book Industry Charitable Foundation (BINC)
3135 S State St, Suite 203, Ann Arbor, MI 48108
Toll Free Tel: 866-733-9064
E-mail: info@bincfoundation.org
Web Site: www.bincfoundation.org/carla-gray/
Key Personnel
Exec Dir: Pamela French *E-mail:* pam@bincfoundation.org
Dir, Devt: Kathy Bartson *E-mail:* kathy@bincfoundation.org
Prog Mgr: Judey Kalchik *E-mail:* judey@bincfoundation.org; Ken White *E-mail:* ken@bincfoundation.org
Commun Coord: Erika Mantz *E-mail:* erika@bincfoundation.org
Devt Coord: Jennifer Rojas *E-mail:* jennifer@bincfoundation.org
Off Coord: Jane Regenstreif *E-mail:* jane@bincfoundation.org
Spec Projs Coord: Kate Weiss *E-mail:* kate@bincfoundation.org
Presented to a single bookseller with fewer than 5 years of experience, working at a store with less than $500K in revenue. The bookseller will be given a scholarship for professional development, including attendance at a key industry trade show. The bookseller will have the opportunity to connect with booksellers, publishers & authors. The bookseller will also be given a stipend to support a community outreach project of his/her own creation.

James H Gray Award for Short Nonfiction
Writers' Guild of Alberta
11759 Groat Rd NW, Edmonton, AB T5M 3K6, Canada
Tel: 780-422-8174 *Toll Free Tel:* 800-665-5354 (AB only)
E-mail: mail@writersguild.ab.ca
Web Site: writersguild.ca
Key Personnel
Exec Dir: Giorgia Severini *E-mail:* gseverini@writersguild.ab.ca
Commmuns & Partnerships Coord: Ellen Kartz *E-mail:* ellen.kartz@writersguild.ab.ca
Memb Servs Coord: Mike Maguire
Prog & Opers Coord: Ashley Mann *E-mail:* ashley.mann@writersguild.ab.ca
Progs & Events Coord: Jason Norman *E-mail:* jason.norman@writersguild.ab.ca
Proj Asst: Sadie MacGillivray *E-mail:* sadie.macgillivray@writersguild.ab.ca
Established: 2009
Open to published pieces on any topic by an Alberta author; no longer than 5,000 words.
Award: $700
Closing Date: Dec 31
Presented: Alberta Book Awards Gala, AB, CN
Branch Office(s)
223 12 Ave SW, No 204, Calgary, AB T2R 0G9, Canada, Prog & Conference Coord: Dorothy Bentley *Tel:* 403-875-8058 *E-mail:* dorothy.bentley@writersguild.ab.ca

Graywolf Press African Fiction Prize
Graywolf Press
212 Third Ave N, Suite 485, Minneapolis, MN 55401
Tel: 651-641-0077 *Fax:* 651-641-0036
E-mail: submissions@graywolfpress.org
Web Site: www.graywolfpress.org/about-us/submissions
Key Personnel
Sales & Opers Mgr: Mattan Comay
Awarded for a first novel ms by an African author primarily residing in Africa. All submissions must be full-length, previously unpublished novel mss. Submissions must be in English, but translations are acceptable. Applicants with prior books are eligible, so long as none of those books is a novel. Only electronic submissions will be considered through Submittable. Please follow these formatting guidelines: a PDF or Word file (.doc & .docx), 12-point font, double-spaced text, numbered pages.
Award: $12,000 advance & publication
Closing Date: Oct 31

Graywolf Press Nonfiction Prize
Graywolf Press
212 Third Ave N, Suite 485, Minneapolis, MN 55401
Tel: 651-641-0077 *Fax:* 651-641-0036
E-mail: submissions@graywolfpress.org
Web Site: www.graywolfpress.org/about-us/submissions
Key Personnel
Sales & Opers Mgr: Mattan Comay
Awarded to the most promising & innovative literary nonfiction project by a writer not yet established in the genre. Awarded biennially, in even-numbered years, to a ms in progress. One submission per person will be considered. Agented submissions are also welcome. Only electronic submissions are considered (upload ms file to Submittable). See web site for submission & contest guidelines.
Award: $12,000 advance & publication by Graywolf

Green Earth Book Award
The Nature Generation
3100 Clarendon Blvd, Suite 400, Arlington, VA 22201
E-mail: info@natgen.org
Web Site: www.natgen.org/green-earth-book-awards
Key Personnel
Dir, Progs: Jenny Newton Schmidt
Established: 2005
Environmental stewardship award for children & young adult books. There are 5 categories: Picture Book (books for young readers in which the visual & verbal narratives tell the story); Children's Fiction (novels for young readers up to age 12); Young Adult Fiction (books for readers age 13-21); Children's Nonfiction (nonfiction books for readers from infancy to age 12); Young Adult Nonfiction (nonfiction books for readers age 12-21).
Award: $1,500 to winning authors & illustrators

The Fletcher M Green & Charles W Ramsdell Award
Southern Historical Association (SHA)
University of Georgia, Dept of History, Athens, GA 30602-1602
Tel: 706-542-8848
Web Site: thesha.org/ramsdell
Key Personnel
Secy/Treas: Dr Stephen Berry *E-mail:* berrys@thesha.org
Awarded biennially, in even-numbered years, for the best article published in the *Journal of Southern History* during the preceding 2 years.
Presented: Annual Meeting

Bess Gresham Memorial
The Poetry Society of Virginia (PSV)
PO Box 36128, North Chesterfield, VA 23235-3533
E-mail: contest@poetrysocietyofvirginia.org; info@poetryvirginia.org
Web Site: www.poetrysocietyofvirginia.org
Key Personnel
Pres: Cherryl T Cooley
E-mail: poetrysocietypresident@gmail.com
All entries must be in English, original & unpublished. Subject: Friends & friendship, 48 line limit. Submit 1 copy of each poem with no identifying information but put the category in the upper right-hand-side, along with a notation as to whether you are a member of PSV (does not matter if you are a lifetime member or just joined for the contest). Submit a cover letter/page that contains the category, the name of the poem, your name & address, phone number & e-mail address. Entries will not be returned. Entry fee: Free to membs, $5 nonmembs.
Award: $50 (1st prize), $30 (2nd prize), $20 (3rd prize)
Closing Date: Feb
Presented: PSV Awards Ceremony, April

Griffin Poetry Prize
The Griffin Trust for Excellence in Poetry
363 Parkridge Crescent, Oakville, ON L6M 1A8, Canada
Tel: 905-618-0420
E-mail: info@griffinpoetryprize.com; publicity@griffinpoetryprize.com
Web Site: griffinpoetryprize.com
Key Personnel
Founder & Chmn: Scott Griffin
E-mail: scottgriffin@griffinpoetryprize.com
Exec Dir: Ruth Smith
Communs Dir: Melissa Shirley *Tel:* 647-389-9510
Established: 2000
Awarded for the best collection of poetry in English published during the preceding year. Two categories: International & Canadian. Entries must come from publishers only. See web site for full eligibility requirements.
Award: 2 winners receive $65,000 each; finalists are awarded $10,000 each for their participation in the Shortlist Readings
Closing Date: June 30 & Dec 31
Presented: Shortlist announced in April; Awards given in June

Grouse Grind Lit Prize for V Short Form
PRISM international
University of British Columbia, Buch E462, 1866 Main Mall, Vancouver, BC V6T 1Z1, Canada
Tel: 604-822-2514 *Fax:* 604-822-3616
E-mail: promotions@prismmagazine.ca
Web Site: www.prismmagazine.ca/contests
Key Personnel
Mng Ed: Emma Cleary
Poetry Ed: Emily Chou
Promos Ed: Alison Barnett
Prose Ed: Vivian Li
Contest for flash fiction & nonfiction, hybrid forms & experimental work. One piece per entry. Maximum 300 words (including title). Entry fee: $15; additional entries $5.
Award: $500 (grand prize), $150 (1st runner up), $50 (2nd runner up)

Guggenheim Fellowships
John Simon Guggenheim Memorial Foundation
90 Park Ave, New York, NY 10016
Tel: 212-687-4470 *Fax:* 212-697-3248
Web Site: www.gf.org/about/fellowship
Established: 1925
Grants to selected individuals for 6-12 months. Application required. Approximately 175 Fellowships awarded each year. Applicants must

make an account on the web site in order to apply. This application process is composed of 8 sections. Please see web site for further instructions. When notified to submit, poets, playwrights, screenwriters, scholars & writers of fiction & general nonfiction should submit examples of published books; do not submit journal articles, edited volumes, book chapters or essays. Submit no more than 3 different titles. Published writing not regarded as appropriate includes self-published works, publications for which the author has paid & publications by publishers who do not engage in a process of critical review of submitted work. In addition, genre work (e.g., mysteries, romance, fantasy, etc) is considered not competitive. We do not consider children's or young adult books.
Closing Date: Sept (applications), Nov (work example submissions)
Presented: Announced early April

The Thom Gunn Award for Gay Poetry
The Publishing Triangle
511 Avenue of the Americas, No D36, New York, NY 10011
E-mail: awards@publishingtriangle.org; info@publishingtriangle.org; publishingtriangle@gmail.com
Web Site: publishingtriangle.org/awards/thom-gunn-gay-poetry
Established: 2001
Award is for books published in the preceding year in the US or Canada. A call for submissions is posted on the web site in early Autumn. Finalists & winners are determined by a panel of judges appointed by the awards committee.
Award: $1,000

Gutekunst Prize
Goethe-Institute New York
30 Irving Place, New York, NY 10003
Tel: 212-439-8700 Fax: 212-439-8705
E-mail: gutekunst@goethe.de
Web Site: www.goethe.de/ins/us/enkul/ser/uef/gut.html
Key Personnel
Libn: Walter Schlect Tel: 212-439-8697
E-mail: walter.schlect@goethe.de
Open to college students & to all translators under the age of 35 who, at the time the prize is awarded, have not yet published, nor are under contract for, a book-length translation. Applications will be accepted only from permanent residents of the US. Team translations will not be accepted. Each applicant is required to translate a literary text of approximately 22 pages, available on request from the Goethe-Institute New York. To receive the text & the application form, please send an e-mail to gutekunst@goethe.de. The translation & application form must be mailed electronically to the Goethe-Institute New York by the deadline. Full information on the submission procedure is included on the application form.
Award: $2,500
Closing Date: Mid-March
Presented: June

Hackmatack Children's Choice Book Award
PO Box 34055, Halifax, NS B3J 3S1, Canada
Tel: 902-424-3774
E-mail: hackmatack@hackmatack.ca
Web Site: hackmatack.ca
Key Personnel
Prog Coord: Stacey Cornelius
Established: 1999
Atlantic Canadian Children's Choice Award for grades 4-6. Four categories: English fiction, English nonfiction, French fiction & French nonfiction.
Other Sponsor(s): Atlantic Provinces Library Association (APLA); Canada Council for the Arts (Conseil des arts du Canada); New Brunswick Public Library Service; Nova Scotia Department of Education; Nova Scotia Public Libraries
Award: Plaques
Closing Date: Oct 15
Presented: Award Ceremony, Spring

Hackney Literary Awards
4650 Old Looney Mill Rd, Birmingham, AL 35243
Web Site: www.hackneyliteraryawards.org
Established: 1969
Short story, poetry & novel awards. Check web site or send SASE for contest guidelines. Entry fee: novels $30, short stories $20, poetry $15. Presented in the *Birmingham Arts Journal*.
Award: $600 (1st place), $400 (2nd place), $250 (3rd place), plus a $5,000 prize sponsored by Morris Hackney for an unpublished novel
Closing Date: Sept 30 for novel entries, Nov 30 for short story & poetry entries
Presented: March 30

Hadada Award
The Paris Review Foundation
544 W 27 St, New York, NY 10001
Tel: 212-343-1333
E-mail: queries@theparisreview.org
Web Site: www.theparisreview.org/about/prizes
Key Personnel
Mng Ed: Hasan Altaf
Presented to a distinguished member of the writing community who has made a strong & unique contribution to literature.
Presented: Spring Revel, April

Raymond Levi Haislip Memorial
The Poetry Society of Virginia (PSV)
PO Box 36128, North Chesterfield, VA 23235-3533
E-mail: contest@poetrysocietyofvirginia.org; info@poetryvirginia.org
Web Site: www.poetrysocietyofvirginia.org
Key Personnel
Pres: Cherryl T Cooley
E-mail: poetrysocietypresident@gmail.com
Any form. Subject: Celebrating technology. 48 line limit. Submit 1 copy of the poem with no identifying information but put the category in the upper right-hand-side, along with a notation as to whether you are a member of PSV (does not matter if you are a lifetime member or just joined for the contest). Submit a cover letter/page that contains the category, the name of the poem, your name & address, phone number & e-mail address. Entries will not be returned. Entry fee: Free to membs, $5 nonmembs.
Other Sponsor(s): Otis L Haislip Jr
Award: $50 (1st prize), $30 (2nd prize), $20 (3rd prize)

Sarah Josepha Hale Award
Trustees of the Richards Library
58 N Main St, Newport, NH 03773
Tel: 603-863-3430
E-mail: rfl@newport.lib.nh.us
Web Site: www.newport.lib.nh.us
Key Personnel
Lib Dir & Award Admin: Andrea Thorpe
E-mail: athorpe@newport.lib.nh.us
Established: 1956
In recognition of a distinguished body of work in the field of literature & letters. Applications are not accepted. A national Board of Judges submit nominations. Nominees must have been born in New England or reside there at least part of the year as a regular practice. If these conditions are not met, nominee must be associated primarily with New England through his/her work.
Other Sponsor(s): Holden-Yeomans Memorial Fund
Award: Bronze medal & $2,500
Presented: Newport, NH

1/2 K Prize
Indiana Review
Indiana University English Dept, Ballantine Hall 554, 1020 E Kirkwood Ave, Bloomington, IN 47405
Tel: 812-855-3439
E-mail: inreview@indiana.edu
Web Site: indianareview.org
Key Personnel
Ed-in-Chief: Shreya Fadia
Assoc Ed: Bernardo Wade
Send up to 3 pieces of no more than 500 words each in any genre. Entry fee: $20 (includes 1-year subscription to *Indiana Review*). See web site for full submission guidelines.
Award: $1,000 & publication
Closing Date: Aug 15

Loretta Dunn Hall Memorial
The Poetry Society of Virginia (PSV)
PO Box 36128, North Chesterfield, VA 23235-3533
E-mail: contest@poetrysocietyofvirginia.org; info@poetryvirginia.org
Web Site: www.poetrysocietyofvirginia.org
Key Personnel
Pres: Cherryl T Cooley
E-mail: poetrysocietypresident@gmail.com
All entries must be in English, original & unpublished. VA residents only. Subject: Family, any form, 24 line limit. Submit 1 copy of the poem with no identifying information but put the category in the upper right-hand-side, along with a notation as to whether you are a member of PSV (does not matter if you are a lifetime member or just joined for the contest). Submit a cover letter/page that contains the category, the name of the poem, your name & address, phone number & e-mail address. Entries will not be returned. Entry fee: Free to membs, $5 nonmembs.
Other Sponsor(s): Phyllis Hall Haislip
Award: $50 (1st prize), $30 (2nd prize), $20 (3rd prize)
Closing Date: Feb
Presented: PSV Awards Ceremony, April

Virginia Hamilton Award for Lifetime Achievement, see Coretta Scott King - Virginia Hamilton Award for Lifetime Achievement

Hammett Prize
International Association of Crime Writers Inc, North American Branch
PO Box 863, Norman, OK 73071
E-mail: crimewritersna@gmail.com
Web Site: www.crimewritersna.org/hammett
Key Personnel
Exec Dir: J Madison Davis
Awarded for literary excellence in the field of crime writing, as reflected in a book published in the English language in the US +/or Canada. Submissions may be made by publishers, agents, or authors by sending 1 copy of the nominated book to each member of the Nominations Committee.
Closing Date: Dec 15

Handy Andy Prize
The Poetry Society of Virginia (PSV)
PO Box 36128, North Chesterfield, VA 23235-3533
E-mail: contest@poetrysocietyofvirginia.org; info@poetryvirginia.org
Web Site: www.poetrysocietyofvirginia.org

Key Personnel
Pres: Cherryl T Cooley
 E-mail: poetrysocietypresident@gmail.com
Awarded for a limerick. Must be in English, original & unpublished. Submit 1 copy of the poem with no identifying information but put the category in the upper right-hand-side, along with a notation as to whether you are a member of PSV (does not matter if you are a lifetime member or just joined for the contest). Submit a cover letter/page that contains the category, the name of the poem, your name & address, phone number & e-mail address. Entries will not be returned. Entry fee: Free to membs, $5 nonmembs.
Award: $25 (1st prize), $15 (2nd prize), $10 (3rd prize)
Closing Date: Feb
Presented: PSV Awards Ceremony, April

The Joseph Hansen Award for LGBTQ Crime Writing
The Publishing Triangle
511 Avenue of the Americas, No D36, New York, NY 10011
E-mail: awards@publishingtriangle.org; info@publishingtriangle.org; publishingtriangle@gmail.com
Web Site: publishingtriangle.org/awards/joseph-hansen-award-lgbtq-crime-writing
Recognizes an outstanding work of crime fiction or nonfiction published in the preceding year. Honors American novelist Joseph Hansen (1923-2004). A call for submissions is posted on the web site in early Autumn. Finalists & winners are determined by a panel of judges appointed by the awards committee.
Award: $1,000

Clarence H Haring Prize in Latin American History
American Historical Association (AHA)
400 "A" St SE, Washington, DC 20003
Tel: 202-544-2422
E-mail: awards@historians.org
Web Site: www.historians.org/award-grant/clarence-h-haring-prize/
Awarded every 5 years to a Latin American author who has published the most outstanding book on Latin American history during the 5 years preceding the year of the award. There is no language limitation on works submitted. Along with an application form, applicants must mail a copy of their book to each prize committee member posted on our web site as the prize deadline approaches. Books with a copyright of 2021 through 2025 will be eligible for the 2026 prize. All updated info on web site.
Award: $1,000
Closing Date: May 15, 2026
Presented: AHA Annual Meeting, New Orleans, LA, Jan 2027

Joy Harjo Poetry Award
CUTTHROAT, A Journal of the Arts
PO Box 2414, Durango, CO 81302
Tel: 970-903-7914
E-mail: cutthroatmag@gmail.com
Web Site: www.cutthroatmag.com
Key Personnel
Ed-in-Chief: Pamela Uschuk
Mng Ed: Andrew Allport
Established: 2005
Submit online up to 3 unpublished poems (100 line limit each), any subject, any style. No poems previously published or that have won contests are eligible. Reading fee: $23.
Award: $1,200 & publication (1st prize), $250 & publication (2nd prize), publication only (honorable mention)
Closing Date: Nov
Presented: Dec

LD & LaVerne Harrell Clark Fiction Prize
Texas State University Department of English
Flowers Hall, Rm 365, 601 University Dr, San Marcos, TX 78666
Tel: 512-245-2163 *Fax:* 512-245-8546
Web Site: www.english.txstate.edu/clarkfictionprize.html
Key Personnel
Chair, English Dept: Victoria L Smith, PhD
 E-mail: vs13@txstate.edu
Established: 2019
Awarded to recognize an exceptional recently published book-length work of fiction. Prize committee solicits nominations. No applications or unsol nominations accepted.
Award: $25,000

Aurand Harris Memorial Playwriting Award
The New England Theatre Conference Inc
167 Cherry St, No 331, Milford, CT 06460
E-mail: harris-award@netconline.org; mail@netconline.org
Web Site: www.netconline.org
Established: 1997
Competition for new plays for young audiences. Scripts must be unpublished & unproduced. For guidelines, go to web site.
Closing Date: May 1
Presented: NETC Annual Convention, Nov

Julie Harris Playwright Award Competition, see BHTG - Julie Harris Playwright Award Competition

Haskins Medal Award
Medieval Academy of America (MAA)
6 Beacon St, Suite 500, Boston, MA 02108
Tel: 617-491-1622 *Fax:* 617-492-3303
E-mail: info@themedievalacademy.org
Web Site: www.medievalacademy.org/page/haskins_medal
Key Personnel
Exec Dir: Lisa Fagin Davis *E-mail:* lfd@themedievalacademy.org
Established: 1940
For a book of outstanding importance in the medieval field.
Award: Gold medal
Closing Date: Oct 15
Presented: Spring

Ellis W Hawley Prize
The Organization of American Historians (OAH)
112 N Bryan Ave, Bloomington, IN 47408-4141
Tel: 812-855-7311
E-mail: oah@oah.org
Web Site: www.oah.org/awards
Key Personnel
Exec Dir: Beth English *Tel:* 812-855-9836
 E-mail: benglish@oah.org
Dir, Communs & Mktg: Kym Robinson *Tel:* 812-855-5430 *E-mail:* kymarobi@oah.org
Awarded to the author of the best book-length historical study of the political economy, politics, or institutions of the US in its domestic or international affairs, from the Civil War to the present. Eligible works shall include book-length historical studies, written in English, published during the calendar year preceding that in which the award is given. One copy of each entry must be mailed directly to the committee members listed on the web site.
Closing Date: Oct 1 (postmarked)
Presented: OAH Conference on American History, Spring

Friedrich Hayek Lecture & Book Prize
Manhattan Institute for Policy Research
52 Vanderbilt Ave, New York, NY 10017
Tel: 212-599-7000
Web Site: www.manhattan-institute.org
Key Personnel
Contact: Dean Ball *E-mail:* dball@manhattan-institute.org
Honors the book published within the past 2 years that best reflects political philosopher & Nobel laureate F A Hayek's vision of economic & individual liberty. The winner of the prize will deliver the annual Hayek Lecture in New York in early June.
Award: $50,000
Presented: Late Feb

Headlands Center for the Arts Residency for Writers
Headlands Center for the Arts
944 Fort Barry, Sausalito, CA 94965
Tel: 415-331-2787 *Fax:* 415-331-3857
Web Site: www.headlands.org
Key Personnel
Residency Mgr: Holly Blake *Tel:* 415-331-2787 ext 24 *E-mail:* hblake@headlands.org
Established: 1982
Residency granted to writers of the Artist in Residency Program. See web site for application, deadline & other information.
Award: 6-week stay, with stipend of $1,000/mo
Closing Date: June 3

Heartland Booksellers Award
Great Lakes Independent Booksellers Association (GLIBA)
3123 Andrea Ct, Woodridge, IL 60517
Tel: 630-841-8129
Web Site: www.gliba.org/heartland-booksellers-award.html
Key Personnel
Exec Dir: Larry Law *E-mail:* larry@gliba.org
Exec Coord: February Spikener
 E-mail: february@gliba.org
Joint awards program with the Midwest Independent Booksellers Association (MIBA). A book's relationship to the Great Lakes region may consist of either the content of the book, the author's hometown, or the author's current residence. Books must be classifiable in one of 5 awarded genres: Fiction, nonfiction, poetry, young adult/middle grade, or children's picture book. Books submitted must have an on-sale date between May 1 of the year prior & April 30 of the award year. Both GLIBA & MIBA are conducting separate submission processes with publishers.
GLIBA submissions: Submit books by authors from the following states or books with content that pertains specifically to these states: Illinois, Indiana, Kentucky, Michigan & Ohio.
MIBA submissions: Submit books by authors from the following states or books with content that pertains specifically to these states: Iowa, Kansas, Minnesota, Missouri, Nebraska, North Dakota, South Dakota & Wisconsin.
Dual submissions: If the theme of your book is broadly Midwestern & pertains to both regions, please submit to both associations. Entry fee: $25 per title.
Other Sponsor(s): Midwest Independent Booksellers Association (MIBA)
Closing Date: June 1
Presented: Heartland Fall Forum, Oct

Heartland Literary Award
Chicago Tribune
160 N Stetson Ave, Chicago, IL 60601
Tel: 312-222-3001
E-mail: ctc-arts@chicagotribune.com
Web Site: www.chicagotribune.com/entertainment/books/literary-awards
Established: 1988
Awarded in 2 categories: fiction & nonfiction.
Presented: Autumn

AWARDS, PRIZE CONTESTS, FELLOWSHIPS & GRANTS

Robert A Heinlein Award
Baltimore Science Fiction Society Inc
PO Box 686, Baltimore, MD 21203-0686
Tel: 410-563-2737
E-mail: webmeister@bsfs.org
Web Site: www.bsfs.org/bsfsheinlein.htm
Key Personnel
Comm Chair: Michael F Flynn
Awarded for outstanding published works in science fiction & technical writings to inspire the human exploration of space.
Other Sponsor(s): Heinlein Society; Dr Yoji Kondo Family
Award: Sterling silver medallion, red-white-blue lanyard & 2 lapel pins

Drue Heinz Literature Prize
University of Pittsburgh Press
7500 Thomas Blvd, Pittsburgh, PA 15260
Tel: 412-383-2456 *Fax:* 412-383-2466
E-mail: info@upress.pitt.edu
Web Site: upittpress.org/prize/drue-heinz-literature-prize; www.upress.pitt.edu
Key Personnel
Dir: Peter W Kracht *E-mail:* pkracht@upress.pitt.edu
Opers Admin: Eileen O'Malley
E-mail: eomalley@upress.pitt.edu
Established: 1980
For a collection of short fiction 150-300 pages in length. Open to all writers who have published a book-length collection of short fiction or who have had 3 short stories or novellas published in commercial magazines or literary journals of national distribution. See web site for complete rules.
Other Sponsor(s): Drue Heinz & The Drue Heinz Trust
Award: $15,000 & publication by the University of Pittsburgh Press
Closing Date: May 1-June 30 (postmark)
Presented: Pittsburgh, PA, Dec or Jan

The Shirley Holden Helberg Grants for Mature Women
National League of American Pen Women Inc
The Pen Arts Bldg & Arts Museum, 1300 17 St NW, Washington, DC 20036-1973
Tel: 202-785-1997 *Fax:* 202-452-6868
E-mail: contact@nlapw.org
Web Site: www.nlapw.org
Key Personnel
Pres: Evelyn B Wofford
Established: 1976
Awarded biennially in even-numbered years. Judges in each category (art, letters, music) change for each award every award year. Must send SASE with inquiry for requirements. Include an $8 fee payable to NLAPW with entry.
Award: $1,000 (1st place), $750 (2nd place), $500 (3rd place); $150 (Photography Award), $150 (Water Media Award), $100 (Jean Baber Memorial Art Fund)
Closing Date: Oct 1, odd-numbered years
Presented: NLAPW Convention, April, even-numbered years; mail notification March 15

Hemingway Award for Debut Novel, see PEN/Hemingway Award for Debut Novel

Cecil Hemley Memorial Award
Poetry Society of America (PSA)
119 Smith St, Brooklyn, NY 11201
Tel: 212-254-9628
E-mail: info@poetrysociety.org
Web Site: poetrysociety.org/awards
Key Personnel
Exec Dir: Matt Brogan *E-mail:* matt@poetrysociety.org
Deputy Dir: Brett Fletcher Lauer *E-mail:* brett@poetrysociety.org
Devt Dir: Madeline Weinfield *E-mail:* madeline@poetrysociety.org
Established: 1969
For a lyric poem that addresses a philosophical or epistemological concern. All submissions must be through Submittable. Entry fee: Free to membs, $10 nonmembs.
Award: $500
Closing Date: Dec 31
Presented: Annual Awards Ceremony, New York, NY, Spring

Brodie Herndon Memorial
The Poetry Society of Virginia (PSV)
PO Box 36128, North Chesterfield, VA 23235-3533
E-mail: contest@poetrysocietyofvirginia.org; info@poetryvirginia.org
Web Site: www.poetrysocietyofvirginia.org
Key Personnel
Pres: Cherryl T Cooley
E-mail: poetrysocietypresident@gmail.com
Poems in any form about heroism, 48 line limit. Must be original, unpublished & in English. Submit 1 copy of the poem with no identifying information but put the category in the upper right-hand-side, along with a notation as to whether you are a member of PSV (does not matter if you are a lifetime member or just joined for the contest). Submit a cover letter/page that contains the category, the name of the poem, your name & address, phone number & e-mail address. Entries will not be returned. Entry fee: Free to membs, $5 nonmembs.
Award: $50 (1st prize), $30 (2nd prize), $20 (3rd prize)
Closing Date: Feb
Presented: PSV Awards Ceremony, April

Hidden River Arts Playwriting Award
Hidden River™ Arts
PO Box 63927, Philadelphia, PA 19147
Tel: 610-764-0813
E-mail: hiddenriverarts@gmail.com
Web Site: www.hiddenriverarts.org; www.hiddenriverarts.com
Key Personnel
Founding Dir: Debra Leigh Scott
Established: 2002
Award for an unpublished, unproduced full-length play. Entry fee: $20. See web site for full submission guidelines (via Submittable).
Award: $1,000 (awarded by mail)
Closing Date: June 30
Presented: Dec

High Plains Book Awards
c/o Billings Public Library, 510 N 28 St, Billings, MT 59101
Tel: 406-672-6223
E-mail: highplainsbookawards@gmail.com
Web Site: highplainsbookawards.org
Key Personnel
Bd Memb: Julie Schultz
Established: 2007
Celebrates literary works which examine & reflect life in the High Plains region, which includes the states of Colorado, Kansas, Montana, Nebraska, North Dakota, South Dakota & Wyoming & the Canadian provinces of Alberta, Manitoba & Saskatchewan. Categories: Art & photography; children's picture book; children's middle grade book; fiction; first book; indigenous writer; nonfiction; memoir/creative nonfiction; poetry; short stories; woman writer; young adult; Big Sky. Nominated books must have been published in the previous calendar year, have an ISBN & be written by an author or writing team currently resident in the High Plains region or be a literary work which examines & reflects life within that region. Entry fee: $75 per category. Submissions must include 4 printed reader copies.
Other Sponsor(s): Billings Junior Woman's Club; Billings Public Library; Mary Alice Fortin Foundation for Youth Enrichment; Friends of Billings Public Library; Kathy & Doug James; Susan Lubbers; Montana State University Billings Foundation & Alumni; Montana State University Billings Library; Rocky Mountain College; Ucross Foundation; Writer's Voice; Yellowstone Art Museum Board of Directors; Zonta Club of Billings
Award: $500 each
Closing Date: March
Presented: Awards Event, Billings, MT, Oct

ASSOCIATIONS, EVENTS

High School Sequoyah Book Award
Oklahoma Library Association
119 Meramec Station Rd, Suite 207, Ballwin, MO 63021-6902
Toll Free Tel: 800-969-6562 (ext 5) *Fax:* 636-529-1396
E-mail: sequoyah@oklibs.org; ola@amigos.org
Web Site: www.oklibs.org
Established: 2010
Student choice award: students in grades 9-12 who have read/listened to at least 3 titles from the High School Masterlist are eligible to vote. Books are considered for Masterlist 2 years prior to the award being given. Voting takes place February 1-March 15 with winner announced by March 31.
Award: Medal
Presented: OLA Annual Conference, March/April

Higher Education Scholarship Program
Book Industry Charitable Foundation (BINC)
3135 S State St, Suite 203, Ann Arbor, MI 48108
Toll Free Tel: 866-733-9064
E-mail: info@bincfoundation.org
Web Site: www.bincfoundation.org/scholarship
Key Personnel
Exec Dir: Pamela French *E-mail:* pam@bincfoundation.org
Dir, Devt: Kathy Bartson *E-mail:* kathy@bincfoundation.org
Prog Mgr: Judey Kalchik *E-mail:* judey@bincfoundation.org; Ken White *E-mail:* ken@bincfoundation.org
Commun Coord: Erika Mantz *E-mail:* erika@bincfoundation.org
Devt Coord: Jennifer Rojas *E-mail:* jennifer@bincfoundation.org
Off Coord: Jane Regenstreif *E-mail:* jane@bincfoundation.org
Spec Projs Coord: Kate Weiss *E-mail:* kate@bincfoundation.org
Established: 2001
Seven awards to the dependents or spouses/partners of booksellers for full-or part-time study at any accredited institution in the US. The booksellers themselves must be currently employed at a brick & mortar bookstore & have been employed there for at least 90 days for their family members to be eligible.
Award: $3,500 each

The Tony Hillerman Prize
Western Writers of America Inc (WWA)
c/o St Martin's Press, 120 Broadway, New York, NY 10271
E-mail: tonyhillermanprize@stmartins.com
Web Site: us.macmillan.com/minotaurbooks/tonyhillermanprize
Established: 2007
Awarded for the best first mystery set in the Southwest. Entrants must submit entry form & ms online or by mail. Limit of 1 entry per person. See web site for full guidelines.
Other Sponsor(s): St Martin's Press
Award: $10,000 & publication by St Martin's Press
Closing Date: Jan 2

Hillman Prizes for Journalism
The Sidney Hillman Foundation
330 W 42 St, Suite 900, New York, NY 10036
Tel: 646-448-6413
Web Site: www.hillmanfoundation.org
Key Personnel
Pres: Bruce Raynor
Exec Dir: Alexandra Lescaze *E-mail:* alex@hillmanfoundation.org
Established: 1950
For investigative journalism that fosters social & economic justice. See web site for categories.
Award: $5,000 & certificate designed by New Yorker cartoonist Edward Sorel
Closing Date: Jan 31
Presented: Award Ceremony & Cocktail Party, New York, NY, Mid-May

Darlene Clark Hine Award
The Organization of American Historians (OAH)
112 N Bryan Ave, Bloomington, IN 47408-4141
Tel: 812-855-7311
E-mail: oah@oah.org
Web Site: www.oah.org/awards
Key Personnel
Exec Dir: Beth English *Tel:* 812-855-9836 *E-mail:* benglish@oah.org
Dir, Communs & Mktg: Kym Robinson *Tel:* 812-855-5430 *E-mail:* kymarobi@oah.org
Presented to the author of the best book in African American women's & gender history. Each entry must be published in the calendar year preceding that in which the award is given. One copy of each entry must be mailed directly to the committee members listed on the web site.
Closing Date: Oct 1 (postmarked)
Presented: OAH Conference on American History, Spring

Theodore C Hines Award
American Society for Indexing Inc (ASI)
1628 E Southern Ave, Suite 9-223, Tempe, AZ 85282
Tel: 480-245-6750
E-mail: info@asindexing.org
Web Site: www.asindexing.org/about/awards/hines-award
Key Personnel
Exec Dir: Gwen Henson *E-mail:* gwen@asindexing.org
Hines Comm Chair: Diana Witt *E-mail:* diana.witt@comcast.net
Established: 1993
To recognize those who have made exceptional contributions to ASI & to the indexing profession. Nominations are gathered each spring.
Award: Lifetime membership in ASI
Closing Date: March 26
Presented: ASI Annual Meeting, May

Eric Hoffer Award
www.HofferAward.com
Subsidiary of The Eric Hoffer Project
PO Box 11, Titusville, NJ 08560
E-mail: info@hofferaward.com
Web Site: www.hofferaward.com
Key Personnel
Chair: Christopher Klim
Coord: Dawn Shows
Established: 2002
Award that honors independent books of exceptional merit. Open to small, academic & independent presses for books published in the last 2 years. Books published before this 2-year window may enter either the Legacy Fiction or Legacy Nonfiction categories. In addition to the grand prize, various other prizes & separate distinctions are given for presses, including the Montaigne Medal, the da Vinci Eye & the First Horizon Award. For each category registration, submit 1 book, registration form & $55 fee. See web site for complete guidelines.
Award: $2,500 grand prize
Closing Date: Jan 21
Presented: April/May

Bess Hokin Prize
Poetry Magazine
61 W Superior St, Chicago, IL 60654
Tel: 312-787-7070
Web Site: www.poetryfoundation.org/poetrymagazine/prizes
Key Personnel
Assoc Ed: Holly Amos *E-mail:* hamos@poetrymagazine.org
Established: 1948
For poetry published during the preceding year in *Poetry* magazine. No application necessary.
Award: $1,000
Presented: Announced in Nov issue

William F Holmes Award
Southern Historical Association (SHA)
University of Georgia, Dept of History, Athens, GA 30602-1602
Tel: 706-542-8848
Web Site: thesha.org/holmes
Key Personnel
Secy/Treas: Dr Stephen Berry *E-mail:* berrys@thesha.org
Awarded for the best paper presented at the annual meeting by a graduate student or junior faculty member (anyone who received his or her PhD within 3 years of the time of presentation). Papers should be submitted via e-mail to Manager, Southern Historical Association. The paper should be no longer than 15 pages of text & must be in the same form as will be delivered at the annual meeting. Each entry should have a cover sheet, which includes the author's name, the paper title & the institution for the PhD with the expected month/year of graduation, or the month/year when the PhD was received.
Award: Cash
Closing Date: Oct 9
Presented: Annual Meeting

Honickman First Book Prize
American Poetry Review
1906 Rittenhouse Sq, Philadelphia, PA 19103
Tel: 215-309-3722
Web Site: www.aprweb.org
Key Personnel
Ed: Elizabeth Scanlon *E-mail:* escanlon@aprweb.org
Established: 1997
Awarded to any US citizen writing in English who has not published a book-length collection of poems with an ISBN. Poems previously published in periodicals or limited-edition chapbooks may be included in the ms, but the ms itself must not have been published as a book-length work exceeding 25 pages. No translations or multiple author entries accepted. Entry fee $25. Now accepting online submissions.
Award: $3,000
Closing Date: Oct 31 (postmark)
Presented: Winner announced in March/April issue of the *American Poetry Review*

Honoring Fatherhood Award
The Poetry Society of Virginia (PSV)
PO Box 36128, North Chesterfield, VA 23235-3533
E-mail: contest@poetrysocietyofvirginia.org; info@poetryvirginia.org
Web Site: www.poetrysocietyofvirginia.org
Key Personnel
Pres: Cherryl T Cooley *E-mail:* poetrysocietypresident@gmail.com
Awarded in memory of Theodore Tomala Jr. Any form. Subject: Honoring fathers +/or their sacrifices. 48 line limit. Submit 1 copy of the poem with no identifying information but put the category in the upper right-hand-side, along with a notation as to whether you are a member of PSV (does not matter if you are a lifetime member or just joined for the contest). Submit a cover letter/page that contains the category, the name of the poem, your name & address, phone number & e-mail address. Entries will not be returned. Entry fee: Free to membs, $5 nonmembs.
Other Sponsor(s): Bill & Michelle O'Hearn
Award: $50 (1st prize), $30 (2nd prize), $20 (3rd prize)

The Hopwood Award Theodore Roethke Prize
University of Michigan, College of Literature, Science & Arts
1176 Angell Hall, 435 S State St, Ann Arbor, MI 48109-1003
Tel: 734-764-6296 *Fax:* 734-764-3128
E-mail: abeauch@umich.edu
Web Site: lsa.umich.edu/hopwood
Awarded to the best long poem or poetic sequence written by a University of Michigan student, undergraduate or graduate.
Award: $5,000
Closing Date: 1st Wednesday in Dec, by 12 noon
Presented: April

Hopwood Underclassmen Contest
University of Michigan, College of Literature, Science & Arts
1176 Angell Hall, 435 S State St, Ann Arbor, MI 48109-1003
Tel: 734-764-6296 *Fax:* 734-764-3128
E-mail: abeauch@umich.edu
Web Site: lsa.umich.edu/hopwood
Open to any first- or second-year student regularly enrolled in qualifying writing courses. Three types of writing are eligible: nonfiction, fiction & poetry. See web site for specific guidelines.
Award: $500-$2,000 each
Closing Date: 1st Wednesday in Dec, by 12 noon
Presented: Early in Winter term

Housatonic Book Awards
Western Connecticut State University MFA in Creative & Professional Writing
Dept of Writing, Linguistics & Creative Process, 181 White St, Higgins Hall, Rm 219, Danbury, CT 06810
Web Site: housatonicbookawards.wordpress.com
Key Personnel
MFA Prog Coord: Dr Anthony D'Aries *Tel:* 203-837-3252 *Fax:* 203-837-3953 *E-mail:* dariesa@wcsu.edu
Graduate Asst: Michaela Lawlor *E-mail:* lawlor033@wcsu.edu
Submissions open January 1 & are accepted in fiction, nonfiction, poetry & young adult/middle grade. All books must have been published in the previous calendar year. Winning authors must attend the WCSU MFA residency & give a public reading & a 1 day, 3 hour workshop with MFA students. Entry fee: $25 per title.
Award: $1,000 honorarium, $500 travel stipend & up to 2 night hotel stay
Closing Date: Mid-June

Tom Howard/John H Reid Fiction & Essay Contest
Winning Writers
351 Pleasant St, Suite B, PMB 222, Northampton, MA 01060-3998
Tel: 413-320-1847 *Toll Free Tel:* 866-WINWRIT (946-9748) *Fax:* 413-280-0539
Web Site: www.winningwriters.com/our-contests/tom-howard-john-h-reid-fiction-essay-contest

AWARDS, PRIZE CONTESTS, FELLOWSHIPS & GRANTS

Key Personnel
Pres: Adam Cohen *E-mail:* adam@winningwriters.com
VP: Jendi Reiter
Established: 1990
Submit short stories, essays or other works of prose, up to 6,000 words each. Must be your own original work. $20 reading fee per entry. Writers of most nations may enter, however, the works you submit should be in English. Both published & unpublished work accepted. Applications accepted October 15-April 30.
Other Sponsor(s): Duotrope
Award: $3,000 (each 1st prize, fiction & essay), $200 (10 honorable mention awards) & publication on web site for all winners. Top 2 winners also receive 2-year gift certificates from Duotrope
Closing Date: April 30 (postmark)
Presented: Winner announced Oct 15 on web site

Tom Howard/Margaret Reid Poetry Contest
Winning Writers
351 Pleasant St, Suite B, PMB 222, Northampton, MA 01060-3998
Tel: 413-320-1847 *Toll Free Tel:* 866-WINWRIT (946-9748) *Fax:* 413-280-0539
Web Site: www.winningwriters.com/our-contests/tom-howard-margaret-reid-poetry-contest
Key Personnel
Pres: Adam Cohen *E-mail:* adam@winningwriters.com
VP: Jendi Reiter
Established: 2002
The Tom Howard Prize is awarded for a poem in any style or genre. The Margaret Reid Prize is awarded for a poem that rhymes or has a traditional style. Entry fee is $15 for 1-2 poems. Each poem may have up to 250 lines. See web site for complete submission details & contest results. Both published & unpublished work accepted. Poets of most nations may enter, however, the works you submit should be in English. Applications are accepted beginning April 15.
Other Sponsor(s): Duotrope
Award: $3,000 each (1st prize, Tom Howard & Margaret Reid), $200 each (10 honorable mention awards) & publication on web site for all winners. Top 2 winners also receive 2-year gift certificates from Duotrope
Closing Date: Sept 30 (postmark)
Presented: Winner announced Oct 15 on web site

Julia Ward Howe Book Awards
Boston Authors Club Inc
c/o Prof Julie Dobrow, 103 Conant Rd, Lincoln, MA 01773
Tel: 781-259-1220
E-mail: bostonauthorsclub2@gmail.com
Web Site: bostonauthorsclub.org
Key Personnel
Pres: Julie Dobrow *E-mail:* jdobrow111@gmail.com
VP: Tracy Geary *Tel:* 781-334-2025 *E-mail:* geary321@hotmail.com
Established: 1997
Books must be published the year prior to the award. Prizes given in fiction, nonfiction, poetry & young reader's categories. Authors must live or have lived, worked or attended college within 100 miles of Boston the year their books are published. Submission fee: $35 per title.
Other Sponsor(s): Boston Public Library (Rare Books Div)
Award: Cash prizes for winners; certificates to finalists & authors of recommended books (number varies). All receive 1-year complimentary membership in the Club
Closing Date: Jan 31
Presented: Boston Public Library, Boston, MA, Sept

The William Dean Howells Medal
American Academy of Arts & Letters
633 W 155 St, New York, NY 10032
Tel: 212-368-5900
E-mail: academy@artsandletters.org
Web Site: artsandletters.org/awards
Key Personnel
Exec Dir: Cody Upton
Established: 1925
Given once every 5 years in recognition of the most distinguished American novel published during that period. Next medal to be presented in 2025. Candidates must be nominated by an Academy member.
Award: Medal

L Ron Hubbard's Writers of the Future Contest
Author Services Inc
7051 Hollywood Blvd, Hollywood, CA 90028
Tel: 323-466-3310 *Fax:* 323-466-6474
E-mail: contests@authorservicesinc.com
Web Site: www.writersofthefuture.com
Key Personnel
Contest Dir: Joni Labaqui
Coordinating Judge: David Farland
Established: 1983
Short stories & novelettes (under 17,000 words) of science fiction & fantasy for new & amateur writers. No entry fee required, entrants retain all publication rights.
Award: Annually: Trophy & $5,000 (Grand prize); Quarterly: $1,000 (1st place), $750 (2nd place), $500 (3rd place)
Closing Date: Quarterly: March 31, June 30, Sept 30, Dec 31

Charlotte Huck Award
National Council of Teachers of English (NCTE)
340 N Neil St, Suite 104, Champaign, IL 61820
Tel: 217-328-3870 *Toll Free Tel:* 877-369-6283 (cust serv) *Fax:* 217-328-9645
E-mail: bookawards@ncte.org
Web Site: ncte.org/awards/ncte-childrens-book-awards
Key Personnel
Prog Coord: Sarah Miller
Established: 2014
Awarded to promote & recognize fiction that has the potential to transform children's lives by inviting compassion, imagination & wonder. Books must have been published +/or distributed in the US during the calendar year. Nominations of individual books may come from publishers, NCTE membership & from the educational community at large. One title is singled out for the award & up to 5 honor books are also recognized. Eight additional recommended books can be named.
Award: Winning author(s) +/or illustrator(s) receive plaque & are the featured speaker(s) at the following year's Children's Book Awards Luncheon; Honor book author(s) +/or illustrator(s) receive certificate & invitation to present at session following the luncheon
Closing Date: Oct 15
Presented: Children's Book Awards Luncheon, NCTE Annual Convention

The Hugo Awards
The World Science Fiction Society
c/o Kevin Lee, Hugo Awards Mktg Comm, PO Box 242, Fernley, NV 89408-0242
E-mail: info@thehugoawards.org
Web Site: www.wsfs.org/awards; www.thehugoawards.org
Established: 1953
Fan-voted awards for science fiction & fantasy literature. During January-March, members of Worldcon can nominate up to 5 people or works from the previous year in 15 categories. Shortlist of 5 finalists announced in April.

ASSOCIATIONS, EVENTS

Worldcon members cast their final ballots in July.
Award: Trophy
Presented: Hugo Award Ceremony, Worldcon

Lynda Hull Memorial Poetry Prize
Crazyhorse
College of Charleston, Dept of English, 66 George St, Charleston, SC 29424
Tel: 843-953-4470
E-mail: crazyhorse@cofc.edu
Web Site: crazyhorse.cofc.edu/prizes
Key Personnel
Mng Ed: Jonathan Heinen
Awarded for best single poem. Enter 3 poems with $20 entry fee, which includes 1-year subscription. Submissions accepted during the month of January. Nationally prominent poet judges. See web site for complete instructions.
Award: $2,000 & publication in *Crazyhorse*
Closing Date: Jan 31
Presented: June 1

Hurston/Wright Award for College Writers
The Zora Neale Hurston/Richard Wright Foundation
10 "G" St NE, Suite 600, Washington, DC 20002
E-mail: info@hurstonwright.org
Web Site: www.hurstonwright.org/awards/hurston-wright-award-for-college-writers
Key Personnel
Exec Dir: Khadijah Z Ali-Coleman *E-mail:* khadijah@hurstonwright.org
Writing Progs Mgr: DeAndrea L Johnson
Events & Programming Coord: Molly Rufus
Established: 1990
Literary award to honor excellence in fiction writing by African-American students enrolled as an undergraduate or graduate student in any college or university. Non-refundable application fee: $10.
Other Sponsor(s): Amistad
Award: $1,000 & story published in literary journal (1st prize), $500 (awarded to 2 runners-up)
Closing Date: Jan
Presented: Announced in May

Hurston/Wright Legacy Awards
The Zora Neale Hurston/Richard Wright Foundation
10 "G" St NE, Suite 600, Washington, DC 20002
E-mail: info@hurstonwright.org
Web Site: www.hurstonwright.org/awards/legacy-awards
Key Personnel
Exec Dir: Khadijah Z Ali-Coleman *E-mail:* khadijah@hurstonwright.org
Writing Progs Mgr: DeAndrea L Johnson
Events & Programming Coord: Molly Rufus
Established: 2001
National literary award for debut fiction, fiction, nonfiction & poetry for published black writers. Application fee: $40.
Award: $10,000 for winners in 3 categories, $5,000 for 6 runners-up (2 in each category)
Closing Date: Dec
Presented: Legacy Awards Gala, Oct

IACP Cookbook Awards
International Association of Culinary Professionals (IACP)
c/o Marshall Jones, 4625 Alexander Dr, Alpharetta, GA 30022
Toll Free Fax: 866-358-2524
E-mail: awards@iacp.com; info@iacp.com
Web Site: www.iacp.com/awards/cookbook-awards
Key Personnel
Exec Dir: Nancy Hopkins
Awards Dir: Paola Briseno-Gonzalez
Established: 1985
Recognizes authors, publishers & other contributors behind the best cookbooks published each

year. Awards are divided into a variety of categories & are open to members & nonmembers. Entry fee: $150 early, $200 regular.
Closing Date: Dec 1 (early), Feb 19 (regular)
Presented: IACP Annual Conference

IBPA Book Awards
Formerly Benjamin Franklin Awards™
The Independent Book Publishers Association (IBPA)
1020 Manhattan Beach Blvd, Suite 204, Manhattan Beach, CA 90266
Tel: 310-546-1818
E-mail: info@ibpa-online.org
Web Site: www.ibpa-online.org
Key Personnel
Chair: Tieshena Davis
CEO: Andrea Fleck-Nisbet *E-mail:* andrea@ibpa-online.org
COO: Terry Nathan *E-mail:* terry@ibpa-online.org
Chief Content Offr: Lee Wind *E-mail:* lee@ibpa-online.org
Dir, Mktg & Communs: Adeline Lui *E-mail:* adeline@ibpa-online.org
Established: 1985
Excellence in independent publishing in specific genre & design (books, audio & video). Categories have been expanded to include: Jan Nathan Lifetime Achievement Award; AAPI Communities; Black/African American Communities; Disabled Communities; First Nations/Indigenous Communities; Latina/o/e Communities; LGBTQIA2+ Communities; Neurodivergent Communities. Entry fee: $95/title/category membs; $229/first title (includes 1-year membership), $95/additional titles non-membs.
Award: Gold winners: Engraved crystal trophy & award certificates with gold stickers. Silver winners: Award certificates with silver stickers
Closing Date: Sept 30 (1st call) & Dec 15 (2nd call)
Presented: Gala Awards Ceremony, May

The Idaho Prize for Poetry
Lost Horse Press
1025 S Garry Rd, Liberty Lake, WA 99019
Tel: 208-597-3008 *Fax:* 208-255-1560
E-mail: losthorsepress@mindspring.com
Web Site: www.losthorsepress.org
Key Personnel
Publr: Christine Holbert
Established: 2003
A national competition for a book-length poetry ms written by an American poet. Accompany ms with $28 reading fee (check or money order only). Books distributed by the University of Washington Press. May also submit online using submittable.com.
Award: $1,000 & publication with 20 free author copies
Closing Date: May 15
Presented: Aug 15

ILA Children's & Young Adults' Book Awards
International Literacy Association (ILA)
PO Box 8139, Newark, DE 19714-8139
Tel: 302-731-1600 *Toll Free Tel:* 800-336-7323 (US & CN)
E-mail: ilaawards@reading.org
Web Site: www.literacyworldwide.org
Key Personnel
Exec Dir: Marcie Craig Post
Established: 1975
Awards for newly published authors who show unusual promise in the children's or young adult book field. Awards will be given for fiction & nonfiction in 3 categories: Primary (ages preschool-8), Intermediate (ages 9-13) & Young Adult (ages 14-17). Books from any country & published in English for the first time during the previous calendar year will be considered.
Award: $800 per book
Closing Date: Nov 1
Presented: Annual Conference, May

Illumination Book Awards
Independent Publisher Online
Division of Jenkins Group Inc
1129 Woodmere Ave, Suite B, Traverse City, MI 49686
Tel: 231-933-0445 *Toll Free Tel:* 800-706-4636
Fax: 231-933-0448
Web Site: illuminationawards.com
Key Personnel
Awards Dir: Amy Shamroe *Tel:* 800-644-0133 ext 1000 *E-mail:* amys@jenkinsgroupinc.com
Established: 2013
With the motto "Shining a Light on Exemplary Christian Books," the Illumination Awards are designed to honor the year's best new titles written & published with a Christian worldview. The contest is for published books only, as our judging criteria include cover design, layout, etc. Books from all methods of publishing are welcome & authors of royalty-published books are welcome to enter their books themselves. Entry fee: $75-$95 per category.
Other Sponsor(s): Jenkins Group Inc
Award: Gold medal (1st place), silver medal (2nd place), bronze medal (3rd place), personalized certificate & 20 sample seals
Closing Date: Dec 30
Presented: Feb

John Phillip Immroth Memorial Award
Intellectual Freedom Round Table (IFRT)
Unit of The American Library Association (ALA)
225 Michigan Ave, Suite 1300, Chicago, IL 60601
Tel: 312-280-4226 *Toll Free Tel:* 800-545-2433
E-mail: ifrt@ala.org
Web Site: www.ala.org/rt/ifrt/immroth
Key Personnel
Comm Chair: Johannah Genett
Asst Dir, Office of Intellectual Freedom: Kristen Pekoll *Tel:* 312-280-4221 *E-mail:* kpekoll@ala.org
Established: 1979
Awarded for notable contribution to intellectual freedom & demonstrations of personal courage in defense of freedom of expression.
Award: $500 & citation
Closing Date: Dec 1
Presented: ALA Annual Conference & Exhibition, June

IMPACT Awards, see The SIIA IMPACT Awards

Independent Artist Awards
Maryland State Arts Council
Affiliate of Maryland Dept of Commerce
175 W Ostend St, Suite E, Baltimore, MD 21230
Tel: 410-767-6555
E-mail: msac.commerce@maryland.gov
Web Site: www.msac.org/programs/independent-artist-award
Key Personnel
Prog Dir, Arts Servs: Emily Sollenberger; Laura Weiss *E-mail:* laura.weiss@maryland.gov
Recognizes achievement by Maryland artists making work independent of an institution or organization. The awards are accompanied by grants that encourage artistic growth & sustained practice. See web site for further details & complete guidelines.
Award: $2,000 Regional Awards-awarded in each region to encourage the pursuit of promising work by an individual artist or collaborative group. $10,000 Regional Awards-awarded in each region to recognize notable artistic achievement by an individual artist or collaborative group. All $10,000 Regional Award winners will be eligible for the State Award(s): $15,000 State Award(s)-awarded to up to 2 artists or collaborative groups per year to recognize outstanding artistic achievement
Closing Date: Summer
Presented: Awards Reception, Early June

Independent Press Award®
63 Clinton Rd, Glen Ridge, NJ 07028
Web Site: www.independentpressaward.com
Key Personnel
Founder: Gabrielle (Gabby) L Olczak *E-mail:* gabby@independentpressaward.com
Mktg Mgr: Ted Olczak *E-mail:* ted@gabbybookawards.com
Celebration of great books by independent presses. Print & audiobooks can be submitted by independent publishers, hybrid publishers, self-published authors, university presses & association presses. Over 150 recognized categories. Entry fee: $125 for first category, $75 for each additional category.
Award: Winners & distinguished favorites receive banners in 2 different sizes, digital certificate of recognition, press release template & self-adhesive book seals (available for purchase)
Closing Date: Rolling submissions: March 1-Aug 30 & Sept 1-Dec 30
Presented: Awards Dinner & Ceremony, May

The Independent Publisher Book Awards
Independent Publisher Online
Division of Jenkins Group Inc
1129 Woodmere Ave, Suite B, Traverse City, MI 49686
Tel: 231-933-0445 *Toll Free Tel:* 800-706-4636
Fax: 231-933-0448
E-mail: ippy@jgibookawards.com
Web Site: ippyawards.com
Key Personnel
Awards Dir: Amy Shamroe *Tel:* 800-644-0133 ext 1000 *E-mail:* amys@jenkinsgroupinc.com
Established: 1996
Recognizes the works of independent publishers in 90 subject categories, for excellence in literary merit, design & production, published during previous calendar year. Ebooks & audiobooks are welcome. Entry fee: $75-$95 per category.
Other Sponsor(s): Jenkins Group Inc
Award: Gold medal (1st place), silver medal (2nd place), bronze medal (3rd place), personalized certificate & 20 foil seals
Closing Date: Feb 19
Presented: May

Independent Publishers of New England Book Awards
Independent Publishers of New England (IPNE)
c/o Eddie Vincent, Encircle Publications, Farmington, ME 04955
Tel: 339-368-8229
E-mail: bookawards@ipne.org
Web Site: www.ipne.org/awards
Key Personnel
Pres: Eddie Vincent
VP: Charlotte R Pierce
Categories: Informational nonfiction, narrative nonfiction, literary nonfiction, genre fiction, design, young adult, children's, book promotional campaign, coffee table & art books. Entry fee: $45 per title (1 category), $25 per additional category, nonmembs $70 per title (1 category).
Closing Date: May 31
Presented: Nov

Indiana Review Creative Nonfiction Prize
Indiana Review

AWARDS, PRIZE CONTESTS, FELLOWSHIPS & GRANTS

Indiana University English Dept, Ballantine Hall 554, 1020 E Kirkwood Ave, Bloomington, IN 47405
Tel: 812-855-3439
E-mail: inreview@indiana.edu
Web Site: indianareview.org
Key Personnel
Ed-in-Chief: Shreya Fadia
Assoc Ed: Bernardo Wade
Send 1 creative nonfiction piece, up to 5,000 words. Entry fee: $20 (includes 1-year subscription to *Indiana Review*). See web site for full submission guidelines.
Award: $1,000 & publication
Closing Date: Oct 31

Indiana Review Fiction Prize
Indiana Review
Indiana University English Dept, Ballantine Hall 554, 1020 E Kirkwood Ave, Bloomington, IN 47405
Tel: 812-855-3439
E-mail: inreview@indiana.edu
Web Site: indianareview.org
Key Personnel
Ed-in-Chief: Shreya Fadia
Assoc Ed: Bernardo Wade
Submit a short story of up to 6,000 words; only 1 story per entry. Previously published works & works forthcoming elsewhere cannot be considered. Entry fee: $20 (includes 1-year subscription to *Indiana Review*). All prize entries are considered for publication.
Award: $1,000 & publication
Closing Date: March 31

Indiana Review Poetry Prize
Indiana Review
Indiana University English Dept, Ballantine Hall 554, 1020 E Kirkwood Ave, Bloomington, IN 47405
Tel: 812-855-3439
E-mail: inreview@indiana.edu
Web Site: indianareview.org
Key Personnel
Ed-in-Chief: Shreya Fadia
Assoc Ed: Bernardo Wade
Submit up to 3 poems. Entry fee: $20 (includes 1-year subscription to *Indiana Review*). See web site for full submission guidelines.
Award: $1,000 & publication
Closing Date: March 31

IndieReader Discovery Awards
IndieReader
PO Box 43121, Montclair, NJ 07043
E-mail: customerservice@indiereader.com
Web Site: indiereader.com/the-discovery-awards/
Key Personnel
Founder & Pres: Amy Edelman *E-mail:* amy@indiereader.com
Established: 2010
Awards open to indie authors who have self-published books. Entry fee: $150 per title plus $50 for each additional category entered. Submit 3 copies of your work or a shareable efile-no matter how many categories you've entered. IndieReader review (value: $250-$275); Publicist consultation session with Smith Publicity (value: $499); Custom author web site & one year of hosting & management provided by Featherlight (value: $1,347); *The Writers Guild* membership (value: $450); Reedsy credit towards any service (value: $100).
Other Sponsor(s): Dystel, Goderich & Bourrett Literary Management; Featherlight; Reedsy; Smith Publicity; The Writers Guild/Jerry Jenkins
Award: Top 2 winners (1 fiction & 1 nonfiction): Professional IndieReader review, tailored publicist consultation session, custom author web site & one year of hosting & management, one-year membership to *The Writers Guild* & Reedsy credit towards any service; Top 6 winners (3 fiction & 3 nonfiction): $250 cash prize (2nd & 3rd place books in fiction & nonfiction), professional IndieReader review & first look consideration with an eye to representation from Dystel, Goderich & Bourret Literary Management
Closing Date: March
Presented: Late May/early June

Individual Artist Fellowships
Maine Arts Commission
Division of State of Maine
25 State House Sta, 193 State St, Augusta, ME 04333-0025
Tel: 207-287-2724 *Fax:* 207-287-2725
Web Site: mainearts.maine.gov
Key Personnel
Grants Dir: Kerstin Gilg *E-mail:* kerstin.gilg@maine.gov
Established: 1987
Three prizes awarded annually to visual, performing & literary artists, craft, multimedia/film, traditional arts.
Other Sponsor(s): Maine Community Foundation
Award: $5,000
Closing Date: May
Presented: Fall

Individual Artist Fellowships
Nebraska Arts Council
Division of State of Nebraska
1004 Farnam, Plaza Level, Omaha, NE 68102
Tel: 402-595-2122
E-mail: nac.info@nebraska.gov
Web Site: www.artscouncil.nebraska.gov
Key Personnel
Artist Servs & Communs Mgr: Meagan Dion *Tel:* 402-595-3935 *E-mail:* meagan.dion@nebraska.gov
Established: 1991
Program recognizes exemplary work by Nebraska artists & provides support for presentations, training, research +/or creation of new art for 1 year through monetary stipends. Professional, out-of-state jurors adjudicate work according to the merit of the artists' work. The program rotates annually, highlighting different artistic disciplines each year.
Award: $1,000-$5,000

Individual Artist Project Grants
Florida Department of State, Division of Cultural Affairs
500 S Bronough St, Tallahassee, FL 32399-0250
Tel: 850-245-6470 *Fax:* 850-245-6497
E-mail: dcagrants@dos.myflorida.com
Web Site: dos.myflorida.com/cultural
Key Personnel
Dir: Sandy Shaughnessy
Arts Consultant: Hillary Crawford
Established: 1976
Fellowship program in support of the general artistic & career advancement of individual artists & recognizes the creation of new artworks by these artists. Projects can be in all artistic disciplines, genres & styles.
Award: Up to $25,000
Closing Date: June 1

Individual Artist's Fellowships
South Carolina Arts Commission (SCAC)
Division of State of South Carolina
1026 Sumter St, Suite 200, Columbia, SC 29201-3746
Tel: 803-734-8696 *Fax:* 803-734-8526
E-mail: info@arts.sc.gov
Web Site: www.southcarolinaarts.com
Key Personnel
Communs Dir: Milly Hough *Tel:* 803-734-8698 *E-mail:* mhough@arts.sc.gov

ASSOCIATIONS, EVENTS

Established: 2007
Non-matching funds for South Carolina residents only. Up to 4 fellowships each year according to rotation cycle. Online submissions only. See commission's web site for details.
Award: $5,000 each
Closing Date: Nov (1st weekday)

Individual Excellence Awards
Ohio Arts Council
30 E Broad St, 33rd fl, Columbus, OH 43215
Tel: 614-466-2613 *Fax:* 614-466-4494
Web Site: www.oac.state.oh.us
Key Personnel
Exec Dir: Donna Collins *E-mail:* donna.collins@oac.ohio.gov
Indiv Artist Prog Dir: Kathy Signorino *E-mail:* kathy.signorino@oac.ohio.gov
Indiv Artist Prog Coord: Katie Davis *E-mail:* katie.davis@oac.ohio.gov
Established: 1978
Available to creative artists who are residents of Ohio. Applicants must have lived in Ohio for 1 year prior to the September 1 deadline & must remain in the state during the grant period. Applications must be submitted online.
Odd-numbered calendar years, applications accepted in the following disciplines: choreography, criticism, fiction/nonfiction, music composition, playwriting/screenplays & poetry.
Even-numbered calendar years, applications accepted in these disciplines: crafts, design arts/illustration, interdisciplinary/performance art, media arts, photography & visual arts.
Award: $4,000 (number of awards given determined by panel)
Closing Date: Sept 1

Innis-Gerin Medal
Royal Society of Canada
Walter House, 282 Somerset W, Ottawa, ON K2P 0J6, Canada
Tel: 613-991-6990 (ext 106) *Fax:* 613-991-6996
E-mail: nominations@rsc-src.ca
Web Site: www.rsc-src.ca
Key Personnel
Mgr, Fellowship & Awards: Marie-Lyne Renaud *E-mail:* mlrenaud@rsc-src.ca
Established: 1966
Biennial award given in even-numbered years for a distinguished & sustained contribution to literature in social science, human geography & social psychology.
Award: Bronze medal
Closing Date: March 1
Presented: RSC Annual Meeting, Nov

Inside Literary Prize
Freedom Reads
2666 State St, Suite 5A, Hamden, CT 06517
E-mail: freedomreads@freedomreads.org
Web Site: freedomreads.org/showing-up/inside-literary-prize
Key Personnel
Founder & CEO: Reginald Dwayne Betts
Chief Communs Offr: Ivan J Dominguez *Tel:* 203-200-0186 *E-mail:* ivan@freedomreads.org
Communs Mgr: Madeline Sklar *Tel:* 203-208-9123 *E-mail:* madelines@freedomreads.org
Established: 2023
Literary prize voted on & awarded by incarcerated people, to honor their insights & add to cultural conversations.
Other Sponsor(s): Center for Justice Innovation; Lori Feathers; National Book Foundation
Award: $4,860 & wood trophy
Presented: Aug

Institute for Immigration Research New American Voices Award
Fall for the Book Inc
4400 University Dr, MS 3E4, Fairfax, VA 22030

Tel: 703-993-3986
E-mail: submissions@fallforthebook.org
Web Site: fallforthebook.
  org/aboutnewamericanvoices
Key Personnel
Festival Dir: Kara Oakleaf *E-mail:* kara@
  fallforthebook.org
Mktg Dir: Kate Lewis *E-mail:* kate@
  fallforthebook.org
Festival Mgr: Suzy Rigdon *Tel:* 703-993-4039
  E-mail: suzy@fallforthebook.org
Established: 2018
Awarded in recognition of recently published works that illuminate the complexity of the human experience as told by immigrants, whose work is historically underrepresented in writing & publishing.
Award: $5,000; $1,000 each to 2 finalists
Presented: Fall for the Book Festival, Oct

Intermediate Sequoyah Book Award
Oklahoma Library Association
119 Meramec Station Rd, Suite 207, Ballwin, MO 63021-6902
Toll Free Tel: 800-969-6562 (ext 5) *Fax:* 636-529-1396
E-mail: sequoyah@oklibs.org; ola@amigos.org
Web Site: www.oklibs.org
Established: 1988
Student choice award; students in grades 6-8 who have read/listened to at least 3 titles from the Intermediate Masterlist are eligible to vote. Books are considered for Masterlist 2 years prior to the award being given. Voting takes place February 1-March 15 with winner announced by March 31.
Award: Medal
Presented: OLA Annual Conference, March/April

International Latino Book Awards
Empowering Latino Futures
624 Hillcrest Lane, Fallbrook, CA 92028
Tel: 760-689-2317
E-mail: awards@empoweringlatinofutures.org
Web Site: www.latinobookawards.org; www.empoweringlatinofutures.org
Key Personnel
Awards Chair: Kirk Whisler *Tel:* 760-579-1696
  E-mail: kirk@whisler.com
Established: 1998
Awards celebrating books by & about Latinos.
Other Sponsor(s): California State University Dominguez Hills; California State University San Bernardino, John M Pfau Library; Entravision; Libros Publishing; Los Angeles Community College District; Scholastic; VISA
Closing Date: March 15
Presented: Los Angeles City College, Los Angeles, CA, Mid-Sept

International Poetry Competition
Atlanta Review
686 Cherry St NW, Suite 333, Atlanta, GA 30332-0161
E-mail: atlantareview@gatech.edu
Web Site: www.atlantareview.com
Key Personnel
Mng Ed: J C Reilly
Ed: Karen J Head, PhD
Established: 1996
Online entry at atlantareview.submittable.com. Contest opens February 1.
Award: $1,000 (grand prize), publication in *Atlanta Review* (20 publication prizes)
Closing Date: May 1

IODE Jean Throop Book Award
IODE Ontario
9-45 Frid St, Hamilton, ON L8P 4M3, Canada
Tel: 905-522-9537 *Fax:* 905-522-3637
E-mail: iodeontario@gmail.com
Web Site: www.iodeontario.ca
Key Personnel
Chair, Selection Comm: Linda Dennis
Convenor: Mary K Anderson
Established: 1974
Awarded for a children's book written by a Canadian author/illustrator residing in the province of Ontario. The book should appeal to children ages 3-7.
Award: $5,000
Closing Date: Dec 31
Presented: IODE Provincial Chapter of Ontario Annual Meeting, April

IODE Violet Downey Book Award
The National Chapter of Canada IODE
40 Orchard View Blvd, Suite 219, Toronto, ON M4R 1B9, Canada
Tel: 416-487-4416 *Toll Free Tel:* 866-827-7428
  Fax: 416-487-4417
E-mail: iodecanada@bellnet.ca
Web Site: www.iode.ca
Key Personnel
Natl Pres: Carol McCall
Established: 1984
Children's book award. Must be a Canadian author with text in English. At least 500 words & printed in Canada during previous calendar year. Suitable for children 13 years & under.
Award: $5,000
Closing Date: Dec 31
Presented: The National Annual Meeting, Late May

Iowa Poetry Prize
University of Iowa Press
119 W Park Rd, 100 Kuhl House, Iowa City, IA 52242-1000
SAN: 282-4868
Tel: 319-335-2000 *Fax:* 319-335-2055
E-mail: uipress@uiowa.edu
Web Site: www.uipress.uiowa.edu
Key Personnel
Dir: James McCoy *Tel:* 319-335-2013
  E-mail: james-mccoy@uiowa.edu
Assoc Dir/Design & Prodn Mgr: Karen Copp
  Tel: 319-335-2014 *E-mail:* karen-copp@uiowa.edu
Mktg Dir: Allison T Means *Tel:* 319-335-3440
  E-mail: allison-means@uiowa.edu
Off Mgr: Angie Dickey *Tel:* 319-335-3424
  E-mail: angela-dickey@uiowa.edu
Open to new as well as established poets for a book-length collection of poems written originally in English. Previous winners, current University of Iowa students & current & former University of Iowa Press employees are not eligible. Reading fee: $20.
Award: Publication by the University of Iowa Press under a standard royalty agreement
Closing Date: April 30 (postmarked)

The Iowa Review Awards
University of Iowa-The Iowa Review
308 EPB, Iowa City, IA 52242-1408
E-mail: iowa-review@uiowa.edu
Web Site: www.iowareview.org
Key Personnel
Mng Ed: Katie Berta
Ed: Lynne Nugent
Established: 2003
Fiction, poetry & nonfiction categories. Submit up to 25 pages of prose (double-spaced) or 10 pages of poetry (1 poem or several, but no more than 1 poem per page). Work must be previously unpublished. Entry fee: $20 (enclose an additional $10 for a optional 1-year subscription to the magazine). Submissions accepted beginning January 1.
Award: $1,500 & publication in December issue of *Iowa Review* (1st place), $750 & publication in December issue of *Iowa Review* (1st runners-up)
Closing Date: Jan 31

The Iowa Short Fiction Award
Writers' Workshop, The University of Iowa
102 Dey House, 507 N Clinton St, Iowa City, IA 52242-1000
Tel: 319-335-0416 *Fax:* 319-335-0420
Web Site: writersworkshop.uiowa.edu/about/iowa-short-fiction-awards
Key Personnel
Dir, Writers' Workshop: Lan Samantha Chang
Prog Admin: Sasha Khmelnik *E-mail:* aleksandra-khmelnik@uiowa.edu
Established: 1970
For a previously unpublished collection of short stories of at least 150 typewritten pages by a writer who has not previously published a volume of prose fiction. Stories previously published in periodicals are eligible for inclusion. Include SASE. Application period begins August 1.
Other Sponsor(s): University of Iowa Press
Award: Publication by University of Iowa Press under the Press's standard contract
Closing Date: Sept 30

IPPY Awards, see The Independent Publisher Book Awards

Italian Prose in Translation Award (IPTA)
American Literary Translators Association (ALTA)
University of Arizona, Esquire Bldg, No 205, 1230 N Park Ave, Tucson, AZ 85721
Tel: 520-621-1757
E-mail: info@literarytranslators.org
Web Site: literarytranslators.org/awards/ipta
Key Personnel
Commns & Awards Mgr: Rachael Daum
  Tel: 413-200-0459 *E-mail:* rachaeldaum@literarytranslators.org
Prog Dir: Kelsi Vanada *E-mail:* kelsi@literarytranslators.org
Established: 2015
Recognizes the importance of contemporary Italian prose (fiction & literary nonfiction) & promotes the translation of Italian works into English. Books must be published in the US in the previous calendar year. Both translators & publishers are invited to submit titles beginning in mid-January each year via Submittable only.
Award: $5,000
Closing Date: Mid-April
Presented: ATLA Annual Conference

Jackie White Memorial National Children's Playwriting Contest
Columbia Entertainment Co
1800 Nelwood Dr, Columbia, MO 65202
Mailing Address: PO Box 953, Columbia, MO 65205
Web Site: www.cectheatre.org
Key Personnel
Exec Dir: Enola-Riann White
Artistic Dir: Elizabeth Alexander *E-mail:* artistic.director@cectheatre.org
Established: 1988
Original or adapted scripts written for young audiences. Entry should be family-friendly & for the following audiences: Children (5-13) or Young Adults (14-21). Entry can be a play or musical. If a musical, music is required & piano track recordings (at minimum) are required. The script should have at least 5 speaking roles & require no more than 10 actors; doubling is encouraged. At least 2 of the roles should be female & one of the female roles must be a major character. Entry must comply with copyright laws. We do not produce scripts that have had an Equity production &

do not review these scripts as part of this contest. Playwrights may submit more than 1 entry in both categories, additional entry fee required for each submission. The following materials are required for an entry to be considered: Entry fee: $30 per submission, full script, character descriptions & scene synopsis.
Other Sponsor(s): City of Columbia, Office of Cultural Affairs
Award: $500 (1st place)

The Jackson Poetry Prize
Poets & Writers Inc
90 Broad St, Suite 2100, New York, NY 10004
Tel: 212-226-3586 *Fax:* 212-226-3963
E-mail: admin@pw.org
Web Site: www.pw.org
Key Personnel
Exec Dir: Melissa Ford Gradel *Tel:* 212-226-3586 ext 223 *E-mail:* mgradel@pw.org
Established: 2006
Honors an American poet of exceptional talent who deserves wider recognition. Eligible poets must have published at least 2 books of acknowledged literary merit. There is no application process. Nominees are identified by a group of poets selected by Poets & Writers who remain anonymous. Final selection is made by a panel of esteemed poets.
Other Sponsor(s): Liana Foundation
Award: $75,000

Jacobs/Jones African-American Literary Prize
North Carolina Writers' Network
PO Box 21591, Winston-Salem, NC 27120-1591
Tel: 336-293-8844
E-mail: mail@ncwriters.org; nclrsubmissions@ecu.edu
Web Site: www.ncwriters.org
Key Personnel
Exec Dir: Ed Southern *E-mail:* ed@ncwriters.org
Honors Harriet Jacobs & Thomas Jones, two pioneering African-American writers from North Carolina & seeks to convey the rich & varied existence of Black North Carolinians. The contest is administered by the Creative Writing Program at UNC-Chapel Hill. The competition is open to any African-American writer whose primary residence is in North Carolina. Entries may be fiction or creative nonfiction, but must be unpublished, no more than 3,000 words & concerned with the lives & experiences of North Carolina African-Americans. Entries may be excerpts from longer works, but must be self-contained. Entries will be judged on literary merit. Entry fee: $10 membs, $20 nonmembs. Entries can be submitted via US Postal Service or online at ncwriters.submittable.com/submit. See web site for full submission guidelines.
Award: $1,000 & possible publication in *The Carolina Quarterly*
Closing Date: Jan 15

The Joan Leiman Jacobson Poetry Prizes, see Discovery Poetry Contest

Japan-US Friendship Commission Translation Prize for the Translation of Japanese Literature
Japan-US Friendship Commission
Affiliate of Donald Keene Center of Japanese Culture, Columbia University
Columbia University, 507 Kent Hall, MC3920, New York, NY 10027
Tel: 212-854-5036 *Fax:* 212-854-4019
E-mail: donald-keene-center@columbia.edu
Web Site: www.keenecenter.org
Established: 1979
Presented for the best translation of a modern work or a classical work. Translators must be citizens or permanent residents of the US.
Award: Up to $6,000 (either to one translator or divided between classical & modern)
Closing Date: June 1
Presented: Columbia University, New York, NY, April

Randall Jarrell Poetry Competition
North Carolina Writers' Network
PO Box 21591, Winston-Salem, NC 27120-1591
Tel: 336-293-8844
E-mail: mail@ncwriters.org; nclrsubmissions@ecu.edu
Web Site: www.ncwriters.org
Key Personnel
Exec Dir: Ed Southern *E-mail:* ed@ncwriters.org
Assoc Dir, MFA Writing Prog: Terry L Kennedy *E-mail:* tlkenned@uncg.edu
The competition is open to any writer who is a legal resident of North Carolina or a member of the North Carolina Writers' Network. Entries can be submitted via US Postal Service or online at ncwriters.submittable.com. Entry fee per poem by mail: $10 membs, $15 nonmembs. Entry fee per poem via Submittable: $15 membs, $25 nonmembs. Submissions should be one poem only (40-line limit), original & previously unpublished. See web site for full submission guidelines.
Award: $200 & publication in *storySouth*
Closing Date: March 1

Jefferson Cup Award
Youth Services Forum
Unit of Virginia Library Association (VLA)
c/o Virginia Library Association (VLA), PO Box 56312, Virginia Beach, VA 23456
Tel: 757-689-0594 *Fax:* 757-447-3478
Web Site: www.vla.org
Key Personnel
VLA Exec Dir: Lisa R Varga *E-mail:* vla.lisav@cox.net
Established: 1983
Honors a distinguished biography, historical fiction or American history book written especially for young people. Two awards given, one for books published for children & one for books published for young adults.
Award: $500 & engraved silver Jefferson Cup for each
Closing Date: Jan 31
Presented: Virginia Library Association (VLA) Annual Conference, Fall

Jerome Award
Catholic Library Association
8550 United Plaza Blvd, Suite 1001, Baton Rouge, LA 70809
Tel: 225-408-4417
E-mail: cla2@cathla.org
Web Site: cathla.org
Key Personnel
Exec Dir: Melanie Talley
Association Coord: Mary Coll
Established: 1992
For outstanding contribution & commitment to excellence in Catholic scholarship; no unsol mss.
Award: Plaque
Closing Date: None; in-house votes
Presented: CLA Annual Convention, April

Jerome Fellowship
Playwrights' Center
2301 Franklin Ave E, Minneapolis, MN 55406-1099
Tel: 612-332-7481 *Fax:* 612-332-6037
E-mail: info@pwcenter.org
Web Site: www.pwcenter.org
Key Personnel
Producing Artistic Dir: Jeremy Cohen *Tel:* 612-332-7481 ext 1113 *E-mail:* jeremyc@pwcenter.org
Assoc Artistic Dir: Hayley Finn *Tel:* 612-332-7481 ext 1119 *E-mail:* hayleyf@pwcenter.org
Artistic Progs Mgr: Julia Brown *Tel:* 612-332-7481 ext 1115 *E-mail:* juliab@pwcenter.org
Established: 1976
Fellowships awarded to early career playwrights. Provides playwrights with funds & services to aid them in the development of their craft. One year in residence required, July 1-June 30. Contact above for application & guidelines, or download from web site.
Award: $18,000 stipend & $2,500 in development support

John Steinbeck Award for Fiction
Reed Magazine
San Jose State University, English Dept, One Washington Sq, San Jose, CA 95192-0090
Tel: 408-924-4441
E-mail: mail@reedmag.org
Web Site: www.reedmag.org; reedmagazine.submittable.com
All submissions must be through the online system. Keep submissions under 5,000 words. Reading fee: $15.
Award: $1,000 & publication in *Reed Magazine*
Closing Date: Nov 1 (submissions accepted beginning June 1)

Anson Jones MD Awards
Texas Medical Association
401 W 15 St, Austin, TX 78701
Tel: 512-370-1300 *Toll Free Tel:* 800-880-7955
E-mail: ansonjones@texmed.org
Web Site: www.texmed.org/ansonjones
Key Personnel
Awards Coord: Tammy Wishard *Tel:* 512-370-1470
Established: 1957
Awarded in recognition of outstanding coverage of health & medical issues to the public by Texas media. Any general-interest print, broadcast, or online news journalist or media outlet based in Texas (no trade or medical professional publications) can enter. Stories must be intended primarily for a Texas audience. Material must be first published or broadcast in the previous calendar year. See web site for categories & entry form.
Award: $500 cash award & plaque for winners
Closing Date: Jan 10

Jesse H Jones Award
Texas Institute of Letters (TIL)
PO Box 130294, Spring, TX 77393
Web Site: texasinstituteofletters.org
Key Personnel
Pres: David Bowles *E-mail:* president@texasinstituteofletters.org
VP: Chris Barton
Secy: Kathryn Jones *E-mail:* secretary@texasinstituteofletters.org
Treas: Cliff Hudder
Award for the best book of fiction by a Texan or about Texas. The author must have been born in Texas or have lived in Texas for at least 5 consecutive years at some time. See web site for guidelines.
Award: $6,000
Closing Date: Jan
Presented: TIL Annual Meeting & Awards Ceremony, Spring

Judah, Sarah, Grace & Tom Memorial
The Poetry Society of Virginia (PSV)
PO Box 36128, North Chesterfield, VA 23235-3533
E-mail: contest@poetrysocietyofvirginia.org; info@poetryvirginia.org
Web Site: www.poetrysocietyofvirginia.org
Key Personnel
Pres: Cherryl T Cooley
E-mail: poetrysocietypresident@gmail.com

COURSES & AWARDS

AWARDS, PRIZE CONTESTS, FELLOWSHIPS & GRANTS

All entries must be in English, original & unpublished. Subject: Encouraging reflection on inter-ethnic relations, any form, 48 line limit. Submit 1 copy of the poem with no identifying information but put the category in the upper right-hand-side, along with a notation as to whether you are a member of PSV (does not matter if you are a lifetime member or just joined for the contest). Submit a cover letter/page that contains the category, the name of the poem, your name & address, phone number & e-mail address. Entries will not be returned. Entry fee: Free to membs, $5 nonmembs.
Other Sponsor(s): Linda Nottingham
Award: $50 (1st prize), $30 (2nd prize), $20 (3rd prize)
Closing Date: Feb
Presented: PSV Awards Ceremony, April

Juniper Prize for Creative Nonfiction
University of Massachusetts Press
New Africa House, 180 Infirmary Way, 4th fl, Amherst, MA 01003-9289
E-mail: juniperprize@umpress.umass.edu
Web Site: www.umasspress.com/juniper-prizes
Key Personnel
Dir: Mary V Dougherty E-mail: mvd@umpress.umass.edu
Mktg & Sales Dir: Courtney J Andree Tel: 413-545-4987 E-mail: cjandree@umpress.umass.edu
Awarded to 1 original ms. Open to all writers in English, whether or not they are US residents. Entry fee: $30. Submit ms online through Submittable (umasspress.submittable.com/submit). Entries accepted beginning August 1.
Award: $1,000 & publication
Closing Date: Sept 30
Presented: Winner announced on web site in April; publication by the following Spring

Juniper Prize for Fiction
University of Massachusetts Press
New Africa House, 180 Infirmary Way, 4th fl, Amherst, MA 01003-9289
E-mail: juniperprize@umpress.umass.edu
Web Site: www.umasspress.com/juniper-prizes
Key Personnel
Dir: Mary V Dougherty E-mail: mvd@umpress.umass.edu
Mktg & Sales Dir: Courtney J Andree Tel: 413-545-4987 E-mail: cjandree@umpress.umass.edu
Established: 2004
Awarded to 2 original mss of fiction: 1 short story collection & 1 novel. Open to all writers in English, whether or not they are US residents. Entry fee: $30. Submit ms online through Submittable (umasspress.submittable.com/submit). Entries accepted beginning August 1.
Award: $1,000 & publication
Closing Date: Sept 30
Presented: Winner announced on web site in April; publication by the following Spring

Juniper Prize for Poetry
University of Massachusetts Press
New Africa House, 180 Infirmary Way, 4th fl, Amherst, MA 01003-9289
E-mail: juniperprize@umpress.umass.edu
Web Site: www.umasspress.com/juniper-prizes
Key Personnel
Dir: Mary V Dougherty E-mail: mvd@umpress.umass.edu
Mktg & Sales Dir: Courtney J Andree Tel: 413-545-4987 E-mail: cjandree@umpress.umass.edu
Established: 1976
Awarded to 2 original mss of poems: 1 first book prize for a previously unpublished author & 1 prize for a previously published author. Open to all writers in English, whether or not they are US residents. Entry fee: $30. Submit ms online through Submittable (umasspress.submittable.com/submit). Entries accepted beginning August 1.
Award: $1,000 & publication
Closing Date: Sept 30
Presented: Winners announced on web site in April; publication by the following Spring

Susan Kamil Award for Emerging Writers
The Center for Fiction
15 Lafayette Ave, Brooklyn, NY 11217
Tel: 212-755-6710
E-mail: info@centerforfiction.org
Web Site: centerforfiction.org
Key Personnel
Writing Progs Mgr: Randy Winston
Supports emerging writers living in New York City whose work shows promise of excellence.
Other Sponsor(s): Jerome Foundation
Award: $5,000 grant
Closing Date: May 30

Susan Kamil Scholarship for Emerging Writers
Book Industry Charitable Foundation (BINC)
3135 S State St, Suite 203, Ann Arbor, MI 48108
Toll Free Tel: 866-733-9064
E-mail: info@bincfoundation.org
Web Site: bincfoundation.org/susankamil-scholarship
Key Personnel
Exec Dir: Pamela French E-mail: pam@bincfoundation.org
Dir, Devt: Kathy Bartson E-mail: kathy@bincfoundation.org
Prog Mgr: Judey Kalchik E-mail: judey@bincfoundation.org; Ken White E-mail: ken@bincfoundation.org
Commun Coord: Erika Mantz E-mail: erika@bincfoundation.org
Devt Coord: Jennifer Rojas E-mail: jennifer@bincfoundation.org
Off Coord: Jane Regenstreif E-mail: jane@bincfoundation.org
Spec Projs Coord: Kate Weiss E-mail: kate@bincfoundation.org
Established: 2024
Scholarships are awarded to 5 booksellers or comic retailers to provide emerging writers-booksellers the financial support to focus on a full-length ms. Eligible writers must be unpublished, over the age of 18, working on a full-length ms, graphic novel, or book-length comic who is also currently employed at (or owns) a physical book or comic store in the US or its territories with a minimum of 3 months of continuous book or comic store employment.
Award: $10,000 each
Closing Date: April

The Michele Karlsberg Leadership Award
The Publishing Triangle
511 Avenue of the Americas, No D36, New York, NY 10011
E-mail: awards@publishingtriangle.org; info@publishingtriangle.org; publishingtriangle@gmail.com
Web Site: publishingtriangle.org/awards/leadership-award
Established: 2002
Honors contributions to LGBTQ literature by those who are not primarily writers, such as editors, literary agents, booksellers & institutions. A call for submissions is posted on the web site in early Autumn.
Award: $500

Sue Kaufman Prize for First Fiction
American Academy of Arts & Letters
633 W 155 St, New York, NY 10032
Tel: 212-368-5900
E-mail: academy@artsandletters.org
Web Site: artsandletters.org/awards
Key Personnel
Exec Dir: Cody Upton
Established: 1979
For the best published 1st novel or collection of short stories of the preceding year. Candidates must be nominated by an Academy member.
Award: $5,000

George Markey Keating Memorial Scholarships
Book Industry Charitable Foundation (BINC)
3135 S State St, Suite 203, Ann Arbor, MI 48108
Toll Free Tel: 866-733-9064
E-mail: info@bincfoundation.org
Web Site: www.bincfoundation.org
Key Personnel
Exec Dir: Pamela French E-mail: pam@bincfoundation.org
Dir, Devt: Kathy Bartson E-mail: kathy@bincfoundation.org
Prog Mgr: Judey Kalchik E-mail: judey@bincfoundation.org; Ken White E-mail: ken@bincfoundation.org
Commun Coord: Erika Mantz E-mail: erika@bincfoundation.org
Devt Coord: Jennifer Rojas E-mail: jennifer@bincfoundation.org
Off Coord: Jane Regenstreif E-mail: jane@bincfoundation.org
Spec Projs Coord: Kate Weiss E-mail: kate@bincfoundation.org
Established: 2021
Scholarships are awarded to a bookseller from each of 3 regional associations, NAIBA, SIBA & NEIBA, for the purpose of professional development. See web site for application details.
Other Sponsor(s): The Friends of George Keating; New Atlantic Independent Booksellers Association (NAIBA); New England Independent Booksellers Association (NEIBA); Southern Independent Booksellers Alliance (SIBA)
Award: $250
Closing Date: April
Presented: June

Ezra Jack Keats Book Award
Ezra Jack Keats Foundation
450 14 St, Brooklyn, NY 11215-5702
E-mail: foundation@ezra-jack-keats.org
Web Site: www.ezra-jack-keats.org
Key Personnel
Exec Dir: Dr Deborah Pope
Awarded to an outstanding new writer & new illustrator to recognize & encourage emerging talent in the field of children's books.
Other Sponsor(s): de Gummond Children's Literature Collection, University of Southern Mississippi
Award: $3,000 & bronze medallion for each winner
Presented: Fay B Kaigler Children's Book Festival, University of Southern Mississippi, Hattiesburg, MS, April

Ezra Jack Keats/Kerlan Memorial Fellowship
Ezra Jack Keats Foundation
University of Minnesota, 113 Andersen Library, 222 21 Ave S, Minneapolis, MN 55455
Tel: 612-624-4576
E-mail: asc-clrc@umn.edu
Web Site: www.lib.umn.edu/clrc
Key Personnel
Curator, Kerlan Collection: Lisa Von Drasek
Awarded to a talented writer +/or illustrator of children's books who wish to use the Kerlan Collection to further his or her artistic development.
Award: $4,000
Closing Date: Jan 30

Joan Kelly Memorial Prize in Women's History
American Historical Association (AHA)

400 "A" St SE, Washington, DC 20003
Tel: 202-544-2422
E-mail: awards@historians.org
Web Site: www.historians.org/award-grant/joan-kelly-memorial-prize/
Established: 1984
Awarded for the book in women's history +/or feminist theory that best reflects the high intellectual & scholarly ideals exemplified by the life & work of Joan Kelly. Submissions shall be books in any chronological period, any geographical location, or in any area of feminist theory that incorporates an historical perspective. Books should demonstrate originality of research, creativity of insight, graceful stylistic presentation, analytical skills & a recognition of the important role of sex & gender in the historical process. The inter-relationship between women & the historical process should be addressed. Books with a 2024 copyright are eligible for the 2025 prize. Along with an application form, a copy of each entry must be received by each of the 5 committee members. All updated info on web site.
Award: $1,000
Closing Date: May 15, 2025
Presented: AHA Annual Meeting, Chicago, IL, Jan 2026

Randall Kenan Prize for Black LGBTQ Fiction
Lambda Literary
PO Box 20186, New York, NY 10014
Tel: 213-277-5755
E-mail: awards@lambdaliterary.org; admin@lambdaliterary.org
Web Site: www.lambdaliterary.org/awards/special-awards
Key Personnel
Awards Mgr: Brian Gentes
Award presented to honor a Black LGBTQ writer whose fiction explores themes of Black LGBTQ life, culture +/or history. To be eligible, the applicant must have written & published (self-published or traditionally published) at least 1 book of fiction & show promise in continuing to produce groundbreaking work. Applicants must submit a sample from an already published book of fiction of no more than 20 pages.
Other Sponsor(s): Cedric Brown; Darnell Moore; Dr L Lamar Wilson
Award: $3,000
Closing Date: Feb 15
Presented: June

The Joanne Scott Kennedy Memorial, see New Voices: The Joanne Scott Kennedy Memorial

Robert F Kennedy Book Awards
Robert F Kennedy Center for Justice & Human Rights
1300 19 St NW, Suite 750, Washington, DC 20036
Tel: 646-553-4750 *Fax:* 202-463-6606
E-mail: info@rfkhumanrights.org
Web Site: rfkhumanrights.org
Key Personnel
Contact: Jae Regala *E-mail:* regala@rfkhumanrights.org
Established: 1980
For a book of fiction or nonfiction that most faithfully & forcefully reflects Robert Kennedy's interests & concerns. Publishers or authors should mail 6 copies of the book published in the previous year. Submit entry form, press release, review, or descriptive letter & $75 entry fee through online submission portal. See web site for further details.
Award: $2,500 & bust of Robert F Kennedy
Closing Date: Feb 2
Presented: May

Kids' Book Choice Awards
Every Child a Reader/The Children's Book Council (CBC)
54 W 39 St, 14th fl, New York, NY 10018
E-mail: cbc.info@cbcbooks.org
Web Site: everychildareader.net/choice
Key Personnel
Assoc Exec Dir: Shaina Birkhead *E-mail:* shaina.birkhead@cbcbooks.org
Established: 2008
The only national book awards voted on only by kids & teens. Not an open application process. Awards given in 15 categories across 3 age ranges.
Presented: Dec

Coretta Scott King Book Awards
The American Library Association (ALA)
225 N Michigan Ave, Suite 1300, Chicago, IL 60601
SAN: 201-0062
Tel: 312-944-6780 *Toll Free Tel:* 800-545-2433
Fax: 312-440-9374
E-mail: diversity@ala.org
Web Site: www.ala.org/awardsgrants/coretta-scott-king-book-awards
Key Personnel
Coretta Scott King Book Awards Coord: Monica Chapman *Tel:* 800-545-2433 ext 4297 *E-mail:* mlchapman@ala.org
Established: 1970
Awarded to outstanding African-American authors & illustrators of books for children & young adults that demonstrate an appreciation of African-American culture & universal human values. Administered by the Ethnic Multicultural Information Exchange Round Table (EMIERT).
Other Sponsor(s): Black Caucus of the American Library Association (BCALA); DEMCO; Encyclopaedia Britannica; World Book Inc
Award: Bronze award seal & $1,000 to both author & illustrator
Closing Date: Dec 1
Presented: Coretta Scott King Awards Breakfast, ALA Annual Conference & Exhibition, June

Coretta Scott King - John Steptoe Award for New Talent
The American Library Association (ALA)
225 N Michigan Ave, Suite 1300, Chicago, IL 60601
SAN: 201-0062
Tel: 312-944-6780 *Toll Free Tel:* 800-545-2433 (ext 4294) *Fax:* 312-280-3256
E-mail: diversity@ala.org
Web Site: www.ala.org/awardsgrants
Key Personnel
Prog Offr, ODLOS: Amber Hayes *Tel:* 800-545-2433 ext 2140 *E-mail:* ahayes@ala.org
Coretta Scott King Book Awards Coord: Monica Chapman *Tel:* 800-545-2433 ext 4297 *E-mail:* mlchapman@ala.org
Awarded to affirm new talent & offer visibility to excellence in writing or illustration at the beginning of a career as a published book creator. Administered by the Ethnic & Multicultural Information Exchange Round Table (EMIERT).
Other Sponsor(s): DEMCO
Award: Plaque
Closing Date: Dec 1
Presented: Coretta Scott King Book Awards Breakfast, ALA Annual Conference & Exhibition, June

Coretta Scott King - Virginia Hamilton Award for Lifetime Achievement
The American Library Association (ALA)
225 N Michigan Ave, Suite 1300, Chicago, IL 60601
SAN: 201-0062
Toll Free Tel: 800-545-2433

E-mail: diversity@ala.org
Web Site: www.ala.org/emiert/virginia-hamilton-award-lifetime-achievement
Key Personnel
Prog Offr, ODLOS: Amber Hayes *Tel:* 800-545-2433 ext 2140 *E-mail:* ahayes@ala.org
Coretta Scott King Book Awards Coord: Monica Chapman *Tel:* 800-545-2433 ext 4297 *E-mail:* mlchapman@ala.org
Established: 2010
Award is presented biennially, in even-numbered years, to an African American author, illustrator or author/illustrator for a body of his or her published books for children +/or young adults & who has made a significant & lasting literary contribution.
In odd years, the award is presented to a practitioner for substantial contributions through active engagement with youth using award-winning African American literature for children +/or young adults, via implementation of reading & reading-related activities/programs. Administered by the Ethnic & Multicultural Information Exchange Round Table (EMIERT). See web site for specific selection criteria.
Award: Medal & $1,500
Closing Date: July 1
Presented: Coretta Scott King Book Awards Breakfast, ALA Annual Conference & Exhibition, June

Jack Temple Kirby Award
Southern Historical Association (SHA)
University of Georgia, Dept of History, Athens, GA 30602-1602
Tel: 706-542-8848
Web Site: thesha.org/kirby
Key Personnel
Secy/Treas: Dr Stephen Berry *E-mail:* berrys@thesha.org
Established: 2010
Awarded biennially, in odd-numbered years, to authors of journal articles in either southern agricultural or environmental history published during the previous 2 years. Submissions can be made by either the article authors or journal editors. Off-prints or articles should be submitted to Manager, Southern Historical Association.
Closing Date: June 1
Presented: Annual Meeting

Kirkus Prize
Kirkus Media LLC
1140 Broadway, Suite 802, New York, NY 10001
Web Site: www.kirkusreviews.com/prize
Key Personnel
Chief Mktg Offr: Sarah Kalina *E-mail:* skalina@kirkus.com
Awarded to authors of fiction, nonfiction & young readers' literature. Both traditionally published & self-published books reviewed by Kirkus that earn the Kirkus Star are eligible.
Award: $50,000 each category
Presented: Oct

Knight Science Journalism Fellowships
Massachusetts Institute of Technology-Knight Science Journalism Program
77 Massachusetts Ave, Cambridge, MA 02139
Tel: 617-452-3513
E-mail: knight-info@mit.edu
Web Site: ksj.mit.edu/fellowship
Key Personnel
Dir: Deborah Blum *Tel:* 617-258-8249 *E-mail:* dblum@mit.edu
Assoc Dir: Ashley Smart *Tel:* 617-253-3442 *E-mail:* asmart@mit.edu
Prog Admin: Myles Crowley *E-mail:* mcrowley@mit.edu
Program recognizes journalists from around the world who demonstrate a high level of professional excellence & accomplishment as

well as a long-term commitment to their craft. Academic-year fellowships are offered to 10 science journalists. Applicants must be full-time journalists, on staff or freelance, with at least 3 consecutive years of experience covering science, health, technology & environmental reporting. They can be reporters, writers, editors, producers, illustrators, filmmakers or photojournalists. See web site for items to be included with application.
Award: $85,000 stipend, relocation allowance & basic health insurance for each fellow & their family
Closing Date: Mid-Jan
Presented: April

Knightville Poetry Contest
The New Guard
PO Box 472, Brunswick, ME 04011
E-mail: info@newguardreview.com; editors@writershotel.com
Web Site: www.newguardreview.com
Key Personnel
Founding Ed & Publr: Shanna McNair
Established: 2009
Up to 3 poems per entry. Up to 150 lines per poem. Submit all 3 poems in a single document. Online submissions only. Entry fee: $20.
Award: $1,500 & publication in The New Guard
Closing Date: Aug 31

Kobo Emerging Writer Prize
Rakuten Kobo Inc
135 Liberty St, Suite 101, Toronto, ON M6K 1A7, Canada
E-mail: pr@kobo.com
Web Site: www.kobo.com/emergingwriterprize
Key Personnel
Sr Mgr, PR: Sinead McElhinney Tel: 416-977-8737 ext 3382 E-mail: sinead.mcelhinney@rakuten.com
Established: 2014
Award with the goal of kick-starting the careers of debut Canadian authors. Three categories: Nonfiction, literary fiction & genre fiction.
Award: $10,000; each winning author receives promotional, marketing & communications support throughout the award year
Closing Date: March
Presented: June

Mary Lynn Kotz Award, see Art In Literature: The Mary Lynn Kotz Award

Katherine Singer Kovacs Prize
Modern Language Association (MLA)
85 Broad St, New York, NY 10004
SAN: 202-6422
Tel: 646-576-5141; 646-576-5000
E-mail: awards@mla.org
Web Site: www.mla.org
Key Personnel
Coord, Book Prizes: Annie M Reiser
 E-mail: areiser@mla.org
Established: 1990
Prize for an outstanding book published in 2024 in English or Spanish in the field of Latin American & Spanish literatures & cultures. Authors need not be members of MLA. For consideration, submit 6 print copies & electronic access.
Award: Cash award & certificate
Closing Date: May 1, 2025
Presented: MLA Annual Convention, Toronto, ON, CN, Jan 2026

The Kraken Book Prize for Middle-Grade Fiction
Fitzroy Books
Imprint of Regal House Publishing
c/o Regal House Publishing, 806 Oberlin Rd, No 12094, Raleigh, NC 27605
E-mail: info@regalhousepublishing.com
Web Site: regalhousepublishing.com/the-kraken-book-award/
Key Personnel
Founder, Publr & Ed-in-Chief: Jaynie Royal
Mng Ed: Pam Van Dyk
Ed: Elizabeth Lowenstein
Established: 2019
Recognizing finely crafted works written for middle grade readers. Submissions through Submittable or by post. Entry fee $25. Fax or e-mail submissions not accepted. See web site for submission guidelines. Five finalists announced May 30.
Award: Publication & $500 honorarium
Closing Date: March 30 (postmark)
Presented: June 30

Michael Kraus Research Grants in American Colonial History
American Historical Association (AHA)
400 "A" St SE, Washington, DC 20003
Tel: 202-544-2422
E-mail: awards@historians.org
Web Site: www.historians.org/award-grant/michael-kraus-research-grants-in-american-colonial-history/
Established: 1994
Grant given to a member of the association to recognize the most deserving proposal relating to works in progress on a research project in American colonial history, with particular reference to the intercultural aspects of American & European relations. The grants are intended to further research in progress & may be used for travel to a library or archive, for microfilms, photographs, or photocopying. Preference will be given to those with specific research needs, such as the completion of a project or completion of a discrete segment thereof. Only members of the association are eligible to apply. See web site for additional submission guidelines & eligibility. Applicants will be notified of the committee's decision by e-mail in mid-May.
Award: Individual grants up to $800
Closing Date: Feb 15
Presented: June

The Robert Kroetsch City of Edmonton Book Prize
Writers' Guild of Alberta
11759 Groat Rd NW, Edmonton, AB T5M 3K6, Canada
Tel: 780-422-8174 Toll Free Tel: 800-665-5354 (AB only)
E-mail: mail@writersguild.ab.ca
Web Site: writersguild.ca
Key Personnel
Exec Dir: Giorgia Severini E-mail: gseverini@writersguild.ab.ca
Communs & Partnerships Coord: Ellen Kartz
 E-mail: ellen.kartz@writersguild.ab.ca
Memb Servs Coord: Mike Maguire
Prog & Opers Coord: Ashley Mann
 E-mail: ashley.mann@writersguild.ab.ca
Progs & Events Coord: Jason Norman
 E-mail: jason.norman@writersguild.ab.ca
Proj Asst: Sadie MacGillivray E-mail: sadie.macgillivray@writersguild.ab.ca
Established: 1995
Entries must deal with some aspect of the City of Edmonton: history, geography, current affairs, its arts or its people, or be written by an Edmonton author.
Other Sponsor(s): Audreys Books; City of Edmonton; Edmonton Arts Council
Award: $10,000 & leather-bound copy of book
Closing Date: Dec 31
Presented: Mayor's Evening for the Arts, Spring

Branch Office(s)
223 12 Ave SW, No 204, Calgary, AB T2R 0G9, Canada, Prog & Conference Coord: Dorothy Bentley Tel: 403-875-8058 E-mail: dorothy.bentley@writersguild.ab.ca

KSJ Fellowship Program, see Knight Science Journalism Fellowships

KTA Journalism & Mass Communication Research Award, see Frank Luther Mott-KTA Journalism & Mass Communication Research Award

Kumu Kahua/UHM Theatre & Dance Department Playwriting Contest
Kumu Kahua/UHM Theatre & Dance Department
46 Merchant St, Honolulu, HI 96813
Tel: 808-536-4441 (box off); 808-536-4222 (off admin) Fax: 808-536-4226
E-mail: officemanager@kumukahua.org
Web Site: www.kumukahua.org
Key Personnel
Artistic Dir: Harry L Wong, III
Hawaii Prize: Open to residents of Hawaii & non-residents; full-length (50 pages or more); play must be set in Hawaii +/or deal with the Hawaii experience.
Pacific Rim Prize: Open to residents of Hawaii & non-residents; full-length (50 pages or more); play must be set in +/or dealing with the Pacific Islands, Pacific Rim, or the Pacific/Asian-American experience.
Resident Prize: Only open to residents of Hawaii; full-length (50 pages or more) or one-acts; play can be on any topic.
Award: $600 (Hawaii Prize), $450 (Pacific Rim Prize), $250 (Resident Prize)
Closing Date: Early Jan
Presented: May

W Kaye Lamb Scholarships
British Columbia Historical Federation
PO Box 448, Fort Langley, BC V1M 2R7, Canada
E-mail: info@bchistory.ca
Web Site: www.bchistory.ca/awards/scholarships
Key Personnel
Recognition Chair: Shannon Bettles
 E-mail: shannon@bchistory.ca
Two scholarships offered for essays written by students in British Columbia colleges or universities on a topic relating to British Columbia history.
Award: $750 (1st or 2nd yr student), $1,000 (3rd or 4th yr student)
Closing Date: March 1
Presented: BCHF Annual Conference Awards Banquet, May/June

Lambda Literary Awards (Lammys)
Lambda Literary
PO Box 20186, New York, NY 10014
Tel: 213-277-5755
E-mail: awards@lambdaliterary.org; admin@lambdaliterary.org
Web Site: www.lambdaliterary.org
Key Personnel
Awards Mgr: Brian Gentes
Established: 1989
Award recognizing excellence in LGBTQ literature. Entry fee required. Guidelines on the web site.
Award: Trophy
Closing Date: Mid-Nov
Presented: June

Lammys, see Lambda Literary Awards (Lammys)

Gerald Lampert Memorial Award
The League of Canadian Poets

2 Carlton St, Suite 1519, Toronto, ON M5B 1J3, Canada
Tel: 416-504-1657
E-mail: info@poets.ca; admin@poets.ca
Web Site: poets.ca/awards/lampert
Key Personnel
Exec Dir: Lesley Fletcher *E-mail:* lesley@poets.ca
Artistic Programming Dir: Nic Brewer
 E-mail: nicole@poets.ca
Admin & Communs Coord: Caitlin Lapena
 E-mail: caitlin@poets.ca
Award intended to recognize the work of a Canadian writer early in his or her career. Awarded for a first book of poetry published in the preceding year. Authors must be Canadian citizens or permanent residents. Submitted titles must be at least 48 pages in length & have 1 author (translators are not eligible). Chapbooks & self-published books are not eligible. Submission fee: $25 per title. See web site for full eligibility guidelines.
Award: $2,000
Closing Date: Nov 13
Presented: Annual Conference, May

David J Langum Sr Prize in American Historical Fiction
The Langum Foundation
c/o David J Langum Sr, 2809 Berkeley Dr, Birmingham, AL 35242
Web Site: langumfoundation.org/about-prizes/american-historical-fiction
Key Personnel
Dir: David J Langum, Sr *E-mail:* djlangum@samford.edu
Established: 2001
Awarded to a book published by any non-subsidy press for American historical fiction set in the colonial or national periods that is both excellent fiction & excellent history.
Award: $1,000
Closing Date: Dec 1
Presented: March

David J Langum Sr Prize in American Legal History or Biography
The Langum Foundation
c/o William G Ross, Cumberland School of Law, 800 Lakeshore Dr, Birmingham, AL 35229
Web Site: langumfoundation.org/about-prizes/american-legal-history-or-biography
Key Personnel
Chmn, Selection Comm: William G Ross
 E-mail: wgross@samford.edu
Established: 2001
Awarded for a book in the area of American legal history or American legal biography that is accessible to the educated general public, rooted in sound scholarship & with themes that touch upon matters of general concern to the American public, past or present. Send 3 copies to the committee chairman.
Award: $1,000
Closing Date: Dec 1
Presented: March

Lannan Literary Awards & Fellowships
Lannan Foundation
313 Read St, Santa Fe, NM 87501-2628
Tel: 505-986-8160
E-mail: info@lannan.org
Web Site: lannan.org
Key Personnel
Pres & Treas: Lawrence P Lannan, Jr
EVP, Secy & Dir, Admin: Frank C Lawler
Prog Dir, Literary & Residency Progs: Martha Jessup
Established: 1989
The awards recognize writers who have made significant contributions to English language literature. The fellowships recognize writers of distinctive literary merit who demonstrate potential for continued outstanding work. Award categories are poetry, fiction, nonfiction, lifetime & notable book. Candidates selected by an anonymous nomination process. Applications & letters of inquiry are not accepted.

Latino Books Into Movies Awards
Empowering Latino Futures
624 Hillcrest Lane, Fallbrook, CA 92028
Tel: 760 645-3455 (submission info); 760-689-2317
E-mail: awards@empoweringlatinofutures.org
Web Site: www.latinobookawards.org
Key Personnel
Awards Chair: Kirk Whisler *Tel:* 760-579-1696
 E-mail: kirk@whisler.com
Established: 2010
Accept books, movie screenplays, plays & television scripts. Send 5 copies of each book or script being nominated. In the movie & television categories, the author or co-author of the book or screenplay must be Latino, Latin American, or Spanish. Categories under Latino themes by non-Latino authors or screenwriters are open only to non-Latino writers, but must be Latino themed. Books & screenplays must be in English language. If in Spanish, must be accompanied by a PDF of English translation. Entry fee: $100 per each individual entry per category.
Award: Winning books distributed to pertinent motion picture studios, television networks, producers & agents, depending on genre

Latner Griffin Writers' Trust Poetry Prize
The Writers' Trust of Canada
600-460 Richmond St W, Toronto, ON M5V 1Y1, Canada
Tel: 416-504-8222 *Toll Free Tel:* 877-906-6548
Fax: 416-504-9090
E-mail: info@writerstrust.com
Web Site: www.writerstrust.com/awards/latner-writers-trust-poetry-prize
Key Personnel
Exec Dir: Charlie Foran *Tel:* 416-504-8222 ext 244 *E-mail:* cforan@writerstrust.com
Mgr, Author Progs: Devon Jackson *Tel:* 416-504-8222 ext 248 *E-mail:* djackson@writerstrust.com
Established: 2014
Awarded to a Canadian poet in recognition of a remarkable body of work & in hope of future contributions to Canadian poetry. All eligible poets in mid-career are considered. No age restrictions apply & no submission process. Jury selection.
Other Sponsor(s): Latner Family Foundation
Award: $25,000
Presented: The Writers' Trust Awards, Toronto, ON, CN, Nov

James Laughlin Award
The Academy of American Poets Inc
75 Maiden Lane, Suite 901, New York, NY 10038
Tel: 212-274-0343
E-mail: awards@poets.org
Web Site: poets.org/academy-american-poets/prizes/james-laughlin-award
Key Personnel
Pres & Exec Dir: Ricardo Alberto Maldonado
VP, Digital Engagement & Content: Jeff Gleaves
Ad & Mktg Dir: Michelle Campagna
Dir, Donor Rel: Molly Walsh
Dir, Progs: Nikay Paredes
Established: 1954
Awarded to recognize & support a second book of poetry forthcoming in the next calendar year. Entries must be at least 48 pages & submitted in ms form (or page proofs). Publishers must send 4 copies of each ms. Submissions are welcome from small presses, university presses & trade publishers that have previously published at least 4 books of poetry. Translations & new editions of previously published books are not eligible.
Award: $5,000, all-expenses-paid weeklong residency at The Betsy Hotel, Miami Beach, FL & approximately 1,000 copies of winning book distributed to Academy members
Closing Date: May 15
Presented: Sept

Lawrence Foundation Prize
Michigan Quarterly Review
University of Michigan, 3277 Angell Hall, 435 S State St, Ann Arbor, MI 48109-1003
Tel: 734-764-9265
E-mail: mqr@umich.edu
Web Site: sites.lsa.umich.edu/mqr/about-us/prizes
Established: 1978
Awarded to the best work of fiction published in MQR each year. No deadline or special application process.
Other Sponsor(s): Leonard S Bernstein; University of Michigan Alumnus
Award: $2,000

The Ursula K Le Guin Prize for Fiction
The Ursula K Le Guin Foundation
9450 SW Gemini Dr, PMB 51842, Beaverton, OR 97008-7105
E-mail: estateofukl@gmail.com
Web Site: www.ursulakleguin.com/prize-overview
Key Personnel
Bd Memb: Elisabeth Le Guin; India Downes-Le Guin; Theo Downes-Le Guin
Awarded to a writer for a single work of imaginative fiction that reflects the concepts & ideas that were central to Ursula's own work, including but not limited to: hope, equity, freedom; non-violence & alternatives to conflict; a holistic view of humanity's place in the natural world. Nominations are open to all. The book must be a book-length work of imaginative fiction written by a single author, available in the US in English or in translation to English & published in the specific window for each year's prize.
Award: $25,000 (in the case of a translated work, the cash prize will be equally divided between author & translator)

Stephen Leacock Memorial Medal for Humour
The Leacock Associates
PO Box 854, Orillia, ON L3V 6K8, Canada
Tel: 705-326-9286
E-mail: info@leacock.ca
Web Site: www.leacock.ca
Key Personnel
Chair, Award Comm: Bette Walker
 E-mail: bettewalkerca@gmail.com
Pres: Mike Hill *E-mail:* mghill@bell.net
Secy: Anne Kallin *E-mail:* fkallin@golden.net
Established: 1946
Humorous writing by Canadian authors. All entries must have been published in the year prior to the year the award is given. Submit 8 copies of each book along with $200 fee & authors bio. No ebooks accepted. Books are non-returnable.
Other Sponsor(s): Dunkley Charitable Foundation
Award: $15,000 Dunkley Charitable Foundation cash award & silver medal. Each of the 2 finalists receive $3,000
Closing Date: Dec 31
Presented: Gala Award Dinner, 1st weekend in June

Leapfrog Global Fiction Prize
Leapfrog Press Inc
PO Box 505, Fredonia, NY 14063
E-mail: leapfrog@leapfrogpress.com

Web Site: leapfrogpress.com/the-leapfrog-global-fiction-prize-contest
Key Personnel
Pres & Publr: Tobias Steed
Mng Ed: Rebecca Cuthbert
Edit & Proj Mgmt: Shannon Clinton-Copeland
Global fiction contest in partnership with Can of Worms Press (UK). Two award categories: Adult novels, novelas & short story collections; young adult & middle grade novels. Entries are accepted from any country as long as ms is in English. Minimum word count: 22,000. Entry fee required. See leapfrogpress.submittable.com/submit.
Other Sponsor(s): Can of Worms Press
Award: Publication contract offer from Leapfrog Press & Can of Worms Press, with an advance payment against royalties, plus the finalist awards (1st prize); Finalists: $150 & critiques of ms from contest judges, permanent listing on Leap Frog Press & Can of Worms web sites as contest finalist; Semi-finalist receives choice of free Leapfrog or Can of Worms book & permanent listing on web sites; Honorable Mention receives listing on web sites
Closing Date: Early May

Harper Lee Prize for Legal Fiction
The University of Alabama School of Law
101 Paul Bryant Dr, Tuscaloosa, AL 35487
Tel: 205-348-5195
Web Site: www.harperleeprize.com
Key Personnel
Contact: Monique Fields E-mail: mfields@law.ua.edu
Established: 2011
Awarded to a published work of fiction that best illuminates the role of lawyers in society & their power to effect change.
Other Sponsor(s): ABA Journal
Closing Date: March 31
Presented: Prize Ceremony, Washington, DC, Sept in conjunction with the National Book Festival

Legacy Award
New Atlantic Independent Booksellers Association (NAIBA)
2667 Hyacinth St, Westbury, NY 11590
Tel: 516-333-0681
E-mail: kit@naiba.com
Web Site: www.naiba.com/page/LegacyAward
Key Personnel
Exec Dir: Eileen Dengler E-mail: eileen@naiba.com
Established: 2004
To recognize those individuals whose body of work contributed significantly to the realm of American arts & letters. Candidates must either reside in the region served by NAIBA, or have created work that reflects the character of the geographical area so represented & the spirit of the independent bookselling community found therin.
Presented: NAIBA Fall Conference, Oct

Waldo G Leland Prize for Reference Tools
American Historical Association (AHA)
400 "A" St SE, Washington, DC 20003
Tel: 202-544-2422
E-mail: awards@historians.org
Web Site: www.historians.org/award-grant/waldo-g-leland-prize/
Established: 1981
Award offered every 5 years for the most outstanding reference tool in the field of history. Reference tool encompasses bibliographies, indexes, encyclopedias & other scholarly apparatus. Books with a copyright between 2021 & 2025 will be eligible for the prize in 2026. Applicant must send a copy of their book to each prize committee member posted on our web site as the prize deadline approaches. All updated info on web site.
Closing Date: May 15, 2026
Presented: AHA Annual Meeting, Jan 2027

Vincent Lemieux Prize
Canadian Political Science Association (CPSA)
260 Dalhousie St, Suite 204, Ottawa, ON K1N 7E4, Canada
Tel: 613-562-1202 Fax: 613-241-0019
E-mail: cpsa-acsp@cpsa-acsp.ca; cpsaprizes@cpsa-acsp.ca
Web Site: www.cpsa-acsp.ca
Key Personnel
Exec Dir: Silvina Danesi
Admin: C Ngako Woktcheu
Established: 1997
A biennial prize, awarded in odd-numbered years, to the author of the best PhD thesis in any subfield of political science submitted at a Canadian University, written in English or French, judged eminently worthy of publication in the form of a book or articles. A thesis is eligible only after nomination by the unit in which it was defended. For the 2025 award, a thesis must have been defended in 2023 or 2024.
Other Sponsor(s): Les Presses de l'Universite Laval
Award: $1,000 & commemorative certificate
Presented: CPSA Annual Conference

John Leonard Prize
National Book Critics Circle (NBCC)
c/o Jacob M Appel, Icahn School of Medicine at Mount Sinai, One Gustave L Levy Place, New York, NY 10029
E-mail: info@bookcritics.org
Web Site: www.bookcritics.org/awards/leonard-prize
Key Personnel
Pres: Heather Scott Partington E-mail: hsp@bookcritics.org
Secy: Colette Bancroft E-mail: bancroft.colette72@gmail.com
Treas: Jacob M Appel E-mail: jacobmappel@gmail.com
VP, Awards: Keetje Kuipers E-mail: keetje@poetrynw.org
VP, Events: Jane Ciabattari E-mail: janeciab@gmail.com
Established: 2013
Awarded for the best first book in any genre. Prize is decided by NBCC membership.
Presented: NBCC Awards Ceremony, March

Leopold-Hidy Award
The Forest History Society Inc
2925 Academy Rd, Durham, NC 27705
Tel: 919-682-9319 Fax: 919-682-2349
Web Site: foresthistory.org/awards-fellowships/leopold-hidy-award
Key Personnel
Admin Asst: Andrea Anderson E-mail: andrea.anderson@foresthistory.org
Established: 2001
Awarded to recognize superior scholarship in the quarterly journal Environmental History, co-published with the American Society for Environmental History.
Other Sponsor(s): American Society for Environmental History

Richard W Leopold Prize
The Organization of American Historians (OAH)
112 N Bryan Ave, Bloomington, IN 47408-4141
Tel: 812-855-7311
E-mail: oah@oah.org
Web Site: www.oah.org/awards
Key Personnel
Exec Dir: Beth English Tel: 812-855-9836 E-mail: benglish@oah.org
Dir, Communs & Mktg: Kym Robinson Tel: 812-855-5430 E-mail: kymarobi@oah.org
Awarded biennially, in even-numbered years, to the author or editor of the best book on foreign policy, military affairs, historical activities of the federal government, documentary histories, or biography written by a US government historian or federal contract historian. Each entry must be published during the 2-year period January 1, 2024-December 31, 2025. The winner must have been employed as a full-time historian or federal contract historian with the US government for a minimum of 5 years prior to the submission. If the author has accepted an academic position, retired, or otherwise left federal service, the book must have been published within 2 years of their separation date. Verification of current or past employment with the US government (in the form of a letter or e-mail sent to the publisher from the office that employs or has employed the author) must be included with each entry. One copy of each entry must be mailed directly to the committee members listed on the web site.
Closing Date: Oct 1, 2025 (postmarked)
Presented: OAH Conference on American History, Philadelphia, PA, April 2026

Fenia & Yaakov Leviant Memorial Prize in Yiddish Studies
Modern Language Association (MLA)
85 Broad St, New York, NY 10004
SAN: 202-6422
Tel: 646-576-5141; 646-576-5000
E-mail: awards@mla.org
Web Site: www.mla.org
Key Personnel
Coord, Book Prizes: Annie M Reiser E-mail: areiser@mla.org
Established: 2000
Awarded alternately to an outstanding scholarly or translation work in the field of Yiddish. The 2026 prize will be awarded to a scholarly work in English published between 2022 & 2025. Authors need not be members of the MLA. For consideration, submit 4 print copies & electronic access.
Award: Cash award & certificate
Closing Date: May 1, 2026
Presented: MLA Annual Convention, New Orleans, LA, Jan 2027

Harry Levin Prize
American Comparative Literature Association (ACLA)
323 E Wacker Dr, No 642, Chicago, IL 60601
Tel: 312-600-8072
E-mail: info@acla.org
Web Site: www.acla.org/prize-awards/harry-levin-prize
Established: 1968
Prize recognizing an outstanding first book in the discipline of comparative literature published during the previous 2 calendar years as the author's first book-length publication. See web site for nomination process.
Award: Complimentary registration for the annual meeting, as well as hotel & airfare accommodations (not including food)
Closing Date: Nov 15
Presented: ACLA Annual Meeting

Kay W Levin Award for Short Nonfiction
Council for Wisconsin Writers (CWW)
c/o 210 N Main St, No 204, Cedar Grove, WI 53013
E-mail: wiswriters@gmail.com
Web Site: wiswriters.org/awards
Key Personnel
Contest Chair: Sylvia Cavanaugh E-mail: bgirl4shadow@gmail.com
Established: 1967

Awarded for the best piece of short nonfiction published by a Wisconsin-based author in the contest year. Entry fee: $25 nonmembs.
Award: $500 & 1-week residency at Shake Rag Alley Center for the Arts
Closing Date: Jan 31
Presented: CWW Annual Award Ceremony & Banquet, May

Lawrence W Levine Award
The Organization of American Historians (OAH)
112 N Bryan Ave, Bloomington, IN 47408-4141
Tel: 812-855-7311
E-mail: oah@oah.org
Web Site: www.oah.org/awards
Key Personnel
Exec Dir: Beth English *Tel:* 812-855-9836
 E-mail: benglish@oah.org
Dir, Communs & Mktg: Kym Robinson *Tel:* 812-855-5430 *E-mail:* kymarobi@oah.org
Awarded to the author of the best book in American cultural history. Each entry must be published during the calendar year preceding that in which the award is given. One copy of each entry must be mailed directly to the committee members listed on the web site.
Closing Date: Oct 1 (postmarked)
Presented: OAH Conference on American History, Spring

Levinson Prize
Poetry Magazine
61 W Superior St, Chicago, IL 60654
Tel: 312-787-7070
Web Site: www.poetryfoundation.org/poetrymagazine/prizes
Key Personnel
Assoc Ed: Holly Amos *E-mail:* hamos@poetrymagazine.org
Established: 1914
For poetry published during the preceding year in *Poetry* magazine. No application necessary.
Award: $500
Presented: Announced in Nov issue

Levis Reading Prize
Virginia Commonwealth University, Dept of English
PO Box 842005, Richmond, VA 23284-2005
Tel: 804-828-1331
E-mail: levis@vcu.edu
Web Site: english.vcu.edu/mfa/levis-reading-prize
Established: 1997
In memory of Larry Levis, awarded for best first or second book of poetry (not for self-published or chapbooks).
Award: $5,000
Closing Date: Feb 1
Presented: VCU Cabell Library, Richmond, VA, Sept/Oct

Lewis Memorial Lifetime Achievement Award
PRINTING United Alliance
10015 Main St, Fairfax, VA 22031
Tel: 703-385-1335 *Toll Free Tel:* 888-385-3588
 Fax: 703-273-0456
E-mail: assist@printing.org; info@printing.org
Web Site: www.printing.org/programs/awards/lewis-memorial-lifetime-achievement-award
Key Personnel
CEO: Ford Bowers *E-mail:* fbowers@printing.org
Established: 1950
Award honors business leaders who have excelled at shaping the business of printed communications. See web site for eligibility requirements & nomination information.
Branch Office(s)
1325 "G" St NW, Suite 500, Washington, DC 20005 *Tel:* 202-627-6925 ext 504
2000 Corporate Dr, Suite 205, Wexford, PA 15090 *Tel:* 412-741-6860 *Toll Free Tel:* 800-910-4283 *Fax:* 412-741-2311

Liberty Legacy Foundation Award
The Organization of American Historians (OAH)
112 N Bryan Ave, Bloomington, IN 47408-4141
Tel: 812-855-7311
E-mail: oah@oah.org
Web Site: www.oah.org/awards
Key Personnel
Exec Dir: Beth English *Tel:* 812-855-9836
 E-mail: benglish@oah.org
Dir, Communs & Mktg: Kym Robinson *Tel:* 812-855-5430 *E-mail:* kymarobi@oah.org
Awarded to the author of the best book by a historian on the civil rights struggle from the beginnings of the nation to the present. Each entry must be published during the calendar year preceding that in which the award is given. One copy of each entry must be mailed directly to the committee members listed on the web site.
Closing Date: Oct 1 (postmarked)
Presented: OAH Conference on American History, Spring

Michael J Libow Youth Theatre Award, see BHTG - Michael J Libow Youth Theatre Award

Library of Congress Literacy Awards
Library of Congress
101 Independence Ave SE, Washington, DC 20540-1400
Tel: 202-707-5221 (Center for the Book)
 Fax: 202-707-0269
Web Site: www.read.gov/literacyawards
Established: 2013
Awards are given to 3 organizations that have made outstanding contributions to increasing literacy in the US or abroad.
Award: Rubenstein Prize $150,000, American Prize $50,000, International Prize $50,000
Presented: Library of Congress National Book Festival

Library of Congress Prize for American Fiction
Library of Congress
101 Independence Ave SE, Washington, DC 20540-1400
Tel: 202-707-5221 (Center for the Book)
 Fax: 202-707-0269
Web Site: www.loc.gov
Key Personnel
Communs Offr: Guy Lamolinara
Prog Asst: Diziree Amaiz
Established: 2013
Award to honor an American literary writer whose body of work is distinguished not only for its mastery of the art but for its originality of thought & imagination. The award seeks to commend strong, unique, enduring voices that, throughout long, consistently accomplished careers, have told us something about the American experience.
Presented: Library of Congress National Book Festival

Library of Virginia Literary Awards
Library of Virginia
800 E Broad St, Richmond, VA 23219
Tel: 804-692-3535
Web Site: www.lva.virginia.gov/public/litawards/
Key Personnel
Exec Asst: Taylor Melton *E-mail:* taylor.melton@lva.virginia.gov
Established: 1997
Awarded to Virginia authors in the categories of fiction & poetry & to nonfiction authors for works about a Virginia subject. Books must have been published & distributed during the previous calendar year. The following types of books are not eligible: reference works, anthologies, documentary editions, essay & short story collections, children's & juvenile literature, photographic books, self-help books & how-to books. Finalists in each category notified by August 1.
Closing Date: March 1
Presented: Oct

The Lieutenant-Governor's Awards for High Achievement in the Arts
New Brunswick Arts Board (Conseil des arts du Nouveau-Brunswick)
225 King St, Suite 201, Fredericton, NB E3B 1E1, Canada
Tel: 506-444-4444 *Toll Free Tel:* 866-460-ARTS (460-2787) *Fax:* 506-444-5543
E-mail: prog@artsnb.ca
Web Site: www.artsnb.ca
Key Personnel
Exec Dir: Joss Richer *Tel:* 506-478-4610
 E-mail: direct@artsnb.ca
Prog Offr: Sarah Jonathan Parker *Tel:* 506-440-0037
Opers Mgr: Tilly Jackson *Tel:* 506-478-4422
 E-mail: tjackson@artsnb.ca
Established: 1989
Awarded biennially, in odd-numbered years, to recognize the outstanding contribution of New Brunswick artists. Three categories: Visual arts; performing arts; literary arts (including literary translation, literary performance, spoken word & storytelling). Awards in literary arts alternate between French & English.
Award: $20,000
Closing Date: June 15
Presented: Fredericton, NB, CN

Lighthouse Poetry Series
Cleveland State University Poetry Center
Rhodes Tower, Rm 1841, 2121 Euclid Ave, Cleveland, OH 44115
Tel: 216-687-3986
E-mail: poetrycenter@csuohio.edu
Web Site: www.csupoetrycenter.com/lighthouse-poetry-series; www.csupoetrycenter.com
Key Personnel
Dir: Caryl Pagel *E-mail:* c.pagel@csuohio.edu
Assoc Dir: Hilary Plum *E-mail:* h.plum@csuohio.edu
Open to poets with any history of publication. Translations are not eligible. Mss should be 55 pages minimum, 150 pages maximum. No biographical information should be included in your submission & your name should not appear in the ms. You may include an acknowledgements page that lists previously published poems. Multiple submissions are welcome & simultaneous submissions are acceptable (please inform us immediately if the ms is accepted elsewhere). Submit ms via Submittable. Reading fee: $25.
Award: $1,000, publication & standard royalty contract
Closing Date: March 31 (digital entry only)
Presented: Late Summer/Early Fall

Ruth Lilly & Dorothy Sargent Rosenberg Poetry Fellowships
Poetry Foundation
61 W Superior St, Chicago, IL 60654
Tel: 312-787-7070 *Fax:* 312-787-6650
E-mail: info@poetryfoundation.org; media@poetryfoundation.org
Web Site: www.poetryfoundation.org
Established: 1989
Awarded to young US poets to encourage the further study & writing of poetry. Five fellowships awarded.
Award: $25,800 each
Presented: Oct

AWARDS, PRIZE CONTESTS, FELLOWSHIPS & GRANTS

Ruth Lilly Poetry Prize
Poetry Foundation
61 W Superior St, Chicago, IL 60654
Tel: 312-787-7070 *Fax:* 312-787-6650
E-mail: editors@poetrymagazine.org
Web Site: poetrymagazine.org
Established: 1986
Awarded to a living US poet to recognize extraordinary artistic accomplishment.
Award: $100,000
Presented: Oct

Abraham Lincoln Institute Book Award
Abraham Lincoln Institute Inc
c/o ALI Treasurer, 4158 Vernoy Hills Rd, Fairfax, VA 22030
Web Site: www.lincoln-institute.org
Key Personnel
Chpn: Michelle A Krowl
Pres: Edna Greene Medford, PhD
VP: John M Barr
Secy: Clark Evans
Treasurer: David Keat
Established: 1998
Given for the previous year's most noteworthy book on the subject of Abraham Lincoln. Prize committee members must each receive 1 copy of the nominated book, accompanied by a brief letter stating its merits.
Award: $1,000
Closing Date: Nov 1
Presented: ALI Symposium, Ford's Theatre, Washington, DC, March

Joseph W Lippincott Award
The American Library Association (ALA)
225 N Michigan Ave, Suite 1300, Chicago, IL 60601
SAN: 201-0062
Tel: 312-280-3247 *Toll Free Tel:* 800-545-2433 (ext 3247) *Fax:* 312-944-3897
E-mail: awards@ala.org
Web Site: www.ala.org
Key Personnel
Prog Offr: Cheryl M Malden *E-mail:* cmalden@ala.org
Established: 1938
Presented to a librarian for distinguished service to the profession of librarianship, such service to include outstanding participation in the activities of professional library association, notable published professional writing, or other significant activity on behalf of the profession & its aims.
Other Sponsor(s): Joseph W Lippincott III
Award: $1,500 & 24 karat gold-framed citation
Closing Date: Feb 1
Presented: ALA Annual Conference & Exhibition, June

Literature Fellowship
Idaho Commission on the Arts
9543 W Emerald St, Suite 204, Boise, ID 83704
Tel: 208-334-2119
E-mail: info@arts.idaho.gov
Web Site: arts.idaho.gov/grants/fellowships
Key Personnel
Lit Dir: Jocelyn Robertson *Tel:* 208-334-2119 ext 108 *E-mail:* jocelyn.robertson@arts.idaho.gov
Three fellowships awarded biennially, in odd-numbered years, for literary excellence. Applicant must be an Idaho resident for at least 1 year.
Award: $5,000
Closing Date: Jan
Presented: July

Literature for Children Awards
Prince Edward Island Writers' Guild
81 Prince St, Charlottetown, PE C1A 4R3, Canada
E-mail: peiliteraryawards@gmail.com
Web Site: www.peiwritersguild.com
Submissions must be a story written for children (maximum 5,000 words). Illustrations may be submitted with the story but are not necessary. Work must be original & unpublished. Entry fee: $25 per submission. Prince Edward Island residents only. See web site for complete entry requirements.
Award: Cash prizes for 1st, 2nd & 3rd place
Closing Date: Changes annually (see web site)
Presented: Island Literary Awards Gala, Spring

Jean Little First Novel Award
The Canadian Children's Book Centre
425 Adelaide St W, Suite 200, Toronto, ON M5V 3C1, Canada
Tel: 416-975-0010
E-mail: info@bookcentre.ca
Web Site: www.bookcentre.ca
Key Personnel
Exec Dir: Sarah Sahagian
Lib Coord: Meghan Howe *E-mail:* meghan@bookcentre.ca
Established: 2021
Awarded to recognize the achievements of a first-time Canadian children's middle-grade novelist.
Award: $5,000 cash
Closing Date: Mid-Dec

Littleton-Griswold Prize in American Law & Society
American Historical Association (AHA)
400 "A" St SE, Washington, DC 20003
Tel: 202-544-2422
E-mail: awards@historians.org
Web Site: www.historians.org/award-grant/littleton-griswold-prize/
Established: 1985
Award for the best book in any subject on the history of American law & society. Only books of high scholarly & literary merit with a 2024 copyright are eligible for the 2025 prize. Along with an application form, applicants must mail a copy of their book to each prize committee member posted on our web site as the prize deadline approaches. All updated info on web site.
Award: $1,000
Closing Date: May 15, 2025
Presented: AHA Annual Meeting, Chicago, IL, Jan 2026

Littleton-Griswold Research Grant for Research in US Legal History
American Historical Association (AHA)
400 "A" St SE, Washington, DC 20003
Tel: 202-544-2422
E-mail: awards@historians.org
Web Site: www.historians.org/award-grant/littleton-griswold-research-grants-in-us-legal-history/
Established: 1994
Awarded for research in US legal history & the field of law & society. Only members of the association are eligible. Applications must include application form with estimated budget, curriculum vitae & statement of no more than 750 words & a one-page bibliography of the most recent, relevant, secondary works on the topic. Preference will be given to advanced doctoral students, non-tenured faculty & unaffiliated scholars, & to those with specific research needs such as completion of a project or a discrete segment thereof. Application form & all updated info on web site. Applicants will be notified of the committee's decision by e-mail in mid-May.
Award: Individual grants up to $1,000
Closing Date: Feb 15
Presented: June

Living Now Book Awards
Independent Publisher Online
Division of Jenkins Group Inc
1129 Woodmere Ave, Suite B, Traverse City, MI 49686
Tel: 231-933-0445 *Toll Free Tel:* 800-706-4636 *Fax:* 231-933-0448
Web Site: livingnowawards.com
Key Personnel
Awards Dir: Amy Shamroe *Tel:* 800-644-0133 ext 1000 *E-mail:* amys@jenkinsgroupinc.com
Established: 2008
Awarded to celebrate the innovation & creativity of newly published books that can help us improve the quality of our lives, from cooking & entertaining to fitness & travel. The awards are open to all books written in English & intended for the North American market. Entry fee: $75-$95 per category.
Other Sponsor(s): Jenkins Group Inc
Award: Gold medal (1st place), silver medal (2nd place), bronze medal (3rd place), foil seals & medals available. Winning books promoted on independentpublisher.com & to national media
Closing Date: June

Sarah Lockwood Memorial
The Poetry Society of Virginia (PSV)
PO Box 36128, North Chesterfield, VA 23235-3533
E-mail: contest@poetrysocietyofvirginia.org; info@poetryvirginia.org
Web Site: www.poetrysocietyofvirginia.org
Key Personnel
Pres: Cherryl T Cooley *E-mail:* poetrysocietypresident@gmail.com
Sonnet in rhyme & meter, any subject. Submit 1 copy of the poem with no identifying information but put the category in the upper right-hand-side, along with a notation as to whether you are a member of PSV (does not matter if you are a lifetime member or just joined for the contest). Submit a cover letter/page that contains the category, the name of the poem, your name & address, phone number & e-mail address. Entries will not be returned. Entry fee: Free to membs, $5 nonmembs.
Award: $100 (1st prize), $75 (2nd prize), $50 (3rd prize)

Locus Awards
Locus Science Fiction Foundation
Division of Locus Publications
655 13 St, Suite 100, Oakland, CA 94612
Tel: 510-339-9196 *Fax:* 510-339-9198
E-mail: locus@locusmag.com
Web Site: www.locusmag.com; lsff.net
Key Personnel
Publr & Ed-in-Chief: Liza Groen Trombi
Mng Ed: Kirsten Gong-Wong
Established: 1971
Awarded in recognition of excellence in science fiction & fantasy literature. Categories: Science fiction novel, fantasy novel, horror novel, young adult novel, first novel, novella, novelette, short story, anthology, collection, magazine, publisher, editor, artist, nonfiction, illustrated & art book.
Award: Trophy & free subn to *Locus* magazine
Presented: June

The Gerald Loeb Awards
Anderson School of Management at UCLA
Gold Hall, Suite B-307, 110 Westwood Plaza, Los Angeles, CA 90095-1481
Tel: 310-825-4478 *Fax:* 310-825-4479
E-mail: loeb@anderson.ucla.edu
Web Site: www.anderson.ucla.edu/gerald-loeb-awards
Key Personnel
Exec Dir: Jonathan Daillak
Established: 1957

Distinguished business & finance journalism in print & broadcast media. See web site for a complete list of categories, eligibility & rules. $100 per entry.
Award: The winning entry in each category receives a $2,000 honorarium. Honorable mentions in each category receive $500. Under certain special circumstances, established by the final judges, a writer or entry may receive a special award
Closing Date: March 31
Presented: Early Summer

Loft-Mentor Series in Poetry & Creative Prose
The Loft Literary Center
Open Book Bldg, Suite 200, 1011 Washington Ave S, Minneapolis, MN 55415
Tel: 612-215-2575 *Fax:* 612-215-2576
E-mail: loft@loft.org
Web Site: loft.org
Key Personnel
Exec & Artistic Dir: Arleta M Little *Tel:* 612-215-2584 *E-mail:* alittle@loft.org
Mktg & Communs Dir: Chris Mackenzie Jones *Tel:* 612-215-2589 *E-mail:* cjones@loft.org
Established: 1980
Annual award for poetry, nonfiction & fiction mss. Must be Minnesota State resident. Six different residencies scheduled throughout the year. Winners announced on web site. Open to poets, fiction writers & nonfiction writers.
Award: Stipend to defray costs of participating in the program & opportunity to study with six nationally known writer-mentors in brief residence during the course of the year
Closing Date: Mid-Spring
Presented: The Loft

Long Poem Prize
The Malahat Review
University of Victoria, PO Box 1700, Sta CSC, Victoria, BC V8W 2Y2, Canada
Tel: 250-721-8524
E-mail: malahat@uvic.ca
Web Site: www.malahatreview.ca/contests/long_poem_prize/info.html; www.malahatreview.ca
Key Personnel
Mng Ed: L'Amour Lisik
Ed: Iain Higgins *E-mail:* malahateditor@uvic.ca
Established: 1988
Two awards for best long poem(s). Submissions must be made online through Submittable. See web site for details & entry fees. Contest runs every other year (odd-numbered years).
Award: $1,250 each & publication in the Summer issue of *The Malahat Review*
Closing Date: Feb 1, odd-numbered years

Barry Lopez Nonfiction Award
CUTTHROAT, A Journal of the Arts
PO Box 2414, Durango, CO 81302
Tel: 970-903-7914
E-mail: cutthroatmag@gmail.com
Web Site: www.cutthroatmag.com
Key Personnel
Ed-in-Chief: Pamela Uschuk
Mng Ed: Andrew Allport
Submit 1 unpublished creative nonfiction piece (5,000 word limit), any subject, any style. Mss must be 12 point font & doubled spaced. No stories previously published or that have won contests are eligible. Reading fee: $23.
Award: $1,200 & publication (1st prize), $250 & publication (2nd prize), publication only (honorable mention)
Closing Date: Nov
Presented: Dec

Judy Lopez Memorial Award For Children's Literature
Women's National Book Association/Los Angeles Chapter
1225 Selby Ave, Los Angeles, CA 90024
Tel: 310-474-9917 *Fax:* 310-474-6436
Web Site: www.wnba-books.org/la; www.judylopezbookaward.org
Key Personnel
Pres: Natalie Obondo
Chair, Lopez Comm: Margaret Flanders
Chair, Selection Comm: Gail Kim
Established: 1986
For best books for young readers 9-12 years of age, submitted by publishers, written by US citizen/US resident in year that precedes the award.
Award: Bronze medal & cash honorarium
Closing Date: Feb 1
Presented: Los Angeles, CA, 3rd Sunday in Sept

The Audre Lorde Award for Lesbian Poetry
The Publishing Triangle
511 Avenue of the Americas, No D36, New York, NY 10011
E-mail: awards@publishingtriangle.org; info@publishingtriangle.org; publishingtriangle@gmail.com
Web Site: publishingtriangle.org/awards/audre-lorde-lesbian-poetry
Established: 2001
Award is for books published in the preceding year in the US or Canada. A call for submissions is posted on the web site in early Autumn. Finalists & winners are determined by a panel of judges appointed by the awards committee.
Award: $1,000

The Audre Lorde Creative Writing Award
Poetry Center & American Poetry Archives at San Francisco State University
511-512 Humanities Bldg, 1600 Holloway Ave, San Francisco, CA 94132
Tel: 415-338-2227 *Fax:* 415-338-0966
E-mail: poetry@sfsu.edu
Web Site: poetry.sfsu.edu
Key Personnel
Dir: Steve Dickison *E-mail:* steved@sfsu.edu
Assoc Dir: Elise Ficarra *E-mail:* eficarra@sfsu.edu
Presented for an original, outstanding work of poetry (hybrid work welcome) by a continuing SF State student that in its artistry expresses a social conscience.
Award: $500
Presented: Fall

Los Angeles Times Book Prizes
Los Angeles Times
2300 E Imperial Hwy, El Segundo, CA 90245
Tel: 213-237-5775 *Toll Free Tel:* 800-528-4637 (ext 75775)
Web Site: events.latimes.com/festivalofbooks
Key Personnel
Publr & CEO: Chris Argentieri
Programming Mgr: Ann Binney *E-mail:* ann.binney@latimes.com
Established: 1980
Awarded to authors in the categories of fiction, first fiction, autobiographical prose (Isherwood Prize), young adult literature, graphic novels/comics, mystery/thriller, biography, current interest, history, poetry, science & technology, science fiction (Bradbury Prize). No submissions accepted; nominations are done by committees of appointed judges. There is also an award for lifetime achievement (Robert Kirsch Award) & innovation in storytelling (Innovator's Award).
Other Sponsor(s): Ray Bradbury Foundation; The Christopher Isherwood Foundation
Award: $500 & citation (in 10 different categories); $1,000 each (Robert Kirsch Award & Innovator's Award); $2,500 & citation (Ray Bradbury Prizes); $10,000 & citation (Christopher Isherwood Prize for Autobiographical Prose)
Presented: The Los Angeles Times Festival of Books, USC Campus, Los Angeles, CA, April

Louise Louis/Emily F Bourne Student Poetry Award
Poetry Society of America (PSA)
119 Smith St, Brooklyn, NY 11201
Tel: 212-254-9628
E-mail: info@poetrysociety.org
Web Site: poetrysociety.org/awards
Key Personnel
Exec Dir: Matt Brogan *E-mail:* matt@poetrysociety.org
Deputy Dir: Brett Fletcher Lauer *E-mail:* brett@poetrysociety.org
Devt Dir: Madeline Weinfield *E-mail:* madeline@poetrysociety.org
Established: 1971
For the best unpublished poem by a student in grades 9-12 from the US. One entry per student. Teachers or administrators may submit an unlimited number of their students' poems, 1 submission per student. A poem that has previously won a PSA Award cannot be resubmitted. No previously published work can be submitted. Translations are ineligible. Poems by more than 1 author will not be accepted. All entries must be sent through Submittable. Entry fee: $5 students (single entry), $20 teachers & administrators (unlimited entries, 1 submission per student).
Award: $250
Closing Date: Dec 31
Presented: Annual Awards Ceremony, New York, NY, Spring

Louisiana Writer Award
Louisiana Center for the Book
Subsidiary of State Library of Louisiana
701 N Fourth St, Baton Rouge, LA 70802
Mailing Address: PO Box 131, Baton Rouge, LA 70821-0131
Tel: 225-342-4913 *Fax:* 225-219-4804
E-mail: admin@state.lib.la.us
Web Site: louisianabookfestival.org/louisiana_writer_award.html; www.state.lib.la.us/literacy-and-reading/louisiana-writer-award
Key Personnel
Asst Dir, Louisiana Book Festival: Robert Wilson *E-mail:* lbf@state.lib.la.us
Established: 2000
Award honoring contemporary Louisiana writers whose published body of work represents a distinguished & enduring contribution to the literary & intellectual heritage of Louisiana.

Louisville Grawemeyer Award in Religion
Louisville Presbyterian Theological Seminary & University of Louisville
1044 Alta Vista Rd, Louisville, KY 40205-1798
Tel: 502-895-3411 *Toll Free Tel:* 800-264-1839
Fax: 502-895-1096
E-mail: grawemeyer@lpts.edu
Web Site: www.grawemeyer.org
Key Personnel
Dir: Tyler Mayfield
Established: 1990
Given for a work presented or published in the 8 years preceding the year of the award. Nominations are invited from religious organizations, appropriate academic associations, religious leaders & scholars, presidents of universities or schools of religion & publishers & editors of scholarly journals. Personal nominations accepted, self-nominations not accepted.
Award: $100,000 one-time payment

COURSES & AWARDS — AWARDS, PRIZE CONTESTS, FELLOWSHIPS & GRANTS

Closing Date: Nominations by Jan 15
Presented: Spring

Amy Lowell Prize
New England Poetry Club
c/o Linda Haviland Conte, 18 Hall Ave, Apt 2, Somerville, MA 02144
E-mail: info@nepoetryclub.org
Web Site: nepoetryclub.org
Key Personnel
Co-Pres: Doug Holder; Denise Provost
VP: Hilary Sallick
Treas: Linda Haviland Conte
 E-mail: nepctreasurer@gmail.com
Awarded for an outstanding poem of any length or style by a poet with strong ties to New England. Only one poem per contest. Entries must be original unpublished (neither print nor online) poems in English. Submissions must be made by post or by Submittable link. See web site for full guidelines. Entry fee: Free to membs, nonmembs $5.
Award: $250, publication of winning poems on NEPC web site & opportunity to read at the NEPC (travel expenses not included)
Closing Date: May 31
Presented: Announced online Aug/Sept

James Russell Lowell Prize
Modern Language Association (MLA)
85 Broad St, New York, NY 10004
SAN: 202-6422
Tel: 646-576-5141; 646-576-5000
E-mail: awards@mla.org
Web Site: www.mla.org
Key Personnel
Coord, Book Prizes: Annie M Reiser
 E-mail: areiser@mla.org
Established: 1969
Prize for an outstanding literary or linguistic study, a critical edition of an important work, or critical biography by a current MLA member published in 2024. Authors or publishers should submit 5 print copies, electronic access & confirmation of the author's membership in the MLA.
Award: Cash award & certificate
Closing Date: March 1, 2025
Presented: MLA Annual Convention, Toronto, ON, CN, Jan 2026

Pat Lowther Memorial Award
The League of Canadian Poets
2 Carlton St, Suite 1519, Toronto, ON M5B 1J3, Canada
Tel: 416-504-1657
E-mail: info@poets.ca
Web Site: poets.ca/awards/lowther
Key Personnel
Exec Dir: Lesley Fletcher *E-mail:* lesley@poets.ca
Artistic Programming Dir: Nic Brewer
 E-mail: nicole@poets.ca
Admin & Communs Coord: Caitlin Lapena
 E-mail: caitlin@poets.ca
Award for the best book of poetry written by a Canadian woman & published in the preceding year. Authors must be Canadian citizens or permanent residents. Submitted titles must be at least 48 pages in length & have 1 author (translators not eligible). Chapbooks & self-published books are not eligible. Submission fee: $25 per title. See web site for full eligibility guidelines.
Award: $2,000
Closing Date: Nov 13
Presented: May

Jeremiah Ludington Award
Educational Book & Media Association (EBMA)
11 Main St, Suite D, Warrenton, VA 20186
Mailing Address: PO Box 3363, Warrenton, VA 20188
Tel: 540-318-7770 *Fax:* 202-962-3939
E-mail: info@edupaperback.org; admin@edupaperback.org
Web Site: www.edupaperback.org
Key Personnel
Exec Dir: Brian Gorg
Established: 1979
Presented to an individual who has made a significant contribution to the educational book & media business.
Award: Framed certificate & EBMA presents a $2,500 check to the charity of their choice
Presented: EBMA Annual Meeting, Jan

J Anthony Lukas Book Prize
Columbia University Graduate School of Journalism
2950 Broadway, New York, NY 10027
Tel: 212-854-6468
E-mail: cjsprizes@gmail.com
Web Site: www.journalism.columbia.edu
Key Personnel
Exec Dir, Prof Prizes: Abi Wright
Established: 1998
Awarded for a book-length work of narrative nonfiction on a topic of American political or social concern that exemplifies the literary grace, commitment to serious research & social concern that characterized the distinguished work of the award's namesake. Submissions must include 4 copies of each book. Entry fee: $75 (non-refundable).
Award: $10,000
Closing Date: Dec 11

J Anthony Lukas Work-in-Progress Award
Columbia University Graduate School of Journalism
2950 Broadway, New York, NY 10027
Tel: 212-854-6468
E-mail: cjsprizes@gmail.com
Web Site: www.journalism.columbia.edu
Key Personnel
Exec Dir, Prof Prizes: Abi Wright
Established: 1998
Awarded to aid in the completion of a significant work of nonfiction on a topic of American political or social concern. Applicants should send copy of their original book proposal, sample chapter from book, photocopy of contract with US-based publisher & explanation of how award will advance progress of the book. No entry fee.
Award: $30,000
Closing Date: Dec 11

Lush Triumphant Literary Awards
subTerrain Magazine
PO Box 3008, MPO, Vancouver, BC V6B 3X5, Canada
Tel: 604-876-8009 *Fax:* 604-879-2667
E-mail: subter@portal.ca
Web Site: www.subterrain.ca
Established: 2003
Literary award presented in 3 categories: Fiction, poetry & nonfiction. Entry fee: $27.50.
Award: $3,000 in cash prizes, plus publication. The winner in each category receives a $1,000 prize plus publication in the Winter issue (plus contributor's payment). The runners-up entries are published in the Spring issue of the following year (& they receive contributor's payment)
Closing Date: May 15
Presented: Vancouver, BC, CN, Aug 15

Mark Lynton History Prize
Columbia University Graduate School of Journalism
2950 Broadway, New York, NY 10027
Tel: 212-854-6468
E-mail: cjsprizes@gmail.com
Web Site: www.journalism.columbia.edu
Key Personnel
Exec Dir, Prof Prizes: Abi Wright
Established: 1998
Awarded to a book-length work of history on any topic that best combines intellectual distinction with felicity of expression. Submissions must include 4 copies of each book. Entry fee: $75 (non-refundable).
Award: $10,000
Closing Date: Dec 11

Thomas J Lyon Book Award in Western American Literary and Cultural Studies
Western Literature Association
PO Box 6815, Logan, UT 84341
E-mail: wlaoperations@gmail.com
Web Site: www.westernlit.org/thomas-j-lyon-book-award-in-western-american-literary-and-cultural-studies; www.westernlit.org
Key Personnel
Dir, Opers: Sabine Barcatta
Established: 1997
Honors outstanding single-author scholarly book on the literature & culture of the American West published in the previous year. Must submit a statement of support & 3 copies of the book.
Award: Certificate
Closing Date: June 1
Presented: Annual Conference

Lyric Poetry Award
Poetry Society of America (PSA)
119 Smith St, Brooklyn, NY 11201
Tel: 212-254-9628
E-mail: info@poetrysociety.org
Web Site: poetrysociety.org/awards
Key Personnel
Exec Dir: Matt Brogan *E-mail:* matt@poetrysociety.org
Deputy Dir: Brett Fletcher Lauer *E-mail:* brett@poetrysociety.org
Devt Dir: Madeline Weinfield *E-mail:* madeline@poetrysociety.org
Established: 1972
For a lyric poem on any subject. All submissions must be through Submittable. Entry fee: Free to membs, $10 nonmembs.
Award: $500
Closing Date: Dec 31
Presented: Annual Awards Ceremony, New York, NY, Spring

Lyric Poetry Prizes
The Lyric Foundation
PO Box 110, Jericho, VT 05465
E-mail: themuse@thelyricmagazine.com
Web Site: thelyricmagazine.com
Key Personnel
Ed: Jean Mellichamp Milliken
Assoc Ed: Nancy Mellichamp Savo
Collegiate Contest Coord: Tanya Cimonetti
 E-mail: tanyacim@aol.com
Established: 1921
The Collegiate contest prize is awarded to undergraduates enrolled full-time in an American or Canadian college. The annual & quarterly prizes are awarded to poems published in *The Lyric*. Winners of annual awards are announced in the winter issue each year. Send SASE or provide e-mail address for guidelines. Individual copy of *The Lyric* $5, subscription $18/yr, $32/2 yrs, $42/3 yrs, $2/yr extra Canadian.
Award: Quarterly prize: $50. Annual awards: Lyric College Poetry Contest: $500 (1st prize), $150 (2nd prize), $100 (3rd prize); Lyric Memorial, Leslie Mellichamp & Roberts Memorial Prizes: $100 each; New England & Fluvanna Prizes: $50 each. Honorable mentions get one-year subn to *The Lyric*

AWARDS, PRIZE CONTESTS, FELLOWSHIPS & GRANTS

Closing Date: Dec 31 (postmark)
Presented: Quarterly prizes awarded in the following issue, annual prizes in the winter issue

MacArthur Fellows Program
John D & Catherine T MacArthur Foundation
Office of Grants Management, 140 S Dearborn St, Chicago, IL 60603-5285
Tel: 312-726-8000 *Fax:* 312-920-6528
E-mail: 4answers@macfound.org
Web Site: www.macfound.org/programs/fellows
Key Personnel
Mng Dir: Cecilia A Conrad
Prog Dir: Marlies A Carruth
Awards unrestricted fellowships to talented individuals who have shown extraordinary originality & dedication in their creative pursuits & a marked capacity for self-direction. Recipients may be writers, scientists, artists, social scientists, humanists, teachers, entrepreneurs or those in other fields, with or without institutional affiliations.
The Fellows Program does not accept applications or unsol nominations.
Award: $625,000 stipend paid in equal quarterly installments over 5 years

Macavity Award
Mystery Readers International
7155 Marlborough Terr, Berkeley, CA 94705
Tel: 510-845-3600
Web Site: www.mysteryreaders.org
Key Personnel
Dir: Janet Rudolph *E-mail:* janet@mysteryreaders.org
Established: 1986
Awarded for works nominated by & voted on by members of Mystery Readers International in categories: Best Novel, Best First Novel, Best Short Story, Best Nonfiction/Critical; Sue Feder Award for the Historical Mystery (all published in the US the previous year).
Award: Crystal plaque
Presented: Bouchercon, the World Mystery Convention, Autumn

MacDowell Fellowships
MacDowell
100 High St, Peterborough, NH 03458
Tel: 603-924-3886
E-mail: info@macdowell.org; admissions@macdowell.org
Web Site: www.macdowell.org
Key Personnel
Exec Dir: Chiwoniso "Chi" Kaitano
Admissions Dir: Courtney Bethel
E-mail: cbethel@macdowell.org
Communs Mgr: Jonathan Gourlay *Tel:* 603-924-3886 ext 114 *E-mail:* jgourlay@macdowell.org
Established: 1907
Fellowships of up to 8 weeks are available for writers, composers, film/video artists, theatre artists, visual artists, architects & interdisciplinary artists. Artists-in-residence receive room, board & exclusive use of a studio. The average length of stay is 6 weeks. Talent is the sole criterion for acceptance. Established artists as well as emerging artists are encouraged to apply. Committees of distinguished professionals donate their time to judge applications, which include work samples, references & a brief project description. There are no residency fees. Grants for travel to & from MacDowell are available based on need. Financial aid for all artists is available through special grants from various foundations. An aid application will be mailed following acceptance. The Edward MacDowell medal is awarded for a career of outstanding contributions to the arts, including musical composition, visual arts or literature, architecture, film & video & interdisciplinary arts.

Closing Date: For fellowships: Jan 15, April 15 & Sept 15, see application form & guidelines online for details
Presented: Peterborough, NH
Branch Office(s)
MacDowell NYC, 521 W 23 St, 2nd fl, New York, NY 10011 *Tel:* 212-535-9690

Machigonne Fiction Contest
The New Guard
PO Box 472, Brunswick, ME 04011
E-mail: info@newguardreview.com; editors@writershotel.com
Web Site: www.newguardreview.com
Key Personnel
Founding Ed & Publr: Shanna McNair
Established: 2009
Submit a short story or novel excerpt up to 5,000 words. Online submissions only. Entry fee: $20.
Award: $1,500 & publication in *The New Guard*
Closing Date: Aug 31

Macmillan Booksellers Professional Development Scholarship
Book Industry Charitable Foundation (BINC)
3135 S State St, Suite 203, Ann Arbor, MI 48108
Toll Free Tel: 866-733-9064
E-mail: info@bincfoundation.org
Web Site: www.bincfoundation.org/scholarship
Key Personnel
Exec Dir: Pamela French *E-mail:* pam@bincfoundation.org
Dir, Devt: Kathy Bartson *E-mail:* kathy@bincfoundation.org
Prog Mgr: Judey Kalchik *E-mail:* judey@bincfoundation.org; Ken White *E-mail:* ken@bincfoundation.org
Commun Coord: Erika Mantz *E-mail:* erika@bincfoundation.org
Devt Coord: Jennifer Rojas *E-mail:* jennifer@bincfoundation.org
Off Coord: Jane Regenstreif *E-mail:* jane@bincfoundation.org
Spec Projs Coord: Kate Weiss *E-mail:* kate@bincfoundation.org
Established: 2017
Aims to strengthen the industry by encouraging a greater number of individuals from underrepresented groups to choose +/or continue careers in bookselling. This scholarship will allow up to one bookseller to attend each of the fall regional trade shows.

C B MacPherson Prize
Canadian Political Science Association (CPSA)
260 Dalhousie St, Suite 204, Ottawa, ON K1N 7E4, Canada
Tel: 613-562-1202 *Fax:* 613-241-0019
E-mail: cpsa-acsp@cpsa-acsp.ca; cpsaprizes@cpsa-acsp.ca
Web Site: www.cpsa-acsp.ca
Key Personnel
Exec Dir: Silvina Danesi
Admin: C Ngako Woktcheu
Established: 1992
Biennial prize, awarded in even-numbered years, to the author(s) of the best book published in English or in French in the field of political theory. A book may be single-authored or multi-authored. Single-authored book: author must be a member of the CPSA in the year the book is considered for the prize. Multi-authored book: at least one of the authors must be a member of the CPSA in the year the book is considered for the prize. For the 2026 award, a book must have a copyright date of 2024 or 2025.
Award: Commemorative plaque & receive/share the set of books submitted to the CPSA office
Presented: CPSA Annual Conference

ASSOCIATIONS, EVENTS

Magazine Merit Awards
Society of Children's Book Writers & Illustrators (SCBWI)
6363 Wilshire Blvd, Suite 425, Los Angeles, CA 90048
Tel: 323-782-1010
E-mail: info@scbwi.org
Web Site: www.scbwi.org/awards/magazine-merit-award
Key Personnel
Exec Dir: Sarah Baker
Assoc Dir, Digital Content & Awards: Sarah Diamond
Assoc Mgr, Awards & Pubns: Danielle Monique
Established: 1988
For outstanding original magazine work for young people in the categories of fiction, nonfiction, illustration & poetry. Applicants must be SCBWI members. Every magazine work for young people—writer, author, or photographer—is eligible during the year of original publication.
Award: Plaque
Closing Date: Dec

Maine Literary Awards
Maine Writers & Publishers Alliance (MWPA)
Glickman Family Library, 314 Forest Ave, Rm 318, Portland, ME 04101
Tel: 207-228-8263
E-mail: info@mainewriters.org
Web Site: www.mainewriters.org/programs/maine-literary-awards
Key Personnel
Prog Dir: Meghan Sterling *Tel:* 207-228-8257
E-mail: meghan@mainewriters.org
Statewide competition for published books as well as drama, short works (either published or unpublished) & student writing. Maine writers may self-nominate or be nominated by others. All nominations must have been published in the previous calendar year.
Submission fees: Book Awards & Excellence in Publishing Award $25 membs, $45 nonmembs; Short Works Awards & Drama Award $10 membs, $25 nonmembs. No fee for Youth Awards. See web site for full submission details & all categories.
Other Sponsor(s): John N Cole Family; Just Write Books; Maine Authors Publishing; Maine Poetry Society; University of Southern Maine
Closing Date: Feb 1
Presented: Mid-June

Major Achievement Award
Council for Wisconsin Writers (CWW)
c/o 3225 N 91 St, Milwaukee, WI 53222
E-mail: wiswriters@gmail.com
Web Site: wiswriters.org/awards
Key Personnel
Contest Chair: Erik Richardson
E-mail: erichardson@wi.rr.com
Awarded biennially, currently in even-numbered years, from the Christopher Latham Sholes Award to honor the work of a Wisconsin writer, without regard to genre or category, who deserves special recognition to his/her literary merit. No entry fee.
Award: $1,000
Closing Date: Jan 31
Presented: CWW Annual Award Ceremony & Banquet, May

J Russell Major Prize in French History
American Historical Association (AHA)
400 "A" St SE, Washington, DC 20003
Tel: 202-544-2422
E-mail: awards@historians.org
Web Site: www.historians.org/award-grant/j-russell-major-prize/
Established: 2000

Awarded for the best work in English on any aspect of French history. Books with a 2024 copyright are eligible for the 2025 prize. Nominations may be made by an author or publisher. Along with an application form, applicants must mail a copy of their book to each prize committee member posted on our web site as the prize deadline approaches. All updated info on web site.
Award: $1,000
Closing Date: May 15, 2025
Presented: AHA Annual Meeting, Chicago, IL, Jan 2026

Gene E & Adele R Malott Prize for Recording Community Activism
The Langum Foundation
c/o Frederick M Shepherd, 3900 Seventh Ave S, Birmingham, AL 35222
Web Site: langumfoundation.org/about-prizes/recording-community-activism
Key Personnel
Chmn, Selection Comm: Frederick M Shepherd
  E-mail: fmshephe@samford.edu
Established: 2007
Awarded biennially, in even-numbered years, to recognize the best literary depiction of an individual or small group of individuals whose efforts resulted in a significant improvement of their local community. Although the work of community improvement must be significant, the basis of the prize will be the skill & power of the literary or film depiction. Eligible media include books, magazine articles, series of newspaper articles, or films, published or released within the past 2 years of a prize cycle. Send 3 copies to the committee chairman.
Award: $1,000 for the writer. If film, divided between the director & screenwriter
Closing Date: Dec 1 for materials published or released the previous 2 calendar years

Ralph Manheim Award for Translation, see PEN/Ralph Manheim Award for Translation

Margaret Mann Citation
Core: Leadership, Infrastructure, Futures Division of The American Library Association (ALA)
c/o The American Library Association, 225 N Michigan Ave, Suite 1300, Chicago, IL 60601
Tel: 312-944-6780 *Toll Free Tel:* 800-545-2433
Fax: 312-440-9374
E-mail: scholarships@ala.org
Web Site: www.ala.org/core
Key Personnel
Exec Dir: Julie Reese *Tel:* 312-280-5030
  E-mail: jreese@ala.org
Established: 1951
Awarded for outstanding professional achievement in cataloging or classification in a significant publication or by participation in a professional organization. Candidates are nominated. Citation recipient selected by jury.
Closing Date: Dec 1
Presented: ALA Annual Conference & Exhibition, June

Many Voices Fellowships & Mentorships
Playwrights' Center
2301 Franklin Ave E, Minneapolis, MN 55406-1099
Tel: 612-332-7481 *Fax:* 612-332-6037
E-mail: info@pwcenter.org
Web Site: www.pwcenter.org
Key Personnel
Producing Artistic Dir: Jeremy Cohen *Tel:* 612-332-7481 ext 1113 *E-mail:* jeremyc@pwcenter.org
Assoc Artistic Dir: Hayley Finn *Tel:* 612-332-7481 ext 1119 *E-mail:* hayleyf@pwcenter.org
Artistic Progs Mgr: Julia Brown *Tel:* 612-332-7481 ext 1115 *E-mail:* juliab@pwcenter.org
For beginning & early career Black writers, Indigenous writers & writers of color.
Award: Many Voices Mentorship: 2 Minnesota-based beginning BIPOC playwrights receive $2,000 stipend plus workshop & educational resources; Many Voices Fellowship: 3 early career BIPOC playwrights receive $18,000 stipend, $2,500 in play development funds & dramaturgical support

Marfield Prize
Arts Club of Washington
2017 "I" St NW, Washington, DC 20006-1804
E-mail: award@artsclubofwashington.org
Web Site: artsclubofwashington.org/awards
Key Personnel
Award Admin: Sass Brown
Established: 2006
Given for nonfiction books about the visual, literary or performing arts written for a broad audience. Works published in the US during the previous calendar year are eligible for consideration. Publishers, agents, or authors may submit books. No entry fee. Submit 3 copies of the book with prize submission form.
Award: $10,000
Closing Date: Oct 15

Margins Fellowship
Asian American Writers' Workshop (AAWW)
112 W 27 St, Suite 600, New York, NY 10001
Tel: 212-494-0061
E-mail: fellowships@aaww.org
Web Site: aaww.org/fellowships/margins
Key Personnel
Progs Mgr: Lily Philpott
Progs Coord: Vandana Pawa
Applications open in the Fall. Fellowship is a year-long program running January-December. Access to AAWW Reading Room & workspace. Mentorship with an established writer during the second half of the fellowship term. Submit statement of purpose, writing sample & CV via Submittable. No submission fee.
Award: $5,000 honoraria, distributed in 3 parts over the fellowship year; residency time at Millay Arts, Austerlitz, NY; publication in *The Margins*; free AAWW membership; 1 free writing workshop

Judith A Markowitz Award for Emerging LGBTQ Writers
Lambda Literary
PO Box 20186, New York, NY 10014
Tel: 213-277-5755
E-mail: awards@lambdaliterary.org; admin@lambdaliterary.org
Web Site: www.lambdaliterary.org/awards/special-awards
Key Personnel
Awards Mgr: Brian Gentes
Two prizes awarded to recognize LGBTQ-identified writers whose work demonstrates their strong potential for promising careers. The applicant must have written & published at least 1 but no more than 2 books of fiction, nonfiction or poetry & must show meaningful engagement with LGBTQ literary communities. Applicants must submit a Core Writing Sample, their strongest representative work. Maximum of 20 pages for prose & 10 pages for poetry. This can be an excerpt to a larger piece or a standalone work. Supplemental literary work will also be considered.
Award: $1,000 each
Closing Date: Feb 15
Presented: June

Helen & Howard R Marraro Prize in Italian History
American Historical Association (AHA)
400 "A" St SE, Washington, DC 20003
Tel: 202-544-2422
E-mail: awards@historians.org
Web Site: www.historians.org/award-grant/helen-howard-r-marraro-prize/
Established: 1973
Award for the best book on Italian history, Italian cultural history, or Italo-American cultural relations published in English by an historian whose usual residence is North America. Books with a 2024 copyright are eligible for the 2025 prize. Nominations may be made by an author or publisher. Along with an application form, applicants must mail a copy of their book together with a curriculum vitae & bibliography of the author to each prize committee member posted on our web site as the prize deadline approaches. All updated info on web site.
Other Sponsor(s): American Catholic Historical Association; Society for Italian Historical Studies
Award: $1,000
Closing Date: May 15, 2025
Presented: AHA Annual Meeting, Chicago, IL, Jan 2026

Howard R Marraro Prize
Modern Language Association (MLA)
85 Broad St, New York, NY 10004
SAN: 202-6422
Tel: 646-576-5141; 646-576-5000
E-mail: awards@mla.org
Web Site: www.mla.org
Key Personnel
Coord, Book Prizes: Annie M Reiser
  E-mail: areiser@mla.org
Established: 1973
Awarded biennially, in even-numbered years, for an outstanding scholarly work on any phase of Italian literature or comparative literature involving Italian by an MLA member. The committee solicits submissions of works published in 2025 by current members. Submit 4 print copies of the work & letter identifyng the work & confirming the author's membership in the MLA along with electronic access.
Award: Cash award & certificate
Closing Date: May 1, 2026
Presented: MLA Annual Convention, Los Angeles, CA, Jan 2027

Lenore Marshall Poetry Prize
The Academy of American Poets Inc
75 Maiden Lane, Suite 901, New York, NY 10038
Tel: 212-274-0343
E-mail: awards@poets.org
Web Site: poets.org/academy-american-poets/prizes/lenore-marshall-poetry-prize
Key Personnel
Pres & Exec Dir: Ricardo Alberto Maldonado
VP, Digital Engagement & Content: Jeff Gleaves
Ad & Mktg Dir: Michelle Campagna
Dir, Donor Rel: Molly Walsh
Dir, Progs: Nikay Paredes
Established: 1975
Awarded in recognition of the most outstanding book of poetry published in the US in the previous calendar year. Self-published books are not eligible. Translations & new editions of previously published books are not eligible. Publishers should send 4 copies of each book along with $75 entry fee & entry form for each title submitted.
Award: $25,000 & 200 copies of winning book distributed to Academy members
Closing Date: May 15
Presented: Sept

AWARDS, PRIZE CONTESTS, FELLOWSHIPS & GRANTS

The Eliud Martinez Prize
Inlandia Institute
4178 Chestnut St, Riverside, CA 92501
SAN: 992-6380
E-mail: inlandia@inlandiainstitute.org
Web Site: inlandinstitute.org/books/the-eliud-martinez-prize
Key Personnel
Exec Dir: Cati Porter
Progs & Mktg Coord: Janine Pourroy Gamblin
Awarded for a first book in fiction or creative nonfiction by a Hispanic, Latino/a/x, or Chicana/o/x writer. Ms page limit 150-300. Electronic submissions only via Submittable.
Award: $1,000 & book publication
Closing Date: Feb

Mass Book Awards, see Massachusetts Book Awards

Massachusetts Book Awards
Massachusetts Center for the Book
Old School Commons, No 302, 17 New South St, Northampton, MA 01060
Tel: 617-872-3718
E-mail: bookawards@massbook.org
Web Site: www.massbook.org
Key Personnel
Exec Dir: Sharon Shaloo *E-mail:* shaloo@massbook.org
Established: 2000
The Mass Book Awards recognize significant achievements by Massachusetts writers in fiction, nonfiction, poetry & literature for young readers from the previous publishing year. See web site for details.
Presented: Massachusetts State House, Boston, MA, Oct

Amy Mathers Teen Book Award
The Canadian Children's Book Centre
425 Adelaide St W, Suite 200, Toronto, ON M5V 3C1, Canada
Tel: 416-975-0010
E-mail: info@bookcentre.ca
Web Site: www.bookcentre.ca
Key Personnel
Exec Dir: Sarah Sahagian
Lib Coord: Meghan Howe *E-mail:* meghan@bookcentre.ca
Established: 2014
Awarded to a Canadian author for excellence in teen/young adult fiction.
Award: $5,000 cash
Closing Date: Mid-Dec

Mathical Book Prize
Mathematical Sciences Research Institute (MSRI)
17 Gauss Way, Berkeley, CA 94720
Tel: 510-499-5181
E-mail: mathical@msri.org
Web Site: www.mathicalbooks.org
Key Personnel
Prize Coord: Kirsten Bohl
Awarded for fiction & nonfiction books that inspire children of all ages to see math in the world around them. Winners are selected in 5 grade-level categories: PreK, K-2, 3-5, 6-8 & 9-12. Publishers may submit up to 3 titles published in the year prior to the award.
Other Sponsor(s): Children's Book Council (CBC); National Council of Teachers of English (NCTE); National Council of Teachers of Mathematics (NCTM)
Presented: National Conference on Mathematics Education, Feb

Matt Cohen Award: In Celebration of a Writing Life
The Writers' Trust of Canada
600-460 Richmond St W, Toronto, ON M5V 1Y1, Canada
Tel: 416-504-8222 *Toll Free Tel:* 877-906-6548
Fax: 416-504-9090
E-mail: info@writerstrust.com
Web Site: www.writerstrust.com
Key Personnel
Exec Dir: Charlie Foran *Tel:* 416-504-8222 ext 244 *E-mail:* cforan@writerstrust.com
Mgr, Author Progs: Devon Jackson *Tel:* 416-504-8222 ext 248 *E-mail:* djackson@writerstrust.com
Established: 2001
Recognizes a lifetime of distinguished work by a Canadian writer, working in either poetry or prose, in either French or English.
Other Sponsor(s): Lorraine Greey
Award: $25,000
Presented: The Writers' Trust Awards, Toronto, ON, CN, Nov

Maxim Mazumdar New Play Competition
Alleyway Theatre
One Curtain Up Alley, Buffalo, NY 14202-1911
Tel: 716-852-2600
E-mail: newplays@alleyway.com; email@alleyway.com
Web Site: www.alleyway.com/playwrights/maxim-mazumdar-new-play-competition
Key Personnel
Exec Artistic Dir: Chris J Handley *E-mail:* chandley@alleyway.com
Mng Dir: Robyn Lee Horn *Tel:* 716-852-2600 ext 202 *E-mail:* rhorn@alleyway.com
Established: 1989
Playwrights around the world (with or without representation) are encouraged to submit their plays & musicals each season to the Mazumdar Competition. Each category is for plays that are ready for production. Outlines or summaries, incomplete or rough drafts will not be accepted. Anyone may submit. Finalists & other promising works will be considered for production in future seasons +/or our development lab. Alleyway is an associate member of the National New Play Network & winning plays may be considered for Rolling World Premier & Showcase submissions. Entry in the Maxim Mazumdar New Play Competition is understood as an indication of the playwright's willingness, in the event of winning, to grant first production rights to Alleyway Theatre. Selection as a winner requires the playwright's prior commitment to grant first production rights under the terms of Alleyway Theatre's Standard Production Agreement. Plays must be unpublished & unproduced at the time of submission (developmental readings & workshops notwithstanding). All entries must be withheld from production during the period of the competition, reserving the premiere production for Alleyway Theatre. Playwrights may submit up to one play in each category. All work must be original & unproduced. The rights to any material used in the script not in the public domain must have been granted to the playwright in writing & must be available to be presented upon request. Playwrights should format submission draft in the following way: Each full length & one act submission must be uploaded as a single PDF document; remove all personally identifying information (name, contact info, agent, agent's contact, etc) from the script; include a character & scene/song breakdown (include character names & any necessary identifying traits, plus doubling plot, etc); if a musical, indicate on title page a URL where demos can be heard. All submissions must be made via form on the web site. There is no fee to enter.
Award: Cash prize & premiere production of entry at Alleyway Theatre to winning script in each category
Closing Date: Aug

ASSOCIATIONS, EVENTS

Mary McCarthy Prize in Short Fiction
Sarabande Books Inc
822 E Market St, Louisville, KY 40206
Tel: 502-458-4028
E-mail: info@sarabandebooks.org
Web Site: www.sarabandebooks.org/mccarthy
Key Personnel
Dir, Mktg & Publicity: Joanna Englert *E-mail:* joanna@sarabandebooks.org
Contest is open to any short fiction writer of English. Submissions may include a collection of short stories, one or more novellas, or a short novel. Works that have previously appeared in magazines or in anthologies may be included. Translations & previously published collections are not eligible. Online submission process. See web site for full details & ms requirements. Submission fee: $28.
Award: $2,000, publication of ms, Sarabande Writing Residency & standard royalty contract
Closing Date: Feb 15
Presented: Sept

McClelland & Stewart Journey Prize, see Writers' Trust McClelland & Stewart Journey Prize

John H McGinnis Memorial Award
Southwest Review
PO Box 750374, Dallas, TX 75275-0374
Fax: 214-768-1408
E-mail: swr@mail.smu.edu
Web Site: southwestreview.com
Key Personnel
Ed-in-Chief: Greg Brownderville
Established: 1960
For the best essay & story appearing in the *Southwest Review* during the preceding year.
Award: $500 (2-4 awards)
Presented: Jan

Harold W McGraw Jr Prize in Education
University of Pennsylvania Graduate School of Education (Penn GSE)
3440 Market St, Suite 500, Philadelphia, PA 19104
E-mail: info@mcgrawprize.com
Web Site: www.mcgrawprize.com
Established: 1988
Honors 3 individuals whose accomplishments, programs & ideas can serve as effective models for the education of future generations. Categories: PreK-12, higher education & learning science research.
Other Sponsor(s): Harold W McGraw Jr Family Foundation
Award: $50,000 & prize sculpture
Closing Date: April 15
Presented: McGraw Prize Celebration, Nov

William Holmes McGuffey Longevity Award
Textbook & Academic Authors Association (TAA)
PO Box 367, Fountain City, WI 54629
E-mail: info@taaonline.net
Web Site: www.taaonline.net/mcguffey-longevity-award
Key Personnel
Exec Dir: Michael Spinella *Tel:* 973-943-0501 *E-mail:* michael.spinella@taaonline.net
Dir, Publg & Opers: Kim Pawlak *Tel:* 507-459-1363 *E-mail:* kim.pawlak@taaonline.net
Dir, Instl Memberships & Meetings: Maureen Foerster *Tel:* 530-864-3538 *E-mail:* maureen.foerster@taaonline.net
Membership Mktg Mgr: Eric Schmieder *Tel:* 919-437-0241 *E-mail:* eric.schmieder@taaonline.net
Membership Coord: Bekky Murphy *Tel:* 608-567-9060 *E-mail:* bekky.murphy@taaonline.net
Recognizes textbooks & learning materials whose excellence has been demonstrated over time. To be nominated, a work must have been in

print 15 years & still be selling. Works are judged for merit in 4 areas: pedagogy; content/scholarship; writing; appearance & design. Nomination fee: $375 (non-refundable). See web site for nomination form & entry guidelines.
Closing Date: Nov 1
Presented: TAA Annual Conference, June

McKnight Artist Fellowship for Writers
The Loft Literary Center
Open Book Bldg, Suite 200, 1011 Washington Ave S, Minneapolis, MN 55415
Tel: 612-215-2575 *Fax:* 612-215-2576
E-mail: loft@loft.org
Web Site: loft.org
Key Personnel
Exec & Artistic Dir: Arleta M Little *Tel:* 612-215-2584 *E-mail:* alittle@loft.org
Mktg & Communs Dir: Chris Mackenzie Jones *Tel:* 612-215-2589 *E-mail:* cjones@loft.org
Established: 1982
Contest for Minnesota residents only.
Award: Four $25,000 awards which alternate between poetry & creative prose; one $25,000 award in children's literature which alternates between writing for children 8 & under & older children
Closing Date: Late Fall
Presented: The Loft, Minneapolis, MN, Spring

McKnight Fellowships in Playwriting
Playwrights' Center
2301 Franklin Ave E, Minneapolis, MN 55406-1099
Tel: 612-332-7481 *Fax:* 612-332-6037
E-mail: info@pwcenter.org
Web Site: www.pwcenter.org
Key Personnel
Producing Artistic Dir: Jeremy Cohen *Tel:* 612-332-7481 ext 1113 *E-mail:* jeremyc@pwcenter.org
Assoc Artistic Dir: Hayley Finn *Tel:* 612-332-7481 ext 1119 *E-mail:* hayleyf@pwcenter.org
Artistic Progs Mgr: Julia Brown *Tel:* 612-332-7481 ext 1115 *E-mail:* juliab@pwcenter.org
Established: 1990
Fellowships that recognize mid-career playwrights whose work demonstrates exceptional artistic merit & potential. Playwright's primary residence must be in the state of Minnesota. Applicants must have had a minimum of one work fully produced by a professional theater at the time of application.
Award: $25,000 stipend, $2,500 in development support & $1,400 in travel support

McKnight National Residency & Commission
Playwrights' Center
2301 Franklin Ave E, Minneapolis, MN 55406-1099
Tel: 612-332-7481 *Fax:* 612-332-6037
E-mail: info@pwcenter.org
Web Site: www.pwcenter.org
Key Personnel
Producing Artistic Dir: Jeremy Cohen *Tel:* 612-332-7481 ext 1113 *E-mail:* jeremyc@pwcenter.org
Assoc Artistic Dir: Hayley Finn *Tel:* 612-332-7481 ext 1119 *E-mail:* hayleyf@pwcenter.org
Artistic Progs Mgr: Julia Brown *Tel:* 612-332-7481 ext 1115 *E-mail:* juliab@pwcenter.org
Established: 1982
Open to nationally recognized playwrights. Applicants must have had a minimum of 2 different works fully produced by professional theaters. Call or check web site for application information & deadline guidelines. Minnesota-based playwrights are not eligible for the award.
Award: $15,000 commission & up to $12,250 in development support

Phillip H McMath Post Publication Book Award
Arkansas Writers MFA Workshop, University of Central Arkansas
Dept of Writing, University of Central Arkansas, 201 Donaghey Ave, Thompson Hall 303, Conway, AR 72035
Web Site: arkansaswriters.wordpress.com
Key Personnel
Dir: Stephanie Vanderslice *Tel:* 501-450-3340 *E-mail:* stephv@uca.edu
Two awards offered, 1 for prose & 1 for poetry. Any publisher, author, agent, or any legal representative of an author may enter full-length books published in the previous calendar year. Submissions may be in any genre & may not be self-published. Entry fee: $25. See web site for detailed guidelines & submission info.
Award: $500 honorarium & travel stipend to Arkatext Literary Festival in the Spring
Closing Date: Oct 15

John McMenemy Prize
Canadian Political Science Association (CPSA)
260 Dalhousie St, Suite 400, Ottawa, ON K1N 7E4, Canada
Tel: 613-562-1202 *Fax:* 613-241-0019
E-mail: cpsaprizes@cpsa-acsp.ca; cpsa-acsp@cpsa-acsp.ca
Web Site: www.cpsa-acsp.ca
Key Personnel
Exec Dir: Silvina Danesi
Admin: C Ngako Woktcheu
Established: 2000
To the author(s) of the best article in English or French, published in the *Canadian Journal of Political Science*.
Other Sponsor(s): Societe Quebecoise de Science Politique
Award: Five memberships in the Canadian Political Science Association & the Societe Quebecoise de Science Politique
Presented: CPSA Annual Conference

Medal for Distinguished Contribution to American Letters
National Book Foundation
90 Broad St, Suite 604, New York, NY 10004
Tel: 212-685-0261 *Fax:* 212-213-6570
E-mail: nationalbook@nationalbook.org
Web Site: www.nationalbook.org/amerletters.html
Key Personnel
Exec Dir: Ruth Dickey *E-mail:* rdickey@nationalbook.org
Sr Mgr, Awards & Honors: Madeleine Shelton *E-mail:* mshelton@nationalbook.org
Sr Mgr, Mktg & Communs: Ale Romero *E-mail:* aromero@nationalbook.org
Awards & Communs Coord: Lilly Santiago *E-mail:* lsantiago@nationalbook.org
Presented by the Board of Directors, in conjunction with the conferring of the National Book Awards to a person who has enriched our literary heritage over a life of service, or a corpus of work.
Award: $10,000
Presented: Autumn

Medal for Editorial Excellence
The Center for Fiction
15 Lafayette Ave, Brooklyn, NY 11217
Tel: 212-755-6710
E-mail: info@centerforfiction.org
Web Site: www.centerforfiction.org/grants-awards/maxwell-e-perkins-award
Key Personnel
Writing Progs Mgr: Randy Winston
Established: 2005
To honor the work of an editor, publisher, or agent who over the course of his or her career has discovered, nurtured & championed writers of fiction in the US.

Medal of Honor for Literature
National Arts Club
15 Gramercy Park S, New York, NY 10003
Tel: 212-475-3424
E-mail: literary@thenationalartsclub.org
Web Site: www.nationalartsclub.org
Key Personnel
Chair, Literary Comm: Cherry Provost
Established: 1967
Presented for a body of work of literary excellence; nominations within the committee only & awarded by the Board of Governors. Recipent chooses gala location.
Award: Gold medal
Presented: Gala Black Tie Dinner

Medieval Academy Book Subvention Program
Medieval Academy of America (MAA)
6 Beacon St, Suite 500, Boston, MA 02108
Tel: 617-491-1622 *Fax:* 617-492-3303
E-mail: info@themedievalacademy.org
Web Site: www.medievalacademy.org/page/maa_book_subvention
Key Personnel
Exec Dir: Lisa Fagin Davis *E-mail:* lfd@themedievalacademy.org
Provides subventions to university or other nonprofit scholarly presses to support the publication of first books by Medieval Academy members. Applications for subventions will be accepted only from the publisher & only for books that have already been approved for publication. See web site for eligibility requirements & application details.
Award: Up to $2,500
Closing Date: May 1

Medieval Academy Inclusivity & Diversity Book Subvention Program
Medieval Academy of America (MAA)
6 Beacon St, Suite 500, Boston, MA 02108
Tel: 617-491-1622 *Fax:* 617-492-3303
E-mail: info@themedievalacademy.org
Web Site: www.medievalacademy.org/page/inclusivitydiversitybooksubvention
Key Personnel
Exec Dir: Lisa Fagin Davis *E-mail:* lfd@themedievalacademy.org
Provides subventions to university or other nonprofit scholarly presses to support the publication of books concerning the study of inclusivity & diversity in the Middle Ages (broadly conceived) by Medieval Academy members. Applications for subventions will be accepted only from the publisher & only for books that have already been approved for publication. See web site for eligibility requirements & application details.
Award: Up to $5,000
Closing Date: May 1

Medieval Academy of America Article Prize in Critical Race Studies
Medieval Academy of America (MAA)
6 Beacon St, Suite 500, Boston, MA 02108
Tel: 617-491-1622 *Fax:* 617-492-3303
E-mail: info@themedievalacademy.org
Web Site: www.medievalacademy.org/page/racestudiesarticleprize
Key Personnel
Exec Dir: Lisa Fagin Davis *E-mail:* lfd@themedievalacademy.org
Established: 2020
Awarded to an article in the field of medieval studies, published in a scholarly journal, that explores questions of race & the medieval world, which is judged by the selection committee to be of outstanding quality. Seeks to highlight contributions that effectively challenge & enable the field of medieval studies to examine the significance of race both in our areas of research & our processes & methods

of scholarship. Articles may be historical or historiographic in nature; scholars of all levels & affiliations are welcome to apply. Articles shall be submitted in the year following their publication. Articles, published in a scholarly journal, must be at least 5 pages in length. A PDF of the article should be sent by e-mail to the Executive Director, together with a CV.
Award: $500 & certificate
Closing Date: Oct 15
Presented: MAA Annual Meeting, Spring

Lucille Medwick Memorial Award
Poetry Society of America (PSA)
119 Smith St, Brooklyn, NY 11201
Tel: 212-254-9628
E-mail: info@poetrysociety.org
Web Site: poetrysociety.org/awards
Key Personnel
Exec Dir: Matt Brogan *E-mail:* matt@poetrysociety.org
Deputy Dir: Brett Fletcher Lauer *E-mail:* brett@poetrysociety.org
Devt Dir: Madeline Weinfield *E-mail:* madeline@poetrysociety.org
Established: 1974
For an original poem in any form on a humanitarian theme. All submissions must be through Submittable. Entry fee: Free to membs, $10 nonmembs.
Award: $500
Closing Date: Dec 31
Presented: Annual Awards Ceremony, New York, NY, Spring

Sonny Mehta Fellowships in Creative Writing
Writers' Workshop, The University of Iowa
102 Dey House, 507 N Clinton St, Iowa City, IA 52242-1000
Tel: 319-335-0416
Web Site: writersworkshop.uiowa.edu/mehta
Key Personnel
Dir, Writers' Workshop: Lan Samantha Chang
Prog Admin: Sasha Khmelnik *E-mail:* aleksandra-khmelnik@uiowa.edu
Established: 2021
Two full fellowships for international students, 1 in fiction & 1 in poetry, with preference given to applicants from underrepresented countries, particularly the Indian subcontinent, the Middle East & North Africa.
Other Sponsor(s): Gita Mehta Endowment
Award: Support for travel & visa costs, tuition, a living stipend & other associated expenses for a year of study at the workshop
Closing Date: Dec 15

Frederic G Melcher Scholarship
Association for Library Service to Children (ALSC)
Division of The American Library Association (ALA)
225 N Michigan Ave, Suite 1300, Chicago, IL 60601
Tel: 312-280-2163 *Toll Free Tel:* 800-545-2433
Fax: 312-280-5271
E-mail: alsc@ala.org
Web Site: www.ala.org/alsc/awardsgrants/scholarships
Key Personnel
Exec Dir: Alena Rivers *Tel:* 800-545-2433 ext 5866 *E-mail:* arivers@ala.org
Awards Coord: Jordan Dubin *Tel:* 800-545-2433 ext 5839 *E-mail:* jdubin@ala.org
Prog Coord: Ann Michaud *Tel:* 800-545-2433 ext 2166 *E-mail:* amichaud@ala.org
Membership/Mktg Specialist: Elizabeth Serrano *Tel:* 800-545-2433 ext 2164 *E-mail:* eserrano@ala.org
Established: 1956
Two scholarships awarded to provide financial assistance for the professional education of men & women who intend to pursue an MLS degree & who plan to work in children's librarianship. This work may be serving children up to & including the age of 14 in any type of library. Applicants must be citizens of the US or Canada.
Award: $8,000 each
Closing Date: March 1
Presented: ALA Annual Conference & Exhibition, June

Louise Meriwether First Book Prize
The Feminist Press at The City University of New York
365 Fifth Ave, Suite 5406, New York, NY 10016
SAN: 213-6813
Tel: 212-817-7915
E-mail: louisemeriwetherprize@gmail.com; info@feministpress.org
Web Site: www.feministpress.org/louise-meriwether-first-book-prize
Established: 2016
The prize honors author Louise Meriwether by publishing a debut work by a woman or nonbinary author of color, between 30,000 & 80,000 words. Open to fiction & nonfiction. No poetry, plays, or academic texts. Submit ms as a PDF along with cover letter as a separate PDF attachment including author statement, brief bio, ms word count, how your work fits with the Feminist Press, brief list of up to 3 writers that you consider part of your writing lineage & if you are represented by a literary agent. The work submitted may not be under contract elsewhere.
Other Sponsor(s): TAYO Literary Magazine
Award: $5,000 advance (half at the time of the initial award & half upon publication) & contract to publish their book

Joyce Meskis Excellence in Bookselling Scholarship
Mountains & Plains Independent Booksellers Association
PO Box 746, Denver, CO 80201
Toll Free Tel: 800-752-0249
E-mail: info@mountainsplains.org
Web Site: www.mountainsplains.org/meskis-scholarship
Key Personnel
Exec Dir: Heather Duncan *E-mail:* heather@mountainsplains.org
Mktg & Communs Mgr: Jeremy Ellis
Opers Mgr: Kelsey Myers
Established: 2023
Program offers scholarships to MPIBA member bookstores to attend the FallCon Trade Show & Conference & the SpringCon Conference. Member applicants must be in good standing, with dues current. One scholarship per store per year.
Award: Airfare & other travel-related expense reimbursement, 3-night hotel room, tickets to all conference events (meals included) & $50 per conference day additional spending stipend
Closing Date: Aug

Addison M Metcalf Award in Literature
American Academy of Arts & Letters
633 W 155 St, New York, NY 10032
Tel: 212-368-5900
E-mail: academy@artsandletters.org
Web Site: artsandletters.org/awards
Key Personnel
Exec Dir: Cody Upton
Established: 1986
Awarded biennially, in odd-numbered years, to honor young writers of great promise. Candidates must be nominated by an Academy member.
Award: $10,000

Edna Meudt Poetry Book Award
Council for Wisconsin Writers (CWW)
c/o 210 N Main St, No 204, Cedar Grove, WI 53013
E-mail: wiswriters@gmail.com
Web Site: wiswriters.org/awards
Key Personnel
Contest Chair: Sylvia Cavanaugh *E-mail:* bgirl4shadow@gmail.com
Established: 1965
Award for the best book of poems published by a Wisconsin-based author in the contest year. Entry fee: $25 nonmembs.
Award: $500 & 1-week residency at Shake Rag Alley Center for the Arts
Closing Date: Jan 31
Presented: CWW Annual Award Ceremony & Banquet, May

Michener Center for Writers Fellowship
Michener Center for Writers
702 E Dean Keeton St, Austin, TX 78705
Tel: 512-471-1601
E-mail: mcw@utexas.edu
Web Site: michener.utexas.edu
MFA in Writing program of the University of Texas at Austin. Full-time residency.
Award: $29,500 per academic year, plus total coverage of tuition & stipend for health insurance

Midwest Bookseller of the Year Award
Midwest Independent Booksellers Association (MIBA)
939 W Seventh St, St Paul, MN 55102
Tel: 612-208-6279
Web Site: www.midwestbooksellers.org/bookseller-of-the-year.html
Key Personnel
Exec Dir: Carrie Obry *E-mail:* carrie@midwestbooksellers.org
Opers Mgr: Kate Scott
Prog Coord: Melissa Peterson
Established: 2018
Awarded to a bookseller in MIBA's region (North Dakota, South Dakota, Wisconsin, Iowa, Minnesota, Michigan's Upper Peninsula, Illinois, Kansas, Missouri & Nebraska) in recognition of excellence in the field of bookselling. Anyone working in a bookstore is eligible for the award. Nomination form opens April 1.
Closing Date: April 30
Presented: Annual Heartland Fall Forum, Winner announced July 1

Kenneth W Mildenberger Prize
Modern Language Association (MLA)
85 Broad St, New York, NY 10004
SAN: 202-6422
Tel: 646-576-5141; 646-576-5000
E-mail: awards@mla.org
Web Site: www.mla.org
Key Personnel
Coord, Book Prizes: Annie M Reiser *E-mail:* areiser@mla.org
Established: 1980
Awarded biennially, in odd-numbered years, for a work in the field of language, culture, literacy or literature with strong application to the teaching of languages other than English. Authors need not be members of the MLA. Awarded for a book published in 2023 or 2024. For consideration, submit 4 print copies & electronic access.
Award: Cash award & certificate
Closing Date: May 1, 2025
Presented: MLA Annual Convention, Toronto, ON, CN, Jan 2026

Milkweed Fellowship
Milkweed Editions
1011 Washington Ave S, Suite 300, Minneapolis, MN 55415-1246

Tel: 612-332-3192 *Toll Free Tel:* 800-520-6455
E-mail: fellowship@milkweed.org
Web Site: milkweed.org/milkweed-fellowship
Key Personnel
Art Dir: Mary Austin Speaker
  E-mail: mary_austin_speaker@milkweed.org
Paid 1- to 2-year immersion program designed to offer the tools, experience & exposure necessary to pursue a career in book publishing. Position seeks to provide entry to those historically underrepresented among workers in book publishing (indigenous, people of color, LGBTQIA+ & those with disabilities). Application must include cover letter, 1- to 2-page resume & writing sample. Materials should be submitted as one combined PDF via Submittable (milkweededitions.submittable.com/submit).
Award: $30,000 salary per year, paid time off, health & dental benefits
Closing Date: June

Millay Colony for the Arts Residency
Millay Colony for the Arts
454 E Hill Rd, Austerlitz, NY 12017
Mailing Address: PO Box 3, Austerlitz, NY 12017-0003
Tel: 518-392-3103
E-mail: apply@millaycolony.org; residency@millaycolony.org
Web Site: www.millaycolony.org
Key Personnel
Co-Dir: Monika Burczyk
Residency Dir: Calliope Nicholas
Established: 1973
Residencies for writers, composers & visual artists. Information available by e-mail or on web site. Applications available via web site portal.
Award: One-month & 2-week residencies offered including room, studio & meals; no cash award
Closing Date: Oct 1 (residencies in May/June/July) & March 1 (residencies in Aug/Sept/Oct)

Patricia Cleary Miller Award for Poetry
New Letters
UMKC, University House, 5101 Rockhill Rd, Kansas City, MO 64110-2499
Tel: 816-235-1169
E-mail: newletters@umkc.edu
Web Site: www.newletters.org
Established: 1986
All entries considered for publication. A poetry entry may contain up to 6 poems & those poems need not be related. Multiple entries are accepted with appropriate fees. No postal entries will be accepted. All entries must be submitted online through Submittable. Please include one cover sheet stating the genre (poetry) & title of each poem. Your personal information should not appear anywhere on the entry. The name of the file you upload should be the title of the first poem in the entry. Entry fee: $24 per ms (includes 1-year subscription to *New Letters*).
Award: $2,500 & publication
Closing Date: May 18

Milner Award
Friends of the Atlanta-Fulton Public Library
One Margaret Mitchell Sq NW, Atlanta, GA 30303
Tel: 404-730-1865
E-mail: info@themilneraward.org
Web Site: www.themilneraward.org
Established: 1983
For living American authors of children's books voted on by the children of Atlanta & Fulton County. No application process.
Other Sponsor(s): Milner Award Committee
Award: Honorarium & glass sculpture (inkwell & pen) by Hans Frabel

Closing Date: April 1
Presented: Atlanta, GA

Minnesota Book Awards
The Friends of the Saint Paul Public Library
1080 Montreal Ave, Suite 2, St Paul, MN 55116
Tel: 651-222-3242 *Fax:* 651-222-1988
E-mail: friends@thefriends.org
Web Site: thefriends.org/events/mnba
Key Personnel
Dir: Alayne Hopkins *Tel:* 651-366-6488
  E-mail: alayne@thefriends.org
Established: 1988
Books created by writers, illustrators, or book artists who are Minnesotans are eligible for the awards through submissions that open in August. Awards are given each year for books published in the previous year.
Award: Cash & physical award
Closing Date: Mid-Nov
Presented: Minnesota Book Awards Ceremony, April

Minotaur Books/Mystery Writers of America First Crime Novel Competition
Mystery Writers of America (MWA)
1140 Broadway, Suite 1507, New York, NY 10001
Tel: 212-888-8171
E-mail: mwa@mysterywriters.org
Web Site: mysterywriters.org/about-mwa/st-martins; us.macmillan.com/minotaurbooks/submit-manuscript
Key Personnel
EVP: Donna Andrews
Exec Dir: Margery Flax
Open to any writer, regardless of nationality, aged 18 or older, who has never been the author of any published novel (in any genre) & is not under contract with a publisher for publication of a novel. Only one ms entry is permitted per writer. Must submit online entry form & upload electronic file of ms; do not mail or e-mail ms submission to Minotaur Books.
Other Sponsor(s): Minotaur Books
Closing Date: Jan 1
Presented: Edgar Awards Banquet, April

The Miranda Family Voces Latinx National Playwriting Competition
The Miranda Family Foundation
138 E 27 St, New York, NY 10016
Tel: 212-225-9950 *Fax:* 212-225-9085
Web Site: www.repertorio.org
Key Personnel
Spec Projs Mgr: Allison Astor Vargas
  E-mail: aav@repertorio.org
Established: 2019
Competition to develop & promote Latinx plays & playwrights. Playwrights may be Latinx or of any other ethnic or racial background as long as the play's subject matter & characters resonate with, & accurately depict, the Latinx/Hispanic experience. Must be 18 years of age & residents of the US or Puerto Rico. All plays must be original & full-length (minimum running time: 75 minutes) & can be written in Spanish +/or English.
Award: $3,000 (1st prize), $2,000 (2nd prize), $1,000 (3rd prize), $500 each (2 runners up); top 5 plays get a staged reading at Repertorio Espanol
Closing Date: Feb 1

Mirrors & Windows Fellowship
The Loft Literary Center
Open Book Bldg, Suite 200, 1011 Washington Ave S, Minneapolis, MN 55415
Tel: 612-215-2575 *Fax:* 612-215-2576
E-mail: loft@loft.org
Web Site: loft.org/awards/mirrors-windows

Key Personnel
Exec & Artistic Dir: Arleta M Little *Tel:* 612-215-2584 *E-mail:* alittle@loft.org
Mktg & Communs Dir: Chris Mackenzie Jones
  Tel: 612-215-2589 *E-mail:* cjones@loft.org
Established: 2018
Six-month mentorships to 10-12 emerging/early career Minnesota indigenous writers & writers of color who are interested in creating children's +/or young adult books.
Other Sponsor(s): Jerome Foundation; Archie D & Bertha H Walker Foundation
Award: Mentoring by diverse published authors of books for children & young readers

Mississippi Review Prize
University of Southern Mississippi Department of English
118 College Dr, Box 5144, Hattiesburg, MS 39406-0001
Tel: 601-266-4321
E-mail: msreview@usm.edu
Web Site: www.usm.edu/mississippi-review/contest.html
Key Personnel
Ed-in-Chief: Adam Clay
Prizes in poetry, fiction & nonfiction. Contest is open to all writers in English except current or former students or employees of the University of Southern Mississippi. Fiction & nonfiction entries should be 1,000-8,000 words; poetry entries should be 3-5 poems totaling 10 pages or less. Entry fee: $16 online, $15 by post.
Award: $1,000 each category & publication in the print issue of *Mississippi Review* next Spring
Closing Date: Jan 1
Presented: Announced in March

H L Mitchell Award
Southern Historical Association (SHA)
University of Georgia, Dept of History, Athens, GA 30602-1602
Tel: 706-542-8848
Web Site: thesha.org/mitchell
Key Personnel
Secy/Treas: Dr Stephen Berry *E-mail:* berrys@thesha.org
Given in recognition of a distinguished book concerning the history of the southern working class, including but not limited to industrial laborers +/or small farmers & agricultural laborers. Awarded in even-numbered years for a book published during the preceding 2 years.
Closing Date: March 1
Presented: Annual Meeting (even-numbered years)

W O Mitchell Book Prize, see The City of Calgary W O Mitchell Book Prize

Lindsley & Masao Miyoshi Translation Prizes & Grants
Japan-US Friendship Commission
Affiliate of Donald Keene Center of Japanese Culture, Columbia University
Columbia University, 507 Kent Hall, MC3920, New York, NY 10027
Tel: 212-854-5036 *Fax:* 212-854-4019
E-mail: donald-keene-center@columbia.edu
Web Site: www.keenecenter.org
Established: 2017
Prizes & grants of varying amounts. These include: prizes given to outstanding translations by non-citizens or non-permanent residents of the US; prizes for translations of particular scholarly merit or significance; grants to promising translations-in-progress; subventions for forthcoming publication of especially deserving translations; in rare cases, lifetime achievement awards for translators with particularly distinguished careers.
Award: Up to $6,000

Closing Date: June 1
Presented: Columbia University, New York, NY, April

MLA Prize for a First Book
Modern Language Association (MLA)
85 Broad St, New York, NY 10004
SAN: 202-6422
Tel: 646-576-5141; 646-576-5000
E-mail: awards@mla.org
Web Site: www.mla.org
Key Personnel
Coord, Book Prizes: Annie M Reiser
    E-mail: areiser@mla.org
Established: 1993
Awarded for an outstanding scholarly work published in the year prior to competition as the first book-length publication by a current member of the MLA. For consideration, submit 5 print copies & electronic access.
Award: Cash award & certificate
Closing Date: March 1, 2025
Presented: MLA Annual Convention, Toronto, ON, CN, Jan 2026

MLA Prize for a Scholarly Edition
Modern Language Association (MLA)
85 Broad St, New York, NY 10004
SAN: 202-6422
Tel: 646-576-5141; 646-576-5000
E-mail: awards@mla.org
Web Site: www.mla.org
Key Personnel
Coord, Book Prizes: Annie M Reiser
    E-mail: areiser@mla.org
Established: 1995
Awarded biennially in odd-numbered years. Committee solicits submissions of editions published in 2023 or 2024. A multivolume edition is eligible if at least one volume has been published during that period. The editor need not be a member of the MLA. Edition should be based on an examination of all available relevant textual sources. The source texts & the edited text's deviation from them should be fully described. The edition should exhibit the highest standards of accuracy in the presentation of its text & apparatus, which should be presented as accessibly & elegantly as possible. For consideration, submit 4 print copies & electronic access.
Award: Cash award & certificate
Closing Date: May 1, 2025
Presented: MLA Annual Convention, Toronto, ON, CN, Jan 2026

MLA Prize for an Edited Collection
Modern Language Association (MLA)
85 Broad St, New York, NY 10004
SAN: 202-6422
Tel: 646-576-5141; 646-576-5000
E-mail: awards@mla.org
Web Site: www.mla.org
Key Personnel
Coord, Book Prizes: Annie M Reiser
    E-mail: areiser@mla.org
Awarded biennially, in odd-numbered years, to recognize the intellectual labor involved in producing edited collections. The prize is given without regard to the language of the text presented in the work as long as the work falls within the subject scope of the MLA (modern languages & literatures, composition theory, folklore, linguistics). Editors must be current MLA members, but contributors to the collections need not be. Edited collections must be published in 2023 or 2024. For consideration, send 4 print copies & electronic access.
Award: Cash award & certificate
Closing Date: May 1, 2025
Presented: MLA Annual Convention, Toronto, ON, CN, Jan 2026

MLA Prize for Bibliographical or Archival Scholarship
Modern Language Association (MLA)
85 Broad St, New York, NY 10004
SAN: 202-6422
Tel: 646-576-5141; 646-576-5000
E-mail: awards@mla.org
Web Site: www.mla.org
Key Personnel
Coord, Book Prizes: Annie M Reiser
    E-mail: areiser@mla.org
Established: 1998
Awarded biennially, in even-numbered years, to recognize enumerative & descriptive bibliographies, archives, digital projects, or collaborative research projects published in 2024 or 2025. Editors or compilers need not be members of MLA. For consideration, editors or publishers should submit 4 print copies, PDF & letter of identification.
Award: Cash award & certificate
Closing Date: May 1, 2026
Presented: MLA Annual Convention, Los Angeles, CA, Jan 2027

MLA Prize for Independent Scholars
Modern Language Association (MLA)
85 Broad St, New York, NY 10004
SAN: 202-6422
Tel: 646-576-5141; 646-576-5000
E-mail: awards@mla.org
Web Site: www.mla.org
Key Personnel
Coord, Book Prizes: Annie M Reiser
    E-mail: areiser@mla.org
Established: 1983
Awarded biennially, in even-numbered years, for a distinguished scholarly book published in 2024 or 2025 in the field of English or another modern language or literature. Author enrolled in a program leading to an academic degree & did not hold a tenured, tenure-accruing, or tenure-track position in post-secondary education at the time of publication is eligible. For consideration, submit 6 print copies & electronic access, plus a completed entry form.
Award: Cash award & certificate
Closing Date: May 1, 2025
Presented: MLA Annual Convention, Los Angeles, CA, Jan 2027

MLA Prize for Studies in Native American Literatures, Cultures & Languages
Modern Language Association (MLA)
85 Broad St, New York, NY 10004
SAN: 202-6422
Tel: 646-576-5141; 646-576-5000
E-mail: awards@mla.org
Web Site: www.mla.org
Key Personnel
Coord, Book Prizes: Annie M Reiser
    E-mail: areiser@mla.org
Established: 2012
Awarded biennially, in even-numbered years, to a current MLA member for an outstanding scholarly work in the field of Native American literatures, cultures & languages published in 2024 or 2025. Selection committee is seeking works that examine & broaden understanding of the cultural expressions of first peoples or nations in the US, CN & Mexico. For consideration, submit 4 print copies & electronic access.
Closing Date: May 1, 2026
Presented: MLA Annual Convention, Los Angeles, CA, Jan 2027

MLA Prize in United States Latina & Latino & Chicana & Chicano Literary & Cultural Studies
Modern Language Association (MLA)
85 Broad St, New York, NY 10004
SAN: 202-6422
Tel: 646-576-5141; 646-576-5000
E-mail: awards@mla.org
Web Site: www.mla.org
Key Personnel
Coord, Book Prizes: Annie M Reiser
    E-mail: areiser@mla.org
Established: 2002
Awarded biennially, in odd-numbered years, to a current member of the association for an outstanding scholarly study in any language of US Latina & Latino or Chicana & Chicano literature or culture published in 2023 or 2024. Books that are primarily translations will not be considered. For consideration, the author or publisher should send 4 print copies & electronic access.
Award: Cash award, certificate & 1 year association membership
Closing Date: May 1, 2025
Presented: MLA Annual Convention, Toronto, ON, CN, Jan 2026

Henry Allen Moe Prize
Fenimore Art Museum
5798 State Hwy 80, Cooperstown, NY 13326
Mailing Address: PO Box 800, Cooperstown, NY 13326-0800
Tel: 607-547-2586
E-mail: publications@fenimoreart.org
Web Site: www.fenimoreartmuseum.org/publication-awards
Key Personnel
Dir, Mktg & Communs: Todd A Kenyon
    E-mail: t.kenyon@fenimoreart.org
Awarded in recognition of excellence in exhibitions & collections-based publishing. Income from an endowment from Mrs Henry Allen Moe, in memory of her husband, is used for substantial cash prizes to foster & recognize scholarship in art history & decorative arts studies in the form of published catalogues of exhibits & collections. Entries must have been published the previous year & be submitted in 4 copies, accompanied by a letter of transmittal stating intent to enter the contest. Only catalogs treating collections located or exhibited in New York State qualify.
Closing Date: Feb 15

Montana Book Award
Friends of Missoula Public Library
PO Box 8732, Missoula, MT 59802-8732
E-mail: montanabookaward@gmail.com
Web Site: montanabookaward.org
Established: 2002
Awarded in recognition of literary +/or artistic excellence in a book published during the award year. Eligible titles are either set in Montana, deal with Montana themes/issues, or are written, edited or illustrated by a Montana author or artist. Books for all ages are considered for the award. See web site for nomination form & full eligibility requirements.
Closing Date: Dec 10 (postmark)

David Montgomery Award
The Organization of American Historians (OAH)
112 N Bryan Ave, Bloomington, IN 47408-4141
Tel: 812-855-7311
E-mail: oah@oah.org
Web Site: www.oah.org/awards
Key Personnel
Exec Dir: Beth English *Tel:* 812-855-9836
    E-mail: benglish@oah.org
Dir, Communs & Mktg: Kym Robinson *Tel:* 812-855-5430 *E-mail:* kymarobi@oah.org
Awarded for the best book on a topic in American labor & working-class history. Eligible works shall be written in English & deal with US history in significant ways but may include comparative or transnational studies that fall within these guidelines. Each entry must be published during the calendar year preceding

that in which the award is given. One copy of each entry must be mailed directly to the committee members listed on the web site.
Closing Date: Oct 1 (postmarked)
Presented: OAH Conference on American History, Spring

Cenie H Moon Prize
The Poetry Society of Virginia (PSV)
PO Box 36128, North Chesterfield, VA 23235-3533
E-mail: contest@poetrysocietyofvirginia.org; info@poetryvirginia.org
Web Site: www.poetrysocietyofvirginia.org
Key Personnel
Pres: Cherryl T Cooley
E-mail: poetrysocietypresident@gmail.com
All entries must be in English, original & unpublished. Subject: Woman or women, 48 line limit, any form. Submit 1 copy of the poem with no identifying information but put the category in the upper right-hand-side, along with a notation as to whether you are a member of PSV (does not matter if you are a lifetime member or just joined for the contest). Submit a cover letter/page that contains the category, the name of the poem, your name & address, phone number & e-mail address. Entries will not be returned. Entry fee: Free to membs, $5 nonmembs.
Award: $50 (1st prize), $30 (2nd prize), $20 (3rd prize)
Closing Date: Feb
Presented: PSV Awards Ceremony, April

Moonbeam Children's Book Awards
Independent Publisher Online
Division of Jenkins Group Inc
1129 Woodmere Ave, Suite B, Traverse City, MI 49686
Tel: 231-933-0445 *Toll Free Tel:* 800-706-4636 *Fax:* 231-933-0448
E-mail: moonbeam@jgibookawards.com
Web Site: moonbeamawards.com
Key Personnel
Awards Dir: Amy Shamroe *Tel:* 800-644-0133 ext 1000 *E-mail:* amys@jenkinsgroupinc.com
Established: 2007
Award celebrating youthful curiosity, discovery & learning through books & reading. Recognizes the best children's books published each year for the North American market. Authors, illustrators, publishers & self-publishers of children's books intended for the North American market may enter. Entry fee: $75-$95 per category.
Other Sponsor(s): Jenkins Group Inc
Award: Gold medal (1st place), silver medal (2nd place), bronze medal (3rd place), personalized certificate & 20 sample seals
Closing Date: Aug
Presented: Traverse City Children's Book Festival, Nov

Jenny McKean Moore Writer-in-Washington
George Washington University
English Dept, Rome Hall, 801 22 St NW, Suite 643, Washington, DC 20052
Tel: 202-994-6180
E-mail: engldept@gwu.edu
Web Site: english.columbian.gwu.edu
Key Personnel
Dir, Creative Writing: Lisa Page
E-mail: lpageinc@gwu.edu
Established: 1976
To be considered, applications must be made by letter indicating publications, teaching experience & a selection of published work. Genre alternates from year to year. Consult AWP job list for advertisement specifying genre.
Award: One-year teaching position for approximately $80,000 plus benefits
Closing Date: Biennially in Dec, odd-numbered years

The William C Morris YA Debut Award
The American Library Association (ALA)
225 N Michigan Ave, Suite 1300, Chicago, IL 60601
SAN: 201-0062
Tel: 312-280-4390 *Toll Free Tel:* 800-545-2433 (ext 4390) *Fax:* 312-280-5276
E-mail: yalsa@ala.org
Web Site: www.ala.org/yalsa/morris
Established: 2009
Honors a debut book published by a first-time author writing for teens & celebrating impressive new voices in young adult literature. Books must have been published November 1-October 31 of the year preceding the award. Nominations by committee.
Presented: ALA Youth Media Awards, Late Jan

Willie Morris Awards for Southern Writing
University of Mississippi
Dept of Writing & Rhetoric, PO Box 1848, University, MS 38677
E-mail: wmawards@olemiss.edu
Web Site: www.williemorrisawards.org; www.williemorrisawards.org/submissions
Key Personnel
Awards Prog Coord: Susan Nicholas
Established: 2008
Funded by Reba White Williams & Dave Williams, the awards honor some of the best literature telling rich, original stories about the US South marked by a strain of honest optimism. The award-winning works reflect a belief that things can be better, that the South, a region marked by systemic racism & economic extraction, can still be a place of opportunity & hope. Awarded in 3 categories. For fiction & nonfiction: books must be published during the submission year & cannot be self-published; poetry: poets may submit 1 original, unpublished poem no longer than 3 pages that evokes the American South. Submissions accepted starting July 1. See web site for complete criteria & submission instructions.
Award: Fiction & Nonfiction: $12,000 each; Poetry: $3,000; winners also receive an expenses-paid trip to Oxford, MS & a trophy
Closing Date: Sept 30
Presented: Oxford Conference for the Book

The Toni Morrison Achievement Award
National Book Critics Circle (NBCC)
c/o Jacob M Appel, Icahn School of Medicine at Mount Sinai, One Gustave L Levy Place, New York, NY 10029
E-mail: info@bookcritics.org
Web Site: www.bookcritics.org/the-toni-morrison-achievement-award
Key Personnel
Pres: Heather Scott Partington *E-mail:* hsp@bookcritics.org
Secy: Colette Bancroft *E-mail:* bancroft.colette72@gmail.com
Treas: Jacob M Appel *E-mail:* jacobmappel@gmail.com
VP, Awards: Keetje Kuipers *E-mail:* keetje@poetrynw.org
VP, Events: Jane Ciabattari *E-mail:* janeciab@gmail.com
Established: 2021
Awarded to an institution that has, over time, made significant contributions to book culture.
Presented: NBCC Awards Ceremony, March

Harold Morton Landon Translation Award
The Academy of American Poets Inc
75 Maiden Lane, Suite 901, New York, NY 10038
Tel: 212-274-0343
E-mail: awards@poets.org
Web Site: poets.org/academy-american-poets/prizes/harold-morton-landon-translation-award
Key Personnel
Pres & Exec Dir: Ricardo Alberto Maldonado
VP, Digital Engagement & Content: Jeff Gleaves
Ad & Mktg Dir: Michelle Campagna
Dir, Donor Rel: Molly Walsh
Dir, Progs: Nikay Paredes
Established: 1976
Award to recognize a poetry collection translated from any language into English & published in the previous calendar year. Books must be published in a standard edition (48 pages or more). Collaborations by up to 2 translators are eligible. Anthologies & self-published books will not be considered.
Award: $1,000
Closing Date: Feb 15

Kathryn A Morton Prize in Poetry
Sarabande Books Inc
822 E Market St, Louisville, KY 40206
Tel: 502-458-4028
E-mail: info@sarabandebooks.org
Web Site: www.sarabandebooks.org/morton
Key Personnel
Dir, Mktg & Publicity: Joanna Englert
E-mail: joanna@sarabandebooks.org
Contest is open to any poet writing in English. Individual poems from the ms may have been published previously in magazines, chapbooks of less than 48 pages, or anthologies, but the collection as a whole must be unpublished. Translations & previously published collections are not eligible. Online submission process. See web site for full details & ms requirements. Submission fee: $28.
Award: $2,000, publication of ms, Sarabande Writing Residency & standard royalty contract
Closing Date: Feb 15
Presented: Sept

George L Mosse Prize in European Intellectual & Cultural History
American Historical Association (AHA)
400 "A" St SE, Washington, DC 20003
Tel: 202-544-2422
E-mail: awards@historians.org
Web Site: www.historians.org/award-grant/george-l-mosse-prize/
Established: 2000
Awarded for an outstanding major work of extraordinary scholarly distinction, creativity & originality in the intellectual & cultural history of Europe since 1500. Only books of a high scholarly distinction should be submitted. Research accuracy, originality & literary merit are important selection factors. Books with a copyright of 2024 are eligible for the 2025 prize. Nominations may be made by an author or publisher. Along with an application form, applicants must mail a copy of their book to each prize committee member posted on our web site as the prize deadline approaches. All updated info on web site.
Award: $1,000
Closing Date: May 15, 2025
Presented: AHA Annual Meeting, Chicago, IL, Jan 2026

Most Promising New Textbook Award
Textbook & Academic Authors Association (TAA)
PO Box 367, Fountain City, WI 54629
E-mail: info@taaonline.net
Web Site: www.taaonline.net/promising-new-textbook-award

AWARDS, PRIZE CONTESTS, FELLOWSHIPS & GRANTS

Key Personnel
Exec Dir: Michael Spinella *Tel:* 973-943-0501 *E-mail:* michael.spinella@taaonline.net
Dir, Publg & Opers: Kim Pawlak *Tel:* 507-459-1363 *E-mail:* kim.pawlak@taaonline.net
Dir, Instl Memberships & Meetings: Maureen Foerster *Tel:* 530-864-3538 *E-mail:* maureen.foerster@taaonline.net
Membership Mktg Mgr: Eric Schmieder *Tel:* 919-437-0241 *E-mail:* eric.schmieder@taaonline.net
Membership Coord: Bekky Murphy *Tel:* 608-567-9060 *E-mail:* bekky.murphy@taaonline.net
Recognizes excellence in 1st edition textbooks & learning materials. Works are judged for merit in 4 areas: pedagogy; content/scholarship; writing; appearance & design. Nomination fee: $375 (non-refundable). See web site for nomination form & entry guidelines.
Closing Date: Dec 15
Presented: TAA Annual Conference, June

Frank Luther Mott-KTA Journalism & Mass Communication Research Award
Kappa Tau Alpha
University of Missouri, School of Journalism, 203 Neff Hall, Columbia, MO 65211-1200
Tel: 573-882-7685
E-mail: umcjourkta@missouri.edu
Web Site: www.kappataualpha.net
Key Personnel
Exec Dir: Beverly J Horvit, PhD *Tel:* 573-882-0880 *E-mail:* horvitb@missouri.edu
Established: 1944
For the best research-based books about journalism or mass communication published each year. Edited volumes, textbooks & revised editions previously entered are not eligible. Paperback editions are acceptable.
Award: $1,000 & plaque
Closing Date: Dec (see web site)
Presented: Aug

Sheila Margaret Motton Book Prize
New England Poetry Club
c/o Linda Haviland Conte, 18 Hall Ave, Apt 2, Somerville, MA 02144
E-mail: info@nepoetryclub.org
Web Site: nepoetryclub.org
Key Personnel
Co-Pres: Doug Holder; Denise Provost
VP: Hilary Sallick
Treas: Linda Haviland Conte
 E-mail: nepctreasurer@gmail.com
Awarded for a book of poems published in the last 2 years. Send 2 copies of your book with a cover page that includes your contact information to Doug Holder, 25 School St, Somerville, MA 02143. Entry by post only. Entry fee: Free to membs, nonmembs $15 per submitted title.
Award: $250, 250 NEPC Award book cover stickers & opportunity to read at the NEPC (travel expenses not included)
Closing Date: May 31
Presented: Winners announced online Aug/Sept

Elizabeth Mrazik-Cleaver Canadian Picture Book Award
IBBY Canada
Unit of International Board on Books for Young People (IBBY)
c/o The Canadian Children's Book Ctr, 425 Adelaide St W, Suite 200, Toronto, ON M5V 3C1, Canada
Fax: 416-975-8970
E-mail: cleaver@ibby-canada.org; info@ibby-canada.org
Web Site: www.ibby-canada.org/awards/elizabeth-mrazik-cleaver-award/
Key Personnel
Treas: Yvette Ghione *E-mail:* treasurer@ibby-canada.org
Established: 1985
Awarded in recognition of outstanding artistic talent in a Canadian picture book. The recipient is a Canadian illustrator of a picture book published in Canada in English or French during the previous calendar year. To be eligible, the book must be a first edition & contain original illustrations by a Canadian illustrator (either a citizen or permanent resident). All genres are considered: fiction, nonfiction, poetry & folk & fairy tales. Entry fee: $25.
Award: $1,000 & certificate
Closing Date: Nov
Presented: Feb

Derrick Murdoch Award
Crime Writers of Canada (CWC)
716 Thicket Way, Ottawa, ON K4A 3B5, Canada
E-mail: info@crimewriterscanada.com
Web Site: www.crimewriterscanada.com/awards
Key Personnel
Exec Dir: Alison Bruce *E-mail:* ed@crimewriterscanada.com
Asst Exec Dir & Awards Mgr: Ludvica Boota *E-mail:* aed@crimewriterscanada.com
Established: 1984
Biennial special achievement award (alternating with the Grand Master Award) for contributions to the crime genre. Awarded in odd-numbered years.

Walter Dean Myers Awards for Outstanding Children's Literature
We Need Diverse Books™
10319 Westlake Dr, No 104, Bethesda, MD 20817
Tel: 701-404-WNDB (404-9632, voicemail only)
E-mail: walteraward@diversebooks.org
Web Site: diversebooks.org/our-programs/walter-award
Key Personnel
Co-Dir: Kathie Weinberg
 E-mail: kathieweinberg@diversebooks.org
Judging Comm Co-Chair: Maria Salvadore
Established: 2016
Awarded in recognition of diverse authors (or co-authors) whose works feature diverse main characters & address diversity in a meaningful way. Applicants must identify as diverse & the main character of the story must also identify as diverse, defined as one or more of the following: person of color; Native American; LGBTQIA+; person with a disability; marginalized religious or cultural minority in the US. Two categories: Teen & Young Reader. See web site for submission guidelines. Self-published titles are not accepted.
Closing Date: Nov 1 (postmarked)
Presented: Awards Ceremony, Library of Congress, Washington, DC, Winners announced Jan, ceremony in March

Walter Dean Myers Grants
We Need Diverse Books™
10319 Westlake Dr, No 104, Bethesda, MD 20817
Tel: 701-404-WNDB (404-9632, voicemail only)
E-mail: waltergrant@diversebooks.org
Web Site: diversebooks.org
Key Personnel
Pres & CEO: Ellen Oh
COO: Dhonielle Clayton
 E-mail: dhonielleclayton@diversebooks.org
CFO: Judy Schricker
Established: 2015
Applicants must identify as diverse, defined as one or more of the following: person of color; Native American; LGBTQIA+; person with a disability; marginalized religious or cultural minority in the US. Applicants must be unpublished illustrators +/or authors & working toward a career as a children's author +/or illustrator. Submit application via e-mail to: waltergrantapplications@diversebooks.org, including cover letter, essay & work sample. See web site for full submission guidelines. Grant is limited to US residents only or refugees living in the US. Ten winners will be selected.
Award: $2,000
Closing Date: June 30

Mythopoeic Awards
Mythopoeic Society
c/o University of Arizona, Dept of English, Rm 445, Tucson, AZ 85721
Mailing Address: PO Box 210067, Tucson, AZ 85721
E-mail: awards@mythsoc.org
Web Site: www.mythsoc.org
Key Personnel
Awards Admin: Dennis Wise
Established: 1967
Four awards. Two scholarship awards honor academic work from the last 3 years. One award is focused on Inklings scholarship & another award honors scholarship in myth & fantasy studies more generally. The 2 awards in the literature category, respectively, honor adult mythopoeic literature as well as children's or young adult mythopoeic literature. Only fiction from the last calendar year is eligible. Members make nominations in January & February. Winners are chosen by late July.
Award: Statuette
Presented: Mythcon, the annual conference of the Mythopoeic Society, Aug

NAREE Bivins Fellowship
National Association of Real Estate Editors (NAREE)
1003 NW Sixth Terr, Boca Raton, FL 33486-3455
Tel: 561-391-3599
Web Site: www.naree.org/bivins-fellowship
Key Personnel
Exec Dir: Mary Doyle-Kimball *Tel:* 561-391-1983 (cell) *E-mail:* mdkimball@naree.org
Professional development fellowship created for independent journalists working for the news division of independent news outlets. Provides travel grants for real estate journalists who want to attend the annual conference. Application fee: Free for membs, $75 nonmembs.
Closing Date: Sept

NAREE Real Estate Journalism Awards Competition
National Association of Real Estate Editors (NAREE)
1003 NW Sixth Terr, Boca Raton, FL 33486-3455
Tel: 561-391-3599
E-mail: nareejcontest@gmail.com
Web Site: www.naree.org/jcontest
Key Personnel
Exec Dir: Mary Doyle-Kimball *Tel:* 561-391-1983 (cell) *E-mail:* mdkimball@naree.org
Entrants must be independent journalists working for the news division of independent news outlets. Awards in more than 25 categories plus 3 overall awards for work published, posted or broadcast in the preceding calendar year. Work must be written or broadcast in English. Entry portal opens February 1. Entry fee: Free to membs, $75 nonmembs (for 1st entry); 2nd & each additional entry is $25.
Closing Date: March
Presented: NAREE Annual Real Estate Journalism Conference, Autumn

Natan Notable Books, see National Jewish Book Award-Natan Notable Books

National Award for Arts Writing, see Marfield Prize

COURSES & AWARDS

AWARDS, PRIZE CONTESTS, FELLOWSHIPS & GRANTS

National Awards for Education Reporting
Education Writers Association (EWA)
1825 "K" St NW, Suite 200, Washington, DC 20006
Tel: 202-452-9830
E-mail: awards@ewa.org
Web Site: ewa.org
Key Personnel
Exec Dir: Kathy Chow *E-mail:* kchow@ewa.org
Asst Dir: Lori Crouch *E-mail:* lcrouch@ewa.org
Established: 1960
Best education reporting in print & broadcast media. Winners & finalists in numerous categories. See web site for complete information.
Award: $1,000 for category prize winners. In the event of a tie, winners will split the prize
Closing Date: Jan
Presented: EWA National Seminar, Announced in the Spring

National Book Awards
National Book Foundation
90 Broad St, Suite 604, New York, NY 10004
Tel: 212-685-0261 *Fax:* 212-213-6570
E-mail: nationalbook@nationalbook.org
Web Site: www.nationalbook.org
Key Personnel
Exec Dir: Ruth Dickey *E-mail:* rdickey@nationalbook.org
Sr Mgr, Awards & Honors: Madeleine Shelton *E-mail:* mshelton@nationalbook.org
Sr Mgr, Mktg & Communs: Ale Romero *E-mail:* aromero@nationalbook.org
Awards & Communs Coord: Lilly Santiago *E-mail:* lsantiago@nationalbook.org
Established: 1950
Awards for living American authors for books in the US. Authors must either hold US citizenship or maintain primary, long-term residency in the US, US territories, or Tribal lands. Five categories: Fiction, nonfiction, poetry, young people's literature & translated literature. Entry fee: $135 per title.
Other Sponsor(s): Amazon Literary Partnership; Barnes & Noble; Hachette Book Group Inc; Lindenmeyr Book Publishing Papers; Penguin Random House; Simon & Schuster
Award: $10,000 & bronze sculpture for winner in each genre; $1,000, medal & Judge's citation to each finalist
Closing Date: May
Presented: New York, NY, Nov

National Book Critics Circle Award
National Book Critics Circle (NBCC)
c/o Jacob M Appel, Icahn School of Medicine at Mount Sinai, One Gustave L Levy Place, New York, NY 10029
E-mail: info@bookcritics.org
Web Site: www.bookcritics.org/awards
Key Personnel
Pres: Heather Scott Partington *E-mail:* hsp@bookcritics.org
Secy: Colette Bancroft *E-mail:* bancroft.colette72@gmail.com
Treas: Jacob M Appel *E-mail:* jacobmappel@gmail.com
VP, Awards: Keetje Kuipers *E-mail:* keetje@poetrynw.org
VP, Events: Jane Ciabattari *E-mail:* janeciab@gmail.com
Awards to honor the best literature published in the US in 6 categories: autobiography, biography, criticism, fiction, nonfiction & poetry. Books published in English (including translations) in the US with publication dates in the calendar year of the award are considered.
Closing Date: Dec 1
Presented: NBCC Awards Ceremony, March

The National Business Book Award (NBBA)
c/o Freedman & Associates Inc, 10 Delisle Ave, Suite 214, Toronto, ON M4V 3C6, Canada
Tel: 416-868-1500
Web Site: www.nbbaward.com
Key Personnel
Contact: Mary Ann Freedman *E-mail:* maf@freedmanandassociates.com
Established: 1985
Excellence in business writing in or about Canada.
Other Sponsor(s): Globe & Mail; Bennett Jones LLP; Miles S Nadal; The Walrus Magazine
Award: $30,000
Closing Date: March 31
Presented: Fall

National City & Regional Magazine Awards
City & Regional Magazine Association (CRMA)
287 Richards Ave, Norwalk, CT 06850
Tel: 203-515-9294
Web Site: citymag.org/awards
Key Personnel
Exec Dir: Cate Sanderson *E-mail:* cate@sandersonmgt.com
Awards for excellence to qualified member organizations in designated categories. Awards are managed on CRMA's behalf by the University of Missouri School of Journalism. Three general excellence categories: Circulation less than 30,000; circulation 30,000-60,000; circulation more than 60,000.

National Federation of State Poetry Societies Annual Poetry Contest
National Federation of State Poetry Societies (NFSPS)
c/o 115 N Wisteria St, Mansfield, TX 76063-1835
E-mail: contestchair@nfsps.com
Web Site: www.nfsps.com
Established: 1959
Fifty poetry contests, 1 for students only; rules & categories vary. Prizes are offered by NFSPS affiliated poetry societies & individual donors. Consult NFSPS web site for specific details for each contest.
Other Sponsor(s): Individual states' poetry society as host society
Closing Date: March 15 (must not be postmarked before Jan 1)
Presented: NFSPS Annual Convention

The National Humanities Medal
National Endowment for the Humanities
400 Seventh St SW, Washington, DC 20506
Tel: 202-606-8400 *Toll Free Tel:* 800-NEH-1121 (634-1121)
E-mail: questions@neh.gov
Web Site: www.neh.gov/about/awards
Key Personnel
Dir, Communs: Carmen Ingwell *E-mail:* cingwell@neh.gov
Established: 1997
Honors individuals or groups whose work has deepened the nation's understanding of the humanities & broadened out citizens' engagement with history, literature, languages, philosophy & other humanities subjects. Up to 12 medals awarded annually.

National Jewish Book Award-Children's Picture Book
Jewish Book Council
520 Eighth Ave, 4th fl, New York, NY 10018
Tel: 212-201-2920 *Fax:* 212-532-4952
E-mail: njba@jewishbooks.org
Web Site: www.jewishbookcouncil.org/awards
Key Personnel
Exec Dir: Carol Kaufman
Assoc Dir: Miri Pomerantz Dauber
Prog Dir: Evie Saphire-Bernstein *E-mail:* evie@jewishbooks.org
Founded: 1944
An illustrated story or nonfiction book designed to be read aloud to children ages 3-8 or a board book intended for children 0-3. This category should also include early readers & chapter books if they are intended for readers in the same age range. The award will be shared by the author & illustrator.
Award: Certificate & publication
Closing Date: Sept
Presented: Center for Jewish History, New York, NY, March

National Jewish Book Award-Natan Notable Books
Jewish Book Council
520 Eighth Ave, 4th fl, New York, NY 10018
Tel: 212-201-2920 *Fax:* 212-532-4952
E-mail: njba@jewishbooks.org; natannotable@jewishbooks.org
Web Site: www.jewishbookcouncil.org/awards
Key Personnel
Exec Dir: Carol Kaufman
Assoc Dir: Miri Pomerantz Dauber
Prog Dir: Evie Saphire-Bernstein *E-mail:* evie@jewishbooks.org
Submissions must be recently published or about to be published nonfiction titles that will catalyze conversations aligned with the themes of Natan's grantmaking: reinventing Jewish life & community for the 21st century, shifting notions of individual & collective Jewish identity, the history & future of Israel & the evolving relationship between Israel & world Jewry. The Natan Notable Books Committee is made up of Natan members & partners. An Advisory Committee made up of journalists, scholars, media figures & former Book Award winners & finalists nominate books for consideration. Publishers & authors can also submit books for consideration. Status update on finalists by May.
Award: Natan Notable Book seal, $5,000 for author, marketing/distribution coaching & promotion, along with customized support to bring the book +/or author to new audiences
Presented: Center for Jewish History, New York, NY

National Jewish Book Award-Young Adult Literature
Jewish Book Council
520 Eighth Ave, 4th fl, New York, NY 10018
Tel: 212-201-2920 *Fax:* 212-532-4952
E-mail: njba@jewishbooks.org
Web Site: www.jewishbookcouncil.org/awards
Key Personnel
Exec Dir: Carol Kaufman
Assoc Dir: Miri Pomerantz Dauber
Prog Dir: Evie Saphire-Bernstein *E-mail:* evie@jewishbooks.org
A book on a Jewish theme for ages 12-18.
Award: Certificate & publication
Closing Date: Sept
Presented: Center for Jewish History, New York, NY, March

National Jewish Book Awards
Jewish Book Council
520 Eighth Ave, 4th fl, New York, NY 10018
Tel: 212-201-2920 *Fax:* 212-532-4952
E-mail: njba@jewishbooks.org
Web Site: www.jewishbookcouncil.org/awards
Key Personnel
Exec Dir: Carol Kaufman
Assoc Dir: Miri Pomerantz Dauber
Prog Dir: Evie Saphire-Bernstein *E-mail:* evie@jewishbooks.org
Established: 1950
Awards program to recognize authors of books of exceptional literary achievement in a variety of Judaic subjects. Submissions open in June for books published in the same calendar year. Handling fee: $165 per title submitted (category as specified by entrant); if title submitted

for multiple categories, an additional $75 is required for each additional category.
Categories: American Jewish Studies (Celebrate 350 Award); Autobiography & Memoir (Krauss Family Award); Biography; Book Club (Miller Family Award); Children's Picture Book; Contemporary Jewish Life & Practice (Myra H Kraft Memorial Award); Debut Fiction (Goldberg Prize); Education & Jewish Identity; Fiction (JJ Greenberg Memorial Award); Food Writing & Cookbooks (Jane & Stuart Weitzman Family Award); History (Gerrard & Ella Berman Memorial Award); Holocaust; Middle Grade Literature; Modern Jewish Thought & Experience (Dorot Foundation Award); Poetry (Berru Award); Scholarship (Nahum M Sarna Memorial Award); Sephardic Culture (Mimi S Frank Award); Visual Arts (occasional award); Women's Studies (Barbara Dobkin Award); Writing Based on Archival Material (JDC-Herbert Katzki Award); Young Adult Literature.
See web site for specific category definitions, full eligibility requirements & submission guidelines. All nonfiction books submitted are automatically eligible for the Everett Family Foundation Jewish Book of the Year Award, which is determined by a select committee. A Special Recognition Award has been created to provide the Jewish Book Council with the flexibility to recognize selection(s) of outstanding merit. A select panel, headed by the Chair of the National Jewish Book Awards, makes this determination.
Award: Certificate & publication
Closing Date: Sept
Presented: Center for Jewish History, New York, NY, March

National Magazine Awards
National Media Awards Foundation
2300 Yonge St, Suite 1600, Toronto, ON M4P 1E4, Canada
Tel: 416-939-6200
E-mail: staff@magazine-awards.com
Web Site: www.magazine-awards.com; x.com/magawards
Key Personnel
Mng Dir: Barbara Gould
Established: 1977
Award to honor excellence in Canadian magazine journalism with awards in 29 categories.
Award: $1,000 Gold Award
Closing Date: Mid-Jan
Presented: Early June

The National Medal of Arts
National Endowment for the Arts
400 Seventh St SW, Washington, DC 20506-0001
Tel: 202-682-5570
Web Site: www.arts.gov/honors/medals
Key Personnel
Chmn: Jane Chu *E-mail:* chairman@arts.gov
Dir, Strategic Communs & Pub Aff: Helen Aguirre Ferre *Tel:* 202-682-5759
 E-mail: ferreh@arts.gov
Established: 1984
Highest award given to artists & arts patrons by the US government. Awarded by the President of the US.

National Outdoor Book Awards (NOBA)
National Outdoor Book Awards Foundation Inc
921 S Eighth Ave, Stop 8128, Pocatello, ID 83209-8128
Tel: 208-282-3912 *Fax:* 208-282-2127
Web Site: www.noba-web.org
Key Personnel
Chair: Ron Watters *E-mail:* wattron@isu.edu
Established: 1995
Award recognizing the work of outstanding writers & publishers of outdoor books. Categories include history/biography, outdoor literature, journeys, outdoor adventure guides, nature guides, children's books, design/artistic merit & nature & environment. Guidelines on the web site.
Other Sponsor(s): Association of Outdoor Recreation & Education; Idaho State University
Closing Date: Aug
Presented: International Conference on Outdoor Recreation & Education, Early Nov

National Poetry Series Open Competition
National Poetry Series
57 Mountain Ave, Princeton, NJ 08540
Tel: 609-430-0999 *Fax:* 609-430-9933
E-mail: npspoetry@gmail.com
Web Site: nationalpoetryseries.org
Key Personnel
Founder/Dir: Daniel Halpern
Coord: Beth Dial *E-mail:* bethdial@nationalpoetryseries.org
Established: 1978
For book-length typed ms of poetry, previously unpublished in book form. Mss are submitted online only via Submittable. Entry fee: $35 per ms. See web site for guidelines.
Award: Five books to be published by trade publishers, small presses & university publishers. $10,000 cash award for each winner
Closing Date: March 15
Presented: Summer

National Translation Award
American Literary Translators Association (ALTA)
University of Arizona, Esquire Bldg, No 205, 1230 N Park Ave, Tucson, AZ 85721
Tel: 520-621-1757
E-mail: info@literarytranslators.org
Web Site: www.literarytranslators.org/awards/national-translation-award
Key Personnel
Communs & Awards Mgr: Rachael Daum
 Tel: 413-200-0459 *E-mail:* rachaeldaum@literarytranslators.org
Prog Dir: Kelsi Vanada *E-mail:* kelsi@literarytranslators.org
Established: 1998
Awarded in poetry & in prose to literary translators who have made an outstanding contribution to literature in English by masterfully recreating the artistic force of a book of consummate quality. Submissions are accepted from publishers only beginning January each year via Submittable only. Publishers are invited to submit translated works of poetry or prose published in the previous calendar year. Hybrid works & drama are welcome & may be submitted to either category as determined appropriate by the publisher. Book must be translated from any language into English; must be a book-length work of literature (poetry, fiction, drama, literary nonfiction & hybrid works are accepted; must have been published in English translation anywhere in the world in the previous calendar year. To submit, complete entry form online & pay submission fee ($30 per entry for publishers with 10 or fewer titles a year, $50 per entry for publishers with more than 10 titles a year); send hard copies of the book(s) submitted to the judges requesting them. Publishers will receive the addresses to use as part of the online entry confirmation e-mail. Please do not send hard copies of the book to ALTA directly as they will not be considered submitted for the award.
Award: $5,000
Closing Date: Mid-April
Presented: ALTA Annual Conference

National Writers Association Novel Contest
National Writers Association
10940 S Parker Rd, Suite 508, Parker, CO 80134
Tel: 303-656-7235
E-mail: natlwritersassn@hotmail.com
Web Site: www.nationalwriters.com
Key Personnel
Exec Dir & Ed: Sandy Whelchel
Established: 1937
Novel contest for unpublished works. Entry fee: $35.
Award: $500 (1st prize), $250 (2nd prize), $150 (3rd prize)
Closing Date: April 1

Nautilus Book Awards
Lifethread Institute LLC
PO Box 2285, Vashon, WA 98070
Tel: 206-304-2250
Web Site: www.nautilusbookawards.com
Key Personnel
Owner & Dir: Mary Belknap, PhD
 E-mail: mbelknap@nautilusbookawards.com
Established: 1997
Award to recognize authors & titles as *Better Books for a Better World*, books that make excellent literary contributions to any of 4 themes, spiritual growth, health & wholeness, conscious living, sustainability, positive social change & social justice. Nautilus welcomes entries for print books, in English, that are intended to help co-create a better future. Author or publisher selects the category of their book's entry from among 35 possible categories/genres.
Award: Each winner receives complimentary JPG of their Nautilus Award (Gold or Silver Seal) for use on author's web site & promotional materials; other digital formats of the Seal are also available. The embossed version of Nautilus Seals to affix to books in inventory is available to purchase. Winners have option for *Author Spotlight* video interview (see sample videos on web site). Several dozen of each year's award winners receive complimentary visibility in "Feature Focus" bulletins that are sent to full Nautilus mail list quarterly
Closing Date: Mid-Feb
Presented: May (option for exhibit at ALA Annual Conference & Exhibition in June)

Phyllis Naylor Grant for Children's & Young Adult Novelists, see PEN/Phyllis Naylor Grant for Children's & Young Adult Novelists

NEA Creative Writing Fellowships
National Endowment for the Arts
400 Seventh St SW, Washington, DC 20506-0001
Tel: 202-682-5400; 202-682-5082 (voice/TTY); 202-682-5034 (lit fellowships hotline)
E-mail: litfellowships@arts.gov
Web Site: www.arts.gov/grants/creative-writing-fellowships
Established: 1967
Given to published writers of prose (fiction & creative nonfiction) & poetry. Variable number of fellowships, based on available program funds. Applications accepted by genre (prose-even years & poetry-odd years). Applicants are restricted to applying in one fellowship category only in the same year. Guidelines available on web site. Electronic application through grants.gov is mandatory.
Award: $25,000
Closing Date: March
Presented: Notifications to be sent by e-mail in Dec

The Jesse H Neal Awards
Software & Information Industry Association (SIIA)
1620 Eye St NW, Washington, DC 20005
Tel: 202-289-7442
E-mail: nealawards@siia.net
Web Site: siia.net/neals

Key Personnel
VP, Awards & Recognition Progs: Amanda McMaster *Tel:* 202-789-4469 *E-mail:* amcmaster@siia.net
Established: 1955
Editorial honors in the field of business journalism. Open to editorial staff of B2B media companies. All entries (print & digital) must have been published in the previous calendar year & be in English. Material that has been published previously in any other publication or edition is not eligible. Only the original published or posted version may be submitted. Entry fee: Early-$195 membs, $325 nonmembs; regular-$225 membs, $350 nonmembs; extended-$260 membs, $395 nonmembs.
Closing Date: Nov (early bird), Dec (regular), Jan (extended)
Presented: Neal Awards Ceremony, April

Barbara Neely Memorial Scholarship Program
Mystery Writers of America (MWA)
1140 Broadway, Suite 1507, New York, NY 10001
Tel: 212-888-8171
E-mail: mwa@mysterywriters.org
Web Site: mysterywriters.org
Key Personnel
EVP: Donna Andrews
Exec Dir: Margery Flax
Established: 2021
Two scholarships for Black crime writers, 1 for an aspiring Black writer who has yet to publish in the crime or mystery field & 1 for Black authors who have already published in crime or mystery. Applicants must be American citizens, age 18 or older. Submit brief bio, completed application form & 300- to 500-word statement on your interest in the mystery genre & in general terms how you would use the scholarship funds.
Award: $2,000 each & 1-year membership to MWA
Closing Date: Sept 30

Nelligan Prize for Short Fiction
Colorado Review
Unit of Colorado State University
Colorado State University, Dept of English, Center for Literary Publishing, 9105 Campus Delivery, Fort Collins, CO 80523-9105
Tel: 970-491-5449
E-mail: creview@colostate.edu
Web Site: coloradoreview.colostate.edu/nelligan-prize
Key Personnel
Dir & Ed: Stephanie G'Schwind
 E-mail: stephanie-gschwind@colostate.edu
Mng Ed: C E Janecek
Established: 2004
Awarded to the author of an outstanding short story, previously unpublished. Entry fee: $15 per story with no limit on number of entries. Stories must be at least 10, but no more than 50 pages. Online entry fee: $17.
Award: $2,000 honorarium & publication in fall/winter issue of *Colorado Review*
Closing Date: March 14
Presented: Winners announced mid-June

Nero Award
The Wolfe Pack
PO Box 230822, Ansonia Sta, New York, NY 10023
Web Site: nerowolfe.org/htm/literary_awards/nero_award/award.htm
Key Personnel
Chair: Stephannie Culbertson
 E-mail: neroawardchair@nerowolfe.org
Established: 1979
Award for the best American mystery written in the tradition of Rex Stout's Nero Wolfe stories. Books must be submitted directly by the publisher; no author-submitted entries are accepted. Books must be originally published in the US in the year preceding the award year. See web site for Mystery Writers of America-approved publishers.
Presented: Black Orchid Banquet, New York, NY, 1st Saturday in Dec

The Pablo Neruda Prize for Poetry
Nimrod International Journal
University of Tulsa, Kendall College of Arts & Sciences, 800 S Tucker Dr, Tulsa, OK 74104
Tel: 918-631-3080
E-mail: nimrod@utulsa.edu
Web Site: artsandsciences.utulsa.edu/nimrod/nimrod-literary-awards/
Key Personnel
Ed-in-Chief: Eilis O'Neal
Mng Ed: Cassidy McCants
Assoc Ed: Diane Burton
Established: 1978
No previously published works. Omit author's name on mss. Must have a US address by October to enter. Works must be in English or translated by the original author. Include a cover sheet containing major title & subtitles of the work, author's name, address & phone along with 3-10 pages of poetry: 1 long poem or several short poems. Mss will not be returned. Winners, selected finalists & semi-finalists will be published. Include SASE & a check for $20 (includes a 1-year subscription & processing). Online submissions: nimrodjournal.submittable.com.
Award: $2,000 (1st prize), $1,000 (2nd prize); published writers receive 2 copies of the journal; winners will be flown to Tulsa for a conference & banquet
Closing Date: April 1
Presented: Oct

Neukom Institute Literary Arts Award for Playwriting
Neukom Institute for Computational Science
Dartmouth College, Sudikoff Bldg, Rm 121, 9 Maynard St, Hanover, NH 03755
Web Site: sites.dartmouth.edu/neukominstitutelitawards
Key Personnel
Dir: Prof Daniel N Rockmore *E-mail:* daniel.n.rockmore@dartmouth.edu
Established: 2018
Full-length plays & other full-length works for the theater considered. Playwrights with either traditional or experimental theater pieces, including multimedia productions, are encouraged to submit works to the award program. Works that have already received a full production are not eligible for the competition. The award is a partnership between the Neukom Institute & Northern Stage based in White River Junction, Vermont. Complete information for submissions, as well as information on previous winners, may be found on the Neukom Awards web site.
Award: $5,000 honorarium, 29-hour workshop & public reading produced by Northern Stage
Closing Date: April 15
Presented: Winner announced in Summer

Neustadt International Prize for Literature
World Literature Today
Affiliate of University of Oklahoma
c/o University of Oklahoma, 630 Parrington Oval, Suite 110, Norman, OK 73019-4033
Tel: 405-325-4531
Web Site: www.worldliteraturetoday.org; www.neustadtprize.org
Key Personnel
Exec Dir: Robert Con Davis-Undiano
 E-mail: rcdavis@ou.edu
Asst Dir & Ed-in-Chief: Daniel Simon
 E-mail: dsimon@ou.edu
Art Dir: Gayle Curry *E-mail:* gayle.curry@ou.edu
Mng Ed: Michelle Johnson *E-mail:* lmjohnson@ou.edu
Book Reviews Ed: Robert Vollmar
 E-mail: robvollmar@ou.edu
Circ & Accts Specialist: Kay Blunck
 E-mail: kblunck@ou.edu
Progs & Devt: Terri Stubblefield
 E-mail: tdstubb@ou.edu
Established: 1969
Prize presented biennially, in even-numbered years, to a living writer for outstanding literary achievement. May honor a single major work or an entire oeuvre. Writer's work must be available in a representative sample in English, Spanish or French. Writer must accept the award in person in ceremonies at the University of Oklahoma. A special issue of *World Literature Today* is devoted to the laureate. Candidates must be nominated by a jury member.
Award: $50,000, eagle feather cast in silver & certificate
Presented: University of Oklahoma, Norman, OK

Elizabeth Neuwirth Memorial
The Poetry Society of Virginia (PSV)
PO Box 36128, North Chesterfield, VA 23235-3533
E-mail: contest@poetrysocietyofvirginia.org; info@poetryvirginia.org
Web Site: www.poetrysocietyofvirginia.org
Key Personnel
Pres: Cherryl T Cooley
 E-mail: poetrysocietypresident@gmail.com
Iambic pentameter. Subject: A specific work of art other than poetry (identify the work in the title or in the poem & in an epigraph). 48 line limit. Submit 1 copy of the poem with no identifying information but put the category in the upper right-hand-side, along with a notation as to whether you are a member of PSV (does not matter if you are a lifetime member or just joined for the contest). Submit a cover letter/page that contains the category, the name of the poem, your name & address, phone number & e-mail address. Entries will not be returned. Entry fee: Free to membs, $5 nonmembs.
Other Sponsor(s): Claudia Gary
Award: $50 (1st prize), $30 (2nd prize), $20 (3rd prize)

Allan Nevins Prize
Society of American Historians (SAH)
Affiliate of American Historical Association
Columbia University, 3009 Broadway MC 802, New York, NY 10027
Tel: 212-854-1919
E-mail: amhistsociety@columbia.edu
Web Site: sah.columbia.edu
Key Personnel
Pres: Martha A Sandweiss
VP: Martha Hodes
Exec Secy: Andrew Lipman
Established: 1961
For the best written doctoral dissertation on an American subject. The dissertation must have been defended or the PhD degree received in the calendar year preceding the award presentation & must not have already been accepted for publication.
Award: $2,000, certificate & publication by an award sponsoring publication house
Closing Date: Dec 31
Presented: New York, NY, May

New England Book Awards
New England Independent Booksellers Association Inc (NEIBA)
One Beacon St, 15th fl, Boston, MA 02108
Tel: 617-547-3642

Web Site: www.newenglandbooks.org/page/book-awards
Key Personnel
Pres & Exec Dir: Beth Ineson *E-mail:* beth@neba.org
Mktg Mgr: Alexandra Schmelzle *E-mail:* ali@neba.org
Mktg Coord: Rachael Conrad
Established: 1990
Award winners are chosen by NEIBA booksellers. Titles submitted must be about New England, set in New England, or by an author residing in New England, published between September 1 of the award year prior & August 31 of the award year. Entry fee: Free for membs, $25 per title nonmembs.
Award: $250 donation to literary charity of their choice
Closing Date: July
Presented: Fall Conference, Sept/Oct

New Hampshire Literary Awards
New Hampshire Writers' Project (NHWP)
2500 N River Rd, Manchester, NH 03106
Tel: 603-270-5466
E-mail: info@nhwritersproject.org
Web Site: www.nhwritersproject.org/new-hampshire-literary-awards
Key Personnel
Chair: Masheri Chappelle
Vice Chair: Dan Pouliot
Secy & Literary Awards Comm Chair: Claudia Decker
Treas: Kathy McKenna
Mktg Dir: Beth D'Ovidio
Established: 1992
Biennial award given in odd-numbered years. Nominees must live in New Hampshire, be a native or deal with subject matter that is deemed by judges to be inherently connected with New Hampshire.
Nomination fee: $50.
Closing Date: Varies. Typically in Spring
Presented: Oct

New Mexico-Arizona Book Awards
New Mexico Book Co-op
925 Salamanca NW, Los Ranchos, NM 87107
Tel: 505-344-9382
E-mail: info@nmbookcoop.com
Web Site: www.nmbookcoop.com/BookAwards/BookAwards.html
Open to authors & publishers anywhere. Books must have a direct connection to Arizona or New Mexico, either as subject, author, or publisher. Books with a publication date or copyright date since January 1 of the preceding year are eligible. Books that won in a category in a previous New Mexico Book Award Program are not eligible for re-submission; finalists can be re-submitted. Books can be entered in more than 1 category. Each title must include the entry form (1 form for multiple categories), payment of entry fee & 3 copies of the book being considered (add 1 copy for each additional category entered for the same book). Entry fee: $50 per entry/per category. Entries received by Feb 28 of the year of the award are eligible for a $10 discount. See web site for information on 56 award categories. For ebooks, entries of fiction or nonfiction are accepted in epub or mobi formats & must be e-mailed. Entry fee: $25 per entry.
Closing Date: July 1
Presented: Awards Banquet, Nov

New Millennium Awards for Fiction, Poetry & Nonfiction
New Millennium Writings
821 Indian Gap Rd, Sevierville, TN 37876
Tel: 865-254-4880
E-mail: hello@newmillenniumwritings.org
Web Site: newmillenniumwritings.org
Key Personnel
Publr & Ed: Alexis Williams *E-mail:* alexis.williams@hotmail.com
Established: 1996
Each fiction or nonfiction prize should total no more than 6,000 words (short-short fiction no more than 1,000 words). Each poetry entry may include up to 3 poems. Reading fee: $20 per entry. See web site for further information.
Award: $1,000 each for poem, fiction, nonfiction & short-short fiction, plus publication
Closing Date: Jan & July

New Voices: The Joanne Scott Kennedy Memorial
The Poetry Society of Virginia (PSV)
PO Box 36128, North Chesterfield, VA 23235-3533
E-mail: contest@poetrysocietyofvirginia.org; info@poetryvirginia.org
Web Site: www.poetrysocietyofvirginia.org
Key Personnel
Pres: Cherryl T Cooley
E-mail: poetrysocietypresident@gmail.com
Open only to poets who have never received a 1st, 2nd or 3rd prize in any PSV contest. Any form, any subject, 48 line limit. Submit 1 copy of the poem with no identifying information but put the category in the upper right-hand-side, along with a notation as to whether you are a member of PSV (does not matter if you are a lifetime member or just joined for the contest). Submit a cover letter/page that contains the category, the name of the poem, your name & address, phone number & e-mail address. Entries will not be returned. Entry fee: Free to membs, $5 nonmembs.
Other Sponsor(s): Williamsburg Poetry Guild
Award: $50 (1st prize), $30 (2nd prize), $20 (3rd prize)

New Women's Voices Chapbook Competition
Finishing Line Press
PO Box 1626, Georgetown, KY 40324
Tel: 502-603-0670
E-mail: finishingbooks@aol.com; flpbookstore@aol.com
Web Site: www.finishinglinepress.com; finishinglinepress.submittable.com/submit
Key Personnel
Publr: Leah Maines
Dir: Christen Kincaid
Mng Ed: Kevin Murphy Maines
Established: 1998
Prize for a poetry chapbook by a writer who identifies as a woman & has not yet published a full-length collection. Submit 16-40 pages of poetry, plus bio, acknowledgments, table of contents & cover letter. Entry fee: $15. Winner announced on web site & in *Poets & Writers Magazine*.
Other Sponsor(s): Duotrope
Award: $1,500, royalty contract, publication & 2-year Duotrope gift certificate
Closing Date: June 30

New York City Big Book Award®, see NYC Big Book Award®

New York City Book Awards
The New York Society Library
53 E 79 St, New York, NY 10075
Tel: 212-288-6900 *Fax:* 212-744-5832
E-mail: events@nysoclib.org
Web Site: www.nysoclib.org
Key Personnel
Events Asst: Katie Fricas *Tel:* 212-288-6900 ext 230
Established: 1996
Awarded to the authors of the best books about New York City. Must submit copy of nominated book the same year of publication. $40 per book fee. Make check payable to The New York Society Library.
Award: Plaque & varied monetary amount
Closing Date: Dec
Presented: The New York Society Library, New York, NY, Early May

The New York Public Library Helen Bernstein Book Award for Excellence in Journalism
The New York Public Library
445 Fifth Ave, 4th fl, New York, NY 10016
Tel: 212-930-9206 *Fax:* 212-930-0983
E-mail: bernsteinawards@nypl.org
Web Site: www.nypl.org
Key Personnel
Helen Bernstein Libn, Periodicals: Shannon Keller
Established: 1987
Requires overall journalistic excellence & a published book that stems from the author's reportage & exemplifies outstanding work. Note: nominations are for books published during the calendar year & are solicited only from publishers & editors-in-chief of major newspapers, news magazines & book publishers nationwide.
Award: $15,000
Closing Date: Aug 31
Presented: The New York Public Library, New York, NY, April/May

New York State Edith Wharton Citation of Merit for Fiction Writers
New York State Writers Institute
Subsidiary of University at Albany
University at Albany, Science Library 320, 1400 Washington Ave, Albany, NY 12222
Tel: 518-442-5620
E-mail: writers@albany.edu
Web Site: www.nyswritersinstitute.org
Key Personnel
Founder & Exec Dir: William Kennedy
Dir: Paul Grondahl
Asst Dir: Mark Koplik
Prog Coord: Jennifer Kowalski
E-mail: jkowalski@albany.edu
Established: 1985
State author designation for a New York State fiction writer. Applications not accepted. Nominations by advisory panel only.
Award: $10,000
Presented: Albany, NY, Biennially, even-numbered years

New York State Walt Whitman Citation of Merit for Poets
New York State Writers Institute
Subsidiary of University at Albany
University at Albany, Science Library 320, 1400 Washington Ave, Albany, NY 12222
Tel: 518-442-5620
E-mail: writers@albany.edu
Web Site: www.nyswritersinstitute.org
Key Personnel
Founder & Exec Dir: William Kennedy
Dir: Paul Grondahl
Asst Dir: Mark Koplik
Prog Coord: Jennifer Kowalski
E-mail: jkowalski@albany.edu
Established: 1985
State author designation for a New York State poet. Applications not accepted. Nominations by advisory panel only.
Award: $10,000
Presented: Albany, NY, Biennially, even-numbered years

John Newbery Medal
Association for Library Service to Children (ALSC)
Division of The American Library Association (ALA)

225 N Michigan Ave, Suite 1300, Chicago, IL 60601
Tel: 312-280-2163 *Toll Free Tel:* 800-545-2433
Fax: 312-280-5271
E-mail: alsc@ala.org
Web Site: www.ala.org/alsc/awardsgrants/bookmedia/newbery
Key Personnel
Exec Dir: Alena Rivers *Tel:* 800-545-2433 ext 5866 *E-mail:* arivers@ala.org
Awards Coord: Jordan Dubin *Tel:* 800-545-2433 ext 5839 *E-mail:* jdubin@ala.org
Prog Coord: Ann Michaud *Tel:* 800-545-2433 ext 2166 *E-mail:* amichaud@ala.org
Membership/Mktg Specialist: Elizabeth Serrano *Tel:* 800-545-2433 ext 2164 *E-mail:* eserrano@ala.org
Established: 1922
Awarded to the author of the most distinguished contribution to American literature for children published by an American publisher in the US in English during the preceding year. Restricted to authors who are citizens or residents of the US.
Award: Medal
Closing Date: Dec 31
Presented: ALA Youth Media Awards, Late Jan

Newfoundland and Labrador Book Awards
Writers' Alliance of Newfoundland and Labrador (WANL)/Literary Arts Foundation of Newfoundland and Labrador
Haymarket Sq, 223 Duckworth St, St John's, NL A1C 6N1, Canada
Tel: 709-739-5215 *Toll Free Tel:* 866-739-5215
E-mail: info@wanl.ca; membership@wanl.ca
Web Site: wanl.ca
Key Personnel
Exec Dir: Jen Winsor *E-mail:* director@wanl.ca
Memb Servs Coord: Wendy Rose
Established: 1996
Honor excellence in Newfoundland and Labrador writing in 4 categories: Fiction & children's/young adult literature (in even years), nonfiction & poetry (in odd years).
Other Sponsor(s): The Bruneau Family (children's/young adult literature); Killick Capital; The E J Pratt Family (poetry)
Award: $1,500 (1st prize), $500 each to 2 runners-up

Newfoundland and Labrador Credit Union Fresh Fish Award for Emerging Writers
Writers' Alliance of Newfoundland and Labrador (WANL)/Literary Arts Foundation of Newfoundland and Labrador
Haymarket Sq, 223 Duckworth St, St John's, NL A1C 6N1, Canada
Tel: 709-739-5215 *Toll Free Tel:* 866-739-5215
E-mail: info@wanl.ca; membership@wanl.ca
Web Site: wanl.ca
Key Personnel
Exec Dir: Jen Winsor *E-mail:* director@wanl.ca
Memb Servs Coord: Wendy Rose
Established: 2006
Biennial award, in even-numbered years, intended to serve as an incentive for emerging writers in Newfoundland and Labrador by providing them with financial support, recognition & professional editing services for a book-length ms in any genre. Must be registered members of WANL; writers may join WANL at the time of submission.
Award: $5,200, plus $1,000 toward professional editing services; $1,200 each to 2 runners-up
Closing Date: Odd-numbered years

Don & Gee Nicholl Fellowships in Screenwriting
Academy of Motion Picture Arts & Sciences (AMPAS)
1313 Vine St, Hollywood, CA 90028
Tel: 310-247-3010 *Fax:* 310-247-3794
E-mail: nicholl@oscars.org
Web Site: www.oscars.org/nicholl
Established: 1986
Screenwriting fellowship. Visit web site for additional information.
Award: Up to 5 awards of $35,000 each
Closing Date: May 1
Presented: Beverly Hills, CA, Nov

Mike Nichols Writing for Performance Award, see PEN/Mike Nichols Writing for Performance Award

Mary Nickliss Prize in US Women's and/or Gender History
The Organization of American Historians (OAH)
112 N Bryan Ave, Bloomington, IN 47408-4141
Tel: 812-855-7311
E-mail: oah@oah.org
Web Site: www.oah.org/awards
Key Personnel
Exec Dir: Beth English *Tel:* 812-855-9836 *E-mail:* benglish@oah.org
Dir, Communs & Mktg: Kym Robinson *Tel:* 812-855-5430 *E-mail:* kymarobi@oah.org
Established: 2015
The prize acknowledges the generations of women whose opportunities were constrained by the historical circumstances in which they lived. It is given for "the most original" book in US women's +/or gender history (including North America & the Caribbean prior to 1776). The OAH defines "the most original" book as one that is a path breaking work or challenges +/or changes widely accepted scholarly interpretations in the field. If no book submitted for the prize meets this criterion, the award shall be given for "the best" book in US women's +/or gender history. "The best" book recognizes the ideas & originality of the significant historical scholarship being done by historians of US women's +/or gender history & makes a significant contribution to the understanding of US women's +/or gender history. Each entry must be published during the calendar year preceding that in which the award is given. One copy of each entry must be mailed directly to the committee members listed on the web site.
Closing Date: Oct 1 (postmarked)
Presented: OAH Conference in American History, Spring

Lorine Niedecker Poetry Award
Council for Wisconsin Writers (CWW)
c/o 3225 N 91 St, Milwaukee, WI 53222
E-mail: wiswriters@gmail.com
Web Site: wiswriters.org/awards
Key Personnel
Contest Chair: Erik Richardson *E-mail:* erichardson@wi.rr.com
Prize awarded for a group of shorter poems (2 of which must be published in the contest year) & which represent a significant achievement commensurate with the quality of Niedecker's work. Submit up to 5 poems, none longer than 50 lines each. All types of poetry are welcome. Entry fee: $25 nonmembs. No entries accepted via e-mail.
Award: $500, $50 honorable mention
Closing Date: Jan 31
Presented: CWW Annual Award Ceremony & Banquet, May

John Frederick Nims Memorial Prize for Translation
Poetry Magazine
61 W Superior St, Chicago, IL 60654
Tel: 312-787-7070
Web Site: www.poetryfoundation.org/poetrymagazine/prizes
Key Personnel
Assoc Ed: Holly Amos *E-mail:* hamos@poetrymagazine.org
Established: 1999
For poetry published during the preceding year in *Poetry* magazine. No application necessary.
Award: $500
Presented: Announced in Nov issue

North Carolina Arts Council Writers Fellowships
North Carolina Arts Council
Division of North Carolina State Government
109 E Jones St, Raleigh, NC 27601
Mailing Address: Dept of Cultural Resources, Mail Service Ctr 4632, Raleigh, NC 27699-4632
Tel: 919-807-6500 *Fax:* 919-807-6532
E-mail: ncarts@ncdcr.gov
Web Site: www.ncarts.org
Key Personnel
Exec Dir: Wayne Martin *Tel:* 919-807-6525 *E-mail:* wayne.martin@ncdcr.gov
Lit & Theatre Dir: David Potorti *Tel:* 919-807-6512 *E-mail:* david.potorti@ncdcr.gov
Established: 1980
Fellowships are given every 2 years to poets & writers of fiction, literary nonfiction, literary translation playwrights & screenwriters. Writers who have lived in the state for at least 1 year as of application deadline & who intend to remain instate during the fellowship year are eligible.
Award: $10,000
Closing Date: Nov 1, even-numbered years
Presented: Summer, odd-numbered years

North Street Book Prize
Winning Writers
351 Pleasant St, Suite B, PMB 222, Northampton, MA 01060-3998
Tel: 413-320-1847 *Toll Free Tel:* 866-WINWRIT (946-9748) *Fax:* 413-280-0539
Web Site: www.winningwriters.com/our-contests/north-street-book-prize
Key Personnel
Pres: Adam Cohen *E-mail:* adam@winningwriters.com
VP: Jendi Reiter
Submit self-published books, any year of publication, in the following categories: Mainstream/literary fiction; genre fiction; creative nonfiction & memoir; poetry; children's picture book; graphic novel & memoir; art book. Up to 200,000 words in length. Entry fee: $65 per book.
Award: $5,000 (grand prize), $1,000 (1st prize in each category), $250 (honorable mention in each category)
Closing Date: June 30
Presented: Winner announced Feb 15 on web site

Northern California Book Awards
Northern California Book Reviewers (NCBR)
c/o Poetry Flash, 1450 Fourth St, Suite 4, Berkeley, CA 94710
Tel: 510-525-5476
E-mail: editor@poetryflash.org; ncbr@poetryflash.org
Web Site: poetryflash.org
Key Personnel
Publr, Exec Dir & Ed: Joyce Jenkins
Established: 1981
Honors the work of northern California authors & California literary translators & recognizes exceptional service to the community by northern California writers & literary leaders through the Fred Cody Lifetime Achievement Award & NCBR Recognition Award. Eligible books are considered in fiction, general nonfiction, creative nonfiction, poetry, translation (poetry & prose) & children's literature (young read-

AWARDS, PRIZE CONTESTS, FELLOWSHIPS & GRANTS

ers, middle grade, young adult). Books written by authors based in northern California & published for the first time in the previous year are eligible for nomination. In the case of children's picture books, the author of the text must live or be based in northern California. Authors may divide their time between two locales. Literary translators may live anywhere in California & may divide their time. There are no fees or forms. Either the publisher or the author may send books for consideration. Send 3 copies of each title to be considered.
Other Sponsor(s): Friends of the San Francisco Public Library; Mechanics' Institute Library; PEN West; Poetry Flash; San Francisco Public Library; Women's National Book Association (San Francisco Chapter)
Award: Fred Cody Award for Lifetime Achievement carries a $1,000 honorarium
Closing Date: Jan 10

Notable Wisconsin Authors
Wisconsin Library Association Inc (WLA)
112 Owen Rd, Unit 6437, Monona, WI 53716
Mailing Address: PO Box 6437, Monona, WI 53716
Tel: 608-245-3640
E-mail: wla@wisconsinlibraries.org
Web Site: www.wisconsinlibraries.org
Key Personnel
Comm Chair: Hannah Majeska
  E-mail: hmajeska@madisonpubliclibrary.org
Established: 1973
Award funded by the WLA Foundation, honoring Wisconsin connected authors for their literary contributions. To be eligible, an author must have written a work or works which are a contribution to the world of literature & ideas. The work must be written or illustrated by a person who was born in Wisconsin, is currently living in Wisconsin, or who lived in Wisconsin for a significant length of time. No more than 3 living authors will be recognized each year. Nominations may be sent via e-mail to wla@wisconsinlibraries.org or to the current chair, Nell Fleming, at nell.fleming@wsd.k12.wi.us.
Award: Printed brochure with biographical information on the notable author, including a list of authors' works
Closing Date: April 15
Presented: WLA Annual Conference, Oct/Nov

Novella Prize
The Malahat Review
University of Victoria, PO Box 1700, Sta CSC, Victoria, BC V8W 2Y2, Canada
Tel: 250-721-8524
E-mail: malahat@uvic.ca
Web Site: www.malahatreview.ca/contests/novella_contest/info.html; www.malahatreview.ca
Key Personnel
Mng Ed: L'Amour Lisik
Ed: Iain Higgins *E-mail:* malahateditor@uvic.ca
Established: 1995
Awarded biennially in even-numbered years. Submissions must be made online through Submittable. See web site for details & entry fees.
Award: $1,750 & publication in the Summer issue of *The Malahat Review*
Closing Date: Feb 1, even-numbered years

n+1 Writers' Fellowship
n+1 Foundation Inc
Cadman Plaza Sta, PO Box 26428, Brooklyn, NY 11202
E-mail: editors@nplusonemag.com; subs@nplusonemag.com (submission queries); submissions@nplusonemag.com
Web Site: www.nplusonemag.com/awards

Key Personnel
Publr: Mark Krotov
Exec Dir: Dayna Tortorici
Mng Ed: Tess Edmonson
Granted to an outstanding print contributor whose writing captures the spirit of n+1 & has been an important part of the magazine's evolution.
Award: $5,000

NSK Neustadt Prize for Children's Literature
World Literature Today
Affiliate of University of Oklahoma
c/o University of Oklahoma, 630 Parrington Oval, Suite 110, Norman, OK 73019-4033
Tel: 405-325-4531
Web Site: www.worldliteraturetoday.org; www.neustadtprize.org
Key Personnel
Exec Dir: Robert Con Davis-Undiano
  E-mail: rcdavis@ou.edu
Asst Dir & Ed-in-Chief: Daniel Simon
  E-mail: dsimon@ou.edu
Art Dir: Gayle Curry *E-mail:* gayle.curry@ou.edu
Mng Ed: Michelle Johnson *E-mail:* lmjohnson@ou.edu
Book Reviews Ed: Robert Vollmar
  E-mail: robvollmar@ou.edu
Circ & Accts Specialist: Kay Blunck
  E-mail: kblunck@ou.edu
Progs & Devt: Terri Stubblefield
  E-mail: tdstubb@ou.edu
Established: 2003
Biennial award, presented in odd-numbered years, intended to enhance the quality of children's literature by promoting writing that contributes to the quality of their lives. Awarded to a living writer with significant achievement, either over a lifetime or in a particular publication. The essential criterion for awarding this prize is that the writer's work is having a positive impact on the quality of children's literature.
Other Sponsor(s): Nancy Barcelo; Kathy Neustadt; Susan Neustadt Schwartz; The University of Oklahoma
Award: $35,000, medal & certificate
Closing Date: No outside nominations accepted, nominations by jury member only
Presented: The University of Oklahoma, Norman, OK, Oct

NYC Big Book Award®
63 Clinton Rd, Glen Ridge, NJ 07028
Tel: 973-969-1899
Web Site: www.nycbigbookaward.com
Key Personnel
Founder: Gabrielle (Gabby) L Olczak
  E-mail: gabby@nycbigbookaward.com
Mktg Mgr: Ted Olczak *E-mail:* ted@gabbybookawards.com
Print & audiobooks can be submitted by any author or publisher, including any of the big 5 publishing houses & their imprints. Entry fee: $99 per book entry/per category, $79 per title for each additional category. Send 1 copy of the book per category, up to 4 books.
Award: Winners & distinguished favorites get national media & industry exposure, downloadable banner promoting winner status, gold or silver foil embossed seals available for purchase & customized promotion
Closing Date: Rolling submissions: Oct 1-March 30 & April 1-Aug 30

NYSCA/NYFA Artist Fellowships
New York Foundation for the Arts (NYFA)
20 Jay St, Suite 740, Brooklyn, NY 11201
Tel: 212-366-6900 *Fax:* 212-366-1778
E-mail: fellowships@nyfa.org
Web Site: www.nyfa.org
Key Personnel
Exec Dir: Michael L Royce *E-mail:* mroyce@nyfa.org

ASSOCIATIONS, EVENTS

Exec Asst: Lisa Fagan *E-mail:* lfagan@nyfa.org
Fellowship applications limited to New York State residents. Applications open in the fall. Grants awarded in 15 artistic disciplines over a 3-year period, 5 categories per year. See web site for categories by year & eligibility requirements.
Award: $7,000
Closing Date: Jan
Presented: New York, NY, Announced in July

Joyce Carol Oates Prize
The New Literary Project
4100 Redwood Rd, Suite 20A-424, Oakland, CA 94619
Tel: 510-919-0970
Web Site: www.newliteraryproject.org/joyce-carol-oates-prize
Key Personnel
Chair: Joseph Di Prisco
Exec Dir: Diane Del Signore
Established: 2017
Award to a writer who has earned a distinguished reputation & the approbation of gratitude of readers. There is an application process & an anonymous jury selects the recipient. The winner has a 10-day residency in UC Berkeley's English Department & will participate in public readings & public appearances in the Bay Area at the time of the residency.
Award: $50,000
Closing Date: Oct 15
Presented: Spring

Eli M Oboler Memorial Award
Intellectual Freedom Round Table (IFRT)
Unit of The American Library Association (ALA)
225 Michigan Ave, Suite 1300, Chicago, IL 60601
Tel: 312-280-4226 *Toll Free Tel:* 800-545-2433
E-mail: ifrt@ala.org
Web Site: www.ala.org/rt/ifrt/oboler
Key Personnel
Comm Chair: Johannah Genett
Asst Dir, Office of Intellectual Freedom: Kristen Pekoll *Tel:* 312-280-4221 *E-mail:* kpekoll@ala.org
Established: 1986
Biennial award given to an author of a published work in English, or an English translation dealing with issues, events, questions or controversies in the area of intellectual freedom. Must have been published within previous 2 calendar years prior to the ALA Annual Conference & Exhibition at which it is granted.
Award: $500 & certificate
Closing Date: Dec 1, odd-numbered years
Presented: ALA Annual Conference & Exhibition, June, even-numbered years

The Flannery O'Connor Award for Short Fiction
University of Georgia Press
Main Library, 3rd fl, 320 S Jackson St, Athens, GA 30602
Fax: 706-542-2558
Web Site: www.ugapress.org
Key Personnel
Series Ed: Roxane Gay
Acqs Ed/Acqs Coord: Beth Snead *Tel:* 706-542-7613 *E-mail:* bsnead@uga.edu
Established: 1981
Collections of original short fiction. Ms should be 40,000-75,000 words & should be accompanied by a $30 submission fee; ms will not be returned. Submissions accepted beginning April 1. Open to both published & unpublished writers. Applicants should visit the press web site for guidelines. No phone calls regarding the award will be accepted. Accepting electronic submissions at georgiapress.submishmash.com.

Award: $1,000 & publication by the University of Georgia Press under a standard publishing contract
Closing Date: May 31

Frank O'Connor Prize for Fiction
Texas Christian University
Dept of English, TCU Box 297270, Fort Worth, TX 76129
E-mail: descant@tcu.edu
Web Site: www.descant.tcu.edu
Established: 1957
Best published fiction in each volume of *descant*. All published submissions are eligible for consideration. There is no application process.
Other Sponsor(s): descant (publication), Dept of English, TCU
Award: $500
Presented: Winner announced in the Summer in *descant*

Scott O'Dell Award for Historical Fiction
c/o Horn Book Inc, 300 The Fenway, Suite P-311, Palace Road Bldg, Boston, MA 02215
Tel: 617-278-0225 *Toll Free Tel:* 888-628-0225
E-mail: scottodellfanpage@gmail.com
Web Site: scottodell.com/the-scott-odell-award
Key Personnel
Chair: Deborah Stevenson
Asst to Chair: Ann Carlson
Established: 1982
Presented for a work of historical fiction published in the previous year for children or young adults, by a US publisher & set in the New World. Winner is selected by O'Dell Award Committee.
Award: $5,000
Closing Date: Dec 31

Odyssey Award for Excellence in Audiobook Production
Young Adult Library Services Association (YALSA)
Division of The American Library Association (ALA)
225 N Michigan Ave, Suite 1300, Chicago, IL 60601
Toll Free Tel: 800-545-2433 (ext 4390)
E-mail: yalsa@ala.org
Web Site: www.ala.org/yalsa/odyssey
Key Personnel
Exec Dir: Tammy Dillard-Steels *Tel:* 800-545-2433 ext 4391 *E-mail:* tdillard@ala.org
Prog Offr, Events & Conferences: Nichole O'Connor *Tel:* 800-545-2433 ext 4387 *E-mail:* noconnor@ala.org
Communs Specialist: Anna Lam *Tel:* 800-545-2433 ext 5849 *E-mail:* alam@ala.org
Awarded to the producer of the best audiobook produced for children +/or young adults, available in English in the US. Administered jointly with the Association for Library Service to Children (ALSC).
Other Sponsor(s): Booklist

Annual Off Off Broadway Short Play Festival
Samuel French, Inc
Imprint of Concord Theatricals
250 W 57 St, 6th fl, New York, NY 10107-0102
Toll Free Tel: 866-979-0447
E-mail: oobfestival@samuelfrench.com; info@concordtheatricals.com
Web Site: oobfestival.com; www.concordtheatricals.com
Key Personnel
Sr Mgr, Acqs & Artistic Devt: Garrett Anderson *E-mail:* garrett.anderson@concord.com
Acqs & Artistic Devt Coord: Rachel Levens *E-mail:* rachel.levens@concord.com
Established: 1975
Four-week submission period beginning in November. Selected plays are presented on the final day of the festival.
Award: Publication of top 6 plays
Closing Date: Mid-Dec
Presented: July/Aug

Karma Deane Ogden Memorial
The Poetry Society of Virginia (PSV)
PO Box 36128, North Chesterfield, VA 23235-3533
E-mail: contest@poetrysocietyofvirginia.org; info@poetryvirginia.org
Web Site: www.poetrysocietyofvirginia.org
Key Personnel
Pres: Cherryl T Cooley *E-mail:* poetrysocietypresident@gmail.com
Any form, any subject, 48 line limit. PSV members only.
Award: $50 (1st prize), $30 (2nd prize), $20 (3rd prize)

Dayne Ogilvie Prize for LGBTQ2S+ Emerging Writers
The Writers' Trust of Canada
600-460 Richmond St W, Toronto, ON M5V 1Y1, Canada
Tel: 416-504-8222 *Toll Free Tel:* 877-906-6548 *Fax:* 416-504-9090
E-mail: info@writerstrust.com
Web Site: www.writerstrust.com
Key Personnel
Exec Dir: Charlie Foran *Tel:* 416-504-8222 ext 244 *E-mail:* cforan@writerstrust.com
Mgr, Author Progs: Devon Jackson *Tel:* 416-504-8222 ext 248 *E-mail:* djackson@writerstrust.com
Established: 2007
Awarded to an emerging LGBTQ writer.
Other Sponsor(s): Robin Pacific
Award: $10,000
Presented: Toronto, ON, CN, Pride Week, early Summer

Howard O'Hagan Award for Short Story
Writers' Guild of Alberta
11759 Groat Rd NW, Edmonton, AB T5M 3K6, Canada
Tel: 780-422-8174 *Toll Free Tel:* 800-665-5354 (AB only)
E-mail: mail@writersguild.ab.ca
Web Site: writersguild.ca
Key Personnel
Exec Dir: Giorgia Severini *E-mail:* gseverini@writersguild.ab.ca
Communs & Partnerships Coord: Ellen Kartz *E-mail:* ellen.kartz@writersguild.ab.ca
Memb Servs Coord: Mike Maguire
Prog & Opers Coord: Ashley Mann *E-mail:* ashley.mann@writersguild.ab.ca
Progs & Events Coord: Jason Norman *E-mail:* jason.norman@writersguild.ab.ca
Proj Asst: Sadie MacGillivray *E-mail:* sadie.macgillivray@writersguild.ab.ca
Established: 1982
Alberta literary award for published short stories only, author must be resident of Alberta; no longer than 5,000 words.
Award: $700
Closing Date: Dec 31
Presented: Alberta Book Awards Gala, AB, CN
Branch Office(s)
223 12 Ave SW, No 204, Calgary, AB T2R 0G9, Canada, Prog & Conference Coord: Dorothy Bentley *Tel:* 403-875-8058 *E-mail:* dorothy.bentley@writersguild.ab.ca

Ohioana Book Awards
Ohioana Library Association
274 E First Ave, Suite 300, Columbus, OH 43201
Tel: 614-466-3831 *Fax:* 614-728-6974
E-mail: ohioana@ohioana.org
Web Site: www.ohioana.org
Key Personnel
Exec Dir, Ohioana Library Association: Kimberlee Kiehl
Established: 1942
For the best books by Ohio authors in various fields of writing or books about Ohio or Ohioans. Submit 2 copies of nominated book. Categories: Fiction, poetry, juvenile literature, middle grade/young adult literature, nonfiction, book about Ohio/Ohioan.
Award: $1,500 cash prize for winning book in each category
Closing Date: Dec 31
Presented: Ohioana Awards Ceremony, Oct

Ohioana Walter Rumsey Marvin Grant
Ohioana Library Association
274 E First Ave, Suite 300, Columbus, OH 43201
Tel: 614-466-3831 *Fax:* 614-728-6974
E-mail: ohioana@ohioana.org
Web Site: www.ohioana.org
Key Personnel
Exec Dir, Ohioana Library Association: Kimberlee Kiehl
Established: 1982
Writing competition; awarded to young (30 years of age or younger), Ohio authors who were born or have lived in Ohio 5 years or more & who have not yet published a book.
Award: $1,000 cash prize & publication of winning submission in the *Ohioana Quarterly*
Closing Date: Jan 31
Presented: Ohioana Awards Ceremony, Oct

Oklahoma Book Awards
Oklahoma Center for the Book (OCB)
200 NE 18 St, Oklahoma City, OK 73105-3205
Tel: 405-522-3383
Web Site: libraries.ok.gov/ocb/ok-book-awards/
Presented for work written by an Oklahoman or about Oklahoma. Categories: Fiction, nonfiction, children/young adult, poetry & design/illustration.
Other Sponsor(s): Friends of the Oklahoma Center for the Book
Presented: April

Nancy Olson Bookseller Award
Southern Independent Booksellers Alliance (SIBA)
51 Pleasant Ridge Dr, Asheville, NC 28805
Tel: 803-994-9530 *Fax:* 309-410-0211
E-mail: siba@sibaweb.com
Web Site: www.sibaweb.com
Key Personnel
Exec Dir: Linda-Marie Barrett *E-mail:* lindamarie@sibaweb.com
Established: 2019
Award to recognize special booksellers. All SIBA booksellers (not owners) are eligible. Nominations accepted from writers, readers & store owners. Individual booksellers may nominate themselves.
Award: 2 awards of $2,000
Closing Date: Dec

Chris O'Malley Fiction Prize
The Madison Review
University of Wisconsin, 6193 Helen C White Hall, English Dept, 600 N Park St, Madison, WI 53706
E-mail: madisonrevw@gmail.com
Web Site: www.themadisonrevw.com
Key Personnel
Dept Chair: Anja Wanner
Faculty Advisor & Prog Coord: Ronald Kuka *Tel:* 608-263-3374 *E-mail:* rfkuka@wisc.edu
Size limit 30 page maximum. Only 1 submission is allowed per person per contest. Ms must be previously unpublished & should be double-spaced with standard 1 inch margins & 12

point font. Entries must be submitted online at madisonreview.submittable.com/submit. Entry fee: $10.
Award: $1,000 & publication in Spring issue of *The Madison Review*
Closing Date: Nov 1
Presented: Announcement in March

On-the-Verge Emerging Voices Award
Society of Children's Book Writers & Illustrators (SCBWI)
6363 Wilshire Blvd, Suite 425, Los Angeles, CA 90048
Tel: 323-782-1010
E-mail: info@scbwi.org
Web Site: www.scbwi.org/awards/grants/on-the-verge-emerging-voices-grant
Key Personnel
Exec Dir: Sarah Baker
Assoc Dir, Digital Content & Awards: Sarah Diamond
Assoc Mgr, Awards & Pubns: Danielle Monique
Established: 2012
Grant to foster the emergence of diverse voices in children's books. To be eligible, a writer or writer/illustrator must be from an ethnic +/or cultural background that is traditionally under-represented in children's literature in America. This includes, but is not limited to: American Indian, Asian, Black or African American, Hispanic, Pacific Islander. Ms must be an original work written in English for young readers & may not be under contract. Applicant must be over 18, be unpublished (self-published is not considered published for this award) & should not yet have representation. Applications accepted via e-mail only to sarah-diamond@scbwi.org. See web site for specific submission guidelines.
Award: 2 writers or writer/illustrators will each receive full tuition to SCBWI Summer Conference, ms consultation, press release, publicity, ms included on secure web site for selected publishing professionals to view & professional career development guidance throughout the winning year
Closing Date: Nov 15
Presented: SCBWI Summer Conference

One-Act Playwriting Competition
Little Theatre of Alexandria
600 Wolfe St, Alexandria, VA 22314
Tel: 703-683-5778 (ext 2) *Fax:* 703-683-1378
E-mail: oneactslta@gmail.com
Web Site: thelittletheatre.com
Key Personnel
Chair: Nick Friedlander; Brittany Huffman
Pres: Frank Shutts
Treas: David B Hale
Busn Off Mgr: Crissy Wilke
PR: Rachel Alberts
Established: 1978
Open to all playwrights. Scripts must be original, unpublished & unproduced (not staged for a playing audience) stage plays. Film & TV scripts are ineligible. Entry fee: $20 per play (limit 2 plays per person). Accept plays beginning mid-August. Prize awarded by mail.
Award: $350 (1st prize), $250 (2nd prize), $150 (3rd prize), usually stage readings of top plays
Closing Date: Sept 30
Presented: Typically Nov/Dec

Open Chapbook Competition
Finishing Line Press
PO Box 1626, Georgetown, KY 40324
Tel: 502-603-0670
E-mail: finishingbooks@aol.com; flpbookstore@aol.com
Web Site: www.finishinglinepress.com
Key Personnel
Publr: Leah Maines
Dir: Christen Kincaid
Mng Ed: Kevin Murphy Maines
Established: 2002
Awarded for a chapbook-length poetry collection. Submit 16-38 pages of poetry, plus bio, acknowledgments, SASE & cover letter. Entry fee: $15. Winner announced on web site & in *Poets & Writers Magazine*.
Award: $1,000 & publication
Closing Date: Oct 31

Open City Fellowship
Asian American Writers' Workshop (AAWW)
112 W 27 St, Suite 600, New York, NY 10001
Tel: 212-494-0061
E-mail: fellowships@aaww.org
Web Site: aaww.org/fellowships/open-city
Key Personnel
Progs Mgr: Lily Philpott
Progs Coord: Vandana Pawa
Nine-month program for emerging writers of color to write about how Asian American & Muslim American lives are being lived in New York City. It is open to writers who are based in New York City, or can claim residency in the city but temporarily relocated due to the pandemic. Six fellows are selected, 3 for the Neighborhoods/Communities Fellowship & 3 for the Muslim Communities Fellowship. Applications via Submittable open in the Fall. Submit project proposal, CV & writing samples.
Award: $2,500 grant, skill-building workshops & publishing opportunities

Open Season Awards
The Malahat Review
University of Victoria, PO Box 1700, Sta CSC, Victoria, BC V8W 2Y2, Canada
Tel: 250-721-8524
E-mail: malahat@uvic.ca
Web Site: www.malahatreview.ca/contests/open_season/info.html; www.malahatreview.ca
Key Personnel
Mng Ed: L'Amour Lisik
Ed: Iain Higgins *E-mail:* malahateditor@uvic.ca
Established: 2009
Awards in 3 categories: poetry, short fiction & creative nonfiction. Submissions must be made online through Submittable. See web site for details & entry fees.
Award: $2,000 in each of 3 categories & publication in the Spring issue of *The Malahat Review*
Closing Date: Nov 1

Iona & Peter Opie Prize
American Folklore Society/Children's Folklore Section
Indiana University, Classroom-Off Bldg, 800 E Third St, Bloomington, IN 47405
Tel: 812-856-2379 *Fax:* 812-856-2483
E-mail: americanfolkloresociety@afsnet.org; cf.section@afsnet.org
Web Site: www.afsnet.org; childrensfolklore.org/opie-prize
Key Personnel
Comm Chair: John McDowell; Elizabeth Tucker
Exec Dir: Jessica A Turner *E-mail:* jturner@afsnet.org
Assoc Dir: Lorraine Walsh Cashman *E-mail:* lcashman@afsnet.org
Award presented approximately every 2 years for the best recently published scholarly book on children's folklore. Edited volumes, collections of folklore & authored studies published in English during previous 2 years are eligible. Authors or publishers should submit 2 copies of the book.
Award: $200
Closing Date: Aug 15
Presented: Oct

Orbis Pictus Award
National Council of Teachers of English (NCTE)
340 N Neil St, Suite 104, Champaign, IL 61820
Tel: 217-328-3870 *Toll Free Tel:* 877-369-6283 (cust serv) *Fax:* 217-328-9645
E-mail: bookawards@ncte.org
Web Site: ncte.org/awards/ncte-childrens-book-awards
Key Personnel
Prog Coord: Sarah Miller
Established: 1989
Awarded to promote & recognize excellence in nonfiction writing for children. Books must have been published +/or distributed in the US during the calendar year. Nominations of individual books may come from publishers, NCTE membership & from the educational community at large. One title is singled out for the award & up to 5 honor books are also recognized. Eight additional recommended books can be named.
Award: Winning author(s) +/or illustrator(s) receive plaque & are the featured speakers(s) at the following year's Children's Book Awards Luncheon; Honor book author(s) +/or illustrator(s) receive certificate & invitation to present at session following the luncheon
Closing Date: Oct 15
Presented: Children's Book Awards Luncheon, NCTE Annual Convention

Oregon Book Awards
Literary Arts
925 SW Washington St, Portland, OR 97205
Tel: 503-227-2583 *Fax:* 503-241-4256
E-mail: la@literary-arts.org
Web Site: literary-arts.org/about/programs/oba/book-awards
Key Personnel
Dir, Progs for Writers: Susan Moore *Tel:* 503-227-2583 ext 107 *E-mail:* susan@literary-arts.org
Established: 1988
Awarded to honor original work by Oregon writers in the following categories: Poetry, fiction, graphic literature, drama, literary nonfiction & literature for young readers. Submission fee: $50. See web site for full eligibility requirements.
Closing Date: Oct 1
Presented: Spring

The Orison Chapbook Prize
Orison Books
PO Box 8385, Asheville, NC 28814
Tel: 828-713-1755
E-mail: editor@orisonbooks.com
Web Site: www.orisonbooks.com/submissions
Key Personnel
Founder & Ed: Luke Hankins
For chapbook mss (20-45 pages) in any genre (poetry, fiction, nonfiction, drama or hybrid). Submission period begins April 1 (electronic only via Duosuma).
Other Sponsor(s): Duotrope
Award: Publication, $300 cash, 2-yr Duotrope membership, 20 copies of chapbook & standard royalties contract
Closing Date: July 1
Presented: Oct

The Orison Prizes in Poetry & Fiction
Orison Books
PO Box 8385, Asheville, NC 28814
Tel: 828-713-1755
E-mail: editor@orisonbooks.com
Web Site: www.orisonbooks.com/submissions
Key Personnel
Founder & Ed: Luke Hankins
For full-length poetry (50-100 pages) & fiction (minimum 30,000 words). Original English work only. Submission period begins Decem-

ber 1 (electronic only via Duosuma). Entry fee: $25.
Award: $1,500 & publication
Closing Date: April 1
Presented: Oct

George Orwell Award
National Council of Teachers of English (NCTE)
340 N Neil St, Suite 104, Champaign, IL 61820
Tel: 217-328-3870 *Toll Free Tel:* 877-369-6283 (cust serv) *Fax:* 217-328-9645
E-mail: publiclangaward@ncte.org
Web Site: ncte.org/awards/george-orwell-award
Key Personnel
Prog Coord: Sarah Miller
Established: 1975
Recognizes people who have made outstanding contributions to the critical analysis of public discourse.
Other Sponsor(s): NCTE Public Language Award Committee
Award: Certificate
Closing Date: Aug 1
Presented: NCTE Annual Conference, Late Nov

James H Ottaway Jr Award for the Promotion of International Literature
Words Without Borders
147 Prince St, Brooklyn, NY 11201
Tel: 347-699-2914
E-mail: info@wordswithoutborders.org
Web Site: www.wordswithoutborders.org/ottaway-award
Key Personnel
Book Review Ed: Miguel Conde
  E-mail: miguel@wordswithoutborders.org
Recognizes individuals who have taken extraordinary steps to advance literature in translation into English.
Presented: Annual Gala, New York, NY, Autumn

Ottoline Prize
Fence Books
Imprint of Fence Magazine Inc
36-09 28 Ave, Apt 3R, Astoria, NY 11103-4518
Tel: 518-567-7006
Web Site: www.fenceportal.org
Key Personnel
Co-Edit Dir: Emily Wallis Hughes *Tel:* 530-220-4373; Jason Zuzga *Tel:* 267-902-0731
Established: 2013
For a book-length work of poetry by a woman writing in English who has previously published one or more full-length books of poetry. Submission fee: $28.
Award: $5,000 & publication, plus complimentary subn to *Fence*

Frank L & Harriet C Owsley Award
Southern Historical Association (SHA)
University of Georgia, Dept of History, Athens, GA 30602-1602
Tel: 706-542-8848
Web Site: thesha.org
Key Personnel
Secy/Treas: Dr Stephen Berry *E-mail:* berrys@thesha.org
Established: 1985
Awarded, in odd-numbered years, for the most distinguished book in southern history published in even-numbered years.
Award: Cash
Closing Date: March 1
Presented: Annual Meeting, Fall

Pacific Northwest Book Awards
Pacific Northwest Booksellers Association (PNBA)
520 W 13 Ave, Eugene, OR 97401-3461
Tel: 541-683-4363 *Fax:* 541-683-3910
E-mail: info@pnba.org; awards@pnba.org
Web Site: www.pnba.org/book-awards.html
Key Personnel
Exec Dir: Brian Juenemann *E-mail:* brian@pnba.org
Established: 1964
Awards to recognize excellence in writing from the Pacific Northwest. Author +/or illustrator must reside within the PNBA region (Washington, Oregon, Idaho, Alaska, Montana & British Columbia).
Award: Plaque & marketing to independent bookstores of the Pacific Northwest
Closing Date: Sept 30

Pacific Northwest Young Reader's Choice Award
Pacific Northwest Library Association (PNLA)
c/o Jocie Wilson, Yellowhead Regional Library, 433 King St, Spruce Grove, AB T7X 2C6, Canada
E-mail: yrcachair@gmail.com
Web Site: www.pnla.org/yrca
Key Personnel
Coord: Jocie Wilson *Tel:* 780-962-2003 ext 223
Established: 1940
Nominations taken only from children, teachers, parents & librarians of the Pacific Northwest (WA, OR, AK, ID, MT, BC & AB) for titles published 3 years before the award year in the US or CN. Only 4th-12th graders in the Pacific Northwest vote on a selected list of titles. The categories are junior grades 4-6, intermediate grades 7-9 & senior grades 10-12. See web site for nomination form.
Award: Silver Medal
Closing Date: Nov 15
Presented: Pacific Northwest Library Association's Annual Conference

The Pacific Spirit Poetry Prize
PRISM international
University of British Columbia, Buch E462, 1866 Main Mall, Vancouver, BC V6T 1Z1, Canada
Tel: 604-822-2514 *Fax:* 604-822-3616
E-mail: promotions@prismmagazine.ca
Web Site: www.prismmagazine.ca/contests
Key Personnel
Mng Ed: Emma Cleary
Poetry Ed: Emily Chou
Promos Ed: Alison Barnett
Prose Ed: Vivian Li
Established: 1986
Awarded for the best original, unpublished poem. Each entry can include 1-3 poems (100 lines maximum each). Entry fee: $35 CN, $40 US, $45 intl; additional entries $5.
Award: $1,500 (grand prize), $600 (1st runner up), $400 (2nd runner up); all entries include 1-year subn to *PRISM international*

PAGE International Screenwriting Awards
Production Arts Group LLC
7190 W Sunset Blvd, Suite 610, Hollywood, CA 90046
E-mail: info@pageawards.com
Web Site: pageawards.com
Key Personnel
Exec Dir: Kristin Overn
Admin Dir: Jennifer Berg
Edit Dir: John Evans
Contest Coord: Zoe Simmons
Established: 2003
Each year, the PAGE judges present a total of 31 awards in 10 genre categories. Entry fee: $45 early, $55 regular, $65 late, $75 last minute, $85 final.
Other Sponsor(s): Filmarket Hub; InkTip; Roadmap Writers
Award: $25,000 (grand prize) plus gold, silver & bronze prizes in all 10 categories
Closing Date: Jan 15 (early), Feb 15 (regular), March 15 (late), April 15 (last minute)
Presented: Hollywood, CA, Oct

Dobie Paisano Fellowship Program
University of Texas at Austin
110 Inner Campus Dr, Stop G0400, Austin, TX 78712-0710
Fax: 512-471-7620
Web Site: dobiepaisano.utexas.edu
Key Personnel
Dir: Dr Michael Adams *E-mail:* adameve@austin.utexas.edu
Established: 1967
Provides an opportunity for creative or nonfiction writers to live & write for an extended period in an environment that offers isolation & tranquility. At the time of application, the applicant must: be a native Texan; have lived in Texas at some time for at least 3 years; or have published significant work with a Texas subject. Criteria for making the awards include quality of work, character of the proposed project & suitability of the applicant for life at Paisano, the late J Frank Dobie's ranch near Austin, TX. Applications are available at the above web site or write for more information. Application fee: $20/1 fellowship; $30/both fellowships.
Other Sponsor(s): Texas Institute of Letters (TIL)
Award: Ralph A Johnston Memorial Fellowship: $25,000 over 4 months; Jesse H Jones Writing Fellowship: $18,000 over 6 months
Closing Date: Dec 15
Presented: May

Mildred & Albert Panowski Playwriting Award
Northern Michigan University
Forest Roberts Theatre, 1401 Presque Isle Ave, Marquette, MI 49855-5364
Tel: 906-227-2553 *Fax:* 906-227-2567
E-mail: theatre@nmu.edu
Web Site: www.nmu.edu/theatre
Key Personnel
Dir: William Digneit *Tel:* 906-227-2044
  E-mail: wdigneit@nmu.edu
Established: 1977
Provides students & faculty the unique opportunity to mount & produce an original work on the university stage. The playwright will benefit from seeing the work on its feet in front of an audience & from professional adjudication by guest critics. Please check the web site for theme or genre. Play must be unproduced. Only one play per playwright may be entered. Electronic submission only.
Award: $2,000 cash, airline fare, room & board for the week of production
Presented: Forest Roberts Theatre, Northern Michigan University, Marquette, MI

William Riley Parker Prize
Modern Language Association (MLA)
85 Broad St, New York, NY 10004
SAN: 202-6422
Tel: 646-576-5141; 646-576-5000
E-mail: awards@mla.org
Web Site: www.mla.org
Key Personnel
Coord, Book Prizes: Annie M Reiser
  E-mail: areiser@mla.org
Awarded for an outstanding article published in *PMLA*. Article must have been submitted by a member of MLA & published in one of the 4 scholarly article issues of *PMLA* that appear in the academic year. There is no need to enter articles in this competition. All eligible articles will be reviewed by the prize selection committee.
Award: Cash award & certificate
Presented: MLA Annual Convention, Toronto, ON, CN, Jan 2026

AWARDS, PRIZE CONTESTS, FELLOWSHIPS & GRANTS

Francis Parkman Prize
Society of American Historians (SAH)
Affiliate of American Historical Association
Columbia University, 3009 Broadway MC 802, New York, NY 10027
Tel: 212-854-1919
E-mail: amhistsociety@columbia.edu
Web Site: sah.columbia.edu
Key Personnel
Pres: Martha A Sandweiss
VP: Martha Hodes
Exec Secy: Andrew Lipman
Established: 1957
For a nonfiction book, including biography, that is distinguished by its literary merit & makes an important contribution to the history of what is now the US. The author need not be a citizen or resident of the US & the book need not be published in the US although must be published & copyrighted in the year preceding the award.
Award: $2,000 & certificate
Closing Date: Dec 1
Presented: New York, NY, May

The Scott Parsons Literary Award
Prince Edward Island Writers' Guild
81 Prince St, Charlottetown, PE C1A 4R3, Canada
E-mail: peiliteraryawards@gmail.com
Web Site: www.peiwritersguild.com
Presented in recognition & celebration of the outstanding literary merit of a Black Island writer. Scott Parsons, Co-Founder & first President of the Black Cultural Society of Prince Edward Island, is a multi-disciplined Island singer/songwriter who has consistently used his voice, through a variety of mediums including music, theatre, film, radio & television, to deepen & enrich our understanding of our Island's history, sparking a new generation of artistic creativity. This prize is designed to recognize literary merit & promote works in all categories including fiction, nonfiction, poetry, writing for children & young adults, plays & scriptwriting. Work must be original & unpublished. Entry fee: $25 per submission. Prince Edward Island residents only. See web site for complete entry requirements.
Award: Cash prize for 1st place
Closing Date: Changes annually (see web site)
Presented: Island Literary Awards Gala, Spring

The Paterson Poetry Prize
The Poetry Center at Passaic County Community College
One College Blvd, Paterson, NJ 07505-1179
Tel: 973-684-6555 *Fax:* 973-523-6085
Web Site: www.poetrycenterpccc.com
Key Personnel
Exec Dir: Maria Mazziotti Gillan
E-mail: mgillan@pccc.edu
Mgr: Susan Balik *E-mail:* sbalik@pccc.edu
For a book of poems, 48 pages or more in length, selected by our judges as the strongest collection of poems published in the previous year. The poet will be asked to participate in an awards ceremony & to give a reading at the Poetry Center. Publisher may submit more than one book for prize consideration.
Award: $1,000
Closing Date: Feb 1

The Paterson Prize for Books for Young People
The Poetry Center at Passaic County Community College
One College Blvd, Paterson, NJ 07505-1179
Tel: 973-684-6555 *Fax:* 973-523-6085
Web Site: www.poetrycenterpccc.com
Key Personnel
Exec Dir: Maria Mazziotti Gillan
E-mail: mgillan@pccc.edu
Mgr: Susan Balik *E-mail:* sbalik@pccc.edu
Awarded for the most outstanding book for young people published in the previous year. One book in each category will be selected: PreK-grade 3, grades 4-6 & grades 7-12.
Award: $1,000 in each category
Closing Date: Feb 1

The Alicia Patterson Foundation Fellowship Program
The Alicia Patterson Foundation
1100 Vermont Ave, Suite 900, Washington, DC 20005
Tel: 202-393-5995 *Fax:* 301-951-8512
E-mail: info@aliciapatterson.org
Web Site: www.aliciapatterson.org
Key Personnel
Exec Dir: Margaret Engel
Established: 1963
Stipend (12 or 6 months), not for academic study, for professional print journalist with 5 years experience & must write/photograph for English language medium. One additional fellowship for science & environmental topics. Submit applications online beginning June 1. See web site for requirements.
Award: $40,000 over 12 months, $20,000 over 6 months. Applicants choose whether they want 6 or 12 month grants
Closing Date: Oct 1
Presented: 2nd week of Dec

The Pattis Family Foundation Book Award
The Newberry Library
60 W Walton St, Chicago, IL 60610
Tel: 312-943-9090
E-mail: pattisprize@newberry.org
Web Site: www.newberry.org/pattis-family-foundation-chicago-book-award
Key Personnel
Pres & Libn: Daniel Greene
Established: 2021
Presented to a book that transforms public understanding of Chicago, its history, or its people. Nominations may be made by authors, publishers, or members of the general public. Titles must be available for purchase by the general public in either hardcover or bound paperback form. All genres are eligible.
Other Sponsor(s): The Pattis Family Foundation
Award: $25,000
Closing Date: Jan 31
Presented: July

Pattis Family Foundation Global Cities Book Award
The Chicago Council on Global Affairs
Prudential Plaza, 180 N Stetson Ave, Suite 1400, Chicago, IL 60601
Tel: 312-726-3860 *Fax:* 312-821-7555
E-mail: gcbookaward@thechicagocouncil.org
Web Site: globalaffairs.org/bookaward
Key Personnel
Global Cities Offr: Rachel Abrams *Tel:* 312-256-8525
Established: 2022
Celebrates books that deepen our understanding of the role cities play in addressing critical global challenges & urban policy. Book must be an original work of fiction, published in English & have a copyright date from January (2 years preceding award year) to December of the year preceding the award. Submissions accepted via e-mail with an attached PDF.
Other Sponsor(s): Pattis Family Foundation
Closing Date: Dec 31
Presented: Sept

Deborah Pease Prize
A Public Space
323 Dean St, Brooklyn, NY 11217
Tel: 718-858-8067
E-mail: general@apublicspace.org
Web Site: apublicspace.org
Key Personnel
Founding Ed: Brigid Hughes
Mktg & Devt Dir: Lauren Cerand *Tel:* 917-533-0103 *E-mail:* lauren@apublicspace.org
Established: 2018
Awarded to a figure who has advanced the art of literature.
Presented: Dec

Jean Pedrick Chapbook Prize
New England Poetry Club
c/o Linda Haviland Conte, 18 Hall Ave, Apt 2, Somerville, MA 02144
E-mail: info@nepoetryclub.org
Web Site: nepoetryclub.org
Key Personnel
Co-Pres: Doug Holder; Denise Provost
VP: Hilary Sallick
Treas: Linda Haviland Conte
E-mail: nepctreasurer@gmail.com
Awarded for a chapbook of poems published in the last 2 years. Entry by post only. Send 2 copies of your book with a cover page the includes your contact information to Doug Holder, 25 School St, Somerville, MA 02143. Entry fee: Free to membs, nonmembs $15 per submitted title.
Award: $250, 250 NEPC Award book cover stickers & opportunity to read at the NEPC (travel expenses not included)
Closing Date: May 31
Presented: Announced online Aug/Sept

Pegasus Award for Poetry Criticism
Poetry Foundation
61 W Superior St, Chicago, IL 60654
Tel: 312-787-7070
E-mail: info@poetryfoundation.org
Web Site: www.poetryfoundation.org/foundation/criticism-award
Prize to honor the best book-length works of criticism published in the US in the prior calendar year, including biographies, essay collections & critical editions that consider the subject of poetry or poets.
Award: $7,500
Presented: Oct

PEN America Literary Awards
PEN America
Affiliate of PEN International
120 Broadway, 26th fl N, New York, NY 10271
Tel: 212-334-1660 *Fax:* 212-334-2181
E-mail: awards@pen.org; info@pen.org
Web Site: pen.org/literary-awards
Key Personnel
Prog Dir, Literary Awards: Donica Bettanin
E-mail: dbettanin@pen.org
Established: 1963
Literary awards presented across diverse genres, including fiction, poetry, science writing, essays, sports writing, biography, children's literature & drama. Annual call for submissions opens each summer. Submissions accepted from publishers or literary agents. Authors may not submit their own books. Entry fee: $85.
Closing Date: Aug
Presented: PEN America Literary Awards Ceremony, New York, NY, Spring

PEN Award for Poetry in Translation
PEN America
Affiliate of PEN International
120 Broadway, 26th fl N, New York, NY 10271
Tel: 212-334-1660 *Fax:* 212-334-2181
E-mail: awards@pen.org; info@pen.org
Web Site: pen.org/pen-award-poetry-translation
Key Personnel
Prog Dir, Literary Awards: Donica Bettanin
E-mail: dbettanin@pen.org
Established: 1996

Award in recognition of book-length translations of poetry from any language into English, published during the current calendar year. Only publishers & literary agents may submit. Entry fee: $85.
Award: $3,000
Closing Date: Aug
Presented: PEN America Literary Awards Ceremony, New York, NY, Spring

PEN/Barbey Freedom to Write Award
PEN America
Affiliate of PEN International
120 Broadway, 26th fl N, New York, NY 10271
Tel: 212-334-1660 *Fax:* 212-334-2181
E-mail: awards@pen.org; info@pen.org
Web Site: pen.org/penbarbey-freedom-to-write-award
Key Personnel
Prog Dir, Literary Awards: Donica Bettanin
 E-mail: dbettanin@pen.org
Established: 2016
Designed to honor a writer imprisoned for his or her work in an effort to end the persecution of writers & defend free expression.

PEN/Bernard & Ann Malamud Award for Excellence in the Short Story
Formerly PEN/Malamud Award for Excellence in Short Fiction
PEN/Faulkner Foundation
6218 Georgia Ave NW, Unit 1062, Washington, DC 20011
Tel: 202-898-9063 *Fax:* 202-675-0360
E-mail: awards@penfaulkner.org; info@penfaulkner.org
Web Site: www.penfaulkner.org/our-awards/the-pen-malamud-award
Key Personnel
Exec Dir: Gwydion Suilebhan *E-mail:* gwydion@penfaulkner.org
Honors excellence in the art of short fiction.

PEN/Diamonstein-Spielvogel Award for the Art of the Essay
PEN America
Affiliate of PEN International
120 Broadway, 26th fl N, New York, NY 10271
Tel: 212-334-1660 *Fax:* 212-334-2181
E-mail: awards@pen.org; info@pen.org
Web Site: pen.org/pen-diamonstein-spielvogel-award-for-the-art-of-the-essay
Key Personnel
Prog Dir, Literary Awards: Donica Bettanin
 E-mail: dbettanin@pen.org
Award to honor a seasoned writer whose collection of essays, published by a US trade publisher in the applicable calendar year, is an expansion on their corpus of work & is not their first collection of essays. Essays may deal with a range of subjects or may explore one specific theme, but the book, taken as a whole, should be a collection of individual essays, not a book-length work of nonfiction. Candidates must be permanent US residents or American citizens & living at the time of the book's publication. First time & debut authors are ineligible. Self-published works are ineligible. Entry fee: $85.
Award: $15,000
Closing Date: Aug
Presented: PEN America Literary Awards Ceremony, New York, NY, Spring

PEN/E O Wilson Literary Science Writing Award
PEN America
Affiliate of PEN International
120 Broadway, 26th fl N, New York, NY 10271
Tel: 212-334-1660 *Fax:* 212-334-2181
E-mail: awards@pen.org; info@pen.org
Web Site: pen.org/pen-eo-wilson-prize-literary-science-writing
Key Personnel
Prog Dir, Literary Awards: Donica Bettanin
 E-mail: dbettanin@pen.org
Established: 2011
Nonfiction award which celebrates writing that exemplifies literary excellence on the subject of the physical or biological sciences & communicates complex scientific concepts to a lay audience. Entry fee: $85.
Other Sponsor(s): Jim & Cathy Stone; E O Wilson Biodiversity Foundation
Award: $10,000
Closing Date: Aug
Presented: PEN America Literary Awards Ceremony, New York, NY, Spring

PEN/Faulkner Award for Fiction
PEN/Faulkner Foundation
6218 Georgia Ave NW, Unit 1062, Washington, DC 20011
Tel: 202-898-9063
E-mail: awards@penfaulkner.org
Web Site: www.penfaulkner.org/our-awards/pen-faulkner-award
Key Personnel
Exec Dir: Gwydion Suilebhan *E-mail:* gwydion@penfaulkner.org
Established: 1980
Honors the best published works of fiction by American permanent residents in a single calendar year. Send PDF of each book via e-mail.
Award: $15,000 (1st prize), $5,000 to each of 4 finalists
Closing Date: Oct 31
Presented: May

PEN/Heim Translation Fund Grants
PEN America
Affiliate of PEN International
120 Broadway, 26th fl N, New York, NY 10271
Tel: 212-334-1660 *Fax:* 212-334-2181
E-mail: awards@pen.org
Web Site: pen.org/pen-heim-grants
Key Personnel
Prog Dir, Literary Awards: Donica Bettanin
 E-mail: dbettanin@pen.org
Established: 2003
Grants to promote the publication & reception of translated world literature into English. Works should be translations-in-progress with up to 2 translators. Only one project can be submitted per year. See web site for full application guidelines & materials required.
Other Sponsor(s): Pricilla Heim; Michael Henry
Award: $2,000-$4,000
Closing Date: June 1

PEN/Hemingway Award for Debut Novel
PEN America
Affiliate of PEN International
120 Broadway, 26th fl N, New York, NY 10271
Tel: 212-334-1660 *Fax:* 212-334-2181
E-mail: awards@pen.org; info@pen.org
Web Site: pen.org/pen-hemingway-award
Key Personnel
Sr Literary Progs Dir: Clarisse Rosaz Shariyf
Established: 1976
Awarded for a debut novel of exceptional literary merit by an American author who has not previously published a book-length work of fiction. Entry fee: $85, directly from a publisher.
Other Sponsor(s): Hemingway Foundation & Society
Closing Date: Aug 1
Presented: PEN America Literary Awards Ceremony, New York, NY; separate celebratory luncheon held at JFK Presidential Museum & Library, Boston, MA, Spring

PEN/Jacqueline Bograd Weld Award for Biography
PEN America
Affiliate of PEN International
120 Broadway, 26th fl N, New York, NY 10271
Tel: 212-334-1660 *Fax:* 212-334-2181
E-mail: awards@pen.org; info@pen.org
Web Site: pen.org/pen-bograd-weld-award-biography
Key Personnel
Prog Dir, Literary Awards: Donica Bettanin
 E-mail: dbettanin@pen.org
For a biography of exceptional literary, narrative & artistic merit, based on scrupulous research. Entry fee: $85.
Award: $5,000
Closing Date: Aug
Presented: PEN America Literary Awards Ceremony, New York, NY, Spring

PEN/Jean Stein Book Award
PEN America
Affiliate of PEN International
120 Broadway, 26th fl N, New York, NY 10271
Tel: 212-334-1660 *Fax:* 212-334-2181
E-mail: awards@pen.org; info@pen.org
Web Site: pen.org/pen-jean-stein-book-award
Key Personnel
Prog Dir, Literary Awards: Donica Bettanin
 E-mail: dbettanin@pen.org
Established: 2016
Award recognizing a book-length work of any genre for its originality, merit & impact. Judging panel will serve anonymously & will nominate candidates internally & without submissions from the public.
Award: $75,000
Closing Date: Aug
Presented: PEN America Literary Awards Ceremony, New York, NY, Spring

PEN/John Kenneth Galbraith Award for Nonfiction
PEN America
Affiliate of PEN International
120 Broadway, 26th fl N, New York, NY 10271
Tel: 212-334-1660 *Fax:* 212-334-2181
E-mail: awards@pen.org; info@pen.org
Web Site: pen.org/pen-galbraith-award-for-nonfiction
Key Personnel
Prog Dir, Literary Awards: Donica Bettanin
 E-mail: dbettanin@pen.org
Biennial prize given, in odd-numbered years, to the author of a distinguished book of general nonfiction possessing notable literary merit & critical perspective that illuminates important contemporary issues & that has been published in the US during the previous 2 calendar years. Biographies, autobiographies & memoirs are not accepted. Self-published books are not eligible. Submissions are only accepted from publishers & literary agents; authors may not submit their own work. See web site for full submission guidelines. Entry fee: $85.
Award: $10,000

PEN/Malamud Award for Excellence in Short Fiction, see PEN/Bernard & Ann Malamud Award for Excellence in the Short Story

PEN/Mike Nichols Writing for Performance Award
PEN America
Affiliate of PEN International
120 Broadway, 26th fl N, New York, NY 10271
Tel: 212-334-1660 *Fax:* 212-334-2181
E-mail: awards@pen.org; info@pen.org
Web Site: pen.org/pen-nichols-award
Key Personnel
Prog Dir, Literary Awards: Donica Bettanin
 E-mail: dbettanin@pen.org

Established: 2019
Award aims to highlight transformative works that enlighten & inspire audiences. No outside nominations. Winner is selected by a panel of judges.
Award: $25,000
Closing Date: Aug
Presented: Feb

PEN/Nabokov Award for Achievement in International Literature
PEN America
Affiliate of PEN International
120 Broadway, 26th fl N, New York, NY 10271
Tel: 212-334-1660 *Fax:* 212-334-2181
E-mail: awards@pen.org; info@pen.org
Web Site: pen.org/pen-nabokov-award
Key Personnel
Prog Dir, Literary Awards: Donica Bettanin
  E-mail: dbettanin@pen.org
Established: 2016
Presented to a living author whose body of work, either written in or translated into English, represents the highest level of achievement in fiction, nonfiction, poetry +/or drama & is of enduring originality & consummate craftsmanship. The winner is selected by a panel of judges. There are no outside nominations.
Other Sponsor(s): Vladimir Nabokov Literary Foundation
Award: $50,000
Presented: PEN America Literary Awards Ceremony, New York, NY, Spring

PEN Open Book Award
PEN America
Affiliate of PEN International
120 Broadway, 26th fl N, New York, NY 10271
Tel: 212-334-1660 *Fax:* 212-334-2181
E-mail: awards@pen.org; info@pen.org
Web Site: pen.org/pen-open-book-award
Key Personnel
Prog Dir, Literary Awards: Donica Bettanin
  E-mail: dbettanin@pen.org
Awarded for an exceptional book-length work of any genre by a writer of color. Entry fee: $85.
Award: $10,000
Closing Date: Aug
Presented: PEN America Literary Awards Ceremony, New York, NY, Spring

PEN/Phyllis Naylor Grant for Children's & Young Adult Novelists
PEN America
Affiliate of PEN International
120 Broadway, 26th fl N, New York, NY 10271
Tel: 212-334-1660 *Fax:* 212-334-2181
E-mail: awards@pen.org; info@pen.org
Web Site: pen.org/literary-awards/grants-fellowships
Key Personnel
Dir, Foundations & Grants: Brandon Stinchfield
  E-mail: bstinchfield@pen.org
Established: 2001
Presented to an author of children's or young adult fiction. Provides a writer with a measure of financial sustenance in order to make possible an extended period of time to complete a book-length work-in-progress & to assist a writer at a crucial moment in his or her career when monetary support is particularly needed.
Award: $5,000
Closing Date: Aug
Presented: PEN America Literary Awards Ceremony, New York, NY, Spring

PEN/Ralph Manheim Award for Translation
PEN America
Affiliate of PEN International
120 Broadway, 26th fl N, New York, NY 10271
Tel: 212-334-1660 *Fax:* 212-334-2181
E-mail: awards@pen.org; info@pen.org
Web Site: pen.org/literary-award/penralph-manheim-medal-for-translation
Key Personnel
Prog Dir, Literary Awards: Donica Bettanin
  E-mail: dbettanin@pen.org
Established: 1982
Awarded triennially to a translator who has demonstrated exceptional commitment to excellence throughout the body of his work. Candidates nominated by PEN America members & the winner is selected by the PEN Translation Committee.
Award: $1,000
Closing Date: Aug
Presented: PEN America Literary Awards Ceremony, New York, NY, Spring

PEN/Robert J Dau Short Story Prize for Emerging Writers
PEN America
Affiliate of PEN International
120 Broadway, 26th fl N, New York, NY 10271
Tel: 212-334-1660 *Fax:* 212-334-2181
E-mail: awards@pen.org; info@pen.org
Web Site: pen.org/pen-dau-short-story-prize
Key Personnel
Prog Dir, Literary Awards: Donica Bettanin
  E-mail: dbettanin@pen.org
Recognizes 12 emerging writers for their debut short stories published in a literary magazine, journal, or cultural web site & aims to support the launch of their careers as fiction writers. Submissions open June 1. Entry fee: $85. See web site for eligibility requirements.
Other Sponsor(s): Robert J Dau Family
Award: $2,000 & publication by Catapult in their annual anthology, *Best Debut Short Stories: The PEN America Dau Prize*
Closing Date: Nov 15
Presented: PEN America Literary Awards Ceremony, New York, NY, Spring

PEN/Robert W Bingham Prize for Debut Short Story Collection
PEN America
Affiliate of PEN International
120 Broadway, 26th fl N, New York, NY 10271
Tel: 212-334-1660 *Fax:* 212-334-2181
E-mail: awards@pen.org; info@pen.org
Web Site: pen.org/pen-bingham-prize
Key Personnel
Prog Dir, Literary Awards: Donica Bettanin
  E-mail: dbettanin@pen.org
Honors an exceptionally talented fiction writer whose debut book, a collection of short stories, represents distinguished literary achievement & suggests great promise for a second work of literary fiction. Candidates must be US residents but American citizenship is not required. Self-published books are not eligible. Entry fee: $85.
Award: $25,000
Closing Date: Aug
Presented: PEN America Literary Awards Ceremony, New York, NY, Spring

PEN/Saul Bellow Award for Achievement in American Fiction
PEN America
Affiliate of PEN International
120 Broadway, 26th fl N, New York, NY 10271
Tel: 212-334-1660 *Fax:* 212-334-2181
E-mail: awards@pen.org; info@pen.org
Web Site: pen.org/pen-saul-bellow-award
Key Personnel
Prog Dir, Literary Awards: Donica Bettanin
  E-mail: dbettanin@pen.org
Established: 2009
Awarded biennially, in even-numbered years, to a living American author whose scale of achievement in fiction, over a sustained career, places him or her in the highest rank of American literature. Administered by internal nomination only.
Award: $25,000

PEN Translation Prize
PEN America
Affiliate of PEN International
120 Broadway, 26th fl N, New York, NY 10271
Tel: 212-334-1660 *Fax:* 212-334-2181
E-mail: awards@pen.org; info@pen.org
Web Site: pen.org/pen-translation-prize
Key Personnel
Prog Dir, Literary Awards: Donica Bettanin
  E-mail: dbettanin@pen.org
Established: 1963
Awarded for the best book-length translation into English from any language published in the US during the previous calendar year. Entry fee: $85.
Award: $3,000
Closing Date: Aug
Presented: PEN America Literary Awards Ceremony, New York, NY, Spring

PEN/Voelcker Award for Poetry Collection
PEN America
Affiliate of PEN International
120 Broadway, 26th fl N, New York, NY 10271
Tel: 212-334-1660 *Fax:* 212-334-2181
E-mail: awards@pen.org; info@pen.org
Web Site: pen.org/pen-voelcker-award-poetry
Key Personnel
Prog Dir, Literary Awards: Donica Bettanin
  E-mail: dbettanin@pen.org
Awarded to a poet whose distinguished & growing body of work to date represents a notable & accomplished presence in American literature. Entry fee: $85.
Award: $5,000
Closing Date: Aug
Presented: PEN America Literary Awards Ceremony, New York, NY, Spring

PEN Writers' Emergency Fund
PEN America
Affiliate of PEN International
120 Broadway, 26th fl N, New York, NY 10271
Tel: 212-334-1660 *Fax:* 212-334-2181
E-mail: writersfund@pen.org; info@pen.org
Web Site: pen.org/writers-emergency-fund
Key Personnel
Dir, Foundations & Grants: Brandon Stinchfield
  E-mail: bstinchfield@pen.org
Established: 1921
Grants intended to assist fiction & nonfiction authors, poets, playwrights, screenwriters, translators & journalists. Applicants must be based in the US & be able to demonstrate that this one-time grant will be meaningful in helping them to address an emergency situation. Application form available online.
Other Sponsor(s): The Haven Foundation; Lannan Foundation
Award: $500 or $1,000

Perkoff Prize
The Missouri Review
357 McReynolds Hall, University of Missouri, Columbia, MO 65211
Tel: 573-882-4474
E-mail: contest_question@moreview.com
Web Site: www.missourireview.com/contests/perkoff-prize
Key Personnel
Contest Ed: Bailey Boyd
Tri-genre contest awarding writers of the best story, set of poems & essay that engage in evocative ways with health & medicine as judged by the editors. Submissions must engage with health & medicine in some way & be previously unpublished. Submissions accepted online & by mail. Entry fee: $15 standard (includes 1-year digital subscription), $30

all access (includes 1-year digital subscription & access to last 10 years of digital issues & audio recordings).
Award: $1,000 & publication
Closing Date: March 15

Aliki Perroti & Seth Frank Most Promising Young Poet Award
The Academy of American Poets Inc
75 Maiden Lane, Suite 901, New York, NY 10038
Tel: 212-274-0343
E-mail: awards@poets.org
Web Site: poets.org/academy-american-poets/american-poets-prizes
Key Personnel
Pres & Exec Dir: Ricardo Alberto Maldonado
VP, Digital Engagement & Content: Jeff Gleaves
Ad & Mktg Dir: Michelle Campagna
Dir, Donor Rel: Molly Walsh
Dir, Progs: Nikay Paredes
Established: 2013
Awarded in recognition of a student poet 23 years old or younger. Only a school's college prize coordinator may submit a student's winning poem to be considered for the prize. No applications are accepted. The prize winner will be featured on the Academy web site & in *American Poets* magazine.
Award: $1,000 cash prize

Perugia Press Prize
Perugia Press
PO Box 60364, Florence, MA 01062
Web Site: www.perugiapress.com; perugiapress.org
Key Personnel
Dir & Ed: Rebecca Olander
Established: 1997
Poets must be women, which is inclusive of transgender women & female-identified individuals & must have no more than 1 previously published full-length book. Submission fee: $30 (with free book), $15 (reduced rate), fee-free (Black, Indigenous & Women of Color). See web site for detailed guidelines.
Award: $1,000 & publication
Closing Date: Nov 15
Presented: Winner announced by April 1

The Petrichor Prize for Finely Crafted Fiction
Regal House Publishing
806 Oberlin Rd, No 12094, Raleigh, NC 27605
E-mail: info@regalhousepublishing.com
Web Site: regalhousepublishing.com/the-petrichor-prize-for-finely-crafted-fiction/
Key Personnel
Founder, Publr & Ed-in-Chief: Jaynie Royal
Mng Ed: Pam Van Dyk
Established: 2019
Recognizes finely crafted works of literary fiction. Submissions through Submittable or by post. Entry fee: $25. Fax or e-mail submissions not accepted. See web site for submission guidelines. Five finalists announced on Sept 10.
Award: Publication & $500 honorarium
Closing Date: July 15 (postmark)
Presented: Oct 10

Pfizer Award
History of Science Society
Affiliate of American Council of Learned Societies
440 Geddes Hall, Notre Dame, IN 46556
Tel: 574-631-1194 Fax: 574-631-1533
E-mail: info@hssonline.org
Web Site: www.hssonline.org
Established: 1958
Award given for an outstanding book in English, published during the preceding 3 years, on a topic related to the history of science.
Award: $2,500 & medal
Closing Date: April 1
Presented: Oct/Nov

Phi Beta Kappa Award in Science
The Phi Beta Kappa Society
1606 New Hampshire Ave NW, Washington, DC 20009
Tel: 202-265-3808 Fax: 202-986-1601
E-mail: awards@pbk.org
Web Site: www.pbk.org/bookawards
Key Personnel
Exec Asst to the Secy: Aurora Sherman Tel: 202-745-3287 E-mail: asherman@pbk.org
Established: 1959
For an outstanding interpretation of science written by a scientist & published in the US during the previous year. Works in the physical & biological sciences & mathematics are eligible for the award. Highly technical works, monographs & reports on research are not eligible. Nominations must come from publisher & be submitted online.
Award: $10,000
Closing Date: Jan
Presented: Washington, DC, Dec

Phoenix Award
Children's Literature Association (ChLA)
140B Purcellville Gateway Dr, Suite 1200, Purcellville, VA 20132
Tel: 630-571-4520
E-mail: info@childlitassn.org
Web Site: www.childlitassn.org
Key Personnel
Association Mgr: Cate Langley
Established: 1985
Awarded to an author, or the estate of an author, to recognize a children's book of exceptional literary merit. The book must have been first published 20 years earlier, in English. It may not have won any major award at the time of publication. Anyone may nominate a book & there is no minimum page count. A maximum of 2 honor books may be designated. The award winner is selected 2 years prior to the conference at which the award is given.
Presented: ChLA Annual Conference, June

Phoenix Picture Book Award
Children's Literature Association (ChLA)
140B Purcellville Gateway Dr, Suite 1200, Purcellville, VA 20132
Tel: 630-571-4520
E-mail: info@childlitassn.org
Web Site: www.childlitassn.org
Key Personnel
Association Mgr: Cate Langley
Established: 2013
Awarded to an author +/or illustrator, or the estate of the author +/or illustrator, in recognition of an exemplary picture book that conveys its story (whether fact or fiction) through the synergy between pictures & text, or through pictures alone if there is no text. The book must have been first published 20 years earlier, in English. It may not have won any major award at the time of publication. Anyone may nominate a book. The award winner must be selected at the annual conference of the year before that in which the award is given.
Presented: ChLA Annual Conference, June

The Bruce Piasecki & Andrea Masters Annual Award on Business & Science Writing
AHC Group Inc
158 Stone Church Rd, Ballston Spa, NY 12020
Tel: 518-583-9615 Fax: 518-583-9726
Web Site: www.ahcgroup.com
Key Personnel
Founder & Pres: Dr Bruce Piasecki
Honors young authors (ages 18–35) who offer solutions to urgent problems facing American society & the world.
Other Sponsor(s): Creative Force Fund
Award: $5,000
Presented: Albany, NY

Robert J Pickering/J R Colbeck Award for Playwriting Excellence
Branch County Community Theatre
14 S Hanchett St, Coldwater, MI 49036
E-mail: president@branchcct.org
Web Site: www.branchcct.org
Key Personnel
Comm Chmn: Jennifer Colbeck
Established: 1984
Playwriting, must be unproduced full-length plays +/or musicals.
Award: $200 & production (1st prize), $50 (2nd prize), $25 (3rd prize)
Closing Date: Dec 31 (entries accepted all year, hard copy only)
Presented: Tibbits Opera House, Coldwater, MI, March +/or Oct

Lorne Pierce Medal
Royal Society of Canada
Walter House, 282 Somerset W, Ottawa, ON K2P 0J6, Canada
Tel: 613-991-6990 (ext 106) Fax: 613-991-6996
E-mail: nominations@rsc-src.ca
Web Site: www.rsc-src.ca
Key Personnel
Mgr, Fellowship & Awards: Marie-Lyne Renaud E-mail: mlrenaud@rsc-src.ca
Established: 1926
Biennial award given in even-numbered years for an achievement of significance & conspicuous merit in imaginative or critical literature.
Award: Medal
Closing Date: March 1
Presented: RSC Annual Meeting, Nov

The Pinch Writing Awards in Fiction
The Pinch Literary Journal
University of Memphis, English Dept, 431 Patterson Hall, Memphis, TN 38152
Tel: 901-678-2651 Fax: 901-678-2226
E-mail: editor@pinchjournal.com
Web Site: www.pinchjournal.com
Key Personnel
Ed-in-Chief: Eric Schlich
Established: 1987
Submit a previously unpublished work not to exceed 5,000 words. Submission fee: $20. No longer accepting paper or e-mail submissions. Send work through online portal via Submittable.
Award: $2,000 & publication in the subsequent issue of *The Pinch* (1st prize), 2nd & 3rd place winners may also be published. All entrants receive 2 free copies of the journal in which the work appears
Presented: Mid-Sept

The Pinch Writing Awards in Poetry
The Pinch Literary Journal
University of Memphis, English Dept, 431 Patterson Hall, Memphis, TN 38152
Tel: 901-678-2651 Fax: 901-678-2226
E-mail: editor@pinchjournal.com
Web Site: www.pinchjournal.com
Key Personnel
Ed-in-Chief: Eric Schlich
Established: 1987
Submit unpublished poems. Submission fee: $20. No longer accepting paper or e-mail submissions. Send work through online portal via Submittable.
Award: $2,000 & publication in the subsequent issue of *The Pinch* (1st prize), 2nd & 3rd place winners may also be published. All entrants re-

AWARDS, PRIZE CONTESTS, FELLOWSHIPS & GRANTS

ceive 2 free copies of the journal in which the work appears
Presented: Mid-Sept

Pinckley Prizes for Crime Fiction
Women's National Book Association of New Orleans
PO Box 13926, New Orleans, LA 70185
E-mail: pinckleyprizes@gmail.com
Web Site: www.pinckleyprizes.org
Key Personnel
Admin: Susan Larson
The prizes honor 2 women writers. The Pinckley Prize for Distinguished Body of Work honors an established woman writer who has created a significant body of work in crime fiction. The winner is nominated & selected by a jury of WNBA-NO members. The Pinckley Prize for Debut Novel honors a woman writer with a first-time published novel in adult crime fiction. The winner is selected from the submissions by a three-judge panel. Entry forms must accompany all submissions for the Debut Novel Prize.
Other Sponsor(s): Greater New Orleans Foundation
Award: $2,500 & trip to New Orleans
Closing Date: Dec 31
Presented: Oct

Pinnacle Book Achievement Awards
National Association of Book Entrepreneurs (NABE)
PO Box 606, Cottage Grove, OR 97424
Tel: 541-942-7455 Fax: 541-942-7455
E-mail: nabe@bookmarketingprofits.com
Web Site: www.bookmarketingprofits.com/PinnacleBookEntryFormE.html
Key Personnel
Exec Dir: Al Galasso
Established: 1995
Awarded in recognition of the finest books published by NABE members based on book content, quality, writing style, presentation & cover design. One free entry form for one book for NABE members. Additional books or additional categories can be entered for $50 per book or category for members. All printed books written in English & published in the previous 2 years or in the year of the awards are eligible.
Award: Honor & mention in upcoming issue of Book Dealers World, Award Winners web page, press releases, book stickers & certificates for their web site

Pinnacle InterTech Awards
PRINTING United Alliance
10015 Main St, Fairfax, VA 22031
Tel: 703-385-1335 Toll Free Tel: 888-385-3588 Fax: 703-273-0456
E-mail: pinnacleintertech@printing.org
Web Site: pinnacleawards.printing.org
Key Personnel
CEO: Ford Bowers E-mail: fbowers@printing.org
Established: 1978
Honors the development of technologies predicted to have a major impact on commercial printing, digital textile, packaging, screen printing, wide format, or related industries. Entry fee: $1,500 membs, $2,000 nonmembs. See web site for full eligibility requirements.
Award: Lucite Star
Closing Date: July 31
Presented: Sept 15
Branch Office(s)
1325 "G" St NW, Suite 500, Washington, DC 20005 Tel: 202-627-6925 ext 504
2000 Corporate Dr, Suite 205, Wexford, PA 15090, Events & Spec Progs Mgr:
Mike Packard Tel: 412-741-6860 Toll Free Tel: 800-910-4283 Fax: 412-741-2311
E-mail: mpackard@printing.org

Playwright Discovery Award, see The Jean Kennedy Smith VSA Playwright Discovery Award

The Plimpton Prize for Fiction
The Paris Review Foundation
544 W 27 St, New York, NY 10001
Tel: 212-343-1333
E-mail: queries@theparisreview.org
Web Site: www.theparisreview.org
Key Personnel
Mng Ed: Hasan Altaf
Established: 1992
Awarded for the best work of fiction published in The Paris Review that year by an emerging or previously unpublished writer.
Award: $10,000
Presented: Spring Revel

Judith Plotz Emerging Scholar Award
Children's Literature Association (ChLA)
140B Purcellville Gateway Dr, Suite 1200, Purcellville, VA 20132
Tel: 630-571-4520
E-mail: info@childlitassn.org
Web Site: www.childlitassn.org
Key Personnel
Association Mgr: Cate Langley
Awarded in recognition of outstanding articles of literary criticism focused on children's literature by new, never-before-published authors. Articles should be submitted online through the web site. The focus of the article should be a literary, historical, theoretical, or cultural examination of children's texts +/or children's culture, although other items may also be included in the analysis. Eligible articles must be the first article published by a given author & must be written in English exclusively by the author(s) or translator(s) whose name(s) appear(s) on the article & must have been published during the year under consideration. Articles should provide new insights into the field, making a distinct or significant scholarly contribution to the understanding of children's literature. Reprints of previously published articles are not eligible.
Closing Date: Nov 1
Presented: ChLA Annual Conference, June

Ploughshares Emerging Writer's Contest
Ploughshares
Emerson College, 120 Boylston St, Boston, MA 02116
Tel: 617-824-3757
E-mail: pshares@pshares.org
Web Site: www.pshares.org
Key Personnel
Exec Dir & Ed-in-Chief: Ladette Randolph
Awarded in recognition of work by an emerging writer in each of 3 genres: fiction, nonfiction & poetry. Authors are considered "emerging" if they haven't published or self-published a book. Fiction & nonfiction: Under 6,000 words; Poetry: 3-5 pages. Submit 1 entry per year via the online submission manager. Entry fee: $24 (waived if subscriber through winter issue of Ploughshares).
Award: $2,000 & publication to 1 winner in each genre
Closing Date: May 15
Presented: Mid-Sept

Plutarch Award
Biographers International Organization (BIO)
PO Box 33020, Santa Fe, NM 87594
Tel: 505-983-4671

ASSOCIATIONS, EVENTS

E-mail: plutarch@biographersinternational.org
Web Site: biographersinternational.org/award/the-plutarch
Key Personnel
Exec Dir: Michael Gately E-mail: execdirector@biographersinternational.org
Established: 2013
Awarded by a committee of distinguished biographers for the best biographical work of the calendar year based on nominations by publishers & BIO members.
Award: $1,000 honorarium
Closing Date: Dec 1
Presented: BIO Annual Conference, May

PNWA Writers' Contest
PNWA - a writer's resource
1420 NW Gilman Blvd, Suite 29, PMB 2717, Issaquah, WA 98027
Tel: 425-673-2665
E-mail: pnwa@pnwa.org
Web Site: www.pnwa.org
Key Personnel
Pres: Pam Binder E-mail: pambinder@pnwa.org
VP: Sandy McCormack E-mail: sandymccormack@pnwa.org
Secy: Robert Dugoni
Treas: Brian Mercer E-mail: brianmercer@pnwa.org
Multiple categories by genre. Entry fee: $47 membs, $62 nonmembs; $10 discount if postmarked by January 31.
Award: $600 (1st prize), $250 (2nd prize), $150 (3rd prize)
Closing Date: March 31 (postmarked)
Presented: PNWA Annual Conference

Edgar Allan Poe Memorial
The Poetry Society of Virginia (PSV)
PO Box 36128, North Chesterfield, VA 23235-3533
E-mail: contest@poetrysocietyofvirginia.org; info@poetryvirginia.org
Web Site: www.poetrysocietyofvirginia.org
Key Personnel
Pres: Cherryl T Cooley E-mail: poetrysocietypresident@gmail.com
All entries must be in English, original & unpublished. Any form, any subject, no line limit. Submit 1 copy of the poem with no identifying information but put the category in the upper right-hand-side, along with a notation as to whether you are a member of PSV (does not matter if you are a lifetime member or just joined for the contest). Submit a cover letter/page that contains the category, the name of the poem, your name & address, phone number & e-mail address. Entries will not be returned. Entry fee: Free to membs, $5 nonmembs.
Award: $100
Closing Date: Feb
Presented: PSV Awards Ceremony, April

Poetry Awards
Prince Edward Island Writers' Guild
81 Prince St, Charlottetown, PE C1A 4R3, Canada
E-mail: peiliteraryawards@gmail.com
Web Site: www.peiwritersguild.com
One entry consists of 8 pages (minimum) to 10 pages (maximum) of poetry. Work must be original & unpublished. Entry fee: $25 per submission. Prince Edward Island residents only. See web site for complete entry requirements.
Award: Cash prizes for 1st, 2nd & 3rd place
Closing Date: Changes annually (see web site)
Presented: Island Literary Awards Gala, Spring

Poetry Center Book Award
Poetry Center & American Poetry Archives at San Francisco State University

511-512 Humanities Bldg, 1600 Holloway Ave,
  San Francisco, CA 94132
Tel: 415-338-2227 *Fax:* 415-338-0966
E-mail: poetry@sfsu.edu
Web Site: poetry.sfsu.edu
Key Personnel
Dir: Steve Dickison *E-mail:* steved@sfsu.edu
Assoc Dir: Elise Ficarra *E-mail:* eficarra@sfsu.edu
Established: 1980
For an outstanding book of poetry published in the previous year by a single author only. Translated works when translated by the author do qualify. Entries can be submitted by publisher, author, or by a reader. Include a cover letter noting author name, book title(s), name of person or publisher issuing check & check number. Entry fee: $15 per book.
Award: Cash prize & invitation to read, along with the award judge, at the Poetry Center
Closing Date: Jan 31
Presented: Fall

Karl Pohrt Tribute Award
Book Industry Charitable Foundation (BINC)
3135 S State St, Suite 203, Ann Arbor, MI 48108
Toll Free Tel: 866-733-9064
E-mail: info@bincfoundation.org
Web Site: www.bincfoundation.org/scholarship
Key Personnel
Exec Dir: Pamela French *E-mail:* pam@bincfoundation.org
Dir, Devt: Kathy Bartson *E-mail:* kathy@bincfoundation.org
Prog Mgr: Judey Kalchik *E-mail:* judey@bincfoundation.org; Ken White *E-mail:* ken@bincfoundation.org
Commun Coord: Erika Mantz *E-mail:* erika@bincfoundation.org
Devt Coord: Jennifer Rojas *E-mail:* jennifer@bincfoundation.org
Off Coord: Jane Regenstreif *E-mail:* jane@bincfoundation.org
Spec Projs Coord: Kate Weiss *E-mail:* kate@bincfoundation.org
Awarded to an independent bookseller who has overcome learning adversity or is a nontraditional student. The bookstore must have a brick & mortar presence in the US & be owned by an entity deriving a substantial portion of its revenue from the sale of physical books.
Award: $5,000

George Polk Awards in Journalism
Long Island University
The Brooklyn Campus, One University Plaza, Brooklyn, NY 11201-5372
Tel: 718-488-1009
Web Site: www.liu.edu/polk
Key Personnel
Curator: John Darnton
Coord: Ralph Engelman *E-mail:* ralph.engelman@liu.edu
Established: 1949
For outstanding discernment & reporting of a news or feature story on the Internet, in newspapers, radio or television. Entries originating from publication offices, newsrooms or individual reporters are considered. Only online submissions are accepted at liu.edu/polk. See web site for entry fee information & submission guidelines.
Award: Plaque & cash award
Closing Date: End of 1st week in Jan for the previous calendar year
Presented: Luncheon in New York, NY, Spring

Porchlight Book Co Business Book Awards
Porchlight Book Co
544 S First St, Milwaukee, WI 53204
Toll Free Tel: 800-236-7323
E-mail: info@porchlightbooks.com
Web Site: porchlightbooks.com
Key Personnel
Owner, Pres & CEO: Rebecca Schwartz *E-mail:* rebecca@porchlightbooks.com
Owner & Chair: Carol Grossmeyer *E-mail:* carol@porchlightbooks.com
Mng Dir: Sally Haldorson *E-mail:* sally@porchlightbooks.com
Opers Dir: Ryan Schleicher *E-mail:* ryan@porchlightbooks.com
Awarded in recognition of the best books in the business genre. Any business book originally published in the prior year & available in the US is eligible. Books must be submitted by the publisher, agent, or author of the book. Categories: Leadership & strategy, management & workplace culture, marketing & sales, innovation & creativity, personal development & human behavior, current events & public affairs, narrative & biography, big ideas & new perspectives.
Closing Date: Sept
Presented: Jan (Business Book of the Year & Jack Covert Award)

Katherine Anne Porter Award
American Academy of Arts & Letters
633 W 155 St, New York, NY 10032
Tel: 212-368-5900
E-mail: academy@artsandletters.org
Web Site: artsandletters.org/awards
Key Personnel
Exec Dir: Cody Upton
Established: 2001
Awarded biennialy, in even-numbered years, to honor a prose writer whose achievements & dedication to the literary profession have been demonstrated. Candidates must be nominated by an Academy member.
Award: $20,000

Katherine Anne Porter Prize for Fiction
Nimrod International Journal
University of Tulsa, Kendall College of Arts & Sciences, 800 S Tucker Dr, Tulsa, OK 74104
Tel: 918-631-3080
E-mail: nimrod@utulsa.edu
Web Site: artsandsciences.utulsa.edu/nimrod/nimrod-literary-awards/
Key Personnel
Ed-in-Chief: Eilis O'Neal
Mng Ed: Cassidy McCants
Assoc Ed: Diane Burton
Established: 1978
Awarded for a 7,500 word maximum work not previously published or accepted for publication elsewhere. Must have a US address by October to enter. Works must be in English or translated by original author. Author's name must not appear on ms. Include a cover sheet containing major title & subtitles, author's name, address, phone number & e-mail address. "Contest Entry" must be on envelope. Mss will not be returned. SASE for results only. $20 entry fee includes processing & 1-year subscription. Online submissions: nimrod-journal.submittable.com.
Award: $2,000 (1st prize), $1,000 (2nd prize); published writers receive 2 copies of the journal; winners are flown to Tulsa for a conference & banquet
Closing Date: April 1
Presented: Oct

Rose Post Creative Nonfiction Competition
North Carolina Writers' Network
PO Box 21591, Winston-Salem, NC 27120-1591
Tel: 336-293-8844
E-mail: mail@ncwriters.org; nclrsubmissions@ecu.edu
Web Site: www.ncwriters.org
Key Personnel
Exec Dir: Ed Southern *E-mail:* ed@ncwriters.org
Encourages the creation of lasting nonfiction that is outside the realm of conventional journalism & has relevance to North Carolinians. Subjects may include traditional categories such as reviews, travel articles, profiles or interviews, place/history pieces, or culture criticism. The competition is open to any writer who is a legal resident of North Carolina or a member of the North Carolina Writer's Network. Entries can be submitted via US Postal Service or online at ncwriters.submittable.com. Entry fee: $10 membs, $12 nonmembs. Each entry must be an original & previously unpublished ms of no more than 2,000 words, typed in a 12-point standard font (i.e., Times New Roman) & double-spaced. See web site for full submission guidelines.
Award: $1,000 (1st prize), $300 (2nd prize), $200 (3rd prize); winning entry considered for publication in *Ecotone*
Closing Date: Jan 15

Prairie Schooner Annual Strousse Award
Prairie Schooner
110 Andrews Hall, University of Nebraska-Lincoln, Lincoln, NE 68588-0334
Tel: 402-472-0911 *Fax:* 402-472-1817
E-mail: psbookprize@unl.edu; prairieschooner@unl.edu
Web Site: prairieschooner.unl.edu
Key Personnel
Book Prize Coord: Nicole Lachat
Established: 1975
For best poetry published in the magazine each year.
Other Sponsor(s): Friends & famliy of Fora Strousse
Award: $500
Presented: Prairie Schooner, Lincoln, NE, March

Prairie Schooner Bernice Slote Award
Prairie Schooner
110 Andrews Hall, University of Nebraska-Lincoln, Lincoln, NE 68588-0334
Tel: 402-472-0911 *Fax:* 402-472-1817
E-mail: psbookprize@unl.edu; prairieschooner@unl.edu
Web Site: prairieschooner.unl.edu
Key Personnel
Book Prize Coord: Nicole Lachat
Established: 1985
Writing prize for best work by a beginning writer published in *Prairie Schooner* in the previous year.
Award: $500
Presented: Winners announced in Spring issue of *Prairie Schooner* magazine

Prairie Schooner Book Prize in Poetry
Prairie Schooner
110 Andrews Hall, University of Nebraska-Lincoln, Lincoln, NE 68588-0334
Tel: 402-472-0911 *Fax:* 402-472-1817
E-mail: psbookprize@unl.edu; prairieschooner@unl.edu
Web Site: prairieschooner.unl.edu
Key Personnel
Book Prize Coord: Nicole Lachat
Welcomes mss from all living writers, including non-US citizens, writing in English. Mss previously published will not be considered. Writers may enter both fiction & poetry contests. For poetry mss, at least 50 pages in length is preferred. Entry fee: $25 per submission. Mss accepted by electronic or hard copy submission beginning January 15.
Award: $3,000 & publication through the University of Nebraska Press
Closing Date: March 15

Prairie Schooner Edward Stanley Award
Prairie Schooner
110 Andrews Hall, University of Nebraska-Lincoln, Lincoln, NE 68588-0334
Tel: 402-472-0911 *Fax:* 402-472-1817
E-mail: psbookprize@unl.edu; prairieschooner@unl.edu
Web Site: prairieschooner.unl.edu
Key Personnel
Book Prize Coord: Nicole Lachat
Established: 1992
Writing award for best poem or group of poems in the volume. Only contributors to the magazine are eligible.
Other Sponsor(s): Friends & family of Marion Edward Stanley (in memorium)
Award: $1,000
Presented: Winners announced in Spring issue of *Prairie Schooner* magazine

Prairie Schooner Glenna Luschei Award
Prairie Schooner
110 Andrews Hall, University of Nebraska-Lincoln, Lincoln, NE 68588-0334
Tel: 402-472-0911 *Fax:* 402-472-1817
E-mail: psbookprize@unl.edu; prairieschooner@unl.edu
Web Site: prairieschooner.unl.edu
Key Personnel
Book Prize Coord: Nicole Lachat
Established: 1989
Writing awards for best work published in the magazine. Only work published in *Prairie Schooner* in the previous year is considered.
Other Sponsor(s): Glenna Luschei
Award: $1,500 (1st place), $250 (10 runners up)
Presented: Winners announced in Spring issue of *Prairie Schooner* magazine

Prairie Schooner Hugh J Luke Award
Prairie Schooner
110 Andrews Hall, University of Nebraska-Lincoln, Lincoln, NE 68588-0334
Tel: 402-472-0911 *Fax:* 402-472-1817
E-mail: psbookprize@unl.edu; prairieschooner@unl.edu
Web Site: prairieschooner.unl.edu
Key Personnel
Book Prize Coord: Nicole Lachat
Established: 1989
Writing prize for best work published in the *Prairie Schooner* magazine in the previous year.
Other Sponsor(s): Friends & family of Hugh J Luke (in memoriam)
Award: $250
Presented: Winners announced in Spring issue of *Prairie Schooner* magazine

Prairie Schooner Jane Geske Award
Prairie Schooner
110 Andrews Hall, University of Nebraska-Lincoln, Lincoln, NE 68588-0334
Tel: 402-472-0911 *Fax:* 402-472-1817
E-mail: psbookprize@unl.edu; prairieschooner@unl.edu
Web Site: prairieschooner.unl.edu
Key Personnel
Book Prize Coord: Nicole Lachat
Established: 2000
Awarded for work in any genre published in *Prairie Schooner* in the previous year.
Other Sponsor(s): Family of Jane Geske
Award: $250
Presented: Winners announced in Spring issue of *Prairie Schooner* magazine

Prairie Schooner Lawrence Foundation Award
Prairie Schooner
110 Andrews Hall, University of Nebraska-Lincoln, Lincoln, NE 68588-0334
Tel: 402-472-0911 *Fax:* 402-472-1817
E-mail: psbookprize@unl.edu; prairieschooner@unl.edu
Web Site: prairieschooner.unl.edu
Key Personnel
Book Prize Coord: Nicole Lachat
Established: 1978
Writing award for the best short story published in *Prairie Schooner* magazine; only work published in the previous year will be considered.
Other Sponsor(s): The Lawrence Foundation of New York City
Award: $2,000
Presented: Winners announced in Spring issue of *Prairie Schooner* magazine

Prairie Schooner Raz-Shumaker Book Prize Contest
Prairie Schooner
110 Andrews Hall, University of Nebraska-Lincoln, Lincoln, NE 68588-0334
Tel: 402-472-0911 *Fax:* 402-472-1817
E-mail: psbookprize@unl.edu; prairieschooner@unl.edu
Web Site: prairieschooner.unl.edu
Key Personnel
Book Prize Coord: Nicole Lachat
Welcomes mss from all living writers, including non-US citizens, writing in English. Mss previously published will not be considered. Writers may enter both fiction & poetry contests. For fiction mss, at least 150 pages in length is preferred. Entry fee: $25 per submission. Mss accepted by electronic or hard copy submission beginning January 15.
Award: $3,000 & publication through the University of Nebraska Press
Closing Date: March 15
Presented: Winners announced online on or before Aug 15

Prairie Schooner Virginia Faulkner Award for Excellence in Writing
Prairie Schooner
110 Andrews Hall, University of Nebraska-Lincoln, Lincoln, NE 68588-0334
Tel: 402-472-0911 *Fax:* 402-472-1817
E-mail: psbookprize@unl.edu; prairieschooner@unl.edu
Web Site: prairieschooner.unl.edu
Key Personnel
Book Prize Coord: Nicole Lachat
Established: 1987
Writing award for work published in *Prairie Schooner* magazine. Only work published in the previous year is considered.
Other Sponsor(s): Friends & family of Virginia Faulkner
Award: $1,000
Presented: Winners announced in Spring issue of *Prairie Schooner* magazine

Premier PRINT Awards
PRINTING United Alliance
10015 Main St, Fairfax, VA 22031
Tel: 703-385-1335 *Toll Free Tel:* 888-385-3588 *Fax:* 703-273-0456
E-mail: assist@printing.org; info@printing.org
Web Site: premierprint.printing.org
Key Personnel
CEO: Ford Bowers *E-mail:* fbowers@printing.org
Established: 1950
All-inclusive industry competition that represents all areas & categories of print. The awards recognize excellence in quality, creative & innovation. See web site for full guidelines & fees.
Award: Winners of Best Of category, Printed Product of the Year category & Best of Show Award receive trophies & digital badges
Closing Date: July
Presented: Aug

Branch Office(s)
1325 "G" St NW, Suite 500, Washington, DC 20005 *Tel:* 202-627-6925 ext 504
2000 Corporate Dr, Suite 205, Wexford, PA 15090, Events & Spec Progs Mgr: Mike Packard *Tel:* 412-741-6860 *Toll Free Tel:* 800-910-4283 *Fax:* 412-741-2311 *E-mail:* mpackard@printing.org

Presidential Master's Prize
American Comparative Literature Association (ACLA)
323 E Wacker Dr, No 642, Chicago, IL 60601
Tel: 312-600-8072
E-mail: info@acla.org
Web Site: www.acla.org/prize-awards/presidential-masters-prize
Awarded to the best thesis, report or substantial essay nominated by a department or program at any institution. Project must be completed by July 1 of the year prior to the award. Each institution may nominate 1 student in the field of comparative literature, identified as the best without regard to actual departmental affiliation.
Award: $500, certificate, complimentary registration for annual meeting, hotel & airfare accommodations

Presidential Undergraduate Prize
American Comparative Literature Association (ACLA)
323 E Wacker Dr, No 642, Chicago, IL 60601
Tel: 312-600-8072
E-mail: info@acla.org
Web Site: www.acla.org/prize-awards/presidential-undergraduate-prize
Awarded to the best substantial essay nominated by a department or program. Project must be completed by July 1 of the year prior to the award. Each institution may nominate 1 student in the field of comparative literature, identified as the best without regard to actual department affiliation.
Award: $250, certificate, complimentary registration for annual meeting, hotel & airfare accommodations

Derek Price/Rod Webster Prize Award
History of Science Society
Affiliate of American Council of Learned Societies
440 Geddes Hall, Notre Dame, IN 46556
Tel: 574-631-1194 *Fax:* 574-631-1533
E-mail: info@hssonline.org
Web Site: www.hssonline.org
Established: 1979
In recognition of excellence in a research article published in *Isis* during the preceding 3 years.
Award: $250 & certificate
Closing Date: April 1
Presented: Annual Meeting, Late Oct/early Nov

Prince Edward Island Association for Newcomers to Canada Award
Prince Edward Island Writers' Guild
81 Prince St, Charlottetown, PE C1A 4R3, Canada
E-mail: peiliteraryawards@gmail.com
Web Site: www.peiwritersguild.com
Recognizes & acknowledges the contribution made to the Prince Edward Island culture by a writer new to Canada. Newcomers help expand our culture awareness & share their unique experience in a number of ways, including the written word. This prize is open to anyone who has immigrated to Canada & made Prince Edward Island their home within the past 5 years. Submissions can be in any category (fiction, nonfiction, poetry, writing for children & young adults, plays & scriptwriting). Work must be original & unpublished. Entry fee: $25 per

submission. See web site for complete entry requirements.
Award: Cash prize for 1st place
Closing Date: Changes annually (see web site)
Presented: Island Literary Awards Gala, Spring

Michael L Printz Award
Young Adult Library Services Association (YALSA)
Division of The American Library Association (ALA)
225 N Michigan Ave, Suite 1300, Chicago, IL 60601
Tel: 312-280-4390 *Toll Free Tel:* 800-545-2433
E-mail: yalsa@ala.org
Web Site: www.ala.org/yalsa/printz-award
Key Personnel
Printz Comm Chair: Janet Hilbin *E-mail:* janet.hilbin@unt.edu
Exec Dir: Tammy Dillard-Steels *Tel:* 800-545-2433 ext 4391 *E-mail:* tdillard@ala.org
Prog Offr, Events & Conferences: Nichole O'Connor *Tel:* 800-545-2433 ext 4387 *E-mail:* noconnor@ala.org
Communs Specialist: Anna Lam *Tel:* 800-545-2433 ext 5849 *E-mail:* alam@ala.org
Established: 1999
Honors excellence in literature written for young adults. May be fiction, nonfiction, poetry or an anthology & must have been published during the preceding year & designated as young adult book or ages 12-18.
Other Sponsor(s): Booklist
Closing Date: Dec 1
Presented: YALSA Printz Reception during ALA Annual Conference & Exhibition, June

PRISM international Creative Nonfiction Contest
PRISM international
University of British Columbia, Buch E462, 1866 Main Mall, Vancouver, BC V6T 1Z1, Canada
Tel: 604-822-2514 *Fax:* 604-822-3616
E-mail: promotions@prismmagazine.ca
Web Site: www.prismmagazine.ca/contests
Key Personnel
Mng Ed: Emma Cleary
Poetry Ed: Emily Chou
Promos Ed: Alison Barnett
Prose Ed: Vivian Li
One piece per entry. Maximum 6,000 words (including title). Entry fee: $35 CN, $40 US, $45 intl; additional entries $5.
Other Sponsor(s): University of British Columbia Bookstore
Award: $1,500 (grand prize), $600 (1st runner up), $400 (2nd runner up); all entries include 1-year subn to PRISM international

Pritzker Military Museum & Library Literature Award for Lifetime Achievement in Military Writing
Pritzker Military Museum & Library
104 S Michigan Ave, Suite 400, Chicago, IL 60603
Tel: 312-374-9333
E-mail: info@pritzkermilitary.org
Web Site: www.pritzkermilitary.org
Established: 2007
Awarded to recognize a living author who has made a significant contribution to the understanding of American military history, including military affairs.
Other Sponsor(s): Pritzker Military Foundation
Award: $100,000, citation & gold medallion
Closing Date: March
Presented: The Pritzker Military Museum & Library Liberty Gala, Oct

The Prix Albertine Jeunesse, see The Albertine Youth Prize

Prix Emile-Nelligan
La Fondation Emile Nelligan
100, rue Sherbrooke, Suite 202, Montreal, QC H2X 1C3, Canada
Tel: 514-278-4657 *Fax:* 514-271-6369
E-mail: info@fondation-nelligan.org
Web Site: www.fondation-nelligan.org
Key Personnel
Pres: Michel Dallaire
VP: Marie-Andree Beaudet
Secy/Treas: Michel Gonneville
Exec Dir: Manon Gagnon
Established: 1979
Collection of poetry must be published in the preceding calendar year. Poets must be 35 years of age or younger.
Award: $7,500 & a bronze medal
Presented: May

Prometheus Awards
Libertarian Futurist Society
650 Castro St, Suite 120-433, Mountain View, CA 94041
Tel: 650-968-6319
E-mail: bestnovel@lfs.org; specialaward@lfs.org
Web Site: www.lfs.org
Key Personnel
Bd Pres: Bill Stoddard
VP: Charles Morrison
Secy: Michael Grossberg
Established: 1979
Recognize works of science fiction & fantasy that champion individual freedom & human rights, that challenge authoritarianism of the Left or Right or that satirically or seriously critique abuses of power. The Best Novel category is limited to science fiction/fantasy novels published during the previous year or so. The Hall of Fame category (for Best Classic Fiction) is broadly inclusive: Novels, novellas, short stories, poems, plays, films, TV shows (individual episodes or entire series), series & trilogies are all eligible for nomination. Works are eligible 20 years after first publication or broadcast. Best Novel & Best Classic Fiction categories are presented annually. Special Awards are occasional & focus on outstanding pro-freedom achievements that fall outside the realm of the Best Novel category.
Award: One ounce gold coin mounted on an engraved plaque for both the Prometheus Best Novel Award & the Hall of Fame Award
Closing Date: Feb 1
Presented: World Science Fiction Convention or NASFIC, Labor Day weekend

PROSE Awards
Association of American Publishers (AAP)
455 Massachusetts Ave NW, Suite 700, Washington, DC 20001-2777
Tel: 202-347-3375 *Fax:* 202-347-3690
E-mail: proseawards@publishers.org
Web Site: proseawards.com; publishers.org
Key Personnel
COO: Syreeta N Swann *E-mail:* sswann@publishers.org
Established: 1976
Awards to recognize the very best in professional & scholarly publishing by celebrating the authors, editors & publishers whose landmark works have made significant advancements in their respective fields of study.
Award: Plaque & crystal cubes
Closing Date: Nov 1
Presented: Feb

Public Scholars
National Endowment for the Humanities, Division of Research Programs
400 Seventh St SW, Washington, DC 20506
Tel: 202-606-8200
E-mail: publicscholar@neh.gov

Web Site: www.neh.gov/grants
Key Personnel
NEH Chmn: Jon Parrish Peede
Grant supporting well-researched books in the humanities intended to reach a broad readership. Fellowship periods last from 6-12 months & must be full-time & continuous. Open to both individuals affiliated with scholarly institutions & independent scholars. All applications to this program must be submitted via Grants.gov. Applications receive peer review & NEH Chairman makes all funding decisions.
Award: $5,000 monthly stipend maximum
Closing Date: Nov 30
Presented: Aug

The Publishing Triangle Award for Trans & Gender-Variant Literature, see The Leslie Feinberg Award for Trans & Gender-Variant Literature

PubWest Book Design Awards
Publishers Association of the West Inc (PubWest)
12727 Highland Ct, Auburn, CA 95603-3634
Tel: 720-443-3637
E-mail: executivedirector@pubwest.org
Web Site: pubwest.org
Key Personnel
Pres: Miriam Warren
Established: 1984
Gold, silver & bronze awards are given in 21 categories: Adult trade book (illustrated); adult trade book (non-illustrated); children's/young adult book (illustrated); children's/young adult book (non-illustrated); children's book (wordless); academic/non-trade book; guide/travel book; how-to/crafts book; cookbook; photography book; art book; sports/fitness/recreation book; reference book; short stories/poetry/anthologies; gift/holiday/specialty book; historical/biographical book; graphic album-new material; graphic album-previously published material; jacket cover-small format; jacket cover-large format; special editions. Entry fee: $75 membs, $100 nonmembs.
Award: Certificates & graphics
Closing Date: Sept 30
Presented: PubWest Conference, Feb

Pulitzer Prizes
Columbia University, 2950 Broadway, New York, NY 10027
Tel: 212-854-3841 *Fax:* 212-854-3342
E-mail: pulitzer@pulitzer.org
Web Site: www.pulitzer.org
Established: 1917
Five book awards in the following categories: Fiction, history, biography, poetry & general nonfiction. Books must have been first published in the US during the calendar year. All entries must be made available for purchase by the general public in either hardcover or bound paperback book form by a US-based press. In the fiction, biography, poetry & general nonfiction categories, authors must be US citizens. In the history category, the author may be of any nationality but the subject of the book must pertain to US history. Anyone (including the author) may submit an eligible book. All entry forms & fees must be submitted electronically. Entry fee: $75.
Award: $15,000 each
Closing Date: Oct 15
Presented: Spring

Pushcart Prize: Best of the Small Presses
Pushcart Press
PO Box 380, Wainscott, NY 11975-0380
SAN: 202-9871
Tel: 631-324-9300
Web Site: www.pushcartprize.com

Key Personnel
Pres: Bill Henderson
Established: 1976
Awarded for works by a small press or literary journal. Nominations may be any combination of poetry, short stories, essays, memoirs, or stand-alone excerpts from novels. Works must have been published (or scheduled to be published) in the current calendar year. Nominations are accepted beginning October 1.
Other Sponsor(s): Pushcart Prize Fellowships Inc
Award: Copies of the book *The Pushcart Prize: Best of the Small Presses*
Closing Date: Dec 1 (postmarked)
Presented: Spring

Pynn-Silverman Lifetime Achievement Award
Textbook & Academic Authors Association (TAA)
PO Box 367, Fountain City, WI 54629
E-mail: info@taaonline.net
Web Site: www.taaonline.net/council-awards#pynn
Key Personnel
Exec Dir: Michael Spinella *Tel:* 973-943-0501 *E-mail:* michael.spinella@taaonline.net
Dir, Publg & Opers: Kim Pawlak *Tel:* 507-459-1363 *E-mail:* kim.pawlak@taaonline.net
Dir, Instl Memberships & Meetings: Maureen Foerster *Tel:* 530-864-3538 *E-mail:* maureen.foerster@taaonline.net
Membership Mktg Mgr: Eric Schmieder *Tel:* 919-437-0241 *E-mail:* eric.schmieder@taaonline.net
Membership Coord: Bekky Murphy *Tel:* 608-567-9060 *E-mail:* bekky.murphy@taaonline.net
Successful candidates authored a considerable body of work in their field that has proven over time to reflect the best understanding of their discipline at the time & to have helped advance knowledge of the discipline. While co-authored works are eligible for consideration, it is expected that the candidate authored a number of works alone. There is no set of number of works required to qualify, but a successful candidate authored a substantial number of article-length works +/or several book-length works. Textbooks, courseware, monographs & journal articles may all be considered, but the essential element is high-quality & proven value over time. Other considerations that may indicate a strong candidate might be having published in more than one discipline or specialty area & evidence of recognition of the quality of the author's work as shown by winning TAA Textbook Awards, or other national awards for teaching or writing. Any TAA member may nominate him or herself or another TAA member. One recipient is selected by the TAA Council via ballot. Submit nominee & documentation via e-mail.
Closing Date: Jan/Feb
Presented: TAA Annual Conference, June

QWF Literary Awards
Quebec Writers' Federation (QWF)
1200 Atwater Ave, Suite 3, Westmount, QC H3Z 1X4, Canada
Tel: 514-933-0878
E-mail: info@qwf.org
Web Site: quebecbooks.qwf.org/awards; www.qwf.org/awards/awards-overview/
Key Personnel
Exec Dir: Lori Schubert *E-mail:* lori@qwf.org
Established: 1988
Literary awards for Quebec, English language authors. Request submission details.
Awards: A M Klein Prize for Poetry; Paragraphe Hugh MacLennan Prize for Fiction; Mavis Gallant Prize for Non-fiction; Concordia University First Book Prize; Cole Foundation Prize for Translation; Janet Savage Blachford Prize for Children's & Young Adult Literature; QWF Prize for Playwriting.
Award: $3,000 each
Closing Date: June 1
Presented: QWF Literary Awards Gala, Nov

Radcliffe Institute Fellowship Program
The Radcliffe Institute for Advanced Study
Byerly Hall, 8 Garden St, Cambridge, MA 02138
Tel: 617-495-8212 *Fax:* 617-495-8136
E-mail: fellowships@radcliffe.harvard.edu
Web Site: www.radcliffe.harvard.edu/fellowship-program
Key Personnel
Exec Dir: Claudia Rizzini *Tel:* 617-495-8213 *E-mail:* claudia_rizzini@radcliffe.harvard.edu
Assoc Dir: Sharon Bromberg-Lim *Tel:* 617-495-3798 *E-mail:* sharon_bromberg-lim@radcliffe.harvard.edu
Admin, Fellowships: Alison Ney *Tel:* 617-495-8234 *E-mail:* alison_ney@radcliffe.harvard.edu
Coord I, Admin for Fellows: Rebecca Haley *Tel:* 617-496-0105 *E-mail:* rebecca_haley@radcliffe.harvard.edu
Prog Asst: Jeffrey Potts *Tel:* 617-495-8237 *E-mail:* jpotts@radcliffe.harvard.edu
Radcliffe Institute fellowships are designed to support scholars, scientists, artists & writers of exceptional promise & demonstrated accomplishments who wish to pursue work in academic & professional fields & in the creative arts.
Award: $78,000 stipend plus $5,000 to cover project expenses; single-semester fellows receive $39,000 stipend plus $2,500 to cover project expenses; fellows also receive relocation funds & office or studio space
Closing Date: Sept 10 for creative arts & humanities & social sciences; Oct 1 for science, engineering & mathematics

Thomas Raddall Atlantic Fiction Award
Writers' Federation of Nova Scotia (WFNS)
1113 Marginal Rd, Halifax, NS B3H 4P7, Canada
Tel: 902-423-8116 *Fax:* 902-422-0881
E-mail: wits@writers.ns.ca (awards)
Web Site: writers.ns.ca
Key Personnel
Prog Mgr, Arts Educ: Linda Hudson
Established: 1991
Awarded for a novel or book of short fiction, published by an Atlantic Canadian writer who has lived in one or a combination of these provinces for at least 2 concurrent years immediately prior to the submission deadline date. Non-refundable $35 administrative fee per entry.
Award: $25,000
Closing Date: Nov 1
Presented: Halifax, NS, CN, Spring

The Ragan Old North State Award Cup for Nonfiction
North Carolina Literary & Historical Association
Affiliate of North Carolina Department of Natural & Cultural Resources
4610 Mail Service Ctr, Raleigh, NC 27699-4610
Web Site: www.ncdcr.gov/about/history/lit-and-hist/awards
Key Personnel
Awards Coord: Joseph Beatty *E-mail:* joseph.beatty@ncdcr.gov
Established: 2003
Awarded in recognition of achievement in nonfiction. The author must have maintained legal or physical residence, or a combination of both, in North Carolina for the 3 years preceding the close of the contest period.
Award: Cup
Closing Date: July 15
Presented: Nov

Raiziss/de Palchi Fellowship
The Academy of American Poets Inc
75 Maiden Lane, Suite 901, New York, NY 10038
Tel: 212-274-0343
E-mail: awards@poets.org
Web Site: poets.org/academy-american-poets/american-poets-prizes
Key Personnel
Pres & Exec Dir: Ricardo Alberto Maldonado
VP, Digital Engagement & Content: Jeff Gleaves
Ad & Mktg Dir: Michelle Campagna
Dir, Donor Rel: Molly Walsh
Dir, Progs: Nikay Paredes
Established: 1995
Awarded to recognize outstanding translations into English of modern Italian poetry. Given to enable an American translator of 20th century Italian poetry to travel, study, or otherwise advance a significant work-in-progress. Book prize is awarded in even-numbered years & fellowship awarded in odd-numbered years.
Award: $10,000 book prize & a $25,000 fellowship
Closing Date: Feb 15
Presented: Sept

Sir Walter Raleigh Award for Fiction
Historical Book Club of North Carolina
Affiliate of North Carolina Literary & Historical Association
4610 Mail Service Ctr, Raleigh, NC 27699-4610
Tel: 919-814-6623
Web Site: www.ncdcr.gov/about/history/lit-and-hist/awards
Key Personnel
Awards Coord: Joseph Beatty *E-mail:* joseph.beatty@ncdcr.gov
Established: 1953
Awarded in recognition of the most significant work of original fiction writing published over the course of the last year by a North Carolina author. Author must be a legal or physical resident of North Carolina for at least 3 years prior to the end of the contest period.
Closing Date: July 15
Presented: Fall

Ramirez Family Award
Texas Institute of Letters (TIL)
PO Box 130294, Spring, TX 77393
Web Site: texasinstituteofletters.org
Key Personnel
Pres: David Bowles *E-mail:* president@texasinstituteofletters.org
VP: Chris Barton
Secy: Kathryn Jones *E-mail:* secretary@texasinstituteofletters.org
Treas: Cliff Hudder
Award for the most useful & informative scholarly book contributing to general knowledge, by a Texan or about Texas. The author must have been born in Texas or have lived in Texas for at least 5 consecutive years at some time. See web site for guidelines.
Award: $2,500
Closing Date: Jan
Presented: TIL Annual Meeting & Awards Ceremony, Spring

James A Rawley Award
Southern Historical Association (SHA)
University of Georgia, Dept of History, Athens, GA 30602-1602
Tel: 706-542-8848
Web Site: thesha.org/rawley
Key Personnel
Secy/Treas: Dr Stephen Berry *E-mail:* berrys@thesha.org
Awarded biennially to a distinguished book dealing with secession +/or the sectional crisis published in the preceding 2 years.
Closing Date: March 1
Presented: Annual Meeting (odd-numbered years)

COURSES & AWARDS

AWARDS, PRIZE CONTESTS, FELLOWSHIPS & GRANTS

James A Rawley Prize
The Organization of American Historians (OAH)
112 N Bryan Ave, Bloomington, IN 47408-4141
Tel: 812-855-7311
E-mail: oah@oah.org
Web Site: www.oah.org/awards
Key Personnel
Exec Dir: Beth English *Tel:* 812-855-9836
 E-mail: benglish@oah.org
Dir, Communs & Mktg: Kym Robinson *Tel:* 812-855-5430 *E-mail:* kymarobi@oah.org
Awarded to the author of the best book dealing with the history of race relations in the US. Each entry must be published during the calendar year preceding that in which the award is given. One copy of each entry must be mailed directly to the committee members listed on the web site.
Closing Date: Oct 1 (postmarked)
Presented: OAH Conference on American History, Spring

RBC Bronwen Wallace Award for Emerging Writers
The Writers' Trust of Canada
600-460 Richmond St W, Toronto, ON M5V 1Y1, Canada
Tel: 416-504-8222 *Toll Free Tel:* 877-906-6548
 Fax: 416-504-9090
E-mail: info@writerstrust.com
Web Site: www.writerstrust.com
Key Personnel
Exec Dir: Charlie Foran *Tel:* 416-504-8222 ext 244 *E-mail:* cforan@writerstrust.com
Mgr, Author Progs: Devon Jackson *Tel:* 416-504-8222 ext 248 *E-mail:* djackson@writerstrust.com
Established: 1994
Awarded to a young author, 35 years of age & under, who has not been previously published in book form. Two awards are given each year, one for achievement in short fiction & one for achievement in poetry.
Other Sponsor(s): RBC Foundation
Award: $10,000 (winner), $2,500 (finalists)
Presented: Spring

Reading the West Book Awards
Mountains & Plains Independent Booksellers Association
PO Box 746, Denver, CO 80201
Tel: 970-484-3939 *Toll Free Tel:* 800-752-0249
 Fax: 970-484-0037
E-mail: info@mountainsplains.org
Web Site: www.mountainsplains.org/reading-the-west-book-awards
Key Personnel
Exec Dir: Heather Duncan *E-mail:* heather@mountainsplains.org
Mktg & Communs Mgr: Jeremy Ellis
Opers Mgr: Kelsey Myers
Assists publishers, authors & booksellers in promoting & building sales for exceptional books & authors in the Mountains & Plains region. These adult & children's titles exemplify the best in writing +/or illustrations whose subject matter is set in the region or invokes the spirit of the region: Arizona, Colorado, Kansas, Montana, Nebraska, Nevada, New Mexico, Oklahoma, South Dakota, Texas, Utah & Wyoming. The author's place of residence is immaterial for this award. Nominations open September 1. Books must be published in the calendar year when submissions open.
Closing Date: Dec 31
Presented: May 31

Reed Environmental Writing Award
Southern Environmental Law Center (SELC)
201 W Main St, Suite 14, Charlottesville, VA 22902
Tel: 434-977-4090 *Fax:* 434-977-1483
Web Site: www.southernenvironment.org
Key Personnel
Exec Dir: Jeff Gleason
Dir, Communs: Erin Malec
Devt Assoc: Jessica Hamilton
 E-mail: jhamilton@selcva.org
Established: 1994
Award to recognize & encourage the writers who most effectively tell the stories of the South. Two categories: Book (nonfiction, not self-published) & Journalism (newspaper, magazine & online articles). Entries must be at least 3,000 words, published in the preceding 12 months & relate to the natural resources or special places in at least one of SELC's states: Alabama, Georgia, North Carolina, South Carolina, Tennessee, or Virginia.
Award: $2,500 each category
Closing Date: Oct 1

Regina Medal Award
Catholic Library Association
8550 United Plaza Blvd, Suite 1001, Baton Rouge, LA 70809
Tel: 225-408-4417
E-mail: cla2@cathla.org
Web Site: cathla.org
Key Personnel
Exec Dir: Melanie Talley
Association Coord: Mary Coll
Established: 1959
For continued distinguished lifetime contribution to children's literature; no unsol mss.
Award: Sterling silver medal
Closing Date: None; in-house votes
Presented: CLA Annual Convention, April

Nathan Reingold Prize
History of Science Society
Affiliate of American Council of Learned Societies
440 Geddes Hall, Notre Dame, IN 46556
Tel: 574-631-1194 *Fax:* 574-631-1533
E-mail: info@hssonline.org
Web Site: www.hssonline.org
Established: 1955
For an original essay, not to exceed 8,000 words, in history of science & its cultural influences. Open to graduate students only. Must send in 3 copies of essay with a detachable author/title page.
Award: $500 (& up to $500 travel reimbursement)
Closing Date: June 1
Presented: Oct/Nov

ReLit Awards
PO Box 250, Burnt Head, Cupids, NL A0A 2B0, Canada
Web Site: www.relitawards.com
Key Personnel
Exec Dir: Katherine Alexandra Harvey
 E-mail: katherineharvey8@gmail.com
Established: 2000
Canadian literary prizes awarded for book-length works in the novel, short story & poetry categories. Books must have been written by Canadian authors while living in Canada & published by an independent Canadian press in the previous calendar year. Books must be submitted by the publisher to be eligible (individuals can not submit their own book). Self-published books are not eligible. Publishers may submit a maximum of 8 books per year. No entry fee.
Award: Silver ring
Closing Date: Jan 30

Arthur Rense Prize
American Academy of Arts & Letters
633 W 155 St, New York, NY 10032
Tel: 212-368-5900
E-mail: academy@artsandletters.org
Web Site: artsandletters.org/awards
Key Personnel
Exec Dir: Cody Upton
Established: 1998
Given triennially to an exceptional poet. Candidates must be nominated by an Academy member.
Award: $20,000

Republic of Consciousness Prize for Small Presses in the USA
c/o Interabang Books, 56 Lovers Lane, No 142, Dallas, TX 75209
E-mail: rofcusa@gmail.com
Web Site: www.republicofconsciousnessprize-usa.com
Key Personnel
Prize Founder & Jury Chair: Lori Feathers
Established: 2021
Awarded in support of small presses for their ongoing commitment to work of high literary merit. A small press is defined as an average of 18 or fewer published titles per year, the majority of which are new, adult literary fiction. Books must be published during the calendar year of the prize in physical form. Only presses from the US & Canada are eligible. See web site for detailed submissions criteria. The prize fund will be divided in half across the long list of 10 & the remaining half is divided between the short list & the winner(s).
Award: $35,000 total; $2,000 each to longlist presses; $3,000 each additional to 5 shortlisted books (split equally between publisher/author/translator)

The Restless Books Prize for New Immigrant Writing
Restless Books
232 Third St, Suite A101, Brooklyn, NY 11215
E-mail: publisher@restlessbooks.com
Web Site: www.restlessbooks.org/prize-for-new-immigrant-writing
Key Personnel
Publr: Ilan Stavans
For an outstanding debut literary work by a first-generation immigrant. Awarded for fiction & nonfiction in alternating years. Only one submission is accepted per candidate per submission period. See full submission guidelines & eligibility requirements on the web site.
Award: $10,000 & publication
Closing Date: March 31 (even-numbered years for fiction, odd-numbered years for nonfiction)

The Harold U Ribalow Prize
Hadassah Magazine
40 Wall St, 8th fl, New York, NY 10005-1387
Tel: 212-451-6289
E-mail: magazine@hadassah.org
Web Site: www.hadassahmagazine.org
Key Personnel
Exec Ed: Lisa Hostein *E-mail:* lhostein@hadassah.org
Established: 1983
Award for an outstanding English-language work of fiction on a Jewish theme by an author deserving of recognition.
Other Sponsor(s): Harold U Ribalow family
Award: $3,000
Closing Date: April of the year following publication
Presented: Autumn

Evelyn Richardson Nonfiction Award
Writers' Federation of Nova Scotia (WFNS)
1113 Marginal Rd, Halifax, NS B3H 4P7, Canada
Tel: 902-423-8116 *Fax:* 902-422-0881
E-mail: wits@writers.ns.ca (awards)
Web Site: writers.ns.ca
Key Personnel
Prog Mgr, Arts Educ: Linda Hudson
Established: 1978

Presented for the best nonfiction book, published by a native or resident Nova Scotian who has lived in the province for at least 2 concurrent years immediately prior to the submission deadline date. Non-refundable $35 administrative fee per entry.
Award: $2,000
Closing Date: Nov 1
Presented: Halifax, NS, CN, Spring

The Ridenhour Book Prize
Type Media Center Inc
116 E 16 St, 8th fl, New York, NY 10003
Tel: 212-822-0250 *Fax:* 212-253-5356
E-mail: ridenhour@typemediacenter.org; admin@ridenhour.org
Web Site: www.ridenhour.org
Key Personnel
Dir, Devt & Spec Progs: Kristine Bruch *Tel:* 212-822-0263 *E-mail:* kristine@typemediacenter.org
Established: 2003
Honors an outstanding work of social significance from the prior publishing year. The prize also recognizes investigative & reportorial distinction.
Other Sponsor(s): The Fertel Foundation
Award: $10,000 stipend

The Ridenhour Courage Prize
Type Media Center Inc
116 E 16 St, 8th fl, New York, NY 10003
Tel: 212-822-0250 *Fax:* 212-253-5356
E-mail: ridenhour@typemediacenter.org; admin@ridenhour.org
Web Site: www.ridenhour.org
Key Personnel
Exec Dir & CEO: Taya Kitman *E-mail:* taya@nationinstitute.org
Dir, Devt & Spec Progs: Kristine Bruch *Tel:* 212-822-0263 *E-mail:* kristine@typemediacenter.org
Established: 2003
Presented to an individual in recognition of his or her courageous & life-long defense of the public interest & passionate commitment to social justice.
Other Sponsor(s): The Fertel Foundation
Award: $10,000 stipend

The Ridenhour Prize for Truth-Telling
Type Media Center Inc
116 E 16 St, 8th fl, New York, NY 10003
Tel: 212-822-0250 *Fax:* 212-253-5356
E-mail: ridenhour@typemediacenter.org; admin@ridenhour.org
Web Site: www.ridenhour.org
Key Personnel
Dir, Devt & Spec Progs: Kristine Bruch *Tel:* 212-822-0263 *E-mail:* kristine@typemediacenter.org
Established: 2003
Presented to a citizen, corporate or government whistleblower, investigative journalist, or organization for bringing a specific issue of social importance to the public's attention.
Other Sponsor(s): The Fertel Foundation
Award: $10,000 stipend

Rilke Prize
University of North Texas Creative Writing Program, Department of English
Auditorium Bldg, Rm 214, 1155 Union Circle, Denton, TX 76203
E-mail: untrilkeprize@unt.edu
Web Site: english.unt.edu/creative-writing/unt-rilke-prize
Key Personnel
Dir, Creative Writing: Corey Marks, PhD *Tel:* 940-565-2126 *E-mail:* corey.marks@unt.edu
Established: 2012
Awarded in recognition of a book that demonstrates exceptional artistry & vision written by a mid-career poet & published in the preceding year.
Award: $10,000
Presented: April

Gwen Pharis Ringwood Award for Drama
Writers' Guild of Alberta
11759 Groat Rd NW, Edmonton, AB T5M 3K6, Canada
Tel: 780-422-8174 *Toll Free Tel:* 800-665-5354 (AB only)
E-mail: mail@writersguild.ab.ca
Web Site: writersguild.ca
Key Personnel
Exec Dir: Giorgia Severini *E-mail:* gseverini@writersguild.ab.ca
Communs & Partnerships Coord: Ellen Kartz *E-mail:* ellen.kartz@writersguild.ab.ca
Memb Servs Coord: Mike Maguire
Prog & Opers Coord: Ashley Mann *E-mail:* ashley.mann@writersguild.ab.ca
Progs & Events Coord: Jason Norman *E-mail:* jason.norman@writersguild.ab.ca
Proj Asst: Sadie MacGillivray *E-mail:* sadie.macgillivray@writersguild.ab.ca
Established: 1982
Created to recognize excellence in writing by Alberta authors.
Award: $1,500 plus leather-bound copy of book
Closing Date: Dec 31
Presented: Alberta Book Awards Gala, AB, CN
Branch Office(s)
223 12 Ave SW, No 204, Calgary, AB T2R 0G9, Canada, Prog & Conference Coord: Dorothy Bentley *Tel:* 403-875-8058 *E-mail:* dorothy.bentley@writersguild.ab.ca

The Ripped Bodice Awards for Excellence in Romantic Fiction
The Ripped Bodice
3806 Main St, Culver City, CA 90232
Tel: 424-603-4776
E-mail: therippedbodicela@gmail.com
Web Site: www.therippedbodicela.com
Key Personnel
Co-Owner: Bea Koch; Leah Koch
Established: 2019
Celebrates the best books of the year in the best-selling romance genre. Twelve honorees will be selected each year. The book must be a romance novel published in the previous year.
Award: $1,000 to each honoree plus $100 donation to charity of their choice
Presented: Valentine's Day

RISING STAR Award
Women's Fiction Writers Association (WFWA)
PO Box 190, Jefferson, OR 97352
E-mail: risingstar@womenfictionwriters.org
Web Site: wfwa.memberclicks.net/rising-star-award
Key Personnel
Pres: Jacki Kelly *E-mail:* president@womensfictionwriters.org
VP, Communs: Sharon Ritchey
VP, Fin & Treas: Kathy Dodson *E-mail:* treasurer@womensfictionwriters.org
VP, Progs: Kristi Leonard
Secy: Michele Montgomery *E-mail:* secretary@womensfictionwriters.org
Events Dir: Jami Sheets
Award for an unpublished writer of women's fiction. Open to all unagented writers who have never been published in the book-length women's fiction of 60,000 words or more. Award is limited to the first 75 entries. Entry fee: $30 membs, $40 nonmembs. See web site for entry submission details & complete eligibility requirements.
Award: Trophy, digital badge & certificate of display within their online presence
Closing Date: April 21
Presented: WFWA Retreat Banquet, Sept

Jack D Rittenhouse Award
Publishers Association of the West Inc (PubWest)
12727 Highland Ct, Auburn, CA 95603-3634
Tel: 720-443-3637
E-mail: executivedirector@pubwest.org
Web Site: pubwest.org
Key Personnel
Pres: Miriam Warren
Honors individuals who have made outstanding contributions to the book community in the West.
Presented: PubWest Annual Conference

Max Ritvo Poetry Prize
Milkweed Editions
1011 Washington Ave S, Suite 300, Minneapolis, MN 55415-1246
Tel: 612-332-3192 *Toll Free Tel:* 800-520-6455
Web Site: milkweed.org/max-ritvo-poetry-prize
Key Personnel
Publr & CEO: Daniel Slager
Assoc Ed: Bailey Hutchinson *E-mail:* bailey_hutchinson@milkweed.org
Established: 2018
Awarded to an outstanding author of a debut collection of poems. Poets may submit one complete, book-length collection, defined as a ms of 48 or more pages. Poems may have been previously published in periodicals, chapbooks, or anthologies, but the poet must not have published, nor committed to publish, a book-length collection of poems. Mss must be of original work by a single poet; translations are not eligible. The submitting poet must reside in the US. Only online submissions via Submittable will be considered. Entry fee: $25.
Award: $10,000 & publication contract
Closing Date: June 30

Riverby Awards
John Burroughs Association Inc
500 Burroughs Dr, at Floyd Ackert, New York, NY 12493
Mailing Address: PO Box 439, West Park, NY 12493
Tel: 845-384-6556
E-mail: info@johnburroughsassociation.org
Web Site: www.johnburroughsassociation.org
Key Personnel
Pres: Joan Burroughs *E-mail:* joan@johnburroughsassociation.org
Established: 1988
Given to authors, artists & publishers of exceptional natural history books for young readers that contains perceptive & artistic accounts of direct experiences in the natural world & demonstrate respect for nature, accuracy of information & quality of prose & illustrations.
Award: Certificate of recognition to authors, illustrators & publishers of each selected book each year
Closing Date: Late Oct/early Nov
Presented: Celebratory Awards Luncheon, Yale Club, New York, NY, 1st Monday in April

Roanoke-Chowan Award for Poetry
North Carolina Literary & Historical Association
Affiliate of North Carolina Department of Natural & Cultural Resources
4610 Mail Service Ctr, Raleigh, NC 27699-4610
Web Site: www.ncdcr.gov/about/history/lit-and-hist/awards
Key Personnel
Awards Coord: Joseph Beatty *E-mail:* joseph.beatty@ncdcr.gov
Established: 1953
Awarded in recognition of the most significant work of original poetry published over the course of the last year by a North Carolina

poet. The poet must have maintained legal or physical residence, or a combination of both, in North Carolina for the 3 years preceding the close of the contest period.
Other Sponsor(s): Roanoke-Chowan Group of Writers & Allied Artists
Award: Cup
Closing Date: July 15
Presented: Nov

John A Robertson Award for Best First Book of Poetry
Texas Institute of Letters (TIL)
PO Box 130294, Spring, TX 77393
Web Site: texasinstituteofletters.org
Key Personnel
Pres: David Bowles *E-mail:* president@texasinstituteofletters.org
VP: Chris Barton
Secy: Kathryn Jones *E-mail:* secretary@texasinstituteofletters.org
Treas: Cliff Hudder
Established: 2017
Award for the first book of poetry by a writer from Texas or writing about Texas. The author must have been born in Texas or have lived in Texas for at least 5 consecutive years at some time.
Award: $1,000
Closing Date: Jan
Presented: TIL Annual Meeting & Awards Ceremony, April

Rocky Mountain Book Award
PO Box 42, Lethbridge, AB T1J 3Y3, Canada
Tel: 403-381-7164
E-mail: rockymountainbookaward@shaw.ca
Web Site: www.rmba.info
Key Personnel
Contact: Michelle Dimnik
Established: 2001
Alberta children's choice book award, grades 4-7.
Other Sponsor(s): Lethbridge Public Library; Lethbridge School Division; United Library Services; University of Lethbridge Bookstore
Closing Date: Jan 31
Presented: Winner announced electronically on April 22

Theodore Roethke Prize, see The Hopwood Award Theodore Roethke Prize

Sami Rohr Prize for Jewish Literature
452 Fifth Ave, 24th fl, New York, NY 10018
Tel: 516-548-3921
Web Site: www.samirohrprize.org
Key Personnel
Dir: Debra Goldberg *E-mail:* debra@samirohrprize.org
Established: 2007
Prize to recognize the unique role of contemporary writers in the transmission & examination of the Jewish experience. Finalists & winners of monetary prizes become Fellows in the Sami Rohr Jewish Literary Institute. Works that are translated into English may be eligible in the fiction category. For nonfiction, eligibility may include works related to Jewish history, scholarship, culture or contemporary Jewish concerns. Fiction & nonfiction awards are granted in alternate years.
Award: $100,000; 3 finalists receive $5,000 each
Presented: New York (fiction), Jerusalem (nonfiction), May

The Frances "Frank" Rollin Fellowship
Biographers International Organization (BIO)
PO Box 33020, Santa Fe, NM 87594
Tel: 505-983-4671
Web Site: biographersinternational.org/award/the-frances-frank-rollin-fellowship

Key Personnel
Exec Dir: Michael Gately *E-mail:* execdirector@biographersinternational.org
Established: 2021
Named for one of the first African American biographers, this award goes to the author of an exceptional biography-in-progress about an African American figure or figures whose story provides a significant contribution to our understanding of the Black experience. The Rollin Fellowship aims to remediate the disproportionate scarcity & even suppression of Black lives & voices in the broad catalog of published biography. Open to all biographers anywhere in the world who are writing in English & who are at any stage in the writing of a book-length biography. See web site for application process.
Award: $2,000, 1-year membership in BIO, registration to annual BIO conference & publicity through BIO marketing channels
Closing Date: March 1
Presented: BIO Annual Conference, May

Eleanor Roosevelt Award for Bravery in Literature
Eleanor Roosevelt Center at Val-Kill
PO Box 255, Hyde Park, NY 12538
Tel: 845-229-5302
E-mail: admin@ervk.org
Web Site: ervk.org/banned-book-awards
Key Personnel
Chair: Anna Eleanor Fierst
Established: 2024
Celebrates authors who have championed intellectual freedom & the fight against censorship. Awards are given to authors whose works focus on racial justice, LGBTQ+ rights & gender equity.
Presented: Fisher Center at Bard College, Annandale-on-Hudson, NY, Feb

Rosenthal Family Foundation Award for Literature
American Academy of Arts & Letters
633 W 155 St, New York, NY 10032
Tel: 212-368-5900
E-mail: academy@artsandletters.org
Web Site: artsandletters.org/awards
Key Personnel
Exec Dir: Cody Upton
Established: 1957
Award to a young writer for a work of fiction published during the previous year that is a considerable literary achievement. Candidates must be nominated by an Academy member.
Other Sponsor(s): The Rosenthal Foundation
Award: $10,000

Margaret W Rossiter History of Women in Science Prize
History of Science Society
Affiliate of American Council of Learned Societies
440 Geddes Hall, Notre Dame, IN 46556
Tel: 574-631-1194 *Fax:* 574-631-1533
E-mail: info@hssonline.org
Web Site: www.hssonline.org
Recognition of an outstanding book (or, in even-numbered years, article) on the history of women in science. Books & articles published in the preceding 4 years are eligible.
Award: $1,000
Closing Date: April 1

Lois Roth Award
Modern Language Association (MLA)
85 Broad St, New York, NY 10004
SAN: 202-6422
Tel: 646-576-5141; 646-576-5000
E-mail: awards@mla.org
Web Site: www.mla.org

Key Personnel
Coord, Book Prizes: Annie M Reiser *E-mail:* areiser@mla.org
Established: 1999
Committee solicits submissions of outstanding translations into English of a book-length literary work. Translations published in 2024 are eligible. Translators need not be members of the association. For consideration, submit 6 print copies & electronic access, plus 12-15 pages of original text in its original language.
Award: Cash award & certificate
Closing Date: April 1, 2025
Presented: MLA Annual Convention, Toronto, ON, CN, Jan 2026

Hazel Rowley Prize
Biographers International Organization (BIO)
PO Box 33020, Santa Fe, NM 87594
Web Site: biographersinternational.org/award/hazel-rowley-prize
Key Personnel
Exec Dir: Michael Gately *E-mail:* execdirector@biographersinternational.org
Established: 2014
Awarded for the best book proposal by a first-time biographer. Open to anyone writing in English who is working on a biography that has not yet been commissioned, contracted, or self-published & who has never published a biography, history, or work of narrative nonfiction. See web site for full details. Application fee: $35.
Award: $2,000, review by an established literary agent, 1-year BIO membership, registration for the BIO Annual Conference & publicity through BIO's marketing channels
Closing Date: Feb 1
Presented: BIO Annual Conference, May

Lexi Rudnitsky First Book Prize in Poetry
Persea Books
90 Broad St, Suite 2100, New York, NY 10004
SAN: 212-8233
Tel: 212-260-9256
E-mail: poetry@perseabooks.com
Web Site: www.perseabooks.com
Key Personnel
Pres & Publr: Michael Braziller
VP & Edit Dir: Karen Braziller
Poetry Ed: Gabriel Fried
Publicity: Jonah Fried
Established: 2006
Open to all female-identifying Americans (no matter where they live in the world), as well as female-identifying individuals of any nationality or immigration status currently living in the US.
Award: $1,000, publication & expenses paid residency at the Civitella Ranieri Foundation in Italy
Closing Date: Oct 31

William B Ruggles Journalism Scholarship
National Institute for Labor Relations Research
5211 Port Royal Rd, Suite 510, Springfield, VA 22151
Tel: 703-321-9606 *Fax:* 703-327-8101
Web Site: www.nilrr.org
Key Personnel
Scholarship Admin: Cathy Jones *E-mail:* clj@nrtw.org
Established: 1974
Scholarship for students majoring in journalism or related majors. Based on scholastic ability demonstrating an understanding of the economic, political & social implications of compulsory unionism. Applications may be submitted online beginning September 1.
Award: $2,000
Closing Date: Jan 31
Presented: April/May

AWARDS, PRIZE CONTESTS, FELLOWSHIPS & GRANTS

Sandy Run Novella Award
Hidden River™ Arts
PO Box 63927, Philadelphia, PA 19147
Tel: 610-764-0813
E-mail: info@hiddenriverarts.org
Web Site: hiddenriverarts.wordpress.com
Key Personnel
Founding Dir: Debra Leigh Scott
Established: 2019
Offered for an unpublished novella. Submissions must be 17,500-40,000 words. Open to international submissions from writers in English. Each ms must be submitted separately online. Entry fee: $20. See web site for full submission guidelines.
Award: $1,000 & publication by Hidden River Press

Frances E Russell Grant
IBBY Canada
Unit of International Board on Books for Young People (IBBY)
c/o The Canadian Children's Book Ctr, 425 Adelaide St W, Suite 200, Toronto, ON M5V 3C1, Canada
Fax: 416-975-8970
E-mail: russell@ibby-canada.org
Web Site: www.ibby-canada.org/awards/frances-e-russell-grant/
Key Personnel
Grant Chair: Dr Deirdre Baker
Established: 1982
Given in support of research for a publishable work (a book or a paper) on Canadian children's literature. The grant supports scholarly work only; works of fiction are not eligible. Proposals may be submitted in English or in French. See web site for criteria & submission guidelines.
Award: $1,000
Closing Date: Jan 15

Stephan Russo Book Prize, see Goddard Riverside Stephan Russo Book Prize for Social Justice

The Cornelius Ryan Award
Overseas Press Club of America (OPC)
40 W 45 St, New York, NY 10036
Tel: 212-626-9220
E-mail: info@opcofamerica.org
Web Site: opcofamerica.org
Key Personnel
Exec Dir: Patricia Kranz *E-mail:* patricia@opcofamerica.org
Awarded for best nonfiction book on international affairs.
Award: Certificate & cash award
Closing Date: Last week of Jan
Presented: New York, NY, Late April

Dr Tony Ryan Book Award
Castleton Lyons
2469 Ironworks Pike, Lexington, KY 40511
Tel: 859-455-9222
Web Site: www.castletonlyons.com
Key Personnel
Commercial Mgr: Stuart Fitzgibbon
  E-mail: sfitzgibbon@castletonlyons.com
Off Mgr: Betsy Hager *E-mail:* bhager@castletonlyons.com
Established: 2007
Awarded to the author of the best book, in any category, on any aspect of thoroughbred horse racing. The book must have been officially released in the previous calendar year. Re-releases or updates of previously published books are not eligible. Six copies of each book must be submitted along with a signed nomination form.
Award: $10,000 & trophy, finalists receive $1,000 & trophy

Closing Date: Dec 31
Presented: April

SAH Prize for Historical Fiction
Society of American Historians (SAH)
Affiliate of American Historical Association
Columbia University, 3009 Broadway MC 802, New York, NY 10027
Tel: 212-854-1919
E-mail: amhistsociety@columbia.edu
Web Site: sah.columbia.edu
Key Personnel
Pres: Martha A Sandweiss
VP: Martha Hodes
Exec Secy: Andrew Lipman
Established: 1993
For a book of historical fiction on an American subject which makes a significant contribution to historical understanding, portrays authentically the people & events of the historical past & displays skills in narrative construction & prose style. Must be published & have a copyright within 2 years prior to prize year. Awarded biennially in odd-numbered years.
Award: $2,000 & certificate
Closing Date: Dec 1
Presented: New York, NY, May

Saint Louis Literary Award
Saint Louis University Library Associates
Pius XII Memorial Library, 3650 Lindell Blvd, St Louis, MO 63108
Tel: 314-977-3100; 314-977-3087 *Fax:* 314-977-3108
E-mail: slula@slu.edu
Web Site: lib.slu.edu/about/associates/literary-award
Key Personnel
Exec Dir: Edward S Ibur
Established: 1967
For body of author's work. No applications; awardee chosen by committee.
Award: Honorarium, Citation
Presented: Award Ceremony, Sheldon Concert Hall, St Louis, MO, Spring

San Francisco Browning Society Award
Poetry Center & American Poetry Archives at San Francisco State University
511-512 Humanities Bldg, 1600 Holloway Ave, San Francisco, CA 94132
Tel: 415-338-2227 *Fax:* 415-338-0966
E-mail: poetry@sfsu.edu
Web Site: poetry.sfsu.edu
Key Personnel
Dir: Steve Dickison *E-mail:* steved@sfsu.edu
Assoc Dir: Elise Ficarra *E-mail:* eficarra@sfsu.edu
Open to SF State creative writing students. All entries must be original, unpublished dramatic monologues. Students may submit up to 3 poems of not more than 5 pages each. Attach cover letter to ms with your name, address, phone number & social security number. Separate cover sheets for each entry. Submit by hand original & 2 copies of work to the Poetry Center, HUM 511 or by mail. No e-mail submission. Poets retain full rights to their work, but mss will not be returned.
Award: $300 (1st place), $200 (2nd place), $100 (3rd place), $50 each (3 honorable mentions); All winners are invited to attend Spring meeting of the Browning Society in March
Closing Date: Nov 1
Presented: Mid-Feb

San Francisco Foundation/Nomadic Press Literary Awards
Nomadic Press
111 Fairmount Ave, Oakland, CA 94611
Tel: 510-500-5162
E-mail: info@nomadicpress.org

ASSOCIATIONS, EVENTS

Web Site: www.nomadicpress.org/sff/nomadicpressliteraryawards; nomadicpress.submittable.com/submit; www.nomadicpress.org
Key Personnel
Exec Dir: J K Fowler *E-mail:* jkfowler@nomadicpress.org
Established: 2021
Individual poetry, fiction & nonfiction awards to 20 writers from Alameda, San Francisco & Contra Costa counties.
Other Sponsor(s): San Francisco Foundation
Award: $5,000 each
Closing Date: Mid-March
Presented: April

San Francisco Writing Contest (SFWC)
San Francisco Writers Conference
1901 Cleveland Ave, Suite D, Santa Rosa, CA 94501
Tel: 415-689-6301
E-mail: contest@sfwriters.org; director@sfwriters.org
Web Site: www.sfwriters.org
Key Personnel
Conference Co-Dir & Busn Devt Dir: Laurie McLean
Conference Co-Dir & Opers/Programming Dir: Lissa Provost
Dir, Mktg: Elisabeth Kauffman
Dir, Registrations/Cust Support: Praveena Raman
Dir, Volunteers: Amanda Clay Traylor
All entries must be original, unpublished work not submitted to this contest in previous years & be in English. Entry forms are available on-line. Entry fee: $30 (includes free copy of contest anthology). Four categories: Adult fiction, nonfiction/memoir, children's/young adult & poetry.
Award: Full conference registration (grand prize), $100 (1st prize in each category). All finalists & winners will get their entries published in the contest anthology
Closing Date: Sept
Presented: Annual Conference

The Carl Sandburg Literary Award
The Chicago Public Library Foundation & Chicago Public Library
200 W Madison, 3rd fl, Chicago, IL 60606
Tel: 312-201-9830
E-mail: info@cplfoundation.org
Web Site: www.cplfoundation.org
Key Personnel
Pres: Brenda Langstraat *Tel:* 312-374-5242
  E-mail: blangstraat@cplfoundation.org
Mgr, Mktg Communs: Rica Bouso *Tel:* 312-201-9830 ext 32 *E-mail:* rbouso@cplfoundation.org
Established: 2000
Presented to an acclaimed author in recognition of outstanding contributions to the literary world & honors a significant work or body of work that has enhanced the public's awareness of the written award.

Ada Sanderson Memorial
The Poetry Society of Virginia (PSV)
PO Box 36128, North Chesterfield, VA 23235-3533
E-mail: contest@poetrysocietyofvirginia.org; info@poetryvirginia.org
Web Site: www.poetrysocietyofvirginia.org
Key Personnel
Pres: Cherryl T Cooley
  E-mail: poetrysocietypresident@gmail.com
All entries must be in English, original & unpublished. Subject: Nature, any form, 48 line limit. Submit 1 copy of the poem with no identifying information but put the category in the upper right-hand-side, along with a notation as to whether you are a member of PSV (does not matter if you are a lifetime member or just joined for the contest). Submit a cover letter/page that contains the category, the name of

the poem, your name & address, phone number & e-mail address. Entries will not be returned.
Entry fee: Free to membs, $5 nonmembs.
Award: $100
Closing Date: Feb
Presented: PSV Awards Ceremony, April

Mari Sandoz Award
Nebraska Library Association (NLA)
PO Box 21756, Lincoln, NE 68542-1756
Web Site: www.nebraskalibraries.org/mari_sandoz_award
Key Personnel
Exec Dir: Ginger Jelinek
  E-mail: nlaexecutivedirector@nebraskalibraries.org
Established: 1971
Given in recognition of significant, enduring contribution to the Nebraska book world through writing, film production or related activity.
Award: Plaque
Closing Date: July 30
Presented: NLA Fall Conference, Late Oct

Ivan Sandrof Lifetime Achievement Award
National Book Critics Circle (NBCC)
c/o Jacob M Appel, Icahn School of Medicine at Mount Sinai, One Gustave L Levy Place, New York, NY 10029
E-mail: info@bookcritics.org
Web Site: www.bookcritics.org/awards/sandrof/
Key Personnel
Pres: Heather Scott Partington *E-mail:* hsp@bookcritics.org
Secy: Colette Bancroft *E-mail:* bancroft.colette72@gmail.com
Treas: Jacob M Appel *E-mail:* jacobmappel@gmail.com
VP, Awards: Keetje Kuipers *E-mail:* keetje@poetrynw.org
VP, Events: Jane Ciabattari *E-mail:* janeciab@gmail.com
Awarded to a person or institution who has, over time, made significant contributions to book culture. Nominations from members only.
Presented: NBCC Awards Ceremony, March

The Sarabande Series in Kentucky Literature
Sarabande Books Inc
822 E Market St, Louisville, KY 40206
Tel: 502-458-4028
E-mail: info@sarabandebooks.org
Web Site: www.sarabandebooks.org/bruckheimer
Key Personnel
Dir, Mktg & Publicity: Joanna Englert
  E-mail: joanna@sarabandebooks.org
Established: 2005
Submissions are open to any writer of English who is a native of Kentucky, has lived in Kentucky for at least 1 year, or whose ms is set in Kentucky, about Kentucky, or about a Kentuckian. In addition, the author must be willing & able to travel to or within Kentucky for readings & public events. Translations & previously self-published collections are not eligible. Electronic submissions via Submittable during the month of July. Must include cover letter, full-length ms of poetry, short fiction, or literary nonfiction & $22 reading fee.
Award: Publication of work by Sarabande & 2-week residency at Blackacre Conservatory
Closing Date: July 31

The William Saroyan International Prize for Writing
The William Saroyan Foundation
1801 Van Ness Ave, Suite 320, San Francisco, CA 94109
E-mail: info@williamsaroyanfoundation.org
Web Site: williamsaroyanfoundation.org/prizes
Established: 2003
Biennial competition, awarded in even-numbered years, for newly published books by new & emerging writers. The 2026 prize will be for books published in 2024 or 2025. Entry form & 5 copies of publication required. Entry fee: $50.
Other Sponsor(s): Stanford Libraries
Award: $5,000 each in fiction & nonfiction
Closing Date: Jan 31, 2026
Presented: Winners announced late Summer/early Fall 2026

May Sarton New Hampshire Poetry Prize
Bauhan Publishing LLC
44 Main St, 2nd fl, Peterborough, NH 03458
Mailing Address: PO Box 117, Peterborough, NH 03458
Tel: 603-567-4430
Web Site: www.bauhanpublishing.com
Key Personnel
Publr: Sarah Bauhan *E-mail:* sbauhan@bauhanpublishing.com
Edit Dir: Mary Ann Faughnan
  E-mail: mafaughnan@bauhanpublishing.com
Established: 2010
Awarded for a book-length collection of poetry. The book must be previously unublished as a whole. Collection must be written or translated into English. The poetry within can be on any topic & in any form. Entry fee: $25 per ms.
Award: $1,000, book publication, 100 complimentary copies & distribution through Casemate | IPM

Sarton Women's Book Awards™
Story Circle Network
PO Box 1616, Bertram, TX 78605-1616
E-mail: sartonprize@storycircle.org
Web Site: www.storycircle.org/SartonLiteraryAward
Available to women authors writing chiefly about women in memoir, biography & fiction published in the US & Canada selected from works submitted. Limited to submissions originally written in English & published by small/independent publishers, university presses & author-publishers (self-publishing authors). Judging is conducted in 2 rounds. Professional librarians not affiliated with SCN select the winner & finalists.
Awards are presented in 5 categories: Memoir; Nonfiction: Biography, Collective biography, Edited diaries, Scholarly studies of women's literature, Anthologies; Contemporary Fiction; Historical Fiction; Young Adult & New Adult Fiction. Lesbian entries are welcome in all categories. Entry fee: $90 early bird, $110 regular.
See web site for full guidelines.
Closing Date: Mid-Nov

Saturnalia Books Poetry Prize & Editors Prize
Saturnalia Books
105 Woodside Rd, Ardmore, PA 19003
Tel: 267-278-9541
Web Site: saturnaliabooks.com
Key Personnel
Publr: Henry Israeli *E-mail:* hisraeli@aol.com
Established: 2003
Recognizes a poetry ms of high merit. All entries are considered for both prizes. Online fee: $30.
Award: $2,000 & publication (poetry), $500 & publication (editors)
Closing Date: April 1

SATW Foundation Lowell Thomas Travel Journalism Competition
Society of American Travel Writers Foundation
306 Summer Hill Dr, Fredericksburg, TX 78624
Tel: 281-217-2872
E-mail: marylua@satwf.com
Web Site: www.satwf.org
Key Personnel
Pres: Catharine M Hamm
Established: 1985
Premier awards for the best work in travel journalism. Competition is open to all North American journalists & is judged by leading schools of journalism. There are 20-plus categories, including individual & publication awards. Among them: Grand Award for Travel Journalist of the Year for a portfolio of work, Best Newspaper Travel Coverage, Best Travel Magazine, Best Travel Coverage in Other Magazines, Best Guidebook, Best Travel Book, Best Online Travel Journalism Site & categories for writing, photography, audio broadcast, video broadcast, multimedia work & more. For entry details & forms, see web site. New materials usually updated mid-February.
Award: More than $20,000 total in prize money: $1,500 (top prize), $500 (1st place)
Closing Date: April 1
Presented: SATW Annual Convention, Fall

Aldo & Jeanne Scaglione Prize for a Translation of a Literary Work
Modern Language Association (MLA)
85 Broad St, New York, NY 10004
SAN: 202-6422
Tel: 646-576-5141; 646-576-5000
E-mail: awards@mla.org
Web Site: www.mla.org
Key Personnel
Coord, Book Prizes: Annie M Reiser
  E-mail: areiser@mla.org
Awarded for an outstanding translation into English of a book-length literary work; books must have been published in 2024. Translators need not be members of the MLA. For consideration, submit 6 print copies & electronic access, plus 12-15 pages of the text in its original language.
Award: Cash award & certificate
Closing Date: April 1, 2025
Presented: MLA Annual Convention, Toronto, ON, CN, Jan 2026

Aldo & Jeanne Scaglione Prize for a Translation of a Scholarly Study of Literature
Modern Language Association (MLA)
85 Broad St, New York, NY 10004
SAN: 202-6422
Tel: 646-576-5141; 646-576-5000
E-mail: awards@mla.org
Web Site: www.mla.org
Key Personnel
Coord, Book Prizes: Annie M Reiser
  E-mail: areiser@mla.org
Established: 1993
Awarded biennially, in odd-numbered years, for an outstanding translation into English of a book-length work of literary history, literary criticism, philology or literary theory published in 2023 or 2024. For consideration, submit 4 print copies & electronic access.
Award: Cash award & certificate
Closing Date: May 1, 2025
Presented: MLA Annual Convention, Toronto, ON, CN, Jan 2026

Aldo & Jeanne Scaglione Prize for Comparative Literary Studies
Modern Language Association (MLA)
85 Broad St, New York, NY 10004
SAN: 202-6422
Tel: 646-576-5141; 646-576-5000
E-mail: awards@mla.org
Web Site: www.mla.org
Key Personnel
Coord, Book Prizes: Annie M Reiser
  E-mail: areiser@mla.org
Established: 1992

Prize awarded for an outstanding scholarly work by a current member of the MLA in the field of comparative literary studies involving at least 2 literatures, published in 2024. For consideration, submit 4 print copies & electronic access.
Award: Cash award & certificate
Closing Date: May 1, 2025
Presented: MLA Annual Convention, Toronto, ON, CN, Jan 2026

Aldo & Jeanne Scaglione Prize for French & Francophone Studies
Modern Language Association (MLA)
85 Broad St, New York, NY 10004
SAN: 202-6422
Tel: 646-576-5141; 646-576-5000
E-mail: awards@mla.org
Web Site: www.mla.org
Key Personnel
Coord, Book Prizes: Annie M Reiser
  E-mail: areiser@mla.org
Established: 1992
Awarded for an outstanding scholarly work by a current member of the MLA in the field of French or Francophone linguistic or literary studies published in 2024. Books that are primarily translations will not be considered. For consideration, submit 4 print copies & electronic access.
Award: Cash award & certificate
Closing Date: May 1, 2025
Presented: MLA Annual Convention, Toronto, ON, CN, Jan 2026

Aldo & Jeanne Scaglione Prize for Italian Studies
Modern Language Association (MLA)
85 Broad St, New York, NY 10004
SAN: 202-6422
Tel: 646-576-5141; 646-576-5000
E-mail: awards@mla.org
Web Site: www.mla.org
Key Personnel
Coord, Book Prizes: Annie M Reiser
  E-mail: areiser@mla.org
Established: 2000
Awarded biennially, in odd-numbered years, to the author of an outstanding scholarly book on any phase of Italian literature or culture or comparative literature involving Italian by a current MLA member for books published in 2024. For consideration, submit 4 print copies & electronic access.
Award: Cash award & certificate
Closing Date: May 1, 2025
Presented: MLA Annual Convention, Toronto, ON, CN, Jan 2026

Aldo & Jeanne Scaglione Prize for Studies in Germanic Languages & Literatures
Modern Language Association (MLA)
85 Broad St, New York, NY 10004
SAN: 202-6422
Tel: 646-576-5141; 646-576-5000
E-mail: awards@mla.org
Web Site: www.mla.org
Key Personnel
Coord, Book Prizes: Annie M Reiser
  E-mail: areiser@mla.org
Established: 1992
Awarded biennially, in even-numbered years, to a current MLA member for an outstanding scholarly work on the linguistics or literatures of the Germanic languages including Danish, Dutch, German, Icelandic, Norwegian, Swedish & Yiddish & published 2024 or 2025. For consideration, submit 4 print copies & electronic access, along with a letter identifying the work & confirming the author's membership.
Award: Cash award & certificate
Closing Date: May 1, 2026
Presented: MLA Annual Convention, Los Angeles, CA, Jan 2027

Aldo & Jeanne Scaglione Prize for Studies in Slavic Languages & Literatures
Modern Language Association (MLA)
85 Broad St, New York, NY 10004
SAN: 202-6422
Tel: 646-576-5141; 646-576-5000
E-mail: awards@mla.org
Web Site: www.mla.org
Key Personnel
Coord, Book Prizes: Annie M Reiser
  E-mail: areiser@mla.org
Established: 1993
Awarded biennially, in odd-numbered years, for an outstanding scholarly work on the linguistics or literatures of the Slavic languages published in 2023 or 2024. Works of literary history, literary criticism, philology & literary theory are eligible. Books that are primarily translations will not be considered. Authors need not be members of the MLA. For consideration, submit 4 print copies & electronic access.
Award: Cash award & certificate
Closing Date: May 1, 2025
Presented: MLA Annual Convention, Toronto, ON, CN, Jan 2026

Aldo & Jeanne Scaglione Publication Award for a Manuscript in Italian Literary Studies
Modern Language Association (MLA)
85 Broad St, New York, NY 10004
SAN: 202-6422
Tel: 646-576-5141; 646-576-5000
E-mail: awards@mla.org
Web Site: www.mla.org
Key Personnel
Coord, Book Prizes: Annie M Reiser
  E-mail: areiser@mla.org
Established: 1998
Awarded to the author of an outstanding ms dealing with any aspect of the languages & literatures of Italy, including medieval Latin & comparative studies or intellectual history of the work's main point is related to the humanities. Ms must be accepted for publication in 2024 or 2025 by a not-for-profit member of the AUPresses; authors must be current members of the MLA residing in the US or CN. For consideration, submit 4 print copies & electronic access, plus contact & biographical information.
Award: Cash award & certificate
Closing Date: July 1, 2025
Presented: MLA Annual Convention, Toronto, ON, CN, Jan 2026

William Sanders Scarborough Prize
Modern Language Association (MLA)
85 Broad St, New York, NY 10004
SAN: 202-6422
Tel: 646-576-5141; 646-576-5000
E-mail: awards@mla.org
Web Site: www.mla.org
Key Personnel
Coord, Book Prizes: Annie M Reiser
  E-mail: areiser@mla.org
Established: 2001
Prize for an outstanding scholarly study of Black American literature or culture published the previous calendar year. Author need not be a member of the MLA. For consideration, submit 4 print copies & electronic access.
Award: Cash award & certificate
Closing Date: May 1, 2025
Presented: MLA Annual Convention, Toronto, ON, CN, Jan 2026

SCBWI Work-In-Progress Awards
Society of Children's Book Writers & Illustrators (SCBWI)
6363 Wilshire Blvd, Suite 425, Los Angeles, CA 90048
Tel: 323-782-1010
E-mail: info@scbwi.org
Web Site: www.scbwi.org/awards/grants/work-in-progress-grants
Key Personnel
Exec Dir: Sarah Baker
Assoc Dir, Digital Content & Awards: Sarah Diamond
Assoc Mgr, Awards & Pubns: Danielle Monique
Established: 1978
Assists children's book writers & illustrators in the publication of a specific project currently not under contract. The award showcases outstanding mss from members of SCBWI. One winner in each of the following 6 categories will be selected: Picture book text; chapter books/early readers; middle grade; young adult fiction; nonfiction (Anna Cross Giblin Nonfiction Award); underrepresented fiction or nonfiction. To be eligible, you must be a current SCBWI member when your work is submitted & when the award is announced. You may not submit work that is under contract. If the work becomes under contract before the award is announced, you will become ineligible. Each member may submit only 1 ms to the WIP Awards each year. Illustrations can apply for one of the Don Freeman Grants. You may not apply for both the Don Freeman & Picture Book category of the WIP Award.
Award: Winning works shown to editors & agents
Closing Date: April 15
Presented: Announced in early Oct

Nicholas Schaffner Award for Music in Literature
Schaffner Press
PO Box 41567, Tucson, AZ 85717
Web Site: www.schaffnerawards.com
Key Personnel
Publr: Tim Schaffner *E-mail:* tim@schaffnerpress.com
Given to the writer of an unpublished ms who submits a literary work in the English language, either fiction, poetry or nonfiction that deals in some way with the subject of music (of any genre or period) & its influence. Entry fee: $25. See web site for submission style & format.
Award: Contract & $1,000 advance for book publication
Closing Date: Jan 28

Bernadotte E Schmitt Grants
American Historical Association (AHA)
400 "A" St SE, Washington, DC 20003
Tel: 202-544-2422
E-mail: awards@historians.org
Web Site: www.historians.org/award-grant/bernadotte-e-schmitt-research-grants-in-european-african-or-asian-history/
Awarded to support research in the history of Europe, Africa & Asia. Only members of the association are eligible. The grants are intended to be used for expenses relating to furthering research in progress & may be used for travel to a library or archive, for microfilms, photographs, or photocopying. Preference will be given to advanced doctoral students, non-tenured faculty & unaffiliated scholars, & to those with specific research needs such as the completion of a project or a discrete segment thereof. All updated info on web site. Applicants will be notified of the committee's decision by e-mail in mid-May.
Award: Individual grants up to $1,500
Closing Date: Feb 15
Presented: June

Schneider Family Book Awards
The American Library Association (ALA)
225 N Michigan Ave, Suite 1300, Chicago, IL 60601
SAN: 201-0062
Tel: 312-280-3247 *Toll Free Tel:* 800-545-2433
Fax: 312-944-3897
E-mail: ala@ala.org
Web Site: www.ala.org/awardsgrants/schneider-family-book-award
Key Personnel
Prog Offr: Cheryl M Malden *E-mail:* cmalden@ala.org
Established: 2003
Awards to honor an author or illustrator for a book that embodies an artistic expression of the disability experience for a child & adolescent audiences. Three awards given annually: younger children (ages 0-8), middle grades (ages 9-13) & teens (ages 14-18). Full eligibility requirements & application instructions on web site.
Award: 3 awards $5,000 each & framed plaque. When a picture book wins, $5,000 is divided equally between author & illustrator
Closing Date: Dec 1

Ruth & Sylvia Schwartz Children's Book Awards
Ruth Schwartz Foundation
c/o Ontario Arts Council, 121 Bloor St E, 7th fl, Toronto, ON M4W 3M5, Canada
Tel: 416-961-1660 *Toll Free Tel:* 800-387-0058 (ON) *Fax:* 416-961-7796 (Ontario Arts Council)
E-mail: info@oafdn.ca (Ontario Arts Foundation); info@arts.on.ca (Ontario Arts Council)
Web Site: www.arts.on.ca; www.oafdn.ca/pages/ruth-sylvia-schwartz-awards
Key Personnel
Exec Dir, Ontario Arts Foundation: Alan F Walker *Tel:* 416-969-7413 *E-mail:* awalker@oafdn.ca
Dir of Admin, Ontario Arts Foundation: Ann Boyd *Tel:* 416-969-7411 *E-mail:* aboyd@oafdn.ca
Awards Offr, Ontario Arts Council: Carolyn Gloude *Tel:* 416-969-7423 *E-mail:* cgloude@arts.on.ca
Established: 1976
Awards to recognize artistic excellence in writing & illustration in Canadian children's literature.
Other Sponsor(s): Ontario Arts Council; Ontario Arts Foundation
Award: $6,000 each for picture book & young adult/middle reader
Presented: An Ontario, CN public school, May

Science + Literature Program
National Book Foundation
90 Broad St, Suite 604, New York, NY 10004
Tel: 212-685-0261 *Fax:* 212-213-6570
E-mail: nationalbook@nationalbook.org
Web Site: www.nationalbook.org/programs/science-literature
Key Personnel
Exec Dir: Ruth Dickey *E-mail:* rdickey@nationalbook.org
Sr Mgr, Awards & Honors: Madeleine Shelton *E-mail:* mshelton@nationalbook.org
Sr Mgr, Mktg & Communs: Ale Romero *E-mail:* aromero@nationalbook.org
Awards & Communs Coord: Lilly Santiago *E-mail:* lsantiago@nationalbook.org
Three books awarded that highlight the diversity of voices in scientific writing.
Other Sponsor(s): Alfred P Sloan Foundation
Award: $10,000 & feature in national public programming
Presented: Award Ceremony (invitation only), March

Science in Society Journalism Awards
National Association of Science Writers Inc (NASW)
PO Box 7905, Berkeley, CA 94707
Tel: 510-859-7229
Web Site: www.nasw.org/awards/sis
Key Personnel
Exec Dir: Tinsley Davis *E-mail:* director@nasw.org
Established: 1972
Awarded to provide recognition for investigative reporting about the sciences & their impact on society, for material published or broadcast between the period of January 1-December 31. Publishers & broadcasters will also receive certificates of recognition.
Award: $2,000, certificate of recognition in each category, travel to awards presentation for 1 author or representative
Closing Date: Feb 1 (postmark)
Presented: Annual Meeting, Oct

Scotiabank Giller Prize
Scotiabank
499 Douglas Ave, Toronto, ON M5M 1H6, Canada
Web Site: www.scotiabankgillerprize.ca
Key Personnel
Exec Dir: Elana Rabinovitch
Submissions Mgr: Daphna Rabinovitch *E-mail:* daphna@scotiabankgillerprize.ca
Established: 1994
Presented to the author of the best Canadian novel, graphic novel or collection of short stories published in English, either originally, or in translation. See web site for full submission guidelines.
Other Sponsor(s): Audible; CBC
Award: $140,000
Closing Date: Aug 14
Presented: Gala Ceremony, Nov

The Robert S Sergeant Memorial
The Poetry Society of Virginia (PSV)
PO Box 36128, North Chesterfield, VA 23235-3533
E-mail: contest@poetrysocietyofvirginia.org; info@poetryvirginia.org
Web Site: www.poetrysocietyofvirginia.org
Key Personnel
Pres: Cherryl T Cooley *E-mail:* poetrysocietypresident@gmail.com
All entries must be in English, original & unpublished. Subject: Birds, any form, 48 line limit. Submit 1 copy of the poem with no identifying information but put the category in the upper right-hand-side, along with a notation as to whether you are a member of PSV (does not matter if you are a lifetime member or just joined for the contest). Submit a cover letter/page that contains the category, the name of the poem, your name & address, phone number & e-mail address. Entries will not be returned.
Entry fee: Free to membs, $5 nonmembs.
Award: $50 (1st prize), $30 (2nd prize), $20 (3rd prize)
Closing Date: Feb
Presented: PSV Awards Ceremony, April

SFWA Nebula Awards
Science Fiction and Fantasy Writers Association, Inc (SFWA)
PO Box 215, San Lorenzo, CA 94580
Tel: 860-698-0536
E-mail: office@sfwa.org; operations@sfwa.org
Web Site: www.sfwa.org
Key Personnel
CFO: Nathan Lowell *E-mail:* cfo@sfwa.org
Pres: Jeffe Kennedy *E-mail:* president@sfwa.org
VP: Tobias S Buckell *E-mail:* vp@sfwa.org
Secy: Adam Rakunas *E-mail:* secretary@sfwa.org
Exec Dir: Kate Baker
Nebula Awards Commissioner: Jim Hosek *E-mail:* nac@sfwa.org
Established: 1965
Voted on & presented by members of SFWA. Given to outstanding novel, novella, novelette & short stories eligible for that year's award. The Andre Norton Nebula Award for Middle Grade & Young Adult Fiction was added in 2005, followed by the Ray Bradbury Nebula Award for Outstanding Dramatic Presentation in 2009 & the Nebula Award for Best Game Writing in 2018. An anthology including the winning pieces of short fiction & several finalists continues to be published every year since 1966. It's now known as the Nebula Awards Showcase.
Award: Lucite trophy for Novel, Novella, Novelette, Short Story, Norton & Game Writing awards; bronze sculpture for the Bradbury award
Presented: Annual Nebula Conference & Awards Ceremony, Spring

Shamus Awards
The Private Eye Writers of America (PWA)
3665 S Needles Hwy, 7G, Laughlin, NV 89029
Web Site: www.privateeyewriters.com
Key Personnel
Awards Chair: Gay Toltl Kinman *E-mail:* gaykinman@gaykinman.com
Awards for private eye novels & short stories first published in the US in the year preceding the award. Eligible works must feature as a main character a person paid for investigative work but not employed for that work by a unit of government. See web site for submission guidelines. Categories: Best Hardcover PI Novel, Best First PI Novel, Best Original Paperback PI Novel, Best PI Short Story.
Closing Date: March 31
Presented: Autumn

Shaughnessy Cohen Prize for Political Writing
The Writers' Trust of Canada
600-460 Richmond St W, Toronto, ON M5V 1Y1, Canada
Tel: 416-504-8222 *Toll Free Tel:* 877-906-6548
Fax: 416-504-9090
E-mail: info@writerstrust.com
Web Site: www.writerstrust.com
Key Personnel
Exec Dir: Charlie Foran *Tel:* 416-504-8222 ext 244 *E-mail:* cforan@writerstrust.com
Mgr, Author Progs: Devon Jackson *Tel:* 416-504-8222 ext 248 *E-mail:* djackson@writerstrust.com
Established: 2000
Awarded for a nonfiction book that captures a political subject of relevance to the Canadian reader & enhances understanding of the issue. The winning work combines compelling new insights with depth of research & is of significant literary merit.
Other Sponsor(s): CN
Award: $25,000 (winner), $2,500 (finalists)
Presented: Politics & the Pen, Ottawa, ON, CN, Spring

Mina P Shaughnessy Prize
Modern Language Association (MLA)
85 Broad St, New York, NY 10004
SAN: 202-6422
Tel: 646-576-5141; 646-576-5000
E-mail: awards@mla.org
Web Site: www.mla.org
Key Personnel
Coord, Book Prizes: Annie M Reiser *E-mail:* areiser@mla.org
Established: 1980
Awarded biennially, in odd-numbered years, for an outstanding scholarly book in the fields of language, culture, literacy & literature with

strong application to the teaching of English, published in 2024 or 2025. Authors need not be a member of the MLA. For consideration, submit 4 print copies & electronic access.
Award: Cash award & certificate
Closing Date: May 1, 2026
Presented: MLA Annual Convention, Los Angeles, CA, Jan 2027

Shelley Memorial Award
Poetry Society of America (PSA)
119 Smith St, Brooklyn, NY 11201
Tel: 212-254-9628
E-mail: info@poetrysociety.org
Web Site: poetrysociety.org/awards
Key Personnel
Exec Dir: Matt Brogan *E-mail:* matt@poetrysociety.org
Deputy Dir: Brett Fletcher Lauer *E-mail:* brett@poetrysociety.org
Devt Dir: Madeline Weinfield *E-mail:* madeline@poetrysociety.org
Awarded to a poet, selected with reference to his or her genius & need, by a jury of 3 poets. By nomination only.
Award: $6,000-$9,000

The Randy Shilts Award for Gay Nonfiction
The Publishing Triangle
511 Avenue of the Americas, No D36, New York, NY 10011
E-mail: awards@publishingtriangle.org; info@publishingtriangle.org; publishingtriangle@gmail.com
Web Site: publishingtriangle.org/awards/randy-shilts-gay-nonfiction
Established: 1997
Recognizes works that are by or about gay men, bisexual men +/or trans men, or that have a significant influence upon the lives of queer men. A call for submissions is posted on the web site in early Autumn. Finalists & winners are determined by a panel of judges appointed by the awards committee.
Award: $1,000

Christopher Latham Sholes Award
Council for Wisconsin Writers (CWW)
c/o 3225 N 91 St, Milwaukee, WI 53222
E-mail: wiswriters@gmail.com
Web Site: wiswriters.org/awards
Key Personnel
Contest Chair: Erik Richardson
 E-mail: erichardson@wi.rr.com
Biennial award currently offered in odd-numbered years to honor an individual or organization for outstanding encouragement of Wisconsin writers. No entry fee.
Award: $500
Closing Date: Jan 31
Presented: CWW Annual Award Ceremony & Banquet, May

Short Prose Competition for Developing Writers
The Writers' Union of Canada (TWUC)
600-460 Richmond St W, Toronto, ON M5V 1Y1, Canada
Tel: 416-703-8982
E-mail: info@writersunion.ca
Web Site: www.writersunion.ca
Key Personnel
Exec Dir: John Degen *Tel:* 416-703-8982 ext 221 *E-mail:* jdegen@writersunion.ca
Assoc Dir: Siobhan O'Connor *Tel:* 416-703-8982 ext 222 *E-mail:* soconnor@writersunion.ca
Short prose up to 2,500 words by an unpublished Canadian writer.
Award: $2,500
Closing Date: March 1

Short Story Awards
Prince Edward Island Writers' Guild
81 Prince St, Charlottetown, PE C1A 4R3, Canada
E-mail: peiliteraryawards@gmail.com
Web Site: www.peiwritersguild.com
A short story, maximum 2,500 words, will constitute as an entry. Work must be original & unpublished. Entry fee: $25 per submission. Prince Edward Island residents only. See web site for complete entry requirements.
Award: Cash prizes for 1st, 2nd & 3rd place
Closing Date: Changes annually (see web site)
Presented: Island Literary Awards Gala, Spring

Edwin "Bud" Shrake Award for Best Short Nonfiction
Texas Institute of Letters (TIL)
PO Box 130294, Spring, TX 77393
Web Site: texasinstituteofletters.org
Key Personnel
Pres: David Bowles *E-mail:* president@texasinstituteofletters.org
VP: Chris Barton
Secy: Kathryn Jones *E-mail:* secretary@texasinstituteofletters.org
Treas: Cliff Hudder
Award for the best short nonfiction writing appearing in a magazine, journal or other periodical or in a newspaper Sunday supplement. Only one story per entrant. The author must have been born in Texas or have lived in Texas for at least 5 consecutive years at some time. See web site for guidelines.
Award: $1,000
Closing Date: Jan
Presented: TIL Annual Meeting & Awards Ceremony, Spring

Joe Shuster Awards
Canadian Comic Book Creator Awards Association (CCBCAA)
305-484 Oriole Pkwy, Toronto, ON M5P 2H8, Canada
E-mail: info@joeshusterawards.com
Web Site: joeshusterawards.com
Key Personnel
Exec Dir/Nominating & Jury Coord: Kevin A Boyd *E-mail:* kevin@joeshusterawards.com
Art Dir: Tyrone Biljan *E-mail:* tyrone@joeshusterawards.com
Established: 2004
Canada's national award that honors & raises the awareness of Canadians that create, publish & sell comics, graphic novels & webcomics. Core categories: Cartoonist (writer/artist), artist, writer, colorist, cover artist, publisher. Awards chosen by jury decision. Five additional specialty awards.
Presented: Late Summer/early Fall

Robert F Sibert Informational Book Award
Association for Library Service to Children (ALSC)
Division of The American Library Association (ALA)
225 N Michigan Ave, Suite 1300, Chicago, IL 60601
Tel: 312-280-2163 *Toll Free Tel:* 800-545-2433
Fax: 312-280-5271
E-mail: alsc@ala.org
Web Site: www.ala.org/alsc/awardsgrants/bookmedia/sibert
Key Personnel
Exec Dir: Alena Rivers *Tel:* 800-545-2433 ext 5866 *E-mail:* arivers@ala.org
Awards Coord: Jordan Dubin *Tel:* 800-545-2433 ext 5839 *E-mail:* jdubin@ala.org
Prog Coord: Ann Michaud *Tel:* 800-545-2433 ext 2166 *E-mail:* amichaud@ala.org
Membership/Mktg Specialist: Elizabeth Serrano *Tel:* 800-545-2433 ext 2164 *E-mail:* eserrano@ala.org
Presented to the author(s) & illustrator(s) of the most distinguished informational book published in the US in English during the preceding year.
Award: Medal
Closing Date: Dec 31
Presented: ALA Youth Media Awards, Late Jan

The SIIA IMPACT Awards
Software & Information Industry Association (SIIA)
1620 Eye St NW, Washington, DC 20005
Tel: 202-289-7442
E-mail: info@siia.net
Web Site: www.siia.net/impact-award
Key Personnel
VP, Awards & Recognition Progs: Amanda McMaster *Tel:* 202-789-4469 *E-mail:* amcmaster@siia.net
Acknowledges leadership in the publishing industry, specifically championing emerging talent & equity. Awards are open to SIIA members & nonmembers. Self-nominations are welcome.
Emerging talent recognizes those aged 35 & under who have 3 or more years of service to the industry & have demonstrated outstanding success & leadership potential.
Equity awards recognize individuals & teams demonstrating significant progress & indentifiable achievement toward efforts related to advancing diversity, equity & inclusion.
Closing Date: Sept
Presented: Nov

Silver Gavel Awards for Media & the Arts
American Bar Association (ABA)
Division for Public Education, 321 N Clark St, MS 17.2, Chicago, IL 60654
Tel: 312-988-5719 *Toll Free Tel:* 800-285-2221
E-mail: gavelawards@americanbar.org
Web Site: www.americanbar.org/groups/public_education/programs/silver_gavel
Key Personnel
Admin Asst: Christina Pluta *E-mail:* christina.pluta@americanbar.org
Established: 1958
Media & arts awards competition to recognize communications media that have been exemplary in fostering public understanding of the law & the legal system during the previous calendar year. Book entries must submit 5 hard copies. Handling fee: $100 per entry.
Award: Silver Gavel, honorable mentions
Closing Date: Jan
Presented: July

The Robert B Silvers Prize for Journalism
The Robert B Silvers Foundation
c/o The New York Review of Books, 435 Hudson St, Suite 300, New York, NY 10014
Tel: 212-757-8070
E-mail: admin@silversfoundation.org
Web Site: silversfoundation.org/about-the-silvers-dudley-prizes
Key Personnel
Admin: Alex Beatty
Recognizes achievement in reporting, long-form political analysis or commentary. There is no application process.
Award: $135,000

The Robert B Silvers Prize for Literary Criticism
The Robert B Silvers Foundation
c/o The New York Review of Books, 435 Hudson St, Suite 300, New York, NY 10014
Tel: 212-757-8070
E-mail: admin@silversfoundation.org

Web Site: silversfoundation.org/about-the-silvers-dudley-prizes
Key Personnel
Admin: Alex Beatty
Recognizes achievement in long-form literary criticism & the intellectual & cultural essay. There is no application process.
Award: $135,000

Francis B Simkins Award
Southern Historical Association (SHA)
University of Georgia, Dept of History, Athens, GA 30602-1602
Tel: 706-542-8848
Web Site: thesha.org/simkins
Key Personnel
Secy/Treas: Dr Stephen Berry *E-mail:* berrys@thesha.org
Established: 1977
Awarded for the most distinguished first book by an author in the field of southern history over a 2-year period. Awarded in odd-numbered years for a book published in the 2 previous calendar years.
Other Sponsor(s): Longwood College
Award: Cash
Closing Date: March 1
Presented: Annual Meeting, Fall

The John Simmons Short Fiction Award
Writers' Workshop, The University of Iowa
102 Dey House, 507 N Clinton St, Iowa City, IA 52242-1000
Tel: 319-335-0416 *Fax:* 319-335-0420
Web Site: writersworkshop.uiowa.edu/about/iowa-short-fiction-awards
Key Personnel
Dir, Writers' Workshop: Lan Samantha Chang
Prog Admin: Sasha Khmelnik *E-mail:* aleksandra-khmelnik@uiowa.edu
Established: 1988
Open to any writer who has not previously published a volume of prose fiction. Revised mss which have been previously entered may be resubmitted as well as writers who have published a volume of poetry are eligible. Mss must be a collection of short stories of at least 150 typewritten pages. Photo copies are acceptable; SASE return packaging must accompany the mss or these will not be returned. No cash, checks, or money orders accepted. Application period begins August 1.
Other Sponsor(s): University of Iowa Press
Award: Publication by University of Iowa Press under the Press's standard contract
Closing Date: Sept 30
Presented: Autumn

Charlie May Simon Children's Book Award
Arkansas State Library
Arkansas State Library, Suite 100, 900 W Capitol Ave, Little Rock, AR 72201-3108
Tel: 501-682-2860
Web Site: www.library.arkansas.gov/programs/book-awards
Key Personnel
Lib Coord, Youth Servs: Ruth Hyatt *E-mail:* ruth.hyatt@arkansas.gov
Established: 1971
State of Arkansas school children in grades 4-6 read books selected by the award committee throughout the year & vote on their favorite choice.
Other Sponsor(s): Arkansas Department of Education; Arkansas Reading Association
Award: CMS Medallion (1st place), Honor Book plaque (2nd place)
Closing Date: Voted on in May
Presented: Little Rock, AR

Skipping Stones Honor Awards
Skipping Stones Inc
166 W 12 Ave, Eugene, OR 97401
Tel: 541-342-4956
E-mail: info@skippingstones.org
Web Site: www.skippingstones.org
Key Personnel
Exec Ed: Arun N Toke *E-mail:* editor@skippingstones.org
Established: 1993
Honors exceptional multicultural & international awareness books, nature/ecology books, bilingual books & teaching resources. A panel of parents, teachers, librarians, students & editors of *Skipping Stones* select the honors list in the above categories. Entry fee: $60. Winners announced in the Autumn issue of *Skipping Stones* & on our web site.
Award: Honor award certificates, award seals, reviews, press releases, e-releases, web site hyperlinks. Also displayed at NAME (National Association for Multicultural Education) Conference in November. Publicity in multicultural education journal each year
Closing Date: Feb 28
Presented: Announced in June on web site

The Skipping Stones Youth Honor Awards
Skipping Stones Inc
166 W 12 Ave, Eugene, OR 97401
Tel: 541-342-4956
E-mail: info@skippingstones.org
Web Site: www.skippingstones.org
Key Personnel
Exec Ed: Arun N Toke *E-mail:* editor@skippingstones.org
Established: 1993
Recognizes 10 creative & artistic works (writing, art, photo, essays, etc) by young people that promote multicultural & nature awareness. Entry fee: $6. Everyone who enters the awards program receives the Autumn issue with 10 winners & a few noteworthy entries. International entrants receive digital copies of the awards issue.
Award: Honor award certificate, subscription to *Skipping Stones* & 5 nature +/or multicultural books
Closing Date: May 5
Presented: Winners announced in Autumn issue of *Skipping Stones*

Slipstream Annual Poetry Chapbook Contest
Slipstream Press
PO Box 2071, Dept W-1, Niagara Falls, NY 14301
Web Site: www.slipstreampress.org/contest.html
Key Personnel
Co-Ed: Dan Sicoli
Established: 1986
Prize awarded to best 40-page ms of poetry. Entry fee: $20.
Award: $1,000 & 50 copies of book
Closing Date: Dec 1
Presented: Announced in late Spring/early Summer

Phyllis Smart-Young Poetry Prize
The Madison Review
University of Wisconsin, 6193 Helen C White Hall, English Dept, 600 N Park St, Madison, WI 53706
E-mail: madisonrevw@gmail.com
Web Site: www.themadisonrevw.com
Key Personnel
Dept Chair: Anja Wanner
Faculty Advisor & Prog Coord: Ronald Kuka *Tel:* 608-263-3374 *E-mail:* rfkuka@wisc.edu
Ed: Kiyoko Reidy
Mss must be previously unpublished & should be double-spaced with standard 1-inch margins. There is a maximum of 15 pages for combined 3 poems. Only 1 submission (3 poems) is allowed per person per contest. Entries must be submitted online at madisonreview.submittable.com/submit. Entry fee: $10.
Award: $1,000 & publication in Spring issue of *The Madison Review*
Closing Date: Nov 1
Presented: Announcement in March

Donald Smiley Prize
Canadian Political Science Association (CPSA)
260 Dalhousie St, Suite 204, Ottawa, ON K1N 7E4, Canada
Tel: 613-562-1202 *Fax:* 613-241-0019
E-mail: cpsaprizes@cpsa-acsp.ca; cpsa-acsp@cpsa-acsp.ca
Web Site: www.cpsa-acsp.ca
Key Personnel
Exec Dir: Silvina Danesi
Admin: C Ngako Woktcheu
Established: 1995
Awarded to the author(s) of the best book published in English or in French in the field relating to the study of government & politics in Canada. To be eligible, a book may be single-authored or multi-authored. Single-authored: author must be a member of the CPSA in the year the book is considered for the prize. Multi-authored: at least one of the authors must be a member of the CPSA in the year the book is considered for the prize. The book must have a copyright date of the year prior to the award year.
Award: Commemorative plaque & receive/share the set of books submitted to the CPSA office
Closing Date: Dec
Presented: CPSA Annual Conference

Helen C Smith Memorial Award
Texas Institute of Letters (TIL)
PO Box 130294, Spring, TX 77393
Web Site: texasinstituteofletters.org
Key Personnel
Pres: David Bowles *E-mail:* president@texasinstituteofletters.org
VP: Chris Barton
Secy: Kathryn Jones *E-mail:* secretary@texasinstituteofletters.org
Treas: Cliff Hudder
Award for the first best book of poetry by a poet with a Texas association. The poet must have been born in Texas or have lived in Texas for at least 5 consecutive years at some time. See web site for guidelines.
Award: $1,200
Closing Date: Jan
Presented: TIL Annual Meeting & Awards Ceremony, Spring

The Jean Kennedy Smith VSA Playwright Discovery Award
VSA
Affiliate of The John F Kennedy Center for the Performing Arts
2700 "F" St NW, Washington, DC 20566
Tel: 202-416-8898 *Fax:* 202-416-4840
E-mail: vsainfo@kennedy-center.org
Web Site: www.kennedy-center.org/education/opportunities-for-artists/competitions-and-commissions
Key Personnel
VSA Progs: Katharine Mead *Tel:* 202-416-8823 *E-mail:* kmead@kennedy-center.org
Established: 1984
Students with disabilities, ages 11 to 18, are invited to submit works written for performance: plays, spoken word poetry, musicals, scripts for video or film & more. Winners receive professional development opportunities provided by the Kennedy Center in Washington, DC.
Award: Attend performance of their script at JFK Center, scholarship funds
Closing Date: March 10
Presented: The John F Kennedy Center for Performing Arts, Washington, DC

AWARDS, PRIZE CONTESTS, FELLOWSHIPS & GRANTS

The Jeffrey E Smith Editors' Prize
The Missouri Review
357 McReynolds Hall, University of Missouri, Columbia, MO 65211
Tel: 573-882-4474 *Toll Free Tel:* 800-949-2505
Fax: 573-884-4671
E-mail: question@moreview.com; contest_question@moreview.com
Web Site: www.missourireview.com/contests/jeffrey-e-smith-editors-prize
Key Personnel
Mng Ed: Marc McKee
Established: 1991
Awarded in 3 genres: fiction, nonfiction & poetry. Submit one piece of fiction or nonfiction up to 8,500 words or any number of poems up to 10 pages. Entries must be previously unpublished. Submit online or by mail. Standard entry fee: $25, includes 1-year digital subscription to Missouri Review & digital copy of *Strange Encounters*; All Access entry fee: $30, includes in addition access to last 10 years of digital issues & audio recordings of each digital issue.
Award: $5,000 each genre, publication & invitation to reception & reading in their honor
Closing Date: Oct 1
Presented: Spring

Kay Snow Writing Contest
Willamette Writers
5331 SW Macadam Ave, Suite 258, PMB 215, Portland, OR 97239
Tel: 971-200-5385
E-mail: wilwrite@willamettewriters.org
Web Site: willamettewriters.org/kay-snow-writing-contest
Key Personnel
Pres: Gail Pasternack
Exec Dir: Kate Ristau
Established: 1971
Writing competition in 5 categories: Fiction; creative nonfiction; poetry; drama & screenplay; students in 2 grade divisions, 1-6 & 7-12.
Award: Winners in fiction, nonfiction, poetry & screenplay: $100 (1st prize), $50 (2nd prize), $25 (3rd prize). Also includes 1-day admission to Willamette Writers Conference; Winners in student categories in each of 2 grade divisions: $50 (1st prize), $20 (2nd prize), $10 (3rd prize)
Presented: Willamette Writers Conference, Aug

The Richard Snyder Memorial Publication Prize
The Ashland Poetry Press
Bixler Center for the Humanities, Ashland University, 401 College Ave, Ashland, OH 44805
E-mail: app@ashland.edu
Web Site: www.ashlandpoetrypress.com/guidelines/snyder-prize
Key Personnel
Dir & Ed: Chuck Carlisle
Poetry book series honoring the memory of Richard Snyder. Ms of original collection of poems from 48 to 96 pages, one poem per page, single sided, single spaced to be submitted electronically through Submittable. Entry fee: $27 (to cover credit card fees). See web site for additional guidelines.
Award: $1,000 plus publication in a paperback edition & 50 copies of the published book (in lieu of royalties)

Anthony Veasna So Fiction Prize
n+1 Foundation Inc
Cadman Plaza Sta, PO Box 26428, Brooklyn, NY 11202
E-mail: editors@nplusonemag.com; subs@nplusonemag.com (submission queries); submissions@nplusonemag.com
Web Site: www.nplusonemag.com/awards
Key Personnel
Publr: Mark Krotov
Exec Dir: Dayna Tortorici
Mng Ed: Tess Edmonson
Established: 2021
Granted to an outstanding fiction writer whose work has appeared in *n+1* magazine or nplusonemag.com, the magazine's online supplement.
Award: $5,000

The Society of Midland Authors Awards
The Society of Midland Authors (SMA)
PO Box 10419, Chicago, IL 60610
Web Site: midlandauthors.org
Established: 1915
Juried award offers prizes in each of 6 literary categories: Adult fiction, adult nonfiction, biography/memoir, poetry, children's fiction & children's nonfiction. Awarded to authors in any of the Midland states: Illinois, Indiana, Iowa, Kansas, Michigan, Minnesota, Missouri, Nebraska, North Dakota, Ohio, South Dakota & Wisconsin. Entry fee: $25. See web site for guidelines & submission requirements.
Award: $500 & recognition award
Closing Date: Jan
Presented: Chicago, IL, 2nd Tuesday in May

The Society of Southwestern Authors Writing Contest
The Society of Southwestern Authors (SSA)
PO Box 30355, Tucson, AZ 85751-0355
E-mail: contest@ssa-az.org
Web Site: www.ssa-az.org/contest.htm
Key Personnel
Pres: Mary Ann Carman *E-mail:* macarman6@gmail.com
VP: Sharon Lashinger *E-mail:* srlashinger@hotmail.com
Treas: David Gilmore *E-mail:* lacroixpublishing@gmail.com
Recording Secy: Solomon Cantanio *E-mail:* scantanio@gmail.com
Established: 1972
SSA members & others can submit their entries. Awards for poetry (up to 80 lines), short story & memoir (up to 2,500 words) & novel 1st chapter (up to 5,000 words). See web site for entry form. Entry fee: $30.
Award: $200 (1st prize), $100 (2nd prize), $50 (3rd prize)
Closing Date: July
Presented: Awards Forum, Oct

Sophie Kerr Prize
Washington College
c/o College Relations Off, 300 Washington Ave, Chestertown, MD 21620
Tel: 410-778-2800 *Toll Free Tel:* 800-422-1782
Fax: 410-810-7150
Web Site: www.washcoll.edu
Key Personnel
Dir, Communs: Marcia Landskroener *Tel:* 410-778-7797 *E-mail:* mlandskroener2@washcoll.edu
Established: 1968
Literary award presented to a graduating senior. Only open to undergraduates of Washington College.
Award: $65,000
Closing Date: April
Presented: Washington College Commencement, Chestertown, MD, May

Raymond Souster Award
The League of Canadian Poets
2 Carlton St, Suite 1519, Toronto, ON M5B 1J3, Canada
Tel: 416-504-1657
E-mail: admin@poets.ca
Web Site: poets.ca/awards/souster

ASSOCIATIONS, EVENTS

Key Personnel
Exec Dir: Lesley Fletcher *E-mail:* lesley@poets.ca
Artistic Programming Dir: Nic Brewer *E-mail:* nicole@poets.ca
Admin & Communs Coord: Caitlin Lapena *E-mail:* caitlin@poets.ca
Established: 2013
To honor a book of poetry by a League of Canadian Poets member. Authors must be Canadian citizens or permanent residents. Submitted titles must be at least 48 pages in length & have 1 author (translators are not eligible). Chapbooks & self-published books are not eligible. Submission fee: $25 per title. See web site for full eligibility guidelines.
Award: $2,000
Presented: May

Southeast Review's Gearhart Poetry Contest
The Southeast Review
Florida State University, Dept of English, Tallahassee, FL 32306
E-mail: southeastreview@gmail.com
Web Site: www.southeastreview.org/writing-contests
Key Personnel
Ed-in-Chief: Zach Linge
Asst Ed: Diamond Forde
Established: 1996
Awarded for best poem. $16 entry fee for up to 3 poems, no more than 10 pages total.
Award: $500 & publication in Spring issue
Closing Date: April 1
Presented: Summer

The Southern Book Prize
Southern Independent Booksellers Alliance (SIBA)
51 Pleasant Ridge Dr, Asheville, NC 28805
Tel: 803-994-9530 *Fax:* 309-410-0211
E-mail: siba@sibaweb.com
Web Site: www.sibaweb.com/siba-book-award
Key Personnel
Exec Dir: Linda-Marie Barrett *E-mail:* lindamarie@sibaweb.com
Nominations accepted from SIBA member booksellers. Books must be Southern in nature, or by a Southern author & published in the previous calendar year.
Presented: Winners announced on Valentine's Day

Southern Books Competition
Southeastern Library Association
PO Box 30703, Savannah, GA 31410
Tel: 912-999-7979
E-mail: selaadminservices@selaonline.org
Web Site: selaonline.org
Key Personnel
Chmn: Camille McCutcheon
Admin Servs: Dr Gordon N Baker *E-mail:* gordonbaker@clayton.edu
Established: 1952
Recognition for excellence in bookmaking awarded biennially, in even-numbered years, for a title published during the previous 2 years. Trade publishers, university presses, specialty publishers & private presses located in Alabama, Arkansas, Florida, Georgia, Kentucky, Louisiana, Mississippi, North Carolina, South Carolina, Tennessee, Virginia, West Virginia or Puerto Rico are eligible to enter the competition. Awards are given based on design, typography & quality of production. Winners are displayed at SELA Conference & in a traveling exhibit available to institutions & organizations. It has been borrowed throughout the South, Canada, Scandinavia, Russia & South Africa.
Award: Published recognition list. Rotating & permanent display of winning books
Presented: SELA Conference, Oct

Southern Playwrights Competition
Jacksonville State University, Dept of English
700 Pelham Rd N, Jacksonville, AL 36265-1602
Tel: 256-782-5412
Web Site: www.jsu.edu/english/southpla.html
Key Personnel
Coord: Joy Maloney *E-mail:* jmaloney@jsu.edu
Established: 1988
Identify & encourage the best of Southern playwriting. Entries accepted beginning September 15.
Award: $1,000 honorarium & possible production of winning entry
Closing Date: Jan 15

Southern Studies Fellowship in Arts & Letters
Hub City Writers Project
186 W Main St, Spartanburg, SC 29306
Tel: 864-577-9349
E-mail: info@hubcity.org
Web Site: southernstudiesfellowship.org
Key Personnel
Exec Dir & Publr: Meg Reid *E-mail:* meg@hubcity.org
Immersive fellowship focused on the culture of the American South. Program brings 1 early-career artist & 1 early-career writer to Spartanburg, SC for a 9-month fellowship of research, creativity, teaching & travel, culminating in a collaborative project informed by the region. Fellowship is for early-career artists, writers, journalists & humanities scholars within 5 years of their latest degree. Apply online.
Other Sponsor(s): Chapman Cultural Center; Watson-Brown Foundation
Award: 9-month fellowship, including housing & monthly stipend; funding for 6-10 days of travel to conduct research at cultural & educational institutions in the southern region
Closing Date: April 30
Presented: June

Terry Southern Prize
The Paris Review Foundation
544 W 27 St, New York, NY 10001
Tel: 212-343-1333
E-mail: queries@theparisreview.org
Web Site: www.theparisreview.org
Key Personnel
Mng Ed: Hasan Altaf
Established: 2010
Honors "humor, wit & sprezzatura" in work from either *The Paris Review* or *The Paris Review Daily*.
Award: $5,000
Presented: Spring Revel

Sovereign Award for Outstanding Writing
The Jockey Club of Canada
Woodbine Sales Pavilion, 555 Rexdale Blvd, Toronto, ON M9W 5L2, Canada
Mailing Address: PO Box 66, Sta B, Toronto, ON M9W 5K9, Canada
Tel: 416-675-7756 *Fax:* 416-675-6378
E-mail: jockeyclubcanada@gmail.com
Web Site: www.jockeyclubcanada.com
Key Personnel
Gen Mgr: Megan Allan
Established: 1975
Must be submitted by the author & be of significant Canadian Thoroughbred racing or breeding content. The piece must have appeared for the first time in a public medium recognized by The Jockey Club of Canada. Works of fiction are not eligible. The Jockey Club of Canada has the right to refuse any submission. No entry fee. See guidelines on web site.
Award: Bronze statue of Saint Simon
Closing Date: Dec 31
Presented: Annual Sovereign Awards Ceremony, Ontario, CN, Date TBD upon confirmation of the first day of racing for that calendar year

Spain-USA Foundation Translation Award
American Literary Translators Association (ALTA)
University of Arizona, Esquire Bldg, No 205, 1230 N Park Ave, Tucson, AZ 85721
Tel: 520-621-1757
E-mail: info@literarytranslators.org
Web Site: literarytranslators.org/awards/spain-usa-award
Key Personnel
Communs & Awards Mgr: Rachael Daum
Tel: 413-200-0459 *E-mail:* rachaeldaum@literarytranslators.org
Prog Dir: Kelsi Vanada *E-mail:* kelsi@literarytranslators.org
Established: 2022
Recognizes translations into English of literary prose works written originally by authors of Spanish (Spain) nationality. Source language of the original text may be Spanish, Catalan, Basque or Galician. Author need not be living for the work to be eligible. The book may be translated by a translator based anywhere in the world, individually or in a team of up to 4 co-translators. Submissions accepted beginning in mid-January each year via Submittable only.
Other Sponsor(s): Spain-USA Foundation
Award: $5,000
Closing Date: Mid-April
Presented: ATLA Annual Conference

Spark Award
Society of Children's Book Writers & Illustrators (SCBWI)
6363 Wilshire Blvd, Suite 425, Los Angeles, CA 90048
Tel: 323-782-1010
E-mail: grants@scbwi.org; info@scbwi.org
Web Site: www.scbwi.org
Key Personnel
Exec Dir: Sarah Baker
Assoc Dir, Digital Content & Awards: Sarah Diamond
Assoc Mgr, Awards & Pubns: Danielle Monique
Established: 2013
Award recognizing excellence in a children's book published through a non-traditional publishing route. One winner & up to 2 Honor Book recipients will be chosen in 2 categories: Books for older readers & illustrated books. See web site for full submission guidelines.
Award: Commemorative plaque, Spark Seal to display on book & other opportunities
Closing Date: Dec 19
Presented: March

SPD Design Awards
The Society of Publication Designers Inc
27 Union Sq W, Suite 207, New York, NY 10003
Tel: 212-223-3332
E-mail: mail@spd.org
Web Site: www.spd.org
Key Personnel
Exec Dir: Keisha Dean
Established: 1965
Awards for continuing excellence in the field of publication design. Approximately 100 categories in design, photography & illustration. Winners include: Magazine of the Year, Brand of the Year, App of the Year, Website of the Year, Video of the Year, Entire Issue, Redesign, Cover, Spread/Single Page & Story.
Presented: Awards Gala, June

The Anne Spencer Memorial
The Poetry Society of Virginia (PSV)
PO Box 36128, North Chesterfield, VA 23235-3533
E-mail: contest@poetrysocietyofvirginia.org; info@poetryvirginia.org
Web Site: www.poetrysocietyofvirginia.org
Key Personnel
Pres: Cherryl T Cooley
E-mail: poetrysocietypresident@gmail.com
Any form. Subject: Overcoming adversity, 64 line limit. Submit 1 copy of the poem with no identifying information but put the category in the upper right-hand-side, along with a notation as to whether you are a member of PSV (does not matter if you are a lifetime member or just joined for the contest). Submit a cover letter/page that contains the category, the name of the poem, your name & address, phone number & e-mail address. Entries will not be returned. Entry fee: Free to membs, $5 nonmembs.
Award: $50 (1st prize), $30 (2nd prize), $20 (3rd prize)

Spur Awards
Western Writers of America Inc (WWA)
271 CR 219, Encampment, WY 82325
Tel: 307-329-8942
Web Site: westernwriters.org/spur-awards
Key Personnel
Pres: Chris Enss *E-mail:* gvcenss@aol.com
Exec Dir & Secy-Treas: Candy Moulton
E-mail: wwa.moulton@gmail.com
Established: 1953
Western fiction/nonfiction (various categories).
Award: Plaques & recognition
Closing Date: Oct 1 (material published Jan 1-Aug 31), Jan 15 (material published Sept 1-Dec 31)
Presented: Annual Convention, June

The Edna Staebler Award for Creative Non-Fiction
Wilfrid Laurier University
Office of the Dean, Faculty of Arts, 75 University Ave W, Waterloo, ON N2L 3C5, Canada
Tel: 519-884-1970 (ext 3361)
E-mail: staebleraward@wlu.ca
Web Site: wlu.ca/staebleraward
Key Personnel
Sr Admin Offr: Joan Leach *Tel:* 519-884-0710 ext 3364 *E-mail:* jleach@wlu.ca
Sr Admin Asst to Dean of Arts: Cathy Mahler
Tel: 519-884-0710 ext 3361 *E-mail:* cmahler@wlu.ca
Established: 1991
Literary award for a first or second published book of creative nonfiction with a Canadian locale +/or significance published in the previous calendar year. Open to works & distinguished by first-hand research, well-crafted interpretive writing & creative use of language or approach to the subject matter. Writer must be Canadian. Award is open to print books & ebooks.
Award: $10,000
Presented: Wilfrid Laurier University

Stanley Drama Award
Wagner College
One Campus Rd, Staten Island, NY 10301
Tel: 718-390-3223 *Fax:* 718-390-3323
Web Site: wagner.edu/theatre/stanley-drama
Key Personnel
Assoc Professor: Todd Alan Price *E-mail:* todd.price@wagner.edu
Established: 1957
Award given for original full-length play or musical which has not been professionally produced or received trade book publication. Writers of musicals are urged to submit music on tape or CD as well as books & lyrics. Consideration will also be given to a series of 2 or 3 thematically related one-act plays. Scripts must be accompanied by a SASE. Former winners are not eligible to compete. Applications are obtained by sending SASE or online. A reading fee of $30 must accompany submission.
Award: $2,000
Closing Date: Oct 31
Presented: April

AWARDS, PRIZE CONTESTS, FELLOWSHIPS & GRANTS

STAR Award
Women's Fiction Writers Association (WFWA)
PO Box 190, Jefferson, OR 97352
E-mail: staraward@womenfictionwriters.org
Web Site: wfwa.memberclicks.net/star-award
Key Personnel
Pres: Jacki Kelly *E-mail:* president@womensfictionwriters.org
VP, Communs: Sharon Ritchey
VP, Fin & Treas: Kathy Dodson
E-mail: treasurer@womensfictionwriters.org
VP, Progs: Kristi Leonard
Secy: Michele Montgomery *E-mail:* secretary@womensfictionwriters.org
Events Dir: Jami Sheets
Awards for published women's fiction authors. Work must be book-length (60,000 words or more), have an ISBN & have a copyright date in the calendar year prior to the award year. Two categories: General & outstanding debut. Contest is limited to the first 50 entries in each category. Entry fee: $40 membs, $50 nonmembs. See web site for entry submission details & complete eligibility requirements.
Award: Trophy, digital badge for web site & stickers for book covers
Closing Date: Jan 30
Presented: Annual WFWA Retreat, Sept

Agnes Lynch Starrett Poetry Prize
University of Pittsburgh Press
7500 Thomas Blvd, Pittsburgh, PA 15260
Tel: 412-383-2456 *Fax:* 412-383-2466
E-mail: info@upress.pitt.edu
Web Site: upittpress.org/prize/agnes-lynch-starrett-poetry-prize/; www.upress.pitt.edu
Key Personnel
Dir: Peter W Kracht *E-mail:* pkracht@upress.pitt.edu
Opers Admin: Eileen O'Malley
E-mail: eomalley@upress.pitt.edu
Established: 1981
Open to any poet who has not had a full-length book previously published. Submit typed 48-100 page poetry mss on white paper with SASE & check or money order of $25 for each ms submitted. See web site for complete rules.
Award: $5,000 & publication
Closing Date: March 1-April 30 (postmark)
Presented: Pittsburgh, PA, Autumn

Stegner Fellowship
Stanford University Creative Writing Program
Stanford University, Dept of English, Stanford, CA 94305-2087
Tel: 650-723-0011
E-mail: stegnerfellowship@stanford.edu
Web Site: creativewriting.stanford.edu
Key Personnel
Prog Coord: Ose Jackson
Residence required for 2 years at Stanford beginning Autumn quarter each year.
Award: $43,000, required tuition, fees & health insurance
Closing Date: Dec 1

Jean Stein Book Award, see PEN/Jean Stein Book Award

Steinberg Memorial Essay Prize
Fourth Genre
Michigan State University Press, 1405 S Harrison Rd, Suite 25, East Lansing, MI 48823
E-mail: 4thgenre@gmail.com
Web Site: duotrope.com/listing/8258/fourth-genre-steinberg-memorial-essay (submissions)
Prize for an essay under 6,000 words. Multiple submissions are accepted. Entry fee: $20. Online submissions via Duotrope beginning January 1.
Award: $1,000 & publication in following year's Spring issue
Closing Date: March 15
Presented: Late Spring

Stephan G Stephansson Award for Poetry
Writers' Guild of Alberta
11759 Groat Rd NW, Edmonton, AB T5M 3K6, Canada
Tel: 780-422-8174 *Toll Free Tel:* 800-665-5354 (AB only)
E-mail: mail@writersguild.ab.ca
Web Site: writersguild.ca
Key Personnel
Exec Dir: Giorgia Severini *E-mail:* gseverini@writersguild.ab.ca
Communs & Partnerships Coord: Ellen Kartz
E-mail: ellen.kartz@writersguild.ab.ca
Memb Servs Coord: Mike Maguire
Prog & Opers Coord: Ashley Mann
E-mail: ashley.mann@writersguild.ab.ca
Progs & Events Coord: Jason Norman
E-mail: jason.norman@writersguild.ab.ca
Proj Asst: Sadie MacGillivray *E-mail:* sadie.macgillivray@writersguild.ab.ca
Established: 1982
Awarded to an author who is a resident of Alberta.
Award: $1,500 plus leather-bound copy of book
Closing Date: Dec 31
Presented: Alberta Book Awards Gala, AB, CN
Branch Office(s)
223 12 Ave SW, No 204, Calgary, AB T2R 0G9, Canada, Prog & Conference Coord: Dorothy Bentley *Tel:* 403-875-8058 *E-mail:* dorothy.bentley@writersguild.ab.ca

John Steptoe Award for New Talent, see Coretta Scott King - John Steptoe Award for New Talent

Wallace Stevens Award
The Academy of American Poets Inc
75 Maiden Lane, Suite 901, New York, NY 10038
Tel: 212-274-0343
E-mail: awards@poets.org
Web Site: poets.org/academy-american-poets/prizes/wallace-stevens-award
Key Personnel
Pres & Exec Dir: Ricardo Alberto Maldonado
VP, Digital Engagement & Content: Jeff Gleaves
Ad & Mktg Dir: Michelle Campagna
Dir, Donor Rel: Molly Walsh
Dir, Progs: Nikay Paredes
Established: 1994
Recognizes outstanding & proven mastery in the art of poetry. Recipients are chosen by the Academy of American Poets Board of Chancellors. No applications are accepted.
Award: $100,000 stipend

Bram Stoker Awards®
Horror Writers Association (HWA)
PO Box 56687, Sherman Oaks, CA 91413
Tel: 818-220-3965
E-mail: stokerchair@horror.org
Web Site: www.thebramstokerawards.com; horror.org
Key Personnel
Award Co-Chair: James Chambers; Jessica Landry
Established: 1988
Twelve award categories: Novel, first novel, short fiction, long fiction, young adult, fiction collection, poetry collection, anthology, screenplay, graphic novel, nonfiction & short nonfiction.
Closing Date: Nov 30 (works to jury), Dec 31 (works published Dec 1-31); Members may recommend works for consideration through Jan 15 of the following year
Presented: HWA Annual Convention, StokerCon

ASSOCIATIONS, EVENTS

Stone Award for Lifetime Literary Achievement
Oregon State University
College of Liberal Arts, 214 Bexell Hall, Corvalis, OR 97331
Tel: 541-737-0561
Web Site: liberalarts.oregonstate.edu/stone-award
Honors a major American author who has created a body of critically acclaimed literary work & has been a dedicated mentor to succeeding generations of young writers. Awarded biennially in even-numbered years.
Other Sponsor(s): Patrick F & Vicki Stone
Award: $20,000

Stonewall Book Awards
Rainbow Round Table (RRT)
Unit of The American Library Association (ALA)
225 N Michigan Ave, Suite 1300, Chicago, IL 60601
Tel: 312-944-6780 *Toll Free Tel:* 800-545-2433
Fax: 312-440-9374
E-mail: diversity@ala.org; ala@ala.org
Web Site: www.ala.org/rt/rrt/award/stonewall; www.ala.org/rt/rrt; www.ala.org
Key Personnel
Staff Liaison: Amber Hayes
Established: 1971
Three awards presented annually to honor books of exceptional merit relating to the LGBTQIA+ experience: Barbara Gittings Literature Award; Israel Fishman Nonfiction Award; Mike Morgan & Larry Romans Children's & Young Adult Literature Award. Award is announced in January.
Award: $1,000 & commemorative plaque
Closing Date: Dec 31
Presented: ALA Annual Conference & Exhibition, June

Story Monsters Approved! Program
Story Monsters LLC
4696 W Tyson St, Chandler, AZ 85226-2903
Tel: 480-940-8182 *Fax:* 480-940-8787
Web Site: www.StoryMonstersBookAwards.com/sma-details
Key Personnel
Pres: Linda F Radke *E-mail:* Linda@StoryMonsters.com
Designation to recognize & honor accomplished authors in the field of children's literature, as well as children's products that inspire, inform, teach, or entertain. Each honoree gains permission to use the seal on book covers, web site, or marketing materials, Story Monsters Book Awards contest winners page listing, a mention on social media & in Book Briefs blog, along with free 1-year subscription.
All titles are considered for the Book of the Year. One book is chosen for this honor & must be outstanding in content, readability, message & overall production.
Program is open to printed children's books published in any calendar year or any products for children. Books entered must be printed in English. Authors age 17 & younger must have parent or guardian permission to enter. Non-refundable entry fee: $65 for 1 title in 1 category.
Award: $500 (grand prize), certificate, 100 seals, digital award seal & 1-hour marketing consulting session with Linda F Radke; 1st prize winners in all categories are put into $100 prize drawing & receive digital certificate & award seal
Closing Date: Nov 1 (early), Feb 1 (final)

Story Monsters® Book Awards
Story Monsters LLC
4696 W Tyson St, Chandler, AZ 85226-2903
Tel: 480-940-8182 *Fax:* 480-940-8787
E-mail: info@StoryMonsters.com
Web Site: www.StoryMonstersBookAwards.com

Key Personnel
Pres: Linda F Radke *E-mail:* Linda@StoryMonsters.com
Established: 2009
The Royal Dragonfly Book Awards honor published authors of all types of literature—fiction & nonfiction—in 68 categories. Entry fees: $60 per category (on or before August 2), $65 per category (after August 4).
The Purple Dragonfly Book Awards honor accomplished authors in the field of children's literature. 54 subject categories. Entry fees: $60 per category (on or before March 1), $65 per category (after March 1).
The awards contests are open to books published in any calendar year & in any country as long as they are available for purchase. Books entered must be printed in English. Provided they adhere to the above criteria, we accept traditionally published, partnership published & self-published books.
Printed Books: Mail one (1) copy of each book for each category in which it is entered. Along with the books, send one (1) printed copy of the e-mail confirmation per title for each category in which the book is entered. When submitting more than one book, all entries can be sent in the same envelope. Mail entries to: Cristy Bertini, Attn: Royal Dragonfly Book Awards (or Purple Dragonfly Book Awards), 1271 Turkey St, Hardwick, MA 01082.
Ebooks: E-mail one (1) electronic copy of the book & a copy of the e-mail confirmation to ebookentry@storymonsters.com with "Royal Dragonfly Book Awards" or "Purple Dragonfly Book Awards: as the subject.
Award: Grand prize winner $500, certificate, 100 seals & digital award seal; 1st place winners receive digital certificate & award seal & go in drawing for $100 (1 winner); 2nd place winners receive digital certificate & award seal; honorable mentions receive digital certificate & award seal
Closing Date: Purple Dragonfly: March 1 (early), May 3 (final); Royal Dragonfly: Aug 2 (early), Oct 1 (final)
Presented: Announced last weekend of Nov

The Story Prize
41 Watchung Plaza, No 384, Montclair, NJ 07042
Tel: 973-932-0324
E-mail: info@thestoryprize.org
Web Site: www.thestoryprize.org
Key Personnel
Dir: Larry Dark *E-mail:* ldark@thestoryprize.org
Established: 2004
Award honoring the author of an outstanding collection of short fiction. Entry fee: $75.
Award: $20,000, $5,000 (runners up)
Closing Date: July 15 (books published Jan-June), Nov 15 (books published July-Dec)
Presented: The New School, 66 W 12 St, New York, NY, March

The Story Prize Spotlight Award
The Story Prize
41 Watchung Plaza, No 384, Montclair, NJ 07042
Tel: 973-932-0324
E-mail: info@thestoryprize.org
Web Site: www.thestoryprize.org
Key Personnel
Dir: Larry Dark *E-mail:* ldark@thestoryprize.org
Awarded for a short story collection of exceptional merit.
Award: $1,000
Closing Date: July 15 (books published Jan-June), Nov 15 (books published July-Dec)
Presented: March

Elizabeth Matchett Stover Memorial Award
Southwest Review
PO Box 750374, Dallas, TX 75275-0374
Fax: 214-768-1408
E-mail: swr@mail.smu.edu
Web Site: southwestreview.com
Key Personnel
Ed-in-Chief: Greg Brownderville
Established: 1978
Awarded to the author of the best poem or group of poems published in the *Southwest Review* during the preceding year.
Award: $300

Lucien Stryk Asian Translation Prize
American Literary Translators Association (ALTA)
University of Arizona, Esquire Bldg, No 205, 1230 N Park Ave, Tucson, AZ 85721
Tel: 520-621-1757
E-mail: info@literarytranslators.org
Web Site: literarytranslators.org/awards/lucien-stryk-prize
Key Personnel
Communs & Awards Mgr: Rachael Daum
Tel: 413-200-0459 *E-mail:* rachaeldaum@literarytranslators.org
Prog Dir: Kelsi Vanada *E-mail:* kelsi@literarytranslators.org
Established: 2009
Recognizes the importance of Asian translation for international literature & to promote the translation of Asian works into English. Both translators & publishers are invited to submit titles. Works must be book-length translations into English of poetry or source texts from, but not solely commentaries on, Zen Buddhism; translations from Chinese, Hindi, Japanese, Kannada, Korean, Sanskrit, Tamil, Thai, or Vietnamese into English; published in the previous calendar year. Submissions accepted beginning in January each year via Submittable only.
Award: $6,000
Closing Date: Mid-April
Presented: ALTA Annual Conference

Ned Stuckey-French Nonfiction Contest
The Southeast Review
Florida State University, Dept of English, Tallahassee, FL 32306
E-mail: southeastreview@gmail.com
Web Site: www.southeastreview.org/writing-contests
Key Personnel
Ed-in-Chief: Zach Linge
Asst Ed: Diamond Forde
Seeks work of nonfiction that prods & pressures expectations; that speaks to the personal against the powerful & most importantly, that prioritizes soul, heart & service. Send one essay, no more than 10 pages total, accompanied by a $16 reading fee for mailed or online submissions.
Award: $500 & publication in Spring issue
Closing Date: March

Jessamy Stursberg Poetry Prize for Canadian Youth
The League of Canadian Poets
2 Carlton St, Suite 1519, Toronto, ON M5B 1J3, Canada
Tel: 416-504-1657
E-mail: info@poets.ca; admin@poets.ca
Web Site: poets.ca
Key Personnel
Exec Dir: Lesley Fletcher *E-mail:* lesley@poets.ca
Artistic Programming Dir: Nic Brewer
E-mail: nicole@poets.ca
Admin & Communs Coord: Caitlin Lapena
E-mail: caitlin@poets.ca
Established: 1995
Seeking poems by young poets across the country. Two age categories with 3 prizes awarded in both: Junior (grades 7-9) & Senior (grades 10-12).
Award: $400 (1st place), $350 (2nd place), $300 (3rd place); selected poems will also be featured in a special edition League of Canadian Poets chapbook for nationwide distribution
Closing Date: April 30

Subaru Prize for Excellence in Science Books, see AAAS/Subaru Prize for Excellence in Science Books

Sudden Fiction Contest
Berkeley Fiction Review
c/o ASUC Publications, Univ of California, 10-B Eshleman Hall, Berkeley, CA 94720-4500
E-mail: berkeleyfictionreview@gmail.com
Web Site: berkeleyfictionreview.org
Key Personnel
Mng Ed: Alex Jimenez; Regina Lim; Madelyn Peterson; Aaron Saliman
All entries must be 1,000 words or less; typed, double-spaced, with a 12-point font; include cover letter & e-mail only. Entry fee: $5 ($4 each additional story).
Award: $150 (1st place), $50 (2nd place), $25 (3rd place) & publication in upcoming newsletter

Ronald Sukenick Innovative Fiction Contest, see The FC2 Ronald Sukenick Innovative Fiction Contest

Hollis Summers Poetry Prize
Ohio University Press
Alden Library, Suite 101, 30 Park Place, Athens, OH 45701-2909
Tel: 740-593-1154
Web Site: www.ohioswallow.com/poetry_prize; ohiouniversitypress.submittable.com/submit (online submissions)
Key Personnel
Dir & Prodn Mgr: Beth Pratt *Tel:* 740-593-1162
E-mail: prattb@ohio.edu
Established: 1997
This competition invites writers to submit unpublished collections of original poems. Individual collections must be the work of a single author. Translations are not accepted. Submit a ms of 60-95 pages of a poetry collection. Entry fee: $30.
Award: $1,000 & publication
Closing Date: Dec 1

Sunburst Award for Excellence in Canadian Literature of the Fantastic
The Sunburst Award Society
2 Farm Greenway, Toronto, ON M3A 3M2, Canada
E-mail: secretary@sunburstaward.org
Web Site: www.sunburstaward.org
Juried award which celebrates exceptional writing in 3 categories: adult, young adult & short story. The awards are presented to the best Canadian speculative fiction novel, book-length collection, or short story published any time during the previous calendar year. See web site for eligibility criteria & submissions info.
Award: $1,000 each adult & young adult, $500 short story, plus Sunburst medallion
Closing Date: Jan 31
Presented: Fall

Supporting Diverse Voices: Book Proposal Development Grants
Princeton University Press
41 William St, Princeton, NJ 08540-5237
Tel: 609-258-4900
E-mail: info@press.princeton.edu
Web Site: press.princeton.edu/book-proposal-development-grants

Key Personnel
Dir: Christie Henry *E-mail:* christie_henry@press.princeton.edu
Grants offer direct support & coaching to scholarly authors preparing to draft a book proposal. Opportunity is to open to previously published & first-time authors alike. Grants are administered twice during the calendar year, with particular disciplines & groups specified for eligibility each cycle.
Closing Date: April & Sept

Sydney Taylor Book Award
Association of Jewish Libraries Inc (AJL)
Affiliate of The American Library Association (ALA)
PO Box 1118, Teaneck, NJ 07666
Tel: 201-371-3255
E-mail: sydneytaylorbookaward@jewishlibraries.org; info@jewishlibraries.org
Web Site: jewishlibraries.org/sydney_taylor_book_award
Key Personnel
Pres: Michelle Margolis
Comm Chair: Martha Simpson
Established: 1968
Literary content for outstanding children's books in field of Jewish literature. Three categories of prizes: Picture books, middle grade, young adult.
Award: Gold medals; honor books receive silver medals
Closing Date: Nov 30
Presented: AJL Annual Convention, June

Sydney Taylor Manuscript Award
Association of Jewish Libraries Inc (AJL)
Affiliate of The American Library Association (ALA)
204 Park St, Montclair, NJ 07042
Tel: 201-371-3255
E-mail: info@jewishlibraries.org
Web Site: jewishlibraries.org
Key Personnel
Pres: Michelle Margolis
Chpn: Aileen Grossberg *E-mail:* stmacajl@aol.com
Established: 1985
Award to encourage outstanding Jewish themed fiction written by an unpublished author. Story will appeal to all children ages 8-13 & to help launch new children's writers in their careers.
Award: $1,000
Closing Date: Sept 30
Presented: AJL Annual Convention, June

Charles S Sydnor Award
Southern Historical Association (SHA)
University of Georgia, Dept of History, Athens, GA 30602-1602
Tel: 706-542-8848
Web Site: thesha.org/sydnor
Key Personnel
Secy/Treas: Dr Stephen Berry *E-mail:* berrys@thesha.org
Established: 1956
Awarded, in even-numbered years, for the most distinguished book in southern history published in odd-numbered years.
Award: Cash
Closing Date: March 1
Presented: Annual Meeting, Fall

TAA Council of Fellows
Textbook & Academic Authors Association (TAA)
PO Box 367, Fountain City, WI 54629
E-mail: info@taaonline.net
Web Site: www.taaonline.net/council-of-fellows
Key Personnel
Exec Dir: Michael Spinella *Tel:* 973-943-0501
  E-mail: michael.spinella@taaonline.net
Dir, Publg & Opers: Kim Pawlak *Tel:* 507-459-1363 *E-mail:* kim.pawlak@taaonline.net
Dir, Instl Memberships & Meetings: Maureen Foerster *Tel:* 530-864-3538 *E-mail:* maureen.foerster@taaonline.net
Membership Mktg Mgr: Eric Schmieder *Tel:* 919-437-0241 *E-mail:* eric.schmieder@taaonline.net
Membership Coord: Bekky Murphy *Tel:* 608-567-9060 *E-mail:* bekky.murphy@taaonline.net
Honors distinguished authors who have a long record of successful publishing. Any author whose textbook or other instructional materials have established his/her presence in the market place over time, who has been innovative in the presentation of material, is qualified for nomination. Members are chosen by a TAA Selection Committee based on a set of criteria which includes their: level of participation in TAA activities; teaching excellence; quality & quantity of textbooks (if textbook authors); quality & quantity of professional journal articles, monographs & edited books (if academic authors).
Closing Date: Feb

The Tamaqua Award for a Collection of Essays
Hidden River™ Arts
PO Box 63927, Philadelphia, PA 19147
Tel: 610-764-0813
E-mail: hiddenriverarts@gmail.com
Web Site: hiddenriverarts.wordpress.com
Key Personnel
Founding Dir: Debra Leigh Scott
Established: 2019
Award for an original collection of essays that mines deep in its search for the truth of the human experience, essays that go beyond safe boundaries to discover deep realities. Open to international submissions from writers in English. Each ms must be submitted separately online. Entry fee: $22. See web site for full submission guidelines.
Award: $1,000 & publication by Hidden River Press
Closing Date: April

The Tampa Review Prize for Poetry
Tampa Review
University of Tampa Press, 401 W Kennedy Blvd, Tampa, FL 33606
Tel: 813-253-6266
E-mail: utpress@ut.edu
Web Site: tampareview.org/the-tampa-review-prize-for-poetry
Key Personnel
Ed: Richard Mathews
Edit Asst: Sean Donnelly
Established: 2001
Mss must be previously unpublished & at least 48 typed pages (preferred length is 60-100 pages). Handling fee: $25 per ms. Submissions must be made online through Submittable & are accepted year-round. See web site for full submission details.
Award: $2,000 & publication; all entries receive 1-year subn to *Tampa Review*
Presented: Summer

Helen Tartar First Book Subvention Award
American Comparative Literature Association (ACLA)
323 E Wacker Dr, No 642, Chicago, IL 60601
Tel: 312-600-8072
E-mail: info@acla.org
Web Site: www.acla.org/prize-awards/helen-tartar-first-book-subvention-award
Awarded on a competitive basis to first-time ACLA-member book authors. Applicants who have already secured provisional contracts from established academic presses will be given special consideration, but a provisional contract is not a requirement for the award. Subventions will be paid directly to the press. Applications should be submitted electronically to the ACLA publications committee chair. See web site for specific guidelines.
Award: Up to 3 awards $3,500 each

Taylor/Blakeslee Graduate Fellowships
Council for the Advancement of Science Writing (CASW)
PO Box 17337, Seattle, WA 98127
Tel: 206-880-0177
E-mail: info@casw.org
Web Site: casw.org/casw/graduate-school-fellowships
Key Personnel
Exec Dir: Rosalind Reid *E-mail:* ros_reid@casw.org
Admin & Communs Mgr: Sylvia Kantor
  E-mail: sylviakantor@casw.org
Established: 1975
Fellowships for students accepted to graduate-level programs in science writing. Online submissions.
Award: $5,000
Closing Date: March
Presented: ScienceWriters Meeting, Oct

Harold Taylor Prize, see The Academy of American Poets Harold Taylor Prize

TD Canadian Children's Literature Award
The Canadian Children's Book Centre
425 Adelaide St W, Suite 200, Toronto, ON M5V 3C1, Canada
Tel: 416-975-0010
E-mail: info@bookcentre.ca
Web Site: www.bookcentre.ca
Key Personnel
Exec Dir: Sarah Sahagian
Lib Coord: Meghan Howe *E-mail:* meghan@bookcentre.ca
Established: 2004
Awarded to a Canadian author/illustrator for the most distinguished book of the year.
Other Sponsor(s): TD Bank Group
Award: $50,000 cash each to one English language & one French language book, $10,000 to an English language honour book (maximum of 4), $10,000 to a French language honour book (maximum of 4), $2,500 to the publishers of the grand prize winning books for promotion & publicity purposes
Closing Date: Mid-Dec

Prix TD de Litterature Canadienne pour l'Enfance et la Jeunesse, see TD Canadian Children's Literature Award

Tennessee Arts Commission Fellowships
Tennessee Arts Commission
401 Charlotte Ave, Nashville, TN 37243-0780
Tel: 615-741-1701 *Fax:* 615-741-8559
Web Site: tnartscommission.org
Key Personnel
Dir, Literary Arts & Grants Analyst: Lee Baird
  Tel: 615-532-0493 *E-mail:* lee.baird@tn.gov
Literary fellowships given to Tennessee writers of every genre. Tennessee residents only.
Award: $5,000
Closing Date: Jan

The Tenth Gate Prize
The Word Works
PO Box 42164, Washington, DC 20015
E-mail: editor@wordworksbooks.org
Web Site: www.wordworksbooks.org
Key Personnel
Chpn, Bd of Dirs: Karren L Alenier
Pres: Nancy White
Series Ed: Kasey Jueds
Established: 2014

For an unpublished ms of poetry written in English, by a poet who has previously published at least 2 full-length collections. Submissions should be 48-80 pages in length. Online submissions only. See web site for guidelines.
Award: $1,000 & publication
Closing Date: July 15

Texas Bluebonnet Award
Texas Library Association (TLA)
3420 Executive Center Dr, Suite 301, Austin, TX 78731
Tel: 512-328-1518 *Fax:* 512-328-8852
E-mail: tla@txla.org
Web Site: txla.org/tools-resources/reading-lists/texas-bluebonnet-award/about/; txla.org
Key Personnel
Coord, Membership & Spec Servs: Christy Reynolds *Tel:* 512-328-1518 ext 153 *E-mail:* christyr@txla.org
Established: 1979
Awarded to favorite title on annual list, voted on by 200,000 children, grades 3-6.
Other Sponsor(s): Children's Round Table; Texas Association of School Librarians
Award: Medallion in desk mount
Closing Date: Aug 1
Presented: April

Textbook Excellence Award
Textbook & Academic Authors Association (TAA)
PO Box 367, Fountain City, WI 54629
E-mail: info@taaonline.net
Web Site: www.taaonline.net/textbook-excellence-award
Key Personnel
Exec Dir: Michael Spinella *Tel:* 973-943-0501 *E-mail:* michael.spinella@taaonline.net
Dir, Publg & Opers: Kim Pawlak *Tel:* 507-459-1363 *E-mail:* kim.pawlak@taaonline.net
Dir, Instl Memberships & Meetings: Maureen Foerster *Tel:* 530-864-3538 *E-mail:* maureen.foerster@taaonline.net
Membership Mktg Mgr: Eric Schmieder *Tel:* 919-437-0241 *E-mail:* eric.schmieder@taaonline.net
Membership Coord: Bekky Murphy *Tel:* 608-567-9060 *E-mail:* bekky.murphy@taaonline.net
Recognizes excellence in current textbooks & learning materials. Works are judged for merit in 4 areas: pedagogy; content/scholarship; writing; appearance & design. Nomination fee: $375 (non-refundable). See web site for nomination form & entry guidelines.
Closing Date: Dec 15
Presented: TAA Annual Conference, June

David Thelen Award
The Organization of American Historians (OAH)
112 N Bryan Ave, Bloomington, IN 47408-4141
Tel: 812-855-7311
E-mail: oah@oah.org
Web Site: www.oah.org/awards
Key Personnel
Exec Dir: Beth English *Tel:* 812-855-9836 *E-mail:* benglish@oah.org
Dir, Communs & Mktg: Kym Robinson *Tel:* 812-855-5430 *E-mail:* kymarobi@oah.org
Awarded biennially, in even-numbered years, to the author of the best article on American history written in a foreign language. To be eligible, an article may have already been published (during January 1, 2023 through December 31, 2024) or may be an original work that broadens the presentation of American history. The winning article will illustrate how the understanding of American history can be approached differently when it is conceived in the scholarly or public debates of a country other than the US. Submissions should be interesting, compelling & highlight a way of thinking or writing about the US that offers a perspective most American readers rarely encounter. The award is open to roundtables, keynote addresses, conference papers, or other types of scholarship. The ms should be framed & communicated to people outside the US & written in a language other than English. See web site for complete submission process.
Award: Winning article will be published in the *Journal of American History*
Closing Date: May 1, 2025 (postmarked)
Presented: OAH Conference on American History, Philadelphia, PA, April 2026

The Piri Thomas Poetry Prize
Poetry Center & American Poetry Archives at San Francisco State University
511-512 Humanities Bldg, 1600 Holloway Ave, San Francisco, CA 94132
Tel: 415-338-2227 *Fax:* 415-338-0966
E-mail: poetry@sfsu.edu
Web Site: poetry.sfsu.edu
Key Personnel
Dir: Steve Dickison *E-mail:* steved@sfsu.edu
Assoc Dir: Elise Ficarra *E-mail:* eficarra@sfsu.edu
Established: 2009
Awarded to an SF State creative writing undergraduate student. The prize is administered by the Academy of American Poets. Candidates for the prize are nominated by SF State faculty.
Award: $100 cash

3-Day Novel Contest
Anvil Press Publishers
PO Box 3008, MPO, Vancouver, BC V6B 3X5, Canada
Tel: 604-876-8710
E-mail: info@3daynovel.com
Web Site: www.3daynovel.com
Established: 1977
International novel writing competition. Entry fee: $50 ($35 early bird) for US & CN entries; may be postmarked up until 1 day before contest.
Award: Publication & cash prize
Closing Date: Friday before Labor Day (postmark)
Presented: Labor Day weekend

Thriller Awards Competition
International Thriller Writers (ITW)
PO Box 311, Eureka, CA 95502
Web Site: thrillerwriters.org
Key Personnel
Exec Dir: Liz Berry
VP, Awards: Anthony Franze *E-mail:* anthony@anthonyfranzebooks.com
To be eligible, all novels must first be published by an ITW recognized publisher or from an ITW active member during the eligibility period. Works must have been published between September 1 & August 31 of the year preceding the award. Works may be submitted to only one category: Hardcover Novel, First Novel, Short Story, Paperback Original Novel, Young Adult Novel, Ebook Original Novel.
Closing Date: Nov 1
Presented: ITW Gala Banquet, New York, NY, July

Jean Throop Book Award, see IODE Jean Throop Book Award

Thurber Prize for American Humor
Thurber House
77 Jefferson Ave, Columbus, OH 43215
Tel: 614-464-1032
E-mail: thurberhouse@thurberhouse.org
Web Site: www.thurberhouse.org
Key Personnel
Exec Dir: Laurie Lathan *Tel:* 614-464-1032 ext 2 *E-mail:* llathan@thurberhouse.org
Deputy Dir: Anne Touvell *Tel:* 614-464-1032 ext 3 *E-mail:* atouvell@thurberhousel.org
Established: 1997
National award for the most outstanding book of humor writing published in the US. The award is presented by Thurber House, a nonprofit literary center in Columbus, OH & the former home of American humorist, author & New Yorker cartoonist James Thurber.
Award: $5,000 & commemorative plaque
Presented: National Awards Ceremony, Columbus, OH, Spring

Lon Tinkle Award for Lifetime Achievement
Texas Institute of Letters (TIL)
PO Box 130294, Spring, TX 77393
Web Site: texasinstituteofletters.org
Key Personnel
Pres: David Bowles *E-mail:* president@texasinstituteofletters.org
VP: Chris Barton
Secy: Kathryn Jones *E-mail:* secretary@texasinstituteofletters.org
Treas: Cliff Hudder
Award for lifetime literary achievement by a writer with a career in letters associatied with the state of Texas. The author must have been born in Texas or have lived in Texas for at least 5 consecutive years at some time. See web site for guidelines.
Award: $1,500
Closing Date: Jan
Presented: TIL Annual Meeting & Awards Ceremony, April

James Tiptree Jr Literary Award
James Tiptree Jr Literary Award Council
173 Anderson St, San Francisco, CA 94110
Tel: 415-641-4103
E-mail: info@tiptree.org
Web Site: tiptree.org
Key Personnel
Founder: Karen Joy Fowler; Pat Murphy
Established: 1991
Literary prize for science fiction or fantasy that expands or explores our understanding of gender. Nominations are accepted throughout the year on the web site.
Presented: WisCon, Madison, WI, Memorial Day weekend

Arthur Tofte/Betty Ren Wright Children's Literature Award
Council for Wisconsin Writers (CWW)
c/o 3225 N 91 St, Milwaukee, WI 53222
E-mail: wiswriters@gmail.com
Web Site: wiswriters.org/awards
Key Personnel
Contest Chair: Erik Richardson *E-mail:* erichardson@wi.rr.com
Established: 1966
Awarded for the best children's book published by a Wisconsin-based writer in the contest year. Entry fee: $25 nonmembs.
Award: $500 & 1-week residency at Shake Rag Alley Center for the Arts
Closing Date: Jan 31
Presented: CWW Annual Award Ceremony & Banquet, May

Toronto Book Awards
Toronto Cultural Partnerships
Division of City of Toronto
c/o Toronto Arts & Culture, City Hall, 9E, 100 Queen St W, Toronto, ON M5H 2N2, Canada
Web Site: www.toronto.ca/book_awards
Key Personnel
Cultural Devt Offr: Christopher Jones *Tel:* 416-392-6832 *E-mail:* christopher.jones@toronto.ca
Established: 1974
To honor authors of books of literary or artistic merit that are evocative of Toronto. Books

must have been published between March 1 of the previous year & May 31 of the award year. Fiction & nonfiction books published in English for adults +/or children are eligible. Ebooks, textbooks, self-published works & ghost-written works are not eligible.
Other Sponsor(s): Toronto Public Library (in partnership)
Award: $10,000; finalists receive $1,000
Closing Date: Last weekday in April
Presented: Toronto, ON, CN, Shortlist announced in Aug & winner in Oct

Towson University Prize for Literature
Towson University
English Dept, 8000 York Rd, Towson, MD 21252
Tel: 410-704-2000
Web Site: www.towson.edu/english
Key Personnel
Chair: Christopher Cain, PhD *E-mail:* ccain@towson.edu
Established: 1979
Award for a single book or book-length ms of fiction, poetry, drama or imaginative nonfiction by a Maryland writer. Applicant must have resided in Maryland at least 3 years prior to applying & must be a Maryland resident when the prize is awarded.
Other Sponsor(s): Alice & Franklin Cooley Endowment
Award: $1,000
Closing Date: June 15
Presented: Spring

Translation Projects
National Endowment for the Arts
400 Seventh St SW, Washington, DC 20506-0001
Tel: 202-682-5400; 202-682-5082 (voice/TTY); 202-682-5034 (lit fellowships hotline)
E-mail: litfellowships@arts.gov
Web Site: www.arts.gov/grants/translation-projects
Fellowships for published translators to support the translation of specific works of prose, poetry, or drama from other languages into English. Electronic application through grants.gov is mandatory.
Award: Up to $25,000
Closing Date: Jan
Presented: Notification by e-mail in Aug

Translation Series
Cleveland State University Poetry Center
Rhodes Tower, Rm 1841, 2121 Euclid Ave, Cleveland, OH 44115
Tel: 216-687-3986
E-mail: poetrycenter@csuohio.edu
Web Site: www.csupoetrycenter.com/translation-series; www.csupoetrycenter.com
Key Personnel
Dir: Caryl Pagel *E-mail:* c.pagel@csuohio.edu
Assoc Dir: Hilary Plum *E-mail:* h.plum@csuohio.edu
The CSU Poetry Center invites submissions of book-length volumes of poetry in translation during an open reading period in winter. Please send a cover letter describing the project & confirming any necessary permissions along with a sample translation of at least 20 pages. Full mss are welcome. Please e-mail materials to Associate Director Hilary Plum at h.plum@csuohio.edu. Reading period opens December 1.
Closing Date: Feb 1
Presented: Early Summer

Treehouse Climate Action Poem Prize
The Academy of American Poets Inc
75 Maiden Lane, Suite 901, New York, NY 10038
Tel: 212-274-0343
E-mail: awards@poets.org
Web Site: poets.org
Key Personnel
Pres & Exec Dir: Ricardo Alberto Maldonado
VP, Digital Engagement & Content: Jeff Gleaves
Ad & Mktg Dir: Michelle Campagna
Dir, Donor Rel: Molly Walsh
Dir, Progs: Nikay Paredes
Established: 2019
To honor exceptional poems that help make real for readers the gravity of the vulnerable state of our environment at present. Poets may submit only 1 poem for consideration. Poems must be original works by the poet submitting & be previously unpublished. Poems may be submitted in Spanish but must be accompanied by an English translation. Submissions accepted online only through Submittable. See web site for full guidelines.
Other Sponsor(s): Treehouse Investments
Award: $1,000 (1st prize), $750 (2nd prize), $500 (3rd prize); poems will be published in the *Poem-a-Day* series
Closing Date: Nov 1

Emma Gray Trigg Memorial
The Poetry Society of Virginia (PSV)
PO Box 36128, North Chesterfield, VA 23235-3533
E-mail: contest@poetrysocietyofvirginia.org; info@poetryvirginia.org
Web Site: www.poetrysocietyofvirginia.org
Key Personnel
Pres: Cherryl T Cooley
 E-mail: poetrysocietypresident@gmail.com
Lyric poem, any subject, 64 line limit. PSV members only.
Award: $50 (1st prize), $30 (2nd prize), $20 (3rd prize)

Trillium Book Award/Prix Trillium
Ontario Creates
Division of Ministry of Culture, Ontario Government
South Tower, Suite 501, 175 Bloor St E, Toronto, ON M4W 3R8, Canada
Tel: 416-314-6858
E-mail: programs2@ontariocreates.ca
Web Site: ontariocreates.ca
Key Personnel
Prog Consultant, Indus Initiatives: Bianca Spence *Tel:* 416-642-6698 *E-mail:* bspence@ontariocreates.ca
Established: 1987
Open to books in any genre; fiction, nonfiction, drama, children's books & poetry. Anthologies & translations are not eligible. For the poetry award, a first, second, or third work by a new or emerging poet is eligible. A jury of writers & figures from the literary community judges all submissions & selects the winning titles.
Award: $20,000 to winning authors in English & French & their publishers receive $2,500 for marketing & promotion; Poetry award recipients receive $10,000 & $2,000 is given to the winning publishers
Closing Date: Dec (titles published Jan-Oct), Jan (titles published Nov-Dec)
Presented: Award Ceremony, Late Spring

Sergio Troncoso Award for Best Book of Fiction
Texas Institute of Letters (TIL)
PO Box 130294, Spring, TX 77393
Web Site: texasinstituteofletters.org
Key Personnel
Pres: David Bowles *E-mail:* president@texasinstituteofletters.org
VP: Chris Barton
Secy: Kathryn Jones *E-mail:* secretary@texasinstituteofletters.org
Treas: Cliff Hudder
Award for the best first fiction book by a Texan or about Texas. The author must have been born in Texas or have lived in Texas for at least 5 consecutive years at some time. See web site for guidelines.
Award: $3,000
Closing Date: Jan
Presented: TIL Annual Meeting & Awards Ceremony, April

Harry S Truman Book Award
Truman Library Institute
5151 Troost Ave, Suite 300, Kansas City, MO 64110
Tel: 816-400-1212 *Toll Free Tel:* 844-358-5400
Web Site: www.trumanlibraryinstitute.org/research-grants/bookaward/; trumanlibraryinstitute.org
Key Personnel
Book Award Admin: Lisa Sullivan *E-mail:* lisa.sullivan@trumanlibraryinstitute.org
Established: 1963
Biennial award, presented in even-numbered years, for recognition of the best book published within a 2-year period prior to the award year dealing primarily & substantially with some aspect of the history of the US between April 12, 1945 & January 20, 1953, or with the life or career of Harry S Truman. Five copies of each book entered must be submitted to the Book Award Administrator.
Award: $2,500
Closing Date: Before Jan 20, 2026
Presented: No later than May 8 (Truman's birthday), 2026

Trustus Playwrights' Festival
Trustus Theatre
520 Lady St, Columbia, SC 29201
Tel: 803-254-9732
E-mail: boxoffice@trustus.org
Web Site: trustus.org/playwrights-festival
Key Personnel
Exec Dir: Jessica Francis Fichter
 E-mail: jessica@trustus.org
Artistic Dir: Dewey Scott-Wiley *E-mail:* dewey@trustus.org
Established: 1988
Accepts submissions nationally from playwrights seeking to develop their script for a full main state production at Trustus Theatre. Submissions should be non-musical plays that have small casts (6 actors or less) & modest design needs. Open to experimental works. Prefers scripts that have not been produced. Submission portal opens in December.
Closing Date: March 1
Presented: Aug, full production

Harriet Tubman Prize
The Lapidus Center for the Historical Analysis of Transatlantic Slavery
515 Malcolm X Blvd, New York, NY 10037
Tel: 212-491-2263
E-mail: lapiduscenter@nypl.org
Web Site: www.lapiduscenter.org/category/tubman
Key Personnel
Assoc Dir & Curator: Dr Michelle Commander
Awarded for a distinguished nonfiction book published in the US on the slave trade, slavery & anti-slavery in the Atlantic world. Anthologies & works of fiction are not eligible. Books must be nominated by publishers & accompanied by the nomination form.
Award: $7,500
Closing Date: Dec 31
Presented: Schomburg Center for Research in Black Culture, New York, NY

Kate Tufts Discovery Award
Claremont Graduate University
Harper East, Unit B-7, 160 E Tenth St, Claremont, CA 91711-6165
Tel: 909-621-8974
E-mail: tufts@cgu.edu

Web Site: www.cgu.edu/tufts
Key Personnel
Poetry Awards Coord: Genevieve Kaplan
Established: 1994
Most worthy first book of poetry published between July 1 & June 30. Award presented for a first book by a poet of genuine promise.
Award: $10,000 cash
Closing Date: July 1
Presented: Claremont Graduate University, Claremont, CA, April

Kingsley Tufts Poetry Award
Claremont Graduate University
Harper East, Unit B-7, 160 E Tenth St, Claremont, CA 91711-6165
Tel: 909-621-8974
E-mail: tufts@cgu.edu
Web Site: www.cgu.edu/tufts
Key Personnel
Poetry Awards Coord: Genevieve Kaplan
Established: 1993
Most worthy book of poetry published between July 1 & June 30. Mss, CDs & chapbooks are not accepted. This annual award honors a poet who is past the very beginning, but has not yet reached the acknowledged pinnacle of his or her career.
Award: $100,000 cash
Closing Date: July 1
Presented: Claremont Graduate University, Claremont, CA, April

Tupelo Press Berkshire Prize for a First or Second Book of Poetry
Tupelo Press Inc
60 Roberts Dr, Suite 308, North Adams, MA 01247
SAN: 254-3281
Tel: 413-664-9611 Fax: 413-664-9711
E-mail: info@tupelopress.org
Web Site: www.tupelopress.org
Key Personnel
Publr: Jeffrey Levine E-mail: publisher@tupelopress.org
Ed-in-Chief: Kristina Marie Darling
  E-mail: kdarling@tupelopress.org
Established: 2000
Competition for first or second books of poetry. Full guidelines on the web site. Entries accepted beginning January 1.
Award: $3,000 & publication & distribution
Closing Date: April 30
Presented: Summer

Tupelo Press Snowbound Series Chapbook Award
Tupelo Press Inc
60 Roberts Dr, Suite 308, North Adams, MA 01247
SAN: 254-3281
Tel: 413-664-9611 Fax: 413-664-9711
E-mail: info@tupelopress.org
Web Site: www.tupelopress.org
Key Personnel
Publr: Jeffrey Levine E-mail: publisher@tupelopress.org
Ed-in-Chief: Kristina Marie Darling
  E-mail: kdarling@tupelopress.org
Established: 2004
Open poetry chapbook competition. Full guidelines on the web site. Entries accepted beginning December 1.
Award: $1,000 & publication
Closing Date: Feb 28
Presented: Spring

Frederick Jackson Turner Award
The Organization of American Historians (OAH)
112 N Bryan Ave, Bloomington, IN 47408-4141
Tel: 812-855-7311
E-mail: oah@oah.org
Web Site: www.oah.org/awards
Key Personnel
Exec Dir: Beth English Tel: 812-855-9836
  E-mail: benglish@oah.org
Dir, Communs & Mktg: Kym Robinson Tel: 812-855-5430 E-mail: kymarobi@oah.org
Awarded to the author of a first scholarly book dealing with some aspect of American history. Eligible books must be published during the calendar year preceding that in which the award is given. The author may not have previously published a book-length work of history. Submissions will be made by publishers, who may submit such books as they deem eligible. Co-authored works are eligible, as long as neither author has previously published a book of history. Authors who have previously co-authored a book of history are not eligible. One copy of each entry must be mailed directly to the committee members listed on the web site & must include a complete list of the author's publications or a statement from the publisher verifying this is the author's first book. No submission will be considered without this proof of eligibility.
Closing Date: Oct 1 (postmarked)
Presented: OAH Conference on American History, Spring

Nancy Byrd Turner Memorial
The Poetry Society of Virginia (PSV)
PO Box 36128, North Chesterfield, VA 23235-3533
E-mail: contest@poetrysocietyofvirginia.org; info@poetryvirginia.org
Web Site: www.poetrysocietyofvirginia.org
Key Personnel
Pres: Cherryl T Cooley
  E-mail: poetrysocietypresident@gmail.com
Sonnet or other traditional form (state the form), any subject. Submit 1 copy of the poem with no identifying information but put the category in the upper right-hand-side, along with a notation as to whether you are a member of PSV (does not matter if you are a lifetime member or just joined for the contest). Submit a cover letter/page that contains the category, the name of the poem, your name & address, phone number & e-mail address. Entries will not be returned. Entry fee: Free to membs, $5 nonmembs.
Award: $50 (1st prize), $30 (2nd prize), $20 (3rd prize)

The Tuscarora Award for Historical Fiction
Hidden River™ Arts
PO Box 63927, Philadelphia, PA 19147
Tel: 610-764-0813
E-mail: hiddenriverarts@gmail.com
Web Site: hiddenriverarts.wordpress.com
Key Personnel
Founding Dir: Debra Leigh Scott
Established: 2018
Award for an unpublished book-length work of historical fiction. Open to international submissions from writers in English. Each ms must be submitted separately online. Entry fee: $22. See web site for full submission guidelines.
Award: $1,000 & publication by Hidden River Press
Closing Date: Jan

The Tusculum Review Poetry Chapbook Prize
The Tusculum Review
60 Shiloh Rd, Greeneville, TN 37745
Mailing Address: PO Box 5113, Greeneville, TN 37743
E-mail: review@tusculum.edu
Web Site: web.tusculum.edu/tusculumreview/contest
Each chapbook ms entered should consist of 20-30 pages of poems in a standard 12-point font. No more than one poem may appear on a page. Entry fee: $20 per chapbook ms. A ms need not be thematically coherent or connected through narrative. Co-authored mss are permitted. Include title page, table of contents & acknowledgements page (if any of the poems have been previously published). Please send a cover letter with your contest entry. See web site for details.
Award: $1,000 & publication in *The Tusculum Review*
Closing Date: April 1

Mark Twain American Voice in Literature Award
The Mark Twain House & Museum
351 Farmington Ave, Hartford, CT 06105
Tel: 860-247-0998
E-mail: info@marktwainhouse.org
Web Site: marktwainhouse.org
Key Personnel
Dir, Public Progs: Jennifer LaRue
  E-mail: jennifer.larue@marktwainhouse.org
Awarded for a work of fiction published during the previous calendar year that best exemplifies or expresses a uniquely American voice. Submissions are accepted from publishers, authors, librarians, agents, instructors & others. Novels & short story collections are both accepted. Works of nonfiction & self-published works are not accepted. Only digital submissions are considered. Entry fee: $50 per title.
Other Sponsor(s): David Baldacci; Bank of America
Award: $25,000
Closing Date: Jan 31
Presented: Fall

21st Century Award
The Chicago Public Library Foundation & Chicago Public Library
200 W Madison, 3rd fl, Chicago, IL 60606
Tel: 312-201-9830
E-mail: info@cplfoundation.org
Web Site: www.cplfoundation.org
Key Personnel
Pres: Brenda Langstraat Tel: 312-374-5242
  E-mail: blangstraat@cplfoundation.org
Mgr, Mktg Communs: Rica Bouso Tel: 312-201-9830 ext 32 E-mail: rbouso@cplfoundation.org
Honors significant recent achievement in writing by a Chicago-based author. In presenting this award, the foundation's directors hope to encourage the creation of new works & increase public awareness of the writer's talents.

The 25 Most "Censored" Stories
Project Censored - Media Freedom Foundation
PO Box 1177, Fair Oaks, CA 95628
Tel: 707-241-4596
E-mail: info@projectcensored.org
Web Site: www.projectcensored.org/censorship/nominate
Key Personnel
Pres, Media Freedom Foundation & Dir, Project Censored: Mickey Huff E-mail: mickey@projectcensored.org
Established: 1976
Project Censored was developed to research & publicize news media censorship in the US & develop students' critical thinking skills & media literacy. Nominations are accepted year-round. A censored news story is one that has been published, either electronically or in print, in a circulated newspaper, journal, magazine, newsletter, or similar online publication from either a foreign or domestic source, but to which there has been limited access. Project Censored identifies & evaluates the independent news stories & brings forth the top 25 stories each year.
Award: Certificate
Presented: Oct 1

AWARDS, PRIZE CONTESTS, FELLOWSHIPS & GRANTS

Cy Twombly Award for Poetry
Foundation for Contemporary Arts
820 Greenwich St, New York, NY 10014
Tel: 212-807-7077
E-mail: info@contemporary-arts.org
Web Site: www.foundationforcontemporaryarts.org/grants/cy-twombly-award-for-poetry
Key Personnel
Exec Dir: Stacy Tenenbaum Stark
Assoc Dir: Sarah Rulfs
Prog Mgr: Alexander Thompson
Established: 2018
Grant given to support a poet. Administered by a confidential nomination & selection process. Applications & unsol nominations are not accepted.
Other Sponsor(s): Cy Twombly Foundation
Award: $40,000
Presented: Jan

Ucross Foundation Residency Program
Ucross Foundation
30 Big Red Lane, Clearmont, WY 82835
Tel: 307-737-2291
E-mail: info@ucross.org
Web Site: www.ucross.org
Key Personnel
Pres, Ucross Foundation: Sharon Dynak
  E-mail: sdynak@ucross.org
Residency Mgr: Tracey Kikut *E-mail:* tkikut@ucross.org
Established: 1983
Artist & writer residency program. Approximately 100 individuals per year for 2-6 week lengths of time. Application fee: $40.
Award: Room, studio & board
Closing Date: March 1 (Fall session) & Oct 1 (Spring session)

Friedrich Ulfers Prize
New York University, Deutsches Haus
42 Washington Mews, New York, NY 10003
E-mail: info@festivalneueliteratur.org
Web Site: festivalneueliteratur.org/prize
Awarded to a leading publisher, writer, critic, translator, or scholar who has championed the advancement of German-language literature in the US.
Award: $5,000 grant
Presented: Festival Neue Literatur, March

Undergraduate Poetry Award
The Poetry Society of Virginia (PSV)
PO Box 36128, North Chesterfield, VA 23235-3533
E-mail: contest@poetrysocietyofvirginia.org; info@poetryvirginia.org
Web Site: www.poetrysocietyofvirginia.org
Key Personnel
Pres: Cherryl T Cooley
  E-mail: poetrysocietypresident@gmail.com
Any form. Any subject such as loss, overcoming a significant setback, or a strong feeling. 36 line limit. Undergraduate Virginia students only.
Award: $50 (1st prize), $30 (2nd prize), $20 (3rd prize)

John Updike Award
American Academy of Arts & Letters
633 W 155 St, New York, NY 10032
Tel: 212-368-5900
E-mail: academy@artsandletters.org
Web Site: artsandletters.org/awards
Key Personnel
Exec Dir: Cody Upton
Awarded biennially, in odd-numbered years, to recognize a writer in mid-career who has demonstrated consistent excellence. Candidates must be nominated by an Academy member.
Award: $20,000

Claudette Upton Scholarship
Editors Canada (Reviseurs Canada)
1507-180 Dundas St W, Toronto, ON M5G 1Z8, Canada
Tel: 416-975-1379
E-mail: info@editors.ca; info@reviseurs.ca; communications@editors.ca
Web Site: www.editors.ca/about/awards/claudette-upton-scholarship
Key Personnel
Exec Dir: Natasha Bood
  E-mail: executivedirector@editors.ca
Sr Communs Mgr: Michelle Ou
Training & Devt Mgr: Caitlin Stewart
Established: 2009
National award to recognize a promising student editor from among Editor Canada's student affiliates.
Other Sponsor(s): Simon Fraser University, Continuing Studies; West Coast Editorial Associates
Award: $1,000 scholarship to help support continuing professional development in editing

The Elizabeth J Urquhart Memorial, see A Sense of Place: The Elizabeth J Urquhart Memorial

Utah Original Writing Competition
Utah Division of Arts & Museums
Subsidiary of Utah State Department of Heritage & Arts
617 E South Temple, Salt Lake City, UT 84102
Tel: 801-236-7555 *Fax:* 801-236-7556
Web Site: arts.utah.gov
Key Personnel
Literary Arts Specialist: Alyssa Hickman Grove
  Tel: 801-236-7548 *E-mail:* agrove@utah.gov
Established: 1958
Applicants must be Utah residents age 18 or older. Guidelines & forms posted on web site in April.
Award: $7,350 in prizes in 7 categories
Closing Date: Last Friday in June
Presented: Salt Lake City, UT, Oct/Nov

The William Van Wert Memorial Fiction Award
Hidden River™ Arts
PO Box 63927, Philadelphia, PA 19147
Tel: 610-764-0813
E-mail: hiddenriverarts@gmail.com
Web Site: www.hiddenriverarts.org; www.hiddenriverarts.com
Key Personnel
Founding Dir: Debra Leigh Scott
Established: 2002
Awarded for a work of unpublished short story or novel excerpt of 25 pages or less. Entry fee: $17. See web site for full submission guidelines (via Submittable).
Award: $1,000 & publication in *Hidden River Review of Arts & Letters*
Closing Date: June 30
Presented: Dec

Vermont Golden Dome Book Award
Vermont Department of Libraries
60 Washington St, Suite 2, Barre, VT 05641
Tel: 802-636-0040
Web Site: libraries.vermont.gov/services/children_and_teens/book_awards/vtgdba
Key Personnel
Chpn: Rebecca Rupp *E-mail:* rebeccarupp@gmail.com
Youth Servs Consultant: Jonathan Clark
  E-mail: jonathan.l.clark@vermont.gov
Lib Advancement Asst: Jennifer Johnson
  E-mail: jennifer.johnson@vermont.gov
Established: 1957
Awarded for a book by a living American or Canadian author published in the previous year, chosen by the children of Vermont, grades 4-8, from a master list of titles.
Other Sponsor(s): Friends of Vermont Golden Dome Book Award
Closing Date: Dec 31
Presented: May/June

ASSOCIATIONS, EVENTS

Vermont Studio Center Writer's Program Fellowships
Vermont Studio Center
80 Pearl St, Johnson, VT 05656
Mailing Address: PO Box 613, Johnson, VT 05656
Tel: 802-635-2727 *Fax:* 802-635-2730
E-mail: writing@vermontstudiocenter.org; info@vermontstudiocenter.org
Web Site: www.vermontstudiocenter.org
Key Personnel
Prog Dir: Kathy Black *E-mail:* kblack@vermontstudiocenter.org
Writing Across Media Facilitator: Sarah Audsley
  E-mail: sarah.audsley@vermontstudiocenter.org
Established: 1984
Writing residency which includes a private studio, 3 meals per day from fresh local produce & private on-campus accommodations.
Award: Two, three & four week residencies

Jill Vickers Prize
Canadian Political Science Association (CPSA)
260 Dalhousie St, Suite 204, Ottawa, ON K1N 7E4, Canada
Tel: 613-562-1202 *Fax:* 613-241-0019
E-mail: cpsaprizes@cpsa-acsp.ca; cpsa-acsp@cpsa-acsp.ca
Web Site: www.cpsa-acsp.ca
Key Personnel
Exec Dir: Silvina Danesi
Admin: C Ngako Woktcheu
Awarded to the author of the best paper presented on the topic of gender & politics.
Award: Commemorative certificate
Closing Date: June
Presented: CPSA Annual Conference

Vicky Metcalf Award for Literature for Young People
The Writers' Trust of Canada
600-460 Richmond St W, Toronto, ON M5V 1Y1, Canada
Tel: 416-504-8222 *Toll Free Tel:* 877-906-6548
  Fax: 416-504-9090
E-mail: info@writerstrust.com
Web Site: www.writerstrust.com
Key Personnel
Exec Dir: Charlie Foran *Tel:* 416-504-8222 ext 244 *E-mail:* cforan@writerstrust.com
Mgr, Author Progs: Devon Jackson *Tel:* 416-504-8222 ext 248 *E-mail:* djackson@writerstrust.com
Awarded to a Canadian writer of young people's literature for a body of work.
Other Sponsor(s): George Cedric Metcalf Charitable Foundation
Award: $25,000
Presented: The Writers' Trust Awards, Toronto, ON, CN, Nov

Village Books Literary Citizenship Award
Village Books & Paper Dreams
1200 11 St, Bellingham, WA 98225
Tel: 360-671-2626
E-mail: biblioinfo@villagebooks.com; marketing@villagebooks.com
Web Site: www.villagebooks.com/literary-citizenship-award
Key Personnel
Owner: Kelly Evert; Paul Hanson; Sarah Hutton
Established: 2023
Recipients are of diverse backgrounds & professions, but have each demonstrated a commitment to engage with the literary community.

AWARDS, PRIZE CONTESTS, FELLOWSHIPS & GRANTS

Award: $1,000 each
Presented: June 20 to coincide with the bookstore's anniversary

Karen Virag Award
Editors Canada (Reviseurs Canada)
1507-180 Dundas St W, Toronto, ON M5G 1Z8, Canada
Tel: 416-975-1379
E-mail: info@editors.ca; info@reviseurs.ca; communications@editors.ca
Web Site: www.editors.ca/about/awards/karen-virag-award-0
Key Personnel
Exec Dir: Natasha Bood
 E-mail: executivedirector@editors.ca
Sr Communs Mgr: Michelle Ou
Training & Devt Mgr: Caitlin Stewart
Recognizes the efforts of an editor or an organization to raise the profile of editing in their community.
Other Sponsor(s): Editors Edmonton
Award: $400

Voelcker Award for Poetry Collection, see PEN/Voelcker Award for Poetry Collection

Harold D Vursell Memorial Award
American Academy of Arts & Letters
633 W 155 St, New York, NY 10032
Tel: 212-368-5900
E-mail: academy@artsandletters.org
Web Site: artsandletters.org/awards
Key Personnel
Exec Dir: Cody Upton
Given to single out recent prose that merits recognition for the quality of its style. Candidates must be nominated by an Academy member.
Award: $20,000

Christopher Lightfoot Walker Award
American Academy of Arts & Letters
633 W 155 St, New York, NY 10032
Tel: 212-368-5900
E-mail: academy@artsandletters.org
Web Site: artsandletters.org/awards
Key Personnel
Lit Coord: Ashley Fedor *E-mail:* afedor@artsandletters.org
Established: 2018
Awarded biennially, in even-numbered years, to recognize a writer of distinction who has made a significant contribution to American literature. Candidates must be nominated by an Academy member.
Award: $100,000

Bennett H Wall Award
Southern Historical Association (SHA)
University of Georgia, Dept of History, Athens, GA 30602-1602
Tel: 706-542-8848
Web Site: thesha.org/wall
Key Personnel
Secy/Treas: Dr Stephen Berry *E-mail:* berrys@thesha.org
Established: 2000
Awarded biennially, in even-numbered years, for the best book on southern business or economic history published in the preceding 2 years.
Closing Date: March 1
Presented: Annual Meeting

Richard Wall Memorial Award
Theatre Library Association (TLA)
c/o The New York Public Library for the Performing Arts, 111 Amsterdam Ave, New York, NY 10023
E-mail: theatrelibraryassociation@gmail.com; tlabookawards@gmail.com
Web Site: www.tla-online.org/awards/bookawards
Key Personnel
Co-Chair, Book Awards Comm: Suzanne Lipkin; Annemarie van Roessel
Established: 1973
Honors books published in US in the field of recorded performance including motion picture, TV & radio. Ineligible books are: directories, collections from previously published sources & reprints.
Award: $500 (1st prize), $250 (Special Jury prize); certificate
Closing Date: Feb 28
Presented: New York, NY, Oct

Edward Lewis Wallant Award
Dr & Mrs Irving Waltman
Maurice Greenberg Center for Judaic Studies, 200 Bloomfield Ave, Harry Jack Gray E 300, West Hartford, CT 06117
Tel: 860-768-4964 *Fax:* 860-768-5044
E-mail: mgcjs@hartford.edu
Web Site: www.hartford.edu/a_and_s/greenberg/wallant
Key Personnel
Sponsor of Award: Fran Waltman; Irving Waltman
Coord, Award Comm: Avinoam Patt, PhD
Established: 1963
Awarded to a Jewish writer, preferably unrecognized, whose published creative work of fiction is deemed to have significance for the American Jew.
Award: $500 & scroll
Closing Date: Nov 1

Walter Grants, see Walter Dean Myers Grants

Jesmyn Ward Prize
Michigan Quarterly Review
University of Michigan, 3277 Angell Hall, 435 S State St, Ann Arbor, MI 48109-1003
Tel: 734-764-9265
E-mail: mqr@umich.edu
Web Site: sites.lsa.umich.edu/mqr/about-us/prizes
Established: 2021
Prize for fiction in honor of Helen Zell Writers' Program alumna Jesmyn Ward & her significant contributions to the literary arts. Entry fee: $25. See web site for submission guidelines.
Award: $2,000 & publication

Jo Warner Award
Business Forms Management Association (BFMA)
1147 Fleetwood Ave, Madison, WI 53716-1417
E-mail: bfma@bfma.org
Web Site: www.bfma.org/page/awardsjowarner
Lifetime award focused on honoring an individual who has made outstanding contributions to the form systems profession. Members are encouraged to nominate an individual who they feel has exhibited outstanding service & accomplishments within the profession. Nominees need not be members of BFMA. See web site for criteria & contact information to submit nominations & supporting documentation.
Award: Lifetime BFMA honorary membership
Closing Date: March 1

George Washington Prize
George Washington's Mount Vernon
c/o Fred W Smith National Library, 3600 Mount Vernon Memorial Hwy, Mount Vernon, VA 22121
Tel: 703-799-8686
Web Site: www.mountvernon.org/library/george-washington-prize
Key Personnel
Dir, Lib Progs: Stephen McLeod
 E-mail: smcleod@mountvernon.org
Established: 2005
Awarded to honor outstanding new works on George Washington & his times (Revolutionary & founding eras circa 1760-1820). Submissions must have a date of first publication during the previous calendar year.
Other Sponsor(s): Gilder Lehrman Institute of American History; Washington College
Award: $50,000
Closing Date: Dec 31
Presented: Mount Vernon Estate & Gardens, 3200 Mount Vernon Memorial Hwy, Mount Vernon, VA, Fall

Washington State Book Awards
Washington Center for the Book
c/o The Seattle Public Library, 1000 Fourth Ave, Seattle, WA 98104-1109
Web Site: washingtoncenterforthebook.org
Key Personnel
Awards Contact: Linda Johns *E-mail:* linda.johns@spl.org
Honors works of outstanding literary merit by Washington authors published in the previous calendar year. Books are judged based on 3 criteria: Quality of writing, lasting importance & quality of the publication (including design & production). Categories for adult books: Biography & memoir; fiction; creative nonfiction; general nonfiction; poetry. Categories for youth books: Picture books; books for young readers (ages 6-12); books for young adults (ages 13+). Complete online submission form & send copies of each final printed title (6 copies for adult categories, 4 copies for youth categories).
Other Sponsor(s): The Seattle Public Library Foundation
Closing Date: Jan 20
Presented: Announced by Oct

The Robert Watson Literary Prizes in Fiction & Poetry
The Greensboro Review
MFA Writing Program, The Greensboro Review, UNC-Greensboro, 3302 MHRA Bldg, Greensboro, NC 27402-6170
Tel: 336-334-5459
Web Site: www.greensbororeview.org
Key Personnel
Ed: Terry L Kennedy *E-mail:* tlkenned@uncg.edu
Assoc Ed: Jessie Van Rheenen
 E-mail: jmvanrhe@uncg.edu
Established: 1984
Short story & poetry.
Other Sponsor(s): MFA Writing Program at UNC Greensboro
Award: $1,000 (each category)
Closing Date: Sept 15

The Weatherford Awards
Berea College
Loyal Jones Appalachian Ctr, 101 Chestnut St, Berea, KY 40404
Tel: 859-985-3000
Web Site: www.berea.edu/centers/loyal-jones-appalachian-center/awards/weatherford-award
Key Personnel
Dir, Loyal Jones Appalachian Ctr: Chris Green
 E-mail: greenchr@berea.edu
Established: 1970
Honors books that best illuminate the challenges, personalities & unique qualities of the Appalachian South. Three categories: Fiction, nonfiction & poetry. Nominations are accepted for books published in the current year. No self-published books. To nominate, e-mail Chris Green & send 7 copies of the book via post by the deadline.

Other Sponsor(s): Appalachian Studies Association
Award: $500 each
Closing Date: Nov 1
Presented: Appalachian Studies Conference, March

Jacqueline Bograd Weld Award for Biography, see PEN/Jacqueline Bograd Weld Award for Biography

Rene Wellek Prize
American Comparative Literature Association (ACLA)
323 E Wacker Dr, No 642, Chicago, IL 60601
Tel: 312-600-8072
E-mail: info@acla.org
Web Site: www.acla.org/prize-awards/rené-wellek-prize
Established: 1968
To recognize the best book published in the field of comparative literature published in the 2 calendar years prior to presentation. See web site for nomination process.
Award: Complimentary registration for the annual meeting as well as hotel & airfare accommodations (not including food)
Closing Date: Nov 1
Presented: ACLA Annual Meeting

Wergle Flomp Humor Poetry Contest
Winning Writers
351 Pleasant St, Suite B, PMB 222, Northampton, MA 01060-3998
Tel: 413-320-1847 *Toll Free Tel:* 866-WINWRIT (946-9748) *Fax:* 413-280-0539
Web Site: www.winningwriters.com/our-contests/wergle-flomp-humor-poetry-contest-free
Key Personnel
Pres: Adam Cohen *E-mail:* adam@winningwriters.com
VP: Jendi Reiter
Established: 2001
Seeks best humor poems. Both published & unpublished works are welcome. Submit poems in English or inspired gibberish. No entry fee. Contestants may enter one poem per year up to 250 lines. Poets from all nations welcome.
Award: $2,000 & Duotrope 2-year gift certificate (1st prize), $500 (2nd prize), $100 (10 honorable mentions), plus publication on web site for all winners
Closing Date: April 1
Presented: Winners announced Aug 15 on web site

Wesley-Logan Prize in African Diaspora History
American Historical Association (AHA)
400 "A" St SE, Washington, DC 20003
Tel: 202-544-2422
E-mail: awards@historians.org
Web Site: www.historians.org/award-grant/wesley-logan-prize/
Established: 1992
Awarded for an outstanding book in African diaspora history. The prize is offered for a book on some aspect of the history of the dispersion, settlement & adjustment +/or return of peoples originally from Africa. Books in any chronological period & any geological location with a 2024 copyright are eligible for the 2025 prize. Only books of high scholarly & literary merit will be considered. Nominations may be made by an author or publisher. Along with an application form, applicants must mail a copy of their book to each prize committee member posted on our web site as the prize deadline approaches. All updated info on web site.
Other Sponsor(s): Association for the Study of African-American Life & History
Award: $1,000
Closing Date: May 15, 2025
Presented: AHA Annual Meeting, Chicago, IL, Jan 2026

Western Heritage Awards (Wrangler Award)
National Cowboy & Western Heritage Museum®
1700 NE 63 St, Oklahoma City, OK 73111
Tel: 405-478-2250 *Fax:* 405-478-4714
E-mail: info@nationalcowboymuseum.org
Web Site: nationalcowboymuseum.org
Key Personnel
Communs Mgr: Melissa Stewart
E-mail: mstewart@nationalcowboymuseum.org
Established: 1961
Awarded to honor creative works in literature, music, television & film that share the great stories of the American West.
Award: Bronze sculpture of a cowboy on horseback
Closing Date: Nov 30 (literary), Dec 31 (TV, film & music)
Presented: Banquet & Awards Ceremonies, National Cowboy & Western Heritage Museum, Oklahoma City, OK, April (must be in attendance to receive bronze sculpture)

Hilary Weston Writers' Trust Prize for Nonfiction
The Writers' Trust of Canada
600-460 Richmond St W, Toronto, ON M5V 1Y1, Canada
Tel: 416-504-8222 *Toll Free Tel:* 877-906-6548 *Fax:* 416-504-9090
E-mail: info@writerstrust.com
Web Site: www.writerstrust.com
Key Personnel
Exec Dir: Charlie Foran *Tel:* 416-504-8222 ext 244 *E-mail:* cforan@writerstrust.com
Mgr, Author Progs: Devon Jackson *Tel:* 416-504-8222 ext 248 *E-mail:* djackson@writerstrust.com
Established: 1997
Awarded for literary exellence in nonfiction, which includes personal or journalistic essays, history, biography, memoirs, commentary & criticism, both social & political.
Other Sponsor(s): The Honourable Hilary M Weston
Award: $60,000 (winner), $5,000 (finalists)
Presented: The Writers' Trust Awards, Toronto, ON, CN, Nov

Weston International Award
The Writers' Trust of Canada
600-460 Richmond St W, Toronto, ON M5V 1Y1, Canada
Tel: 416-504-8222 *Toll Free Tel:* 877-906-6548 *Fax:* 416-504-9090
E-mail: info@writerstrust.com
Web Site: westoninternationalaward.com
Key Personnel
Exec Dir: Charlie Foran *Tel:* 416-504-8222 ext 244 *E-mail:* cforan@writerstrust.com
Established: 2023
Honors career achievement of an international author whose body of nonfiction work, written in English or widely available in translation, has advanced our understanding of the world. There is no submission process. Winners are selected following a peer-review process.
Other Sponsor(s): Hilary & Galen Weston Foundation
Award: $75,000

Charles A Weyerhauser Book Award
The Forest History Society Inc
2925 Academy Rd, Durham, NC 27705
Tel: 919-682-9319 *Fax:* 919-682-2349
Web Site: foresthistory.org/awards-fellowships/weyerhaeuser-award
Key Personnel
Admin Asst: Andrea Anderson *E-mail:* andrea.anderson@foresthistory.org
Established: 1977
Rewards superior scholarship in forest & conservation history. Award goes to an author who has exhibited fresh insight into a topic & whose narrative analysis is clear, inventive & thought-provoking. A committee comprised of the previous recipient & 2 other scholars working in the field chooses the winner.

E B White Award
American Academy of Arts & Letters
633 W 155 St, New York, NY 10032
Tel: 212-368-5900
E-mail: academy@artsandletters.org
Web Site: artsandletters.org/awards
Key Personnel
Exec Dir: Cody Upton
Established: 2013
Given to a writer for achievement in children's literature. Candidates must be nominated by an Academy member.
Award: $10,000

The Edmund White Award for Debut Fiction
The Publishing Triangle
511 Avenue of the Americas, No D36, New York, NY 10011
E-mail: awards@publishingtriangle.org; info@publishingtriangle.org; publishingtriangle@gmail.com
Web Site: publishingtriangle.org/awards/edmund-white-debut-fiction
Established: 2006
Recognizes outstanding first novels or story collections by LGBTQ authors. The award is open to first-book authors of any age whose work contains queer themes. Writers can have published works of nonfiction & their short fiction can have previously appeared in a published anthology. The book nominated must be the author's first work of book-length fiction & have been published in the preceding year. A call for submissions is posted on the web site in early Autumn. Finalists & winners are determined by a panel of judges appointed by the awards committee.
Award: $1,000

White, Jackie, Memorial National Children's Playwriting Contest, see Jackie White Memorial National Children's Playwriting Contest

William Allen White Children's Book Awards
Emporia State University Libraries & Archives
One Kellogg Circle, Emporia, KS 66801-5092
Mailing Address: Emporia State University, Campus Box 4051, Emporia, KS 66801-5092
Tel: 620-341-5040
E-mail: wawbookaward@emporia.edu
Web Site: wawchildrensbookaward.com
Key Personnel
Exec Dir: Michelle Hammond
E-mail: mhammon2@emporia.edu
Established: 1952
Two children's books are selected by the children of Kansas, grades 3-5 & 6-8, from 2 master lists of books chosen by a selection committee. When a student has read 2 books from either of the master lists, he or she is eligible to vote at their school (homeschooled vote at their local public library) for the annual White Award winners. Votes are recorded by each school, district or public library & submitted to the William Allen White Children Book Awards Program.
Other Sponsor(s): Trusler Foundation
Award: Two bronze medals, one for each grade level, & a $2,500 check for each winner

Closing Date: Votes must be received by April 15
Presented: Emporia State University, Webb Hall, Emporia, KS, Winners announced in May, awards presented in Autumn

The Bill Whitehead Award for Lifetime Achievement
The Publishing Triangle
511 Avenue of the Americas, No D36, New York, NY 10011
E-mail: awards@publishingtriangle.org; info@publishingtriangle.org; publishingtriangle@gmail.com
Web Site: publishingtriangle.org/awards/bill-whitehead-award/
Established: 1989
Awarded in celebration of an author's lifetime of work & their commitment to fostering queer culture. A panel of judges selects the winner & will consider authors who identify anywhere on the LGBTQ spectrum.
Award: $3,000 & invitation to deliver an address on LGBTQ literary culture at the annual awards ceremony

Fred Whitehead Award for Best Design of a Trade Book
Texas Institute of Letters (TIL)
PO Box 130294, Spring, TX 77393
Web Site: texasinstituteofletters.org
Key Personnel
Pres: David Bowles E-mail: president@texasinstituteofletters.org
VP: Chris Barton
Secy: Kathryn Jones E-mail: secretary@texasinstituteofletters.org
Treas: Cliff Hudder
Awarded biennially, in odd-numbered years, for the best design of a trade book by a Texan or about Texas. The author must have been born in Texas or have lived in Texas for at least 5 consecutive years at some time. See web site for guidelines.
Award: $1,500
Closing Date: Jan
Presented: TIL Awards Ceremony, April

Whiting Awards
Mrs Giles Whiting Foundation
16 Court St, Suite 2308, Brooklyn, NY 11241
Tel: 718-701-5962
E-mail: info@whiting.org
Web Site: www.whiting.org
Key Personnel
Pres: Peter Pennoyer
Exec Dir: Daniel Reid
Dir, Literary Progs: Courtney Hodell
Prog Offr: Katy Einerson
Prog Assoc: Adina Applebaum
Established: 1985
For creative writing in fiction, nonfiction, poetry & drama. Applications not accepted by the foundation; confidential nominators propose candidates for selection committee consideration.
Award: Ten awards of $50,000 each
Presented: March

Whiting Creative Nonfiction Grant
Mrs Giles Whiting Foundation
16 Court St, Suite 2308, Brooklyn, NY 11241
Tel: 718-701-5962
E-mail: nonfiction@whiting.org; info@whiting.org
Web Site: www.whiting.org
Key Personnel
Pres: Peter Pennoyer
Exec Dir: Daniel Reid
Dir, Literary Progs: Courtney Hodell
Prog Offr: Katy Einerson
Prog Assoc: Adina Applebaum
Established: 2016
Program offers allocations to as many as 8 works in progress to enable authors to complete their books. To be eligible, writers must be under contract with a publisher. Submissions welcome for nonfiction works of history, cultural or political reportage, biography, memoir, the sciences, philosophy, criticism, food or travel writing & personal essays, among other categories, for a general, not academic, readership. To apply, writers should submit their original proposal that led to the contract, as many as 3 sample chapters, a list of grants, funds & fellowships received for the book, a budget & schedule for completion & a letter of support from their publisher. Writers can submit applications online at www.whiting.org/nonfiction/application.
Award: $40,000
Closing Date: April
Presented: Announced in the Fall

Whiting Literary Magazine Prizes
Mrs Giles Whiting Foundation
16 Court St, Suite 2308, Brooklyn, NY 11241
Tel: 718-701-5962
E-mail: info@whiting.org
Web Site: www.whiting.org/writers/whiting-literary-magazine-prizes
Key Personnel
Exec Dir: Daniel Reid
Dir, Literary Progs: Courtney Hodell
Prog Offr: Katy Einerson
Awards in print & digital categories to smaller & mid-sized journals with budgets of up to $500,000. Each prize includes an outright gift in the first year followed by substantial matching grants in the next 2 years & capacity building opportunities. Applicants must be not-for-profit in the US & have published at least annually for at least the last 3 years.
Closing Date: Dec

Jon Whyte Memorial Essay Prize
Writers' Guild of Alberta
11759 Groat Rd NW, Edmonton, AB T5M 3K6, Canada
Tel: 780-422-8174 Toll Free Tel: 800-665-5354 (AB only)
E-mail: mail@writersguild.ab.ca
Web Site: writersguild.ca
Key Personnel
Exec Dir: Giorgia Severini E-mail: gseverini@writersguild.ab.ca
Communs & Partnerships Coord: Ellen Kartz E-mail: ellen.kartz@writersguild.ab.ca
Memb Servs Coord: Mike Maguire
Prog & Opers Coord: Ashley Mann E-mail: ashley.mann@writersguild.ab.ca
Progs & Events Coord: Jason Norman E-mail: jason.norman@writersguild.ab.ca
Proj Asst: Sadie MacGillivray E-mail: sadie.macgillivray@writersguild.ab.ca
Established: 1992
Awarded to an outstanding unpublished essay by an Alberta author; no longer than 3,000 words.
Award: $700
Closing Date: Dec 31
Presented: Alberta Book Awards Gala, AB, CN
Branch Office(s)
223 12 Ave SW, No 204, Calgary, AB T2R 0G9, Canada, Prog & Conference Coord: Dorothy Bentley Tel: 403-875-8058 E-mail: dorothy.bentley@writersguild.ab.ca

Wichita State University Playwriting Contest
Wichita State University School of Performing Arts
1845 Fairmount St, Box 153, Wichita, KS 67260-0153
Tel: 316-978-3360
Web Site: www.wichita.edu
Key Personnel
Assoc Educator, Theatre: Jeannine Russell Tel: 316-285-4743 E-mail: jeannine.russell@wichita.edu
Established: 1974
Contest open to all graduate & undergraduate students enrolled at any college or university in the US. All submissions must be original, unpublished & unproduced. Both full-length & one-act plays may be submitted.
Award: Production of play, transportation & housing for playwright to attend performance
Closing Date: Jan 15
Presented: Welsbacher Theatre, Wichita State University, Wichita, KS, March 15

Thornton Wilder Prize for Translation
American Academy of Arts & Letters
633 W 155 St, New York, NY 10032
Tel: 212-368-5900
E-mail: academy@artsandletters.org
Web Site: artsandletters.org/awards
Key Personnel
Exec Dir: Cody Upton
Established: 2009
Recognizes a practitioner, scholar, or patron who has made a significant contribution to the art of literary translation. Candidates must be nominated by an Academy member.
Award: $20,000

William Flanagan Memorial Creative Persons Center
Edward F Albee Foundation
14 Harrison St, New York, NY 10013
Tel: 212-226-2020 Fax: 212-226-5551
E-mail: info@albeefoundation.org
Web Site: www.albeefoundation.org
Key Personnel
Exec Dir: Jakob Holder
Residency program for writers & visual artists. The only requirements are talent & need.
Award: Room (writers); Room & Studio (visual artists)
Closing Date: Jan 1-March 1 for Summer season
Presented: The Barn, Montauk, Long Island, NY, Mid-May through mid-Oct, every writer or artist can choose 4 or 6 weeks, depending on availability

Oscar Williams/Gene Derwood Award
NY Community Trust
909 Third Ave, New York, NY 10022
Tel: 212-686-0010 Fax: 212-532-8528
E-mail: info@nycommunitytrust.org
Web Site: www.nycommunitytrust.org
Key Personnel
Pres: Lorie Slutsky Tel: 212-686-2565
VP, Grants: Shawn V Morehead Tel: 212-686-7069
Dir, Communs: Marty Lipp Tel: 212-889-3963
Dir, Grants Budgeting: Liza Lagunoff Tel: 212-686-7196 E-mail: ll@nyct-cfi.org
Asst to Pres: Barbara Wybraniec Tel: 212-686-0010 ext 229
Established: 1971
Award intended to help worthy poets & artists in need who have had long & distinguished careers. Nominations or applications are not accepted in any form.
Award: Cash varies in amount

William Carlos Williams Award
Poetry Society of America (PSA)
119 Smith St, Brooklyn, NY 11201
Tel: 212-254-9628
E-mail: info@poetrysociety.org
Web Site: poetrysociety.org/awards
Key Personnel
Exec Dir: Matt Brogan E-mail: matt@poetrysociety.org
Deputy Dir: Brett Fletcher Lauer E-mail: brett@poetrysociety.org

AWARDS, PRIZE CONTESTS, FELLOWSHIPS & GRANTS

Devt Dir: Madeline Weinfield *E-mail:* madeline@poetrysociety.org
For a book of poetry written by a living author who lives in the US or is a US citizen. The book must be published by a small press, non-profit, or university press in a standard edition. Translations & chapbooks are ineligible. Books must be submitted directly by publishers. Entry forms required. Entry fee: $20 per book.
Award: $500
Closing Date: Dec 31 (postmark)
Presented: Annual Awards Ceremony, New York, NY, Spring

E O Wilson Literary Science Writing Award, see PEN/E O Wilson Literary Science Writing Award

Gary Wilson Award for Short Fiction
Texas Christian University
Dept of English, TCU Box 297270, Fort Worth, TX 76129
E-mail: descant@tcu.edu
Web Site: www.descant.tcu.edu
Established: 2005
Award for an outstanding story in an issue of *descant*. All published submissions are eligible for prize consideration. There is no application process.
Other Sponsor(s): descant (publication), Dept of English, TCU
Award: $250 cash
Presented: Winner announced in the Summer in *descant*

Sheri-D Wilson Golden Beret Award
The League of Canadian Poets
2 Carlton St, Suite 1519, Toronto, ON M5B 1J3, Canada
Tel: 416-504-1657
E-mail: admin@poets.ca
Web Site: poets.ca/awards/goldenberet
Key Personnel
Exec Dir: Lesley Fletcher *E-mail:* lesley@poets.ca
Artistic Programming Dir: Nic Brewer
  E-mail: nicole@poets.ca
Admin & Communs Coord: Caitlin Lapena
  E-mail: caitlin@poets.ca
Established: 2007
Honors an established Canadian poet with a history of achievement & performance in spoken word. Poets must be nominated (no self-nominations). Open to league members & non-members.
Award: $2,000

Herbert Warren Wind Book Award
USGA Museum & Archives
77 Liberty Corner Rd, Liberty Corner, NJ 07931-0708
Tel: 908-326-1207
Web Site: www.usga.org
Key Personnel
Libn: Tara Valente *E-mail:* tvalente@usga.org
Established: 1987
Recognizes & honors outstanding contributions to golf literature. Named in honor of the famed golf writer, the annual award acknowledges & encourages outstanding research, writing & publishing about golf in an attempt to broaden the public's interest in & knowledge of the game. USGA's top literary prize.
Award: Silver inkwell with feather
Closing Date: Oct 31
Presented: USGA Annual Meeting, Feb

Windham-Campbell Prizes
Yale University, Windham-Campbell Prizes Endowment
Beinecke Rare Book & Manuscript Library, 121 Wall St, New Haven, CT 06511
Fax: 203-432-9033
Web Site: windhamcampbell.org
Key Personnel
Prog Dir: Michael Kelleher
Global English language awards that call attention to literary achievement & provide writers with the opportunity to focus on their work independent of financial concerns. Nomination only. Eight prizes available each year. Categories: Fiction, nonfiction, drama & poetry.
Award: $165,000 unrestricted grant
Presented: Spring

Justin Winsor Library History Essay Award
Library History Round Table (LHRT)
Unit of The American Library Association (ALA)
225 N Michigan Ave, Suite 1300, Chicago, IL 60601
Tel: 312-944-6780 *Toll Free Tel:* 800-545-2433
  Fax: 312-440-9374
E-mail: ala@ala.org
Web Site: www.ala.org/rt/lhrt/awards/windsor-essay-award; www.ala.org/rt/lhrt; www.ala.org
Key Personnel
LHRT Liaison: Danielle Ponton
  E-mail: dponton@ala.org
Established: 1978
Awarded to recognize the best essay written in English on library history. The award is named in honor of the distinguished 19th century librarian, historian & bibliographer who was also ALA's first president.
Award: Certificate, $500 cash & invitation to have paper considered for publication in *Libraries: Culture, History, and Society*
Closing Date: Feb 1

Charlotte Wise Memorial
The Poetry Society of Virginia (PSV)
PO Box 36128, North Chesterfield, VA 23235-3533
E-mail: contest@poetrysocietyofvirginia.org; info@poetryvirginia.org
Web Site: www.poetrysocietyofvirginia.org
Key Personnel
Pres: Cherryl T Cooley
  E-mail: poetrysocietypresident@gmail.com
Any form, any subject, 64 line limit. Submit 1 copy of the poem with no identifying information but put the category in the upper right-hand-side, along with a notation as to whether you are a member of PSV (does not matter if you are a lifetime member or just joined for the contest). Submit a cover letter/page that contains the category, the name of the poem, your name & address, phone number & e-mail address. Entries will not be returned. Entry fee: Free to membs, $5 nonmembs.
Award: $50 (1st prize), $30 (2nd prize), $20 (3rd prize)

WLA Literary Award
Wisconsin Library Association Inc (WLA)
112 Owen Rd, Unit 6437, Monona, WI 53716
Mailing Address: PO Box 6437, Monona, WI 53716
Tel: 608-245-3640
E-mail: wla@wisconsinlibraries.org
Web Site: www.wisconsinlibraries.org
Key Personnel
Comm Chair: Hannah Majeska
  E-mail: hmajeska@madisonpubliclibrary.org
Established: 1974
To honor a work by an author with a Wisconsin connection for a work published in the preceding year that contributes to the world of literature & ideas. Nominations may be sent via e-mail to wla@wisconsinlibraries.org or to the current chair, Nell Fleming, at nell.fleming@wsd.k12.wi.us.

ASSOCIATIONS, EVENTS

Award: Monetary award
Closing Date: March 31
Presented: WLA Annual Conference, Oct/Nov

WNBA Pannell Award for Excellence in Children's Bookselling
Women's National Book Association Inc
PO Box 237, FDR Sta, New York, NY 10150-0231
Toll Free Tel: 866-610-WNBA (610-9622)
E-mail: pannell@wnba-books.org
Web Site: wnba-books.org/pannell-award
Key Personnel
Co-Chair: Susan Knopf; Susan Koster
Established: 1981
Recognizes retail bookstores that excel at creatively bringing books & children together & inspiring children's interest in books & reading. Nominations come from customers, sales & marketing people & other book industry professionals & stores themselves. One general book store with a children's section & one children's specialty store are selected each year by a jury of 5 book industry professionals based on creativity, responsiveness to community needs, passion & understanding of children's books & young readers.
Other Sponsor(s): Estate of Lucile Micheels Pannell; Penguin Young Readers Group
Award: $2,000 (2 at $1,000 each) plus 1 piece of original art for each recipient
Closing Date: Feb
Presented: Late May/early June

WNBA Writing Contest
Women's National Book Association Inc
PO Box 237, FDR Sta, New York, NY 10150-0231
Toll Free Tel: 866-610-WNBA (610-9622)
E-mail: contest@wnba-books.org; info@wnba-books.org
Web Site: wnba-books.org/contest
Key Personnel
Chair: Andrea Autin
Entries accepted in 4 categories: Fiction (3,000 words maximum), creative nonfiction (2,500 words maximum), flash prose (750 words maximum), poetry (3-5 pages maximum). Open to all adults 18 years or older writing in English. International submissions are welcome if the author is able to accept the winning prize in US dollars. Multiple entries accepted but each requires a fee & separate entry. Entry fee: $15 membs, $20 nonmembs. All entries must be submitted online via Submittable.
Award: $250 cash prize for winner in each category & publication in *Bookwoman Newsletter*. Each category will also have 2nd & 3rd place award winners

WNDB Internship Grants
We Need Diverse Books™
10319 Westlake Dr, No 104, Bethesda, MD 20817
Tel: 701-404-WNDB (404-9632, voicemail only)
E-mail: internships@diversebooks.org
Web Site: diversebooks.org/our-programs/internship-grants
Key Personnel
Head, Internship Grants Comm: Jennifer Mann
  E-mail: jennifermann@diversebooks.org
Communs Mgr: Alaina Leary
  E-mail: alainaleary@diversebooks.org
Supplemental grants to students from diverse backgrounds to help further their goals of pursuing a career in children's publishing. Applicant must identify as coming from a diverse background, be a high school graduate/GED, or currently enrolled college/university student, or college graduate, have received a paid internship offer from a participating publisher or from a qualifying literary agent. The posi-

Thomas Wolfe Fiction Prize
North Carolina Writers' Network
PO Box 21591, Winston-Salem, NC 27120-1591
Tel: 336-293-8844
E-mail: mail@ncwriters.org
Web Site: www.ncwriters.org
Key Personnel
Exec Dir: Ed Southern *E-mail:* ed@ncwriters.org
Exec Dir, Great Smokies Writing Prog: Tommy Hays *E-mail:* thays@unca.edu
Competition is open to all writers regardless of geographical location or prior publication. Submit 2 copies of an unpublished fiction ms not to exceed 3,000 words. Entry fee: $15 membs, $25 nonmembs. Submission period begins December 1. Entries can be submitted via US Postal Service or online at ncwriters.submittable.com/submit. Mail submissions to Thomas Wolfe Fiction Prize, Great Smokies Writing Program, UNC Asheville, One University Heights, CPO 1915, Asheville, NC 28804.
Award: $1,000 & possible publication in *The Thomas Wolfe Review*
Closing Date: Jan 30

Helen & Kurt Wolff Translator's Prize
Goethe-Institute New York
30 Irving Place, New York, NY 10003
Tel: 212-439-8700 *Fax:* 212-439-8705
E-mail: info-newyork@goethe.de
Web Site: www.goethe.de/ins/us/enkul/ser/uef/hkw.html
Key Personnel
Libn: Walter Schlect *Tel:* 212-439-8697 *E-mail:* walter.schlect@goethe.de
Established: 1996
Awarded to honor an outstanding literary translation from German into English published in the US the previous year. American publishers are invited to submit 6 copies.
Award: $10,000
Closing Date: Jan 31
Presented: June (winning translation announced mid-April)

Tobias Wolff Award for Fiction
The Bellingham Review
Mail Stop 9053, Western Washington University, Bellingham, WA 98225
Tel: 360-650-4863
E-mail: bellingham.review@wwu.edu
Web Site: bhreview.org; bhreview.submittable.com
Key Personnel
Ed-in-Chief: Susanne Paola Antonetta
Mng Ed: Stephen Haines
Asst Mng Ed: Keegan Lawler
Established: 1993
Entry consists of 1 essay, 1 story, up to 3 pieces of flash, or up to 3 poems. Please limit prose to 4,000 words. For prose that is 1,500 words or fewer, submit up to 3 in one entry. Upload entries via Submittable beginning December 1. Paper submissions are not accepted. All submissions must be previously unpublished in North America. Entry fee: $20, $30 international.
Award: $1,000 & publication in *The Bellingham Review* (1st prize); considered for publication (2nd, 3rd & finalists)
Closing Date: March 15
Presented: June

Women's National Book Association Award
Women's National Book Association Inc
PO Box 237, FDR Sta, New York, NY 10150-0231
Toll Free Tel: 866-610-WNBA (610-9622)
Web Site: wnba-books.org/wnba-award
Key Personnel
Natl Co-VP & Chair, Award Comm: NC Weil
Natl Treas: Karen Holly
NYC Pres: Rachel Slaiman *E-mail:* president@wnba-nyc.org
Established: 1940
Presented to a living American woman who derives part or all of her income from books & allied arts & who has done meritorious work in the world of books beyond the duties or responsibilities of her profession or occupation. Offered biennially in even-numbered years.
Award: Citation
Presented: Varies

The J Howard & Barbara M J Wood Prize
Poetry Magazine
61 W Superior St, Chicago, IL 60654
Tel: 312-787-7070
Web Site: www.poetryfoundation.org/poetrymagazine/prizes
Key Personnel
Assoc Ed: Holly Amos *E-mail:* hamos@poetrymagazine.org
Established: 1994
For poetry published during the preceding year in *Poetry* magazine. No application necessary.
Award: $5,000
Presented: Announced in Nov issue

Carter G Woodson Book Awards
National Council for the Social Studies
8555 16 St, Suite 500, Silver Spring, MD 20910
Tel: 301-588-1800
E-mail: ncss@ncss.org
Web Site: www.socialstudies.org/membership/awards/carter-g-woodson-book-awards
Key Personnel
Exec Dir: Lawrence Paska *E-mail:* lpaska@ncss.org
Dir, Mktg, Communs & Membership: Joy D Lindsey *Tel:* 301-850-7458 *E-mail:* jlindsey@ncss.org
Dir, Meetings & Exhibits: David Bailor *E-mail:* dbailor@ncss.org
Dir, Pubns & Resources: Michael Simpson *Tel:* 301-850-7453 *E-mail:* msimpson@ncss.org
Established: 1974
Awards presented to exceptional books written for children & young people. Three books, one each elementary (K-6), middle (5-6) & secondary (7-12) will receive the Carter G Woodson Book Award. Three outstanding runner-up books will be designated Carter G Woodson Honor Books. Award winning books will be reviewed in the NCSS journal *Social Education* in the year following the recognition.
Award: Commemorative gift & medallion presented at the NCSS Meet-the-Author Panel Session followed by a book signing
Closing Date: Oct
Presented: Awards Reception, NCSS Annual Conference

The Jacqueline Woodson Award for LGBTQ+ Children's/YA Literature
The Publishing Triangle
511 Avenue of the Americas, No D36, New York, NY 10011
E-mail: awards@publishingtriangle.org; info@publishingtriangle.org; publishingtriangle@gmail.com
Web Site: publishingtriangle.org/awards/the-jacqueline-woodson-award-for-lgbtq-childrens-ya-literature
Celebrates outstanding works of literature, published in the preceding year, geared toward children & young adults that explore themes related to LGBTQ+ experiences, identities & issues. Finalists & winners are determined by a panel of judges appointed by the awards committee.
Award: $1,000

C Vann Woodward Award
Southern Historical Association (SHA)
University of Georgia, Dept of History, Athens, GA 30602-1602
Tel: 706-542-8848
Web Site: thesha.org/woodward
Key Personnel
Secy/Treas: Dr Stephen Berry *E-mail:* berrys@thesha.org
To recognize the best dissertation in southern history defended in the previous calendar year. Authors of eligible dissertations should submit the following information in a single PDF file via e-mail to Manager, Southern Historical Association (manager@thesha.org): cover letter with full contact information; title page, abstract & table of contents; along with sample chapter. The full dissertation should not be submitted. The author should also make arrangements with their dissertation advisor to send in a letter of support containing the dissertator's name in the e-mail subject line, along with a reference to the Woodward Prize.
Other Sponsor(s): Woodward Fund
Award: $3,000 stipend
Closing Date: May 1

Word Works Washington Prize
The Word Works
PO Box 42164, Washington, DC 20015
E-mail: editor@wordworksbooks.org
Web Site: www.wordworksbooks.org
Key Personnel
Chpn, Bd of Dirs: Karren L Alenier
Pres: Nancy White
Series Ed: Andrea Carter Brown *E-mail:* andrea@wordworksbooks.org
Established: 1981
Prize for an unpublished ms of original poetry in English. Submission may be made by any living American or Canadian poet. Submissions should be 48-80 pages. Entry fee: $25.
Award: $1,500 & publication
Closing Date: March 15

World Fantasy Awards
World Fantasy Awards Association
3519 Glen Ave, Palmer Township, PA 18045-5812
Web Site: www.worldfantasy.org
Key Personnel
Pres: Peter Dennis Pautz *E-mail:* sfexecsec@gmail.com
To acknowledge excellence in fantasy writing & art.
Award: Trophy
Closing Date: June 1
Presented: World Fantasy Convention, Halloween weekend

World's Best Short-Short Story Contest
The Southeast Review
Florida State University, Dept of English, Tallahassee, FL 32306
E-mail: southeastreview@gmail.com
Web Site: www.southeastreview.org/writing-contests
Key Personnel
Ed-in-Chief: Zach Linge
Asst Ed: Diamond Forde
Established: 1986

Awarded for best 500 word (maximum) previously unpublished short-short story. Entry fee: $16 for up to 3 stories.
Award: $500 & publication in Spring issue
Closing Date: April 1
Presented: Summer

Doug Wright Awards
PO Box 611, Sta P, Toronto, ON M5S 2Y4, Canada
E-mail: dougwrightawards@gmail.com
Web Site: dougwrightawards.com
Key Personnel
Exec Dir: Conan Tobias
Established: 2004
Four awards given for best book, emerging talent, best small or micro-press book & best kids' book. Entries must have been published during the previous calendar year. The Doug Wright Awards is broad minded in what it considers a book (graphic novel, single comic, mini-comic, zine, etc), but reserves the right to make the final call on a publication's qualification. Books must be published in English. Books originally published in another language & translated into English are eligible, provided the English edition was published during the current calendar year. Creators must be a Canadian citizen or permanent resident/landed immigrant (i.e. legally allowed to work in Canada). For books with more than one creator (i.e. writer & artist team), each creator must be a Canadian citizen or permanent resident. Entries may be published by a non-Canadian publisher, provided creator(s) is a Canadian citizen or permanent resident. There is no limit to how many individual titles a creator or group of creators submit in a single year. Books may be submitted by creators or publishers. Entry fee: $15 per submission for best book & best kids' book. No entry fee for emerging talent or best small or micro-press book.
Award: Cash prize
Closing Date: Jan

Write Now
Childsplay
900 S Mitchell Dr, Tempe, AZ 85281
Tel: 480-921-5700 *Fax:* 480-921-5777
E-mail: info@writenow.co
Web Site: www.writenow.co
Key Personnel
Founder: Dorothy Webb
Artistic Dir: Jenny Millinger *Tel:* 480-921-5770 *E-mail:* jmillinger@childsplayaz.org
Established: 1988
New plays competition & biennial workshop (odd-numbered years) to encourage writers to create strikingly original scripts for young audiences.
Award: $1,000, development workshop & rehearsed reading (up to 4 winners); all scripts receive dramaturgical feedback
Closing Date: May 31

Writer in Residence
Idaho Commission on the Arts
9543 W Emerald St, Suite 204, Boise, ID 83704
Tel: 208-334-2119
E-mail: info@arts.idaho.gov
Web Site: arts.idaho.gov/writer-in-residence
Key Personnel
Lit Dir: Jocelyn Robertson *Tel:* 208-334-2119 ext 108 *E-mail:* jocelyn.robertson@arts.idaho.gov
Awarded biennially, in even-numbered years, for artistic excellence. Applicant must be a resident of Idaho for at least 1 year. Recipient serves a 2-year term, tours the state & gives at least 4 annual readings (6 of 8 in rural communities).
Award: $10,000 ($5,000 annually) plus allowable travel expenses
Closing Date: Jan
Presented: July

The Writer Magazine/Emily Dickinson Award
Poetry Society of America (PSA)
119 Smith St, Brooklyn, NY 11201
Tel: 212-254-9628
E-mail: info@poetrysociety.org
Web Site: poetrysociety.org/awards
Key Personnel
Exec Dir: Matt Brogan *E-mail:* matt@poetrysociety.org
Deputy Dir: Brett Fletcher Lauer *E-mail:* brett@poetrysociety.org
Devt Dir: Madeline Weinfield *E-mail:* madeline@poetrysociety.org
Established: 1971
For a poem inspired by Emily Dickinson (though not necessarily in her style). All submissions must be through Submittable. Entry fee: Free to membs, $10 nonmembs.
Award: $250
Closing Date: Dec 31
Presented: Annual Awards Ceremony, New York, NY, Spring

Writer's Digest Annual Writing Competition
Active Interest Media (AIM)
5720 Flatiron Pkwy, Boulder, CO 80301
Web Site: www.writersdigest.com/writing-competitions
Original, unpublished mss in 10 categories: Inspirational/spiritual; memoirs/personal essay; print or online article; genre short story (mystery, romance, etc); mainstream/literary short story; rhyming poetry; non-rhyming poetry; script (stage play/television/movie script/short film); children's/young adult fiction.
Poetry entry fees: Early $20 first entry, $15 each additional entry; Regular $25 first entry, $20 each additional entry.
Ms entry fees: Early $30 first entry, $25 each additional entry; Regular $35 first entry, $30 each additional entry.
Award: Paid trip to Writer's Digest Conference with (grand prize) $5,000 cash & more, interview in *Writer's Digest*, one-year subn to magazine. See web site for additional prizes for 1st-10th place & honorable mentions
Presented: May (early), June (regular)

Writers Guild of America Awards
Writers Guild of America West (WGAW)
7000 W Third St, Los Angeles, CA 90048
Tel: 323-951-4000; 323-782-4569
   Toll Free Tel: 800-548-4532 *Fax:* 323-782-4801
Web Site: www.wga.org; awards.wga.org
Key Personnel
Pres: Meredith Stiehm
VP: Michele Mulroney
Secy-Treas: Betsy Thomas
Established: 1948
Honors outstanding writing in film, television, new media, news, radio & promotional categories. Theatrical screenplay submissions must have been exhibited for 1 week during the eligibility period. Original & adapted screenplays. Only members can enter.
Award: Statuette
Closing Date: Dec
Presented: Annual Writer's Guild Award Show

Writers' League of Texas Book Awards
Writers' League of Texas (WLT)
611 S Congress Ave, Suite 200 A-3, Austin, TX 78704
Mailing Address: PO Box 41355, Austin, TX 78704
Tel: 512-499-8914
E-mail: wlt@writersleague.org
Web Site: www.writersleague.org
Key Personnel
Exec Dir: Becka Oliver *E-mail:* becka@writersleague.org
Prog Dir: Samantha Babiak *E-mail:* sam@writersleague.org
Memb Servs Mgr/Digital Media Mgr: J Evan Parks
Office Coord: Lore Arnold
Established: 1991
Members of the Writers' League of Texas annually recognize outstanding books (fiction, nonfiction, poetry & literary prose, children's long & children's short) published in the year prior to presentation. Membership is not required. See web site for complete submission details.
Award: $1,000 each award, commemorative award & appearance at the Texas Book Festival
Closing Date: Late Feb
Presented: Autumn

Writers' Trust Engel Findley Award
The Writers' Trust of Canada
600-460 Richmond St W, Toronto, ON M5V 1Y1, Canada
Tel: 416-504-8222 *Toll Free Tel:* 877-906-6548
   Fax: 416-504-9090
E-mail: info@writerstrust.com
Web Site: www.writerstrust.com
Key Personnel
Exec Dir: Charlie Foran *Tel:* 416-504-8222 ext 244 *E-mail:* cforan@writerstrust.com
Mgr, Author Progs: Devon Jackson *Tel:* 416-504-8222 ext 248 *E-mail:* djackson@writerstrust.com
Established: 1986
Presented to a Canadian writer in mid-career. Writers are judged on their body of work—no less than 3 works of literary merit which are predominantly fiction rather than a single book. All Canadian writers are considered.
Award: $25,000
Presented: The Writers' Trust Awards, Toronto, ON, CN, Nov

Writers' Trust McClelland & Stewart Journey Prize
The Writers' Trust of Canada
600-460 Richmond St W, Toronto, ON M5V 1Y1, Canada
Tel: 416-504-8222 *Toll Free Tel:* 877-906-6548
   Fax: 416-504-9090
E-mail: info@writerstrust.com
Web Site: www.writerstrust.com
Key Personnel
Exec Dir: Charlie Foran *Tel:* 416-504-8222 ext 244 *E-mail:* cforan@writerstrust.com
Mgr, Author Progs: Devon Jackson *Tel:* 416-504-8222 ext 248 *E-mail:* djackson@writerstrust.com
Established: 1988
Awarded to a new & developing writer of distinction for a short story published in a Canadian literary publication.
Other Sponsor(s): James A Michener (donation of his Canadian royalty earnings from his novel *Journey*)
Award: $10,000 (winner), $2,500 (finalists)
Presented: The Writers' Trust Awards, Toronto, ON, CN, Nov

WritersWeekly.com's 24-Hour Short Story Contest
WritersWeekly
200 Second Ave S, Unit 526, St Petersburg, FL 33701
Tel: 305-768-0261
Web Site: 24hourshortstorycontest.com
Key Personnel
Publr: Angela Hoy *E-mail:* angela@writersweekly.com
Held quarterly & limited to 500 entrants. You must be entered in the contest before the topic

is posted in order to submit your story. Late stories are disqualified. Entry fee: $5.
Award: $300 & a free print & ebook publishing package from booklocker.com valued at $875 (1st prize), $250 (2nd prize), $200 (3rd prize); plus 85 other prizes
Closing Date: 24 hours after contest start

Wyoming Arts Council Creative Writing Fellowships
Wyoming Arts Council
Division of Wyoming Department of Parks & Cultural Resources
Barrett Bldg, 2nd fl, 2301 Central Ave, Cheyenne, WY 82002
Tel: 307-777-7742
Web Site: wyoarts.state.wy.us
Key Personnel
Creative Arts Specialist: Taylor Craig
 E-mail: taylor.craig@wyo.gov
Established: 1986
Award honoring Wyoming's literary artists whose work reflects serious & exceptional writing. The 3 categories are: Poetry, fiction & nonfiction. Blind judges & one juror. Submissions open in April.
Award: $3,000 each
Closing Date: June

Yale Series of Younger Poets
Yale University Press
302 Temple St, New Haven, CT 06511
Mailing Address: PO Box 209040, New Haven, CT 06520-9040
Tel: 203-432-0960 *Fax:* 203-432-0948
E-mail: ysyp@yale.edu
Web Site: youngerpoets.yupnet.org
Established: 1919
Awarded for poetry mss, 48-64 pages, by early-career American poets who have not previously had a volume of verse published. Submission fee: $25. Mss accepted October 1-November 15. See web site for further details.
Award: Publication & royalties
Closing Date: Nov 15

YALSA Conference Grants
Young Adult Library Services Association (YALSA)
Division of The American Library Association (ALA)
225 N Michigan Ave, Suite 1300, Chicago, IL 60601
Tel: 312-280-4390 *Toll Free Tel:* 800-545-2433
E-mail: yalsa@ala.org
Web Site: www.ala.org/yalsa/awardsandgrants.bakertaloryalsa
Key Personnel
Exec Dir: Tammy Dillard-Steels *Tel:* 800-545-2433 ext 4391 *E-mail:* tdillard@ala.org
Prog Offr, Events & Conferences: Nichole O'Connor *Tel:* 800-545-2433 ext 4387 *E-mail:* noconnor@ala.org
Communs Specialist: Anna Lam *Tel:* 800-545-2433 ext 5849 *E-mail:* alam@ala.org
Established: 1983
Awarded to librarians who work directly with or for young adults to enable them to attend the annual conference for the first time. Two grants given, one to a school librarian & one to a librarian whose focus is public libraries. Applicants must hold YALSA personal membership (preferably for at least 2 years) & have 1-2 years experience working with teenagers.
Other Sponsor(s): Baker & Taylor
Award: $1,000 each
Closing Date: Dec 1

YALSA Research Grant, see Frances Henne/YALSA Research Grant

Anne & Philip Yandle Best Article Award
British Columbia Historical Federation
PO Box 448, Fort Langley, BC V1M 2R7, Canada
E-mail: info@bchistory.ca
Web Site: www.bchistory.ca/awards
Key Personnel
Recognition Chair: Shannon Bettles
 E-mail: shannon@bchistory.ca
Awarded to the author of an article published in *British Columbia History* that best enhances knowledge of the history of British Columbia & provides enjoyable reading. Judging is based upon subject development, writing skill, freshness of material & its appeal to a general readership interested in all aspects of the history of the province.
Award: $250 cash prize & certificate
Closing Date: Dec 31
Presented: BCHF Annual Conference Awards Banquet

YES New Play Festival
Northern Kentucky University
205 FA Theatre Dept, Nunn Dr, Highland Heights, KY 41099-1007
Tel: 859-572-7622
Web Site: www.nku.edu/yesfestival
Key Personnel
Proj Dir: Corrie Danieley *E-mail:* daneileyc1@nku.edu; Michael King *E-mail:* mking@nku.edu
Established: 1983
New play contest (biennial).
Award: $400 & expense-paid (travel & accommodations) visit to NKU to see their plays in production
Closing Date: June 1

Jake Adam York Poetry Prize
Milkweed Editions
1011 Washington Ave S, Suite 300, Minneapolis, MN 55415-1246
Tel: 612-332-3192 *Toll Free Tel:* 800-520-6455
E-mail: thanks@milkweed.org
Web Site: copper-nickel.org/bookprize; milkweed.org/submissions
Accept online submissions of book-length (more than 48 pages) poetry mss. Poets cannot have published, or have under contract, more than one full-length book of poetry. Previously self-published books & co-authored books are ineligible. Poets must be US citizens or must live in the US & be writing in English. Submissions accepted via Submittable beginning July 1, see coppernickel.submittable.com/submit.
Other Sponsor(s): Copper Nickel
Award: $2,000 & publication
Closing Date: Oct 15

Young Lions Fiction Award
The New York Public Library
445 Fifth Ave, 4th fl, New York, NY 10016
Tel: 212-930-0887 *Fax:* 212-930-0983
E-mail: younglions@nypl.org
Web Site: www.nypl.org/ylfa
Key Personnel
Assoc Mgr, Young Lions Fiction Award: Kayla Ponturo *E-mail:* kaylaponturo@nypl.org
Established: 2001
Given to an American writer age 35 or younger for either a novel or collection of short stories.
Award: $10,000
Closing Date: Aug
Presented: The New York Public Library, New York, NY, June

Young Writers Award
Council for Wisconsin Writers (CWW)
c/o 3225 N 91 St, Milwaukee, WI 53222
E-mail: wiswriters@gmail.com
Web Site: wiswriters.org/awards

Key Personnel
Contest Chair: Erik Richardson
 E-mail: erichardson@wi.rr.com
Award to recognize Wisconsin high school students who excel at creative writing. An entry is a single written work in any literary genre on any topic. Genres include poetry, drama, short fiction, essay, humor & memoir.
Award: $250, $50 honorable mention
Closing Date: Jan 31
Presented: CWW Annual Award Ceremony & Banquet, May

YoungArts
National YoungArts Foundation
2100 Biscayne Blvd, Miami, FL 33137
Tel: 305-377-1140 *Toll Free Tel:* 800-970-ARTS (970-2787)
E-mail: info@youngarts.org; apply@youngarts.org
Web Site: www.youngarts.org
Key Personnel
Sr PR Mgr: Heike Dempster *E-mail:* hdempster@youngarts.org
Established: 1981
Cash award & scholarship opportunities for 15-18 year old artists (or in grades 10-12) with demonstrated talent in classical music, dance, design arts, film, jazz, photography, theater, visual arts, voice & writing. Registration fee: $35. Applicants must be US citizens or have permanent resident status.
Other Sponsor(s): Carnival Foundation
Award: Up to $10,000 in individual awards with potential for Presidential Scholar in the Arts Award
Closing Date: Oct 15
Presented: Public performances & exhibitions in Miami, Los Angeles & New York, Jan-April (National YoungArts Week takes place in Miami in Jan)

Morton Dauwen Zabel Award
American Academy of Arts & Letters
633 W 155 St, New York, NY 10032
Tel: 212-368-5900
E-mail: academy@artsandletters.org
Web Site: artsandletters.org/awards
Key Personnel
Exec Dir: Cody Upton
Awarded biennially, in even-numbered years, in rotation to a poet, writer of fiction, or critic, of progressive, original & experimental tendencies. Candidates must be nominated by an academy member.
Award: $10,000

Barbara & David Zalaznick Book Prize in American History
New-York Historical Society
170 Central Park W, New York, NY 10024
Tel: 212-873-3400 *Fax:* 212-595-5707
E-mail: info@nyhistory.org
Web Site: www.nyhistory.org/news/book-prize
Key Personnel
SVP & Dir, Patricia D Klingenstein Library: Valerie Paley
Awarded for a nonfiction book on American history or biography that is distinguished by its scholarship, its literary style & its appeal to a general, as well as an academic, audience. Publishers may submit as many titles as they wish, but must send 7 copies of each submission.
Award: Engraved medal, $50,000 cash prize to author & title of American Historian Laureate
Presented: Chairman's Council Weekend with History, April

The Jacob Zilber Prize for Short Fiction
PRISM international
University of British Columbia, Buch E462, 1866 Main Mall, Vancouver, BC V6T 1Z1, Canada
Tel: 604-822-2514 *Fax:* 604-822-3616

AWARDS, PRIZE CONTESTS, FELLOWSHIPS & GRANTS

E-mail: promotions@prismmagazine.ca
Web Site: www.prismmagazine.ca/contests
Key Personnel
Mng Ed: Emma Cleary
Poetry Ed: Emily Chou
Promos Ed: Alison Barnett
Prose Ed: Vivian Li
Established: 1986
One piece per entry. Maximum 4,000 words (including title). Entry fee: $35 CN, $40 US, $45 intl; additional entries $5.
Award: $1,500 (grand prize), $600 (1st runner up), $400 (2nd runner up); all entries include 1-year subn to *PRISM international*

Charlotte Zolotow Award
Cooperative Children's Book Center (CCBC)
225 N Mills St, Rm 401, Madison, WI 53706
Tel: 608-263-3720
E-mail: ccbcinfo@education.wisc.edu
Web Site: ccbs.education.wisc.edu/books/zolotow.asp
Key Personnel
Comm Chair: Megan Schliesman *Tel:* 608-262-9503 *E-mail:* schliesman@education.wisc.edu
Established: 1998
Awarded to the author of the best picture book text published in the US in the preceding year. Book may be fiction, nonfiction or folklore, as long as it is presented in picture book form & aimed at children from birth to age 7. Must be printed book originally written in English. Books published only as ebooks/digital books are not eligible.
Award: Bronze medallion
Closing Date: Dec
Presented: Spring

Anna Zornio Memorial Children's Theatre Playwriting Award
University of New Hampshire Department of Theatre & Dance
D22 Paul Creative Arts Center, 30 Academic Way, Durham, NH 03824
Tel: 603-862-2919 *Fax:* 603-862-0298
E-mail: theatre.dance@unh.edu
Web Site: cola.unh.edu/theatre-dance/opportunities/competitions
Key Personnel
Chair, Dept of Theatre & Dance: Raina Ames
Admin Mgr: Michael Wood *Tel:* 603-862-3038
  E-mail: mike.wood@unh.edu
Established: 1980
Award for a well written play or musical appropriate for young audiences, PreK-12.
Award: Cash award, up to $500 & play underwritten & produced by the UNH Theatre Department
Closing Date: March 1, 2025
Presented: University of New Hampshire, Durham, NH, Winner announced in Nov

Books & Magazines for the Trade

Reference Books for the Trade

A Dictionary of Modern English Usage
Published by Oxford University Press USA
198 Madison Ave, New York, NY 10016
SAN: 202-5892
Toll Free Tel: 800-445-9714 (cust serv)
E-mail: custserv.us@oup.com
Web Site: global.oup.com
Key Personnel
Author: H W Fowler
Ed: David Crystal
Resource on the correct use of English in matters of style, grammar & syntax.
1st ed, 2010: 832 pp, $17.95 paper
ISBN(s): 978-0-19-958589-2

A Guide to Academic Writing
Published by Praeger
Imprint of ABC-CLIO
147 Castiliane Dr, Santa Barbara, CA 93117
Tel: 805-968-1911 *Toll Free Tel:* 800-368-6868
  Toll Free Fax: 866-270-3856
E-mail: customerservice@abc-clio.com; rights@abc-clio.com
Web Site: www.abc-clio.com
Key Personnel
Edit Dir, Print: Kevin Downing
Author: Jeffery A Cantor
A comprehensive guide to academic writing & publishing.
200 pp, $63 hardcover
ISBN(s): 978-0-313-29017-6

American Book Prices Current
Published by Bancroft-Parkman Inc
PO Box 1236, Washington, CT 06793-0236
Tel: 860-868-7408
E-mail: writeabpc@gmail.com
Web Site: www.bookpricescurrent.com
Key Personnel
Ed-in-Chief: Katharine Kyes Leab
Assoc Ed: Abigail Leab Martin
Research price guide detailing prices realized at auction in the US & abroad in the world of books, mss, autographs, maps & broadsides. Now online only, continually updated.
Online price: Libn, appraiser or dealer $595, others $800, annual update $185
First published 1895

American Book Publishing Record® Annual
Published by Grey House Publishing Inc™
4919 Rte 22, Amenia, NY 12501
Mailing Address: PO Box 56, Amenia, NY 12501-0056
Tel: 518-789-8700 *Toll Free Tel:* 800-562-2139
  Fax: 518-789-0556
E-mail: books@greyhouse.com
Web Site: greyhouse.com
Provides access to approximately 50,000 cataloging records for the entire previous year, for books published or distributed in the US.
Annual.
2023 ed, March 2024: 3,800 pp, $1,170/2 vol set
ISBN(s): 978-1-63700-983-3 (2 vol set)

American Book Trade Directory™
Published by Information Today, Inc
121 Chanlon Rd, Suite G-20, New Providence, NJ 07974-2195
Toll Free Tel: 800-824-2470
E-mail: custserv@infotoday.com
Key Personnel
Mgr, Tampa Edit Opers: Debra James *Tel:* 800-824-2470 option 1 *E-mail:* djames@infotoday.com
Comprehensive directory of over 10,150 booksellers & wholesalers in the US & Canada, arranged by state/province & city; includes information on sidelines, appraisers, auctioneers & dealers in foreign language books.
Annual.
70th ed, 2024-2025: 908 pp, $399.50
ISBN(s): 978-1-57387-598-1

American Library Directory™
Published by Information Today, Inc
121 Chanlon Rd, Suite G-20, New Providence, NJ 07974-2195
Toll Free Tel: 800-300-9868 (cust serv); 800-409-4929 (press 4)
E-mail: custserv@infotoday.com
Web Site: www.americanlibrarydirectory.com
Key Personnel
Consulting Ed: Stephen L Torpie *Tel:* 908-219-0278 *E-mail:* storpie@infotoday.com
Comprehensive directory of over 29,000 libraries (public, academic & special) throughout the US & Canada. Also includes listings of library schools, networks & systems, consortia & state library agencies. Automation information, as well as URLs for libraries & e-mails for library personnel included. Entries arranged geographically. Personnel Index section arranged alphabetically.
Annual.
77th ed, 2024-2025: 3,808 pp, $429 vol set cloth
ISBN(s): 978-1-57387-599-8 (2 vol set)

American Reference Books Annual (2019 ed)
Published by Libraries Unlimited
Imprint of ABC-CLIO
147 Castilian Dr, Santa Barbara, CA 93117
Tel: 805-968-1911 *Toll Free Tel:* 800-368-6868
  Toll Free Fax: 866-270-3856
E-mail: customerservice@abc-clio.com
Web Site: www.abc-clio.com
Key Personnel
Assoc Ed: Juneal M Chenoweth
The premier sources of information for the library & information community for more than 3 decades. Includes descriptive & evaluative entries for recent reference publications. Reviews by subject experts of materials from more than 300 publishers & in nearly 500 subject areas. ARBA assists in answering everyday reference questions & in building a reference collection. Also available online.
Vol 50, 2019: 552 pp, $155 hardcover
ISBN(s): 978-1-4408-6913-6 (hardcover); 978-1-4408-6914-3 (ebook)

The Art & Science of Book Publishing
Published by Ohio University Press
Alden Library, Suite 101, 30 Park Place, Athens, OH 45701-2909
Tel: 740-593-1154
Web Site: www.ohioswallow.com
Key Personnel
Dir & Prodn Mgr: Beth Pratt *Tel:* 740-593-1162
  E-mail: prattb@ohio.edu
Mng Ed: Tyler Balli *E-mail:* tylerballi@ohio.edu
Author: Herbert S Bailey, Jr
Introduction to basics of book publishing.
1990 ed: 234 pp, $24.95 paper
First published 1970
ISBN(s): 978-0-8214-0970-1

Association of University Presses Directory
Published by Association of University Presses (AUPresses)
1412 Broadway, Suite 2135, New York, NY 10018
Tel: 212-989-1010 *Toll Free Tel:* 800-621-2736 (orders) *Fax:* 212-989-0275 *Toll Free Fax:* 800-621-8476 (orders)
E-mail: info@aupresses.org
Web Site: www.aupresses.org
A detailed introduction to the structure & staff of the AUPresses & to the publishing programs & personnel of member presses.
2021: 260 pp, $30 print, $30 full-access digital, $9 30-day access digital
ISBN(s): 978-0-945103-42-4 (digital); 978-0-945103-44-8 (print)

Associations Unlimited
Published by Gale
27555 Executive Dr, Suite 270, Farmington Hills, MI 48331
SAN: 213-4373
Toll Free Tel: 800-877-4253 *Toll Free Fax:* 877-363-4253
E-mail: gale.customerexperience@cengage.com
Web Site: www.gale.com/c/associations-unlimited

Combines data from the entire *Encyclopedia of Associations* series & includes additional IRS information on nonprofit organizations, for a total of more than 456,000 organizations. Useful resource for public & academic librarians, library users, business people & staff of non-profit associations. Online database.

AUPresses Directory, see Association of University Presses Directory

Author in Progress
Published by Writer's Digest Books
Imprint of Penguin Publishing Group
1745 Broadway, New York, NY 10019
Web Site: www.penguinrandomhouse.com
No-nonsense guide for excelling at every step of the novel writing process, from setting goals, researching & drafting to giving & receiving critiques, polishing prose & seeking publication.
2016: 352 pp, $24 paper, $15.99 ebook
ISBN(s): 978-1-4403-4671-2 (paper); 978-1-4403-4673-6 (ebook)

Authors, Copyright, and Publishing in the Digital Era
Published by IGI Global
701 E Chocolate Ave, Hershey, PA 17033
Tel: 717-533-8845 (ext 100) *Toll Free Tel:* 866-342-6657 *Fax:* 717-533-8661; 717-533-7115
E-mail: cust@igi-global.com
Web Site: www.igi-global.com
2014: 262 pp, $195
ISBN(s): 978-1-4666-5214-9; 978-1-4666-5215-6 (ebook)

Awards & Prizes Online
Published by The Children's Book Council (CBC)
54 W 39 St, 14th fl, New York, NY 10018
E-mail: cbc.info@cbcbooks.org
Web Site: www.cbcbooks.org
Key Personnel
Exec Dir: Carl Lennertz *E-mail:* carl.lennertz@cbcbooks.org
Assoc Exec Dir: Shaina Birkhead *E-mail:* shaina.birkhead@cbcbooks.org
Lists over 300 major US, British Commonwealth & international children's & young adult book awards; for teachers, librarians & universities with English, library or education schools teaching children's literature or creative writing. Includes indices, appendix & a list of information resources.
$150 online

Banned in the USA: A Reference Guide to Book Censorship in Schools and Public Libraries
Published by Greenwood
Imprint of ABC-CLIO LLC
147 Castilian Dr, Santa Barbara, CA 93117
Tel: 805-968-1911 *Toll Free Tel:* 800-368-6868
Toll Free Fax: 866-270-3856
E-mail: customerservice@abc-clio.com; rights@abc-clio.com
Web Site: www.abc-clio.com
Key Personnel
Edit Dir, Print: Kevin Downing
Author: Herbert N Foerstel
Foerstel's book is the perfect book to hand to students writing papers on censorship or anyone doing research on the subject.
2nd ed, 2002: 328 pp, $72 hardcover
ISBN(s): 978-0-313-00670-8 (ebook); 978-0-313-31166-6 (hardcover)

Be the Media
Published by Natural E Creative Group LLC
10 W Broadway, Suite 10J, Long Beach, NY 11561
Tel: 516-488-1143 *Fax:* 516-889-1493
E-mail: info@bethemedia.com
Web Site: www.bethemedia.com
1st ed: 536 pp, $34.95 US
First published 2008
ISBN(s): 978-0-9760814-5-6

Biography and Genealogy Master Index (BGMI)
Published by Gale
Division of Cengage Learning
27555 Executive Dr, Suite 270, Farmington Hills, MI 48331
SAN: 213-4373
Toll Free Tel: 800-877-4253 *Toll Free Fax:* 877-363-4253
E-mail: gale.customerexperience@cengage.com
Web Site: www.gale.com
Provides more than 17 million citations compiled from more than 2,000 publications, covering over 5 million people. Available online, updated twice annually.

Book Review Digest
Published by Grey House Publishing Inc™
4919 Rte 22, Amenia, NY 12501
Mailing Address: PO Box 56, Amenia, NY 12501-0056
Tel: 518-789-8700 *Toll Free Tel:* 800-562-2139
Fax: 518-789-0556
E-mail: books@greyhouse.com
Web Site: greyhouse.com
Concise critical evaluations, including citations & excerpts from more than 5,000 book reviews, from more than 100 selected American, British & Canadian periodicals.
Annual.
2023 annual cumulation, Jan 2024, $695
ISBN(s): 978-1-63700-873-7

Book Review Index
Published by Gale
Division of Cengage Learning
27555 Executive Dr, Suite 270, Farmington Hills, MI 48331
SAN: 213-4373
Toll Free Tel: 800-877-4253 *Toll Free Fax:* 877-363-4253
E-mail: gale.customerexperience@cengage.com
Web Site: www.gale.com
Provides access to reviews of books, periodicals, books on tape & electronic media representing a wide range of popular, academic & professional interests. Includes the entire backfile of *Book Review Index* print content from 1965 to present with more than 5.6 million reviews on more than 2.5 million titles. Online database, OpenURL compliant.

Bookbinding Materials & Techniques 1700-1920
Published by Canadian Bookbinders and Book Artists Guild (CBBAG)
82809-467 Parliament St, Toronto, ON M5A 3Y2, Canada
E-mail: cbbag@cbbag.ca
Web Site: www.cbbag.ca
Key Personnel
Author: Margaret Lock
160 pp, $20
First published 2003
ISBN(s): 978-0-9695091-9-6

Bookman's Price Index: A Guide to the Values of Rare & Other Out-of-Print Books
Published by Gale
Division of Cengage Learning
27555 Executive Dr, Suite 270, Farmington Hills, MI 48331
SAN: 213-4373
Toll Free Tel: 800-877-4253 *Toll Free Fax:* 877-363-4253
E-mail: gale.customerexperience@cengage.com
Web Site: www.gale.com
Gathers the most recent listings in the antiquarian book world in order to create a catalog of recent trends & pricing in the field of collectible books. Volumes do not supersede previous volumes. Each volume covers catalogs from the previous 4-6 months. Each entry includes title, author, edition, year published, physical description (size, binding, illustrations), condition of the book & price.
Vol 105, 2018, $1,229 hardcover
First published 1964
ISBN(s): 978-1-4103-1796-4

Books in Print®
Published by Grey House Publishing Inc™
4919 Rte 22, Amenia, NY 12501
Mailing Address: PO Box 56, Amenia, NY 12501-0056
Tel: 518-789-8700 *Toll Free Tel:* 800-562-2139
Fax: 518-789-0556
E-mail: books@greyhouse.com
Web Site: greyhouse.com
Serves the library & book trade communities as the definitive bibliographic resource. Features more than 2 million titles from more than 75,000 US publishers, to offer unparalleled coverage of the full range of books currently published or distributed in the US.
Annual.
77th ed, 2024/2025, July 2024: 18,000 pp, $1,999/7 vol set
ISBN(s): 978-1-63700-938-3 (7 vol set)

Books in Print® Supplement
Published by Grey House Publishing Inc™
4919 Rte 22, Amenia, NY 12501
Mailing Address: PO Box 56, Amenia, NY 12501-0056
Tel: 518-789-8700 *Toll Free Tel:* 800-562-2139
Fax: 518-789-0556
E-mail: books@greyhouse.com
Web Site: greyhouse.com
This essential mid-year companion to *Books In Print®* provides the latest book publishing updates for the past 6 months. This resource is crucial in ensuring that libraries & bookstores have access to the most accurate information throughout the year.
Annual.
60th ed, 2023-2024, Feb 2024: 8,400 pp, $1,235/3 vol set
ISBN(s): 978-1-63700-617-3 (3 vol set)

Books Out Loud™: Bowker's Guide to Audiobooks
Published by Grey House Publishing Inc™
4919 Rte 22, Amenia, NY 12501
Mailing Address: PO Box 56, Amenia, NY 12501-0056
Tel: 518-789-8700 *Toll Free Tel:* 800-562-2139
Fax: 518-789-0556
E-mail: books@greyhouse.com
Web Site: greyhouse.com
Must-have collection development & reference tool for your library or bookstore. Offers bibliographic information on over 300,000 audiobooks from over 10,000 producers & 2,100 distributors & wholesalers.
Annual.
2024, Dec 2023: 5,800 pp, $875/2 vol set
ISBN(s): 978-1-63700-628-3 (2 vol set)

Business & Legal Forms for Authors & Self-Publishers
Published by Allworth Press
Imprint of Skyhorse Publishing Inc
307 W 36 St, 11th fl, New York, NY 10018

FOR THE TRADE

Tel: 212-643-6816 Fax: 212-643-6819
Web Site: www.allworth.com
Key Personnel
Founder & Publr: Tad Crawford
  E-mail: tcrawford@skyhorsepublishing.com
Busn Mgr: Marrissa Jones E-mail: mjones@skyhorsepublishing.com
Contains 32 ready-to-use forms, negotiation checklist & extra tear-out forms; digital forms available online.
4th ed, 2015: 176 pp, $24.99
ISBN(s): 978-1-62153-464-2

Business Information Resources
Published by Grey House Publishing Inc™
4919 Rte 22, Amenia, NY 12501
Mailing Address: PO Box 56, Amenia, NY 12501-0056
Tel: 518-789-8700 Toll Free Tel: 800-562-2139
  Fax: 518-789-0556
E-mail: books@greyhouse.com
Web Site: greyhouse.com
With comprehensive coverage of 104 industries, detailed & informative entries include contact names, phone & fax numbers, web sites & e-mail addresses along with descriptions, membership information, ordering details & more.
Annual.
31st ed, 2024: 1,800 pp, $195 (includes online access)
First published 1992
ISBN(s): 978-1-63700-811-9

Butcher's Copy-editing: The Cambridge Handbook for Editors, Copy-editors and Proofreaders
Published by Cambridge University Press
One Liberty Plaza, 20th fl, New York, NY 10006
SAN: 200-206X
Tel: 212-337-5000
E-mail: customer_service@cambridge.org
Web Site: www.cambridge.org/us
Key Personnel
Author: Judith Butcher; Caroline Drake; Maureen Leach
Covers all aspects of the editorial process, from the basics of how to prepare text & illustrations for the designer & typesetter, through the ground rules of house style, to how to read & correct proofs.
4th ed, 2006: 558 pp, $121 hardcover, $92 ebook
First published 1975
ISBN(s): 978-0-511-24772-9 (ebook); 978-0-521-84713-1 (hardcover)

The Byline Bible
Published by Writer's Digest Books
Imprint of Penguin Publishing Group
1745 Broadway, New York, NY 10019
Web Site: www.penguinrandomhouse.com
Everything you need to learn to write & sell your short nonfiction story in 5 weeks or less.
2018: 272 pp, $19.99 paper, $14.99 ebook
ISBN(s): 978-1-4403-5368-0 (paper); 978-1-4403-5370-3 (ebook)

Careers in Communications & Media
Published by Grey House Publishing Inc™
4919 Rte 22, Amenia, NY 12501
Mailing Address: PO Box 56, Amenia, NY 12501-0056
Tel: 518-789-8700 Toll Free Tel: 800-562-2139
  Fax: 518-789-0556
E-mail: csr@salempress.com
Web Site: salempress.com
Key Personnel
Ed: Michael Shally-Jensen, PhD
Provides a current overview & future outlook of specific occupations in communications & media industries. Companies in this field are involved in television & radio broadcasting, motion picture/video production, publishing, advertising & telecommunications.
Jan 2014: 375 pp, $125 (includes online access with print purchase)
ISBN(s): 978-1-61925-230-1; 978-1-61925-231-8 (ebook)

Careers in Writing & Editing
Published by Grey House Publishing Inc™
4919 Rte 22, Amenia, NY 12501
Mailing Address: PO Box 56, Amenia, NY 12501-0056
Tel: 518-789-8700 Toll Free Tel: 800-562-2139
  Fax: 518-789-0556
E-mail: csr@salempress.com
Web Site: salempress.com
Considers the changing landscape of work opportunities for writers & editors, including freelance, remote & contract work for writers & editors; photo & video editing; copy-editing & proofreading; scriptwriting; assessment writing; grant writing; indexing & more.
Feb 2020: 350 pp, $125 (includes online access)
ISBN(s): 978-1-64265-395-3; 978-1-64265-396-0 (ebook)

Catholic Media Association Directory
Published by Catholic Media Association (CMA)
10 S Riverside Plaza, Suite 875, Chicago, IL 60606
Tel: 312-380-6789
Web Site: www.catholicmediaassociation.org
Key Personnel
Exec Dir: Rob DeFrancesco
  E-mail: rdefrancesco@CatholicMediaAssociation.org
Features information about all CMA members, including contact information, services offered, circulation & more.
Annual.
2024, $35 membs, $80 for nonmembs

CCOD, see Consultants & Consulting Organizations Directory (CCOD)

The Chicago Guide to Fact-Checking
Published by University of Chicago Press
1427 E 60 St, Chicago, IL 60637-2954
SAN: 202-5280
Tel: 773-702-7700; 773-702-7000 (cust serv, print); 773-753-3347 Toll Free Tel: 800-621-2736 (orders); 877-705-1878 (US & CN)
  Fax: 773-702-9756
E-mail: custserv@press.uchicago.edu; marketing@press.uchicago.edu
Web Site: www.press.uchicago.edu
Key Personnel
Exec Ed, Ref & Writing Guides: Mary Laur
  Tel: 773-702-7326 E-mail: mlaur@uchicago.edu
This book is an accessible, one-stop guide to the why, what & how of contemporary fact-checking. Brooke Borel covers best practices for fact-checking in a variety of media—from magazine articles, both print & online, to books & documentaries—& from the perspective of both in-house & freelance checkers. She also offers advice on navigating relationships with writers, editors & sources; considers the realities of fact-checking on a budget & checking one's own work; & reflects on the place of fact-checking in today's media landscape.
2nd ed: 192 pp, $18 paper, $17.99 epub or PDF
First published 2016
ISBN(s): 978-0-226-29109-3 (epub or PDF); 978-0-226-81789-7 (paper)

The Chicago Manual of Style
Published by University of Chicago Press
1427 E 60 St, Chicago, IL 60637-2954
SAN: 202-5280
Tel: 773-702-7700; 773-702-7000 (cust serv, print); 773-753-3347 Toll Free Tel: 800-621-2736 (orders); 877-705-1878 (US & CN)
  Fax: 773-702-9756
E-mail: custserv@press.uchicago.edu; marketing@press.uchicago.edu; cmoshelpdesk@press.uchicago.edu
Web Site: www.press.uchicago.edu; www.chicagomanualofstyle.org
Key Personnel
Exec Ed, Ref & Writing Guides: Mary Laur
  Tel: 773-702-7326 E-mail: mlaur@uchicago.edu
Style manual for authors, editors & copywriters. Also available as an online subscription.
Revised every 7-10 yrs.
18th ed, 2024: 1,192 pp, $75
ISBN(s): 978-0-226-81797-2

Children's Books in Print®
Published by Grey House Publishing Inc™
4919 Rte 22, Amenia, NY 12501
Mailing Address: PO Box 56, Amenia, NY 12501-0056
Tel: 518-789-8700 Toll Free Tel: 800-562-2139
  Fax: 518-789-0556
E-mail: books@greyhouse.com
Web Site: greyhouse.com
Vital resource for locating children's & young adult titles in the US, offering immediate access to over 275,000 children's books from over 20,000 U.S. Publishers.
Annual.
55th ed, 2024, Nov 2023: 3,500 pp, $990/3 vol set
ISBN(s): 978-1-63700-639-9 (3 vol set)

Children's Core Collection
Published by Grey House Publishing Inc™
4919 Rte 22, Amenia, NY 12501
Mailing Address: PO Box 56, Amenia, NY 12501-0056
Tel: 518-789-8700 Toll Free Tel: 800-562-2139
  Fax: 518-789-0556
E-mail: books@greyhouse.com
Web Site: greyhouse.com
Guide to approximately 12,000 books, covering fiction & nonfiction works, story collections, picture books, easy readers, graphic novels & biographies recommended for readers from preschool through grade 6.
26th ed, Oct 2023: 3,000 pp, $240
ISBN(s): 978-1-63700-509-5

Children's Literature Review
Published by Gale
Division of Cengage Learning
27555 Executive Dr, Suite 270, Farmington Hills, MI 48331
SAN: 213-4373
Toll Free Tel: 800-877-4253 Toll Free Fax: 877-363-4253
E-mail: gale.customerexperience@cengage.com
Web Site: www.gale.com
Online resource providing critical information from English language sources in the field of children's & young adult literature. The series currently covers more than 750 authors.

Children's Writer's & Illustrator's Market
Published by Writer's Digest Books
Imprint of Penguin Publishing Group
1745 Broadway, New York, NY 10019
Web Site: www.penguinrandomhouse.com
More than 500 listings for children's book markets, including publishers, literary agents, magazines, contests & more. Listings include point of contact, how to properly submit your work & what categories each market accepts.
33rd ed, 2022: 416 pp, $30 paper, $14.99 ebook
ISBN(s): 978-0-593-33205-4 (paper); 978-0-593-33206-1 (ebook)

REFERENCE BOOKS FOR THE TRADE

Children's Writer's Word Book
Published by Writer's Digest Books
Imprint of Penguin Publishing Group
1745 Broadway, New York, NY 10019
Web Site: www.penguinrandomhouse.com
Find appropriate words & discover substitute words for children of various ages to address your young audience with a vocabulary & style they will understand & improve your chances with children's publishers.
2nd ed, 2006: 400 pp, $19.99 paper, $14.99 ebook
First published 1999
ISBN(s): 978-1-58297-413-2 (paper); 978-1-58297-688-4 (ebook)

Complete Broadcasting Industry Guide: Television, Radio, Cable & Streaming
Published by Grey House Publishing Inc™
4919 Rte 22, Amenia, NY 12501
Mailing Address: PO Box 56, Amenia, NY 12501-0056
Tel: 518-789-8700 *Toll Free Tel:* 800-562-2139
Fax: 518-789-0556
E-mail: books@greyhouse.com
Web Site: greyhouse.com
Station data & industry contacts in the U.S. & Canadian television, radio & cable marketplace.
Annual.
2024: 1,700 pp, $350 (includes online access)
ISBN(s): 978-1-63700-563-7

The Complete Guide to Book Marketing
Published by Allworth Press
Imprint of Skyhorse Publishing Inc
307 W 36 St, 11th fl, New York, NY 10018
Tel: 212-643-6816 *Fax:* 212-643-6819
Web Site: www.allworth.com
Key Personnel
Founder & Publr: Tad Crawford
  E-mail: tcrawford@skyhorsepublishing.com
Busn Mgr: Marrissa Jones *E-mail:* mjones@skyhorsepublishing.com
Author: David Cole
Comprehensive resource book covering all aspects of book marketing.
2004 (revised): 256 pp, $26.99
ISBN(s): 978-1-62153-661-1

The Complete Guide to Book Publicity
Published by Allworth Press
Imprint of Skyhorse Publishing Inc
307 W 36 St, 11th fl, New York, NY 10018
Tel: 212-643-6816 *Fax:* 212-643-6819
Web Site: www.allworth.com
Key Personnel
Founder & Publr: Tad Crawford
  E-mail: tcrawford@skyhorsepublishing.com
Busn Mgr: Marrissa Jones *E-mail:* mjones@skyhorsepublishing.com
Author: Jodee Blanco
A comprehensive resource book covering all aspects of book publicity.
2nd ed, 2004: 304 pp, $19.95
ISBN(s): 978-1-58115-349-1

The Complete Guide to Successful Publishing
Published by Cardoza Publishing
1916 E Charleston Blvd, Las Vegas, NV 89104
Tel: 702-870-7200
E-mail: cardozaent@aol.com
Web Site: cardozapublishing.com
Key Personnel
Publr & Author: Avery Cardoza
This step-by-step guide shows beginning & established publishers how to successfully produce professional-looking books that not only look good, but sell in the open market; readers learn how to find & develop ideas; set up the business from the ground up; design & layout a book; find authors, work contracts & negotiate deals; get distribution; expand a publishing company into a large enterprise & more.
3rd ed, April 2003: 416 pp, $12.97
First published 1995
ISBN(s): 978-1-58042-097-6

The Complete Handbook of Novel Writing
Published by Writer's Digest Books
Imprint of Penguin Publishing Group
1745 Broadway, New York, NY 10019
Web Site: www.penguinrandomhouse.com
Everything you need to know about creating & selling your work.
3rd ed, 2017: 528 pp, $22.99 paper, $10.99 ebook
First published 2002
ISBN(s): 978-1-4403-4839-6 (paper); 978-1-4403-4845-7 (ebook)

Complete Video Directory™
Published by Grey House Publishing Inc™
4919 Rte 22, Amenia, NY 12501
Mailing Address: PO Box 56, Amenia, NY 12501-0056
Tel: 518-789-8700 *Toll Free Tel:* 800-562-2139
Fax: 518-789-0556
E-mail: books@greyhouse.com
Web Site: greyhouse.com
Extensive listing of over 72,000 entertainment & performance titles along with educational & special interest videos & educational programs.
Annual.
2024: 7,900 pp, $1,245/4 vol set
ISBN(s): 978-1-63700-960-4 (4 vol set)

Concise Dictionary of British Literary Biography
Published by Gale
Division of Cengage Learning
27555 Executive Dr, Suite 270, Farmington Hills, MI 48331
SAN: 213-4373
Toll Free Tel: 800-877-4253 *Toll Free Fax:* 877-363-4253
E-mail: gale.customerexperience@cengage.com
Web Site: www.gale.com
Key Personnel
Ed: Matthew J Bruccoli; Richard Layman
Illustrated set provides thorough coverage of major British literary figures of all eras. Each volume covers 20-30 writers from all genres who were active during a single historical period.
Vol 1: *Writers of the Middle Ages and Renaissance Before 1660*
Vol 2: *Writers of the Restoration and 18th Century 1660-1789*
Vol 3: *Writers of the Romantic Period, 1789-1832*
Vol 4: *Victorian Writers, 1832-1890*
Vol 5: *Late Victorian and Edwardian Writers, 1890-1914*
Vol 6: *Modern Writers, 1914-1945*
Vol 7: *Writers After World War II, 1945-1960*
Vol 8: *Contemporary Writers, 1960-Present*.
1st ed, 1992: 24,000 pp, $1,786/8-vol set hardcover
ISBN(s): 978-0-8103-7980-0

Concise Major 21st-Century Writers
Published by Gale
Division of Cengage Learning
27555 Executive Dr, Suite 270, Farmington Hills, MI 48331
SAN: 213-4373
Toll Free Tel: 800-877-4253 *Toll Free Fax:* 877-363-4253
E-mail: gale.customerexperience@cengage.com
Web Site: www.gale.com
Detailed biographical & bibliographical information on approximately 700 authors who are most often studied in college & high school. Sketches typically include personal information, addresses, career history, writings, works in progress, biographical/critical sources & authors' comments +/or informative essays about their lives & work. Available as ebook only.
3rd ed, 2006
ISBN(s): 978-1-4144-1048-7

Consultants & Consulting Organizations Directory (CCOD)
Published by Gale
Division of Cengage Learning
27555 Executive Dr, Suite 270, Farmington Hills, MI 48331
SAN: 213-4373
Toll Free Tel: 800-877-4253 *Toll Free Fax:* 877-363-4253
E-mail: gale.customerexperience@cengage.com
Web Site: www.gale.com
Important details, including services offered, full contact information, date founded & principal business executives. More than 26,000 firms & individuals listed are arranged in subject sections under 14 general fields of consulting activity ranging from agriculture to marketing. More than 400 specialties are represented, including finance, computers, fund raising & others. Available as ebook only.
48th ed, 2023
ISBN(s): 978-0-0286-7631-9

Contemporary Authors
Published by Gale
Division of Cengage Learning
27555 Executive Dr, Suite 270, Farmington Hills, MI 48331
SAN: 213-4373
Toll Free Tel: 800-877-4253 *Toll Free Fax:* 877-363-4253
E-mail: gale.customerexperience@cengage.com
Web Site: www.gale.com
Current biographical & bibliographical data on more than 164,500 modern authors. All 770 volumes of *Contemporary Authors & Contemporary Authors New Revision* are included along with select autobiographies, author-provided updates, expanded entries, bibliographies & awards. Online database updated monthly.

Contemporary Literary Criticism
Published by Gale
Division of Cengage Learning
27555 Executive Dr, Suite 270, Farmington Hills, MI 48331
SAN: 213-4373
Toll Free Tel: 800-877-4253 *Toll Free Fax:* 877-363-4253
E-mail: gale.customerexperience@cengage.com
Web Site: www.gale.com
Series provides readers with critical commentary & general information on more than 3,000 authors from 91 countries, currently living or who died after December 31, 1999. Online database.

Creating Characters
Published by Writer's Digest Books
Imprint of Penguin Publishing Group
1745 Broadway, New York, NY 10019
Web Site: www.penguinrandomhouse.com
Comprehensive reference to every stage of character development to populate your fiction series, novel, short story, or flash fiction.
2014: 352 pp, $19.99 paper, $9.99 ebook
ISBN(s): 978-1-59963-876-8 (paper); 978-1-59963-880-5 (ebook)

Critical Approaches to Literature
Published by Grey House Publishing Inc™
4919 Rte 22, Amenia, NY 12501
Mailing Address: PO Box 56, Amenia, NY 12501-0056
Tel: 518-789-8700 *Toll Free Tel:* 800-562-2139
Fax: 518-789-0556
E-mail: csr@salempress.com

Web Site: salempress.com
Key Personnel
Ed: Robert C Evans
Each volume provides literature students with the tools necessary to study each approach to literary criticism using a unique combination of critical contexts & analysis of several works. Also includes in-depth critical readings of popular works.
Individual volumes:
Feminist, published Jan 2018, 359 pp
Moral, published April 2017, 300 pp
Multicultural, published July 2017, 336 pp
Psychological, published March 2017, 350 pp.
$125/vol (includes online access)
ISBN(s): 978-1-68217-272-8 (Psychological); 978-1-68217-273-5 (Psychological ebook); 978-1-68217-274-2 (Moral); 978-1-68217-275-9 (Moral ebook); 978-1-68217-575-0 (Multicultural); 978-1-68217-576-7 (Multicultural ebook); 978-1-68217-577-4 (Feminist); 978-1-68217-578-1 (Feminist ebook)

Critical Insights: Authors
Published by Grey House Publishing Inc™
4919 Rte 22, Amenia, NY 12501
Mailing Address: PO Box 56, Amenia, NY 12501-0056
Tel: 518-789-8700 *Toll Free Tel:* 800-562-2139
Fax: 518-789-0556
E-mail: csr@salempress.com
Web Site: salempress.com
Key Personnel
Ed, The Bronte Sisters & Edgar Allen Poe: Robert C Evans
Ed, J D Salinger: Peter J Bailey
Ed, Amy Tan: Linda Trinh Moser; Kathryn West
Ed, Virginia Woolf: James F Nicosia; Laura Nicosia
Each volume includes: General bibliography, chronology of author's life, complete list of author's works, publication dates of works, detailed bio of the editor & general subject index.
Volumes published Aug-Oct 2021:
Thomas Hardy, 300 pp
Amy Tan, 258 pp
Volumes published Jan-Oct 2022:
The Bronte Sisters, 300 pp
J D Salinger, 300 pp
Edgar Allen Poe, 300 pp
Virginia Woolf, 300 pp
Volumes published Feb-Sept 2023:
C S Lewis, 300 pp
Ralph Waldo Emerson, 300 pp.
$105/vol (includes online access with print purchase)
ISBN(s): 978-1-63700-002-1 (Thomas Hardy); 978-1-63700-003-8 (Thomas Hardy ebook); 978-1-63700-073-1 (The Bronte Sisters); 978-1-63700-074-8 (The Bronte Sisters ebook); 978-1-63700-075-5 (J D Salinger); 978-1-63700-076-2 (J D Salinger ebook); 978-1-63700-347-3 (Edgar Allen Poe); 978-1-63700-348-0 (Edgar Allen Poe ebook); 978-1-63700-351-3 (Virginia Woolf); 978-1-63700-352-7 (Virginia Woolf ebook); 978-1-63700-434-0 (C S Lewis); 978-1-63700-435-7 (C S Lewis ebook); 978-1-63700-440-1 (Ralph Waldo Emerson); 978-1-63700-441-8 (Ralph Waldo Emerson ebook); 978-1-64265-994-8 (Amy Tan); 978-1-64265-995-5 (Amy Tan ebook)

Critical Insights: Themes
Published by Grey House Publishing Inc™
4919 Rte 22, Amenia, NY 12501
Mailing Address: PO Box 56, Amenia, NY 12501-0056
Tel: 518-789-8700 *Toll Free Tel:* 800-562-2139
Fax: 518-789-0556
E-mail: csr@salempress.com
Web Site: salempress.com
Key Personnel
Ed, Truth & Lies: Robert C Evans
Each volume explores a popular literary theme.
Volume published July 2021:
Patriotism, 300 pp
Volumes published Feb-Oct 2022:
Love, 300 pp
Truth & Lies, 300 pp
Volume published Oct 2023:
Power & Corruption, 400 pp.
$105/vol (includes online access with print purchase)
ISBN(s): 978-1-63700-000-7 (Patriotism); 978-1-63700-001-4 (Patriotism ebook); 978-1-63700-077-9 (Love); 978-1-63700-078-6 (Love ebook); 978-1-63700-349-7 (Truth & Lies); 978-1-63700-350-3 (Truth & Lies ebook); 978-1-63700-442-5 (Power & Corruption); 978-1-63700-443-2 (Power & Corruption ebook)

Critical Insights: Works
Published by Grey House Publishing Inc™
4919 Rte 22, Amenia, NY 12501
Mailing Address: PO Box 56, Amenia, NY 12501-0056
Tel: 518-789-8700 *Toll Free Tel:* 800-562-2139
Fax: 518-789-0556
E-mail: csr@salempress.com
Web Site: salempress.com
Key Personnel
Ed, Catch-22: James F Nicosia, PhD; Laura Nicosia, PhD
Ed, Julius Caesar, On the Road, The Lord of the Rings & The Old Man and the Sea: Robert C Evans
Ed, The Adventures of Tom Sawyer: R Kent Rasmussen
Ed, The Color Purple: Jericho Williams
Each essay is 5,000 words in length & offers comprehensive, in-depth coverage of a single work. Each volume contains essays that break down the work from several different perspectives & includes a brief biography of the author.
Volumes published Aug-Dec 2021:
A Tale of Two Cities by Charles Dickens, 300 pp
Catch-22 by Joseph Heller, 300 pp
Julius Caesar by William Shakespeare, 300 pp
Volumes published Jan-Dec 2022:
The Lord of the Rings by JRR Tolkien, 300 pp
The Color Purple by Alice Walker, 300 pp
On the Road by Jack Kerouac, 300 pp
The Adventures of Tom Sawyer by Mark Twain, 300 pp
The Old Man and the Sea by Ernest Hemingway, 300 pp
The Merchant of Venice by William Shakespeare, 300 pp
Volumes published Jan-Aug 2023:
A Raisin in the Sun by Lorraine Hansberry, 300 pp
The Plague by Albert Camus, 300 pp
All the Pretty Horses by Cormac McCarthy, 400 pp
Sense and Sensibility by Jane Austen, 400 pp.
$105/vol (includes online access with print purchase)
ISBN(s): 978-1-61925-525-8 (On the Road); 978-1-61925-526-5 (On the Road ebook); 978-1-63700-067-0 (Julius Caesar); 978-1-63700-068-7 (Julius Caesar ebook); 978-1-63700-069-4 (The Color Purple); 978-1-63700-070-0 (The Color Purple ebook); 978-1-63700-071-7 (The Lord of the Rings); 978-1-63700-072-4 (The Lord of the Rings ebook); 978-1-63700-343-5 (The Adventures of Tom Sawyer); 978-1-63700-344-2 (The Adventures of Tom Sawyer ebook); 978-1-63700-345-9 (The Old Man and the Sea); 978-1-63700-346-6 (The Old Man and the Sea ebook); 978-1-63700-428-9 (A Raisin in the Sun); 978-1-63700-429-6 (A Raisin in the Sun ebook); 978-1-63700-430-2 (The Merchant of Venice); 978-1-63700-431-9 (The Merchant of Venice ebook); 978-1-63700-432-6 (The Plague); 978-1-63700-433-3 (The Plague ebook); 978-1-63700-436-4 (All the Pretty Horses); 978-1-63700-437-1 (All the Pretty Horses ebook); 978-1-63700-438-8 (Sense and Sensibility); 978-1-63700-439-5 (Sense and Sensibility ebook); 978-1-64265-992-4 (A Tale of Two Cities); 978-1-64265-993-1 (A Tale of Two Cities ebook); 978-1-64265-996-2 (Catch-22); 978-1-64265-997-9 (Catch-22 ebook)

Critical Survey of American Literature
Published by Grey House Publishing Inc™
4919 Rte 22, Amenia, NY 12501
Mailing Address: PO Box 56, Amenia, NY 12501-0056
Tel: 518-789-8700 *Toll Free Tel:* 800-562-2139
Fax: 518-789-0556
E-mail: csr@salempress.com
Web Site: salempress.com
Key Personnel
Ed: Steven G Kellman, PhD
Detailed profiles of over 400 major American authors of fiction, drama & poetry, each with sections on biography, general analysis & analysis of the author's most important works. Originally published as *Magill's Survey of American Literature*.
Dec 2016: 3,422 pp, $499/6 vol set (includes online access with print purchase)
First published 2006
ISBN(s): 978-1-68217-128-8 (6 vol set); 978-1-68217-147-9 (ebook set)

Critical Survey of Drama
Published by Grey House Publishing Inc™
4919 Rte 22, Amenia, NY 12501
Mailing Address: PO Box 56, Amenia, NY 12501-0056
Tel: 518-789-8700 *Toll Free Tel:* 800-562-2139
Fax: 518-789-0556
E-mail: csr@salempress.com
Web Site: salempress.com
Contains 638 essays that discuss both individual dramatists & overview topics. Also contains a listing of major dramatic awards, time line of drama history, glossary & bibliography.
3rd ed, Dec 2017: 4,438 pp, $599/8 vol set (includes online access with print purchase)
ISBN(s): 978-1-68217-622-1 (8 vol set); 978-1-68217-639-9 (ebook set)

Critical Survey of Graphic Novels: Heroes & Superheroes
Published by Grey House Publishing Inc™
4919 Rte 22, Amenia, NY 12501
Mailing Address: PO Box 56, Amenia, NY 12501-0056
Tel: 518-789-8700 *Toll Free Tel:* 800-562-2139
Fax: 518-789-0556
E-mail: csr@salempress.com
Web Site: salempress.com
Key Personnel
Ed: Bart H Beaty; Stephen Weiner
Provides in-depth insight into over 150 of the most popular & studied graphic novels. Arranged alphabetically.
2nd ed, Sept 2018: 948 pp, $295/2 vol set (includes online access with print purchase)
ISBN(s): 978-1-68217-908-6 (2 vol set); 978-1-68217-956-7 (ebook set)

Critical Survey of Graphic Novels: History, Theme & Technique
Published by Grey House Publishing Inc™
4919 Rte 22, Amenia, NY 12501
Mailing Address: PO Box 56, Amenia, NY 12501-0056
Tel: 518-789-8700 *Toll Free Tel:* 800-562-2139
Fax: 518-789-0556
E-mail: csr@salempress.com
Web Site: salempress.com
Key Personnel
Ed: Bart H Beaty; Stephen Weiner

Contains over 80 essays covering themes & concepts in graphic novels, including genres, time periods, foreign language traditions, social relevance & craftsmanship such as lettering & inking.
2nd ed, April 2019: 524 pp, $195 (includes online access with print purchase)
ISBN(s): 978-1-68217-911-6; 978-1-68217-959-8 (ebook)

Critical Survey of Graphic Novels: Independents & Underground Classics
Published by Grey House Publishing Inc™
4919 Rte 22, Amenia, NY 12501
Mailing Address: PO Box 56, Amenia, NY 12501-0056
Tel: 518-789-8700 *Toll Free Tel:* 800-562-2139
Fax: 518-789-0556
E-mail: csr@salempress.com
Web Site: salempress.com
Key Personnel
Ed: Bart H Beaty; Stephen Weiner
215 essays covering graphic novels & core comics series, focusing on the independents & underground genre.
May 2019: 1,110 pp, $395 (includes online access with print purchase)
ISBN(s): 978-1-68217-913-0 (3 vol set); 978-1-68217-958-1 (ebook set)

Critical Survey of Graphic Novels: Manga
Published by Grey House Publishing Inc™
4919 Rte 22, Amenia, NY 12501
Mailing Address: PO Box 56, Amenia, NY 12501-0056
Tel: 518-789-8700 *Toll Free Tel:* 800-562-2139
Fax: 518-789-0556
E-mail: csr@salempress.com
Web Site: salempress.com
Key Personnel
Ed: Bart H Beaty; Stephen Weiner
Provides in-depth insight into more than 65 of the most popular & studied manga graphic novels, ranging from metaseries to stand-alone books.
Oct 2018: 412 pp, $195 (includes online access with print purchase)
ISBN(s): 978-1-68217-912-3; 978-1-68217-957-4 (ebook)

Critical Survey of Long Fiction
Published by Grey House Publishing Inc™
4919 Rte 22, Amenia, NY 12501
Mailing Address: PO Box 56, Amenia, NY 12501-0056
Tel: 518-789-8700 *Toll Free Tel:* 800-562-2139
Fax: 518-789-0556
E-mail: csr@salempress.com
Web Site: salempress.com
Key Personnel
Ed: Carl Rollyson, PhD
Profiles of major writers of long fiction throughout history & the world, including critical analyses of their significant novels & novellas. Single hardcover & paperback volumes with the most popular content also available, each profiling authors & works in a particular genre or geography.
Original 10 volume set profiles 678 writers & is available for $995, contact publisher for details (ISBN: 978-1-58765-535-7 hardcover, ISBN: 978-1-58765-546-3 ebook).
6,056 pp, $39.95 or $105/vol (depending on individual volume title); hardcover titles include online access
First published 1983
ISBN(s): 978-1-4298-3675-3 (Detective & Mystery Novelists); 978-1-4298-3676-0 (Fantasy Novelists); 978-1-4298-3677-7 (Novelists with Gay & Lesbian Themes); 978-1-4298-3680-7 (Picaresque Novelists); 978-1-4298-3681-4 (Political Novelists); 978-1-4298-3682-1 (Psychological Novelists); 978-1-4298-3685-2 (Satirical Novelists); 978-1-4298-3686-9 (Religious Novelists); 978-1-4298-3691-3 (German Novelists); 978-1-4298-3693-7 (Italian Novelists); 978-1-4298-3694-4 (Novelists of the Jewish Culture); 978-1-4298-3698-2 (Spanish Novelists); 978-1-58765-926-3 (Detective & Mystery Novelists ebook); 978-1-58765-927-0 (Fantasy Novelists ebook); 978-1-58765-928-7 (Novelists with Gay & Lesbian Themes ebook); 978-1-58765-929-4 (Gothic Novelists ebook); 978-1-58765-930-0 (Naturalist Novelists ebook); 978-1-58765-931-7 (Picaresque Novelists ebook); 978-1-58765-932-4 (Political Novelists ebook); 978-1-58765-933-1 (Psychological Novelists ebook); 978-1-58765-934-8 (Science Fiction Novelists ebook); 978-1-58765-935-5 (Novelists with Feminist Themes ebook); 978-1-58765-936-2 (Satirical Novelists ebook); 978-1-58765-937-9 (Religious Novelists ebook); 978-1-58765-938-6 (African American Culture ebook); 978-1-58765-939-3 (Asian Novelists ebook); 978-1-58765-940-9 (English Novelists ebook); 978-1-58765-941-6 (French Novelists ebook); 978-1-58765-942-3 (German Novelists ebook); 978-1-58765-943-0 (Irish Novelists ebook); 978-1-58765-944-7 (Italian Novelists ebook); 978-1-58765-945-4 (Novelists of the Jewish Culture ebook); 978-1-58765-946-1 (Latin American Novelists ebook); 978-1-58765-947-8 (Native American Novelists ebook); 978-1-58765-948-5 (Russian Novelists ebook); 978-1-58765-949-2 (Spanish Novelists ebook); 978-1-61925-717-7 (African American Culture); 978-1-61925-718-4 (Asian Novelists); 978-1-61925-719-1 (English Novelists); 978-1-61925-720-7 (French Novelists); 978-1-61925-721-4 (Gothic Novelists); 978-1-61925-722-1 (Irish Novelists); 978-1-61925-723-8 (Latin American Novelists); 978-1-61925-724-5 (Native American Novelists); 978-1-61925-725-2 (Naturalist Novelists); 978-1-61925-726-9 (Novelists with Feminist Themes); 978-1-61925-727-6 (Russian Novelists); 978-1-61925-728-3 (Science Fiction Novelists)

Critical Survey of Mystery & Detective Fiction
Published by Grey House Publishing Inc™
4919 Rte 22, Amenia, NY 12501
Mailing Address: PO Box 56, Amenia, NY 12501-0056
Tel: 518-789-8700 *Toll Free Tel:* 800-562-2139
Fax: 518-789-0556
E-mail: csr@salempress.com
Web Site: salempress.com
Key Personnel
Ed: Carl Rollyson, PhD
Provides detailed analyses of the lives & writings of major contributors to mystery & detective fiction.
Jan 2008: 2,400 pp, $399/5 vol set or ebook set
ISBN(s): 978-1-64265-707-4 (5 vol set); 978-1-68765-444-2 (ebook set)

Critical Survey of Mythology & Folklore: Creation Myths
Published by Grey House Publishing Inc™
4919 Rte 22, Amenia, NY 12501
Mailing Address: PO Box 56, Amenia, NY 12501-0056
Tel: 518-789-8700 *Toll Free Tel:* 800-562-2139
Fax: 518-789-0556
E-mail: csr@salempress.com
Web Site: salempress.com
Articles focus on archetypal creation myths that reflect the profound wrestling of civilizations around the world with the most important facets of human existence.
July 2023: 600 pp, $295/2 vol set (includes online access)
ISBN(s): 978-1-63700-452-4 (2 vol set); 978-1-63700-455-5 (ebook set)

Critical Survey of Mythology & Folklore: Deadly Battles & Warring Enemies
Published by Grey House Publishing Inc™
4919 Rte 22, Amenia, NY 12501
Mailing Address: PO Box 56, Amenia, NY 12501-0056
Tel: 518-789-8700 *Toll Free Tel:* 800-562-2139
Fax: 518-789-0556
E-mail: csr@salempress.com
Web Site: salempress.com
Focus on famous clashes & renowned heroes & heroines in folklore & mythology. These struggles chronicled suffering, bravery & patriotism as well as indifference, cowardice & duplicity. This compilation features not only battles that are already well known, but battles from African, Asian, Polynesian, East European & other marginalized cultures, along with an abundance of essays on female warriors from all around the world.
April 2023: 600 pp, $295/2 vol set (includes online access)
ISBN(s): 978-1-63700-448-7 (2 vol set); 978-1-63700-451-7 (ebook set)

Critical Survey of Mythology & Folklore: Gods & Goddesses
Published by Grey House Publishing Inc™
4919 Rte 22, Amenia, NY 12501
Mailing Address: PO Box 56, Amenia, NY 12501-0056
Tel: 518-789-8700 *Toll Free Tel:* 800-562-2139
Fax: 518-789-0556
E-mail: csr@salempress.com
Web Site: salempress.com
Key Personnel
Ed: Michael Shally-Jensen, PhD
Examines the major & minor deities from a broad range of regions & cultures throughout the world. Collection includes 524 essays organized into 10 world regions.
2019: 1,048 pp, $295/2 vol set (includes online access with print purchase)
ISBN(s): 978-1-64265-115-7; 978-1-64265-116-4 (ebook set)

Critical Survey of Mythology & Folklore: Heroes & Heroines
Published by Grey House Publishing Inc™
4919 Rte 22, Amenia, NY 12501
Mailing Address: PO Box 56, Amenia, NY 12501-0056
Tel: 518-789-8700 *Toll Free Tel:* 800-562-2139
Fax: 518-789-0556
E-mail: csr@salempress.com
Web Site: salempress.com
Covers a diverse range of countries & cultures, as well as important retellings in the modern tradition. Articles cover: *Birth & Prophecy*, *The Host of Heroines*, *The Culture Hero*, *Trial & Quest*, *Myth & Monstrosity*, *Survey of Myth & Folklore*.
Sept 2013: 516 pp, $175 (includes online access)
ISBN(s): 978-1-61925-181-6; 978-1-61925-186-1 (ebook)

Critical Survey of Mythology & Folklore: Love, Sexuality & Desire
Published by Grey House Publishing Inc™
4919 Rte 22, Amenia, NY 12501
Mailing Address: PO Box 56, Amenia, NY 12501-0056
Tel: 518-789-8700 *Toll Free Tel:* 800-562-2139
Fax: 518-789-0556
E-mail: csr@salempress.com
Web Site: salempress.com
Each title examines familiar & unfamiliar myths, from a diverse range of countries & cultures, as well as important retellings in the modern tradition. Topics covered include: *Gods & Goddesses in Love*, *The Myth of Ideal Love*, *Loss of the Beloved*, *Tales of Transformation*, *Animal Loves*, *Love, Sexuality & Creation*.

Jan 2013: 984 pp, $295/2 vol set (includes online access with print purchase)
ISBN(s): 978-1-4298-3765-1 (2 vol set); 978-1-4298-3768-2 (ebook set)

Critical Survey of Mythology & Folklore: World Mythology
Published by Grey House Publishing Inc™
4919 Rte 22, Amenia, NY 12501
Mailing Address: PO Box 56, Amenia, NY 12501-0056
Tel: 518-789-8700 *Toll Free Tel:* 800-562-2139
Fax: 518-789-0556
E-mail: csr@salempress.com
Web Site: salempress.com
Presents articles on myths, folktales, legends & other traditional literature. Covers a diverse range of authors, countries & cultures that span the globe. Articles begin with a summary that offers readers the major actions & characters in the tale followed by an analysis of the important cultural & social interpretations of the author & myth.
Dec 2013: 326 pp, $175 (includes online access with print purchase)
ISBN(s): 978-1-61925-182-3; 978-1-61925-187-8 (ebook)

Critical Survey of Poetry
Published by Grey House Publishing Inc™
4919 Rte 22, Amenia, NY 12501
Mailing Address: PO Box 56, Amenia, NY 12501-0056
Tel: 518-789-8700 *Toll Free Tel:* 800-562-2139
Fax: 518-789-0556
E-mail: csr@salempress.com
Web Site: salempress.com
An in-depth resource covering over 900 poets throughout history & the world. Organized into 6 subsets by geography & essay type.
American Poets, 4 vol set, 2,414 pp, $495
British, Irish & Commonwealth Poets, 3 vol set, 1,470 pp, $395
European Poets, 3 vol set, 1,262 pp, $395
World Poets, 1 vol, 442 pp, $150
Topical Essays, 2 vol set, 924 pp, $295
Cumulative Indexes, 1 vol, 266 pp, free with purchase of more than one subset.
4th ed, Jan 2011: 6,778 pp, $1,295/14 vol set (includes online access with print purchase)
First published 2002
ISBN(s): 978-1-58765-582-1 (14 vol set); 978-1-58765-583-8 (American Poets set); 978-1-58765-588-3 (British, Irish & Commonwealth Poets set); 978-1-58765-592-0 (American Poets ebook set); 978-1-58765-593-7 (14 vol ebook set); 978-1-58765-755-9 (British, Irish & Commonwealth Poets ebook set); 978-1-58765-756-6 (European Poets set); 978-1-58765-760-3 (European Poets ebook set); 978-1-58765-761-0 (World Poets); 978-1-58765-762-7 (World Poets ebook); 978-1-58765-763-4 (Topical Essays set); 978-1-58765-766-5 (Topical Essays ebook set); 978-1-58765-767-2 (Cumulative Indexes); 978-1-64265-279-6 (Contemporary Poets set)

Critical Survey of Science Fiction & Fantasy Literature
Published by Grey House Publishing Inc™
4919 Rte 22, Amenia, NY 12501
Mailing Address: PO Box 56, Amenia, NY 12501-0056
Tel: 518-789-8700 *Toll Free Tel:* 800-562-2139
Fax: 518-789-0556
E-mail: csr@salempress.com
Web Site: salempress.com
Key Personnel
Ed: Paul Di Filippo
Provides descriptions of hundreds of important works of science fiction & fantasy, summarizing plots & analyzing the works in terms of their contributions to literature.

3rd ed, March 2017: 1,572 pp, $295/3 vol set (includes online access with print purchase)
ISBN(s): 978-1-68217-278-0 (3 vol set); 978-1-68217-279-7 (ebook set)

Critical Survey of Shakespeare's Plays
Published by Grey House Publishing Inc™
4919 Rte 22, Amenia, NY 12501
Mailing Address: PO Box 56, Amenia, NY 12501-0056
Tel: 518-789-8700 *Toll Free Tel:* 800-562-2139
Fax: 518-789-0556
E-mail: csr@salempress.com
Web Site: salempress.com
Key Personnel
Ed: Joseph Rosenblum
Examines all 39 of Shakespeare's most influential plays, as well as his life, style, technique & influences.
Oct 2015: 381 pp, $125 (includes online access with print purchase)
ISBN(s): 978-1-61925-864-8; 978-1-61925-865-5 (ebook)

Critical Survey of Shakespeare's Sonnets
Published by Grey House Publishing Inc™
4919 Rte 22, Amenia, NY 12501
Mailing Address: PO Box 56, Amenia, NY 12501-0056
Tel: 518-789-8700 *Toll Free Tel:* 800-562-2139
Fax: 518-789-0556
E-mail: csr@salempress.com
Web Site: salempress.com
Collection of 25 essays on the most popular sonnets written by William Shakespeare, each providing an in-depth analysis of its historical significance, literary technique & discusses its meaning to a contemporary audience.
July 2014: 355 pp, $125 (includes online access with print purchase)
ISBN(s): 978-1-61925-499-2; 978-1-61925-500-5 (ebook)

Critical Survey of Short Fiction
Published by Grey House Publishing Inc™
4919 Rte 22, Amenia, NY 12501
Mailing Address: PO Box 56, Amenia, NY 12501-0056
Tel: 518-789-8700 *Toll Free Tel:* 800-562-2139
Fax: 518-789-0556
E-mail: csr@salempress.com
Web Site: salempress.com
Key Personnel
Ed: Charles E May
625 essays providing in-depth overviews of short story writers throughout history & the world. Organized into 5 subsets by geography & essay type.
American Writers, 4 vol set, 1,600 pp, $495
British, Irish & Commonwealth Writers, 2 vol set, 800 pp, $295
European Writers, 1 vol, 400 pp, $175
World Writers, 1 vol, 400 pp, $175
Topical Essays, 1 vol, 400 pp, $175
Cumulative Indexes, 1 vol, 400 pp, free with purchase of more than one subset.
4th ed, Jan 2012: 4,000 pp, $1,095/10 vol set (includes online access with print purchase)
ISBN(s): 978-1-58765-789-4 (10 vol set); 978-1-58765-790-0 (American Writers set); 978-1-58765-795-5 (British, Irish & Commonwealth Writers set); 978-1-58765-798-6 (European Writers); 978-1-58765-799-3 (World Writers); 978-1-58765-800-6 (Topical Essays); 978-1-58765-803-7 (Cumulative Indexes); 978-1-58765-804-4 (10 vol ebook set); 978-1-58765-805-1 (American Writers ebook set); 978-1-58765-806-8 (British, Irish & Commonwealth Writers ebook set); 978-1-58765-807-5 (European Writers ebook); 978-1-58765-808-2 (World Writers ebook); 978-1-58765-809-9 (Topical Essays ebook)

Critical Survey of World Literature
Published by Grey House Publishing Inc™
4919 Rte 22, Amenia, NY 12501
Mailing Address: PO Box 56, Amenia, NY 12501-0056
Tel: 518-789-8700 *Toll Free Tel:* 800-562-2139
Fax: 518-789-0556
E-mail: csr@salempress.com
Web Site: salempress.com
Key Personnel
Ed: Robert C Evans
Profiles major authors of fiction, drama, poetry & essays, each with sections on biography, general analysis & analysis of the author's most important works.
Jan 2018: 3,366 pp, $499/6 vol set (includes online access with print purchase)
ISBN(s): 978-1-68217-615-3 (6 vol set); 978-1-68217-638-2 (ebook set)

Critical Survey of Young Adult Literature
Published by Grey House Publishing Inc™
4919 Rte 22, Amenia, NY 12501
Mailing Address: PO Box 56, Amenia, NY 12501-0056
Tel: 518-789-8700 *Toll Free Tel:* 800-562-2139
Fax: 518-789-0556
E-mail: csr@salempress.com
Web Site: salempress.com
Key Personnel
Ed: Amy Pattee
Author biographies, genre overviews, plot summaries, theme overviews & film analysis for the young adult genre.
April 2016: 694 pp, $185 (includes online access with print purchase)
ISBN(s): 978-1-61925-971-3; 978-1-61925-972-0 (ebook)

Current Biography Cumulated Index 1940-2021
Published by Grey House Publishing Inc™
4919 Rte 22, Amenia, NY 12501
Mailing Address: PO Box 56, Amenia, NY 12501-0056
Tel: 518-789-8700 *Toll Free Tel:* 800-562-2139
Fax: 518-789-0556
E-mail: books@greyhouse.com
Web Site: greyhouse.com
Name & profession indexes to late issues in which biographies appear in *Current Biography Yearbook*.
2021: 800 pp, $199
ISBN(s): 978-1-64265-807-1

Current Biography Yearbook
Published by Grey House Publishing Inc™
4919 Rte 22, Amenia, NY 12501
Mailing Address: PO Box 56, Amenia, NY 12501-0056
Tel: 518-789-8700 *Toll Free Tel:* 800-562-2139
Fax: 518-789-0556
E-mail: books@greyhouse.com
Web Site: greyhouse.com
Contemporary profiles of accomplished & rising stars of politics, industry, entertainment & the arts from the US & around the world.
Annual.
2024: 1,000 pp, $199
ISBN(s): 978-1-63700-7-112

Cyclopedia of Literary Characters
Published by Grey House Publishing Inc™
4919 Rte 22, Amenia, NY 12501
Mailing Address: PO Box 56, Amenia, NY 12501-0056
Tel: 518-789-8700 *Toll Free Tel:* 800-562-2139
Fax: 518-789-0556
E-mail: csr@salempress.com
Web Site: salempress.com
Key Personnel
Ed: Frank N Magill

Provides critical descriptions of more than 29,000 major characters that appear in 3,500 important works of literature. New to this edition are 245 characters published in popular works of fiction from 2000 to 2013.
4th ed, Feb 2015: 3,344 pp, $495/5 vol set (includes online access with print purchase)
ISBN(s): 978-1-61925-497-8 (5 vol set); 978-1-61925-498-5 (ebook set)

Cyclopedia of Literary Places
Published by Grey House Publishing Inc™
4919 Rte 22, Amenia, NY 12501
Mailing Address: PO Box 56, Amenia, NY 12501-0056
Tel: 518-789-8700 *Toll Free Tel:* 800-562-2139
Fax: 518-789-0556
E-mail: csr@salempress.com
Web Site: salempress.com
Key Personnel
Ed: Denise Lenchner
In-depth discussion of the use of place in over 1,400 popular literary works. Each article provides the full title of the work, author's name & vital dates, type of work, type of plot, time of plot & date of original publication.
2nd ed, April 2016: 1,304 pp, $395/3 vol set (includes online access with print purchase)
ISBN(s): 978-1-61925-884-6 (3 vol set); 978-1-61925-885-3 (ebook set)

Developmental Editing: A Handbook for Freelancers, Authors, and Publishers
Published by University of Chicago Press
1427 E 60 St, Chicago, IL 60637-2954
SAN: 202-5280
Tel: 773-702-7700; 773-702-7000 (cust serv, print); 773-753-3347 *Toll Free Tel:* 800-621-2736 (orders); 877-705-1878 (US & CN)
Fax: 773-702-9756
E-mail: custserv@press.uchicago.edu; marketing@press.uchicago.edu
Web Site: www.press.uchicago.edu
Key Personnel
Exec Ed, Ref & Writing Guides: Mary Laur
  Tel: 773-702-7326 *E-mail:* mlaur@uchicago.edu
Transforming a mss into a book that edifies, inspires & sells is the job of the developmental editor. Author Scott Norton starts with the core tasks of shaping the proposal, finding the hook & building the narrative or argument & then turns to the hard work of executing the plan & establishing a style. The book also includes detailed case studies featuring a variety of nonfiction books & authors ranging from first-timer to veteran, journalist to scholar.
2nd ed, 2023: 320 pp, $32 paper; $31.99 epub or PDF
First published 2009
ISBN(s): 978-0-226-79363-4 (paper); 978-0-226-79377-1 (epub or PDF)

Dictionary of Literary Biography
Published by Gale
Division of Cengage Learning
27555 Executive Dr, Suite 270, Farmington Hills, MI 48331
SAN: 213-4373
Toll Free Tel: 800-877-4253 *Toll Free Fax:* 877-363-4253
E-mail: gale.customerexperience@cengage.com
Web Site: www.gale.com
Biographical & critical essays on the lives, works & careers of the world's most influential literary figures. More than 16,000 articles & thousands of images. Online database.

A Directory of American Poets & Writers
Published by Poets & Writers Inc
90 Broad St, Suite 2100, New York, NY 10004
Tel: 212-226-3586 *Fax:* 212-226-3963

E-mail: directory@pw.org
Web Site: www.pw.org/directory
Key Personnel
Exec Dir: Melissa Ford Gradel *Tel:* 212-226-3586 ext 223 *E-mail:* mgradel@pw.org
Names, addresses, telephone numbers & e-mail addresses of over 10,000 contemporary American writers & poets. Available online only.
Free

The Directory of Mail Order Catalogs
Published by Grey House Publishing Inc™
4919 Rte 22, Amenia, NY 12501
Mailing Address: PO Box 56, Amenia, NY 12501-0056
Tel: 518-789-8700 *Toll Free Tel:* 800-562-2139
Fax: 518-789-0556
E-mail: books@greyhouse.com
Web Site: greyhouse.com
Complete listing of direct-to-consumer & business-to-business mail order catalogs, including detailed contact information available as an online database.
34th ed, 2020: 1,000 pp, $250 (includes online access)
ISBN(s): 978-1-64265-106-5

Directory of Special Libraries and Information Centers (DSL)
Published by Gale
Division of Cengage Learning
27555 Executive Dr, Suite 270, Farmington Hills, MI 48331
SAN: 213-4373
Toll Free Tel: 800-877-4253 *Toll Free Fax:* 877-363-4253
E-mail: gale.customerexperience@cengage.com
Web Site: www.gale.com
Identifies & describes special libraries, special collections & documentation centers located in the United States, Canada & throughout the world. DSL provides information on subject-specific resource collections maintained by government agencies, businesses, publishers, educational institutions, nonprofit organizations & associations.
51st ed, 2023
ISBN(s): 978-0-0286-7632-6 (ebook)

Drama Criticism
Published by Gale
Division of Cengage Learning
27555 Executive Dr, Suite 270, Farmington Hills, MI 48331
SAN: 213-4373
Toll Free Tel: 800-877-4253 *Toll Free Fax:* 877-363-4253
E-mail: gale.customerexperience@cengage.com
Web Site: www.gale.com
The series is designed to introduce readers to the most frequently studied playwrights of all time periods & nationalities & to present discerning commentary on dramatic works of enduring interest. Covers approximately 150 writers & includes numerous entries focusing on individual works & topics. Each entry includes a set of previously published reviews, essays & other critical responses from sources that include scholarly books & journals, literary magazines, interviews, letters & diaries. Online database.

E-Publishing and Digital Libraries: Legal and Organizational Issues
Published by IGI Global
701 E Chocolate Ave, Hershey, PA 17033
Tel: 717-533-8845 (ext 100) *Toll Free Tel:* 866-342-6657 *Fax:* 717-533-8661; 717-533-7115
E-mail: cust@igi-global.com
Web Site: www.igi-global.com
2011: 552 pp, $180
ISBN(s): 978-1-60960-031-0; 978-1-60960-033-4 (ebook)

EFA Member Directory
Published by Editorial Freelancers Association (EFA)
266 W 37 St, 20th fl, New York, NY 10018
Tel: 212-920-4816 *Toll Free Tel:* 866-929-5425
E-mail: info@the-efa.org
Web Site: www.the-efa.org
Key Personnel
Co-Exec: Katy Grenfell *E-mail:* co-executives@the-efa.org; Cody Sisco *E-mail:* co-executives@the-efa.org
Secy: Ronane Lloyd *E-mail:* secretary@the-efa.org
Treas: Marcina Zaccaria *E-mail:* treasurer@the-efa.org
National, nonprofit professional organization comprising editors, writers, indexers, proofreaders, researchers, translators & other self-employed workers in the publishing industry. Online directory searchable by skills, subject matter, expertise & location. Members may post descriptions of services, resumes & contact information. Clients can directly hire the freelance help they need.
free (online)

El-Hi Textbooks & Serials in Print®
Published by Grey House Publishing Inc™
4919 Rte 22, Amenia, NY 12501
Mailing Address: PO Box 56, Amenia, NY 12501-0056
Tel: 518-789-8700 *Toll Free Tel:* 800-562-2139
Fax: 518-789-0556
E-mail: books@greyhouse.com
Web Site: greyhouse.com
Includes the in-print titles of publishers of textbooks & related materials. Coverage includes over 103,000 elementary, junior high & high school textbooks from over 17,000 US publishers.
Annual.
152nd ed, 2024: 4,000 pp, $875/2 vol set
ISBN(s): 978-1-63700-965-9 (2 vol set)

The Emotional Craft of Fiction
Published by Writer's Digest Books
Imprint of Penguin Publishing Group
1745 Broadway, New York, NY 10019
Web Site: www.penguinrandomhouse.com
Veteran literary agent & expert fiction instructor Donald Maass shows you how to use story to provoke a visceral & emotional experience in readers.
2016: 224 pp, $19.99 paper, $14.99 ebook
ISBN(s): 978-1-4403-4837-2 (paper); 978-1-4403-4843-3 (ebook)

Encyclopedia of African-American Writing
Published by Grey House Publishing Inc™
4919 Rte 22, Amenia, NY 12501
Mailing Address: PO Box 56, Amenia, NY 12501-0056
Tel: 518-789-8700 *Toll Free Tel:* 800-562-2139
Fax: 518-789-0556
E-mail: books@greyhouse.com
Web Site: greyhouse.com
Highlights the role & influence of African-American authors from the 18th century to the present. 722 author biographies, with illustrations, cover the important events in each writer's life, education, major works, honors & awards, family & important associates.
4th ed, 2022: 1,134 pp, $220 hardcover (includes online access), $275 ebook
ISBN(s): 978-1-63700-165-3; 978-1-63700-166-0 (ebook)

Encyclopedia of Associations: National Organizations
Published by Gale
Division of Cengage Learning

27555 Executive Dr, Suite 270, Farmington Hills, MI 48331
SAN: 213-4373
Toll Free Tel: 800-877-4253 *Toll Free Fax:* 877-363-4253
E-mail: gale.customerexperience@cengage.com
Web Site: www.gale.com
A guide to more than 24,000 nonprofit American membership organizations of national & international scope. Detailed entries furnish association name & complete contact information. Name & keyword indexes accompany each volume. Two companion volumes: Vol 2: *Geographic & Executive Indexes* & Vol 3: *Supplement*. Available as ebook only.
59th ed, 2020
ISBN(s): 978-1-4103-8221-4

Essential Writing Skills for College and Beyond
Published by Writer's Digest Books
Imprint of Penguin Publishing Group
1745 Broadway, New York, NY 10019
Web Site: www.penguinrandomhouse.com
Guide to writing a successful college paper, including term papers, essays, creative assignments & more, along with advice on writing effectively after graduation & on the job.
2014: 304 pp, $18 paper, $13.99 ebook
ISBN(s): 978-1-59963-759-4 (paper); 978-1-59963-765-5 (ebook)

Everyone Has What It Takes
Published by Writer's Digest Books
Imprint of Penguin Publishing Group
1745 Broadway, New York, NY 10019
Web Site: www.penguinrandomhouse.com
Relatable stories, wisdom & best practices to spark renewed purpose & joy on your writing journey.
2021: 240 pp, $19 paper, $10.99 ebook, $17.50 audiobook
ISBN(s): 978-0-593-33078-4 (paper); 978-0-593-33079-1 (ebook); 978-0-593-60928-6 (audiobook)

Fiction Core Collection
Published by Grey House Publishing Inc™
4919 Rte 22, Amenia, NY 12501
Mailing Address: PO Box 56, Amenia, NY 12501-0056
Tel: 518-789-8700 *Toll Free Tel:* 800-562-2139
Fax: 518-789-0556
E-mail: books@greyhouse.com
Web Site: greyhouse.com
Recommends works of classic & contemporary fiction. Includes over 6,600 titles plus review sources & other professional aids for librarians.
22nd ed, 2024: 1,300 pp, $295
ISBN(s): 978-1-63700-726-6

45 Master Characters
Published by Writer's Digest Books
Imprint of Penguin Publishing Group
1745 Broadway, New York, NY 10019
Web Site: www.penguinrandomhouse.com
Gives all the information you need to develop believable characters that resonate with every reader.
2012 (revised): 288 pp, $18.99 paper, $13.99 ebook
First published 2001
ISBN(s): 978-1-59963-534-7 (paper); 978-1-59963-536-1 (ebook)

Funny You Should Ask
Published by Writer's Digest Books
Imprint of Penguin Publishing Group
1745 Broadway, New York, NY 10019
Web Site: www.penguinrandomhouse.com
Assists to deconstruct, inform & illuminate the path to publication & beyond.
2020: 224 pp, $18.99 paper, $13.99 ebook
ISBN(s): 978-0-593-32783-8 (ebook); 978-1-4403-5507-3 (paper)

Gale Directory of Databases (GDD)
Published by Gale
Division of Cengage Learning
27555 Executive Dr, Suite 270, Farmington Hills, MI 48331
SAN: 213-4373
Toll Free Tel: 800-877-4253 *Toll Free Fax:* 877-363-4253
E-mail: gale.customerexperience@cengage.com
Web Site: www.gale.com
Current information about more than 14,000 databases & more than 3,000 producers, online services & vendors/distributors available worldwide in a variety of formats.
40th ed, 2017: 2,556 pp, $1,176 paper
ISBN(s): 978-1-4103-2675-1

Gale Directory of Publications and Broadcast Media (GDPBM)
Published by Gale
Division of Cengage Learning
27555 Executive Dr, Suite 270, Farmington Hills, MI 48331
SAN: 213-4373
Toll Free Tel: 800-877-4253 *Toll Free Fax:* 877-363-4253
E-mail: gale.customerexperience@cengage.com
Web Site: www.gale.com
Each edition contains approximately 60,000 listings for radio & television stations, cable companies & print/online companies as well as more than 18,000 international entries. Includes phone & fax number, e-mail addresses & web site URLs, listing of key personnel & more. Available as ebook only.
158th ed, 2022
First published 1869
ISBN(s): 978-0-02-866910-6 (ebook)

General Issues in Literacy/Illiteracy in the World: A Bibliography
Published by Greenwood
Imprint of ABC-CLIO LLC
147 Castilian Dr, Santa Barbara, CA 93117
Tel: 805-968-1911 *Toll Free Tel:* 800-368-6868
Toll Free Fax: 866-270-3856
E-mail: customerservice@abc-clio.com; rights@abc-clio.com
Web Site: www.abc-clio.com
Key Personnel
Edit Dir, Print: Kevin Downing
Author: William Eller; John Hladczuk; Sharon Hladczuk
Literacy-illiteracy; bibliography.
1st ed, 1990: 435 pp, $96.25 hardcover
ISBN(s): 978-0-313-27327-8

Gentle Writing Advice
Published by Writer's Digest Books
Imprint of Penguin Publishing Group
1745 Broadway, New York, NY 10019
Web Site: www.penguinrandomhouse.com
Book of writing advice, with sections on debunking popular advice, self-care tips & footnotes.
2023: 256 pp, $18 paper, $13.99 ebook, $17.50 audiobook
ISBN(s): 978-0-593-53997-2 (ebook); 978-0-593-68472-6 (audiobook); 978-1-4403-0120-9 (paper)

Getting It Published: A Guide for Scholars & Anyone Else Serious About Serious Books
Published by University of Chicago Press
1427 E 60 St, Chicago, IL 60637-2954
SAN: 202-5280
Tel: 773-702-7700; 773-702-7000 (cust serv, print); 773-753-3347 *Toll Free Tel:* 800-621-2736 (orders); 877-705-1878 (US & CN)
Fax: 773-702-9756
E-mail: custserv@press.uchicago.edu; marketing@press.uchicago.edu
Web Site: www.press.uchicago.edu
Key Personnel
Edit Dir, Humanities & Sci: Alan G Thomas
Tel: 773-702-7644 *E-mail:* athomas2@uchicago.edu
A professor, author & 30-year veteran of the book industry, William Germano, knows what editors want & what writers need to know to get their work published. This 3rd edition of *Getting It Published* offers clear, practicable guidance on developing a compelling book proposal, finding the right publisher, evaluating a contract, negotiating the production process & emerging as a published author.
3rd ed, 2016: 304 pp, $23 paper, $22.99 epub or PDF
First published 2001
ISBN(s): 978-0-226-28140-7 (paper); 978-0-226-28154-4 (epub or PDF)

Gordon's Radio List
Published by North Ridge Books
38972 Camino Buendia, Indio, CA 92203
Tel: 949-533-5106 (cell)
E-mail: nrbooks@aol.com
Web Site: www.radiopublicity.net
Key Personnel
Publr & Ed: William A Gordon
Book-length database of over 700 radio shows that interview authors, updated on a day-to-day basis. Available in Excel.
$369 includes free e-mailed updates for 3 months with the option to purchase additional updates

Grammatically Correct
Published by Writer's Digest Books
Imprint of Penguin Publishing Group
1745 Broadway, New York, NY 10019
Web Site: www.penguinrandomhouse.com
Easy to use guide covering 4 essential aspects of good writing: Individual words; punctuation; syntax & structure; style.
2nd ed, 2010: 352 pp, $19.99 paper, $14.99 ebook
First published 1997
ISBN(s): 978-1-58297-616-7 (paper); 978-1-59963-173-8 (ebook)

Graphic Novels Core Collection
Published by Grey House Publishing Inc™
4919 Rte 22, Amenia, NY 12501
Mailing Address: PO Box 56, Amenia, NY 12501-0056
Tel: 518-789-8700 *Toll Free Tel:* 800-562-2139
Fax: 518-789-0556
E-mail: books@greyhouse.com
Web Site: greyhouse.com
Essential resource for library & media specialists looking to energize, enhance & enrich their collection with 2,500 important & highly recommended fiction & nonfiction graphic novel titles.
5th ed, Dec 2024: 1,000 pp, $295
ISBN(s): 978-1-63700-910-9

Guide to Literary Agents
Published by Writer's Digest Books
Imprint of Penguin Publishing Group
1745 Broadway, New York, NY 10019
Web Site: www.penguinrandomhouse.com
Go-to resource for finding a literary agent & earning a contract from a reputable publisher.
30th ed, Dec 2021: 320 pp, $31 paper, $19.99 ebook
ISBN(s): 978-0-5933-3209-2 (paper); 978-0-5933-3210-8 (ebook)

REFERENCE BOOKS FOR THE TRADE

Guide to Writers Conferences & Writing Workshops
Published by ShawGuides
PO Box 61569, Staten Island, NY 10306-7569
Tel: 718-874-3311
E-mail: support@shawguides.com
Web Site: shawguides.com
Online directory of writing conferences, writers workshops, creative career writing programs & literary retreats. 1,466 programs available at writing.shawguides.com.

How to Write a Book Proposal
Published by Writer's Digest Books
Imprint of Penguin Publishing Group
1745 Broadway, New York, NY 10019
Web Site: www.penguinrandomhouse.com
Essential resource for presenting a book proposal to agents & publishers. Understanding how publishers work, how to brand yourself, build a platform & structure your book.
5th ed, 2017: 336 pp, $19.99 paper, $15.99 ebook
First published 2003
ISBN(s): 978-1-4403-4817-4 (paper); 978-1-4403-4821-1 (ebook)

How to Write a Page Turner
Published by Writer's Digest Books
Imprint of Penguin Publishing Group
1745 Broadway, New York, NY 10019
Web Site: www.penguinrandomhouse.com
Key areas that need tension building, from character to plot.
2019: 240 pp, $18.99 paper, $13.99 ebook
ISBN(s): 978-1-4403-5434-2 (paper); 978-1-4403-5450-2 (ebook)

Hudson's Washington News Media Contacts Guide
Published by Grey House Publishing Inc™
4919 Rte 22, Amenia, NY 12501
Mailing Address: PO Box 56, Amenia, NY 12501-0056
Tel: 518-789-8700 *Toll Free Tel:* 800-562-2139
Fax: 518-789-0556
E-mail: books@greyhouse.com
Web Site: greyhouse.com
Comprehensive listing of over 3,000 news organizations & their holdings & more than 4,000 key media contacts in the Washington, DC metropolitan area.
Annual.
57th ed, 2024: 400 pp, $289, online database available (see web site for quote)
ISBN(s): 978-8-89179-007-0

Index to Legal Periodicals & Books
Published by Grey House Publishing Inc™
4919 Rte 22, Amenia, NY 12501
Mailing Address: PO Box 56, Amenia, NY 12501-0056
Tel: 518-789-8700 *Toll Free Tel:* 800-562-2139
Fax: 518-789-0556
E-mail: books@greyhouse.com
Web Site: greyhouse.com
A cumulative author-subject index to legal publications with a table of cases & statutes & listing of book reviews.
62nd ed, 2024 (2023 annual cumulation): 1,400 pp, $695
ISBN(s): 978-1-63700-911-6 (hardcover)

Indexing from A to Z
Published by Grey House Publishing Inc™
4919 Rte 22, Amenia, NY 12501
Mailing Address: PO Box 56, Amenia, NY 12501-0056
Tel: 518-789-8700 *Toll Free Tel:* 800-562-2139
Fax: 518-789-0556
E-mail: books@greyhouse.com
Web Site: greyhouse.com
Includes the latest national & international standards & recommended practices pertaining to indexes & indexing.
Available for purchase at www.hwwilsoninprint.com/index_AZ.php.
2nd ed, 1996: 569 pp, $80
First published 1991
ISBN(s): 978-0-8242-0882-0

International Literary Market Place™ (ILMP)
Published by Information Today, Inc
121 Chanlon Rd, Suite G-20, New Providence, NJ 07974-2195
Tel: 908-795-3755 *Toll Free Tel:* 800-409-4929 (press 3); 800-300-9868 (cust serv)
E-mail: custserv@infotoday.com
Web Site: www.literarymarketplace.com
Key Personnel
Mng Ed: Karen Hallard *Tel:* 908-219-0277
E-mail: khallard@infotoday.com
A comprehensive directory of data on the book trade industry in over 175 countries outside the US & Canada, with 8,471 publishers & over 3,200 book organizations including, among others, agents, booksellers & library associations. Includes information basic to conducting business in each country. The US & Canada are covered by *Literary Market Place*™. Web version, which includes *Literary Market Place*™, also available.
Annual.
58th ed, 2025: 1,824 pp, $399.50 paper, $459.50 online subn
ISBN(s): 978-1-57387-602-5

Introduction to Literary Context
Published by Grey House Publishing Inc™
4919 Rte 22, Amenia, NY 12501
Mailing Address: PO Box 56, Amenia, NY 12501-0056
Tel: 518-789-8700 *Toll Free Tel:* 800-562-2139
Fax: 518-789-0556
E-mail: csr@salempress.com
Web Site: salempress.com
Each volume explores literary content. Each essay examines works through the following categories: content synopsis, religious context, historical context, societal context, biographical context, scientific & technological context. Includes discussion questions, essay ideas, works cited, bibliography & general index.
Volumes published Nov 2013:
American Post-Modernist Novels, 340 pp
American Short Fiction, 290 pp.
Volumes published April-Dec 2014:
American Poetry of the 20th Century, 265 pp
English Literature, 274 pp
Plays, 262 pp
World Literature, 369 pp.
$165/vol (includes online access with print purchase)
ISBN(s): 978-1-61925-210-3 (American Post-Modernist Novels); 978-1-61925-211-0 (American Post-Modernist Novels ebook); 978-1-61925-212-7 (American Short Fiction); 978-1-61925-213-4 (American Short Fiction ebook); 978-1-61925-483-1 (World Literature); 978-1-61925-484-8 (World Literature ebook); 978-1-61925-485-5 (English Literature); 978-1-61925-486-2 (English Literature ebook); 978-1-61925-713-9 (American Poetry of the 20th Century); 978-1-61925-714-6 (American Poetry of the 20th Century ebook); 978-1-61925-715-3 (Plays); 978-1-61925-716-0 (Plays ebook)

Jeff Herman's Guide to Book Publishers, Editors and Literary Agents: Who They Are, What They Want, How to Win Them Over
Published by New World Library
Division of Whatever Publishing Inc
14 Pamaron Way, Novato, CA 94949
SAN: 211-8777
Tel: 415-884-2100 *Fax:* 415-884-2199
Web Site: www.newworldlibrary.com
Key Personnel
Author: Jeff Herman
Writing/reference book. Directory of US publishers & literary agents. Includes abundant information about how to succeed as a published author.
29th ed, 2022: 672 pp, $32.95 paper
First published 1990
ISBN(s): 978-1-60868-788-6

Journalytics Academic & Predatory Reports
Published by Cabell Publishing Co
2615 Calder Ave, Suite 665, Beaumont, TX 77702
Mailing Address: PO Box 5428, Beaumont, TX 77726-5428
E-mail: sales@cabells.com; support@cabells.com (tech support)
Web Site: cabells.com
Key Personnel
Founder, Owner & Pres: David Cabell
CEO: Lacey Earle
Exec Dir: Sheree Crosby
Curated journal database providing decision data, benchmarks & context for thousands of reputable academic journals. Covering journals of all sizes, specialties & from every field, Journalytics Academic is used by faculty, university leadership, research funders & libraries among others. Through partnerships with major academic publishers, journal editors, scholarly societies, accreditation agencies, & other independent databases, Cabells provides accurate, up-to-date information about academic journals to universities worldwide.

Journalytics Medicine & Predatory Reports
Published by Cabell Publishing Co
2615 Calder Ave, Suite 665, Beaumont, TX 77702
Mailing Address: PO Box 5428, Beaumont, TX 77726-5428
E-mail: sales@cabells.com; support@cabells.com (tech support)
Web Site: cabells.com
Key Personnel
Founder, Owner & Pres: David Cabell
CEO: Lacey Earle
Exec Dir: Sheree Crosby
Search platform dedicated to the medical research community. Publications included adhere to industry best-practices & will be recognized by the academic community. Included are 37 medical disciplines & 26,000+ verified & predatory journals, along with other important information. Manage your publishing opportunities & risks. Journalytics Medicine, with integrated Predatory Reports, gives you a complete picture of the publishing landscape. Avoid threats to your scholarly output by ensuring you rely on the most reputable journals.

Keys to Great Writing
Published by Writer's Digest Books
Imprint of Penguin Publishing Group
1745 Broadway, New York, NY 10019
Web Site: www.penguinrandomhouse.com
Provides invaluable instruction on every aspect of the craft, from word choice & sentence structure to organization & revision.
2nd ed, 2016 (revised): 288 pp, $24 paper, $14.99 ebook
ISBN(s): 978-1-4403-4580-7 (paper); 978-1-4403-4582-1 (ebook)

Law Books & Serials in Print™
Published by Grey House Publishing Inc™
4919 Rte 22, Amenia, NY 12501
Mailing Address: PO Box 56, Amenia, NY 12501-0056

Tel: 518-789-8700 *Toll Free Tel:* 800-562-2139
Fax: 518-789-0556
E-mail: books@greyhouse.com
Web Site: greyhouse.com
Provides immediate access to current legal books, serials & multimedia publications distributed or published in the US.
Annual.
49th ed, 2024: 3,900 pp, $2,185/3 vol set
ISBN(s): 978-1-63700-975-8 (3 vol set)

Library and Book Trade Almanac™
Published by Information Today, Inc
121 Chanlon Rd, Suite G-20, New Providence, NJ 07974-2195
Tel: 908-219-0279 *Toll Free Tel:* 800-300-9868 (cust serv)
E-mail: custserv@infotoday.com
Key Personnel
Ed: Kathy Bayer
Almanac of US library & book trade statistics, standards, programs & major events of the year, as well as international statistics & developments. Includes lists of library & literary awards & prizes, notable books, library schools, scholarship sources; directory of book trade & library associations at state, regional, national & international levels; employment sources; calendar of events.
Annual.
69th ed: 634 pp, $329.50 hardbound
ISBN(s): 978-1-57387-600-1

Literary Market Place™ (LMP)
Published by Information Today, Inc
121 Chanlon Rd, Suite G-20, New Providence, NJ 07974-2195
Tel: 908-795-3755 *Toll Free Tel:* 800-409-4929 (press 3); 800-300-9868 (cust serv)
E-mail: custserv@infotoday.com
Web Site: www.literarymarketplace.com
Key Personnel
Mng Ed: Karen Hallard *Tel:* 908-219-0277
E-mail: khallard@infotoday.com
Directory of over 23,000 companies & individuals in US & Canadian publishing. Areas covered include book publishers; associations; book trade events; courses, conferences & contests; agents & agencies; services & suppliers; direct-mail promotion; review, selection & reference; radio & television; wholesale, export & import & book manufacturing. A 2 volume set, each containing 2 alphabetical names & numbers indexes, one for key companies listed & one for individuals. The rest of the world is covered by *International Literary Market Place™*. Web version, which also includes *International Literary Market Place™*, also available.
Annual.
85th ed, 2025: 1,548 pp, $489.50/2 vol set paper, $459.50 online subn
ISBN(s): 978-1-57387-604-9 (2 vol set)

Magazines for Libraries™
Published by ProQuest LLC, part of Clarivate PLC
789 E Eisenhower Pkwy, Ann Arbor, MI 48106
E-mail: info@proquest.com
Web Site: www.proquest.com
Key Personnel
Gen Ed: Cheryl LaGuardia
Creator: Bill Katz
A critically annotated guide to magazine selection for public, college, school & special libraries, with approximately 5,000 periodicals critically evaluated by more than 160 subject specialists & classified under more than 160 subject headings. Includes journals (print & electronic) & newspapers.
2022, $1,670 cloth
First published 1969
ISBN(s): 978-1-60030-688-4

Magill's Choice: American Ethnic Writers
Published by Grey House Publishing Inc™
4919 Rte 22, Amenia, NY 12501
Mailing Address: PO Box 56, Amenia, NY 12501-0056
Tel: 518-789-8700 *Toll Free Tel:* 800-562-2139
Fax: 518-789-0556
E-mail: csr@salempress.com
Web Site: salempress.com
Coverage of 225 ethnic writers, including summary descriptions of the writer's significance, associated ethnicities, birth/death dates, biography & thorough analysis of the writer's works.
Aug 2008: 1,000 pp, $217/3 vol set (includes online access with print purchase)
ISBN(s): 978-1-58765-462-6; 978-1-58765-466-4 (ebook)

Magill's Choice: Holocaust Literature
Published by Grey House Publishing Inc™
4919 Rte 22, Amenia, NY 12501
Mailing Address: PO Box 56, Amenia, NY 12501-0056
Tel: 518-789-8700 *Toll Free Tel:* 800-562-2139
Fax: 518-789-0556
E-mail: csr@salempress.com
Web Site: salempress.com
Key Personnel
Ed: John K Roth; Edward J Sexton
More than 100 in-depth reviews of the classics of Holocaust literature, including histories, biographies, memoirs, diaries, testimonials, philosophy, social criticism, novels, short fiction, poetry & plays.
March 2008: 960 pp, $130/2 vol set (includes online access with print purchase)
ISBN(s): 978-1-58765-375-9 (2 vol set); 978-1-58765-443-5 (ebook set)

Magill's Choice: Notable African American Writers
Published by Grey House Publishing Inc™
4919 Rte 22, Amenia, NY 12501
Mailing Address: PO Box 56, Amenia, NY 12501-0056
Tel: 518-789-8700 *Toll Free Tel:* 800-562-2139
Fax: 518-789-0556
E-mail: csr@salempress.com
Web Site: salempress.com
Biographical essays on 80 important African American writers in all genres.
April 2006: 1,350 pp, $217/3 vol set (includes online access with print purchase)
ISBN(s): 978-1-58765-272-1 (3 vol set); 978-1-58765-362-9 (ebook set)

Magill's Choice: Notable American Novelists
Published by Grey House Publishing Inc™
4919 Rte 22, Amenia, NY 12501
Mailing Address: PO Box 56, Amenia, NY 12501-0056
Tel: 518-789-8700 *Toll Free Tel:* 800-562-2139
Fax: 518-789-0556
E-mail: csr@salempress.com
Web Site: salempress.com
Presents biographical sketches & analytical overviews of 145 of the best known American & Canadian writers of long fiction from the 19th & 20th centuries that are studied in the core curricula of high school & undergraduate literature studies.
Aug 2007 (revised): 1,536 pp, $217/3 vol set (includes online access with print purchase)
ISBN(s): 978-1-58765-393-3 (3 vol set); 978-1-58765-410-7 (ebook set)

Magill's Choice: Notable Playwrights
Published by Grey House Publishing Inc™
4919 Rte 22, Amenia, NY 12501
Mailing Address: PO Box 56, Amenia, NY 12501-0056
Tel: 518-789-8700 *Toll Free Tel:* 800-562-2139
Fax: 518-789-0556
E-mail: csr@salempress.com
Web Site: salempress.com
Biographical sketches & critical studies of 106 of the most important & best-known dramatists, from the development of drama in ancient Greece & Rome to European, American, Asian & African writers of the present century.
Aug 2004: 1,131 pp, $217/3 vol set (includes online access with print purchase)
ISBN(s): 978-1-58765-195-3 (3 vol set); 978-1-58765-316-2 (ebook set)

Magill's Choice: Short Story Writers
Published by Grey House Publishing Inc™
4919 Rte 22, Amenia, NY 12501
Mailing Address: PO Box 56, Amenia, NY 12501-0056
Tel: 518-789-8700 *Toll Free Tel:* 800-562-2139
Fax: 518-789-0556
E-mail: csr@salempress.com
Web Site: salempress.com
Key Personnel
Ed: Charles May
Covers 146 of the most frequently taught, read & researched short fiction writers studied in American schools & colleges.
Oct 2007 (revised): 1,164 pp, $217/3 vol set (includes online access with print purchase)
ISBN(s): 978-1-58765-389-6 (3 vol set); 978-1-58765-411-4 (ebook set)

Magill's Literary Annual
Published by Grey House Publishing Inc™
4919 Rte 22, Amenia, NY 12501
Mailing Address: PO Box 56, Amenia, NY 12501-0056
Tel: 518-789-8700 *Toll Free Tel:* 800-562-2139
Fax: 518-789-0556
E-mail: csr@salempress.com
Web Site: salempress.com
Offers over 150 major examples of serious literature published during the previous calendar year, covering the best of the best in fiction & nonfiction.
Annual.
April 2024: 700 pp, $210/2 vol set (includes online access with print purchase)
First published 1954
ISBN(s): 978-1-63700-478-4 (ebook set); 978-1-63700-807-2 (2 vol set)

Managing the Publishing Process: An Annotated Bibliography
Published by Greenwood
Imprint of ABC-CLIO LLC
147 Castilian Dr, Santa Barbara, CA 93117
Tel: 805-968-1911 *Toll Free Tel:* 800-368-6868
Toll Free Fax: 866-270-3856
E-mail: customerservice@abc-clio.com; rights@abc-clio.com
Web Site: www.abc-clio.com
Key Personnel
Edit Dir, Print: Kevin Downing
Author: Bruce W Speck
Cites & annotates more than 1,200 books & articles on how to manage the publishing process.
1995: 360 pp, $75 hardcover
ISBN(s): 978-0-313-27956-0

Manufacturing Standards & Specifications for (El-Hi) Textbooks (MSST)
Published by Book Manufacturers' Institute Inc (BMI)
7282 55 Ave E, No 147, Bradenton, FL 34203
Tel: 386-986-4552 *Fax:* 386-986-4553
E-mail: info@bmibook.com
Web Site: www.bmibook.com/msst
Key Personnel
Exec Dir: Matt Baehr *Tel:* 703-939-0679
The official Advisory Commission on Textbook Specifications (ACTS) publication detailing the

approved guidelines for the manufacture of elementary & high school textbooks.
Jan 2020: 92 pp

Mastering Suspense, Structure & Plot
Published by Writer's Digest Books
Imprint of Penguin Publishing Group
1745 Broadway, New York, NY 10019
Web Site: www.penguinrandomhouse.com
Hands-on guide to navigate genre conventions, write for your audience & build gripping tension to craft an irresistible page-turner.
2016: 240 pp, $18.99 paper, $13.99 ebook
ISBN(s): 978-1-59963-967-3 (paper); 978-1-59963-969-7 (ebook)

Masterplots
Published by Grey House Publishing Inc™
4919 Rte 22, Amenia, NY 12501
Mailing Address: PO Box 56, Amenia, NY 12501-0056
Tel: 518-789-8700 *Toll Free Tel:* 800-562-2139
Fax: 518-789-0556
E-mail: csr@salempress.com
Web Site: salempress.com
Key Personnel
Ed: Laurence W Mazzeno
Fundamental reference data, plot synopses & critical evaluations of a comprehensive selection of English language & world literature that has been translated into English.
4th ed, Nov 2010: 7,316 pp, $1,200/12 vol set (includes online access)
First published 1976
ISBN(s): 978-1-58765-568-5 (12 vol set)

Masterplots 2010-2018 Supplement
Published by Grey House Publishing Inc™
4919 Rte 22, Amenia, NY 12501
Mailing Address: PO Box 56, Amenia, NY 12501-0056
Tel: 518-789-8700 *Toll Free Tel:* 800-562-2139
Fax: 518-789-0556
E-mail: csr@salempress.com
Web Site: salempress.com
Critically evaluates 187 major examples of serious fiction, published in English from 2010-2018, from writers in the US & around the world.
Dec 2018: 616 pp, $225/2 vol set (includes online access with print purchase)
ISBN(s): 978-1-64265-032-7; 978-1-64265-033-4 (ebook)

Medical & Health Care Books & Serials in Print™
Published by Grey House Publishing Inc™
4919 Rte 22, Amenia, NY 12501
Mailing Address: PO Box 56, Amenia, NY 12501-0056
Tel: 518-789-8700 *Toll Free Tel:* 800-562-2139
Fax: 518-789-0556
E-mail: books@greyhouse.com
Web Site: greyhouse.com
Bibliographic information on thousands of highly specialized health science & allied health titles published or distributed in the US. Provides immediate access to over 107,000 ISBNs.
Annual.
49th ed, 2024: 6,300 pp, $1,060/3 vol set
ISBN(s): 978-1-63700-979-6 (3 vol set)

Middle & Junior High Core Collection
Published by Grey House Publishing Inc™
4919 Rte 22, Amenia, NY 12501
Mailing Address: PO Box 56, Amenia, NY 12501-0056
Tel: 518-789-8700 *Toll Free Tel:* 800-562-2139
Fax: 518-789-0556
E-mail: books@greyhouse.com
Web Site: greyhouse.com

Guide to over 11,000 fiction & nonfiction books recommended for children & young adolescents, grades 5-9.
16th ed, Dec 2023: 1,500 pp, $295
ISBN(s): 978-1-63700-510-1

MLRC 50-State Survey: Employment Libel & Privacy Law
Published by Media Law Resource Center Inc (MLRC)
266 W 37 St, 20th fl, New York, NY 10018
Tel: 212-337-0200 *Fax:* 212-337-9893
E-mail: medialaw@medialaw.org
Web Site: www.medialaw.org
Key Personnel
Exec Dir: George Freeman
Easy-to-use compendiums of the law in all US jurisdictions, state & federal, used by journalists, lawyers, judges & law schools nationwide. Each state's chapter, prepared by experts in that jurisdiction, is presented in a uniform outline format. Also available as an ebook. See store.lexisnexis.com for purchasing options.
Annual.
2024, $284

MLRC 50-State Survey: Media Libel Law
Published by Media Law Resource Center Inc (MLRC)
266 W 37 St, 20th fl, New York, NY 10018
Tel: 212-337-0200 *Fax:* 212-337-9893
E-mail: medialaw@medialaw.org
Web Site: www.medialaw.org
Key Personnel
Exec Dir: George Freeman
Easy-to-use compendiums of the law in all US jurisdictions, state & federal, used by journalists, lawyers, judges & law schools nationwide. Each state's chapter, prepared by experts in that jurisdiction, is presented in a uniform outline format. Also available as an ebook. See store.lexisnexis.com for purchasing options.
Annual.
2023-2024, $284

MLRC 50-State Survey: Media Privacy & Related Law
Published by Media Law Resource Center Inc (MLRC)
266 W 37 St, 20th fl, New York, NY 10018
Tel: 212-337-0200 *Fax:* 212-337-9893
E-mail: medialaw@medialaw.org
Web Site: www.medialaw.org
Key Personnel
Exec Dir: George Freeman
Easy-to-use compendiums of the law in all US jurisdictions, state & federal, used by journalists, lawyers, judges & law schools nationwide. Each state's chapter, prepared by experts in that jurisdiction, is presented in a uniform outline format. Also available as an ebook. See store.lexisnexis.com for purchasing options.
Annual.
2023-2024, $284

National Trade and Professional Associations of the United States
Published by Columbia Books & Information Services (CBIS)
1530 Wilson Blvd, Suite 400, Arlington, VA 22209
Tel: 202-464-1662 *Fax:* 301-664-9600
E-mail: info@columbiabooks.com
Web Site: www.columbiabooks.com; www.associationexecs.com/National-Trade-and-Professional-Associations-Directory
Key Personnel
Dir Prod & Serv Mktg: Sami Marshall
 E-mail: smarshall@columbiabooks.com
Covers over 8,000 trade associations, professional societies & labor unions with national memberships with such data as chief executive, size of membership & staff, budget, telephone, facsimile number, e-mail address, publications, meeting data & historical background. Includes indexes by subject, geography, budget, acronym, chief executive officer & annual meeting location. Also available online at www.associationexecs.com.
2019: 1,920 pp, $349
First published 1965
ISBN(s): 978-1-938939-83-9 (paper)

The New York Times Manual of Style and Usage
Published by Crown Publishing Group
Imprint of Penguin Random House LLC
c/o Penguin Random House LLC, 1745 Broadway, New York, NY 10019
Tel: 212-782-9000 *Toll Free Tel:* 800-733-3000 (cust serv)
Web Site: www.penguinrandomhouse.com
Key Personnel
Author: William G Connolly; Allan M Siegal
Alphabetical guide used by writers & editors, including guidelines to hyphenation, punctuation, capitalization & spelling. This edition is updated with solutions on how to cite links/blogs, how to handle social media content & how to thoughtfully use current terminology.
5th ed, 2015, $18.99 paper, $11.99 ebook
ISBN(s): 978-1-101-90322-8 (ebook); 978-1-101-90544-9 (paper)

Nineteenth-Century Literature Criticism
Published by Gale
Division of Cengage Learning
27555 Executive Dr, Suite 270, Farmington Hills, MI 48331
SAN: 213-4373
Toll Free Tel: 800-877-4253 *Toll Free Fax:* 877-363-4253
E-mail: gale.customerexperience@cengage.com
Web Site: www.gale.com
Assembles critical responses to the works of 19th century authors from every region of the world. Each of the more than 300 volumes profiles 3-6 novelists, poets, playwrights, journalists, philosophers or other creative & nonfiction writers by profiling full-text or excerpted criticism reproduced from books, magazines, literary reviews, newspapers & scholarly journals. Online database.

Notable African American Writers
Published by Grey House Publishing Inc™
4919 Rte 22, Amenia, NY 12501
Mailing Address: PO Box 56, Amenia, NY 12501-0056
Tel: 518-789-8700 *Toll Free Tel:* 800-562-2139
Fax: 518-789-0556
E-mail: csr@salempress.com
Web Site: salempress.com
Highlights African Americans who wrote centuries ago, as well as modern storytellers whose work reflects the changing global landscape. 500 author biographies cover the important events in a writer's life, education, major works, honors & awards, family & important associations.
2nd ed, March 2020: 900 pp, $295/3 vol set (includes online access)
ISBN(s): 978-1-64265-407-3 (3 vol set); 978-1-64265-408-0 (ebook set)

Notable American Women Writers
Published by Grey House Publishing Inc™
4919 Rte 22, Amenia, NY 12501
Mailing Address: PO Box 56, Amenia, NY 12501-0056
Tel: 518-789-8700 *Toll Free Tel:* 800-562-2139
Fax: 518-789-0556
E-mail: csr@salempress.com
Web Site: salempress.com

Key Personnel
Ed: James F Nicosia, PhD; Laura Nicosia, PhD
Overviews & in-depth analysis of hundreds of American women writers of literature, from Colonial America to present day. Features more than 415 biographies. Each essay includes name, description of each woman's contributions & the type of writing she is best known for, along with birth/death dates & locations.
March 2020: 600 pp, $225/2 vol set (includes online access)
ISBN(s): 978-1-64265-423-3 (2 vol set); 978-1-64265-424-0 (ebook set)

Notable Crime Fiction Writers
Published by Grey House Publishing Inc™
4919 Rte 22, Amenia, NY 12501
Mailing Address: PO Box 56, Amenia, NY 12501-0056
Tel: 518-789-8700 *Toll Free Tel:* 800-562-2139
Fax: 518-789-0556
E-mail: csr@salempress.com
Web Site: salempress.com
Key Personnel
Ed: Robert C Evans, PhD
Features the best crime & mystery fiction writers, both classic & contemporary. Includes survey essays which cover crime writers whose detectives fall into various groups, including LGBTQ detectives, African American detectives, Asian detectives, Scandinavian detectives & detectives with disabilities. Each essay includes name, description of each author's contributions & the type of writing they are best known for, as well as birth/death dates & locations.
Oct 2021: 930 pp, $225/2 vol set (includes online access)
ISBN(s): 978-1-63700-031-1 (2 vol set); 978-1-63700-032-8 (ebook set)

Notable Writers of LGBTQ+ Literature
Published by Grey House Publishing Inc™
4919 Rte 22, Amenia, NY 12501
Mailing Address: PO Box 56, Amenia, NY 12501-0056
Tel: 518-789-8700 *Toll Free Tel:* 800-562-2139
Fax: 518-789-0556
E-mail: csr@salempress.com
Web Site: salempress.com
Collection of analytic, scholarly, encyclopedic essays of LGBTQ+ literature, examining poems, plays, novels & short fiction from ancient times to present day. Each essay identifies relevant genres & biographical data.
Sept 2023: 600 pp, $225/2 vol set (includes online access)
ISBN(s): 978-1-63700-719-8 (2 vol set); 978-1-63700-722-8 (ebook set)

Notable Writers of the American West & the Native American Experience
Published by Grey House Publishing Inc™
4919 Rte 22, Amenia, NY 12501
Mailing Address: PO Box 56, Amenia, NY 12501-0056
Tel: 518-789-8700 *Toll Free Tel:* 800-562-2139
Fax: 518-789-0556
E-mail: csr@salempress.com
Web Site: salempress.com
Key Personnel
Ed: James F Nicosia, PhD; Laura Nicosia, PhD
Overview & in-depth context to the stories of over 100 acclaimed writers. Each entry includes a comprehensive overview of each author's biography & literary career as well as a ready-reference listing of their major works in all genres. Introduces readers to the rich world of Native Americans & the vivid literature of the American West.

Nov 2021: 662 pp, $175 (includes online access)
ISBN(s): 978-1-63700-004-5; 978-1-63700-005-2 (ebook)

Novel & Short Story Writer's Market
Published by Writer's Digest Books
Imprint of Penguin Publishing Group
1745 Broadway, New York, NY 10019
Web Site: www.penguinrandomhouse.com
Go-to resource to get your short stories, novellas & novels published. Hundreds of listings for book publishers, literary agents, fiction publications, contests & more, including contact information, submission guidelines & other essential tips.
40th ed, 2021: 512 pp, $31 paper, $19.99 ebook
ISBN(s): 978-0-593-33207-8 (paper); 978-0-593-33208-5 (ebook)

Novels Into Film: Adaptations & Interpretations
Published by Grey House Publishing Inc™
4919 Rte 22, Amenia, NY 12501
Mailing Address: PO Box 56, Amenia, NY 12501-0056
Tel: 518-789-8700 *Toll Free Tel:* 800-562-2139
Fax: 518-789-0556
E-mail: csr@salempress.com
Web Site: salempress.com
Key Personnel
Ed: D Alan Dean, PhD
128 concise essays on significant novels & movie adaptations, ranging from classics to contemporary favorites. Providing authoritative information & scholarly analysis with a focus on narrative elements & adaptation strategies. The essays also introduce fundamental concepts in literary & film criticism & address the qualities that are specific to the two media of literature & film.
Vol 2, Sept 2021: 448 pp, $185 (includes online access with print purchase)
ISBN(s): 978-1-63700-036-6; 978-1-63700-037-3 (ebook)

O'Dwyer's Directory of Public Relations Firms
Published by J R O'Dwyer Co Inc
271 Madison Ave, No 1500, New York, NY 10016
Tel: 212-679-2471 *Fax:* 212-683-2750
Web Site: www.odwyerpr.com
Key Personnel
Publr: John O'Dwyer *E-mail:* john@odwyerpr.com
Dir, Opers & Fin: Jane Landers *E-mail:* jane@odwyerpr.com
Dir, Mktg: Christine O'Dwyer *E-mail:* christine@odwyerpr.com
Dir, Res: Melissa Werbell *E-mail:* melissa@odwyerpr.com
Sr Ed: Fraser P Seitel *E-mail:* yusake@aol.com
Contains listings firms in the US & abroad.
54th ed, 2024: 330 pp, $95
First published 1970
ISBN(s): 978-0-9976910-8-5

1,001 Tips for Writers: Words of Wisdom About Writing, Getting Published, and Living the Literary Life
Published by North Ridge Books
38972 Camino Buendia, Indio, CA 92203
Tel: 949-533-5106 (cell)
E-mail: nrbooks@aol.com
Key Personnel
Publr & Ed: William A Gordon
1,001 Tips for Writers is a quotation book offering "Words of Wisdom About Writing, Getting Published, and Living the Literary Life." The book quotes literary greats; working writers, publishers, editors on subjects such as "How to Get Traditionally Published", "Self-Publishing", "Book Publicity" & writing history, humor, novels, & journalism.
1st ed, 2014, $16.95 paper, $8.95 ebook
ISBN(s): 978-0-937813-09-6 (ebook); 978-0-937813-10-2 (paper)

Poetry Criticism
Published by Gale
Division of Cengage Learning
27555 Executive Dr, Suite 270, Farmington Hills, MI 48331
SAN: 213-4373
Toll Free Tel: 800-877-4253 *Toll Free Fax:* 877-363-4253
E-mail: gale.customerexperience@cengage.com
Web Site: www.gale.com
Assembles critical responses to the writings of the world's most renowned poets & provides supplementary biographical context & bibliographic material to guide the reader to a greater understanding of the genre & its creators. The series covers more than 500 poets & authors & includes numerous entries focused on individual works. Online database.

Poet's Market
Published by Writer's Digest Books
Imprint of Penguin Publishing Group
1745 Broadway, New York, NY 10019
Web Site: www.penguinrandomhouse.com
Includes hundreds of publishing opportunities specifically for poets, including listings for book & chapbook publishers, print & online poetry publications, contests & more.
34th ed, 2021: 480 pp, $32 paper, $16.99 ebook
ISBN(s): 978-0-5933-3211-5 (paper); 978-0-5934-1909-0 (ebook)

Professional Writing: Processes, Strategies & Tips for Publishing in Education Journals
Published by Krieger Publishing Co
1725 Krieger Lane, Malabar, FL 32950
SAN: 202-6562
Tel: 321-724-9542 *Fax:* 321-951-3671
E-mail: info@krieger-publishing.com
Web Site: www.krieger-publishing.com
Key Personnel
Author: Roger Hiemstra
Provides insights, tips, strategies & recommendations for publishing in educational periodicals.
1994: 152 pp, $27.50 cloth
First published 1994
ISBN(s): 978-0-89464-660-7

Public Library Core Collection: Nonfiction
Published by Grey House Publishing Inc™
4919 Rte 22, Amenia, NY 12501
Mailing Address: PO Box 56, Amenia, NY 12501-0056
Tel: 518-789-8700 *Toll Free Tel:* 800-562-2139
Fax: 518-789-0556
E-mail: books@greyhouse.com
Web Site: greyhouse.com
Recommends reference & nonfiction books for the general adult audience. Guide to over 12,000 books, plus review sources & other professional aids for librarians & media specialists.
19th ed, March 2023: 3,000 pp, $420
ISBN(s): 978-1-63700-395-4

Publish, Don't Perish: The Scholar's Guide to Academic Writing & Publishing
Published by Praeger
Imprint of ABC-CLIO
147 Castiliane Dr, Santa Barbara, CA 93117
Tel: 805-968-1911 *Toll Free Tel:* 800-368-6868
Toll Free Fax: 866-270-3856
E-mail: customerservice@abc-clio.com; rights@abc-clio.com
Web Site: www.abc-clio.com

Key Personnel
Edit Dir, Print: Kevin Downing
Author: Joseph M Moxley
Expressing a strongly positive view of the value of academic publishing that reaches far beyond what is implied by the book title, Moxley offers informed suggestions to faculty members for conceiving, developing & publishing scholarly documents as books or journal articles.
224 pp, $40 hardcover
First published 1992
ISBN(s): 978-0-313-27735-1

Publishers Directory (PD)
Published by Gale
Division of Cengage Learning
27555 Executive Dr, Suite 270, Farmington Hills, MI 48331
SAN: 213-4373
Toll Free Tel: 800-877-4253 *Toll Free Fax:* 877-363-4253
E-mail: gale.customerexperience@cengage.com
Web Site: www.gale.com
Contains over 20,000 US & Canadian publishers & distributors. Entries contain full organization contact information, including corporate e-mails & web sites when provided. In addition, most entries feature a wealth of descriptive (when available), including principal officers with personal e-mails; year founded; annual sales; number of titles per year, including an estimate for current year; total title count; discount policy; percentage of sales. Available as ebook only.
36th ed, 2011
ISBN(s): 978-1-4144-6061-1

Publishers, Distributors & Wholesalers of the United States™
Published by Grey House Publishing Inc™
4919 Rte 22, Amenia, NY 12501
Mailing Address: PO Box 56, Amenia, NY 12501-0056
Tel: 518-789-8700 *Toll Free Tel:* 800-562-2139 *Fax:* 518-789-0556
E-mail: books@greyhouse.com
Web Site: greyhouse.com
Offers detailed data on active US publishers, distributors, wholesalers, video producers, manufacturers, audio producers, museums with publishing programs & other related businesses. Immediate access to over 500,000 publishers & over 15,000 distributors & wholesalers.
Annual.
45th ed, 2024: 5,400 pp, $995/2 vol set hardcover
ISBN(s): 978-1-63700-986-4 (2 vol set)

Publishers' International ISBN Directory
Published by De Gruyter Saur
Imprint of Walter de Gruyter GmbH
Genthiner Str 13, 10785 Berlin, Germany
Tel: (030) 260 05-0 *Fax:* (030) 260 05-251
E-mail: service@degruyter.com
Web Site: www.degruyter.com
Seven volume set containing the names of more than 1,000,000 active publishing houses & more than 1,100,000 ISBN prefixes from 221 countries & territories.
41st ed, 2015: 9,217 pp, $2,366 hardcover, $2,239 PDF
ISBN(s): 978-3-11-033619-1 (hardcover/7-vol set); 978-3-11-033735-8 (ebook)

Publishing for the PreK-12 Market
Published by Simba Information
Division of Market Research.com
6116 Executive Blvd, Suite 550, Rockville, MD 20852
SAN: 210-2021
Tel: 240-747-3091 *Toll Free Tel:* 888-297-4622 (cust serv) *Fax:* 240-747-3004
E-mail: customerservice@simbainformation.com
Web Site: www.simbainformation.com
Key Personnel
Sr Analyst/Mng Ed: Kathy Mickey
Sr Ed/Analyst: Daniel Strempel
Ed/Analyst: Karen Meaney
Up-to-date descriptions & statistics on enrollments, demographic trends, in several categories; publishers' sales, forecasts, expenditures & profiles of the leading publishers in the K-12 market place.
Annual.
2023-2024: 140 pp, $3,900 online download

Publishing in the Information Age: A New Management Framework for the Digital Era
Published by Praeger
Imprint of ABC-CLIO
147 Castiliane Dr, Santa Barbara, CA 93117
Tel: 805-968-1911 *Toll Free Tel:* 800-368-6868 *Toll Free Fax:* 866-270-3856
E-mail: customerservice@abc-clio.com; rights@abc-clio.com
Web Site: www.abc-clio.com
Key Personnel
Edit Dir, Print: Kevin Downing
Author: Douglas M Eisenhart
A comprehensive single-volume study of the transformations underway in the publishing industry attributable to the penetration of digital information technologies & how publishers can benefit from them.
312 pp, $84 hardcover
First published 1994
ISBN(s): 978-0-89930-847-0 (hardcover); 978-1-56750-753-9 (ebook)

Putting the Fact in Fantasy
Published by Writer's Digest Books
Imprint of Penguin Publishing Group
1745 Broadway, New York, NY 10019
Web Site: www.penguinrandomhouse.com
A collection of essays from historians, linguists, martial artists & other experts to help you write more inspired & convincing fantasy.
2022: 352 pp, $20 paper, $14.99 ebook, $20 audiobook
ISBN(s): 978-0-593-33199-6 (paper); 978-0-593-33200-9 (ebook); 978-0-593-55821-8 (audiobook)

Recommended Reading: 600 Classics Reviewed
Published by Grey House Publishing Inc™
4919 Rte 22, Amenia, NY 12501
Mailing Address: PO Box 56, Amenia, NY 12501-0056
Tel: 518-789-8700 *Toll Free Tel:* 800-562-2139 *Fax:* 518-789-0556
E-mail: csr@salempress.com
Web Site: salempress.com
Covers 600 noteworthy works of literature (fiction, nonfiction, poetry or drama) & introduces brief, ready-reference data for the user's convenience: title, author, date of first publication, type of work & brief extract of book's content or impact.
2nd ed, Oct 2015: 406 pp, $125 (includes online access with print purchase)
First published 1995
ISBN(s): 978-1-61925-867-9; 978-1-61925-868-6 (ebook)

Research Centers Directory (RCD)
Published by Gale
Division of Cengage Learning
27555 Executive Dr, Suite 270, Farmington Hills, MI 48331
SAN: 213-4373
Toll Free Tel: 800-877-4253 *Toll Free Fax:* 877-363-4253
E-mail: gale.customerexperience@cengage.com
Web Site: www.gale.com
Directory describes university affiliated & other nonprofit research institutes in North America. Indexes: subject, geographic, personal name & master. Available as ebook only.
48th ed, 2018
ISBN(s): 978-1-4103-6477-7 (ebook)

Sears List of Subject Headings
Published by Grey House Publishing Inc™
4919 Rte 22, Amenia, NY 12501
Mailing Address: PO Box 56, Amenia, NY 12501-0056
Tel: 518-789-8700 *Toll Free Tel:* 800-562-2139 *Fax:* 518-789-0556
E-mail: books@greyhouse.com
Web Site: greyhouse.com
Standard thesaurus of subject terminology for small & medium-sized libraries. Also includes *Principles of the Sears List*, outlining theoretical foundations of the *Sears List* & the general principles of subject cataloging.
23rd ed, July 2022: 950 pp, $195 (includes online access)
First published 1923
ISBN(s): 978-1-63700-307-7

The Secrets of Character
Published by Writer's Digest Books
Imprint of Penguin Publishing Group
1745 Broadway, New York, NY 10019
Web Site: www.penguinrandomhouse.com
Guide to making characters embraceable & unforgettable with insider tips & tricks for writers of all levels & genres.
2022: 304 pp, $19 paper, $13.99 ebook, $20 audiobook
ISBN(s): 978-0-593-33122-4 (paper); 978-0-593-33123-1 (ebook); 978-0-593-63415-8 (audiobook)

The Secrets of Story
Published by Writer's Digest Books
Imprint of Penguin Publishing Group
1745 Broadway, New York, NY 10019
Web Site: www.penguinrandomhouse.com
Provides comprehensive, audience-focused strategies for becoming a master storyteller.
2016: 368 pp, $19.99 paper, $15.99 ebook
ISBN(s): 978-1-4403-4823-5 (paper); 978-1-4403-4829-7 (ebook)

Senior High Core Collection
Published by Grey House Publishing Inc™
4919 Rte 22, Amenia, NY 12501
Mailing Address: PO Box 56, Amenia, NY 12501-0056
Tel: 518-789-8700 *Toll Free Tel:* 800-562-2139 *Fax:* 518-789-0556
E-mail: books@greyhouse.com
Web Site: greyhouse.com
Guide to over 4,500 fiction & nonfiction books recommended for adolescents & young adults, grades 9-12.
24th ed, Nov 2024: 1,500 pp, $295
ISBN(s): 978-1-63700-909-3

Shakespearean Criticism
Published by Gale
Division of Cengage Learning
27555 Executive Dr, Suite 270, Farmington Hills, MI 48331
SAN: 213-4373
Toll Free Tel: 800-877-4253 *Toll Free Fax:* 877-363-4253
E-mail: gale.customerexperience@cengage.com
Web Site: www.gale.com
Provides students, educators, theatergoers & other interested readers with valuable insights into Shakespeare's drama & poetry. Volumes 1-10 present critical overviews of each play & feature criticism from the 17th century to the present. Volumes 11-26 focus on the history of Shakespeare's plays on the stage & in ma-

jor film adaptations. Volumes 27-56 focus on criticism published after 1960 & include topic entries that deliver thematic approaches to Shakespeare's works. Starting with Volume 57, the series provides general criticism published since 1990 & historical criticism not featured in previous volumes on 4-5 plays or works per volume. Select volumes contain topic entries. Online database.

Short Story Criticism: Excerpts from Criticism of the Works of Short Fiction Writers
Published by Gale
Division of Cengage Learning
27555 Executive Dr, Suite 270, Farmington Hills, MI 48331
SAN: 213-4373
Toll Free Tel: 800-877-4253 *Toll Free Fax:* 877-363-4253
E-mail: gale.customerexperience@cengage.com
Web Site: www.gale.com
Assembles critical responses to the writings of the world's most renowned short fiction writers & provides supplementary biographical context & bibliographical material to guide the reader to a greater understanding of the genre & its creators. Each of the more than 250 volumes in this series profiles approximately 3-6 writers of short fiction from all time periods & all parts of the world. Entries provide an introductory biographical essay, a primary bibliography, a selection of full-text or excerpted critical essays reproduced from books, magazines, literary reviews, newspapers & scholarly journals & sources for additional research; many entries include an author portrait. A full citation & annotation precede each of the approximately 50 essays per volume. The series currently covers more than 500 authors & also includes numerous entries focusing on individual works & topics.
Vol 306, 2022, $384 hardcover
ISBN(s): 978-1-4103-9784-3

Short Story Index
Published by Grey House Publishing Inc™
4919 Rte 22, Amenia, NY 12501
Mailing Address: PO Box 56, Amenia, NY 12501-0056
Tel: 518-789-8700 *Toll Free Tel:* 800-562-2139
Fax: 518-789-0556
E-mail: books@greyhouse.com
Web Site: greyhouse.com
Indexing coverage of short stories written in or translated into English & published in collections, covering all styles & genres, from classics to experimental fiction.
Annual.
2023 ed (2022 annual cumulation): 300 pp, $295
ISBN(s): 978-1-63700-874-4

Software and Intellectual Property Protection: Copyright and Patent Issues for Computer and Legal Professionals
Published by Praeger
Imprint of ABC-CLIO
147 Castiliane Dr, Santa Barbara, CA 93117
Tel: 805-968-1911 *Toll Free Tel:* 800-368-6868
Toll Free Fax: 866-270-3856
E-mail: customerservice@abc-clio.com; rights@abc-clio.com
Web Site: www.abc-clio.com
Key Personnel
Edit Dir, Print: Kevin Downing
Author: Bernard A Galler
A succinct, readable survey of the critical issues & cases in copyright & patent law applied to computer software, intended for computer professionals, academics & lawyers.
224 pp, $84 hardcover
First published 1995
ISBN(s): 978-0-89930-974-3

Something About the Author
Published by Gale
Division of Cengage Learning
27555 Executive Dr, Suite 270, Farmington Hills, MI 48331
SAN: 213-4373
Toll Free Tel: 800-877-4253 *Toll Free Fax:* 877-363-4253
E-mail: gale.customerexperience@cengage.com
Web Site: www.gale.com
Examines the lives & works of authors & illustrators for children & young adults. The collection includes both the main series & *Something About the Author Autobiography Series*, totaling more than 217 volumes, 12,000 entries & nearly 17,000 images. Each volume provides illustrated biographical profiles of approximately 75 children's authors & artists, typically covering personal life, career, writings, works in progress, adaptations & additional sources. A cumulative author index is included in each odd-numbered volume. Online database.

The Standard Periodical Directory
Published by Oxbridge® Communications Inc
301 W 29 St, No 301, New York, NY 10001
Key Personnel
CEO: Louis Hagood *Tel:* 212-741-0231
Over 63,000 US & Canadian periodicals arranged by subject matter into 262 classifications & indexed by title. Listings include publishing company, address, telephone number; names of editor, publisher, ad director; annotations; frequency, circulation, advertising & subscription rates; year established; trim size, print method, page count.
42nd ed, 2019: 2,112 pp, $1,995 hardcover, $995 digital, $1,995 single user CD-ROM, $2,995 print & CD-ROM
First published 1964
ISBN(s): 978-1-891783-69-2 (hardcover)

Subject Guide to Books in Print®
Published by Grey House Publishing Inc™
4919 Rte 22, Amenia, NY 12501
Mailing Address: PO Box 56, Amenia, NY 12501-0056
Tel: 518-789-8700 *Toll Free Tel:* 800-562-2139
Fax: 518-789-0556
E-mail: books@greyhouse.com
Web Site: greyhouse.com
Master subject reference to titles, authors, publishers, wholesalers & distributors in the US.
Annual.
2024-2025: 15,400 pp, $1,599/6 vol set
ISBN(s): 978-1-63700-950-5 (6 vol set)

Subject Guide to Children's Books in Print®
Published by Grey House Publishing Inc™
4919 Rte 22, Amenia, NY 12501
Mailing Address: PO Box 56, Amenia, NY 12501-0056
Tel: 518-789-8700 *Toll Free Tel:* 800-562-2139
Fax: 518-789-0556
E-mail: books@greyhouse.com
Web Site: greyhouse.com
A natural complement to *Children's Books in Print®* & valuable tool when expanding children's literature collections & new curriculum areas. Coverage includes over 500,000 titles organized by 10,000 Library of Congress subject headings.
Annual.
55th ed, 2024: 2,900 pp, $850
ISBN(s): 978-1-63700-643-6

The Subversive Copy Editor: Advice from Chicago (Or, How to Negotiate Good Relationships with Your Writers, Your Colleagues, and Yourself)
Published by University of Chicago Press
1427 E 60 St, Chicago, IL 60637-2954
SAN: 202-5280
Tel: 773-702-7700; 773-702-7000 (cust serv, print); 773-753-3347 *Toll Free Tel:* 800-621-2736 (orders); 877-705-1878 (US & CN)
Fax: 773-702-9756
E-mail: custserv@press.uchicago.edu; marketing@press.uchicago.edu
Web Site: www.press.uchicago.edu
Key Personnel
Exec Ed, Ref & Writing Guides: Mary Laur *Tel:* 773-702-7326 *E-mail:* mlaur@uchicago.edu
Longtime mss editor & *Chicago Manual of Style* guru Carol Fisher Saller brings a refreshingly levelheaded approach to the classic battle between writers & editors. The 2nd edition reflects today's publishing practices while retaining the self-deprecating tone & sharp humor that helped make the 1st edition so popular. Saller's sage advice will prove useful & entertaining to anyone charged with the sometimes perilous task of improving the writing of others.
2nd ed, 2016: 200 pp, $45 cloth, $15 paper or ebook
First published 2009
ISBN(s): 978-0-226-23990-3 (cloth); 978-0-226-24007-7 (paper); 978-0-226-24010-7 (ebook)

Training Guide to Frontline Bookselling
Published by Paz & Associates
1417 Sadler Rd, PMB 274, Fernandina Beach, FL 32034
Tel: 904-277-2664
E-mail: mkaufman@pazbookbiz.com
Web Site: www.openingabookstore.com
Key Personnel
Partner: Donna Paz Kaufman *E-mail:* dpaz@pazbookbiz.com
12 chapters on all aspects of bookstore operations, includes trainers outline & contents in Word format for easy customization.
11th ed, Jan 2021: 125 pp, $189 plus shipping
First published 1993

Troubleshooting Your Novel
Published by Writer's Digest Books
Imprint of Penguin Publishing Group
1745 Broadway, New York, NY 10019
Web Site: www.penguinrandomhouse.com
Helpful techniques & checklists, timesaving tricks of the trade & hundreds of questions for ms analysis & revision.
2016: 368 pp, $25 paper, $15.99 ebook
ISBN(s): 978-1-59963-980-2 (paper); 978-1-59963-984-0 (ebook)

TRUMATCH Colorfinder
Published by TRUMATCH Inc
122 Mill Pond Lane, Water Mill, NY 11976
Mailing Address: PO Box 501, Water Mill, NY 11976-0501
Tel: 631-204-9100 *Toll Free Tel:* 800-TRU-9100 (878-9100, US & CN)
E-mail: info@trumatch.com
Web Site: www.trumatch.com
Key Personnel
Pres: Steven J Abramson *E-mail:* stevea@trumatch.com
VP: Jane E Nichols *E-mail:* janen@trumatch.com
Digital guides for 4-color printing.
$85 paper for coated ed or uncoated ed

Twentieth-Century Literary Criticism
Published by Gale
Division of Cengage Learning
27555 Executive Dr, Suite 270, Farmington Hills, MI 48331
SAN: 213-4373
Toll Free Tel: 800-877-4253 *Toll Free Fax:* 877-363-4253
E-mail: gale.customerexperience@cengage.com

Web Site: www.gale.com
Assembles critical responses to the works of 20th century authors of all genres. The series currently covers nearly 1,200 authors & includes thousands of entries on literary topics & individual works. Close to 95% of critical essays from the print version series are reproduced in full in this version. Online database.

20 Master Plots
Published by Writer's Digest Books
Imprint of Penguin Publishing Group
1745 Broadway, New York, NY 10019
Web Site: www.penguinrandomhouse.com
How to take timeless storytelling structures & make them immediate, now, for fiction that's universal in how it speaks to the reader's heart.
2012: 288 pp, $18.99 paper, $13.99 ebook
First published 2003
ISBN(s): 978-1-59963-537-8 (paper); 978-1-59963-539-2 (ebook)

Ulrich's Periodicals Directory™
Published by ProQuest LLC, part of Clarivate PLC
789 E Eisenhower Pkwy, Ann Arbor, MI 48106
Tel: 734-761-4700 *Toll Free Tel:* 800-521-0600
E-mail: ulrichs@proquest.com
Web Site: www.ulrichsweb.com; www.proquest.com
Bibliographic & publisher information on more than 300,00 periodicals of all types academic & scholarly journals, Open Access publications, peer-reviewed titles, popular magazines, newspapers, newsletters & more from around the world. It covers all subjects & includes publications that are published regularly or irregularly. Online only.
First published 1932

Walden's Paper Catalog
Published by Walden-Mott Corp
225 N Franklin Tpke, Ramsey, NJ 07446-1600
Tel: 201-818-8630 *Fax:* 201-818-8720
Web Site: www.waldenmott.com
Key Personnel
Ed: Alfred F Walden *Tel:* 201-818-8630 ext 11
National directory for information on commercial printing & writing papers. Brand names are listed alphabetically & by classification of paper. Paper distributors are listed geographically to help printers source from a local supplier.
2 issues/yr.
$85/yr
First published 1914

Walden's Paper Handbook
Published by Walden-Mott Corp
225 N Franklin Tpke, Ramsey, NJ 07446-1600
Tel: 201-818-8630 *Fax:* 201-818-8720
Web Site: www.waldenmott.com
Key Personnel
Ed: Alfred F Walden *Tel:* 201-818-8630 ext 11
Pulp & paper industry pocket guide.
3rd ed: 277 pp, $25

What Editors Do: The Art, Craft, and Business of Book Editing
Published by University of Chicago Press
1427 E 60 St, Chicago, IL 60637-2954
SAN: 202-5280
Tel: 773-702-7700; 773-702-7000 (cust serv, print); 773-753-3347 *Toll Free Tel:* 800-621-2736 (orders); 877-705-1878 (US & CN)
Fax: 773-702-9756
E-mail: custserv@press.uchicago.edu; marketing@press.uchicago.edu
Web Site: www.press.uchicago.edu
Key Personnel
Exec Ed, Ref & Writing Guides: Mary Laur
Tel: 773-702-7326 *E-mail:* mlaur@uchicago.edu
In this volume, Peter Ginna gathers essays from 27 leading editors in book publishing about their work. Representing both large houses & small & encompassing trade, textbook, academic & children's publishing, the contributors shed light on such issues as how editors acquire books, what constitutes a strong author-editor relationship & the editor's vital role at each stage of the publishing process. The book serves as a resource both for those entering the profession (or already in it) & for those outside publishing who seek an understanding of it.
1st ed: 320 pp, $75 cloth, $25 paper, $18 ebook
First published 2017
ISBN(s): 978-0-226-29983-9 (cloth); 978-0-226-29997-6 (paper); 978-0-226-30003-0 (ebook)

Word Painting
Published by Writer's Digest Books
Imprint of Penguin Publishing Group
1745 Broadway, New York, NY 10019
Web Site: www.penguinrandomhouse.com
Combines direct instruction with intriguing word exercises to teach you how to "paint" evocative descriptions that capture the images of your mind's eye & improve your writing.
2014 (revised): 272 pp, $18.99 paper, $13.99 ebook
First published 2000
ISBN(s): 978-1-59963-868-3 (paper); 978-1-59963-872-0 (ebook)

World Authors 2000-2005
Published by Grey House Publishing Inc™
4919 Rte 22, Amenia, NY 12501
Mailing Address: PO Box 56, Amenia, NY 12501-0056
Tel: 518-789-8700 *Toll Free Tel:* 800-562-2139
Fax: 518-789-0556
E-mail: books@greyhouse.com
Web Site: greyhouse.com
Covers some 300 novelists, poets, dramatists, essayists, scientists, biographers & other authors whose books, published 2000 through 2005, represent the dawn of a new millenium of great literature.
Available for purchase at www.hwwilsoninprint.com/world_authors05.php.
2007: 800 pp, $170
ISBN(s): 978-0-8242-1077-9

Write Naked
Published by Writer's Digest Books
Imprint of Penguin Publishing Group
1745 Broadway, New York, NY 10019
Web Site: www.penguinrandomhouse.com
Lessons & craft advice every writer needs in order to carve out a rewarding career in the romance genre.
2017: 240 pp, $17.99 paper, $13.99 ebook
ISBN(s): 978-1-4403-4734-4 (paper); 978-1-4403-4746-7 (ebook)

Writer's Digest Guide to Magazine Article Writing
Published by Writer's Digest Books
Imprint of Penguin Publishing Group
1745 Broadway, New York, NY 10019
Web Site: www.penguinrandomhouse.com
Sample articles, expert advice from magazine editors & successful freelance writers, practical tips on researching potential publications & instructions on crafting compelling query letters.
2018: 240 pp, $19.99 paper, $14.99 ebook
ISBN(s): 978-1-4403-5124-2 (paper); 978-1-4403-5132-7 (ebook)

Writer's Guide to Character Traits
Published by Writer's Digest Books
Imprint of Penguin Publishing Group
1745 Broadway, New York, NY 10019
Web Site: www.penguinrandomhouse.com
Profiles the mental, emotional & physical qualities of different personality types to help authors create distinctive characters.
2nd ed, 2006: 384 pp, $18.99 paper (retail)
First published 1999
ISBN(s): 978-1-58297-390-6

The Writer's Guide to Crafting Stories for Children
Published by Writer's Digest Books
Imprint of Penguin Publishing Group
1745 Broadway, New York, NY 10019
Web Site: www.penguinrandomhouse.com
Insightful advice for mastering storytelling basics with dozens of examples that illustrate a variety of plot-building techniques.
2001: 240 pp, $20 paper (retail)
ISBN(s): 978-1-58297-052-3

The Writer's Idea Book 10th Anniversary Edition
Published by Writer's Digest Books
Imprint of Penguin Publishing Group
1745 Broadway, New York, NY 10019
Web Site: www.penguinrandomhouse.com
Helps you to jump-start your creativity & develop original ideas.
10th ed, 2012: 352 pp, $26 paper, $16.99 ebook
First published 2002
ISBN(s): 978-1-59963-386-2 (paper); 978-1-59963-388-6 (ebook)

Writer's Market
Published by Writer's Digest Books
Imprint of Penguin Publishing Group
1745 Broadway, New York, NY 10019
Web Site: www.penguinrandomhouse.com
Includes thousands of publishing opportunities for writers, including listings for book publishers, consumer & trade magazines, contests & awards & literary agents, as well as new playwriting & screenwriting sections.
100th ed, 2021: 912 pp, $32 paper, $20.99 ebook
ISBN(s): 978-0-5933-3203-0 (paper); 978-0-5933-3204-7 (ebook)

Writing Creative Nonfiction
Published by Writer's Digest Books
Imprint of Penguin Publishing Group
1745 Broadway, New York, NY 10019
Web Site: www.penguinrandomhouse.com
More than thirty essays examining every key element of the craft, from researching ideas & structuring the story, to reportage & personal reflection.
384 pp, $24 paper (retail)
First published 2001
ISBN(s): 978-1-884910-50-0

Writing Down the Bones: Freeing the Writer Within
Published by Shambhala Publications Inc
2129 13 St, Boulder, CO 80302
SAN: 203-2481
Tel: 978-829-2599 (intl callers)
Toll Free Tel: 888-424-2329 (orders & cust serv); 866-424-0030 (off) *Fax:* 617-236-1563
E-mail: editorialdept@shambhala.com
Web Site: www.shambhala.com
Key Personnel
Owner & EVP: Sara Bercholz
Pres: Nikko Odiseos
Sales & Edit Opers Mgr: John Golebiewski
E-mail: jgolebiewski@shambhala.com
Mng Ed: Liz Shaw *E-mail:* lshaw@shambhala.com
Author: Natalie Goldberg
Brings together Zen meditation & writing.
224 pp, $14.95 paper, $11.99 ebook

First published 2005
ISBN(s): 978-1-61180-308-2 (paper); 987-0-8348-2113-2 (ebook)

Writing Fantasy & Science Fiction
Published by Writer's Digest Books
Imprint of Penguin Publishing Group
1745 Broadway, New York, NY 10019
Web Site: www.penguinrandomhouse.com
Advice from master authors offering definitive instructions on word building, character creation & storytelling in the many styles & possibilities available to writers of speculative fiction.
2013: 416 pp, $21.99 paper
ISBN(s): 978-1-59963-140-0

Writing Life Stories
Published by Writer's Digest Books
Imprint of Penguin Publishing Group
1745 Broadway, New York, NY 10019
Web Site: www.penguinrandomhouse.com
How to capture your own experiences & turn them into personal essays & book-length memoirs.
2008: 304 pp, $17.99 paper, $10.99 ebook
First published 1998
ISBN(s): 978-1-58297-527-6 (paper); 978-1-59963-452-4 (ebook)

Writing Picture Books
Published by Writer's Digest Books
Imprint of Penguin Publishing Group
1745 Broadway, New York, NY 10019
Web Site: www.penguinrandomhouse.com
Go-to resource for writers crafting stories for children ages 2-8.
2018 (revised): 272 pp, $18.99 paper, $13.99 ebook
ISBN(s): 978-1-4403-5132-7 (ebook); 978-1-4403-5375-8 (paper)

Writing the Breakout Novel
Published by Writer's Digest Books
Imprint of Penguin Publishing Group
1745 Broadway, New York, NY 10019
Web Site: www.penguinrandomhouse.com
How to take your prose to the next level & write a breakout novel.
2002: 272 pp, $18.99 paper, $13.99 ebook
ISBN(s): 978-1-58297-182-7 (paper); 978-1-59963-325-1 (ebook)

Young Adult Fiction Core Collection
Published by Grey House Publishing Inc™
4919 Rte 22, Amenia, NY 12501
Mailing Address: PO Box 56, Amenia, NY 12501-0056
Tel: 518-789-8700 *Toll Free Tel:* 800-562-2139
Fax: 518-789-0556
E-mail: books@greyhouse.com
Web Site: greyhouse.com
Essential resource for library & media specialists looking to enhance & enrich their collection with more than 2,500 important & highly recommended titles for young adult readers.
5th ed, July 2023: 500 pp, $255
ISBN(s): 978-1-63700-511-8

Magazines for the Trade

The magazines listed have been selected because they are published specifically for the book trade industry (apart from book review and index journals, which are listed in **Book Review & Index Journals & Services** in volume 2) or because they are widely used in the industry for reference. Also included in this section are literary journals.

For a comprehensive international directory of periodicals, see *Ulrich's Periodicals Directory* (online only, compiled by ProQuest LLC, part of Clarivate PLC, 789 East Eisenhower Parkway, Ann Arbor, MI 48108), which lists magazines by subject and includes notations indicating those that carry book reviews.

Ad Age
Published by Crain Communications Inc
685 Third Ave, New York, NY 10017-4024
Tel: 212-210-0100 *Toll Free Tel:* 877-320-1721
E-mail: adageeditor@adage.com; info@adage.com; customerservice@adage.com
Web Site: adage.com
Key Personnel
Pres & Publr: Josh Golden *E-mail:* jgolden@adage.com
Assoc Publr, Gen Mgr, Mktg & Brand: Heidi Waldusky *E-mail:* hwaldusky@adage.com
Exec Ed: Judann Pollack *E-mail:* jpollack@adage.com
Ed: Brian Braiker *E-mail:* bbraiker@adage.com
Covers advertising in business, media, trade newspapers & magazines. Print & digital.
First published 1930
Frequency: 24 issues/yr
Circulation: 58,000
$109/yr (All Access), $279/yr (Insider), $1,199/yr (Editor's Circle)
ISSN: 0001-8899 (print); 1557-7414 (online)
Trim Size: 10 x 13
Ad Rates: 4-color full page (1-5x) $35,190; B&W full page (1-5x) $27,060

Adweek
Published by Adweek LLC
261 Madison Ave, 8th fl, New York, NY 10016
Tel: 212-493-4262
Web Site: www.adweek.com
Subscription Address: PO Box 15, Congers, NY 10920 *Toll Free Tel:* 877-674-8161 (US); 845-267-3007 (outside US) *E-mail:* subscriptions@adweek.com
Key Personnel
Ed & SVP, Programming: Lisa Granatstein *E-mail:* lisa.granatstein@adweek.com
Edit Dir: James Cooper *E-mail:* james.cooper@adweek.com
First published 1979
Frequency: 33 issues/yr
$99/yr digital, $149/yr digital & print
ISSN: 1549-9553
Trim Size: 9 x 10 3/4
Ad Rates: Full page $29,400 (1x); 1/2 page $17,600 (1x)

American Poetry Review
1906 Rittenhouse Sq, Philadelphia, PA 19103
Tel: 215-309-3722
Web Site: www.aprweb.org
Key Personnel
Busn Mgr: Michael Duffy
Ed: Elizabeth Scanlon *E-mail:* escanlon@aprweb.org
Poetry, general essays, fiction, translations, columns & interviews.
First published 1972
Book Use: Excerpts & serial rights, reviews
Frequency: 6 issues/yr
Avg pages per issue: 44
Circulation: 8,000
$5/issue, $28/yr
ISSN: 0360-3709
Ad Rates: B&W full page $950; see web site for additional rates

The American Spectator
Published by The American Spectator Foundation
122 S Royal St, Suite 1, Alexandria, VA 22314
Tel: 703-807-2011
E-mail: editor@spectator.org
Web Site: spectator.org
Key Personnel
Publr: Melissa Mackenzie
Edit Dir: Wladyslaw Pleszczynski
Ed-in-Chief: R Emmett Tyrrell, Jr
Occasional book reviews & articles featuring books. Online only.
First published 1924

ANQ: A Quarterly Journal of Short Articles, Notes & Reviews
Published by Taylor & Francis Inc
530 Walnut St, Suite 850, Philadelphia, PA 19106
Tel: 215-625-8900 (ext 4) *Toll Free Tel:* 800-354-1420 *Fax:* 215-207-0050; 215-207-0046 (cust serv)
E-mail: support@tandfonline.com
Web Site: www.tandfonline.com; www.routledge.com
Key Personnel
Global Publg Dir, Journals: Leon Heward-Mills
Mng Ed: Geraldine Richards
Short, incisive research-based articles about the literature of the English-speaking world & the language of literature. Contributors unravel obscure allusions, explain sources & analogues & supply variant ms readings. Also included are Old English word studies, textual emendations & rare correspondence from neglected archives. The journal is an essential source for professors & students, as well as archivists, bibliographers, biographers, editors, lexicographers & textual scholars. Also available online.
First published 1987
Book Use: Reviews
Frequency: Quarterly
Avg pages per issue: 72
Circulation: 500
Indivs: $108/yr (print only or print & online); Instns: $276/yr (online only), $325/yr (print & online)
ISSN: 0895-769X (print); 1940-3364 (online)
Trim Size: 7 x 10
Ad Rates: Full page $550; 1/2 page $350
Ad Closing Date(s): Winter, Dec 1; Spring, March 21; Summer, June 18; Fall, Sept 19

Artists Magazine
Published by Golden Peak Media
9912 Carver Rd, Blue Ash, OH 45242
E-mail: info@artistsnetwork.com
Web Site: www.artistsnetwork.com
Subscription Address: PO Box 421751, Palm Coast, FL 32142-1751 *Tel:* 386-246-3370 *Toll Free Tel:* 800-333-0440 (US only)
Key Personnel
Sr Art Dir: Brian Roeth
Mng Ed: Brian Riley
Sr Ed: Holly Davis
Ed: Maureen Bloomfield
Assoc Ed: McKenzie Graham; Michael Woodson
Art instruction & advice for the working artist.
First published 1984
Book Use: Occasional book reviews (art-related titles only)
Frequency: 10 issues/yr
Avg pages per issue: 100
Circulation: 60,000
$17.99/yr digital, $21.99/yr US print only, $23.99/yr US print & digital, $31.99/yr CN print only, $33.99/yr CN print & digital, $36.99/yr intl print only, $39.99/yr intl print & digital
ISSN: 0741-3351
Trim Size: 7 3/4 x 10 1/2

AudioFile®
Published by AudioFile® Publications Inc
37 Silver St, Portland, ME 04101
Tel: 207-774-7563 *Toll Free Tel:* 800-506-1212 *Fax:* 207-775-3744
E-mail: info@audiofilemagazine.com; editorial@audiofilemagazine.com
Web Site: www.audiofilemagazine.com
Key Personnel
Founder & Ed: Robin F Whitten *E-mail:* robin@audiofilemagazine.com
Publr: Michele L Cobb *E-mail:* michele@audiofilemagazine.com
Art Dir: Jennifer Steele
Mng Ed: Jennifer M Dowell *E-mail:* jennifer@audiofilemagazine.com
Review Ed: Elizabeth K Dodge
Edit Asst: Alisha Langerman; Joanne Simonean
Audiobook reviews & recommendations. Focus on the listening experience & the unique aspects of the audio performance. Reviews published weekly on web site. Also narrator & author profiles. Award exceptional performances with AudioFile's Earphone Awards.
First published 1992
Frequency: 6 issues/yr
Avg pages per issue: 72
Circulation: 20,000
$19.95/yr, $26.95/2 yrs, $60/yr (prof subn with annual "Audiobook Reference Guide"); $10/issue
ISSN: 1063-0244
Avg reviews per issue: 400
Trim Size: 8 3/8 x 10 7/8
Ad Rates: Full page $3,250

Authorship
Published by National Writers Association
10940 S Parker Rd, Suite 508, Parker, CO 80134
Tel: 303-656-7235
E-mail: natlwritersassn@hotmail.com
Web Site: www.nationalwriters.com
Key Personnel
Exec Dir & Ed: Sandy Whelchel
Only take submissions dealing with writing. Also available online.
Book Use: Review books for writers (in-house staff)
Frequency: Quarterly
Avg pages per issue: 28
Circulation: 8,000
$20/yr
ISSN: 1092-9347

MAGAZINES FOR THE TRADE

Book Dealers World
Published by National Association of Book Entrepreneurs (NABE)
PO Box 606, Cottage Grove, OR 97424
Tel: 541-942-7455 *Fax:* 541-942-7455
E-mail: bookdealersworld@bookmarketingprofits.com
Web Site: www.bookmarketingprofits.com
Key Personnel
Exec Dir: Al Galasso
Assoc Dir: Ingrid Crawford
Features the latest marketing ideas, publisher profiles, advertising tips, prime contacts & promotional strategies.
First published 1980
Book Use: From NABE members
Frequency: 3 issues/yr (Jan, May & Sept)
Avg pages per issue: 32
Circulation: 5,000
$50/yr US, $55/yr CN, $70/yr foreign; free to membs
ISSN: 1098-8521
Ad Rates: Full page $500; 1/2 page $250; 1/4 page $150

BookPage
Published by ProMotion Inc
2143 Belcourt Ave, Nashville, TN 37212
Tel: 615-292-8926 *Fax:* 615-292-8249
Web Site: bookpage.com
Key Personnel
Founder & Pres: Michael A Zibart
Publr & Ed-in-Chief: Trisha Ping *E-mail:* trisha@bookpage.com
Assoc Publr: Elizabeth Grace Herbert *Tel:* 615-292-8926 ext 34 *E-mail:* elizabeth@bookpage.com
Book reviews, author interviews; focus on general interest new releases. Columns on romance, mystery, audio & paperback, plus individual reviews on books in all categories. Focus is completely on new releases; no backlist reviewed. Hardcover & paperback titles reviewed.
First published 1988
Book Use: Reviews
Frequency: Monthly
Avg pages per issue: 32
Circulation: 400,000
Trim Size: 9 x 10.9
Ad Rates: Full page color $9,650; 1/2 page $5,600

Bookselling This Week
Published by American Booksellers Association
600 Mamaroneck Ave, Suite 400, Harrison, NY 10528
Tel: 914-406-7500 *Toll Free Tel:* 800-637-0037 *Fax:* 914-417-4013
E-mail: info@bookweb.org
Web Site: www.bookweb.org
Book industry & ABA membership news. Available online only.
Frequency: Weekly
Circulation: 12,000

Canadian Children's Book News
Published by The Canadian Children's Book Centre
425 Adelaide St W, Suite 200, Toronto, ON M5V 3C1, Canada
Tel: 416-975-0010
E-mail: info@bookcentre.ca
Web Site: www.bookcentre.ca
Key Personnel
Ed: Sandra O'Brien *E-mail:* sandra@bookcentre.ca
News, book reviews (only reviews books by Canadian authors & illustrators), author & illustrator profiles & information about the world of children's books in Canada. Visit web site for media kit. CCBN is available with membership to the Canadian Children's Book Centre; also available in bulk subns & on newsstands across Canada.
First published 1977
Frequency: Quarterly
Avg pages per issue: 40
Circulation: 4,000
$4.95/issue; $24.95/single-copy subn (add $25 shipping for intl orders); contact CCBC for bulk rates
ISSN: 1705-7809
Trim Size: 8 1/8 x 10 7/8

Catholic Library World
Published by Catholic Library Association
8550 United Plaza Blvd, Suite 1001, Baton Rouge, LA 70809
Tel: 225-408-4417
E-mail: cla2@cathla.org
Web Site: cathla.org
Key Personnel
Gen Ed: Sigrid Kelsey *E-mail:* sigridkelsey@gmail.com
Articles, book & media reviews for library information professionals.
First published 1929
Book Use: Regularly publish reviews of books & other media
Frequency: 3 issues/yr
Avg pages per issue: 90
$15/issue, $55/yr membs, $100/yr nonmembs US, $125/yr nonmembs outside US
ISSN: 0008-820X
Trim Size: 6 7/8 x 9 1/2
Ad Rates: Full page $425; 2/3 page $360; 1/2 page $295; 1/3 page $230; 1/6 page $185; preferred space also available, color additional
Ad Closing Date(s): Feb 1 (March issue), Aug 1 (Sept issue), Nov 1 (Dec issue)

The Bulletin of the Center for Children's Books
Published by Johns Hopkins University Press
2715 N Charles St, Baltimore, MD 21218-4363
SAN: 202-7348
Tel: 410-516-6900; 410-516-6987 (journal orders outside US & CN); 217-244-0324 (bulletin info) *Toll Free Tel:* 800-548-1784 (journal orders) *Fax:* 410-516-6968
E-mail: bccb@illinois.edu; jlorder@jhupress.jhu.edu
Web Site: bccb.ischool.illinois.edu; www.press.jhu.edu/journals/bulletin-center-childrens-books
Key Personnel
Ed: Deborah Stevenson
Asst Ed: Kate Quealy-Gainer
For teachers, librarians, parents & booksellers.
First published 1947
Book Use: Reviews of children's & young adult books for teachers, librarians, parents & booksellers
Frequency: 11 issues/yr
Avg pages per issue: 40
Circulation: 6,500
Indivs: $55/yr, $99/2 yrs (print), $64.82/yr, $117/2 yrs (electronic); Instns: $120/yr, $240/2 yrs (print)
ISSN: 0008-9036

Christian Retailing
Published by Charisma Media
1150 Greenwood Blvd, Lake Mary, FL 32746
Tel: 407-333-0600 *Fax:* 407-333-7133
E-mail: retailing@charismamedia.com
Web Site: www.christianretailing.com; www.charismamedia.com
Key Personnel
Ed: Christine D Johnson *E-mail:* chris.johnson@charismamedia.com
This trade publication for the Christian products industry includes industry news, bestseller lists, industry expert Q&As & columns & Christian retail features. Advertising targets Christian retail store owners & buyers.
First published 1955
Book Use: News & reviews of new releases
Frequency: 3 issues/yr
Avg pages per issue: 50
Circulation: 4,300
$40/yr, $65/yr CN, $80/yr foreign, free to qualified readers
ISSN: 0892-0281

The Chronicle of Higher Education
1255 23 St NW, Suite 700, Washington, DC 20037
Tel: 202-466-1000 *Fax:* 202-452-1033
E-mail: editor@chronicle.com
Web Site: www.chronicle.com
Key Personnel
Pres & Ed-in-Chief: Michael G Riley *E-mail:* michael.riley@chronicle.com
Mng Ed: Brock Read
Deputy Mng Ed: Jennifer Ruark *E-mail:* jennifer.ruark@chronicle.com
Weekly newspaper covering higher education, including scholarly & publishing news.
First published 1966
Book Use: Articles on books of interest to an academic audience & on academic aspects of the publishing industry. Lists new books on higher education & new scholarly books; short- & medium-length excerpts from books on academic & literary issues
Frequency: Weekly (except for 2 issues in Dec & 1 in Aug)
Avg pages per issue: 100
Circulation: 350,000
$6.99/issue; digital & print: $99.95/yr, $169.95/2 yrs
ISSN: 0009-5982

College & Research Libraries (C&RL)
Published by Association of College & Research Libraries (ACRL)
Division of The American Library Association (ALA)
225 N Michigan Ave, Suite 1300, Chicago, IL 60601
Tel: 312-280-2516 *Toll Free Tel:* 800-545-2433 (ext 2516) *Fax:* 312-280-2520
E-mail: acrl@ala.org
Web Site: crl.acrl.org/index.php/crl; www.ala.org/acrl
Key Personnel
Sr Prodn Ed: Dawn Mueller *E-mail:* dmueller@ala.org
Ed: Wendi Arant Kaspar
Online only scholarly research journal. Theory & research relevant to academic & research librarians. See web site for submission guidelines.
First published 1939
Book Use: Reviews
Frequency: 6 issues/yr
Free

Columbia Journalism Review
Published by Columbia Graduate School of Journalism
Affiliate of Columbia University
801 Pulitzer Hall, 2950 Broadway, New York, NY 10027
Tel: 212-854-1881; 212-854-2718 (busn) *Toll Free Tel:* 888-425-7782 (US subns) *Fax:* 212-854-8367
E-mail: editors@cjr.org
Web Site: www.cjr.org
Key Personnel
Ed-in-Chief & Publr: Kyle Pope
Mng Ed: Betsy Morais
Sr Digital Ed: Justin Ray
Assoc Ed: Brendan Fitzgerald
Sr Writer & Sr Delacorte Fellow: Alexandria Neason

CJR's mission is to be the intellectual leader in the rapidly changing world of journalism. It is the most respected voice on press criticism & it shapes the ideas that make media leaders & journalists smarter about their work. Through its fast-turn analysis & deep reporting, CJR is an essential venue not just for journalists, but also for the thousands of professionals in communications, technology, academia & other fields reliant on solid media industry knowledge.
First published 1961
Frequency: 2 issues/yr
Circulation: 30,000
Free online; print: $50/yr US, $75/yr CN & intl
ISSN: 0010-194X
Ad Rates: E-mail for rates

Connections
Published by Printing Industries of New England
5 Crystal Pond Rd, Southborough, MA 01772-1758
Tel: 508-804-4171 *Toll Free Tel:* 800-365-7463
Web Site: www.pine.org
Key Personnel
Pres & Publr: Christine Hadopian
Members only trade magazine for printing & graphic communication companies in New England.
First published 1938
Frequency: 6 issues/yr
Avg pages per issue: 48
Circulation: 1,200
Free to membs
ISSN: 0162-8771
Trim Size: 8 1/2 x 11
Ad Closing Date(s): 10th of the month preceding publication

Consequence Magazine
PO Box 323, Cohasset, MA 02025-0323
E-mail: consequence.mag@gmail.com
Web Site: www.consequencemagazine.org
Key Personnel
Ed: Catherine Parnell
Art Feature Ed: Anne Kovach
Layout Ed: Jane Widiger
Reviews Ed: John R Coats
Independent nonprofit literary magazine focusing on the culture & consequences of war. Publishes short fiction, poetry, nonfiction, interviews, visual art & reviews. Also available online.
Frequency: Annual
$10/yr, $19/2 yrs, $28/3 yrs; Intl: $20/yr, $39/2 yrs, $58/3 yrs

Editors Canada - Online Directory of Editors
Published by Editors Canada (Reviseurs Canada)
1507-180 Dundas St W, Toronto, ON M5G 1Z8, Canada
Tel: 416-975-1379
E-mail: info@editors.ca; communications@editors.ca
Web Site: www.editors.ca
Key Personnel
Exec Dir: Natasha Bood
  E-mail: executivedirector@editors.ca
Sr Communs Mgr: Michelle Ou
Training & Devt Mgr: Caitlin Stewart
Online directory of descriptive listings of current association members indexed by specialty.
Free to membs

Educational Marketer
Published by Simba Information
Division of Market Research.com
6116 Executive Blvd, Suite 550, Rockville, MD 20852
SAN: 210-2021
Tel: 240-747-3091 *Toll Free Tel:* 888-297-4622 (cust serv) *Fax:* 240-747-3004
E-mail: customerservice@simbainformation.com
Web Site: www.simbainformation.com; www.educationalmarketer.net
Key Personnel
Sr Analyst/Mng Ed: Kathy Mickey
Sr Ed/Analyst: Daniel Strempel
Ed/Analyst: Karen Meaney
Newsletter; reports on educational publishing field (el-hi & college): enrollments, demographics, funding, mergers & acquisitions, new product developments & personnel changes. For publishers, suppliers & dealers in the educational market.
First published 1968
Frequency: 24 issues/yr
Avg pages per issue: 8
$695/yr
ISSN: 1013-1806

Electronic Education Report
Published by Simba Information
Division of Market Research.com
6116 Executive Blvd, Suite 550, Rockville, MD 20852
SAN: 210-2021
Tel: 240-747-3091 *Toll Free Tel:* 888-297-4622 (cust serv) *Fax:* 240-747-3004
E-mail: customerservice@simbainformation.com
Web Site: www.simbainformation.com
Key Personnel
Sr Analyst/Mng Ed: Kathy Mickey
Sr Ed/Analyst: Daniel Strempel
Ed/Analyst: Karen Meaney
Published twice each month to provide industry top executives & decision-makers with critical news & informed perspective on the K-12 electronic instructional materials market. Each issue contains insight into the current opportunities & challenges facing instructional software providers, as well as relevant analysis of emergent technology.
First published 1994
Frequency: 24 issues/yr
$650/yr PDF download
ISSN: 1077-9949
Trim Size: 8 1/2 x 11

Event
Published by Douglas College
700 Royal Ave, New Westminster, BC V3M 5Z5, Canada
Mailing Address: PO Box 2503, New Westminster, BC V3L 5B2, Canada
Tel: 604-527-5293 *Fax:* 604-527-5095
E-mail: event@douglascollege.ca
Web Site: www.eventmagazine.ca
Key Personnel
Mng Ed: Ian Cockfield
Ed: Shashi Bhat
Fiction Ed: Christine Dewar
Poetry Ed: Joanne Arnott
Reviews Ed: Susan Wasserman
Literary journal. Occasionally publish unsol reviews but should query first. Publish mostly Canadian writers, but are open to anyone writing in English. Do not read mss in Jan, July, August or December. Buy fiction, poetry, creative nonfiction.
First published 1971
Frequency: 3 issues/yr
Avg pages per issue: 128
Circulation: 950
$11.95/issue, $29.95/yr
ISSN: 0315-3770
Trim Size: 6 x 9
Ad Rates: Full page $200; 1/2 page $100
Ad Closing Date(s): March 15 (Summer), July 15 (Fall/Winter), Nov 15 (Spring)

Facilities & Destinations
Published by Facilities Media Group
55 E 59 St, 20th fl, New York, NY 10022
Tel: 212-532-4150 *Fax:* 212-213-6382
Web Site: facilitiesonline.com
Key Personnel
Assoc Publr: Michael Caffin *E-mail:* mcaffin@facilitiesonline.com
Edit Dir: George Seli *E-mail:* gseli@facilitiesonline.com
Trade magazine chronicling the facility, event & convention marketplace.
First published 1991
Frequency: Quarterly
Avg pages per issue: 48
Circulation: 29,000
Free to qualified readers

Facilities & Event Management
Published by Facilities Media Group
55 E 59 St, 20th fl, New York, NY 10022
Tel: 212-532-4150 *Fax:* 212-213-6382
Web Site: facilitiesonline.com
Key Personnel
Assoc Publr: Michael Caffin *E-mail:* mcaffin@facilitiesonline.com
Edit Dir: George Seli *E-mail:* gseli@facilitiesonline.com
Trade magazine chronicling the facility, event & convention marketplace.
First published 1991
Frequency: 2 issues/yr
Free to qualified readers

Folio: The Magazine for Magazine Management
Published by Access Intelligence
761 Main Ave, 2nd fl, Norwalk, CT 06851
Tel: 203-854-6730; 203-899-8433
Web Site: www.foliomag.com
Key Personnel
Publr: Robbie Caploe *Tel:* 917-974-0640
  E-mail: rcaploe@accessintel.com
Assoc Publr: Danielle Sikes *E-mail:* dsikes@accessintel.com
Content Dir: Caysey Welton *Tel:* 203-899-8431
  E-mail: cwelton@accessintel.com
Sr Ed: Greg Dool *Tel:* 212-621-4979
  E-mail: gdool@accessintel.com
Asst Ed: Kayleigh Barber *Tel:* 203-899-8455
  E-mail: kbarber@accessintel.com
News & articles for the magazine publishing executive.
First published 1972
Book Use: Excerpts & condensations
Frequency: Monthly
Avg pages per issue: 60
Circulation: 8,500
ISSN: 0046-4333

Forecast
Published by Baker & Taylor LLC
2550 W Tyvola Rd, Suite 300, Charlotte, NC 28217
Mailing Address: PO Box 6885, Bridgewater, NJ 08807-0855
Tel: 704-998-3100 *Toll Free Tel:* 800-775-1800 (info servs); 800-775-1700 (cust serv)
Toll Free Fax: 866-557-3396 (cust serv)
E-mail: btinfo@baker-taylor.com
Web Site: www.baker-taylor.com
Key Personnel
Dir, Mdsg, Ad Sales & Edit: Lynn Bond
Ed: Charles Pizar
Mktg Specialist: Donna Heffner
Promotes new & forthcoming adult hardcover, paperback & spoken word audio titles. Digital only.
Avg pages per issue: 87
Free

Foreword Reviews
Division of Foreword Magazine Inc
12935 W Bay Shore Rd, Suite 380, Traverse City, MI 49684
Tel: 231-933-3699

Web Site: www.forewordreviews.com
Key Personnel
Publr: Victoria Sutherland *E-mail:* victoria@forewordreviews.com
Assoc Publr: Barbara Hodge *E-mail:* barbara@forewordreviews.com
Ed-in-Chief: Michelle Anne Schingler *E-mail:* mschingler@forewordreviews.com
Mng Ed: Matt Sutherland *E-mail:* matt@forewordreviews.com
Review journal of books from independent presses, university presses & self-publishers. Distributed to librarians & booksellers for collection development.
First published 1998
Frequency: 6 issues/yr
Avg pages per issue: 68
Circulation: 30,000
$5.99/issue, $29.95/yr, $59.95/yr intl
ISSN: 1099-2642
Avg reviews per issue: 100
Trim Size: 8 3/8 x 10 7/8
Ad Rates: 4-color full page (1x) $3,575; 1/2 page (1x) $2,145
Ad Closing Date(s): 5 weeks prior to issue date

Gateway Journalism Review/St Louis Journalism Review
Published by Southern Illinois University Carbondale, School of Journalism, College of Mass Communication & Media Arts
Communications Bldg, 1100 Lincoln Dr, Mail Code 6601, Carbondale, IL 62901
Tel: 618-453-3262; 618-536-3361 (subns)
E-mail: gatewayjr@siu.edu (subns)
Web Site: gatewayjr.org
Key Personnel
Publr: William Freivogel *E-mail:* wfreivogel@gmail.com
Ed: Jackie Spinner *Tel:* 202-441-0228 *E-mail:* jspinner@colum.edu
Critically analyzes the mass media in the Midwest. The publication's goal is to regularly review journalism new media, photojournalism, advertising, public relations & entertainment media to help ensure the public has the most credible, fair media possible.
First published 1970
Book Use: Book review & excerpts
Frequency: Quarterly
Avg pages per issue: 36
Circulation: 1,250
$20/yr, $35/2 yrs, $45/3 yrs
ISSN: 0036-2972
Trim Size: 8 1/2 x 11
Ad Closing Date(s): 20th of each month

Geist
Published by The Geist Foundation
201-111 W Hastings St, Vancouver, BC V6B 1H4, Canada
Tel: 604-681-9161 *Toll Free Tel:* 888-GEIST-EH (434-7834) *Fax:* 604-677-6319
E-mail: geist@geist.com
Web Site: www.geist.com
Key Personnel
Publr: Michal Kozlowski
Assoc Publr: AnnMarie MacKinnon
Canadian ideas & culture with a strong literary focus. The 'Geist' tone is intelligent, plain-talking, inclusive & offbeat. Submissions must have a Canadian angle content or author. Mail-in submissions only (except for contests).
First published 1990
Frequency: Quarterly
Avg pages per issue: 72
Circulation: 7,000
$24.95/yr CN, $40/yr US, $45/yr intl, $39.95/2 yrs CN, $54.95/3 yrs CN
ISSN: 1181-6554
Ad Rates: Full page $970; 2/3 page $735; 1/2 page $685; 1/3 page $425; 1/6 page $270; ad rates decrease with frequent advertisement

Graphic Monthly
Published by North Island Publishing Ltd
1606 Sedlescomb Dr, Suite 8, Mississauga, ON L4X 1M6, Canada
Tel: 905-625-7070 *Toll Free Tel:* 800-331-7408 (US only) *Fax:* 905-625-4856
E-mail: editor@graphicmonthly.ca; circulation@graphicmonthly.ca
Web Site: www.graphicmonthly.ca
Key Personnel
Publr: Alexander (Sandy) Donald *E-mail:* s.donald@northisland.ca
Online printing industry reference tool for owners & managers delivering expert how-to advice, product & service information & insightful analysis.
First published 1980
Frequency: 6 issues/yr

Growing Minds
Published by Baker & Taylor LLC
2550 W Tyvola Rd, Suite 300, Charlotte, NC 28217
Mailing Address: PO Box 6885, Bridgewater, NJ 08807-0855
Tel: 704-998-3100 *Toll Free Tel:* 800-775-1800 (info servs); 800-775-1700 (cust serv) *Toll Free Fax:* 866-557-3396 (cust serv)
E-mail: btinfo@baker-taylor.com
Web Site: www.baker-taylor.com
Key Personnel
Dir, Mdsg, Ad Sales & Edit: Lynn Bond
Ed: Pamela Day
Mktg Specialist: Donna Heffner
Comprehensive guide to children's & teen selections featuring titles of interest to all levels, from toddlers to young adults. Digital only.
Frequency: 10 issues/yr (combined June/July & Nov/Dec issues)
Free

Guild of Book Workers Newsletter
Published by Guild of Book Workers
521 Fifth Ave, New York, NY 10175
E-mail: newsletter@guildofbookworkers.org; communications@guildofbookworkers.org
Web Site: www.guildofbookworkers.org
Key Personnel
Pres: Bexx Caswell *E-mail:* president@guildofbookworkers.org
VP: Henry Hebert *E-mail:* vicepresident@guildofbookworkers.org
Secy: Lindsey Jackson *E-mail:* secretary@guildofbookworkers.org
Treas: Lawrence Houston *E-mail:* treasurer@guildofbookworkers.org
Newsletter Ed: Lang Ingalls
Articles, calendar of activities related to the book arts.
Frequency: 6 issues/yr
Avg pages per issue: 24
Circulation: 900
Free with membership
Trim Size: 8 1/2 x 11
Ad Rates: Full page $265; 1/2 page $140; 1/4 page $75; 1/8 page $40
Ad Closing Date(s): First Fri of month prior to publication

The Horn Book Magazine
Published by Horn Book Inc
7858 Industrial Pkwy, Plain City, OH 43064
Toll Free Tel: 800-325-9558
E-mail: info@hbook.com
Web Site: www.hbook.com
Subscription Address: PO Box 460965, Escondido, CA 92046 *Toll Free Tel:* 877-523-6072 *Fax:* 760-738-4805
Key Personnel
Group Publr: Rebecca T Miller *Tel:* 646-380-0738 *E-mail:* rmiller@mediasourceinc.com
Ed-in-Chief: Elissa Gershowitz *E-mail:* egershowitz@hbook.com
Reviews Ed: Kitty Flynn *E-mail:* kflynn@hbook.com
Asst Ed: Monica de los Reyes *E-mail:* mdelosreyes@hbook.com
Children's literature journal featuring reviews, articles, essays, columns, interviews with children's book authors & illustrators, current announcements.
First published 1924
Book Use: Reviews & occasional excerpts
Frequency: 6 issues/yr
Avg pages per issue: 128
Circulation: 5,500
$72/yr
ISSN: 0018-5078
Trim Size: 6 x 9
Ad Rates: Color covers 2, 3 & 4 $2,577/each; full page interior $2,150
Ad Closing Date(s): 2 months before publication date

Independent Publisher
Published by Jenkins Group Inc
1129 Woodmere Ave, Suite B, Traverse City, MI 49686
Tel: 231-933-0445; 213-883-5365
Web Site: www.independentpublisher.com
Key Personnel
CEO: Jerrold R Jenkins *Tel:* 231-933-0445 ext 1008 *E-mail:* jrj@jenkinsgroupinc.com
Pres & COO: James Kalajian *Tel:* 231-933-0445 ext 1006 *E-mail:* jjk@jenkinsgroupinc.com
Ed, Independent Publisher Online: Jim Barnes *E-mail:* editor@independentpublisher.com
Article topics relevant to the business of independent book publishing & retailing, including marketing, book awards, promotion & distribution. Available online since 2000.
First published 1983
Book Use: Featured reviews & individual reviews from independently published works of the current year
Frequency: Monthly
Avg pages per issue: 80
Circulation: 10,000
Free online; sent monthly via e-mail
ISSN: 1098-5735
Avg reviews per issue: 40

Indiana Review
Indiana University English Dept, Ballantine Hall 554, 1020 E Kirkwood Ave, Bloomington, IN 47405
Tel: 812-855-3439
E-mail: inreview@indiana.edu
Web Site: indianareview.org
Key Personnel
Ed-in-Chief: Shreya Fadia
Assoc Ed: Bernardo Wade
Fiction Ed: Sophie Stein
Nonfiction Ed: Tyler Raso
Poetry Ed: S J Ghaus
Nonprofit literary magazine dedicated to showcasing the talents of emerging & established writers.
First published 1976
Frequency: 2 issues/yr (Summer & Winter)
$12/issue

Information Today
Published by Information Today, Inc
143 Old Marlton Pike, Medford, NJ 08055-8750
Tel: 609-654-6266 *Toll Free Tel:* 800-300-9868 (cust serv) *Fax:* 609-654-4309
E-mail: jwelsh@infotoday.com (cust serv)
Web Site: www.infotoday.com/IT/default.asp; store.infotoday.com/brand/it-mag/ (subns)
Key Personnel
Publr/Pres & CEO: Thomas H Hogan
Ed: Brandi Scardilli *E-mail:* bscardilli@infotoday.com

Newsmagazine designed to meet the needs of the information professional, delivering coverage of recent news & long-term trends in the information industry. Accurate, timely news articles inform the reader of the people, products, services, & events that impact the industry, while topical articles explain significant developments in the field. Subscription options include print, PDF or print + PDF.
First published 1983
Frequency: 9 issues/yr
Avg pages per issue: 32
Print: $99.95/yr, $188/2 yrs, $288/3 yrs US; $128/yr CN & MX; $143/yr other; $69.95/yr personal use (US only); Digital: $99.95/yr, $188/2 yrs, $288/3 yrs, $69.95/yr personal use; Print + Digital: $124.95/yr, $234/2 yrs, $360/3 yrs US; $160/yr CN & MX; $179/yr other, $89.95/yr personal use (US only)
ISSN: 8755-6286
Trim Size: 8 1/2 x 11
Ad Rates: See web site for complete details

Journal of International Marketing
Published by American Marketing Association
130 E Randolph St, 22nd fl, Chicago, IL 60601
Tel: 312-542-9000 *Toll Free Tel:* 800-AMA-1150 (262-1150)
E-mail: jim@ama.org; customersupport@ama.org; amasubs@subscriptionoffice.com
Web Site: www.ama.org
Key Personnel
VP, Pubns: David W Stewart
Ed-in-Chief: Constantine S Katsikeas
International peer-reviewed journal dedicated to advancing international marketing practice, research & theory. Contributions addressing any aspects of international marketing are welcome. The journal presents scholarly & managerially relevant articles on international marketing. Aimed at both international marketing/business scholars & practitioners at senior- & mid-level international marketing positions, the journal's prime objective is to bridge the gap between theory & practice in international marketing.
Frequency: Quarterly
Avg pages per issue: 144
Circulation: 1,300
Indivs: $50/issue, $140/yr online only, $152/yr print only, $155/yr print & online; Instns: $81/issue, $294/yr print or online only, $353/yr print & online
ISSN: 1069-031X (print); 1547-7215 (online)

Journal of Marketing
Published by American Marketing Association
130 E Randolph St, 22nd fl, Chicago, IL 60601
Tel: 312-542-9000 *Toll Free Tel:* 800-AMA-1150 (262-1150)
E-mail: jom@ama.org; amasubs@subscriptionoffice.com
Web Site: www.ama.org/journal-of-marketing
Key Personnel
VP, Pubns: David W Stewart
Ed-in-Chief: Christine Moorman
Develops & disseminates knowledge about real-world marketing questions useful to scholars, educators, managers, policy makers, consumers & other societal stakeholders around the world. It is the premier outlet for substantive research in marketing.
First published 1936
Book Use: Some reviews & excerpts
Frequency: 6 issues/yr
Avg pages per issue: 144
Circulation: 8,200
Indivs: $41/issue, $171/yr online only, $186/yr print only, $190/yr print & online; Instns: $82/issue, $449/yr print or online only, $540/yr print & online
ISSN: 0022-2429 (print); 1547-7185 (online)

Journal of Marketing Research
Published by American Marketing Association
130 E Randolph St, 22nd fl, Chicago, IL 60601
Tel: 312-542-9000 *Toll Free Tel:* 800-AMA-1150 (262-1150)
E-mail: jmr@ama.org; customersupport@ama.org; amasubs@subscriptionoffice.com
Web Site: www.ama.org
Key Personnel
VP, Pubns: David W Stewart
Ed: Rajdeep Grewal
Articles representing the entire spectrum of topics in marketing. It welcomes diverse theoretical perspectives & a wide variety of data & methodological approaches. Seeks papers that make methodological, substantive +/or theoretical contributions. Empirical studies in papers that seek to make a theoretical +/or substantive contribution may involve experimental +/or observational designs & rely on primary data (including qualitative date) +/or secondary data (including meta-analytic data sets).
First published 1963
Book Use: Some reviews
Frequency: 6 issues/yr
Avg pages per issue: 128
Circulation: 4,400
Indivs: $41/issue, $171/yr online only, $186/yr print only, $190/yr print & online; Instns: $82/issue, $449/yr print or online only, $540/yr print & online
ISSN: 0022-2437 (print); 1547-7193 (online)

Journal of Scholarly Publishing
Published by University of Toronto Press Journals Division
Division of University of Toronto Press Inc
5201 Dufferin St, Toronto, ON M3H 5T8, Canada
Tel: 416-667-7810 *Toll Free Tel:* 800-221-9985 (CN) *Fax:* 416-667-7832
E-mail: jsp@utpress.utoronto.ca; journals@utpress.utoronto.ca
Web Site: utpjournals.press/loi/jsp
Key Personnel
Dir, Journals: Antonia Pop *Tel:* 416-667-7838
  E-mail: apop@utpress.utoronto.ca
Ed-in-Chief: Robert Brown; Alex Holzman
Sales & Ad Rep, Journals: Lauren Gowing
  Tel: 416-667-7806 *E-mail:* lgowing@utpress.utoronto.ca
Articles on the writing, publication & use of serious nonfiction addressed to scholars, authors, publishers, reviewers, editors & librarians. Also available online.
First published 1969
Book Use: Reviews of books relating to publishing
Frequency: Quarterly
Avg pages per issue: 64
Circulation: 800
Indivs: $48/yr (student, print & online), $40/yr (online only), $60/yr (print only), $77/yr (print & online); Instns: $140/yr (online only), $180/yr (print only), $199/yr (print & online)
ISSN: 1198-9742 (print); 1710-1166 (online)
Trim Size: 6 x 9

Journalism & Mass Communication Quarterly
Published by SAGE Publishing
2455 Teller Rd, Thousand Oaks, CA 91320
Toll Free Tel: 800-818-7243 *Toll Free Fax:* 800-583-2665
E-mail: jmcq.electronic@gmail.com; journals@sagepub.com
Web Site: www.sagepub.com
Key Personnel
Book Review Ed: Daniel C Hallin
Ed: Louisa Ha
Research in journalism & mass communication. Also available online.
First published 1924
Frequency: Quarterly
Avg pages per issue: 300
Circulation: 5,000
Indivs: $185 (print only); Instns: $370 (electronic only), $403 (print only), $411 (print & electronic)
ISSN: 1077-6990 (print); 2161-430X (online)

The Kenyon Review
Subsidiary of Kenyon College
Finn House, 102 W Wiggin St, Gambier, OH 43022-9623
Tel: 740-427-5208 *Fax:* 740-427-5417
E-mail: kenyonreview@kenyon.edu
Web Site: www.kenyonreview.org
Key Personnel
Mng Ed: Jackson Saul
Asst Mng Ed: Danilo John Thomas
The David H Lynn Ed: Nicole Terez Dutton
Assoc Ed: Sergei Lobanov-Rostovsky
Fiction, poetry, essays, book reviews, drama.
First published 1939
Book Use: Reviews of 12 books
Frequency: 6 issues/yr
Avg pages per issue: 120
Circulation: 7,500
$35/yr, $60/2 yrs, $85/3 yrs
ISSN: 0163-075X
Trim Size: 6 1/8 x 10
Ad Rates: Full page $375
Ad Closing Date(s): Nov 10, Jan 10, March 10, May 10, July 10, Sept 10

Knowledge Quest
Published by American Association of School Librarians (AASL)
Division of The American Library Association (ALA)
225 N Michigan Ave, Suite 1300, Chicago, IL 60601
Tel: 312-944-6780 *Toll Free Tel:* 800-545-2433 *Fax:* 312-280-5276
E-mail: aasl@ala.org
Web Site: knowledgequest.aasl.org
Key Personnel
Ed: Meg Featheringham *Tel:* 312-280-1396
Devoted to offering substantive information to assist in building-level school librarians, supervisors, library educators & other decision makers concerned with the development of school library programs & services. Articles address the integration of theory & practice in school librarianship & new developments in education, learning theory & relevant disciplines.
First published 1997
Frequency: 5 issues/yr
Avg pages per issue: 80
Circulation: 7,000
$12/issue, $50/yr nonmembs US, $60/yr nonmembs foreign
ISSN: 1094-9046
Trim Size: 8 x 10 1/2
Ad Rates: 4-color full page (1x) $1,480; B&W full page (1x) $830

LARB Quarterly Journal
Published by Los Angeles Review of Books
6671 Sunset Blvd, Suite 1521, Los Angeles, CA 90028
Tel: 323-952-3950
E-mail: info@lareviewofbooks.org; editorial@lareviewofbooks.org
Web Site: lareviewofbooks.org
Key Personnel
Publr & Ed-in-Chief: Tom Lutz *E-mail:* tom@lareviewofbooks.org
Mng Dir: Jessica Kubinec *E-mail:* jessica@lareviewofbooks.org
Exec Ed: Boris Dralyuk *E-mail:* boris@lareviewofbooks.org
Mng Ed: Medaya Ocher *E-mail:* medaya@lareviewofbooks.org
Literary journal featuring original art, essays, poetry & fiction.

First published 2013
Frequency: Quarterly
Avg pages per issue: 144
Circulation: 1,250
$10/mo or $100/yr (LARB membership)
Trim Size: 7.5 x 9.2
Ad Rates: Contact Bill Harper, bill@lareviewofbooks.org for ad rates & closing dates

Latin American Literary Review
Published by Ubiquity Press
Cornell University, Dept Comparative Literature, Goldwin Smith Hall, Ithaca, NY 14853
Web Site: www.lalrp.net; lalronline.wordpress.com
Key Personnel
Ed: Debra A Castillo E-mail: dac9@cornell.edu
Book Review Ed: Luis Carcamo Huechante E-mail: carcamohuechante@austin.utexas.edu
Ed, Creative Writing Section: Lina Meruane E-mail: lina.meruane@nyu.edu
Peer-reviewed scholarly journal devoted to the literature of Latin America (including the US) & Brazil. Published in English, Spanish & Portuguese. Bringing to its readers the most recent writing of some of the leading scholars & critics in the fields of Hispanic & Portuguese literature, the *Latin American Literary Review* is of interest to all libraries & institutions of higher learning, especially to all departments of English, Modern Languages, Latin American Studies & Comparative Literature. Back content can be found on JSTOR or PROQUEST. See www.lalrp.net/about/submissions for complete submission guidelines.
First published 1972
Frequency: 2 issues/yr
Avg pages per issue: 150
Circulation: 1,500
Print copies of back issues: $32 indiv domestic, $55 instl domestic, $42 indiv foreign, $58 instl foreign; for airmail add $12
ISSN: 0047-4134
Trim Size: 9 x 6

Library Journal
Published by Media Source Inc
123 William St, Suite 802, New York, NY 10038
Tel: 646-380-0700 Toll Free Tel: 800-588-1030
Fax: 646-380-0756
E-mail: ljinfo@mediasourceinc.com
Web Site: www.libraryjournal.com
Key Personnel
Pres & CEO: Steve Zales Tel: 614-873-7940 E-mail: szales@mediasourceinc.com
Group Publr: Rebecca T Miller Tel: 646-380-0738 E-mail: rmiller@mediasourceinc.com
Ed-in-Chief: Hallie Rich
Mng Ed: Bette-Lee Fox Tel: 646-380-0717 E-mail: blfox@mediasourceinc.com
Reviews Ed: Neal Wyatt
Reviews over 8,000 books, audiobooks, DVDs, databases & web sites annually & provides coverage of technology, management, policy & other professional concerns through our print journal, weekly newsletters, online reporting & digital & live events. Over 75,000 library directors, administrators & staff in public, academic & special libraries read *Library Journal*.
First published 1876
Book Use: Reviews, news, technology, best practices
Frequency: Semimonthly (exc monthly during Jan, July, Aug & Dec)
Avg pages per issue: 104
Circulation: 12,000
$157.99/yr US, $199.99/yr CN & Mexico, $219.99/yr foreign
ISSN: 0363-0277

The Library Quarterly
Published by University of Chicago Press, Journals Division
University of Maryland, College of Information Studies, 4105 Hornbake Bldg, South Wing, College Park, MD 20742
Fax: 301-314-9145
E-mail: lq@press.uchicago.edu
Web Site: www.journals.uchicago.edu
Subscription Address: 1427 E 60 St, Chicago, IL 60637 Tel: 773-753-3347 (subns) Toll Free Tel: 877-705-1878 (subns)
Key Personnel
Mng Ed: Karen Kettnich E-mail: kkettnic@umd.edu
Ed: Ursula Gorham; Paul Jaeger; Natalie Greene Taylor
Reviews Ed: Lindsay Inge Carpenter; Rachel Gammons
Library & information science & related subjects. Also available online.
First published 1931
Book Use: Reviews
Frequency: Quarterly
Avg pages per issue: 128
Circulation: 432 (print)
Indivs: $17/issue, $48/yr (electronic only), $49/yr (print only), $54/yr (electronic & print); Students: $17/issue, $27/yr (electronic only); Instns: $84/issue, $280/yr (print only), see web site for pricing by instn type
ISSN: 0024-2519 (print); 1549-652X (online)
Trim Size: 6 x 9
Ad Rates: Full page $760

Locus: The Magazine of the Science Fiction & Fantasy Field
Published by Locus Science Fiction Foundation
655 13 St, Suite 100, Oakland, CA 94612
Tel: 510-339-9196
E-mail: locus@locusmag.com
Web Site: www.locusmag.com
Key Personnel
Publr & Ed-in-Chief: Liza Groen Trombi
Mng Ed: Kirsten Gong-Wong
Includes publishing news, book reviews, literary awards, author interviews & annual analysis of the science fiction, fantasy, horror & young-adult field, monthly bestseller list & a complete monthly listing of new publications. Primarily a trade magazine for publishing professionals, writers, booksellers & libraries.
First published 1968
Book Use: Reviews
Frequency: Monthly
Avg pages per issue: 72
Circulation: 6,000
$8.99/issue + S&H, $75/yr (print & digital)
ISSN: 0047-4959
Trim Size: 8 3/8 x 10 7/8
Ad Rates: Color full page $1,500; 2/3 page $1,050; 1/2 page $800; 1/3 page $525; 1/4 page $400; 1/6 page $275
Ad Closing Date(s): 20th of the month, 6 weeks before issue date

Medical Reference Services Quarterly
Published by Routledge
Member of Taylor & Francis Group, an Informa Business
530 Walnut St, Suite 850, Philadelphia, PA 19106
Tel: 215-625-8900 Toll Free Tel: 800-354-1420
Web Site: www.tandfonline.com
Key Personnel
Ed: Jonquil D Feldman
Working tool journal for medical & health sciences librarians. Regularly publishes brief practice-oriented articles relating to medical reference services, with an emphasis on user education, database searching & electronic information.
First published 1982
Book Use: Reviews
Frequency: Quarterly
Avg pages per issue: 116
Indivs: $170/yr online only, $194/yr print & online; Instns: $618/yr online only, $727/yr print & online
ISSN: 0276-3869 (print); 1540-9597 (online)

Mergers & Acquisitions
Published by SourceMedia LLC
One State Street Plaza, 27th fl, New York, NY 10004
Tel: 212-803-8200; 212-803-6079 (subns); 212-803-8500 (cust serv)
E-mail: help@sourcemedia.com
Web Site: www.themiddlemarket.com
Key Personnel
Publr: Harry Nikpour E-mail: harry.nikpour@sourcemedia.com
Ed-in-Chief: Mary Kathleen Flynn Tel: 212-803-3871 E-mail: marykathleen.flynn@sourcemedia.com
Asst Mng Ed: Demitri Diakantonis Tel: 212-803-8704 E-mail: demitri.diakantonis@sourcemedia.com
Professional journal; covers the latest trends & influences impacting the buying & selling of businesses. Articles cover how to make money, save money & avoid disaster in the constantly changing merger & acquisition environment.
First published 1965
Frequency: Monthly
Avg pages per issue: 56
Circulation: 20,000
$449/yr (print & digital), free 2-wk trial available
ISSN: 0026-0010

MLQ (Modern Language Quarterly): A Journal of Literary History
Published by Duke University Press
c/o University of Washington, English Dept, Box 354330, Seattle, WA 98195-4430
Tel: 206-543-6827 Fax: 206-685-2673
E-mail: mlq@u.washington.edu
Web Site: www.dukeupress.edu/modern-language-quarterly
Subscription Address: Duke University Press, 905 W Main St, Suite 18-B, Durham, NC 27701 Tel: 919-688-5134 Toll Free Tel: 888-651-0122 US Toll Free Fax: 888-651-0124 US
E-mail: subscriptions@dukeupress.edu
Key Personnel
Journals Dir: Rob Dilworth E-mail: journalsdirector@dukeupress.edu
Dir, Mktg & Sales: Cason Lynley
Ed: Marshall Brown
Assoc Ed: Jeffrey Knight; Juliet Shields
Asst Ed: Matthew Poland
Scholarly articles on literary history.
First published 1940
Book Use: Reviews
Frequency: Quarterly
Avg pages per issue: 130
Circulation: 1,350
Indivs: $20/yr online only, $35/yr print & online; Students: $18/yr print & online; Instns: $334/yr online only, $416/yr print only, $436/yr print & online; add $14 postage CN, $18 postage intl
ISSN: 0026-7929 (print); 1527-1943 (online)
Ad Rates: B&W full page $300; 1/2 page $225

Network
Published by The International Women's Writing Guild (IWWG)
888 Eighth Ave, No 537, New York, NY 10019
Tel: 917-720-6959
E-mail: iwwgquestions@iwwg.org
Web Site: www.iwwg.org
Key Personnel
Exec Dir: Michelle Miller E-mail: michelle@iwwg.org
Member news, regional clusters, correspondence corner, letters to the editor, environmental, special offerings, profile of guild members. Several

hundred opportunities for publication & submission in every issue.
First published 1978
Frequency: Quarterly
Avg pages per issue: 32
Circulation: 3,000
Free to membs

New Millennium Writings
821 Indian Gap Rd, Sevierville, TN 37876
Tel: 865-254-4880
E-mail: hello@newmillenniumwritings.org
Web Site: newmillenniumwritings.org
Key Personnel
Publr & Ed: Alexis Williams *E-mail:* alexis.williams@hotmail.com
Contains fiction, poetry & creative nonfiction by both emerging & well known writers. Regularly features profiles, interviews & essay on famous writers. Also includes writing tips & commentary by the editor.
First published 1996

News & Tech, see Newspapers & Technology

Newspapers & Technology
Published by Conley Magazines LLC
PO Box 478, Beaver Dam, WI 53916
Tel: 303-575-9595
E-mail: editor@newsandtech.com
Web Site: www.newsandtech.com
Key Personnel
Publr & Editor-in-Chief: Mary Van Meter
 E-mail: vanmeternt@aol.com
Trade publication for newspaper publishers & department managers involved in applying & integrating technology. Written by industry experts who provide regular coverage of the following departments: prepress, press, postpress & new media.
First published 1988
Frequency: 6 issues/yr
Avg pages per issue: 48
Circulation: 15,000
Free to qualified personnel
ISSN: 1052-5572

North Carolina Literary Review (NCLR)
Published by East Carolina University/North Carolina Literary & Historical Association/University of North Carolina Press
East Carolina University, English Dept, ECU Mailstop 555 English, Greenville, NC 27858-4353
Tel: 252-328-1537 *Fax:* 252-328-4889
E-mail: nclrstaff@ecu.edu
Web Site: nclr.ecu.edu
Key Personnel
Mng Ed: Lyra Thomas
Ed: Margaret Bauer *E-mail:* bauerm@ecu.edu
Articles, essays, interviews, fiction/poetry by & about North Carolina writers & literature, culture & history. Essay reviews only; excerpts from forthcoming books when relevant & appropriate. *North Carolina Literary Review Online* also available quarterly.
First published 1992
Book Use: Excerpts from forthcoming books when relevant & appropriate; essay reviews only - 2 or more books treated thematically
Frequency: Annual
Avg pages per issue: 200
Circulation: 750
$18/yr indiv, $30/2 yrs indiv, $27/yr instl, $50/2 yrs instl
ISSN: 1063-0724
Avg reviews per issue: 8-12
Ad Rates: Full page $250; 1/2 page $150; 1/4 page $100
Ad Closing Date(s): Feb 1

n+1
Published by n+1 Foundation Inc
Cadman Plaza Sta, PO Box 26428, Brooklyn, NY 11202
E-mail: editors@nplusonemag.com; subs@nplusonemag.com (submission queries); submissions@nplusonemag.com
Web Site: www.nplusonemag.com
Key Personnel
Publr: Mark Krotov
Exec Dir: Dayna Tortorici
Mng Ed: Tess Edmonson
Print & digital magazine of literature, culture & politics.
First published 2004
Frequency: 3 issues/yr
Avg pages per issue: 200
Circulation: 12,000
Basic digital: $4.50/mo, $36/yr; print & digital: $5/mo, $45/yr
Trim Size: 7 x 10

Poetics Today
Published by Duke University Press
Ohio State University, Dept of English, 164 W Annie & John Glenn Ave, Columbus, OH 43210
Tel: 614-292-6065 *Fax:* 614-292-7816
E-mail: poeticstoday@osu.edu
Web Site: www.dukeupress.edu/poetics-today
Subscription Address: Duke University Press, 905 W Main St, Suite 18-B, Durham, NC 27701 *Tel:* 919-688-5134 *Toll Free Tel:* 888-651-0122 US *Toll Free Fax:* 888-651-0124 US
E-mail: subscriptions@dukeupress.edu
Key Personnel
Journals Dir: Rob Dilworth
 E-mail: journalsdirector@dukeupress.edu
Dir, Mktg & Sales: Cason Lynley
Ed: Brian McHale
Book Review Ed: Eyal Segal
International journal for theory & analysis of literature & communication.
Book Use: Book reviews
Frequency: Quarterly
Avg pages per issue: 200
Circulation: 800
Indivs: $25/yr online only, $40/yr print & online; Students: $20/yr print & online; Instns: $422/yr online only, $524/yr print only, $556/yr print & online; add $14 postage CN, $18 postage intl
ISSN: 0333-5372 (print); 1527-5507 (online)
Ad Rates: B&W full page $300; 1/2 page $225

Poetry
Published by Poetry Foundation
61 W Superior St, Chicago, IL 60654
Tel: 312-787-7070 *Fax:* 312-787-6650
E-mail: editors@poetrymagazine.org
Web Site: www.poetryfoundation.org/poetrymagazine
Subscription Address: PO Box 421141, Palm Coast, FL 32142-1141
Key Personnel
Ed: Adrian Matejka; Don Share
Asst Ed: Holly Amos *E-mail:* hamos@poetrymagazine.org
Poetry, essays & book reviews. Complete submission guidelines can be found on the web site.
First published 1912
Frequency: Monthly
Avg pages per issue: 100
Circulation: 25,000
US: $3.75/issue, $35/yr indivs, $38/yr instns; Foreign: $47/yr indivs, $50/yr instns
ISSN: 0032-2032
Trim Size: 5 1/2 x 9
Ad Rates: Full page $800; 1/2 page $500; 1/4 page $375
Ad Closing Date(s): 15th of the 3rd month before issue date

Poets & Writers Magazine
Published by Poets & Writers Inc
90 Broad St, Suite 2100, New York, NY 10004
Tel: 212-226-3586 *Fax:* 212-226-3963
E-mail: editor@pw.org
Web Site: www.pw.org
Key Personnel
Ed-in-Chief: Kevin Larimer
Prodn Ed: Ariel Davis
News for & about the contemporary literary community in the US. Pertinent articles, grants & awards, publishing opportunities, essays, interviews with writers.
First published 1973
Book Use: First serial, excerpts, author interviews
Frequency: 6 issues/yr
Avg pages per issue: 132
Circulation: 60,000
$5.95/issue, $12.95/yr, $19.95/2 yrs
ISSN: 0891-6136

PRISM international
Published by University of British Columbia
Creative Writing Program UBC, 1866 Main Mall, Buch E-462, Vancouver, BC V6T 1Z1, Canada
Tel: 604-822-2514 *Fax:* 604-822-3616
E-mail: circulation@prismmagazine.ca; promotions@prismmagazine.ca; reviews@prismmagazine.ca
Web Site: prismmagazine.ca
Key Personnel
Exec Ed, Circ: Molly Cross-Blanchard
Exec Ed, Promos: Olga Holin
Exec Ed, Reviews: Cara Nelissen
Contemporary writing & translation from Canada & around the world.
First published 1959
Frequency: Quarterly
Avg pages per issue: 90
Circulation: 1,200
$35/yr CN, $40/yr US, $45/yr intl, $55/2 yrs CN, $63/2 yrs US, $69/2 yrs intl
Trim Size: 6 x 9
Ad Rates: Full page $220; 1/2 page $160; inside cover front or back $295

Professional Photographer - The Magazine
Published by PPA Publications & Events Inc
229 Peachtree St NE, Suite 2300, Atlanta, GA 30303
Tel: 404-522-8600 *Toll Free Tel:* 800-786-6277
E-mail: csc@ppa.com
Web Site: www.ppa.com; ppmag.com
Key Personnel
Dir, Sales & Strategic Alliances: Wayne Jones
 Tel: 404-522-8600 ext 248 *E-mail:* wjones@ppa.com
Illustrated feature articles about photographers, business & photographic techniques & trends; for practicing professional photographers (portrait, wedding, commercial, illustration, freelance, industrial, biomedical & scientific).
First published 1907
Frequency: Monthly
Avg pages per issue: 80
$19.95/yr US (print or digital), $29.95/yr US (print & digital), $19.95/yr CN (digital only), $35.95/yr CN (print only), $45.95/yr CN (print & digital)

Publishers Weekly
Published by PWxyz LLC
49 W 23 St, 9th fl, New York, NY 10010
Tel: 212-377-5500 *Fax:* 212-377-2733
Web Site: www.publishersweekly.com
Key Personnel
Pres: George Slowik, Jr *E-mail:* george@publishersweekly.com
Pres & COO, BookLife: Carl Pritzkat
 E-mail: cpritzkat@publishersweekly.com
Publr & CEO, BookLife: Cevin Bryerman
 Tel: 917-941-1879 *E-mail:* cbryerman@publishersweekly.com

SVP & Edit Dir: Jonathan Segura
  E-mail: jsegura@publishersweekly.com
SVP & Children's Book Ed: Diane Roback
  E-mail: roback@publishersweekly.com
VP, Opers: Ryk Hsieh *E-mail:* rhsieh@
  publishersweekly.com
Art Dir: Clive Chiu *E-mail:* cchiu@
  publishersweekly.com
Dir, Branded Content: Rachel Deahl
  E-mail: rdeahl@publishersweekly.com
Reviews Dir: David Adams *E-mail:* dadams@
  publishersweekly.com
Exec Ed: Andrew R Albanese
  E-mail: aalbanese@publishersweekly.com
Mng Ed: Daniel Berchenko *E-mail:* dberchenko@
  publishersweekly.com
Sr Bookselling & Intl News Ed: Ed Nawotka
  E-mail: enawotka@publishersweekly.com
Sr Digital & News Ed: John Maher
  E-mail: jmaher@publishersweekly.com
Sr Ed: Adam Boretz *E-mail:* aboretz@
  publishersweekly.com; Mark Rotella
  E-mail: mrotella@publishersweekly.com
Sr Religion Ed: Lynn Garrett *E-mail:* lgarrett@
  publishersweekly.com
Sr Reviews Ed: Rose Fox
Copy Ed: Hannah Kushnick *E-mail:* hkushnick@
  publishersweekly.com
Ed, BookLife: Matia Burnett *E-mail:* mburnett@
  publishersweekly.com
Features Ed: Carolyn Juris *E-mail:* cjuris@
  publishersweekly.com
Religion Ed: Emma Koonse *E-mail:* ekoonse@
  publishersweekly.com
Religion Reviews Ed: Seth Satterlee
  E-mail: ssatterlee@publishersweekly.com
Reviews Ed: Phoebe Cramer *E-mail:* pcramer@
  publishersweekly.com; Alex Crowley; Annie Coreno; Everett Jones; David Varno
  E-mail: dvarno@publishersweekly.com
Ed-at-Large: Louisa Ermelino
  E-mail: lermelino@publishersweekly.com; Jim Milliot *E-mail:* jmilliot@publishersweekly.com
Deputy Children's Book Ed: Emma Kantor
  E-mail: ekantor@publishersweekly.com
Licensing, Rts & Perms: Christi Cassidy
  E-mail: ccassidy@publishersweekly.com
News for the book trade.
First published 1872
Book Use: Reviews, excerpts, news, features & statistics
Frequency: Weekly (51 issues/yr)
Avg pages per issue: 112
Circulation: 64,000 print + digital
Print, digital & online: $289.99/yr US, $339.99/yr CN; Digital & online: $229.99/yr US & CN
ISSN: 0000-0019 (print); 2150-4008 (digital)
Trim Size: 7 7/8 x 10 1/2
Ad Rates: See web site
Ad Closing Date(s): See web site

Publishing Perspectives
30 Irving Place, 4th fl, New York, NY 10003
Tel: 212-794-2851
Web Site: publishingperspectives.com
Key Personnel
Publr: Hannah Johnson *E-mail:* hannah@
  publishingperspectives.com
Ed-in-Chief: Porter Anderson
Online trade magazine for the international publishing industry.
First published 2009
Frequency: Daily (Mon-Fri)
Free

Quill & Quire
Published by St Joseph Communications
111 Queen St E, Suite 320, Toronto, ON M5C 1S2, Canada
Tel: 416-364-3333 *Fax:* 416-595-5415
Web Site: www.quillandquire.com
Key Personnel
Publr: Alison Jones *Tel:* 416-364-3333 ext 3119
  E-mail: ajones@quillandquire.com
Ed: Sue Carter
Articles & features on book selling, publishing & Canadian libraries for writers, booksellers, publishers & librarians. Includes section, *Books for Young People*, with news & reviews of children's books & authors; review section for books for adults.
First published 1935
Book Use: Reviews
Frequency: 10 issues/yr
Avg pages per issue: 42
Circulation: 2,500
$89.50/yr CN, $150/2 yrs CN, $125/yr outside CN
ISSN: 0033-6491

Quill & Scroll
Published by Quill and Scroll Society
University of Iowa, School of Journalism, W111 Adler Journalism Bldg, Iowa City, IA 52242
Tel: 319-335-3457
E-mail: quill-scroll@uiowa.edu
Web Site: quillandscroll.org
Key Personnel
Exec Dir: Jeffrey Browne
Off Mgr: Judy M Hauge
Scholastic journalism publishing, editing, writing, design, legal, ethics, broadcast & multimedia production. Digital only.
First published 1926
Frequency: 2 issues/yr during school yr
Avg pages per issue: 24
ISSN: 0033-6505

Quill Magazine
Published by Society of Professional Journalists (SPJ)
PO Box 441748, Indianapolis, IN 46244
Tel: 317-927-8000 *Fax:* 317-920-4789
E-mail: quill@spj.org
Web Site: www.quillmag.com
Key Personnel
Quill Ed/Mgr, Pubns & Awards: Lou Harry
  Tel: 317-927-8000 ext 202 *E-mail:* lharry@
  spj.org
Examines the issues, changes & trends that influence the journalism profession.
First published 1912
Book Use: Book reviews, excerpts from books with journalism themes
Frequency: Quarterly
Avg pages per issue: 32
Circulation: 5,000 paid
$75/yr, free for membs
ISSN: 0033-6475
Trim Size: 8 1/4 x 10 3/4
Ad Rates: Full page color: $2,000 (1x), $1,900 (2x), $1,800 (4x); 1/2 page: $1,000 (1x), $900 (2x), $800 (4x); 1/4 page: $600 (1x), $500 (2x), $400 (4x); back inside cover: $2,500 (1x), $2,400 (2x), $2,300 (4x); front inside cover: $2,500 (1x), $2,400 (2x), $2,300 (4x)

Radio-TV Interview Report (RTIR)
Published by Bradley Communications Corp
390 Reed Rd, Broomall, PA 19008
Tel: 484-477-4220
E-mail: info@rtir.com
Web Site: www.rtir.com; rtironline.com
Key Personnel
Publr: Steve Harrison
Lists authors, experts, celebrities, entrepreneurs & others available for live & in-studio interviews. Electronic only.
Frequency: 2 issues/wk
Circulation: 4,000
Free to qualified personnel

Reference & User Services Quarterly, see RUSQ: A Journal of Reference and User Experience

Rosebud Magazine
Published by Rosebud Inc
PO Box 459, Cambridge, WI 53523
Tel: 608-423-9780
Web Site: www.rsbd.net
Key Personnel
Publr & Mng Ed: Roderick Clark
  E-mail: jrodclark@rsbd.net
Short story, poetry & nonfiction.
First published 1993
Book Use: Excerpts
Frequency: 2 issues/yr
Avg pages per issue: 136
Circulation: 6,000
$7.95/issue, $24/2 yrs, $40/4 yrs
ISSN: 1072-1681
Ad Rates: Full page $750; 1/2 page $400; 1/4 page $250

RUSQ: A Journal of Reference and User Experience
Formerly Reference & User Services Quarterly
Published by Reference & User Services Association (RUSA)
Division of The American Library Association (ALA)
225 N Michigan Ave, Suite 1300, Chicago, IL 60601
SAN: 201-0062
Tel: 312-280-4395 *Toll Free Tel:* 800-545-2433
Fax: 312-280-5273
E-mail: rusq@ala.org
Web Site: www.ala.org/rusa/rusq-journal
Key Personnel
Exec Dir: Bill Ladewski *E-mail:* bladewski@ala.org
Open access journal.
First published 1960
Frequency: Quarterly
ISSN: 2163-5242
Avg reviews per issue: 35-40

Sales & Marketing Management Magazine
Published by Mach1 Business Media LLC
27020 Noble Rd, Excelsior, MN 55331
Mailing Address: PO Box 247, Excelsior, MN 55331-0247
Tel: 952-401-1283 *Fax:* 952-401-7899
Web Site: www.salesandmarketing.com
Key Personnel
Pres & Publr: Mike Murrell *Tel:* 952-401-1283
  E-mail: mike@salesandmarketing.com
Audience Mktg Dir: Vicki Blomquist
  E-mail: vicki@salesandmarketing.com
Ed-in-Chief: Paul Nolan *Tel:* 763-350-3411
  E-mail: paul@salesandmarketing.com
Print & online magazine providing information on major marketing, sales & management trends.
First published 1918
Book Use: Reviews
Frequency: Updated 2-3 times a week
Avg pages per issue: 36
Circulation: 25,000 print
Free online. Print free to qualified recipients. Otherwise $48 US; $67 CN; $146 other countries
ISSN: 0163-7517
Trim Size: 8 x 10 3/4
Ad Rates: 2-page spread: $13,995 (1x), $13,695 (3x), $13,265 (6x); full page: $9,395 (1x), $8,695 (3x), $8,265 (6x); 1/2 page $6,075 (1x), $5,765 (3x), $5,460 (6x)
Ad Closing Date(s): See media kit online

School Library Connection
Published by Libraries Unlimited
147 Castilian Dr, Santa Barbara, CA 93117
Toll Free Tel: 800-368-6868 *Toll Free Fax:* 866-270-3856

E-mail: customerservice@abc-clio.com
Web Site: schoollibraryconnection.com
Key Personnel
Mng Ed: David Paige
K-12 school librarians & educators. See web site for information regarding ad rates & ad closing dates as well as submission & reviewer information.
First published 1982
Book Use: Reviews; articles written by school librarians
Frequency: 6 print issues/school yr plus 4 online issues
Avg pages per issue: 84
$89/yr
ISSN: 1542-4715

School Library Journal
Published by Media Source Inc
123 William St, Suite 802, New York, NY 10038
Tel: 646-380-0752 *Toll Free Tel:* 800-595-1066 *Fax:* 646-380-0756
E-mail: slj@mediasourceinc.com; sljsubs@pcspublink.com
Web Site: www.slj.com; www.facebook.com/schoollibraryjournal; x.com/sljournal
Subscription Address: PO Box 461119, Escondido, CA 92046
Key Personnel
Group Publr: Rebecca T Miller *Tel:* 646-380-0738 *E-mail:* rmiller@mediasourceinc.com
Reviews Dir: Kiera Parrott *E-mail:* kparrott@mediasourceinc.com
Ed-in-Chief: Kathy Ishizuka *E-mail:* kishizuka@mediasourceinc.com
Mng Ed, SLJ Reviews: Luann Toth *Tel:* 646-380-0749 *E-mail:* ltoth@mediasourceinc.com
Articles about library service to children & young adults; reviews of new books & multimedia products for children & young adults by school & public librarians.
First published 1954
Book Use: Reviews
Frequency: Monthly
Avg pages per issue: 115
Circulation: 38,000
$15/issue newsstand; Indivs: $136.99/yr (print or digital), $159.99/yr (print & digital); Instns: $136.99/yr (print only), $249.99/yr (digital only), $349.99/yr (print & digital)
ISSN: 0362-8930

Science & Technology Libraries
Published by Routledge
Member of Taylor & Francis Group, an Informa Business
530 Walnut St, Suite 850, Philadelphia, PA 19106
Tel: 215-625-8900 *Toll Free Tel:* 800-354-1420
Web Site: www.tandfonline.com
Key Personnel
Ed-in-Chief: Tony Stankus *E-mail:* tstankus@uark.edu
Topics relevant to management, operations, collections, services & staffing of specialized libraries in science & technology fields.
First published 1980
Book Use: Reviews
Frequency: Quarterly
Avg pages per issue: 105
Circulation: 343
Indivs: $176/yr online only, $200/yr print & online or print only; Instns: $710/yr online only, $835/yr print & online
ISSN: 0194-262X (print); 1541-1109 (online)

The Serials Librarian
Published by Routledge
Member of Taylor & Francis Group, an Informa Business
530 Walnut St, Suite 850, Philadelphia, PA 19106
Tel: 215-625-8900 *Toll Free Tel:* 800-354-1420
Web Site: www.tandfonline.com

Key Personnel
Ed-in-Chief: Sharon Dyas-Correia
Assoc Ed: Courtney McAllister
Serials librarianship in academic, public, medical, law & other special libraries.
First published 1976
Book Use: Reviews
Frequency: Quarterly
Avg pages per issue: 154
Circulation: 712
Indivs: $332/yr online only, $379/yr print & online; Instns: $1,202/yr online only, $1,414/yr print & online
ISSN: 0361-526X (print); 1541-1095 (online)

Story Monsters Ink®
Published by Story Monsters Press
Imprint of Story Monsters LLC
4696 W Tyson St, Chandler, AZ 85226-2903
Tel: 480-940-8182 *Fax:* 480-940-8787
Web Site: www.StoryMonsters.com; www.StoryMonstersInk.com
Key Personnel
Pres: Linda F Radke *E-mail:* Linda@StoryMonsters.com
Ed-in-Chief: Cristy Bertini *Tel:* 413-687-0733 *E-mail:* cristy@storymonsters.com
E-mail article submissions to cristy@storymonsters.com
First published 2014
Frequency: Monthly
Avg pages per issue: 64
Circulation: 130,000
$15/issue, $150/yr print, free digital subn
ISSN: 2374-4413
Trim Size: 8.375 x 10.875
Ad Rates: $75-$1,600
Ad Closing Date(s): 1st of each month

subTerrain Magazine
Published by subTerrain Literary Collective Society
PO Box 3008, MPO, Vancouver, BC V6B 3X5, Canada
Tel: 604-876-8710
E-mail: subter@portal.ca
Web Site: www.subterrain.ca
Key Personnel
Ed-in-Chief: Brian Kaufman
Literary magazine with the motto "Strong Words for a Polite Nation".
First published 1988
Frequency: 3 issues/yr
Avg pages per issue: 80
Circulation: 4,000
$7/issue US, $8 issue/CN; $18/yr, $32/2 yrs (US & CN)
ISSN: 0840-7533
Trim Size: 6 1/2 x 9
Ad Rates: Back cover-color $900; inside front/back cover $800; inside full page color $847; 1/2 page color $575. Prices in Canadian dollars. For other sizes & B&W rates, see web site
Ad Closing Date(s): Feb 13, June 15, Oct 15

The Wordsworth Circle
Published by University of Chicago Press
1427 E 60 St, Chicago, IL 60637-2954
SAN: 202-5280
Tel: 773-753-3347 *Toll Free Tel:* 877-705-1878 (US & CN) *Fax:* 773-753-0811
Toll Free Fax: 877-705-1879 (US & CN)
E-mail: subscriptions@press.uchicago.edu; journalsupport@press.uchicago.edu
Web Site: www.journals.uchicago.edu/twc
Key Personnel
Ed: Marilyn Gaull *E-mail:* mgaull@bu.edu
Peer-reviewed essays on all areas of British Romanticism.
First published 1970
Frequency: Quarterly

Avg pages per issue: 125
Circulation: 4,600
Indiv: $45/yr; Instl: $120-$210 tiered electronic only, $193-$339 tiered print & electronic
ISSN: 0043-8006 (print); 2640-7310 (online)
Trim Size: 6 x 9
Ad Rates: Full page $724; 1/2 page $546
Ad Closing Date(s): Feb 1 (Spring), May 1 (Summer), Aug 1 (Autumn), Nov 1 (Winter)

World Literature Today
Published by University of Oklahoma
630 Parrington Oval, Suite 110, Norman, OK 73019-4033
Tel: 405-325-4531
E-mail: wlt@ou.edu
Web Site: www.worldliteraturetoday.org
Key Personnel
Exec Dir: Robert Con Davis-Undiano
E-mail: rcdavis@ou.edu
Asst Dir & Ed-in-Chief: Daniel Simon
E-mail: dsimon@ou.edu
Art Dir: Parker Buske *E-mail:* pbuske@ou.edu
Mktg Dir, Progs & Devt: Terri D Stubblefield
E-mail: tdstubb@ou.edu
Mng Ed: Michelle Johnson *E-mail:* lmjohnson@ou.edu
Book Reviews Ed: Robert Vollmar
E-mail: robvollmar@ou.edu
Circ & Accts Specialist: Kay Blunck
E-mail: kblunck@ou.edu
Critical essays & reviews covering all the major & most of the smaller languages & literatures of the world. Also available online.
First published 1927
Frequency: 6 issues/yr
Avg pages per issue: 80
Circulation: 300,000
Indivs: $45/yr US, $55/yr CN, $75/yr elsewhere (print), $30/yr (online); Instns: $170/yr US, $245/yr CN, $265/yr elsewhere (print), $155/yr (online)
ISSN: 0196-3570 (print); 1945-8134 (online)
Trim Size: 7 1/2 x 9 7/8
Ad Rates: Full page $700; 1/2 page $500; inside cover (front or back) $800; back cover $1,250
Ad Closing Date(s): 5 weeks prior to issue date

The Writer
Published by Madavor Media LLC
25 Braintree Hill Office Park, Suite 404, Braintree, MA 02184
Tel: 903-636-1120 (cust serv) *Toll Free Tel:* 877-252-8139 (cust serv) *Fax:* 617-536-0102
E-mail: customerservice@the-writer.us
Web Site: www.writermag.com
Key Personnel
Sr Ed: Nicki Porter *E-mail:* nporter@madavor.com
Instructional articles on fiction, nonfiction & freelance writing, plus markets for ms sales. See guidelines on web site. Accept unsol mss.
First published 1887
Book Use: Regular book review section
Frequency: Monthly
Avg pages per issue: 60
Circulation: 30,000
$8/issue, $28.95/yr US, $38.95/yr CN, $43.95/yr elsewhere
ISSN: 0043-9517 (print); 2163-0046 (online)
Trim Size: 8 x 10 1/2
Ad Rates: 4-color full page $2,794; 1/2 page $1,649; 1/4 page $894

Writer's Digest Magazine
Published by Active Interest Media (AIM)
5720 Flatiron Pkwy, Boulder, CO 80301
E-mail: wdsubmissions@aimmedia.com
Web Site: www.writersdigest.com
Key Personnel
Mng Content Dir: Amy Jones
Ed-in-Chief: Ericka McIntyre
Assoc Mng Ed: Cassie Lipp

MAGAZINES FOR THE TRADE

Sr Ed: Jeanne Veillette Bowerman; Robert Lee Brewer
Focus is on the craft & business of writing.
First published 1920
Book Use: Excerpts, profiles of authors, tips & techniques
Frequency: 8 issues/yr
Circulation: 60,000 paid
$19.96/yr, $29.96/2 yrs
ISSN: 0043-9525
Trim Size: 7 3/4 x 10 1/2

The Yale Review
Published by Yale University
314 Prospect St, New Haven, CT 06511
Mailing Address: PO Box 208343, New Haven, CT 06520-8243
Tel: 203-432-0499 *Fax:* 203-432-0510
Web Site: yalereview.yale.edu
Subscription Address: John Wiley & Sons Inc, Wiley Subscription Services, 111 River St, Hoboken, NJ 07030-5774 *Toll Free Tel:* 800-835-6770 *E-mail:* cs-journals@wiley.com
Key Personnel
Ed: Meghan O'Rourke
Deputy Ed: Elliott Holt
Literary work, essays & reviews.
First published 1911
Frequency: Quarterly
Indivs: $43/yr print & online North & South America, 46 GBP/yr UK & rest of world; Instns: $244/yr print & online North & South America, 189 GBP/yr UK & rest of world
Ad Rates: Full page $425; 1/2 page $300; inside back cover $475; series discount 10% (3x or more)

ZYZZYVA
57 Post St, Suite 708, San Francisco, CA 94104
E-mail: ads@zyzzyva.org
Web Site: www.zyzzyva.org
Key Personnel
Copy Ed: Regan McMahon
Ed: Oscar Villalon
Ed-at-Large: Laura Cogan
Print Prodn: Keith Kinsella
Publg: Laura Howard
Publishes fiction, nonfiction, poetry & visual art from the best contemporary writers & artists.
First published 1985
Frequency: 3 issues/yr
$35/yr, $30/yr (students)
ISSN: 8756-5633

Company Index

Included in this index are the names, addresses, telecommunication numbers and electronic addresses of the organizations included in this volume of *LMP*. Entries also include the page number(s) on which the listings appear.

Sections not represented in this index are **Imprints, Subsidiaries & Distributors; Calendar of Book Trade & Promotional Events; Reference Books for the Trade** and **Magazines for the Trade**.

A Public Space Fellowships, 323 Dean St, Brooklyn, NY 11217 Tel: 718-858-8067 E-mail: general@apublicspace.org Web Site: apublicspace.org, pg 569

A-R Editions Inc, 1600 Aspen Commons, Suite 100, Middleton, WI 53562 Tel: 608-836-9000 Toll Free Tel: 800-736-0070 (North America book orders only) Fax: 608-831-8200 E-mail: info@areditions.com; orders@areditions.com Web Site: www.areditions.com, pg 1

A Sense of Place: The Elizabeth J Urquhart Memorial, PO Box 36128, North Chesterfield, VA 23235-3533 E-mail: contest@poetrysocietyofvirginia.org; info@poetryvirginia.org Web Site: www.poetrysocietyofvirginia.org, pg 569

A 2 Z Press LLC, 3670 Woodbridge Rd, Deland, FL 32720 Tel: 440-241-3126 E-mail: sizemore3630@aol.com Web Site: www.a2zpress.com; www.bestlittleonlinebookstore.com, pg 1

AAA Books Unlimited, 3060 Blackthorn Rd, Riverwoods, IL 60015 Tel: 847-444-1220 Fax: 847-607-8335 Web Site: www.aaabooksunlimited.com, pg 447

AAAI Press, 2275 E Bayshore Rd, Suite 160, Palo Alto, CA 94303 Tel: 650-328-3123 Fax: 650-321-4457 E-mail: publications21@aaai.org Web Site: www.aaai.org/Press/press.php, pg 1

AAAS/Subaru Prize for Excellence in Science Books, 1200 New York Ave NW, Washington, DC 20005 Tel: 202-326-6400 E-mail: sbf@aaas.org Web Site: www.sbfprize.org, pg 569

AAH Graphics Inc, 9293 Fort Valley Rd, Fort Valley, VA 22652 Tel: 540-933-6210 Fax: 540-933-6523 E-mail: aah@aahgraphics.com Web Site: www.aahgraphics.com, pg 435

The Aaland Agency, PO Box 849, Inyokern, CA 93527-0849 Tel: 760-384-3910 E-mail: anniejo41@gmail.com Web Site: www.the-aaland-agency.com, pg 447

AAPG (American Association of Petroleum Geologists), 1444 S Boulder Ave, Tulsa, OK 74119 Tel: 918-584-2555 Toll Free Tel: 800-364-AAPG (364-2274) Fax: 918-580-2665 E-mail: info@aapg.org Web Site: www.aapg.org, pg 1

Aaron-Spear, PO Box 42, Brooksville, ME 04617 Tel: 207-326-8764, pg 435

ABAC/ALAC, c/o 1938 Bloor St W, Toronto, ON M6P 3K8, Canada E-mail: info@abac.org Web Site: www.abac.org, pg 493

Abbeville Press, 655 Third Ave, New York, NY 10017 Tel: 212-366-5585 Toll Free Tel: 800-ART-BOOK (278-2665); 800-343-4499 (orders) E-mail: abbeville@abbeville.com; sales@abbeville.com; marketing@abbeville.com; rights@abbeville.com Web Site: www.abbeville.com, pg 1

Abbeville Publishing Group, 655 Third Ave, New York, NY 10017 Tel: 646-375-2136 E-mail: abbeville@abbeville.com; rights@abbeville.com Web Site: www.abbeville.com, pg 2

ABC-CLIO, 147 Castilian Dr, Santa Barbara, CA 93117 Tel: 805-968-1911 Toll Free Tel: 800-368-6868 Toll Free Fax: 866-270-3856 E-mail: customerservice@abc-clio.com Web Site: www.abc-clio.com, pg 2

ABDO, 8000 W 78 St, Suite 310, Edina, MN 55439 Tel: 952-698-2403 Toll Free Tel: 800-800-1312 Fax: 952-831-1632 Toll Free Fax: 800-862-3480 E-mail: customerservice@abdobooks.com; info@abdobooks.com Web Site: abdobooks.com, pg 2

Dominick Abel Literary Agency Inc, 146 W 82 St, Suite 1-A, New York, NY 10024 Tel: 212-877-0710 Fax: 212-595-3133 E-mail: agency@dalainc.com Web Site: www.dalainc.com, pg 448

Abingdon Press, 810 12 Ave S, Nashville, TN 37203 Toll Free Tel: 800-251-3320 E-mail: orders@abingdonpress.com; permissions@abingdonpress.com Web Site: www.abingdonpress.com, pg 2

J M Abraham Poetry Award, 1113 Marginal Rd, Halifax, NS B3H 4P7, Canada Tel: 902-423-8116 Fax: 902-422-0881 E-mail: wits@writers.ns.ca (awards) Web Site: writers.ns.ca, pg 569

Abrams Amplify Award, 195 Broadway, 9th fl, New York, NY 10007 E-mail: childrenspublicity@abramsbooks.com Web Site: www.abramsbooks.com/abramsamplifyaward, pg 569

Harry N Abrams Inc, 195 Broadway, 9th fl, New York, NY 10007 Tel: 212-206-7715 Toll Free Tel: 800-345-1359 Fax: 212-645-8437 E-mail: abrams@abramsbooks.com; publicity@abramsbooks.com; sales@abramsbooks.com Web Site: www.abramsbooks.com, pg 2

Acacia House Publishing Services Ltd, 687 Oliver St, Oak Bay, BC V8S 4W2, Canada Tel: 226-387-4757, pg 448

Academic Press, 50 & 60 Hampshire St, 5th fl, Cambridge, MA 02139 Web Site: www.elsevier.com/books-and-journals/academic-press, pg 3

Academica Press, 1727 Massachusetts Ave NW, Suite 507, Washington, DC 20036 E-mail: editorial@academicapress.com Web Site: www.academicapress.com, pg 3

Academy Chicago Publishers, 814 N Franklin St, Chicago, IL 60610 Tel: 312-337-0747 Toll Free Tel: 800-888-4741 (orders) Fax: 312-337-5110 E-mail: frontdesk@chicagoreviewpress.com Web Site: www.chicagoreviewpress.com, pg 3

Academy of American Poets Fellowship, 75 Maiden Lane, Suite 901, New York, NY 10038 Tel: 212-274-0343 E-mail: awards@poets.org Web Site: poets.org/academy-american-poets/prizes/academy-american-poets-fellowship, pg 569

Academy of American Poets First Book Award, 75 Maiden Lane, Suite 901, New York, NY 10038 Tel: 212-274-0343 E-mail: awards@poets.org Web Site: poets.org/academy-american-poets/prizes/first-book-award, pg 569

The Academy of American Poets Harold Taylor Prize, 511-512 Humanities Bldg, 1600 Holloway Ave, San Francisco, CA 94132 Tel: 415-338-2227 Fax: 415-338-0966 E-mail: poetry@sfsu.edu Web Site: poetry.sfsu.edu, pg 569

The Academy of American Poets Inc, 75 Maiden Lane, Suite 901, New York, NY 10038 Tel: 212-274-0343 E-mail: academy@poets.org Web Site: poets.org, pg 493

Academy of Motion Picture Arts & Sciences (AMPAS), 8949 Wilshire Blvd, Beverly Hills, CA 90211 Tel: 310-247-3000 Fax: 310-859-9619 E-mail: ampas@oscars.org Web Site: www.oscars.org, pg 493

Academy of Nutrition & Dietetics, 120 S Riverside Plaza, Suite 2190, Chicago, IL 60606-6995 Tel: 312-899-0040 (ext 5000) Toll Free Tel: 800-877-1600 E-mail: publications@eatright.org; sales@eatright.org Web Site: www.eatrightstore.org, pg 3

ACC Art Books, 6 W 18 St, Suite 4B, New York, NY 10011 Tel: 212-645-1111 Toll Free Tel: 800-252-5231 Fax: 212-989-3205 E-mail: ussales@accpublishinggroup.com Web Site: www.accartbooks.com/us/, pg 3

Access Copyright, The Canadian Copyright Licensing Agency, 69 Younge St, Suite 1100, Toronto, ON M5E 1K3, Canada Tel: 416-868-1620 Toll Free Tel: 800-893-5777 Fax: 416-868-1621 E-mail: info@accesscopyright.ca Web Site: www.accesscopyright.ca, pg 493

Accurate Writing & More, 16 Barstow Lane, Hadley, MA 01035 Tel: 413-586-2388 Web Site: www.accuratewriting.com; frugalmarketing.com, pg 435

The Acheven Book Prize for Young Adult Fiction, c/o Regal House Publishing, 806 Oberlin Rd, No 12094, Raleigh, NC 27605 E-mail: info@regalhousepublishing.com Web Site: regalhousepublishing.com/the-acheven-book-prize-for-young-adult-fiction/, pg 570

ACM Books, 1601 Broadway, 10th fl, New York, NY 10019-7434 Tel: 212-869-7440 E-mail: acmbooks-info@acm.org Web Site: www.acm.org; books.acm.org, pg 4

ACMRS Press, Arizona State University, PO Box 874402, Tempe, AZ 85287-4402 Tel: 480-727-6503 Toll Free Tel: 800-621-2736 (orders) Fax: 480-965-1681 Toll Free Fax: 800-621-8476 (orders) E-mail: acmrs@asu.edu Web Site: acmrspress.com, pg 4

ACP Best of the Best Awards, 104 Westland Dr, Columbia, TN 38401 Toll Free Tel: 877-203-2327 E-mail: info@communitypublishers.com Web Site: www.communitypublishers.com/awards, pg 570

Acres USA, 603 Eighth St, Greeley, CO 80631 Tel: 970-392-4464 Toll Free Tel: 800-355-5313 E-mail: info@acresusa.com Web Site: www.acresusa.com, pg 4

ACS Publications, 1155 16 St NW, Washington, DC 20036 Tel: 202-872-4600 Toll Free Tel: 800-227-5558 (US) Fax: 202-872-6067 E-mail: help@acs.org Web Site: pubs.acs.org; publish.acs.org/publish, pg 4

ACTA Press, 200-4040 Bowness Rd NW, Calgary, AB T3B 3R7, Canada Tel: 403-288-1195 Fax: 403-247-6851 E-mail: journals@actapress.com; publish@actapress.com; sales@actapress.com Web Site: www.actapress.com, pg 395

ACTA Publications, 7135 W Keeney St, Niles, IL 60714 Toll Free Tel: 800-397-2282 E-mail: actapublications@actapublications.com Web Site: www.actapublications.com, pg 4

ACU Press, ACU Box 29138, Abilene, TX 79699 Tel: 325-674-2720 Toll Free Tel: 877-816-4455 E-mail: acupressoffice@groupmail.acu.edu Web Site: www.acupressbooks.com; www.leafwoodpublishers.com, pg 4

Adams & Ambrose Publishing, 1622 Capital Ave, Madison, WI 53705-1228 Tel: 608-572-2471 E-mail: info@adamsambrose.com, pg 4

Herbert Baxter Adams Prize in European History, 400 "A" St SE, Washington, DC 20003 Tel: 202-544-2422 E-mail: awards@historians.org Web Site: www.historians.org/award-grant/herbert-baxter-adams-prize/, pg 570

Adams Media, 100 Technology Center Dr, Suite 501, Stoughton, MA 02072 *Tel:* 508-427-7100 *Web Site:* www.simonandschuster.com, pg 4

Willi Paul Adams Award, 112 N Bryan Ave, Bloomington, IN 47408-4141 *Tel:* 812-855-7311 *E-mail:* oah@oah.org *Web Site:* www.oah.org/awards, pg 570

Jane Addams Children's Book Award, 276 Fifth Ave, Suite 704, PMB 45, New York, NY 10001 *Tel:* 212-682-8830 *E-mail:* info@janeaddamspeace.org *Web Site:* www.janeaddamspeace.org, pg 570

Addicus Books Inc, PO Box 45327, Omaha, NE 68145 *Tel:* 402-330-7493 *Fax:* 402-330-1707 *E-mail:* info@addicusbooks.com *Web Site:* www.addicusbooks.com, pg 5

J Adel Art & Design, 586 Ramapo Rd, Teaneck, NJ 07666 *Tel:* 201-836-2606 *E-mail:* jadelnj@aol.com, pg 435

Adirondack Mountain Club (ADK), 4833 Cascade Rd, Lake Placid, NY 12946-4113 *Tel:* 518-837-5047 *Toll Free Tel:* 800-395-8080 *E-mail:* info@adk.org *Web Site:* www.adk.org, pg 5

Adult Writers Workshops, Finn House, 102 W Wiggin St, Gambier, OH 43022-9623 *Tel:* 740-427-5196 *Fax:* 740-427-5417 *E-mail:* writers@kenyonreview.org *Web Site:* kenyonreview.org/adult-writers, pg 553

Advance Publishing Inc, 6950 Fulton St, Houston, TX 77022 *Tel:* 713-695-0600 *Toll Free Tel:* 800-917-9630 *Fax:* 713-695-8585 *E-mail:* info@advancepublishing.com *Web Site:* www.advancepublishing.com, pg 5

AdventureKEEN, 2204 First Ave S, Suite 102, Birmingham, AL 35233 *Tel:* 763-689-9800 *Toll Free Tel:* 800-678-7006 *Fax:* 763-689-9039 *Toll Free Fax:* 877-374-9016 *E-mail:* info@adventurewithkeen.com *Web Site:* adventurewithkeen.com, pg 5

Adventures Unlimited Press (AUP), One Adventure Place, Kempton, IL 60946 *Tel:* 815-253-6390 *Fax:* 815-253-6300 *E-mail:* info@adventuresunlimitedpress.com *Web Site:* www.adventuresunlimitedpress.com, pg 5

Advertising Research Foundation (ARF), 432 Park Ave S, 4th fl, New York, NY 10016 *Tel:* 212-751-5656 *Fax:* 212-689-1859 *E-mail:* membership@thearf.org; new-member-info@thearf.org *Web Site:* thearf.org, pg 493, 525

The AEI Press, 1789 Massachusetts Ave NW, Washington, DC 20036 *Tel:* 202-862-5800 *Fax:* 202-862-7177 *Web Site:* www.aei.org, pg 5

AEIOU Inc, 894 Piermont Ave, Piermont, NY 10968 *Tel:* 845-359-1911, pg 435

Aevitas Creative Management LLC, 19 W 21 St, Suite 501, New York, NY 10010 *Tel:* 212-765-6900 *Web Site:* www.aevitascreative.com, pg 448

Africa World Press Inc, 541 W Ingham Ave, Suite B, Trenton, NJ 08638 *Tel:* 609-695-3200 *Fax:* 609-695-6466 *E-mail:* customerservice@africaworldpressbooks.com *Web Site:* www.africaworldpressbooks.com, pg 5

African American Images Inc (AAI), 3126 E Fruitvale Ct, Gilbert, AZ 85297 *Tel:* 480-621-8307 *Fax:* 480-621-7794 *E-mail:* customersvc@africanamericanimages.com *Web Site:* africanamericanimages.com, pg 5

Agate Publishing Academy, 1328 Greenleaf St, Evanston, IL 60202 *Tel:* 847-475-4457 *E-mail:* help@agatepublishingacademy.com *Web Site:* agatepublishingacademy.com, pg 561

Agatha Awards, PO Box 8007, Gaithersburg, MD 20898 *Tel:* 301-730-1675 *E-mail:* mdregservices@gmail.com *Web Site:* malicedomestic.org, pg 570

Agency Chicago, 7000 Phoenix Ave NE, Suite 202, Albuquerque, NM 87110 *Tel:* 505-299-1911 *E-mail:* agency.chicago@usa.com, pg 448

Aggiornamento Award, 8550 United Plaza Blvd, Suite 1001, Baton Rouge, LA 70809 *Tel:* 225-408-4417 *E-mail:* cla2@cathla.org *Web Site:* cathla.org, pg 570

AHA Prize in American History, 400 "A" St SE, Washington, DC 20003 *Tel:* 202-544-2422 *E-mail:* awards@historians.org *Web Site:* www.historians.org/award-grant/aha-prize-in-american-history/, pg 570

AHA Prize in European International History, 400 "A" St SE, Washington, DC 20003 *Tel:* 202-544-2422 *E-mail:* awards@historians.org *Web Site:* www.historians.org/award-grant/aha-prize-in-european-international-history/, pg 570

AHA Prize in History prior to CE 1000, 400 "A" St SE, Washington, DC 20003 *Tel:* 202-544-2422 *E-mail:* awards@historians.org *Web Site:* www.historians.org/award-grant/aha-prize-in-history-prior-to-ce-1000/, pg 571

AICPA® & CIMA®, 220 Leigh Farm Rd, Durham, NC 27707 *Tel:* 919-402-4500 *Toll Free Tel:* 888-777-7077 (memb serv ctr) *Web Site:* www.aicpa-cima.com/cpe-learning, pg 5

AIGA 50 Books | 50 Covers, 228 Park Ave S, Suite 58603, New York, NY 10003 *Tel:* 212-807-1990 *E-mail:* competitions@aiga.org *Web Site:* www.aiga.org, pg 571

AIGA, the professional association for design, 228 Park Ave S, Suite 58603, New York, NY 10003 *Tel:* 212-807-1990 *E-mail:* general@aiga.org *Web Site:* www.aiga.org, pg 493

AIHA (American Industrial Hygiene Association), 3141 Fairview Park Dr, Suite 777, Falls Church, VA 22042 *Tel:* 703-849-8888 *Fax:* 703-207-3561 *E-mail:* infonet@aiha.org *Web Site:* www.aiha.org, pg 6

AIP Publishing LLC, 1305 Walt Whitman Rd, Suite 110, Melville, NY 11747 *Tel:* 516-576-2200 *E-mail:* help@aip.org; press@aip.org; rights@aip.org *Web Site:* www.aip.org; publishing.aip.org, pg 6

AJL Jewish Fiction Award, PO Box 1118, Teaneck, NJ 07666 *Tel:* 201-371-3255 *E-mail:* info@jewishlibraries.org *Web Site:* jewishlibraries.org/AJL_Jewish_Fiction_Award, pg 571

AJL Judaica Bibliography Award, PO Box 1118, Teaneck, NJ 07666 *Tel:* 201-371-3255 *E-mail:* info@jewishlibraries.org *Web Site:* jewishlibraries.org, pg 571

AJL Judaica Reference Award, PO Box 1118, Teaneck, NJ 07666 *Tel:* 201-371-3255 *E-mail:* info@jewishlibraries.org *Web Site:* jewishlibraries.org, pg 571

AJL Scholarship, PO Box 1118, Teaneck, NJ 07666 *Tel:* 201-371-3255 *E-mail:* scholarship@jewishlibraries.org; info@jewishlibraries.org *Web Site:* jewishlibraries.org/student-scholarship-award, pg 571

AK Press, 370 Ryan Ave, Unit 100, Chico, CA 95973 *Tel:* 510-208-1700 *Fax:* 510-208-1701 *E-mail:* info@akpress.org *Web Site:* www.akpress.org, pg 6

AKA Literary Management, 11445 Dallas Rd, Peyton, CO 80831 *Tel:* 646-846-2478 *E-mail:* hello@akaliterary.com *Web Site:* akalm.net, pg 448

Akashic Books, 232 Third St, Suite A115, Brooklyn, NY 11215 *Tel:* 718-643-9193 *E-mail:* info@akashicbooks.com *Web Site:* www.akashicbooks.com, pg 6

Akron Poetry Prize, 120 E Mill St, Suite 415, Akron, OH 44308 *Tel:* 330-972-2795 *E-mail:* uapress@uakron.edu *Web Site:* www.uakron.edu/uapress/akron-poetry-prize, pg 571

ALA Neal-Schuman, 225 N Michigan Ave, Suite 1300, Chicago, IL 60601 *Toll Free Tel:* 800-545-2433 *Fax:* 312-280-5860 *E-mail:* editionsmarketing@ala.org *Web Site:* www.alastore.ala.org, pg 6

Alabama Artists Fellowship Awards, 201 Monroe St, Suite 110, Montgomery, AL 36130-1800 *Tel:* 334-242-4076 *Fax:* 334-240-3269 *Web Site:* arts.alabama.gov/programs/literary_arts/literary_fellowships.aspx, pg 571

Alaska Native Language Center (ANLC), PO Box 757680, Fairbanks, AK 99775-7680 *Tel:* 907-474-7874 *E-mail:* uaf-anlc@alaska.edu (orders) *Web Site:* www.uaf.edu/anlc, pg 6

Albert Whitman & Company, 250 S Northwest Hwy, Suite 320, Park Ridge, IL 60068 *Tel:* 847-232-2800 *Toll Free Tel:* 800-255-7675 (orders) *Fax:* 847-581-0039 *E-mail:* mail@albertwhitman.com; orders@albertwhitman.com *Web Site:* www.albertwhitman.com, pg 6

Alberta Book Publishing Awards, 11759 Groat Rd NW, 2nd fl, Edmonton, AB T5M 3K6, Canada *Tel:* 780-424-5060 *E-mail:* info@bookpublishers.ab.ca *Web Site:* bookpublishers.ab.ca; www.readalberta.ca, pg 571

The Albertine Youth Prize, 972 Fifth Ave, New York, NY 10075 *Tel:* 332-228-2238 *E-mail:* info@albertine.com *Web Site:* www.albertine.com/prix-albertine-jeunesse-2024/; www.albertine.com, pg 571

Rodelinde Albrecht, 274 Bradley St, Lee, MA 01238 *Tel:* 413-243-4350 *E-mail:* rodelinde@gmail.com, pg 435

Alcuin Society, PO Box 3216, Sta Terminal, Vancouver, BC V6B 3X8, Canada *Tel:* 604-732-5403 *E-mail:* info@alcuinsociety.com; awards@alcuinsociety.com *Web Site:* alcuinsociety.com, pg 493

Alcuin Society Awards for Excellence in Book Design in Canada, PO Box 3216, Sta Terminal, Vancouver, BC V6B 3X8, Canada *Tel:* 604-732-5403 *E-mail:* awards@alcuinsociety.com *Web Site:* alcuinsociety.com, pg 571

A Owen Aldridge Prize, 323 E Wacker Dr, No 642, Chicago, IL 60601 *Tel:* 312-600-8072 *E-mail:* info@acla.org *Web Site:* www.acla.org/prize-awards/owen-aldridge-prize, pg 572

Alex Awards, 225 N Michigan Ave, Suite 1300, Chicago, IL 60601 *Tel:* 312-280-4390 *Toll Free Tel:* 800-545-2433 *E-mail:* yalsa@ala.org *Web Site:* www.ala.org/yalsa/alex-awards, pg 572

Alexander Street, part of Clarivate PLC, 789 E Eisenhower Pkwy, Ann Arbor, MI 48108 *Toll Free Tel:* 800-521-0600; 888-963-2071 (sales) *E-mail:* sales@alexanderstreet.com; marketing@alexanderstreet.com; support@alexanderstreet.com *Web Site:* alexanderstreet.com, pg 6

Alfred Music, 285 Century Place, Louisville, CO 80027 *Tel:* 818-891-5999 (dealer sales, intl) *Toll Free Tel:* 800-292-6122 (dealer sales, US & CN); 800-628-1528 (cust serv) *Fax:* 818-893-5560 (dealer sales); 818-830-6252 (cust serv) *Toll Free Fax:* 800-632-1928 (dealer sales) *E-mail:* customerservice@alfred.com; sales@alfred.com *Web Site:* www.alfred.com, pg 6

Algora Publishing, 1632 First Ave, No 20330, New York, NY 10028-4305 *Tel:* 212-678-0232 *Fax:* 212-202-5488 *E-mail:* editors@algora.com *Web Site:* www.algora.com, pg 7

Nelson Algren Literary Awards, 160 N Stetson Ave, Chicago, IL 60601 *Tel:* 312-222-3001 *E-mail:* ctc-arts@chicagotribune.com *Web Site:* www.chicagotribune.com/entertainment/books/literary-awards; algren.submittable.com, pg 572

Alice Award, 518 Warren St, Hudson, NY 12534 *Tel:* 518-828-8900 *Web Site:* www.furthermore.org, pg 572

All About Kids Publishing, PO Box 159, Gilroy, CA 95021 *Tel:* 408-337-1152 *E-mail:* info@allaboutkidspub.com *Web Site:* www.allaboutkidspub.com, pg 7

All Things That Matter Press, 79 Jones Rd, Somerville, ME 04348 *E-mail:* allthingsthatmatterpress@gmail.com *Web Site:* www.allthingsthatmatterpress.com, pg 7

Samuel Washington Allen Prize, c/o Linda Haviland Conte, 18 Hall Ave, Apt 2, Somerville, MA 02144 *E-mail:* info@nepoetryclub.org *Web Site:* nepoetryclub.org, pg 572

Alliance for Audited Media (AAM), 4513 Lincoln Ave, Suite 105B, Lisle, IL 60532 *Tel:* 224-366-6939 *Toll Free Tel:* 800-285-2220 *E-mail:* corpcomm@auditedmedia.com *Web Site:* auditedmedia.com, pg 493

COMPANY INDEX

Alliance for Women in Media (AWM), 2365 Harrodsburg Rd, A325, Lexington, KY 40504 *Tel:* 202-750-3664 *Fax:* 202-750-3664 *E-mail:* info@allwomeninmedia.org *Web Site:* allwomeninmedia.org, pg 494

Alloy Entertainment LLC, 30 Hudson Yards, 22nd fl, New York, NY 10001, pg 7

Allworth Press, 307 W 36 St, 11th fl, New York, NY 10018 *Tel:* 212-643-6816 *Fax:* 212-643-6819 *Web Site:* www.allworth.com, pg 7

AllWrite Publishing, PO Box 1071, Atlanta, GA 30301 *Tel:* 770-284-8983 *Fax:* 770-284-8983 *E-mail:* questions@allwritepublishing.com; support@allwritepublishing.com (orders & returns) *Web Site:* allwritepublishing.com, pg 7

Jeanette Almada, 452 W Aldine, Unit 215, Chicago, IL 60657 *Tel:* 773-404-9350 *E-mail:* jmalmada@sbcglobal.net, pg 435

ALSC Baker & Taylor Summer Reading Grant, 225 N Michigan Ave, Suite 1300, Chicago, IL 60601 *Tel:* 312-280-2163 *Toll Free Tel:* 800-545-2433 *Fax:* 312-280-5271 *E-mail:* alsc@ala.org *Web Site:* www.ala.org/alsc/awardsgrants/profawards/bakertaylor, pg 572

Prix Alvine-Belisle, 2065 rue Parthenais, Bureau 387, Montreal, QC H2K 3T1, Canada *Tel:* 514-281-5012 *E-mail:* info@fmdoc.org *Web Site:* www.fmdoc.org/activities/prix-alvine-belisle, pg 572

Amadeus Press, 4501 Forbes Blvd, Suite 200, Lanham, MD 20706 *Tel:* 212-529-3888 *Fax:* 212-529-4223 *Web Site:* www.rowman.com, pg 7

Amakella Publishing, PO Box 9445, Arlington, VA 22219 *Tel:* 202-239-8660 *E-mail:* info@amakella.com *Web Site:* www.amakella.com, pg 7

AM&P Network, 1620 "I" St NW, Suite 501, Washington, DC 20005 *Tel:* 202-289-7442 *Fax:* 202-289-7097 *Web Site:* www.siia.net/amp-network, pg 494

Amateur Writing Contest, PO Box 686, Baltimore, MD 21203-0686 *Tel:* 410-563-2737 *E-mail:* bsfs-amc@bsfs.org *Web Site:* www.bsfs.org/bsfsssc.htm, pg 572

Ambassador International, 411 University Ridge, Suite B14, Greenville, SC 29601 *Tel:* 864-751-4844 *E-mail:* info@emeraldhouse.com; publisher@emeraldhouse.com (ms submissions); sales@emeraldhouse.com (orders/order inquiries); media@emeraldhouse.com; design@emeraldhouse.com *Web Site:* ambassador-international.com; www.facebook.com/AmbassadorIntl; x.com/ambassadorintl, pg 7

The Ambassador Richard C Holbrooke Distinguished Achievement Award, PO Box 461, Wright Brothers Branch, Dayton, OH 45409-0461 *Tel:* 937-298-5072 *E-mail:* sharon.rab@daytonliterarypeaceprize.org *Web Site:* www.daytonliterarypeaceprize.org, pg 572

Amber Lotus Publishing, PO Box 11329, Portland, OR 97211 *Tel:* 503-284-6400 *Toll Free Tel:* 800-326-2375 (orders only) *Fax:* 503-284-6417 *E-mail:* info@amberlotus.com; neworder@amberlotus.com *Web Site:* www.amberlotus.com, pg 8

Ambroggio Prize, 75 Maiden Lane, Suite 901, New York, NY 10038 *Tel:* 212-274-0343 *E-mail:* awards@poets.org *Web Site:* poets.org/academy-american-poets/prizes/ambroggio-prize, pg 572

American Academy of Arts & Sciences (AAAS), 136 Irving St, Cambridge, MA 02138 *Tel:* 617-576-5000 *Fax:* 617-576-5050 *E-mail:* aaas@amacad.org *Web Site:* www.amacad.org, pg 494

American Academy of Environmental Engineers & Scientists®, 147 Old Solomons Island Rd, Suite 303, Annapolis, MD 21401 *Tel:* 410-266-3311 *Fax:* 410-266-7653 *E-mail:* info@aaees.org *Web Site:* www.aaees.org, pg 8

American Academy of Pediatrics, 345 Park Blvd, Itasca, IL 60143 *Toll Free Tel:* 888-227-1770 *Fax:* 847-228-1281 *Web Site:* www.aap.org; shop.aap.org; publishing.aap.org, pg 8

American Academy of Political & Social Science (AAPSS), 220 S 40 St, Suite 201-E, Philadelphia, PA 19104-3543 *Tel:* 215-746-6500 *Fax:* 215-573-2667 *Web Site:* www.aapss.org, pg 494

American Alpine Club, 710 Tenth St, Suite 100, Golden, CO 80401 *Tel:* 303-384-0110 *Fax:* 303-384-0111 *E-mail:* info@americanalpineclub.org *Web Site:* americanalpineclub.org, pg 8

American Anthropological Association (AAA), 2300 Clarendon Blvd, Suite 1301, Arlington, VA 22201 *E-mail:* pubs@americananthro.org *Web Site:* www.americananthro.org, pg 8

American Antiquarian Society (AAS), 185 Salisbury St, Worcester, MA 01609-1634 *Tel:* 508-755-5221 *Fax:* 508-754-9069 *E-mail:* library@mwa.org *Web Site:* www.americanantiquarian.org, pg 494

American Association for the Advancement of Science (AAAS), 1200 New York Ave NW, Washington, DC 20005 *Tel:* 202-326-6400 *E-mail:* membership@aaas.org *Web Site:* www.aaas.org, pg 494

American Association of Collegiate Registrars & Admissions Officers (AACRAO), 1108 16 St NW, Washington, DC 20011 *Tel:* 202-293-9161 *Fax:* 202-872-8857 *E-mail:* pubs@aacrao.org *Web Site:* www.aacrao.org, pg 8

American Association of University Women of NC Young People's Literature Award, 4610 Mail Service Ctr, Raleigh, NC 27699-4610 *Tel:* 919-814-6623 *Web Site:* www.ncdcr.gov/about/history/lit-and-hist/awards; www.aauw.org, pg 573

American Auto Racing Writers & Broadcasters (AARWBA), 922 N Pass Ave, Burbank, CA 91505-2703 *Tel:* 818-842-7005 *Fax:* 818-842-7020 *E-mail:* aarwba.pres@gmail.com *Web Site:* aarwba.org, pg 494

American Bar Association Publishing, 321 N Clark St, Chicago, IL 60654 *Tel:* 312-988-5000 *Toll Free Tel:* 800-285-2221 (orders) *Tel:* 312-988-5850 (orders) *E-mail:* service@americanbar.org *Web Site:* www.americanbar.org/groups/departments_offices/publishing, pg 8

American Bible Society, 101 N Independence Mall E, 8th fl, Philadelphia, PA 19106-2112 *Tel:* 215-309-0900 *Toll Free Tel:* 800-322-4253 (cust serv); 888-596-6296 *E-mail:* info@americanbible.org *Web Site:* www.americanbible.org, pg 8

American Book Awards, The Raymond House, 655 13 St, Suite 302, Oakland, CA 94612 *Tel:* 916-425-7916 *E-mail:* beforecolumbusfoundation@gmail.com *Web Site:* www.beforecolumbusfoundation.com, pg 573

American Book Producers Association (ABPA), 7 Peter Cooper Rd, No 7G, New York, NY 10010 *E-mail:* office@abpaonline.org *Web Site:* www.abpaonline.org, pg 494

American Booksellers Association, 600 Mamaroneck Ave, Suite 400, Harrison, NY 10528 *Tel:* 914-406-7500 *Toll Free Tel:* 800-637-0037 *Fax:* 914-417-4013 *E-mail:* info@bookweb.org *Web Site:* www.bookweb.org, pg 494

American Carriage House Publishing (ACHP), PO Box 1900, Pen Valley, CA 95946 *Tel:* 530-432-8860 *Toll Free Tel:* 866-986-2665 *E-mail:* editor@carriagehousepublishing.com *Web Site:* www.americancarriagehousepublishing.com, pg 8

American Catholic Press (ACP), 16565 S State St, South Holland, IL 60473 *Tel:* 708-331-5485 *Fax:* 708-331-5484 *E-mail:* acp@acpress.org *Web Site:* www.acpress.org, pg 9

The American Ceramic Society, 550 Polaris Pkwy, Suite 510, Westerville, OH 43082 *Tel:* 240-646-7054 *Toll Free Tel:* 866-721-3322 *Fax:* 240-396-5637 *E-mail:* customerservice@ceramics.org *Web Site:* ceramics.org, pg 9

American Christian Writers, 4854 Aster Dr, Nashville, TN 37211 *Tel:* 615-331-8668; 615-498-8630 *E-mail:* acwriters@aol.com *Web Site:* acwriters.com, pg 494

AMERICAN INDIAN YOUTH LITERATURE AWARD

American Civil Liberties Union (ACLU), 125 Broad St, 18th fl, New York, NY 10004 *Tel:* 212-549-2500 *E-mail:* media@aclu.org *Web Site:* www.aclu.org, pg 495

The American College of Financial Services, 630 Allendale Rd, Suite 400, King of Prussia, PA 19406 *Tel:* 610-526-1000 *Toll Free Tel:* 866-883-5640 *Web Site:* www.theamericancollege.edu, pg 9

American College of Surgeons, 633 N Saint Clair St, Chicago, IL 60611-3211 *Tel:* 312-202-5000 *Fax:* 312-202-5001 *E-mail:* postmaster@facs.org *Web Site:* www.facs.org, pg 9

American Correctional Association, 206 N Washington St, Suite 200, Alexandria, VA 22314 *Tel:* 703-224-0000 *Toll Free Tel:* 800-222-5646 *Fax:* 703-224-0179 *E-mail:* publications@aca.org *Web Site:* www.aca.org, pg 9

American Council on Education (ACE), One Dupont Circle NW, Washington, DC 20036 *Tel:* 202-939-9300 *Web Site:* www.acenet.edu, pg 9, 495

American Counseling Association (ACA), 6101 Stevenson Ave, Suite 600, Alexandria, VA 22304 *Tel:* 703-823-9800 *Toll Free Tel:* 800-298-2276 *Toll Free Fax:* 800-473-2329 *E-mail:* orders@counseling.org (book orders) *Web Site:* www.counseling.org, pg 9

American Diabetes Association, 2451 Crystal Dr, Suite 900, Arlington, VA 22202 *Tel:* 703-549-1500 *Toll Free Tel:* 800-342-2383 *E-mail:* booksales@diabetes.org; ada_pubs@diabetes.org *Web Site:* diabetes.org; diabetesjournals.org/books; www.facebook.com/adapublications, pg 9

American Federation of Arts, 305 E 47 St, 10th fl, New York, NY 10017 *Tel:* 212-988-7700 *Toll Free Tel:* 800-232-0270 *Fax:* 212-861-2487 *E-mail:* pubinfo@amfedarts.org *Web Site:* www.amfedarts.org, pg 9

American Federation of Astrologers Inc, 6535 S Rural Rd, Tempe, AZ 85283-3746 *Tel:* 480-838-1751 *Toll Free Tel:* 888-301-7630 *E-mail:* info@astrologers.com *Web Site:* www.astrologers.com, pg 9

American Fisheries Society, 425 Barlow Place, Suite 110, Bethesda, MD 20814-2144 *Tel:* 301-897-8616; 703-661-1570 (book orders) *Fax:* 301-897-8096; 703-996-1010 (book orders) *E-mail:* main@fisheries.org *Web Site:* fisheries.org/books-journals, pg 9

American Forest & Paper Association (AF&PA), 1101 "K" St NW, Suite 700, Washington, DC 20005 *Tel:* 202-463-2700 *E-mail:* info@afandpa.org; comm@afandpa.org *Web Site:* www.afandpa.org, pg 495

American Geophysical Union (AGU), 2000 Florida Ave NW, Washington, DC 20009 *Tel:* 202-462-6900 *Toll Free Tel:* 800-966-2481 (North America) *Fax:* 202-328-0566 *E-mail:* service@agu.org (cust serv) *Web Site:* www.agu.org, pg 10

American Geosciences Institute (AGI), 4220 King St, Alexandria, VA 22302-1502 *Tel:* 703-379-2480 (ext 246) *E-mail:* agi@americangeosciences.org *Web Site:* www.americangeosciences.org; www.geosciencestore.org, pg 10

American Girl Publishing, 2330 Eagle Dr, Middleton, WI 53562 *Tel:* 608-830-4444 *Toll Free Tel:* 800-845-0005 (US & CN) *Fax:* 608-836-1999 *Web Site:* www.americangirl.com/pages/books; www.americangirl.com, pg 10

American Historical Association (AHA), 400 "A" St SE, Washington, DC 20003 *Tel:* 202-544-2422 *E-mail:* info@historians.org; awards@historians.org *Web Site:* www.historians.org, pg 10

American Illustration/American Photography, 225 W 36 St, Suite 602, New York, NY 10018 *Tel:* 646-669-8111 *E-mail:* info@ai-ap.com *Web Site:* www.ai-ap.com, pg 573

American Indian Youth Literature Award, PO Box 41296, San Jose, CA 95160 *E-mail:* ailawebsite@gmail.com *Web Site:* ailanet.org/activities/american-indian-youth-literature-award, pg 573

American Institute for Economic Research (AIER), 250 Division St, Great Barrington, MA 01230 *Tel:* 413-528-1216 *Toll Free Tel:* 888-528-1216 (orders) *Fax:* 413-528-0103 *E-mail:* press@aier.org; submissions@aier.org *Web Site:* www.aier.org, pg 10

American Institute of Aeronautics and Astronautics (AIAA), 12700 Sunrise Valley Dr, Suite 200, Reston, VA 20191-5807 *Tel:* 703-264-7500 *Toll Free Tel:* 800-639-AIAA (639-2422) *Fax:* 703-264-7551 *E-mail:* custserv@aiaa.org *Web Site:* www.aiaa.org; arc.aiaa.org (orders), pg 10

American Institute of Chemical Engineers (AIChE), 120 Wall St, 23rd fl, New York, NY 10005-4020 *Tel:* 203-702-7660 *Toll Free Tel:* 800-242-4363 *E-mail:* customerservice@aiche.org *Web Site:* www.aiche.org/publications, pg 10

American Jewish Committee (AJC), Mail Code 6760, PO Box 7247, Philadelphia, PA 19170-0001 *Tel:* 212-751-4000 *Fax:* 212-891-1450 *E-mail:* social@ajc.org *Web Site:* www.ajc.org, pg 495

American Law Institute, 4025 Chestnut St, Philadelphia, PA 19104-3099 *Tel:* 215-243-1600 *Toll Free Tel:* 800-253-6397 *E-mail:* custserv@ali.org *Web Site:* www.ali.org, pg 10

American Law Institute Continuing Legal Education (ALI CLE), 4025 Chestnut St, Philadelphia, PA 19104 *Tel:* 215-243-1600 *Toll Free Tel:* 800-CLE-NEWS (253-6397) *Fax:* 215-243-1664 *E-mail:* custserv@ali-cle.org; press@ali-cle.org *Web Site:* www.ali-cle.org, pg 10

The American Library Association (ALA), 225 N Michigan Ave, Suite 1300, Chicago, IL 60601 *Tel:* 312-944-6780 *Toll Free Tel:* 800-545-2433; 866-SHOP-ALA (746-7252, orders) *Fax:* 312-280-5275; 312-440-9374; 312-280-5860 (orders) *E-mail:* ala@ala.org; alastore@ala.org *Web Site:* www.alastore.ala.org; www.ala.org, pg 10

The American Library Association (ALA), 225 N Michigan Ave, Suite 1300, Chicago, IL 60601 *Tel:* 312-944-6780; 312-280-4299 (memb & cust serv) *Toll Free Tel:* 800-545-2433 *Fax:* 312-440-9374 *E-mail:* ala@ala.org; customerservice@ala.org *Web Site:* www.ala.org, pg 495

American Literacy Council, c/o Los Alamos National Laboratory, Los Alamos, NM 87545 *E-mail:* questions@americanliteracy.com *Web Site:* www.americanliteracy.com, pg 495

American Literary Translators Association (ALTA), University of Arizona, Esquire Bldg, No 205, 1230 N Park Ave, Tucson, AZ 85721 *Tel:* 520-621-1757 *E-mail:* info@literarytranslators.org *Web Site:* www.literarytranslators.org, pg 495

American Marketing Association, 130 E Randolph St, 22nd fl, Chicago, IL 60601 *Tel:* 312-542-9000 *Toll Free Tel:* 800-AMA-1150 (262-1150) *Web Site:* www.ama.org, pg 495

American Mathematical Society (AMS), 201 Charles St, Providence, RI 02904-2213 *Tel:* 401-455-4000 *Toll Free Tel:* 800-321-4267 *Fax:* 401-331-3842; 401-455-4046 (cust serv) *E-mail:* ams@ams.org; cust-serv@ams.org *Web Site:* www.ams.org, pg 11

American Medical Association (AMA), AMA Plaza, 330 N Wabash, Suite 39300, Chicago, IL 60611-5885 *Tel:* 312-464-5000; 312-464-4430 (media & edit) *Toll Free Tel:* 800-621-8335 *E-mail:* media@ama-assn.org (media & edit); bookandonlinesales@ama-assn.org (volume book/ebook sales) *Web Site:* www.ama-assn.org, pg 11

American Medical Association (AMA), AMA Plaza, 330 N Wabash, Suite 39300, Chicago, IL 60611-5885 *Tel:* 312-464-5000 *Toll Free Tel:* 800-621-8335 *E-mail:* media@ama-assn.org (media & edit) *Web Site:* www.ama-assn.org; www.jamanetwork.org, pg 495

American Medical Writers Association (AMWA), 9841 Washingtonian Blvd, Suite 500-26, Gaithersburg, MD 20878 *Tel:* 240-238-0940 *Fax:* 301-294-9006 *E-mail:* amwa@amwa.org *Web Site:* www.amwa.org, pg 495

American Numismatic Society, 75 Varick St, 11th fl, New York, NY 10013 *Tel:* 212-571-4470 *Fax:* 212-571-4479 *E-mail:* ans@numismatics.org *Web Site:* www.numismatics.org, pg 11

American Philosophical Society Press, 104 S Fifth St, Philadelphia, PA 19106 *Tel:* 215-440-3425 *Fax:* 215-440-3450 *Web Site:* www.amphilsoc.org, pg 11

American Photographic Artists (APA), 5042 Wilshire Blvd, No 321, Los Angeles, CA 90036 *E-mail:* membershiprep@apanational.org *Web Site:* apanational.org, pg 496

American Political Science Association (APSA), 1527 New Hampshire Ave NW, Washington, DC 20036-1203 *Tel:* 202-483-2512 *Fax:* 202-483-2657 *E-mail:* apsa@apsanet.org; membership@apsanet.org; press@apsanet.org *Web Site:* www.apsanet.org, pg 496

American Press, 75 State St, Suite 100, Boston, MA 02109 *Tel:* 617-247-0022 *E-mail:* americanpress@flash.net *Web Site:* www.americanpresspublishers.com, pg 11

American Printing History Association, PO Box 4519, Grand Central Sta, New York, NY 10163 *E-mail:* secretary@printinghistory.org *Web Site:* printinghistory.org, pg 496

American Printing History Association Award, PO Box 4519, Grand Central Sta, New York, NY 10163 *E-mail:* secretary@printinghistory.org *Web Site:* printinghistory.org/programs/awards, pg 573

American Program Bureau Inc, One Gateway Center, Suite 751, Newton, MA 02458 *Tel:* 617-614-1600 *E-mail:* apb@apbspeakers.com *Web Site:* www.apbspeakers.com, pg 487

American Psychiatric Association Publishing, 800 Maine Ave SW, Suite 900, Washington, DC 20024 *Tel:* 202-459-9722 *Toll Free Tel:* 800-368-5777 *Fax:* 202-403-3094 *E-mail:* appi@psych.org *Web Site:* www.appi.org; www.psychiatryonline.org, pg 11

American Psychological Association, 750 First St NE, Washington, DC 20002 *Tel:* 202-336-5510 *Toll Free Tel:* 800-374-2721 *Fax:* 202-336-5502 *E-mail:* order@apa.org; booksales@apa.org *Web Site:* www.apa.org/books, pg 11

American Public Human Services Association (APHSA), 1300 17 St N, Suite 340, Arlington, VA 22209-3801 *Tel:* 202-682-0100 *Fax:* 202-289-6555 *E-mail:* memberservice@aphsa.org *Web Site:* www.aphsa.org, pg 496

American Public Works Association (APWA), 1200 Main St, Suite 1400, Kansas City, MO 64105-2100 *Tel:* 816-472-6100 *Toll Free Tel:* 800-848-APWA (848-2792) *Fax:* 816-472-1610 *Web Site:* www.apwa.org, pg 12

American Quilter's Society (AQS), 5801 Kentucky Dam Rd, Paducah, KY 42003-9323 *Tel:* 270-898-7903 *Toll Free Tel:* 800-626-5420 (orders) *Fax:* 270-898-8890 *E-mail:* orders@americanquilter.com; info@aqsquilt.com *Web Site:* www.americanquilter.com, pg 12

American Society for Indexing Inc (ASI), 1628 E Southern Ave, Suite 9-223, Tempe, AZ 85282 *Tel:* 480-245-6750 *E-mail:* info@asindexing.org *Web Site:* www.asindexing.org, pg 496

American Society for Nondestructive Testing, 1201 Dublin Rd, Suite G04, Columbus, OH 43215 *Tel:* 800-222-2768 *E-mail:* customersupport@asnt.org *Web Site:* www.asnt.org; source.asnt.org (orders); asntmediaplanner.com (ad & sponsored content), pg 12

American Society for Quality (ASQ), 600 N Plankinton Ave, Milwaukee, WI 53203 *Tel:* 414-272-8575 *Toll Free Tel:* 800-248-1946 (US & CN); 800-514-1564 (Mexico) *E-mail:* help@asq.org; books@asq.org *Web Site:* www.asq.org, pg 12

American Society of Agricultural & Biological Engineers (ASABE), 2950 Niles Rd, St Joseph, MI 49085-9659 *Tel:* 269-429-0300 *Toll Free Tel:* 800-371-2723 *Fax:* 269-429-3852 *E-mail:* hq@asabe.org *Web Site:* www.asabe.org, pg 12

American Society of Agronomy (ASA), 5585 Guilford Rd, Madison, WI 53711-5801 *Tel:* 608-273-8080 *E-mail:* books@sciencesocieties.org *Web Site:* www.agronomy.org, pg 12

American Society of Civil Engineers (ASCE), 1801 Alexander Bell Dr, Reston, VA 20191-4400 *Tel:* 703-295-6300 *Toll Free Tel:* 800-548-ASCE (548-2723) *Toll Free Fax:* 866-913-6085 *E-mail:* ascelibrary@asce.org; pubsful@asce.org *Web Site:* www.asce.org, pg 12

American Society of Composers, Authors & Publishers (ASCAP), 250 W 57 St, New York, NY 10107 *Tel:* 212-621-6000 *Toll Free Tel:* 800-952-7227 (cust serv) *Fax:* 212-621-6595 *Web Site:* www.ascap.com, pg 496

American Society of Journalists and Authors (ASJA), 355 Lexington Ave, 15th fl, New York, NY 10017-6603 *Tel:* 212-997-0947 *E-mail:* asjaoffice@asja.org *Web Site:* asja.org, pg 496

American Society of Journalists and Authors Annual Writers Conference, 355 Lexington Ave, 15th fl, New York, NY 10017-6603 *Tel:* 212-997-0947 *E-mail:* asjaoffice@asja.org *Web Site:* asja.org, pg 553

American Society of Magazine Editors (ASME), 23 Barnabas Rd, Suite 34, Hawleyville, CT 06440-0034 *Tel:* 212-872-3737 *E-mail:* asme@asme.media *Web Site:* www.asme.media, pg 496

American Society of Mechanical Engineers (ASME), 2 Park Ave, New York, NY 10016-5990 *Tel:* 646-616-3100 *Toll Free Tel:* 800-843-2763 (cust serv-CN, Mexico & US) *Fax:* 973-882-1717 (orders & inquiries) *E-mail:* customercare@asme.org *Web Site:* www.asme.org, pg 12

American Society of Media Photographers Inc, Four Embarcadero Ctr, Suite 1400, San Francisco, CA 94111 *Toll Free Tel:* 844-762-3386 *Web Site:* asmp.org, pg 496

American Society of Plant Taxonomists, c/o Missouri Botanical Garden, 4344 Shaw Blvd, St Louis, MO 63110 *E-mail:* businessoffice@aspt.net *Web Site:* www.aspt.net, pg 13

American Sociological Association (ASA), 1430 "K" St NW, Suite 600, Washington, DC 20005-4701 *Tel:* 202-383-9005 *E-mail:* asa@asanet.org; communications@asanet.org; membership@asanet.org *Web Site:* www.asanet.org, pg 497

American Speech-Language-Hearing Association (ASHA), 2200 Research Blvd, Rockville, MD 20850-3289 *Tel:* 301-296-5700 *Toll Free Tel:* 800-638-8255 (nonmembs); 800-498-2071 (membs) *Fax:* 301-296-5777; 301-296-8580 *E-mail:* actioncenter@asha.org *Web Site:* www.asha.org, pg 497

American Technical Publishers, 10100 Orland Pkwy, Suite 200, Orland Park, IL 60467-5756 *Toll Free Tel:* 800-323-3471 *Fax:* 708-957-1101 *E-mail:* service@atplearning.com; order@atplearning.com *Web Site:* www.atplearning.com; www.atpcanada.com (CN orders), pg 13

American Translators Association (ATA), 211 N Union St, Suite 100, Alexandria, VA 22314 *Tel:* 703-683-6100 *Fax:* 703-778-7222 *E-mail:* ata@atanet.org *Web Site:* www.atanet.org, pg 497

American Water Works Association (AWWA), 6666 W Quincy Ave, Denver, CO 80235-3098 *Tel:* 303-794-7711 *Toll Free Tel:* 800-926-7337 *E-mail:* service@awwa.org (cust serv); aws@awwa.org; books@awwa.org *Web Site:* www.awwa.org/publications, pg 13

Amicus, PO Box 227, Mankato, MN 56002 *Tel:* 507-388-9357 *Toll Free Tel:* 800-445-6209 (cust serv/orders) *E-mail:* info@thecreativecompany.us (gen inquiries); orders@thecreativecompany.us (cust serv) *Web Site:* amicuspublishing.us, pg 13

AMMO Books LLC, 3653 Primavera Ave, Los Angeles, CA 90065 *Tel:* 323-223-AMMO (223-2666) *Fax:* 323-978-4200 *E-mail:* weborders@ammobooks.com; orders@ammobooks.com *Web Site:* ammobooks.com, pg 13

Ampersand Group, 1136 Maritime Way, Suite 717, Kanata, ON K2K 0M1, Canada *Tel:* 613-435-5066, pg 435

COMPANY INDEX

Ampersand Inc/Professional Publishing Services, 515 Madison St, New Orleans, LA 70116 Tel: 312-280-8905 Fax: 312-944-1582 E-mail: info@ampersandworks.com Web Site: www.ampersandworks.com, pg 13

Betsy Amster Literary Enterprises, 607 Foothill Blvd, No 1061, La Canada Flintridge, CA 91012 E-mail: rights@amsterlit.com; b.amster.assistant@gmail.com (book queries) Web Site: amsterlit.com, pg 448

The Amy Award, 90 Broad St, Suite 2100, New York, NY 10004 Tel: 212-226-3586 Fax: 212-226-3963 E-mail: admin@pw.org Web Site: www.pw.org, pg 573

Anaphora Literary Press, 1108 W Third St, Quanah, TX 79252 Tel: 470-289-6395 Web Site: anaphoraliterary.com, pg 13

Ancient Faith Publishing, PO Box 748, Chesterton, IN 46304 Tel: 219-728-2216 Toll Free Tel: 800-967-7377 E-mail: general@ancientfaith.com; support@ancientfaith.com Web Site: www.ancientfaith.com/publishing, pg 13

Barbara S Anderson, 706 W Davis Ave, Ann Arbor, MI 48103-4855 Tel: 734-995-0125 E-mail: bsa@watercolorbarbara.com, pg 435

Anderson Literary Management LLC, 244 Fifth Ave, 2nd fl, Suite F166, New York, NY 10001 Tel: 212-645-6045 Fax: 212-741-1936 E-mail: info@andersonliterary.com Web Site: www.andersonliterary.com, pg 449

Sara Anderson Children's Books, PO Box 47182, Seattle, WA 98146 Tel: 206-285-1520 Web Site: www.saraandersonchildrensbooks.com, pg 13

Andrews McMeel Publishing LLC, 1130 Walnut St, Kansas City, MO 64106-2109 Tel: 816-581-7500 Toll Free Tel: 800-851-8923 Web Site: www.andrewsmcmeel.com; publishing.andrewsmcmeel.com, pg 14

Andrews University Press, Sutherland House, 8360 W Campus Circle Dr, Berrien Springs, MI 49104-1700 Tel: 269-471-6134 Toll Free Tel: 800-467-6369 (Visa, MC & American Express orders only) Fax: 269-471-6224 E-mail: aupo@andrews.edu; aup@andrews.edu Web Site: www.universitypress.andrews.edu, pg 14

Andy Ross Literary Agency, 767 Santa Ray Ave, Oakland, CA 94610 Tel: 510-238-8965 E-mail: andyrossagency@hotmail.com Web Site: www.andyrossagency.com, pg 449

Angel City Press, 2118 Wilshire Blvd, Suite 880, Santa Monica, CA 90403 Tel: 310-395-9982 E-mail: info@angelcitypress.com Web Site: www.angelcitypress.com, pg 14

Angel Editing Services, PO Box 752, Mountain Ranch, CA 95246 Tel: 209-728-8364 E-mail: info@stephaniemarohn.com Web Site: www.stephaniemarohn.com, pg 435

Angels Editorial Services, 1630 Main St, No 41, Coventry, CT 06238 Tel: 860-742-5279 E-mail: angelsus@aol.com, pg 435

Angelus Press, 522 W Bertrand St, St Marys, KS 66536 Tel: 816-753-3150 Toll Free Tel: 800-966-7337 E-mail: support@angeluspress.org Web Site: www.angeluspress.org, pg 14

Anhinga Press Inc, PO Box 3665, Tallahassee, FL 32315 E-mail: info@anhinga.org Web Site: www.anhingapress.org; www.facebook.com/anhingapress, pg 14

Anhinga Prize for Poetry, PO Box 3665, Tallahassee, FL 32315 E-mail: info@anhinga.org Web Site: www.anhingapress.org, pg 573

The Anisfield-Wolf Book Awards, 1422 Euclid Ave, Suite 1300, Cleveland, OH 44115 Tel: 216-861-3810 Fax: 216-861-1729 E-mail: awinfo@clevefdn.org Web Site: www.anisfield-wolf.org; www.clevelandfoundation.org, pg 573

R Ross Annett Award for Children's Literature, 11759 Groat Rd NW, Edmonton, AB T5M 3K6, Canada Tel: 780-422-8174 Toll Free Tel: 800-665-5354 (AB only) E-mail: mail@writersguild.ab.ca Web Site: writersguild.ca, pg 573

Annick Press Ltd, 388 Carlaw Ave, Suite 200, Toronto, ON M4M 2T4, Canada Tel: 416-221-4802 Fax: 416-221-8400 E-mail: annickpress@annickpress.com Web Site: www.annickpress.com, pg 395

Annual & Rolling Grants for Artists, 136 State St, Montpelier, VT 05633 Tel: 802-828-3291 E-mail: info@vermontartscouncil.org Web Site: www.vermontartscouncil.org, pg 573

Annual Reviews, 1875 S Grant St, Suite 700, San Mateo, CA 94402 Tel: 650-493-4400 Toll Free Tel: 800-523-8635 Fax: 650-424-0910; 650-855-9815 E-mail: service@annualreviews.org Web Site: www.annualreviews.org, pg 14

ANR Publications University of California, 2801 Second St, Davis, CA 95618 Tel: 530-400-0725 (cust serv) Toll Free Tel: 800-994-8849 E-mail: anrcatalog@ucanr.edu Web Site: anrcatalog.ucanr.edu, pg 14

Antiquarian Booksellers' Association of America (ABAA), 155 Water St, 6th fl, Suite 7, Brooklyn, NY 11201 Tel: 212-944-8291 Fax: 212-944-8293 E-mail: hq@abaa.org Web Site: www.abaa.org, pg 497

Anvil Press Publishers, PO Box 3008, MPO, Vancouver, BC V6B 3X5, Canada Tel: 604-876-8710 E-mail: info@anvilpress.com Web Site: www.anvilpress.com, pg 395

AOTA Press, 6116 Executive Blvd, Suite 200, North Bethesda, MD 20852-4929 Tel: 301-652-6611 Fax: 770-238-0414 (orders) E-mail: aotapress@aota.org; customerservice@aota.org Web Site: store.aota.org; www.aota.org, pg 14

APA Talent & Literary Agency, 405 S Beverly Dr, Beverly Hills, CA 90212 Tel: 310-888-4200 Web Site: www.apa-agency.com, pg 449

APC Publishing, PO Box 461166, Aurora, CO 80046-1166 Tel: 303-660-2158 Toll Free Tel: 800-660-5107 (sales & orders) E-mail: mail@4wdbooks.com; orders@4wdbooks.com Web Site: www.4wdbooks.com, pg 15

Aperture Books, 548 W 28 St, 4th fl, New York, NY 10001 Tel: 212-505-5555 Toll Free Fax: 888-623-6908 E-mail: customerservice@aperture.org Web Site: aperture.org, pg 15

APH Press, 1839 Frankfort Ave, Louisville, KY 40206 Tel: 502-895-2405 Toll Free Tel: 800-223-1839 E-mail: press@aph.org Web Site: aph.org/shop, pg 15

The Apocryphile Press, 1700 Shattuck Ave, Suite 81, Berkeley, CA 94709 Tel: 510-290-4349 E-mail: apocryphile@me.com Web Site: www.apocryphilepress.com, pg 15

Apogee Press, PO Box 10066, Berkeley, CA 94709 E-mail: apogeelibri@gmail.com Web Site: www.apogeepress.com, pg 15

APPA - Leadership in Education Facilities, 1643 Prince St, Alexandria, VA 22314-2818 Tel: 703-684-1446; 703-542-3837 (bookshop) E-mail: webmaster@appa.org Web Site: www.appa.org, pg 15

Appalachian Mountain Club Books, 10 City Sq, Boston, MA 02129 Tel: 617-523-0655 E-mail: amcbooks@outdoors.org; amcpublications@outdoors.org Web Site: www.outdoors.org, pg 15

Appalachian Writers' Workshop, 51 Center St, Hindman, KY 41822 Tel: 606-785-5475 E-mail: info@hindman.org Web Site: www.hindman.org, pg 553

Applause Theatre & Cinema Books, 64 S Main St, Essex, CT 06426 Tel: 973-223-5039 E-mail: info@applausepub.com Web Site: www.applausepub.com, pg 15

Applewood Books, 210 Wingo Way, Suite 200, Mount Pleasant, SC 29464 Tel: 843-853-2070 E-mail: retailers@arcadiapublishing.com; publishing@arcadiapublishing.com Web Site: www.arcadiapublishing.com, pg 15

Appraisal Institute, 200 W Madison, Suite 1500, Chicago, IL 60606 Tel: 312-335-4100 Toll Free Tel: 888-756-4624 E-mail: aiservice@appraisalinstitute.org Web Site: www.appraisalinstitute.org, pg 15

Apress Media LLC, One New York Plaza, Suite 4600, New York, NY 10004-1562 Tel: 212-460-1500 E-mail: editorial@apress.com; customerservice@springernature.com Web Site: www.apress.com, pg 15

APS PRESS, 3340 Pilot Knob Rd, St Paul, MN 55121 Tel: 651-454-7250 Toll Free Tel: 800-328-7560 Fax: 651-454-0766 E-mail: aps@scisoc.org Web Site: my.apsnet.org/apsstore, pg 16

Aptara Inc, 2901 Telestar Ct, Suite 522, Falls Church, VA 22042 Tel: 703-352-0001 E-mail: moreinfo@aptaracorp.com Web Site: www.aptaracorp.com, pg 435

Aquila Communications Inc, 176 Beacon Hill, Montreal, QC H9W 1T6, Canada Toll Free Tel: 800-667-7071 Web Site: www.aquilacommunications.com, pg 395

The Arab American Book Awards, 13624 Michigan Ave, Dearborn, MI 48126 Tel: 313-429-2535 Fax: 313-582-1086 E-mail: librarian@accesscommunity.org Web Site: arabamericanmuseum.org/book-awards, pg 573

Arbordale Publishing, 612 Johnnie Dodds Blvd, Suite A2, Mount Pleasant, SC 29464 Tel: 843-971-6722 Toll Free Tel: 877-243-3457 Fax: 843-216-3804 E-mail: info@arbordalepublishing.com Web Site: www.arbordalepublishing.com, pg 16

Arcade Publishing Inc, 307 W 36 St, 11th fl, New York, NY 10018 Tel: 212-643-6816 Fax: 212-643-6819 E-mail: info@skyhorsepublishing.com (subs & foreign rts) Web Site: www.arcadepub.com, pg 16

Arcadia, 159 Lake Place S, Danbury, CT 06810-7261 Tel: 203-797-0993 E-mail: arcadialit@gmail.com, pg 449

Arcadia Publishing Inc, 210 Wingo Way, Suite 200, Mount Pleasant, SC 29464 Tel: 843-853-2070 E-mail: retailers@arcadiapublishing.com Web Site: www.arcadiapublishing.com, pg 16

ARE Press, 215 67 St, Virginia Beach, VA 23451 Tel: 757-428-3588 Toll Free Tel: 800-333-4499 Web Site: www.edgarcayce.org, pg 16

Ariadne Press, 270 Goins Ct, Riverside, CA 92507 Tel: 951-684-9202 E-mail: ariadnepress@aol.com Web Site: www.ariadnebooks.com, pg 16

Ariel Press, 2317 Quail Cove Dr, Jasper, GA 30143 Tel: 770-894-4226 E-mail: lig201@lightariel.com Web Site: www.lightariel.com, pg 16

The Arion Press, The Presidio, 1802 Hays St, San Francisco, CA 94129 Tel: 415-668-2542 Fax: 415-668-2550 E-mail: arionpress@arionpress.com Web Site: www.arionpress.com, pg 16

Arizona State University Creative Writing Program, 1102 S McAllister Ave, Rm 170, Tempe, AZ 85281 Tel: 480-965-3168 Fax: 480-965-3451 Web Site: www.asu.edu/clas/english/creativewriting, pg 561

Arkansas Diamond Primary Book Award, Arkansas State Library, Suite 100, 900 W Capitol Ave, Little Rock, AR 72201-3108 Tel: 501-682-2860 Web Site: www.library.arkansas.gov/programs/book-awards, pg 574

Arkansas State University Graphic Communications Program, Dept of Media, PO Box 1930, State University, AR 72467-1930 Tel: 870-972-3114 Fax: 870-972-3321 Web Site: www.astate.edu, pg 561

Jason Aronson Inc, 4501 Forbes Blvd, Suite 200, Lanham, MD 20706 Tel: 301-459-3366 Toll Free Tel: 800-462-6420 ext 3024 (cust serv) Fax: 301-429-5748 Toll Free Fax: 800-338-4550 (cust serv) E-mail: orders@rowman.com; customercare@rowman.com Web Site: www.rowman.com, pg 17

Arsenal Pulp Press, 211 E Georgia St, No 202, Vancouver, BC V6A 1Z6, Canada Tel: 604-687-4233 Toll Free Tel: 888-600-PULP (600-7857) Fax: 604-687-4283 E-mail: info@arsenalpulp.com Web Site: www.arsenalpulp.com, pg 395

Art Image Publications, PO Box 160, Derby Line, VT 05830 *Tel Free Tel:* 800-361-2598 *Toll Free Fax:* 800-559-2598 *E-mail:* info@artimagepublications.com; customer.service@artimagepublications.com *Web Site:* www.artimagepublications.com, pg 17

Art In Literature: The Mary Lynn Kotz Award, 800 E Broad St, Richmond, VA 23219 *Tel:* 804-692-3535 *Web Site:* www.lva.virginia.gov/public/litawards/kotz.htm; lvafoundation.org/home/literaryawards/, pg 574

The Art Institute of Chicago, 111 S Michigan Ave, Chicago, IL 60603-6404 *Tel:* 312-443-3600 *Toll Free Tel:* 855-301-9612 *E-mail:* aicshop@artic.edu *Web Site:* www.artic.edu/print-publications; shop.artic.edu, pg 17

Art of Living, PrimaMedia Inc, 1250 Bethlehem Pike, Suite 241, Hatfield, PA 19440 *Tel:* 267-421-7326 *E-mail:* info@artoflivingprimamedia.com *Web Site:* artoflivingprimamedia.com, pg 17

ArtAge Publications, PO Box 19955, Portland, OR 97280 *Tel:* 503-246-3000 *Toll Free Tel:* 800-858-4998 *Web Site:* www.seniortheatre.com, pg 17

Arte Publico Press, 4902 Gulf Fwy, Bldg 19, Rm 100, Houston, TX 77204-2004 *Tel:* 713-743-2998 (orders) *E-mail:* appinfo@uh.edu; bkorders@uh.edu *Web Site:* artepublicopress.com, pg 17

Artech House®, 685 Canton St, Norwood, MA 02062 *Tel:* 781-769-9750 *Toll Free Tel:* 800-225-9977 *Fax:* 781-769-6334 *E-mail:* artech@artechhouse.com *Web Site:* us.artechhouse.com, pg 17

Artist Fellowships, One Capital Hill, 3rd fl, Providence, RI 02908 *Tel:* 401-222-3880 *Fax:* 401-222-3018 *Web Site:* risca.online/grants/artist-fellowships, pg 574

Artist Grants, 711 E Wells Ave, Pierre, SD 57501-3369 *Tel:* 605-773-3301 *Fax:* 605-773-5977 *E-mail:* sdac@state.sd.us *Web Site:* www.artscouncil.sd.gov/grants, pg 574

Artist-in-Residence Program, 225 King St, Suite 201, Fredericton, NB E3B 1E1, Canada *Tel:* 506-444-4444 *Toll Free Tel:* 866-460-ARTS (460-2787) *Fax:* 506-444-5543 *E-mail:* prog@artsnb.ca *Web Site:* www.artsnb.ca, pg 574

Artist Research & Development Grants, 417 W Roosevelt St, Phoenix, AZ 85003-1326 *Tel:* 602-771-6501 *Fax:* 602-256-0282 *E-mail:* info@azarts.gov *Web Site:* azarts.gov/grant/artist-research-and-development, pg 574

Artists & Writers Summer Fellowships, 435 Ellis Hollow Creek Rd, Ithaca, NY 14850 *Tel:* 607-539-3146 *E-mail:* artscolony@saltonstall.org *Web Site:* www.saltonstall.org, pg 553

Arts & Letters Awards in Literature, 633 W 155 St, New York, NY 10032 *Tel:* 212-368-5900 *E-mail:* academy@artsandletters.org *Web Site:* artsandletters.org/awards, pg 574

Arts Scholarships, 225 King St, Suite 201, Fredericton, NB E3B 1E1, Canada *Tel:* 506-444-4444 *Toll Free Tel:* 866-460-ARTS (460-2787) *Fax:* 506-444-5543 *E-mail:* prog@artsnb.ca *Web Site:* www.artsnb.ca, pg 574

ArtWrite Productions, 1555 Gardena Ave NE, Minneapolis, MN 55432-5848 *Tel:* 612-803-0436 *Web Site:* artwriteproductions.com; adaptedclassics.com, pg 18

ASCD, 2800 Shirlington Rd, Suite 1001, Arlington, VA 22206 *Tel:* 703-578-9600 *Toll Free Tel:* 800-933-2723 *Fax:* 703-575-5400 *E-mail:* member@ascd.org; books@ascd.org *Web Site:* www.ascd.org, pg 18

Ascend Books LLC, 11722 W 91 St, Overland Park, KS 66214 *Tel:* 913-948-5500 *Web Site:* www.ascendbooks.com, pg 18

Ascension Press, PO Box 1990, West Chester, PA 19380 *Tel:* 484-875-4550 (admin) *Toll Free Tel:* 800-376-0520 (sales & cust serv) *Fax:* 484-875-4555 *E-mail:* orders@ascensionpress.com; newsroom@ascensionpress.com; sales@ascensionpress.com *Web Site:* ascensionpress.com, pg 18

ASCP Press, 33 W Monroe St, Suite 1600, Chicago, IL 60603 *Tel:* 312-541-4999 *Toll Free Tel:* 800-267-2727 *Fax:* 312-541-4998 *Web Site:* www.ascp.org, pg 18

ASCSA Publications, 321 Wall St, Princeton, NJ 08540-1515 *Tel:* 609-683-0800 *Web Site:* www.ascsa.edu.gr/publications, pg 18

ASET - The Neurodiagnostic Society, 402 E Bannister Rd, Suite A, Kansas City, MO 64131-3019 *Tel:* 816-931-1120 *Fax:* 816-931-1145 *E-mail:* info@aset.org *Web Site:* www.aset.org, pg 18

ASF Translation Awards, Scandinavia House, 58 Park Ave, New York, NY 10016 *Tel:* 212-779-3587 *E-mail:* grants@amscan.org *Web Site:* www.amscan.org, pg 574

Ash Tree Publishing, PO Box 64, Woodstock, NY 12498 *Tel:* 845-246-8081 *Fax:* 845-246-8081 *Web Site:* www.ashtreepublishing.com, pg 18

Ashland Creek Press, 2305 Ashland St, Suite C417, Ashland, OR 97520 *Tel:* 760-300-3620 *E-mail:* editors@ashlandcreekpress.com *Web Site:* www.ashlandcreekpress.com, pg 18

The Ashland Poetry Press, Bixler Center for the Humanities, Ashland University, 401 College Ave, Ashland, OH 44805 *E-mail:* app@ashland.edu *Web Site:* www.ashlandpoetrypress.com, pg 19

ASI Excellence in Indexing Award, 1628 E Southern Ave, Suite 9-223, Tempe, AZ 85282 *Tel:* 480-245-6750 *E-mail:* info@asindexing.org *Web Site:* www.asindexing.org/about/awards/asi-indexing-award, pg 574

Asian American Writers' Workshop (AAWW), 112 W 27 St, Suite 600, New York, NY 10001 *Tel:* 212-494-0061 *E-mail:* desk@aaww.org *Web Site:* aaww.org; facebook.com/AsianAmericanWritersWorkshop, pg 497

Asian/Pacific American Award for Literature, PO Box 677593, Orlando, FL 32867-7593 *Web Site:* www.apalaweb.org/awards/literature-awards, pg 575

ASIS International, 1625 Prince St, Alexandria, VA 22314 *Tel:* 703-519-6200 *Fax:* 703-519-6299 *E-mail:* asis@asisonline.org *Web Site:* www.asisonline.org, pg 19

ASJA Freelance Writer Search, 355 Lexington Ave, 15th fl, New York, NY 10017-6603 *Tel:* 212-997-0947 *E-mail:* asjaoffice@asja.org *Web Site:* www.asja.org/finder, pg 435

ASLE Book Awards, PO Box 502, Keene, NH 03431-0502 *Tel:* 603-357-7411 *Fax:* 603-357-7411 *E-mail:* info@asle.org *Web Site:* www.asle.org/research-write/asle-book-paper-awards, pg 575

ASLE Graduate Student Paper Awards, PO Box 502, Keene, NH 03431-0502 *Tel:* 603-357-7411 *Fax:* 603-357-7411 *Web Site:* www.asle.org/research-write/asle-book-paper-awards, pg 575

ASM International, 9639 Kinsman Rd, Materials Park, OH 44073-0002 *Tel:* 440-338-5151 *Toll Free Tel:* 800-336-5152; 800-368-9800 (Europe) *Fax:* 440-338-4634 *E-mail:* memberservicecenter@asminternational.org *Web Site:* www.asminternational.org, pg 19

ASM Publishing, 1752 "N" St NW, Washington, DC 20036-2904 *Tel:* 202-737-3600 *E-mail:* communications@asmusa.org; service@asmusa.org *Web Site:* www.asm.org; journals.asm.org, pg 19

ASME Award for Fiction, 23 Barnabas Rd, Suite 34, Hawleyville, CT 06440-0034 *Tel:* 212-872-3737 *E-mail:* asme@asme.media *Web Site:* www.asme.media, pg 575

Aspatore Books, 610 Opperman Dr, Eagan, MN 55123 *Tel:* 651-687-7000 *Toll Free Tel:* 844-209-1086 *E-mail:* globallegalproducts@thomson.com *Web Site:* store.legal.thomsonreuters.com, pg 19

Aspen Words, 110 E Hallam St, Suite 116, Aspen, CO 81611 *Tel:* 970-925-3122 *Fax:* 970-920-5700 *E-mail:* aspenwords@aspeninstitute.org *Web Site:* www.aspenwords.org, pg 497

Aspen Words Literary Prize, 110 E Hallam St, Suite 116, Aspen, CO 81611 *Tel:* 970-925-3122 *Fax:* 970-920-5700 *E-mail:* literary.prize@aspeninstitute.org *Web Site:* www.aspenwords.org/programs/literary-prize/; www.aspenwords.org, pg 575

Associated Editors, 27 W 96 St, New York, NY 10025 *Tel:* 917-744-3481; 212-662-9703, pg 435

Association des Libraires du Quebec (ALQ), 483, blvd St Joseph E, Montreal, QC H2J 1J8, Canada *Tel:* 514-526-3349 *Fax:* 514-526-3340 *E-mail:* info@alq.qc.ca *Web Site:* www.alq.qc.ca, pg 498

Association for Information Science & Technology (ASIS&T), 673 Potomac Station Dr, Suite 155, Leesburg, VA 20176 *Tel:* 301-495-0900 *Fax:* 301-495-0810 *E-mail:* asist@asist.org *Web Site:* www.asist.org, pg 19

Association for Information Science & Technology (ASIS&T), 673 Potomac Station Dr, Suite 155, Leesburg, VA 20176 *Tel:* 301-495-0900 *Fax:* 301-495-0810 *E-mail:* asist@asist.org; membership@asist.org *Web Site:* www.asist.org, pg 498

Association for Intelligent Information Management (AIIM), 8403 Colesville Rd, No 1100, Silver Spring, MD 20910 *Tel:* 301-587-8202 *Toll Free Tel:* 800-477-2446 *Fax:* 301-587-2711 *E-mail:* hello@aiim.org *Web Site:* www.aiim.org, pg 498

Association for PRINT Technologies (APTech), 113 Seaboard Lane, Suite C-250, Franklin, TN 37067 *Tel:* 703-264-7200 *E-mail:* aptech@aptech.org *Web Site:* printtechnologies.org, pg 498

Association for Talent Development (ATD) Press, 1640 King St, Box 1443, Alexandria, VA 22314-1443 *Tel:* 703-683-8100 *Toll Free Tel:* 800-628-2783 *Fax:* 703-299-8723; 703-683-1523 (cust care) *E-mail:* customercare@td.org *Web Site:* www.td.org, pg 19

Association for the Advancement of Blood & Biotherapies, North Tower, 4550 Montgomery Ave, Suite 700, Bethesda, MD 20814 *Tel:* 301-907-6977; 301-215-6499 (orders outside US) *Toll Free Tel:* 866-222-2498 (sales) *Fax:* 301-907-6895 *E-mail:* aabb@aabb.org; sales@aabb.org (ordering); publications1@aabb.org (catalog) *Web Site:* www.aabb.org, pg 19

Association for the Study of Literature and Environment (ASLE), PO Box 502, Keene, NH 03431-0502 *Tel:* 603-357-7411 *Fax:* 603-357-7411 *E-mail:* info@asle.org *Web Site:* www.asle.org, pg 498

Association nationale des editeurs de livres-ANEL (The National Association of Book Publishers), 2514, blvd Rosemont, Montreal, QC H1Y 1K4, Canada *Tel:* 514-273-8130 *Toll Free Tel:* 866-900-ANEL (900-2635) *E-mail:* info@anel.qc.ca *Web Site:* www.anel.qc.ca, pg 498

Association of American Editorial Cartoonists (AAEC), PO Box 160314, Sacramento, CA 95816 *Tel:* 954-356-4945 *E-mail:* editorialcartoonists@gmail.com *Web Site:* www.editorialcartoonists.com, pg 498

Association of American Literary Agents Inc (AALA), 302A W 12 St, No 122, New York, NY 10014 *Tel:* 212-840-5770 *E-mail:* info@aalitagents.org *Web Site:* aalitagents.org, pg 498

Association of American Publishers (AAP), 455 Massachusetts Ave NW, Suite 700, Washington, DC 20001-2777 *Tel:* 202-347-3375 *Fax:* 202-347-3690 *E-mail:* info@publishers.org *Web Site:* publishers.org, pg 498

The Association of Book Publishers of British Columbia (ABPBC), 600-402 W Pender St, Vancouver, BC V6B 1T6, Canada *Tel:* 604-684-0228 *E-mail:* admin@books.bc.ca *Web Site:* www.books.bc.ca, pg 499

Association of Canadian Publishers (ACP), 401 Richmond St W, Studio 257A, Toronto, ON M5V 3A8, Canada *Tel:* 416-487-6116 *E-mail:* admin@canbook.org *Web Site:* publishers.ca, pg 499

Association of Canadian University Presses, 542 King Edward, Ottawa, ON K1N 6N5, Canada *Tel:* 780-288-2697 *Web Site:* acup-apuc.ca, pg 499

COMPANY INDEX

Association of Catholic Publishers Inc, 4725 Dorsey Hall Dr, Suite A, PMB 709, Ellicott City, MD 21042 *Tel:* 410-988-2926 *Fax:* 410-571-4946 *E-mail:* info@catholicpublishers.org *Web Site:* www.catholicsread.org; www.catholicpublishers.org; www.midatlanticcongress.org, pg 499

Association of College & Research Libraries (ACRL), 225 N Michigan Ave, Suite 1300, Chicago, IL 60601 *Tel:* 312-280-2523; 312-280-2516 *Toll Free Tel:* 800-545-2433 (ext 2523) *Fax:* 312-280-2520 *E-mail:* acrl@ala.org; alastore@ala.org *Web Site:* www.ala.org/acrl; alastore.ala.org, pg 19

Association of College & University Printers, 2006 E Marlboro Ave, Suite 104, Hyattsville, MD 20785 *Tel:* 571-409-3533 *Web Site:* www.acup-edu.org, pg 499

Association of Community Publishers Inc (ACP), 8119 Circuit Rider Path, Cicero, NY 13039 *Toll Free Tel:* 877-203-2327 *Fax:* 315-670-3121 (memb registration) *E-mail:* info@communitypublishers.com *Web Site:* www.communitypublishers.com, pg 499

The Association of English-Language Publishers of Quebec-AELAQ (Association des Editeurs de Langue Anglaise du Quebec), Atwater Library, 1200 Atwater Ave, Suite 3, Westmount, QC H3Z 1X4, Canada *Tel:* 514-932-5633 *E-mail:* admin@aelaq.org *Web Site:* aelaq.org, pg 499

Association of Jewish Libraries Inc (AJL), PO Box 1118, Teaneck, NJ 07666 *Tel:* 201-371-3255 *E-mail:* info@jewishlibraries.org *Web Site:* jewishlibraries.org, pg 499

Association of Manitoba Book Publishers (AMBP), 100 Arthur St, Suite 404, Winnipeg, MB R3B 1H3, Canada *Tel:* 204-947-3335 *E-mail:* ambp@mymts.net *Web Site:* ambp.ca, pg 499

The Association of Medical Illustrators (AMI), 201 E Main St, Suite 810, Lexington, KY 40507 *Toll Free Tel:* 866-393-4AMI (393-4264) *E-mail:* hq@ami.org *Web Site:* www.ami.org, pg 499

Association of National Advertisers Inc (ANA), 155 E 44 St, New York, NY 10017 *Tel:* 212-697-5950 *Fax:* 212-687-7310 *E-mail:* info@ana.net *Web Site:* www.ana.net, pg 499

Association of Publishers for Special Sales (APSS), PO Box 715, Avon, CT 06001-0715 *Tel:* 860-675-1344 *Web Site:* www.bookapss.org, pg 500

Association of Research Libraries (ARL), 21 Dupont Circle NW, Suite 800, Washington, DC 20036 *Tel:* 202-296-2296 *Fax:* 202-872-0884 *E-mail:* webmgr@arl.org *Web Site:* www.arl.org, pg 20

Association of School Business Officials International, 44790 Maynard Sq, Suite 200, Ashburn, VA 20147 *Tel:* 703-478-0405 *Toll Free Tel:* 866-682-2729 *Fax:* 703-478-0205; 703-708-7060 (membership) *E-mail:* asboreq@asbointl.org; membership@asbointl.org *Web Site:* www.asbointl.org, pg 20

Association of University Presses (AUPresses), 1412 Broadway, Suite 2135, New York, NY 10018 *Tel:* 212-989-1010 *Fax:* 212-989-0275 *E-mail:* info@aupresses.org *Web Site:* www.aupresses.org, pg 500

Association of Writers & Writing Programs (AWP), 440 Monticello Ave, Suite 1802, PMB 73708, Norfolk, VA 23510-2670 *Tel:* 240-696-7700 *E-mail:* awp@awpwriter.org; press@awpwriter.org *Web Site:* www.awpwriter.org, pg 500

Asta Publications LLC, 3 E Evergreen Rd, No 1112, New York, NY 10956 *Tel:* 678-814-1320 *Toll Free Tel:* 800-482-4190 *Fax:* 678-814-1370 *E-mail:* info@astapublications.com *Web Site:* www.astapublications.com, pg 20

ASTM International, 100 Barr Harbor Dr, West Conshohocken, PA 19428-2959 *Tel:* 610-832-9500; 610-832-9585 (intl) *Toll Free Tel:* 877-909-2786 (sales & cust support) *Fax:* 610-832-9555 *E-mail:* sales@astm.org *Web Site:* www.astm.org, pg 20

Astor Indexers, 22 S Commons, Kent, CT 06757 *Tel:* 860-592-0225; 570-534-8951 (cell), pg 435

Astounding Award for Best New Writer, PO Box 61363, Sunnyvale, CA 94088 *Web Site:* www.wsfs.org/awards, pg 575

Astra Books for Young Readers, 19 W 21 St, No 1201, New York, NY 10010 *Tel:* 646-844-3485 *E-mail:* ahinfo@astrahouse.com; permissions@astrapublishinghouse.com *Web Site:* astrapublishinghouse.com, pg 20

Astra International Picture Book Writing Contest, 19 W 21 St, No 1201, New York, NY 10010 *E-mail:* astrawritingcontest@readinglife.com *Web Site:* www.readinglife.com/writingcontest, pg 575

Astragal Press, 31 E Main St, New Kingstown, PA 17072 *Tel:* 717-590-8974 *Web Site:* astragalpress.com, pg 20

The Astronomical Society of the Pacific, 390 Ashton Ave, San Francisco, CA 94112 *Tel:* 415-337-1100; 415-715-1414 (cust serv) *Toll Free Tel:* 800-335-2624 (cust serv) *Fax:* 415-337-5205 *E-mail:* service@astrosociety.org *Web Site:* astrosociety.org, pg 20

Athabasca University Press, Edmonton Learning Ctr, Peace Hills Trust Tower, 1200, 10011-109 St, Edmonton, AB T5J 3S8, Canada *Tel:* 780-497-3412 *Fax:* 780-421-3298 *E-mail:* aupress@athabascau.ca *Web Site:* www.aupress.ca, pg 395

The Athenaeum Literary Award, 219 S Sixth St, Philadelphia, PA 19106-3794 *Tel:* 215-925-2688 *Web Site:* www.philaathenaeum.org/literary.html, pg 575

Atlantic Center for the Arts Mentoring Artist-in-Residence Program, 1414 Art Center Ave, New Smyrna Beach, FL 32168 *Tel:* 386-427-6975 *E-mail:* program@atlanticcenterforthearts.org *Web Site:* atlanticcenterforthearts.org, pg 553

Atlantic Provinces Library Association (APLA), Dalhouse University, Kenneth C Rowe Management Bldg, 6100 University Ave, Suite 4010, Halifax, NS B3H 4R2, Canada *Web Site:* www.apla.ca, pg 500

Atlantic Publishing Group Inc, 1210 SW 23 Place, Ocala, FL 34471 *Tel:* 352-622-1825 *E-mail:* sales@atlantic-pub.com *Web Site:* www.atlantic-pub.com, pg 21

Atlas Publishing, 16050 Circa de Lindo, Rancho Santa Fe, CA 92091 *Tel:* 858-790-1944 *E-mail:* permissions@atlaspublishing.biz *Web Site:* www.atlaspublishing.biz, pg 21

Atria Books, 1230 Avenue of the Americas, New York, NY 10020 *Tel:* 212-698-7000 *Fax:* 212-698-7007 *Web Site:* www.simonandschuster.com, pg 21

Atwood Gibson Writers' Trust Fiction Prize, 600-460 Richmond St W, Toronto, ON M5V 1Y1, Canada *Tel:* 416-504-8222 *Toll Free Tel:* 877-906-6548 *Fax:* 416-504-9090 *E-mail:* info@writerstrust.com *Web Site:* www.writerstrust.com, pg 575

Claude Aubry Award, c/o The Canadian Children's Book Ctr, 425 Adelaide St W, Suite 200, Toronto, ON M5V 3C1, Canada *Tel:* 416-975-8970 *E-mail:* aubry@ibby-canada.org *Web Site:* www.ibby-canada.org/awards/claude-aubry-award/, pg 575

The Audies®, 333 Hudson St, Suite 503, New York, NY 10013 *E-mail:* audies@audiopub.org *Web Site:* www.audiopub.org/members/audies, pg 576

Audrey Owen, 494 Eaglecrest Dr, Gibsons, BC V0N 1V8, Canada *E-mail:* editor@writershelper.com *Web Site:* www.writershelper.com, pg 436

Augsburg Fortress Publishers, Publishing House of the Evangelical Lutheran Church in America, 411 Washington Ave N, 3rd fl, Minneapolis, MN 55401 *Tel:* 612-330-3300 *Toll Free Tel:* 800-426-0115 (ext 639, subns); 800-328-4648 (orders) *Fax:* 612-330-3455 *E-mail:* info@augsburgfortress.org; copyright@augsburgfortress.org (reprint permission requests); customercare@augsburgfortress.org *Web Site:* www.augsburgfortress.org; www.1517.media, pg 22

August House Inc, 3500 Piedmont Rd NE, Suite 310, Atlanta, GA 30305 *Tel:* 404-442-4420 *Toll Free Tel:* 800-284-8784 *Fax:* 404-442-4435 *E-mail:* ahinfo@augusthouse.com *Web Site:* www.augusthouse.com, pg 22

AUPresses Book, Jacket & Journal Show, 1412 Broadway, Suite 2135, New York, NY 10018 *Tel:* 212-989-1010 *Fax:* 212-989-0275 *E-mail:* info@aupresses.org *Web Site:* www.aupresses.org, pg 576

Aurous Inc, PO Box 20490, New York, NY 10017 *Tel:* 212-628-9729 *Fax:* 212-535-7861, pg 449

Austin Area Translators & Interpreters Association (AATIA), PO Box 92334, Austin, TX 78709-2334 *E-mail:* info@aatia.org; communications@aatia.org; membership@aatia.org; finance@aatia.org; profdev@aatia.org *Web Site:* aatia.org, pg 500

AuthorHouse, 1663 Liberty Dr, Bloomington, IN 47403 *Toll Free Tel:* 833-262-8899; 888-519-5121 *E-mail:* sales@authorhouse.com; vip@authorhouse.com *Web Site:* www.authorhouse.com, pg 22

Authorlink® Press, 103 Guadalupe Dr, Irving, TX 75039-3334 *Tel:* 972-402-0101 *E-mail:* admin@authorlink.com *Web Site:* www.authorlink.com, pg 22

Authors Alliance, 2705 Webster St, No 5805, Berkeley, CA 94705 *E-mail:* info@authorsalliance.org *Web Site:* www.authorsalliance.org, pg 500

The Authors Guild®, 31 E 32 St, Suite 901, New York, NY 10016 *Tel:* 212-563-5904 *Fax:* 212-564-5363 *E-mail:* staff@authorsguild.org *Web Site:* www.authorsguild.org, pg 500

The Authors Guild® Foundation, 31 E 32 St, Suite 901, New York, NY 10016 *Tel:* 212-563-5904 *Fax:* 212-564-5363 *E-mail:* staff@authorsguild.org *Web Site:* authorsguild.org/foundation, pg 525

Authors League Fund, 155 Water St, Brooklyn, NY 11201 *Tel:* 212-268-1208 *E-mail:* staff@authorsleaguefund.org *Web Site:* www.authorsleaguefund.org, pg 500

The Authors Registry Inc, 31 E 32 St, 7th fl, New York, NY 10016 *Tel:* 212-563-6920 *E-mail:* staff@authorsregistry.org *Web Site:* www.authorsregistry.org, pg 500

Autumn House Poetry, Fiction & Nonfiction Prizes, 5530 Penn Ave, Pittsburgh, PA 15206 *Tel:* 412-362-2665 *E-mail:* info@autumnhouse.org *Web Site:* www.autumnhouse.org; autumnhousepress.submittable.com/submit, pg 576

Autumn House Press, 5530 Penn Ave, Pittsburgh, PA 15206 *Tel:* 412-362-2665 *E-mail:* info@autumnhouse.org *Web Site:* www.autumnhouse.org, pg 22

Avant-Guide, 244 Fifth Ave, Suite 2053, New York, NY 10001-7604 *Tel:* 917-512-3881 *Fax:* 212-202-7757 *E-mail:* info@avantguide.com; communications@avantguide.com; editor@avantguide.com *Web Site:* www.avantguide.com, pg 22

Ave Maria Press Inc, PO Box 428, Notre Dame, IN 46556 *Toll Free Tel:* 800-282-1865 *Toll Free Fax:* 800-282-5681 *E-mail:* avemariapress.1@nd.edu *Web Site:* www.avemariapress.com, pg 22

Avery, c/o Penguin Random House LLC, 1745 Broadway, New York, NY 10019 *Tel:* 212-366-2000 *Web Site:* www.penguin.com/avery-overview/, pg 23

Avery Color Studios, 511 "D" Ave, Gwinn, MI 49841 *Tel:* 906-346-3908 *Toll Free Tel:* 800-722-9925 *Fax:* 906-346-3015 *E-mail:* averycolor@averycolorstudios.com *Web Site:* www.averycolorstudios.com, pg 23

Avid Reader Press, 1230 Avenue of the Americas, New York, NY 10020 *Web Site:* avidreaderpress.com, pg 23

Avotaynu Books LLC, 10 Sunset Rd, Needham, MA 02494 *Tel:* 781-449-2131 *E-mail:* info@avotaynubooks.com *Web Site:* www.avotaynubooks.com, pg 23

Award for Excellence in Poetry for Children, 340 N Neil St, Suite 104, Champaign, IL 61820 *Tel:* 217-328-3870 *Toll Free Tel:* 877-369-6283 (cust serv) *Fax:* 217-328-9645 *Web Site:* ncte.org/awards/ncte-childrens-book-awards, pg 576

AWARD OF MERIT MEDAL — COMPANY INDEX

Award of Merit Medal, 633 W 155 St, New York, NY 10032 *Tel:* 212-368-5900 *E-mail:* academy@artsandletters.org *Web Site:* artsandletters.org/awards, pg 576

AWP Award Series, 440 Monticello Ave, Suite 1802, PMB 73708, Norfolk, VA 23510-2670 *Tel:* 240-696-7700 *E-mail:* awp@awpwriter.org; press@awpwriter.org *Web Site:* www.awpwriter.org, pg 576

The Axelrod Agency, 55 Main St, Chatham, NY 12037 *Tel:* 518-392-2100, pg 449

Axiom Business Book Awards, 1129 Woodmere Ave, Suite B, Traverse City, MI 49686 *Tel:* 231-933-0445 *Toll Free Tel:* 800-706-4636 *Fax:* 231-933-0448 *E-mail:* info@axiomawards.com *Web Site:* www.axiomawards.com, pg 576

Baby Tattoo Books, 6045 Longridge Ave, Van Nuys, CA 91401 *Tel:* 818-416-5314 *E-mail:* info@babytattoo.com *Web Site:* www.babytattoo.com, pg 23

Backbeat Books, PO Box 1520, Wayne, NJ 07042-1520 *Tel:* 973-987-5363 *E-mail:* submissions@halleonardbooks.com *Web Site:* www.backbeatbooks.com, pg 23

Elizabeth H Backman, 86 Johnnycake Hollow Rd, Pine Plains, NY 12567 *Tel:* 518-398-9344 *E-mail:* bethcountry@gmail.com, pg 449

Baen Books, PO Box 1188, Wake Forest, NC 27588 *Tel:* 919-570-1640 *Fax:* 919-570-1644 *E-mail:* info@baen.com *Web Site:* www.baen.com, pg 23

Baha'i Publishing Trust, 1233 Central St, Evanston, IL 60201 *Tel:* 847-853-7899 *Toll Free Tel:* 800-999-9019 (orders) *E-mail:* bds@usbnc.org; acquisitions@usbnc.org *Web Site:* www.bahaibookstore.com, pg 23

Marilyn Baillie Picture Book Award, 425 Adelaide St W, Suite 200, Toronto, ON M5V 3C1, Canada *Tel:* 416-975-0010 *E-mail:* info@bookcentre.ca *Web Site:* www.bookcentre.ca, pg 576

Baker Books, 6030 E Fulton Rd, Ada, MI 49301 *Tel:* 616-676-9185 *Toll Free Tel:* 877-877-2665 (orders) *Fax:* 616-676-9573 *Toll Free Fax:* 800-398-3111 (orders) *E-mail:* media@bakerpublishinggroup.com; orders@bakerpublishinggroup.com; sales@bakerpublishinggroup.com *Web Site:* www.bakerpublishinggroup.com, pg 23

The Baker Street Irregulars (BSI), 3040 Sloat Rd, Pebble Beach, CA 93953 *Tel:* 831-372-8852 *E-mail:* service@bakerstreetirregulars.com *Web Site:* www.bakerstreetirregulars.com, pg 500

Nona Balakian Citation for Excellence in Reviewing, c/o Jacob M Appel, Icahn School of Medicine at Mount Sinai, One Gustave L Levy Place, New York, NY 10029 *E-mail:* info@bookcritics.org *Web Site:* www.bookcritics.org/awards/balakian/, pg 576

The Balcones Fiction Prize, Dept of Creative Writing, 6101 Highland Campus Dr, Austin, TX 78752 *Tel:* 512-223-7196; 512-223-3255 *E-mail:* balcones@austincc.edu *Web Site:* sites.austincc.edu/crw/balcones-prizes, pg 576

The Balcones Poetry Prize, Dept of Creative Writing, 6101 Highland Campus Dr, Austin, TX 78752 *Tel:* 512-223-7196; 512-223-3255 *E-mail:* balcones@austincc.edu *Web Site:* sites.austincc.edu/crw/balcones-prizes, pg 577

Malaga Baldi Literary Agency, 233 W 99, Suite 19C, New York, NY 10025 *Tel:* 212-222-3213 *E-mail:* baldibooks@gmail.com *Web Site:* www.baldibooks.com, pg 449

Ballard Spahr Prize for Poetry, 1011 Washington Ave S, Suite 300, Minneapolis, MN 55415-1246 *Tel:* 612-332-3192 *Toll Free Tel:* 800-520-6455 *Web Site:* milkweed.org/ballard-spahr-prize-for-poetry, pg 577

Ballinger Publishing, 21 E Garden St, Suite 205, Pensacola, FL 32502 *Tel:* 850-433-1166 *Fax:* 850-435-9174 *E-mail:* info@ballingerpublishing.com *Web Site:* www.ballingerpublishing.com, pg 24

Balsillie Prize for Public Policy, 600-460 Richmond St W, Toronto, ON M5V 1Y1, Canada *Tel:* 416-504-8222 *Toll Free Tel:* 877-906-6548 *Fax:* 416-504-9090 *E-mail:* info@writerstrust.com *Web Site:* www.writerstrust.com, pg 577

Carol Bancroft & Friends, PO Box 2030, Danbury, CT 06813 *Tel:* 203-730-8270 *Fax:* 203-730-8275 *E-mail:* cbfriends@sbcglobal.net; artists@carolbancroft.com *Web Site:* www.carolbancroft.com, pg 485

Bancroft Press, 4527 Glenwood Ave, La Crescenta, CA 91214 *Tel:* 818-275-3061 *Fax:* 410-764-1967 *E-mail:* bruceb@bancroftpress.com *Web Site:* www.bancroftpress.com, pg 24

Bancroft Prizes, 517 Butler Library, Mail Code 1101, 535 W 114 St, New York, NY 10027 *Tel:* 212-854-3051 *E-mail:* bancroft-prize@library.columbia.edu *Web Site:* library.columbia.edu/about/awards/bancroft.html, pg 577

B&A, 433 Broadway, Suite 420, New York, NY 10013 *Tel:* 212-682-1490 *E-mail:* info@ba-reps.com *Web Site:* www.ba-reps.com, pg 485

B&H Publishing Group, 200 Powell Place, Suite 100, Brentwood, TN 37027-7707 *Toll Free Tel:* 800-251-3225 (retailers); 800-448-8032 (consumers); 800-458-2772 (churches) *Fax:* 615-251-3914 (consumers); 615-251-5933 (churches) *Toll Free Fax:* 800-296-4036 (retailers) *E-mail:* customerservice@lifeway.com *Web Site:* www.bhpublishinggroup.com, pg 24

A Richard Barber & Associates, 80 N Main St, Kent, CT 06757 *Tel:* 860-927-4911; 212-737-7266 (cell) *Fax:* 860-927-3942 *E-mail:* barberrich@aol.com, pg 449

Barbour Publishing Inc, 1810 Barbour Dr, Uhrichsville, OH 44683 *Tel:* 740-922-6045 *Fax:* 740-922-5948 *E-mail:* info@barbourbooks.com *Web Site:* www.barbourbooks.com, pg 24

Barcelona Publishers LLC, 10231 N Plano Rd, Dallas, TX 75238 *Tel:* 214-553-9785 *E-mail:* warehouse@barcelonapublishers.com *Web Site:* www.barcelonapublishers.com, pg 24

Bard Fiction Prize, Campus Rd, PO Box 5000, Annandale-on-Hudson, NY 12504-5000 *Tel:* 845-758-7087 *E-mail:* bfp@bard.edu *Web Site:* www.bard.edu/bfp, pg 577

Barefoot Books, 23 Bradford St, 2nd fl, Concord, MA 01742 *Tel:* 617-576-0660 *Toll Free Tel:* 866-215-1756 (cust serv); 866-417-2369 (orders) *Fax:* 617-576-0049 *E-mail:* help@barefootbooks.com *Web Site:* www.barefootbooks.com, pg 24

Barnes & Noble Writers for Writers Award, 90 Broad St, Suite 2100, New York, NY 10004 *Tel:* 212-226-3586 *Fax:* 212-226-3963 *E-mail:* admin@pw.org *Web Site:* www.pw.org, pg 577

Kathleen Barnes, 238 W Fourth St, Suite 3-C, New York, NY 10014 *Tel:* 212-924-8084 *E-mail:* kbarnes@compasscommunications.org, pg 436

Baror International Inc, PO Box 868, Armonk, NY 10504-0868 *Tel:* 914-273-9199 *Fax:* 914-273-5058 *Web Site:* www.barorint.com, pg 449

Barranca Press, 17 Rockridge Rd, Mount Vernon, NY 10552 *Tel:* 347-820-2363 *E-mail:* editor@barrancapress.com *Web Site:* www.barrancapress.com, pg 24

Loretta Barrett Books, Inc, Brooklyn, NY 11231 *Tel:* 212-242-3420 *E-mail:* lbbagency@gmail.com *Web Site:* www.lorettabarrettbooks.com, pg 449

Barringer Publishing, 16398 Barclay Ct, Naples, FL 34110 *Tel:* 239-920-1668 *E-mail:* schlesadv@gmail.com *Web Site:* www.barringerpublishing.com, pg 24

Gregg Barrios Book in Translation Prize, c/o Jacob M Appel, Icahn School of Medicine at Mount Sinai, One Gustave L Levy Place, New York, NY 10029 *E-mail:* info@bookcritics.org *Web Site:* www.bookcritics.org/gregg-barrios-book-in-translation-prize/, pg 577

Barrytown/Station Hill Press, 120 Station Hill Rd, Barrytown, NY 12507 *Tel:* 845-758-5293 *E-mail:* publishers@stationhill.org *Web Site:* www.stationhill.org, pg 24

Diana Barth, 535 W 51 St, Suite 3-A, New York, NY 10019 *Tel:* 212-307-5465 *E-mail:* diabarth99@gmail.com, pg 436

Anita Bartholomew, 16650 SE Sunridge Lane, Portland, OR 97267 *Tel:* 774-264-8205 *E-mail:* anita@anitabartholomew.com *Web Site:* www.anitabartholomew.com, pg 436

Bartleby Press, 8926 Baltimore St, No 858, Savage, MD 20763 *Tel:* 301-589-5831 *Toll Free Tel:* 800-953-9929 *E-mail:* inquiries@bartlebythepublisher.com *Web Site:* www.bartlebythepublisher.com, pg 24

Basic Books Group, 1290 Avenue of the Americas, New York, NY 10104 *Tel:* 212-340-8100 *Toll Free Tel:* 800-343-4499 (cust serv) *Fax:* 212-340-8105 *E-mail:* customer.service@hbgusa.com; orders@hbgusa.com *Web Site:* www.hachettebookgroup.com/imprint/basic-books/, pg 25

Basic Health Publications Inc, 4507 Charlotte Ave, Suite 100, Nashville, TN 37209 *Tel:* 615-255-2665 *E-mail:* marketing@turnerpublishing.com, pg 25

Baskerville Publishers Poetry Award, Dept of English, TCU Box 297270, Fort Worth, TX 76129 *E-mail:* descant@tcu.edu *Web Site:* www.descant.tcu.edu, pg 577

The Mildred L Batchelder Award, 225 N Michigan Ave, Suite 1300, Chicago, IL 60601 *Tel:* 312-280-2163 *Toll Free Tel:* 800-545-2433 *Fax:* 312-280-5271 *E-mail:* alsc@ala.org *Web Site:* www.ala.org/alsc/awardsgrants/bookmedia/batchelder, pg 577

Baton Rouge Area Foundation, 100 North St, Suite 900, Baton Rouge, LA 70802 *Tel:* 225-387-6126 *Web Site:* www.braf.org, pg 525

Mark E Battersby, PO Box 527, Ardmore, PA 19003-0527 *Tel:* 610-924-9157 *Fax:* 610-924-9159 *E-mail:* mebatt12@earthlink.net *Web Site:* www.thetaxscribe.com, pg 436

Bay Area Women in Publishing (BAWiP), 680 Second St, San Francisco, CA 94107 *E-mail:* bayareawomeninpublishing@gmail.com *Web Site:* www.bayareawomeninpublishing.com, pg 500

Bayeux Arts Inc, 2403, 510-Sixth Ave SE, Calgary, AB T2G 1L7, Canada *E-mail:* mail@bayeux.com *Web Site:* bayeux.com, pg 396

Baylor University Press, Baylor University, One Bear Place, Waco, TX 76798-7363 *Tel:* 254-710-3164 *E-mail:* bup_marketing@baylor.edu *Web Site:* www.baylorpress.com, pg 25

Baylor University, Professional Writing & Rhetoric, Dept of English, One Bear Place, Unit 97404, Waco, TX 76798-7404 *Tel:* 254-710-1768 *Web Site:* english.artsandsciences.baylor.edu/undergraduate/professional-writing-rhetoric, pg 561

The BC & Yukon Book Prizes, 201-145 Keefer St, Vancouver, BC V6B 1H7, Canada *E-mail:* info@bcyukonbookprizes.com *Web Site:* www.bcyukonbookprizes.com, pg 577

BCHF Historical Writing Competition, PO Box 448, Fort Langley, BC V1M 2R7, Canada *E-mail:* info@bchistory.ca *Web Site:* www.bchistory.ca/awards/historical-writing, pg 578

Beacon Hill Press of Kansas City, PO Box 419527, Kansas City, MO 64141 *Tel:* 816-931-1900 *Toll Free Tel:* 800-877-0700 (cust serv) *Fax:* 816-531-0923 *Toll Free Fax:* 800-849-9827 *E-mail:* orders@thefoundrypublishing.com; customercare@thefoundrypublishing.com *Web Site:* www.thefoundrypublishing.com, pg 25

Beacon Press, 24 Farnsworth St, Boston, MA 02210-1409 *Tel:* 617-742-2110 *Fax:* 617-723-3097 *E-mail:* production@beacon.org *Web Site:* www.beacon.org, pg 25

Bear & Bobcat Books, 5212 Venice Blvd, Los Angeles, CA 90019 *Toll Free Tel:* 866-918-6173 *Fax:* 858-369-5201 *E-mail:* info@hameraypublishing.com (cust serv); sales@hameraypublishing.com (sales) *Web Site:* www.bearandbobcat.com, pg 26

COMPANY INDEX

Bear & Co Inc, One Park St, Rochester, VT 05767 *Tel:* 802-767-3174 *Toll Free Tel:* 800-932-3277 *Fax:* 802-767-3726 *E-mail:* customerservice@InnerTraditions.com *Web Site:* InnerTraditions.com, pg 26

James Beard Foundation Book Awards, 167 W 12 St, New York, NY 10011 *Tel:* 212-627-2308 *E-mail:* awards@jamesbeard.org *Web Site:* www.jamesbeard.org/awards, pg 578

BearManor Media, 1317 Edgewater Dr, No 110, Orlando, FL 32804 *Tel:* 760-709-9696 *Web Site:* www.bearmanormedia.com, pg 26

Bearport Publishing, 5357 Penn Ave S, Minneapolis, MN 55419 *Tel:* 212-337-8577 *Toll Free Tel:* 877-337-8577 *Fax:* 212-337-8557 *Toll Free Fax:* 866-337-8557 *E-mail:* service@bearportpublishing.com *Web Site:* www.bearportpublishing.com, pg 26

Beaver's Pond Press Inc, 939 Seventh St W, St Paul, MN 55102 *Tel:* 952-829-8818 *E-mail:* submissions@beaverspondpress.com *Web Site:* www.beaverspondpress.com, pg 26

Bedford/St Martin's, One New York Plaza, 46th fl, New York, NY 10004 *Tel:* 212-576-9400; 212-375-7000 *E-mail:* press.inquiries@macmillan.com *Web Site:* www.macmillanlearning.com/college/us, pg 26

Beehive Books, 4700 Kingsessing Ave, Suite C, Philadelphia, PA 19143 *E-mail:* beehivebook@gmail.com *Web Site:* www.beehivebooks.net, pg 26

Before Columbus Foundation, The Raymond House, 655 13 St, Suite 302, Oakland, CA 94612 *Tel:* 916-425-7916 *E-mail:* beforecolumbusfoundation@gmail.com *Web Site:* www.beforecolumbusfoundation.com, pg 525

Begell House Inc Publishers, 50 North St, Danbury, CT 06810 *Tel:* 203-456-6161 *Fax:* 203-456-6167 *E-mail:* orders@begellhouse.com *Web Site:* www.begellhouse.com, pg 27

Behrman House Inc, 241B Millburn Ave, Millburn, NJ 07041 *Tel:* 973-379-7200 *Toll Free Tel:* 800-221-2755 *Fax:* 973-379-7280 *E-mail:* customersupport@behrmanhouse.com *Web Site:* store.behrmanhouse.com, pg 27

Frederic C Beil Publisher Inc, 609 Whitaker St, Savannah, GA 31401 *Tel:* 912-233-2446 *E-mail:* fcb@beil.com *Web Site:* www.beil.com, pg 27

Hannah Beiter Graduate Student Research Grants, 140B Purcellville Gateway Dr, Suite 1200, Purcellville, VA 20132 *Tel:* 630-571-4520 *E-mail:* info@childlitassn.org *Web Site:* www.childlitassn.org, pg 578

Beliveau Editeur, 567 rue Bienville, Boucherville, QC J4B 4Z5, Canada *Tel:* 450-679-1933 *Web Site:* www.beliveauediteur.com, pg 396

Bella Books, PO Box 10543, Tallahassee, FL 32302 *Tel:* 850-576-2370 *Toll Free Tel:* 800-729-4992 *E-mail:* info@bellabooks.com; orders@bellabooks.com; ebooks@bellabooks.com *Web Site:* www.bellabooks.com, pg 27

BelleBooks, PO Box 300921, Memphis, TN 38130 *Tel:* 901-344-9024 *Fax:* 901-344-9068 *E-mail:* bellebooks@bellebooks.com *Web Site:* www.bellebooks.com, pg 27

Bellerophon Books, PO Box 21307, Santa Barbara, CA 93121-1307 *Tel:* 805-965-7034 *Toll Free Tel:* 800-253-9943 *Fax:* 805-965-8286 *E-mail:* sales.bellerophon@gmail.com *Web Site:* www.bellerophonbooks.com, pg 27

Bellevue Literary Press, 90 Broad St, Suite 2100, New York, NY 10004 *Tel:* 917-732-3603 *Web Site:* blpress.org, pg 27

The Pura Belpre Award, 225 N Michigan Ave, Suite 1300, Chicago, IL 60601 *Tel:* 312-280-2163 *Toll Free Tel:* 800-545-2433 *Fax:* 312-280-5271 *E-mail:* alsc@ala.org *Web Site:* www.ala.org/alsc/awardsgrants/bookmedia/belpre, pg 578

Don Belton Fiction Reading Period, Indiana University English Dept, Ballantine Hall 554, 1020 E Kirkwood Ave, Bloomington, IN 47405 *Tel:* 812-855-3439 *E-mail:* inreview@indiana.edu *Web Site:* indianareview.org, pg 578

Ben Yehuda Press, 122 Ayers Ct, No 1B, Teaneck, NJ 07666 *E-mail:* orders@benyehudapress.com; yudel@benyehudapress.com *Web Site:* www.benyehudapress.com, pg 27

BenBella Books Inc, 10440 N Central Expwy, Suite 800, Dallas, TX 75231-2264 *Tel:* 214-750-3600 *Web Site:* www.benbellabooks.com; www.smartpopbooks.com, pg 27

John Benjamins Publishing Co, 10 Meadowbrook Rd, Brunswick, ME 04011 *Toll Free Tel:* 800-562-5666 (orders) *Web Site:* www.benjamins.com, pg 28

George Bennett Fellowship, Phillips Exeter Academy, Off of the Dean of Faculty, 20 Main St, Exeter, NH 03833-2460 *Tel:* 603-777-3714 *E-mail:* lhearon@exeter.edu *Web Site:* www.exeter.edu/about-us/career-opportunities/fellowships/george-bennett-fellowship, pg 578

Bentley Publishers, 1734 Massachusetts Ave, Cambridge, MA 02138-1804 *Tel:* 617-547-4170 *E-mail:* sales@bentleypubs.com *Web Site:* www.bentleypublishers.com, pg 28

BePuzzled, 2030 Harrison St, San Francisco, CA 94110 *Tel:* 415-934-3705 *Toll Free Tel:* 800-347-4818 *E-mail:* info@ugames.com; consumer@ugames.com *Web Site:* universitygames.com, pg 28

Berghahn Books, 20 Jay St, Suite 512, Brooklyn, NY 11201 *Tel:* 212-233-6004 *Fax:* 212-233-6007 *E-mail:* info@berghahnbooks.com; salesus@berghahnbooks.com; editorial@journals.berghahnbooks.com *Web Site:* www.berghahnbooks.com, pg 28

Berkley, c/o Penguin Random House LLC, 1745 Broadway, 19th fl, New York, NY 10019 *Tel:* 212-366-2000 *Web Site:* www.penguin.com/publishers/berkley/; www.penguin.com/ace-overview/, pg 28

Berkshire Publishing Group LLC, 122 Castle St, Great Barrington, MA 01230 *E-mail:* info@berkshirepublishing.com; cservice@berkshirepublishing.com; rights@berkshirepublishing.com *Web Site:* www.berkshirepublishing.com, pg 28

Bernan, 4501 Forbes Blvd, Suite 200, Lanham, MD 20706 *Tel:* 717-794-3800 (cust serv & orders) *Toll Free Tel:* 800-462-6420 (cust serv & orders) *Fax:* 717-794-3803 *Toll Free Fax:* 800-338-4550 *E-mail:* customercare@rowman.com; orders@rowman.com; publicity@rowman.com *Web Site:* rowman.com/page/bernan, pg 28

Jessie Bernard Award, c/o Governance Off, 1430 "K" St NW, Suite 600, Washington, DC 20005 *Tel:* 202-383-9005 *E-mail:* asa@asanet.org; nominations@asanet.org *Web Site:* www.asanet.org/about/awards, pg 578

The Charles Bernheimer Prize, 323 E Wacker Dr, No 642, Chicago, IL 60601 *Tel:* 312-600-8072 *E-mail:* info@acla.org *Web Site:* www.acla.org/prize-awards/charles-bernheimer-prize, pg 578

Meredith Bernstein Literary Agency Inc, 2095 Broadway, Suite 505, New York, NY 10023 *Tel:* 212-799-1007 *Fax:* 212-799-1145 *E-mail:* MGoodBern@aol.com *Web Site:* www.meredithbernsteinliteraryagency.com, pg 449

Berrett-Koehler Publishers Inc, 1333 Broadway, Suite 1000, Oakland, CA 94612 *Tel:* 510-817-2277 *Fax:* 510-817-2278 *E-mail:* bkpub@bkpub.com *Web Site:* www.bkconnection.com, pg 29

The Betty Berzon Emerging Writer Award, 511 Avenue of the Americas, No D36, New York, NY 10011 *E-mail:* awards@publishingtriangle.org; info@publishingtriangle.org; publishingtriangle@gmail.com *Web Site:* publishingtriangle.org/awards/betty-berzon-award, pg 578

Bess Press Inc, 3565 Harding Ave, Honolulu, HI 96816 *Tel:* 808-734-7159 *Fax:* 808-732-3627 *E-mail:* customerservice@besspress.com *Web Site:* www.besspress.com, pg 29

Best in Business Book Award, Walter Cronkite School of Journalism & Mass Communication, Arizona State University, 555 N Central Ave, Suite 406E, Phoenix, AZ 85004-1248 *Tel:* 602-496-7862 *E-mail:* sabew@sabew.org *Web Site:* sabew.org/best-in-business-book-awards, pg 578

The Best Spiritual Literature Awards, PO Box 8385, Asheville, NC 28814 *Tel:* 828-713-1755 *E-mail:* editor@orisonbooks.com *Web Site:* www.orisonbooks.com/submissions, pg 579

Best Translated Book Award, c/o Open Letter, University of Rochester, Dewey Hall 1-219, Box 278968, Rochester, NY 14627 *Tel:* 585-319-0823 *E-mail:* contact@openletterbooks.org *Web Site:* besttranslatedbook.org, pg 579

Best Workplace in the Americas (MWA), 10015 Main St, Fairfax, VA 22031 *Tel:* 703-385-1335 *Toll Free Tel:* 888-385-3588 *Fax:* 703-273-0456 *E-mail:* assist@printing.org; info@printing.org *Web Site:* www.printing.org/programs/awards/best-workplace-in-the-americas, pg 579

Bethany House Publishers, 11400 Hampshire Ave S, Bloomington, MN 55438 *Tel:* 952-829-2500 *Toll Free Tel:* 800-877-2665 (orders) *Fax:* 952-829-2568 *Toll Free Fax:* 800-398-3111 (orders) *Web Site:* www.bethanyhouse.com; www.bakerpublishinggroup.com, pg 29

Bethlehem Books, 10194 Garfield St S, Bathgate, ND 58216 *Toll Free Tel:* 800-757-6831 *Fax:* 701-265-3716 *E-mail:* contact@bethlehembooks.com *Web Site:* www.bethlehembooks.com, pg 29

Doris Betts Fiction Prize, PO Box 21591, Winston-Salem, NC 27120-1591 *Tel:* 336-293-8844 *E-mail:* mail@ncwriters.org; nclrsubmissions@ecu.edu *Web Site:* www.ncwriters.org, pg 579

Between the Lines, 401 Richmond St W, No 281, Toronto, ON M5V 3A8, Canada *Tel:* 416-535-9914 *Toll Free Tel:* 800-718-7201 *E-mail:* info@btlbooks.com *Web Site:* btlbooks.com, pg 396

Beullah Rose Poetry Prize, 2221 Lake Ave, Baltimore, MD 21213 *E-mail:* smartishpace@gmail.com *Web Site:* www.smartishpace.com/poetry-prizes, pg 579

Beveridge Family Prize in American History, 400 "A" St SE, Washington, DC 20003 *Tel:* 202-544-2422 *E-mail:* awards@historians.org *Web Site:* www.historians.org/award-grant/beveridge-family-prize-in-american-history/, pg 579

Beveridge Family Research Grants in Western Hemisphere History, 400 "A" St SE, Washington, DC 20003 *Tel:* 202-544-2422 *E-mail:* awards@historians.org *Web Site:* www.historians.org/award-grant/beveridge-family-research-grants-in-western-hemisphere-history/, pg 579

BFMA Award of Excellence, 1147 Fleetwood Ave, Madison, WI 53716-1417 *E-mail:* bfma@bfma.org *Web Site:* www.bfma.org/page/awardsexcellence, pg 579

BFMA Professional Awards Program, 1147 Fleetwood Ave, Madison, WI 53716-1417 *E-mail:* bfma@bfma.org *Web Site:* www.bfma.org/page/awardsprofessional, pg 579

Bhaktivedanta Book Trust (BBT), 9701 Venice Blvd, Suite 3, Los Angeles, CA 90034 *Tel:* 310-837-5283 *Toll Free Tel:* 800-927-4152 *Fax:* 310-837-1056 *E-mail:* store@krishna.com *Web Site:* www.krishna.com, pg 29

BHTG - Julie Harris Playwright Award Competition, PO Box 148, Beverly Hills, CA 90213 *Tel:* 310-765-1605 *E-mail:* submissions@beverlyhillstheatreguild.com *Web Site:* www.beverlyhillstheatreguild.com, pg 580

BHTG - Michael J Libow Youth Theatre Award, PO Box 148, Beverly Hills, CA 90213 *Tel:* 310-765-1605 *E-mail:* submissions@beverlyhillstheatreguild.com *Web Site:* www.beverlyhillstheatreguild.com, pg 580

Biblio Award, PO Box 33020, Santa Fe, NM 87594 *Web Site:* biographersinternational.org/award/biblio-award, pg 580

BiblioGenesis, 152 Coddington Rd, Ithaca, NY 14850 *Tel:* 607-277-9660 *Web Site:* www.bibliogenesis.com, pg 436

Bibliographical Society of America (BSA), 67 West St, Suite 401, Unit C17, Brooklyn, NY 11222 *E-mail:* bsa@bibsocamer.org *Web Site:* bibsocamer.org, pg 500

Bibliographical Society of the University of Virginia, 2014 Hessian Rd, Charlottesville, VA 22903 *Tel:* 434-996-8663 *E-mail:* bibsoc@virginia.edu *Web Site:* bsuva.org, pg 501

BiG GUY BOOKS, 6866 Embarcadero Lane, Carlsbad, CA 92011 *Tel:* 760-652-5360 *Toll Free Tel:* 800-536-3030 (booksellers' cust serv) *E-mail:* info@greatbooksforboys.com *Web Site:* www.bigguybooks.com, pg 29

Vicky Bijur Literary Agency, 333 West End Ave, No 5B, New York, NY 10023 *Tel:* 212-580-4108 *E-mail:* queries@vickybijuragency.com *Web Site:* www.vickybijuragency.com, pg 449

Ray Allen Billington Prize, 112 N Bryan Ave, Bloomington, IN 47408-4141 *Tel:* 812-855-7311 *E-mail:* oah@oah.org *Web Site:* www.oah.org/awards, pg 580

The Geoffrey Bilson Award for Historical Fiction for Young People, 425 Adelaide St W, Suite 200, Toronto, ON M5V 3C1, Canada *Tel:* 416-975-0010 *E-mail:* info@bookcentre.ca *Web Site:* www.bookcentre.ca, pg 580

Binghamton University Creative Writing Program, c/o Dept of English, General Literature & Rhetoric, PO Box 6000, Binghamton, NY 13902-6000 *Tel:* 607-777-2168 *Fax:* 607-777-2408 *E-mail:* cwpro@binghamton.edu *Web Site:* www.binghamton.edu/english/creative-writing/index.html, pg 561

Binghamton University John Gardner Fiction Book Award, Dept of English, General Literature & Rhetoric, Bartle Library N, Rm 1149, Vestal Pkwy E, Binghamton, NY 13902 *Tel:* 607-777-2713 *Web Site:* www2.binghamton.edu/english/creative-writing, pg 580

Binghamton University Milt Kessler Poetry Book Award, Dept of English, General Literature & Rhetoric, Bartle Library N, Rm 1149, Vestal Pkwy E, Binghamton, NY 13902 *Tel:* 607-777-2713 *Web Site:* www2.binghamton.edu/english/creative-writing, pg 580

Binkley-Stephenson Award, 112 N Bryan Ave, Bloomington, IN 47408-4141 *Tel:* 812-855-7311 *E-mail:* oah@oah.org *Web Site:* www.oah.org/awards, pg 580

BIO Award, PO Box 33020, Santa Fe, NM 87594 *Web Site:* biographersinternational.org/award/the-bio-award, pg 580

Biographical Publishing Co, 95 Sycamore Dr, Prospect, CT 06712-1011 *Tel:* 203-758-3661 *Fax:* 253-793-2618 *E-mail:* biopub@aol.com *Web Site:* www.biopub.us, pg 29

Biography Fellowships, 365 Fifth Ave, Rm 6200, New York, NY 10016 *Tel:* 212-817-2025 *E-mail:* biography@gc.cuny.edu *Web Site:* llcb.ws.gc.cuny.edu/fellowships, pg 580

Paul Birdsall Prize in European Military & Strategic History, 400 "A" St SE, Washington, DC 20003 *Tel:* 202-544-2422 *E-mail:* awards@historians.org *Web Site:* www.historians.org/award-grant/paul-birdsall-prize/, pg 580

George T Bisel Co Inc, 710 S Washington Sq, Philadelphia, PA 19106-3519 *Tel:* 215-922-5760 *Toll Free Tel:* 800-247-3526 *Fax:* 215-922-2235 *E-mail:* gbisel@bisel.com *Web Site:* www.bisel.com, pg 29

BISG Industry Awards, 232 Madison Ave, Suite 1200, New York, NY 10016 *Tel:* 646-336-7141 *E-mail:* info@bisg.org *Web Site:* www.bisg.org, pg 581

Chip Bishop Fellowship, PO Box 33020, Santa Fe, NM 87594 *Web Site:* biographersinternational.org/award/chip-bishop-fellowship, pg 581

Bisk Education, 9417 Princess Palm Ave, Suite 400, Tampa, FL 33619 *Tel:* 813-621-6200 *E-mail:* media@bisk.com *Web Site:* www.bisk.com, pg 29

Bitingduck Press LLC, 1262 Sunnyoaks Circle, Altadena, CA 91001 *Tel:* 626-507-8033 *E-mail:* notifications@bitingduckpress.com *Web Site:* bitingduckpress.com, pg 30

BJU Press, 1430 Wade Hampton Blvd, Greenville, SC 29609-5046 *Tel:* 864-770-1317; 864-546-4600 *Toll Free Tel:* 800-845-5731 *E-mail:* bjupinfo@bju.edu *Web Site:* www.bjupress.com, pg 30

BkMk Press Inc, 5 W Third St, Parkville, MO 64152 *Tel:* 816-200-7895 *E-mail:* info@bkmkpress.org *Web Site:* www.bkmkpress.org, pg 30

Black Classic Press, 3921 Vero Rd, Suite F, Baltimore, MD 21203-3414 *Tel:* 410-242-6954 *Toll Free Tel:* 800-476-8870 *E-mail:* email@blackclassicbooks.com; blackclassicpress@yahoo.com *Web Site:* www.blackclassicbooks.com; www.agooddaytoprint.com, pg 30

David Black Agency, 335 Adams St, 27th fl, Suite 2707, Brooklyn, NY 11201 *Tel:* 718-852-5500 *Fax:* 718-852-5539 *Web Site:* www.davidblackagency.com, pg 450

Black Dome Press Corp, PO Box 64, Catskill, NY 12414 *Tel:* 518-577-5238 *E-mail:* blackdomep@aol.com *Web Site:* www.blackdomepress.com, pg 30

Prix Harry Black, 425 Adelaide St W, Suite 200, Toronto, ON M5V 3C1, Canada *Tel:* 416-975-0010 *E-mail:* info@bookcentre.ca *Web Site:* www.bookcentre.ca, pg 581

Black Heron Press, PO Box 614, Anacortes, WA 98221 *Tel:* 360-899-9335 *Web Site:* blackheronpress.com, pg 30

Irma Simonton & James H Black Award, 610 W 112 St, New York, NY 10025 *Tel:* 212-875-4458 *E-mail:* bookcom@bankstreet.edu *Web Site:* www.bankstreet.edu/library/center-for-childrens-literature/irma-black-award, pg 581

Black Literary Publishing Award, 154 Christopher St, Suite 3C, New York, NY 10014-9110 *Tel:* 212-741-9110 *E-mail:* info@clmp.org *Web Site:* www.clmp.org, pg 581

Black Mountain Press, PO Box 9907, Asheville, NC 28815 *Tel:* 828-273-3332 *Web Site:* www.theblackmountainpress.com, pg 30

Black Orchid Novella Award, PO Box 230822, Ansonia Sta, New York, NY 10023 *E-mail:* blackorchidaward@nerowolfe.org *Web Site:* nerowolfe.org/htm/literary_awards/black_orchid_award/Black_Orchid_award_intro.htm, pg 581

Black Rabbit Books, 2140 Howard Dr W, North Mankato, MN 56003 *Tel:* 507-388-1609 *Fax:* 507-388-2746 *E-mail:* info@blackrabbitbooks.com; orders@blackrabbitbooks.com *Web Site:* www.blackrabbitbooks.com, pg 30

Black Rose Books Ltd, CP 35788, succursale Leo-Pariseau, Montreal, QC H2X 0A4, Canada *Tel:* 514-844-4076 *E-mail:* info@blackrosebooks.com *Web Site:* blackrosebooks.com, pg 396

Black Warrior Review Fiction, Nonfiction & Poetry Contest, University of Alabama, Off of Student Media, 414 Campus Dr E, Tuscaloosa, AL 35487 *Tel:* 205-348-4518 *Fax:* 205-348-8036 *E-mail:* blackwarriorreview@gmail.com; bwr@ua.edu *Web Site:* www.bwr.ua.edu, pg 581

The Blackburn Press, PO Box 287, Caldwell, NJ 07006-0287 *Tel:* 973-228-7077 *Fax:* 973-228-7276 *Web Site:* www.blackburnpress.com, pg 30

Blair, 905 W Main St, Suite 19 D-1, Durham, NC 27701 *Tel:* 919-682-0555 *E-mail:* customersupport@blair.com *Web Site:* www.blairpub.com, pg 30

Blake-Dodd Prize, 633 W 155 St, New York, NY 10032 *Tel:* 212-368-5900 *E-mail:* academy@artsandletters.org *Web Site:* artsandletters.org/awards, pg 581

Neltje Blanchan Memorial Award, Barrett Bldg, 2nd fl, 2301 Central Ave, Cheyenne, WY 82002 *Tel:* 307-777-7742 *Web Site:* wyoarts.state.wy.us, pg 581

Eleanor Taylor Bland Crime Fiction Writers of Color Award, PO Box 442124, Lawrence, KS 66044 *Tel:* 785-842-1325 *Fax:* 785-856-6314 *E-mail:* admin@sistersincrime.org *Web Site:* www.sistersincrime.org, pg 581

Theodore C Blegen Award, 2925 Academy Rd, Durham, NC 27705 *Tel:* 919-682-9319 *Fax:* 919-682-2349 *Web Site:* foresthistory.org/awards-fellowships/blegen-award, pg 582

Norbert Blei/August Derleth Nonfiction Book Award, c/o 4414 W Fillmore Dr, Milwaukee, WI 53219 *E-mail:* wiswriters@gmail.com *Web Site:* wiswriters.org/awards, pg 582

Blood Moon Productions Ltd, 75 Saint Marks Place, Staten Island, NY 10301-1606 *Tel:* 718-556-9410 *Web Site:* bloodmoonproductions.com, pg 31

Bloom Ink, 6437 Maple Hills Dr, Bloomfield Hills, MI 48301 *E-mail:* info@bloomwriting.com *Web Site:* www.bloomwriting.com, pg 436

Bloom's Literary Criticism, 132 W 31 St, 16th fl, New York, NY 10001 *Toll Free Tel:* 800-322-8755 *Toll Free Fax:* 800-678-3633 *E-mail:* custserv@infobase.com *Web Site:* www.infobasepublishing.com; www.infobase.com (online resources), pg 31

Bloomsbury Academic, 1385 Broadway, 5th fl, New York, NY 10018 *Tel:* 212-419-5300 *Web Site:* www.bloomsbury.com/us/academic, pg 31

Bloomsbury Publishing Inc, 1385 Broadway, 5th fl, New York, NY 10018 *Tel:* 212-419-5300 *E-mail:* marketingusa@bloomsbury.com; adultpublicityusa@bloomsbury.com; askacademic@bloomsbury.com *Web Site:* www.bloomsbury.com, pg 31

Heidi Blough, Book Indexer, 732 Violet Ave, Copley, OH 44321 *Tel:* 904-806-3923 *E-mail:* indexing@heidiblough.com *Web Site:* www.heidiblough.com, pg 436

BLR®—Business & Legal Resources, 5511 Virginia Way, Suite 150, Brentwood, TN 37027 *Tel:* 860-510-0100 *Toll Free Tel:* 800-727-5257 *Toll Free Fax:* 800-785-9212 *E-mail:* media@blr.com; sales@blr.com; service@blr.com; techsupport@blr.com *Web Site:* blr.com, pg 32

Blue & Ude Writers' Services, 4249 Nuthatch Way, Clinton, WA 98236 *Tel:* 360-341-1630 *E-mail:* blue@whidbey.com *Web Site:* www.sunbreakpress.com, pg 436

Blue Bike Books, 317 Fairway Dr, Stony Plain, AB T7Z 2X2, Canada *Tel:* 780-435-2376 *Web Site:* www.bluebikebooks.com, pg 396

Blue Book Publications Inc, PO Box 184, Eva, AL 35621 *Tel:* 952-854-5229 *Toll Free Tel:* 800-877-4867 *Fax:* 952-853-1486 *E-mail:* support@bluebookinc.com *Web Site:* www.bluebookofgunvalues.com; www.bluebookofguitarvalues.com, pg 32

Blue Crane Books Inc, 36 Hazel St, Watertown, MA 02472 *Tel:* 617-926-8989, pg 32

Blue Light Books Prize, Indiana University English Dept, Ballantine Hall 554, 1020 E Kirkwood Ave, Bloomington, IN 47405 *Tel:* 812-855-3439 *E-mail:* inreview@indiana.edu *Web Site:* indianareview.org, pg 582

Blue Mountain Arts Inc, PO Box 4549, Boulder, CO 80306-4549 *Tel:* 303-449-0536 *Toll Free Tel:* 800-525-0642 *Toll Free Fax:* 800-545-8573 *E-mail:* info@sps.com; bmpbooks@sps.com (submissions) *Web Site:* www.sps.com, pg 32

The Blue Mountain Novel Award, PO Box 63927, Philadelphia, PA 19147 *Tel:* 610-764-0813 *E-mail:* hiddenriverarts@gmail.com *Web Site:* hiddenriverarts.wordpress.com, pg 582

COMPANY INDEX

Blue Note Publications Inc, 721 North Dr, Suite D, Melbourne, FL 32934 *Tel:* 321-799-2583; 321-622-6289 *Toll Free Tel:* 800-624-0401 (orders) *Fax:* 321-799-1942; 321-622-6830 *E-mail:* bluenotebooks@gmail.com *Web Site:* bluenotepublications.com, pg 32

Blue Poppy Press, 4824 SE 69 Ave, Portland, OR 97206 *Tel:* 503-650-6077 *Toll Free Tel:* 800-487-9296 *Fax:* 503-650-6076 *E-mail:* info@bluepoppy.com *Web Site:* www.bluepoppy.com, pg 32

Blue Whale Press, 237 Rainbow Dr, No 13702, Livingston, TX 77399-2037 *Toll Free Tel:* 800-848-1631 *E-mail:* info@bluewhalepress.com; sales@bluewhalepress.com *Web Site:* www.bluewhalepress.com, pg 32

BlueBridge, 8 Cottage Place, Katonah, NY 10536 *Tel:* 914-301-5901 *Web Site:* www.bluebridgebooks.com, pg 32

Bluestocking Press, 3045 Sacramento St, No 1014, Placerville, CA 95667-1014 *Tel:* 530-622-8586 *Toll Free Tel:* 800-959-8586 *Fax:* 530-642-9222 *E-mail:* customerservice@bluestockingpress.com; orders@bluestockingpress.com *Web Site:* www.bluestockingpress.com, pg 33

BMI®, 7 World Trade Center, 250 Greenwich St, New York, NY 10007-0030 *Tel:* 212-220-3000 *Toll Free Tel:* 888-689-5264 (sales) *E-mail:* newyork@bmi.com *Web Site:* www.bmi.com, pg 501

BMO Winterset Award, Newman Bldg, 2nd fl, One Springdale St, St John's, NL A1C 5H5, Canada *Tel:* 709-726-2212 *Toll Free Tel:* 866-726-2212 (NL only) *Fax:* 709-726-0619 *Web Site:* www.nlac.ca/awards/winterset.htm, pg 582

BNi Building News, 990 Park Center Dr, Suite E, Vista, CA 92081-8352 *Tel:* 760-734-1113 (pubn dept) *Toll Free Tel:* 888-BNI-BOOK (264-2665) *Web Site:* www.bnibooks.com, pg 33

BOA Editions Ltd, 250 N Goodman St, Suite 306, Rochester, NY 14607 *Tel:* 585-546-3410 *Fax:* 585-546-3913 *E-mail:* contact@boaeditions.org *Web Site:* www.boaeditions.org, pg 33

BOA Short Fiction Prize, 250 N Goodman St, Suite 306, Rochester, NY 14607 *Tel:* 585-546-3410 *E-mail:* contact@boaeditions.org *Web Site:* www.boaeditions.org/pages/boa-short-fiction-prize, pg 582

BoardSource, 750 Ninth St NW, Suite 520, Washington, DC 20001-4793 *Tel:* 202-349-2500 *E-mail:* members@boardsource.org; mediarelations@boardsource.org *Web Site:* www.boardsource.org, pg 33

Reid Boates Literary Agency, 69 Cooks Crossroad, Pittstown, NJ 08867-0328 *Tel:* 908-797-8087 *E-mail:* reid.boates@gmail.com, pg 450

Rebekah Johnson Bobbitt National Prize for Poetry, 101 Independence Ave SE, Washington, DC 20540-4861 *Tel:* 202-707-5000 *Web Site:* www.loc.gov/programs/poetry-and-literature/prizes/bobbitt-prize, pg 582

Frederick Bock Prize, 61 W Superior St, Chicago, IL 60654 *Tel:* 312-787-7070 *Web Site:* www.poetryfoundation.org/poetrymagazine/prizes, pg 582

George Bogin Memorial Award, 119 Smith St, Brooklyn, NY 11201 *Tel:* 212-254-9628 *E-mail:* info@poetrysociety.org *Web Site:* poetrysociety.org/awards, pg 582

Bogle Pratt International Library Travel Fund, c/o The American Library Association, 225 N Michigan Ave, Suite 1300, Chicago, IL 60601-7757 *Tel:* 312-280-3201 *Toll Free Tel:* 800-545-2433 (ext 3201) *Fax:* 312-280-4392 *E-mail:* intl@ala.org *Web Site:* www.ala.org, pg 582

Editions du Bois-de-Coulonge, 1142 Ave de Montigny, Quebec, QC G1S 3T7, Canada *Web Site:* www.ebc.qc.ca, pg 396

Bolchazy-Carducci Publishers Inc, 1000 Brown St, Unit 301, Wauconda, IL 60084 *Tel:* 847-526-4344 *Fax:* 847-526-2867 *E-mail:* info@bolchazy.com; orders@bolchazy.com *Web Site:* www.bolchazy.com, pg 33

Bold Strokes Books Inc, 648 S Cambridge Rd, Bldg A, Johnsonville, NY 12094 *Tel:* 518-859-8965 *E-mail:* service@boldstrokesbooks.com *Web Site:* www.boldstrokesbooks.com, pg 33

Laura Day Boggs Bolling Memorial, PO Box 36128, North Chesterfield, VA 23235-3533 *E-mail:* contest@poetrysocietyofvirginia.org; info@poetryvirginia.org *Web Site:* www.poetrysocietyofvirginia.org, pg 582

Bollingen Prize for American Poetry, 121 Wall St, New Haven, CT 06511 *Tel:* 203-432-2977 *Fax:* 203-432-4047 *E-mail:* beinecke.library@yale.edu *Web Site:* beinecke.library.yale.edu, pg 582

Bond Literary Agency, 201 Milwaukee St, Suite 200, Denver, CO 80206 *Tel:* 303-781-9305 *Web Site:* bondliteraryagency.com, pg 450

Book & Periodical Council (BPC), 36 Springhurst Ave, Toronto, ON M6K 1B6, Canada *Tel:* 416-975-9366 *E-mail:* info@thebpc.ca *Web Site:* www.thebpc.ca, pg 501

The Book Group (TBG), 20 W 20 St, Suite 601, New York, NY 10011 *E-mail:* info@thebookgroup.com; submissions@thebookgroup.com *Web Site:* www.thebookgroup.com, pg 450

Book Industry Charitable Foundation (BINC), 3135 S State St, Suite 203, Ann Arbor, MI 48108 *Toll Free Tel:* 866-733-9064 *E-mail:* info@bincfoundation.org *Web Site:* www.bincfoundation.org, pg 525

Book Industry Study Group Inc (BISG), 232 Madison Ave, Suite 1200, New York, NY 10016 *Tel:* 646-336-7141 *E-mail:* info@bisg.org *Web Site:* www.bisg.org, pg 501

Book Manufacturers' Institute Inc (BMI), 7282 55 Ave E, No 147, Bradenton, FL 34203 *Tel:* 386-986-4552 *Web Site:* bmibook.com, pg 501

Book Marketing Works LLC, 50 Lovely St (Rte 177), Avon, CT 06001 *Tel:* 860-675-1344 *Web Site:* www.bookmarketingworks.com, pg 33

Book of the Year Award, 600 Maryland Ave SW, Suite 1000W, Washington, DC 20024 *Toll Free Tel:* 800-443-8456 *Fax:* 202-314-5121 *E-mail:* foundation@fb.org *Web Site:* www.agfoundation.org/projects/book-of-the-year-award, pg 583

Book of the Year Award, William F Winter Archives & History Bldg, 200 North St, Jackson, MS 39201 *Tel:* 601-576-6936 *Fax:* 601-576-6975 *E-mail:* mhs@mdah.ms.gov *Web Site:* www.mdah.ms.gov, pg 583

Book of the Year Awards, 2667 Hyacinth St, Westbury, NY 11590 *Tel:* 516-333-0681 *E-mail:* kit@naiba.com *Web Site:* www.naiba.com/page/BooksoftheYear, pg 583

Book Publicists of Southern California, 357 S Fairfax, No 232, Los Angeles, CA 90036 *Web Site:* www.bookpublicists.org, pg 501

The Book Publishers Association of Alberta (BPAA), 11759 Groat Rd NW, 2nd fl, Edmonton, AB T5M 3K6, Canada *Tel:* 780-424-5060 *E-mail:* info@bookpublishers.ab.ca *Web Site:* bookpublishers.ab.ca; www.readalberta.ca, pg 501

Book Sales, 142 W 36 St, 4th fl, New York, NY 10018 *Tel:* 212-779-4972; 212-779-4971 *Fax:* 212-779-6058 *Web Site:* www.quartoknows.com, pg 33

The Book Tree, 3316 Adams Ave, Suite A, San Diego, CA 92116 *Tel:* 619-280-1263 *Toll Free Tel:* 800-700-8733 (orders) *Fax:* 619-280-1285 *E-mail:* orders@thebooktree.com; info@thebooktree.com *Web Site:* thebooktree.com, pg 34

BookBaby, 7905 N Crescent Blvd, Pennsauken, NJ 08110 *Tel:* 856-554-2316 *Toll Free Tel:* 877-961-6878 *E-mail:* info@bookbaby.com *Web Site:* www.bookbaby.com/book-editing-services, pg 436

Bookcase Literary Agency, 5062 Lankershim Blvd, PMB 3046, North Hollywood, CA 91601 *Web Site:* www.bookcaseagency.com, pg 450

BookCrafters LLC Editing, 24 Old Glen Rd, Morristown, NJ 07960 *Tel:* 973-984-3868 *Web Site:* bookcraftersllc.com, pg 436

BookEnds Literary Agency, 136 Long Hill Rd, Gillette, NJ 07933 *Web Site:* www.bookendsliterary.com, pg 450

Bookhaven Press LLC, 302 Scenic Ct, Moon Township, PA 15108 *Tel:* 412-494-6926 *E-mail:* info@bookhavenpress.com; orders@bookhavenpress.com *Web Site:* bookhavenpress.com, pg 34

BookLogix, 1264 Old Alpharetta Rd, Alpharetta, GA 30005 *Tel:* 470-239-8547 *E-mail:* publishing@booklogix.com; info@booklogix.com; customerservice@booklogix.com *Web Site:* www.booklogix.com, pg 34

Bookmark Literary, 189 Berdan Ave, No 101, Wayne, NJ 07470 *E-mail:* bookmarkliterary@gmail.com *Web Site:* bookmarkliterary.com, pg 451

The Bookmill, 501 Palisades Dr, No 315, Pacific Palisades, CA 90272-2848 *Tel:* 310-459-0190 *E-mail:* thebookmill1@verizon.net *Web Site:* www.thebookmill.us, pg 436

Books & Such, 2222 Queen Anne Ave, No 1005, Santa Rosa, CA 95403 *Tel:* 707-538-4184 *Web Site:* booksandsuch.com, pg 451

Books In Motion, 9922 E Montgomery Dr, Suite 31, Spokane Valley, WA 99206 *Tel:* 509-922-1646 *Toll Free Tel:* 800-752-3199 *Fax:* 509-922-1445 *E-mail:* info@booksinmotion.com *Web Site:* www.booksinmotion.com, pg 34

Books Like Us First Novel Contest, 1230 Avenue of the Americas, New York, NY 10020 *Tel:* 212-698-7000 *Web Site:* www.simonandschuster.com/p/simon-and-schuster-books-like-us, pg 583

Books on Tape™, 1745 Broadway, New York, NY 10019 *Toll Free Tel:* 800-733-3000 (cust serv) *Toll Free Fax:* 800-940-7046 *Web Site:* PenguinRandomHouseLibrary.com, pg 34

BookStop Literary Agency LLC, 67 Meadow View Rd, Orinda, CA 94563 *E-mail:* info@bookstopliterary.com *Web Site:* www.bookstopliterary.com, pg 451

BOOM! Studios, 5670 Wilshire Blvd, Suite 400, Los Angeles, CA 90036 *E-mail:* contact@boom-studios.com; customerservice@boom-studios.com; press@boom-studios.com *Web Site:* www.boom-studios.com, pg 34

Georges Borchardt Inc, 136 E 57 St, New York, NY 10022 *Tel:* 212-753-5785 *E-mail:* georges@gbagency.com *Web Site:* www.gbagency.com, pg 451

Borealis Press Ltd, 8 Mohawk Crescent, Nepean, ON K2H 7G6, Canada *Tel:* 613-829-0150 *Toll Free Tel:* 877-696-2585 *Fax:* 613-829-7783 *E-mail:* drt@borealispress.com *Web Site:* www.borealispress.com, pg 396

Boson Books™, 1262 Sunnyoaks Circle, Altadena, CA 91001 *Tel:* 626-507-8033 *Fax:* 626-818-1842 *Web Site:* bitingduckpress.com, pg 34

Boston Authors Club Inc, c/o Prof Julie Dobrow, 103 Conant Rd, Lincoln, MA 01773 *Tel:* 781-259-1220 *E-mail:* bostonauthorsclub2@gmail.com *Web Site:* bostonauthorsclub.org, pg 34

Boston Globe-Horn Book Award, c/o Book Reviews, The Horn Book Inc, Palace Road Bldg, 300 The Fenway, Suite P-311, Boston, MA 02115-5820 *Tel:* 617-278-0225 *Toll Free Tel:* 888-628-0225 *E-mail:* bghb@hbook.com *Web Site:* www.hbook.com, pg 583

The Boston Mills Press, 50 Staples Ave, Unit 1, Richmond Hill, ON L4B 0A7, Canada *Tel:* 416-499-8412 *Toll Free Tel:* 800-387-6192 *Fax:* 416-499-8313 *Toll Free Fax:* 800-450-0391 *E-mail:* service@fireflybooks.com *Web Site:* www.fireflybooks.com, pg 397

Boston University Creative Writing Program, 236 Bay State Rd, Boston, MA 02215 *Tel:* 617-353-2510 *E-mail:* crwr@bu.edu *Web Site:* www.bu.edu/creativewriting, pg 561

Bottom Dog Press, 813 Seneca Ave, Huron, OH 44839 *Tel:* 419-602-1556 *Fax:* 419-616-3966 *Web Site:* smithdocs.net, pg 34

Boulevard Magazine Short Fiction Contest for Emerging Writers, 3829 Hartford St, St Louis, MO 63116 E-mail: editors@boulevardmagazine.org Web Site: www.boulevardmagazine.org, pg 583

Bound to Stay Bound Books Scholarship, 225 N Michigan Ave, Suite 1300, Chicago, IL 60601 Tel: 312-280-2163 Toll Free Tel: 800-545-2433 Fax: 312-280-5271 E-mail: alsc@ala.org Web Site: www.ala.org/alsc/awardsgrants/scholarships; www.btsb.com/about-us/scholarships, pg 583

R R Bowker LLC, 26 Main St, Suite 102, Chatham, NJ 07928 Tel: 734-761-4700 Toll Free Tel: 888-269-5372 (edit & cust serv); 800-521-0600 Toll Free Fax: 877-337-7015 (US & CN) E-mail: isbn-san@bowker.com; isbn-san@proquest.com Web Site: www.bowker.com, pg 34

Bowling Green State University Creative Writing Program, Dept of English, 212 East Hall, Bowling Green, OH 43403-0001 Tel: 419-372-6864; 419-372-2576 Fax: 419-372-0333 E-mail: english@bgsu.edu Web Site: www.bgsu.edu/academics/creative-writing, pg 561

Boydell & Brewer Inc, 668 Mount Hope Ave, Rochester, NY 14620-2731 Tel: 585-275-0419 Fax: 585-271-8778 E-mail: boydell@boydellusa.net Web Site: www.boydellandbrewer.com, pg 35

Boys Town Press, 13603 Flanagan Blvd, 2nd fl, Boys Town, NE 68010 Tel: 531-355-1320 Toll Free Tel: 800-282-6657 Fax: 531-355-1310 E-mail: btpress@boystown.org Web Site: www.boystownpress.org, pg 35

BPA Worldwide, 100 Beard Sawmill Rd, 6th fl, Shelton, CT 06484 Tel: 203-447-2800 Fax: 203-447-2900 E-mail: info@bpaww.com Web Site: www.bpaww.com, pg 501

BPC, 415 Farm Rd, Summertown, TN 38483 Tel: 931-964-3571 Toll Free Tel: 888-260-8458 Fax: 931-964-3518 E-mail: info@bookpubco.com Web Site: www.bookpubco.com, pg 35

BPS Books, 47 Anderson Ave, Toronto, ON M5P 1H6, Canada Tel: 416-609-2004 Web Site: www.bpsbooks.com, pg 397

Bradford Literary Agency, 5694 Mission Center Rd, Suite 347, San Diego, CA 92108 Tel: 619-521-1201 E-mail: hillary@bradfordlit.com Web Site: www.bradfordlit.com, pg 451

Brady Literary Management, PO Box 64, Hartland Four Corners, VT 05049 Tel: 802-436-2455, pg 436

BrainStorm Poetry Contest for Mental Health Consumers, 36 Elgin St, 2nd fl, Sudbury, ON P3C 5B4, Canada Tel: 705-222-6472 (ext 303) E-mail: openminds@nisa.on.ca Web Site: www.openmindsquarterly.com/poetry-contest, pg 583

Brandt & Hochman Literary Agents Inc, 1501 Broadway, Suite 2310, New York, NY 10036 Tel: 212-840-5760 Fax: 212-840-5776 Web Site: brandthochman.com, pg 452

Brandylane Publishers Inc, 5 S First St, Richmond, VA 23219 Tel: 804-644-3090 Web Site: brandylanepublishers.com, pg 35

Michael Braude Award, 633 W 155 St, New York, NY 10032 Tel: 212-368-5900 E-mail: academy@artsandletters.org Web Site: artsandletters.org/awards, pg 583

Brault & Bouthillier, 700 ave Beaumont, Montreal, QC H3N 1V5, Canada Tel: 514-273-0178 Fax: 514-273-8627 Toll Free Fax: 800-361-0378 E-mail: communicationbb@bb.ca Web Site: bb.ca, pg 397

Barbara Braun Associates Inc, 7 E 14 St, Suite 19F, New York, NY 10003 Tel: 917-414-3022 Web Site: barbarabraunagency.com, pg 452

Lilian Jackson Braun Award, 1140 Broadway, Suite 1507, New York, NY 10001 Tel: 212-888-8171 E-mail: mwa@mysterywriters.org Web Site: mysterywriters.org/edgars/lilian-jackson-braun-award, pg 583

BRAVE Books, 13614 Poplar Circle, Suite 302, Conroe, TX 77304 Tel: 932-380-5648 E-mail: info@brave.us Web Site: bravebooks.us, pg 35

George Braziller Inc, 90 Broad St, Suite 2100, New York, NY 10004 Tel: 212-260-9256 E-mail: editorial@georgebraziller.com Web Site: www.georgebraziller.com, pg 35

Bread Loaf Fellowships & Scholarships, Middlebury College, 204 College St, Middlebury, VT 05753 Tel: 802-443-5286 Fax: 802-443-2087 E-mail: blwc@middlebury.edu Web Site: www.middlebury.edu/blwc, pg 584

Bread Loaf Writers' Conference, 204 College St, Middlebury, VT 05753 Tel: 802-443-5286 Fax: 802-443-2087 E-mail: blwc@middlebury.edu Web Site: www.middlebury.edu/blwc, pg 553

Breakaway Books, PO Box 24, Halcottsville, NY 12438-0024 E-mail: breakawaybooks@gmail.com Web Site: www.breakawaybooks.com, pg 36

Breakthrough Publications Inc, 3 Iroquois St, Emmaus, PA 18049 Tel: 610-928-4062 E-mail: dot@booksonhorses.com; ruth@booksonhorses.com Web Site: www.booksonhorses.com, pg 36

Breakwater Books Ltd, One Stamp's Lane, St John's, NL A1C 6E6, Canada Tel: 709-722-6680 Toll Free Tel: 800-563-3333 (orders) Fax: 709-753-0708 E-mail: info@breakwaterbooks.com; orders@breakwaterbooks.com Web Site: www.breakwaterbooks.com, pg 397

Nicholas Brealey Publishing, 53 State St, 9th fl, Boston, MA 02109 Tel: 617-523-3801 E-mail: sales-us@nicholasbrealey.com Web Site: nbuspublishing.com, pg 36

Brentwood Christian Press, PO Box 4773, Columbus, GA 31914-4773 Toll Free Tel: 800-334-8861 E-mail: brentwood@aol.com Web Site: www.brentwoodbooks.com, pg 36

Brethren Press, 1451 Dundee Ave, Elgin, IL 60120 Tel: 847-742-5100 Toll Free Tel: 800-441-3712 Toll Free Fax: 800-667-8188 E-mail: brethrenpress@brethren.org Web Site: www.brethrenpress.com, pg 36

Brewers Publications, 1327 Spruce St, Boulder, CO 80302 Tel: 303-447-0816 Toll Free Tel: 888-822-6273 (CN & US) Fax: 303-447-2825 E-mail: info@brewersassociation.org Web Site: www.brewersassociation.org, pg 36

The Briar Cliff Review Fiction, Poetry & Creative Nonfiction Contest, 3303 Rebecca St, Sioux City, IA 51104-2100 Tel: 712-279-1651 Fax: 712-279-5486 Web Site: www.bcreview.org, pg 584

Brick Books, 22 Spencer Ave, Toronto, ON M6K 2J6, Canada Tel: 416-455-8385 Web Site: www.brickbooks.ca, pg 397

Brick Road Poetry Book Contest, 341 Lee Rd 553, Phenix City, AL 36867 Web Site: www.brickroadpoetrypress.com/poetry-book-contest, pg 584

Brick Tower Press, Manhanset House, PO Box 342, Shelter Island Heights, NY 11965-0342 Tel: 212-427-7139 Toll Free Tel: 800-68-BRICK (682-7425) E-mail: bricktower@aol.com Web Site: bricktowerpress.com, pg 36

Bridge Logos Inc, 14260 W Newberry Rd, Newberry, FL 32669-2765 E-mail: info@bridgelogos.com Web Site: www.bridgelogos.com, pg 36

Bridge Publications Inc, 5600 E Olympic Blvd, Commerce, CA 90022 Tel: 323-888-6200 Toll Free Tel: 800-722-1733 Fax: 323-888-6202 E-mail: info@bridgepub.com Web Site: www.bridgepub.com, pg 36

Bridge to Asia, 1505 Juanita Way, Berkeley, CA 94702, pg 525

Brigantine Media, 211 North Ave, St Johnsbury, VT 05819 Tel: 802-751-8802 Fax: 802-751-8804 Web Site: brigantinemedia.com, pg 37

Brill Inc, 10 Liberty Sq, 3rd fl, Boston, MA 02109 Tel: 617-263-2323 Fax: 617-263-2324 E-mail: sales@brill.com Web Site: www.brill.com, pg 37

Brilliance Publishing Inc, 1704 Eaton Dr, Grand Haven, MI 49417 Tel: 616-846-5256 Toll Free Tel: 800-648-2312 (orders only) E-mail: brilliance-publishing@amazon.com; customerservice@brilliancepublishing.com; media@brilliancepublishing.com; publicity@brilliancepublishing.com Web Site: www.brilliancepublishing.com, pg 37

Ann Conner Brimer Award for Atlantic Canadian Children's Literature, 1113 Marginal Rd, Halifax, NS B3H 4P7, Canada Tel: 902-423-8116 Fax: 902-422-0881 E-mail: wits@writers.ns.ca (awards) Web Site: writers.ns.ca, pg 584

Brindle & Glass Publishing Ltd, 103-1075 Pendergast St, Victoria, BC V8V 0A1, Canada Tel: 250-360-0829 Fax: 250-386-0829 E-mail: info@touchwoodeditions.com Web Site: www.touchwoodeditions.com, pg 397

Bristol Park Books, 252 W 38 St, Suite 206, New York, NY 10018 Tel: 212-842-0700 Fax: 212-842-1771 E-mail: info@bristolparkbooks.com Web Site: www.bristolparkbooks.com, pg 37

Brittingham & Pollak Prizes in Poetry, Dept of English, 600 N Park St, Madison, WI 53706 Web Site: creativewriting.wisc.edu/submit.html, pg 584

Broadview Press, 280 Perry St, Unit 5, Peterborough, ON K9J 2J4, Canada Tel: 705-482-5915 Fax: 705-743-8353 E-mail: customerservice@broadviewpress.com Web Site: www.broadviewpress.com, pg 397

Brockman Inc, 260 Fifth Ave, 10th fl, New York, NY 10001 Tel: 212-935-8900 E-mail: rights@brockman.com Web Site: www.brockman.com, pg 452

Sophie Brody Medal, 225 N Michigan Ave, Suite 1300, Chicago, IL 60601 Web Site: rusaupdate.org/awards/sophie-brody-medal, pg 584

Paul H Brookes Publishing Co Inc, PO Box 10624, Baltimore, MD 21285-0624 Tel: 410-337-9580 (outside US & CN) Toll Free Tel: 800-638-3775 (US & CN) Fax: 410-337-8539 E-mail: custserv@brookespublishing.com Web Site: www.brookespublishing.com, pg 37

The Brookings Institution Press, 1775 Massachusetts Ave NW, Washington, DC 20036-2188 Tel: 202-797-6000 E-mail: permissions@brookings.edu Web Site: www.brookings.edu, pg 37

Brookline Books, 8 Trumbull Rd, Suite B-001, Northampton, MA 01060 Fax: 413-584-6184 E-mail: brbooks@yahoo.com, pg 37

Brooklyn Public Library Literary Prize, 10 Grand Army Plaza, Brooklyn, NY 11238 Tel: 718-230-2100 E-mail: brooklyneagles@bklynlibrary.org Web Site: www.bklynlibrary.org/support/bpl-literary-prize, pg 584

Brooklyn Publishers LLC, PO Box 248, Cedar Rapids, IA 52406 Tel: 319-368-8012 Toll Free Tel: 888-473-8521 Fax: 319-368-8011 E-mail: customerservice@brookpub.com; editor@brookpub.com Web Site: www.brookpub.com, pg 37

Broquet Inc, 97-B, Montee des Bouleaux, St-Constant, QC J5A 1A9, Canada Tel: 450-638-3338 Fax: 450-638-4338 E-mail: info@broquet.qc.ca Web Site: www.broquet.qc.ca, pg 397

Brower Literary & Management Inc, 13720 Old St Augustine Rd, Suite 8-512, Jacksonville, FL 32258 Tel: 646-854-6073 E-mail: admin@browerliterary.com; foreign@browerliterary.com (foreign publr inquiries); queries@browerliterary.com; subrights@browerliterary.com (busn inquiries) Web Site: browerliterary.com, pg 452

Brown Books Publishing Group (BBPG), 16250 Knoll Trail, Suite 205, Dallas, TX 75248 Tel: 972-381-0009 E-mail: publishing@brownbooks.com Web Site: www.brownbooks.com, pg 38

Curtis Brown, Ltd, 228 E 45 St, Suite 310, New York, NY 10017 Tel: 212-473-5400 Fax: 212-598-0917 E-mail: info@cbltd.com Web Site: www.curtisbrown.com, pg 452

COMPANY INDEX

John Nicholas Brown Prize, 6 Beacon St, Suite 500, Boston, MA 02108 *Tel:* 617-491-1622 *Fax:* 617-492-3303 *E-mail:* info@themedievalacademy.org *Web Site:* www.medievalacademy.org/page/brown_prize, pg 584

Kurt Brown Prizes, 440 Monticello Ave, Suite 1802, PMB 73708, Norfolk, VA 23510-2670 *Tel:* 240-696-7700 *E-mail:* awp@awpwriter.org *Web Site:* www.awpwriter.org/contests/kurt_brown_prizes_overview, pg 584

Marie Brown Associates, 412 W 154 St, New York, NY 10032 *Tel:* 212-939-9725 *E-mail:* mbrownlit@gmail.com, pg 452

Browne & Miller Literary Associates, 52 Village Place, Hinsdale, IL 60521 *Tel:* 312-922-3063 *E-mail:* mail@browneandmiller.com *Web Site:* www.browneandmiller.com, pg 452

John Brubaker Award, 8550 United Plaza Blvd, Suite 1001, Baton Rouge, LA 70809 *Tel:* 225-408-4417 *E-mail:* cla2@cathla.org *Web Site:* cathla.org, pg 584

Brush Education Inc, 6531-111 St NW, Edmonton, AB T6H 4R5, Canada *Tel:* 780-989-0910 *Toll Free Tel:* 855-283-0900 *Fax:* 780-989-0930 *Toll Free Fax:* 855-283-6947 *E-mail:* contact@brusheducation.ca *Web Site:* www.brusheducation.ca, pg 397

Robert Bruss Real Estate Book Awards, 1003 NW Sixth Terr, Boca Raton, FL 33486-3455 *Tel:* 561-391-3599 *E-mail:* nareeprograms@gmail.com *Web Site:* www.naree.org/bookcontest, pg 584

BSFS Poetry Contest, PO Box 686, Baltimore, MD 21203-0686 *Tel:* 410-563-2737 *E-mail:* poetry@bsfs.org *Web Site:* www.bsfs.org/bsfspoetry.htm, pg 585

Buchwald, 10 E 44 St, New York, NY 10017 *Tel:* 212-867-1200 *E-mail:* info@buchwald.com *Web Site:* www.buchwald.com, pg 453

Bucknell University Press, One Dent Dr, Lewisburg, PA 17837 *Tel:* 570-577-1049 *E-mail:* universitypress@bucknell.edu *Web Site:* www.bucknell.edu/universitypress, pg 38

Sally Buckner Emerging Writers' Fellowship, PO Box 21591, Winston-Salem, NC 27120-1591 *Tel:* 336-293-8844 *E-mail:* mail@ncwriters.org; nclrsubmissions@ecu.edu *Web Site:* www.ncwriters.org, pg 585

Georges Bugnet Award for Fiction, 11759 Groat Rd NW, Edmonton, AB T5M 3K6, Canada *Tel:* 780-422-8174 *Toll Free Tel:* 800-665-5354 (AB only) *E-mail:* mail@writersguild.ab.ca *Web Site:* writersguild.ca, pg 585

BuilderBooks, 1201 15 St NW, Washington, DC 20005 *Toll Free Tel:* 800-368-5242 *E-mail:* info@nahb.com *Web Site:* builderbooks.com, pg 38

The Bukowski Agency Ltd, 20 Prince Arthur Ave, Suite 12-I, Toronto, ON M5R 1B1, Canada *Tel:* 416-928-6728 *Fax:* 416-963-9978 *E-mail:* info@bukowskiagency.com *Web Site:* www.bukowskiagency.com, pg 453

Bull Publishing Co, PO Box 1377, Boulder, CO 80306 *Tel:* 303-545-6350 *Toll Free Tel:* 800-676-2855 *E-mail:* sales@bullpub.com *Web Site:* www.bullpub.com, pg 38

The Bureau for At-Risk Youth, 40 Aero Rd, Unit 2, Bohemia, NY 11716 *Toll Free Tel:* 800-99YOUTH (999-6884) *Toll Free Fax:* 800-262-1886 *Web Site:* www.at-risk.com, pg 38

Bureau of Economic Geology, c/o The University of Texas at Austin, 10100 Burnet Rd, Bldg 130, Austin, TX 78758 *Tel:* 512-471-1534 *Fax:* 512-471-0140 *E-mail:* pubsales@beg.utexas.edu *Web Site:* www.beg.utexas.edu, pg 38

Burford Books, 101 E State St, No 301, Ithaca, NY 14850 *Tel:* 607-319-4373 *Fax:* 607-319-4373 *Toll Free Fax:* 866-212-7750 *E-mail:* info@burfordbooks.com *Web Site:* www.burfordbooks.com, pg 38

Hilary R Burke, 59 Sparks St, Ottawa, ON K1P 6C3, Canada *Tel:* 613-237-4658 *E-mail:* hburke99@yahoo.com, pg 436

Burns Archive Press, 140 E 38 St, New York, NY 10016 *Tel:* 212-889-1938 *E-mail:* info@burnsarchive.com *Web Site:* www.burnsarchive.com, pg 38

Burns Entertainment, 3637 Westfield Lane, Glenview, IL 60026 *Tel:* 847-866-9400 *Web Site:* burnsent.com, pg 487

John Burroughs Medal, 500 Burroughs Dr, at Floyd Ackert, New York, NY 12493 *Tel:* 845-384-6556 *E-mail:* info@johnburroughsassociation.org *Web Site:* www.johnburroughsassociation.org, pg 585

John Burroughs Nature Essay Award, 500 Burroughs Dr, at Floyd Ackert, New York, NY 12493 *Tel:* 845-384-6556 *E-mail:* info@johnburroughsassociation.org *Web Site:* www.johnburroughsassociation.org, pg 585

Business Expert Press, 222 E 46 St, Suite 203, New York, NY 10017-2906 *Tel:* 212-661-8810 *Fax:* 646-478-8107 *E-mail:* sales@businessexpertpress.com *Web Site:* www.businessexpertpress.com, pg 38

Business Forms Management Association (BFMA), 1147 Fleetwood Ave, Madison, WI 53716-1417 *E-mail:* bfma@bfma.org *Web Site:* www.bfma.org, pg 502

Business Marketing NYC, 155 E 44 St, New York, NY 10017 *Tel:* 212-697-5950 *Fax:* 212-687-7310 *E-mail:* info@ana.net *Web Site:* www.anab2b.nyc; www.marketing.org, pg 502

Business Research Services Inc, PO Box 42674, Washington, DC 20015 *Tel:* 301-229-5561 *Toll Free Fax:* 877-516-0818 *E-mail:* brspubs@sba8a.com *Web Site:* www.sba8a.com; www.setasidealert.com, pg 38

BWL Publishing Inc, 5030 44 St, Drayton Valley, AB T7A 1B9, Canada *Tel:* 780-833-1215 *E-mail:* bookswelove@telus.net *Web Site:* bookswelove.net; bwlpublishing.ca, pg 398

Byer-Sprinzeles Agency, 5800 Arlington Ave, Suite 16-C, Riverdale, NY 10471 *Tel:* 718-543-9399 *Web Site:* www.maggiebyersprinzeles.com, pg 485

Sheree Bykofsky Associates Inc, PO Box 706, Brigantine, NJ 08203 *E-mail:* shereebee@aol.com *Web Site:* www.shereebee.com, pg 453

Bywater Books Inc, 3415 Porter Rd, Ann Arbor, MI 48103 *Tel:* 734-662-8815 *Web Site:* bywaterbooks.com, pg 39

BZ/Rights & Permissions Inc, 145 W 86 St, New York, NY 10024 *Tel:* 212-924-3000 *Fax:* 212-924-2525 *E-mail:* info@bzrights.com *Web Site:* www.bzrights.com, pg 436

CAA Speakers, 2000 Avenue of the Stars, Los Angeles, CA 90067 *Tel:* 424-288-2000 *Fax:* 424-288-2900 *E-mail:* speakers@caa.com *Web Site:* www.caa.com/caaspeakers, pg 487

Cabell First Novelist Award, 901 Park Ave, Richmond, VA 23284 *Tel:* 804-828-0593 *E-mail:* cabellfn@vcu.edu *Web Site:* firstnovelist.vcu.edu, pg 585

Gerald Cable Book Award, PO Box 3541, Eugene, OR 97403 *Tel:* 541-228-0422 *E-mail:* sfrpress@gmail.com *Web Site:* www.silverfishreviewpress.com, pg 585

The Randolph Caldecott Medal, 225 N Michigan Ave, Suite 1300, Chicago, IL 60601 *Tel:* 312-280-2163 *Toll Free Tel:* 800-545-2433 *Fax:* 312-280-5271 *E-mail:* alsc@ala.org *Web Site:* www.ala.org/alsc/awardsgrants/bookmedia/caldecott, pg 585

CALIBA Golden Poppy Awards, 100 Black Diamond Rd, Stonyford, CA 95979 *Tel:* 415-561-7686 *E-mail:* info@caliballiance.org *Web Site:* caliballiance.org/golden-poppy-awards.html, pg 585

California Book Awards, 110 The Embarcadero, San Francisco, CA 94105 *Tel:* 415-597-6700 *Fax:* 415-597-6729 *E-mail:* bookawards@commonwealthclub.org *Web Site:* www.commonwealthclub.org/bookawards, pg 585

California Independent Booksellers Alliance (CALIBA), 100 Black Diamond Rd, Stonyford, CA 95979 *Tel:* 415-561-7686 *E-mail:* info@caliballiance.org *Web Site:* caliballiance.org, pg 502

California Writers Club (CWC), PO Box 201, Danville, CA 94526 *E-mail:* membership@calwriters.org; advertising-promotion@calwriters.org *Web Site:* calwriters.org, pg 502

California Young Playwrights Contest, 3675 Ruffin Rd, Suite 330, San Diego, CA 92123 *Tel:* 858-384-2970 *Fax:* 858-384-2974 *E-mail:* write@playwrightsproject.org *Web Site:* www.playwrightsproject.org, pg 586

Matei Calinescu Prize, 85 Broad St, New York, NY 10004 *Tel:* 646-576-5141; 646-576-5000 *E-mail:* awards@mla.org *Web Site:* www.mla.org, pg 586

Callawind Publications Inc, 3551 St Charles Blvd, Suite 179, Kirkland, QC H9H 3C4, Canada *Tel:* 514-685-9109 *E-mail:* info@callawind.com *Web Site:* www.callawind.com, pg 398

Calligraph LLC, 45 Main St, No 850, Brooklyn, NY 11201 *Tel:* 212-253-1074 *E-mail:* mail@calligraphlit.com; rights@calligraphlit.com; submissions@calligraphlit.com *Web Site:* www.calligraphlit.com, pg 453

Cambridge University Press, One Liberty Plaza, 20th fl, New York, NY 10006 *Tel:* 212-924-3900; 212-337-5000 *Fax:* 212-691-3239; 845-353-4141 *E-mail:* customer_service@cambridge.org; orders@cambridge.org; subscriptions_newyork@cambridge.org *Web Site:* www.cambridge.org/us, pg 39

Kimberley Cameron & Associates LLC, 1550 Tiburon Blvd, Suite 704, Tiburon, CA 94920 *E-mail:* info@kimberleycameron.com *Web Site:* www.kimberleycameron.com, pg 453

Camino Books Inc, PO Box 59026, Philadelphia, PA 19102-9026 *Tel:* 215-413-1917 *Fax:* 215-413-3255 *E-mail:* camino@caminobooks.com *Web Site:* www.caminobooks.com, pg 39

Joe Pendleton Campbell Narrative Contest, PO Box 36128, North Chesterfield, VA 23235-3533 *E-mail:* contest@poetrysocietyofvirginia.org; info@poetryvirginia.org *Web Site:* www.poetrysocietyofvirginia.org, pg 586

Campfield & Campfield Publishing LLC, 6521 Cutler St, Philadelphia, PA 19126 *Toll Free Tel:* 888-518-2440 *Fax:* 215-224-6696 *E-mail:* info@campfieldspublishing.com *Web Site:* www.campfieldspublishing.com, pg 39

Canada Council for the Arts (Conseil des arts du Canada), 150 Elgin St, 2nd fl, Ottawa, ON K2P 1L4, Canada *Tel:* 613-566-4414 *Toll Free Tel:* 800-263-5588 (CN only) *Fax:* 613-566-4390 *E-mail:* info@canadacouncil.ca; media@canadacouncil.ca *Web Site:* canadacouncil.ca, pg 502

Canada-Japan Literary Awards, 150 Elgin St, 2nd fl, Ottawa, ON K2P 1L4, Canada *Tel:* 613-566-4414 *Toll Free Tel:* 800-263-5588 (CN only) *Fax:* 613-566-4390 *E-mail:* canadajapan-prizes@canadacouncil.ca *Web Site:* canadacouncil.ca/funding/prizes/canada-japan-literary-awards, pg 586

Canadian Authors Association (CAA), 45 Penetang St, Orillia, ON L3V 3N3, Canada *Tel:* 705-955-0716 *E-mail:* office@canadianauthors.org *Web Site:* www.canadianauthors.org, pg 502

Canadian Bible Society, 10 Carnforth Rd, Toronto, ON M4A 2S4, Canada *Tel:* 416-757-4171 *Toll Free Tel:* 800-465-2425 *Fax:* 416-757-3376 *E-mail:* customerservice@biblesociety.ca *Web Site:* www.biblescanada.com; www.biblesociety.ca, pg 398

Canadian Bookbinders and Book Artists Guild (CBBAG), 82809-467 Parliament St, Toronto, ON M5A 3Y2, Canada *E-mail:* cbbag@cbbag.ca *Web Site:* www.cbbag.ca, pg 502

Canadian Cataloguing in Publication Program, Library & Archives Canada, 395 Wellington St, Ottawa, ON K1A 0N4, Canada *Tel:* 819-994-6881 *Toll Free Tel:* 866-578-7777 (CN) *Fax:* 819-934-6777 *E-mail:* bac.cip.lac@canada.ca *Web Site:* www.bac-lac.gc.ca/eng/services/cip/pages/cip.aspx, pg 502

The Canadian Children's Book Centre, 425 Adelaide St W, Suite 200, Toronto, ON M5V 3C1, Canada *Tel:* 416-975-0010 *E-mail:* info@bookcentre.ca *Web Site:* www.bookcentre.ca, pg 502

The Canadian Circulations Audit Board (CCAB), 111 Queen St E, Suite 450, Toronto, ON M5C 1S2, Canada *Toll Free Tel:* 877-302-8348 *Web Site:* www.bpaww.com, pg 502

Canadian Circumpolar Institute (CCI) Press, 1-16 Rutherford Library South, 11204 89 Ave NW, Edmonton, AB T6G 2J4, Canada *Tel:* 780-492-3662 *Web Site:* www.uap.ualberta.ca, pg 398

Canadian First Book Prize, 363 Parkridge Crescent, Oakville, ON L6M 1A8, Canada *Tel:* 905-618-0420 *E-mail:* info@griffinpoetryprize.com; publicity@griffinpoetryprize.com *Web Site:* griffinpoetryprize.com, pg 586

Canadian Independent Booksellers Association (CIBA), 188 Dublin St N, Guelph, ON N1H 4P2, Canada *E-mail:* info@cibabooks.ca *Web Site:* cibabooks.ca, pg 502

Canadian Institute for Studies in Publishing (CISP), Simon Fraser University at Harbour Centre, 515 W Hastings St, Suite 3576, Vancouver, BC V6B 5K3, Canada *Tel:* 778-782-5242 *E-mail:* pub-info@sfu.ca *Web Site:* publishing.sfu.ca/research-2, pg 502

Canadian Institute of Resources Law (L'Institut canadien du droit des ressources), Faculty of Law, University of Calgary, 2500 University Dr NW, MFH 3353, Calgary, AB T2N 1N4, Canada *Tel:* 403-220-3200 *Fax:* 403-282-6182 *E-mail:* cirl@ucalgary.ca *Web Site:* www.cirl.ca, pg 398

Canadian Institute of Ukrainian Studies Press, University of Toronto, 47 Queen's Park Crescent E, Suite B-12, Toronto, ON M5S 2C3, Canada *Tel:* 416-946-7326 *E-mail:* cius@ualberta.ca *Web Site:* www.ciuspress.com, pg 398

The Canadian Jewish Literary Awards, Koschitzy Centre for Jewish Studies, 763 Kaneff Tower, York University, 4700 Keele St, Toronto, ON M3J 1P3, Canada *E-mail:* info@cjlawards.ca; cjs@yorku.ca (digital submissions) *Web Site:* www.cjlawards.ca, pg 586

Canadian Museum of History (Musee canadien de l'histoire), 100 Laurier St, Gatineau, QC K1A 0M8, Canada *Tel:* 819-776-7000 *Toll Free Tel:* 800-555-5621 (North American orders only) *Fax:* 819-776-7187 *Web Site:* www.historymuseum.ca, pg 398

Canadian Publishers' Council (CPC), 3080 Yonge St, Suite 6060, Toronto, ON M4N 3N1, Canada *Tel:* 647-255-8880 *Web Site:* pubcouncil.ca, pg 502

Canadian Scholars, 425 Adelaide St W, Suite 200, Toronto, ON M5V 3C1, Canada *Tel:* 416-929-2774 *Toll Free Tel:* 800-463-1998 *E-mail:* info@canadianscholars.ca; editorial@canadianscholars.ca *Web Site:* www.canadianscholars.ca; www.womenspress.ca, pg 398

Canadian Society of Children's Authors, Illustrators & Performers (CANSCAIP), 720 Bathurst St, Suite 503, Toronto, ON M5S 2R4, Canada *Tel:* 416-515-1559 *E-mail:* office@canscaip.org *Web Site:* www.canscaip.org, pg 503

The Canadian Writers' Foundation Inc (La Fondation des Ecrivains Canadiens), PO Box 13281, Kanata Sta, Ottawa, ON K2K 1X4, Canada *Tel:* 613-978-2723 *Fax:* 613-900-6393 *E-mail:* info@canadianwritersfoundation.org *Web Site:* www.canadianwritersfoundation.org, pg 525

Candid, 32 Old Slip, 24th fl, New York, NY 10005-3500 *Tel:* 212-620-4230 *Toll Free Tel:* 800-424-9836 *Fax:* 212-807-3677 *Web Site:* candid.org, pg 39

Candied Plums, 7548 Ravenna Ave NE, Seattle, WA 98115 *E-mail:* candiedplums@gmail.com *Web Site:* www.candiedplums.com, pg 39

Candlewick Press, 99 Dover St, Somerville, MA 02144-2825 *Tel:* 617-661-3330 *Fax:* 617-661-0565 *E-mail:* bigbear@candlewick.com; salesinfo@candlewick.com *Web Site:* candlewick.com, pg 39

C&T Publishing Inc, 1651 Challenge Dr, Concord, CA 94520-5206 *Tel:* 925-677-0377 *E-mail:* ctinfo@ctpub.com *Web Site:* www.ctpub.com, pg 40

Cape Cod Writers Center Conference, 919 Main St, Osterville, MA 02655 *Tel:* 508-420-0200 *E-mail:* writers@capecodwriterscenter.org *Web Site:* capecodwriterscenter.org, pg 553

Capen Publishing Co Inc, 4440 Edison St, San Diego, CA 92117 *Toll Free Tel:* 800-358-0560 *E-mail:* info@capenpublishingco.com *Web Site:* capenpubco.com, pg 40

Capitol Enquiry Inc, 1034 Emerald Bay Rd, No 435, South Lake Tahoe, CA 96150 *Tel:* 916-442-1434 *Toll Free Tel:* 800-922-7486 *Fax:* 916-244-2704 *E-mail:* info@capenq.com *Web Site:* govbuddy.com, pg 40

Truman Capote Award for Literary Criticism in Honor of Newton Arvin, 102 Dey House, 507 N Clinton St, Iowa City, IA 52242-1000 *Tel:* 319-335-0416 *Web Site:* writersworkshop.uiowa.edu, pg 586

Capstone Publishers™, 1710 Roe Crest Dr, North Mankato, MN 56003 *Toll Free Tel:* 800-747-4992 (cust serv) *Toll Free Fax:* 888-262-0705 *E-mail:* customer.service@capstonepub.com *Web Site:* www.capstonepub.com, pg 40

Captain Fiddle Music & Publications, 94 Wiswall Rd, Lee, NH 03861 *Tel:* 603-659-2658 *E-mail:* cfiddle@tiac.net *Web Site:* captainfiddle.com, pg 40

Captus Press Inc, 1600 Steeles Ave W, Units 14 & 15, Concord, ON L4K 4M2, Canada *Tel:* 905-760-2723 *Fax:* 905-760-7523 *E-mail:* info@captus.com *Web Site:* www.captus.com, pg 399

Cardiotext Publishing, 750 Second St NE, Suite 102, Hopkins, MN 55343 *Tel:* 612-925-2053 *Fax:* 612-922-7556 *E-mail:* info@cardiotext.com *Web Site:* www.cardiotextpublishing.com, pg 40

Cardoza Publishing, 1916 E Charleston Blvd, Las Vegas, NV 89104 *Tel:* 702-870-7200 *E-mail:* cardozaent@aol.com *Web Site:* cardozapublishing.com, pg 40

Career Development Program, 225 King St, Suite 201, Fredericton, NB E3B 1E1, Canada *Tel:* 506-444-4444 *Toll Free Tel:* 866-460-ARTS (460-2787) *Fax:* 506-444-5543 *E-mail:* prog@artsnb.ca *Web Site:* www.artsnb.ca, pg 586

The Carle Honors, 125 W Bay Rd, Amherst, MA 01002 *Tel:* 413-559-6300 *E-mail:* info@carlemuseum.org *Web Site:* www.carlemuseum.org/content/carle-honors, pg 586

Carlisle Press - Walnut Creek, 2593 Township Rd 421, Sugarcreek, OH 44681 *Tel:* 330-852-1900 *Toll Free Tel:* 800-852-4482 *Fax:* 330-852-3285 *E-mail:* cpress@cprinting.com, pg 40

Andrew Carnegie Medals for Excellence in Fiction & Nonfiction, 225 N Michigan Ave, Suite 1300, Chicago, IL 60601 *Tel:* 312-944-6780 *Toll Free Tel:* 800-545-2433 *Fax:* 312-440-9374 *E-mail:* ala@ala.org *Web Site:* www.ala.org/awardsgrants/carnegieadult, pg 587

Carnegie Mellon University Press, 5032 Forbes Ave, Pittsburgh, PA 15289-1021 *Tel:* 412-268-2861 *E-mail:* cmupress@andrew.cmu.edu *Web Site:* www.cmu.edu/universitypress, pg 41

Carnegie-Whitney Award, 225 N Michigan Ave, Suite 1300, Chicago, IL 60601 *Tel:* 312-280-5416 *Toll Free Tel:* 800-545-2433 *Web Site:* www.ala.org, pg 587

The Robert & Ina Caro Research/Travel Fellowship, PO Box 33020, Santa Fe, NM 87594 *Web Site:* biographersinternational.org/award/the-robert-and-ina-caro-research-travel-fellowship, pg 587

Carolina Academic Press, 700 Kent St, Durham, NC 27701 *Tel:* 919-489-7486 *Toll Free Tel:* 800-489-7486 *Fax:* 919-493-5668 *E-mail:* cap@cap-press.com *Web Site:* www.cap-press.com; www.caplaw.com, pg 41

Carolrhoda Books Inc, 241 First Ave N, Minneapolis, MN 55401 *Tel:* 612-332-3344 *Toll Free Tel:* 800-328-4929 *Fax:* 612-332-7615 *Toll Free Fax:* 800-332-1132 *E-mail:* info@lernerbooks.com; custserve@lernerbooks.com *Web Site:* www.lernerbooks.com; www.facebook.com/lernerbooks, pg 41

Carolrhoda Lab™, 241 First Ave N, Minneapolis, MN 55401 *Tel:* 612-332-3344 *Toll Free Tel:* 800-328-4929 *Fax:* 612-332-7615 *Toll Free Fax:* 800-332-1132 *E-mail:* info@lernerbooks.com; custserve@lernerbooks.com *Web Site:* www.lernerbooks.com; www.facebook.com/lernerbooks, pg 41

Carpe Indexum, 1960 Deer Run Rd, LaFayette, NY 13084 *Tel:* 315-677-3030 *E-mail:* info@carpeindexum.com *Web Site:* www.carpeindexum.com, pg 436

R E Carsch, MS-Consultant, 1453 Rhode Island St, San Francisco, CA 94107-3248 *Tel:* 415-533-8356 (cell) *E-mail:* recarsch@mzinfo.com, pg 436

Carson Dellosa Publishing LLC, PO Box 35665, Greensboro, NC 27425-5665 *Tel:* 336-632-0084 *Toll Free Tel:* 800-321-0943 *Fax:* 336-632-0084 *E-mail:* custsvc@carsondellosa.com *Web Site:* www.carsondellosa.com, pg 41

Carswell, One Corporate Plaza, 2075 Kennedy Rd, Toronto, ON M1T 3V4, Canada *Tel:* 416-609-5811 (sales); 416-609-3800 *Toll Free Tel:* 800-387-5164 (CN & US) *Fax:* 416-298-5094 (sales); 416-298-5082 *Toll Free Fax:* 877-750-9041 (CN only) *E-mail:* customersupport.legaltaxcanada@tr.com *Web Site:* store.thomsonreuters.ca, pg 399

Carol Cartaino, 2000 Flat Run Rd, Seaman, OH 45679 *Tel:* 937-764-1303 *Fax:* 937-764-1303 *E-mail:* cartaino@aol.com, pg 437

CarTech Inc, 6118 Main St, North Branch, MN 55056 *Tel:* 651-277-1200 *Toll Free Tel:* 800-551-4754 *Fax:* 651-277-1203 *E-mail:* info@cartechbooks.com *Web Site:* www.cartechbooks.com, pg 41

Claudia Caruana, 1333 Union Ave, New York, NY 11003 *E-mail:* ccaruana29@hotmail.com, pg 437

Maria Carvainis Agency Inc, Rockefeller Center, 1270 Avenue of the Americas, Suite 2915, New York, NY 10020 *Tel:* 212-245-6365 *Fax:* 212-245-7196 *E-mail:* mca@mariacarvainisagency.com *Web Site:* mariacarvainisagency.com, pg 453

Casa Bautista de Publicaciones, 130 Montoya Rd, El Paso, TX 79932 *Tel:* 915-566-9656 *Toll Free Tel:* 800-755-5958 (cust serv & orders) *E-mail:* orders@editorialmh.org *Web Site:* www.editorialmh.org, pg 41

Cascade Christian Writers (CCW), PO Box 22, Gladstone, OR 97027 *Tel:* 503-393-3356 *E-mail:* contact@oregonchristianwriters.org *Web Site:* oregonchristianwriters.org, pg 503

Cascade Christian Writers Conference, PO Box 22, Gladstone, OR 97027 *Tel:* 503-393-3356 *E-mail:* business@cascadechristianwriters.org *Web Site:* cascadechristianwriters.org, pg 553

Casemate | publishers, 1950 Lawrence Rd, Havertown, PA 19083 *Tel:* 610-853-9131 *Fax:* 610-853-9146 *E-mail:* casemate@casematepublishers.com *Web Site:* www.casematepublishers.com, pg 41

The CAT Agency Inc, 345 Old Oaks Rd, Fairfield, CT 06825 *Tel:* 917-434-3141 *Web Site:* catagencyinc.com, pg 485

Catholic Book Awards, 10 S Riverside Plaza, Suite 875, Chicago, IL 60606 *Tel:* 312-380-6789 *E-mail:* awards@catholicmediaassociation.org *Web Site:* www.catholicmediaassociation.org, pg 587

Catholic Book Publishing Corp, 77 West End Rd, Totowa, NJ 07512 *Tel:* 973-890-2400 *Toll Free Tel:* 877-228-2665 *Fax:* 973-890-2410 *E-mail:* info@catholicbookpublishing.com *Web Site:* www.catholicbookpublishing.com, pg 42

The Catholic Health Association of the United States, 4455 Woodson Rd, St Louis, MO 63134-3797 *Tel:* 314-427-2500 *Fax:* 314-427-0029 *E-mail:* servicecenter@chausa.org *Web Site:* www.chausa.org, pg 42

COMPANY INDEX

Catholic Library Association, 8550 United Plaza Blvd, Suite 1001, Baton Rouge, LA 70809 *Tel:* 225-408-4417 *E-mail:* cla2@cathla.org *Web Site:* cathla.org, pg 503

Catholic Media Association (CMA), 10 S Riverside Plaza, Suite 875, Chicago, IL 60606 *Tel:* 312-380-6789 *Web Site:* www.catholicmediaassociation.org, pg 503

Catholic Media Awards, 10 S Riverside Plaza, Suite 875, Chicago, IL 60606 *Tel:* 312-380-6789 *E-mail:* awards@catholicmediaassociation.org *Web Site:* www.catholicmediaassociation.org, pg 587

The Catholic University of America Press, 240 Leahy Hall, 620 Michigan Ave NE, Washington, DC 20064 *Tel:* 202-319-5052 *Toll Free Tel:* 800-537-5487 (orders only) *Fax:* 202-319-4985 *E-mail:* cua-press@cua.edu *Web Site:* cuapress.org, pg 42

Cato Institute, 1000 Massachusetts Ave NW, Washington, DC 20001-5403 *Tel:* 202-842-0200 *Web Site:* www.cato.org, pg 42

Kay Cattarulla Award for Best Short Story, PO Box 130294, Spring, TX 77393 *Web Site:* texasinstituteofletters.org, pg 587

Cave Canem Foundation Inc, 20 Jay St, Suite 310-A, Brooklyn, NY 11201-8301 *Tel:* 718-858-0000 *Fax:* 718-858-0002 *E-mail:* info@ccpoets.org *Web Site:* cavecanempoets.org, pg 525

Cave Canem Northwestern University Press Poetry Prize, 20 Jay St, Suite 310-A, Brooklyn, NY 11201-8301 *Tel:* 718-858-0000 *Fax:* 718-858-0002 *E-mail:* info@ccpoets.org *Web Site:* cavecanempoets.org/prizes/cave-canem-northwestern-university-press-poetry-prize/, pg 587

Cave Canem Poetry Prize, 20 Jay St, Suite 310-A, Brooklyn, NY 11201-8301 *Tel:* 718-858-0000 *Fax:* 718-858-0002 *E-mail:* info@ccpoets.org *Web Site:* cavecanempoets.org/prizes/cave-canem-poetry-prize/, pg 587

Jeanne Cavelos Editorial Services, PO Box 75, Mont Vernon, NH 03057 *Tel:* 603-673-6234 *Web Site:* jeannecavelos.com, pg 437

Caxton Press, 312 Main St, Caldwell, ID 83605-3299 *Tel:* 208-459-7421 *Toll Free Tel:* 800-657-6465 *Fax:* 208-459-7450 *E-mail:* publish@caxtonpress.com *Web Site:* www.caxtonpress.com, pg 42

CBC Diversity Outstanding Achievement Awards, 54 W 39 St, 14th fl, New York, NY 10018 *E-mail:* cbc.info@cbcbooks.org *Web Site:* www.cbcbooks.org, pg 587

CCH, a Wolters Kluwer business, 2700 Lake Cook Rd, Riverwoods, IL 60015 *Tel:* 847-267-7000 *Web Site:* www.cch.com, pg 42

CeciBooks Editorial & Publishing Consultation, 7057 26 Ave NW, Seattle, WA 98117 *E-mail:* info@cecibooks.com *Web Site:* www.cecibooks.com, pg 437

Cedar Fort Inc, 2373 W 700 S, Suite 100, Springville, UT 84663 *Tel:* 801-489-4084 *Toll Free Tel:* 800-SKY-BOOK (759-2665) *E-mail:* marketinginfo@cedarfort.com *Web Site:* cedarfort.com, pg 43

Cedar Grove Publishing, 3205 Elmhurst St, Rowlett, TX 75088 *Tel:* 415-364-8292 *E-mail:* queries@cedargrovebooks.com *Web Site:* www.cedargrovebooks.com, pg 43

Cedar Tree Books, PO Box 4256, Wilmington, DE 19807 *Tel:* 302-998-4171 *Fax:* 302-998-4185 *E-mail:* books@ctpress.com *Web Site:* www.cedartreebooks.com, pg 43

CEF Press, 17482 State Hwy M, Warrenton, MO 63383-0348 *Tel:* 636-456-4321 *Toll Free Tel:* 800-748-7710 (cust serv) *E-mail:* info@cefonline.com *Web Site:* www.cefonline.com; www.cefpress.com, pg 43

Cengage Learning, 20 Channel Center St, Boston, MA 02210 *Tel:* 617-289-7700 *Toll Free Tel:* 800-354-9706 *Fax:* 617-289-7844 *E-mail:* esales@cengage.com *Web Site:* www.cengage.com, pg 43

The Center for Book Arts, 28 W 27 St, 3rd fl, New York, NY 10001 *Tel:* 212-481-0295 *E-mail:* info@centerforbookarts.org *Web Site:* www.centerforbookarts.org, pg 503, 561

Center for Creative Leadership LLC, One Leadership Place, Greensboro, NC 27410-9427 *Tel:* 336-545-2810; 336-288-7210 *Fax:* 336-282-3284 *E-mail:* info@ccl.org *Web Site:* shop.ccl.org/usa/books, pg 43

The Center for Exhibition Industry Research (CEIR), 12700 Park Central Dr, Suite 308, Dallas, TX 75251 *Tel:* 972-687-9242 *Fax:* 972-692-6020 *E-mail:* info@ceir.org *Web Site:* www.ceir.org, pg 503

The Center for Fiction, 15 Lafayette Ave, Brooklyn, NY 11217 *Tel:* 212-755-6710 *E-mail:* info@centerforfiction.org *Web Site:* centerforfiction.org, pg 503

The Center for Fiction First Novel Prize, 15 Lafayette Ave, Brooklyn, NY 11217 *Tel:* 212-755-6710 *E-mail:* info@centerforfiction.org *Web Site:* www.centerforfiction.org/awards/the-first-novel-prize, pg 587

Center for Futures Education Inc, 345 Erie St, Grove City, PA 16127 *Tel:* 724-458-5860 *Fax:* 724-458-5962 *E-mail:* info@thectr.com *Web Site:* www.thectr.com, pg 43

The Center for Learning, PO Box 802, Culver City, CA 90232 *Tel:* 310-839-2436 *Toll Free Tel:* 800-421-4246 *Fax:* 310-839-2249 *Toll Free Tel:* 800-944-5432 *E-mail:* access@socialstudies.com; customerservice@socialstudies.com; submissions@socialstudies.com *Web Site:* www.centerforlearning.org, pg 43

Center for Publishing Departmental Scholarships, Midtown Ctr, Rm 429, 11 W 42 St, New York, NY 10036 *Tel:* 212-992-3232 *Fax:* 212-992-3233 *E-mail:* pub.center@nyu.edu *Web Site:* www.scps.nyu.edu, pg 588

Center for Strategic & International Studies (CSIS), 1616 Rhode Island Ave NW, Washington, DC 20036 *Tel:* 202-887-0200 *Fax:* 202-775-3199 *Web Site:* www.csis.org, pg 44

Center for the Collaborative Classroom, 1001 Marina Village Pkwy, Suite 110, Alameda, CA 94501-1042 *Tel:* 510-533-0213 *Toll Free Tel:* 800-666-7270 *Fax:* 510-464-3670 *E-mail:* info@collaborativeclassroom.org; clientsupport@collaborativeclassroom.org *Web Site:* www.collaborativeclassroom.org, pg 44

Centering Corp, 6406 Maple St, Omaha, NE 68104 *Tel:* 402-553-1200 *Toll Free Tel:* 866-218-0101 *Fax:* 402-553-0507 *E-mail:* orders@centeringcorp.com *Web Site:* www.centering.org, pg 44

Centerstream Publishing LLC, PO Box 17878, Anaheim Hills, CA 92817-7878 *Tel:* 714-779-9390 *E-mail:* centerstrm@aol.com *Web Site:* www.centerstream-usa.com, pg 44

Central Conference of American Rabbis/CCAR Press, 355 Lexington Ave, New York, NY 10017 *Tel:* 212-972-3636 *E-mail:* info@ccarpress.org; info@ccarnet.org *Web Site:* www.ccarpress.org, pg 44

Central Recovery Press (CRP), 3321 N Buffalo Dr, Suite 200, Las Vegas, NV 89129 *Tel:* 702-868-5830 *Fax:* 702-868-5831 *E-mail:* sales@recoverypress.com *Web Site:* centralrecoverypress.com, pg 44

Centre for Reformation & Renaissance Studies (CRRS), 71 Queen's Park Crescent E, Toronto, ON M5S 1K7, Canada *Tel:* 416-585-4465 *Fax:* 416-585-4430 (attn: CRRS) *E-mail:* crrs.publications@utoronto.ca *Web Site:* crrs.ca, pg 399

Centre Franco-Ontarien de Ressources en Alphabétisation (Centre FORA), 4800 rue Notre-Dame, Hanmer, ON P3P 1X5, Canada *Tel:* 705-524-3672 *Toll Free Tel:* 888-814-4422 (orders, CN only) *Fax:* 705-524-8535 *E-mail:* info@centrefora.on.ca *Web Site:* centrefora.on.ca, pg 399

Cercador Prize, c/o Third Place Books, 6504 20 Ave NE, Seattle, WA 98115 *E-mail:* info@cercadorprize.com *Web Site:* www.cercadorprize.com, pg 588

Cereals & Grains Association, 3285 Northwood Circle, Suite 100, St Paul, MN 55121 *Tel:* 651-454-7250 *E-mail:* info@cerealsgrains.org *Web Site:* cerealsgrains.org, pg 44

Eugene Cervi Award, Missouri Southern State University, 3950 E Newman Rd, Joplin, MO 64801-1595 *Web Site:* www.iswne.org/contests, pg 588

The CHA Best Scholarly Book in Canadian History Prize, 130 Albert St, Suite 1201, Ottawa, ON K1P 5G4, Canada *Tel:* 613-233-7885 *Fax:* 613-565-5445 *E-mail:* cha-shc@cha-shc.ca *Web Site:* cha-shc.ca, pg 588

Chain Store Guide (CSG), 3710 Corporex Park Dr, Suite 310, Tampa, FL 33619 *Toll Free Tel:* 800-927-9292 (orders) *Fax:* 813-627-6888 *E-mail:* webmaster@chainstoreguide.com *Web Site:* www.chainstoreguide.com, pg 44

Chalice Press, 11939 Manchester Rd, No 100, St Louis, MO 63131 *Tel:* 314-231-8500 *Toll Free Tel:* 800-366-3383 *E-mail:* customerservice@chalicepress.com *Web Site:* www.chalicepress.com, pg 44

Jack L Chalker Young Writers' Contest, PO Box 686, Baltimore, MD 21203-0686 *Tel:* 410-563-2737 *E-mail:* ywc@balticon.org *Web Site:* www.bsfs.org/bsfsywc.htm, pg 588

Jane Chambers Playwriting Award, Georgetown University, 108 David Performing Arts Ctr, Box 571063, 37 & "O" St, NW, Washington, DC 20057-1063 *Web Site:* www.athe.org/page/jane_chambers; www.womenandtheatreprogram.com/jane-chambers, pg 588

The Alfred & Fay Chandler Book Award, c/o Harvard Business School, Connell House 301A, Boston, MA 02163 *Tel:* 617-495-1003 *Fax:* 617-495-2705 *E-mail:* bhr@hbs.edu *Web Site:* www.hbs.edu/businesshistory/fellowships, pg 588

G S Sharat Chandra Prize for Short Fiction, 5 W Third St, Parkville, MO 64152 *Tel:* 816-200-7895 *E-mail:* info@bkmkpress.org *Web Site:* www.bkmkpress.org, pg 588

Chaosium Inc, 3450 Wooddale Ct, Ann Arbor, MI 48104 *Tel:* 734-972-9551 *E-mail:* customerservice@chaosium.com *Web Site:* www.chaosium.com, pg 45

Charisma Media, 1150 Greenwood Blvd, Lake Mary, FL 32746 *Tel:* 407-333-0600 (all imprints) *Fax:* 407-333-7100 (all imprints) *E-mail:* info@charismamedia.com; customerservice@charismamedia.com *Web Site:* www.charismamedia.com, pg 45

Charles Press Publishers, 1754 Wylie St, No 4, Philadelphia, PA 19130 *Tel:* 215-470-5977 *E-mail:* mail@charlespresspub.com *Web Site:* charlespresspub.com, pg 45

Charles River Media, 20 Channel Center St, Boston, MA 02210 *Tel:* 617-289-7700 *Fax:* 617-289-7844 *Web Site:* www.cengage.com; www.delmarlearning.com/charlesriver, pg 45

Charlesbridge Publishing Inc, 85 Main St, Watertown, MA 02472 *Tel:* 617-926-0329 *Toll Free Tel:* 800-225-3214 *Fax:* 617-926-5720 *Toll Free Fax:* 800-926-5775 *E-mail:* books@charlesbridge.com *Web Site:* www.charlesbridge.com, pg 45

The Charlton Press Corp, 645 Ave Lepine, Dorval, QC H9P 2R2, Canada *Tel:* 416-962-2665 *Toll Free Tel:* 866-663-8827 *Fax:* 514-954-3618 *E-mail:* chpress@charltonpress.com; info@charltonpress.com *Web Site:* www.charltonpress.com, pg 399

Chartered Professional Accountants of Canada (CPA Canada), 277 Wellington St W, Toronto, ON M5V 3H2, Canada *Tel:* 416-977-3222 *Toll Free Tel:* 800-268-3793 *Fax:* 416-977-8585 *E-mail:* member.services@cpacanada.ca; customerservice@cpacanada.ca *Web Site:* www.cpacanada.ca; www.facebook.com/cpacanada; cpastore.ca, pg 399

The Chautauqua Prize, One Ames Ave, Chautauqua, NY 14722 *Toll Free Tel:* 800-836-ARTS (836-2787) *Web Site:* www.chq.org/prize, pg 588

Chautauqua Writers' Workshop, One Ames Ave, Chautauqua, NY 14722 *Tel:* 716-357-6255 *Web Site:* www.chq.org, pg 553

Margaret Cheasebro PhD, 5709 Holmes Dr, Farmington, NM 87402 *Tel:* 505-325-1557 *E-mail:* mwriter4571@yahoo.com *Web Site:* www.margaretcheasebro.com; www.ifiwereatreewhatwouldibe.com, pg 437

Chelsea Green Publishing Co, 85 N Main St, Suite 120, White River Junction, VT 05001 *Tel:* 802-295-6300 *Toll Free Tel:* 800-639-4099 (cust serv & orders) *Fax:* 802-295-6444 *E-mail:* customerservice@chelseagreen.com; editorial@chelseagreen.com; publicity@chelseagreen.com; rights@chelseagreen.com *Web Site:* www.chelseagreen.com, pg 45

Chelsea House, 132 W 31 St, 16th fl, New York, NY 10001 *Toll Free Tel:* 800-322-8755 *Toll Free Fax:* 800-678-3633 *E-mail:* custserv@infobase.com; info@infobase.com *Web Site:* www.infobasepublishing.com; www.infobase.com (online resources), pg 45

ChemTec Publishing, 38 Earswick Dr, Toronto, ON M1E 1C6, Canada *Tel:* 416-265-2603 *E-mail:* orderdesk@chemtec.org *Web Site:* www.chemtec.org, pg 399

Cheneliere Education Inc, 5800, rue St Denis, bureau 900, Montreal, QC H2S 3L5, Canada *Tel:* 514-273-1066 *Toll Free Tel:* 800-565-5531 *Fax:* 514-276-0324 *Toll Free Fax:* 800-814-0324 *E-mail:* info@cheneliere.ca *Web Site:* www.cheneliere.ca, pg 399

Cheng & Tsui Co Inc, 25 West St, 2nd fl, Boston, MA 02111-1213 *Tel:* 617-988-2400 *Toll Free Tel:* 800-554-1963 *Fax:* 617-426-3669 *E-mail:* service@cheng-tsui.com; orders@cheng-tsui.com; marketing@cheng-tsui.com *Web Site:* www.cheng-tsui.com, pg 46

Ruth Chernia, 198 Victor Ave, Toronto, ON M4K 1B2, Canada *Tel:* 416-466-0164 *E-mail:* rchernia@editors.ca; rchernia@sympatico.ca *Web Site:* www.editors.ca/profile/444/ruth-chernia, pg 437

Cherry Hill Publishing LLC, 24344 Del Amo Rd, Ramona, CA 92065 *Tel:* 858-868-1260 *Toll Free Tel:* 800-407-1072 *Fax:* 760-203-1200 *E-mail:* operations@cherryhillpublishing.com; sales@cherryhillpublishing.com *Web Site:* www.cherryhillpublishing.com, pg 46

Linda Chester Literary Agency, 630 Fifth Ave, Suite 2000, New York, NY 10111 *Tel:* 212-218-3350 *E-mail:* submissions@lindachester.com *Web Site:* www.lindachester.com, pg 453

Chicago Review Press, 814 N Franklin St, Chicago, IL 60610 *Tel:* 312-337-0747 *Toll Free Tel:* 800-888-4741 *Fax:* 312-337-5110 *E-mail:* frontdesk@chicagoreviewpress.com *Web Site:* www.chicagoreviewpress.com, pg 46

Chicago Women in Publishing (CWIP), PO Box 60363, Chicago, IL 60660 *Tel:* 773-508-0351 *Fax:* 303-942-7164 *E-mail:* info@cwip.org *Web Site:* www.cwip.org, pg 503

Chickadee Prince Books LLC, 1030 Lake Ave, Greenwich, CT 06830 *Tel:* 212-808-5500 *E-mail:* submissions@chickadeeprince.com *Web Site:* chickadeeprince.com, pg 46

Child Welfare League of America (CWLA), 727 15 St NW, Suite 1200, Washington, DC 20005 *Tel:* 202-590-8748 *E-mail:* cwla@cwla.org *Web Site:* www.cwla.org/pubs, pg 46

The Children's Book Council (CBC), 54 W 39 St, 14th fl, New York, NY 10018 *E-mail:* cbc.info@cbcbooks.org *Web Site:* www.cbcbooks.org, pg 503

Children's Book Press, 95 Madison Ave, Suite 1205, New York, NY 10016 *Tel:* 212-779-4400 *Fax:* 212-683-1894 *E-mail:* editorial@leeandlow.com; orders@leeandlow.com; customer.support@leeandlow.com *Web Site:* www.leeandlow.com/imprints/children-s-book-press, pg 46

Children's History Book Prize, 170 Central Park W, New York, NY 10024 *Tel:* 212-873-3400 *Fax:* 212-595-5707 *E-mail:* info@nyhistory.org *Web Site:* www.nyhistory.org/childrens-museum/connect/book-prize, pg 588

Children's Literature Association Article Award, 140B Purcellville Gateway Dr, Suite 1200, Purcellville, VA 20132 *Tel:* 630-571-4520 *E-mail:* info@childlitassn.org *Web Site:* www.childlitassn.org, pg 588

Children's Literature Association Book Award, 140B Purcellville Gateway Dr, Suite 1200, Purcellville, VA 20132 *Tel:* 630-571-4520 *E-mail:* info@childlitassn.org *Web Site:* www.childlitassn.org, pg 589

Children's Literature Association Edited Book Award, 140B Purcellville Gateway Dr, Suite 1200, Purcellville, VA 20132 *Tel:* 630-571-4520 *E-mail:* info@childlitassn.org *Web Site:* www.childlitassn.org, pg 589

Children's Literature Association Graduate Student Essay Award, 140B Purcellville Gateway Dr, Suite 1200, Purcellville, VA 20132 *Tel:* 630-571-4520 *E-mail:* info@childlitassn.org *Web Site:* www.childlitassn.org, pg 589

Children's Literature Lecture Award, 225 N Michigan Ave, Suite 1300, Chicago, IL 60601 *Tel:* 312-280-2163 *Toll Free Tel:* 800-545-2433 *Fax:* 312-280-5271 *E-mail:* alsc@ala.org *Web Site:* www.ala.org/alsc/awardsgrants/profawards/chll, pg 589

Children's Literature Legacy Award, 225 N Michigan Ave, Suite 1300, Chicago, IL 60601 *Tel:* 312-280-2163 *Toll Free Tel:* 800-545-2433 *Fax:* 312-280-5271 *E-mail:* alsc@ala.org *Web Site:* www.ala.org/awardsgrants/childrens-literature-legacy-award; www.ala.org/alsc/awardsgrants/bookmedia/clla, pg 589

Children's Sequoyah Book Award, 119 Meramec Station Rd, Suite 207, Ballwin, MO 63021-6902 *Toll Free Tel:* 800-969-6562 (ext 5) *Fax:* 636-529-1396 *E-mail:* sequoyah@oklibs.org; ola@amigos.org *Web Site:* www.oklibs.org, pg 589

Faith Childs Literary Agency Inc, 915 Broadway, Suite 1009, New York, NY 10010 *Tel:* 212-995-9600 *Web Site:* faithchildsliteraryagency.com, pg 454

Child's Play® Inc, 250 Minot Ave, Auburn, ME 04210 *Tel:* 207-784-7252 *Toll Free Tel:* 800-639-6404 *Fax:* 207-784-7358 *Toll Free Fax:* 800-854-6989 *E-mail:* chpmaine@aol.com *Web Site:* www.childs-play.com, pg 46

The Child's World Inc, 21735 E Idyllwilde Dr, Parker, CO 80138-8892 *Toll Free Tel:* 800-599-READ (599-7323) *Toll Free Fax:* 888-320-2329 *E-mail:* info@childsworld.com *Web Site:* www.childsworld.com, pg 46

China Books, 360 Swift Ave, Suite 48, South San Francisco, CA 94080 *Fax:* 650-872-7808 *E-mail:* editor.sinomedia@gmail.com, pg 47

Chocorua Writing Workshop, PO Box 2280, Conway, NH 03818-2280 *Tel:* 603-447-2280 *E-mail:* office@worldfellowship.org *Web Site:* www.worldfellowship.org; www.facebook.com/World.Fellowship.Center, pg 553

Chosen Books, 7808 Creekridge Circle, Suite 250, Bloomington, MN 55439 *Tel:* 952-829-2500 *Toll Free Tel:* 800-877-2665 (orders only) *Web Site:* www.chosenbooks.com, pg 47

Christian Book Award®, 5801 S McClintock Dr, Suite 104, Tempe, AZ 85283 *Tel:* 480-966-3998 *Fax:* 480-966-1944 *E-mail:* info@ecpa.org *Web Site:* christianbookawards.com, pg 589

Christian Liberty Press, 502 W Euclid Ave, Arlington Heights, IL 60004-5402 *Toll Free Tel:* 800-348-0899 *Fax:* 847-259-2941 *E-mail:* custserv@christianlibertypress.com *Web Site:* www.shopchristianliberty.com, pg 47

Christian Light Publications Inc, 1051 Mount Clinton Pike, Harrisonburg, VA 22802 *Tel:* 540-434-1003 *Toll Free Tel:* 800-776-0478 *Fax:* 540-433-8896 *E-mail:* info@clp.org; orders@clp.org *Web Site:* www.clp.org, pg 47

Christian Retail Association Inc (CRA), 200 West Bay Dr, Largo, FL 33770 *Tel:* 727-596-7625 *Toll Free Tel:* 800-868-4388 *Fax:* 727-593-3523 *Toll Free Fax:* 855-815-9277 *E-mail:* service@munce.com *Web Site:* www.christianretailassociation.org, pg 503

Christian Schools International (CSI), 99 Monroe Ave NW, Suite 200, Grand Rapids, MI 49503 *Tel:* 616-957-1070 *Toll Free Tel:* 800-635-8288 *Web Site:* www.csionline.org, pg 47

The Christian Science Publishing Society, 210 Massachusetts Ave, Boston, MA 02115 *Tel:* 617-450-2000 *E-mail:* info@christianscience.com *Web Site:* christianscience.com, pg 47

The Christopher Awards, 5 Hanover Sq, 22nd fl, New York, NY 10004-2751 *Tel:* 212-759-4050 *Toll Free Tel:* 888-298-4050 (orders) *Fax:* 212-838-5073 *E-mail:* mail@christophers.org *Web Site:* www.christophers.org, pg 589

Chronicle Books LLC, 680 Second St, San Francisco, CA 94107 *Tel:* 415-537-4200 *Fax:* 415-537-4460 (perms) *E-mail:* hello@chroniclebooks.com; subrights@chroniclebooks.com *Web Site:* www.chroniclebooks.com, pg 47

John Ciardi Prize for Poetry, 5 W Third St, Parkville, MO 64152 *Tel:* 816-200-7895 *E-mail:* info@bkmkpress.org *Web Site:* www.bkmkpress.org, pg 589

Cider Mill Press Book Publishers LLC, 501 Nelson Place, Nashville, TN 37214 *Toll Free Tel:* 800-250-5308 *E-mail:* focuscc@harpercollins.com *Web Site:* www.cidermillpress.com, pg 48

Cine/Lit Representation, PO Box 802918, Santa Clarita, CA 91380-2918 *E-mail:* cinelit@att.net, pg 454

Circlet Press, 5676 Riverdale Ave, Suite 101, Riverdale, NY 10471 *Tel:* 212-279-6418 *E-mail:* customerservice@riverdaleavebooks.com; rab@riverdaleavebooks.com; customerservice@riverdaleavebooks.com (orders) *Web Site:* www.circlet.com; riverdaleavebooks.com (orders & edit), pg 48

Cistercian Publications, Saint John's Abbey, PO Box 7500, Collegeville, MN 56321 *Tel:* 320-363-2213 *Toll Free Tel:* 800-436-8431 *Fax:* 320-363-3299 *Toll Free Fax:* 800-445-5899 *E-mail:* sales@litpress.org *Web Site:* www.cistercianpublications.org, pg 48

City & Regional Magazine Association (CRMA), 287 Richards Ave, Norwalk, CT 06850 *Tel:* 203-515-9294 *Web Site:* citymag.org, pg 504

City Lights Publishers, 261 Columbus Ave, San Francisco, CA 94133 *Tel:* 415-362-8193 *E-mail:* staff@citylights.com *Web Site:* citylights.com, pg 48

The City of Calgary W O Mitchell Book Prize, 11759 Groat Rd NW, Edmonton, AB T5M 3K6, Canada *Tel:* 780-422-8174 *Toll Free Tel:* 800-665-5354 (AB only) *E-mail:* mail@writersguild.ab.ca *Web Site:* writersguild.ca, pg 590

City of Vancouver Book Award, Woodward's Heritage Bldg, Suite 501, 111 W Hastings St, Vancouver, BC V6B 1H4, Canada *Tel:* 604-871-6634 *Fax:* 604-871-6005 *E-mail:* culture@vancouver.ca *Web Site:* vancouver.ca/bookaward, pg 590

Civil War and Reconstruction Book Award, 112 N Bryan Ave, Bloomington, IN 47408-4141 *Tel:* 812-855-7311 *E-mail:* oah@oah.org *Web Site:* www.oah.org/awards, pg 590

Clarion Books, 195 Broadway, New York, NY 10007 *Tel:* 212-207-7000 *Toll Free Tel:* 800-242-7737 *E-mail:* consumercare@harpercollins.com *Web Site:* www.harpercollins.com/collections/books-by-clarion-books, pg 48

The Clarion Science Fiction & Fantasy Writers' Workshop, Arthur C Clarke Ctr for Human Imagination, UC San Diego, 9500 Gilman Dr, MC0445, La Jolla, CA 92093-0445 *Tel:* 858-534-6875 *E-mail:* clarion@ucsd.edu *Web Site:* clarion.ucsd.edu; imagination.ucsd.edu, pg 553

Clarity Press Inc, 2625 Piedmont Rd NE, Suite 56, Atlanta, GA 30324 *Tel:* 404-647-6501 *E-mail:* claritypress@usa.net (foreign rts & perms) *Web Site:* www.claritypress.com, pg 49

Ev Clark/Seth Payne Award for Young Science Journalists, PO Box 17337, Seattle, WA 98127 *Tel:* 206-880-0177 *E-mail:* info@casw.org

Web Site: casw.org/casw/evert-clarkseth-payne-award-young-science-journalists; casw.submittable.com/submit, pg 590

Wm Clark Associates, 54 W 21 St, Suite 809, New York, NY 10010 *Tel:* 212-675-2784 *E-mail:* general@wmclark.com *Web Site:* www.wmclark.com, pg 454

Classical Academic Press, 515 S 32 St, Camp Hill, PA 17011 *Tel:* 717-730-0711 *Toll Free Tel:* 866-730-0711 *Fax:* 717-730-0721 *Toll Free Fax:* 866-730-0721 *E-mail:* info@classicalsubjects.com; orders@classicalsubjects.com *Web Site:* classicalacademicpress.com, pg 49

Page Davidson Clayton Prize for Emerging Poets, University of Michigan, 3277 Angell Hall, 435 S State St, Ann Arbor, MI 48109-1003 *Tel:* 734-764-9265 *E-mail:* mqr@umich.edu *Web Site:* sites.lsa.umich.edu/mqr/about-us/prizes, pg 590

Clear Concepts, 1329 Federal Ave, Suite 6, Los Angeles, CA 90025 *Tel:* 323-285-0325, pg 437

Clear Light Publishers, 823 Don Diego Ave, Santa Fe, NM 87501 *Tel:* 505-989-9590 *Toll Free Tel:* 800-253-2747 (orders) *E-mail:* info@clearlightbooks.com *Web Site:* www.clearlightbooks.com, pg 49

Clearfield Co Inc, 3600 Clipper Mill Rd, Suite 229, Baltimore, MD 21211 *Tel:* 410-837-8271 *Toll Free Tel:* 800-296-6687 (orders & cust serv) *Fax:* 410-752-8492 *E-mail:* sales@genealogical.com *Web Site:* www.genealogical.com, pg 49

Cleis Press, 221 River St, 9th fl, Hoboken, NJ 07030 *Tel:* 212-431-5455 *E-mail:* cleis@cleispress.com *Web Site:* cleispress.com; www.vivaeditions.com, pg 49

Clerical Plus, 97 Blueberry Lane, Shelton, CT 06484 *Tel:* 203-225-0879 *Fax:* 203-225-0879 *E-mail:* clericalplus@aol.com, pg 437

Clerisy Press, 306 Greenup St, Covington, KY 41011 *Tel:* 859-815-7204 *E-mail:* info@clerisypress.com *Web Site:* www.clerisypress.com, pg 49

David H Clift Scholarship, 225 N Michigan Ave, Suite 1300, Chicago, IL 60601 *Tel:* 800-545-2433 (ext 4279) *Fax:* 312-280-4279 *E-mail:* scholarships@ala.org *Web Site:* www.ala.org/scholarships, pg 590

Clinical and Laboratory Standards Institute (CLSI), 1055 Westlakes Dr, Suite 300, Berwyn, PA 19312 *Tel:* 610-688-0100 *Toll Free Tel:* 877-447-1888 (orders) *Fax:* 610-688-0700 *E-mail:* customerservice@clsi.org *Web Site:* www.clsi.org, pg 49

Close Up Publishing, 671 N Glebe Rd, Suite 900, Arlington, VA 22203 *Tel:* 703-706-3300 *Toll Free Tel:* 800-CLOSE-UP (256-7387) *E-mail:* info@closeup.org *Web Site:* www.closeup.org, pg 49

Closson Press, 257 Delilah St, Apollo, PA 15613-1933 *Tel:* 724-337-4482 *E-mail:* clossonpress@comcast.net *Web Site:* www.clossonpress.com, pg 49

Clotilde's Secretarial & Management Services, PO Box 871926, New Orleans, LA 70187 *Tel:* 504-242-2912 *E-mail:* elcsy58@att.net, pg 437

Dwight Clough, PO Box 670, Wyocena, WI 53969 *E-mail:* lmp@dwightclough.com *Web Site:* dwightclough.com, pg 437

CN Times Books, 100 Jericho Quadrangle, Suite 337, Jericho, NY 11791 *Tel:* 516-719-0886 *E-mail:* yanliu@cntimesbooks.com *Web Site:* www.cntimesbooks.com, pg 50

Coach House Books, 80 bpNichol Lane, Toronto, ON M5S 3J4, Canada *Tel:* 416-979-2217 *Toll Free Tel:* 800-367-6360 (outside Toronto) *Fax:* 416-977-1158 *E-mail:* mail@chbooks.com *Web Site:* www.chbooks.com, pg 399

Coaches Choice, PO Box 1828, Monterey, CA 93942 *Toll Free Tel:* 888-229-5745 *E-mail:* info@coacheschoice.com *Web Site:* www.coacheschoice.com, pg 50

Coastside Editorial, PO Box 181, Moss Beach, CA 94038 *E-mail:* bevjoe@pacific.net, pg 437

Codhill Press, 420 E 23 St, Suite 3H, New York, NY 10010 *E-mail:* info@codhill.com *Web Site:* www.codhill.com, pg 50

CODiE Awards, PO Box 34340, Washington, DC 20043 *Tel:* 202-789-4446 *Fax:* 202-289-7097 *Web Site:* www.siia.net, pg 590

Coe College Playwriting Festival, 1220 First Ave NE, Cedar Rapids, IA 52402 *Tel:* 319-399-8624 *Fax:* 319-399-8557 *Web Site:* www.theatre.coe.edu; www.coe.edu/academics/theatrearts/theatrearts_playwritingfestival, pg 590

Coffee House Press, 79 13 Ave NE, Suite 110, Minneapolis, MN 55413 *Tel:* 612-338-0125 *Fax:* 612-338-4004 *E-mail:* info@coffeehousepress.org *Web Site:* coffeehousepress.org, pg 50

Cognizant Communication Corp, PO Box 37, Putnam Valley, NY 10579-0037 *Tel:* 845-603-6440 *Fax:* 845-603-6442 *E-mail:* inquiries@cognizantcommunication.com; sales@cognizantcommunication.com *Web Site:* www.cognizantcommunication.com, pg 50

Carla Cohen Free Speech Award, 2667 Hyacinth St, Westbury, NY 11590 *Tel:* 516-333-0681 *E-mail:* kit@naiba.com *Web Site:* www.naiba.com/page/cohenfreespeechaward, pg 590

Morton N Cohen Award for a Distinguished Edition of Letters, 85 Broad St, New York, NY 10004 *Tel:* 646-576-5141; 646-576-5000 *E-mail:* awards@mla.org *Web Site:* www.mla.org, pg 590

Robert L Cohen, 182-12 Horace Harding Expwy, Suite 2M, Fresh Meadows, NY 11365 *Tel:* 718-762-1195 *Toll Free Tel:* 866-EDITING (334-8464) *Fax:* 917-781-0703 *E-mail:* wordsmith@sterlingmp.com *Web Site:* www.rlcwordsandmusic.com; www.linkedin.com/in/robertcohen17, pg 437

Cohesion®, 511 W Bay St, Suite 480, Tampa, FL 33606 *Tel:* 813-999-3111 *Toll Free Tel:* 866-727-6800 *Web Site:* www.cohesion.com, pg 437

The Victor Cohn Prize for Excellence in Medical Science Reporting, PO Box 17337, Seattle, WA 98127 *Tel:* 206-880-0177 *E-mail:* info@casw.org *Web Site:* casw.org/casw/victor-cohn-prize-excellence-medical-science-reporting-0, pg 590

William E Colby Award, 158 Harmon Dr, Box 60, Northfield, VT 05663 *Tel:* 802-485-2965 *Web Site:* colby.norwich.edu/award, pg 591

Cold Spring Harbor Laboratory Press, 500 Sunnyside Blvd, Woodbury, NY 11797-2924 *Tel:* 516-422-4100 *Toll Free Tel:* 800-843-4388 *E-mail:* cshpress@cshl.edu *Web Site:* www.cshlpress.com, pg 50

The College Board, 250 Vesey St, New York, NY 10281 *Tel:* 212-713-8000 *Toll Free Tel:* 866-630-9305 *Web Site:* www.collegeboard.com, pg 50

College of Liberal & Professional Studies, University of Pennsylvania, 3440 Market St, Suite 100, Philadelphia, PA 19104-3335 *Tel:* 215-898-7326 *Fax:* 215-573-2053 *E-mail:* lps@sas.upenn.edu *Web Site:* www.upenn.edu/lps, pg 561

College Publishing, 12309 Lynwood Dr, Glen Allen, VA 23059 *Tel:* 804-364-8410 *Fax:* 804-364-8408 *E-mail:* collegepub@mindspring.com *Web Site:* www.collegepublishing.us, pg 50

Collier Associates, 309 Kelsey Park Circle, Palm Beach Gardens, FL 33410 *Tel:* 561-514-6548 *E-mail:* dmccabooks@gmail.com, pg 454

John M Collier Award for Forest History Journalism, 2925 Academy Rd, Durham, NC 27705 *Tel:* 919-682-9319 *Fax:* 919-682-2349 *Web Site:* foresthistory.org/awards-fellowships/collier-award, pg 591

Carr P Collins Award, PO Box 130294, Spring, TX 77393 *Web Site:* texasinstituteofletters.org, pg 591

Colorado Authors' League, 700 Colorado Blvd, Denver, CO 80206 *Tel:* 913-369-5040 *Web Site:* www.coloradoauthors.org, pg 504

Colorado Book Awards, 7935 E Prentice Ave, Suite 450, Greenwood Village, CO 80111 *Tel:* 303-894-7951 (ext 19) *Fax:* 303-864-9361 *E-mail:* info@coloradohumanities.org *Web Site:* coloradohumanities.org, pg 591

Colorado Prize for Poetry, 9105 Campus Delivery, Colorado State University, Fort Collins, CO 80523-9105 *Tel:* 970-491-5449 *E-mail:* creview@colostate.edu *Web Site:* coloradoreview.colostate.edu/colorado-prize-for-poetry, pg 591

Betsy Colquitt Award for Poetry, Dept of English, TCU Box 297270, Fort Worth, TX 76129 *E-mail:* descant@tcu.edu *Web Site:* www.descant.tcu.edu, pg 591

Columbia Books & Information Services (CBIS), 1530 Wilson Blvd, Suite 400, Arlington, VA 22209 *Tel:* 202-464-1662 *Fax:* 301-664-9600 *E-mail:* info@columbiabooks.com *Web Site:* www.columbiabooks.com; www.association-insight.com; www.ceoupdate.com; www.thealmanacofamericanpolitics.com; www.thompsongrants.com, pg 50

Columbia Publishing Course at Columbia University, 2950 Broadway, MC 3801, New York, NY 10027 *Tel:* 212-854-1898; 212-854-9775 *E-mail:* publishing-jrn@columbia.edu *Web Site:* journalism.columbia.edu/columbia-publishing-course, pg 561

Columbia University Press, 61 W 62 St, New York, NY 10023 *Tel:* 212-459-0600 *Toll Free Tel:* 800-944-8648 *Fax:* 212-459-3678 *Web Site:* cup.columbia.edu, pg 51

Columbia University School of the Arts Creative Writing Program, 609 Kent Hall, New York, NY 10027 *Tel:* 212-854-3774 *E-mail:* writingprogram@columbia.edu *Web Site:* arts.columbia.edu/writing, pg 562

Comex Systems Inc, 9380 Nastrand Circle, Port Charlotte, FL 33981 *Tel:* 908-881-6301 *E-mail:* mail@comexsystems.com *Web Site:* www.comexsystems.com, pg 51

Committee on Scholarly Editions, c/o Modern Language Association of America, 85 Broad St, Suite 500, New York, NY 10004-2434 *Tel:* 646-646-5000 *E-mail:* cse@mla.org *Web Site:* www.mla.org, pg 504

Commonwealth Editions, 210 Wingo Way, Suite 200, Mount Pleasant, SC 29464 *Tel:* 843-853-2070 *E-mail:* retailers@arcadiapublishing.com; publishing@arcadiapublishing.com *Web Site:* www.arcadiapublishing.com, pg 51

Community of Literary Magazines & Presses (CLMP), 154 Christopher St, Suite 3C, New York, NY 10014-9110 *Tel:* 212-741-9110 *E-mail:* info@clmp.org *Web Site:* www.clmp.org, pg 504

Community of Writers Summer Workshops, PO Box 1416, Nevada City, CA 95959 *Tel:* 530-470-8440 *E-mail:* info@communityofwriters.org *Web Site:* www.communityofwriters.org, pg 553

Company's Coming Publishing Ltd, 7735 Wagner Rd, Edmonton, AB T6E 5B1, Canada *Toll Free Tel:* 800-661-9017 (CN) *Fax:* 780-450-1857 *Toll Free Fax:* 800-424-7133 *E-mail:* accounts@companyscoming.com *Web Site:* companyscoming.com, pg 400

Concordia Publishing House, 3558 S Jefferson Ave, St Louis, MO 63118-3968 *Tel:* 314-268-1000; 314-268-1268 (bookshop) *Toll Free Tel:* 800-325-3040 (cust serv) *Toll Free Fax:* 800-490-9889 (cust serv) *E-mail:* order@cph.org *Web Site:* www.cph.org, pg 51

The Conference Board Inc, 845 Third Ave, New York, NY 10022-6600 *Tel:* 212-759-0900; 212-339-0345 (cust serv) *E-mail:* customer.service@tcb.org *Web Site:* www.conference-board.org/us; www.linkedin.com/company/the-conference-board, pg 51

Conference on Poetry & Teaching, 158 Ridge Rd, Franconia, NH 03580 *Tel:* 603-823-5510 *E-mail:* frost@frostplace.org *Web Site:* frostplace.org, pg 554

Don Congdon Associates Inc, 110 William St, Suite 2202, New York, NY 10038-3914 *Tel:* 212-645-1229 *Fax:* 212-727-2688 *E-mail:* dca@doncongdon.com *Web Site:* www.doncongdon.com, pg 454

Beasley Conger Jr Award for Nonfiction, UMKC, University House, 5101 Rockhill Rd, Kansas City, MO 64110-2499 *Tel:* 816-235-1169 *E-mail:* newletters@umkc.edu *Web Site:* www.newletters.org, pg 591

Connecticut Authors & Publishers Association (CAPA), PO Box 715, Avon, CT 06001-0715 Tel: 860-675-1344 Web Site: ctauthorsandpublishers.com, pg 504

The Connecticut Law Tribune, c/o 10 Talcott Ridge Rd, Unit A3, Farmington, CT 06032 Toll Free Tel: 877-256-2472 E-mail: editorial@alm.com Web Site: www.law.com/ctlawtribune/, pg 52

Miles Conrad Award, 3600 Clipper Mill Rd, Suite 302, Baltimore, MD 21211-1948 Tel: 301-654-2512 Fax: 410-685-5278 E-mail: nisohq@niso.org Web Site: www.niso.org, pg 591

Constance Rooke Creative Nonfiction Prize, University of Victoria, PO Box 1700, Sta CSC, Victoria, BC V8W 2Y2, Canada Tel: 250-721-8524 E-mail: malahat@uvic.ca Web Site: www.malahatreview.ca/contests/creative_non-fiction_prize/info.html; www.malahatreview.ca, pg 591

Consumer Press, 13326 SW 28 St, Suite 102, Fort Lauderdale, FL 33330-1102 Tel: 954-370-9153 E-mail: info@consumerpress.com Web Site: www.consumerpress.com, pg 52

Continental AfrikaPublishers, 182 Stribling Circle, Spartanburg, SC 29301 E-mail: afrikalion@aol.com; profafrikadzatadeku@yahoo.com; profafrikadzatadeku@facebook.com Web Site: www.afrikacentricity.com, pg 52

The Continuing Legal Education Society of British Columbia (CLEBC), 500-1155 W Pender St, Vancouver, BC V6E 2P4, Canada Tel: 604-669-3544; 604-893-2121 (cust serv) Toll Free Tel: 800-663-0437 (CN) Fax: 604-669-9260 E-mail: custserv@cle.bc.ca Web Site: www.cle.bc.ca, pg 400

David C Cook, 4050 Lee Vance Dr, Colorado Springs, CO 80918 Tel: 719-536-0100 Toll Free Tel: 800-323-7543 (orders & cust serv) Toll Free Fax: 800-430-0726 (cust serv) E-mail: bookstores@davidccook.org; customercare@davidccook.org Web Site: www.davidccook.org, pg 52

The Cook Prize, 610 W 112 St, New York, NY 10025 Web Site: www.bankstreet.edu/library/center-for-childrens-literature/the-cook-prize, pg 591

The Doe Coover Agency, PO Box 668, Winchester, MA 01890 Tel: 781-721-6000 Fax: 781-721-6727 E-mail: info@doecooveragency.com Web Site: www.doecooveragency.com, pg 454

Copper Canyon Press, Fort Worden State Park, Bldg 313, Port Townsend, WA 98368 Tel: 360-385-4925 E-mail: poetry@coppercanyonpress.org; publicity@coppercanyonpress.org; digitalcontent@coppercanyonpress.org Web Site: www.coppercanyonpress.org, pg 52

Cordon d' Or - Gold Ribbon International Culinary Academy Awards, 7312 Sixth Ave N, St Petersburg, FL 33710 Tel: 727-347-2437 E-mail: cordondor@aol.com Web Site: www.cordondorcuisine.com; www.florida-americasculinaryparadise.com; www.culinaryambassadorofireland.com, pg 591

Jeanne Cordova Prize for Lesbian/Queer Nonfiction, PO Box 20186, New York, NY 10014 Tel: 213-277-5755 E-mail: awards@lambdaliterary.org; admin@lambdaliterary.org Web Site: www.lambdaliterary.org/awards/special-awards, pg 592

Core/Christian Larew Memorial Scholarship in Library & Information Technology, c/o The American Library Association, 225 N Michigan Ave, Suite 1300, Chicago, IL 60601 Tel: 312-944-6780 Toll Free Tel: 800-545-2433 Fax: 312-440-9374 E-mail: scholarships@ala.org Web Site: www.ala.org/core, pg 592

Core/OCLC Spectrum Scholarship in Library & Information Technology, c/o The American Library Association, 225 N Michigan Ave, Suite 1300, Chicago, IL 60601 Tel: 312-944-6780 Toll Free Tel: 800-545-2433 Fax: 312-440-9374 E-mail: scholarships@ala.org Web Site: www.ala.org/core, pg 592

Albert B Corey Prize, c/o American Historical Association, 400 "A" St SE, Washington, DC 20003-3889 Tel: 202-544-2422 E-mail: awards@historians.org; cha-shc@cha-shc.ca Web Site: www.historians.org/awards-and-grants/awards-and-prizes/albert-b-corey-prize; www.cha-shc.ca, pg 592

Cormorant Books Inc, 260 Spadina Ave, Suite 502, Toronto, ON M5T 1E5, Canada Tel: 416-925-8887 E-mail: info@cormorantbooks.com Web Site: www.cormorantbooks.com, pg 400

Cornell & Company, LLC, 44 Jog Hill Rd, Trumbull, CT 06611 Tel: 203-454-4210 Web Site: www.cornellandco.com, pg 485

Cornell Maritime Press, 4880 Lower Valley Rd, Atglen, PA 19310 Tel: 610-593-1777 Fax: 610-593-2002 E-mail: info@schifferbooks.com Web Site: www.schifferbooks.com, pg 52

Cornell University Press, Sage House, 512 E State St, Ithaca, NY 14850 Tel: 607-253-2338 E-mail: cupressinfo@cornell.edu; cupress-sales@cornell.edu; cupress-perms@cornell.edu (reprint/class use permissions) Web Site: www.cornellpress.cornell.edu, pg 52

Cornerstone Book Publishers, PO Box 8423, Hot Springs Village, AR 71910 Tel: 504-215-6258 E-mail: 1cornerstonebooks@gmail.com Web Site: cornerstonepublishers.com, pg 53

Corporation for Public Broadcasting (CPB), 401 Ninth St NW, Washington, DC 20004-2129 Tel: 202-879-9600 E-mail: press@cpb.org Web Site: cpb.org, pg 504

Corporation of Professional Librarians of Quebec, 2065, rue Parthenais, Bureau 387, Montreal, QC H2K 3T1, Canada Tel: 514-845-3327 E-mail: info@cbpq.qc.ca Web Site: www.cbpq.qc.ca, pg 504

Corwin, 2455 Teller Rd, Thousand Oaks, CA 91320 Tel: 805-499-9734 Toll Free Tel: 800-233-9936 Fax: 805-499-5323 Toll Free Fax: 800-417-2466 E-mail: info@corwin.com; order@corwin.com Web Site: www.corwin.com, pg 53

Cosimo Inc, Old Chelsea Sta, PO Box 416, New York, NY 10011-0416 Tel: 212-989-3616 Fax: 212-989-3662 E-mail: info@cosimobooks.com Web Site: www.cosimobooks.com, pg 53

Cotsen Institute of Archaeology Press, 308 Charles E Young Dr N, Fowler A210, Box 951510, Los Angeles, CA 90095 Tel: 310-206-9384 Fax: 310-206-4723 E-mail: cioapress@ioa.ucla.edu Web Site: www.ioa.ucla.edu, pg 53

Council for Advancement & Support of Education (CASE), 1201 Eye St NW, Suite 300, Washington, DC 20005 Tel: 202-328-CASE (328-2273) Fax: 202-387-4973 E-mail: membersupportcenter@case.org Web Site: www.case.org, pg 504

Council for Exceptional Children (CEC), 3100 Clarendon Blvd, Suite 600, Arlington, VA 22201 Toll Free Tel: 888-232-7733 E-mail: service@exceptionalchildren.org Web Site: www.exceptionalchildren.org, pg 53

Council for Research in Values & Philosophy, The Catholic University of America, Gibbons Hall, B-20, 620 Michigan Ave NE, Washington, DC 20064 Tel: 202-319-6089 E-mail: cua-rvp@cua.edu Web Site: www.crvp.org, pg 53

Council for the Advancement of Science Writing (CASW), PO Box 17337, Seattle, WA 98127 Tel: 206-880-0177 E-mail: info@casw.org Web Site: casw.org, pg 504

The Council of State Governments, 1776 Avenue of the States, Lexington, KY 40511 Tel: 859-244-8000 Fax: 859-244-8001 E-mail: membership@csg.org Web Site: www.csg.org, pg 53

Council on Foreign Relations Press, The Harold Pratt House, 58 E 68 St, New York, NY 10065 Tel: 212-434-9400 Fax: 212-434-9800 E-mail: publications@cfr.org Web Site: www.cfr.org, pg 53

Counterpath Press, 7935 E 14 Ave, Denver, CO 80220 E-mail: counterpath@counterpathpress.org Web Site: www.counterpathpress.org, pg 54

Counterpoint Press LLC, 2560 Ninth St, Suite 318, Berkeley, CA 94710 Tel: 510-704-0230 Fax: 510-704-0268 E-mail: info@counterpointpress.com Web Site: counterpointpress.com; softskull.com, pg 54

Country Music Foundation Press, 222 Rep John Lewis Way S, Nashville, TN 37203 Tel: 615-416-2001 E-mail: info@countrymusichalloffame.org Web Site: www.countrymusichalloffame.org, pg 54

Countryman Press, c/o W W Norton & Company Inc, 500 Fifth Ave, New York, NY 10110 Tel: 212-354-5500 Fax: 212-869-0856 E-mail: countrymanpress@wwnorton.com Web Site: wwnorton.com/countryman-press, pg 54

La Courte Echelle, 4388, rue Saint-Denis, Suite 315, Montreal, QC H2J 2L1, Canada Tel: 514-312-6950 E-mail: info@courteechelle.com Web Site: www.groupecourteechelle.com/la-courte-echelle, pg 400

Covenant Communications Inc, 1226 S 630 E, Suite 4, American Fork, UT 84003 Tel: 801-756-1041 E-mail: info@covenant-lds.com; covenantorders@covenant-lds.com Web Site: www.covenant-lds.com, pg 54

COVR Visionary Awards, PO Box 1397, Palmer Lake, CO 80133 Tel: 719-487-0424 E-mail: info@covr.org Web Site: covr.org/awards, pg 592

The Terry J Cox Poetry Award, 806 Oberlin Rd, No 12094, Raleigh, NC 27605 E-mail: info@regalhousepublishing.com Web Site: regalhousepublishing.com/the-terry-j-cox-poetry-award/, pg 592

Marie Coyoteblanc Award for Indigenous Writing, 81 Prince St, Charlottetown, PE C1A 4R3, Canada E-mail: peiliteraryawards@gmail.com Web Site: www.peiwritersguild.com, pg 592

CPSA Prize in Comparative Politics, 260 Dalhousie St, Suite 204, Ottawa, ON K1N 7E4, Canada Tel: 613-562-1202 Fax: 613-241-0019 E-mail: cpsaprizes@cpsa-acsp.ca; cpsa-acsp@cpsa-acsp.ca Web Site: www.cpsa-acsp.ca, pg 592

CPSA Prize in International Relations, 260 Dalhousie St, Suite 204, Ottawa, ON K1N 7E4, Canada Tel: 613-562-1202 Fax: 613-241-0019 E-mail: cpsaprizes@cpsa-acsp.ca; cpsa-acsp@cpsa-acsp.ca Web Site: www.cpsa-acsp.ca, pg 592

CQ Press, 2600 Virginia Ave NW, Suite 600, Washington, DC 20037 Tel: 202-729-1900; 202-729-1800 Toll Free Tel: 866-4CQ-PRESS (427-7737) E-mail: customerservice@cqpress.com Web Site: www.cqpress.com; library.cqpress.com, pg 54

Crabtree Publishing Co, 347 Fifth Ave, Suite 1402-145, New York, NY 10016 Tel: 212-496-5040 Toll Free Tel: 800-387-7650 Toll Free Fax: 800-355-7166 E-mail: custserv@crabtreebooks.com Web Site: www.crabtreebooks.com, pg 54

Crabtree Publishing Co Ltd, 616 Welland Ave, St Catharines, ON L2M 5V6, Canada Tel: 905-682-5221 Toll Free Tel: 800-387-7650 Fax: 905-682-7166 Toll Free Fax: 800-355-7166 E-mail: custserv@crabtreebooks.com; sales@crabtreebooks.com; orders@crabtreebooks.com Web Site: www.crabtreebooks.ca, pg 400

Craftsman Book Co, 6058 Corte Del Cedro, Carlsbad, CA 92011 Tel: 760-438-7828 Toll Free Tel: 800-829-8123 Fax: 760-438-0398 Web Site: www.craftsman-book.com, pg 54

Craven Design Inc, 229 E 85 St, New York, NY 10028 Tel: 212-288-1022 Fax: 212-249-9910 E-mail: cravendesign@mac.com Web Site: www.cravendesignstudios.com, pg 485

The Crazyhorse Fiction Prize, College of Charleston, Dept of English, 66 George St, Charleston, SC 29424 Tel: 843-953-4470 E-mail: crazyhorse@cofc.edu Web Site: crazyhorse.cofc.edu/prizes, pg 593

CRC Press, 2385 Executive Center Dr, Suite 320, Boca Raton, FL 33431 Toll Free Tel: 800-354-1420; 800-634-7064 (orders) E-mail: orders@taylorandfrancis.com Web Site: www.routledge.com/go/crc-press, pg 55

COMPANY INDEX

Creation Grant Program, 225 King St, Suite 201, Fredericton, NB E3B 1E1, Canada *Tel:* 506-444-4444 *Toll Free Tel:* 866-460-ARTS (460-2787) *Fax:* 506-444-5543 *E-mail:* prog@artsnb.ca *Web Site:* www.artsnb.ca, pg 593

Creative Editions, 2140 Howard Dr W, North Mankato, MN 56003 *Tel:* 507-388-6273 *Toll Free Tel:* 800-445-6209 *Fax:* 507-388-2746 *E-mail:* info@thecreativecompany.us; orders@thecreativecompany.us *Web Site:* www.thecreativecompany.us, pg 55

Creative Homeowner, 903 Square St, Mount Joy, PA 17552 *Tel:* 717-560-4703 *Toll Free Tel:* 844-307-3677 *Toll Free Fax:* 888-369-2885 *E-mail:* customerservice@foxchapelpublishing.com; sales@foxchapelpublishing.com *Web Site:* www.foxchapelB2B.com, pg 55

Creative Non-Fiction Awards, 81 Prince St, Charlottetown, PE C1A 4R3, Canada *E-mail:* peiliteraryawards@gmail.com *Web Site:* www.peiwritersguild.com, pg 593

Creative Residencies-Quebec, 225 King St, Suite 201, Fredericton, NB E3B 1E1, Canada *Tel:* 506-444-4444 *Toll Free Tel:* 866-460-ARTS (460-2787) *Fax:* 506-444-5543 *E-mail:* prog@artsnb.ca *Web Site:* www.artsnb.ca, pg 593

Creative Writing Awards for Young People, 81 Prince St, Charlottetown, PE C1A 4R3, Canada *E-mail:* peiliteraryawards@gmail.com *Web Site:* www.peiwritersguild.com, pg 593

CreativeWell Inc, PO Box 3130, Memorial Sta, Upper Montclair, NJ 07043 *Tel:* 973-783-7575 *E-mail:* info@creativewell.com *Web Site:* www.creativewell.com, pg 454, 487

Creston Books, PO Box 9369, Berkeley, CA 94709 *Web Site:* www.crestonbooks.co, pg 55

Crichton & Associates Inc, 6940 Carroll Ave, Takoma, MD 20912 *Tel:* 301-495-9663 *E-mail:* cricht1@aol.com, pg 455

Cricket Cottage Publishing LLC, 275 Medical Dr, No 4773, Carmel, IN 46082 *E-mail:* thecricketpublishing@gmail.com *Web Site:* thecricketpublishing.com; www.facebook.com/CricketCottagePublishing, pg 55

Crime Writers of Canada (CWC), 4C-240 Westwood Rd, Guelph, ON N1H 7W9, Canada *E-mail:* info@crimewriterscanada.com *Web Site:* www.crimewriterscanada.com, pg 504

Crime Writers of Canada Awards of Excellence, 716 Thicket Way, Ottawa, ON K4A 3B5, Canada *E-mail:* awards@crimewriterscanada.com *Web Site:* www.crimewriterscanada.com/awards, pg 593

Compton Crook Award, PO Box 686, Baltimore, MD 21203-0686 *Tel:* 410-563-2737 *E-mail:* webmeister@bsfs.org *Web Site:* www.bsfs.org/CCA/bsfsccnu2014.htm, pg 593

Crook's Corner Book Prize, 313 Country Club Rd, Chapel Hill, NC 27514 *E-mail:* info@crookscornerbookprize.com *Web Site:* crookscornerbookprize.com, pg 593

Cross-Cultural Communications, 239 Wynsum Ave, Merrick, NY 11566-4725 *Tel:* 516-868-5635 *Fax:* 516-379-1901 *E-mail:* cccpoetry@aol.com *Web Site:* www.facebook.com/CrossCulturalCommunications.NY, pg 55

The Crossroad Publishing Co, 831 Chestnut Ridge Rd, Chestnut Ridge, NY 10977 *Tel:* 845-517-0180 *E-mail:* info@crossroadpublishing.com; office@crossroadpublishing.com *Web Site:* crossroadpublishing.com, pg 55

Crossway, 1300 Crescent St, Wheaton, IL 60187 *Tel:* 630-682-4300 *Toll Free Tel:* 800-635-7993 (orders); 800-543-1659 (cust serv) *Fax:* 630-682-4785 *E-mail:* info@crossway.org *Web Site:* www.crossway.org, pg 55

Crown House Publishing Co LLC, 81 Brook Hills Circle, White Plains, NY 10605 *Tel:* 914-946-3517 *Toll Free Tel:* 877-925-1213 (cust serv) *Fax:* 914-946-1160 *E-mail:* info@chpus.com *Web Site:* www.crownhousepublishing.com, pg 56

Crown Publishing Group, c/o Penguin Random House LLC, 1745 Broadway, New York, NY 10019 *Tel:* 212-782-9000 *Toll Free Tel:* 888-264-1745 *Fax:* 212-940-7408 *E-mail:* crownosm@penguinrandomhouse.com *Web Site:* crownpublishing.com, pg 56

Crystal Clarity Publishers, 14618 Tyler Foote Rd, Nevada City, CA 95959 *Toll Free Tel:* 800-424-1055 *E-mail:* info@crystalclarity.com *Web Site:* www.crystalclarity.com, pg 56

Crystal Kite Awards, 6363 Wilshire Blvd, Suite 425, Los Angeles, CA 90048 *Tel:* 323-782-1010 *E-mail:* info@scbwi.org *Web Site:* www.scbwi.org/awards/crystal-kite-member-choice-award, pg 593

CSLI Publications, Stanford University, Cordura Hall, 220 Panama St, Stanford, CA 94305-4115 *Tel:* 650-723-1839 *Fax:* 650-725-2166 *E-mail:* pubs@csli.stanford.edu *Web Site:* cslipublications.stanford.edu, pg 56

CSWE Press, 333 John Carlyle St, Suite 400, Alexandria, VA 22314-3457 *Tel:* 703-683-8080 *Fax:* 703-683-8493 *E-mail:* publications@cswe.org; info@cswe.org *Web Site:* www.cswe.org, pg 56

Cullman Center Fellowships, New York Public Library, Stephen A Schwarzman Bldg, Fifth Ave & 42 St, Rm 225, New York, NY 10018-2788 *Tel:* 917-275-6975 *E-mail:* csw@nypl.org *Web Site:* www.nypl.org/help/about-nypl/fellowships-institutes, pg 594

Cultural Studies & Analysis, 1123 Montrose St, Philadelphia, PA 19147-3721 *Tel:* 215-592-8544 *E-mail:* info@culturalanalysis.com *Web Site:* www.culturalanalysis.com, pg 437

E E Cummings Prize, c/o Linda Haviland Conte, 18 Hall Ave, Apt 2, Somerville, MA 02144 *E-mail:* info@nepoetryclub.org *Web Site:* nepoetryclub.org, pg 594

Cundill History Prize, 840 Dr Penfield Ave, Rm 233, Montreal, QC H3A 1A4, Canada *Tel:* 514-398-4400 (ext 00468) *E-mail:* cundill.prize@mcgill.ca *Web Site:* www.cundillprize.com, pg 594

Cunningham Commission for Youth Theatre, Lincoln Park Campus, 2350 N Racine Ave, Chicago, IL 60614-4100 *Tel:* 773-325-7999 *E-mail:* cunninghamcommission@depaul.edu *Web Site:* theatre.depaul.edu, pg 594

Merle Curti Intellectual History Award, 112 N Bryan Ave, Bloomington, IN 47408-4141 *Tel:* 812-855-7311 *E-mail:* oah@oah.org *Web Site:* www.oah.org/awards, pg 594

Merle Curti Social History Award, 112 N Bryan Ave, Bloomington, IN 47408-4141 *Tel:* 812-855-7311 *E-mail:* oah@oah.org *Web Site:* www.oah.org/awards, pg 594

C Michael Curtis Short Story Book Prize, 186 W Main St, Spartanburg, SC 29306 *Tel:* 864-577-9349 *Fax:* 864-577-0188 *E-mail:* info@hubcity.org; submit@hubcity.org *Web Site:* hubcity.org/press/c-michael-curtis-short-story-book-prize, pg 594

Richard Curtis Associates Inc, 286 Madison Ave, Suite 1002, New York, NY 10017 *Tel:* 212-772-7363 *E-mail:* curtisagency@haroldober.com *Web Site:* ilpliterary.com, pg 455

Karen & Philip Cushman Late Bloomer Award, 6363 Wilshire Blvd, Suite 425, Los Angeles, CA 90048 *Tel:* 323-782-1010 *E-mail:* info@scbwi.org *Web Site:* www.scbwi.org/awards-and-grants-new, pg 594

CWA/SCA Canada, 2200 Prince of Wales Dr, Suite 301, Ottawa, ON K2E 6Z9, Canada *Tel:* 613-820-9777 *Toll Free Tel:* 877-486-4292 *Fax:* 613-820-8188 *E-mail:* info@cwacanada.ca *Web Site:* www.cwacanada.ca, pg 504

Cypress House, 155 Cypress St, Suite A, Fort Bragg, CA 95437 *Tel:* 707-964-9520 *Toll Free Tel:* 800-773-7782 *Fax:* 707-964-7531 *E-mail:* office@cypresshouse.com *Web Site:* www.cypresshouse.com, pg 56, 437

Dalkey Archive Press, c/o Deep Vellum Publishing, 3000 Commerce St, Dallas, TX 75226 *E-mail:* admin@deepvellum.org *Web Site:* www.dalkeyarchive.com, pg 56

LIZA DAWSON ASSOCIATES

The Danahy Fiction Prize, University of Tampa Press, 401 W Kennedy Blvd, Tampa, FL 33606 *Tel:* 813-253-6266 *E-mail:* utpress@ut.edu *Web Site:* tampareview.org/the-danahy-fiction-prize, pg 594

Dancing Dakini Press, 2935 NE 77 Ave, Portland, OR 97213 *Tel:* 503-415-0229 *E-mail:* editor@dancingdakinipress.com *Web Site:* www.dancingdakinipress.com, pg 57

Dancing Lemur Press LLC, PO Box 383, Pikeville, NC 27863-0383 *E-mail:* admin@dancinglemurpress.com *Web Site:* www.dancinglemurpressllc.com, pg 57

D&B Hoovers™, 7700 W Parmer Lane, Bldg A, Austin, TX 78729 *Tel:* 512-374-4500 *Toll Free Tel:* 855-858-5974 *Web Site:* www.dnb.com/products/marketing-sales/dnb-hoovers.html, pg 57

John M Daniel Literary Services, PO Box 2790, McKinleyville, CA 95519 *Tel:* 707-839-3495 *E-mail:* jmd@danielpublishing.com *Web Site:* www.danielpublishing.com/litserv.htm, pg 438

Benjamin H Danks Award, 633 W 155 St, New York, NY 10032 *Tel:* 212-368-5900 *E-mail:* academy@artsandletters.org *Web Site:* artsandletters.org/awards, pg 594

Darhansoff & Verrill, 529 11 St, 3rd fl, Brooklyn, NY 11215 *Tel:* 917-305-1300 *E-mail:* permissions@dvagency.com *Web Site:* www.dvagency.com, pg 455

Dark Horse Comics, 10956 SE Main St, Milwaukie, OR 97222 *Tel:* 503-652-8815 *Fax:* 503-654-9440 *E-mail:* dhcomics@darkhorse.com *Web Site:* www.darkhorse.com, pg 57

Data Trace Publishing Co (DTP), 110 West Rd, Suite 227, Towson, MD 21204-2316 *Tel:* 410-494-4994 *Toll Free Tel:* 800-342-0454 *Fax:* 410-494-0515 *E-mail:* info@datatrace.com; customerservice@datatrace.com; salesandmarketing@datatrace.com; editorial@datatrace.com *Web Site:* www.datatrace.com, pg 57

Database Directories Inc, 96-320 Westminster Ave, London, ON N6C 5H5, Canada *Tel:* 519-433-1666 *E-mail:* mail@databasedirectory.com *Web Site:* www.databasedirectory.com, pg 400

Davies Publishing Inc, 32 S Raymond Ave, Suites 4 & 5, Pasadena, CA 91105-1961 *Tel:* 626-792-3046 *Toll Free Tel:* 877-792-0005 *Fax:* 626-792-5308 *E-mail:* info@daviespublishing.com *Web Site:* daviespublishing.com, pg 57

F A Davis Co, 1915 Arch St, Philadelphia, PA 19103 *Tel:* 215-568-2270; 215-440-3001 *Toll Free Tel:* 800-523-4049 *Fax:* 215-568-5065; 215-440-3016 *E-mail:* info@fadavis.com; orders@fadavis.com *Web Site:* www.fadavis.com, pg 57

Watson Davis & Helen Miles Davis Prize, 440 Geddes Hall, Notre Dame, IN 46556 *Tel:* 574-631-1194 *Fax:* 574-631-1533 *E-mail:* info@hssonline.org *Web Site:* www.hssonline.org, pg 594

DAW Books, 19 W 21 St, No 1201, New York, NY 10010 *E-mail:* info@astrapublishinghouse.com *Web Site:* astrapublishinghouse.com/imprints/daw-books, pg 57

The Dawn Horse Press, 12040 N Seigler Rd, Middletown, CA 95461 *Tel:* 707-928-6590 *Toll Free Tel:* 877-770-0772 *Fax:* 707-928-5068 *E-mail:* dhp@adidam.org *Web Site:* www.dawnhorsepress.com, pg 57

DawnSignPress, 6130 Nancy Ridge Dr, San Diego, CA 92121-3223 *Tel:* 858-625-0600 *Toll Free Tel:* 800-549-5350 *Fax:* 858-625-2336 *E-mail:* contactus@dawnsign.com *Web Site:* www.dawnsign.com, pg 58

Liza Dawson Associates, 121 W 27 St, Suite 1201, New York, NY 10001 *Tel:* 212-465-9071 *Web Site:* www.lizadawsonassociates.com, pg 455

Robert Day Award for Fiction, UMKC, University House, 5101 Rockhill Rd, Kansas City, MO 64110-2499 Tel: 816-235-1169 E-mail: newletters@umkc.edu Web Site: www.newletters.org, pg 595

Dayton Literary Peace Prize, PO Box 461, Wright Brothers Branch, Dayton, OH 45409-0461 Tel: 937-298-5072 Web Site: www.daytonliterarypeaceprize.org, pg 595

Dayton Playhouse FutureFest, PO Box 3017, Dayton, OH 45401-3017 Tel: 937-424-8477 Fax: 937-424-0062 E-mail: futurefest@daytonplayhouse.com Web Site: wordpress.thedaytonplayhouse.com/futurefest-2, pg 595

dbS Productions, PO Box 94, Charlottesville, VA 22902 Tel: 434-293-5502 Toll Free Tel: 800-745-1581 E-mail: info@dbs-sar.com Web Site: www.dbs-sar.com, pg 58

DC Canada Education Publishing (DCCED), 170 Laurier Ave W, Unit 603, Ottawa, ON K1P 5V5, Canada Tel: 613-565-8885 Toll Free Tel: 888-565-0262 Fax: 613-565-8881 E-mail: info@dc-canada.ca Web Site: www.dc-canada.ca, pg 400

DC Comics Inc, 4000 Warner Blvd, Burbank, CA 91522 Web Site: www.dc.com, pg 58

Walter De Gruyter Inc, 121 High St, 3rd fl, Boston, MA 02110 Tel: 857-284-7073; 617-377-4392 Fax: 857-284-7358 E-mail: service@degruyter.com; orders@degruyter.com Web Site: www.degruyter.com, pg 58

J de S Associates Inc, 9 Shagbark Rd, South Norwalk, CT 06854 Tel: 203-838-7571 Fax: 203-866-2713 Web Site: www.jdesassociates.com, pg 455

Deadline Club, c/o Salmagundi Club, 47 Fifth Ave, New York, NY 10003 Tel: 646-481-7584 E-mail: info@deadlineclub.org Web Site: www.deadlineclub.org, pg 504

The Jennifer DeChiara Literary Agency, 245 Park Ave, 39th fl, New York, NY 10167 Tel: 212-372-8989 Web Site: www.jdlit.com, pg 455

Deep River Books LLC, PO Box 310, Sisters, OR 97759 Tel: 541-549-1139 E-mail: info@deepriverbooks.com Web Site: deepriverbooks.com, pg 58

DeFiore and Company Literary Management Inc, 47 E 19 St, 3rd fl, New York, NY 10003 Tel: 212-925-7744 Fax: 212-925-9803 E-mail: info@defliterary.com; submissions@defliterary.com Web Site: www.defliterary.com, pg 455

Delaware Division of the Arts Individual Artist Fellowships, Carvel State Off Bldg, 4th fl, 820 N French St, Wilmington, DE 19801 Tel: 302-577-8278 Fax: 302-577-6561 E-mail: delarts@delaware.gov Web Site: arts.delaware.gov/grants-for-artists, pg 595

Joelle Delbourgo Associates Inc, 101 Park St, Montclair, NJ 07042 Tel: 973-773-0836 (call only during standard business hours) Web Site: www.delbourgo.com, pg 456

Delphinium Books, 16350 Ventura Blvd, Suite D, Encino, CA 91436 Tel: 917-301-7496 (e-mail first) Web Site: www.delphiniumbooks.com, pg 58

Rick DeMarinis Short Story Award, PO Box 2414, Durango, CO 81302 Tel: 970-903-7914 E-mail: cutthroatmag@gmail.com Web Site: www.cutthroatmag.com, pg 595

Demos Medical Publishing, 902 Carnegie Center Dr, Princeton, NJ 08540 Tel: 212-431-4370 E-mail: info@springerpub.com; cs@springerpub.com Web Site: www.springerpub.com/medicine, pg 58

Denver Publishing Institute Scholarship, 3135 S State St, Suite 203, Ann Arbor, MI 48108 Toll Free Tel: 866-733-9064 E-mail: info@bincfoundation.org Web Site: www.bincfoundation.org/denver-publishing-institute/, pg 595

Der Hovanessian Prize, c/o Linda Haviland Conte, 18 Hall Ave, Apt 2, Somerville, MA 02144 E-mail: info@nepoetryclub.org Web Site: nepoetryclub.org, pg 595

Deseret Book Co, 55 N 300 W, 3rd fl, Salt Lake City, UT 84101-3502 Tel: 801-517-3369; 801-534-1515 (corp) Toll Free Tel: 800-453-4532 (orders); 888-846-7302 (orders) Fax: 801-517-3126 E-mail: service@deseretbook.com Web Site: www.deseretbook.com, pg 58

DEStech Publications Inc, 439 N Duke St, Lancaster, PA 17602-4967 Tel: 717-290-1660 Toll Free Tel: 877-500-4DES (500-4337) Fax: 717-509-6100 E-mail: info@destechpub.com; orders@destechpub.com Web Site: www.destechpub.com, pg 59

Destiny Image Inc, 167 Walnut Bottom Rd, Shippensburg, PA 17257 Tel: 717-532-3040 Toll Free Tel: 800-722-6774 (orders only) Fax: 717-532-9291 Web Site: www.destinyimage.com, pg 59

Anne Devereaux Jordan Award, 140B Purcellville Gateway Dr, Suite 1200, Purcellville, VA 20132 Tel: 630-571-4520 E-mail: info@childlitassn.org Web Site: www.childlitassn.org, pg 595

DeVorss & Co, 1100 Flynn Rd, Unit 104, Camarillo, CA 93012 Tel: 805-322-9010 Toll Free Tel: 800-843-5743 Fax: 805-322-9011 E-mail: service@devorss.com Web Site: www.devorss.com, pg 59

Anna Dewdney Read Together Award, 54 W 39 St, 14th fl, New York, NY 10018 Web Site: everychildareader.net/anna, pg 595

Dewey Publications Inc, 1840 Wilson Blvd, Suite 203, Arlington, VA 22201 Tel: 703-524-1355 Web Site: deweypub.com, pg 59

Dharma Publishing, 35788 Hauser Bridge Rd, Cazadero, CA 95421 Tel: 707-847-3717 Fax: 707-847-3380 E-mail: contact@dharmapublishing.com Web Site: www.dharmapublishing.com, pg 59

Alice Fay Di Castagnola Award, 119 Smith St, Brooklyn, NY 11201 Tel: 212-254-9628 E-mail: info@poetrysociety.org Web Site: poetrysociety.org/awards, pg 595

Christina Di Martino Literary Services, 87 Hamilton Place, No 7G, New York, NY 10031 Tel: 212-996-9086; 561-283-1549 E-mail: writealotmail@gmail.com, pg 438

diacriTech Inc, 4 S Market St, 4th fl, Boston, MA 02109 Tel: 617-600-3366 Fax: 617-848-2938 Web Site: www.diacritech.com, pg 438

Dial Books for Young Readers, c/o Penguin Random House LLC, 1745 Broadway, New York, NY 10019 Tel: 212-782-9000 Web Site: www.penguin.com/dial-overview/, pg 59

Philip K Dick Award, PO Box 3447, Hoboken, NJ 07030 Tel: 201-876-2551 Web Site: www.philipkdickaward.org, pg 595

D4EO Literary Agency, 13206 Treviso Dr, Lakewood Ranch, FL 34211 Tel: 203-545-7180 (cell) Web Site: www.d4eoliteraryagency.com; www.publishersmarketplace.com/members/d4eo/; x.com/d4eo, pg 456

Sandra Dijkstra Literary Agency, 1155 Camino del Mar, PMB 515, Del Mar, CA 92014-2605 Web Site: dijkstraagency.com, pg 456

Annie Dillard Award for Creative Nonfiction, Mail Stop 9053, Western Washington University, Bellingham, WA 98225 Tel: 360-650-4863 E-mail: bellingham.review@wwu.edu Web Site: bhreview.org; bhreview.submittable.com, pg 596

Gordon W Dillon/Richard C Peterson Memorial Essay Contest, PO Box 565477, Miami, FL 33156-5477 Tel: 305-740-2010 Fax: 305-747-7154 E-mail: theaos@aos.org Web Site: www.aos.org, pg 596

DiscoverNet Publishing, 1000 N Main St, Suite 102, Fuquay Varina, NC 27526 Tel: 919-301-0109 Fax: 919-557-2261 E-mail: info@discovernet.com Web Site: www.discovernet.com, pg 59

Discovery Poetry Contest, 1395 Lexington Ave, New York, NY 10128 Tel: 212-415-5760 E-mail: unterberg@92y.org Web Site: www.92y.org/discovery, pg 596

Disney-Hyperion Books, 1101 Flower St, Glendale, CA 91201 Web Site: books.disney.com/imprint/disney-hyperion, pg 59

Disney Press, 1101 Flower St, Glendale, CA 91201 Web Site: books.disney.com, pg 59

Disney Publishing Worldwide, 1101 Flower St, Glendale, CA 91201 Web Site: books.disney.com, pg 60

Dissertation.com, 200 Spectrum Center Dr, 3rd fl, Irvine, CA 92618 Tel: 561-750-4344 Toll Free Tel: 800-636-8329 Fax: 561-750-6797 Web Site: www.dissertation.com, pg 60

Distinguished Scholarly Book Award, c/o Governance Off, 1430 "K" St NW, Suite 600, Washington, DC 20005 Tel: 202-383-9005 E-mail: asa@asanet.org; nominations@asanet.org Web Site: www.asanet.org/about/awards, pg 596

Diversion Books, 11 E 44 St, Suite 1603, New York, NY 10017 Tel: 212-961-6390 E-mail: info@diversionbooks.com Web Site: www.diversionbooks.com, pg 60

Djerassi Resident Artists Program, 2325 Bear Gulch Rd, Woodside, CA 94062 Tel: 650-747-0691 E-mail: info@djerassi.org Web Site: www.djerassi.org, pg 554

DK, c/o Penguin Random House LLC, 1745 Broadway, 20th fl, New York, NY 10019 Tel: 646-674-4000 Toll Free Tel: 800-733-3000 Fax: 646-674-4020 E-mail: marketing@dk.com (lib servs); publicity@dk.com; csorders@penguinrandomhouse.com; customerservice@penguinrandomhouse.com Web Site: www.dk.com, pg 60

DK Research Inc, 9 Wicks Dr, Commack, NY 11725-3921 Tel: 631-543-5537 Fax: 631-543-5549 E-mail: dkresearch@optimum.net Web Site: www.dkresearchinc.com, pg 438

Documentation Grant Program, 225 King St, Suite 201, Fredericton, NB E3B 1E1, Canada Tel: 506-444-4444 Toll Free Tel: 866-460-ARTS (460-2787) Fax: 506-444-5543 E-mail: prog@artsnb.ca Web Site: www.artsnb.ca, pg 596

Dog Writers Association of America Inc (DWAA), PO Box 787, Hughesville, MD 20637 Web Site: dogwriters.org, pg 505

Dog Writers Association of America Inc (DWAA) Annual Writing Competition, PO Box 787, Hughesville, MD 20637 Web Site: dogwriters.org, pg 596

Dogwise Publishing, 403 S Mission St, Wenatchee, WA 98801 Tel: 509-663-9115 Toll Free Tel: 800-776-2665 E-mail: mail@dogwise.com Web Site: www.dogwise.com, pg 60

Janis A Donnaud & Associates Inc, 77 Bleecker St, No C1-25, New York, NY 10012 Tel: 212-431-2663 Fax: 212-431-2667 E-mail: jdonnaud@aol.com, pg 456

Donner Canadian Foundation, 8 Prince Arthur Ave, 3rd fl, Toronto, ON M5R 1A9, Canada Tel: 416-920-6400 Fax: 416-920-5577 Web Site: www.donnerfoundation.org, pg 525

Donner Prize, c/o Naylor and Associates, 23 Empire Ave, Toronto, ON M4M 2L3, Canada Tel: 416-368-8253 E-mail: donnerprize@naylorandassociates.com Web Site: donnerbookprize.com, pg 596

The Donning Company Publishers, 731 S Brunswick St, Brookfield, MO 64628 Toll Free Tel: 800-369-2646 (ext 3377) Web Site: www.donning.com, pg 60

Jim Donovan Literary, 5635 SMU Blvd, Suite 201, Dallas, TX 75206 Tel: 214-696-9411 E-mail: jdlqueries@sbcglobal.net, pg 456

Doodle and Peck Publishing, 413 Cedarburg Ct, Yukon, OK 73099 Tel: 405-354-7422 E-mail: mjones@doodleandpeck.com Web Site: www.doodleandpeck.com, pg 60

Dordt Press, 700 Seventh St NE, Sioux Center, IA 51250-1671 Tel: 712-722-6420 Toll Free Tel: 800-343-6738 Fax: 712-722-6035 E-mail: dordtpress@dordt.edu; bookstore@dordt.edu Web Site: www.dordt.edu/about-dordt/publications/dordt-press-catalog, pg 60

COMPANY INDEX

Dorrance Publishing Co Inc, 585 Alpha Dr, Suite 103, Pittsburgh, PA 15238 *Toll Free Tel:* 800-695-9599; 800-788-7654 (gen cust orders) *Fax:* 412-387-1319 *E-mail:* dorrinfo@dorrancepublishing.com *Web Site:* www.dorrancepublishing.com, pg 61

Dorset Press, 60 Roberts Dr, Suite 308, North Adams, MA 01247 *Tel:* 413-664-9611 *Fax:* 413-664-9711 *E-mail:* info@tupelopress.org *Web Site:* www.tupelopress.org, pg 596

John Dos Passos Prize for Literature, Dept of English & Modern Languages, 201 High St, Farmville, VA 23909 *Tel:* 434-395-2155 *Web Site:* www.longwood.edu/english/dos-passos-prize, pg 596

Double Play, 303 Hillcrest Rd, Belton, MO 64012-1852 *Tel:* 816-651-7118, pg 438

Doubleday, c/o Penguin Random House LLC, 1745 Broadway, New York, NY 10019 *Tel:* 212-751-2600 *Fax:* 212-940-7390 (dom rts); 212-572-2662 (foreign rts) *Web Site:* knopfdoubleday.com/imprint/doubleday/; knopfdoubleday.com, pg 61

Doubleday Canada, 320 Front St W, Suite 1400, Toronto, ON M5V 3B6, Canada *Tel:* 416-364-4449 *Fax:* 416-598-7764 *Web Site:* www.penguinrandomhouse.ca, pg 401

Frank Nelson Doubleday Memorial Award, Barrett Bldg, 2nd fl, 2301 Central Ave, Cheyenne, WY 82002 *Tel:* 307-777-7742 *Web Site:* wyoarts.state.wy.us, pg 597

Douglas & McIntyre (2013) Ltd, 4437 Rondeview Rd, Madeira Park, BC V0N 2H1, Canada *E-mail:* info@douglas-mcintyre.com *Web Site:* www.douglas-mcintyre.com, pg 401

Dover Publications Inc, 1325 Franklin Ave, Suite 250, Garden City, NY 11530 *Tel:* 516-294-7000 *Toll Free Tel:* 800-223-3130 (orders) *Fax:* 516-742-6953 *E-mail:* rights@doverpublications.com *Web Site:* store.doverpublications.com; store.doverdirect.com, pg 61

Down East Books, 4501 Forbes Blvd, Suite 200, Lanham, MD 20706 *Web Site:* rowman.com/page/downeastbooks, pg 61

Down The Shore Publishing, 106 Forge Rd, West Creek, NJ 08092 *Tel:* 609-812-5076 *Fax:* 609-812-5098 *E-mail:* downshore@gmail.com *Web Site:* www.down-the-shore.com, pg 61

Dragon Door Publications, 2999 Yorkton Blvd, Suite 2, Little Canada, MN 55117 *Tel:* 651-487-2180 *E-mail:* support@dragondoor.com *Web Site:* www.dragondoor.com, pg 61

Dramatic Publishing Co, 311 Washington St, Woodstock, IL 60098-3308 *Tel:* 815-338-7170 *Toll Free Tel:* 800-448-7469 *Fax:* 815-338-8981 *Toll Free Fax:* 800-334-5302 *E-mail:* customerservice@dpcplays.com *Web Site:* www.dramaticpublishing.com, pg 61

Dramatists Play Service Inc, 440 Park Ave S, New York, NY 10016 *E-mail:* dpsinfo@broadwaylicensing.com; publications@broadwaylicensing.com *Web Site:* www.dramatists.com, pg 61

Dreamscape Media LLC, 1417 Timberwolf Dr, Holland, OH 43528 *Tel:* 419-867-6965 *Toll Free Tel:* 877-983-7326 *E-mail:* info@dreamscapeab.com *Web Site:* www.dreamscapepublishing.com, pg 62

Carleton Drewry Memorial, PO Box 36128, North Chesterfield, VA 23235-3533 *E-mail:* contest@poetrysocietyofvirginia.org; info@poetryvirginia.org *Web Site:* www.poetrysocietyofvirginia.org, pg 597

Saint Katharine Drexel Award, 8550 United Plaza Blvd, Suite 1001, Baton Rouge, LA 70809 *Tel:* 225-408-4417 *E-mail:* cla2@cathla.org *Web Site:* cathla.org, pg 597

Drury University One-Act Play Competition, 900 N Benton Ave, Springfield, MO 65802-3344 *Tel:* 417-873-6821 *Web Site:* www.drury.edu, pg 597

Dubuque Fine Arts Players Annual One Act Play Festival, PO Box 1160, Dubuque, IA 52004-1160 *Tel:* 563-581-6521 *E-mail:* contact_dbqoneacts@iowa706.com *Web Site:* www.dbqoneacts.org, pg 597

The Grace Dudley Prize for Arts Writing, c/o The New York Review of Books, 435 Hudson St, Suite 300, New York, NY 10014 *Tel:* 212-757-8070 *E-mail:* admin@silversfoundation.org *Web Site:* silversfoundation.org/about-the-silvers-dudley-prizes, pg 597

Duende-Word BIPOC Bookseller Award, 757 E 20 Ave, Suite 370-335, Denver, CO 80205 *E-mail:* info@thewordfordiversity.org *Web Site:* www.thewordfordiversity.org/booksselleraward, pg 597

Jim Duggins PhD Outstanding Mid-Career Novelist Prize, PO Box 20186, New York, NY 10014 *Tel:* 213-277-5755 *E-mail:* awards@lambdaliterary.org; admin@lambdaliterary.org *Web Site:* www.lambdaliterary.org/awards/special-awards, pg 597

Duke University Press, 905 W Main St, Suite 18B, Durham, NC 27701 *Tel:* 919-688-5134 *Toll Free Tel:* 888-651-0122 (US) *Fax:* 919-688-2615 *Toll Free Fax:* 888-651-0124 *E-mail:* orders@dukeupress.edu *Web Site:* www.dukepress.edu, pg 62

Dumbarton Oaks, 1703 32 St NW, Washington, DC 20007 *Tel:* 202-339-6400 *Fax:* 202-339-6401; 202-298-8407 *E-mail:* doaksbooks@doaks.org; press@doaks.org *Web Site:* www.doaks.org, pg 62

Dun & Bradstreet, 103 JFK Pkwy, Short Hills, NJ 07078 *Tel:* 973-921-5500 *Toll Free Tel:* 844-869-8244; 800-234-3867 (cust serv) *Web Site:* www.dnb.com, pg 62

Dundurn Press Ltd, PO Box 19510, RPO Manulife, Toronto, ON M4W 3T9, Canada *Tel:* 416-214-5544 *E-mail:* info@dundurn.com; publicity@dundurn.com; sales@dundurn.com *Web Site:* www.dundurn.com, pg 401

Dunham Literary Inc, 487 Hardscrabble Rd, North Salem, NY 10560 *Tel:* 914-669-5535 *E-mail:* dunhamlit@gmail.com *Web Site:* dunhamlit.com, pg 456

The Joseph R Dunlap Memorial Fellowship, PO Box 53263, Washington, DC 20009 *E-mail:* us@morrissociety.org *Web Site:* www.morrissociety.org, pg 597

Dunow, Carlson & Lerner Literary Agency Inc, 27 W 20 St, Suite 1107, New York, NY 10011 *Tel:* 212-645-7606 *E-mail:* mail@dclagency.com *Web Site:* www.dclagency.com, pg 457

Dupree, Miller & Associates Inc, 4311 Oak Lawn Ave, Suite 650, Dallas, TX 75219 *Tel:* 214-559-2665 *E-mail:* editorial@dupreemiller.com *Web Site:* www.dupreemiller.com, pg 457

Dutton, c/o Penguin Random House LLC, 1745 Broadway, New York, NY 10019 *Tel:* 212-366-2000 *Web Site:* www.penguin.com/dutton-overview/; www.penguin.com/plume-books-overview/; www.penguin.com/tiny-reparations-overview/, pg 62

Dutton Children's Books, c/o Penguin Random House LLC, 1745 Broadway, New York, NY 10019 *Tel:* 212-782-9000 *Web Site:* www.penguin.com/dutton-childrens-overview/, pg 62

Dystel, Goderich & Bourret LLC, One Union Sq W, Suite 904, New York, NY 10003 *Tel:* 212-627-9100 *Fax:* 212-627-9313 *Web Site:* www.dystel.com, pg 457

Eakin Press, PO Box 331779, Fort Worth, TX 76163 *Tel:* 817-344-7036 *Toll Free Tel:* 888-982-8270 *Fax:* 817-344-7036 *Web Site:* www.eakinpress.com, pg 62

Earth Edit, PO Box 114, Maiden Rock, WI 54750 *Tel:* 715-448-3009, pg 438

East Mountain Editing Services, PO Box 1895, Tijeras, NM 87059-1895 *Tel:* 505-281-8422 *Web Site:* www.spanishindexing.com, pg 438

East West Discovery Press, PO Box 3585, Manhattan Beach, CA 90266 *Tel:* 310-545-3730 *Fax:* 310-545-3731 *E-mail:* info@eastwestdiscovery.com *Web Site:* www.eastwestdiscovery.com, pg 63

Eastland Press, 2421 29 Ave W, Seattle, WA 98199 *Tel:* 206-931-6957 (cust serv) *Fax:* 206-283-7084 (orders) *E-mail:* info@eastlandpress.com; orders@eastlandpress.com *Web Site:* www.eastlandpress.com, pg 63

LES EDITIONS ALIRE

Easy Money Press, 82-5800 Napo'opo'o Rd, Captain Cook, HI 96704 *Tel:* 808-313-2808 *E-mail:* easymoneypress@yahoo.com, pg 63

Eaton Literary Associates Literary Awards, PO Box 49795, Sarasota, FL 34230-6795 *Tel:* 941-366-6589 *E-mail:* eatonlit@aol.com *Web Site:* www.eatonliterary.com, pg 597

EBSCO Information Services Library Staff Development Award, 225 N Michigan Ave, Suite 1300, Chicago, IL 60601 *Tel:* 312-280-3247 *Toll Free Tel:* 800-545-2433 (ext 3247) *Fax:* 312-944-3897 *E-mail:* awards@ala.org *Web Site:* www.ala.org/awardsgrants, pg 597

Ecrits des Forges, 992-A rue Royale, Trois-Rivieres, QC G9A 4H9, Canada *Tel:* 819-840-8492 *E-mail:* ecritsdesforges@gmail.com *Web Site:* www.ecritsdesforges.com, pg 401

ECS Publishing Group, 1727 Larkin Williams Rd, Fenton, MO 63026 *Tel:* 636-305-0100 *Toll Free Tel:* 800-647-2117 *Web Site:* ecspublishing.com; www.facebook.com/ecspublishing, pg 63

ECW Press, 665 Gerrard St E, Toronto, ON M4M 1Y2, Canada *Tel:* 416-694-3348 *E-mail:* info@ecwpress.com *Web Site:* www.ecwpress.com, pg 401

EDC Publishing, 5402 S 122 E Ave, Tulsa, OK 74146 *Tel:* 918-622-4522 *Toll Free Tel:* 800-475-4522 *Fax:* 918-663-2525 *Toll Free Fax:* 800-743-5660 *E-mail:* orders@edcpub.com *Web Site:* www.edcpub.com, pg 63

EdCan Network, 60 St Clair Ave E, Suite 703, Toronto, ON M4T 1N5, Canada *Tel:* 416-591-6300 *Toll Free Tel:* 866-803-9549 *Fax:* 416-591-5345 *Toll Free Fax:* 866-803-9549 *E-mail:* info@edcan.ca *Web Site:* www.edcan.ca, pg 505

Anne Edelstein Literary Agency LLC, 258 Riverside Dr, No 8D, New York, NY 10025 *Tel:* 212-414-4923 *E-mail:* info@aeliterary.com *Web Site:* www.aeliterary.com, pg 457

The Edgar Awards®, 1140 Broadway, Suite 1507, New York, NY 10001 *Tel:* 212-888-8171 *E-mail:* mwa@mysterywriters.org *Web Site:* theedgars.com; mysterywriters.org, pg 598

EDGE Science Fiction & Fantasy Publishing Inc, PO Box 1714, Calgary, AB T2P 2L7, Canada *Tel:* 403-254-0102 *Fax:* 403-254-0456 *E-mail:* admin@hadespublications.com *Web Site:* www.edgewebsite.com, pg 401

Edgewise Press Inc, 24 Fifth Ave, Suite 224, New York, NY 10011 *Tel:* 212-387-0931 *E-mail:* epinc@mindspring.com *Web Site:* www.edgewisepress.org, pg 63

ediciones Lerner, 241 First Ave N, Minneapolis, MN 55401 *Tel:* 612-332-3344 *Toll Free Tel:* 800-328-4929 *Fax:* 612-332-7615 *Toll Free Fax:* 800-332-1132 *E-mail:* info@lernerbooks.com; custserve@lernerbooks.com *Web Site:* www.lernerbooks.com; www.facebook.com/lernerbooks, pg 63

Edit Etc, 26 Country Lane, Brunswick, ME 04011 *Tel:* 914-715-5849 *E-mail:* atkedit@cs.com *Web Site:* www.anntkeene.com, pg 438

Edit Resource LLC, 19265 Lincoln Green Lane, Monument, CO 80132 *Tel:* 719-290-0757 *E-mail:* info@editresource.com *Web Site:* www.editresource.com, pg 438

EditAmerica, 115 Jacobs Creek Rd, Ewing, NJ 08628-1014 *Tel:* 609-882-5852 *Web Site:* www.EditAmerica.com; www.linkedin.com/in/PaulaPlantier, pg 438

Editcetera, 2034 Blake St, Suite 5, Berkeley, CA 94704 *Tel:* 510-849-1110 *E-mail:* info@editcetera.com *Web Site:* www.editcetera.com, pg 438

EditCraft Editorial Services, 422 Pine St, Grass Valley, CA 95945 *Tel:* 530-273-3934 *Web Site:* www.editcraft.com, pg 438

Les Editions Alire, 120 cote du Passage, Levis, QC G6V 5S9, Canada *Tel:* 418-835-4441 *Fax:* 418-838-4443 *E-mail:* info@alire.com *Web Site:* www.alire.com, pg 401

Les Editions ASTED, 2065 rue Parthenais, Bureau 387, Montreal, QC H2K 3T1, Canada *Tel:* 514-281-5012 *Fax:* 514-281-8219 *E-mail:* editions@asted.org; info@asted.org *Web Site:* www.asted.org, pg 401

Les Editions Caractere, 5800, rue St-Denis, bureau 900, Montreal, QC H2S 3L5, Canada *Toll Free Tel:* 855-861-2782 *E-mail:* caractere@tc.tc *Web Site:* www.tcmedialivres.com, pg 401

Les Editions Chouette, 2515, avenue de la Renaissance, Boisbriand, QC J7H 1T9, Canada *Tel:* 514-925-3325 *E-mail:* info@editions-chouette.com; serviceclient@editions-chouette.com; foreignrights@editions-chouette.com *Web Site:* www.editions-chouette.com, pg 402

Editions de la Pleine Lune, 223 34 Ave, Lachine, QC H8T 1Z4, Canada *Tel:* 514-634-7954 *E-mail:* editpllune@videotron.ca *Web Site:* www.pleinelune.qc.ca, pg 402

Les Editions de l'Hexagone, 4545, rue Frontenac, 3rd fl, Montreal, QC H2H 2R7, Canada *Tel:* 514-523-1182 *Fax:* 514-521-4434 *Web Site:* editionshexagone.groupelivre.com, pg 402

Les Editions de Mortagne, CP 116, Boucherville, QC J4B 5E6, Canada *Tel:* 450-641-2387 *E-mail:* info@editionsdemortagne.com *Web Site:* editionsdemortagne.com, pg 402

Les Editions du Ble, 340, blvd Provencher, St Boniface, MB R2H 0G7, Canada *Tel:* 204-237-8200 *E-mail:* direction@editionsduble.ca *Web Site:* ble.avoslivres.ca, pg 402

Les Editions du Boreal, 4447, rue St-Denis, Montreal, QC H2J 2L2, Canada *Tel:* 514-287-7401 *Fax:* 514-287-7664 *E-mail:* info@editionsboreal.qc.ca; boreal@editionsboreal.qc.ca; communications@editionsboreal.qc.ca *Web Site:* www.editionsboreal.qc.ca, pg 402

Editions du CHU Sainte-Justine, 3175, chemin de la Cote-Sainte-Catherine, Montreal, QC H3T 1C5, Canada *Tel:* 514-345-4671 *Fax:* 514-345-4631 *E-mail:* edition.hsj@ssss.gouv.qc.ca *Web Site:* www.editions-chu-sainte-justine.org, pg 402

Les Editions du Noroit, 4609, rue D'Iberville, espace 202, Montreal, QC H2H 2L9, Canada *Tel:* 514-727-0005 *E-mail:* poesie@lenoroit.com *Web Site:* lenoroit.com, pg 403

Les Editions du Remue-Menage, 469, Jean-Talon Ouest, bureau 401, Montreal, QC H3N 1R4, Canada *Tel:* 514-876-0097 *E-mail:* info@editions-rm.ca *Web Site:* www.editions-rm.ca, pg 403

Les Editions du Septentrion, 86, Cote de la Montagne, bureau 200, Quebec, QC G1K 4E3, Canada *Tel:* 418-688-3556 *Fax:* 418-527-4978 *E-mail:* info@septentrion.qc.ca *Web Site:* www.septentrion.qc.ca, pg 403

Les Editions Fides, 7333 place des Roseraies, bureau 501, Anjou, QC H1M 2X6, Canada *Tel:* 514-745-4290 *Fax:* 514-745-4299 *E-mail:* editions@groupefides.com *Web Site:* www.editionsfides.com, pg 403

Editions FouLire, 4339, rue des Becassines, Quebec, QC G1G 1V5, Canada *Tel:* 418-628-4029 *Toll Free Tel:* 877-628-4029 (CN & US) *Fax:* 418-628-4801 *E-mail:* edition@foulire.com *Web Site:* www.foulire.com, pg 403

Les Editions Ganesha Inc, CP 484, Succursale Chabanel, Montreal, QC H2N 0A7, Canada *E-mail:* courriel@editions-ganesha.qc.ca; email@editions-ganesha.qc.ca *Web Site:* www.editions-ganesha.qc.ca, pg 403

Les Editions Goelette et Coup d-oeil Inc, 1350, rue Marie-Victorin, St-Bruno-de-Montarville, QC J3V 6B9, Canada *Tel:* 450-653-1337 *Toll Free Tel:* 800-463-4961 *Fax:* 450-653-9924 *E-mail:* info@boutiquegoelette.com; rights@goelette.ca *Web Site:* boutiquegoelette.com, pg 403

Les Editions Heritage Inc, 1101, ave Victoria, St-Lambert, QC J4R 1P8, Canada *Tel:* 514-875-0327 *E-mail:* dominiqueetcie@editionsheritage.com; info@editionsheritage.com *Web Site:* www.dominiqueetcompagnie.com, pg 403

Editions Hurtubise, 1815, ave de Lorimier, Montreal, QC H2K 3W6, Canada *Tel:* 514-523-1523 *Toll Free Tel:* 800-361-1664 *Web Site:* editionshurtubise.com, pg 403

Les Editions JCL, 348, 9e Ave, St-Jean-sur-Richelieu, QC J2X 1K3, Canada *Tel:* 450-515-4438 *E-mail:* info@jcl.qc.ca *Web Site:* www.jcl.qc.ca, pg 404

Editions Le Dauphin Blanc Inc, 825, blvd Lebourgneuf, Suite 125, Quebec, QC G2J 0B9, Canada *Tel:* 418-845-4045 *Fax:* 418-845-1933 *E-mail:* info@dauphinblanc.com *Web Site:* dauphinblanc.com, pg 404

Editions Marie-France, CP 32263 BP Waverly, Montreal, QC H3L 3X1, Canada *Tel:* 514-329-3700 *Toll Free Tel:* 800-563-6644 (CN) *Fax:* 514-329-0630 *E-mail:* editions@marie-france.qc.ca *Web Site:* www.marie-france.qc.ca, pg 404

Editions Mediaspaul, 3965, blvd Henri-Bourassa E, Montreal, QC H1H 1L1, Canada *Tel:* 514-322-7341 *Fax:* 514-322-4281 *E-mail:* mediaspaul@mediaspaul.ca *Web Site:* mediaspaul.ca, pg 404

Editions Michel Quintin, 2259 Papineau Ave, Suite 104, Montreal, QC H2K 4J5, Canada *Tel:* 514-379-3774 *Fax:* 450-539-4905 *E-mail:* info@editionsmichelquintin.ca; commande@editionsmichelquintin.ca (orders) *Web Site:* www.editionsmichelquintin.ca, pg 404

Editions MultiMondes, 1815, Avenue de Lorimier, Montreal, QC H2K 3W6, Canada *Tel:* 514-523-1523 *Toll Free Tel:* 800-361-1664 *Web Site:* editionsmultimondes.com, pg 404

Les Editions Phidal Inc, 5740 Ferrier St, Montreal, QC H4P 1M7, Canada *Tel:* 514-738-0202 *Toll Free Tel:* 800-738-7349 *Fax:* 514-738-5102 *E-mail:* info@phidal.com; orders@phidal.com (sales & export) *Web Site:* phidal.com, pg 404

Les Editions Pierre Tisseyre, 155, rue Maurice, Rosemere, QC J7A 2S8, Canada *Tel:* 514-335-0777 *Fax:* 514-335-6723 *E-mail:* info@edtisseyre.ca *Web Site:* www.tisseyre.ca, pg 404

Editions Prise de parole, 359-27 rue Larch, Sudbury, ON P3E 1B7, Canada *Tel:* 705-675-6491 *E-mail:* info@prisedeparole.ca *Web Site:* www.prisedeparole.ca, pg 405

Editions Trecarre, 4545, rue Frontenac, 3rd fl, Montreal, QC H2H 2R7, Canada *Tel:* 514-849-5259 *Fax:* 514-849-1388 *Web Site:* www.editions-trecarre.com, pg 405

Les Editions Un Monde Different, 3905 Isabelle, bureau 101, Brossard, QC J4Y 2R2, Canada *Tel:* 450-656-2660 *Toll Free Tel:* 800-443-2582 *Fax:* 450-659-9328 *E-mail:* info@umd.ca *Web Site:* umd.ca, pg 405

Les Editions XYZ inc, 1815, ave De Lorimier, Montreal, QC H2K 3W6, Canada *Tel:* 514-525-2170 *Fax:* 514-525-7537 *E-mail:* info@editionsxyz.com *Web Site:* editionsxyz.com, pg 405

Editions Yvon Blais, 75 rue Queen, bureau 4700, Montreal, QC H3C 2N6, Canada *Toll Free Tel:* 800-363-3047 *E-mail:* editionsyvonblais.commandes@tr.com (cust serv) *Web Site:* store.thomsonreuters.ca/fr-ca/nouveautes, pg 405

Editorial Bautista Independiente, 3417 Kenilworth Blvd, Sebring, FL 33870-4469 *Tel:* 863-382-6350 *Toll Free Tel:* 800-398-7187 (US) *Fax:* 863-382-8650 *E-mail:* info@ebi-bmm.org *Web Site:* www.ebi-bmm.org, pg 63

Editorial de la Universidad de Puerto Rico, PO Box 23322, San Juan, PR 00931-3322 *Tel:* 787-525-7654 *Web Site:* www.facebook.com/editorialupr, pg 63

The Editorial Department LLC, 8476 E Speedway Blvd, Suite 202, Tucson, AZ 85710 *Tel:* 520-546-9992 *E-mail:* admin@editorialdepartment.com *Web Site:* www.editorialdepartment.com, pg 438

Editorial Excellence Award, PO Box 33020, Santa Fe, NM 87594 *Web Site:* biographersinternational.org/award/editorial-excellence, pg 598

Editorial Freelancers Association (EFA), 266 W 37 St, 20th fl, New York, NY 10018 *Tel:* 212-920-4816 *Toll Free Tel:* 866-929-5425 *E-mail:* info@the-efa.org; membership@the-efa.org *Web Site:* www.the-efa.org, pg 505

Editorial Portavoz, 2450 Oak Industrial Dr NE, Grand Rapids, MI 49505 *Toll Free Tel:* 877-733-2607 (ext 206) *E-mail:* kregelbooks@kregel.com *Web Site:* www.portavoz.com, pg 64

Editorial Unilit, 8167 NW 84 St, Medley, FL 33166 *Tel:* 305-592-6136; 305-592-6135 *Toll Free Tel:* 800-767-7726 *Fax:* 305-592-0087 *E-mail:* info@editorialunilit.com; ventas@editorialunilit.com (sales) *Web Site:* www.editorialunilit.com, pg 64

Editor's Award, 90 Broad St, Suite 2100, New York, NY 10004 *Tel:* 212-226-3586 *Fax:* 212-226-3963 *E-mail:* admin@pw.org *Web Site:* www.pw.org/about-us/sponsored-prizes, pg 598

Editors Canada (Reviseurs Canada), 1507-180 Dundas St W, Toronto, ON M5G 1Z8, Canada *Tel:* 416-975-1379 *E-mail:* info@editors.ca; info@reviseurs.ca; communications@editors.ca *Web Site:* www.editors.ca; www.reviseurs.ca, pg 505

Editor's Choice Award, UMKC, University House, 5101 Rockhill Rd, Kansas City, MO 64110-2499 *Tel:* 816-235-1169 *E-mail:* newletters@umkc.edu *Web Site:* www.newletters.org, pg 598

The Editors Circle, 24 Holly Circle, Easthampton, MA 01027 *Tel:* 862-596-9709 *E-mail:* query@theeditorscircle.com *Web Site:* www.theeditorscircle.com, pg 438

Editors Prize for Feature Article, 61 W Superior St, Chicago, IL 60654 *Tel:* 312-787-7070 *Web Site:* www.poetryfoundation.org/poetrymagazine/prizes, pg 598

Editors Prize for Reviewing, 61 W Superior St, Chicago, IL 60654 *Tel:* 312-787-7070 *Web Site:* www.poetryfoundation.org/poetrymagazine/prizes, pg 598

Editors Prize for Visual Poetry, 61 W Superior St, Chicago, IL 60654 *Tel:* 312-787-7070 *Web Site:* www.poetryfoundation.org/poetrymagazine/prizes, pg 598

Education Writers Association (EWA), 1825 "K" St NW, Suite 200, Washington, DC 20006 *Tel:* 202-452-9830 *Web Site:* ewa.org, pg 505

Education Writers Association Workshops, 1825 "K" St NW, Suite 200, Washington, DC 20006 *Tel:* 202-452-9830 *Web Site:* ewa.org, pg 554

Educational Book & Media Association (EBMA), 11 Main St, Suite D, Warrenton, VA 20186 *Tel:* 540-318-7770 *Fax:* 202-962-3939 *E-mail:* info@edupaperback.org; admin@edupaperback.org *Web Site:* www.edupaperback.org, pg 505

Educational Insights®, 152 W Walnut St, Suite 201, Gardena, CA 90248 *Toll Free Tel:* 800-995-4436 *Toll Free Fax:* 888-892-8731 *E-mail:* info@educationalinsights.com; cs@educationalinsights.com *Web Site:* www.educationalinsights.com, pg 64

Educators Book Award, 1801 E 51 St, Suite 365-163, Austin, TX 78701 *Tel:* 512-478-5748 *Toll Free Tel:* 888-762-4685 *Fax:* 512-478-3961 *Web Site:* www.dkg.org, pg 598

Educator's International Press Inc (EIP), 756 Linderman Ave, Kingston, NY 12401 *Tel:* 518-334-0276 *Toll Free Tel:* 800-758-3756 *Fax:* 703-661-1547 *E-mail:* info@edint.com, pg 64

Edupress Inc, 12621 Western Ave, Garden Grove, CA 92841 *Toll Free Tel:* 800-662-4321 *Toll Free Fax:* 800-525-1254 *E-mail:* custserv@teachercreated.com *Web Site:* www.teachercreated.com, pg 64

Margaret A Edwards Award, 225 N Michigan Ave, Suite 1300, Chicago, IL 60601 *Tel:* 312-280-4390 *Toll Free Tel:* 800-545-2433 *E-mail:* yalsa@ala.org *Web Site:* www.ala.org/yalsa/edwards-award, pg 598

Edwin Markham Prize for Poetry, San Jose State University, English Dept, One Washington Sq, San Jose, CA 95192-0090 *Tel:* 408-924-4441 *E-mail:* mail@reedmag.org *Web Site:* www.reedmag.org; reedmagazine.submittable.com, pg 598

COMPANY INDEX

Wm B Eerdmans Publishing Co, 4035 Park East Ct SE, Grand Rapids, MI 49546 Tel: 616-459-4591 Toll Free Tel: 800-253-7521 E-mail: customerservice@eerdmans.com; sales@eerdmans.com Web Site: www.eerdmans.com, pg 64

The Maureen Egen Writers Exchange Award, 90 Broad St, Suite 2100, New York, NY 10004 Tel: 212-226-3586 Fax: 212-226-3963 E-mail: wex@pw.org; admin@pw.org Web Site: www.pw.org, pg 598

Wilfrid Eggleston Award for Nonfiction, 11759 Groat Rd NW, Edmonton, AB T5M 3K6, Canada Tel: 780-422-8174 Toll Free Tel: 800-665-5354 (AB only) E-mail: mail@writersguild.ab.ca Web Site: writersguild.ca, pg 598

Eifrig Publishing LLC, PO Box 66, Lemont, PA 16851 Tel: 814-954-9445 E-mail: info@eifrigpublishing.com Web Site: www.eifrigpublishing.com, pg 64

Eisenbrauns, 820 N University Dr, USB 1, Suite C, University Park, PA 16802-1003 Tel: 814-865-1327 Toll Free Tel: 800-326-9180 (orders & cust serv) Fax: 814-863-1408 Toll Free Fax: 877-778-2665 (orders) E-mail: orders@psupress.org; customerservice@psupress.org Web Site: www.eisenbrauns.org, pg 64

Ekphrastic Poetry Award, PO Box 36128, North Chesterfield, VA 23235-3533 E-mail: contest@poetrysocietyofvirginia.org; info@poetryvirginia.org Web Site: www.poetrysocietyofvirginia.org, pg 599

Ekus Group LLC, 57 North St, Hatfield, MA 01038 Tel: 413-247-9325 E-mail: info@ekusgroup.com Web Site: ekusgroup.com, pg 457, 562

Elderberry Press Inc, 1393 Old Homestead Dr, Oakland, OR 97462-9690 Tel: 541-459-6043 E-mail: editor@elderberrypress.com Web Site: www.elderberrypress.com, pg 65

The Electrochemical Society (ECS), 65 S Main St, Bldg D, Pennington, NJ 08534-2839 Tel: 609-737-1902 Fax: 609-737-0629 E-mail: publications@electrochem.org; customerservice@electrochem.org; ecs@ioppublishing.org Web Site: www.electrochem.org, pg 65

Edward Elgar Publishing Inc, The William Pratt House, 9 Dewey Ct, Northampton, MA 01060-3815 Tel: 413-584-5551 Toll Free Tel: 800-390-3149 (orders) Fax: 413-584-9933 E-mail: elgarinfo@e-elgar.com; elgarsales@e-elgar.com; elgarsubmissions@e-elgar.com (edit) Web Site: www.e-elgar.com; www.elgaronline.com (ebooks & journals), pg 65

eLit Awards, 1129 Woodmere Ave, Suite B, Traverse City, MI 49686 Tel: 231-933-0445 Toll Free Tel: 800-706-4636 Fax: 231-933-0448 E-mail: info@elitawards.com Web Site: elitawards.com, pg 599

Elite Books, PO Box 222, Petaluma, CA 94953-0222 Tel: 707-525-9292 Toll Free Fax: 800-330-9798 E-mail: support@eftuniverse.com Web Site: www.elitebooksonline.com, pg 65

Ethan Ellenberg Literary Agency, 548 Broadway, Apt 5C, New York, NY 10012 Tel: 212-431-4554 E-mail: agent@ethanellenberg.com Web Site: www.ethanellenberg.com, pg 458

Van Courtlandt Elliott Prize, 6 Beacon St, Suite 500, Boston, MA 02108 Tel: 617-491-1622 Fax: 617-492-3303 E-mail: info@themedievalacademy.org Web Site: www.medievalacademy.org/page/elliott_prize, pg 599

Ralph Ellison Award, 200 NE 18 St, Oklahoma City, OK 73105-3205 Tel: 405-522-3383 Web Site: libraries.ok.gov/ocb/oklahoma-book-awards, pg 599

Elsevier Health Sciences, 1600 John F Kennedy Blvd, Suite 1800, Philadelphia, PA 19103-2899 Tel: 215-239-3900 Toll Free Tel: 800-523-1649 Fax: 215-239-3990 Web Site: www.us.elsevierhealth.com, pg 65

Elsevier Inc, 230 Park Ave, Suite 800, New York, NY 10169 Tel: 212-989-5800 Fax: 212-633-3990 Web Site: www.elsevier.com, pg 65

Elva Resa Publishing, 8362 Tamarack Village, Suite 119-106, St Paul, MN 55125 Tel: 651-357-8770 Fax: 501-641-0777 E-mail: staff@elvaresa.com Web Site: elvaresa.com; www.militaryfamilybooks.com, pg 65

Catherine C Elverston ELS, 3242 NW Fifth St, Gainesville, FL 32609 Tel: 352-222-0625 (cell) E-mail: celverston@gmail.com Web Site: www.celverston.com/CatherineElverstonEditingService.html, pg 439

R Elwell Indexing, 193 Main St, Cold Spring, NY 10516 Tel: 845-667-1036 E-mail: r.elwell.indexing@gmail.com, pg 439

Embolden Literary, PO Box 953607, Lake Mary, FL 32795-3607 E-mail: info@emboldenmediagroup.com; submissions@emboldenmediagroup.com Web Site: emboldenmediagroup.com/literary-representation, pg 458

Emerald Books, PO Box 55787, Seattle, WA 98155 Tel: 425-771-1153 Toll Free Tel: 800-922-2143 Fax: 425-775-2383 E-mail: books@ywampublishing.com Web Site: www.ywampublishing.com, pg 66

Emerging Critics Fellowship, c/o Jacob M Appel, Icahn School of Medicine at Mount Sinai, One Gustave L Levy Place, New York, NY 10029 E-mail: info@bookcritics.org Web Site: www.bookcritics.org/awards, pg 599

Emerging Playwright Award, 555 Eighth Ave, Suite 1800, New York, NY 10018 Tel: 212-421-1380 Fax: 212-421-1387 E-mail: urbanstage@aol.com Web Site: urbanstages.org, pg 599

Emerging Voices Fellowship, 1370 N St Andrews Place, Los Angeles, CA 90028 Tel: 323-424-4939 E-mail: ev@pen.org; awards@pen.org; info@pen.org Web Site: pen.org/emerging-voices-fellowship, pg 599

Emerson College Department of Writing, Literature & Publishing, 180 Tremont St, 10th fl, Boston, MA 02116-4624 Tel: 617-824-8750 Web Site: www.emerson.edu; www.emerson.edu/writing-literature-publishing, pg 562

The Ralph Waldo Emerson Award, 1606 New Hampshire Ave NW, Washington, DC 20009 Tel: 202-265-3808 Fax: 202-986-1601 E-mail: awards@pbk.org Web Site: www.pbk.org/bookawards, pg 599

Emmaus Road Publishing Inc, 1468 Parkview Circle, Steubenville, OH 43952 Tel: 750-264-9535 Fax: 740-475-0230 (orders) E-mail: questions@emmausroad.org Web Site: stpaulcenter.com/emmaus-road-publishing, pg 66

Emond Montgomery Publications Ltd, One Eglinton Ave E, Toronto, ON M4P 3A1, Canada Tel: 416-975-3925 Toll Free Tel: 888-837-0815 Fax: 416-975-3924 E-mail: orders@emond.ca Web Site: www.emond.ca, pg 405

Empire State Award for Excellence in Literature for Young People, 6021 State Farm Rd, Guilderland, NY 12084 Tel: 518-432-6952 Toll Free Tel: 800-252-6952 Fax: 518-427-1697 E-mail: info@nyla.org; marketing@nyla.org Web Site: www.nyla.org, pg 599

Enchanted Lion Books, 248 Creamer St, Studio 4, Brooklyn, NY 11231 Tel: 646-785-9272 E-mail: enchantedlion@gmail.com Web Site: www.enchantedlion.com, pg 66

Encounter Books, 900 Broadway, Suite 601, New York, NY 10003 Tel: 212-871-6310 Toll Free Tel: 855-203-7220 E-mail: publicity@encounterbooks.com Web Site: www.encounterbooks.com, pg 66

Encyclopaedia Britannica Inc, 325 N La Salle St, Suite 200, Chicago, IL 60654 Tel: 312-347-7000 (all other countries) Toll Free Tel: 800-323-1229 (US & CN) Fax: 312-294-2104 E-mail: contact@eb.com Web Site: www.britannica.com, pg 66

Endless Mountains Publishing Co, 72 Glenmaura National Blvd, Suite 104B, Moosic, PA 18507 Tel: 862-251-2296 E-mail: info@endlessmountainspublishing.com Web Site: kalaniotbooks.com, pg 66

Energy Psychology Press, PO Box 222, Petaluma, CA 94953-0222 Tel: 707-525-9292 Toll Free Fax: 800-330-9798 E-mail: energypsychologypress@gmail.com; support@eftuniverse.com Web Site: www.energypsychologypress.com; www.elitebooksonline.com, pg 66

EUROPA EDITIONS

Paul Engle Prize, 123 S Linn St, Iowa City, IA 52240 E-mail: info@iowacityofliterature.org Web Site: www.iowacityofliterature.org/paul-engle-prize, pg 599

Enough Said: Editing, Writing, Research, Project Management, 3959 NW 29 Lane, Gainesville, FL 32606 Tel: 352-262-2971 E-mail: enoughsaid@cox.net, pg 439

The Gerald Ensley Developing Writer Award, 116 Honors Way, Suite 314, Tallahassee, FL 32306 Tel: 850-644-5211 E-mail: floridabookawards@gmail.com Web Site: www.floridabookawards.org/index.php/ensley-award, pg 600

Enslow Publishing LLC, 101 W 23 St, Suite 240, New York, NY 10011 Toll Free Tel: 800-398-2504 Fax: 908-771-0925 Toll Free Fax: 877-980-4454 E-mail: customercare@enslow.com Web Site: www.enslow.com, pg 66

Entangled Publishing LLC, 644 Shrewsbury Commons Ave, Suite 181, Shrewsbury, PA 17361 Toll Free Tel: 877-677-9451 E-mail: publisher@entangledpublishing.com Web Site: www.entangledpublishing.com, pg 67

Entomological Society of America, 170 Jennifer Rd, Suite 230, Annapolis, MD 21401 Tel: 301-731-4535 Fax: 301-731-4538 E-mail: esa@entsoc.org Web Site: www.entsoc.org, pg 67

Environmental Law Institute, 1730 "M" St NW, Suite 700, Washington, DC 20036 Tel: 202-939-3800 Toll Free Tel: 800-433-5120 Fax: 202-939-3868 E-mail: law@eli.org Web Site: www.eli.org, pg 67

Epicenter Press Inc, 6524 NE 181 St, Suite 2, Kenmore, WA 98028 Tel: 425-485-6822 (edit, mktg, busn off) Fax: 425-481-8253 E-mail: info@epicenterpress.com Web Site: www.epicenterpress.com, pg 67

EPS School Specialty, 625 Mount Auburn St, Suite 202, Cambridge, MA 02138-3039 Toll Free Tel: 800-225-5750 Toll Free Fax: 888-440-2665 E-mail: curriculumcare@schoolspecialty.com; curriculumorders@schoolspecialty.com Web Site: eps.schoolspecialty.com, pg 67

Norma Epstein Foundation Awards in Creative Writing, 15 King's College Circle, UC 165, Toronto, ON M5S 3H7, Canada Tel: 416-946-0271 E-mail: uc.programs@utoronto.ca Web Site: www.uc.utoronto.ca/norma-epstein, pg 600

Equity Fellowship, 1507-180 Dundas St W, Toronto, ON M5G 1Z8, Canada Tel: 416-975-1379 E-mail: info@editors.ca; info@reviseurs.ca; communications@editors.ca Web Site: www.editors.ca/about/awards/equity-fellowship, pg 600

Ernest Sandeen Prize in Poetry & Richard Sullivan Prize in Short Fiction, 310 Flanner Hall, Notre Dame, IN 46556 Tel: 574-631-6346 Fax: 574-631-8148 E-mail: undpress@nd.edu; creativewriting@nd.edu Web Site: english.nd.edu/creative-writing/awards-and-prizes/; undpress.nd.edu, pg 600

ERPI, 1611 Cremazie Blvd E, 10th fl, Montreal, QC H2M 2P2, Canada Tel: 514-334-2690 Toll Free Tel: 800-263-3678 Fax: 514-334-4720 Toll Free Fax: 800-643-4720 E-mail: bienvenue@pearsonerpi.com Web Site: pearsonerpi.com; pearsonplc.ca, pg 405

Erskine J Poetry Prize, 2221 Lake Ave, Baltimore, MD 21213 E-mail: smartishpace@gmail.com Web Site: www.smartishpace.com/poetry-prizes, pg 600

Felicia Eth Literary Representation, 555 Bryant St, Suite 350, Palo Alto, CA 94301 Tel: 415-970-9717 E-mail: feliciaeth.literary@gmail.com Web Site: www.ethliterary.com, pg 458

Etruscan Press, Wilkes University, 84 W South St, Wilkes-Barre, PA 18766 Tel: 570-408-4546 Fax: 570-408-3333 E-mail: books@etruscanpress.org Web Site: www.etruscanpress.org, pg 67

Europa Editions, 27 Union Sq W, Suite 302, New York, NY 10003 Tel: 212-868-6844 Fax: 212-868-6845 E-mail: info@europaeditions.com; books@europaeditions.com; publicity@europaeditions.com Web Site: www.europaeditions.com, pg 67

Evan-Moor Educational Publishers, 10 Harris Ct, Suite C-3, Monterey, CA 93940 *Tel:* 831-649-5901 *Toll Free Tel:* 800-777-4362 (orders) *Fax:* 831-649-6256 *Toll Free Fax:* 800-777-4332 (orders) *E-mail:* sales@evan-moor.com; marketing@evan-moor.com *Web Site:* www.evan-moor.com, pg 68

Evangelical Christian Publishers Association (ECPA), 5801 S McClintock Dr, Suite 104, Tempe, AZ 85283 *Tel:* 480-966-3998 *Fax:* 480-966-1944 *E-mail:* info@ecpa.org *Web Site:* www.ecpa.org, pg 505

Evangelical Press Association (EPA), PO Box 1787, Queen Creek, AZ 85142 *Toll Free Tel:* 888-311-1731 *E-mail:* info@evangelicalpress.com *Web Site:* www.evangelicalpress.com, pg 505

David W & Beatrice C Evans Biography & Handcart Awards, 0735 Old Main Hill, Logan, UT 84322-0735 *Tel:* 435-797-0299 *Fax:* 435-797-1092 *E-mail:* mwc@usu.edu *Web Site:* mountainwest.usu.edu, pg 600

M Evans & Company, c/o Rowman & Littlefield Publishing Group, 4501 Forbes Blvd, Suite 200, Lanham, MD 20706 *Tel:* 301-459-3366 *Fax:* 301-429-5748 *Web Site:* rowman.com, pg 68

Mary Evans Inc, 242 E Fifth St, New York, NY 10003-8501 *Fax:* 212-979-5344 *E-mail:* info@maryevansinc.com *Web Site:* maryevansinc.com, pg 458

Evergreen Pacific Publishing Ltd, 10114 19 Ave SE, Suite 8, PMB 703, Everett, WA 98208 *Tel:* 425-493-1451 *E-mail:* sales@evergreenpacific.com *Web Site:* www.evergreenpacific.com, pg 68

Everyman's Library, c/o Penguin Random House LLC, 1745 Broadway, New York, NY 10019 *Tel:* 212-751-2600 *Fax:* 212-940-7390 (dom rts); 212-572-2662 (foreign rts) *Web Site:* knopfdoubleday.com/imprint/everymans-library/; knopfdoubleday.com, pg 68

Everything Goes Media LLC, PO Box 1524, Milwaukee, WI 53201 *Tel:* 312-226-8400 *E-mail:* info@everythinggoesmedia.com *Web Site:* www.everythinggoesmedia.com, pg 68

EWA Reporting Fellowships, 1825 "K" St NW, Suite 200, Washington, DC 20006 *Tel:* 202-452-9830 *Web Site:* ewa.org, pg 600

Excalibur Publications, 6855 W Ina Rd, Tucson, AZ 85743-9633 *Tel:* 520-575-9057 *E-mail:* excaliburpublications@centurylink.net, pg 68

EXCEL Awards, 1620 "I" St NW, Suite 501, Washington, DC 20005 *Tel:* 202-289-7442 *Fax:* 202-289-7097 *E-mail:* excelawards@siia.net *Web Site:* siia.net/excel, pg 600

Excellence in Graphic Literature Awards, 2760 W Fifth Ave, Denver, CO 80204 *Tel:* 303-325-1236 *E-mail:* egl@popcultureclassroom.org *Web Site:* www.popcultureclassroom.org/events, pg 600

Excellence in Nonfiction for Young Adults, 225 N Michigan Ave, Suite 1300, Chicago, IL 60601 *Toll Free Tel:* 800-545-2433 (ext 4390) *E-mail:* yalsa@ala.org *Web Site:* www.ala.org/yalsa/nonfiction-award, pg 601

Excellence in Teaching Fellowships, Open Book Bldg, Suite 200, 1011 Washington Ave S, Minneapolis, MN 55415 *Tel:* 612-215-2575 *Fax:* 612-215-2576 *E-mail:* loft@loft.org *Web Site:* loft.org/awards/excellence-teaching-fellowships, pg 601

Excelsior Editions, 10 N Pearl St, 4th fl, Albany, NY 12207 *Tel:* 518-944-2800 *Toll Free Tel:* 866-430-7869 *Fax:* 518-320-1592 *E-mail:* info@sunypress.edu *Web Site:* www.sunypress.edu, pg 68

The Experiment, 220 E 23 St, Suite 600, New York, NY 10010-4658 *Tel:* 212-889-1659 *E-mail:* info@theexperimentpublishing.com *Web Site:* www.theexperimentpublishing.com, pg 68

Facts On File, 1000 N West St, Suite 1281-230, Wilmington, DE 19801 *Tel:* 212-967-8800 *Toll Free Tel:* 800-322-8755 *Toll Free Fax:* 800-678-3633 *E-mail:* custserv@factsonfile.com *Web Site:* infobasepublishing.com, pg 69

Fair Winds Press, 100 Cummings Ctr, Suite 265-D, Beverly, MA 01915 *Tel:* 978-282-9590 *Fax:* 978-282-7765 *E-mail:* sales@quarto.com *Web Site:* www.quartoknows.com, pg 69

John K Fairbank Prize in East Asian History, 400 "A" St SE, Washington, DC 20003 *Tel:* 202-544-2422 *E-mail:* awards@historians.org *Web Site:* www.historians.org/award-grant/john-k-fairbank-prize/, pg 601

Fairchild Books, 1385 Broadway, 5th fl, New York, NY 10018 *Tel:* 212-419-5300 *Toll Free Tel:* 800-932-4724; 888-330-8477 (orders) *Web Site:* www.bloomsbury.com/us/discover/bloomsbury-academic/fairchild-books/, pg 69

Linda Fairchild & Company LLC, 101 Lucas Valley Rd, Suite 363, San Rafael, CA 94903 *Tel:* 415-336-6407 *Web Site:* www.lindafairchild.com, pg 439

Fairleigh Dickinson University Press, 842 Cambie St, Vancouver, BC V6B 2P6, Canada *Tel:* 604-648-4476 *Fax:* 604-648-4489 *E-mail:* fdupress@fdu.edu *Web Site:* www.fdupress.org, pg 405

Tom Fairley Award for Editorial Excellence, 1507-180 Dundas St W, Toronto, ON M5G 1Z8, Canada *Tel:* 416-975-1379 *E-mail:* fairley_award@editors.ca; info@editors.ca; communications@editors.ca *Web Site:* www.editors.ca/about/awards/tom-fairley-award, pg 601

Faith & Fellowship Publishing, 1020 W Alcott Ave, Fergus Falls, MN 56537 *Tel:* 218-736-7357 *Toll Free Tel:* 800-332-9232 *E-mail:* ffpublishing@clba.org *Web Site:* www.clba.org, pg 69

Faith Library Publications, PO Box 50126, Tulsa, OK 74150-0126 *Tel:* 918-258-1588 *Toll Free Tel:* 888-258-0999 (orders) *Fax:* 918-872-7710 (orders) *E-mail:* flp@rhema.org *Web Site:* www.rhema.org/store, pg 69

Faithlife Corp, 1313 Commercial St, Bellingham, WA 98225 *Tel:* 360-527-1700 *Toll Free Tel:* 888-563-0382 *E-mail:* support@faithlife.com; customerservice@logos.com *Web Site:* faithlife.com, pg 69

Familius, PO Box 1249, Reedley, CA 93654 *Tel:* 559-876-2170 *Fax:* 559-876-2180 *E-mail:* orders@familius.com *Web Site:* www.familius.com, pg 69

Far Horizons Award for Poetry, University of Victoria, PO Box 1700, Sta CSC, Victoria, BC V8W 2Y2, Canada *Tel:* 250-721-8524 *E-mail:* malahat@uvic.ca *Web Site:* www.malahatreview.ca/contests/far_horizons_poetry/info.html; www.malahatreview.ca, pg 601

Far Horizons Award for Short Fiction, University of Victoria, PO Box 1700, Sta CSC, Victoria, BC V8W 2Y2, Canada *Tel:* 250-721-8524 *E-mail:* malahat@uvic.ca *Web Site:* www.malahatreview.ca/contests/far_horizons_fiction/info.html; www.malahatreview.ca, pg 601

Norma Farber First Book Award, 119 Smith St, Brooklyn, NY 11201 *Tel:* 212-254-9628 *E-mail:* info@poetrysociety.org *Web Site:* poetrysociety.org/awards, pg 601

Farcountry Press, 2750 Broadwater Ave, Helena, MT 59602-9202 *Tel:* 406-422-1263 *Toll Free Tel:* 800-821-3874 (sales off) *Fax:* 406-443-5480 *E-mail:* books@farcountrypress.com; sales@farcountrypress.com *Web Site:* www.farcountrypress.com, pg 69

Farrar, Straus & Giroux Books for Young Readers, 120 Broadway, New York, NY 10271 *Tel:* 212-741-6900 *Toll Free Tel:* 888-330-8477 (orders) *E-mail:* childrens.publicity@macmillanusa.com; childrensrights@macmillanusa.com *Web Site:* us.macmillan.com/mackids, pg 69

Farrar, Straus & Giroux, LLC, 120 Broadway, New York, NY 10271 *Tel:* 212-741-6900 *E-mail:* fsg.publicity@fsgbooks.com; sales@fsgbooks.com *Web Site:* us.macmillan.com/fsg, pg 70

Farrar Writing & Editing, 4638 Manchester Rd, Mound, MN 55364 *Tel:* 952-451-5982 *Web Site:* www.writeandedit.net, pg 439

Father & Son Publishing Inc, 4909 N Monroe St, Tallahassee, FL 32303-7015 *Tel:* 850-562-2712 *Toll Free Tel:* 800-741-2712 (orders only) *Fax:* 850-562-0916 *Web Site:* www.fatherson.com, pg 70

The FC2 Catherine Doctorow Innovative Fiction Prize, c/o University of Alabama Press, Box 870380, Tuscaloosa, AL 35487-0380 *E-mail:* fc2@gmail.com *Web Site:* fc2.org, pg 601

The FC2 Ronald Sukenick Innovative Fiction Contest, c/o University of Alabama Press, Box 870380, Tuscaloosa, AL 35487-0380 *E-mail:* fc2@gmail.com *Web Site:* fc2.org, pg 601

FC&A Publishing, 103 Clover Green, Peachtree City, GA 30269 *Tel:* 770-487-6307 *Toll Free Tel:* 800-226-8024 *Web Site:* www.fca.com, pg 70

Federal Street Press, 47 Federal St, Springfield, MA 01102 *Tel:* 413-734-3134 (ext 8158) *Toll Free Tel:* 800-828-1880 *Fax:* 413-731-5979 *E-mail:* sales@federalstreetpress.com; customerservice@federalstreetpress.com; orders@federalstreetpress.com *Web Site:* federalstreetpress.com, pg 70

Federation des Milieux Documentaires, 2065 rue Parthenais, Bureau 387, Montreal, QC H2K 3T1, Canada *Tel:* 514-281-5012 *E-mail:* info@fmdoc.org *Web Site:* fmdoc.org, pg 505

Federation of BC Writers, PO Box 3503, Courtenay, BC V9N 6Z9, Canada *E-mail:* hello@bcwriters.ca *Web Site:* bcwriters.ca, pg 505

Feigenbaum Publishing Consultants Inc, 61 Bounty Lane, Jericho, NY 11753 *Tel:* 516-647-8314 (cell), pg 458

The Leslie Feinberg Award for Trans & Gender-Variant Literature, 511 Avenue of the Americas, No D36, New York, NY 10011 *E-mail:* awards@publishingtriangle.org; info@publishingtriangle.org; publishingtriangle@gmail.com *Web Site:* publishingtriangle.org/awards/trans-gender-variant-literature, pg 601

Betsy Feist Resources, 140 E 81 St, Unit 7-E, New York, NY 10028-1875 *Tel:* 212-861-2014 *E-mail:* betsyfeist@gmail.com, pg 439

Feldheim Publishers, 208 Airport Executive Park, Nanuet, NY 10954 *Tel:* 845-356-2282 *Toll Free Tel:* 800-237-7149 (orders) *Fax:* 845-425-1908 *E-mail:* sales@feldheim.com *Web Site:* www.feldheim.com, pg 70

Fellowships for Creative & Performing Artists & Writers, 185 Salisbury St, Worcester, MA 01609-1634 *Tel:* 508-755-5221 *Fax:* 508-754-9069 *E-mail:* library@mwa.org *Web Site:* www.americanantiquarian.org, pg 602

Fellowships for Historical Research, 185 Salisbury St, Worcester, MA 01609-1634 *Tel:* 508-755-5221 *Fax:* 508-754-9069 *Web Site:* www.americanantiquarian.org, pg 602

Jerry Felsen, 3960 NW 196 St, Miami Gardens, FL 33055-1869 *Tel:* 305-625-5012 *E-mail:* jf0@mail.com, pg 439

The Feminist Press at The City University of New York, 365 Fifth Ave, Suite 5406, New York, NY 10016 *Tel:* 212-817-7915 *Fax:* 212-817-1593 *E-mail:* info@feministpress.org *Web Site:* www.feministpress.org, pg 71

Fence Books, 36-09 28 Ave, Apt 3R, Astoria, NY 11103-4518 *Tel:* 518-567-7006 *Web Site:* www.fenceportal.org, pg 71

Fence Modern Poets Series, 36-09 28 Ave, Apt 3R, Astoria, NY 11103-4518 *Tel:* 518-567-7006 *Web Site:* www.fenceportal.org, pg 602

Shubert Fendrich Memorial Playwriting Contest, PO Box 4267, Englewood, CO 80155-4267 *Tel:* 303-779-4035 *Toll Free Tel:* 800-333-7262 *Fax:* 303-779-4315 *Web Site:* www.pioneerdrama.com/playwrights/contest.asp, pg 602

Feral House, 1240 W Sims Way, Suite 124, Port Townsend, WA 98368 *Tel:* 323-666-3311 *E-mail:* info@feralhouse.com *Web Site:* feralhouse.com, pg 71

Edna Ferber Fiction Book Award, c/o 210 N Main St, No 204, Cedar Grove, WI 53013 E-mail: wiswriters@gmail.com Web Site: wiswriters.org/awards, pg 602

Ferguson Publishing, 132 W 31 St, 16 fl, New York, NY 10001 Tel: 212-967-8800 Toll Free Tel: 800-322-8755 Toll Free Fax: 800-678-3633 E-mail: custserv@infobase.com Web Site: infobasepublishing.com, pg 71

Fernwood Publishing, 2970 Oxford St, Halifax, NS B3L 2W4, Canada Tel: 902-857-1388 E-mail: info@fernpub.ca Web Site: fernwoodpublishing.ca, pg 405

The Ferro-Grumley Award for LGBTQ Fiction, 511 Avenue of the Americas, No D36, New York, NY 10011 E-mail: awards@publishingtriangle.org; info@publishingtriangle.org; publishingtriangle@gmail.com Web Site: publishingtriangle.org/awards/ferro-grumley-awards, pg 602

Fiction Collective 2 (FC2), c/o University of Alabama Press, Box 870380, Tuscaloosa, AL 35487-0380 Web Site: fc2.org, pg 71

Fifth Estate Publishing, 2795 County Hwy 57, Blountsville, AL 35031 Tel: 256-631-5107 E-mail: josephlumpkin@hotmail.com Web Site: fifthestatepub.com, pg 71

Fifth House Publishers, 209 Wicksteed Ave, Unit 51, Toronto, ON M4G 0B1, Canada Tel: 905-477-9700 Toll Free Tel: 800-387-9776 E-mail: godwit@fitzhenry.ca; bookinfo@fitzhenry.ca (cust serv) Web Site: www.fifthhousepublishers.ca, pg 406

Filter Press LLC, PO Box 95, Palmer Lake, CO 80133 Tel: 719-481-2420 Toll Free Tel: 888-570-2663 Fax: 719-481-2420 E-mail: info@filterpressbooks.com; orders@filterpressbooks.com Web Site: filterpressbooks.com, pg 71

Financial Times Press, 221 River St, Hoboken, NJ 07030 E-mail: customer-service@informit.com; community@informit.com Web Site: www.informit.com/promotions/pearson-ft-press-141135, pg 71

Fine Arts Work Center in Provincetown, 24 Pearl St, Provincetown, MA 02657 Tel: 508-487-9960 E-mail: fellowship@fawc.org Web Site: www.fawc.org, pg 602

Fine Creative Media, Inc, 589 Eighth Ave, 6th fl, New York, NY 10018 Tel: 212-595-3500 Fax: 212-202-4195 E-mail: info@mjfbooks.com, pg 71

Fine Wordworking, PO Box 3041, Monterey, CA 93942-3041 Tel: 831-375-6278 E-mail: info@finewordworking.com Web Site: marilynch.com, pg 439

FineEdge.com LLC, 910 25 St, Unit B, Anacortes, WA 98221 Tel: 360-299-8500 Fax: 360-299-0535 E-mail: orders@fineedge.com; info@waggonerguide.com Web Site: www.waggonerguidebooks.com; waggonerguide.com, pg 72

FinePrint Literary Management, 207 W 106 St, Suite 1D, New York, NY 10025 Tel: 212-279-6214 E-mail: info@fineprintlit.com; submissions@fineprint.com Web Site: www.fineprintlit.com, pg 458

Fire Engineering Books & Videos, Clarion Events LLC, 110 S Hartford, Suite 220, Tulsa, OK 74120 Tel: 918-831-9421 Toll Free Tel: 800-752-9764 Fax: 918-831-9555 E-mail: info@fireengineeringbooks.com Web Site: fireengineeringbooks.com, pg 72

Firecracker Awards, 154 Christopher St, Suite 3C, New York, NY 10014-9110 Tel: 212-741-9110 E-mail: info@clmp.org Web Site: www.clmp.org/firecracker, pg 602

Firefall Editions, 4905 Tunlaw St, Alexandria, VA 22312 Tel: 510-549-2461 E-mail: literary@att.net Web Site: www.firefallmedia.com, pg 72

Firefly Books Ltd, 50 Staples Ave, Unit 1, Richmond Hill, ON L4B 0A7, Canada Tel: 416-499-8412 Toll Free Tel: 800-387-6192 (CN); 800-387-5085 (US) Fax: 416-499-8313 Toll Free Fax: 800-450-0391 (CN); 800-565-6034 (US) E-mail: service@fireflybooks.com Web Site: www.fireflybooks.com, pg 406

First Avenue Editions, 241 First Ave N, Minneapolis, MN 55401 Tel: 612-332-3344 Toll Free Tel: 800-328-4929 Fax: 612-332-7615 Toll Free Fax: 800-332-1132 E-mail: info@lernerbooks.com; custserve@lernerbooks.com Web Site: www.lernerbooks.com; www.facebook.com/lernerbooks.com, pg 72

The Fischer-Harbage Agency Inc, 237 36 St, Brooklyn, NY 11232 Tel: 212-695-7105 E-mail: submissions@fischerharbage.com Web Site: www.fischerharbage.com, pg 458

The Fischer Ross Group Inc, 2 Greenwich Off Park, Suite 300, Greenwich, CT 06831 Tel: 203-622-4950 Fax: 203-531-4132 E-mail: frgstaff@earthlink.net Web Site: frg-speakers.com, pg 487

Fitzhenry & Whiteside Limited, 209 Wicksteed Ave, Unit 51, Markham, ON M4G 0B1, Canada Tel: 905-477-9700 Toll Free Tel: 800-387-9776 Fax: 905-477-2834 E-mail: bookinfo@fitzhenry.ca Web Site: www.fitzhenry.ca, pg 406

Fitzroy Books, c/o Regal House Publishing, 806 Oberlin Rd, No 12094, Raleigh, NC 27605 E-mail: info@regalhousepublishing.com Web Site: fitzroybooks.com, pg 72

5 Under 35, 90 Broad St, Suite 604, New York, NY 10004 Tel: 212-685-0261 Fax: 212-213-6570 E-mail: nationalbook@nationalbook.org Web Site: www.nationalbook.org, pg 602

FJH Music Co Inc, 100 SE Third Ave, Suite 1000, Fort Lauderdale, FL 33394 Tel: 954-382-6061 Fax: 954-382-3073 E-mail: sales@fjhmusic.com Web Site: www.fjhmusic.com, pg 72

Flamingo Books, c/o Penguin Random House LLC, 1745 Broadway, New York, NY 10019 Tel: 212-782-9000 Web Site: www.penguin.com/flamingo-overview/, pg 72

Flammarion Quebec, 3700A, Blvd Saint-Laurent, Montreal, QC H2X 2V4, Canada Tel: 514-499-1002 Fax: 514-499-1002 E-mail: info@flammarion.qc.ca Web Site: www.flammarionquebec.com, pg 406

Flanker Press Ltd, 1243 Kenmount Rd, Unit 1, Paradise, NL A1L 0V8, Canada Tel: 709-739-4477 Toll Free Tel: 800-739-4420 Fax: 709-739-4447 E-mail: info@flankerpress.com; sales@flankerpress.com Web Site: www.flankerpress.com, pg 406

Flannery Literary, 1140 Wickfield Ct, Naperville, IL 60563 E-mail: jennifer@flanneryliterary.com Web Site: flanneryliterary.com, pg 459

Flashlight Press, 527 Empire Blvd, Brooklyn, NY 11225 Tel: 718-288-8300 Fax: 718-972-6307 Web Site: www.flashlightpress.com, pg 72

Norma Fleck Award for Canadian Children's Non-Fiction, 425 Adelaide St W, Suite 200, Toronto, ON M5V 3C1, Canada Tel: 416-975-0010 E-mail: info@bookcentre.ca Web Site: www.bookcentre.ca, pg 602

Florida Antiquarian Booksellers Association (FABA), c/o Lighthouse Books, ABAA, 14046 Fifth St, Dade City, FL 33525 Tel: 727-234-7759 E-mail: floridabooksellers@gmail.com Web Site: floridabooksellers.com, pg 506

Florida Authors and Publishers Association Inc (FAPA), 6237 Presidential Ct, Suite 140, Fort Myers, FL 33919 E-mail: admin@myfapa.org Web Site: myfapa.org, pg 506

The Florida Book Awards, 116 Honors Way, Suite 314, Tallahassee, FL 32306 Tel: 850-644-5211 E-mail: floridabookawards@gmail.com Web Site: www.floridabookawards.org, pg 602

Florida Freelance Writers Association, 45 Main St, North Stratford, NH 03590 Tel: 603-922-8338 Fax: 603-922-8339 E-mail: ffwa@writers-editors.com Web Site: www.writers-editors.com; writerseditorsnetwork.com, pg 506

Florida Graphics Alliance (FGA), 10524 Mosspark Rd, Suite 204, PMB 334, Orlando, FL 32832 Tel: 407-240-8009 E-mail: info@floridagraphics.org Web Site: www.floridagraphics.org, pg 506

Florida Outdoor Writers Association Inc (FOWA), 235 Apollo Beach Blvd, Unit 271, Apollo Beach, FL 33572 Tel: 813-579-0990 E-mail: info@fowa.org Web Site: www.fowa.org, pg 506

Florida Writers Association Inc, 127 W Fairbanks Ave, No 407, Winter Park, FL 32789 E-mail: contactus@floridawriters.org Web Site: www.floridawriters.org, pg 506

Florida WritersCon, 127 W Fairbanks Ave, No 407, Winter Park, FL 32789 E-mail: contactus@floridawriters.org Web Site: www.floridawriters.org, pg 554

Flowerpot Press, 2160 S Service Rd W, Oakville, ON L6L 5N1, Canada Tel: 416-479-0695 Toll Free Tel: 866-927-5001 E-mail: info@flowerpotpress.com; order@flowerpotpress.com Web Site: www.flowerpotpress.com, pg 406

Brigid Erin Flynn Award for Best Picture Book, PO Box 130294, Spring, TX 77393 Web Site: texasinstituteofletters.org, pg 603

Jean Flynn Award for Best Young Adult Book, PO Box 130294, Spring, TX 77393 Web Site: texasinstituteofletters.org, pg 603

Deirdre Siobhan FlynnBass Award for Best Middle Grade Book, PO Box 130294, Spring, TX 77393 Web Site: texasinstituteofletters.org, pg 603

Focus, PO Box 390007, Cambridge, MA 02139-0001 Tel: 317-635-9250 Fax: 317-635-9292 E-mail: customer@hackettpublishing.com; editorial@hackettpublishing.com Web Site: focusbookstore.com; www.hackettpublishing.com, pg 73

Focus on the Family, 8605 Explorer Dr, Colorado Springs, CO 80920-1051 Tel: 719-531-5181 Toll Free Tel: 800-A-FAMILY (232-6459) Fax: 719-531-3424 Web Site: www.focusonthefamily.com; www.facebook.com/focusonthefamily, pg 73

Focus Strategic Communications Inc, 15 Hunter Way, Brantford, ON N3T 6S3, Canada Tel: 519-756-3265 E-mail: info@focussc.com Web Site: www.focussc.com, pg 439

Sheldon Fogelman Agency Inc, 420 E 72 St, New York, NY 10021 Tel: 212-532-7250 Fax: 212-685-8939 E-mail: info@sheldonfogelmanagency.com; submissions@sheldonfogelmanagency.com Web Site: sheldonfogelmanagency.com, pg 459

Foil & Specialty Effects Association (FSEA), 2150 SW Westport Dr, Suite 101, Topeka, KS 66614 Tel: 785-271-5816 Fax: 785-271-6404 Web Site: fsea.com, pg 506

Folio Literary Management, The Film Center Bldg, 630 Ninth Ave, Suite 1101, New York, NY 10036 Tel: 212-400-1494 Fax: 212-967-0977 Web Site: www.foliolit.com, pg 459

Folklore Publishing, 11717-9B Ave NW, Unit 2, Edmonton, AB T6J 7B7, Canada Tel: 780-435-2376 Web Site: www.folklorepublishing.com, pg 406

La Fondation Emile Nelligan, 100, rue Sherbrooke, Suite 202, Montreal, QC H2X 1C3, Canada Tel: 514-278-4657 E-mail: info@fondation-nelligan.org Web Site: www.fondation-nelligan.org, pg 506

Fons Vitae, 49 Mockingbird Valley Dr, Louisville, KY 40207-1366 Tel: 502-897-3641 Fax: 502-893-7373 E-mail: fonsvitaeky@aol.com Web Site: www.fonsvitae.com, pg 73

Fordham University, Gabelli School of Business, 140 W 62 St, Rm 440, New York, NY 10023 Web Site: www.fordham.edu, pg 73

Fordham University Press, Joseph A Martino Hall, 45 Columbus Ave, 3rd fl, New York, NY 10023 Fax: 347-842-3083 Web Site: www.fordhampress.com, pg 73

Foreword's INDIES Awards, 12935 W Bay Shore Rd, Suite 380, Traverse City, MI 49684 Tel: 231-933-3699 Web Site: www.forewordreviews.com, pg 603

Morris D Forkosch Prize in British History, 400 "A" St SE, Washington, DC 20003 Tel: 202-544-2422 E-mail: awards@historians.org Web Site: www.historians.org/awards-and-grants/awards-and-prizes/morris-d-forkosch-prize, pg 603

E M Forster Award, 633 W 155 St, New York, NY 10032 Tel: 212-368-5900 E-mail: academy@artsandletters.org Web Site: artsandletters.org/awards, pg 603

Fort Ross Inc - International Representation for Artists, 26 Arthur Place, Yonkers, NY 10701 Tel: 914-375-6448, pg 459, 485

49th Parallel Poetry Award, Mail Stop 9053, Western Washington University, Bellingham, WA 98225 Tel: 360-650-4863 E-mail: bellingham.review@wwu.edu Web Site: bhreview.org; bhreview.submittable.com, pg 603

Forum Publishing Co, 383 E Main St, Centerport, NY 11721 Tel: 631-754-5000 Toll Free Tel: 800-635-7654 Fax: 631-754-0630 E-mail: forumpublishing@aol.com Web Site: www.forum123.com, pg 73

Forward Movement, 412 Sycamore St, Cincinnati, OH 45202-4110 Tel: 513-721-6659 Toll Free Tel: 800-543-1813 Fax: 513-721-0729 (orders) E-mail: orders@forwardmovement.org (orders & cust serv) Web Site: www.forwardmovement.org, pg 73

Foster City International Writers Contest, 650 Shell Blvd, Foster City, CA 94404 Tel: 650-286-3380 E-mail: fostercity_writers@yahoo.com Web Site: www.fostercity.org, pg 603

Foster Travel Publishing, 1623 Martin Luther King Jr Way, Berkeley, CA 94709 Tel: 510-549-2202 Web Site: www.fostertravel.com, pg 439

Walter Foster Publishing, 26391 Crown Valley Pkwy, Suite 220, Mission Viejo, CA 92691 Tel: 949-380-7510 Fax: 949-380-7575 E-mail: walterfoster@quarto.com Web Site: www.quartoknows.com/walter-foster, pg 74

Foundation Press, c/o West Academic, 860 Blue Gentian Rd, Eagan, MN 55121 Toll Free Tel: 877-888-1330 E-mail: support@westacademic.com Web Site: www.westacademic.com, pg 74

Four Quartets Prize, 119 Smith St, Brooklyn, NY 11201 Tel: 212-254-9628 E-mail: info@poetrysociety.org Web Site: poetrysociety.org/awards, pg 603

4A's (American Association of Advertising Agencies), 25 W 45 St, 16th fl, New York, NY 10036 Tel: 212-682-2500 E-mail: media@4as.org; membership@4as.org Web Site: www.aaaa.org, pg 506

Fowler Museum at UCLA, PO Box 951549, Los Angeles, CA 90095-1549 Tel: 310-825-4361 Fax: 310-206-7007 E-mail: fowlerws@arts.ucla.edu Web Site: www.fowler.ucla.edu, pg 74

Fox Chapel Publishing Co Inc, 1970 Broad St, East Petersburg, PA 17520 Tel: 717-560-4703 Toll Free Tel: 800-457-9112 Fax: 717-560-4702 E-mail: customerservice@foxchapelpublishing.com Web Site: www.foxchapelpublishing.com, pg 74

Frances Henne/YALSA Research Grant, 225 N Michigan Ave, Suite 1300, Chicago, IL 60601 Tel: 312-280-4390 Toll Free Tel: 800-545-2433 E-mail: yalsa@ala.org Web Site: www.ala.org/yalsa/awardsandgrants/franceshenne, pg 604

Franciscan Media, 28 W Liberty St, Cincinnati, OH 45202 Tel: 513-241-5615 E-mail: admin@franciscanmedia.org Web Site: www.franciscanmedia.org, pg 74

Prix Francophone de l'ACSP, 260 Dalhousie St, Suite 204, Ottawa, ON K1N 7E4, Canada Tel: 613-562-1202 Fax: 613-241-0019 E-mail: cpsaprizes@cpsa-acsp.ca; cpsa-acsp@cpsa-acsp.ca Web Site: www.cpsa-acsp.ca, pg 604

Sandi Frank, 8 Fieldcrest Ct, Cortlandt Manor, NY 10567 Tel: 914-739-7088 E-mail: sfrankmail@aol.com, pg 439

Franklin, Beedle & Associates Inc, 10350 N Vancouver Way, No 5012, Portland, OR 97217 Tel: 503-284-6348 Toll Free Tel: 800-322-2665 Fax: 503-625-4434 Web Site: www.fbeedle.com, pg 74

Soeurette Diehl Fraser Translation Award, PO Box 130294, Spring, TX 77393 Web Site: texasinstituteofletters.org, pg 604

Frederick Fell Publishers Inc, 1403 Shoreline Way, Hollywood, FL 33019 Tel: 954-925-5242 E-mail: fellpub@aol.com (admin only) Web Site: www.fellpub.com, pg 74

Free Spirit Publishing Inc, 9850 51 Ave N, Suite 100, Minneapolis, MN 55442 Tel: 714-891-2273 Toll Free Tel: 800-858-7339 Fax: 714-230-7070 Toll Free Fax: 888-877-7606 E-mail: customerservice@tcmpub.com Web Site: www.teachercreatedmaterials.com/free-spirit-publishing, pg 74

George Freedley Memorial Award, c/o The New York Public Library for the Performing Arts, 111 Amsterdam Ave, New York, NY 10023 E-mail: tlabookawards@gmail.com; theatrelibraryassociation@gmail.com Web Site: www.tla-online.org/awards/bookawards, pg 604

Robert A Freedman Dramatic Agency Inc, PO Box 3544, New York, NY 10163 Tel: 718-897-0950, pg 459

The Don Freeman Work-in-Progress Grant, 6363 Wilshire Blvd, Suite 425, Los Angeles, CA 90048 Tel: 323-782-1010 E-mail: info@scbwi.org Web Site: www.scbwi.org, pg 604

W H Freeman, c/o Macmillan Learning, One New York Plaza, Suite 46, New York, NY 10004 Tel: 212-576-9400 Web Site: www.macmillanlearning.com/college/us, pg 75

The French-American Foundation & Florence Gould Foundation Annual Translation Prize, 28 W 44 St, Suite 812, New York, NY 10036 Web Site: www.frenchamerican.org, pg 604

Samuel French, Inc, 250 W 57 St, 6th fl, New York, NY 10107-0102 Toll Free Tel: 866-979-0447 E-mail: info@concordtheatricals.com Web Site: www.concordtheatricals.com/a/4346/samuel-a-french, pg 75

Horst Frenz Prize, 323 E Wacker Dr, No 642, Chicago, IL 60601 Tel: 312-660-8072 E-mail: info@acla.org Web Site: www.acla.org/prize-awards/horst-frenz-prize, pg 604

Fresh Air Books, 1908 Grand Ave, Nashville, TN 37212 Tel: 615-340-7200 Toll Free Tel: 800-972-0433 (orders) Web Site: books.upperroom.org, pg 75

Sarah Jane Freymann Literary Agency LLC, 59 W 71 St, Suite 9-B, New York, NY 10023 Tel: 212-362-9277 E-mail: submissions@sarahjanefreymann.com Web Site: www.sarahjanefreymann.com, pg 459

Fredrica S Friedman & Co Inc, 857 Fifth Ave, New York, NY 10065 Tel: 212-639-9455 E-mail: info@fredricafriedman.com Web Site: www.fredricafriedman.com, pg 459

Friends of American Writers (FAW), c/o 506 Rose Ave, Des Plaines, IL 60016 E-mail: info@fawchicago.org Web Site: www.fawchicago.org, pg 506

Friends of American Writers Literature Awards, c/o 506 Rose Ave, Des Plaines, IL 60016 Tel: 847-827-8339 E-mail: info@fawchicago.org Web Site: www.fawchicago.org, pg 604

Friends of American Writers Young People's Literature Awards, c/o 506 Rose Ave, Des Plaines, IL 60016 Tel: 847-827-8339 E-mail: info@fawchicago.org Web Site: www.fawchicago.org, pg 604

Friends of Literature Prize, 61 W Superior St, Chicago, IL 60654 Tel: 312-787-7070 Web Site: www.poetryfoundation.org/poetrymagazine/prizes, pg 605

Friends United Press, 101 Quaker Hill Dr, Richmond, IN 47374 Tel: 765-962-7573 Fax: 765-966-1293 E-mail: friendspress@fum.org; orders@fum.org Web Site: www.friendsunitedmeeting.org; bookstore.friendsunitedmeeting.org, pg 75

Fromer, 1606 Noyes Dr, Silver Spring, MD 20910-2224 Tel: 301-585-8827, pg 439

Frost Medal, 119 Smith St, Brooklyn, NY 11201 Tel: 212-254-9628 E-mail: info@poetrysociety.org Web Site: poetrysociety.org/awards, pg 605

FSG Writer's Fellowship, 120 Broadway, New York, NY 10271 Tel: 212-741-6900 E-mail: fsg.publicity@fsgbooks.com Web Site: fsgfellowship.com, pg 605

Candice Fuhrman Literary Agency, 10 Cypress Hollow Dr, Tiburon, CA 94920 Tel: 415-383-1014 E-mail: fuhrmancandice@gmail.com, pg 459

Fulbright Scholar Program, 1400 "K" St NW, Washington, DC 20005 Tel: 202-686-4000 E-mail: scholars@iie.org Web Site: www.cies.org; www.iie.org, pg 605

Fulcrum Publishing Inc, 3970 Youngfield St, Wheat Ridge, CO 80033 Tel: 303-277-1623 Toll Free Tel: 800-888-4741 (orders) E-mail: info@fulcrumbooks.com Web Site: www.fulcrumbooks.com, pg 75

Future Horizons Inc, 107 W Randol Mill Rd, Suite 100, Arlington, TX 76011 Tel: 817-277-0727 Toll Free Tel: 800-489-0727 E-mail: info@fhautism.com Web Site: www.fhautism.com, pg 75

Gabelli School of Business Communications & Media Management Program, 140 W 62 St, Rm 440, New York, NY 10023 Tel: 212-636-6150 Fax: 718-817-4999 Web Site: www.fordham.edu/gabelli-school-of-business, pg 562

Gabriele Rico Challenge for Nonfiction, San Jose State University, English Dept, One Washington Sq, San Jose, CA 95192-0090 Tel: 408-924-4441 E-mail: mail@reedmag.org Web Site: www.reedmag.org; reedmagazine.submittable.com, pg 605

Gaetan Morin Editeur, 5800, rue St-Denis, bureau 900, Montreal, QC H2S 3L5, Canada Tel: 514-273-1066 Toll Free Tel: 800-565-5531 Fax: 514-276-0324 Toll Free Fax: 800-814-0324 E-mail: info@cheneliere.ca Web Site: www.cheneliere.ca, pg 407

Gagosian Gallery, 980 Madison Ave, New York, NY 10075 Tel: 212-744-2313 Fax: 212-772-7962 E-mail: newyork@gagosian.com Web Site: www.gagosian.com, pg 75

Ernest J Gaines Award for Literary Excellence, 100 North St, Suite 900, Baton Rouge, LA 70802 Tel: 225-387-6126 E-mail: gainesaward@braf.org Web Site: www.ernestjgainesaward.org, pg 605

Lewis Galantiere Translation Award, 211 N Union St, Suite 100, Alexandria, VA 22314 Tel: 703-683-6100 Fax: 703-778-7222 E-mail: honors_awards@atanet.org Web Site: www.atanet.org, pg 605

Galaxy Press Inc, 7051 Hollywood Blvd, Los Angeles, CA 90028 Tel: 323-466-3310 Toll Free Tel: 877-8GALAXY (842-5299) E-mail: info@galaxypress.com; customers@galaxypress.com Web Site: www.galaxypress.com, pg 75

Galde Press Inc, PO Box 774, Hendersonville, NC 28793 Tel: 828-702-3032 Web Site: www.galdepress.com, pg 75

Gale, 27555 Executive Dr, Suite 270, Farmington Hills, MI 48331 Toll Free Tel: 800-877-4253 Toll Free Fax: 877-363-4253 E-mail: gale.customerexperience@cengage.com Web Site: www.gale.com, pg 75

Zona Gale Award for Short Fiction, c/o 4414 W Fillmore Dr, Milwaukee, WI 53219 E-mail: wiswriters@gmail.com Web Site: wiswriters.org/awards, pg 605

Gallaudet University Press, 800 Florida Ave NE, Washington, DC 20002-3695 Tel: 202-651-5488 Fax: 202-651-5489 E-mail: gupress@gallaudet.edu Web Site: gupress.gallaudet.edu, pg 76

Gallery Books, 1230 Avenue of the Americas, New York, NY 10020 Toll Free Tel: 800-456-6798 Fax: 212-698-7284 E-mail: consumer.customerservice@simonandschuster.com Web Site: www.simonandschuster.com, pg 76

Diane Gallo, 49 Hilton St, Gilbertsville, NY 13776 Tel: 607-783-2386 Fax: 607-783-2386 E-mail: dgallo@stny.rr.com Web Site: www.dianegallo.com, pg 439

Gallopade International Inc, 611 Hwy 74 S, Suite 2000, Peachtree City, GA 30269 Tel: 770-631-4222 Toll Free Tel: 800-536-2438 Fax: 770-631-4810 Toll Free Fax: 800-871-2979 E-mail: customerservice@gallopade.com Web Site: www.gallopade.com, pg 76

COMPANY INDEX

Gannon University's High School Poetry Contest, Gannon University, 109 University Sq, Erie, PA 16541 *Tel:* 814-871-5583 *Web Site:* www.gannon.edu/poetrycontest, pg 605

The Garamond Agency Inc, 12 Horton St, Newburyport, MA 01950 *E-mail:* query@garamondagency.com *Web Site:* www.garamondagency.com, pg 459

GardenComm: Garden Communicators International, 9825 Magnolia Ave, Suite B-415, Riverside, CA 92503 *Tel:* 951-899-5015 *E-mail:* info@gardencomm.org *Web Site:* gardencomm.org, pg 506

Gareth Stevens Publishing, 29 E 21 St, New York, NY 10010 *Tel:* 212-777-3017 *Toll Free Tel:* 800-542-2595 *Toll Free Tel:* 877-542-2596 *E-mail:* customerservice@gspub.com *Web Site:* garethstevens.com, pg 76

Francois-Xavier Garneau Medal, 130 Albert St, Suite 1201, Ottawa, ON K1P 5G4, Canada *Tel:* 613-233-7885 *Fax:* 613-565-5445 *E-mail:* cha-shc@cha-shc.ca *Web Site:* cha-shc.ca, pg 605

Max Gartenberg Literary Agency, 912 N Pennsylvania Ave, Yardley, PA 19067 *Tel:* 215-295-9230 *Web Site:* www.maxgartenberg.com, pg 459

The Gary-Paul Agency (GPA), 1549 Main St, Stratford, CT 06615 *Tel:* 203-345-6167 *Web Site:* www.thegarypaulagency.com, pg 439

John Gassner Memorial Playwriting Award, 167 Cherry St, No 331, Milford, CT 06460 *E-mail:* gassner-award@netconline.org; mail@netconline.org *Web Site:* www.netconline.org, pg 605

Gatekeeper Press, 7853 Gunn Hwy, Suite 209, Tampa, FL 33626 *Toll Free Tel:* 866-535-0913 *Fax:* 216-803-0350 *E-mail:* info@gatekeeperpress.com *Web Site:* www.gatekeeperpress.com, pg 77

Gateways Books & Tapes, PO Box 370, Nevada City, CA 95959-0370 *Tel:* 530-271-2239 *Toll Free Tel:* 800-869-0658 *Web Site:* www.gatewaysbooksandtapes.com, pg 77

The Christian Gauss Award; 1606 New Hampshire Ave NW, Washington, DC 20009 *Tel:* 202-265-3808 *Fax:* 202-986-1601 *E-mail:* awards@pbk.org *Web Site:* www.pbk.org/bookawards, pg 605

Gauthier Publications Inc, PO Box 806241, St Clair Shores, MI 48080 *Tel:* 313-458-7141 *Fax:* 586-279-1515 *E-mail:* info@gauthierpublications.com *Web Site:* www.gauthierpublications.com, pg 77

Carol Gay Award, 140B Purcellville Gateway Dr, Suite 1200, Purcellville, VA 20132 *Tel:* 630-571-4520 *E-mail:* info@childlitassn.org *Web Site:* www.childlitassn.org, pg 605

The Gaylactic Spectrum Awards, 1425 "S" St NW, Washington, DC 20009 *E-mail:* nominations@spectrumawards.org *Web Site:* www.spectrumawards.org, pg 606

Gaylord College of Journalism & Mass Communication, Professional Writing Program, c/o University of Oklahoma, 395 W Lindsey St, Rm 3000, Norman, OK 73019-0270 *Tel:* 405-325-2721 *Web Site:* www.ou.edu/gaylord; www.ou.edu/gaylord/undergraduate/professional-writing, pg 563

Fred Gebhart, PO Box 111, Gold Hill, OR 97525 *Tel:* 415-596-5819 *E-mail:* fgebhart@pobox.com *Web Site:* www.fredgebhart.com, pg 439

Theodor Seuss Geisel Award, 225 N Michigan Ave, Suite 1300, Chicago, IL 60601 *Toll Free Tel:* 800-545-2433 *E-mail:* alsc@ala.org *Web Site:* www.ala.org/alsc/awardsgrants/bookmedia/geisel, pg 606

Lionel Gelber Prize, University of Toronto, Munk School of Global Affairs & Public Policy, One Devonshire Place, Toronto, ON M5S 3K7, Canada *Tel:* 416-946-5670 *Fax:* 416-946-8915 *E-mail:* gelberprize.munk@utoronto.ca *Web Site:* munkschool.utoronto.ca/gelber; www.facebook.com/GelberPrize, pg 606

Gelfman Schneider Literary Agents Inc, 850 Seventh Ave, Suite 903, New York, NY 10019 *Tel:* 212-245-1993 *E-mail:* mail@gelfmanschneider.com *Web Site:* gelfmanschneider.com, pg 460

Gell: A Finger Lakes Creative Retreat, 740 University Ave, Rochester, NY 14607-1259 *Tel:* 585-473-2590 *Fax:* 585-442-9333 *Web Site:* www.wab.org, pg 554

Gelles-Cole Literary Enterprises, 2163 Lima Loop, PMB 01-408, Laredo, TX 78045-9452 *Tel:* 845-810-0029 *Web Site:* www.literaryenterprises.com, pg 439

GemStone Press, 4507 Charlotte Ave, Suite 100, Nashville, TN 37209 *Tel:* 615-255-BOOK (255-2665) *Fax:* 615-255-5081 *E-mail:* marketing@turnerpublishing.com *Web Site:* gemstonepress.com; www.turnerpublishing.com, pg 77

Genealogical Publishing Co, 3600 Clipper Mill Rd, Suite 229, Baltimore, MD 21211 *Tel:* 410-837-8271 *Toll Free Tel:* 800-296-6687 *Fax:* 410-752-8492 *Toll Free Fax:* 800-599-9561 *E-mail:* info@genealogical.com; web@genealogical.com *Web Site:* www.genealogical.com, pg 77

The Geological Society of America Inc (GSA), 3300 Penrose Place, Boulder, CO 80301-1806 *Tel:* 303-357-1000 *Toll Free Tel:* 800-472-1988 *Fax:* 303-357-1070 *E-mail:* pubs@geosociety.org (prodn); editing@geosociety.org (edit); books@geosociety.org; gsaservice@geosociety.org (sales & serv) *Web Site:* www.geosociety.org, pg 77

GeoLytics Inc, 507 Horizon Way, Branchburg, NJ 08853 *Tel:* 908-707-1505 *Toll Free Tel:* 800-577-6717 *E-mail:* support@geolytics.com; questions@geolytics.com *Web Site:* www.geolytics.com, pg 77

Georgetown University Press, 3520 Prospect St NW, Suite 140, Washington, DC 20007 *Tel:* 202-687-5889 (busn) *Fax:* 202-687-6340 (edit) *E-mail:* gupress@georgetown.edu *Web Site:* press.georgetown.edu, pg 77

The Gersh Agency (TGA), 41 Madison Ave, 29th fl, New York, NY 10010 *Tel:* 212-997-1818 *Web Site:* gersh.com/books, pg 460

Leo Gershoy Award in Western European History, 400 "A" St SE, Washington, DC 20003 *Tel:* 202-544-2422 *E-mail:* awards@historians.org *Web Site:* www.historians.org/awards-and-grants/awards-and-prizes/leo-gershoy-award, pg 606

Nancy C Gerth PhD, 1431 Harlan's Trail, Sagle, ID 83860 *Tel:* 208-304-9066 *E-mail:* docnangee@nancygerth.com *Web Site:* www.nancygerth.com, pg 440

Charles M Getchell New Play Contest, 5710 W Gate City Blvd, Suite K, Box 186, Greensboro, NC 27407 *Tel:* 336-265-6148 *E-mail:* info@setc.org *Web Site:* www.setc.org, pg 606

Getty Publications, 1200 Getty Center Dr, Suite 500, Los Angeles, CA 90049-1682 *Tel:* 310-440-7365 *Toll Free Tel:* 800-223-3431 (orders) *Fax:* 310-440-7758 *E-mail:* pubsinfo@getty.edu *Web Site:* www.getty.edu/publications, pg 77

GGP Publishing Inc, Larchmont, NY 10538 *Tel:* 914-834-8896 *Fax:* 914-834-7566 *Web Site:* www.GGPPublishing.com, pg 440, 460

GIA Publications Inc, 7404 S Mason Ave, Chicago, IL 60638 *Tel:* 708-496-3800 *Toll Free Tel:* 800-GIA-1358 (442-1358) *E-mail:* custserv@giamusic.com *Web Site:* www.giamusic.com, pg 78

Gibbs Smith Publisher, 1877 E Gentile St, Layton, UT 84041 *Tel:* 801-544-9800 *Toll Free Tel:* 800-748-5439; 800-835-4993 (orders) *Fax:* 801-544-5582 *Toll Free Fax:* 800-213-3023 (orders only) *E-mail:* info@gibbs-smith.com; orders@gibbs-smith.com *Web Site:* gibbs-smith.com, pg 78

Arrell Gibson Lifetime Achievement Award, 200 NE 18 St, Oklahoma City, OK 73105-3205 *Tel:* 405-522-3383 *Web Site:* libraries.ok.gov/ocb/arrell-gibson/, pg 606

Gifted Unlimited LLC, 12340 US Hwy 42, No 453, Goshen, KY 40026 *Tel:* 502-715-6306 *E-mail:* info@giftedunlimitedllc.com; orders@giftedunlimitedllc.com *Web Site:* www.giftedunlimitedllc.com, pg 78

Sheri Gilbert, 123 Van Voorhis Ave, Rochester, NY 14617 *Tel:* 585-342-0331 *E-mail:* shergilb@aol.com *Web Site:* www.permissionseditor.com, pg 440

Gilder Lehrman Lincoln Prize, 300 N Washington St, Campus Box 435, Gettysburg, PA 17325 *Tel:* 717-337-8255 *E-mail:* lincolnprize@gettysburg.edu *Web Site:* www.gilderlehrman.org, pg 606

Gilder Lehrman Prize for Military History, 49 W 45 St, 2nd fl, New York, NY 10036 *Tel:* 646-366-9666 *E-mail:* info@gilderlehrman.org *Web Site:* www.gilderlehrman.org, pg 606

Gingko Press Inc, 2332 Fourth St, Suite E, Berkeley, CA 94710 *Tel:* 510-898-1195 *Fax:* 510-898-1196 *E-mail:* books@gingkopress.com *Web Site:* www.gingkopress.com, pg 78

Allen Ginsberg Poetry Award, One College Blvd, Paterson, NJ 07505-1179 *Tel:* 973-684-6555 *Fax:* 973-523-6085 *Web Site:* www.poetrycenterpccc.com, pg 606

Gival Press Oscar Wilde Award, PO Box 3812, Arlington, VA 22203 *Tel:* 703-351-0079 *Fax:* 703-351-0079 (call first) *E-mail:* givalpress@yahoo.com *Web Site:* www.givalpress.com; givalpress.submittable.com, pg 606

Gival Press Short Story Award, PO Box 3812, Arlington, VA 22203 *Tel:* 703-351-0079 *Fax:* 703-351-0079 (call first) *E-mail:* givalpress@yahoo.com *Web Site:* www.givalpress.com; givalpress.submittable.com, pg 606

John Glassco Translation Prize, Concordia University, LB 601, 1455 De Maisonneuve W, Montreal, QC H3G 1M8, Canada *Tel:* 514-848-2424 (ext 8702) *E-mail:* info@attlc-ltac.org *Web Site:* www.attlc-ltac.org, pg 607

GLCA New Writers Awards, 535 W William St, Suite 301, Ann Arbor, MI 48103 *Tel:* 734-661-2350 *Fax:* 734-661-2349 *Web Site:* www.glca.org, pg 607

Susan Gleason, 325 Riverside Dr, Suite 41, New York, NY 10025 *Tel:* 212-662-3876 *E-mail:* sgleasonliteraryagent@gmail.com, pg 460

The Danuta Gleed Literary Award, 600-460 Richmond St W, Toronto, ON M5V 1Y1, Canada *Tel:* 416-703-8982 *E-mail:* info@writersunion.ca *Web Site:* www.writersunion.ca, pg 607

The Glen Workshop, 3307 Third Ave W, Seattle, WA 98119 *Tel:* 206-281-2988 *E-mail:* image@imagejournal.org *Web Site:* www.imagejournal.org, pg 554

Eugene & Marilyn Glick Indiana Authors Awards, 1500 N Delaware St, Indianapolis, IN 46202 *Tel:* 317-638-1500 *Toll Free Tel:* 800-675-8897 *E-mail:* info@indianaauthorsawards.org *Web Site:* www.indianaauthorsawards.org, pg 607

Glitterati Inc, PO Box 3781, New York, NY 10163 *Tel:* 212-810-7519 *E-mail:* info@glitteratiincorporated.com; media@glitteratiincorporated.com; sales@glitteratiincorporated.com; trade@glitteratiincorporated.com *Web Site:* glitteratiinc.com, pg 78

Global Authors Publications (GAP), 38 Bluegrass, Middleberg, FL 32068 *Tel:* 904-425-1608 *E-mail:* gapbook@yahoo.com *Web Site:* www.globalauthorspublications.com, pg 78

Global Lion Intellectual Property Management Inc, PO Box 669238, Pompano Beach, FL 33066 *Tel:* 754-222-6948 *Fax:* 754-222-6948 *E-mail:* queriesgloballionmgt@gmail.com *Web Site:* www.globallionmanagement.com, pg 460

Global Publishing Solutions LLC, PO Box 2043, Matteson, IL 60443 *Toll Free Tel:* 888-351-2411 *E-mail:* info@globalpublishingsolutions.com *Web Site:* globalpublishingsolutions.com, pg 79

Global Training Center, 550 S Mesa Hills Dr, Suite E4, El Paso, TX 79912 *Tel:* 915-534-7900 *Toll Free Tel:* 800-860-5030 *Fax:* 915-534-7903 *E-mail:* contact@globaltrainingcenter.com *Web Site:* www.globaltrainingcenter.com, pg 79

The Globe Pequot Press, 64 S Main St, Essex, CT 06426 *Tel:* 203-458-4500 *Toll Free Tel:* 800-243-0495 (orders only); 888-249-7586 (cust serv) *Fax:* 203-458-4601 *Toll Free Fax:* 800-820-2329 (orders & cust serv)

E-mail: editorial@globepequot.com; info@rowman.com; orders@rowman.com *Web Site:* rowman.com, pg 79

Globo Libros Literary Management, 450 E 63 St, New York, NY 10065 *Web Site:* www.globo-libros.com; www.publishersmarketplace.com/members/dstockwell, pg 460

Goddard Riverside CBC Youth Book Prize for Social Justice, 593 Columbus Ave, New York, NY 10024 *Tel:* 212-873-6600 *E-mail:* cbcprize@goddard.org *Web Site:* goddard.org/bookprizes, pg 607

Goddard Riverside Stephan Russo Book Prize for Social Justice, 593 Columbus Ave, New York, NY 10024 *E-mail:* russoprize@goddard.org *Web Site:* goddard.org/bookprizes, pg 607

Godine, 184 Belknap St, Concord, MA 01742 *E-mail:* info@godine.com *Web Site:* www.godine.com, pg 79

Gold Medal, 633 W 155 St, New York, NY 10032 *Tel:* 212-368-5900 *E-mail:* academy@artsandletters.org *Web Site:* artsandletters.org/awards, pg 607

Golden Cylinder Awards, 150 Executive Center Dr, Suite 201, Greenville, SC 29615 *Tel:* 803-948-9470 *Fax:* 803-948-9471 *E-mail:* aimcal@aimcal.org *Web Site:* gaa.org/awards/golden-cylinder-awards, pg 607

Golden Kite Awards, 6363 Wilshire Blvd, Suite 425, Los Angeles, CA 90048 *Tel:* 323-782-1010 *E-mail:* info@scbwi.org *Web Site:* www.scbwi.org/awards/golden-kite-award, pg 607

Golden Meteorite Press, 11919 82 St NW, Suite 103, Edmonton, AB T5B 2W4, Canada *Tel:* 587-783-0059 *Web Site:* goldenmeteoritepress.com, pg 407

Golden Quill Award, Missouri Southern State University, 3950 E Newman Rd, Joplin, MO 64801-1595 *Web Site:* www.iswne.org/contests, pg 607

Golden Rose Award, c/o Linda Haviland Conte, 18 Hall Ave, Apt 2, Somerville, MA 02144 *E-mail:* info@nepoetryclub.org *Web Site:* nepoetryclub.org, pg 608

Golden West Cookbooks, 5738 N Central Ave, Phoenix, AZ 85012-1316 *Tel:* 602-234-1574 *Toll Free Tel:* 602-521-9221 *Fax:* 602-234-3062 *E-mail:* info@americantravelerpress.com *Web Site:* www.americantravelerpress.com, pg 79

Goldfarb & Associates, 721 Gibbon St, Alexandria, VA 22314 *Tel:* 202-466-3030 *E-mail:* rlglawlit@gmail.com *Web Site:* www.ronaldgoldfarb.com, pg 460

Frances Goldin Literary Agency, Inc, 214 W 29 St, Suite 410, New York, NY 10001 *Tel:* 212-777-0047 *Fax:* 212-228-1660 *E-mail:* agency@goldinlit.com *Web Site:* www.goldinlit.com, pg 460

Laurence Goldstein Poetry Prize, University of Michigan, 3277 Angell Hall, 435 S State St, Ann Arbor, MI 48109-1003 *Tel:* 734-764-9265 *E-mail:* mqr@umich.edu *Web Site:* sites.lsa.umich.edu/mqr/about-us/prizes, pg 608

Goodheart-Willcox Publisher, 18604 W Creek Dr, Tinley Park, IL 60477-6243 *Tel:* 708-687-5000 *Toll Free Tel:* 800-323-0440 *Toll Free Fax:* 888-409-3900 *E-mail:* custserv@g-w.com; orders@g-w.com *Web Site:* www.g-w.com, pg 79

Irene Goodman Literary Agency, 27 W 24 St, Suite 700B, New York, NY 10010 *Tel:* 212-604-0330 *E-mail:* queries@irenegoodman.com *Web Site:* www.irenegoodman.com, pg 460

Robert M Goodman, 140 West End Ave, Unit 11-J, New York, NY 10023 *Tel:* 917-439-1097 *E-mail:* bobbybgood@gmail.com, pg 440

Goodreads Choice Awards, 188 Spear St, 3rd fl, San Francisco, CA 94105 *E-mail:* press@goodreads.com *Web Site:* www.goodreads.com/award, pg 608

Goose Lane Editions, 500 Beaverbrook Ct, Suite 330, Fredericton, NB E3B 5X4, Canada *Tel:* 506-450-4251 *Toll Free Tel:* 888-926-8377 *Fax:* 506-459-4991 *E-mail:* orders@gooselane.com *Web Site:* www.gooselane.com, pg 407

Goose River Press, 3400 Friendship Rd, Waldoboro, ME 04572-6337 *Tel:* 207-832-6665 *E-mail:* gooseriverpress@gmail.com *Web Site:* gooseriverpress.com, pg 79

P M Gordon Associates Inc, 2115 Wallace St, Philadelphia, PA 19130 *Tel:* 215-769-2525 *Web Site:* www.pmgordonassociates.com, pg 440

Gorgias Press LLC, PO Box 6939, Piscataway, NJ 08854-6939 *Tel:* 732-885-8900 *Fax:* 732-885-8908 *E-mail:* helpdesk@gorgiaspress.com *Web Site:* www.gorgiaspress.com, pg 80

Amanda Gorman Award for Poetry, 1745 Broadway, New York, NY 10019 *Tel:* 212-782-9348 *Fax:* 212-782-5157 *E-mail:* creativewriting@penguinrandomhouse.com *Web Site:* social-impact.penguinrandomhouse.com/creativewriting, pg 608

Gospel Publishing House, 1445 Boonville Ave, Springfield, MO 65802-1894 *Tel:* 417-866-8014 *Toll Free Tel:* 855-642-2011 *Fax:* 417-862-0414 *Toll Free Fax:* 877-840-5100 *E-mail:* custsrv@myhealthychurch.com *Web Site:* myhealthychurch.com/store, pg 80

Gotham Book Prize, 251 Park Ave S, New York, NY 10010 *Web Site:* www.gothambookprize.org, pg 608

Gotham Writers' Workshop, 555 Eighth Ave, Suite 1402, New York, NY 10018-4358 *Tel:* 212-974-8377 *E-mail:* contact@gothamwriters.com *Web Site:* www.gothamwriters.com, pg 554

Sherry Gottlieb, 300 W Ninth St, No 126, Oxnard, CA 93030-7098 *Tel:* 805-382-3425 *E-mail:* writer@wordservices.com *Web Site:* www.wordservices.com, pg 440

Karen Gould Prize in Art History, 6 Beacon St, Suite 500, Boston, MA 02108 *Tel:* 617-491-1622 *Fax:* 617-492-3303 *E-mail:* info@themedievalacademy.org *Web Site:* www.medievalacademy.org/page/gouldprize, pg 608

Governor General's Literary Awards, 150 Elgin St, 2nd fl, Ottawa, ON K2P 1L4, Canada *Tel:* 613-566-4414 *Toll Free Tel:* 800-263-5588 (CN only) *Fax:* 613-566-4390 *E-mail:* ggbooks@canadacouncil.ca *Web Site:* ggbooks.ca, pg 608

The Gracies®, 2365 Harrodsburg Rd, Suite A325, Lexington, KY 40504 *Tel:* 202-750-3664 *Fax:* 202-750-3664 *E-mail:* info@allwomeninmedia.org *Web Site:* allwomeninmedia.org, pg 608

Doug Grad Literary Agency Inc, 156 Prospect Park W, No 3L, Brooklyn, NY 11215 *Tel:* 718-788-6067 *E-mail:* query@dgliterary.com *Web Site:* www.dgliterary.com, pg 460

Graduate & Undergraduate Hopwood Contest, 1176 Angell Hall, 435 S State St, Ann Arbor, MI 48109-1003 *Tel:* 734-764-6296 *Fax:* 734-764-3128 *E-mail:* abeauch@umich.edu *Web Site:* lsa.umich.edu/hopwood, pg 608

The Graduate Group/Booksellers, 86 Norwood Rd, West Hartford, CT 06117-2236 *Tel:* 860-233-2330 *E-mail:* graduategroup@hotmail.com *Web Site:* www.graduategroup.com, pg 80

The Judy Grahn Award for Lesbian Nonfiction, 511 Avenue of the Americas, No D36, New York, NY 10011 *E-mail:* awards@publishingtriangle.org; info@publishingtriangle.org; publishingtriangle@gmail.com *Web Site:* publishingtriangle.org/awards/judy-grahn-lesbian-nonfiction, pg 608

Grand & Archer Publishing, 463 Coyote, Cathedral City, CA 92234 *Tel:* 323-493-2785 *E-mail:* grandandarcher@gmail.com, pg 80

Grand Central Publishing, 1290 Avenue of the Americas, New York, NY 10104 *Tel:* 212-364-1100 *Web Site:* www.hachettebookgroup.com/imprint/grand-central-publishing/, pg 80

Grand Master Award, 716 Thicket Way, Ottawa, ON K4A 3B5, Canada *E-mail:* info@crimewriterscanada.com *Web Site:* www.crimewriterscanada.com/awards, pg 608

Donald M Grant Publisher Inc, 19 Surrey Lane, Hampton Falls, NH 03844 *Tel:* 603-778-7191 *Fax:* 603-778-7191 *Web Site:* secure.grantbooks.com, pg 80

Grant Program for Diverse Voices, One Broadway, 12th fl, Cambridge, MA 02142 *Web Site:* mitpress.mit.edu/grant-program-diverse-voices, pg 608

The Graphic Artists Guild Inc, 2248 Broadway, Suite 1341, New York, NY 10024 *Tel:* 212-791-3400 *E-mail:* admin@graphicartistsguild.org; membership@graphicartistsguild.org *Web Site:* www.graphicartistsguild.org, pg 506, 563

Graphic Arts Education & Research Foundation (GAERF), 1899 Preston White Dr, Reston, VA 20191 *Tel:* 703-264-7200 *E-mail:* gaerf@npes.org *Web Site:* www.gaerf.org, pg 525

Graphic Universe™, 241 First Ave N, Minneapolis, MN 55401 *Tel:* 612-332-3344 *Toll Free Tel:* 800-328-4929 *Fax:* 612-332-7615 *Toll Free Fax:* 800-332-1132 *E-mail:* info@lernerbooks.com; custserve@lernerbooks.com *Web Site:* www.lernerbooks.com; www.facebook.com/lernerbooks, pg 80

The Hillary Gravendyk Prize, 4178 Chestnut St, Riverside, CA 92501 *E-mail:* inlandia@inlandiainstitute.org *Web Site:* inlandiainstitute.org/books/the-hillary-gravendyk-prize, pg 608

Gravure AIMCAL Alliance (GAA), 150 Executive Center Dr, Suite 201, Greenville, SC 29615 *Tel:* 803-948-9470 *Fax:* 803-948-9471 *E-mail:* aimcal@aimcal.org *Web Site:* gaa.org, pg 507

Gray & Company Publishers, 1588 E 40 St, Suite 1B, Cleveland, OH 44103 *Tel:* 216-431-2665 *Toll Free Tel:* 800-915-3609 *E-mail:* sales@grayco.com; editorial@grayco.com; publicity@grayco.com *Web Site:* www.grayco.com, pg 80

Carla Gray Memorial Scholarship, 3135 S State St, Suite 203, Ann Arbor, MI 48108 *Toll Free Tel:* 866-733-9064 *E-mail:* info@bincfoundation.org *Web Site:* www.bincfoundation.org/carla-gray/, pg 609

James H Gray Award for Short Nonfiction, 11759 Groat Rd NW, Edmonton, AB T5M 3K6, Canada *Tel:* 780-422-8174 *Toll Free Tel:* 800-665-5354 (AB only) *E-mail:* mail@writersguild.ab.ca *Web Site:* writersguild.ca, pg 609

Graywolf Press, 212 Third Ave N, Suite 485, Minneapolis, MN 55401 *Tel:* 651-641-0077 *Fax:* 651-641-0036 *E-mail:* wolves@graywolfpress.org (no ms queries, sample chapters or proposals) *Web Site:* www.graywolfpress.org, pg 81

Graywolf Press African Fiction Prize, 212 Third Ave N, Suite 485, Minneapolis, MN 55401 *Tel:* 651-641-0077 *Fax:* 651-641-0036 *E-mail:* submissions@graywolfpress.org *Web Site:* www.graywolfpress.org/about-us/submissions, pg 609

Graywolf Press Nonfiction Prize, 212 Third Ave N, Suite 485, Minneapolis, MN 55401 *Tel:* 651-641-0077 *Fax:* 651-641-0036 *E-mail:* submissions@graywolfpress.org *Web Site:* www.graywolfpress.org/about-us/submissions, pg 609

Great Lakes Graphics Association (GLGA), N27 W23960 Paul Rd, Suite 200, Pewaukee, WI 53072 *Tel:* 262-522-2210 *Toll Free Tel:* 855-522-2210 *Fax:* 262-522-2211 *E-mail:* info@glga.info *Web Site:* glga.info, pg 507

Great Lakes Independent Booksellers Association (GLIBA), 3123 Andrea Ct, Woodridge, IL 60517 *Tel:* 630-841-8129 *Web Site:* www.gliba.org, pg 507

Green Dragon Books, 2275 Ibis Isle Rd W, Palm Beach, FL 33480 *Tel:* 561-533-6231 *Toll Free Tel:* 800-874-8844 *Fax:* 561-533-6233 *Toll Free Fax:* 888-874-8844 *E-mail:* info@greendragonbooks.com *Web Site:* greendragonbooks.com, pg 81

Green Earth Book Award, 3100 Clarendon Blvd, Suite 400, Arlington, VA 22201 *E-mail:* info@natgen.org *Web Site:* www.natgen.org/green-earth-book-awards, pg 609

The Fletcher M Green & Charles W Ramsdell Award, University of Georgia, Dept of History, Athens, GA 30602-1602 *Tel:* 706-542-8848 *Web Site:* thesha.org/ramsdell, pg 609

Green Integer, 750 S Spaulding Ave, Suite 112, Los Angeles, CA 90036 *E-mail:* info@greeninteger.com *Web Site:* www.greeninteger.com, pg 81

Sanford J Greenburger Associates Inc, 55 Fifth Ave, New York, NY 10003 *Tel:* 212-206-5600 *Web Site:* greenburger.com, pg 461

Greenhaven Publishing, 2544 Clinton St, Buffalo, NY 14224 *Toll Free Tel:* 844-317-7404 *Toll Free Fax:* 844-317-7405 *Web Site:* greenhavenpublishing.com; www.rosenpublishing.com, pg 81

Paul Greenland Communications Inc, 5062 Rockrose Ct, Suite 209, Roscoe, IL 61073 *Tel:* 815-240-4108 *Web Site:* www.paulgreenland.com, pg 440

Greenleaf Book Group LLC, PO Box 91869, Austin, TX 78709 *Tel:* 512-891-6100 *Fax:* 512-891-6150 *E-mail:* contact@greenleafbookgroup.com; orders@greenleafbookgroup.com; foreignrights@greenleafbookgroup.com; media@greenleafbookgroup.com *Web Site:* greenleafbookgroup.com, pg 81

Bess Gresham Memorial, PO Box 36128, North Chesterfield, VA 23235-3533 *E-mail:* contest@poetrysocietyofvirginia.org; info@poetryvirginia.org *Web Site:* www.poetrysocietyofvirginia.org, pg 609

Grey House Publishing Inc™, 4919 Rte 22, Amenia, NY 12501 *Tel:* 518-789-8700 *Toll Free Tel:* 800-562-2139 *Fax:* 518-789-0556 *E-mail:* books@greyhouse.com; customerservice@greyhouse.com *Web Site:* greyhouse.com, pg 81

Greystone Books Ltd, 343 Railway St, Suite 302, Vancouver, BC V6A 1A4, Canada *Tel:* 604-875-1550 *Fax:* 604-875-1556 *E-mail:* info@greystonebooks.com; rights@greystonebooks.com *Web Site:* www.greystonebooks.com, pg 407

Griffin Poetry Prize, 363 Parkridge Crescent, Oakville, ON L6M 1A8, Canada *Tel:* 905-618-0420 *E-mail:* info@griffinpoetryprize.com; publicity@griffinpoetryprize.com *Web Site:* griffinpoetryprize.com, pg 609

Joan K Griffitts Indexing, 3909 W 71 St, Indianapolis, IN 46268-2257 *Tel:* 317-297-7312 *E-mail:* jkgriffitts@gmail.com *Web Site:* www.joankgriffittsindexing.com, pg 440

Jill Grinberg Literary Management LLC, 392 Vanderbilt Ave, Brooklyn, NY 11238 *Tel:* 212-620-5883 *E-mail:* info@jillgrinbergliterary.com *Web Site:* www.jillgrinbergliterary.com, pg 461

Jill Grosjean Literary Agency, 1390 Millstone Rd, Sag Harbor, NY 11963 *Tel:* 631-725-7419 *Fax:* 631-725-8632 *E-mail:* JillLit310@aol.com, pg 461

Laura Gross Literary Agency, PO Box 610326, Newton Highlands, MA 02461 *Tel:* 617-964-2977 *E-mail:* query@lg-la.com; rights@lg-la.com *Web Site:* www.lg-la.com, pg 461

Groundwood Books, 128 Sterling Rd, Lower Level, Toronto, ON M6R 2B7, Canada *Tel:* 416-363-4343 *Fax:* 416-363-1017 *E-mail:* customerservice@houseofanansi.com *Web Site:* www.houseofanansi.com, pg 407

Group Publishing Inc, 1515 Cascade Ave, Loveland, CO 80538 *Tel:* 970-669-3836 *Toll Free Tel:* 800-447-1070 *E-mail:* puorgbus@group.com (submissions) *Web Site:* www.group.com, pg 82

Groupe Educalivres Inc, 1699, blvd le Corbusier, bureau 350, Laval, QC H7S 1Z3, Canada *Tel:* 514-334-8466 *Toll Free Tel:* 800-567-3671 (info serv) *Fax:* 514-334-8387 *Toll Free Fax:* 800-267-4387 *E-mail:* infoservice@grandduc.com *Web Site:* www.educalivres.com, pg 408

Groupe Modulo Inc, c/o TC Media Books Inc, 5800 St Denis St, Suite 900, Montreal, QC H2S 3L5, Canada *Tel:* 514-273-1066 *Toll Free Tel:* 800-565-5531 *Fax:* 514-276-0234 *Toll Free Fax:* 800-814-0324 *E-mail:* clientele@tc.tc *Web Site:* www.groupemodulo.com, pg 408

Groupe Sogides Inc, 955 rue Amherst, Montreal, QC H2L 3K4, Canada *Tel:* 514-523-1182 *Fax:* 514-597-0370 *Web Site:* sogides.com, pg 408

Grouse Grind Lit Prize for V Short Form, University of British Columbia, Buch E462, 1866 Main Mall, Vancouver, BC V6T 1Z1, Canada *Tel:* 604-822-2514 *Fax:* 604-822-3616 *E-mail:* promotions@prismmagazine.ca *Web Site:* www.prismmagazine.ca/contests, pg 609

Grove Atlantic Inc, 154 W 14 St, 12th fl, New York, NY 10011 *Tel:* 212-614-7850 *Toll Free Tel:* 800-521-0178 *Fax:* 212-614-7886 *E-mail:* info@groveatlantic.com; sales@groveatlantic.com; publicity@groveatlantic.com; rights@groveatlantic.com *Web Site:* www.groveatlantic.com, pg 82

Gryphon Editions, PO Box 241823, Omaha, NE 68124 *Tel:* 402-298-5385 (intl) *Toll Free Tel:* 888-655-0134 (US & CN) *E-mail:* customerservice@gryphoneditions.com *Web Site:* www.gryphoneditions.com, pg 82

Gryphon House Inc, 6848 Leon's Way, Lewisville, NC 27023 *Toll Free Tel:* 800-638-0928 *Toll Free Fax:* 877-638-7576 *E-mail:* info@ghbooks.com *Web Site:* www.gryphonhouse.com, pg 82

Carol Guenzi Agents Inc, 865 Delaware St, Denver, CO 80204 *Tel:* 303-820-2599 *Toll Free Tel:* 800-417-5120 *E-mail:* art@artagent.com *Web Site:* artagent.com, pg 485

Guerin Editeur Ltee, 800, Blvd Industriel, bureau 200, St-Jean-sur-Richelieu, QC J3B 8G4, Canada *Tel:* 514-842-3481 *Toll Free Tel:* 800-398-8337 *Fax:* 514-842-4923 *E-mail:* info@guerin-editeur.qc.ca *Web Site:* www.guerin-editeur.qc.ca, pg 408

Guernica Editions Inc, 287 Templemead Dr, Hamilton, ON L8W 2W4, Canada *Tel:* 905-599-5304 *E-mail:* info@guernicaeditions.com *Web Site:* www.guernicaeditions.com; www.facebook.com/guernicaed, pg 408

Guggenheim Fellowships, 90 Park Ave, New York, NY 10016 *Tel:* 212-687-4470 *Fax:* 212-697-3248 *Web Site:* www.gf.org/about/fellowship, pg 609

John Simon Guggenheim Memorial Foundation, 90 Park Ave, New York, NY 10016 *Tel:* 212-687-4470 *Fax:* 212-697-3248 *Web Site:* www.gf.org, pg 525

Guideposts Book & Inspirational Media, 100 Reserve Rd, Suite E200, Danbury, CT 06810 *Tel:* 203-749-0200 *Toll Free Tel:* 800-932-2145 (cust serv) *E-mail:* gpsprod@cdsfulfillment.com; gdpcustserv@cdsfulfillment.com *Web Site:* guideposts.org, pg 82

Guild of Book Workers, 521 Fifth Ave, New York, NY 10175 *E-mail:* communications@guildofbookworkers.org; membership@guildofbookworkers.org *Web Site:* www.guildofbookworkers.org, pg 507

The Guilford Press, 370 Seventh Ave, Suite 1200, New York, NY 10001-1020 *Tel:* 212-431-9800 *Toll Free Tel:* 800-365-7006 *Fax:* 212-966-6708 *E-mail:* info@guilford.com; orders@guilford.com *Web Site:* www.guilford.com, pg 82

Gulf Energy Information, 2 Greenway Plaza, Suite 1020, Houston, TX 77046 *Tel:* 713-520-4498; 713-529-4301 *E-mail:* store@gulfpub.com; customerservice@gulfenergyinfo.com *Web Site:* www.gulfenergyinfo.com, pg 83

The Thom Gunn Award for Gay Poetry, 511 Avenue of the Americas, No D36, New York, NY 10011 *E-mail:* awards@publishingtriangle.org; info@publishingtriangle.org; publishingtriangle@gmail.com *Web Site:* publishingtriangle.org/awards/thom-gunn-gay-poetry, pg 610

The Charlotte Gusay Literary Agency, 10532 Blythe Ave, Los Angeles, CA 90064 *Tel:* 310-559-0831 *E-mail:* gusayagency1@gmail.com *Web Site:* www.gusay.com, pg 461

Gutekunst Prize, 30 Irving Place, New York, NY 10003 *Tel:* 212-439-8700 *Fax:* 212-439-8705 *E-mail:* gutekunst@goethe.de *Web Site:* www.goethe.de/ins/us/enkul/ser/uef/gut.html, pg 610

GW Inc, 2290 Ball Dr, St Louis, MO 63146 *Tel:* 314-567-9854 *E-mail:* media@gwinc.com *Web Site:* www.gwinc.com, pg 440

Hachai Publishing, 527 Empire Blvd, Brooklyn, NY 11225 *Tel:* 718-633-0100 *Fax:* 718-633-0103 *E-mail:* info@hachai.com *Web Site:* www.hachai.com, pg 83

Hachette Audio, 1290 Avenue of the Americas, New York, NY 10104 *Tel:* 212-364-1100 *Web Site:* www.hachettebookgroup.com/imprint/hachette-audio/, pg 83

Hachette Book Group Inc, 1290 Avenue of the Americas, New York, NY 10104 *Tel:* 212-364-1100 *Toll Free Tel:* 800-759-0190 (cust serv) *Fax:* 212-364-0933 (intl orders) *Toll Free Fax:* 800-286-9471 (cust serv) *E-mail:* customer.service@hbgusa.com; orders@hbgusa.com *Web Site:* www.hachettebookgroup.com, pg 83

Hachette Nashville, 6100 Tower Circle, Room 210, Franklin, TN 37067 *Tel:* 615-221-0996 *Fax:* 615-221-0962 *Web Site:* www.hachettebookgroup.com/imprint/hachette-nashville/, pg 83

Hackett Publishing Co Inc, 3333 Massachusetts Ave, Indianapolis, IN 46218 *Tel:* 317-635-9250 (orders & cust serv); 617-497-6303 (edit off & sales) *Fax:* 317-635-9292; 617-661-8703 (edit off) *Toll Free Fax:* 800-783-9213 *E-mail:* customer@hackettpublishing.com; editorial@hackettpublishing.com *Web Site:* www.hackettpublishing.com, pg 83

Hackmatack Children's Choice Book Award, PO Box 34055, Halifax, NS B3J 3S1, Canada *Tel:* 902-424-3774 *E-mail:* hackmatack@hackmatack.ca *Web Site:* hackmatack.ca, pg 610

Hackney Literary Awards, 4650 Old Looney Mill Rd, Birmingham, AL 35243 *Web Site:* www.hackneyliteraryawards.org, pg 610

Hadada Award, 544 W 27 St, New York, NY 10001 *Tel:* 212-343-1333 *E-mail:* queries@theparisreview.org *Web Site:* www.theparisreview.org/about/prizes, pg 610

Lisa Hagan Literary, 110 Martin Dr, Bracey, VA 23919 *Tel:* 434-636-4138 *E-mail:* Lisa@lisahaganbooks.com *Web Site:* www.publishersmarketplace.com/members/LisaHagan, pg 462

Raymond Levi Haislip Memorial, PO Box 36128, North Chesterfield, VA 23235-3533 *E-mail:* contest@poetrysocietyofvirginia.org; info@poetryvirginia.org *Web Site:* www.poetrysocietyofvirginia.org, pg 610

Hal Leonard LLC, 7777 W Bluemound Rd, Milwaukee, WI 53213 *Tel:* 414-774-3630 *E-mail:* info@halleonard.com; sales@halleonard.com *Web Site:* www.halleonard.com, pg 84

Sarah Josepha Hale Award, 58 N Main St, Newport, NH 03773 *Tel:* 603-863-3430 *E-mail:* rfl@newport.lib.nh.us *Web Site:* www.newport.lib.nh.us, pg 610

1/2 K Prize, Indiana University English Dept, Ballantine Hall 554, 1020 E Kirkwood Ave, Bloomington, IN 47405 *Tel:* 812-855-3439 *E-mail:* inreview@indiana.edu *Web Site:* indianareview.org, pg 610

Loretta Dunn Hall Memorial, PO Box 36128, North Chesterfield, VA 23235-3533 *E-mail:* contest@poetrysocietyofvirginia.org; info@poetryvirginia.org *Web Site:* www.poetrysocietyofvirginia.org, pg 610

Hameray Publishing Group Inc, 5212 Venice Blvd, Los Angeles, CA 90019 *Toll Free Tel:* 866-918-6173 *Fax:* 858-369-5201 *E-mail:* info@hameraypublishing.com (cust serv); sales@hameraypublishing.com (sales) *Web Site:* www.hameraypublishing.com, pg 84

Hamilton Books, 4501 Forbes Blvd, Suite 200, Lanham, MD 20706 *Tel:* 301-459-3366 *Toll Free Tel:* 800-462-6420 (cust serv) *Fax:* 301-429-5748 *Toll Free Fax:* 800-388-4550 (cust serv), pg 84

Hamilton College, Literature & Creative Writing, Literature & Creative Writing Dept, 198 College Hill Rd, Clinton, NY 13323 *Tel:* 315-859-4370 *Fax:* 315-859-4390 *Web Site:* www.hamilton.edu, pg 563

Hamilton Stone Editions, PO Box 43, Maplewood, NJ 07040 *Tel:* 973-378-8361 *E-mail:* hstone@hamiltonstone.org *Web Site:* www.hamiltonstone.org, pg 84

Hammett Prize, PO Box 863, Norman, OK 73071 *E-mail:* crimewritersna@gmail.com *Web Site:* www.crimewritersna.org/hammett, pg 610

Hampton Roads Publishing, 65 Parker St, Suite 7, Newburyport, MA 01950-4600 Tel: 978-465-0504 Toll Free Tel: 800-423-7087 (orders) Fax: 978-465-0243 Toll Free Fax: 877-337-3309 E-mail: orders@rwwbooks.com; rights@rwwbooks.com Web Site: redwheelweiser.com, pg 84

Hancock House Publishers, 4550 Birch Bay Lynden Rd, Suite 104, Blaine, WA 98230-9436 Tel: 604-538-1114 Toll Free Tel: 800-938-1114 Fax: 604-538-2262 Toll Free Fax: 800-983-2262 E-mail: sales@hancockhouse.com Web Site: www.hancockhouse.com, pg 84

Hancock House Publishers Ltd, 19313 Zero Ave, Surrey, BC V3S 9R9, Canada Tel: 604-538-1114 Toll Free Tel: 800-938-1114 Fax: 604-538-2262 Toll Free Fax: 800-983-2262 E-mail: sales@hancockhouse.com; info@hancockhouse.com Web Site: www.hancockhouse.com, pg 408

Handprint Books Inc, 413 Sixth Ave, Brooklyn, NY 11215 Tel: 718-768-3696 Toll Free Tel: 800-759-0190 (orders) E-mail: hello@chroniclebooks.com (orders); publicity@chroniclebooks.com Web Site: www.handprintbooks.com, pg 84

Handy Andy Prize, PO Box 36128, North Chesterfield, VA 23235-3533 E-mail: contest@poetrysocietyofvirginia.org; info@poetryvirginia.org Web Site: www.poetrysocietyofvirginia.org, pg 610

Hanging Loose Press, 231 Wyckoff St, Brooklyn, NY 11217 Tel: 347-529-4738 Fax: 347-227-8215 E-mail: print225@aol.com Web Site: www.hangingloosepress.com, pg 85

Hannacroix Creek Books Inc, 1127 High Ridge Rd, PMB 110, Stamford, CT 06905 Tel: 203-968-8098 E-mail: hannacroix@aol.com, pg 85

The Joseph Hansen Award for LGBTQ Crime Writing, 511 Avenue of the Americas, No D36, New York, NY 10011 E-mail: awards@publishingtriangle.org; info@publishingtriangle.org; publishingtriangle@gmail.com Web Site: publishingtriangle.org/awards/joseph-hansen-award-lgbtq-crime-writing, pg 611

Hanser Publications LLC, c/o CFAS, 5667 Kyles Lane, Liberty Township, OH 45044 Toll Free Tel: 800-950-8977; 888-558-2632 (orders) E-mail: info@hanserpublications.com Web Site: www.hanserpublications.com, pg 85

Harbour Publishing Co Ltd, 4437 Rondeview Rd, Madeira Park, BC V0N 2H0, Canada Tel: 604-883-2730 Toll Free Tel: 800-667-2988 Fax: 604-883-9451 Toll Free Fax: 877-604-9449 E-mail: info@harbourpublishing.com; orders@harbourpublishing.com Web Site: www.harbourpublishing.com, pg 408

Clarence H Haring Prize in Latin American History, 400 "A" St SE, Washington, DC 20003 Tel: 202-544-2422 E-mail: awards@historians.org Web Site: www.historians.org/award-grant/clarence-h-haring-prize/, pg 611

Joy Harjo Poetry Award, PO Box 2414, Durango, CO 81302 Tel: 970-903-7914 E-mail: cutthroatmag@gmail.com Web Site: www.cutthroatmag.com, pg 611

Harlequin Enterprises Ltd, 195 Broadway, 24th fl, New York, NY 10007 Tel: 212-207-7000 Toll Free Tel: 888-432-4879; 800-370-5838 (ebooks) E-mail: customerservice@harlequin.com Web Site: www.harlequin.com/shop/index.html; corporate.harlequin.com, pg 85

Harlequin Enterprises Ltd, Bay Adelaide Centre, East Tower, 22 Adelaide St W, 41st fl, Toronto, ON M5H 4E3, Canada Tel: 416-445-5860 Toll Free Tel: 888-432-4879; 800-370-5838 (ebook inquiries) E-mail: customerservice@harlequin.com Web Site: www.harlequin.com, pg 409

HarperCollins Canada Ltd, 22 Adelaide St W, 41st fl, Toronto, ON M5H 4E3, Canada Tel: 416-975-9334 E-mail: hcorder@harpercollins.com Web Site: www.harpercollins.ca, pg 409

HarperCollins Children's Books, 195 Broadway, New York, NY 10007 Tel: 212-207-7000 Web Site: www.harpercollins.com/childrens, pg 85

HarperCollins Publishers LLC, 195 Broadway, New York, NY 10007 Tel: 212-207-7000 Web Site: www.harpercollins.com, pg 86

LD & LaVerne Harrell Clark Fiction Prize, Flowers Hall, Rm 365, 601 University Dr, San Marcos, TX 78666 Tel: 512-245-2163 Fax: 512-245-8546 Web Site: www.english.txstate.edu/clarkfictionprize.html, pg 611

Harrington Park Press, 9 E Eighth St, Box 331, New York, NY 10003 Tel: 347-882-3545 (edit & publicity) Fax: 646-602-1349 (edit & publicity) Web Site: harringtonparkpress.com, pg 87

Aurand Harris Memorial Playwriting Award, 167 Cherry St, No 331, Milford, CT 06460 E-mail: harris-award@netconline.org; mail@netconline.org Web Site: www.netconline.org, pg 611

The Joy Harris Literary Agency Inc, 1501 Broadway, Suite 2310, New York, NY 10036 Tel: 212-924-6269 Fax: 212-840-5776 E-mail: contact@joyharrisliterary.com Web Site: www.joyharrisliterary.com, pg 462

Harrison House, 167 Walnut Bottom Rd, Shippensburg, PA 17257 Tel: 717-532-3040 Web Site: norimediagroup.com, pg 87

Hartline Literary Agency LLC, 123 Queenston Dr, Pittsburgh, PA 15235 Tel: 412-829-2483 Toll Free Fax: 888-279-6007 Web Site: www.hartlineliterary.com, pg 462

Hartman Publishing Inc, 1313 Iron Ave SW, Albuquerque, NM 87102 Tel: 505-291-1274 Toll Free Tel: 800-999-9534 Toll Free Fax: 800-474-6106 E-mail: info@hartmanonline.com Web Site: www.hartmanonline.com, pg 87

Harvard Art Museums, 32 Quincy St, Cambridge, MA 02138 Tel: 617-495-9400 Web Site: www.harvardartmuseums.org, pg 87

Harvard Business Review Press, 20 Guest St, Suite 700, Brighton, MA 02135 Tel: 617-783-7400 Fax: 617-783-7489 E-mail: custserv@hbsp.harvard.edu Web Site: www.harvardbusiness.org, pg 87

Harvard Common Press, 100 Cummings Ctr, Suite 265-D, Beverly, MA 01915 Tel: 978-282-9590 Fax: 978-282-7765 Web Site: www.quartoknows.com/harvard-common-press, pg 87

Harvard Education Publishing Group, 8 Story St, 1st fl, Cambridge, MA 02138 Tel: 617-495-3432 Fax: 617-496-3584 Web Site: www.hepg.org, pg 88

Harvard Square Editions, Beachwood Terr, Hollywood, CA 90068 Tel: 323-203-0233 E-mail: submissions@harvardsquareeditions.org Web Site: harvardsquareeditions.org, pg 88

Harvard Summer School Writing Center, 51 Brattle St, Cambridge, MA 02138 Tel: 617-495-4024 E-mail: dcewriting@gmail.com; inquiry@summerharvard.edu Web Site: summer.harvard.edu, pg 554

Harvard Ukrainian Research Institute, 34 Kirkland St, Cambridge, MA 02138 Tel: 617-495-4053 Fax: 617-495-8097 E-mail: huripubs@fas.harvard.edu Web Site: books.huri.harvard.edu, pg 88

Harvard University Press, 79 Garden St, Cambridge, MA 02138-1499 Tel: 617-495-2600; 401-531-2800 (intl orders) Toll Free Tel: 800-405-1619 (orders) Fax: 617-495-5898 (gen); 617-496-4677 (edit & rts); 401-531-2801 (intl orders) Toll Free Fax: 800-406-9145 (orders) E-mail: contact_hup@harvard.edu Web Site: www.hup.harvard.edu, pg 88

Harvest House Publishers Inc, PO Box 41210, Eugene, OR 97404-0322 Tel: 541-343-0123 Toll Free Tel: 888-501-6991 Fax: 541-343-9711 E-mail: admin@harvesthousepublishers.com; permissions@harvesthousepublishers.com Web Site: harvesthousepublishers.com, pg 88

Haskins Medal Award, 6 Beacon St, Suite 500, Boston, MA 02108 Tel: 617-491-1622 Fax: 617-492-3303 E-mail: info@themedievalacademy.org Web Site: www.medievalacademy.org/page/haskins_medal, pg 611

Hatherleigh Press Ltd, 62545 State Hwy 10, Hobart, NY 13788 Toll Free Tel: 800-528-2550 E-mail: info@hatherleighpress.com; publicity@hatherleighpress.com Web Site: www.hatherleighpress.com, pg 88

John Hawkins and Associates Inc, 80 Maiden Lane, Suite 1503, New York, NY 10038 Tel: 212-807-7040 E-mail: jha@jhalit.com Web Site: jhalit.com, pg 462

Ellis W Hawley Prize, 112 N Bryan Ave, Bloomington, IN 47408-4141 Tel: 812-855-7311 E-mail: oah@oah.org Web Site: www.oah.org/awards, pg 611

Hay House LLC, PO Box 5100, Carlsbad, CA 92018-5100 Tel: 760-431-7695 (ext 1, intl) Toll Free Tel: 800-654-5126 (ext 1, US) Toll Free Fax: 800-650-5115 Web Site: www.hayhouse.com, pg 89

Friedrich Hayek Lecture & Book Prize, 52 Vanderbilt Ave, New York, NY 10017 Tel: 212-599-7000 Web Site: www.manhattan-institute.org, pg 611

Haynes North America Inc, 2801 Townsgate Rd, Suite 340, Westlake Village, CA 91361 Tel: 805-498-6703 Toll Free Tel: 800-4-HAYNES (442-9637) Fax: 805-498-2867 E-mail: customerservice.haynes@infopro-digital.com Web Site: www.haynes.com, pg 89

Hazelden Publishing, 15251 Pleasant Valley Rd, Center City, MN 55012-0011 Tel: 651-213-4200 Toll Free Tel: 800-257-7810; 866-328-9000 Fax: 651-213-4793 Web Site: www.hazelden.org, pg 89

Hazy Dell Press, 1001 SE Water Ave, Suite 132, Portland, OR 97214 Tel: 971-279-5779 E-mail: info@hazydellpress.com Web Site: www.hazydellpress.com, pg 89

HCPro/DecisionHealth, 5511 Virginia Way, Suite 150, Brentwood, TN 37027 Tel: 800-650-6787 Toll Free Fax: 800-785-9212 E-mail: customer@hcpro.com Web Site: www.hcpro.com, pg 89

Headlands Center for the Arts Residency for Writers, 944 Fort Barry, Sausalito, CA 94965 Tel: 415-331-2787 Fax: 415-331-3857 Web Site: www.headlands.org, pg 611

Health Administration Press, 300 S Riverside Plaza, Suite 1900, Chicago, IL 60606 Tel: 312-424-2800 Fax: 312-424-0014 E-mail: hapbooks@ache.org Web Site: www.ache.org/hap (orders), pg 89

Health Communications Inc, 301 Crawford Blvd, Suite 200, Boca Raton, FL 33432 Tel: 561-453-0696 Toll Free Tel: 800-441-5569 (cust serv & orders) Fax: 561-453-1009 Toll Free Fax: 800-943-9831 (orders) E-mail: editorial@hcibooks.com Web Site: hcibooks.com, pg 89

Health Forum Inc, 155 N Wacker Dr, Suite 400, Chicago, IL 60606 Tel: 312-893-6800 Toll Free Tel: 800-242-2626 Web Site: www.ahaonlinestore.com; www.aha.org, pg 90

Health Professions Press, 409 Washington Ave, Suite 500, Towson, MD 21204 Tel: 410-337-9585 Toll Free Tel: 888-337-8808 Fax: 410-337-8539 Web Site: www.healthpropress.com, pg 90

Heartland Booksellers Award, 3123 Andrea Ct, Woodridge, IL 60517 Tel: 630-841-8129 Web Site: www.gliba.org/heartland-booksellers-award.html, pg 611

Heartland Literary Award, 160 N Stetson Ave, Chicago, IL 60601 Tel: 312-222-3001 E-mail: ctc-arts@chicagotribune.com Web Site: www.chicagotribune.com/entertainment/books/literary-awards, pg 611

HeartMath LLC, 14700 W Park Ave, Boulder Creek, CA 95006 Tel: 831-338-8500 Toll Free Tel: 800-711-6221 Fax: 831-338-8504 E-mail: info@heartmath.org; service@heartmath.org Web Site: www.heartmath.org, pg 90

Hearts 'n Tummies Cookbook Co, 3544 Blakslee St, Wever, IA 52658 Tel: 319-372-7480 Toll Free Tel: 800-571-2665 E-mail: quixotepress@gmail.com; heartsntummies@gmail.com Web Site: www.heartsntummies.com, pg 90

Anne Hebenstreit, 20 Tip Top Way, Berkeley Heights, NJ 07922 Tel: 908-665-0536, pg 440

Hebrew Union College Press, 3101 Clifton Ave, Cincinnati, OH 45220 Tel: 513-221-1875 Fax: 513-221-0321 Web Site: press.huc.edu, pg 90

Hedgebrook Radical Craft Retreats, PO Box 1231, Freeland, WA 98249 Tel: 360-321-4786 E-mail: hedgebrook@hedgebrook.org Web Site: www.hedgebrook.org/radical-craft-retreats; www.facebook.com/hedgebrook, pg 554

Hedgebrook VorTEXT Intensives Writing Retreat, PO Box 1231, Freeland, WA 98249 Tel: 360-321-4786 E-mail: hedgebrook@hedgebrook.org; programs@hedgebrook.org Web Site: www.hedgebrook.org/vortext; www.facebook.com/hedgebrook, pg 554

Hedgebrook Writers in Residence Program, PO Box 1231, Freeland, WA 98249 Tel: 360-321-4786 E-mail: hedgebrook@hedgebrook.org; programs@hedgebrook.org Web Site: www.hedgebrook.org/writers-in-residence; www.facebook.com/hedgebrook, pg 554

Heimburger House Publishing Co, 7236 W Madison St, Forest Park, IL 60130 Tel: 708-366-1973 Fax: 708-366-1973 E-mail: info@heimburgerhouse.com Web Site: www.heimburgerhouse.com, pg 90

William S Hein & Co Inc, 2350 N Forest Rd, Suite 10A, Getzville, NY 14068 Tel: 716-882-2600 Toll Free Tel: 800-828-7571 Fax: 716-883-8100 E-mail: mail@wshein.com; marketing@wshein.com; customerservice@wshein.com Web Site: home.heinonline.org, pg 90

Heinemann, 145 Maplewood Ave, Suite 300, Portsmouth, NH 03801 Tel: 603-431-7894 Toll Free Tel: 800-225-5800 (US) Fax: 603-547-9917 E-mail: custserv@heinemann.com Web Site: www.heinemann.com, pg 90

Robert A Heinlein Award, PO Box 686, Baltimore, MD 21203-0686 Tel: 410-563-2737 E-mail: webmeister@bsfs.org Web Site: www.bsfs.org/bsfsheinlein.htm, pg 612

Drue Heinz Literature Prize, 7500 Thomas Blvd, Pittsburgh, PA 15260 Tel: 412-383-2456 Fax: 412-383-2466 E-mail: info@upress.pitt.edu Web Site: upittpress.org/prize/drue-heinz-literature-prize; www.upress.pitt.edu, pg 612

The Shirley Holden Helberg Grants for Mature Women, The Pen Arts Bldg & Arts Museum, 1300 17 St NW, Washington, DC 20036-1973 Tel: 202-785-1997 Fax: 202-452-6868 E-mail: contact@nlapw.org Web Site: www.nlapw.org, pg 612

Hellgate Press, PO Box 3531, Ashland, OR 97520 Tel: 541-973-5154 E-mail: sales@hellgatepress.com Web Site: www.hellgatepress.com, pg 91

Helm Editorial Services, 300 Canopy Walk Lane, Unit 325, Palm Coast, FL 32137 Tel: 954-525-5626 E-mail: lynnehelm12@aol.com, pg 440

Cecil Hemley Memorial Award, 119 Smith St, Brooklyn, NY 11201 Tel: 212-254-9628 E-mail: info@poetrysociety.org Web Site: poetrysociety.org/awards, pg 612

Hendrickson Publishers Inc, c/o Tyndale House Publishers, 351 Executive Dr, Carol Stream, IL 60188 Toll Free Tel: 855-277-9400 Toll Free Fax: 866-622-9474 E-mail: consumers@tyndale.com Web Site: www.hendricksonrose.com, pg 91

Her Own Words LLC, PO Box 5264, Madison, WI 53705-0264 Tel: 608-271-7083 Fax: 608-271-0209 Web Site: www.herownwords.com; www.nontraditionalcareers.com, pg 91

Herald Press, PO Box 866, Harrisonburg, VA 22803 Toll Free Tel: 800-245-7894 (orders) Fax: 540-242-4476 Toll Free Fax: 877-271-0760 E-mail: info@mennomedia.org; customerservice@mennomedia.org Web Site: www.heraldpress.com; store.mennomedia.org, pg 91

Heritage Books Inc, 5810 Ruatan St, Berwyn Heights, MD 20740 Toll Free Tel: 800-876-6103 Toll Free Fax: 800-876-6103; 800-297-9954 E-mail: orders@heritagebooks.com; submissions@heritagebooks.com Web Site: www.heritagebooks.com, pg 91

The Heritage Foundation, 214 Massachusetts Ave NE, Washington, DC 20002-4999 Tel: 202-546-4400 Toll Free Tel: 800-546-2843 Fax: 202-546-8328 E-mail: info@heritage.org Web Site: www.heritage.org, pg 91

Heritage House Publishing Co Ltd, 1075 Pendergast St, No 103, Victoria, BC V8V 0A1, Canada Tel: 250-360-0829 Fax: 250-386-0829 E-mail: heritage@heritagehouse.ca; info@heritagehouse.ca; orders@heritagehouse.ca Web Site: www.heritagehouse.ca, pg 409

Herman Agency, 350 Central Park W, Apt 4I, New York, NY 10025 Tel: 212-749-4907 Web Site: www.hermanagencyinc.com, pg 485

The Jeff Herman Agency LLC, 29 Park St, Stockbridge, MA 01262 Tel: 413-298-0077 Web Site: www.jeffherman.com, pg 462

Brodie Herndon Memorial, PO Box 36128, North Chesterfield, VA 23235-3533 E-mail: contest@poetrysocietyofvirginia.org; info@poetryvirginia.org Web Site: www.poetrysocietyofvirginia.org, pg 612

Herr's Indexing Service, 76-340 Kealoha St, Kailua Kona, HI 96740-2915 Tel: 808-365-4348 Web Site: www.herrsindexing.com, pg 440

Heuer Publishing LLC, PO Box 248, Cedar Rapids, IA 52406 Tel: 319-368-8008 Toll Free Tel: 800-950-7529 Fax: 319-368-8011 E-mail: orders@heuerpub.com; customerservice@heuerpub.com Web Site: www.hitplays.com, pg 91

Les Heures bleues, 4455 Coolbrook Ave, No 2, Montreal, QC H4A 3G1, Canada Tel: 438-399-2077 Fax: 450-671-7718 E-mail: editions.lesheuresbleues@gmail.com Web Site: www.heuresbleues.com, pg 409

Hewitt Homeschooling Resources, 8117 N Division, Suite D, Spokane, WA 99208 Toll Free Tel: 800-348-1750 Fax: 360-835-8697 E-mail: sales@hewitthomeschooling.com Web Site: hewitthomeschooling.com, pg 91

Heyday, 1808 San Pablo Ave, Suite A, Berkeley, CA 94702 Tel: 510-549-3564 E-mail: heyday@heydaybooks.com Web Site: heydaybooks.com, pg 91

HG Literary, 6 W 18 St, Suite 7R, New York, NY 10011 E-mail: foreign@hgliterary.com; rights@hgliterary.com Web Site: www.hgliterary.com, pg 463

Hi Willow Research & Publishing, 146 S 700 E, Provo, UT 84601 Tel: 801-755-1122 E-mail: lmcsourceutah@gmail.com Web Site: www.lmcsource.com; www.davidvl.org, pg 91

Hidden River Arts Playwriting Award, PO Box 63927, Philadelphia, PA 19147 Tel: 610-764-0813 E-mail: hiddenriverarts@gmail.com Web Site: www.hiddenriverarts.org; www.hiddenriverarts.com, pg 612

Higginson Book Company LLC, 219 Mill Rd, Morgantown, PA 19543 Tel: 484-249-0378 Web Site: www.higginsonbooks.com, pg 91

High Plains Book Awards, c/o Billings Public Library, 510 N 28 St, Billings, MT 59101 Tel: 406-672-6223 E-mail: highplainsbookawards@gmail.com Web Site: highplainsbookawards.org, pg 612

High Plains Press, PO Box 123, Glendo, WY 82213 Tel: 307-735-4370 Toll Free Tel: 800-552-7819 Fax: 307-735-4590 E-mail: editor@highplainspress.com Web Site: highplainspress.com, pg 91

High School Sequoyah Book Award, 119 Meramec Station Rd, Suite 207, Ballwin, MO 63021-6902 Toll Free Tel: 800-969-6562 (ext 5) Fax: 636-529-1396 E-mail: sequoyah@oklibs.org; ola@amigos.org Web Site: www.oklibs.org, pg 612

High Tide Press, 101 Hempstead Place, Suite 1A, Joliet, IL 60433 Tel: 779-702-5540 E-mail: orders@hightidepress.org; award@hightidepress.org Web Site: hightidepress.org, pg 92

Higher Education Scholarship Program, 3135 S State St, Suite 203, Ann Arbor, MI 48108 Toll Free Tel: 866-733-9064 E-mail: info@bincfoundation.org Web Site: www.bincfoundation.org/scholarship, pg 612

Highland Summer Writers' Conference, Radford University, Cook Hall 229, Radford, VA 24142 Tel: 540-831-5366 Web Site: www.radford.edu/content/cehd/home/appalachian-studies.html, pg 554

Highlights for Children Inc, 815 Church St, Honesdale, PA 18431 Tel: 570-253-1164 Toll Free Tel: 800-490-5111 Fax: 570-253-0179 E-mail: salesandmarketing@highlightspress.com Web Site: www.highlightspress.com; www.highlights.com; www.facebook.com/HighlightsforChildren, pg 92

Hill & Wang, 120 Broadway, New York, NY 10271 Tel: 212-741-6900 E-mail: fsg.publicity@fsgbooks.com; sales@fsgbooks.com Web Site: us.macmillan.com/fsg, pg 92

Hill Nadell Literary Agency, 6442 Santa Monica Blvd, Suite 200A, Los Angeles, CA 90038 Tel: 310-860-9605 E-mail: queries@hillnadell.com; rights@hillnadell.com (rts & perms) Web Site: www.hillnadell.com, pg 463

The Tony Hillerman Prize, c/o St Martin's Press, 120 Broadway, New York, NY 10271 E-mail: tonyhillermanprize@stmartins.com Web Site: us.macmillan.com/minotaurbooks/tonyhillermanprize, pg 612

Hillman Prizes for Journalism, 330 W 42 St, Suite 900, New York, NY 10036 Tel: 646-448-6413 Web Site: www.hillmanfoundation.org, pg 613

Hillsdale College Press, 33 E College St, Hillsdale, MI 49242 Tel: 517-437-7341 Toll Free Tel: 800-437-2268 Fax: 517-607-2658 E-mail: pr@hillsdale.edu Web Site: www.hillsdale.edu, pg 92

Hilton Publishing Co, 5261-A Fountain Dr, Crown Point, IN 46307 Tel: 219-922-4868 Fax: 219-924-6811 E-mail: info@hpcinternationalinc.com Web Site: www.hpcinternationalinc.com; www.hpcinternationalinc.com/bookstore (orders), pg 92

Himalayan Institute Press, 952 Bethany Tpke, Honesdale, PA 18431 Tel: 570-253-5551 Toll Free Tel: 800-822-4547 E-mail: trade@himalayaninstitute.org Web Site: www.himalayaninstitute.org, pg 92

Darlene Clark Hine Award, 112 N Bryan Ave, Bloomington, IN 47408-4141 Tel: 812-855-7311 E-mail: oah@oah.org Web Site: www.oah.org/awards, pg 613

Theodore C Hines Award, 1628 E Southern Ave, Suite 9-223, Tempe, AZ 85282 Tel: 480-245-6750 E-mail: info@asindexing.org Web Site: www.asindexing.org/about/awards/hines-award, pg 613

Hippocrene Books Inc, 171 Madison Ave, Suite 1605, New York, NY 10016 Tel: 212-685-4373 E-mail: info@hippocrenebooks.com; orderdept@hippocrenebooks.com (orders) Web Site: www.hippocrenebooks.com, pg 92

L Anne Hirschel DDS, 5990 Highgate Ave, East Lansing, MI 48823 Tel: 517-333-1748 E-mail: alicerichard@comcast.net, pg 440

The Historic New Orleans Collection, 533 Royal St, New Orleans, LA 70130 Tel: 504-523-4662 Fax: 504-598-7108 E-mail: wrc@hnoc.org Web Site: www.hnoc.org, pg 93

Historical Novel Society North American Conference, PO Box 1146, Jacksonville, AL 36265 E-mail: hnsnorthamerica@gmail.com Web Site: hns-conference.com; historicalnovelsociety.org/event/hns-north-american-conference; historicalnovelsociety.org, pg 554

History Publishing Co LLC, PO Box 700, Palisades, NY 10964 Tel: 845-359-1765 Fax: 845-818-3730 (sales) E-mail: info@historypublishingco.com Web Site: www.historypublishingco.com, pg 93

Histria Books, 7181 N Hualapai Way, Suite 130-86, Las Vegas, NV 89166 Tel: 561-299-0802 E-mail: info@histriabooks.com; orders@histriabooks.com; rights@histriabooks.com Web Site: histriabooks.com, pg 93

W D Hoard & Sons Co, 28 W Milwaukee Ave, Fort Atkinson, WI 53538 Tel: 920-563-5551 E-mail: hdbooks@hoards.com; editors@hoards.com Web Site: www.hoards.com, pg 93

Hobblebush Books, PO Box 1285, Concord, NH 03302 Tel: 603-715-9615 E-mail: info@hobblebush.com Web Site: www.hobblebush.com, pg 93

Eric Hoffer Award, PO Box 11, Titusville, NJ 08560 *E-mail:* info@hofferaward.com *Web Site:* www.hofferaward.com, pg 613

Hofstra University, Department of English, 204 Mason Hall, Hempstead, NY 11549 *Tel:* 516-463-5454 *E-mail:* english@hofstra.edu *Web Site:* www.hofstra.edu/english, pg 563

The Barbara Hogenson Agency Inc, 165 West End Ave, Suite 19-C, New York, NY 10023 *Tel:* 212-874-8084 *E-mail:* barbarahogenson@gmail.com, pg 463

Hogrefe Publishing Corp, 44 Merrimac St, Suite 207, Newburyport, MA 01950 *Tel:* 978-255-3700 (off) *E-mail:* customersupport@hogrefe.com *Web Site:* www.hogrefe.com/us, pg 93

Hohm Press, PO Box 4410, Chino Valley, AZ 86323 *Tel:* 928-636-3331 *Toll Free Tel:* 800-381-2700 *Fax:* 928-636-7519 *E-mail:* publisher@hohmpress.com *Web Site:* www.hohmpress.com, pg 93

Bess Hokin Prize, 61 W Superior St, Chicago, IL 60654 *Tel:* 312-787-7070 *Web Site:* www.poetryfoundation.org/poetrymagazine/prizes, pg 613

Holiday House Publishing Inc, 50 Broad St, New York, NY 10004 *Tel:* 212-688-0085 *Fax:* 212-421-6134 *E-mail:* info@holidayhouse.com *Web Site:* www.holidayhouse.com, pg 94

Hollins University-Jackson Center for Creative Writing, 7916 Williamson Rd, Roanoke, VA 24020 *Tel:* 540-362-6317 *E-mail:* creative.writing@hollins.edu *Web Site:* www.hollins.edu; www.hollins.edu/jacksoncenter/index.shtml, pg 563

Hollym International Corp, 2647 Gateway Rd, No 105-223, Carlsbad, CA 92009 *Tel:* 760-814-9880 *Fax:* 908-353-0255 *E-mail:* contact@hollym.com *Web Site:* www.hollym.com, pg 94

Burnham Holmes, 182 Lakeview Hill Rd, Poultney, VT 05764-9179 *Tel:* 802-287-9707 *Fax:* 802-287-9707 (computer fax/modem) *E-mail:* burnham.holmes@castleton.edu, pg 440

Holmes Publishing Group LLC, PO Box 2370, Sequim, WA 98382 *Tel:* 360-681-2900 *E-mail:* holmespub@fastmail.fm *Web Site:* www.jdholmes.com, pg 94

William F Holmes Award, University of Georgia, Dept of History, Athens, GA 30602-1602 *Tel:* 706-542-8848 *Web Site:* thesha.org/holmes, pg 613

Henry Holt and Company, LLC, 120 Broadway, 23rd fl, New York, NY 10271 *Tel:* 646-307-5151 *Toll Free Tel:* 888-330-8477 (orders) *Fax:* 646-307-5285 *Web Site:* www.henryholt.com, pg 94

Holy Cow! Press, PO Box 3170, Mount Royal Sta, Duluth, MN 55803 *Tel:* 218-606-2792 *E-mail:* holycow@holycowpress.org *Web Site:* www.holycowpress.org, pg 95

Holy Cross Orthodox Press, 50 Goddard Ave, Brookline, MA 02445 *Tel:* 617-731-3500; 617-850-1303 *E-mail:* press@hchc.edu *Web Site:* www.hchc.edu, pg 95

Homa & Sekey Books, Mack-Cali Ctr II, N Tower, 3rd fl, 140 E Ridgewood Ave, Paramus, NJ 07652 *Tel:* 201-261-8810 *Fax:* 201-261-8890 *E-mail:* info@homabooks.com *Web Site:* www.homabooks.com, pg 95

Homestead Publishing, Box 193, Moose, WY 83012-0193 *Tel:* 307-733-6248 *Fax:* 307-733-6248 *E-mail:* info@homesteadpublishing.com; orders@homesteadpublishing.net *Web Site:* www.homesteadpublishing.net, pg 95

Honickman First Book Prize, 1906 Rittenhouse Sq, Philadelphia, PA 19103 *Tel:* 215-309-3722 *Web Site:* www.aprweb.org, pg 613

Honoring Fatherhood Award, PO Box 36128, North Chesterfield, VA 23235-3533 *E-mail:* contest@poetrysocietyofvirginia.org; info@poetryvirginia.org *Web Site:* www.poetrysocietyofvirginia.org, pg 613

Hoover Institution Press, Stanford University, 434 Galvez Mall, Stanford, CA 94305-6003 *Tel:* 650-723-3373 *Toll Free Tel:* 800-935-2882 (US only); 877-466-8374 (US only) *Fax:* 650-723-8626 *E-mail:* hooverpress@stanford.edu *Web Site:* www.hoover.org/publications/hooverpress, pg 95

Hope Publishing Co, 380 S Main Place, Carol Stream, IL 60188 *Tel:* 630-665-3200 *Toll Free Tel:* 800-323-1049 *E-mail:* hope@hopepublishing.com *Web Site:* www.hopepublishing.com, pg 95

The Hopwood Award Theodore Roethke Prize, 1176 Angell Hall, 435 S State St, Ann Arbor, MI 48109-1003 *Tel:* 734-764-6296 *Fax:* 734-764-3128 *E-mail:* abeauch@umich.edu *Web Site:* lsa.umich.edu/hopwood, pg 613

Hopwood Underclassmen Contest, 1176 Angell Hall, 435 S State St, Ann Arbor, MI 48109-1003 *Tel:* 734-764-6296 *Fax:* 734-764-3128 *E-mail:* abeauch@umich.edu *Web Site:* lsa.umich.edu/hopwood, pg 613

Horizon Publishers & Distributors Inc, 191 N 650 E, Bountiful, UT 84010-3628 *Tel:* 801-292-7102 *E-mail:* ldshorizonpublishers1@gmail.com *Web Site:* www.ldshorizonpublishers.com, pg 95

Hornfischer Literary Management LP, PO Box 50544, Austin, TX 78763 *Tel:* 512-472-0011 *E-mail:* queries@hornfischerlit.com *Web Site:* www.hornfischerlit.com, pg 463

Horror Writers Association (HWA), PO Box 56687, Sherman Oaks, CA 91413 *Tel:* 818-220-3965 *E-mail:* admin@horror.org; membership@horror.org *Web Site:* horror.org, pg 507

Hospital & Healthcare Compensation Service, 3 Post Rd, Suite 3, Oakland, NJ 07436 *Tel:* 201-405-0075 *Fax:* 201-405-2110 *E-mail:* allinfo@hhcsinc.com *Web Site:* www.hhcsinc.com, pg 95

Host Publications, 3408 West Ave, Austin, TX 78705 *E-mail:* editors@hostpublications.com *Web Site:* www.hostpublications.com, pg 95

Houghton Mifflin Harcourt, 125 High St, Boston, MA 02110 *Tel:* 617-351-5000 *Toll Free Tel:* 855-969-4642; 800-225-5425 (K-12 educ materials); 800-323-9540 (assessment materials); 877-219-1537 (SkillsTutor); 888-242-6747 (Innovation in Educ Group); 800-225-3362 (Trade & Ref Div) *Toll Free Tel:* 800-269-5232 *E-mail:* myhmco@hmco.com *Web Site:* www.hmhco.com, pg 95

Houghton Mifflin Harcourt Assessments, One Pierce Place, Itasca, IL 60143 *Tel:* 630-467-7000 *Toll Free Tel:* 800-323-9540 *Fax:* 630-467-7192 (cust serv) *E-mail:* assessmentsorders@hmhco.com *Web Site:* www.hmhco.com/classroom-solutions/assessment, pg 96

Houghton Mifflin Harcourt K-12 Publishers, 125 High St, Boston, MA 02110 *Tel:* 617-351-5020 *E-mail:* corporate.communications@hmhco.com *Web Site:* www.hmhco.com/classroom (solutions); www.hmhco.com, pg 96

Houghton Mifflin Harcourt Trade & Reference Division, 125 High St, Boston, MA 02110 *Tel:* 617-351-5000 *Web Site:* www.hmhco.com, pg 96

Housatonic Book Awards, Dept of Writing, Linguistics & Creative Process, 181 White St, Higgins Hall, Rm 219, Danbury, CT 06810 *Web Site:* housatonicbookawards.wordpress.com, pg 613

House of Anansi Press Inc, 128 Sterling Rd, Lower Level, Toronto, ON M6R 2B7, Canada *Tel:* 416-363-4343 *Fax:* 416-363-1017 *E-mail:* customerservice@houseofanansi.com *Web Site:* houseofanansi.com, pg 409

House to House Publications, 11 Toll Gate Rd, Lititz, PA 17543 *Tel:* 717-627-1996 *Toll Free Tel:* 800-848-5892 *Fax:* 717-627-4004 *E-mail:* h2hp@dcfi.org *Web Site:* www.h2hp.com, pg 97

Housing Assistance Council, 1025 Vermont Ave NW, Suite 606, Washington, DC 20005 *Tel:* 202-842-8600 *Fax:* 202-347-3441 *E-mail:* hac@ruralhome.org *Web Site:* www.ruralhome.org, pg 97

Tom Howard/John H Reid Fiction & Essay Contest, 351 Pleasant St, Suite B, PMB 222, Northampton, MA 01060-3998 *Tel:* 413-320-1847 *Toll Free Tel:* 866-WINWRIT (946-9748) *Fax:* 413-280-0539 *Web Site:* www.winningwriters.com/our-contests/tom-howard-john-h-reid-fiction-essay-contest, pg 613

Tom Howard/Margaret Reid Poetry Contest, 351 Pleasant St, Suite B, PMB 222, Northampton, MA 01060-3998 *Tel:* 413-320-1847 *Toll Free Tel:* 866-WINWRIT (946-9748) *Fax:* 413-280-0539 *Web Site:* www.winningwriters.com/our-contests/tom-howard-margaret-reid-poetry-contest, pg 614

C D Howe Institute, 67 Yonge St, Suite 300, Toronto, ON M5E 1J8, Canada *Tel:* 416-865-1904 *Fax:* 416-865-1866 *E-mail:* cdhowe@cdhowe.org *Web Site:* www.cdhowe.org, pg 410

Julia Ward Howe Book Awards, c/o Prof Julie Dobrow, 103 Conant Rd, Lincoln, MA 01773 *Tel:* 781-259-1220 *E-mail:* bostonauthorsclub2@gmail.com *Web Site:* bostonauthorsclub.org, pg 614

The William Dean Howells Medal, 633 W 155 St, New York, NY 10032 *Tel:* 212-368-5900 *E-mail:* academy@artsandletters.org *Web Site:* artsandletters.org/awards, pg 614

HRD Press, PO Box 2600, Amherst, MA 01004 *Tel:* 413-253-3488 *Toll Free Tel:* 800-822-2801 *E-mail:* info@hrdpress.com; customerservice@hrdpress.com *Web Site:* www.hrdpress.com, pg 97

Hub City Writing in Place Conference, 186 W Main St, Spartanburg, SC 29306 *Tel:* 864-577-9349 *E-mail:* info@hubcity.org *Web Site:* www.hubcity.org/annual-writing-in-place-conference, pg 554

L Ron Hubbard's Writers of the Future Contest, 7051 Hollywood Blvd, Hollywood, CA 90028 *Tel:* 323-466-3310 *Fax:* 323-466-6474 *E-mail:* contests@authorservicesinc.com *Web Site:* www.writersofthefuture.com, pg 614

Charlotte Huck Award, 340 N Neil St, Suite 104, Champaign, IL 61820 *Tel:* 217-328-3870 *Toll Free Tel:* 877-369-6283 (cust serv) *Fax:* 217-328-9645 *E-mail:* bookawards@ncte.org *Web Site:* ncte.org/awards/ncte-childrens-book-awards, pg 614

Hudson Institute, 1201 Pennsylvania Ave NW, 4th fl, Washington, DC 20004 *Tel:* 202-974-2400 *Fax:* 202-974-2410 *E-mail:* info@hudson.org *Web Site:* www.hudson.org, pg 97

The Hugo Awards, c/o Kevin Lee, Hugo Awards Mktg Comm, PO Box 242, Fernley, NV 89408-0242 *E-mail:* info@thehugoawards.org *Web Site:* www.wsfs.org/awards; www.thehugoawards.org, pg 614

Lynda Hull Memorial Poetry Prize, College of Charleston, Dept of English, 66 George St, Charleston, SC 29424 *Tel:* 843-953-4470 *E-mail:* crazyhorse@cofc.edu *Web Site:* crazyhorse.cofc.edu/prizes, pg 614

Human Kinetics Inc, 1607 N Market St, Champaign, IL 61820 *Tel:* 217-351-5076 *Toll Free Tel:* 800-747-4457 *Fax:* 217-351-1549 (orders/cust serv) *E-mail:* info@hkusa.com *Web Site:* us.humankinetics.com, pg 97

Human Rights Watch, 350 Fifth Ave, 34th fl, New York, NY 10118-3299 *Tel:* 212-290-4700 *Fax:* 212-736-1300 *E-mail:* hrwpress@hrw.org *Web Site:* www.hrw.org, pg 97

Humanix Books LLC, 805 Third Ave, New York, NY 10022 *Toll Free Tel:* 855-371-7810 *E-mail:* info@humanixbooks.com *Web Site:* www.humanixbooks.com, pg 97

Huntington Press Publishing, 3665 Procyon St, Las Vegas, NV 89103-1907 *Tel:* 702-252-0655 *Toll Free Tel:* 800-244-2224 *Fax:* 702-252-0675 *E-mail:* editor@huntingtonpress.com *Web Site:* www.huntingtonpress.com, pg 97

Hurston/Wright Award for College Writers, 10 "G" St NE, Suite 600, Washington, DC 20002 *E-mail:* info@hurstonwright.org *Web Site:* www.hurstonwright.org/awards/hurston-wright-award-for-college-writers, pg 614

Hurston/Wright Legacy Awards, 10 "G" St NE, Suite 600, Washington, DC 20002 *E-mail:* info@hurstonwright.org *Web Site:* www.hurstonwright.org/awards/legacy-awards, pg 614

COMPANY INDEX

Hurston/Wright Writers Week Workshops, 10 "G" St NE, Suite 600, Washington, DC 20002 *E-mail:* info@hurstonwright.org *Web Site:* www.hurstonwright.org/workshops/writers-week-workshops, pg 554

The Zora Neale Hurston/Richard Wright Foundation, 10 "G" St NE, Suite 600, Washington, DC 20002 *E-mail:* info@hurstonwright.org *Web Site:* www.hurstonwright.org, pg 525

Hutton Publishing, 12 Golden Hill St, Norwalk, CT 06854 *Tel:* 203-558-4478 *E-mail:* huttonbooks@hotmail.com, pg 97

IACP Cookbook Awards, c/o Marshall Jones, 4625 Alexander Dr, Alpharetta, GA 30022 *Toll Free Fax:* 866-358-2524 *E-mail:* awards@iacp.com; info@iacp.com *Web Site:* www.iacp.com/awards/cookbook-awards, pg 614

IBBY Canada, c/o The Canadian Children's Book Ctr, 425 Adelaide St W, Suite 200, Toronto, ON M5V 3C1, Canada *Fax:* 416-975-8970 *E-mail:* info@ibby-canada.org *Web Site:* www.ibby-canada.org, pg 507

Ibex Publishers, PO Box 30087, Bethesda, MD 20824 *Tel:* 301-718-8188 *Toll Free Tel:* 888-718-8188 *Fax:* 301-907-8707 *E-mail:* info@ibexpub.com *Web Site:* ibexpub.com, pg 98

IBFD North America Inc (International Bureau of Fiscal Documentation), 8300 Boone Blvd, Suite 380, Vienna, VA 22182 *Tel:* 703-442-7757 *E-mail:* info@ibfd.org *Web Site:* www.ibfd.org, pg 98

IBPA Book Awards, 1020 Manhattan Beach Blvd, Suite 204, Manhattan Beach, CA 90266 *Tel:* 310-546-1818 *E-mail:* info@ibpa-online.org *Web Site:* www.ibpa-online.org, pg 615

The Ibsen Society of America (ISA), c/o Indiana University, Global & Intl Studies Bldg 3111, 355 N Jordan Ave, Bloomington, IN 47405-1105 *Web Site:* www.ibsensociety.org, pg 507

The Idaho Prize for Poetry, 1025 S Garry Rd, Liberty Lake, WA 99019 *Tel:* 208-597-3008 *Fax:* 208-255-1560 *E-mail:* losthorsepress@mindspring.com *Web Site:* www.losthorsepress.org, pg 615

Idyll Arbor Inc, 2432 39 St, Bedford, IN 47421 *Tel:* 812-675-6623 *E-mail:* sales@idyllarbor.com *Web Site:* www.idyllarbor.com, pg 98

Idyllwild Arts Summer Program, 52500 Temecula Rd, No 38, Idyllwild, CA 92549 *Tel:* 951-659-2171 *E-mail:* summer@idyllwildarts.org; adultprograms@idyllwildarts.org *Web Site:* idyllwildarts.org/summer, pg 555

IEEE Computer Society, 2001 "L" St NW, Suite 700, Washington, DC 20036-4928 *Tel:* 202-371-0101 *Toll Free Tel:* 800-678-4333 (memb info) *Fax:* 202-728-9614 *E-mail:* help@computer.org *Web Site:* www.computer.org, pg 98

IEEE Press, 445 Hoes Lane, Piscataway, NJ 08854 *Tel:* 732-981-0060 *Fax:* 732-867-9946 *E-mail:* pressbooks@ieee.org (proposals & info) *Web Site:* www.ieee.org/press, pg 98

IET USA Inc, 379 Thornall St, Edison, NJ 08837 *Tel:* 732-321-5575 *Fax:* 732-321-5702 *E-mail:* ietusa@theiet.org *Web Site:* www.theiet.org, pg 98

Ignatius Press, 1348 Tenth Ave, San Francisco, CA 94122-2304 *Toll Free Tel:* 800-651-1531 (orders); 888-615-3186 (cust serv) *Fax:* 415-387-0896 *E-mail:* info@ignatius.com *Web Site:* www.ignatius.com, pg 98

IHS Press, 222 W 21 St, Suite F-122, Norfolk, VA 23517 *Toll Free Tel:* 877-447-7737 *Toll Free Fax:* 877-447-7737 *E-mail:* query@ihspress.com; tradesales@ihspress.com (wholesale sales); order@ihspress.com; pr@ihspress.com *Web Site:* www.ihspress.com, pg 98

ILA Children's & Young Adults' Book Awards, PO Box 8139, Newark, DE 19714-8139 *Tel:* 302-731-1600 *Toll Free Tel:* 800-336-7323 (US & CN) *E-mail:* ilaawards@reading.org *Web Site:* www.literacyworldwide.org, pg 615

iLEARNING+ - Orientation to the Graphic Arts, 10015 Main St, Fairfax, VA 22031 *Tel:* 703-385-1335 *Toll Free Tel:* 888-385-3588 *Fax:* 703-273-0456 *E-mail:* info@printing.org; assist@printing.org *Web Site:* www.printing.org; www.ilearningplus.org, pg 555

Illinois State Museum Society, 502 S Spring St, Springfield, IL 62706-5000 *Tel:* 217-782-7386 *Fax:* 217-782-1254 *E-mail:* subscriptions@museum.state.il.us *Web Site:* www.illinoisstatemuseum.org, pg 99

Illuminating Engineering Society of North America (IES), 120 Wall St, 17th fl, New York, NY 10005-4001 *Tel:* 212-248-5000 *Fax:* 212-248-5017; 212-248-5018 *E-mail:* ies@ies.org *Web Site:* www.ies.org, pg 99

Illumination Book Awards, 1129 Woodmere Ave, Suite B, Traverse City, MI 49686 *Tel:* 231-933-0445 *Toll Free Tel:* 800-706-4636 *Fax:* 231-933-0448 *Web Site:* illuminationawards.com, pg 615

Illustration Online LLC, 13 Wingstone Lane, Devon, PA 19333 *Tel:* 215-232-6666 *Web Site:* www.illustrationonline.com, pg 485

ImaJinn Books, PO Box 300921, Memphis, TN 38130 *E-mail:* bellebooks@bellebooks.com *Web Site:* www.imajinnbooks.com, pg 99

Immedium, 535 Rockdale Dr, San Francisco, CA 94127 *Tel:* 415-452-8546 *Fax:* 360-937-6272 *E-mail:* orders@immedium.com; sales@immedium.com *Web Site:* www.immedium.com, pg 99

John Phillip Immroth Memorial Award, 225 Michigan Ave, Suite 1300, Chicago, IL 60601 *Tel:* 312-280-4226 *Toll Free Tel:* 800-545-2433 *E-mail:* ifrt@ala.org *Web Site:* www.ala.org/rt/ifrt/immroth, pg 615

Impact Publications/Development Concepts Inc, 7820 Sudley Rd, Suite 100, Manassas, VA 20109 *Tel:* 703-361-7300 *Toll Free Tel:* 800-361-1055 (cust serv) *Fax:* 703-335-9486 *E-mail:* query2@impactpublications.com *Web Site:* www.impactpublications.com, pg 99

In-Plant Printing & Mailing Association (IPMA), 103 N Jefferson St, Kearney, MO 64060 *Tel:* 816-919-1691 *E-mail:* ipmainfo@ipma.org *Web Site:* www.ipma.org, pg 507

In the Garden Publishing, 6460 E Grant Rd, No 31944, Tucson, AZ 85715 *Tel:* 937-317-0859 *E-mail:* admin@inthegardenpublishing.com *Web Site:* www.inthegardenpublishing.com, pg 99

Incentive Publications by World Book, 180 N LaSalle St, Suite 900, Chicago, IL 60101 *Toll Free Tel:* 800-967-5325; 800-975-3250; 888-482-9764 (trade dept) *Toll Free Fax:* 888-922-3766 *E-mail:* tradeorders@worldbook.com *Web Site:* www.incentivepublications.com, pg 99

Inclusion Press International, 47 Indian Trail, Toronto, ON M6R 1Z8, Canada *Tel:* 416-658-5363 *Fax:* 416-658-5067 *E-mail:* inclusionpress@inclusion.com *Web Site:* inclusion.com, pg 410

Independent Artist Awards, 175 W Ostend St, Suite E, Baltimore, MD 21230 *Tel:* 410-767-6555 *E-mail:* msac.commerce@maryland.gov *Web Site:* www.msac.org/programs/independent-artist-award, pg 615

The Independent Book Publishers Association (IBPA), 1020 Manhattan Beach Blvd, Suite 204, Manhattan Beach, CA 90266 *Tel:* 310-546-1818 *E-mail:* info@ibpa-online.org *Web Site:* www.ibpa-online.org, pg 507

Independent Institute, 100 Swan Way, Oakland, CA 94621-1428 *Tel:* 510-632-1366 *Fax:* 510-568-6040 *Web Site:* www.independent.org, pg 99

Independent Press Award®, 63 Clinton Rd, Glen Ridge, NJ 07028 *Web Site:* www.independentpressaward.com, pg 615

The Independent Publisher Book Awards, 1129 Woodmere Ave, Suite B, Traverse City, MI 49686 *Tel:* 231-933-0445 *Toll Free Tel:* 800-706-4636 *Fax:* 231-933-0448 *E-mail:* ippy@jgibookawards.com *Web Site:* ippyawards.com, pg 615

INDIVIDUAL ARTIST'S FELLOWSHIPS

Independent Publishers Caucus (IPC), c/o Seven Stories Press, 140 Watts St, New York, NY 10013 *E-mail:* info@indiepubs.org *Web Site:* www.indiepubs.org, pg 507

Independent Publishers of New England (IPNE), c/o Eddie Vincent, Encircle Publications, Farmington, ME 04955 *Tel:* 339-368-8229 *E-mail:* talktous@ipne.org *Web Site:* www.ipne.org, pg 508

Independent Publishers of New England Book Awards, c/o Eddie Vincent, Encircle Publications, Farmington, ME 04955 *Tel:* 339-368-8229 *E-mail:* bookawards@ipne.org *Web Site:* www.ipne.org/awards, pg 615

Independent Writers of Chicago (IWOC), 332 S Michigan Ave, Suite 121-W686, Chicago, IL 60604-4434 *E-mail:* info@iwoc.org; membership@iwoc.org *Web Site:* www.iwoc.org, pg 508

Indexing by the Book, 5912 E Eastland St, Tucson, AZ 85711-4636 *Tel:* 520-405-8083 *E-mail:* indextran@cox.net *Web Site:* www.indexingbythebook.com, pg 440

Indiana Historical Society Press, 450 W Ohio St, Indianapolis, IN 46202-3269 *Tel:* 317-232-1882; 317-234-0026 (orders); 317-234-2716 (edit) *Toll Free Tel:* 800-447-1830 (orders) *Fax:* 317-234-0562 (orders); 317-233-0857 (edit) *E-mail:* ihspress@indianahistory.org; orders@indianahistory.org (orders) *Web Site:* www.indianahistory.org; shop.indianahistory.org (orders), pg 99

Indiana Review Creative Nonfiction Prize, Indiana University English Dept, Ballantine Hall 554, 1020 E Kirkwood Ave, Bloomington, IN 47405 *Tel:* 812-855-3439 *E-mail:* inreview@indiana.edu *Web Site:* indianareview.org, pg 615

Indiana Review Fiction Prize, Indiana University English Dept, Ballantine Hall 554, 1020 E Kirkwood Ave, Bloomington, IN 47405 *Tel:* 812-855-3439 *E-mail:* inreview@indiana.edu *Web Site:* indianareview.org, pg 616

Indiana Review Poetry Prize, Indiana University English Dept, Ballantine Hall 554, 1020 E Kirkwood Ave, Bloomington, IN 47405 *Tel:* 812-855-3439 *E-mail:* inreview@indiana.edu *Web Site:* indianareview.org, pg 616

Indiana University African Studies Program, Indiana University, 355 N Eagleson Ave, Rm GA 3072, Bloomington, IN 47405-1105 *Tel:* 812-855-8284 *Fax:* 812-855-6734 *E-mail:* afrist@indiana.edu *Web Site:* www.indiana.edu/~afrist; www.go.iu.edu/afrist, pg 100

Indiana University Press, Off of Scholarly Publg, Herman B Wells Library 350, 1320 E Tenth St, Bloomington, IN 47405-3907 *Tel:* 812-855-8817 *Fax:* 812-855-7931; 812-855-8507 *E-mail:* iupress@indiana.edu *Web Site:* iupress.org, pg 100

Indiana University Writers' Conference, Ballantine Hall 440, 1020 E Kirkwood Ave, Bloomington, IN 47405-7103 *E-mail:* writecon@indiana.edu *Web Site:* www.iuwc.indiana.edu, pg 555

IndieReader Discovery Awards, PO Box 43121, Montclair, NJ 07043 *E-mail:* customerservice@indiereader.com *Web Site:* indiereader.com/the-discovery-awards/, pg 616

Individual Artist Fellowships, 1004 Farnam, Plaza Level, Omaha, NE 68102 *Tel:* 402-595-2122 *E-mail:* nac.info@nebraska.gov *Web Site:* www.artscouncil.nebraska.gov, pg 616

Individual Artist Fellowships, 25 State House Sta, 193 State St, Augusta, ME 04333-0025 *Tel:* 207-287-2724 *Fax:* 207-287-2725 *Web Site:* mainearts.maine.gov, pg 616

Individual Artist Project Grants, 500 S Bronough St, Tallahassee, FL 32399-0250 *Tel:* 850-245-6470 *Fax:* 850-245-6497 *E-mail:* dcagrants@dos.myflorida.com *Web Site:* dos.myflorida.com/cultural, pg 616

Individual Artist's Fellowships, 1026 Sumter St, Suite 200, Columbia, SC 29201-3746 *Tel:* 803-734-8696 *Fax:* 803-734-8526 *E-mail:* info@arts.sc.gov *Web Site:* www.southcarolinaarts.com, pg 616

Individual Excellence Awards, 30 E Broad St, 33rd fl, Columbus, OH 43215 *Tel:* 614-466-2613 *Fax:* 614-466-4494 *Web Site:* www.oac.state.oh.us, pg 616

Industrial Press Inc, One Chestnut St, South Norwalk, CT 06854 *Tel:* 203-956-5593 *Toll Free Tel:* 888-528-7852 (ext 1, cust serv) *E-mail:* info@industrialpress.com *Web Site:* books.industrialpress.com; ebooks.industrialpress.com, pg 100

Information Age Publishing Inc, PO Box 79049, Charlotte, NC 28271-7047 *Tel:* 704-752-9125 *Fax:* 704-752-9113 *E-mail:* infoage@infoagepub.com *Web Site:* www.infoagepub.com, pg 100

Information Gatekeepers Inc (IGI), PO Box 606, Winchester, MA 01890 *Tel:* 617-782-5033 *Fax:* 617-507-8338 *E-mail:* info@igigroup.com *Web Site:* www.igigroup.com, pg 100

Information Today, Inc, 143 Old Marlton Pike, Medford, NJ 08055-8750 *Tel:* 609-654-6266 *Toll Free Tel:* 800-300-9868 (cust serv) *Fax:* 609-654-4309 *E-mail:* custserv@infotoday.com *Web Site:* informationtodayinc.com, pg 100

Infosources Publishing, 140 Norma Rd, Teaneck, NJ 07666 *Tel:* 201-836-7072 *Web Site:* www.infosourcespub.com, pg 100

InkWell Management, 521 Fifth Ave, Suite 2600, New York, NY 10175 *Tel:* 212-922-3500 *Fax:* 212-922-0535 *E-mail:* info@inkwellmanagement.com; submissions@inkwellmanagement.com; permissions@inkwellmanagement.com *Web Site:* inkwellmanagement.com, pg 463

Inner Traditions International Ltd, One Park St, Rochester, VT 05767 *Tel:* 802-767-3174 *Toll Free Tel:* 800-246-8648 *Fax:* 802-767-3726 *E-mail:* customerservice@InnerTraditions.com *Web Site:* www.InnerTraditions.com, pg 101

Innis-Gerin Medal, Walter House, 282 Somerset W, Ottawa, ON K2P 0J6, Canada *Tel:* 613-991-6990 (ext 106) *Fax:* 613-991-6996 *E-mail:* nominations@rsc-src.ca *Web Site:* www.rsc-src.ca, pg 616

The Innovation Press, 7511 Greenwood Ave N, No 4132, Seattle, WA 98103 *Tel:* 360-870-9988 *E-mail:* info@theinnovationpress.com *Web Site:* www.theinnovationpress.com, pg 101

InScribe Christian Writers' Fellowship (ICWF), PO Box 68025, Edmonton, AB T6C 4N6, Canada *Tel:* 780-646-3068 *E-mail:* inscribe.mail@gmail.com *Web Site:* inscribe.org, pg 508

Inside Literary Prize, 2666 State St, Suite 5A, Hamden, CT 06517 *E-mail:* freedomreads@freedomreads.org *Web Site:* freedomreads.org/showing-up/inside-literary-prize, pg 616

Insight Editions, 800 "A" St, San Rafael, CA 94901 *Tel:* 415-526-1370 *Toll Free Tel:* 800-809-3792 *Toll Free Fax:* 866-509-0515 *E-mail:* info@insighteditions.com; marketing@insighteditions.com *Web Site:* insighteditions.com, pg 101

Institut de cooperation pour l'education des adultes-ICEA (The Institute for Cooperation on Adult Education), 5000 D'Iberville, Suite 304, Montreal, QC H2H 2S6, Canada *Tel:* 514-948-2044 *E-mail:* icae@icea.qc.ca *Web Site:* www.icea.qc.ca, pg 508

Institute for Immigration Research New American Voices Award, 4400 University Dr, MS 3E4, Fairfax, VA 22030 *Tel:* 703-993-3986 *E-mail:* submissions@fallforthebook.org *Web Site:* fallforthebook.org/aboutnewamericanvoices, pg 616

Institute for Research on Public Policy (IRPP), 1470 Peel St, No 200, Montreal, QC H3A 1T1, Canada *Tel:* 514-985-2461 *Fax:* 514-985-2559 *E-mail:* irpp@irpp.org *Web Site:* irpp.org, pg 410

Institute of Continuing Legal Education, 1020 Greene St, Ann Arbor, MI 48109-1444 *Tel:* 734-764-0533 *Toll Free Tel:* 877-229-4350 *Fax:* 734-763-2412 *Toll Free Fax:* 877-229-4351 *E-mail:* icle@umich.edu *Web Site:* www.icle.org, pg 101

Institute of Environmental Sciences & Technology - IEST, 1827 Walden Office Sq, Suite 400, Schaumburg, IL 60173 *Tel:* 847-981-0100 *Fax:* 847-981-4130 *E-mail:* information@iest.org *Web Site:* www.iest.org, pg 101

Institute of Governmental Studies, 109 Moses Hall, No 2370, Berkeley, CA 94720-2370 *Tel:* 510-642-1428 *E-mail:* igspress@berkeley.edu *Web Site:* www.igs.berkeley.edu, pg 101

Institute of Intergovernmental Relations, Queen's University, Robert Sutherland Hall, Rm 412, Kingston, ON K7L 3N6, Canada *Tel:* 613-533-2080 *E-mail:* iigr@queensu.ca *Web Site:* www.queensu.ca/iigr, pg 410

Institute of Jesuit Sources (IJS), Boston College Institute for Advanced Jesuit Studies, 140 Commonwealth Ave, Chestnut Hill, MA 02467 *Tel:* 617-552-2568 *Fax:* 617-552-2575 *E-mail:* jesuitsources@bc.edu *Web Site:* jesuitsources.bc.edu, pg 102

Institute of Police Technology & Management (IPTM), 12000 Alumni Dr, Jacksonville, FL 32224-2678 *Tel:* 904-620-4786 *Fax:* 904-620-2453 *E-mail:* info@iptm.unf.edu *Web Site:* iptm.unf.edu, pg 102

Institute of Public Administration of Canada, 1075 Bay St, Suite 401, Toronto, ON M5S 2B1, Canada *Tel:* 416-924-8787 *Fax:* 416-924-4992 *E-mail:* ntl@ipac.ca *Web Site:* www.ipac.ca, pg 410

The Institutes™, 720 Providence Rd, Suite 100, Malvern, PA 19355-3433 *Tel:* 610-644-2100 *Toll Free Tel:* 800-644-2101 *Fax:* 610-640-9576 *E-mail:* customerservice@theinstitutes.org *Web Site:* www.theinstitutes.org, pg 102

Integra Software Services Inc, 2021 Midwest Rd, Suite 200, Oak Brook, IL 60523 *Web Site:* www.integranxt.com, pg 441

Intensive Novel Architects Writing Workshop, 1809 Indiana St, Lawrence, KS 66044 *Tel:* 785-766-7039 *Web Site:* adastra-sf.com/Workshop-stuff/Johnson-Webb-Workshops.htm, pg 555

Inter-American Development Bank, 1300 New York Ave NW, Washington, DC 20577 *Tel:* 202-623-1000 *Fax:* 202-623-3096 *E-mail:* pic@iadb.org *Web Site:* publications.iadb.org, pg 102

Inter American Press Association (IAPA), PO Box 226606, Doral, FL 33222 *Tel:* 305-987-3363 *Fax:* 305-860-4264 *E-mail:* info@sipiapa.org *Web Site:* www.sipiapa.org, pg 508

Inter-University Consortium for Political & Social Research (ICPSR), 330 Packard St, Ann Arbor, MI 48104 *Tel:* 734-647-5000; 734-647-2200 *Fax:* 734-647-8200 *E-mail:* icpsr-help@umich.edu *Web Site:* www.icpsr.umich.edu, pg 102

Intercultural Development Research Association (IDRA), 5815 Callaghan Rd, Suite 101, San Antonio, TX 78228 *Tel:* 210-444-1710 *Fax:* 210-444-1714 *E-mail:* contact@idra.org *Web Site:* www.idra.org, pg 102

InterLicense Ltd, 110 Country Club Dr, Suite A, Mill Valley, CA 94941 *Tel:* 415-381-9780 *Fax:* 415-381-6485 *E-mail:* foreignrights@interlicense.net *Web Site:* interlicense.net, pg 463

Interlink Publishing Group Inc, 46 Crosby St, Northampton, MA 01060 *Tel:* 413-582-7054 *Toll Free Tel:* 800-238-LINK (238-5465) *E-mail:* info@interlinkbooks.com; publicity@interlinkbooks.com; sales@interlinkbooks.com *Web Site:* www.interlinkbooks.com, pg 102

Intermediate Sequoyah Book Award, 119 Meramec Station Rd, Suite 207, Ballwin, MO 63021-6902 *Toll Free Tel:* 800-969-6562 (ext 5) *Fax:* 636-529-1396 *E-mail:* sequoyah@oklibs.org; ola@amigos.org *Web Site:* www.oklibs.org, pg 617

International Association of Business Communicators (IABC), 330 N Wabash Ave, Suite 2000, Chicago, IL 60611 *Tel:* 312-321-6868 *Toll Free Tel:* 800-218-8097 *Fax:* 312-673-6708 *E-mail:* member_relations@iabc.com *Web Site:* www.iabc.com, pg 508

International Association of Crime Writers Inc, North American Branch, PO Box 863, Norman, OK 73071 *E-mail:* crimewritersna@gmail.com *Web Site:* www.crimewritersna.org, pg 508

International Book Centre Inc, 2391 Auburn Rd, Shelby Township, MI 48317 *Tel:* 586-254-7230 *Fax:* 586-254-7230 *E-mail:* ibc@ibcbooks.com *Web Site:* www.ibcbooks.com, pg 102

International City/County Management Association (ICMA), 777 N Capitol St NE, Suite 500, Washington, DC 20002-4201 *Tel:* 202-962-3680 *Toll Free Tel:* 800-745-8780 *Fax:* 202-962-3500 *E-mail:* customerservices@icma.org *Web Site:* icma.org/about-icma-publications, pg 102

International Code Council Inc, 3060 Saturn St, Suite 100, Brea, CA 92821 *Tel:* 562-699-0541 *Toll Free Tel:* 888-422-7233 *Fax:* 562-908-5524 *Toll Free Fax:* 866-891-1695 *E-mail:* order@icc-es.org *Web Site:* www.iccsafe.org, pg 102

International Council of Shopping Centers (ICSC), 1251 Avenue of the Americas, 41st fl, New York, NY 10020-1099 *Web Site:* www.icsc.com, pg 102

International Entertainment Bureau, 3618 N Washington Blvd, Indianapolis, IN 46205 *Tel:* 317-926-7566 *E-mail:* ieb@prodigy.net, pg 487

International Food Policy Research Institute, 1201 Eye St NW, Washington, DC 20005-3915 *Tel:* 202-862-5600 *Fax:* 202-862-5606 *E-mail:* ifpri@cgiar.org *Web Site:* www.ifpri.org, pg 103

International Foundation of Employee Benefit Plans, 18700 W Bluemound Rd, Brookfield, WI 53045 *Tel:* 262-786-6700 *Toll Free Tel:* 888-334-3327 *Fax:* 262-786-8780 *E-mail:* editor@ifebp.org *Web Site:* www.ifebp.org, pg 103

The International Institute of Islamic Thought, 500 Grove St, Suite 200, Herndon, VA 20170 *Tel:* 703-471-1133 *Fax:* 703-471-3922 *E-mail:* iiit@iiit.org *Web Site:* www.iiit.org, pg 103

International Latino Book Awards, 624 Hillcrest Lane, Fallbrook, CA 92028 *Tel:* 760-689-2317 *E-mail:* awards@empoweringlatinofutures.org *Web Site:* www.latinobookawards.org; www.empoweringlatinofutures.org, pg 617

International Linguistics Corp, 12220 Blue Ridge Blvd, Suite G, Kansas City, MO 64030 *Tel:* 816-765-8855 *Toll Free Tel:* 800-237-1830 (orders) *E-mail:* learnables@sbcglobal.net *Web Site:* www.learnables.com, pg 103

International Literacy Association (ILA), PO Box 8139, Newark, DE 19714-8139 *Tel:* 302-731-1600 *Toll Free Tel:* 800-336-7323 (US & CN) *E-mail:* customerservice@reading.org *Web Site:* www.literacyworldwide.org; www.reading.org, pg 103, 508

International Monetary Fund (IMF), Editorial & Publications Division, 700 19 St NW, HQ1-5-355, Washington, DC 20431 *Tel:* 202-623-7430 *E-mail:* publications@imf.org *Web Site:* bookstore.imf.org; elibrary.imf.org (online collection); www.imf.org/publications, pg 103

International Poetry Competition, 686 Cherry St NW, Suite 333, Atlanta, GA 30332-0161 *E-mail:* atlantareview@gatech.edu *Web Site:* www.atlantareview.com, pg 617

International Press of Boston Inc, 387 Somerville Ave, Somerville, MA 02143 *Tel:* 617-623-3016 (orders & cust serv) *Fax:* 617-623-3101 *E-mail:* ipb-orders@intlpress.com *Web Site:* www.intlpress.com, pg 103

International Publishers Co Inc, 235 W 23 St, New York, NY 10011 *Tel:* 212-366-9816 *Fax:* 212-366-9820 *E-mail:* service@intpubnyc.com *Web Site:* www.intpubnyc.com, pg 103

International Risk Management Institute Inc, 12222 Merit Dr, Suite 1600, Dallas, TX 75251-2266 *Tel:* 972-960-7693 *Fax:* 972-371-5120 *E-mail:* info27@irmi.com *Web Site:* www.irmi.com, pg 103

International Self-Counsel Press Ltd, 1481 Charlotte Rd, North Vancouver, BC V7J 1H1, Canada *Tel:* 604-986-3366 *Toll Free Tel:* 800-663-3007 *E-mail:* orders@self-counsel.com; sales@self-counsel.com *Web Site:* www.self-counsel.com, pg 410

COMPANY INDEX

International Society for Technology in Education, 2111 Wilson Blvd, Suite 300, Arlington, VA 22201 *Tel:* 503-342-2848 (intl) *Toll Free Tel:* 800-336-5191 (US & CN) *Fax:* 541-302-3778 *E-mail:* iste@iste.org *Web Site:* www.iste.org, pg 103

International Society of Automation (ISA), 3252 S Miami Blvd, Suite 102, Durham, NC 27703 *Tel:* 919-549-8411 *Fax:* 919-549-8288 *E-mail:* info@isa.org *Web Site:* www.isa.org/standards-and-publications/isa-publications, pg 103

International Society of Latino Authors (ISLA), c/o Empowering Latino Futures, 624 Hillcrest Lane, Fallbrook, CA 92084 *Tel:* 760-689-2317 *Fax:* 760-434-7476 *Web Site:* isla.news, pg 508

International Society of Weekly Newspaper Editors (ISWNE), Missouri Southern State University, 3950 E Newman Rd, Joplin, MO 64801-1595 *Web Site:* www.iswne.org, pg 508

International Standard Book Numbering (ISBN) US Agency, A Cambridge Information Group Co, PO Box 8134, Bridgewater, NJ 08807 *Toll Free Tel:* 877-310-7333 *Fax:* 908-219-0188 *E-mail:* isbn-san@bowker.com *Web Site:* www.isbn.org, pg 508

International Titles, 931 E 56 St, Austin, TX 78751-1724 *Tel:* 512-909-2447 *Web Site:* www.internationaltitles.com, pg 464

International Transactions Inc, 28 Alope Way, Gila, NM 88038 *Tel:* 845-373-9696 *Fax:* 520-300-7248 *E-mail:* info@internationaltransactions.us *Web Site:* www.intltrans.com, pg 464

International Wealth Success (IWS), 332 Center St, Wilkes-Barre, PA 18702 *Tel:* 570-825-3598 *E-mail:* admin@iwsmoney.com *Web Site:* iwealthsuccess.com, pg 104

The International Women's Writing Guild (IWWG), 888 Eighth Ave, No 537, New York, NY 10019 *Tel:* 917-720-6959 *E-mail:* iwwgquestions@iwwg.org *Web Site:* www.iwwg.org, pg 508

InterVarsity Press, 430 Plaza Dr, Westmont, IL 60559-1234 *Tel:* 630-734-4000 *Toll Free Tel:* 800-843-9487 *Fax:* 630-734-4200 *E-mail:* email@ivpress.com *Web Site:* www.ivpress.com, pg 104

Interweave Press LLC, 4868 Innovation Dr, Fort Collins, CO 80525 *Web Site:* www.interweave.com, pg 104

Intimate & Inspiring Workshops for Children's Authors & Illustrators, 814 Court St, Honesdale, PA 18431 *Tel:* 570-253-1192 *E-mail:* support@highlightsfoundation.zendesk.com *Web Site:* www.highlightsfoundation.org, pg 555

Investigative Reporters & Editors, Missouri School of Journalism, Lee Hills Hall, 221 S Eighth St, Columbia, MO 65201 *Tel:* 573-882-2042 *E-mail:* info@ire.org *Web Site:* www.ire.org, pg 509

IODE Jean Throop Book Award, 9-45 Frid St, Hamilton, ON L8P 4M3, Canada *Tel:* 905-522-9537 *Fax:* 905-522-3637 *E-mail:* iodeontario@gmail.com *Web Site:* www.iodeontario.ca, pg 617

IODE Violet Downey Book Award, 40 Orchard View Blvd, Suite 219, Toronto, ON M4R 1B9, Canada *Tel:* 416-487-4416 *Toll Free Tel:* 866-827-7428 *Fax:* 416-487-4417 *E-mail:* iodecanada@bellnet.ca *Web Site:* www.iode.ca, pg 617

Iowa Poetry Prize, 119 W Park Rd, 100 Kuhl House, Iowa City, IA 52242-1000 *Tel:* 319-335-2000 *Fax:* 319-335-2055 *E-mail:* uipress@uiowa.edu *Web Site:* www.uipress.uiowa.edu, pg 617

The Iowa Review Awards, 308 EPB, Iowa City, IA 52242-1408 *E-mail:* iowa-review@uiowa.edu *Web Site:* www.iowareview.org, pg 617

The Iowa Short Fiction Award, 102 Dey House, 507 N Clinton St, Iowa City, IA 52242-1000 *Tel:* 319-335-0416 *Fax:* 319-335-0420 *Web Site:* writersworkshop.uiowa.edu/about/iowa-short-fiction-awards, pg 617

Iowa Summer Writing Festival, 24E Phillips Hall, University of Iowa, Iowa City, IA 52242 *Tel:* 319-335-4160 *E-mail:* iswfestival@uiowa.edu *Web Site:* iowasummerwritingfestival.uiowa.edu, pg 555

Iowa Writers' Workshop, Graduate Program in Creative Writing, 102 Dey House, Iowa City, IA 52242-1000 *Tel:* 319-335-0416 *Web Site:* writersworkshop.uiowa.edu, pg 555

Iris Press, 969 Oak Ridge Tpke, No 328, Oak Ridge, TN 37830 *Web Site:* www.irisbooks.com, pg 104

Iron Gate Publishing, PO Box 999, Niwot, CO 80544 *Tel:* 303-530-2551 *E-mail:* editor@irongate.com *Web Site:* www.irongate.com, pg 104

Iron Stream Media, 100 Missionary Ridge, Birmingham, AL 35242 *E-mail:* info@ironstreammedia.com *Web Site:* ironstreammedia.com, pg 104

IRP editeur, CP 68, succursale St-Dominique, Montreal, QC H2S 3K6, Canada *Tel:* 514-382-3000 *E-mail:* info@irpcanada.com *Web Site:* www.irpcanada.com, pg 410

Irwin Law Inc, 14 Duncan St, Suite 206, Toronto, ON M5H 3G8, Canada *Tel:* 416-862-7690 *Toll Free Tel:* 888-314-9014 *Fax:* 416-862-9236 *E-mail:* info@irwinlaw.com; contact@irwinlaw.com *Web Site:* www.irwinlaw.com, pg 410

ISBN Canada, Library & Archives Canada, 550, blvd de la Cit, Gatineau, QC J8T 0A7, Canada *Tel:* 819-994-6872 *Toll Free Tel:* 866-578-7777 (CN & US) *Fax:* 819-934-7535 *E-mail:* isbn@bac-lac.gc.ca *Web Site:* www.bac-lac.gc.ca/eng/services/isbn-canada/pages/isbn-canada.aspx, pg 509

Island Press, 2000 "M" St NW, Suite 480-B, Washington, DC 20036 *Tel:* 202-232-7933 *Toll Free Tel:* 800-621-2736 *Fax:* 202-234-1328 *E-mail:* info@islandpress.org *Web Site:* www.islandpress.org, pg 104

Islandport Press, 247 Portland St, Bldg C, Yarmouth, ME 04096 *Tel:* 207-846-3344 *E-mail:* info@islandportpress.com; orders@islandportpress.com *Web Site:* www.islandportpress.com, pg 105

Italian Prose in Translation Award (IPTA), University of Arizona, Esquire Bldg, No 205, 1230 N Park Ave, Tucson, AZ 85721 *Tel:* 520-621-1757 *E-mail:* info@literarytranslators.org *Web Site:* literarytranslators.org/awards/ipta, pg 617

Italica Press, 99 Wall St, Suite 650, New York, NY 10005 *Tel:* 917-371-0563 *E-mail:* inquiries@italicapress.com *Web Site:* www.italicapress.com, pg 105

Italics Publishing, 100 Northcliffe Dr, No 223, Gulf Breeze, FL 32561 *E-mail:* submissions@italicspublishing.com (submissions) *Web Site:* italicspublishing.com, pg 105

ITMB Publishing Ltd, 12300 Bridgeport Rd, Richmond, BC V6V 1J5, Canada *Tel:* 604-273-1400 *Fax:* 604-273-1488 *E-mail:* itmb@itmb.com *Web Site:* www.itmb.com, pg 410

iUniverse, 1663 Liberty Dr, Bloomington, IN 47403 *Toll Free Tel:* 800-AUTHORS (288-4677); 844-349-9409 *E-mail:* media@iuniverse.com *Web Site:* www.iuniverse.com, pg 105

Ivey Publishing, Ivey Business School Foundation, Western University, 1255 Western Rd, London, ON N6G 0N1, Canada *Tel:* 519-661-3206; 519-661-3208 *Toll Free Tel:* 800-649-6355 *Fax:* 519-661-3485; 519-661-3882 *E-mail:* cases@ivey.ca *Web Site:* www.iveypublishing.ca, pg 411

IWWG Annual Summer Conference, 888 Eighth Ave, No 537, New York, NY 10019 *Tel:* 917-720-6959 *E-mail:* iwwgquestions@iwwg.org *Web Site:* www.iwwg.org, pg 555

IWWG Annual Writing Conference, 888 Eighth Ave, No 537, New York, NY 10019 *Tel:* 617-792-7272 *E-mail:* iwwgquestions@iwwg.org *Web Site:* www.iwwg.org, pg 555

JABberwocky Literary Agency Inc, 49 W 45 St, 5th fl, New York, NY 10036 *Tel:* 917-388-3010 *Fax:* 917-388-2998 *Web Site:* www.awfulagent.com, pg 464

Jackie White Memorial National Children's Playwriting Contest, 1800 Nelwood Dr, Columbia, MO 65202 *Web Site:* www.cectheatre.org, pg 617

Melanie Jackson Agency LLC, 41 W 72 St, Suite 3F, New York, NY 10023 *Web Site:* www.mjalit.com, pg 464

The Jackson Poetry Prize, 90 Broad St, Suite 2100, New York, NY 10004 *Tel:* 212-226-3586 *Fax:* 212-226-3963 *E-mail:* admin@pw.org *Web Site:* www.pw.org, pg 618

Jacobs/Jones African-American Literary Prize, PO Box 21591, Winston-Salem, NC 27120-1591 *Tel:* 336-293-8844 *E-mail:* mail@ncwriters.org; nclrsubmissions@ecu.edu *Web Site:* www.ncwriters.org, pg 618

Jain Publishing Co, 164 Concho Dr, Fremont, CA 94539 *Tel:* 510-659-8272 *E-mail:* mail@jainpub.com *Web Site:* www.jainpub.com, pg 105

Alice James Books, 60 Pineland Dr, Suite 206, New Gloucester, ME 04260 *Tel:* 207-926-8283 *E-mail:* info@alicejamesbooks.org *Web Site:* alicejamesbooks.org, pg 105

Janklow & Nesbit Associates, 285 Madison Ave, 21st fl, New York, NY 10017 *Tel:* 212-421-1700 *Fax:* 212-355-1403 *E-mail:* info@janklow.com; submissions@janklow.com; filmtvrights@janklow.com *Web Site:* www.janklowandnesbit.com, pg 464

Janus Literary Agency, PO Box 837, Methuen, MA 01844 *Tel:* 978-273-4227 *E-mail:* janusliteraryagency@gmail.com *Web Site:* janusliteraryagency.blogspot.com, pg 464

Japan-US Friendship Commission Translation Prize for the Translation of Japanese Literature, Columbia University, 507 Kent Hall, MC3920, New York, NY 10027 *Tel:* 212-854-5036 *Fax:* 212-854-4019 *E-mail:* donald-keene-center@columbia.edu *Web Site:* www.keenecenter.org, pg 618

Randall Jarrell Poetry Competition, PO Box 21591, Winston-Salem, NC 27120-1591 *Tel:* 336-293-8844 *E-mail:* mail@ncwriters.org; nclrsubmissions@ecu.edu *Web Site:* www.ncwriters.org, pg 618

Jefferson Cup Award, c/o Virginia Library Association (VLA), PO Box 56312, Virginia Beach, VA 23456 *Tel:* 757-689-0594 *Fax:* 757-447-3478 *Web Site:* www.vla.org, pg 618

Jellinek & Murray Literary Agency, 47-231 Kamakoi Rd, Kaneohe, HI 96744 *Tel:* 808-239-8451, pg 464

Jenkins Group Inc, 1129 Woodmere Ave, Suite B, Traverse City, MI 49686 *Tel:* 231-933-0445; 213-883-5365 *E-mail:* info@jenkinsgroupinc.com *Web Site:* www.jenkinsgroupinc.com, pg 441

Carolyn Jenks Agency, 30 Cambridge Park Dr, Suite 5115, Cambridge, MA 02140 *Tel:* 617-233-9130 *Web Site:* www.carolynjenksagency.com, pg 464

Jentel Artist Residency, 130 Lower Piney Rd, Banner, WY 82832 *Tel:* 307-737-2311 *Fax:* 307-737-2305 *E-mail:* jentel@jentelarts.org *Web Site:* www.jentelarts.org, pg 555

Jerome Award, 8550 United Plaza Blvd, Suite 1001, Baton Rouge, LA 70809 *Tel:* 225-408-4417 *E-mail:* cla2@cathla.org *Web Site:* cathla.org, pg 618

Jerome Fellowship, 2301 Franklin Ave E, Minneapolis, MN 55406-1099 *Tel:* 612-332-7481 *Fax:* 612-332-6037 *E-mail:* info@pwcenter.org *Web Site:* www.pwcenter.org, pg 618

JET Literary Associates Inc, 941 Calle Mejia, Suite 507, Santa Fe, NM 87501 *Tel:* 505-780-0721 *E-mail:* jetliterary@gmail.com *Web Site:* www.jetliterary.wordpress.com, pg 464

Jewish Book Council, 520 Eighth Ave, 4th fl, New York, NY 10018 *Tel:* 212-201-2920 *Fax:* 212-532-4952 *E-mail:* info@jewishbooks.org *Web Site:* www.jewishbookcouncil.org, pg 509

Jewish Lights Publishing, 4507 Charlotte Ave, Suite 100, Nashville, TN 37209 *Tel:* 615-255-BOOK (255-2665) *Fax:* 615-255-5081 *E-mail:* marketing@turnerpublishing.com *Web Site:* jewishlights.com; www.turnerpublishing.com, pg 105

The Jewish Publication Society, c/o Gratz College, 7605 Old York Rd, Melrose Park, PA 19027 *Tel:* 215-832-0600 *Web Site:* www.jps.org; www.nebraskapress.unl.edu/jps/, pg 105

JFE Editorial, 190 Ocean Dr, Gun Barrel City, TX 75156 *Tel:* 817-560-7018 *E-mail:* jford@jfe-editorial.com, pg 441

Jhpiego, 1615 Thames St, Baltimore, MD 21231-3492 *Tel:* 410-537-1800 *E-mail:* info@jhpiego.org *Web Site:* www.jhpiego.org, pg 106

JIST Publishing, 4050 Westmark Dr, Dubuque, IA 52002 *Tel:* 563-589-1000 *Toll Free Tel:* 800-328-1452; 800-228-0810 *Fax:* 563-589-1046 *Toll Free Fax:* 800-772-9165 *E-mail:* orders@kendallhunt.com *Web Site:* www.paradigmeducation.com, pg 106

JL Communications, 10205 Green Holly Terr, Silver Spring, MD 20902 *Tel:* 301-593-0640, pg 441

JMW Group Inc, 346 Rte 6, No 867, Mahopac, NY 10541 *Tel:* 914-841-7105 *Fax:* 914-248-8861 *E-mail:* jmwgroup@jmwgroup.net *Web Site:* jmwforlife.com, pg 465

John Steinbeck Award for Fiction, San Jose State University, English Dept, One Washington Sq, San Jose, CA 95192-0090 *Tel:* 408-924-4441 *E-mail:* mail@reedmag.org *Web Site:* www.reedmag.org; reedmagazine.submittable.com, pg 618

Johns Hopkins University Press, 2715 N Charles St, Baltimore, MD 21218-4363 *Tel:* 410-516-6900; 410-516-6987 *Toll Free Tel:* 800-537-5487 (book orders & cust serv); 800-548-1784 (journal orders) *Fax:* 410-516-6968; 410-516-6998 (orders) *E-mail:* hfscustserv@press.jhu.edu (cust serv); jrnlcirc@jh.edu (journal orders) *Web Site:* www.press.jhu.edu; muse.jhu.edu, pg 106

Lyndon B Johnson School of Public Affairs, University of Texas at Austin, 2300 Red River St, Stop E2700, Austin, TX 78712-1536 *Tel:* 512-471-3200 *E-mail:* lbjdeansoffice@austin.utexas.edu *Web Site:* lbj.utexas.edu, pg 106

Jones & Bartlett Learning LLC, 25 Mall Rd, Burlington, MA 01803 *Tel:* 978-443-5000 *Toll Free Tel:* 800-832-0034 *Fax:* 978-443-8000 *E-mail:* info@jblearning.com; customerservice@jblearning.com *Web Site:* www.jblearning.com, pg 107

Anson Jones MD Awards, 401 W 15 St, Austin, TX 78701 *Tel:* 512-370-1300 *Toll Free Tel:* 800-880-7955 *E-mail:* ansonjones@texmed.org *Web Site:* www.texmed.org/ansonjones, pg 618

Jones Hutton Literary Associates, 140D Heritage Village, Southbury, CT 06488 *Tel:* 203-558-4478 *E-mail:* huttonbooks@hotmail.com, pg 465

Jesse H Jones Award, PO Box 130294, Spring, TX 77393 *Web Site:* texasinstituteofletters.org, pg 618

Joshua Tree Publishing, 3 Golf Ctr, Suite 201, Hoffman Estates, IL 60169 *Tel:* 312-893-7525 *E-mail:* info@joshuatreepublishing.com; info@centaurbooks.com *Web Site:* www.joshuatreepublishing.com; www.centaurbooks.com, pg 107

Judah, Sarah, Grace & Tom Memorial, PO Box 36128, North Chesterfield, VA 23235-3533 *E-mail:* contest@poetrysocietyofvirginia.org; info@poetryvirginia.org *Web Site:* www.poetrysocietyofvirginia.org, pg 618

Judaica Press Inc, 123 Ditmas Ave, Brooklyn, NY 11218 *Tel:* 718-972-6200 *Toll Free Tel:* 800-972-6201 *Fax:* 718-972-6204 *E-mail:* info@judaicapress.com; orders@judaicapress.com; submissions@judaicapress.com *Web Site:* www.judaicapress.com, pg 107

Judson Press, 1075 First Ave, King of Prussia, PA 19406 *Toll Free Tel:* 800-458-3766 *Fax:* 610-768-2107 *E-mail:* publisher@judsonpress.com; editor@judsonpress.com; marketing@judsonpress.com *Web Site:* www.judsonpress.com, pg 107

Jump!, 5357 Penn Ave, Minneapolis, MN 55419 *Toll Free Tel:* 888-799-1860 *Toll Free Fax:* 800-675-6679 *E-mail:* customercare@jumplibrary.com *Web Site:* www.jumplibrary.com, pg 107

Jump at the Sun, 125 West End Ave, 3rd fl, New York, NY 10023 *Web Site:* books.disney.com, pg 107

Juniper Prize for Creative Nonfiction, New Africa House, 180 Infirmary Way, 4th fl, Amherst, MA 01003-9289 *E-mail:* juniperprize@umpress.umass.edu *Web Site:* www.umasspress.com/juniper-prizes, pg 619

Juniper Prize for Fiction, New Africa House, 180 Infirmary Way, 4th fl, Amherst, MA 01003-9289 *E-mail:* juniperprize@umpress.umass.edu *Web Site:* www.umasspress.com/juniper-prizes, pg 619

Juniper Prize for Poetry, New Africa House, 180 Infirmary Way, 4th fl, Amherst, MA 01003-9289 *E-mail:* juniperprize@umpress.umass.edu *Web Site:* www.umasspress.com/juniper-prizes, pg 619

Juniper Summer Writing Institute, c/o University Conference Services, 810 Campus Center, One Campus Center Way, Amherst, MA 01003 *Tel:* 413-545-5503 *E-mail:* juniperinstitute@hfa.umass.edu *Web Site:* www.umass.edu/juniperinstitute, pg 555

Just Creative Writing & Indexing Services (JCR), 301 Wood Duck Dr, Greensboro, MD 21639 *Tel:* 443-262-2136 *E-mail:* judy@justcreativewriting.com *Web Site:* www.justcreativewriting.com, pg 441

Just World Books LLC, PO Box 57075, Washington, DC 20037 *Toll Free Tel:* 888-506-3769 *E-mail:* sales@justworldbooks.com; info@justworldbooks.com; rights@justworldbooks.com *Web Site:* justworldbooks.com, pg 107

Kaeden Publishing, 24700 Center Ridge Rd, Suite 240, Westlake, OH 44145 *Tel:* 440-617-1400 *Toll Free Tel:* 800-890-7323 *Fax:* 440-617-1403 *E-mail:* sales@kaeden.com *Web Site:* www.kaeden.com, pg 107

Kalaniot Books, 72 Glenmaura National Blvd, Suite 104B, Moosic, PA 18507 *Tel:* 862-251-2296; 570-451-6095 *E-mail:* info@kalaniotbooks.com *Web Site:* www.kalaniotbooks.com, pg 107

Kallisti Publishing Inc, 332 Center St, Wilkes-Barre, PA 18702 *Tel:* 570-825-3598 *E-mail:* editor@kallistipublishing.com *Web Site:* www.kallistipublishing.com; arisbooks.com, pg 108

Kalmbach Media Co, 21027 Crossroads Circle, Waukesha, WI 53186 *Tel:* 262-796-8776 *Web Site:* www.kalmbach.com, pg 108

Kamehameha Publishing, 567 S King St, Honolulu, HI 96813 *E-mail:* publishing@ksbe.edu *Web Site:* kamehamehapublishing.org, pg 108

Susan Kamil Award for Emerging Writers, 15 Lafayette Ave, Brooklyn, NY 11217 *Tel:* 212-755-6710 *E-mail:* info@centerforfiction.org *Web Site:* centerforfiction.org, pg 619

Susan Kamil Scholarship for Emerging Writers, 3135 S State St, Suite 203, Ann Arbor, MI 48108 *Toll Free Tel:* 866-733-9064 *E-mail:* info@bincfoundation.org *Web Site:* bincfoundation.org/susankamil-scholarship, pg 619

Kapp Books LLC, 3602 Rocky Meadow Ct, Fairfax, VA 22033 *Tel:* 703-261-9171 *Fax:* 703-621-7162 *E-mail:* info@kappbooks.com *Web Site:* www.kappbooks.com, pg 108

Kar-Ben Publishing, 241 First Ave N, Minneapolis, MN 55401 *Tel:* 612-332-3344 *Toll Free Tel:* 800-4-KARBEN (452-7236) *Fax:* 612-332-7615 *Toll Free Fax:* 800-332-1132 *E-mail:* custserve@karben.com *Web Site:* www.karben.com, pg 108

The Michele Karlsberg Leadership Award, 511 Avenue of the Americas, No D36, New York, NY 10011 *E-mail:* awards@publishingtriangle.org; info@publishingtriangle.org; publishingtriangle@gmail.com *Web Site:* publishingtriangle.org/awards/leadership-award, pg 619

The Karpfinger Agency, 357 W 20 St, New York, NY 10011-3379 *Tel:* 212-691-2690 *Fax:* 212-691-7129 *E-mail:* info@karpfinger.com (no queries or submissions) *Web Site:* karpfinger.com, pg 465

Sue Kaufman Prize for First Fiction, 633 W 155 St, New York, NY 10032 *Tel:* 212-368-5900 *E-mail:* academy@artsandletters.org *Web Site:* artsandletters.org/awards, pg 619

Kazi Publications Inc, 3023 W Belmont Ave, Chicago, IL 60618 *Tel:* 773-267-7001 *Fax:* 773-267-7002 *E-mail:* info@kazi.org *Web Site:* www.kazi.org, pg 108

George Markey Keating Memorial Scholarships, 3135 S State St, Suite 203, Ann Arbor, MI 48108 *Toll Free Tel:* 866-733-9064 *E-mail:* info@bincfoundation.org *Web Site:* www.bincfoundation.org, pg 619

Ezra Jack Keats Book Award, 450 14 St, Brooklyn, NY 11215-5702 *E-mail:* foundation@ezra-jack-keats.org *Web Site:* www.ezra-jack-keats.org, pg 619

Ezra Jack Keats/Kerlan Memorial Fellowship, University of Minnesota, 113 Andersen Library, 222 21 Ave S, Minneapolis, MN 55455 *Tel:* 612-624-4576 *E-mail:* asc-clrc@umn.edu *Web Site:* www.lib.umn.edu/clrc, pg 619

Keim Publishing, 66 Main St, Suite 807, Yonkers, NY 10701 *Tel:* 917-655-7190, pg 441

J J Keller & Associates, Inc®, 3003 Breezewood Lane, Neenah, WI 54957 *Tel:* 920-722-2848 *Toll Free Tel:* 877-564-2333 *Toll Free Fax:* 800-727-7516 *E-mail:* customerservice@jjkeller.com; sales@jjkeller.com *Web Site:* www.jjkeller.com, pg 108

Keller Media Inc, 578 Washington Blvd, No 745, Marina del Rey, CA 90292 *Toll Free Tel:* 800-278-8706 *E-mail:* query@kellermedia.com *Web Site:* kellermedia.com/submission-guidelines, pg 465

Joan Kelly Memorial Prize in Women's History, 400 "A" St SE, Washington, DC 20003 *Tel:* 202-544-2422 *E-mail:* awards@historians.org *Web Site:* www.historians.org/award-grant/joan-kelly-memorial-prize/, pg 619

Kelsey Street Press, 2824 Kelsey St, Berkeley, CA 94705 *E-mail:* info@kelseystreetpress.org *Web Site:* www.kelseystreetpress.org, pg 108

Randall Kenan Prize for Black LGBTQ Fiction, PO Box 20186, New York, NY 10014 *Tel:* 213-277-5755 *E-mail:* awards@lambdaliterary.org; admin@lambdaliterary.org *Web Site:* www.lambdaliterary.org/awards/special-awards, pg 620

Kendall Hunt Publishing Co, 4050 Westmark Dr, Dubuque, IA 52002-2624 *Tel:* 563-589-1000 *Toll Free Tel:* 800-228-0810 (orders) *Fax:* 563-589-1071 *Toll Free Fax:* 800-772-9165 *E-mail:* ordernow@kendallhunt.com *Web Site:* www.kendallhunt.com, pg 108

Kennedy Information LLC, 24 Railroad St, Keene, NH 03431 *Tel:* 603-357-8103 *Toll Free Tel:* 800-531-0140, pg 108

Robert F Kennedy Book Awards, 1300 19 St NW, Suite 750, Washington, DC 20036 *Tel:* 646-553-4750 *Fax:* 202-463-6606 *E-mail:* info@rfkhumanrights.org *Web Site:* rfkhumanrights.org, pg 620

Kensington Publishing Corp, 900 Third Ave, 26th fl, New York, NY 10022 *Tel:* 212-407-1500 *Toll Free Tel:* 800-221-2647 *Fax:* 212-935-0699 *Web Site:* www.kensingtonbooks.com, pg 109

Kent State University Press, 1118 University Library Bldg, 1125 Risman Dr, Kent, OH 44242 *Tel:* 330-672-7913 *Fax:* 330-672-3104 *E-mail:* ksupress@kent.edu *Web Site:* www.kentstateuniversitypress.com, pg 109

Kentucky Writers Conference, c/o Warren Public Library, 1225 State St, Bowling Green, KY 42101 *E-mail:* sokybookfest@warrenpl.org *Web Site:* sokybookfest.org/programs/ky-writers-conference, pg 555

Natasha Kern Literary Agency Inc, PO Box 1069, White Salmon, WA 98672 *Tel:* 509-493-3803 *Web Site:* www.natashakernliterary.com, pg 465

Kessinger Publishing LLC, PO Box 1404, Whitefish, MT 59937 *Web Site:* www.kessingerpublishing.com, pg 109

Louise B Ketz Agency, 414 E 78 St, Suite 1B, New York, NY 10075 *Tel:* 212-249-0668 *E-mail:* ketzagency@aol.com, pg 465

COMPANY INDEX

Key West Literary Seminar, 717 Love Lane, Key West, FL 33040 *Tel:* 305-293-9291 *E-mail:* mail@kwls.org *Web Site:* www.kwls.org/seminar, pg 555

Key West Literary Seminar's Writers' Workshop Program, 717 Love Lane, Key West, FL 33040 *Tel:* 305-293-9291 *E-mail:* mail@kwls.org *Web Site:* www.kwls.org, pg 555

Virginia Kidd Agency Inc, 538 E Harford St, PO Box 278, Milford, PA 18337 *Tel:* 570-296-6205 *Web Site:* vk-agency.com, pg 465

Kids' Book Choice Awards, 54 W 39 St, 14th fl, New York, NY 10018 *E-mail:* cbc.info@cbcbooks.org *Web Site:* everychildareader.net/choice, pg 620

Kids Can Press Ltd, 25 Dockside Dr, Toronto, ON M5A 0B5, Canada *Tel:* 416-479-7000 *Toll Free Tel:* 800-265-0884 *Fax:* 416-960-5437 *E-mail:* info@kidscan.com; customerservice@kidscan.com *Web Site:* www.kidscanpress.com; www.kidscanpress.ca, pg 411

Kidsbooks® Publishing, 5306 Ballard Ave NW, Suite 311, Seattle, WA 98107 *E-mail:* customerservice@kidsbookspublishing.com *Web Site:* www.kidsbookspublishing.com, pg 109

Kindred Productions, 1310 Taylor Ave, Winnipeg, MB R3M 3Z6, Canada *Tel:* 204-669-6575 *Toll Free Tel:* 800-545-7322 *E-mail:* kindred@mbchurches.ca *Web Site:* www.kindredproductions.com, pg 411

Kinesis Education Inc, 4823 Sherbrooke St W, Suite 275, Westmount, QC H3Z 1G7, Canada *Tel:* 514-932-9466 *Toll Free Tel:* 866-750-9466 *E-mail:* editions@ebbp.ca *Web Site:* ebbp.ca, pg 411

Coretta Scott King Book Awards, 225 N Michigan Ave, Suite 1300, Chicago, IL 60601 *Tel:* 312-944-6780 *Toll Free Tel:* 800-545-2433 *Fax:* 312-440-9374 *E-mail:* diversity@ala.org *Web Site:* www.ala.org/awardsgrants/coretta-scott-king-book-awards, pg 620

Coretta Scott King - John Steptoe Award for New Talent, 225 N Michigan Ave, Suite 1300, Chicago, IL 60601 *Tel:* 312-944-6780 *Toll Free Tel:* 800-545-2433 (ext 4294) *Fax:* 312-280-3256 *E-mail:* diversity@ala.org *Web Site:* www.ala.org/awardsgrants, pg 620

Coretta Scott King - Virginia Hamilton Award for Lifetime Achievement, 225 N Michigan Ave, Suite 1300, Chicago, IL 60601 *Toll Free Tel:* 800-545-2433 *E-mail:* diversity@ala.org *Web Site:* www.ala.org/emiert/virginia-hamilton-award-lifetime-achievement, pg 620

Jessica Kingsley Publishers Inc, 123 S Broad St, Suite 2750, Philadelphia, PA 19109 *Tel:* 215-922-1161 *Toll Free Tel:* 866-416-1078 (cust serv) *Fax:* 215-922-1474 *E-mail:* hello.usa@jkp.com *Web Site:* us.jkp.com, pg 110

Jack Temple Kirby Award, University of Georgia, Dept of History, Athens, GA 30602-1602 *Tel:* 706-542-8848 *Web Site:* thesha.org/kirby, pg 620

Kirchoff/Wohlberg Inc, 897 Boston Post Rd, Madison, CT 06443 *Tel:* 203-245-7308 *Fax:* 203-245-3218 *E-mail:* info@kirchoffwohlberg.com *Web Site:* www.kirchoffwohlberg.com, pg 465

Kirkus Prize, 1140 Broadway, Suite 802, New York, NY 10001 *Web Site:* www.kirkusreviews.com/prize, pg 620

Kiva Publishing Inc, 10 Bella Loma, Santa Fe, NM 87506 *Tel:* 909-896-0518 *E-mail:* kivapub@aol.com *Web Site:* www.kivapub.com, pg 110

Harvey Klinger Inc, 300 W 55 St, Suite 11V, New York, NY 10019 *Tel:* 212-581-7068 *Fax:* 212-315-3823 *E-mail:* queries@harveyklinger.com *Web Site:* www.harveyklinger.com, pg 465

Klutz®, 557 Broadway, New York, NY 10012 *Tel:* 212-343-6360 *Toll Free Tel:* 800-737-4123 (cust serv) *E-mail:* scholasticmarketing@scholastic.com; scholasticstore@scholastic.com *Web Site:* www.scholastic.com/parents/klutz.html; store.scholastic.com, pg 110

The Knight Agency Inc, 232 W Washington St, Madison, GA 30650 *E-mail:* admin@knightagency.net *Web Site:* www.knightagency.net, pg 466

Knight Science Journalism Fellowships, 77 Massachusetts Ave, Cambridge, MA 02139 *Tel:* 617-452-3513 *E-mail:* knight-info@mit.edu *Web Site:* ksj.mit.edu/fellowship, pg 620

Knightville Poetry Contest, PO Box 472, Brunswick, ME 04011 *E-mail:* info@newguardreview.com; editors@writershotel.com *Web Site:* www.newguardreview.com, pg 621

Alfred A Knopf, c/o Penguin Random House LLC, 1745 Broadway, New York, NY 10019 *Tel:* 212-751-2600 *Fax:* 212-940-7390 (dom rts); 212-572-2662 (foreign rts) *Web Site:* knopfdoubleday.com/imprint/knopf/; knopfdoubleday.com, pg 110

Knopf Canada, 320 Front St W, Suite 1400, Toronto, ON M5V 3B6, Canada *Tel:* 416-364-4449 *Toll Free Tel:* 888-523-9292 *Fax:* 416-598-7764 *Web Site:* www.penguinrandomhouse.ca, pg 411

Knopf Doubleday Publishing Group, c/o Penguin Random House LLC, 1745 Broadway, New York, NY 10019 *Tel:* 212-751-2600 *Fax:* 212-940-7390 (dom rts); 212-572-2662 (foreign rts) *Web Site:* knopfdoubleday.com, pg 110

KO Media Management, 2817 Wetmore Ave, Everett, WA 98201 *E-mail:* info@komediamanagement.com; query@komediamanagement.com *Web Site:* komediamanagement.com, pg 466

Kobo Emerging Writer Prize, 135 Liberty St, Suite 101, Toronto, ON M6K 1A7, Canada *E-mail:* pr@kobo.com *Web Site:* www.kobo.com/emergingwriterprize, pg 621

Kodansha USA Inc, 451 Park Ave S, 7th fl, New York, NY 10016 *Tel:* 917-322-6200 *Fax:* 212-935-6929 *E-mail:* info@kodansha.com *Web Site:* kodansha.us, pg 110

Barry R Koffler, Featherside, 14 Ginger Rd, High Falls, NY 12440 *Tel:* 845-687-9851 *E-mail:* barkof@feathersite.com, pg 441

Kogan Page, 8 W 38 St, Suite 902, New York, NY 10018 *Tel:* 212-812-4414 *E-mail:* info@koganpage.com *Web Site:* www.koganpage.com, pg 111

The Kohner Agency, 9300 Wilshire Blvd, Suite 300, Beverly Hills, CA 90212 *Tel:* 310-550-1060 *Web Site:* kohneragency.com, pg 466

Koho Pono LLC, 15024 SE Pinegrove Loop, Clackamas, OR 97015 *Tel:* 503-723-7392 *E-mail:* info@kohopono.com; orders@ingrambook.com *Web Site:* kohopono.com, pg 111

KOK Edit, 15 Hare Lane, East Setauket, NY 11733-3606 *Tel:* 631-997-8191 *E-mail:* editor@kokedit.com *Web Site:* www.kokedit.com; x.com/kokedit; www.facebook.com/K.OmooreKlopf; www.linkedin.com/in/kokedit; www.editor-mom.blogspot.com, pg 441

Kokila, c/o Penguin Random House LLC, 1745 Broadway, New York, NY 10019 *Tel:* 212-782-9000 *Web Site:* www.penguin.com/kokila-books-overview/, pg 111

Konecky & Konecky LLC, 72 Ayers Point Rd, Old Saybrook, CT 06475 *Tel:* 860-388-0878 *E-mail:* sean.konecky@gmail.com *Web Site:* www.koneckyandkonecky.com, pg 111

Linda Konner Literary Agency (LKLA), 10 W 15 St, Suite 1918, New York, NY 10011 *Web Site:* www.lindakonnerliteraryagency.com, pg 466

Katherine Singer Kovacs Prize, 85 Broad St, New York, NY 10004 *Tel:* 646-576-5141; 646-576-5000 *E-mail:* awards@mla.org *Web Site:* www.mla.org, pg 621

The Kraken Book Prize for Middle-Grade Fiction, c/o Regal House Publishing, 806 Oberlin Rd, No 12094, Raleigh, NC 27605 *E-mail:* info@regalhousepublishing.com *Web Site:* regalhousepublishing.com/the-kraken-book-award/, pg 621

Eileen Kramer, 336 Great Rd, Stow, MA 01775 *Tel:* 978-897-4121 *E-mail:* kramer@tiac.net, pg 441

Michael Kraus Research Grants in American Colonial History, 400 "A" St SE, Washington, DC 20003 *Tel:* 202-544-2422 *E-mail:* awards@historians.org *Web Site:* www.historians.org/award-grant/michael-kraus-research-grants-in-american-colonial-history/, pg 621

Krause Publications Inc, 1745 Broadway, New York, NY 10019 *Tel:* 212-782-9000 *Web Site:* www.penguinrandomhouse.com, pg 111

Kregel Publications, 2450 Oak Industrial Dr NE, Grand Rapids, MI 49505 *Tel:* 616-451-4775 *Toll Free Tel:* 800-733-2607 *Fax:* 616-451-9330 *E-mail:* kregelbooks@kregel.com *Web Site:* www.kregel.com, pg 111

Stuart Krichevsky Literary Agency Inc, 118 E 28 St, Suite 908, New York, NY 10016 *Tel:* 212-725-5288 *Fax:* 212-725-5275 *E-mail:* query@skagency.com *Web Site:* skagency.com, pg 466

Krieger Publishing Co, 1725 Krieger Lane, Malabar, FL 32950 *Tel:* 321-724-9542 *Fax:* 321-951-3671 *E-mail:* info@krieger-publishing.com *Web Site:* www.krieger-publishing.com, pg 111

The Robert Kroetsch City of Edmonton Book Prize, 11759 Groat Rd NW, Edmonton, AB T5M 3K6, Canada *Tel:* 780-422-8174 *Toll Free Tel:* 800-665-5354 (AB only) *E-mail:* mail@writersguild.ab.ca *Web Site:* writersguild.ca, pg 621

Lynn C Kronzek, Richard A Flom & Robert Flom, 145 S Glenoaks Blvd, Suite 240, Burbank, CA 91502 *Tel:* 818-768-7688, pg 441

KTAV Publishing House Inc, 527 Empire Blvd, Brooklyn, NY 11225 *Tel:* 201-963-9524; 718-972-5449 *Fax:* 718-972-6307 *E-mail:* orders@ktav.com *Web Site:* www.ktav.com, pg 111

Kumarian Press, 1800 30 St, Suite 314, Boulder, CO 80301 *Tel:* 303-444-6684 *Fax:* 303-444-0824 *E-mail:* questions@rienner.com *Web Site:* www.rienner.com, pg 112

Polly Kummel LLC, 624 Boardman Rd, Aiken, SC 29803 *Tel:* 803-641-6831 *E-mail:* editor@amazinphrasin.com; pollyk1@msn.com *Web Site:* www.amazinphrasin.com, pg 441

Kumon Publishing North America Inc (KPNA), 301 Rte 17 N, Suite 704, Rutherford, NJ 07070-2581 *Tel:* 201-836-2105; 201-836-1559; 703-661-1501 (orders) *Toll Free Tel:* 800-657-7970 (cust serv) *Fax:* 201-836-1559 *E-mail:* books@kumon.com; kumon@presswarehouse.com *Web Site:* kumonbooks.com, pg 112

Kumu Kahua/UHM Theatre & Dance Department Playwriting Contest, 46 Merchant St, Honolulu, HI 96813 *Tel:* 808-536-4441 (box off); 808-536-4222 (off admin) *Fax:* 808-536-4226 *E-mail:* officemanager@kumukahua.org *Web Site:* www.kumukahua.org, pg 621

Kundiman Retreat, Fordham University, English Dept, 113 W 60 St, Rm 924, New York, NY 10023 *E-mail:* info@kundiman.org *Web Site:* www.kundiman.org, pg 556

The LA Literary Agency, 1264 N Hayworth Ave, Los Angeles, CA 90046 *Tel:* 323-654-5288 *E-mail:* laliteraryagency@mac.com *Web Site:* www.laliteraryagency.com, pg 466

Lachina Creative Inc, 3791 S Green Rd, Cleveland, OH 44122 *Tel:* 216-292-7959 *E-mail:* info@lachina.com *Web Site:* www.lachina.com, pg 441

Ladderbird Literary Agency, 460 Yellow Brick Rd, Orange, CT 06477 *Tel:* 203-290-1703 *Web Site:* www.ladderbird.com, pg 466

Lake Superior Publishing LLC, 109 W Superior St, Suite 200, Duluth, MN 55802 *Tel:* 218-722-5002 *Toll Free Tel:* 888-BIG-LAKE (244-5253) *Fax:* 218-722-4096 *E-mail:* edit@lakesuperior.com *Web Site:* www.lakesuperior.com, pg 112

LAMA Books, 2381 Sleepy Hollow Ave, Hayward, CA 94545 *Tel:* 510-785-1091 *Toll Free Tel:* 888-452-6244 *Fax:* 510-785-1099 *Web Site:* www.lamabooks.com, pg 112

W Kaye Lamb Scholarships, PO Box 448, Fort Langley, BC V1M 2R7, Canada *E-mail:* info@bchistory.ca *Web Site:* www.bchistory.ca/awards/scholarships, pg 621

Lambda Literary Awards (Lammys), PO Box 20186, New York, NY 10014 *Tel:* 213-277-5755 *E-mail:* awards@lambdaliterary.org; admin@lambdaliterary.org *Web Site:* www.lambdaliterary.org, pg 621

Peter Lampack Agency Inc, 350 Fifth Ave, Suite 5300, New York, NY 10118 *Tel:* 212-687-9106 *Fax:* 212-687-9109 *Web Site:* www.peterlampackagency.com, pg 467

Gerald Lampert Memorial Award, 2 Carlton St, Suite 1519, Toronto, ON M5B 1J3, Canada *Tel:* 416-504-1657 *E-mail:* info@poets.ca; admin@poets.ca *Web Site:* poets.ca/awards/lampert, pg 621

Lanahan Publishers Inc, 324 Hawthorne Rd, Baltimore, MD 21210-2303 *Tel:* 410-366-2434 *Toll Free Tel:* 866-345-1949 *Fax:* 410-366-8798 *E-mail:* lanahan@aol.com *Web Site:* www.lanahanpublishers.com, pg 112

Land on Demand, 1003 Lakeview Pkwy, Locust Grove, VA 22508 *Tel:* 423-366-0513 *E-mail:* landondemand@gmail.com *Web Site:* boblandedits.blogspot.com, pg 441

Landauer Publishing, 903 Square St, Mount Joy, PA 17552 *Tel:* 717-560-4703 *Toll Free Tel:* 800-457-9112 *Fax:* 717-560-4702 *E-mail:* customerservice@foxchapelpublishing.com *Web Site:* landauerpub.com, pg 112

Peter Lang Publishing Inc, 80 Broadway, 5th fl, New York, NY 10004 *Tel:* 703-661-1584 *Toll Free Tel:* 800-770-5264 (cust serv) *Fax:* 703-996-1010 *E-mail:* info@peterlang.com; newyork.editorial@peterlang.com; customerservice@plang.com *Web Site:* www.peterlang.com, pg 112

David J Langum Sr Prize in American Historical Fiction, c/o David J Langum Sr, 2809 Berkeley Dr, Birmingham, AL 35242 *Web Site:* langumfoundation.org/about-prizes/american-historical-fiction, pg 622

David J Langum Sr Prize in American Legal History or Biography, c/o William G Ross, Cumberland School of Law, 800 Lakeshore Dr, Birmingham, AL 35229 *Web Site:* langumfoundation.org/about-prizes/american-legal-history-or-biography, pg 622

Lannan Foundation, 313 Read St, Santa Fe, NM 87501-2628 *Tel:* 505-986-8160 *E-mail:* info@lannan.org *Web Site:* lannan.org, pg 525

Lannan Literary Awards & Fellowships, 313 Read St, Santa Fe, NM 87501-2628 *Tel:* 505-986-8160 *E-mail:* info@lannan.org *Web Site:* lannan.org, pg 622

Lantern Publishing & Media, 128 Second Place, Garden Suite, Brooklyn, NY 11231 *Web Site:* lanternpm.org, pg 112

LARB Books, 6671 Sunset Blvd, Suite 1521, Los Angeles, CA 90028 *Tel:* 323-952-3950 *E-mail:* larbbooks@lareviewofbooks.org *Web Site:* larbbooks.org, pg 113

LARB/USC Publishing Workshop, 6671 Sunset Blvd, Suite 1521, Los Angeles, CA 90028 *E-mail:* publishingworkshop@lareviewofbooks.org *Web Site:* thepublishingworkshop.com, pg 556

Laredo Publishing Co, 465 Westview Ave, Englewood, NJ 07631 *Tel:* 201-408-4048 *E-mail:* info@laredopublishing.com *Web Site:* www.laredopublishing.com, pg 113

Larson Publications, 4936 State Rte 414, Burdett, NY 14818 *Tel:* 607-546-9342 *Toll Free Tel:* 800-828-2197 *Fax:* 607-546-9344 *E-mail:* custserv@larsonpublications.com *Web Site:* www.larsonpublications.com, pg 113

Lasaria Creative Publishing, 4094 Majestic Lane, Suite 352, Fairfax, VA 22033 *E-mail:* info@lasariacreative.com *Web Site:* www.lasariacreative.com, pg 113

Latino Books Into Movies Awards, 624 Hillcrest Lane, Fallbrook, CA 92028 *Tel:* 760 645-3455 (submission info); 760-689-2317 *E-mail:* awards@empoweringlatinofutures.org *Web Site:* www.latinobookawards.org, pg 622

Latner Griffin Writers' Trust Poetry Prize, 600-460 Richmond St W, Toronto, ON M5V 1Y1, Canada *Tel:* 416-504-8222 *Toll Free Tel:* 877-906-6548 *Fax:* 416-504-9090 *E-mail:* info@writerstrust.com *Web Site:* www.writerstrust.com/awards/latner-writers-trust-poetry-prize, pg 622

Laughing Elephant Books, 3645 Interlake N, Seattle, WA 98103 *Tel:* 206-447-9229 *Toll Free Tel:* 800-354-0400 *Fax:* 206-447-9189 *E-mail:* support@laughingelephant.com *Web Site:* www.laughingelephant.com, pg 113

James Laughlin Award, 75 Maiden Lane, Suite 901, New York, NY 10038 *Tel:* 212-274-0343 *E-mail:* awards@poets.org *Web Site:* poets.org/academy-american-poets/prizes/james-laughlin-award, pg 622

Law School Admission Council (LSAC), 662 Penn St, Newtown, PA 18940 *Tel:* 215-968-1101 *Toll Free Tel:* 800-336-3982 *E-mail:* lsacinfo@lsac.org *Web Site:* www.lsac.org, pg 113

The Lawbook Exchange, Ltd, 33 Terminal Ave, Clark, NJ 07066-1321 *Tel:* 732-382-1800 *Toll Free Tel:* 800-422-6686 *Fax:* 732-382-1887 *E-mail:* law@lawbookexchange.com *Web Site:* www.lawbookexchange.com, pg 113

Lawrence Foundation Prize, University of Michigan, 3277 Angell Hall, 435 S State St, Ann Arbor, MI 48109-1003 *Tel:* 734-764-9265 *E-mail:* mqr@umich.edu *Web Site:* sites.lsa.umich.edu/mqr/about-us/prizes, pg 622

Lawyers & Judges Publishing Co Inc, 917 N Swan Rd, Suite 300, Tucson, AZ 85711 *Tel:* 520-323-1500 *Fax:* 520-323-0055 *E-mail:* sales@lawyersandjudges.com *Web Site:* www.lawyersandjudges.com, pg 113

The Ursula K Le Guin Prize for Fiction, 9450 SW Gemini Dr, PMB 51842, Beaverton, OR 97008-7105 *E-mail:* estateofukl@gmail.com *Web Site:* www.ursulakleguin.com/prize-overview, pg 622

Stephen Leacock Memorial Medal for Humour, PO Box 854, Orillia, ON L3V 6K8, Canada *Tel:* 705-326-9286 *E-mail:* info@leacock.ca *Web Site:* www.leacock.ca, pg 622

Leadership Ministries Worldwide, 1928 Central Ave, Chattanooga, TN 37408 *Tel:* 423-855-1181 *Toll Free Tel:* 800-987-8790 *E-mail:* info@lmw.org *Web Site:* lmw.org; store.lmw.org, pg 113

Leaf Storm Press, PO Box 4670, Santa Fe, NM 87502-4670 *Tel:* 505-216-6155 *E-mail:* leafstormpress@gmail.com *Web Site:* www.leafstormpress.com, pg 113

The League of Canadian Poets, 2 Carlton St, Suite 1519, Toronto, ON M5B 1J3, Canada *Tel:* 416-504-1657 *E-mail:* info@poets.ca *Web Site:* poets.ca, pg 509

League of Vermont Voters Inc, PO Box 5046, Burlington, VT 05402 *E-mail:* lvw@leagueofvermontwriters.org *Web Site:* leagueofvermontwriters.org, pg 509

Leapfrog Global Fiction Prize, PO Box 505, Fredonia, NY 14063 *E-mail:* leapfrog@leapfrogpress.com *Web Site:* leapfrogpress.com/the-leapfrog-global-fiction-prize-contest, pg 622

THE Learning Connection®, 4100 Silverstar Rd, Suite D, Orlando, FL 32808 *Toll Free Tel:* 800-218-8489 *Fax:* 407-292-2123 *E-mail:* tlc@tlconnection.com *Web Site:* www.tlconnection.com, pg 113

Learning Links-USA Inc, 18 Haypress Rd, Suite 414, Cranbury, NJ 08512 *Tel:* 516-437-9071 *Toll Free Tel:* 800-724-2616 *Fax:* 732-329-6994 *E-mail:* info@learninglinks.com *Web Site:* www.learninglinks.com, pg 114

The Learning Source Ltd, 644 Tenth St, Brooklyn, NY 11215 *E-mail:* info@learningsourceltd.com *Web Site:* www.learningsourceltd.com, pg 441

LearningExpress, 224 W 29 St, 3rd fl, New York, NY 10001 *Toll Free Tel:* 800-295-9556 (ext 2) *Web Site:* learningexpresshub.com, pg 114

The Ned Leavitt Agency, 752 Creeklocks Rd, Rosendale, NY 12472 *Tel:* 845-658-3333 *Web Site:* www.nedleavittagency.com, pg 467

Lectorum Publications Inc, 10 New Maple Ave, Suite 303, Pine Brook, NJ 07058 *Tel:* 201-559-2200 *Toll Free Tel:* 800-345-5946 *E-mail:* lectorum@lectorum.com *Web Site:* www.lectorum.com, pg 114

Lederer Books, 6120 Day Long Lane, Clarksville, MD 21029 *Tel:* 410-531-6644 *Toll Free Tel:* 800-410-7367 (orders) *Web Site:* www.messianicjewish.net, pg 114

Lee & Low Books Inc, 95 Madison Ave, Suite 1205, New York, NY 10016 *Tel:* 212-779-4400 *Toll Free Tel:* 888-320-3190 (ext 28, orders only) *Fax:* 212-683-1894 (orders only); 212-532-6035 *E-mail:* general@leeandlow.com *Web Site:* www.leeandlow.com, pg 114

Harper Lee Prize for Legal Fiction, 101 Paul Bryant Dr, Tuscaloosa, AL 35487 *Tel:* 205-348-5195 *Web Site:* www.harperleeprize.com, pg 623

Legacy Award, 2667 Hyacinth St, Westbury, NY 11590 *Tel:* 516-333-0681 *E-mail:* kit@naiba.com *Web Site:* www.naiba.com/page/LegacyAward, pg 623

Legacy Bound, 5 N Central Ave, Ely, MN 55731 *Tel:* Legacy Bound *Toll Free Tel:* 800-909-9698 *E-mail:* orders@legacybound.net *Web Site:* www.legacybound.net, pg 114

Lehigh University Press, B-040 Christmas-Saucon Hall, 14 E Packer Ave, Bethlehem, PA 18015 *Tel:* 610-758-3933 *Fax:* 610-758-6331 *E-mail:* inlup@lehigh.edu *Web Site:* lupress.cas2.lehigh.edu, pg 114

Leisure Arts Inc, 104 Champs Blvd, Suite 100, Maumelle, AR 72113 *Tel:* 501-868-8800 *Toll Free Tel:* 800-643-8030 *Toll Free Fax:* 877-710-5603 (catalog) *E-mail:* customer_service@leisurearts.com *Web Site:* www.leisurearts.com, pg 114

Waldo G Leland Prize for Reference Tools, 400 "A" St SE, Washington, DC 20003 *Tel:* 202-544-2422 *E-mail:* awards@historians.org *Web Site:* www.historians.org/award-grant/waldo-g-leland-prize/, pg 623

Vincent Lemieux Prize, 260 Dalhousie St, Suite 204, Ottawa, ON K1N 7E4, Canada *Tel:* 613-562-1202 *Fax:* 613-241-0019 *E-mail:* cpsa-acsp@cpsa-acsp.ca; cpsaprizes@cpsa-acsp.ca *Web Site:* www.cpsa-acsp.ca, pg 623

Debra Lemonds, PO Box 5516, Pasadena, CA 91117-0516 *Tel:* 626-844-9363 *E-mail:* dlemonds@zoho.com, pg 442

The Lentz Leadership Institute LLC, 540 Arlington Lane, Grayslake, IL 60030 *Tel:* 702-719-9214 *E-mail:* orders@lentzleadership.com *Web Site:* www.lentzleadership.com; www.refractivethinker.com; www.pensieropress.com; www.narratorepress.com, pg 115

John Leonard Prize, c/o Jacob M Appel, Icahn School of Medicine at Mount Sinai, One Gustave L Levy Place, New York, NY 10029 *E-mail:* info@bookcritics.org *Web Site:* www.bookcritics.org/awards/leonard-prize, pg 623

Leopold-Hidy Award, 2925 Academy Rd, Durham, NC 27705 *Tel:* 919-682-9319 *Fax:* 919-682-2349 *Web Site:* foresthistory.org/awards-fellowships/leopold-hidy-award, pg 623

Richard W Leopold Prize, 112 N Bryan Ave, Bloomington, IN 47408-4141 *Tel:* 812-855-7311 *E-mail:* oah@oah.org *Web Site:* www.oah.org/awards, pg 623

Lerner Publications, 241 First Ave N, Minneapolis, MN 55401 *Tel:* 612-332-3344 *Toll Free Tel:* 800-328-4929 *Fax:* 612-332-7615 *Toll Free Fax:* 800-332-1132 *E-mail:* info@lernerbooks.com; custserve@lernerbooks.com *Web Site:* www.lernerbooks.com; www.facebook.com/lernerbooks, pg 115

Lerner Publishing Group Inc, 241 First Ave N, Minneapolis, MN 55401 *Tel:* 612-332-3344 *Toll Free Tel:* 800-328-4929 *Fax:* 612-332-7615 *Toll Free Fax:* 800-332-1132 *E-mail:* info@lernerbooks.com; custserve@lernerbooks.com *Web Site:* www.lernerbooks.com; www.facebook.com/lernerbooks, pg 115

LernerClassroom, 241 First Ave N, Minneapolis, MN 55401 *Tel:* 612-332-3344 *Toll Free Tel:* 800-328-4929 *Fax:* 612-332-7615 *Toll Free Fax:* 800-332-1132 *E-mail:* info@lernerbooks.com; custserve@lernerbooks.com *Web Site:* www.lernerbooks.com; www.facebook.com/lernerbooks, pg 115

Fenia & Yaakov Leviant Memorial Prize in Yiddish Studies, 85 Broad St, New York, NY 10004 *Tel:* 646-576-5141; 646-576-5000 *E-mail:* awards@mla.org *Web Site:* www.mla.org, pg 623

Harry Levin Prize, 323 E Wacker Dr, No 642, Chicago, IL 60601 *Tel:* 312-600-8072 *E-mail:* info@acla.org *Web Site:* www.acla.org/prize-awards/harry-levin-prize, pg 623

Kay W Levin Award for Short Nonfiction, c/o 210 N Main St, No 204, Cedar Grove, WI 53013 *E-mail:* wiswriters@gmail.com *Web Site:* wiswriters.org/awards, pg 623

Levine|Greenberg|Rostan Literary Agency, 307 Seventh Ave, Suite 2407, New York, NY 10001 *Tel:* 212-337-0934 *Fax:* 212-337-0948 *E-mail:* submit@lgrliterary.com *Web Site:* lgrliterary.com, pg 467

Lawrence W Levine Award, 112 N Bryan Ave, Bloomington, IN 47408-4141 *Tel:* 812-855-7311 *E-mail:* oah@oah.org *Web Site:* www.oah.org/awards, pg 624

Levinson Prize, 61 W Superior St, Chicago, IL 60654 *Tel:* 312-787-7070 *Web Site:* www.poetryfoundation.org/poetrymagazine/prizes, pg 624

Levis Reading Prize, PO Box 842005, Richmond, VA 23284-2005 *Tel:* 804-828-1331 *E-mail:* levis@vcu.edu *Web Site:* english.vcu.edu/mfa/levis-reading-prize, pg 624

Levy Creative Management LLC, 425 E 58 St, Suite 37F, New York, NY 10022 *Tel:* 212-687-6463 *E-mail:* info@levycreative.com *Web Site:* www.levycreative.com, pg 485

Lewis Memorial Lifetime Achievement Award, 10015 Main St, Fairfax, VA 22031 *Tel:* 703-385-1335 *Toll Free Tel:* 888-385-3588 *Fax:* 703-273-0456 *E-mail:* assist@printing.org; info@printing.org *Web Site:* www.printing.org/programs/awards/lewis-memorial-lifetime-achievement-award, pg 624

Lexington Books, 4501 Forbes Blvd, Suite 200, Lanham, MD 20706 *Tel:* 301-459-3366 *Web Site:* rowman.com/page/lexington, pg 115

LexisNexis®, 230 Park Ave, Suite 7, New York, NY 10169 *Tel:* 212-309-8100 *Toll Free Fax:* 800-437-8674 *Web Site:* www.lexisnexis.com, pg 116

LexisNexis® Canada Inc, 111 Gordon Baker Rd, Suite 900, Toronto, ON M2H 3R1, Canada *Tel:* 905-479-2665 *Toll Free Tel:* 800-668-6481; 800-387-0899 (cust care); 800-255-5174 (sales) *E-mail:* service@lexisnexis.ca (cust serv); sales@lexisnexis.ca *Web Site:* www.lexisnexis.ca, pg 411

LexisNexis® Matthew Bender®, 701 E Water St, Charlottesville, VA 22902 *Tel:* 434-972-7600 *Toll Free Tel:* 800-223-1940 (sales) *Web Site:* www.lexisnexis.com; store.lexisnexis.com/categories/publishers/matthew-bender-850, pg 116

Liberty Fund Inc, 11301 N Meridian St, Carmel, IN 46032-4564 *Tel:* 317-842-0880 *Toll Free Tel:* 800-955-8335; 800-866-3520 *Fax:* 317-579-6060 (cust serv); 708-534-7803 *E-mail:* books@libertyfund.org; info@libertyfund.org *Web Site:* www.libertyfund.org, pg 116

Liberty Legacy Foundation Award, 112 N Bryan Ave, Bloomington, IN 47408-4141 *Tel:* 812-855-7311 *E-mail:* oah@oah.org *Web Site:* www.oah.org/awards, pg 624

Libraries Unlimited, 1385 Broadway, 5th fl, New York, NY 10018 *Tel:* 212-419-5300 *Web Site:* www.bloomsbury.com/us/, pg 116

Library Association of Alberta (LAA), c/o The Alberta Library, 7 Sir Winston Churchill Sq NW, No 623, Edmonton, AB T5J 2V5, Canada *E-mail:* info@laa.ca *Web Site:* www.laa.ca, pg 509

Library of America, 14 E 60 St, New York, NY 10022-1006 *Tel:* 212-308-3360 *Fax:* 212-750-8352 *E-mail:* info@loa.org *Web Site:* www.loa.org, pg 116

Library of American Broadcasting (LAB), University of Maryland, Hornbake Library, College Park, MD 20742 *Web Site:* exhibitions.lib.umd.edu/libraryofamericanbroadcasting, pg 509

The Library of Congress Center for the Book, The Library of Congress, 101 Independence Ave SE, Washington, DC 20540-4920 *Tel:* 202-707-5221 *Fax:* 202-707-0269 *E-mail:* cfbook@loc.gov *Web Site:* www.read.gov/cfb, pg 509

Library of Congress Literacy Awards, 101 Independence Ave SE, Washington, DC 20540-1400 *Tel:* 202-707-5221 (Center for the Book) *Fax:* 202-707-0269 *Web Site:* www.read.gov/literacyawards, pg 624

Library of Congress Prize for American Fiction, 101 Independence Ave SE, Washington, DC 20540-1400 *Tel:* 202-707-5221 (Center for the Book) *Fax:* 202-707-0269 *Web Site:* www.loc.gov, pg 624

Library of Virginia Literary Awards, 800 E Broad St, Richmond, VA 23219 *Tel:* 804-692-3535 *Web Site:* www.lva.virginia.gov/public/litawards/, pg 624

Lidec Inc, 800, blvd Industriel, bureau 202, St-Jean-sur-Richlieu, QC J3B 8G4, Canada *Tel:* 514-843-5991 *Toll Free Tel:* 800-350-5991 (CN only) *Fax:* 514-843-5252 *E-mail:* lidec@lidec.qc.ca *Web Site:* www.lidec.qc.ca, pg 411

Robert Lieberman Agency, 475 Nelson Rd, Ithaca, NY 14850 *Tel:* 607-273-8801 *Web Site:* roberthlieberman.com, pg 467

Mary Ann Liebert Inc, 140 Huguenot St, 3rd fl, New Rochelle, NY 10801-5215 *Tel:* 914-740-2100 *Toll Free Tel:* 800-654-3237 *Fax:* 914-740-2101 *E-mail:* info@liebertpub.com *Web Site:* www.liebertonline.com, pg 116

The Lieutenant-Governor's Awards for High Achievement in the Arts, 225 King St, Suite 201, Fredericton, NB E3B 1E1, Canada *Tel:* 506-444-4444 *Toll Free Tel:* 866-460-ARTS (460-2787) *Fax:* 506-444-5543 *E-mail:* prog@artsnb.ca *Web Site:* www.artsnb.ca, pg 624

Life Cycle Books, PO Box 799, Fort Collins, CO 80522 *Toll Free Tel:* 800-214-5849 *E-mail:* orders@lifecyclebooks.com *Web Site:* www.lifecyclebooks.com, pg 116

Life Cycle Books Ltd, 11 Progress Ave, Unit 6, Toronto, ON M1P 4S7, Canada *E-mail:* orders@lifecyclebooks.ca; billing@lifecyclebooks.ca; support@lifecyclebooks.ca *Web Site:* www.lifecyclebooks.com, pg 412

Light-Beams Publishing, 36 Blandings Way, Biddeford, ME 04005 *Tel:* 603-659-1300 *E-mail:* info@light-beams.com *Web Site:* www.light-beams.com, pg 116

Light Publications, 306 Thayer St, Suite 2462, Providence, RI 02906 *Tel:* 401-484-0228 *E-mail:* info@lightpublications.com; pr@lightpublications.com (media rel) *Web Site:* lightpublications.com, pg 116

Light Technology Publishing LLC, 4030 E Huntington Dr, Flagstaff, AZ 86004 *Tel:* 928-526-1345 *Toll Free Tel:* 800-450-0985 *Fax:* 928-714-1132 *E-mail:* publishing@lighttechnology.com *Web Site:* www.lighttechnology.com, pg 116

Lighthouse Poetry Series, Rhodes Tower, Rm 1841, 2121 Euclid Ave, Cleveland, OH 44115 *Tel:* 216-687-3986 *E-mail:* poetrycenter@csuohio.edu *Web Site:* www.csupoetrycenter.com/lighthouse-poetry-series; www.csupoetrycenter.com, pg 624

Liguori Publications, One Liguori Dr, Liguori, MO 63057-1000 *Tel:* 636-464-2500 *Toll Free Tel:* 800-325-9521 *Toll Free Fax:* 800-325-9526 (sales) *E-mail:* liguori@liguori.org (sales & cust serv) *Web Site:* www.liguori.org, pg 117

Ruth Lilly & Dorothy Sargent Rosenberg Poetry Fellowships, 61 W Superior St, Chicago, IL 60654 *Tel:* 312-787-7070 *Fax:* 312-787-6650 *E-mail:* info@poetryfoundation.org; media@poetryfoundation.org *Web Site:* www.poetryfoundation.org, pg 624

Ruth Lilly Poetry Prize, 61 W Superior St, Chicago, IL 60654 *Tel:* 312-787-7070 *Fax:* 312-787-6650 *E-mail:* editors@poetrymagazine.org *Web Site:* poetrymagazine.org, pg 625

Limelight Editions, 64 S Main St, Essex, CT 06426 *Tel:* 973-223-5039 *Web Site:* limelighteditions.com, pg 117

Abraham Lincoln Institute Book Award, c/o ALI Treasurer, 4158 Vernoy Hills Rd, Fairfax, VA 22030 *Web Site:* www.lincoln-institute.org, pg 625

Linden Publishing Co Inc, 2006 S Mary St, Fresno, CA 93721 *Tel:* 559-233-6633 *Toll Free Tel:* 800-345-4447 (orders) *Fax:* 559-233-6933 *Web Site:* lindenpub.com; quilldriverbooks.com, pg 117

Lindgren & Smith, 888C Eighth Ave, No 329, New York, NY 10019 *Tel:* 212-397-7330 *E-mail:* info@lindgrensmith.com; hello@lindgrensmith.com *Web Site:* lindgrensmith.com, pg 485

LinguaText LLC, 103 Walker Way, Newark, DE 19711 *Tel:* 302-453-8695 *E-mail:* text@linguatextbooks.com *Web Site:* www.linguatextbooks.com, pg 117

Linguistic Society of America (LSA), 522 21 St NW, Suite 120, Washington, DC 20006-5012 *Tel:* 202-835-1714 *Fax:* 202-835-1717 *E-mail:* lsa@lsadc.org; membership@lsadc.org *Web Site:* www.linguisticsociety.org, pg 509

Elliot Linzer, 126-10 Powells Cove Blvd, College Point, NY 11356 *Tel:* 718-353-1261 *E-mail:* elinzer@juno.com, pg 442

Joseph W Lippincott Award, 225 N Michigan Ave, Suite 1300, Chicago, IL 60601 *Tel:* 312-280-3247 *Toll Free Tel:* 800-545-2433 (ext 3247) *Fax:* 312-944-3897 *E-mail:* awards@ala.org *Web Site:* www.ala.org, pg 625

Lippincott Williams & Wilkins, 333 Seventh Ave, New York, NY 10001 *Toll Free Tel:* 800-933-6525 *E-mail:* orders@lww.com *Web Site:* www.lww.com, pg 117

Listen & Live Audio Inc, 803 13 St, Union City, NJ 07087 *Tel:* 201-558-9000 *Web Site:* www.listenandlive.com, pg 117

Literacy Texas, PO Box 111, Texarkana, TX 75504-0111 *Tel:* 903-392-9802 *E-mail:* info@literacytexas.org *Web Site:* literacytexas.org; www.facebook.com/LiteracyTX, pg 509

Literary & Creative Artists Inc, 3543 Albemarle St NW, Washington, DC 20008-4213 *Tel:* 202-362-4688 *Fax:* 202-362-8875 *E-mail:* lca9643@lcadc.com (queries, no attachments) *Web Site:* www.lcadc.com, pg 467

Literary Artists Representatives, 575 West End Ave, Suite GRC, New York, NY 10024-2711 *Tel:* 212-679-7788 *E-mail:* litartists@aol.com, pg 467

Literary Management Group LLC, 1020 San Antonio Lane, Lady Lake, FL 32159 *Tel:* 615-812-4445 *Web Site:* www.literarymanagementgroup.com, pg 467

The Literary Press Group of Canada, 234 Eglinton Ave E, Suite 401, Toronto, ON M4P 1K5, Canada *Tel:* 416-483-1321 *Fax:* 416-483-2510 *E-mail:* sales@lpg.ca *Web Site:* www.lpg.ca, pg 509

Literary Translators' Association of Canada, Concordia University, LB 601, 1455 De Maisonneuve W, Montreal, QC H3G 1M8, Canada *Tel:* 514-848-2424 (ext 8702) *E-mail:* info@attlc-ltac.org *Web Site:* www.attlc-ltac.org, pg 509

Literature Fellowship, 9543 W Emerald St, Suite 204, Boise, ID 83704 *Tel:* 208-334-2119 *E-mail:* info@arts.idaho.gov *Web Site:* arts.idaho.gov/grants/fellowships, pg 625

Literature for Children Awards, 81 Prince St, Charlottetown, PE C1A 4R3, Canada *E-mail:* peiliteraryawards@gmail.com *Web Site:* www.peiwritersguild.com, pg 625

little bee books, 598 Broadway, 7th fl, New York, NY 10012 *Tel:* 212-321-0237 *Toll Free Tel:* 844-321-0237 *E-mail:* info@littlebeebooks.com; sales@littlebeebooks.com; publicity@littlebeebooks.com *Web Site:* littlebeebooks.com, pg 117

Little, Brown and Company, 1290 Avenue of the Americas, New York, NY 10104 *Tel:* 212-364-1100 *Fax:* 212-364-0952 *E-mail:* firstname.lastname@hbgusa.com *Web Site:* www.hachettebookgroup.com/imprint/little-brown-and-company/, pg 118

Little, Brown Books for Young Readers (LBYR), 1290 Avenue of the Americas, New York, NY 10104 *Tel:* 212-364-1100 *Toll Free Tel:* 800-759-0190 (cust serv) *E-mail:* rights@lbchildrens.com *Web Site:* www.hachettebookgroup.com/imprint/little-brown-books-for-young-readers/, pg 118

Little Chicago Editorial Services, 154 Natural Tpke, Ripton, VT 05766 *Tel:* 802-388-9782 *Web Site:* andreachesman.com, pg 442

The Little Entrepreneur, c/o Harper Arrington Media, 33228 W 12 Mile Rd, Suite 105, Farmington Hills, MI 48334 *Toll Free Tel:* 888-435-9234 *Fax:* 248-281-0373 *E-mail:* support@digitalfashionpro.com, pg 118

Jean Little First Novel Award, 425 Adelaide St W, Suite 200, Toronto, ON M5V 3C1, Canada *Tel:* 416-975-0010 *E-mail:* info@bookcentre.ca *Web Site:* www.bookcentre.ca, pg 625

Littleton-Griswold Prize in American Law & Society, 400 "A" St SE, Washington, DC 20003 *Tel:* 202-544-2422 *E-mail:* awards@historians.org *Web Site:* www.historians.org/award-grant/littleton-griswold-prize/, pg 625

Littleton-Griswold Research Grant for Research in US Legal History, 400 "A" St SE, Washington, DC 20003 *Tel:* 202-544-2422 *E-mail:* awards@historians.org *Web Site:* www.historians.org/award-grant/littleton-griswold-research-grants-in-us-legal-history/, pg 625

Liturgical Press, PO Box 7500, St John's Abbey, Collegeville, MN 56321-7500 *Tel:* 320-363-2213 *Toll Free Tel:* 800-858-5450 *Fax:* 320-363-3299 *Toll Free Fax:* 800-445-5899 *E-mail:* sales@litpress.org *Web Site:* www.litpress.org, pg 118

Liturgy Training Publications, 3949 S Racine Ave, Chicago, IL 60609-2523 *Tel:* 773-579-4900 *Toll Free Tel:* 800-933-1800 (US & CN only orders) *Fax:* 773-579-4929 *E-mail:* orders@ltp.org *Web Site:* www.ltp.org, pg 119

Livestock Publications Council (LPC), 301 Main St, Courtland, KS 66939 *Tel:* 785-614-5371 *Web Site:* livestockpublications.com, pg 510

Living Language, c/o Penguin Random House LLC, 1745 Broadway, New York, NY 10019 *Tel:* 212-782-9000 *Toll Free Tel:* 800-733-3000 (orders) *E-mail:* support@livinglanguage.com *Web Site:* www.livinglanguage.com, pg 119

Living Now Book Awards, 1129 Woodmere Ave, Suite B, Traverse City, MI 49686 *Tel:* 231-933-0445 *Toll Free Tel:* 800-706-4636 *Fax:* 231-933-0448 *Web Site:* livingnowawards.com, pg 625

Living Stream Ministry (LSM), 2431 W La Palma Ave, Anaheim, CA 92801 *Tel:* 714-236-6050 *Toll Free Tel:* 800-549-5164 *Fax:* 714-236-6054 *E-mail:* books@lsm.org *Web Site:* www.lsm.org, pg 119

Livingston Press, University of West Alabama, Sta 22, Livingston, AL 35470 *Tel:* 205-652-3470 *Web Site:* livingstonpress.uwa.edu, pg 119

Livres Canada Books, One Nicholas, Suite 504, Ottawa, ON K1N 7B7, Canada *Tel:* 613-562-2324 *Fax:* 613-562-2329 *E-mail:* info@livrescanadabooks.com *Web Site:* www.livrescanadabooks.com, pg 510

Llewellyn Publications, 2143 Wooddale Dr, Woodbury, MN 55125 *Tel:* 651-291-1970 *Toll Free Tel:* 800-843-6666 *Fax:* 651-291-1908 *E-mail:* publicity@llewellyn.com; customerservice@llewellyn.com *Web Site:* www.llewellyn.com, pg 119

The Local History Co, 112 N Woodland Rd, Pittsburgh, PA 15232-2849 *Tel:* 412-362-2294 *Toll Free Tel:* 866-362-0789 (orders) *Fax:* 412-362-8192 *E-mail:* info@thelocalhistorycompany.com; sales@thelocalhistorycompany.com; editor@thelocalhistorycompany.com *Web Site:* www.thelocalhistorycompany.com, pg 119

The Lockman Foundation, 900 S Euclid St, Unit A, La Habra, CA 90631 *Tel:* 714-879-3055 *E-mail:* lockman@lockman.org *Web Site:* www.lockman.org, pg 119

Locks Art Publications/Locks Gallery, 600 Washington Sq S, Philadelphia, PA 19106 *Tel:* 215-629-1000 *E-mail:* info@locksgallery.com *Web Site:* locksgallery.com, pg 119

Sarah Lockwood Memorial, PO Box 36128, North Chesterfield, VA 23235-3533 *E-mail:* contest@poetrysocietyofvirginia.org; info@poetryvirginia.org *Web Site:* www.poetrysocietyofvirginia.org, pg 625

Locus Awards, 655 13 St, Suite 100, Oakland, CA 94612 *Tel:* 510-339-9196 *Fax:* 510-339-9198 *E-mail:* locus@locusmag.com *Web Site:* www.locusmag.com; lsff.net, pg 625

The Gerald Loeb Awards, Gold Hall, Suite B-307, 110 Westwood Plaza, Los Angeles, CA 90095-1481 *Tel:* 310-825-4478 *Fax:* 310-825-4479 *E-mail:* loeb@anderson.ucla.edu *Web Site:* www.anderson.ucla.edu/gerald-loeb-awards, pg 625

Loft-Mentor Series in Poetry & Creative Prose, Open Book Bldg, Suite 200, 1011 Washington Ave S, Minneapolis, MN 55415 *Tel:* 612-215-2575 *Fax:* 612-215-2576 *E-mail:* loft@loft.org *Web Site:* loft.org, pg 626

Loft Press Inc, 9293 Fort Valley Rd, Fort Valley, VA 22652 *Tel:* 540-933-6210 *Fax:* 540-933-6523 *E-mail:* Books@LoftPress.com *Web Site:* www.loftpress.com, pg 119

Logos Press, 3909 Witmer Rd, Suite 416, Niagara Falls, NY 14305 *Tel:* 815-346-3514 *E-mail:* info@logos-press.com *Web Site:* www.logos-press.com, pg 119

Lone Pine Publishing, 87 E Pender, Vancouver, BC V6A 1S9, Canada *Tel:* 780-433-9333 *Toll Free Tel:* 800-661-9017 *Fax:* 780-433-9646 *Toll Free Fax:* 800-424-7173 *E-mail:* info@lonepinepublishing.com *Web Site:* www.lonepinepublishing.com, pg 412

Lonely Planet Publications Inc, 124 Linden St, Oakland, CA 94607 *Tel:* 510-250-6400 *Toll Free Tel:* 800-275-8555 (orders) *E-mail:* info@lonelyplanet.com *Web Site:* www.lonelyplanet.com, pg 120

Long Poem Prize, University of Victoria, PO Box 1700, Sta CSC, Victoria, BC V8W 2Y2, Canada *Tel:* 250-721-8524 *E-mail:* malahat@uvic.ca *Web Site:* www.malahatreview.ca/contests/long_poem_prize/info.html; www.malahatreview.ca, pg 626

Long River Press, 360 Swift Ave, Suite 48, South San Francisco, CA 94080 *Tel:* 650-872-7718 (ext 312) *Fax:* 650-872-7808 *E-mail:* editor@sinomediausa.com, pg 120

Looseleaf Law Publications Inc, 43-08 162 St, Flushing, NY 11358 *Tel:* 718-359-5559 *Toll Free Tel:* 800-647-5547 *Fax:* 718-539-0941 *E-mail:* info@looseleaflaw.com *Web Site:* www.looseleaflaw.com, pg 120

Barry Lopez Nonfiction Award, PO Box 2414, Durango, CO 81302 *Tel:* 970-903-7914 *E-mail:* cutthroatmag@gmail.com *Web Site:* www.cutthroatmag.com, pg 626

Judy Lopez Memorial Award For Children's Literature, 1225 Selby Ave, Los Angeles, CA 90024 *Tel:* 310-474-9917 *Fax:* 310-474-6436 *Web Site:* www.wnba-books.org/la; www.judylopezbookaward.org, pg 626

The Audre Lorde Award for Lesbian Poetry, 511 Avenue of the Americas, No D36, New York, NY 10011 *E-mail:* awards@publishingtriangle.org; publishingtriangle.org; publishingtriangle.gmail.com *Web Site:* publishingtriangle.org/awards/audre-lorde-lesbian-poetry/, pg 626

The Audre Lorde Creative Writing Award, 511-512 Humanities Bldg, 1600 Holloway Ave, San Francisco, CA 94132 *Tel:* 415-338-2227 *Fax:* 415-338-0966 *E-mail:* poetry@sfsu.edu *Web Site:* poetry.sfsu.edu, pg 626

Lorenz Educational Press, 501 E Third St, Dayton, OH 45402 *Toll Free Tel:* 800-444-1144 *Fax:* 937-223-2042 *E-mail:* service@lorenz.com *Web Site:* www.lorenzeducationalpress.com, pg 120

James Lorimer & Co Ltd, Publishers, 117 Peter St, Suite 304, Toronto, ON M5V 0M3, Canada *Tel:* 416-362-4762 *Fax:* 416-362-3939 *E-mail:* sales@lorimer.ca; promotion@lorimer.ca; rights@lorimer.ca *Web Site:* www.lorimer.ca, pg 412

Los Angeles Times Book Prizes, 2300 E Imperial Hwy, El Segundo, CA 90245 *Tel:* 213-237-5775 *Toll Free Tel:* 800-528-4637 (ext 75775) *Web Site:* events.latimes.com/festivalofbooks, pg 626

Lost Classics Book Company LLC, 411 N Wales Dr, Lake Wales, FL 33853-3881 *Tel:* 863-632-1981 (edit off) *E-mail:* mgeditor@lostclassicsbooks.com *Web Site:* www.lostclassicsbooks.com, pg 120

Lost Horse Press, 1025 S Garry Rd, Liberty Lake, WA 99019 *Tel:* 208-597-3008 *Fax:* 208-255-1560 *E-mail:* losthorsepress@mindspring.com *Web Site:* www.losthorsepress.org, pg 120

Lost Lake Writers Retreat, 627 Lloyd Ave, Royal Oak, MI 48073 *Tel:* 248-589-3913 *E-mail:* info@springfed.org *Web Site:* www.springfed.org, pg 556

Lott Representatives Ltd, PO Box 3607, New York, NY 10163 *Tel:* 212-755-5737 *Web Site:* www.lottreps.com, pg 485

Lotus Press, 1100 E Lotus Dr, Silver Lake, WI 53170 *Tel:* 262-889-8561 *Toll Free Tel:* 800-824-6396 (orders) *Fax:* 262-889-2461; 262-889-8591 *E-mail:* lotuspress@lotuspress.com *Web Site:* www.lotuspress.com, pg 120

Louise Louis/Emily F Bourne Student Poetry Award, 119 Smith St, Brooklyn, NY 11201 *Tel:* 212-254-9628 *E-mail:* info@poetrysociety.org *Web Site:* poetrysociety.org/awards, pg 626

Louisiana State University Creative Writing Program MFA, English Dept, 260 Allen Hall, Baton Rouge, LA 70803 *Tel:* 225-578-4086 *Fax:* 225-578-4129 *E-mail:* lsucrwriting@lsu.edu *Web Site:* www.lsu.edu; lsu.edu/hss/english/creative_writing, pg 563

Louisiana State University Press, 338 Johnston Hall, Baton Rouge, LA 70803 *Tel:* 225-578-6294 *E-mail:* lsupress@lsu.edu *Web Site:* lsupress.org, pg 120

Louisiana Writer Award, 701 N Fourth St, Baton Rouge, LA 70802 *Tel:* 225-342-4913 *Fax:* 225-219-4804 *E-mail:* admin@state.lib.la.us *Web Site:* louisianabookfestival.org/louisiana_writer_award.html; www.state.lib.la.us/literacy-and-reading/louisiana-writer-award, pg 626

Louisville Grawemeyer Award in Religion, 1044 Alta Vista Rd, Louisville, KY 40205-1798 *Tel:* 502-895-3411 *Toll Free Tel:* 800-264-1839 *Fax:* 502-895-1096 *E-mail:* grawemeyer@lpts.edu *Web Site:* www.grawemeyer.org, pg 626

Love Inspired Books, 233 Broadway, Suite 1001, New York, NY 10279 *Tel:* 212-553-4200 *Toll Free Tel:* 888-432-4879 *Fax:* 212-227-8969 *E-mail:* customerservice@harlequin.ca *Web Site:* www.harlequin.com, pg 120

Loving Healing Press Inc, 5145 Pontiac Trail, Ann Arbor, MI 48105 *Tel:* 734-417-4266 *Toll Free Tel:* 888-761-6268 (US & CN) *Fax:* 734-663-6861 *E-mail:* info@lovinghealing.com; info@lhpress.com *Web Site:* www.lovinghealing.com; www.modernhistorypress.com (imprint), pg 121

Amy Lowell Prize, c/o Linda Haviland Conte, 18 Hall Ave, Apt 2, Somerville, MA 02144 *E-mail:* info@nepoetryclub.org *Web Site:* nepoetryclub.org, pg 627

James Russell Lowell Prize, 85 Broad St, New York, NY 10004 *Tel:* 646-576-5141; 646-576-5000 *E-mail:* awards@mla.org *Web Site:* www.mla.org, pg 627

Lowenstein Associates Inc, 115 E 23 St, 4th fl, New York, NY 10010 Tel: 212-206-1630 E-mail: assistant@bookhaven.com (queries, no attachments) Web Site: www.lowensteinassociates.com, pg 467

Pat Lowther Memorial Award, 2 Carlton St, Suite 1519, Toronto, ON M5B 1J3, Canada Tel: 416-504-1657 E-mail: info@poets.ca Web Site: poets.ca/awards/lowther, pg 627

Loyola Press, 8770 W Bryn Mawr Ave, Suite 1125, Chicago, IL 60631 Tel: 773-281-1818 Toll Free Tel: 800-621-1008 Fax: 773-281-0555 (cust serv); 773-281-4129 (edit) E-mail: customerservice@loyolapress.com Web Site: www.loyolapress.com, pg 121

LPD Press/Rio Grande Books, 925 Salamanca NW, Los Ranchos de Albuquerque, NM 87107-5647 Tel: 505-269-8324 Web Site: nmsantos.com, pg 121

LRP Publications, 360 Hiatt Dr, Palm Beach Gardens, FL 33418 Tel: 561-622-6520 Toll Free Tel: 800-341-7874 Fax: 561-622-2423 E-mail: custserve@lrp.com Web Site: www.lrp.com; www.shoplrp.com, pg 121

LRS, 6150 Little Willow Rd, Payette, ID 83661 Toll Free Tel: 800-255-5002 E-mail: largeprint@lrsbooks.com Web Site: www.lrsbooks.com, pg 121

Lucent Press, 2544 Clinton St, Buffalo, NY 14224 Toll Free Tel: 844-317-7404 Toll Free Fax: 844-317-7405 Web Site: greenhavenpublishing.com, pg 121

Jeremiah Ludington Award, 11 Main St, Suite D, Warrenton, VA 20186 Tel: 540-318-7770 Fax: 202-962-3939 E-mail: info@edupaperback.org; admin@edupaperback.org Web Site: www.edupaperback.org, pg 627

J Anthony Lukas Book Prize, 2950 Broadway, New York, NY 10027 Tel: 212-854-6468 E-mail: cjsprizes@gmail.com Web Site: www.journalism.columbia.edu, pg 627

J Anthony Lukas Work-in-Progress Award, 2950 Broadway, New York, NY 10027 Tel: 212-854-6468 E-mail: cjsprizes@gmail.com Web Site: www.journalism.columbia.edu, pg 627

Lumina Datamatics Inc, 600 Cordwainer Dr, Unit 103, Norwell, MA 02061 Tel: 508-746-0300 Fax: 508-746-3233 E-mail: marketing@luminad.com Web Site: luminadatamatics.com, pg 442

Luna Bisonte Prods, 137 Leland Ave, Columbus, OH 43214 Tel: 614-846-4126 Web Site: www.johnmbennett.net; www.lulu.com/spotlight/lunabisonteprods, pg 121

Lush Triumphant Literary Awards, PO Box 3008, MPO, Vancouver, BC V6B 3X5, Canada Tel: 604-876-8009 Fax: 604-879-2667 E-mail: subter@portal.ca Web Site: www.subterrain.ca, pg 627

Lutheran Braille Workers Inc, 13471 California St, Yucaipa, CA 92399 Tel: 909-795-8977 Toll Free Tel: 800-925-6092 E-mail: lbw@lbwloveworks.org Web Site: www.lbwloveworks.org, pg 121

Mark Lynton History Prize, 2950 Broadway, New York, NY 10027 Tel: 212-854-6468 E-mail: cjsprizes@gmail.com Web Site: www.journalism.columbia.edu, pg 627

Lynx House Press, 420 W 24 St, Spokane, WA 99203 Tel: 509-624-4894 E-mail: lynxhousepress@gmail.com Web Site: www.lynxhousepress.org, pg 121

Elizabeth Lyon, 1980 Cleveland St, Eugene, OR 97405 Tel: 541-357-4181 E-mail: elyon123@comcast.net Web Site: www.elizabethlyon.com, pg 442

Thomas J Lyon Book Award in Western American Literary and Cultural Studies, PO Box 6815, Logan, UT 84341 E-mail: wlaoperations@gmail.com Web Site: www.westernlit.org/thomas-j-lyon-book-award-in-western-american-literary-and-cultural-studies; www.westernlit.org, pg 627

The Lyons Press, 64 S Main St, Essex, CT 06426 Tel: 203-458-4500 E-mail: info@rowman.com Web Site: rowman.com/page/lyonspress, pg 121

Lyric Poetry Award, 119 Smith St, Brooklyn, NY 11201 Tel: 212-254-9628 E-mail: info@poetrysociety.org Web Site: poetrysociety.org/awards, pg 627

Lyric Poetry Prizes, PO Box 110, Jericho, VT 05465 E-mail: themuse@thelyricmagazine.com Web Site: thelyricmagazine.com, pg 627

Donald Maass Literary Agency, 1000 Dean St, Suite 331, Brooklyn, NY 11238 Tel: 212-727-8383 E-mail: info@maassagency.com Web Site: www.maassagency.com, pg 468

MacArthur Fellows Program, Office of Grants Management, 140 S Dearborn St, Chicago, IL 60603-5285 Tel: 312-726-8000 Fax: 312-920-6528 E-mail: 4answers@macfound.org Web Site: www.macfound.org/programs/fellows, pg 628

Macavity Award, 7155 Marlborough Terr, Berkeley, CA 94705 Tel: 510-845-3600 Web Site: www.mysteryreaders.org, pg 628

Gina Maccoby Literary Agency, PO Box 60, Chappaqua, NY 10514-0060 Tel: 914-238-5630 E-mail: query@maccobylit.com Web Site: www.publishersmarketplace.com/members/GinaMaccoby, pg 468

MacDowell Fellowships, 100 High St, Peterborough, NH 03458 Tel: 603-924-3886 E-mail: info@macdowell.org; admissions@macdowell.org Web Site: www.macdowell.org, pg 628

Machigonne Fiction Contest, PO Box 472, Brunswick, ME 04011 E-mail: info@newguardreview.com; editors@writershotel.com Web Site: www.newguardreview.com, pg 628

Macmillan, 120 Broadway, 22nd fl, New York, NY 10271 E-mail: press.inquiries@macmillan.com Web Site: us.macmillan.com, pg 121

Macmillan Audio, 120 Broadway, 22nd fl, New York, NY 10271 Tel: 646-600-7856 Toll Free Tel: 888-330-8477 (cust serv) Toll Free Fax: 800-672-7703 E-mail: macmillan.audio@macmillanusa.com Web Site: us.macmillan.com/audio, pg 123

Macmillan Booksellers Professional Development Scholarship, 3135 S State St, Suite 203, Ann Arbor, MI 48108 Toll Free Tel: 866-733-9064 E-mail: info@bincfoundation.org Web Site: www.bincfoundation.org/scholarship, pg 628

Macmillan Learning, One New York Plaza, Suite 46, New York, NY 10004 Tel: 212-576-9400 E-mail: salesoperations@macmillanusa.com Web Site: www.macmillanlearning.com/college/us, pg 123

Macmillan Reference USA™, 27500 Drake Rd, Farmington Hills, MI 48331-3535 Tel: 248-699-4253 Toll Free Tel: 800-877-4253 Toll Free Fax: 877-363-4253 E-mail: gale.customercare@cengage.com Web Site: www.gale.cengage.com/macmillan, pg 123

C B MacPherson Prize, 260 Dalhousie St, Suite 204, Ottawa, ON K1N 7E4, Canada Tel: 613-562-1202 Fax: 613-241-0019 E-mail: cpsa-acsp@cpsa-acsp.ca; cpsaprizes@cpsa-acsp.ca Web Site: www.cpsa-acsp.ca, pg 628

Madonna House Publications, 2888 Dafoe Rd, Combermere, ON K0J 1L0, Canada Tel: 613-756-3728 Toll Free Tel: 888-703-7110 Fax: 613-756-0103 E-mail: publications@madonnahouse.org Web Site: publications.madonnahouse.org; www.madonnahouse.org/publications, pg 412

Magazine Merit Awards, 6363 Wilshire Blvd, Suite 425, Los Angeles, CA 90048 Tel: 323-782-1010 E-mail: info@scbwi.org Web Site: www.scbwi.org/awards/magazine-merit-award, pg 628

Magazines Canada (MC), 555 Richmond St W, Suite 604, Mailbox 201, Toronto, ON M5V 3B1, Canada Tel: 416-994-6471 Toll Free Tel: 877-238-8354 Fax: 416-504-0437 E-mail: info@magazinescanada.ca Web Site: magazinescanada.ca, pg 510

Mage Publishers Inc, 5600 Wisconsin Ave, No 1408, Chevy Chase, MD 20815 Web Site: www.mage.com, pg 123

The Magni Co, 7106 Wellington Point Rd, McKinney, TX 75072 Tel: 972-540-2050 Fax: 972-540-1057 E-mail: sales@magnico.com; info@magnico.com Web Site: www.magnico.com, pg 123

Maharishi International University Press, MIU Press Marketing, MR 785, Fairfield, IA 52557 Tel: 641-472-1101 Toll Free Tel: 800-831-6523 E-mail: miupress@miu.edu Web Site: miupress.org, pg 123

Maine Literary Awards, Glickman Family Library, 314 Forest Ave, Rm 318, Portland, ME 04101 Tel: 207-228-8263 E-mail: info@mainewriters.org Web Site: www.mainewriters.org/programs/maine-literary-awards, pg 628

Maine Writers & Publishers Alliance (MWPA), Glickman Family Library, 314 Forest Ave, Rm 318, Portland, ME 04101 Tel: 207-228-8263 E-mail: info@mainewriters.org Web Site: www.mainewriters.org, pg 510

Maine Writers Conference at Ocean Park, 14 Temple Ave, Ocean Park, ME 04063 Tel: 401-598-1424 E-mail: www.opa@oceanpark.org Web Site: oceanpark.org, pg 556

Major Achievement Award, c/o 3225 N 91 St, Milwaukee, WI 53222 E-mail: wiswriters@gmail.com Web Site: wiswriters.org/awards, pg 628

J Russell Major Prize in French History, 400 "A" St SE, Washington, DC 20003 Tel: 202-544-2422 E-mail: awards@historians.org Web Site: www.historians.org/award-grant/j-russell-major-prize/, pg 628

Gene E & Adele R Malott Prize for Recording Community Activism, c/o Frederick M Shepherd, 3900 Seventh Ave S, Birmingham, AL 35222 Web Site: langumfoundation.org/about-prizes/recording-community-activism, pg 629

Management Advisory Services & Publications (MASP), PO Box 81151, Wellesley Hills, MA 02481-0001 Tel: 781-235-2895 Fax: 781-235-5446 E-mail: info@masp.com Web Site: www.masp.com, pg 123

Management Sciences for Health, 200 Rivers Edge Dr, Medford, MA 02155 Tel: 617-250-9500 Fax: 617-250-9090 E-mail: bookstore@msh.org Web Site: www.msh.org, pg 123

Mandala Earth, 800 "A" St, San Rafael, CA 94901 Tel: 415-526-1370 Toll Free Tel: 866-509-0515 E-mail: info@mandalapublishing.com Web Site: www.mandalaeartheditions.com, pg 124

Mandel Vilar Press, 19 Oxford Ct, Simsbury, CT 06070 Tel: 806-790-4731 E-mail: info@mvpress.org Web Site: www.mvpublishers.org, pg 124

Manhattanville College Master of Fine Arts in Creative Writing Program, 2900 Purchase St, Purchase, NY 10577 Web Site: www.mville.edu/programs/masters-creative-writing.php, pg 563

Manic D Press Inc, 250 Banks St, San Francisco, CA 94110 Tel: 415-648-8288 E-mail: info@manicdpress.com Web Site: www.manicdpress.com, pg 124

Manitoba Arts Council (MAC), 525-93 Lombard Ave, Winnipeg, MB R3B 3B1, Canada Tel: 204-945-2237 Toll Free Tel: 866-994-2787 Fax: 204-945-5925 Web Site: artscouncil.mb.ca, pg 510

The Manitoba Writers' Guild Inc (MWG), 218-100 Arthur St, Winnipeg, MB R3B 1H3, Canada Tel: 204-944-8013 E-mail: manitobawritersguild3@gmail.com Web Site: www.mbwriter.mb.ca, pg 510

Carol Mann Agency, 55 Fifth Ave, 18th fl, New York, NY 10003 Tel: 212-206-5635 Fax: 212-675-4809 E-mail: submissions@carolmannagency.com Web Site: www.carolmannagency.com, pg 468

Margaret Mann Citation, c/o The American Library Association, 225 N Michigan Ave, Suite 1300, Chicago, IL 60601 Tel: 312-944-6780 Toll Free Tel: 800-545-2433 Fax: 312-440-9374 E-mail: scholarships@ala.org Web Site: www.ala.org/core, pg 629

Phyllis Manner, 17 Springdale Rd, New Rochelle, NY 10804 Tel: 914-834-4707 Fax: 914-834-4707 E-mail: pmanner@aol.com; manneredit@gmail.com, pg 442

Manning Publications Co, 20 Baldwin Rd, PO Box 761, Shelter Island, NY 11964 Tel: 203-626-1510 E-mail: sales@manning.com; support@manning.com (cust serv) Web Site: www.manning.com, pg 124

ManuscriptCritique.com, PO Box 362, Clay, AL 35048 Web Site: manuscriptcritique.com, pg 442

Many Voices Fellowships & Mentorships, 2301 Franklin Ave E, Minneapolis, MN 55406-1099 Tel: 612-332-7481 Fax: 612-332-6037 E-mail: info@pwcenter.org Web Site: www.pwcenter.org, pg 629

MapEasy Inc, PO Box 80, Wainscott, NY 11975-0080 Tel: 631-537-6213 Fax: 631-537-4541 E-mail: info@mapeasy.com Web Site: www.mapeasy.com, pg 124

MAR*CO Products Inc, PO Box 686, Hatfield, PA 19440 Tel: 215-956-0313 Toll Free Tel: 800-448-2197 Fax: 215-956-9041 E-mail: help@marcoproducts.com; sales@marcoproducts.com Web Site: www.marcoproducts.com, pg 124

Marathon Press, 1500 Square Turn Blvd, Norfolk, NE 68701 Tel: 402-371-5040 Toll Free Tel: 800-228-0629 Fax: 402-371-9382 E-mail: info@marathonpress.net Web Site: www.marathonpress.com, pg 124

Denise Marcil Literary Agency LLC, 483 Westover Rd, Stamford, CT 06902 Tel: 203-327-9970 Fax: 203-327-9970 Web Site: www.marcilofarrellagency.com, pg 468

Danny Marcus Word Worker, 201 Captains Row, Apt 220, Chelsea, MA 02150 Tel: 781-290-9174 E-mail: emildanelle@yahoo.com, pg 442

Maren Green Publishing Inc, 7900 Excelsior Blvd, Suite 105K, Hopkins, MN 55343 Tel: 651-439-4500 Toll Free Tel: 800-287-1512 Fax: 651-439-4532 E-mail: info@marengreen.com Web Site: www.marengreen.com, pg 125

Marfield Prize, 2017 "I" St NW, Washington, DC 20006-1804 E-mail: award@artsclubofwashington.org Web Site: artsclubofwashington.org/awards, pg 629

Margins Fellowship, 112 W 27 St, Suite 600, New York, NY 10001 Tel: 212-494-0061 E-mail: fellowships@aaww.org Web Site: aaww.org/fellowships/margins, pg 629

Marick Press, 1342 Three Mile Dr, Grosse Pointe Park, MI 48230 Tel: 313-407-9236 E-mail: orders@marickpress.com; info@marickpress.com Web Site: www.marickpress.com, pg 125

Marine Education Textbooks, 124 N Van Ave, Houma, LA 70363-5895 Tel: 985-879-3866 Fax: 985-879-3911 E-mail: email@marineeducationtextbooks.com Web Site: www.marineeducationtextbooks.com, pg 125

Marine Techniques Publishing, 311 W River Rd, Augusta, ME 04330-3991 Tel: 207-622-7984 E-mail: promariner@roadrunner.com

Judith A Markowitz Award for Emerging LGBTQ Writers, PO Box 20186, New York, NY 10014 Tel: 213-277-5755 E-mail: awards@lambdaliterary.org; admin@lambdaliterary.org Web Site: www.lambdaliterary.org/awards/special-awards, pg 629

Markowski International Publishers, One Oakglade Circle, Hummelstown, PA 17036-9525 Tel: 717-566-0468 E-mail: info@possibilitypress.com Web Site: www.possibilitypress.com; www.aeronauticalpublishers.com, pg 125

Mildred Marmur Associates Ltd, 2005 Palmer Ave, PMB 127, Larchmont, NY 10538 Tel: 914-843-5582 Fax: 914-833-1175 E-mail: marmur@westnet.com, pg 468

Marquette University Press, 1415 W Wisconsin Ave, Milwaukee, WI 53233 Tel: 414-288-1564 Web Site: www.marquette.edu/mupress, pg 125

Marquis Who's Who, 350 RXR Plaza, Uniondale, NY 11556 Tel: 908-673-0100; 908-279-0100 Toll Free Tel: 844-394-6946 Fax: 908-356-0184 E-mail: info@marquisww.com; customerservice@marquisww.com (cust serv, sales) Web Site: marquiswhoswho.com, pg 125

Helen & Howard R Marraro Prize in Italian History, 400 "A" St SE, Washington, DC 20003 Tel: 202-544-2422 E-mail: awards@historians.org Web Site: www.historians.org/award-grant/helen-howard-r-marraro-prize/, pg 629

Howard R Marraro Prize, 85 Broad St, New York, NY 10004 Tel: 646-576-5141; 646-576-5000 E-mail: awards@mla.org Web Site: www.mla.org, pg 629

Marriage Transformation LLC, PO Box 249, Harrison, TN 37341 Tel: 423-599-0153 E-mail: staff@marriagetransformation.com Web Site: www.marriagetransformation.com; www.transformationlearningcenter.com, pg 125

Marsal Lyon Literary Agency LLC, 665 San Rodolfo Dr, Suite 124, PMB 121, Solana Beach, CA 92075 Tel: 760-814-8507 Web Site: www.marsallyonliteraryagency.com, pg 468

Marshall Cavendish Education, 99 White Plains Rd, Tarrytown, NY 10591-9001 Tel: 914-332-8888 Toll Free Tel: 800-821-9881 Fax: 914-332-1082 E-mail: mce@marshallcavendish.com; customerservice@marshallcavendish.com Web Site: www.mceducation.us, pg 125

The Evan Marshall Agency, One Pacio Ct, Roseland, NJ 07068-1121 Tel: 973-287-6216 Web Site: www.evanmarshallagency.com, pg 469

Lenore Marshall Poetry Prize, 75 Maiden Lane, Suite 901, New York, NY 10038 Tel: 212-274-0343 E-mail: awards@poets.org Web Site: poets.org/academy-american-poets/prizes/lenore-marshall-poetry-prize, pg 629

The Martell Agency, 1350 Avenue of the Americas, Suite 1205, New York, NY 10019 Tel: 212-317-2672 Web Site: www.themartellagency.com, pg 469

Martin Literary Management, 914 164 St SE, Suite B12, Box 307, Mill Creek, WA 98012 Tel: 206-466-1773 (no phone queries) Web Site: www.martinliterarymanagement.com, pg 469

Martindale LLC, 121 Chanlon Rd, Suite 110, New Providence, NJ 07974 Tel: 908-464-6800; 908-771-7777 (intl) Toll Free Tel: 800-526-4902 Fax: 908-771-8704 E-mail: info@martindale.com Web Site: www.martindale.com, pg 126

The Eliud Martinez Prize, 4178 Chestnut St, Riverside, CA 92501 E-mail: inlandia@inlandiainstitute.org Web Site: inlandinstitute.org/books/the-eliud-martinez-prize, pg 630

Maryland Center for History & Culture (MCHC), 610 Park Ave, Baltimore, MD 21201 Tel: 410-685-3750; 410-685-3750 ext 377 (orders) Fax: 410-385-2105 E-mail: shop@mdhistory.org Web Site: www.mdhistory.org; shop.mdhistory.org, pg 126

Maryland History Press, 6913 Seneca Dr, Snow Hill, MD 21863 Tel: 443-397-0912 Web Site: www.marylandhistorypress.com, pg 126

Mason Crest Publishers, 450 Parkway Dr, Suite D, Broomall, PA 19008 Tel: 610-543-6200 Toll Free Tel: 866-MCP-BOOK (627-2665) Fax: 610-543-3878 Web Site: www.masoncrest.com, pg 126

Massachusetts Book Awards, Old School Commons, No 302, 17 New South St, Northampton, MA 01060 Tel: 617-872-3718 E-mail: bookawards@massbook.org Web Site: www.massbook.org, pg 630

The Massachusetts Historical Society, 1154 Boylston St, Boston, MA 02215-3695 Tel: 617-536-1608 Fax: 617-859-0074 E-mail: publications@masshist.org Web Site: www.masshist.org, pg 126

Massie & McQuilkin, 27 W 20 St, Suite 305, New York, NY 10011 Tel: 212-352-2055 E-mail: info@mmqlit.com Web Site: www.mmqlit.com, pg 469

Master Books®, 3142 Hwy 103 N, Green Forest, AR 72638 Tel: 870-438-5288 Toll Free Tel: 800-999-3777 E-mail: sales@masterbooks.com; nlp@nlpg.com; submissions@newleafpress.net Web Site: www.masterbooks.com; www.nlpg.com, pg 126

Master Point Press, 214 Merton St, Suite 205, Toronto, ON M4S 1A6, Canada Tel: 647-956-4933 E-mail: info@masterpointpress.com Web Site: www.masterpointpress.com; www.ebooksbridge.com (ebook sales), pg 412

Mastery Education, 25 Philips Pkwy, Suite 105, Montvale, NJ 07645 Tel: 201-708-2349 Toll Free Tel: 800-822-1080 Fax: 201-712-0045 E-mail: cs@masteryeducation.com Web Site: masteryeducation.com; www.measuringuplive2.com, pg 126

Materials Research Society, 506 Keystone Dr, Warrendale, PA 15086-7537 Tel: 724-779-3003 Fax: 724-779-8313 E-mail: info@mrs.org Web Site: www.mrs.org, pg 126

Math Solutions®, One Harbor Dr, Suite 101, Sausalito, CA 94965 Toll Free Tel: 877-234-7323 Toll Free Fax: 800-724-4716 E-mail: info@mathsolutions.com; orders@mathsolutions.com Web Site: www.mathsolutions.com; store.mathsolutions.com, pg 127

Math Teachers Press Inc, 4850 Park Glen Rd, Minneapolis, MN 55416 Tel: 952-545-6535 Toll Free Tel: 800-852-2435 Fax: 952-546-7502 E-mail: info@movingwithmath.com Web Site: www.movingwithmath.com, pg 127

The Mathematical Association of America, 1529 18 St NW, Washington, DC 20036-1358 Tel: 202-387-5200 Toll Free Tel: 800-741-9415 Fax: 202-265-2384 E-mail: maahq@maa.org; advertising@maa.org (pubns) Web Site: www.maa.org, pg 127

Amy Mathers Teen Book Award, 425 Adelaide St W, Suite 200, Toronto, ON M5V 3C1, Canada Tel: 416-975-0010 E-mail: info@bookcentre.ca Web Site: www.bookcentre.ca, pg 630

Mathical Book Prize, 17 Gauss Way, Berkeley, CA 94720 Tel: 510-499-5181 E-mail: mathical@msri.org Web Site: www.mathicalbooks.org, pg 630

Matt Cohen Award: In Celebration of a Writing Life, 600-460 Richmond St W, Toronto, ON M5V 1Y1, Canada Tel: 416-504-8222 Toll Free Tel: 877-906-6548 Fax: 416-504-9090 E-mail: info@writerstrust.com Web Site: www.writerstrust.com, pg 630

Mawenzi House Publishers Ltd, 39 Woburn Ave (B), Toronto, ON M5W 1K5, Canada Tel: 416-483-7191 E-mail: info@mawenzihouse.com Web Site: www.mawenzihouse.com, pg 412

Peter Mayeux, 8148 Regent Dr, Lincoln, NE 68507-3366 Tel: 402-466-8547 E-mail: pm41923@windstream.net, pg 442

Mazda Publishers Inc, PO Box 2603, Costa Mesa, CA 92628 Tel: 714-751-5252 Fax: 714-751-4805 E-mail: mazdapub@aol.com Web Site: www.mazdapublishers.com, pg 127

Maxim Mazumdar New Play Competition, One Curtain Up Alley, Buffalo, NY 14202-1911 Tel: 716-852-2600 E-mail: newplays@alleyway.com; email@alleyway.com Web Site: www.alleyway.com/playwrights/maxim-mazumdar-new-play-competition, pg 630

MB Artists, 775 Sixth Ave, Suite 6, New York, NY 10001 Tel: 212-689-7830 Web Site: www.mbartists.com, pg 485

McBooks Press, 246 Goose Lane, Guildord, CT 06357 Tel: 203-458-4500 E-mail: info@rowman.com Web Site: www.mcbooks.com, pg 127

Margret McBride Literary Agency, PO Box 9128, La Jolla, CA 92038 Tel: 858-454-1550 E-mail: staff@mcbridelit.com Web Site: www.mcbrideliterary.com, pg 469

E J McCarthy Agency, 405 Maple St, Suite H, Mill Valley, CA 94941 Tel: 415-383-6639 E-mail: ejmagency@gmail.com Web Site: www.publishersmarketplace.com/members/ejmccarthy, pg 470

Mary McCarthy Prize in Short Fiction, 822 E Market St, Louisville, KY 40206 Tel: 502-458-4028 E-mail: info@sarabandebooks.org Web Site: www.sarabandebooks.org/mccarthy, pg 630

Gerard McCauley Agency Inc, PO Box 844, Katonah, NY 10536-0844 Tel: 914-232-5700, pg 470

COMPANY INDEX

McClelland & Stewart Ltd, 320 Front St W, Suite 1400, Toronto, ON M5V 3B6, Canada *Tel:* 416-364-4449 *Toll Free Tel:* 888-523-9292 *E-mail:* customerservicescanada@penguinrandomhouse.com; mcclellandsubmissions@prh.com *Web Site:* penguinrandomhouse.ca/imprints/mcclelland-stewart, pg 412

The McDonald & Woodward Publishing Co, 695 Tall Oaks Dr, Newark, OH 43055 *Tel:* 740-641-2691 *Toll Free Tel:* 800-233-8787 *Fax:* 740-641-2692 *E-mail:* mwpubco@mwpubco.com *Web Site:* www.mwpubco.com, pg 127

McFarland, 960 NC Hwy 88 W, Jefferson, NC 28640 *Tel:* 336-246-4460 *Toll Free Tel:* 800-253-2187 (orders) *Fax:* 336-246-5018; 336-246-4403 (orders) *E-mail:* info@mcfarlandpub.com *Web Site:* mcfarlandbooks.com, pg 127

McGill-Queen's University Press, 1010 Sherbrooke W, Suite 1720, Montreal, QC H3A 2R7, Canada *Tel:* 514-398-3750 *Fax:* 514-398-4333 *E-mail:* mqup@mcgill.ca *Web Site:* www.mqup.ca, pg 412

John H McGinnis Memorial Award, PO Box 750374, Dallas, TX 75275-0374 *Fax:* 214-768-1408 *E-mail:* swr@mail.smu.edu *Web Site:* southwestreview.com, pg 630

Harold W McGraw Jr Prize in Education, 3440 Market St, Suite 500, Philadelphia, PA 19104 *E-mail:* info@mcgrawprize.com *Web Site:* www.mcgrawprize.com, pg 630

McGraw-Hill Create, 2 Penn Plaza, New York, NY 10121 *Toll Free Tel:* 800-962-9342 *E-mail:* mhhe.create@mheducation.com *Web Site:* create.mheducation.com; shop.mheducation.com, pg 127

McGraw-Hill Education, 2 Penn Plaza, New York, NY 10121-2298 *Tel:* 212-904-2000 *E-mail:* international_cs@mheducation.com; seg_customerservice@mheducation.com (PreK-12); hep_customerservice@mheducation.com (higher education) *Web Site:* www.mheducation.com, pg 127

McGraw-Hill Higher Education, 1325 Avenue of the Americas, New York, NY 10019 *Toll Free Tel:* 800-338-3987 (cust serv) *Toll Free Fax:* 800-953-8691 (cust serv) *Web Site:* www.mheducation.com/highered, pg 128

McGraw-Hill Professional Publishing Group, 2 Penn Plaza, New York, NY 10121 *Tel:* 646-766-2000 *Web Site:* www.mhprofessional.com; www.mheducation.com, pg 128

McGraw-Hill Ryerson, 300 Water St, Whitby, ON L1N 9B6, Canada *Tel:* 905-430-5000 *Toll Free Tel:* 800-565-5758 (cust serv) *Fax:* 905-430-5020 *Toll Free Fax:* 800-463-5885 *Web Site:* www.mheducation.ca, pg 413

McGraw-Hill School Education Group, 8787 Orion Place, Columbus, OH 43240 *Tel:* 614-430-4000 *Toll Free Tel:* 800-848-1567 *Web Site:* www.mheducation.com, pg 128

William Holmes McGuffey Longevity Award, PO Box 367, Fountain City, WI 54629 *E-mail:* info@taaonline.net *Web Site:* www.taaonline.net/mcguffey-longevity-award, pg 630

McIntosh and Otis Inc, 235 Main St, Suite 318, White Plains, NY 10601 *Tel:* 212-687-7400 *Fax:* 212-687-6894 *E-mail:* info@mcintoshandotis.com *Web Site:* www.mcintoshandotis.com, pg 470

McKnight Artist Fellowship for Writers, Open Book Bldg, Suite 200, 1011 Washington Ave S, Minneapolis, MN 55415 *Tel:* 612-215-2575 *Fax:* 612-215-2576 *E-mail:* loft@loft.org *Web Site:* loft.org, pg 631

McKnight Fellowships in Playwriting, 2301 Franklin Ave E, Minneapolis, MN 55406-1099 *Tel:* 612-332-7481 *Fax:* 612-332-6037 *E-mail:* info@pwcenter.org *Web Site:* www.pwcenter.org, pg 631

McKnight National Residency & Commission, 2301 Franklin Ave E, Minneapolis, MN 55406-1099 *Tel:* 612-332-7481 *Fax:* 612-332-6037 *E-mail:* info@pwcenter.org *Web Site:* www.pwcenter.org, pg 631

Pamela Dittmer McKuen, 87 Tanglewood Dr, Glen Ellyn, IL 60137 *Tel:* 630-730-1340 *E-mail:* pmckuen@gmail.com *Web Site:* www.pamelamckuen.com; www.allthewriteplaces.com, pg 442

Phillip H McMath Post Publication Book Award, Dept of Writing, University of Central Arkansas, 201 Donaghey Ave, Thompson Hall 303, Conway, AR 72035 *Web Site:* arkansaswriters.wordpress.com, pg 631

John McMenemy Prize, 260 Dalhousie St, Suite 204, Ottawa, ON K1N 7E4, Canada *Tel:* 613-562-1202 *Fax:* 613-241-0019 *E-mail:* cpsaprizes@cpsa-acsp.ca; cpsa-acsp@cpsa-acsp.ca *Web Site:* www.cpsa-acsp.ca, pg 631

Pat McNees, 10643 Weymouth St, Suite 204, Bethesda, MD 20814 *Tel:* 301-897-8557 *E-mail:* patmcnees@gmail.com *Web Site:* www.patmcnees.com; www.writersandeditors.com, pg 442

McNeese State University MFA in Creative Writing Program, PO Box 92655, Lake Charles, LA 70609-0001 *Tel:* 337-475-5325; 337-475-5327 *Web Site:* www.mcneese.edu/academics/graduate/creative-writing, pg 563

McPherson & Co, 148 Smith Ave, Kingston, NY 12401 *Tel:* 845-331-5807 *E-mail:* bmcphersonco@gmail.com *Web Site:* www.mcphersonco.com, pg 128

McSweeney's Publishing, 849 Valencia St, San Francisco, CA 94110 *E-mail:* custserv@mcsweeneys.net *Web Site:* www.mcsweeneys.net, pg 128

MC2 Solutions LLC, 5101 Violet Lane, Madison, WI 53714, pg 442

me+mi publishing inc, 2600 Beverly Dr, Unit 113, Aurora, IL 60502 *Tel:* 630-588-9801 *Toll Free Tel:* 888-251-1444 *Web Site:* www.memima.com, pg 128

R S Means from The Gordian Group, 1099 Hingham St, Suite 201, Rockland, MA 02370 *Toll Free Tel:* 800-448-8182 (cust serv); 800-334-3509 (sales) *Toll Free Fax:* 800-632-6732 *Web Site:* www.rsmeans.com, pg 128

Medal for Distinguished Contribution to American Letters, 90 Broad St, Suite 604, New York, NY 10004 *Tel:* 212-685-0261 *Fax:* 212-213-6570 *E-mail:* nationalbook@nationalbook.org *Web Site:* www.nationalbook.org/amerletters.html, pg 631

Medal for Editorial Excellence, 15 Lafayette Ave, Brooklyn, NY 11217 *Tel:* 212-755-6710 *E-mail:* info@centerforfiction.org *Web Site:* www.centerforfiction.org/grants-awards/maxwell-e-perkins-award, pg 631

Medal of Honor for Literature, 15 Gramercy Park S, New York, NY 10003 *Tel:* 212-475-3424 *E-mail:* literary@thenationalartsclub.org *Web Site:* www.nationalartsclub.org, pg 631

Medals of America Press, 114 Southchase Blvd, Fountain Inn, SC 29644 *Toll Free Tel:* 800-605-4001 *Toll Free Fax:* 800-407-8640 *Web Site:* moapress.com, pg 128

Media Alliance, 2830 20 St, Suite 102, San Francisco, CA 94110 *Tel:* 415-746-9475 *E-mail:* information@media-alliance.org; info@media-alliance.org *Web Site:* www.media-alliance.org, pg 510

Media Coalition Inc, 19 Fulton St, Suite 407, New York, NY 10038 *Tel:* 212-587-4025 *E-mail:* info@mediacoalition.org *Web Site:* mediacoalition.org, pg 510

Medical Group Management Association (MGMA), 104 Inverness Terr E, Englewood, CO 80112-5306 *Tel:* 303-799-1111; 303-799-1111 (ext 1888, book orders) *Toll Free Tel:* 877-275-6462 *E-mail:* support@mgma.com; infocenter@mgma.com *Web Site:* www.mgma.com, pg 128

Medical Physics Publishing Corp (MPP), 4555 Helgesen Dr, Madison, WI 53718 *Tel:* 608-224-4508 (returns) *Toll Free Tel:* 800-442-5778 (cust serv) *Fax:* 608-224-5016 *E-mail:* mpp@medicalphysics.org *Web Site:* www.medicalphysics.org, pg 129

Medical Writing & Communication Conference, 9841 Washingtonian Blvd, Suite 500-26, Gaithersburg, MD 20878 *Tel:* 240-238-0940 *Fax:* 301-294-9006 *E-mail:* amwa@amwa.org; conference@amwa.org *Web Site:* www.amwa.org, pg 556

Medieval Academy Book Subvention Program, 6 Beacon St, Suite 500, Boston, MA 02108 *Tel:* 617-491-1622 *Fax:* 617-492-3303 *E-mail:* info@themedievalacademy.org *Web Site:* www.medievalacademy.org/page/maa_book_subvention, pg 631

Medieval Academy Inclusivity & Diversity Book Subvention Program, 6 Beacon St, Suite 500, Boston, MA 02108 *Tel:* 617-491-1622 *Fax:* 617-492-3303 *E-mail:* info@themedievalacademy.org *Web Site:* www.medievalacademy.org/page/inclusivitydiversitybooksubvention, pg 631

Medieval Academy of America Article Prize in Critical Race Studies, 6 Beacon St, Suite 500, Boston, MA 02108 *Tel:* 617-491-1622 *Fax:* 617-492-3303 *E-mail:* info@themedievalacademy.org *Web Site:* www.medievalacademy.org/page/racestudiesarticleprize, pg 631

Medieval Institute Publications (MIP), Western Michigan University, Walwood Hall, 1903 W Michigan Ave, Mail Stop 5432, Kalamazoo, MI 49008-5432 *Tel:* 269-387-8755 *Web Site:* wmich.edu/medievalpublications, pg 129

MedMaster Inc, 360 NE 191 St, Miami, FL 33179 *Tel:* 954-962-8414 *E-mail:* info@medmaster.net *Web Site:* www.medmaster.net, pg 129

Lucille Medwick Memorial Award, 119 Smith St, Brooklyn, NY 11201 *Tel:* 212-254-9628 *E-mail:* info@poetrysociety.org *Web Site:* poetrysociety.org/awards, pg 632

Sonny Mehta Fellowships in Creative Writing, 102 Dey House, 507 N Clinton St, Iowa City, IA 52242-1000 *Tel:* 319-335-0416 *Web Site:* writersworkshop.uiowa.edu/mehta, pg 632

Mel Bay Publications Inc, 16 N Gore Ave, Suite 203, Webster Groves, MO 63119-2315 *Tel:* 636-257-3970 *Toll Free Tel:* 800-863-5229 *E-mail:* email@melbay.com *Web Site:* www.melbay.com, pg 129

Frederic G Melcher Scholarship, 225 N Michigan Ave, Suite 1300, Chicago, IL 60601 *Tel:* 312-280-2163 *Toll Free Tel:* 800-545-2433 *Fax:* 312-280-5271 *E-mail:* alsc@ala.org *Web Site:* www.ala.org/alsc/awardsgrants/scholarships, pg 632

Melissa Turk & the Artist Network, 9 Babbling Brook Lane, Suffern, NY 10901 *Tel:* 845-368-8606 *E-mail:* melissa@melissaturk.com *Web Site:* www.melissaturk.com, pg 486

The Edwin Mellen Press, 450 Ridge St, Lewiston, NY 14092 *Tel:* 716-754-2266; 716-754-2788 (order fulfillment) *E-mail:* editor@mellenpress.com; librarian@mellenpress.com *Web Site:* www.mellenpress.com, pg 129

The Melville Society, Johns Hopkins University Press, 2715 N Charles St, Baltimore, MD 21218-4363 *Web Site:* melvillesociety.org, pg 510

Menasha Ridge Press, 2204 First Ave S, Suite 102, Birmingham, AL 35233 *Toll Free Tel:* 888-604-4537 *Fax:* 205-326-1012 *E-mail:* info@adventurewithkeen.com *Web Site:* www.menasharidge.com; www.adventurewithkeen.com, pg 129

Mendel Media Group LLC, PO Box 5032, East Hampton, NY 11937 *Tel:* 646-239-9896 *Web Site:* www.mendelmedia.com, pg 470

MennoMedia, 841 Mount Clinton Pike, Harrisonburg, VA 22802 *Toll Free Tel:* 800-245-7894 (orders & cust serv US) *Toll Free Fax:* 877-271-0760 *E-mail:* info@mennomedia.org *Web Site:* www.mennomedia.org, pg 129

Mercer University Press, 368 Orange St, Macon, GA 31201 *Tel:* 478-301-2880 *Toll Free Tel:* 866-895-1472 *Fax:* 478-301-2585 *E-mail:* mupressorders@mercer.edu *Web Site:* www.mupress.org, pg 129

Scott Meredith Literary Agency LP, 1035 Park Ave, Apt 3-A, New York, NY 10028 *Tel:* 917-685-1064 *E-mail:* info@scottmeredith.com *Web Site:* www.scottmeredith.com, pg 470

Louise Meriwether First Book Prize, 365 Fifth Ave, Suite 5406, New York, NY 10016 *Tel:* 212-817-7915 *E-mail:* louisemeriwetherprize@gmail.com; info@feministpress.org *Web Site:* www.feministpress.org/louise-meriwether-first-book-prize, pg 632

Meriwether Publishing, c/o Pioneer Drama Service, 109 Inverness Dr E, Suite H, Centennial, CO 80112 *Tel:* 303-779-4035 *Toll Free Tel:* 800-333-7262 *Fax:* 303-779-4315 *Web Site:* meriwetherpublishing.com; www.pioneerdrama.com, pg 129

Merriam-Webster Inc, 47 Federal St, Springfield, MA 01102 *Tel:* 413-734-3134 *Toll Free Tel:* 800-828-1880 (orders & cust serv) *Fax:* 413-731-5979 (sales) *E-mail:* support@merriam-webster.com *Web Site:* www.merriam-webster.com, pg 129

Joyce Meskis Excellence in Bookselling Scholarship, PO Box 746, Denver, CO 80201 *Toll Free Tel:* 800-752-0249 *E-mail:* info@mountainsplains.org *Web Site:* www.mountainsplains.org/meskis-scholarship, pg 632

Mesorah Publications Ltd, 313 Regina Ave, Rahway, NJ 07065 *Tel:* 718-921-9000 *Toll Free Tel:* 800-637-6724 *Fax:* 718-680-1875 *E-mail:* info@artscroll.com; orders@artscroll.com *Web Site:* www.artscroll.com, pg 130

Messianic Jewish Publishers, 6120 Day Long Lane, Clarksville, MD 21029 *Tel:* 410-531-6644; 616-970-2449 *Toll Free Tel:* 800-410-7367 (orders) *Fax:* 410-531-9440; 717-761-7273 (orders) *Toll Free Fax:* 800-327-0048 (orders) *E-mail:* editor@messianicjewish.net; customerservice@messianicjewish.net *Web Site:* messianicjewish.net/publish, pg 130

Metamorphosis Literary Agency, 12410 S Acuff Ct, Olathe, KS 66062 *Tel:* 646-397-1640 *E-mail:* info@metamorphosisliteraryagency.com *Web Site:* www.metamorphosisliteraryagency.com, pg 470

Addison M Metcalf Award in Literature, 633 W 155 St, New York, NY 10032 *Tel:* 212-368-5900 *E-mail:* academy@artsandletters.org *Web Site:* artsandletters.org/awards, pg 632

Metropolitan Classics, 26 Arthur Place, Yonkers, NY 10701 *Tel:* 914-375-6448 *Web Site:* www.fortrossinc.com, pg 130

The Metropolitan Museum of Art, 1000 Fifth Ave, New York, NY 10028 *Tel:* 212-535-7710 *E-mail:* editorial@metmuseum.org *Web Site:* www.metmuseum.org, pg 130

Edna Meudt Poetry Book Award, c/o 210 N Main St, No 204, Cedar Grove, WI 53013 *E-mail:* wiswriters@gmail.com *Web Site:* wiswriters.org/awards, pg 632

MFA Publications, 465 Huntington Ave, Boston, MA 02115 *Tel:* 617-369-4233 *E-mail:* publications@mfa.org *Web Site:* www.mfa.org/publications, pg 130

Michelin Maps & Guides, One Parkway S, Greenville, SC 29615-5022 *E-mail:* michelin.guides@michelin.com *Web Site:* guide.michelin.com; michelinmedia.com, pg 130

Michener Center for Writers Fellowship, 702 E Dean Keeton St, Austin, TX 78705 *Tel:* 512-471-1601 *E-mail:* mcw@utexas.edu *Web Site:* michener.utexas.edu, pg 632

Michigan Library Association (MLA), 3410 Belle Chase Way, Lansing, MI 48911 *Tel:* 517-394-2774 *E-mail:* mla@milibraries.org *Web Site:* www.milibraries.org, pg 510

Michigan State University Press (MSU Press), Manly Miles Bldg, Suite 25, 1405 S Harrison Rd, East Lansing, MI 48823-5245 *Tel:* 517-355-9543 *Fax:* 517-432-2611 *Web Site:* msupress.org, pg 130

Susan T Middleton, 366A Norton Hill Rd, Ashfield, MA 01330-9601 *Tel:* 413-628-4039 *E-mail:* smiddle23@icloud.com, pg 442

Midnight Marquee Press Inc, 9721 Britinay Lane, Baltimore, MD 21234 *Tel:* 410-665-1198 *E-mail:* mmarquee@aol.com *Web Site:* www.midmar.com, pg 130

Midwest Bookseller of the Year Award, 939 W Seventh St, St Paul, MN 55102 *Tel:* 612-208-6279 *Web Site:* www.midwestbooksellers.org/bookseller-of-the-year.html, pg 632

Midwest Independent Booksellers Association (MIBA), 939 W Seventh St, St Paul, MN 55102 *Tel:* 612-208-6279 *Web Site:* www.midwestbooksellers.org, pg 510

Midwest Travel Journalists Association Inc (MTJA), PO Box 185, Jessup, IA 50648 *Tel:* 319-529-1109 *E-mail:* admin@mtja.us *Web Site:* www.mtja.us, pg 511

Mighty Media Press, 1201 Currie Ave, Minneapolis, MN 55403 *Tel:* 612-455-0252; 612-399-1969 *Fax:* 612-338-4817 *E-mail:* info@mightymedia.com *Web Site:* www.mightymediapress.com, pg 131

Mike Murach & Associates Inc, 3730 W Swift, Fresno, CA 93722 *Tel:* 559-440-9071 *Toll Free Tel:* 800-221-5528 *Fax:* 559-440-0963 *E-mail:* murachbooks@murach.com *Web Site:* www.murach.com, pg 131

Milady, 5191 Natorp Blvd, Mason, OH 45040 *Toll Free Tel:* 866-848-5143 *Fax:* 518-373-6309 *E-mail:* info@milady.com *Web Site:* www.milady.com, pg 131

Kenneth W Mildenberger Prize, 85 Broad St, New York, NY 10004 *Tel:* 646-576-5141; 646-576-5000 *E-mail:* awards@mla.org *Web Site:* www.mla.org, pg 632

Milford Books™, 243 W Lafayette St, Milford, MI 48381 *Tel:* 734-255-9530 *E-mail:* eic@milfordbooks.com *Web Site:* milfordbooks.com, pg 131

Military Info Publishing, PO Box 41211, Plymouth, MN 55442 *Tel:* 763-533-8627 *E-mail:* publisher@military-info.com *Web Site:* www.military-info.com, pg 131

Military Living Publications, 333 Maple Ave E, Suite 3130, Vienna, VA 22180-4717 *Tel:* 703-237-0203 *Fax:* 703-552-8855 *E-mail:* customerservice@militaryliving.com; sales@militaryliving.com; editor@militaryliving.com *Web Site:* www.militaryliving.com, pg 131

Milkweed Editions, 1011 Washington Ave S, Suite 300, Minneapolis, MN 55415-1246 *Tel:* 612-332-3192 *Toll Free Tel:* 800-520-6455 *E-mail:* orders@milkweed.org *Web Site:* milkweed.org, pg 131

Milkweed Fellowship, 1011 Washington Ave S, Suite 300, Minneapolis, MN 55415-1246 *Tel:* 612-332-3192 *Toll Free Tel:* 800-520-6455 *E-mail:* fellowship@milkweed.org *Web Site:* milkweed.org/milkweed-fellowship, pg 632

Millay Colony for the Arts Residency, 454 E Hill Rd, Austerlitz, NY 12017 *Tel:* 518-392-3103 *E-mail:* apply@millaycolony.org; residency@millaycolony.org *Web Site:* www.millaycolony.org, pg 633

Millbrook Press, 241 First Ave N, Minneapolis, MN 55401 *Tel:* 612-332-3344 *Toll Free Tel:* 800-328-4929 *Fax:* 612-332-7615 *Toll Free Fax:* 800-332-1132 *E-mail:* info@lernerbooks.com; custserve@lernerbooks.com *Web Site:* www.lernerbooks.com; www.facebook.com/millbrookpress, pg 131

Patricia Cleary Miller Award for Poetry, UMKC, University House, 5101 Rockhill Rd, Kansas City, MO 64110-2499 *Tel:* 816-235-1169 *E-mail:* newletters@umkc.edu *Web Site:* www.newletters.org, pg 633

Richard K Miller Associates, 2413 Main St, Suite 331, Miramar, FL 33025 *Tel:* 404-276-3376 *Fax:* 404-581-5335 *Web Site:* rkma.com, pg 132

Stephen M Miller Inc, 15727 S Madison Dr, Olathe, KS 66062 *Tel:* 913-945-0200 *Web Site:* www.stephenmillerbooks.com, pg 442

Milliken Publishing Co, 501 E Third St, Dayton, OH 45402 *Toll Free Tel:* 800-444-1144 *Fax:* 937-223-2042 *E-mail:* service@lorenz.com *Web Site:* www.lorenzeducationalpress.com, pg 132

Kathleen Mills Editorial Services, 327 E King St, Chardon, OH 44024 *Tel:* 440-285-4347 *E-mail:* mills_edit@yahoo.com, pg 442

Milner Award, One Margaret Mitchell Sq NW, Atlanta, GA 30303 *Tel:* 404-730-1865 *E-mail:* info@themilneraward.org *Web Site:* www.themilneraward.org, pg 633

The Minerals, Metals & Materials Society (TMS), 5700 Corporate Dr, Suite 750, Pittsburgh, PA 15237 *Tel:* 724-776-9000 *Toll Free Tel:* 800-759-4867 *Fax:* 724-776-3770 *E-mail:* publications@tms.org (orders) *Web Site:* www.tms.org/bookstore (orders); www.tms.org, pg 132

Miniature Book Society Inc, 518 High St, Fall River, MA 02720 *Web Site:* www.mbs.org, pg 511

Minnesota Book Awards, 1080 Montreal Ave, Suite 2, St Paul, MN 55116 *Tel:* 651-222-3242 *Fax:* 651-222-1988 *E-mail:* friends@thefriends.org *Web Site:* thefriends.org/events/mnba, pg 633

Minnesota Historical Society Press, 345 Kellogg Blvd W, St Paul, MN 55102-1906 *Tel:* 651-259-3205 *Fax:* 651-297-1345 *E-mail:* info-mnhspress@mnhs.org *Web Site:* www.mnhs.org/mnhspress, pg 132

Minotaur Books/Mystery Writers of America First Crime Novel Competition, 1140 Broadway, Suite 1507, New York, NY 10001 *Tel:* 212-888-8171 *E-mail:* mwa@mysterywriters.org *Web Site:* mysterywriters.org/about-mwa/st-martins; us.macmillan.com/minotaurbooks/submit-manuscript, pg 633

The Miranda Family Voces Latinx National Playwriting Competition, 138 E 27 St, New York, NY 10016 *Tel:* 212-225-9950 *Fax:* 212-225-9085 *Web Site:* www.repertorio.org, pg 633

Mirrors & Windows Fellowship, Open Book Bldg, Suite 200, 1011 Washington Ave S, Minneapolis, MN 55415 *Tel:* 612-215-2575 *Fax:* 612-215-2576 *E-mail:* loft@loft.org *Web Site:* loft.org/awards/mirrors-windows, pg 633

Mississippi Review Prize, 118 College Dr, Box 5144, Hattiesburg, MS 39406-0001 *Tel:* 601-266-4321 *E-mail:* msreview@usm.edu *Web Site:* www.usm.edu/mississippi-review/contest.html, pg 633

Mississippi Review/University of Southern Mississippi, Center for Writers, 118 College Dr 5144, Hattiesburg, MS 39406-1000 *Tel:* 601-266-1000 *Web Site:* www.usm.edu/humanities/center-writers.php; sites.usm.edu/mississippi-review/index.html, pg 563

MIT List Visual Arts Center, MIT E 15-109, 20 Ames St, Cambridge, MA 02139 *Tel:* 617-253-4680 *E-mail:* listinfo@mit.edu *Web Site:* listart.mit.edu, pg 132

The MIT Press, One Broadway, 12th fl, Cambridge, MA 02142 *Tel:* 617-253-5255 *Toll Free Tel:* 800-405-1619 (orders) *Fax:* 617-258-6779; 617-577-1545 (orders) *Web Site:* mitpress.mit.edu, pg 132

H L Mitchell Award, University of Georgia, Dept of History, Athens, GA 30602-1602 *Tel:* 706-542-8848 *Web Site:* thesha.org/mitchell, pg 633

Mitchell Lane Publishers Inc, 2001 SW 31 Ave, Hallandale, FL 33009 *Tel:* 954-985-9400 *Toll Free Tel:* 800-223-3251 *Fax:* 954-987-2200 *E-mail:* customerservice@mitchelllane.com *Web Site:* www.mitchelllane.com, pg 133

Lindsley & Masao Miyoshi Translation Prizes & Grants, Columbia University, 507 Kent Hall, MC3920, New York, NY 10027 *Tel:* 212-854-5036 *Fax:* 212-854-4019 *E-mail:* donald-keene-center@columbia.edu *Web Site:* www.keenecenter.org, pg 633

MLA Prize for a First Book, 85 Broad St, New York, NY 10004 *Tel:* 646-576-5141; 646-576-5000 *E-mail:* awards@mla.org *Web Site:* www.mla.org, pg 634

MLA Prize for a Scholarly Edition, 85 Broad St, New York, NY 10004 *Tel:* 646-576-5141; 646-576-5000 *E-mail:* awards@mla.org *Web Site:* www.mla.org, pg 634

COMPANY INDEX

MLA Prize for an Edited Collection, 85 Broad St, New York, NY 10004 *Tel:* 646-576-5141; 646-576-5000 *E-mail:* awards@mla.org *Web Site:* www.mla.org, pg 634

MLA Prize for Bibliographical or Archival Scholarship, 85 Broad St, New York, NY 10004 *Tel:* 646-576-5141; 646-576-5000 *E-mail:* awards@mla.org *Web Site:* www.mla.org, pg 634

MLA Prize for Independent Scholars, 85 Broad St, New York, NY 10004 *Tel:* 646-576-5141; 646-576-5000 *E-mail:* awards@mla.org *Web Site:* www.mla.org, pg 634

MLA Prize for Studies in Native American Literatures, Cultures & Languages, 85 Broad St, New York, NY 10004 *Tel:* 646-576-5141; 646-576-5000 *E-mail:* awards@mla.org *Web Site:* www.mla.org, pg 634

MLA Prize in United States Latina & Latino & Chicana & Chicano Literary & Cultural Studies, 85 Broad St, New York, NY 10004 *Tel:* 646-576-5141; 646-576-5000 *E-mail:* awards@mla.org *Web Site:* www.mla.org, pg 634

Sondra Mochson, 18 Overlook Dr, Port Washington, NY 11050 *Tel:* 516-883-0961, pg 443

Modern Language Association (MLA), 85 Broad St, New York, NY 10004 *Tel:* 646-576-5000 *E-mail:* help@mla.org *Web Site:* www.mla.org; x.com/MLAnews; www.facebook.com/modernlanguageassociation; www.linkedin.com/company/modern-language-association, pg 133

Modern Language Association (MLA), 85 Broad St, New York, NY 10004 *Tel:* 646-576-5000 *E-mail:* help@mla.org; membership@mla.org *Web Site:* www.mla.org; x.com/MLAnews; www.facebook.com/modernlanguageassociation; www.linkedin.com/company/modern-language-association, pg 511

Modern Memoirs Inc, 417 West St, Suite 104, Amherst, MA 01002 *Tel:* 413-253-2353 *Web Site:* www.modernmemoirs.com, pg 133

Modus Vivendi Publishing Inc, 55, rue Jean-Talon Ouest, Montreal, QC H2R 2W8, Canada *Tel:* 514-272-0433 *Fax:* 514-272-7234 *E-mail:* info@groupemodus.com *Web Site:* www.groupemodus.com, pg 413

Henry Allen Moe Prize, 5798 State Hwy 80, Cooperstown, NY 13326 *Tel:* 607-547-2586 *E-mail:* publications@fenimoreart.org *Web Site:* www.fenimoreartmuseum.org/publication-awards, pg 634

The Monacelli Press, 65 Bleecker St, 8th fl, New York, NY 10012 *Tel:* 212-652-5400 *E-mail:* contact@monacellipress.com *Web Site:* www.phaidon.com/monacelli, pg 133

Mondial, 203 W 107 St, Suite 6-C, New York, NY 10025 *Tel:* 646-807-8031 *Fax:* 208-361-2863 *E-mail:* contact@mondialbooks.com *Web Site:* www.mondialbooks.com, pg 133

The Mongolia Society Inc, Indiana University, 703 Eigenmann Hall, 1900 E Tenth St, Bloomington, IN 47406-7512 *Tel:* 812-855-4078 *Fax:* 812-855-4078 *E-mail:* monsoc@indiana.edu *Web Site:* mongoliasociety.org, pg 133

Monkfish Book Publishing Co, 22 E Market St, Suite 304, Rhinebeck, NY 12572 *Tel:* 845-876-4861 *Web Site:* www.monkfishpublishing.com, pg 133

Montana Book Award, PO Box 8732, Missoula, MT 59802-8732 *E-mail:* montanabookaward@gmail.com *Web Site:* montanabookaward.org, pg 634

Montemayor Press, 663 Hyland Hill Rd, Washington, VT 05675 *Tel:* 802-552-0750 *E-mail:* mail@montemayorpress.com *Web Site:* www.montemayorpress.com, pg 133

David Montgomery Award, 112 N Bryan Ave, Bloomington, IN 47408-4141 *Tel:* 812-855-7311 *E-mail:* oah@oah.org *Web Site:* www.oah.org/awards, pg 634

Monthly Review Press, 134 W 29 St, Suite 706, New York, NY 10001 *Tel:* 212-691-2555 *E-mail:* social@monthlyreview.org *Web Site:* monthlyreview.org, pg 134

Moody Publishers, 820 N La Salle Blvd, Chicago, IL 60610 *Tel:* 312-329-2101 *Toll Free Tel:* 800-678-8812 *Fax:* 312-329-2144 *Toll Free Fax:* 800-678-3329 *E-mail:* mpcustomerservice@moody.edu; mporders@moody.edu; publicity@moody.edu *Web Site:* www.moodypublishers.com, pg 134

Cenie H Moon Prize, PO Box 36128, North Chesterfield, VA 23235-3533 *E-mail:* contest@poetrysocietyofvirginia.org *Web Site:* www.poetrysocietyofvirginia.org, pg 635

Moonbeam Children's Book Awards, 1129 Woodmere Ave, Suite B, Traverse City, MI 49686 *Tel:* 231-933-0445 *Toll Free Tel:* 800-706-4636 *Fax:* 231-933-0448 *E-mail:* moonbeam@jgibookawards.com *Web Site:* moonbeamawards.com, pg 635

Moonshine Cove Publishing LLC, 150 Willow Point, Abbeville, SC 29620 *E-mail:* publisher@moonshinecovepublishing.com *Web Site:* moonshinecovepublishing.com, pg 134

Jenny McKean Moore Writer-in-Washington, English Dept, Rome Hall, 801 22 St NW, Suite 643, Washington, DC 20052 *Tel:* 202-994-6180 *E-mail:* engldept@gwu.edu *Web Site:* english.columbian.gwu.edu, pg 635

Moose Hide Books, 684 Walls Rd, Prince Township, ON P6A 6K4, Canada *Tel:* 705-779-3331 *Fax:* 705-779-3331 *E-mail:* mooseenterprises@on.aibn.com *Web Site:* www.moosehidebooks.com, pg 413

Morehouse Publishing, 19 E 34 St, New York, NY 10016 *Tel:* 212-592-1800 *Toll Free Tel:* 800-242-1918 (retail orders only) *E-mail:* churchpublishingorders@pbd.com *Web Site:* www.churchpublishing.org, pg 134

Morgan Gaynin, 41 N Main St, Norwalk, CT 06854 *Tel:* 212-475-0440 *E-mail:* info@morgangaynin.com *Web Site:* www.morgangaynin.com, pg 486

Morgan James Publishing, 5 Penn Plaza, 23rd fl, New York, NY 10001 *Tel:* 212-655-5470 *Fax:* 516-908-4496 *E-mail:* support@morganjamespublishing.com *Web Site:* www.morganjamespublishing.com, pg 134

Morgan Kaufmann, 50 & 60 Hampshire St, 5th fl, Cambridge, MA 02139 *Web Site:* www.elsevier.com/books-and-journals/morgan-kaufmann, pg 134

Howard Morhaim Literary Agency Inc, 30 Pierrepont St, Brooklyn, NY 11201-3371 *Tel:* 718-222-8400 *E-mail:* info@morhaimliterary.com *Web Site:* www.morhaimliterary.com, pg 470

Moriah Books, PO Box 1094, Casper, WY 82602 *Web Site:* moriahbook.com, pg 134

Morning Sun Books Inc, 1200 County Rd 523, Flemington, NJ 08822 *Tel:* 908-806-6216 *Fax:* 908-237-2407 *E-mail:* sales@morningsunbooks.com *Web Site:* morningsunbooks.com, pg 134

The William C Morris YA Debut Award, 225 N Michigan Ave, Suite 1300, Chicago, IL 60601 *Tel:* 312-280-4390 *Toll Free Tel:* 800-545-2433 (ext 4390) *Fax:* 312-280-5276 *E-mail:* yalsa@ala.org *Web Site:* www.ala.org/yalsa/morris, pg 635

Willie Morris Awards for Southern Writing, Dept of Writing & Rhetoric, PO Box 1848, University, MS 38677 *E-mail:* wmawards@olemiss.edu *Web Site:* www.williemorrisawards.org; www.williemorrisawards.org/submissions, pg 635

The Toni Morrison Achievement Award, c/o Jacob M Appel, Icahn School of Medicine at Mount Sinai, One Gustave L Levy Place, New York, NY 10029 *E-mail:* info@bookcritics.org *Web Site:* www.bookcritics.org/the-toni-morrison-achievement-award, pg 635

Harold Morton Landon Translation Award, 75 Maiden Lane, Ste 901, New York, NY 10038 *Tel:* 212-274-0343 *E-mail:* awards@poets.org *Web Site:* poets.org/academy-american-poets/prizes/harold-morton-landon-translation-award, pg 635

Kathryn A Morton Prize in Poetry, 822 E Market St, Louisville, KY 40206 *Tel:* 502-458-4028 *E-mail:* info@sarabandebooks.org *Web Site:* www.sarabandebooks.org/morton, pg 635

Morton Publishing Co, 925 W Kenyon Ave, Unit 12, Englewood, CO 80110 *Tel:* 303-761-4805 *Fax:* 303-762-9923 *E-mail:* contact@morton-pub.com; returns@morton-pub.com *Web Site:* www.morton-pub.com, pg 134

Mosaic Press, 1252 Speers Rd, Units 1 & 2, Oakville, ON L6L 5N9, Canada *Tel:* 905-825-2130 *Fax:* 905-825-2130 *E-mail:* info@mosaic-press.com *Web Site:* www.mosaic-press.com, pg 413

George L Mosse Prize in European Intellectual & Cultural History, 400 "A" St SE, Washington, DC 20003 *Tel:* 202-544-2422 *E-mail:* awards@historians.org *Web Site:* www.historians.org/award-grant/george-l-mosse-prize/, pg 635

Most Promising New Textbook Award, PO Box 367, Fountain City, WI 54629 *E-mail:* info@taaonline.net *Web Site:* www.taaonline.net/promising-new-textbook-award, pg 635

Frank Luther Mott-KTA Journalism & Mass Communication Research Award, University of Missouri, School of Journalism, 203 Neff Hall, Columbia, MO 65211-1200 *Tel:* 573-882-7685 *E-mail:* umcjourkta@missouri.edu *Web Site:* www.kappataualpha.net, pg 636

Sheila Margaret Motton Book Prize, c/o Linda Haviland Conte, 18 Hall Ave, Apt 2, Somerville, MA 02144 *E-mail:* info@nepoetryclub.org *Web Site:* nepoetryclub.org, pg 636

Mountain Press Publishing Co, 1301 S Third W, Missoula, MT 59801 *Tel:* 406-728-1900 *Toll Free Tel:* 800-234-5308 *Fax:* 406-728-1635 *E-mail:* info@mtnpress.com *Web Site:* www.mountain-press.com, pg 135

Mountain Writers Series, 2804 SE 27 Ave, Suite 2, Portland, OR 97202 *E-mail:* pdxmws@mountainwriters.org *Web Site:* www.mountainwriters.org, pg 556

Mountaineers Books, 1001 SW Klickitat Way, Suite 201, Seattle, WA 98134 *Tel:* 206-223-6303 *Fax:* 206-223-6306 *E-mail:* mbooks@mountaineersbooks.org; customerservice@mountaineersbooks.org *Web Site:* www.mountaineers.org/books, pg 135

De Gruyter Mouton, 125 Pearl St, Boston, MA 02110 *Tel:* 857-284-7073 *Fax:* 857-284-7358 *E-mail:* service@degruyter.com *Web Site:* www.degruyter.com, pg 135

Movable Type Management, 244 Madison Ave, Suite 334, New York, NY 10016 *Web Site:* www.movabletm.com, pg 470

Moznaim Publishing Corp, 4304 12 Ave, Brooklyn, NY 11219 *Tel:* 718-438-7680 *Fax:* 718-438-1305 *E-mail:* info@moznaim.com *Web Site:* www.moznaim.com, pg 135

Elizabeth Mrazik-Cleaver Canadian Picture Book Award, c/o The Canadian Children's Book Ctr, 425 Adelaide St W, Suite 200, Toronto, ON M5V 3C1, Canada *Fax:* 416-975-8970 *E-mail:* cleaver@ibby-canada.org; info@ibby-canada.org *Web Site:* www.ibby-canada.org/awards/elizabeth-mrazik-cleaver-award/, pg 636

Mary Mueller, 516 Bartram Rd, Moorestown, NJ 08057 *Tel:* 856-778-4769 *E-mail:* mamam49@aol.com, pg 443

Multicultural Publications Inc, 1939 Manchester Rd, Akron, OH 44314 *Tel:* 330-865-9578 *Fax:* 330-865-9578 *E-mail:* multiculturalpub@prodigy.net *Web Site:* www.multiculturalpub.net, pg 135

Multnomah, 10807 New Allegiance Dr, Suite 500, Colorado Springs, CO 80921 *Tel:* 719-590-4999 *Toll Free Tel:* 800-603-7051 (orders) *Fax:* 719-590-8977 *E-mail:* info@waterbrookmultnomah.com *Web Site:* waterbrookmultnomah.com, pg 135

Derrick Murdoch Award, 716 Thicket Way, Ottawa, ON K4A 3B5, Canada *E-mail:* info@crimewriterscanada.com *Web Site:* www.crimewriterscanada.com/awards, pg 636

The Museum of Modern Art (MoMA), Publications Dept, 11 W 53 St, New York, NY 10019 *Tel:* 212-708-9400 *E-mail:* moma_publications@moma.org *Web Site:* www.moma.org, pg 135

Museum of New Mexico Press, 725 Camino Lejo, Suite C, Santa Fe, NM 87505 *Tel:* 505-476-1155; 505-272-7777 (orders) *Toll Free Tel:* 800-249-7737 (orders) *Fax:* 505-476-1156 *Toll Free Fax:* 800-622-8667 (orders) *Web Site:* www.mnmpress.org, pg 135

Music Publishers Association (MPA), 442 Fifth Ave, Suite 1137, New York, NY 10018 *E-mail:* admin@mpa.org *Web Site:* www.mpa.org, pg 511

Mutual Publishing LLC, 1215 Center St, Suite 210, Honolulu, HI 96816 *Tel:* 808-732-1709 *Fax:* 808-734-4094 *E-mail:* info@mutualpublishing.com *Web Site:* www.mutualpublishing.com, pg 136

Walter Dean Myers Awards for Outstanding Children's Literature, 10319 Westlake Dr, No 104, Bethesda, MD 20817 *Tel:* 701-404-WNDB (404-9632, voicemail only) *E-mail:* walteraward@diversebooks.org *Web Site:* diversebooks.org/our-programs/walter-award, pg 636

Walter Dean Myers Grants, 10319 Westlake Dr, No 104, Bethesda, MD 20817 *Tel:* 701-404-WNDB (404-9632, voicemail only) *E-mail:* waltergrant@diversebooks.org *Web Site:* diversebooks.org, pg 636

Mystery Writers of America (MWA), 1140 Broadway, Suite 1507, New York, NY 10001 *Tel:* 212-888-8171 *E-mail:* mwa@mysterywriters.org *Web Site:* mysterywriters.org, pg 511

Mythopoeic Awards, c/o University of Arizona, Dept of English, Rm 445, Tucson, AZ 85721 *E-mail:* awards@mythsoc.org *Web Site:* www.mythsoc.org, pg 636

NACE International, 15835 Park Ten Place, Houston, TX 77084 *Tel:* 281-228-6200; 281-228-6223 *Toll Free Tel:* 800-797-NACE (797-6223) *Fax:* 281-228-6300 *E-mail:* firstservice@nace.org *Web Site:* www.nace.org, pg 136

Jean V Naggar Literary Agency Inc (JVNLA), 216 E 75 St, Suite 1-E, New York, NY 10021 *Tel:* 212-794-1082 *E-mail:* jvnla@jvnla.com *Web Site:* www.jvnla.com, pg 471

Napa Valley Writers' Conference, 2277 Napa-Vallejo Hwy, Off 1753, Napa, CA 94558 *Tel:* 707-256-7113 *E-mail:* info@napawritersconference.org; fiction@napawritersconference.org; poetry@napawritersconference.org *Web Site:* www.napawritersconference.org, pg 556

Narada Press, 591 Leighland Dr, Waterloo, ON N2T 2J9, Canada *Tel:* 519-886-1969, pg 413

NAREE Bivins Fellowship, 1003 NW Sixth Terr, Boca Raton, FL 33486-3455 *Tel:* 561-391-3599 *Web Site:* www.naree.org/bivins-fellowship, pg 636

NAREE Real Estate Journalism Awards Competition, 1003 NW Sixth Terr, Boca Raton, FL 33486-3455 *Tel:* 561-391-3599 *E-mail:* nareejcontest@gmail.com *Web Site:* www.naree.org/jcontest, pg 636

NASW Press, 750 First St NE, Suite 800, Washington, DC 20002 *Tel:* 202-408-8600 *Fax:* 203-336-8312 *E-mail:* press@naswdc.org *Web Site:* www.naswpress.org, pg 136

Nataraj Books, 7967 Twist Lane, Springfield, VA 22153 *Tel:* 703-455-4996 *E-mail:* orders@natarajbooks.com; natarajbooks@gmail.com *Web Site:* www.natarajbooks.com, pg 136

National Academies Press (NAP), 500 Fifth St NW, Washington, DC 20001 *Toll Free Tel:* 800-624-6242 *Fax:* 202-334-2451 (cust serv); 202-334-2793 (mktg dept) *E-mail:* customer_service@nap.edu *Web Site:* www.nap.edu, pg 136

National Association of Black Journalists (NABJ), 1100 Knight Hall, Suite 3101, College Park, MD 20742 *Tel:* 301-405-0248 *E-mail:* contact@nabj.org; press@nabj.org *Web Site:* nabjonline.org, pg 511

National Association of Book Entrepreneurs (NABE), PO Box 606, Cottage Grove, OR 97424 *Tel:* 541-942-7455 *Fax:* 541-942-7455 *E-mail:* nabe@bookmarketingprofits.com *Web Site:* www.bookmarketingprofits.com, pg 511

National Association of Broadcasters (NAB), One "M" St SE, Washington, DC 20003 *Tel:* 202-429-5300 *E-mail:* nab@nab.org *Web Site:* www.nab.org, pg 136, 511

National Association of College Stores (NACS), 528 E Lorain St, Oberlin, OH 44074 *Toll Free Tel:* 800-622-7498 *Fax:* 440-775-4769 *E-mail:* info@nacs.org *Web Site:* www.nacs.org, pg 511

National Association of Hispanic Publications Inc (NAHP), National Press Bldg, 529 14 St NW, Suite 923, Washington, DC 20045 *Web Site:* nahp.org, pg 511

National Association of Insurance Commissioners, 1100 Walnut St, Suite 1500, Kansas City, MO 64106-2197 *Tel:* 816-842-3600 *Fax:* 816-783-8175 *E-mail:* prodserv@naic.org *Web Site:* www.naic.org, pg 136

National Association of Printing Ink Manufacturers (NAPIM), National Press Bldg, 529 14 St NW, Suite 1280, Washington, DC 20045 *Tel:* 410-940-6589 *E-mail:* info@napim.org *Web Site:* www.napim.org, pg 512

National Association of Real Estate Editors (NAREE), 1003 NW Sixth Terr, Boca Raton, FL 33486-3455 *Tel:* 561-391-3599 *Web Site:* www.naree.org, pg 512

National Association of Science Writers Inc (NASW), PO Box 7905, Berkeley, CA 94707 *Tel:* 510-859-7229 *Web Site:* www.nasw.org, pg 512

National Awards for Education Reporting, 1825 "K" St NW, Suite 200, Washington, DC 20006 *Tel:* 202-452-9830 *E-mail:* awards@ewa.org *Web Site:* ewa.org, pg 637

National Book Awards, 90 Broad St, Suite 604, New York, NY 10004 *Tel:* 212-685-0261 *Fax:* 212-213-6570 *E-mail:* nationalbook@nationalbook.org *Web Site:* www.nationalbook.org, pg 637

National Book Co, PO Box 3428, Hillsboro, OR 97123-1943 *Tel:* 503-245-1500 *Fax:* 810-885-5811 *E-mail:* info@eralearning.com *Web Site:* www.eralearning.com, pg 136

National Book Critics Circle (NBCC), c/o Jacob M Appel, Icahn School of Medicine at Mount Sinai, One Gustave L Levy Place, New York, NY 10029 *E-mail:* info@bookcritics.org; membership@bookcritics.org *Web Site:* www.bookcritics.org, pg 512

National Book Critics Circle Award, c/o Jacob M Appel, Icahn School of Medicine at Mount Sinai, One Gustave L Levy Place, New York, NY 10029 *E-mail:* info@bookcritics.org *Web Site:* www.bookcritics.org/awards, pg 637

National Book Foundation, 90 Broad St, Suite 604, New York, NY 10004 *Tel:* 212-685-0261 *Fax:* 212-213-6570 *E-mail:* nationalbook@nationalbook.org *Web Site:* www.nationalbook.org, pg 526

National Braille Press, 88 Saint Stephen St, Boston, MA 02115-4312 *Tel:* 617-266-6160 *Toll Free Tel:* 800-548-7323 (cust serv); 888-965-8965 *Fax:* 617-437-0456 *E-mail:* contact@nbp.org *Web Site:* www.nbp.org, pg 137

The National Business Book Award (NBBA), c/o Freedman & Associates Inc, 10 Delisle Ave, Suite 214, Toronto, ON M4V 3C6, Canada *Tel:* 416-868-1500 *Web Site:* www.nbbaward.com, pg 637

National Cartoonists Society (NCS), PO Box 592927, Orlando, FL 32859-2927 *Tel:* 407-994-6703 *E-mail:* info@nationalcartoonists.com; membership@nationalcartoonists.com *Web Site:* www.nationalcartoonists.com, pg 512

National Catholic Educational Association, 200 N Glebe Rd, Suite 310, Arlington, VA 22203 *Tel:* 571-257-0010 *Toll Free Tel:* 800-711-6232 *Fax:* 703-243-0025 *E-mail:* nceaadmin@ncea.org *Web Site:* www.ncea.org, pg 137

National Center for Children in Poverty, 722 W 168 St, New York, NY 10032 *Tel:* 646-284-9600; 212-304-6073 *E-mail:* info@nccp.org *Web Site:* www.nccp.org, pg 137

National Center For Employee Ownership (NCEO), 440 N Barranca Ave, Suite 3554, Covina, CA 91723 *Tel:* 510-208-1300 *E-mail:* customerservice@nceo.org *Web Site:* www.nceo.org, pg 137

National City & Regional Magazine Awards, 287 Richards Ave, Norwalk, CT 06850 *Tel:* 203-515-9294 *Web Site:* citymag.org/awards, pg 637

National Coalition Against Censorship (NCAC), 19 Fulton St, Suite 407, New York, NY 10038 *Tel:* 212-807-6222 *Fax:* 212-807-6245 *E-mail:* ncac@ncac.org *Web Site:* www.ncac.org, pg 512

National Coalition for Literacy (NCL), PO Box 2932, Washington, DC 20013-2932 *E-mail:* ncl@ncladvocacy.org *Web Site:* www.national-coalition-literacy.org, pg 512

National Communication Association, 1765 "N" St NW, Washington, DC 20036 *Tel:* 202-464-4622 *Fax:* 202-464-4600 *E-mail:* inbox@natcom.org *Web Site:* www.natcom.org, pg 512

National Conference of State Legislatures (NCSL), 7700 E First Place, Denver, CO 80230 *Tel:* 303-364-7700 *E-mail:* press-room@ncsl.org *Web Site:* www.ncsl.org, pg 137

National Council of Teachers of English (NCTE), 340 N Neil St, Suite 104, Champaign, IL 61820 *Tel:* 217-328-3870 *Toll Free Tel:* 877-369-6283 (cust serv) *Fax:* 217-328-9645 *E-mail:* customerservice@ncte.org *Web Site:* ncte.org, pg 137, 512

National Council of Teachers of Mathematics (NCTM), 1906 Association Dr, Reston, VA 20191-1502 *Tel:* 703-620-9840 *Toll Free Tel:* 800-235-7566 *Fax:* 703-476-2970 *E-mail:* nctm@nctm.org *Web Site:* www.nctm.org, pg 137

National Education Association (NEA), 1201 16 St NW, Washington, DC 20036-3290 *Tel:* 202-833-4000 *Fax:* 202-822-7974 *Web Site:* www.nea.org, pg 137

National Education Association (NEA), 1201 16 St NW, Washington, DC 20036-3290 *Tel:* 202-833-4000 *Fax:* 202-822-7974 *E-mail:* media-relations-team@nea.org *Web Site:* www.nea.org, pg 513

National Endowment for the Arts, 400 Seventh St SW, Washington, DC 20506-0001 *Tel:* 202-682-5400 *Web Site:* www.arts.gov, pg 526

National Federation of Press Women Inc (NFPW), 140B Purcellville Gateway Dr, Suite 120, Purcellville, VA 20132 *Tel:* 571-295-5900 *E-mail:* info@nfpw.org *Web Site:* www.nfpw.org, pg 513

National Federation of State Poetry Societies Annual Poetry Contest, c/o 115 N Wisteria St, Mansfield, TX 76063-1835 *E-mail:* contestchair@nfsps.com *Web Site:* www.nfsps.com, pg 637

National Freedom of Information Coalition (NFOIC), PO Box 405, Williamsburg, VA 23187 *Tel:* 757-276-1413 *E-mail:* nfoic@nfoic.org *Web Site:* www.nfoic.org, pg 513

National Gallery of Art, Sixth & Constitution Ave NW, Washington, DC 20565 *Tel:* 202-842-6280 *E-mail:* thecenter@nga.gov *Web Site:* www.nga.gov, pg 137

National Gallery of Canada Boutique, 380 Sussex Dr, Ottawa, ON K1N 9N4, Canada *Tel:* 613-990-0962 (mail order sales) *E-mail:* ngcbook@gallery.ca *Web Site:* www.gallery.ca, pg 413

National Geographic Books, 1145 17 St NW, Washington, DC 20036-4688 *Tel:* 202-857-7000 *Toll Free Tel:* 877-866-6486 *E-mail:* ngbooks@cdsfulfillment.com *Web Site:* www.nationalgeographic.com/books/; ngbooks.buysub.com, pg 137

National Geographic Learning, 20 Channel Center St, Boston, MA 02210 *Tel:* 617-289-7900 *E-mail:* schoolcustomerservice@cengage.com *Web Site:* www.ngl.cengage.com/school, pg 138

National Golf Foundation, 501 N Hwy A1A, Jupiter, FL 33477-4577 *Tel:* 561-744-6006 *Toll Free Tel:* 888-275-4643 *Fax:* 561-744-9085 *E-mail:* general@ngf.org *Web Site:* www.ngf.org, pg 138

The National Humanities Medal, 400 Seventh St SW, Washington, DC 20506 *Tel:* 202-606-8400 *Toll Free Tel:* 800-NEH-1121 (634-1121) *E-mail:* questions@neh.gov *Web Site:* www.neh.gov/about/awards, pg 637

National Information Standards Organization (NISO), 3600 Clipper Mill Rd, Suite 302, Baltimore, MD 21211-1948 *Tel:* 301-654-2512 *Fax:* 410-685-5278 *E-mail:* nisohq@niso.org *Web Site:* www.niso.org, pg 138, 513

National Institute for Trial Advocacy (NITA), 1685 38 St, Suite 200, Boulder, CO 80301-2735 *Tel:* 720-890-4860 *Toll Free Tel:* 877-648-2632; 800-225-6482 (orders & returns) *Fax:* 720-890-7069 *E-mail:* customerservice@nita.org; sales@nita.org *Web Site:* www.nita.org, pg 138

National Jewish Book Award-Children's Picture Book, 520 Eighth Ave, 4th fl, New York, NY 10018 *Tel:* 212-201-2920 *Fax:* 212-532-4952 *E-mail:* njba@jewishbooks.org *Web Site:* www.jewishbookcouncil.org/awards, pg 637

National Jewish Book Award-Natan Notable Books, 520 Eighth Ave, 4th fl, New York, NY 10018 *Tel:* 212-201-2920 *Fax:* 212-532-4952 *E-mail:* njba@jewishbooks.org; natannotable@jewishbooks.org *Web Site:* www.jewishbookcouncil.org/awards, pg 637

National Jewish Book Award-Young Adult Literature, 520 Eighth Ave, 4th fl, New York, NY 10018 *Tel:* 212-201-2920 *Fax:* 212-532-4952 *E-mail:* njba@jewishbooks.org *Web Site:* www.jewishbookcouncil.org/awards, pg 637

National Jewish Book Awards, 520 Eighth Ave, 4th fl, New York, NY 10018 *Tel:* 212-201-2920 *Fax:* 212-532-4952 *E-mail:* njba@jewishbookcouncil.org *Web Site:* www.jewishbookcouncil.org/awards, pg 637

National Latino Press Association (NLPA), 1841 Columbia Rd NW, Suite 614, Washington, DC 20009 *Tel:* 202-489-9516; 509-545-3055 (off of the Pres) *E-mail:* info@nationallatinopressassoc.org *Web Site:* nationallatinopressassoc.org, pg 513

National League of American Pen Women Inc, The Pen Arts Bldg & Arts Museum, 1300 17 St NW, Washington, DC 20036-1973 *Tel:* 202-785-1997 *Fax:* 202-452-6868 *E-mail:* contact@nlapw.org *Web Site:* www.nlapw.org, pg 513

National Learning Corp, 212 Michael Dr, Syosset, NY 11791 *Tel:* 516-921-8888 *Toll Free Tel:* 800-632-8888 *Fax:* 516-921-8743 *E-mail:* info@passbooks.com *Web Site:* www.passbooks.com, pg 138

National Magazine Awards, 2300 Yonge St, Suite 1600, Toronto, ON M4P 1E4, Canada *Tel:* 416-939-6200 *E-mail:* staff@magazine-awards.com *Web Site:* www.magazine-awards.com; x.com/magawards, pg 638

The National Medal of Arts, 400 Seventh St SW, Washington, DC 20506-0001 *Tel:* 202-682-5570 *Web Site:* www.arts.gov/honors/medals, pg 638

National Music Publishers' Association (NMPA), 1900 "N" St NW, Suite 500, Washington, DC 20036 *Tel:* 202-393-6672 *E-mail:* members@nmpa.org *Web Site:* nmpa.org, pg 513

National Newspaper Association (NNA), PO Box 13323, Pensacola, FL 32591 *Tel:* 850-542-7087 *Web Site:* www.nna.org; nnaweb.org, pg 513

National Newspaper Publishers Association (NNPA), 1816 12 St NW, Washington, DC 20009 *Tel:* 202-588-8764 *E-mail:* info@nnpa.org *Web Site:* nnpa.org; blackpressusa.com, pg 513

National Notary Association (NNA), 9350 De Soto Ave, Chatsworth, CA 91311-4926 *Tel:* 818-739-4000 *Toll Free Tel:* 800-876-6827 *Toll Free Fax:* 800-833-1211 *E-mail:* services@nationalnotary.org *Web Site:* nationalnotary.org, pg 138

National Outdoor Book Awards (NOBA), 921 S Eighth Ave, Stop 8128, Pocatello, ID 83209-8128 *Tel:* 208-282-3912 *Fax:* 208-282-2127 *Web Site:* www.noba-web.org, pg 638

National Paper Trade Association (NPTA), 330 N Wabash Ave, Suite 2000, Chicago, IL 60611 *Tel:* 312-321-4092 *Toll Free Tel:* 800-355-NPTA (355-6782) *Fax:* 312-673-6736 *Web Site:* www.gonpta.com, pg 513

National Poetry Series Open Competition, 57 Mountain Ave, Princeton, NJ 08540 *Tel:* 609-430-0999 *Fax:* 609-430-9933 *E-mail:* npspoetry@gmail.com *Web Site:* nationalpoetryseries.org, pg 638

National Press Club (NPC), 529 14 St NW, 13th fl, Washington, DC 20045 *Tel:* 202-662-7500 *Web Site:* www.press.org, pg 513

National Press Foundation, 1211 Connecticut Ave NW, Suite 310, Washington, DC 20036 *Tel:* 202-663-7286 *Web Site:* nationalpress.org, pg 526

National Press Photographers Association Inc (NPPA), 120 Hooper St, Athens, GA 30602-3018 *Tel:* 706-542-2506 *E-mail:* info@nppa.org; director@nppa.org *Web Site:* nppa.org, pg 514

National Resource Center for Youth Services, Schusterman Ctr, Bldg 4W, 4502 E 41 St, Tulsa, OK 74135-2512 *Tel:* 918-660-3700 *Toll Free Tel:* 800-274-2687 *E-mail:* nrcys@ou.edu *Web Site:* www.nrcys.ou.edu, pg 138

National Science Teachers Association (NSTA), 1840 Wilson Blvd, Arlington, VA 22201-3000 *Tel:* 703-243-7100 *Toll Free Tel:* 800-277-5300 (orders) *Fax:* 703-243-7177 *Toll Free Fax:* 888-433-0526 (orders) *E-mail:* nstapress@nsta.org (edit); orders@nsta.org; pubsales@nsta.org *Web Site:* www.nsta.org/bookstore, pg 138

National Society of Newspaper Columnists (NSNC), 205 Gun Hill St, Milton, MA 02186 *Tel:* 617-697-6854 *Web Site:* www.columnists.com, pg 514

National Society of Newspaper Columnists Annual Conference, 205 Gun Hill St, Milton, MA 02186 *Tel:* 617-697-6854 *Web Site:* www.columnists.com, pg 556

National Translation Award, University of Arizona, Esquire Bldg, No 205, 1230 N Park Ave, Tucson, AZ 85721 *Tel:* 520-621-1757 *E-mail:* info@literarytranslators.org *Web Site:* www.literarytranslators.org/awards/national-translation-award, pg 638

The National Underwriter Co, 4157 Olympic Blvd, Suite 225, Erlanger, KY 41018 *Tel:* 859-692-2100 *Toll Free Tel:* 800-543-0874 *E-mail:* customerservice@nuco.com *Web Site:* www.nationalunderwriter.com, pg 138

National Wildlife Federation, 11100 Wildlife Center Dr, Reston, VA 20190-5362 *Toll Free Tel:* 800-477-5034 *Web Site:* www.zoobooks.com, pg 139

National Writers Association, 10940 S Parker Rd, Suite 508, Parker, CO 80134 *Tel:* 303-656-7235 *E-mail:* natlwritersassn@hotmail.com *Web Site:* www.nationalwriters.com, pg 514

National Writers Association Novel Contest, 10940 S Parker Rd, Suite 508, Parker, CO 80134 *Tel:* 303-656-7235 *E-mail:* natlwritersassn@hotmail.com *Web Site:* www.nationalwriters.com, pg 638

National Writers Union (NWU), 61 Broadway, Suite 1630, New York, NY 10006 *Tel:* 315-545-5034 *E-mail:* nwu@nwu.org *Web Site:* nwu.org, pg 514

Nautilus Book Awards, PO Box 2285, Vashon, WA 98070 *Tel:* 206-304-2250 *Web Site:* www.nautilusbookawards.com, pg 638

Naval Institute Press, 291 Wood Rd, Annapolis, MD 21402-5034 *Tel:* 410-268-6110 *Toll Free Tel:* 800-233-8764 *Fax:* 410-295-1084 *E-mail:* customer@usni.org (cust inquiries) *Web Site:* www.usni.org/press/books; www.usni.org, pg 139

NavPress Publishing Group, 3820 N 30 St, Colorado Springs, CO 80904 *Web Site:* www.navpress.com, pg 139

NBM Publishing Inc, 300 E 54 St, No 12C, New York, NY 10022-5021 *Tel:* 917-628-6777 *E-mail:* nbmgn@nbmpub.com *Web Site:* www.nbmpub.com, pg 139

NEA Creative Writing Fellowships, 400 Seventh St SW, Washington, DC 20506-0001 *Tel:* 202-682-5400; 202-682-5082 (voice/TTY); 202-682-5034 (lit fellowships hotline) *E-mail:* litfellowships@arts.gov *Web Site:* www.arts.gov/grants/creative-writing-fellowships, pg 638

The Jesse H Neal Awards, 1620 Eye St NW, Washington, DC 20005 *Tel:* 202-289-7442 *E-mail:* nealawards@siia.net *Web Site:* siia.net/neals, pg 638

Barbara Neely Memorial Scholarship Program, 1140 Broadway, Suite 1507, New York, NY 10001 *Tel:* 212-888-8171 *E-mail:* mwa@mysterywriters.org *Web Site:* mysterywriters.org, pg 639

Nina Neimark Editorial Services, 543 Third St, Brooklyn, NY 11215 *Tel:* 718-499-6804 *E-mail:* pneimark@hotmail.com, pg 443

Nelligan Prize for Short Fiction, Colorado State University, Dept of English, Center for Literary Publishing, 9105 Campus Delivery, Fort Collins, CO 80523-9105 *Tel:* 970-491-5449 *E-mail:* creview@colostate.edu *Web Site:* coloradoreview.colostate.edu/nelligan-prize, pg 639

Nelson Education Ltd, 1120 Birchmount Rd, Scarborough, ON M1K 5G4, Canada *Tel:* 416-752-9448 *Toll Free Tel:* 800-268-2222 (cust serv) *Fax:* 416-752-9646 *E-mail:* peopleandengagement@nelson.com *Web Site:* www.nelson.com, pg 413

Nelson Literary Agency LLC, 700 Colorado Blvd, No 352, Denver, CO 80206 *Tel:* 303-292-2805 *E-mail:* info@nelsonagency.com *Web Site:* www.nelsonagency.com, pg 471

Nero Award, PO Box 230822, Ansonia Sta, New York, NY 10023 *Web Site:* nerowolfe.org/htm/literary_awards/nero_award/award.htm, pg 639

The Pablo Neruda Prize for Poetry, University of Tulsa, Kendall College of Arts & Sciences, 800 S Tucker Dr, Tulsa, OK 74104 *Tel:* 918-631-3080 *E-mail:* nimrod@utulsa.edu *Web Site:* artsandsciences.utulsa.edu/nimrod/nimrod-literary-awards/, pg 639

Neukom Institute Literary Arts Award for Playwriting, Dartmouth College, Sudikoff Bldg, Rm 121, 9 Maynard St, Hanover, NH 03755 *Web Site:* sites.dartmouth.edu/neukominstitutelitawards, pg 639

Neustadt International Prize for Literature, c/o University of Oklahoma, 630 Parrington Oval, Suite 110, Norman, OK 73019-4033 *Tel:* 405-325-4531 *Web Site:* www.worldliteraturetoday.org; www.neustadtprize.org, pg 639

Elizabeth Neuwirth Memorial, PO Box 36128, North Chesterfield, VA 23235-3533 *E-mail:* contest@poetrysocietyofvirginia.org; info@poetryvirginia.org *Web Site:* www.poetrysocietyofvirginia.org, pg 639

Allan Nevins Prize, Columbia University, 3009 Broadway MC 802, New York, NY 10027 *Tel:* 212-854-1919 *E-mail:* amhistsociety@columbia.edu *Web Site:* sah.columbia.edu, pg 639

New Atlantic Independent Booksellers Association (NAIBA), 2667 Hyacinth St, Westbury, NY 11590 *Tel:* 516-333-0681 *E-mail:* kit@naiba.com *Web Site:* www.naiba.com, pg 514

New Author Publishing, 4 E Fulford Place, Brockville, ON K6V 2Z8, Canada *Tel:* 613-865-7471 *Web Site:* www.newauthorpublishing.com, pg 413

New City Press, 202 Comforter Blvd, Hyde Park, NY 12538 *Tel:* 845-229-0335 *Toll Free Tel:* 800-462-5980 (orders only) *Fax:* 845-229-0351 *E-mail:* info@newcitypress.com; orders@newcitypress.com *Web Site:* www.newcitypress.com, pg 139

New Concepts Publishing, 5265 Humphreys Rd, Lake Park, GA 31636 *E-mail:* newconcepts@newconceptspublishing.com *Web Site:* www.newconceptspublishing.com, pg 139

New Directions Publishing Corp, 80 Eighth Ave, 19th fl, New York, NY 10011 *Tel:* 212-255-0230 *E-mail:* editorial@ndbooks.com; publicity@ndbooks.com *Web Site:* ndbooks.com, pg 139

New England Book Awards, One Beacon St, 15th fl, Boston, MA 02108 *Tel:* 617-547-3642 *Web Site:* www.newenglandbooks.org/page/book-awards, pg 639

New England Independent Booksellers Association Inc (NEIBA), One Beacon St, 15th fl, Boston, MA 02108 *Tel:* 617-547-3642 *Web Site:* www.newenglandbooks.org, pg 514

New England Poetry Club, c/o Linda Haviland Conte, 18 Hall Ave, Apt 2, Somerville, MA 02144 *E-mail:* info@nepoetryclub.org; president@nepoetryclub.org *Web Site:* nepoetryclub.org, pg 514

New Forums Press Inc, 1018 S Lewis St, Stillwater, OK 74074 *Tel:* 405-372-6158 *Toll Free Tel:* 800-606-3766 *Fax:* 405-377-2237 *Web Site:* www.newforums.com, pg 139

New Hampshire Literary Awards, 2500 N River Rd, Manchester, NH 03106 *Tel:* 603-270-5466 *E-mail:* info@nhwritersproject.org *Web Site:* www.nhwritersproject.org/new-hampshire-literary-awards, pg 640

New Hampshire Writers' Project (NHWP), 2500 N River Rd, Manchester, NH 03106 *Tel:* 603-270-5466 *E-mail:* info@nhwritersproject.org *Web Site:* www.nhwritersproject.org, pg 514

New Harbinger Publications Inc, 5674 Shattuck Ave, Oakland, CA 94609 *Tel:* 510-652-0215 *Toll Free Tel:* 800-748-6273 (orders only) *Fax:* 510-652-5472 *Toll Free Fax:* 800-652-1613 *E-mail:* customerservice@newharbinger.com *Web Site:* www.newharbinger.com, pg 140

New Issues Poetry & Prose, c/o Western Michigan University, 1903 W Michigan Ave, Kalamazoo, MI 49008-5463 *Tel:* 269-387-8185 *E-mail:* new-issues@wmich.edu *Web Site:* newissuespress.com, pg 140

New Jersey Business & Industry Association (NJBIA), 10 W Lafayette St, Trenton, NJ 08608-2002 *Tel:* 609-393-7707 *Web Site:* njbia.org, pg 514

New Leaf Press, 3142 Hwy 103 N, Green Forest, AR 72638-2233 *Tel:* 870-438-5288 *Toll Free Tel:* 800-999-3777 *Fax:* 870-438-5120 *E-mail:* submissions@nlpg.com *Web Site:* www.nlpg.com, pg 140

New Mexico-Arizona Book Awards, 925 Salamanca NW, Los Ranchos, NM 87107 *Tel:* 505-344-9382 *E-mail:* info@nmbookcoop.com *Web Site:* www.nmbookcoop.com/BookAwards/BookAwards.html, pg 640

New Mexico Book Association (NMBA), PO Box 1285, Santa Fe, NM 87504 *E-mail:* libroentry@gmail.com *Web Site:* www.nmbookassociation.org, pg 514

New Millennium Awards for Fiction, Poetry & Nonfiction, 821 Indian Gap Rd, Sevierville, TN 37876 *Tel:* 865-254-4880 *E-mail:* hello@newmillenniumwritings.org *Web Site:* newmillenniumwritings.org, pg 640

The New Press, 120 Wall St, 31st fl, New York, NY 10005 *Tel:* 212-629-8802 *Fax:* 212-629-8617 *E-mail:* newpress@thenewpress.com *Web Site:* thenewpress.com, pg 140

New Readers Press, 104 Marcellus, Syracuse, NY 13204 *Tel:* 315-422-9121 *Toll Free Tel:* 800-448-8878 *Toll Free Fax:* 866-894-2100 *E-mail:* nrp@proliteracy.org *Web Site:* www.newreaderspress.com, pg 140

New Star Books Ltd, 107-3477 Commercial St, Vancouver, BC V5N 4E8, Canada *Tel:* 604-738-9429 *E-mail:* customerservice@newstarbooks.com *Web Site:* www.newstarbooks.com, pg 413

New Voices: The Joanne Scott Kennedy Memorial, PO Box 36128, North Chesterfield, VA 23235-3533 *E-mail:* contest@poetrysocietyofvirginia.org; info@poetryvirginia.org *Web Site:* www.poetrysocietyofvirginia.org, pg 640

New Women's Voices Chapbook Competition, PO Box 1626, Georgetown, KY 40324 *Tel:* 502-603-0670 *E-mail:* finishingbooks@aol.com; flpbookstore@aol.com *Web Site:* www.finishinglinepress.com; finishinglinepress.submittable.com/submit, pg 640

New World Library, 14 Pamaron Way, Novato, CA 94949 *Tel:* 415-884-2100 *Fax:* 415-884-2199 *E-mail:* escort@newworldlibrary.com *Web Site:* www.newworldlibrary.com, pg 140

New World Publishing (Canada), PO Box 36075, Halifax, NS B3J 3S9, Canada *Tel:* 902-576-2055 (inquiries) *Toll Free Tel:* 877-211-3334 (orders) *Fax:* 902-576-2095 *Web Site:* www.newworldpublishing.com, pg 414

New York Academy of Sciences (NYAS), 7 World Trade Center, 40th fl, 250 Greenwich St, New York, NY 10007-2157 *Tel:* 212-298-8600 *Toll Free Tel:* 800-843-6927 *Fax:* 212-298-3650 *E-mail:* nyas@nyas.org; annals@nyas.org; customerservice@nyas.org *Web Site:* www.nyas.org, pg 140

The New York Botanical Garden Press, 2900 Southern Blvd, Bronx, NY 10458-5126 *Tel:* 718-817-8721 *Fax:* 718-817-8842 *E-mail:* nybgpress@nybg.org *Web Site:* www.nybgpress.org, pg 140

New York City Book Awards, 53 E 79 St, New York, NY 10075 *Tel:* 212-288-6900 *Fax:* 212-744-5832 *E-mail:* events@nysoclib.org *Web Site:* www.nysoclib.org, pg 640

New York City College of Technology Professional & Technical Writing Program, Namm Hall 512, 300 Jay St, Brooklyn, NY 11201 *Tel:* 718-260-5392 *E-mail:* english@citytech.cuny.edu *Web Site:* www.citytech.cuny.edu/english/technical-writing-bs.aspx, pg 563

The New York Public Library Helen Bernstein Book Award for Excellence in Journalism, 445 Fifth Ave, 4th fl, New York, NY 10016 *Tel:* 212-930-9206 *Fax:* 212-930-0983 *E-mail:* bernsteinawards@nypl.org *Web Site:* www.nypl.org, pg 640

New York State Bar Association, One Elk St, Albany, NY 12207 *Tel:* 518-463-3200 *Toll Free Tel:* 800-582-2452 *Fax:* 518-463-5993 *E-mail:* mrc@nysba.org *Web Site:* nysba.org, pg 141

New York State Edith Wharton Citation of Merit for Fiction Writers, University at Albany, Science Library 320, 1400 Washington Ave, Albany, NY 12222 *Tel:* 518-442-5620 *E-mail:* writers@albany.edu *Web Site:* www.nyswritersinstitute.org, pg 640

New York State Walt Whitman Citation of Merit for Poets, University at Albany, Science Library 320, 1400 Washington Ave, Albany, NY 12222 *Tel:* 518-442-5620 *E-mail:* writers@albany.edu *Web Site:* www.nyswritersinstitute.org, pg 640

New York State Writers Institute, University at Albany, Science Library 320, 1400 Washington Ave, Albany, NY 12222 *Tel:* 518-442-5620 *Fax:* 518-442-5621 *E-mail:* writers@albany.edu *Web Site:* www.nyswritersinstitute.org, pg 556

New York University, Center for Publishing & Applied Liberal Arts, 7 E 12 St, New York, NY 10003 *Tel:* 212-998-7200 *E-mail:* sps.info@nyu.edu *Web Site:* www.scps.nyu.edu/professional-pathways/topics.html, pg 563

New York University Press, 838 Broadway, 3rd fl, New York, NY 10003-4812 *Tel:* 212-998-2575 (edit) *Toll Free Tel:* 800-996-6987 (orders) *Fax:* 212-995-4798 (orders) *E-mail:* nyupressinfo@nyu.edu (cust care) *Web Site:* www.nyupress.org, pg 141

John Newbery Medal, 225 N Michigan Ave, Suite 1300, Chicago, IL 60601 *Tel:* 312-280-2163 *Toll Free Tel:* 800-545-2433 *Fax:* 312-280-5271 *E-mail:* alsc@ala.org *Web Site:* www.ala.org/alsc/awardsgrants/bookmedia/newbery, pg 640

Newbury Street Press, 99-101 Newbury St, Boston, MA 02116 *Tel:* 617-226-1206 *Toll Free Tel:* 888-296-3447 (NEHGS membership) *Fax:* 617-536-7307 *E-mail:* thebookstore@nehgs.org *Web Site:* www.americanancestors.org, pg 141

NeWest Press, 8540 109 St, No 201, Edmonton, AB T6G 1E6, Canada *Tel:* 780-432-9427 *Fax:* 780-433-3179 *E-mail:* info@newestpress.com; orders@newestpress.com *Web Site:* www.newestpress.com, pg 414

Newfoundland and Labrador Book Awards, Haymarket Sq, 223 Duckworth St, St John's, NL A1C 6N1, Canada *Tel:* 709-739-5215 *Toll Free Tel:* 866-739-5215 *E-mail:* info@wanl.ca; membership@wanl.ca *Web Site:* wanl.ca, pg 641

Newfoundland and Labrador Credit Union Fresh Fish Award for Emerging Writers, Haymarket Sq, 223 Duckworth St, St John's, NL A1C 6N1, Canada *Tel:* 709-739-5215 *Toll Free Tel:* 866-739-5215 *E-mail:* info@wanl.ca; membership@wanl.ca *Web Site:* wanl.ca, pg 641

Newgen North America Inc, 2714 Bee Cave Rd, Suite 201, Austin, TX 78746 *Tel:* 512-478-5341 *Fax:* 512-476-4756 *E-mail:* sales@newgen.co *Web Site:* www.newgen.co, pg 443

News Leaders Association (NLA), 209 Reynolds Journalism Institute, Missouri School of Journalism, Columbia, MO 65211 *Tel:* 202-964-0912 *E-mail:* contact@newsleaders.org *Web Site:* www.newsleaders.org, pg 514

News/Media Alliance, 4401 N Fairfax Dr, Suite 300, Arlington, VA 22203 *Tel:* 571-366-1000 *E-mail:* info@newsmediaalliance.org *Web Site:* www.newsmediaalliance.org, pg 514

News Media Canada, 37 Front St E, Suite 200, Toronto, ON M5E 1B3, Canada *Tel:* 416-923-3567 *Toll Free Tel:* 877-305-2262 *Fax:* 416-923-7206 *E-mail:* info@newsmediacanada.ca *Web Site:* nmc-mic.ca, pg 515

The NewsGuild - CWA, 501 Third St NW, 6th fl, Washington, DC 20001-2797 *Tel:* 202-434-7177 *Fax:* 202-434-1472 *E-mail:* guild@cwa-union.org *Web Site:* www.newsguild.org, pg 515

NewSouth Books, 105 S Court St, Montgomery, AL 36104 *Tel:* 334-834-3556 *E-mail:* info@newsouthbooks.com *Web Site:* www.newsouthbooks.com, pg 141

Sue Newton, 1397 Cypress Point Lane, Apt 106, Ventura, CA 93003 *Tel:* 805-765-4412; 805-864-3065 *E-mail:* sue.edit@gmail.com, pg 443

NFB Publishing, 119 Dorchester Rd, Buffalo, NY 14213 *Tel:* 716-510-0520 *E-mail:* submissions@nfbpublishing.com *Web Site:* www.nfbpublishing.com, pg 141

Don & Gee Nicholl Fellowships in Screenwriting, 1313 Vine St, Hollywood, CA 90028 *Tel:* 310-247-3010 *Fax:* 310-247-3794 *E-mail:* nicholl@oscars.org *Web Site:* www.oscars.org/nicholl, pg 641

Donald Nicholson-Smith, 50 Plaza St E, Apt 1D, Brooklyn, NY 11238 *Tel:* 718-636-4732 *E-mail:* mnr.dns@verizon.net, pg 443

Mary Nickliss Prize in US Women's and/or Gender History, 112 N Bryan Ave, Bloomington, IN 47408-4141 *Tel:* 812-855-7311 *E-mail:* oah@oah.org *Web Site:* www.oah.org/awards, pg 641

Lorine Niedecker Poetry Award, c/o 3225 N 91 St, Milwaukee, WI 53222 *E-mail:* wiswriters@gmail.com *Web Site:* wiswriters.org/awards, pg 641

Nilgiri Press, 3600 Tomales Rd, Tomales, CA 94971 *Tel:* 707-878-2369 *E-mail:* info@easwaran.org *Web Site:* www.easwaran.org, pg 141

Nimbus Publishing Ltd, 3660 Strawberry Hill, Halifax, NS B3K 5A9, Canada *Tel:* 902-455-4286 *Toll Free Tel:* 800-NIMBUS9 (646-2879) *Fax:* 902-455-5440 *Toll Free Fax:* 888-253-3133 *E-mail:* customerservice@nimbus.ca *Web Site:* www.nimbus.ca, pg 414

John Frederick Nims Memorial Prize for Translation, 61 W Superior St, Chicago, IL 60654 *Tel:* 312-787-7070 *Web Site:* www.poetryfoundation.org/poetrymagazine/prizes, pg 641

No Starch Press, 245 Eighth St, San Francisco, CA 94103 *Tel:* 415-863-9900 *Toll Free Tel:* 800-420-7240 *Fax:* 415-863-9950 *E-mail:* info@nostarch.

com; sales@nostarch.com; editors@nostarch.com; marketing@nostarch.com Web Site: www.nostarch.com, pg 141

The Betsy Nolan Literary Agency, 112 E 17 St, Suite 1W, New York, NY 10003 Tel: 212-967-8200 Web Site: www.nolanlehrgroup.com, pg 471

NOLO, 909 N Pacific Coast Hwy, 11th fl, El Segundo, CA 90245 Web Site: www.nolo.com, pg 141

Norilana Books, PO Box 209, Highgate Center, VT 05459-0209 E-mail: service@norilana.com Web Site: www.norilana.com, pg 142

North American Agricultural Journalists (NAAJ), c/o Jacqui Fatka, 6866 County Rd, 183, Fredericktown, OH 43019 Tel: 979-324-4302 E-mail: naajnews@yahoo.com Web Site: www.naaj.net, pg 515

North American Snowsports Journalists Association (NASJA), 290 Laramie Blvd, Boulder, CO 80304 E-mail: execsec@nasja.org Web Site: nasja.org, pg 515

North Atlantic Books (NAB), 2526 Martin Luther King Jr Way, Berkeley, CA 94704 Tel: 510-549-4270 Web Site: www.northatlanticbooks.com, pg 142

North Carolina Arts Council Writers Fellowships, 109 E Jones St, Raleigh, NC 27601 Tel: 919-807-6500 Fax: 919-807-6532 E-mail: ncarts@ncdcr.gov Web Site: www.ncarts.org, pg 641

North Carolina Office of Archives & History, Historical Publications Branch, 4622 Mail Service Ctr, Raleigh, NC 27699-4622 Tel: 919-733-7442 E-mail: historical.publications@ncdcr.gov Web Site: www.dncr.nc.gov/about-us/office-archives-and-history, pg 142

North Carolina Writers' Network, PO Box 21591, Winston-Salem, NC 27120-1591 Tel: 336-293-8844 E-mail: mail@ncwriters.org Web Site: www.ncwriters.org, pg 515

North Carolina Writers' Network Annual Fall Conference, PO Box 21591, Winston-Salem, NC 27120-1591 Tel: 336-293-8844 E-mail: mail@ncwriters.org Web Site: www.ncwriters.org, pg 556

North Country Press, 126 Main St, Unity, ME 04988 Tel: 207-948-2208 E-mail: info@northcountrypress.com Web Site: www.northcountrypress.com, pg 142

North Point Press, 120 Broadway, New York, NY 10271 Tel: 212-741-6900 E-mail: sales@fsgbooks.com Web Site: us.macmillan.com/fsg, pg 142

North River Press Publishing Corp, 27 Rosseter St, Great Barrington, MA 01230 Tel: 413-528-0034 Toll Free: 800-486-2665 Fax: 413-528-3163 Toll Free Fax: 800-BOOK-FAX (266-5329) E-mail: info@northriverpress.com Web Site: www.northriverpress.com, pg 142

North Star Editions Inc, 2297 Waters Dr, Mendota Heights, MN 55120 Toll Free Tel: 888-417-0195 Fax: 952-582-1000 E-mail: sales@northstareditions.com; publicity@northstareditions.com Web Site: www.northstareditions.com, pg 142

North Star Press of Saint Cloud Inc, 19485 Estes Rd, Clearwater, MN 55320 Tel: 320-558-9062 E-mail: info@northstarpress.com Web Site: www.northstarpress.com, pg 142

North Street Book Prize, 351 Pleasant St, Suite B, PMB 222, Northampton, MA 01060-3998 Tel: 413-320-1847 Toll Free Tel: 866-WINWRIT (946-9748) Fax: 413-280-0539 Web Site: www.winningwriters.com/our-contests/north-street-book-prize, pg 641

Northern California Book Awards, c/o Poetry Flash, 1450 Fourth St, Suite 4, Berkeley, CA 94710 Tel: 510-525-5476 E-mail: editor@poetryflash.org; ncbr@poetryflash.org Web Site: poetryflash.org, pg 641

Northern California Translators Association, 2261 Market St, Suite 160, San Francisco, CA 94114-1600 Tel: 510-845-8712 E-mail: ncta@ncta.org Web Site: ncta.org, pg 515

Northern Illinois University Press, Sage House, 512 E State St, Ithaca, NY 14850 Tel: 607-253-2338 Web Site: cornellpress.cornell.edu/imprints/northern-illinois-university-press, pg 143

Northwest Independent Editors Guild, 7511 Greenwood Ave N, No 307, Seattle, WA 98103 E-mail: info@edsguild.org Web Site: www.edsguild.org, pg 515

Northwest Territories Public Library Services, 75 Woodland Dr, Hay River, NT X0E 1G1, Canada Tel: 867-874-6531 Toll Free Tel: 866-297-0232 (CN) Fax: 867-874-3321 Web Site: ece.gov.nt.ca/en/services/nwt-public-libraries, pg 515

Northwestern University Press, 629 Noyes St, Evanston, IL 60208-4210 Tel: 847-491-2046 Toll Free Tel: 800-621-2736 (orders only) Fax: 847-491-8150 E-mail: nupress@northwestern.edu Web Site: www.nupress.northwestern.edu, pg 143

W W Norton & Company Inc, 500 Fifth Ave, New York, NY 10110-0017 Tel: 212-354-5500 Toll Free Tel: 800-233-4830 (orders & cust serv) Fax: 212-869-0856 Toll Free Fax: 800-458-6515 E-mail: orders@wwnorton.com Web Site: wwnorton.com, pg 143

Norwood House Press, PO Box 1306, Fairport, NY 14450 Tel: 773-467-0837 Toll Free Tel: 866-565-2900 Fax: 773-467-9686 Toll Free Fax: 866-565-2901 E-mail: customerservice@norwoodhousepress.com Web Site: www.norwoodhousepress.com, pg 143

Nosy Crow Inc, 145 Lincoln Rd, Lincoln, MA 01773 E-mail: nosycrowinc@nosycrow.com; salesinfo@nosycrow.com; export@nosycrow.com (export sales); rights@nosycrow.com Web Site: nosycrow.us, pg 144

Notable Wisconsin Authors, 112 Owen Rd, Unit 6437, Monona, WI 53716 Tel: 608-245-3640 E-mail: wla@wisconsinlibraries.org Web Site: www.wisconsinlibraries.org, pg 642

Nova Press, PO Box 692023, West Hollywood, CA 90069 Tel: 310-601-8551 E-mail: novapress@aol.com Web Site: www.novapress.net, pg 144

Nova Science Publishers Inc, 400 Oser Ave, Suite 1600, Hauppauge, NY 11788-3619 Tel: 631-231-7269 Fax: 631-231-8175 E-mail: nova.main@novapublishers.com Web Site: www.novapublishers.com, pg 144

Novalis Publishing, One Eglinton Ave E, Suite 800, Toronto, ON M4P 3A1, Canada Tel: 416-363-3303 Toll Free Tel: 877-702-7773 Fax: 416-363-9409 Toll Free Fax: 877-702-7775 E-mail: books@novalis.ca Web Site: www.novalis.ca, pg 414

Novella Prize, University of Victoria, PO Box 1700, Sta CSC, Victoria, BC V8W 2Y2, Canada Tel: 250-721-8524 E-mail: malahat@uvic.ca Web Site: www.malahatreview.ca/contests/novella_contest/info.html; www.malahatreview.ca, pg 642

Wanda Nowak Creative Illustrators Agency, 231 E 76 St, Suite 5-D, New York, NY 10021 Tel: 212-535-0438 E-mail: wanda@wandanow.com Web Site: www.wandanow.com, pg 486

n+1 Writers' Fellowship, Cadman Plaza Sta, PO Box 26428, Brooklyn, NY 11202 E-mail: editors@nplusonemag.com; subs@nplusonemag.com (submission queries); submissions@nplusonemag.com Web Site: www.nplusonemag.com/awards, pg 642

NRP Direct, 220 College Ave, Suite 618, Athens, GA 30601-9801 Tel: 908-517-0780 Toll Free Tel: 844-592-4197 E-mail: info@nrpdirect.com Web Site: www.nrpdirect.com, pg 144

NSK Neustadt Prize for Children's Literature, c/o University of Oklahoma, 630 Parrington Oval, Suite 110, Norman, OK 73019-4033 Tel: 405-325-4531 Web Site: www.worldliteraturetoday.org; www.neustadtprize.org, pg 642

Nursesbooks.org, The Publishing Program of ANA, 8515 Georgia Ave, Suite 400, Silver Spring, MD 20910-3492 Tel: 301-628-5000 Toll Free Tel: 800-274-4262; 800-637-0323 (orders) Fax: 301-628-5342 E-mail: anp@ana.org Web Site: www.Nursesbooks.org; www.NursingWorld.org, pg 144

NYC Big Book Award®, 63 Clinton Rd, Glen Ridge, NJ 07028 Tel: 973-969-1899 Web Site: www.nycbigbookaward.com, pg 642

NYSCA/NYFA Artist Fellowships, 20 Jay St, Suite 740, Brooklyn, NY 11201 Tel: 212-366-6900 Fax: 212-366-1778 E-mail: fellowships@nyfa.org Web Site: www.nyfa.org, pg 642

Nystrom Education, PO Box 802, Culver City, CA 90232 Tel: 310-839-2436 Toll Free Tel: 800-421-4246 Fax: 310-839-2249 Toll Free Fax: 800-944-5432 E-mail: access@socialstudies.com; customerservice@socialstudies.com Web Site: www.socialstudies.com, pg 144

NYU Advanced Publishing Institute, NYU SPS Center for Publishing & Applied Liberal Arts, 7 E 12 St, Suite 921, New York, NY 10003 E-mail: nyu.api@nyu.edu Web Site: www.sps.nyu.edu, pg 564

OAG Worldwide, 801 Warrenville Rd, Suite 555, Lisle, IL 60532 Tel: 630-515-5300 Toll Free Tel: 800-342-5624 (cust serv) E-mail: contactus@oag.com Web Site: www.oag.com, pg 144

Oak Knoll Press, 310 Delaware St, New Castle, DE 19720 Tel: 302-328-7232 Fax: 302-328-7274 E-mail: oakknoll@oakknoll.com; orders@oakknoll.com; publishing@oakknoll.com Web Site: www.oakknoll.com, pg 144

The Oaklea Press Inc, 41 Old Mill Rd, Richmond, VA 23226-3111 Tel: 804-218-2394 Web Site: oakleapress.com, pg 145

Joyce Carol Oates Prize, 4100 Redwood Rd, Suite 20A-424, Oakland, CA 94619 Tel: 510-919-0970 Web Site: www.newliteraryproject.org/joyce-carol-oates-prize, pg 642

Objective Entertainment, 609 Greenwich St, 6th fl, New York, NY 10014 Tel: 212-431-5454 Web Site: www.objectiveent.com, pg 471

Eli M Oboler Memorial Award, 225 Michigan Ave, Suite 1300, Chicago, IL 60601 Tel: 312-280-4226 Toll Free Tel: 800-545-2433 E-mail: ifrt@ala.org Web Site: www.ala.org/rt/ifrt/oboler, pg 642

Ocean Tree Books, 1325 Cerro Gordo Rd, Santa Fe, NM 87501 Tel: 505-983-1412 Fax: 505-983-0899 E-mail: richard@oceantree.com Web Site: www.oceantree.com, pg 145

Oceanview Publishing Inc, PO Box 3168, Sarasota, FL 34230 Tel: 941-387-8500 Web Site: oceanviewpub.com, pg 145

The Flannery O'Connor Award for Short Fiction, Main Library, 3rd fl, 320 S Jackson St, Athens, GA 30602 Fax: 706-542-2558 Web Site: www.ugapress.org, pg 642

Frank O'Connor Prize for Fiction, Dept of English, TCU Box 297270, Fort Worth, TX 76129 E-mail: descant@tcu.edu Web Site: www.descant.tcu.edu, pg 643

OCP, 340 Oswego Pointe Dr, Lake Oswego, OR 97034 Tel: 503-281-1191 Toll Free Tel: 800-LITURGY (548-8749) Fax: 503-282-3486 Toll Free Fax: 800-843-8181 E-mail: liturgy@ocp.org Web Site: www.ocp.org, pg 145

Octane Press, 1211 W Sixth St, Suite 600-144, Austin, TX 78703 Tel: 512-334-9441; 512-761-4555 (sales) E-mail: info@octanepress.com; sales@octanepress.com Web Site: octanepress.com/content/submissions, pg 145

Scott O'Dell Award for Historical Fiction, c/o Horn Book Inc, 300 The Fenway, Suite P-311, Palace Road Bldg, Boston, MA 02215 Tel: 617-278-0225 Toll Free Tel: 888-628-0225 E-mail: scottodellfanpage@gmail.com Web Site: scottodell.com/the-scott-odell-award, pg 643

Odyssey Award for Excellence in Audiobook Production, 225 N Michigan Ave, Suite 1300, Chicago, IL 60601 Toll Free Tel: 800-545-2433 (ext 4390) E-mail: yalsa@ala.org Web Site: www.ala.org/yalsa/odyssey, pg 643

Odyssey Books, 2421 Redwood Ct, Longmont, CO 80503-8155 Tel: 720-494-1473 Fax: 720-494-1471 E-mail: books@odysseybooks.net, pg 145

OECD Washington Center, 1776 "I" St NW, Suite 450, Washington, DC 20006 Tel: 202-785-6323 Toll Free Tel: 800-456-6323 (dist ctr/pubns orders) Fax: 202-

785-0350 E-mail: washington.contact@oecd.org; oecdilibrary@oecd.org (sales) Web Site: www.oecd-ilibrary.org, pg 145

Annual Off Off Broadway Short Play Festival, 250 W 57 St, 6th fl, New York, NY 10107-0102 Toll Free Tel: 866-979-0447 E-mail: oobfestival@samuelfrench.com; info@concordtheatricals.com Web Site: oobfestival.com; www.concordtheatricals.com, pg 643

Karma Deane Ogden Memorial, PO Box 36128, North Chesterfield, VA 23235-3533 E-mail: contest@poetrysocietyofvirginia.org; info@poetryvirginia.org Web Site: www.poetrysocietyofvirginia.org, pg 643

Dayne Ogilvie Prize for LGBTQ2S+ Emerging Writers, 600-460 Richmond St W, Toronto, ON M5V 1Y1, Canada Tel: 416-504-8222 Toll Free Tel: 877-906-6548 Fax: 416-504-9090 E-mail: info@writerstrust.com Web Site: www.writerstrust.com, pg 643

Howard O'Hagan Award for Short Story, 11759 Groat Rd NW, Edmonton, AB T5M 3K6, Canada Tel: 780-422-8174 Toll Free Tel: 800-665-5354 (AB only) E-mail: mail@writersguild.ab.ca Web Site: writersguild.ca, pg 643

Ohio Genealogical Society, 611 State Rte 97 W, Bellville, OH 44813-8813 Tel: 419-886-1903 E-mail: ogs@ogs.org Web Site: www.ogs.org, pg 145

The Ohio State University Press, 180 Pressey Hall, 1070 Carmack Rd, Columbus, OH 43210-1002 Tel: 614-292-6930 Fax: 614-292-2065 Toll Free Fax: 800-621-8476 E-mail: OSUPInfo@osu.edu Web Site: ohiostatepress.org, pg 145

Ohio University, English Department, Creative Writing Program, Ohio University, English Dept, Ellis Hall, Athens, OH 45701 E-mail: english.department@ohio.edu Web Site: www.ohio.edu/cas/english, pg 564

Ohio University Press, Alden Library, Suite 101, 30 Park Place, Athens, OH 45701-2909 Tel: 740-593-1154 Web Site: www.ohioswallow.com, pg 145

Ohioana Book Awards, 274 E First Ave, Suite 300, Columbus, OH 43201 Tel: 614-466-3831 Fax: 614-728-6974 E-mail: ohioana@ohioana.org Web Site: www.ohioana.org, pg 643

Ohioana Walter Rumsey Marvin Grant, 274 E First Ave, Suite 300, Columbus, OH 43201 Tel: 614-466-3831 Fax: 614-728-6974 E-mail: ohioana@ohioana.org Web Site: www.ohioana.org, pg 643

Oklahoma Book Awards, 200 NE 18 St, Oklahoma City, OK 73105-3205 Tel: 405-522-3383 Web Site: libraries.ok.gov/ocb/ok-book-awards/, pg 643

Olde & Oppenheim Publishers, 3219 N Margate Place, Chandler, AZ 85224 E-mail: olde_oppenheim@hotmail.com, pg 146

Veronica Oliva, 304 Lily St, San Francisco, CA 94102-5608 Tel: 415-337-7707 E-mail: veronicaoliva@sbcglobal.net, pg 443

Nancy Olson Bookseller Award, 51 Pleasant Ridge Dr, Asheville, NC 28805 Tel: 803-994-9530 Fax: 309-410-0211 E-mail: siba@sibaweb.com Web Site: www.sibaweb.com, pg 643

Chris O'Malley Fiction Prize, University of Wisconsin, 6193 Helen C White Hall, English Dept, 600 N Park St, Madison, WI 53706 E-mail: madisonrevw@gmail.com Web Site: www.themadisonrevw.com, pg 643

Omnibus Press, 180 Madison Ave, 24th fl, New York, NY 10016 Tel: 212-254-2100 Toll Free Tel: 800-431-7187 Fax: 212-254-2013 Toll Free Fax: 800-345-6842 E-mail: info@omnibuspress.com Web Site: www.omnibuspress.com; www.musicsales.com, pg 146

Omnidawn, 1632 Elm Ave, Richmond, CA 94805 Tel: 510-439-6285 E-mail: manager@omnidawn.com Web Site: www.omnidawn.com, pg 146

Omnigraphics Inc, 615 Griswold, Suite 520, Detroit, MI 48226 Tel: 610-461-3548 Toll Free Tel: 800-234-1340 (cust serv) Fax: 610-532-9001 Toll Free Fax: 800-875-1340 (cust serv) E-mail: contact@omnigraphics.com; customerservice@omnigraphics.com Web Site: omnigraphics.com, pg 146

Omohundro Institute of Early American History & Culture, Swem Library, Ground fl, 400 Landrum Dr, Williamsburg, VA 23185 Tel: 757-221-1114 Fax: 757-221-1047 E-mail: ieahc1@wm.edu Web Site: oieahc.wm.edu, pg 146

On-the-Verge Emerging Voices Award, 6363 Wilshire Blvd, Suite 425, Los Angeles, CA 90048 Tel: 323-782-1010 E-mail: info@scbwi.org Web Site: www.scbwi.org/awards/grants/on-the-verge-emerging-voices-grant, pg 644

On the Write Path Publishing, 5023 W 120 Ave, Suite 228, Broomfield, CO 80020 Tel: 303-465-2056 Fax: 303-465-2056, pg 146

One Act Play Depot, Box 335, Spiritwood, SK S0J 2M0, Canada E-mail: plays@oneactplays.net; orders@oneactplays.net Web Site: oneactplays.net, pg 414

One-Act Playwriting Competition, 600 Wolfe St, Alexandria, VA 22314 Tel: 703-683-5778 (ext 2) Fax: 703-683-1378 E-mail: oneactslta@gmail.com Web Site: thelittletheatre.com, pg 644

One On One Book Publishing/Film-Video Publications, 7944 Capistrano Ave, West Hills, CA 91304 Tel: 818-340-6620; 818-340-0175 Fax: 818-340-6620 E-mail: onebookpro@aol.com, pg 146

Ontario Book Publishers Organization (OBPO), 2 Amelia St, Picton, ON K0K 2T0, Canada Tel: 416-536-7584 Web Site: obpo.ca, pg 515

Ontario Library Association (OLA), 2080 Danforth Ave, Toronto, ON M4C 1J9, Canada Toll Free Tel: 877-340-1730 E-mail: info@accessola.com Web Site: accessola.com, pg 515

Oolichan Books, PO Box 2278, Fernie, BC V0B 1M0, Canada Tel: 250-423-6113 E-mail: info@oolichan.com Web Site: www.oolichan.com, pg 414

Ooligan Press, Portland State University, PO Box 751, Portland, OR 97207 Tel: 503-725-9748 Fax: 503-725-3561 E-mail: ooligan@ooliganpress.pdx.edu Web Site: www.ooliganpress.com, pg 146

Open Book Literary, 1500 Chestnut St, Suite 2, No 1436, Philadelphia, PA 19102 E-mail: info@openbooklit.com Web Site: www.openbooklit.com, pg 471

Open Books Press, 4719 Holly Hills Ave, St Louis, MO 63116 Tel: 314-827-6567 E-mail: info@openbookspress.com Web Site: openbookspress.com, pg 146

Open Chapbook Competition, PO Box 1626, Georgetown, KY 40324 Tel: 502-603-0670 E-mail: finishingbooks@aol.com; flpbookstore@aol.com Web Site: www.finishinglinepress.com, pg 644

Open City Fellowship, 112 W 27 St, Suite 600, New York, NY 10001 Tel: 212-494-0061 E-mail: fellowships@aaww.org Web Site: aaww.org/fellowships/open-city, pg 644

Open Court Publishing Co, 1751 Pinnacle Dr, Suite 600, McLean, VA 22102 Tel: 703-885-3400 E-mail: mediarelations@cricketmedia.com; licensing@cricketmedia.com; support@cricketmedia.com Web Site: cricketmedia.com/open-court-publishing, pg 147

Open Horizons Publishing Co, PO Box 271, Dolan Springs, NM 86441 Tel: 575-741-1581 E-mail: books@bookmarketingbestsellers.com Web Site: bookmarketingbestsellers.com, pg 147

Open Letter, University of Rochester, Dewey Hall, 1-219, Box 278968, Rochester, NY 14627 Tel: 585-319-0823 Fax: 585-273-1097 E-mail: contact@openletterbooks.org Web Site: www.openletterbooks.org, pg 147

Open Season Awards, University of Victoria, PO Box 1700, Sta CSC, Victoria, BC V8W 2Y2, Canada Tel: 250-721-8524 E-mail: malahat@uvic.ca Web Site: www.malahatreview.ca/contests/open_season/info.html; www.malahatreview.ca, pg 644

Iona & Peter Opie Prize, Indiana University, Classroom-Off Bldg, 800 E Third St, Bloomington, IN 47405 Tel: 812-856-2379 Fax: 812-856-2483

E-mail: americanfolkloresociety@afsnet.org; cf. section@afsnet.org Web Site: www.afsnet.org; childrensfolklore.org/opie-prize, pg 644

Optometric Extension Program Foundation (OEPF), 2300 York Rd, Suite 113, Timonium, MD 21093 Tel: 410-561-3791 Fax: 410-252-1719 Web Site: www.oepf.org, pg 147

OptumInsight™, 11000 Optum Circle, Eden Prairie, MN 55344 Tel: 952-833-7100 Toll Free Tel: 888-445-8745 Web Site: www.optum.com, pg 147

Orange Frazer Press Inc, 37 1/2 W Main St, Wilmington, OH 45177 Tel: 937-382-3196 Fax: 937-383-3159 E-mail: ofrazer@erinet.com Web Site: www.orangefrazer.com, pg 147

Orbis Books, PO Box 302, Maryknoll, NY 10545-0302 Tel: 914-941-7636 Toll Free Tel: 800-258-5838 (orders, Mon-Fri 8AM-4PM EST) Fax: 914-941-7005 E-mail: orbisbooks@maryknoll.org Web Site: orbisbooks.com, pg 147

Orbis Pictus Award, 340 N Neil St, Suite 104, Champaign, IL 61820 Tel: 217-328-3870 Toll Free Tel: 877-369-6283 (cust serv) Fax: 217-328-9645 E-mail: bookawards@ncte.org Web Site: ncte.org/awards/ncte-childrens-book-awards, pg 644

Orbit, 1290 Avenue of the Americas, New York, NY 10104 Tel: 212-364-1100 Toll Free Tel: 800-759-0190 Web Site: www.orbitbooks.net; www.hachettebookgroup.com/imprint/orbit, pg 147

Orca Book Publishers, 1016 Balmoral Rd, Victoria, BC V8T 1A8, Canada Toll Free Tel: 800-210-5277 Toll Free Fax: 877-408-1551 E-mail: orca@orcabook.com Web Site: www.orcabook.com, pg 415

Ordre des traducteurs, terminologues et interpretes agrees du quebec (OTTIAQ), 1108-2021 Ave Union, Montreal, QC H3A 2S9, Canada Tel: 514-845-4411 Toll Free Tel: 800-265-4815 Fax: 514-845-9903 E-mail: info@ottiaq.org; direction@ottiaq.org; reception@ottiaq.org; communications@ottiaq.org Web Site: www.ottiaq.org, pg 515

Oregon Book Awards, 925 SW Washington St, Portland, OR 97205 Tel: 503-227-2583 Fax: 503-241-4256 E-mail: la@literary-arts.org Web Site: literary-arts.org/about/programs/oba/book-awards, pg 644

Oregon State University Press, 121 The Valley Library, Corvallis, OR 97331-4501 Tel: 541-737-3166, pg 147

O'Reilly Media Inc, 1005 Gravenstein Hwy N, Sebastopol, CA 95472 Tel: 707-827-7000; 707-827-7019 (cust support) Toll Free Tel: 800-998-9938; 800-889-8969 Fax: 707-829-0104; 707-824-8268 E-mail: orders@oreilly.com; support@oreilly.com Web Site: www.oreilly.com, pg 147

Oriental Institute Publications, 1155 E 58 St, Chicago, IL 60637 Tel: 773-702-5967 E-mail: oi-publications@uchicago.edu Web Site: oi.uchicago.edu, pg 148

The Original Falcon Press, 1753 E Broadway Rd, No 101-277, Tempe, AZ 85282 Tel: 602-708-1409 E-mail: info@originalfalcon.com Web Site: www.originalfalcon.com, pg 148

The Orison Chapbook Prize, PO Box 8385, Asheville, NC 28814 Tel: 828-713-1755 E-mail: editor@orisonbooks.com Web Site: www.orisonbooks.com/submissions, pg 644

The Orison Prizes in Poetry & Fiction, PO Box 8385, Asheville, NC 28814 Tel: 828-713-1755 E-mail: editor@orisonbooks.com Web Site: www.orisonbooks.com/submissions, pg 644

ORO editions, 31 Commercial Blvd, Suite F, Novato, CA 94949 Tel: 415-883-3300 Fax: 415-883-3309 E-mail: info@oroeditions.com Web Site: www.oroeditions.com, pg 148

George Orwell Award, 340 N Neil St, Suite 104, Champaign, IL 61820 Tel: 217-328-3870 Toll Free Tel: 877-369-6283 (cust serv) Fax: 217-328-9645 E-mail: publiclangaward@ncte.org Web Site: ncte.org/awards/george-orwell-award, pg 645

COMPANY INDEX

Fifi Oscard Agency Inc, 1140 Avenue of the Americas, 9th fl, New York, NY 10036 Tel: 212-764-1100 E-mail: agency@fifioscard.com Web Site: fifioscard.com, pg 471

Other Press, 267 Fifth Ave, 6th fl, New York, NY 10016 Tel: 212-414-0054 Toll Free Tel: 877-THEOTHER (843-6843) Fax: 212-414-0939 E-mail: editor@otherpress.com; marketing@otherpress.com; publicity@otherpress.com Web Site: otherpress.com, pg 148

James H Ottaway Jr Award for the Promotion of International Literature, 147 Prince St, Brooklyn, NY 11201 Tel: 347-699-2914 E-mail: info@wordswithoutborders.org Web Site: www.wordswithoutborders.org/ottaway-award, pg 645

Ottoline Prize, 36-09 28 Ave, Apt 3R, Astoria, NY 11103-4518 Tel: 518-567-7006 Web Site: www.fenceportal.org, pg 645

Our Daily Bread Publishing, 3000 Kraft Ave SE, Grand Rapids, MI 49512 Toll Free Tel: 800-653-8333 (cust serv) E-mail: customerservice@odb.org Web Site: ourdailybreadpublishing.org, pg 148

Our Sunday Visitor Publishing, 200 Noll Plaza, Huntington, IN 46750 Tel: 260-356-8400 Toll Free Tel: 800-348-2440 (orders) Toll Free Fax: 800-498-6709 E-mail: osvbooks@osv.com (book orders); customerservice@osv.com Web Site: www.osv.com, pg 148

Outdoor Writers Association of America (OWAA), 2814 Brooks St, Box 442, Missoula, MT 59801 Tel: 406-728-7434 E-mail: info@owaa.org Web Site: owaa.org, pg 516

Outdoor Writers Association of America Annual Conference, 2814 Brooks St, Box 442, Missoula, MT 59801 Tel: 406-728-7434 E-mail: info@owaa.org Web Site: owaa.org, pg 556

The Overlook Press, 195 Broadway, 9th fl, New York, NY 10007 Tel: 212-206-7715 E-mail: abrams@abramsbooks.com; sales@abramsbooks.com (orders) Web Site: www.abramsbooks.com/imprints/overlookpress, pg 148

Overseas Press Club of America (OPC), 40 W 45 St, New York, NY 10036 Tel: 212-626-9220 E-mail: info@opcofamerica.org Web Site: opcofamerica.org, pg 516

Richard C Owen Publishers Inc, PO Box 585, Katonah, NY 10536-0585 Tel: 914-232-3903 Toll Free Tel: 800-336-5588 Fax: 914-232-3977 Web Site: www.rcowen.com, pg 149

Owlkids Books Inc, 10 Lower Spadina Ave, Suite 400, Toronto, ON M5V 2Z2, Canada Tel: 416-340-2700 Fax: 416-340-9769 E-mail: owlkids@owlkids.com Web Site: www.owlkidsbooks.com, pg 415

Frank L & Harriet C Owsley Award, University of Georgia, Dept of History, Athens, GA 30602-1602 Tel: 706-542-8848 Web Site: thesha.org, pg 645

Oxford University Press USA, 198 Madison Ave, New York, NY 10016 Toll Free Tel: 800-451-7556 (orders); 800-445-9714 (cust serv) Fax: 919-677-1303 E-mail: custserv.us@oup.com Web Site: global.oup.com, pg 149

Ozark Creative Writers Inc Annual Conference, c/o 900 W Dixson St, Rogers, AR 72758 E-mail: ozarkcreativewriters@ozarkcreativewriters.com Web Site: www.ozarkcreativewriters.com, pg 556

Ozark Mountain Publishing Inc, PO Box 754, Huntsville, AR 72740-0754 Tel: 479-738-2348 Toll Free Tel: 800-935-0045 Fax: 479-738-2448 E-mail: info@ozarkmt.com Web Site: www.ozarkmt.com, pg 149

P & R Publishing Co, 1102 Marble Hill Rd, Phillipsburg, NJ 08865 Tel: 908-454-0505 Toll Free Tel: 800-631-0094 E-mail: sales@prpbooks.com; info@prpbooks.com Web Site: www.prpbooks.com, pg 149

PA Press, 202 Warren St, Hudson, NY 12534 Tel: 518-671-6100 Toll Free Tel: 800-722-6657 (dist); 800-759-0190 (sales) E-mail: sales@papress.com Web Site: www.papress.com, pg 149

Pace University, Master of Science in Publishing, 163 William St, 18th fl, New York, NY 10038 Tel: 212-346-1431 E-mail: puboffice@pace.edu Web Site: www.pace.edu/program/publishing-ms, pg 564

Pace University Press, Pace University, One Pace Plaza, New York, NY 10038 Tel: 212-346-1417 Fax: 212-346-1417 E-mail: paceupress@gmail.com Web Site: www.pace.edu/press, pg 149

Pacific Educational Press, c/o UBC Press, 2029 West Mall, Vancouver, BC V6T 1Z2, Canada Tel: 604-822-5959 Toll Free Tel: 877-377-9378 E-mail: pep.admin@ubc.ca; pep.sales@ubc.ca Web Site: pacificedpress.ca, pg 415

Pacific Northwest Book Awards, 520 W 13 Ave, Eugene, OR 97401-3461 Tel: 541-683-4363 Fax: 541-683-3910 E-mail: info@pnba.org; awards@pnba.org Web Site: www.pnba.org/book-awards.html, pg 645

Pacific Northwest Booksellers Association (PNBA), 520 W 13 Ave, Eugene, OR 97401-3461 Tel: 541-683-4363 Toll Free Tel: 800-353-6764 Fax: 541-683-3910 E-mail: info@pnba.org Web Site: www.pnba.org, pg 516

Pacific Northwest Young Reader's Choice Award, c/o Jocie Wilson, Yellowhead Regional Library, 433 King St, Spruce Grove, AB T7X 2C6, Canada E-mail: yrcachair@gmail.com Web Site: www.pnla.org/yrca, pg 645

Pacific Press® Publishing Association, 1350 N Kings Rd, Nampa, ID 83687-3193 Tel: 208-465-2500 Fax: 208-465-2531 E-mail: booksubmissions@pacificpress.com Web Site: www.pacificpress.com, pg 149

The Pacific Spirit Poetry Prize, University of British Columbia, Buch E462, 1866 Main Mall, Vancouver, BC V6T 1Z1, Canada Tel: 604-822-2514 Fax: 604-822-3616 E-mail: promotions@prismmagazine.ca Web Site: www.prismmagazine.ca/contests, pg 645

Pact Press, c/o Regal House Publishing, 806 Oberlin Rd, No 12094, Raleigh, NC 27605 E-mail: info@regalhousepublishing.com Web Site: pactpress.com, pg 150

PAGE International Screenwriting Awards, 7190 W Sunset Blvd, Suite 610, Hollywood, CA 90046 E-mail: info@pageawards.com Web Site: pageawards.com, pg 645

Paintbox Press, 275 Madison Ave, Suite 600, New York, NY 10016 Tel: 212-878-6610 E-mail: info@paintboxpress.com Web Site: www.paintboxpress.com, pg 150

Painted-Words Inc, 310 W 97 St, Suite 24, New York, NY 10025 Tel: 212-663-2311 E-mail: info@painted-words.com Web Site: painted-words.com, pg 486

Dobie Paisano Fellowship Program, 110 Inner Campus Dr, Stop G0400, Austin, TX 78712-0710 Fax: 512-471-7620 Web Site: dobiepaisano.utexas.edu, pg 645

Palgrave Macmillan, One New York Plaza, Suite 4500, New York, NY 10004-1562 Tel: 212-726-9200 E-mail: sales-ny@springernature.com Web Site: www.palgrave.com; www.springernature.com, pg 150

Palimpsest Press, 1171 Eastlawn Ave, Windsor, ON N8S 3J1, Canada Tel: 519-259-2112 E-mail: publicity@palimpsestpress.ca Web Site: www.palimpsestpress.ca, pg 415

Palladium Books Inc, 39074 Webb Ct, Westland, MI 48185 Tel: 734-721-2903 (orders) Web Site: www.palladiumbooks.com, pg 150

Palm Island Press, 2039 Geogia St, Sebring, FL 33870 Tel: 305-296-3102 E-mail: pipress2@gmail.com, pg 150

Palm Springs Writers Guild, 44489 Town Center Way, Suite D, 369, Palm Desert, CA 92260 E-mail: pswg@geographilia.com Web Site: palmspringswritersguild.org, pg 516

Pangaea Publications, 110183 Friendship Lane S, Chaska, MN 55318 Tel: 651-226-2032 E-mail: info@pangaea.org Web Site: pangaea.org, pg 150

Mildred & Albert Panowski Playwriting Award, Forest Roberts Theatre, 1401 Presque Isle Ave, Marquette, MI 49855-5364 Tel: 906-227-2553 Fax: 906-227-2567 E-mail: theatre@nmu.edu Web Site: www.nmu.edu/theatre, pg 645

Pantheon Books, c/o Penguin Random House LLC, 1745 Broadway, New York, NY 10019 Tel: 212-751-2600 Fax: 212-940-7390 (dom rts); 212-572-2662 (foreign rts) Web Site: knopfdoubleday.com/imprint/pantheon/; knopfdoubleday.com, pg 150

Pants On Fire Press, 10441 Waterbird Way, Bradenton, FL 34209 Tel: 941-405-3078 E-mail: submission@pantsonfirepress.com Web Site: www.pantsonfirepress.com, pg 150

Papercutz, 8838 SW 129 St, Miami, FL 33176 Tel: 786-953-4195 E-mail: contact@papercutz.com; snellis@madcavestudios.com Web Site: www.papercutz.com, pg 150

Parachute Publishing LLC, PO Box 320249, Fairfield, CT 06825 Tel: 203-255-1303, pg 151

Paraclete Press Inc, 100 Southern Eagle Cartway, Brewster, MA 02631 Tel: 508-255-4685 Toll Free Tel: 800-451-5006 E-mail: mail@paracletepress.com; customerservice@paracletepress.com Web Site: www.paracletepress.com, pg 151

Paradigm Publications, 202 Bendix Dr, Taos, NM 87571 Tel: 575-758-7758 Toll Free Tel: 800-873-3946 (US); 888-873-3947 (CN) Fax: 575-758-7768 E-mail: info@paradigm-pubs.com Web Site: www.paradigm-pubs.com; www.redwingbooks.com, pg 151

Paradise Cay Publications Inc, 120 Monda Way, Blue Lake, CA 95525 Tel: 707-822-9063 Toll Free Tel: 800-736-4509 Fax: 707-822-9163 E-mail: info@paracay.com; orders@paracay.com Web Site: www.paracay.com, pg 151

Paragon House, 3600 Labore Rd, Suite 1, St Paul, MN 55110-4144 Tel: 651-644-3087 Toll Free Tel: 800-447-3709 Fax: 651-644-0997 E-mail: paragon@paragonhouse.com Web Site: www.paragonhouse.com, pg 151

Parallax Press, 2236B Sixth St, Berkeley, CA 94710 Tel: 510-325-2945 Toll Free Tel: 800-863-5290 (orders) Web Site: www.parallax.org, pg 151

Paramount Market Publishing Inc, 274 N Goodman St, Suite D214, Rochester, NY 14607 Tel: 607-275-8100 E-mail: editors@paramountbooks.com Web Site: www.paramountbooks.com, pg 151

Parenting Press, 13751 Lake City Way NE, Suite 110, Seattle, WA 98125 Tel: 206-364-2900 Toll Free Tel: 800-99-BOOKS (992-6657) Fax: 206-364-0702 E-mail: office@parentingpress.com; marketing@parentingpress.com Web Site: www.parentingpress.com, pg 151

Park Place Publications, 410 Central Ave, No 3, Pacific Grove, CA 93950-2836 Tel: 831-649-6640 E-mail: publishingbiz@sbcglobal.net Web Site: www.parkplacepublications.com, pg 152

Mel Parker Books LLC, 215 E 68 St, 10-O, New York, NY 10065 Tel: 917-696-6105 E-mail: info@melparkerbooks.com Web Site: melparkerbooks.com, pg 471

William Riley Parker Prize, 85 Broad St, New York, NY 10004 Tel: 646-576-5141; 646-576-5000 E-mail: awards@mla.org Web Site: www.mla.org, pg 645

Francis Parkman Prize, Columbia University, 3009 Broadway MC 802, New York, NY 10027 Tel: 212-854-1919 E-mail: amhistsociety@columbia.edu Web Site: sah.columbia.edu, pg 646

Parmenides Publishing, 3753 Howard Hughes Pkwy, Suite 200, Las Vegas, NV 89169 Tel: 702-892-3934 Fax: 702-892-3939 E-mail: info@parmenides.com; editor@parmenides.com Web Site: www.parmenides.com, pg 152

Parsons School of Design, Continuing & Professional Education, 66 W 12 St, New York, NY 10011 *Tel:* 212-229-8933 ext 4076 *E-mail:* continuinged@newschool.edu *Web Site:* www.newschool.edu/parsons, pg 564

The Scott Parsons Literary Award, 81 Prince St, Charlottetown, PE C1A 4R3, Canada *E-mail:* peiliteraryawards@gmail.com *Web Site:* www.peiwritersguild.com, pg 646

The Paterson Poetry Prize, One College Blvd, Paterson, NJ 07505-1179 *Tel:* 973-684-6555 *Fax:* 973-523-6085 *Web Site:* www.poetrycenterpccc.com, pg 646

The Paterson Prize for Books for Young People, One College Blvd, Paterson, NJ 07505-1179 *Tel:* 973-684-6555 *Fax:* 973-523-6085 *Web Site:* www.poetrycenterpccc.com, pg 646

Path Press Inc, 708 Washington St, Evanston, IL 60202 *Tel:* 847-492-0177 *E-mail:* pathpressinc@aol.com, pg 152

Pathfinder Publishing Inc, 120 S Houghton Rd, Suite 138, Tucson, AZ 85748 *Tel:* 520-647-0158 *Web Site:* www.pathfinderpublishing.com, pg 152

Kathi J Paton Literary Agency, Box 2044, Radio City Sta, New York, NY 10101-2044 *Tel:* 212-265-6586 *E-mail:* kjplitbiz@optonline.net *Web Site:* www.patonliterary.com, pg 471

Diane Patrick, 140 Carver Loop, No 21A, Bronx, NY 10475-2954 *E-mail:* dpatrickediting@aol.com *Web Site:* dianepatrick.wordpress.com, pg 443

The Alicia Patterson Foundation Fellowship Program, 1100 Vermont Ave, Suite 900, Washington, DC 20005 *Tel:* 202-393-5995 *Fax:* 301-951-8512 *E-mail:* info@aliciapatterson.org *Web Site:* www.aliciapatterson.org, pg 646

The Pattis Family Foundation Book Award, 60 W Walton St, Chicago, IL 60610 *Tel:* 312-943-9090 *E-mail:* pattisprize@newberry.org *Web Site:* www.newberry.org/pattis-family-foundation-chicago-book-award, pg 646

Pattis Family Foundation Global Cities Book Award, Prudential Plaza, 180 N Stetson Ave, Suite 1400, Chicago, IL 60601 *Tel:* 312-726-3860 *Fax:* 312-821-7555 *E-mail:* gcbookaward@thechicagocouncil.org *Web Site:* globalaffairs.org/bookaward, pg 646

Paul Dry Books, 1700 Sansom St, Suite 700, Philadelphia, PA 19103 *Tel:* 215-231-9939 *E-mail:* editor@pauldrybooks.com *Web Site:* www.pauldrybooks.com, pg 152

Pauline Books & Media, 50 Saint Paul's Ave, Boston, MA 02130 *Tel:* 617-522-8911 *Toll Free Tel:* 800-876-4463 (orders); 800-836-9723 (cust serv) *Fax:* 617-541-9805 *E-mail:* editorial@paulinemedia.com (ms submissions); orderentry@pauline.org (cust serv) *Web Site:* www.pauline.org/pbmpublishing pg 152

Paulines Editions, 5610 rue Beaubien est, Montreal, QC H1T 1X5, Canada *Tel:* 514-253-5610 *Fax:* 514-253-1907 *E-mail:* editions@paulines.qc.ca; fsp-paulines@videotron.ca *Web Site:* www.editions.paulines.qc.ca, pg 415

Paulist Press, 997 Macarthur Blvd, Mahwah, NJ 07430-9990 *Tel:* 201-825-7300 *Toll Free Tel:* 800-218-1903 *Fax:* 201-825-6921 *E-mail:* info@paulistpress.com; publicity@paulistpress.com *Web Site:* www.paulistpress.com, pg 152

Nancy Paulsen Books, c/o Penguin Random House LLC, 1745 Broadway, New York, NY 10019 *Tel:* 212-782-9000 *Web Site:* www.penguin.com/nancy-paulsen-books-overview/, pg 152

Peabody Museum Press, 11 Divinity Ave, Cambridge, MA 02138 *Tel:* 617-495-4255; 617-495-3938 (edit) *E-mail:* peapub@fas.harvard.edu *Web Site:* www.peabody.harvard.edu/publications, pg 153

Peachpit Press, 1301 Sansome St, San Francisco, CA 94111 *Toll Free Tel:* 800-283-9444 *E-mail:* info@peachpit.com; ask@peachpit.com *Web Site:* www.peachpit.com, pg 153

Peachtree Publishing Co Inc, 1700 Chattahoochee Ave, Atlanta, GA 30318-2112 *Tel:* 404-876-8761 *Toll Free Tel:* 800-241-0113 *Fax:* 404-875-2578 *Toll Free Fax:* 800-875-8909 *E-mail:* hello@peachtree-online.com; orders@peachtree-online.com; sales@peachtree-online.com *Web Site:* www.peachtreebooks.com; www.peachtree-online.com, pg 153

PearlCo Literary Agency, LLC, 6596 Heronswood Cove, Memphis, TN 38119 *Tel:* 901-754-5276 *Web Site:* www.pearlcoliteraryagency.com, pg 472

Pearson Business Publishing, 221 River St, Hoboken, NJ 07030-4772 *Tel:* 201-236-7000 *Web Site:* www.pearsonhighered.com, pg 153

Pearson Education Canada, 26 Prince Andrew Place, North York, ON M3C 2H4, Canada *Toll Free Tel:* 800-567-3800 *Fax:* 416-447-7755 *Toll Free Fax:* 800-263-7733 *E-mail:* cdn.ordr@pearsoned.com *Web Site:* www.pearson.com/ca; www.mypearsonstore.ca, pg 415

Pearson Education Ltd, 225 River St, Hoboken, NJ 07030-4772 *Tel:* 201-236-7000 *Fax:* 201-236-6549 *Web Site:* www.pearson.com, pg 153

Pearson ELT, 221 River St, Hoboken, NJ 07030 *Tel:* 815-862-4472 *Web Site:* www.pearson.com/languages, pg 153

Pearson Higher Education, 221 River St, Hoboken, NJ 07030 *Tel:* 201-236-7000 *Web Site:* www.pearson.com/en-us/highered-education.html, pg 153

Pearson Learning Solutions, 501 Boylston St, Suite 900, Boston, MA 02116 *Tel:* 617-671-3300 *Toll Free Tel:* 800-428-4466 (orders); 800-635-1579 *E-mail:* pcp@pearson.com *Web Site:* www.pearsoned.com, pg 153

Deborah Pease Prize, 323 Dean St, Brooklyn, NY 11217 *Tel:* 718-858-8067 *E-mail:* general@apublicspace.org *Web Site:* apublicspace.org, pg 646

Jean Pedrick Chapbook Prize, c/o Linda Haviland Conte, 18 Hall Ave, Apt 2, Somerville, MA 02144 *E-mail:* info@nepoetryclub.org *Web Site:* nepoetryclub.org, pg 646

Pegasus Award for Poetry Criticism, 61 W Superior St, Chicago, IL 60654 *Tel:* 312-787-7070 *E-mail:* info@poetryfoundation.org *Web Site:* www.poetryfoundation.org/foundation/criticism-award, pg 646

Pelican Publishing, 990 N Corporate Dr, Suite 100, New Orleans, LA 70123 *Tel:* 504-684-8976 *Toll Free Tel:* 844-868-1798 (orders) *E-mail:* editorial@pelicanpub.com (submissions) *Web Site:* www.pelicanpub.com; www.arcadiapublishing.com/imprints/pelican-publishing, pg 153

Pembroke Publishers Ltd, 538 Hood Rd, Markham, ON L3R 3K9, Canada *Tel:* 905-477-0650 *Toll Free Tel:* 800-997-9807 *Fax:* 905-477-3691 *Toll Free Fax:* 800-339-5568 *Web Site:* www.pembrokepublishers.com, pg 415

PEN America, 120 Broadway, 26th fl N, New York, NY 10271 *Tel:* 212-334-1660 *Fax:* 212-334-2181 *E-mail:* info@pen.org; membership@pen.org; education@pen.org *Web Site:* pen.org, pg 516

PEN America Literary Awards, 120 Broadway, 26th fl N, New York, NY 10271 *Tel:* 212-334-1660 *Fax:* 212-334-2181 *E-mail:* awards@pen.org; info@pen.org *Web Site:* pen.org/literary-awards, pg 646

PEN America Los Angeles, 1370 N St Andrews Place, Los Angeles, CA 90028 *Tel:* 323-607-1867 *E-mail:* info@pen.org *Web Site:* pen.org, pg 516

PEN America Washington, DC, 1100 13 St NW, Suite 800, Washington, DC 20005 *E-mail:* info@pen.org *Web Site:* pen.org/region/washington-dc, pg 516

Pen & Publish LLC, 4719 Holly Hills Ave, St Louis, MO 63116 *Tel:* 314-827-6567 *E-mail:* info@penandpublish.com *Web Site:* www.penandpublish.com, pg 153

PEN Award for Poetry in Translation, 120 Broadway, 26th fl N, New York, NY 10271 *Tel:* 212-334-1660 *Fax:* 212-334-2181 *E-mail:* awards@pen.org; info@pen.org *Web Site:* pen.org/pen-award-poetry-translation, pg 646

PEN/Barbey Freedom to Write Award, 120 Broadway, 26th fl N, New York, NY 10271 *Tel:* 212-334-1660 *Fax:* 212-334-2181 *E-mail:* awards@pen.org; info@pen.org *Web Site:* pen.org/penbarbey-freedom-to-write-award, pg 647

PEN/Bernard & Ann Malamud Award for Excellence in the Short Story, 6218 Georgia Ave NW, Unit 1062, Washington, DC 20011 *Tel:* 202-898-9063 *Fax:* 202-675-0360 *E-mail:* awards@penfaulkner.org; info@penfaulkner.org *Web Site:* www.penfaulkner.org/our-awards/the-pen-malamud-award, pg 647

PEN Canada, 401 Richmond St W, Suite 244, Toronto, ON M5V 3A8, Canada *Tel:* 416-703-8448 *E-mail:* queries@pencanada.ca *Web Site:* www.pencanada.ca, pg 516

PEN/Diamonstein-Spielvogel Award for the Art of the Essay, 120 Broadway, 26th fl N, New York, NY 10271 *Tel:* 212-334-1660 *Fax:* 212-334-2181 *E-mail:* awards@pen.org; info@pen.org *Web Site:* pen.org/pen-diamonstein-spielvogel-award-for-the-art-of-the-essay, pg 647

PEN/E O Wilson Literary Science Writing Award, 120 Broadway, 26th fl N, New York, NY 10271 *Tel:* 212-334-1660 *Fax:* 212-334-2181 *E-mail:* awards@pen.org; info@pen.org *Web Site:* pen.org/pen-eo-wilson-prize-literary-science-writing, pg 647

PEN/Faulkner Award for Fiction, 6218 Georgia Ave NW, Unit 1062, Washington, DC 20011 *Tel:* 202-898-9063 *E-mail:* awards@penfaulkner.org *Web Site:* www.penfaulkner.org/our-awards/pen-faulkner-award, pg 647

PEN/Heim Translation Fund Grants, 120 Broadway, 26th fl N, New York, NY 10271 *Tel:* 212-334-1660 *Fax:* 212-334-2181 *E-mail:* awards@pen.org *Web Site:* pen.org/pen-heim-grants, pg 647

PEN/Hemingway Award for Debut Novel, 120 Broadway, 26th fl N, New York, NY 10271 *Tel:* 212-334-1660 *Fax:* 212-334-2181 *E-mail:* awards@pen.org; info@pen.org *Web Site:* pen.org/pen-hemingway-award, pg 647

PEN/Jacqueline Bograd Weld Award for Biography, 120 Broadway, 26th fl N, New York, NY 10271 *Tel:* 212-334-1660 *Fax:* 212-334-2181 *E-mail:* awards@pen.org; info@pen.org *Web Site:* pen.org/pen-bograd-weld-award-biography, pg 647

PEN/Jean Stein Book Award, 120 Broadway, 26th fl N, New York, NY 10271 *Tel:* 212-334-1660 *Fax:* 212-334-2181 *E-mail:* awards@pen.org; info@pen.org *Web Site:* pen.org/pen-jean-stein-book-award, pg 647

PEN/John Kenneth Galbraith Award for Nonfiction, 120 Broadway, 26th fl N, New York, NY 10271 *Tel:* 212-334-1660 *Fax:* 212-334-2181 *E-mail:* awards@pen.org; info@pen.org *Web Site:* pen.org/pen-galbraith-award-for-nonfiction, pg 647

Pen-L Publishing, 12 W Dickson St, No 4455, Fayetteville, AR 72702 *E-mail:* info@pen-l.com *Web Site:* www.pen-l.com, pg 153

PEN/Mike Nichols Writing for Performance Award, 120 Broadway, 26th fl N, New York, NY 10271 *Tel:* 212-334-1660 *Fax:* 212-334-2181 *E-mail:* awards@pen.org; info@pen.org *Web Site:* pen.org/pen-nichols-award, pg 647

PEN/Nabokov Award for Achievement in International Literature, 120 Broadway, 26th fl N, New York, NY 10271 *Tel:* 212-334-1660 *Fax:* 212-334-2181 *E-mail:* awards@pen.org; info@pen.org *Web Site:* pen.org/pen-nabokov-award, pg 648

PEN Open Book Award, 120 Broadway, 26th fl N, New York, NY 10271 *Tel:* 212-334-1660 *Fax:* 212-334-2181 *E-mail:* awards@pen.org; info@pen.org *Web Site:* pen.org/pen-open-book-award, pg 648

PEN/Phyllis Naylor Grant for Children's & Young Adult Novelists, 120 Broadway, 26th fl N, New York, NY 10271 *Tel:* 212-334-1660 *Fax:* 212-334-2181 *E-mail:* awards@pen.org; info@pen.org *Web Site:* pen.org/literary-awards/grants-fellowships, pg 648

PEN/Ralph Manheim Award for Translation, 120 Broadway, 26th fl N, New York, NY 10271 Tel: 212-334-1660 Fax: 212-334-2181 E-mail: awards@pen.org; info@pen.org Web Site: pen.org/literary-award/penralph-manheim-medal-for-translation, pg 648

PEN/Robert J Dau Short Story Prize for Emerging Writers, 120 Broadway, 26th fl N, New York, NY 10271 Tel: 212-334-1660 Fax: 212-334-2181 E-mail: awards@pen.org; info@pen.org Web Site: pen.org/pen-dau-short-story-prize, pg 648

PEN/Robert W Bingham Prize for Debut Short Story Collection, 120 Broadway, 26th fl N, New York, NY 10271 Tel: 212-334-1660 Fax: 212-334-2181 E-mail: awards@pen.org; info@pen.org Web Site: pen.org/pen-bingham-prize, pg 648

PEN/Saul Bellow Award for Achievement in American Fiction, 120 Broadway, 26th fl N, New York, NY 10271 Tel: 212-334-1660 Fax: 212-334-2181 E-mail: awards@pen.org; info@pen.org Web Site: pen.org/pen-saul-bellow-award, pg 648

PEN Translation Prize, 120 Broadway, 26th fl N, New York, NY 10271 Tel: 212-334-1660 Fax: 212-334-2181 E-mail: awards@pen.org; info@pen.org Web Site: pen.org/pen-translation-prize, pg 648

PEN/Voelcker Award for Poetry Collection, 120 Broadway, 26th fl N, New York, NY 10271 Tel: 212-334-1660 Fax: 212-334-2181 E-mail: awards@pen.org; info@pen.org Web Site: pen.org/pen-voelcker-award-poetry, pg 648

PEN Writers' Emergency Fund, 120 Broadway, 26th fl N, New York, NY 10271 Tel: 212-334-1660 Fax: 212-334-2181 E-mail: writersfund@pen.org; info@pen.org Web Site: pen.org/writers-emergency-fund, pg 648

Pendragon Press, 52 White Hill Rd, Hillsdale, NY 12529-5839 Tel: 518-325-6100 Toll Free Tel: 877-656-6381 (orders) E-mail: editor@pendragonpress.com; orders@pendragonpress.com Web Site: www.pendragonpress.com, pg 154

Penfield Books, 215 Brown St, Iowa City, IA 52245 Tel: 319-337-9998 Toll Free Tel: 800-728-9998 Fax: 319-351-6846 E-mail: penfield@penfieldbooks.com; orders@penfieldbooks.com Web Site: www.penfieldbooks.com, pg 154

Penguin Press, c/o Penguin Random House LLC, 1745 Broadway, New York, NY 10019 Tel: 212-782-9000 E-mail: penguinpress@penguinrandomhouse.com Web Site: www.penguin.com/penguin-press-overview/, pg 154

Penguin Publishing Group, c/o Penguin Random House LLC, 1745 Broadway, New York, NY 10019 Tel: 212-782-9000 Web Site: www.penguin.com, pg 154

Penguin Random House Audio Publishing Group, 1745 Broadway, New York, NY 10019 Toll Free Tel: 800-793-2665 (cust serv) E-mail: audio@penguinrandomhouse.com; ecustomerservice@penguinrandomhouse.com Web Site: www.penguinrandomhouseaudio.com, pg 154

Penguin Random House Canada, a Penguin Random House company, 320 Front St W, Suite 1100, Toronto, ON M5V 3B6, Canada Tel: 416-364-4449 Toll Free Tel: 888-523-9292 (cust serv) E-mail: canadaweb@penguinrandomhouse.com; customerservicescanada@penguinrandomhouse.com Web Site: www.penguinrandomhouse.ca, pg 415

Penguin Random House LLC, 1745 Broadway, New York, NY 10019 Tel: 212-782-9000 Toll Free Tel: 800-726-0600 Web Site: www.penguinrandomhouse.com, pg 155

Penguin Random House Speakers Bureau, a Penguin Random House company, 1745 Broadway, Mail Drop 13-1, New York, NY 10019 Tel: 212-572-2013 E-mail: speakers@penguinrandomhouse.com Web Site: www.prhspeakers.com, pg 487

Penguin Workshop, c/o Penguin Random House LLC, 1745 Broadway, New York, NY 10019 Tel: 212-782-9000 Web Site: www.penguin.com/publishers/penguinworkshop/, pg 156

Penguin Young Readers Group, c/o Penguin Random House LLC, 1745 Broadway, New York, NY 10019 Tel: 212-782-9000 Web Site: www.penguin.com/penguin-young-readers-overview, pg 156

Penn State University Press, University Support Bldg 1, Suite C, 820 N University Dr, University Park, PA 16802-1003 Tel: 814-865-1327 Toll Free Tel: 800-326-9180 (orders & cust serv) Fax: 814-863-1408 Toll Free Fax: 877-778-2665 (book orders) E-mail: orders@psupress.org; customerservice@psupress.org Web Site: www.psupress.org, pg 157

Pennsylvania Historical & Museum Commission, State Museum Bldg, 300 North St, Harrisburg, PA 17120-0053 Tel: 717-787-3362; 717-787-5526 (orders) E-mail: ra-shoppaheritage@pa.gov Web Site: www.phmc.pa.gov; www.shoppaheritage.com, pg 157

Pennsylvania State Data Center, Penn State Harrisburg, 777 W Harrisburg Pike, Middletown, PA 17057-4898 Tel: 717-948-6336 Fax: 717-948-6754 E-mail: pasdc@psu.edu Web Site: pasdc.hbg.psu.edu, pg 157

PennWell Books, 10050 E 52 St, Tulsa, OK 74146 Toll Free Tel: 866-777-1814 Fax: 918-550-8962 E-mail: sales@pennwellbooks.com Web Site: www.pennwellbooks.com, pg 157

Pennwriters Conference, PO Box 685, Dalton, PA 18414 E-mail: conferencecoordinator@pennwriters.org; info@pennwriters.org Web Site: pennwriters.org, pg 556

Penny-Farthing Productions, One Sugar Creek Center Blvd, Suite 820, Sugar Land, TX 77478 Tel: 713-780-0300 Toll Free Tel: 800-926-2669 Fax: 713-780-4004 E-mail: corp@pfproductions.com Web Site: www.pfproductions.com, pg 157

Pentecostal Resources Group, 36 Research Park Ct, Weldon Spring, MO 63304 Tel: 636-229-7900 Toll Free Tel: 866-819-7667 Web Site: www.pentecostalpublishing.com, pg 157

PeopleSpeak, 24338 El Toro Rd, No E227, Laguna Woods, CA 92637 Tel: 949-581-6190 Fax: 949-581-4958 E-mail: pplspeak@att.net Web Site: www.peoplespeakservices.com, pg 443

Rebecca Pepper, 434 NE Floral Place, Portland, OR 97232 Tel: 503-236-5802 E-mail: rpepper@rpepper.net, pg 443

Peradam Press, PO Box 6, North San Juan, CA 95960-0006 Tel: 530-277-9324 Fax: 530-559-0754 E-mail: peradam@earthlink.net, pg 158

Dan Peragine Literary Agency, PO Box 5032, South Hackensack, NJ 07606 Tel: 201-390-0468 E-mail: dannyperagine@aol.com, pg 472

Perfection Learning®, 1000 N Second Ave, Logan, IA 51546-1061 Tel: 712-644-2831 Toll Free Tel: 800-831-4190 Toll Free Fax: 800-543-2745 E-mail: orders@perfectionlearning.com Web Site: www.perfectionlearning.com, pg 158

Perkoff Prize, 357 McReynolds Hall, University of Missouri, Columbia, MO 65211 Tel: 573-882-4474 E-mail: contest_question@moreview.com Web Site: www.missourireview.com/contests/perkoff-prize, pg 648

The Permanent Press, 4170 Noyac Rd, Sag Harbor, NY 11963 Tel: 631-725-1101 E-mail: info@thepermanentpress.com Web Site: www.thepermanentpress.com, pg 158

Aliki Perroti & Seth Frank Most Promising Young Poet Award, 75 Maiden Lane, Suite 901, New York, NY 10038 Tel: 212-274-0343 E-mail: awards@poets.org Web Site: poets.org/academy-american-poets/american-poets-prizes, pg 649

Persea Books, 90 Broad St, Suite 2100, New York, NY 10004 Tel: 212-260-9256 E-mail: info@perseabooks.com; poetry@perseabooks.com; publicity@perseabooks.com Web Site: www.perseabooks.com, pg 158

Perugia Press Prize, PO Box 60364, Florence, MA 01062 Web Site: www.perugiapress.com; perugiapress.org, pg 649

Peter Pauper Press, Inc, 202 Mamaroneck Ave, Suite 400, White Plains, NY 10601-5376 Tel: 914-681-0144 Fax: 914-681-0389 E-mail: customerservice@peterpauper.com; orders@peterpauper.com; marketing@peterpauper.com Web Site: www.peterpauper.com, pg 158

Elsa Peterson Ltd, 41 East Ave, Norwalk, CT 06851-3919 Tel: 203-846-8331 E-mail: elsa@epltd.com, pg 443

Peterson Institute for International Economics (PIIE), 1750 Massachusetts Ave NW, Washington, DC 20036-1903 Tel: 202-328-9000 E-mail: media@piie.com Web Site: piie.com, pg 158

Peterson's, 8740 Lucent Blvd, Suite 400, Highlands Ranch, CO 80129 Tel: 609-896-1800 Toll Free Tel: 800-338-3282 E-mail: pubmarketing@petersons.com Web Site: www.petersons.com, pg 158

The Petrichor Prize for Finely Crafted Fiction, 806 Oberlin Rd, No 12094, Raleigh, NC 27605 E-mail: info@regalhousepublishing.com Web Site: regalhousepublishing.com/the-petrichor-prize-for-finely-crafted-fiction/, pg 649

Petroleum Extension Service (PETEX), JJ Pickle Research Campus, 10100 Burnet Rd, Bldg 2, Austin, TX 78758-4445 Tel: 512-471-5940 Toll Free Tel: 800-687-4132 Fax: 512-471-9410 Toll Free Fax: 800-687-7839 E-mail: info@petex.utexas.edu Web Site: cee.utexas.edu/ce/petex, pg 159

Pfizer Award, 440 Geddes Hall, Notre Dame, IN 46556 Tel: 574-631-1194 Fax: 574-631-1533 E-mail: info@hssonline.org Web Site: www.hssonline.org, pg 649

Pflaum Publishing Group, 3055 Kettering Blvd, Suite 100, Dayton, OH 45439 Toll Free Tel: 800-523-4625; 800-543-4383 (ext 1136, cust serv) Toll Free Fax: 800-370-4450 E-mail: service@pflaum.com Web Site: www.pflaum.com, pg 159

Phaidon, 65 Bleecker St, 8th fl, New York, NY 10012 Tel: 212-652-5400 Toll Free Tel: 800-759-0190 (cust serv) Fax: 212-652-5410 Toll Free Fax: 800-286-9471 (cust serv) E-mail: enquiries@phaidon.com Web Site: www.phaidon.com, pg 159

Phi Beta Kappa Award in Science, 1606 New Hampshire Ave NW, Washington, DC 20009 Tel: 202-265-3808 Fax: 202-986-1601 E-mail: awards@pbk.org Web Site: www.pbk.org/bookawards, pg 649

Philadelphia Museum of Art, PO Box 7646, Philadelphia, PA 19101-7646 Tel: 215-763-8100 Fax: 215-236-4465 Web Site: www.philamuseum.org, pg 159

Meredith Phillips, 4127 Old Adobe Rd, Palo Alto, CA 94306 Tel: 650-857-9555 E-mail: mphillips0743@comcast.net, pg 443

Philomel Books, c/o Penguin Random House LLC, 1745 Broadway, New York, NY 10019 Tel: 212-782-9000 Web Site: www.penguin.com/philomel/, pg 159

Philosophical Library Inc, 275 Central Park W, Suite 12D, New York, NY 10024 Tel: 212-873-6070 Fax: 212-873-6070 E-mail: editors@philosophicallibrary.com Web Site: philosophicallibrary.com, pg 159

Philosophy Documentation Center, PO Box 7147, Charlottesville, VA 22906-7147 Tel: 434-220-3300 Toll Free Tel: 800-444-2419 Fax: 434-220-3301 E-mail: order@pdcnet.org Web Site: www.pdcnet.org, pg 159

Phoenix Award, 140B Purcellville Gateway Dr, Suite 1200, Purcellville, VA 20132 Tel: 630-571-4520 E-mail: info@childlitassn.org Web Site: www.childlitassn.org, pg 649

Phoenix Picture Book Award, 140B Purcellville Gateway Dr, Suite 1200, Purcellville, VA 20132 Tel: 630-571-4520 E-mail: info@childlitassn.org Web Site: www.childlitassn.org, pg 649

Photographic Society of America® (PSA®), 8241 S Walker Ave, Suite 104, Oklahoma City, OK 73139 Tel: 405-843-1437 Toll Free Tel: 855-PSA-INFO (772-4636) E-mail: hq@psa-photo.org Web Site: psa-photo.org, pg 516

Piano Press, 1425 Ocean Ave, Suite 5, Del Mar, CA 92014 Tel: 619-884-1401 E-mail: pianopress@pianopress.com Web Site: www.pianopress.com, pg 159

The Bruce Piasecki & Andrea Masters Annual Award on Business & Science Writing, 158 Stone Church Rd, Ballston Spa, NY 12020 Tel: 518-583-9615 Fax: 518-583-9726 Web Site: www.ahcgroup.com, pg 649

Picador, 120 Broadway, New York, NY 10271 Tel: 646-307-5151 Fax: 212-253-9627 E-mail: publicity@picadorusa.com Web Site: us.macmillan.com/picador, pg 159

Alison Picard Literary Agent, PO Box 2000, Cotuit, MA 02635 Tel: 508-477-7192 Fax: 508-477-7192 (call first) E-mail: ajpicard@aol.com, pg 472

The Picasso Project, 1109 Geary Blvd, San Francisco, CA 94109 Tel: 415-292-6500 Fax: 415-292-6594 E-mail: editeur@earthlink.net (edit); picasso@art-books.com (orders) Web Site: www.art-books.com, pg 160

Robert J Pickering/J R Colbeck Award for Playwriting Excellence, 14 S Hanchett St, Coldwater, MI 49036 E-mail: president@branchcct.org Web Site: www.branchcct.org, pg 649

Pictures & Words Editorial Services, 3100 "B" Ave, Anacortes, WA 98221 Tel: 360-293-8476 Web Site: www.picturesandwords.com/words, pg 443

Pieces of Learning Inc, 1112 N Carbon St, Suite A, Marion, IL 62959-8976 Tel: 618-964-9426 Toll Free Tel: 800-729-5137 Toll Free Fax: 800-844-0455 E-mail: info@piecesoflearning.com Web Site: piecesoflearning.com, pg 160

Lorne Pierce Medal, Walter House, 282 Somerset W, Ottawa, ON K2P 0J6, Canada Tel: 613-991-6990 (ext 106) Fax: 613-991-6996 E-mail: nominations@rsc-src.ca Web Site: www.rsc-src.ca, pg 649

The Pilgrim Press/United Church Press, 700 Prospect Ave, Cleveland, OH 44115-1100 Tel: 216-736-2100 Toll Free Tel: 800-537-3394 (orders) E-mail: permissions@thepilgrimpress.com; store@ucc.org (orders) Web Site: www.thepilgrimpress.com, pg 160

The Pinch Writing Awards in Fiction, University of Memphis, English Dept, 431 Patterson Hall, Memphis, TN 38152 Tel: 901-678-2651 Fax: 901-678-2226 E-mail: editor@pinchjournal.com Web Site: www.pinchjournal.com, pg 649

The Pinch Writing Awards in Poetry, University of Memphis, English Dept, 431 Patterson Hall, Memphis, TN 38152 Tel: 901-678-2651 Fax: 901-678-2226 E-mail: editor@pinchjournal.com Web Site: www.pinchjournal.com, pg 649

Pinckley Prizes for Crime Fiction, PO Box 13926, New Orleans, LA 70185 E-mail: pinckleyprizes@gmail.com Web Site: www.pinckleyprizes.org, pg 650

Caroline Pincus Book Midwife, 101 Wool St, San Francisco, CA 94110 Tel: 415-516-6206 E-mail: cpincus1958@gmail.com Web Site: www.carolinepincus.com, pg 443

Pinder Lane & Garon-Brooke Associates Ltd, 2136 NE 58 Ct, Fort Lauderdale, FL 33308 Tel: 212-489-0880 Fax: 212-489-7104 Web Site: www.pinderlaneandgaronbrooke.com, pg 472

Pineapple Press, c/o The Globe Pequot Press, 64 S Main St, Essex, CT 06426 E-mail: pineappleedit@rowman.com Web Site: www.pineapplepress.com, pg 160

Pinnacle Book Achievement Awards, PO Box 606, Cottage Grove, OR 97424 Tel: 541-942-7455 Fax: 541-942-7455 E-mail: nabe@bookmarketingprofits.com Web Site: www.bookmarketingprofits.com/PinnacleBookEntryFormE.html, pg 650

Pinnacle InterTech Awards, 10015 Main St, Fairfax, VA 22031 Tel: 703-385-1335 Toll Free Tel: 888-385-3588 Fax: 703-273-0456 E-mail: pinnacleintertech@printing.org Web Site: pinnacleawards.printing.org, pg 650

Pippin Properties Inc, 110 W 40 St, Suite 1704, New York, NY 10018 Tel: 212-338-9310 E-mail: info@pippinproperties.com Web Site: www.pippinproperties.com; www.facebook.com/pippinproperties, pg 472

Planert Creek Press, E4843 395 Ave, Menomonie, WI 54751 Tel: 715-235-4110 E-mail: publisher@planertcreekpress.com Web Site: www.planertcreekpress.com, pg 160

Planners Press, 205 N Michigan Ave, Suite 1200, Chicago, IL 60601 Tel: 312-431-9100 Fax: 312-786-6700 E-mail: customerservice@planning.org Web Site: www.planning.org, pg 160

Platypus Media LLC, 725 Eighth St SE, Washington, DC 20003 Tel: 202-546-1674 Toll Free Tel: 877-PLATYPS (752-8977) Fax: 202-546-2356 E-mail: info@platypusmedia.com Web Site: www.platypusmedia.com, pg 160

Playwrights Guild of Canada, 401 Richmond St W, Suite 350, Toronto, ON M5V 3A8, Canada Tel: 416-703-0201 E-mail: info@playwrightsguild.ca; marketing@playwrightsguild.ca; orders@playwrightsguild.ca; membership@playwrightsguild.ca Web Site: playwrightsguild.ca, pg 516

Pleasure Boat Studio: A Literary Press, 3710 SW Barton St, Seattle, WA 98126 Tel: 206-962-0460 E-mail: pleasboatpublishing@gmail.com Web Site: www.pleasureboatstudio.com, pg 160

Plexus Publishing, Inc, 143 Old Marlton Pike, Medford, NJ 08055 Tel: 609-654-6500 Fax: 609-654-4309 E-mail: info@plexuspublishing.com Web Site: www.plexuspublishing.com, pg 160

The Plimpton Prize for Fiction, 544 W 27 St, New York, NY 10001 Tel: 212-343-1333 E-mail: queries@theparisreview.org Web Site: www.theparisreview.org, pg 650

Judith Plotz Emerging Scholar Award, 140B Purcellville Gateway Dr, Suite 1200, Purcellville, VA 20132 Tel: 630-571-4520 E-mail: info@childlitassn.org Web Site: www.childlitassn.org, pg 650

Plough Publishing House, 151 Bowne Dr, Walden, NY 12586-2832 Tel: 845-572-3455 Toll Free Tel: 800-521-8011 E-mail: info@plough.com; editor@plough.com Web Site: www.plough.com, pg 161

Ploughshares, Emerson College, 120 Boylston St, Boston, MA 02116 Tel: 617-824-3757 E-mail: pshares@pshares.org Web Site: www.pshares.org, pg 161

Ploughshares Emerging Writer's Contest, Emerson College, 120 Boylston St, Boston, MA 02116 Tel: 617-824-3757 E-mail: pshares@pshares.org Web Site: www.pshares.org, pg 650

Plowshare Media, 405 Vincente Way, La Jolla, CA 92037 Tel: 858-454-5446 E-mail: sales@plowsharemedia.com Web Site: plowsharemedia.com, pg 161

Plum Tree Books, 2151 Market St, Camp Hill, PA 17011 Tel: 717-730-0711 E-mail: info@classicalsubjects.com Web Site: www.plumtreebooks.com, pg 161

Plunkett Research Ltd, PO Drawer 541737, Houston, TX 77254-1737 Tel: 713-932-0000 Fax: 713-932-7080 E-mail: customersupport@plunkettresearch.com Web Site: www.plunkettresearch.com, pg 161

Plutarch Award, PO Box 33020, Santa Fe, NM 87594 Tel: 505-983-4671 E-mail: plutarch@biographersinternational.org Web Site: biographersinternational.org/award/the-plutarch, pg 650

PNWA Writers' Contest, 1420 NW Gilman Blvd, Suite 29, PMB 2717, Issaquah, WA 98027 Tel: 425-673-2665 E-mail: pnwa@pnwa.org Web Site: www.pnwa.org, pg 650

PNWA - a writer's resource, 1420 NW Gilman Blvd, Suite 29, PMB 2717, Issaquah, WA 98027 Tel: 425-673-2665 E-mail: pnwa@pnwa.org Web Site: www.pnwa.org, pg 517

Pocket Press Inc, PO Box 25124, Portland, OR 97298-0124 Toll Free Tel: 888-237-2110 Toll Free Fax: 877-643-3732 E-mail: sales@pocketpressinc.com Web Site: www.pocketpressinc.com, pg 161

Pocol Press, 320 Sutton St, Punxsutawney, PA 15767 Tel: 703-870-9611 E-mail: chrisandtom@erols.com Web Site: www.pocolpress.com, pg 161

Edgar Allan Poe Memorial, PO Box 36128, North Chesterfield, VA 23235-3533 E-mail: contest@poetrysocietyofvirginia.org; info@poetryvirginia.org Web Site: www.poetrysocietyofvirginia.org, pg 650

Poetry Awards, 81 Prince St, Charlottetown, PE C1A 4R3, Canada E-mail: peiliteraryawards@gmail.com Web Site: www.peiwritersguild.com, pg 650

Poetry Center Book Award, 511-512 Humanities Bldg, 1600 Holloway Ave, San Francisco, CA 94132 Tel: 415-338-2227 Fax: 415-338-0966 E-mail: poetry@sfsu.edu Web Site: poetry.sfsu.edu, pg 650

Poetry Flash Reading Series, 1450 Fourth St, Suite 4, Berkeley, CA 94710 Tel: 510-525-5476 E-mail: editor@poetryflash.org Web Site: poetryflash.org, pg 556

Poetry Foundation, 61 W Superior St, Chicago, IL 60654 Tel: 312-787-7070 E-mail: info@poetryfoundation.org Web Site: www.poetryfoundation.org, pg 526

Poetry Society of America (PSA), 119 Smith St, Brooklyn, NY 11201 Tel: 212-254-9628 E-mail: info@poetrysociety.org Web Site: poetrysociety.org, pg 517

Poets & Writers Inc, 90 Broad St, Suite 2100, New York, NY 10004 Tel: 212-226-3586 Fax: 212-226-3963 E-mail: admin@pw.org Web Site: www.pw.org, pg 517

Karl Pohrt Tribute Award, 3135 S State St, Suite 203, Ann Arbor, MI 48108 Toll Free Tel: 866-733-9064 E-mail: info@bincfoundation.org Web Site: www.bincfoundation.org/scholarship, pg 651

Pointed Leaf Press, 136 Baxter St, New York, NY 10013 Tel: 212-941-1800 Fax: 212-941-1822 E-mail: info@pointedleafpress.com Web Site: www.pointedleafpress.com, pg 161

Poisoned Pen Press, 4014 N Goldwater Blvd, Suite 201, Scottsdale, AZ 85251 Tel: 480-945-3375 Toll Free Tel: 800-421-3976 Fax: 480-949-1707 E-mail: info@poisonedpenpress.com Web Site: www.poisonedpenpress.com, pg 161

Polar Bear & Company, 8 Brook St, Solon, ME 04979 Tel: 207-319-4727 Web Site: polarbearandco.com, pg 161

Polebridge Press, Willamette University, 900 State St, Salem, OR 97301 Tel: 651-200-2372 E-mail: orders@westarinstitute.org Web Site: www.westarinstitute.org, pg 161

Wendy Polhemus-Annibell, PO Box 464, Peconic, NY 11958 Tel: 631-833-6942 E-mail: wannibell@gmail.com, pg 443

Police Executive Research Forum, 1120 Connecticut Ave NW, Suite 930, Washington, DC 20036 Tel: 202-466-7820 Web Site: www.policeforum.org, pg 162

Polis Books, 1201 Hudson St, No 211S, Hoboken, NJ 07030 E-mail: info@polisbooks.com; submissions@polisbooks.com Web Site: www.polisbooks.com; facebook.com/PolisBooks; x.com/PolisBooks, pg 162

George Polk Awards in Journalism, The Brooklyn Campus, One University Plaza, Brooklyn, NY 11201-5372 Tel: 718-488-1009 Web Site: www.liu.edu/polk, pg 651

Pom Inc, 18-15 215 St, Bayside, NY 11360, pg 472

Pomegranate Communications Inc, 105 SE 18 Ave, Portland, OR 97214 Tel: 503-328-6500 Toll Free Tel: 800-227-1428 Fax: 503-328-9330 Toll Free Fax: 800-848-4376 E-mail: hello@pomegranate.com Web Site: www.pomegranate.com, pg 162

Pontifical Institute of Mediaeval Studies, Department of Publications, 59 Queen's Park Crescent E, Toronto, ON M5S 2C4, Canada Tel: 416-926-7142 Fax: 416-926-7292 Web Site: www.pims.ca, pg 416

COMPANY INDEX

Porchlight Book Co Business Book Awards, 544 S First St, Milwaukee, WI 53204 *Toll Free Tel:* 800-236-7323 *E-mail:* info@porchlightbooks.com *Web Site:* porchlightbooks.com, pg 651

Porcupine's Quill Inc, 68 Main St, Erin, ON N0B 1T0, Canada *Tel:* 519-833-9158 *E-mail:* pql@sentex.net *Web Site:* porcupinesquill.ca; www.facebook.com/theporcupinesquill, pg 416

Port Townsend Writers Conference, 223 Battery Way, Port Townsend, WA 98368 *Tel:* 360-385-3102 *Fax:* 360-385-2470 *E-mail:* info@centrum.org *Web Site:* centrum.org, pg 557

Portage & Main Press, 318 McDermot Ave, Suite 100, Winnipeg, MB R3A 0A2, Canada *Tel:* 204-987-3500 *Toll Free Tel:* 800-667-9673 *Fax:* 204-947-0080 *Toll Free Fax:* 866-734-8477 *E-mail:* customerservice@portageandmainpress.com *Web Site:* www.portageandmainpress.com, pg 416

Katherine Anne Porter Award, 633 W 155 St, New York, NY 10032 *Tel:* 212-368-5900 *E-mail:* academy@artsandletters.org *Web Site:* artsandletters.org/awards, pg 651

Katherine Anne Porter Prize for Fiction, University of Tulsa, Kendall College of Arts & Sciences, 800 S Tucker Dr, Tulsa, OK 74104 *Tel:* 918-631-3080 *E-mail:* nimrod@utulsa.edu *Web Site:* artsandsciences.utulsa.edu/nimrod/nimrod-literary-awards/, pg 651

Portfolio, c/o Penguin Random House LLC, 1745 Broadway, New York, NY 10019 *Tel:* 212-782-9000 *Web Site:* www.penguin.com/portfolio-overview/; www.penguin.com/sentinel-overview/; www.penguin.com/thesis/, pg 162

Rose Post Creative Nonfiction Competition, PO Box 21591, Winston-Salem, NC 27120-1591 *Tel:* 336-293-8844 *E-mail:* mail@ncwriters.org; nclrsubmissions@ecu.edu *Web Site:* www.ncwriters.org, pg 651

Potomac Books, c/o University of Nebraska Press, 1225 "L" St, Suite 200, Lincoln, NE 68588-0630 *Tel:* 402-472-5937 *Web Site:* www.nebraskapress.unl.edu/potomac/, pg 162

Clarkson Potter, 1745 Broadway, New York, NY 10019 *Tel:* 212-782-9000 *Web Site:* crownpublishing.com/archives/imprint/clarkson-potter, pg 162

Pottersfield Press, 248 Leslie Rd, East Lawrencetown, NS B2Z 1T4, Canada *Toll Free Tel:* 800-646-2879 (orders only) *E-mail:* pottersfieldcreative@gmail.com *Web Site:* www.pottersfieldpress.com, pg 416

powerHouse Books, 32 Adams St, Brooklyn, NY 11201 *Tel:* 212-604-9074 *E-mail:* sales@powerhousebooks.com; publicity@powerhousebooks.com *Web Site:* www.powerhousebooks.com; www.powerhousebookstores.com, pg 162

PPI, A Kaplan Company, 332 Front St, Suite 501, La Crosse, WI 54601 *Tel:* 650-593-9119 *Fax:* 650-592-4519 *E-mail:* info@ppi2pass.com *Web Site:* ppi2pass.com, pg 162

Practice Management Information Corp (PMIC), 4727 Wilshire Blvd, Suite 302, Los Angeles, CA 90010 *Tel:* 323-954-0224 *Fax:* 323-954-0253 *E-mail:* customer.service@pmionline.com *Web Site:* pmionline.stores.yahoo.net, pg 163

Practising Law Institute (PLI), 1177 Avenue of the Americas, 2nd fl, New York, NY 10036 *Tel:* 212-824-5710 (cust serv) *Toll Free Tel:* 800-260-4PLI (260-4754) *Toll Free Fax:* 800-321-0093 (cust serv) *E-mail:* info@pli.edu; membership@pli.edu *Web Site:* www.pli.edu, pg 163

Prairie Schooner Annual Strousse Award, 110 Andrews Hall, University of Nebraska-Lincoln, Lincoln, NE 68588-0334 *Tel:* 402-472-0911 *Fax:* 402-472-1817 *E-mail:* psbookprize@unl.edu; prairieschooner@unl.edu *Web Site:* prairieschooner.unl.edu, pg 651

Prairie Schooner Bernice Slote Award, 110 Andrews Hall, University of Nebraska-Lincoln, Lincoln, NE 68588-0334 *Tel:* 402-472-0911 *Fax:* 402-472-1817 *E-mail:* psbookprize@unl.edu; prairieschooner@unl.edu *Web Site:* prairieschooner.unl.edu, pg 651

Prairie Schooner Book Prize in Poetry, 110 Andrews Hall, University of Nebraska-Lincoln, Lincoln, NE 68588-0334 *Tel:* 402-472-0911 *Fax:* 402-472-1817 *E-mail:* psbookprize@unl.edu; prairieschooner@unl.edu *Web Site:* prairieschooner.unl.edu, pg 651

Prairie Schooner Edward Stanley Award, 110 Andrews Hall, University of Nebraska-Lincoln, Lincoln, NE 68588-0334 *Tel:* 402-472-0911 *Fax:* 402-472-1817 *E-mail:* psbookprize@unl.edu; prairieschooner@unl.edu *Web Site:* prairieschooner.unl.edu, pg 652

Prairie Schooner Glenna Luschei Award, 110 Andrews Hall, University of Nebraska-Lincoln, Lincoln, NE 68588-0334 *Tel:* 402-472-0911 *Fax:* 402-472-1817 *E-mail:* psbookprize@unl.edu; prairieschooner@unl.edu *Web Site:* prairieschooner.unl.edu, pg 652

Prairie Schooner Hugh J Luke Award, 110 Andrews Hall, University of Nebraska-Lincoln, Lincoln, NE 68588-0334 *Tel:* 402-472-0911 *Fax:* 402-472-1817 *E-mail:* psbookprize@unl.edu; prairieschooner@unl.edu *Web Site:* prairieschooner.unl.edu, pg 652

Prairie Schooner Jane Geske Award, 110 Andrews Hall, University of Nebraska-Lincoln, Lincoln, NE 68588-0334 *Tel:* 402-472-0911 *Fax:* 402-472-1817 *E-mail:* psbookprize@unl.edu; prairieschooner@unl.edu *Web Site:* prairieschooner.unl.edu, pg 652

Prairie Schooner Lawrence Foundation Award, 110 Andrews Hall, University of Nebraska-Lincoln, Lincoln, NE 68588-0334 *Tel:* 402-472-0911 *Fax:* 402-472-1817 *E-mail:* psbookprize@unl.edu; prairieschooner@unl.edu *Web Site:* prairieschooner.unl.edu, pg 652

Prairie Schooner Raz-Shumaker Book Prize Contest, 110 Andrews Hall, University of Nebraska-Lincoln, Lincoln, NE 68588-0334 *Tel:* 402-472-0911 *Fax:* 402-472-1817 *E-mail:* psbookprize@unl.edu; prairieschooner@unl.edu *Web Site:* prairieschooner.unl.edu, pg 652

Prairie Schooner Virginia Faulkner Award for Excellence in Writing, 110 Andrews Hall, University of Nebraska-Lincoln, Lincoln, NE 68588-0334 *Tel:* 402-472-0911 *Fax:* 402-472-1817 *E-mail:* psbookprize@unl.edu; prairieschooner@unl.edu *Web Site:* prairieschooner.unl.edu, pg 652

PrairieView Press, 625 Seventh St, Gretna, MB R0G 0V0, Canada *Tel:* 204-327-6543 *Toll Free Tel:* 800-477-7377 *Toll Free Fax:* 866-480-0253 *Web Site:* prairieviewpress.com, pg 417

PRB Productions, 963 Peralta Ave, Albany, CA 94706-2144 *Tel:* 510-526-0722 *E-mail:* prbprdns@aol.com *Web Site:* www.prbmusic.com, pg 163

Premier PRINT Awards, 10015 Main St, Fairfax, VA 22031 *Tel:* 703-385-1335 *Toll Free Tel:* 888-385-3588 *Fax:* 703-273-0456 *E-mail:* assist@printing.org; info@printing.org *Web Site:* premierprint.printing.org, pg 652

Presbyterian Publishing Corp (PPC), 100 Witherspoon St, Louisville, KY 40202 *Tel:* 502-569-5000 *Toll Free Tel:* 800-533-4371; 800-523-1631 (US only) *Fax:* 502-569-5113 *E-mail:* customerservice@presbypub.com *Web Site:* www.ppcbooks.com; www.wjkbooks.com, pg 163

Presidential Master's Prize, 323 E Wacker Dr, No 642, Chicago, IL 60601 *Tel:* 312-600-8072 *E-mail:* info@acla.org *Web Site:* www.acla.org/prize-awards/presidential-masters-prize, pg 652

Presidential Undergraduate Prize, 323 E Wacker Dr, No 642, Chicago, IL 60601 *Tel:* 312-600-8072 *E-mail:* info@acla.org *Web Site:* www.acla.org/prize-awards/presidential-undergraduate-prize, pg 652

The Press at California State University, Fresno, 2380 E Keats, M/S MB 99, Fresno, CA 93740-8024 *Tel:* 559-278-4103 *E-mail:* press@csufresno.edu, pg 163

Les Presses de l'Universite de Montreal, 5450, chemin de la Cote-des-Neiges, bureau 100, Montreal, QC H3T 1Y6, Canada *Tel:* 514-343-6933 *Fax:* 514-343-2232 *E-mail:* pum@umontreal.ca *Web Site:* www.pum.umontreal.ca, pg 417

Les Presses de l'Universite du Quebec, 2875 blvd Laurier, Suite 450, Quebec, QC G1V 2M2, Canada *Tel:* 418-657-4399 *Fax:* 418-657-2096 *E-mail:* puq@puq.ca *Web Site:* www.puq.ca, pg 417

Les Presses de l'Universite Laval, 2180, Chemin Sainte-Foy, 1st fl, Quebec, QC G1V 0A6, Canada *Tel:* 418-656-2803 *Fax:* 418-656-3305 *E-mail:* presses@pul.ulaval.ca *Web Site:* www.pulaval.com, pg 417

Derek Price/Rod Webster Prize Award, 440 Geddes Hall, Notre Dame, IN 46556 *Tel:* 574-631-1194 *Fax:* 574-631-1533 *E-mail:* info@hssonline.org *Web Site:* www.hssonline.org, pg 652

The Aaron M Priest Literary Agency Inc, 370 Lexington Ave, Suite 1202, New York, NY 10017 *Tel:* 212-818-0344 *Fax:* 212-573-9417 *E-mail:* info@aaronpriest.com *Web Site:* www.aaronpriest.com, pg 472

Primary Research Group Inc, 2585 Broadway, Suite 156, New York, NY 10025 *Tel:* 212-736-2316 *Fax:* 212-412-9097 *E-mail:* primaryresearchgroup@gmail.com *Web Site:* www.primaryresearch.com, pg 163

Prince Edward Island Association for Newcomers to Canada Award, 81 Prince St, Charlottetown, PE C1A 4R3, Canada *E-mail:* peiliteraryawards@gmail.com *Web Site:* www.peiwritersguild.com, pg 652

Princeton Book Co Publishers, 15 W Front St, Trenton, NJ 08608 *Tel:* 609-426-0602 *Toll Free Tel:* 800-220-7149 *Fax:* 609-426-1344 *E-mail:* pbc@dancehorizons.com *Web Site:* www.dancehorizons.com, pg 163

The Princeton Review, 110 E 42 St, 7th fl, New York, NY 10017 *Toll Free Tel:* 800-273-8439 (orders only) *Web Site:* www.princetonreview.com, pg 164

Princeton University Press, 41 William St, Princeton, NJ 08540-5237 *Tel:* 609-258-4900 *Fax:* 609-258-6305 *E-mail:* info@press.princeton.edu *Web Site:* press.princeton.edu, pg 164

Print Industries Market Information and Research Organization (PRIMIR), 1899 Preston White Dr, Reston, VA 20191 *Tel:* 703-264-7200 *E-mail:* aptech@aptech.org *Web Site:* www.printtechnologies.org; www.npes.org/primirresearch/primir.aspx, pg 517

Printing & Graphics Association MidAtlantic (PGAMA), 9160 Red Branch Rd, Suite E-9, Columbia, MD 21045 *Tel:* 410-319-0900 *Toll Free Tel:* 877-319-0906 *Fax:* 410-319-0905 *E-mail:* info@pgama.com *Web Site:* www.pgama.com, pg 517

Printing Brokerage/Buyers Association International (PBBA), 74-5576 Pawai Place, No 599, Kailua Kona, HI 96740 *Tel:* 808-339-0880 *E-mail:* contactus@pbba.org *Web Site:* pbba.org, pg 517

Printing Industries Alliance, 636 N French Rd, Suite 1, Amherst, NY 14228 *Tel:* 716-691-3211 *Toll Free Tel:* 800-777-4742 *Fax:* 716-691-4249 *E-mail:* info@pialliance.org *Web Site:* pialliance.org, pg 517

Printing Industries Association Inc of Southern California (PIASC), 5800 S Eastern Ave, Suite 400, Los Angeles, CA 90040 *Tel:* 323-728-9500 *E-mail:* info@piasc.org *Web Site:* www.piasc.org, pg 517

Printing Industry Association of the South (PIAS), 305 Plus Park Blvd, Nashville, TN 37217 *Tel:* 615-366-1094 *Fax:* 615-366-4192 *Web Site:* www.pias.org, pg 517

PRINTING United Alliance, 10015 Main St, Fairfax, VA 22031 *Tel:* 703-385-1335 *Toll Free Tel:* 888-385-3588 *Fax:* 703-273-0456 *E-mail:* assist@printing.org; info@printing.org *Web Site:* www.printing.org, pg 165

PRINTING United Alliance, 10015 Main St, Fairfax, VA 22031 *Tel:* 703-385-1335 *Toll Free Tel:* 888-385-3588 *Fax:* 703-273-0456; 703-691-7492 (membership) *E-mail:* assist@printing.org; info@printing.org *Web Site:* www.printing.org, pg 517

Michael L Printz Award, 225 N Michigan Ave, Suite 1300, Chicago, IL 60601 *Tel:* 312-280-4390 *Toll Free Tel:* 800-545-2433 *E-mail:* yalsa@ala.org *Web Site:* www.ala.org/yalsa/printz-award, pg 653

PRISM international Creative Nonfiction Contest, University of British Columbia, Buch E462, 1866 Main Mall, Vancouver, BC V6T 1Z1,

Canada *Tel:* 604-822-2514 *Fax:* 604-822-3616 *E-mail:* promotions@prismmagazine.ca *Web Site:* www.prismmagazine.ca/contests, pg 653

Pritzker Military Museum & Library Literature Award for Lifetime Achievement in Military Writing, 104 S Michigan Ave, Suite 400, Chicago, IL 60603 *Tel:* 312-374-9333 *E-mail:* info@pritzkermilitary.org *Web Site:* www.pritzkermilitary.org, pg 653

The Private Eye Writers of America (PWA), 3665 S Needles Hwy, 7G, Laughlin, NV 89029 *Web Site:* www.privateeyewriters.com, pg 518

Prix Emile-Nelligan, 100, rue Sherbrooke, Suite 202, Montreal, QC H2X 1C3, Canada *Tel:* 514-278-4657 *Fax:* 514-271-6369 *E-mail:* info@fondation-nelligan.org *Web Site:* www.fondation-nelligan.org, pg 653

PRO-ED Inc, 8700 Shoal Creek Blvd, Austin, TX 78757-6897 *Tel:* 512-451-3246 *Toll Free Tel:* 800-897-3202 *Fax:* 512-451-8542 *Toll Free Fax:* 800-397-7633 *E-mail:* info@proedinc.com *Web Site:* www.proedinc.com, pg 165

Pro Lingua Associates Inc, 74 Cotton Mill Hill, Suite A-315, Brattleboro, VT 05301 *Tel:* 802-257-7779 *Toll Free Tel:* 800-366-4775 *Fax:* 802-257-5117 *E-mail:* info@prolinguaassociates.com *Web Site:* www.prolinguaassociates.com, pg 165

Productive Publications, 380 Brooke Ave, Lower Level, North York, ON M5M 2L6, Canada *Tel:* 416-483-0634 *Toll Free Tel:* 877-879-2669 (orders) *Fax:* 416-322-7434 *E-mail:* productivepublications@rogers.com *Web Site:* www.productivepublications.ca, pg 417

Productivity Press, 605 Third Ave, 22nd fl, New York, NY 10158 *Tel:* 800-634-7064 (orders); 800-797-3803 *E-mail:* orders@taylorandfrancis.com *Web Site:* www.crcpress.com, pg 165

Professional Booksellers School Inc, 2667 Hyacinth St, Westbury, NY 11590 *Tel:* 516-333-0681 *E-mail:* hello@professionalbooksellers.com *Web Site:* www.professionalbooksellers.com, pg 564

Professional Communications Inc, 1223 W Main, Suite 1427, Durant, OK 74702-1427 *Tel:* 580-745-9838 *Toll Free Tel:* 800-337-9838 *Fax:* 580-745-9837 *E-mail:* info@pcibooks.com *Web Site:* www.pcibooks.com, pg 165

The Professional Education Group LLC (PEG), 700 Twelve Oaks Center Dr, Suite 104, Wayzata, MN 55391 *Tel:* 952-933-9990 *Toll Free Tel:* 800-229-2531 *E-mail:* orders@proedgroup.com *Web Site:* www.proedgroup.com, pg 165

Professional Resource Press, 5864 Elegant Orchid Way, Sarasota, FL 34232 *Tel:* 941-343-9601 *Toll Free Tel:* 800-443-3364 (orders & cust serv) *Fax:* 941-343-9201 *Toll Free Fax:* 866-804-4843 (orders only) *E-mail:* cs@prpress.com *Web Site:* www.prpress.com, pg 165

Progressive Press, 4028 Texas St, No 7, San Diego, CA 92104 *E-mail:* info@progressivepress.com *Web Site:* www.progressivepress.com, pg 165

Prometheus Awards, 650 Castro St, Suite 120-433, Mountain View, CA 94041 *Tel:* 650-968-6319 *E-mail:* bestnovel@lfs.org; specialaward@lfs.org *Web Site:* www.lfs.org, pg 653

Prometheus Books, 59 John Glenn Dr, Amherst, NY 14228-2119 *Fax:* 716-691-0137 *E-mail:* marketing@prometheusbooks.com; editorial@prometheusbooks.com; rights@prometheusbooks.com *Web Site:* www.prometheusbooks.com, pg 166

Pronk Media Inc, 16 Glen Davis Crescent, Toronto, ON M4E 1X5, Canada *Tel:* 416-716-9660 (cell) *E-mail:* info@pronk.com; hello@pronk.com *Web Site:* www.pronk.com; www.h5engines.com; www.html5alive.com, pg 443

Proofed to Perfection Editing Services, 6519 Sherrill Baggett Rd, Godwin, NC 28344 *Tel:* 910-980-0832 *E-mail:* inquiries@proofedtoperfection.com *Web Site:* www.proofedtoperfection.com, pg 443

ProQuest LLC, part of Clarivate PLC, 789 E Eisenhower Pkwy, Ann Arbor, MI 48108 *Tel:* 734-761-4700 *Toll Free Tel:* 800-521-0600; 877-779-6768 (sales) *E-mail:* sales@proquest.com *Web Site:* www.proquest.com, pg 166

PROSE Awards, 455 Massachusetts Ave NW, Suite 700, Washington, DC 20001-2777 *Tel:* 202-347-3375 *Fax:* 202-347-3690 *E-mail:* proseawards@publishers.org *Web Site:* proseawards.com; publishers.org, pg 653

Prospect Agency, 551 Valley Rd, PMB 337, Upper Montclair, NJ 07043 *Tel:* 718-788-3217 *Web Site:* www.prospectagency.com, pg 472

ProStar Publications Inc, 226 W Florence Ave, Inglewood, CA 90301 *Toll Free Tel:* 800-481-6277 *E-mail:* editor@prostarpublications.com *Web Site:* www.prostarpublications.com, pg 166

Protestant Church-Owned Publishers Association, 841 Mount Clinton Pike, Suite D, Harrisonburg, VA 22802 *Web Site:* www.pcpaonline.org, pg 518

The PRS Group Inc, 5800 Heritage Landing Dr, Suite E, East Syracuse, NY 13057-9358 *Tel:* 315-431-0511 *Fax:* 315-431-0200 *E-mail:* custserv@prsgroup.com *Web Site:* www.prsgroup.com, pg 166

PSMJ Resources Inc, 10 Midland Ave, Newton, MA 02458 *Tel:* 617-965-0055 *Toll Free Tel:* 800-537-PSMJ (537-7765) *Fax:* 617-965-5152 *Web Site:* www.psmj.com, pg 166

Psychological Assessment Resources Inc (PAR), 16204 N Florida Ave, Lutz, FL 33549 *Tel:* 813-449-4065 *Toll Free Tel:* 800-331-8378 *Fax:* 813-961-2196 *Toll Free Fax:* 800-727-9329 *Web Site:* www.parinc.com, pg 166

Public Citizen, 1600 20 St NW, Washington, DC 20009 *Tel:* 202-588-1000 *Web Site:* www.citizen.org, pg 167

Public Library Association (PLA), 225 N Michigan Ave, Suite 1300, Chicago, IL 60601 *Toll Free Tel:* 800-545-2433 (ext 5752) *Fax:* 312-280-5029 *E-mail:* pla@ala.org *Web Site:* www.ala.org/pla/, pg 518

Public Relations Society of America Inc, 120 Wall St, 21st fl, New York, NY 10005 *Tel:* 212-460-1400 *E-mail:* membership@prsa.org *Web Site:* www.prsa.org, pg 518

Public Scholars, 400 Seventh St SW, Washington, DC 20506 *Tel:* 202-606-8200 *E-mail:* publicscholar@neh.gov *Web Site:* www.neh.gov/grants, pg 653

Publication Consultants, 8370 Eleusis Dr, Anchorage, AK 99502 *Tel:* 907-349-2424 *Fax:* 907-349-2426 *E-mail:* books@publicationconsultants.com *Web Site:* www.publicationconsultants.com, pg 167

Les Publications du Quebec, 425, rue Jacques-Parizeau, 5e etage, Quebec, QC G1R 4Z1, Canada *Tel:* 418-643-5150 *Toll Free Tel:* 800-463-2100 (Quebec province only) *Fax:* 418-643-6177 *Toll Free Fax:* 800-561-3479 *E-mail:* publicationsduquebec@cspq.gouv.qc.ca *Web Site:* www.publicationsduquebec.gouv.qc.ca, pg 417

Publications International Ltd (PIL), 8140 N Lehigh Ave, Morton Grove, IL 60053 *Tel:* 847-676-3470 *Fax:* 847-676-3671 *E-mail:* customer_service@pubint.com *Web Site:* pilbooks.com, pg 167

Publishers Association of the West Inc (PubWest), 12727 Highland Ct, Auburn, CA 95603-3634 *Tel:* 720-443-3637 *E-mail:* executivedirector@pubwest.org *Web Site:* pubwest.org, pg 518

Publishers' Publicity Association (PPA), PO Box 2437, New York, NY 10017 *Tel:* 212-790-7259 *E-mail:* publisherspublicity@gmail.com *Web Site:* publisherspublicityassociation.square.site, pg 518

Publishing Certificate Program at City College of New York, Division of Humanities NAC 5225, City College of New York, New York, NY 10031 *Tel:* 212-650-7925 *Fax:* 212-650-7912 *E-mail:* ccnypub@aol.com *Web Site:* english.ccny.cuny.edu/publishing-program, pg 565

Publishing Professionals Network, c/o Postal Annex, 274 Redwood Shores Pkwy, Redwood City, CA 94065-1173 *E-mail:* operations@pubpronetwork.org *Web Site:* pubpronetwork.org, pg 518

PubWest Book Design Awards, 12727 Highland Ct, Auburn, CA 95603-3634 *Tel:* 720-443-3637 *E-mail:* executivedirector@pubwest.org *Web Site:* pubwest.org, pg 653

Puddingstone Literary, Authors' Agents, 11 Mabro Dr, Denville, NJ 07834-9607 *Tel:* 973-366-3622, pg 472

Puffin Books, c/o Penguin Random House LLC, 1745 Broadway, New York, NY 10019 *Tel:* 212-782-9000 *Web Site:* www.penguin.com/puffin-overview/, pg 167

Pulitzer Prizes, Columbia University, 2950 Broadway, New York, NY 10027 *Tel:* 212-854-3841 *Fax:* 212-854-3342 *E-mail:* pulitzer@pulitzer.org *Web Site:* www.pulitzer.org, pg 653

Purdue University Press, Stewart Ctr 190, 504 W State St, West Lafayette, IN 47907-2058 *Tel:* 765-494-2038 *Fax:* 765-496-2442 *E-mail:* pupress@purdue.edu *Web Site:* www.thepress.purdue.edu, pg 167

Purple House Press, 8100 US Hwy 62 E, Cynthiana, KY 41031 *Tel:* 859-235-9970 *Web Site:* www.purplehousepress.com, pg 167

Pushcart Press, PO Box 380, Wainscott, NY 11975-0380 *Tel:* 631-324-9300 *Web Site:* www.pushcartprize.com/pushcartpress, pg 167

Pushcart Prize: Best of the Small Presses, PO Box 380, Wainscott, NY 11975-0380 *Tel:* 631-324-9300 *Web Site:* www.pushcartprize.com, pg 653

GP Putnam's Sons, c/o Penguin Random House LLC, 1745 Broadway, New York, NY 10019 *Tel:* 212-782-9000 *Web Site:* www.penguin.com/putnam/, pg 167

GP Putnam's Sons Books for Young Readers, c/o Penguin Random House LLC, 1745 Broadway, New York, NY 10019 *Tel:* 212-782-9000 *Web Site:* www.penguin.com/putnam-young-readers/, pg 167

PNWA Writers Conference, 1420 NW Gilman Blvd, Suite 29, PMB 2717, Issaquah, WA 98027 *Tel:* 425-673-2665 *E-mail:* pnwa@pnwa.org *Web Site:* www.pnwa.org, pg 557

Pyncheon House, 6 University Dr, Suite 105, Amherst, MA 01002, pg 167

Pynn-Silverman Lifetime Achievement Award, PO Box 367, Fountain City, WI 54629 *E-mail:* info@taaonline.net *Web Site:* www.taaonline.net/council-awards#pynn, pg 654

QA International (QAI), 7240 Rue Saint-Hubert, Montreal, QC H2R 2N1, Canada *Tel:* 514-499-3000 *Fax:* 514-499-3010 *Web Site:* www.qa-international.com, pg 417

Quail Ridge Press (QRP), 2451 Atrium Way, Nashville, TN 37214 *Toll Free Tel:* 800-358-0560 *Fax:* 615-391-2815 *Web Site:* www.swphbooks.com/quail-ridge-press.html, pg 168

Quarto Publishing Group USA Inc, 100 Cummings Ctr, Suite 265D, Beverly, MA 01915 *Tel:* 978-282-9590 *Toll Free Tel:* 800-328-0590 (sales) *Fax:* 978-283-2742 *E-mail:* sales@quartous.com *Web Site:* www.quartoknows.com, pg 168

Quattro Books Inc, 12 Concord Ave, 2nd fl, Toronto, ON M6H 2P1, Canada *Tel:* 416-893-7979 *E-mail:* info@quattrobooks.ca *Web Site:* www.quattrobooks.ca, pg 417

Quebec Writers' Federation (QWF), 1200 Atwater Ave, Suite 3, Westmount, QC H3Z 1X4, Canada *Tel:* 514-933-0878 *E-mail:* info@qwf.org *Web Site:* www.qwf.org; www.hireawriter.ca; quebecbooks.qwf.org, pg 518

Quincannon Publishing Group, PO Box 8100, Glen Ridge, NJ 07028-8100 *Tel:* 973-380-9942 *E-mail:* editors@quincannongroup.com (query first via e-mail) *Web Site:* www.quincannongroup.com, pg 168

Quintessence Publishing Co Inc, 411 N Raddant Rd, Batavia, IL 60510 *Tel:* 630-736-3600 *Toll Free Tel:* 800-621-0387 *Fax:* 630-736-3633 *E-mail:* contact@quintbook.com; service@quintbook.com *Web Site:* www.quintpub.com, pg 168

Quirk Books, 215 Church St, Philadelphia, PA 19106 *Tel:* 215-627-3581 *Fax:* 215-627-5220 *E-mail:* general@quirkbooks.com *Web Site:* www.quirkbooks.com, pg 168

Quite Specific Media Group Ltd, 7373 Pyramid Place, Hollywood, CA 90046 *E-mail:* info@quitespecificmedia.com *Web Site:* quitespecificmedia.com, pg 168

Quixote Press, 3544 Blakslee St, Wever, IA 52658 *Tel:* 319-372-4383 *Toll Free Tel:* 800-571-2665 *E-mail:* heartsntummies@gmail.com *Web Site:* heartsntummies.com, pg 169

QWF Literary Awards, 1200 Atwater Ave, Suite 3, Westmount, QC H3Z 1X4, Canada *Tel:* 514-933-0878 *E-mail:* info@qwf.org *Web Site:* quebecbooks.qwf.org/awards; www.qwf.org; qwf.org/awards/awards-overview/, pg 654

Radcliffe Institute Fellowship Program, Byerly Hall, 8 Garden St, Cambridge, MA 02138 *Tel:* 617-495-8212 *Fax:* 617-495-8136 *E-mail:* fellowships@radcliffe.harvard.edu *Web Site:* www.radcliffe.harvard.edu/fellowship-program, pg 654

Thomas Raddall Atlantic Fiction Award, 1113 Marginal Rd, Halifax, NS B3H 4P7, Canada *Tel:* 902-423-8116 *Fax:* 902-422-0881 *E-mail:* wits@writers.ns.ca (awards) *Web Site:* writers.ns.ca, pg 654

Radix Press, 11715 Bandlon Dr, Houston, TX 77072 *Tel:* 281-879-5688 *Web Site:* www.vvfh.org; www.specialforcesbooks.com; vinabooks.us, pg 169

The Ragan Old North State Award Cup for Nonfiction, 4610 Mail Service Ctr, Raleigh, NC 27699-4610 *Web Site:* www.ncdcr.gov/about/history/lit-and-hist/awards, pg 654

Raiziss/de Palchi Fellowship, 75 Maiden Lane, Suite 901, New York, NY 10038 *Tel:* 212-274-0343 *E-mail:* awards@poets.org *Web Site:* poets.org/academy-american-poets/american-poets-prizes, pg 654

Sir Walter Raleigh Award for Fiction, 4610 Mail Service Ctr, Raleigh, NC 27699-4610 *Tel:* 919-814-6623 *Web Site:* www.ncdcr.gov/about/history/lit-and-hist/awards, pg 654

Jerry Ralya, 7909 Vt Rte 14, Craftsbury Common, VT 05827 *Tel:* 802-586-7514 *E-mail:* jerryralya@gmail.com, pg 444

Ramirez Family Award, PO Box 130294, Spring, TX 77393 *Web Site:* texasinstituteofletters.org, pg 654

RAND Corp, 1776 Main St, Santa Monica, CA 90407-2138 *Tel:* 310-393-0411 *Fax:* 310-393-4818 *Web Site:* www.rand.org, pg 169

Rand McNally, 9855 Woods Dr, Skokie, IL 60077 *Tel:* 847-329-8100 *Toll Free Tel:* 877-446-4863 *Toll Free Fax:* 877-469-1298 *E-mail:* mediarelations@randmcnally.com; tndsupport@randmcnally.com *Web Site:* www.randmcnally.com, pg 169

Rand-Smith Publishing, 204 College Ave, Ashland, VA 23005 *Tel:* 804-874-6012 *E-mail:* randsmithllc@gmail.com *Web Site:* www.rand-smith.com, pg 169

Peter E Randall Publisher, 5 Greenleaf Woods Dr, Suite 102, Portsmouth, NH 03801 *Tel:* 603-431-5667 *Fax:* 603-431-3566 *E-mail:* media@perpublisher.com *Web Site:* www.perpublisher.com, pg 169

Random House Children's Books, c/o Penguin Random House LLC, 1745 Broadway, New York, NY 10019 *Tel:* 212-782-9000 *Web Site:* www.rhcbooks.com, pg 169

Random House Large Print, 1745 Broadway, New York, NY 10019 *Tel:* 212-782-9000 *Web Site:* www.penguinrandomhouse.com, pg 170

Random House Publishing Group, 1745 Broadway, New York, NY 10019 *Toll Free Tel:* 800-200-3552 *Web Site:* www.randomhousebooks.com, pg 170

Random House Reference/Random House Puzzles & Games, c/o Penguin Random House LLC, 1745 Broadway, New York, NY 10019 *Tel:* 212-782-9000 *Web Site:* www.penguinrandomhouse.com, pg 171

Gerald & Cullen Rapp, 41 N Main St, Suite 103, South Norwalk, CT 06854 *Tel:* 212-889-3337 *E-mail:* info@rappart.com *Web Site:* www.rappart.com, pg 486

Rational Island Publishers, 719 Second Ave N, Seattle, WA 98109 *Tel:* 206-284-0311 *E-mail:* ircc@rc.org *Web Site:* www.rc.org, pg 171

Rattapallax Press, 532 La Guadia Place, Suite 353, New York, NY 10012 *Web Site:* www.rattapallax.com, pg 172

Raven Publishing Inc, 125 Cherry Creek Rd, Norris, MT 59745 *Tel:* 406-685-3545 *Toll Free Tel:* 866-685-3545 *E-mail:* info@ravenpublishing.net *Web Site:* www.ravenpublishing.net, pg 172

Ravenhawk™ Books, 311 E Drowsey Circle, Payson, AZ 85541 *Tel:* 520-402-9033 *Fax:* 520-402-9033 *Web Site:* www.facebook.com/6DOFRavenhawk, pg 172

James A Rawley Award, University of Georgia, Dept of History, Athens, GA 30602-1602 *Tel:* 706-542-8848 *Web Site:* thesha.org/rawley, pg 654

James A Rawley Prize, 112 N Bryan Ave, Bloomington, IN 47408-4141 *Tel:* 812-855-7311 *E-mail:* oah@oah.org *Web Site:* www.oah.org/awards, pg 655

RBC Bronwen Wallace Award for Emerging Writers, 600-460 Richmond St W, Toronto, ON M5V 1Y1, Canada *Tel:* 416-504-8222 *Toll Free Tel:* 877-906-6548 *Fax:* 416-504-9090 *E-mail:* info@writerstrust.com *Web Site:* www.writerstrust.com, pg 655

Reader's Digest Select Editions, 44 S Broadway, White Plains, NY 10601 *Tel:* 914-238-1000 *Toll Free Tel:* 877-732-4438 (cust serv) *Web Site:* www.rd.com/article/select-editions/; www.facebook.com/selecteditions, pg 172

Reader's Digest Trade Publishing, 44 S Broadway, White Plains, NY 10601 *Tel:* 914-238-1000 *Web Site:* rdtradepublishing.com, pg 172

Reading the West Book Awards, PO Box 746, Denver, CO 80201 *Tel:* 970-484-3939 *Toll Free Tel:* 800-752-0249 *Fax:* 970-484-0037 *E-mail:* info@mountainsplains.org *Web Site:* www.mountainsplains.org/reading-the-west-book-awards, pg 655

Recorded Books Inc, an RBmedia company, 8400 Corporate Dr, Landover, MD 20785 *Toll Free Tel:* 800-305-3450 *Web Site:* rbmediaglobal.com/recorded-books, pg 172

Red Chair Press, PO Box 333, South Egremont, MA 01258-0333 *Tel:* 413-528-2398 (edit off) *Toll Free Tel:* 800-328-4929 (orders & cust serv) *E-mail:* info@redchairpress.com *Web Site:* www.redchairpress.com, pg 172

Red Deer Press Inc, 209 Wicksteed Ave, Unit 51, Toronto, ON M4G 0B1, Canada *Tel:* 905-477-9700 *Toll Free Tel:* 800-387-9776 *E-mail:* bookinfo@fitzhenry.ca *Web Site:* www.reddeerpress.com, pg 417

Red Hen Press, PO Box 40820, Pasadena, CA 91114 *Tel:* 626-356-4760 *Fax:* 626-356-9974 *Web Site:* www.redhen.org, pg 172

Red Moon Press, PO Box 2461, Winchester, VA 22604-1661 *Tel:* 540-722-2156 *Web Site:* www.redmoonpress.com, pg 172

Red Pencil Conference, 7511 Greenwood Ave N, No 307, Seattle, WA 98103 *E-mail:* conference@edsguild.org *Web Site:* www.edsguild.org/red-pencil-conferences, pg 557

The Red Sea Press Inc, 541 W Ingham Ave, Suite B, Trenton, NJ 08638 *Tel:* 609-695-3200 *Fax:* 609-695-6466 *E-mail:* customerservice@africaworldpressbooks.com *Web Site:* www.africaworldpressbooks.com, pg 173

Red Wheel/Weiser, 65 Parker St, Suite 7, Newburyport, MA 01950 *Tel:* 978-465-0504 *Toll Free Tel:* 800-423-7087 (orders) *Fax:* 978-465-0243 *E-mail:* info@rwwbooks.com *Web Site:* www.redwheelweiser.com, pg 173

Redleaf Press®, 10 Yorkton Ct, St Paul, MN 55117 *Tel:* 651-641-0508 *Toll Free Tel:* 800-423-8309 *Fax:* 651-641-0115 *E-mail:* customerservice@redleafpress.org; info@redleafpress.org; marketing@redleafpress.org *Web Site:* www.redleafpress.org, pg 173

Reed Environmental Writing Award, 201 W Main St, Suite 14, Charlottesville, VA 22902 *Tel:* 434-977-4090 *Fax:* 434-977-1483 *Web Site:* www.southernenvironment.org, pg 655

Robert D Reed Publishers, PO Box 1992, Bandon, OR 97411-1192 *Tel:* 541-347-9882 *Fax:* 541-347-9883 *E-mail:* 4bobreed@msn.com *Web Site:* rdrpublishers.com, pg 173

Reedswain Inc, 88 Wells Rd, Spring City, PA 19475 *Tel:* 610-495-9578 *Toll Free Tel:* 800-331-5191 *Fax:* 610-495-6632 *E-mail:* orders@reedswain.com *Web Site:* www.reedswain.com, pg 173

Rees Literary Agency, One Westinghouse Plaza, Suite A203, Boston, MA 02136 *Tel:* 617-227-9014 *Web Site:* www.reesagency.com, pg 473

Referee Books, 2017 Lathrop Ave, Racine, WI 53405 *Tel:* 262-632-8855 *Toll Free Tel:* 800-733-6100 *Fax:* 262-632-5460 *E-mail:* customerservice@referee.com *Web Site:* www.referee.com, pg 173

Reference Publications Inc, 5419 Fawn Lake Rd, Shelbyville, MI 49344, pg 173

ReferencePoint Press Inc, 17150 Via del Campo, Suite 205, San Diego, CA 92127 *Tel:* 858-618-1314 *Toll Free Tel:* 888-479-6436 *Fax:* 858-618-1730 *E-mail:* info@referencepointpress.com *Web Site:* www.referencepointpress.com, pg 173

Reformation Heritage Books, 2965 Leonard St NE, Grand Rapids, MI 49525 *Tel:* 616-977-0889 *Fax:* 616-285-3246 *E-mail:* orders@heritagebooks.org *Web Site:* www.heritagebooks.org, pg 173

Regal Hoffmann & Associates LLC, 157 13 St, Brooklyn, NY 11215 *Tel:* 212-684-7900 *E-mail:* info@rhaliterary.com; submissions@rhaliterary.com *Web Site:* www.rhaliterary.com, pg 473

Regal House Publishing, 806 Oberlin Rd, No 12094, Raleigh, NC 27605 *E-mail:* info@regalhousepublishing.com *Web Site:* regalhousepublishing.com, pg 173

Regent Press Printers & Publishers, 2747 Regent St, Berkeley, CA 94705 *Tel:* 510-845-1196 *E-mail:* regentpress@mindspring.com *Web Site:* www.regentpress.net, pg 174

Regina Medal Award, 8550 United Plaza Blvd, Suite 1001, Baton Rouge, LA 70809 *Tel:* 225-408-4417 *E-mail:* cla2@cathla.org *Web Site:* cathla.org, pg 655

Regnery Publishing, 122 "C" St NW, Suite 515, Washington, DC 20001 *Tel:* 202-216-0600 *Web Site:* www.regnery.com, pg 174

Regular Baptist Press, 3715 N Ventura Dr, Arlington Heights, IL 60004 *Tel:* 847-843-1600 *Toll Free Tel:* 800-727-4440 (cust serv) *Fax:* 847-843-3757 *E-mail:* orders@rbpstore.org *Web Site:* regularbaptistpress.org, pg 174

Kerry Reilly: Representatives, 1826 Asheville Place, Charlotte, NC 28203 *Tel:* 704-372-6007; 704-281-5007 (cell) *E-mail:* kerry@reillyreps.com *Web Site:* www.reillyreps.com, pg 486

Nathan Reingold Prize, 440 Geddes Hall, Notre Dame, IN 46556 *Tel:* 574-631-1194 *Fax:* 574-631-1533 *E-mail:* info@hssonline.org *Web Site:* www.hssonline.org, pg 655

ReLit Awards, PO Box 250, Burnt Head, Cupids, NL A0A 2B0, Canada *Web Site:* www.relitawards.com, pg 655

Remember Point Inc, PO Box 1448, Pacific Palisades, CA 90272 *Tel:* 310-896-8716 *E-mail:* info@rememberpoint.com *Web Site:* www.rememberpoint.com; www.longfellowfindsahome.com, pg 174

Renaissance House, 465 Westview Ave, Englewood, NJ 07631 *Tel:* 201-408-4048 *Web Site:* www.renaissancehouse.net, pg 174, 486

Renaissance Literary & Talent, PO Box 17379, Beverly Hills, CA 90209 *Tel:* 323-848-8305 *E-mail:* query@renaissancemgmt.net *Web Site:* renaissancemgmt.net, pg 473

The Amy Rennert Agency Inc, 1880 Century Park E, No 1600, Los Angeles, CA 90067 Tel: 415-789-8955 E-mail: queries@amyrennert.com (no unsol queries), pg 473

Arthur Rense Prize, 633 W 155 St, New York, NY 10032 Tel: 212-368-5900 E-mail: academy@artsandletters.org Web Site: artsandletters.org/awards, pg 655

Reporters Committee for Freedom of the Press, 1156 15 St NW, Suite 1020, Washington, DC 20005-1779 Tel: 202-795-9300 Toll Free Tel: 800-336-4243 (legal hotline for journalists) E-mail: info@rcfp.org Web Site: www.rcfp.org, pg 518

Republic of Consciousness Prize for Small Presses in the USA, c/o Interabang Books, 56 Lovers Lane, No 142, Dallas, TX 75209 E-mail: rofcusa@gmail.com Web Site: www.republicofconsciousnessprize-usa.com, pg 655

Research & Education Association (REA), 258 Prospect Plains Rd, Cranbury, NJ 08512 Toll Free Tel: 833-591-2798 (cust care) Fax: 516-742-5049 (orders) E-mail: info@rea.com Web Site: www.rea.com, pg 174

Research Press, 2612 N Mattis Ave, Champaign, IL 61822 Tel: 217-352-3273 Toll Free Tel: 800-519-2707 Fax: 217-352-1221 E-mail: rp@researchpress.com; orders@researchpress.com Web Site: www.researchpress.com, pg 174

Research Research, 240 E 27 St, Suite 20-K, New York, NY 10016-9238 Tel: 212-779-9540 Fax: 212-779-9540 E-mail: ehtac@msn.com, pg 444

The Restless Books Prize for New Immigrant Writing, 232 Third St, Suite A101, Brooklyn, NY 11215 E-mail: publisher@restlessbooks.com Web Site: www.restlessbooks.org/prize-for-new-immigrant-writing, pg 655

Revell, Publishing Div, 6030 E Fulton Rd, Ada, MI 49301 Tel: 616-676-9185 Toll Free Tel: 800-877-2665 (orders only) Fax: 616-676-9573 Toll Free Fax: 800-398-3111 (orders only) E-mail: media@bakerpublishinggroup.com; orders@bakerpublishinggroup.com; sales@bakerpublishinggroup.com Web Site: www.bakerpublishinggroup.com/revell, pg 174

The Harold U Ribalow Prize, 40 Wall St, 8th fl, New York, NY 10005-1387 Tel: 212-451-6289 E-mail: magazine@hadassah.org Web Site: www.hadassahmagazine.org, pg 655

Evelyn Richardson Nonfiction Award, 1113 Marginal Rd, Halifax, NS B3H 4P7, Canada Tel: 902-423-8116 Fax: 902-422-0881 E-mail: wits@writers.ns.ca (awards) Web Site: writers.ns.ca, pg 655

The Ridenhour Book Prize, 116 E 16 St, 8th fl, New York, NY 10003 Tel: 212-822-0250 Fax: 212-253-5356 E-mail: ridenhour@typemediacenter.org; admin@ridenhour.org Web Site: www.ridenhour.org, pg 656

The Ridenhour Courage Prize, 116 E 16 St, 8th fl, New York, NY 10003 Tel: 212-822-0250 Fax: 212-253-5356 E-mail: ridenhour@typemediacenter.org; admin@ridenhour.org Web Site: www.ridenhour.org, pg 656

The Ridenhour Prize for Truth-Telling, 116 E 16 St, 8th fl, New York, NY 10003 Tel: 212-822-0250 Fax: 212-253-5356 E-mail: ridenhour@typemediacenter.org; admin@ridenhour.org Web Site: www.ridenhour.org, pg 656

Lynne Rienner Publishers Inc, 1800 30 St, Suite 314, Boulder, CO 80301 Tel: 303-444-6684 Fax: 303-444-0824 E-mail: questions@rienner.com; cservice@rienner.com Web Site: www.rienner.com, pg 174

Rilke Prize, Auditorium Bldg, Rm 214, 1155 Union Circle, Denton, TX 76203 E-mail: untrilkeprize@unt.edu Web Site: english.unt.edu/creative-writing/unt-rilke-prize, pg 655

Gwen Pharis Ringwood Award for Drama, 11759 Groat Rd NW, Edmonton, AB T5M 3K6, Canada Tel: 780-422-8174 Toll Free Tel: 800-665-5354 (AB only) E-mail: mail@writersguild.ab.ca Web Site: writersguild.ca, pg 656

Rio Nuevo Publishers, 451 N Bonita Ave, Tucson, AZ 85745 Tel: 520-623-9558 Toll Free Tel: 800-969-9558 Fax: 520-624-5888 Toll Free Fax: 800-715-5888 E-mail: info@rionuevo.com (cust serv) Web Site: www.rionuevo.com, pg 175

The Ripped Bodice Awards for Excellence in Romantic Fiction, 3806 Main St, Culver City, CA 90232 Tel: 424-603-4776 E-mail: therippedbodicela@gmail.com Web Site: www.therippedbodicela.com, pg 656

RISING STAR Award, PO Box 190, Jefferson, OR 97352 E-mail: risingstar@womenfictionwriters.org Web Site: wfwa.memberclicks.net/rising-star-award, pg 656

Rising Sun Publishing, PO Box 70906, Marietta, GA 30007-0906 Tel: 770-518-0369 Fax: 770-587-0862 E-mail: info@rspublishing.com Web Site: www.rspublishing.com, pg 175

Ann Rittenberg Literary Agency Inc, 15 Maiden Lane, Suite 206, New York, NY 10038 Tel: 212-684-6936 Fax: 212-684-6929 E-mail: info@rittlit.com Web Site: www.rittlit.com, pg 473

Jack D Rittenhouse Award, 12727 Highland Ct, Auburn, CA 95603-3634 Tel: 720-443-3637 E-mail: executivedirector@pubwest.org Web Site: pubwest.org, pg 656

Max Ritvo Poetry Prize, 1011 Washington Ave S, Suite 300, Minneapolis, MN 55415-1246 Tel: 612-332-3192 Toll Free Tel: 800-520-6455 Web Site: milkweed.org/max-ritvo-poetry-prize, pg 656

Judith Riven Literary Agent LLC, 250 W 16 St, Suite 4F, New York, NY 10011, pg 444, 473

River City Publishing, 1719 Mulberry St, Montgomery, AL 36106 Tel: 334-265-6753, pg 175

Riverby Awards, 500 Burroughs Dr, at Floyd Ackert, New York, NY 12493 Tel: 845-384-6556 E-mail: info@johnburroughsassociation.org Web Site: www.johnburroughsassociation.org, pg 656

Riverdale Avenue Books (RAB), 5676 Riverdale Ave, Bronx, NY 10471 Tel: 212-279-6418 E-mail: customerservice@riverdaleavebooks.com Web Site: www.riverdaleavebooks.com, pg 175

Riverhead Books, c/o Penguin Random House LLC, 1745 Broadway, New York, NY 10019 Tel: 212-782-9000 Web Site: www.penguin.com/riverhead-overview/, pg 175

Riverside Literary Agency, 41 Simon Keets Rd, Leyden, MA 01337 Tel: 413-772-0067 Fax: 413-772-0969 E-mail: rivlit@sover.net Web Site: www.riversideliteraryagency.com, pg 473

Rizzoli International Publications Inc, 300 Park Ave S, 4th fl, New York, NY 10010-5399 Tel: 212-387-3400 Toll Free Tel: 800-522-6657 (orders only) Fax: 212-387-3535 E-mail: publicity@rizzoliusa.com Web Site: www.rizzoliusa.com, pg 175

RMA, 47 Tiffany Way, Plattsburgh, NY 12901 Tel: 718-434-1893 Fax: 518-310-0668 Web Site: ricia.com, pg 473

The RoadRunner Press, 124 NW 32 St, Oklahoma City, OK 73118 Tel: 405-524-6205 Fax: 405-524-6312 E-mail: info@theroadrunnerpress.com; orders@theroadrunnerpress.com Web Site: www.theroadrunnerpress.com, pg 175

Roam Agency, 45 Main St, Suite 727, Brooklyn, NY 11201-1076 E-mail: roam@roamagency.com Web Site: www.roamagency.com, pg 473

Roanoke-Chowan Award for Poetry, 4610 Mail Service Ctr, Raleigh, NC 27699-4610 Web Site: www.ncdcr.gov/about/history/lit-and-hist/awards, pg 656

Roaring Brook Press, 120 Broadway, New York, NY 10271 Tel: 646-307-5151 Web Site: us.macmillan.com/publishers/roaring-brook-press, pg 175

B J Robbins Literary Agency, 5130 Bellaire Ave, North Hollywood, CA 91607 E-mail: robbinsliterary@gmail.com, pg 474

John A Robertson Award for Best First Book of Poetry, PO Box 130294, Spring, TX 77393 Web Site: texasinstituteofletters.org, pg 657

Rochester Institute of Technology, Department of Packaging & Graphic Media Science, 69 Lomb Memorial Dr, Rochester, NY 14623-5603 Tel: 585-475-2728; 585-475-5336 Fax: 585-475-5336 E-mail: spmofc@rit.edu Web Site: rit.edu/engineeringtechnology/department-packaging-and-graphic-media-science, pg 565

The Rockefeller University Press, 950 Third Ave, 2nd fl, New York, NY 10022 Tel: 212-327-7938 E-mail: rupress@rockefeller.edu Web Site: www.rupress.org, pg 176

RockHill Publishing LLC, PO Box 62523, Virginia Beach, VA 23466-2523 Tel: 757-692-2021 Web Site: rockhillpublishing.com, pg 176

Rocky Mountain Book Award, PO Box 42, Lethbridge, AB T1J 3Y3, Canada Tel: 403-381-7164 E-mail: rockymountainbookaward@shaw.ca Web Site: www.rmba.info, pg 657

Rocky Mountain Books Ltd (RMB), 103-1075 Pendergast St, Victoria, BC V8V 0A1, Canada Tel: 250-360-0829 Fax: 250-386-0829 Web Site: rmbooks.com, pg 418

Rocky Mountain Mineral Law Foundation, 9191 Sheridan Blvd, Suite 203, Westminster, CO 80031 Tel: 303-321-8100 Fax: 303-321-7657 E-mail: info@rmmlf.org Web Site: www.rmmlf.org, pg 176

Rocky Pond Books, c/o Penguin Random House LLC, 1745 Broadway, New York, NY 10019 Tel: 212-782-9000 Web Site: www.penguin.com/rocky-pond-overview/, pg 176

Rod & Staff Publishers Inc, 14193 Hwy 172, Crockett, KY 41413 Tel: 606-522-4348 Fax: 606-522-4896, pg 176

Rodin Books, 666 Old Country Rd, Suite 510, Garden City, NY 11530 Tel: 917-685-1064 Web Site: www.rodinbooks.com, pg 176

Rogers & Weil Literary, 530 Divisadero St, No 169, San Francisco, CA 94117 Web Site: www.rwliterary.com, pg 474

Linda Roghaar Literary Agency LLC, 133 High Point Dr, Amherst, MA 01002 Tel: 413-256-1921 Web Site: www.lindaroghaar.com, pg 474

Sami Rohr Prize for Jewish Literature, 452 Fifth Ave, 24th fl, New York, NY 10018 Tel: 516-548-3921 Web Site: www.samirohrprize.org, pg 657

The Roistacher Literary Agency, 545 W 111 St, Suite 7J, New York, NY 10025-1965 Tel: 212-222-1405, pg 474

The Frances "Frank" Rollin Fellowship, PO Box 33020, Santa Fe, NM 87594 Tel: 505-983-4671 Web Site: biographersinternational.org/award/the-frances-frank-rollin-fellowship, pg 657

Roman Catholic Books, PO Box 2286, Fort Collins, CO 80522-2286 Tel: 970-490-2735 Fax: 904-493-8781 Web Site: www.booksforcatholics.com, pg 176

Romance Writers of America®, 2455 E Sunrise Blvd, Suite 816, Fort Lauderdale, FL 33304 Tel: 832-717-5200 E-mail: info@rwa.org Web Site: www.rwa.org, pg 518

Roncorp Music, PO Box 1210, Coatesville, PA 19320 Tel: 610-679-5400 E-mail: info@nemusicpub.com Web Site: www.nemusicpub.com, pg 176

Ronin Publishing Inc, PO Box 3436, Oakland, CA 94609 Tel: 510-420-3669 Fax: 510-420-3672 E-mail: ronin@roninpub.com Web Site: www.roninpub.com, pg 176

Ronsdale Press Ltd, 125A-1030 Denman St, Vancouver, BC V6G 2M6, Canada Tel: 604-738-4688 E-mail: ronsdalepress@gmail.com Web Site: ronsdalepress.com, pg 418

COMPANY INDEX

Peter Rooney, 135 Hudson St, New York, NY 10013 *Tel:* 917-376-1792 *Fax:* 212-226-8047 *E-mail:* magneticreports@gmail.com *Web Site:* www.magneticreports.xyz, pg 444

Eleanor Roosevelt Award for Bravery in Literature, PO Box 255, Hyde Park, NY 12538 *Tel:* 845-229-5302 *E-mail:* admin@ervk.org *Web Site:* ervk.org/banned-book-awards, pg 657

Rootstock Publishing, 27 Main St, Suite 6, Montpelier, VT 05602 *Tel:* 802-839-0371 *E-mail:* info@rootstockpublishing.com *Web Site:* www.rootstockpublishing.com, pg 176

Robert Rose Inc, 120 Eglinton Ave E, Suite 800, Toronto, ON M4P 1E2, Canada *Tel:* 416-322-6552 *Fax:* 416-322-6936 *Web Site:* www.robertrose.ca, pg 418

Rosemont College, Graduate Publg Prog, 1400 Montgomery Ave, Rosemont, PA 19010 *Tel:* 610-527-0200 (ext 2431) *Web Site:* www.rosemont.edu, pg 565

The Rosen Publishing Group Inc, 29 E 21 St, New York, NY 10010 *Tel:* 800-237-9932 *Toll Free Tel:* 888-436-4643 *E-mail:* info@rosenpub.com *Web Site:* www.rosenpublishing.com, pg 177

The Rosenberg Group, 23 Lincoln Ave, Marblehead, MA 01945 *E-mail:* rosenberglitsubmit@icloud.com *Web Site:* www.rosenberggroup.com, pg 474

Rita Rosenkranz Literary Agency, 440 West End Ave, Suite 15D, New York, NY 10024-5358 *Tel:* 212-873-6333 *Fax:* 212-873-5225 *Web Site:* www.ritarosenkranzliteraryagency.com, pg 474

Rosenthal Family Foundation Award for Literature, 633 W 155 St, New York, NY 10032 *Tel:* 212-368-5900 *E-mail:* academy@artsandletters.org *Web Site:* artsandletters.org/awards, pg 657

RosettaBooks, 1035 Park Ave, No 3A, New York, NY 10028-0912 *Tel:* 917-685-1064 *Web Site:* www.rosettabooks.com; www.rosettaebooks.com, pg 177

Ross Books, PO Box 4340, Berkeley, CA 94704-0340 *Tel:* 510-841-2474 *Fax:* 510-295-2531 *E-mail:* sales@rossbooks.com *Web Site:* www.rossbooks.com, pg 177

Margaret W Rossiter History of Women in Science Prize, 440 Geddes Hall, Notre Dame, IN 46556 *Tel:* 574-631-1194 *Fax:* 574-631-1533 *E-mail:* info@hssonline.org *Web Site:* www.hssonline.org, pg 657

Lois Roth Award, 85 Broad St, New York, NY 10004 *Tel:* 646-576-5141; 646-576-5000 *E-mail:* awards@mla.org *Web Site:* www.mla.org, pg 657

Rothstein Associates Inc, 4 Arapaho Rd, Brookfield, CT 06804-3104 *Tel:* 203-740-7400 *Toll Free Tel:* 888-768-4783 *Fax:* 203-740-7401 *E-mail:* info@rothstein.com *Web Site:* www.rothstein.com; www.rothsteinpublishing.com, pg 177

Jane Rotrosen Agency LLC, 318 E 51 St, New York, NY 10022-7803 *Tel:* 212-593-4330 *E-mail:* info@janerotrosen.com *Web Site:* janerotrosen.com, pg 474

The Rough Notes Co Inc, 11690 Technology Dr, Carmel, IN 46032-5600 *Tel:* 317-582-1600 *Toll Free Tel:* 800-428-4384 (cust serv) *Fax:* 317-816-1000 *Toll Free Fax:* 800-321-1909 *E-mail:* rnc@roughnotes.com *Web Site:* www.roughnotes.com, pg 177

Round Table Companies, PO Box 1603, Deerfield, IL 60015 *Toll Free Tel:* 833-750-5683 *Web Site:* www.roundtablecompanies.com, pg 177

Routledge, 711 Third Ave, New York, NY 10017 *Tel:* 212-216-7800 *Toll Free Tel:* 800-634-7064 (order enquiries, cust serv) *Fax:* 212-564-7854 *Web Site:* www.routledge.com, pg 177

Rowe Publishing LLC, 655 Old Lifsey Springs Rd, Molena, GA 30258 *Tel:* 785-302-0451 *E-mail:* info@rowepub.com *Web Site:* www.rowepub.com, pg 178

Hazel Rowley Prize, PO Box 33020, Santa Fe, NM 87594 *Web Site:* biographersinternational.org/award/hazel-rowley-prize, pg 657

Rowman & Littlefield, 4501 Forbes Blvd, Suite 200, Lanham, MD 20706 *Tel:* 301-459-3366 *Toll Free Tel:* 800-462-6420 (ext 3024, cust serv) *Fax:* 301-429-5748 *Web Site:* rowman.com, pg 178

Royal Fireworks Press, 41 First Ave, Unionville, NY 10988 *Tel:* 845-726-4444 *E-mail:* mail@rfwp.com *Web Site:* www.rfwp.com, pg 178

Royal Ontario Museum Press, 100 Queen's Park, Toronto, ON M5S 2C6, Canada *Tel:* 416-586-8000 *E-mail:* info@rom.on.ca *Web Site:* www.rom.on.ca, pg 418

Lexi Rudnitsky First Book Prize in Poetry, 90 Broad St, Suite 2100, New York, NY 10004 *Tel:* 212-260-9256 *E-mail:* poetry@perseabooks.com *Web Site:* www.perseabooks.com, pg 657

William B Ruggles Journalism Scholarship, 5211 Port Royal Rd, Suite 510, Springfield, VA 22151 *Tel:* 703-321-9606 *Fax:* 703-327-8101 *Web Site:* www.nilrr.org, pg 657

Sandy Run Novella Award, PO Box 63927, Philadelphia, PA 19147 *Tel:* 610-764-0813 *E-mail:* info@hiddenriverarts.org *Web Site:* hiddenriverarts.wordpress.com, pg 658

Running Press, 1290 Avenue of the Americas, New York, NY 10104 *Tel:* 212-364-1100 *Toll Free Tel:* 800-759-0190 (cust serv) *Fax:* 212-364-0933 (intl orders) *Toll Free Fax:* 800-286-9471 (cust serv) *E-mail:* customer.service@hbgusa.com; orders@hbgusa.com *Web Site:* www.hachettebookgroup.com/imprint/running-press/; www.moon.com (Moon Travel Guides), pg 178

Frances E Russell Grant, c/o The Canadian Children's Book Ctr, 425 Adelaide St W, Suite 200, Toronto, ON M5V 3C1, Canada *Fax:* 416-975-8970 *E-mail:* russell@ibby-canada.org *Web Site:* www.ibby-canada.org/awards/frances-e-russell-grant/, pg 658

Russell Sage Foundation, 112 E 64 St, New York, NY 10065 *Tel:* 212-750-6000 *Toll Free Tel:* 800-524-6401 *Fax:* 212-371-4761 *E-mail:* info@rsage.org *Web Site:* www.russellsage.org, pg 178

Rutgers University Press, 106 Somerset St, 3rd fl, New Brunswick, NJ 08901 *Tel:* 848-445-7762; 848-445-7761 (sales) *Fax:* 732-745-4935 *E-mail:* sales@rutgersuniversitypress.org *Web Site:* www.rutgersuniversitypress.org, pg 178

The Cornelius Ryan Award, 40 W 45 St, New York, NY 10036 *Tel:* 212-626-9220 *E-mail:* info@opcofamerica.org *Web Site:* opcofamerica.org, pg 658

Dr Tony Ryan Book Award, 2469 Ironworks Pike, Lexington, KY 40511 *Tel:* 859-455-9222 *Web Site:* www.castletonlyons.com, pg 658

Regina Ryan Books, 251 Central Park W, Suite 7-D, New York, NY 10024 *Tel:* 212-787-5589 *E-mail:* queries@reginaryanbooks.com *Web Site:* www.reginaryanbooks.com, pg 474

Sachem Publishing Associates Inc, 402 W Lyon Farm Dr, Greenwich, CT 06831 *Tel:* 203-813-3077 *E-mail:* sachempub@optonline.net, pg 444

Saddleback Educational Publishing, 151 Kalmus Dr, Suite J-1, Costa Mesa, CA 92626 *Tel:* 714-640-5200 *Toll Free Tel:* 888-SDLBACK (735-2225); 800-637-8715 *Fax:* 714-640-5297 *Toll Free Fax:* 888-734-4010 *E-mail:* contact@sdlback.com *Web Site:* www.sdlback.com, pg 179

William H Sadlier Inc, 9 Pine St, New York, NY 10005 *Tel:* 212-227-2120 *Toll Free Tel:* 800-221-5175 (cust serv) *Fax:* 212-312-6080 *E-mail:* customerservice@sadlier.com *Web Site:* www.sadlier.com, pg 179

SAE (Society of Automotive Engineers International), 400 Commonwealth Dr, Warrendale, PA 15096-0001 *Tel:* 724-776-4841; 724-776-4970 (outside US & CN) *Toll Free Tel:* 877-606-7323 (cust serv) *Fax:* 724-776-0790 (cust serv) *E-mail:* publications@sae.org; customerservice@sae.org *Web Site:* www.sae.org, pg 179

Safari Press, 15621 Chemical Lane, Bldg B, Huntington Beach, CA 92649 *Tel:* 714-894-9080 *Toll Free Tel:* 800-451-4788 *Fax:* 714-894-4949 *E-mail:* info@safaripress.com *Web Site:* www.safaripress.com, pg 179

Safer Society Press, PO Box 340, Brandon, VT 05733-0340 *Tel:* 802-247-3132 *Fax:* 802-247-4233 *E-mail:* info@safersociety.org *Web Site:* safersocietypress.org, pg 179

Sagamore Publishing LLC, 3611 N Staley Rd, Suite B, Champaign, IL 61822 *Tel:* 217-359-5940 *Toll Free Tel:* 800-327-5557 (orders) *Fax:* 217-359-5975 *E-mail:* web@sagamorepub.com *Web Site:* www.sagamorepub.com, pg 179

SAGE Publishing, 2455 Teller Rd, Thousand Oaks, CA 91320 *Toll Free Tel:* 800-818-7243 *Toll Free Fax:* 800-583-2665 *E-mail:* info@sagepub.com; orders@sagepub.com *Web Site:* www.sagepublishing.com, pg 180

SAH Prize for Historical Fiction, Columbia University, 3009 Broadway MC 802, New York, NY 10027 *Tel:* 212-854-1919 *E-mail:* amhistsociety@columbia.edu *Web Site:* sah.columbia.edu, pg 658

St Augustine's Press Inc, PO Box 2285, South Bend, IN 46680-2285 *Tel:* 574-291-3500 *Fax:* 574-291-3700 *Web Site:* www.staugustine.net, pg 180

St Herman Press, 4430 Mushroom Lane, Platina, CA 96076 *Tel:* 530-352-4430 *Fax:* 530-352-4432 *E-mail:* stherman@stherman.com *Web Site:* www.sainthermanmonastery.com, pg 180

St James Press®, 27500 Drake Rd, Farmington Hills, MI 48331-3535 *Tel:* 248-699-4253 *Toll Free Tel:* 800-877-4253 (orders) *Toll Free Fax:* 877-363-4253 *E-mail:* gale.customerservice@cengage.com *Web Site:* www.gale.com, pg 180

Saint-Jean Editeur Inc, 4490, rue Garand, Laval, QC H7L 5Z6, Canada *Tel:* 450-663-1777 *E-mail:* info@saint-jeanediteur.com *Web Site:* saint-jeanediteur.com, pg 418

St Johann Press, 315 Schraalenburgh Rd, Haworth, NJ 07641 *Tel:* 201-387-1529 *Fax:* 201-501-0698 *Web Site:* www.stjohannpress.com, pg 180

St Joseph's University Press, 5600 City Ave, Philadelphia, PA 19131-1395 *Tel:* 610-660-3402 *Fax:* 610-660-3412 *E-mail:* sjupress@sju.edu *Web Site:* www.sjupress.com, pg 180

Saint Louis Literary Award, Pius XII Memorial Library, 3650 Lindell Blvd, St Louis, MO 63108 *Tel:* 314-977-3100; 314-977-3087 *Fax:* 314-977-3108 *E-mail:* slula@slu.edu *Web Site:* lib.slu.edu/about/associates/literary-award, pg 658

St Martin's Press, LLC, 120 Broadway, New York, NY 10271 *E-mail:* publicity@stmartins.com; trademarketing@stmartins.com; foreignrights@stmartins.com *Web Site:* us.macmillan.com/smp, pg 180

Saint Mary's Press, 702 Terrace Heights, Winona, MN 55987-1320 *Tel:* 507-457-7900 *Toll Free Tel:* 800-533-8095 *Toll Free Fax:* 800-344-9225 *E-mail:* smpress@smp.org *Web Site:* www.smp.org, pg 181

St Nectarios Press, 10300 Ashworth Ave N, Seattle, WA 98133-9410 *Tel:* 206-522-4471 *Toll Free Tel:* 800-643-4233 *E-mail:* orders@stnectariospress.com *Web Site:* www.stnectariospress.com, pg 181

St Pauls, 2187 Victory Blvd, Staten Island, NY 10314-6603 *Tel:* 718-761-0047 (edit & prodn); 718-698-2759 (mktg & billing) *Toll Free Tel:* 800-343-2522 *Fax:* 718-761-0057 *E-mail:* sales@stpauls.us; marketing@stpauls.us *Web Site:* www.stpauls.us, pg 181

Salem Press, 2 University Plaza, Suite 310, Hackensack, NJ 07601 *Tel:* 201-968-0500 *Toll Free Tel:* 800-221-1592 *Fax:* 201-968-0511 *E-mail:* csr@salempress.com *Web Site:* salempress.com, pg 181

Salina Bookshelf Inc, 1120 W University Ave, Suite 102, Flagstaff, AZ 86001 *Toll Free Tel:* 877-527-0070 *Fax:* 928-526-0386 *Web Site:* www.salinabookshelf.com, pg 181

Salmon Bay Indexing, 26026 Wax Orchard Rd SW, Vashon, WA 98070 *Tel:* 206-612-3993 *Web Site:* salmonbayindexing.com, pg 444

Barbara S Salz LLC Photo Research, 127 Prospect Place, South Orange, NJ 07079 Tel: 646-734-5949 E-mail: bsalz.photo@gmail.com, pg 444

Salzman International, 1751 Charles Ave, Arcata, CA 95521 Tel: 707-822-5500 Fax: 707-825-6600 Web Site: salzmanart.com, pg 486

SAMS Technical Publishing LLC, 9850 E 30 St, Indianapolis, IN 46229 Toll Free Tel: 800-428-7267 E-mail: customercare@samswebsite.com Web Site: www.samswebsite.com, pg 181

San Diego State University Press, Arts & Letters 283/MC 6020, 5500 Campanile Dr, San Diego, CA 92182-6020 Tel: 619-594-6220 (orders); 619-594-1524 (returns) E-mail: memo@sdsu.edu Web Site: sdsupress.sdsu.edu, pg 182

San Francisco Browning Society Award, 511-512 Humanities Bldg, 1600 Holloway Ave, San Francisco, CA 94132 Tel: 415-338-2227 Fax: 415-338-0966 E-mail: poetry@sfsu.edu Web Site: poetry.sfsu.edu, pg 658

San Francisco Foundation/Nomadic Press Literary Awards, 111 Fairmount Ave, Oakland, CA 94611 Tel: 510-500-5162 E-mail: info@nomadicpress.org Web Site: www.nomadicpress.org/sff/nomadicpressliteraryawards; nomadicpress.submittable.com/submit; www.nomadicpress.org, pg 658

San Francisco Writers Conference, 1901 Cleveland Ave, Suite D, Santa Rosa, CA 94501 Tel: 415-689-6301 E-mail: registrations@sfwriters.org; director@sfwriters.org; bizdev@sfwriters.org Web Site: www.sfwriters.org, pg 557

San Francisco Writing Contest (SFWC), 1901 Cleveland Ave, Suite D, Santa Rosa, CA 94501 Tel: 415-689-6301 E-mail: contest@sfwriters.org; director@sfwriters.org Web Site: www.sfwriters.org, pg 658

The Carl Sandburg Literary Award, 200 W Madison, 3rd fl, Chicago, IL 60606 Tel: 312-201-9830 E-mail: info@cplfoundation.org Web Site: www.cplfoundation.org, pg 658

Victoria Sanders & Associates LLC, 440 Buck Rd, Stone Ridge, NY 12484 Tel: 212-633-8811 Web Site: www.victoriasanders.com, pg 474

Ada Sanderson Memorial, PO Box 36128, North Chesterfield, VA 23235-3533 E-mail: contest@poetrysocietyofvirginia.org; info@poetryvirginia.org Web Site: www.poetrysocietyofvirginia.org, pg 658

Mari Sandoz Award, PO Box 21756, Lincoln, NE 68542-1756 Web Site: www.nebraskalibraries.org/mari_sandoz_award, pg 659

Ivan Sandrof Lifetime Achievement Award, c/o Jacob M Appel, Icahn School of Medicine at Mount Sinai, One Gustave L Levy Place, New York, NY 10029 E-mail: info@bookcritics.org Web Site: www.bookcritics.org/awards/sandrof/, pg 659

Santa Monica Press LLC, 249 S Hwy 101, No 301, Solana Beach, CA 92075 Tel: 858-832-7906 Toll Free Tel: 800-784-9553 E-mail: books@santamonicapress.com; acquisitions@santamonicapress.com (edit submissions) Web Site: www.santamonicapress.com, pg 182

Sara Jordan Publishing, RPO Lakeport Box 28105, St Catharines, ON L2N 7P8, Canada Tel: 905-938-5050 Toll Free Tel: 800-567-7733 Fax: 905-938-9970 Toll Free Fax: 800-229-3855 Web Site: www.sara-jordan.com; www.songsthatteach.com, pg 418

Sarabande Books Inc, 822 E Market St, Louisville, KY 40206 Tel: 502-458-4028 Fax: 502-458-4065 E-mail: info@sarabandebooks.org Web Site: www.sarabandebooks.org, pg 182

The Sarabande Series in Kentucky Literature, 822 E Market St, Louisville, KY 40206 Tel: 502-458-4028 E-mail: info@sarabandebooks.org Web Site: www.sarabandebooks.org/bruckheimer, pg 659

The William Saroyan International Prize for Writing, 1801 Van Ness Ave, Suite 320, San Francisco, CA 94109 E-mail: info@williamsaroyanfoundation.org Web Site: williamsaroyanfoundation.org/prizes, pg 659

May Sarton New Hampshire Poetry Prize, 44 Main St, 2nd fl, Peterborough, NH 03458 Tel: 603-567-4430 Web Site: www.bauhanpublishing.com, pg 659

Sarton Women's Book Awards™, PO Box 1616, Bertram, TX 78605-1616 E-mail: sartonprize@storycircle.org Web Site: www.storycircle.org/SartonLiteraryAward, pg 659

SAS Press, 100 SAS Campus Dr, Cary, NC 27513-2414 Tel: 919-677-8000 Toll Free Tel: 800-727-0025 Fax: 919-677-4444 E-mail: saspress@sas.com Web Site: support.sas.com/en/books.html, pg 182

Sasquatch Books, 1904 S Third Ave, Suite 710, Seattle, WA 98101 Tel: 206-467-4300 Toll Free Tel: 800-775-0817 Fax: 206-467-4301 E-mail: custserv@sasquatchbooks.com Web Site: sasquatchbooks.com, pg 182

Saturnalia Books Poetry Prize & Editors Prize, 105 Woodside Rd, Ardmore, PA 19003 Tel: 267-278-9541 Web Site: saturnaliabooks.com, pg 659

SATW Foundation Lowell Thomas Travel Journalism Competition, 306 Summer Hill Dr, Fredericksburg, TX 78624 Tel: 281-217-2872 E-mail: marylua@satwf.com Web Site: www.satwf.org, pg 659

Satya House Publications, 22 Turkey St, Hardwick, MA 01037 Web Site: www.satyahouse.com, pg 182

Savant Books & Publications LLC, 2630 Kapiolani Blvd, Suite 1601, Honolulu, HI 96826 Tel: 808-941-3927 (9AM-noon HST) E-mail: savantbooks@gmail.com; savantdistribution@gmail.com Web Site: www.savantbooksandpublications.com; www.savantdistribution.com, pg 182

Savvas Learning Co LLC, 15 E Midland Ave, Suite 502, Paramus, NJ 07652 Toll Free Tel: 800-848-9500 Web Site: www.savvas.com, pg 183

SBL Press, The Luce Ctr, Suite 350, 825 Houston Mill Rd, Atlanta, GA 30329 Tel: 404-727-3100 Fax: 404-727-3101 (corp) E-mail: sbl@sbl-site.org Web Site: www.sbl-site.org, pg 183

Aldo & Jeanne Scaglione Prize for a Translation of a Literary Work, 85 Broad St, New York, NY 10004 Tel: 646-576-5141; 646-576-5000 E-mail: awards@mla.org Web Site: www.mla.org, pg 659

Aldo & Jeanne Scaglione Prize for a Translation of a Scholarly Study of Literature, 85 Broad St, New York, NY 10004 Tel: 646-576-5141; 646-576-5000 E-mail: awards@mla.org Web Site: www.mla.org, pg 659

Aldo & Jeanne Scaglione Prize for Comparative Literary Studies, 85 Broad St, New York, NY 10004 Tel: 646-576-5141; 646-576-5000 E-mail: awards@mla.org Web Site: www.mla.org, pg 659

Aldo & Jeanne Scaglione Prize for French & Francophone Studies, 85 Broad St, New York, NY 10004 Tel: 646-576-5141; 646-576-5000 E-mail: awards@mla.org Web Site: www.mla.org, pg 660

Aldo & Jeanne Scaglione Prize for Italian Studies, 85 Broad St, New York, NY 10004 Tel: 646-576-5141; 646-576-5000 E-mail: awards@mla.org Web Site: www.mla.org, pg 660

Aldo & Jeanne Scaglione Prize for Studies in Germanic Languages & Literatures, 85 Broad St, New York, NY 10004 Tel: 646-576-5141; 646-576-5000 E-mail: awards@mla.org Web Site: www.mla.org, pg 660

Aldo & Jeanne Scaglione Prize for Studies in Slavic Languages & Literatures, 85 Broad St, New York, NY 10004 Tel: 646-576-5141; 646-576-5000 E-mail: awards@mla.org Web Site: www.mla.org, pg 660

Aldo & Jeanne Scaglione Publication Award for a Manuscript in Italian Literary Studies, 85 Broad St, New York, NY 10004 Tel: 646-576-5141; 646-576-5000 E-mail: awards@mla.org Web Site: www.mla.org, pg 660

William Sanders Scarborough Prize, 85 Broad St, New York, NY 10004 Tel: 646-576-5141; 646-576-5000 E-mail: awards@mla.org Web Site: www.mla.org, pg 660

Scarsdale Publishing Ltd, 333 Mamaroneck Ave, White Plains, NY 10607 E-mail: scarsdale@scarsdalepublishing.com Web Site: scarsdalepublishing.com, pg 183

SCBWI Work-In-Progress Awards, 6363 Wilshire Blvd, Suite 425, Los Angeles, CA 90048 Tel: 323-782-1010 E-mail: info@scbwi.org Web Site: www.scbwi.org/awards/grants/work-in-progress-grants, pg 660

Scepter Publishers, PO Box 360694, Strongsville, OH 44149 Tel: 212-354-0670 Toll Free Tel: 800-322-8773 Fax: 646-417-7707 E-mail: info@scepterpublishers.org Web Site: www.scepterpublishers.org, pg 183

Nicholas Schaffner Award for Music in Literature, PO Box 41567, Tucson, AZ 85717 Web Site: www.schaffnerawards.com, pg 660

Schaffner Press, PO Box 41567, Tucson, AZ 85717 Web Site: www.schaffnerpress.com, pg 183

C J Scheiner Books, 275 Linden Blvd, Unit B2, Brooklyn, NY 11226 Tel: 718-469-1089, pg 444

Schiffer Publishing Ltd, 4880 Lower Valley Rd, Atglen, PA 19310 Tel: 610-593-1777 Fax: 610-593-2002 E-mail: info@schifferbooks.com; customercare@schifferbooks.com; sales@schifferbooks.com; marketing@schifferbooks.com Web Site: www.schifferbooks.com, pg 183

G Schirmer Inc/Associated Music Publishers Inc, 180 Madison Ave, 24th fl, New York, NY 10016 Tel: 212-254-2100 Fax: 212-254-2013 E-mail: schirmer@schirmer.com Web Site: www.musicsalesclassical.com, pg 183

Schlager Group Inc, 10228 E Northwest Hwy, No 1151, Dallas, TX 75238 Toll Free Tel: 888-416-5727 Fax: 469-325-3700 E-mail: info@schlagergroup.com; sales@schlagergroup.com Web Site: www.schlagergroup.com, pg 183

Harold Schmidt Literary Agency, 415 W 23 St, Suite 6-F, New York, NY 10011 Tel: 212-727-7473, pg 475

Bernadotte E Schmitt Grants, 400 "A" St SE, Washington, DC 20003 Tel: 202-544-2422 E-mail: awards@historians.org Web Site: www.historians.org/award-grant/bernadotte-e-schmitt-research-grants-in-european-african-or-asian-history/, pg 660

Schneider Family Book Awards, 225 N Michigan Ave, Suite 1300, Chicago, IL 60601 Tel: 312-280-3247 Toll Free Tel: 800-545-2433 Fax: 312-944-3897 E-mail: ala@ala.org Web Site: www.ala.org/awardsgrants/schneider-family-book-award, pg 661

Schocken Books, c/o Penguin Random House LLC, 1745 Broadway, New York, NY 10019 Tel: 212-751-2600 Fax: 212-940-7390 (dom rts); 212-572-2662 (foreign rts) Web Site: knopfdoubleday.com/imprint/schocken/; knopfdoubleday.com, pg 183

Scholastic Canada Ltd, 175 Hillmount Rd, Markham, ON L6C 1Z7, Canada Tel: 905-887-7323 Toll Free Tel: 800-268-3860 (CN) Toll Free Fax: 800-387-4944 E-mail: custserve@scholastic.ca Web Site: www.scholastic.ca, pg 418

Scholastic Education Solutions, 557 Broadway, New York, NY 10012 Tel: 212-343-6100 Fax: 212-343-6189 Web Site: www.scholastic.com, pg 184

Scholastic Inc, 557 Broadway, New York, NY 10012 Tel: 212-343-6100 Toll Free Tel: 800-SCHOLASTIC (724-6527) Web Site: www.scholastic.com, pg 184

Scholastic International, 557 Broadway, New York, NY 10012 Tel: 212-343-6100; 646-330-5288 (intl cust serv) Toll Free Tel: 800-SCHOLASTIC (724-6527) Fax: 646-837-7878 E-mail: international@scholastic.com, pg 184

Scholastic Trade Publishing, 557 Broadway, New York, NY 10012 Tel: 212-343-6100; 212-343-4685 (export sales) Fax: 212-343-4714 (export sales) Web Site: www.scholastic.com, pg 184

Schonfeld & Associates Inc, 1932 Terramar Lane, Virginia Beach, VA 23456 *Toll Free Tel:* 800-205-0030 *E-mail:* saiinfo@saibooks.com *Web Site:* www.saibooks.com, pg 184

School for Advanced Research Press, 660 Garcia St, Santa Fe, NM 87505 *E-mail:* press@sarsf.org *Web Site:* sarweb.org, pg 185

School Guide Publications, 420 Railroad Way, Mamaroneck, NY 10543 *Tel:* 914-632-1220 *Toll Free Tel:* 800-433-7771 *E-mail:* info@schoolguides.com *Web Site:* www.graduateguide.com; www.schoolguides.com; www.religiousministries.com, pg 185

School of Visual Arts Continuing Education Programs, 209 E 23 St, New York, NY 10010-3994 *Tel:* 212-592-2000 *E-mail:* registrar@sva.edu *Web Site:* www.sva.edu, pg 565

School Zone Publishing Co, 1819 Industrial Dr, Grand Haven, MI 49417 *Tel:* 616-846-5030 *Toll Free Tel:* 800-253-0564 *Fax:* 616-846-6181 *Web Site:* www.schoolzone.com, pg 185

Schoolhouse Indexing, 10-B Parade Ground Rd, Etna, NH 03750 *Tel:* 603-359-5826 *Web Site:* schoolhouseindexing.com, pg 444

Schoolhouse Network, PO Box 1518, Northampton, MA 01061 *Tel:* 480-427-4836 *E-mail:* schoolhousenetwork@gmail.com, pg 444

Schreiber Publishing, PO Box 858, Savage, MD 20763 *Tel:* 301-589-5831 *Toll Free Tel:* 800-296-1961 (sales) *E-mail:* language@schreiberpublishing.net *Web Site:* schreiberlanguage.com; shengold.com; elstreeteducational.com, pg 185

Schroeder Indexing Services, 23 Camilla Pink Ct, Bluffton, SC 29909 *Tel:* 843-415-3900 *E-mail:* sanindex@schroederindexing.com *Web Site:* www.schroederindexing.com, pg 444

Franklin L Schulaner, PO Box 507, Kealakekua, HI 96750-0507 *Tel:* 808-322-3785 *E-mail:* fschulaner@hawaii.rr.com, pg 444

Susan Schulman Literary Agency LLC, 454 W 44 St, New York, NY 10036 *Tel:* 212-713-1633; 917-488-0906 (direct line) *E-mail:* queries@schulmanagency.com *Web Site:* www.schulmanagency.com, pg 475

Sherri Schultz/Words with Grace, 1810 Alder St, No 105, Eugene, OR 97401 *Tel:* 206-928-2015 *E-mail:* WordsWithGraceEditorial@gmail.com, pg 444

Laurens R Schwartz, Esquire, 5 E 22 St, Suite 15-D, New York, NY 10010-5325 *Tel:* 212-228-2614 *E-mail:* lschwartz@nyc.rr.com, pg 475

Ruth & Sylvia Schwartz Children's Book Awards, c/o Ontario Arts Council, 121 Bloor St E, 7th fl, Toronto, ON M4W 3M5, Canada *Tel:* 416-961-1660 *Toll Free Tel:* 800-387-0058 (ON) *Fax:* 416-961-7796 (Ontario Arts Council) *E-mail:* info@oafdn.ca (Ontario Arts Foundation); info@arts.on.ca (Ontario Arts Council) *Web Site:* www.arts.on.ca; www.oafdn.ca/pages/ruth-sylvia-schwartz-awards, pg 661

Science & Humanities Press, 63 Summit Point, St Charles, MO 63301-0571, pg 185

Science + Literature Program, 90 Broad St, Suite 604, New York, NY 10004 *Tel:* 212-685-0261 *Fax:* 212-213-6570 *E-mail:* nationalbook@nationalbook.org *Web Site:* www.nationalbook.org/programs/science-literature, pg 661

Science Fiction and Fantasy Writers Association, Inc (SFWA), PO Box 215, San Lorenzo, CA 94580 *Tel:* 860-698-0536 *E-mail:* office@sfwa.org; operations@sfwa.org *Web Site:* www.sfwa.org, pg 518

Science History Publications USA Inc, 349 Old Plymouth Rd, Sagamore Beach, MA 02562 *E-mail:* orders@shpusa.com *Web Site:* www.shpusa.com, pg 185

Science in Society Journalism Awards, PO Box 7905, Berkeley, CA 94707 *Tel:* 510-859-7229 *Web Site:* www.nasw.org/awards/sis, pg 661

"Science into Fiction" Speculative Fiction Writing Workshop Series, 1809 Indiana St, Lawrence, KS 66044 *Tel:* 785-766-7039 *Web Site:* adastra-sf.com/Workshop-stuff/AdAstranauts-workshop.htm, pg 557

Science, Naturally, 725 Eighth St SE, Washington, DC 20003 *Tel:* 202-465-4798 *Fax:* 202-558-2132 *E-mail:* info@sciencenaturally.com *Web Site:* www.sciencenaturally.com, pg 185

Sciendex, 1388 Leisure Dr, Summerville, SC 29486 *Tel:* 843-693-6689 *Web Site:* www.sciendex.com, pg 444

Scotiabank Giller Prize, 499 Douglas Ave, Toronto, ON M5M 1H6, Canada *Web Site:* www.scotiabankgillerprize.ca, pg 661

S©ott Treimel NY, 434 Lafayette St, New York, NY 10003-6943 *Tel:* 212-505-8353 *E-mail:* general@scotttreimelny.com *Web Site:* scotttreimelny.com; www.linkedin.com/in/scott-treimel-46658727/, pg 475

Scovil Galen Ghosh Literary Agency Inc, 348 W 57 St, New York, NY 10019 *Tel:* 212-679-8686 *E-mail:* info@sgglit.com *Web Site:* www.sgglit.com, pg 475

Scribendi Inc, 405 Riverview Dr, Chatham, ON N7M 0N3, Canada *Tel:* 519-351-1626 (cust serv) *Fax:* 519-354-0192 *E-mail:* customerservice@scribendi.com *Web Site:* www.scribendi.com, pg 444

Scribner, 1230 Avenue of the Americas, New York, NY 10020 *Web Site:* www.simonandschusterpublishing.com/scribner/, pg 185

Scripta Humanistica Publishing International, 1383 Kersey Lane, Potomac, MD 20854 *Tel:* 301-294-7949 *Fax:* 301-424-9584 *E-mail:* info@scriptahumanistica.com *Web Site:* www.scriptahumanistica.com, pg 185

SDP Publishing Solutions LLC, 36 Captain's Way, East Bridgewater, MA 02333 *Tel:* 617-775-0656 *Web Site:* www.sdppublishingsolutions.com, pg 444

Seal Books, 320 Front St W, Suite 1400, Toronto, ON M5V 3B6, Canada *Tel:* 416-364-4449 *Toll Free Tel:* 888-523-9292 (order desk) *Fax:* 416-598-7764 *Web Site:* www.penguinrandomhouse.ca, pg 419

Second Story Press, 20 Maud St, Suite 401, Toronto, ON M5V 2M5, Canada *Tel:* 416-537-7850 *Fax:* 416-537-0588 *E-mail:* info@secondstorypress.ca *Web Site:* secondstorypress.ca, pg 419

See-More's Workshop Arts & Education Workshops, 325 West End Ave, New York, NY 10023 *Tel:* 212-724-0677 *E-mail:* sbt@shadowboxtheatre.org *Web Site:* shadowboxtheatre.org/workshops, pg 557

Seedling Publications Inc, 520 E Bainbridge St, Elizabethtown, PA 17022 *Toll Free Tel:* 800-233-0759 *Toll Free Fax:* 888-834-1303 *E-mail:* edcsr@continentalpress.com *Web Site:* www.continentalpress.com, pg 186

SelectBooks Inc, 325 W 38 St, Suite 306, New York, NY 10018 *Tel:* 212-206-1997 *Fax:* 212-206-3815 *E-mail:* info@selectbooks.com *Web Site:* www.selectbooks.com, pg 186

Self-Realization Fellowship Publishers, 3208 Humboldt St, Los Angeles, CA 90031 *Tel:* 323-276-6002 *Toll Free Tel:* 888-773-8680 *E-mail:* sales@yogananda-srf.org *Web Site:* www.yogananda-srf.org; bookstore.yogananda-srf.org (online retail orders), pg 186

Lynn Seligman, 400 Highland Ave, Upper Montclair, NJ 07043 *Tel:* 973-783-3631 *Fax:* 973-783-3691 *E-mail:* seliglit@aol.com, pg 475

Alexa Selph, 4300 McClatchey Circle, Atlanta, GA 30342 *Tel:* 404-256-3717 *E-mail:* lexa101@aol.com, pg 444

Sentient Publications LLC, PO Box 1851, Boulder, CO 80306 *Tel:* 303-443-2188 *E-mail:* contact@sentientpublications.com *Web Site:* www.sentientpublications.com, pg 186

The Robert S Sergeant Memorial, PO Box 36128, North Chesterfield, VA 23235-3533 *E-mail:* contest@poetrysocietyofvirginia.org; info@poetryvirginia.org *Web Site:* www.poetrysocietyofvirginia.org, pg 661

Serindia Publications, PO Box 10335, Chicago, IL 60610-0335 *E-mail:* info@serindia.com *Web Site:* www.serindia.com, pg 186

Seven Stories Press, 140 Watts St, New York, NY 10013 *Tel:* 212-226-8760 *Toll Free Tel:* 800-733-3000 (orders) *Fax:* 212-226-1411 *E-mail:* sevenstories@sevenstories.com *Web Site:* www.sevenstories.com, pg 186

1765 Productions, 2911 Hunting Hills Ct, Oakton, VA 22124-1752 *Tel:* 202-813-9421 *E-mail:* 1765productions@gmail.com, pg 186

Seventh Avenue Literary Agency, 6318 Rimrock Rd, Sechelt, BC V7Z 0L1, Canada *Tel:* 604-538-7252 *E-mail:* info@seventhavenuelit.com *Web Site:* www.seventhavenuelit.com, pg 475

Sewanee Writers' Conference, 735 University Ave, Sewanee, TN 37383 *Tel:* 931-598-1654 *E-mail:* swc@sewanee.edu *Web Site:* www.sewaneewriters.org, pg 557

The Seymour Agency, 475 Miner Street Rd, Canton, NY 13617 *Tel:* 239-398-8209 *Web Site:* www.theseymouragency.com, pg 475

SF Canada, c/o Jane Glatt, 35 Southshore Crescent, No 103, Hamilton, ON L8E 0J2, Canada *Web Site:* www.sfcanada.org, pg 519

SFWA Nebula Awards, PO Box 215, San Lorenzo, CA 94580 *Tel:* 860-698-0536 *E-mail:* office@sfwa.org; operations@sfwa.org *Web Site:* www.sfwa.org, pg 661

Shadow Mountain Publishing, PO Box 30178, Salt Lake City, UT 84130-0178 *Tel:* 801-534-1515 *Toll Free Tel:* 800-453-3876 *E-mail:* info@shadowmountain.com; submissions@shadowmountain.com *Web Site:* shadowmountain.com, pg 187

Shambhala Publications Inc, 2129 13 St, Boulder, CO 80302 *Tel:* 978-829-2599 (intl callers) *Toll Free Tel:* 866-424-0030 (off); 888-424-2329 (orders & cust serv) *Fax:* 617-236-1563 *E-mail:* customercare@shambhala.com; royalties@shambhala.com *Web Site:* www.shambhala.com, pg 187

Shamus Awards, 3665 S Needles Hwy, 7G, Laughlin, NV 89029 *Web Site:* www.privateeyewriters.com, pg 661

Denise Shannon Literary Agency Inc, 280 Madison Ave, Suite 308, New York, NY 10016 *E-mail:* info@deniseshannonagency.com; submissions@deniseshannonagency.com *Web Site:* deniseshannonagency.com, pg 475

Shaughnessy Cohen Prize for Political Writing, 600-460 Richmond St W, Toronto, ON M5V 1Y1, Canada *Tel:* 416-504-8222 *Toll Free Tel:* 877-906-6548 *Fax:* 416-504-9090 *E-mail:* info@writerstrust.com *Web Site:* www.writerstrust.com, pg 661

Mina P Shaughnessy Prize, 85 Broad St, New York, NY 10004 *Tel:* 646-576-5141; 646-576-5000 *E-mail:* awards@mla.org *Web Site:* www.mla.org, pg 661

Charlotte Sheedy Literary Agency Inc, 928 Broadway, Suite 901, New York, NY 10010 *Tel:* 212-780-9800 *Web Site:* www.sheedylit.com, pg 476

Barry Sheinkopf, c/o The Writing Ctr, 601 Palisade Ave, Englewood Cliffs, NJ 07632 *Tel:* 201-567-4017 *Fax:* 201-567-7202 *E-mail:* bsheinkopf@optonline.net, pg 444

Shelley Memorial Award, 119 Smith St, Brooklyn, NY 11201 *Tel:* 212-254-9628 *E-mail:* info@poetrysociety.org *Web Site:* poetrysociety.org/awards, pg 662

Shen's Books, 95 Madison Ave, Suite 1205, New York, NY 10016 *Tel:* 212-779-4400 *Fax:* 212-683-1894 *E-mail:* general@leeandlow.com *Web Site:* www.leeandlow.com, pg 187

Shepard Publications, 1117 N Garden St, Apt 302, Bellingham, WA 98225 *Web Site:* www.shepardpub.com, pg 187

Sherman Asher Publishing, 126 Candelario St, Santa Fe, NM 87501 *Tel:* 505-988-7214 *E-mail:* westernedge@santa-fe.net *Web Site:* www.shermanasher.com; www.westernedgepress.com, pg 187

Ken Sherman & Associates, 8530 Holloway Dr, Suite 220, West Hollywood, CA 90069 *Tel:* 310-273-8840 *E-mail:* kenshermanassociates@gmail.com *Web Site:* www.kenshermanassociates.com, pg 476

Wendy Sherman Associates Inc, 138 W 25 St, Suite 1018, New York, NY 10001 *Tel:* 212-279-9027 *E-mail:* submissions@wsherman.com *Web Site:* www.wsherman.com, pg 476

J Gordon Shillingford Publishing Inc, PO Box 86, RPO Corydon Ave, Winnipeg, MB R3M 3S3, Canada *Tel:* 204-779-6967 *E-mail:* jgshill2@mymts.net *Web Site:* www.jgshillingford.com, pg 419

The Randy Shilts Award for Gay Nonfiction, 511 Avenue of the Americas, No D36, New York, NY 10011 *E-mail:* awards@publishingtriangle.org; info@publishingtriangle.org; publishingtriangle@gmail.com *Web Site:* publishingtriangle.org/awards/randy-shilts-gay-nonfiction, pg 662

Monika Shoffman-Graves, 70 Transylvania Ave, Key Largo, FL 33037 *Tel:* 305-451-1462 *E-mail:* mograv@gmail.com, pg 445

Christopher Latham Sholes Award, c/o 3225 N 91 St, Milwaukee, WI 53222 *E-mail:* wiswriters@gmail.com *Web Site:* wiswriters.org/awards, pg 662

Short Prose Competition for Developing Writers, 600-460 Richmond St W, Toronto, ON M5V 1Y1, Canada *Tel:* 416-703-8982 *E-mail:* info@writersunion.ca *Web Site:* www.writersunion.ca, pg 662

Short Story Awards, 81 Prince St, Charlottetown, PE C1A 4R3, Canada *E-mail:* peiliteraryawards@gmail.com *Web Site:* www.peiwritersguild.com, pg 662

Edwin "Bud" Shrake Award for Best Short Nonfiction, PO Box 130294, Spring, TX 77393 *Web Site:* texasinstituteofletters.org, pg 662

Joe Shuster Awards, 305-484 Oriole Pkwy, Toronto, ON M5P 2H8, Canada *E-mail:* info@joeshusterawards.com *Web Site:* www.joeshusterawards.com, pg 662

Robert F Sibert Informational Book Award, 225 N Michigan Ave, Suite 1300, Chicago, IL 60601 *Tel:* 312-280-2163 *Toll Free Tel:* 800-545-2433 *Fax:* 312-280-5271 *E-mail:* alsc@ala.org *Web Site:* www.ala.org/alsc/awardsgrants/bookmedia/sibert, pg 662

Side by Side Literary Productions Inc, 145 E 35 St, Suite 7FE, New York, NY 10016 *Tel:* 212-685-6831 *Web Site:* sidebysidelit.com, pg 476

Siglio, PO Box 111, Catskill, NY 12414 *Tel:* 310-857-6935 *E-mail:* publisher@sigliopress.com *Web Site:* sigliopress.com, pg 187

Signalman Publishing, 3700 Commerce Blvd, Kissimmee, FL 34741 *Tel:* 407-504-4103 *Toll Free Tel:* 888-907-4423 *E-mail:* info@signalmanpublishing.com *Web Site:* www.signalmanpublishing.com, pg 187

Signature Books Publishing LLC, 564 W 400 N, Salt Lake City, UT 84116-3411 *Toll Free Tel:* 800-356-5687 *E-mail:* people@signaturebooks.com *Web Site:* www.signaturebooks.com; www.signaturebookslibrary.org, pg 187

Signature Editions, PO Box 206, RPO Corydon, Winnipeg, MB R3M 3S7, Canada *Tel:* 204-779-7803 *E-mail:* signature@allstream.net; orders@signature-editions.com *Web Site:* www.signature-editions.com, pg 419

The SIIA IMPACT Awards, 1620 Eye St NW, Washington, DC 20005 *Tel:* 202-289-7442 *E-mail:* info@siia.net *Web Site:* www.siia.net/impact-award, pg 662

SIL International, 7500 W Camp Wisdom Rd, Dallas, TX 75236-5629 *E-mail:* publications_intl@sil.org *Web Site:* www.sil.org; www.sil.org/resources/publications; www.ethnologue.com, pg 188

Silman-James Press Inc, 141 N Clark Dr, Unit 1, West Hollywood, CA 90048 *Tel:* 310-205-0665 *E-mail:* info@silmanjamespress.com *Web Site:* www.silmanjamespress.com, pg 188

Silver Gavel Awards for Media & the Arts, Division for Public Education, 321 N Clark St, MS 17.2, Chicago, IL 60654 *Tel:* 312-988-5719 *Toll Free Tel:* 800-285-2221 *E-mail:* gavelawards@americanbar.org *Web Site:* www.americanbar.org/groups/public_education/programs/silver_gavel, pg 662

Silver Leaf Books LLC, 1661 Washington St, Suite 6460, Holliston, MA 01746-6460 *E-mail:* sales@silverleafbooks.com; editor@silverleafbooks.com; customerservice@silverleafbooks.com *Web Site:* www.silverleafbooks.com, pg 188

The Robert B Silvers Prize for Journalism, c/o The New York Review of Books, 435 Hudson St, Suite 300, New York, NY 10014 *Tel:* 212-757-8070 *E-mail:* admin@silversfoundation.org *Web Site:* silversfoundation.org/about-the-silvers-dudley-prizes, pg 662

The Robert B Silvers Prize for Literary Criticism, c/o The New York Review of Books, 435 Hudson St, Suite 300, New York, NY 10014 *Tel:* 212-757-8070 *E-mail:* admin@silversfoundation.org *Web Site:* silversfoundation.org/about-the-silvers-dudley-prizes, pg 662

Francis B Simkins Award, University of Georgia, Dept of History, Athens, GA 30602-1602 *Tel:* 706-542-8848 *Web Site:* thesha.org/simkins, pg 663

The John Simmons Short Fiction Award, 102 Dey House, 507 N Clinton St, Iowa City, IA 52242-1000 *Tel:* 319-335-0416 *Fax:* 319-335-0420 *Web Site:* writersworkshop.uiowa.edu/about/iowa-short-fiction-awards, pg 663

Simon & Schuster, 1230 Avenue of the Americas, New York, NY 10020 *Tel:* 212-698-7000 *Toll Free Tel:* 800-223-2348 (cust serv); 800-223-2336 (orders) *Toll Free Fax:* 800-943-9831 (orders) *Web Site:* simonandschusterpublishing.com/simonandschuster/, pg 188

Simon & Schuster Audio, 1230 Avenue of the Americas, New York, NY 10020 *Web Site:* audio.simonandschuster.com, pg 189

Simon & Schuster Canada, 166 King St E, Suite 300, Toronto, ON M5A 1J3, Canada *Tel:* 647-427-8882 *Toll Free Tel:* 800-387-0446; 800-268-3216 (orders) *Fax:* 647-430-9446 *Toll Free Fax:* 888-849-8151 (orders) *E-mail:* info@simonandschuster.ca *Web Site:* www.simonandschuster.ca, pg 419

Simon & Schuster Children's Publishing, 1230 Avenue of the Americas, New York, NY 10020 *Tel:* 212-698-7000 *Web Site:* www.simonandschuster.com/kids; www.simonandschuster.com/teen; simonandschuster.net; simonandschuster.biz, pg 189

Simon & Schuster, LLC, 1230 Avenue of the Americas, New York, NY 10020 *Tel:* 212-698-7000 *Toll Free Tel:* 800-223-2336 (orders) *Fax:* 212-698-7007 *Toll Free Fax:* 800-943-9831 (orders) *E-mail:* firstname.lastname@simonandschuster.com; purchaseorders@simonandschuster.com (orders) *Web Site:* www.simonandschuster.com, pg 189

Charlie May Simon Children's Book Award, Arkansas State Library, Suite 100, 900 W Capitol Ave, Little Rock, AR 72201-3108 *Tel:* 501-682-2860 *Web Site:* www.library.arkansas.gov/programs/book-awards, pg 663

Simply Read Books, 501-5525 West Blvd, Vancouver, BC V6M 3W6, Canada *E-mail:* go@simplyreadbooks.com; orders@simplyreadbooks.com; rights@simplyreadbooks.com *Web Site:* www.simplyreadbooks.com, pg 419

Sinauer Associates, Oxford University Press Higher Education, 2001 Evans Rd, Cary, NC 27513 *Toll Free Tel:* 800-280-0280 *Fax:* 919-678-1435 *E-mail:* highered.us@oup.com; custserv.us@oup.com *Web Site:* sinauer.com, pg 190

SK Arts, 1355 Broad St, Regina, SK S4R 7V1, Canada *Tel:* 306-787-4056 *Toll Free Tel:* 800-667-7526 (CN) *E-mail:* info@sk-arts.ca *Web Site:* sk-arts.ca, pg 519

SkillPath Publications, 6900 Squibb Rd, Mission, KS 66202 *Tel:* 913-362-3900 *Toll Free Tel:* 800-873-7545 *Fax:* 913-362-4241 *E-mail:* customercare@skillpath.com; products@skillpath.com *Web Site:* www.skillpath.com, pg 190

Skinner House Books, c/o Unitarian Universalist Assn, 24 Farnsworth St, Boston, MA 02210-1409 *Tel:* 617-742-2100 *Fax:* 617-948-6466 *E-mail:* skinnerhouse@uua.org *Web Site:* www.uua.org/publications/skinnerhouse, pg 190

Skipping Stones Honor Awards, 166 W 12 Ave, Eugene, OR 97401 *Tel:* 541-342-4956 *E-mail:* info@skippingstones.org *Web Site:* www.skippingstones.org, pg 663

The Skipping Stones Youth Honor Awards, 166 W 12 Ave, Eugene, OR 97401 *Tel:* 541-342-4956 *E-mail:* info@skippingstones.org *Web Site:* www.skippingstones.org, pg 663

Sky Pony Press, 307 W 36 St, 11th fl, New York, NY 10018 *Tel:* 212-643-6816 *Fax:* 212-643-6819 *E-mail:* info@skyhorsepublishing.com; skyponysubmissions@skyhorsepublishing.com *Web Site:* www.skyhorsepublishing.com/sky-pony-press, pg 191

SkyLight Paths® Publishing, 4507 Charlotte Ave, Suite 100, Nashville, TN 37209 *Tel:* 615-255-BOOK (255-2665) *Fax:* 615-255-5081 *E-mail:* marketing@turnerpublishing.com *Web Site:* www.skylightpaths.com; www.turnerpublishing.com, pg 191

SLACK® Incorporated, A Wyanoke Group Company, 6900 Grove Rd, Thorofare, NJ 08086-9447 *Tel:* 856-848-1000 *Toll Free Tel:* 800-257-8290 *Fax:* 856-848-6091 *E-mail:* sales@slackinc.com; editor@slackinc.com; customerservice@slackinc.com *Web Site:* www.healio.com/books, pg 191

Sleeping Bear Press™, 2395 S Huron Pkwy, Suite 200, Ann Arbor, MI 48104 *Toll Free Tel:* 800-487-2323 *Fax:* 734-794-0004 *E-mail:* customerservice@sleepingbearpress.com *Web Site:* www.sleepingbearpress.com, pg 191

Slipstream Annual Poetry Chapbook Contest, PO Box 2071, Dept W-1, Niagara Falls, NY 14301 *Web Site:* www.slipstreampress.org/contest.html, pg 663

Beverley Slopen Literary Agency, 131 Bloor St W, Suite 711, Toronto, ON M5S 1S3, Canada *Tel:* 416-964-9598 *Fax:* 416-964-9598 *Web Site:* www.slopenagency.com, pg 476

Small Beer Press, 150 Pleasant St, No 306, Easthampton, MA 01027 *Tel:* 413-240-4197 *E-mail:* info@smallbeerpress.com *Web Site:* smallbeerpress.com, pg 191

Small Business Advisors Inc, 2005 Park St, Atlantic Beach, NY 11509 *Tel:* 516-374-1184 *Fax:* 516-374-1175 *E-mail:* info@smallbusinessadvice.com *Web Site:* www.smallbusinessadvice.com, pg 191

Phyllis Smart-Young Poetry Prize, University of Wisconsin, 6193 Helen C White Hall, English Dept, 600 N Park St, Madison, WI 53706 *E-mail:* madisonrevw@gmail.com *Web Site:* www.themadisonrevw.com, pg 663

SME (Society of Manufacturing Engineers), 1000 Town Ctr, Suite 1910, Southfield, MI 48075 *Tel:* 313-425-3000 *Toll Free Tel:* 800-733-4763 (cust serv) *Fax:* 313-425-3400 *E-mail:* publications@sme.org *Web Site:* www.sme.org, pg 191

Donald Smiley Prize, 260 Dalhousie St, Suite 204, Ottawa, ON K1N 7E4, Canada *Tel:* 613-562-1202 *Fax:* 613-241-0019 *E-mail:* cpsaprizes@cpsa-acsp.ca; cpsa-acsp@cpsa-acsp.ca *Web Site:* www.cpsa-acsp.ca, pg 663

Smith & Kraus Publishers Inc, 177 Lyme Rd, Hanover, NH 03755 *Tel:* 618-783-0519 *Toll Free Tel:* 877-668-8680 *Fax:* 618-783-0520 *E-mail:* editor@smithandkraus.com; info@smithandkraus.com; customerservice@smithandkraus.com *Web Site:* www.smithandkraus.com, pg 192

Helen C Smith Memorial Award, PO Box 130294, Spring, TX 77393 *Web Site:* texasinstituteofletters.org, pg 663

The Jean Kennedy Smith VSA Playwright Discovery Award, 2700 "F" St NW, Washington, DC 20566 *Tel:* 202-416-8898 *Fax:* 202-416-4840

E-mail: vsainfo@kennedy-center.org *Web Site:* www.kennedy-center.org/education/opportunities-for-artists/competitions-and-commissions, pg 663

The Jeffrey E Smith Editors' Prize, 357 McReynolds Hall, University of Missouri, Columbia, MO 65211 *Tel:* 573-882-4474 *Toll Free Tel:* 800-949-2505 *Fax:* 573-884-4671 *E-mail:* question@moreview.com; contest_question@moreview.com *Web Site:* www.missourireview.com/contests/jeffrey-e-smith-editors-prize, pg 664

M Lee Smith Publishers, 100 Winners Circle, Suite 300, Brentwood, TN 37027 *Tel:* 615-373-7517 *Toll Free Tel:* 800-274-6774; 800-727-5257 *E-mail:* custserv@mleesmith.com; service@blr.com *Web Site:* www.mleesmith.com; www.blr.com, pg 192

Roger W Smith, 59-67 58 Rd, Maspeth, NY 11378-3211 *Tel:* 718-416-1334 *E-mail:* brandeis106@gmail.com, pg 445

Smithsonian Institution Scholarly Press, Aerospace Bldg, 704-A, MRC 957, Washington, DC 20013 *Tel:* 202-633-3017 *Fax:* 202-633-6877 *E-mail:* schol_press@si.edu *Web Site:* scholarlypress.si.edu, pg 192

Smyth & Helwys Publishing Inc, 6316 Peake Rd, Macon, GA 31210-3960 *Tel:* 478-757-0564 *Toll Free Tel:* 800-747-3016 (orders only) *Fax:* 478-757-1305 *E-mail:* information@helwys.com *Web Site:* www.helwys.com, pg 192

Michael Snell Literary Agency, PO Box 1206, Truro, MA 02666-1206 *Tel:* 508-349-3718 *Web Site:* www.michaelsnellagency.com, pg 476

Kay Snow Writing Contest, 5331 SW Macadam Ave, Suite 258, PMB 215, Portland, OR 97239 *Tel:* 971-200-5385 *E-mail:* wilwrite@willamettewriters.org *Web Site:* willamettewriters.org/kay-snow-writing-contest, pg 664

Snow Lion, 4720 Walnut St, Boulder, CO 80301 *E-mail:* customercare@shambhala.com *Web Site:* www.shambhala.com/snowlion, pg 192

The Richard Snyder Memorial Publication Prize, Bixler Center for the Humanities, Ashland University, 401 College Ave, Ashland, OH 44805 *E-mail:* app@ashland.edu *Web Site:* www.ashlandpoetrypress.com/guidelines/snyder-prize, pg 664

Anthony Veasna So Fiction Prize, Cadman Plaza Sta, PO Box 26428, Brooklyn, NY 11202 *E-mail:* editors@nplusonemag.com; subs@nplusonemag.com (submission queries); submissions@nplusonemag.com *Web Site:* www.nplusonemag.com/awards, pg 664

Sobel Weber Associates Inc, 146 E 19 St, New York, NY 10003-2404 *Tel:* 212-420-8585 *E-mail:* info@sobelweber.com *Web Site:* www.sobelweber.com, pg 476

Social Sciences & Humanities Research Council (SSHRC), 350 Albert St, Ottawa, ON K1P 6G4, Canada *Tel:* 613-995-4273 *Toll Free Tel:* 855-275-2861 *E-mail:* research@sshrc-crsh.gc.ca *Web Site:* www.sshrc-crsh.gc.ca, pg 519

Society for Advancing Business Editing and Writing (SABEW), Walter Cronkite School of Journalism & Mass Communication, Arizona State University, 555 N Central Ave, Suite 406E, Phoenix, AZ 85004-1248 *Tel:* 602-496-7862 *E-mail:* sabew@sabew.org *Web Site:* www.sabew.org, pg 519

Society for Features Journalism (SFJ), Eugene S Pulliam National Journalism Ctr, 3909 N Meridian St, Indianapolis, IN 46208 *E-mail:* wearesfj@gmail.com *Web Site:* featuresjournalism.org, pg 519

Society for Human Resource Management (SHRM), 1800 Duke St, Alexandria, VA 22314 *Tel:* 703-548-3440 *Toll Free Tel:* 800-283-7476 (orders) *E-mail:* books@shrm.org *Web Site:* www.shrm.org, pg 192

Society for Industrial & Applied Mathematics, 3600 Market St, 6th fl, Philadelphia, PA 19104-2688 *Tel:* 215-382-9800 *Toll Free Tel:* 800-447-7426 *E-mail:* siam@siam.org *Web Site:* www.siam.org, pg 192

Society for Mining, Metallurgy & Exploration, 12999 E Adam Aircraft Circle, Englewood, CO 80112 *Tel:* 303-948-4200 *Toll Free Tel:* 800-763-3132 *Fax:* 303-973-3845 *E-mail:* cs@smenet.org; books@smenet.org *Web Site:* www.smenet.org, pg 192

Society for Scholarly Publishing (SSP), 1120 Rte 73, Suite 200, Mount Laurel, NJ 08054 *Tel:* 856-439-1385 *Fax:* 856-439-0525 *E-mail:* info@sspnet.org *Web Site:* www.sspnet.org, pg 519

Society for Technical Communication (STC), 3251 Blenheim Blvd, Suite 406, Fairfax, VA 22030 *Tel:* 703-522-4114 *Fax:* 703-522-2075 *E-mail:* stc@stc.org *Web Site:* www.stc.org, pg 519

Society for the History of Authorship, Reading & Publishing Inc (SHARP), c/o Johns Hopkins University Press, Journals Publishing Div, PO Box 19966, Baltimore, MD 21211-0966 *Tel:* 410-516-6987 *Toll Free Tel:* 800-548-1784 *Fax:* 410-516-3866 *E-mail:* members@sharpweb.org *Web Site:* www.sharpweb.org, pg 519

Society of American Archivists, 17 N State St, Suite 1425, Chicago, IL 60602-4061 *Tel:* 312-606-0722 *Toll Free Tel:* 866-722-7858 *Fax:* 312-606-0728 *Web Site:* www.archivists.org, pg 192

Society of American Travel Writers (SATW), 355 Lexington Ave, 15th fl, New York, NY 10017 *E-mail:* info@satw.org *Web Site:* www.satw.org, pg 519

Society of Children's Book Writers & Illustrators (SCBWI), 6363 Wilshire Blvd, Suite 425, Los Angeles, CA 90048 *Tel:* 323-782-1010 *E-mail:* membership@scbwi.org *Web Site:* www.scbwi.org, pg 520

Society of Environmental Toxicology & Chemistry (SETAC), 229 S Baylen St, 2nd fl, Pensacola, FL 32502 *Tel:* 850-469-1500 *Toll Free Fax:* 888-296-4136 *E-mail:* setac@setac.org *Web Site:* www.setac.org, pg 192

Society of Exploration Geophysicists, 8801 S Yale Ave, Suite 500, Tulsa, OK 74137 *Tel:* 918-497-5500 *Fax:* 918-497-5557 *E-mail:* web@seg.org *Web Site:* www.seg.org, pg 520

Society of Illustrators (SI), 128 E 63 St, New York, NY 10065 *Tel:* 212-838-2560 *Fax:* 212-838-2561 *E-mail:* info@societyillustrators.org *Web Site:* www.societyillustrators.org, pg 520

The Society of Midland Authors (SMA), PO Box 10419, Chicago, IL 60610 *Web Site:* midlandauthors.org, pg 520

The Society of Midland Authors Awards, PO Box 10419, Chicago, IL 60610 *Web Site:* midlandauthors.org, pg 664

Society of Motion Picture and Television Engineers® (SMPTE®), White Plains Plaza, 445 Hamilton Ave, Suite 601, White Plains, NY 10601-1827 *Tel:* 914-761-1100 *E-mail:* hello@smpte.org (mktg) *Web Site:* www.smpte.org, pg 520

The Society of Naval Architects & Marine Engineers (SNAME), 99 Canal Center Plaza, Suite 310, Alexandria, VA 22314 *Tel:* 703-997-6701 *Toll Free Tel:* 800-798-2188 *Fax:* 703-997-6702 *Web Site:* www.sname.org, pg 193

Society of Professional Journalists (SPJ), PO Box 441748, Indianapolis, IN 46244 *Tel:* 317-927-8000 *Fax:* 317-920-4789 *E-mail:* communications@spj.org *Web Site:* www.spj.org, pg 520

The Society of Southwestern Authors (SSA), PO Box 30355, Tucson, AZ 85751-0355 *Web Site:* www.ssa-az.org, pg 520

The Society of Southwestern Authors Writing Contest, PO Box 30355, Tucson, AZ 85751-0355 *E-mail:* contest@ssa-az.org *Web Site:* www.ssa-az.org/contest.htm, pg 664

Software & Information Industry Association (SIIA), 1620 Eye St NW, Washington, DC 20005 *Tel:* 202-289-7442 *Fax:* 202-289-7097 *E-mail:* info@siia.net *Web Site:* www.siia.net, pg 520

Soho Press Inc, 853 Broadway, New York, NY 10003 *Tel:* 212-260-1900 *E-mail:* soho@sohopress.com; publicity@sohopress.com *Web Site:* sohopress.com, pg 193

Soil Science Society of America (SSSA), 5585 Guilford Rd, Madison, WI 53711-5801 *Tel:* 608-273-8080 *Fax:* 608-273-2021 *Web Site:* www.soils.org, pg 193

Solano Press Books, PO Box 773, Point Arena, CA 95468 *Tel:* 707-884-4508 *Toll Free Tel:* 800-931-9373 *E-mail:* spbooks@solano.com *Web Site:* www.solano.com, pg 193

Jodi F Solomon Speakers Bureau Inc, PO Box 302123, Boston, MA 02130 *Tel:* 617-266-9450 *Fax:* 617-266-5660 *E-mail:* inquiries@jodisolomonspeakers.com *Web Site:* www.jodisolomonspeakers.com, pg 487

Solution Tree, 555 N Morton St, Bloomington, IN 47404 *Tel:* 812-336-7700 *Toll Free Tel:* 800-733-6786 *Fax:* 812-336-7790 *E-mail:* pubs@solutiontree.com; orders@solutiontree.com *Web Site:* www.solutiontree.com, pg 193

Somerset Hall Press, 416 Commonwealth Ave, Suite 612, Boston, MA 02215 *Tel:* 617-236-5126 *E-mail:* info@somersethallpress.com *Web Site:* www.somersethallpress.com, pg 193

Soncino Press Ltd, 123 Ditmas Ave, Brooklyn, NY 11218 *Tel:* 718-972-6200 *Toll Free Tel:* 800-972-6201 *Fax:* 718-972-6204 *E-mail:* info@soncino.com *Web Site:* www.soncino.com, pg 193

Sophia Institute Press®, 18 Celina Ave, Unit 1, Nashua, NH 03063 *Tel:* 603-641-9344 *Toll Free Tel:* 800-888-9344 *Fax:* 603-641-8108 *Toll Free Fax:* 888-288-2259 *E-mail:* orders@sophiainstitute.com *Web Site:* www.sophiainstitute.com, pg 193

Sophie Kerr Prize, c/o College Relations Off, 300 Washington Ave, Chestertown, MD 21620 *Tel:* 410-778-2800 *Toll Free Tel:* 800-422-1782 *Fax:* 410-810-7150 *Web Site:* www.washcoll.edu, pg 664

Soul Mate Publishing, 3210 Sherwood Dr, Walworth, NY 14568 *Web Site:* www.soulmatepublishing.com, pg 194

Sound Feelings Publishing, 18375 Ventura Blvd, No 8000, Tarzana, CA 91356 *Tel:* 818-757-0600 *E-mail:* information@soundfeelings.com *Web Site:* www.soundfeelings.com, pg 194

Sounds True Inc, 413 S Arthur Ave, Louisville, CO 80027 *Tel:* 303-665-3151 *Toll Free Tel:* 800-333-9185 (US); 888-303-9185 (US & CN) *E-mail:* customerservice@soundstrue.com; stpublicity@soundstrue.com *Web Site:* www.soundstrue.com, pg 194

Sourcebooks LLC, 1935 Brookdale Rd, Suite 139, Naperville, IL 60563 *Tel:* 630-961-3900 *Toll Free Tel:* 800-432-7444 *Fax:* 630-961-2168 *E-mail:* info@sourcebooks.com *Web Site:* www.sourcebooks.com, pg 194

Sourced Media Books, 15 Via Picato, San Clemente, CA 92673 *Tel:* 949-813-0182 *E-mail:* editor@sourcedmediabooks.com *Web Site:* sourcedmediabooks.com, pg 195

Raymond Souster Award, 2 Carlton St, Suite 1519, Toronto, ON M5B 1J3, Canada *Tel:* 416-504-1657 *E-mail:* admin@poets.ca *Web Site:* poets.ca/awards/souster, pg 664

South Carolina Bar, 1501 Park St, Columbia, SC 29201 *Tel:* 803-799-6653 *Toll Free Tel:* 800-768-7787 *E-mail:* scbar-info@scbar.org *Web Site:* www.scbar.org, pg 195

South Dakota Historical Society Press, 900 Governors Dr, Pierre, SD 57501 *Tel:* 605-773-6009 *Fax:* 605-773-6041 *E-mail:* info@sdhspress.com; orders@sdhspress.com *Web Site:* www.sdhspress.com, pg 195

South Platte Press, PO Box 163, David City, NE 68632-0163 *Tel:* 402-367-3554 *E-mail:* railroads@windstream.net *Web Site:* www.southplattepress.net, pg 195

Southampton Writers' Conference, 239 Montauk Hwy, Southampton, NY 11968 *Tel:* 631-632-5007 *Web Site:* www.stonybrook.edu/writers, pg 557

Southeast Review's Gearhart Poetry Contest, Florida State University, Dept of English, Tallahassee, FL 32306 *E-mail:* southeastreview@gmail.com *Web Site:* www.southeastreview.org/writing-contests, pg 664

The Southern Book Prize, 51 Pleasant Ridge Dr, Asheville, NC 28805 *Tel:* 803-994-9530 *Fax:* 309-410-0211 *E-mail:* siba@sibaweb.com *Web Site:* www.sibaweb.com/siba-book-award, pg 664

Southern Books Competition, PO Box 30703, Savannah, GA 31410 *Tel:* 912-999-7979 *E-mail:* selaadminservices@selaonline.org *Web Site:* selaonline.org, pg 664

Southern California Writers' Conference (SCWC), PO Box 433, Redmond, OR 97756 *Tel:* 619-303-8185 *Fax:* 619-906-7462 *E-mail:* msg@writersconference.com *Web Site:* www.writersconference.com; www.facebook.com/SouthernCaliforniaWritersConference/, pg 557

Southern Historical Press Inc, 375 W Broad St, Greenville, SC 29601 *Tel:* 864-233-2346 *E-mail:* southernhistoricalpress@gmail.com *Web Site:* www.southernhistoricalpress.com, pg 195

Southern Illinois University Press, 1915 University Press Dr, SIUC Mail Code 6806, Carbondale, IL 62901-4323 *Tel:* 618-453-2281 *Fax:* 618-453-1221 *E-mail:* rights@siu.edu *Web Site:* www.siupress.com, pg 195

Southern Independent Booksellers Alliance (SIBA), 51 Pleasant Ridge Dr, Asheville, NC 28805 *Tel:* 803-994-9530 *Fax:* 309-410-0211 *E-mail:* siba@sibaweb.com *Web Site:* www.sibaweb.com, pg 520

Southern Playwrights Competition, 700 Pelham Rd N, Jacksonville, AL 36265-1602 *Tel:* 256-782-5412 *Web Site:* www.jsu.edu/english/southpla.html, pg 665

Southern Studies Fellowship in Arts & Letters, 186 W Main St, Spartanburg, SC 29306 *Tel:* 864-577-9349 *E-mail:* info@hubcity.org *Web Site:* southernstudiesfellowship.org, pg 665

Terry Southern Prize, 544 W 27 St, New York, NY 10001 *Tel:* 212-343-1333 *E-mail:* queries@theparisreview.org *Web Site:* www.theparisreview.org, pg 665

SouthWest Writers Conference Series, 3200 Carlisle Blvd NE, Suite 114, Albuquerque, NM 87110-1663 *Tel:* 505-830-6034 *E-mail:* info@swwriters.com *Web Site:* www.southwestwriters.com, pg 557

Sovereign Award for Outstanding Writing, Woodbine Sales Pavilion, 555 Rexdale Blvd, Toronto, ON M9W 5L2, Canada *Tel:* 416-675-7756 *Fax:* 416-675-6378 *E-mail:* jockeyclubcanada@gmail.com *Web Site:* www.jockeyclubcanada.com, pg 665

Soyinfo Center, 1021 Dolores Dr, Lafayette, CA 94549-0234 *Tel:* 925-283-2991 *Web Site:* www.soyinfocenter.com, pg 196

Spain-USA Foundation Translation Award, University of Arizona, Esquire Bldg, No 205, 1230 N Park Ave, Tucson, AZ 85721 *Tel:* 520-621-1757 *E-mail:* info@literarytranslators.org *Web Site:* literarytranslators.org/awards/spain-usa-award, pg 665

Spark Award, 6363 Wilshire Blvd, Suite 425, Los Angeles, CA 90048 *Tel:* 323-782-1010 *E-mail:* grants@scbwi.org; info@scbwi.org *Web Site:* www.scbwi.org, pg 665

SPD Design Awards, 27 Union Sq W, Suite 207, New York, NY 10003 *Tel:* 212-223-3332 *E-mail:* mail@spd.org *Web Site:* www.spd.org, pg 665

Speakers Unlimited, 7532 Courtyard Place, Cary, NC 27519 *Tel:* 919-466-7676 *E-mail:* prospeak@aol.com *Web Site:* www.speakersunlimited.com, pg 487

Special Libraries Association (SLA), 7918 Jones Branch Dr, Suite 300, McLean, VA 22102 *Tel:* 703-647-4900 *Fax:* 703-506-3266 *E-mail:* info@sla.org *Web Site:* www.sla.org, pg 520

Spectrum Literary Agency, 320 Central Park W, Suite 1-D, New York, NY 10025 *Tel:* 212-362-4323 *Fax:* 212-362-4562 *Web Site:* www.spectrumliteraryagency.com, pg 477

Speculative Fiction Writing Workshop, 1809 Indiana St, Lawrence, KS 66044 *Tel:* 785-766-7039 *Web Site:* adastra-sf.com/Workshop-stuff/Spec-Fic-Workshop.htm, pg 557

The Anne Spencer Memorial, PO Box 36128, North Chesterfield, VA 23235-3533 *E-mail:* contest@poetrysocietyofvirginia.org; info@poetryvirginia.org *Web Site:* www.poetrysocietyofvirginia.org, pg 665

SPIE, 1000 20 St, Bellingham, WA 98225-6705 *Tel:* 360-676-3290 *Toll Free Tel:* 888-504-8171 (orders) *Fax:* 360-647-1445 *E-mail:* help@spie.org; customerservice@spie.org (orders) *Web Site:* www.spie.org, pg 196

The Spieler Agency, 75 Broad St, Suite 304, New York, NY 10004 *Tel:* 212-757-4439 *E-mail:* thespieleragency@gmail.com *Web Site:* thespieleragency.com, pg 477

Philip G Spitzer Literary Agency Inc, 50 Talmage Farm Lane, East Hampton, NY 11937 *Tel:* 631-329-3650 *Fax:* 631-329-3651 *Web Site:* www.spitzeragency.com, pg 477

Spizzirri Publishing Inc, PO Box 9397, Rapid City, SD 57709-9397 *Tel:* 605-348-2749 *Toll Free Tel:* 800-325-9819 *Fax:* 605-348-6251 *Toll Free Fax:* 800-322-9819 *E-mail:* spizzpub@aol.com *Web Site:* www.spizzirri.com, pg 196

Springer, One New York Plaza, Suite 4600, New York, NY 10004-1562 *Tel:* 212-460-1500 *Toll Free Tel:* 800-SPRINGER (777-4643) *Fax:* 212-460-1700 *E-mail:* customerservice@springernature.com *Web Site:* www.springer.com, pg 196

Springer Publishing Co, 11 W 42 St, 15th fl, New York, NY 10036-8002 *Tel:* 212-431-4370 *Toll Free Tel:* 877-687-7476 *E-mail:* marketing@springerpub.com; cs@springerpub.com (orders); textbook@springerpub.com; specialsales@springerpub.com *Web Site:* www.springerpub.com, pg 196

Spur Awards, 271 CR 219, Encampment, WY 82325 *Tel:* 307-329-8942 *Web Site:* westernwriters.org/spur-awards, pg 665

Square One Publishers Inc, 115 Herricks Rd, Garden City Park, NY 11040 *Tel:* 516-535-2010 *Toll Free Tel:* 877-900-BOOK (900-2665) *Fax:* 516-535-2014 *E-mail:* sq1publish@aol.com *Web Site:* www.squareonepublishers.com, pg 196

Stackler Editorial, 200 Woodland Ave, Summit, NJ 07901 *Tel:* 510-912-9187 *E-mail:* ed.stackler@gmail.com *Web Site:* www.fictioneditor.com, pg 445

Stackpole Books, 31 E Main St, New Kingstown, PA 17072 *Tel:* 717-590-8974 *Web Site:* www.stackpolebooks.com, pg 196

The Edna Staebler Award for Creative Non-Fiction, Office of the Dean, Faculty of Arts, 75 University Ave W, Waterloo, ON N2L 3C5, Canada *Tel:* 519-884-1970 (ext 3361) *E-mail:* staebleraward@wlu.ca *Web Site:* wlu.ca/staebleraward, pg 665

Standard Publishing, 4050 Lee Vance Dr, Colorado Springs, CO 80918 *Tel:* 719-536-0100 *Toll Free Tel:* 800-323-7543 (orders & cust serv) *Toll Free Fax:* 800-430-0726 (cust serv), pg 197

Standard Publishing Corp, 10 High St, Boston, MA 02110 *Tel:* 617-457-0600 *Toll Free Tel:* 800-682-5759 *Fax:* 617-457-0608 *Web Site:* www.spcpub.com, pg 197

Stanford University Press, 425 Broadway St, Redwood City, CA 94063-3126 *Tel:* 650-723-9434 *Fax:* 650-725-3457 *E-mail:* info@www.sup.org; publicity@www.sup.org; sales@www.sup.org *Web Site:* www.sup.org, pg 197

Stanley Drama Award, One Campus Rd, Staten Island, NY 10301 *Tel:* 718-390-3223 *Fax:* 718-390-3323 *Web Site:* wagner.edu/theatre/stanley-drama, pg 665

STAR Award, PO Box 190, Jefferson, OR 97352 *E-mail:* staraward@womenfictionwriters.org *Web Site:* wfwa.memberclicks.net/star-award, pg 666

Star Bright Books Inc, 13 Landsdowne St, Cambridge, MA 02139 *Tel:* 617-354-1300 *Fax:* 617-354-1399 *E-mail:* info@starbrightbooks.com; orders@starbrightbooks.com *Web Site:* www.starbrightbooks.org, pg 197

Star Publishing Co Inc, PO Box 5165, Belmont, CA 94002-5165 *Tel:* 650-591-3505 *E-mail:* starpublishing@gmail.com *Web Site:* www.starpublishing.com, pg 197

STARbooks Press, PO Box 711612, Herndon, VA 20171 *E-mail:* publish@starbookspress.com; contact@starbookspress.com *Web Site:* www.starbookspress.com, pg 197

Starcrafts LLC, 68A Fogg Rd, Epping, NH 03042 *Tel:* 603-734-4300 *Toll Free Tel:* 866-953-8458 (24/7 message ctr) *Fax:* 603-734-4311 *E-mail:* astrosales@astrocom.com *Web Site:* www.astrocom.com, pg 197

Stargazer Publishing Co, 958 Stanislaus Dr, Corona, CA 92881 *Tel:* 951-898-4619 *E-mail:* stargazer@stargazerpub.com; orders@stargazerpub.com *Web Site:* www.stargazerpub.com, pg 197

StarGroup International Inc, 1194 Old Dixie Hwy, Suite 201, West Palm Beach, FL 33413 *Tel:* 561-547-0667 *Fax:* 561-843-8530 *E-mail:* info@stargroupinternational.com *Web Site:* stargroupinternational.com, pg 197

Agnes Lynch Starrett Poetry Prize, 7500 Thomas Blvd, Pittsburgh, PA 15260 *Tel:* 412-383-2456 *Fax:* 412-383-2466 *E-mail:* info@upress.pitt.edu *Web Site:* upittpress.org/prize/agnes-lynch-starrett-poetry-prize/; www.upress.pitt.edu, pg 666

State University of New York Press, 10 N Pearl St, 4th fl, Albany, NY 12207 *Tel:* 518-944-2800 *Toll Free Tel:* 877-204-6073 (orders) *Fax:* 518-320-1592 *Toll Free Fax:* 877-204-6074 (orders) *E-mail:* info@sunypress.edu (edit off); suny@presswarehouse.com (orders) *Web Site:* www.sunypress.edu, pg 198

Nancy Stauffer Associates, PO Box 1203, Darien, CT 06820 *Tel:* 203-202-2500 *Web Site:* www.publishersmarketplace.com/members/nstauffer/, pg 477

STC Technical Communication Summit, 3251 Blenheim Blvd, Suite 406, Fairfax, VA 22030 *Tel:* 703-522-4114 *Fax:* 703-522-2075 *E-mail:* stc@stc.org; summit@stc.org *Web Site:* summit.stc.org; www.stc.org, pg 557

Steerforth Press & Services, 31 Hanover St, Suite 1, Lebanon, NH 03766 *Tel:* 603-643-4787 *Fax:* 603-643-4788 *E-mail:* info@steerforth.com *Web Site:* www.steerforth.com, pg 198

Stegner Fellowship, Stanford University, Dept of English, Stanford, CA 94305-2087 *Tel:* 650-723-0011 *E-mail:* stegnerfellowship@stanford.edu *Web Site:* creativewriting.stanford.edu, pg 666

Steinberg Memorial Essay Prize, Michigan State University Press, 1405 S Harrison Rd, Suite 25, East Lansing, MI 48823 *E-mail:* 4thgenre@gmail.com *Web Site:* duotrope.com/listing/8258/fourth-genre-steinberg-memorial-essay (submissions), pg 666

Michael Steinberg Literary Agent, PO Box 274, Glencoe, IL 60022-0274 *Tel:* 847-626-1000 *E-mail:* michael14steinberg@comcast.net, pg 477

SteinerBooks Inc, 610 Main St, Suite 1, Great Barrington, MA 01230 *Tel:* 413-528-8233 *E-mail:* service@steinerbooks.org; friends@steinerbooks.org *Web Site:* steiner.presswarehouse.com, pg 198

Stellar Publishing, 2114 S Live Oak Pkwy, Wilmington, NC 28403 *Tel:* 910-269-7444 *Web Site:* www.stellar-publishing.com, pg 198

Stenhouse Publishers, 1400 Goodale Blvd, Suite 200, Grandview Heights, OH 43212 *Toll Free Tel:* 800-988-9812 *Toll Free Fax:* 800-992-6087 *E-mail:* customerservice@stenhouse.com; editors@stenhouse.com *Web Site:* www.stenhouse.com, pg 198

Stephan G Stephansson Award for Poetry, 11759 Groat Rd NW, Edmonton, AB T5M 3K6, Canada *Tel:* 780-422-8174 *Toll Free Tel:* 800-665-5354 (AB only) *E-mail:* mail@writersguild.ab.ca *Web Site:* writersguild.ca, pg 666

COMPANY INDEX

Sterling Lord Literistic Inc, 594 Broadway, Suite 205, New York, NY 10012 *Tel:* 212-780-6050 *Fax:* 212-780-6095 *E-mail:* info@sll.com *Web Site:* www.sll.com, pg 477

Wallace Stevens Award, 75 Maiden Lane, Suite 901, New York, NY 10038 *Tel:* 212-274-0343 *E-mail:* awards@poets.org *Web Site:* poets.org/academy-american-poets/prizes/wallace-stevens-award, pg 666

Stewart, Tabori & Chang, 195 Broadway, 9th fl, New York, NY 10007 *Tel:* 212-206-7715 *Fax:* 212-519-1210 *E-mail:* abrams@abramsbooks.com *Web Site:* www.abramsbooks.com/imprints/stc, pg 198

Stimola Literary Studio Inc, 11 Briarwood Lane, West Tisbury, MA 02575 *Tel:* 201-945-9353 *Fax:* 201-490-5920 *E-mail:* info@stimolaliterarystudio.com *Web Site:* www.stimolaliterarystudio.com, pg 477

Stipes Publishing LLC, 204 W University Ave, Champaign, IL 61820 *Tel:* 217-356-8391 *Fax:* 217-356-5753 *E-mail:* stipes01@sbcglobal.net *Web Site:* www.stipes.com, pg 198

STM Learning Inc, 1220 Paddock Dr, Florissant, MO 63033 *Tel:* 314-434-2424 *E-mail:* info@stmlearning.com; orders@stmlearning.com *Web Site:* www.stmlearning.com, pg 199

STOCKCERO Inc, 3785 NW 82 Ave, Suite 314, Doral, FL 33166 *Tel:* 305-722-7628 *Fax:* 305-722-7628 *E-mail:* academicservices@stockcero.com; sales@stockcero.com *Web Site:* www.stockcero.com, pg 199

Brooke C Stoddard, 111 S Columbus St, Alexandria, VA 22314 *E-mail:* stoddardbc@gmail.com *Web Site:* brookecstoddard.com, pg 445

Bram Stoker Awards®, PO Box 56687, Sherman Oaks, CA 91413 *Tel:* 818-220-3965 *E-mail:* stokerchair@horror.org *Web Site:* www.thebramstokerawards.com; horror.org, pg 666

Jeri L Stolk, 8 Rush Vine Ct, Owings Mills, MD 21117 *Tel:* 410-864-8109 *E-mail:* jeristolk@gmail.com, pg 445

Stone Award for Lifetime Literary Achievement, College of Liberal Arts, 214 Bexell Hall, Corvalis, OR 97331 *Tel:* 541-737-0561 *Web Site:* liberalarts.oregonstate.edu/stone-award, pg 666

Stone Bridge Press Inc, 1393 Solano Ave, Suite C, Albany, CA 94706 *Tel:* 510-524-8732 *E-mail:* sbp@stonebridge.com; sbpedit@stonebridge.com *Web Site:* www.stonebridge.com, pg 199

Stone Pier Press, PO Box 170572, San Francisco, CA 94117 *Tel:* 415-484-2821 *E-mail:* hello@stonepierpress.org *Web Site:* www.stonepierpress.org, pg 199

Stonesong, 270 W 39 St, Suite 201, New York, NY 10018 *Tel:* 212-929-4600 *E-mail:* editors@stonesong.com *Web Site:* www.stonesong.com, pg 478

Stonewall Book Awards, 225 N Michigan Ave, Suite 1300, Chicago, IL 60601 *Tel:* 312-944-6780 *Toll Free Tel:* 800-545-2433 *Fax:* 312-440-9374 *E-mail:* diversity@ala.org; ala@ala.org *Web Site:* www.ala.org/rt/rrt/award/stonewall; www.ala.org/rt/rrt; www.ala.org, pg 666

Stoneydale Press Publishing Co, 523 Main St, Stevensville, MT 59870-2839 *Tel:* 406-777-2729 *Toll Free Tel:* 800-735-7006 *Fax:* 406-777-2521 *E-mail:* stoneydale@stoneydale.com *Web Site:* www.stoneydale.com, pg 199

Story Monsters Approved! Program, 4696 W Tyson St, Chandler, AZ 85226-2903 *Tel:* 480-940-8182 *Fax:* 480-940-8787 *Web Site:* www.StoryMonstersBookAwards.com/sma-details, pg 666

Story Monsters® Book Awards, 4696 W Tyson St, Chandler, AZ 85226-2903 *Tel:* 480-940-8182 *Fax:* 480-940-8787 *E-mail:* info@StoryMonsters.com *Web Site:* www.StoryMonstersBookAwards.com, pg 666

Story Monsters LLC, 4696 W Tyson St, Chandler, AZ 85226-2903 *Tel:* 480-940-8182 *Fax:* 480-940-8787 *Web Site:* www.StoryMonsters.com; www.StoryMonstersBookAwards.com; www.AuthorBookings.com; www.StoryMonstersBookAwards.com/sma-details; www.StoryMonstersInk.com, pg 199

The Story Plant, 1270 Caroline St, Suite D120-381, Atlanta, GA 30307 *Tel:* 203-722-7920 *E-mail:* thestoryplant@thestoryplant.com *Web Site:* www.thestoryplant.com, pg 199

The Story Prize, 41 Watchung Plaza, No 384, Montclair, NJ 07042 *Tel:* 973-932-0324 *E-mail:* info@thestoryprize.org *Web Site:* www.thestoryprize.org, pg 667

The Story Prize Spotlight Award, 41 Watchung Plaza, No 384, Montclair, NJ 07042 *Tel:* 973-932-0324 *E-mail:* info@thestoryprize.org *Web Site:* www.thestoryprize.org, pg 667

Storybook Arts Inc, 414 Poplar Hill Rd, Dover Plains, NY 12522 *Tel:* 845-877-3305 *Web Site:* www.storybookartsinc.com, pg 486

Storyworkz Inc, PO Box 567, Montpelier, VT 05601 *Tel:* 802-223-4955 *E-mail:* orders@storyworkz.com *Web Site:* www.storyworkz.com, pg 199

Elizabeth Matchett Stover Memorial Award, PO Box 750374, Dallas, TX 75275-0374 *Fax:* 214-768-1408 *E-mail:* swr@mail.smu.edu *Web Site:* southwestreview.com, pg 667

Strategic Book Publishing (SBP), Durham, CT 06422 *Tel:* 860-331-1201; 361-244-1058 *E-mail:* bookorder@sbpra.net; support@sbpra.net *Web Site:* sbpra.net; www.facebook.com/sbpra.us, pg 199

Strategic Media Books LLC, 782 Wofford St, Rock Hill, SC 29730 *Tel:* 803-366-5440 *E-mail:* contact@strategicmediabooks.com *Web Site:* strategicmediabooks.com, pg 200

Straus Literary, 77 Van Ness Ave, Suite 101, San Francisco, CA 94102 *Tel:* 646-843-9950 *Web Site:* www.strausliterary.com, pg 478

Robin Straus Agency, Inc, 229 E 79 St, Suite 5A, New York, NY 10075 *Tel:* 212-472-3282 *Fax:* 212-472-3833 *E-mail:* info@robinstrausagency.com *Web Site:* www.robinstrausagency.com, pg 478

Stress Free Kids®, 2561 Chimney Springs Dr, Marietta, GA 30062 *Tel:* 678-642-9555 *Toll Free Tel:* 866-302-2759 *E-mail:* media@stressfreekids.com *Web Site:* www.stressfreekids.com, pg 200

Lucien Stryk Asian Translation Prize, University of Arizona, Esquire Bldg, No 205, 1230 N Park Ave, Tucson, AZ 85721 *Tel:* 520-621-1757 *E-mail:* info@literarytranslators.org *Web Site:* literarytranslators.org/awards/lucien-stryk-prize, pg 667

The Stuart Agency, 450 North End Ave, 25C, New York, NY 10282 *Tel:* 917-842-7589 *Web Site:* www.stuartagency.com, pg 479

The Jesse Stuart Foundation (JSF), 4440 13 St, Ashland, KY 41102 *Tel:* 606-326-1667 *Fax:* 606-325-2519 *E-mail:* jsf@jsfbooks.com *Web Site:* www.jsfbooks.com, pg 200

Ned Stuckey-French Nonfiction Contest, Florida State University, Dept of English, Tallahassee, FL 32306 *E-mail:* southeastreview@gmail.com *Web Site:* www.southeastreview.org/writing-contests, pg 667

Jessamy Stursberg Poetry Prize for Canadian Youth, 2 Carlton St, Suite 1519, Toronto, ON M5B 1J3, Canada *Tel:* 416-504-1657 *E-mail:* info@poets.ca; admin@poets.ca *Web Site:* poets.ca, pg 667

Stylus Publishing LLC, 22883 Quicksilver Dr, Sterling, VA 20166-2019 *Tel:* 703-661-1504 (edit & sales) *Toll Free Tel:* 800-232-0223 (orders & cust serv) *Fax:* 703-661-1547 *E-mail:* stylusmail@styluspub.com (orders & cust serv); stylusinfo@styluspub.com *Web Site:* styluspub.com, pg 200

Sudden Fiction Contest, c/o ASUC Publications, Univ of California, 10-B Eshleman Hall, Berkeley, CA 94720-4500 *E-mail:* berkeleyfictionreview@gmail.com *Web Site:* berkeleyfictionreview.org, pg 667

Vivian Sudhalter, 1202 Loma Dr, No 117, Ojai, CA 93023 *Tel:* 805-640-9737 *E-mail:* vivians09@att.net, pg 445

Summer Words Writing Conference & Literary Festival, 110 E Hallam St, Suite 116, Aspen, CO 81611 *Tel:* 970-925-3122 *Fax:* 970-920-5700 *E-mail:* aspenwords@aspeninstitute.org *Web Site:* www.aspenwords.org, pg 557

Summer Writing Courses, 1831 College Ave, Suite 324, Regina, SK S4P 4V5, Canada *Tel:* 306-537-7243 *E-mail:* sage.hill@sasktel.net; info.sagehill@sasktel.net *Web Site:* www.sagehillwriting.ca, pg 557

Summer Writing Seminar, 7 E Pasture Rd, Aquinnah, MA 02535 *Tel:* 954-242-2903 *Web Site:* mvicw.com, pg 558

Hollis Summers Poetry Prize, Alden Library, Suite 101, 30 Park Place, Athens, OH 45701-2909 *Tel:* 740-593-1154 *Web Site:* www.ohioswallow.com/poetry_prize; ohiouniversitypress.submittable.com/submit (online submissions), pg 667

Summerthought Publishing, PO Box 2309, Banff, AB T1L 1C1, Canada *Tel:* 403-762-0535 *E-mail:* info@summerthought.com *Web Site:* summerthought.com, pg 420

Summertime Publications Inc, 4115 E Palo Verde Dr, Phoenix, AZ 85018 *E-mail:* summertime.publications@gmail.com *Web Site:* www.summertimepublications.com, pg 200

Summit University Press, 63 Summit Way, Gardiner, MT 59030 *Tel:* 406-848-9292; 406-848-9500 (retail orders) *Fax:* 406-848-9555 *E-mail:* info@tsl.org; rights@summituniversitypress.com *Web Site:* www.summituniversitypress.com, pg 200

Sun Publishing Company, PO Box 5588, Santa Fe, NM 87502-5588 *Tel:* 505-471-5177; 505-660-0704 *Toll Free Tel:* 877-849-0051 *E-mail:* info@sunbooks.com *Web Site:* www.sunbooks.com; abooksource.com, pg 200

Sun Valley Writers' Conference (SVWC), Galleria Bldg, 2nd fl, 351 Leadville Ave N, Ketchum, ID 83340 *Tel:* 208-726-5454 *E-mail:* info@svwc.com *Web Site:* svwc.com, pg 558

Sunbelt Publications Inc, 664 Marsat Ct, Suite A, Chula Vista, CA 91911 *Tel:* 619-258-4911 *Toll Free Tel:* 800-626-6579 (cust serv) *Fax:* 619-258-4916 *E-mail:* info@sunbeltpub.com; service@sunbeltpub.com *Web Site:* sunbeltpublications.com, pg 200

Sunburst Award for Excellence in Canadian Literature of the Fantastic, 2 Farm Greenway, Toronto, ON M3A 3M2, Canada *E-mail:* secretary@sunburstaward.org *Web Site:* www.sunburstaward.org, pg 667

Sundance/Newbridge Publishing, 33 Boston Post Rd W, Suite 440, Marlborough, MA 01752 *Toll Free Tel:* 888-200-2720; 800-343-8204 *Toll Free Fax:* 800-456-2419 (orders) *E-mail:* info@sundancenewbridge.com; orders@sundancenewbridge.com *Web Site:* www.sundancenewbridge.com, pg 200

Sunrise River Press, 838 Lake St S, Forrest Lake, MN 55025 *Tel:* 651-277-1400 *Toll Free Tel:* 800-895-4585 *E-mail:* info@sunriseriverpress.com; sales@sunriseriverpress.com *Web Site:* www.sunriseriverpress.com, pg 201

Sunstone Press, PO Box 2321, Santa Fe, NM 87504-2321 *Tel:* 505-988-4418 *E-mail:* orders@sunstonepress.com *Web Site:* sunstonepress.com, pg 201

Supporting Diverse Voices: Book Proposal Development Grants, 41 William St, Princeton, NJ 08540-5237 *Tel:* 609-258-4900 *E-mail:* info@press.princeton.edu *Web Site:* press.princeton.edu/book-proposal-development-grants, pg 667

Surrey Books, 1328 Greenleaf St, Evanston, IL 60202 *Tel:* 847-475-4457 *Toll Free Tel:* 800-326-4430 *Web Site:* agatepublishing.com/surrey, pg 201

Susquehanna University, Department of English & Creative Writing, 514 University Ave, Selinsgrove, PA 17870 *Tel:* 570-372-4196 *Web Site:* www.susqu.edu, pg 565

Fraser Sutherland, 39 Helena Ave, Toronto, ON M6G 2H3, Canada *Tel:* 416-652-5735 *E-mail:* rodfrasers@gmail.com, pg 445

Swallow Press, Alden Library, Suite 101, 30 Park Place, Athens, OH 45701-2909 *Tel:* 740-593-1154 *Web Site:* www.ohioswallow.com, pg 201

Swan Isle Press, c/o Chicago Distribution Ctr, 11030 S Langley Ave, Chicago, IL 60628 *Tel:* 773-636-1818 (edit) *E-mail:* info@swanislepress.com *Web Site:* www.swanislepress.com, pg 201

Swedenborg Foundation, 320 N Church St, West Chester, PA 19380 *Tel:* 610-430-3222 *Toll Free Tel:* 800-355-3222 (cust serv) *Fax:* 610-430-7982 *E-mail:* info@swedenborg.com *Web Site:* swedenborg.com, pg 201

SYBEX, 111 River St, Suite 300, Hoboken, NJ 07030-5774 *Tel:* 201-748-6000 *Fax:* 201-748-6088 *Toll Free Fax:* 800-565-6802 *Web Site:* www.wiley.com/en-us/Sybex, pg 201

Sydney Taylor Book Award, PO Box 1118, Teaneck, NJ 07666 *Tel:* 201-371-3255 *E-mail:* sydneytaylorbookaward@jewishlibraries.org; info@jewishlibraries.org *Web Site:* jewishlibraries.org/sydney_taylor_book_award, pg 668

Sydney Taylor Manuscript Award, 204 Park St, Montclair, NJ 07042 *Tel:* 201-371-3255 *E-mail:* info@jewishlibraries.org *Web Site:* jewishlibraries.org, pg 668

Charles S Sydnor Award, University of Georgia, Dept of History, Athens, GA 30602-1602 *Tel:* 706-542-8848 *Web Site:* thesha.org/sydnor, pg 668

Syracuse University Creative Writing Program, 401 Hall of Languages, Syracuse, NY 13244-1170 *Tel:* 315-443-2173 *Fax:* 315-443-3660 *Web Site:* artsandsciences.syracuse.edu/english-department/creative-writing-mf-program; artsandsciences.syracuse.edu/english-department/cw-undergraduate-program, pg 565

Syracuse University Press, 621 Skytop Rd, Suite 110, Syracuse, NY 13244-5290 *Tel:* 315-443-5534 *Toll Free Tel:* 800-365-8929 (cust serv) *Fax:* 315-443-5545 *E-mail:* supress@syr.edu *Web Site:* press.syr.edu, pg 201

Syracuse University, SI Newhouse School of Public Communications, 215 University Place, Syracuse, NY 13244 *Tel:* 315-443-3627 *E-mail:* newhouse@syr.edu *Web Site:* newhouse.syr.edu/academics/programs, pg 565

TAA Council of Fellows, PO Box 367, Fountain City, WI 54629 *E-mail:* info@taaonline.net *Web Site:* www.taaonline.net/council-of-fellows, pg 668

Tachyon Publications LLC, 1459 18 St, No 139, San Francisco, CA 94107 *Tel:* 415-285-5615 *E-mail:* tachyon@tachyonpublications.com; submissions@tachyonpublications.com *Web Site:* www.tachyonpublications.com, pg 202

Tahrike Tarsile Qur'an Inc, 8008 51 Ave, Elmhurst, NY 11373 *Tel:* 718-446-6472 *Fax:* 718-446-4370 *E-mail:* read@koranusa.org *Web Site:* www.koranusa.org, pg 202

Talcott Notch Literary, 127 Broad St, 2P, Milford, CT 06460 *Tel:* 203-876-4959 *Web Site:* talcottnotch.net, pg 479

Nan A Talese, c/o Penguin Random House LLC, 1745 Broadway, New York, NY 10019 *Tel:* 212-751-2600 *Fax:* 212-940-7390 (dom rts); 212-572-2662 (foreign rts) *Web Site:* knopfdoubleday.com/imprint/nan-a-talese/; knopfdoubleday.com, pg 202

The Tamaqua Award for a Collection of Essays, PO Box 63927, Philadelphia, PA 19147 *Tel:* 610-764-0813 *E-mail:* hiddenriverarts@gmail.com *Web Site:* hiddenriverarts.wordpress.com, pg 668

The Tampa Review Prize for Poetry, University of Tampa Press, 401 W Kennedy Blvd, Tampa, FL 33606 *Tel:* 813-253-6266 *E-mail:* utpress@ut.edu *Web Site:* tampareview.org/the-tampa-review-prize-for-poetry, pg 668

TAN Books, PO Box 269, Gastonia, NC 28053 *Tel:* 704-731-0651 *Toll Free Tel:* 800-437-5876 *Fax:* 815-226-7770 *E-mail:* customerservice@tanbooks.com *Web Site:* www.tanbooks.com, pg 202

T&T Clark International, 1385 Broadway, 5th fl, New York, NY 10018 *E-mail:* askacademic@bloomsbury.com *Web Site:* www.bloomsbury.com/us/academic/academic-subjects/theology/t-t-clark, pg 202

Tanenbaum International Literary Agency Ltd (TILA), 1035 Fifth Ave, Suite 15D, New York, NY 10028 *Tel:* 212-371-4120 *Fax:* 212-988-0457 *E-mail:* hello@tanenbauminternational.com *Web Site:* tanenbauminternational.com, pg 479

Tanglewood Publishing, 1060 N Capitol Ave, Suite E-395, Indianapolis, IN 46204 *Tel:* 812-877-9488 *Toll Free Tel:* 800-788-3123 (orders) *E-mail:* info@tanglewoodbooks.com; orders@tanglewoodbooks.com; submission@tanglewoodbooks.com *Web Site:* www.tanglewoodbooks.com, pg 202

Tantor Media Inc, 6 Business Park, Old Saybrook, CT 06475 *Tel:* 860-395-1155 *Toll Free Tel:* 877-782-6867 *Toll Free Fax:* 888-782-7821 *E-mail:* service@tantor.com; rights@tantor.com *Web Site:* www.tantor.com, pg 202

Tapestry Press Ltd, 19 Nashoba Rd, Littleton, MA 01460 *Tel:* 978-486-0200 *Toll Free Tel:* 800-535-2007 *E-mail:* publish@tapestrypress.com *Web Site:* www.tapestrypress.com, pg 202

TarcherPerigee, c/o Penguin Random House LLC, 1745 Broadway, New York, NY 10019 *Tel:* 212-782-9000 *Web Site:* www.penguin.com/tarcherperigee-overview/; www.facebook.com/TarcherPerigee, pg 202

Helen Tartar First Book Subvention Award, 323 E Wacker Dr, No 642, Chicago, IL 60601 *Tel:* 312-600-8072 *E-mail:* info@acla.org *Web Site:* www.acla.org/prize-awards/helen-tartar-first-book-subvention-award, pg 668

Taschen America, NeueHouse, 6121 Sunset Blvd, Los Angeles, CA 90028 *Tel:* 323-463-4441 *Toll Free Tel:* 888-TASCHEN (827-2436) *E-mail:* contact-us@taschen.com *Web Site:* www.taschen.com, pg 203

Taunton Books, 63 S Main St, Newtown, CT 06470 *Tel:* 203-426-8171 *Toll Free Tel:* 866-505-4689 (orders) *Fax:* 203-270-9373, pg 203

Taylor & Francis Inc, 530 Walnut St, Suite 850, Philadelphia, PA 19106 *Tel:* 215-625-8900 *Toll Free Tel:* 800-354-1420 *Fax:* 215-207-0050; 215-207-0046 (cust serv) *E-mail:* support@tandfonline.com *Web Site:* www.taylorandfrancis.com, pg 203

Taylor/Blakeslee Graduate Fellowships, PO Box 17337, Seattle, WA 98127 *Tel:* 206-880-0177 *E-mail:* info@casw.org *Web Site:* casw.org/casw/graduate-school-fellowships, pg 668

TCP Press, 20200 Marsh Hill Rd, Uxbridge, ON L9P 1R3, Canada *Tel:* 905-852-3777 *Toll Free Tel:* 800-772-7765 *E-mail:* tcp@tcpnow.com *Web Site:* www.tcppress.com, pg 420

TCU Press, 3000 Sandage Ave, Fort Worth, TX 76109 *Tel:* 817-257-7822 *E-mail:* tcupress@tcu.edu *Web Site:* www.tcupress.com, pg 203

TD Canadian Children's Literature Award, 425 Adelaide St W, Suite 200, Toronto, ON M5V 3C1, Canada *Tel:* 416-975-0010 *E-mail:* info@bookcentre.ca *Web Site:* www.bookcentre.ca, pg 668

Teacher Created Resources Inc, 12621 Western Ave, Garden Grove, CA 92481 *Tel:* 714-891-7895 *Toll Free Tel:* 800-662-4321; 888-343-4335 *Toll Free Fax:* 800-525-1254 *E-mail:* custserv@teachercreated.com *Web Site:* www.teachercreated.com, pg 203

Teachers & Writers Collaborative (T&W), 20 W 20 St, Suite 801, New York, NY 10011 *Tel:* 212-691-6590 *E-mail:* info@twc.org *Web Site:* www.twc.org, pg 520

Teachers College Press, 1234 Amsterdam Ave, New York, NY 10027 *Tel:* 212-678-3929 *Fax:* 212-678-4149 *E-mail:* tcpress@tc.edu *Web Site:* www.tcpress.com, pg 203

Teacher's Discovery®, 2741 Paldan Dr, Auburn Hills, MI 48326 *Toll Free Tel:* 800-TEACHER (832-2437) *Toll Free Fax:* 800-287-4509 *E-mail:* help@teachersdiscovery.com; orders@teachersdiscovery.com *Web Site:* www.teachersdiscovery.com, pg 203

Teaching & Learning Co, 501 E Third St, Dayton, OH 45402 *Toll Free Tel:* 800-444-1144 *Fax:* 937-223-2042 *E-mail:* service@lorenz.com *Web Site:* www.lorenzeducationalpress.com, pg 204

Teaching Strategies LLC, 4500 East-West Hwy, Suite 300, Bethesda, MD 20814 *Tel:* 301-634-0818 *Toll Free Tel:* 800-637-3652 *E-mail:* info@teachingstrategies.com; support@teachingstrategies.com *Web Site:* teachingstrategies.com, pg 204

Technical Association of the Pulp & Paper Industry (TAPPI), 15 Technology Pkwy S, Suite 115, Peachtree Corners, GA 30092 *Tel:* 770-446-1400 *Toll Free Tel:* 800-332-8686 (US); 800-446-9431 (CN) *Fax:* 770-446-6947 *E-mail:* memberconnection@tappi.org *Web Site:* www.tappi.org, pg 521

Television Academy, 5220 Lankershim Blvd, North Hollywood, CA 91601-3109 *Tel:* 818-754-2800 *Web Site:* www.emmys.com, pg 521

Temple University Press, 1852 N Tenth St, Philadelphia, PA 19122-6099 *Tel:* 215-926-2140 *Toll Free Tel:* 800-621-2736 *Fax:* 215-926-2141 *E-mail:* tempress@temple.edu *Web Site:* tupress.temple.edu, pg 204

Temporal Mechanical Press, 6760 Hwy 7, Estes Park, CO 80517-6404 *Tel:* 970-586-4706 *E-mail:* info@enosmills.com *Web Site:* www.enosmills.com, pg 204

Ten Speed Press, 6001 Shellmound St, Suite 600, Emeryville, CA 94608 *Tel:* 510-285-3000 *Toll Free Tel:* 800-841-BOOK (841-2665) *Web Site:* www.randomhousebooks.com/imprint/ten-speed-press/; crownpublishing.com/archives/imprint/ten-speed-press, pg 204

Tennessee Arts Commission Fellowships, 401 Charlotte Ave, Nashville, TN 37243-0780 *Tel:* 615-741-1701 *Fax:* 615-741-8559 *Web Site:* tnartscommission.org, pg 668

The Tenth Gate Prize, PO Box 42164, Washington, DC 20015 *E-mail:* editor@wordworksbooks.org *Web Site:* www.wordworksbooks.org, pg 668

Teora USA LLC, 9443 Rosehill Dr, Bethesda, MD 20817 *Tel:* 301-986-6990 *E-mail:* teorausa@gmail.com *Web Site:* www.teora.com, pg 204

Terra Nova Books, 33 Alondra Rd, Santa Fe, NM 87508 *Tel:* 505-670-9319 *Fax:* 509-461-9333 *E-mail:* publisher@terranovabooks.com; marketing@terranovabooks.com *Web Site:* www.terranovabooks.com, pg 204

TESOL Press, 1925 Ballenger Ave, Suite 550, Alexandria, VA 22314-6820 *Tel:* 703-518-2500; 703-518-2501 (cust serv) *Toll Free Tel:* 888-891-0041 (cust serv) *Fax:* 703-691-5327 *E-mail:* publications@tesol.org; press@tesol.org; members@tesol.org *Web Site:* www.tesol.org, pg 204

Tessler Literary Agency LLC, 155 W 68 St, No 27F, New York, NY 10023 *Tel:* 212-242-0466 *Web Site:* www.tessleragency.com, pg 479

Teton NewMedia Inc, 5286 Dunewood Dr, Florence, OR 97439 *Tel:* 541-991-3342 *E-mail:* lodgepole@tetonnm.com *Web Site:* www.tetonnm.com, pg 205

Texas A&M University Press, John H Lindsey Bldg, Lewis St, 4354 TAMU, College Station, TX 77843-4354 *Tel:* 979-845-1436 *Toll Free Tel:* 800-826-8911 (orders) *Fax:* 979-847-8752 *Toll Free Fax:* 888-617-2421 (orders) *E-mail:* bookorders@tamu.edu *Web Site:* www.tamupress.com, pg 205

Texas Bluebonnet Award, 3420 Executive Center Dr, Suite 301, Austin, TX 78731 *Tel:* 512-328-1518 *Fax:* 512-328-8852 *E-mail:* tla@txla.org *Web Site:* txla.org/tools-resources/reading-lists/texas-bluebonnet-award/about/; txla.org, pg 669

Texas Institute of Letters (TIL), PO Box 130294, Spring, TX 77393 *Web Site:* texasinstituteofletters.org, pg 521

COMPANY INDEX

Texas Library Association (TLA), 3420 Executive Center Dr, Suite 301, Austin, TX 78731 *Tel:* 512-328-1518 *Fax:* 512-328-8852 *E-mail:* tla@txla.org *Web Site:* txla.org, pg 521

Texas State Historical Association, 3001 Lake Austin Blvd, Suite 3.116, Austin, TX 78703 *Tel:* 512-471-2600 *Fax:* 512-473-8691 *Web Site:* www.tshaonline.org, pg 205

Texas Tech University Press, 1120 Main St, 2nd fl, Lubbock, TX 79401 *Tel:* 806-742-2982 *Toll Free Tel:* 800-832-4042 *E-mail:* ttup@ttu.edu *Web Site:* www.ttupress.org, pg 205

University of Texas Press, 3001 Lake Austin Blvd, 2.200, Austin, TX 78703 *Tel:* 512-471-7233 *Fax:* 512-232-7178 *E-mail:* utpress@uts.cc.utexas.edu; info@utpress.utexas.edu *Web Site:* utpress.utexas.edu, pg 205

Texas Western Press, c/o University of Texas at El Paso, 500 W University Ave, El Paso, TX 79968-0633 *Tel:* 915-747-5688 *Toll Free Tel:* 800-488-3798 (orders only) *Fax:* 915-747-5345 *E-mail:* twpress@utep.edu *Web Site:* twp.utep.edu, pg 205

Textbook Excellence Award, PO Box 367, Fountain City, WI 54629 *E-mail:* info@taaonline.net *Web Site:* www.taaonline.net/textbook-excellence-award, pg 669

Thames & Hudson, 500 Fifth Ave, New York, NY 10110 *Tel:* 212-354-3763 *Toll Free Tel:* 800-233-4830 *Fax:* 212-398-1252 *E-mail:* bookinfo@thames.wwnorton.com *Web Site:* www.thamesandhudsonusa.com, pg 205

Theatre Communications Group, 520 Eighth Ave, 24th fl, New York, NY 10018-4156 *Tel:* 212-609-5900 *Fax:* 212-609-5901 *E-mail:* info@tcg.org *Web Site:* www.tcg.org, pg 205

Theatre Library Association (TLA), c/o The New York Public Library for the Performing Arts, 40 Lincoln Center Plaza, New York, NY 10023 *E-mail:* theatrelibraryassociation@gmail.com *Web Site:* www.tla-online.org, pg 521

David Thelen Award, 112 N Bryan Ave, Bloomington, IN 47408-4141 *Tel:* 812-855-7311 *E-mail:* oah@oah.org *Web Site:* www.oah.org/awards, pg 669

Theosophical University Press, PO Box C, Pasadena, CA 91109-7107 *Tel:* 626-798-3378 *E-mail:* tupress@theosociety.org *Web Site:* www.theosociety.org, pg 206

Theytus Books Ltd, 154 Enowkin Trail, RR 2, Site 50, Comp 8, Penticton, BC V2A 6J7, Canada *Tel:* 250-493-7181 *Fax:* 250-493-5302 *E-mail:* order@theytus.com; marketing@theytus.com *Web Site:* www.theytus.com, pg 420

Thieme Medical Publishers Inc, 333 Seventh Ave, 18th fl, New York, NY 10001 *Tel:* 212-760-0888 *Toll Free Tel:* 800-782-3488 *Fax:* 212-947-1112 *E-mail:* customerservice@thieme.com *Web Site:* www.thieme.com, pg 206

Third World Press Foundation, 7822 S Dobson Ave, Chicago, IL 60619 *Tel:* 773-651-0700 *E-mail:* twpbooks@thirdworldpressfoundation.org *Web Site:* thirdworldpressfoundation.org, pg 206

Thistledown Press, 220 20 St W, Unit 222, Saskatoon, SK S7M 0W9, Canada *Tel:* 306-244-1722 *E-mail:* tdpress@thistledownpress.com *Web Site:* www.thistledownpress.com, pg 420

Thodestool Fiction Editing, 40 McDougall Rd, Waterloo, ON N2L 2W5, Canada *Web Site:* www.thodestool.ca, pg 445

Charles C Thomas Publisher Ltd, 2600 S First St, Springfield, IL 62704 *Tel:* 217-789-8980 *Toll Free Tel:* 800-258-8980 *Fax:* 217-789-9130 *E-mail:* books@ccthomas.com *Web Site:* www.ccthomas.com, pg 206

Thomas Nelson, 501 Nelson Place, Nashville, TN 37214 *Tel:* 615-889-9000 *Toll Free Tel:* 800-251-4000 *Web Site:* www.thomasnelson.com, pg 206

The Piri Thomas Poetry Prize, 511-512 Humanities Bldg, 1600 Holloway Ave, San Francisco, CA 94132 *Tel:* 415-338-2227 *Fax:* 415-338-0966 *E-mail:* poetry@sfsu.edu *Web Site:* poetry.sfsu.edu, pg 669

Thompson Educational Publishing Inc, 20 Ripley Ave, Toronto, ON M6S 3N9, Canada *Tel:* 416-766-2763 (admin & orders) *Toll Free Tel:* 877-366-2763 *Fax:* 416-766-0398 (admin & orders) *E-mail:* info@thompsonbooks.com; support@thompsonbooks.com *Web Site:* www.thompsonbooks.com, pg 420

Thomson West, 610 Opperman Dr, Eagan, MN 55123 *Tel:* 651-687-7000 *Toll Free Tel:* 888-728-7677 (cust serv) *Web Site:* store.legal.thomsonreuters.com/law-products/brands/thomson-west/c/20287, pg 206

Thorndike Press®, 10 Water St, Suite 310, Waterville, ME 04901 *Tel:* 207-861-1514 *Toll Free Tel:* 800-877-4253 (option 1) *Toll Free Fax:* 800-558-4676 (orders) *E-mail:* gale.printorders@cengage.com; gale.customerservice@cengage.com *Web Site:* www.gale.com/thorndike, pg 206

3-Day Novel Contest, PO Box 3008, MPO, Vancouver, BC V6B 3X5, Canada *Tel:* 604-876-8710 *E-mail:* info@3daynovel.com *Web Site:* www.3daynovel.com, pg 669

3 Seas Literary Agency, PO Box 444, Sun Prairie, WI 53590 *Tel:* 608-834-9317 *E-mail:* threeseaslit@aol.com *Web Site:* threeseasagency.com, pg 479

Thriller Awards Competition, PO Box 311, Eureka, CA 95502 *Web Site:* thrillerwriters.org, pg 669

ThunderStone Books, 6575 Horse Dr, Las Vegas, NV 89131 *E-mail:* info@thunderstonebooks.com *Web Site:* www.thunderstonebooks.com, pg 207

Thurber Prize for American Humor, 77 Jefferson Ave, Columbus, OH 43215 *Tel:* 614-464-1032 *E-mail:* thurberhouse@thurberhouse.org *Web Site:* www.thurberhouse.org, pg 669

Tide-mark Press, 207 Oakwood Ave, West Hartford, CT 06119 *Tel:* 860-310-3370 *Toll Free Tel:* 800-338-2508 *Fax:* 860-310-3654 *E-mail:* customerservice@tide-mark.com, pg 207

Tiger Tales, 5 River Rd, Suite 128, Wilton, CT 06897-4069 *Tel:* 920-387-2333 *Fax:* 920-387-9994 *Web Site:* www.tigertalesbooks.com, pg 207

Tilbury House Publishers, 12 Starr St, Thomaston, ME 04861 *Tel:* 207-582-1899 *Toll Free Tel:* 800-582-1899 (orders) *Fax:* 207-582-8227 *E-mail:* tilbury@tilburyhouse.com *Web Site:* www.tilburyhouse.com, pg 207

Tin House Summer Workshop, 2617 NW Thurman St, Portland, OR 97210 *Tel:* 503-473-8663 *Web Site:* tinhouse.com/workshop/summer-workshop, pg 558

Tin House Winter Workshop, 2617 NW Thurman St, Portland, OR 97210 *Tel:* 503-473-8663 *Web Site:* tinhouse.com/winter-workshop, pg 558

Lon Tinkle Award for Lifetime Achievement, PO Box 130294, Spring, TX 77393 *Web Site:* texasinstituteofletters.org, pg 669

James Tiptree Jr Literary Award, 173 Anderson St, San Francisco, CA 94110 *Tel:* 415-641-4103 *E-mail:* info@tiptree.org *Web Site:* tiptree.org, pg 669

The Toby Press LLC, PO Box 8531, New Milford, CT 06776-8531 *Tel:* 203-830-8508 *Fax:* 203-830-8512 *E-mail:* info@tobypress.com; orders@korenpub.com *Web Site:* www.korenpub.com/collections/toby, pg 207

Todd Publications, 15494 Fiorenza Circle, Delray Beach, FL 33446 *Tel:* 561-910-0440 *Fax:* 561-910-0440 *E-mail:* toddpub@yahoo.com, pg 207

Arthur Tofte/Betty Ren Wright Children's Literature Award, c/o 3225 N 91 St, Milwaukee, WI 53222 *E-mail:* wiswriters@gmail.com *Web Site:* wiswriters.org/awards, pg 669

Tommy Nelson®, 501 Nelson Place, Nashville, TN 37214 *Tel:* 615-889-9000; 615-902-1485 (cust serv) *Toll Free Tel:* 800-251-4000 *Web Site:* www.tommynelson.com, pg 207

Top Publications Ltd, 5101 Brouette Ct, Plano, TX 75023 *Tel:* 972-628-6414 *Fax:* 972-233-0713 *E-mail:* bill@topfiction.net (sales & admin) *Web Site:* toppub.com, pg 207

TRANSLATION PROJECTS

Tor Publishing Group, 120 Broadway, New York, NY 10271 *Toll Free Tel:* 800-455-0340 (Macmillan) *E-mail:* torpublicity@tor.com; forgepublicity@forgebooks.com *Web Site:* us.macmillan.com/torpublishinggroup, pg 207

Torah Umesorah Publications, 620 Foster Ave, Brooklyn, NY 11230 *Tel:* 718-259-1223 *E-mail:* publications@torahumesorah.org *Web Site:* www.torahumesorah.org/publications, pg 208

Toronto Book Awards, c/o Toronto Arts & Culture, City Hall, 9E, 100 Queen St W, Toronto, ON M5H 2N2, Canada *Web Site:* www.toronto.ca/book_awards, pg 669

Tortuga Press, 2777 Yulupa Ave, PMB 181, Santa Rosa, CA 95405 *Tel:* 707-544-4720 *Fax:* 707-595-5331 *E-mail:* info@tortugapress.com *Web Site:* www.tortugapress.com, pg 208

TotalRecall Publications Inc, 1103 Middlecreek, Friendswood, TX 77546 *Tel:* 281-992-3131 *E-mail:* sales@totalrecallpress.com *Web Site:* www.totalrecallpress.com, pg 208

TouchWood Editions, 103-1075 Pendergast St, Victoria, BC V8V 0A1, Canada *Tel:* 250-360-0829 *Fax:* 250-386-0829 *E-mail:* info@touchwoodeditions.com *Web Site:* www.touchwoodeditions.com, pg 420

Tower Publishing Co, 650 Cape Rd, Standish, ME 04084 *Tel:* 207-642-5400 *Toll Free Tel:* 800-969-8693 *E-mail:* info@towerpub.com *Web Site:* www.towerpub.com, pg 208

Townson Publishing Co Ltd, PO Box 1404, Sta A, Vancouver, BC V6C 2P7, Canada *Tel:* 604-886-0594 *E-mail:* gpubinc@gmail.com; translationrights@gmail.com *Web Site:* generalpublishing.com, pg 420

Towson University Prize for Literature, English Dept, 8000 York Rd, Towson, MD 21252 *Tel:* 410-704-2000 *Web Site:* www.towson.edu/english, pg 670

Tracks Publishing, 458 Dorothy Ave, Ventura, CA 93003 *Tel:* 805-754-0248 *E-mail:* tracks@cox.net *Web Site:* www.startupsports.com, pg 208

Tradewind Books, 202-1807 Maritime Mews, Vancouver, BC V6H 3W7, Canada *Tel:* 604-662-4405 *E-mail:* tradewindbooks@yahoo.com; tradewindbooks@gmail.com *Web Site:* www.tradewindbooks.com, pg 421

Trafalgar Square Books, 388 Howe Hill Rd, North Pomfret, VT 05053 *Tel:* 802-457-1911 *Toll Free Tel:* 800-423-4525 *Fax:* 802-457-1913 *E-mail:* contact@trafalgarbooks.com *Web Site:* www.trafalgarbooks.com; www.horseandriderbooks.com, pg 208

Trafford Publishing, 1663 Liberty Dr, Bloomington, IN 47403 *Toll Free Tel:* 844-688-6899 *E-mail:* customersupport@trafford.com; sales@trafford.com *Web Site:* www.trafford.com, pg 208

Trans-Atlantic Publications Inc, 33 Ashley Dr, Schwenksville, PA 19473 *Tel:* 215-925-2762 *Fax:* 215-925-1912 *Web Site:* www.transatlanticpub.com; www.businesstitles.com, pg 209

Transatlantic Agency, 2 Bloor St E, Suite 3500, Toronto, ON M4W 1A8, Canada *Tel:* 416-488-9214 *E-mail:* info@transatlanticagency.com; royalties@transatlanticagency.com *Web Site:* www.transatlanticagency.com, pg 479

Transcontinental Music Publications (TMP), 1375 Remington Rd, Suite M, Schaumburg, IL 60173-4844 *Tel:* 847-781-7800 *Fax:* 847-781-7801 *E-mail:* tmp@accantors.org *Web Site:* www.transcontinentalmusic.com, pg 209

Translation Projects, 400 Seventh St SW, Washington, DC 20506-0001 *Tel:* 202-682-5400; 202-682-5082 (voice/TTY); 202-682-5034 (lit fellowships hotline) *E-mail:* litfellowships@arts.gov *Web Site:* www.arts.gov/grants/translation-projects, pg 670

TRANSLATION SERIES

Translation Series, Rhodes Tower, Rm 1841, 2121 Euclid Ave, Cleveland, OH 44115 Tel: 216-687-3986 E-mail: poetrycenter@csuohio.edu Web Site: www.csupoetrycenter.com/translation-series; www.csupoetrycenter.com, pg 670

Transportation Research Board (TRB), 500 Fifth St NW, Washington, DC 20001 Tel: 202-334-2934; 202-334-3213 (bookshop) E-mail: trbsales@nas.edu; mytrb@nas.edu Web Site: www.nationalacademies.org/trb/transportation-research-board, pg 209

Travelers' Tales, 2320 Bowdoin St, Palo Alto, CA 94306 Tel: 650-462-2110 E-mail: ttales@travelerstales.com; info@travelerstales.com Web Site: travelerstales.com, pg 209

Treasure Bay Inc, PO Box 119, Novato, CA 94948 Tel: 415-884-2888 Fax: 415-884-2840 E-mail: customerservice@treasurebaybooks.com Web Site: www.treasurebaybooks.com, pg 209

Treehaus Communications Inc, PO Box 249, Loveland, OH 45140-0249 Tel: 513-683-5716 Toll Free Tel: 800-638-4287 (orders) Fax: 513-683-2882 (orders) E-mail: treehaus@treehaus1.com; treehauscommunications@gmail.com Web Site: www.treehaus1.com, pg 209

Treehouse Climate Action Poem Prize, 75 Maiden Lane, Suite 901, New York, NY 10038 Tel: 212-274-0343 E-mail: awards@poets.org Web Site: poets.org, pg 670

TriadaUS Literary Agency, PO Box 561, Sewickley, PA 15143 Tel: 412-401-3376 Web Site: www.triadaus.com, pg 480

Trident Media Group LLC, 355 Lexington Ave, 12th fl, New York, NY 10017 Tel: 212-333-1511 E-mail: info@tridentmediagroup.com; press@tridentmediagroup.com; foreignrights@tridentmediagroup.com; office.assistant@tridentmediagroup.com Web Site: www.tridentmediagroup.com, pg 480

Emma Gray Trigg Memorial, PO Box 36128, North Chesterfield, VA 23235-3533 E-mail: contest@poetrysocietyofvirginia.org; info@poetryvirginia.org Web Site: www.poetrysocietyofvirginia.org, pg 670

Trillium Book Award/Prix Trillium, South Tower, Suite 501, 175 Bloor St E, Toronto, ON M4W 3R8, Canada Tel: 416-314-6858 E-mail: programs2@ontariocreates.ca Web Site: ontariocreates.ca, pg 670

The Trinity Foundation, PO Box 68, Unicoi, TN 37692-0068 Tel: 423-743-0199 Web Site: www.trinityfoundation.org, pg 209

Trinity University Press, One Trinity Place, San Antonio, TX 78212-7200 Tel: 210-999-8884 Fax: 210-999-8838 E-mail: books@trinity.edu Web Site: www.tupress.org, pg 209

TriQuarterly Books, 629 Noyes St, Evanston, IL 60208 Tel: 847-491-7420 Toll Free Tel: 800-621-2736 (orders only) Fax: 847-491-8150 E-mail: nupress@northwestern.edu Web Site: www.nupress.northwestern.edu, pg 209

TRISTAN Publishing, 2355 Louisiana Ave N, Minneapolis, MN 55427 Tel: 763-545-1383 Toll Free Tel: 866-545-1383 Fax: 763-545-1387 E-mail: info@tristanpublishing.com Web Site: www.tristanpublishing.com, pg 209

Triumph Books LLC, 814 N Franklin St, Chicago, IL 60610 Tel: 312-337-0747 Toll Free Tel: 800-888-4741 (cust serv) Fax: 312-280-5470; 312-337-5985 Web Site: www.triumphbooks.com, pg 209

Sergio Troncoso Award for Best Book of Fiction, PO Box 130294, Spring, TX 77393 Web Site: texasinstituteofletters.org, pg 670

Harry S Truman Book Award, 5151 Troost Ave, Suite 300, Kansas City, MO 64110 Tel: 816-400-1212 Toll Free Tel: 844-358-5400 Web Site: www.trumanlibraryinstitute.org/research-grants/bookaward/; trumanlibraryinstitute.org, pg 670

Trusted Media Brands Inc, 750 Third Ave, 3rd fl, New York, NY 10017 Tel: 646-293-6299 Toll Free Tel: 877-732-4438 (cust serv) Fax: 646-293-6251 E-mail: customercare@trustedmediabrands.com; press@trustedmediabrands.com Web Site: www.trustedmediabrands.com; www.rd.com, pg 210

Trustus Playwrights' Festival, 520 Lady St, Columbia, SC 29201 Tel: 803-254-9732 E-mail: boxoffice@trustus.org Web Site: trustus.org/playwrights-festival, pg 670

TSG Publishing Foundation Inc, 8685 E Stagecoach Pass Rd, Scottsdale, AZ 85266 Tel: 480-502-1909 E-mail: info@tsgfoundation.org Web Site: www.tsgfoundation.org, pg 210

Harriet Tubman Prize, 515 Malcolm X Blvd, New York, NY 10037 Tel: 212-491-2263 E-mail: lapiduscenter@nypl.org Web Site: www.lapiduscenter.org/category/tubman, pg 670

The Tuesday Agency, 404 E College St, Suite 408, Iowa City, IA 52240 Tel: 319-338-7080; 319-400-9031 (cell) E-mail: info@tuesdayagency.com Web Site: tuesdayagency.com, pg 487

Kate Tufts Discovery Award, Harper East, Unit B-7, 160 E Tenth St, Claremont, CA 91711-6165 Tel: 909-621-8974 E-mail: tufts@cgu.edu Web Site: www.cgu.edu/tufts, pg 670

Kingsley Tufts Poetry Award, Harper East, Unit B-7, 160 E Tenth St, Claremont, CA 91711-6165 Tel: 909-621-8974 E-mail: tufts@cgu.edu Web Site: www.cgu.edu/tufts, pg 671

Tugeau 2 Inc, 2231 Grandview Ave, Cleveland Heights, OH 44106 Tel: 216-513-4047 Web Site: www.tugeau2.com, pg 486

Tughra Books, 335 Clifton Ave, Clifton, NJ 07011 Tel: 646-415-9331 Fax: 646-827-6228 E-mail: info@tughrabooks.com Web Site: www.tughrabooks.com, pg 210

Tumblehome Learning Inc, 201 Newbury St, Suite 201, Boston, MA 02116 E-mail: info@tumblehomelearning.com Web Site: www.tumblehomelearning.com, pg 210

Tundra Book Group, 320 Front St W, Suite 1400, Toronto, ON M5V 3B6, Canada Tel: 416-364-4449 Toll Free Tel: 888-523-9292 (orders); 800-588-1074 E-mail: youngreaders@penguinrandomhouse.com Web Site: www.tundrabooks.com, pg 421

Tupelo Press Berkshire Prize for a First or Second Book of Poetry, 60 Roberts Dr, Suite 308, North Adams, MA 01247 Tel: 413-664-9611 Fax: 413-664-9711 E-mail: info@tupelopress.org Web Site: www.tupelopress.org, pg 671

Tupelo Press Inc, 60 Roberts Dr, Suite 308, North Adams, MA 01247 Tel: 413-664-9611 Fax: 413-664-9711 E-mail: info@tupelopress.org Web Site: www.tupelopress.org, pg 210

Tupelo Press Snowbound Series Chapbook Award, 60 Roberts Dr, Suite 308, North Adams, MA 01247 Tel: 413-664-9611 Fax: 413-664-9711 E-mail: info@tupelopress.org Web Site: www.tupelopress.org, pg 671

Frederick Jackson Turner Award, 112 N Bryan Ave, Bloomington, IN 47408-4141 Tel: 812-855-7311 E-mail: oah@oah.org Web Site: www.oah.org/awards, pg 671

Nancy Byrd Turner Memorial, PO Box 36128, North Chesterfield, VA 23235-3533 E-mail: contest@poetrysocietyofvirginia.org; info@poetryvirginia.org Web Site: www.poetrysocietyofvirginia.org, pg 671

Turner Publishing Co LLC, 4507 Charlotte Ave, Suite 100, Nashville, TN 37209 Tel: 615-255-BOOK (255-2665) Fax: 615-255-5081 E-mail: info@turnerpublishing.com; marketing@turnerpublishing.com; submissions@turnerpublishing.com; editorial@turnerpublishing.com; admin@turnerpublishing.com; orders@turnerpublishing.com Web Site: turnerpublishing.com; www.facebook.com/turner.publishing, pg 210

Turnstone Press, Artspace Bldg, 206-100 Arthur St, Winnipeg, MB R3B 1H3, Canada Tel: 204-947-1555 Toll Free Tel: 888-363-7718 Fax: 204-942-1555 E-mail: info@turnstonepress.com Web Site: www.turnstonepress.com, pg 421

COMPANY INDEX

Turtle Point Press, 208 Java St, 5th fl, Brooklyn, NY 11222-5748 Tel: 212-741-1393 E-mail: info@turtlepointpress.com Web Site: www.turtlepointpress.com, pg 210

The Tuscarora Award for Historical Fiction, PO Box 63927, Philadelphia, PA 19147 Tel: 610-764-0813 E-mail: hiddenriverarts@gmail.com Web Site: hiddenriverarts.wordpress.com, pg 671

The Tusculum Review Poetry Chapbook Prize, 60 Shiloh Rd, Greeneville, TN 37745 E-mail: review@tusculum.edu Web Site: web.tusculum.edu/tusculumreview/contest, pg 671

Tuttle Publishing, Airport Business Park, 364 Innovation Dr, North Clarendon, VT 05759-9436 Tel: 802-773-8930 Toll Free Tel: 800-526-2778 Fax: 802-773-6993 Toll Free Fax: 800-FAX-TUTL (329-8885) E-mail: info@tuttlepublishing.com; orders@tuttlepublishing.com Web Site: www.tuttlepublishing.com, pg 211

Tuxedo Press, 546 E Springville Rd, Carlisle, PA 17015 Tel: 717-258-9733 Fax: 717-243-0074 E-mail: info@tuxedo-press.com Web Site: tuxedo-press.com, pg 211

Mark Twain American Voice in Literature Award, 351 Farmington Ave, Hartford, CT 06105 Tel: 860-247-0998 E-mail: info@marktwainhouse.org Web Site: marktwainhouse.org, pg 671

21st Century Award, 200 W Madison, 3rd fl, Chicago, IL 60606 Tel: 312-201-9830 E-mail: info@cplfoundation.org Web Site: www.cplfoundation.org, pg 671

Twenty-First Century Books, 241 First Ave N, Minneapolis, MN 55401 Tel: 612-332-3344 Toll Free Tel: 800-328-4929 Fax: 612-332-7615 Toll Free Fax: 800-332-1132 E-mail: info@lernerbooks.com; custserve@lernerbooks.com Web Site: www.lernerbooks.com; www.facebook.com/lernerbooks, pg 211

The 25 Most "Censored" Stories Annual, PO Box 1177, Fair Oaks, CA 95628 Tel: 707-241-4596 E-mail: info@projectcensored.org Web Site: www.projectcensored.org/censorship/nominate, pg 671

Twenty-Third Publications, One Montauk Ave, Suite 200, New London, CT 06320 Tel: 860-437-3012 Toll Free Tel: 800-321-0411 (orders) Toll Free Fax: 800-572-0788 E-mail: resources@twentythirdpublications.com Web Site: www.twentythirdpublications.com, pg 211

Twilight Times Books, PO Box 3340, Kingsport, TN 37664-0340 Tel: 423-390-1111 Fax: 423-390-1111 E-mail: publisher@twilighttimes.com Web Site: www.twilighttimesbooks.com, pg 211

Twin Oaks Indexing, 138 Twin Oaks Rd, Suite W, Louisa, VA 23093 Tel: 540-894-5126 E-mail: twinoaksindexing@gmail.com Web Site: www.twinoakscommunity.org, pg 445

2M Communications Ltd, 263 West End Ave, Suite 21A, New York, NY 10023 Tel: 212-741-1509 Fax: 212-691-4460 Web Site: www.2mcommunications.com, pg 480

Cy Twombly Award for Poetry, 820 Greenwich St, New York, NY 10014 Tel: 212-807-7077 E-mail: info@contemporary-arts.org Web Site: www.foundationforcontemporaryarts.org/grants/cy-twombly-award-for-poetry, pg 672

Tyndale House Publishers Inc, 351 Executive Dr, Carol Stream, IL 60188 Tel: 630-668-8300 Toll Free Tel: 800-323-9400; 855-277-9400 Toll Free Fax: 866-622-9474 Web Site: www.tyndale.com, pg 211

UCLA Latin American Center Publications, UCLA Latin American Institute, 10343 Bunche Hall, Los Angeles, CA 90095 Tel: 310-825-4571 Fax: 310-206-6859 E-mail: latinamctr@international.ucla.edu Web Site: www.international.ucla.edu/lai, pg 212

Ucross Foundation Residency Program, 30 Big Red Lane, Clearmont, WY 82835 Tel: 307-737-2291 E-mail: info@ucross.org Web Site: www.ucross.org, pg 672

COMPANY INDEX

Ugly Duckling Presse, The Old American Can Factory, 232 Third St, Suite E303, Brooklyn, NY 11215 *Tel:* 347-948-5170 *E-mail:* office@uglyducklingpresse.org; orders@uglyducklingpresse.org; publicity@uglyducklingpresse.org; rights@uglyducklingpresse.org *Web Site:* uglyducklingpresse.org, pg 212

Friedrich Ulfers Prize, 42 Washington Mews, New York, NY 10003 *E-mail:* info@festivalneueliteratur.org *Web Site:* festivalneueliteratur.org/prize, pg 672

Ulysses Press, 195 Montague St, 14th fl, Brooklyn, NY 11201 *Tel:* 510-601-8301 *Toll Free Tel:* 800-377-2542 *Fax:* 510-601-8307 *E-mail:* ulysses@ulyssespress.com *Web Site:* www.ulyssespress.com, pg 212

Ulysses Travel Guides, 4176, rue Saint-Denis, Montreal, QC H2W 2M5, Canada *Tel:* 514-843-9882 (ext 2232); 514-843-9447 (bookstore) *Fax:* 514-843-9448 *E-mail:* info@ulysse.ca; st-denis@ulysse.ca *Web Site:* www.guidesulysse.com, pg 421

Unarius Academy of Science Publications, 145 S Magnolia Ave, El Cajon, CA 92020-4522 *Tel:* 619-444-7062 *Toll Free Tel:* 800-475-7062 *E-mail:* uriel@unarius.org *Web Site:* www.unarius.org, pg 212

Undergraduate Poetry Award, PO Box 36128, North Chesterfield, VA 23235-3533 *E-mail:* contest@poetrysocietyofvirginia.org; info@poetryvirginia.org *Web Site:* www.poetrysocietyofvirginia.org, pg 672

Union Literary, 30 Vandam St, Suite 5A, New York, NY 10013 *Tel:* 212-255-2112 *Web Site:* www.unionliterary.com, pg 480

Union Square & Co, 1166 Avenue of the Americas, 17th fl, New York, NY 10036-2715 *Tel:* 212-532-7160 *Toll Free Tel:* 800-367-9692 *Fax:* 212-213-2495 *Toll Free Fax:* 800-542-7567 *E-mail:* custservice@sterlingpublishing.com; customerservice@sterlingpublishing.com; editorial@sterlingpublishing.com; tradesales@sterlingpublishing.com *Web Site:* www.sterlingpublishing.com, pg 212

United for Libraries, 225 N Michigan Ave, Suite 1300, Chicago, IL 60601 *Tel:* 312-280-2161 *Toll Free Tel:* 800-545-2433 (ext 2161) *E-mail:* united@ala.org *Web Site:* www.ala.org/united, pg 521

United Nations Publications, 405 E 42 St, 11th fl, New York, NY 10017 *Tel:* 703-661-1571 *E-mail:* publications@un.org *Web Site:* shop.un.org, pg 213

United States Board on Books for Young People (USBBY), National Luis University, Ctr for Teaching through Children's Books, 1000 Capitol Dr, Wheeling, IL 60090 *Tel:* 224-233-2798 *E-mail:* secretariat@usbby.org *Web Site:* www.usbby.org, pg 521

United States Holocaust Memorial Museum, 100 Raoul Wallenberg Place SW, Washington, DC 20024-2126 *Tel:* 202-488-0400; 202-488-6144 (orders) *Toll Free Tel:* 800-259-9998 (orders) *E-mail:* academicpublications@ushmm.org *Web Site:* www.ushmm.org, pg 213

United States Institute of Peace Press, 2301 Constitution Ave NW, Washington, DC 20037 *Tel:* 703-661-1590 (cust serv) *Toll Free Tel:* 800-868-8064 (cust serv) *E-mail:* usipmail@presswarehouse.com (orders) *Web Site:* bookstore.usip.org, pg 213

United States Pharmacopeia (USP), 12601 Twinbrook Pkwy, Rockville, MD 20852-1790 *Tel:* 301-881-0666 *Toll Free Tel:* 800-227-8772 *E-mail:* marketing@usp.org *Web Site:* www.usp.org, pg 213

United Talent Agency LLC, 9336 Civic Center Dr, Beverly Hills, CA 90210 *Tel:* 310-273-6700 *Web Site:* www.unitedtalent.com, pg 480

Univelt Inc, 740 Metcalf St, No 13, Escondido, CA 92025 *Tel:* 760-746-4005 *Fax:* 760-746-3139 *E-mail:* sales@univelt.com *Web Site:* www.univelt.com; www.astronautical.org, pg 213

Universal-Publishers Inc, 200 Spectrum Center Dr, Suite 300, Irvine, CA 92618-5004 *Tel:* 561-750-4344 *Toll Free Tel:* 800-636-8329 (US only) *Fax:* 561-750-6797 *Web Site:* www.universal-publishers.com, pg 213

Universe Publishing, 300 Park Ave S, 4th fl, New York, NY 10010 *Tel:* 212-387-3400 *Fax:* 212-387-3535 *Web Site:* www.rizzoliusa.com, pg 214

University Council for Educational Administration (UCEA), Michigan State University, College of Education, 620 Farm Lane, 432 Erickson Hall, East Lansing, MI 48824 *Tel:* 434-243-1041 *E-mail:* ucea@msu.edu *Web Site:* www.ucea.org, pg 214

University of Alabama Press, 200 Hackberry Lane, 2nd fl, Tuscaloosa, AL 35487 *Tel:* 205-348-5180 *Fax:* 205-348-9201 *Web Site:* www.uapress.ua.edu, pg 214

University of Alabama Program in Creative Writing, PO Box 870244, Tuscaloosa, AL 35487-0244 *Tel:* 205-348-5065 *Fax:* 205-348-1388 *E-mail:* english@ua.edu *Web Site:* www.as.ua.edu/english, pg 566

University of Alaska Press, Elmer E Rasmuson Library, 1732 Tanana Loop, Suite 420, Fairbanks, AK 99775 *Tel:* 907-474-5831 *Toll Free Tel:* 888-252-6657 (US only) *Fax:* 907-474-5502 *Web Site:* www.alaska.edu/uapress, pg 214

University of Alberta Press, Ring House 2, Edmonton, AB T6G 2E1, Canada *Tel:* 780-492-3662 *Fax:* 780-492-0719 *Web Site:* www.uap.ualberta.ca, pg 421

The University of Arizona Press, 1510 E University Blvd, Tucson, AZ 85721 *Tel:* 520-621-1441 *Toll Free Tel:* 800-621-2736 (orders) *Fax:* 520-621-8899 *Toll Free Fax:* 800-621-8476 (orders) *E-mail:* uap@uapress.arizona.edu *Web Site:* www.uapress.arizona.edu, pg 214

The University of Arkansas Press, McIlroy House, 105 N McIlroy Ave, Fayetteville, AR 72701 *Tel:* 479-575-7544 *E-mail:* info@uapress.com *Web Site:* www.uapress.com, pg 214

University of Baltimore - Yale Gordon College of Arts & Sciences, Liberal Arts & Policy Bldg, 10 W Preston St, Rm 107, Baltimore, MD 21201 *Web Site:* www.ubalt.edu/cas/about-the-college/schools-and-divisions/school-of-communications-design, pg 566

University of British Columbia Creative Writing Program, Buchanan Rm E-462, 1866 Main Mall, Vancouver, BC V6T 1Z1, Canada *Tel:* 604-822-0699 *Web Site:* creativewriting.ubc.ca, pg 566

University of British Columbia Press, 2029 West Mall, Vancouver, BC V6T 1Z2, Canada *Tel:* 604-822-5959 *Toll Free Tel:* 877-377-9378 *Fax:* 604-822-6083 *Toll Free Fax:* 800-668-0821 *E-mail:* frontdesk@ubcpress.ca *Web Site:* www.ubcpress.ca, pg 422

University of Calgary Press, 2500 University Dr NW, Calgary, AB T2N 1N4, Canada *Tel:* 403-220-7578 *E-mail:* ucpbooks@ucalgary.ca *Web Site:* press.ucalgary.ca, pg 422

University of California Extension - Writing, Editing & Humanities, 1995 University Ave, Suite 110, Berkeley, CA 94720-7000 *Tel:* 510-643-8916 *Fax:* 510-643-0216 *E-mail:* extension-letters@berkeley.edu *Web Site:* www.extension.berkeley.edu, pg 566

University of California Institute on Global Conflict & Cooperation, 9500 Gilman Dr, MC 0518, La Jolla, CA 92093-0518 *Tel:* 858-534-6106 *Fax:* 858-534-7655 *E-mail:* igcc-communications@ucsd.edu *Web Site:* igcc.ucsd.edu, pg 215

University of California Press, 155 Grand Ave, Suite 400, Oakland, CA 94612-3758 *Tel:* 510-883-8232 *Fax:* 510-836-8910 *E-mail:* customerservice@ucpress.edu *Web Site:* www.ucpress.edu, pg 215

University of Chicago, Graham School Writer's Studio, 1427 E 60 St, Chicago, IL 60637 *Tel:* 773-702-1731 *Web Site:* graham.uchicago.edu/programs-courses/writers-studio, pg 566

University of Chicago Press, 1427 E 60 St, Chicago, IL 60637-2954 *Tel:* 773-702-7700; 773-702-7600 *Toll Free Tel:* 800-621-2736 (orders) *Fax:* 773-702-9756; 773-660-2235 (orders); 773-702-2708 *E-mail:* custserv@press.uchicago.edu; marketing@press.uchicago.edu *Web Site:* www.press.uchicago.edu, pg 215

University of Delaware Press, 200A Morris Library, 181 S College Ave, Newark, DE 19717-5267 *Tel:* 302-831-1149 *Toll Free Tel:* 800-462-6420 *Fax:* 302-831-6549 *E-mail:* ud-press@udel.edu; orders@rowman.com *Web Site:* library.udel.edu/udpress, pg 215

UNIVERSITY OF NEBRASKA PRESS

University of Denver Publishing Institute, 2000 E Asbury Ave, Denver, CO 80208 *Tel:* 303-871-2570 *Fax:* 303-871-2501 *E-mail:* pi-info@du.edu *Web Site:* liberalarts.du.edu/publishing, pg 566

University of Georgia Press, Main Library, 3rd fl, 320 S Jackson St, Athens, GA 30602 *Fax:* 706-542-2558; 706-542-6770 *Web Site:* www.ugapress.org, pg 216

University of Hawaii Press, 2840 Kolowalu St, Honolulu, HI 96822-1888 *Tel:* 808-956-8255 *Toll Free Tel:* 888-UHPRESS (847-7377) *Toll Free Fax:* 800-650-7811 *E-mail:* uhpbooks@hawaii.edu *Web Site:* www.uhpress.hawaii.edu, pg 216

University of Houston Creative Writing Program, Dept of English/College of Liberal Arts & Social Science, 3687 Cullen Blvd, Rm 229, Houston, TX 77204-5008 *Tel:* 713-743-3015 *E-mail:* cwp@uh.edu *Web Site:* uh.edu/class/english/programs/graduate-studies/index, pg 566

University of Illinois at Chicago, Program for Writers, College of Liberal Arts & Sciences, 601 S Morgan St, Chicago, IL 60607 *Tel:* 312-413-2200 (Eng dept) *E-mail:* english@uic.edu *Web Site:* engl.uic.edu/graduate-studies/program-for-writers, pg 566

University of Illinois, Department of Journalism, 119 Gregory Hall, 810 S Wright St, Urbana, IL 61801 *Tel:* 217-333-0709 *E-mail:* journ@illinois.edu *Web Site:* catalog.illinois.edu/graduate/media/journalism-ms; media.illinois.edu/journalism/degrees-programs/masters, pg 567

University of Illinois Press, 1325 S Oak St, MC-566, Champaign, IL 61820-6903 *Tel:* 217-333-0950 *Fax:* 217-244-8082 *E-mail:* uipress@uillinois.edu; journals@uillinois.edu *Web Site:* www.press.uillinois.edu, pg 216

University of Iowa Press, 119 W Park Rd, 100 Kuhl House, Iowa City, IA 52242-1000 *Tel:* 319-335-2000 *Toll Free Tel:* 800-621-2736 (orders only) *Fax:* 319-335-2055 *Toll Free Fax:* 800-621-8476 (orders only) *E-mail:* uipress@uiowa.edu *Web Site:* www.uipress.uiowa.edu, pg 216

University of Iowa, Writers' Workshop, Graduate Creative Writing Program, 102 Dey House, 507 N Clinton St, Iowa City, IA 52242-1000 *Tel:* 319-335-0416 *Fax:* 319-335-0420 *Web Site:* writersworkshop.uiowa.edu, pg 567

University of Louisiana at Lafayette Press, PO Box 43558, Lafayette, LA 70504-3558 *Tel:* 337-482-6027 *E-mail:* press.submissions@louisiana.edu *Web Site:* ulpress.org, pg 217

University of Manitoba Press, University of Manitoba, 301 St Johns College, 92 Dysart Rd, Winnipeg, MB R3T 2M5, Canada *Tel:* 204-474-9495 *Fax:* 204-474-7566 *E-mail:* uofmpress@umanitoba.ca *Web Site:* uofmpress.ca, pg 422

University of Massachusetts Press, New Africa House, 180 Infirmary Way, 4th fl, Amherst, MA 01003-9289 *Web Site:* www.umasspress.com, pg 217

University of Michigan Press, 839 Greene St, Ann Arbor, MI 48104-3209 *Tel:* 734-764-4388 *Fax:* 734-615-1540 *E-mail:* um.press@umich.edu *Web Site:* www.press.umich.edu, pg 217

University of Minnesota Press, 111 Third Ave S, Suite 290, Minneapolis, MN 55401-2520 *Tel:* 612-301-1990 *Fax:* 612-301-1980 *E-mail:* ump@umn.edu *Web Site:* www.upress.umn.edu, pg 217

University of Missouri Press, 113 Heinkel Bldg, 201 S Seventh St, Columbia, MO 65211 *Tel:* 573-882-7641; 573-882-9672 (publicity & sales enquiries) *Toll Free Tel:* 800-621-2736 (orders) *Fax:* 573-884-4498 *Toll Free Fax:* 800-621-8476 (orders) *E-mail:* upress@missouri.edu; umpmarketing@missouri.edu (publicity & sales enquiries) *Web Site:* upress.missouri.edu, pg 217

University of Nebraska Press, 1225 "L" St, Suite 200, Lincoln, NE 68588-0630 *Tel:* 402-472-3581; 919-966-7449 (cust serv & foreign orders) *Toll Free Tel:* 800-848-6224 (cust serv & US orders) *Fax:* 402-472-

6214; 919-962-2704 (cust serv & foreign orders) *Toll Free Fax:* 800-272-6817 (cust serv & US orders) *E-mail:* presswebmail@unl.edu *Web Site:* www.nebraskapress.unl.edu, pg 217

University of Nevada Press, c/o University of Nevada, Continuing Educ Bldg, MS 0166, Reno, NV 89557-0166 *Tel:* 775-784-6573 *Fax:* 775-784-6200 *Web Site:* www.unpress.nevada.edu, pg 218

University of New Mexico Press, One University of New Mexico, Albuquerque, NM 87131-0001 *Tel:* 505-272-7777 *Fax:* 505-277-3343 *E-mail:* custserv@unm.edu (order dept) *Web Site:* unmpress.com, pg 218

University of New Orleans Press, 2000 Lakeshore Dr, New Orleans, LA 70148 *Tel:* 504-280-7457 *E-mail:* unopress@uno.edu *Web Site:* www.uno.edu/unopress, pg 218

The University of North Carolina Press, 116 S Boundary St, Chapel Hill, NC 27514-3808 *Tel:* 919-966-3561; 919-966-7449 (orders) *Toll Free Tel:* 800-848-3224 (orders) *Fax:* 919-962-2704 (orders) *Toll Free Fax:* 800-272-6817 (orders) *E-mail:* uncpress@unc.edu *Web Site:* uncpress.org, pg 218

University of North Texas Press, 941 Precision Dr, Denton, TX 76207 *Tel:* 940-565-2142 *Fax:* 940-369-8760 *Web Site:* untpress.unt.edu, pg 218

University of Notre Dame Press, 310 Flanner Hall, Notre Dame, IN 46556 *Tel:* 574-631-6346 *Fax:* 574-631-8148 *E-mail:* undpress@nd.edu *Web Site:* www.undpress.nd.edu, pg 219

University of Oklahoma Press, 2800 Venture Dr, Norman, OK 73069-8216 *Tel:* 405-325-2000 *Web Site:* www.oupress.com, pg 219

University of Ottawa Press (Presses de l'Université d'Ottawa), 542 King Edward Ave, Ottawa, ON K1N 6N5, Canada *Tel:* 613-562-5246 *Fax:* 613-562-5247 *E-mail:* puo-uop@uottawa.ca; acquisitions@uottawa.ca *Web Site:* press.uottawa.ca, pg 422

University of Pennsylvania Museum of Archaeology & Anthropology, 3260 South St, Philadelphia, PA 19104-6324 *Tel:* 215-898-4119; 215-898-4000 *E-mail:* publications@pennmuseum.org *Web Site:* www.penn.museum, pg 219

University of Pennsylvania Press, 3905 Spruce St, Philadelphia, PA 19104 *Tel:* 215-898-6261 *Fax:* 215-898-0404 *E-mail:* custserv@pobox.upenn.edu *Web Site:* www.pennpress.org, pg 219

University of Pittsburgh Press, 7500 Thomas Blvd, Pittsburgh, PA 15260 *Tel:* 412-383-2456 *Fax:* 412-383-2466 *E-mail:* info@upress.pitt.edu *Web Site:* www.upress.pitt.edu, pg 219

University of Regina Press, 2 Research Dr, Suite 160, Regina, SK S4S 7H9, Canada *Tel:* 306-585-4758 *Fax:* 306-585-4699 *E-mail:* uofrpress@uregina.ca *Web Site:* uofrpress.ca, pg 423

University of Rochester Press, 668 Mount Hope Ave, Rochester, NY 14620-2731 *Tel:* 585-275-0419 *Fax:* 585-271-8778 *E-mail:* boydell@boydellusa.net *Web Site:* www.urpress.com, pg 220

University of South Carolina Press, 1600 Hampton St, Suite 544, Columbia, SC 29208 *Tel:* 803-777-5245 *Toll Free Tel:* 800-768-2500 (orders) *Fax:* 803-777-0160 *Toll Free Fax:* 800-868-0740 (orders) *Web Site:* uscpress.com, pg 220

University of Tennessee Press, 323 Hodges Library, 1015 Volunteer Blvd, Knoxville, TN 37996 *Tel:* 865-974-3321 *Toll Free Tel:* 800-621-2736 (orders) *Toll Free Fax:* 800-621-2736 (orders) *E-mail:* custserv@utpress.org *Web Site:* www.utpress.org, pg 220

University of Texas at Austin, New Writers Project, Dept of English, 204 W 21 St, B-5000, Austin, TX 78712-1164 *Tel:* 512-471-4991 *Fax:* 512-471-4909 *E-mail:* newwritersproject@utexas.edu *Web Site:* liberalarts.utexas.edu/nwp, pg 567

University of Texas at El Paso, Department of Creative Writing, MFA/Department of Creative Writing, M520, University Towers, Oregon St, El Paso, TX 79968 *E-mail:* creativewriting@utep.edu *Web Site:* www.utep.edu/liberalarts/creative-writing, pg 567

University of Toronto Press, Book Publishing Div, 800 Bay St, Mezzanine, Toronto, ON M5S 3A9, Canada *Tel:* 416-978-2239 *Fax:* 416-978-4736 *E-mail:* utpbooks@utorontopress.com (orders) *Web Site:* utorontopress.com, pg 423

The University of Utah Press, J Willard Marriott Library, Suite 5400, 295 S 1500 E, Salt Lake City, UT 84112-0860 *Tel:* 801-585-9786 *Fax:* 801-581-3365 *E-mail:* hannah.new@utah.edu *Web Site:* www.uofupress.com, pg 220

University of Virginia Press, PO Box 400318, Charlottesville, VA 22904-4318 *Tel:* 434-924-3469 (cust serv) *Toll Free Tel:* 800-831-3406 *Fax:* 434-982-2655 *Toll Free Fax:* 877-288-6400 *E-mail:* vapress@virginia.edu *Web Site:* www.upress.virginia.edu, pg 220

University of Washington Press, 4333 Brooklyn Ave NE, Seattle, WA 98105-9570 *Toll Free Tel:* 800-537-5487 (orders) *Fax:* 206-543-3932; 410-516-6998 (orders) *E-mail:* uwapress@uw.edu *Web Site:* www.uwapress.uw.edu, pg 220

University of Wisconsin Press, 728 State St, Suite 443, Madison, WI 53706-1418 *Tel:* 608-263-1110; 608-263-0668 (journal orders) *Toll Free Tel:* 800-621-2736 (book orders) *Fax:* 608-263-1173 *Toll Free Fax:* 800-621-2736 (book orders) *E-mail:* uwiscpress@uwpress.wisc.edu *Web Site:* uwpress.wisc.edu, pg 221

University Press of America Inc, 4501 Forbes Blvd, Suite 200, Lanham, MD 20706 *Tel:* 301-459-3366 *Toll Free Tel:* 800-462-6420 *Web Site:* www.univpress.com, pg 221

University Press of Colorado, 1580 N Logan St, Suite 660, PMB 39883, Denver, CO 80203-1942 *Tel:* 720-406-8849 *Toll Free Tel:* 800-621-2736 (orders) *Fax:* 720-406-3443 *Web Site:* www.upcolorado.com, pg 221

University Press of Florida, 2046 NE Waldo Rd, Suite 2100, Gainesville, FL 32609 *Tel:* 352-392-1351 *Toll Free Tel:* 800-226-3822 (orders only) *Fax:* 352-392-0590 *Toll Free Fax:* 800-680-1955 (orders only) *E-mail:* press@upress.ufl.edu; orders@upress.ufl.edu *Web Site:* www.upf.com, pg 221

University Press of Kansas, 2502 Westbrooke Circle, Lawrence, KS 66045-4444 *Tel:* 785-864-4154 *Fax:* 785-864-4586 *E-mail:* upress@ku.edu *Web Site:* www.kansaspress.ku.edu, pg 221

The University Press of Kentucky, 663 S Limestone St, Lexington, KY 40508-4008 *Tel:* 859-257-8400 *Fax:* 859-323-1873 *Web Site:* www.kentuckypress.com, pg 222

University Press of Mississippi, 3825 Ridgewood Rd, Jackson, MS 39211-6492 *Tel:* 601-432-6205 *Toll Free Tel:* 800-737-7788 (orders & cust serv) *Fax:* 601-432-6217 *E-mail:* press@mississippi.edu *Web Site:* www.upress.state.ms.us, pg 222

University Publishing House, PO Box 1664, Mannford, OK 74044 *Tel:* 918-865-4726 *E-mail:* upub5@outlook.com *Web Site:* www.universitypublishinghouse.net, pg 222

University Science Books, 1305 Walt Whitman Rd, Suite 110, Melville, NY 11747 *Tel:* 703-661-1572 (cust serv & orders) *Fax:* 703-661-1501 *E-mail:* usbmail@presswarehouse.com (cust serv, orders) *Web Site:* uscibooks.aip.org, pg 222

UnKnownTruths.com Publishing Co, 8815 Conroy Windermere Rd, Suite 190, Orlando, FL 32835 *Tel:* 407-929-9207 *E-mail:* info@unknowntruths.com *Web Site:* unknowntruths.com, pg 222

John Updike Award, 633 W 155 St, New York, NY 10032 *Tel:* 212-368-5900 *E-mail:* academy@artsandletters.org *Web Site:* artsandletters.org/awards, pg 672

Upper Room Books, 1908 Grand Ave, Nashville, TN 37212 *Tel:* 615-340-7200 *Toll Free Tel:* 800-972-0433 *Web Site:* books.upperroom.org, pg 223

Upstart Books™, PO Box 7488, Madison, WI 53707 *Tel:* 608-241-1201 *Toll Free Tel:* 800-356-1200 (orders); 800-962-4463 (cust serv) *Toll Free Fax:* 800-245-1329 (orders) *E-mail:* custserv@demco.com; order@demco.com *Web Site:* www.demco.com/upstart, pg 223

Claudette Upton Scholarship, 1507-180 Dundas St W, Toronto, ON M5G 1Z8, Canada *Tel:* 416-975-1379 *E-mail:* info@editors.ca; info@reviseurs.ca; communications@editors.ca *Web Site:* www.editors.ca/about/awards/claudette-upton-scholarship, pg 672

Urim Publications, 527 Empire Blvd, Brooklyn, NY 11225-3121 *Tel:* 718-972-5449 *Fax:* 718-972-6307 *E-mail:* urimpublisher@gmail.com; orders@urimpublications.com *Web Site:* www.urimpublications.com, pg 223

US Conference of Catholic Bishops, USCCB Publishing, 3211 Fourth St NE, Washington, DC 20017 *Toll Free Tel:* 800-235-8722 *Fax:* 301-779-8596 (orders) *E-mail:* css@usccb.org *Web Site:* store.usccb.org, pg 223

US Games Systems Inc, 179 Ludlow St, Stamford, CT 06902 *Tel:* 203-353-8400 *Toll Free Tel:* 800-54-GAMES (544-2637) *Fax:* 203-353-8431 *E-mail:* info@usgamesinc.com *Web Site:* www.usgamesinc.com, pg 223

US Government Publishing Office (GPO), Superintendent of Documents, 732 N Capitol St NW, Washington, DC 20401 *Tel:* 202-512-1800 *Toll Free Tel:* 866-512-1800 (orders) *Fax:* 202-512-1998 *E-mail:* contactcenter@gpo.gov *Web Site:* www.gpo.gov; bookstore.gpo.gov (sales), pg 223

UTA Speakers, 888 Seventh Ave, Suite 922, New York, NY 10106 *Tel:* 212-659-2600; 212-645-4200 *E-mail:* utaspeakers@unitedtalent.com *Web Site:* www.utaspeakers.com, pg 487

Utah Geological Survey, 1594 W North Temple, Suite 3110, Salt Lake City, UT 84116-3154 *Tel:* 801-537-3300 *Toll Free Tel:* 888-UTAH-MAP (882-4627, bookshop) *Fax:* 801-537-3400 *E-mail:* geostore@utah.gov *Web Site:* geology.utah.gov, pg 223

Utah Original Writing Competition, 617 E South Temple, Salt Lake City, UT 84102 *Tel:* 801-236-7555 *Fax:* 801-236-7556 *Web Site:* arts.utah.gov, pg 672

Utah State University Press, 3078 Old Main Hill, Logan, UT 84322-3078 *Tel:* 435-797-1362 *Web Site:* www.usupress.com, pg 223

The William Van Wert Memorial Fiction Award, PO Box 63927, Philadelphia, PA 19147 *Tel:* 610-764-0813 *E-mail:* hiddenriverarts@gmail.com *Web Site:* www.hiddenriverarts.org; www.hiddenriverarts.com, pg 672

VanDam Inc, The VanDam Bldg, 121 W 27 St, New York, NY 10001 *Tel:* 917-297-5445 *E-mail:* info@vandam.com *Web Site:* www.vandam.com, pg 223

Vandamere Press, 3580 Morris St N, St Petersburg, FL 33713 *Tel:* 727-556-0950 *Toll Free Tel:* 800-551-7776 *Fax:* 727-556-2560 *E-mail:* orders@vandamere.com *Web Site:* www.vandamere.com, pg 223

Vanderbilt University Press, 2301 Vanderbilt Place, PMB 401813, Nashville, TN 37240-1813 *Tel:* 615-322-3585 *Toll Free Tel:* 800-848-6224 (orders only) *Fax:* 615-343-0308 *E-mail:* vupress@vanderbilt.edu *Web Site:* www.vanderbiltuniversitypress.com, pg 224

Vault.com Inc, 132 W 31 St, 16th fl, New York, NY 10001 *Tel:* 212-366-4212 *Toll Free Tel:* 800-535-2074 *Fax:* 212-366-6117 *E-mail:* mediainquiries@vault.com; customerservice@vault.com *Web Site:* www.vault.com, pg 224

Vedanta Press, 1946 Vedanta Place, Hollywood, CA 90068 *Tel:* 323-960-1728; 323-960-1736 (catalog) *Fax:* 323-465-9568 *E-mail:* vpress@vedanta.com *Web Site:* www.vedanta.com, pg 224

Vehicule Press, PO Box 42094, CP Roy, Montreal, QC H2W 2T3, Canada *Tel:* 514-844-6073 *E-mail:* vp@vehiculepress.com; admin@vehiculepress.com *Web Site:* www.vehiculepress.com, pg 424

Velazquez Press, 9682 Telstar Ave, Suite 110, El Monte, CA 91731 *Tel:* 626-448-3448 *Fax:* 626-602-3817 *E-mail:* info@academiclearningcompany.com *Web Site:* www.velazquezpress.com, pg 224

COMPANY INDEX

The Vendome Press, 244 Fifth Ave, Suite 2043, New York, NY 10001 Tel: 212-737-1857 E-mail: info@vendomepress.com Web Site: www.vendomepress.com, pg 224

Vermont College of Fine Arts MFA in Writing for Children & Young Adults Program, 36 College St, Montpelier, VT 05602 Toll Free Tel: 866-934-VCFA (934-8232) Web Site: vcfa.edu/mfa-writing-for-children-and-young-adults, pg 567

Vermont College of Fine Arts, MFA in Writing Program, 36 College St, Montpelier, VT 05602 Tel: 802-828-8840; 802-828-8839 Toll Free Tel: 866-934-VCFA (934-8232) Fax: 802-828-8649 Web Site: www.vcfa.edu, pg 567

Vermont Golden Dome Book Award, 60 Washington St, Suite 2, Barre, VT 05641 Tel: 802-636-0040 Web Site: libraries.vermont.gov/services/children_and_teens/book_awards/vtgdba, pg 672

Vermont Studio Center Writer's Program Fellowships, 80 Pearl St, Johnson, VT 05656 Tel: 802-635-2727 Fax: 802-635-2730 E-mail: writing@vermontstudiocenter.org; info@vermontstudiocenter.org Web Site: www.vermontstudiocenter.org, pg 672

Vernon Press, 1000 N West St, Suite 1200, Wilmington, DE 19801 Tel: 302-250-4440 E-mail: info@vernonpress.com Web Site: www.vernonpress.com, pg 224

Verso Books, 388 Atlantic Ave, Brooklyn, NY 11217 Tel: 718-246-8160 Fax: 718-246-8165 E-mail: verso@versobooks.com Web Site: www.versobooks.com, pg 224

Vesuvian Books, 711 Dolly Parton Pkwy, No 4313, Sevierville, TN 37864 E-mail: info@vesuvianmedia.com Web Site: www.vesuvianmedia.com, pg 224

Jill Vickers Prize, 260 Dalhousie St, Suite 204, Ottawa, ON K1N 7E4, Canada Tel: 613-562-1202 Fax: 613-241-0019 E-mail: cpsaprizes@cpsa-acsp.ca; cpsa-acsp@cpsa-acsp.ca Web Site: www.cpsa-acsp.ca, pg 672

Vicky Metcalf Award for Literature for Young People, 600-460 Richmond St W, Toronto, ON M5V 1Y1, Canada Tel: 416-504-8222 Toll Free Tel: 877-906-6548 Fax: 416-504-9090 E-mail: info@writerstrust.com Web Site: www.writerstrust.com, pg 672

Vigliano Associates Ltd, 575 Madison Ave, Suite 1006, New York, NY 10022 Tel: 212-888-8525 E-mail: info@viglianoassociates.com Web Site: viglianoassociates.com, pg 481

Viking Children's Books, c/o Penguin Random House LLC, 1745 Broadway, New York, NY 10019 Tel: 212-782-9000 Web Site: www.penguin.com/viking-childrens-books-overview/, pg 224

Viking Penguin, c/o Penguin Random House LLC, 1745 Broadway, New York, NY 10019 Tel: 212-782-9000 Web Site: www.penguin.com/overview-vikingbooks/; www.penguin.com/pamela-dorman-books-overview/; www.penguin.com/penguin-classics-overview/; www.penguin.com/penguin-life-overview/, pg 224

Village Books Literary Citizenship Award, 1200 11 St, Bellingham, WA 98225 Tel: 360-671-2626 E-mail: biblioinfo@villagebooks.com; marketing@villagebooks.com Web Site: www.villagebooks.com/literary-citizenship-award, pg 672

Vintage Books, c/o Penguin Random House LLC, 1745 Broadway, New York, NY 10019 Tel: 212-572-2420 Fax: 212-940-7390 (dom rts); 212-572-2662 (foreign rts) E-mail: vintageanchorpublicity@randomhouse.com Web Site: knopfdoubleday.com/imprint/vintage; knopfdoubleday.com, pg 225

Karen Virag Award, 1507-180 Dundas St W, Toronto, ON M5G 1Z8, Canada Tel: 416-975-1379 E-mail: info@editors.ca; info@reviseurs.ca; communications@editors.ca Web Site: www.editors.ca/about/awards/karen-virag-award-0, pg 673

Visible Ink Press®, 43311 Joy Rd, Suite 414, Canton, MI 48187-2075 Tel: 734-667-3211 Fax: 734-667-4311 E-mail: info@visibleinkpress.com Web Site: www.visibleinkpress.com, pg 225

Visual Media Alliance (VMA), 665 Third St, Suite 500, San Francisco, CA 94107-1926 Tel: 415-495-8242 Toll Free Tel: 800-659-3363 Fax: 415-520-1126 E-mail: info@vma.bz Web Site: main.vma.bz, pg 521

Visual Profile Books Inc, 389 Fifth Ave, Suite 1105, New York, NY 10016 Tel: 516-445-0116 Web Site: www.visualprofilebooks.com, pg 225

VLB editeur, 4545, rue Frontenac, 3rd fl, Montreal, QC H2H 2R7, Canada Tel: 514-849-5259 Web Site: www.edvlb.com, pg 424

Ludwig von Mises Institute, 518 W Magnolia Ave, Auburn, AL 36832 Tel: 334-321-2100 Fax: 334-321-2119 E-mail: info@mises.org Web Site: www.mises.org, pg 225

VONA Voices Summer Writing Workshops, 2820 SW 20 St, Miami, FL 33145 E-mail: info@vonavoices.org Web Site: www.vonavoices.org, pg 558

Voyager Sopris Learning Inc, 17855 Dallas Pkwy, Suite 400, Dallas, TX 75287 Tel: 303-651-2829 Toll Free Tel: 800-547-6747 Fax: 303-776-5934 Toll Free Fax: 888-819-7767 E-mail: customerservice@voyagersopris.com Web Site: www.voyagersopris.com, pg 225

Harold D Vursell Memorial Award, 633 W 155 St, New York, NY 10032 Tel: 212-368-5900 E-mail: academy@artsandletters.org Web Site: artsandletters.org/awards, pg 673

Wake Forest University Press, 2518 Reynolda Rd, Winston-Salem, NC 27106 Tel: 336-758-5448 Fax: 336-842-3853 E-mail: wfupress@wfu.edu Web Site: wfupress.wfu.edu, pg 225

Walch Education, 40 Walch Dr, Portland, ME 04103-1286 Tel: 207-772-2846 Toll Free Tel: 800-558-2846; 800-341-6094 (cust serv) Fax: 207-772-3105 Toll Free Fax: 888-991-5755 E-mail: customerservice@walch.com Web Site: www.walch.com, pg 225

Waldorf Publishing LLC, 2140 Hall Johnson Rd, No 102-345, Grapevine, TX 76051 Tel: 972-674-3131 E-mail: info@waldorfpublishing.com Web Site: www.waldorfpublishing.com, pg 226

Wales Literary Agency Inc, 1508 Tenth Ave E, No 401, Seattle, WA 98102 Tel: 206-553-9684 E-mail: waleslit@waleslit.com Web Site: www.waleslit.com, pg 481

Christopher Lightfoot Walker Award, 633 W 155 St, New York, NY 10032 Tel: 212-368-5900 E-mail: academy@artsandletters.org Web Site: artsandletters.org/awards, pg 673

Bennett H Wall Award, University of Georgia, Dept of History, Athens, GA 30602-1602 Tel: 706-542-8848 Web Site: thesha.org/wall, pg 673

Richard Wall Memorial Award, c/o The New York Public Library for the Performing Arts, 111 Amsterdam Ave, New York, NY 10023 E-mail: theatrelibraryassociation@gmail.com; tlabookawards@gmail.com Web Site: www.tla-online.org/awards/bookawards, pg 673

Edward Lewis Wallant Award, Maurice Greenberg Center for Judaic Studies, 200 Bloomfield Ave, Harry Jack Gray E 300, West Hartford, CT 06117 Tel: 860-768-4964 Fax: 860-768-5044 E-mail: mgcjs@hartford.edu Web Site: www.hartford.edu/a_and_s/greenberg/wallant, pg 673

Wambtac Communications LLC, 1512 E Santa Clara Ave, Santa Ana, CA 92705 Tel: 714-954-0580 Toll Free Tel: 800-641-3936 E-mail: wambtac@wambtac.com Web Site: www.wambtac.com; claudiasuzanne.com (prof servs), pg 445

Jesmyn Ward Prize, University of Michigan, 3277 Angell Hall, 435 S State St, Ann Arbor, MI 48109-1003 Tel: 734-764-9265 E-mail: mqr@umich.edu Web Site: sites.lsa.umich.edu/mqr/about-us/prizes, pg 673

Jo Warner Award, 1147 Fleetwood Ave, Madison, WI 53716-1417 E-mail: bfma@bfma.org Web Site: www.bfma.org/page/awardsjowarner, pg 673

WAYNE STATE UNIVERSITY PRESS

Warner Press, 2902 Enterprise Dr, Anderson, IN 46013 Tel: 765-644-7721 Toll Free Tel: 800-741-7721 (orders) Fax: 765-640-8005 E-mail: wporders@warnerpress.org Web Site: www.warnerpress.org, pg 226

Warren Wilson College, MFA Program for Writers, 701 Warren Wilson Rd, Swannanoa, NC 28778 Tel: 828-771-3717 E-mail: mfa@warren-wilson.edu Web Site: www.warren-wilson.edu/programs/mfa-in-creative-writing/, pg 567

Warwick Associates, 18340 Sonoma Hwy, Sonoma, CA 95476 Tel: 707-939-9212 Fax: 707-938-3515 E-mail: warwick@vom.com Web Site: www.warwickassociates.com, pg 481

George Washington Prize, c/o Fred W Smith National Library, 3600 Mount Vernon Memorial Hwy, Mount Vernon, VA 22121 Tel: 703-799-8686 Web Site: www.mountvernon.org/library/george-washington-prize, pg 673

Washington State Book Awards, c/o The Seattle Public Library, 1000 Fourth Ave, Seattle, WA 98104-1109 Web Site: washingtoncenterforthebook.org, pg 673

Washington State University Press, Cooper Publications Bldg, 2300 Grimes Way, Pullman, WA 99164-5910 Tel: 509-335-7880 Toll Free Tel: 800-354-7360 (orders) E-mail: wsupress@wsu.edu Web Site: wsupress.wsu.edu, pg 226

Water Environment Federation, 601 Wythe St, Alexandria, VA 22314-1994 Tel: 703-684-2400 Toll Free Tel: 800-666-0206 (cust serv) Fax: 703-684-2492 E-mail: inquiry@wef.org Web Site: www.wef.org, pg 226

Water Resources Publications LLC, PO Box 630026, Highlands Ranch, CO 80163-0026 Tel: 720-873-0171 Toll Free Tel: 800-736-2405 Fax: 720-873-0173 Toll Free Fax: 800-616-1971 E-mail: info@wrpllc.com Web Site: www.wrpllc.com, pg 226

WaterBrook, 10807 New Allegiance Dr, Suite 500, Colorado Springs, CO 80921 Tel: 719-590-4999 Toll Free Tel: 800-603-7051 (orders) Fax: 719-590-8977 E-mail: info@waterbrookmultnomah.com Web Site: waterbrookmultnomah.com, pg 226

Watermark Publishing, 1000 Bishop St, Suite 806, Honolulu, HI 96813 Tel: 808-587-7766 Toll Free Tel: 866-900-BOOK (900-2665) Fax: 808-521-3461 E-mail: info@bookshawaii.net Web Site: www.bookshawaii.net, pg 226

Waterside Productions Inc, 2055 Oxford Ave, Cardiff, CA 92007 Tel: 760-632-9190 Fax: 760-632-9295 E-mail: admin@waterside.com Web Site: www.waterside.com, pg 481

Watkins/Loomis Agency Inc, PO Box 20925, New York, NY 10025 Tel: 212-532-0080 Fax: 646-383-2449 E-mail: assistant@watkinsloomis.com; permissions@watkinsloomis.com Web Site: watkins-loomis.squarespace.com, pg 481

Watson-Guptill, c/o Ten Speed Press, 6001 Shellmount St, Suite 600, Emeryville, CA 94608 Web Site: crownpublishing.com/archives/imprint/watson-guptill, pg 226

The Robert Watson Literary Prizes in Fiction & Poetry, MFA Writing Program, The Greensboro Review, UNC-Greensboro, 3302 MHRA Bldg, Greensboro, NC 27402-6170 Tel: 336-334-5459 Web Site: www.greensbororeview.org, pg 673

Waveland Press Inc, 4180 IL Rte 83, Suite 101, Long Grove, IL 60047-9580 Tel: 847-634-0081 Fax: 847-634-9501 E-mail: info@waveland.com Web Site: www.waveland.com, pg 226

Waxman Literary Agency, 443 Park Ave S, No 1004, New York, NY 10016 Tel: 212-675-5556 Web Site: www.waxmanliteraryagency.com, pg 481

Wayne State University Press, Leonard N Simons Bldg, 4809 Woodward Ave, Detroit, MI 48201-1309 Tel: 313-577-6120 Toll Free Tel: 800-978-7323 Fax: 313-577-6131 E-mail: bookorders@wayne.edu Web Site: www.wsupress.wayne.edu, pg 226

Wayside Publishing, 2 Stonewood Dr, Freeport, ME 04032 *Toll Free Tel:* 888-302-2519 *E-mail:* info@waysidepublishing.com; support@waysidepublishing.com *Web Site:* waysidepublishing.com, pg 227

The Weatherford Awards, Loyal Jones Appalachian Ctr, 101 Chestnut St, Berea, KY 40404 *Tel:* 859-985-3000 *Web Site:* www.berea.edu/centers/loyal-jones-appalachian-center/awards/weatherford-award, pg 673

Weigl Educational Publishers Ltd, 6325 Tenth St SE, Calgary, AB T2H 2Z9, Canada *Tel:* 403-233-7747 *Toll Free Tel:* 800-668-0766 *Fax:* 403-233-7769 *E-mail:* orders@weigl.com *Web Site:* www.weigl.ca, pg 424

Cherry Weiner Literary Agency, 925 Oak Bluff Ct, Dacula, GA 30019-6660 *Tel:* 732-446-2096 *E-mail:* cwliteraryagency@gmail.com, pg 481

The Weingel-Fidel Agency, 310 E 46 St, Suite 21-E, New York, NY 10017 *Tel:* 212-599-2959, pg 481

Welcome Books, 300 Park Ave S, New York, NY 10010 *Tel:* 212-387-3400 *Fax:* 212-387-3535 *Web Site:* www.rizzoliusa.com/publisher/rizzoli/imprint/wb, pg 227

Welcome Rain Publishers LLC, 217 Thompson St, Suite 473, New York, NY 10012 *Tel:* 212-686-1909 *Web Site:* welcomerain.com, pg 227

Well-Trained Mind Press, 18021 The Glebe Lane, Charles City, VA 23030 *Tel:* 804-593-0306 *Toll Free Tel:* 877-322-3445 *Fax:* 804-829-5704 *E-mail:* support@welltrainedmind.com *Web Site:* welltrainedmind.com, pg 227

Rene Wellek Prize, 323 E Wacker Dr, No 642, Chicago, IL 60601 *Tel:* 312-600-8072 *E-mail:* info@acla.org *Web Site:* www.acla.org/prize-awards/rené-wellek-prize, pg 674

Wellington Press, 3811 Long & Winding Rd, Tallahassee, FL 32309 *E-mail:* peacegames@aol.com *Web Site:* www.peacegames.com, pg 227

WendyLynn & Co, 2705 Willow Hill Rd, Annapolis, MD 21403 *Tel:* 410-533-5766 *Web Site:* wendylynn.com, pg 486

Wergle Flomp Humor Poetry Contest, 351 Pleasant St, Suite B, PMB 222, Northampton, MA 01060-3998 *Tel:* 413-320-1847 *Toll Free Tel:* 866-WINWRIT (946-9748) *Fax:* 413-280-0539 *Web Site:* www.winningwriters.com/our-contests/wergle-flomp-humor-poetry-contest-free, pg 674

Eliot Werner Publications Inc, 31 Willow Lane, Clinton Corners, NY 12514 *Tel:* 845-266-4241 *Fax:* 845-266-3317 *E-mail:* eliotwerner217@gmail.com *Web Site:* www.eliotwerner.com, pg 227

Toby Wertheim, 240 E 76 St, New York, NY 10021 *Tel:* 212-472-8587 *E-mail:* tobywertheim@yahoo.com, pg 445

Wesley-Logan Prize in African Diaspora History, 400 "A" St SE, Washington, DC 20003 *Tel:* 202-544-2422 *E-mail:* awards@historians.org *Web Site:* www.historians.org/award-grant/wesley-logan-prize/, pg 674

Wesleyan Publishing House, 13300 Olio Rd, Fishers, IN 46037 *Tel:* 317-774-3853 *Toll Free Tel:* 800-493-7539 *Fax:* 317-774-3865 *Toll Free Fax:* 800-788-3535 *E-mail:* wph@wesleyan.org *Web Site:* www.wesleyan.org/books, pg 227

Wesleyan University Press, 215 Long Lane, Middletown, CT 06459-0433 *Tel:* 860-685-7712 *Fax:* 860-685-7712 *Web Site:* www.wesleyan.edu/wespress, pg 227

West Academic, 444 Cedar St, Suite 700, St Paul, MN 55101 *Toll Free Tel:* 877-888-1330 *E-mail:* customerservice@westacademic.com; support@westacademic.com; media@westacademic.com *Web Site:* www.westacademic.com, pg 227

West Margin Press, 4507 Charlotte Ave, Suite 100, Nashville, TN 37209 *Tel:* 612-255-BOOK (255-2665) *E-mail:* info@turnerpublishing.com; admin@turnerpublishing.com; marketing@turnerpublishing.com; orders@turnerpublishing.com *Web Site:* turnerpublishing.com, pg 227

West Virginia University Press, West Virginia University, PO Box 6295, Morgantown, WV 26506-6295 *Tel:* 304-293-8400 *Web Site:* www.wvupress.com, pg 228

Western Edge Press, 126 Candelario St, Santa Fe, NM 87501 *Tel:* 505-988-7214 *E-mail:* westernedge@santa-fe.net *Web Site:* www.westernedgepress.com; www.shermanasher.com, pg 228

Western Heritage Awards (Wrangler Award), 1700 NE 63 St, Oklahoma City, OK 73111 *Tel:* 405-478-2250 *Fax:* 405-478-4714 *E-mail:* info@nationalcowboymuseum.org *Web Site:* nationalcowboymuseum.org, pg 674

Western Pennsylvania Genealogical Society, 4400 Forbes Ave, Pittsburgh, PA 15213-4007 *Tel:* 412-687-6811 (answering machine) *E-mail:* info@wpgs.org *Web Site:* www.wpgs.org, pg 228

Western Reflections Publishing Co, 951B N Hwy 149, Lake City, CO 81235 *Tel:* 970-944-0110 *E-mail:* publisher@westernreflectionspublishing.com; westernreflectionspublishing@gmail.com *Web Site:* www.westernreflectionspublishing.com, pg 228

Western States Arts Federation (WESTAF), 1536 Wynkoop St, Suite 522, Denver, CO 80202 *Tel:* 303-629-1166 *E-mail:* staff@westaf.org *Web Site:* www.westaf.org, pg 526

Western Writers of America Inc (WWA), 271 CR 219, Encampment, WY 82325 *Tel:* 307-329-8942 *Web Site:* westernwriters.org, pg 521

Westernlore Press, PO Box 35305, Tucson, AZ 85740-5305 *Tel:* 520-297-5491, pg 228

Westminster John Knox Press (WJK), 100 Witherspoon St, Louisville, KY 40202-1396 *Tel:* 502-569-5052 *Toll Free Tel:* 800-523-1631 (US & CN) *Fax:* 502-569-8308 *Toll Free Fax:* 800-541-5113 (US & CN) *E-mail:* customer_service@wjkbooks.com; orders@wjkbooks.com *Web Site:* www.wjkbooks.com, pg 228

Hilary Weston Writers' Trust Prize for Nonfiction, 600-460 Richmond St W, Toronto, ON M5V 1Y1, Canada *Tel:* 416-504-8222 *Toll Free Tel:* 877-906-6548 *Fax:* 416-504-9090 *E-mail:* info@writerstrust.com *Web Site:* www.writerstrust.com, pg 674

Weston International Award, 600-460 Richmond St W, Toronto, ON M5V 1Y1, Canada *Tel:* 416-504-8222 *Toll Free Tel:* 877-906-6548 *Fax:* 416-504-9090 *E-mail:* info@writerstrust.com *Web Site:* westoninternationalaward.com, pg 674

Westwood Creative Artists Ltd, 386 Huron St, Toronto, ON M5S 2G6, Canada *Tel:* 416-964-3302 *Fax:* 416-964-3302 *E-mail:* wca_office@wcaltd.com *Web Site:* www.wcaltd.com, pg 481

Charles A Weyerhauser Book Award, 2925 Academy Rd, Durham, NC 27705 *Tel:* 919-682-9319 *Fax:* 919-682-2349 *Web Site:* foresthistory.org/awards-fellowships/weyerhaeuser-award, pg 674

Wheatherstone Press, PO Box 257, Portland, OR 97207 *Tel:* 503-244-8929 *Fax:* 503-244-9795 *Web Site:* www.wheatherstonepress.com; www.relocationbooks.com, pg 228

Barbara Mlotek Whelehan, 7064 SE Cricket Ct, Stuart, FL 34997 *Tel:* 954-554-0765 (cell); 772-463-0818 (home) *E-mail:* barbarawhelehan@bellsouth.net, pg 445

Whiskey Creek Press, 221 River St, 9th fl, Suite 9137, Hoboken, NJ 07030 *Tel:* 212-431-5455 *E-mail:* publisher@whiskeycreekpress.com *Web Site:* whiskeycreekpress.com, pg 228

Whitaker House, 1030 Hunt Valley Circle, New Kensington, PA 15068 *Tel:* 724-334-7000 *Toll Free Tel:* 800-444-4484 (sales) *Fax:* 724-334-1200 *E-mail:* publisher@whitakerhouse.com; sales@whitakerhouse.com *Web Site:* www.whitakerhouse.com, pg 228

E B White Award, 633 W 155 St, New York, NY 10032 *Tel:* 212-368-5900 *E-mail:* academy@artsandletters.org *Web Site:* artsandletters.org/awards, pg 674

The Edmund White Award for Debut Fiction, 511 Avenue of the Americas, No D36, New York, NY 10011 *E-mail:* awards@publishingtriangle.org; info@publishingtriangle.org; publishingtriangle@gmail.com *Web Site:* publishingtriangle.org/awards/edmund-white-debut-fiction, pg 674

White Pine Press, PO Box 236, Buffalo, NY 14201 *Tel:* 716-573-8202 *E-mail:* wpine@whitepine.org *Web Site:* www.whitepine.org, pg 228

William Allen White Children's Book Awards, One Kellogg Circle, Emporia, KS 66801-5092 *Tel:* 620-341-5040 *E-mail:* wawbookaward@emporia.edu *Web Site:* wawchildrensbookaward.com, pg 674

Whitecap Books, 314 W Cordova St, Suite 209, Vancouver, BC V6B 1E8, Canada *Tel:* 604-681-6181 *Web Site:* www.whitecap.ca, pg 424

The Bill Whitehead Award for Lifetime Achievement, 511 Avenue of the Americas, No D36, New York, NY 10011 *E-mail:* awards@publishingtriangle.org; info@publishingtriangle.org; publishingtriangle@gmail.com *Web Site:* publishingtriangle.org/awards/bill-whitehead-award/, pg 675

Fred Whitehead Award for Best Design of a Trade Book, PO Box 130294, Spring, TX 77393 *Web Site:* texasinstituteofletters.org, pg 675

Whiting Awards, 16 Court St, Suite 2308, Brooklyn, NY 11241 *Tel:* 718-701-5962 *E-mail:* info@whiting.org *Web Site:* www.whiting.org, pg 675

Whiting Creative Nonfiction Grant, 16 Court St, Suite 2308, Brooklyn, NY 11241 *Tel:* 718-701-5962 *E-mail:* nonfiction@whiting.org; info@whiting.org *Web Site:* www.whiting.org, pg 675

Whiting Literary Magazine Prizes, 16 Court St, Suite 2308, Brooklyn, NY 11241 *Tel:* 718-701-5962 *E-mail:* info@whiting.org *Web Site:* www.whiting.org/writers/whiting-literary-magazine-prizes, pg 675

Whittier Publications Inc, 121 Regent Dr, Lido Beach, NY 11561 *Tel:* 516-432-8120 *Toll Free Tel:* 800-897-TEXT (897-8398) *Fax:* 516-889-0341 *E-mail:* info@whitbooks.com *Web Site:* www.whitbooks.com, pg 229

Whole Person Associates Inc, 101 W Second St, Suite 203, Duluth, MN 55802 *Tel:* 218-727-0500 *Toll Free Tel:* 800-247-6789 *Fax:* 218-727-0505 *E-mail:* books@wholeperson.com *Web Site:* www.wholeperson.com, pg 229

Jon Whyte Memorial Essay Prize, 11759 Groat Rd NW, Edmonton, AB T5M 3K6, Canada *Tel:* 780-422-8174 *Toll Free Tel:* 800-665-5354 (AB only) *E-mail:* mail@writersguild.ab.ca *Web Site:* writersguild.ca, pg 675

Wichita State University Playwriting Contest, 1845 Fairmount St, Box 153, Wichita, KS 67260-0153 *Tel:* 316-978-3360 *Web Site:* www.wichita.edu, pg 675

Wide World of Maps Inc, 2133 E Indian School Rd, Phoenix, AZ 85016 *Tel:* 602-279-2323 *Toll Free Tel:* 800-279-7654 *Web Site:* www.maps4u.com, pg 229

Wide World Publishing, PO Box 476, San Carlos, CA 94070-0476 *Tel:* 650-593-2839 *E-mail:* wwpbl@aol.com *Web Site:* wideworldpublishing.com, pg 229

Markus Wiener Publishers Inc, 231 Nassau St, Princeton, NJ 08542 *Tel:* 609-921-1141 *E-mail:* publisher@markuswiener.com *Web Site:* www.markuswiener.com, pg 229

Michael Wiese Productions, 12400 Ventura Blvd, No 1111, Studio City, CA 91604 *Tel:* 818-379-8799 *Toll Free Tel:* 800-833-5738 (orders) *Fax:* 818-986-3408 *E-mail:* mwpsales@earthlink.net; fulfillment@portcity.com *Web Site:* www.mwp.com, pg 229

Thornton Wilder Prize for Translation, 633 W 155 St, New York, NY 10032 *Tel:* 212-368-5900 *E-mail:* academy@artsandletters.org *Web Site:* artsandletters.org/awards, pg 675

Wilderness Adventures Press Inc, 45 Buckskin Rd, Belgrade, MT 59714 *Tel:* 406-388-0112 *Toll Free Tel:* 866-400-2012 *Toll Free Fax:* 866-400-2013 *E-mail:* books@wildadvpress.com *Web Site:* store.wildadvpress.com, pg 229

COMPANY INDEX

Wildflower Press, c/o Oakbrook Press, 3301 S Valley Dr, Rapid City, SD 57703 *Tel:* 605-381-6385 *E-mail:* info@wildflowerpress.org *Web Site:* www.wildflowerpress.org, pg 229

Wildside Press LLC, 7945 MacArthur Blvd, Suite 215, Cabin John, MD 20818 *Tel:* 301-762-1305 *E-mail:* wildside@wildsidepress.com *Web Site:* wildsidepress.com, pg 229

Wiley-Blackwell, 111 River St, Suite 300, Hoboken, NJ 07030-5774 *Tel:* 201-748-6000 *Toll Free Tel:* 800-567-4797 *Fax:* 201-748-6088 *Toll Free Fax:* 800-565-6802 *E-mail:* info@wiley.com *Web Site:* www.wiley.com, pg 229

John Wiley & Sons Canada Ltd, 90 Eglinton Ave E, Suite 300, Toronto, ON M4P 2Y3, Canada *Tel:* 416-236-4433 *Toll Free Tel:* 800-567-4797 *Fax:* 416-236-4446 *Toll Free Fax:* 800-565-6802 (orders) *E-mail:* canada@wiley.com *Web Site:* www.wiley.com, pg 424

John Wiley & Sons Inc, 111 River St, Hoboken, NJ 07030-5774 *Tel:* 201-748-6000 *Toll Free Tel:* 800-225-5945 (cust serv) *Fax:* 201-748-6088 *Web Site:* www.wiley.com, pg 230

John Wiley & Sons Inc Global Education, 111 River St, Suite 300, Hoboken, NJ 07030-5774 *Tel:* 201-748-6000 *Toll Free Tel:* 800-567-4797 *Fax:* 201-748-6008 *Toll Free Fax:* 800-565-6802 *E-mail:* info@wiley.com *Web Site:* www.wiley.com, pg 230

John Wiley & Sons Inc Professional Development, 111 River St, Suite 300, Hoboken, NJ 07030-5774 *Tel:* 201-748-6000 *Toll Free Tel:* 800-567-4797 *Fax:* 201-748-6088 *Toll Free Fax:* 800-565-6802 *E-mail:* info@wiley.com *Web Site:* www.wiley.com, pg 230

Wilfrid Laurier University Press, 75 University Ave W, Waterloo, ON N2L 3C5, Canada *Tel:* 519-884-0710 *Toll Free Tel:* 866-836-5551 (CN & US) *Fax:* 519-725-1399 *E-mail:* press@wlu.ca *Web Site:* www.wlupress.wlu.ca, pg 424

Willamette Writers, 5331 SW Macadam Ave, Suite 258, PMB 215, Portland, OR 97239 *Tel:* 971-200-5385 *E-mail:* wilwrite@willamettewriters.org *Web Site:* willamettewriters.org, pg 521

Willamette Writers' Conference, 5331 SW Macadam Ave, Suite 258, PMB 215, Portland, OR 97239 *Tel:* 971-200-5385 *E-mail:* wilwrite@willamettewriters.org *Web Site:* willamettewriters.org, pg 558

William Carey Publishing, 10 W Dry Creek Circle, Littleton, CO 80120 *Tel:* 720-372-7036 *E-mail:* publishing@wclbooks.com *Web Site:* www.missionbooks.org, pg 230

William Flanagan Memorial Creative Persons Center, 14 Harrison St, New York, NY 10013 *Tel:* 212-226-2020 *Fax:* 212-226-5551 *E-mail:* info@albeefoundation.org *Web Site:* www.albeefoundation.org, pg 675

Williams & Company Book Publishers, 1317 Pine Ridge Dr, Savannah, GA 31406 *Tel:* 912-352-0404 *E-mail:* bookpub@comcast.net, pg 230

Oscar Williams/Gene Derwood Award, 909 Third Ave, New York, NY 10022 *Tel:* 212-686-0010 *Fax:* 212-532-8528 *E-mail:* info@nycommunitytrust.org *Web Site:* www.nycommunitytrust.org, pg 675

Roger Williams Agency, 17 Paddock Dr, Lawrence Twp, NJ 08648 *Tel:* 860-973-2439 *E-mail:* roger@rogerwilliamsagency.com *Web Site:* www.rogerwilliamsagency.com, pg 482

William Carlos Williams Award, 119 Smith St, Brooklyn, NY 11201 *Tel:* 212-254-9628 *E-mail:* info@poetrysociety.org *Web Site:* poetrysociety.org/awards, pg 675

Willow Creek Press, 9931 Hwy 70 W, Minocqua, WI 54548 *Tel:* 715-358-7010 *Toll Free Tel:* 800-850-9453 *Fax:* 715-358-2807 *E-mail:* info@willowcreekpress.com *Web Site:* www.willowcreekpress.com; www.wcpretail.com, pg 230

Lydia Wills LLC, 5344 N Paulina, 3F, Chicago, IL 60660 *Tel:* 917-292-8314 *E-mail:* lydiawills@gmail.com *Web Site:* www.lydiawills.com, pg 482

Wilshire Book Co, 22647 Ventura Blvd, No 314, Woodland Hills, CA 91364-1416 *Tel:* 818-700-1522 *E-mail:* sales@mpowers.com *Web Site:* www.mpowers.com, pg 230

Gary Wilson Award for Short Fiction, Dept of English, TCU Box 297270, Fort Worth, TX 76129 *E-mail:* descant@tcu.edu *Web Site:* www.descant.tcu.edu, pg 676

The H W Wilson Foundation, 750 Third Ave, 13th fl, New York, NY 10017 *Tel:* 212-418-8473 *Web Site:* www.thwwf.org, pg 526

Sheri-D Wilson Golden Beret Award, 2 Carlton St, Suite 1519, Toronto, ON M5B 1J3, Canada *Tel:* 416-504-1657 *E-mail:* admin@poets.ca *Web Site:* poets.ca/awards/goldenberet, pg 676

Herbert Warren Wind Book Award, 77 Liberty Corner Rd, Liberty Corner, NJ 07931-0708 *Tel:* 908-326-1207 *Web Site:* www.usga.org, pg 676

Windham-Campbell Prizes, Beinecke Rare Book & Manuscript Library, 121 Wall St, New Haven, CT 06511 *Fax:* 203-432-9033 *Web Site:* windhamcampbell.org, pg 676

Windhaven®, 466 Rte 10, Orford, NH 03777 *Tel:* 603-512-9251 (cell) *Web Site:* www.windhavenpress.com, pg 445

Windsor Books, 260 W Main St, Suite 5, Bayshore, NY 11706 *Tel:* 631-665-6688 *Toll Free Tel:* 800-321-5934 *E-mail:* windsor.books@att.net *Web Site:* www.windsorpublishing.com, pg 230

Wings Press, PO Box 591176, San Antonio, TX 78259 *E-mail:* wingspresspublishing@gmail.com *Web Site:* www.wingspress.com, pg 231

Justin Winsor Library History Essay Award, 225 N Michigan Ave, Suite 1300, Chicago, IL 60601 *Tel:* 312-944-6780 *Toll Free Tel:* 800-545-2433 *Fax:* 312-440-9374 *E-mail:* ala@ala.org *Web Site:* www.ala.org/rt/lhrt/awards/windsor-essay-award; www.ala.org/rt/lhrt; www.ala.org, pg 676

Winter Words Author Series, 110 E Hallam St, Suite 116, Aspen, CO 81611 *Tel:* 970-925-3122 *Fax:* 970-920-5700 *E-mail:* aspenwords@aspeninstitute.org *Web Site:* www.aspenwords.org, pg 558

Winters Publishing, 705 E Washington St, Greensburg, IN 47240 *Tel:* 812-663-4948 *Toll Free Tel:* 800-457-3230 *Fax:* 812-663-4948 *E-mail:* winterspublishing@gmail.com *Web Site:* www.winterspublishing.com, pg 231

Winterthur Museum, Garden & Library, 5105 Kennett Pike, Winterthur, DE 19735 *Tel:* 302-888-4663 *Toll Free Tel:* 800-448-3883 *Fax:* 302-888-4950 *Web Site:* www.winterthur.org, pg 231

Winterwolf Press, 8635 W Sahara Ave, Suite 425, Las Vegas, NV 89117 *Tel:* 725-222-3442 *E-mail:* info@winterwolfpress.com *Web Site:* www.winterwolfpress.com, pg 231

Wisconsin Department of Public Instruction, 125 S Webster St, Madison, WI 53703 *Tel:* 608-266-2188 *Toll Free Tel:* 800-441-4563 (US only); 800-243-8782 (US only) *E-mail:* pubsales@dpi.wi.gov *Web Site:* pubsales.dpi.wi.gov, pg 231

Wisdom Publications Inc, 199 Elm St, Somerville, MA 02144 *Tel:* 617-776-7416 *Toll Free Tel:* 800-272-4050 (orders) *Fax:* 617-776-7841 *E-mail:* submission@wisdompubs.org *Web Site:* wisdomexperience.org, pg 231

Charlotte Wise Memorial, PO Box 36128, North Chesterfield, VA 23235-3533 *E-mail:* contest@poetrysocietyofvirginia.org; info@poetryvirginia.org *Web Site:* www.poetrysocietyofvirginia.org, pg 676

Wizards of the Coast LLC, 1600 Lind Ave SW, Suite 400, Renton, WA 98057-3305 *Tel:* 425-226-6500; 425-204-8069 *Toll Free Tel:* 800-324-6496 *E-mail:* press@wizards.com *Web Site:* company.wizards.com, pg 231

WLA Literary Award, 112 Owen Rd, Unit 6437, Monona, WI 53716 *Tel:* 608-245-3640 *E-mail:* wla@wisconsinlibraries.org *Web Site:* www.wisconsinlibraries.org, pg 676

WME, 11 Madison Ave, New York, NY 10010 *Tel:* 212-586-5100 *Web Site:* www.wmeagency.com, pg 482

WNBA Pannell Award for Excellence in Children's Bookselling, PO Box 237, FDR Sta, New York, NY 10150-0231 *Toll Free Tel:* 866-610-WNBA (610-9622) *E-mail:* pannell@wnba-books.org *Web Site:* wnba-books.org/pannell-award, pg 676

WNBA Writing Contest, PO Box 237, FDR Sta, New York, NY 10150-0231 *Toll Free Tel:* 866-610-WNBA (610-9622) *E-mail:* contest@wnba-books.org; info@wnba-books.org *Web Site:* wnba-books.org/contest, pg 676

WNDB Internship Grants, 10319 Westlake Dr, No 104, Bethesda, MD 20817 *Tel:* 701-404-WNDB (404-9632, voicemail only) *E-mail:* internships@diversebooks.org *Web Site:* diversebooks.org/our-programs/internship-grants, pg 676

Alan Wofsy Fine Arts, 1109 Geary Blvd, San Francisco, CA 94109 *Tel:* 415-292-6500 *Toll Free Tel:* 800-660-6403 *Fax:* 415-292-6594 (off & cust serv); 510-251-1840 (acctg) *E-mail:* order@art-books.com (orders); editeur@earthlink.net (edit); beauxarts@earthlink.net (cust serv) *Web Site:* www.art-books.com, pg 231

Thomas Wolfe Fiction Prize, PO Box 21591, Winston-Salem, NC 27120-1591 *Tel:* 336-293-8844 *E-mail:* mail@ncwriters.org *Web Site:* www.ncwriters.org, pg 677

Helen & Kurt Wolff Translator's Prize, 30 Irving Place, New York, NY 10003 *Tel:* 212-439-8700 *Fax:* 212-439-8705 *E-mail:* info-newyork@goethe.de *Web Site:* www.goethe.de/ins/us/enkul/ser/uef/hkw.html, pg 677

Tobias Wolff Award for Fiction, Mail Stop 9053, Western Washington University, Bellingham, WA 98225 *Tel:* 360-650-4863 *E-mail:* bellingham.review@wwu.edu *Web Site:* bhreview.org; bhreview.submittable.com, pg 677

Wolfman Books, 410 13 St, Oakland, CA 94612 *Tel:* 510-679-4650 *E-mail:* hello@wolfmanhomerepair.com *Web Site:* wolfmanhomerepair.com, pg 232

Wolters Kluwer Law & Business, 76 Ninth Ave, 7th fl, New York, NY 10011-5201 *Tel:* 212-771-0600; 301-698-7100 (cust serv outside US) *Toll Free Tel:* 800-234-1660 (cust serv) *E-mail:* customer.service@wolterskluwer.com; lrusmedia@wolterskluwer.com *Web Site:* lrus.wolterskluwer.com, pg 232

Wolters Kluwer US Corp, 2700 Lake Cook Rd, Riverwoods, IL 60015 *Tel:* 847-267-7000 *E-mail:* info@wolterskluwer.com *Web Site:* www.wolterskluwer.com, pg 232

Women Who Write Inc, PO Box 652, Madison, NJ 07940-0652 *Web Site:* www.womenwhowrite.org, pg 522

Women's Fiction Writers Association (WFWA), PO Box 190, Jefferson, OR 97352 *E-mail:* communications@womensfictionwriters.org; membership@womensfictionwriters.org; programs@womensfictionwriters.org *Web Site:* www.womensfictionwriters.org, pg 522

Women's National Book Association Award, PO Box 237, FDR Sta, New York, NY 10150-0231 *Toll Free Tel:* 866-610-WNBA (610-9622) *Web Site:* wnba-books.org/wnba-award, pg 677

Women's National Book Association Inc, PO Box 237, FDR Sta, New York, NY 10150-0231 *Toll Free Tel:* 866-610-WNBA (610-9622) *E-mail:* info@wnba-books.org *Web Site:* wnba-books.org, pg 522

The J Howard & Barbara M J Wood Prize, 61 W Superior St, Chicago, IL 60654 *Tel:* 312-787-7070 *Web Site:* www.poetryfoundation.org/poetrymagazine/prizes, pg 677

Wood Lake Publishing Inc, 485 Beaver Lake Rd, Kelowna, BC V4V 1S5, Canada *Tel:* 250-766-2778 *Toll Free Tel:* 800-663-2775 (orders & cust serv) *Fax:* 250-766-2736 *Toll Free Fax:* 888-841-9991 (orders & cust serv) E-mail: info@woodlake.com; customerservice@woodlake.com Web Site: www.woodlake.com, pg 425

Woodbine House, 6510 Bells Mill Rd, Bethesda, MD 20817 Tel: 301-897-3570 Toll Free Tel: 800-843-7323 Fax: 301-897-5838 E-mail: info@woodbinehouse.com Web Site: www.woodbinehouse.com, pg 232

Woodrow Wilson Center Press, One Woodrow Wilson Plaza, 1300 Pennsylvania Ave NW, Washington, DC 20004-3027 Tel: 202-691-4122 Web Site: wilsoncenter.org/woodrow-wilson-center-press, pg 232

Carter G Woodson Book Awards, 8555 16 St, Suite 500, Silver Spring, MD 20910 Tel: 301-588-1800 E-mail: ncss@ncss.org Web Site: www.socialstudies.org/membership/awards/carter-g-woodson-book-awards, pg 677

The Jacqueline Woodson Award for LGBTQ+ Children's/YA Literature, 511 Avenue of the Americas, No D36, New York, NY 10011 E-mail: awards@publishingtriangle.org; info@publishingtriangle.org; publishingtriangle@gmail.com Web Site: publishingtriangle.org/awards/the-jacqueline-woodson-award-for-lgbtq-childrens-ya-literature, pg 677

WoodstockArts, PO Box 1342, Woodstock, NY 12498 Tel: 845-679-8111; 845-679-8555 Fax: 419-793-3452 E-mail: info@woodstockarts.com Web Site: woodstockarts.com, pg 232

C Vann Woodward Award, University of Georgia, Dept of History, Athens, GA 30602-1602 Tel: 706-542-8848 Web Site: thesha.org/woodward, pg 677

The Word, A Storytelling Sanctuary Inc, 757 E 20 Ave, Suite 370-335, Denver, CO 80205 E-mail: info@thewordfordiversity.org Web Site: www.thewordfordiversity.org, pg 522

Word Works Washington Prize, PO Box 42164, Washington, DC 20015 E-mail: editor@wordworksbooks.org Web Site: www.wordworksbooks.org, pg 677

WordCo Indexing Services Inc, 66 Franklin St, Norwich, CT 06360 E-mail: office@wordco.com Web Site: www.wordco.com, pg 445

Words into Print, 208 Java St, 5th fl, Brooklyn, NY 11222 E-mail: query@wordsintoprint.org Web Site: wordsintoprint.org, pg 445

Wordsmith, Open Book Bldg, Suite 200, 1011 Washington Ave S, Minneapolis, MN 55415 Tel: 612-215-2575 Fax: 612-215-2576 E-mail: loft@loft.org Web Site: loft.org/conference/about-wordsmith, pg 558

Workers Compensation Research Institute, 955 Massachusetts Ave, Cambridge, MA 02139 Tel: 617-661-9274 Fax: 617-661-9284 E-mail: wcri@wcrinet.org Web Site: www.wcrinet.org, pg 232

Working With Words, 5320 SW Mayfair Ct, Beaverton, OR 97005 Tel: 503-626-4998 E-mail: editor@zzz.com, pg 445

Workman Publishing, 1290 Avenue of the Americas, New York, NY 10104 Toll Free Tel: 800-759-0190 Fax: 212-364-0950 E-mail: workman-inquiry@hbgusa.com Web Site: www.hachettebookgroup.com/imprint/workman-publishing-company/, pg 232

World Almanac®, 307 W 36 St, 11 fl, New York, NY 10018 Tel: 212-643-6816 Fax: 212-643-6819 E-mail: info@skyhorsepublishing.com Web Site: skyhorsepublishing.com, pg 233

World Bank Publications, 1818 "H" St NW, Washington, DC 20433 Tel: 202-473-1000 Toll Free Tel: 800-645-7247 (cust serv) E-mail: books@worldbank.org; pubrights@worldbank.org (foreign rts) Web Site: www.worldbank.org/en/research, pg 233

World Book Inc, 180 N LaSalle, Suite 900, Chicago, IL 60601 Tel: 312-729-5800 Toll Free Tel: 800-967-5325 (consumer sales, US); 800-975-3250 (school & lib sales, US); 800-837-5365 (school & lib sales, CN) Toll Free Fax: 888-922-3766 E-mail: customerservice@worldbook.com Web Site: www.worldbook.com, pg 233

World Citizens, PO Box 131, Mill Valley, CA 94942-0131 Tel: 415-380-8020; 415-233-2822 (direct), pg 233

World Class Speakers & Entertainers, 5158 Clareton Dr, Suite 1034, Agoura Hills, CA 91376 Tel: 818-991-5400 E-mail: wcse@wcspeakers.com Web Site: www.wcspeakers.com, pg 487

World Fantasy Awards, 3519 Glen Ave, Palmer Township, PA 18045-5812 Web Site: www.worldfantasy.org, pg 677

World Resources Institute, 10 "G" St NE, Suite 800, Washington, DC 20002 Tel: 202-729-7600 Fax: 202-729-7610 Web Site: www.wri.org, pg 233

World Scientific Publishing Co Inc, 27 Warren St, Suite 401-402, Hackensack, NJ 07601 Tel: 201-487-9655 Fax: 201-487-9656 E-mail: sales@wspc.com; mkt@wspc.com; editor@wspc.com; customercare@wspc.com Web Site: www.worldscientific.com, pg 233

World Trade Press LLC, 616 E Eighth St, Suite 7, Traverse City, MI 49686 Tel: 707-778-1124 Toll Free Tel: 800-833-8586 Fax: 231-642-5300 Web Site: www.worldtradepress.com, pg 234

World's Best Short-Short Story Contest, Florida State University, Dept of English, Tallahassee, FL 32306 E-mail: southeastreview@gmail.com Web Site: www.southeastreview.org/writing-contests, pg 677

Worldwide Library, Bay Adelaide Centre, East Tower, 22 Adelaide St W, 41st fl, Toronto, ON M5H 4E3, Canada Tel: 416-445-5860 Toll Free Tel: 888-432-4879 E-mail: customerservice@harlequin.com Web Site: www.harlequin.com, pg 425

Worth Publishers, One New York Plaza, 46th fl, New York, NY 10004 Tel: 212-576-9400; 212-375-7000 E-mail: press.inquiries@macmillan.com Web Site: www.macmillanlearning.com/college/us, pg 234

Doug Wright Awards, PO Box 611, Sta P, Toronto, ON M5S 2Y4, Canada E-mail: dougwrightawards@gmail.com Web Site: dougwrightawards.com, pg 678

Wright Information Indexing Services, Sandia Park, NM 87047 Web Site: www.wrightinformation.com, pg 445

Write for Success Editing Services, PO Box 292153, Los Angeles, CA 90029-8653 Tel: 323-356-8833 E-mail: writeforsuccessediting@gmail.com Web Site: www.writeforsuccessediting.com, pg 445

Write Now, 900 S Mitchell Dr, Tempe, AZ 85281 Tel: 480-921-5700 Fax: 480-921-5777 E-mail: info@writenow.co Web Site: www.writenow.co, pg 678

Write on the Sound Writers' Conference, Frances Anderson Center, 700 Main St, Edmonds, WA 98020 Tel: 425-771-0228 Fax: 425-771-0253 E-mail: wots@edmondswa.gov Web Site: www.writeonthesound.com, pg 558

Write Stuff Enterprises LLC, 1001 S Andrews Ave, Suite 200, Fort Lauderdale, FL 33316 Tel: 954-462-6657 Fax: 954-462-6023 E-mail: info@writestuffbooks.com Web Site: www.writestuffbooks.com, pg 234

WriteLife Publishing, Wilkinson Pass Lane, Waynesville, NC 28786 E-mail: writelife@boutiqueofqualitybooks.com Web Site: www.facebook.com/writelife, pg 234

Writer in Residence, 9543 W Emerald St, Suite 204, Boise, ID 83704 Tel: 208-334-2119 E-mail: info@arts.idaho.gov Web Site: arts.idaho.gov/writer-in-residence, pg 678

The Writer Magazine/Emily Dickinson Award, 119 Smith St, Brooklyn, NY 11201 Tel: 212-254-9628 E-mail: info@poetrysociety.org Web Site: poetrysociety.org/awards, pg 678

Writer's Digest Annual Writing Competition, 5720 Flatiron Pkwy, Boulder, CO 80301 Web Site: www.writersdigest.com/writing-competitions, pg 678

Writers' Alliance of Newfoundland & Labrador, Haymarket Sq, 223 Duckworth St, Suite 202, St John's, NL A1C 6N1, Canada Tel: 709-739-5215 Toll Free Tel: 866-739-5215 E-mail: info@wanl.ca; membership@wanl.ca Web Site: wanl.ca, pg 522

Writers & Publishers Network (WPN), 1129 Maricopa Hwy, No 142, Ojai, CA 93023 Web Site: writersandpublishersnetwork.com, pg 522

Writers & Readers Days, PO Box 801, Abingdon, VA 24212 Tel: 276-623-5266 E-mail: info@vahighlandsfestival.org Web Site: www.vahighlandsfestival.com, pg 558

Writer's AudioShop, 1316 Overland Stage Rd, Dripping Springs, TX 78620 Tel: 512-476-1616 E-mail: wrtaudshop@aol.com Web Site: www.writersaudio.com, pg 234

The Writers' Colony at Dairy Hollow, 515 Spring St, Eureka Springs, AR 72632 Tel: 479-253-7444 E-mail: director@writerscolony.org Web Site: www.writerscolony.org, pg 558

Writer's Digest Books, 1745 Broadway, New York, NY 10019 Tel: 212-782-9000 Web Site: sites.prh.com/writersdigestbooks, pg 234

Writer's Digest University, 5720 Flatiron Pkwy, Boulder, CO 80301 Toll Free Tel: 800-759-0963; 800-333-5441 E-mail: writersdigestuniversity@aimmedia.com Web Site: www.writersonlineworkshops.com, pg 567

Writers' Federation of Nova Scotia (WFNS), 1113 Marginal Rd, Halifax, NS B3H 4P7, Canada Tel: 902-423-8116 Fax: 902-422-0881 E-mail: contact@writers.ns.ca; wits@writers.ns.ca (awards); programs@writers.ns.ca; communications@writers.ns.ca Web Site: writers.ns.ca, pg 522

Writers' Guild of Alberta, 11759 Groat Rd NW, Edmonton, AB T5M 3K6, Canada Tel: 780-422-8174 Toll Free Tel: 800-665-5354 (AB only) E-mail: mail@writersguild.ab.ca Web Site: writersguild.ca, pg 522

Writers Guild of America Awards, 7000 W Third St, Los Angeles, CA 90048 Tel: 323-951-4000; 323-782-4569 Toll Free Tel: 800-548-4532 Fax: 323-782-4801 Web Site: www.wga.org; awards.wga.org, pg 678

Writers Guild of America, East (WGAE), 250 Hudson St, Suite 700, New York, NY 10013 Tel: 212-767-7800 Fax: 212-582-1909 Web Site: www.wgaeast.org, pg 522

Writers Guild of America West (WGAW), 7000 W Third St, Los Angeles, CA 90048 Tel: 323-951-4000 Toll Free Tel: 800-548-4532 Fax: 323-782-4801 Web Site: www.wga.org, pg 522

Writers House, 21 W 26 St, New York, NY 10010 Tel: 212-685-2400 Web Site: www.writershouse.com, pg 482

Writers' League of Texas (WLT), 611 S Congress Ave, Suite 200 A-3, Austin, TX 78704 Tel: 512-499-8914 E-mail: wlt@writersleague.org Web Site: www.writersleague.org, pg 488, 523, 558

Writers' League of Texas Book Awards, 611 S Congress Ave, Suite 200 A-3, Austin, TX 78704 Tel: 512-499-8914 E-mail: wlt@writersleague.org Web Site: www.writersleague.org, pg 678

The Writers Lifeline Inc, a Story Merchant company, 400 S Burnside Ave, Suite 11B, Los Angeles, CA 90036 Tel: 310-968-1607 Web Site: www.thewriterslifeline.com, pg 446

Writers' Productions, PO Box 630, Westport, CT 06881-0630 Tel: 203-227-8199, pg 482

Writer's Relief, Inc, 18766 John J Williams Hwy, Unit 4, Box 335, Rehoboth Beach, DE 19971 Toll Free Tel: 866-405-3003 Fax: 201-641-1253 E-mail: info@writersrelief.com Web Site: www.WritersRelief.com, pg 446

Writers' Representatives LLC, 116 W 14 St, 11th fl, New York, NY 10011-7305 Tel: 212-620-9009 E-mail: transom@writersreps.com Web Site: www.writersreps.com, pg 482

Writers' Trust Engel Findley Award, 600-460 Richmond St W, Toronto, ON M5V 1Y1, Canada Tel: 416-504-8222 Toll Free Tel: 877-906-6548 Fax: 416-504-9090 E-mail: info@writerstrust.com Web Site: writerstrust.com, pg 678

COMPANY INDEX

Writers' Trust McClelland & Stewart Journey Prize, 600-460 Richmond St W, Toronto, ON M5V 1Y1, Canada *Tel:* 416-504-8222 *Toll Free Tel:* 877-906-6548 *Fax:* 416-504-9090 *E-mail:* info@writerstrust.com *Web Site:* www.writerstrust.com, pg 678

The Writers' Union of Canada (TWUC), 600-460 Richmond St W, Toronto, ON M5V 1Y1, Canada *Tel:* 416-703-8982 *E-mail:* info@writersunion.ca *Web Site:* www.writersunion.ca, pg 523

Writer's Workshop at Balticon, PO Box 686, Baltimore, MD 21203-0686 *Tel:* 410-563-2737 *E-mail:* writersworkshop@bsfs.org *Web Site:* bsfs.org/bsfswriterwork.htm, pg 558

Writer's Workshop at BSFS, PO Box 686, Baltimore, MD 21203-0686 *Tel:* 410-563-2737 *E-mail:* bsfsevents@bsfs.org *Web Site:* bsfs.org/bsfswriterwork.htm, pg 558

WritersWeekly.com's 24-Hour Short Story Contest, 200 Second Ave S, Unit 526, St Petersburg, FL 33701 *Tel:* 305-768-0261 *Web Site:* 24hourshortstorycontest.com, pg 678

The Writing Center, 601 E Palisade Ave, Suite 4, Englewood Cliffs, NJ 07632 *Tel:* 201-567-4017 *Fax:* 201-567-7202 *E-mail:* writingcenter@optonline.net *Web Site:* www.writingcenternj.com, pg 559

The Wylie Agency LLC, 250 W 57 St, Suite 2114, New York, NY 10107 *Tel:* 212-246-0069 *E-mail:* mail@wylieagency.com *Web Site:* www.wylieagency.com, pg 483

Wyman Indexing, 1311 Delaware Ave SW, Suite S332, Washington, DC 20024 *Tel:* 443-336-5497 *Web Site:* www.wymanindexing.com, pg 446

Wyndham Hall Press, 10372 W Munro Lake Dr, Levering, MI 49755 *Tel:* 419-648-9124 *E-mail:* orders@wyndhamhallpress.com *Web Site:* www.wyndhamhallpress.com, pg 234

Wyoming Arts Council Creative Writing Fellowships, Barrett Bldg, 2nd fl, 2301 Central Ave, Cheyenne, WY 82002 *Tel:* 307-777-7742 *Web Site:* wyoarts.state.wy.us, pg 679

Xist Publishing, 24200 Southwest Fwy, Suite 402, PMB 290, Rosenberg, TX 77471 *Tel:* 949-478-2568 *E-mail:* info@xistpublishing.com *Web Site:* www.xistpublishing.com, pg 234

Xlibris Corp, 1663 Liberty Dr, Suite 200, Bloomington, IN 47403 *Toll Free Tel:* 844-714-8691; 888-795-4274 *Fax:* 610-915-0294 *E-mail:* info@xlibris.com; media@xlibris.com *Web Site:* www.xlibris.com; www.authorsolutions.com/our-imprints/xlibris, pg 234

XML Press, 458 Dallas St, Denver, CO 80230 *Tel:* 970-231-3624 *E-mail:* publisher@xmlpress.net *Web Site:* xmlpress.net, pg 235

YA Fiction Workshop, 2617 NW Thurman St, Portland, OR 97210 *Tel:* 503-473-8663 *Web Site:* tinhouse.com/ya-workshop, pg 559

Yaddo Artists Residency, 312 Union Ave, Saratoga Springs, NY 12866 *Tel:* 518-584-0746 *Fax:* 518-584-1312 *Web Site:* www.yaddo.org, pg 559

Yale Center for British Art, 1080 Chapel St, New Haven, CT 06510-2302 *Tel:* 203-432-8929 *Fax:* 203-432-1626 *E-mail:* ycba.publications@yale.edu *Web Site:* britishart.yale.edu, pg 235

Yale Series of Younger Poets, 302 Temple St, New Haven, CT 06511 *Tel:* 203-432-0960 *Fax:* 203-432-0948 *E-mail:* ysyp@yale.edu *Web Site:* youngerpoets.yupnet.org, pg 679

Yale University Press, 302 Temple St, New Haven, CT 06511-8909 *Tel:* 203-432-0960; 203-432-0966 (sales); 401-531-2800 (cust serv) *Toll Free Tel:* 800-405-1619 (cust serv) *Fax:* 203-432-0948; 203-432-8485 (sales); 401-531-2801 (cust serv) *Toll Free Fax:* 800-406-9145 (cust serv) *E-mail:* sales.press@yale.edu (sales); customer.care@triliteral.org (cust serv) *Web Site:* www.yalebooks.com; yalepress.yale.edu/yupbooks, pg 235

YALSA Conference Grants, 225 N Michigan Ave, Suite 1300, Chicago, IL 60601 *Tel:* 312-280-4390 *Toll Free Tel:* 800-545-2433 *E-mail:* yalsa@ala.org *Web Site:* www.ala.org/yalsa/awardsandgrants.bakertayloryalsa, pg 679

Anne & Philip Yandle Best Article Award, PO Box 448, Fort Langley, BC V1M 2R7, Canada *E-mail:* info@bchistory.ca *Web Site:* www.bchistory.ca/awards, pg 679

The Yao Enterprises (Literary Agents) LLC, 67 Banksville Rd, Armonk, NY 10504 *Tel:* 914-765-0296 *E-mail:* yaollc@gmail.com, pg 483

Yard Dog Press, 710 W Redbud Lane, Alma, AR 72921-7247 *Tel:* 479-632-4693 *Fax:* 479-632-4693 *Web Site:* www.yarddogpress.com, pg 235

YBK Publishers Inc, 39 Crosby St, New York, NY 10013 *Tel:* 212-219-0135 *E-mail:* readmybook@ybkpublishers.com; info@ybkpublishers.com *Web Site:* www.ybkpublishers.com, pg 235

YES New Play Festival, 205 FA Theatre Dept, Nunn Dr, Highland Heights, KY 41099-1007 *Tel:* 859-572-7622 *Web Site:* www.nku.edu/yesfestival, pg 679

Yeshiva University Press, 500 W 185 St, New York, NY 10033 *Tel:* 212-960-5400 *Web Site:* www.yu.edu/books, pg 235

YMAA Publication Center Inc, PO Box 480, Wolfeboro, NH 03894 *Tel:* 603-569-7988 *Toll Free Tel:* 800-669-8892 *Fax:* 603-569-1889 *E-mail:* info@ymaa.com *Web Site:* www.ymaa.com, pg 235

Jake Adam York Poetry Prize, 1011 Washington Ave S, Suite 300, Minneapolis, MN 55415-1246 *Tel:* 612-332-3192 *Toll Free Tel:* 800-520-6455 *E-mail:* thanks@milkweed.org *Web Site:* coppernickel.org/bookprize; milkweed.org/submissions, pg 679

Yotzeret Publishing, PO Box 18662, St Paul, MN 55118-0662 *Tel:* 651-647-0900 *E-mail:* info@yotzeretpublishing.com; orders@yotzeretpublishing.com *Web Site:* yotzeretpublishing.com, pg 236

The Young Agency, 213 Bennett Ave, No 3H, New York, NY 10040 *Tel:* 212-229-2612, pg 483

Young Lions Fiction Award, 445 Fifth Ave, 4th fl, New York, NY 10016 *Tel:* 212-930-0887 *Fax:* 212-930-0983 *E-mail:* younglions@nypl.org *Web Site:* www.nypl.org/ylfa, pg 679

Young Writers Award, c/o 3225 N 91 St, Milwaukee, WI 53222 *E-mail:* wiswriters@gmail.com *Web Site:* wiswriters.org/awards, pg 679

Young Writers' Workshop, 919 Main St, Osterville, MA 02655 *Tel:* 508-420-0200 *E-mail:* writers@capecodwriterscenter.org *Web Site:* capecodwriterscenter.org, pg 559

Young Writers Workshops, Finn House, 102 W Wiggin St, Gambier, OH 43022-9623 *Tel:* 740-427-5391 *Fax:* 740-427-5417 *E-mail:* youngwriters@kenyonreview.org *Web Site:* kenyonreview.org/highschool-workshops, pg 559

YoungArts, 2100 Biscayne Blvd, Miami, FL 33137 *Tel:* 305-377-1140 *Toll Free Tel:* 800-970-ARTS (970-2787) *E-mail:* info@youngarts.org; apply@youngarts.org *Web Site:* www.youngarts.org, pg 679

Your Personal Odyssey Writing Workshop, PO Box 75, Mont Vernon, NH 03057 *Tel:* 603-673-6234 *Fax:* 603-673-6234 *Web Site:* www.odysseyworkshop.org, pg 559

YWAM Publishing, PO Box 55787, Seattle, WA 98155-0787 *Tel:* 425-771-1153 *Toll Free Tel:* 800-922-2143 *E-mail:* books@ywampublishing.com; marketing@ywampublishing.com *Web Site:* www.ywampublishing.com, pg 236

Morton Dauwen Zabel Award, 633 W 155 St, New York, NY 10032 *Tel:* 212-368-5900 *E-mail:* academy@artsandletters.org *Web Site:* artsandletters.org/awards, pg 679

Zagat Inc, 424 Broadway, 5th fl, New York, NY 10013 *E-mail:* feedback@zagat.com *Web Site:* www.zagat.com, pg 236

Barbara & David Zalaznick Book Prize in American History, 170 Central Park W, New York, NY 10024 *Tel:* 212-873-3400 *Fax:* 212-595-5707 *E-mail:* info@nyhistory.org *Web Site:* www.nyhistory.org/news/book-prize, pg 679

Zaner-Bloser Inc, 1400 Goodale Blvd, Suite 200, Grandview Heights, OH 43212 *Toll Free Tel:* 800-421-3018 (cust serv) *Toll Free Fax:* 800-992-6087 (orders) *E-mail:* customerexperience@zaner-bloser.com *Web Site:* www.zaner-bloser.com, pg 236

Zebra Communications, 13682 Hwy 92, No 3005, Woodstock, GA 30188-4734 *Tel:* 404-433-7507 *E-mail:* bobbie@zebraeditor.com *Web Site:* www.zebraeditor.com, pg 446

Zeig, Tucker & Theisen Inc, 2632 E Thomas Rd, Suite 201, Phoenix, AZ 85016 *Tel:* 480-389-4342 *Web Site:* www.zeigtucker.com, pg 236

Zest Books, 241 First Ave N, Minneapolis, MN 55401 *Tel:* 612-332-3344 *Toll Free Tel:* 800-328-4929 *Toll Free Fax:* 800-332-1132 *E-mail:* info@lernerbooks.com; publicity@lernerbooks.com; custserve@lernerbooks.com (orders) *Web Site:* lernerbooks.com, pg 236

The Jacob Zilber Prize for Short Fiction, University of British Columbia, Buch E462, 1866 Main Mall, Vancouver, BC V6T 1Z1, Canada *Tel:* 604-822-2514 *Fax:* 604-822-3616 *E-mail:* promotions@prismmagazine.ca *Web Site:* www.prismmagazine.ca/contests, pg 679

Barbara J Zitwer Agency, 525 West End Ave, Unit 11-H, New York, NY 10024 *Tel:* 212-501-8423 *E-mail:* zitwer@gmail.com *Web Site:* www.barbarajzitweragency.com, pg 483

Charlotte Zolotow Award, 225 N Mills St, Rm 401, Madison, WI 53706 *Tel:* 608-263-3720 *E-mail:* ccbcinfo@education.wisc.edu *Web Site:* ccbs.education.wisc.edu/books/zolotow.asp, pg 680

Zondervan, 3900 Sparks Dr SE, Grand Rapids, MI 49546 *Tel:* 616-698-6900 *Toll Free Tel:* 800-226-1122; 800-727-1309 (retail orders) *Fax:* 616-698-3350 *Toll Free Fax:* 800-698-3256 (retail orders) *E-mail:* customercare@harpercollins.com *Web Site:* www.zondervan.com, pg 236

Zone Books, 633 Vanderbilt St, Brooklyn, NY 11218 *Tel:* 718-686-0048 *E-mail:* info@zonebooks.org *Web Site:* www.zonebooks.org, pg 237

Anna Zornio Memorial Children's Theatre Playwriting Award, D22 Paul Creative Arts Center, 30 Academic Way, Durham, NH 03824 *Tel:* 603-862-2919 *Fax:* 603-862-0298 *E-mail:* theatre.dance@unh.edu *Web Site:* cola.unh.edu/theatre-dance/opportunities/competitions, pg 680

Zumaya Publications LLC, 3209 S Interstate 35, Suite 1086, Austin, TX 78741 *Tel:* 512-333-4055 (scheduled calls only) *Fax:* 512-276-6745 *E-mail:* publisher@zumayapublications.com; acquisitions@zumayapublications.com *Web Site:* www.zumayapublications.com, pg 237

Personnel Index

Included in this index are the personnel included in the entries in this volume of *LMP*, along with the page number(s) on which they appear. Not included in this index are those individuals associated with listings in the **Calendar of Book Trade & Promotional Events; Reference Books for the Trade** and **Magazines for the Trade** sections. Also, personnel associated with secondary addresses within listings (such as branch offices, sales offices, editorial offices, etc.) are not included.

Aalto, Helena, Canadian Society of Children's Authors, Illustrators & Performers (CANSCAIP), 720 Bathurst St, Suite 503, Toronto, ON M5S 2R4, Canada *Tel:* 416-515-1559 *E-mail:* office@canscaip.org *Web Site:* www.canscaip.org, pg 503

Aardema, John, Sourcebooks LLC, 1935 Brookdale Rd, Suite 139, Naperville, IL 60563 *Tel:* 630-961-3900 *Toll Free Tel:* 800-432-7444 *Fax:* 630-961-2168 *E-mail:* info@sourcebooks.com *Web Site:* www.sourcebooks.com, pg 194

Aaronson, Deborah, Phaidon, 65 Bleecker St, 8th fl, New York, NY 10012 *Tel:* 212-652-5400 *Toll Free Tel:* 800-759-0190 (cust serv) *Fax:* 212-652-5410 *Toll Free Fax:* 800-286-9471 (cust serv) *E-mail:* enquiries@phaidon.com *Web Site:* www.phaidon.com, pg 159

Aaronson, Jordan, Penguin Publishing Group, c/o Penguin Random House LLC, 1745 Broadway, New York, NY 10019 *Tel:* 212-782-9000 *Web Site:* www.penguin.com, pg 154

Aaronson, Whitney, Random House Children's Books, c/o Penguin Random House LLC, 1745 Broadway, New York, NY 10019 *Tel:* 212-782-9000 *Web Site:* www.rhcbooks.com, pg 170

Abad, Ariana, Bloomsbury Publishing Inc, 1385 Broadway, 5th fl, New York, NY 10018 *Tel:* 212-419-5300 *E-mail:* marketingusa@bloomsbury.com; adultpublicityusa@bloomsbury.com; askacademic@bloomsbury.com *Web Site:* www.bloomsbury.com, pg 32

Abballe, Sabrina, HarperCollins Children's Books, 195 Broadway, New York, NY 10007 *Tel:* 212-207-7000 *Web Site:* www.harpercollins.com/childrens, pg 85

Abbate, Gabriella, Houghton Mifflin Harcourt Trade & Reference Division, 125 High St, Boston, MA 02110 *Tel:* 617-351-5000 *Web Site:* www.hmhco.com, pg 96

Abbate, James, Kensington Publishing Corp, 900 Third Ave, 26th fl, New York, NY 10022 *Tel:* 212-407-1500 *Toll Free Tel:* 800-221-2647 *Fax:* 212-935-0699 *Web Site:* www.kensingtonbooks.com, pg 109

Abbate, Megan, Bloomsbury Publishing Inc, 1385 Broadway, 5th fl, New York, NY 10018 *Tel:* 212-419-5300 *E-mail:* marketingusa@bloomsbury.com; adultpublicityusa@bloomsbury.com; askacademic@bloomsbury.com *Web Site:* www.bloomsbury.com, pg 31

Abbene, Darcie, Health Communications Inc, 301 Crawford Blvd, Suite 200, Boca Raton, FL 33432 *Tel:* 561-453-0696 *Toll Free Tel:* 800-441-5569 (cust serv & orders) *Fax:* 561-453-1009 *Toll Free Fax:* 800-943-9831 (orders) *E-mail:* editorial@hcibooks.com *Web Site:* hcibooks.com, pg 90

Abbey, Caroline, Random House Children's Books, c/o Penguin Random House LLC, 1745 Broadway, New York, NY 10019 *Tel:* 212-782-9000 *Web Site:* www.rhcbooks.com, pg 169

Abbott, Charlotte, Bay Area Women in Publishing (BAWiP), 680 Second St, San Francisco, CA 94107 *E-mail:* bayareawomeninpublishing@gmail.com *Web Site:* www.bayareawomeninpublishing.com, pg 500

Abbott, Joseph P Jr, Houghton Mifflin Harcourt, 125 High St, Boston, MA 02110 *Tel:* 617-351-5000 *Toll Free Tel:* 855-969-4642; 800-225-5425 (K-12 educ materials); 800-323-9540 (assessment materials); 877-219-1537 (SkillsTutor); 888-242-6747 (Innovation in Educ Group); 800-225-3362 (Trade & Ref Div) *Toll Free Fax:* 800-269-5232 *E-mail:* myhmhco@hmhco.com *Web Site:* www.hmhco.com, pg 95

Abdelmoumen, Melikah, Les Editions de l'Hexagone, 4545, rue Frontenac, 3rd fl, Montreal, QC H2H 2R7, Canada *Tel:* 514-523-1182 *Fax:* 514-521-4434 *Web Site:* editionshexagone.groupelivre.com, pg 402

Abdi, Zahra, Penguin Random House Canada, a Penguin Random House company, 320 Front St W, Suite 1400, Toronto, ON M5V 3B6, Canada *Tel:* 416-364-4449 *Toll Free Tel:* 888-523-9292 (cust serv) *E-mail:* canadaweb@penguinrandomhouse.com; customerservicescanada@penguinrandomhouse.com *Web Site:* www.penguinrandomhouse.ca, pg 416

Abdo, Jim, ABDO, 8000 W 78 St, Suite 310, Edina, MN 55439 *Tel:* 952-698-2403 *Toll Free Tel:* 800-800-1312 *Fax:* 952-831-1632 *Toll Free Fax:* 800-862-3480 *E-mail:* customerservice@abdobooks.com *Web Site:* abdobooks.com, pg 2

Abdo, Paul, ABDO, 8000 W 78 St, Suite 310, Edina, MN 55439 *Tel:* 952-698-2403 *Toll Free Tel:* 800-800-1312 *Fax:* 952-831-1632 *Toll Free Fax:* 800-862-3480 *E-mail:* customerservice@abdobooks.com *Web Site:* abdobooks.com, pg 2

Abdul-Azeez, Fajr, Johns Hopkins University Press, 2715 N Charles St, Baltimore, MD 21218-4363 *Tel:* 410-516-6900; 410-516-6987 *Toll Free Tel:* 800-537-5487 (book orders & cust serv); 800-548-1784 (journal orders) *Fax:* 410-516-6968; 410-516-6998 (orders) *E-mail:* hfscustserv@press.jhu.edu (cust serv); jrnlcirc@jh.edu (journal orders) *Web Site:* www.press.jhu.edu; muse.jhu.edu, pg 106

Abdullah, Chelsea, Astra Books for Young Readers, 19 W 21 St, No 1201, New York, NY 10010 *Tel:* 646-844-3485 *E-mail:* ahinfo@astrahouse.com; permissions@astrapublishinghouse.com *Web Site:* astrapublishinghouse.com, pg 20

Abe, Carol, University of Hawaii Press, 2840 Kolowalu St, Honolulu, HI 96822-1888 *Tel:* 808-956-8255 *Toll Free Tel:* 888-UHPRESS (847-7377) *Toll Free Fax:* 800-650-7811 *E-mail:* uhpbooks@hawaii.edu *Web Site:* www.uhpress.hawaii.edu, pg 216

Abel, Dominick, Dominick Abel Literary Agency Inc, 146 W 82 St, Suite 1-A, New York, NY 10024 *Tel:* 212-877-0710 *Fax:* 212-595-3133 *E-mail:* agency@dalainc.com *Web Site:* www.dalainc.com, pg 448

Abel, Jess, HarperCollins Children's Books, 195 Broadway, New York, NY 10007 *Tel:* 212-207-7000 *Web Site:* www.harpercollins.com/childrens, pg 85

Abel, Jess, HarperCollins Publishers LLC, 195 Broadway, New York, NY 10007 *Tel:* 212-207-7000 *Web Site:* www.harpercollins.com, pg 86

Abel, Lydia, Candlewick Press, 99 Dover St, Somerville, MA 02144-2825 *Tel:* 617-661-3330 *Fax:* 617-661-0565 *E-mail:* bigbear@candlewick.com; salesinfo@candlewick.com *Web Site:* candlewick.com, pg 40

Abell, Anna Gjesteby, Holiday House Publishing Inc, 50 Broad St, New York, NY 10004 *Tel:* 212-688-0085 *Fax:* 212-421-6134 *E-mail:* info@holidayhouse.com *Web Site:* www.holidayhouse.com, pg 94

Abell, Anna Gjesteby, Peachtree Publishing Co Inc, 1700 Chattahoochee Ave, Atlanta, GA 30318-2112 *Tel:* 404-876-8761 *Toll Free Tel:* 800-241-0113 *Fax:* 404-875-2578 *Toll Free Fax:* 800-875-8909 *E-mail:* hello@peachtree-online.com; orders@peachtree-online.com; sales@peachtree-online.com *Web Site:* www.peachtreebooks.com; www.peachtree-online.com, pg 153

Abell, Whitley, The Jennifer DeChiara Literary Agency, 245 Park Ave, 39th fl, New York, NY 10167 *Tel:* 212-372-8989 *Web Site:* www.jdlit.com, pg 455

Abellera, Lisa, Kimberley Cameron & Associates LLC, 1550 Tiburon Blvd, Suite 704, Tiburon, CA 94920 *E-mail:* info@kimberleycameron.com *Web Site:* www.kimberleycameron.com, pg 453

Abfier, Mel, StarGroup International Inc, 1194 Old Dixie Hwy, Suite 201, West Palm Beach, FL 33413 *Tel:* 561-547-0667 *Fax:* 561-843-8530 *E-mail:* info@stargroupinternational.com *Web Site:* stargroupinternational.com, pg 197

Abkemeier, Laurie, DeFiore and Company Literary Management Inc, 47 E 19 St, 3rd fl, New York, NY 10003 *Tel:* 212-925-7744 *Fax:* 212-925-9803 *E-mail:* info@defliterary.com; submissions@defliterary.com *Web Site:* www.defliterary.com, pg 455

Ableman, Brian, The Learning Source Ltd, 644 Tenth St, Brooklyn, NY 11215 *E-mail:* info@learningsourceltd.com *Web Site:* www.learningsourceltd.com, pg 441

Ables, Anna, Cunningham Commission for Youth Theatre, Lincoln Park Campus, 2350 N Racine Ave, Chicago, IL 60614-4100 *Tel:* 773-325-7999 *E-mail:* cunninghamcommission@depaul.edu *Web Site:* theatre.depaul.edu, pg 594

Abouali, Diana, The Arab American Book Awards, 13624 Michigan Ave, Dearborn, MI 48126 *Tel:* 313-429-2535 *Fax:* 313-582-1086 *E-mail:* librarian@accesscommunity.org *Web Site:* arabamericanmuseum.org/book-awards, pg 573

Abraham, Jeff, Penguin Random House LLC, 1745 Broadway, New York, NY 10019 *Tel:* 212-782-9000 *Toll Free Tel:* 800-726-0600 *Web Site:* www.penguinrandomhouse.com, pg 155

Abraham, Rozana, Software & Information Industry Association (SIIA), 1620 Eye St NW, Washington, DC 20005 *Tel:* 202-289-7442 *Fax:* 202-289-7097 *E-mail:* info@siia.net *Web Site:* www.siia.net, pg 520

Abraham, Shawn, Sourcebooks LLC, 1935 Brookdale Rd, Suite 139, Naperville, IL 60563 *Tel:* 630-961-3900 *Toll Free Tel:* 800-432-7444 *Fax:* 630-961-2168 *E-mail:* info@sourcebooks.com *Web Site:* www.sourcebooks.com, pg 194

Abrahamsen, Eric, Candied Plums, 7548 Ravenna Ave NE, Seattle, WA 98115 *E-mail:* candiedplums@gmail.com *Web Site:* www.candiedplums.com, pg 39

Abrami, Jenny, Sasquatch Books, 1904 S Third Ave, Suite 710, Seattle, WA 98101 *Tel:* 206-467-4300 *Toll Free Tel:* 800-775-0817 *Fax:* 206-467-4301 *E-mail:* custserv@sasquatchbooks.com *Web Site:* sasquatchbooks.com, pg 182

Abramo, Lauren E, Dystel, Goderich & Bourret LLC, One Union Sq W, Suite 904, New York, NY 10003 *Tel:* 212-627-9100 *Fax:* 212-627-9313 *Web Site:* www.dystel.com, pg 457

Abramowitz, Jenne, Sourcebooks LLC, 1935 Brookdale Rd, Suite 139, Naperville, IL 60563 *Tel:* 630-961-3900 *Toll Free Tel:* 800-432-7444 *Fax:* 630-961-2168 *E-mail:* info@sourcebooks.com *Web Site:* www.sourcebooks.com, pg 194

Abrams, Joanne, Square One Publishers Inc, 115 Herricks Rd, Garden City Park, NY 11040 *Tel:* 516-535-2010 *Toll Free Tel:* 877-900-BOOK (900-2665) *Fax:* 516-535-2014 *E-mail:* sq1publish@aol.com *Web Site:* www.squareonepublishers.com, pg 196

Abrams, Liesa, Random House Children's Books, c/o Penguin Random House LLC, 1745 Broadway, New York, NY 10019 *Tel:* 212-782-9000 *Web Site:* www.rhcbooks.com, pg 169

Abrams, Rachel, Pattis Family Foundation Global Cities Book Award, Prudential Plaza, 180 N Stetson Ave, Suite 1400, Chicago, IL 60601 Tel: 312-726-3860 Fax: 312-821-7555 E-mail: gcbookaward@thechicagocouncil.org Web Site: globalaffairs.org/bookaward, pg 646

Abrams, Stacy Cantor, Entangled Publishing LLC, 644 Shrewsbury Commons Ave, Suite 181, Shrewsbury, PA 17361 Toll Free Tel: 877-677-9451 E-mail: publisher@entangledpublishing.com Web Site: www.entangledpublishing.com, pg 67

Abramson, Rob, Bisk Education, 9417 Princess Palm Ave, Suite 400, Tampa, FL 33619 Tel: 813-621-6200 E-mail: media@bisk.com Web Site: www.bisk.com, pg 29

Abramson, Talia, Penguin Random House Canada, a Penguin Random House company, 320 Front St W, Suite 1400, Toronto, ON M5V 3B6, Canada Tel: 416-364-4449 Toll Free Tel: 888-523-9292 (cust serv) E-mail: canadaweb@penguinrandomhouse.com; customerservicescanada@penguinrandomhouse.com Web Site: www.penguinrandomhouse.ca, pg 416

Acevedo Quinones, Claudia, Graywolf Press, 212 Third Ave N, Suite 485, Minneapolis, MN 55401 Tel: 651-641-0077 Fax: 651-641-0036 E-mail: wolves@graywolfpress.org (no ms queries, sample chapters or proposals) Web Site: www.graywolfpress.org, pg 81

Aceves, Alexandra, Holiday House Publishing Inc, 50 Broad St, New York, NY 10004 Tel: 212-688-0085 Fax: 212-421-6134 E-mail: info@holidayhouse.com Web Site: www.holidayhouse.com, pg 94

Achenbaum, Anne, Alfred A Knopf, c/o Penguin Random House LLC, 1745 Broadway, New York, NY 10019 Tel: 212-751-2600 Fax: 212-940-7390 (dom rts); 212-572-2662 (foreign rts) Web Site: knopfdoubleday.com/imprint/knopf/; knopfdoubleday.com, pg 110

Ackell, Melinda, Random House Children's Books, c/o Penguin Random House LLC, 1745 Broadway, New York, NY 10019 Tel: 212-782-9000 Web Site: www.rhcbooks.com, pg 169

Ackerman, Larissa, Kensington Publishing Corp, 900 Third Ave, 26th fl, New York, NY 10022 Tel: 212-407-1500 Toll Free Tel: 800-221-2647 Fax: 212-935-0699 Web Site: www.kensingtonbooks.com, pg 109

Ackroyd, Cameron, Macmillan, 120 Broadway, 22nd fl, New York, NY 10271 E-mail: press.inquiries@macmillan.com Web Site: us.macmillan.com, pg 122

Acosta, Rob, Macmillan, 120 Broadway, 22nd fl, New York, NY 10271 E-mail: press.inquiries@macmillan.com Web Site: us.macmillan.com, pg 122

Acquarola, Amy, Swedenborg Foundation, 320 N Church St, West Chester, PA 19380 Tel: 610-430-3222 Toll Free Tel: 800-355-3222 (cust serv) Fax: 610-430-7982 E-mail: info@swedenborg.com Web Site: swedenborg.com, pg 201

Acquaviva, Stef, Grand Central Publishing, 1290 Avenue of the Americas, New York, NY 10104 Tel: 212-364-1100 Web Site: www.hachettebookgroup.com/imprint/grand-central-publishing/, pg 80

Adair, Kaylan, Candlewick Press, 99 Dover St, Somerville, MA 02144-2825 Tel: 617-661-3330 Fax: 617-661-0565 E-mail: bigbear@candlewick.com; salesinfo@candlewick.com Web Site: candlewick.com, pg 39

Adame, Ivan, National Association of Hispanic Publications Inc (NAHP), National Press Bldg, 529 14 St NW, Suite 923, Washington, DC 20045 Web Site: nahp.org, pg 511

Adames, Brittany, Simon & Schuster, 1230 Avenue of the Americas, New York, NY 10020 Tel: 212-698-7000 Toll Free Tel: 800-223-2348 (cust servs); 800-223-2336 (orders) Toll Free Fax: 800-943-9831 (orders) Web Site: simonandschusterpublishing.com/simonandschuster/, pg 188

Adamo, John, Random House Children's Books, c/o Penguin Random House LLC, 1745 Broadway, New York, NY 10019 Tel: 212-782-9000 Web Site: www.rhcbooks.com, pg 169

Adams, Austin, St Martin's Press, LLC, 120 Broadway, New York, NY 10271 E-mail: publicity@stmartins.com; trademarketing@stmartins.com; foreignrights@stmartins.com Web Site: us.macmillan.com/smp, pg 181

Adams, Benjamin, Basic Books Group, 1290 Avenue of the Americas, New York, NY 10104 Tel: 212-340-8100 Toll Free Tel: 800-343-4499 (cust serv) Fax: 212-340-8105 E-mail: customer.service@hbgusa; orders@hbgusa.com Web Site: www.hachettebookgroup.com/imprint/basic-books/, pg 25

Adams, Beth, Hachette Nashville, 6100 Tower Circle, Room 210, Franklin, TN 37067 Tel: 615-221-0996 Fax: 615-221-0962 Web Site: www.hachettebookgroup.com/imprint/hachette-nashville/, pg 83

Adams, Craig, Random House Publishing Group, 1745 Broadway, New York, NY 10019 Toll Free Tel: 800-200-3552 Web Site: www.randomhousebooks.com, pg 171

Adams, Jen, Sounds True Inc, 413 S Arthur Ave, Louisville, CO 80027 Tel: 303-665-3151 Toll Free Tel: 800-333-9185 (US); 888-303-9185 (US & CN) E-mail: customerservice@soundstrue.com; stpublicity@soundstrue.com Web Site: www.soundstrue.com, pg 194

Adams, John, Bartleby Press, 8926 Baltimore St, No 858, Savage, MD 20763 Tel: 301-589-5831 Toll Free Tel: 800-953-9929 E-mail: inquiries@bartlebythepublisher.com Web Site: www.bartlebythepublisher.com, pg 24

Adams, Katie Henderson, W W Norton & Company Inc, 500 Fifth Ave, New York, NY 10110-0017 Tel: 212-354-5500 Toll Free Tel: 800-233-4830 (orders & cust serv) Fax: 212-869-0856 Toll Free Fax: 800-458-6515 E-mail: orders@wwnorton.com Web Site: wwnorton.com, pg 143

Adams, Kelli, Counterpoint Press LLC, 2560 Ninth St, Suite 318, Berkeley, CA 94710 Tel: 510-704-0230 Fax: 510-704-0268 E-mail: info@counterpointpress.com Web Site: counterpointpress.com; softskull.com, pg 54

Adams, Lisa, The Garamond Agency Inc, 12 Horton St, Newburyport, MA 01950 E-mail: query@garamondagency.com Web Site: www.garamondagency.com, pg 459

Adams, Martha, Leisure Arts Inc, 104 Champs Blvd, Suite 100, Maumelle, AR 72113 Tel: 501-868-8800 Toll Free Tel: 800-643-8030 Toll Free Fax: 877-710-5603 (catalog) E-mail: customer_service@leisurearts.com Web Site: www.leisurearts.com, pg 114

Adams, Dr Michael, Dobie Paisano Fellowship Program, 110 Inner Campus Dr, Stop G0400, Austin, TX 78712-0710 Fax: 512-471-7620 Web Site: dobiepaisano.utexas.edu, pg 645

Adams Mireles, Jacob, Gulf Energy Information, 2 Greenway Plaza, Suite 1020, Houston, TX 77046 Tel: 713-520-4498; 713-529-4301 E-mail: store@gulfpub.com; customerservice@gulfenergyinfo.com Web Site: www.gulfenergyinfo.com, pg 83

Adams, Stephanie, Stanford University Press, 425 Broadway St, Redwood City, CA 94063-3126 Tel: 650-723-9434 Fax: 650-725-3457 E-mail: info@www.sup.org; publicity@www.sup.org; sales@www.sup.org Web Site: www.sup.org, pg 197

Adams, Wesley, Farrar, Straus & Giroux Books for Young Readers, 120 Broadway, New York, NY 10271 Tel: 212-741-6900 Toll Free Tel: 888-330-8477 (orders) E-mail: childrens.publicity@macmillanusa.com; childrensrights@macmillanusa.com Web Site: us.macmillan.com/mackids, pg 70

Adcox, John, The Story Plant, 1270 Caroline St, Suite D120-381, Atlanta, GA 30307 Tel: 203-722-7920 E-mail: thestoryplant@thestoryplant.com Web Site: www.thestoryplant.com, pg 199

Addison, Tonia, Penguin Random House Canada, a Penguin Random House company, 320 Front St W, Suite 1400, Toronto, ON M5V 3B6, Canada Tel: 416-364-4449 Toll Free Tel: 888-523-9292 (cust serv) E-mail: canadaweb@penguinrandomhouse.com; customerservicescanada@penguinrandomhouse.com Web Site: www.penguinrandomhouse.ca, pg 416

Addo-Chazet, Michelle, Kensington Publishing Corp, 900 Third Ave, 26th fl, New York, NY 10022 Tel: 212-407-1500 Toll Free Tel: 800-221-2647 Fax: 212-935-0699 Web Site: www.kensingtonbooks.com, pg 109

Ade, Robert, Independent Institute, 100 Swan Way, Oakland, CA 94621-1428 Tel: 510-632-1366 Fax: 510-568-6040 Web Site: www.independent.org, pg 99

Adel, Judith, J Adel Art & Design, 586 Ramapo Rd, Teaneck, NJ 07666 Tel: 201-836-2606 E-mail: jadelnj@aol.com, pg 435

Adero, Malaika, Farrar, Straus & Giroux, LLC, 120 Broadway, New York, NY 10271 Tel: 212-741-6900 E-mail: fsg.publicity@fsgbooks.com; sales@fsgbooks.com Web Site: us.macmillan.com/fsg, pg 70

Adjemian, Robert, Vedanta Press, 1946 Vedanta Place, Hollywood, CA 90068 Tel: 323-960-1728; 323-960-1736 (catalog) Fax: 323-465-9568 E-mail: vpress@vedanta.com Web Site: www.vedanta.com, pg 224

Adkins, David, The Council of State Governments, 1776 Avenue of the States, Lexington, KY 40511 Tel: 859-244-8000 Fax: 859-244-8001 E-mail: membership@csg.org Web Site: www.csg.org, pg 53

Adler, Allison, Chronicle Books LLC, 680 Second St, San Francisco, CA 94107 Tel: 415-537-4200 Fax: 415-537-4460 (perms) E-mail: hello@chroniclebooks.com; subrights@chroniclebooks.com Web Site: www.chroniclebooks.com, pg 47

Adler, Alyssa, Avery, c/o Penguin Random House LLC, 1745 Broadway, New York, NY 10019 Tel: 212-366-2000 Web Site: www.penguin.com/avery-overview/, pg 23

Adler, Alyssa, TarcherPerigee, c/o Penguin Random House LLC, 1745 Broadway, New York, NY 10019 Tel: 212-782-9000 Web Site: www.penguin.com/tarcherperigee-overview/; www.facebook.com/TarcherPerigee, pg 203

Adler, Jared, Macmillan, 120 Broadway, 22nd fl, New York, NY 10271 E-mail: press.inquiries@macmillan.com Web Site: us.macmillan.com, pg 122

Adler, Laina, HarperCollins Publishers LLC, 195 Broadway, New York, NY 10007 Tel: 212-207-7000 Web Site: www.harpercollins.com, pg 86

Adler-Kozak, Mary, National Association of College Stores (NACS), 528 E Lorain St, Oberlin, OH 44074 Toll Free Tel: 800-622-7498 Fax: 440-775-4769 E-mail: info@nacs.org Web Site: www.nacs.org, pg 511

Adydan, Eric, Close Up Publishing, 671 N Glebe Rd, Suite 900, Arlington, VA 22203 Tel: 703-706-3300 Toll Free Tel: 800-CLOSE-UP (256-7387) E-mail: info@closeup.org Web Site: www.closeup.org, pg 49

Afghani, Nora, Macmillan, 120 Broadway, 22nd fl, New York, NY 10271 E-mail: press.inquiries@macmillan.com Web Site: us.macmillan.com, pg 122

Agarwal, Koki, Jhpiego, 1615 Thames St, Baltimore, MD 21231-3492 Tel: 410-537-1800 E-mail: info@jhpiego.org Web Site: www.jhpiego.org, pg 106

Agro, Janine, Soho Press Inc, 853 Broadway, New York, NY 10003 Tel: 212-260-1900 E-mail: soho@sohopress.com; publicity@sohopress.com Web Site: sohopress.com, pg 193

Agte-Studier, Montana, Community of Literary Magazines & Presses (CLMP), 154 Christopher St, Suite 3C, New York, NY 10014-9110 Tel: 212-741-9110 E-mail: info@clmp.org Web Site: www.clmp.org, pg 504

Aguilar, Juan, Penguin Random House Canada, a Penguin Random House company, 320 Front St W, Suite 1400, Toronto, ON M5V 3B6, Canada Tel: 416-364-4449 Toll Free Tel: 888-523-9292 (cust serv)

E-mail: canadaweb@penguinrandomhouse.com; customerservicescanada@penguinrandomhouse.com Web Site: www.penguinrandomhouse.ca, pg 416

Aguirre, Andrew, HarperCollins Children's Books, 195 Broadway, New York, NY 10007 Tel: 212-207-7000 Web Site: www.harpercollins.com/childrens, pg 86

Aguirre, Danielle, National Music Publishers' Association (NMPA), 1900 "N" St NW, Suite 500, Washington, DC 20036 Tel: 202-393-6672 E-mail: members@nmpa.org Web Site: nmpa.org, pg 513

Aguirre, Vanessa, St Martin's Press, LLC, 120 Broadway, New York, NY 10271 E-mail: publicity@stmartins.com; trademarketing@stmartins.com; foreignrights@stmartins.com Web Site: us.macmillan.com/smp, pg 181

Agurto, Tonya, Disney Publishing Worldwide, 1101 Flower St, Glendale, CA 91201 Web Site: books.disney.com, pg 60

Ahadi, Julia, Penny-Farthing Productions, One Sugar Creek Center Blvd, Suite 820, Sugar Land, TX 77478 Tel: 713-780-0300 Toll Free Tel: 800-926-2669 Fax: 713-780-4004 E-mail: corp@pfproductions.com Web Site: www.pfproductions.com, pg 157

Aherne, Tavy, Indiana University African Studies Program, Indiana University, 355 N Eagleson Ave, Rm GA 3072, Bloomington, IN 47405-1105 Tel: 812-855-8284 Fax: 812-855-6734 E-mail: afrist@indiana.edu Web Site: www.indiana.edu/~afrist; www.go.iu.edu/afrist, pg 100

Ahmad, Ibrahim, Viking Penguin, c/o Penguin Random House LLC, 1745 Broadway, New York, NY 10019 Tel: 212-782-9000 Web Site: www.penguin.com/overview-vikingbooks/; www.penguin.com/pamela-dorman-books-overview/; www.penguin.com/penguin-classics-overview/; www.penguin.com/penguin-life-overview/, pg 225

Ahmed, Asiya, Kokila, c/o Penguin Random House LLC, 1745 Broadway, New York, NY 10019 Tel: 212-782-9000 Web Site: www.penguin.com/kokila-books-overview/, pg 111

Ahmed, Rosie, Dial Books for Young Readers, c/o Penguin Random House LLC, 1745 Broadway, New York, NY 10019 Tel: 212-782-9000 Web Site: www.penguin.com/dial-overview/, pg 59

Ahuja, Parveen, Kapp Books LLC, 3602 Rocky Meadow Ct, Fairfax, VA 22033 Tel: 703-261-9171 Fax: 703-621-7162 E-mail: info@kappbooks.com Web Site: www.kappbooks.com, pg 108

Aippersbach, Kim, Tradewind Books, 202-1807 Maritime Mews, Vancouver, BC V6H 3W7, Canada Tel: 604-662-4405 E-mail: tradewindbooks@yahoo.com; tradewindbooks@gmail.com Web Site: www.tradewindbooks.com, pg 421

Aitken, Daniel T, Wisdom Publications Inc, 199 Elm St, Somerville, MA 02144 Tel: 617-776-7416 Toll Free Tel: 800-272-4050 (orders) Fax: 617-776-7841 E-mail: submission@wisdompubs.org Web Site: wisdomexperience.org, pg 231

Aitken, Lisa, McGill-Queen's University Press, 1010 Sherbrooke W, Suite 1720, Montreal, QC H3A 2R7, Canada Tel: 514-398-3750 Fax: 514-398-4333 E-mail: mqup@mcgill.ca Web Site: www.mqup.ca, pg 412

Aiwuyor, Jessica, Association of Research Libraries (ARL), 21 Dupont Circle NW, Suite 800, Washington, DC 20036 Tel: 202-296-2296 Fax: 202-872-0884 E-mail: webmgr@arl.org Web Site: www.arl.org, pg 20

Akers, Terrie, Other Press, 267 Fifth Ave, 6th fl, New York, NY 10016 Tel: 212-414-0054 Toll Free Tel: 877-THEOTHER (843-6843) Fax: 212-414-0939 E-mail: editor@otherpress.com; marketing@otherpress.com; publicity@otherpress.com Web Site: otherpress.com, pg 148

Akey, Katherine, Little, Brown and Company, 1290 Avenue of the Americas, New York, NY 10104 Tel: 212-364-1100 Fax: 212-364-0952 E-mail: firstname.lastname@hbgusa.com Web Site: www.hachettebookgroup.com/imprint/little-brown-and-company/, pg 118

Akinaka, James, Penguin Young Readers Group, c/o Penguin Random House LLC, 1745 Broadway, New York, NY 10019 Tel: 212-782-9000 Web Site: www.penguin.com/penguin-young-readers-overview, pg 156

Akoury-Ross, Lisa, SDP Publishing Solutions LLC, 36 Captain's Way, East Bridgewater, MA 02333 Tel: 617-775-0656 Web Site: www.sdppublishingsolutions.com, pg 444

Akturk, Ceylan, Princeton University Press, 41 William St, Princeton, NJ 08540-5237 Tel: 609-258-4900 Fax: 609-258-6305 E-mail: info@press.princeton.edu Web Site: press.princeton.edu, pg 164

Al-Hillal, Semareh, Groundwood Books, 128 Sterling Rd, Lower Level, Toronto, ON M6R 2B7, Canada Tel: 416-363-4343 Fax: 416-363-1017 E-mail: customerservice@houseofanansi.com Web Site: www.houseofanansi.com, pg 407

Al-Hillal, Semareh, House of Anansi Press Inc, 128 Sterling Rd, Lower Level, Toronto, ON M6R 2B7, Canada Tel: 416-363-4343 Fax: 416-363-1017 E-mail: customerservice@houseofanansi.com Web Site: houseofanansi.com, pg 409

Al-Nima, Sahar, Sounds True Inc, 413 S Arthur Ave, Louisville, CO 80027 Tel: 303-665-3151 Toll Free Tel: 800-333-9185 (US); 888-303-9185 (US & CN) E-mail: customerservice@soundstrue.com; stpublicity@soundstrue.com Web Site: www.soundstrue.com, pg 194

Al-Sayed, Mary, University of Chicago Press, 1427 E 60 St, Chicago, IL 60637-2954 Tel: 773-702-7700; 773-702-7600 Toll Free Tel: 800-621-2736 (orders) Fax: 773-702-9756; 773-660-2235 (orders); 773-702-2708 E-mail: custserv@press.uchicago.edu; marketing@press.uchicago.edu Web Site: www.press.uchicago.edu, pg 215

Alain, Louise, Les Editions Alire, 120 cote du Passage, Levis, QC G6V 5S9, Canada Tel: 418-835-4441 Fax: 418-838-4443 E-mail: info@alire.com Web Site: www.alire.com, pg 401

Alain, Marc, Modus Vivendi Publishing Inc, 55, rue Jean-Talon Ouest, Montreal, QC H2R 2W8, Canada Tel: 514-272-0433 Fax: 514-272-7234 E-mail: info@groupemodus.com Web Site: www.groupemodus.com, pg 413

Albanese, Frank, Harry N Abrams Inc, 195 Broadway, 9th fl, New York, NY 10007 Tel: 212-206-7715 Toll Free Tel: 800-345-1359 Fax: 212-645-8437 E-mail: abrams@abramsbooks.com; publicity@abramsbooks.com; sales@abramsbooks.com Web Site: www.abramsbooks.com, pg 2

Alben, Spencer, HarperCollins Children's Books, 195 Broadway, New York, NY 10007 Tel: 212-207-7000 Web Site: www.harpercollins.com/childrens, pg 85

Albers, Wes, Southern California Writers' Conference (SCWC), PO Box 433, Redmond, OR 97756 Tel: 619-303-8185 Fax: 619-906-7462 E-mail: msg@writersconference.com Web Site: www.writersconference.com; www.facebook.com/SouthernCaliforniaWritersConference/, pg 557

Albert, Ashley, Harry N Abrams Inc, 195 Broadway, 9th fl, New York, NY 10007 Tel: 212-206-7715 Toll Free Tel: 800-345-1359 Fax: 212-645-8437 E-mail: abrams@abramsbooks.com; publicity@abramsbooks.com; sales@abramsbooks.com Web Site: www.abramsbooks.com, pg 3

Albert, Ayana, Harry N Abrams Inc, 195 Broadway, 9th fl, New York, NY 10007 Tel: 212-206-7715 Toll Free Tel: 800-345-1359 Fax: 212-645-8437 E-mail: abrams@abramsbooks.com; publicity@abramsbooks.com; sales@abramsbooks.com Web Site: www.abramsbooks.com, pg 2

Albert, Kelly, Penguin Random House Canada, a Penguin Random House company, 320 Front St W, Suite 1400, Toronto, ON M5V 3B6, Canada Tel: 416-364-4449 Toll Free Tel: 888-523-9292 (cust serv) E-mail: canadaweb@penguinrandomhouse.com; customerservicescanada@penguinrandomhouse.com Web Site: www.penguinrandomhouse.ca, pg 416

Albert, Suzanne, Barefoot Books, 23 Bradford St, 2nd fl, Concord, MA 01742 Tel: 617-576-0660 Toll Free Tel: 866-215-1756 (cust serv); 866-417-2369 (orders) Fax: 617-576-0049 E-mail: help@barefootbooks.com Web Site: www.barefootbooks.com, pg 24

Alberts, Rachel, One-Act Playwriting Competition, 600 Wolfe St, Alexandria, VA 22314 Tel: 703-683-5778 (ext 2) Fax: 703-683-1378 E-mail: oneactslta@gmail.com Web Site: thelittletheatre.com, pg 644

Albiniak, Mike, Teton NewMedia Inc, 5286 Dunewood Dr, Florence, OR 97439 Tel: 541-991-3342 E-mail: lodgepole@tetonnm.com Web Site: www.tetonnm.com, pg 205

Alcala, Rosa, University of Texas at El Paso, Department of Creative Writing, MFA/Department of Creative Writing, M520, University Towers, Oregon St, El Paso, TX 79968 E-mail: creativewriting@utep.edu Web Site: www.utep.edu/liberalarts/creative-writing, pg 567

Alcid, Edmond, Moose Hide Books, 684 Walls Rd, Prince Township, ON P6A 6K4, Canada Tel: 705-779-3331 Fax: 705-779-3331 E-mail: mooseenterprises@on.aibn.com Web Site: www.moosehidebooks.com, pg 413

Aldana, Patsy, Greystone Books Ltd, 343 Railway St, Suite 302, Vancouver, BC V6A 1A4, Canada Tel: 604-875-1550 Fax: 604-875-1556 E-mail: info@greystonebooks.com; rights@greystonebooks.com Web Site: www.greystonebooks.com, pg 407

Alderman, Joe, University of North Texas Press, 941 Precision Dr, Denton, TX 76207 Tel: 940-565-2142 Fax: 940-369-8760 Web Site: untpress.unt.edu, pg 219

Alders, Pam, Random House Publishing Group, 1745 Broadway, New York, NY 10019 Toll Free Tel: 800-200-3552 Web Site: www.randomhousebooks.com, pg 171

Alenier, Karren L, The Tenth Gate Prize, PO Box 42164, Washington, DC 20015 E-mail: editor@wordworksbooks.org Web Site: www.wordworksbooks.org, pg 668

Alenier, Karren L, Word Works Washington Prize, PO Box 42164, Washington, DC 20015 E-mail: editor@wordworksbooks.org Web Site: www.wordworksbooks.org, pg 677

Alessi, Ana Maria, Hachette Book Group Inc, 1290 Avenue of the Americas, New York, NY 10104 Tel: 212-364-1100 Toll Free Tel: 800-759-0190 (cust serv) Fax: 212-364-0933 (intl orders) Toll Free Fax: 800-286-9471 (cust serv) E-mail: customer.service@hbgusa.com; orders@hbgusa.com Web Site: www.hachettebookgroup.com, pg 83

Alessi, Darren, Running Press, 1290 Avenue of the Americas, New York, NY 10104 Tel: 212-364-1100 Toll Free Tel: 800-759-0190 (cust serv) Fax: 212-364-0933 (intl orders) Toll Free Fax: 800-286-9471 (cust serv) E-mail: customer.service@hbgusa.com; orders@hbgusa.com Web Site: www.hachettebookgroup.com/imprint/running-press/; www.moon.com (Moon Travel Guides), pg 178

Alewel, Max, Marathon Press, 1500 Square Turn Blvd, Norfolk, NE 68701 Tel: 402-371-5040 Toll Free Tel: 800-228-0629 Fax: 402-371-9382 E-mail: info@marathonpress.net Web Site: www.marathonpress.com, pg 124

Alexander, Elizabeth, Jackie White Memorial National Children's Playwriting Contest, 1800 Nelwood Dr, Columbia, MO 65202 Web Site: www.cectheatre.org, pg 617

Alexander, Isabelle, Viking Penguin, c/o Penguin Random House LLC, 1745 Broadway, New York, NY 10019 Tel: 212-782-9000 Web Site: www.penguin.com/overview-vikingbooks/; www.penguin.com/pamela-dorman-books-overview/; www.penguin.com/penguin-classics-overview/; www.penguin.com/penguin-life-overview/, pg 225

Alexander, J Trent, Inter-University Consortium for Political & Social Research (ICPSR), 330 Packard St, Ann Arbor, MI 48104 *Tel:* 734-647-5000; 734-647-2200 *Fax:* 734-647-8200 *E-mail:* icpsr-help@umich.edu *Web Site:* www.icpsr.umich.edu, pg 102

Alexander, Jeff, Words into Print, 208 Java St, 5th fl, Brooklyn, NY 11222 *E-mail:* query@wordsintoprint.org *Web Site:* wordsintoprint.org, pg 445

Alexander, Lee Ann, Pentecostal Resources Group, 36 Research Park Ct, Weldon Spring, MO 63304 *Tel:* 636-229-7900 *Toll Free Tel:* 866-819-7667 *Web Site:* www.pentecostalpublishing.com, pg 157

Alexander, Patrick, Eisenbrauns, 820 N University Dr, USB 1, Suite C, University Park, PA 16802-1003 *Tel:* 814-865-1327 *Toll Free Tel:* 800-326-9180 (orders & cust serv) *Fax:* 814-863-1408 *Toll Free Fax:* 877-778-2665 (orders) *E-mail:* orders@psupress.org; customerservice@psupress.org *Web Site:* www.eisenbrauns.org, pg 64

Alexander, Richard, Bristol Park Books, 252 W 38 St, Suite 206, New York, NY 10018 *Tel:* 212-842-0700 *Fax:* 212-842-1771 *E-mail:* info@bristolparkbooks.com *Web Site:* bristolparkbooks.com, pg 37

Alexander, Ms Sandy, University Press of Mississippi, 3825 Ridgewood Rd, Jackson, MS 39211-6492 *Tel:* 601-432-6205 *Toll Free Tel:* 800-737-7788 (orders & cust serv) *Fax:* 601-432-6217 *E-mail:* press@mississippi.edu *Web Site:* www.upress.state.ms.us, pg 222

Alexander, Shara, Houghton Mifflin Harcourt Trade & Reference Division, 125 High St, Boston, MA 02110 *Tel:* 617-351-5000 *Web Site:* www.hmhco.com, pg 96

Alexander, Susanne, Goose Lane Editions, 500 Beaverbrook Ct, Suite 330, Fredericton, NB E3B 5X4, Canada *Tel:* 506-450-4251 *Toll Free Tel:* 888-926-8377 *Fax:* 506-459-4991 *E-mail:* orders@gooselane.com *Web Site:* www.gooselane.com, pg 407

Alexander, Susanne M, Marriage Transformation LLC, PO Box 249, Harrison, TN 37341 *Tel:* 423-599-0153 *E-mail:* staff@marriagetransformation.com *Web Site:* www.marriagetransformation.com; www.transformationlearningcenter.com, pg 125

Alexandrov, Steve, Scholastic Trade Publishing, 557 Broadway, New York, NY 10012 *Tel:* 212-343-6100; 212-343-4685 (export sales) *Fax:* 212-343-4714 (export sales) *Web Site:* www.scholastic.com, pg 184

Alfano, Alex, Andrews McMeel Publishing LLC, 1130 Walnut St, Kansas City, MO 64106-2109 *Tel:* 816-581-7500 *Toll Free Tel:* 800-851-8923 *Web Site:* www.andrewsmcmeel.com; publishing.andrewsmcmeel.com, pg 14

Alfaro, Nicole, Penguin Random House Canada, a Penguin Random House company, 320 Front St W, Suite 1400, Toronto, ON M5V 3B6, Canada *Tel:* 416-364-4449 *Toll Free Tel:* 888-523-9292 (cust serv) *E-mail:* canadaweb@penguinrandomhouse.com; customerservicescanada@penguinrandomhouse.com *Web Site:* www.penguinrandomhouse.ca, pg 416

Alfred, Valerie, Workman Publishing, 1290 Avenue of the Americas, New York, NY 10104 *Toll Free Tel:* 800-759-0190 *Fax:* 212-364-0950 *E-mail:* workman-inquiry@hbgusa.com *Web Site:* www.hachettebookgroup.com/imprint/workman-publishing-company/, pg 233

Alguire, Julie, Crabtree Publishing Co, 347 Fifth Ave, Suite 1402-145, New York, NY 10016 *Tel:* 212-496-5040 *Toll Free Tel:* 800-387-7650 *Toll Free Fax:* 800-355-7166 *E-mail:* custserv@crabtreebooks.com *Web Site:* www.crabtreebooks.com, pg 54

Alguire, Julie, Crabtree Publishing Co Ltd, 616 Welland Ave, St Catharines, ON L2M 5V6, Canada *Tel:* 905-682-5221 *Toll Free Tel:* 800-387-7650 *Fax:* 905-682-7166 *Toll Free Fax:* 800-355-7166 *E-mail:* custserv@crabtreebooks.com; sales@crabtreebooks.com; orders@crabtreebooks.com *Web Site:* www.crabtreebooks.ca, pg 400

Ali, Liaquat, Kazi Publications Inc, 3023 W Belmont Ave, Chicago, IL 60618 *Tel:* 773-267-7001 *Fax:* 773-267-7002 *E-mail:* info@kazi.org *Web Site:* www.kazi.org, pg 108

Ali, Sonia, LARB/USC Publishing Workshop, 6671 Sunset Blvd, Suite 1521, Los Angeles, CA 90028 *E-mail:* publishingworkshop@lareviewofbooks.org *Web Site:* thepublishingworkshop.com, pg 556

Ali-Coleman, Khadijah Z, Hurston/Wright Award for College Writers, 10 "G" St NE, Suite 600, Washington, DC 20002 *E-mail:* info@hurstonwright.org *Web Site:* www.hurstonwright.org/awards/hurston-wright-award-for-college-writers, pg 614

Ali-Coleman, Khadijah Z, Hurston/Wright Legacy Awards, 10 "G" St NE, Suite 600, Washington, DC 20002 *E-mail:* info@hurstonwright.org *Web Site:* www.hurstonwright.org/awards/legacy-awards, pg 614

Ali-Coleman, Khadijah Z, Hurston/Wright Writers Week Workshops, 10 "G" St NE, Suite 600, Washington, DC 20002 *E-mail:* info@hurstonwright.org *Web Site:* www.hurstonwright.org/workshops/writers-week-workshops, pg 555

Ali-Coleman, Khadijah Z, The Zora Neale Hurston/Richard Wright Foundation, 10 "G" St NE, Suite 600, Washington, DC 20002 *E-mail:* info@hurstonwright.org *Web Site:* www.hurstonwright.org, pg 525

Ali-Virani, Sanaa, Tor Publishing Group, 120 Broadway, New York, NY 10271 *Toll Free Tel:* 800-455-0340 (Macmillan) *E-mail:* torpublicity@tor.com; forgepublicity@forgebooks.com *Web Site:* us.macmillan.com/torpublishinggroup, pg 208

Allahverdi, Layla, International Society for Technology in Education, 2111 Wilson Blvd, Suite 300, Arlington, VA 22201 *Tel:* 503-342-2848 (intl) *Toll Free Tel:* 800-336-5191 (US & CN) *Fax:* 541-302-3778 *E-mail:* iste@iste.org *Web Site:* www.iste.org, pg 103

Allan, Megan, Sovereign Award for Outstanding Writing, Woodbine Sales Pavilion, 555 Rexdale Blvd, Toronto, ON M9W 5L2, Canada *Tel:* 416-675-7756 *Fax:* 416-675-6378 *E-mail:* jockeyclubcanada@gmail.com *Web Site:* www.jockeyclubcanada.com, pg 665

Allan, Richard, The Aaland Agency, PO Box 849, Inyokern, CA 93527-0849 *Tel:* 760-384-3910 *E-mail:* anniejo41@gmail.com *Web Site:* www.the-aaland-agency.com, pg 447

Allannic, Rica, David Black Agency, 335 Adams St, 27th fl, Suite 2707, Brooklyn, NY 11201 *Tel:* 718-852-5500 *Fax:* 718-852-5539 *Web Site:* www.davidblackagency.com, pg 450

Allen, Anaka, Macmillan, 120 Broadway, 22nd fl, New York, NY 10271 *E-mail:* press.inquiries@macmillan.com *Web Site:* us.macmillan.com, pg 122

Allen, Ben, St Martin's Press, LLC, 120 Broadway, New York, NY 10271 *E-mail:* publicity@stmartins.com; trademarketing@stmartins.com; foreignrights@stmartins.com *Web Site:* us.macmillan.com/smp, pg 181

Allen, Charlie, Princeton University Press, 41 William St, Princeton, NJ 08540-5237 *Tel:* 609-258-4900 *Fax:* 609-258-6305 *E-mail:* info@press.princeton.edu *Web Site:* press.princeton.edu, pg 164

Allen, Heather, Harry N Abrams Inc, 195 Broadway, 9th fl, New York, NY 10007 *Tel:* 212-206-7715 *Toll Free Tel:* 800-345-1359 *Fax:* 212-645-8437 *E-mail:* abrams@abramsbooks.com; publicity@abramsbooks.com; sales@abramsbooks.com *Web Site:* www.abramsbooks.com, pg 3

Allen, Johanna, Farrar, Straus & Giroux Books for Young Readers, 120 Broadway, New York, NY 10271 *Tel:* 212-741-6900 *Toll Free Tel:* 888-330-8477 (orders) *E-mail:* childrens.publicity@macmillanusa.com; childrensrights@macmillanusa.com *Web Site:* us.macmillan.com/mackids, pg 70

Allen, Johanna, Roaring Brook Press, 120 Broadway, New York, NY 10271 *Tel:* 646-307-5151 *Web Site:* us.macmillan.com/publishers/roaring-brook-press, pg 176

Allen, Josyann, Les Presses de l'Universite Laval, 2180, Chemin Sainte-Foy, 1st fl, Quebec, QC G1V 0A6, Canada *Tel:* 418-656-2803 *Fax:* 418-656-3305 *E-mail:* presses@pul.ulaval.ca *Web Site:* www.pulaval.com, pg 417

Allen, Kathleen, Les Presses de l'Universite Laval, 2180, Chemin Sainte-Foy, 1st fl, Quebec, QC G1V 0A6, Canada *Tel:* 418-656-2803 *Fax:* 418-656-3305 *E-mail:* presses@pul.ulaval.ca *Web Site:* www.pulaval.com, pg 417

Allen, Kini, Little, Brown and Company, 1290 Avenue of the Americas, New York, NY 10104 *Tel:* 212-364-1100 *Fax:* 212-364-0952 *E-mail:* firstname.lastname@hbgusa.com *Web Site:* www.hachettebookgroup.com/imprint/little-brown-and-company/, pg 118

Allen, Marc, New World Library, 14 Pamaron Way, Novato, CA 94949 *Tel:* 415-884-2100 *Fax:* 415-884-2199 *E-mail:* escort@newworldlibrary.com *Web Site:* www.newworldlibrary.com, pg 140

Allen, Pete, JMW Group Inc, 346 Rte 6, No 867, Mahopac, NY 10541 *Tel:* 914-841-7105 *Fax:* 914-248-8861 *E-mail:* jmwgroup@jmwgroup.net *Web Site:* www.jmwforlife.com, pg 465

Allen, Robert, Macmillan Audio, 120 Broadway, 22nd fl, New York, NY 10271 *Tel:* 646-600-7856 *Toll Free Tel:* 888-330-8477 (cust serv) *Toll Free Fax:* 800-672-7703 *E-mail:* macmillan.audio@macmillanusa.com *Web Site:* us.macmillan.com/audio, pg 123

Allen, Ron, International Risk Management Institute Inc, 12222 Merit Dr, Suite 1600, Dallas, TX 75251-2266 *Tel:* 972-960-7693 *Fax:* 972-371-5120 *E-mail:* info27@irmi.com *Web Site:* www.irmi.com, pg 103

Allen, Samantha, Chronicle Books LLC, 680 Second St, San Francisco, CA 94107 *Tel:* 415-537-4200 *Fax:* 415-537-4460 (perms) *E-mail:* hello@chroniclebooks.com; subrights@chroniclebooks.com *Web Site:* www.chroniclebooks.com, pg 47

Allen, Simon, McGraw-Hill Education, 2 Penn Plaza, New York, NY 10121-2298 *Tel:* 212-904-2000 *E-mail:* international_cs@mheducation.com; seg_customerservice@mheducation.com (PreK-12); hep_customerservice@mheducation.com (higher education) *Web Site:* www.mheducation.com, pg 127

Allen, Thomas M, Union Square & Co, 1166 Avenue of the Americas, 17th fl, New York, NY 10036-2715 *Tel:* 212-532-7160 *Toll Free Tel:* 800-367-9692 *Fax:* 212-213-2495 *Toll Free Fax:* 800-542-7567 *E-mail:* custservice@sterlingpublishing.com; customerservice@sterlingpublishing.com; editorial@sterlingpublishing.com; tradesales@sterlingpublishing.com *Web Site:* www.sterlingpublishing.com, pg 212

Allen, Tom, Sophia Institute Press®, 18 Celina Ave, Unit 1, Nashua, NH 03063 *Tel:* 603-641-9344 *Toll Free Tel:* 800-888-9344 *Fax:* 603-641-8108 *Toll Free Fax:* 888-288-2259 *E-mail:* orders@sophiainstitute.com *Web Site:* www.sophiainstitute.com, pg 193

Allender, David, Godine, 184 Belknap St, Concord, MA 01742 *E-mail:* info@godine.com *Web Site:* www.godine.com, pg 79

Aller, Gary, Gallaudet University Press, 800 Florida Ave NE, Washington, DC 20002-3695 *Tel:* 202-651-5488 *Fax:* 202-651-5489 *E-mail:* gupress@gallaudet.edu *Web Site:* gupress.gallaudet.edu, pg 76

Allessi, Ana Maria, Hachette Audio, 1290 Avenue of the Americas, New York, NY 10104 *Tel:* 212-364-1100 *Web Site:* www.hachettebookgroup.com/imprint/hachette-audio/, pg 83

Allgood, Evan, Beaver's Pond Press Inc, 939 Seventh St W, St Paul, MN 55102 *Tel:* 952-829-8818 *E-mail:* submissions@beaverspondpress.com *Web Site:* www.beaverspondpress.com, pg 26

Allman, Karen, Rowman & Littlefield, 4501 Forbes Blvd, Suite 200, Lanham, MD 20706 *Tel:* 301-459-3366 *Toll Free Tel:* 800-462-6420 (ext 3024, cust serv) *Fax:* 301-429-5748 *Web Site:* rowman.com, pg 178

Allport, Andrew, Rick DeMarinis Short Story Award, PO Box 2414, Durango, CO 81302 *Tel:* 970-903-7914 *E-mail:* cutthroatmag@gmail.com *Web Site:* www.cutthroatmag.com, pg 595

Allport, Andrew, Joy Harjo Poetry Award, PO Box 2414, Durango, CO 81302 *Tel:* 970-903-7914 *E-mail:* cutthroatmag@gmail.com *Web Site:* www.cutthroatmag.com, pg 611

Allport, Andrew, Barry Lopez Nonfiction Award, PO Box 2414, Durango, CO 81302 *Tel:* 970-903-7914 *E-mail:* cutthroatmag@gmail.com *Web Site:* www.cutthroatmag.com, pg 626

Almahdi, Nadia, Simon & Schuster Children's Publishing, 1230 Avenue of the Americas, New York, NY 10020 *Tel:* 212-698-7000 *Web Site:* www.simonandschuster.com/kids; www.simonandschuster.com/teen; simonandschuster.net; simonandschuster.biz, pg 189

Alonzo, Melissa, HarperCollins Publishers LLC, 195 Broadway, New York, NY 10007 *Tel:* 212-207-7000 *Web Site:* www.harpercollins.com, pg 87

Alperen, Jenny, The Betsy Nolan Literary Agency, 112 E 17 St, Suite 1W, New York, NY 10003 *Tel:* 212-967-8200 *Web Site:* www.nolanlehrgroup.com, pg 471

Alps, Marisa, Harbour Publishing Co Ltd, 4437 Rondeview Rd, Madeira Park, BC V0N 2H0, Canada *Tel:* 604-883-2730 *Toll Free Tel:* 800-667-2988 *Fax:* 604-883-9451 *Toll Free Fax:* 877-604-9449 *E-mail:* info@harbourpublishing.com; orders@harbourpublishing.com *Web Site:* harbourpublishing.com, pg 408

Alquist, Pierce, Skinner House Books, c/o Unitarian Universalist Assn, 24 Farnsworth St, Boston, MA 02210-1409 *Tel:* 617-742-2100 *Fax:* 617-948-6466 *E-mail:* skinnerhouse@uua.org *Web Site:* www.uua.org/publications/skinnerhouse, pg 190

Alsdorf, Debbie, Books & Such, 2222 Cleveland Ave, No 1005, Santa Rosa, CA 95403 *Tel:* 707-538-4184 *Web Site:* booksandsuch.com, pg 451

Altaf, Hasan, Hadada Award, 544 W 27 St, New York, NY 10001 *Tel:* 212-343-1333 *E-mail:* queries@theparisreview.org *Web Site:* www.theparisreview.org/about/prizes, pg 610

Altaf, Hasan, The Plimpton Prize for Fiction, 544 W 27 St, New York, NY 10001 *Tel:* 212-343-1333 *E-mail:* queries@theparisreview.org *Web Site:* www.theparisreview.org, pg 650

Altaf, Hasan, Terry Southern Prize, 544 W 27 St, New York, NY 10001 *Tel:* 212-343-1333 *E-mail:* queries@theparisreview.org *Web Site:* www.theparisreview.org, pg 665

Altman, David, Hudson Institute, 1201 Pennsylvania Ave NW, 4th fl, Washington, DC 20004 *Tel:* 202-974-2400 *Fax:* 202-974-2410 *E-mail:* info@hudson.org *Web Site:* www.hudson.org, pg 97

Altman, David G, Center for Creative Leadership LLC, One Leadership Place, Greensboro, NC 27410-9427 *Tel:* 336-545-2810; 336-288-7210 *Fax:* 336-282-3284 *E-mail:* info@ccl.org *Web Site:* shop.ccl.org/usa/books, pg 43

Altman, Mary, Sourcebooks LLC, 1935 Brookdale Rd, Suite 139, Naperville, IL 60563 *Tel:* 630-961-3900 *Toll Free Tel:* 800-432-7444 *Fax:* 630-961-2168 *E-mail:* info@sourcebooks.com *Web Site:* www.sourcebooks.com, pg 194

Altschuler, Miriam, DeFiore and Company Literary Management Inc, 47 E 19 St, 3rd fl, New York, NY 10003 *Tel:* 212-925-7744 *Fax:* 212-925-9803 *E-mail:* info@defliterary.com; submissions@defliterary.com *Web Site:* www.defliterary.com, pg 456

Alvarado, Veronica (Ronnie), Atria Books, 1230 Avenue of the Americas, New York, NY 10020 *Tel:* 212-698-7000 *Fax:* 212-698-7007 *Web Site:* www.simonandschuster.com, pg 21

Alvarez, Awilda, Hippocrene Books Inc, 171 Madison Ave, Suite 1605, New York, NY 10016 *Tel:* 212-685-4373 *E-mail:* info@hippocrenebooks.com; orderdept@hippocrenebooks.com (orders) *Web Site:* www.hippocrenebooks.com, pg 92

Alvarez, Brian, Harry N Abrams Inc, 195 Broadway, 9th fl, New York, NY 10007 *Tel:* 212-206-7715 *Toll Free Tel:* 800-345-1359 *Fax:* 212-645-8437 *E-mail:* abrams@abramsbooks.com; publicity@abramsbooks.com; sales@abramsbooks.com *Web Site:* www.abramsbooks.com, pg 2

Alvarez, Iria, Penguin Random House LLC, 1745 Broadway, New York, NY 10019 *Tel:* 212-782-9000 *Toll Free Tel:* 800-726-0600 *Web Site:* www.penguinrandomhouse.com, pg 155

Alvarez, Jessica, BookEnds Literary Agency, 136 Long Hill Rd, Gillette, NJ 07933 *Web Site:* www.bookendsliterary.com, pg 451

Alvarez, Lisa, Community of Writers Summer Workshops, PO Box 1416, Nevada City, CA 95959 *Tel:* 530-470-8440 *E-mail:* info@communityofwriters.org *Web Site:* www.communityofwriters.org, pg 553

Alves, Elissa, Folio Literary Management, The Film Center Bldg, 630 Ninth Ave, Suite 1101, New York, NY 10036 *Tel:* 212-400-1494 *Fax:* 212-967-0977 *Web Site:* www.foliolit.com, pg 459

Alward, Kathy, Piano Press, 1425 Ocean Ave, Suite 5, Del Mar, CA 92014 *Tel:* 619-884-1401 *E-mail:* pianopress@pianopress.com *Web Site:* www.pianopress.com, pg 159

Amadi-obi, Nneoma, W W Norton & Company Inc, 500 Fifth Ave, New York, NY 10110-0017 *Tel:* 212-354-5500 *Toll Free Tel:* 800-233-4830 (orders & cust serv) *Fax:* 212-869-0856 *Toll Free Fax:* 800-458-6515 *E-mail:* orders@wwnorton.com *Web Site:* wwnorton.com, pg 143

Amaiz, Diziree, Library of Congress Prize for American Fiction, 101 Independence Ave SE, Washington, DC 20540-1400 *Tel:* 202-707-5221 (Center for the Book) *Fax:* 202-707-0269 *Web Site:* www.loc.gov, pg 624

Amatucci, Danielle, Princeton University Press, 41 William St, Princeton, NJ 08540-5237 *Tel:* 609-258-4900 *Fax:* 609-258-6305 *E-mail:* info@press.princeton.edu *Web Site:* press.princeton.edu, pg 164

Amatullo, Mariana, Parsons School of Design, Continuing & Professional Education, 66 W 12 St, New York, NY 10011 *Tel:* 212-229-8933 ext 4076 *E-mail:* continuinged@newschool.edu *Web Site:* www.newschool.edu/parsons, pg 564

Ambrose, Ann, Princeton University Press, 41 William St, Princeton, NJ 08540-5237 *Tel:* 609-258-4900 *Fax:* 609-258-6305 *E-mail:* info@press.princeton.edu *Web Site:* press.princeton.edu, pg 164

Amendolara, Paula, Sourcebooks LLC, 1935 Brookdale Rd, Suite 139, Naperville, IL 60563 *Tel:* 630-961-3900 *Toll Free Tel:* 800-432-7444 *Fax:* 630-961-2168 *E-mail:* info@sourcebooks.com *Web Site:* www.sourcebooks.com, pg 194

Ames, Bill, Triumph Books LLC, 814 N Franklin St, Chicago, IL 60610 *Tel:* 312-337-0747 *Toll Free Tel:* 800-888-4741 (cust serv) *Fax:* 312-280-5470; 312-337-5985 *Web Site:* www.triumphbooks.com, pg 209

Ames, Joanna, Canadian Publishers' Council (CPC), 3080 Yonge St, Suite 6060, Toronto, ON M4N 3N1, Canada *Tel:* 647-255-8880 *Web Site:* pubcouncil.ca, pg 502

Ames, Leah, Perfection Learning®, 1000 N Second Ave, Logan, IA 51546-1061 *Tel:* 712-644-2831 *Toll Free Tel:* 800-831-4190 *Toll Free Fax:* 800-543-2745 *E-mail:* orders@perfectionlearning.com *Web Site:* www.perfectionlearning.com, pg 158

Ames, Raina, Anna Zornio Memorial Children's Theatre Playwriting Award, D22 Paul Creative Arts Center, 30 Academic Way, Durham, NH 03824 *Tel:* 603-862-2919 *Fax:* 603-862-0298 *E-mail:* theatre.dance@unh.edu *Web Site:* cola.unh.edu/theatre-dance/opportunities/competitions, pg 680

Ames, Steve, World Citizens, PO Box 131, Mill Valley, CA 94942-0131 *Tel:* 415-380-8020; 415-233-2822 (direct), pg 233

Amini, Christina Maheen, Chronicle Books LLC, 680 Second St, San Francisco, CA 94107 *Tel:* 415-537-4200 *Fax:* 415-537-4460 (perms) *E-mail:* hello@chroniclebooks.com; subrights@chroniclebooks.com *Web Site:* www.chroniclebooks.com, pg 47

Amling, Eric, Darhansoff & Verrill, 529 11 St, 3rd fl, Brooklyn, NY 11215 *Tel:* 917-305-1300 *E-mail:* permissions@dvagency.com *Web Site:* www.dvagency.com, pg 455

Amodei, Michael, Ave Maria Press Inc, PO Box 428, Notre Dame, IN 46556 *Toll Free Tel:* 800-282-1865 *Toll Free Fax:* 800-282-5681 *E-mail:* avemariapress.1@nd.edu *Web Site:* www.avemariapress.com, pg 22

Amodeo, Paul, New York University, Center for Publishing & Applied Liberal Arts, 7 E 12 St, New York, NY 10003 *Tel:* 212-998-7200 *E-mail:* sps.info@nyu.edu *Web Site:* www.scps.nyu.edu/professional-pathways/topics.html, pg 563

Amoroso, Connie, Carnegie Mellon University Press, 5032 Forbes Ave, Pittsburgh, PA 15289-1021 *Tel:* 412-268-2861 *E-mail:* cmupress@andrew.cmu.edu *Web Site:* www.cmu.edu/universitypress, pg 41

Amos, Holly, Frederick Bock Prize, 61 W Superior St, Chicago, IL 60654 *Tel:* 312-787-7070 *Web Site:* www.poetryfoundation.org/poetrymagazine/prizes, pg 582

Amos, Holly, Editors Prize for Feature Article, 61 W Superior St, Chicago, IL 60654 *Tel:* 312-787-7070 *Web Site:* www.poetryfoundation.org/poetrymagazine/prizes, pg 598

Amos, Holly, Editors Prize for Reviewing, 61 W Superior St, Chicago, IL 60654 *Tel:* 312-787-7070 *Web Site:* www.poetryfoundation.org/poetrymagazine/prizes, pg 598

Amos, Holly, Editors Prize for Visual Poetry, 61 W Superior St, Chicago, IL 60654 *Tel:* 312-787-7070 *Web Site:* www.poetryfoundation.org/poetrymagazine/prizes, pg 598

Amos, Holly, Friends of Literature Prize, 61 W Superior St, Chicago, IL 60654 *Tel:* 312-787-7070 *Web Site:* www.poetryfoundation.org/poetrymagazine/prizes, pg 605

Amos, Holly, Bess Hokin Prize, 61 W Superior St, Chicago, IL 60654 *Tel:* 312-787-7070 *Web Site:* www.poetryfoundation.org/poetrymagazine/prizes, pg 613

Amos, Holly, Levinson Prize, 61 W Superior St, Chicago, IL 60654 *Tel:* 312-787-7070 *Web Site:* www.poetryfoundation.org/poetrymagazine/prizes, pg 624

Amos, Holly, John Frederick Nims Memorial Prize for Translation, 61 W Superior St, Chicago, IL 60654 *Tel:* 312-787-7070 *Web Site:* www.poetryfoundation.org/poetrymagazine/prizes, pg 641

Amos, Holly, The J Howard & Barbara M J Wood Prize, 61 W Superior St, Chicago, IL 60654 *Tel:* 312-787-7070 *Web Site:* www.poetryfoundation.org/poetrymagazine/prizes, pg 677

Amphlett, Nick, HarperCollins Publishers LLC, 195 Broadway, New York, NY 10007 *Tel:* 212-207-7000 *Web Site:* www.harpercollins.com, pg 87

Amstadter, Noah, Triumph Books LLC, 814 N Franklin St, Chicago, IL 60610 *Tel:* 312-337-0747 *Toll Free Tel:* 800-888-4741 (cust serv) *Fax:* 312-280-5470; 312-337-5985 *Web Site:* www.triumphbooks.com, pg 209

Amster, Betsy, Betsy Amster Literary Enterprises, 607 Foothill Blvd, No 1061, La Canada Flintridge, CA 91012 *E-mail:* rights@amsterlit.com; b.amster.assistant@gmail.com (book queries) *Web Site:* amsterlit.com, pg 448

Amstutz, Nicolette, Hamilton Books, 4501 Forbes Blvd, Suite 200, Lanham, MD 20706 *Tel:* 301-459-3366 *Toll Free Tel:* 800-462-6420 (cust serv) *Fax:* 301-429-5748 *Toll Free Fax:* 800-388-4550 (cust serv), pg 84

Amstutz, Nicolette, Lexington Books, 4501 Forbes Blvd, Suite 200, Lanham, MD 20706 *Tel:* 301-459-3366 *Web Site:* rowman.com/page/lexington, pg 115

Amstutz, Nicolette, University Press of America Inc, 4501 Forbes Blvd, Suite 200, Lanham, MD 20706 *Tel:* 301-459-3366 *Toll Free Tel:* 800-462-6420 *Web Site:* www.univpress.com, pg 221

Anakwah, Lashanda, Dutton, c/o Penguin Random House LLC, 1745 Broadway, New York, NY 10019 *Tel:* 212-366-2000 *Web Site:* www.penguin.com/dutton-overview/; www.penguin.com/plume-books-overview/; www.penguin.com/tiny-reparations-overview/, pg 62

Anand, Rajit, Scholastic International, 557 Broadway, New York, NY 10012 *Tel:* 212-343-6100; 646-330-5288 (intl cust serv) *Toll Free Tel:* 800-SCHOLASTIC (724-6527) *Fax:* 646-837-7878 *E-mail:* international@scholastic.com, pg 184

Anand, Ritu, D4EO Literary Agency, 13206 Treviso Dr, Lakewood Ranch, FL 34211 *Tel:* 203-545-7180 (cell) *Web Site:* www.d4eoliteraryagency.com; www.publishersmarketplace.com/members/d4eo/; x.com/d4eo, pg 456

Anastas, Margaret, Flamingo Books, c/o Penguin Random House LLC, 1745 Broadway, New York, NY 10019 *Tel:* 212-782-9000 *Web Site:* www.penguin.com/flamingo-overview/, pg 72

Andadari, Chalista, Penguin Random House Canada, a Penguin Random House company, 320 Front St W, Suite 1400, Toronto, ON M5V 3B6, Canada *Tel:* 416-364-4449 *Toll Free Tel:* 888-523-9292 (cust serv) *E-mail:* canadaweb@penguinrandomhouse.com; customerservicescanada@penguinrandomhouse.com *Web Site:* www.penguinrandomhouse.ca, pg 416

Anders, Tim, FC&A Publishing, 103 Clover Green, Peachtree City, GA 30269 *Tel:* 770-487-6307 *Toll Free Tel:* 800-226-8024 *Web Site:* www.fca.com, pg 70

Anderson, Andrea, Theodore C Blegen Award, 2925 Academy Rd, Durham, NC 27705 *Tel:* 919-682-9319 *Fax:* 919-682-2349 *Web Site:* foresthistory.org/awards-fellowships/blegen-award, pg 582

Anderson, Andrea, John M Collier Award for Forest History Journalism, 2925 Academy Rd, Durham, NC 27705 *Tel:* 919-682-9319 *Fax:* 919-682-2349 *Web Site:* foresthistory.org/awards-fellowships/collier-award, pg 591

Anderson, Andrea, Leopold-Hidy Award, 2925 Academy Rd, Durham, NC 27705 *Tel:* 919-682-9319 *Fax:* 919-682-2349 *Web Site:* foresthistory.org/awards-fellowships/leopold-hidy-award, pg 623

Anderson, Andrea, Charles A Weyerhauser Book Award, 2925 Academy Rd, Durham, NC 27705 *Tel:* 919-682-9319 *Fax:* 919-682-2349 *Web Site:* foresthistory.org/awards-fellowships/weyerhaeuser-award, pg 674

Anderson, Chris, HarperCollins Publishers LLC, 195 Broadway, New York, NY 10007 *Tel:* 212-207-7000 *Web Site:* www.harpercollins.com, pg 86

Anderson, Dawn, Our Daily Bread Publishing, 3000 Kraft Ave SE, Grand Rapids, MI 49512 *Toll Free Tel:* 800-653-8333 (cust serv) *E-mail:* customerservice@odb.org *Web Site:* ourdailybreadpublishing.org, pg 148

Anderson, Derrick, American Council on Education (ACE), One Dupont Circle NW, Washington, DC 20036 *Tel:* 202-939-9300 *Web Site:* www.acenet.edu, pg 9, 495

Anderson, Devery S, Signature Books Publishing LLC, 564 W 400 N, Salt Lake City, UT 84116-3411 *Toll Free Tel:* 800-356-5687 *E-mail:* people@signaturebooks.com *Web Site:* www.signaturebooks.com; www.signaturebookslibrary.org, pg 188

Anderson, Duane, ACU Press, ACU Box 29138, Abilene, TX 79699 *Tel:* 325-674-2720 *Toll Free Tel:* 877-816-4455 *E-mail:* acupressoffice@groupmail.acu.edu *Web Site:* www.acupressbooks.com; www.leafwoodpublishers.com, pg 4

Anderson, Elizabeth, Chronicle Books LLC, 680 Second St, San Francisco, CA 94107 *Tel:* 415-537-4200 *Fax:* 415-537-4460 (perms) *E-mail:* hello@chroniclebooks.com; subrights@chroniclebooks.com *Web Site:* www.chroniclebooks.com, pg 47

Anderson, Ellie, HarperCollins Publishers LLC, 195 Broadway, New York, NY 10007 *Tel:* 212-207-7000 *Web Site:* www.harpercollins.com, pg 87

Anderson, Erik, University of Minnesota Press, 111 Third Ave S, Suite 290, Minneapolis, MN 55401-2520 *Tel:* 612-301-1990 *Fax:* 612-301-1980 *E-mail:* ump@umn.edu *Web Site:* www.upress.umn.edu, pg 217

Anderson, Garrett, Annual Off Off Broadway Short Play Festival, 250 W 57 St, 6th fl, New York, NY 10107-0102 *Toll Free Tel:* 866-979-0447 *E-mail:* oobfestival@samuelfrench.com; info@concordtheatricals.com *Web Site:* oobfestival.com; www.concordtheatricals.com, pg 643

Anderson, Dr Gordon L, Paragon House, 3600 Labore Rd, Suite 1, St Paul, MN 55110-4144 *Tel:* 651-644-3087 *Toll Free Tel:* 800-447-3709 *Fax:* 651-644-0997 *E-mail:* paragon@paragonhouse.com *Web Site:* www.paragonhouse.com, pg 151

Anderson, Jon, Simon & Schuster Children's Publishing, 1230 Avenue of the Americas, New York, NY 10020 *Tel:* 212-698-7000 *Web Site:* www.simonandschuster.com/kids; www.simonandschuster.com/teen; simonandschuster.net; simonandschuster.biz, pg 189

Anderson, Jon, Simon & Schuster, LLC, 1230 Avenue of the Americas, New York, NY 10020 *Tel:* 212-698-7000 *Toll Free Tel:* 800-223-2336 (orders) *Fax:* 212-698-7007 *Toll Free Fax:* 800-943-9831 (orders) *E-mail:* firstname.lastname@simonandschuster.com; purchaseorders@simonandschuster.com (orders) *Web Site:* www.simonandschuster.com, pg 189

Anderson, Kathleen, Anderson Literary Management LLC, 244 Fifth Ave, 2nd fl, Suite F166, New York, NY 10001 *Tel:* 212-645-6045 *Fax:* 212-741-1936 *E-mail:* info@andersonliterary.com *Web Site:* www.andersonliterary.com, pg 449

Anderson, Kim A, National Education Association (NEA), 1201 16 St NW, Washington, DC 20036-3290 *Tel:* 202-833-4000 *Fax:* 202-822-7974 *Web Site:* www.nea.org, pg 137

Anderson, Kim A, National Education Association (NEA), 1201 16 St NW, Washington, DC 20036-3290 *Tel:* 202-833-4000 *Fax:* 202-822-7974 *E-mail:* media-relations-team@nea.org *Web Site:* www.nea.org, pg 513

Anderson, Kimberly Bolton, Chronicle Books LLC, 680 Second St, San Francisco, CA 94107 *Tel:* 415-537-4200 *Fax:* 415-537-4460 *E-mail:* hello@chroniclebooks.com; subrights@chroniclebooks.com *Web Site:* www.chroniclebooks.com, pg 47

Anderson, Mary K, IODE Jean Throop Book Award, 9-45 Frid St, Hamilton, ON L8P 4M3, Canada *Tel:* 905-522-9537 *Fax:* 905-522-3637 *E-mail:* iodeontario@gmail.com *Web Site:* www.iodeontario.ca, pg 617

Anderson, Mindy, Springer Publishing Co, 11 W 42 St, 15th fl, New York, NY 10036-8002 *Tel:* 212-431-4370 *Toll Free Tel:* 877-687-7476 *E-mail:* marketing@springerpub.com; cs@springerpub.com (orders); textbook@springerpub.com; specialsales@springerpub.com *Web Site:* www.springerpub.com, pg 196

Anderson, Monty, Presbyterian Publishing Corp (PPC), 100 Witherspoon St, Louisville, KY 40202 *Tel:* 502-569-5000 *Toll Free Tel:* 800-533-4371; 800-523-1631 (US only) *Fax:* 502-569-5113 *E-mail:* customerservice@presbypub.com *Web Site:* www.ppcbooks.com; www.wjkbooks.com, pg 163

Anderson, Monty, Westminster John Knox Press (WJK), 100 Witherspoon St, Louisville, KY 40202-1396 *Tel:* 502-569-5052 *Toll Free Tel:* 800-523-1631 (US & CN) *Fax:* 502-569-8308 *Toll Free Fax:* 800-541-5113 (US & CN) *E-mail:* customer_service@wjkbooks.com; orders@wjkbooks.com *Web Site:* www.wjkbooks.com, pg 228

Anderson, Nikki, Princeton University Press, 41 William St, Princeton, NJ 08540-5237 *Tel:* 609-258-4900 *Fax:* 609-258-6305 *E-mail:* info@press.princeton.edu *Web Site:* press.princeton.edu, pg 164

Anderson, Roshe, Avery, c/o Penguin Random House LLC, 1745 Broadway, New York, NY 10019 *Tel:* 212-366-2000 *Web Site:* www.penguin.com/avery-overview/, pg 23

Anderson, Roshe, TarcherPerigee, c/o Penguin Random House LLC, 1745 Broadway, New York, NY 10019 *Tel:* 212-782-9000 *Web Site:* www.penguin.com/tarcherperigee-overview/; www.facebook.com/TarcherPerigee, pg 202

Anderson, Sara, Sara Anderson Children's Books, PO Box 47182, Seattle, WA 98146 *Tel:* 206-285-1520 *Web Site:* www.saraandersonchildrensbooks.com, pg 13

Anderson-Kenkpen, Tenisha, Kokila, c/o Penguin Random House LLC, 1745 Broadway, New York, NY 10019 *Tel:* 212-782-9000 *Web Site:* www.penguin.com/kokila-books-overview/, pg 111

Anderton, Trish, Goddard Riverside CBC Youth Book Prize for Social Justice, 593 Columbus Ave, New York, NY 10024 *Tel:* 212-873-6600 *E-mail:* cbcprize@goddard.org *Web Site:* goddard.org/bookprizes, pg 607

Anderton, Trish, Goddard Riverside Stephan Russo Book Prize for Social Justice, 593 Columbus Ave, New York, NY 10024 *E-mail:* russoprize@goddard.org *Web Site:* goddard.org/bookprizes, pg 607

Andonian, Mr Aramais, Blue Crane Books Inc, 36 Hazel St, Watertown, MA 02472 *Tel:* 617-926-8989, pg 32

Andrade, Hannah, Bradford Literary Agency, 5694 Mission Center Rd, Suite 347, San Diego, CA 92108 *Tel:* 619-521-1201 *E-mail:* hillary@bradfordlit.com *Web Site:* www.bradfordlit.com, pg 451

Andrade, Jamie, Running Press, 1290 Avenue of the Americas, New York, NY 10104 *Tel:* 212-364-1100 *Toll Free Tel:* 800-759-0190 (cust serv) *Fax:* 212-364-0933 (intl orders) *Toll Free Fax:* 800-286-9471 (cust serv) *E-mail:* customer.service@hbgusa.com; orders@hbgusa.com *Web Site:* www.hachettebookgroup.com/imprint/running-press/; www.moon.com (Moon Travel Guides), pg 178

Andre, Laura, Ohio University Press, Alden Library, Suite 101, 30 Park Place, Athens, OH 45701-2909 *Tel:* 740-593-1154 *Web Site:* www.ohioswallow.com, pg 146

Andreadis, Tina, HarperCollins Publishers LLC, 195 Broadway, New York, NY 10007 *Tel:* 212-207-7000 *Web Site:* www.harpercollins.com, pg 86

Andree, Courtney J, Juniper Prize for Creative Nonfiction, New Africa House, 180 Infirmary Way, 4th fl, Amherst, MA 01003-9289 *E-mail:* juniperprize@umpress.umass.edu *Web Site:* www.umasspress.com/juniper-prizes, pg 619

Andree, Courtney J, Juniper Prize for Fiction, New Africa House, 180 Infirmary Way, 4th fl, Amherst, MA 01003-9289 *E-mail:* juniperprize@umpress.umass.edu *Web Site:* www.umasspress.com/juniper-prizes, pg 619

Andree, Courtney J, Juniper Prize for Poetry, New Africa House, 180 Infirmary Way, 4th fl, Amherst, MA 01003-9289 *E-mail:* juniperprize@umpress.umass.edu *Web Site:* www.umasspress.com/juniper-prizes, pg 619

Andree, Courtney J, University of Massachusetts Press, New Africa House, 180 Infirmary Way, 4th fl, Amherst, MA 01003-9289 *Web Site:* www.umasspress.com, pg 217

Andreoni, Edoardo, Europa Editions, 27 Union Sq W, Suite 302, New York, NY 10003 *Tel:* 212-868-6844 *Fax:* 212-868-6845 *E-mail:* info@europaeditions.com; books@europaeditions.com; publicity@europaeditions.com *Web Site:* www.europaeditions.com, pg 67

Andreoni, Regina, GP Putnam's Sons, c/o Penguin Random House LLC, 1745 Broadway, New York, NY 10019 *Tel:* 212-782-9000 *Web Site:* www.penguin.com/putnam/, pg 167

Andreou, George, Harvard University Press, 79 Garden St, Cambridge, MA 02138-1499 *Tel:* 617-495-2600; 401-531-2800 (intl orders) *Toll Free Tel:* 800-405-1619 (orders); 617-495-5898 (pg); 617-496-4677 (edit & rts); 401-531-2801 (intl orders) *Toll Free Fax:* 800-406-9145 (orders) *E-mail:* contact_hup@harvard.edu *Web Site:* www.hup.harvard.edu, pg 88

Andrews, Donna, Lilian Jackson Braun Award, 1140 Broadway, Suite 1507, New York, NY 10001 *Tel:* 212-888-8171 *E-mail:* mwa@mysterywriters.org *Web Site:* mysterywriters.org/edgars/lilian-jackson-braun-award, pg 583

Andrews, Donna, The Edgar Awards®, 1140 Broadway, Suite 1507, New York, NY 10001 *Tel:* 212-888-8171 *E-mail:* mwa@mysterywriters.org *Web Site:* theedgars.com; mysterywriters.org, pg 598

Andrews, Donna, Minotaur Books/Mystery Writers of America First Crime Novel Competition, 1140 Broadway, Suite 1507, New York, NY 10001 *Tel:* 212-888-8171 *E-mail:* mwa@mysterywriters.org *Web Site:* mysterywriters.org/about-mwa/st-martins; us.macmillan.com/minotaurbooks/submit-manuscript, pg 633

Andrews, Donna, Mystery Writers of America (MWA), 1140 Broadway, Suite 1507, New York, NY 10001 *Tel:* 212-888-8171 *E-mail:* mwa@mysterywriters.org *Web Site:* mysterywriters.org, pg 511

Andrews, Donna, Barbara Neely Memorial Scholarship Program, 1140 Broadway, Suite 1507, New York, NY 10001 *Tel:* 212-888-8171 *E-mail:* mwa@mysterywriters.org *Web Site:* mysterywriters.org, pg 639

Andrews, Hugh, Andrews McMeel Publishing LLC, 1130 Walnut St, Kansas City, MO 64106-2109 *Tel:* 816-581-7500 *Toll Free Tel:* 800-851-8923 *Web Site:* www.andrewsmcmeel.com; publishing.andrewsmcmeel.com, pg 14

Andrews, James, Andrews McMeel Publishing LLC, 1130 Walnut St, Kansas City, MO 64106-2109 *Tel:* 816-581-7500 *Toll Free Tel:* 800-851-8923 *Web Site:* www.andrewsmcmeel.com; publishing.andrewsmcmeel.com, pg 14

Andrews, Meredith, National Book Foundation, 90 Broad St, Suite 604, New York, NY 10004 *Tel:* 212-685-0261 *Fax:* 212-213-6570 *E-mail:* nationalbook@nationalbook.org *Web Site:* www.nationalbook.org, pg 526

Andrews, Michael, Access Copyright, The Canadian Copyright Licensing Agency, 69 Yonge St, Suite 1100, Toronto, ON M5E 1K3, Canada *Tel:* 416-868-1620 *Toll Free Tel:* 800-893-5777 *Fax:* 416-868-1621 *E-mail:* info@accesscopyright.ca *Web Site:* www.accesscopyright.ca, pg 493

Andrews, Sydney, Book of the Year Award, 600 Maryland Ave SW, Suite 1000W, Washington, DC 20024 *Toll Free Tel:* 800-443-8456 *Fax:* 202-314-5121 *E-mail:* foundation@fb.org *Web Site:* www.agfoundation.org/projects/book-of-the-year-award, pg 583

Andrews, Tom, Adirondack Mountain Club (ADK), 4833 Cascade Rd, Lake Placid, NY 12946-4113 *Tel:* 518-837-5047 *Toll Free Tel:* 800-395-8080 *E-mail:* info@adk.org *Web Site:* www.adk.org, pg 5

Andrus, Raven, HarperCollins Publishers LLC, 195 Broadway, New York, NY 10007 *Tel:* 212-207-7000 *Web Site:* www.harpercollins.com, pg 87

Angel, Mitzi, Farrar, Straus & Giroux, LLC, 120 Broadway, New York, NY 10271 *Tel:* 212-741-6900 *E-mail:* fsg.publicity@fsgbooks.com; sales@fsgbooks.com *Web Site:* us.macmillan.com/fsg, pg 70

Angel, Mitzi, FSG Writer's Fellowship, 120 Broadway, New York, NY 10271 *Tel:* 212-741-6900 *E-mail:* fsg.publicity@fsgbooks.com *Web Site:* fsgfellowship.com, pg 605

Angel, Mitzi, Macmillan, 120 Broadway, 22nd fl, New York, NY 10271 *Tel:* 646 *E-mail:* press.inquiries@macmillan.com *Web Site:* us.macmillan.com, pg 122

Angeles, Janella, Candlewick Press, 99 Dover St, Somerville, MA 02144-2825 *Tel:* 617-661-3330 *Fax:* 617-661-0565 *E-mail:* bigbear@candlewick.com; salesinfo@candlewick.com *Web Site:* candlewick.com, pg 40

Angeloro, Nicole, HarperCollins Publishers LLC, 195 Broadway, New York, NY 10007 *Tel:* 212-207-7000 *Web Site:* www.harpercollins.com, pg 86

Angle, Lisa, Writers & Publishers Network (WPN), 1129 Maricopa Hwy, No 142, Ojai, CA 93023 *Web Site:* writersandpublishersnetwork.com, pg 522

Angress, Miriam, Duke University Press, 905 W Main St, Suite 18B, Durham, NC 27701 *Tel:* 919-688-5134 *Toll Free Tel:* 888-651-0122 (US) *Fax:* 919-688-2615 *Toll Free Fax:* 888-651-0124 *E-mail:* orders@dukeupress.edu *Web Site:* www.dukeupress.edu, pg 62

Angulo, Albert, Running Press, 1290 Avenue of the Americas, New York, NY 10104 *Tel:* 212-364-1100 *Toll Free Tel:* 800-759-0190 (cust serv) *Fax:* 212-364-0933 (intl orders) *Toll Free Fax:* 800-286-9471 (cust serv) *E-mail:* customer.service@hbgusa.com; orders@hbgusa.com *Web Site:* www.hachettebookgroup.com/imprint/running-press/; www.moon.com (Moon Travel Guides), pg 178

Angulo, Mari, New Mexico Book Association (NMBA), PO Box 1285, Santa Fe, NM 87504 *E-mail:* libroentry@gmail.com *Web Site:* www.nmbookassociation.org, pg 514

Annis, Amanda, Trident Media Group LLC, 355 Lexington Ave, 12th fl, New York, NY 10017 *Tel:* 212-333-1511 *E-mail:* info@tridentmediagroup.com; press@tridentmediagroup.com; foreignrights@tridentmediagroup.com; office.assistant@tridentmediagroup.com *Web Site:* www.tridentmediagroup.com, pg 480

Anthony, Graham, August House Inc, 3500 Piedmont Rd NE, Suite 310, Atlanta, GA 30305 *Tel:* 404-442-4420 *Toll Free Tel:* 800-284-8784 *Fax:* 404-442-4435 *E-mail:* ahinfo@augusthouse.com *Web Site:* www.augusthouse.com, pg 22

Anthony, Jason, Massie & McQuilkin, 27 W 20 St, Suite 305, New York, NY 10011 *Tel:* 212-352-2055 *E-mail:* info@mmqlit.com *Web Site:* www.mmqlit.com, pg 469

Antippas, Frank, Candlewick Press, 99 Dover St, Somerville, MA 02144-2825 *Tel:* 617-661-3330 *Fax:* 617-661-0565 *E-mail:* bigbear@candlewick.com; salesinfo@candlewick.com *Web Site:* candlewick.com, pg 40

Antoine, Marie-Claire, Lynne Rienner Publishers Inc, 1800 30 St, Suite 314, Boulder, CO 80301 *Tel:* 303-444-6684 *Fax:* 303-444-0824 *E-mail:* questions@rienner.com; cservice@rienner.com *Web Site:* www.rienner.com, pg 174

Antonetta, Susanne Paola, Annie Dillard Award for Creative Nonfiction, Mail Stop 9053, Western Washington University, Bellingham, WA 98225 *Tel:* 360-650-4863 *E-mail:* bellingham.review@wwu.edu *Web Site:* bhreview.org; bhreview.submittable.com, pg 596

Antonetta, Susanne Paola, 49th Parallel Poetry Award, Mail Stop 9053, Western Washington University, Bellingham, WA 98225 *Tel:* 360-650-4863 *E-mail:* bellingham.review@wwu.edu *Web Site:* bhreview.org; bhreview.submittable.com, pg 603

Antonetta, Susanne Paola, Tobias Wolff Award for Fiction, Mail Stop 9053, Western Washington University, Bellingham, WA 98225 *Tel:* 360-650-4863 *E-mail:* bellingham.review@wwu.edu *Web Site:* bhreview.org; bhreview.submittable.com, pg 677

Antonson, Lori, The Axelrod Agency, 55 Main St, Chatham, NY 12037 *Tel:* 518-392-2100, pg 449

Antony, Peter, The Metropolitan Museum of Art, 1000 Fifth Ave, New York, NY 10028 *Tel:* 212-535-7710 *E-mail:* editorial@metmuseum.org *Web Site:* www.metmuseum.org, pg 130

Anzuoni, Nicole, Pauline Books & Media, 50 Saint Paul's Ave, Boston, MA 02130 *Tel:* 617-522-8911 *Toll Free Tel:* 800-876-4463 (orders); 800-836-9723 (cust serv) *Fax:* 617-541-9805 *E-mail:* editorial@paulinemedia.com (ms submissions); orderentry@pauline.org (cust serv) *Web Site:* www.pauline.org/pbmpublishing, pg 152

Aoyagi, Nora, Chronicle Books LLC, 680 Second St, San Francisco, CA 94107 *Tel:* 415-537-4200 *Fax:* 415-537-4460 (perms) *E-mail:* hello@chroniclebooks.com; subrights@chroniclebooks.com *Web Site:* www.chroniclebooks.com, pg 48

Apampa, Praise, PEN America, 120 Broadway, 26th fl N, New York, NY 10271 *Tel:* 212-334-1660 *Fax:* 212-334-2181 *E-mail:* hello@pen.org; membership@pen.org; education@pen.org *Web Site:* pen.org, pg 516

Apelian, Bill, BJU Press, 1430 Wade Hampton Blvd, Greenville, SC 29609-5046 *Tel:* 864-770-1317; 864-546-4600 *Toll Free Tel:* 800-845-5731 *E-mail:* bjupinfo@bju.edu *Web Site:* www.bjupress.com, pg 30

Appel, Amelia, TriadaUS Literary Agency, PO Box 561, Sewickley, PA 15143 *Tel:* 412-401-3376 *Web Site:* www.triadaus.com, pg 480

Appel, Celeste, Unarius Academy of Science Publications, 145 S Magnolia Ave, El Cajon, CA 92020-4522 *Tel:* 619-444-7062 *Toll Free Tel:* 800-475-7062 *E-mail:* uriel@unarius.org *Web Site:* www.unarius.org, pg 212

Appel, Fred, Princeton University Press, 41 William St, Princeton, NJ 08540-5237 *Tel:* 609-258-4900 *Fax:* 609-258-6305 *E-mail:* info@press.princeton.edu *Web Site:* press.princeton.edu, pg 164

Appel, Jacob M, Nona Balakian Citation for Excellence in Reviewing, c/o Jacob M Appel, Icahn School of Medicine at Mount Sinai, One Gustave L Levy Place, New York, NY 10029 *E-mail:* info@bookcritics.org *Web Site:* www.bookcritics.org/awards/balakian/, pg 576

Appel, Jacob M, Gregg Barrios Book in Translation Prize, c/o Jacob M Appel, Icahn School of Medicine at Mount Sinai, One Gustave L Levy Place, New York, NY 10029 *E-mail:* info@bookcritics.org *Web Site:* www.bookcritics.org/gregg-barrios-book-in-translation-prize/, pg 577

Appel, Jacob M, Emerging Critics Fellowship, c/o Jacob M Appel, Icahn School of Medicine at Mount Sinai, One Gustave L Levy Place, New York, NY 10029 *E-mail:* info@bookcritics.org *Web Site:* www.bookcritics.org/awards, pg 599

Appel, Jacob M, John Leonard Prize, c/o Jacob M Appel, Icahn School of Medicine at Mount Sinai, One Gustave L Levy Place, New York, NY 10029 *E-mail:* info@bookcritics.org *Web Site:* www.bookcritics.org/awards/leonard-prize, pg 623

Appel, Jacob M, The Toni Morrison Achievement Award, c/o Jacob M Appel, Icahn School of Medicine at Mount Sinai, One Gustave L Levy Place, New York, NY 10029 *E-mail:* info@bookcritics.org *Web Site:* www.bookcritics.org/the-toni-morrison-achievement-award, pg 635

Appel, Jacob M, National Book Critics Circle (NBCC), c/o Jacob M Appel, Icahn School of Medicine at Mount Sinai, One Gustave L Levy Place, New York, NY 10029 *E-mail:* info@bookcritics.org; membership@bookcritics.org *Web Site:* www.bookcritics.org, pg 512

Appel, Jacob M, National Book Critics Circle Award, c/o Jacob M Appel, Icahn School of Medicine at Mount Sinai, One Gustave L Levy Place, New York, NY 10029 *E-mail:* info@bookcritics.org *Web Site:* www.bookcritics.org/awards, pg 637

Appel, Jacob M, Ivan Sandrof Lifetime Achievement Award, c/o Jacob M Appel, Icahn School of Medicine at Mount Sinai, One Gustave L Levy Place, New York, NY 10029 *E-mail:* info@bookcritics.org *Web Site:* www.bookcritics.org/awards/sandrof/, pg 659

Appelbaum, David, Codhill Press, 420 E 23 St, Suite 3H, New York, NY 10010 *E-mail:* info@codhill.com *Web Site:* www.codhill.com, pg 50

Appelbaum, Susannah, Codhill Press, 420 E 23 St, Suite 3H, New York, NY 10010 *E-mail:* info@codhill.com *Web Site:* www.codhill.com, pg 50

Appelbaum, Adina, Whiting Awards, 16 Court St, Suite 2308, Brooklyn, NY 11241 *Tel:* 718-701-5962 *E-mail:* info@whiting.org *Web Site:* www.whiting.org, pg 675

Applebaum, Adina, Whiting Creative Nonfiction Grant, 16 Court St, Suite 2308, Brooklyn, NY 11241 *Tel:* 718-701-5962 *E-mail:* nonfiction@whiting.org; info@whiting.org *Web Site:* www.whiting.org, pg 675

Appleton, Lauren, TarcherPerigee, c/o Penguin Random House LLC, 1745 Broadway, New York, NY 10019 *Tel:* 212-782-9000 *Web Site:* www.penguin.com/tarcherperigee-overview/; www.facebook.com/TarcherPerigee, pg 202

Appolloni, Simon, Novalis Publishing, One Eglinton Ave E, Suite 800, Toronto, ON M4P 3A1, Canada *Tel:* 416-363-3303 *Toll Free Tel:* 877-702-7773 *Fax:* 416-363-9409 *Toll Free Fax:* 877-702-7775 *E-mail:* books@novalis.ca *Web Site:* www.novalis.ca, pg 414

Aquilina, Drew, National Cartoonists Society (NCS), PO Box 592927, Orlando, FL 32859-2927 *Tel:* 407-994-6703 *E-mail:* info@nationalcartoonists.com; membership@nationalcartoonists.com *Web Site:* www.nationalcartoonists.com, pg 512

Araujo, Camila, Atria Books, 1230 Avenue of the Americas, New York, NY 10020 *Tel:* 212-698-7000 *Fax:* 212-698-7007 *Web Site:* www.simonandschuster.com, pg 21

Arbuckle, Michelle, Ontario Library Association (OLA), 2080 Danforth Ave, Toronto, ON M4C 1J9, Canada *Toll Free Tel:* 877-340-1730 *E-mail:* info@accessola.com *Web Site:* accessola.com, pg 515

Arbus, Michelle, Penguin Random House Canada, a Penguin Random House company, 320 Front St W, Suite 1400, Toronto, ON M5V 3B6, Canada *Tel:* 416-364-4449 *Toll Free Tel:* 888-523-9292 (cust serv) *E-mail:* canadaweb@penguinrandomhouse.com; customerservicescanada@penguinrandomhouse.com *Web Site:* www.penguinrandomhouse.ca, pg 416

Archbold, Emily, Penguin Random House LLC, 1745 Broadway, New York, NY 10019 *Tel:* 212-782-9000 *Toll Free Tel:* 800-726-0600 *Web Site:* www.penguinrandomhouse.com, pg 155

Archer, Deborah, American Civil Liberties Union (ACLU), 125 Broad St, 18th fl, New York, NY 10004 *Tel:* 212-549-2500 *E-mail:* media@aclu.org *Web Site:* www.aclu.org, pg 495

Archer, Ellen, Houghton Mifflin Harcourt Trade & Reference Division, 125 High St, Boston, MA 02110 *Tel:* 617-351-5000 *Web Site:* www.hmhco.com, pg 96

Arcuri, Meghan, Horror Writers Association (HWA), PO Box 56687, Sherman Oaks, CA 91413 *Tel:* 818-220-3965 *E-mail:* admin@horror.org; membership@horror.org *Web Site:* horror.org, pg 507

Areheart, Shaye, Columbia Publishing Course at Columbia University, 2950 Broadway, MC 3801, New York, NY 10027 *Tel:* 212-854-1898; 212-854-9775 *E-mail:* publishing-jrn@columbia.edu *Web Site:* journalism.columbia.edu/columbia-publishing-course, pg 561

Arellano, Barbara, Hoover Institution Press, Stanford University, 434 Galvez Mall, Stanford, CA 94305-6003 *Tel:* 650-723-3373 *Toll Free Tel:* 800-935-2882 (US only); 877-466-8374 (US only) *Fax:* 650-723-8626 *E-mail:* hooverpress@stanford.edu *Web Site:* www.hoover.org/publications/hooverpress, pg 95

Arens, Andrew, Macmillan, 120 Broadway, 22nd fl, New York, NY 10271 *E-mail:* press.inquiries@macmillan.com *Web Site:* us.macmillan.com, pg 122

Argentieri, Chris, Los Angeles Times Book Prizes, 2300 E Imperial Hwy, El Segundo, CA 90245 *Tel:* 213-237-5775 *Toll Free Tel:* 800-528-4637 (ext 75775) *Web Site:* events.latimes.com/festivalofbooks, pg 626

Argiropoulos, Matie, Penguin Random House Audio Publishing Group, 1745 Broadway, New York, NY 10019 *Toll Free Tel:* 800-793-2665 (cust serv) *E-mail:* audio@penguinrandomhouse.com; ecustomerservice@penguinrandomhouse.com *Web Site:* www.penguinrandomhouseaudio.com, pg 154

Argyres, Nichole, St Martin's Press, LLC, 120 Broadway, New York, NY 10271 *E-mail:* publicity@stmartins.com; trademarketing@stmartins.com; foreignrights@stmartins.com *Web Site:* us.macmillan.com/smp, pg 181

Arian, Amir Ahmadi, Binghamton University Creative Writing Program, c/o Dept of English, General Literature & Rhetoric, PO Box 6000, Binghamton, NY 13902-6000 *Tel:* 607-777-2168 *Fax:* 607-777-2408 *E-mail:* cwpro@binghamton.edu *Web Site:* www.binghamton.edu/english/creative-writing/index.html, pg 561

Arjune, Ray, Penguin Random House LLC, 1745 Broadway, New York, NY 10019 *Tel:* 212-782-9000 *Toll Free Tel:* 800-726-0600 *Web Site:* www.penguinrandomhouse.com, pg 155

Armato, Doug, University of Minnesota Press, 111 Third Ave S, Suite 290, Minneapolis, MN 55401-2520 *Tel:* 612-301-1990 *Fax:* 612-301-1980 *E-mail:* ump@umn.edu *Web Site:* www.upress.umn.edu, pg 217

Armijo, Dan, Milford Books™, 243 W Lafayette St, Milford, MI 48381 *Tel:* 734-255-9530 *E-mail:* eic@milfordbooks.com *Web Site:* milfordbooks.com, pg 131

Armstrong, Gail Paul, SK Arts, 1355 Broad St, Regina, SK S4R 7V1, Canada *Tel:* 306-787-4056 *Toll Free Tel:* 800-667-7526 (CN) *E-mail:* info@sk-arts.ca *Web Site:* sk-arts.ca, pg 519

Armstrong, Janeen, Copper Canyon Press, Fort Worden State Park, Bldg 313, Port Townsend, WA 98368 *Tel:* 360-385-4925 *E-mail:* poetry@coppercanyonpress.org; publicity@coppercanyonpress.org; digitalcontent@coppercanyonpress.org *Web Site:* www.coppercanyonpress.org, pg 52

Armstrong, Jessica-Lynn, Workman Publishing, 1290 Avenue of the Americas, New York, NY 10104 *Toll Free Tel:* 800-759-0190 *Fax:* 212-364-0950 *E-mail:* workman-inquiry@hbgusa.com *Web Site:* www.hachettebookgroup.com/imprint/workman-publishing-company/, pg 232

Armstrong, Kevin, Chronicle Books LLC, 680 Second St, San Francisco, CA 94107 *Tel:* 415-537-4200 *Fax:* 415-537-4460 (perms) *E-mail:* hello@chroniclebooks.com; subrights@chroniclebooks.com *Web Site:* www.chroniclebooks.com, pg 48

Armstrong, Kirsten, Penguin Random House Canada, a Penguin Random House company, 320 Front St W, Suite 1400, Toronto, ON M5V 3B6, Canada *Tel:* 416-364-4449 *Toll Free Tel:* 888-523-9292 (cust serv) *E-mail:* canadaweb@penguinrandomhouse.com; customerservicescanada@penguinrandomhouse.com *Web Site:* www.penguinrandomhouse.ca, pg 416

Armstrong, Taylor, Macmillan, 120 Broadway, 22nd fl, New York, NY 10271 *E-mail:* press.inquiries@macmillan.com *Web Site:* us.macmillan.com, pg 122

Armstrong-Frank, Amanda, Simon & Schuster, LLC, 1230 Avenue of the Americas, New York, NY 10020 *Tel:* 212-698-7000 *Toll Free Tel:* 800-223-2336 (orders) *Fax:* 212-698-7007 *Toll Free Fax:* 800-943-9831 (orders) *E-mail:* firstname.lastname@simonandschuster.com; purchaseorders@simonandschuster.com (orders) *Web Site:* www.simonandschuster.com, pg 190

Arnold, Alex, Quirk Books, 215 Church St, Philadelphia, PA 19106 *Tel:* 215-627-3581 *Fax:* 215-627-5220 *E-mail:* general@quirkbooks.com *Web Site:* www.quirkbooks.com, pg 168

Arnold, Andrew, HarperCollins Children's Books, 195 Broadway, New York, NY 10007 *Tel:* 212-207-7000 *Web Site:* www.harpercollins.com/childrens, pg 85

Arnold, Carol, Catholic Media Association (CMA), 10 S Riverside Plaza, Suite 875, Chicago, IL 60606 *Tel:* 312-380-6789 *Web Site:* www.catholicmediaassociation.org, pg 503

Arnold, David, CarTech Inc, 6118 Main St, North Branch, MN 55056 *Tel:* 651-277-1200 *Toll Free Tel:* 800-551-4754 *Fax:* 651-277-1203 *E-mail:* info@cartechbooks.com *Web Site:* www.cartechbooks.com, pg 41

Arnold, Lore, Writers' League of Texas (WLT), 611 S Congress Ave, Suite 200 A-3, Austin, TX 78704 *Tel:* 512-499-8914 *E-mail:* wlt@writersleague.org *Web Site:* www.writersleague.org, pg 488, 523, 558

Arnold, Lore, Writers' League of Texas Book Awards, 611 S Congress Ave, Suite 200 A-3, Austin, TX 78704 *Tel:* 512-499-8914 *E-mail:* wlt@writersleague.org *Web Site:* www.writersleague.org, pg 678

Arnone, Shannon, HarperCollins Publishers LLC, 195 Broadway, New York, NY 10007 *Tel:* 212-207-7000 *Web Site:* www.harpercollins.com, pg 87

Arnove, Anthony, Roam Agency, 45 Main St, Suite 727, Brooklyn, NY 11201-1076 *E-mail:* roam@roamagency.com *Web Site:* www.roamagency.com, pg 473

Arnow, Ann, Bridge Publications Inc, 5600 E Olympic Blvd, Commerce, CA 90022 *Tel:* 323-888-6200 *Toll Free Tel:* 800-722-1733 *Fax:* 323-888-6202 *E-mail:* info@bridgepub.com *Web Site:* www.bridgepub.com, pg 36

Arocho, Caite, Random House Children's Books, c/o Penguin Random House LLC, 1745 Broadway, New York, NY 10019 *Tel:* 212-782-9000 *Web Site:* www.rhcbooks.com, pg 170

Aronica, Lou, The Story Plant, 1270 Caroline St, Suite D120-381, Atlanta, GA 30307 *Tel:* 203-722-7920 *E-mail:* thestoryplant@thestoryplant.com *Web Site:* www.thestoryplant.com, pg 199

Aronson, Rosa PhD, TESOL Press, 1925 Ballenger Ave, Suite 550, Alexandria, VA 22314-6820 *Tel:* 703-518-2500; 703-518-2501 (cust serv) *Toll Free Tel:* 888-891-0041 (cust serv) *Fax:* 703-691-5327 *E-mail:* publications@tesol.org; press@tesol.org; members@tesol.org *Web Site:* www.tesol.org, pg 204

Arredondo, Joey, Penguin Random House Canada, a Penguin Random House company, 320 Front St W, Suite 1400, Toronto, ON M5V 3B6, Canada *Tel:* 416-364-4449 *Toll Free Tel:* 888-523-9292 (cust serv) *E-mail:* canadaweb@penguinrandomhouse.com; customerservicescanada@penguinrandomhouse.com *Web Site:* www.penguinrandomhouse.ca, pg 416

Arreguin, Maryn, Sourcebooks LLC, 1935 Brookdale Rd, Suite 139, Naperville, IL 60563 *Tel:* 630-961-3900 *Toll Free Tel:* 800-432-7444 *Fax:* 630-961-2168 *E-mail:* info@sourcebooks.com *Web Site:* www.sourcebooks.com, pg 194

Arreola, Cristina, Sourcebooks LLC, 1935 Brookdale Rd, Suite 139, Naperville, IL 60563 *Tel:* 630-961-3900 *Toll Free Tel:* 800-432-7444 *Fax:* 630-961-2168 *E-mail:* info@sourcebooks.com *Web Site:* www.sourcebooks.com, pg 194

Arrington, Jay, The Little Entrepreneur, c/o Harper Arrington Media, 33228 W 12 Mile Rd, Suite 105, Farmington Hills, MI 48334 *Toll Free Tel:* 888-435-9234 *Fax:* 248-281-0373 *E-mail:* support@digitalfashionpro.com, pg 118

Arrow, Kevin, GW Inc, 2290 Ball Dr, St Louis, MO 63146 *Tel:* 314-567-9854 *E-mail:* media@gwinc.com *Web Site:* www.gwinc.com, pg 440

Arsenault, Jessica, Bear & Co Inc, One Park St, Rochester, VT 05767 *Tel:* 802-767-3174 *Toll Free Tel:* 800-932-3277 *Fax:* 802-767-3726 *E-mail:* customerservice@InnerTraditions.com *Web Site:* InnerTraditions.com, pg 26

Arsenault, Jessica, Inner Traditions International Ltd, One Park St, Rochester, VT 05767 *Tel:* 802-767-3174 *Toll Free Tel:* 800-246-8648 *Fax:* 802-767-3726 *E-mail:* customerservice@InnerTraditions.com *Web Site:* www.InnerTraditions.com, pg 101

Arter, Jen, Editcetera, 2034 Blake St, Suite 5, Berkeley, CA 94704 *Tel:* 510-849-1110 *E-mail:* info@editcetera.com *Web Site:* www.editcetera.com, pg 438

Arthur, David, American Institute of Aeronautics and Astronautics (AIAA), 12700 Sunrise Valley Dr, Suite 200, Reston, VA 20191-5807 *Tel:* 703-264-7500 *Toll Free Tel:* 800-639-AIAA (639-2422) *Fax:* 703-264-7551 *E-mail:* custserv@aiaa.org *Web Site:* www.aiaa.org; arc.aiaa.org (orders), pg 10

Arthur, Jonathan D, American Geosciences Institute (AGI), 4220 King St, Alexandria, VA 22302-1502 Tel: 703-379-2480 (ext 246) E-mail: agi@americangeosciences.org Web Site: www.americangeosciences.org; www.geosciencestore.org, pg 10

Arthur, Reagan, Hachette Book Group Inc, 1290 Avenue of the Americas, New York, NY 10104 Tel: 212-364-1100 Toll Free Tel: 800-759-0190 (cust serv) Fax: 212-364-0933 (intl orders) Toll Free Fax: 800-286-9471 (cust serv) E-mail: customer.service@hbgusa.com; orders@hbgusa.com Web Site: www.hachettebookgroup.com, pg 83

Arvelo, Jason, Macmillan, 120 Broadway, 22nd fl, New York, NY 10271 E-mail: press.inquiries@macmillan.com Web Site: us.macmillan.com, pg 122

Arzeno, Emily, Gallery Books, 1230 Avenue of the Americas, New York, NY 10020 Toll Free Tel: 800-456-6798 Fax: 212-698-7284 E-mail: consumer.customerservice@simonandschuster.com Web Site: www.simonandschuster.com, pg 76

Ascher, David, Scholastic Trade Publishing, 557 Broadway, New York, NY 10012 Tel: 212-343-6100; 212-343-4685 (export sales) Fax: 212-343-4714 (export sales) Web Site: www.scholastic.com, pg 184

Ash, Rachel, Michigan Library Association (MLA), 3410 Belle Chase Way, Lansing, MI 48911 Tel: 517-394-2774 E-mail: mla@milibraries.org Web Site: www.milibraries.org, pg 510

Ash-Milby, Edward, Insight Editions, 800 "A" St, San Rafael, CA 94901 Tel: 415-526-1370 Toll Free Tel: 800-809-3792 Toll Free Fax: 866-509-0515 E-mail: info@insighteditions.com; marketing@insighteditions.com Web Site: insighteditions.com, pg 101

Ashcraft, Aimee, Brower Literary & Management Inc, 13720 Old St Augustine Rd, Suite 8-512, Jacksonville, FL 32258 Tel: 646-854-6073 E-mail: admin@browerliterary.com; foreign@browerliterary.com (foreign publr inquiries); queries@browerliterary.com; subrights@browerliterary.com (busn inquiries) Web Site: browerliterary.com, pg 452

Ashenfelter, Paul, University of Notre Dame Press, 310 Flanner Hall, Notre Dame, IN 46556 Tel: 574-631-6346 Fax: 574-631-8148 E-mail: undpress@nd.edu Web Site: www.undpress.nd.edu, pg 219

Ashford, Brittain, Music Publishers Association (MPA), 442 Fifth Ave, Suite 1137, New York, NY 10018 E-mail: admin@mpa.org Web Site: www.mpa.org, pg 511

Ashley, Bennett, Janklow & Nesbit Associates, 285 Madison Ave, 21st fl, New York, NY 10017 Tel: 212-421-1700 Fax: 212-355-1403 E-mail: info@janklow.com; submissions@janklow.com; filmtvrights@janklow.com Web Site: www.janklowandnesbit.com, pg 464

Ashley, Kris, Northwest Independent Editors Guild, 7511 Greenwood Ave N, No 307, Seattle, WA 98103 E-mail: info@edsguild.org Web Site: www.edsguild.org, pg 515

Ashley, Kris, Red Pencil Conference, 7511 Greenwood Ave N, No 307, Seattle, WA 98103 E-mail: conference@edsguild.org Web Site: www.edsguild.org/red-pencil-conferences, pg 557

Ashton, David, Nelson Education Ltd, 1120 Birchmount Rd, Scarborough, ON M1K 5G4, Canada Tel: 416-752-9448 Toll Free Tel: 800-268-2222 (cust serv) Fax: 416-752-9646 E-mail: peopleandengagement@nelson.com Web Site: www.nelson.com, pg 413

Ashton, Emily, Brooklyn Public Library Literary Prize, 10 Grand Army Plaza, Brooklyn, NY 11238 Tel: 718-230-2100 E-mail: brooklyneagles@bklynlibrary.org Web Site: www.bklynlibrary.org/support/bpl-literary-prize, pg 584

Ashwood-Viala, Shana, LearningExpress, 224 W 29 St, 3rd fl, New York, NY 10001 Toll Free Tel: 800-295-9556 (ext 2) Web Site: learningexpresshub.com, pg 114

Aspey, Susan, Cengage Learning, 20 Channel Center St, Boston, MA 02210 Tel: 617-289-7700 Toll Free Tel: 800-354-9706 Fax: 617-289-7844 E-mail: esales@cengage.com Web Site: www.cengage.com, pg 43

Assathiany, Pascal, Les Editions du Boreal, 4447, rue St-Denis, Montreal, QC H2J 2L2, Canada Tel: 514-287-7401 Fax: 514-287-7664 E-mail: info@editionsboreal.qc.ca; boreal@editionsboreal.qc.ca; communications@editionsboreal.qc.ca Web Site: www.editionsboreal.qc.ca, pg 402

Assogba, Benedicte, Ordre des traducteurs, terminologues et interpretes agrees du quebec (OTTIAQ), 1108-2021 Ave Union, Montreal, QC H3A 2S9, Canada Tel: 514-845-4411 Toll Free Tel: 800-265-4815 Fax: 514-845-9903 E-mail: info@ottiaq.org; direction@ottiaq.org; reception@ottiaq.org; communications@ottiaq.org Web Site: www.ottiaq.org, pg 516

Assouad, Maya, Vehicule Press, PO Box 42094, CP Roy, Montreal, QC H2W 2T3, Canada Tel: 514-844-6073 E-mail: vp@vehiculepress.com; admin@vehiculepress.com Web Site: www.vehiculepress.com, pg 424

Aster, Howard, Mosaic Press, 1252 Speers Rd, Units 1 & 2, Oakville, ON L6L 5N9, Canada Tel: 905-825-2130 Fax: 905-825-2130 E-mail: info@mosaic-press.com Web Site: www.mosaic-press.com, pg 413

Asteriou, Michael, The Apocryphile Press, 1700 Shattuck Ave, Suite 81, Berkeley, CA 94709 Tel: 510-290-4349 E-mail: apocryphile@me.com Web Site: www.apocryphilepress.com, pg 15

Astle, Robert, SDP Publishing Solutions LLC, 36 Captain's Way, East Bridgewater, MA 02333 Tel: 617-775-0656 Web Site: www.sdppublishingsolutions.com, pg 444

Astley, Edie, HarperCollins Publishers LLC, 195 Broadway, New York, NY 10007 Tel: 212-207-7000 Web Site: www.harpercollins.com, pg 87

Astras, Alex, Chronicle Books LLC, 680 Second St, San Francisco, CA 94107 Tel: 415-537-4200 Fax: 415-537-4460 (perms) E-mail: hello@chroniclebooks.com; subrights@chroniclebooks.com Web Site: www.chroniclebooks.com, pg 48

Astrella, Kait, Grove Atlantic Inc, 154 W 14 St, 12th fl, New York, NY 10011 Tel: 212-614-7850 Toll Free Tel: 800-521-0178 Fax: 212-614-7886 E-mail: info@groveatlantic.com; sales@groveatlantic.com; publicity@groveatlantic.com; rights@groveatlantic.com Web Site: www.groveatlantic.com, pg 82

Asuquo, Joie, Scribner, 1230 Avenue of the Americas, New York, NY 10020 Web Site: www.simonandschusterpublishing.com/scribner/, pg 185

Atchison, Faye, Margret McBride Literary Agency, PO Box 9128, La Jolla, CA 92038 Tel: 858-454-1550 E-mail: staff@mcbridelit.com Web Site: www.mcbrideliterary.com, pg 469

Atchity, Kenneth PhD, The Writers Lifeline Inc, a Story Merchant company, 400 S Burnside Ave, Suite 11B, Los Angeles, CA 90036 Tel: 310-968-1607 Web Site: www.thewriterslifeline.com, pg 446

Atkinson, Marisa, Graywolf Press, 212 Third Ave N, Suite 485, Minneapolis, MN 55401 Tel: 651-641-0077 Fax: 651-641-0036 E-mail: wolves@graywolfpress.org (no ms queries, sample chapters or proposals) Web Site: www.graywolfpress.org, pg 81

Atkinson, Rebecca, Sourcebooks LLC, 1935 Brookdale Rd, Suite 139, Naperville, IL 60563 Tel: 630-961-3900 Toll Free Tel: 800-432-7444 Fax: 630-961-2168 E-mail: info@sourcebooks.com Web Site: sourcebooks.com, pg 195

Atkinson, Wendy, Ronsdale Press Ltd, 125A-1030 Denman St, Vancouver, BC V6G 2M6, Canada Tel: 604-738-4688 E-mail: ronsdalepress@gmail.com Web Site: ronsdalepress.com, pg 418

Atoria, Anna, Brower Literary & Management Inc, 13720 Old St Augustine Rd, Suite 8-512, Jacksonville, FL 32258 Tel: 646-854-6073 E-mail: admin@browerliterary.com; foreign@browerliterary.com (foreign publr inquiries); queries@browerliterary.com; subrights@browerliterary.com (busn inquiries) Web Site: browerliterary.com, pg 452

Atsma, Helen, HarperCollins Publishers LLC, 195 Broadway, New York, NY 10007 Tel: 212-207-7000 Web Site: www.harpercollins.com, pg 86

Attebery, Gerilyn, City Lights Publishers, 261 Columbus Ave, San Francisco, CA 94133 Tel: 415-362-8193 E-mail: staff@citylights.com Web Site: citylights.com, pg 48

Attermann, Eve, WME, 11 Madison Ave, New York, NY 10010 Tel: 212-586-5100 Web Site: www.wmeagency.com, pg 482

Attlee, James, University of Chicago Press, 1427 E 60 St, Chicago, IL 60637-2954 Tel: 773-702-7700; 773-702-7600 Toll Free Tel: 800-621-2736 (orders) Fax: 773-702-9756; 773-660-2235 (orders); 773-702-2708 E-mail: custserv@press.uchicago.edu; marketing@press.uchicago.edu Web Site: www.press.uchicago.edu, pg 219

Atwell, Margot, The Feminist Press at The City University of New York, 365 Fifth Ave, Suite 5406, New York, NY 10016 Tel: 212-817-7915 Fax: 212-817-1593 E-mail: info@feministpress.org Web Site: www.feministpress.org, pg 71

Atwood, Akiva, KTAV Publishing House Inc, 527 Empire Blvd, Brooklyn, NY 11225 Tel: 201-963-9524; 718-972-5449 Fax: 718-972-6307 E-mail: orders@ktav.com Web Site: www.ktav.com, pg 111

Atwood, Dr Christopher, The Mongolia Society Inc, Indiana University, 703 Eigenmann Hall, 1900 E Tenth St, Bloomington, IN 47406-7512 Tel: 812-855-4078 Fax: 812-855-4078 E-mail: monsoc@indiana.edu Web Site: mongoliasociety.org, pg 133

Auch, Allison, Fulcrum Publishing Inc, 3970 Youngfield St, Wheat Ridge, CO 80033 Tel: 303-277-1623 Toll Free Tel: 800-888-4741 (orders) E-mail: info@fulcrumbooks.com Web Site: www.fulcrumbooks.com, pg 75

Aucoin, Cassandra, Flanker Press Ltd, 1243 Kenmount Rd, Unit 1, Paradise, NL A1L 0V8, Canada Tel: 709-739-4477 Toll Free Tel: 866-739-4420 Fax: 709-739-4420 E-mail: info@flankerpress.com; sales@flankerpress.com Web Site: www.flankerpress.com, pg 406

Audet, Janice, The MIT Press, One Broadway, 12th fl, Cambridge, MA 02142 Tel: 617-253-5255 Toll Free Tel: 800-405-1619 (orders) Fax: 617-258-6779; 617-577-1545 (orders) Web Site: mitpress.mit.edu, pg 132

Audsley, Sarah, Vermont Studio Center Writer's Program Fellowships, 80 Pearl St, Johnson, VT 05656 Tel: 802-635-2727 Fax: 802-635-2730 E-mail: writing@vermontstudiocenter.org; info@vermontstudiocenter.org Web Site: www.vermontstudiocenter.org, pg 672

Auerbach, Scott, Farrar, Straus & Giroux, LLC, 120 Broadway, New York, NY 10271 Tel: 212-741-6900 E-mail: fsg.publicity@fsgbooks.com; sales@fsgbooks.com Web Site: us.macmillan.com/fsg, pg 70

Auffarth, Maggie, Folio Literary Management, The Film Center Bldg, 630 Ninth Ave, Suite 1101, New York, NY 10036 Tel: 212-400-1494 Fax: 212-967-0977 Web Site: www.foliolit.com, pg 459

Aughavin, Maria, Writers House, 21 W 26 St, New York, NY 10010 Tel: 212-685-2400 Web Site: www.writershouse.com, pg 482

Augusto, Andy, Sourcebooks LLC, 1935 Brookdale Rd, Suite 139, Naperville, IL 60563 Tel: 630-961-3900 Toll Free Tel: 800-432-7444 Fax: 630-961-2168 E-mail: info@sourcebooks.com Web Site: www.sourcebooks.com, pg 194

Auh, Jin, The Wylie Agency LLC, 250 W 57 St, Suite 2114, New York, NY 10107 Tel: 212-246-0069 E-mail: mail@wylieagency.com Web Site: www.wylieagency.com, pg 483

Auld, Dorothy, Penguin Random House LLC, 1745 Broadway, New York, NY 10019 Tel: 212-782-9000 Toll Free Tel: 800-726-0600 Web Site: www.penguinrandomhouse.com, pg 155

Ault, Elizabeth, Duke University Press, 905 W Main St, Suite 18B, Durham, NC 27701 *Tel:* 919-688-5134 *Toll Free Tel:* 888-651-0122 (US) *Fax:* 919-688-2615 *Toll Free Fax:* 888-651-0124 *E-mail:* orders@dukeupress.edu *Web Site:* www.dukeupress.edu, pg 62

Auren, Taber, Math Solutions®, One Harbor Dr, Suite 101, Sausalito, CA 94965 *Toll Free Tel:* 877-234-7323 *Toll Free Fax:* 800-724-4716 *E-mail:* info@mathsolutions.com; orders@mathsolutions.com *Web Site:* www.mathsolutions.com; store.mathsolutions.com, pg 127

Ausenda, Marco, Rizzoli International Publications Inc, 300 Park Ave S, 4th fl, New York, NY 10010-5399 *Tel:* 212-387-3400 *Toll Free Tel:* 800-522-6657 (orders only) *Fax:* 212-387-3535 *E-mail:* publicity@rizzoliusa.com *Web Site:* www.rizzoliusa.com, pg 175

Austin, Jay, Environmental Law Institute, 1730 "M" St NW, Suite 700, Washington, DC 20036 *Tel:* 202-939-3800 *Toll Free Tel:* 800-433-5120 *Fax:* 202-939-3868 *E-mail:* law@eli.org *Web Site:* www.eli.org, pg 67

Austin, Kurt, National Council of Teachers of English (NCTE), 340 N Neil St, Suite 104, Champaign, IL 61820 *Tel:* 217-328-3870 *Toll Free Tel:* 877-369-6283 (cust serv) *Fax:* 217-328-9645 *E-mail:* customerservice@ncte.org *Web Site:* ncte.org, pg 137, 512

Autin, Andrea, WNBA Writing Contest, PO Box 237, FDR Sta, New York, NY 10150-0231 *Toll Free Tel:* 866-610-WNBA (610-9622) *E-mail:* contest@wnba-books.org; info@wnba-books.org *Web Site:* wnba-books.org/contest, pg 676

Avery, Gayley, DK, c/o Penguin Random House LLC, 1745 Broadway, 20th fl, New York, NY 10019 *Tel:* 646-674-4000 *Toll Free Tel:* 800-733-3000 *Fax:* 646-674-4020 *E-mail:* marketing@dk.com (lib servs); publicity@dk.com; csorders@penguinrandomhouse.com; customerservice@penguinrandomhouse.com *Web Site:* www.dk.com, pg 60

Avis, Ed, National Latino Press Association (NLPA), 1841 Columbia Rd NW, Suite 614, Washington, DC 20009 *Tel:* 202-489-9516; 509-545-3055 (off of the Pres) *E-mail:* info@nationallatinopressassoc.org *Web Site:* nationallatinopressassoc.org, pg 513

Awe, Alyssa, Macmillan, 120 Broadway, 22nd fl, New York, NY 10271 *E-mail:* press.inquiries@macmillan.com *Web Site:* us.macmillan.com, pg 122

Axelrod, Steven, The Axelrod Agency, 55 Main St, Chatham, NY 12037 *Tel:* 518-392-2100, pg 449

Axford, Elizabeth C, Piano Press, 1425 Ocean Ave, Suite 5, Del Mar, CA 92014 *Tel:* 619-884-1401 *E-mail:* pianopress@pianopress.com *Web Site:* www.pianopress.com, pg 159

Ayala, Jasmin, Penguin Random House Audio Publishing Group, 1745 Broadway, New York, NY 10019 *Toll Free Tel:* 800-793-2665 (cust serv) *E-mail:* audio@penguinrandomhouse.com; ecustomerservice@penguinrandomhouse.com *Web Site:* www.penguinrandomhouseaudio.com, pg 154

Aycock, David, Baylor University Press, Baylor University, One Bear Place, Waco, TX 76798-7363 *Tel:* 254-710-3164 *E-mail:* bup_marketing@baylor.edu *Web Site:* www.baylorpress.com, pg 25

Aydinian, Chelly-Ann, Penguin Random House Audio Publishing Group, 1745 Broadway, New York, NY 10019 *Toll Free Tel:* 800-793-2665 (cust serv) *E-mail:* audio@penguinrandomhouse.com; ecustomerservice@penguinrandomhouse.com *Web Site:* www.penguinrandomhouseaudio.com, pg 154

Ayer, Paula, Greystone Books Ltd, 343 Railway St, Suite 302, Vancouver, BC V6A 1A4, Canada *Tel:* 604-875-1550 *Fax:* 604-875-1556 *E-mail:* info@greystonebooks.com; rights@greystonebooks.com *Web Site:* www.greystonebooks.com, pg 407

Ayers, James, University of New Mexico Press, One University of New Mexico, Albuquerque, NM 87131-0001 *Tel:* 505-272-7777 *Fax:* 505-277-3343 *E-mail:* custserv@unm.edu (order dept) *Web Site:* unmpress.com, pg 218

Ayubi, Emily, American Psychological Association, 750 First St NE, Washington, DC 20002 *Tel:* 202-336-5510 *Toll Free Tel:* 800-374-2721 *Fax:* 202-336-5502 *E-mail:* order@apa.org; booksales@apa.org *Web Site:* www.apa.org/books, pg 11

Ayuso, Daniela, Doubleday, c/o Penguin Random House LLC, 1745 Broadway, New York, NY 10019 *Tel:* 212-751-2600 *Fax:* 212-940-7390 (dom rts); 212-572-2662 (foreign rts) *Web Site:* knopfdoubleday.com/imprint/doubleday/; knopfdoubleday.com, pg 61

Aziz, Duriya, Scholastic International, 557 Broadway, New York, NY 10012 *Tel:* 212-343-6100; 646-330-5288 (intl cust serv) *Toll Free Tel:* 800-SCHOLASTIC (724-6527) *Fax:* 646-837-7878 *E-mail:* international@scholastic.com, pg 184

Aziz, Ms Nurjehan, Mawenzi House Publishers Ltd, 39 Woburn Ave (B), Toronto, ON M5W 1K5, Canada *Tel:* 416-483-7191 *E-mail:* info@mawenzihouse.com *Web Site:* www.mawenzihouse.com, pg 412

Azouz, Nora, Ordre des traducteurs, terminologues et interpretes agrees du quebec (OTTIAQ), 1108-2021 Ave Union, Montreal, QC H3A 2S9, Canada *Tel:* 514-845-4411 *Toll Free Tel:* 800-265-4815 *Fax:* 514-845-9903 *E-mail:* info@ottiaq.org; direction@ottiaq.org; reception@ottiaq.org; communications@ottiaq.org *Web Site:* www.ottiaq.org, pg 515

Azze, Nicole, Bloomsbury Academic, 1385 Broadway, 5th fl, New York, NY 10018 *Tel:* 212-419-5300 *Web Site:* www.bloomsbury.com/us/academic, pg 31

Baake, Mike, Self-Realization Fellowship Publishers, 3208 Humboldt St, Los Angeles, CA 90031 *Tel:* 323-276-6002 *Toll Free Tel:* 888-773-8680 *E-mail:* sales@yogananda-srf.org *Web Site:* www.yogananda-srf.org; bookstore.yogananda-srf.org (online retail orders), pg 186

Babad, Jake, Westwood Creative Artists Ltd, 386 Huron St, Toronto, ON M5S 2G6, Canada *Tel:* 416-964-3302 *Fax:* 416-964-3302 *E-mail:* wca_office@wcaltd.com *Web Site:* www.wcaltd.com, pg 481

Babakhan, Jen, Books & Such, 2222 Cleveland Ave, No 1005, Santa Rosa, CA 95403 *Tel:* 707-538-4184 *Web Site:* booksandsuch.com, pg 451

Babb-Rosenfeld, Leah, Bloomsbury Academic, 1385 Broadway, 5th fl, New York, NY 10018 *Tel:* 212-419-5300 *Web Site:* www.bloomsbury.com/us/academic, pg 31

Babcock, Hannah, Random House Children's Books, c/o Penguin Random House LLC, 1745 Broadway, New York, NY 10019 *Tel:* 212-782-9000 *Web Site:* www.rhcbooks.com, pg 169

Babiak, Samantha, Writers' League of Texas (WLT), 611 S Congress Ave, Suite 200 A-3, Austin, TX 78704 *Tel:* 512-499-8914 *E-mail:* wlt@writersleague.org *Web Site:* www.writersleague.org, pg 488, 523, 558

Babiak, Samantha, Writers' League of Texas Book Awards, 611 S Congress Ave, Suite 200 A-3, Austin, TX 78704 *Tel:* 512-499-8914 *E-mail:* wlt@writersleague.org *Web Site:* www.writersleague.org, pg 678

Baccam, Mike, University of Washington Press, 4333 Brooklyn Ave NE, Seattle, WA 98105-9570 *Toll Free Tel:* 800-537-5487 (orders) *Tel:* 206-543-3932; 410-516-6998 (orders) *E-mail:* uwapress@uw.edu *Web Site:* uwapress.uw.edu, pg 220

Bace, Marjan, Manning Publications Co, 20 Baldwin Rd, PO Box 761, Shelter Island, NY 11964 *Tel:* 203-626-1510 *E-mail:* sales@manning.com; support@manning.com (cust serv) *Web Site:* www.manning.com, pg 124

Bachmann, Elizabeth, Encounter Books, 900 Broadway, Suite 601, New York, NY 10003 *Tel:* 212-871-6310 *Toll Free Tel:* 855-203-7220 *E-mail:* publicity@encounterbooks.com *Web Site:* www.encounterbooks.com, pg 66

Bachmann, Lorin, Clinical and Laboratory Standards Institute (CLSI), 1055 Westlakes Dr, Suite 300, Berwyn, PA 19312 *Tel:* 610-688-0100 *Toll Free Tel:* 877-447-1888 (orders) *Fax:* 610-688-0700 *E-mail:* customerservice@clsi.org *Web Site:* www.clsi.org, pg 49

Bacigalupi, John, Taunton Books, 63 S Main St, Newtown, CT 06470 *Tel:* 203-426-8171 *Toll Free Tel:* 866-505-4689 (orders) *Fax:* 203-270-9373, pg 203

Backowski, Therese, Dog Writers Association of America Inc (DWAA), PO Box 787, Hughesville, MD 20637 *Web Site:* dogwriters.org, pg 505

Backowski, Therese, Dog Writers Association of America Inc (DWAA) Annual Writing Competition, PO Box 787, Hughesville, MD 20637 *Web Site:* dogwriters.org, pg 596

Badalian, Alvart, Blue Crane Books Inc, 36 Hazel St, Watertown, MA 02472 *Tel:* 617-926-8989, pg 32

Bader, Bonnie, Golden Kite Awards, 6363 Wilshire Blvd, Suite 425, Los Angeles, CA 90048 *Tel:* 323-782-1010 *E-mail:* info@scbwi.org *Web Site:* www.scbwi.org/awards/golden-kite-award, pg 607

Bader, Rachel, Random House Children's Books, c/o Penguin Random House LLC, 1745 Broadway, New York, NY 10019 *Tel:* 212-782-9000 *Web Site:* www.rhcbooks.com, pg 169

Badowski, Keith, Brick Road Poetry Book Contest, 341 Lee Rd 553, Phenix City, AL 36867 *Web Site:* www.brickroadpoetrypress.com/poetry-book-contest, pg 584

Baehr, Matt, Book Manufacturers' Institute Inc (BMI), 7282 55 Ave E, No 147, Bradenton, FL 34203 *Tel:* 386-986-4552 *Web Site:* bmibook.com, pg 501

Baez, Lara, HarperCollins Publishers LLC, 195 Broadway, New York, NY 10007 *Tel:* 212-207-7000 *Web Site:* www.harpercollins.com, pg 87

Bagatella, Andrew, Whitecap Books, 314 W Cordova St, Suite 209, Vancouver, BC V6B 1E8, Canada *Tel:* 604-681-6181 *Web Site:* www.whitecap.ca, pg 424

Baggett, Chris, David C Cook, 4050 Lee Vance Dr, Colorado Springs, CO 80918 *Tel:* 719-536-0100 *Toll Free Tel:* 800-323-7543 (orders & cust serv) *Toll Free Fax:* 800-430-0726 (cust serv) *E-mail:* bookstores@davidccook.org; customercare@davidccook.org *Web Site:* www.davidccook.org, pg 52

Bagley, Jennifer, American College of Surgeons, 633 N Saint Clair St, Chicago, IL 60611-3211 *Tel:* 312-202-5000 *Fax:* 312-202-5001 *E-mail:* postmaster@facs.org *Web Site:* www.facs.org, pg 9

Bagnall, Roger, American Philosophical Society Press, 104 S Fifth St, Philadelphia, PA 19106 *Tel:* 215-440-3425 *Fax:* 215-440-3450 *Web Site:* www.amphilsoc.org, pg 11

Bahr, Ed, Pacific Press® Publishing Association, 1350 N Kings Rd, Nampa, ID 83687-3193 *Tel:* 208-465-2500 *Fax:* 208-465-2531 *E-mail:* booksubmissions@pacificpress.com *Web Site:* www.pacificpress.com, pg 150

Bailey, Anne G, Westernlore Press, PO Box 35305, Tucson, AZ 85740-5305 *Tel:* 520-297-5491, pg 228

Bailey, Deanna, HarperCollins Publishers LLC, 195 Broadway, New York, NY 10007 *Tel:* 212-207-7000 *Web Site:* www.harpercollins.com, pg 87

Bailey, Emma, Bloomsbury Academic, 1385 Broadway, 5th fl, New York, NY 10018 *Tel:* 212-419-5300 *Web Site:* www.bloomsbury.com/us/academic, pg 31

Bailey, Jocelyn, Thomas Nelson, 501 Nelson Place, Nashville, TN 37214 *Tel:* 615-889-9000 *Toll Free Tel:* 800-251-4000 *Web Site:* www.thomasnelson.com, pg 206

Bailey, Jocelyn, Zondervan, 3900 Sparks Dr SE, Grand Rapids, MI 49546 *Tel:* 616-698-6900 *Toll Free Tel:* 800-226-1122; 800-727-1309 (retail orders) *Fax:* 616-698-3350 *Toll Free Fax:* 800-698-3256 (retail orders) *E-mail:* customercare@harpercollins.com *Web Site:* www.zondervan.com, pg 237

Bailey, Keondra, Miles Conrad Award, 3600 Clipper Mill Rd, Suite 302, Baltimore, MD 21211-1948 *Tel:* 301-654-2512 *Fax:* 410-685-5278 *E-mail:* nisohq@niso.org *Web Site:* www.niso.org, pg 591

Bailey, Keondra, National Information Standards Organization (NISO), 3600 Clipper Mill Rd, Suite 302, Baltimore, MD 21211-1948 *Tel:* 301-654-2512 *Fax:* 410-685-5278 *E-mail:* nisohq@niso.org *Web Site:* www.niso.org, pg 138, 513

Bailey, Lynn R, Westernlore Press, PO Box 35305, Tucson, AZ 85740-5305 *Tel:* 520-297-5491, pg 228

Bailor, David, Carter G Woodson Book Awards, 8555 16 St, Suite 500, Silver Spring, MD 20910 *Tel:* 301-588-1800 *E-mail:* ncss@ncss.org *Web Site:* www.socialstudies.org/membership/awards/carter-g-woodson-book-awards, pg 677

Baines, Rebecca, National Geographic Books, 1145 17 St NW, Washington, DC 20036-4688 *Tel:* 202-857-7000 *Toll Free Tel:* 877-866-6486 *E-mail:* ngbooks@cdsfulfillment.com *Web Site:* www.nationalgeographic.com/books/; ngbooks.buysub.com, pg 138

Bains, Pritpaul, Macmillan, 120 Broadway, 22nd fl, New York, NY 10271 *E-mail:* press.inquiries@macmillan.com *Web Site:* us.macmillan.com, pg 122

Baird, Ashley, Naval Institute Press, 291 Wood Rd, Annapolis, MD 21402-5034 *Tel:* 410-268-6110 *Toll Free Tel:* 800-233-8764 *Fax:* 410-295-1084 *E-mail:* customer@usni.org (cust inquiries) *Web Site:* www.usni.org/press/books; www.usni.org, pg 139

Baird, Lee, Tennessee Arts Commission Fellowships, 401 Charlotte Ave, Nashville, TN 37243-0780 *Tel:* 615-741-1701 *Fax:* 615-741-8559 *Web Site:* tnartscommission.org, pg 668

Baird, Michele, David C Cook, 4050 Lee Vance Dr, Colorado Springs, CO 80918 *Tel:* 719-536-0100 *Toll Free Tel:* 800-323-7543 (orders & cust serv) *Toll Free Fax:* 800-430-0726 (cust serv) *E-mail:* bookstores@davidccook.org; customercare@davidccook.org *Web Site:* www.davidccook.org, pg 52

Baitch, Tzipora, Simon & Schuster, 1230 Avenue of the Americas, New York, NY 10020 *Tel:* 212-698-7000 *Toll Free Tel:* 800-223-2348 (cust serv); 800-223-2336 (orders) *Toll Free Fax:* 800-943-9831 (orders) *Web Site:* simonandschusterpublishing.com/simonandschuster/, pg 188

Bajek, Lauren, Liza Dawson Associates, 121 W 27 St, Suite 1201, New York, NY 10001 *Tel:* 212-465-9071 *Web Site:* www.lizadawsonassociates.com, pg 455

Bak, Jenny, Viking Children's Books, c/o Penguin Random House LLC, 1745 Broadway, New York, NY 10019 *Tel:* 212-782-9000 *Web Site:* www.penguin.com/viking-childrens-books-overview/, pg 224

Bakamjian, Ted, Society of Exploration Geophysicists, 8801 S Yale Ave, Suite 500, Tulsa, OK 74137 *Tel:* 918-497-5500 *Fax:* 918-497-5557 *E-mail:* web@seg.org *Web Site:* www.seg.org, pg 192

Bakeman, Karl, W W Norton & Company Inc, 500 Fifth Ave, New York, NY 10110-0017 *Tel:* 212-354-5500 *Toll Free Tel:* 800-233-4830 (orders & cust serv) *Fax:* 212-869-0856 *Toll Free Fax:* 800-458-6515 *E-mail:* orders@wwnorton.com *Web Site:* wwnorton.com, pg 143

Baker, Alice, Macmillan, 120 Broadway, 22nd fl, New York, NY 10271 *E-mail:* press.inquiries@macmillan.com *Web Site:* us.macmillan.com, pg 122

Baker, Amy, HarperCollins Publishers LLC, 195 Broadway, New York, NY 10007 *Tel:* 212-207-7000 *Web Site:* www.harpercollins.com, pg 86

Baker, Daniel W, Library of America, 14 E 60 St, New York, NY 10022-1006 *Tel:* 212-308-3360 *Fax:* 212-750-8352 *E-mail:* info@loa.org *Web Site:* www.loa.org, pg 116

Baker, Dr Deirdre, Frances E Russell Grant, c/o The Canadian Children's Book Ctr, 425 Adelaide St W, Suite 200, Toronto, ON M5V 3C1, Canada *Fax:* 416-975-8970 *E-mail:* russell@ibby-canada.org *Web Site:* www.ibby-canada.org/awards/frances-e-russell-grant/, pg 658

Baker, Doris, Filter Press LLC, PO Box 95, Palmer Lake, CO 80133 *Tel:* 719-481-2420 *Toll Free Tel:* 888-570-2663 *Fax:* 719-481-2420 *E-mail:* info@filterpressbooks.com; orders@filterpressbooks.com *Web Site:* filterpressbooks.com, pg 71

Baker, Dwight, Baker Books, 6030 E Fulton Rd, Ada, MI 49301 *Tel:* 616-676-9185 *Toll Free Tel:* 800-877-2665 (orders) *Fax:* 616-676-9573 *Toll Free Fax:* 800-398-3111 (orders) *E-mail:* media@bakerpublishinggroup.com; orders@bakerpublishinggroup.com; sales@bakerpublishinggroup.com *Web Site:* www.bakerpublishinggroup.com, pg 23

Baker, Dwight, Bethany House Publishers, 11400 Hampshire Ave S, Bloomington, MN 55438 *Tel:* 952-829-2500 *Toll Free Tel:* 800-877-2665 (orders) *Fax:* 952-829-2568 *Toll Free Fax:* 800-398-3111 (orders) *Web Site:* www.bethanyhouse.com; www.bakerpublishinggroup.com, pg 29

Baker, Dr Gordon N, Southern Books Competition, PO Box 30703, Savannah, GA 31410 *Tel:* 912-999-7979 *E-mail:* selaadminservices@selaonline.org *Web Site:* selaonline.org, pg 664

Baker, John F, Barbara Braun Associates Inc, 7 E 14 St, Suite 19F, New York, NY 10003 *Tel:* 917-414-3022 *Web Site:* www.barbarabraunagency.com, pg 452

Baker, Karen, Temple University Press, 1852 N Tenth St, Philadelphia, PA 19122-6099 *Tel:* 215-926-2140 *Toll Free Tel:* 800-621-2736 *Fax:* 215-926-2141 *E-mail:* tempress@temple.edu *Web Site:* tupress.temple.edu, pg 204

Baker, Kate, Science Fiction and Fantasy Writers Association, Inc (SFWA), PO Box 215, San Lorenzo, CA 94580 *Tel:* 860-698-0536 *E-mail:* office@sfwa.org; operations@sfwa.org *Web Site:* www.sfwa.org, pg 519

Baker, Kate, SFWA Nebula Awards, PO Box 215, San Lorenzo, CA 94580 *Tel:* 860-698-0536 *E-mail:* office@sfwa.org; operations@sfwa.org *Web Site:* www.sfwa.org, pg 661

Baker, Katie, University of Oklahoma Press, 2800 Venture Dr, Norman, OK 73069-8216 *Tel:* 405-325-2000 *Web Site:* www.oupress.com, pg 219

Baker, Lisa-Jo, Thomas Nelson, 501 Nelson Place, Nashville, TN 37214 *Tel:* 615-889-9000 *Toll Free Tel:* 800-251-4000 *Web Site:* www.thomasnelson.com, pg 206

Baker, Liza, Scholastic Trade Publishing, 557 Broadway, New York, NY 10012 *Tel:* 212-343-6100; 212-343-4685 (export sales) *Fax:* 212-343-4714 (export sales) *Web Site:* www.scholastic.com, pg 184

Baker, Lucy Childs, The Aaron M Priest Literary Agency Inc, 370 Lexington Ave, Suite 1202, New York, NY 10017 *Tel:* 212-818-0344 *Fax:* 212-573-9417 *E-mail:* info@aaronpriest.com *Web Site:* www.aaronpriest.com, pg 472

Baker, Mary, Berkley, c/o Penguin Random House LLC, 1745 Broadway, 19th fl, New York, NY 10019 *Tel:* 212-366-2000 *Web Site:* www.penguin.com/publishers/berkley/; www.penguin.com/ace-overview/, pg 28

Baker, Matt, The Minerals, Metals & Materials Society (TMS), 5700 Corporate Dr, Suite 750, Pittsburgh, PA 15237 *Tel:* 724-776-9000 *Toll Free Tel:* 800-759-4867 *Fax:* 724-776-3770 *E-mail:* publications@tms.org (orders) *Web Site:* www.tms.org/bookstore (orders); www.tms.org, pg 132

Baker, Patrick, Artist Grants, 711 E Wells Ave, Pierre, SD 57501-3369 *Tel:* 605-773-3301 *Fax:* 605-773-5977 *E-mail:* sdac@state.sd.us *Web Site:* www.artscouncil.sd.gov/grants, pg 574

Baker, Sarah, Crystal Kite Awards, 6363 Wilshire Blvd, Suite 425, Los Angeles, CA 90048 *Tel:* 323-782-1010 *E-mail:* info@scbwi.org *Web Site:* www.scbwi.org/awards/crystal-kite-member-choice-award, pg 593

Baker, Sarah, Karen & Philip Cushman Late Bloomer Award, 6363 Wilshire Blvd, Suite 425, Los Angeles, CA 90048 *Tel:* 323-782-1010 *E-mail:* info@scbwi.org *Web Site:* www.scbwi.org/awards-and-grants-new, pg 594

Baker, Sarah, The Don Freeman Work-in-Progress Grant, 6363 Wilshire Blvd, Suite 425, Los Angeles, CA 90048 *Tel:* 323-782-1010 *E-mail:* info@scbwi.org *Web Site:* www.scbwi.org, pg 604

Baker, Sarah, Golden Kite Awards, 6363 Wilshire Blvd, Suite 425, Los Angeles, CA 90048 *Tel:* 323-782-1010 *E-mail:* info@scbwi.org *Web Site:* www.scbwi.org/awards/golden-kite-award, pg 607

Baker, Sarah, Magazine Merit Awards, 6363 Wilshire Blvd, Suite 425, Los Angeles, CA 90048 *Tel:* 323-782-1010 *E-mail:* info@scbwi.org *Web Site:* www.scbwi.org/awards/magazine-merit-award, pg 628

Baker, Sarah, On-the-Verge Emerging Voices Award, 6363 Wilshire Blvd, Suite 425, Los Angeles, CA 90048 *Tel:* 323-782-1010 *E-mail:* info@scbwi.org *Web Site:* www.scbwi.org/awards/grants/on-the-verge-emerging-voices-grant, pg 644

Baker, Sarah, SCBWI Work-In-Progress Awards, 6363 Wilshire Blvd, Suite 425, Los Angeles, CA 90048 *Tel:* 323-782-1010 *E-mail:* info@scbwi.org *Web Site:* www.scbwi.org/awards/grants/work-in-progress-grants, pg 660

Baker, Sarah, Society of Children's Book Writers & Illustrators (SCBWI), 6363 Wilshire Blvd, Suite 425, Los Angeles, CA 90048 *Tel:* 323-782-1010 *E-mail:* membership@scbwi.org *Web Site:* www.scbwi.org, pg 520

Baker, Sarah, Spark Award, 6363 Wilshire Blvd, Suite 425, Los Angeles, CA 90048 *Tel:* 323-782-1010 *E-mail:* grants@scbwi.org; info@scbwi.org *Web Site:* www.scbwi.org, pg 665

Baker, Scottie, Andrews University Press, Sutherland House, 8360 W Campus Circle Dr, Berrien Springs, MI 49104-1700 *Tel:* 269-471-6134 *Toll Free Tel:* 800-467-6369 (Visa, MC & American Express orders only) *Fax:* 269-471-6224 *E-mail:* aupo@andrews.edu; aup@andrews.edu *Web Site:* www.universitypress.andrews.edu, pg 14

Baker, Steven, University of Oklahoma Press, 2800 Venture Dr, Norman, OK 73069-8216 *Tel:* 405-325-2000 *Web Site:* www.oupress.com, pg 219

Baker-Baughman, Bernadette, Victoria Sanders & Associates LLC, 440 Buck Rd, Stone Ridge, NY 12484 *Tel:* 212-633-8811 *Web Site:* www.victoriasanders.com, pg 475

Bakhtiar, Mary, Kazi Publications Inc, 3023 W Belmont Ave, Chicago, IL 60618 *Tel:* 773-267-7001 *Fax:* 773-267-7002 *E-mail:* info@kazi.org *Web Site:* www.kazi.org, pg 108

Balabanlilar, Sara, Dalkey Archive Press, c/o Deep Vellum Publishing, 3000 Commerce St, Dallas, TX 75226 *E-mail:* admin@deepvellum.org *Web Site:* www.dalkeyarchive.com, pg 56

Balash, Kristen, American Antiquarian Society (AAS), 185 Salisbury St, Worcester, MA 01609-1634 *Tel:* 508-755-5221 *Fax:* 508-754-9069 *E-mail:* library@mwa.org *Web Site:* www.americanantiquarian.org, pg 494

Balash, Kristen, Fellowships for Creative & Performing Artists & Writers, 185 Salisbury St, Worcester, MA 01609-1634 *Tel:* 508-755-5221 *Fax:* 508-754-9069 *E-mail:* library@mwa.org *Web Site:* www.americanantiquarian.org, pg 602

Balash, Kristen, Fellowships for Historical Research, 185 Salisbury St, Worcester, MA 01609-1634 *Tel:* 508-755-5221 *Fax:* 508-754-9069 *Web Site:* www.americanantiquarian.org, pg 602

Balazs, Kirsi, St Martin's Press, LLC, 120 Broadway, New York, NY 10271 *E-mail:* publicity@stmartins.com; trademarketing@stmartins.com; foreignrights@stmartins.com *Web Site:* us.macmillan.com/smp, pg 181

Baldi, Malaga, Malaga Baldi Literary Agency, 233 W 99, Suite 19C, New York, NY 10025 *Tel:* 212-222-3213 *E-mail:* baldibooks@gmail.com *Web Site:* www.baldibooks.com, pg 449

Baldwin, Robin, IEEE Computer Society, 2001 "L" St NW, Suite 700, Washington, DC 20036-4928 *Tel:* 202-371-0101 *Toll Free Tel:* 800-678-4333 (memb info) *Fax:* 202-728-9614 *E-mail:* help@computer.org *Web Site:* www.computer.org, pg 98

Balestrino, Logan, Penguin Random House LLC, 1745 Broadway, New York, NY 10019 *Tel:* 212-782-9000 *Toll Free Tel:* 800-726-0600 *Web Site:* www.penguinrandomhouse.com, pg 155

Balfour, Kate, The Association of Book Publishers of British Columbia (ABPBC), 600-402 W Pender St, Vancouver, BC V6B 1T6, Canada *Tel:* 604-684-0228 *E-mail:* admin@books.bc.ca *Web Site:* www.books.bc.ca, pg 499

Balik, Susan, Allen Ginsberg Poetry Award, One College Blvd, Paterson, NJ 07505-1179 *Tel:* 973-684-6555 *Fax:* 973-523-6085 *Web Site:* www.poetrycenterpccc.com, pg 606

Balik, Susan, The Paterson Poetry Prize, One College Blvd, Paterson, NJ 07505-1179 *Tel:* 973-684-6555 *Fax:* 973-523-6085 *Web Site:* www.poetrycenterpccc.com, pg 646

Balik, Susan, The Paterson Prize for Books for Young People, One College Blvd, Paterson, NJ 07505-1179 *Tel:* 973-684-6555 *Fax:* 973-523-6085 *Web Site:* www.poetrycenterpccc.com, pg 646

Ball, Christine, Berkley, c/o Penguin Random House LLC, 1745 Broadway, 19th fl, New York, NY 10019 *Tel:* 212-366-2000 *Web Site:* www.penguin.com/publishers/berkley/; www.penguin.com/ace-overview/, pg 28

Ball, Dean, Friedrich Hayek Lecture & Book Prize, 52 Vanderbilt Ave, New York, NY 10017 *Tel:* 212-599-7000 *Web Site:* www.manhattan-institute.org, pg 611

Ball, Don, National Endowment for the Arts, 400 Seventh St SW, Washington, DC 20506-0001 *Tel:* 202-682-5400 *Web Site:* www.arts.gov, pg 526

Ball, Elizabeth (Liz), HarperCollins Publishers LLC, 195 Broadway, New York, NY 10007 *Tel:* 212-207-7000 *Web Site:* www.harpercollins.com, pg 86

Ball, Lillian, Avery, c/o Penguin Random House LLC, 1745 Broadway, New York, NY 10019 *Tel:* 212-366-2000 *Web Site:* www.penguin.com/avery-overview/, pg 23

Ball, Lillian, TarcherPerigee, c/o Penguin Random House LLC, 1745 Broadway, New York, NY 10019 *Tel:* 212-782-9000 *Web Site:* www.penguin.com/tarcherperigee-overview/; www.facebook.com/TarcherPerigee, pg 202

Ballantyne, Robert, Arsenal Pulp Press, 211 E Georgia St, No 202, Vancouver, BC V6A 1Z6, Canada *Tel:* 604-687-4233 *Toll Free Tel:* 888-600-PULP (600-7857) *Fax:* 604-687-4283 *E-mail:* info@arsenalpulp.com *Web Site:* www.arsenalpulp.com, pg 395

Ballard, Holly, Data Trace Publishing Co (DTP), 110 West Rd, Suite 227, Towson, MD 21204-2316 *Tel:* 410-494-4994 *Toll Free Tel:* 800-342-6454 *Fax:* 410-494-0515 *E-mail:* info@datatrace.com; customerservice@datatrace.com; salesandmarketing@datatrace.com; editorial@datatrace.com *Web Site:* www.datatrace.com, pg 57

Ballard, John, World Citizens, PO Box 131, Mill Valley, CA 94942-0131 *Tel:* 415-380-8020; 415-233-2822 (direct), pg 233

Ballas, Toula, Union Square & Co, 1166 Avenue of the Americas, 17th fl, New York, NY 10036-2715 *Tel:* 212-532-7160 *Toll Free Tel:* 800-367-9692 *Fax:* 212-213-2495 *Toll Free Fax:* 800-542-7567 *E-mail:* custservice@sterlingpublishing.com; customerservice@sterlingpublishing.com; editorial@sterlingpublishing.com; tradesales@sterlingpublishing.com *Web Site:* www.sterlingpublishing.com, pg 212

Ballast, Matthew, Grand Central Publishing, 1290 Avenue of the Americas, New York, NY 10104 *Tel:* 212-364-1100 *Web Site:* www.hachettebookgroup.com/imprint/grand-central-publishing/, pg 80

Ballenger, Seale, Scholastic Trade Publishing, 557 Broadway, New York, NY 10012 *Tel:* 212-343-6100; 212-343-4685 (export sales) *Fax:* 212-343-4714 (export sales) *Web Site:* www.scholastic.com, pg 184

Balli, Tyler, Ohio University Press, Alden Library, Suite 101, 30 Park Place, Athens, OH 45701-2909 *Tel:* 740-593-1154 *Web Site:* www.ohioswallow.com, pg 146

Balliett, Will, Thames & Hudson, 500 Fifth Ave, New York, NY 10110 *Tel:* 212-354-3763 *Toll Free Tel:* 800-233-4830 *Fax:* 212-398-1252 *E-mail:* bookinfo@thames.wwnorton.com *Web Site:* www.thamesandhudsonusa.com, pg 205

Ballinger, Malcolm, Ballinger Publishing, 21 E Garden St, Suite 205, Pensacola, FL 32502 *Tel:* 850-433-1166 *Fax:* 850-435-9174 *E-mail:* info@ballingerpublishing.com *Web Site:* www.ballingerpublishing.com, pg 24

Ballinger, Peter R, PRB Productions, 963 Peralta Ave, Albany, CA 94706-2144 *Tel:* 510-526-0722 *E-mail:* prbprdns@aol.com *Web Site:* www.prbmusic.com, pg 163

Balthazar, Martin, Les Editions de l'Hexagone, 4545, rue Frontenac, 3rd fl, Montreal, QC H2H 2R7, Canada *Tel:* 514-523-1182 *Fax:* 514-521-4434 *Web Site:* editionshexagone.groupelivre.com, pg 402

Balthazar, Martin, VLB editeur, 4545, rue Frontenac, 3rd fl, Montreal, QC H2H 2R7, Canada *Tel:* 514-849-5259 *Web Site:* www.edvlb.com, pg 424

Baltzer, Keren, Zondervan, 3900 Sparks Dr SE, Grand Rapids, MI 49546 *Tel:* 616-698-6900 *Toll Free Tel:* 800-226-1122; 800-727-1309 (retail orders) *Fax:* 616-698-3350 *Toll Free Fax:* 800-698-3256 (retail orders) *E-mail:* customercare@harpercollins.com *Web Site:* www.zondervan.com, pg 236

Balvenie, K, One Act Play Depot, Box 335, Spiritwood, SK S0J 2M0, Canada *E-mail:* plays@oneactplays.net; orders@oneactplays.net *Web Site:* oneactplays.net, pg 414

Balwinski, Scott, Teaching Strategies LLC, 4500 East-West Hwy, Suite 300, Bethesda, MD 20814 *Tel:* 301-634-0818 *Toll Free Tel:* 800-637-3652 *E-mail:* info@teachingstrategies.com; support@teachingstrategies.com *Web Site:* teachingstrategies.com, pg 204

Balzer, Jesse, Indiana University Press, Off of Scholarly Publg, Herman B Wells Library 350, 1320 E Tenth St, Bloomington, IN 47405-3907 *Tel:* 812-855-8817 *Fax:* 812-855-7931; 812-855-8507 *E-mail:* iupress@indiana.edu *Web Site:* iupress.org, pg 100

Bamford, Christopher, SteinerBooks Inc, 610 Main St, Suite 1, Great Barrington, MA 01230 *Tel:* 413-528-8233 *E-mail:* service@steinerbooks.org; friends@steinerbooks.org *Web Site:* steiner.presswarehouse.com, pg 198

Ban, Ana, Trident Media Group LLC, 355 Lexington Ave, 12th fl, New York, NY 10017 *Tel:* 212-333-1511 *E-mail:* info@tridentmediagroup.com; press@tridentmediagroup.com; foreignrights@tridentmediagroup.com; office.assistant@tridentmediagroup.com *Web Site:* www.tridentmediagroup.com, pg 480

Banales, Anney, Evan-Moor Educational Publishers, 10 Harris Ct, Suite C-3, Monterey, CA 93940 *Tel:* 831-649-5901 *Toll Free Tel:* 800-777-4362 (orders) *Fax:* 831-649-6256 *Toll Free Fax:* 800-777-4332 (orders) *E-mail:* sales@evan-moor.com; marketing@evan-moor.com *Web Site:* www.evan-moor.com, pg 68

Banci, Amanda, Harry N Abrams Inc, 195 Broadway, 9th fl, New York, NY 10007 *Tel:* 212-206-7715 *Toll Free Tel:* 800-345-1359 *Fax:* 212-645-8437 *E-mail:* abrams@abramsbooks.com; publicity@abramsbooks.com; sales@abramsbooks.com *Web Site:* www.abramsbooks.com, pg 3

Bancroft, Colette, Nona Balakian Citation for Excellence in Reviewing, c/o Jacob M Appel, Icahn School of Medicine at Mount Sinai, One Gustave L Levy Place, New York, NY 10029 *E-mail:* info@bookcritics.org *Web Site:* www.bookcritics.org/awards/balakian/, pg 576

Bancroft, Colette, Gregg Barrios Book in Translation Prize, c/o Jacob M Appel, Icahn School of Medicine at Mount Sinai, One Gustave L Levy Place, New York, NY 10029 *E-mail:* info@bookcritics.org *Web Site:* www.bookcritics.org/gregg-barrios-book-in-translation-prize/, pg 577

Bancroft, Colette, Emerging Critics Fellowship, c/o Jacob M Appel, Icahn School of Medicine at Mount Sinai, One Gustave L Levy Place, New York, NY 10029 *E-mail:* info@bookcritics.org *Web Site:* www.bookcritics.org/awards, pg 599

Bancroft, Colette, John Leonard Prize, c/o Jacob M Appel, Icahn School of Medicine at Mount Sinai, One Gustave L Levy Place, New York, NY 10029 *E-mail:* info@bookcritics.org *Web Site:* www.bookcritics.org/awards/leonard-prize, pg 623

Bancroft, Colette, The Toni Morrison Achievement Award, c/o Jacob M Appel, Icahn School of Medicine at Mount Sinai, One Gustave L Levy Place, New York, NY 10029 *E-mail:* info@bookcritics.org *Web Site:* www.bookcritics.org/the-toni-morrison-achievement-award, pg 635

Bancroft, Colette, National Book Critics Circle (NBCC), c/o Jacob M Appel, Icahn School of Medicine at Mount Sinai, One Gustave L Levy Place, New York, NY 10029 *E-mail:* info@bookcritics.org; membership@bookcritics.org *Web Site:* www.bookcritics.org, pg 512

Bancroft, Colette, National Book Critics Circle Award, c/o Jacob M Appel, Icahn School of Medicine at Mount Sinai, One Gustave L Levy Place, New York, NY 10029 *E-mail:* info@bookcritics.org *Web Site:* www.bookcritics.org/awards, pg 637

Bancroft, Colette, Ivan Sandrof Lifetime Achievement Award, c/o Jacob M Appel, Icahn School of Medicine at Mount Sinai, One Gustave L Levy Place, New York, NY 10029 *E-mail:* info@bookcritics.org *Web Site:* www.bookcritics.org/awards/sandrof/, pg 659

Bandler, Kenneth, American Jewish Committee (AJC), Mail Code 6760, PO Box 7247, Philadelphia, PA 19170-0001 *Tel:* 212-751-4000 *Fax:* 212-891-1450 *E-mail:* social@ajc.org *Web Site:* www.ajc.org, pg 495

Banducci, JoAnne, University of Nevada Press, c/o University of Nevada, Continuing Educ Bldg, MS 0166, Reno, NV 89557-0166 *Tel:* 775-784-6573 *Fax:* 775-784-6200 *Web Site:* www.unpress.nevada.edu, pg 218

Bandy, Emily Snyder, University Press of Mississippi, 3825 Ridgewood Rd, Jackson, MS 39211-6492 *Tel:* 601-432-6205 *Toll Free Tel:* 800-737-7788 (orders & cust serv) *Fax:* 601-432-6217 *E-mail:* press@mississippi.edu *Web Site:* www.upress.state.ms.us, pg 222

Banerjee, Rita, Warren Wilson College, MFA Program for Writers, 701 Warren Wilson Rd, Swannanoa, NC 28778 *Tel:* 828-771-3717 *E-mail:* mfa@warren-wilson.edu *Web Site:* www.warren-wilson.edu/programs/mfa-in-creative-writing, pg 567

Bangs, Kim, Chosen Books, 7808 Creekridge Circle, Suite 250, Bloomington, MN 55439 *Tel:* 952-829-2500 *Toll Free Tel:* 800-877-2665 (orders only) *Web Site:* www.chosenbooks.com, pg 47

Banis, Robert (Bud) J, Science & Humanities Press, 63 Summit Point, St Charles, MO 63301-0571, pg 185

Bank, Josh, Alloy Entertainment LLC, 30 Hudson Yards, 22nd fl, New York, NY 10001, pg 7

Banks, Clare, Beullah Rose Poetry Prize, 2221 Lake Ave, Baltimore, MD 21213 *E-mail:* smartishpace@gmail.com *Web Site:* www.smartishpace.com/poetry-prizes, pg 579

Banks, Clare, Erskine J Poetry Prize, 2221 Lake Ave, Baltimore, MD 21213 *E-mail:* smartishpace@gmail.com *Web Site:* www.smartishpace.com/poetry-prizes, pg 600

Banks, Jennifer, Yale University Press, 302 Temple St, New Haven, CT 06511-8909 *Tel:* 203-432-0960; 203-432-0966 (sales); 401-531-2800 (cust serv) *Toll Free Tel:* 800-405-1619 (cust serv) *Fax:* 203-432-0948; 203-432-8485 (sales); 401-531-2801 (cust serv) *Toll Free Fax:* 800-406-9145 (cust serv) *E-mail:* sales.press@yale.edu (sales); customer.care@triliteral.org (cust serv) *Web Site:* www.yalebooks.com; yalepress.yale.edu/yupbooks, pg 235

Banks, Jerry, Printing Industries Alliance, 636 N French Rd, Suite 1, Amherst, NY 14228 Tel: 716-691-3211 Toll Free Tel: 800-777-4742 Fax: 716-691-4249 E-mail: info@pialliance.org Web Site: pialliance.org, pg 517

Banning, Lisa, Rutgers University Press, 106 Somerset St, 3rd fl, New Brunswick, NJ 08901 Tel: 848-445-7762; 848-445-7761 (sales) Fax: 732-745-4935 E-mail: sales@rutgersuniversitypress.org Web Site: www.rutgersuniversitypress.org, pg 179

Bannon, Dr Joseph J Sr, Sagamore Publishing LLC, 3611 N Staley Rd, Suite B, Champaign, IL 61822 Tel: 217-359-5940 Toll Free Tel: 800-327-5557 (orders) Fax: 217-359-5975 E-mail: web@sagamorepub.com Web Site: www.sagamorepub.com, pg 179

Bannon, Peter L, Sagamore Publishing LLC, 3611 N Staley Rd, Suite B, Champaign, IL 61822 Tel: 217-359-5940 Toll Free Tel: 800-327-5557 (orders) Fax: 217-359-5975 E-mail: web@sagamorepub.com Web Site: www.sagamorepub.com, pg 179

Banta, Bel, HarperCollins Publishers LLC, 195 Broadway, New York, NY 10007 Tel: 212-207-7000 Web Site: www.harpercollins.com, pg 87

Banta, Tess, Roaring Brook Press, 120 Broadway, New York, NY 10271 Tel: 646-307-5151 Web Site: us.macmillan.com/publishers/roaring-brook-press, pg 176

Banyard, Toni, Greystone Books Ltd, 343 Railway St, Suite 302, Vancouver, BC V6A 1A4, Canada Tel: 604-875-1550 Fax: 604-875-1556 E-mail: info@greystonebooks.com; rights@greystonebooks.com Web Site: www.greystonebooks.com, pg 407

Banyon, Alexis, Sourcebooks LLC, 1935 Brookdale Rd, Suite 139, Naperville, IL 60563 Tel: 630-961-3900 Toll Free Tel: 800-432-7444 Fax: 630-961-2168 E-mail: info@sourcebooks.com Web Site: www.sourcebooks.com, pg 194

Baran, Maya, HarperCollins Publishers LLC, 195 Broadway, New York, NY 10007 Tel: 212-207-7000 Web Site: www.harpercollins.com, pg 86

Baranczyk, Susan, J J Keller & Associates, Inc®, 3003 Breezewood Lane, Neenah, WI 54957 Tel: 920-722-2848 Toll Free Tel: 877-564-2333 Toll Free Fax: 800-727-7516 E-mail: customerservice@jjkeller.com; sales@jjkeller.com Web Site: www.jjkeller.com, pg 108

Baranowski, Jennifer, CODiE Awards, PO Box 34340, Washington, DC 20043 Tel: 202-789-4446 Fax: 202-289-7097 Web Site: www.siia.net, pg 590

Barba, Alex, The Jennifer DeChiara Literary Agency, 245 Park Ave, 39th fl, New York, NY 10167 Tel: 212-372-8989 Web Site: www.jdlit.com, pg 455

Barbara, Stephen, InkWell Management, 521 Fifth Ave, Suite 2600, New York, NY 10175 Tel: 212-922-3500 Fax: 212-922-0535 E-mail: info@inkwellmanagement.com; submissions@inkwellmanagement.com; permissions@inkwellmanagement.com Web Site: inkwellmanagement.com, pg 463

Barbasa, Santos, University of Hawaii Press, 2840 Kolowalu St, Honolulu, HI 96822-1888 Tel: 808-956-8255 Toll Free Tel: 888-UHPRESS (847-7377) Toll Free Fax: 800-650-7811 E-mail: uhpbooks@hawaii.edu Web Site: www.uhpress.hawaii.edu, pg 216

Barber, A Richard, A Richard Barber & Associates, 80 N Main St, Kent, CT 06757 Tel: 860-927-4911; 212-737-7266 (cell) Fax: 860-927-3942 E-mail: barberrich@aol.com, pg 449

Barber, Terry, Parallax Press, 2236B Sixth St, Berkeley, CA 94710 Tel: 510-325-2945 Toll Free Tel: 800-863-5290 (orders) Web Site: www.parallax.org, pg 151

Barbiea, Laura, Alloy Entertainment LLC, 30 Hudson Yards, 22nd fl, New York, NY 10001, pg 7

Barbieri, William, Council for Research in Values & Philosophy, The Catholic University of America, Gibbons Hall, B-20, 620 Michigan Ave NE, Washington, DC 20064 Tel: 202-319-6089 E-mail: cua-rvp@cua.edu Web Site: www.crvp.org, pg 53

Barbo, Maria, HarperCollins Children's Books, 195 Broadway, New York, NY 10007 Tel: 212-207-7000 Web Site: www.harpercollins.com/childrens, pg 85

Barbour, Bruce R, Literary Management Group LLC, 1020 San Antonio Lane, Lady Lake, FL 32159 Tel: 615-812-4445 Web Site: www.literarymanagementgroup.com, pg 467

Barcatta, Sabine, Thomas J Lyon Book Award in Western American Literary and Cultural Studies, PO Box 6815, Logan, UT 84341 E-mail: wlaoperations@gmail.com Web Site: www.westernlit.org/thomas-j-lyon-book-award-in-western-american-literary-and-cultural-studies; www.westernlit.org, pg 627

Barer, Julie, The Book Group (TBG), 20 W 20 St, Suite 601, New York, NY 10011 E-mail: info@thebookgroup.com; submissions@thebookgroup.com Web Site: www.thebookgroup.com, pg 450

Barich, Steven, Alan Wofsy Fine Arts, 1109 Geary Blvd, San Francisco, CA 94109 Tel: 415-292-6500 Toll Free Tel: 800-660-6403 Fax: 415-292-6594 (off & cust serv); 510-251-1840 (acctg) E-mail: order@art-books.com (orders); editeur@earthlink.net (edit); beauxarts@earthlink.net (cust serv) Web Site: www.art-books.com, pg 231

Baril, Daniel, Institut de cooperation pour l'education des adultes-ICEA (The Institute for Cooperation on Adult Education), 5000 D'Iberville, Suite 304, Montreal, QC H2H 2S6, Canada Tel: 514-948-2044 E-mail: icae@icea.qc.ca Web Site: www.icea.qc.ca, pg 508

Barilla, Mary Beth, Miles Conrad Award, 3600 Clipper Mill Rd, Suite 302, Baltimore, MD 21211-1948 Tel: 301-654-2512 Fax: 410-685-5278 E-mail: nisohq@niso.org Web Site: www.niso.org, pg 591

Barilla, Mary Beth, National Information Standards Organization (NISO), 3600 Clipper Mill Rd, Suite 302, Baltimore, MD 21211-1948 Tel: 301-654-2512 Fax: 410-685-5278 E-mail: nisohq@niso.org Web Site: www.niso.org, pg 138, 513

Barkan, Bebe, Cross-Cultural Communications, 239 Wynsum Ave, Merrick, NY 11566-4725 Tel: 516-868-5635 Fax: 516-379-1901 E-mail: cccpoetry@aol.com Web Site: www.facebook.com/CrossCulturalCommunications.NY, pg 55

Barkan, Stanley H, Cross-Cultural Communications, 239 Wynsum Ave, Merrick, NY 11566-4725 Tel: 516-868-5635 Fax: 516-379-1901 E-mail: cccpoetry@aol.com Web Site: www.facebook.com/CrossCulturalCommunications.NY, pg 55

Barker, Donnie, Institute of Police Technology & Management (IPTM), 12000 Alumni Dr, Jacksonville, FL 32224-2678 Tel: 904-620-4786 Fax: 904-620-2453 E-mail: info@iptm.org Web Site: iptm.unf.edu, pg 102

Barker, Kathy, Florida Outdoor Writers Association Inc (FOWA), 235 Apollo Beach Blvd, Unit 271, Apollo Beach, FL 33572 Tel: 813-579-0990 E-mail: info@fowa.org Web Site: www.fowa.org, pg 506

Barker, Leah, Dramatists Play Service Inc, 440 Park Ave S, New York, NY 10016 E-mail: dpsinfo@broadwaylicensing.com; publications@broadwaylicensing.com Web Site: www.dramatists.com, pg 61

Barker, Ryan, The Tuesday Agency, 404 E College St, Suite 408, Iowa City, IA 52240 Tel: 319-338-7080; 319-400-9031 (cell) E-mail: info@tuesdayagency.com Web Site: tuesdayagency.com, pg 487

Barks, Brenna, The Press at California State University, Fresno, 2380 E Keats, M/S MB 99, Fresno, CA 93740-8024 Tel: 559-278-4103 E-mail: press@csufresno.edu, pg 163

Barks, Daniel, Beacon Press, 24 Farnsworth St, Boston, MA 02210-1409 Tel: 617-742-2110 Fax: 617-723-3097 E-mail: production@beacon.org Web Site: www.beacon.org, pg 25

Barley, Dawn, Macmillan, 120 Broadway, 22nd fl, New York, NY 10271 E-mail: press.inquiries@macmillan.com Web Site: us.macmillan.com, pg 122

Barley, Sarah, Simon & Schuster Children's Publishing, 1230 Avenue of the Americas, New York, NY 10020 Tel: 212-698-7000 Web Site: www.simonandschuster.com/kids; www.simonandschuster.com/teen; simonandschuster.net; simonandschuster.biz, pg 189

Barlow, Greg, Merriam-Webster Inc, 47 Federal St, Springfield, MA 01102 Tel: 413-734-3134 Toll Free Tel: 800-828-1880 (orders & cust serv) Fax: 413-731-5979 (sales) E-mail: support@merriam-webster.com Web Site: www.merriam-webster.com, pg 130

Barlow, Randy, Rizzoli International Publications Inc, 300 Park Ave S, 4th fl, New York, NY 10010-5399 Tel: 212-387-3400 Toll Free Tel: 800-522-6657 (orders only) Fax: 212-387-3535 E-mail: publicity@rizzoliusa.com Web Site: www.rizzoliusa.com, pg 175

Barmash, Erica, Bloomsbury Publishing Inc, 1385 Broadway, 5th fl, New York, NY 10018 Tel: 212-419-5300 E-mail: marketingusa@bloomsbury.com; adultpublicityusa@bloomsbury.com; askacademic@bloomsbury.com Web Site: www.bloomsbury.com, pg 31

Barnard, Megan, The Jennifer DeChiara Literary Agency, 245 Park Ave, 39th fl, New York, NY 10167 Tel: 212-372-8989 Web Site: www.jdlit.com, pg 455

Barnard, Megan, Tor Publishing Group, 120 Broadway, New York, NY 10271 Toll Free Tel: 800-455-0340 (Macmillan) E-mail: torpublicity@tor.com; forgepublicity@forgebooks.com Web Site: us.macmillan.com/torpublishinggroup, pg 208

Barnes, Janet, Bentley Publishers, 1734 Massachusetts Ave, Cambridge, MA 02138-1804 Tel: 617-547-4170 E-mail: sales@bentleypubs.com Web Site: www.bentleypublishers.com, pg 28

Barnes, Jeff, Abingdon Press, 810 12 Ave S, Nashville, TN 37203 Toll Free Tel: 800-251-3320 E-mail: orders@abingdonpress.com; permissions@abingdonpress.com Web Site: www.abingdonpress.com, pg 2

Barnes, Jim, Jenkins Group Inc, 1129 Woodmere Ave, Suite B, Traverse City, MI 49686 Tel: 231-933-0445; 213-883-5365 E-mail: info@jenkinsgroupinc.com Web Site: www.jenkinsgroupinc.com, pg 441

Barnes, Jonathan, The Astronomical Society of the Pacific, 390 Ashton Ave, San Francisco, CA 94112 Tel: 415-337-1100; 415-715-1414 (cust serv) Toll Free Tel: 800-335-2624 (cust serv) Fax: 415-337-5205 E-mail: service@astrosociety.org Web Site: astrosociety.org, pg 20

Barnes, Lori, Idyll Arbor Inc, 2432 39 St, Bedford, IN 47421 Tel: 812-675-6623 E-mail: sales@idyllarbor.com Web Site: www.idyllarbor.com, pg 98

Barnes, Lyndsi, American Printing History Association, PO Box 4519, Grand Central Sta, New York, NY 10163 E-mail: secretary@printinghistory.org Web Site: printinghistory.org, pg 496

Barnes, Lyndsi, American Printing History Association Award, PO Box 4519, Grand Central Sta, New York, NY 10163 E-mail: secretary@printinghistory.org Web Site: printinghistory.org/programs/awards, pg 573

Barnes, Marcy, Beacon Press, 24 Farnsworth St, Boston, MA 02210-1409 Tel: 617-742-2110 Fax: 617-723-3097 E-mail: production@beacon.org Web Site: www.beacon.org, pg 25

Barnes, Natalie, Transportation Research Board (TRB), 500 Fifth St NW, Washington, DC 20001 Tel: 202-334-2934; 202-334-3213 (bookshop) E-mail: trbsales@nas.edu; mytrb@nas.edu Web Site: www.nationalacademies.org/trb/transportation-research-board, pg 209

Barnes, Nisha, Chronicle Books LLC, 680 Second St, San Francisco, CA 94107 Tel: 415-537-4200 Fax: 415-537-4460 (perms) E-mail: hello@chroniclebooks.com; subrights@chroniclebooks.com Web Site: www.chroniclebooks.com, pg 48

Barnet, Anna Kyoko, American Federation of Arts, 305 E 47 St, 10th fl, New York, NY 10017 Tel: 212-988-7700 Toll Free Tel: 800-232-0270 Fax: 212-861-2487 E-mail: pubinfo@amfedarts.org Web Site: www.amfedarts.org, pg 9

Barnet, Tamara, Deep River Books LLC, PO Box 310, Sisters, OR 97759 *Tel:* 541-549-1139 *E-mail:* info@deepriverbooks.com *Web Site:* deepriverbooks.com, pg 58

Barnett, Alison, Grouse Grind Lit Prize for V Short Form, University of British Columbia, Buch E462, 1866 Main Mall, Vancouver, BC V6T 1Z1, Canada *Tel:* 604-822-2514 *Fax:* 604-822-3616 *E-mail:* promotions@prismmagazine.ca *Web Site:* www.prismmagazine.ca/contests, pg 609

Barnett, Alison, The Pacific Spirit Poetry Prize, University of British Columbia, Buch E462, 1866 Main Mall, Vancouver, BC V6T 1Z1, Canada *Tel:* 604-822-2514 *Fax:* 604-822-3616 *E-mail:* promotions@prismmagazine.ca *Web Site:* www.prismmagazine.ca/contests, pg 645

Barnett, Alison, PRISM international Creative Nonfiction Contest, University of British Columbia, Buch E462, 1866 Main Mall, Vancouver, BC V6T 1Z1, Canada *Tel:* 604-822-2514 *Fax:* 604-822-3616 *E-mail:* promotions@prismmagazine.ca *Web Site:* www.prismmagazine.ca/contests, pg 653

Barnett, Alison, The Jacob Zilber Prize for Short Fiction, University of British Columbia, Buch E462, 1866 Main Mall, Vancouver, BC V6T 1Z1, Canada *Tel:* 604-822-2514 *Fax:* 604-822-3616 *E-mail:* promotions@prismmagazine.ca *Web Site:* www.prismmagazine.ca/contests, pg 680

Barnett, Bob, University of Texas Press, 3001 Lake Austin Blvd, 2.200, Austin, TX 78703 *Tel:* 512-471-7233 *Fax:* 512-232-7178 *E-mail:* utpress@uts.cc.utexas.edu; info@utpress.utexas.edu *Web Site:* utpress.utexas.edu, pg 205

Barnett, Kathy, Global Authors Publications (GAP), 38 Bluegrass, Middleberg, FL 32068 *Tel:* 904-425-1608 *E-mail:* gapbook@yahoo.com *Web Site:* www.globalauthorspublications.com, pg 78

Barnett, Robin, Zondervan, 3900 Sparks Dr SE, Grand Rapids, MI 49546 *Tel:* 616-698-6900 *Toll Free Tel:* 800-226-1122; 800-727-1309 (retail orders) *Fax:* 616-698-3350 *Toll Free Fax:* 800-698-3256 (retail orders) *E-mail:* customercare@harpercollins.com *Web Site:* www.zondervan.com, pg 236

Barney, Jenny, Publications International Ltd (PIL), 8140 N Lehigh Ave, Morton Grove, IL 60053 *Tel:* 847-676-3470 *Fax:* 847-676-3671 *E-mail:* customer_service@pubint.com *Web Site:* pilbooks.com, pg 167

Barney, Stacey, Nancy Paulsen Books, c/o Penguin Random House LLC, 1745 Broadway, New York, NY 10019 *Tel:* 212-782-9000 *Web Site:* www.penguin.com/nancy-paulsen-books-overview/, pg 152

Baron, Carole, Alfred A Knopf, c/o Penguin Random House LLC, 1745 Broadway, New York, NY 10019 *Tel:* 212-751-2600 *Fax:* 212-940-7390 (dom rts); 212-572-2662 (foreign rts) *Web Site:* knopfdoubleday.com/imprint/knopf/; knopfdoubleday.com, pg 110

Baron, Eva, Phaidon, 65 Bleecker St, 8th fl, New York, NY 10012 *Tel:* 212-652-5400 *Toll Free Tel:* 800-759-0190 (cust serv) *Fax:* 212-652-5410 *Toll Free Fax:* 800-286-9471 (cust serv) *E-mail:* enquiries@phaidon.com *Web Site:* www.phaidon.com, pg 159

Baron, Kaley, Penguin Random House Speakers Bureau, a Penguin Random House company, 1745 Broadway, Mail Drop 13-1, New York, NY 10019 *Tel:* 212-572-2013 *E-mail:* speakers@penguinrandomhouse.com *Web Site:* www.prhspeakers.com, pg 487

Baroni, Diana, Random House Publishing Group, 1745 Broadway, New York, NY 10019 *Toll Free Tel:* 800-200-3552 *Web Site:* www.randomhousebooks.com, pg 170

Baror, Danny, Baror International Inc, PO Box 868, Armonk, NY 10504-0868 *Tel:* 914-273-9199 *Fax:* 914-273-5058 *Web Site:* www.barorint.com, pg 449

Baror-Shapiro, Heather, Baror International Inc, PO Box 868, Armonk, NY 10504-0868 *Tel:* 914-273-9199 *Fax:* 914-273-5058 *Web Site:* www.barorint.com, pg 449

Barot, Len, Bold Strokes Books Inc, 648 S Cambridge Rd, Bldg A, Johnsonville, NY 12094 *Tel:* 518-859-8965 *E-mail:* service@boldstrokesbooks.com *Web Site:* www.boldstrokesbooks.com, pg 33

Barr, Anjanette, Dunham Literary Inc, 487 Hardscrabble Rd, North Salem, NY 10560 *Tel:* 914-669-5535 *E-mail:* dunhamlit@gmail.com *Web Site:* dunhamlit.com, pg 457

Barr, John M, Abraham Lincoln Institute Book Award, c/o ALI Treasurer, 4158 Vernoy Hills Rd, Fairfax, VA 22030 *Web Site:* www.lincoln-institute.org, pg 625

Barr, Shannon, Sourcebooks LLC, 1935 Brookdale Rd, Suite 139, Naperville, IL 60563 *Tel:* 630-961-3900 *Toll Free Tel:* 800-432-7444 *Fax:* 630-961-2168 *E-mail:* info@sourcebooks.com *Web Site:* www.sourcebooks.com, pg 194

Barr, Stephen, Writers House, 21 W 26 St, New York, NY 10010 *Tel:* 212-685-2400 *Web Site:* www.writershouse.com, pg 482

Barrales-Saylor, Kelly, Sourcebooks LLC, 1935 Brookdale Rd, Suite 139, Naperville, IL 60563 *Tel:* 630-961-3900 *Toll Free Tel:* 800-432-7444 *Fax:* 630-961-2168 *E-mail:* info@sourcebooks.com *Web Site:* www.sourcebooks.com, pg 194

Barrett, Linda-Marie, Nancy Olson Bookseller Award, 51 Pleasant Ridge Dr, Asheville, NC 28805 *Tel:* 803-994-9530 *Fax:* 309-410-0211 *E-mail:* siba@sibaweb.org *Web Site:* www.sibaweb.com, pg 643

Barrett, Linda-Marie, The Southern Book Prize, 51 Pleasant Ridge Dr, Asheville, NC 28805 *Tel:* 803-994-9530 *Fax:* 309-410-0211 *E-mail:* siba@sibaweb.org *Web Site:* www.sibaweb.com/siba-book-award, pg 664

Barrett, Linda-Marie, Southern Independent Booksellers Alliance (SIBA), 51 Pleasant Ridge Dr, Asheville, NC 28805 *Tel:* 803-994-9530 *Fax:* 309-410-0211 *E-mail:* siba@sibaweb.org *Web Site:* www.sibaweb.com, pg 520

Barrett, Michael, Adirondack Mountain Club (ADK), 4833 Cascade Rd, Lake Placid, NY 12946-4113 *Tel:* 518-837-5047 *Toll Free Tel:* 800-395-8080 *E-mail:* info@adk.org *Web Site:* www.adk.org, pg 5

Barricklow, Pamela, HarperCollins Publishers LLC, 195 Broadway, New York, NY 10007 *Tel:* 212-207-7000 *Web Site:* www.harpercollins.com, pg 86

Barrow, Bebe, Chronicle Books LLC, 680 Second St, San Francisco, CA 94107 *Tel:* 415-537-4200 *Fax:* 415-537-4460 (perms) *E-mail:* hello@chroniclebooks.com; subrights@chroniclebooks.com *Web Site:* www.chroniclebooks.com, pg 48

Barrow, Kiara, Penguin Press, c/o Penguin Random House LLC, 1745 Broadway, New York, NY 10019 *Tel:* 212-782-9000 *E-mail:* penguinpress@penguinrandomhouse.com *Web Site:* www.penguin.com/penguin-press-overview/, pg 154

Barrs, Michael, Little, Brown and Company, 1290 Avenue of the Americas, New York, NY 10104 *Tel:* 212-364-1100 *Fax:* 212-364-0952 *E-mail:* firstname.lastname@hbgusa.com *Web Site:* www.hachettebookgroup.com/imprint/little-brown-and-company/, pg 118

Barry, Bridget, University of Nebraska Press, 1225 "L" St, Suite 200, Lincoln, NE 68588-0630 *Tel:* 402-472-3581; 919-966-7449 (cust serv & foreign orders) *Toll Free Tel:* 800-848-6224 (cust serv & US orders) *Fax:* 402-472-6214; 919-962-2704 (cust serv & foreign orders) *Toll Free Fax:* 800-272-6817 (cust serv & US orders) *E-mail:* presswebmail@unl.edu *Web Site:* www.nebraskapress.unl.edu, pg 218

Barry, Graham, Chronicle Books LLC, 680 Second St, San Francisco, CA 94107 *Tel:* 415-537-4200 *Fax:* 415-537-4460 (perms) *E-mail:* hello@chroniclebooks.com; subrights@chroniclebooks.com *Web Site:* www.chroniclebooks.com, pg 47

Barry, Natassja, House of Anansi Press Inc, 128 Sterling Rd, Lower Level, Toronto, ON M6R 2B7, Canada *Tel:* 416-363-4343 *Fax:* 416-363-1017 *E-mail:* customerservice@houseofanansi.com *Web Site:* houseofanansi.com, pg 409

Barry, Rachel, Highlights for Children Inc, 815 Church St, Honesdale, PA 18431 *Tel:* 570-253-1164 *Toll Free Tel:* 800-490-5111 *Fax:* 570-253-0179 *E-mail:* salesandmarketing@highlightspress.com *Web Site:* www.highlightspress.com; www.highlights.com; www.facebook.com/HighlightsforChildren, pg 92

Barry, Thalia, Johns Hopkins University Press, 2715 N Charles St, Baltimore, MD 21218-4363 *Tel:* 410-516-6900; 410-516-6987 *Toll Free Tel:* 800-537-5487 (book orders & cust serv); 800-548-1784 (journal orders) *Fax:* 410-516-6968; 410-516-6998 (orders) *E-mail:* hfscustserv@press.jhu.edu (cust serv); jrnlcirc@jh.edu (journal orders) *Web Site:* www.press.jhu.edu; muse.jhu.edu, pg 106

Barsella, Audrey, Sourcebooks LLC, 1935 Brookdale Rd, Suite 139, Naperville, IL 60563 *Tel:* 630-961-3900 *Toll Free Tel:* 800-432-7444 *Fax:* 630-961-2168 *E-mail:* info@sourcebooks.com *Web Site:* www.sourcebooks.com, pg 194

Barth, Jennifer, Alfred A Knopf, c/o Penguin Random House LLC, 1745 Broadway, New York, NY 10019 *Tel:* 212-751-2600 *Fax:* 212-940-7390 (dom rts); 212-572-2662 (foreign rts) *Web Site:* knopfdoubleday.com/imprint/knopf/; knopfdoubleday.com, pg 110

Barthel, Anne, Hay House LLC, PO Box 5100, Carlsbad, CA 92018-5100 *Tel:* 760-431-7695 (ext 1, intl) *Toll Free Tel:* 800-654-5126 (ext 1, US) *Toll Free Fax:* 800-650-5115 *Web Site:* www.hayhouse.com, pg 89

Bartholomew, Marie, Kids Can Press Ltd, 25 Dockside Dr, Toronto, ON M5A 0B5, Canada *Tel:* 416-479-7000 *Toll Free Tel:* 800-265-0884 *Fax:* 416-960-5437 *E-mail:* info@kidscan; customerservice@kidscan.com *Web Site:* www.kidscanpress.com; www.kidscanpress.ca, pg 411

Bartleson, Katelynn, Jessica Kingsley Publishers Inc, 123 S Broad St, Suite 2750, Philadelphia, PA 19109 *Tel:* 215-922-1161 *Toll Free Tel:* 866-416-1078 (cust serv) *Fax:* 215-922-1474 *E-mail:* hello.usa@jkp.com *Web Site:* us.jkp.com, pg 110

Bartlett, Amy, Whitaker House, 1030 Hunt Valley Circle, New Kensington, PA 15068 *Tel:* 724-334-7000 *Toll Free Tel:* 800-444-4484 (sales) *Fax:* 724-334-1200 *E-mail:* publisher@whitakerhouse.com; sales@whitakerhouse.com *Web Site:* www.whitakerhouse.com, pg 228

Bartlett, Danielle, HarperCollins Publishers LLC, 195 Broadway, New York, NY 10007 *Tel:* 212-207-7000 *Web Site:* www.harpercollins.com, pg 86

Bartlett, Sydney, Princeton University Press, 41 William St, Princeton, NJ 08540-5237 *Tel:* 609-258-4900 *Fax:* 609-258-6305 *E-mail:* info@press.princeton.edu *Web Site:* press.princeton.edu, pg 164

Bartok, Josh, Wisdom Publications Inc, 199 Elm St, Somerville, MA 02144 *Tel:* 617-776-7416 *Toll Free Tel:* 800-272-4050 (orders) *Fax:* 617-776-7841 *E-mail:* submission@wisdompubs.org *Web Site:* wisdomexperience.org, pg 231

Barton, Beth, Simon & Schuster Children's Publishing, 1230 Avenue of the Americas, New York, NY 10020 *Tel:* 212-698-7000 *Web Site:* www.simonandschuster.com/kids; www.simonandschuster.com/teen; simonandschuster.net; simonandschuster.biz, pg 189

Barton, Chris, Kay Cattarulla Award for Best Short Story, PO Box 130294, Spring, TX 77393 *Web Site:* texasinstituteofletters.org, pg 587

Barton, Chris, Carr P Collins Award, PO Box 130294, Spring, TX 77393 *Web Site:* texasinstituteofletters.org, pg 591

Barton, Chris, Fire Engineering Books & Videos, Clarion Events LLC, 110 S Hartford, Suite 220, Tulsa, OK 74120 *Tel:* 918-831-9421 *Toll Free Tel:* 800-752-9764 *Fax:* 918-831-9555 *E-mail:* info@fireengineeringbooks.com *Web Site:* fireengineeringbooks.com, pg 72

Barton, Chris, Brigid Erin Flynn Award for Best Picture Book, PO Box 130294, Spring, TX 77393 *Web Site:* texasinstituteofletters.org, pg 603

Barton, Chris, Jean Flynn Award for Best Young Adult Book, PO Box 130294, Spring, TX 77393 *Web Site:* texasinstituteofletters.org, pg 603

Barton, Chris, Deirdre Siobhan FlynnBass Award for Best Middle Grade Book, PO Box 130294, Spring, TX 77393 *Web Site:* texasinstituteofletters.org, pg 603

Barton, Chris, Soeurette Diehl Fraser Translation Award, PO Box 130294, Spring, TX 77393 *Web Site:* texasinstituteofletters.org, pg 604

Barton, Chris, Jesse H Jones Award, PO Box 130294, Spring, TX 77393 *Web Site:* texasinstituteofletters.org, pg 618

Barton, Chris, Ramirez Family Award, PO Box 130294, Spring, TX 77393 *Web Site:* texasinstituteofletters.org, pg 654

Barton, Chris, John A Robertson Award for Best First Book of Poetry, PO Box 130294, Spring, TX 77393 *Web Site:* texasinstituteofletters.org, pg 657

Barton, Chris, Edwin "Bud" Shrake Award for Best Short Nonfiction, PO Box 130294, Spring, TX 77393 *Web Site:* texasinstituteofletters.org, pg 662

Barton, Chris, Helen C Smith Memorial Award, PO Box 130294, Spring, TX 77393 *Web Site:* texasinstituteofletters.org, pg 663

Barton, Chris, Texas Institute of Letters (TIL), PO Box 130294, Spring, TX 77393 *Web Site:* texasinstituteofletters.org, pg 521

Barton, Chris, Lon Tinkle Award for Lifetime Achievement, PO Box 130294, Spring, TX 77393 *Web Site:* texasinstituteofletters.org, pg 669

Barton, Chris, Sergio Troncoso Award for Best Book of Fiction, PO Box 130294, Spring, TX 77393 *Web Site:* texasinstituteofletters.org, pg 670

Barton, Chris, Fred Whitehead Award for Best Design of a Trade Book, PO Box 130294, Spring, TX 77393 *Web Site:* texasinstituteofletters.org, pg 675

Barton, Jeff, Insight Editions, 800 "A" St, San Rafael, CA 94901 *Tel:* 415-526-1370 *Toll Free Tel:* 800-809-3792 *Toll Free Fax:* 866-509-0515 *E-mail:* info@insighteditions.com; marketing@insighteditions.com *Web Site:* insighteditions.com, pg 101

Barton, Kate, Louisiana State University Press, 338 Johnston Hall, Baton Rouge, LA 70803 *Tel:* 225-578-6294 *E-mail:* lsupress@lsu.edu *Web Site:* lsupress.org, pg 120

Barton, Ken, Princeton University Press, 41 William St, Princeton, NJ 08540-5237 *Tel:* 609-258-4900 *Fax:* 609-258-6305 *E-mail:* info@press.princeton.edu *Web Site:* press.princeton.edu, pg 164

Bartram, Brent, Andrews McMeel Publishing LLC, 1130 Walnut St, Kansas City, MO 64106-2109 *Tel:* 816-581-7500 *Toll Free Tel:* 800-851-8923 *Web Site:* www.andrewsmcmeel.com; publishing.andrewsmcmeel.com, pg 14

Bartson, Kathy, Book Industry Charitable Foundation (BINC), 3135 S State St, Suite 203, Ann Arbor, MI 48108 *Toll Free Tel:* 866-733-9064 *E-mail:* info@bincfoundation.org *Web Site:* www.bincfoundation.org, pg 525

Bartson, Kathy, Denver Publishing Institute Scholarship, 3135 S State St, Suite 203, Ann Arbor, MI 48108 *Toll Free Tel:* 866-733-9064 *E-mail:* info@bincfoundation.org *Web Site:* www.bincfoundation.org/denver-publishing-institute/, pg 595

Bartson, Kathy, Carla Gray Memorial Scholarship, 3135 S State St, Suite 203, Ann Arbor, MI 48108 *Toll Free Tel:* 866-733-9064 *E-mail:* info@bincfoundation.org *Web Site:* www.bincfoundation.org/carla-gray/, pg 609

Bartson, Kathy, Higher Education Scholarship Program, 3135 S State St, Suite 203, Ann Arbor, MI 48108 *Toll Free Tel:* 866-733-9064 *E-mail:* info@bincfoundation.org *Web Site:* www.bincfoundation.org/scholarship, pg 612

Bartson, Kathy, Susan Kamil Scholarship for Emerging Writers, 3135 S State St, Suite 203, Ann Arbor, MI 48108 *Toll Free Tel:* 866-733-9064 *E-mail:* info@bincfoundation.org *Web Site:* bincfoundation.org/susankamil-scholarship, pg 619

Bartson, Kathy, George Markey Keating Memorial Scholarships, 3135 S State St, Suite 203, Ann Arbor, MI 48108 *Toll Free Tel:* 866-733-9064 *E-mail:* info@bincfoundation.org *Web Site:* www.bincfoundation.org, pg 619

Bartson, Kathy, Macmillan Booksellers Professional Development Scholarship, 3135 S State St, Suite 203, Ann Arbor, MI 48108 *Toll Free Tel:* 866-733-9064 *E-mail:* info@bincfoundation.org *Web Site:* www.bincfoundation.org/scholarship, pg 628

Bartson, Kathy, Karl Pohrt Tribute Award, 3135 S State St, Suite 203, Ann Arbor, MI 48108 *Toll Free Tel:* 866-733-9064 *E-mail:* info@bincfoundation.org *Web Site:* www.bincfoundation.org/scholarship, pg 651

Bartz, Olivia, Houghton Mifflin Harcourt Trade & Reference Division, 125 High St, Boston, MA 02110 *Tel:* 617-351-5000 *Web Site:* www.hmhco.com, pg 96

Barz, Otto, YBK Publishers Inc, 39 Crosby St, New York, NY 10013 *Tel:* 212-219-0135 *E-mail:* readmybook@ybkpublishers.com; info@ybkpublishers.com *Web Site:* www.ybkpublishers.com, pg 235

Basalmo, Mike, National Press Club (NPC), 529 14 St NW, 13th fl, Washington, DC 20045 *Tel:* 202-662-7500 *Web Site:* www.press.org, pg 513

Basco, Buenaventura "Ven", Asian/Pacific American Award for Literature, PO Box 677593, Orlando, FL 32867-7593 *Web Site:* www.apalaweb.org/awards/literature-awards, pg 575

Bashirrad, Avideh, Penguin Random House LLC, 1745 Broadway, New York, NY 10019 *Tel:* 212-782-9000 *Toll Free Tel:* 800-726-0600 *Web Site:* www.penguinrandomhouse.com, pg 155

Baskin, John, Orange Frazer Press Inc, 37 1/2 W Main St, Wilmington, OH 45177 *Tel:* 937-382-3196 *Fax:* 937-383-3159 *E-mail:* ofrazer@erinet.com *Web Site:* www.orangefrazer.com, pg 147

Bass, Anderson, Candlewick Press, 99 Dover St, Somerville, MA 02144-2825 *Tel:* 617-661-3330 *Fax:* 617-661-0565 *E-mail:* bigbear@candlewick.com; salesinfo@candlewick.com *Web Site:* candlewick.com, pg 40

Bass, Chonise, Simon & Schuster, 1230 Avenue of the Americas, New York, NY 10020 *Tel:* 212-698-7000 *Toll Free Tel:* 800-223-2348 (cust serv); 800-223-2336 (orders) *Toll Free Fax:* 800-943-9831 (orders) *Web Site:* simonandschusterpublishing.com/simonandschuster/, pg 188

Bass, Judy, Industrial Press Inc, One Chestnut St, South Norwalk, CT 06854 *Tel:* 203-956-5593 *Toll Free Tel:* 888-528-7852 (ext 1, cust serv) *E-mail:* info@industrialpress.com *Web Site:* books.industrialpress.com; ebooks.industrialpress.com, pg 100

Bass, Patrik, HarperCollins Publishers LLC, 195 Broadway, New York, NY 10007 *Tel:* 212-207-7000 *Web Site:* www.harpercollins.com, pg 86

Basseches, John, Royal Ontario Museum Press, 100 Queen's Park, Toronto, ON M5S 2C6, Canada *Tel:* 416-586-8000 *E-mail:* info@rom.on.ca *Web Site:* www.rom.on.ca, pg 418

Bassel, Katie, St Martin's Press, LLC, 120 Broadway, New York, NY 10271 *E-mail:* publicity@stmartins.com; trademarketing@stmartins.com; foreignrights@stmartins.com *Web Site:* us.macmillan.com/smp, pg 181

Bastagli, Alessandra, Atria Books, 1230 Avenue of the Americas, New York, NY 10020 *Tel:* 212-698-7000 *Fax:* 212-698-7007 *Web Site:* www.simonandschuster.com, pg 21

Bastian, Donald G, BPS Books, 47 Anderson Ave, Toronto, ON M5P 1H6, Canada *Tel:* 416-609-2004 *Web Site:* www.bpsbooks.com, pg 397

Basu, Anwesha, HarperCollins Publishers LLC, 195 Broadway, New York, NY 10007 *Tel:* 212-207-7000 *Web Site:* www.harpercollins.com, pg 86

Basu, Nita, Hachette Audio, 1290 Avenue of the Americas, New York, NY 10104 *Tel:* 212-364-1100 *Web Site:* www.hachettebookgroup.com/imprint/hachette-audio/, pg 83

Batana, Rosario, Vernon Press, 1000 N West St, Suite 1200, Wilmington, DE 19801 *Tel:* 302-250-4440 *E-mail:* info@vernonpress.com *Web Site:* www.vernonpress.com, pg 224

Batcheller, Susan, Candlewick Press, 99 Dover St, Somerville, MA 02144-2825 *Tel:* 617-661-3330 *Fax:* 617-661-0565 *E-mail:* bigbear@candlewick.com; salesinfo@candlewick.com *Web Site:* candlewick.com, pg 39

Batchelor, Justina, Grove Atlantic Inc, 154 W 14 St, 12th fl, New York, NY 10011 *Tel:* 212-614-7850 *Toll Free Tel:* 800-521-0178 *Fax:* 212-614-7886 *E-mail:* info@groveatlantic.com; sales@groveatlantic.com; publicity@groveatlantic.com; rights@groveatlantic.com *Web Site:* www.groveatlantic.com, pg 82

Batcher, Bradley, Simon & Schuster, LLC, 1230 Avenue of the Americas, New York, NY 10020 *Tel:* 212-698-7000 *Toll Free Tel:* 800-223-2336 (orders) *Fax:* 212-698-7007 *Toll Free Fax:* 800-943-9831 (orders) *E-mail:* firstname.lastname@simonandschuster.com; purchaseorders@simonandschuster.com (orders) *Web Site:* www.simonandschuster.com, pg 189

Bate, Ellie, Macmillan, 120 Broadway, 22nd fl, New York, NY 10271 *E-mail:* press.inquiries@macmillan.com *Web Site:* us.macmillan.com, pg 122

Bates, Chris, National Music Publishers' Association (NMPA), 1900 "N" St NW, Suite 500, Washington, DC 20036 *Tel:* 202-393-6672 *E-mail:* members@nmpa.org *Web Site:* nmpa.org, pg 513

Bathgate, Linda, Washington State University Press, Cooper Publications Bldg, 2300 Grimes Way, Pullman, WA 99164-5910 *Tel:* 509-335-7880 *Toll Free Tel:* 800-354-7360 (orders) *E-mail:* wsupress@wsu.edu *Web Site:* wsupress.wsu.edu, pg 226

Batiz-Benet, Mercedes, Bayeux Arts Inc, 2403, 510-Sixth Ave SE, Calgary, AB T2G 1L7, Canada *E-mail:* mail@bayeux.com *Web Site:* bayeux.com, pg 396

Batmanglij, Mohammad, Mage Publishers Inc, 5600 Wisconsin Ave, No 1408, Chevy Chase, MD 20815 *Web Site:* www.mage.com, pg 123

Batmanglij, Najmieh, Mage Publishers Inc, 5600 Wisconsin Ave, No 1408, Chevy Chase, MD 20815 *Web Site:* www.mage.com, pg 123

Battaglia, Dana, Paul H Brookes Publishing Co Inc, PO Box 10624, Baltimore, MD 21285-0624 *Tel:* 410-337-9580 (outside US & CN) *Toll Free Tel:* 800-638-3775 (US & CN) *Fax:* 410-337-8539 *E-mail:* custserv@brookespublishing.com *Web Site:* www.brookespublishing.com, pg 37

Batten, Candace, Kennedy Information LLC, 24 Railroad St, Keene, NH 03431 *Tel:* 603-357-8103 *Toll Free Tel:* 800-531-0140, pg 108

Battista, Dino, The University of North Carolina Press, 116 S Boundary St, Chapel Hill, NC 27514-3808 *Tel:* 919-966-3561; 919-966-7449 (orders) *Toll Free Tel:* 800-848-3224 (orders) *Fax:* 919-962-2704 (orders) *Toll Free Fax:* 800-272-6817 (orders) *E-mail:* uncpress@unc.edu *Web Site:* uncpress.org, pg 218

Battista, Garth, Breakaway Books, PO Box 24, Halcottsville, NY 12438-0024 *E-mail:* breakawaybooks@gmail.com *Web Site:* www.breakawaybooks.com, pg 36

Battle, Maya, Macmillan, 120 Broadway, 22nd fl, New York, NY 10271 *E-mail:* press.inquiries@macmillan.com *Web Site:* us.macmillan.com, pg 122

Batura, Paul, Focus on the Family, 8605 Explorer Dr, Colorado Springs, CO 80920-1051 *Tel:* 719-531-5181 *Toll Free Tel:* 800-A-FAMILY (232-6459) *Fax:* 719-531-3424 *Web Site:* www.focusonthefamily.com; www.facebook.com/focusonthefamily, pg 73

Bauer, Abby, W D Hoard & Sons Co, 28 W Milwaukee Ave, Fort Atkinson, WI 53538 *Tel:* 920-563-5551 *E-mail:* hdbooks@hoards.com; editors@hoards.com *Web Site:* www.hoards.com, pg 93

Bauer, Margaret, Doris Betts Fiction Prize, PO Box 21591, Winston-Salem, NC 27120-1591 *Tel:* 336-293-8844 *E-mail:* mail@ncwriters.org; nclrsubmissions@ecu.edu *Web Site:* www.ncwriters.org, pg 579

Bauer, Mike, Recorded Books Inc, an RBmedia company, 8400 Corporate Dr, Landover, MD 20785 *Toll Free Tel:* 800-305-3450 *Web Site:* rbmediaglobal.com/recorded-books, pg 172

Bauer, Nate, University of Alaska Press, Elmer E Rasmuson Library, 1732 Tanana Loop, Suite 402, Fairbanks, AK 99775 *Tel:* 907-474-5831 *Toll Free Tel:* 888-252-6657 (US only) *Fax:* 907-474-5502 *Web Site:* www.alaska.edu/uapress, pg 214

Bauer, Susan Wise, Well-Trained Mind Press, 18021 The Glebe Lane, Charles City, VA 23030 *Tel:* 804-593-0306 *Toll Free Tel:* 877-322-3445 *Fax:* 804-829-5704 *E-mail:* support@welltrainedmind.com *Web Site:* welltrainedmind.com, pg 227

Bauerle, Chris, Highlights for Children Inc, 815 Church St, Honesdale, PA 18431 *Tel:* 570-253-1164 *Toll Free Tel:* 800-490-5111 *Fax:* 570-253-0179 *E-mail:* salesandmarketing@highlightspress.com *Web Site:* www.highlightspress.com; www.highlights.com; www.facebook.com/HighlightsforChildren, pg 92

Baughman, Emelise, Dog Writers Association of America Inc (DWAA), PO Box 787, Hughesville, MD 20637 *Web Site:* dogwriters.org, pg 505

Baughman, Emelise, Dog Writers Association of America Inc (DWAA) Annual Writing Competition, PO Box 787, Hughesville, MD 20637 *Web Site:* dogwriters.org, pg 596

Baughman, Jeff, Fox Chapel Publishing Co Inc, 1970 Broad St, East Petersburg, PA 17520 *Tel:* 717-560-4703 *Toll Free Tel:* 800-457-9112 *Fax:* 717-560-4702 *E-mail:* customerservice@foxchapelpublishing.com *Web Site:* www.foxchapelpublishing.com, pg 74

Bauhan, Sarah, May Sarton New Hampshire Poetry Prize, 44 Main St, 2nd fl, Peterborough, NH 03458 *Tel:* 603-567-4430 *Web Site:* www.bauhanpublishing.com, pg 659

Baule, Deirdre, Hachette Nashville, 6100 Tower Circle, Room 210, Franklin, TN 37067 *Tel:* 615-221-0996 *Fax:* 615-221-0962 *Web Site:* www.hachettebookgroup.com/imprint/hachette-nashville/, pg 83

Baum, Geraldine, PEN America, 120 Broadway, 26th fl N, New York, NY 10271 *Tel:* 212-334-1660 *Fax:* 212-334-2181 *E-mail:* info@pen.org; membership@pen.org; education@pen.org *Web Site:* pen.org, pg 516

Bauman, Erica, Aevitas Creative Management LLC, 19 W 21 St, Suite 501, New York, NY 10010 *Tel:* 212-765-6900 *Web Site:* www.aevitascreative.com, pg 448

Bauman, Liz, Round Table Companies, PO Box 1603, Deerfield, IL 60015 *Toll Free Tel:* 833-750-5683 *Web Site:* www.roundtablecompanies.com, pg 177

Baumann, Andrew, Oriental Institute Publications, 1155 E 58 St, Chicago, IL 60637 *Tel:* 773-702-5967 *E-mail:* oi-publications@uchicago.edu *Web Site:* oi.uchicago.edu, pg 148

Baumann, David, University of Pittsburgh Press, 7500 Thomas Blvd, Pittsburgh, PA 15260 *Tel:* 412-383-2456 *Fax:* 412-383-2466 *E-mail:* info@upress.pitt.edu *Web Site:* www.upress.pitt.edu, pg 219

Baumeister, Quinn, Casemate | publishers, 1950 Lawrence Rd, Havertown, PA 19083 *Tel:* 610-853-9131 *Fax:* 610-853-9146 *E-mail:* casemate@casematepublishers.com *Web Site:* www.casematepublishers.com, pg 42

Baumer, Jan, Folio Literary Management, The Film Center Bldg, 630 Ninth Ave, Suite 1101, New York, NY 10036 *Tel:* 212-400-1494 *Fax:* 212-967-0977 *Web Site:* www.foliolit.com, pg 459

Baumgartner, Jenny, Hachette Nashville, 6100 Tower Circle, Room 210, Franklin, TN 37067 *Tel:* 615-221-0996 *Fax:* 615-221-0962 *Web Site:* www.hachettebookgroup.com/imprint/hachette-nashville/, pg 83

Bause Mason, Thomas, Society of Motion Picture and Television Engineers® (SMPTE®), White Plains Plaza, 445 Hamilton Ave, Suite 601, White Plains, NY 10601-1827 *Tel:* 914-761-1100 *E-mail:* hello@smpte.org (mktg) *Web Site:* www.smpte.org, pg 520

Bautista, Fr Tony, St Pauls, 2187 Victory Blvd, Staten Island, NY 10314-6603 *Tel:* 718-761-0047 (edit & prodn); 718-698-2759 (mktg & billing) *Toll Free Tel:* 800-343-2522 *Fax:* 718-761-0057 *E-mail:* sales@stpauls.us; marketing@stpauls.us *Web Site:* www.stpauls.us, pg 181

Baxter, Carol, The Mathematical Association of America, 1529 18 St NW, Washington, DC 20036-1358 *Tel:* 202-387-5200 *Toll Free Tel:* 800-741-9415 *Fax:* 202-265-2384 *E-mail:* maahq@maa.org; advertising@maa.org (pubns) *Web Site:* www.maa.org, pg 127

Baxter, Kelli C, American Translators Association (ATA), 211 N Union St, Suite 100, Alexandria, VA 22314 *Tel:* 703-683-6100 *Fax:* 703-778-7222 *E-mail:* ata@atanet.org *Web Site:* www.atanet.org, pg 497

Bay, Bill, Mel Bay Publications Inc, 16 N Gore Ave, Suite 203, Webster Groves, MO 63119-2315 *Tel:* 636-257-3970 *Toll Free Tel:* 800-863-5229 *E-mail:* email@melbay.com *Web Site:* www.melbay.com, pg 129

Bay, Stephanie, Random House Children's Books, c/o Penguin Random House LLC, 1745 Broadway, New York, NY 10019 *Tel:* 212-782-9000 *Web Site:* www.rhcbooks.com, pg 170

Bayer, Lisa, University of Georgia Press, Main Library, 3rd fl, 320 S Jackson St, Athens, GA 30602 *Fax:* 706-542-2558; 706-542-6770 *Web Site:* www.ugapress.org, pg 216

Bayers, William, Houghton Mifflin Harcourt, 125 High St, Boston, MA 02110 *Tel:* 617-351-5000 *Toll Free Tel:* 855-969-4642; 800-225-5425 (K-12 educ materials); 800-323-9540 (assessment materials); 877-219-1537 (SkillsTutor); 888-242-6747 (Innovation in Educ Group); 800-225-3362 (Trade & Ref Div) *Toll Free Fax:* 800-269-5232 *E-mail:* myhmco@hmhco.com *Web Site:* www.hmhco.com, pg 96

Bayrami, Mandy, The Literary Press Group of Canada, 234 Eglinton Ave E, Suite 401, Toronto, ON M4P 1K5, Canada *Tel:* 416-483-1321 *Fax:* 416-483-2510 *E-mail:* sales@lpg.ca *Web Site:* www.lpg.ca, pg 509

Bayuk, Michelle, Berghahn Books, 20 Jay St, Suite 512, Brooklyn, NY 11201 *Tel:* 212-233-6004 *Fax:* 212-233-6007 *E-mail:* info@berghahnbooks.com; salesus@berghahnbooks.com; editorial@journals.berghahnbooks.com *Web Site:* www.berghahnbooks.com, pg 28

Bazzy, William M, Artech House®, 685 Canton St, Norwood, MA 02062 *Tel:* 781-769-9750 *Toll Free Tel:* 800-225-9977 *Fax:* 781-769-6334 *E-mail:* artech@artechhouse.com *Web Site:* us.artechhouse.com, pg 17

Beale, Asari, Teachers & Writers Collaborative (T&W), 20 W 20 St, Suite 801, New York, NY 10011 *Tel:* 212-691-6590 *E-mail:* info@twc.org *Web Site:* www.twc.org, pg 520

Bean, Daniel, Bloomsbury Publishing Inc, 1385 Broadway, 5th fl, New York, NY 10018 *Tel:* 212-419-5300 *E-mail:* marketingusa@bloomsbury.com; adultpublicityusa@bloomsbury.com; askacademic@bloomsbury.com *Web Site:* www.bloomsbury.com, pg 31

Beard, Amber, Penguin Random House Audio Publishing Group, 1745 Broadway, New York, NY 10019 *Toll Free Tel:* 800-793-2665 (cust serv) *E-mail:* audio@penguinrandomhouse.com; ecustomerservice@penguinrandomhouse.com *Web Site:* www.penguinrandomhouseaudio.com, pg 154

Beard, Elliott, The Brookings Institution Press, 1775 Massachusetts Ave NW, Washington, DC 20036-2188 *Tel:* 202-797-6000 *E-mail:* permissions@brookings.edu *Web Site:* www.brookings.edu, pg 37

Beard, Morgan, Swedenborg Foundation, 320 N Church St, West Chester, PA 19380 *Tel:* 610-430-3222 *Toll Free Tel:* 800-355-3222 (cust serv) *Fax:* 610-430-7982 *E-mail:* info@swedenborg.com *Web Site:* swedenborg.com, pg 201

Beardow, Jim, International Monetary Fund (IMF), Editorial & Publications Division, 700 19 St NW, HQ1-5-355, Washington, DC 20431 *Tel:* 202-623-7430 *E-mail:* publications@imf.org *Web Site:* bookstore.imf.org; elibrary.imf.org (online collection); www.imf.org/publications, pg 103

Bearse, Kristen, Knopf Doubleday Publishing Group, c/o Penguin Random House LLC, 1745 Broadway, New York, NY 10019 *Tel:* 212-751-2600 *Fax:* 212-940-7390 (dom rts); 212-572-2662 (foreign rts) *Web Site:* knopfdoubleday.com, pg 110

Bearse, Kristen, Penguin Random House LLC, 1745 Broadway, New York, NY 10019 *Tel:* 212-782-9000 *Toll Free Tel:* 800-726-0600 *Web Site:* www.penguinrandomhouse.com, pg 155

Beasley, J Malcolm, Professional Communications Inc, 1223 W Main, Suite 1427, Durant, OK 74702-1427 *Tel:* 580-745-9838 *Toll Free Tel:* 800-337-9838 *Fax:* 580-745-9837 *E-mail:* info@pcibooks.com *Web Site:* www.pcibooks.com, pg 165

Beatty, Alex, The Grace Dudley Prize for Arts Writing, c/o The New York Review of Books, 435 Hudson St, Suite 300, New York, NY 10014 *Tel:* 212-757-8070 *E-mail:* admin@silversfoundation.org *Web Site:* silversfoundation.org/about-the-silvers-dudley-prizes, pg 597

Beatty, Alex, The Robert B Silvers Prize for Journalism, c/o The New York Review of Books, 435 Hudson St, Suite 300, New York, NY 10014 *Tel:* 212-757-8070 *E-mail:* admin@silversfoundation.org *Web Site:* silversfoundation.org/about-the-silvers-dudley-prizes, pg 662

Beatty, Alex, The Robert B Silvers Prize for Literary Criticism, c/o The New York Review of Books, 435 Hudson St, Suite 300, New York, NY 10014 *Tel:* 212-757-8070 *E-mail:* admin@silversfoundation.org *Web Site:* silversfoundation.org/about-the-silvers-dudley-prizes, pg 663

Beatty, Cory, HarperCollins Canada Ltd, 22 Adelaide St W, 41st fl, Toronto, ON M5H 4E3, Canada *Tel:* 416-975-9334 *E-mail:* hcorder@harpercollins.com *Web Site:* www.harpercollins.ca, pg 409

Beatty, Joseph, American Association of University Women of NC Young People's Literature Award, 4610 Mail Service Ctr, Raleigh, NC 27699-4610 *Tel:* 919-814-6623 *Web Site:* www.ncdcr.gov/about/history/lit-and-hist/awards; www.aauw.org, pg 573

Beatty, Joseph, The Ragan Old North State Award Cup for Nonfiction, 4610 Mail Service Ctr, Raleigh, NC 27699-4610 *Web Site:* www.ncdcr.gov/about/history/lit-and-hist/awards, pg 654

Beatty, Joseph, Sir Walter Raleigh Award for Fiction, 4610 Mail Service Ctr, Raleigh, NC 27699-4610 *Tel:* 919-814-6623 *Web Site:* www.ncdcr.gov/about/history/lit-and-hist/awards, pg 654

Beatty, Joseph, Roanoke-Chowan Award for Poetry, 4610 Mail Service Ctr, Raleigh, NC 27699-4610 *Web Site:* www.ncdcr.gov/about/history/lit-and-hist/awards, pg 656

Beaudet, Marie-Andree, La Fondation Emile Nelligan, 100, rue Sherbrooke, Suite 202, Montreal, QC H2X 1C3, Canada *Tel:* 514-278-4657 *E-mail:* info@fondation-nelligan.org *Web Site:* www.fondation-nelligan.org, pg 506

Beaudet, Marie-Andree, Prix Emile-Nelligan, 100, rue Sherbrooke, Suite 202, Montreal, QC H2X 1C3, Canada *Tel:* 514-278-4657 *Fax:* 514-271-6369 *E-mail:* info@fondation-nelligan.org *Web Site:* www.fondation-nelligan.org, pg 653

Beaudin-Quintin, Sophane, Editions Michel Quintin, 2259 Papineau Ave, Suite 104, Montreal, QC H2K 4J5, Canada *Tel:* 514-379-3774 *Fax:* 450-539-4905

E-mail: info@editionsmichelquintin.ca; commande@editionsmichelquintin.ca (orders) *Web Site:* www.editionsmichelquintin.ca, pg 404

Beaudoin, Andre, Les Editions Ganesha Inc, CP 484, Succursale Chabanel, Montreal, QC H2N 0A7, Canada *E-mail:* courriel@editions-ganesha.qc.ca; email@editions-ganesha.qc.ca *Web Site:* www.editions-ganesha.qc.ca, pg 403

Beaudry, Christopher, Island Press, 2000 "M" St NW, Suite 480-B, Washington, DC 20036 *Tel:* 202-232-7933 *Toll Free Tel:* 800-621-2736 *Fax:* 202-234-1328 *E-mail:* info@islandpress.org *Web Site:* www.islandpress.org, pg 104

Beaudry, Veronique, Les Editions Fides, 7333 place des Roseraies, bureau 501, Anjou, QC H1M 2X6, Canada *Tel:* 514-745-4290 *Fax:* 514-745-4299 *E-mail:* editions@groupefides.com *Web Site:* www.editionsfides.com, pg 403

Beaumier, Fr Casey, Institute of Jesuit Sources (IJS), Boston College Institute for Advanced Jesuit Studies, 140 Commonwealth Ave, Chestnut Hill, MA 02467 *Tel:* 617-552-2568 *Fax:* 617-552-2575 *E-mail:* jesuitsources@bc.edu *Web Site:* jesuitsources.bc.edu, pg 102

Becerra, Natalia, Macmillan, 120 Broadway, 22nd fl, New York, NY 10271 *E-mail:* press.inquiries@macmillan.com *Web Site:* us.macmillan.com, pg 122

Becher, Bill, AuthorHouse, 1663 Liberty Dr, Bloomington, IN 47403 *Toll Free Tel:* 833-262-8899; 888-519-5121 *E-mail:* sales@authorhouse.com; vip@authorhouse.com *Web Site:* www.authorhouse.com, pg 22

Becher, Bill, iUniverse, 1663 Liberty Dr, Bloomington, IN 47403 *Toll Free Tel:* 800-AUTHORS (288-4677); 844-349-9409 *E-mail:* media@iuniverse.com *Web Site:* www.iuniverse.com, pg 105

Becher, Bill, Trafford Publishing, 1663 Liberty Dr, Bloomington, IN 47403 *Toll Free Tel:* 844-688-6899 *E-mail:* customersupport@trafford.com; sales@trafford.com *Web Site:* www.trafford.com, pg 208

Becher, Bill, Xlibris Corp, 1663 Liberty Dr, Suite 200, Bloomington, IN 47403 *Toll Free Tel:* 844-714-8691; 888-795-4274 *Fax:* 610-915-0294 *E-mail:* info@xlibris.com; media@xlibris.com *Web Site:* www.xlibris.com; www.authorsolutions.com/our-imprints/xlibris, pg 234

Bechunas, Gwyneth, Macmillan, 120 Broadway, 22nd fl, New York, NY 10271 *E-mail:* press.inquiries@macmillan.com *Web Site:* us.macmillan.com, pg 122

Beck, Eric, Seedling Publications Inc, 520 E Bainbridge St, Elizabethtown, PA 17022 *Toll Free Tel:* 800-233-0759 *Toll Free Tel:* 888-834-1303 *E-mail:* edcsr@continentalpress.com *Web Site:* www.continentalpress.com, pg 186

Beck, Rachel, Liza Dawson Associates, 121 W 27 St, Suite 1201, New York, NY 10001 *Tel:* 212-465-9071 *Web Site:* www.lizadawsonassociates.com, pg 455

Becker, Janet Besso, American Jewish Committee (AJC), Mail Code 6760, PO Box 7247, Philadelphia, PA 19170-0001 *Tel:* 212-751-4000 *Fax:* 212-891-1450 *E-mail:* social@ajc.org *Web Site:* www.ajc.org, pg 495

Becker, Matt, University of Massachusetts Press, New Africa House, 180 Infirmary Way, 4th fl, Amherst, MA 01003-9289 *Web Site:* www.umasspress.com, pg 217

Becker, Ulrich, Mondial, 203 W 107 St, Suite 6-C, New York, NY 10025 *Tel:* 646-807-8031 *Fax:* 208-361-2863 *E-mail:* contact@mondialbooks.com *Web Site:* www.mondialbooks.com, pg 133

Beckerman, Chad W, The CAT Agency Inc, 345 Old Oaks Rd, Fairfield, CT 06825 *Tel:* 917-434-3141 *Web Site:* catagencyinc.com, pg 485

Beckwith, Lori, Savvas Learning Co LLC, 15 E Midland Ave, Suite 502, Paramus, NJ 07652 *Toll Free Tel:* 800-848-9500 *Web Site:* www.savvas.com, pg 183

Bedard, Patricia, Novalis Publishing, One Eglinton Ave E, Suite 800, Toronto, ON M4P 3A1, Canada *Tel:* 416-363-3303 *Toll Free Tel:* 877-702-7773 *Fax:* 416-363-9409 *Toll Free Fax:* 877-702-7775 *E-mail:* books@novalis.ca *Web Site:* www.novalis.ca, pg 414

Bedard, Rachel, Les Editions du Remue-Menage, 469, Jean-Talon Ouest, bureau 401, Montreal, QC H3N 1R4, Canada *Tel:* 514-876-0097 *E-mail:* info@editions-rm.ca *Web Site:* www.editions-rm.ca, pg 403

Bedenbaugh, Thomas, The University of North Carolina Press, 116 S Boundary St, Chapel Hill, NC 27514-3808 *Tel:* 919-966-3561; 919-966-7449 (orders) *Toll Free Tel:* 800-848-3224 (orders) *Fax:* 919-962-2704 (orders) *Toll Free Fax:* 800-272-6817 (orders) *E-mail:* uncpress@unc.edu *Web Site:* uncpress.org, pg 218

Bedford, Stephen, Simon & Schuster, 1230 Avenue of the Americas, New York, NY 10020 *Tel:* 212-698-7000 *Toll Free Tel:* 800-223-2348 (cust serv); 800-223-2336 (orders) *Toll Free Fax:* 800-943-9831 (orders) *Web Site:* simonandschusterpublishing.com/simonandschuster/, pg 188

Bedi, Bharti, Tundra Book Group, 320 Front St W, Suite 1400, Toronto, ON M5V 3B6, Canada *Tel:* 416-364-4449 *Toll Free Tel:* 888-523-9292 (orders); 800-588-1074 *E-mail:* youngreaders@penguinrandomhouse.com *Web Site:* www.tundrabooks.com, pg 421

Bedick, Cara, Little, Brown and Company, 1290 Avenue of the Americas, New York, NY 10104 *Tel:* 212-364-1100 *Fax:* 212-364-0952 *E-mail:* firstname.lastname@hbgusa.com *Web Site:* www.hachettebookgroup.com/imprint/little-brown-and-company/, pg 118

Bedingfield, Sarah, Levine|Greenberg|Rostan Literary Agency, 307 Seventh Ave, Suite 2407, New York, NY 10001 *Tel:* 212-337-0934 *Fax:* 212-337-0948 *E-mail:* submit@lgrliterary.com *Web Site:* lgrliterary.com, pg 467

Beditz, Dr Joseph, National Golf Foundation, 501 N Hwy A1A, Jupiter, FL 33477-4577 *Tel:* 561-744-6006 *Toll Free Tel:* 888-275-4643 *Fax:* 561-744-9085 *E-mail:* general@ngf.org *Web Site:* www.ngf.org, pg 138

Bedrick, Claudia Zoe, Enchanted Lion Books, 248 Creamer St, Studio 4, Brooklyn, NY 11231 *Tel:* 646-785-9272 *E-mail:* enchantedlion@gmail.com *Web Site:* www.enchantedlion.com, pg 66

Beech, Lisa, Thomas Nelson, 501 Nelson Place, Nashville, TN 37214 *Tel:* 615-889-9000 *Toll Free Tel:* 800-251-4000 *Web Site:* www.thomasnelson.com, pg 206

Beech, Mary, Scholastic Inc, 557 Broadway, New York, NY 10012 *Tel:* 212-343-6100 *Toll Free Tel:* 800-SCHOLASTIC (724-6527) *Web Site:* www.scholastic.com, pg 184

Beehler, Grace, Penguin Random House LLC, 1745 Broadway, New York, NY 10019 *Tel:* 212-782-9000 *Toll Free Tel:* 800-726-0600 *Web Site:* www.penguinrandomhouse.com, pg 155

Beehler, Katy, Bay Area Women in Publishing (BAWiP), 680 Second St, San Francisco, CA 94107 *E-mail:* bayareawomeninpublishing@gmail.com *Web Site:* www.bayareawomeninpublishing.com, pg 500

Beeke, Joel R, Reformation Heritage Books, 2965 Leonard St NE, Grand Rapids, MI 49525 *Tel:* 616-977-0889 *Fax:* 616-285-3246 *E-mail:* orders@heritagebooks.org *Web Site:* www.heritagebooks.org, pg 173

Beeny, Martyn, Cornell University Press, Sage House, 512 E State St, Ithaca, NY 14850 *Tel:* 607-253-2338 *E-mail:* cupressinfo@cornell.edu; cupress-sales@cornell.edu; cupress-perms@cornell.edu (reprint/class use permissions) *Web Site:* www.cornellpress.cornell.edu, pg 52

Beer, Molly, Writers Guild of America, East (WGAE), 250 Hudson St, Suite 700, New York, NY 10013 *Tel:* 212-767-7800 *Fax:* 212-582-1909 *Web Site:* www.wgaeast.org, pg 522

Beers, Ron, Tyndale House Publishers Inc, 351 Executive Dr, Carol Stream, IL 60188 *Tel:* 630-668-8300 *Toll Free Tel:* 800-323-9400; 855-277-9400 *Toll Free Fax:* 866-622-9474 *Web Site:* www.tyndale.com, pg 211

Beery, Josef, American Printing History Association, PO Box 4519, Grand Central Sta, New York, NY 10163 *E-mail:* secretary@printinghistory.org *Web Site:* printinghistory.org, pg 496

Beery, Josef, American Printing History Association Award, PO Box 4519, Grand Central Sta, New York, NY 10163 *E-mail:* secretary@printinghistory.org *Web Site:* printinghistory.org/programs/awards, pg 573

Begay, Corey, Salina Bookshelf Inc, 1120 W University Ave, Suite 102, Flagstaff, AZ 86001 *Toll Free Tel:* 877-527-0070 *Fax:* 928-526-0386 *Web Site:* www.salinabookshelf.com, pg 181

Begler, Henry, Agate Publishing Academy, 1328 Greenleaf St, Evanston, IL 60202 *Tel:* 847-475-4457 *E-mail:* help@agatepublishingacademy.com *Web Site:* agatepublishingacademy.com, pg 561

Beguiristain, Luisa, Roaring Brook Press, 120 Broadway, New York, NY 10271 *Tel:* 646-307-5151 *Web Site:* us.macmillan.com/publishers/roaring-brook-press, pg 176

Behar, Ann, Scovil Galen Ghosh Literary Agency Inc, 348 W 57 St, New York, NY 10019 *Tel:* 212-679-8686 *E-mail:* info@sgglit.com *Web Site:* www.sgglit.com, pg 475

Behar, Tracy, Avery, c/o Penguin Random House LLC, 1745 Broadway, New York, NY 10019 *Tel:* 212-366-2000 *Web Site:* www.penguin.com/avery-overview/, pg 23

Behar, Tracy, TarcherPerigee, c/o Penguin Random House LLC, 1745 Broadway, New York, NY 10019 *Tel:* 212-782-9000 *Web Site:* www.penguin.com/tarcherperigee-overview/; www.facebook.com/TarcherPerigee, pg 202

Beharry, Oma, Penguin Random House LLC, 1745 Broadway, New York, NY 10019 *Tel:* 212-782-9000 *Toll Free Tel:* 800-726-0600 *Web Site:* www.penguinrandomhouse.com, pg 155

Behm, Melissa, Health Professions Press, 409 Washington Ave, Suite 500, Towson, MD 21204 *Tel:* 410-337-9585 *Toll Free Tel:* 888-337-8808 *Fax:* 410-337-8539 *Web Site:* www.healthpropress.com, pg 90

Behm, Melissa A, Paul H Brookes Publishing Co Inc, PO Box 10624, Baltimore, MD 21285-0624 *Tel:* 410-337-9580 (outside US & CN) *Toll Free Tel:* 800-638-3775 (US & CN) *Fax:* 410-337-8539 *E-mail:* custserv@brookespublishing.com *Web Site:* www.brookespublishing.com, pg 37

Behning, Janet, PA Press, 202 Warren St, Hudson, NY 12534 *Tel:* 518-671-6100 *Toll Free Tel:* 800-722-6657 (dist); 800-759-0190 (sales) *E-mail:* sales@papress.com *Web Site:* www.papress.com, pg 149

Behrend-Wilcox, Talia, Harry N Abrams Inc, 195 Broadway, 9th fl, New York, NY 10007 *Tel:* 212-206-7715 *Toll Free Tel:* 800-345-1359 *Fax:* 212-645-8437 *E-mail:* abrams@abramsbooks.com; publicity@abramsbooks.com; sales@abramsbooks.com *Web Site:* www.abramsbooks.com, pg 3

Behrman, David, Behrman House Inc, 241B Millburn Ave, Millburn, NJ 07041 *Tel:* 973-379-7200 *Toll Free Tel:* 800-221-2755 *Fax:* 973-379-7280 *E-mail:* customersupport@behrmanhouse.com *Web Site:* store.behrmanhouse.com, pg 27

Beier, Betsy, Hay House LLC, PO Box 5100, Carlsbad, CA 92018-5100 *Tel:* 760-431-7695 (ext 1, intl) *Toll Free Tel:* 800-654-5126 (ext 1, US) *Toll Free Fax:* 800-650-5115 *Web Site:* www.hayhouse.com, pg 89

Beil, Frederic C, Frederic C Beil Publisher Inc, 609 Whitaker St, Savannah, GA 31401 *Tel:* 912-233-2446 *E-mail:* fcb@beil.com *Web Site:* www.beil.com, pg 27

Beilenson, Esther, Peter Pauper Press, Inc, 202 Mamaroneck Ave, Suite 400, White Plains, NY 10601-5376 *Tel:* 914-681-0144 *Fax:* 914-681-0389

E-mail: customerservice@peterpauper.com; orders@peterpauper.com; marketing@peterpauper.com Web Site: www.peterpauper.com, pg 158

Beilenson, Laurence, Peter Pauper Press, Inc, 202 Mamaroneck Ave, Suite 400, White Plains, NY 10601-5376 Tel: 914-681-0144 Fax: 914-681-0389 E-mail: customerservice@peterpauper.com; orders@peterpauper.com; marketing@peterpauper.com Web Site: www.peterpauper.com, pg 158

Belan, Allison, Duke University Press, 905 W Main St, Suite 18B, Durham, NC 27701 Tel: 919-688-5134 Toll Free Tel: 888-651-0122 (US) Fax: 919-688-2615 Toll Free Fax: 888-651-0124 E-mail: orders@dukeupress.edu Web Site: www.dukeupress.edu, pg 62

Belden, Kathryn, Scribner, 1230 Avenue of the Americas, New York, NY 10020 Web Site: www.simonandschusterpublishing.com/scribner/, pg 185

Belderis, Ina, Theosophical University Press, PO Box C, Pasadena, CA 91109-7107 Tel: 626-798-3378 E-mail: tupress@theosociety.org Web Site: www.theosociety.org, pg 206

Belfiglio, Brian, Scribner, 1230 Avenue of the Americas, New York, NY 10020 Web Site: www.simonandschusterpublishing.com/scribner/, pg 185

Belisle-Kennedy, Marie-Piere, North American Snowsports Journalists Association (NASJA), 290 Laramie Blvd, Boulder, CO 80304 E-mail: execsec@nasja.org Web Site: nasja.org, pg 515

Beliveau, Mathieu, Beliveau Editeur, 567 rue Bienville, Boucherville, QC J4B 2Z5, Canada Tel: 450-679-1933 Web Site: www.beliveauediteur.com, pg 396

Belkas, Julia, Adams Media, 100 Technology Center Dr, Suite 501, Stoughton, MA 02072 Tel: 508-427-7100 Web Site: www.simonandschuster.com, pg 4

Belknap, Mary PhD, Nautilus Book Awards, PO Box 2285, Vashon, WA 98070 Tel: 206-304-2250 Web Site: www.nautilusbookawards.com, pg 638

Bell, Aimee, Gallery Books, 1230 Avenue of the Americas, New York, NY 10020 Toll Free Tel: 800-456-6798 Fax: 212-698-7284 E-mail: consumer.customerservice@simonandschuster.com Web Site: www.simonandschuster.com, pg 76

Bell, Aurora, University of South Carolina Press, 1600 Hampton St, Suite 544, Columbia, SC 29208 Tel: 803-777-5245 Toll Free Tel: 800-768-2500 (orders) Fax: 803-777-0160 Toll Free Fax: 800-868-0740 (orders) Web Site: uscpress.com, pg 220

Bell, Jessica, Association for Intelligent Information Management (AIIM), 8403 Colesville Rd, No 1100, Silver Spring, MD 20910 Tel: 301-587-8202 Toll Free Tel: 800-477-2446 Fax: 301-587-2711 E-mail: hello@aiim.org Web Site: www.aiim.org, pg 498

Bell, John, Nelson Education Ltd, 1120 Birchmount Rd, Scarborough, ON M1K 5G4, Canada Tel: 416-752-9448 Toll Free Tel: 800-268-2222 (cust serv) Fax: 416-752-9646 E-mail: peopleandengagement@nelson.com Web Site: www.nelson.com, pg 413

Bell, Justin, Spectrum Literary Agency, 320 Central Park W, Suite 1-D, New York, NY 10025 Tel: 212-362-4323 Fax: 212-362-4562 Web Site: www.spectrumliteraryagency.com, pg 477

Bell, Zach, BRAVE Books, 13614 Poplar Circle, Suite 302, Conroe, TX 77304 Tel: 932-380-5648 E-mail: info@brave.us Web Site: bravebooks.us, pg 35

Bellemare, Stacie, Lionel Gelber Prize, University of Toronto, Munk School of Global Affairs & Public Policy, One Devonshire Place, Toronto, ON M5S 3K7, Canada Tel: 416-946-5670 Fax: 416-946-8915 E-mail: gelberprize.munk@utoronto.ca Web Site: munkschool.utoronto.ca/gelber; www.facebook.com/GelberPrize, pg 606

Belleris, Christine, Health Communications Inc, 301 Crawford Blvd, Suite 200, Boca Raton, FL 33432 Tel: 561-453-0696 Toll Free Tel: 800-441-5569 (cust serv & orders) Fax: 561-453-1009 Toll Free Fax: 800-943-9831 (orders) E-mail: editorial@hcibooks.com Web Site: hcibooks.com, pg 90

Belnap, Penelope, Alfred A Knopf, c/o Penguin Random House LLC, 1745 Broadway, New York, NY 10019 Tel: 212-751-2600 Fax: 212-940-7390 (dom rts); 212-572-2662 (foreign rts) Web Site: knopfdoubleday.com/imprint/knopf/; knopfdoubleday.com, pg 110

Belozerskaya, Marina, Fowler Museum at UCLA, PO Box 951549, Los Angeles, CA 90095-1549 Tel: 310-825-4361 Fax: 310-206-7007 E-mail: fowlerws@arts.ucla.edu Web Site: www.fowler.ucla.edu, pg 74

Ben, Crystal, Orbit, 1290 Avenue of the Americas, New York, NY 10104 Tel: 212-364-1100 Toll Free Tel: 800-759-0190 Web Site: www.orbitbooks.net; www.hachettebookgroup.com/imprint/orbit, pg 147

Benamy, Talia, Philomel Books, c/o Penguin Random House LLC, 1745 Broadway, New York, NY 10019 Tel: 212-782-9000 Web Site: www.penguin.com/philomel/, pg 159

Benard, Mary, Skinner House Books, c/o Unitarian Universalist Assn, 24 Farnsworth St, Boston, MA 02210-1409 Tel: 617-742-2100 Fax: 617-948-6466 E-mail: skinnerhouse@uua.org Web Site: www.uua.org/publications/skinnerhouse, pg 190

Benatar, Raquel, Laredo Publishing Co, 465 Westview Ave, Englewood, NJ 07631 Tel: 201-408-4048 E-mail: info@laredopublishing.com Web Site: www.laredopublishing.com, pg 113

Benatar, Raquel, Renaissance House, 465 Westview Ave, Englewood, NJ 07631 Tel: 201-408-4048 Web Site: www.renaissancehouse.net, pg 174, 486

Benavides, Yvette, Trinity University Press, One Trinity Place, San Antonio, TX 78212-7200 Tel: 210-999-8884 Fax: 210-999-8838 E-mail: books@trinity.edu Web Site: www.tupress.org, pg 209

Benayoun, Julian, Harry N Abrams Inc, 195 Broadway, 9th fl, New York, NY 10007 Tel: 212-206-7715 Toll Free Tel: 800-345-1359 Fax: 212-645-8437 E-mail: abrams@abramsbooks.com; publicity@abramsbooks.com; sales@abramsbooks.com Web Site: www.abramsbooks.com, pg 3

Bender, Faye, The Book Group (TBG), 20 W 20 St, Suite 601, New York, NY 10011 E-mail: info@thebookgroup.com; submissions@thebookgroup.com Web Site: www.thebookgroup.com, pg 450

Bender, Robyn, Penguin Young Readers Group, c/o Penguin Random House LLC, 1745 Broadway, New York, NY 10019 Tel: 212-782-9000 Web Site: www.penguin.com/penguin-young-readers-overview, pg 156

Bendiy, Anna, Kids Can Press Ltd, 25 Dockside Dr, Toronto, ON M5A 0B5, Canada Tel: 416-479-7000 Toll Free Tel: 800-265-0884 Fax: 416-960-5437 E-mail: info@kidscan.com; customerservice@kidscan.com Web Site: www.kidscanpress.com; www.kidscanpress.ca, pg 411

Benedict, Holly, Quincannon Publishing Group, PO Box 8100, Glen Ridge, NJ 07028-8100 Tel: 973-380-9942 E-mail: editors@quincannongroup.com (query first via e-mail) Web Site: www.quincannongroup.com, pg 168

Beninato, Alison, American Philosophical Society Press, 104 S Fifth St, Philadelphia, PA 19106 Tel: 215-440-3425 Fax: 215-440-3450 E-mail: books@amphilsoc.org, pg 11

Benincase, Joe, Grand Central Publishing, 1290 Avenue of the Americas, New York, NY 10104 Tel: 212-364-1100 Web Site: www.hachettebookgroup.com/imprint/grand-central-publishing/, pg 80

Benjey, Thomas R, Tuxedo Press, 546 E Springville Rd, Carlisle, PA 17015 Tel: 717-258-9733 Fax: 717-243-0074 E-mail: info@tuxedo-press.com Web Site: tuxedo-press.com, pg 211

Benne, Susan, Antiquarian Booksellers' Association of America (ABAA), 155 Water St, 6th fl, Suite 7, Brooklyn, NY 11201 Tel: 212-944-8291 Fax: 212-944-8293 E-mail: hq@abaa.org Web Site: www.abaa.org, pg 497

Benner, Deborah J, Goose River Press, 3400 Friendship Rd, Waldoboro, ME 04572-6337 Tel: 207-832-6665 E-mail: gooseriverpress@gmail.com Web Site: gooseriverpress.com, pg 79

Bennett, Barbara, Kensington Publishing Corp, 900 Third Ave, 26th fl, New York, NY 10022 Tel: 212-407-1500 Toll Free Tel: 800-221-2647 Fax: 212-935-0699 Web Site: www.kensingtonbooks.com, pg 109

Bennett, Elizabeth, Transatlantic Agency, 2 Bloor St E, Suite 3500, Toronto, ON M4W 1A8, Canada Tel: 416-488-9214 E-mail: info@transatlanticagency.com; royalties@transatlanticagency.com Web Site: www.transatlanticagency.com, pg 479

Bennett, Jed, Penguin Young Readers Group, c/o Penguin Random House LLC, 1745 Broadway, New York, NY 10019 Tel: 212-782-9000 Web Site: www.penguin.com/penguin-young-readers-overview, pg 156

Bennett, John M, Luna Bisonte Prods, 137 Leland Ave, Columbus, OH 43214 Tel: 614-846-4126 Web Site: www.johnmbennett.net; www.lulu.com/spotlight/lunabisonteprods, pg 121

Bennett, Katherine, Running Press, 1290 Avenue of the Americas, New York, NY 10104 Tel: 212-364-1100 Toll Free Tel: 800-759-0190 (cust serv) Fax: 212-364-0933 (intl orders) Toll Free Fax: 800-286-9471 (cust serv) E-mail: customer.service@hbgusa.com; orders@hbgusa.com Web Site: www.hachettebookgroup.com/imprint/running-press/; www.moon.com (Moon Travel Guides), pg 178

Bennett, Matt, HarperCollins Publishers LLC, 195 Broadway, New York, NY 10007 Tel: 212-207-7000 Web Site: www.harpercollins.com, pg 86

Bennett, Millicent, Houghton Mifflin Harcourt Trade & Reference Division, 125 High St, Boston, MA 02110 Tel: 617-351-5000 Web Site: www.hmhco.com, pg 96

Bennie, Dale, University of Oklahoma Press, 2800 Venture Dr, Norman, OK 73069-8216 Tel: 405-325-2000 Web Site: www.oupress.com, pg 219

Bensaid, Barbara, US Games Systems Inc, 179 Ludlow St, Stamford, CT 06902 Tel: 203-353-8400 Toll Free Tel: 800-54-GAMES (544-2637) Fax: 203-353-8431 E-mail: info@usgamesinc.com Web Site: www.usgamesinc.com, pg 223

Benshoff, Kirk, Farrar, Straus & Giroux Books for Young Readers, 120 Broadway, New York, NY 10271 Tel: 212-741-6900 Toll Free Tel: 888-330-8477 (orders) E-mail: childrens.publicity@macmillanusa.com; childrensrights@macmillanusa.com Web Site: us.macmillan.com/mackids, pg 70

Benshoff, Kirk, Henry Holt and Company, LLC, 120 Broadway, 23rd fl, New York, NY 10271 Tel: 646-307-5151 Toll Free Tel: 888-330-8477 (orders) Fax: 646-307-5285 Web Site: www.henryholt.com, pg 94

Benshoff, Kirk, Roaring Brook Press, 120 Broadway, New York, NY 10271 Tel: 646-307-5151 Web Site: us.macmillan.com/publishers/roaring-brook-press, pg 175

Bensky, Dan, Eastland Press, 2421 29 Ave W, Seattle, WA 98199 Tel: 206-931-6957 (cust serv) Fax: 206-283-7084 (orders) E-mail: info@eastlandpress.com; orders@eastlandpress.com Web Site: www.eastlandpress.com, pg 63

Bent, Siobhan, Phaidon, 65 Bleecker St, 8th fl, New York, NY 10012 Tel: 212-652-5400 Toll Free Tel: 800-759-0190 (cust serv) Fax: 212-652-5410 Toll Free Fax: 800-286-9471 (cust serv) E-mail: enquiries@phaidon.com Web Site: www.phaidon.com, pg 159

Bentley, Michael, Bentley Publishers, 1734 Massachusetts Ave, Cambridge, MA 02138-1804 Tel: 617-547-4170 E-mail: sales@bentleypubs.com Web Site: www.bentleypublishers.com, pg 28

Benton, Carla, St Martin's Press, LLC, 120 Broadway, New York, NY 10271 E-mail: publicity@stmartins.com; trademarketing@stmartins.com; foreignrights@stmartins.com Web Site: us.macmillan.com/smp, pg 181

Benton, Lori, Scholastic Trade Publishing, 557 Broadway, New York, NY 10012 Tel: 212-343-6100; 212-343-4685 (export sales) Fax: 212-343-4714 (export sales) Web Site: www.scholastic.com, pg 184

Benton, Michael, Macmillan, 120 Broadway, 22nd fl, New York, NY 10271 *E-mail:* press.inquiries@macmillan.com *Web Site:* us.macmillan.com, pg 122

Benvenuto, Kerri, Random House Children's Books, c/o Penguin Random House LLC, 1745 Broadway, New York, NY 10019 *Tel:* 212-782-9000 *Web Site:* www.rhcbooks.com, pg 169

Benyam, Kleopatra, HarperCollins Publishers LLC, 195 Broadway, New York, NY 10007 *Tel:* 212-207-7000 *Web Site:* www.harpercollins.com, pg 86

Benz, Sophia, Simon & Schuster, 1230 Avenue of the Americas, New York, NY 10020 *Tel:* 212-698-7000 *Toll Free Tel:* 800-223-2348 (cust serv); 800-223-2336 (orders) *Toll Free Fax:* 800-943-9831 (orders) *Web Site:* simonandschusterpublishing.com/simonandschuster/, pg 188

Bercholz, Ivan, Shambhala Publications Inc, 2129 13 St, Boulder, CO 80302 *Tel:* 978-829-2599 (intl callers) *Toll Free Tel:* 866-424-0030 (off); 888-424-2329 (orders & cust serv) *Fax:* 617-236-1563 *E-mail:* customercare@shambhala.com; royalties@shambhala.com *Web Site:* www.shambhala.com, pg 187

Bercholz, Samuel, Shambhala Publications Inc, 2129 13 St, Boulder, CO 80302 *Tel:* 978-829-2599 (intl callers) *Toll Free Tel:* 866-424-0030 (off); 888-424-2329 (orders & cust serv) *Fax:* 617-236-1563 *E-mail:* customercare@shambhala.com; royalties@shambhala.com *Web Site:* www.shambhala.com, pg 187

Bercholz, Sara, Shambhala Publications Inc, 2129 13 St, Boulder, CO 80302 *Tel:* 978-829-2599 (intl callers) *Toll Free Tel:* 866-424-0030 (off); 888-424-2329 (orders & cust serv) *Fax:* 617-236-1563 *E-mail:* customercare@shambhala.com; royalties@shambhala.com *Web Site:* www.shambhala.com, pg 187

Berdinsky, Kendall, Dystel, Goderich & Bourret LLC, One Union Sq W, Suite 904, New York, NY 10003 *Tel:* 212-627-9100 *Fax:* 212-627-9313 *Web Site:* www.dystel.com, pg 457

Berendson, Laura, Apress Media LLC, One New York Plaza, Suite 4600, New York, NY 10004-1562 *Tel:* 212-460-1500 *E-mail:* editorial@apress.com; customerservice@springernature.com *Web Site:* www.apress.com, pg 16

Berg, Jennifer, PAGE International Screenwriting Awards, 7190 W Sunset Blvd, Suite 610, Hollywood, CA 90046 *E-mail:* info@pageawards.com *Web Site:* pageawards.com, pg 645

Bergan, Josh, Wilderness Adventures Press Inc, 45 Buckskin Rd, Belgrade, MT 59714 *Tel:* 406-388-0112 *Toll Free Tel:* 866-400-2012 *Toll Free Fax:* 866-400-2013 *E-mail:* books@wildadvpress.com *Web Site:* store.wildadvpress.com, pg 229

Berge, Pablo Agrest, STOCKCERO Inc, 3785 NW 82 Av, Suite 314, Doral, FL 33166 *Tel:* 305-722-7628 *Fax:* 305-722-7628 *E-mail:* academicservices@stockcero.com; sales@stockcero.com *Web Site:* www.stockcero.com, pg 199

Bergels, Dan, ASTM International, 100 Barr Harbor Dr, West Conshohocken, PA 19428-2959 *Tel:* 610-832-9500; 610-832-9585 (intl) *Toll Free Tel:* 877-909-2786 (sales & cust support) *Fax:* 610-832-9555 *E-mail:* sales@astm.org *Web Site:* www.astm.org, pg 20

Bergen, Glenn, University of Manitoba Press, University of Manitoba, 301 St Johns College, 92 Dysart Rd, Winnipeg, MB R3T 2M5, Canada *Tel:* 204-474-9495 *Fax:* 204-474-7566 *E-mail:* uofmpress@umanitoba.ca *Web Site:* uofmpress.ca, pg 422

Bergen, Julia, Tor Publishing Group, 120 Broadway, New York, NY 10271 *Toll Free Tel:* 800-455-0340 (Macmillan) *E-mail:* torpublicity@tor.com; forgepublicity@forgebooks.com *Web Site:* us.macmillan.com/torpublishinggroup, pg 208

Berger, Annie, Sourcebooks LLC, 1935 Brookdale Rd, Suite 139, Naperville, IL 60563 *Tel:* 630-961-3900 *Toll Free Tel:* 800-432-7444 *Fax:* 630-961-2168 *E-mail:* info@sourcebooks.com *Web Site:* www.sourcebooks.com, pg 194

Berger, Courtney, Duke University Press, 905 W Main St, Suite 18B, Durham, NC 27701 *Tel:* 919-688-5134 *Toll Free Tel:* 888-651-0122 (US) *Fax:* 919-688-2615 *Toll Free Fax:* 888-651-0124 *E-mail:* orders@dukeupress.edu *Web Site:* www.dukeupress.edu, pg 62

Berger, Ellie, Scholastic Inc, 557 Broadway, New York, NY 10012 *Tel:* 212-343-6100 *Toll Free Tel:* 800-SCHOLASTIC (724-6527) *Web Site:* www.scholastic.com, pg 184

Berger, Ellie, Scholastic Trade Publishing, 557 Broadway, New York, NY 10012 *Tel:* 212-343-6100; 212-343-4685 (export sales) *Fax:* 212-343-4714 (export sales) *Web Site:* www.scholastic.com, pg 184

Berger, Erin M, Scholastic Trade Publishing, 557 Broadway, New York, NY 10012 *Tel:* 212-343-6100; 212-343-4685 (export sales) *Fax:* 212-343-4714 (export sales) *Web Site:* www.scholastic.com, pg 184

Berger, Whitney, Sasquatch Books, 1904 S Third Ave, Suite 710, Seattle, WA 98101 *Tel:* 206-467-4300 *Toll Free Tel:* 800-775-0817 *Fax:* 206-467-4301 *E-mail:* custserv@sasquatchbooks.com *Web Site:* sasquatchbooks.com, pg 182

Bergera, Gary James, Signature Books Publishing LLC, 564 W 400 N, Salt Lake City, UT 84116-3411 *Toll Free Tel:* 800-356-5687 *E-mail:* people@signaturebooks.com *Web Site:* www.signaturebooks.com, www.signaturebookslibrary.org, pg 188

Bergeron, Amanda, Berkley, c/o Penguin Random House LLC, 1745 Broadway, 19th fl, New York, NY 10019 *Tel:* 212-366-2000 *Web Site:* www.penguin.com/publishers/berkley/; www.penguin.com/ace-overview/, pg 28

Bergeron, Catherine, Johns Hopkins University Press, 2715 N Charles St, Baltimore, MD 21218-4363 *Tel:* 410-516-6900; 410-516-6987 *Toll Free Tel:* 800-537-5487 (book orders & cust serv); 800-548-1784 (journal orders) *Fax:* 410-516-6968; 410-516-6998 (orders) *E-mail:* hfscustserv@press.jhu.edu (cust serv); jrnlcirc@jh.edu (journal orders) *Web Site:* www.press.jhu.edu; muse.jhu.edu, pg 106

Bergeron, Laura, Science History Publications USA Inc, 349 Old Plymouth Rd, Sagamore Beach, MA 02562 *E-mail:* orders@shpusa.com *Web Site:* www.shpusa.com, pg 185

Bergeron, Patricia, IRP editeur, CP 68, succursale St-Dominique, Montreal, QC H2S 3K6, Canada *Tel:* 514-382-3000 *E-mail:* info@irpcanada.com *Web Site:* www.irpcanada.com, pg 410

Bergh, Lily, Canadian Scholars, 425 Adelaide St W, Suite 200, Toronto, ON M5V 3C1, Canada *Tel:* 416-929-2774 *Toll Free Tel:* 800-463-1998 *E-mail:* info@canadianscholars.ca; editorial@canadianscholars.ca *Web Site:* www.canadianscholars.ca; www.womenspress.ca, pg 398

Berghahn, Dr Marion, Berghahn Books, 20 Jay St, Suite 512, Brooklyn, NY 11201 *Tel:* 212-233-6004 *Fax:* 212-233-6007 *E-mail:* info@berghahnbooks.com; salesus@berghahnbooks.com; editorial@journals.berghahnbooks.com *Web Site:* www.berghahnbooks.com, pg 28

Berghahn, Vivian, Berghahn Books, 20 Jay St, Suite 512, Brooklyn, NY 11201 *Tel:* 212-233-6004 *Fax:* 212-233-6007 *E-mail:* info@berghahnbooks.com; salesus@berghahnbooks.com; editorial@journals.berghahnbooks.com *Web Site:* www.berghahnbooks.com, pg 28

Bergkamp, Will, Wm B Eerdmans Publishing Co, 4035 Park East Ct SE, Grand Rapids, MI 49546 *Tel:* 616-459-4591 *Toll Free Tel:* 800-253-7521 *E-mail:* customerservice@eerdmans.com; sales@eerdmans.com *Web Site:* www.eerdmans.com, pg 64

Bergonzi, Megan, Seedling Publications Inc, 520 E Bainbridge St, Elizabethtown, PA 17022 *Toll Free Tel:* 800-233-0759 *Toll Free Fax:* 888-834-1303 *E-mail:* edcsr@continentalpress.com *Web Site:* www.continentalpress.com, pg 186

Bergstrom, Jennifer, Gallery Books, 1230 Avenue of the Americas, New York, NY 10020 *Toll Free Tel:* 800-456-6798 *Fax:* 212-698-7284 *E-mail:* consumer.customerservice@simonandschuster.com *Web Site:* www.simonandschuster.com, pg 76

Bergstrom, Jennifer, Simon & Schuster, LLC, 1230 Avenue of the Americas, New York, NY 10020 *Tel:* 212-698-7000 *Toll Free Tel:* 800-223-2336 (orders) *Fax:* 212-698-7007 *Toll Free Fax:* 800-943-9831 (orders) *E-mail:* firstname.lastname@simonandschuster.com; purchaseorders@simonandschuster.com (orders) *Web Site:* www.simonandschuster.com, pg 189

Bergstrom, Krista, University of British Columbia Press, 2029 West Mall, Vancouver, BC V6T 1Z2, Canada *Tel:* 604-822-5959 *Toll Free Tel:* 877-377-9378 *Fax:* 604-822-6083 *Toll Free Fax:* 800-668-0821 *E-mail:* frontdesk@ubcpress.ca *Web Site:* www.ubcpress.ca, pg 422

Berk, Adina Popescu, Yale University Press, 302 Temple St, New Haven, CT 06511-8909 *Tel:* 203-432-0960; 203-432-0966 (sales); 401-531-2800 (cust serv) *Toll Free Tel:* 800-405-1619 (cust serv) *Fax:* 203-432-0948; 203-432-8485 (sales); 401-531-2801 (cust serv) *Toll Free Fax:* 800-406-9145 (cust serv) *E-mail:* sales.press@yale.edu (sales); customer.care@triliteral.org (cust serv) *Web Site:* www.yalebooks.com; yalepress.yale.edu/yupbooks, pg 235

Berkery, Peter, Association of University Presses (AUPresses), 1412 Broadway, Suite 2135, New York, NY 10018 *Tel:* 212-989-1010 *Fax:* 212-989-0275 *E-mail:* info@aupresses.org *Web Site:* www.aupresses.org, pg 500

Berkery, Peter, AUPresses Book, Jacket & Journal Show, 1412 Broadway, Suite 2135, New York, NY 10018 *Tel:* 212-989-1010 *Fax:* 212-989-0275 *E-mail:* info@aupresses.org *Web Site:* www.aupresses.org, pg 576

Berkey, Jane Rotrosen, Jane Rotrosen Agency LLC, 318 E 51 St, New York, NY 10022-7803 *Tel:* 212-593-4330 *E-mail:* info@janerotrosen.com *Web Site:* janerotrosen.com, pg 474

Berkhofer, Robert F III, Medieval Institute Publications (MIP), Western Michigan University, Walwood Hall, 1903 W Michigan Ave, Mail Stop 5432, Kalamazoo, MI 49008-5432 *Tel:* 269-387-8755 *Web Site:* wmich.edu/medievalpublications, pg 129

Berkley, Bri, National Music Publishers' Association (NMPA), 1900 "N" St NW, Suite 500, Washington, DC 20036 *Tel:* 202-393-6672 *E-mail:* members@nmpa.org *Web Site:* nmpa.org, pg 513

Berkman, Hilary, Candlewick Press, 99 Dover St, Somerville, MA 02144-2825 *Tel:* 617-661-3330 *Fax:* 617-661-0565 *E-mail:* bigbear@candlewick.com; salesinfo@candlewick.com *Web Site:* candlewick.com, pg 39

Berkower, Amy, Writers House, 21 W 26 St, New York, NY 10010 *Tel:* 212-685-2400 *Web Site:* www.writershouse.com, pg 482

Berliner, Marlo, The Jennifer DeChiara Literary Agency, 245 Park Ave, 39th fl, New York, NY 10167 *Tel:* 212-372-8989 *Web Site:* www.jdlit.com, pg 455

Berman, Ari, Yeshiva University Press, 500 W 185 St, New York, NY 10033 *Tel:* 212-960-5400 *Web Site:* www.yu.edu/books, pg 235

Berman, Sam, The Rough Notes Co Inc, 11690 Technology Dr, Carmel, IN 46032-5600 *Tel:* 317-582-1600 *Toll Free Tel:* 800-428-4384 (cust serv) *Fax:* 317-816-1000 *Toll Free Fax:* 800-321-1909 *E-mail:* rnc@roughnotes.com *Web Site:* www.roughnotes.com, pg 177

Berman, Todd, Penguin Random House LLC, 1745 Broadway, New York, NY 10019 *Tel:* 212-782-9000 *Toll Free Tel:* 800-726-0600 *Web Site:* www.penguinrandomhouse.com, pg 155

Bermudez, Melanie, Random House Children's Books, c/o Penguin Random House LLC, 1745 Broadway, New York, NY 10019 *Tel:* 212-782-9000 *Web Site:* www.rhcbooks.com, pg 170

Bernal, Jennifer, University of Notre Dame Press, 310 Flanner Hall, Notre Dame, IN 46556 *Tel:* 574-631-6346 *Fax:* 574-631-8148 *E-mail:* undpress@nd.edu *Web Site:* www.undpress.nd.edu, pg 219

Bernard, Alec, Puddingstone Literary, Authors' Agents, 11 Mabro Dr, Denville, NJ 07834-9607 *Tel:* 973-366-3622, pg 472

Bernard, Anna, HarperCollins Children's Books, 195 Broadway, New York, NY 10007 *Tel:* 212-207-7000 *Web Site:* www.harpercollins.com/childrens, pg 85

Berndt, Alice, Trident Media Group LLC, 355 Lexington Ave, 12th fl, New York, NY 10017 *Tel:* 212-333-1511 *E-mail:* info@tridentmediagroup.com; press@tridentmediagroup.com; foreignrights@tridentmediagroup.com; office.assistant@tridentmediagroup.com *Web Site:* www.tridentmediagroup.com, pg 480

Berndt, Kirstin, Portfolio, c/o Penguin Random House LLC, 1745 Broadway, New York, NY 10019 *Tel:* 212-782-9000 *Web Site:* www.penguin.com/portfolio-overview/; www.penguin.com/sentinel-overview/; www.penguin.com/thesis/, pg 162

Berner, Kate, Penguin Random House Speakers Bureau, a Penguin Random House company, 1745 Broadway, Mail Drop 13-1, New York, NY 10019 *Tel:* 212-572-2013 *E-mail:* speakers@penguinrandomhouse.com *Web Site:* www.prhspeakers.com, pg 487

Bernier, Jean, Les Editions du Boreal, 4447, rue St-Denis, Montreal, QC H2J 2L2, Canada *Tel:* 514-287-7401 *Fax:* 514-287-7664 *E-mail:* info@editionsboreal.qc.ca; boreal@editionsboreal.qc.ca; communications@editionsboreal.qc.ca *Web Site:* www.editionsboreal.qc.ca, pg 402

Berniker, Amy, Candlewick Press, 99 Dover St, Somerville, MA 02144-2825 *Tel:* 617-661-3330 *Fax:* 617-661-0565 *E-mail:* bigbear@candlewick.com; salesinfo@candlewick.com *Web Site:* candlewick.com, pg 39

Bernstein, Laurie, Side by Side Literary Productions Inc, 145 E 35 St, Suite 7FE, New York, NY 10016 *Tel:* 212-685-6831 *Web Site:* sidebysidelit.com, pg 476

Bernstein, Meredith, Meredith Bernstein Literary Agency Inc, 2095 Broadway, Suite 505, New York, NY 10023 *Tel:* 212-799-1007 *Fax:* 212-799-1145 *E-mail:* MGoodBern@aol.com *Web Site:* www.meredithbernsteinliteraryagency.com, pg 449

Bernstein, Tracy, Berkley, c/o Penguin Random House LLC, 1745 Broadway, 19th fl, New York, NY 10019 *Tel:* 212-366-2000 *Web Site:* www.penguin.com/publishers/berkley/; www.penguin.com/ace-overview/, pg 28

Berquist, Rachel, HarperCollins Publishers LLC, 195 Broadway, New York, NY 10007 *Tel:* 212-207-7000 *Web Site:* www.harpercollins.com, pg 87

Berrigan, Delia, Martin Literary Management, 914 164 St SE, Suite B12, Box 307, Mill Creek, WA 98012 *Tel:* 206-466-1773 (no phone queries) *Web Site:* www.martinliterarymanagement.com, pg 469

Berrios, Frank, Random House Children's Books, c/o Penguin Random House LLC, 1745 Broadway, New York, NY 10019 *Tel:* 212-782-9000 *Web Site:* www.rhcbooks.com, pg 170

Berry, Crystal, National Catholic Educational Association, 200 N Glebe Rd, Suite 310, Arlington, VA 22203 *Tel:* 571-257-0010 *Toll Free Tel:* 800-711-6232 *Fax:* 703-243-0025 *E-mail:* nceaadmin@ncea.org *Web Site:* www.ncea.org, pg 137

Berry, Drew, National Association of Black Journalists (NABJ), 1100 Knight Hall, Suite 3101, College Park, MD 20742 *Tel:* 301-405-0248 *E-mail:* contact@nabj.org; press@nabj.org *Web Site:* nabjonline.org, pg 511

Berry, Jon, University of Alabama Press, 200 Hackberry Lane, 2nd fl, Tuscaloosa, AL 35487 *Tel:* 205-348-5180 *Fax:* 205-348-9201 *Web Site:* www.uapress.ua.edu, pg 214

Berry, Liz, Thriller Awards Competition, PO Box 311, Eureka, CA 95502 *Web Site:* thrillerwriters.org, pg 669

Berry, Dr Stephen, The Fletcher M Green & Charles W Ramsdell Award, University of Georgia, Dept of History, Athens, GA 30602-1602 *Tel:* 706-542-8848 *Web Site:* thesha.org/ramsdell, pg 609

Berry, Dr Stephen, William F Holmes Award, University of Georgia, Dept of History, Athens, GA 30602-1602 *Tel:* 706-542-8848 *Web Site:* thesha.org/holmes, pg 613

Berry, Dr Stephen, Jack Temple Kirby Award, University of Georgia, Dept of History, Athens, GA 30602-1602 *Tel:* 706-542-8848 *Web Site:* thesha.org/kirby, pg 620

Berry, Dr Stephen, H L Mitchell Award, University of Georgia, Dept of History, Athens, GA 30602-1602 *Tel:* 706-542-8848 *Web Site:* thesha.org/mitchell, pg 633

Berry, Dr Stephen, Frank L & Harriet C Owsley Award, University of Georgia, Dept of History, Athens, GA 30602-1602 *Tel:* 706-542-8848 *Web Site:* thesha.org, pg 645

Berry, Dr Stephen, James A Rawley Award, University of Georgia, Dept of History, Athens, GA 30602-1602 *Tel:* 706-542-8848 *Web Site:* thesha.org/rawley, pg 654

Berry, Dr Stephen, Francis B Simkins Award, University of Georgia, Dept of History, Athens, GA 30602-1602 *Tel:* 706-542-8848 *Web Site:* thesha.org/simkins, pg 663

Berry, Dr Stephen, Charles S Sydnor Award, University of Georgia, Dept of History, Athens, GA 30602-1602 *Tel:* 706-542-8848 *Web Site:* thesha.org/sydnor, pg 668

Berry, Dr Stephen, Bennett H Wall Award, University of Georgia, Dept of History, Athens, GA 30602-1602 *Tel:* 706-542-8848 *Web Site:* thesha.org/wall, pg 673

Berry, Dr Stephen, C Vann Woodward Award, University of Georgia, Dept of History, Athens, GA 30602-1602 *Tel:* 706-542-8848 *Web Site:* thesha.org/woodward, pg 677

Berry, Taylor, Penguin Random House Canada, a Penguin Random House company, 320 Front St W, Suite 1400, Toronto, ON M5V 3B6, Canada *Tel:* 416-364-4449 *Toll Free Tel:* 888-523-9292 (cust serv) *E-mail:* canadaweb@penguinrandomhouse.com; customerservicescanada@penguinrandomhouse.com *Web Site:* www.penguinrandomhouse.ca, pg 416

Bershtel, Sara, Penguin Press, c/o Penguin Random House LLC, 1745 Broadway, New York, NY 10019 *Tel:* 212-782-9000 *E-mail:* penguinpress@penguinrandomhouse.com *Web Site:* www.penguin.com/penguin-press-overview/, pg 154

Berta, Katie, The Iowa Review Awards, 308 EPB, Iowa City, IA 52242-1408 *E-mail:* iowa-review@uiowa.edu *Web Site:* www.iowareview.org, pg 617

Bertrand, Alfred, Georgetown University Press, 3520 Prospect St NW, Suite 140, Washington, DC 20007 *Tel:* 202-687-5889 (busn) *Fax:* 202-687-6340 (edit) *E-mail:* gupress@georgetown.edu *Web Site:* press.georgetown.edu, pg 77

Bertrand, Daniel, Les Editions JCL, 348, 9e Ave, St-Jean-sur-Richelieu, QC J2X 1K3, Canada *Tel:* 450-515-4438 *E-mail:* info@jcl.qc.ca *Web Site:* www.jcl.qc.ca, pg 404

Bertrand, Kiera, Berkley, c/o Penguin Random House LLC, 1745 Broadway, 19th fl, New York, NY 10019 *Tel:* 212-366-2000 *Web Site:* www.penguin.com/publishers/berkley/; www.penguin.com/ace-overview/, pg 28

Berube, Dr Brenda, Bisk Education, 9417 Princess Palm Ave, Suite 400, Tampa, FL 33619 *Tel:* 813-621-6200 *E-mail:* media@bisk.com *Web Site:* www.bisk.com, pg 30

Berube, Dominique, Social Sciences & Humanities Research Council (SSHRC), 350 Albert St, Ottawa, ON K1P 6G4, Canada *Tel:* 613-995-4273 *Toll Free Tel:* 855-275-2861 *E-mail:* research@sshrc-crsh.gc.ca *Web Site:* www.sshrc-crsh.gc.ca, pg 519

Berube, Patty, Wood Lake Publishing Inc, 485 Beaver Lake Rd, Kelowna, BC V4V 1S5, Canada *Tel:* 250-766-2778 *Toll Free Tel:* 800-663-2775 (orders & cust serv) *Fax:* 250-766-2736 *Toll Free Fax:* 888-841-9991 (orders & cust serv) *E-mail:* info@woodlake.com; customerservice@woodlake.com *Web Site:* www.woodlake.com, pg 425

Bervig, David, David C Cook, 4050 Lee Vance Dr, Colorado Springs, CO 80918 *Tel:* 719-536-0100 *Toll Free Tel:* 800-323-7543 (orders & cust serv) *Toll Free Fax:* 800-430-0726 (cust serv) *E-mail:* bookstores@davidccook.org; customercare@davidccook.org *Web Site:* www.davidccook.org, pg 52

Berzanskis, Andrew, University of Washington Press, 4333 Brooklyn Ave NE, Seattle, WA 98105-9570 *Toll Free Tel:* 800-537-5487 (orders) *Fax:* 206-543-3932; 410-516-6998 (orders) *E-mail:* uwapress@uw.edu *Web Site:* uwapress.uw.edu, pg 220

Besel, Jen, Black Rabbit Books, 2140 Howard Dr W, North Mankato, MN 56003 *Tel:* 507-388-1609 *Fax:* 507-388-2746 *E-mail:* info@blackrabbitbooks.com; orders@blackrabbitbooks.com *Web Site:* www.blackrabbitbooks.com, pg 30

Bess, Benjamin E, Bess Press Inc, 3565 Harding Ave, Honolulu, HI 96816 *Tel:* 808-734-7159 *Fax:* 808-732-3627 *E-mail:* customerservice@besspress.com *Web Site:* www.besspress.com, pg 29

Besser, Jennifer, Farrar, Straus & Giroux Books for Young Readers, 120 Broadway, New York, NY 10271 *Tel:* 212-741-6900 *Toll Free Tel:* 888-330-8477 (orders) *E-mail:* childrens.publicity@macmillanusa.com; childrensrights@macmillanusa.com *Web Site:* us.macmillan.com/mackids, pg 69

Besser, Jennifer, Macmillan, 120 Broadway, 22nd fl, New York, NY 10271 *E-mail:* press.inquiries@macmillan.com *Web Site:* us.macmillan.com, pg 122

Besser, Jennifer, Roaring Brook Press, 120 Broadway, New York, NY 10271 *Tel:* 646-307-5151 *Web Site:* us.macmillan.com/publishers/roaring-brook-press, pg 175

Best, Kirby, Penguin Random House Canada, a Penguin Random House company, 320 Front St W, Suite 1400, Toronto, ON M5V 3B6, Canada *Tel:* 416-364-4449 *Toll Free Tel:* 888-523-9292 (cust serv) *E-mail:* canadaweb@penguinrandomhouse.com; customerservicescanada@penguinrandomhouse.com *Web Site:* www.penguinrandomhouse.ca, pg 416

Best, Macey, Macmillan, 120 Broadway, 22nd fl, New York, NY 10271 *E-mail:* press.inquiries@macmillan.com *Web Site:* us.macmillan.com, pg 122

Bestler, Emily, Atria Books, 1230 Avenue of the Americas, New York, NY 10020 *Tel:* 212-698-7000 *Fax:* 212-698-7007 *Web Site:* www.simonandschuster.com, pg 21

Betancourt, John, Wildside Press LLC, 7945 MacArthur Blvd, Suite 215, Cabin John, MD 20818 *Tel:* 301-762-1305 *E-mail:* wildside@wildsidepress.com *Web Site:* wildsidepress.com, pg 229

Betancourt, Lorraine, Oxford University Press USA, 198 Madison Ave, New York, NY 10016 *Toll Free Tel:* 800-451-7556 (orders); 800-445-9714 (cust serv) *Fax:* 919-677-1303 *E-mail:* custserv.us@oup.com *Web Site:* global.oup.com, pg 149

Bethel, Courtney, MacDowell Fellowships, 100 High St, Peterborough, NH 03458 *Tel:* 603-924-3886 *E-mail:* info@macdowell.org; admissions@macdowell.org *Web Site:* www.macdowell.org, pg 628

Bettanin, Donica, PEN America, 120 Broadway, 26th fl N, New York, NY 10271 *Tel:* 212-334-1660 *Fax:* 212-334-2181 *E-mail:* info@pen.org; membership@pen.org; education@pen.org *Web Site:* pen.org, pg 516

Bettanin, Donica, PEN America Literary Awards, 120 Broadway, 26th fl N, New York, NY 10271 *Tel:* 212-334-1660 *Fax:* 212-334-2181 *E-mail:* awards@pen.org; info@pen.org *Web Site:* pen.org/literary-awards, pg 646

Bettanin, Donica, PEN Award for Poetry in Translation, 120 Broadway, 26th fl N, New York, NY 10271 *Tel:* 212-334-1660 *Fax:* 212-334-2181 *E-mail:* awards@pen.org; info@pen.org *Web Site:* pen.org/pen-award-poetry-translation, pg 646

Bettanin, Donica, PEN/Barbey Freedom to Write Award, 120 Broadway, 26th fl N, New York, NY 10271 *Tel:* 212-334-1660 *Fax:* 212-334-2181 *E-mail:* awards@pen.org; info@pen.org *Web Site:* pen.org/penbarbey-freedom-to-write-award, pg 647

Bettanin, Donica, PEN/Diamonstein-Spielvogel Award for the Art of the Essay, 120 Broadway, 26th fl N, New York, NY 10271 *Tel:* 212-334-1660 *Fax:* 212-334-2181 *E-mail:* awards@pen.org; info@pen.org *Web Site:* pen.org/pen-diamonstein-spielvogel-award-for-the-art-of-the-essay, pg 647

Bettanin, Donica, PEN/E O Wilson Literary Science Writing Award, 120 Broadway, 26th fl N, New York, NY 10271 *Tel:* 212-334-1660 *Fax:* 212-334-2181 *E-mail:* awards@pen.org; info@pen.org *Web Site:* pen.org/pen-eo-wilson-prize-literary-science-writing, pg 647

Bettanin, Donica, PEN/Heim Translation Fund Grants, 120 Broadway, 26th fl N, New York, NY 10271 *Tel:* 212-334-1660 *Fax:* 212-334-2181 *E-mail:* awards@pen.org *Web Site:* pen.org/pen-heim-grants, pg 647

Bettanin, Donica, PEN/Jacqueline Bograd Weld Award for Biography, 120 Broadway, 26th fl N, New York, NY 10271 *Tel:* 212-334-1660 *Fax:* 212-334-2181 *E-mail:* awards@pen.org; info@pen.org *Web Site:* pen.org/pen-bograd-weld-award-biography, pg 647

Bettanin, Donica, PEN/Jean Stein Book Award, 120 Broadway, 26th fl N, New York, NY 10271 *Tel:* 212-334-1660 *Fax:* 212-334-2181 *E-mail:* awards@pen.org; info@pen.org *Web Site:* pen.org/pen-jean-stein-book-award, pg 647

Bettanin, Donica, PEN/John Kenneth Galbraith Award for Nonfiction, 120 Broadway, 26th fl N, New York, NY 10271 *Tel:* 212-334-1660 *Fax:* 212-334-2181 *E-mail:* awards@pen.org; info@pen.org *Web Site:* pen.org/pen-galbraith-award-for-nonfiction, pg 647

Bettanin, Donica, PEN/Mike Nichols Writing for Performance Award, 120 Broadway, 26th fl N, New York, NY 10271 *Tel:* 212-334-1660 *Fax:* 212-334-2181 *E-mail:* awards@pen.org; info@pen.org *Web Site:* pen.org/pen-nichols-award, pg 647

Bettanin, Donica, PEN/Nabokov Award for Achievement in International Literature, 120 Broadway, 26th fl N, New York, NY 10271 *Tel:* 212-334-1660 *Fax:* 212-334-2181 *E-mail:* awards@pen.org; info@pen.org *Web Site:* pen.org/pen-nabokov-award, pg 648

Bettanin, Donica, PEN Open Book Award, 120 Broadway, 26th fl N, New York, NY 10271 *Tel:* 212-334-1660 *Fax:* 212-334-2181 *E-mail:* awards@pen.org; info@pen.org *Web Site:* pen.org/pen-open-book-award, pg 648

Bettanin, Donica, PEN/Ralph Manheim Award for Translation, 120 Broadway, 26th fl N, New York, NY 10271 *Tel:* 212-334-1660 *Fax:* 212-334-2181 *E-mail:* awards@pen.org; info@pen.org *Web Site:* pen.org/literary-award/penralph-manheim-medal-for-translation, pg 648

Bettanin, Donica, PEN/Robert J Dau Short Story Prize for Emerging Writers, 120 Broadway, 26th fl N, New York, NY 10271 *Tel:* 212-334-1660 *Fax:* 212-334-2181 *E-mail:* awards@pen.org; info@pen.org *Web Site:* pen.org/pen-dau-short-story-prize, pg 648

Bettanin, Donica, PEN/Robert W Bingham Prize for Debut Short Story Collection, 120 Broadway, 26th fl N, New York, NY 10271 *Tel:* 212-334-1660 *Fax:* 212-334-2181 *E-mail:* awards@pen.org; info@pen.org *Web Site:* pen.org/pen-bingham-prize, pg 648

Bettanin, Donica, PEN/Saul Bellow Award for Achievement in American Fiction, 120 Broadway, 26th fl N, New York, NY 10271 *Tel:* 212-334-1660 *Fax:* 212-334-2181 *E-mail:* awards@pen.org; info@pen.org *Web Site:* pen.org/pen-saul-bellow-award, pg 648

Bettanin, Donica, PEN Translation Prize, 120 Broadway, 26th fl N, New York, NY 10271 *Tel:* 212-334-1660 *Fax:* 212-334-2181 *E-mail:* awards@pen.org; info@pen.org *Web Site:* pen.org/pen-translation-prize, pg 648

Bettanin, Donica, PEN/Voelcker Award for Poetry Collection, 120 Broadway, 26th fl N, New York, NY 10271 *Tel:* 212-334-1660 *Fax:* 212-334-2181 *E-mail:* awards@pen.org; info@pen.org *Web Site:* pen.org/pen-voelcker-award-poetry, pg 648

Bettles, Shannon, W Kaye Lamb Scholarships, PO Box 448, Fort Langley, BC V1M 2R7, Canada *E-mail:* info@bchistory.ca *Web Site:* www.bchistory.ca/awards/scholarships, pg 621

Bettles, Shannon, Anne & Philip Yandle Best Article Award, PO Box 448, Fort Langley, BC V1M 2R7, Canada *E-mail:* info@bchistory.ca *Web Site:* www.bchistory.ca/awards, pg 679

Betts, Amanda, Knopf Canada, 320 Front St W, Suite 1400, Toronto, ON M5V 3B6, Canada *Tel:* 416-364-4449 *Toll Free Tel:* 888-523-9292 *Fax:* 416-598-7764 *Web Site:* www.penguinrandomhouse.ca, pg 411

Betts, Reginald Dwayne, Inside Literary Prize, 2666 State St, Suite 5A, Hamden, CT 06517 *E-mail:* freedomreads@freedomreads.org *Web Site:* freedomreads.org/showing-up/inside-literary-prize, pg 616

Bevington, Stan, Coach House Books, 80 bpNichol Lane, Toronto, ON M5S 3J4, Canada *Tel:* 416-979-2217 *Toll Free Tel:* 800-367-6360 (outside Toronto) *Fax:* 416-977-1158 *E-mail:* mail@chbooks.com *Web Site:* www.chbooks.com, pg 400

Bewick, Andrea, Napa Valley Writers' Conference, 2277 Napa-Vallejo Hwy, Off 1753, Napa, CA 94558 *Tel:* 707-256-7113 *E-mail:* info@napawritersconference.org; fiction@napawritersconference.org; poetry@napawritersconference.org *Web Site:* www.napawritersconference.org, pg 556

Bewley, Elizabeth, Sterling Lord Literistic Inc, 594 Broadway, Suite 205, New York, NY 10012 *Tel:* 212-780-6050 *Fax:* 212-780-6095 *E-mail:* info@sll.com *Web Site:* www.sll.com, pg 477

Beyette, Claire, Macmillan Audio, 120 Broadway, 22nd fl, New York, NY 10271 *Tel:* 646-600-7856 *Toll Free Tel:* 888-330-8477 (cust serv) *Toll Free Fax:* 800-672-7703 *E-mail:* macmillan.audio@macmillanusa.com *Web Site:* us.macmillan.com/audio, pg 123

Beynon, Almeda, HarperCollins Publishers LLC, 195 Broadway, New York, NY 10007 *Tel:* 212-207-7000 *Web Site:* www.harpercollins.com, pg 87

Bhasin, Abhi, Jhpiego, 1615 Thames St, Baltimore, MD 21231-3492 *Tel:* 410-537-1800 *E-mail:* info@jhpiego.org *Web Site:* www.jhpiego.org, pg 106

Bhatnagar, Supriya, Association of Writers & Writing Programs (AWP), 440 Monticello Ave, Suite 1802, PMB 73708, Norfolk, VA 23510-2670 *Tel:* 240-696-7700 *E-mail:* awp@awpwriter.org; press@awpwriter.org *Web Site:* www.awpwriter.org, pg 500

Bhatnagar, Supriya, AWP Award Series, 440 Monticello Ave, Suite 1802, PMB 73708, Norfolk, VA 23510-2670 *Tel:* 240-696-7700 *E-mail:* awp@awpwriter.org; press@awpwriter.org *Web Site:* www.awpwriter.org, pg 576

Bhotla, Vish, Columbia Books & Information Services (CBIS), 1530 Wilson Blvd, Suite 400, Arlington, VA 22209 *Tel:* 202-464-1662 *Fax:* 301-664-9600 *E-mail:* info@columbiabooks.com *Web Site:* www.columbiabooks.com; www.association-insight.com; www.ceoupdate.com; www.thealmanacofamericanpolitics.com; www.thompsongrants.com, pg 51

Bi, Faye, Bloomsbury Publishing Inc, 1385 Broadway, 5th fl, New York, NY 10018 *Tel:* 212-419-5300 *E-mail:* marketingusa@bloomsbury.com; adultpublicityusa@bloomsbury.com; askacademic@bloomsbury.com *Web Site:* www.bloomsbury.com, pg 31

Bialer, Matt, Sanford J Greenburger Associates Inc, 55 Fifth Ave, New York, NY 10003 *Tel:* 212-206-5600 *Web Site:* greenburger.com, pg 461

Bialosky, Jill, W W Norton & Company Inc, 500 Fifth Ave, New York, NY 10110-0017 *Tel:* 212-354-5500 *Toll Free Tel:* 800-233-4830 (orders & cust serv) *Fax:* 212-869-0856 *Toll Free Fax:* 800-458-6515 *E-mail:* orders@wwnorton.com *Web Site:* wwnorton.com, pg 143

Bianchini, Bob, Random House Children's Books, c/o Penguin Random House LLC, 1745 Broadway, New York, NY 10019 *Tel:* 212-782-9000 *Web Site:* www.rhcbooks.com, pg 170

Bianco, Kristen, GP Putnam's Sons, c/o Penguin Random House LLC, 1745 Broadway, New York, NY 10019 *Tel:* 212-782-9000 *Web Site:* www.penguin.com/putnam/, pg 167

Bibbins-Domingo, Kirsten PhD, American Medical Association (AMA), AMA Plaza, 330 N Wabash, Suite 39300, Chicago, IL 60611-5885 *Tel:* 312-464-5000; 312-464-4430 (media & edit) *Toll Free Tel:* 800-621-8335 *E-mail:* media@ama-assn.org (media & edit); bookandonlinesales@ama-assn.org (volume book/ebook sales) *Web Site:* www.ama-assn.org, pg 11

Bibbins-Domingo, Kirsten PhD, American Medical Association (AMA), AMA Plaza, 330 N Wabash, Suite 39300, Chicago, IL 60611-5885 *Tel:* 312-464-5000 *Toll Free Tel:* 800-621-8335 *E-mail:* media@ama-assn.org (media & edit) *Web Site:* www.ama-assn.org; www.jamanetwork.org, pg 495

Biddinger, Mary, Akron Poetry Prize, 120 E Mill St, Suite 415, Akron, OH 44308 *Tel:* 330-972-2795 *E-mail:* uapress@uakron.edu *Web Site:* www.uakron.edu/uapress/akron-poetry-prize, pg 571

Biderman, Marilyn, Transatlantic Agency, 2 Bloor St E, Suite 3500, Toronto, ON M4W 1A8, Canada *Tel:* 416-488-9214 *E-mail:* info@transatlanticagency.com; royalties@transatlanticagency.com *Web Site:* www.transatlanticagency.com, pg 479

Biedenharn, Isabella, Random House Publishing Group, 1745 Broadway, New York, NY 10019 *Toll Free Tel:* 800-200-3552 *Web Site:* www.randomhousebooks.com, pg 171

Bieker, Lauren, FinePrint Literary Management, 207 W 106 St, Suite 1D, New York, NY 10025 *Tel:* 212-279-6214 *E-mail:* info@fineprintlit.com; submissions@fineprint.com *Web Site:* www.fineprintlit.com, pg 458

Bieker, Mike, The University of Arkansas Press, McIlroy House, 105 N McIlroy Ave, Fayetteville, AR 72701 *Tel:* 479-575-7544 *E-mail:* info@uapress.com *Web Site:* www.uapress.com, pg 214

Biesel, David, St Johann Press, 315 Schraalenburgh Rd, Haworth, NJ 07641 *Tel:* 201-387-1529 *Fax:* 201-501-0698 *Web Site:* www.stjohannpress.com, pg 180

Biesel, Diane, St Johann Press, 315 Schraalenburgh Rd, Haworth, NJ 07641 *Tel:* 201-387-1529 *Fax:* 201-501-0698 *Web Site:* www.stjohannpress.com, pg 180

Biggins, Walter, University of Pennsylvania Press, 3905 Spruce St, Philadelphia, PA 19104 *Tel:* 215-898-6261 *Fax:* 215-898-0404 *E-mail:* custserv@pobox.upenn.edu *Web Site:* www.pennpress.org, pg 219

Bigham, Lori, Sourcebooks LLC, 1935 Brookdale Rd, Suite 139, Naperville, IL 60563 *Tel:* 630-961-3900 *Toll Free Tel:* 800-432-7444 *Fax:* 630-961-2168 *E-mail:* info@sourcebooks.com *Web Site:* sourcebooks.com, pg 195

Bigler, Amy, Zondervan, 3900 Sparks Dr SE, Grand Rapids, MI 49546 *Tel:* 616-698-6900 *Toll Free Tel:* 800-226-1122; 800-727-1309 (retail orders) *Fax:* 616-698-3350 *Toll Free Fax:* 800-698-3256 (retail orders) *E-mail:* customercare@harpercollins.com *Web Site:* www.zondervan.com, pg 237

Bigman, Michelle, HarperCollins Children's Books, 195 Broadway, New York, NY 10007 *Tel:* 212-207-7000 *Web Site:* www.harpercollins.com/childrens, pg 85

Bijur, Vicky, Vicky Bijur Literary Agency, 333 West End Ave, No 5B, New York, NY 10023 *Tel:* 212-580-4108 *E-mail:* queries@vickybijuragency.com *Web Site:* www.vickybijuragency.com, pg 450

Bilis, Shavon, Macmillan, 120 Broadway, 22nd fl, New York, NY 10271 *E-mail:* press.inquiries@macmillan.com *Web Site:* us.macmillan.com, pg 122

Biljan, Tyrone, Joe Shuster Awards, 305-484 Oriole Pkwy, Toronto, ON M5P 2H8, Canada *E-mail:* info@joeshusterawards.com *Web Site:* joeshusterawards.com, pg 662

Billingsley, Sarah, Chronicle Books LLC, 680 Second St, San Francisco, CA 94107 *Tel:* 415-537-4200 *Fax:* 415-537-4460 (perms) *E-mail:* hello@chroniclebooks.com; subrights@chroniclebooks.com *Web Site:* www.chroniclebooks.com, pg 47

Bily, Beth, Lake Superior Publishing LLC, 109 W Superior St, Suite 200, Duluth, MN 55802 *Tel:* 218-722-5002 *Toll Free Tel:* 888-BIG-LAKE (244-5253) *Fax:* 218-722-4096 *E-mail:* edit@lakesuperior.com *Web Site:* www.lakesuperior.com, pg 112

Binder, Amelia, National Music Publishers' Association (NMPA), 1900 "N" St NW, Suite 500, Washington, DC 20036 *Tel:* 202-393-6672 *E-mail:* members@nmpa.org *Web Site:* nmpa.org, pg 513

Binder, Connie, ASI Excellence in Indexing Award, 1628 E Southern Ave, Suite 9-223, Tempe, AZ 85282 *Tel:* 480-245-6750 *E-mail:* info@asindexing.org *Web Site:* www.asindexing.org/about/awards/asi-indexing-award, pg 574

Binder, Pam, PNWA Writers' Contest, 1420 NW Gilman Blvd, Suite 29, PMB 2717, Issaquah, WA 98027 *Tel:* 425-673-2665 *E-mail:* pnwa@pnwa.org *Web Site:* www.pnwa.org, pg 650

Binder, Pam, PNWA - a writer's resource, 1420 NW Gilman Blvd, Suite 29, PMB 2717, Issaquah, WA 98027 *Tel:* 425-673-2665 *E-mail:* pnwa@pnwa.org *Web Site:* www.pnwa.org, pg 517

Binder, Pam, PNWA Writers Conference, 1420 NW Gilman Blvd, Suite 29, PMB 2717, Issaquah, WA 98027 *Tel:* 425-673-2665 *E-mail:* pnwa@pnwa.org *Web Site:* www.pnwa.org, pg 557

Bingham, Tony, Association for Talent Development (ATD) Press, 1640 King St, Box 1443, Alexandria, VA 22314-1443 *Tel:* 703-683-8100 *Toll Free Tel:* 800-628-2783 *Fax:* 703-299-8723; 703-683-1523 (cust care) *E-mail:* customercare@td.org *Web Site:* www.td.org, pg 19

Binney, Ann, Los Angeles Times Book Prizes, 2300 E Imperial Hwy, El Segundo, CA 90245 *Tel:* 213-237-5775 *Toll Free Tel:* 800-528-4637 (ext 75775) *Web Site:* events.latimes.com/festivalofbooks, pg 626

Binns, Beth, Woodbine House, 6510 Bells Mill Rd, Bethesda, MD 20817 *Tel:* 301-897-3570 *Toll Free Tel:* 800-843-7323 *Fax:* 301-897-5838 *E-mail:* info@woodbinehouse.com *Web Site:* www.woodbinehouse.com, pg 232

Binyominson, Yerachmiel, Hachai Publishing, 527 Empire Blvd, Brooklyn, NY 11225 *Tel:* 718-633-0100 *Fax:* 718-633-0103 *E-mail:* info@hachai.com *Web Site:* www.hachai.com, pg 83

Birch, Alessandra, Writers House, 21 W 26 St, New York, NY 10010 *Tel:* 212-685-2400 *Web Site:* www.writershouse.com, pg 482

Birckmayer, Ann, Alice Award, 518 Warren St, Hudson, NY 12534 *Tel:* 518-828-8900 *Web Site:* www.furthermore.org, pg 572

Bird, Kai, Biography Fellowships, 365 Fifth Ave, Rm 6200, New York, NY 10016 *Tel:* 212-817-2025 *E-mail:* biography@gc.cuny.edu *Web Site:* llcb.ws.gc.cuny.edu/fellowships, pg 580

Birkey, Mark, Random House Publishing Group, 1745 Broadway, New York, NY 10019 *Toll Free Tel:* 800-200-3552 *Web Site:* www.randomhousebooks.com, pg 171

Birkhead, Shaina, CBC Diversity Outstanding Achievement Awards, 54 W 39 St, 14th fl, New York, NY 10018 *E-mail:* cbc.info@cbcbooks.org *Web Site:* www.cbcbooks.org, pg 587

Birkhead, Shaina, The Children's Book Council (CBC), 54 W 39 St, 14th fl, New York, NY 10018 *E-mail:* cbc.info@cbcbooks.org *Web Site:* www.cbcbooks.org, pg 503

Birkhead, Shaina, Anna Dewdney Read Together Award, 54 W 39 St, 14th fl, New York, NY 10018 *Web Site:* everychildareader.net/anna, pg 595

Birkhead, Shaina, Kids' Book Choice Awards, 54 W 39 St, 14th fl, New York, NY 10018 *E-mail:* cbc.info@cbcbooks.org *Web Site:* everychildareader.net/choice, pg 620

Birkholz, Linda, Peradam Press, PO Box 6, North San Juan, CA 95960-0006 *Tel:* 530-277-9324 *Fax:* 530-559-0754 *E-mail:* peradam@earthlink.net, pg 158

Birkner, Kay, Sourcebooks LLC, 1935 Brookdale Rd, Suite 139, Naperville, IL 60563 *Tel:* 630-961-3900 *Toll Free Tel:* 800-432-7444 *Fax:* 630-961-2168 *E-mail:* info@sourcebooks.com *Web Site:* www.sourcebooks.com, pg 194

Birmingham, Sara, Random House Publishing Group, 1745 Broadway, New York, NY 10019 *Toll Free Tel:* 800-200-3552 *Web Site:* www.randomhousebooks.com, pg 171

Birzer, Dedra McDonald PhD, South Dakota Historical Society Press, 900 Governors Dr, Pierre, SD 57501 *Tel:* 605-773-6009 *Fax:* 605-773-6041 *E-mail:* info@sdhspress; orders@sdhspress.com *Web Site:* sdhspress.com, pg 195

Bisch, Florence, Groupe Sogides Inc, 955 rue Amherst, Montreal, QC H2L 3K4, Canada *Tel:* 514-523-1182 *Fax:* 514-597-0370 *Web Site:* sogides.com, pg 408

Bishop, Hannah, Simon & Schuster, 1230 Avenue of the Americas, New York, NY 10020 *Tel:* 212-698-7000 *Toll Free Tel:* 800-223-2348 (cust serv); 800-223-2336 (orders) *Toll Free Fax:* 800-943-9831 (orders) *Web Site:* simonandschusterpublishing.com/simonandschuster/, pg 188

Bishop, Jordan, Random House Children's Books, c/o Penguin Random House LLC, 1745 Broadway, New York, NY 10019 *Tel:* 212-782-9000 *Web Site:* www.rhcbooks.com, pg 170

Bishop, Megan, Alberta Book Publishing Awards, 11759 Groat Rd NW, 2nd fl, Edmonton, AB T5M 3K6, Canada *Tel:* 780-424-5060 *E-mail:* info@bookpublishers.ab.ca *Web Site:* bookpublishers.ab.ca; www.readalberta.ca, pg 571

Bishop, Megan, The Book Publishers Association of Alberta (BPAA), 11759 Groat Rd NW, 2nd fl, Edmonton, AB T5M 3K6, Canada *Tel:* 780-424-5060 *E-mail:* info@bookpublishers.ab.ca *Web Site:* bookpublishers.ab.ca; www.readalberta.ca, pg 501

Bishop, Sandra, Transatlantic Agency, 2 Bloor St E, Suite 3500, Toronto, ON M4W 1A8, Canada *Tel:* 416-488-9214 *E-mail:* info@transatlanticagency.com; royalties@transatlanticagency.com *Web Site:* www.transatlanticagency.com, pg 479

Bishop, Sean, Brittingham & Pollak Prizes in Poetry, Dept of English, 600 N Park St, Madison, WI 53706 *Web Site:* creativewriting.wisc.edu/submit.html, pg 584

Bisk, Mike, Bisk Education, 9417 Princess Palm Ave, Suite 400, Tampa, FL 33619 *Tel:* 813-621-6200 *E-mail:* media@bisk.com *Web Site:* www.bisk.com, pg 29

Bismuth, Mona, Other Press, 267 Fifth Ave, 6th fl, New York, NY 10016 *Tel:* 212-414-0054 *Toll Free Tel:* 877-THEOTHER (843-6843) *Fax:* 212-414-0939 *E-mail:* editor@otherpress.com; marketing@otherpress.com; publicity@otherpress.com *Web Site:* otherpress.com, pg 148

Bissonnette, Melanie, Les Editions Alire, 120 cote du Passage, Levis, QC G6V 5S9, Canada *Tel:* 418-835-4441 *Fax:* 418-838-4443 *E-mail:* info@alire.com *Web Site:* www.alire.com, pg 401

Biton, Nicole, GP Putnam's Sons, c/o Penguin Random House LLC, 1745 Broadway, New York, NY 10019 *Tel:* 212-782-9000 *Web Site:* www.penguin.com/putnam/, pg 167

Bittrich, Lauren, Candlewick Press, 99 Dover St, Somerville, MA 02144-2825 *Tel:* 617-661-3330 *Fax:* 617-661-0565 *E-mail:* bigbear@candlewick.com; salesinfo@candlewick.com *Web Site:* candlewick.com, pg 40

Bivens, Collin, Concordia Publishing House, 3558 S Jefferson Ave, St Louis, MO 63118-3968 *Tel:* 314-268-1000; 314-268-1268 (bookshop) *Toll Free Tel:* 800-325-3040 (cust serv) *Toll Free Fax:* 800-490-9889 (cust serv) *E-mail:* order@cph.org *Web Site:* www.cph.org, pg 51

Bixler, Bryan, Penguin Random House LLC, 1745 Broadway, New York, NY 10019 *Tel:* 212-782-9000 *Toll Free Tel:* 800-726-0600 *Web Site:* www.penguinrandomhouse.com, pg 155

Bjerke, Paisius, St Herman Press, 4430 Mushroom Lane, Platina, CA 96076 *Tel:* 530-352-4430 *Fax:* 530-352-4432 *E-mail:* stherman@stherman.com *Web Site:* www.sainthermanmonastery.com, pg 180

Black, Adam PhD, Macmillan Learning, One New York Plaza, Suite 46, New York, NY 10004 *Tel:* 212-576-9400 *E-mail:* salesoperations@macmillanusa.com *Web Site:* www.macmillanlearning.com/college/us, pg 123

Black, Amy, Doubleday Canada, 320 Front St W, Suite 1400, Toronto, ON M5V 3B6, Canada *Tel:* 416-364-4449 *Fax:* 416-598-7764 *Web Site:* www.penguinrandomhouse.ca, pg 401

Black, Brittanie, Penguin Random House Audio Publishing Group, 1745 Broadway, New York, NY 10019 *Toll Free Tel:* 800-793-2665 (cust serv) *E-mail:* audio@penguinrandomhouse.com; ecustomerservice@penguinrandomhouse.com *Web Site:* www.penguinrandomhouseaudio.com, pg 154

Black, Charlie, Concordia Publishing House, 3558 S Jefferson Ave, St Louis, MO 63118-3968 *Tel:* 314-268-1000; 314-268-1268 (bookshop) *Toll Free Tel:* 800-325-3040 (cust serv) *Toll Free Fax:* 800-490-9889 (cust serv) *E-mail:* order@cph.org *Web Site:* www.cph.org, pg 51

Black, David, David Black Agency, 335 Adams St, 27th fl, Suite 2707, Brooklyn, NY 11201 *Tel:* 718-852-5500 *Fax:* 718-852-5539 *Web Site:* www.davidblackagency.com, pg 450

Black, Erick, Dreamscape Media LLC, 1417 Timberwolf Dr, Holland, OH 43528 *Tel:* 419-867-6965 *Toll Free Tel:* 877-983-7326 *E-mail:* info@dreamscapeab.com *Web Site:* www.dreamscapepublishing.com, pg 62

Black, Hilary, National Geographic Books, 1145 17 St NW, Washington, DC 20036-4688 *Tel:* 202-857-7000 *Toll Free Tel:* 877-866-6486 *E-mail:* ngbooks@cdsfulfillment.com *Web Site:* www.nationalgeographic.com/books/; ngbooks.buysub.com, pg 138

Black, Julie, Penguin Random House LLC, 1745 Broadway, New York, NY 10019 *Tel:* 212-782-9000 *Toll Free Tel:* 800-726-0600 *Web Site:* www.penguinrandomhouse.com, pg 155

Black, Kathy, Vermont Studio Center Writer's Program Fellowships, 80 Pearl St, Johnson, VT 05656 *Tel:* 802-635-2727 *Fax:* 802-635-2730 *E-mail:* writing@vermontstudiocenter.org *Web Site:* www.vermontstudiocenter.org, pg 672

Black, Lindsay, David C Cook, 4050 Lee Vance Dr, Colorado Springs, CO 80918 *Tel:* 719-536-0100 *Toll Free Tel:* 800-323-7543 (orders & cust serv) *Toll Free Fax:* 800-430-0726 (cust serv) *E-mail:* bookstores@davidccook.org; customercare@davidccook.org *Web Site:* www.davidccook.org, pg 52

Black, Lisa, Princeton University Press, 41 William St, Princeton, NJ 08540-5237 *Tel:* 609-258-4900 *Fax:* 609-258-6305 *E-mail:* info@press.princeton.edu *Web Site:* press.princeton.edu, pg 164

Black, Ron, George T Bisel Co Inc, 710 S Washington Sq, Philadelphia, PA 19106-3519 *Tel:* 215-922-5760 *Toll Free Tel:* 800-247-3526 *Fax:* 215-922-2235 *E-mail:* gbisel@bisel.com *Web Site:* www.bisel.com, pg 29

Blackbriar, Shannon, Penguin Random House Audio Publishing Group, 1745 Broadway, New York, NY 10019 *Toll Free Tel:* 800-793-2665 (cust serv) *E-mail:* audio@penguinrandomhouse.com;

ecustomerservice@penguinrandomhouse.com *Web Site:* www.penguinrandomhouseaudio.com, pg 154

Blackburn, Heather Norton, American Diabetes Association, 2451 Crystal Dr, Suite 900, Arlington, VA 22202 *Tel:* 703-549-1500 *Toll Free Tel:* 800-342-2383 *E-mail:* booksales@diabetes.org; ada_pubs@diabetes.org; diabetesjournals.org/books; www.facebook.com/adapublications, pg 9

Blackburn, Kacie, Poisoned Pen Press, 4014 N Goldwater Blvd, Suite 201, Scottsdale, AZ 85251 *Tel:* 480-945-3375 *Toll Free Tel:* 800-421-3976 *Fax:* 480-949-1707 *E-mail:* info@poisonedpenpress.com *Web Site:* www.poisonedpenpress.com, pg 161

Blackman, Justin, Macmillan, 120 Broadway, 22nd fl, New York, NY 10271 *E-mail:* press.inquiries@macmillan.com *Web Site:* us.macmillan.com, pg 122

Blackman, Lara, Simon & Schuster Audio, 1230 Avenue of the Americas, New York, NY 10020 *Web Site:* audio.simonandschuster.com, pg 189

Blackmer, Shannon, Milkweed Editions, 1011 Washington Ave S, Suite 300, Minneapolis, MN 55415-1246 *Tel:* 612-332-3192 *Toll Free Tel:* 800-520-6455 *E-mail:* orders@milkweed.org *Web Site:* milkweed.org, pg 131

Blackstock, Peter, Grove Atlantic Inc, 154 W 14 St, 12th fl, New York, NY 10011 *Tel:* 212-614-7850 *Toll Free Tel:* 800-521-0178 *Fax:* 212-614-7886 *E-mail:* info@groveatlantic.com; sales@groveatlantic.com; publicity@groveatlantic.com; rights@groveatlantic.com *Web Site:* www.groveatlantic.com, pg 82

Blaifeder, Rachael, Cambridge University Press, One Liberty Plaza, 20th fl, New York, NY 10006 *Tel:* 212-924-3900; 212-337-5000 *Fax:* 212-691-3239; 845-353-4141 *E-mail:* customer_service@cambridge.org; orders@cambridge.org; subscriptions_newyork@cambridge.org *Web Site:* www.cambridge.org/us, pg 39

Blain, Phyllis, Summit University Press, 63 Summit Way, Gardiner, MT 59030 *Tel:* 406-848-9292; 406-848-9500 (retail orders) *Tel:* 406-848-9555 *E-mail:* ts@tsl.org; rights@summituniversitypress.com *Web Site:* www.summituniversitypress.com, pg 200

Blair, Kelly, Alfred A Knopf, c/o Penguin Random House LLC, 1745 Broadway, New York, NY 10019 *Tel:* 212-751-2600 *Fax:* 212-940-7390 (dom rts); 212-572-2662 (foreign rts) *Web Site:* knopfdoubleday.com/imprint/knopf/; knopfdoubleday.com, pg 110

Blais, Melanie, Candlewick Press, 99 Dover St, Somerville, MA 02144-2825 *Tel:* 617-661-3330 *Fax:* 617-661-0565 *E-mail:* bigbear@candlewick.com; salesinfo@candlewick.com *Web Site:* candlewick.com, pg 40

Blaise, Lizz, St Martin's Press, LLC, 120 Broadway, New York, NY 10271 *E-mail:* publicity@stmartins.com; trademarketing@stmartins.com; foreignrights@stmartins.com *Web Site:* us.macmillan.com/smp, pg 181

Blaize-Hopkins, Ashanti, Society of Professional Journalists (SPJ), PO Box 441748, Indianapolis, IN 46244 *Tel:* 317-927-8000 *Fax:* 317-920-4789 *E-mail:* communications@spj.org *Web Site:* www.spj.org, pg 520

Blake, Anthony, Johns Hopkins University Press, 2715 N Charles St, Baltimore, MD 21218-4363 *Tel:* 410-516-6900; 410-516-6987 *Toll Free Tel:* 800-537-5487 (book orders & cust serv); 800-548-1784 (journal orders) *Fax:* 410-516-6968; 410-516-6998 (orders) *E-mail:* hfscustserv@press.jhu.edu (cust serv); jrnlcirc@jh.edu (journal orders) *Web Site:* www.press.jhu.edu; muse.jhu.edu, pg 106

Blake, Corey Michael, Round Table Companies, PO Box 1603, Deerfield, IL 60015 *Toll Free Tel:* 833-750-5683 *Web Site:* www.roundtablecompanies.com, pg 177

Blake, Holly, Headlands Center for the Arts Residency for Writers, 944 Fort Barry, Sausalito, CA 94965 *Tel:* 415-331-2787 *Fax:* 415-331-3857 *Web Site:* www.headlands.org, pg 611

Blake, Tammy, Random House Publishing Group, 1745 Broadway, New York, NY 10019 *Toll Free Tel:* 800-200-3552 *Web Site:* www.randomhousebooks.com, pg 170

Blake-Linn, Elizabeth, Simon & Schuster Children's Publishing, 1230 Avenue of the Americas, New York, NY 10020 *Tel:* 212-698-7000 *Web Site:* www.simonandschuster.com/kids; www.simonandschuster.com/teen; simonandschuster.net; simonandschuster.biz, pg 189

Blakeslee, Kristine M, Michigan State University Press (MSU Press), Manly Miles Bldg, Suite 25, 1405 S Harrison Rd, East Lansing, MI 48823-5245 *Tel:* 517-355-9543 *Fax:* 517-432-2611 *Web Site:* msupress.org, pg 130

Blanc-Tal, Jennifer, Rutgers University Press, 106 Somerset St, 3rd fl, New Brunswick, NJ 08901 *Tel:* 848-445-7762; 848-445-7761 (sales) *Fax:* 732-745-4935 *E-mail:* sales@rutgersuniversitypress.org *Web Site:* www.rutgersuniversitypress.org, pg 178

Blanchard, Marshall, Hoover Institution Press, Stanford University, 434 Galvez Mall, Stanford, CA 94305-6003 *Tel:* 650-723-3373 *Toll Free Tel:* 800-935-2882 (US only); 877-466-8374 (US only) *Fax:* 650-723-8626 *E-mail:* hooverpress@stanford.edu *Web Site:* www.hoover.org/publications/hooverpress, pg 95

Blanco, Jordan, Random House Children's Books, c/o Penguin Random House LLC, 1745 Broadway, New York, NY 10019 *Tel:* 212-782-9000 *Web Site:* www.rhcbooks.com, pg 170

Blanco, Miguel, National Latino Press Association (NLPA), 1841 Columbia Rd NW, Suite 614, Washington, DC 20009 *Tel:* 202-489-9516; 509-545-3055 (off of the Pres) *E-mail:* info@nationallatinopressassoc.org *Web Site:* nationallatinopressassoc.org, pg 513

Blank, Julie Bonn, Cascade Christian Writers (CCW), PO Box 22, Gladstone, OR 97027 *Tel:* 503-393-3356 *E-mail:* contact@oregonchristianwriters.org *Web Site:* oregonchristianwriters.org, pg 503

Blankenship, Jody, Indiana Historical Society Press, 450 W Ohio St, Indianapolis, IN 46202-3269 *Tel:* 317-232-1882; 317-234-0026 (orders); 317-234-2716 (edit) *Toll Free Tel:* 800-447-1830 (orders) *Fax:* 317-234-0562 (orders); 317-233-0857 (edit) *E-mail:* ihspress@indianahistory.org; orders@indianahistory.org (orders) *Web Site:* www.indianahistory.org; shop.indianahistory.org (orders), pg 99

Blasdell, Caitlin, Liza Dawson Associates, 121 W 27 St, Suite 1201, New York, NY 10001 *Tel:* 212-465-9071 *Web Site:* www.lizadawsonassociates.com, pg 455

Bledsoe, Bob, Indiana University Writers' Conference, Ballantine Hall 440, 1020 E Kirkwood Ave, Bloomington, IN 47405-7103 *E-mail:* writecon@indiana.edu *Web Site:* www.iuwc.indiana.edu, pg 555

Bledsoe, Kristen, Coffee House Press, 79 13 Ave NE, Suite 110, Minneapolis, MN 55413 *Tel:* 612-338-0125 *Fax:* 612-338-4004 *E-mail:* info@coffeehousepress.org *Web Site:* coffeehousepress.org, pg 50

Blelock, Julia, WoodstockArts, PO Box 1342, Woodstock, NY 12498 *Tel:* 845-679-8111; 845-679-8555 *Fax:* 419-793-3452 *E-mail:* info@woodstockarts.com *Web Site:* woodstockarts.com, pg 232

Blelock, Weston, WoodstockArts, PO Box 1342, Woodstock, NY 12498 *Tel:* 845-679-8111; 845-679-8555 *Fax:* 419-793-3452 *E-mail:* info@woodstockarts.com *Web Site:* woodstockarts.com, pg 232

Blessing, Lyndsey, InkWell Management, 521 Fifth Ave, Suite 2600, New York, NY 10175 *Tel:* 212-922-3500 *Fax:* 212-922-0535 *E-mail:* info@inkwellmanagement.com; submissions@inkwellmanagement.com; permissions@inkwellmanagement.com *Web Site:* inkwellmanagement.com, pg 463

Blevins, Tim, Augsburg Fortress Publishers, Publishing House of the Evangelical Lutheran Church in America, 411 Washington Ave N, 3rd fl, Minneapolis, MN 55401 *Tel:* 612-330-3300 *Toll Free Tel:* 800-426-0115 (ext 639, subns); 800-328-4648 (orders) *Fax:* 612-330-3455 *E-mail:* info@augsburgfortress.org; copyright@augsburgfortress.org (reprint permission requests); customercare@augsburgfortress.org *Web Site:* www.augsburgfortress.org; www.1517.media, pg 22

Bleyer, Craig, Macmillan Learning, One New York Plaza, Suite 46, New York, NY 10004 *Tel:* 212-576-9400 *E-mail:* salesoperations@macmillanusa.com *Web Site:* www.macmillanlearning.com/college/us, pg 123

Bliss, Eric, Penguin Random House Speakers Bureau, a Penguin Random House company, 1745 Broadway, Mail Drop 13-1, New York, NY 10019 *Tel:* 212-572-2013 *E-mail:* speakers@penguinrandomhouse.com *Web Site:* www.prhspeakers.com, pg 487

Blizard, Freesia, Chronicle Books LLC, 680 Second St, San Francisco, CA 94107 *Tel:* 415-537-4200 *Fax:* 415-537-4460 (perms) *E-mail:* hello@chroniclebooks.com; subrights@chroniclebooks.com *Web Site:* www.chroniclebooks.com, pg 47

Block, Gwen M, Marine Education Textbooks, 124 N Van Ave, Houma, LA 70363-5895 *Tel:* 985-879-3866 *Fax:* 985-879-3911 *E-mail:* email@marineeducationtextbooks.com *Web Site:* www.marineeducationtextbooks.com, pg 125

Block, Richard A, Marine Education Textbooks, 124 N Van Ave, Houma, LA 70363-5895 *Tel:* 985-879-3866 *Fax:* 985-879-3911 *E-mail:* email@marineeducationtextbooks.com *Web Site:* www.marineeducationtextbooks.com, pg 125

Block, Ruthie, Beacon Press, 24 Farnsworth St, Boston, MA 02210-1409 *Tel:* 617-742-2110 *Fax:* 617-723-3097 *E-mail:* production@beacon.org *Web Site:* www.beacon.org, pg 25

Blom, Harry, Springer, One New York Plaza, Suite 4600, New York, NY 10004-1562 *Tel:* 212-460-1500 *Toll Free Tel:* 800-SPRINGER (777-4643) *Fax:* 212-460-1700 *E-mail:* customerservice@springernature.com *Web Site:* www.springer.com, pg 196

Blom, Madlyn, Florida Antiquarian Booksellers Association (FABA), c/o Lighthouse Books, ABAA, 14046 Fifth St, Dade City, FL 33525 *Tel:* 727-234-7759 *E-mail:* floridabooksellers@gmail.com *Web Site:* floridabooksellers.com, pg 506

Blonshine, Christian, Health Communications Inc, 301 Crawford Blvd, Suite 200, Boca Raton, FL 33432 *Tel:* 561-453-0696 *Toll Free Tel:* 800-441-5569 (cust serv & orders) *Fax:* 561-453-1009 *Toll Free Fax:* 800-943-9831 (orders) *E-mail:* editorial@hcibooks.com *Web Site:* hcibooks.com, pg 90

Bloom, Anna, Scholastic Trade Publishing, 557 Broadway, New York, NY 10012 *Tel:* 212-343-6100; 212-343-4685 (export sales) *Fax:* 212-343-4714 (export sales) *Web Site:* www.scholastic.com, pg 184

Bloom, Barbara, Bloom Ink, 6437 Maple Hills Dr, Bloomfield Hills, MI 48301 *E-mail:* info@bloomwriting.com *Web Site:* www.bloomwriting.com, pg 436

Bloom, Brettne, The Book Group (TBG), 20 W 20 St, Suite 601, New York, NY 10011 *E-mail:* info@thebookgroup.com; submissions@thebookgroup.com *Web Site:* www.thebookgroup.com, pg 450

Bloom, Diem, Johns Hopkins University Press, 2715 N Charles St, Baltimore, MD 21218-4363 *Tel:* 410-516-6900; 410-516-6987 *Toll Free Tel:* 800-537-5487 (book orders & cust serv); 800-548-1784 (journal orders) *Fax:* 410-516-6968; 410-516-6998 (orders) *E-mail:* hfscustserv@press.jhu.edu (cust serv); jrnlcirc@jh.edu (journal orders) *Web Site:* www.press.jhu.edu; muse.jhu.edu, pg 106

Bloom, Lexy, Alfred A Knopf, c/o Penguin Random House LLC, 1745 Broadway, New York, NY 10019 *Tel:* 212-751-2600 *Fax:* 212-940-7390 (dom rts); 212-572-2662 (foreign rts) *Web Site:* knopfdoubleday.com/imprint/knopf/; knopfdoubleday.com, pg 110

Blough, Diana, Random House Children's Books, c/o Penguin Random House LLC, 1745 Broadway, New York, NY 10019 *Tel:* 212-782-9000 *Web Site:* www.rhcbooks.com, pg 169

Blough, Heidi, Heidi Blough, Book Indexer, 732 Violet Ave, Copley, OH 44321 Tel: 904-806-3923 E-mail: indexing@heidiblough.com Web Site: www.heidiblough.com, pg 436

Bloxham, Saville, Bloomsbury Academic, 1385 Broadway, 5th fl, New York, NY 10018 Tel: 212-419-5300 Web Site: www.bloomsbury.com/us/academic, pg 31

Bloxson, Carrie, Hachette Book Group Inc, 1290 Avenue of the Americas, New York, NY 10104 Tel: 212-364-1100 Toll Free Tel: 800-759-0190 (cust serv) Fax: 212-364-0933 (intl orders) Toll Free Fax: 800-286-9471 (cust serv) E-mail: customer.service@hbgusa.com; orders@hbgusa.com Web Site: www.hachettebookgroup.com, pg 83

Blue, Marian, Blue & Ude Writers' Services, 4249 Nuthatch Way, Clinton, WA 98236 Tel: 360-341-1630 E-mail: blue@whidbey.com Web Site: www.sunbreakpress.com, pg 436

Blum, Deborah, Knight Science Journalism Fellowships, 77 Massachusetts Ave, Cambridge, MA 02139 Tel: 617-452-3513 E-mail: knight-info@mit.edu Web Site: ksj.mit.edu/fellowship, pg 620

Blum, Michele, Westminster John Knox Press (WJK), 100 Witherspoon St, Louisville, KY 40202-1396 Tel: 502-569-5052 Toll Free Tel: 800-523-1631 (US & CN) Fax: 502-569-8308 Toll Free Fax: 800-541-5113 (US & CN) E-mail: customer_service@wjkbooks.com; orders@wjkbooks.com Web Site: www.wjkbooks.com, pg 228

Blumenfeld, Jeff, North American Snowsports Journalists Association (NASJA), 290 Laramie Blvd, Boulder, CO 80304 E-mail: execsec@nasja.org Web Site: nasja.org, pg 515

Blumenstock, Sarah, Berkley, c/o Penguin Random House LLC, 1745 Broadway, 19th fl, New York, NY 10019 Tel: 212-366-2000 Web Site: www.penguin.com/publishers/berkley/; www.penguin.com/ace-overview/, pg 28

Blunck, Kay, Neustadt International Prize for Literature, c/o University of Oklahoma, 630 Parrington Oval, Suite 110, Norman, OK 73019-4033 Tel: 405-325-4531 Web Site: www.worldliteraturetoday.org; www.neustadtprize.org, pg 639

Blunck, Kay, NSK Neustadt Prize for Children's Literature, c/o University of Oklahoma, 630 Parrington Oval, Suite 110, Norman, OK 73019-4033 Tel: 405-325-4531 Web Site: www.worldliteraturetoday.org; www.neustadtprize.org, pg 642

Blythe, Heather, Society for Industrial & Applied Mathematics, 3600 Market St, 6th fl, Philadelphia, PA 19104-2688 Tel: 215-382-9800 Toll Free Tel: 800-447-7426 E-mail: siam@siam.org Web Site: www.siam.org, pg 192

Boates, Reid, Reid Boates Literary Agency, 69 Cooks Crossroad, Pittstown, NJ 08867-0328 Tel: 908-797-8087 E-mail: reid.boates@gmail.com, pg 450

Bob, Tammie, Friends of American Writers (FAW), c/o 506 Rose Ave, Des Plaines, IL 60016 E-mail: info@fawchicago.org Web Site: www.fawchicago.org, pg 506

Bob, Tammie, Friends of American Writers Literature Awards, c/o 506 Rose Ave, Des Plaines, IL 60016 Tel: 847-827-8339 E-mail: info@fawchicago.org Web Site: www.fawchicago.org, pg 604

Bob, Tammie, Friends of American Writers Young People's Literature Awards, c/o 506 Rose Ave, Des Plaines, IL 60016 Tel: 847-827-8339 E-mail: info@fawchicago.org Web Site: www.fawchicago.org, pg 604

Bobowicz, Pamela, Workman Publishing, 1290 Avenue of the Americas, New York, NY 10104 Toll Free Tel: 800-759-0190 Fax: 212-364-0950 E-mail: workman-inquiry@hbgusa.com Web Site: www.hachettebookgroup.com/imprint/workman-publishing-company/, pg 232

Boccardi, Paul, Astra Books for Young Readers, 19 W 21 St, No 1201, New York, NY 10010 Tel: 646-844-3485 E-mail: ahinfo@astrahouse.com; permissions@astrapublishinghouse.com Web Site: astrapublishinghouse.com, pg 20

Bode, Jaime McNutt, Macmillan, 120 Broadway, 22nd fl, New York, NY 10271 E-mail: press.inquiries@macmillan.com Web Site: us.macmillan.com, pg 122

Bode, Sarah, Random House Publishing Group, 1745 Broadway, New York, NY 10019 Toll Free Tel: 800-200-3552 Web Site: www.randomhousebooks.com, pg 171

Boden, Natalie, American College of Surgeons, 633 N Saint Clair St, Chicago, IL 60611-3211 Tel: 312-202-5000 Fax: 312-202-5001 E-mail: postmaster@facs.org Web Site: www.facs.org, pg 9

Bodwell, Joshua, Godine, 184 Belknap St, Concord, MA 01742 E-mail: info@godine.com Web Site: www.godine.com, pg 79

Boecher, Sarah, Sourcebooks LLC, 1935 Brookdale Rd, Suite 139, Naperville, IL 60563 Tel: 630-961-3900 Toll Free Tel: 800-432-7444 Fax: 630-961-2168 E-mail: info@sourcebooks.com Web Site: www.sourcebooks.com, pg 194

Boehmer, Gabriella, HeartMath LLC, 14700 W Park Ave, Boulder Creek, CA 95006 Tel: 831-338-8500 Toll Free Tel: 800-711-6221 Fax: 831-338-8504 E-mail: info@heartmath.com; service@heartmath.org Web Site: www.heartmath.org, pg 90

Boer, Faye, Folklore Publishing, 11717-9B Ave NW, Unit 2, Edmonton, AB T6J 7B7, Canada Tel: 780-435-2376 Web Site: www.folklorepublishing.com, pg 406

Boer, Peter J, Blue Bike Books, 317 Fairway Dr, Stony Plain, AB T7Z 2X2, Canada Tel: 780-435-2376 Web Site: www.bluebikebooks.com, pg 396

Boersma, Karen, Owlkids Books Inc, 10 Lower Spadina Ave, Suite 400, Toronto, ON M5V 2Z2, Canada Tel: 416-340-2700 Fax: 416-340-9769 E-mail: owlkids@owlkids.com Web Site: www.owlkidsbooks.com, pg 415

Boesch, William, US Government Publishing Office (GPO), Superintendent of Documents, 732 N Capitol St NW, Washington, DC 20401 Tel: 202-512-1800 Toll Free Tel: 866-512-1800 (orders) Fax: 202-512-1998 E-mail: contactcenter@gpo.gov Web Site: www.gpo.gov; bookstore.gpo.gov (sales), pg 223

Boggs, Kate, Writers House, 21 W 26 St, New York, NY 10010 Tel: 212-685-2400 Web Site: www.writershouse.com, pg 482

Boghosian, Taline, Random House Children's Books, c/o Penguin Random House LLC, 1745 Broadway, New York, NY 10019 Tel: 212-782-9000 Web Site: www.rhcbooks.com, pg 170

Bogin, Catherine, Macmillan, 120 Broadway, 22nd fl, New York, NY 10271 E-mail: press.inquiries@macmillan.com Web Site: us.macmillan.com, pg 122

Bohl, Kirsten, Mathical Book Prize, 17 Gauss Way, Berkeley, CA 94720 Tel: 510-499-5181 E-mail: mathical@msri.org Web Site: www.mathicalbooks.org, pg 630

Bohlin, Kaitlyn, Wordsmith, Open Book Bldg, Suite 200, 1011 Washington Ave S, Minneapolis, MN 55415 Tel: 612-215-2575 Fax: 612-215-2576 E-mail: loft@loft.org Web Site: loft.org/conference/about-wordsmith, pg 558

Boilard, Melanie, La Courte Echelle, 4388, rue Saint-Denis, Suite 315, Montreal, QC H2J 2L1, Canada Tel: 514-312-6950 E-mail: info@courteechelle.com Web Site: www.groupecourteechelle.com/la-courte-echelle, pg 400

Boileau, Kendra, Penn State University Press, University Support Bldg 1, Suite C, 820 N University Dr, University Park, PA 16802-1003 Tel: 814-865-1327 Toll Free Tel: 800-326-9180 (orders & cust serv) Fax: 814-863-1408 Toll Free Fax: 877-778-2665 (book orders) E-mail: orders@psupress.org; customerservice@psupress.org Web Site: www.psupress.org, pg 157

Boivin, Lucie, Brault & Bouthillier, 700 ave Beaumont, Montreal, QC H3N 1V5, Canada Tel: 514-273-9186 Toll Free Tel: 800-361-0378 Fax: 514-273-8627 Toll Free Fax: 800-361-0378 E-mail: communicationbb@bb.ca Web Site: bb.ca, pg 397

Bolan, Michael, LinguaText LLC, 103 Walker Way, Newark, DE 19711 Tel: 302-453-8695 E-mail: text@linguatextbooks.com Web Site: www.linguatextbooks.com, pg 117

Boland, John, Trusted Media Brands Inc, 750 Third Ave, 3rd fl, New York, NY 10017 Tel: 646-293-6299 Toll Free Tel: 877-732-4438 (cust serv) Fax: 646-293-6251 E-mail: customercare@trustedmediabrands.com; press@trustedmediabrands.com Web Site: www.trustedmediabrands.com; www.rd.com, pg 210

Bolchazy, Allan, Bolchazy-Carducci Publishers Inc, 1000 Brown St, Unit 301, Wauconda, IL 60084 Tel: 847-526-4344 Fax: 847-526-2867 E-mail: info@bolchazy.com; orders@bolchazy.com Web Site: www.bolchazy.com, pg 33

Bolden, Jevon, Embolden Literary, PO Box 953607, Lake Mary, FL 32795-3607 E-mail: info@emboldenmediagroup.com; submissions@emboldenmediagroup.com Web Site: emboldenmediagroup.com/literary-representation, pg 458

Boldrick, Penelope, Ignatius Press, 1348 Tenth Ave, San Francisco, CA 94122-2304 Toll Free Tel: 800-651-1531 (orders); 888-615-3186 (cust serv) Fax: 415-387-0896 E-mail: info@ignatius.com Web Site: www.ignatius.com, pg 98

Bolduc, Mary Jo, The American Library Association (ALA), 225 N Michigan Ave, Suite 1300, Chicago, IL 60601 Tel: 312-944-6780 Toll Free Tel: 800-545-2433; 866-SHOP-ALA (746-7252, orders) Fax: 312-280-5275; 312-440-9374; 312-280-5860 (orders) E-mail: ala@ala.org; alastore@ala.org Web Site: www.alastore.ala.org; www.ala.org, pg 10

Bolduc, Mary Jo, Carnegie-Whitney Award, 225 N Michigan Ave, Suite 1300, Chicago, IL 60601 Tel: 312-280-5416 Toll Free Tel: 800-545-2433 Web Site: www.ala.org, pg 587

Bolinao, Mela, MB Artists, 775 Sixth Ave, Suite 6, New York, NY 10001 Tel: 212-689-7830 Web Site: www.mbartists.com, pg 485

Boling, John Mark, Grove Atlantic Inc, 154 W 14 St, 12th fl, New York, NY 10011 Tel: 212-614-7850 Toll Free Tel: 800-521-0178 Fax: 212-614-7886 E-mail: customercare@groveatlantic.com; sales@groveatlantic.com; publicity@groveatlantic.com; rights@groveatlantic.com Web Site: www.groveatlantic.com, pg 82

Bolinger, Becke, Indiana Historical Society Press, 450 W Ohio St, Indianapolis, IN 46202-3269 Tel: 317-232-1882; 317-234-0026 (orders); 317-234-2716 (edit) Toll Free Tel: 800-447-1830 (orders) Fax: 317-234-0562 (orders); 317-233-0857 (edit) E-mail: ihspress@indianahistory.org; orders@indianahistory.org (orders) Web Site: www.indianahistory.org; shop.indianahistory.org (orders), pg 99

Boller, Katherine, Yale University Press, 302 Temple St, New Haven, CT 06511-8909 Tel: 203-432-0960; 203-432-0966 (sales); 401-531-2800 (cust serv) Toll Free Tel: 800-405-1619 (cust serv) Fax: 203-432-0948; 203-432-8485 (sales); 401-531-2801 (cust serv) Toll Free Fax: 800-406-9145 (cust serv) E-mail: sales.press@yale.edu (sales); customer.care@triliteral.org (cust serv) Web Site: www.yalebooks.com; yalepress.yale.edu/yupbooks, pg 235

Bolm, Jennifer, Adventures Unlimited Press (AUP), One Adventure Place, Kempton, IL 60946 Tel: 815-253-6390 Fax: 815-253-6300 E-mail: info@adventuresunlimitedpress.com Web Site: www.adventuresunlimitedpress.com, pg 5

Bomier, John, Public Relations Society of America Inc, 120 Wall St, 21st fl, New York, NY 10005 Tel: 212-460-1400 E-mail: membership@prsa.org Web Site: www.prsa.org, pg 518

Bonacum, Leslie, CCH, a Wolters Kluwer business, 2700 Lake Cook Rd, Riverwoods, IL 60015 Tel: 847-267-7000 Web Site: www.cch.com, pg 42

Bonadio, Sylvia, Brill Inc, 10 Liberty Sq, 3rd fl, Boston, MA 02109 Tel: 617-263-2323 Fax: 617-263-2324 E-mail: sales@brill.com Web Site: www.brill.com, pg 37

Bonaparte, Ian, Janklow & Nesbit Associates, 285 Madison Ave, 21st fl, New York, NY 10017 Tel: 212-421-1700 Fax: 212-355-1403 E-mail: info@janklow.com; submissions@janklow.com; filmtvrights@janklow.com Web Site: www.janklowandnesbit.com, pg 464

Bonar, Jake, Prometheus Books, 59 John Glenn Dr, Amherst, NY 14228-2119 Fax: 716-691-0137 E-mail: marketing@prometheusbooks.com; editorial@prometheusbooks.com; rights@prometheusbooks.com Web Site: www.prometheusbooks.com, pg 166

Bonaventura, Philip T, Public Relations Society of America Inc, 120 Wall St, 21st fl, New York, NY 10005 Tel: 212-460-1400 E-mail: membership@prsa.org Web Site: www.prsa.org, pg 518

Boncha, Sara, Chronicle Books LLC, 680 Second St, San Francisco, CA 94107 Tel: 415-537-4200 Fax: 415-537-4460 (perms) E-mail: hello@chroniclebooks.com; subrights@chroniclebooks.com Web Site: www.chroniclebooks.com, pg 48

Bonczek, Sonya, The University of North Carolina Press, 116 S Boundary St, Chapel Hill, NC 27514-3808 Tel: 919-966-3561; 919-966-7449 (orders) Toll Free Tel: 800-848-3224 (orders) Fax: 919-962-2704 (orders) Toll Free Fax: 800-272-6817 (orders) E-mail: uncpress@unc.edu Web Site: uncpress.org, pg 218

Bond, Nicole, Simon & Schuster, LLC, 1230 Avenue of the Americas, New York, NY 10020 Tel: 212-698-7000 Toll Free Tel: 800-223-2336 (orders) Fax: 212-698-7007 Toll Free Fax: 800-943-9831 (orders) E-mail: firstname.lastname@simonandschuster.com; purchaseorders@simonandschuster.com (orders) Web Site: www.simonandschuster.com, pg 190

Bond, Sandra, Bond Literary Agency, 201 Milwaukee St, Suite 200, Denver, CO 80206 Tel: 303-781-9305 Web Site: bondliteraryagency.com, pg 450

Bonelli, Kristen Hornyak, Ave Maria Press Inc, PO Box 428, Notre Dame, IN 46556 Toll Free Tel: 800-282-1865 Toll Free Fax: 800-282-5681 E-mail: avemariapress.1@nd.edu Web Site: www.avemariapress.com, pg 22

Bonfiglio, Alana, Workman Publishing, 1290 Avenue of the Americas, New York, NY 10104 Toll Free Tel: 800-759-0190 Fax: 212-364-0950 E-mail: workman-inquiry@hbgusa.com Web Site: www.hachettebookgroup.com/imprint/workman-publishing-company/, pg 233

Boni, Alexis, Sourcebooks LLC, 1935 Brookdale Rd, Suite 139, Naperville, IL 60563 Tel: 630-961-3900 Toll Free Tel: 800-432-7444 Fax: 630-961-2168 E-mail: info@sourcebooks.com Web Site: www.sourcebooks.com, pg 195

Boni, Katie, HarperCollins Children's Books, 195 Broadway, New York, NY 10007 Tel: 212-207-7000 Web Site: www.harpercollins.com/childrens, pg 85

Bonikowski, Janna, The Knight Agency Inc, 232 W Washington St, Madison, GA 30650 E-mail: admin@knightagency.net Web Site: www.knightagency.net, pg 466

Bonk, Rich, Philadelphia Museum of Art, PO Box 7646, Philadelphia, PA 19101-7646 Tel: 215-763-8100 Fax: 215-236-4465 Web Site: www.philamuseum.org, pg 159

Bonner, Erin, Penguin Random House Canada, a Penguin Random House company, 320 Front St W, Suite 1400, Toronto, ON M5V 3B6, Canada Tel: 416-364-4449 Toll Free Tel: 888-523-9292 (cust serv) E-mail: canadaweb@penguinrandomhouse.com; customerservicescanada@penguinrandomhouse.com Web Site: www.penguinrandomhouse.ca, pg 416

Bonner, Laura, WME, 11 Madison Ave, New York, NY 10010 Tel: 212-586-5100 Web Site: www.wmeagency.com, pg 482

Bonnett, Carol, McGill-Queen's University Press, 1010 Sherbrooke W, Suite 1720, Montreal, QC H3A 2R7, Canada Tel: 514-398-3750 Fax: 514-398-4333 E-mail: mqup@mcgill.ca Web Site: www.mqup.ca, pg 412

Bono, Garry, International Publishers Co Inc, 235 W 23 St, New York, NY 10011 Tel: 212-366-9816 Fax: 212-366-9820 E-mail: service@intpubnyc.com Web Site: www.intpubnyc.com, pg 103

Bonthrone, Robin, Austin Area Translators & Interpreters Association (AATIA), PO Box 92334, Austin, TX 78709-2334 E-mail: info@aatia.org; communications@aatia.org; membership@aatia.org; finance@aatia.org; profdev@aatia.org Web Site: aatia.org, pg 500

Bonthrone, Waleska, Austin Area Translators & Interpreters Association (AATIA), PO Box 92334, Austin, TX 78709-2334 E-mail: info@aatia.org; communications@aatia.org; membership@aatia.org; finance@aatia.org; profdev@aatia.org Web Site: aatia.org, pg 500

Bontrager, Kristi, Europa Editions, 27 Union Sq W, Suite 302, New York, NY 10003 Tel: 212-868-6844 Fax: 212-868-6845 E-mail: info@europaeditions.com; books@europaeditions.com; publicity@europaeditions.com Web Site: www.europaeditions.com, pg 67

Bonvissuto, Lisa, Berkley, c/o Penguin Random House LLC, 1745 Broadway, 19th fl, New York, NY 10019 Tel: 212-366-2000 Web Site: www.penguin.com/publishers/berkley/; www.penguin.com/ace-overview/, pg 28

Bood, Natasha, Editors Canada (Reviseurs Canada), 1507-180 Dundas St W, Toronto, ON M5G 1Z8, Canada Tel: 416-975-1379 Fax: 416-975-1379 E-mail: info@editors.ca; info@reviseurs.ca; communications@editors.ca Web Site: www.editors.ca; www.reviseurs.ca, pg 505

Bood, Natasha, Equity Fellowship, 1507-180 Dundas St W, Toronto, ON M5G 1Z8, Canada Tel: 416-975-1379 E-mail: info@editors.ca; info@reviseurs.ca; communications@editors.ca Web Site: www.editors.ca/about/awards/equity-fellowship, pg 600

Bood, Natasha, Tom Fairley Award for Editorial Excellence, 1507-180 Dundas St W, Toronto, ON M5G 1Z8, Canada Tel: 416-975-1379 E-mail: fairley_award@editors.ca; info@editors.ca; communications@editors.ca Web Site: www.editors.ca/about/awards/tom-fairley-award, pg 601

Bood, Natasha, Claudette Upton Scholarship, 1507-180 Dundas St W, Toronto, ON M5G 1Z8, Canada Tel: 416-975-1379 E-mail: info@editors.ca; info@reviseurs.ca; communications@editors.ca Web Site: www.editors.ca/about/awards/claudette-upton-scholarship, pg 672

Bood, Natasha, Karen Virag Award, 1507-180 Dundas St W, Toronto, ON M5G 1Z8, Canada Tel: 416-975-1379 E-mail: info@editors.ca; info@reviseurs.ca; communications@editors.ca Web Site: www.editors.ca/about/awards/karen-virag-award-0, pg 673

Booker, Darryl, Mountaineers Books, 1001 SW Klickitat Way, Suite 201, Seattle, WA 98134 Tel: 206-223-6303 Fax: 206-223-6306 E-mail: mbooks@mountaineersbooks.org; customerservice@mountaineersbooks.org Web Site: www.mountaineers.org/books, pg 135

Boomer, Carlee, Chronicle Books LLC, 680 Second St, San Francisco, CA 94107 Tel: 415-537-4200 Fax: 415-537-4460 (perms) E-mail: hello@chroniclebooks.com; subrights@chroniclebooks.com Web Site: www.chroniclebooks.com, pg 48

Boomer, Helen, Penguin Random House LLC, 1745 Broadway, New York, NY 10019 Tel: 212-782-9000 Toll Free Tel: 800-726-0600 Web Site: www.penguinrandomhouse.com, pg 155

Boomhower, Ray, Indiana Historical Society Press, 450 W Ohio St, Indianapolis, IN 46202-3269 Tel: 317-232-1882; 317-234-0026 (orders); 317-234-2716 (edit) Toll Free Tel: 800-447-1830 (orders); 317-234-0562 (orders); 317-233-0857 (edit) E-mail: ihspress@indianahistory.org; orders@indianahistory.org (orders) Web Site: www.indianahistory.org; shop.indianahistory.org (orders), pg 99

Boota, Ludvica, Crime Writers of Canada (CWC), 4C-240 Westwood Rd, Guelph, ON N1H 7W9, Canada E-mail: info@crimewriterscanada.com Web Site: www.crimewriterscanada.com, pg 504

Boota, Ludvica, Crime Writers of Canada Awards of Excellence, 716 Thicket Way, Ottawa, ON K4A 3B5, Canada E-mail: awards@crimewriterscanada.com Web Site: www.crimewriterscanada.com/awards, pg 593

Boota, Ludvica, Grand Master Award, 716 Thicket Way, Ottawa, ON K4A 3B5, Canada E-mail: info@crimewriterscanada.com Web Site: www.crimewriterscanada.com/awards, pg 608

Boota, Ludvica, Derrick Murdoch Award, 716 Thicket Way, Ottawa, ON K4A 3B5, Canada E-mail: info@crimewriterscanada.com Web Site: www.crimewriterscanada.com/awards, pg 636

Booth, Doris, Authorlink® Press, 103 Guadalupe Dr, Irving, TX 75039-3334 Tel: 972-402-0101 E-mail: admin@authorlink.com Web Site: www.authorlink.com, pg 22

Booth, Jessica, The University of Utah Press, J Willard Marriott Library, Suite 5400, 295 S 1500 E, Salt Lake City, UT 84112-0860 Tel: 801-585-9786 Fax: 801-581-3365 E-mail: hannah.new@utah.edu Web Site: www.uofupress.com, pg 220

Booth, Tom, Oregon State University Press, 121 The Valley Library, Corvallis, OR 97331-4501 Tel: 541-737-3166, pg 147

Boran, Kristin, Macmillan, 120 Broadway, 22nd fl, New York, NY 10271 E-mail: press.inquiries@macmillan.com Web Site: us.macmillan.com, pg 122

Borbolla, Alex, Bloomsbury Publishing Inc, 1385 Broadway, 5th fl, New York, NY 10018 Tel: 212-419-5300 E-mail: marketingusa@bloomsbury.com; adultpublicityusa@bloomsbury.com; askacademic@bloomsbury.com Web Site: www.bloomsbury.com, pg 31

Borchardt, Anne, Georges Borchardt Inc, 136 E 57 St, New York, NY 10022 Tel: 212-753-5785 E-mail: georges@gbagency.com Web Site: www.gbagency.com, pg 451

Borchardt, Georges, Georges Borchardt Inc, 136 E 57 St, New York, NY 10022 Tel: 212-753-5785 E-mail: georges@gbagency.com Web Site: www.gbagency.com, pg 451

Borchardt, Valerie, Georges Borchardt Inc, 136 E 57 St, New York, NY 10022 Tel: 212-753-5785 E-mail: georges@gbagency.com Web Site: www.gbagency.com, pg 451

Boren, Laura, Sourcebooks LLC, 1935 Brookdale Rd, Suite 139, Naperville, IL 60563 Tel: 630-961-3900 Toll Free Tel: 800-432-7444 Fax: 630-961-2168 E-mail: info@sourcebooks.com Web Site: www.sourcebooks.com, pg 195

Borgenicht, David, Quirk Books, 215 Church St, Philadelphia, PA 19106 Tel: 215-627-3581 Fax: 215-627-5220 E-mail: general@quirkbooks.com Web Site: www.quirkbooks.com, pg 168

Boriack, Steven, Random House Publishing Group, 1745 Broadway, New York, NY 10019 Toll Free Tel: 800-200-3552 Web Site: www.randomhousebooks.com, pg 171

Borland, Peter, Atria Books, 1230 Avenue of the Americas, New York, NY 10020 Tel: 212-698-7000 Fax: 212-698-7007 Web Site: www.simonandschuster.com, pg 21

Born, Bob, Pocket Press Inc, PO Box 25124, Portland, OR 97298-0124 Toll Free Tel: 888-237-2110 Toll Free Fax: 877-643-3732 E-mail: sales@pocketpressinc.com Web Site: www.pocketpressinc.com, pg 161

Borne, Joell Smith, Vanderbilt University Press, 2301 Vanderbilt Place, PMB 401813, Nashville, TN 37240-1813 Tel: 615-322-3585 Toll Free Tel: 800-848-6224 (orders only) Fax: 615-343-0308 E-mail: vupress@vanderbilt.edu Web Site: www.vanderbiltuniversitypress.com, pg 224

Bornhoft, Elsa, Transatlantic Agency, 2 Bloor St E, Suite 3500, Toronto, ON M4W 1A8, Canada Tel: 416-488-9214 E-mail: info@transatlanticagency.com; royalties@transatlanticagency.com Web Site: www.transatlanticagency.com, pg 480

Borodyanskaya, Yulia, Harry N Abrams Inc, 195 Broadway, 9th fl, New York, NY 10007 Tel: 212-206-7715 Toll Free Tel: 800-345-1359 Fax: 212-645-8437 E-mail: abrams@abramsbooks.com; publicity@abramsbooks.com; sales@abramsbooks.com Web Site: www.abramsbooks.com, pg 2

Boron, Ben, William S Hein & Co Inc, 2350 N Forest Rd, Suite 10A, Getzville, NY 14068 Tel: 716-882-2600 Toll Free Tel: 800-828-7571 Fax: 716-883-8100 E-mail: mail@wshein.com; marketing@wshein.com; customerservice@wshein.com Web Site: home.heinonline.org, pg 90

Boros, Betty, New Jersey Business & Industry Association (NJBIA), 10 W Lafayette St, Trenton, NJ 08608-2002 Tel: 609-393-7707 Web Site: njbia.org, pg 514

Borzumato-Greenberg, Terry, Holiday House Publishing Inc, 50 Broad St, New York, NY 10004 Tel: 212-688-0085 Fax: 212-421-6134 E-mail: info@holidayhouse.com Web Site: www.holidayhouse.com, pg 94

Borzutzky, Daniel, University of Illinois at Chicago, Program for Writers, College of Liberal Arts & Sciences, 601 S Morgan St, Chicago, IL 60607 Tel: 312-413-2200 (Eng dept) E-mail: english@uic.edu Web Site: engl.uic.edu/graduate-studies/program-for-writers, pg 566

Bosch, Sammy, Mighty Media Press, 1201 Currie Ave, Minneapolis, MN 55403 Tel: 612-455-0252; 612-399-1969 Fax: 612-338-4817 E-mail: info@mightymedia.com Web Site: www.mightymediapress.com, pg 131

Boskovic, Zoya, Sourcebooks LLC, 1935 Brookdale Rd, Suite 139, Naperville, IL 60563 Tel: 630-961-3900 Toll Free Tel: 800-432-7444 Fax: 630-961-2168 E-mail: info@sourcebooks.com Web Site: www.sourcebooks.com, pg 195

Bossemeyer, Debora, Jhpiego, 1615 Thames St, Baltimore, MD 21231-3492 Tel: 410-537-1800 E-mail: info@jhpiego.org Web Site: www.jhpiego.org, pg 106

Bostic, Amanda, Thomas Nelson, 501 Nelson Place, Nashville, TN 37214 Tel: 615-889-9000 Toll Free Tel: 800-251-4000 Web Site: www.thomasnelson.com, pg 206

Bostic, Amanda, Zondervan, 3900 Sparks Dr SE, Grand Rapids, MI 49546 Tel: 616-698-6900 Toll Free Tel: 800-226-1122; 800-727-1309 (retail orders) Fax: 616-698-3350 Toll Free Fax: 800-698-3256 (retail orders) E-mail: customercare@harpercollins.com Web Site: www.zondervan.com, pg 236

Botero, Juan, Candlewick Press, 99 Dover St, Somerville, MA 02144-2825 Tel: 617-661-3330 Fax: 617-661-0565 E-mail: bigbear@candlewick.com; salesinfo@candlewick.com Web Site: candlewick.com, pg 40

Botsford, Marj, CWA/SCA Canada, 2200 Prince of Wales Dr, Suite 301, Ottawa, ON K2E 6Z9, Canada Tel: 613-820-9777 Toll Free Tel: 877-486-4292 Fax: 613-820-8188 E-mail: info@cwacanada.ca Web Site: www.cwacanada.ca, pg 504

Botton, Maury, The New Press, 120 Wall St, 31st fl, New York, NY 10005 Tel: 212-629-8802 Fax: 212-629-8617 E-mail: newpress@thenewpress.com Web Site: thenewpress.com, pg 140

Bottorff, Todd, GemStone Press, 4507 Charlotte Ave, Suite 100, Nashville, TN 37209 Tel: 615-255-BOOK (255-2665) Fax: 615-255-5081 E-mail: marketing@turnerpublishing.com Web Site: gemstonepress.com; www.turnerpublishing.com, pg 77

Bottorff, Todd, Jewish Lights Publishing, 4507 Charlotte Ave, Suite 100, Nashville, TN 37209 Tel: 615-255-BOOK (255-2665) Fax: 615-255-5081 E-mail: marketing@turnerpublishing.com Web Site: jewishlights.com; www.turnerpublishing.com, pg 105

Bottorff, Todd, SkyLight Paths® Publishing, 4507 Charlotte Ave, Suite 100, Nashville, TN 37209 Tel: 615-255-BOOK (255-2665) Fax: 615-255-5081 E-mail: marketing@turnerpublishing.com Web Site: www.skylightpaths.com; www.turnerpublishing.com, pg 191

Bottorff, Todd, Turner Publishing Co LLC, 4507 Charlotte Ave, Suite 100, Nashville, TN 37209 Tel: 615-255-BOOK (255-2665) Fax: 615-255-5081 E-mail: info@turnerpublishing.com; marketing@turnerpublishing.com; submissions@turnerpublishing.com; editorial@turnerpublishing.com; admin@turnerpublishing.com; orders@turnerpublishing.com Web Site: turnerpublishing.com; www.facebook.com/turner.publishing, pg 210

Bottorff, Todd, West Margin Press, 4507 Charlotte Ave, Suite 100, Nashville, TN 37209 Tel: 612-255-BOOK (255-2665) E-mail: info@turnerpublishing.com; admin@turnerpublishing.com; marketing@turnerpublishing.com; orders@turnerpublishing.com Web Site: turnerpublishing.com, pg 228

Bouchard, Jean-Francois, Les Editions Fides, 7333 place des Roseraies, bureau 501, Anjou, QC H1M 2X6, Canada Tel: 514-745-4290 Fax: 514-745-4299 E-mail: editions@groupefides.com Web Site: www.editionsfides.com, pg 403

Boucher, Marie-Helene, Les Presses de l'Universite Laval, 2180, Chemin Sainte-Foy, 1st fl, Quebec, QC G1V 0A6, Canada Tel: 418-656-2803 Fax: 418-656-3305 E-mail: presses@pul.ulaval.ca Web Site: www.pulaval.com, pg 417

Boudreau, Eden, Transatlantic Agency, 2 Bloor St E, Suite 3500, Toronto, ON M4W 1A8, Canada Tel: 416-488-9214 E-mail: info@transatlanticagency.com; royalties@transatlanticagency.com Web Site: www.transatlanticagency.com, pg 479

Boudreaux, Lee, Doubleday, c/o Penguin Random House LLC, 1745 Broadway, New York, NY 10019 Tel: 212-751-2600 Fax: 212-940-7390 (dom rts); 212-572-2662 (foreign rts) Web Site: knopfdoubleday.com/imprint/doubleday/; knopfdoubleday.com, pg 61

Boughton, Simon, W W Norton & Company Inc, 500 Fifth Ave, New York, NY 10110-0017 Tel: 212-354-5500 Toll Free Tel: 800-233-4830 (orders & cust serv) Fax: 212-869-0856 Toll Free Fax: 800-458-6515 E-mail: orders@wwnorton.com Web Site: wwnorton.com, pg 143

Boulerice, Yvan, Art Image Publications, PO Box 160, Derby Line, VT 05830 Toll Free Tel: 800-361-2598 Toll Free Fax: 800-559-2598 E-mail: info@artimagepublications.com; customer.service@artimagepublications.com Web Site: www.artimagepublications.com, pg 17

Bouma, Melinda, Zondervan, 3900 Sparks Dr SE, Grand Rapids, MI 49546 Tel: 616-698-6900 Toll Free Tel: 800-226-1122; 800-727-1309 (retail orders) Fax: 616-698-3350 Toll Free Fax: 800-698-3256 (retail orders) E-mail: customercare@harpercollins.com Web Site: www.zondervan.com, pg 236

Bourgoyne, Barbara, Louisiana State University Press, 338 Johnston Hall, Baton Rouge, LA 70803 Tel: 225-578-6294 E-mail: lsupress@lsu.edu Web Site: lsupress.org, pg 120

Bourret, Michael, Dystel, Goderich & Bourret LLC, One Union Sq W, Suite 904, New York, NY 10003 Tel: 212-627-9100 Fax: 212-627-9313 Web Site: www.dystel.com, pg 457

Bouso, Rica, The Carl Sandburg Literary Award, 200 W Madison, 3rd fl, Chicago, IL 60606 Tel: 312-201-9830 E-mail: info@cplfoundation.org Web Site: www.cplfoundation.org, pg 658

Bouso, Rica, 21st Century Award, 200 W Madison, 3rd fl, Chicago, IL 60606 Tel: 312-201-9830 E-mail: info@cplfoundation.org Web Site: www.cplfoundation.org, pg 671

Boutillier, Katie Shea, Donald Maass Literary Agency, 1000 Dean St, Suite 331, Brooklyn, NY 11238 Tel: 212-727-8383 E-mail: info@maassagency.com Web Site: www.maassagency.com, pg 468

Boutin, Carole, Editions Trecarre, 4545, rue Frontenac, 3rd fl, Montreal, QC H2H 2R7, Canada Tel: 514-849-5259 Fax: 514-849-1388 Web Site: www.editions-trecarre.com, pg 405

Boutros, Tristan, American Society of Composers, Authors & Publishers (ASCAP), 250 W 57 St, New York, NY 10107 Tel: 212-621-6000 Toll Free Tel: 800-952-7227 (cust serv) Fax: 212-621-6595 Web Site: www.ascap.com, pg 496

Boutross, Kathryn Hough, St Martin's Press, LLC, 120 Broadway, New York, NY 10271 E-mail: publicity@stmartins.com; trademarketing@stmartins.com; foreignrights@stmartins.com Web Site: us.macmillan.com/smp, pg 181

Bovay, Nicolas, United Nations Publications, 405 E 42 St, 11th fl, New York, NY 10017 Tel: 703-661-1571 E-mail: publications@un.org Web Site: shop.un.org, pg 213

Bowe, Hannah, Bloomsbury Publishing Inc, 1385 Broadway, 5th fl, New York, NY 10018 Tel: 212-419-5300 E-mail: marketingusa@bloomsbury.com; adultpublicityusa@bloomsbury.com; askacademic@bloomsbury.com Web Site: www.bloomsbury.com, pg 32

Bowe, Taryn, Maine Writers & Publishers Alliance (MWPA), Glickman Family Library, 314 Forest Ave, Rm 318, Portland, ME 04101 Tel: 207-228-8263 E-mail: info@mainewriters.org Web Site: www.mainewriters.org, pg 510

Bowen, Brenda, The Book Group (TBG), 20 W 20 St, Suite 601, New York, NY 10011 E-mail: info@thebookgroup.com; submissions@thebookgroup.com Web Site: www.thebookgroup.com, pg 450

Bowen, Deborah J, Health Administration Press, 300 S Riverside Plaza, Suite 1900, Chicago, IL 60606 Tel: 312-424-2800 Fax: 312-424-0014 E-mail: hapbooks@ache.org Web Site: www.ache.org/hap (orders), pg 89

Bowen, Stephanie, Penguin Random House LLC, 1745 Broadway, New York, NY 10019 Tel: 212-782-9000 Toll Free Tel: 800-726-0600 Web Site: www.penguinrandomhouse.com, pg 155

Bower, Kimberly, Indiana University Press, Off of Scholarly Publg, Herman B Wells Library 350, 1320 E Tenth St, Bloomington, IN 47405-3907 Tel: 812-855-8817 Fax: 812-855-7931; 812-855-8507 E-mail: iupress@indiana.edu Web Site: iupress.org, pg 100

Bower, Thomas, Perfection Learning®, 1000 N Second Ave, Logan, IA 51546-1061 Tel: 712-644-2831 Toll Free Tel: 800-831-4190 Toll Free Fax: 800-543-2745 E-mail: orders@perfectionlearning.com Web Site: www.perfectionlearning.com, pg 158

Bowers, Ford, Best Workplace in the Americas (MWA), 10015 Main St, Fairfax, VA 22031 Tel: 703-385-1335 Toll Free Tel: 888-385-3588 Fax: 703-273-0456 E-mail: assist@printing.org; info@printing.org Web Site: www.printing.org/programs/awards/best-workplace-in-the-americas, pg 579

Bowers, Ford, iLEARNING+ - Orientation to the Graphic Arts, 10015 Main St, Fairfax, VA 22031 Tel: 703-385-1335 Toll Free Tel: 888-385-3588 Fax: 703-273-0456 E-mail: info@printing.org; assist@printing.org Web Site: www.printing.org; www.ilearningplus.org, pg 555

Bowers, Ford, Lewis Memorial Lifetime Achievement Award, 10015 Main St, Fairfax, VA 22031 Tel: 703-385-1335 Toll Free Tel: 888-385-3588 Fax: 703-273-0456 E-mail: assist@printing.org; info@printing.org Web Site: www.printing.org/programs/awards/lewis-memorial-lifetime-achievement-award, pg 624

Bowers, Ford, Pinnacle InterTech Awards, 10015 Main St, Fairfax, VA 22031 Tel: 703-385-1335 Toll Free Tel: 888-385-3588 Fax: 703-273-0456 E-mail: pinnacleintertech@printing.org Web Site: pinnacleawards.printing.org, pg 650

Bowers, Ford, Premier PRINT Awards, 10015 Main St, Fairfax, VA 22031 Tel: 703-385-1335 Toll Free Tel: 888-385-3588 Fax: 703-273-0456 E-mail: assist@printing.org; info@printing.org Web Site: premierprint.printing.org, pg 652

Bowers, Ford, PRINTING United Alliance, 10015 Main St, Fairfax, VA 22031 *Tel:* 703-385-1335 *Toll Free Tel:* 888-385-3588 *Fax:* 703-273-0456; 703-691-7492 (membership) *E-mail:* assist@printing.org; info@printing.org *Web Site:* www.printing.org, pg 517

Bowers, John, Sanford J Greenburger Associates Inc, 55 Fifth Ave, New York, NY 10003 *Tel:* 212-206-5600 *Web Site:* greenburger.com, pg 461

Bowers, Sharon, Folio Literary Management, The Film Center Bldg, 630 Ninth Ave, Suite 1101, New York, NY 10036 *Tel:* 212-400-1494 *Fax:* 212-967-0977 *Web Site:* www.foliolit.com, pg 459

Bowersox, Jodi, Colorado Authors' League, 700 Colorado Blvd, Denver, CO 80206 *Tel:* 913-369-5040 *Web Site:* coloradoauthors.org, pg 504

Bowes, Matt, NeWest Press, 8540 109 St, No 201, Edmonton, AB T6G 1E6, Canada *Tel:* 780-432-9427 *Fax:* 780-433-3179 *E-mail:* info@newestpress.com; orders@newestpress.com *Web Site:* www.newestpress.com, pg 414

Bowles, David, Kay Cattarulla Award for Best Short Story, PO Box 130294, Spring, TX 77393 *Web Site:* texasinstituteofletters.org, pg 587

Bowles, David, Carr P Collins Award, PO Box 130294, Spring, TX 77393 *Web Site:* texasinstituteofletters.org, pg 591

Bowles, David, Brigid Erin Flynn Award for Best Picture Book, PO Box 130294, Spring, TX 77393 *Web Site:* texasinstituteofletters.org, pg 603

Bowles, David, Jean Flynn Award for Best Young Adult Book, PO Box 130294, Spring, TX 77393 *Web Site:* texasinstituteofletters.org, pg 603

Bowles, David, Deirdre Siobhan FlynnBass Award for Best Middle Grade Book, PO Box 130294, Spring, TX 77393 *Web Site:* texasinstituteofletters.org, pg 603

Bowles, David, Soeurette Diehl Fraser Translation Award, PO Box 130294, Spring, TX 77393 *Web Site:* texasinstituteofletters.org, pg 604

Bowles, David, Jesse H Jones Award, PO Box 130294, Spring, TX 77393 *Web Site:* texasinstituteofletters.org, pg 618

Bowles, David, Ramirez Family Award, PO Box 130294, Spring, TX 77393 *Web Site:* texasinstituteofletters.org, pg 654

Bowles, David, John A Robertson Award for Best First Book of Poetry, PO Box 130294, Spring, TX 77393 *Web Site:* texasinstituteofletters.org, pg 657

Bowles, David, Edwin "Bud" Shrake Award for Best Short Nonfiction, PO Box 130294, Spring, TX 77393 *Web Site:* texasinstituteofletters.org, pg 662

Bowles, David, Helen C Smith Memorial Award, PO Box 130294, Spring, TX 77393 *Web Site:* texasinstituteofletters.org, pg 663

Bowles, David, Texas Institute of Letters (TIL), PO Box 130294, Spring, TX 77393 *Web Site:* texasinstituteofletters.org, pg 521

Bowles, David, Lon Tinkle Award for Lifetime Achievement, PO Box 130294, Spring, TX 77393 *Web Site:* texasinstituteofletters.org, pg 669

Bowles, David, Sergio Troncoso Award for Best Book of Fiction, PO Box 130294, Spring, TX 77393 *Web Site:* texasinstituteofletters.org, pg 670

Bowles, David, Fred Whitehead Award for Best Design of a Trade Book, PO Box 130294, Spring, TX 77393 *Web Site:* texasinstituteofletters.org, pg 675

Bowlin, Sarah, Aevitas Creative Management LLC, 19 W 21 St, Suite 501, New York, NY 10010 *Tel:* 212-765-6900 *Web Site:* www.aevitascreative.com, pg 448

Bowling, Kivmars H, Society for Industrial & Applied Mathematics, 3600 Market St, 6th fl, Philadelphia, PA 19104-2688 *Tel:* 215-382-9800 *Toll Free Tel:* 800-447-7426 *E-mail:* siam@siam.org *Web Site:* www.siam.org, pg 192

Bowman, Amy, Random House Children's Books, c/o Penguin Random House LLC, 1745 Broadway, New York, NY 10019 *Tel:* 212-782-9000 *Web Site:* www.rhcbooks.com, pg 169

Bowman, Anne, Chelsea Green Publishing Co, 85 N Main St, Suite 120, White River Junction, VT 05001 *Tel:* 802-295-6300 *Toll Free Tel:* 800-639-4099 (cust serv & orders) *Fax:* 802-295-6444 *E-mail:* customerservice@chelseagreen.com; editorial@chelseagreen.com; publicity@chelseagreen.com; rights@chelseagreen.com *Web Site:* www.chelseagreen.com, pg 45

Bowman, Claire, Host Publications, 3408 West Ave, Austin, TX 78705 *E-mail:* editors@hostpublications.com *Web Site:* www.hostpublications.com, pg 95

Bowman, Hannah, Liza Dawson Associates, 121 W 27 St, Suite 1201, New York, NY 10001 *Tel:* 212-465-9071 *Web Site:* www.lizadawsonassociates.com, pg 455

Bowman, Rae, Macmillan, 120 Broadway, 22nd fl, New York, NY 10271 *E-mail:* press.inquiries@macmillan.com *Web Site:* us.macmillan.com, pg 122

Bowman, Ryland, Carolina Academic Press, 700 Kent St, Durham, NC 27701 *Tel:* 919-489-7486 *Toll Free Tel:* 800-489-7486 *Fax:* 919-493-5668 *E-mail:* cap@cap-press.com *Web Site:* www.cap-press.com; www.caplaw.com, pg 41

Bowyer, Clifford B, Silver Leaf Books LLC, 1661 Washington St, Suite 6460, Holliston, MA 01746-6460 *E-mail:* sales@silverleafbooks.com; editor@silverleafbooks.com; customerservice@silverleafbooks.com *Web Site:* www.silverleafbooks.com, pg 188

Boxleiter, Thomas, Dubuque Fine Arts Players Annual One Act Play Festival, PO Box 1160, Dubuque, IA 52004-1160 *Tel:* 563-581-6521 *E-mail:* contact_dbqoneacts@iowa706.com *Web Site:* www.dbqoneacts.org, pg 597

Boyd, Ann, Ruth & Sylvia Schwartz Children's Book Awards, c/o Ontario Arts Council, 121 Bloor St E, 7th fl, Toronto, ON M4W 3M5, Canada *Tel:* 416-961-1660 *Toll Free Tel:* 800-387-0058 (ON) *Fax:* 416-961-7796 (Ontario Arts Council) *E-mail:* info@oafdn.ca (Ontario Arts Foundation); info@arts.on.ca (Ontario Arts Council) *Web Site:* www.arts.on.ca; www.oafdn.ca/pages/ruth-sylvia-schwartz-awards, pg 661

Boyd, Bailey, Perkoff Prize, 357 McReynolds Hall, University of Missouri, Columbia, MO 65211 *Tel:* 573-882-4474 *E-mail:* contest_question@moreview.com *Web Site:* www.missourireview.com/contests/perkoff-prize, pg 648

Boyd, Betsy, University of Baltimore - Yale Gordon College of Arts & Sciences, Liberal Arts & Policy Bldg, 10 W Preston St, Rm 107, Baltimore, MD 21201 *Web Site:* www.ubalt.edu/cas/about-the-college/schools-and-divisions/school-of-communications-design, pg 566

Boyd, Cat, Simon & Schuster, 1230 Avenue of the Americas, New York, NY 10020 *Tel:* 212-698-7000 *Toll Free Tel:* 800-223-2348 (cust serv); 800-223-2336 (orders) *Toll Free Fax:* 800-943-9831 (orders) *Web Site:* simonandschusterpublishing.com/simonandschuster/, pg 188

Boyd, Emily, North Atlantic Books (NAB), 2526 Martin Luther King Jr Way, Berkeley, CA 94704 *Tel:* 510-549-4270 *Web Site:* www.northatlanticbooks.com, pg 142

Boyd, Jon, InterVarsity Press, 430 Plaza Dr, Westmont, IL 60559-1234 *Tel:* 630-734-4000 *Toll Free Tel:* 800-843-9487 *Fax:* 630-734-4200 *E-mail:* email@ivpress.com *Web Site:* www.ivpress.com, pg 104

Boyd, Kevin A, Joe Shuster Awards, 305-484 Oriole Pkwy, Toronto, ON M5P 2H8, Canada *E-mail:* info@joeshusterawards.com *Web Site:* joeshusterawards.com, pg 662

Boyd, Matt, Penguin Press, c/o Penguin Random House LLC, 1745 Broadway, New York, NY 10019 *Tel:* 212-782-9000 *E-mail:* penguinpress@penguinrandomhouse.com *Web Site:* www.penguin.com/penguin-press-overview/, pg 154

Boyd, Taryn, Brindle & Glass Publishing Ltd, 103-1075 Pendergast St, Victoria, BC V8V 0A1, Canada *Tel:* 250-360-0829 *Fax:* 250-386-0829 *E-mail:* info@touchwoodeditions.com *Web Site:* www.touchwoodeditions.com, pg 397

Boyd, Taryn, TouchWood Editions, 103-1075 Pendergast St, Victoria, BC V8V 0A1, Canada *Tel:* 250-360-0829 *Fax:* 250-386-0829 *E-mail:* info@touchwoodeditions.com *Web Site:* www.touchwoodeditions.com, pg 420

Boyd, Vicki, Houghton Mifflin Harcourt, 125 High St, Boston, MA 02110 *Tel:* 617-351-5000 *Toll Free Tel:* 855-969-4642; 800-225-5425 (K-12 educ materials); 800-323-9540 (assessment materials); 877-219-1537 (SkillsTutor); 888-242-6747 (Innovation in Educ Group); 800-225-3362 (Trade & Ref Div) *Toll Free Fax:* 800-269-5232 *E-mail:* myhmhco@hmhco.com *Web Site:* www.hmhco.com, pg 96

Boyer, Heather, Island Press, 2000 "M" St NW, Suite 480-B, Washington, DC 20036 *Tel:* 202-232-7933 *Toll Free Tel:* 800-621-2736 *Fax:* 202-234-1328 *E-mail:* info@islandpress.org *Web Site:* www.islandpress.org, pg 104

Boyer, Jennifer, Association for the Advancement of Blood & Biotherapies, North Tower, 4550 Montgomery Ave, Suite 700, Bethesda, MD 20814 *Tel:* 301-907-6977; 301-215-6499 (orders outside US) *Toll Free Tel:* 866-222-2498 (sales) *Fax:* 301-907-6895 *E-mail:* aabb@aabb.org; sales@aabb.org (ordering); publications1@aabb.org (catalog) *Web Site:* www.aabb.org, pg 19

Boylan, Jennifer Finney, PEN America, 120 Broadway, 26th fl N, New York, NY 10271 *Tel:* 212-334-1660 *Fax:* 212-334-2181 *E-mail:* info@pen.org; membership@pen.org; education@pen.org *Web Site:* pen.org, pg 516

Boyle, Corinne, Peradam Press, PO Box 6, North San Juan, CA 95960-0006 *Tel:* 530-277-9324 *Fax:* 530-559-0754 *E-mail:* peradam@earthlink.net, pg 158

Boyne, Natalie, Scholastic Education Solutions, 557 Broadway, New York, NY 10012 *Tel:* 212-343-6100 *Fax:* 212-343-6189 *Web Site:* www.scholastic.com, pg 184

Bozzi, Debra, Yale University Press, 302 Temple St, New Haven, CT 06511-8909 *Tel:* 203-432-0960; 203-432-0966 (sales); 401-531-2800 (cust serv) *Toll Free Tel:* 800-405-1619 (cust serv) *Fax:* 203-432-0948; 203-432-8485 (sales); 401-531-2801 (cust serv) *Toll Free Fax:* 800-406-9145 (cust serv) *E-mail:* sales.press@yale.edu (sales); customer.care@triliteral.org (cust serv) *Web Site:* www.yalebooks.com; yalepress.yale.edu/yupbooks, pg 235

Braaten, Douglas PhD, New York Academy of Sciences (NYAS), 7 World Trade Center, 40th fl, 250 Greenwich St, New York, NY 10007-2157 *Tel:* 212-298-8600 *Toll Free Tel:* 800-843-6927 *Fax:* 212-298-3650 *E-mail:* nyas@nyas.org; annals@nyas.org; customerservice@nyas.org *Web Site:* www.nyas.org, pg 140

Braaten, Hannah, Gallery Books, 1230 Avenue of the Americas, New York, NY 10020 *Toll Free Tel:* 800-456-6798 *Fax:* 212-698-7284 *E-mail:* consumer.customerservice@simonandschuster.com *Web Site:* www.simonandschuster.com, pg 76

Brabec, Kimberly, Waterside Productions Inc, 2055 Oxford Ave, Cardiff, CA 92007 *Tel:* 760-632-9190 *Fax:* 760-632-9295 *E-mail:* admin@waterside.com *Web Site:* www.waterside.com, pg 481

Brach, Courtney, Rutgers University Press, 106 Somerset St, 3rd fl, New Brunswick, NJ 08901 *Tel:* 848-445-7762; 848-445-7761 (sales) *Fax:* 732-745-4935 *E-mail:* sales@rutgersuniversitypress.org *Web Site:* www.rutgersuniversitypress.org, pg 179

Bracken, Don, History Publishing Co LLC, PO Box 700, Palisades, NY 10964 *Tel:* 845-359-1765 *Fax:* 845-818-3730 (sales) *E-mail:* info@historypublishingco.com *Web Site:* www.historypublishingco.com, pg 93

Brackob, Kurt, Histria Books, 7181 N Hualapai Way, Suite 130-86, Las Vegas, NV 89166 *Tel:* 561-299-0802 *E-mail:* info@histriabooks.com; orders@histriabooks.com; rights@histriabooks.com *Web Site:* histriabooks.com, pg 93

Bradford, Laura, Bradford Literary Agency, 5694 Mission Center Rd, Suite 347, San Diego, CA 92108 Tel: 619-521-1201 E-mail: hillary@bradfordlit.com Web Site: www.bradfordlit.com, pg 451

Bradley, Cheryl, NASW Press, 750 First St NE, Suite 800, Washington, DC 20002 Tel: 202-408-8600 Fax: 203-336-8312 E-mail: press@naswdc.org Web Site: www.naswpress.org, pg 136

Bradley, Fern Marshall, Chelsea Green Publishing Co, 85 N Main St, Suite 120, White River Junction, VT 05001 Tel: 802-295-6300 Toll Free Tel: 800-639-4099 (cust serv & orders) Fax: 802-295-6444 E-mail: customerservice@chelseagreen.com; editorial@chelseagreen.com; publicity@chelseagreen.com; rights@chelseagreen.com Web Site: www.chelseagreen.com, pg 45

Bradley, Sharon, The BC & Yukon Book Prizes, 201-145 Keefer St, Vancouver, BC V6B 1H7, Canada E-mail: info@bcyukonbookprizes.com Web Site: www.bcyukonbookprizes.com, pg 577

Brady, Laura, House of Anansi Press Inc, 128 Sterling Rd, Lower Level, Toronto, ON M6R 2B7, Canada Tel: 416-363-4343 Fax: 416-363-1017 E-mail: customerservice@houseofanansi.com Web Site: houseofanansi.com, pg 409

Brady, Dr Philip, Etruscan Press, Wilkes University, 84 W South St, Wilkes-Barre, PA 18766 Tel: 570-408-4546 Fax: 570-408-3333 E-mail: books@etruscanpress.org Web Site: www.etruscanpress.org, pg 67

Brady, Sally R, Brady Literary Management, PO Box 64, Hartland Four Corners, VT 05049 Tel: 802-436-2455, pg 436

Braeckel, Maria, Random House Publishing Group, 1745 Broadway, New York, NY 10019 Toll Free Tel: 800-200-3552 Web Site: www.randomhousebooks.com, pg 170

Brailsford, Karen, Aevitas Creative Management LLC, 19 W 21 St, Suite 501, New York, NY 10010 Tel: 212-765-6900 Web Site: www.aevitascreative.com, pg 448

Brainard, Georgia, Scribner, 1230 Avenue of the Americas, New York, NY 10020 Web Site: www.simonandschusterpublishing.com/scribner/, pg 185

Branch, Justin, Greenleaf Book Group LLC, PO Box 91869, Austin, TX 78709 Tel: 512-891-6100 Fax: 512-891-6150 E-mail: contact@greenleafbookgroup.com; orders@greenleafbookgroup.com; foreignrights@greenleafbookgroup.com; media@greenleafbookgroup.com Web Site: greenleafbookgroup.com, pg 81

Brand, Amy, The MIT Press, One Broadway, 12th fl, Cambridge, MA 02142 Tel: 617-253-5255 Toll Free Tel: 800-405-1619 (orders) Fax: 617-258-6779; 617-577-1545 (orders) Web Site: mitpress.mit.edu, pg 132

Brand, Lana M, University of Georgia Press, Main Library, 3rd fl, 320 S Jackson St, Athens, GA 30602 Fax: 706-542-2558; 706-542-6770 Web Site: www.ugapress.org, pg 216

Brand, Megan, University of British Columbia Press, 2029 West Mall, Vancouver, BC V6T 1Z2, Canada Tel: 604-822-5959 Toll Free Tel: 877-377-9378 Fax: 604-822-6083 Toll Free Fax: 800-668-0821 E-mail: frontdesk@ubcpress.ca Web Site: www.ubcpress.ca, pg 422

Brandel, Ms Dusty, American Auto Racing Writers & Broadcasters (AARWBA), 922 N Pass Ave, Burbank, CA 91505-2703 Tel: 818-842-7005 Fax: 818-842-7020 E-mail: aarwba.pres@gmail.com Web Site: aarwba.org, pg 494

Brander, Jacob, Mesorah Publications Ltd, 313 Regina Ave, Rahway, NJ 07065 Tel: 718-921-9000 Toll Free Tel: 800-637-6724 Fax: 718-680-1875 E-mail: info@artscroll.com; orders@artscroll.com Web Site: www.artscroll.com, pg 130

Brandon, Josh, Black Warrior Review Fiction, Nonfiction & Poetry Contest, University of Alabama, Off of Student Media, 414 Campus Dr E, Tuscaloosa, AL 35487 Tel: 205-348-4518 Fax: 205-348-8036 E-mail: blackwarriorreview@gmail.com; bwr@ua.edu Web Site: www.bwr.ua.edu, pg 581

Brandsdorfer, Mara, Paul Dry Books, 1700 Sansom St, Suite 700, Philadelphia, PA 19103 Tel: 215-231-9939 E-mail: editor@pauldrybooks.com Web Site: www.pauldrybooks.com, pg 152

Brandt, Eric, University of Virginia Press, PO Box 400318, Charlottesville, VA 22904-4318 Tel: 434-924-3469 (cust serv) Toll Free Tel: 800-831-3406 Fax: 434-982-2655 Toll Free Fax: 877-288-6400 E-mail: vapress@virginia.edu Web Site: www.upress.virginia.edu, pg 220

Brandt, Suzanne, Feldheim Publishers, 208 Airport Executive Park, Nanuet, NY 10954 Tel: 845-356-2282 Toll Free Tel: 800-237-7149 (orders) Fax: 845-425-1908 E-mail: sales@feldheim.com Web Site: www.feldheim.com, pg 70

Brandt, William, Arcadia Publishing Inc, 210 Wingo Way, Suite 200, Mount Pleasant, SC 29464 Tel: 843-853-2070 E-mail: retailers@arcadiapublishing.com Web Site: www.arcadiapublishing.com, pg 16

Brannigan, James, American Society of Journalists and Authors (ASJA), 355 Lexington Ave, 15th fl, New York, NY 10017-6603 Tel: 212-997-0947 E-mail: asjaoffice@asja.org Web Site: asja.org, pg 496

Brannigan, James, American Society of Journalists and Authors Annual Writers Conference, 355 Lexington Ave, 15th fl, New York, NY 10017-6603 Tel: 212-997-0947 E-mail: asjaoffice@asja.org Web Site: asja.org, pg 553

Bransbourg, Dr Gilles, American Numismatic Society, 75 Varick St, 11th fl, New York, NY 10013 Tel: 212-571-4470 Fax: 212-571-4479 E-mail: ans@numismatics.org Web Site: www.numismatics.org, pg 11

Brashem, Mara, Little, Brown Books for Young Readers (LBYR), 1290 Avenue of the Americas, New York, NY 10104 Tel: 212-364-1100 Toll Free Tel: 800-759-0190 (cust serv) E-mail: rights@lbchildrens.com Web Site: www.hachettebookgroup.com/imprint/little-brown-books-for-young-readers/, pg 118

Brassard, Kirsten, House of Anansi Press Inc, 128 Sterling Rd, Lower Level, Toronto, ON M6R 2B7, Canada Tel: 416-363-4343 Fax: 416-363-1017 E-mail: customerservice@houseofanansi.com Web Site: houseofanansi.com, pg 409

Braswell, Bess, Farrar, Straus & Giroux Books for Young Readers, 120 Broadway, New York, NY 10271 Tel: 212-741-6900 Toll Free Tel: 888-330-8477 (orders) E-mail: childrens.publicity@macmillanusa.com; childrensrights@macmillanusa.com Web Site: us.macmillan.com/mackids, pg 69

Braswell, Bess, Roaring Brook Press, 120 Broadway, New York, NY 10271 Tel: 646-307-5151 Web Site: us.macmillan.com/publishers/roaring-brook-press, pg 175

Bratcher, Sally, Candlewick Press, 99 Dover St, Somerville, MA 02144-2825 Tel: 617-661-3330 Fax: 617-661-0565 E-mail: bigbear@candlewick.com; salesinfo@candlewick.com Web Site: candlewick.com, pg 39

Brault, Pierre, Brault & Bouthillier, 700 ave Beaumont, Montreal, QC H3N 1V5, Canada Tel: 514-273-9186 Toll Free Tel: 800-361-0378 Fax: 514-273-8627 Toll Free Fax: 800-361-0378 E-mail: communicationbb@bb.ca Web Site: bb.ca, pg 397

Braun, Barbara, Barbara Braun Associates Inc, 7 E 14 St, Suite 19F, New York, NY 10003 Tel: 917-414-3022 Web Site: www.barbarabraunagency.com, pg 452

Braunstein, Bruce, Book Publicists of Southern California, 357 S Fairfax, No 222 Los Angeles, CA 90036 Web Site: www.bookpublicists.org, pg 501

Braverman, Louise, HarperCollins Publishers LLC, 195 Broadway, New York, NY 10007 Tel: 212-207-7000 Web Site: www.harpercollins.com, pg 86

Brayda, Stephen, HarperCollins Publishers LLC, 195 Broadway, New York, NY 10007 Tel: 212-207-7000 Web Site: www.harpercollins.com, pg 86

Braziller, Joel, George Braziller Inc, 90 Broad St, Suite 2100, New York, NY 10004 Tel: 212-260-9256 E-mail: editorial@georgebraziller.com Web Site: www.georgebraziller.com, pg 35

Braziller, Karen, Persea Books, 90 Broad St, Suite 2100, New York, NY 10004 Tel: 212-260-9256 E-mail: info@perseabooks.com; poetry@perseabooks.com; publicity@perseabooks.com Web Site: www.perseabooks.com, pg 158

Braziller, Karen, Lexi Rudnitsky First Book Prize in Poetry, 90 Broad St, Suite 2100, New York, NY 10004 Tel: 212-260-9256 E-mail: poetry@perseabooks.com Web Site: www.perseabooks.com, pg 657

Braziller, Michael, George Braziller Inc, 90 Broad St, Suite 2100, New York, NY 10004 Tel: 212-260-9256 E-mail: editorial@georgebraziller.com Web Site: www.georgebraziller.com, pg 35

Braziller, Michael, Persea Books, 90 Broad St, Suite 2100, New York, NY 10004 Tel: 212-260-9256 E-mail: info@perseabooks.com; poetry@perseabooks.com; publicity@perseabooks.com Web Site: www.perseabooks.com, pg 158

Braziller, Michael, Lexi Rudnitsky First Book Prize in Poetry, 90 Broad St, Suite 2100, New York, NY 10004 Tel: 212-260-9256 E-mail: poetry@perseabooks.com Web Site: www.perseabooks.com, pg 657

Brazis, Tamar, Philomel Books, c/o Penguin Random House LLC, 1745 Broadway, New York, NY 10019 Tel: 212-782-9000 Web Site: www.penguin.com/philomel/, pg 159

Brebner, Nicole, Harlequin Enterprises Ltd, Bay Adelaide Centre, East Tower, 22 Adelaide St W, 41st fl, Toronto, ON M5H 4E3, Canada Tel: 416-445-5860 Toll Free Tel: 888-432-4879; 800-370-5838 (ebook inquiries) E-mail: customerservice@harlequin.com Web Site: www.harlequin.com, pg 409

Breckenridge, Savannah, Simon & Schuster, 1230 Avenue of the Americas, New York, NY 10020 Tel: 212-698-7000 Toll Free Tel: 800-223-2348 (cust serv); 800-223-2336 (orders) Toll Free Fax: 800-943-9831 (orders) Web Site: simonandschusterpublishing.com/simonandschuster/, pg 188

Breden, Cathy, The Center for Exhibition Industry Research (CEIR), 12700 Park Central Dr, Suite 308, Dallas, TX 75251 Tel: 972-687-9242 Fax: 972-692-6020 E-mail: info@ceir.org Web Site: www.ceir.org, pg 503

Breeden, Elizabeth, Atria Books, 1230 Avenue of the Americas, New York, NY 10020 Tel: 212-698-7000 Fax: 212-698-7007 Web Site: www.simonandschuster.com, pg 21

Breeden, Vickie, AuthorHouse, 1663 Liberty Dr, Bloomington, IN 47403 Toll Free Tel: 833-262-8899; 888-519-5121 E-mail: sales@authorhouse.com; vip@authorhouse.com Web Site: www.authorhouse.com, pg 22

Breen, Jessica, Basic Books Group, 1290 Avenue of the Americas, New York, NY 10104 Tel: 212-340-8100 Toll Free Tel: 800-343-4499 (cust serv) Fax: 212-340-8105 E-mail: customer.service@hbgusa.com; orders@hbgusa.com Web Site: www.hachettebookgroup.com/imprint/basic-books/, pg 25

Breichner, William M, Johns Hopkins University Press, 2715 N Charles St, Baltimore, MD 21218-4363 Tel: 410-516-6900; 410-516-6987 Toll Free Tel: 800-537-5487 (book orders & cust serv); 800-548-1784 (journal orders) Fax: 410-516-6968; 410-516-6998 (orders) E-mail: hfscustserv@press.jhu.edu (cust serv); jrnlcirc@jh.edu (journal orders) Web Site: www.press.jhu.edu; muse.jhu.edu, pg 106

Breier, Davida, Johns Hopkins University Press, 2715 N Charles St, Baltimore, MD 21218-4363 Tel: 410-516-6900; 410-516-6987 Toll Free Tel: 800-537-5487 (book orders & cust serv); 800-548-1784 (journal orders) Fax: 410-516-6968; 410-516-6998 (orders) E-mail: hfscustserv@press.jhu.edu (cust serv); jrnlcirc@jh.edu (journal orders) Web Site: www.press.jhu.edu; muse.jhu.edu, pg 106

Brekelmans, Ashley, Signature Editions, PO Box 206, RPO Corydon, Winnipeg, MB R3M 3S7, Canada *Tel:* 204-779-7803 *E-mail:* signature@allstream. net; orders@signature-editions.com *Web Site:* www.signature-editions.com, pg 419

Brendan, Stephen, Light Publications, 306 Thayer St, Suite 2462, Providence, RI 02906 *Tel:* 401-484-0228 *E-mail:* info@lightpublications.com; pr@lightpublications.com (media rel) *Web Site:* lightpublications.com, pg 116

Brengelman, Laura, Industrial Press Inc, One Chestnut St, South Norwalk, CT 06854 *Tel:* 203-956-5593 *Toll Free Tel:* 888-528-7852 (ext 1, cust serv) *E-mail:* info@industrialpress.com *Web Site:* books.industrialpress.com; ebooks.industrialpress.com, pg 100

Brenna, Beverley, Red Deer Press Inc, 209 Wicksteed Ave, Unit 51, Toronto, ON M4G 0B1, Canada *Tel:* 905-477-9700 *Toll Free Tel:* 800-387-9776 *E-mail:* bookinfo@fitzhenry.ca *Web Site:* www.reddeerpress.com, pg 417

Brennan, Kate, American Booksellers Association, 600 Mamaroneck Ave, Suite 400, Harrison, NY 10528 *Tel:* 914-406-7500 *Toll Free Tel:* 800-637-0037 *Fax:* 914-417-4013 *E-mail:* info@bookweb.org *Web Site:* www.bookweb.org, pg 494

Brennan, Nancy, Candlewick Press, 99 Dover St, Somerville, MA 02144-2825 *Tel:* 617-661-3330 *Fax:* 617-661-0565 *E-mail:* bigbear@candlewick.com; salesinfo@candlewick.com *Web Site:* candlewick.com, pg 39

Brennan, Tom, Candlewick Press, 99 Dover St, Somerville, MA 02144-2825 *Tel:* 617-661-3330 *Fax:* 617-661-0565 *E-mail:* bigbear@candlewick.com; salesinfo@candlewick.com *Web Site:* candlewick.com, pg 40

Bresson, Hugo, Penguin Random House LLC, 1745 Broadway, New York, NY 10019 *Tel:* 212-782-9000 *Toll Free Tel:* 800-726-0600 *Web Site:* www.penguinrandomhouse.com, pg 155

Breton, Charles, Institute for Research on Public Policy (IRPP), 1470 Peel St, No 200, Montreal, QC H3A 1T1, Canada *Tel:* 514-985-2461 *Fax:* 514-985-2559 *E-mail:* irpp@irpp.org *Web Site:* irpp.org, pg 410

Breuer, Mitch, Galaxy Press Inc, 7051 Hollywood Blvd, Los Angeles, CA 90028 *Tel:* 323-466-3310 *Toll Free Tel:* 877-8GALAXY (842-5299) *E-mail:* info@galaxypress.com; customers@galaxypress.com *Web Site:* www.galaxypress.com, pg 75

Brewer, Amy, Metamorphosis Literary Agency, 12410 S Acuff Ct, Olathe, KS 66062 *Tel:* 646-397-1640 *E-mail:* info@metamorphosisliteraryagency.com *Web Site:* www.metamorphosisliteraryagency.com, pg 470

Brewer, Andrew, Princeton University Press, 41 William St, Princeton, NJ 08540-5237 *Tel:* 609-258-4900 *Fax:* 609-258-6305 *E-mail:* info@press.princeton.edu *Web Site:* press.princeton.edu, pg 164

Brewer, Nic, Gerald Lampert Memorial Award, 2 Carlton St, Suite 1519, Toronto, ON M5B 1J3, Canada *Tel:* 416-504-1657 *E-mail:* info@poets.ca; admin@poets.ca *Web Site:* poets.ca/awards/lampert, pg 622

Brewer, Nic, The League of Canadian Poets, 2 Carlton St, Suite 1519, Toronto, ON M5B 1J3, Canada *Tel:* 416-504-1657 *E-mail:* info@poets.ca *Web Site:* poets.ca, pg 509

Brewer, Nic, Pat Lowther Memorial Award, 2 Carlton St, Suite 1519, Toronto, ON M5B 1J3, Canada *Tel:* 416-504-1657 *E-mail:* info@poets.ca *Web Site:* poets.ca/awards/lowther, pg 627

Brewer, Nic, Raymond Souster Award, 2 Carlton St, Suite 1519, Toronto, ON M5B 1J3, Canada *Tel:* 416-504-1657 *E-mail:* admin@poets.ca *Web Site:* poets.ca/awards/souster, pg 664

Brewer, Nic, Jessamy Stursberg Poetry Prize for Canadian Youth, 2 Carlton St, Suite 1519, Toronto, ON M5B 1J3, Canada *Tel:* 416-504-1657 *E-mail:* info@poets.ca; admin@poets.ca *Web Site:* poets.ca, pg 667

Brewer, Nic, Sheri-D Wilson Golden Beret Award, 2 Carlton St, Suite 1519, Toronto, ON M5B 1J3, Canada *Tel:* 416-504-1657 *E-mail:* admin@poets.ca *Web Site:* poets.ca/awards/goldenberet, pg 676

Brezack, Hannah, Running Press, 1290 Avenue of the Americas, New York, NY 10104 *Tel:* 212-364-1100 *Toll Free Tel:* 800-759-0190 (cust serv) *Fax:* 212-364-0933 (intl orders) *Toll Free Fax:* 800-286-9471 (cust serv) *E-mail:* customer.service@hbgusa.com; orders@hbgusa.com *Web Site:* www.hachettebookgroup.com/imprint/running-press/; www.moon.com (Moon Travel Guides), pg 178

Brezenoff, Beth, Capstone Publishers™, 1710 Roe Crest Dr, North Mankato, MN 56003 *Toll Free Tel:* 800-747-4992 (cust serv) *Toll Free Fax:* 888-262-0705 *E-mail:* customer.service@capstonepub.com *Web Site:* www.capstonepub.com, pg 40

Brianik, Christina, Teachers College Press, 1234 Amsterdam Ave, New York, NY 10027 *Tel:* 212-678-3929 *Fax:* 212-678-4149 *E-mail:* tcpress@tc.edu *Web Site:* www.tcpress.com, pg 203

Bridges, Blaire, The Word, A Storytelling Sanctuary Inc, 757 E 20 Ave, Suite 370-335, Denver, CO 80205 *E-mail:* info@thewordfordiversity.org *Web Site:* www.thewordfordiversity.org, pg 522

Briel, Barbara, Sourcebooks LLC, 1935 Brookdale Rd, Suite 139, Naperville, IL 60563 *Tel:* 630-961-3900 *Toll Free Tel:* 800-432-7444 *Fax:* 630-961-2168 *E-mail:* info@sourcebooks.com *Web Site:* www.sourcebooks.com, pg 194

Briggs, Christopher B, Independent Institute, 100 Swan Way, Oakland, CA 94621-1428 *Tel:* 510-632-1366 *Fax:* 510-568-6040 *Web Site:* www.independent.org, pg 99

Bright, Jocelyn, Tor Publishing Group, 120 Broadway, New York, NY 10271 *Toll Free Tel:* 800-455-0340 (Macmillan) *E-mail:* torpublicity@tor.com; forgepublicity@forgebooks.com *Web Site:* us.macmillan.com/torpublishinggroup, pg 208

Bright, Rebecca, Island Press, 2000 "M" St NW, Suite 480-B, Washington, DC 20036 *Tel:* 202-232-7933 *Toll Free Tel:* 800-621-2736 *Fax:* 202-234-1328 *E-mail:* info@islandpress.org *Web Site:* www.islandpress.org, pg 104

Brigido, Adrianne, Springer Publishing Co, 11 W 42 St, 15th fl, New York, NY 10036-8002 *Tel:* 212-431-4370 *Toll Free Tel:* 877-687-7476 *E-mail:* marketing@springerpub.com; cs@springerpub.com (orders); textbook@springerpub.com; specialsales@springerpub.com *Web Site:* www.springerpub.com, pg 57

Briglia, Jillian, Doubleday, c/o Penguin Random House LLC, 1745 Broadway, New York, NY 10019 *Tel:* 212-751-2600 *Fax:* 212-940-7390 (dom rts); 212-572-2662 (foreign rts) *Web Site:* knopfdoubleday.com/imprint/doubleday/; knopfdoubleday.com, pg 61

Briglia, Jillian, Farrar, Straus & Giroux, LLC, 120 Broadway, New York, NY 10271 *Tel:* 212-741-6900 *E-mail:* fsg.publicity@fsgbooks.com; sales@fsgbooks.com *Web Site:* us.macmillan.com/fsg, pg 70

Brigman, Jess, Candlewick Press, 99 Dover St, Somerville, MA 02144-2825 *Tel:* 617-661-3330 *Fax:* 617-661-0565 *E-mail:* bigbear@candlewick.com; salesinfo@candlewick.com *Web Site:* candlewick.com, pg 39

Brigman, Jess, Holiday House Publishing Inc, 50 Broad St, New York, NY 10004 *Tel:* 212-688-0085 *Fax:* 212-421-6134 *E-mail:* info@holidayhouse.com *Web Site:* www.holidayhouse.com, pg 94

Brigman, Jess, Peachtree Publishing Co Inc, 1700 Chattahoochee Ave, Atlanta, GA 30318-2112 *Tel:* 404-876-8761 *Toll Free Tel:* 800-241-0113 *Fax:* 404-875-2578 *Toll Free Fax:* 800-875-8909 *E-mail:* hello@peachtree-online.com; orders@peachtree-online.com; sales@peachtree-online.com *Web Site:* www.peachtreebooks.com; www.peachtree-online.com, pg 153

Brill, Calista, Roaring Brook Press, 120 Broadway, New York, NY 10271 *Tel:* 646-307-5151 *Web Site:* us.macmillan.com/publishers/roaring-brook-press, pg 176

Brings, Kent, Educational Insights®, 152 W Walnut St, Suite 201, Gardena, CA 90248 *Toll Free Tel:* 800-995-4436 *Toll Free Fax:* 888-892-8731 *E-mail:* info@educationalinsights.com; cs@educationalinsights.com *Web Site:* www.educationalinsights.com, pg 64

Briseno-Gonzalez, Paola, IACP Cookbook Awards, c/o Marshall Jones, 4625 Alexander Dr, Alpharetta, GA 30022 *Toll Free Tel:* 866-358-2524 *E-mail:* awards@iacp.com; info@iacp.com *Web Site:* www.iacp.com/awards/cookbook-awards, pg 614

Brissie, Eugene F Jr, The Lyons Press, 64 S Main St, Essex, CT 06426 *Tel:* 203-458-4500 *E-mail:* info@rowman.com *Web Site:* rowman.com/page/lyonspress, pg 121

Brito, Mariner, HarperCollins Children's Books, 195 Broadway, New York, NY 10007 *Tel:* 212-207-7000 *Web Site:* www.harpercollins.com/childrens, pg 85

Britton, Gregory M, Johns Hopkins University Press, 2715 N Charles St, Baltimore, MD 21218-4363 *Tel:* 410-516-6900; 410-516-6987 *Toll Free Tel:* 800-537-5487 (book orders & cust serv); 800-548-1784 (journal orders) *Fax:* 410-516-6968; 410-516-6998 (orders) *E-mail:* hfscustserv@press.jhu.edu (cust serv); jrnlcirc@jh.edu (journal orders) *Web Site:* www.press.jhu.edu; muse.jhu.edu, pg 106

Britton, Laurel, The Metropolitan Museum of Art, 1000 Fifth Ave, New York, NY 10028 *Tel:* 212-535-7710 *E-mail:* editorial@metmuseum.org *Web Site:* www.metmuseum.org, pg 130

Brochu, Karen, Groundwood Books, 128 Sterling Rd, Lower Level, Toronto, ON M6R 2B7, Canada *Tel:* 416-363-4343 *Fax:* 416-363-1017 *E-mail:* customerservice@houseofanansi.com *Web Site:* www.houseofanansi.com, pg 407

Brochu, Karen, House of Anansi Press Inc, 128 Sterling Rd, Lower Level, Toronto, ON M6R 2B7, Canada *Tel:* 416-363-4343 *Fax:* 416-363-1017 *E-mail:* customerservice@houseofanansi.com *Web Site:* houseofanansi.com, pg 409

Brochu, Ron, Lake Superior Publishing LLC, 109 W Superior St, Suite 200, Duluth, MN 55802 *Tel:* 218-722-5002 *Toll Free Tel:* 888-BIG-LAKE (244-5253) *Fax:* 218-722-4096 *E-mail:* edit@lakesuperior.com *Web Site:* www.lakesuperior.com, pg 112

Brochu, Yvon, Editions FouLire, 4339, rue des Becassines, Quebec, QC G1G 1V5, Canada *Tel:* 418-628-4029 *Toll Free Tel:* 877-628-4029 (CN & US) *Fax:* 418-628-4801 *E-mail:* edition@foulire.com *Web Site:* www.foulire.com, pg 403

Brock, Heidi, American Forest & Paper Association (AF&PA), 1101 "K" St NW, Suite 700, Washington, DC 20005 *Tel:* 202-463-2700 *E-mail:* info@afandpa.org; comm@afandpa.org *Web Site:* www.afandpa.org, pg 495

Brock, John, Texas Tech University Press, 1120 Main St, 2nd fl, Lubbock, TX 79401 *Tel:* 806-742-2982 *Toll Free Tel:* 800-832-4042 *E-mail:* ttup@ttu.edu *Web Site:* www.ttupress.org, pg 205

Brock, Maddie, Harry N Abrams Inc, 195 Broadway, 9th fl, New York, NY 10007 *Tel:* 212-206-7715 *Toll Free Tel:* 800-345-1359 *Fax:* 212-645-8437 *E-mail:* abrams@abramsbooks.com; publicity@abramsbooks.com; sales@abramsbooks.com *Web Site:* www.abramsbooks.com, pg 3

Brockenbrough, Gina, SLACK® Incorporated, A Wyanoke Group Company, 6900 Grove Rd, Thorofare, NJ 08086-9447 *Tel:* 856-848-1000 *Toll Free Tel:* 800-257-8290 *Fax:* 856-848-6091 *E-mail:* sales@slackinc.com; editor@slackinc.com; customerservice@slackinc.com *Web Site:* www.healio.com/books, pg 191

Brockett, Louise, W W Norton & Company Inc, 500 Fifth Ave, New York, NY 10110-0017 *Tel:* 212-354-5500 *Toll Free Tel:* 800-233-4830 (orders & cust serv) *Fax:* 212-869-0856 *Toll Free Fax:* 800-458-6515 *E-mail:* orders@wwnorton.com *Web Site:* wwnorton.com, pg 143

Brockman, John, Brockman Inc, 260 Fifth Ave, 10th fl, New York, NY 10001 Tel: 212-935-8900 E-mail: rights@brockman.com Web Site: www.brockman.com, pg 452

Brockman, Max, Brockman Inc, 260 Fifth Ave, 10th fl, New York, NY 10001 Tel: 212-935-8900 E-mail: rights@brockman.com Web Site: www.brockman.com, pg 452

Broderick, Geoff, World Book Inc, 180 N LaSalle, Suite 900, Chicago, IL 60601 Tel: 312-729-5800 Toll Free Tel: 800-967-5325 (consumer sales, US); 800-975-3250 (school & lib sales, US); 800-837-5365 (school & lib sales, CN) Toll Free Fax: 888-922-3766 E-mail: customerservice@worldbook.com Web Site: www.worldbook.com, pg 233

Broderick, Kim, BenBella Books Inc, 10440 N Central Expwy, Suite 800, Dallas, TX 75231-2264 Tel: 214-750-3600 Web Site: www.benbellabooks.com; www.smartpopbooks.com, pg 27

Brodeur, Adrienne, Aspen Words, 110 E Hallam St, Suite 116, Aspen, CO 81611 Tel: 970-925-3122 Fax: 970-920-5700 E-mail: aspenwords@aspeninstitute.org Web Site: www.aspenwords.org, pg 497

Brodeur, Adrienne, Aspen Words Literary Prize, 110 E Hallam St, Suite 116, Aspen, CO 81611 Tel: 970-925-3122 Fax: 970-920-5700 E-mail: literary.prize@aspeninstitute.org Web Site: www.aspenwords.org/programs/literary-prize/; www.aspenwords.org, pg 575

Brodeur, Adrienne, Summer Words Writing Conference & Literary Festival, 110 E Hallam St, Suite 116, Aspen, CO 81611 Tel: 970-925-3122 Fax: 970-920-5700 E-mail: aspenwords@aspeninstitute.org Web Site: www.aspenwords.org, pg 557

Brodeur, Adrienne, Winter Words Author Series, 110 E Hallam St, Suite 116, Aspen, CO 81611 Tel: 970-925-3122 Fax: 970-920-5700 E-mail: aspenwords@aspeninstitute.org Web Site: www.aspenwords.org, pg 558

Brodeur, Kristin, Houghton Mifflin Harcourt Trade & Reference Division, 125 High St, Boston, MA 02110 Tel: 617-351-5000 Web Site: www.hmhco.com, pg 96

Brodine, Dianna, Foil & Specialty Effects Association (FSEA), 2150 SW Westport Dr, Suite 101, Topeka, KS 66614 Tel: 785-271-5816 Fax: 785-271-6404 Web Site: fsea.com, pg 506

Brodsky, Steve, Encyclopaedia Britannica Inc, 325 N La Salle St, Suite 200, Chicago, IL 60654 Tel: 312-347-7000 (all other countries) Toll Free Tel: 800-323-1229 (US & CN) Fax: 312-294-2104 E-mail: contact@eb.com Web Site: www.britannica.com, pg 66

Brodsly, Eve, Chronicle Books LLC, 680 Second St, San Francisco, CA 94107 Tel: 415-537-4200 Fax: 415-537-4460 (perms) E-mail: hello@chroniclebooks.com; subrights@chroniclebooks.com Web Site: www.chroniclebooks.com, pg 48

Brody, Deb, HarperCollins Publishers LLC, 195 Broadway, New York, NY 10007 Tel: 212-207-7000 Web Site: www.harpercollins.com, pg 86

Brody, Sarah, Sourcebooks LLC, 1935 Brookdale Rd, Suite 139, Naperville, IL 60563 Tel: 630-961-3900 Toll Free Tel: 800-432-7444 Fax: 630-961-2168 E-mail: info@sourcebooks.com Web Site: www.sourcebooks.com, pg 194

Brody, Stefanie Rosenblum, Portfolio, c/o Penguin Random House LLC, 1745 Broadway, New York, NY 10019 Tel: 212-782-9000 Web Site: www.penguin.com/portfolio-overview/; www.penguin.com/sentinel-overview/; www.penguin.com/thesis/, pg 162

Broelis, Allison, Little, Brown Books for Young Readers (LBYR), 1290 Avenue of the Americas, New York, NY 10104 Tel: 212-364-1100 Toll Free Tel: 800-759-0190 (cust serv) E-mail: rights@lbchildrens.com Web Site: www.hachettebookgroup.com/imprint/little-brown-books-for-young-readers/, pg 118

Brogan, Matt, George Bogin Memorial Award, 119 Smith St, Brooklyn, NY 11201 Tel: 212-254-9628 E-mail: info@poetrysociety.org Web Site: poetrysociety.org/awards, pg 582

Brogan, Matt, Alice Fay Di Castagnola Award, 119 Smith St, Brooklyn, NY 11201 Tel: 212-254-9628 E-mail: info@poetrysociety.org Web Site: poetrysociety.org/awards, pg 595

Brogan, Matt, Norma Farber First Book Award, 119 Smith St, Brooklyn, NY 11201 Tel: 212-254-9628 E-mail: info@poetrysociety.org Web Site: poetrysociety.org/awards, pg 601

Brogan, Matt, Four Quartets Prize, 119 Smith St, Brooklyn, NY 11201 Tel: 212-254-9628 E-mail: info@poetrysociety.org Web Site: poetrysociety.org/awards, pg 603

Brogan, Matt, Frost Medal, 119 Smith St, Brooklyn, NY 11201 Tel: 212-254-9628 E-mail: info@poetrysociety.org Web Site: poetrysociety.org/awards, pg 605

Brogan, Matt, Cecil Hemley Memorial Award, 119 Smith St, Brooklyn, NY 11201 Tel: 212-254-9628 E-mail: info@poetrysociety.org Web Site: poetrysociety.org/awards, pg 612

Brogan, Matt, Louise Louis/Emily F Bourne Student Poetry Award, 119 Smith St, Brooklyn, NY 11201 Tel: 212-254-9628 E-mail: info@poetrysociety.org Web Site: poetrysociety.org/awards, pg 626

Brogan, Matt, Lyric Poetry Award, 119 Smith St, Brooklyn, NY 11201 Tel: 212-254-9628 E-mail: info@poetrysociety.org Web Site: poetrysociety.org/awards, pg 627

Brogan, Matt, Lucille Medwick Memorial Award, 119 Smith St, Brooklyn, NY 11201 Tel: 212-254-9628 E-mail: info@poetrysociety.org Web Site: poetrysociety.org/awards, pg 632

Brogan, Matt, Poetry Society of America (PSA), 119 Smith St, Brooklyn, NY 11201 Tel: 212-254-9628 E-mail: info@poetrysociety.org Web Site: poetrysociety.org, pg 517

Brogan, Matt, Shelley Memorial Award, 119 Smith St, Brooklyn, NY 11201 Tel: 212-254-9628 E-mail: info@poetrysociety.org Web Site: poetrysociety.org/awards, pg 662

Brogan, Matt, William Carlos Williams Award, 119 Smith St, Brooklyn, NY 11201 Tel: 212-254-9628 E-mail: info@poetrysociety.org Web Site: poetrysociety.org/awards, pg 675

Brogan, Matt, The Writer Magazine/Emily Dickinson Award, 119 Smith St, Brooklyn, NY 11201 Tel: 212-254-9628 E-mail: info@poetrysociety.org Web Site: poetrysociety.org/awards, pg 678

Broich, Alexander, Cengage Learning, 20 Channel Center St, Boston, MA 02210 Tel: 617-289-7700 Toll Free Tel: 800-354-9706 Fax: 617-289-7844 E-mail: esales@cengage.com Web Site: www.cengage.com, pg 43

Bromberg-Lim, Sharon, Radcliffe Institute Fellowship Program, Byerly Hall, 8 Garden St, Cambridge, MA 02138 Tel: 617-495-8212 Fax: 617-495-8136 E-mail: fellowships@radcliffe.harvard.edu Web Site: www.radcliffe.harvard.edu/fellowship-program, pg 654

Bronersky, Corrin, Sourcebooks LLC, 1935 Brookdale Rd, Suite 139, Naperville, IL 60563 Tel: 630-961-3900 Toll Free Tel: 800-432-7444 Fax: 630-961-2168 E-mail: info@sourcebooks.com Web Site: www.sourcebooks.com, pg 195

Bronson, Andrea, The Authors Guild®, 31 E 32 St, Suite 901, New York, NY 10016 Tel: 212-563-5904 Fax: 212-564-5363 E-mail: staff@authorsguild.org Web Site: www.authorsguild.org, pg 500

Brook, Matt, Johns Hopkins University Press, 2715 N Charles St, Baltimore, MD 21218-4363 Tel: 410-516-6900; 410-516-6987 Toll Free Tel: 800-537-5487 (book orders & cust serv); 800-548-1784 (journal orders) Fax: 410-516-6968; 410-516-6998 (orders) E-mail: hfscustserv@press.jhu.edu (cust serv); jrnlcirc@jh.edu (journal orders) Web Site: www.press.jhu.edu; muse.jhu.edu, pg 106

Brook, Susan Todd, Naval Institute Press, 291 Wood Rd, Annapolis, MD 21402-5034 Tel: 410-268-6110 Toll Free Tel: 800-233-8764 Fax: 410-295-1084 E-mail: customer@usni.org (cust inquiries) Web Site: www.usni.org/press/books; www.usni.org, pg 139

Brookes, Jeffrey D, Paul H Brookes Publishing Co Inc, PO Box 10624, Baltimore, MD 21285-0624 Tel: 410-337-9580 (outside US & CN) Toll Free Tel: 800-638-3775 (US & CN) Fax: 410-337-8539 E-mail: custserv@brookespublishing.com Web Site: www.brookespublishing.com, pg 37

Brookes, Paul H, Paul H Brookes Publishing Co Inc, PO Box 10624, Baltimore, MD 21285-0624 Tel: 410-337-9580 (outside US & CN) Toll Free Tel: 800-638-3775 (US & CN) Fax: 410-337-8539 E-mail: custserv@brookespublishing.com Web Site: www.brookespublishing.com, pg 37

Brooks, Alicia, Jean V Naggar Literary Agency Inc (JVNLA), 216 E 75 St, Suite 1-E, New York, NY 10021 Tel: 212-794-1082 E-mail: jvnla@jvnla.com Web Site: www.jvnla.com, pg 471

Brooks, Becky, Alliance for Women in Media (AWM), 2365 Harrodsburg Rd, A325, Lexington, KY 40504 Tel: 202-750-3664 Fax: 202-750-3664 E-mail: info@allwomeninmedia.org Web Site: allwomeninmedia.org, pg 494

Brooks, Becky, The Gracies®, 2365 Harrodsburg Rd, Suite A325, Lexington, KY 40504 Tel: 202-750-3664 Fax: 202-750-3664 E-mail: info@allwomeninmedia.org Web Site: allwomeninmedia.org, pg 608

Brooks, Ben, Farrar, Straus & Giroux, LLC, 120 Broadway, New York, NY 10271 Tel: 212-741-6900 E-mail: fsg.publicity@fsgbooks.com; sales@fsgbooks.com Web Site: us.macmillan.com/fsg, pg 70

Brooks, Christine, Kent State University Press, 1118 University Library Bldg, 1125 Risman Dr, Kent, OH 44242 Tel: 330-672-7913 Fax: 330-672-3104 E-mail: ksupress@kent.edu Web Site: www.kentstateuniversitypress.com, pg 109

Brooks, Gabrielle, Alfred A Knopf, c/o Penguin Random House LLC, 1745 Broadway, New York, NY 10019 Tel: 212-751-2600 Fax: 212-940-7390 (dom rts); 212-572-2662 (foreign rts) Web Site: knopfdoubleday.com/imprint/knopf/; knopfdoubleday.com, pg 110

Brooks, Gabrielle, Knopf Doubleday Publishing Group, c/o Penguin Random House LLC, 1745 Broadway, New York, NY 10019 Tel: 212-751-2600 Fax: 212-940-7390 (dom rts); 212-572-2662 (foreign rts) Web Site: knopfdoubleday.com, pg 110

Brooks, Gabrielle, Vintage Books, c/o Penguin Random House LLC, 1745 Broadway, New York, NY 10019 Tel: 212-572-2420 Fax: 212-940-7390 (dom rts); 212-572-2662 (foreign rts) E-mail: vintageanchorpublicity@randomhouse.com Web Site: knopfdoubleday.com/imprint/vintage; knopfdoubleday.com, pg 225

Brooks, Joan, Solution Tree, 555 N Morton St, Bloomington, IN 47404 Tel: 812-336-7700 Toll Free Tel: 800-733-6786 Fax: 812-336-7790 E-mail: pubs@solutiontree.com; orders@solutiontree.com Web Site: www.solutiontree.com, pg 193

Brooks, Linda Thomas, Public Relations Society of America Inc, 120 Wall St, 21st fl, New York, NY 10005 Tel: 212-460-1400 E-mail: membership@prsa.org Web Site: www.prsa.org, pg 518

Brooks, Rachel, BookEnds Literary Agency, 136 Long Hill Rd, Gillette, NJ 07933 Web Site: www.bookendsliterary.com, pg 450

Brooks, Regina, Association of American Literary Agents Inc (AALA), 302A W 12 St, No 122, New York, NY 10014 Tel: 212-840-5770 E-mail: info@aalitagents.org Web Site: aalitagents.org, pg 498

Brooks, Susette, Penguin Random House LLC, 1745 Broadway, New York, NY 10019 Tel: 212-782-9000 Toll Free Tel: 800-726-0600 Web Site: www.penguinrandomhouse.com, pg 155

Brophy, Philippa, Sterling Lord Literistic Inc, 594 Broadway, Suite 205, New York, NY 10012 Tel: 212-780-6050 Fax: 212-780-6095 E-mail: info@sll.com Web Site: www.sll.com, pg 477

Broquet, Antoine, Broquet Inc, 97-B, Montee des Bouleaux, St-Constant, QC J5A 1A9, Canada *Tel:* 450-638-3338 *Fax:* 450-638-4338 *E-mail:* info@broquet.qc.ca *Web Site:* www.broquet.qc.ca, pg 397

Brosnan, Dr Jim, Maine Writers Conference at Ocean Park, 14 Temple Ave, Ocean Park, ME 04063 *Tel:* 401-598-1424 *E-mail:* www.opa@oceanpark.org *Web Site:* oceanpark.org, pg 556

Brosnan, Joe, Grove Atlantic Inc, 154 W 14 St, 12th fl, New York, NY 10011 *Tel:* 212-614-7850 *Toll Free Tel:* 800-521-0178 *Fax:* 212-614-7886 *E-mail:* info@groveatlantic.com; sales@groveatlantic.com; publicity@groveatlantic.com; rights@groveatlantic.com *Web Site:* www.groveatlantic.com, pg 82

Brosnan, Rosemary, HarperCollins Children's Books, 195 Broadway, New York, NY 10007 *Tel:* 212-207-7000 *Web Site:* www.harpercollins.com/childrens, pg 85

Brouckaert, Justin, Aevitas Creative Management LLC, 19 W 21 St, Suite 501, New York, NY 10010 *Tel:* 212-765-6900 *Web Site:* www.aevitascreative.com, pg 448

Broucksou, Tom, Penguin Random House LLC, 1745 Broadway, New York, NY 10019 *Tel:* 212-782-9000 *Toll Free Tel:* 800-726-0600 *Web Site:* www.penguinrandomhouse.com, pg 155

Broughton, Paul, Life Cycle Books, PO Box 799, Fort Collins, CO 80522 *Toll Free Tel:* 800-214-5849 *E-mail:* orders@lifecyclebooks.com *Web Site:* www.lifecyclebooks.com, pg 116

Broughton, Paul, Life Cycle Books Ltd, 11 Progress Ave, Unit 6, Toronto, ON M1P 4S7, Canada *E-mail:* orders@lifecyclebooks.ca; billing@lifecyclebooks.ca; support@lifecyclebooks.ca *Web Site:* www.lifecyclebooks.com, pg 412

Brouwer, Joel, University of Alabama Program in Creative Writing, PO Box 870244, Tuscaloosa, AL 35487-0244 *Tel:* 205-348-5065 *Fax:* 205-348-1388 *E-mail:* english@ua.edu *Web Site:* www.as.ua.edu/english, pg 566

Brow, Dorothy, Shambhala Publications Inc, 2129 13 St, Boulder, CO 80302 *Tel:* 978-829-2599 (intl callers) *Toll Free Tel:* 866-424-0030 (off); 888-424-2329 (orders & cust serv) *Fax:* 617-236-1563 *E-mail:* customercare@shambhala.com; royalties@shambhala.com *Web Site:* www.shambhala.com, pg 187

Brower, Kimberly, Brower Literary & Management Inc, 13720 Old St Augustine Rd, Suite 8-512, Jacksonville, FL 32258 *Tel:* 646-854-6073 *E-mail:* admin@browerliterary.com; foreign@browerliterary.com (foreign publr inquiries); queries@browerliterary.com; subrights@browerliterary.com (busn inquiries) *Web Site:* browerliterary.com, pg 452

Browler, Daryl, Rutgers University Press, 106 Somerset St, 3rd fl, New Brunswick, NJ 08901 *Tel:* 848-445-7762; 848-445-7761 (sales) *Fax:* 732-745-4935 *E-mail:* sales@rutgersuniversitypress.org *Web Site:* www.rutgersuniversitypress.org, pg 178

Brown, Alex, St Martin's Press, LLC, 120 Broadway, New York, NY 10271 *E-mail:* publicity@stmartins.com; trademarketing@stmartins.com; foreignrights@stmartins.com *Web Site:* us.macmillan.com/smp, pg 181

Brown, Alexandra, Chronicle Books LLC, 680 Second St, San Francisco, CA 94107 *Tel:* 415-537-4200 *Fax:* 415-537-4460 (perms) *E-mail:* hello@chroniclebooks.com; subrights@chroniclebooks.com *Web Site:* www.chroniclebooks.com, pg 47

Brown, Allison, HarperCollins Children's Books, 195 Broadway, New York, NY 10007 *Tel:* 212-207-7000 *Web Site:* www.harpercollins.com/childrens, pg 85

Brown, Amelia, Laura Gross Literary Agency, PO Box 610326, Newton Highlands, MA 02461 *Tel:* 617-964-2977 *E-mail:* query@lg-la.com; rights@lg-la.com *Web Site:* www.lg-la.com, pg 461

Brown, Andrea Carter, Word Works Washington Prize, PO Box 42164, Washington, DC 20015 *E-mail:* editor@wordworksbooks.org *Web Site:* www.wordworksbooks.org, pg 677

Brown, Arthur, Vandamere Press, 3580 Morris St N, St Petersburg, FL 33713 *Tel:* 727-556-0950 *Toll Free Tel:* 800-551-7776 *Fax:* 727-556-2560 *E-mail:* orders@vandamere.com *Web Site:* www.vandamere.com, pg 224

Brown, Bruce, Reporters Committee for Freedom of the Press, 1156 15 St NW, Suite 1020, Washington, DC 20005-1779 *Tel:* 202-795-9300 *Toll Free Tel:* 800-336-4243 (legal hotline for journalists) *E-mail:* info@rcfp.org *Web Site:* www.rcfp.org, pg 518

Brown, Cheri, Hackett Publishing Co Inc, 3333 Massachusetts Ave, Indianapolis, IN 46218 *Tel:* 317-635-9250 (orders & cust serv); 617-497-6303 (edit off & sales) *Fax:* 317-635-9292; 617-661-8703 (edit off) *Toll Free Fax:* 800-783-9213 *E-mail:* customer@hackettpublishing.com; editorial@hackettpublishing.com *Web Site:* www.hackettpublishing.com, pg 84

Brown, Christine, Texas A&M University Press, John H Lindsey Bldg, Lewis St, 4354 TAMU, College Station, TX 77843-4354 *Tel:* 979-845-1436 *Toll Free Tel:* 800-826-8911 (orders) *Fax:* 979-847-8752 *Toll Free Fax:* 888-617-2421 (orders) *E-mail:* bookorders@tamu.edu *Web Site:* www.tamupress.com, pg 205

Brown, Curtis, Dun & Bradstreet, 103 JFK Pkwy, Short Hills, NJ 07078 *Tel:* 973-921-5500 *Toll Free Tel:* 844-869-8244; 800-234-3867 (cust serv) *Web Site:* www.dnb.com, pg 62

Brown, Dave, Shadow Mountain Publishing, PO Box 30178, Salt Lake City, UT 84130-0178 *Tel:* 801-534-1515 *Toll Free Tel:* 800-453-3876 *E-mail:* info@shadowmountain.com; submissions@shadowmountain.com *Web Site:* shadowmountain.com, pg 187

Brown, David, Atria Books, 1230 Avenue of the Americas, New York, NY 10020 *Tel:* 212-698-7000 *Fax:* 212-698-7007 *Web Site:* www.simonandschuster.com, pg 21

Brown, Douglas R, Atlantic Publishing Group Inc, 1210 SW 23 Place, Ocala, FL 34471 *Tel:* 352-622-1825 *E-mail:* sales@atlantic-pub.com *Web Site:* www.atlantic-pub.com, pg 21

Brown, Eric, Workman Publishing, 1290 Avenue of the Americas, New York, NY 10104 *Toll Free Tel:* 800-759-0190 *Fax:* 212-364-0950 *E-mail:* workman-inquiry@hbgusa.com *Web Site:* www.hachettebookgroup.com/imprint/workman-publishing-company/, pg 233

Brown, Evan, Transatlantic Agency, 2 Bloor St E, Suite 3500, Toronto, ON M4W 1A8, Canada *Tel:* 416-488-9214 *E-mail:* info@transatlanticagency.com; royalties@transatlanticagency.com *Web Site:* www.transatlanticagency.com, pg 479

Brown, George, Intimate & Inspiring Workshops for Children's Authors & Illustrators, 814 Court St, Honesdale, PA 18431 *Tel:* 570-253-1192 *E-mail:* support@highlightsfoundation.zendesk.com *Web Site:* www.highlightsfoundation.org, pg 555

Brown, Heather, Penguin Random House Speakers Bureau, a Penguin Random House company, 1745 Broadway, Mail Drop 13-1, New York, NY 10019 *Tel:* 212-572-2013 *E-mail:* speakers@penguinrandomhouse.com *Web Site:* www.prhspeakers.com, pg 487

Brown, Janel, Macmillan, 120 Broadway, 22nd fl, New York, NY 10271 *E-mail:* press.inquiries@macmillan.com *Web Site:* us.macmillan.com, pg 122

Brown, Jennifer, Sounds True Inc, 413 S Arthur Ave, Louisville, CO 80027 *Tel:* 303-665-3151 *Toll Free Tel:* 800-333-9185 (US); 888-303-9185 (US & CN) *E-mail:* customerservice@soundstrue.com; stpublicity@soundstrue.com *Web Site:* www.soundstrue.com, pg 194

Brown, Jessie, American Council on Education (ACE), One Dupont Circle NW, Washington, DC 20036 *Tel:* 202-939-9300 *Web Site:* www.acenet.edu, pg 9, 495

Brown, Jonathan, David C Cook, 4050 Lee Vance Dr, Colorado Springs, CO 80918 *Tel:* 719-536-0100 *Toll Free Tel:* 800-323-7543 (orders & cust serv) *Toll Free Fax:* 800-430-0726 (cust serv) *E-mail:* bookstores@davidccook.org; customercare@davidccook.org *Web Site:* www.davidccook.org, pg 52

Brown, Julia, Jerome Fellowship, 2301 Franklin Ave E, Minneapolis, MN 55406-1099 *Tel:* 612-332-7481 *Fax:* 612-332-6037 *E-mail:* info@pwcenter.org *Web Site:* www.pwcenter.org, pg 618

Brown, Julia, Many Voices Fellowships & Mentorships, 2301 Franklin Ave E, Minneapolis, MN 55406-1099 *Tel:* 612-332-7481 *Fax:* 612-332-6037 *E-mail:* info@pwcenter.org *Web Site:* www.pwcenter.org, pg 629

Brown, Julia, McKnight Fellowships in Playwriting, 2301 Franklin Ave E, Minneapolis, MN 55406-1099 *Tel:* 612-332-7481 *Fax:* 612-332-6037 *E-mail:* info@pwcenter.org *Web Site:* www.pwcenter.org, pg 631

Brown, Julia, McKnight National Residency & Commission, 2301 Franklin Ave E, Minneapolis, MN 55406-1099 *Tel:* 612-332-7481 *Fax:* 612-332-6037 *E-mail:* info@pwcenter.org *Web Site:* www.pwcenter.org, pg 631

Brown, Kate, Quirk Books, 215 Church St, Philadelphia, PA 19106 *Tel:* 215-627-3581 *Fax:* 215-627-5220 *E-mail:* general@quirkbooks.com *Web Site:* www.quirkbooks.com, pg 168

Brown, Kate, Yale University Press, 302 Temple St, New Haven, CT 06511-8909 *Tel:* 203-432-0960; 203-432-0966 (sales); 401-531-2800 (cust serv) *Toll Free Tel:* 800-405-1619 (cust serv) *Fax:* 203-432-0948; 203-432-8485 (sales); 401-531-2801 (cust serv) *Toll Free Fax:* 800-406-9145 (cust serv) *E-mail:* sales.press@yale.edu (sales); customer.care@triliteral.org (cust serv) *Web Site:* www.yalebooks.com; yalepress.yale.edu/yupbooks, pg 235

Brown, Laini, Hachette Nashville, 6100 Tower Circle, Room 210, Franklin, TN 37067 *Tel:* 615-221-0996 *Fax:* 615-221-0962 *Web Site:* www.hachettebookgroup.com/imprint/hachette-nashville/, pg 83

Brown, Laura, Atria Books, 1230 Avenue of the Americas, New York, NY 10020 *Tel:* 212-698-7000 *Fax:* 212-698-7007 *Web Site:* www.simonandschuster.com, pg 21

Brown, Lucia, The Feminist Press at The City University of New York, 365 Fifth Ave, Suite 5406, New York, NY 10016 *Tel:* 212-817-7915 *Fax:* 212-817-1593 *E-mail:* info@feministpress.org *Web Site:* www.feministpress.org, pg 71

Brown, Madeleine, Sourcebooks LLC, 1935 Brookdale Rd, Suite 139, Naperville, IL 60563 *Tel:* 630-961-3900 *Toll Free Tel:* 800-432-7444 *Fax:* 630-961-2168 *E-mail:* info@sourcebooks.com *Web Site:* www.sourcebooks.com, pg 195

Brown, Marian, Henry Holt and Company, LLC, 120 Broadway, 23rd fl, New York, NY 10271 *Tel:* 646-307-5151 *Toll Free Tel:* 888-330-8477 (orders) *Fax:* 646-307-5285 *Web Site:* www.henryholt.com, pg 94

Brown, Marie D, Marie Brown Associates, 412 W 154 St, New York, NY 10032 *Tel:* 212-939-9725 *E-mail:* mbrownlit@gmail.com, pg 452

Brown, Marissa, Pippin Properties Inc, 110 W 40 St, Suite 1704, New York, NY 10018 *Tel:* 212-338-9310 *E-mail:* info@pippinproperties.com *Web Site:* www.pippinproperties.com; www.facebook.com/pippinproperties, pg 472

Brown, Mark, Beacon Hill Press of Kansas City, PO Box 419527, Kansas City, MO 64141 *Tel:* 816-931-1900 *Toll Free Tel:* 800-877-0700 (cust serv) *Fax:* 816-531-0923 *Toll Free Fax:* 800-849-9827 *E-mail:* orders@thefoundrypublishing.com; customercare@thefoundrypublishing.com *Web Site:* www.thefoundrypublishing.com, pg 25

Brown, Marty, Oregon State University Press, 121 The Valley Library, Corvallis, OR 97331-4501 *Tel:* 541-737-3166, pg 147

Brown, Merle, Harry N Abrams Inc, 195 Broadway, 9th fl, New York, NY 10007 *Tel:* 212-206-7715 *Toll Free Tel:* 800-345-1359 *Fax:* 212-645-8437

E-mail: abrams@abramsbooks.com; publicity@abramsbooks.com; sales@abramsbooks.com Web Site: www.abramsbooks.com, pg 2

Brown, Milena, Doubleday, c/o Penguin Random House LLC, 1745 Broadway, New York, NY 10019 Tel: 212-751-2600 Fax: 212-940-7390 (dom rts); 212-572-2662 (foreign rts) Web Site: knopfdoubleday.com/imprint/doubleday/; knopfdoubleday.com, pg 61

Brown, Milli, Brown Books Publishing Group (BBPG), 16250 Knoll Trail, Suite 205, Dallas, TX 75248 Tel: 972-381-0009 E-mail: publishing@brownbooks.com Web Site: www.brownbooks.com, pg 38

Brown, Richard, Rowman & Littlefield, 4501 Forbes Blvd, Suite 200, Lanham, MD 20706 Tel: 301-459-3366 Toll Free Tel: 800-462-6420 (ext 3024, cust serv) Fax: 301-429-5748 Web Site: rowman.com, pg 178

Brown, Robert, Farrar, Straus & Giroux Books for Young Readers, 120 Broadway, New York, NY 10271 Tel: 212-741-6900 Toll Free Tel: 888-330-8477 (orders) E-mail: childrens.publicity@macmillanusa.com; childrensrights@macmillanusa.com Web Site: us.macmillan.com/mackids, pg 70

Brown, Robert, Roaring Brook Press, 120 Broadway, New York, NY 10271 Tel: 646-307-5151 Web Site: us.macmillan.com/publishers/roaring-brook-press, pg 176

Brown, Rose, Clerical Plus, 97 Blueberry Lane, Shelton, CT 06484 Tel: 203-225-0879 Fax: 203-225-0879 E-mail: clericalplus@aol.com, pg 437

Brown, Sally, Library of American Broadcasting (LAB), University of Maryland, Hornbake Library, College Park, MD 20742 Web Site: exhibitions.lib.umd.edu/libraryofamericanbroadcasting, pg 509

Brown, Samantha Ruth, HarperCollins Children's Books, 195 Broadway, New York, NY 10007 Tel: 212-207-7000 Web Site: www.harpercollins.com/childrens, pg 85

Brown, Sass, Marfield Prize, 2017 "I" St NW, Washington, DC 20006-1804 E-mail: award@artsclubofwashington.org Web Site: artsclubofwashington.org/awards, pg 629

Brown, Sherri L, Atlantic Publishing Group Inc, 1210 SW 23 Place, Ocala, FL 34471 Tel: 352-622-1825 E-mail: sales@atlantic-pub.com Web Site: www.atlantic-pub.com, pg 21

Brown, Stephanie, Vandamere Press, 3580 Morris St N, St Petersburg, FL 33713 Tel: 727-556-0950 Toll Free Tel: 800-551-7776 Fax: 727-556-2560 E-mail: orders@vandamere.com Web Site: www.vandamere.com, pg 224

Brown, Steven, Nelson Education Ltd, 1120 Birchmount Rd, Scarborough, ON M1K 5G4, Canada Tel: 416-752-9448 Toll Free Tel: 800-268-2222 (cust serv) Fax: 416-752-9646 E-mail: peopleengagement@nelson.com Web Site: www.nelson.com, pg 413

Brown, Tammy, Society of Children's Book Writers & Illustrators (SCBWI), 6363 Wilshire Blvd, Suite 425, Los Angeles, CA 90048 Tel: 323-782-1010 E-mail: membership@scbwi.org Web Site: www.scbwi.org, pg 520

Brown, Therese, Association of Catholic Publishers Inc, 4725 Dorsey Hall Dr, Suite A, PMB 709, Ellicott City, MD 21042 Tel: 410-988-2926 Fax: 410-571-4946 E-mail: info@catholicpublishers.org Web Site: catholicsread.org; www.catholicpublishers.org; www.midatlanticcongress.org, pg 499

Brown, William, James Lorimer & Co Ltd, Publishers, 117 Peter St, Suite 304, Toronto, ON M5V 0M3, Canada Tel: 416-362-4762 Fax: 416-362-3939 E-mail: sales@lorimer.ca; promotion@lorimer.ca; rights@lorimer.ca Web Site: www.lorimer.ca, pg 412

Brownderville, Greg, John H McGinnis Memorial Award, PO Box 750374, Dallas, TX 75275-0374 Fax: 214-768-1408 E-mail: swr@mail.smu.edu Web Site: southwestreview.com, pg 630

Brownderville, Greg, Elizabeth Matchett Stover Memorial Award, PO Box 750374, Dallas, TX 75275-0374 Fax: 214-768-1408 E-mail: swr@mail.smu.edu Web Site: southwestreview.com, pg 667

Browne, Anne, Scholastic Canada Ltd, 175 Hillmount Rd, Markham, ON L6C 1Z7, Canada Tel: 905-887-7323 Toll Free Tel: 800-268-3860 (CN) Toll Free Fax: 800-387-4944 E-mail: custserve@scholastic.ca Web Site: www.scholastic.ca, pg 418

Browne, Dylan, Penguin Random House Canada, a Penguin Random House company, 320 Front St W, Suite 1400, Toronto, ON M5V 3B6, Canada Tel: 416-364-4449 Toll Free Tel: 888-523-9292 (cust serv) E-mail: canadaweb@penguinrandomhouse.com; customerservicescanada@penguinrandomhouse.com Web Site: www.penguinrandomhouse.ca, pg 416

Browne, Jennifer, Holiday House Publishing Inc, 50 Broad St, New York, NY 10004 Tel: 212-688-0085 Fax: 212-421-6134 E-mail: info@holidayhouse.com Web Site: www.holidayhouse.com, pg 94

Browne, Jennifer, Peachtree Publishing Co Inc, 1700 Chattahoochee Ave, Atlanta, GA 30318-2112 Tel: 404-876-8761 Toll Free Tel: 800-241-0113 Fax: 404-875-2578 Toll Free Fax: 800-875-8909 E-mail: hello@peachtree-online.com; orders@peachtree-online.com; sales@peachtree-online.com Web Site: www.peachtreebooks.com; www.peachtree-online.com, pg 153

Browne, Renni, The Editorial Department LLC, 8476 E Speedway Blvd, Suite 202, Tucson, AZ 85710 Tel: 520-546-9992 E-mail: admin@editorialdepartment.com Web Site: www.editorialdepartment.com, pg 438

Browne, Ross, The Editorial Department LLC, 8476 E Speedway Blvd, Suite 202, Tucson, AZ 85710 Tel: 520-546-9992 E-mail: admin@editorialdepartment.com Web Site: www.editorialdepartment.com, pg 438

Brownfield, Renee, National Association of Insurance Commissioners, 1100 Walnut St, Suite 1500, Kansas City, MO 64106-2197 Tel: 816-842-3600 Fax: 816-783-8175 E-mail: prodserv@naic.org Web Site: www.naic.org, pg 136

Brownoff, Alan, University of Alberta Press, Ring House 2, Edmonton, AB T6G 2E1, Canada Tel: 780-492-3662 Fax: 780-492-0719 Web Site: www.uap.ualberta.ca, pg 421

Bruce, Alison, Crime Writers of Canada (CWC), 4C-240 Westwood Rd, Guelph, ON N1H 7W9, Canada E-mail: info@crimewriterscanada.com Web Site: www.crimewriterscanada.com, pg 504

Bruce, Alison, Crime Writers of Canada Awards of Excellence, 716 Thicket Way, Ottawa, ON K4A 3B5, Canada E-mail: awards@crimewriterscanada.com Web Site: www.crimewriterscanada.com/awards, pg 593

Bruce, Alison, Grand Master Award, 716 Thicket Way, Ottawa, ON K4A 3B5, Canada E-mail: info@crimewriterscanada.com Web Site: www.crimewriterscanada.com/awards, pg 608

Bruce, Alison, Derrick Murdoch Award, 716 Thicket Way, Ottawa, ON K4A 3B5, Canada E-mail: info@crimewriterscanada.com Web Site: www.crimewriterscanada.com/awards, pg 636

Bruce, Emily, DK, c/o Penguin Random House LLC, 1745 Broadway, 20th fl, New York, NY 10019 Tel: 646-674-4000 Toll Free Tel: 800-733-3000 Fax: 646-674-4020 E-mail: marketing@dk.com (lib servs); publicity@dk.com; csorders@penguinrandomhouse.com; customerservice@penguinrandomhouse.com Web Site: www.dk.com, pg 60

Bruce, Emily, Random House Children's Books, c/o Penguin Random House LLC, 1745 Broadway, New York, NY 10019 Tel: 212-782-9000 Web Site: www.rhcbooks.com, pg 169

Bruce, Kesha, Artist Research & Development Grants, 417 W Roosevelt St, Phoenix, AZ 85003-1326 Tel: 602-771-6501 Fax: 602-256-0282 E-mail: info@azarts.gov Web Site: azarts.gov/grant/artist-research-and-development, pg 574

Bruce, Sandra, Milady, 5191 Natorp Blvd, Mason, OH 45040 Toll Free Tel: 866-848-5143 Fax: 518-373-6309 E-mail: info@milady.com Web Site: www.milady.com, pg 131

Bruce-Eddings, Carla, Random House Publishing Group, 1745 Broadway, New York, NY 10019 Toll Free Tel: 800-200-3552 Web Site: www.randomhousebooks.com, pg 171

Bruch, Kristine, The Ridenhour Book Prize, 116 E 16 St, 8th fl, New York, NY 10003 Tel: 212-822-0250 Fax: 212-253-5356 E-mail: ridenhour@typemediacenter.org; admin@ridenhour.org Web Site: www.ridenhour.org, pg 656

Bruch, Kristine, The Ridenhour Courage Prize, 116 E 16 St, 8th fl, New York, NY 10003 Tel: 212-822-0250 Fax: 212-253-5356 E-mail: ridenhour@typemediacenter.org; admin@ridenhour.org Web Site: www.ridenhour.org, pg 656

Bruch, Kristine, The Ridenhour Prize for Truth-Telling, 116 E 16 St, 8th fl, New York, NY 10003 Tel: 212-822-0250 Fax: 212-253-5356 E-mail: ridenhour@typemediacenter.org; admin@ridenhour.org Web Site: www.ridenhour.org, pg 656

Bruckman, Nancy, Candlewick Press, 99 Dover St, Somerville, MA 02144-2825 Tel: 617-661-3330 Fax: 617-661-0565 E-mail: bigbear@candlewick.com; salesinfo@candlewick.com Web Site: candlewick.com, pg 40

Bruder, Mikyla, Chronicle Books LLC, 680 Second St, San Francisco, CA 94107 Tel: 415-537-4200 Fax: 415-537-4460 (perms) E-mail: hello@chroniclebooks.com; subrights@chroniclebooks.com Web Site: www.chroniclebooks.com, pg 47

Brugger, Deborah, St Johann Press, 315 Schraalenburgh Rd, Haworth, NJ 07641 Tel: 201-387-1529 Fax: 201-501-0698 Web Site: www.stjohannpress.com, pg 180

Brule, Micheline, Prix Alvine-Belisle, 2065 rue Parthenais, Bureau 387, Montreal, QC H2K 3T1, Canada Tel: 514-281-5012 E-mail: info@fmdoc.org Web Site: www.fmdoc.org/activities/prix-alvine-belisle, pg 572

Brule, Micheline, Les Editions ASTED, 2065 rue Parthenais, Bureau 387, Montreal, QC H2K 3T1, Canada Tel: 514-281-5012 Fax: 514-281-8219 E-mail: editions@asted.org; info@asted.org Web Site: www.asted.org, pg 401

Brule, Micheline, Federation des Milieux Documentaires, 2065 rue Parthenais, Bureau 387, Montreal, QC H2K 3T1, Canada Tel: 514-281-5012 E-mail: info@fmdoc.org Web Site: fmdoc.org, pg 505

Brumley, Mark, Ignatius Press, 1348 Tenth Ave, San Francisco, CA 94122-2304 Toll Free Tel: 800-651-1531 (orders); 888-615-3186 (cust serv) Fax: 415-387-0896 E-mail: info@ignatius.com Web Site: www.ignatius.com, pg 98

Brumwell, Barbara, LexisNexis® Canada Inc, 111 Gordon Baker Rd, Suite 900, Toronto, ON M2H 3R1, Canada Tel: 905-479-2665 Toll Free Tel: 800-668-6481; 800-387-0899 (cust care); 800-255-5174 (sales) E-mail: service@lexisnexis.ca (cust serv); sales@lexisnexis.ca Web Site: www.lexisnexis.ca, pg 411

Brunn, Jennifer, DK, c/o Penguin Random House LLC, 1745 Broadway, 20th fl, New York, NY 10019 Tel: 646-674-4000 Toll Free Tel: 800-733-3000 Fax: 646-674-4020 E-mail: marketing@dk.com (lib servs); publicity@dk.com; csorders@penguinrandomhouse.com; customerservice@penguinrandomhouse.com Web Site: www.dk.com, pg 60

Brunnhuber, Mackenzie, Eisenbrauns, 820 N University Dr, USB 1, Suite C, University Park, PA 16802-1003 Tel: 814-865-1327 Toll Free Tel: 800-326-9180 (orders & cust serv) Fax: 814-863-1408 Toll Free Fax: 877-778-2665 (orders) E-mail: orders@psupress.org; customerservice@psupress.org Web Site: www.eisenbrauns.org, pg 65

Bruno, Matthew, National Paper Trade Association (NPTA), 330 N Wabash Ave, Suite 2000, Chicago, IL 60611 Tel: 312-321-4092 Toll Free Tel: 800-355-NPTA (355-6782) Fax: 312-673-6736 Web Site: www.gonpta.com, pg 513

Brunsek, Judy, Owlkids Books Inc, 10 Lower Spadina Ave, Suite 400, Toronto, ON M5V 2Z2, Canada *Tel:* 416-340-2700 *Fax:* 416-340-9769 *E-mail:* owlkids@owlkids.com *Web Site:* www.owlkidsbooks.com, pg 415

Bruscia, Kenneth E, Barcelona Publishers LLC, 10231 N Plano Rd, Dallas, TX 75238 *Tel:* 214-553-9785 *E-mail:* warehouse@barcelonapublishers.com *Web Site:* www.barcelonapublishers.com, pg 24

Brussel, Gail, Penguin Press, c/o Penguin Random House LLC, 1745 Broadway, New York, NY 10019 *Tel:* 212-782-9000 *E-mail:* penguinpress@penguinrandomhouse.com *Web Site:* www.penguin.com/penguin-press-overview/, pg 154

Brutus, Rebecca, Cornell University Press, Sage House, 512 E State St, Ithaca, NY 14850 *Tel:* 607-253-2338 *E-mail:* cupressinfo@cornell.edu; cupress-sales@cornell.edu; cupress-perms@cornell.edu (reprint/class use permissions) *Web Site:* www.cornellpress.cornell.edu, pg 52

Bryan, Heather, Nimbus Publishing Ltd, 3660 Strawberry Hill, Halifax, NS B3K 5A9, Canada *Tel:* 902-455-4286 *Toll Free Tel:* 800-NIMBUS9 (646-2879) *Fax:* 902-455-5440 *Toll Free Fax:* 888-253-3133 *E-mail:* customerservice@nimbus.ca *Web Site:* www.nimbus.ca, pg 414

Bryan, Nancy, University of Texas Press, 3001 Lake Austin Blvd, 2.200, Austin, TX 78703 *Tel:* 512-471-7233 *Fax:* 512-232-7178 *E-mail:* utpress@uts.cc.utexas.edu; info@utpress.utexas.edu *Web Site:* utpress.utexas.edu, pg 205

Bryant, Kim, The University of North Carolina Press, 116 S Boundary St, Chapel Hill, NC 27514-3808 *Tel:* 919-966-3561; 919-966-7449 (orders) *Toll Free Tel:* 800-848-3224 (orders) *Fax:* 919-962-2704 (orders) *Toll Free Fax:* 800-272-6817 (orders) *E-mail:* uncpress@unc.edu *Web Site:* uncpress.org, pg 218

Bryant, L J, Wildflower Press, c/o Oakbrook Press, 3301 S Valley Dr, Rapid City, SD 57703 *Tel:* 605-381-6385 *E-mail:* info@wildflowerpress.org *Web Site:* www.wildflowerpress.org, pg 229

Bryant, Travis, Menasha Ridge Press, 2204 First Ave S, Suite 102, Birmingham, AL 35233 *Toll Free Tel:* 888-604-4537 *Fax:* 205-326-1012 *E-mail:* info@adventurewithkeen.com *Web Site:* www.menasharidge.com; www.adventurewithkeen.com, pg 129

Bryant, Virginia Veiga, Georgetown University Press, 3520 Prospect St NW, Suite 140, Washington, DC 20007 *Tel:* 202-687-5889 (busn) *Fax:* 202-687-6340 (edit) *E-mail:* gupress@georgetown.edu *Web Site:* press.georgetown.edu, pg 77

Bryniarski, Ali, Creative Editions, 2140 Howard Dr W, North Mankato, MN 56003 *Tel:* 507-388-6273 *Toll Free Tel:* 800-445-6209 *Fax:* 507-388-2746 *E-mail:* info@thecreativecompany.us; orders@thecreativecompany.us *Web Site:* www.thecreativecompany.us, pg 55

Bucaria, Catherine, Penguin Random House Audio Publishing Group, 1745 Broadway, New York, NY 10019 *Toll Free Tel:* 800-793-2665 (cust serv) *E-mail:* audio@penguinrandomhouse.com; ecustomerservice@penguinrandomhouse.com *Web Site:* www.penguinrandomhouseaudio.com, pg 154

Bucca, Lauren, Princeton University Press, 41 William St, Princeton, NJ 08540-5237 *Tel:* 609-258-4900 *Fax:* 609-258-6305 *E-mail:* info@press.princeton.edu *Web Site:* press.princeton.edu, pg 164

Bucci, Chris, Aevitas Creative Management LLC, 19 W 21 St, Suite 501, New York, NY 10010 *Tel:* 212-765-6900 *Web Site:* www.aevitascreative.com, pg 448

Bucci, Martha, Quarto Publishing Group USA Inc, 100 Cummings Ctr, Suite 265D, Beverly, MA 01915 *Tel:* 978-282-9590 *Toll Free Tel:* 800-328-0590 (sales) *Fax:* 978-283-2742 *E-mail:* sales@quartous.com *Web Site:* www.quartoknows.com, pg 168

Buchanan, Amy Ruth, Duke University Press, 905 W Main St, Suite 18B, Durham, NC 27701 *Tel:* 919-688-5134 *Toll Free Tel:* 888-651-0122 (US) *Fax:* 919-688-2615 *Toll Free Fax:* 888-651-0124 *E-mail:* orders@dukeupress.edu *Web Site:* www.dukeupress.edu, pg 62

Buchanan, Matt, Tanglewood Publishing, 1060 N Capitol Ave, Suite E-395, Indianapolis, IN 46204 *Tel:* 812-877-9488 *Toll Free Tel:* 800-788-3123 (orders) *E-mail:* info@tanglewoodbooks.com; orders@tanglewoodbooks.com; submission@tanglewoodbooks.com *Web Site:* www.tanglewoodbooks.com, pg 202

Buchanan, Melissa, University of Georgia Press, Main Library, 3rd fl, 320 S Jackson St, Athens, GA 30602 *Fax:* 706-542-2558; 706-542-6770 *Web Site:* www.ugapress.org, pg 216

Buchwald, Don, Buchwald, 10 E 44 St, New York, NY 10017 *Tel:* 212-867-1200 *E-mail:* info@buchwald.com *Web Site:* www.buchwald.com, pg 453

Buckell, Tobias S, Science Fiction and Fantasy Writers Association, Inc (SFWA), PO Box 215, San Lorenzo, CA 94580 *Tel:* 860-698-0536 *E-mail:* office@sfwa.org; operations@sfwa.org *Web Site:* www.sfwa.org, pg 519

Buckell, Tobias S, SFWA Nebula Awards, PO Box 215, San Lorenzo, CA 94580 *Tel:* 860-698-0536 *E-mail:* office@sfwa.org; operations@sfwa.org *Web Site:* www.sfwa.org, pg 661

Buckles, Kristen, The University of Arizona Press, 1510 E University Blvd, Tucson, AZ 85721 *Tel:* 520-621-1441 *Toll Free Tel:* 800-621-2736 (orders) *Fax:* 520-621-8899 *Toll Free Fax:* 800-621-8476 (orders) *E-mail:* uap@uapress.arizona.edu *Web Site:* www.uapress.arizona.edu, pg 214

Buckley, Carol, Piano Press, 1425 Ocean Ave, Suite 5, Del Mar, CA 92014 *Tel:* 619-884-1401 *E-mail:* pianopress@pianopress.com *Web Site:* www.pianopress.com, pg 159

Buckley, Kerri, Dreamscape Media LLC, 1417 Timberwolf Dr, Holland, OH 43528 *Tel:* 419-867-6965 *Toll Free Tel:* 877-983-7326 *E-mail:* info@dreamscapeab.com *Web Site:* www.dreamscapepublishing.com, pg 62

Buckner, Richard E, Beacon Hill Press of Kansas City, PO Box 419527, Kansas City, MO 64141 *Tel:* 816-931-1900 *Toll Free Tel:* 800-877-0700 (cust serv) *Fax:* 816-531-0923 *Toll Free Fax:* 800-849-9827 *E-mail:* orders@thefoundrypublishing.com; customercare@thefoundrypublishing.com *Web Site:* www.thefoundrypublishing.com, pg 25

Budak, Melissa, Liturgy Training Publications, 3949 S Racine Ave, Chicago, IL 60609-2523 *Tel:* 773-579-4900 *Toll Free Tel:* 800-933-1800 (US & CN only orders) *Fax:* 773-579-4929 *E-mail:* orders@ltp.org *Web Site:* www.ltp.org, pg 119

Budde, Mark, Carolrhoda Books Inc, 241 First Ave N, Minneapolis, MN 55401 *Tel:* 612-332-3344 *Toll Free Tel:* 800-328-4929 *Fax:* 612-332-7615 *Toll Free Fax:* 800-332-1132 *E-mail:* info@lernerbooks.com; custserve@lernerbooks.com *Web Site:* www.lernerbooks.com; www.facebook.com/lernerbooks, pg 41

Budde, Mark, Carolrhoda Lab™, 241 First Ave N, Minneapolis, MN 55401 *Tel:* 612-332-3344 *Toll Free Tel:* 800-328-4929 *Fax:* 612-332-7615 *Toll Free Fax:* 800-332-1132 *E-mail:* info@lernerbooks.com; custserve@lernerbooks.com *Web Site:* www.lernerbooks.com; www.facebook.com/lernerbooks, pg 41

Budde, Mark, ediciones Lerner, 241 First Ave N, Minneapolis, MN 55401 *Tel:* 612-332-3344 *Toll Free Tel:* 800-328-4929 *Fax:* 612-332-7615 *Toll Free Fax:* 800-332-1132 *E-mail:* info@lernerbooks.com; custserve@lernerbooks.com *Web Site:* www.lernerbooks.com; www.facebook.com/lernerbooks, pg 63

Budde, Mark, First Avenue Editions, 241 First Ave N, Minneapolis, MN 55401 *Tel:* 612-332-3344 *Toll Free Tel:* 800-328-4929 *Fax:* 612-332-7615 *Toll Free Fax:* 800-332-1132 *E-mail:* info@lernerbooks.com; custserve@lernerbooks.com *Web Site:* www.lernerbooks.com; www.facebook.com/lernerbooks, pg 72

Budde, Mark, Graphic Universe™, 241 First Ave N, Minneapolis, MN 55401 *Tel:* 612-332-3344 *Toll Free Tel:* 800-328-4929 *Fax:* 612-332-7615 *Toll Free Fax:* 800-332-1132 *E-mail:* info@lernerbooks.com; custserve@lernerbooks.com *Web Site:* www.lernerbooks.com; www.facebook.com/lernerbooks, pg 80

Budde, Mark, Lerner Publications, 241 First Ave N, Minneapolis, MN 55401 *Tel:* 612-332-3344 *Toll Free Tel:* 800-328-4929 *Fax:* 612-332-7615 *Toll Free Fax:* 800-332-1132 *E-mail:* info@lernerbooks.com; custserve@lernerbooks.com *Web Site:* www.lernerbooks.com; www.facebook.com/lernerbooks, pg 115

Budde, Mark, Lerner Publishing Group Inc, 241 First Ave N, Minneapolis, MN 55401 *Tel:* 612-332-3344 *Toll Free Tel:* 800-328-4929 *Fax:* 612-332-7615 *Toll Free Fax:* 800-332-1132 *E-mail:* info@lernerbooks.com; custserve@lernerbooks.com *Web Site:* www.lernerbooks.com; www.facebook.com/lernerbooks, pg 115

Budde, Mark, LernerClassroom, 241 First Ave N, Minneapolis, MN 55401 *Tel:* 612-332-3344 *Toll Free Tel:* 800-328-4929 *Fax:* 612-332-7615 *Toll Free Fax:* 800-332-1132 *E-mail:* info@lernerbooks.com; custserve@lernerbooks.com *Web Site:* www.lernerbooks.com; www.facebook.com/lernerbooks, pg 115

Budde, Mark, Millbrook Press, 241 First Ave N, Minneapolis, MN 55401 *Tel:* 612-332-3344 *Toll Free Tel:* 800-328-4929 *Fax:* 612-332-7615 *Toll Free Fax:* 800-332-1132 *E-mail:* info@lernerbooks.com; custserve@lernerbooks.com *Web Site:* www.lernerbooks.com; www.facebook.com/millbrookpress, pg 131

Budde, Mark, Twenty-First Century Books, 241 First Ave N, Minneapolis, MN 55401 *Tel:* 612-332-3344 *Toll Free Tel:* 800-328-4929 *Fax:* 612-332-7615 *Toll Free Fax:* 800-332-1132 *E-mail:* info@lernerbooks.com; custserve@lernerbooks.com *Web Site:* www.lernerbooks.com; www.facebook.com/lernerbooks, pg 211

Budde, Mark, Zest Books, 241 First Ave N, Minneapolis, MN 55401 *Tel:* 612-332-3344 *Toll Free Tel:* 800-328-4929 *Toll Free Fax:* 800-332-1132 *E-mail:* info@lernerbooks.com; publicity@lernerbooks.com; custserve@lernerbooks.com (orders) *Web Site:* lernerbooks.com, pg 236

Budhu, Adrian, Theatre Communications Group, 520 Eighth Ave, 24th fl, New York, NY 10018-4156 *Tel:* 212-609-5900 *Fax:* 212-609-5901 *E-mail:* info@tcg.org *Web Site:* www.tcg.org, pg 206

Bugler, Beth, The Experiment, 220 E 23 St, Suite 600, New York, NY 10010-4658 *Tel:* 212-889-1659 *E-mail:* info@theexperimentpublishing.com *Web Site:* www.theexperimentpublishing.com, pg 68

Bui, Sr Maria Kim-Ngan, Pauline Books & Media, 50 Saint Paul's Ave, Boston, MA 02130 *Tel:* 617-522-8911 *Toll Free Tel:* 800-876-4463 (orders); 800-836-9723 (cust serv) *Fax:* 617-541-9805 *E-mail:* editorial@paulinemedia.com (ms submissions); orderentry@pauline.org (cust serv) *Web Site:* www.pauline.org/pbmpublishing, pg 152

Buis, Micah, Harvard Art Museums, 32 Quincy St, Cambridge, MA 02138 *Tel:* 617-495-9400 *Web Site:* www.harvardartmuseums.org, pg 87

Bukowski, Danielle, Sterling Lord Literistic Inc, 594 Broadway, Suite 205, New York, NY 10012 *Tel:* 212-780-6050 *Fax:* 212-780-6095 *E-mail:* info@sll.com *Web Site:* www.sll.com, pg 477

Bukowski, Denise, The Bukowski Agency Ltd, 20 Prince Arthur Ave, Suite 12-I, Toronto, ON M5R 1B1, Canada *Tel:* 416-928-6728 *Fax:* 416-963-9978 *E-mail:* info@bukowskiagency.com *Web Site:* www.bukowskiagency.com, pg 453

Bulger, Joe, Simon & Schuster, LLC, 1230 Avenue of the Americas, New York, NY 10020 *Tel:* 212-698-7000 *Toll Free Tel:* 800-223-2336 (orders) *Fax:* 212-698-7007 *Toll Free Fax:* 800-943-9831 (orders)

Bulger, Terrilee, Nimbus Publishing Ltd, 3660 Strawberry Hill, Halifax, NS B3K 5A9, Canada *Tel:* 902-455-4286 *Toll Free Tel:* 800-NIMBUS9 (646-2879) *Fax:* 902-455-5440 *Toll Free Fax:* 888-253-3133 *E-mail:* customerservice@nimbus.ca *Web Site:* www.nimbus.ca, pg 414

Bull, James, Bull Publishing Co, PO Box 1377, Boulder, CO 80306 *Tel:* 303-545-6350 *Toll Free Tel:* 800-676-2855 *E-mail:* sales@bullpub.com *Web Site:* www.bullpub.com, pg 38

Bullard, Tiffany, The Seymour Agency, 475 Miner Street Rd, Canton, NY 13617 *Tel:* 239-398-8209 *Web Site:* www.theseymouragency.com, pg 475

Buller, Bob, SBL Press, The Luce Ctr, Suite 350, 825 Houston Mill Rd, Atlanta, GA 30329 *Tel:* 404-727-3100 *Fax:* 404-727-3101 (corp) *E-mail:* sbl@sbl-site.org *Web Site:* www.sbl-site.org, pg 183

Bullett, Alexander, Chelsea Green Publishing Co, 85 N Main St, Suite 120, White River Junction, VT 05001 *Tel:* 802-295-6300 *Toll Free Tel:* 800-639-4099 (cust serv & orders) *Fax:* 802-295-6444 *E-mail:* customerservice@chelseagreen.com; editorial@chelseagreen.com; publicity@chelseagreen.com; rights@chelseagreen.com *Web Site:* www.chelseagreen.com, pg 45

Bultman, Gail, Redleaf Press®, 10 Yorkton Ct, St Paul, MN 55117 *Tel:* 651-641-0508 *Toll Free Tel:* 800-423-8309 *Fax:* 651-641-0115 *E-mail:* customerservice@redleafpress.org; info@redleafpress.org; marketing@redleafpress.org *Web Site:* www.redleafpress.org, pg 173

Bumps, Susan, North Atlantic Books (NAB), 2526 Martin Luther King Jr Way, Berkeley, CA 94704 *Tel:* 510-549-4270 *Web Site:* www.northatlanticbooks.com, pg 142

Bunch, Cindy, InterVarsity Press, 430 Plaza Dr, Westmont, IL 60559-1234 *Tel:* 630-734-4000 *Toll Free Tel:* 800-843-9487 *Fax:* 630-734-4200 *E-mail:* email@ivpress.com *Web Site:* www.ivpress.com, pg 104

Bunker, Jane, Cornell University Press, Sage House, 512 E State St, Ithaca, NY 14850 *Tel:* 607-253-2338 *E-mail:* cupressinfo@cornell.edu; cupress-sales@cornell.edu; cupress-perms@cornell.edu (reprint/class use permissions) *Web Site:* www.cornellpress.cornell.edu, pg 52

Bunzel, Mark, FineEdge.com LLC, 910 25 St, Unit B, Anacortes, WA 98221 *Tel:* 360-299-8500 *Fax:* 360-299-0535 *E-mail:* orders@fineedge.com; info@waggonerguide.com *Web Site:* www.waggonerguidebooks.com; waggonerguide.com, pg 72

Burch, Ciera, HarperCollins Children's Books, 195 Broadway, New York, NY 10007 *Tel:* 212-207-7000 *Web Site:* www.harpercollins.com/childrens, pg 85

Burch, Martin, Ocean Tree Books, 1325 Cerro Gordo Rd, Santa Fe, NM 87501 *Tel:* 505-983-1412 *Fax:* 505-983-0899 *E-mail:* richard@oceantree.com *Web Site:* www.oceantree.com, pg 145

Burcher, Jessica, ECS Publishing Group, 1727 Larkin Williams Rd, Fenton, MO 63026 *Tel:* 636-305-0100 *Toll Free Tel:* 800-647-2117 *Web Site:* ecspublishing.com; www.facebook.com/ecspublishing, pg 63

Burczyk, Monika, Millay Colony for the Arts Residency, 454 E Hill Rd, Austerlitz, NY 12017 *Tel:* 518-392-3103 *E-mail:* apply@millaycolony.org; residency@millaycolony.org *Web Site:* www.millaycolony.org, pg 633

Burdette, Mathew, Penguin Random House LLC, 1745 Broadway, New York, NY 10019 *Tel:* 212-782-9000 *Toll Free Tel:* 800-726-0600 *Web Site:* www.penguinrandomhouse.com, pg 155

Bures, Brooke, Hamilton Books, 4501 Forbes Blvd, Suite 200, Lanham, MD 20706 *Tel:* 301-459-3366 *Toll Free Tel:* 800-462-6420 (cust serv) *Fax:* 301-429-5748 *Toll Free Fax:* 800-388-4550 (cust serv), pg 84

Burfield, Maria, Jane Rotrosen Agency LLC, 318 E 51 St, New York, NY 10022-7803 *Tel:* 212-593-4330 *E-mail:* info@janerotrosen.com *Web Site:* janerotrosen.com, pg 474

Burford, Peter, Burford Books, 101 E State St, No 301, Ithaca, NY 14850 *Tel:* 607-319-4373 *Fax:* 607-319-4373 *Toll Free Fax:* 866-212-7750 *E-mail:* info@burfordbooks.com *Web Site:* www.burfordbooks.com, pg 38

Burgener, Kathleen, Human Kinetics Inc, 1607 N Market St, Champaign, IL 61820 *Tel:* 217-351-5076 *Toll Free Tel:* 800-747-4457 *Fax:* 217-351-1549 (orders/cust serv) *E-mail:* info@hkusa.com *Web Site:* us.humankinetics.com, pg 97

Burgess, Grace, Ozark Mountain Publishing Inc, PO Box 754, Huntsville, AR 72740-0754 *Tel:* 479-738-2348 *Toll Free Tel:* 800-935-0045 *Fax:* 479-738-2448 *E-mail:* info@ozarkmt.com *Web Site:* www.ozarkmt.com, pg 149

Burgess, Kathy, University Press of Mississippi, 3825 Ridgewood Rd, Jackson, MS 39211-6492 *Tel:* 601-432-6205 *Toll Free Tel:* 800-737-7788 (orders & cust serv) *Fax:* 601-432-6217 *E-mail:* press@mississippi.edu *Web Site:* www.upress.state.ms.us, pg 222

Burgess, Olenka, Counterpoint Press LLC, 2560 Ninth St, Suite 318, Berkeley, CA 94710 *Tel:* 510-704-0230 *Fax:* 510-704-0268 *E-mail:* info@counterpointpress.com *Web Site:* counterpointpress.com; softskull.com, pg 54

Burghardt, Jordan, Special Libraries Association (SLA), 7918 Jones Branch Dr, Suite 300, McLean, VA 22102 *Tel:* 703-647-4900 *Fax:* 703-506-3266 *E-mail:* info@sla.org *Web Site:* www.sla.org, pg 520

Burk, Dale A, Stoneydale Press Publishing Co, 523 Main St, Stevensville, MT 59870-2839 *Tel:* 406-777-2729 *Toll Free Tel:* 800-735-7006 *Fax:* 406-777-2521 *E-mail:* stoneydale@stoneydale.com *Web Site:* www.stoneydale.com, pg 199

Burke, Aliya, Insight Editions, 800 "A" St, San Rafael, CA 94901 *Tel:* 415-526-1370 *Toll Free Tel:* 800-809-3792 *Toll Free Fax:* 866-509-0515 *E-mail:* info@insighteditions.com; marketing@insighteditions.com *Web Site:* insighteditions.com, pg 101

Burke, Colleen, Binghamton University Creative Writing Program, c/o Dept of English, General Literature & Rhetoric, PO Box 6000, Binghamton, NY 13902-6000 *Tel:* 607-777-2168 *Fax:* 607-777-2408 *E-mail:* cwpro@binghamton.edu *Web Site:* www.binghamton.edu/english/creative-writing/index.html, pg 561

Burke, Craig, Berkley, c/o Penguin Random House LLC, 1745 Broadway, 19th fl, New York, NY 10019 *Tel:* 212-366-2000 *Web Site:* www.penguin.com/publishers/berkley/; www.penguin.com/ace-overview/, pg 28

Burke, Darius, Pomegranate Communications Inc, 105 SE 18 Ave, Portland, OR 97214 *Tel:* 503-328-6500 *Toll Free Tel:* 800-227-1428 *Fax:* 503-328-9330 *Toll Free Fax:* 800-848-4376 *E-mail:* hello@pomegranate.com *Web Site:* www.pomegranate.com, pg 162

Burke, Karen, Scholastic Education Solutions, 557 Broadway, New York, NY 10012 *Tel:* 212-343-6100 *Fax:* 212-343-6189 *Web Site:* www.scholastic.com, pg 184

Burke, Penny, Rutgers University Press, 106 Somerset St, 3rd fl, New Brunswick, NJ 08901 *Tel:* 848-445-7762; 848-445-7761 (sales) *Fax:* 732-745-4935 *E-mail:* sales@rutgersuniversitypress.org *Web Site:* www.rutgersuniversitypress.org, pg 179

Burke, Porscha, Random House Publishing Group, 1745 Broadway, New York, NY 10019 *Toll Free Tel:* 800-200-3552 *Web Site:* www.randomhousebooks.com, pg 171

Burke, Suzanne, Augsburg Fortress Publishers, Publishing House of the Evangelical Lutheran Church in America, 411 Washington Ave N, 3rd fl, Minneapolis, MN 55401 *Tel:* 612-330-3300 *Toll Free Tel:* 800-426-0115 (ext 639, subns); 800-328-4648 (orders) *Fax:* 612-330-3455 *E-mail:* info@augsburgfortress.org; copyright@augsburgfortress.org (reprint permission requests); customercare@augsburgfortress.org *Web Site:* www.augsburgfortress.org; www.1517.media, pg 22

Burke, Thomas F, Pomegranate Communications Inc, 105 SE 18 Ave, Portland, OR 97214 *Tel:* 503-328-6500 *Toll Free Tel:* 800-227-1428 *Fax:* 503-328-9330 *Toll Free Fax:* 800-848-4376 *E-mail:* hello@pomegranate.com *Web Site:* www.pomegranate.com, pg 162

Burkholder, Bruce, Editorial Bautista Independiente, 3417 Kenilworth Blvd, Sebring, FL 33870-4469 *Tel:* 863-382-6350 *Toll Free Tel:* 800-398-7187 (US) *Fax:* 863-382-8650 *E-mail:* info@ebi-bmm.org *Web Site:* www.ebi-bmm.org, pg 63

Burkle, Sharon, Random House Children's Books, c/o Penguin Random House LLC, 1745 Broadway, New York, NY 10019 *Tel:* 212-782-9000 *Web Site:* www.rhcbooks.com, pg 169

Burl, Emelie, Susan Schulman Literary Agency LLC, 454 W 44 St, New York, NY 10036 *Tel:* 212-713-1633; 917-488-0906 (direct line) *E-mail:* queries@schulmanagency.com *Web Site:* www.schulmanagency.com, pg 475

Burnett, Karen, Friends of American Writers (FAW), c/o 506 Rose Ave, Des Plaines, IL 60016 *E-mail:* info@fawchicago.org *Web Site:* www.fawchicago.org, pg 506

Burnett, Terry, South Carolina Bar, 1501 Park St, Columbia, SC 29201 *Tel:* 803-799-6653 *Toll Free Tel:* 800-768-7787 *E-mail:* scbar-info@scbar.org *Web Site:* www.scbar.org, pg 195

Burnham, Jonathan, HarperCollins Publishers LLC, 195 Broadway, New York, NY 10007 *Tel:* 212-207-7000 *Web Site:* www.harpercollins.com, pg 86

Burns, Anne, The Donning Company Publishers, 731 S Brunswick St, Brookfield, MO 64628 *Toll Free Tel:* 800-369-2646 (ext 3377) *Web Site:* www.donning.com, pg 60

Burns, Emily, Grove Atlantic Inc, 154 W 14 St, 12th fl, New York, NY 10011 *Tel:* 212-614-7850 *Toll Free Tel:* 800-521-0178 *Fax:* 212-614-7886 *E-mail:* info@groveatlantic.com; sales@groveatlantic.com; publicity@groveatlantic.com; rights@groveatlantic.com *Web Site:* www.groveatlantic.com, pg 82

Burns, Katie, Pantheon Books, c/o Penguin Random House LLC, 1745 Broadway, New York, NY 10019 *Tel:* 212-751-2600 *Fax:* 212-940-7390 (dom rts); 212-572-2662 (foreign rts) *Web Site:* knopfdoubleday.com/imprint/pantheon/; knopfdoubleday.com, pg 150

Burns, Katie, Schocken Books, c/o Penguin Random House LLC, 1745 Broadway, New York, NY 10019 *Tel:* 212-751-2600 *Fax:* 212-940-7390 (dom rts); 212-572-2662 (foreign rts) *Web Site:* knopfdoubleday.com/imprint/schocken/; knopfdoubleday.com, pg 183

Burns, Marilyn, Math Solutions®, One Harbor Dr, Suite 101, Sausalito, CA 94965 *Toll Free Tel:* 877-234-7323 *Toll Free Fax:* 800-724-4716 *E-mail:* info@mathsolutions.com; orders@mathsolutions.com *Web Site:* www.mathsolutions.com; store.mathsolutions.com, pg 127

Burns, Mary, Barbour Publishing Inc, 1810 Barbour Dr, Uhrichsville, OH 44683 *Tel:* 740-922-6045 *Fax:* 740-922-5948 *E-mail:* info@barbourbooks.com *Web Site:* www.barbourbooks.com, pg 24

Burns, Penelope, Gelfman Schneider Literary Agents Inc, 850 Seventh Ave, Suite 903, New York, NY 10019 *Tel:* 212-245-1993 *E-mail:* mail@gelfmanschneider.com *Web Site:* gelfmanschneider.com, pg 460

Burns, Shona, Andrews McMeel Publishing LLC, 1130 Walnut St, Kansas City, MO 64106-2109 *Tel:* 816-581-7500 *Toll Free Tel:* 800-851-8923 *Web Site:* www.andrewsmcmeel.com; publishing.andrewsmcmeel.com, pg 14

Burns, Stanley B MD, Burns Archive Press, 140 E 38 St, New York, NY 10016 *Tel:* 212-889-1938 *E-mail:* info@burnsarchive.com *Web Site:* www.burnsarchive.com, pg 38

Burns, Susan, Doubleday Canada, 320 Front St W, Suite 1400, Toronto, ON M5V 3B6, Canada *Tel:* 416-364-4449 *Fax:* 416-598-7764 *Web Site:* www.penguinrandomhouse.ca, pg 401

Burns, Susan, Penguin Random House Canada, a Penguin Random House company, 320 Front St W, Suite 1400, Toronto, ON M5V 3B6, Canada *Tel:* 416-364-4449 *Toll Free Tel:* 888-523-9292 (cust serv) *E-mail:* canadaweb@penguinrandomhouse.com; customerservicescanada@penguinrandomhouse.com *Web Site:* www.penguinrandomhouse.ca, pg 416

Burnstein, Lauren, Berkley, c/o Penguin Random House LLC, 1745 Broadway, 19th fl, New York, NY 10019 *Tel:* 212-366-2000 *Web Site:* www.penguin.com/publishers/berkley/; www.penguin.com/ace-overview/, pg 28

Burr, Jim, University of Texas Press, 3001 Lake Austin Blvd, 2.200, Austin, TX 78703 *Tel:* 512-471-7233 *Fax:* 512-232-7178 *E-mail:* utpress@uts.cc.utexas.edu; info@utpress.utexas.edu *Web Site:* utpress.utexas.edu, pg 205

Burr, Lacee, Simon & Schuster, 1230 Avenue of the Americas, New York, NY 10020 *Tel:* 212-698-7000 *Toll Free Tel:* 800-223-2348 (cust serv); 800-223-2336 (orders) *Toll Free Fax:* 800-943-9831 (orders) *Web Site:* simonandschusterpublishing.com/simonandschuster/, pg 188

Burr, Scott, Koho Pono LLC, 15024 SE Pinegrove Loop, Clackamas, OR 97015 *Tel:* 503-723-7392 *E-mail:* info@kohopono.com; orders@ingrambook.com *Web Site:* kohopono.com, pg 111

Burri, Peter, The Experiment, 220 E 23 St, Suite 600, New York, NY 10010-4658 *Tel:* 212-889-1659 *E-mail:* info@theexperimentpublishing.com *Web Site:* www.theexperimentpublishing.com, pg 68

Burriss, Dr Theresa, Highland Summer Writers' Conference, Radford University, Cook Hall 229, Radford, VA 24142 *Tel:* 540-831-5366 *Web Site:* www.radford.edu/content/cehd/home/appalachian-studies.html, pg 554

Burroughs, Joan, John Burroughs Medal, 500 Burroughs Dr, at Floyd Ackert, New York, NY 12493 *Tel:* 845-384-6556 *E-mail:* info@johnburroughsassociation.org *Web Site:* www.johnburroughsassociation.org, pg 585

Burroughs, Joan, John Burroughs Nature Essay Award, 500 Burroughs Dr, at Floyd Ackert, New York, NY 12493 *Tel:* 845-384-6556 *E-mail:* info@johnburroughsassociation.org *Web Site:* www.johnburroughsassociation.org, pg 585

Burroughs, Joan, Riverby Awards, 500 Burroughs Dr, at Floyd Ackert, New York, NY 12493 *Tel:* 845-384-6556 *E-mail:* info@johnburroughsassociation.org *Web Site:* www.johnburroughsassociation.org, pg 656

Burrows, Arthur A, Pro Lingua Associates Inc, 74 Cotton Mill Hill, Suite A-315, Brattleboro, VT 05301 *Tel:* 802-257-7779 *Toll Free Tel:* 800-366-4775 *Fax:* 802-257-5117 *E-mail:* info@prolinguaassociates.com *Web Site:* www.prolinguaassociates.com, pg 165

Burrows, Elise C, Pro Lingua Associates Inc, 74 Cotton Mill Hill, Suite A-315, Brattleboro, VT 05301 *Tel:* 802-257-7779 *Toll Free Tel:* 800-366-4775 *Fax:* 802-257-5117 *E-mail:* info@prolinguaassociates.com *Web Site:* www.prolinguaassociates.com, pg 165

Burrus, Abigail, Macmillan, 120 Broadway, 22nd fl, New York, NY 10271 *E-mail:* press.inquiries@macmillan.com *Web Site:* us.macmillan.com, pg 122

Burson, Kayla, Macmillan, 120 Broadway, 22nd fl, New York, NY 10271 *E-mail:* press.inquiries@macmillan.com *Web Site:* us.macmillan.com, pg 122

Burt, Madelyn, Stonesong, 270 W 39 St, Suite 201, New York, NY 10018 *Tel:* 212-929-4600 *E-mail:* editors@stonesong.com *Web Site:* www.stonesong.com, pg 478

Burt, Staci, Grand Central Publishing, 1290 Avenue of the Americas, New York, NY 10104 *Tel:* 212-364-1100 *Web Site:* www.hachettebookgroup.com/imprint/grand-central-publishing/, pg 80

Burton, Amy, Alliance for Women in Media (AWM), 2365 Harrodsburg Rd, A325, Lexington, KY 40504 *Tel:* 202-750-3664 *Fax:* 202-750-3664 *E-mail:* info@allwomeninmedia.org *Web Site:* allwomeninmedia.org, pg 494

Burton, Connie, Free Spirit Publishing Inc, 9850 51 Ave N, Suite 100, Minneapolis, MN 55442 *Tel:* 714-891-2273 *Toll Free Tel:* 800-858-7339 *Fax:* 714-230-7070 *Toll Free Fax:* 888-877-7606 *E-mail:* customerservice@tcmpub.com *Web Site:* www.teachercreatedmaterials.com/free-spirit-publishing, pg 74

Burton, David, Brooklyn Publishers LLC, PO Box 248, Cedar Rapids, IA 52406 *Tel:* 319-368-8012 *Toll Free Tel:* 888-473-8521 *Fax:* 319-368-8011 *E-mail:* customerservice@brookpub.com; editor@brookpub.com *Web Site:* www.brookpub.com, pg 37

Burton, Diane, The Pablo Neruda Prize for Poetry, University of Tulsa, Kendall College of Arts & Sciences, 800 S Tucker Dr, Tulsa, OK 74104 *Tel:* 918-631-3080 *E-mail:* nimrod@utulsa.edu *Web Site:* artsandsciences.utulsa.edu/nimrod/nimrod-literary-awards/, pg 639

Burton, Diane, Katherine Anne Porter Prize for Fiction, University of Tulsa, Kendall College of Arts & Sciences, 800 S Tucker Dr, Tulsa, OK 74104 *Tel:* 918-631-3080 *E-mail:* nimrod@utulsa.edu *Web Site:* artsandsciences.utulsa.edu/nimrod/nimrod-literary-awards/, pg 651

Burton, Elizabeth K, Zumaya Publications LLC, 3209 S Interstate 35, Suite 1086, Austin, TX 78741 *Tel:* 512-333-4055 (scheduled calls only) *Fax:* 512-276-6745 *E-mail:* publisher@zumayapublications.com; acquisitions@zumayapublications.com *Web Site:* www.zumayapublications.com, pg 237

Burton, Harry, Thames & Hudson, 500 Fifth Ave, New York, NY 10110 *Tel:* 212-354-3763 *Toll Free Tel:* 800-233-4830 *Fax:* 212-398-1252 *E-mail:* bookinfo@thames.wwnorton.com *Web Site:* www.thamesandhudsonusa.com, pg 205

Burton, Katie, Random House Children's Books, c/o Penguin Random House LLC, 1745 Broadway, New York, NY 10019 *Tel:* 212-782-9000 *Web Site:* www.rhcbooks.com, pg 170

Burton, Melissa, Princeton University Press, 41 William St, Princeton, NJ 08540-5237 *Tel:* 609-258-4900 *Fax:* 609-258-6305 *E-mail:* info@press.princeton.edu *Web Site:* press.princeton.edu, pg 164

Burton, Rebecca, Playwrights Guild of Canada, 401 Richmond St W, Suite 350, Toronto, ON M5V 3A8, Canada *Tel:* 416-703-0201 *E-mail:* info@playwrightsguild.ca; marketing@playwrightsguild.ca; orders@playwrightsguild.ca; membership@playwrightsguild.ca *Web Site:* playwrightsguild.ca, pg 516

Busanet, Angelica, Harry N Abrams Inc, 195 Broadway, 9th fl, New York, NY 10007 *Tel:* 212-206-7715 *Toll Free Tel:* 800-345-1359 *Fax:* 212-645-8437 *E-mail:* abrams@abramsbooks.com; publicity@abramsbooks.com; sales@abramsbooks.com *Web Site:* www.abramsbooks.com, pg 3

Busby, Colin, Institute for Research on Public Policy (IRPP), 1470 Peel St, No 200, Montreal, QC H3A 1T1, Canada *Tel:* 514-985-2461 *Fax:* 514-985-2559 *E-mail:* irpp@irpp.org *Web Site:* irpp.org, pg 410

Bush, Jonathan, St Martin's Press, LLC, 120 Broadway, New York, NY 10271 *E-mail:* publicity@stmartins.com; trademarketing@stmartins.com; foreignrights@stmartins.com *Web Site:* us.macmillan.com/smp, pg 181

Bush, Lisa, Math Solutions®, One Harbor Dr, Suite 101, Sausalito, CA 94965 *Toll Free Tel:* 877-234-7323 *Toll Free Fax:* 800-724-4716 *E-mail:* info@mathsolutions.com; orders@mathsolutions.com *Web Site:* www.mathsolutions.com; store.mathsolutions.com, pg 127

Bushell, Krystal, Linguistic Society of America (LSA), 522 21 St NW, Suite 120, Washington, DC 20006-5012 *Tel:* 202-835-1714 *Fax:* 202-835-1717 *E-mail:* lsa@lsadc.org; membership@lsadc.org *Web Site:* www.linguisticsociety.org, pg 509

Buskirk, Amy, Donner Canadian Foundation, 8 Prince Arthur Ave, 3rd fl, Toronto, ON M5R 1A9, Canada *Tel:* 416-920-6400 *Fax:* 416-920-5577 *Web Site:* www.donnerfoundation.org, pg 525

Busse, Heidi, Twenty-Third Publications, One Montauk Ave, Suite 200, New London, CT 06320 *Tel:* 860-437-3012 *Toll Free Tel:* 800-321-0411 (orders) *Toll Free Fax:* 800-572-0788 *E-mail:* resources@twentythirdpublications.com *Web Site:* www.twentythirdpublications.com, pg 211

Bustillo, Karina, American Institute of Aeronautics and Astronautics (AIAA), 12700 Sunrise Valley Dr, Suite 200, Reston, VA 20191-5807 *Tel:* 703-264-7500 *Toll Free Tel:* 800-639-AIAA (639-2422) *Fax:* 703-264-7551 *E-mail:* custserv@aiaa.org *Web Site:* www.aiaa.org; arc.aiaa.org (orders), pg 10

Buteas, Christine, New Jersey Business & Industry Association (NJBIA), 10 W Lafayette St, Trenton, NJ 08608-2002 *Tel:* 609-393-7707 *Web Site:* njbia.org, pg 514

Butler, Adios, The Picasso Project, 1109 Geary Blvd, San Francisco, CA 94109 *Tel:* 415-292-6500 *Fax:* 415-292-6594 *E-mail:* editeur@earthlink.net (edit); picasso@art-books.com (orders) *Web Site:* www.art-books.com, pg 160

Butler, Adios, Alan Wofsy Fine Arts, 1109 Geary Blvd, San Francisco, CA 94109 *Tel:* 415-292-6500 *Toll Free Tel:* 800-660-6403 *Fax:* 415-292-6594 (off & cust serv); 510-251-1840 (acctg) *E-mail:* order@art-books.com (orders); editeur@earthlink.net (edit); beauxarts@earthlink.net (cust serv) *Web Site:* www.art-books.com, pg 231

Butler, Butch, StarGroup International Inc, 1194 Old Dixie Hwy, Suite 201, West Palm Beach, FL 33413 *Tel:* 561-547-0667 *Fax:* 561-843-8530 *E-mail:* info@stargroupinternational.com *Web Site:* stargroupinternational.com, pg 198

Butler, Shannon M, Islandport Press, 247 Portland St, Bldg C, Yarmouth, ME 04096 *Tel:* 207-846-3344 *E-mail:* info@islandportpress.com; orders@islandportpress.com *Web Site:* www.islandportpress.com, pg 105

Butterfield, Heather, BenBella Books Inc, 10440 N Central Expwy, Suite 800, Dallas, TX 75231-2264 *Tel:* 214-750-3600 *Web Site:* www.benbellabooks.com; www.smartpopbooks.com, pg 27

Butterfield, Natalie, Chronicle Books LLC, 680 Second St, San Francisco, CA 94107 *Tel:* 415-537-4200 *Fax:* 415-537-4460 (perms) *E-mail:* hello@chroniclebooks.com; subrights@chroniclebooks.com *Web Site:* www.chroniclebooks.com, pg 47

Button, Lana, Canadian Society of Children's Authors, Illustrators & Performers (CANSCAIP), 720 Bathurst St, Suite 503, Toronto, ON M5S 2R4, Canada *Tel:* 416-515-1559 *E-mail:* office@canscaip.org *Web Site:* www.canscaip.org, pg 503

Byer, Mike, University of Toronto Press, Book Publishing Div, 800 Bay St, Mezzanine, Toronto, ON M5S 3A9, Canada *Tel:* 416-978-2239 *Fax:* 416-978-4736 *E-mail:* utpbooks@utorontopress.com (orders) *Web Site:* utorontopress.com, pg 423

Byer-Sprinzeles, Maggie, Byer-Sprinzeles Agency, 5800 Arlington Ave, Suite 16-C, Riverdale, NY 10471 *Tel:* 718-543-9399 *Web Site:* www.maggiebyersprinzeles.com, pg 485

Bykofsky, Sheree, Sheree Bykofsky Associates Inc, PO Box 706, Brigantine, NJ 08203 *E-mail:* shereebee@aol.com *Web Site:* www.shereebee.com, pg 453

Bylander, John, Teachers College Press, 1234 Amsterdam Ave, New York, NY 10027 *Tel:* 212-678-3929 *Fax:* 212-678-4149 *E-mail:* tcpress@tc.edu *Web Site:* www.tcpress.com, pg 203

Byrd, Elizabeth, Princeton University Press, 41 William St, Princeton, NJ 08540-5237 *Tel:* 609-258-4900 *Fax:* 609-258-6305 *E-mail:* info@press.princeton.edu *Web Site:* press.princeton.edu, pg 164

Byrd, Maggie, Macmillan, 120 Broadway, 22nd fl, New York, NY 10271 *E-mail:* press.inquiries@macmillan.com *Web Site:* us.macmillan.com, pg 122

Byrne-Jimenez, Monica, University Council for Educational Administration (UCEA), Michigan State University, College of Education, 620 Farm Lane, 432 Erickson Hall, East Lansing, MI 48824 *Tel:* 434-243-1041 *E-mail:* ucea@msu.edu *Web Site:* www.ucea.org, pg 214

Byrnes, Annie, Island Press, 2000 "M" St NW, Suite 480-B, Washington, DC 20036 *Tel:* 202-232-7933 *Toll Free Tel:* 800-621-2736 *Fax:* 202-234-1328 *E-mail:* info@islandpress.org *Web Site:* www.islandpress.org, pg 104

Caban, Isa, Tor Publishing Group, 120 Broadway, New York, NY 10271 *Toll Free Tel:* 800-455-0340 (Macmillan) *E-mail:* torpublicity@tor.com; forgepublicity@forgebooks.com *Web Site:* us.macmillan.com/torpublishinggroup, pg 208

Cabaza, Becky, Words into Print, 208 Java St, 5th fl, Brooklyn, NY 11222 *E-mail:* query@wordsintoprint.org *Web Site:* wordsintoprint.org, pg 445

Cabin, John, Vandamere Press, 3580 Morris St N, St Petersburg, FL 33713 *Tel:* 727-556-0950 *Toll Free Tel:* 800-551-7776 *Fax:* 727-556-2560 *E-mail:* orders@vandamere.com *Web Site:* www.vandamere.com, pg 224

Cable, Colleen, Association of Writers & Writing Programs (AWP), 440 Monticello Ave, Suite 1802, PMB 73708, Norfolk, VA 23510-2670 *Tel:* 240-696-7700 *E-mail:* awp@awpwriter.org; press@awpwriter.org *Web Site:* www.awpwriter.org, pg 500

Cable, Colleen, AWP Award Series, 440 Monticello Ave, Suite 1802, PMB 73708, Norfolk, VA 23510-2670 *Tel:* 240-696-7700 *E-mail:* awp@awpwriter.org; press@awpwriter.org *Web Site:* www.awpwriter.org, pg 576

Cabrera, Jorge, Princeton University Press, 41 William St, Princeton, NJ 08540-5237 *Tel:* 609-258-4900 *Fax:* 609-258-6305 *E-mail:* info@press.princeton.edu *Web Site:* press.princeton.edu, pg 164

Caffery, Dr Joshua, University of Louisiana at Lafayette Press, PO Box 43558, Lafayette, LA 70504-3558 *Tel:* 337-482-6027 *E-mail:* press.submissions@louisiana.edu *Web Site:* ulpress.org, pg 217

Caggiula, Sam, Naval Institute Press, 291 Wood Rd, Annapolis, MD 21402-5034 *Tel:* 410-268-6110 *Toll Free Tel:* 800-233-8764 *Fax:* 410-295-1084 *E-mail:* customer@usni.org (cust inquiries) *Web Site:* www.usni.org/press/books; www.usni.org, pg 139

Cahill, Kerry, American Psychological Association, 750 First St NE, Washington, DC 20002 *Tel:* 202-336-5510 *Toll Free Tel:* 800-374-2721 *Fax:* 202-336-5502 *E-mail:* order@apa.org; booksales@apa.org *Web Site:* www.apa.org/books, pg 12

Cahill, Martin, Kensington Publishing Corp, 900 Third Ave, 26th fl, New York, NY 10022 *Tel:* 212-407-1500 *Toll Free Tel:* 800-221-2647 *Fax:* 212-935-0699 *Web Site:* www.kensingtonbooks.com, pg 109

Cahoon, Nancy Stauffer, Nancy Stauffer Associates, PO Box 1203, Darien, CT 06820 *Tel:* 203-202-2500 *Web Site:* www.publishersmarketplace.com/members/nstauffer/, pg 477

Cai, Shirley, Kundiman Retreat, Fordham University, English Dept, 113 W 60 St, Rm 924, New York, NY 10023 *E-mail:* info@kundiman.org *Web Site:* www.kundiman.org, pg 556

Caiati, Michael, Random House Children's Books, c/o Penguin Random House LLC, 1745 Broadway, New York, NY 10019 *Tel:* 212-782-9000 *Web Site:* www.rhcbooks.com, pg 170

Cain, Christopher PhD, Towson University Prize for Literature, English Dept, 8000 York Rd, Towson, MD 21252 *Tel:* 410-704-2000 *Web Site:* www.towson.edu/english, pg 670

Cain, Rosie, United States Holocaust Memorial Museum, 100 Raoul Wallenberg Place SW, Washington, DC 20024-2126 *Tel:* 202-488-0400; 202-488-6144 (orders) *Toll Free Tel:* 800-259-9998 *E-mail:* academicpublications@ushmm.org *Web Site:* www.ushmm.org, pg 213

Caine, Rebecca, Picador, 120 Broadway, New York, NY 10271 *Tel:* 646-307-5151 *Fax:* 212-253-9627 *E-mail:* publicity@picadorusa.com *Web Site:* us.macmillan.com/picador, pg 159

Cajahuaringa, Esther, Penguin Random House LLC, 1745 Broadway, New York, NY 10019 *Tel:* 212-782-9000 *Toll Free Tel:* 800-726-0600 *Web Site:* www.penguinrandomhouse.com, pg 155

Calabrese, Gabbi, Sourcebooks LLC, 1935 Brookdale Rd, Suite 139, Naperville, IL 60563 *Tel:* 630-961-3900 *Toll Free Tel:* 800-432-7444 *Fax:* 630-961-2168 *E-mail:* info@sourcebooks.com *Web Site:* www.sourcebooks.com, pg 194

Calamia, Joseph, University of Chicago Press, 1427 E 60 St, Chicago, IL 60637-2954 *Tel:* 773-702-7700; 773-702-7600 *Toll Free Tel:* 800-621-2736 (orders) *Fax:* 773-702-9756; 773-660-2235 (orders); 773-702-2708 *E-mail:* custserv@press.uchicago.edu; marketing@press.uchicago.edu *Web Site:* www.press.uchicago.edu, pg 215

Calcasola, Lisa, HarperCollins Children's Books, 195 Broadway, New York, NY 10007 *Tel:* 212-207-7000 *Web Site:* www.harpercollins.com/childrens, pg 86

Calder, Kayla, Canadian Independent Booksellers Association (CIBA), 188 Dublin St N, Guelph, ON N1H 4P2, Canada *E-mail:* info@cibabooks.ca *Web Site:* cibabooks.ca, pg 502

Calderara, Theo, Oxford University Press USA, 198 Madison Ave, New York, NY 10016 *Toll Free Tel:* 800-451-7556 (orders); 800-445-9714 (cust serv) *Fax:* 919-677-1303 *E-mail:* custserv.us@oup.com *Web Site:* global.oup.com, pg 149

Calderon, Mariana, American Booksellers Association, 600 Mamaroneck Ave, Suite 400, Harrison, NY 10528 *Tel:* 914-406-7500 *Toll Free Tel:* 800-637-0037 *Fax:* 914-417-4013 *E-mail:* info@bookweb.org *Web Site:* www.bookweb.org, pg 494

Caldwell, Amy, Beacon Press, 24 Farnsworth St, Boston, MA 02210-1409 *Tel:* 617-742-2110 *Fax:* 617-723-3097 *E-mail:* production@beacon.org *Web Site:* www.beacon.org, pg 25

Caldwell, Claire, Annick Press Ltd, 388 Carlaw Ave, Suite 200, Toronto, ON M4M 2T4, Canada *Tel:* 416-221-4802 *Fax:* 416-221-8400 *E-mail:* annickpress@annickpress.com *Web Site:* www.annickpress.com, pg 395

Caldwell, Maddie, Grand Central Publishing, 1290 Avenue of the Americas, New York, NY 10104 *Tel:* 212-364-1100 *Web Site:* www.hachettebookgroup.com/imprint/grand-central-publishing/, pg 80

Calella, Christine, Simon & Schuster, 1230 Avenue of the Americas, New York, NY 10020 *Tel:* 212-698-7000 *Toll Free Tel:* 800-223-2348 (cust serv); 800-223-2336 (orders) *Toll Free Fax:* 800-943-9831 (orders) *Web Site:* simonandschusterpublishing.com/simonandschuster/, pg 188

Calip, Accalia, Berrett-Koehler Publishers Inc, 1333 Broadway, Suite 1000, Oakland, CA 94612 *Tel:* 510-817-2277 *Fax:* 510-817-2278 *E-mail:* bkpub@bkpub.com *Web Site:* www.bkconnection.com, pg 29

Calistro, Paddy, Angel City Press, 2118 Wilshire Blvd, Suite 880, Santa Monica, CA 90403 *Tel:* 310-395-9982 *E-mail:* info@angelcitypress.com *Web Site:* www.angelcitypress.com, pg 14

Callahan, Alison, Gallery Books, 1230 Avenue of the Americas, New York, NY 10020 *Toll Free Tel:* 800-456-6798 *Fax:* 212-698-7284 *E-mail:* consumer.customerservice@simonandschuster.com *Web Site:* www.simonandschuster.com, pg 76

Callahan, Kevin, Harry N Abrams Inc, 195 Broadway, 9th fl, New York, NY 10007 *Tel:* 212-206-7715 *Toll Free Tel:* 800-345-1359 *Fax:* 212-645-8437 *E-mail:* abrams@abramsbooks.com; publicity@abramsbooks.com; sales@abramsbooks.com *Web Site:* www.abramsbooks.com, pg 2

Callahan, Laurie, New Directions Publishing Corp, 80 Eighth Ave, 19th fl, New York, NY 10011 *Tel:* 212-255-0230 *E-mail:* editorial@ndbooks.com; publicity@ndbooks.com *Web Site:* ndbooks.com, pg 139

Callahan, Pat, University of South Carolina Press, 1600 Hampton St, Suite 544, Columbia, SC 29208 *Tel:* 803-777-5245 *Toll Free Tel:* 800-768-2500 (orders) *Fax:* 803-777-0160 *Toll Free Fax:* 800-868-0740 (orders) *Web Site:* uscpress.com, pg 220

Callahan, Sabrina, Little, Brown and Company, 1290 Avenue of the Americas, New York, NY 10104 *Tel:* 212-364-1100 *Fax:* 212-364-0952 *E-mail:* firstname.lastname@hbgusa.com *Web Site:* www.hachettebookgroup.com/imprint/little-brown-and-company/, pg 118

Callahan, William, InkWell Management, 521 Fifth Ave, Suite 2600, New York, NY 10175 *Tel:* 212-922-3500 *Fax:* 212-922-0535 *E-mail:* info@inkwellmanagement.com; submissions@inkwellmanagement.com; permissions@inkwellmanagement.com *Web Site:* inkwellmanagement.com, pg 463

Callan, Lacie, J J Keller & Associates, Inc®, 3003 Breezewood Lane, Neenah, WI 54957 *Tel:* 920-722-2848 *Toll Free Tel:* 877-564-2333 *Toll Free Fax:* 800-727-7516 *E-mail:* customerservice@jjkeller.com; sales@jjkeller.com *Web Site:* www.jjkeller.com, pg 108

Callanan, Annie, Taylor & Francis Inc, 530 Walnut St, Suite 850, Philadelphia, PA 19106 *Tel:* 215-625-8900 *Toll Free Tel:* 800-354-1420 *Fax:* 215-207-0050; 215-207-0046 (cust serv) *E-mail:* support@tandfonline.com *Web Site:* www.taylorandfrancis.com, pg 203

Callaway, Jaimee, Running Press, 1290 Avenue of the Americas, New York, NY 10104 *Tel:* 212-364-1100 *Toll Free Tel:* 800-759-0190 (cust serv) *Fax:* 212-364-0933 (intl orders) *Toll Free Fax:* 800-286-9471 (cust serv) *E-mail:* customer.service@hbgusa.com; orders@hbgusa.com *Web Site:* www.hachettebookgroup.com/imprint/running-press/; www.moon.com (Moon Travel Guides), pg 178

Callery, Maryann, Plowshare Media, 405 Vincente Way, La Jolla, CA 92037 *Tel:* 858-454-5446 *E-mail:* sales@plowsharemedia.com *Web Site:* plowsharemedia.com, pg 161

Callow, Phil, OAG Worldwide, 801 Warrenville Rd, Suite 555, Lisle, IL 60532 *Tel:* 630-515-5300 *Toll Free Tel:* 800-342-5624 (cust serv) *E-mail:* contactus@oag.com *Web Site:* www.oag.com, pg 144

Calusine, Lyndsay, Houghton Mifflin Harcourt Trade & Reference Division, 125 High St, Boston, MA 02110 *Tel:* 617-351-5000 *Web Site:* www.hmhco.com, pg 96

Calvano, Ashley, Cleis Press, 221 River St, 9th fl, Hoboken, NJ 07030 *Tel:* 212-431-5455 *E-mail:* cleis@cleispress.com *Web Site:* cleispress.com; www.vivaeditions.com, pg 49

Calvello, John, The Princeton Review, 110 E 42 St, 7th fl, New York, NY 10017 *Toll Free Tel:* 800-273-8439 (orders only) *Web Site:* www.princetonreview.com, pg 164

Calvert, Cordelia, HarperCollins Publishers LLC, 195 Broadway, New York, NY 10007 *Tel:* 212-207-7000 *Web Site:* www.harpercollins.com, pg 86

Calvi, Paul, Annual Reviews, 1875 S Grant St, Suite 700, San Mateo, CA 94402 *Tel:* 650-493-4400 *Toll Free Tel:* 800-523-8635 *Fax:* 650-424-0910; 650-855-9815 *E-mail:* service@annualreviews.org *Web Site:* www.annualreviews.org, pg 14

Cameron, Alazane, Penguin Random House Audio Publishing Group, 1745 Broadway, New York, NY 10019 *Toll Free Tel:* 800-793-2665 (cust serv) *E-mail:* audio@penguinrandomhouse.com; ecustomerservice@penguinrandomhouse.com *Web Site:* www.penguinrandomhouseaudio.com, pg 154

Cameron, Alex, Tor Publishing Group, 120 Broadway, New York, NY 10271 *Toll Free Tel:* 800-455-0340 (Macmillan) *E-mail:* torpublicity@tor.com; forgepublicity@forgebooks.com *Web Site:* us.macmillan.com/torpublishinggroup, pg 208

Cameron, Claire, Bull Publishing Co, PO Box 1377, Boulder, CO 80306 Tel: 303-545-6350 Toll Free Tel: 800-676-2855 E-mail: sales@bullpub.com Web Site: www.bullpub.com, pg 38

Cameron, Kimberley, Kimberley Cameron & Associates LLC, 1550 Tiburon Blvd, Suite 704, Tiburon, CA 94920 E-mail: info@kimberleycameron.com Web Site: www.kimberleycameron.com, pg 453

Cameron, Laura, Transatlantic Agency, 2 Bloor St E, Suite 3500, Toronto, ON M4W 1A8, Canada Tel: 416-488-9214 E-mail: info@transatlanticagency.com; royalties@transatlanticagency.com Web Site: www.transatlanticagency.com, pg 479

Camfiord, Liz, Penguin Random House LLC, 1745 Broadway, New York, NY 10019 Tel: 212-782-9000 Toll Free Tel: 800-726-0600 Web Site: www.penguinrandomhouse.com, pg 155

Camma, Tina, Running Press, 1290 Avenue of the Americas, New York, NY 10104 Tel: 212-364-1100 Toll Free Tel: 800-759-0190 (cust serv) Fax: 212-364-0933 (intl orders) Toll Free Fax: 800-286-9471 (cust serv) E-mail: customer.service@hbgusa.com; orders@hbgusa.com Web Site: www.hachettebookgroup.com/imprint/running-press/; www.moon.com (Moon Travel Guides), pg 178

Camp, Aaron, Crossway, 1300 Crescent St, Wheaton, IL 60187 Tel: 630-682-4300 Toll Free Tel: 800-635-7993 (orders); 800-543-1659 (cust serv) Fax: 630-682-4785 E-mail: info@crossway.org Web Site: www.crossway.org, pg 56

Camp, Martha, Princeton University Press, 41 William St, Princeton, NJ 08540-5237 Tel: 609-258-4900 Fax: 609-258-6305 E-mail: info@press.princeton.edu Web Site: press.princeton.edu, pg 164

Campagna, Michelle, Academy of American Poets Fellowship, 75 Maiden Lane, Suite 901, New York, NY 10038 Tel: 212-274-0343 E-mail: awards@poets.org Web Site: poets.org/academy-american-poets/prizes/academy-american-poets-fellowship, pg 569

Campagna, Michelle, Academy of American Poets First Book Award, 75 Maiden Lane, Suite 901, New York, NY 10038 Tel: 212-274-0343 E-mail: awards@poets.org Web Site: poets.org/academy-american-poets/prizes/first-book-award, pg 569

Campagna, Michelle, The Academy of American Poets Inc, 75 Maiden Lane, Suite 901, New York, NY 10038 Tel: 212-274-0343 E-mail: academy@poets.org Web Site: poets.org, pg 493

Campagna, Michelle, Ambroggio Prize, 75 Maiden Lane, Suite 901, New York, NY 10038 Tel: 212-274-0343 E-mail: awards@poets.org Web Site: poets.org/academy-american-poets/prizes/ambroggio-prize, pg 572

Campagna, Michelle, James Laughlin Award, 75 Maiden Lane, Suite 901, New York, NY 10038 Tel: 212-274-0343 E-mail: awards@poets.org Web Site: poets.org/academy-american-poets/prizes/james-laughlin-award, pg 622

Campagna, Michelle, Lenore Marshall Poetry Prize, 75 Maiden Lane, Suite 901, New York, NY 10038 Tel: 212-274-0343 E-mail: awards@poets.org Web Site: poets.org/academy-american-poets/prizes/lenore-marshall-poetry-prize, pg 629

Campagna, Michelle, Harold Morton Landon Translation Award, 75 Maiden Lane, Suite 901, New York, NY 10038 Tel: 212-274-0343 E-mail: awards@poets.org Web Site: poets.org/academy-american-poets/prizes/harold-morton-landon-translation-award, pg 635

Campagna, Michelle, Aliki Perroti & Seth Frank Most Promising Young Poet Award, 75 Maiden Lane, Suite 901, New York, NY 10038 Tel: 212-274-0343 E-mail: awards@poets.org Web Site: poets.org/academy-american-poets/american-poets-prizes, pg 649

Campagna, Michelle, Raiziss/de Palchi Fellowship, 75 Maiden Lane, Suite 901, New York, NY 10038 Tel: 212-274-0343 E-mail: awards@poets.org Web Site: poets.org/academy-american-poets/american-poets-prizes, pg 654

Campagna, Michelle, Wallace Stevens Award, 75 Maiden Lane, Suite 901, New York, NY 10038 Tel: 212-274-0343 E-mail: awards@poets.org Web Site: poets.org/academy-american-poets/prizes/wallace-stevens-award, pg 666

Campagna, Michelle, Treehouse Climate Action Poem Prize, 75 Maiden Lane, Suite 901, New York, NY 10038 Tel: 212-274-0343 E-mail: awards@poets.org Web Site: poets.org, pg 670

Campbell, Anna, Sourcebooks LLC, 1935 Brookdale Rd, Suite 139, Naperville, IL 60563 Tel: 630-961-3900 Toll Free Tel: 800-432-7444 Fax: 630-961-2168 E-mail: info@sourcebooks.com Web Site: www.sourcebooks.com, pg 195

Campbell, Beth, ACS Publications, 1155 16 St NW, Washington, DC 20036 Tel: 202-872-4600 Toll Free Tel: 800-227-5558 (US) Fax: 202-872-6067 E-mail: help@acs.org Web Site: pubs.acs.org; publish.acs.org/publish, pg 4

Campbell, Bruce, Capitol Enquiry Inc, 1034 Emerald Bay Rd, No 435, South Lake Tahoe, CA 96150 Tel: 916-442-1434 Toll Free Tel: 800-922-7486 Fax: 916-244-2704 E-mail: info@capenq.com Web Site: govbuddy.com, pg 40

Campbell, Daniel, James Lorimer & Co Ltd, Publishers, 117 Peter St, Suite 304, Toronto, ON M5V 0M3, Canada Tel: 416-362-4762 Fax: 416-362-3939 E-mail: sales@lorimer.ca; promotion@lorimer.ca; rights@lorimer.ca Web Site: www.lorimer.ca, pg 412

Campbell, David, Princeton University Press, 41 William St, Princeton, NJ 08540-5237 Tel: 609-258-4900 Fax: 609-258-6305 E-mail: info@press.princeton.edu Web Site: press.princeton.edu, pg 164

Campbell, Duncan, University of Regina Press, 2 Research Dr, Suite 160, Regina, SK S4S 7H9, Canada Tel: 306-585-4758 Fax: 306-585-4699 E-mail: uofrpress@uregina.ca Web Site: uofrpress.ca, pg 423

Campbell, Jim, American Literacy Council, c/o Los Alamos National Laboratory, Los Alamos, NM 87545 E-mail: questions@americanliteracy.com Web Site: www.americanliteracy.com, pg 495

Campbell, Michelle, Random House Children's Books, c/o Penguin Random House LLC, 1745 Broadway, New York, NY 10019 Tel: 212-782-9000 Web Site: www.rhcbooks.com, pg 170

Campbell, Scott, Pelican Publishing, 990 N Corporate Dr, Suite 100, New Orleans, LA 70123 Tel: 504-684-8976 Toll Free Tel: 844-868-1798 (orders) E-mail: editorial@pelicanpub.com (submissions) Web Site: www.pelicanpub.com; www.arcadiapublishing.com/imprints/pelican-publishing, pg 153

Campbell, Tim, Amber Lotus Publishing, PO Box 11329, Portland, OR 97211 Tel: 503-284-6400 Toll Free Tel: 800-326-2375 (orders only) Fax: 503-284-6417 E-mail: info@amberlotus.com; neworder@amberlotus.com Web Site: www.amberlotus.com, pg 8

Campbell-Schwartz, Ainslie, Candlewick Press, 99 Dover St, Somerville, MA 02144-2825 Tel: 617-661-3330 Fax: 617-661-0565 E-mail: bigbear@candlewick.com; salesinfo@candlewick.com Web Site: candlewick.com, pg 40

Campfield, Charlene M, Campfield & Campfield Publishing LLC, 6521 Cutler St, Philadelphia, PA 19126 Toll Free Tel: 888-518-2440 Fax: 215-224-6696 E-mail: info@campfieldpublishing.com Web Site: www.campfieldpublishing.com, pg 39

Campi, Dr Alicia, The Mongolia Society Inc, Indiana University, 703 Eigenmann Hall, 1900 E Tenth St, Bloomington, IN 47406-7512 Tel: 812-855-4078 Fax: 812-855-4078 E-mail: monsoc@indiana.edu Web Site: mongoliasociety.org, pg 133

Campion, Melissa, Macmillan, 120 Broadway, 22nd fl, New York, NY 10271 E-mail: press.inquiries@macmillan.com Web Site: us.macmillan.com, pg 122

Campo, Joan, Art of Living, PrimaMedia Inc, 1250 Bethlehem Pike, Suite 241, Hatfield, PA 19440 Tel: 267-421-7326 E-mail: info@artoflivingprimamedia.com Web Site: artoflivingprimamedia.com, pg 17

Campoli, Leila, Stonesong, 270 W 39 St, Suite 201, New York, NY 10018 Tel: 212-929-4600 E-mail: editors@stonesong.com Web Site: www.stonesong.com, pg 478

Campos, Vanessa, D4EO Literary Agency, 13206 Treviso Dr, Lakewood Ranch, FL 34211 Tel: 203-545-7180 (cell) Web Site: www.d4eoliteraryagency.com; www.publishersmarketplace.com/members/d4eo/; x.com/d4eo, pg 456

Canada, Alyea, Orbit, 1290 Avenue of the Americas, New York, NY 10104 Tel: 212-364-1100 Toll Free Tel: 800-759-0190 Web Site: www.orbitbooks.net; www.hachettebookgroup.com/imprint/orbit, pg 147

Canada, Toni, American Medical Association (AMA), AMA Plaza, 330 N Wabash, Suite 39300, Chicago, IL 60611-5885 Tel: 312-464-5000 Toll Free Tel: 800-621-8335 E-mail: media@ama-assn.org (media & edit) Web Site: www.ama-assn.org; www.jamanetwork.org, pg 495

Canales, Chantal, Viking Penguin, c/o Penguin Random House LLC, 1745 Broadway, New York, NY 10019 Tel: 212-782-9000 Web Site: www.penguin.com/overview-vikingbooks/; www.penguin.com/pamela-dorman-books-overview/; www.penguin.com/penguin-classics-overview/; www.penguin.com/penguin-life-overview/, pg 225

Canales, Michael J, Vesuvian Books, 711 Dolly Parton Pkwy, No 4313, Sevierville, TN 37864 E-mail: info@vesuvianmedia.com Web Site: www.vesuvianmedia.com, pg 224

Canavan, Susan, Waxman Literary Agency, 443 Park Ave S, No 1004, New York, NY 10016 Tel: 212-675-5556 Web Site: www.waxmanliteraryagency.com, pg 481

Cancellaro, Cecelia, Cambridge University Press, One Liberty Plaza, 20th fl, New York, NY 10006 Tel: 212-924-3900; 212-337-5000 Fax: 212-691-3239; 845-353-4141 E-mail: customer_service@cambridge.org; orders@cambridge.org; subscriptions_newyork@cambridge.org Web Site: www.cambridge.org/us, pg 39

Candelaria, Noel, National Education Association (NEA), 1201 16 St NW, Washington, DC 20036-3290 Tel: 202-833-4000 Fax: 202-822-7974 Web Site: www.nea.org, pg 137

Candelaria, Noel, National Education Association (NEA), 1201 16 St NW, Washington, DC 20036-3290 Tel: 202-833-4000 Fax: 202-822-7974 E-mail: media-relations-team@nea.org Web Site: www.nea.org, pg 513

Candelario, Ashley, HarperCollins Publishers LLC, 195 Broadway, New York, NY 10007 Tel: 212-207-7000 Web Site: www.harpercollins.com, pg 87

Canders, Emily Brock, Dutton, c/o Penguin Random House LLC, 1745 Broadway, New York, NY 10019 Tel: 212-366-2000 Web Site: www.penguin.com/dutton-overview/; www.penguin.com/plume-books-overview/; www.penguin.com/tiny-reparations-overview/, pg 62

Canfield, Thomas, Starcrafts LLC, 68A Fogg Rd, Epping, NH 03042 Tel: 603-734-4300 Toll Free Tel: 866-953-8458 (24/7 message ctr) Fax: 603-734-4311 E-mail: astrosales@astrocom.com Web Site: www.astrocom.com, pg 197

Cangioli, Pamela, Proofed to Perfection Editing Services, 6519 Sherrill Baggett Rd, Godwin, NC 28344 Tel: 910-980-0832 E-mail: inquiries@proofedtoperfection.com Web Site: www.proofedtoperfection.com, pg 443

Cannarella, Deborah, Yale Center for British Art, 1080 Chapel St, New Haven, CT 06510-2302 Tel: 203-432-8929 Fax: 203-432-1626 E-mail: ycba.publications@yale.edu Web Site: britishart.yale.edu, pg 235

Cannon, Molly B, David W & Beatrice C Evans Biography & Handcart Awards, 0735 Old Main Hill, Logan, UT 84322-0735 Tel: 435-797-0299 Fax: 435-797-1092 E-mail: mwc@usu.edu Web Site: mountainwest.usu.edu, pg 600

Cannon, Pamela, Gallery Books, 1230 Avenue of the Americas, New York, NY 10020 *Toll Free Tel:* 800-456-6798 *Fax:* 212-698-7284 *E-mail:* consumer.customerservice@simonandschuster.com *Web Site:* www.simonandschuster.com, pg 76

Canonico, Amy, Yale University Press, 302 Temple St, New Haven, CT 06511-8909 *Tel:* 203-432-0960; 203-432-0966 (sales); 401-531-2800 (cust serv) *Toll Free Tel:* 800-405-1619 (cust serv) *Fax:* 203-432-0948; 203-432-8485 (sales); 401-531-2801 (cust serv) *Toll Free Fax:* 800-406-9145 (cust serv) *E-mail:* sales.press@yale.edu (sales); customer.care@triliteral.org (cust serv) *Web Site:* www.yalebooks.com; yalepress.yale.edu/yupbooks, pg 235

Cantada, Daniel, Running Press, 1290 Avenue of the Americas, New York, NY 10104 *Tel:* 212-364-1100 *Toll Free Tel:* 800-759-0190 (cust serv) *Fax:* 212-364-0933 (intl orders) *Toll Free Fax:* 800-286-9471 (cust serv) *E-mail:* customer.service@hbgusa.com; orders@hbgusa.com *Web Site:* www.hachettebookgroup.com/imprint/running-press/; www.moon.com (Moon Travel Guides), pg 178

Cantanio, Solomon, The Society of Southwestern Authors (SSA), PO Box 30355, Tucson, AZ 85751-0355 *Web Site:* www.ssa-az.org, pg 520

Cantanio, Solomon, The Society of Southwestern Authors Writing Contest, PO Box 30355, Tucson, AZ 85751-0355 *E-mail:* contest@ssa-az.org *Web Site:* www.ssa-az.org/contest.htm, pg 664

Cantin, Sarah, St Martin's Press, LLC, 120 Broadway, New York, NY 10271 *E-mail:* publicity@stmartins.com; trademarketing@stmartins.com; foreignrights@stmartins.com *Web Site:* us.macmillan.com/smp, pg 181

Cantor, Carrie, Joelle Delbourgo Associates Inc, 101 Park St, Montclair, NJ 07042 *Tel:* 973-773-0836 (call only during standard business hours) *Web Site:* www.delbourgo.com, pg 456

Cantor, Renee, Random House Children's Books, c/o Penguin Random House LLC, 1745 Broadway, New York, NY 10019 *Tel:* 212-782-9000 *Web Site:* www.rhcbooks.com, pg 170

Cantu, Laura, Winterwolf Press, 8635 W Sahara Ave, Suite 425, Las Vegas, NV 89117 *Tel:* 725-222-3442 *E-mail:* info@winterwolfpress.com *Web Site:* winterwolfpress.com, pg 231

Canzoneri, Jennifer, BenBella Books Inc, 10440 N Central Expwy, Suite 800, Dallas, TX 75231-2264 *Tel:* 214-750-3600 *Web Site:* www.benbellabooks.com; www.smartpopbooks.com, pg 27

Capan, Theresa, Penguin Random House Audio Publishing Group, 1745 Broadway, New York, NY 10019 *Toll Free Tel:* 800-793-2665 (cust serv) *E-mail:* audio@penguinrandomhouse.com; ecustomerservice@penguinrandomhouse.com *Web Site:* www.penguinrandomhouseaudio.com, pg 154

Capen, Christopher, Capen Publishing Co Inc, 4440 Edison St, San Diego, CA 92117 *Toll Free Tel:* 800-358-0560 *E-mail:* info@capenpublishingco.com *Web Site:* capenpubco.com, pg 40

Caplan, David, Little, Brown Books for Young Readers (LBYR), 1290 Avenue of the Americas, New York, NY 10104 *Tel:* 212-364-1100 *Toll Free Tel:* 800-759-0190 (cust serv) *E-mail:* rights@lbchildrens.com *Web Site:* www.hachettebookgroup.com/imprint/little-brown-books-for-young-readers/, pg 118

Capogrossi, Natalie, Random House Children's Books, c/o Penguin Random House LLC, 1745 Broadway, New York, NY 10019 *Tel:* 212-782-9000 *Web Site:* www.rhcbooks.com, pg 170

Capozza, Shana, The Globe Pequot Press, 64 S Main St, Essex, CT 06426 *Tel:* 203-458-4500 *Toll Free Tel:* 800-243-0495 (orders only); 888-249-7586 (cust serv) *Fax:* 203-458-4601 *Toll Free Fax:* 800-820-2329 (orders & cust serv) *E-mail:* editorial@globepequot.com; info@rowman.com; orders@rowman.com *Web Site:* rowman.com, pg 79

Capozzi, Suzy, Union Square & Co, 1166 Avenue of the Americas, 17th fl, New York, NY 10036-2715 *Tel:* 212-532-7160 *Toll Free Tel:* 800-367-9692 *Fax:* 212-213-2495 *Toll Free Fax:* 800-542-7567 *E-mail:* custservice@sterlingpublishing.com; customerservice@sterlingpublishing.com; editorial@sterlingpublishing.com; tradesales@sterlingpublishing.com *Web Site:* www.sterlingpublishing.com, pg 212

Capps, Karen, Concordia Publishing House, 3558 S Jefferson Ave, St Louis, MO 63118-3968 *Tel:* 314-268-1000; 314-268-1268 (bookshop) *Toll Free Tel:* 800-325-3040 (cust serv) *Toll Free Fax:* 800-490-9889 (cust serv) *E-mail:* order@cph.org *Web Site:* www.cph.org, pg 51

Capra, Juliette, Chronicle Books LLC, 680 Second St, San Francisco, CA 94107 *Tel:* 415-537-4200 *Fax:* 415-537-4460 (perms) *E-mail:* hello@chroniclebooks.com; subrights@chroniclebooks.com *Web Site:* www.chroniclebooks.com, pg 47

Capron, Elise, Sandra Dijkstra Literary Agency, 1155 Camino del Mar, PMB 515, Del Mar, CA 92014-2605 *Web Site:* www.dijkstraagency.com, pg 456

Caputo, Nicole, Counterpoint Press LLC, 2560 Ninth St, Suite 318, Berkeley, CA 94710 *Tel:* 510-704-0230 *Fax:* 510-704-0268 *E-mail:* info@counterpointpress.com *Web Site:* counterpointpress.com; softskull.com, pg 54

Carabulea, Ingrid, Atria Books, 1230 Avenue of the Americas, New York, NY 10020 *Tel:* 212-698-7000 *Fax:* 212-698-7007 *Web Site:* www.simonandschuster.com, pg 21

Caranante, Giuliana, Quarto Publishing Group USA Inc, 100 Cummings Ctr, Suite 265D, Beverly, MA 01915 *Tel:* 978-282-9590 *Toll Free Tel:* 800-328-0590 (sales) *Fax:* 978-283-2742 *E-mail:* sales@quartous.com *Web Site:* www.quartoknows.com, pg 168

Caratozzolo, Marie, Square One Publishers Inc, 115 Herricks Rd, Garden City Park, NY 11040 *Tel:* 516-535-2010 *Toll Free Tel:* 877-900-BOOK (900-2665) *Fax:* 516-535-2014 *E-mail:* sq1publish@aol.com *Web Site:* www.squareonepublishers.com, pg 196

Carattini, Morgan, Random House Publishing Group, 1745 Broadway, New York, NY 10019 *Toll Free Tel:* 800-200-3552 *Web Site:* www.randomhousebooks.com, pg 171

Carden, Gwen, StarGroup International Inc, 1194 Old Dixie Hwy, Suite 201, West Palm Beach, FL 33413 *Tel:* 561-547-0667 *Fax:* 561-843-8530 *E-mail:* info@stargroupinternational.com *Web Site:* stargroupinternational.com, pg 198

Cardenas, Joanna, Kokila, c/o Penguin Random House LLC, 1745 Broadway, New York, NY 10019 *Tel:* 212-782-9000 *Web Site:* www.penguin.com/kokila-books-overview/, pg 111

Cardenas, Yvonne, Other Press, 267 Fifth Ave, 6th fl, New York, NY 10016 *Tel:* 212-414-0054 *Toll Free Tel:* 877-THEOTHER (843-6843) *Fax:* 212-414-0939 *E-mail:* editor@otherpress.com; marketing@otherpress.com; publicity@otherpress.com *Web Site:* otherpress.com, pg 148

Carder, Justin, Wolfman Books, 410 13 St, Oakland, CA 94612 *Tel:* 510-679-4650 *E-mail:* hello@wolfmanhomerepair.com *Web Site:* wolfmanhomerepair.com, pg 232

Cardillo, Sarah, Sourcebooks LLC, 1935 Brookdale Rd, Suite 139, Naperville, IL 60563 *Tel:* 630-961-3900 *Toll Free Tel:* 800-432-7444 *Fax:* 630-961-2168 *E-mail:* info@sourcebooks.com *Web Site:* www.sourcebooks.com, pg 194

Cardinal, Chyla, Rocky Mountain Books Ltd (RMB), 103-1075 Pendergast St, Victoria, BC V8V 0A1, Canada *Tel:* 250-360-0829 *Fax:* 250-386-0829 *Web Site:* rmbooks.com, pg 418

Cardona, Moses, John Hawkins and Associates Inc, 80 Maiden Lane, Suite 1503, New York, NY 10038 *Tel:* 212-807-7040 *E-mail:* jha@jhalit.com *Web Site:* jhalit.com, pg 462

Cardoza, Avery, Cardoza Publishing, 1916 E Charleston Blvd, Las Vegas, NV 89104 *Tel:* 702-870-7200 *E-mail:* cardozaent@aol.com *Web Site:* cardozapublishing.com, pg 40

Carey, Dana, Random House Children's Books, c/o Penguin Random House LLC, 1745 Broadway, New York, NY 10019 *Tel:* 212-782-9000 *Web Site:* www.rhcbooks.com, pg 170

Carey, Edward, University of Texas at Austin, New Writers Project, Dept of English, 204 W 21 St, B-5000, Austin, TX 78712-1164 *Tel:* 512-471-4991 *Fax:* 512-471-4909 *E-mail:* newwritersproject@utexas.edu *Web Site:* liberalarts.utexas.edu/nwp, pg 567

Carey, Jennifer, Mountain Press Publishing Co, 1301 S Third W, Missoula, MT 59801 *Tel:* 406-728-1900 *Toll Free Tel:* 800-234-5308 *Fax:* 406-728-1635 *E-mail:* info@mtnpress.com *Web Site:* www.mountain-press.com, pg 135

Cargill, Noreen, Bread Loaf Fellowships & Scholarships, Middlebury College, 204 College St, Middlebury, VT 05753 *Tel:* 802-443-5286 *Fax:* 802-443-2087 *E-mail:* blwc@middlebury.edu *Web Site:* www.middlebury.edu/blwc, pg 584

Cargill, Noreen, Bread Loaf Writers' Conference, 204 College St, Middlebury, VT 05753 *Tel:* 802-443-5286 *Fax:* 802-443-2087 *E-mail:* blwc@middlebury.edu *Web Site:* www.middlebury.edu/blwc, pg 553

Caridi, Christopher, John Wiley & Sons Inc, 111 River St, Hoboken, NJ 07030-5774 *Tel:* 201-748-6000 *Toll Free Tel:* 800-225-5945 (cust serv) *Fax:* 201-748-6088 *Web Site:* www.wiley.com, pg 230

Carispat, Gia, Art of Living, PrimaMedia Inc, 1250 Bethlehem Pike, Suite 241, Hatfield, PA 19440 *Tel:* 267-421-7326 *E-mail:* info@artoflivingprimamedia.com *Web Site:* artoflivingprimamedia.com, pg 17

Carkhuff, Robert W, HRD Press, PO Box 2600, Amherst, MA 01004 *Tel:* 413-253-3488 *Toll Free Tel:* 800-822-2801 *E-mail:* info@hrdpress.com; customerservice@hrdpress.com *Web Site:* www.hrdpress.com, pg 97

Carl, Melissa, Nicholas Brealey Publishing, 53 State St, 9th fl, Boston, MA 02109 *Tel:* 617-523-3801 *E-mail:* sales-us@nicholasbrealey.com *Web Site:* nbuspublishing.com, pg 36

Carlin, Pat, Naval Institute Press, 291 Wood Rd, Annapolis, MD 21402-5034 *Tel:* 410-268-6110 *Toll Free Tel:* 800-233-8764 *Fax:* 410-295-1084 *E-mail:* customer@usni.org (cust inquiries) *Web Site:* www.usni.org/press/books; www.usni.org, pg 139

Carlisle, Chuck, The Ashland Poetry Press, Bixler Center for the Humanities, Ashland University, 401 College Ave, Ashland, OH 44805 *E-mail:* app@ashland.edu *Web Site:* www.ashlandpoetrypress.com, pg 19

Carlisle, Chuck, The Richard Snyder Memorial Publication Prize, Bixler Center for the Humanities, Ashland University, 401 College Ave, Ashland, OH 44805 *E-mail:* app@ashland.edu *Web Site:* www.ashlandpoetrypress.com/guidelines/snyder-prize, pg 664

Carlisle, Michael V, InkWell Management, 521 Fifth Ave, Suite 2600, New York, NY 10175 *Tel:* 212-922-3500 *Fax:* 212-922-0535 *E-mail:* info@inkwellmanagement.com; submissions@inkwellmanagement.com; permissions@inkwellmanagement.com *Web Site:* www.inkwellmanagement.com, pg 463

Carlisle, Rebecca, Workman Publishing, 1290 Avenue of the Americas, New York, NY 10104 *Toll Free Tel:* 800-759-0190 *Fax:* 212-364-0950 *E-mail:* workman-inquiry@hbgusa.com *Web Site:* www.hachettebookgroup.com/imprint/workman-publishing-company/, pg 232

Carlos, Francesca, Atria Books, 1230 Avenue of the Americas, New York, NY 10020 *Tel:* 212-698-7000 *Fax:* 212-698-7007 *Web Site:* www.simonandschuster.com, pg 21

Carlson, Ann, Scott O'Dell Award for Historical Fiction, c/o Horn Book Inc, 300 The Fenway, Suite P-311, Palace Road Bldg, Boston, MA

02215 *Tel:* 617-278-0225 *Toll Free Tel:* 888-628-0225 *E-mail:* scottodellfanpage@gmail.com *Web Site:* scottodell.com/the-scott-odell-award, pg 643

Carlson, Bruce, Hearts 'n Tummies Cookbook Co, 3544 Blakslee St, Wever, IA 52658 *Tel:* 319-372-7480 *Toll Free Tel:* 800-571-2665 *E-mail:* quixotepress@gmail.com; heartsntummies@gmail.com *Web Site:* www.heartsntummies.com, pg 90

Carlson, Bryce, BOOM! Studios, 5670 Wilshire Blvd, Suite 400, Los Angeles, CA 90036 *E-mail:* contact@boom-studios.com; customerservice@boom-studios.com; press@boom-studios.com *Web Site:* www.boom-studios.com, pg 34

Carlson, Jennifer, Dunow, Carlson & Lerner Literary Agency Inc, 27 W 20 St, Suite 1107, New York, NY 10011 *Tel:* 212-645-7606 *E-mail:* mail@dclagency.com *Web Site:* www.dclagency.com, pg 457

Carlson, Jennifer, Nystrom Education, PO Box 802, Culver City, CA 90232 *Tel:* 310-839-2436 *Toll Free Tel:* 800-421-4246 *Fax:* 310-839-2249 *Toll Free Fax:* 800-944-5432 *E-mail:* access@socialstudies.com; customerservice@socialstudies.com *Web Site:* www.socialstudies.com, pg 144

Carlson, John, Chronicle Books LLC, 680 Second St, San Francisco, CA 94107 *Tel:* 415-537-4200 *Fax:* 415-537-4460 (perms) *E-mail:* hello@chroniclebooks.com; subrights@chroniclebooks.com *Web Site:* www.chroniclebooks.com, pg 47

Carlson, Megan, Harry N Abrams Inc, 195 Broadway, 9th fl, New York, NY 10007 *Tel:* 212-206-7715 *Toll Free Tel:* 800-345-1359 *Fax:* 212-645-8437 *E-mail:* abrams@abramsbooks.com; publicity@abramsbooks.com; sales@abramsbooks.com *Web Site:* www.abramsbooks.com, pg 3

Carlson, Rachael, Paul Engle Prize, 123 S Linn St, Iowa City, IA 52240 *E-mail:* info@iowacityofliterature.org *Web Site:* www.iowacityofliterature.org/paul-engle-prize, pg 600

Carlson, Tara Singh, GP Putnam's Sons, c/o Penguin Random House LLC, 1745 Broadway, New York, NY 10019 *Tel:* 212-782-9000 *Web Site:* www.penguin.com/putnam/, pg 167

Carlton, Kat, Indiana University Writers' Conference, Ballantine Hall 440, 1020 E Kirkwood Ave, Bloomington, IN 47405-7103 *E-mail:* writecon@indiana.edu *Web Site:* www.iuwc.indiana.edu, pg 555

Carman, Mary Ann, The Society of Southwestern Authors (SSA), PO Box 30355, Tucson, AZ 85751-0355 *Web Site:* www.ssa-az.org, pg 520

Carman, Mary Ann, The Society of Southwestern Authors Writing Contest, PO Box 30355, Tucson, AZ 85751-0355 *E-mail:* contest@ssa-az.org *Web Site:* www.ssa-az.org/contest.htm, pg 664

Carmichael, Andy, Deep River Books LLC, PO Box 310, Sisters, OR 97759 *Tel:* 541-549-1139 *E-mail:* info@deepriverbooks.com *Web Site:* deepriverbooks.com, pg 58

Carmichael, Bill, Deep River Books LLC, PO Box 310, Sisters, OR 97759 *Tel:* 541-549-1139 *E-mail:* info@deepriverbooks.com *Web Site:* deepriverbooks.com, pg 58

Carmichael, Nancie, Deep River Books LLC, PO Box 310, Sisters, OR 97759 *Tel:* 541-549-1139 *E-mail:* info@deepriverbooks.com *Web Site:* deepriverbooks.com, pg 58

Carmona, Lisa, Zaner-Bloser Inc, 1400 Goodale Blvd, Suite 200, Grandview Heights, OH 43212 *Toll Free Tel:* 800-421-3018 (cust serv) *Toll Free Fax:* 800-992-6087 (orders) *E-mail:* customerexperience@zaner-bloser.com *Web Site:* www.zaner-bloser.com, pg 236

Carner, Susan, Macmillan, 120 Broadway, 22nd fl, New York, NY 10271 *E-mail:* press.inquiries@macmillan.com *Web Site:* us.macmillan.com, pg 122

Carney, Allison, HarperCollins Publishers LLC, 195 Broadway, New York, NY 10007 *Tel:* 212-207-7000 *Web Site:* www.harpercollins.com, pg 86

Carney, Allison, Henry Holt and Company, LLC, 120 Broadway, 23rd fl, New York, NY 10271 *Tel:* 646-307-5151 *Toll Free Tel:* 888-330-8477 (orders) *Fax:* 646-307-5285 *Web Site:* www.henryholt.com, pg 94

Caron, David, ECW Press, 665 Gerrard St E, Toronto, ON M4M 1Y2, Canada *Tel:* 416-694-3348 *E-mail:* info@ecwpress.com *Web Site:* www.ecwpress.com, pg 401

Caron, Lou, Printing Industries Association Inc of Southern California (PIASC), 5800 S Eastern Ave, Suite 400, Los Angeles, CA 90040 *Tel:* 323-728-9500 *E-mail:* info@piasc.org *Web Site:* www.piasc.org, pg 517

Caron-Lacoste, Ariane, Les Editions de l'Hexagone, 4545, rue Frontenac, 3rd fl, Montreal, QC H2H 2R7, Canada *Tel:* 514-523-1182 *Fax:* 514-521-4434 *Web Site:* editionshexagone.groupelivre.com, pg 402

Caron-Lacoste, Ariane, VLB editeur, 4545, rue Frontenac, 3rd fl, Montreal, QC H2H 2R7, Canada *Tel:* 514-849-5259 *Web Site:* www.edvlb.com, pg 424

Carosi, Chris, City Lights Publishers, 261 Columbus Ave, San Francisco, CA 94133 *Tel:* 415-362-8193 *E-mail:* staff@citylights.com *Web Site:* citylights.com, pg 48

Carpenter, Emily, Chautauqua Writers' Workshop, One Ames Ave, Chautauqua, NY 14722 *Tel:* 716-357-6255 *Web Site:* www.chq.org, pg 553

Carpenter, Ken, Harvard University Press, 79 Garden St, Cambridge, MA 02138-1499 *Tel:* 617-495-2600; 401-531-2800 (intl orders) *Toll Free Tel:* 800-405-1619 (orders) *Fax:* 617-495-5898 (gen); 617-496-4677 (edit & rts); 401-531-2801 (intl orders) *Toll Free Fax:* 800-406-9145 (orders) *E-mail:* contact_hup@harvard.edu *Web Site:* www.hup.harvard.edu, pg 88

Carpenter, Manzanita, Bear & Co Inc, One Park St, Rochester, VT 05767 *Tel:* 802-767-3174 *Toll Free Tel:* 800-932-3277 *Fax:* 802-767-3726 *E-mail:* customerservice@InnerTraditions.com *Web Site:* InnerTraditions.com, pg 26

Carpenter, Manzanita, Inner Traditions International Ltd, One Park St, Rochester, VT 05767 *Tel:* 802-767-3174 *Toll Free Tel:* 800-246-8648 *Fax:* 802-767-3726 *E-mail:* customerservice@InnerTraditions.com *Web Site:* www.InnerTraditions.com, pg 101

Carpenter, Todd, Miles Conrad Award, 3600 Clipper Mill Rd, Suite 302, Baltimore, MD 21211-1948 *Tel:* 301-654-2512 *Fax:* 410-685-5278 *E-mail:* nisohq@niso.org *Web Site:* www.niso.org, pg 591

Carpenter, Todd, National Information Standards Organization (NISO), 3600 Clipper Mill Rd, Suite 302, Baltimore, MD 21211-1948 *Tel:* 301-654-2512 *Fax:* 410-685-5278 *E-mail:* nisohq@niso.org *Web Site:* www.niso.org, pg 138, 513

Carpentier, Patrick, Federation des Milieux Documentaires, 2065 rue Parthenais, Bureau 387, Montreal, QC H2K 3T1, Canada *Tel:* 514-281-5012 *E-mail:* info@fmdoc.org *Web Site:* fmdoc.org, pg 505

Carpentieri, Ariana, Tor Publishing Group, 120 Broadway, New York, NY 10271 *Toll Free Tel:* 800-455-0340 (Macmillan) *E-mail:* torpublicity@tor.com; forgepublicity@forgebooks.com *Web Site:* us.macmillan.com/torpublishinggroup, pg 208

Carpino, Christina, HarperCollins Children's Books, 195 Broadway, New York, NY 10007 *Tel:* 212-207-7000 *Web Site:* www.harpercollins.com/childrens, pg 86

Carr, David, University of Manitoba Press, University of Manitoba, 301 St Johns College, 92 Dysart Rd, Winnipeg, MB R3T 2M5, Canada *Tel:* 204-474-9495 *Fax:* 204-474-7566 *E-mail:* uofmpress@umanitoba.ca *Web Site:* uofmpress.ca, pg 422

Carr, Gale, Parmenides Publishing, 3753 Howard Hughes Pkwy, Suite 200, Las Vegas, NV 89169 *Tel:* 702-892-3934 *Fax:* 702-892-3939 *E-mail:* info@parmenides.com; editor@parmenides.com *Web Site:* www.parmenides.com, pg 152

Carr, Jamie, The Book Group (TBG), 20 W 20 St, Suite 601, New York, NY 10011 *E-mail:* info@thebookgroup.com; submissions@thebookgroup.com *Web Site:* www.thebookgroup.com, pg 450

Carr, Julie, Counterpath Press, 7935 E 14 Ave, Denver, CO 80220 *E-mail:* counterpath@counterpathpress.org *Web Site:* www.counterpathpress.org, pg 54

Carr, Lauren, Gallery Books, 1230 Avenue of the Americas, New York, NY 10020 *Toll Free Tel:* 800-456-6798 *Fax:* 212-698-7284 *E-mail:* consumer.customerservice@simonandschuster.com *Web Site:* www.simonandschuster.com, pg 76

Carr, Micaela, Henry Holt and Company, LLC, 120 Broadway, 23rd fl, New York, NY 10271 *Tel:* 646-307-5151 *Toll Free Tel:* 888-330-8477 (orders) *Fax:* 646-307-5285 *Web Site:* www.henryholt.com, pg 94

Carr, Rosalyn, University of Alabama Press, 200 Hackberry Lane, 2nd fl, Tuscaloosa, AL 35487 *Tel:* 205-348-5180 *Fax:* 205-348-9201 *Web Site:* www.uapress.ua.edu, pg 214

Carr, Shida, Atria Books, 1230 Avenue of the Americas, New York, NY 10020 *Tel:* 212-698-7000 *Fax:* 212-698-7007 *Web Site:* www.simonandschuster.com, pg 21

Carreno-Bernard, Regina, Ladderbird Literary Agency, 460 Yellow Brick Rd, Orange, CT 06477 *Tel:* 203-290-1703 *Web Site:* www.ladderbird.com, pg 466

Carrera, Monica, Teachers College Press, 1234 Amsterdam Ave, New York, NY 10027 *Tel:* 212-678-3929 *Fax:* 212-678-4149 *E-mail:* tcpress@tc.edu *Web Site:* www.tcpress.com, pg 203

Carrick, Christina, The Massachusetts Historical Society, 1154 Boylston St, Boston, MA 02215-3695 *Tel:* 617-536-1608 *Fax:* 617-859-0074 *E-mail:* publications@masshist.org *Web Site:* www.masshist.org, pg 126

Carrillo, Koraima, Albert Whitman & Company, 250 S Northwest Hwy, Suite 320, Park Ridge, IL 60068 *Tel:* 847-232-2800 *Toll Free Tel:* 800-255-7675 (orders) *Fax:* 847-581-0039 *E-mail:* mail@albertwhitman.com; orders@albertwhitman.com *Web Site:* www.albertwhitman.com, pg 6

Carroll, Kent, Europa Editions, 27 Union Sq W, Suite 302, New York, NY 10003 *Tel:* 212-868-6844 *Fax:* 212-868-6845 *E-mail:* info@europaeditions.com; books@europaeditions.com; publicity@europaeditions.com *Web Site:* www.europaeditions.com, pg 67

Carroll, Sheena, University of Pittsburgh Press, 7500 Thomas Blvd, Pittsburgh, PA 15260 *Tel:* 412-383-2456 *Fax:* 412-383-2466 *E-mail:* info@upress.pitt.edu *Web Site:* www.upress.pitt.edu, pg 219

Carrow, Jenny, Atria Books, 1230 Avenue of the Americas, New York, NY 10020 *Tel:* 212-698-7000 *Fax:* 212-698-7007 *Web Site:* www.simonandschuster.com, pg 21

Carruth, Marlies A, MacArthur Fellows Program, Office of Grants Management, 140 S Dearborn St, Chicago, IL 60603-5285 *Tel:* 312-726-8000 *Fax:* 312-920-6528 *E-mail:* 4answers@macfound.org *Web Site:* www.macfound.org/programs/fellows, pg 628

Carson, Dina C, Iron Gate Publishing, PO Box 999, Niwot, CO 80544 *Tel:* 303-530-2551 *E-mail:* editor@irongate.com *Web Site:* www.irongate.com, pg 104

Carson, Ken, Cengage Learning, 20 Channel Center St, Boston, MA 02210 *Tel:* 617-289-7700 *Toll Free Tel:* 800-354-9706 *Fax:* 617-289-7844 *E-mail:* esales@cengage.com *Web Site:* www.cengage.com, pg 43

Carstens, Sarah, Rizzoli International Publications Inc, 300 Park Ave S, 4th fl, New York, NY 10010-5399 *Tel:* 212-387-3400 *Toll Free Tel:* 800-522-6657 (orders only) *Fax:* 212-387-3535 *E-mail:* publicity@rizzoliusa.com *Web Site:* www.rizzoliusa.com, pg 175

Carter, Dr Allyson, The University of Arizona Press, 1510 E University Blvd, Tucson, AZ 85721 *Tel:* 520-621-1441 *Toll Free Tel:* 800-621-2736 (orders) *Fax:* 520-621-8899 *Toll Free Fax:* 800-621-8476 (orders) *E-mail:* uap@uapress.arizona.edu *Web Site:* www.uapress.arizona.edu, pg 214

Carter, Brittany, Columbia Books & Information Services (CBIS), 1530 Wilson Blvd, Suite 400, Arlington, VA 22209 *Tel:* 202-464-1662 *Fax:* 301-664-9600 *E-mail:* info@columbiabooks.com *Web Site:* www.columbiabooks.com; www.association-insight.com; www.ceoupdate.com; www.thealmanacofamericanpolitics.com; www.thompsongrants.com, pg 51

Carter Eaton, Eryn, Hampton Roads Publishing, 65 Parker St, Suite 7, Newburyport, MA 01950-4600 *Tel:* 978-465-0504 *Toll Free Tel:* 800-423-7087 (orders) *Fax:* 978-465-0243 *Toll Free Fax:* 877-337-3309 *E-mail:* orders@rwwbooks.com; rights@rwwbooks.com *Web Site:* redwheelweiser.com, pg 84

Carter, Jill, Crossway, 1300 Crescent St, Wheaton, IL 60187 *Tel:* 630-682-4300 *Toll Free Tel:* 800-635-7993 (orders); 800-543-1659 (cust serv) *Fax:* 630-682-4785 *E-mail:* info@crossway.org *Web Site:* www.crossway.org, pg 56

Carter, La'Toya, Health Administration Press, 300 S Riverside Plaza, Suite 1900, Chicago, IL 60606 *Tel:* 312-424-2800 *Fax:* 312-424-0014 *E-mail:* hapbooks@ache.org *Web Site:* www.ache.org/hap (orders), pg 89

Carter, Laura, Canadian Independent Booksellers Association (CIBA), 188 Dublin St N, Guelph, ON N1H 4P2, Canada *E-mail:* info@cibabooks.ca *Web Site:* cibabooks.ca, pg 502

Carty-Sipp, April, National Association of Broadcasters (NAB), One "M" St SE, Washington, DC 20003 *Tel:* 202-429-5300 *E-mail:* nab@nab.org *Web Site:* www.nab.org, pg 136, 511

Caruso, Emma, Random House Publishing Group, 1745 Broadway, New York, NY 10019 *Toll Free Tel:* 800-200-3552 *Web Site:* www.randomhousebooks.com, pg 171

Carvainis, Maria, Maria Carvainis Agency Inc, Rockefeller Center, 1270 Avenue of the Americas, Suite 2915, New York, NY 10020 *Tel:* 212-245-6365 *Fax:* 212-245-7196 *E-mail:* mca@mariacarvainisagency.com *Web Site:* mariacarvainisagency.com, pg 453

Carver, Andrew, Penguin Random House LLC, 1745 Broadway, New York, NY 10019 *Tel:* 212-782-9000 *Toll Free Tel:* 800-726-0600 *Web Site:* www.penguinrandomhouse.com, pg 155

Casares, Isabel, Simon & Schuster, 1230 Avenue of the Americas, New York, NY 10020 *Tel:* 212-698-7000 *Toll Free Tel:* 800-223-2348 (cust serv); 800-223-2336 (orders) *Toll Free Fax:* 800-943-9831 (orders) *Web Site:* simonandschusterpublishing.com/simonandschuster/, pg 188

Casares, Oscar, University of Texas at Austin, New Writers Project, Dept of English, 204 W 21 St, B-5000, Austin, TX 78712-1164 *Tel:* 512-471-4991 *Fax:* 512-471-4909 *E-mail:* newwritersproject@utexas.edu *Web Site:* liberalarts.utexas.edu/nwp, pg 567

Cascardi, Andrea, Transatlantic Agency, 2 Bloor St E, Suite 3500, Toronto, ON M4W 1A8, Canada *Tel:* 416-488-9214 *E-mail:* info@transatlanticagency.com; royalties@transatlanticagency.com *Web Site:* www.transatlanticagency.com, pg 479

Casement, Alex, HarperCollins Publishers LLC, 195 Broadway, New York, NY 10007 *Tel:* 212-207-7000 *Web Site:* www.harpercollins.com, pg 87

Casey, Alec, Trusted Media Brands Inc, 750 Third Ave, 3rd fl, New York, NY 10017 *Tel:* 646-293-6299 *Toll Free Tel:* 877-732-4438 (cust serv) *Fax:* 646-293-6251 *E-mail:* customercare@trustedmediabrands.com; press@trustedmediabrands.com *Web Site:* trustedmediabrands.com; www.rd.com, pg 210

Casey, Barbara, Strategic Media Books LLC, 782 Wofford St, Rock Hill, SC 29730 *Tel:* 803-366-5440 *E-mail:* contact@strategicmediabooks.com *Web Site:* strategicmediabooks.com, pg 200

Casey, Maribeth, Workman Publishing, 1290 Avenue of the Americas, New York, NY 10104 *Toll Free Tel:* 800-759-0190 *Fax:* 212-364-0950 *E-mail:* workman-inquiry@hbgusa.com *Web Site:* www.hachettebookgroup.com/imprint/workman-publishing-company/, pg 232

Cash, Amy Opperman, Larson Publications, 4936 State Rte 414, Burdett, NY 14818 *Tel:* 607-546-9342 *Toll Free Tel:* 800-828-2197 *Fax:* 607-546-9344 *E-mail:* custserv@larsonpublications.com *Web Site:* www.larsonpublications.com, pg 113

Cash, Mary, Holiday House Publishing Inc, 50 Broad St, New York, NY 10004 *Tel:* 212-688-0085 *Fax:* 212-421-6134 *E-mail:* info@holidayhouse.com *Web Site:* www.holidayhouse.com, pg 94

Cash, Paul R, Larson Publications, 4936 State Rte 414, Burdett, NY 14818 *Tel:* 607-546-9342 *Toll Free Tel:* 800-828-2197 *Fax:* 607-546-9344 *E-mail:* custserv@larsonpublications.com *Web Site:* www.larsonpublications.com, pg 113

Cashman, Ann, The LA Literary Agency, 1264 N Hayworth Ave, Los Angeles, CA 90046 *Tel:* 323-654-5288 *E-mail:* laliteraryagency@mac.com *Web Site:* www.laliteraryagency.com, pg 466

Cashman, Jessica, Random House Publishing Group, 1745 Broadway, New York, NY 10019 *Toll Free Tel:* 800-200-3552 *Web Site:* www.randomhousebooks.com, pg 171

Cashman, Lorraine Walsh, Iona & Peter Opie Prize, Indiana University, Classroom-Off Bldg, 800 E Third St, Bloomington, IN 47405 *Tel:* 812-856-2379 *Fax:* 812-856-2483 *E-mail:* americanfolkloresociety@afsnet.org; cf.section@afsnet.org *Web Site:* www.afsnet.org; childrensfolklore.org/opie-prize, pg 644

Cashman, Michelle, St Martin's Press, LLC, 120 Broadway, New York, NY 10271 *E-mail:* publicity@stmartins.com; trademarketing@stmartins.com; foreignrights@stmartins.com *Web Site:* us.macmillan.com/smp, pg 181

Casolaro, Frank, Hachette Book Group Inc, 1290 Avenue of the Americas, New York, NY 10104 *Tel:* 212-364-1100 *Toll Free Tel:* 800-759-0190 (cust serv) *Fax:* 212-364-0933 (intl orders) *Toll Free Fax:* 800-286-9471 (cust serv) *E-mail:* customer.service@hbgusa.com; orders@hbgusa.com *Web Site:* www.hachettebookgroup.com, pg 83

Cason, Mary, Philadelphia Museum of Art, PO Box 7646, Philadelphia, PA 19101-7646 *Tel:* 215-763-8100 *Fax:* 215-236-4465 *Web Site:* www.philamuseum.org, pg 159

Casper, Scott E, American Antiquarian Society (AAS), 185 Salisbury St, Worcester, MA 01609-1634 *Tel:* 508-755-5221 *Fax:* 508-754-9069 *E-mail:* library@mwa.org *Web Site:* www.americanantiquarian.org, pg 494

Casper, Scott E, Fellowships for Creative & Performing Artists & Writers, 185 Salisbury St, Worcester, MA 01609-1634 *Tel:* 508-755-5221 *Fax:* 508-754-9069 *E-mail:* library@mwa.org *Web Site:* www.americanantiquarian.org, pg 602

Casper, Scott E, Fellowships for Historical Research, 185 Salisbury St, Worcester, MA 01609-1634 *Tel:* 508-755-5221 *Fax:* 508-754-9069 *Web Site:* www.americanantiquarian.org, pg 602

Cass, Celeste, Macmillan, 120 Broadway, 22nd fl, New York, NY 10271 *E-mail:* press.inquiries@macmillan.com *Web Site:* us.macmillan.com, pg 122

Cass, Curtis, Chelsea Green Publishing Co, 85 N Main St, Suite 120, White River Junction, VT 05001 *Tel:* 802-295-6300 *Toll Free Tel:* 800-639-4099 (cust serv & orders) *Fax:* 802-295-6444 *E-mail:* customerservice@chelseagreen.com; editorial@chelseagreen.com; publicity@chelseagreen.com; rights@chelseagreen.com *Web Site:* www.chelseagreen.com, pg 45

Cassagnol, Allene, Macmillan, 120 Broadway, 22nd fl, New York, NY 10271 *E-mail:* press.inquiries@macmillan.com *Web Site:* us.macmillan.com, pg 122

Cassell, Dana K, Florida Freelance Writers Association, 45 Main St, North Stratford, NH 03590 *Tel:* 603-922-8338 *Fax:* 603-922-8339 *E-mail:* ffwa@writers-editors.com; info@writers-editors.com *Web Site:* www.writers-editors.com; writerseditorsnetwork.com, pg 506

Cassion, Maggie, Macmillan, 120 Broadway, 22nd fl, New York, NY 10271 *E-mail:* press.inquiries@macmillan.com *Web Site:* us.macmillan.com, pg 122

Cassity, Liza, Penguin Publishing Group, c/o Penguin Random House LLC, 1745 Broadway, New York, NY 10019 *Tel:* 212-782-9000 *Web Site:* www.penguin.com, pg 154

Castaldo, John, G Schirmer Inc/Associated Music Publishers Inc, 180 Madison Ave, 24th fl, New York, NY 10016 *Tel:* 212-254-2100 *Fax:* 212-254-2013 *E-mail:* schirmer@schirmer.com *Web Site:* www.musicsalesclassical.com, pg 183

Castellani, Mary Kate, Bloomsbury Publishing Inc, 1385 Broadway, 5th fl, New York, NY 10018 *Tel:* 212-419-5300 *E-mail:* marketingusa@bloomsbury.com; adultpublicityusa@bloomsbury.com; askacademic@bloomsbury.com *Web Site:* www.bloomsbury.com, pg 31

Castellanos, Manny, BOOM! Studios, 5670 Wilshire Blvd, Suite 400, Los Angeles, CA 90036 *E-mail:* contact@boom-studios.com; customerservice@boom-studios.com; press@boom-studios.com *Web Site:* www.boom-studios.com, pg 34

Castillanes, John, Penguin Random House Canada, a Penguin Random House company, 320 Front St W, Suite 1400, Toronto, ON M5V 3B6, Canada *Tel:* 416-364-4449 *Toll Free Tel:* 888-523-9292 (cust serv) *E-mail:* canadaweb@penguinrandomhouse.com; customerservicescanada@penguinrandomhouse.com *Web Site:* www.penguinrandomhouse.ca, pg 416

Castillo, Johanna V, Writers House, 21 W 26 St, New York, NY 10010 *Tel:* 212-685-2400 *Web Site:* www.writershouse.com, pg 482

Castle, Sara, JMW Group Inc, 346 Rte 6, No 867, Mahopac, NY 10541 *Tel:* 914-841-7105 *Fax:* 914-248-8861 *E-mail:* jmwgroup@jmwgroup.net *Web Site:* jmwforlife.com, pg 465

Castner, Lauren, Simon & Schuster, 1230 Avenue of the Americas, New York, NY 10020 *Tel:* 212-698-7000 *Toll Free Tel:* 800-223-2348 (cust serv); 800-223-2336 (orders) *Toll Free Fax:* 800-943-9831 (orders) *Web Site:* simonandschusterpublishing.com/simonandschuster/, pg 188

Castorena, Valeria, Tor Publishing Group, 120 Broadway, New York, NY 10271 *Toll Free Tel:* 800-455-0340 (Macmillan) *E-mail:* torpublicity@tor.com; forgepublicity@forgebooks.com *Web Site:* us.macmillan.com/torpublishinggroup, pg 208

Castro, Adam, Random House Children's Books, c/o Penguin Random House LLC, 1745 Broadway, New York, NY 10019 *Tel:* 212-782-9000 *Web Site:* www.rhcbooks.com, pg 170

Castro, Christina, Publishing Certificate Program at City College of New York, Division of Humanities NAC 5225, City College of New York, New York, NY 10031 *Tel:* 212-650-7925 *Fax:* 212-650-7912 *E-mail:* ccnypub@aol.com *Web Site:* english.ccny.cuny.edu/publishing-program, pg 565

Castro, Evelyn, National Association of Hispanic Publications Inc (NAHP), National Press Bldg, 529 14 St NW, Suite 923, Washington, DC 20045 *Web Site:* nahp.org, pg 511

Caswell, Ashley, Farrar, Straus & Giroux Books for Young Readers, 120 Broadway, New York, NY 10271 *Tel:* 212-741-6900 *Toll Free Tel:* 888-330-8477 (orders) *E-mail:* childrens.publicity@macmillanusa.com; childrensrights@macmillanusa.com *Web Site:* us.macmillan.com/mackids, pg 70

Caswell, Ashley, Roaring Brook Press, 120 Broadway, New York, NY 10271 *Tel:* 646-307-5151 *Web Site:* us.macmillan.com/publishers/roaring-brook-press, pg 176

Caswell, Bexx, Guild of Book Workers, 521 Fifth Ave, New York, NY 10175 *E-mail:* communications@guildofbookworkers.org; membership@guildofbookworkers.org *Web Site:* www.guildofbookworkers.org, pg 507

Cataffo, Caitlin, Farrar, Straus & Giroux, LLC, 120 Broadway, New York, NY 10271 *Tel:* 212-741-6900 *E-mail:* fsg.publicity@fsgbooks.com; sales@fsgbooks.com *Web Site:* us.macmillan.com/fsg, pg 70

Catalano, Kim, Galaxy Press Inc, 7051 Hollywood Blvd, Los Angeles, CA 90028 *Tel:* 323-466-3310 *Toll Free Tel:* 877-8GALAXY (842-5299) *E-mail:* info@galaxypress.com; customers@galaxypress.com *Web Site:* www.galaxypress.com, pg 75

Catalano, Pierre, Editions Mediaspaul, 3965, blvd Henri-Bourassa E, Montreal, QC H1H 1L1, Canada *Tel:* 514-322-7341 *Fax:* 514-322-4281 *E-mail:* mediaspaul@mediaspaul.ca *Web Site:* mediaspaul.ca, pg 404

Catalano, Steve, Naval Institute Press, 291 Wood Rd, Annapolis, MD 21402-5034 *Tel:* 410-268-6110 *Toll Free Tel:* 800-233-8764 *Fax:* 410-295-1084 *E-mail:* customer@usni.org (cust inquiries) *Web Site:* www.usni.org/press/books; www.usni.org, pg 139

Catalano, Steve, Stanford University Press, 425 Broadway St, Redwood City, CA 94063-3126 *Tel:* 650-723-9434 *Fax:* 650-725-3457 *E-mail:* info@www.sup.org; publicity@www.sup.org; sales@www.sup.org *Web Site:* www.sup.org, pg 197

Catlin-Legutko, Cinnamon, Illinois State Museum Society, 502 S Spring St, Springfield, IL 62706-5000 *Tel:* 217-782-7386 *Fax:* 217-782-1254 *E-mail:* subscriptions@museum.state.il.us *Web Site:* www.illinoisstatemuseum.org, pg 99

Caulfield, Charlene, Wildflower Press, c/o Oakbrook Press, 3301 S Valley Dr, Rapid City, SD 57703 *Tel:* 605-381-6385 *E-mail:* info@wildflowerpress.org *Web Site:* www.wildflowerpress.org, pg 229

Cauz, Jorge, Encyclopaedia Britannica Inc, 325 N La Salle St, Suite 200, Chicago, IL 60654 *Tel:* 312-347-7000 (all other countries) *Toll Free Tel:* 800-323-1229 (US & CN) *Fax:* 312-294-2104 *E-mail:* contact@eb.com *Web Site:* www.britannica.com, pg 66

Cavallaro, Andrea, Sandra Dijkstra Literary Agency, 1155 Camino del Mar, PMB 515, Del Mar, CA 92014-2605 *Web Site:* dijkstraagency.com, pg 456

Cavallaro, Lenny, Janus Literary Agency, PO Box 837, Methuen, MA 01844 *Tel:* 978-273-4227 *E-mail:* janusliteraryagency@gmail.com *Web Site:* janusliteraryagency.blogspot.com, pg 464

Cavanagh, Natali, Random House Children's Books, c/o Penguin Random House LLC, 1745 Broadway, New York, NY 10019 *Tel:* 212-782-9000 *Web Site:* www.rhcbooks.com, pg 170

Cavanagh, Sean, HarperCollins Children's Books, 195 Broadway, New York, NY 10007 *Tel:* 212-207-7000 *Web Site:* www.harpercollins.com/childrens, pg 86

Cavanah, Lex, The Donning Company Publishers, 731 S Brunswick St, Brookfield, MO 64628 *Toll Free Tel:* 800-369-2646 (ext 3377) *Web Site:* www.donning.com, pg 60

Cavanaugh, Drew, North Atlantic Books (NAB), 2526 Martin Luther King Jr Way, Berkeley, CA 94704 *Tel:* 510-549-4270 *Web Site:* www.northatlanticbooks.com, pg 142

Cavanaugh, Sylvia, Edna Ferber Fiction Book Award, c/o 210 N Main St, No 204, Cedar Grove, WI 53013 *E-mail:* wiswriters@gmail.com *Web Site:* wiswriters.org/awards, pg 602

Cavanaugh, Sylvia, Kay W Levin Award for Short Nonfiction, c/o 210 N Main St, No 204, Cedar Grove, WI 53013 *E-mail:* wiswriters@gmail.com *Web Site:* wiswriters.org/awards, pg 623

Cavanaugh, Sylvia, Edna Meudt Poetry Book Award, c/o 210 N Main St, No 204, Cedar Grove, WI 53013 *E-mail:* wiswriters@gmail.com *Web Site:* wiswriters.org/awards, pg 632

Cave, Tricia, Doubleday, c/o Penguin Random House LLC, 1745 Broadway, New York, NY 10019 *Tel:* 212-751-2600 *Fax:* 212-940-7390 (dom rts); 212-572-2662 (foreign rts) *Web Site:* knopfdoubleday.com/imprint/doubleday/; knopfdoubleday.com, pg 61

Cave, Tricia, Alfred A Knopf, c/o Penguin Random House LLC, 1745 Broadway, New York, NY 10019 *Tel:* 212-751-2600 *Fax:* 212-940-7390 (dom rts); 212-572-2662 (foreign rts) *Web Site:* knopfdoubleday.com/imprint/knopf/; knopfdoubleday.com, pg 110

Cavelos, Jeanne, Jeanne Cavelos Editorial Services, PO Box 75, Mont Vernon, NH 03057 *Tel:* 603-673-6234 *Web Site:* jeannecavelos.com, pg 437

Cavelos, Jeanne, Your Personal Odyssey Writing Workshop, PO Box 75, Mont Vernon, NH 03057 *Tel:* 603-673-6234 *Fax:* 603-673-6234 *Web Site:* www.odysseyworkshop.org, pg 559

Caviness, Mary, The University of North Carolina Press, 116 S Boundary St, Chapel Hill, NC 27514-3808 *Tel:* 919-966-3561; 919-966-7449 (orders) *Toll Free Tel:* 800-848-3224 (orders) *Fax:* 919-962-2704 (orders) *Toll Free Fax:* 800-272-6817 (orders) *E-mail:* uncpress@unc.edu *Web Site:* uncpress.org, pg 218

Ceballos, Wendy, HarperCollins Publishers LLC, 195 Broadway, New York, NY 10007 *Tel:* 212-207-7000 *Web Site:* www.harpercollins.com, pg 86

Cebik, Stephen, Yale University Press, 302 Temple St, New Haven, CT 06511-8909 *Tel:* 203-432-0960; 203-432-0966 (sales); 401-531-2800 (cust serv) *Toll Free Tel:* 800-405-1619 (cust serv) *Fax:* 203-432-0948; 203-432-8485 (sales); 401-531-2801 (cust serv) *Toll Free Fax:* 800-406-9145 (cust serv) *E-mail:* sales.press@yale.edu (sales); customer.care@triliteral.org (cust serv) *Web Site:* www.yalebooks.com; yalepress.yale.edu/yupbooks, pg 235

Cedillos, Felicia, University of New Mexico Press, One University of New Mexico, Albuquerque, NM 87131-0001 *Tel:* 505-272-7777 *Fax:* 505-277-3343 *E-mail:* custserv@unm.edu (order dept) *Web Site:* unmpress.com, pg 218

Cepero, Lauren, Entangled Publishing LLC, 644 Shrewsbury Commons Ave, Suite 181, Shrewsbury, PA 17361 *Toll Free Tel:* 877-677-9451 *E-mail:* publisher@entangledpublishing.com *Web Site:* www.entangledpublishing.com, pg 67

Ceppos, Robin, The Brookings Institution Press, 1775 Massachusetts Ave NW, Washington, DC 20036-2188 *Tel:* 202-797-6000 *E-mail:* permissions@brookings.edu *Web Site:* www.brookings.edu, pg 37

Cerand, Lauren, A Public Space Fellowships, 323 Dean St, Brooklyn, NY 11217 *Tel:* 718-858-8067 *E-mail:* general@apublicspace.org *Web Site:* apublicspace.org, pg 569

Cerand, Lauren, Deborah Pease Prize, 323 Dean St, Brooklyn, NY 11217 *Tel:* 718-858-8067 *E-mail:* general@apublicspace.org *Web Site:* apublicspace.org, pg 646

Cerbone, Will, Fordham University Press, Joseph A Martino Hall, 45 Columbus Ave, 3rd fl, New York, NY 10023 *Fax:* 347-842-3083 *Web Site:* www.fordhampress.com, pg 73

Cercone, Philip, McGill-Queen's University Press, 1010 Sherbrooke W, Suite 1720, Montreal, QC H3A 2R7, Canada *Tel:* 514-398-3750 *Fax:* 514-398-4333 *E-mail:* mqup@mcgill.ca *Web Site:* www.mqup.ca, pg 412

Cercone, Sean, Dramatists Play Service Inc, 440 Park Ave S, New York, NY 10016 *E-mail:* dpsinfo@broadwaylicensing.com; publications@broadwaylicensing.com *Web Site:* www.dramatists.com, pg 61

Cerda, Jessy, VanDam Inc, The VanDam Bldg, 121 W 27 St, New York, NY 10001 *Tel:* 917-297-5445 *E-mail:* info@vandam.com *Web Site:* www.vandam.com, pg 223

Cerri, Alison, HarperCollins Publishers LLC, 195 Broadway, New York, NY 10007 *Tel:* 212-207-7000 *Web Site:* www.harpercollins.com, pg 87

Cerullo, Clare, Rowman & Littlefield, 4501 Forbes Blvd, Suite 200, Lanham, MD 20706 *Tel:* 301-459-3366 *Toll Free Tel:* 800-462-6420 (ext 3024, cust serv) *Fax:* 301-429-5748 *Web Site:* rowman.com, pg 178

Cerullo, John, Applause Theatre & Cinema Books, 64 S Main St, Essex, CT 06426 *Tel:* 973-223-5039 *E-mail:* info@applausepub.com *Web Site:* www.applausepub.com, pg 15

Cerullo, John, Backbeat Books, PO Box 1520, Wayne, NJ 07042-1520 *Tel:* 973-987-5363 *E-mail:* submissions@halleonardbooks.com *Web Site:* www.backbeatbooks.com, pg 23

Cerullo, John, Limelight Editions, 64 S Main St, Essex, CT 06426 *Tel:* 973-223-5039 *Web Site:* limelighteditions.com, pg 117

Cerullo, John, Rowman & Littlefield, 4501 Forbes Blvd, Suite 200, Lanham, MD 20706 *Tel:* 301-459-3366 *Toll Free Tel:* 800-462-6420 (ext 3024, cust serv) *Fax:* 301-429-5748 *Web Site:* rowman.com, pg 178

Cervantes, Analieze, Harvey Klinger Inc, 300 W 55 St, Suite 11V, New York, NY 10019 *Tel:* 212-581-7068 *Fax:* 212-315-3823 *E-mail:* queries@harveyklinger.com *Web Site:* www.harveyklinger.com, pg 465

Cervantes, Analieze, Rees Literary Agency, One Westinghouse Plaza, Suite A203, Boston, MA 02136 *Tel:* 617-227-9014 *Web Site:* www.reesagency.com, pg 473

Cervone, Emily, Chronicle Books LLC, 680 Second St, San Francisco, CA 94107 *Tel:* 415-537-4200 *Fax:* 415-537-4460 (perms) *E-mail:* hello@chroniclebooks.com; subrights@chroniclebooks.com *Web Site:* www.chroniclebooks.com, pg 47

Cesare, Kara, Random House Publishing Group, 1745 Broadway, New York, NY 10019 *Toll Free Tel:* 800-200-3552 *Web Site:* www.randomhousebooks.com, pg 170

Chaban, Enid, Random House Children's Books, c/o Penguin Random House LLC, 1745 Broadway, New York, NY 10019 *Tel:* 212-782-9000 *Web Site:* www.rhcbooks.com, pg 169

Chacon, Daniel, University of Texas at El Paso, Department of Creative Writing, MFA/Department of Creative Writing, M520, University Towers, Oregon St, El Paso, TX 79968 *E-mail:* creativewriting@utep.edu *Web Site:* www.utep.edu/liberalarts/creative-writing, pg 567

Chadwick, Sacha, Lee & Low Books Inc, 95 Madison Ave, Suite 1205, New York, NY 10016 *Tel:* 212-779-4400 *Toll Free Tel:* 888-320-3190 (ext 28, orders only) *Fax:* 212-683-1894 (orders only); 212-532-6035 *E-mail:* general@leeandlow.com *Web Site:* www.leeandlow.com, pg 114

Chaffa, Mandana, Gregg Barrios Book in Translation Prize, c/o Jacob M Appel, Icahn School of Medicine at Mount Sinai, One Gustave L Levy Place, New York, NY 10029 *E-mail:* info@bookcritics.org *Web Site:* www.bookcritics.org/gregg-barrios-book-in-translation-prize/, pg 577

Chaghatzbanian, Sonya, Simon & Schuster Children's Publishing, 1230 Avenue of the Americas, New York, NY 10020 *Tel:* 212-698-7000 *Web Site:* www.simonandschuster.com/kids; www.simonandschuster.com/teen; simonandschuster.net; simonandschuster.biz, pg 189

Chagnot, Annie, Random House Publishing Group, 1745 Broadway, New York, NY 10019 *Toll Free Tel:* 800-200-3552 *Web Site:* www.randomhousebooks.com, pg 171

Chahal, Mandy, Poisoned Pen Press, 4014 N Goldwater Blvd, Suite 201, Scottsdale, AZ 85251 *Tel:* 480-945-3375 *Toll Free Tel:* 800-421-3976 *Fax:* 480-949-1707 *E-mail:* info@poisonedpenpress.com *Web Site:* www.poisonedpenpress.com, pg 161

Chaiken, Rafael, Central Conference of American Rabbis/CCAR Press, 355 Lexington Ave, New York, NY 10017 *Tel:* 212-972-3636 *E-mail:* info@ccarpress.org; info@ccarnet.org *Web Site:* www.ccarpress.org, pg 44

Chakars, Dr Melissa, The Mongolia Society Inc, Indiana University, 703 Eigenmann Hall, 1900 E Tenth St, Bloomington, IN 47406-7512 *Tel:* 812-855-4078 *Fax:* 812-855-4078 *E-mail:* monsoc@indiana.edu *Web Site:* mongoliasociety.org, pg 133

Chalfant, Sarah, The Wylie Agency LLC, 250 W 57 St, Suite 2114, New York, NY 10107 *Tel:* 212-246-0069 *E-mail:* mail@wylieagency.com *Web Site:* www.wylieagency.com, pg 483

Chalifoux, Ed, Printing Industry Association of the South (PIAS), 305 Plus Park Blvd, Nashville, TN 37217 *Tel:* 615-366-1094 *Fax:* 615-366-4192 *Web Site:* www.pias.org, pg 517

Chalker, Bob, NACE International, 15835 Park Ten Place, Houston, TX 77084 *Tel:* 281-228-6200; 281-228-6223 *Toll Free Tel:* 800-797-NACE (797-6223) *Fax:* 281-228-6300 *E-mail:* firstservice@nace.org *Web Site:* www.nace.org, pg 136

Challender, Gary, Books In Motion, 9922 E Montgomery Dr, Suite 31, Spokane Valley, WA 99206 *Tel:* 509-922-1646 *Toll Free Tel:* 800-752-3199 *Fax:* 509-922-1445 *E-mail:* info@booksinmotion.com *Web Site:* www.booksinmotion.com, pg 34

Cham, Jesmine, Arsenal Pulp Press, 211 E Georgia St, No 202, Vancouver, BC V6A 1Z6, Canada *Tel:* 604-687-4233 *Toll Free Tel:* 888-600-PULP (600-7857) *Fax:* 604-687-4283 *E-mail:* info@arsenalpulp.com *Web Site:* www.arsenalpulp.com, pg 395

Chamberlain, Daphne, Book of the Year Award, William F Winter Archives & History Bldg, 200 North St, Jackson, MS 39201 *Tel:* 601-576-6936 *Fax:* 601-576-6975 *E-mail:* mhs@mdah.ms.gov *Web Site:* www.mdah.ms.gov, pg 583

Chambers, Andrea, New York University, Center for Publishing & Applied Liberal Arts, 7 E 12 St, New York, NY 10003 *Tel:* 212-998-7200 *E-mail:* sps.info@nyu.edu *Web Site:* www.scps.nyu.edu/professional-pathways/topics.html, pg 563

Chambers, Andrea, NYU Advanced Publishing Institute, NYU SPS Center for Publishing & Applied Liberal Arts, 7 E 12 St, Suite 921, New York, NY 10003 *E-mail:* nyu.api@nyu.edu *Web Site:* www.sps.nyu.edu, pg 564

Chambers, Brett, Council for Advancement & Support of Education (CASE), 1201 Eye St NW, Suite 300, Washington, DC 20005 *Tel:* 202-328-CASE (328-2273) *Fax:* 202-387-4973 *E-mail:* membersupportcenter@case.org *Web Site:* www.case.org, pg 504

Chambers, Chris, Magazines Canada (MC), 555 Richmond St W, Suite 604, Mailbox 201, Toronto, ON M5V 3B1, Canada *Tel:* 416-994-6471 *Toll Free Tel:* 877-238-8354 *Fax:* 416-504-0437 *E-mail:* info@magazinescanada.ca *Web Site:* magazinescanada.ca, pg 510

Chambers, James, Ferguson Publishing, 132 W 31 St, 16 fl, New York, NY 10001 *Tel:* 212-967-8800 *Toll Free Tel:* 800-322-8755 *Toll Free Fax:* 800-678-3633 *E-mail:* custserv@infobase.com *Web Site:* infobasepublishing.com, pg 71

Chambers, James, Bram Stoker Awards®, PO Box 56687, Sherman Oaks, CA 91413 *Tel:* 818-220-3965 *E-mail:* stokerchair@horror.org *Web Site:* www.thebramstokerawards.com; horror.org, pg 666

Chambers, Jennifer, In-Plant Printing & Mailing Association (IPMA), 103 N Jefferson St, Kearney, MO 64060 *Tel:* 816-919-1691 *E-mail:* ipmainfo@ipma.org *Web Site:* www.ipma.org, pg 507

Chambers, Nathaniel, National Association of Black Journalists (NABJ), 1100 Knight Hall, Suite 3101, College Park, MD 20742 *Tel:* 301-405-0248 *E-mail:* contact@nabj.org; press@nabj.org *Web Site:* nabjonline.org, pg 511

Chamblee, Ruth, National Geographic Books, 1145 17 St NW, Washington, DC 20036-4688 *Tel:* 202-857-7000 *Toll Free Tel:* 877-866-6486 *E-mail:* ngbooks@cdsfulfillment.com *Web Site:* www.nationalgeographic.com/books/; ngbooks.buysub.com, pg 138

Chambliss, Jamie, Folio Literary Management, The Film Center Bldg, 630 Ninth Ave, Suite 1101, New York, NY 10036 *Tel:* 212-400-1494 *Fax:* 212-967-0977 *Web Site:* www.foliolit.com, pg 459

Chamenko, Tiffany, Information Today, Inc, 143 Old Marlton Pike, Medford, NJ 08055-8750 *Tel:* 609-654-6266 *Toll Free Tel:* 800-300-9868 (cust serv) *Fax:* 609-654-4309 *E-mail:* custserv@infotoday.com *Web Site:* informationtodayinc.com, pg 100

Chan, Darlene, Linda Chester Literary Agency, 630 Fifth Ave, Suite 2000, New York, NY 10111 *Tel:* 212-218-3350 *E-mail:* submissions@lindachester.com *Web Site:* www.lindachester.com, pg 454

Chan, Erica, Bloomsbury Publishing Inc, 1385 Broadway, 5th fl, New York, NY 10018 *Tel:* 212-419-5300 *E-mail:* marketingusa@bloomsbury.com; adultpublicityusa@bloomsbury.com; askacademic@bloomsbury.com *Web Site:* www.bloomsbury.com, pg 32

Chan, Erin, Arsenal Pulp Press, 211 E Georgia St, No 202, Vancouver, BC V6A 1Z6, Canada *Tel:* 604-687-4233 *Toll Free Tel:* 888-600-PULP (600-7857) *Fax:* 604-687-4283 *E-mail:* info@arsenalpulp.com *Web Site:* www.arsenalpulp.com, pg 395

Chan, Katelyn, Penguin Random House Canada, a Penguin Random House company, 320 Front St W, Suite 1400, Toronto, ON M5V 3B6, Canada *Tel:* 416-364-4449 *Toll Free Tel:* 888-523-9292 (cust serv) *E-mail:* canadaweb@penguinrandomhouse.com; customerservicescanada@penguinrandomhouse.com *Web Site:* www.penguinrandomhouse.ca, pg 416

Chan, Randy, Harlequin Enterprises Ltd, Bay Adelaide Centre, East Tower, 22 Adelaide St W, 41st fl, Toronto, ON M5H 4E3, Canada *Tel:* 416-445-5860 *Toll Free Tel:* 888-432-4879; 800-370-5838 (ebook inquiries) *E-mail:* customerservice@harlequin.com *Web Site:* www.harlequin.com, pg 409

Chan, Sylvia, Penguin Random House Canada, a Penguin Random House company, 320 Front St W, Suite 1400, Toronto, ON M5V 3B6, Canada *Tel:* 416-364-4449 *Toll Free Tel:* 888-523-9292 (cust serv) *E-mail:* canadaweb@penguinrandomhouse.com; customerservicescanada@penguinrandomhouse.com *Web Site:* www.penguinrandomhouse.ca, pg 416

Chance, Rachel, The American Library Association (ALA), 225 N Michigan Ave, Suite 1300, Chicago, IL 60601 *Tel:* 312-944-6780 *Toll Free Tel:* 800-545-2433; 866-SHOP-ALA (746-7252, orders) *Fax:* 312-280-5275; 312-440-9374; 312-280-5860 (orders) *E-mail:* ala@ala.org; alastore@ala.org *Web Site:* www.alastore.ala.org; www.ala.org, pg 10

Chanda, Justin, Simon & Schuster Children's Publishing, 1230 Avenue of the Americas, New York, NY 10020 *Tel:* 212-698-7000 *Web Site:* www.simonandschuster.com/kids; www.simonandschuster.com/teen; simonandschuster.net; simonandschuster.biz, pg 189

Chandlee, Chad M, Kendall Hunt Publishing Co, 4050 Westmark Dr, Dubuque, IA 52002-2624 *Tel:* 563-589-1000 *Toll Free Tel:* 800-228-0810 (orders) *Fax:* 563-589-1071 *Toll Free Fax:* 800-772-9165 *E-mail:* ordernow@kendallhunt.com *Web Site:* www.kendallhunt.com, pg 108

Chandler, Pamela Siege, Foundation Press, c/o West Academic, 860 Blue Gentian Rd, Eagan, MN 55121 *Toll Free Tel:* 877-888-1330 *E-mail:* support@westacademic.com *Web Site:* www.westacademic.com, pg 74

Chaney, Margo, University of Illinois Press, 1325 S Oak St, MC-566, Champaign, IL 61820-6903 *Tel:* 217-333-0950 *Fax:* 217-244-8082 *E-mail:* uipress@uillinois.edu; journals@uillinois.edu *Web Site:* www.press.uillinois.edu, pg 216

Chang, Adelynne, Macmillan, 120 Broadway, 22nd fl, New York, NY 10271 *E-mail:* press.inquiries@macmillan.com *Web Site:* us.macmillan.com, pg 122

Chang, Ann Mei, Candid, 32 Old Slip, 24th fl, New York, NY 10005-3500 *Tel:* 212-620-4230 *Toll Free Tel:* 800-424-9836 *Fax:* 212-807-3677 *Web Site:* candid.org, pg 39

Chang, Anna, Modern Language Association (MLA), 85 Broad St, New York, NY 10004 *Tel:* 646-576-5000 *E-mail:* help@mla.org *Web Site:* www.mla.org; x.com/MLAnews; www.facebook.com/modernlanguageassociation; www.linkedin.com/company/modern-language-association, pg 133

Chang, Anna, Modern Language Association (MLA), 85 Broad St, New York, NY 10004 *Tel:* 646-576-5000 *E-mail:* help@mla.org; membership@mla.org *Web Site:* www.mla.org; x.com/MLAnews; www.facebook.com/modernlanguageassociation; www.linkedin.com/company/modern-language-association, pg 511

Chang, Jennifer, University of Texas at Austin, New Writers Project, Dept of English, 204 W 21 St, B-5000, Austin, TX 78712-1164 *Tel:* 512-471-4991 *Fax:* 512-471-4909 *E-mail:* newwritersproject@utexas.edu *Web Site:* liberalarts.utexas.edu/nwp, pg 567

Chang, Lan Samantha, Truman Capote Award for Literary Criticism in Honor of Newton Arvin, 102 Dey House, 507 N Clinton St, Iowa City, IA 52242-1000 *Tel:* 319-335-0416 *Web Site:* writersworkshop.uiowa.edu, pg 586

Chang, Lan Samantha, The Iowa Short Fiction Award, 102 Dey House, 507 N Clinton St, Iowa City, IA 52242-1000 *Tel:* 319-335-0416 *Fax:* 319-335-0420 *Web Site:* writersworkshop.uiowa.edu/about/iowa-short-fiction-awards, pg 617

Chang, Lan Samantha, Iowa Writers' Workshop, Graduate Program in Creative Writing, 102 Dey House, Iowa City, IA 52242-1000 *Tel:* 319-335-0416 *Web Site:* writersworkshop.uiowa.edu, pg 555

Chang, Lan Samantha, Sonny Mehta Fellowships in Creative Writing, 102 Dey House, 507 N Clinton St, Iowa City, IA 52242-1000 *Tel:* 319-335-0416 *Web Site:* writersworkshop.uiowa.edu/mehta, pg 632

Chang, Lan Samantha, The John Simmons Short Fiction Award, 102 Dey House, 507 N Clinton St, Iowa City, IA 52242-1000 *Tel:* 319-335-0416 *Fax:* 319-335-0420 *Web Site:* writersworkshop.uiowa.edu/about/iowa-short-fiction-awards, pg 663

Chang, Lan Samantha, University of Iowa, Writers' Workshop, Graduate Creative Writing Program, 102 Dey House, 507 N Clinton St, Iowa City, IA 52242-1000 *Tel:* 319-335-0416 *Fax:* 319-335-0420 *Web Site:* writersworkshop.uiowa.edu, pg 567

Chang, Melanie, Harry N Abrams Inc, 195 Broadway, 9th fl, New York, NY 10007 *Tel:* 212-206-7715 *Toll Free Tel:* 800-345-1359 *Fax:* 212-645-8437 *E-mail:* abrams@abramsbooks.com; publicity@abramsbooks.com; sales@abramsbooks.com *Web Site:* www.abramsbooks.com, pg 2

Chang, Melanie, Stewart, Tabori & Chang, 195 Broadway, 9th fl, New York, NY 10007 *Tel:* 212-206-7715 *Fax:* 212-519-1210 *E-mail:* abrams@abramsbooks.com *Web Site:* www.abramsbooks.com/imprints/stc, pg 198

Chang, Ms Minju, BookStop Literary Agency LLC, 67 Meadow View Rd, Orinda, CA 94563 *E-mail:* info@bookstopliterary.com *Web Site:* www.bookstopliterary.com, pg 451

Chang, Tina, Binghamton University Creative Writing Program, c/o Dept of English, General Literature & Rhetoric, PO Box 6000, Binghamton, NY 13902-6000 *Tel:* 607-777-2168 *Fax:* 607-777-2408 *E-mail:* cwpro@binghamton.edu *Web Site:* www.binghamton.edu/english/creative-writing/index.html, pg 561

Chang, Tina, Binghamton University John Gardner Fiction Book Award, Dept of English, General Literature & Rhetoric, Bartle Library N, Rm 1149, Vestal Pkwy E, Binghamton, NY 13902 *Tel:* 607-777-2713 *Web Site:* www2.binghamton.edu/english/creative-writing, pg 580

Chang, Tina, Binghamton University Milt Kessler Poetry Book Award, Dept of English, General Literature & Rhetoric, Bartle Library N, Rm 1149, Vestal Pkwy E, Binghamton, NY 13902 *Tel:* 607-777-2713 *Web Site:* www2.binghamton.edu/english/creative-writing, pg 580

Chang, Wah-Ming, Counterpoint Press LLC, 2560 Ninth St, Suite 318, Berkeley, CA 94710 *Tel:* 510-704-0230 *Fax:* 510-704-0268 *E-mail:* info@counterpointpress.com *Web Site:* counterpointpress.com; softskull.com, pg 54

Channer, Bernadette, Jhpiego, 1615 Thames St, Baltimore, MD 21231-3492 Tel: 410-537-1800 E-mail: info@jhpiego.org Web Site: www.jhpiego.org, pg 106

Chanter, Dr Carol, Scholastic Education Solutions, 557 Broadway, New York, NY 10012 Tel: 212-343-6100 Fax: 212-343-6189 Web Site: www.scholastic.com, pg 184

Chapin, Ms Frances, Write on the Sound Writers' Conference, Frances Anderson Center, 700 Main St, Edmonds, WA 98020 Tel: 425-771-0228 Fax: 425-771-0253 E-mail: wots@edmondswa.gov Web Site: www.writeonthesound.com, pg 558

Chaplin, Allison, Indiana University Press, Off of Scholarly Publg, Herman B Wells Library 350, 1320 E Tenth St, Bloomington, IN 47405-3907 Tel: 812-855-8817 Fax: 812-855-7931; 812-855-8507 E-mail: iupress@indiana.edu Web Site: iupress.org, pg 100

Chapman, Amy, AIGA 50 Books | 50 Covers, 228 Park Ave S, Suite 58603, New York, NY 10003 Tel: 212-807-1990 E-mail: competitions@aiga.org Web Site: www.aiga.org, pg 571

Chapman, Amy, AIGA, the professional association for design, 228 Park Ave S, Suite 58603, New York, NY 10003 Tel: 212-807-1990 E-mail: general@aiga.org Web Site: www.aiga.org, pg 493

Chapman, Eric, Macmillan, 120 Broadway, 22nd fl, New York, NY 10271 E-mail: press.inquiries@macmillan.com Web Site: us.macmillan.com, pg 122

Chapman, Ian, Simon & Schuster, LLC, 1230 Avenue of the Americas, New York, NY 10020 Tel: 212-698-7000 Toll Free Tel: 800-223-2336 (orders) Fax: 212-698-7007 Toll Free Fax: 800-943-9831 (orders) E-mail: firstname.lastname@simonandschuster.com; purchaseorders@simonandschuster.com (orders) Web Site: www.simonandschuster.com, pg 189

Chapman, Monica, Coretta Scott King Book Awards, 225 N Michigan Ave, Suite 1300, Chicago, IL 60601 Tel: 312-944-6780 Toll Free Tel: 800-545-2433 Fax: 312-440-9374 E-mail: diversity@ala.org Web Site: www.ala.org/awardsgrants/coretta-scott-king-book-awards, pg 620

Chapman, Monica, Coretta Scott King - John Steptoe Award for New Talent, 225 N Michigan Ave, Suite 1300, Chicago, IL 60601 Tel: 312-944-6780 Toll Free Tel: 800-545-2433 (ext 4294) Fax: 312-280-3256 E-mail: diversity@ala.org Web Site: www.ala.org/awardsgrants, pg 620

Chapman, Monica, Coretta Scott King - Virginia Hamilton Award for Lifetime Achievement, 225 N Michigan Ave, Suite 1300, Chicago, IL 60601 Toll Free Tel: 800-545-2433 E-mail: diversity@ala.org Web Site: www.ala.org/emiert/virginia-hamilton-award-lifetime-achievement, pg 620

Chapman, Robyn, Roaring Brook Press, 120 Broadway, New York, NY 10271 Tel: 646-307-5151 Web Site: us.macmillan.com/publishers/roaring-brook-press, pg 176

Chapman, Sharon, Society for Features Journalism (SFJ), Eugene S Pulliam National Journalism Ctr, 3909 N Meridian St, Indianapolis, IN 46208 E-mail: wearesfj@gmail.com Web Site: featuresjournalism.org, pg 519

Chapnick, Laura, Groundwood Books, 128 Sterling Rd, Lower Level, Toronto, ON M6R 2B7, Canada Tel: 416-363-4343 Fax: 416-363-1017 E-mail: customerservice@houseofanansi.com Web Site: www.houseofanansi.com, pg 407

Chapnick, Laura, House of Anansi Press Inc, 128 Sterling Rd, Lower Level, Toronto, ON M6R 2B7, Canada Tel: 416-363-4343 Fax: 416-363-1017 E-mail: customerservice@houseofanansi.com Web Site: houseofanansi.com, pg 409

Chappell, Chris, Applause Theatre & Cinema Books, 64 S Main St, Essex, CT 06426 Tel: 973-223-5039 E-mail: info@applausepub.com Web Site: www.applausepub.com, pg 15

Chappelle, Masheri, New Hampshire Literary Awards, 2500 N River Rd, Manchester, NH 03106 Tel: 603-270-5466 E-mail: info@nhwritersproject.org Web Site: www.nhwritersproject.org/new-hampshire-literary-awards, pg 640

Chappelle, Masheri, New Hampshire Writers' Project (NHWP), 2500 N River Rd, Manchester, NH 03106 Tel: 603-270-5466 E-mail: info@nhwritersproject.org Web Site: www.nhwritersproject.org, pg 514

Charbonneau, Amelie, QA International (QAI), 7240 Rue Saint-Hubert, Montreal, QC H2R 2N1, Canada Tel: 514-499-3000 Fax: 514-499-3010 Web Site: www.qa-international.com, pg 417

Charbonneau, Annie-Pier, University of Ottawa Press (Presses de l'Université d'Ottawa), 542 King Edward Ave, Ottawa, ON K1N 6N5, Canada Tel: 613-562-5246 Fax: 613-562-5247 E-mail: puo-uop@uottawa.ca; acquisitions@uottawa.ca Web Site: press.uottawa.ca, pg 423

Charbonneau, Catherine, La Courte Echelle, 4388, rue Saint-Denis, Suite 315, Montreal, QC H2J 2L1, Canada Tel: 514-312-6950 E-mail: info@courteechelle.com Web Site: www.groupecourteechelle.com/la-courte-echelle, pg 400

Charette, Francois, Livres Canada Books, One Nicholas, Suite 504, Ottawa, ON K1N 7B7, Canada Tel: 613-562-2324 Fax: 613-562-2329 E-mail: info@livrescanadabooks.com Web Site: www.livrescanadabooks.com, pg 510

Charles, Kristi, National Resource Center for Youth Services, Schusterman Ctr, Bldg 4W, 4502 E 41 St, Tulsa, OK 74135-2512 Tel: 918-660-3700 Toll Free Tel: 800-274-2687 E-mail: nrcys@ou.edu Web Site: www.nrcys.ou.edu, pg 138

Charles, Perpetua, Beacon Press, 24 Farnsworth St, Boston, MA 02210-1409 Tel: 617-742-2110 Fax: 617-723-3097 E-mail: production@beacon.org Web Site: www.beacon.org, pg 25

Charles, Walkie, Alaska Native Language Center (ANLC), PO Box 757680, Fairbanks, AK 99775-7680 Tel: 907-474-7874 E-mail: uaf-anlc@alaska.edu (orders) Web Site: www.uaf.edu/anlc, pg 6

Chasan, Gail, Harlequin Enterprises Ltd, 195 Broadway, 24th fl, New York, NY 10007 Tel: 212-207-7000 Toll Free Tel: 888-432-4879; 800-370-5838 (ebooks) E-mail: customerservice@harlequin.com Web Site: www.harlequin.com/shop/index.html; corporate.harlequin.com, pg 85

Chatfield, Jason, National Cartoonists Society (NCS), PO Box 592927, Orlando, FL 32859-2927 Tel: 407-994-6703 E-mail: info@nationalcartoonists.com; membership@nationalcartoonists.com Web Site: www.nationalcartoonists.com, pg 512

Chatoredussy, Nikita, Macmillan, 120 Broadway, 22nd fl, New York, NY 10271 E-mail: press.inquiries@macmillan.com Web Site: us.macmillan.com, pg 122

Chatterjee, Jaya Aninda, Yale University Press, 302 Temple St, New Haven, CT 06511-8909 Tel: 203-432-0960; 203-432-0966 (sales); 401-531-2800 (cust serv) Toll Free Tel: 800-405-1619 (cust serv) Fax: 203-432-0948; 203-432-8485 (sales); 401-531-2801 (cust serv) Toll Free Fax: 800-406-9145 (cust serv) E-mail: sales.press@yale.edu (sales); customer.care@triliteral.org (cust serv) Web Site: www.yalebooks.com; yalepress.yale.edu/yupbooks, pg 235

Chau, Karen, Macmillan, 120 Broadway, 22nd fl, New York, NY 10271 E-mail: press.inquiries@macmillan.com Web Site: us.macmillan.com, pg 122

Chaudhari, Sameer, Macmillan, 120 Broadway, 22nd fl, New York, NY 10271 E-mail: press.inquiries@macmillan.com Web Site: us.macmillan.com, pg 122

Chauhan, Bhavna, Doubleday Canada, 320 Front St W, Suite 1400, Toronto, ON M5V 3B6, Canada Tel: 416-364-4449 Fax: 416-598-7764 Web Site: www.penguinrandomhouse.ca, pg 401

Chavern, David, News/Media Alliance, 4401 N Fairfax Dr, Suite 300, Arlington, VA 22203 Tel: 571-366-1000 E-mail: info@newsmediaalliance.org Web Site: www.newsmediaalliance.org, pg 514

Chavis, Dr Benjamin F Jr, National Newspaper Publishers Association (NNPA), 1816 12 St NW, Washington, DC 20009 Tel: 202-588-8764 E-mail: info@nnpa.org Web Site: nnpa.org; blackpressusa.com, pg 513

Chawla, Michelle, Canada Council for the Arts (Conseil des arts du Canada), 150 Elgin St, 2nd fl, Ottawa, ON K2P 1L4, Canada Toll Free Tel: 800-263-5588 (CN only) Fax: 613-566-4390 E-mail: info@canadacouncil.ca; media@canadacouncil.ca Web Site: canadacouncil.ca, pg 502

Che, Cathy Linh, Kundiman Retreat, Fordham University, English Dept, 113 W 60 St, Rm 924, New York, NY 10023 E-mail: info@kundiman.org Web Site: www.kundiman.org, pg 556

Checole, Kassahun, Africa World Press Inc, 541 W Ingham Ave, Suite B, Trenton, NJ 08638 Tel: 609-695-3200 Fax: 609-695-6466 E-mail: customerservice@africaworldpressbooks.com Web Site: www.africaworldpressbooks.com, pg 5

Checole, Senait Kassahun, The Red Sea Press Inc, 541 W Ingham Ave, Suite B, Trenton, NJ 08638 Tel: 609-695-3200 Fax: 609-695-6466 E-mail: customerservice@africaworldpressbooks.com Web Site: www.africaworldpressbooks.com, pg 173

Cheek, Claire, St Martin's Press, LLC, 120 Broadway, New York, NY 10271 E-mail: publicity@stmartins.com; trademarketing@stmartins.com; foreignrights@stmartins.com Web Site: us.macmillan.com/smp, pg 181

Cheema, Tia Resham, Random House Children's Books, c/o Penguin Random House LLC, 1745 Broadway, New York, NY 10019 Tel: 212-782-9000 Web Site: www.rhcbooks.com, pg 170

Cheluri, Vasudevareddy, Macmillan, 120 Broadway, 22nd fl, New York, NY 10271 E-mail: press.inquiries@macmillan.com Web Site: us.macmillan.com, pg 122

Chen, Catharine, Arsenal Pulp Press, 211 E Georgia St, No 202, Vancouver, BC V6A 1Z6, Canada Tel: 604-687-4233 Toll Free Tel: 888-600-PULP (600-7857) Fax: 604-687-4283 E-mail: info@arsenalpulp.com Web Site: www.arsenalpulp.com, pg 395

Chen, Cheryl, Penguin Random House Canada, a Penguin Random House company, 320 Front St W, Suite 1400, Toronto, ON M5V 3B6, Canada Tel: 416-364-4449 Toll Free Tel: 888-523-9292 (cust serv) E-mail: canadaweb@penguinrandomhouse.com; customerservicescanada@penguinrandomhouse.com Web Site: www.penguinrandomhouse.ca, pg 416

Chen, Jenny, Random House Publishing Group, 1745 Broadway, New York, NY 10019 Toll Free Tel: 800-200-3552 Web Site: www.randomhousebooks.com, pg 171

Chen, May, HarperCollins Publishers LLC, 195 Broadway, New York, NY 10007 Tel: 212-207-7000 Web Site: www.harpercollins.com, pg 86

Chen, Tania, University of British Columbia Creative Writing Program, Buchanan Rm E-462, 1866 Main Mall, Vancouver, BC V6T 1Z1, Canada Tel: 604-822-0699 Web Site: creativewriting.ubc.ca, pg 566

Chenault, Earlita K, Parallax Press, 2236B Sixth St, Berkeley, CA 94710 Tel: 510-325-2945 Toll Free Tel: 800-863-5290 (orders) Web Site: www.parallax.org, pg 151

Cheng, Christopher, Crystal Kite Awards, 6363 Wilshire Blvd, Suite 425, Los Angeles, CA 90048 Tel: 323-782-1010 E-mail: info@scbwi.org Web Site: www.scbwi.org/awards/crystal-kite-member-choice-award, pg 593

Cheng, Donna, Random House Publishing Group, 1745 Broadway, New York, NY 10019 Toll Free Tel: 800-200-3552 Web Site: www.randomhousebooks.com, pg 171

Cheng, Ivy, Viking Penguin, c/o Penguin Random House LLC, 1745 Broadway, New York, NY 10019 Tel: 212-782-9000 Web Site: www.penguin.com/overview-vikingbooks/; www.penguin.com/pamela-dorman-

Cheng, Jessamine, The New Press, 120 Wall St, 31st fl, New York, NY 10005 Tel: 212-629-8802 Fax: 212-629-8617 E-mail: newpress@thenewpress.com Web Site: thenewpress.com, pg 140

Cheng, Jill, Cheng & Tsui Co Inc, 25 West St, 2nd fl, Boston, MA 02111-1213 Tel: 617-988-2400 Toll Free Tel: 800-554-1963 Fax: 617-426-3669 E-mail: service@cheng-tsui.com; orders@cheng-tsui.com; marketing@cheng-tsui.com Web Site: www.cheng-tsui.com, pg 46

Cheng, Lisa, Hay House LLC, PO Box 5100, Carlsbad, CA 92018-5100 Tel: 760-431-7695 (ext 1, intl) Toll Free Tel: 800-654-5126 (ext 1, US) Toll Free Fax: 800-650-5115 Web Site: www.hayhouse.com, pg 89

Cheng, Melanie, Penguin Random House Canada, a Penguin Random House company, 320 Front St W, Suite 1400, Toronto, ON M5V 3B6, Canada Tel: 416-364-4449 Toll Free Tel: 888-523-9292 (cust serv) E-mail: canadaweb@penguinrandomhouse.com; customerservicescanada@penguinrandomhouse.com Web Site: www.penguinrandomhouse.ca, pg 416

Cheng, Vivian, Marshall Cavendish Education, 99 White Plains Rd, Tarrytown, NY 10591-9001 Tel: 914-332-8888 Toll Free Tel: 800-821-9881 Fax: 914-332-1082 E-mail: mce@marshallcavendish.com; customerservice@marshallcavendish.com Web Site: www.mceducation.us, pg 125

Chepesiuk, Ron, Strategic Media Books LLC, 782 Wofford St, Rock Hill, SC 29730 Tel: 803-366-5440 E-mail: contact@strategicmediabooks.com Web Site: strategicmediabooks.com, pg 200

Chernoff, Mitch, Society for Industrial & Applied Mathematics, 3600 Market St, 6th fl, Philadelphia, PA 19104-2688 Tel: 215-382-9800 Toll Free Tel: 800-447-7426 E-mail: siam@siam.org Web Site: www.siam.org, pg 192

Cherry, Amy, W W Norton & Company Inc, 500 Fifth Ave, New York, NY 10110-0017 Tel: 212-354-5500 Toll Free Tel: 800-233-4830 (orders & cust serv) Fax: 212-869-0856 Toll Free Fax: 800-458-6515 E-mail: orders@wwnorton.com Web Site: wwnorton.com, pg 143

Cherullo, Helen, Mountaineers Books, 1001 SW Klickitat Way, Suite 201, Seattle, WA 98134 Tel: 206-223-6303 Fax: 206-223-6306 E-mail: mbooks@mountaineersbooks.org; customerservice@mountaineersbooks.org Web Site: www.mountaineers.org/books, pg 135

Chesak, Chez, Outdoor Writers Association of America (OWAA), 2814 Brooks St, Box 442, Missoula, MT 59801 Tel: 406-728-7434 E-mail: info@owaa.org Web Site: owaa.org, pg 516

Chesak, Chez, Outdoor Writers Association of America Annual Conference, 2814 Brooks St, Box 442, Missoula, MT 59801 Tel: 406-728-7434 E-mail: info@owaa.org Web Site: owaa.org, pg 556

Chesman, Andrea, Little Chicago Editorial Services, 154 Natural Tpke, Ripton, VT 05766 Tel: 802-388-9782 Web Site: andreachesman.com, pg 442

Chester, Sarah, Phaidon, 65 Bleecker St, 8th fl, New York, NY 10012 Tel: 212-652-5400 Toll Free Tel: 800-759-0190 (cust serv) Fax: 212-652-5410 Toll Free Fax: 800-286-9471 (cust serv) E-mail: enquiries@phaidon.com Web Site: www.phaidon.com, pg 159

Cheuse, Sonya, HarperCollins Publishers LLC, 195 Broadway, New York, NY 10007 Tel: 212-207-7000 Web Site: www.harpercollins.com, pg 86

Chew, Mieke, New Directions Publishing Corp, 80 Eighth Ave, 19th fl, New York, NY 10011 Tel: 212-255-0230 E-mail: editorial@ndbooks.com; publicity@ndbooks.com Web Site: ndbooks.com, pg 139

Chi, Youngsuk "YS", Association of American Publishers (AAP), 455 Massachusetts Ave NW, Suite 700, Washington, DC 20001-2777 Tel: 202-347-3375 Fax: 202-347-3690 E-mail: info@publishers.org Web Site: publishers.org, pg 498

Chia, Jonathan-Cheehong, Macmillan, 120 Broadway, 22nd fl, New York, NY 10271 E-mail: press.inquiries@macmillan.com Web Site: us.macmillan.com, pg 122

Chidiac, Dana, Henry Holt and Company, LLC, 120 Broadway, 23rd fl, New York, NY 10271 Tel: 646-307-5151 Toll Free Tel: 888-330-8477 (orders) Fax: 646-307-5285 Web Site: www.henryholt.com, pg 94

Chidley, Sam, The Karpfinger Agency, 357 W 20 St, New York, NY 10011-3379 Tel: 212-691-2690 Fax: 212-691-7129 E-mail: info@karpfinger.com (no queries or submissions) Web Site: karpfinger.com, pg 465

Childre, Sara, HeartMath LLC, 14700 W Park Ave, Boulder Creek, CA 95006 Tel: 831-338-8500 Toll Free Tel: 800-711-6221 Fax: 831-338-8504 E-mail: info@heartmath.org; service@heartmath.org Web Site: www.heartmath.org, pg 90

Childress, David H, Adventures Unlimited Press (AUP), One Adventure Place, Kempton, IL 60946 Tel: 815-253-6390 Fax: 815-253-6300 E-mail: info@adventuresunlimitedpress.com Web Site: www.adventuresunlimitedpress.com, pg 5

Childs, Faith Hampton, Faith Childs Literary Agency Inc, 915 Broadway, Suite 1009, New York, NY 10010 Tel: 212-995-9600 Web Site: faithchildsliteraryagency.com, pg 454

Childs, Jennifer, Penguin Random House LLC, 1745 Broadway, New York, NY 10019 Tel: 212-782-9000 Toll Free Tel: 800-726-0600 Web Site: www.penguinrandomhouse.com, pg 155

Chillot, Rick, BenBella Books Inc, 10440 N Central Expwy, Suite 800, Dallas, TX 75231-2264 Tel: 214-750-3600 Web Site: www.benbellabooks.com; www.smartpopbooks.com, pg 27

Chin, Brenda, BelleBooks, PO Box 300921, Memphis, TN 38130 Tel: 901-344-9024 Fax: 901-344-9068 E-mail: bellebooks@bellebooks.com Web Site: www.bellebooks.com, pg 27

Chin, Jeffrey, HarperCollins Publishers LLC, 195 Broadway, New York, NY 10007 Tel: 212-207-7000 Web Site: www.harpercollins.com, pg 87

Chin, Lauren Kiri, Chronicle Books LLC, 680 Second St, San Francisco, CA 94107 Tel: 415-537-4200 Fax: 415-537-4460 (perms) E-mail: hello@chroniclebooks.com; subrights@chroniclebooks.com Web Site: www.chroniclebooks.com, pg 48

Chin, Oliver, Immedium, 535 Rockdale Dr, San Francisco, CA 94127 Tel: 415-452-8546 Fax: 360-937-6272 E-mail: orders@immedium.com; sales@immedium.com Web Site: www.immedium.com, pg 99

Ching, Emma, University of Hawaii Press, 2840 Kolowalu St, Honolulu, HI 96822-1888 Tel: 808-956-8255 Toll Free Tel: 888-UHPRESS (847-7377) Toll Free Fax: 800-650-7811 E-mail: uhpbooks@hawaii.edu Web Site: www.uhpress.hawaii.edu, pg 216

Chinn, Jane, Penguin Random House LLC, 1745 Broadway, New York, NY 10019 Tel: 212-782-9000 Toll Free Tel: 800-726-0600 Web Site: www.penguinrandomhouse.com, pg 155

Chinski, Eric, Farrar, Straus & Giroux, LLC, 120 Broadway, New York, NY 10271 Tel: 212-741-6900 E-mail: fsg.publicity@fsgbooks.com; sales@fsgbooks.com Web Site: us.macmillan.com/fsg, pg 70

Chipponeri, Kelli, American Book Producers Association (ABPA), 7 Peter Cooper Rd, No 7G, New York, NY 10010 E-mail: office@abpaonline.org Web Site: www.abpaonline.org, pg 494

Chiriboga, Mireya, HarperCollins Publishers LLC, 195 Broadway, New York, NY 10007 Tel: 212-207-7000 Web Site: www.harpercollins.com, pg 87

Chirichella, Cara, Macmillan, 120 Broadway, 22nd fl, New York, NY 10271 E-mail: press.inquiries@macmillan.com Web Site: us.macmillan.com, pg 122

Chmiel, Barbara, The Blackburn Press, PO Box 287, Caldwell, NJ 07006-0287 Tel: 973-228-7077 Fax: 973-228-7276 Web Site: www.blackburnpress.com, pg 30

Choi, Jennifer, Bloomsbury Publishing Inc, 1385 Broadway, 5th fl, New York, NY 10018 Tel: 212-419-5300 E-mail: marketingusa@bloomsbury.com; adultpublicityusa@bloomsbury.com; askacademic@bloomsbury.com Web Site: www.bloomsbury.com, pg 31

Choi, Lydia, BenBella Books Inc, 10440 N Central Expwy, Suite 800, Dallas, TX 75231-2264 Tel: 214-750-3600 Web Site: www.benbellabooks.com; www.smartpopbooks.com, pg 27

Choi, Min, Gallery Books, 1230 Avenue of the Americas, New York, NY 10020 Toll Free Tel: 800-456-6798 Fax: 212-698-7284 E-mail: consumer.customerservice@simonandschuster.com Web Site: www.simonandschuster.com, pg 76

Choix, Paul, Gallery Books, 1230 Avenue of the Americas, New York, NY 10020 Toll Free Tel: 800-456-6798 Fax: 212-698-7284 E-mail: consumer.customerservice@simonandschuster.com Web Site: www.simonandschuster.com, pg 76

Chong, Anita, McClelland & Stewart Ltd, 320 Front St W, Suite 1400, Toronto, ON M5V 3B6, Canada Tel: 416-364-4449 Toll Free Tel: 888-523-9292 E-mail: customerservicescanada@penguinrandomhouse.com; mcclellandsubmissions@prh.com Web Site: penguinrandomhouse.ca/imprints/mcclelland-stewart, pg 412

Chong, Michele, Michael Wiese Productions, 12400 Ventura Blvd, No 1111, Studio City, CA 91604 Tel: 818-379-8799 Toll Free Tel: 800-833-5738 (orders) Fax: 818-986-3408 E-mail: mwpsales@earthlink.net; fulfillment@portcity.com Web Site: www.mwp.com, pg 229

Chong, Suet, Workman Publishing, 1290 Avenue of the Americas, New York, NY 10104 Toll Free Tel: 800-759-0190 Fax: 212-364-0950 E-mail: workman-inquiry@hbgusa.com Web Site: www.hachettebookgroup.com/imprint/workman-publishing-company/, pg 232

Chorpenning, Rev Joseph F, St Joseph's University Press, 5600 City Ave, Philadelphia, PA 19131-1395 Tel: 610-660-3402 Fax: 610-660-3412 E-mail: sjupress@sju.edu Web Site: www.sjupress.com, pg 180

Chou, Arthur, Velazquez Press, 9682 Telstar Ave, Suite 110, El Monte, CA 91731 Tel: 626-448-3448 Fax: 626-602-3817 E-mail: info@academiclearningcompany.com Web Site: www.velazquezpress.com, pg 224

Chou, Emily, Grouse Grind Lit Prize for V Short Form, University of British Columbia, Buch E462, 1866 Main Mall, Vancouver, BC V6T 1Z1, Canada Tel: 604-822-2514 Fax: 604-822-3616 E-mail: promotions@prismmagazine.ca Web Site: www.prismmagazine.ca/contests, pg 609

Chou, Emily, The Pacific Spirit Poetry Prize, University of British Columbia, Buch E462, 1866 Main Mall, Vancouver, BC V6T 1Z1, Canada Tel: 604-822-2514 Fax: 604-822-3616 E-mail: promotions@prismmagazine.ca Web Site: www.prismmagazine.ca/contests, pg 645

Chou, Emily, PRISM international Creative Nonfiction Contest, University of British Columbia, Buch E462, 1866 Main Mall, Vancouver, BC V6T 1Z1, Canada Tel: 604-822-2514 Fax: 604-822-3616 E-mail: promotions@prismmagazine.ca Web Site: www.prismmagazine.ca/contests, pg 653

Chou, Emily, The Jacob Zilber Prize for Short Fiction, University of British Columbia, Buch E462, 1866 Main Mall, Vancouver, BC V6T 1Z1, Canada Tel: 604-822-2514 Fax: 604-822-3616 E-mail: promotions@prismmagazine.ca Web Site: www.prismmagazine.ca/contests, pg 680

Chou, Shelly, Agency Chicago, 7000 Phoenix Ave NE, Suite 202, Albuquerque, NM 87110 E-mail: agency.chicago@usa.com, pg 448

Chow, Kathy, Education Writers Association (EWA), 1825 "K" St NW, Suite 200, Washington, DC 20006 Tel: 202-452-9830 Web Site: ewa.org, pg 505

Chow, Kathy, Education Writers Association Workshops, 1825 "K" St NW, Suite 200, Washington, DC 20006 Tel: 202-452-9830 Web Site: ewa.org, pg 554

Chow, Kathy, EWA Reporting Fellowships, 1825 "K" St NW, Suite 200, Washington, DC 20006 Tel: 202-452-9830 Web Site: ewa.org, pg 600

Chow, Kathy, National Awards for Education Reporting, 1825 "K" St NW, Suite 200, Washington, DC 20006 Tel: 202-452-9830 E-mail: awards@ewa.org Web Site: ewa.org, pg 637

Choy, May, Doubleday, c/o Penguin Random House LLC, 1745 Broadway, New York, NY 10019 Tel: 212-751-2600 Fax: 212-940-7390 (dom rts); 212-572-2662 (foreign rts) Web Site: knopfdoubleday.com/imprint/doubleday/; knopfdoubleday.com, pg 61

Choy, May, Alfred A Knopf, c/o Penguin Random House LLC, 1745 Broadway, New York, NY 10019 Tel: 212-751-2600 Fax: 212-940-7390 (dom rts); 212-572-2662 (foreign rts) Web Site: knopfdoubleday.com/imprint/knopf/; knopfdoubleday.com, pg 110

Choy, May, Penguin Random House LLC, 1745 Broadway, New York, NY 10019 Tel: 212-782-9000 Toll Free Tel: 800-726-0600 Web Site: www.penguinrandomhouse.com, pg 155

Choyce, Lesley, Pottersfield Press, 248 Leslie Rd, East Lawrencetown, NS B2Z 1T4, Canada Toll Free Tel: 800-646-2879 (orders only) E-mail: pottersfieldcreative@gmail.com Web Site: www.pottersfieldpress.com, pg 416

Chrisant, William, Florida Antiquarian Booksellers Association (FABA), c/o Lighthouse Books, ABAA, 14046 Fifth St, Dade City, FL 33525 Tel: 727-234-7759 E-mail: floridabooksellers@gmail.com Web Site: floridabooksellers.com, pg 506

Chrisman, Ronald, University of North Texas Press, 941 Precision Dr, Denton, TX 76207 Tel: 940-565-2142 Fax: 940-369-8760 Web Site: untpress.unt.edu, pg 218

Christensen, Daniel, Random House Publishing Group, 1745 Broadway, New York, NY 10019 Toll Free Tel: 800-200-3552 Web Site: www.randomhousebooks.com, pg 171

Christensen, Erica, Metamorphosis Literary Agency, 12410 S Acuff Ct, Olathe, KS 66062 Tel: 646-397-1640 E-mail: info@metamorphosisliteraryagency.com Web Site: www.metamorphosisliteraryagency.com, pg 470

Christensen, Karen, Berkshire Publishing Group LLC, 122 Castle St, Great Barrington, MA 01230 E-mail: info@berkshirepublishing.com; cservice@berkshirepublishing.com; rights@berkshirepublishing.com Web Site: www.berkshirepublishing.com, pg 28

Christian, Abigail, Society of American Archivists, 17 N State St, Suite 1425, Chicago, IL 60602-4061 Tel: 312-606-0722 Toll Free Tel: 866-722-7858 Fax: 312-606-0728 Web Site: www.archivists.org, pg 192

Christian, Alayne Kay, Blue Whale Press, 237 Rainbow Dr, No 13702, Livingston, TX 77399-2037 Toll Free Tel: 800-848-1631 E-mail: info@bluewhalepress.com; sales@bluewhalepress.com Web Site: www.bluewhalepress.com, pg 32

Christian, Bryan, Little, Brown and Company, 1290 Avenue of the Americas, New York, NY 10104 Tel: 212-364-1100 Fax: 212-364-0952 E-mail: firstname.lastname@hbgusa.com Web Site: www.hachettebookgroup.com/imprint/little-brown-and-company/, pg 118

Christian, Clark, Thomas Nelson, 501 Nelson Place, Nashville, TN 37214 Tel: 615-889-9000 Toll Free Tel: 800-251-4000 Web Site: www.thomasnelson.com, pg 206

Christmas, Bobbie, Zebra Communications, 13682 Hwy 92, No 3005, Woodstock, GA 30188-4734 Tel: 404-433-7507 E-mail: bobbie@zebraeditor.com Web Site: www.zebraeditor.com, pg 446

Christopher, Danielle Fiorella, St Martin's Press, LLC, 120 Broadway, New York, NY 10271 E-mail: publicity@stmartins.com; trademarketing@stmartins.com; foreignrights@stmartins.com Web Site: us.macmillan.com/smp, pg 180

Christopher, Jared, Macmillan, 120 Broadway, 22nd fl, New York, NY 10271 E-mail: press.inquiries@macmillan.com Web Site: us.macmillan.com, pg 122

Christopher, Rob, ALA Neal-Schuman, 225 N Michigan Ave, Suite 1300, Chicago, IL 60601 Toll Free Tel: 800-545-2433 Fax: 312-280-5860 E-mail: editionsmarketing@ala.org Web Site: www.alastore.ala.org, pg 6

Christy, Stephen, BOOM! Studios, 5670 Wilshire Blvd, Suite 400, Los Angeles, CA 90036 E-mail: contact@boom-studios.com; customerservice@boom-studios.com; press@boom-studios.com Web Site: www.boom-studios.com, pg 34

Chromy, Adam, Movable Type Management, 244 Madison Ave, Suite 334, New York, NY 10016 Web Site: www.movabletm.com, pg 471

Chu, Carol, Beacon Press, 24 Farnsworth St, Boston, MA 02210-1409 Tel: 617-742-2110 Fax: 617-723-3097 E-mail: production@beacon.org Web Site: www.beacon.org, pg 25

Chu, Jane, The National Medal of Arts, 400 Seventh St SW, Washington, DC 20506-0001 Tel: 202-682-5570 Web Site: www.arts.gov/honors/medals, pg 638

Chu, Lily, Captus Press Inc, 1600 Steeles Ave W, Units 14 & 15, Concord, ON L4K 4M2, Canada Tel: 905-760-2723 Fax: 905-760-7523 E-mail: info@captus.com Web Site: www.captus.com, pg 399

Chu, Lynn, Writers' Representatives LLC, 116 W 14 St, 11th fl, New York, NY 10011-7305 Tel: 212-620-9009 E-mail: transom@writersreps.com Web Site: www.writersreps.com, pg 482

Chudnow, Sharon, InkWell Management, 521 Fifth Ave, Suite 2600, New York, NY 10175 Tel: 212-922-3500 Fax: 212-922-0535 E-mail: info@inkwellmanagement.com; submissions@inkwellmanagement.com; permissions@inkwellmanagement.com Web Site: inkwellmanagement.com, pg 463

Chum, Soriya K, Random House Publishing Group, 1745 Broadway, New York, NY 10019 Toll Free Tel: 800-200-3552 Web Site: www.randomhousebooks.com, pg 171

Chun, Jane, Transatlantic Agency, 2 Bloor St E, Suite 3500, Toronto, ON M4W 1A8, Canada Tel: 416-488-9214 E-mail: info@transatlanticagency.com; royalties@transatlanticagency.com Web Site: www.transatlanticagency.com, pg 479

Chun, Jessica, Little, Brown and Company, 1290 Avenue of the Americas, New York, NY 10104 Tel: 212-364-1100 Fax: 212-364-0952 E-mail: firstname.lastname@hbgusa.com Web Site: www.hachettebookgroup.com/imprint/little-brown-and-company/, pg 118

Chun, Stephanie, University of Hawaii Press, 2840 Kolowalu St, Honolulu, HI 96822-1888 Tel: 808-956-8255 Toll Free Tel: 888-UHPRESS (847-7377) Toll Free Fax: 800-650-7811 E-mail: uhpbooks@hawaii.edu Web Site: www.uhpress.hawaii.edu, pg 216

Chung, Gina, Kundiman Retreat, Fordham University, English Dept, 113 W 60 St, Rm 924, New York, NY 10023 E-mail: info@kundiman.org Web Site: www.kundiman.org, pg 556

Chung-Castillo, Jennifer, Random House Children's Books, c/o Penguin Random House LLC, 1745 Broadway, New York, NY 10019 Tel: 212-782-9000 Web Site: www.rhcbooks.com, pg 170

Chupka, Karen, National Association of Broadcasters (NAB), One "M" St SE, Washington, DC 20003 Tel: 202-429-5300 E-mail: nab@nab.org Web Site: www.nab.org, pg 136, 511

Church, Dawson, Energy Psychology Press, PO Box 222, Petaluma, CA 94953-0222 Tel: 707-525-9292 Toll Free Tel: 800-330-9798 E-mail: energypsychologypress@gmail.com; support@eftuniverse.com Web Site: www.energypsychologypress.com; www.elitebooksonline.com, pg 66

Church, Doug, Pacific Press® Publishing Association, 1350 N Kings Rd, Nampa, ID 83687-3193 Tel: 208-465-2500 Fax: 208-465-2531 E-mail: booksubmissions@pacificpress.com Web Site: www.pacificpress.com, pg 150

Church, Lucas, The University of North Carolina Press, 116 S Boundary St, Chapel Hill, NC 27514-3808 Tel: 919-966-3561; 919-966-7449 (orders) Toll Free Tel: 800-848-3224 (orders) Fax: 919-962-2704 (orders) Toll Free Fax: 800-272-6817 (orders) E-mail: uncpress@unc.edu Web Site: uncpress.org, pg 218

Church, Natalie, Grove Atlantic Inc, 154 W 14 St, 12th fl, New York, NY 10011 Tel: 212-614-7850 Toll Free Tel: 800-521-0178 Fax: 212-614-7886 E-mail: info@groveatlantic.com; sales@groveatlantic.com; publicity@groveatlantic.com; rights@groveatlantic.com Web Site: www.groveatlantic.com, pg 82

Ciabattari, Jane, Nona Balakian Citation for Excellence in Reviewing, c/o Jacob M Appel, Icahn School of Medicine at Mount Sinai, One Gustave L Levy Place, New York, NY 10029 E-mail: info@bookcritics.org Web Site: www.bookcritics.org/awards/balakian/, pg 576

Ciabattari, Jane, Gregg Barrios Book in Translation Prize, c/o Jacob M Appel, Icahn School of Medicine at Mount Sinai, One Gustave L Levy Place, New York, NY 10029 E-mail: info@bookcritics.org Web Site: www.bookcritics.org/gregg-barrios-book-in-translation-prize/, pg 577

Ciabattari, Jane, Emerging Critics Fellowship, c/o Jacob M Appel, Icahn School of Medicine at Mount Sinai, One Gustave L Levy Place, New York, NY 10029 E-mail: info@bookcritics.org Web Site: www.bookcritics.org/awards, pg 599

Ciabattari, Jane, John Leonard Prize, c/o Jacob M Appel, Icahn School of Medicine at Mount Sinai, One Gustave L Levy Place, New York, NY 10029 E-mail: info@bookcritics.org Web Site: www.bookcritics.org/awards/leonard-prize, pg 623

Ciabattari, Jane, The Toni Morrison Achievement Award, c/o Jacob M Appel, Icahn School of Medicine at Mount Sinai, One Gustave L Levy Place, New York, NY 10029 E-mail: info@bookcritics.org Web Site: www.bookcritics.org/the-toni-morrison-achievement-award, pg 635

Ciabattari, Jane, National Book Critics Circle (NBCC), c/o Jacob M Appel, Icahn School of Medicine at Mount Sinai, One Gustave L Levy Place, New York, NY 10029 E-mail: info@bookcritics.org; membership@bookcritics.org Web Site: www.bookcritics.org, pg 512

Ciabattari, Jane, National Book Critics Circle Award, c/o Jacob M Appel, Icahn School of Medicine at Mount Sinai, One Gustave L Levy Place, New York, NY 10029 E-mail: info@bookcritics.org Web Site: www.bookcritics.org/awards, pg 637

Ciabattari, Jane, Ivan Sandrof Lifetime Achievement Award, c/o Jacob M Appel, Icahn School of Medicine at Mount Sinai, One Gustave L Levy Place, New York, NY 10029 E-mail: info@bookcritics.org Web Site: www.bookcritics.org/awards/sandrof/, pg 659

Cianfrone, Amy, Running Press, 1290 Avenue of the Americas, New York, NY 10104 Tel: 212-364-1100 Toll Free Tel: 800-759-0190 (cust serv) Fax: 212-364-0933 (intl orders) Toll Free Fax: 800-286-9471 (cust serv) E-mail: customer.service@hbgusa.com; orders@hbgusa.com Web Site: www.hachettebookgroup.com/imprint/running-press/; www.moon.com (Moon Travel Guides), pg 178

Ciani, Nicholas, Atria Books, 1230 Avenue of the Americas, New York, NY 10020 Tel: 212-698-7000 Fax: 212-698-7007 Web Site: www.simonandschuster.com, pg 21

Ciccaglione, Lynne, Phaidon, 65 Bleecker St, 8th fl, New York, NY 10012 Tel: 212-652-5400 Toll Free Tel: 800-759-0190 (cust serv) Fax: 212-652-5410 Toll Free Fax: 800-286-9471 (cust serv) E-mail: enquiries@phaidon.com Web Site: www.phaidon.com, pg 159

Cicchitelli, Melissa, HarperCollins Children's Books, 195 Broadway, New York, NY 10007 Tel: 212-207-7000 Web Site: www.harpercollins.com/childrens, pg 85

Cicchitelli, Melissa, Houghton Mifflin Harcourt Trade & Reference Division, 125 High St, Boston, MA 02110 Tel: 617-351-5000 Web Site: www.hmhco.com, pg 96

Cicciarelli, Joellyn, Loyola Press, 8770 W Bryn Mawr Ave, Suite 1125, Chicago, IL 60631 Tel: 773-281-1818 Toll Free Tel: 800-621-1008 Fax: 773-281-0555 (cust serv); 773-281-4129 (edit) E-mail: customerservice@loyolapress.com Web Site: www.loyolapress.com, pg 121

Cicel, Terezia, Viking Penguin, c/o Penguin Random House LLC, 1745 Broadway, New York, NY 10019 Tel: 212-782-9000 Web Site: www.penguin.com/overview-vikingbooks/; www.penguin.com/pamela-dorman-books-overview/; www.penguin.com/penguin-classics-overview/; www.penguin.com/penguin-life-overview/, pg 225

Ciecierski, Andrea, Stylus Publishing LLC, 22883 Quicksilver Dr, Sterling, VA 20166-2019 Tel: 703-661-1504 (edit & sales) Toll Free Tel: 800-232-0223 (orders & cust serv) Fax: 703-661-1547 E-mail: stylusmail@styluspub.com (orders & cust serv); stylusinfo@styluspub.com Web Site: styluspub.com, pg 200

Cigich, Bradley, Alexander Street, part of Clarivate PLC, 789 E Eisenhower Pkwy, Ann Arbor, MI 48108 Toll Free Tel: 800-521-0600; 888-963-2071 (sales) E-mail: sales@alexanderstreet.com; marketing@alexanderstreet.com; support@alexanderstreet.com Web Site: alexanderstreet.com, pg 6

Cihlar, Jim, Minnesota Historical Society Press, 345 Kellogg Blvd W, St Paul, MN 55102-1906 Tel: 651-259-3205 Fax: 651-297-1345 E-mail: info-mnhspress@mnhs.org Web Site: www.mnhs.org/mnhspress, pg 132

Ciletti, Barbara, Odyssey Books, 2421 Redwood Ct, Longmont, CO 80503-8155 Tel: 720-494-1473 Fax: 720-494-1471 E-mail: books@odysseybooks.net, pg 145

Cimina, Dominique, Random House Children's Books, c/o Penguin Random House LLC, 1745 Broadway, New York, NY 10019 Tel: 212-782-9000 Web Site: www.rhcbooks.com, pg 169

Ciminera, Siobhan, Simon & Schuster Children's Publishing, 1230 Avenue of the Americas, New York, NY 10020 Tel: 212-698-7000 Web Site: www.simonandschuster.com/kids; www.simonandschuster.com/teen; simonandschuster.net; simonandschuster.biz, pg 189

Cimino, Antoinette, Springer, One New York Plaza, Suite 4600, New York, NY 10004-1562 Tel: 212-460-1500 Toll Free Tel: 800-SPRINGER (777-4643) Fax: 212-460-1700 E-mail: customerservice@springernature.com Web Site: www.springer.com, pg 196

Cimonetti, Tanya, Lyric Poetry Prizes, PO Box 110, Jericho, VT 05465 E-mail: themuse@thelyricmagazine.com Web Site: thelyricmagazine.com, pg 627

Cipolla, Kristin, Berkley, c/o Penguin Random House LLC, 1745 Broadway, 19th fl, New York, NY 10019 Tel: 212-366-2000 Web Site: www.penguin.com/publishers/berkley/; www.penguin.com/ace-overview/, pg 28

Cipolla, Kristin, Penguin Random House Canada, a Penguin Random House company, 320 Front St W, Suite 1400, Toronto, ON M5V 3B6, Canada Tel: 416-364-4449 Toll Free Tel: 888-523-9292 (cust serv) E-mail: canadaweb@penguinrandomhouse.com; customerservicescanada@penguinrandomhouse.com Web Site: www.penguinrandomhouse.ca, pg 416

Circosta, Karey, Ave Maria Press Inc, PO Box 428, Notre Dame, IN 46556 Toll Free Tel: 800-282-1865 Toll Free Fax: 800-282-5681 E-mail: avemariapress.1@nd.edu Web Site: www.avemariapress.com, pg 22

Cirillo, Andrea, Jane Rotrosen Agency LLC, 318 E 51 St, New York, NY 10022-7803 Tel: 212-593-4330 E-mail: info@janerotrosen.com Web Site: janerotrosen.com, pg 474

Cirone, Kathy, Cold Spring Harbor Laboratory Press, 500 Sunnyside Blvd, Woodbury, NY 11797-2924 Tel: 516-422-4100 Toll Free Tel: 800-843-4388 E-mail: cshpress@cshl.edu Web Site: www.cshlpress.com, pg 50

Citro, Asia, The Innovation Press, 7511 Greenwood Ave N, No 4132, Seattle, WA 98103 Tel: 360-870-9988 E-mail: info@theinnovationpress.com Web Site: www.theinnovationpress.com, pg 101

Civiletto, Jennifer, HarperCollins Publishers LLC, 195 Broadway, New York, NY 10007 Tel: 212-207-7000 Web Site: www.harpercollins.com, pg 86

Cizek, Nick, The Experiment, 220 E 23 St, Suite 600, New York, NY 10010-4658 Tel: 212-889-1659 E-mail: info@theexperimentpublishing.com Web Site: www.theexperimentpublishing.com, pg 68

Clain, Judy, Simon & Schuster, 1230 Avenue of the Americas, New York, NY 10020 Tel: 212-698-7000 Toll Free Tel: 800-223-2348 (cust serv); 800-223-2336 (orders) Toll Free Fax: 800-943-9831 (orders) Web Site: simonandschusterpublishing.com/simonandschuster/, pg 188

Clain, Judy, Simon & Schuster, LLC, 1230 Avenue of the Americas, New York, NY 10020 Tel: 212-698-7000 Toll Free Tel: 800-223-2336 (orders) Fax: 212-698-7007 Toll Free Fax: 800-943-9831 (orders) E-mail: firstname.lastname@simonandschuster.com; purchaseorders@simonandschuster.com (orders) Web Site: www.simonandschuster.com, pg 189

Clair, Michelle, Chronicle Books LLC, 680 Second St, San Francisco, CA 94107 Tel: 415-537-4200 Fax: 415-537-4460 (perms) E-mail: hello@chroniclebooks.com; subrights@chroniclebooks.com Web Site: www.chroniclebooks.com, pg 48

Claman, Marcy, Callawind Publications Inc, 3551 St Charles Blvd, Suite 179, Kirkland, QC H9H 3C4, Canada Tel: 514-685-9109 E-mail: info@callawind.com Web Site: www.callawind.com, pg 398

Clancy, Devin, Between the Lines, 401 Richmond St W, No 281, Toronto, ON M5V 3A8, Canada Tel: 416-535-9914 Toll Free Tel: 800-718-7201 E-mail: info@btlbooks.com Web Site: btlbooks.com, pg 396

Clancy, Julianne, Pantheon Books, c/o Penguin Random House LLC, 1745 Broadway, New York, NY 10019 Tel: 212-751-2600 Fax: 212-940-7390 (dom rts); 212-572-2662 (foreign rts) Web Site: knopfdoubleday.com/imprint/pantheon/; knopfdoubleday.com, pg 150

Clapps, Bobbi, Syracuse University Press, 621 Skytop Rd, Suite 110, Syracuse, NY 13244-5290 Tel: 315-443-5534 Toll Free Tel: 800-365-8929 (cust serv) Fax: 315-443-5545 E-mail: supress@syr.edu Web Site: press.syr.edu, pg 201

Clapsadl, Katie, Entangled Publishing LLC, 644 Shrewsbury Commons Ave, Suite 181, Shrewsbury, PA 17361 Toll Free Tel: 877-677-9451 E-mail: publisher@entangledpublishing.com Web Site: www.entangledpublishing.com, pg 67

Clare, Jennifer, Penguin Random House LLC, 1745 Broadway, New York, NY 10019 Tel: 212-782-9000 Toll Free Tel: 800-726-0600 Web Site: www.penguinrandomhouse.com, pg 155

Clark, Beth, Farrar, Straus & Giroux Books for Young Readers, 120 Broadway, New York, NY 10271 Tel: 212-741-6900 Toll Free Tel: 888-330-8477 (orders) E-mail: childrens.publicity@macmillanusa.com; childrensrights@macmillanusa.com Web Site: us.macmillan.com/mackids, pg 70

Clark, Beth, Henry Holt and Company, LLC, 120 Broadway, 23rd fl, New York, NY 10271 Tel: 646-307-5151 Toll Free Tel: 888-330-8477 (orders) Fax: 646-307-5285 Web Site: www.henryholt.com, pg 94

Clark, Beth, Roaring Brook Press, 120 Broadway, New York, NY 10271 Tel: 646-307-5151 Web Site: us.macmillan.com/publishers/roaring-brook-press, pg 175

Clark, Billy, Hachette Nashville, 6100 Tower Circle, Room 210, Franklin, TN 37067 Tel: 615-221-0996 Fax: 615-221-0962 Web Site: www.hachettebookgroup.com/imprint/hachette-nashville/, pg 83

Clark, Brian, Penguin Workshop, c/o Penguin Random House LLC, 1745 Broadway, New York, NY 10019 Tel: 212-782-9000 Web Site: www.penguin.com/publishers/penguinworkshop/, pg 156

Clark, Bryn, Little, Brown and Company, 1290 Avenue of the Americas, New York, NY 10104 Tel: 212-364-1100 Fax: 212-364-0952 E-mail: firstname.lastname@hbgusa.com Web Site: www.hachettebookgroup.com/imprint/little-brown-and-company/, pg 118

Clark, Cana, Sourcebooks LLC, 1935 Brookdale Rd, Suite 139, Naperville, IL 60563 Tel: 630-961-3900 Toll Free Tel: 800-432-7444 Fax: 630-961-2168 E-mail: info@sourcebooks.com Web Site: www.sourcebooks.com, pg 195

Clark, John, American Diabetes Association, 2451 Crystal Dr, Suite 900, Arlington, VA 22202 Tel: 703-549-1500 Toll Free Tel: 800-342-2383 E-mail: booksales@diabetes.org; ada_pubs@diabetes.org Web Site: diabetes.org; diabetesjournals.org/books; www.facebook.com/adapublications, pg 9

Clark, Jonathan, Vermont Golden Dome Book Award, 60 Washington St, Suite 2, Barre, VT 05641 Tel: 802-636-0040 Web Site: libraries.vermont.gov/services/children_and_teens/book_awards/vtgdba, pg 672

Clark, June, FinePrint Literary Management, 207 W 106 St, Suite 1D, New York, NY 10025 Tel: 212-279-6214 E-mail: info@fineprintlit.com; submissions@fineprint.com Web Site: www.fineprintlit.com, pg 458

Clark, Karen, University of Regina Press, 2 Research Dr, Suite 160, Regina, SK S4S 7H9, Canada Tel: 306-585-4758 Fax: 306-585-4699 E-mail: uofrpress@uregina.ca Web Site: uofrpress.ca, pg 423

Clark, Laura, St Martin's Press, LLC, 120 Broadway, New York, NY 10271 E-mail: publicity@stmartins.com; trademarketing@stmartins.com; foreignrights@stmartins.com Web Site: us.macmillan.com/smp, pg 180

Clark, Michael, Macmillan, 120 Broadway, 22nd fl, New York, NY 10271 E-mail: press.inquiries@macmillan.com Web Site: us.macmillan.com, pg 122

Clark, Michiko, Pantheon Books, c/o Penguin Random House LLC, 1745 Broadway, New York, NY 10019 Tel: 212-751-2600 Fax: 212-940-7390 (dom rts); 212-572-2662 (foreign rts) Web Site: knopfdoubleday.com/imprint/pantheon/; knopfdoubleday.com, pg 150

Clark, Patty, Math Solutions®, One Harbor Dr, Suite 101, Sausalito, CA 94965 Toll Free Tel: 877-234-7323 Toll Free Fax: 800-724-4716 E-mail: info@mathsolutions.com; orders@mathsolutions.com Web Site: www.mathsolutions.com; store.mathsolutions.com, pg 127

Clark, Rakia, HarperCollins Publishers LLC, 195 Broadway, New York, NY 10007 Tel: 212-207-7000 Web Site: www.harpercollins.com, pg 86

Clark, Rakia, Houghton Mifflin Harcourt Trade & Reference Division, 125 High St, Boston, MA 02110 Tel: 617-351-5000 Web Site: www.hmhco.com, pg 96

Clark, Raymond C, Pro Lingua Associates Inc, 74 Cotton Mill Hill, Suite A-315, Brattleboro, VT 05301 Tel: 802-257-7779 Toll Free Tel: 800-366-4775 Fax: 802-257-5117 E-mail: info@prolinguaassociates.com Web Site: www.prolinguaassociates.com, pg 165

Clark, Rob, National Notary Association (NNA), 9350 De Soto Ave, Chatsworth, CA 91311-4926 Tel: 818-739-4000 Toll Free Tel: 800-876-6827 Toll Free Fax: 800-833-1211 E-mail: services@nationalnotary.org Web Site: www.nationalnotary.org, pg 138

Clark, Rochelle, Random House Publishing Group, 1745 Broadway, New York, NY 10019 *Toll Free Tel:* 800-200-3552 *Web Site:* www.randomhousebooks.com, pg 171

Clark, Stephanie, Orbit, 1290 Avenue of the Americas, New York, NY 10104 *Tel:* 212-364-1100 *Toll Free Tel:* 800-759-0190 *Web Site:* www.orbitbooks.net; www.hachettebookgroup.com/imprint/orbit, pg 147

Clark, William, Wm Clark Associates, 54 W 21 St, Suite 809, New York, NY 10010 *Tel:* 212-675-2784 *E-mail:* general@wmclark.com *Web Site:* www.wmclark.com, pg 454

Clarke, Ayisha, Penguin Random House LLC, 1745 Broadway, New York, NY 10019 *Tel:* 212-782-9000 *Toll Free Tel:* 800-726-0600 *Web Site:* www.penguinrandomhouse.com, pg 155

Clarke, Brandon, Society of Children's Book Writers & Illustrators (SCBWI), 6363 Wilshire Blvd, Suite 425, Los Angeles, CA 90048 *Tel:* 323-782-1010 *E-mail:* membership@scbwi.org *Web Site:* www.scbwi.org, pg 520

Clarke, Breana, Well-Trained Mind Press, 18021 The Glebe Lane, Charles City, VA 23030 *Tel:* 804-593-0306 *Toll Free Tel:* 877-322-3445 *Fax:* 804-829-5704 *E-mail:* support@welltrainedmind.com *Web Site:* welltrainedmind.com, pg 227

Clarke, Erin, Clarion Books, 195 Broadway, New York, NY 10007 *Tel:* 212-207-7000 *Toll Free Tel:* 800-242-7737 *E-mail:* consumercare@harpercollins.com *Web Site:* www.harpercollins.com/collections/books-by-clarion-books, pg 49

Clarke, Kamilah, American Booksellers Association, 600 Mamaroneck Ave, Suite 400, Harrison, NY 10528 *Tel:* 914-406-7500 *Toll Free Tel:* 800-637-0037 *Fax:* 914-417-4013 *E-mail:* info@bookweb.org *Web Site:* www.bookweb.org, pg 494

Clarke, Meghan, Chronicle Books LLC, 680 Second St, San Francisco, CA 94107 *Tel:* 415-537-4200 *Fax:* 415-537-4460 (perms) *E-mail:* hello@chroniclebooks.com; subrights@chroniclebooks.com *Web Site:* www.chroniclebooks.com, pg 47

Clarke, Meghan, Taschen America, NeueHouse, 6121 Sunset Blvd, Los Angeles, CA 90028 *Tel:* 323-463-4441 *Toll Free Tel:* 888-TASCHEN (827-2436) *E-mail:* contact-us@taschen.com *Web Site:* www.taschen.com, pg 203

Clarke, Mia Barkan, Cross-Cultural Communications, 239 Wynsum Ave, Merrick, NY 11566-4725 *Tel:* 516-868-5635 *Fax:* 516-379-1901 *E-mail:* cccpoetry@aol.com *Web Site:* www.facebook.com/CrossCulturalCommunications.NY, pg 55

Classic, Lesley, Database Directories Inc, 96-320 Westminster Ave, London, ON N6C 5H5, Canada *Tel:* 519-433-1666 *E-mail:* mail@databasedirectory.com *Web Site:* www.databasedirectory.com, pg 400

Clauss, Lauren, Random House Children's Books, c/o Penguin Random House LLC, 1745 Broadway, New York, NY 10019 *Tel:* 212-782-9000 *Web Site:* www.rhcbooks.com, pg 170

Clay, Adam, Mississippi Review Prize, 118 College Dr, Box 5144, Hattiesburg, MS 39406-0001 *Tel:* 601-266-4321 *E-mail:* msreview@usm.edu *Web Site:* www.usm.edu/mississippi-review/contest.html, pg 633

Clay, Adam, Mississippi Review/University of Southern Mississippi, Center for Writers, 118 College Dr 5144, Hattiesburg, MS 39406-0001 *Tel:* 601-266-1000 *Web Site:* www.usm.edu/humanities/center-writers.php; sites.usm.edu/mississippi-review/index.html, pg 563

Clay, Molly, Bucknell University Press, One Dent Dr, Lewisburg, PA 17837 *Tel:* 570-577-1049 *E-mail:* universitypress@bucknell.edu *Web Site:* www.bucknell.edu/universitypress, pg 38

Clayton, Dhonielle, Walter Dean Myers Grants, 10319 Westlake Dr, No 104, Bethesda, MD 20817 *Tel:* 701-404-WNDB (404-9632, voicemail only) *E-mail:* waltergrant@diversebooks.org *Web Site:* diversebooks.org, pg 636

Clayton, Keith, Penguin Random House LLC, 1745 Broadway, New York, NY 10019 *Tel:* 212-782-9000 *Toll Free Tel:* 800-726-0600 *Web Site:* www.penguinrandomhouse.com, pg 155

Clayton, Keith, Random House Publishing Group, 1745 Broadway, New York, NY 10019 *Toll Free Tel:* 800-200-3552 *Web Site:* www.randomhousebooks.com, pg 170

Clayton, Patricia Mulrane, Peter Lang Publishing Inc, 80 Broadway, 5th fl, New York, NY 10004 *Tel:* 703-661-1584 *Toll Free Tel:* 800-770-5264 (cust serv) *Fax:* 703-996-1010 *E-mail:* info@peterlang.com; newyork.editorial@peterlang.com; customerservice@plang.com *Web Site:* www.peterlang.com, pg 112

Cleary, Emma, Grouse Grind Lit Prize for V Short Form, University of British Columbia, Buch E462, 1866 Main Mall, Vancouver, BC V6T 1Z1, Canada *Tel:* 604-822-2514 *Fax:* 604-822-3616 *E-mail:* promotions@prismmagazine.ca *Web Site:* www.prismmagazine.ca/contests, pg 609

Cleary, Emma, The Pacific Spirit Poetry Prize, University of British Columbia, Buch E462, 1866 Main Mall, Vancouver, BC V6T 1Z1, Canada *Tel:* 604-822-2514 *Fax:* 604-822-3616 *E-mail:* promotions@prismmagazine.ca *Web Site:* www.prismmagazine.ca/contests, pg 645

Cleary, Emma, PRISM international Creative Nonfiction Contest, University of British Columbia, Buch E462, 1866 Main Mall, Vancouver, BC V6T 1Z1, Canada *Tel:* 604-822-2514 *Fax:* 604-822-3616 *E-mail:* promotions@prismmagazine.ca *Web Site:* www.prismmagazine.ca/contests, pg 653

Cleary, Emma, The Jacob Zilber Prize for Short Fiction, University of British Columbia, Buch E462, 1866 Main Mall, Vancouver, BC V6T 1Z1, Canada *Tel:* 604-822-2514 *Fax:* 604-822-3616 *E-mail:* promotions@prismmagazine.ca *Web Site:* www.prismmagazine.ca/contests, pg 680

Cleary, Kenneth J, Scholastic Inc, 557 Broadway, New York, NY 10012 *Tel:* 212-343-6100 *Toll Free Tel:* 800-SCHOLASTIC (724-6527) *Web Site:* www.scholastic.com, pg 184

Cleary, Kenneth J, Scholastic International, 557 Broadway, New York, NY 10012 *Tel:* 212-343-6100; 646-330-5288 (intl cust serv) *Toll Free Tel:* 800-SCHOLASTIC (724-6527) *Fax:* 646-837-7878 *E-mail:* international@scholastic.com, pg 184

Cleland, Jane K, Black Orchid Novella Award, PO Box 230822, Ansonia Sta, New York, NY 10023 *E-mail:* blackorchidaward@nerowolfe.org *Web Site:* nerowolfe.org/htm/literary_awards/black_orchid_award/Black_Orchid_award_intro.htm, pg 581

Cleland, Lance, Tin House Summer Workshop, 2617 NW Thurman St, Portland, OR 97210 *Tel:* 503-473-8663 *Web Site:* tinhouse.com/workshop/summer-workshop, pg 558

Cleland, Lance, Tin House Winter Workshop, 2617 NW Thurman St, Portland, OR 97210 *Tel:* 503-473-8663 *Web Site:* tinhouse.com/winter-workshop, pg 558

Cleland, Lance, YA Fiction Workshop, 2617 NW Thurman St, Portland, OR 97210 *Tel:* 503-473-8663 *Web Site:* tinhouse.com/ya-workshop, pg 559

Cleland, Lucy, Calligraph LLC, 45 Main St, No 850, Brooklyn, NY 11201 *Tel:* 212-253-1074 *E-mail:* mail@calligraphlit.com; rights@calligraphlit.com; submissions@calligraphlit.com *Web Site:* www.calligraphlit.com, pg 453

Clelland, Georgina, Association for Intelligent Information Management (AIIM), 8403 Colesville Rd, No 1100, Silver Spring, MD 20910 *Tel:* 301-587-8202 *Toll Free Tel:* 800-477-2446 *Fax:* 301-587-2711 *E-mail:* hello@aiim.org *Web Site:* www.aiim.org, pg 498

Clemans, Chris, Janklow & Nesbit Associates, 285 Madison Ave, 21st fl, New York, NY 10017 *Tel:* 212-421-1700 *Fax:* 212-355-1403 *E-mail:* info@janklow.com; submissions@janklow.com; filmtvrights@janklow.com *Web Site:* www.janklowandnesbit.com, pg 464

Clement, Sahara, Penguin Random House LLC, 1745 Broadway, New York, NY 10019 *Tel:* 212-782-9000 *Toll Free Tel:* 800-726-0600 *Web Site:* www.penguinrandomhouse.com, pg 155

Clemons, G Scott, Bibliographical Society of America (BSA), 67 West St, Suite 401, Unit C17, Brooklyn, NY 11222 *E-mail:* bsa@bibsocamer.org *Web Site:* bibsocamer.org, pg 501

Clemons, Kim, Cedar Fort Inc, 2373 W 700 S, Suite 100, Springville, UT 84663 *Tel:* 801-489-4084 *Toll Free Tel:* 800-SKY-BOOK (759-2665) *E-mail:* marketinginfo@cedarfort.com *Web Site:* cedarfort.com, pg 43

Clerk, Emma, Penguin Random House Canada, a Penguin Random House company, 320 Front St W, Suite 1400, Toronto, ON M5V 3B6, Canada *Tel:* 416-364-4449 *Toll Free Tel:* 888-523-9292 (cust serv) *E-mail:* canadaweb@penguinrandomhouse.com; customerservicescanada@penguinrandomhouse.com *Web Site:* www.penguinrandomhouse.ca, pg 416

Clerkley, Cheretta, International Society for Technology in Education, 2111 Wilson Blvd, Suite 300, Arlington, VA 22201 *Tel:* 503-342-2848 (intl) *Toll Free Tel:* 800-336-5191 (US & CN) *Fax:* 541-302-3778 *E-mail:* iste@iste.org *Web Site:* www.iste.org, pg 103

Cleveland, Marisa, The Seymour Agency, 475 Miner Street Rd, Canton, NY 13617 *Tel:* 239-398-8209 *Web Site:* www.theseymouragency.com, pg 475

Cleveland, Rob, August House Inc, 3500 Piedmont Rd NE, Suite 310, Atlanta, GA 30305 *Tel:* 404-442-4420 *Toll Free Tel:* 800-284-8784 *Fax:* 404-442-4435 *E-mail:* ahinfo@augusthouse.com *Web Site:* www.augusthouse.com, pg 22

Clevenger, Beth, The MIT Press, One Broadway, 12th fl, Cambridge, MA 02142 *Tel:* 617-253-5255 *Toll Free Tel:* 800-405-1619 (orders) *Fax:* 617-258-6779; 617-577-1545 (orders) *Web Site:* mitpress.mit.edu, pg 132

Clifford, Christina, Harlequin Enterprises Ltd, Bay Adelaide Centre, East Tower, 22 Adelaide St W, 41st fl, Toronto, ON M5H 4E3, Canada *Tel:* 416-445-5860 *Toll Free Tel:* 888-432-4879; 800-370-5838 (ebook inquiries) *E-mail:* customerservice@harlequin.com *Web Site:* www.harlequin.com, pg 409

Clifford, Christina, Union Literary, 30 Vandam St, Suite 5A, New York, NY 10013 *Tel:* 212-255-2112 *Web Site:* www.unionliterary.com, pg 480

Clinch, Court, Penguin Random House LLC, 1745 Broadway, New York, NY 10019 *Tel:* 212-782-9000 *Toll Free Tel:* 800-726-0600 *Web Site:* www.penguinrandomhouse.com, pg 155

Clinton, John, Penguin Random House LLC, 1745 Broadway, New York, NY 10019 *Tel:* 212-782-9000 *Toll Free Tel:* 800-726-0600 *Web Site:* www.penguinrandomhouse.com, pg 155

Clinton-Copeland, Shannon, Leapfrog Global Fiction Prize, PO Box 505, Fredonia, NY 14063 *E-mail:* leapfrog@leapfrogpress.com *Web Site:* leapfrogpress.com/the-leapfrog-global-fiction-prize-contest, pg 623

Clockel, William, Educator's International Press Inc (EIP), 756 Linderman Ave, Kingston, NY 12401 *Tel:* 518-334-0276 *Toll Free Tel:* 800-758-3756 *Fax:* 703-661-1547 *E-mail:* info@edint.com, pg 64

Closson, Marietta, Closson Press, 257 Delilah St, Apollo, PA 15613-1933 *Tel:* 724-337-4482 *E-mail:* clossonpress@comcast.net *Web Site:* www.clossonpress.com, pg 49

Cloud, Amy, Clarion Books, 195 Broadway, New York, NY 10007 *Tel:* 212-207-7000 *Toll Free Tel:* 800-242-7737 *E-mail:* consumercare@harpercollins.com *Web Site:* www.harpercollins.com/collections/books-by-clarion-books, pg 49

Cloughly, Amy, Kimberley Cameron & Associates LLC, 1550 Tiburon Blvd, Suite 704, Tiburon, CA 94920 *E-mail:* info@kimberleycameron.com *Web Site:* www.kimberleycameron.com, pg 453

Cloutier, Suzanne, University of Ottawa Press (Presses de l'Université d'Ottawa), 542 King Edward Ave, Ottawa, ON K1N 6N5, Canada *Tel:* 613-562-5246 *Fax:* 613-562-5247 *E-mail:* puo-uop@uottawa.ca; acquisitions@uottawa.ca *Web Site:* press.uottawa.ca, pg 422

Clucas, Tori, National Paper Trade Association (NPTA), 330 N Wabash Ave, Suite 2000, Chicago, IL 60611 *Tel:* 312-321-4092 *Toll Free Tel:* 800-355-NPTA (355-6782) *Fax:* 312-673-6736 *Web Site:* www.gonpta.com, pg 513

Clunie, Paige, Princeton University Press, 41 William St, Princeton, NJ 08540-5237 *Tel:* 609-258-4900 *Fax:* 609-258-6305 *E-mail:* info@press.princeton.edu *Web Site:* press.princeton.edu, pg 164

Clute, Sharla, State University of New York Press, 10 N Pearl St, 4th fl, Albany, NY 12207 *Tel:* 518-944-2800 *Toll Free Tel:* 877-204-6073 (orders) *Fax:* 518-320-1592 *Toll Free Fax:* 877-204-6074 (orders) *E-mail:* info@sunypress.edu (edit off); suny@presswarehouse.com (orders) *Web Site:* www.sunypress.edu, pg 198

Coalson, Lance, Father & Son Publishing Inc, 4909 N Monroe St, Tallahassee, FL 32303-7015 *Tel:* 850-562-2712 *Toll Free Tel:* 800-741-2712 (orders only) *Fax:* 850-562-0916 *Web Site:* www.fatherson.com, pg 70

Coan, Cynthia J, Indexing by the Book, 5912 E Eastland St, Tucson, AZ 85711-4636 *Tel:* 520-405-8083 *E-mail:* indextran@cox.net *Web Site:* www.indexingbythebook.com, pg 440

Coates, Damani, Black Classic Press, 3921 Vero Rd, Suite F, Baltimore, MD 21203-3414 *Tel:* 410-242-6954 *Toll Free Tel:* 800-476-8870 *E-mail:* email@blackclassicbooks.com; blackclassicpress@yahoo.com *Web Site:* www.blackclassicbooks.com; www.agooddaytoprint.com, pg 30

Coates, Laraine, University of British Columbia Press, 2029 West Mall, Vancouver, BC V6T 1Z2, Canada *Tel:* 604-822-5959 *Toll Free Tel:* 877-377-9378 *Fax:* 604-822-6083 *Toll Free Fax:* 800-668-0821 *E-mail:* frontdesk@ubcpress.ca *Web Site:* www.ubcpress.ca, pg 422

Coates, Lawrence, Bowling Green State University Creative Writing Program, Dept of English, 212 East Hall, Bowling Green, OH 43403-0001 *Tel:* 419-372-6864; 419-372-2576 *Fax:* 419-372-0333 *E-mail:* english@bgsu.edu *Web Site:* www.bgsu.edu/academics/creative-writing, pg 561

Coates, W Paul, Black Classic Press, 3921 Vero Rd, Suite F, Baltimore, MD 21203-3414 *Tel:* 410-242-6954 *Toll Free Tel:* 800-476-8870 *E-mail:* email@blackclassicbooks.com; blackclassicpress@yahoo.com *Web Site:* www.blackclassicbooks.com; www.agooddaytoprint.com, pg 30

Cobb, Caelyn, Columbia University Press, 61 W 62 St, New York, NY 10023 *Tel:* 212-459-0600 *Toll Free Tel:* 800-944-8648 *Fax:* 212-459-3678 *Web Site:* cup.columbia.edu, pg 51

Cobb, David, The University Press of Kentucky, 663 S Limestone St, Lexington, KY 40508-4008 *Tel:* 859-257-8400 *Fax:* 859-323-1873 *Web Site:* www.kentuckypress.com, pg 222

Cobb, Debbie, Roaring Brook Press, 120 Broadway, New York, NY 10271 *Tel:* 646-307-5151 *Web Site:* us.macmillan.com/publishers/roaring-brook-press, pg 176

Cobb, Jennifer, Society of Exploration Geophysicists, 8801 S Yale Ave, Suite 500, Tulsa, OK 74137 *Tel:* 918-497-5500 *Fax:* 918-497-5557 *E-mail:* web@seg.org *Web Site:* www.seg.org, pg 193

Cobb, Jon, HG Literary, 6 W 18 St, Suite 7R, New York, NY 10011 *E-mail:* foreign@hgliterary.com; rights@hgliterary.com *Web Site:* www.hgliterary.com, pg 463

Cobb, Mara, Martin Literary Management, 914 164 St SE, Suite B12, Box 307, Mill Creek, WA 98012 *Tel:* 206-466-1773 (no phone queries) *Web Site:* www.martinliterarymanagement.com, pg 469

Cobb, Michele, The Audies®, 333 Hudson St, Suite 503, New York, NY 10013 *E-mail:* audies@audiopub.org *Web Site:* www.audiopub.org/members/audies, pg 576

Cobban, Helena, Just World Books LLC, PO Box 57075, Washington, DC 20037 *Toll Free Tel:* 888-506-3769 *E-mail:* sales@justworldbooks.com; info@justworldbooks.com; rights@justworldbooks.com *Web Site:* justworldbooks.com, pg 107

Cobra, Alison, University of Calgary Press, 2500 University Dr NW, Calgary, AB T2N 1N4, Canada *Tel:* 403-220-7578 *E-mail:* ucpbooks@ucalgary.ca *Web Site:* press.ucalgary.ca, pg 422

Coburn, Tristram, Tilbury House Publishers, 12 Starr St, Thomaston, ME 04861 *Tel:* 207-582-1899 *Toll Free Tel:* 800-582-1899 (orders) *Fax:* 207-582-8227 *E-mail:* tilbury@tilburyhouse.com *Web Site:* www.tilburyhouse.com, pg 207

Coccia, Miek, Levine|Greenberg|Rostan Literary Agency, 307 Seventh Ave, Suite 2407, New York, NY 10001 *Tel:* 212-337-0934 *Fax:* 212-337-0948 *E-mail:* submit@lgrliterary.com *Web Site:* lgrliterary.com, pg 467

Coccia, Paul, Canadian Society of Children's Authors, Illustrators & Performers (CANSCAIP), 720 Bathurst St, Suite 503, Toronto, ON M5S 2R4, Canada *Tel:* 416-515-1559 *E-mail:* office@canscaip.org *Web Site:* www.canscaip.org, pg 503

Cochran, Angela, American Society of Civil Engineers (ASCE), 1801 Alexander Bell Dr, Reston, VA 20191-4400 *Tel:* 703-295-6300 *Toll Free Tel:* 800-548-ASCE (548-2723) *Toll Free Fax:* 866-913-6085 *E-mail:* ascelibrary@asce.org; pubsful@asce.org *Web Site:* www.asce.org, pg 12

Cochran, Heather, Television Academy, 5220 Lankershim Blvd, North Hollywood, CA 91601-3109 *Tel:* 818-754-2800 *Web Site:* www.emmys.com, pg 521

Cochran, Marnie, Random House Publishing Group, 1745 Broadway, New York, NY 10019 *Toll Free Tel:* 800-200-3552 *Web Site:* www.randomhousebooks.com, pg 170

Cochrane, Kristin, Doubleday Canada, 320 Front St W, Suite 1400, Toronto, ON M5V 3B6, Canada *Tel:* 416-364-4449 *Fax:* 416-598-7764 *Web Site:* www.penguinrandomhouse.ca, pg 401

Cochrane, Kristin, Knopf Canada, 320 Front St W, Suite 1400, Toronto, ON M5V 3B6, Canada *Tel:* 416-364-4449 *Toll Free Tel:* 888-523-9292 *Fax:* 416-598-7764 *Web Site:* www.penguinrandomhouse.ca, pg 411

Cochrane, Kristin, Penguin Random House Canada, a Penguin Random House company, 320 Front St W, Suite 1400, Toronto, ON M5V 3B6, Canada *Tel:* 416-364-4449 *Toll Free Tel:* 888-523-9292 (cust serv) *E-mail:* canadaweb@penguinrandomhouse.com; customerservicescanada@penguinrandomhouse.com *Web Site:* www.penguinrandomhouse.ca, pg 415

Cochrane, Kristin, Seal Books, 320 Front St W, Suite 1400, Toronto, ON M5V 3B6, Canada *Tel:* 416-364-4449 *Toll Free Tel:* 888-523-9292 (order desk) *Fax:* 416-598-7764 *Web Site:* www.penguinrandomhouse.ca, pg 419

Cockeram, Beth, Penguin Random House Canada, a Penguin Random House company, 320 Front St W, Suite 1400, Toronto, ON M5V 3B6, Canada *Tel:* 416-364-4449 *Toll Free Tel:* 888-523-9292 (cust serv) *E-mail:* canadaweb@penguinrandomhouse.com; customerservicescanada@penguinrandomhouse.com *Web Site:* www.penguinrandomhouse.ca, pg 416

Code, Courtney, Harry N Abrams Inc, 195 Broadway, 9th fl, New York, NY 10007 *Tel:* 212-206-7715 *Toll Free Tel:* 800-345-1359 *Fax:* 212-645-8437 *E-mail:* abrams@abramsbooks.com; publicity@abramsbooks.com; sales@abramsbooks.com *Web Site:* www.abramsbooks.com, pg 3

Codega, Katherine, Candlewick Press, 99 Dover St, Somerville, MA 02144-2825 *Tel:* 617-661-3330 *Fax:* 617-661-0565 *E-mail:* bigbear@candlewick.com; salesinfo@candlewick.com *Web Site:* candlewick.com, pg 40

Coelho, Tiffany, Holiday House Publishing Inc, 50 Broad St, New York, NY 10004 *Tel:* 212-688-0085 *Fax:* 212-421-6134 *E-mail:* info@holidayhouse.com *Web Site:* www.holidayhouse.com, pg 94

Coelho, Tiffany, Peachtree Publishing Co Inc, 1700 Chattahoochee Ave, Atlanta, GA 30318-2112 *Tel:* 404-876-8761 *Toll Free Tel:* 800-241-0113 *Fax:* 404-875-2578 *Toll Free Fax:* 800-875-8909 *E-mail:* hello@peachtree-online.com; orders@peachtree-online.com; sales@peachtree-online.com *Web Site:* www.peachtreebooks.com; www.peachtree-online.com, pg 153

Coffee, Margaret, Sourcebooks LLC, 1935 Brookdale Rd, Suite 139, Naperville, IL 60563 *Tel:* 630-961-3900 *Toll Free Tel:* 800-432-7444 *Fax:* 630-961-2168 *E-mail:* info@sourcebooks.com *Web Site:* www.sourcebooks.com, pg 194

Coffey, Avery, HarperCollins Children's Books, 195 Broadway, New York, NY 10007 *Tel:* 212-207-7000 *Web Site:* www.harpercollins.com/childrens, pg 86

Coffey, Darla Spence PhD, CSWE Press, 333 John Carlyle St, Suite 400, Alexandria, VA 22314-3457 *Tel:* 703-683-8080 *Fax:* 703-683-8493 *E-mail:* publications@cswe.org; info@cswe.org *Web Site:* www.cswe.org, pg 56

Coffey, Laura, Society for Features Journalism (SFJ), Eugene S Pulliam National Journalism Ctr, 3909 N Meridian St, Indianapolis, IN 46208 *E-mail:* wearesfj@gmail.com *Web Site:* featuresjournalism.org, pg 519

Coffey, Roland, Yale University Press, 302 Temple St, New Haven, CT 06511-8909 *Tel:* 203-432-0960; 203-432-0966 (sales); 401-531-2800 (cust serv) *Toll Free Tel:* 800-405-1619 (cust serv) *Fax:* 203-432-0948; 203-432-8485 (sales); 401-531-2801 (cust serv) *Toll Free Fax:* 800-406-9145 (cust serv) *E-mail:* sales.press@yale.edu (sales); customer.care@triliteral.org (cust serv) *Web Site:* www.yalebooks.com; yalepress.yale.edu/yupbooks, pg 235

Cogbill, Monet, Theatre Communications Group, 520 Eighth Ave, 24th fl, New York, NY 10018-4156 *Tel:* 212-609-5900 *Fax:* 212-609-5901 *E-mail:* info@tcg.org *Web Site:* www.tcg.org, pg 206

Coggins, Cara, Houghton Mifflin Harcourt, 125 High St, Boston, MA 02110 *Tel:* 617-351-5000 *Toll Free Tel:* 855-969-4642; 800-225-5425 (K-12 educ materials); 800-323-9540 (assessment materials); 877-219-1537 (SkillsTutor); 888-242-6747 (Innovation in Educ Group); 800-225-3362 (Trade & Ref Div) *Toll Free Fax:* 800-269-5232 *E-mail:* myhmhco@hmhco.com *Web Site:* www.hmhco.com, pg 96

Coggins, Joel, University of Pittsburgh Press, 7500 Thomas Blvd, Pittsburgh, PA 15260 *Tel:* 412-383-2456 *Fax:* 412-383-2466 *E-mail:* info@upress.pitt.edu *Web Site:* www.upress.pitt.edu, pg 219

Cohen, Adam, Tom Howard/John H Reid Fiction & Essay Contest, 351 Pleasant St, Suite B, PMB 222, Northampton, MA 01060-3998 *Tel:* 413-320-1847 *Toll Free Tel:* 866-WINWRIT (946-9748) *Fax:* 413-280-0539 *Web Site:* www.winningwriters.com/our-contests/tom-howard-john-h-reid-fiction-essay-contest, pg 614

Cohen, Adam, Tom Howard/Margaret Reid Poetry Contest, 351 Pleasant St, Suite B, PMB 222, Northampton, MA 01060-3998 *Tel:* 413-320-1847 *Toll Free Tel:* 866-WINWRIT (946-9748) *Fax:* 413-280-0539 *Web Site:* www.winningwriters.com/our-contests/tom-howard-margaret-reid-poetry-contest, pg 614

Cohen, Adam, North Street Book Prize, 351 Pleasant St, Suite B, PMB 222, Northampton, MA 01060-3998 *Tel:* 413-320-1847 *Toll Free Tel:* 866-WINWRIT (946-9748) *Fax:* 413-280-0539 *Web Site:* www.winningwriters.com/our-contests/north-street-book-prize, pg 641

Cohen, Adam, Wergle Flomp Humor Poetry Contest, 351 Pleasant St, Suite B, PMB 222, Northampton, MA 01060-3998 *Tel:* 413-320-1847 *Toll Free Tel:* 866-WINWRIT (946-9748) *Fax:* 413-280-0539 *Web Site:* www.winningwriters.com/our-contests/wergle-flomp-humor-poetry-contest-free, pg 674

Cohen, Alan G, Practising Law Institute (PLI), 1177 Avenue of the Americas, 2nd fl, New York, NY 10036 *Tel:* 212-824-5710 (cust serv) *Toll Free Tel:* 800-260-4PLI (260-4754) *Toll Free Fax:* 800-321-0093 (cust serv) *E-mail:* info@pli.edu; membership@pli.edu *Web Site:* www.pli.edu, pg 163

Cohen, Allison, Running Press, 1290 Avenue of the Americas, New York, NY 10104 *Tel:* 212-364-1100 *Toll Free Tel:* 800-759-0190 (cust serv) *Fax:* 212-364-0933 (intl orders) *Toll Free Fax:* 800-286-9471 (cust serv) *E-mail:* customer.service@hbgusa.com; orders@hbgusa.com *Web Site:* www.hachettebookgroup.com/imprint/running-press/; www.moon.com (Moon Travel Guides), pg 178

Cohen, Bill, Harrington Park Press, 9 E Eighth St, Box 331, New York, NY 10003 *Tel:* 347-882-3545 (edit & publicity) *Fax:* 646-602-1349 (edit & publicity) *Web Site:* harringtonparkpress.com, pg 87

Cohen, Christine M, Virginia Kidd Agency Inc, 538 E Harford St, PO Box 278, Milford, PA 18337 *Tel:* 570-296-6205 *Web Site:* vk-agency.com, pg 465

Cohen, Dakota, Penguin Random House Audio Publishing Group, 1745 Broadway, New York, NY 10019 *Toll Free Tel:* 800-793-2665 (cust serv) *E-mail:* audio@penguinrandomhouse.com; ecustomerservice@penguinrandomhouse.com *Web Site:* www.penguinrandomhouseaudio.com, pg 154

Cohen, Elana, Entangled Publishing LLC, 644 Shrewsbury Commons Ave, Suite 181, Shrewsbury, PA 17361 *Toll Free Tel:* 877-677-9451 *E-mail:* publisher@entangledpublishing.com *Web Site:* www.entangledpublishing.com, pg 67

Cohen, Jeremy, Jerome Fellowship, 2301 Franklin Ave E, Minneapolis, MN 55406-1099 *Tel:* 612-332-7481 *E-mail:* info@pwcenter.org *Web Site:* www.pwcenter.org, pg 618

Cohen, Jeremy, Many Voices Fellowships & Mentorships, 2301 Franklin Ave E, Minneapolis, MN 55406-1099 *Tel:* 612-332-7481 *Fax:* 612-332-6037 *E-mail:* info@pwcenter.org *Web Site:* www.pwcenter.org, pg 629

Cohen, Jeremy, McKnight Fellowships in Playwriting, 2301 Franklin Ave E, Minneapolis, MN 55406-1099 *Tel:* 612-332-7481 *Fax:* 612-332-6037 *E-mail:* info@pwcenter.org *Web Site:* www.pwcenter.org, pg 631

Cohen, Jeremy, McKnight National Residency & Commission, 2301 Franklin Ave E, Minneapolis, MN 55406-1099 *Tel:* 612-332-7481 *Fax:* 612-332-6037 *E-mail:* info@pwcenter.org *Web Site:* www.pwcenter.org, pg 631

Cohen, Jonathan, Kensington Publishing Corp, 900 Third Ave, 26th fl, New York, NY 10022 *Tel:* 212-407-1500 *Toll Free Tel:* 800-221-2647 *Fax:* 212-935-0699 *Web Site:* www.kensingtonbooks.com, pg 109

Cohen, Katia Segre, GeoLytics Inc, 507 Horizon Way, Branchburg, NJ 08853 *Tel:* 908-707-1505 *Toll Free Tel:* 800-577-6717 *E-mail:* support@geolytics.com; questions@geolytics.com *Web Site:* www.geolytics.com, pg 77

Cohen, Katie, Zagat Inc, 424 Broadway, 5th fl, New York, NY 10013 *E-mail:* feedback@zagat.com *Web Site:* www.zagat.com, pg 236

Cohen, Leslie, Chronicle Books LLC, 680 Second St, San Francisco, CA 94107 *Tel:* 415-537-4200 *Fax:* 415-537-4460 (perms) *E-mail:* hello@chroniclebooks.com; subrights@chroniclebooks.com *Web Site:* www.chroniclebooks.com, pg 47

Cohen, Lord, Alan Wofsy Fine Arts, 1109 Geary Blvd, San Francisco, CA 94109 *Tel:* 415-292-6500 *Toll Free Tel:* 800-660-6403 *Fax:* 415-292-6550 (off & cust serv); 510-251-1840 (acctg) *E-mail:* order@art-books.com (orders); editeur@earthlink.net (edit); beauxarts@earthlink.net (cust serv) *Web Site:* www.art-books.com, pg 273

Cohen, Louis, Mason Crest Publishers, 450 Parkway Dr, Suite D, Broomall, PA 19008 *Tel:* 610-543-6200 *Toll Free Tel:* 866-MCP-BOOK (627-2665) *Fax:* 610-543-3878 *Web Site:* www.masoncrest.com, pg 126

Cohen, Michael R, Puddingstone Literary, Authors' Agents, 11 Mabro Dr, Denville, NJ 07834-9607 *Tel:* 973-366-3622, pg 472

Cohen, Nan, Napa Valley Writers' Conference, 2277 Napa-Vallejo Hwy, Off 1753, Napa, CA 94558 *Tel:* 707-256-7113 *E-mail:* info@napawritersconference.org; fiction@napawritersconference.org; poetry@napawritersconference.org *Web Site:* www.napawritersconference.org, pg 556

Cohen, Paul, Monkfish Book Publishing Co, 22 E Market St, Suite 304, Rhinebeck, NY 12572 *Tel:* 845-876-4861 *Web Site:* www.monkfishpublishing.com, pg 133

Cohen, Samantha, Simon & Schuster, LLC, 1230 Avenue of the Americas, New York, NY 10020 *Tel:* 212-698-7000 *Toll Free Tel:* 800-223-2336 (orders) *Fax:* 212-698-7007 *Toll Free Fax:* 800-943-9831 (orders) *E-mail:* firstname.lastname@simonandschuster.com; purchaseorders@simonandschuster.com (orders) *Web Site:* www.simonandschuster.com, pg 189

Cohen, Steve, St Martin's Press, LLC, 120 Broadway, New York, NY 10271 *E-mail:* publicity@stmartins.com; trademarketing@stmartins.com; foreignrights@stmartins.com *Web Site:* us.macmillan.com/smp, pg 180

Cohen, Susan, Writers House, 21 W 26 St, New York, NY 10010 *Tel:* 212-685-2400 *Web Site:* www.writershouse.com, pg 482

Cohen, Susan Lee, Riverside Literary Agency, 41 Simon Keets Rd, Leyden, MA 01337 *Tel:* 413-772-0067 *Fax:* 413-772-0969 *E-mail:* rivlit@sover.net *Web Site:* www.riversideliteraryagency.com, pg 473

Cohen, Susan Perlman, PearlCo Literary Agency, LLC, 6596 Heronswood Cove, Memphis, TN 38119 *Tel:* 901-754-5276 *Web Site:* www.pearlcoliteraryagency.com, pg 472

Coke, Allison Hedge, Idyllwild Arts Summer Program, 52500 Temecula Rd, No 38, Idyllwild, CA 92549 *Tel:* 951-659-2171 *E-mail:* summer@idyllwildarts.org; adultprograms@idyllwildarts.org *Web Site:* idyllwildarts.org/summer, pg 555

Colavita, Madeleine, Grand Central Publishing, 1290 Avenue of the Americas, New York, NY 10104 *Tel:* 212-364-1100 *Web Site:* www.hachettebookgroup.com/imprint/grand-central-publishing/, pg 80

Colbeck, Jennifer, Robert J Pickering/J R Colbeck Award for Playwriting Excellence, 14 S Hanchett St, Coldwater, MI 49036 *E-mail:* president@branchcct.org *Web Site:* www.branchcct.org, pg 649

Colbert, Jaimee Wriston, Binghamton University Creative Writing Program, c/o Dept of English, General Literature & Rhetoric, PO Box 6000, Binghamton, NY 13902-6000 *Tel:* 607-777-2168 *Fax:* 607-777-2408 *E-mail:* cwpro@binghamton.edu *Web Site:* www.binghamton.edu/english/creative-writing/index.html, pg 561

Colburn, Loren, Association of Community Publishers Inc (ACP), 8119 Circuit Rider Path, Cicero, NY 13039 *Toll Free Tel:* 877-203-2327 *Fax:* 315-670-3121 (memb registration) *E-mail:* info@communitypublishers.com *Web Site:* www.communitypublishers.com, pg 499

Colby, John T Jr, Brick Tower Press, Manhanset House, PO Box 342, Shelter Island Heights, NY 11965-0342 *Tel:* 212-427-7139 *Toll Free Tel:* 800-68-BRICK (682-7425) *E-mail:* bricktower@aol.com *Web Site:* bricktowerpress.com, pg 36

Colding, Robert, Information Today, Inc, 143 Old Marlton Pike, Medford, NJ 08055-8750 *Tel:* 609-654-6266 *Toll Free Tel:* 800-300-9868 (cust serv) *Fax:* 609-654-4309 *E-mail:* custserv@infotoday.com *Web Site:* www.informationtodayinc.com, pg 100

Colding, Robert, Plexus Publishing, Inc, 143 Old Marlton Pike, Medford, NJ 08055 *Tel:* 609-654-6500 *Fax:* 609-654-4309 *E-mail:* info@plexuspublishing.com *Web Site:* www.plexuspublishing.com, pg 160

Cole, Deirdre, Writers & Readers Days, PO Box 801, Abingdon, VA 24212 *Tel:* 276-623-5266 *E-mail:* info@vahighlandsfestival.org *Web Site:* www.vahighlandsfestival.com, pg 558

Cole, Emma, Harlequin Enterprises Ltd, Bay Adelaide Centre, East Tower, 22 Adelaide St W, 41st fl, Toronto, ON M5H 4E3, Canada *Tel:* 416-445-5860 *Toll Free Tel:* 888-432-4879; 800-370-5838 (ebook inquiries) *E-mail:* customerservice@harlequin.com *Web Site:* www.harlequin.com, pg 409

Cole, Maureen, HarperCollins Publishers LLC, 195 Broadway, New York, NY 10007 *Tel:* 212-207-7000 *Web Site:* www.harpercollins.com, pg 86

Coleman, Christian, Beacon Press, 24 Farnsworth St, Boston, MA 02210-1409 *Tel:* 617-742-2110 *Fax:* 617-723-3097 *E-mail:* production@beacon.org *Web Site:* www.beacon.org, pg 25

Coleman, David, The College Board, 250 Vesey St, New York, NY 10281 *Tel:* 212-713-8000 *Toll Free Tel:* 866-630-9305 *Web Site:* www.collegeboard.com, pg 50

Coleman, Jason, University of Virginia Press, PO Box 400318, Charlottesville, VA 22904-4318 *Tel:* 434-924-3469 (cust serv) *Toll Free Tel:* 800-831-3406 *Fax:* 434-982-2655 *Toll Free Fax:* 877-288-6400 *E-mail:* vapress@virginia.edu *Web Site:* www.upress.virginia.edu, pg 220

Coleman, Natalie, Penguin Press, c/o Penguin Random House LLC, 1745 Broadway, New York, NY 10019 *Tel:* 212-782-9000 *E-mail:* penguinpress@penguinrandomhouse.com *Web Site:* www.penguin.com/penguin-press-overview/, pg 154

Coleman, Patrick, The Clarion Science Fiction & Fantasy Writers' Workshop, Arthur C Clarke Ctr for Human Imagination, UC San Diego, 9500 Gilman Dr, MC0445, La Jolla, CA 92093-0445 *Tel:* 858-534-6875 *E-mail:* clarion@ucsd.edu *Web Site:* clarion.ucsd.edu; imagination.ucsd.edu, pg 553

Coleman, Robin W, Johns Hopkins University Press, 2715 N Charles St, Baltimore, MD 21218-4363 *Tel:* 410-516-6900; 410-516-6987 *Toll Free Tel:* 800-537-5487 (book orders & cust serv); 800-548-1784 (journal orders) *Fax:* 410-516-6968; 410-516-6998 (orders) *E-mail:* hfscustserv@press.jhu.edu (cust serv); jrnlcirc@jh.edu (journal orders) *Web Site:* www.press.jhu.edu; muse.jhu.edu, pg 106

Coles, Kim, Magazines Canada (MC), 555 Richmond St W, Suite 604, Mailbox 201, Toronto, ON M5V 3B1, Canada *Tel:* 416-994-6471 *Toll Free Tel:* 877-238-8354 *Fax:* 416-504-0437 *E-mail:* info@magazinescanada.ca *Web Site:* magazinescanada.ca, pg 510

Colgan, Mary, Chronicle Books LLC, 680 Second St, San Francisco, CA 94107 *Tel:* 415-537-4200 *Fax:* 415-537-4460 (perms) *E-mail:* hello@chroniclebooks.com; subrights@chroniclebooks.com *Web Site:* www.chroniclebooks.com, pg 47

Colgan, Tom, Berkley, c/o Penguin Random House LLC, 1745 Broadway, 19th fl, New York, NY 10019 *Tel:* 212-366-2000 *Web Site:* www.penguin.com/publishers/berkley/; www.penguin.com/ace-overview/, pg 28

Colin, Graciela Patron, Penguin Random House Canada, a Penguin Random House company, 320 Front St W, Suite 1400, Toronto, ON M5V 3B6, Canada *Tel:* 416-364-4449 *Toll Free Tel:* 888-523-9292 (cust serv) *E-mail:* canadaweb@penguinrandomhouse.com; customerservicescanada@penguinrandomhouse.com *Web Site:* www.penguinrandomhouse.ca, pg 416

Coll, Mary, Aggiornamento Award, 8550 United Plaza Blvd, Suite 1001, Baton Rouge, LA 70809 *Tel:* 225-408-4417 *E-mail:* cla2@cathla.org *Web Site:* cathla.org, pg 570

Coll, Mary, John Brubaker Award, 8550 United Plaza Blvd, Suite 1001, Baton Rouge, LA 70809 *Tel:* 225-408-4417 *E-mail:* cla2@cathla.org *Web Site:* cathla.org, pg 584

Coll, Mary, Catholic Library Association, 8550 United Plaza Blvd, Suite 1001, Baton Rouge, LA 70809 *Tel:* 225-408-4417 *E-mail:* cla2@cathla.org *Web Site:* cathla.org, pg 503

Coll, Mary, Saint Katharine Drexel Award, 8550 United Plaza Blvd, Suite 1001, Baton Rouge, LA 70809 Tel: 225-408-4417 E-mail: cla2@cathla.org Web Site: cathla.org, pg 597

Coll, Mary, Jerome Award, 8550 United Plaza Blvd, Suite 1001, Baton Rouge, LA 70809 Tel: 225-408-4417 E-mail: cla2@cathla.org Web Site: cathla.org, pg 618

Coll, Mary, Regina Medal Award, 8550 United Plaza Blvd, Suite 1001, Baton Rouge, LA 70809 Tel: 225-408-4417 E-mail: cla2@cathla.org Web Site: cathla.org, pg 655

Collicelli, Gilles, Editions Mediaspaul, 3965, blvd Henri-Bourassa E, Montreal, QC H1H 1L1, Canada Tel: 514-322-7341 Fax: 514-322-4281 E-mail: mediaspaul@mediaspaul.ca Web Site: mediaspaul.ca, pg 404

Collier, Abby, University of Pittsburgh Press, 7500 Thomas Blvd, Pittsburgh, PA 15260 Tel: 412-383-2456 Fax: 412-383-2466 E-mail: info@upress.pitt.edu Web Site: www.upress.pitt.edu, pg 219

Collier, Diana G, Clarity Press Inc, 2625 Piedmont Rd NE, Suite 56, Atlanta, GA 30324 Tel: 404-647-6501 E-mail: claritypress@usa.net (foreign rts & perms) Web Site: www.claritypress.com, pg 49

Collier, Dianna, Collier Associates, 309 Kelsey Park Circle, Palm Beach Gardens, FL 33410 Tel: 561-514-6548 E-mail: dmccabooks@gmail.com, pg 454

Collier, James, Princeton University Press, 41 William St, Princeton, NJ 08540-5237 Tel: 609-258-4900 Fax: 609-258-6305 E-mail: info@press.princeton.edu Web Site: press.princeton.edu, pg 164

Collier, Theresa, Workman Publishing, 1290 Avenue of the Americas, New York, NY 10104 Toll Free Tel: 800-759-0190 Fax: 212-364-0950 E-mail: workman-inquiry@hbgusa.com Web Site: www.hachettebookgroup.com/imprint/workman-publishing-company/, pg 232

Colligan, Thomas, Farrar, Straus & Giroux, LLC, 120 Broadway, New York, NY 10271 Tel: 212-741-6900 E-mail: fsg.publicity@fsgbooks.com; sales@fsgbooks.com Web Site: us.macmillan.com/fsg, pg 70

Collignon, Kimberly, Data Trace Publishing Co (DTP), 110 West Rd, Suite 227, Towson, MD 21204-2316 Tel: 410-494-4994 Toll Free Tel: 800-342-0454 Fax: 410-494-0515 E-mail: info@datatrace.com; customerservice@datatrace.com; salesandmarketing@datatrace.com; editorial@datatrace.com Web Site: www.datatrace.com, pg 57

Collin, Rachel, Mitchell Lane Publishers Inc, 2001 SW 31 Ave, Hallandale, FL 33009 Tel: 954-985-9400 Toll Free Tel: 800-223-3251 Fax: 954-987-2200 E-mail: customerservice@mitchelllane.com Web Site: www.mitchelllane.com, pg 133

Collins, Amy, Talcott Notch Literary, 127 Broad St, 2P, Milford, CT 06460 Tel: 203-876-4959 Web Site: talcottnotch.net, pg 479

Collins, Anne, Knopf Canada, 320 Front St W, Suite 1400, Toronto, ON M5V 3B6, Canada Tel: 416-364-4449 Toll Free Tel: 888-523-9292 Fax: 416-598-7764 Web Site: www.penguinrandomhouse.ca, pg 411

Collins, Beth, Beacon Press, 24 Farnsworth St, Boston, MA 02210-1409 Tel: 617-742-2110 Fax: 617-723-3097 E-mail: production@beacon.org Web Site: www.beacon.org, pg 25

Collins, Camille, HarperCollins Publishers LLC, 195 Broadway, New York, NY 10007 Tel: 212-207-7000 Web Site: www.harpercollins.com, pg 87

Collins, Donna, Individual Excellence Awards, 30 E Broad St, 33rd fl, Columbus, OH 43215 Tel: 614-466-2613 Fax: 614-466-4494 Web Site: www.oac.state.oh.us, pg 616

Collins, Elise Marie, Women's National Book Association Inc, PO Box 237, FDR Sta, New York, NY 10150-0231 Toll Free Tel: 866-610-WNBA (610-9622) E-mail: info@wnba-books.org Web Site: wnba-books.org, pg 522

Collins, Kelly, Macmillan, 120 Broadway, 22nd fl, New York, NY 10271 E-mail: press.inquiries@macmillan.com Web Site: us.macmillan.com, pg 122

Collins, Lesley, Simon & Schuster, 1230 Avenue of the Americas, New York, NY 10020 Tel: 212-698-7000 Toll Free Tel: 800-223-2348 (cust serv); 800-223-2336 (orders) Toll Free Fax: 800-943-9831 (orders) Web Site: simonandschusterpublishing.com/simonandschuster/, pg 188

Collins, Libby, Tor Publishing Group, 120 Broadway, New York, NY 10271 Toll Free Tel: 800-455-0340 (Macmillan) E-mail: torpublicity@tor.com; forgepublicity@forgebooks.com Web Site: us.macmillan.com/torpublishinggroup, pg 208

Collins, Malia, University of Hawaii Press, 2840 Kolowalu St, Honolulu, HI 96822-1888 Tel: 808-956-8255 Toll Free Tel: 888-UHPRESS (847-7377) Toll Free Fax: 800-650-7811 E-mail: uhpbooks@hawaii.edu Web Site: www.uhpress.hawaii.edu, pg 216

Collins, Meg, Macmillan, 120 Broadway, 22nd fl, New York, NY 10271 E-mail: press.inquiries@macmillan.com Web Site: us.macmillan.com, pg 122

Collins, Naja Pulliam, University of California Press, 155 Grand Ave, Suite 400, Oakland, CA 94612-3758 Tel: 510-883-8232 Fax: 510-836-8910 E-mail: customerservice@ucpress.edu Web Site: www.ucpress.edu, pg 215

Collins, Patty, Random House Children's Books, c/o Penguin Random House LLC, 1745 Broadway, New York, NY 10019 Tel: 212-782-9000 Web Site: www.rhcbooks.com, pg 169

Collins, Sydney, Random House Publishing Group, 1745 Broadway, New York, NY 10019 Toll Free Tel: 800-200-3552 Web Site: www.randomhousebooks.com, pg 171

Collins, Teresa, The University Press of Kentucky, 663 S Limestone St, Lexington, KY 40508-4008 Tel: 859-257-8400 Fax: 859-323-1873 Web Site: www.kentuckypress.com, pg 222

Colon, Beth, University of Virginia Press, PO Box 400318, Charlottesville, VA 22904-4318 Tel: 434-924-3469 (cust serv) Toll Free Tel: 800-831-3406 Fax: 434-982-2655 Toll Free Fax: 877-288-6400 E-mail: vapress@virginia.edu Web Site: www.upress.virginia.edu, pg 220

Columbus, Nadya, Nova Science Publishers Inc, 400 Oser Ave, Suite 1600, Hauppauge, NY 11788-3619 Tel: 631-231-7269 Fax: 631-231-8175 E-mail: nova.main@novapublishers.com Web Site: www.novapublishers.com, pg 144

Colvin, Andrea, Little, Brown Books for Young Readers (LBYR), 1290 Avenue of the Americas, New York, NY 10104 Tel: 212-364-1100 Toll Free Tel: 800-759-0190 (cust serv) E-mail: rights@lbchildrens.com Web Site: www.hachettebookgroup.com/imprint/little-brown-books-for-young-readers/, pg 118

Colvin, Rod, Addicus Books Inc, PO Box 45327, Omaha, NE 68145 Tel: 402-330-7493 Fax: 402-330-1707 E-mail: info@addicusbooks.com Web Site: www.addicusbooks.com, pg 5

Comay, Mattan, Graywolf Press, 212 Third Ave N, Suite 485, Minneapolis, MN 55401 Tel: 651-641-0077 Fax: 651-641-0036 E-mail: wolves@graywolfpress.org (no ms queries, sample chapters or proposals) Web Site: www.graywolfpress.org, pg 81

Comay, Mattan, Graywolf Press African Fiction Prize, 212 Third Ave N, Suite 485, Minneapolis, MN 55401 Tel: 651-641-0077 Fax: 651-641-0036 E-mail: submissions@graywolfpress.org Web Site: www.graywolfpress.org/about-us/submissions, pg 609

Comay, Mattan, Graywolf Press Nonfiction Prize, 212 Third Ave N, Suite 485, Minneapolis, MN 55401 Tel: 651-641-0077 Fax: 651-641-0036 E-mail: submissions@graywolfpress.org Web Site: www.graywolfpress.org/about-us/submissions, pg 609

Combemale, Chris, Sterling Lord Literistic Inc, 594 Broadway, Suite 205, New York, NY 10012 Tel: 212-780-6050 Fax: 212-780-6095 E-mail: info@sll.com Web Site: www.sll.com, pg 477

Combs, Michele, Carpe Indexum, 1960 Deer Run Rd, LaFayette, NY 13084 Tel: 315-677-3030 E-mail: info@carpeindexum.com Web Site: www.carpeindexum.com, pg 436

Combs, Tyiana, Penguin Workshop, c/o Penguin Random House LLC, 1745 Broadway, New York, NY 10019 Tel: 212-782-9000 Web Site: www.penguin.com/publishers/penguinworkshop/, pg 156

Comeau, Jennifer, University of Illinois Press, 1325 S Oak St, MC-566, Champaign, IL 61820-6903 Tel: 217-333-0950 Fax: 217-244-8082 E-mail: uipress@uillinois.edu; journals@uillinois.edu Web Site: www.press.uillinois.edu, pg 216

Comeau, Kimberly, Scarsdale Publishing Ltd, 333 Mamaroneck Ave, White Plains, NY 10607 E-mail: scarsdale@scarsdalepublishing.com Web Site: scarsdalepublishing.com, pg 183

Comeaux, Kristen, Jane Rotrosen Agency LLC, 318 E 51 St, New York, NY 10022-7803 Tel: 212-593-4330 E-mail: info@janerotrosen.com Web Site: janerotrosen.com, pg 474

Comerford, Rachel, Macmillan Learning, One New York Plaza, Suite 46, New York, NY 10004 Tel: 212-576-9400 E-mail: salesoperations@macmillanusa.com Web Site: www.macmillanlearning.com/college/us, pg 123

Commander, Dr Michelle, Harriet Tubman Prize, 515 Malcolm X Blvd, New York, NY 10037 Tel: 212-491-2263 E-mail: lapiduscenter@nypl.org Web Site: www.lapiduscenter.org/category/tubman, pg 670

Comrie, Tim, YMAA Publication Center Inc, PO Box 480, Wolfeboro, NH 03894 Tel: 603-569-7988 Toll Free Tel: 800-669-8892 Fax: 603-569-1889 E-mail: info@ymaa.com Web Site: www.ymaa.com, pg 235

Conary, Lori, Meriwether Publishing, c/o Pioneer Drama Service, 109 Inverness Dr E, Suite H, Centennial, CO 80112 Tel: 303-779-4035 Toll Free Tel: 800-333-7262 Fax: 303-779-4315 Web Site: meriwetherpublishing.com; www.pioneerdrama.com, pg 129

Conaway, Dan, Writers House, 21 W 26 St, New York, NY 10010 Tel: 212-685-2400 Web Site: www.writershouse.com, pg 482

Concepcion, Cristina, Don Congdon Associates Inc, 110 William St, Suite 2202, New York, NY 10038-3914 Tel: 212-645-1229 Fax: 212-727-2688 E-mail: dca@doncongdon.com Web Site: www.doncongdon.com, pg 454

Conde, Miguel, James H Ottaway Jr Award for the Promotion of International Literature, 147 Prince St, Brooklyn, NY 11201 Tel: 347-699-2914 E-mail: info@wordswithoutborders.org Web Site: www.wordswithoutborders.org/ottaway-award, pg 645

Conde, Sidney, St Martin's Press, LLC, 120 Broadway, New York, NY 10271 E-mail: publicity@stmartins.com; trademarketing@stmartins.com; foreignrights@stmartins.com Web Site: us.macmillan.com/smp, pg 180

Condit, Carl Daniel, Sunstone Press, PO Box 2321, Santa Fe, NM 87504-2321 Tel: 505-988-4418 E-mail: orders@sunstonepress.com Web Site: sunstonepress.com, pg 201

Condon, Brian, Alliance for Audited Media (AAM), 4513 Lincoln Ave, Suite 105B, Lisle, IL 60532 Tel: 224-366-6939 Toll Free Tel: 800-285-2220 E-mail: corpcomm@auditedmedia.com Web Site: auditedmedia.com, pg 493

Congdon, David, University Press of Kansas, 2502 Westbrooke Circle, Lawrence, KS 66045-4444 Tel: 785-864-4154 Fax: 785-864-4586 E-mail: upress@ku.edu Web Site: www.kansaspress.ku.edu, pg 221

Congdon, Michael, Don Congdon Associates Inc, 110 William St, Suite 2202, New York, NY 10038-3914 *Tel:* 212-645-1229 *Fax:* 212-727-2688 *E-mail:* dca@doncongdon.com *Web Site:* www.doncongdon.com, pg 454

Congdon, Sarah, Grand Central Publishing, 1290 Avenue of the Americas, New York, NY 10104 *Tel:* 212-364-1100 *Web Site:* www.hachettebookgroup.com/imprint/grand-central-publishing/, pg 80

Conklin, Kevin, Scholastic Inc, 557 Broadway, New York, NY 10012 *Tel:* 212-343-6100 *Toll Free Tel:* 800-SCHOLASTIC (724-6527) *Web Site:* www.scholastic.com, pg 184

Conley, Michael C, Gallopade International Inc, 611 Hwy 74 S, Suite 2000, Peachtree City, GA 30269 *Tel:* 770-631-4222 *Toll Free Tel:* 800-536-2438 *Fax:* 770-631-4810 *Toll Free Fax:* 800-871-2979 *E-mail:* customerservice@gallopade.com *Web Site:* www.gallopade.com, pg 76

Conlisk, Carrie, Sourcebooks LLC, 1935 Brookdale Rd, Suite 139, Naperville, IL 60563 *Tel:* 630-961-3900 *Toll Free Tel:* 800-432-7444 *Fax:* 630-961-2168 *E-mail:* info@sourcebooks.com *Web Site:* www.sourcebooks.com, pg 195

Conlon, Michael, Red Wheel/Weiser, 65 Parker St, Suite 7, Newburyport, MA 01950 *Tel:* 978-465-0504 *Toll Free Tel:* 800-423-7087 (orders) *Fax:* 978-465-0243 *E-mail:* info@rwwbooks.com *Web Site:* www.redwheelweiser.com, pg 173

Connelly, Prof Claire PhD, Angels Editorial Services, 1630 Main St, No 41, Coventry, CT 06238 *Tel:* 860-742-5279 *E-mail:* angelsus@aol.com, pg 435

Conners, Jim, Encyclopaedia Britannica Inc, 325 N La Salle St, Suite 200, Chicago, IL 60654 *Tel:* 312-347-7000 (all other countries) *Toll Free Tel:* 800-323-1229 (US & CN) *Fax:* 312-294-2104 *E-mail:* contact@eb.com *Web Site:* www.britannica.com, pg 66

Conners, Peter, BOA Editions Ltd, 250 N Goodman St, Suite 306, Rochester, NY 14607 *Tel:* 585-546-3410 *Fax:* 585-546-3913 *E-mail:* contact@boaeditions.org *Web Site:* www.boaeditions.org, pg 33

Conners, Peter, BOA Short Fiction Prize, 250 N Goodman St, Suite 306, Rochester, NY 14607 *Tel:* 585-546-3410 *E-mail:* contact@boaeditions.org *Web Site:* www.boaeditions.org/pages/boa-short-fiction-prize, pg 582

Conniff, Casey, Jane Rotrosen Agency LLC, 318 E 51 St, New York, NY 10022-7803 *Tel:* 212-593-4330 *E-mail:* info@janerotrosen.com *Web Site:* janerotrosen.com, pg 474

Connolly, Chris, HarperCollins Publishers LLC, 195 Broadway, New York, NY 10007 *Tel:* 212-207-7000 *Web Site:* www.harpercollins.com, pg 87

Connolly, Claudia, Pembroke Publishers Ltd, 538 Hood Rd, Markham, ON L3R 3K9, Canada *Tel:* 905-477-0650 *Toll Free Tel:* 800-997-9807 *Fax:* 905-477-3691 *Toll Free Fax:* 800-339-5568 *Web Site:* www.pembrokepublishers.com, pg 415

Connolly, Jim, The Massachusetts Historical Society, 1154 Boylston St, Boston, MA 02215-3695 *Tel:* 617-536-1608 *Fax:* 617-859-0074 *E-mail:* publications@masshist.org *Web Site:* www.masshist.org, pg 126

Connolly, John, Swedenborg Foundation, 320 N Church St, West Chester, PA 19380 *Tel:* 610-430-3222 *Toll Free Tel:* 800-355-3222 (cust serv) *Fax:* 610-430-7982 *E-mail:* info@swedenborg.com *Web Site:* swedenborg.com, pg 201

Connolly, Kevin, House of Anansi Press Inc, 128 Sterling Rd, Lower Level, Toronto, ON M6R 2B7, Canada *Tel:* 416-363-4343 *Fax:* 416-363-1017 *E-mail:* customerservice@houseofanansi.com *Web Site:* houseofanansi.com, pg 409

Connor, Heather, Harlequin Enterprises Ltd, 195 Broadway, 24th fl, New York, NY 10007 *Tel:* 212-207-7000 *Toll Free Tel:* 888-432-4879; 800-370-5838 (ebooks) *E-mail:* customerservice@harlequin.com *Web Site:* www.harlequin.com/shop/index.html; corporate.harlequin.com, pg 85

Connor, Leah, University of Toronto Press, Book Publishing Div, 800 Bay St, Mezzanine, Toronto, ON M5S 3A9, Canada *Tel:* 416-978-2239 *Fax:* 416-978-4736 *E-mail:* utpbooks@utorontopress.com (orders) *Web Site:* utorontopress.com, pg 423

Connors, Becca, New England Poetry Club, c/o Linda Haviland Conte, 18 Hall Ave, Apt 2, Somerville, MA 02144 *E-mail:* info@nepoetryclub.org; president@nepoetryclub.org *Web Site:* nepoetryclub.org, pg 514

Connors, Dan, Twenty-Third Publications, One Montauk Ave, Suite 200, New London, CT 06320 *Tel:* 860-437-3012 *Toll Free Tel:* 800-321-0411 (orders) *Toll Free Fax:* 800-572-0788 *E-mail:* resources@twentythirdpublications.com *Web Site:* www.twentythirdpublications.com, pg 211

Connors, Kaitlyn, Macmillan, 120 Broadway, 22nd fl, New York, NY 10271 *E-mail:* press.inquiries@macmillan.com *Web Site:* us.macmillan.com, pg 122

Conrad, Cecilia A, MacArthur Fellows Program, Office of Grants Management, 140 S Dearborn St, Chicago, IL 60603-5285 *Tel:* 312-726-8000 *Fax:* 312-920-6528 *E-mail:* 4answers@macfound.org *Web Site:* www.macfound.org/programs/fellows, pg 628

Conrad, Joanna, Texas Tech University Press, 1120 Main St, 2nd fl, Lubbock, TX 79401 *Tel:* 806-742-2982 *Toll Free Tel:* 800-832-4042 *E-mail:* ttup@ttu.edu *Web Site:* www.ttupress.org, pg 205

Conrad, Kathryn, The University of Arizona Press, 1510 E University Blvd, Tucson, AZ 85721 *Tel:* 520-621-1441 *Toll Free Tel:* 800-621-2736 *Fax:* 520-621-8899 *Toll Free Fax:* 800-621-8476 (orders) *E-mail:* uap@uapress.arizona.edu *Web Site:* www.uapress.arizona.edu, pg 214

Conrad, Rachael, New England Book Awards, One Beacon St, 15th fl, Boston, MA 02108 *Tel:* 617-547-3642 *Web Site:* www.newenglandbooks.org/page/book-awards, pg 640

Conrad, Rachael, New England Independent Booksellers Association Inc (NEIBA), One Beacon St, 15th fl, Boston, MA 02108 *Tel:* 617-547-3642 *Web Site:* www.newenglandbooks.org, pg 514

Considine, Bob, New Jersey Business & Industry Association (NJBIA), 10 W Lafayette St, Trenton, NJ 08608-2002 *Tel:* 609-393-7707 *Web Site:* njbia.org, pg 514

Considine, Lisa, Penguin Random House Speakers Bureau, a Penguin Random House company, 1745 Broadway, Mail Drop 13-1, New York, NY 10019 *Tel:* 212-572-2013 *E-mail:* speakers@penguinrandomhouse.com *Web Site:* www.prhspeakers.com, pg 487

Consolazio, Pam, Candlewick Press, 99 Dover St, Somerville, MA 02144-2825 *Tel:* 617-661-3330 *Fax:* 617-661-0565 *E-mail:* bigbear@candlewick.com; salesinfo@candlewick.com *Web Site:* candlewick.com, pg 39

Constantinou, Meghan, American Printing History Association, PO Box 4519, Grand Central Sta, New York, NY 10163 *E-mail:* secretary@printinghistory.org *Web Site:* printinghistory.org, pg 496

Constantinou, Meghan, American Printing History Association Award, PO Box 4519, Grand Central Sta, New York, NY 10163 *E-mail:* secretary@printinghistory.org *Web Site:* printinghistory.org/programs/awards, pg 573

Contardo, Nick, Trusted Media Brands Inc, 750 Third Ave, 3rd fl, New York, NY 10017 *Tel:* 646-293-6299 *Toll Free Tel:* 877-732-4438 (cust serv) *Fax:* 646-293-6251 *E-mail:* customercare@trustedmediabrands.com; press@trustedmediabrands.com *Web Site:* www.trustedmediabrands.com; www.rd.com, pg 210

Conte, Beth, Random House Children's Books, c/o Penguin Random House LLC, 1745 Broadway, New York, NY 10019 *Tel:* 212-782-9000 *Web Site:* www.rhcbooks.com, pg 169

Conte, Francesca, Penguin Random House Canada, a Penguin Random House company, 320 Front St W, Suite 1400, Toronto, ON M5V 3B6, Canada *Tel:* 416-364-4449 *Toll Free Tel:* 888-523-9292 (cust serv) *E-mail:* canadaweb@penguinrandomhouse.com; customerservicescanada@penguinrandomhouse.com *Web Site:* www.penguinrandomhouse.ca, pg 416

Conte, Kristin, Random House Publishing Group, 1745 Broadway, New York, NY 10019 *Toll Free Tel:* 800-200-3552 *Web Site:* www.randomhousebooks.com, pg 171

Conte, Linda Haviland, Samuel Washington Allen Prize, c/o Linda Haviland Conte, 18 Hall Ave, Apt 2, Somerville, MA 02144 *E-mail:* info@nepoetryclub.org *Web Site:* nepoetryclub.org, pg 572

Conte, Linda Haviland, E E Cummings Prize, c/o Linda Haviland Conte, 18 Hall Ave, Apt 2, Somerville, MA 02144 *E-mail:* info@nepoetryclub.org *Web Site:* nepoetryclub.org, pg 594

Conte, Linda Haviland, Der Hovanessian Prize, c/o Linda Haviland Conte, 18 Hall Ave, Apt 2, Somerville, MA 02144 *E-mail:* info@nepoetryclub.org *Web Site:* nepoetryclub.org, pg 595

Conte, Linda Haviland, Golden Rose Award, c/o Linda Haviland Conte, 18 Hall Ave, Apt 2, Somerville, MA 02144 *E-mail:* info@nepoetryclub.org *Web Site:* nepoetryclub.org, pg 608

Conte, Linda Haviland, Amy Lowell Prize, c/o Linda Haviland Conte, 18 Hall Ave, Apt 2, Somerville, MA 02144 *E-mail:* info@nepoetryclub.org *Web Site:* nepoetryclub.org, pg 627

Conte, Linda Haviland, Sheila Margaret Motton Book Prize, c/o Linda Haviland Conte, 18 Hall Ave, Apt 2, Somerville, MA 02144 *E-mail:* info@nepoetryclub.org *Web Site:* nepoetryclub.org, pg 636

Conte, Linda Haviland, New England Poetry Club, c/o Linda Haviland Conte, 18 Hall Ave, Apt 2, Somerville, MA 02144 *E-mail:* info@nepoetryclub.org; president@nepoetryclub.org *Web Site:* nepoetryclub.org, pg 514

Conte, Linda Haviland, Jean Pedrick Chapbook Prize, c/o Linda Haviland Conte, 18 Hall Ave, Apt 2, Somerville, MA 02144 *E-mail:* info@nepoetryclub.org *Web Site:* nepoetryclub.org, pg 646

Contini, Christine, Winterwolf Press, 8635 W Sahara Ave, Suite 425, Las Vegas, NV 89117 *Tel:* 725-222-3442 *E-mail:* info@winterwolfpress.com *Web Site:* winterwolfpress.com, pg 231

Contreras, Raquel, Casa Bautista de Publicaciones, 130 Montoya Rd, El Paso, TX 79932 *Tel:* 915-566-9656 *Toll Free Tel:* 800-755-5958 (cust serv & orders) *E-mail:* orders@editorialmh.org *Web Site:* www.editorialmh.org, pg 41

Contreras, Viridiana, Sourcebooks LLC, 1935 Brookdale Rd, Suite 139, Naperville, IL 60563 *Tel:* 630-961-3900 *Toll Free Tel:* 800-432-7444 *Fax:* 630-961-2168 *E-mail:* info@sourcebooks.com *Web Site:* www.sourcebooks.com, pg 194

Conway, Jennie, St Martin's Press, LLC, 120 Broadway, New York, NY 10271 *E-mail:* publicity@stmartins.com; trademarketing@stmartins.com; foreignrights@stmartins.com *Web Site:* us.macmillan.com/smp, pg 181

Conway, JM, University of Chicago, Graham School Writer's Studio, 1427 E 60 St, Chicago, IL 60637 *Tel:* 773-702-1731 *Web Site:* graham.uchicago.edu/programs-courses/writers-studio, pg 566

Conway, Michael, Chronicle Books LLC, 680 Second St, San Francisco, CA 94107 *Tel:* 415-537-4200 *Fax:* 415-537-4460 (perms) *E-mail:* hello@chroniclebooks.com; subrights@chroniclebooks.com *Web Site:* www.chroniclebooks.com, pg 47

Conway, Michelle, Linda Chester Literary Agency, 630 Fifth Ave, Suite 2000, New York, NY 10111 *Tel:* 212-218-3350 *E-mail:* submissions@lindachester.com *Web Site:* www.lindachester.com, pg 453

Cook, Amy PhD, Sourced Media Books, 15 Via Picato, San Clemente, CA 92673 *Tel:* 949-813-0182 *E-mail:* editor@sourcedmediabooks.com *Web Site:* sourcedmediabooks.com, pg 195

Cook, Avery, Nosy Crow Inc, 145 Lincoln Rd, Lincoln, MA 01773 E-mail: nosycrowinc@nosycrow.com; salesinfo@nosycrow.com; export@nosycrow.com (export sales); rights@nosycrow.com Web Site: nosycrow.us, pg 144

Cook, Charles, Kendall Hunt Publishing Co, 4050 Westmark Dr, Dubuque, IA 52002-2624 Tel: 563-589-1000 Toll Free Tel: 800-228-0810 (orders) Fax: 563-589-1071 Toll Free Fax: 800-772-9165 E-mail: ordernow@kendallhunt.com Web Site: www.kendallhunt.com, pg 108

Cook, Chris, University of California Press, 155 Grand Ave, Suite 400, Oakland, CA 94612-3758 Tel: 510-883-8232 Fax: 510-836-8910 E-mail: customerservice@ucpress.edu Web Site: www.ucpress.edu, pg 215

Cook, Dorothy M, W W Norton & Company Inc, 500 Fifth Ave, New York, NY 10110-0017 Tel: 212-354-5500 Toll Free Tel: 800-233-4830 (orders & cust serv) Fax: 212-869-0856 Toll Free Fax: 800-458-6515 E-mail: orders@wwnorton.com Web Site: wwnorton.com, pg 143

Cook, Ian, Sourcebooks LLC, 1935 Brookdale Rd, Suite 139, Naperville, IL 60563 Tel: 630-961-3900 Toll Free Tel: 800-432-7444 Fax: 630-961-2168 E-mail: info@sourcebooks.com Web Site: www.sourcebooks.com, pg 195

Cook, Jazz, Association of Canadian Publishers (ACP), 401 Richmond St W, Studio 257A, Toronto, ON M5V 3A8, Canada Tel: 416-487-6116 E-mail: admin@canbook.org Web Site: publishers.ca, pg 499

Cook, Katie, Piano Press, 1425 Ocean Ave, Suite 5, Del Mar, CA 92014 Tel: 619-884-1401 E-mail: pianopress@pianopress.com Web Site: www.pianopress.com, pg 159

Cook, Kelli, Math Solutions®, One Harbor Dr, Suite 101, Sausalito, CA 94965 Toll Free Tel: 877-234-7323 Toll Free Fax: 800-724-4716 E-mail: info@mathsolutions.com; orders@mathsolutions.com Web Site: www.mathsolutions.com; store.mathsolutions.com, pg 127

Cook, Kenneth, Berrett-Koehler Publishers Inc, 1333 Broadway, Suite 1000, Oakland, CA 94612 Tel: 510-817-2277 Fax: 510-817-2278 E-mail: bkpub@bkpub.com Web Site: www.bkconnection.com, pg 29

Cook, Laura, Transatlantic Agency, 2 Bloor St E, Suite 3500, Toronto, ON M4W 1A8, Canada Tel: 416-488-9214 E-mail: info@transatlanticagency.com; royalties@transatlanticagency.com Web Site: www.transatlanticagency.com, pg 479

Cook, Martha, Trafalgar Square Books, 388 Howe Hill Rd, North Pomfret, VT 05053 Tel: 802-457-1911 Toll Free Tel: 800-423-4525 Fax: 802-457-1913 E-mail: contact@trafalgarbooks.com Web Site: www.trafalgarbooks.com; www.horseandriderbooks.com, pg 208

Cook, Tonya, Cornell University Press, Sage House, 512 E State St, Ithaca, NY 14850 Tel: 607-253-2338 E-mail: cupressinfo@cornell.edu; cupress-sales@cornell.edu; cupress-perms@cornell.edu (reprint/class use permissions) Web Site: www.cornellpress.cornell.edu, pg 52

Cooke, Bridget, Chronicle Books LLC, 680 Second St, San Francisco, CA 94107 Tel: 415-537-4200 Fax: 415-537-4460 (perms) E-mail: hello@chroniclebooks.com; subrights@chroniclebooks.com Web Site: www.chroniclebooks.com, pg 48

Cooke, Max, EdCan Network, 60 St Clair Ave E, Suite 703, Toronto, ON M4T 1N5, Canada Tel: 416-591-6300 Toll Free Tel: 866-803-9549 Fax: 416-591-5345 Toll Free Fax: 866-803-9549 E-mail: info@edcan.ca Web Site: www.edcan.ca, pg 505

Cooley, Cherryl T, A Sense of Place: The Elizabeth J Urquhart Memorial, PO Box 36128, North Chesterfield, VA 23235-3533 E-mail: contest@poetrysocietyofvirginia.org; info@poetryvirginia.org Web Site: www.poetrysocietyofvirginia.org, pg 569

Cooley, Cherryl T, Laura Day Boggs Bolling Memorial, PO Box 36128, North Chesterfield, VA 23235-3533 E-mail: contest@poetrysocietyofvirginia.org; info@poetryvirginia.org Web Site: www.poetrysocietyofvirginia.org, pg 582

Cooley, Cherryl T, Joe Pendleton Campbell Narrative Contest, PO Box 36128, North Chesterfield, VA 23235-3533 E-mail: contest@poetrysocietyofvirginia.org; info@poetryvirginia.org Web Site: www.poetrysocietyofvirginia.org, pg 586

Cooley, Cherryl T, Carleton Drewry Memorial, PO Box 36128, North Chesterfield, VA 23235-3533 E-mail: contest@poetrysocietyofvirginia.org; info@poetryvirginia.org Web Site: www.poetrysocietyofvirginia.org, pg 597

Cooley, Cherryl T, Ekphrastic Poetry Award, PO Box 36128, North Chesterfield, VA 23235-3533 E-mail: contest@poetrysocietyofvirginia.org; info@poetryvirginia.org Web Site: www.poetrysocietyofvirginia.org, pg 599

Cooley, Cherryl T, Bess Gresham Memorial, PO Box 36128, North Chesterfield, VA 23235-3533 E-mail: contest@poetrysocietyofvirginia.org; info@poetryvirginia.org Web Site: www.poetrysocietyofvirginia.org, pg 609

Cooley, Cherryl T, Raymond Levi Haislip Memorial, PO Box 36128, North Chesterfield, VA 23235-3533 E-mail: contest@poetrysocietyofvirginia.org; info@poetryvirginia.org Web Site: www.poetrysocietyofvirginia.org, pg 610

Cooley, Cherryl T, Loretta Dunn Hall Memorial, PO Box 36128, North Chesterfield, VA 23235-3533 E-mail: contest@poetrysocietyofvirginia.org; info@poetryvirginia.org Web Site: www.poetrysocietyofvirginia.org, pg 610

Cooley, Cherryl T, Handy Andy Prize, PO Box 36128, North Chesterfield, VA 23235-3533 E-mail: contest@poetrysocietyofvirginia.org; info@poetryvirginia.org Web Site: www.poetrysocietyofvirginia.org, pg 611

Cooley, Cherryl T, Brodie Herndon Memorial, PO Box 36128, North Chesterfield, VA 23235-3533 E-mail: contest@poetrysocietyofvirginia.org; info@poetryvirginia.org Web Site: www.poetrysocietyofvirginia.org, pg 612

Cooley, Cherryl T, Honoring Fatherhood Award, PO Box 36128, North Chesterfield, VA 23235-3533 E-mail: contest@poetrysocietyofvirginia.org; info@poetryvirginia.org Web Site: www.poetrysocietyofvirginia.org, pg 613

Cooley, Cherryl T, Judah, Sarah, Grace & Tom Memorial, PO Box 36128, North Chesterfield, VA 23235-3533 E-mail: contest@poetrysocietyofvirginia.org; info@poetryvirginia.org Web Site: www.poetrysocietyofvirginia.org, pg 618

Cooley, Cherryl T, Sarah Lockwood Memorial, PO Box 36128, North Chesterfield, VA 23235-3533 E-mail: contest@poetrysocietyofvirginia.org; info@poetryvirginia.org Web Site: www.poetrysocietyofvirginia.org, pg 625

Cooley, Cherryl T, Cenie H Moon Prize, PO Box 36128, North Chesterfield, VA 23235-3533 E-mail: contest@poetrysocietyofvirginia.org; info@poetryvirginia.org Web Site: www.poetrysocietyofvirginia.org, pg 635

Cooley, Cherryl T, Elizabeth Neuwirth Memorial, PO Box 36128, North Chesterfield, VA 23235-3533 E-mail: contest@poetrysocietyofvirginia.org; info@poetryvirginia.org Web Site: www.poetrysocietyofvirginia.org, pg 639

Cooley, Cherryl T, New Voices: The Joanne Scott Kennedy Memorial, PO Box 36128, North Chesterfield, VA 23235-3533 E-mail: contest@poetrysocietyofvirginia.org; info@poetryvirginia.org Web Site: www.poetrysocietyofvirginia.org, pg 640

Cooley, Cherryl T, Karma Deane Ogden Memorial, PO Box 36128, North Chesterfield, VA 23235-3533 E-mail: contest@poetrysocietyofvirginia.org; info@poetryvirginia.org Web Site: www.poetrysocietyofvirginia.org, pg 643

Cooley, Cherryl T, Edgar Allan Poe Memorial, PO Box 36128, North Chesterfield, VA 23235-3533 E-mail: contest@poetrysocietyofvirginia.org; info@poetryvirginia.org Web Site: www.poetrysocietyofvirginia.org, pg 650

Cooley, Cherryl T, Ada Sanderson Memorial, PO Box 36128, North Chesterfield, VA 23235-3533 E-mail: contest@poetrysocietyofvirginia.org; info@poetryvirginia.org Web Site: www.poetrysocietyofvirginia.org, pg 658

Cooley, Cherryl T, The Robert S Sergeant Memorial, PO Box 36128, North Chesterfield, VA 23235-3533 E-mail: contest@poetrysocietyofvirginia.org; info@poetryvirginia.org Web Site: www.poetrysocietyofvirginia.org, pg 661

Cooley, Cherryl T, The Anne Spencer Memorial, PO Box 36128, North Chesterfield, VA 23235-3533 E-mail: contest@poetrysocietyofvirginia.org; info@poetryvirginia.org Web Site: www.poetrysocietyofvirginia.org, pg 665

Cooley, Cherryl T, Emma Gray Trigg Memorial, PO Box 36128, North Chesterfield, VA 23235-3533 E-mail: contest@poetrysocietyofvirginia.org; info@poetryvirginia.org Web Site: www.poetrysocietyofvirginia.org, pg 670

Cooley, Cherryl T, Nancy Byrd Turner Memorial, PO Box 36128, North Chesterfield, VA 23235-3533 E-mail: contest@poetrysocietyofvirginia.org; info@poetryvirginia.org Web Site: www.poetrysocietyofvirginia.org, pg 671

Cooley, Cherryl T, Undergraduate Poetry Award, PO Box 36128, North Chesterfield, VA 23235-3533 E-mail: contest@poetrysocietyofvirginia.org; info@poetryvirginia.org Web Site: www.poetrysocietyofvirginia.org, pg 672

Cooley, Cherryl T, Charlotte Wise Memorial, PO Box 36128, North Chesterfield, VA 23235-3533 E-mail: contest@poetrysocietyofvirginia.org; info@poetryvirginia.org Web Site: www.poetrysocietyofvirginia.org, pg 676

Coolidge, Alison, HarperCollins Publishers LLC, 195 Broadway, New York, NY 10007 Tel: 212-207-7000 Web Site: www.harpercollins.com, pg 87

Coolman, Marie, Bloomsbury Publishing Inc, 1385 Broadway, 5th fl, New York, NY 10018 Tel: 212-419-5300 E-mail: marketingusa@bloomsbury.com; adultpublicityusa@bloomsbury.com; askacademic@bloomsbury.com Web Site: www.bloomsbury.com, pg 31

Cooper, Alex, Greystone Books Ltd, 343 Railway St, Suite 302, Vancouver, BC V6A 1A4, Canada Tel: 604-875-1550 Fax: 604-875-1556 E-mail: info@greystonebooks.com; rights@greystonebooks.com Web Site: www.greystonebooks.com, pg 407

Cooper, Doris, Atria Books, 1230 Avenue of the Americas, New York, NY 10020 Tel: 212-698-7000 Fax: 212-698-7007 Web Site: www.simonandschuster.com, pg 21

Cooper, Karen, Adams Media, 100 Technology Center Dr, Suite 501, Stoughton, MA 02072 Tel: 508-427-7100 Web Site: www.simonandschuster.com, pg 4

Cooper, Karen, Simon & Schuster, LLC, 1230 Avenue of the Americas, New York, NY 10020 Tel: 212-698-7000 Toll Free Tel: 800-223-2336 (orders) Fax: 212-698-7007 Toll Free Fax: 800-943-9831 (orders) E-mail: firstname.lastname@simonandschuster.com; purchaseorders@simonandschuster.com (orders) Web Site: www.simonandschuster.com, pg 189

Cooper, Katie, Sourcebooks LLC, 1935 Brookdale Rd, Suite 139, Naperville, IL 60563 Tel: 630-961-3900 Toll Free Tel: 800-432-7444 Fax: 630-961-2168 E-mail: info@sourcebooks.com Web Site: www.sourcebooks.com, pg 195

Cooper, Kevin, New York University Press, 838 Broadway, 3rd fl, New York, NY 10003-4812 Tel: 212-998-2575 (edit) Toll Free Tel: 800-996-6987 (orders) Fax: 212-995-4798 (orders) E-mail: nyupressinfo@nyu.edu (cust care) Web Site: www.nyupress.org, pg 141

Cooper, Maggie, Aevitas Creative Management LLC, 19 W 21 St, Suite 501, New York, NY 10010 Tel: 212-765-6900 Web Site: www.aevitascreative.com, pg 448

Cooper, Paul, The Electrochemical Society (ECS), 65 S Main St, Bldg D, Pennington, NJ 08534-2839 *Tel:* 609-737-1902 *Fax:* 609-737-0629 *E-mail:* publications@electrochem.org; customerservice@electrochem.org; ecs@ioppublishing.org *Web Site:* www.electrochem.org, pg 65

Cooper, Sarah, Cormorant Books Inc, 260 Spadina Ave, Suite 502, Toronto, ON M5T 1E5, Canada *Tel:* 416-925-8887 *E-mail:* info@cormorantbooks.com *Web Site:* www.cormorantbooks.com, pg 400

Cooper, Stephanie, Dutton, c/o Penguin Random House LLC, 1745 Broadway, New York, NY 10019 *Tel:* 212-366-2000 *Web Site:* www.penguin.com/dutton-overview/; www.penguin.com/plume-books-overview/; www.penguin.com/tiny-reparations-overview/, pg 62

Cooperberg, Anna, Hay House LLC, PO Box 5100, Carlsbad, CA 92018-5100 *Tel:* 760-431-7695 (ext 1, intl) *Toll Free Tel:* 800-654-5126 (ext 1, US) *Toll Free Fax:* 800-650-5115 *Web Site:* www.hayhouse.com, pg 89

Coorpender, Bruce, Pocket Press Inc, PO Box 25124, Portland, OR 97298-0124 *Toll Free Tel:* 888-237-2110 *Toll Free Fax:* 877-643-3732 *E-mail:* sales@pocketpressinc.com *Web Site:* www.pocketpressinc.com, pg 161

Coote, Candice, Berkley, c/o Penguin Random House LLC, 1745 Broadway, 19th fl, New York, NY 10019 *Tel:* 212-366-2000 *Web Site:* www.penguin.com/publishers/berkley/; www.penguin.com/ace-overview/, pg 28

Coover, Doe, The Doe Coover Agency, PO Box 668, Winchester, MA 01890 *Tel:* 781-721-6000 *Fax:* 781-721-6727 *E-mail:* info@doecooveragency.com *Web Site:* www.doecooveragency.com, pg 454

Copp, Karen, Iowa Poetry Prize, 119 W Park Rd, 100 Kuhl House, Iowa City, IA 52242-1000 *Tel:* 319-335-2000 *Fax:* 319-335-2055 *E-mail:* uipress@uiowa.edu *Web Site:* www.uipress.uiowa.edu, pg 617

Copp, Karen, University of Iowa Press, 119 W Park Rd, 100 Kuhl House, Iowa City, IA 52242-1000 *Tel:* 319-335-2000 *Toll Free Tel:* 800-621-2736 (orders only) *Fax:* 319-335-2055 *Toll Free Fax:* 800-621-8476 (orders only) *E-mail:* uipress@uiowa.edu *Web Site:* www.uipress.uiowa.edu, pg 216

Copps, Elizabeth, Maria Carvainis Agency Inc, Rockefeller Center, 1270 Avenue of the Americas, Suite 2915, New York, NY 10020 *Tel:* 212-245-6365 *Fax:* 212-245-7196 *E-mail:* mca@mariacarvainisagency.com *Web Site:* mariacarvainisagency.com, pg 453

Corbett, Sara, Workman Publishing, 1290 Avenue of the Americas, New York, NY 10104 *Toll Free Tel:* 800-759-0190 *Fax:* 212-364-0950 *E-mail:* workman-inquiry@hbgusa.com *Web Site:* www.hachettebookgroup.com/imprint/workman-publishing-company/, pg 232

Corbia, Thomas, Marshall Cavendish Education, 99 White Plains Rd, Tarrytown, NY 10591-9001 *Tel:* 914-332-8888 *Toll Free Tel:* 800-821-9881 *Fax:* 914-332-1082 *E-mail:* mce@marshallcavendish.com; customerservice@marshallcavendish.com *Web Site:* www.mceducation.us, pg 126

Corbin, Kim, New World Library, 14 Pamaron Way, Novato, CA 94949 *Tel:* 415-884-2100 *Fax:* 415-884-2199 *E-mail:* escort@newworldlibrary.com *Web Site:* www.newworldlibrary.com, pg 140

Corcoran, Jennifer, HarperCollins Children's Books, 195 Broadway, New York, NY 10007 *Tel:* 212-207-7000 *Web Site:* www.harpercollins.com/childrens, pg 85

Corcoran, Susan, Penguin Random House LLC, 1745 Broadway, New York, NY 10019 *Tel:* 212-782-9000 *Toll Free Tel:* 800-726-0600 *Web Site:* www.penguinrandomhouse.com, pg 155

Corcoran, Susan, Random House Publishing Group, 1745 Broadway, New York, NY 10019 *Toll Free Tel:* 800-200-3552 *Web Site:* www.randomhousebooks.com, pg 170

Corcoran-Lytle, Katherine, Adams Media, 100 Technology Center Dr, Suite 501, Stoughton, MA 02072 *Tel:* 508-427-7100 *Web Site:* www.simonandschuster.com, pg 4

Corday, Josh, National Coalition Against Censorship (NCAC), 19 Fulton St, Suite 407, New York, NY 10038 *Tel:* 212-807-6222 *Fax:* 212-807-6245 *E-mail:* ncac@ncac.org *Web Site:* www.ncac.org, pg 512

Cordova, Andrea, Counterpoint Press LLC, 2560 Ninth St, Suite 318, Berkeley, CA 94710 *Tel:* 510-704-0230 *Fax:* 510-704-0268 *E-mail:* info@counterpointpress.com *Web Site:* counterpointpress.com; softskull.com, pg 54

Cordova, Melanie, Candlewick Press, 99 Dover St, Somerville, MA 02144-2825 *Tel:* 617-661-3330 *Fax:* 617-661-0565 *E-mail:* bigbear@candlewick.com; salesinfo@candlewick.com *Web Site:* candlewick.com, pg 40

Corey, David, Jessica Kingsley Publishers Inc, 123 S Broad St, Suite 2750, Philadelphia, PA 19109 *Tel:* 215-922-1161 *Toll Free Tel:* 866-416-1078 (cust serv) *Fax:* 215-922-1474 *E-mail:* hello.usa@jkp.com *Web Site:* us.jkp.com, pg 110

Corey, Shana, Random House Children's Books, c/o Penguin Random House LLC, 1745 Broadway, New York, NY 10019 *Tel:* 212-782-9000 *Web Site:* www.rhcbooks.com, pg 169

Cormier, Ellen, Dial Books for Young Readers, c/o Penguin Random House LLC, 1745 Broadway, New York, NY 10019 *Tel:* 212-782-9000 *Web Site:* www.penguin.com/dial-overview/, pg 59

Cormier, Helene, Les Presses de l'Universite Laval, 2180, Chemin Sainte-Foy, 1st fl, Quebec, QC G1V 0A6, Canada *Tel:* 418-656-2803 *Fax:* 418-656-3305 *E-mail:* presses@pul.ulaval.ca *Web Site:* www.pulaval.com, pg 417

Cormier, Stephane, Editions Prise de parole, 359-27 rue Larch, Sudbury, ON P3E 1B7, Canada *Tel:* 705-675-6491 *E-mail:* info@prisedeparole.ca *Web Site:* www.prisedeparole.ca, pg 405

Cornelius, Stacey, Hackmatack Children's Choice Book Award, PO Box 34055, Halifax, NS B3J 3S1, Canada *Tel:* 902-424-3774 *E-mail:* hackmatack@hackmatack.ca *Web Site:* hackmatack.ca, pg 610

Cornell, Merial, Cornell & Company, LLC, 44 Jog Hill Rd, Trumbull, CT 06611 *Tel:* 203-454-4210 *Web Site:* www.cornellandco.com, pg 485

Cornell, Michaela, Kids Can Press Ltd, 25 Dockside Dr, Toronto, ON M5A 0B5, Canada *Tel:* 416-479-7000 *Toll Free Tel:* 800-265-0884 *Fax:* 416-960-5437 *E-mail:* info@kidscan.com; customerservice@kidscan.com *Web Site:* www.kidscanpress.com; www.kidscanpress.ca, pg 411

Cornew, Krista, Society for Technical Communication (STC), 3251 Blenheim Blvd, Suite 406, Fairfax, VA 22030 *Tel:* 703-522-4114 *Fax:* 703-522-2075 *E-mail:* stc@stc.org *Web Site:* www.stc.org, pg 519

Corpus, Angela, Quarto Publishing Group USA Inc, 100 Cummings Ctr, Suite 265D, Beverly, MA 01915 *Tel:* 978-282-9590 *Toll Free Tel:* 800-328-0590 (sales) *Fax:* 978-283-2742 *E-mail:* sales@quartous.com *Web Site:* www.quartoknows.com, pg 168

Corrado, Susan, Naval Institute Press, 291 Wood Rd, Annapolis, MD 21402-5034 *Tel:* 410-268-6110 *Toll Free Tel:* 800-233-8764 *Fax:* 410-295-1084 *E-mail:* customer@usni.org (cust inquiries) *Web Site:* www.usni.org/press/books; www.usni.org, pg 139

Correa, Alex, Lectorum Publications Inc, 10 New Maple Ave, Suite 303, Pine Brook, NJ 07058 *Tel:* 201-559-2200 *Toll Free Tel:* 800-345-5946 *E-mail:* lectorum@lectorum.com *Web Site:* www.lectorum.com, pg 114

Correa, Maria, Random House Children's Books, c/o Penguin Random House LLC, 1745 Broadway, New York, NY 10019 *Tel:* 212-782-9000 *Web Site:* www.rhcbooks.com, pg 170

Corrie, Jalissa, Children's Book Press, 95 Madison Ave, Suite 1205, New York, NY 10016 *Tel:* 212-779-4400 *Fax:* 212-683-1894 *E-mail:* editorial@leeandlow.com; orders@leeandlow.com; customer.support@leeandlow.com *Web Site:* www.leeandlow.com/imprints/childrens-book-press, pg 46

Corrin, Dean, Cunningham Commission for Youth Theatre, Lincoln Park Campus, 2350 N Racine Ave, Chicago, IL 60614-4100 *Tel:* 773-325-7999 *E-mail:* cunninghamcommission@depaul.edu *Web Site:* theatre.depaul.edu, pg 594

Cortez, Rio, HarperCollins Publishers LLC, 195 Broadway, New York, NY 10007 *Tel:* 212-207-7000 *Web Site:* www.harpercollins.com, pg 87

Cortinas, David G, National Latino Press Association (NLPA), 1841 Columbia Rd NW, Suite 614, Washington, DC 20009 *Tel:* 202-489-9516; 509-545-3055 (off the Pres) *E-mail:* info@nationallatinopressassoc.org *Web Site:* nationallatinopressassoc.org, pg 513

Cortner, Sierra, Phaidon, 65 Bleecker St, 8th fl, New York, NY 10012 *Tel:* 212-652-5400 *Toll Free Tel:* 800-759-0190 (cust serv) *Fax:* 212-652-5410 *Toll Free Fax:* 800-286-9471 (cust serv) *E-mail:* enquiries@phaidon.com *Web Site:* www.phaidon.com, pg 159

Corvello, Karen, Princeton University Press, 41 William St, Princeton, NJ 08540-5237 *Tel:* 609-258-4900 *Fax:* 609-258-6305 *E-mail:* info@press.princeton.edu *Web Site:* press.princeton.edu, pg 164

Corzine, Rev Jacob, Concordia Publishing House, 3558 S Jefferson Ave, St Louis, MO 63118-3968 *Tel:* 314-268-1000; 314-268-1268 (bookshop) *Toll Free Tel:* 800-325-3040 (cust serv) *Toll Free Fax:* 800-490-9889 (cust serv) *E-mail:* order@cph.org *Web Site:* www.cph.org, pg 51

Cosgrove, Cynthia, Miniature Book Society Inc, 518 High St, Fall River, MA 02720 *Web Site:* www.mbs.org, pg 511

Coskun, Esin, Portfolio, c/o Penguin Random House LLC, 1745 Broadway, New York, NY 10019 *Tel:* 212-782-9000 *Web Site:* www.penguin.com/portfolio-overview/; www.penguin.com/sentinel-overview/; www.penguin.com/thesis/, pg 162

Cosper, Cary, The Geological Society of America Inc (GSA), 3300 Penrose Place, Boulder, CO 80301-1806 *Tel:* 303-357-1000 *Toll Free Tel:* 800-472-1988 *Fax:* 303-357-1070 *E-mail:* pubs@geosociety.org (prodn); editing@geosociety.org (edit); books@geosociety.org; gsaservice@geosociety.org (sales & serv) *Web Site:* www.geosociety.org, pg 77

Costa, Matteo, Penguin Random House LLC, 1745 Broadway, New York, NY 10019 *Tel:* 212-782-9000 *Toll Free Tel:* 800-726-0600 *Web Site:* www.penguinrandomhouse.com, pg 155

Costa, Megan, Penguin Random House Canada, a Penguin Random House company, 320 Front St W, Suite 1400, Toronto, ON M5V 3B6, Canada *Tel:* 416-364-4449 *Toll Free Tel:* 888-523-9292 (cust serv) *E-mail:* canadaweb@penguinrandomhouse.com; customerservicescanada@penguinrandomhouse.com *Web Site:* www.penguinrandomhouse.ca, pg 416

Costanzo, Gerald, Carnegie Mellon University Press, 5032 Forbes Ave, Pittsburgh, PA 15289-1021 *Tel:* 412-268-2861 *E-mail:* cmupress@andrew.cmu.edu *Web Site:* www.cmu.edu/universitypress, pg 41

Costello, John, The MIT Press, One Broadway, 12th fl, Cambridge, MA 02142 *Tel:* 617-253-5255 *Toll Free Tel:* 800-405-1619 (orders) *Fax:* 617-258-6779; 617-577-1545 (orders) *Web Site:* mitpress.mit.edu, pg 132

Cote, Marc, Cormorant Books Inc, 260 Spadina Ave, Suite 502, Toronto, ON M5T 1E5, Canada *Tel:* 416-925-8887 *E-mail:* info@cormorantbooks.com *Web Site:* www.cormorantbooks.com, pg 400

Cote, Melissa, Les Presses de l'Universite Laval, 2180, Chemin Sainte-Foy, 1st fl, Quebec, QC G1V 0A6, Canada *Tel:* 418-656-2803 *Fax:* 418-656-3305 *E-mail:* presses@pul.ulaval.ca *Web Site:* www.pulaval.com, pg 417

Cote-Botero, Andrea, University of Texas at El Paso, Department of Creative Writing, MFA/Department of Creative Writing, M520, University Towers, Oregon St, El Paso, TX 79968 *E-mail:* creativewriting@utep.edu *Web Site:* www.utep.edu/liberalarts/creative-writing, pg 567

Cott, Sharon, The Metropolitan Museum of Art, 1000 Fifth Ave, New York, NY 10028 *Tel:* 212-535-7710 *E-mail:* editorial@metmuseum.org *Web Site:* www.metmuseum.org, pg 130

Cotter, Glenda, The University of Utah Press, J Willard Marriott Library, Suite 5400, 295 S 1500 E, Salt Lake City, UT 84112-0860 *Tel:* 801-585-9786 *Fax:* 801-581-3365 *E-mail:* hannah.new@utah.edu *Web Site:* www.uofupress.com, pg 220

Cotter, Lindsey, Scholastic Inc, 557 Broadway, New York, NY 10012 *Tel:* 212-343-6100 *Toll Free Tel:* 800-SCHOLASTIC (724-6527) *Web Site:* www.scholastic.com, pg 184

Cotti, Sara La, St Martin's Press, LLC, 120 Broadway, New York, NY 10271 *E-mail:* publicity@stmartins.com; trademarketing@stmartins.com; foreignrights@stmartins.com *Web Site:* us.macmillan.com/smp, pg 181

Cotumaccio, Adam, 4A's (American Association of Advertising Agencies), 25 W 45 St, 16th fl, New York, NY 10036 *Tel:* 212-682-2500 *E-mail:* media@4as.org; membership@4as.org *Web Site:* www.aaaa.org, pg 506

Couch, Mora, Holiday House Publishing Inc, 50 Broad St, New York, NY 10004 *Tel:* 212-688-0085 *Fax:* 212-421-6134 *E-mail:* info@holidayhouse.com *Web Site:* www.holidayhouse.com, pg 94

Couch, Peg, Leisure Arts Inc, 104 Champs Blvd, Suite 100, Maumelle, AR 72113 *Tel:* 501-868-8800 *Toll Free Tel:* 800-643-8030 *Toll Free Fax:* 877-710-5603 (catalog) *E-mail:* customer_service@leisurearts.com *Web Site:* www.leisurearts.com, pg 114

Coughlan, Robert, Capstone Publishers™, 1710 Roe Crest Dr, North Mankato, MN 56003 *Toll Free Tel:* 800-747-4992 (cust serv) *Toll Free Fax:* 888-262-0705 *E-mail:* customer.service@capstonepub.com *Web Site:* www.capstonepub.com, pg 40

Coughlin, Kara, HarperCollins Publishers LLC, 195 Broadway, New York, NY 10007 *Tel:* 212-207-7000 *Web Site:* www.harpercollins.com, pg 86

Coughlin, Kathleen, Poetry Foundation, 61 W Superior St, Chicago, IL 60654 *Tel:* 312-787-7070 *E-mail:* info@poetryfoundation.org *Web Site:* www.poetryfoundation.org, pg 526

Coulter, Barbara Quincer, Perfection Learning®, 1000 N Second Ave, Logan, IA 51546-1061 *Tel:* 712-644-2831 *Toll Free Tel:* 800-831-4190 *Toll Free Fax:* 800-543-2745 *E-mail:* orders@perfectionlearning.com *Web Site:* www.perfectionlearning.com, pg 158

Coulton, Valerie, Apogee Press, PO Box 10066, Berkeley, CA 94709 *E-mail:* apogeelibri@gmail.com *Web Site:* www.apogeepress.com, pg 15

Coumbis, Alex, Phaidon, 65 Bleecker St, 8th fl, New York, NY 10012 *Tel:* 212-652-5400 *Toll Free Tel:* 800-759-0190 (cust serv) *Fax:* 212-652-5410 *Toll Free Fax:* 800-286-9471 (cust serv) *E-mail:* enquiries@phaidon.com *Web Site:* www.phaidon.com, pg 159

Council, Mia, Penguin Press, c/o Penguin Random House LLC, 1745 Broadway, New York, NY 10019 *Tel:* 212-782-9000 *E-mail:* penguinpress@penguinrandomhouse.com *Web Site:* www.penguin.com/penguin-press-overview/, pg 154

Counts, Nicole, Random House Publishing Group, 1745 Broadway, New York, NY 10019 *Toll Free Tel:* 800-200-3552 *Web Site:* www.randomhousebooks.com, pg 171

Courage, Rachel Ekstrom, Folio Literary Management, The Film Center Bldg, 630 Ninth Ave, Suite 1101, New York, NY 10036 *Tel:* 212-400-1494 *Fax:* 212-967-0977 *Web Site:* www.foliolit.com, pg 459

Couto, Ana, St Martin's Press, LLC, 120 Broadway, New York, NY 10271 *E-mail:* publicity@stmartins.com; trademarketing@stmartins.com; foreignrights@stmartins.com *Web Site:* us.macmillan.com/smp, pg 181

Coveney, Chris, The Massachusetts Historical Society, 1154 Boylston St, Boston, MA 02215-3695 *Tel:* 617-536-1608 *Fax:* 617-859-0074 *E-mail:* publications@masshist.org *Web Site:* www.masshist.org, pg 126

Covrett, Katya, Zondervan, 3900 Sparks Dr SE, Grand Rapids, MI 49546 *Tel:* 616-698-6900 *Toll Free Tel:* 800-226-1122; 800-727-1309 (retail orders) *Fax:* 616-698-3350 *Toll Free Fax:* 800-698-3256 (retail orders) *E-mail:* customercare@harpercollins.com *Web Site:* www.zondervan.com, pg 236

Cowles, Lauren, Cambridge University Press, One Liberty Plaza, 20th fl, New York, NY 10006 *Tel:* 212-924-3900; 212-337-5000 *Fax:* 212-691-3239; 845-353-4141 *E-mail:* customer_service@cambridge.org; orders@cambridge.org; subscriptions_newyork@cambridge.org *Web Site:* www.cambridge.org/us, pg 39

Cox, Clare, Rowman & Littlefield, 4501 Forbes Blvd, Suite 200, Lanham, MD 20706 *Tel:* 301-459-3366 *Toll Free Tel:* 800-462-6420 (ext 3024, cust serv) *Fax:* 301-429-5748 *Web Site:* rowman.com, pg 178

Cox, Ron, Kamehameha Publishing, 567 S King St, Honolulu, HI 96813 *E-mail:* publishing@ksbe.edu *Web Site:* kamehamehapublishing.org, pg 108

Cox, Scott, Publications International Ltd (PIL), 8140 N Lehigh Ave, Morton Grove, IL 60053 *Tel:* 847-676-3470 *Fax:* 847-676-3671 *E-mail:* customer_service@pubint.com *Web Site:* pilbooks.com, pg 167

Cox, Shannon, HarperCollins Children's Books, 195 Broadway, New York, NY 10007 *Tel:* 212-207-7000 *Web Site:* www.harpercollins.com/childrens, pg 86

Cox, Tom, Penguin Random House LLC, 1745 Broadway, New York, NY 10019 *Tel:* 212-782-9000 *Toll Free Tel:* 800-726-0600 *Web Site:* www.penguinrandomhouse.com, pg 155

Coxon, Khadija, McGill-Queen's University Press, 1010 Sherbrooke W, Suite 1720, Montreal, QC H3A 2R7, Canada *Tel:* 514-398-3750 *Fax:* 514-398-4333 *E-mail:* mqup@mcgill.ca *Web Site:* www.mqup.ca, pg 412

Coy, Ben, Dreamscape Media LLC, 1417 Timberwolf Dr, Holland, OH 43528 *Tel:* 419-867-6965 *Toll Free Tel:* 877-983-7326 *E-mail:* info@dreamscapeab.com *Web Site:* www.dreamscapepublishing.com, pg 62

Coy, Chloe, Princeton University Press, 41 William St, Princeton, NJ 08540-5237 *Tel:* 609-258-4900 *Fax:* 609-258-6305 *E-mail:* info@press.princeton.edu *Web Site:* press.princeton.edu, pg 164

Coyle, Lily, Beaver's Pond Press Inc, 939 Seventh St W, St Paul, MN 55102 *Tel:* 952-829-8818 *E-mail:* submissions@beaverspondpress.com *Web Site:* www.beaverspondpress.com, pg 26

Coyne, Brendan, Eisenbrauns, 820 N University Dr, USB 1, Suite C, University Park, PA 16802-1003 *Tel:* 814-865-1327 *Toll Free Tel:* 800-326-9180 (orders & cust serv) *Fax:* 814-863-1408 *Toll Free Fax:* 877-778-2665 (orders) *E-mail:* orders@psupress.org; customerservice@psupress.org *Web Site:* www.eisenbrauns.org, pg 64

Coyne, Charlotte, Princeton University Press, 41 William St, Princeton, NJ 08540-5237 *Tel:* 609-258-4900 *Fax:* 609-258-6305 *E-mail:* info@press.princeton.edu *Web Site:* press.princeton.edu, pg 164

Coyne, Christopher, Marshall Cavendish Education, 99 White Plains Rd, Tarrytown, NY 10591-9001 *Tel:* 914-332-8888 *Toll Free Tel:* 800-821-9881 *Fax:* 914-332-1082 *E-mail:* mce@marshallcavendish.com; customerservice@marshallcavendish.com *Web Site:* www.mceducation.us, pg 125

Coyne, Frank, George T Bisel Co Inc, 710 S Washington Sq, Philadelphia, PA 19106-3519 *Tel:* 215-922-5760 *Toll Free Tel:* 800-247-3526 *Fax:* 215-922-2235 *E-mail:* gbisel@bisel.com *Web Site:* www.bisel.com, pg 29

Cozzi, Jessica, HarperCollins Publishers LLC, 195 Broadway, New York, NY 10007 *Tel:* 212-207-7000 *Web Site:* www.harpercollins.com, pg 87

Crab, Jillian, Houghton Mifflin Harcourt Trade & Reference Division, 125 High St, Boston, MA 02110 *Tel:* 617-351-5000 *Web Site:* www.hmhco.com, pg 96

Crabtree, Andrea, Crabtree Publishing Co, 347 Fifth Ave, Suite 1402-145, New York, NY 10016 *Tel:* 212-496-5040 *Toll Free Tel:* 800-387-7650 *Toll Free Fax:* 800-355-7166 *E-mail:* custserv@crabtreebooks.com *Web Site:* www.crabtreebooks.com, pg 54

Crabtree, Andrea, Crabtree Publishing Co Ltd, 616 Welland Ave, St Catharines, ON L2M 5V6, Canada *Tel:* 905-682-5221 *Toll Free Tel:* 800-387-7650 *Fax:* 905-682-7166 *Toll Free Fax:* 800-355-7166 *E-mail:* custserv@crabtreebooks.com; sales@crabtreebooks.com; orders@crabtreebooks.com *Web Site:* www.crabtreebooks.ca, pg 400

Crabtree, Peter A, Crabtree Publishing Co, 347 Fifth Ave, Suite 1402-145, New York, NY 10016 *Tel:* 212-496-5040 *Toll Free Tel:* 800-387-7650 *Toll Free Fax:* 800-355-7166 *E-mail:* custserv@crabtreebooks.com *Web Site:* www.crabtreebooks.com, pg 54

Crabtree, Peter A, Crabtree Publishing Co Ltd, 616 Welland Ave, St Catharines, ON L2M 5V6, Canada *Tel:* 905-682-5221 *Toll Free Tel:* 800-387-7650 *Fax:* 905-682-7166 *Toll Free Fax:* 800-355-7166 *E-mail:* custserv@crabtreebooks.com; sales@crabtreebooks.com; orders@crabtreebooks.com *Web Site:* www.crabtreebooks.ca, pg 400

Crabtree, Tamara, Abingdon Press, 810 12 Ave S, Nashville, TN 37203 *Toll Free Tel:* 800-251-3320 *E-mail:* orders@abingdonpress.com; permissions@abingdonpress.com *Web Site:* www.abingdonpress.com, pg 2

Cracchiolo, Rachelle, Free Spirit Publishing Inc, 9850 51 Ave N, Suite 100, Minneapolis, MN 55442 *Tel:* 714-891-2273 *Toll Free Tel:* 800-858-7339 *Fax:* 714-230-7070 *Toll Free Fax:* 888-877-7606 *E-mail:* customerservice@tcmpub.com *Web Site:* www.teachercreatedmaterials.com/free-spirit-publishing, pg 74

Craciunescu, Miruna, VLB editeur, 4545, rue Frontenac, 3rd fl, Montreal, QC H2H 2R7, Canada *Tel:* 514-849-5259 *Web Site:* www.edvlb.com, pg 424

Craft, Angela, Bloomsbury Publishing Inc, 1385 Broadway, 5th fl, New York, NY 10018 *Tel:* 212-419-5300 *E-mail:* marketingusa@bloomsbury.com; adultpublicityusa@bloomsbury.com; askacademic@bloomsbury.com *Web Site:* www.bloomsbury.com, pg 31

Crago, Jonathan, McGill-Queen's University Press, 1010 Sherbrooke W, Suite 1720, Montreal, QC H3A 2R7, Canada *Tel:* 514-398-3750 *Fax:* 514-398-4333 *E-mail:* mqup@mcgill.ca *Web Site:* www.mqup.ca, pg 412

Crahan, Eric, Princeton University Press, 41 William St, Princeton, NJ 08540-5237 *Tel:* 609-258-4900 *Fax:* 609-258-6305 *E-mail:* info@press.princeton.edu *Web Site:* press.princeton.edu, pg 164

Craig, Annie, Simon & Schuster, 1230 Avenue of the Americas, New York, NY 10020 *Tel:* 212-698-7000 *Toll Free Tel:* 800-223-2348 (cust serv); 800-223-2336 (orders) *Toll Free Fax:* 800-943-9831 (orders) *Web Site:* simonandschusterpublishing.com/simonandschuster/, pg 188

Craig, Brittany, Red Wheel/Weiser, 65 Parker St, Suite 7, Newburyport, MA 01950 *Tel:* 978-465-0504 *Toll Free Tel:* 800-423-7087 (orders) *Fax:* 978-465-0243 *E-mail:* info@rwwbooks.com *Web Site:* www.redwheelweiser.com, pg 173

Craig, Bryce H, P & R Publishing Co, 1102 Marble Hill Rd, Phillipsburg, NJ 08865 *Tel:* 908-454-0505 *Toll Free Tel:* 800-631-0094 *E-mail:* sales@prpbooks.com; info@prpbooks.com *Web Site:* www.prpbooks.com, pg 149

Craig, Shawnda, Cedar Fort Inc, 2373 W 700 S, Suite 100, Springville, UT 84663 *Tel:* 801-489-4084 *Toll Free Tel:* 800-SKY-BOOK (759-2665) *E-mail:* marketinginfo@cedarfort.com *Web Site:* cedarfort.com, pg 43

Craig, Taylor, Neltje Blanchan Memorial Award, Barrett Bldg, 2nd fl, 2301 Central Ave, Cheyenne, WY 82002 *Tel:* 307-777-7742 *Web Site:* wyoarts.state.wy.us, pg 581

Craig, Taylor, Frank Nelson Doubleday Memorial Award, Barrett Bldg, 2nd fl, 2301 Central Ave, Cheyenne, WY 82002 *Tel:* 307-777-7742 *Web Site:* wyoarts.state.wy.us, pg 597

Craig, Taylor, Wyoming Arts Council Creative Writing Fellowships, Barrett Bldg, 2nd fl, 2301 Central Ave, Cheyenne, WY 82002 *Tel:* 307-777-7742 *Web Site:* wyoarts.state.wy.us, pg 679

Crandell, Leslie, Berrett-Koehler Publishers Inc, 1333 Broadway, Suite 1000, Oakland, CA 94612 *Tel:* 510-817-2277 *Fax:* 510-817-2278 *E-mail:* bkpub@bkpub.com *Web Site:* www.bkconnection.com, pg 29

Crane, Sharon L, Practising Law Institute (PLI), 1177 Avenue of the Americas, 2nd fl, New York, NY 10036 *Tel:* 212-824-5710 (cust serv) *Toll Free Tel:* 800-260-4PLI (260-4754) *Toll Free Fax:* 800-321-0093 (cust serv) *E-mail:* info@pli.edu; membership@pli.edu *Web Site:* www.pli.edu, pg 163

Cranford, Garry, Flanker Press Ltd, 1243 Kenmount Rd, Unit 1, Paradise, NL A1L 0V8, Canada *Tel:* 709-739-4477 *Toll Free Tel:* 866-739-4420 *Fax:* 709-739-4420 *E-mail:* info@flankerpress.com; sales@flankerpress.com *Web Site:* www.flankerpress.com, pg 406

Cranford, Jerry, Flanker Press Ltd, 1243 Kenmount Rd, Unit 1, Paradise, NL A1L 0V8, Canada *Tel:* 709-739-4477 *Toll Free Tel:* 866-739-4420 *Fax:* 709-739-4420 *E-mail:* info@flankerpress.com; sales@flankerpress.com *Web Site:* www.flankerpress.com, pg 406

Crassons, Kate, Lehigh University Press, B-040 Christmas-Saucon Hall, 14 E Packer Ave, Bethlehem, PA 18015 *Tel:* 610-758-3933 *Fax:* 610-758-6331 *E-mail:* inlup@lehigh.edu *Web Site:* lupress.cas2.lehigh.edu, pg 114

Craven, Robert H Jr, F A Davis Co, 1915 Arch St, Philadelphia, PA 19103 *Tel:* 215-568-2270; 215-440-3001 *Toll Free Tel:* 800-523-4049 *Fax:* 215-568-5065; 215-440-3016 *E-mail:* info@fadavis.com; orders@fadavis.com *Web Site:* www.fadavis.com, pg 57

Cravens, Greg, National Cartoonists Society (NCS), PO Box 592927, Orlando, FL 32859-2927 *Tel:* 407-994-6703 *E-mail:* info@nationalcartoonists.com; membership@nationalcartoonists.com *Web Site:* www.nationalcartoonists.com, pg 512

Crawford, Ann H, The Geological Society of America Inc (GSA), 3300 Penrose Place, Boulder, CO 80301-1806 *Tel:* 303-357-1000 *Toll Free Tel:* 800-472-1988 *Fax:* 303-357-1070 *E-mail:* pubs@geosociety.org (prodn); editing@geosociety.org (edit); books@geosociety.org; gsaservice@geosociety.org (sales & serv) *Web Site:* www.geosociety.org, pg 77

Crawford, Chandler, Transatlantic Agency, 2 Bloor St E, Suite 3500, Toronto, ON M4W 1A8, Canada *Tel:* 416-488-9214 *E-mail:* info@transatlanticagency.com; royalties@transatlanticagency.com *Web Site:* www.transatlanticagency.com, pg 479

Crawford, Edward, Hachette Nashville, 6100 Tower Circle, Room 210, Franklin, TN 37067 *Tel:* 615-221-0996 *Fax:* 615-221-0962 *Web Site:* www.hachettebookgroup.com/imprint/hachette-nashville/, pg 83

Crawford, Hillary, Individual Artist Project Grants, 500 S Bronough St, Tallahassee, FL 32399-0250 *Tel:* 850-245-6470 *Fax:* 850-245-6497 *E-mail:* dcagrants@dos.myflorida.com *Web Site:* dos.myflorida.com/cultural, pg 616

Crawford, Ingrid, National Association of Book Entrepreneurs (NABE), PO Box 606, Cottage Grove, OR 97424 *Tel:* 541-942-7455 *Fax:* 541-942-7455 *E-mail:* nabe@bookmarketingprofits.com *Web Site:* www.bookmarketingprofits.com, pg 511

Crawford, Kelly, Paintbox Press, 275 Madison Ave, Suite 600, New York, NY 10016 *Tel:* 212-878-6610 *E-mail:* info@paintboxpress.com *Web Site:* www.paintboxpress.com, pg 150

Crawford, Mark, MC2 Solutions LLC, 5101 Violet Lane, Madison, WI 53714, pg 442

Crawford, Patty, Franciscan Media, 28 W Liberty St, Cincinnati, OH 45202 *Tel:* 513-241-5615 *E-mail:* admin@franciscanmedia.org *Web Site:* www.franciscanmedia.org, pg 74

Crawford, Tad, Allworth Press, 307 W 36 St, 11th fl, New York, NY 10018 *Tel:* 212-643-6816 *Fax:* 212-643-6819 *Web Site:* www.allworth.com, pg 7

Crawford, William R Sr, Military Living Publications, 333 Maple Ave E, Suite 3130, Vienna, VA 22180-4717 *Tel:* 703-237-0203 *Fax:* 703-552-8855 *E-mail:* customerservice@militaryliving.com; sales@militaryliving.com; editor@militaryliving.com *Web Site:* www.militaryliving.com, pg 131

Crean, Patrick, HarperCollins Canada Ltd, 22 Adelaide St W, 41st fl, Toronto, ON M5H 4E3, Canada *Tel:* 416-975-9334 *E-mail:* hcorder@harpercollins.com *Web Site:* www.harpercollins.ca, pg 409

Crespo, Paola, Penguin Random House LLC, 1745 Broadway, New York, NY 10019 *Tel:* 212-782-9000 *Toll Free Tel:* 800-726-0600 *Web Site:* www.penguinrandomhouse.com, pg 155

Crewe, Jennifer, Columbia University Press, 61 W 62 St, New York, NY 10023 *Tel:* 212-459-0600 *Toll Free Tel:* 800-944-8648 *Fax:* 212-459-3678 *Web Site:* cup.columbia.edu, pg 51

Crews, Shaquona, Quirk Books, 215 Church St, Philadelphia, PA 19106 *Tel:* 215-627-3581 *Fax:* 215-627-5220 *E-mail:* general@quirkbooks.com *Web Site:* www.quirkbooks.com, pg 168

Crichton, Sarah, Henry Holt and Company, LLC, 120 Broadway, 23rd fl, New York, NY 10271 *Tel:* 646-307-5151 *Toll Free Tel:* 888-330-8477 (orders) *Fax:* 646-307-5285 *Web Site:* www.henryholt.com, pg 94

Crichton, Sha-Shana, Crichton & Associates Inc, 6940 Carroll Ave, Takoma, MD 20912 *Tel:* 301-495-9663 *E-mail:* cricht1@aol.com, pg 455

Crider, Andrew K, Christian Light Publications Inc, 1051 Mount Clinton Pike, Harrisonburg, VA 22802 *Tel:* 540-434-1003 *Toll Free Tel:* 800-776-0478 *Fax:* 540-433-8896 *E-mail:* info@clp.org; orders@clp.org *Web Site:* www.clp.org, pg 47

Crimarco, Amanda, Macmillan, 120 Broadway, 22nd fl, New York, NY 10271 *E-mail:* press.inquiries@macmillan.com *Web Site:* us.macmillan.com, pg 122

Crimmins, Kem, Fordham University Press, Joseph A Martino Hall, 45 Columbus Ave, 3rd fl, New York, NY 10023 *Tel:* 347-842-3083 *Web Site:* www.fordhampress.com, pg 73

Crippen, Cynthia, AEIOU Inc, 894 Piermont Ave, Piermont, NY 10968 *Tel:* 845-359-1911, pg 435

Criscitelli, Michael, St Martin's Press, LLC, 120 Broadway, New York, NY 10271 *E-mail:* publicity@stmartins.com; trademarketing@stmartins.com; foreignrights@stmartins.com *Web Site:* us.macmillan.com/smp, pg 180

Crisp, Laura, Doubleday, c/o Penguin Random House LLC, 1745 Broadway, New York, NY 10019 *Tel:* 212-751-2600 *Fax:* 212-940-7390 (dom rts); 212-572-2662 (foreign rts) *Web Site:* knopfdoubleday.com/imprint/doubleday/; knopfdoubleday.com, pg 61

Crisp, Laura, Alfred A Knopf, c/o Penguin Random House LLC, 1745 Broadway, New York, NY 10019 *Tel:* 212-751-2600 *Fax:* 212-940-7390 (dom rts); 212-572-2662 (foreign rts) *Web Site:* knopfdoubleday.com/imprint/knopf/; knopfdoubleday.com, pg 110

Crissman, Dan, University of Wisconsin Press, 728 State St, Suite 443, Madison, WI 53706-1418 *Tel:* 608-263-1110; 608-263-0668 (journal orders) *Toll Free Tel:* 800-621-2736 (book orders) *Fax:* 608-263-1173 *Toll Free Fax:* 800-621-2736 (book orders) *E-mail:* uwiscpress@uwpress.wisc.edu *Web Site:* uwpress.wisc.edu, pg 221

Crist, Mo, Bloomsbury Publishing Inc, 1385 Broadway, 5th fl, New York, NY 10018 *Tel:* 212-419-5300 *E-mail:* marketingusa@bloomsbury.com; adultpublicityusa@bloomsbury.com; askacademic@bloomsbury.com *Web Site:* www.bloomsbury.com, pg 31

Crist, Mo, W W Norton & Company Inc, 500 Fifth Ave, New York, NY 10110-0017 *Tel:* 212-354-5500 *Toll Free Tel:* 800-233-4830 (orders & cust serv) *Fax:* 212-869-0856 *Toll Free Fax:* 800-458-6515 *E-mail:* orders@wwnorton.com *Web Site:* wwnorton.com, pg 143

Crist, Steve, Chronicle Books LLC, 680 Second St, San Francisco, CA 94107 *Tel:* 415-537-4200 *Fax:* 415-537-4460 (perms) *E-mail:* hello@chroniclebooks.com; subrights@chroniclebooks.com *Web Site:* www.chroniclebooks.com, pg 47

Cristofaro, Joe, Groupe Educalivres Inc, 1699, blvd le Corbusier, bureau 350, Laval, QC H7S 1Z3, Canada *Tel:* 514-334-8466 *Toll Free Tel:* 800-567-3671 (info serv) *Fax:* 514-334-8387 *Toll Free Fax:* 800-267-4387 *E-mail:* infoservice@grandduc.com *Web Site:* www.educalivres.com, pg 408

Croce, Mr Carmen R, St Joseph's University Press, 5600 City Ave, Philadelphia, PA 19131-1395 *Tel:* 610-660-3402 *Fax:* 610-660-3412 *E-mail:* sjupress@sju.edu *Web Site:* www.sjupress.com, pg 180

Croce, Melissa, Simon & Schuster, 1230 Avenue of the Americas, New York, NY 10020 *Tel:* 212-698-7000 *Toll Free Tel:* 800-223-2348 (cust serv); 800-223-2336 (orders) *Toll Free Fax:* 800-943-9831 (orders) *Web Site:* simonandschusterpublishing.com/simonandschuster/, pg 188

Croce, Nicholas, Stimola Literary Studio Inc, 11 Briarwood Lane, West Tisbury, MA 02575 *Tel:* 201-945-9353 *Fax:* 201-490-5920 *E-mail:* info@stimolaliterarystudio.com *Web Site:* www.stimolaliterarystudio.com, pg 478

Crocker, Amanda, Between the Lines, 401 Richmond St W, No 281, Toronto, ON M5V 3A8, Canada *Tel:* 416-535-9914 *Toll Free Tel:* 800-718-7201 *E-mail:* info@btlbooks.com *Web Site:* btlbooks.com, pg 396

Crockett, Laura, TriadaUS Literary Agency, PO Box 561, Sewickley, PA 15143 *Tel:* 412-401-3376 *Web Site:* www.triadaus.com, pg 480

Croft, Merilee, Macmillan, 120 Broadway, 22nd fl, New York, NY 10271 *E-mail:* press.inquiries@macmillan.com *Web Site:* us.macmillan.com, pg 122

Croll, Jennifer, Greystone Books Ltd, 343 Railway St, Suite 302, Vancouver, BC V6A 1A4, Canada *Tel:* 604-875-1550 *Fax:* 604-875-1556 *E-mail:* info@greystonebooks.com; rights@greystonebooks.com *Web Site:* www.greystonebooks.com, pg 407

Cromie, Eric, Chronicle Books LLC, 680 Second St, San Francisco, CA 94107 *Tel:* 415-537-4200 *Fax:* 415-537-4460 (perms) *E-mail:* hello@chroniclebooks.com; subrights@chroniclebooks.com *Web Site:* www.chroniclebooks.com, pg 48

Cronig, Lily, St Martin's Press, LLC, 120 Broadway, New York, NY 10271 *E-mail:* publicity@stmartins.com; trademarketing@stmartins.com; foreignrights@stmartins.com *Web Site:* us.macmillan.com/smp, pg 181

Cronin, Adelaide, Holiday House Publishing Inc, 50 Broad St, New York, NY 10004 *Tel:* 212-688-0085 *Fax:* 212-421-6134 *E-mail:* info@holidayhouse.com *Web Site:* www.holidayhouse.com, pg 94

Cronin, Adelaide, Peachtree Publishing Co Inc, 1700 Chattahoochee Ave, Atlanta, GA 30318-2112 *Tel:* 404-876-8761 *Toll Free Tel:* 800-241-0113 *Fax:* 404-875-2578 *Toll Free Fax:* 800-875-8909 *E-mail:* hello@peachtree-online.com; orders@peachtree-online.com; sales@peachtree-online.com *Web Site:* www.peachtreebooks.com, pg 153

Cronin, Denise, Random House Publishing Group, 1745 Broadway, New York, NY 10019 *Toll Free Tel:* 800-200-3552 *Web Site:* www.randomhousebooks.com, pg 170

Cronin, Kelly, HarperCollins Publishers LLC, 195 Broadway, New York, NY 10007 *Tel:* 212-207-7000 *Web Site:* www.harpercollins.com, pg 87

Cronin, Sam, Nelson Literary Agency LLC, 700 Colorado Blvd, No 352, Denver, CO 80206 *Tel:* 303-292-2805 *E-mail:* info@nelsonagency.com *Web Site:* www.nelsonagency.com, pg 471

Cronin-Jackman, Rose, Pantheon Books, c/o Penguin Random House LLC, 1745 Broadway, New York, NY 10019 *Tel:* 212-751-2600 *Fax:* 212-940-7390 (dom rts); 212-572-2662 (foreign rts) *Web Site:* knopfdoubleday.com/imprint/pantheon/; knopfdoubleday.com, pg 150

Cronshaw, Francine, East Mountain Editing Services, PO Box 1895, Tijeras, NM 87059-1895 *Tel:* 505-281-8422 *Web Site:* www.spanishindexing.com, pg 438

Crooks, Audrey, Trident Media Group LLC, 355 Lexington Ave, 12th fl, New York, NY 10017 *Tel:* 212-333-1511 *E-mail:* info@tridentmediagroup.com; press@tridentmediagroup.com; foreignrights@tridentmediagroup.com; office.assistant@tridentmediagroup.com *Web Site:* www.tridentmediagroup.com, pg 480

Crooks, Cathie, University of Alberta Press, Ring House 2, Edmonton, AB T6G 2E1, Canada *Tel:* 780-492-3662 *Fax:* 780-492-0719 *Web Site:* www.uap.ualberta.ca, pg 421

Crooms, Sandy, University of Pittsburgh Press, 7500 Thomas Blvd, Pittsburgh, PA 15260 *Tel:* 412-383-2456 *Fax:* 412-383-2466 *E-mail:* info@upress.pitt.edu *Web Site:* www.upress.pitt.edu, pg 219

Crosby, Darryl, Kent State University Press, 1118 University Library Bldg, 1125 Risman Dr, Kent, OH 44242 *Tel:* 330-672-7913 *Fax:* 330-672-3104 *E-mail:* ksupress@kent.edu *Web Site:* www.kentstateuniversitypress.com, pg 109

Crosby, Jeff, Christian Book Award®, 5801 S McClintock Dr, Suite 104, Tempe, AZ 85283 *Tel:* 480-966-3998 *Fax:* 480-966-1944 *E-mail:* info@ecpa.org *Web Site:* christianbookawards.com, pg 589

Crosby, Jeff, Evangelical Christian Publishers Association (ECPA), 5801 S McClintock Dr, Suite 104, Tempe, AZ 85283 *Tel:* 480-966-3998 *Fax:* 480-966-1944 *E-mail:* info@ecpa.org *Web Site:* www.ecpa.org, pg 505

Cross, Claudia, Folio Literary Management, The Film Center Bldg, 630 Ninth Ave, Suite 1101, New York, NY 10036 *Tel:* 212-400-1494 *Fax:* 212-967-0977 *Web Site:* www.foliolit.com, pg 459

Cross, Jamie, Math Solutions®, One Harbor Dr, Suite 101, Sausalito, CA 94965 *Toll Free Tel:* 877-234-7323 *Toll Free Fax:* 800-724-4716 *E-mail:* info@mathsolutions.com; orders@mathsolutions.com *Web Site:* www.mathsolutions.com; store.mathsolutions.com, pg 127

Cross, John C Esq, Standard Publishing Corp, 10 High St, Boston, MA 02110 *Tel:* 617-457-0600 *Toll Free Tel:* 800-682-5759 *Fax:* 617-457-0608 *Web Site:* www.spcpub.com, pg 197

Cross, Mark, Redleaf Press®, 10 Yorkton Ct, St Paul, MN 55117 *Tel:* 651-641-0508 *Toll Free Tel:* 800-423-8309 *Fax:* 651-641-0115 *E-mail:* customerservice@redleafpress.org; info@redleafpress.org; marketing@redleafpress.org *Web Site:* www.redleafpress.org, pg 173

Crouch, Lori, Education Writers Association (EWA), 1825 "K" St NW, Suite 200, Washington, DC 20006 *Tel:* 202-452-9830 *Web Site:* ewa.org, pg 505

Crouch, Lori, National Awards for Education Reporting, 1825 "K" St NW, Suite 200, Washington, DC 20006 *Tel:* 202-452-9830 *E-mail:* awards@ewa.org *Web Site:* ewa.org, pg 637

Crouchet, Mike, Cardiotext Publishing, 750 Second St NE, Suite 102, Hopkins, MN 55343 *Tel:* 612-925-2053 *Fax:* 612-922-7556 *E-mail:* info@cardiotext.com *Web Site:* www.cardiotextpublishing.com, pg 40

Crowe, Michelle, Random House Children's Books, c/o Penguin Random House LLC, 1745 Broadway, New York, NY 10019 *Tel:* 212-782-9000 *Web Site:* www.rhcbooks.com, pg 170

Crowe, Perry, Chronicle Books LLC, 680 Second St, San Francisco, CA 94107 *Tel:* 415-537-4200 *Fax:* 415-537-4460 (perms) *E-mail:* hello@chroniclebooks.com; subrights@chroniclebooks.com *Web Site:* www.chroniclebooks.com, pg 47

Crowell, Dee, Piano Press, 1425 Ocean Ave, Suite 5, Del Mar, CA 92014 *Tel:* 619-884-1401 *E-mail:* pianopress@pianopress.com *Web Site:* www.pianopress.com, pg 159

Crowley, Eleanor, Scribner, 1230 Avenue of the Americas, New York, NY 10020 *Web Site:* www.simonandschusterpublishing.com/scribner/, pg 185

Crowley, Myles, Knight Science Journalism Fellowships, 77 Massachusetts Ave, Cambridge, MA 02139 *Tel:* 617-452-3513 *E-mail:* knight-info@mit.edu *Web Site:* ksj.mit.edu/fellowship, pg 620

Crowther, Duane S, Horizon Publishers & Distributors Inc, 191 N 650 E, Bountiful, UT 84010-3628 *Tel:* 801-292-7102 *E-mail:* ldshorizonpublishers1@gmail.com *Web Site:* www.ldshorizonpublishers.com, pg 95

Crowther, Jean D, Horizon Publishers & Distributors Inc, 191 N 650 E, Bountiful, UT 84010-3628 *Tel:* 801-292-7102 *E-mail:* ldshorizonpublishers1@gmail.com *Web Site:* www.ldshorizonpublishers.com, pg 95

Crummer, Robin, Ooligan Press, Portland State University, PO Box 751, Portland, OR 97207 *Tel:* 503-725-9748 *Fax:* 503-725-3561 *E-mail:* ooligan@ooliganpress.pdx.edu *Web Site:* www.ooliganpress.com, pg 146

Cruz, Jesse, Kensington Publishing Corp, 900 Third Ave, 26th fl, New York, NY 10022 *Tel:* 212-407-1500 *Toll Free Tel:* 800-221-2647 *Fax:* 212-935-0699 *Web Site:* www.kensingtonbooks.com, pg 109

Cruz, Ricky, US Games Systems Inc, 179 Ludlow St, Stamford, CT 06902 *Tel:* 203-353-8400 *Toll Free Tel:* 800-54-GAMES (544-2637) *Fax:* 203-353-8431 *E-mail:* info@usgamesinc.com *Web Site:* www.usgamesinc.com, pg 223

Cruz-Jimenez, Alex, Viking Penguin, c/o Penguin Random House LLC, 1745 Broadway, New York, NY 10019 *Tel:* 212-782-9000 *Web Site:* www.penguin.com/overview-vikingbooks/; www.penguin.com/pamela-dorman-books-overview/; www.penguin.com/penguin-classics-overview/; www.penguin.com/penguin-life-overview/, pg 225

Cseh, Viktoria, Tradewind Books, 202-1807 Maritime Mews, Vancouver, BC V6H 3W7, Canada *Tel:* 604-662-4405 *E-mail:* tradewindbooks@yahoo.com; tradewindbooks@gmail.com *Web Site:* www.tradewindbooks.com, pg 421

Csizmadia, Rita, Candlewick Press, 99 Dover St, Somerville, MA 02144-2825 *Tel:* 617-661-3330 *Fax:* 617-661-0565 *E-mail:* bigbear@candlewick.com; salesinfo@candlewick.com *Web Site:* candlewick.com, pg 40

Cuadrado, Dana, Grand Central Publishing, 1290 Avenue of the Americas, New York, NY 10104 *Tel:* 212-364-1100 *Web Site:* www.hachettebookgroup.com/imprint/grand-central-publishing/, pg 80

Cudahy, Jim, American Society of Agronomy (ASA), 5585 Guilford Rd, Madison, WI 53711-5801 *Tel:* 608-273-8080 *E-mail:* books@sciencesocieties.org *Web Site:* www.agronomy.org, pg 12

Cudd, Sophie, The Book Group (TBG), 20 W 20 St, Suite 601, New York, NY 10011 *E-mail:* info@thebookgroup.com; submissions@thebookgroup.com *Web Site:* www.thebookgroup.com, pg 450

Cuevas, Alyssa, Workman Publishing, 1290 Avenue of the Americas, New York, NY 10104 *Toll Free Tel:* 800-759-0190 *Fax:* 212-364-0950 *E-mail:* workman-inquiry@hbgusa.com *Web Site:* www.hachettebookgroup.com/imprint/workman-publishing-company/, pg 233

Cuevas, Lismarie, Sourcebooks LLC, 1935 Brookdale Rd, Suite 139, Naperville, IL 60563 *Tel:* 630-961-3900 *Toll Free Tel:* 800-432-7444 *Fax:* 630-961-2168 *E-mail:* info@sourcebooks.com *Web Site:* www.sourcebooks.com, pg 195

Culatta, Richard, International Society for Technology in Education, 2111 Wilson Blvd, Suite 300, Arlington, VA 22201 *Tel:* 503-342-2848 (intl) *Toll Free Tel:* 800-336-5191 (US & CN) *Fax:* 541-302-3778 *E-mail:* iste@iste.org *Web Site:* www.iste.org, pg 103

Culbertson, Stephannie, Nero Award, PO Box 230822, Ansonia Sta, New York, NY 10023 *Web Site:* nerowolfe.org/htm/literary_awards/nero_award/award.htm, pg 639

Cull, Jody, Bolchazy-Carducci Publishers Inc, 1000 Brown St, Unit 301, Wauconda, IL 60084 *Tel:* 847-526-4344 *Fax:* 847-526-2867 *E-mail:* info@bolchazy.com; orders@bolchazy.com *Web Site:* www.bolchazy.com, pg 33

Cull, Mark E, Red Hen Press, PO Box 40820, Pasadena, CA 91114 *Tel:* 626-356-4760 *Fax:* 626-356-9974 *Web Site:* www.redhen.org, pg 172

Cullen, Darcy, University of British Columbia Press, 2029 West Mall, Vancouver, BC V6T 1Z2, Canada *Tel:* 604-822-5959 *Toll Free Tel:* 877-377-9378 *Fax:* 604-822-6083 *Toll Free Fax:* 800-668-0821 *E-mail:* frontdesk@ubcpress.ca *Web Site:* www.ubcpress.ca, pg 422

Cullen, Kerry, Henry Holt and Company, LLC, 120 Broadway, 23rd fl, New York, NY 10271 *Tel:* 646-307-5151 *Toll Free Tel:* 888-330-8477 (orders) *Fax:* 646-307-5285 *Web Site:* www.henryholt.com, pg 94

Culliford, Craig, Crabtree Publishing Co, 347 Fifth Ave, Suite 1402-145, New York, NY 10016 *Tel:* 212-496-5040 *Toll Free Tel:* 800-387-7650 *Toll Free Fax:* 800-355-7166 *E-mail:* custserv@crabtreebooks.com *Web Site:* www.crabtreebooks.com, pg 54

Culliford, Craig, Crabtree Publishing Co Ltd, 616 Welland Ave, St Catharines, ON L2M 5V6, Canada *Tel:* 905-682-5221 *Toll Free Tel:* 800-387-7650 *Fax:* 905-682-7166 *Toll Free Fax:* 800-355-7166 *E-mail:* custserv@crabtreebooks.com; sales@crabtreebooks.com; orders@crabtreebooks.com *Web Site:* www.crabtreebooks.ca, pg 400

Cullingham, Haley, McClelland & Stewart Ltd, 320 Front St W, Suite 1400, Toronto, ON M5V 3B6, Canada *Tel:* 416-364-4449 *Toll Free Tel:* 888-523-9292 *E-mail:* customerservicescanada@penguinrandomhouse.com; mcclellandsubmissions@prh.com *Web Site:* penguinrandomhouse.ca/imprints/mcclelland-stewart, pg 412

Cullingham, Haley, Penguin Random House Canada, a Penguin Random House company, 320 Front St W, Suite 1400, Toronto, ON M5V 3B6, Canada *Tel:* 416-364-4449 *Toll Free Tel:* 888-523-9292 (cust serv) *E-mail:* canadaweb@penguinrandomhouse.com; customerservicescanada@penguinrandomhouse.com *Web Site:* www.penguinrandomhouse.ca, pg 416

Cullmann, Erica, New York Academy of Sciences (NYAS), 7 World Trade Center, 40th fl, 250 Greenwich St, New York, NY 10007-2157 *Tel:* 212-298-8600 *Toll Free Tel:* 800-843-6927 *Fax:* 212-298-3650 *E-mail:* nyas@nyas.org; annals@nyas.org; customerservice@nyas.org *Web Site:* www.nyas.org, pg 140

Cully, Lynn, Kensington Publishing Corp, 900 Third Ave, 26th fl, New York, NY 10022 *Tel:* 212-407-1500 *Toll Free Tel:* 800-221-2647 *Fax:* 212-935-0699 *Web Site:* www.kensingtonbooks.com, pg 109

Culp, Lianna, Farrar, Straus & Giroux, LLC, 120 Broadway, New York, NY 10271 *Tel:* 212-741-6900 *E-mail:* fsg.publicity@fsgbooks.com; sales@fsgbooks.com *Web Site:* us.macmillan.com/fsg, pg 70

Cumberland, Brian, Faith Library Publications, PO Box 50126, Tulsa, OK 74150-0126 *Tel:* 918-258-1588 *Toll Free Tel:* 888-258-0999 (orders) *Fax:* 918-872-7710 (orders) *E-mail:* flp@rhema.org *Web Site:* www.rhema.org/store, pg 69

Cumming, Beto, Iris Press, 969 Oak Ridge Tpke, No 328, Oak Ridge, TN 37830 *Web Site:* www.irisbooks.com, pg 104

Cumming, Robert, Iris Press, 969 Oak Ridge Tpke, No 328, Oak Ridge, TN 37830 *Web Site:* www.irisbooks.com, pg 104

Cummings, Andy, Carolrhoda Books Inc, 241 First Ave N, Minneapolis, MN 55401 *Tel:* 612-332-3344 *Toll Free Tel:* 800-328-4929 *Fax:* 612-332-7615 *Toll Free Fax:* 800-332-1132 *E-mail:* info@lernerbooks.com; custserve@lernerbooks.com *Web Site:* www.lernerbooks.com; www.facebook.com/lernerbooks, pg 41

Cummings, Andy, Carolrhoda Lab™, 241 First Ave N, Minneapolis, MN 55401 *Tel:* 612-332-3344 *Toll Free Tel:* 800-328-4929 *Fax:* 612-332-7615 *Toll Free Fax:* 800-332-1132 *E-mail:* info@lernerbooks.com; custserve@lernerbooks.com *Web Site:* www.lernerbooks.com; www.facebook.com/lernerbooks, pg 41

Cummings, Andy, ediciones Lerner, 241 First Ave N, Minneapolis, MN 55401 *Tel:* 612-332-3344 *Toll Free Tel:* 800-328-4929 *Fax:* 612-332-7615 *Toll Free Fax:* 800-332-1132 *E-mail:* info@lernerbooks.com; custserve@lernerbooks.com *Web Site:* www.lernerbooks.com; www.facebook.com/lernerbooks, pg 63

Cummings, Andy, First Avenue Editions, 241 First Ave N, Minneapolis, MN 55401 *Tel:* 612-332-3344 *Toll Free Tel:* 800-328-4929 *Fax:* 612-332-7615 *Toll Free Fax:* 800-332-1132 *E-mail:* info@lernerbooks.com; custserve@lernerbooks.com *Web Site:* www.lernerbooks.com; www.facebook.com/lernerbooks, pg 72

Cummings, Andy, Graphic Universe™, 241 First Ave N, Minneapolis, MN 55401 *Tel:* 612-332-3344 *Toll Free Tel:* 800-328-4929 *Fax:* 612-332-7615 *Toll Free Fax:* 800-332-1132 *E-mail:* info@lernerbooks.com; custserve@lernerbooks.com *Web Site:* www.lernerbooks.com; www.facebook.com/lernerbooks, pg 80

Cummings, Andy, Lerner Publications, 241 First Ave N, Minneapolis, MN 55401 *Tel:* 612-332-3344 *Toll Free Tel:* 800-328-4929 *Fax:* 612-332-7615 *Toll Free Fax:* 800-332-1132 *E-mail:* info@lernerbooks.com; custserve@lernerbooks.com *Web Site:* www.lernerbooks.com; www.facebook.com/lernerbooks, pg 115

Cummings, Andy, Lerner Publishing Group Inc, 241 First Ave N, Minneapolis, MN 55401 *Tel:* 612-332-3344 *Toll Free Tel:* 800-328-4929 *Fax:* 612-332-7615 *Toll Free Fax:* 800-332-1132 *E-mail:* info@lernerbooks.com; custserve@lernerbooks.com *Web Site:* www.lernerbooks.com; www.facebook.com/lernerbooks, pg 115

Cummings, Andy, LernerClassroom, 241 First Ave N, Minneapolis, MN 55401 *Tel:* 612-332-3344 *Toll Free Tel:* 800-328-4929 *Fax:* 612-332-7615 *Toll Free Fax:* 800-332-1132 *E-mail:* info@lernerbooks.com; custserve@lernerbooks.com *Web Site:* www.lernerbooks.com; www.facebook.com/lernerbooks, pg 115

Cummings, Andy, Millbrook Press, 241 First Ave N, Minneapolis, MN 55401 *Tel:* 612-332-3344 *Toll Free Tel:* 800-328-4929 *Fax:* 612-332-7615 *Toll Free Fax:* 800-332-1132 *E-mail:* info@lernerbooks.com; custserve@lernerbooks.com *Web Site:* www.lernerbooks.com; www.facebook.com/millbrookpress, pg 131

Cummings, Andy, Twenty-First Century Books, 241 First Ave N, Minneapolis, MN 55401 *Tel:* 612-332-3344 *Toll Free Tel:* 800-328-4929 *Fax:* 612-332-7615 *Toll Free Fax:* 800-332-1132 *E-mail:* info@lernerbooks.com; custserve@lernerbooks.com *Web Site:* www.lernerbooks.com; www.facebook.com/lernerbooks, pg 211

Cummings, Andy, Zest Books, 241 First Ave N, Minneapolis, MN 55401 *Tel:* 612-332-3344 *Toll Free Tel:* 800-328-4929 *Toll Free Fax:* 800-332-1132 *E-mail:* info@lernerbooks.com; publicity@lernerbooks.com; custserve@lernerbooks.com (orders) *Web Site:* lernerbooks.com, pg 236

Cummings, Breanna, Candlewick Press, 99 Dover St, Somerville, MA 02144-2825 *Tel:* 617-661-3330 *Fax:* 617-661-0565 *E-mail:* bigbear@candlewick.com; salesinfo@candlewick.com *Web Site:* candlewick.com, pg 40

Cummings, Brennin, GP Putnam's Sons, c/o Penguin Random House LLC, 1745 Broadway, New York, NY 10019 *Tel:* 212-782-9000 *Web Site:* www.penguin.com/putnam/, pg 167

Cummins, Lucy, Simon & Schuster Children's Publishing, 1230 Avenue of the Americas, New York, NY 10020 *Tel:* 212-698-7000 *Web Site:* www.simonandschuster.com/kids; www.simonandschuster.com/teen; simonandschuster.net; simonandschuster.biz, pg 189

Cunningham, Caitrin, Applewood Books, 210 Wingo Way, Suite 200, Mount Pleasant, SC 29464 *Tel:* 843-853-2070 *E-mail:* retailers@arcadiapublishing.com; publishing@arcadiapublishing.com *Web Site:* www.arcadiapublishing.com, pg 15

Cunningham, David Scott, The University of Arkansas Press, McIlroy House, 105 N McIlroy Ave, Fayetteville, AR 72701 *Tel:* 479-575-7544 *E-mail:* info@uapress.com *Web Site:* www.uapress.com, pg 214

Cunningham, Diane, Sourcebooks LLC, 1935 Brookdale Rd, Suite 139, Naperville, IL 60563 *Tel:* 630-961-3900 *Toll Free Tel:* 800-432-7444 *Fax:* 630-961-2168 *E-mail:* info@sourcebooks.com *Web Site:* www.sourcebooks.com, pg 195

Cunningham, Emily, Alfred A Knopf, c/o Penguin Random House LLC, 1745 Broadway, New York, NY 10019 *Tel:* 212-751-2600 *Fax:* 212-940-7390 (dom rts); 212-572-2662 (foreign rts) *Web Site:* knopfdoubleday.com/imprint/knopf/; knopfdoubleday.com, pg 110

Cunningham, Katie, Candlewick Press, 99 Dover St, Somerville, MA 02144-2825 *Tel:* 617-661-3330 *Fax:* 617-661-0565 *E-mail:* bigbear@candlewick.com; salesinfo@candlewick.com *Web Site:* candlewick.com, pg 39

Cunningham, Laura, Wisdom Publications Inc, 199 Elm St, Somerville, MA 02144 *Tel:* 617-776-7416 *Toll Free Tel:* 800-272-4050 (orders) *Fax:* 617-776-7841 *E-mail:* submission@wisdompubs.org *Web Site:* wisdomexperience.org, pg 231

Cunningham, Michael, Health Administration Press, 300 S Riverside Plaza, Suite 1900, Chicago, IL 60606 *Tel:* 312-424-2800 *Fax:* 312-424-0014 *E-mail:* hapbooks@ache.org *Web Site:* www.ache.org/hap (orders), pg 89

Cunningham, Michelle, Random House Children's Books, c/o Penguin Random House LLC, 1745 Broadway, New York, NY 10019 *Tel:* 212-782-9000 *Web Site:* www.rhcbooks.com, pg 170

Cunningham, Nicole, The Book Group (TBG), 20 W 20 St, Suite 601, New York, NY 10011 *E-mail:* info@thebookgroup.com; submissions@thebookgroup.com *Web Site:* www.thebookgroup.com, pg 450

Cunningham, Ryan, Chronicle Books LLC, 680 Second St, San Francisco, CA 94107 *Tel:* 415-537-4200 *Fax:* 415-537-4460 (perms) *E-mail:* hello@chroniclebooks.com; subrights@chroniclebooks.com *Web Site:* www.chroniclebooks.com, pg 48

Cunningham, Sue, Council for Advancement & Support of Education (CASE), 1201 Eye St NW, Suite 300, Washington, DC 20005 *Tel:* 202-328-CASE (328-2273) *Fax:* 202-387-4973 *E-mail:* membersupportcenter@case.org *Web Site:* www.case.org, pg 504

Cunningham, Tammy, LearningExpress, 224 W 29 St, 3rd fl, New York, NY 10001 *Toll Free Tel:* 800-295-9556 (ext 2) *Web Site:* learningexpresshub.com, pg 114

Cuocci, Kerri, Union Square & Co, 1166 Avenue of the Americas, 17th fl, New York, NY 10036-2715 *Tel:* 212-532-7160 *Toll Free Tel:* 800-367-9692 *Fax:* 212-213-2495 *Toll Free Fax:* 800-542-7567 *E-mail:* custservice@sterlingpublishing.com; customerservice@sterlingpublishing.com; editorial@sterlingpublishing.com; tradesales@sterlingpublishing.com *Web Site:* www.sterlingpublishing.com, pg 212

Curelas, Margaret, SF Canada, c/o Jane Glatt, 35 Southshore Crescent, No 103, Hamilton, ON L8E 0J2, Canada *Web Site:* www.sfcanada.org, pg 519

Curley, Maggie, Orbit, 1290 Avenue of the Americas, New York, NY 10104 *Tel:* 212-364-1100 *Toll Free Tel:* 800-759-0190 *Web Site:* www.orbitbooks.net; www.hachettebookgroup.com/imprint/orbit, pg 147

Curnin, Kate Collins, Random House Publishing Group, 1745 Broadway, New York, NY 10019 *Toll Free Tel:* 800-200-3552 *Web Site:* www.randomhousebooks.com, pg 171

Curr, Judith, HarperCollins Publishers LLC, 195 Broadway, New York, NY 10007 *Tel:* 212-207-7000 *Web Site:* www.harpercollins.com, pg 86

Curran, Gigi, Sourcebooks LLC, 1935 Brookdale Rd, Suite 139, Naperville, IL 60563 *Tel:* 630-961-3900 *Toll Free Tel:* 800-432-7444 *Fax:* 630-961-2168 *E-mail:* info@sourcebooks.com *Web Site:* www.sourcebooks.com, pg 194

Curran, Kathleen, Independent Institute, 100 Swan Way, Oakland, CA 94621-1428 *Tel:* 510-632-1366 *Fax:* 510-568-6040 *Web Site:* www.independent.org, pg 99

Currans-Sheehan, Tricia, The Briar Cliff Review Fiction, Poetry & Creative Nonfiction Contest, 3303 Rebecca St, Sioux City, IA 51104-2100 *Tel:* 712-279-1651 *Fax:* 712-279-5486 *Web Site:* www.bcreview.org, pg 584

Currigan, Louisa, HarperCollins Children's Books, 195 Broadway, New York, NY 10007 *Tel:* 212-207-7000 *Web Site:* www.harpercollins.com/childrens, pg 85

Curry, Ariel, Sourcebooks LLC, 1935 Brookdale Rd, Suite 139, Naperville, IL 60563 *Tel:* 630-961-3900 *Toll Free Tel:* 800-432-7444 *Fax:* 630-961-2168 *E-mail:* info@sourcebooks.com *Web Site:* www.sourcebooks.com, pg 194

Curry, Brendan, W W Norton & Company Inc, 500 Fifth Ave, New York, NY 10110-0017 *Tel:* 212-354-5500 *Toll Free Tel:* 800-233-4830 (orders & cust serv) *Fax:* 212-869-0856 *Toll Free Fax:* 800-458-6515 *E-mail:* orders@wwnorton.com *Web Site:* wwnorton.com, pg 143

Curry, Gayle, Neustadt International Prize for Literature, c/o University of Oklahoma, 630 Parrington Oval, Suite 110, Norman, OK 73019-4033 *Tel:* 405-325-4531 *Web Site:* www.worldliteraturetoday.org; www.neustadtprize.org, pg 639

Curry, Gayle, NSK Neustadt Prize for Children's Literature, c/o University of Oklahoma, 630 Parrington Oval, Suite 110, Norman, OK 73019-4033 *Tel:* 405-325-4531 *Web Site:* www.worldliteraturetoday.org; www.neustadtprize.org, pg 642

Curry, Michael, Donald Maass Literary Agency, 1000 Dean St, Suite 331, Brooklyn, NY 11238 *Tel:* 212-727-8383 *E-mail:* info@maassagency.com *Web Site:* www.maassagency.com, pg 468

Curtis, Anthony, Huntington Press Publishing, 3665 Procyon St, Las Vegas, NV 89103-1907 *Tel:* 702-252-0655 *Toll Free Tel:* 800-244-2224 *Fax:* 702-252-0675 *E-mail:* editor@huntingtonpress.com *Web Site:* www.huntingtonpress.com, pg 97

Curtis, David, HarperCollins Children's Books, 195 Broadway, New York, NY 10007 *Tel:* 212-207-7000 *Web Site:* www.harpercollins.com/childrens, pg 85

Curtis, Erica, Penguin Random House LLC, 1745 Broadway, New York, NY 10019 *Tel:* 212-782-9000 *Toll Free Tel:* 800-726-0600 *Web Site:* www.penguinrandomhouse.com, pg 155

Curtis, Kelsey, Vintage Books, c/o Penguin Random House LLC, 1745 Broadway, New York, NY 10019 *Tel:* 212-572-2420 *Fax:* 212-940-7390 (dom rts); 212-572-2662 (foreign rts) *E-mail:* vintageanchorpublicity@randomhouse.com *Web Site:* knopfdoubleday.com/imprint/vintage; knopfdoubleday.com, pg 225

Curtis, Nancy, High Plains Press, PO Box 123, Glendo, WY 82213 *Tel:* 307-735-4370 *Toll Free Tel:* 800-552-7819 *Fax:* 307-735-4590 *E-mail:* editor@highplainspress.com *Web Site:* highplainspress.com, pg 92

Curtis, Richard, Richard Curtis Associates Inc, 286 Madison Ave, Suite 1002, New York, NY 10017 *Tel:* 212-772-7363 *E-mail:* curtisagency@haroldober.com *Web Site:* ilpliterary.com, pg 455

Cusack, John, St Martin's Press, LLC, 120 Broadway, New York, NY 10271 *E-mail:* publicity@stmartins.com; trademarketing@stmartins.com; foreignrights@stmartins.com *Web Site:* us.macmillan.com/smp, pg 180

Cusano, Melina, University of Calgary Press, 2500 University Dr NW, Calgary, AB T2N 1N4, Canada *Tel:* 403-220-7578 *E-mail:* ucpbooks@ucalgary.ca *Web Site:* press.ucalgary.ca, pg 422

Cushing, Cristina, Macmillan, 120 Broadway, 22nd fl, New York, NY 10271 *E-mail:* press.inquiries@macmillan.com *Web Site:* us.macmillan.com, pg 122

Cusick, John, Folio Literary Management, The Film Center Bldg, 630 Ninth Ave, Suite 1101, New York, NY 10036 *Tel:* 212-400-1494 *Fax:* 212-967-0977 *Web Site:* www.foliolit.com, pg 459

Cuthbert, Rebecca, Leapfrog Global Fiction Prize, PO Box 505, Fredonia, NY 14063 *E-mail:* leapfrog@leapfrogpress.com *Web Site:* leapfrogpress.com/the-leapfrog-global-fiction-prize-contest, pg 623

Cutler, Mary Levin, BHTG - Julie Harris Playwright Award Competition, PO Box 148, Beverly Hills, CA 90213 *Tel:* 310-765-1605 *E-mail:* submissions@beverlyhillstheatreguild.com *Web Site:* www.beverlyhillstheatreguild.com, pg 580

Cutler, Mary Levin, BHTG - Michael J Libow Youth Theatre Award, PO Box 148, Beverly Hills, CA 90213 *Tel:* 310-765-1605 *E-mail:* submissions@beverlyhillstheatreguild.com *Web Site:* www.beverlyhillstheatreguild.com, pg 580

Cutrone, Ali, Simon & Schuster, LLC, 1230 Avenue of the Americas, New York, NY 10020 *Tel:* 212-698-7000 *Toll Free Tel:* 800-223-2336 (orders) *Fax:* 212-698-7007 *Toll Free Fax:* 800-943-9831 (orders) *E-mail:* firstname.lastname@simonandschuster.com; purchaseorders@simonandschuster.com (orders) *Web Site:* www.simonandschuster.com, pg 190

Cutts, Kate, Women Who Write Inc, PO Box 652, Madison, NJ 07940-0652 *Web Site:* www.womenwhowrite.org, pg 522

Cygielman, Jamie, American Girl Publishing, 2330 Eagle Dr, Middleton, WI 53562 *Tel:* 608-830-4444 *Toll Free Tel:* 800-845-0005 (US & CN) *Fax:* 608-836-1999 *Web Site:* www.americangirl.com/pages/books; www.americangirl.com, pg 10

Cyphers, Tara, The Ohio State University Press, 180 Pressey Hall, 1070 Carmack Rd, Columbus, OH 43210-1002 *Tel:* 614-292-6930 *Fax:* 614-292-2065 *Toll Free Fax:* 800-621-8476 *E-mail:* OSUPInfo@osu.edu *Web Site:* ohiostatepress.org, pg 145

Cywinski, David, Hal Leonard LLC, 7777 W Bluemound Rd, Milwaukee, WI 53213 *Tel:* 414-774-3630 *E-mail:* info@halleonard.com; sales@halleonard.com *Web Site:* www.halleonard.com, pg 84

D'Acierno, Amanda, Books on Tape™, 1745 Broadway, New York, NY 10019 *Toll Free Tel:* 800-733-3000 (cust serv) *Toll Free Fax:* 800-940-7046 *Web Site:* PenguinRandomHouseLibrary.com, pg 34

D'Acierno, Amanda, Living Language, c/o Penguin Random House LLC, 1745 Broadway, New York, NY 10019 *Tel:* 212-782-9000 *Toll Free Tel:* 800-733-3000 (orders) *E-mail:* support@livinglanguage.com *Web Site:* www.livinglanguage.com, pg 119

D'Acierno, Amanda, Penguin Random House Audio Publishing Group, 1745 Broadway, New York, NY 10019 *Toll Free Tel:* 800-793-2665 (cust serv) *E-mail:* audio@penguinrandomhouse.com; ecustomerservice@penguinrandomhouse.com *Web Site:* www.penguinrandomhouseaudio.com, pg 154

D'Acierno, Amanda, Random House Reference/Random House Puzzles & Games, c/o Penguin Random House LLC, 1745 Broadway, New York, NY 10019 *Tel:* 212-782-9000 *Web Site:* www.penguinrandomhouse.com, pg 171

D'Addona, David, Springer Publishing Co, 11 W 42 St, 15th fl, New York, NY 10036-8002 *Tel:* 212-431-4370 *Toll Free Tel:* 877-687-7476 *E-mail:* marketing@springerpub.com; cs@springerpub.com (orders); textbook@springerpub.com; specialsales@springerpub.com *Web Site:* www.springerpub.com, pg 196

D'Agostino, Kerry, Curtis Brown, Ltd, 228 E 45 St, Suite 310, New York, NY 10017 *Tel:* 212-473-5400 *Fax:* 212-598-0917 *E-mail:* info@cbltd.com *Web Site:* www.curtisbrown.com, pg 452

D'Agostino, Sonia, Quattro Books Inc, 12 Concord Ave, 2nd fl, Toronto, ON M6H 2P1, Canada *Tel:* 416-893-7979 *E-mail:* info@quattrobooks.ca *Web Site:* www.quattrobooks.ca, pg 417

D'Amato, Sally-Ann, Society of Motion Picture and Television Engineers® (SMPTE®), White Plains Plaza, 445 Hamilton Ave, Suite 601, White Plains, NY 10601-1827 *Tel:* 914-761-1100 *E-mail:* hello@smpte.org (mktg) *Web Site:* www.smpte.org, pg 520

D'Amico, Alexandra, Transatlantic Agency, 2 Bloor St E, Suite 3500, Toronto, ON M4W 1A8, Canada *Tel:* 416-488-9214 *E-mail:* info@transatlanticagency.com; royalties@transatlanticagency.com *Web Site:* www.transatlanticagency.com, pg 479

D'Angelo, Michael, HarperCollins Children's Books, 195 Broadway, New York, NY 10007 *Tel:* 212-207-7000 *Web Site:* www.harpercollins.com/childrens, pg 85

D'Aries, Dr Anthony, Housatonic Book Awards, Dept of Writing, Linguistics & Creative Process, 181 White St, Higgins Hall, Rm 219, Danbury, CT 06810 *Web Site:* housatonicbookawards.wordpress.com, pg 613

D'Auria, Heather, Yale University Press, 302 Temple St, New Haven, CT 06511-8909 *Tel:* 203-432-0960; 203-432-0966 (sales); 401-531-2800 (cust serv) *Toll Free Tel:* 800-405-1619 (cust serv) *Fax:* 203-432-0948; 203-432-8485 (sales); 401-531-2801 (cust serv) *Toll Free Fax:* 800-406-9145 (cust serv) *E-mail:* sales.press@yale.edu (sales); customer.care@triliteral.org (cust serv) *Web Site:* www.yalebooks.com; yalepress.yale.edu/yupbooks, pg 235

D'Orlando, Danielle, Princeton University Press, 41 William St, Princeton, NJ 08540-5237 *Tel:* 609-258-4900 *Fax:* 609-258-6305 *E-mail:* info@press.princeton.edu *Web Site:* press.princeton.edu, pg 164

D'Ovidio, Beth, New Hampshire Literary Awards, 2500 N River Rd, Manchester, NH 03106 *Tel:* 603-270-5466 *E-mail:* info@nhwritersproject.org *Web Site:* www.nhwritersproject.org/new-hampshire-literary-awards, pg 640

D'Ovidio, Beth, New Hampshire Writers' Project (NHWP), 2500 N River Rd, Manchester, NH 03106 *Tel:* 603-270-5466 *E-mail:* info@nhwritersproject.org *Web Site:* www.nhwritersproject.org, pg 514

Dadah, Jordan, Wildflower Press, c/o Oakbrook Press, 3301 S Valley Dr, Rapid City, SD 57703 *Tel:* 605-381-6385 *E-mail:* info@wildflowerpress.org *Web Site:* www.wildflowerpress.org, pg 229

Daddona, Matthew, HarperCollins Publishers LLC, 195 Broadway, New York, NY 10007 *Tel:* 212-207-7000 *Web Site:* www.harpercollins.com, pg 86

Daffron, Stephen C, Dun & Bradstreet, 103 JFK Pkwy, Short Hills, NJ 07078 *Tel:* 973-921-5500 *Toll Free Tel:* 844-869-8244; 800-234-3867 (cust serv) *Web Site:* www.dnb.com, pg 62

Daileda, Kyle, Harry N Abrams Inc, 195 Broadway, 9th fl, New York, NY 10007 *Tel:* 212-206-7715 *Toll Free Tel:* 800-345-1359 *Fax:* 212-645-8437 *E-mail:* abrams@abramsbooks.com; publicity@abramsbooks.com; sales@abramsbooks.com *Web Site:* www.abramsbooks.com, pg 3

Dailey, Pam, Bucknell University Press, One Dent Dr, Lewisburg, PA 17837 *Tel:* 570-577-1049 *E-mail:* universitypress@bucknell.edu *Web Site:* www.bucknell.edu/universitypress, pg 38

Daillak, Jonathan, The Gerald Loeb Awards, Gold Hall, Suite B-307, 110 Westwood Plaza, Los Angeles, CA 90095-1481 *Tel:* 310-825-4478 *Fax:* 310-825-4479 *E-mail:* loeb@anderson.ucla.edu *Web Site:* www.anderson.ucla.edu/gerald-loeb-awards, pg 625

Daito, Yasuaki, Insight Editions, 800 "A" St, San Rafael, CA 94901 *Tel:* 415-526-1370 *Toll Free Tel:* 800-809-3792 *Toll Free Fax:* 866-509-0515 *E-mail:* info@insighteditions.com; marketing@insighteditions.com *Web Site:* insighteditions.com, pg 101

Dale, Brigitte, St Martin's Press, LLC, 120 Broadway, New York, NY 10271 *E-mail:* publicity@stmartins.com; trademarketing@stmartins.com; foreignrights@stmartins.com *Web Site:* us.macmillan.com/smp, pg 181

Dalit, Meilina, Milkweed Editions, 1011 Washington Ave S, Suite 300, Minneapolis, MN 55415-1246 *Tel:* 612-332-3192 *Toll Free Tel:* 800-520-6455 *E-mail:* orders@milkweed.org *Web Site:* milkweed.org, pg 131

Dallaire, Michel, La Fondation Emile Nelligan, 100, rue Sherbrooke, Suite 202, Montreal, QC H2X 1C3, Canada *Tel:* 514-278-4657 *E-mail:* info@fondation-nelligan.org *Web Site:* www.fondation-nelligan.org, pg 506

Dallaire, Michel, Prix Emile-Nelligan, 100, rue Sherbrooke, Suite 202, Montreal, QC H2X 1C3, Canada *Tel:* 514-278-4657 *Fax:* 514-271-6369 *E-mail:* info@fondation-nelligan.org *Web Site:* www.fondation-nelligan.org, pg 653

Dallal, Neda, Avery, c/o Penguin Random House LLC, 1745 Broadway, New York, NY 10019 *Tel:* 212-366-2000 *Web Site:* www.penguin.com/avery-overview/, pg 23

Dallal, Neda, TarcherPerigee, c/o Penguin Random House LLC, 1745 Broadway, New York, NY 10019 *Tel:* 212-782-9000 *Web Site:* www.penguin.com/tarcherperigee-overview/; www.facebook.com/TarcherPerigee, pg 202

Dallam, Josie, HarperCollins Children's Books, 195 Broadway, New York, NY 10007 *Tel:* 212-207-7000 *Web Site:* www.harpercollins.com/childrens, pg 86

Dallanegra-Sanger, Joy, American Booksellers Association, 600 Mamaroneck Ave, Suite 400, Harrison, NY 10528 *Tel:* 914-406-7500 *Toll Free Tel:* 800-637-0037 *Fax:* 914-417-4013 *E-mail:* info@bookweb.org *Web Site:* www.bookweb.org, pg 494

Dalpe, Marianne, La Courte Echelle, 4388, rue Saint-Denis, Suite 315, Montreal, QC H2J 2L1, Canada *Tel:* 514-312-6950 *E-mail:* info@courteechelle.com *Web Site:* www.groupecourteechelle.com/la-courte-echelle, pg 400

Dalton, Emily, Northwestern University Press, 629 Noyes St, Evanston, IL 60208-4210 *Tel:* 847-491-2046 *Toll Free Tel:* 800-621-2736 (orders only) *Fax:* 847-491-8150 *E-mail:* nupress@northwestern.edu *Web Site:* www.nupress.northwestern.edu, pg 143

Dalton, Heather, Living Language, c/o Penguin Random House LLC, 1745 Broadway, New York, NY 10019 *Tel:* 212-782-9000 *Toll Free Tel:* 800-733-3000 (orders) *E-mail:* support@livinglanguage.com *Web Site:* www.livinglanguage.com, pg 119

Dalton, Heather, Penguin Random House Audio Publishing Group, 1745 Broadway, New York, NY 10019 *Toll Free Tel:* 800-793-2665 (cust serv) *E-mail:* audio@penguinrandomhouse.com; ecustomerservice@penguinrandomhouse.com *Web Site:* www.penguinrandomhouseaudio.com, pg 154

Daluga, Emily, Chronicle Books LLC, 680 Second St, San Francisco, CA 94107 *Tel:* 415-537-4200 *Fax:* 415-537-4460 (perms) *E-mail:* hello@chroniclebooks.com; subrights@chroniclebooks.com *Web Site:* www.chroniclebooks.com, pg 47

Daly, Brendan, Corporation for Public Broadcasting (CPB), 401 Ninth St NW, Washington, DC 20004-2129 *Tel:* 202-879-9600 *E-mail:* press@cpb.org *Web Site:* cpb.org, pg 504

Daly, Emma, Human Rights Watch, 350 Fifth Ave, 34th fl, New York, NY 10118-3299 *Tel:* 212-290-4700 *Fax:* 212-736-1300 *E-mail:* hrwpress@hrw.org *Web Site:* www.hrw.org, pg 97

Daly, John, WriteLife Publishing, Wilkinson Pass Lane, Waynesville, NC 28786 *E-mail:* writelife@boutiqueofqualitybooks.com *Web Site:* www.writelife.com; www.facebook.com/writelife, pg 234

Daly, Laura, Adams Media, 100 Technology Center Dr, Suite 501, Stoughton, MA 02072 *Tel:* 508-427-7100 *Web Site:* www.simonandschuster.com, pg 4

Daly, Peter H, Naval Institute Press, 291 Wood Rd, Annapolis, MD 21402-5034 *Tel:* 410-268-6110 *Toll Free Tel:* 800-233-8764 *Fax:* 410-295-1084 *E-mail:* customer@usni.org (cust inquiries) *Web Site:* www.usni.org/press/books; www.usni.org, pg 139

Daly, Trish, Portfolio, c/o Penguin Random House LLC, 1745 Broadway, New York, NY 10019 *Tel:* 212-782-9000 *Web Site:* www.penguin.com/portfolio-overview/; www.penguin.com/sentinel-overview/; www.penguin.com/thesis/, pg 162

Damascene, Abbott, St Herman Press, 4430 Mushroom Lane, Platina, CA 96076 *Tel:* 530-352-4430 *Fax:* 530-352-4432 *E-mail:* stherman@stherman.com *Web Site:* www.sainthermanmonastery.com, pg 180

Damasco, Elise, HarperCollins Children's Books, 195 Broadway, New York, NY 10007 *Tel:* 212-207-7000 *Web Site:* www.harpercollins.com/childrens, pg 86

Damiani, Andrea, Greystone Books Ltd, 343 Railway St, Suite 302, Vancouver, BC V6A 1A4, Canada *Tel:* 604-875-1550 *Fax:* 604-875-1556 *E-mail:* info@greystonebooks.com; rights@greystonebooks.com *Web Site:* www.greystonebooks.com, pg 407

Damiba, Audree, Phaidon, 65 Bleecker St, 8th fl, New York, NY 10012 *Tel:* 212-652-5400 *Toll Free Tel:* 800-759-0190 (cust serv) *Fax:* 212-652-5410 *Toll Free Fax:* 800-286-9471 (cust serv) *E-mail:* enquiries@phaidon.com *Web Site:* www.phaidon.com, pg 159

Damkoehler, Katrina, Random House Children's Books, c/o Penguin Random House LLC, 1745 Broadway, New York, NY 10019 *Tel:* 212-782-9000 *Web Site:* www.rhcbooks.com, pg 169

Damle, Vaishali, IEEE Press, 445 Hoes Lane, Piscataway, NJ 08854 *Tel:* 732-981-0060 *Fax:* 732-867-9946 *E-mail:* pressbooks@ieee.org (proposals & info) *Web Site:* www.ieee.org/press, pg 98

Damond, Marietta, American Association for the Advancement of Science (AAAS), 1200 New York Ave NW, Washington, DC 20005 *Tel:* 202-326-6400 *E-mail:* membership@aaas.org *Web Site:* www.aaas.org, pg 494

Damp, Dennis V, Bookhaven Press LLC, 302 Scenic Ct, Moon Township, PA 15108 *Tel:* 412-494-6926 *E-mail:* info@bookhavenpress.com; orders@bookhavenpress.com *Web Site:* bookhavenpress.com, pg 34

Danaczko, Melissa, Stuart Krichevsky Literary Agency Inc, 118 E 28 St, Suite 908, New York, NY 10016 *Tel:* 212-725-5288 *Fax:* 212-725-5275 *E-mail:* query@skagency.com *Web Site:* skagency.com, pg 466

Dancer, Janetta, St Martin's Press, LLC, 120 Broadway, New York, NY 10271 *E-mail:* publicity@stmartins.com; trademarketing@stmartins.com; foreignrights@stmartins.com *Web Site:* us.macmillan.com/smp, pg 181

Danenbarger, Winnie, Quarto Publishing Group USA Inc, 100 Cummings Ctr, Suite 265D, Beverly, MA 01915 *Tel:* 978-282-9590 *Toll Free Tel:* 800-328-0590 (sales) *Fax:* 978-283-2742 *E-mail:* sales@quartous.com *Web Site:* www.quartoknows.com, pg 168

Danes, Tracy, Counterpoint Press LLC, 2560 Ninth St, Suite 318, Berkeley, CA 94710 *Tel:* 510-704-0230 *Fax:* 510-704-0268 *E-mail:* info@counterpointpress.com *Web Site:* counterpointpress.com; softskull.com, pg 54

Danesi, Silvina, CPSA Prize in Comparative Politics, 260 Dalhousie St, Suite 204, Ottawa, ON K1N 7E4, Canada *Tel:* 613-562-1202 *Fax:* 613-241-0019 *E-mail:* cpsaprizes@cpsa-acsp.ca; cpsa-acsp@cpsa-acsp.ca *Web Site:* www.cpsa-acsp.ca, pg 592

Danesi, Silvina, CPSA Prize in International Relations, 260 Dalhousie St, Suite 204, Ottawa, ON K1N 7E4, Canada *Tel:* 613-562-1202 *Fax:* 613-241-0019 *E-mail:* cpsaprizes@cpsa-acsp.ca; cpsa-acsp@cpsa-acsp.ca *Web Site:* www.cpsa-acsp.ca, pg 592

Danesi, Silvina, Prix Francophone de l'ACSP, 260 Dalhousie St, Suite 204, Ottawa, ON K1N 7E4, Canada *Tel:* 613-562-1202 *Fax:* 613-241-0019 *E-mail:* cpsaprizes@cpsa-acsp.ca; cpsa-acsp@cpsa-acsp.ca *Web Site:* www.cpsa-acsp.ca, pg 604

Danesi, Silvina, Vincent Lemieux Prize, 260 Dalhousie St, Suite 204, Ottawa, ON K1N 7E4, Canada *Tel:* 613-562-1202 *Fax:* 613-241-0019 *E-mail:* cpsaprizes@cpsa-acsp.ca; cpsaprizes@cpsa-acsp.ca *Web Site:* www.cpsa-acsp.ca, pg 623

Danesi, Silvina, C B MacPherson Prize, 260 Dalhousie St, Suite 204, Ottawa, ON K1N 7E4, Canada *Tel:* 613-562-1202 *Fax:* 613-241-0019 *E-mail:* cpsaprizes@cpsa-acsp.ca; cpsaprizes@cpsa-acsp.ca *Web Site:* www.cpsa-acsp.ca, pg 628

Danesi, Silvina, John McMenemy Prize, 260 Dalhousie St, Suite 204, Ottawa, ON K1N 7E4, Canada *Tel:* 613-562-1202 *Fax:* 613-241-0019 *E-mail:* cpsaprizes@cpsa-acsp.ca; cpsa-acsp@cpsa-acsp.ca *Web Site:* www.cpsa-acsp.ca, pg 631

Danesi, Silvina, Donald Smiley Prize, 260 Dalhousie St, Suite 204, Ottawa, ON K1N 7E4, Canada *Tel:* 613-562-1202 *Fax:* 613-241-0019 *E-mail:* cpsaprizes@cpsa-acsp.ca; cpsa-acsp@cpsa-acsp.ca *Web Site:* www.cpsa-acsp.ca, pg 663

Danesi, Silvina, Jill Vickers Prize, 260 Dalhousie St, Suite 204, Ottawa, ON K1N 7E4, Canada *Tel:* 613-562-1202 *Fax:* 613-241-0019 *E-mail:* cpsaprizes@cpsa-acsp.ca; cpsa-acsp@cpsa-acsp.ca *Web Site:* www.cpsa-acsp.ca, pg 672

Danforth, Randi, Cotsen Institute of Archaeology Press, 308 Charles E Young Dr N, Fowler A210, Box 951510, Los Angeles, CA 90095 *Tel:* 310-206-9384 *Fax:* 310-206-4723 *E-mail:* cioapress@ioa.ucla.edu *Web Site:* www.ioa.ucla.edu, pg 53

Danforth, Scott, University of Tennessee Press, 323 Hodges Library, 1015 Volunteer Blvd, Knoxville, TN 37996 *Tel:* 865-974-3321 *Toll Free Tel:* 800-621-2736 (orders) *Toll Free Fax:* 800-621-2736 (orders) *E-mail:* custserv@utpress.org *Web Site:* www.utpress.org, pg 220

Dang, Mei, DC Canada Education Publishing (DCCED), 170 Laurier Ave W, Unit 603, Ottawa, ON K1P 5V5, Canada *Tel:* 613-565-8885 *Toll Free Tel:* 888-565-0262 *Fax:* 613-565-8881 *E-mail:* info@dc-canada.ca *Web Site:* www.dc-canada.ca, pg 401

Daniel, John M, John M Daniel Literary Services, PO Box 2790, McKinleyville, CA 95519 *Tel:* 707-839-3495 *E-mail:* jmd@danielpublishing.com *Web Site:* www.danielpublishing.com/litserv.htm, pg 438

Daniel, Tina, Human Kinetics Inc, 1607 N Market St, Champaign, IL 61820 *Tel:* 217-351-5076 *Toll Free Tel:* 800-747-4457 *Fax:* 217-351-1549 (orders/cust serv) *E-mail:* info@hkusa.com *Web Site:* us.humankinetics.com, pg 97

Danieley, Corrie, YES New Play Festival, 205 FA Theatre Dept, Nunn Dr, Highland Heights, KY 41099-1007 *Tel:* 859-572-7622 *Web Site:* www.nku.edu/yesfestival, pg 679

Daniels, Diana, Mason Crest Publishers, 450 Parkway Dr, Suite D, Broomall, PA 19008 *Tel:* 610-543-6200 *Toll Free Tel:* 866-MCP-BOOK (627-2665) *Fax:* 610-543-3878 *Web Site:* www.masoncrest.com, pg 126

Daniels, Ray, American Booksellers Association, 600 Mamaroneck Ave, Suite 400, Harrison, NY 10528 *Tel:* 914-406-7500 *Toll Free Tel:* 800-637-0037 *Fax:* 914-417-4013 *E-mail:* info@bookweb.org *Web Site:* www.bookweb.org, pg 494

Dannis, Joe, DawnSignPress, 6130 Nancy Ridge Dr, San Diego, CA 92121-3223 *Tel:* 858-625-0600 *Toll Free Tel:* 800-549-5350 *Fax:* 858-625-2336 *E-mail:* contactus@dawnsign.com *Web Site:* www.dawnsign.com, pg 58

Danzinger, Sheldon, Russell Sage Foundation, 112 E 64 St, New York, NY 10065 *Tel:* 212-750-6000 *Toll Free Tel:* 800-524-6401 *Fax:* 212-371-4761 *E-mail:* info@rsage.org *Web Site:* www.russellsage.org, pg 178

Daoud, Ghada, Macmillan, 120 Broadway, 22nd fl, New York, NY 10271 *E-mail:* press.inquiries@macmillan.com *Web Site:* us.macmillan.com, pg 122

Darby, George, University of New Orleans Press, 2000 Lakeshore Dr, New Orleans, LA 70148 *Tel:* 504-280-7457 *E-mail:* unopress@uno.edu *Web Site:* www.uno.edu/unopress, pg 218

Dardick, Simon, Vehicule Press, PO Box 42094, CP Roy, Montreal, QC H2W 2T3, Canada *Tel:* 514-844-6073 *E-mail:* vp@vehiculepress.com; admin@vehiculepress.com *Web Site:* www.vehiculepress.com, pg 424

Darga, Jon Michael, Aevitas Creative Management LLC, 19 W 21 St, Suite 501, New York, NY 10010 *Tel:* 212-765-6900 *Web Site:* www.aevitascreative.com, pg 448

Darhansoff, Liz, Darhansoff & Verrill, 529 11 St, 3rd fl, Brooklyn, NY 11215 *Tel:* 917-305-1300 *E-mail:* permissions@dvagency.com *Web Site:* www.dvagency.com, pg 455

Dark, Elizabeth, Adult Writers Workshops, Finn House, 102 W Wiggin St, Gambier, OH 43022-9623 *Tel:* 740-427-5196 *Fax:* 740-427-5417 *E-mail:* writers@kenyonreview.org *Web Site:* kenyonreview.org/adult-writers, pg 553

Dark, Elizabeth, Young Writers Workshops, Finn House, 102 W Wiggin St, Gambier, OH 43022-9623 *Tel:* 740-427-5391 *Fax:* 740-427-5417 *E-mail:* youngwriters@kenyonreview.org *Web Site:* kenyonreview.org/high-school-workshops, pg 559

Dark, Larry, The Story Prize, 41 Watchung Plaza, No 384, Montclair, NJ 07042 *Tel:* 973-932-0324 *E-mail:* info@thestoryprize.org *Web Site:* www.thestoryprize.org, pg 667

Dark, Larry, The Story Prize Spotlight Award, 41 Watchung Plaza, No 384, Montclair, NJ 07042 *Tel:* 973-932-0324 *E-mail:* info@thestoryprize.org *Web Site:* www.thestoryprize.org, pg 667

Darko, Barbara, Bloomsbury Publishing Inc, 1385 Broadway, 5th fl, New York, NY 10018 *Tel:* 212-419-5300 *E-mail:* marketingusa@bloomsbury.com; adultpublicityusa@bloomsbury.com; askacademic@bloomsbury.com *Web Site:* www.bloomsbury.com, pg 31

Darling, Benjamin, Laughing Elephant Books, 3645 Interlake N, Seattle, WA 98103 *Tel:* 206-447-9229 *Toll Free Tel:* 800-354-0400 *Fax:* 206-447-9189 *E-mail:* support@laughingelephant.com *Web Site:* www.laughingelephant.com, pg 113

Darling, Karen Merikangas, University of Chicago Press, 1427 E 60 St, Chicago, IL 60637-2954 *Tel:* 773-702-7700; 773-702-7600 *Toll Free Tel:* 800-621-2736 (orders); 773-702-9756; 773-660-2235 (orders); 773-702-2708 *E-mail:* custserv@press.uchicago.edu; marketing@press.uchicago.edu *Web Site:* www.press.uchicago.edu, pg 215

Darling, Kristina Marie, Dorset Prize, 60 Roberts Dr, Suite 308, North Adams, MA 01247 *Tel:* 413-664-9611 *Fax:* 413-664-9711 *E-mail:* info@tupelopress.org *Web Site:* www.tupelopress.org, pg 596

Darling, Kristina Marie, Tupelo Press Berkshire Prize for a First or Second Book of Poetry, 60 Roberts Dr, Suite 308, North Adams, MA 01247 *Tel:* 413-664-9611 *Fax:* 413-664-9711 *E-mail:* info@tupelopress.org *Web Site:* www.tupelopress.org, pg 671

Darling, Kristina Marie, Tupelo Press Inc, 60 Roberts Dr, Suite 308, North Adams, MA 01247 Tel: 413-664-9611 Fax: 413-664-9711 E-mail: info@tupelopress.org Web Site: www.tupelopress.org, pg 210

Darling, Kristina Marie, Tupelo Press Snowbound Series Chapbook Award, 60 Roberts Dr, Suite 308, North Adams, MA 01247 Tel: 413-664-9611 Fax: 413-664-9711 E-mail: info@tupelopress.org Web Site: www.tupelopress.org, pg 671

Darling-Kuria, Nikki, Redleaf Press®, 10 Yorkton Ct, St Paul, MN 55117 Tel: 651-641-0508 Toll Free Tel: 800-423-8309 Fax: 651-641-0115 E-mail: customerservice@redleafpress.org; info@redleafpress.org; marketing@redleafpress.org Web Site: www.redleafpress.org, pg 173

Darlington, Gary, Springer Publishing Co, 11 W 42 St, 15th fl, New York, NY 10036-8002 Tel: 212-431-4370 Toll Free Tel: 877-687-7476 E-mail: marketing@springerpub.com; cs@springerpub.com (orders); textbook@springerpub.com; specialsales@springerpub.com Web Site: www.springerpub.com, pg 196

Darnall, Kerry, Washington State University Press, Cooper Publications Bldg, 2300 Grimes Way, Pullman, WA 99164-5910 Tel: 509-335-7880 Toll Free Tel: 800-354-7360 (orders) E-mail: wsupress@wsu.edu Web Site: wsupress.wsu.edu, pg 226

Darnton, John, George Polk Awards in Journalism, The Brooklyn Campus, One University Plaza, Brooklyn, NY 11201-5372 Tel: 718-488-1009 Web Site: www.liu.edu/polk, pg 651

Das, Shouvik, BMI®, 7 World Trade Center, 250 Greenwich St, New York, NY 10007-0030 Tel: 212-220-3000 Toll Free Tel: 888-689-5264 (sales) E-mail: newyork@bmi.com Web Site: www.bmi.com, pg 501

DaSilva, Isabel, Dutton, c/o Penguin Random House LLC, 1745 Broadway, New York, NY 10019 Tel: 212-366-2000 Web Site: www.penguin.com/dutton-overview/; www.penguin.com/plume-books-overview/; www.penguin.com/tiny-reparations-overview/, pg 62

Dasta, Kelly, HarperCollins Publishers LLC, 195 Broadway, New York, NY 10007 Tel: 212-207-7000 Web Site: www.harpercollins.com, pg 87

Datri, James Edmund, American Society of Media Photographers Inc, Four Embarcadero Ctr, Suite 1400, San Francisco, CA 94111 Toll Free Tel: 844-762-3386 Web Site: asmp.org, pg 497

Dattorre, Michael, Ash Tree Publishing, PO Box 64, Woodstock, NY 12498 Tel: 845-246-8081 Fax: 845-246-8081 Web Site: www.ashtreepublishing.com, pg 18

Datz, Arielle, Dunow, Carlson & Lerner Literary Agency Inc, 27 W 20 St, Suite 1107, New York, NY 10011 Tel: 212-645-7606 E-mail: mail@dclagency.com Web Site: www.dclagency.com, pg 457

Datz, Jim, Grand Central Publishing, 1290 Avenue of the Americas, New York, NY 10104 Tel: 212-364-1100 Web Site: www.hachettebookgroup.com/imprint/grand-central-publishing/, pg 80

Dauber, Miri Pomerantz, Jewish Book Council, 520 Eighth Ave, 4th fl, New York, NY 10018 Tel: 212-201-2920 Fax: 212-532-4952 E-mail: info@jewishbooks.org Web Site: www.jewishbookcouncil.org, pg 509

Dauber, Miri Pomerantz, National Jewish Book Award-Children's Picture Book, 520 Eighth Ave, 4th fl, New York, NY 10018 Tel: 212-201-2920 Fax: 212-532-4952 E-mail: njba@jewishbooks.org Web Site: www.jewishbookcouncil.org/awards, pg 637

Dauber, Miri Pomerantz, National Jewish Book Award-Natan Notable Books, 520 Eighth Ave, 4th fl, New York, NY 10018 Tel: 212-201-2920 Fax: 212-532-4952 E-mail: njba@jewishbooks.org; natannotable@jewishbooks.org Web Site: www.jewishbookcouncil.org/awards, pg 637

Dauber, Miri Pomerantz, National Jewish Book Award-Young Adult Literature, 520 Eighth Ave, 4th fl, New York, NY 10018 Tel: 212-201-2920 Fax: 212-532-4952 E-mail: njba@jewishbooks.org Web Site: www.jewishbookcouncil.org/awards, pg 637

Dauber, Miri Pomerantz, National Jewish Book Awards, 520 Eighth Ave, 4th fl, New York, NY 10018 Tel: 212-201-2920 Fax: 212-532-4952 E-mail: njba@jewishbooks.org Web Site: www.jewishbookcouncil.org/awards, pg 637

Daudistel, Marcia Hatfield, Texas Institute of Letters (TIL), PO Box 130294, Spring, TX 77393 Web Site: texasinstituteofletters.org, pg 521

Dauer, Sam, Macmillan, 120 Broadway, 22nd fl, New York, NY 10271 E-mail: press.inquiries@macmillan.com Web Site: us.macmillan.com, pg 122

Daugherty, Peter, Princeton University Press, 41 William St, Princeton, NJ 08540-5237 Tel: 609-258-4900 Fax: 609-258-6305 E-mail: info@press.princeton.edu Web Site: press.princeton.edu, pg 164

Daugherty, Sage, Macmillan, 120 Broadway, 22nd fl, New York, NY 10271 E-mail: press.inquiries@macmillan.com Web Site: us.macmillan.com, pg 122

Daum, Rachael, American Literary Translators Association (ALTA), University of Arizona, Esquire Bldg, No 205, 1230 N Park Ave, Tucson, AZ 85721 Tel: 520-621-1757 E-mail: info@literarytranslators.org Web Site: www.literarytranslators.org, pg 495

Daum, Rachael, Italian Prose in Translation Award (IPTA), University of Arizona, Esquire Bldg, No 205, 1230 N Park Ave, Tucson, AZ 85721 Tel: 520-621-1757 E-mail: info@literarytranslators.org Web Site: literarytranslators.org/awards/ipta, pg 617

Daum, Rachael, National Translation Award, University of Arizona, Esquire Bldg, No 205, 1230 N Park Ave, Tucson, AZ 85721 Tel: 520-621-1757 E-mail: info@literarytranslators.org Web Site: www.literarytranslators.org/awards/national-translation-award, pg 638

Daum, Rachael, Spain-USA Foundation Translation Award, University of Arizona, Esquire Bldg, No 205, 1230 N Park Ave, Tucson, AZ 85721 Tel: 520-621-1757 E-mail: info@literarytranslators.org Web Site: literarytranslators.org/awards/spain-usa-award, pg 665

Daum, Rachael, Lucien Stryk Asian Translation Prize, University of Arizona, Esquire Bldg, No 205, 1230 N Park Ave, Tucson, AZ 85721 Tel: 520-621-1757 E-mail: info@literarytranslators.org Web Site: literarytranslators.org/awards/lucien-stryk-prize, pg 667

Davenport, Elaine, Writer's AudioShop, 1316 Overland Stage Rd, Dripping Springs, TX 78620 Tel: 512-476-1616 E-mail: wrtaudshop@aol.com Web Site: www.writersaudio.com, pg 234

David, Jack, ECW Press, 665 Gerrard St E, Toronto, ON M4M 1Y2, Canada Tel: 416-694-3348 E-mail: info@ecwpress.com Web Site: www.ecwpress.com, pg 401

Davidovic, Maja, Society of Motion Picture and Television Engineers® (SMPTE®), White Plains Plaza, 445 Hamilton Ave, Suite 601, White Plains, NY 10601-1827 Tel: 914-761-1100 E-mail: hello@smpte.org (mktg) Web Site: www.smpte.org, pg 520

Davidson, Andrew J, University of Missouri Press, 113 Heinkel Bldg, 201 S Seventh St, Columbia, MO 65211 Tel: 573-882-7641; 573-882-9672 (publicity & sales enquiries) Toll Free Tel: 800-621-2736 (orders) Fax: 573-884-4498 Toll Free Fax: 800-621-8476 (orders) E-mail: upress@missouri.edu; umpmarketing@missouri.edu (publicity & sales enquiries) Web Site: upress.missouri.edu, pg 217

Davidson, Brian, Association of National Advertisers Inc (ANA), 155 E 44 St, New York, NY 10017 Tel: 212-697-5950 Fax: 212-687-7310 E-mail: info@ana.net Web Site: www.ana.net, pg 499

Davidson, Ray, American Public Human Services Association (APHSA), 1300 17 St N, Suite 340, Arlington, VA 22209-3801 Tel: 202-682-0100 Fax: 202-289-6555 E-mail: memberservice@aphsa.org Web Site: www.aphsa.org, pg 496

Davies, Jeremy M, Coffee House Press, 79 13 Ave NE, Suite 110, Minneapolis, MN 55413 Tel: 612-338-0125 Fax: 612-338-4004 E-mail: info@coffeehousepress.org Web Site: coffeehousepress.org, pg 50

Davies, John G, Baton Rouge Area Foundation, 100 North St, Suite 900, Baton Rouge, LA 70802 Tel: 225-387-6126 Web Site: www.braf.org, pg 525

Davies, Jon, University of Georgia Press, Main Library, 3rd fl, 320 S Jackson St, Athens, GA 30602 Fax: 706-542-2558; 706-542-6770 Web Site: www.ugapress.org, pg 216

Davies, Michael, Davies Publishing Inc, 32 S Raymond Ave, Suites 4 & 5, Pasadena, CA 91105-1961 Tel: 626-792-3046 Toll Free Tel: 877-792-0005 Fax: 626-792-5308 E-mail: info@daviespublishing.com Web Site: daviespublishing.com, pg 57

Daving, Kyle, William S Hein & Co Inc, 2350 N Forest Rd, Suite 10A, Getzville, NY 14068 Tel: 716-882-2600 Toll Free Tel: 800-828-7571 Fax: 716-883-8100 E-mail: mail@wshein.com; marketing@wshein.com; customerservice@wshein.com Web Site: home.heinonline.org, pg 90

Davis, Alex, Random House Publishing Group, 1745 Broadway, New York, NY 10019 Toll Free Tel: 800-200-3552 Web Site: www.randomhousebooks.com, pg 171

Davis, Barry, John Wiley & Sons Inc, 111 River St, Hoboken, NJ 07030-5774 Tel: 201-748-6000 Toll Free Tel: 800-225-5945 (cust serv) Fax: 201-748-6088 Web Site: www.wiley.com, pg 230

Davis, Caitlyn, Candlewick Press, 99 Dover St, Somerville, MA 02144-2825 Tel: 617-661-3330 Fax: 617-661-0565 E-mail: bigbear@candlewick.com; salesinfo@candlewick.com Web Site: candlewick.com, pg 40

Davis, Caitlyn, Holiday House Publishing Inc, 50 Broad St, New York, NY 10004 Tel: 212-688-0085 Fax: 212-421-6134 E-mail: info@holidayhouse.com Web Site: www.holidayhouse.com, pg 94

Davis, Caitlyn, Peachtree Publishing Co Inc, 1700 Chattahoochee Ave, Atlanta, GA 30318-2112 Tel: 404-876-8761 Toll Free Tel: 800-241-0113 Fax: 404-875-2578 Toll Free Fax: 800-875-8909 E-mail: hello@peachtree-online.com; orders@peachtree-online.com; sales@peachtree-online.com Web Site: www.peachtreebooks.com; www.peachtree-online.com, pg 153

Davis, Cheryl L, The Authors Guild®, 31 E 32 St, Suite 901, New York, NY 10016 Tel: 212-563-5904 Fax: 212-564-5363 E-mail: staff@authorsguild.org Web Site: www.authorsguild.org, pg 500

Davis, Christina, Northern California Translators Association, 2261 Market St, Suite 160, San Francisco, CA 94114-1600 Tel: 510-845-8712 E-mail: ncta@ncta.org Web Site: ncta.org, pg 515

Davis, Christine, Institute of Environmental Sciences & Technology - IEST, 1827 Walden Office Sq, Suite 400, Schaumburg, IL 60173 Tel: 847-981-0100 Fax: 847-981-4130 E-mail: information@iest.org Web Site: www.iest.org, pg 101

Davis, Dawn, Simon & Schuster, 1230 Avenue of the Americas, New York, NY 10020 Tel: 212-698-7000 Toll Free Tel: 800-223-2348 (cust serv); 800-223-2336 (orders) Toll Free Fax: 800-943-9831 (orders) Web Site: simonandschusterpublishing.com/simonandschuster/, pg 188

Davis, Dawn, Simon & Schuster, LLC, 1230 Avenue of the Americas, New York, NY 10020 Tel: 212-698-7000 Toll Free Tel: 800-223-2336 (orders) Fax: 212-698-7007 Toll Free Fax: 800-943-9831 (orders) E-mail: firstname.lastname@simonandschuster.com; purchaseorders@simonandschuster.com (orders) Web Site: www.simonandschuster.com, pg 189

Davis, Deanna, University of Missouri Press, 113 Heinkel Bldg, 201 S Seventh St, Columbia, MO 65211 Tel: 573-882-7641; 573-882-9672 (publicity & sales enquiries) Toll Free Tel: 800-621-2736 (orders) Fax: 573-884-4498 Toll Free Fax: 800-621-8476 (orders) E-mail: upress@missouri.edu; umpmarketing@missouri.edu (publicity & sales enquiries) Web Site: upress.missouri.edu, pg 217

Davis, Dina, Harlequin Enterprises Ltd, 195 Broadway, 24th fl, New York, NY 10007 Tel: 212-207-7000 Toll Free Tel: 888-432-4879; 800-370-5838 (ebooks) E-mail: customerservice@harlequin.com Web Site: www.harlequin.com/shop/index.html; corporate.harlequin.com, pg 85

Davis, Gailda Pitre, American Council on Education (ACE), One Dupont Circle NW, Washington, DC 20036 Tel: 202-939-9300 Web Site: www.acenet.edu, pg 9, 495

Davis, Gary, The Learning Source Ltd, 644 Tenth St, Brooklyn, NY 11215 E-mail: info@learningsourceltd.com Web Site: www.learningsourceltd.com, pg 441

Davis, J Madison, Hammett Prize, PO Box 863, Norman, OK 73071 E-mail: crimewritersna@gmail.com Web Site: www.crimewritersna.org/hammett, pg 610

Davis, J Madison, International Association of Crime Writers Inc, North American Branch, PO Box 863, Norman, OK 73071 E-mail: crimewritersna@gmail.com Web Site: www.crimewritersna.org, pg 508

Davis, Jaleesa, Penguin Young Readers Group, c/o Penguin Random House LLC, 1745 Broadway, New York, NY 10019 Tel: 212-782-9000 Web Site: www.penguin.com/penguin-young-readers-overview, pg 156

Davis, James B, Practice Management Information Corp (PMIC), 4727 Wilshire Blvd, Suite 302, Los Angeles, CA 90010 Tel: 323-954-0224 Fax: 323-954-0253 E-mail: customer.service@pmiconline.com Web Site: pmiconline.stores.yahoo.net, pg 163

Davis, Jenny, Random House Publishing Group, 1745 Broadway, New York, NY 10019 Toll Free Tel: 800-200-3552 Web Site: www.randomhousebooks.com, pg 171

Davis, Jill, Astra Books for Young Readers, 19 W 21 St, No 1201, New York, NY 10010 Tel: 646-844-3485 E-mail: ahinfo@astrahouse.com; permissions@astrapublishinghouse.com Web Site: astrapublishinghouse.com, pg 20

Davis, John, Central Recovery Press (CRP), 3321 N Buffalo Dr, Suite 200, Las Vegas, NV 89129 Tel: 702-868-5830 Fax: 702-868-5831 E-mail: sales@recoverypress.com Web Site: centralrecoverypress.com, pg 44

Davis, Karen, David C Cook, 4050 Lee Vance Dr, Colorado Springs, CO 80918 Tel: 719-536-0100 Toll Free Tel: 800-323-7543 (orders & cust serv) Toll Free Fax: 800-430-0726 (cust serv) E-mail: bookstores@davidccook.org; customercare@davidccook.org Web Site: www.davidccook.org, pg 52

Davis, Katie, Individual Excellence Awards, 30 E Broad St, 33rd fl, Columbus, OH 43215 Tel: 614-466-2613 Fax: 614-466-4494 Web Site: www.oac.state.oh.us, pg 616

Davis, Kimberly, Ambassador International, 411 University Ridge, Suite B14, Greenville, SC 29601 Tel: 864-751-4844 E-mail: info@emeraldhouse.com; publisher@emeraldhouse.com (ms submissions); sales@emeraldhouse.com (orders/order inquiries); media@emeraldhouse.com; design@emeraldhouse.com Web Site: ambassador-international.com; www.facebook.com/AmbassadorIntl; x.com/ambassadorintl, pg 7

Davis, Lanie, Alloy Entertainment LLC, 30 Hudson Yards, 22nd fl, New York, NY 10001, pg 7

Davis, Lisa, University of Tennessee Press, 323 Hodges Library, 1015 Volunteer Blvd, Knoxville, TN 37996 Tel: 865-974-3321 Toll Free Tel: 800-621-2736 (orders) Toll Free Fax: 800-621-2736 (orders) E-mail: custserv@utpress.org, pg 220

Davis, Lisa Fagin, John Nicholas Brown Prize, 6 Beacon St, Suite 500, Boston, MA 02108 Tel: 617-491-1622 Fax: 617-492-3303 E-mail: info@themedievalacademy.org Web Site: www.medievalacademy.org/page/brown_prize, pg 584

Davis, Lisa Fagin, Van Courtlandt Elliott Prize, 6 Beacon St, Suite 500, Boston, MA 02108 Tel: 617-491-1622 Fax: 617-492-3303 E-mail: info@themedievalacademy.org Web Site: www.medievalacademy.org/page/elliott_prize, pg 599

Davis, Lisa Fagin, Karen Gould Prize in Art History, 6 Beacon St, Suite 500, Boston, MA 02108 Tel: 617-491-1622 Fax: 617-492-3303 E-mail: info@themedievalacademy.org Web Site: www.medievalacademy.org/page/gouldprize, pg 608

Davis, Lisa Fagin, Haskins Medal Award, 6 Beacon St, Suite 500, Boston, MA 02108 Tel: 617-491-1622 Fax: 617-492-3303 E-mail: info@themedievalacademy.org Web Site: www.medievalacademy.org/page/haskins_medal, pg 611

Davis, Lisa Fagin, Medieval Academy Book Subvention Program, 6 Beacon St, Suite 500, Boston, MA 02108 Tel: 617-491-1622 Fax: 617-492-3303 E-mail: info@themedievalacademy.org Web Site: www.medievalacademy.org/page/maa_book_subvention, pg 631

Davis, Lisa Fagin, Medieval Academy Inclusivity & Diversity Book Subvention Program, 6 Beacon St, Suite 500, Boston, MA 02108 Tel: 617-491-1622 Fax: 617-492-3303 E-mail: info@themedievalacademy.org Web Site: www.medievalacademy.org/page/inclusivitydiversitybooksubvention, pg 631

Davis, Lisa Fagin, Medieval Academy of America Article Prize in Critical Race Studies, 6 Beacon St, Suite 500, Boston, MA 02108 Tel: 617-491-1622 Fax: 617-492-3303 E-mail: info@themedievalacademy.org Web Site: www.medievalacademy.org/page/racestudiesarticleprize, pg 631

Davis, Matt, Beacon Press, 24 Farnsworth St, Boston, MA 02210-1409 Tel: 617-742-2110 Fax: 617-723-3097 E-mail: production@beacon.org Web Site: www.beacon.org, pg 25

Davis, Matthew, Society for Human Resource Management (SHRM), 1800 Duke St, Alexandria, VA 22314 Tel: 703-548-3440 Toll Free Tel: 800-283-7476 (orders) E-mail: books@shrm.org Web Site: www.shrm.org, pg 192

Davis, Naomi, BookEnds Literary Agency, 136 Long Hill Rd, Gillette, NJ 07933 Web Site: www.bookendsliterary.com, pg 450

Davis, Patti, The PRS Group Inc, 5800 Heritage Landing Dr, Suite E, East Syracuse, NY 13057-9358 Tel: 315-431-0511 Fax: 315-431-0200 E-mail: custserv@prsgroup.com Web Site: www.prsgroup.com, pg 166

Davis, Rebecca, Astra Books for Young Readers, 19 W 21 St, No 1201, New York, NY 10010 Tel: 646-844-3485 E-mail: ahinfo@astrahouse.com; permissions@astrapublishinghouse.com Web Site: astrapublishinghouse.com, pg 20

Davis, Reiko, DeFiore and Company Literary Management Inc, 47 E 19 St, 3rd fl, New York, NY 10003 Tel: 212-925-7744 Fax: 212-925-9803 E-mail: info@defliterary.com; submissions@defliterary.com Web Site: www.defliterary.com, pg 456

Davis, Riley Jay, Minnesota Historical Society Press, 345 Kellogg Blvd W, St Paul, MN 55102-1906 Tel: 651-259-3205 Fax: 651-297-1345 E-mail: info-mnhspress@mnhs.org Web Site: www.mnhs.org/mnhspress, pg 132

Davis, Robert, Tor Publishing Group, 120 Broadway, New York, NY 10271 Toll Free Tel: 800-455-0340 (Macmillan) E-mail: torpublicity@tor.com; forgepublicity@forgebooks.com Web Site: us.macmillan.com/torpublishinggroup, pg 208

Davis, Rowen, St Martin's Press, LLC, 120 Broadway, New York, NY 10271 E-mail: publicity@stmartins.com; trademarketing@stmartins.com; foreignrights@stmartins.com Web Site: us.macmillan.com/smp, pg 181

Davis, Sean, Berrett-Koehler Publishers Inc, 1333 Broadway, Suite 1000, Oakland, CA 94612 Tel: 510-817-2277 Fax: 510-817-2278 E-mail: bkpub@bkpub.com Web Site: www.bkconnection.com, pg 29

Davis, Susan M, Sagamore Publishing LLC, 3611 N Staley Rd, Suite B, Champaign, IL 61822 Tel: 217-359-5940 Toll Free Tel: 800-327-5557 (orders) Fax: 217-359-5975 E-mail: web@sagamorepub.com Web Site: www.sagamorepub.com, pg 179

Davis, Tieshena, IBPA Book Awards, 1020 Manhattan Beach Blvd, Suite 204, Manhattan Beach, CA 90266 Tel: 310-546-1818 E-mail: info@ibpa-online.org Web Site: www.ibpa-online.org, pg 615

Davis, Tieshena, The Independent Book Publishers Association (IBPA), 1020 Manhattan Beach Blvd, Suite 204, Manhattan Beach, CA 90266 Tel: 310-546-1818 E-mail: info@ibpa-online.org Web Site: www.ibpa-online.org, pg 507

Davis, Tinsley, National Association of Science Writers Inc (NASW), PO Box 7905, Berkeley, CA 94707 Tel: 510-859-7229 Web Site: www.nasw.org, pg 512

Davis, Tinsley, Science in Society Journalism Awards, PO Box 7905, Berkeley, CA 94707 Tel: 510-859-7229 Web Site: www.nasw.org/awards/sis, pg 661

Davis, Wendy, The Learning Source Ltd, 644 Tenth St, Brooklyn, NY 11215 E-mail: info@learningsourceltd.com Web Site: www.learningsourceltd.com, pg 441

Davis-Undiano, Robert Con, Neustadt International Prize for Literature, c/o University of Oklahoma, 630 Parrington Oval, Suite 110, Norman, OK 73019-4033 Tel: 405-325-4531 Web Site: www.worldliteraturetoday.org; www.neustadtprize.org, pg 639

Davis-Undiano, Robert Con, NSK Neustadt Prize for Children's Literature, c/o University of Oklahoma, 630 Parrington Oval, Suite 110, Norman, OK 73019-4033 Tel: 405-325-4531 Web Site: www.worldliteraturetoday.org; www.neustadtprize.org, pg 642

Davison, Dale, Friends of American Writers (FAW), c/o 506 Rose Ave, Des Plaines, IL 60016 E-mail: info@fawchicago.org Web Site: www.fawchicago.org, pg 506

Davisson, Leslie, Chronicle Books LLC, 680 Second St, San Francisco, CA 94107 Tel: 415-537-4200 Fax: 415-537-4460 (perms) E-mail: hello@chroniclebooks.com; subrights@chroniclebooks.com Web Site: www.chroniclebooks.com, pg 47

Davulis, Laura, Johns Hopkins University Press, 2715 N Charles St, Baltimore, MD 21218-4363 Tel: 410-516-6900; 410-516-6987 Toll Free Tel: 800-537-5487 (book orders & cust serv); 800-548-1784 (journal orders) Fax: 410-516-6968; 410-516-6998 (orders) E-mail: hfscustserv@press.jhu.edu (cust serv); jrnlcirc@jh.edu (journal orders) Web Site: www.press.jhu.edu; muse.jhu.edu, pg 106

Dawes, John, Piano Press, 1425 Ocean Ave, Suite 5, Del Mar, CA 92014 Tel: 619-884-1401 E-mail: pianopress@pianopress.com Web Site: www.pianopress.com, pg 159

Dawkins, Khari, Doubleday, c/o Penguin Random House LLC, 1745 Broadway, New York, NY 10019 Tel: 212-751-2600 Fax: 212-940-7390 (dom rts); 212-572-2662 (foreign rts) Web Site: knopfdoubleday.com/imprint/doubleday/; knopfdoubleday.com, pg 61

Dawson, Brian, Northwest Territories Public Library Services, 75 Woodland Dr, Hay River, NT X0E 1G1, Canada Tel: 867-874-6531 Toll Free Tel: 866-297-0232 (CN) Fax: 867-874-3321 Web Site: ece.gov.nt.ca/en/services/nwt-public-libraries, pg 515

Dawson, Erin, Workman Publishing, 1290 Avenue of the Americas, New York, NY 10104 Toll Free Tel: 800-759-0190 Fax: 212-364-0950 E-mail: workman-inquiry@hbgusa.com Web Site: www.hachettebookgroup.com/imprint/workman-publishing-company/, pg 233

Dawson, Havis, Liza Dawson Associates, 121 W 27 St, Suite 1201, New York, NY 10001 Tel: 212-465-9071 Web Site: www.lizadawsonassociates.com, pg 455

Dawson, Liza, Liza Dawson Associates, 121 W 27 St, Suite 1201, New York, NY 10001 Tel: 212-465-9071 Web Site: www.lizadawsonassociates.com, pg 455

Dawson, Mariel, Farrar, Straus & Giroux Books for Young Readers, 120 Broadway, New York, NY 10271 Tel: 212-741-6900 Toll Free Tel: 888-330-8477 (orders) *E-mail:* childrens.publicity@macmillanusa.com; childrensrights@macmillanusa.com *Web Site:* us.macmillan.com/mackids, pg 70

Dawson, Mariel, Roaring Brook Press, 120 Broadway, New York, NY 10271 *Tel:* 646-307-5151 *Web Site:* us.macmillan.com/publishers/roaring-brook-press, pg 175

Dawson, Robert, SF Canada, c/o Jane Glatt, 35 Southshore Crescent, No 103, Hamilton, ON L8E 0J2, Canada *Web Site:* www.sfcanada.org, pg 519

Day, Alyson, HarperCollins Children's Books, 195 Broadway, New York, NY 10007 *Tel:* 212-207-7000 *Web Site:* www.harpercollins.com/childrens, pg 85

Day, Emily, Macmillan, 120 Broadway, 22nd fl, New York, NY 10271 *E-mail:* press.inquiries@macmillan.com *Web Site:* us.macmillan.com, pg 122

Day, Laurel, Deseret Book Co, 55 N 300 W, 3rd fl, Salt Lake City, UT 84101-3502 *Tel:* 801-517-3369; 801-534-1515 (corp) *Toll Free Tel:* 800-453-4532 (orders); 888-846-7302 (orders) *Fax:* 801-517-3126 *E-mail:* service@deseretbook.com *Web Site:* www.deseretbook.com, pg 58

Day, Lawson, Amber Lotus Publishing, PO Box 11329, Portland, OR 97211 *Tel:* 503-284-6400 *Toll Free Tel:* 800-326-2375 (orders only) *Fax:* 503-284-6417 *E-mail:* info@amberlotus.com; neworder@amberlotus.com *Web Site:* www.amberlotus.com, pg 8

Day, Madeline, Picador, 120 Broadway, New York, NY 10271 *Tel:* 646-307-5151 *Fax:* 212-253-9627 *E-mail:* publicity@picadorusa.com *Web Site:* us.macmillan.com/picador, pg 160

Day, Patricia, HarperCollins Publishers LLC, 195 Broadway, New York, NY 10007 *Tel:* 212-207-7000 *Web Site:* www.harpercollins.com, pg 87

Dayem, Rafik, Sourcebooks LLC, 1935 Brookdale Rd, Suite 139, Naperville, IL 60563 *Tel:* 630-961-3900 *Toll Free Tel:* 800-432-7444 *Fax:* 630-961-2168 *E-mail:* info@sourcebooks.com *Web Site:* www.sourcebooks.com, pg 195

Dayman, Kim, PA Press, 202 Warren St, Hudson, NY 12534 *Tel:* 518-671-6100 *Toll Free Tel:* 800-722-6657 (dist); 800-759-0190 (sales) *E-mail:* sales@papress.com *Web Site:* www.papress.com, pg 149

De Armas, Pedro, National Association of Hispanic Publications Inc (NAHP), National Press Bldg, 529 14 St NW, Suite 923, Washington, DC 20045 *Web Site:* nahp.org, pg 511

de Beaupre, Lara, McGill-Queen's University Press, 1010 Sherbrooke W, Suite 1720, Montreal, QC H3A 2R7, Canada *Tel:* 514-398-3750 *Fax:* 514-398-4333 *E-mail:* mqup@mcgill.ca *Web Site:* www.mqup.ca, pg 412

de Botton, Gen, American Booksellers Association, 600 Mamaroneck Ave, Suite 400, Harrison, NY 10528 *Tel:* 914-406-7500 *Toll Free Tel:* 800-637-0037 *Fax:* 914-417-4013 *E-mail:* info@bookweb.org *Web Site:* www.bookweb.org, pg 494

de Caires, Brendan, PEN Canada, 401 Richmond St W, Suite 244, Toronto, ON M5V 3A8, Canada *Tel:* 416-703-8448 *E-mail:* queries@pencanada.ca *Web Site:* www.pencanada.ca, pg 516

De Carlo, Janet, Storybook Arts Inc, 414 Poplar Hill Rd, Dover Plains, NY 12522 *Tel:* 845-877-3305 *E-mail:* info@storybookartsinc.com, pg 486

De Chant, Katherine, Bloomsbury Academic, 1385 Broadway, 5th fl, New York, NY 10018 *Tel:* 212-419-5300 *Web Site:* www.bloomsbury.com/us/academic, pg 31

de Groot, Ali, Modern Memoirs Inc, 417 West St, Suite 104, Amherst, MA 01002 *Tel:* 413-253-2353 *Web Site:* www.modernmemoirs.com, pg 133

De Guire, Eileen, The American Ceramic Society, 550 Polaris Pkwy, Suite 510, Westerville, OH 43082 *Tel:* 240-646-7054 *Toll Free Tel:* 866-721-3322 *Fax:* 240-396-5637 *E-mail:* customerservice@ceramics.org *Web Site:* ceramics.org, pg 9

de Guzman, Trish, Farrar, Straus & Giroux, LLC, 120 Broadway, New York, NY 10271 *Tel:* 212-741-6900 *E-mail:* fsg.publicity@fsgbooks.com; sales@fsgbooks.com *Web Site:* us.macmillan.com/fsg, pg 70

de Guzman, Trisha, Farrar, Straus & Giroux Books for Young Readers, 120 Broadway, New York, NY 10271 *Tel:* 212-741-6900 *Toll Free Tel:* 888-330-8477 (orders) *E-mail:* childrens.publicity@macmillanusa.com; childrensrights@macmillanusa.com *Web Site:* us.macmillan.com/mackids, pg 70

De Jackmo, Nicole, Quirk Books, 215 Church St, Philadelphia, PA 19106 *Tel:* 215-627-3581 *Fax:* 215-627-5220 *E-mail:* general@quirkbooks.com *Web Site:* www.quirkbooks.com, pg 168

de la Campa, Cecilia, Writers House, 21 W 26 St, New York, NY 10010 *Tel:* 212-685-2400 *Web Site:* www.writershouse.com, pg 482

de la Cruz, Miguel, New Mexico Book Association (NMBA), PO Box 1285, Santa Fe, NM 87504 *E-mail:* libroentry@gmail.com *Web Site:* www.nmbookassociation.org, pg 514

de las Heras, Nicole, Random House Children's Books, c/o Penguin Random House LLC, 1745 Broadway, New York, NY 10019 *Tel:* 212-782-9000 *Web Site:* www.rhcbooks.com, pg 169

de Leon, Concepcion, Pantheon Books, c/o Penguin Random House LLC, 1745 Broadway, New York, NY 10019 *Tel:* 212-751-2600 *Fax:* 212-940-7390 (dom rts); 212-572-2662 (foreign rts) *Web Site:* knopfdoubleday.com/imprint/pantheon/; knopfdoubleday.com, pg 150

De Marchi, Valerie, Les Editions Fides, 7333 place des Roseraies, bureau 501, Anjou, QC H1M 2X6, Canada *Tel:* 514-745-4290 *Fax:* 514-745-4299 *E-mail:* editions@groupefides.com *Web Site:* www.editionsfides.com, pg 403

de Menil, Joy, Avid Reader Press, 1230 Avenue of the Americas, New York, NY 10020 *Web Site:* www.avidreaderpress.com, pg 23

De Mers, Martin, Algora Publishing, 1632 First Ave, No 20330, New York, NY 10028-4305 *Tel:* 212-678-0232 *Fax:* 212-202-5488 *E-mail:* editors@algora.com *Web Site:* www.algora.com, pg 7

De Pasture, Madris, New Concepts Publishing, 5265 Humphreys Rd, Lake Park, GA 31636 *E-mail:* newconcepts@newconceptspublishing.com *Web Site:* www.newconceptspublishing.com, pg 139

de Pierola, Jose, University of Texas at El Paso, Department of Creative Writing, MFA/Department of Creative Writing, M520, University Towers, Oregon St, El Paso, TX 79968 *E-mail:* creativewriting@utep.edu *Web Site:* www.utep.edu/liberalarts/creative-writing, pg 567

De Reza, Lori, Penguin Random House LLC, 1745 Broadway, New York, NY 10019 *Tel:* 212-782-9000 *Toll Free Tel:* 800-726-0600 *Web Site:* www.penguinrandomhouse.com, pg 155

de Ridder, Anthony, Penguin Random House Canada, a Penguin Random House company, 320 Front St W, Suite 1400, Toronto, ON M5V 3B6, Canada *Tel:* 416-364-4449 *Toll Free Tel:* 888-523-9292 (cust serv) *E-mail:* canadaweb@penguinrandomhouse.com; customerservicescanada@penguinrandomhouse.com *Web Site:* www.penguinrandomhouse.ca, pg 416

De Souza, Kathleen, Mary Ann Liebert Inc, 140 Huguenot St, 3rd fl, New Rochelle, NY 10801-5215 *Tel:* 914-740-2100 *Toll Free Tel:* 800-654-3237 *Fax:* 914-740-2101 *E-mail:* info@liebertpub.com *Web Site:* www.liebertonline.com, pg 128

De Spirito, Sal, Encyclopaedia Britannica Inc, 325 N La Salle St, Suite 200, Chicago, IL 60654 *Tel:* 312-347-7000 (all other countries) *Toll Free Tel:* 800-323-1229 (US & CN) *Fax:* 312-294-2104 *E-mail:* contact@eb.com *Web Site:* www.britannica.com, pg 66

de Spoelberch, Jacques, J de S Associates Inc, 9 Shagbark Rd, South Norwalk, CT 06854 *Tel:* 203-838-7571 *Fax:* 203-866-2713 *Web Site:* www.jdesassociates.com, pg 455

de Stefano, Mary Ann, Florida Writers Association Inc, 127 W Fairbanks Ave, No 407, Winter Park, FL 32789 *E-mail:* contactus@floridawriters.org *Web Site:* www.floridawriters.org, pg 506

de Stefano, Mary Ann, Florida WritersCon, 127 W Fairbanks Ave, No 407, Winter Park, FL 32789 *E-mail:* contactus@floridawriters.org *Web Site:* www.floridawriters.org, pg 554

De Vera, Joy, International Monetary Fund (IMF), Editorial & Publications Division, 700 19 St NW, HQ1-5-355, Washington, DC 20431 *Tel:* 202-623-7430 *E-mail:* publications@imf.org *Web Site:* bookstore.imf.org; elibrary.imf.org (online collection); www.imf.org/publications, pg 103

De Vos, Sarah, No Starch Press, 245 Eighth St, San Francisco, CA 94103 *Tel:* 415-863-9900 *Toll Free Tel:* 800-420-7240 *Fax:* 415-863-9950 *E-mail:* info@nostarch.com; sales@nostarch.com; editors@nostarch.com; marketing@nostarch.com *Web Site:* www.nostarch.com, pg 141

De Young, Michele McGonigle, Hachette Audio, 1290 Avenue of the Americas, New York, NY 10104 *Tel:* 212-364-1100 *Web Site:* www.hachettebookgroup.com/imprint/hachette-audio/, pg 83

Dean, Bridget PhD, Bolchazy-Carducci Publishers Inc, 1000 Brown St, Unit 301, Wauconda, IL 60084 *Tel:* 847-526-4344 *Fax:* 847-526-2867 *E-mail:* info@bolchazy.com; orders@bolchazy.com *Web Site:* www.bolchazy.com, pg 33

Dean, Keisha, SPD Design Awards, 27 Union Sq W, Suite 207, New York, NY 10003 *Tel:* 212-223-3332 *E-mail:* mail@spd.org *Web Site:* www.spd.org, pg 665

Deane, Chuck, Arcadia Publishing Inc, 210 Wingo Way, Suite 200, Mount Pleasant, SC 29464 *Tel:* 843-853-2070 *E-mail:* retailers@arcadiapublishing.com *Web Site:* www.arcadiapublishing.com, pg 16

Deans, Meghan, HarperCollins Publishers LLC, 195 Broadway, New York, NY 10007 *Tel:* 212-207-7000 *Web Site:* www.harpercollins.com, pg 86

Dearborn, Rhonda, Springer Publishing Co, 11 W 42 St, 15th fl, New York, NY 10036-8002 *Tel:* 212-431-4370 *Toll Free Tel:* 877-687-7476 *E-mail:* marketing@springerpub.com; cs@springerpub.com (orders); textbook@springerpub.com; specialsales@springerpub.com *Web Site:* www.springerpub.com, pg 196

Deaton, Kathryn, Roaring Brook Press, 120 Broadway, New York, NY 10271 *Tel:* 646-307-5151 *Web Site:* us.macmillan.com/publishers/roaring-brook-press, pg 176

DeBin, Lydah Pyles, The Center for Fiction, 15 Lafayette Ave, Brooklyn, NY 11217 *Tel:* 212-755-6710 *E-mail:* info@centerforfiction.org *Web Site:* centerforfiction.org, pg 503

DeBois, Jena, Random House Children's Books, c/o Penguin Random House LLC, 1745 Broadway, New York, NY 10019 *Tel:* 212-782-9000 *Web Site:* www.rhcbooks.com, pg 170

DeCaires, Angela, BookLogix, 1264 Old Alpharetta Rd, Alpharetta, GA 30005 *Tel:* 470-239-8547 *E-mail:* publishing@booklogix.com; info@booklogix.com; customerservice@booklogix.com *Web Site:* www.booklogix.com, pg 34

DeChiara, Jennifer, The Jennifer DeChiara Literary Agency, 245 Park Ave, 39th fl, New York, NY 10167 *Tel:* 212-372-8989 *Web Site:* www.jdlit.com, pg 455

DeCillo, Carolynn, Candlewick Press, 99 Dover St, Somerville, MA 02144-2825 *Tel:* 617-661-3330 *Fax:* 617-661-0565 *E-mail:* bigbear@candlewick.com; salesinfo@candlewick.com *Web Site:* candlewick.com, pg 40

Decker, Claudia, New Hampshire Literary Awards, 2500 N River Rd, Manchester, NH 03106 *Tel:* 603-270-5466 *E-mail:* info@nhwritersproject.org *Web Site:* www.nhwritersproject.org/new-hampshire-literary-awards, pg 640

Decker, Claudia, New Hampshire Writers' Project (NHWP), 2500 N River Rd, Manchester, NH 03106 *Tel:* 603-270-5466 *E-mail:* info@nhwritersproject.org *Web Site:* www.nhwritersproject.org, pg 514

Decker, Kate, National Newspaper Association (NNA), PO Box 13323, Pensacola, FL 32591 *Tel:* 850-542-7087 *Web Site:* www.nna.org; nnaweb.org, pg 513

Decker, Olivia, Alfred A Knopf, c/o Penguin Random House LLC, 1745 Broadway, New York, NY 10019 *Tel:* 212-751-2600 *Fax:* 212-940-7390 (dom rts); 212-572-2662 (foreign rts) *Web Site:* knopfdoubleday.com/imprint/knopf/; knopfdoubleday.com, pg 110

Decker, Stacia, Dunow, Carlson & Lerner Literary Agency Inc, 27 W 20 St, Suite 1107, New York, NY 10011 *Tel:* 212-645-7606 *E-mail:* mail@dclagency.com *Web Site:* www.dclagency.com, pg 457

DeCosta, Yanique, The Graphic Artists Guild Inc, 2248 Broadway, Suite 1341, New York, NY 10024 *Tel:* 212-791-3400 *E-mail:* admin@graphicartistsguild.org; membership@graphicartistsguild.org *Web Site:* www.graphicartistsguild.org, pg 507, 563

Decter, Jackuelen, The Vendome Press, 244 Fifth Ave, Suite 2043, New York, NY 10001 *Tel:* 212-737-1857 *E-mail:* info@vendomepress.com *Web Site:* www.vendomepress.com, pg 224

Dee, Jonathan, Syracuse University Creative Writing Program, 401 Hall of Languages, Syracuse, NY 13244-1170 *Tel:* 315-443-2173 *Fax:* 315-443-3660 *Web Site:* artsandsciences.syracuse.edu/english-department/creative-writing-mf-program; artsandsciences.syracuse.edu/english-department/cw-undergraduate-program, pg 565

Dee, Seoling, HarperCollins Children's Books, 195 Broadway, New York, NY 10007 *Tel:* 212-207-7000 *Web Site:* www.harpercollins.com/childrens, pg 86

Deegan, Paul, News Media Canada, 37 Front St E, Suite 200, Toronto, ON M5E 1B3, Canada *Tel:* 416-923-3567 *Toll Free Tel:* 877-305-2262 *Fax:* 416-923-7206 *E-mail:* info@newsmediacanada.ca *Web Site:* nmc-mic.ca, pg 515

Deen, John, Rizzoli International Publications Inc, 300 Park Ave S, 4th fl, New York, NY 10010-5399 *Tel:* 212-387-3400 *Toll Free Tel:* 800-522-6657 (orders only) *Fax:* 212-387-3535 *E-mail:* publicity@rizzoliusa.com *Web Site:* www.rizzoliusa.com, pg 175

Dees, Jenn, Emerging Voices Fellowship, 1370 N St Andrews Place, Los Angeles, CA 90028 *Tel:* 323-424-4939 *E-mail:* ev@pen.org; awards@pen.org; info@pen.org *Web Site:* pen.org/emerging-voices-fellowship, pg 599

Dees, Jenn, PEN America Los Angeles, 1370 N St Andrews Place, Los Angeles, CA 90028 *Tel:* 323-607-1867 *E-mail:* info@pen.org *Web Site:* pen.org, pg 516

Deey, Cara, Penguin Random House LLC, 1745 Broadway, New York, NY 10019 *Tel:* 212-782-9000 *Toll Free Tel:* 800-726-0600 *Web Site:* www.penguinrandomhouse.com, pg 155

DeFazio, Michael, Penguin Random House LLC, 1745 Broadway, New York, NY 10019 *Tel:* 212-782-9000 *Toll Free Tel:* 800-726-0600 *Web Site:* www.penguinrandomhouse.com, pg 155

DeFiore, Brian, DeFiore and Company Literary Management Inc, 47 E 19 St, 3rd fl, New York, NY 10003 *Tel:* 212-925-7744 *Fax:* 212-925-9803 *E-mail:* info@defliterary.com; submissions@defliterary.com *Web Site:* www.defliterary.com, pg 455

DeFord-Minerva, Debra, Random House Children's Books, c/o Penguin Random House LLC, 1745 Broadway, New York, NY 10019 *Tel:* 212-782-9000 *Web Site:* www.rhcbooks.com, pg 170

DeFrancesco, Rob, Catholic Book Awards, 10 S Riverside Plaza, Suite 875, Chicago, IL 60606 *Tel:* 312-380-6789 *E-mail:* awards@catholicmediaassociation.org *Web Site:* www.catholicmediaassociation.org, pg 587

DeFrancesco, Rob, Catholic Media Association (CMA), 10 S Riverside Plaza, Suite 875, Chicago, IL 60606 *Tel:* 312-380-6789 *Web Site:* www.catholicmediaassociation.org, pg 503

DeFrancesco, Rob, Catholic Media Awards, 10 S Riverside Plaza, Suite 875, Chicago, IL 60606 *Tel:* 312-380-6789 *E-mail:* awards@catholicmediaassociation.org *Web Site:* www.catholicmediaassociation.org, pg 587

DeGasperis, Abby, Gallery Books, 1230 Avenue of the Americas, New York, NY 10020 *Toll Free Tel:* 800-456-6798 *Fax:* 212-698-7284 *E-mail:* consumer.customerservice@simonandschuster.com *Web Site:* www.simonandschuster.com, pg 76

Degen, John, The Danuta Gleed Literary Award, 600-460 Richmond St W, Toronto, ON M5V 1Y1, Canada *Tel:* 416-703-8982 *E-mail:* info@writersunion.ca *Web Site:* www.writersunion.ca, pg 607

Degen, John, Short Prose Competition for Developing Writers, 600-460 Richmond St W, Toronto, ON M5V 1Y1, Canada *Tel:* 416-703-8982 *E-mail:* info@writersunion.ca *Web Site:* www.writersunion.ca, pg 662

Degen, John, The Writers' Union of Canada (TWUC), 600-460 Richmond St W, Toronto, ON M5V 1Y1, Canada *Tel:* 416-703-8982 *E-mail:* info@writersunion.ca *Web Site:* www.writersunion.ca, pg 523

DeGenaro, Angelo T, McGraw-Hill Education, 2 Penn Plaza, New York, NY 10121-2298 *Tel:* 212-904-2000 *E-mail:* international_cs@mheducation.com; seg_customerservice@mheducation.com (PreK-12); hep_customerservice@mheducation.com (higher education) *Web Site:* www.mheducation.com, pg 127

DeGiglio, Peter, Entangled Publishing LLC, 644 Shrewsbury Commons Ave, Suite 181, Shrewsbury, PA 17361 *Toll Free Tel:* 877-677-9451 *E-mail:* publisher@entangledpublishing.com *Web Site:* www.entangledpublishing.com, pg 67

Degler, Mike, Insight Editions, 800 "A" St, San Rafael, CA 94901 *Tel:* 415-526-1370 *Toll Free Tel:* 800-809-3792 *Toll Free Fax:* 866-509-0515 *E-mail:* info@insighteditions.com; marketing@insighteditions.com *Web Site:* insighteditions.com, pg 101

deGuzman, Beth, Grand Central Publishing, 1290 Avenue of the Americas, New York, NY 10104 *Tel:* 212-364-1100 *Web Site:* www.hachettebookgroup.com/imprint/grand-central-publishing/, pg 80

Dehmler, Mari Lynch, Fine Wordworking, PO Box 3041, Monterey, CA 93942-3041 *Tel:* 831-375-6278 *E-mail:* info@finewordworking.com *Web Site:* marilynch.com, pg 439

Deisinger, Robert D, American Technical Publishers, 10100 Orland Pkwy, Suite 200, Orland Park, IL 60467-5756 *Toll Free Tel:* 800-323-3471 *Fax:* 708-957-1101 *E-mail:* service@atplearning.com; order@atplearning.com *Web Site:* www.atplearning.com; www.atpcanada.com (CN orders), pg 13

Deist, Jeff, Ludwig von Mises Institute, 518 W Magnolia Ave, Auburn, AL 36832 *Tel:* 334-321-2100 *Fax:* 334-321-2119 *E-mail:* info@mises.org *Web Site:* www.mises.org, pg 225

Deitcher, Jess, Doubleday, c/o Penguin Random House LLC, 1745 Broadway, New York, NY 10019 *Tel:* 212-751-2600 *Fax:* 212-940-7390 (dom rts); 212-572-2662 (foreign rts) *Web Site:* knopfdoubleday.com/imprint/doubleday/; knopfdoubleday.com, pg 61

Deitrick, Callie, Wendy Sherman Associates Inc, 138 W 25 St, Suite 1018, New York, NY 10001 *Tel:* 212-279-9027 *E-mail:* submissions@wsherman.com *Web Site:* www.wsherman.com, pg 476

DeJesus, Vanessa, Random House Publishing Group, 1745 Broadway, New York, NY 10019 *Toll Free Tel:* 800-200-3552 *Web Site:* www.randomhousebooks.com, pg 171

Deku, Prof Afrikadzata PhD, Continental AfrikaPublishers, 182 Stribling Circle, Spartanburg, SC 29301 *E-mail:* afrikalion@aol.com; profafrikadzatadeku@yahoo.com; profafrikadzatadeku@facebook.com *Web Site:* www.afrikacentricity.com, pg 52

del Carmen Amado, Maria, National Latino Press Association (NLPA), 1841 Columbia Rd NW, Suite 614, Washington, DC 20009 *Tel:* 202-489-9516; 509-545-3055 (off of the Pres) *E-mail:* info@nationallatinopressassoc.org *Web Site:* nationallatinopressassoc.org, pg 513

Del Col, Anna Maria, University of Toronto Press, Book Publishing Div, 800 Bay St, Mezzanine, Toronto, ON M5S 3A9, Canada *Tel:* 416-978-2239 *Fax:* 416-978-4736 *E-mail:* utpbooks@utpress.com (orders) *Web Site:* utorontopress.com, pg 423

Del Mar, Zoe, Houghton Mifflin Harcourt Trade & Reference Division, 125 High St, Boston, MA 02110 *Tel:* 617-351-5000 *Web Site:* www.hmhco.com, pg 96

Del Priore, Lucy, Roaring Brook Press, 120 Broadway, New York, NY 10271 *Tel:* 646-307-5151 *Web Site:* us.macmillan.com/publishers/roaring-brook-press, pg 176

Del Saz, Rosa, The New Press, 120 Wall St, 31st fl, New York, NY 10005 *Tel:* 212-629-8802 *Fax:* 212-629-8617 *E-mail:* newpress@thenewpress.com *Web Site:* thenewpress.com, pg 140

Del Signore, Diane, Joyce Carol Oates Prize, 4100 Redwood Rd, Suite 20A-424, Oakland, CA 94619 *Tel:* 510-919-0970 *Web Site:* www.newliteraryproject.org/joyce-carol-oates-prize, pg 642

del Valle, Daniel, Farrar, Straus & Giroux, LLC, 120 Broadway, New York, NY 10271 *Tel:* 212-741-6900 *E-mail:* fsg.publicity@fsgbooks.com; sales@fsgbooks.com *Web Site:* us.macmillan.com/fsg, pg 70

del Valle, Daniel, Picador, 120 Broadway, New York, NY 10271 *Tel:* 646-307-5151 *Fax:* 212-253-9627 *E-mail:* publicity@picadorusa.com *Web Site:* us.macmillan.com/picador, pg 159

Delaney, Ashley, Sourcebooks LLC, 1935 Brookdale Rd, Suite 139, Naperville, IL 60563 *Tel:* 630-961-3900 *Toll Free Tel:* 800-432-7444 *Fax:* 630-961-2168 *E-mail:* info@sourcebooks.com *Web Site:* www.sourcebooks.com, pg 195

Delaney, Jacqueline, Princeton University Press, 41 William St, Princeton, NJ 08540-5237 *Tel:* 609-258-4900 *Fax:* 609-258-6305 *E-mail:* info@press.princeton.edu *Web Site:* press.princeton.edu, pg 164

Delaney, Kelly, Random House Children's Books, c/o Penguin Random House LLC, 1745 Broadway, New York, NY 10019 *Tel:* 212-782-9000 *Web Site:* www.rhcbooks.com, pg 170

DeLappe, Kathryn, Firefall Editions, 4905 Tunlaw St, Alexandria, VA 22312 *Tel:* 510-549-2461 *E-mail:* literary@att.net *Web Site:* www.firefallmedia.com, pg 72

Delbourgo, Joelle, Joelle Delbourgo Associates Inc, 101 Park St, Montclair, NJ 07042 *Tel:* 973-773-0836 (call only during standard business hours) *Web Site:* www.delbourgo.com, pg 456

Delgado, Hannah, Chronicle Books LLC, 680 Second St, San Francisco, CA 94107 *Tel:* 415-537-4200 *Fax:* 415-537-4460 (perms) *E-mail:* hello@chroniclebooks.com; subrights@chroniclebooks.com *Web Site:* www.chroniclebooks.com, pg 48

Delgado-Sanchez, Mara, St Martin's Press, LLC, 120 Broadway, New York, NY 10271 *E-mail:* publicity@stmartins.com; trademarketing@stmartins.com; foreignrights@stmartins.com *Web Site:* us.macmillan.com/smp, pg 181

Delia, Nancy, Random House Publishing Group, 1745 Broadway, New York, NY 10019 *Toll Free Tel:* 800-200-3552 *Web Site:* www.randomhousebooks.com, pg 171

Delices, Anne-Christel, Ordre des traducteurs, terminologues et interpretes agrees du quebec (OTTIAQ), 1108-2021 Ave Union, Montreal, QC H3A 2S9, Canada *Tel:* 514-845-4411 *Toll Free Tel:* 800-265-4815 *Fax:* 514-845-9903 *E-mail:* info@ottiaq.org; direction@ottiaq.org; reception@ottiaq.org; communications@ottiaq.org *Web Site:* www.ottiaq.org, pg 516

Dell'Era, Greg, Alfred Music, 285 Century Place, Louisville, CO 80027 *Tel:* 818-891-5999 (dealer sales, intl) *Toll Free Tel:* 800-292-6122 (dealer sales, US & CN); 800-628-1528 (cust serv) *Fax:* 818-893-5560 (dealer sales); 818-830-6252 (cust serv) *Toll Free Fax:* 800-632-1928 (dealer sales) *E-mail:* customerservice@alfred.com; sales@alfred.com *Web Site:* www.alfred.com, pg 7

Delman, Scott, ACM Books, 1601 Broadway, 10th fl, New York, NY 10019-7434 Tel: 212-869-7440 E-mail: acmbooks-info@acm.org Web Site: www.acm.org; books.acm.org, pg 4

Delman, Stephanie, Sanford J Greenburger Associates Inc, 55 Fifth Ave, New York, NY 10003 Tel: 212-206-5600 Web Site: greenburger.com, pg 461

deLone, Sean, Atria Books, 1230 Avenue of the Americas, New York, NY 10020 Tel: 212-698-7000 Fax: 212-698-7007 Web Site: www.simonandschuster.com, pg 21

Delorme, Alain, Les Editions Goelette et Coup d-oeil Inc, 1350, rue Marie-Victorin, St-Bruno-de-Montarville, QC J3V 6B9, Canada Tel: 450-653-1337 Toll Free Tel: 800-463-4961 Fax: 450-653-9924 E-mail: info@boutiquegoelette.com; rights@goelette.ca Web Site: boutiquegoelette.com, pg 403

DeLozier, Sara, Viking Penguin, c/o Penguin Random House LLC, 1745 Broadway, New York, NY 10019 Tel: 212-782-9000 Web Site: www.penguin.com/overview-vikingbooks/; www.penguin.com/pamela-dorman-books-overview/; www.penguin.com/penguin-classics-overview/; www.penguin.com/penguin-life-overview/, pg 225

DeLuca, Anthony, Sourcebooks LLC, 1935 Brookdale Rd, Suite 139, Naperville, IL 60563 Tel: 630-961-3900 Toll Free Tel: 800-432-7444 Fax: 630-961-2168 E-mail: info@sourcebooks.com Web Site: www.sourcebooks.com, pg 194

DeLuca, David, Bess Press Inc, 3565 Harding Ave, Honolulu, HI 96816 Tel: 808-734-7159 Fax: 808-732-3627 E-mail: customerservice@besspress.com Web Site: www.besspress.com, pg 29

Deluca, Michael J, Small Beer Press, 150 Pleasant St, No 306, Easthampton, MA 01027 Tel: 413-240-4197 E-mail: info@smallbeerpress.com Web Site: smallbeerpress.com, pg 191

DeLucci, Theresa, Grand Central Publishing, 1290 Avenue of the Americas, New York, NY 10104 Tel: 212-364-1100 Web Site: www.hachettebookgroup.com/imprint/grand-central-publishing/, pg 80

DeLuise, Janelle, Little, Brown Books for Young Readers (LBYR), 1290 Avenue of the Americas, New York, NY 10104 Tel: 212-364-1100 Toll Free Tel: 800-759-0190 (cust serv) E-mail: rights@lbchildrens.com Web Site: www.hachettebookgroup.com/imprint/little-brown-books-for-young-readers/, pg 118

Delwaide, Charlotte, Editions Michel Quintin, 2259 Papineau Ave, Suite 104, Montreal, QC H2K 4J5, Canada Tel: 514-379-3774 Fax: 450-539-4905 E-mail: info@editionsmichelquintin.ca; commande@editionsmichelquintin.ca (orders) Web Site: www.editionsmichelquintin.ca, pg 404

Dema, Leslie, Broadview Press, 280 Perry St, Unit 5, Peterborough, ON K9J 2J4, Canada Tel: 705-482-5915 Fax: 705-743-8353 E-mail: customerservice@broadviewpress.com Web Site: www.broadviewpress.com, pg 397

Demallie, Katie, The French-American Foundation & Florence Gould Foundation Annual Translation Prize, 28 W 44 St, Suite 812, New York, NY 10036 Web Site: www.frenchamerican.org, pg 604

DeMarco, Karah, Water Environment Federation, 601 Wythe St, Alexandria, VA 22314-1994 Tel: 703-684-2400 Toll Free Tel: 800-666-0206 (cust serv) Fax: 703-684-2492 E-mail: inquiry@wef.org Web Site: www.wef.org, pg 226

Demary, Mensah, Counterpoint Press LLC, 2560 Ninth St, Suite 318, Berkeley, CA 94710 Tel: 510-704-0230 Fax: 510-704-0268 E-mail: info@counterpointpress.com Web Site: counterpointpress.com; softskull.com, pg 54

DeMatteo, Patti, JMW Group Inc, 346 Rte 6, No 867, Mahopac, NY 10541 Tel: 914-841-7105 Fax: 914-248-8861 E-mail: jmwgroup@jmwgroup.net Web Site: jmwforlife.com, pg 465

DeMazza, Matt, Macmillan Audio, 120 Broadway, 22nd fl, New York, NY 10271 Tel: 646-600-7856 Toll Free Tel: 888-330-8477 (cust serv) Toll Free Tel: 800-672-7703 E-mail: macmillan.audio@macmillanusa.com Web Site: us.macmillan.com/audio, pg 123

Dembowczyk, Brian, Thomas Nelson, 501 Nelson Place, Nashville, TN 37214 Tel: 615-889-9000 Toll Free Tel: 800-251-4000 Web Site: www.thomasnelson.com, pg 206

Demick, Nora Alice, Riverhead Books, c/o Penguin Random House LLC, 1745 Broadway, New York, NY 10019 Tel: 212-782-9000 Web Site: www.penguin.com/riverhead-overview/, pg 175

DeMier, Chrissy, Morton Publishing Co, 925 W Kenyon Ave, Unit 12, Englewood, CO 80110 Tel: 303-761-4805 Fax: 303-762-9923 E-mail: contact@morton-pub.com; returns@morton-pub.com Web Site: www.morton-pub.com, pg 134

DeMonico, Rick, Albert Whitman & Company, 250 S Northwest Hwy, Suite 320, Park Ridge, IL 60068 Tel: 847-232-2800 Toll Free Tel: 800-255-7675 (orders) Fax: 847-581-0039 E-mail: mail@albertwhitman.com; orders@albertwhitman.com Web Site: www.albertwhitman.com, pg 6

DeMont, Maggie, Heinemann, 145 Maplewood Ave, Suite 300, Portsmouth, NH 03801 Tel: 603-431-7894 Toll Free Tel: 800-225-5800 (US) Fax: 603-547-9917 E-mail: custserv@heinemann.com Web Site: www.heinemann.com, pg 91

Dempsey, Luke, HarperCollins Publishers LLC, 195 Broadway, New York, NY 10007 Tel: 212-207-7000 Web Site: www.harpercollins.com, pg 86

Dempsey, Nora, Quincannon Publishing Group, PO Box 8100, Glen Ridge, NJ 07028-8100 Tel: 973-380-9942 E-mail: editors@quincannongroup.com (query first via e-mail) Web Site: www.quincannongroup.com, pg 168

Dempster, Heike, YoungArts, 2100 Biscayne Blvd, Miami, FL 33137 Tel: 305-377-1140 Toll Free Tel: 800-970-ARTS (970-2787) E-mail: info@youngarts.org; apply@youngarts.org Web Site: www.youngarts.org, pg 679

DeMuzio, Stephanie, Jessica Kingsley Publishers Inc, 123 S Broad St, Suite 2750, Philadelphia, PA 19109 Tel: 215-922-1161 Toll Free Tel: 866-416-1078 (cust serv) Fax: 215-922-1474 E-mail: hello.usa@jkp.com Web Site: us.jkp.com, pg 110

den Boon, Saskia, Holiday House Publishing Inc, 50 Broad St, New York, NY 10004 Tel: 212-688-0085 Fax: 212-421-6134 E-mail: info@holidayhouse.com Web Site: www.holidayhouse.com, pg 94

den Boon, Saskia, Peachtree Publishing Co Inc, 1700 Chattahoochee Ave, Atlanta, GA 30318-2112 Tel: 404-876-8761 Toll Free Tel: 800-241-0113 Fax: 404-875-2578 Toll Free Fax: 800-875-8909 E-mail: hello@peachtree-online.com; orders@peachtree-online.com; sales@peachtree-online.com Web Site: www.peachtreebooks.com; www.peachtree-online.com, pg 153

DeNardo, Melanie, Random House Publishing Group, 1745 Broadway, New York, NY 10019 Toll Free Tel: 800-200-3552 Web Site: www.randomhousebooks.com, pg 171

Denato, Sr Maria Grace, Pauline Books & Media, 50 Saint Paul's Ave, Boston, MA 02130 Tel: 617-522-8911 Toll Free Tel: 800-876-4463 (orders); 800-836-9723 (cust serv) Fax: 617-541-9805 E-mail: editorial@paulinemedia.com (ms submissions); orderentry@pauline.org (cust serv) Web Site: www.pauline.org/pbmpublishing, pg 152

Denehy, Debby, Petroleum Extension Service (PETEX), JJ Pickle Research Campus, 10100 Burnet Rd, Bldg 2, Austin, TX 78758-4445 Tel: 512-471-5940 Toll Free Tel: 800-687-4132 Fax: 512-471-9410 Toll Free Fax: 800-687-7839 E-mail: info@petex.utexas.edu Web Site: cee.utexas.edu/ce/petex, pg 159

Dengler, Eileen, Book of the Year Awards, 2667 Hyacinth St, Westbury, NY 11590 Tel: 516-333-0681 E-mail: kit@naiba.com Web Site: www.naiba.com/page/BooksoftheYear, pg 583

Dengler, Eileen, Carla Cohen Free Speech Award, 2667 Hyacinth St, Westbury, NY 11590 Tel: 516-333-0681 E-mail: kit@naiba.com Web Site: www.naiba.com/page/cohenfreespeechaward, pg 590

Dengler, Eileen, Legacy Award, 2667 Hyacinth St, Westbury, NY 11590 Tel: 516-333-0681 E-mail: kit@naiba.com Web Site: www.naiba.com/page/LegacyAward, pg 623

Dengler, Eileen, New Atlantic Independent Booksellers Association (NAIBA), 2667 Hyacinth St, Westbury, NY 11590 Tel: 516-333-0681 E-mail: kit@naiba.com Web Site: www.naiba.com, pg 514

Denien, Tracy, AIP Publishing LLC, 1305 Walt Whitman Rd, Suite 110, Melville, NY 11747 Tel: 516-576-2200 E-mail: help@aip.org; press@aip.org; rights@aip.org Web Site: www.aip.org; publishing.aip.org, pg 6

Denis, Casey, Penguin Press, c/o Penguin Random House LLC, 1745 Broadway, New York, NY 10019 Tel: 212-782-9000 E-mail: penguinpress@penguinrandomhouse.com Web Site: www.penguin.com/penguin-press-overview/, pg 154

Denman, Madeleine, Penguin Random House Speakers Bureau, a Penguin Random House company, 1745 Broadway, Mail Drop 13-1, New York, NY 10019 Tel: 212-572-2013 E-mail: speakers@penguinrandomhouse.com Web Site: www.prhspeakers.com, pg 487

Denneny, Samantha, American Psychological Association, 750 First St NE, Washington, DC 20002 Tel: 202-336-5510 Toll Free Tel: 800-374-2721 Fax: 202-336-5502 E-mail: order@apa.org; booksales@apa.org Web Site: www.apa.org/books, pg 12

Denney, Michelle, Sourcebooks LLC, 1935 Brookdale Rd, Suite 139, Naperville, IL 60563 Tel: 630-961-3900 Toll Free Tel: 800-432-7444 Fax: 630-961-2168 E-mail: info@sourcebooks.com Web Site: www.sourcebooks.com, pg 195

Dennis, Josh, Crossway, 1300 Crescent St, Wheaton, IL 60187 Tel: 630-682-4300 Toll Free Tel: 800-635-7993 (orders); 800-543-1659 (cust serv) Fax: 630-682-4785 E-mail: info@crossway.org Web Site: www.crossway.org, pg 56

Dennis, Linda, IODE Jean Throop Book Award, 9-45 Frid St, Hamilton, ON L8P 4M3, Canada Tel: 905-522-9537 Fax: 905-522-3637 E-mail: iodeontario@gmail.com Web Site: www.iodeontario.ca, pg 617

Dennison, Brittany, New Directions Publishing Corp, 80 Eighth Ave, 19th fl, New York, NY 10011 Tel: 212-255-0230 E-mail: editorial@ndbooks.com; publicity@ndbooks.com Web Site: ndbooks.com, pg 139

Denoncourt, Estelle, Editions Hurtubise, 1815, ave de Lorimier, Montreal, QC H2K 3W6, Canada Tel: 514-523-1523 Toll Free Tel: 800-361-1664 Web Site: editionshurtubise, pg 404

Denson, Kelly L, Association of American Publishers (AAP), 455 Massachusetts Ave NW, Suite 700, Washington, DC 20001-2777 Tel: 202-347-3375 Fax: 202-347-3690 E-mail: info@publishers.org Web Site: publishers.org, pg 498

Dent, Catherine Zobal PhD, Susquehanna University, Department of English & Creative Writing, 514 University Ave, Selinsgrove, PA 17870 Tel: 570-372-4196 Web Site: www.susqu.edu, pg 565

Deol, Amar, Grand Central Publishing, 1290 Avenue of the Americas, New York, NY 10104 Tel: 212-364-1100 Web Site: www.hachettebookgroup.com/imprint/grand-central-publishing/, pg 80

DePalma, Michael-John, Baylor University, Professional Writing & Rhetoric, Dept of English, One Bear Place, Unit 97404, Waco, TX 76798-7404 Tel: 254-710-1768 Web Site: english.artsandsciences.baylor.edu/undergraduate/professional-writing-rhetoric, pg 561

Depp, Kirsiah, Grand Central Publishing, 1290 Avenue of the Americas, New York, NY 10104 Tel: 212-364-1100 Web Site: www.hachettebookgroup.com/imprint/grand-central-publishing/, pg 80

DeProfio, Shannon, Goodheart-Willcox Publisher, 18604 W Creek Dr, Tinley Park, IL 60477-6243 *Tel:* 708-687-5000 *Toll Free Tel:* 800-323-0440 *Toll Free Fax:* 888-409-3900 *E-mail:* custserv@g-w.com; orders@g-w.com *Web Site:* www.g-w.com, pg 79

Deraco, Anthony A, DEStech Publications Inc, 439 N Duke St, Lancaster, PA 17602-4967 *Tel:* 717-290-1660 *Toll Free Tel:* 877-500-4DES (500-4337) *Fax:* 717-509-6100 *E-mail:* info@destechpub.com; orders@destechpub.com *Web Site:* www.destechpub.com, pg 59

Dercole, Alicia, Penguin Random House Speakers Bureau, a Penguin Random House company, 1745 Broadway, Mail Drop 13-1, New York, NY 10019 *Tel:* 212-572-2013 *E-mail:* speakers@penguinrandomhouse.com *Web Site:* www.prhspeakers.com, pg 487

Derdall, Alexandra, Sourcebooks LLC, 1935 Brookdale Rd, Suite 139, Naperville, IL 60563 *Tel:* 630-961-3900 *Toll Free Tel:* 800-432-7444 *Fax:* 630-961-2168 *E-mail:* info@sourcebooks.com *Web Site:* www.sourcebooks.com, pg 194

Derevjanik, Debbie, Macmillan, 120 Broadway, 22nd fl, New York, NY 10271 *E-mail:* press.inquiries@macmillan.com *Web Site:* us.macmillan.com, pg 122

DeRose, Christina, Society for Technical Communication (STC), 3251 Blenheim Blvd, Suite 406, Fairfax, VA 22030 *Tel:* 703-522-4114 *Fax:* 703-522-2075 *E-mail:* stc@stc.org *Web Site:* www.stc.org, pg 519

Derr, Matthew, Chelsea Green Publishing Co, 85 N Main St, Suite 120, White River Junction, VT 05001 *Tel:* 802-295-6300 *Toll Free Tel:* 800-639-4099 (cust serv & orders) *Fax:* 802-295-6444 *E-mail:* customerservice@chelseagreen.com; editorial@chelseagreen.com; publicity@chelseagreen.com; rights@chelseagreen.com *Web Site:* www.chelseagreen.com, pg 45

Derviskadic, Dado, Folio Literary Management, The Film Center Bldg, 630 Ninth Ave, Suite 1101, New York, NY 10036 *Tel:* 212-400-1494 *Fax:* 212-967-0977 *Web Site:* www.foliolit.com, pg 459

Desai, Amit, DC Comics Inc, 4000 Warner Blvd, Burbank, CA 91522 *Web Site:* www.dc.com, pg 58

Desai-Geller, Ishan, The New Press, 120 Wall St, 31st fl, New York, NY 10005 *Tel:* 212-629-8802 *Fax:* 212-629-8617 *E-mail:* newpress@thenewpress.com *Web Site:* thenewpress.com, pg 140

Desautels, Jon, Bear & Co Inc, One Park St, Rochester, VT 05767 *Tel:* 802-767-3174 *Toll Free Tel:* 800-932-3277 *Fax:* 802-767-3726 *E-mail:* customerservice@InnerTraditions.com *Web Site:* InnerTraditions.com, pg 26

Desautels, Jon, Inner Traditions International Ltd, One Park St, Rochester, VT 05767 *Tel:* 802-767-3174 *Toll Free Tel:* 800-246-8648 *Fax:* 802-767-3726 *E-mail:* customerservice@InnerTraditions.com *Web Site:* www.InnerTraditions.com, pg 101

Deschenes, Danielle, Penguin Random House LLC, 1745 Broadway, New York, NY 10019 *Tel:* 212-782-9000 *Toll Free Tel:* 800-726-0600 *Web Site:* www.penguinrandomhouse.com, pg 155

Deschenes, Sophie, Les Editions de l'Hexagone, 4545, rue Frontenac, 3rd fl, Montreal, QC H2H 2R7, Canada *Tel:* 514-523-1182 *Fax:* 514-521-4434 *Web Site:* editionshexagone.groupelivre.com, pg 402

DeSena, Juliette, Penguin Random House Audio Publishing Group, 1745 Broadway, New York, NY 10019 *Toll Free Tel:* 800-793-2665 (cust serv) *E-mail:* audio@penguinrandomhouse.com; ecustomerservice@penguinrandomhouse.com *Web Site:* www.penguinrandomhouseaudio.com, pg 154

DeSilva, Guy, American Public Human Services Association (APHSA), 1300 17 St N, Suite 340, Arlington, VA 22209-3801 *Tel:* 202-682-0100 *Fax:* 202-289-6555 *E-mail:* memberservice@aphsa.org *Web Site:* www.aphsa.org, pg 496

Desir, Christa, Sourcebooks LLC, 1935 Brookdale Rd, Suite 139, Naperville, IL 60563 *Tel:* 630-961-3900 *Toll Free Tel:* 800-432-7444 *Fax:* 630-961-2168 *E-mail:* info@sourcebooks.com *Web Site:* www.sourcebooks.com, pg 194

Desjardins, Francoise, Art Image Publications, PO Box 160, Derby Line, VT 05830 *Toll Free Tel:* 800-361-2598 *Toll Free Fax:* 800-559-2598 *E-mail:* info@artimagepublications.com; customer.service@artimagepublications.com *Web Site:* www.artimagepublications.com, pg 17

Desjardins, Maia, Wilfrid Laurier University Press, 75 University Ave W, Waterloo, ON N2L 3C5, Canada *Tel:* 519-884-0710 *Toll Free Tel:* 866-836-5551 (CN & US) *Fax:* 519-725-1399 *E-mail:* press@wlu.ca *Web Site:* www.wlupress.wlu.ca, pg 424

Desmond, Sean, HarperCollins Publishers LLC, 195 Broadway, New York, NY 10007 *Tel:* 212-207-7000 *Web Site:* www.harpercollins.com, pg 86

DeSmyter, DJ, HarperCollins Publishers LLC, 195 Broadway, New York, NY 10007 *Tel:* 212-207-7000 *Web Site:* www.harpercollins.com, pg 86

Despain, Ashley, Chronicle Books LLC, 680 Second St, San Francisco, CA 94107 *Tel:* 415-537-4200 *Fax:* 415-537-4460 (perms) *E-mail:* hello@chroniclebooks.com; subrights@chroniclebooks.com *Web Site:* www.chroniclebooks.com, pg 47

Despins, Paul, Savvas Learning Co LLC, 15 E Midland Ave, Suite 502, Paramus, NJ 07652 *Toll Free Tel:* 800-848-9500 *Web Site:* www.savvas.com, pg 183

Desrochers, Pascale, Les Editions Fides, 7333 place des Roseraies, bureau 501, Anjou, QC H1M 2X6, Canada *Tel:* 514-745-4290 *Fax:* 514-745-4299 *E-mail:* editions@groupefides.com *Web Site:* www.editionsfides.com, pg 403

Desroches, Claire, Beacon Press, 24 Farnsworth St, Boston, MA 02210-1409 *Tel:* 617-742-2110 *Fax:* 617-723-3097 *E-mail:* production@beacon.org *Web Site:* www.beacon.org, pg 25

Desser, Gage, Other Press, 267 Fifth Ave, 6th fl, New York, NY 10016 *Tel:* 212-414-0054 *Toll Free Tel:* 877-THEOTHER (843-6843) *Fax:* 212-414-0939 *E-mail:* editor@otherpress.com; marketing@otherpress.com; publicity@otherpress.com *Web Site:* otherpress.com, pg 148

Detaeye, Lily, Soho Press Inc, 853 Broadway, New York, NY 10003 *Tel:* 212-260-1900 *E-mail:* soho@sohopress.com; publicity@sohopress.com *Web Site:* sohopress.com, pg 193

Dettlinger, Madison, Random House Publishing Group, 1745 Broadway, New York, NY 10019 *Toll Free Tel:* 800-200-3552 *Web Site:* www.randomhousebooks.com, pg 171

Dettman, Tracey, Fifth House Publishers, 209 Wicksteed Ave, Unit 51, Toronto, ON M4G 0B1, Canada *Tel:* 905-477-9700 *Toll Free Tel:* 800-387-9776 *E-mail:* godwit@fitzhenry.ca; bookinfo@fitzhenry.ca (cust serv) *Web Site:* www.fifthhousepublishers.ca, pg 406

Detweiler, Katelyn, Jill Grinberg Literary Management LLC, 392 Vanderbilt Ave, Brooklyn, NY 11238 *Tel:* 212-620-5883 *E-mail:* info@jillgrinbergliterary.com *Web Site:* www.jillgrinbergliterary.com, pg 461

Devanzo, Teresa, Sourcebooks LLC, 1935 Brookdale Rd, Suite 139, Naperville, IL 60563 *Tel:* 630-961-3900 *Toll Free Tel:* 800-432-7444 *Fax:* 630-961-2168 *E-mail:* info@sourcebooks.com *Web Site:* www.sourcebooks.com, pg 194

Devendorf, Katherine, Simon & Schuster Children's Publishing, 1230 Avenue of the Americas, New York, NY 10020 *Tel:* 212-698-7000 *Web Site:* www.simonandschuster.com/kids; www.simonandschuster.com/teen; simonandschuster.net; simonandschuster.biz, pg 189

Devens, Robert, University of Texas Press, 3001 Lake Austin Blvd, 2.200, Austin, TX 78703 *Tel:* 512-471-7233 *Fax:* 512-232-7178 *E-mail:* utpress@uts.cc.utexas.edu; info@utpress.utexas.edu *Web Site:* utpress.utexas.edu, pg 205

Devine, Tracy, Random House Publishing Group, 1745 Broadway, New York, NY 10019 *Toll Free Tel:* 800-200-3552 *Web Site:* www.randomhousebooks.com, pg 171

Devine-Hardy, Heather, American Indian Youth Literature Award, PO Box 41296, San Jose, CA 95160 *E-mail:* ailawebsite@gmail.com *Web Site:* ailanet.org/activities/american-indian-youth-literature-award, pg 573

Devineni, Ram, Rattapallax Press, 532 La Guadia Place, Suite 353, New York, NY 10012 *Web Site:* www.rattapallax.com, pg 172

Devlin, Anne G, Max Gartenberg Literary Agency, 912 N Pennsylvania Ave, Yardley, PA 19067 *Tel:* 215-295-9230 *Web Site:* www.maxgartenberg.com, pg 459

Devlin, Aria, Harry N Abrams Inc, 195 Broadway, 9th fl, New York, NY 10007 *Tel:* 212-206-7715 *Toll Free Tel:* 800-345-1359 *Fax:* 212-645-8437 *E-mail:* abrams@abramsbooks.com; publicity@abramsbooks.com; sales@abramsbooks.com *Web Site:* www.abramsbooks.com, pg 3

Devlin, Jeanne, The RoadRunner Press, 124 NW 32 St, Oklahoma City, OK 73118 *Tel:* 405-524-6205 *Fax:* 405-524-6312 *E-mail:* info@theroadrunnerpress.com; orders@theroadrunnerpress.com *Web Site:* www.theroadrunnerpress.com, pg 175

Devling, Chris, Corwin, 2455 Teller Rd, Thousand Oaks, CA 91320 *Tel:* 805-499-9734 *Toll Free Tel:* 800-233-9936 *Fax:* 805-499-5323 *Toll Free Fax:* 800-417-2466 *E-mail:* info@corwin; order@corwin.com *Web Site:* www.corwin.com, pg 53

Devoll, Julie, Harvard Business Review Press, 20 Guest St, Suite 700, Brighton, MA 02135 *Tel:* 617-783-7400 *Fax:* 617-783-7489 *E-mail:* custserv@hbsp.harvard.edu *Web Site:* www.harvardbusiness.org, pg 87

deVries, Anna, Picador, 120 Broadway, New York, NY 10271 *Tel:* 646-307-5151 *Fax:* 212-253-9627 *E-mail:* publicity@picadorusa.com *Web Site:* us.macmillan.com/picador, pg 159

DeVries, Catherine, Kregel Publications, 2450 Oak Industrial Dr NE, Grand Rapids, MI 49505 *Tel:* 616-451-4775 *Toll Free Tel:* 800-733-2607 *Fax:* 616-451-9330 *E-mail:* kregelbooks@kregel.com *Web Site:* www.kregel.com, pg 111

DeVries, Tom, Wm B Eerdmans Publishing Co, 4035 Park East Ct SE, Grand Rapids, MI 49546 *Tel:* 616-459-4591 *Toll Free Tel:* 800-253-7521 *E-mail:* customerservice@eerdmans.com; sales@eerdmans.com *Web Site:* www.eerdmans.com, pg 64

Dew, Dr Jay, Texas A&M University Press, John H Lindsey Bldg, Lewis St, 4354 TAMU, College Station, TX 77843-4354 *Tel:* 979-845-1436 *Toll Free Tel:* 800-826-8911 (orders) *Fax:* 979-847-8752 *Toll Free Fax:* 888-617-2421 (orders) *E-mail:* bookorders@tamu.edu *Web Site:* www.tamupress.com, pg 205

DeWerd, Andrea, HarperCollins Publishers LLC, 195 Broadway, New York, NY 10007 *Tel:* 212-207-7000 *Web Site:* www.harpercollins.com, pg 86

Dewey, Arthur J, Polebridge Press, Willamette University, 900 State St, Salem, OR 97301 *Tel:* 651-200-2372 *E-mail:* orders@westarinstitute.org *Web Site:* www.westarinstitute.org, pg 162

Dewing-Vallejo, Camille, Random House Publishing Group, 1745 Broadway, New York, NY 10019 *Toll Free Tel:* 800-200-3552 *Web Site:* www.randomhousebooks.com, pg 171

Dextre, Natalia, Random House Children's Books, c/o Penguin Random House LLC, 1745 Broadway, New York, NY 10019 *Tel:* 212-782-9000 *Web Site:* www.rhcbooks.com, pg 170

Deyirmenjian, Ani, University of Toronto Press, Book Publishing Div, 800 Bay St, Mezzanine, Toronto, ON M5S 3A9, Canada *Tel:* 416-978-2239 *Fax:* 416-978-4736 *E-mail:* utpbooks@utorontopress.com (orders) *Web Site:* utorontopress.com, pg 423

Deyoe, Cori, 3 Seas Literary Agency, PO Box 444, Sun Prairie, WI 53590 *Tel:* 608-834-9317 *E-mail:* threeseaslit@aol.com *Web Site:* threeseasagency.com, pg 479

DeYoung, Andrew, Augsburg Fortress Publishers, Publishing House of the Evangelical Lutheran Church in America, 411 Washington Ave N, 3rd fl, Minneapolis, MN 55401 Tel: 612-330-3300 Toll Free Tel: 800-426-0115 (ext 639, subns); 800-328-4648 (orders) Fax: 612-330-3455 E-mail: info@augsburgfortress.org; copyright@augsburgfortress.org (reprint permission requests); customercare@augsburgfortress.org Web Site: www.augsburgfortress.org; www.1517.media, pg 22

DeYoung, Emily, Council for Advancement & Support of Education (CASE), 1201 Eye St NW, Suite 300, Washington, DC 20005 Tel: 202-328-CASE (328-2273) Fax: 202-387-4973 E-mail: membersupportcenter@case.org Web Site: www.case.org, pg 504

Dhar, Uday K, Mondial, 203 W 107 St, Suite 6-C, New York, NY 10025 Tel: 646-807-8031 Fax: 208-361-2863 E-mail: contact@mondialbooks.com Web Site: www.mondialbooks.com, pg 133

Dhawan, Sandeep, Lumina Datamatics Inc, 600 Cordwainer Dr, Unit 103, Norwell, MA 02061 Tel: 508-746-0300 Fax: 508-746-3233 E-mail: marketing@luminad.com Web Site: luminadatamatics.com, pg 442

Di Dio, Ashley, GP Putnam's Sons, c/o Penguin Random House LLC, 1745 Broadway, New York, NY 10019 Tel: 212-782-9000 Web Site: www.penguin.com/putnam/, pg 167

Di Gioia, Tony, George T Bisel Co Inc, 710 S Washington Sq, Philadelphia, PA 19106-3519 Tel: 215-922-5760 Toll Free Tel: 800-247-3526 Fax: 215-922-2235 E-mail: gbisel@bisel.com Web Site: www.bisel.com, pg 29

Di Martino, Christina, Christina Di Martino Literary Services, 87 Hamilton Place, No 7G, New York, NY 10031 Tel: 212-996-9086; 561-283-1549 E-mail: writealotmail@gmail.com, pg 438

Di Prisco, Joseph, Joyce Carol Oates Prize, 4100 Redwood Rd, Suite 20A-424, Oakland, CA 94619 Tel: 510-919-0970 Web Site: www.newliteraryproject.org/joyce-carol-oates-prize, pg 642

Dial, Beth, National Poetry Series Open Competition, 57 Mountain Ave, Princeton, NJ 08540 Tel: 609-430-0999 Fax: 609-430-9933 E-mail: npspoetry@gmail.com Web Site: nationalpoetryseries.org, pg 638

Diallo, Fanta, W W Norton & Company Inc, 500 Fifth Ave, New York, NY 10110-0017 Tel: 212-354-5500 Toll Free Tel: 800-233-4830 (orders & cust serv) Fax: 212-869-0856 Toll Free Fax: 800-458-6515 E-mail: orders@wwnorton.com Web Site: wwnorton.com, pg 143

Diamond, Jordan, Environmental Law Institute, 1730 "M" St NW, Suite 700, Washington, DC 20036 Tel: 202-939-3800 Toll Free Tel: 800-433-5120 Fax: 202-939-3868 E-mail: law@eli.org Web Site: www.eli.org, pg 67

Diamond, Sarah, Crystal Kite Awards, 6363 Wilshire Blvd, Suite 425, Los Angeles, CA 90048 Tel: 323-782-1010 E-mail: info@scbwi.org Web Site: www.scbwi.org/awards/crystal-kite-member-choice-award, pg 593

Diamond, Sarah, Karen & Philip Cushman Late Bloomer Award, 6363 Wilshire Blvd, Suite 425, Los Angeles, CA 90048 Tel: 323-782-1010 E-mail: info@scbwi.org Web Site: www.scbwi.org/awards-and-grants-new, pg 594

Diamond, Sarah, Golden Kite Awards, 6363 Wilshire Blvd, Suite 425, Los Angeles, CA 90048 Tel: 323-782-1010 E-mail: info@scbwi.org Web Site: www.scbwi.org/awards/golden-kite-award, pg 607

Diamond, Sarah, Magazine Merit Awards, 6363 Wilshire Blvd, Suite 425, Los Angeles, CA 90048 Tel: 323-782-1010 E-mail: info@scbwi.org Web Site: www.scbwi.org/awards/magazine-merit-award, pg 628

Diamond, Sarah, On-the-Verge Emerging Voices Award, 6363 Wilshire Blvd, Suite 425, Los Angeles, CA 90048 Tel: 323-782-1010 E-mail: info@scbwi.org Web Site: www.scbwi.org/awards/grants/on-the-verge-emerging-voices-grant, pg 644

Diamond, Sarah, SCBWI Work-In-Progress Awards, 6363 Wilshire Blvd, Suite 425, Los Angeles, CA 90048 Tel: 323-782-1010 E-mail: info@scbwi.org Web Site: www.scbwi.org/awards/grants/work-in-progress-grants, pg 660

Diamond, Sarah, Society of Children's Book Writers & Illustrators (SCBWI), 6363 Wilshire Blvd, Suite 425, Los Angeles, CA 90048 Tel: 323-782-1010 E-mail: membership@scbwi.org Web Site: www.scbwi.org, pg 520

Diamond, Sarah, Spark Award, 6363 Wilshire Blvd, Suite 425, Los Angeles, CA 90048 Tel: 323-782-1010 E-mail: grants@scbwi.org; info@scbwi.org Web Site: www.scbwi.org, pg 665

Diana, Maralee, Penguin Publishing Group, c/o Penguin Random House LLC, 1745 Broadway, New York, NY 10019 Tel: 212-782-9000 Web Site: www.penguin.com, pg 154

DiAngelis, Heather, Transportation Research Board (TRB), 500 Fifth St NW, Washington, DC 20001 Tel: 202-334-2934; 202-334-3213 (bookshop) E-mail: trbsales@nas.edu; mytrb@nas.edu Web Site: www.nationalacademies.org/trb/transportation-research-board, pg 209

Dias, Meire, Bookcase Literary Agency, 5062 Lankershim Blvd, PMB 3046, North Hollywood, CA 91601 Web Site: www.bookcaseagency.com, pg 450

Dias-Mandoly, Melissa, University of Pittsburgh Press, 7500 Thomas Blvd, Pittsburgh, PA 15260 Tel: 412-383-2456 Fax: 412-383-2466 E-mail: info@upress.pitt.edu Web Site: www.upress.pitt.edu, pg 219

Diaz, Dannalie, Random House Publishing Group, 1745 Broadway, New York, NY 10019 Toll Free Tel: 800-200-3552 Web Site: www.randomhousebooks.com, pg 171

Diaz Morgan, Lauren, Books on Tape™, 1745 Broadway, New York, NY 10019 Toll Free Tel: 800-733-3000 (cust serv) Toll Free Fax: 800-940-7046 Web Site: PenguinRandomHouseLibrary.com, pg 34

Diaz Morgan, Lauren, Penguin Random House Audio Publishing Group, 1745 Broadway, New York, NY 10019 Toll Free Tel: 800-793-2665 (cust serv) E-mail: audio@penguinrandomhouse.com; ecustomerservice@penguinrandomhouse.com Web Site: www.penguinrandomhouseaudio.com, pg 154

DiBiase, Diane, Poisoned Pen Press, 4014 N Goldwater Blvd, Suite 201, Scottsdale, AZ 85251 Tel: 480-945-3375 Toll Free Tel: 800-421-3976 Fax: 480-949-1707 E-mail: info@poisonedpenpress.com Web Site: www.poisonedpenpress.com, pg 161

DiCecco, Andrew, HarperCollins Publishers LLC, 195 Broadway, New York, NY 10007 Tel: 212-207-7000 Web Site: www.harpercollins.com, pg 86

Dick, Janet L, Museum of New Mexico Press, 725 Camino Lejo, Suite C, Santa Fe, NM 87505 Tel: 505-476-1155; 505-272-7777 (orders) Toll Free Tel: 800-249-7737 (orders) Fax: 505-476-1156 Toll Free Fax: 800-622-8667 (orders) Web Site: www.mnmpress.org, pg 136

Dickemper, Cheryl, HarperCollins Publishers LLC, 195 Broadway, New York, NY 10007 Tel: 212-207-7000 Web Site: www.harpercollins.com, pg 86

Dickerman, Colin, Grand Central Publishing, 1290 Avenue of the Americas, New York, NY 10104 Tel: 212-364-1100 Web Site: www.hachettebookgroup.com/imprint/grand-central-publishing/, pg 80

Dickerson, Donya, Aevitas Creative Management LLC, 19 W 21 St, Suite 501, New York, NY 10010 Tel: 212-765-6900 Web Site: www.aevitascreative.com, pg 448

Dickey, Angie, Iowa Poetry Prize, 119 W Park Rd, 100 Kuhl House, Iowa City, IA 52242-1000 Tel: 319-335-2000 Fax: 319-335-2055 E-mail: uipress@uiowa.edu Web Site: www.uipress.uiowa.edu, pg 617

Dickey, Angie, University of Iowa Press, 119 W Park Rd, 100 Kuhl House, Iowa City, IA 52242-1000 Tel: 319-335-2000 Toll Free Tel: 800-621-2736

(orders only) Fax: 319-335-2055 Toll Free Fax: 800-621-8476 (orders only) E-mail: uipress@uiowa.edu Web Site: www.uipress.uiowa.edu, pg 216

Dickey, Ruth, 5 Under 35, 90 Broad St, Suite 604, New York, NY 10004 Tel: 212-685-0261 Fax: 212-213-6570 E-mail: nationalbook@nationalbook.org Web Site: www.nationalbook.org, pg 602

Dickey, Ruth, Medal for Distinguished Contribution to American Letters, 90 Broad St, Suite 604, New York, NY 10004 Tel: 212-685-0261 Fax: 212-213-6570 E-mail: nationalbook@nationalbook.org Web Site: www.nationalbook.org/amerletters.html, pg 631

Dickey, Ruth, National Book Awards, 90 Broad St, Suite 604, New York, NY 10004 Tel: 212-685-0261 Fax: 212-213-6570 E-mail: nationalbook@nationalbook.org Web Site: www.nationalbook.org, pg 637

Dickey, Ruth, National Book Foundation, 90 Broad St, Suite 604, New York, NY 10004 Tel: 212-685-0261 Fax: 212-213-6570 E-mail: nationalbook@nationalbook.org Web Site: www.nationalbook.org, pg 526

Dickey, Ruth, Science + Literature Program, 90 Broad St, Suite 604, New York, NY 10004 Tel: 212-685-0261 Fax: 212-213-6570 E-mail: nationalbook@nationalbook.org Web Site: www.nationalbook.org/programs/science-literature, pg 661

Dickey, Sonia, University of New Mexico Press, One University of New Mexico, Albuquerque, NM 87131-0001 Tel: 505-272-7777 Fax: 505-277-3343 E-mail: custserv@unm.edu (order dept) Web Site: unmpress.com, pg 218

Dickinson, Jan, Wheatherstone Press, PO Box 257, Portland, OR 97207 Tel: 503-244-8929 Fax: 503-244-9795 Web Site: www.wheatherstonepress.com; www.relocationbooks.com, pg 228

Dickison, Steve, The Academy of American Poets Harold Taylor Prize, 511-512 Humanities Bldg, 1600 Holloway Ave, San Francisco, CA 94132 Tel: 415-338-2227 Fax: 415-338-0966 E-mail: poetry@sfsu.edu Web Site: poetry.sfsu.edu, pg 569

Dickison, Steve, The Audre Lorde Creative Writing Award, 511-512 Humanities Bldg, 1600 Holloway Ave, San Francisco, CA 94132 Tel: 415-338-2227 Fax: 415-338-0966 E-mail: poetry@sfsu.edu Web Site: poetry.sfsu.edu, pg 626

Dickison, Steve, Poetry Center Book Award, 511-512 Humanities Bldg, 1600 Holloway Ave, San Francisco, CA 94132 Tel: 415-338-2227 Fax: 415-338-0966 E-mail: poetry@sfsu.edu Web Site: poetry.sfsu.edu, pg 651

Dickison, Steve, San Francisco Browning Society Award, 511-512 Humanities Bldg, 1600 Holloway Ave, San Francisco, CA 94132 Tel: 415-338-2227 Fax: 415-338-0966 E-mail: poetry@sfsu.edu Web Site: poetry.sfsu.edu, pg 658

Dickison, Steve, The Piri Thomas Poetry Prize, 511-512 Humanities Bldg, 1600 Holloway Ave, San Francisco, CA 94132 Tel: 415-338-2227 Fax: 415-338-0966 E-mail: poetry@sfsu.edu Web Site: poetry.sfsu.edu, pg 669

Dickman, Katie, BenBella Books Inc, 10440 N Central Expwy, Suite 800, Dallas, TX 75231-2264 Tel: 214-750-3600 Web Site: www.benbellabooks.com; www.smartpopbooks.com, pg 27

Dickson, Alexander, New York State Bar Association, One Elk St, Albany, NY 12207 Tel: 518-463-3200 Toll Free Tel: 800-582-2452 Fax: 518-463-5993 E-mail: mrc@nysba.org Web Site: nysba.org, pg 141

Dickson, Barbara, University Science Books, 1305 Walt Whitman Rd, Suite 110, Melville, NY 11747 Tel: 703-661-1572 (cust serv & orders) Fax: 703-661-1501 E-mail: usbmail@presswarehouse.com (cust serv, orders) Web Site: uscibooks.aip.org, pg 222

Dickson, Johanna, Basic Books Group, 1290 Avenue of the Americas, New York, NY 10104 *Tel:* 212-340-8100 *Toll Free Tel:* 800-343-4499 (cust serv) *Fax:* 212-340-8105 *E-mail:* customer.service@hbgusa.com; orders@hbgusa.com *Web Site:* www.hachettebookgroup.com/imprint/basic-books/, pg 25

Didier, Rebecca, Trafalgar Square Books, 388 Howe Hill Rd, North Pomfret, VT 05053 *Tel:* 802-457-1911 *Toll Free Tel:* 800-423-4525 *Fax:* 802-457-1913 *E-mail:* contact@trafalgarbooks.com *Web Site:* www.trafalgarbooks.com; www.horseandriderbooks.com, pg 208

Didik, Jennifer, Macmillan, 120 Broadway, 22nd fl, New York, NY 10271 *E-mail:* press.inquiries@macmillan.com *Web Site:* us.macmillan.com, pg 122

Didio, Dan, DC Comics Inc, 4000 Warner Blvd, Burbank, CA 91522 *Web Site:* www.dc.com, pg 58

Diemont, Kirin, Little, Brown and Company, 1290 Avenue of the Americas, New York, NY 10104 *Tel:* 212-364-1100 *Fax:* 212-364-0952 *E-mail:* firstname.lastname@hbgusa.com *Web Site:* www.hachettebookgroup.com/imprint/little-brown-and-company/, pg 118

Dienstfrey, Patricia, Kelsey Street Press, 2824 Kelsey St, Berkeley, CA 94705 *E-mail:* info@kelseystreetpress.org *Web Site:* www.kelseystreetpress.org, pg 108

Dierbeck, Lisa, Yaddo Artists Residency, 312 Union Ave, Saratoga Springs, NY 12866 *Tel:* 518-584-0746 *Fax:* 518-584-1312 *Web Site:* www.yaddo.org, pg 559

Diestelkamp, Audrey, HarperCollins Children's Books, 195 Broadway, New York, NY 10007 *Tel:* 212-207-7000 *Web Site:* www.harpercollins.com/childrens, pg 85

Dieter, George, Education Writers Association (EWA), 1825 "K" St NW, Suite 200, Washington, DC 20006 *Tel:* 202-452-9830 *Web Site:* ewa.org, pg 505

Dieterich, Danielle, HarperCollins Publishers LLC, 195 Broadway, New York, NY 10007 *Tel:* 212-207-7000 *Web Site:* www.harpercollins.com, pg 87

Diez, Corina, Random House Publishing Group, 1745 Broadway, New York, NY 10019 *Tel:* 212-782-9000 *Toll Free Tel:* 800-200-3552 *Web Site:* www.randomhousebooks.com, pg 171

DiFazio, Daphne, Coffee House Press, 79 13 Ave NE, Suite 110, Minneapolis, MN 55413 *Tel:* 612-338-0125 *Fax:* 612-338-4004 *E-mail:* info@coffeehousepress.org *Web Site:* coffeehousepress.org, pg 50

Diforio, Robert (Bob) G, D4EO Literary Agency, 13206 Treviso Dr, Lakewood Ranch, FL 34211 *Tel:* 203-545-7180 (cell) *Web Site:* www.d4eoliteraryagency.com; www.publishersmarketplace.com/members/d4eo/; x.com/d4eo, pg 456

Dignard, Herve, Institut de cooperation pour l'education des adultes-ICEA (The Institute for Cooperation on Adult Education), 5000 D'Iberville, Suite 304, Montreal, QC H2H 2S6, Canada *Tel:* 514-948-2044 *E-mail:* icae@icea.qc.ca *Web Site:* www.icea.qc.ca, pg 508

Digneit, William, Mildred & Albert Panowski Playwriting Award, Forest Roberts Theatre, 1401 Presque Isle Ave, Marquette, MI 49855-5364 *Tel:* 906-227-2553 *Fax:* 906-227-2567 *E-mail:* theatre@nmu.edu *Web Site:* www.nmu.edu/theatre, pg 645

Dijkstra, Sandra, Sandra Dijkstra Literary Agency, 1155 Camino del Mar, PMB 515, Del Mar, CA 92014-2605 *Web Site:* dijkstraagency.com, pg 456

Diklich-Newell, Thea, Little, Brown and Company, 1290 Avenue of the Americas, New York, NY 10104 *Tel:* 212-364-1100 *Fax:* 212-364-0952 *E-mail:* firstname.lastname@hbgusa.com *Web Site:* www.hachettebookgroup.com/imprint/little-brown-and-company/, pg 118

Dilanyan, Rema, Peter Lampack Agency Inc, 350 Fifth Ave, Suite 5300, New York, NY 10118 *Tel:* 212-687-9106 *Fax:* 212-687-9109 *Web Site:* www.peterlampackagency.com, pg 467

Dillard-Steels, Tammy, Alex Awards, 225 N Michigan Ave, Suite 1300, Chicago, IL 60601 *Tel:* 312-280-4390 *Toll Free Tel:* 800-545-2433 *E-mail:* yalsa@ala.org *Web Site:* www.ala.org/yalsa/alex-awards, pg 572

Dillard-Steels, Tammy, Margaret A Edwards Award, 225 N Michigan Ave, Suite 1300, Chicago, IL 60601 *Tel:* 312-280-4390 *Toll Free Tel:* 800-545-2433 *E-mail:* yalsa@ala.org *Web Site:* www.ala.org/yalsa/edwards-award, pg 598

Dillard-Steels, Tammy, Excellence in Nonfiction for Young Adults, 225 N Michigan Ave, Suite 1300, Chicago, IL 60601 *Toll Free Tel:* 800-545-2433 (ext 4390) *E-mail:* yalsa@ala.org *Web Site:* www.ala.org/yalsa/nonfiction-award, pg 601

Dillard-Steels, Tammy, Frances Henne/YALSA Research Grant, 225 N Michigan Ave, Suite 1300, Chicago, IL 60601 *Tel:* 312-280-4390 *Toll Free Tel:* 800-545-2433 *E-mail:* yalsa@ala.org *Web Site:* www.ala.org/yalsa/awardsandgrants/franceshenne, pg 604

Dillard-Steels, Tammy, Odyssey Award for Excellence in Audiobook Production, 225 N Michigan Ave, Suite 1300, Chicago, IL 60601 *Toll Free Tel:* 800-545-2433 (ext 4390) *E-mail:* yalsa@ala.org *Web Site:* www.ala.org/yalsa/odyssey, pg 643

Dillard-Steels, Tammy, Michael L Printz Award, 225 N Michigan Ave, Suite 1300, Chicago, IL 60601 *Tel:* 312-280-4390 *Toll Free Tel:* 800-545-2433 *E-mail:* yalsa@ala.org *Web Site:* www.ala.org/yalsa/printz-award, pg 653

Dillard-Steels, Tammy, YALSA Conference Grants, 225 N Michigan Ave, Suite 1300, Chicago, IL 60601 *Tel:* 312-280-4390 *Toll Free Tel:* 800-545-2433 *E-mail:* yalsa@ala.org *Web Site:* www.ala.org/yalsa/awardsandgrants.bakertayloryalsa, pg 679

Dilley, Andrea Palpant, Zondervan, 3900 Sparks Dr SE, Grand Rapids, MI 49546 *Tel:* 616-698-6900 *Toll Free Tel:* 800-226-1122; 800-727-1309 (retail orders) *Fax:* 616-698-3350 *Toll Free Fax:* 800-698-3256 (retail orders) *E-mail:* customercare@harpercollins.com *Web Site:* www.zondervan.com, pg 236

Dillman, Susanne Edes, Standard Publishing Corp, 10 High St, Boston, MA 02110 *Tel:* 617-457-0600 *Toll Free Tel:* 800-682-5759 *Fax:* 617-457-0608 *Web Site:* www.spcpub.com, pg 197

Dillon, Christine, Penguin Random House LLC, 1745 Broadway, New York, NY 10019 *Tel:* 212-782-9000 *Toll Free Tel:* 800-726-0600 *Web Site:* www.penguinrandomhouse.com, pg 155

Dillon Fried, Rachel, Sanford J Greenburger Associates Inc, 55 Fifth Ave, New York, NY 10003 *Tel:* 212-206-5600 *Web Site:* greenburger.com, pg 461

Dillon, Sanyu, Random House Publishing Group, 1745 Broadway, New York, NY 10019 *Toll Free Tel:* 800-200-3552 *Web Site:* www.randomhousebooks.com, pg 170

Dilluvio, Diane, Macmillan, 120 Broadway, 22nd fl, New York, NY 10271 *E-mail:* press.inquiries@macmillan.com *Web Site:* us.macmillan.com, pg 122

DiLoreto, Hilary, Alfred A Knopf, c/o Penguin Random House LLC, 1745 Broadway, New York, NY 10019 *Tel:* 212-751-2600 *Fax:* 212-940-7390 (dom rts); 212-572-2662 (foreign rts) *Web Site:* knopfdoubleday.com/imprint/knopf/; knopfdoubleday.com, pg 110

Dilworth, Rob, Duke University Press, 905 W Main St, Suite 18B, Durham, NC 27701 *Tel:* 919-688-5134 *Toll Free Tel:* 888-651-0122 (US) *Fax:* 919-688-2615 *Toll Free Fax:* 888-651-0124 *E-mail:* orders@dukepress.edu *Web Site:* www.dukepress.edu, pg 62

DiMartino, Sunny, Round Table Companies, PO Box 1603, Deerfield, IL 60015 *Toll Free Tel:* 833-750-5683 *Web Site:* www.roundtablecompanies.com, pg 177

Dimbleby, Robert, Hogrefe Publishing Corp, 44 Merrimac St, Suite 207, Newburyport, MA 01950 *Tel:* 978-255-3700 (off) *E-mail:* customersupport@hogrefe.com *Web Site:* www.hogrefe.com/us, pg 93

Dimnik, Michelle, Rocky Mountain Book Award, PO Box 42, Lethbridge, AB T1J 3Y3, Canada *Tel:* 403-381-7164 *E-mail:* rockymountainbookaward@shaw.ca *Web Site:* www.rmba.info, pg 657

Dimock, Kate, Springer Publishing Co, 11 W 42 St, 15th fl, New York, NY 10036-8002 *Tel:* 212-431-4370 *Toll Free Tel:* 877-687-7476 *E-mail:* marketing@springerpub.com; cs@springerpub.com (orders); textbook@springerpub.com; specialsales@springerpub.com *Web Site:* www.springerpub.com, pg 196

DiMona, Lisa, Writers House, 21 W 26 St, New York, NY 10010 *Tel:* 212-685-2400 *Web Site:* www.writershouse.com, pg 482

Dinardo, Jeff, Red Chair Press, PO Box 333, South Egremont, MA 01258-0333 *Tel:* 413-528-2398 (edit off) *Toll Free Tel:* 800-328-4929 (orders & cust serv) *E-mail:* info@redchairpress.com *Web Site:* www.redchairpress.com, pg 172

Dinas, Jackie, Kensington Publishing Corp, 900 Third Ave, 26th fl, New York, NY 10022 *Tel:* 212-407-1500 *Toll Free Tel:* 800-221-2647 *Fax:* 212-935-0699 *Web Site:* www.kensingtonbooks.com, pg 109

Ding, Kristine, University of Illinois Press, 1325 S Oak St, MC-566, Champaign, IL 61820-6903 *Tel:* 217-333-0950 *Fax:* 217-244-8082 *E-mail:* uipress@uillinois.edu; journals@uillinois.edu *Web Site:* www.press.uillinois.edu, pg 216

Dinger, Angela, William H Sadlier Inc, 9 Pine St, New York, NY 10005 *Tel:* 212-227-2120 *Toll Free Tel:* 800-221-5175 (cust serv) *Fax:* 212-312-6080 *E-mail:* customerservice@sadlier.com *Web Site:* www.sadlier.com, pg 179

Dinger, Frank S, William H Sadlier Inc, 9 Pine St, New York, NY 10005 *Tel:* 212-227-2120 *Toll Free Tel:* 800-221-5175 (cust serv) *Fax:* 212-312-6080 *E-mail:* customerservice@sadlier.com *Web Site:* www.sadlier.com, pg 179

Dinizulu, Kwabena, Penguin Random House Speakers Bureau, a Penguin Random House company, 1745 Broadway, Mail Drop 13-1, New York, NY 10019 *Tel:* 212-572-2013 *E-mail:* speakers@penguinrandomhouse.com *Web Site:* www.prhspeakers.com, pg 487

Dinkins, Joyce, Our Daily Bread Publishing, 3000 Kraft Ave SE, Grand Rapids, MI 49512 *Toll Free Tel:* 800-653-8333 (cust serv) *E-mail:* customerservice@odb.org *Web Site:* ourdailybreadpublishing.org, pg 148

Dinovis, Marisa, Random House Children's Books, c/o Penguin Random House LLC, 1745 Broadway, New York, NY 10019 *Tel:* 212-782-9000 *Web Site:* www.rhcbooks.com, pg 170

Dinstman, Lee, APA Talent & Literary Agency, 405 S Beverly Dr, Beverly Hills, CA 90212 *Tel:* 310-888-4200 *Web Site:* www.apa-agency.com, pg 449

Dion, Meagan, Individual Artist Fellowships, 1004 Farnam, Plaza Level, Omaha, NE 68102 *Tel:* 402-595-2122 *E-mail:* nac.info@nebraska.gov *Web Site:* www.artscouncil.nebraska.gov, pg 616

DiPasquale, Erika, HarperCollins Children's Books, 195 Broadway, New York, NY 10007 *Tel:* 212-207-7000 *Web Site:* www.harpercollins.com/childrens, pg 85

DiPasquale, Megan, Quirk Books, 215 Church St, Philadelphia, PA 19106 *Tel:* 215-627-3581 *Fax:* 215-627-5220 *E-mail:* general@quirkbooks.com *Web Site:* www.quirkbooks.com, pg 168

diPierro, Alyssa, Atria Books, 1230 Avenue of the Americas, New York, NY 10020 *Tel:* 212-698-7000 *Fax:* 212-698-7007 *Web Site:* www.simonandschuster.com, pg 21

DiPietro, Hannah, Sourcebooks LLC, 1935 Brookdale Rd, Suite 139, Naperville, IL 60563 *Tel:* 630-961-3900 *Toll Free Tel:* 800-432-7444 *Fax:* 630-961-2168 *E-mail:* info@sourcebooks.com *Web Site:* www.sourcebooks.com, pg 195

DiPreta, Mauro, HarperCollins Publishers LLC, 195 Broadway, New York, NY 10007 *Tel:* 212-207-7000 *Web Site:* www.harpercollins.com, pg 86

DiRienzo, Katy, Macmillan, 120 Broadway, 22nd fl, New York, NY 10271 *E-mail:* press.inquiries@macmillan.com *Web Site:* us.macmillan.com, pg 122

DiSabatino, Nicholas, The MIT Press, One Broadway, 12th fl, Cambridge, MA 02142 Tel: 617-253-5255 Toll Free Tel: 800-405-1619 (orders) Fax: 617-258-6779; 617-577-1545 (orders) Web Site: mitpress.mit.edu, pg 132

DiSalvo, Sara, Holiday House Publishing Inc, 50 Broad St, New York, NY 10004 Tel: 212-688-0085 Fax: 212-421-6134 E-mail: info@holidayhouse.com Web Site: www.holidayhouse.com, pg 94

DiSalvo, Sara, Peachtree Publishing Co Inc, 1700 Chattahoochee Ave, Atlanta, GA 30318-2112 Tel: 404-876-8761 Toll Free Tel: 800-241-0113 Fax: 404-875-2578 Toll Free Fax: 800-875-8909 E-mail: hello@peachtree-online.com; orders@peachtree-online.com; sales@peachtree-online.com Web Site: www.peachtreebooks.com; www.peachtree-online.com, pg 153

DiSanto, Drohan, Vanderbilt University Press, 2301 Vanderbilt Place, PMB 401813, Nashville, TN 37240-1813 Tel: 615-322-3585 Toll Free Tel: 800-848-6224 (orders only) Fax: 615-343-0308 E-mail: vupress@vanderbilt.edu Web Site: www.vanderbiltuniversitypress.com, pg 224

DiSanto, Phil, Harry N Abrams Inc, 195 Broadway, 9th fl, New York, NY 10007 Tel: 212-206-7715 Toll Free Tel: 800-345-1359 Fax: 212-645-8437 E-mail: abrams@abramsbooks.com; publicity@abramsbooks.com; sales@abramsbooks.com Web Site: www.abramsbooks.com, pg 2

Dishmon, Kade, Holiday House Publishing Inc, 50 Broad St, New York, NY 10004 Tel: 212-688-0085 Fax: 212-421-6134 E-mail: info@holidayhouse.com Web Site: www.holidayhouse.com, pg 94

Dissen, Matthew, Melanie Jackson Agency LLC, 41 W 72 St, Suite 3F, New York, NY 10023 Web Site: www.mjalit.com, pg 464

Dissinger, Amanda, Bloomsbury Publishing Inc, 1385 Broadway, 5th fl, New York, NY 10018 Tel: 212-419-5300 E-mail: marketingusa@bloomsbury.com; adultpublicityusa@bloomsbury.com; askacademic@bloomsbury.com Web Site: www.bloomsbury.com, pg 32

Dissinger, Deanne, American Law Institute, 4025 Chestnut St, Philadelphia, PA 19104-3099 Tel: 215-243-1600 Toll Free Tel: 800-253-6397 E-mail: custserv@ali.org Web Site: www.ali.org, pg 10

Distelberg, Brian, Basic Books Group, 1290 Avenue of the Americas, New York, NY 10104 Tel: 212-340-8100 Toll Free Tel: 800-343-4499 (cust serv) Fax: 212-340-8105 E-mail: customer.service@hbgusa.com; orders@hbgusa.com Web Site: www.hachettebookgroup.com/imprint/basic-books/, pg 25

Ditchburn, Jennifer, Institute for Research on Public Policy (IRPP), 1470 Peel St, No 200, Montreal, QC H3A 1T1, Canada Tel: 514-985-2461 Fax: 514-985-2559 E-mail: irpp@irpp.org Web Site: irpp.org, pg 410

Ditchik, Seth, Yale University Press, 302 Temple St, New Haven, CT 06511-8909 Tel: 203-432-0960; 203-432-0966 (sales); 401-531-2800 (cust serv) Toll Free Tel: 800-405-1619 (cust serv) Fax: 203-432-0948; 203-432-8485 (sales); 401-531-2801 (cust serv) Toll Free Fax: 800-406-9145 (cust serv) E-mail: sales.press@yale.edu (sales); customer.care@triliteral.org (cust serv) Web Site: www.yalebooks.com; yalepress.yale.edu/yupbooks, pg 235

Divelbiss, Andie, Little, Brown Books for Young Readers (LBYR), 1290 Avenue of the Americas, New York, NY 10104 Tel: 212-364-1100 Toll Free Tel: 800-759-0190 (cust serv) E-mail: rights@lbchildrens.com Web Site: www.hachettebookgroup.com/imprint/little-brown-books-for-young-readers/, pg 118

Diver, Lucienne, The Knight Agency Inc, 232 W Washington St, Madison, GA 30650 E-mail: admin@knightagency.net Web Site: www.knightagency.net, pg 466

Dixon, Debra, BelleBooks, PO Box 300921, Memphis, TN 38130 Tel: 901-344-9024 Fax: 901-344-9068 E-mail: bellebooks@bellebooks.com Web Site: www.bellebooks.com, pg 27

DJangi, Taraneh, Penguin Random House Audio Publishing Group, 1745 Broadway, New York, NY 10019 Toll Free Tel: 800-793-2665 (cust serv) E-mail: audio@penguinrandomhouse.com; ecustomerservice@penguinrandomhouse.com Web Site: www.penguinrandomhouseaudio.com, pg 154

Dlouhy, Caitlyn, Simon & Schuster Children's Publishing, 1230 Avenue of the Americas, New York, NY 10020 Tel: 212-698-7000 Web Site: www.simonandschuster.com/kids; www.simonandschuster.com/teen; simonandschuster.net; simonandschuster.biz, pg 189

Do, Quynh, Alfred A Knopf, c/o Penguin Random House LLC, 1745 Broadway, New York, NY 10019 Tel: 212-751-2600 Fax: 212-940-7390 (dom rts); 212-572-2662 (foreign rts) Web Site: knopfdoubleday.com/imprint/knopf/; knopfdoubleday.com, pg 110

Dobday, Kate, James Beard Foundation Book Awards, 167 W 12 St, New York, NY 10011 Tel: 212-627-2308 E-mail: awards@jamesbeard.org Web Site: www.jamesbeard.org/awards, pg 578

Dobinick, Susan, Astra Books for Young Readers, 19 W 21 St, No 1201, New York, NY 10010 Tel: 646-844-3485 E-mail: ahinfo@astrahouse.com; permissions@astrapublishinghouse.com Web Site: astrapublishinghouse.com, pg 20

Dobles, Gustavo, Wolters Kluwer Law & Business, 76 Ninth Ave, 7th fl, New York, NY 10011-5201 Tel: 212-771-0600; 301-698-7100 (cust serv outside US) Toll Free Tel: 800-234-1660 (cust serv) E-mail: customer.service@wolterskluwer.com; lrusmedia@wolterskluwer.com Web Site: lrus.wolterskluwer.com, pg 232

Dobrenis, Dylan, Macmillan, 120 Broadway, 22nd fl, New York, NY 10271 E-mail: press.inquiries@macmillan.com Web Site: us.macmillan.com, pg 122

Dobrow, Julie, Boston Authors Club Inc, c/o Prof Julie Dobrow, 103 Conant Rd, Lincoln, MA 01773 Tel: 781-259-1220 E-mail: bostonauthorsclub2@gmail.com Web Site: bostonauthorsclub.org, pg 501

Dobrow, Julie, Julia Ward Howe Book Awards, c/o Prof Julie Dobrow, 103 Conant Rd, Lincoln, MA 01773 Tel: 781-259-1220 E-mail: bostonauthorsclub2@gmail.com Web Site: bostonauthorsclub.org, pg 614

Dobson, Allison, Penguin Publishing Group, c/o Penguin Random House LLC, 1745 Broadway, New York, NY 10019 Tel: 212-782-9000 Web Site: www.penguin.com, pg 154

Dobson, David, Presbyterian Publishing Corp (PPC), 100 Witherspoon St, Louisville, KY 40202 Tel: 502-569-5000 Toll Free Tel: 800-533-4371; 800-523-1631 (US only) Fax: 502-569-5113 E-mail: customerservice@presbypub.com Web Site: www.ppcbooks.com; www.wjkbooks.com, pg 163

Dobson, David, Westminster John Knox Press (WJK), 100 Witherspoon St, Louisville, KY 40202-1396 Tel: 502-569-5052 Toll Free Tel: 800-523-1631 (US & CN) Fax: 502-569-8308 Toll Free Fax: 800-541-5113 (US & CN) E-mail: customer_service@wjkbooks.com; orders@wjkbooks.com Web Site: www.wjkbooks.com, pg 228

Dobson, Megan, Zondervan, 3900 Sparks Dr SE, Grand Rapids, MI 49546 Tel: 616-698-6900 Toll Free Tel: 800-226-1122; 800-727-1309 (retail orders) Fax: 616-698-3350 Toll Free Fax: 800-698-3256 (retail orders) E-mail: customercare@harpercollins.com Web Site: www.zondervan.com, pg 236

Dobson, Paige, Wood Lake Publishing Inc, 485 Beaver Lake Rd, Kelowna, BC V4V 1S5, Canada Tel: 250-766-2778 Toll Free Tel: 800-663-2775 (orders & cust serv) Fax: 250-766-2736 Toll Free Fax: 888-841-9991 (orders & cust serv) E-mail: info@woodlake.com; customerservice@woodlake.com Web Site: www.woodlake.com, pg 425

Dockrill, Dawn, Research Press, 2612 N Mattis Ave, Champaign, IL 61822 Tel: 217-352-3273 Toll Free Tel: 800-519-2707 Fax: 217-352-1221 E-mail: rp@researchpress.com; orders@researchpress.com Web Site: www.researchpress.com, pg 174

Dodd, Michael A, Liturgy Training Publications, 3949 S Racine Ave, Chicago, IL 60609-2523 Tel: 773-579-4900 Toll Free Tel: 800-933-1800 (US & CN only orders) Fax: 773-579-4929 E-mail: orders@ltp.org Web Site: www.ltp.org, pg 119

Dodds, Andy, Grand Central Publishing, 1290 Avenue of the Americas, New York, NY 10104 Tel: 212-364-1100 Web Site: www.hachettebookgroup.com/imprint/grand-central-publishing/, pg 80

Dodes, Jeff, St Martin's Press, LLC, 120 Broadway, New York, NY 10271 E-mail: publicity@stmartins.com; trademarketing@stmartins.com; foreignrights@stmartins.com Web Site: us.macmillan.com/smp, pg 180

Dodillet, Katie, Tyndale House Publishers Inc, 351 Executive Dr, Carol Stream, IL 60188 Tel: 630-668-8300 Toll Free Tel: 800-323-9400; 855-277-9400 Toll Free Fax: 866-622-9474 Web Site: www.tyndale.com, pg 211

Dodson, Kathy, RISING STAR Award, PO Box 190, Jefferson, OR 97352 E-mail: risingstar@womenfictionwriters.org Web Site: wfwa.memberclicks.net/rising-star-award, pg 656

Dodson, Kathy, STAR Award, PO Box 190, Jefferson, OR 97352 E-mail: staraward@womenfictionwriters.org Web Site: wfwa.memberclicks.net/star-award, pg 666

Dodson, Kathy, Women's Fiction Writers Association (WFWA), PO Box 190, Jefferson, OR 97352 E-mail: communications@womensfictionwriters.org; membership@womensfictionwriters.org; programs@womensfictionwriters.org Web Site: www.womensfictionwriters.org, pg 522

Dodson, Lyric, Sounds True Inc, 413 S Arthur Ave, Louisville, CO 80027 Tel: 303-665-3151 Toll Free Tel: 800-333-9185 (US); 888-303-9185 (US & CN) E-mail: customerservice@soundstrue.com; stpublicity@soundstrue.com Web Site: www.soundstrue.com, pg 194

Dodson, Veronique, National Association of Black Journalists (NABJ), 1100 Knight Hall, Suite 3101, College Park, MD 20742 Tel: 301-405-0248 E-mail: contact@nabj.org; press@nabj.org Web Site: nabjonline.org, pg 511

Doebler, Julie, Simon & Schuster Children's Publishing, 1230 Avenue of the Americas, New York, NY 10020 Tel: 212-698-7000 Web Site: www.simonandschuster.com/kids; www.simonandschuster.com/teen; simonandschuster.net; simonandschuster.biz, pg 189

Doerr, Jennifer, Yale University Press, 302 Temple St, New Haven, CT 06511-8909 Tel: 203-432-0960; 203-432-0966 (sales); 401-531-2800 (cust serv) Toll Free Tel: 800-405-1619 (cust serv) Fax: 203-432-0948; 203-432-8485 (sales); 401-531-2801 (cust serv) Toll Free Fax: 800-406-9145 (cust serv) E-mail: sales.press@yale.edu (sales); customer.care@triliteral.org (cust serv) Web Site: www.yalebooks.com; yalepress.yale.edu/yupbooks, pg 235

Doerr, Susan, University of Minnesota Press, 111 Third Ave S, Suite 290, Minneapolis, MN 55401-2520 Tel: 612-301-1990 Fax: 612-301-1980 E-mail: ump@umn.edu Web Site: www.upress.umn.edu, pg 217

Doherty, Garrett, Association for Information Science & Technology (ASIS&T), 673 Potomac Station Dr, Suite 155, Leesburg, VA 20176 Tel: 301-495-0900 Fax: 301-495-0810 E-mail: asist@asist.org Web Site: www.asist.org, pg 19

Doherty, Garrett, Association for Information Science & Technology (ASIS&T), 673 Potomac Station Dr, Suite 155, Leesburg, VA 20176 Tel: 301-495-0900 Fax: 301-495-0810 E-mail: asist@asist.org; membership@asist.org Web Site: www.asist.org, pg 498

Doherty, Patricia, Macmillan, 120 Broadway, 22nd fl, New York, NY 10271 E-mail: press.inquiries@macmillan.com Web Site: us.macmillan.com, pg 122

Doig, Stephanie, Harlequin Enterprises Ltd, 195 Broadway, 24th fl, New York, NY 10007 Tel: 212-207-7000 Toll Free Tel: 888-432-4879; 800-370-

5838 (ebooks) *E-mail:* customerservice@harlequin. com *Web Site:* www.harlequin.com/shop/index.html; corporate.harlequin.com, pg 85

Doig, Stephanie, Harlequin Enterprises Ltd, Bay Adelaide Centre, East Tower, 22 Adelaide St W, 41st fl, Toronto, ON M5H 4E3, Canada *Tel:* 416-445-5860 *Toll Free Tel:* 888-432-4879; 800-370-5838 (ebook inquiries) *E-mail:* customerservice@harlequin.com *Web Site:* www.harlequin.com, pg 409

Dokos, Janna, St Martin's Press, LLC, 120 Broadway, New York, NY 10271 *E-mail:* publicity@stmartins. com; trademarketing@stmartins.com; foreignrights@ stmartins.com *Web Site:* us.macmillan.com/smp, pg 181

Dolan, Eamon, Simon & Schuster, 1230 Avenue of the Americas, New York, NY 10020 *Tel:* 212-698-7000 *Toll Free Tel:* 800-223-2348 (cust serv); 800-223-2336 (orders) *Toll Free Fax:* 800-943-9831 (orders) *Web Site:* simonandschusterpublishing.com/ simonandschuster/, pg 188

Dolan, Emma, Penguin Random House Canada, a Penguin Random House company, 320 Front St W, Suite 1400, Toronto, ON M5V 3B6, Canada *Tel:* 416-364-4449 *Toll Free Tel:* 888-523-9292 (cust serv) *E-mail:* canadaweb@penguinrandomhouse.com; customerservicescanada@penguinrandomhouse.com *Web Site:* www.penguinrandomhouse.ca, pg 416

Dolce, Holly, Harry N Abrams Inc, 195 Broadway, 9th fl, New York, NY 10007 *Tel:* 212-206-7715 *Toll Free Tel:* 800-345-1359 *Fax:* 212-645-8437 *E-mail:* abrams@abramsbooks.com; publicity@ abramsbooks.com; sales@abramsbooks.com *Web Site:* www.abramsbooks.com, pg 2

Dole, Jason, World Book Inc, 180 N LaSalle, Suite 900, Chicago, IL 60601 *Tel:* 312-729-5800 *Toll Free Tel:* 800-967-5325 (consumer sales, US); 800-975-3250 (school & lib sales, US); 800-837-5365 (school & lib sales, CN) *Toll Free Fax:* 888-922-3766 *E-mail:* customerservice@worldbook.com *Web Site:* www.worldbook.com, pg 233

Dolechek, Melanie, Society for Scholarly Publishing (SSP), 1120 Rte 73, Suite 200, Mount Laurel, NJ 08054 *Tel:* 856-439-1385 *Fax:* 856-439-0525 *E-mail:* info@sspnet.org *Web Site:* www.sspnet.org, pg 519

Doliveux, Maelle, Beehive Books, 4700 Kingsessing Ave, Suite C, Philadelphia, PA 19143 *E-mail:* beehivebook@gmail.com *Web Site:* www. beehivebooks.net, pg 26

Doll, Holly, Fitzhenry & Whiteside Limited, 209 Wicksteed Ave, Unit 51, Markham, ON M4G 0B1, Canada *Tel:* 905-477-9700 *Toll Free Tel:* 800-387-9776 *Fax:* 905-477-2834 *E-mail:* bookinfo@fitzhenry. ca *Web Site:* www.fitzhenry.ca, pg 406

Doll, Holly, Red Deer Press Inc, 209 Wicksteed Ave, Unit 51, Toronto, ON M4G 0B1, Canada *Tel:* 905-477-9700 *Toll Free Tel:* 800-387-9776 *E-mail:* bookinfo@fitzhenry.ca *Web Site:* www. reddeerpress.com, pg 417

Doll, Holly, Whitecap Books, 314 W Cordova St, Suite 209, Vancouver, BC V6B 1E8, Canada *Tel:* 604-681-6181 *Web Site:* www.whitecap.ca, pg 424

Dollar, Douglas, New Forums Press Inc, 1018 S Lewis St, Stillwater, OK 74074 *Tel:* 405-372-6158 *Toll Free Tel:* 800-606-3766 *Fax:* 405-377-2237 *Web Site:* www. newforums.com, pg 139

Dollar, Emma, Viking Penguin, c/o Penguin Random House LLC, 1745 Broadway, New York, NY 10019 *Tel:* 212-782-9000 *Web Site:* www.penguin.com/ overview-vikingbooks/; www.penguin.com/pamela-dorman-books-overview/; www.penguin.com/penguin-classics-overview/; www.penguin.com/penguin-life-overview/, pg 225

Dollins, Christy, Christian Retail Association Inc (CRA), 200 West Bay Dr, Largo, FL 33770 *Tel:* 727-596-7625 *Toll Free Tel:* 800-868-4388 *Fax:* 727-593-3523 *Toll Free Fax:* 855-815-9277 *E-mail:* service@munce.com *Web Site:* www.christianretailassociation.org, pg 503

Dols, Amy, The Child's World Inc, 21735 E Idyllwilde Dr, Parker, CO 80138-8892 *Toll Free Tel:* 800-599-READ (599-7323) *Toll Free Fax:* 888-320-2329 *E-mail:* info@childsworld.com *Web Site:* www. childsworld.com, pg 46

Domantey, Paige, Bloomsbury Academic, 1385 Broadway, 5th fl, New York, NY 10018 *Tel:* 212-419-5300 *Web Site:* www.bloomsbury.com/us/academic, pg 31

Dombroski, Angela, Candlewick Press, 99 Dover St, Somerville, MA 02144-2825 *Tel:* 617-661-3330 *Fax:* 617-661-0565 *E-mail:* bigbear@candlewick.com; salesinfo@candlewick.com *Web Site:* candlewick.com, pg 40

Domenech, Marisa, HarperCollins Publishers LLC, 195 Broadway, New York, NY 10007 *Tel:* 212-207-7000 *Web Site:* www.harpercollins.com, pg 86

Dominguez, Adriana, Aevitas Creative Management LLC, 19 W 21 St, Suite 501, New York, NY 10010 *Tel:* 212-765-6900 *Web Site:* www.aevitascreative.com, pg 448

Dominguez, Ginny, Henry Holt and Company, LLC, 120 Broadway, 23rd fl, New York, NY 10271 *Tel:* 646-307-5151 *Toll Free Tel:* 888-330-8477 (orders) *Fax:* 646-307-5285 *Web Site:* www.henryholt.com, pg 94

Dominguez, Ginny, Roaring Brook Press, 120 Broadway, New York, NY 10271 *Tel:* 646-307-5151 *Web Site:* us. macmillan.com/publishers/roaring-brook-press, pg 176

Dominguez, Ivan J, Inside Literary Prize, 2666 State St, Suite 5A, Hamden, CT 06517 *E-mail:* freedomreads@ freedomreads.org *Web Site:* freedomreads.org/showing-up/inside-literary-prize, pg 616

Dominguez, Maria, Scholastic Trade Publishing, 557 Broadway, New York, NY 10012 *Tel:* 212-343-6100; 212-343-4685 (export sales) *Fax:* 212-343-4714 (export sales) *Web Site:* www.scholastic.com, pg 184

Dominguez, Michelle, Knopf Doubleday Publishing Group, c/o Penguin Random House LLC, 1745 Broadway, New York, NY 10019 *Tel:* 212-751-2600 *Fax:* 212-940-7390 (dom rts); 212-572-2662 (foreign rts) *Web Site:* knopfdoubleday.com, pg 110

Dominguez, Michelle, Penguin Random House LLC, 1745 Broadway, New York, NY 10019 *Tel:* 212-782-9000 *Toll Free Tel:* 800-726-0600 *Web Site:* www. penguinrandomhouse.com, pg 155

Dominguez, Sonia, DeVorss & Co, 1100 Flynn Rd, Unit 104, Camarillo, CA 93012 *Tel:* 805-322-9010 *Toll Free Tel:* 800-843-5743 *Fax:* 805-322-9011 *E-mail:* service@devorss.com *Web Site:* www.devorss. com, pg 59

Dominiak, Michele, American Institute of Aeronautics and Astronautics (AIAA), 12700 Sunrise Valley Dr, Suite 200, Reston, VA 20191-5807 *Tel:* 703-264-7500 *Toll Free Tel:* 800-639-AIAA (639-2422) *Fax:* 703-264-7551 *E-mail:* custserv@aiaa.org *Web Site:* www. aiaa.org; arc.aiaa.org (orders), pg 10

Dommert, Abby, HarperCollins Children's Books, 195 Broadway, New York, NY 10007 *Tel:* 212-207-7000 *Web Site:* www.harpercollins.com/childrens, pg 85

Donaher, Br Edward, St Pauls, 2187 Victory Blvd, Staten Island, NY 10314-6603 *Tel:* 718-761-0047 (edit & prodn); 718-698-2759 (mktg & billing) *Toll Free Tel:* 800-343-2522 *Fax:* 718-761-0057 *E-mail:* sales@ stpauls.us; marketing@stpauls.us *Web Site:* www. stpauls.us, pg 181

Donahue, Bevin, North Atlantic Books (NAB), 2526 Martin Luther King Jr Way, Berkeley, CA 94704 *Tel:* 510-549-4270 *Web Site:* www.northatlanticbooks. com, pg 142

Donahue, Suzanne, Atria Books, 1230 Avenue of the Americas, New York, NY 10020 *Tel:* 212-698-7000 *Fax:* 212-698-7007 *Web Site:* www.simonandschuster. com, pg 21

Donalty, Alison, HarperCollins Children's Books, 195 Broadway, New York, NY 10007 *Tel:* 212-207-7000 *Web Site:* www.harpercollins.com/childrens, pg 85

Donatich, John, Yale University Press, 302 Temple St, New Haven, CT 06511-8909 *Tel:* 203-432-0960; 203-432-0966 (sales); 401-531-2800 (cust serv) *Toll Free Tel:* 800-405-1619 (cust serv) *Fax:* 203-432-0948; 203-432-8485 (sales); 401-531-2801 (cust serv) *Toll Free Fax:* 800-406-9145 (cust serv) *E-mail:* sales. press@yale.edu (sales); customer.care@triliteral.org (cust serv) *Web Site:* www.yalebooks.com; yalepress. yale.edu/yupbooks, pg 235

Donato, Paul, Advertising Research Foundation (ARF), 432 Park Ave S, 4th fl, New York, NY 10016 *Tel:* 212-751-5656 *Fax:* 212-689-1859 *E-mail:* membership@thearf.org; new-member-info@ thearf.org *Web Site:* thearf.org, pg 493, 525

Donato, Tony, Golden Cylinder Awards, 150 Executive Center Dr, Suite 201, Greenville, SC 29615 *Tel:* 803-948-9470 *Fax:* 803-948-9471 *E-mail:* aimcal@aimcal. org *Web Site:* gaa.org/awards/golden-cylinder-awards, pg 607

Donato, Tony, Gravure AIMCAL Alliance (GAA), 150 Executive Center Dr, Suite 201, Greenville, SC 29615 *Tel:* 803-948-9470 *Fax:* 803-948-9471 *E-mail:* aimcal@aimcal.org *Web Site:* gaa.org, pg 507

Donilon, Shawn, National Association of Broadcasters (NAB), One "M" St SE, Washington, DC 20003 *Tel:* 202-429-5300 *E-mail:* nab@nab.org *Web Site:* www.nab.org, pg 136, 511

Donlon, Anne, Committee on Scholarly Editions, c/o Modern Language Association of America, 85 Broad St, Suite 500, New York, NY 10004-2434 *Tel:* 646-646-5000 *E-mail:* cse@mla.org *Web Site:* www.mla. org, pg 504

Donnaud, Janis A, Janis A Donnaud & Associates Inc, 77 Bleecker St, No C1-25, New York, NY 10012 *Tel:* 212-431-2663 *Fax:* 212-431-2667 *E-mail:* jdonnaud@aol.com, pg 456

Donnelly, Sean, The Danahy Fiction Prize, University of Tampa Press, 401 W Kennedy Blvd, Tampa, FL 33606 *Tel:* 813-253-6266 *E-mail:* utpress@ut.edu *Web Site:* tampareview.org/the-danahy-fiction-prize, pg 594

Donnelly, Sean, The Tampa Review Prize for Poetry, University of Tampa Press, 401 W Kennedy Blvd, Tampa, FL 33606 *Tel:* 813-253-6266 *E-mail:* utpress@ ut.edu *Web Site:* tampareview.org/the-tampa-review-prize-for-poetry, pg 668

Donnelly, Shannon, Diversion Books, 11 E 44 St, Suite 1603, New York, NY 10017 *Tel:* 212-961-6390 *E-mail:* info@diversionbooks.com *Web Site:* www. diversionbooks.com, pg 60

Donoghue, John, Facts On File, 1000 N West St, Suite 1281-230, Wilmington, DE 19801 *Tel:* 212-967-8800 *Toll Free Tel:* 800-322-8755 *Toll Free Fax:* 800-678-3633 *E-mail:* custserv@factsonfile.com *Web Site:* infobasepublishing.com, pg 69

Donoghue, John, Ferguson Publishing, 132 W 31 St, 16 fl, New York, NY 10001 *Tel:* 212-967-8800 *Toll Free Tel:* 800-322-8755 *Toll Free Fax:* 800-678-3633 *E-mail:* custserv@infobase.com *Web Site:* infobasepublishing.com, pg 71

Donovan, Danica, The Experiment, 220 E 23 St, Suite 600, New York, NY 10010-4658 *Tel:* 212-889-1659 *E-mail:* info@theexperimentpublishing.com *Web Site:* www.theexperimentpublishing.com, pg 68

Donovan, Jennifer, Penguin Random House Audio Publishing Group, 1745 Broadway, New York, NY 10019 *Toll Free Tel:* 800-793-2665 (cust serv) *E-mail:* audio@penguinrandomhouse.com; ecustomerservice@penguinrandomhouse.com *Web Site:* www.penguinrandomhouseaudio.com, pg 154

Donovan, Jim, Jim Donovan Literary, 5635 SMU Blvd, Suite 201, Dallas, TX 75206 *Tel:* 214-696-9411 *E-mail:* jdlqueries@sbcglobal.net, pg 456

Donovan, Kerry, Berkley, c/o Penguin Random House LLC, 1745 Broadway, 19th fl, New York, NY 10019 *Tel:* 212-366-2000 *Web Site:* www.penguin.com/ publishers/berkley/; www.penguin.com/ace-overview/, pg 28

Donovan, Lauren, Scholastic Trade Publishing, 557 Broadway, New York, NY 10012 Tel: 212-343-6100; 212-343-4685 (export sales) Fax: 212-343-4714 (export sales) Web Site: www.scholastic.com, pg 184

Donovan, Mary Lee, Candlewick Press, 99 Dover St, Somerville, MA 02144-2825 Tel: 617-661-3330 Fax: 617-661-0565 E-mail: bigbear@candlewick.com; salesinfo@candlewick.com Web Site: candlewick.com, pg 39

Doob, Gabriella, HarperCollins Publishers LLC, 195 Broadway, New York, NY 10007 Tel: 212-207-7000 Web Site: www.harpercollins.com, pg 86

Dooley, Lauren, Scribner, 1230 Avenue of the Americas, New York, NY 10020 Web Site: www.simonandschusterpublishing.com/scribner/, pg 185

Dooley, Theresa, HarperCollins Publishers LLC, 195 Broadway, New York, NY 10007 Tel: 212-207-7000 Web Site: www.harpercollins.com, pg 86

Dooley-Dorocke, Erica, Solution Tree, 555 N Morton St, Bloomington, IN 47404 Tel: 812-336-7700 Toll Free Tel: 800-733-6786 Fax: 812-336-7790 E-mail: pubs@solutiontree.com; orders@solutiontree.com Web Site: www.solutiontree.com, pg 193

Dore, Juliet, Harry N Abrams Inc, 195 Broadway, 9th fl, New York, NY 10007 Tel: 212-206-7715 Toll Free Tel: 800-345-1359 Fax: 212-645-8437 E-mail: abrams@abramsbooks.com; publicity@abramsbooks.com; sales@abramsbooks.com Web Site: www.abramsbooks.com, pg 3

Dorff, Patricia, Council on Foreign Relations Press, The Harold Pratt House, 58 E 68 St, New York, NY 10065 Tel: 212-434-9400 Fax: 212-434-9800 E-mail: publications@cfr.org Web Site: www.cfr.org, pg 53

Dorfman, Debra, Scholastic Trade Publishing, 557 Broadway, New York, NY 10012 Tel: 212-343-6100; 212-343-4685 (export sales) Fax: 212-343-4714 (export sales) Web Site: www.scholastic.com, pg 184

Dorman, Dr Jessica, The Historic New Orleans Collection, 533 Royal St, New Orleans, LA 70130 Tel: 504-523-4662 Fax: 504-598-7108 E-mail: wrc@hnoc.org Web Site: www.hnoc.org, pg 93

Dorman, Pamela, Viking Penguin, c/o Penguin Random House LLC, 1745 Broadway, New York, NY 10019 Tel: 212-782-9000 Web Site: www.penguin.com/overview-vikingbooks/; www.penguin.com/pamela-dorman-books-overview/; www.penguin.com/penguin-classics-overview/; www.penguin.com/penguin-life-overview/, pg 225

Dorresteyn, Windy, Random House Publishing Group, 1745 Broadway, New York, NY 10019 Toll Free Tel: 800-200-3552 Web Site: www.randomhousebooks.com, pg 170

Dos Santos, Alexandra, Vintage Books, c/o Penguin Random House LLC, 1745 Broadway, New York, NY 10019 Tel: 212-572-2420 Fax: 212-940-7390 (dom rts); 212-572-2662 (foreign rts) E-mail: vintageanchorpublicity@randomhouse.com Web Site: knopfdoubleday.com/imprint/vintage; knopfdoubleday.com, pg 225

Dosik, Anita, APPA - Leadership in Education Facilities, 1643 Prince St, Alexandria, VA 22314-2818 Tel: 703-684-1446; 703-542-3837 (bookshop) E-mail: webmaster@appa.org Web Site: www.appa.org, pg 15

Doten, Mark, Soho Press Inc, 853 Broadway, New York, NY 10003 Tel: 212-260-1900 E-mail: soho@sohopress.com; publicity@sohopress.com Web Site: sohopress.com, pg 193

Dotolo, Christie, American Public Works Association (APWA), 1200 Main St, Suite 1400, Kansas City, MO 64105-2100 Tel: 816-472-6100 Toll Free Tel: 800-848-APWA (848-2792) Fax: 816-472-1610 Web Site: www.apwa.org, pg 12

Dotson, Rand, Louisiana State University Press, 338 Johnston Hall, Baton Rouge, LA 70803 Tel: 225-578-6294 E-mail: lsupress@lsu.edu Web Site: lsupress.org, pg 120

Dotto, Gabriel, Michigan State University Press (MSU Press), Manly Miles Bldg, Suite 25, 1405 S Harrison Rd, East Lansing, MI 48823-5245 Tel: 517-355-9543 Fax: 517-432-2611 Web Site: msupress.org, pg 130

Doucet, Christy, Livres Canada Books, One Nicholas, Suite 504, Ottawa, ON K1N 7B7, Canada Tel: 613-562-2324 Fax: 613-562-2329 E-mail: info@livrescanadabooks.com Web Site: www.livrescanadabooks.com, pg 510

Dougan, Jill, Beacon Press, 24 Farnsworth St, Boston, MA 02210-1409 Tel: 617-742-2110 Fax: 617-723-3097 E-mail: production@beacon.org Web Site: www.beacon.org, pg 25

Dougherty, Adria, Union Square & Co, 1166 Avenue of the Americas, 17th fl, New York, NY 10036-2715 Tel: 212-532-7160 Toll Free Tel: 800-367-9692 Fax: 212-213-2495 Toll Free Fax: 800-542-7567 E-mail: custservice@sterlingpublishing.com; customerservice@sterlingpublishing.com; editorial@sterlingpublishing.com; tradesales@sterlingpublishing.com Web Site: www.sterlingpublishing.com, pg 212

Dougherty, Mary V, Juniper Prize for Creative Nonfiction, New Africa House, 180 Infirmary Way, 4th fl, Amherst, MA 01003-9289 E-mail: juniperprize@umpress.umass.edu Web Site: www.umasspress.com/juniper-prizes, pg 619

Dougherty, Mary V, Juniper Prize for Fiction, New Africa House, 180 Infirmary Way, 4th fl, Amherst, MA 01003-9289 E-mail: juniperprize@umpress.umass.edu Web Site: www.umasspress.com/juniper-prizes, pg 619

Dougherty, Mary V, Juniper Prize for Poetry, New Africa House, 180 Infirmary Way, 4th fl, Amherst, MA 01003-9289 E-mail: juniperprize@umpress.umass.edu Web Site: www.umasspress.com/juniper-prizes, pg 619

Dougherty, Mary V, University of Massachusetts Press, New Africa House, 180 Infirmary Way, 4th fl, Amherst, MA 01003-9289 Web Site: www.umasspress.com, pg 217

Dougherty, Oliver, Tor Publishing Group, 120 Broadway, New York, NY 10271 Toll Free Tel: 800-455-0340 (Macmillan) E-mail: torpublicity@tor.com; forgepublicity@forgebooks.com Web Site: us.macmillan.com/torpublishinggroup, pg 208

Dougherty, Peter, American Philosophical Society Press, 104 S Fifth St, Philadelphia, PA 19106 Tel: 215-440-3425 Fax: 215-440-3450 Web Site: www.amphilsoc.org, pg 11

Dougherty, Terence, American Civil Liberties Union (ACLU), 125 Broad St, 18th fl, New York, NY 10004 Tel: 212-549-2500 E-mail: media@aclu.org Web Site: www.aclu.org, pg 495

Doughty, Sarah, Adams Media, 100 Technology Center Dr, Suite 501, Stoughton, MA 02072 Tel: 508-427-7100 Web Site: www.simonandschuster.com, pg 4

Doughty, Todd, Knopf Doubleday Publishing Group, c/o Penguin Random House LLC, 1745 Broadway, New York, NY 10019 Tel: 212-751-2600 Fax: 212-940-7390 (dom rts); 212-572-2662 (foreign rts) Web Site: knopfdoubleday.com, pg 110

Doughty, Todd, Penguin Random House LLC, 1745 Broadway, New York, NY 10019 Tel: 212-782-9000 Toll Free Tel: 800-726-0600 Web Site: www.penguinrandomhouse.com, pg 155

Douglass, Jackie, Sourcebooks LLC, 1935 Brookdale Rd, Suite 139, Naperville, IL 60563 Tel: 630-961-3900 Toll Free Tel: 800-432-7444 Fax: 630-961-2168 E-mail: info@sourcebooks.com Web Site: www.sourcebooks.com, pg 195

Douvris, Mara, Institute of Environmental Sciences & Technology - IEST, 1827 Walden Office Sq, Suite 400, Schaumburg, IL 60173 Tel: 847-981-0100 Fax: 847-981-4130 E-mail: information@iest.org Web Site: www.iest.org, pg 101

Dove, Dawn, Association for Intelligent Information Management (AIIM), 8403 Colesville Rd, No 1100, Silver Spring, MD 20910 Tel: 301-587-8202 Toll Free Tel: 800-477-2446 Fax: 301-587-2711 E-mail: hello@aiim.org Web Site: www.aiim.org, pg 498

Dove, Veronica M, Bernan, 4501 Forbes Blvd, Suite 200, Lanham, MD 20706 Tel: 717-794-3800 (cust serv & orders) Toll Free Tel: 800-462-6420 (cust serv & orders) Fax: 717-794-3803 Toll Free Fax: 800-338-4550 E-mail: customercare@rowman.com; orders@rowman.com; publicity@rowman.com Web Site: rowman.com/page/bernan, pg 28

Dowd, Matthew, University of Notre Dame Press, 310 Flanner Hall, Notre Dame, IN 46556 Tel: 574-631-6346 Fax: 574-631-8148 E-mail: undpress@nd.edu Web Site: www.undpress.nd.edu, pg 219

Dowling, Michael, Bogle Pratt International Library Travel Fund, c/o The American Library Association, 225 N Michigan Ave, Suite 1300, Chicago, IL 60601-7757 Tel: 312-280-3201 Toll Free Tel: 800-545-2433 (ext 3201) Fax: 312-280-4392 E-mail: intl@ala.org Web Site: www.ala.org, pg 582

Downes, Stephan, Shambhala Publications Inc, 2129 13 St, Boulder, CO 80302 Tel: 978-829-2599 (intl callers) Toll Free Tel: 866-424-0030 (off); 888-424-2329 (orders & cust serv) Fax: 617-236-1563 E-mail: customercare@shambhala.com; royalties@shambhala.com Web Site: www.shambhala.com, pg 187

Downes-Le Guin, India, The Ursula K Le Guin Prize for Fiction, 9450 SW Gemini Dr, PMB 51842, Beaverton, OR 97008-7105 E-mail: estateofukl@gmail.com Web Site: www.ursulakleguin.com/prize-overview, pg 622

Downes-Le Guin, India, Tin House Summer Workshop, 2617 NW Thurman St, Portland, OR 97210 Tel: 503-473-8663 Web Site: tinhouse.com/workshop/summer-workshop, pg 558

Downes-Le Guin, India, Tin House Winter Workshop, 2617 NW Thurman St, Portland, OR 97210 Tel: 503-473-8663 Web Site: tinhouse.com/winter-workshop, pg 558

Downes-Le Guin, India, YA Fiction Workshop, 2617 NW Thurman St, Portland, OR 97210 Tel: 503-473-8663 Web Site: tinhouse.com/ya-workshop, pg 559

Downes-Le Guin, Theo, The Ursula K Le Guin Prize for Fiction, 9450 SW Gemini Dr, PMB 51842, Beaverton, OR 97008-7105 E-mail: estateofukl@gmail.com Web Site: www.ursulakleguin.com/prize-overview, pg 622

Downey, Naomi Giges, Jhpiego, 1615 Thames St, Baltimore, MD 21231-3492 Tel: 410-537-1800 E-mail: info@jhpiego.org Web Site: www.jhpiego.org, pg 106

Downing, Kevin, Bloomsbury Academic, 1385 Broadway, 5th fl, New York, NY 10018 Tel: 212-419-5300 Web Site: www.bloomsbury.com/us/academic, pg 31

Doyle, Kate, Tundra Book Group, 320 Front St W, Suite 1400, Toronto, ON M5V 3B6, Canada Tel: 416-364-4449 Toll Free Tel: 888-523-9292 (orders); 800-588-1074 E-mail: youngreaders@penguinrandomhouse.com Web Site: www.tundrabooks.com, pg 421

Doyle, Kelly, Penguin Random House LLC, 1745 Broadway, New York, NY 10019 Tel: 212-782-9000 Toll Free Tel: 800-726-0600 Web Site: www.penguinrandomhouse.com, pg 155

Doyle, Miles, HarperCollins Publishers LLC, 195 Broadway, New York, NY 10007 Tel: 212-207-7000 Web Site: www.harpercollins.com, pg 86

Doyle-Kimball, Mary, Robert Bruss Real Estate Book Awards, 1003 NW Sixth Terr, Boca Raton, FL 33486-3455 Tel: 561-391-3599 E-mail: nareeprograms@gmail.com Web Site: www.naree.org/bookcontest, pg 584

Doyle-Kimball, Mary, NAREE Bivins Fellowship, 1003 NW Sixth Terr, Boca Raton, FL 33486-3455 Tel: 561-391-3599 Web Site: www.naree.org/bivins-fellowship, pg 636

Doyle-Kimball, Mary, NAREE Real Estate Journalism Awards Competition, 1003 NW Sixth Terr, Boca Raton, FL 33486-3455 *Tel:* 561-391-3599 *E-mail:* nareejcontest@gmail.com *Web Site:* www.naree.org/jcontest, pg 636

Doyle-Kimball, Mary, National Association of Real Estate Editors (NAREE), 1003 NW Sixth Terr, Boca Raton, FL 33486-3455 *Tel:* 561-391-3599 *Web Site:* www.naree.org, pg 512

Doyon, Ann, Theytus Books Ltd, 154 Enowkin Trail, RR 2, Site 50, Comp 8, Penticton, BC V2A 6J7, Canada *Tel:* 250-493-7181 *Fax:* 250-493-5302 *E-mail:* order@theytus.com; marketing@theytus.com *Web Site:* www.theytus.com, pg 420

Dozier, Laura, Harry N Abrams Inc, 195 Broadway, 9th fl, New York, NY 10007 *Tel:* 212-206-7715 *Toll Free Tel:* 800-345-1359 *Fax:* 212-645-8437 *E-mail:* abrams@abramsbooks.com; publicity@abramsbooks.com; sales@abramsbooks.com *Web Site:* www.abramsbooks.com, pg 3

Drackett, Donna, Psychological Assessment Resources Inc (PAR), 16204 N Florida Ave, Lutz, FL 33549 *Tel:* 813-449-4065 *Toll Free Tel:* 800-331-8378 *Fax:* 813-961-2196 *Toll Free Fax:* 800-727-9329 *Web Site:* www.parinc.com, pg 166

Drake, Mark, The Charlton Press Corp, 645 Ave Lepine, Dorval, QC H9P 2R2, Canada *Tel:* 416-962-2665 *Toll Free Tel:* 866-663-8827 *Fax:* 514-954-3618 *E-mail:* chpress@charltonpress.com; info@charltonpress.com *Web Site:* www.charltonpress.com, pg 399

Dralyuk, Boris, LARB Books, 6671 Sunset Blvd, Suite 1521, Los Angeles, CA 90028 *Tel:* 323-952-3950 *E-mail:* larbbooks@lareviewofbooks.org *Web Site:* larbbooks.org, pg 113

Drayton, Catherine, InkWell Management, 521 Fifth Ave, Suite 2600, New York, NY 10175 *Tel:* 212-922-3500 *Fax:* 212-922-0535 *E-mail:* info@inkwellmanagement.com; submissions@inkwellmanagement.com; permissions@inkwellmanagement.com *Web Site:* inkwellmanagement.com, pg 463

Dreesen, Robert, Cambridge University Press, One Liberty Plaza, 20th fl, New York, NY 10006 *Tel:* 212-924-3900; 212-337-5000 *Fax:* 212-691-3239; 845-353-4141 *E-mail:* customer_service@cambridge.org; orders@cambridge.org; subscriptions_newyork@cambridge.org *Web Site:* www.cambridge.org/us, pg 39

Drehs, Shana, Sourcebooks LLC, 1935 Brookdale Rd, Suite 139, Naperville, IL 60563 *Tel:* 630-961-3900 *Toll Free Tel:* 800-432-7444 *Fax:* 630-961-2168 *E-mail:* info@sourcebooks.com *Web Site:* www.sourcebooks.com, pg 194

Dresher, Matthew, PennWell Books, 10050 E 52 St, Tulsa, OK 74146 *Toll Free Tel:* 866-777-1814 *Fax:* 918-550-8962 *E-mail:* sales@pennwellbooks.com *Web Site:* www.pennwellbooks.com, pg 157

Dresner, Liz, Random House Children's Books, c/o Penguin Random House LLC, 1745 Broadway, New York, NY 10019 *Tel:* 212-782-9000 *Web Site:* www.rhcbooks.com, pg 169

Dresser, Kate, GP Putnam's Sons, c/o Penguin Random House LLC, 1745 Broadway, New York, NY 10019 *Tel:* 212-782-9000 *Web Site:* www.penguin.com/putnam/, pg 167

Drew, Kirsten, Chelsea Green Publishing Co, 85 N Main St, Suite 120, White River Junction, VT 05001 *Tel:* 802-295-6300 *Toll Free Tel:* 800-639-4099 (cust serv & orders) *Fax:* 802-295-6444 *E-mail:* customerservice@chelseagreen.com; editorial@chelseagreen.com; publicity@chelseagreen.com; rights@chelseagreen.com *Web Site:* www.chelseagreen.com, pg 45

Drexler, Wendy, New England Poetry Club, c/o Linda Haviland Conte, 18 Hall Ave, Apt 2, Somerville, MA 02144 *E-mail:* info@nepoetryclub.org; president@nepoetryclub.org *Web Site:* nepoetryclub.org, pg 514

Drinkard, Annie, Council for Exceptional Children (CEC), 3100 Clarendon Blvd, Suite 600, Arlington, VA 22201 *Toll Free Tel:* 888-232-7733 *E-mail:* service@exceptionalchildren.org *Web Site:* www.exceptionalchildren.org, pg 53

Driscoll, Zora, Chronicle Books LLC, 680 Second St, San Francisco, CA 94107 *Tel:* 415-537-4200 *Fax:* 415-537-4460 (perms) *E-mail:* hello@chroniclebooks.com; subrights@chroniclebooks.com *Web Site:* www.chroniclebooks.com, pg 48

Driskell, Maudelle, Conference on Poetry & Teaching, 158 Ridge Rd, Franconia, NH 03580 *Tel:* 603-823-5510 *E-mail:* frost@frostplace.org *Web Site:* frostplace.org, pg 554

Droege, Christy, Sourcebooks LLC, 1935 Brookdale Rd, Suite 139, Naperville, IL 60563 *Tel:* 630-961-3900 *Toll Free Tel:* 800-432-7444 *Fax:* 630-961-2168 *E-mail:* info@sourcebooks.com *Web Site:* www.sourcebooks.com, pg 194

Drollinger, Darrin, American Society of Agricultural & Biological Engineers (ASABE), 2950 Niles Rd, St Joseph, MI 49085-9659 *Tel:* 269-429-0300 *Toll Free Tel:* 800-371-2723 *Fax:* 269-429-3852 *E-mail:* hq@asabe.org *Web Site:* www.asabe.org, pg 12

Drooby, Elizabeth, Workman Publishing, 1290 Avenue of the Americas, New York, NY 10104 *Toll Free Tel:* 800-759-0190 *Fax:* 212-364-0950 *E-mail:* workman-inquiry@hbgusa.com *Web Site:* www.hachettebookgroup.com/imprint/workman-publishing-company/, pg 233

Dros, Meredith, Knopf Doubleday Publishing Group, c/o Penguin Random House LLC, 1745 Broadway, New York, NY 10019 *Tel:* 212-751-2600 *Fax:* 212-940-7390 (dom rts); 212-572-2662 (foreign rts) *Web Site:* knopfdoubleday.com, pg 110

Dros, Meredith, Penguin Publishing Group, c/o Penguin Random House LLC, 1745 Broadway, New York, NY 10019 *Tel:* 212-782-9000 *Web Site:* www.penguin.com, pg 154

Dros, Meredith, Penguin Random House LLC, 1745 Broadway, New York, NY 10019 *Tel:* 212-782-9000 *Toll Free Tel:* 800-726-0600 *Web Site:* www.penguinrandomhouse.com, pg 155

Drost, Susie, The Mongolia Society Inc, Indiana University, 703 Eigenmann Hall, 1900 E Tenth St, Bloomington, IN 47406-7512 *Tel:* 812-855-4078 *Fax:* 812-855-4078 *E-mail:* monsoc@indiana.edu *Web Site:* mongoliasociety.org, pg 133

Droth, Martina, Yale Center for British Art, 1080 Chapel St, New Haven, CT 06510-2302 *Tel:* 203-432-8929 *Fax:* 203-432-1626 *E-mail:* ycba.publications@yale.edu *Web Site:* britishart.yale.edu, pg 235

Drouillard, Tom, Alliance for Audited Media (AAM), 4513 Lincoln Ave, Suite 105B, Lisle, IL 60532 *Tel:* 224-366-6939 *Toll Free Tel:* 800-285-2220 *E-mail:* corpcomm@auditedmedia.com *Web Site:* auditedmedia.com, pg 493

Drucker, Heather, HarperCollins Publishers LLC, 195 Broadway, New York, NY 10007 *Tel:* 212-207-7000 *Web Site:* www.harpercollins.com, pg 86

Druskin, Julia, W W Norton & Company Inc, 500 Fifth Ave, New York, NY 10110-0017 *Tel:* 212-354-5500 *Toll Free Tel:* 800-233-4830 (orders & cust serv) *Fax:* 212-869-0856 *Toll Free Fax:* 800-458-6515 *E-mail:* orders@wwnorton.com *Web Site:* wwnorton.com, pg 143

Dry, Paul, Paul Dry Books, 1700 Sansom St, Suite 700, Philadelphia, PA 19103 *Tel:* 215-231-9939 *E-mail:* editor@pauldrybooks.com *Web Site:* www.pauldrybooks.com, pg 152

Du Cane, John, Dragon Door Publications, 2999 Yorkton Blvd, Suite 2, Little Canada, MN 55117 *Tel:* 651-487-2180 *E-mail:* support@dragondoor.com *Web Site:* www.dragondoor.com, pg 61

du Houx, Paul, Polar Bear & Company, 8 Brook St, Solon, ME 04979 *Tel:* 207-319-4727 *Web Site:* polarbearandco.com, pg 161

du Quenoy, Dr Paul, Academica Press, 1727 Massachusetts Ave NW, Suite 507, Washington, DC 20036 *E-mail:* editorial@academicapress.com *Web Site:* www.academicapress.com, pg 3

Dube, Jessie, Willow Creek Press, 9931 Hwy 70 W, Minocqua, WI 54548 *Tel:* 715-358-7010 *Toll Free Tel:* 800-850-9453 *Fax:* 715-358-2807 *E-mail:* info@willowcreekpress.com *Web Site:* www.willowcreekpress.com; www.wcpretail.com, pg 230

Dube, Matthew, Merriam-Webster Inc, 47 Federal St, Springfield, MA 01102 *Tel:* 413-734-3134 *Toll Free Tel:* 800-828-1880 (orders & cust serv) *Fax:* 413-731-5979 (sales) *E-mail:* support@merriam-webster.com *Web Site:* www.merriam-webster.com, pg 130

Dubey, Gayatri, Macmillan, 120 Broadway, 22nd fl, New York, NY 10271 *E-mail:* press.inquiries@macmillan.com *Web Site:* us.macmillan.com, pg 122

Dubin, Jordan, ALSC Baker & Taylor Summer Reading Grant, 225 N Michigan Ave, Suite 1300, Chicago, IL 60601 *Tel:* 312-280-2163 *Toll Free Tel:* 800-545-2433 *Fax:* 312-280-5271 *E-mail:* alsc@ala.org *Web Site:* www.ala.org/alsc/awardsgrants/profawards/bakertaylor, pg 572

Dubin, Jordan, The Mildred L Batchelder Award, 225 N Michigan Ave, Suite 1300, Chicago, IL 60601 *Tel:* 312-280-2163 *Toll Free Tel:* 800-545-2433 *Fax:* 312-280-5271 *E-mail:* alsc@ala.org *Web Site:* www.ala.org/alsc/awardsgrants/bookmedia/batchelder, pg 577

Dubin, Jordan, The Pura Belpre Award, 225 N Michigan Ave, Suite 1300, Chicago, IL 60601 *Tel:* 312-280-2163 *Toll Free Tel:* 800-545-2433 *Fax:* 312-280-5271 *E-mail:* alsc@ala.org *Web Site:* www.ala.org/alsc/awardsgrants/bookmedia/belpre, pg 578

Dubin, Jordan, Bound to Stay Bound Books Scholarship, 225 N Michigan Ave, Suite 1300, Chicago, IL 60601 *Tel:* 312-280-2163 *Toll Free Tel:* 800-545-2433 *Fax:* 312-280-5271 *E-mail:* alsc@ala.org *Web Site:* www.ala.org/alsc/awardsgrants/scholarships; www.btsb.com/about-us/scholarships, pg 583

Dubin, Jordan, The Randolph Caldecott Medal, 225 N Michigan Ave, Suite 1300, Chicago, IL 60601 *Tel:* 312-280-2163 *Toll Free Tel:* 800-545-2433 *Fax:* 312-280-5271 *E-mail:* alsc@ala.org *Web Site:* www.ala.org/alsc/awardsgrants/bookmedia/caldecott, pg 585

Dubin, Jordan, Children's Literature Lecture Award, 225 N Michigan Ave, Suite 1300, Chicago, IL 60601 *Tel:* 312-280-2163 *Toll Free Tel:* 800-545-2433 *Fax:* 312-280-5271 *E-mail:* alsc@ala.org *Web Site:* www.ala.org/alsc/awardsgrants/profawards/chll, pg 589

Dubin, Jordan, Children's Literature Legacy Award, 225 N Michigan Ave, Suite 1300, Chicago, IL 60601 *Tel:* 312-280-2163 *Toll Free Tel:* 800-545-2433 *Fax:* 312-280-5271 *E-mail:* alsc@ala.org *Web Site:* www.ala.org/awardsgrants/childrens-literature-legacy-award; www.ala.org/alsc/awardsgrants/bookmedia/clla, pg 589

Dubin, Jordan, Theodor Seuss Geisel Award, 225 N Michigan Ave, Suite 1300, Chicago, IL 60601 *Toll Free Tel:* 800-545-2433 *E-mail:* alsc@ala.org *Web Site:* www.ala.org/alsc/awardsgrants/bookmedia/geisel, pg 606

Dubin, Jordan, Frederic G Melcher Scholarship, 225 N Michigan Ave, Suite 1300, Chicago, IL 60601 *Tel:* 312-280-2163 *Toll Free Tel:* 800-545-2433 *Fax:* 312-280-5271 *E-mail:* alsc@ala.org *Web Site:* www.ala.org/alsc/awardsgrants/scholarships, pg 632

Dubin, Jordan, John Newbery Medal, 225 N Michigan Ave, Suite 1300, Chicago, IL 60601 *Tel:* 312-280-2163 *Toll Free Tel:* 800-545-2433 *Fax:* 312-280-5271 *E-mail:* alsc@ala.org *Web Site:* www.ala.org/alsc/awardsgrants/bookmedia/newbery, pg 641

Dubin, Jordan, Robert F Sibert Informational Book Award, 225 N Michigan Ave, Suite 1300, Chicago, IL 60601 *Tel:* 312-280-2163 *Toll Free Tel:* 800-545-2433 *Fax:* 312-280-5271 *E-mail:* alsc@ala.org *Web Site:* www.ala.org/alsc/awardsgrants/bookmedia/sibert, pg 662

Dublinski, Katie, Graywolf Press, 212 Third Ave N, Suite 485, Minneapolis, MN 55401 *Tel:* 651-641-0077 *Fax:* 651-641-0036 *E-mail:* wolves@graywolfpress.org (no ms queries, sample chapters or proposals) *Web Site:* www.graywolfpress.org, pg 81

Ducasse, Bianca, Pantheon Books, c/o Penguin Random House LLC, 1745 Broadway, New York, NY 10019 *Tel:* 212-751-2600 *Fax:* 212-940-7390 (dom rts); 212-572-2662 (foreign rts) *Web Site:* knopfdoubleday.com/imprint/pantheon/; knopfdoubleday.com, pg 150

Ducasse, Bianca, Schocken Books, c/o Penguin Random House LLC, 1745 Broadway, New York, NY 10019 *Tel:* 212-751-2600 *Fax:* 212-940-7390 (dom rts); 212-572-2662 (foreign rts) *Web Site:* knopfdoubleday.com/imprint/schocken/; knopfdoubleday.com, pg 183

Duchesne, Susane, Claude Aubry Award, c/o The Canadian Children's Book Ctr, 425 Adelaide St W, Suite 200, Toronto, ON M5V 3C1, Canada *Fax:* 416-975-8970 *E-mail:* aubry@ibby-canada.org *Web Site:* www.ibby-canada.org/awards/claude-aubry-award/, pg 575

Duchesneau, Monique, Les Editions Un Monde Different, 3905 Isabelle, bureau 101, Brossard, QC J4Y 2R2, Canada *Tel:* 450-656-2660 *Toll Free Tel:* 800-443-2582 *Fax:* 450-659-9328 *E-mail:* info@umd.ca *Web Site:* umd.ca, pg 405

Duckson, Scott, West Academic, 444 Cedar St, Suite 700, St Paul, MN 55101 *Toll Free Tel:* 877-888-1330 *E-mail:* customerservice@westacademic.com; support@westacademic.com; media@westacademic.com *Web Site:* www.westacademic.com, pg 227

Duckworth, Jennifer, The Association of Medical Illustrators (AMI), 201 E Main St, Suite 810, Lexington, KY 40507 *Toll Free Tel:* 866-393-4AMI (393-4264) *E-mail:* hq@ami.org *Web Site:* www.ami.org, pg 499

Duckworth, Tim, ARE Press, 215 67 St, Virginia Beach, VA 23451 *Tel:* 757-428-3588 *Toll Free Tel:* 800-333-4499 *Web Site:* www.edgarcayce.org, pg 16

Dudding, Michael, Tor Publishing Group, 120 Broadway, New York, NY 10271 *Toll Free Tel:* 800-455-0340 (Macmillan) *E-mail:* torpublicity@tor.com; forgepublicity@forgebooks.com *Web Site:* us.macmillan.com/torpublishinggroup, pg 208

Dudley, Andy, Penguin Publishing Group, c/o Penguin Random House LLC, 1745 Broadway, New York, NY 10019 *Tel:* 212-782-9000 *Web Site:* www.penguin.com, pg 154

Dudzik, Andy, Leaf Storm Press, PO Box 4670, Santa Fe, NM 87502-4670 *Tel:* 505-216-6155 *E-mail:* leafstormpress@gmail.com *Web Site:* leafstormpress.com, pg 113

Dufault, Christopher, Knopf Doubleday Publishing Group, c/o Penguin Random House LLC, 1745 Broadway, New York, NY 10019 *Tel:* 212-751-2600 *Fax:* 212-940-7390 (dom rts); 212-572-2662 (foreign rts) *Web Site:* knopfdoubleday.com, pg 110

Dufault, Christopher, Penguin Random House LLC, 1745 Broadway, New York, NY 10019 *Tel:* 212-782-9000 *Toll Free Tel:* 800-726-0600 *Web Site:* www.penguinrandomhouse.com, pg 155

Dufficy, Nicola, Canadian Independent Booksellers Association (CIBA), 188 Dublin St N, Guelph, ON N1H 4P2, Canada *E-mail:* info@cibabooks.ca *Web Site:* cibabooks.ca, pg 502

Duffy, Valerie, Warner Press, 2902 Enterprise Dr, Anderson, IN 46013 *Tel:* 765-644-7721 *Toll Free Tel:* 800-741-7721 (orders) *Fax:* 765-640-8005 *E-mail:* wporders@warnerpress.org *Web Site:* www.warnerpress.org, pg 226

Dufresne, Collette, Editions Michel Quintin, 2259 Papineau Ave, Suite 104, Montreal, QC H2K 4J5, Canada *Tel:* 514-379-3774 *Fax:* 450-539-4905 *E-mail:* info@editionsmichelquintin.ca; commande@editionsmichelquintin.ca (orders) *Web Site:* www.editionsmichelquintin.ca, pg 404

Duft, Todd, RAND Corp, 1776 Main St, Santa Monica, CA 90407-2138 *Tel:* 310-393-0411 *Fax:* 310-393-4818 *Web Site:* www.rand.org, pg 169

Duggan, Tim, Henry Holt and Company, LLC, 120 Broadway, 23rd fl, New York, NY 10271 *Tel:* 646-307-5151 *Toll Free Tel:* 888-330-8477 (orders) *Fax:* 646-307-5285 *Web Site:* www.henryholt.com, pg 94

Dugoni, Robert, PNWA Writers' Contest, 1420 NW Gilman Blvd, Suite 29, PMB 2717, Issaquah, WA 98027 *Tel:* 425-673-2665 *E-mail:* pnwa@pnwa.org *Web Site:* www.pnwa.org, pg 650

Dugoni, Robert, PNWA - a writer's resource, 1420 NW Gilman Blvd, Suite 29, PMB 2717, Issaquah, WA 98027 *Tel:* 425-673-2665 *E-mail:* pnwa@pnwa.org *Web Site:* www.pnwa.org, pg 517

Dugoni, Robert, PNWA Writers Conference, 1420 NW Gilman Blvd, Suite 29, PMB 2717, Issaquah, WA 98027 *Tel:* 425-673-2665 *E-mail:* pnwa@pnwa.org *Web Site:* www.pnwa.org, pg 557

Duhe, Mary, University of Louisiana at Lafayette Press, PO Box 43558, Lafayette, LA 70504-3558 *Tel:* 337-482-6027 *E-mail:* press.submissions@louisiana.edu *Web Site:* ulpress.org, pg 217

Dujack, Stephen, Environmental Law Institute, 1730 "M" St NW, Suite 700, Washington, DC 20036 *Tel:* 202-939-3800 *Toll Free Tel:* 800-433-5120 *Fax:* 202-939-3868 *E-mail:* law@eli.org *Web Site:* www.eli.org, pg 67

Dujan, Patricio, Math Solutions®, One Harbor Dr, Suite 101, Sausalito, CA 94965 *Toll Free Tel:* 877-234-7323 *Toll Free Fax:* 800-724-4716 *E-mail:* info@mathsolutions.com; orders@mathsolutions.com *Web Site:* www.mathsolutions.com; store.mathsolutions.com, pg 127

Duke, Michelle, National Association of Broadcasters (NAB), One "M" St SE, Washington, DC 20003 *Tel:* 202-429-5300 *E-mail:* nab@nab.org *Web Site:* www.nab.org, pg 136, 511

Dukeshire, Deborah, Standard Publishing Corp, 10 High St, Boston, MA 02110 *Tel:* 617-457-0600 *Toll Free Tel:* 800-682-5759 *Fax:* 617-457-0608 *Web Site:* www.spcpub.com, pg 197

Dulaney, Kristin, Farrar, Straus & Giroux Books for Young Readers, 120 Broadway, New York, NY 10271 *Tel:* 212-741-6900 *Toll Free Tel:* 888-330-8477 (orders) *E-mail:* childrens.publicity@macmillanusa.com; childrensrights@macmillanusa.com *Web Site:* us.macmillan.com/mackids, pg 70

Dulaney, Kristin, Roaring Brook Press, 120 Broadway, New York, NY 10271 *Tel:* 646-307-5151 *Web Site:* us.macmillan.com/publishers/roaring-brook-press, pg 175

Dumbacher, Daniel L, American Institute of Aeronautics and Astronautics (AIAA), 12700 Sunrise Valley Dr, Suite 200, Reston, VA 20191-5807 *Tel:* 703-264-7500 *Toll Free Tel:* 800-639-AIAA (639-2422) *Fax:* 703-264-7551 *E-mail:* custserv@aiaa.org *Web Site:* www.aiaa.org; arc.aiaa.org (orders), pg 10

Dunbar, Christine, Columbia University Press, 61 W 62 St, New York, NY 10023 *Tel:* 212-459-0600 *Toll Free Tel:* 800-944-8648 *Fax:* 212-459-3678 *Web Site:* cup.columbia.edu, pg 51

Duncan, Andrew, Grand Central Publishing, 1290 Avenue of the Americas, New York, NY 10104 *Tel:* 212-364-1100 *Web Site:* www.hachettebookgroup.com/imprint/grand-central-publishing/, pg 80

Duncan, D'Kela, Macmillan, 120 Broadway, 22nd fl, New York, NY 10271 *E-mail:* press.inquiries@macmillan.com *Web Site:* us.macmillan.com, pg 122

Duncan, Heather, Joyce Meskis Excellence in Bookselling Scholarship, PO Box 746, Denver, CO 80201 *Toll Free Tel:* 800-752-0249 *E-mail:* info@mountainsplains.org *Web Site:* www.mountainsplains.org/meskis-scholarship, pg 632

Duncan, Heather, Reading the West Book Awards, PO Box 746, Denver, CO 80201 *Tel:* 970-484-3939 *Toll Free Tel:* 800-752-0249 *Fax:* 970-484-0037 *E-mail:* info@mountainsplains.org *Web Site:* www.mountainsplains.org/reading-the-west-book-awards, pg 655

Duncan, Sarah, Playwrights Guild of Canada, 401 Richmond St W, Suite 350, Toronto, ON M5V 3A8, Canada *Tel:* 416-703-0201 *E-mail:* info@playwrightsguild.ca; marketing@playwrightsguild.ca; orders@playwrightsguild.ca; membership@playwrightsguild.ca *Web Site:* playwrightsguild.ca, pg 516

Duncan, Virginia, HarperCollins Children's Books, 195 Broadway, New York, NY 10007 *Tel:* 212-207-7000 *Web Site:* www.harpercollins.com/childrens, pg 85

Dundas, Jeff, Wm B Eerdmans Publishing Co, 4035 Park East Ct SE, Grand Rapids, MI 49546 *Tel:* 616-459-4591 *Toll Free Tel:* 800-253-7521 *E-mail:* customerservice@eerdmans.com; sales@eerdmans.com *Web Site:* www.eerdmans.com, pg 64

Dunham, Gary, Indiana University Press, Off of Scholarly Publg, Herman B Wells Library 350, 1320 E Tenth St, Bloomington, IN 47405-3907 *Tel:* 812-855-8817 *Fax:* 812-855-7931; 812-855-8507 *E-mail:* iupress@indiana.edu *Web Site:* iupress.org, pg 100

Dunham, Jennie, Dunham Literary Inc, 487 Hardscrabble Rd, North Salem, NY 10560 *Tel:* 914-669-5535 *E-mail:* dunhamlit@gmail.com *Web Site:* dunhamlit.com, pg 457

Dunkin, Amy, Houghton Mifflin Harcourt, 125 High St, Boston, MA 02110 *Tel:* 617-351-5000 *Toll Free Tel:* 855-969-4642; 800-225-5425 (K-12 educ materials); 800-323-9540 (assessment materials); 877-219-1537 (SkillsTutor); 888-242-6747 (Innovation in Educ Group); 800-225-3362 (Trade & Ref Div) *Toll Free Fax:* 800-269-5232 *E-mail:* myhmco@hmhco.com *Web Site:* www.hmhco.com, pg 96

Dunkle, Iris, Napa Valley Writers' Conference, 2277 Napa-Vallejo Hwy, Off 1753, Napa, CA 94558 *Tel:* 707-256-7113 *E-mail:* info@napawritersconference.org; fiction@napawritersconference.org; poetry@napawritersconference.org *Web Site:* www.napawritersconference.org, pg 556

Dunlop, Shea, Harry N Abrams Inc, 195 Broadway, 9th fl, New York, NY 10007 *Tel:* 212-206-7715 *Toll Free Tel:* 800-345-1359 *Fax:* 212-645-8437 *E-mail:* abrams@abramsbooks.com; publicity@abramsbooks.com; sales@abramsbooks.com *Web Site:* www.abramsbooks.com, pg 3

Dunn, Aimee Parent, Palimpsest Press, 1171 Eastlawn Ave, Windsor, ON N8S 3J1, Canada *Tel:* 519-259-2112 *E-mail:* publicity@palimpsestpress.ca *Web Site:* www.palimpsestpress.ca, pg 415

Dunn, Dinah, American Book Producers Association (ABPA), 7 Peter Cooper Rd, No 7G, New York, NY 10010 *E-mail:* office@abpaonline.org *Web Site:* www.abpaonline.org, pg 494

Dunn, Kathy, Random House Children's Books, c/o Penguin Random House LLC, 1745 Broadway, New York, NY 10019 *Tel:* 212-782-9000 *Web Site:* www.rhcbooks.com, pg 169

Dunn, Shaun, Palimpsest Press, 1171 Eastlawn Ave, Windsor, ON N8S 3J1, Canada *Tel:* 519-259-2112 *E-mail:* publicity@palimpsestpress.ca *Web Site:* www.palimpsestpress.ca, pg 415

Dunn, Stephen P, W W Norton & Company Inc, 500 Fifth Ave, New York, NY 10110-0017 *Tel:* 212-354-5500 *Toll Free Tel:* 800-233-4830 (orders & cust serv) *Fax:* 212-869-0856 *Toll Free Fax:* 800-458-6515 *E-mail:* orders@wwnorton.com *Web Site:* wwnorton.com, pg 143

Dunnington, Jack, The Experiment, 220 E 23 St, Suite 600, New York, NY 10010-4658 *Tel:* 212-889-1659 *E-mail:* info@theexperimentpublishing.com *Web Site:* www.theexperimentpublishing.com, pg 68

Dunow, Henry, Dunow, Carlson & Lerner Literary Agency Inc, 27 W 20 St, Suite 1107, New York, NY 10011 *Tel:* 212-645-7606 *E-mail:* mail@dclagency.com *Web Site:* www.dclagency.com, pg 457

Dunton, David, Harvey Klinger Inc, 300 W 55 St, Suite 11V, New York, NY 10019 *Tel:* 212-581-7068 *Fax:* 212-315-3823 *E-mail:* queries@harveyklinger.com *Web Site:* www.harveyklinger.com, pg 465

DuPont, Charles, Alan Wofsy Fine Arts, 1109 Geary Blvd, San Francisco, CA 94109 *Tel:* 415-292-6500 *Toll Free Tel:* 800-660-6403 *Fax:* 415-292-6594 (off & cust serv); 510-251-1840 (acctg) *E-mail:* order@art-books.com (orders); editeur@earthlink.net (edit); beauxarts@earthlink.net (cust serv) *Web Site:* www.art-books.com, pg 231

Dupuis, Andrew, Kids Can Press Ltd, 25 Dockside Dr, Toronto, ON M5A 0B5, Canada *Tel:* 416-479-7000 *Toll Free Tel:* 800-265-0884 *Fax:* 416-960-5437 *E-mail:* info@kidscan.com; customerservice@kidscan.com *Web Site:* www.kidscanpress.com; www.kidscanpress.ca, pg 411

Duquet, Michel, The CHA Best Scholarly Book in Canadian History Prize, 130 Albert St, Suite 1201, Ottawa, ON K1P 5G4, Canada *Tel:* 613-233-7885 *Fax:* 613-565-5445 *E-mail:* cha-shc@cha-shc.ca *Web Site:* cha-shc.ca, pg 588

Duquet, Michel, Francois-Xavier Garneau Medal, 130 Albert St, Suite 1201, Ottawa, ON K1P 5G4, Canada *Tel:* 613-233-7885 *Fax:* 613-565-5445 *E-mail:* cha-shc@cha-shc.ca *Web Site:* cha-shc.ca, pg 605

Duquette, Brett, little bee books, 598 Broadway, 7th fl, New York, NY 10012 *Tel:* 212-321-0237 *Toll Free Tel:* 800-421-0237 *E-mail:* info@littlebeebooks.com; sales@littlebeebooks.com; publicity@littlebeebooks.com *Web Site:* littlebeebooks.com, pg 117

Duran, Bernardo, NACE International, 15835 Park Ten Place, Houston, TX 77084 *Tel:* 281-228-6200; 281-228-6223 *Toll Free Tel:* 800-797-NACE (797-6223) *Fax:* 281-228-6300 *E-mail:* firstservice@nace.org *Web Site:* www.nace.org, pg 136

Durante, Dawn, The University of North Carolina Press, 116 S Boundary St, Chapel Hill, NC 27514-3808 *Tel:* 919-966-3561; 919-966-7449 (orders) *Toll Free Tel:* 800-848-3224 (orders) *Fax:* 919-962-2704 (orders) *Toll Free Fax:* 800-272-6817 (orders) *E-mail:* uncpress@unc.edu *Web Site:* uncpress.org, pg 218

Durantt, Ayelet, Random House Publishing Group, 1745 Broadway, New York, NY 10019 *Toll Free Tel:* 800-200-3552 *Web Site:* www.randomhousebooks.com, pg 171

Durbin, Dean, Trusted Media Brands Inc, 750 Third Ave, 3rd fl, New York, NY 10017 *Tel:* 646-293-6299 *Toll Free Tel:* 877-732-4438 (cust serv) *Fax:* 646-293-6251 *E-mail:* customercare@trustedmediabrands.com; press@trustedmediabrands.com *Web Site:* www.trustedmediabrands.com; www.rd.com, pg 210

Durbin, Jon, W W Norton & Company Inc, 500 Fifth Ave, New York, NY 10110-0017 *Tel:* 212-354-5500 *Toll Free Tel:* 800-233-4830 (orders & cust serv) *Fax:* 212-869-0856 *Toll Free Fax:* 800-458-6515 *E-mail:* orders@wwnorton.com *Web Site:* wwnorton.com, pg 143

Durham, Daphne Ming, GP Putnam's Sons, c/o Penguin Random House LLC, 1745 Broadway, New York, NY 10019 *Tel:* 212-782-9000 *Web Site:* www.penguin.com/putnam/, pg 167

Durham, Judith B, Graphic Arts Education & Research Foundation (GAERF), 1899 Preston White Dr, Reston, VA 20191 *Tel:* 703-264-7200 *E-mail:* gaerf@npes.org *Web Site:* www.gaerf.org, pg 525

Durham, Rusty, StarGroup International Inc, 1194 Old Dixie Hwy, Suite 201, West Palm Beach, FL 33413 *Tel:* 561-547-0667 *Fax:* 561-843-8530 *E-mail:* info@stargroupinternational.com *Web Site:* stargroupinternational.com, pg 198

Durkin, Cletus, Penguin Random House LLC, 1745 Broadway, New York, NY 10019 *Tel:* 212-782-9000 *Toll Free Tel:* 800-726-0600 *Web Site:* www.penguinrandomhouse.com, pg 155

Durning, Gretchen, GP Putnam's Sons Books for Young Readers, c/o Penguin Random House LLC, 1745 Broadway, New York, NY 10019 *Tel:* 212-782-9000 *Web Site:* www.penguin.com/putnam-young-readers/, pg 167

Duroselle-Melish, Caroline, Bibliographical Society of America (BSA), 67 West St, Suite 401, Unit C17, Brooklyn, NY 11222 *E-mail:* bsa@bibsocamer.org *Web Site:* bibsocamer.org, pg 501

Durrant, Jennifer, Sourced Media Books, 15 Via Picato, San Clemente, CA 92673 *Tel:* 949-813-0182 *E-mail:* editor@sourcedmediabooks.com *Web Site:* sourcedmediabooks.com, pg 195

Dussel, Tom, Penguin Publishing Group, c/o Penguin Random House LLC, 1745 Broadway, New York, NY 10019 *Tel:* 212-782-9000 *Web Site:* www.penguin.com, pg 154

Dussold, Hannah, Andrews McMeel Publishing LLC, 1130 Walnut St, Kansas City, MO 64106-2109 *Tel:* 816-581-7500 *Toll Free Tel:* 800-851-8923 *Web Site:* www.andrewsmcmeel.com; publishing.andrewsmcmeel.com, pg 14

Dutton, Katie, Random House Children's Books, c/o Penguin Random House LLC, 1745 Broadway, New York, NY 10019 *Tel:* 212-782-9000 *Web Site:* www.rhcbooks.com, pg 170

Duval, Nathalie, Alexander Street, part of Clarivate PLC, 789 E Eisenhower Pkwy, Ann Arbor, MI 48108 *Toll Free Tel:* 800-521-0600; 888-963-2071 (sales) *E-mail:* sales@alexanderstreet.com; marketing@alexanderstreet.com; support@alexanderstreet.com *Web Site:* alexanderstreet.com, pg 6

Duverglas, Donna, Random House Publishing Group, 1745 Broadway, New York, NY 10019 *Toll Free Tel:* 800-200-3552 *Web Site:* www.randomhousebooks.com, pg 171

Dwyer, Liz, North Star Press of Saint Cloud Inc, 19485 Estes Rd, Clearwater, MN 55320 *Tel:* 320-558-9062 *E-mail:* info@northstarpress.com *Web Site:* www.northstarpress.com, pg 143

Dye, Ann, Harlequin Enterprises Ltd, 195 Broadway, 24th fl, New York, NY 10007 *Tel:* 212-207-7000 *Toll Free Tel:* 888-432-4879; 800-370-5838 (ebooks) *E-mail:* customerservice@harlequin.com *Web Site:* www.harlequin.com/shop/index.html; corporate.harlequin.com, pg 85

Dye, Ann, HarperCollins Children's Books, 195 Broadway, New York, NY 10007 *Tel:* 212-207-7000 *Web Site:* www.harpercollins.com/childrens, pg 85

Dye, Ann, Houghton Mifflin Harcourt Trade & Reference Division, 125 High St, Boston, MA 02110 *Tel:* 617-351-5000 *Web Site:* www.hmhco.com, pg 96

Dye, Madison, Macmillan, 120 Broadway, 22nd fl, New York, NY 10271 *E-mail:* press.inquiries@macmillan.com *Web Site:* us.macmillan.com, pg 122

Dye, Skip, Books on Tape™, 1745 Broadway, New York, NY 10019 *Toll Free Tel:* 800-733-3000 (cust serv) *Toll Free Fax:* 800-940-7046 *Web Site:* PenguinRandomHouseLibrary.com, pg 34

Dye, Skip, Penguin Random House LLC, 1745 Broadway, New York, NY 10019 *Tel:* 212-782-9000 *Toll Free Tel:* 800-726-0600 *Web Site:* www.penguinrandomhouse.com, pg 155

Dyer, Emily, Macmillan Audio, 120 Broadway, 22nd fl, New York, NY 10271 *Tel:* 646-600-7856 *Toll Free Tel:* 888-330-8477 (cust serv) *Toll Free Fax:* 800-672-7703 *E-mail:* macmillan.audio@macmillanusa.com *Web Site:* us.macmillan.com/audio, pg 123

Dyer, Maris, Alfred A Knopf, c/o Penguin Random House LLC, 1745 Broadway, New York, NY 10019 *Tel:* 212-751-2600 *Fax:* 212-940-7390 (dom rts); 212-572-2662 (foreign rts) *Web Site:* knopfdoubleday.com/imprint/knopf/; knopfdoubleday.com, pg 110

Dyer, Meagan, University of British Columbia Press, 2029 West Mall, Vancouver, BC V6T 1Z2, Canada *Tel:* 604-822-5959 *Toll Free Tel:* 877-377-9378 *Fax:* 604-822-6083 *Toll Free Fax:* 800-668-0821 *E-mail:* frontdesk@ubcpress.ca *Web Site:* www.ubcpress.ca, pg 422

Dyer, Phoebe, Bloomsbury Publishing Inc, 1385 Broadway, 5th fl, New York, NY 10018 *Tel:* 212-419-5300 *E-mail:* marketingusa@bloomsbury.com; adultpublicityusa@bloomsbury.com; askacademic@bloomsbury.com *Web Site:* www.bloomsbury.com, pg 32

Dyke, George, Earth Edit, PO Box 114, Maiden Rock, WI 54750 *Tel:* 715-448-3009, pg 438

Dykstra, LeeAnna, Broadview Press, 280 Perry St, Unit 5, Peterborough, ON K9J 2J4, Canada *Tel:* 705-482-5915 *Fax:* 705-743-8353 *E-mail:* customerservice@broadviewpress.com *Web Site:* www.broadviewpress.com, pg 397

Dynak, Sharon, Ucross Foundation Residency Program, 30 Big Red Lane, Clearmont, WY 82835 *Tel:* 307-737-2291 *E-mail:* info@ucross.org *Web Site:* www.ucross.org, pg 672

Dyrdahl, Link, Kidsbooks® Publishing, 5306 Ballard Ave NW, Suite 311, Seattle, WA 98107 *E-mail:* customerservice@kidsbookspublishing.com *Web Site:* www.kidsbookspublishing.com, pg 109

Dyson, Elizabeth Branch, University of Chicago Press, 1427 E 60 St, Chicago, IL 60637-2954 *Tel:* 773-702-7700; 773-702-7600 *Toll Free Tel:* 800-621-2736 (orders); 773-702-9756; 773-660-2235 (orders); 773-702-2708 *E-mail:* custserv@press.uchicago.edu; marketing@press.uchicago.edu *Web Site:* www.press.uchicago.edu, pg 215

Dyssegaard, Elisabeth, St Martin's Press, LLC, 120 Broadway, New York, NY 10271 *E-mail:* publicity@stmartins.com; trademarketing@stmartins.com; foreignrights@stmartins.com *Web Site:* us.macmillan.com/smp, pg 181

Dyssou, Nanda, LARB Books, 6671 Sunset Blvd, Suite 1521, Los Angeles, CA 90028 *Tel:* 323-952-3950 *E-mail:* larbbooks@lareviewofbooks.org *Web Site:* larbbooks.org, pg 113

Dystel, Jane, Dystel, Goderich & Bourret LLC, One Union Sq W, Suite 904, New York, NY 10003 *Tel:* 212-627-9100 *Fax:* 212-627-9313 *Web Site:* www.dystel.com, pg 457

Dziena, David, Pflaum Publishing Group, 3055 Kettering Blvd, Suite 100, Dayton, OH 45439 *Toll Free Tel:* 800-523-4625; 800-543-4383 (ext 1136, cust serv) *Toll Free Fax:* 800-370-4450 *E-mail:* service@pflaum.com *Web Site:* www.pflaum.com, pg 159

Dzienkonski, Karen, Penguin Random House Audio Publishing Group, 1745 Broadway, New York, NY 10019 *Toll Free Tel:* 800-793-2665 (cust serv) *E-mail:* audio@penguinrandomhouse.com; ecustomerservice@penguinrandomhouse.com *Web Site:* www.penguinrandomhouseaudio.com, pg 154

Eagle, Sara, Alfred A Knopf, c/o Penguin Random House LLC, 1745 Broadway, New York, NY 10019 *Tel:* 212-751-2600 *Fax:* 212-940-7390 (dom rts); 212-572-2662 (foreign rts) *Web Site:* knopfdoubleday.com/imprint/knopf/; knopfdoubleday.com, pg 110

Eagle, Sara, Pantheon Books, c/o Penguin Random House LLC, 1745 Broadway, New York, NY 10019 *Tel:* 212-751-2600 *Fax:* 212-940-7390 (dom rts); 212-572-2662 (foreign rts) *Web Site:* knopfdoubleday.com/imprint/pantheon/; knopfdoubleday.com, pg 150

Eagle, Sara, Schocken Books, c/o Penguin Random House LLC, 1745 Broadway, New York, NY 10019 *Tel:* 212-751-2600 *Fax:* 212-940-7390 (dom rts); 212-572-2662 (foreign rts) *Web Site:* knopfdoubleday.com/imprint/schocken/; knopfdoubleday.com, pg 183

Eaker, Noah, HarperCollins Publishers LLC, 195 Broadway, New York, NY 10007 *Tel:* 212-207-7000 *Web Site:* www.harpercollins.com, pg 86

Earley, Diane, Charlesbridge Publishing Inc, 85 Main St, Watertown, MA 02472 *Tel:* 617-926-0329 *Toll Free Tel:* 800-225-3214 *Fax:* 617-926-5720 *Toll Free Fax:* 800-926-5775 *E-mail:* books@charlesbridge.com *Web Site:* www.charlesbridge.com, pg 45

Earnest, Hayley, Harry N Abrams Inc, 195 Broadway, 9th fl, New York, NY 10007 *Tel:* 212-206-7715 *Toll Free Tel:* 800-345-1359 *Fax:* 212-645-8437 *E-mail:* abrams@abramsbooks.com; publicity@abramsbooks.com; sales@abramsbooks.com *Web Site:* www.abramsbooks.com, pg 3

Earnheardt, Adam, National Society of Newspaper Columnists Annual Conference, 205 Gun Hill St, Milton, MA 02186 *Tel:* 617-697-6854 *Web Site:* www.columnists.com, pg 556

Easby, Richard, American Society of Agronomy (ASA), 5585 Guilford Rd, Madison, WI 53711-5801 *Tel:* 608-273-8080 *E-mail:* books@sciencesocieties.org *Web Site:* www.agronomy.org, pg 12

Easley, Thomas J, American Medical Association (AMA), AMA Plaza, 330 N Wabash, Suite 39300, Chicago, IL 60611-5885 *Tel:* 312-464-5000; 312-464-4430 (media & edit) *Toll Free Tel:* 800-621-8335 *E-mail:* media@ama-assn.org (media & edit); bookandonlinesales@ama-assn.org (volume book/ebook sales) *Web Site:* www.ama-assn.org, pg 11

Easley, Thomas J, American Medical Association (AMA), AMA Plaza, 330 N Wabash, Suite 39300, Chicago, IL 60611-5885 *Tel:* 312-464-5000 *Toll Free Tel:* 800-621-8335 *E-mail:* media@ama-assn.org (media & edit) *Web Site:* www.ama-assn.org; www.jamanetwork.org, pg 495

Eason, Tracee, Education Writers Association (EWA), 1825 "K" St NW, Suite 200, Washington, DC 20006 *Tel:* 202-452-9830 *Web Site:* ewa.org, pg 505

Easter, Katherine, Zondervan, 3900 Sparks Dr SE, Grand Rapids, MI 49546 *Tel:* 616-698-6900 *Toll Free Tel:* 800-226-1122; 800-727-1309 (retail orders) *Fax:* 616-698-3350 *Toll Free Fax:* 800-698-3256 (retail orders) *E-mail:* customercare@harpercollins.com *Web Site:* www.zondervan.com, pg 237

Eastwood, Hilary, Mazda Publishers Inc, PO Box 2603, Costa Mesa, CA 92628 *Tel:* 714-751-5252 *Fax:* 714-751-4805 *E-mail:* mazdapub@aol.com *Web Site:* www.mazdapublishers.com, pg 127

Eatherly, Alyssa, Random House Children's Books, c/o Penguin Random House LLC, 1745 Broadway, New York, NY 10019 *Tel:* 212-782-9000 *Web Site:* www.rhcbooks.com, pg 170

Eaton, Dena, Bitingduck Press LLC, 1262 Sunnyoaks Circle, Altadena, CA 91001 *Tel:* 626-507-8033 *E-mail:* notifications@bitingduckpress.com *Web Site:* bitingduckpress.com, pg 30

Eaton, Eryn, Red Wheel/Weiser, 65 Parker St, Suite 7, Newburyport, MA 01950 *Tel:* 978-465-0504 *Toll Free Tel:* 800-423-7087 (orders) *Fax:* 978-465-0243 *E-mail:* info@rwwbooks.com *Web Site:* www.redwheelweiser.com, pg 173

Eaton, Jonathan, Tilbury House Publishers, 12 Starr St, Thomaston, ME 04861 *Tel:* 207-582-1899 *Toll Free Tel:* 800-582-1899 (orders) *Fax:* 207-582-8227 *E-mail:* tilbury@tilburyhouse.com *Web Site:* tilburyhouse.com, pg 207

Eaton, Sandi, Chelsea Green Publishing Co, 85 N Main St, Suite 120, White River Junction, VT 05001 *Tel:* 802-295-6300 *Toll Free Tel:* 800-639-4099 (cust serv & orders) *Fax:* 802-295-6444 *E-mail:* customerservice@chelseagreen.com; editorial@chelseagreen.com; publicity@chelseagreen.com; rights@chelseagreen.com *Web Site:* www.chelseagreen.com, pg 45

Eberle, Corina, Greystone Books Ltd, 343 Railway St, Suite 302, Vancouver, BC V6A 1A4, Canada *Tel:* 604-875-1550 *Fax:* 604-875-1556 *E-mail:* info@greystonebooks.com; rights@greystonebooks.com *Web Site:* www.greystonebooks.com, pg 407

Eberle, Katie, Parallax Press, 2236B Sixth St, Berkeley, CA 94710 *Tel:* 510-325-2945 *Toll Free Tel:* 800-863-5290 (orders) *Web Site:* www.parallax.org, pg 151

Ebershoff, David, Penguin Random House LLC, 1745 Broadway, New York, NY 10019 *Tel:* 212-782-9000 *Toll Free Tel:* 800-726-0600 *Web Site:* www.penguinrandomhouse.com, pg 155

Ebershoff, David, Random House Publishing Group, 1745 Broadway, New York, NY 10019 *Toll Free Tel:* 800-200-3552 *Web Site:* www.randomhousebooks.com, pg 170

Ebner, Tim, American Forest & Paper Association (AF&PA), 1101 "K" St NW, Suite 700, Washington, DC 20005 *Tel:* 202-463-2700 *E-mail:* info@afandpa.org; comm@afandpa.org *Web Site:* www.afandpa.org, pg 495

Ebrahimi, Parisa, Random House Publishing Group, 1745 Broadway, New York, NY 10019 *Toll Free Tel:* 800-200-3552 *Web Site:* www.randomhousebooks.com, pg 171

Ebro, Casey, Portfolio, c/o Penguin Random House LLC, 1745 Broadway, New York, NY 10019 *Tel:* 212-782-9000 *Web Site:* www.penguin.com/portfolio-overview/; www.penguin.com/sentinel-overview/; www.penguin.com/thesis/, pg 162

Echeverria, Jessica, Lee & Low Books Inc, 95 Madison Ave, Suite 1205, New York, NY 10016 *Tel:* 212-779-4400 *Toll Free Tel:* 888-320-3190 (ext 28, orders only) *Fax:* 212-683-1894 (orders only); 212-532-6035 *E-mail:* general@leeandlow.com *Web Site:* www.leeandlow.com, pg 114

Echols, Terumi, InterVarsity Press, 430 Plaza Dr, Westmont, IL 60559-1234 *Tel:* 630-734-4000 *Toll Free Tel:* 800-843-9487 *Fax:* 630-734-4200 *E-mail:* email@ivpress.com *Web Site:* www.ivpress.com, pg 104

Ecker, Bev, World Book Inc, 180 N LaSalle, Suite 900, Chicago, IL 60601 *Tel:* 312-729-5800 *Toll Free Tel:* 800-967-5325 (consumer sales, US); 800-975-3250 (school & lib sales, US); 800-837-5365 (school & lib sales, CN) *Toll Free Fax:* 888-922-3766 *E-mail:* customerservice@worldbook.com *Web Site:* www.worldbook.com, pg 233

Eckes, Laura, Simon & Schuster Children's Publishing, 1230 Avenue of the Americas, New York, NY 10020 *Tel:* 212-698-7000 *Web Site:* www.simonandschuster.com/kids; www.simonandschuster.com/teen; simonandschuster.net; simonandschuster.biz, pg 189

Eckhardt, Kristen, HarperCollins Children's Books, 195 Broadway, New York, NY 10007 *Tel:* 212-207-7000 *Web Site:* www.harpercollins.com/childrens, pg 85

Ecklebarger, Timothy, Editorial Unilit, 8167 NW 84 St, Medley, FL 33166 *Tel:* 305-592-6136; 305-592-6135 *Toll Free Tel:* 800-767-7726 *Fax:* 305-592-0087 *E-mail:* info@editorialunilit.com; ventas@editorialunilit.com (sales) *Web Site:* www.editorialunilit.com, pg 64

Eckstut, Arielle, Levine|Greenberg|Rostan Literary Agency, 307 Seventh Ave, Suite 2407, New York, NY 10001 *Tel:* 212-337-0934 *Fax:* 212-337-0948 *E-mail:* submit@lgrliterary.com *Web Site:* lgrliterary.com, pg 467

Economou, Randi, Capstone Publishers™, 1710 Roe Crest Dr, North Mankato, MN 56003 *Toll Free Tel:* 800-747-4992 (cust serv) *Toll Free Fax:* 888-262-0705 *E-mail:* customer.service@capstonepub.com *Web Site:* www.capstonepub.com, pg 40

Eddy, Claire, Tor Publishing Group, 120 Broadway, New York, NY 10271 *Toll Free Tel:* 800-455-0340 (Macmillan) *E-mail:* torpublicity@tor.com; forgepublicity@forgebooks.com *Web Site:* us.macmillan.com/torpublishinggroup, pg 208

Eddy, Holly K, Islandport Press, 247 Portland St, Bldg C, Yarmouth, ME 04096 *Tel:* 207-846-3344 *E-mail:* info@islandportpress.com; orders@islandportpress.com *Web Site:* www.islandportpress.com, pg 105

Eddy, Jim, Psychological Assessment Resources Inc (PAR), 16204 N Florida Ave, Lutz, FL 33549 *Tel:* 813-449-4065 *Toll Free Tel:* 800-331-8378 *Fax:* 813-961-2196 *Toll Free Fax:* 800-727-9329 *Web Site:* www.parinc.com, pg 166

Eddy, Lynn, Strategic Book Publishing (SBP), Durham, CT 06422 *Tel:* 860-331-1201; 361-244-1058 *E-mail:* bookorder@sbpra.net; support@sbpra.net *Web Site:* sbpra.net; www.facebook.com/sbpra.us, pg 199

Edelman, Amy, IndieReader Discovery Awards, PO Box 43121, Montclair, NJ 07043 *E-mail:* customerservice@indiereader.com *Web Site:* indiereader.com/the-discovery-awards/, pg 616

Edelman, Maggie, Chronicle Books LLC, 680 Second St, San Francisco, CA 94107 *Tel:* 415-537-4200 *Fax:* 415-537-4460 (perms) *E-mail:* hello@chroniclebooks.com; subrights@chroniclebooks.com *Web Site:* www.chroniclebooks.com, pg 48

Edelson, Libby, HarperCollins Publishers LLC, 195 Broadway, New York, NY 10007 *Tel:* 212-207-7000 *Web Site:* www.harpercollins.com, pg 86

Edelson, Samantha, Macmillan Audio, 120 Broadway, 22nd fl, New York, NY 10271 *Tel:* 646-600-7856 *Toll Free Tel:* 888-330-8477 (cust serv) *Toll Free Fax:* 800-672-7703 *E-mail:* macmillan.audio@macmillanusa.com *Web Site:* us.macmillan.com/audio, pg 123

Edelstein, Anne, Anne Edelstein Literary Agency LLC, 258 Riverside Dr, No 8D, New York, NY 10025 *Tel:* 212-414-4923 *E-mail:* info@aeliterary.com *Web Site:* www.aeliterary.com, pg 457

Edgar, Lisa, Macmillan, 120 Broadway, 22nd fl, New York, NY 10271 *E-mail:* press.inquiries@macmillan.com *Web Site:* us.macmillan.com, pg 122

Edgecombe, Lindsay, Levine|Greenberg|Rostan Literary Agency, 307 Seventh Ave, Suite 2407, New York, NY 10001 *Tel:* 212-337-0934 *Fax:* 212-337-0948 *E-mail:* submit@lgrliterary.com *Web Site:* lgrliterary.com, pg 467

Edmiston, Aaron, BenBella Books Inc, 10440 N Central Expwy, Suite 800, Dallas, TX 75231-2264 *Tel:* 214-750-3600 *Web Site:* www.benbellabooks.com; www.smartpopbooks.com, pg 27

Edmonson, Tess, n+1 Writers' Fellowship, Cadman Plaza Sta, PO Box 26428, Brooklyn, NY 11202 *E-mail:* editors@nplusonemag.com; subs@nplusonemag.com (submission queries); submissions@nplusonemag.com *Web Site:* www.nplusonemag.com/awards, pg 642

Edmonson, Tess, Anthony Veasna So Fiction Prize, Cadman Plaza Sta, PO Box 26428, Brooklyn, NY 11202 *E-mail:* editors@nplusonemag.com; subs@nplusonemag.com (submission queries); submissions@nplusonemag.com *Web Site:* www.nplusonemag.com/awards, pg 664

Edmunds, Page, Workman Publishing, 1290 Avenue of the Americas, New York, NY 10104 *Toll Free Tel:* 800-759-0190 *Fax:* 212-364-0950 *E-mail:* workman-inquiry@hbgusa.com *Web Site:* www.hachettebookgroup.com/imprint/workman-publishing-company/, pg 232

Edwards, Adrianna, Focus Strategic Communications Inc, 15 Hunter Way, Brantford, ON N3T 6S3, Canada *Tel:* 519-756-3265 *E-mail:* info@focussc.com *Web Site:* www.focussc.com, pg 439

Edwards, Alicia, Penguin Random House Canada, a Penguin Random House company, 320 Front St W, Suite 1400, Toronto, ON M5V 3B6, Canada *Tel:* 416-364-4449 *Toll Free Tel:* 888-523-9292 (cust serv) *E-mail:* canadaweb@penguinrandomhouse.com; customerservicecanada@penguinrandomhouse.com *Web Site:* www.penguinrandomhouse.ca, pg 416

Edwards, Brittany, Houghton Mifflin Harcourt Trade & Reference Division, 125 High St, Boston, MA 02110 *Tel:* 617-351-5000 *Web Site:* www.hmhco.com, pg 96

Edwards, Christine, Harry N Abrams Inc, 195 Broadway, 9th fl, New York, NY 10007 *Tel:* 212-206-7715 *Toll Free Tel:* 800-345-1359 *Fax:* 212-645-8437 *E-mail:* abrams@abramsbooks.com; publicity@abramsbooks.com; sales@abramsbooks.com *Web Site:* www.abramsbooks.com, pg 2

Edwards, Harold, Scholastic Education Solutions, 557 Broadway, New York, NY 10012 *Tel:* 212-343-6100 *Fax:* 212-343-6189 *Web Site:* www.scholastic.com, pg 184

Edwards, Jennifer, Macmillan, 120 Broadway, 22nd fl, New York, NY 10271 *E-mail:* press.inquiries@macmillan.com *Web Site:* us.macmillan.com, pg 122

Edwards, John, Macmillan, 120 Broadway, 22nd fl, New York, NY 10271 *E-mail:* press.inquiries@macmillan.com *Web Site:* us.macmillan.com, pg 122

Edwards, Karen, Workman Publishing, 1290 Avenue of the Americas, New York, NY 10104 *Toll Free Tel:* 800-759-0190 *Fax:* 212-364-0950 *E-mail:* workman-inquiry@hbgusa.com *Web Site:* www.hachettebookgroup.com/imprint/workman-publishing-company/, pg 232

Edwards, Karen Gray, American Sociological Association (ASA), 1430 "K" St NW, Suite 600, Washington, DC 20005-4701 *Tel:* 202-383-9005 *E-mail:* asa@asanet.org; communications@asanet.org; membership@asanet.org *Web Site:* www.asanet.org, pg 497

Edwards, Mary Jane, Jentel Artist Residency, 130 Lower Piney Rd, Banner, WY 82832 *Tel:* 307-737-2311 *Fax:* 307-737-2305 *E-mail:* jentel@jentelarts.org *Web Site:* www.jentelarts.org, pg 555

Edwards, Melissa, Stonesong, 270 W 39 St, Suite 201, New York, NY 10018 *Tel:* 212-929-4600 *E-mail:* editors@stonesong.com *Web Site:* www.stonesong.com, pg 478

Edwards, Omesha, Simon & Schuster, 1230 Avenue of the Americas, New York, NY 10020 *Tel:* 212-698-7000 *Toll Free Tel:* 800-223-2348 (cust serv); 800-223-2336 (orders) *Toll Free Fax:* 800-943-9831 (orders) *Web Site:* simonandschusterpublishing.com/simonandschuster/, pg 188

Edwards, Rebecca Lowell, American Civil Liberties Union (ACLU), 125 Broad St, 18th fl, New York, NY 10004 *Tel:* 212-549-2500 *E-mail:* media@aclu.org *Web Site:* www.aclu.org, pg 495

Edwards, Ron, Focus Strategic Communications Inc, 15 Hunter Way, Brantford, ON N3T 6S3, Canada *Tel:* 519-756-3265 *E-mail:* info@focussc.com *Web Site:* www.focussc.com, pg 439

Eerdmans, Anita, Wm B Eerdmans Publishing Co, 4035 Park East Ct SE, Grand Rapids, MI 49546 *Tel:* 616-459-4591 *Toll Free Tel:* 800-253-7521 *E-mail:* customerservice@eerdmans.com; sales@eerdmans.com *Web Site:* www.eerdmans.com, pg 64

Eerdmans, Karl, Wm B Eerdmans Publishing Co, 4035 Park East Ct SE, Grand Rapids, MI 49546 *Tel:* 616-459-4591 *Toll Free Tel:* 800-253-7521 *E-mail:* customerservice@eerdmans.com; sales@eerdmans.com *Web Site:* www.eerdmans.com, pg 64

Efron, Sonni, National Press Foundation, 1211 Connecticut Ave NW, Suite 310, Washington, DC 20036 *Tel:* 202-663-7286 *Web Site:* nationalpress.org, pg 526

Egan, Neil, Chronicle Books LLC, 680 Second St, San Francisco, CA 94107 *Tel:* 415-537-4200 *Fax:* 415-537-4460 (perms) *E-mail:* hello@chroniclebooks.com; subrights@chroniclebooks.com *Web Site:* www.chroniclebooks.com, pg 47

Egan-Miller, Danielle, Browne & Miller Literary Associates, 52 Village Place, Hinsdale, IL 60521 *Tel:* 312-922-3063 *E-mail:* mail@browneandmiller.com *Web Site:* www.browneandmiller.com, pg 452

Eglash, Joe, Transcontinental Music Publications (TMP), 1375 Remington Rd, Suite M, Schaumburg, IL 60173-4844 *Tel:* 847-781-7800 *Fax:* 847-781-7801 *E-mail:* tmp@accantors.org *Web Site:* www.transcontinentalmusic.com, pg 209

Ehart, Kimberly A, Workman Publishing, 1290 Avenue of the Americas, New York, NY 10104 *Toll Free Tel:* 800-759-0190 *Fax:* 212-364-0950 *E-mail:* workman-inquiry@hbgusa.com *Web Site:* www.hachettebookgroup.com/imprint/workman-publishing-company/, pg 233

Ehle, Robert, Stanford University Press, 425 Broadway St, Redwood City, CA 94063-3126 *Tel:* 650-723-9434 *Fax:* 650-725-3457 *E-mail:* info@www.sup.org; publicity@www.sup.org; sales@www.sup.org *Web Site:* www.sup.org, pg 197

Ehlers, Lance, St Martin's Press, LLC, 120 Broadway, New York, NY 10271 *E-mail:* publicity@stmartins.com; trademarketing@stmartins.com; foreignrights@stmartins.com *Web Site:* us.macmillan.com/smp, pg 181

Ehmann, Stephanie, Penguin Random House Canada, a Penguin Random House company, 320 Front St W, Suite 1400, Toronto, ON M5V 3B6, Canada *Tel:* 416-364-4449 *Toll Free Tel:* 888-523-9292 (cust serv) *E-mail:* canadaweb@penguinrandomhouse.com; customerservicescanada@penguinrandomhouse.com *Web Site:* www.penguinrandomhouse.ca, pg 416

Ehrlich, Dorothy M, American Civil Liberties Union (ACLU), 125 Broad St, 18th fl, New York, NY 10004 *Tel:* 212-549-2500 *E-mail:* media@aclu.org *Web Site:* www.aclu.org, pg 495

Eichacker, Shane, Random House Children's Books, c/o Penguin Random House LLC, 1745 Broadway, New York, NY 10019 *Tel:* 212-782-9000 *Web Site:* www.rhcbooks.com, pg 170

Eickelbeck, Nikolaas, St Martin's Press, LLC, 120 Broadway, New York, NY 10271 *E-mail:* publicity@stmartins.com; trademarketing@stmartins.com; foreignrights@stmartins.com *Web Site:* us.macmillan.com/smp, pg 181

Eidsmo, Robin, Sun Valley Writers' Conference (SVWC), Galleria Bldg, 2nd fl, 351 Leadville Ave N, Ketchum, ID 83340 *Tel:* 208-726-5454 *E-mail:* info@svwc.com *Web Site:* svwc.com, pg 558

Eifrig, Penelope, Eifrig Publishing LLC, PO Box 66, Lemont, PA 16851 *Tel:* 814-954-9445 *E-mail:* info@eifrigpublishing.com *Web Site:* www.eifrigpublishing.com, pg 64

Einerson, Katy, Whiting Awards, 16 Court St, Suite 2308, Brooklyn, NY 11241 *Tel:* 718-701-5962 *E-mail:* info@whiting.org *Web Site:* www.whiting.org, pg 675

Einerson, Katy, Whiting Creative Nonfiction Grant, 16 Court St, Suite 2308, Brooklyn, NY 11241 *Tel:* 718-701-5962 *E-mail:* nonfiction@whiting.org; info@whiting.org *Web Site:* www.whiting.org, pg 675

Einerson, Katy, Whiting Literary Magazine Prizes, 16 Court St, Suite 2308, Brooklyn, NY 11241 *Tel:* 718-701-5962 *E-mail:* info@whiting.org *Web Site:* www.whiting.org/writers/whiting-literary-magazine-prizes, pg 675

Eis, Arlene L, Infosources Publishing, 140 Norma Rd, Teaneck, NJ 07666 *Tel:* 201-836-7072 *Web Site:* www.infosourcespub.com, pg 101

Eisele, Tracy, Macmillan, 120 Broadway, 22nd fl, New York, NY 10271 *E-mail:* press.inquiries@macmillan.com *Web Site:* us.macmillan.com, pg 122

Eisenbeiss, Naomi, InkWell Management, 521 Fifth Ave, Suite 2600, New York, NY 10175 *Tel:* 212-922-3500 *Fax:* 212-922-0535 *E-mail:* info@inkwellmanagement.com; submissions@inkwellmanagement.com; permissions@inkwellmanagement.com *Web Site:* inkwellmanagement.com, pg 463

Eisenberg, Michael, Highlights for Children Inc, 815 Church St, Honesdale, PA 18431 *Tel:* 570-253-1164 *Toll Free Tel:* 800-490-5111 *Fax:* 570-253-0179 *E-mail:* salesandmarketing@highlightspress.com *Web Site:* www.highlightspress.com; www.highlights.com; www.facebook.com/HighlightsforChildren, pg 92

Eisenmann, Caroline, Frances Goldin Literary Agency, Inc, 214 W 29 St, Suite 410, New York, NY 10001 *Tel:* 212-777-0047 *Fax:* 212-228-1660 *E-mail:* agency@goldinlit.com *Web Site:* www.goldinlit.com, pg 460

Eisenstark, Reyna, New York State Bar Association, One Elk St, Albany, NY 12207 *Tel:* 518-463-3200 *Toll Free Tel:* 800-582-2452 *Fax:* 518-463-5993 *E-mail:* mrc@nysba.org *Web Site:* nysba.org, pg 141

Eisenstark, Stacy, Island Press, 2000 "M" St NW, Suite 480-B, Washington, DC 20036 *Tel:* 202-232-7933 *Toll Free Tel:* 800-621-2736 *Fax:* 202-234-1328 *E-mail:* info@islandpress.org *Web Site:* www.islandpress.org, pg 104

Eissing, Cheryl, Flamingo Books, c/o Penguin Random House LLC, 1745 Broadway, New York, NY 10019 *Tel:* 212-782-9000 *Web Site:* www.penguin.com/flamingo-overview/, pg 72

Eiynck, Sandra, Liturgical Press, PO Box 7500, St John's Abbey, Collegeville, MN 56321-7500 *Tel:* 320-363-2213 *Toll Free Tel:* 800-858-5450 *Fax:* 320-363-3299 *Toll Free Fax:* 800-445-5899 *E-mail:* sales@litpress.org *Web Site:* www.litpress.org, pg 118

Ek, Caitlin, Chronicle Books LLC, 680 Second St, San Francisco, CA 94107 *Tel:* 415-537-4200 *Fax:* 415-537-4460 (perms) *E-mail:* hello@chroniclebooks.com; subrights@chroniclebooks.com *Web Site:* www.chroniclebooks.com, pg 47

Ekle, Emily, American Psychological Association, 750 First St NE, Washington, DC 20002 *Tel:* 202-336-5510 *Toll Free Tel:* 800-374-2721 *Fax:* 202-336-5502 *E-mail:* order@apa.org; booksales@apa.org *Web Site:* www.apa.org/books, pg 12

Ekus, Sally, Ekus Group LLC, 57 North St, Hatfield, MA 01038 *Tel:* 413-247-9325 *E-mail:* info@ekusgroup.com *Web Site:* ekusgroup.com, pg 457, 562

Elancheran, Maran, Newgen North America Inc, 2714 Bee Cave Rd, Suite 201, Austin, TX 78746 *Tel:* 512-478-5341 *Fax:* 512-476-4756 *E-mail:* sales@newgen.co *Web Site:* www.newgen.co, pg 443

Elbadawi, Sofia, Candlewick Press, 99 Dover St, Somerville, MA 02144-2825 *Tel:* 617-661-3330 *Fax:* 617-661-0565 *E-mail:* bigbear@candlewick.com; salesinfo@candlewick.com *Web Site:* candlewick.com, pg 40

Elblonk, Matthew, DeFiore and Company Literary Management Inc, 47 E 19 St, 3rd fl, New York, NY 10003 *Tel:* 212-925-7744 *Fax:* 212-925-9803 *E-mail:* info@defliterary.com; submissions@defliterary.com *Web Site:* www.defliterary.com, pg 456

Eldred, Jake, Random House Children's Books, c/o Penguin Random House LLC, 1745 Broadway, New York, NY 10019 *Tel:* 212-782-9000 *Web Site:* www.rhcbooks.com, pg 170

Elias, Lindsey, Penguin Random House LLC, 1745 Broadway, New York, NY 10019 *Tel:* 212-782-9000 *Toll Free Tel:* 800-726-0600 *Web Site:* www.penguinrandomhouse.com, pg 155

Elias Rowley, Kristen, The Ohio State University Press, 180 Pressey Hall, 1070 Carmack Rd, Columbus, OH 43210-1002 *Tel:* 614-292-6930 *Fax:* 614-292-2065 *Toll Free Fax:* 800-621-8476 *E-mail:* OSUPInfo@osu.edu *Web Site:* ohiostatepress.org, pg 145

Elkin, Jillian, ACM Books, 1601 Broadway, 10th fl, New York, NY 10019-7434 *Tel:* 212-869-7440 *E-mail:* acmbooks-info@acm.org *Web Site:* www.acm.org; books.acm.org, pg 4

Ellen, Joan, World Citizens, PO Box 131, Mill Valley, CA 94942-0131 *Tel:* 415-380-8020; 415-233-2822 (direct), pg 233

Ellenberg, Ethan, Ethan Ellenberg Literary Agency, 548 Broadway, Apt 5C, New York, NY 10012 *Tel:* 212-431-4554 *E-mail:* agent@ethanellenberg.com *Web Site:* www.ethanellenberg.com, pg 458

Ellenberg, Ezra, Ethan Ellenberg Literary Agency, 548 Broadway, Apt 5C, New York, NY 10012 *Tel:* 212-431-4554 *E-mail:* agent@ethanellenberg.com *Web Site:* www.ethanellenberg.com, pg 458

Eller, Beth, Bloomsbury Publishing Inc, 1385 Broadway, 5th fl, New York, NY 10018 *Tel:* 212-419-5300 *E-mail:* marketingusa@bloomsbury.com; adultpublicityusa@bloomsbury.com; askacademic@bloomsbury.com *Web Site:* www.bloomsbury.com, pg 31

Ellerbeck, Brian, Teachers College Press, 1234 Amsterdam Ave, New York, NY 10027 *Tel:* 212-678-3929 *Fax:* 212-678-4149 *E-mail:* tcpress@tc.edu *Web Site:* www.tcpress.com, pg 203

Ellery, Nina, Candlewick Press, 99 Dover St, Somerville, MA 02144-2825 *Tel:* 617-661-3330 *Fax:* 617-661-0565 *E-mail:* bigbear@candlewick.com; salesinfo@candlewick.com *Web Site:* candlewick.com, pg 40

Elliot, Billy, AuthorHouse, 1663 Liberty Dr, Bloomington, IN 47403 *Toll Free Tel:* 833-262-8899; 888-519-5121 *E-mail:* sales@authorhouse.com; vip@authorhouse.com *Web Site:* www.authorhouse.com, pg 22

Elliott, Bill, iUniverse, 1663 Liberty Dr, Bloomington, IN 47403 Toll Free Tel: 800-AUTHORS (288-4677); 844-349-9409 E-mail: media@iuniverse.com Web Site: www.iuniverse.com, pg 105

Elliott, Bill, Trafford Publishing, 1663 Liberty Dr, Bloomington, IN 47403 Toll Free Tel: 844-688-6899 E-mail: customersupport@trafford.com; sales@trafford.com Web Site: www.trafford.com, pg 208

Elliott, Bill, Xlibris Corp, 1663 Liberty Dr, Suite 200, Bloomington, IN 47403 Toll Free Tel: 844-714-8691; 888-795-4274 Fax: 610-915-0294 E-mail: info@xlibris.com; media@xlibris.com Web Site: www.xlibris.com; www.authorsolutions.com/our-imprints/xlibris, pg 234

Elliott, Gracie, Workman Publishing, 1290 Avenue of the Americas, New York, NY 10104 Toll Free Tel: 800-759-0190 Fax: 212-364-0950 E-mail: workman-inquiry@hbgusa.com Web Site: www.hachettebookgroup.com/imprint/workman-publishing-company/, pg 233

Elliott, Jasmine, Simon & Schuster Canada, 166 King St E, Suite 300, Toronto, ON M5A 1J3, Canada Tel: 647-427-8882 Toll Free Tel: 800-387-0446; 800-268-3216 (orders) Fax: 647-430-9446 Toll Free Fax: 888-849-8151 (orders) E-mail: info@simonandschuster.ca Web Site: www.simonandschuster.ca, pg 419

Elliott, Jennifer, International Linguistics Corp, 12220 Blue Ridge Blvd, Suite G, Kansas City, MO 64030 Tel: 816-765-8855 Toll Free Tel: 800-237-1830 (orders) E-mail: learnables@sbcglobal.net Web Site: www.learnables.com, pg 103

Elliott, Jess, Sourcebooks LLC, 1935 Brookdale Rd, Suite 139, Naperville, IL 60563 Tel: 630-961-3900 Toll Free Tel: 800-432-7444 Fax: 630-961-2168 E-mail: info@sourcebooks.com Web Site: www.sourcebooks.com, pg 194

Elliott, Julia, HarperCollins Publishers LLC, 195 Broadway, New York, NY 10007 Tel: 212-207-7000 Web Site: www.harpercollins.com, pg 87

Elliott, Richard, Sundance/Newbridge Publishing, 33 Boston Post Rd W, Suite 440, Marlborough, MA 01752 Toll Free Tel: 888-200-2720; 800-343-8204 Toll Free Fax: 800-456-2419 (orders) E-mail: info@sundancenewbridge.com; orders@sundancenewbridge.com Web Site: www.sundancenewbridge.com, pg 200

Elliott, Stephanie, Wesleyan University Press, 215 Long Lane, Middletown, CT 06459-0433 Tel: 860-685-7712 Fax: 860-685-7712 Web Site: www.wesleyan.edu/wespress, pg 227

Elliott, Stephen P, Sachem Publishing Associates Inc, 402 W Lyon Farm Dr, Greenwich, CT 06831 Tel: 203-813-3077 E-mail: sachempub@optonline.net, pg 444

Ellis, Clare, Stone Pier Press, PO Box 170572, San Francisco, CA 94117 Tel: 415-484-2821 E-mail: hello@stonepierpress.org Web Site: www.stonepierpress.org, pg 199

Ellis, Jane, University Science Books, 1305 Walt Whitman Rd, Suite 110, Melville, NY 11747 Tel: 703-661-1572 (cust serv & orders) Fax: 703-661-1501 E-mail: usbmail@presswarehouse.com (cust serv, orders) Web Site: uscibooks.aip.org, pg 222

Ellis, Jeremy, Joyce Meskis Excellence in Bookselling Scholarship, PO Box 746, Denver, CO 80201 Toll Free Tel: 800-752-0249 E-mail: info@mountainsplains.org Web Site: www.mountainsplains.org/meskis-scholarship, pg 632

Ellis, Jeremy, Reading the West Book Awards, PO Box 746, Denver, CO 80201 Tel: 970-484-3939 Toll Free Tel: 800-752-0249 Fax: 970-484-0037 E-mail: info@mountainsplains.org Web Site: www.mountainsplains.org/reading-the-west-book-awards, pg 655

Ellis, Molly, Farrar, Straus & Giroux Books for Young Readers, 120 Broadway, New York, NY 10271 Tel: 212-741-6900 Toll Free Tel: 888-330-8477 (orders) E-mail: childrens.publicity@macmillanusa.com; childrensrights@macmillanusa.com Web Site: us.macmillan.com/mackids, pg 69

Ellis, Molly, Roaring Brook Press, 120 Broadway, New York, NY 10271 Tel: 646-307-5151 Web Site: us.macmillan.com/publishers/roaring-brook-press, pg 175

Ellsberg, Robert, Orbis Books, PO Box 302, Maryknoll, NY 10545-0302 Tel: 914-941-7636 Toll Free Tel: 800-258-5838 (orders, Mon-Fri 8AM-4PM EST) Fax: 914-941-7005 E-mail: orbisbooks@maryknoll.org Web Site: orbisbooks.com, pg 147

Ellsworth, Kate, Tanenbaum International Literary Agency Ltd (TILA), 1035 Fifth Ave, Suite 15D, New York, NY 10028 Tel: 212-371-4120 Fax: 212-988-0457 E-mail: hello@tanenbauminternational.com Web Site: tanenbauminternational.com, pg 479

Ellsworth, Thomas N, Vesuvian Books, 711 Dolly Parton Pkwy, No 4313, Sevierville, TN 37864 E-mail: info@vesuvianmedia.com Web Site: www.vesuvianmedia.com, pg 224

Ellul, Nicole, Simon & Schuster Children's Publishing, 1230 Avenue of the Americas, New York, NY 10020 Tel: 212-698-7000 Web Site: www.simonandschuster.com/kids; www.simonandschuster.com/teen; simonandschuster.net; simonandschuster.biz, pg 189

Ellwood, Nancy, Arcadia Publishing Inc, 210 Wingo Way, Suite 200, Mount Pleasant, SC 29464 Tel: 843-853-2070 E-mail: retailers@arcadiapublishing.com Web Site: www.arcadiapublishing.com, pg 16

Elmer, Derek, Random House Children's Books, c/o Penguin Random House LLC, 1745 Broadway, New York, NY 10019 Tel: 212-782-9000 Web Site: www.rhcbooks.com, pg 169

Elnan, Hannah, Sasquatch Books, 1904 S Third Ave, Suite 710, Seattle, WA 98101 Tel: 206-467-4300 Toll Free Tel: 800-775-0817 Fax: 206-467-4301 E-mail: custserv@sasquatchbooks.com Web Site: sasquatchbooks.com, pg 182

Elroubi, Sara, Farrar, Straus & Giroux Books for Young Readers, 120 Broadway, New York, NY 10271 Tel: 212-741-6900 Toll Free Tel: 888-330-8477 (orders) E-mail: childrens.publicity@macmillanusa.com; childrensrights@macmillanusa.com Web Site: us.macmillan.com/mackids, pg 70

Elroubi, Sara, Roaring Brook Press, 120 Broadway, New York, NY 10271 Tel: 646-307-5151 Web Site: us.macmillan.com/publishers/roaring-brook-press, pg 176

Elsayed, Danya, Penguin Random House Canada, a Penguin Random House company, 320 Front St W, Suite 1400, Toronto, ON M5V 3B6, Canada Tel: 416-364-4449 Toll Free Tel: 888-523-9292 (cust serv) E-mail: canadaweb@penguinrandomhouse.com; customerservicescanada@penguinrandomhouse.com Web Site: www.penguinrandomhouse.ca, pg 416

Elwell, James, Tyndale House Publishers Inc, 351 Executive Dr, Carol Stream, IL 60188 Tel: 630-668-8300 Toll Free Tel: 800-323-9400; 855-277-9400 Toll Free Fax: 866-622-9474 Web Site: www.tyndale.com, pg 211

Emeran, Christine, National Coalition Against Censorship (NCAC), 19 Fulton St, Suite 407, New York, NY 10038 Tel: 212-807-6222 Fax: 212-807-6245 E-mail: ncac@ncac.org Web Site: www.ncac.org, pg 512

Emerson, Brady, Penguin Random House Audio Publishing Group, 1745 Broadway, New York, NY 10019 Toll Free Tel: 800-793-2665 (cust serv) E-mail: audio@penguinrandomhouse.com; ecustomerservice@penguinrandomhouse.com Web Site: www.penguinrandomhouseaudio.com, pg 154

Emmett, Jennifer, National Geographic Books, 1145 17 St NW, Washington, DC 20036-4688 Tel: 202-857-7000 Toll Free Tel: 877-866-6486 E-mail: ngbooks@cdsfulfillment.com Web Site: www.nationalgeographic.com/books/; ngbooks.buysub.com, pg 138

Encarnacion, Ely, Baylor University Press, Baylor University, One Bear Place, Waco, TX 76798-7363 Tel: 254-710-3164 E-mail: bup_marketing@baylor.edu Web Site: www.baylorpress.com, pg 25

Enderle, Kristine, American Psychological Association, 750 First St NE, Washington, DC 20002 Tel: 202-336-5510 Toll Free Tel: 800-374-2721 Fax: 202-336-5502 E-mail: order@apa.org; booksales@apa.org Web Site: www.apa.org/books, pg 12

Enderlin, Jennifer, St Martin's Press, LLC, 120 Broadway, New York, NY 10271 E-mail: publicity@stmartins.com; trademarketing@stmartins.com; foreignrights@stmartins.com Web Site: us.macmillan.com/smp, pg 180

Endler, Abby, Alfred A Knopf, c/o Penguin Random House LLC, 1745 Broadway, New York, NY 10019 Tel: 212-751-2600 Fax: 212-940-7390 (dom rts); 212-572-2662 (foreign rts) Web Site: knopfdoubleday.com/imprint/knopf/; knopfdoubleday.com, pg 110

Engebretson, George, Watermark Publishing, 1000 Bishop St, Suite 806, Honolulu, HI 96813 Tel: 808-587-7766 Toll Free Tel: 866-900-BOOK (900-2665) Fax: 808-521-3461 E-mail: info@bookshawaii.net Web Site: www.bookshawaii.net, pg 226

Engel, Jackie, Little, Brown Books for Young Readers (LBYR), 1290 Avenue of the Americas, New York, NY 10104 Tel: 212-364-1100 Toll Free Tel: 800-759-0190 (cust serv) E-mail: rights@lbchildrens.com Web Site: www.hachettebookgroup.com/imprint/little-brown-books-for-young-readers/, pg 118

Engel, Margaret, The Alicia Patterson Foundation Fellowship Program, 1100 Vermont Ave, Suite 900, Washington, DC 20005 Tel: 202-393-5995 Fax: 301-951-8512 E-mail: info@aliciapatterson.org Web Site: www.aliciapatterson.org, pg 646

Engelman, Ralph, George Polk Awards in Journalism, The Brooklyn Campus, One University Plaza, Brooklyn, NY 11201-5372 Tel: 718-488-1009 Web Site: www.liu.edu/polk, pg 651

Engelmann, Sarah, Knopf Doubleday Publishing Group, c/o Penguin Random House LLC, 1745 Broadway, New York, NY 10019 Tel: 212-751-2600 Fax: 212-940-7390 (dom rts); 212-572-2662 (foreign rts) Web Site: knopfdoubleday.com, pg 110

Engelsma, Jonathan, Reformation Heritage Books, 2965 Leonard St NE, Grand Rapids, MI 49525 Tel: 616-977-0889 Fax: 616-285-3246 E-mail: orders@heritagebooks.org Web Site: www.heritagebooks.org, pg 173

Englander, Amanda, Union Square & Co, 1166 Avenue of the Americas, 17th fl, New York, NY 10036-2715 Tel: 212-532-7160 Toll Free Tel: 800-367-9692 Fax: 212-213-2495 Toll Free Fax: 800-542-7567 E-mail: custservice@sterlingpublishing.com; customerservice@sterlingpublishing.com; editorial@sterlingpublishing.com; tradesales@sterlingpublishing.com Web Site: www.sterlingpublishing.com, pg 212

Engle-Laird, Carl, Tor Publishing Group, 120 Broadway, New York, NY 10271 Toll Free Tel: 800-455-0340 (Macmillan) E-mail: torpublicity@tor.com; forgepublicity@forgebooks.com Web Site: us.macmillan.com/torpublishinggroup, pg 208

Engler, Hannah, Doubleday, c/o Penguin Random House LLC, 1745 Broadway, New York, NY 10019 Tel: 212-751-2600 Fax: 212-940-7390 (dom rts); 212-572-2662 (foreign rts) Web Site: knopfdoubleday.com/imprint/doubleday/; knopfdoubleday.com, pg 61

Englert, Bradley, Orbit, 1290 Avenue of the Americas, New York, NY 10104 Tel: 212-364-1100 Toll Free Tel: 800-759-0190 Web Site: www.orbitbooks.net; www.hachettebookgroup.com/imprint/orbit, pg 147

Englert, Joanna, Mary McCarthy Prize in Short Fiction, 822 E Market St, Louisville, KY 40206 Tel: 502-458-4028 E-mail: info@sarabandebooks.org Web Site: www.sarabandebooks.org/mccarthy, pg 630

Englert, Joanna, Kathryn A Morton Prize in Poetry, 822 E Market St, Louisville, KY 40206 Tel: 502-458-4028 E-mail: info@sarabandebooks.org Web Site: www.sarabandebooks.org/morton, pg 635

Englert, Joanna, Sarabande Books Inc, 822 E Market St, Louisville, KY 40206 Tel: 502-458-4028 Fax: 502-458-4065 E-mail: info@sarabandebooks.org Web Site: www.sarabandebooks.org, pg 182

Englert, Joanna, The Sarabande Series in Kentucky Literature, 822 E Market St, Louisville, KY 40206 *Tel:* 502-458-4028 *E-mail:* info@sarabandebooks.org *Web Site:* www.sarabandebooks.org/bruckheimer, pg 659

Engles, Eric W PhD, EditCraft Editorial Services, 422 Pine St, Grass Valley, CA 95945 *Tel:* 530-273-3934 *Web Site:* www.editcraft.com, pg 438

English, Beth, Willi Paul Adams Award, 112 N Bryan Ave, Bloomington, IN 47408-4141 *Tel:* 812-855-7311 *E-mail:* oah@oah.org *Web Site:* www.oah.org/awards, pg 570

English, Beth, Ray Allen Billington Prize, 112 N Bryan Ave, Bloomington, IN 47408-4141 *Tel:* 812-855-7311 *E-mail:* oah@oah.org *Web Site:* www.oah.org/awards, pg 580

English, Beth, Binkley-Stephenson Award, 112 N Bryan Ave, Bloomington, IN 47408-4141 *Tel:* 812-855-7311 *E-mail:* oah@oah.org *Web Site:* www.oah.org/awards, pg 580

English, Beth, Civil War and Reconstruction Book Award, 112 N Bryan Ave, Bloomington, IN 47408-4141 *Tel:* 812-855-7311 *E-mail:* oah@oah.org *Web Site:* www.oah.org/awards, pg 590

English, Beth, Merle Curti Intellectual History Award, 112 N Bryan Ave, Bloomington, IN 47408-4141 *Tel:* 812-855-7311 *E-mail:* oah@oah.org *Web Site:* www.oah.org/awards, pg 594

English, Beth, Merle Curti Social History Award, 112 N Bryan Ave, Bloomington, IN 47408-4141 *Tel:* 812-855-7311 *E-mail:* oah@oah.org *Web Site:* www.oah.org/awards, pg 594

English, Beth, Ellis W Hawley Prize, 112 N Bryan Ave, Bloomington, IN 47408-4141 *Tel:* 812-855-7311 *E-mail:* oah@oah.org *Web Site:* www.oah.org/awards, pg 611

English, Beth, Darlene Clark Hine Award, 112 N Bryan Ave, Bloomington, IN 47408-4141 *Tel:* 812-855-7311 *E-mail:* oah@oah.org *Web Site:* www.oah.org/awards, pg 613

English, Beth, Richard W Leopold Prize, 112 N Bryan Ave, Bloomington, IN 47408-4141 *Tel:* 812-855-7311 *E-mail:* oah@oah.org *Web Site:* www.oah.org/awards, pg 623

English, Beth, Lawrence W Levine Award, 112 N Bryan Ave, Bloomington, IN 47408-4141 *Tel:* 812-855-7311 *E-mail:* oah@oah.org *Web Site:* www.oah.org/awards, pg 624

English, Beth, Liberty Legacy Foundation Award, 112 N Bryan Ave, Bloomington, IN 47408-4141 *Tel:* 812-855-7311 *E-mail:* oah@oah.org *Web Site:* www.oah.org/awards, pg 624

English, Beth, David Montgomery Award, 112 N Bryan Ave, Bloomington, IN 47408-4141 *Tel:* 812-855-7311 *E-mail:* oah@oah.org *Web Site:* www.oah.org/awards, pg 634

English, Beth, Mary Nickliss Prize in US Women's and/or Gender History, 112 N Bryan Ave, Bloomington, IN 47408-4141 *Tel:* 812-855-7311 *E-mail:* oah@oah.org *Web Site:* www.oah.org/awards, pg 641

English, Beth, James A Rawley Prize, 112 N Bryan Ave, Bloomington, IN 47408-4141 *Tel:* 812-855-7311 *E-mail:* oah@oah.org *Web Site:* www.oah.org/awards, pg 655

English, Beth, David Thelen Award, 112 N Bryan Ave, Bloomington, IN 47408-4141 *Tel:* 812-855-7311 *E-mail:* oah@oah.org *Web Site:* www.oah.org/awards, pg 669

English, Beth, Frederick Jackson Turner Award, 112 N Bryan Ave, Bloomington, IN 47408-4141 *Tel:* 812-855-7311 *E-mail:* oah@oah.org *Web Site:* www.oah.org/awards, pg 671

English, Joe, Random House Children's Books, c/o Penguin Random House LLC, 1745 Broadway, New York, NY 10019 *Tel:* 212-782-9000 *Web Site:* www.rhcbooks.com, pg 169

English-Loeb, Brenna, Transatlantic Agency, 2 Bloor St E, Suite 3500, Toronto, ON M4W 1A8, Canada *Tel:* 416-488-9214 *E-mail:* info@transatlanticagency.com; royalties@transatlanticagency.com *Web Site:* www.transatlanticagency.com, pg 479

Engstrand, Vida, Kensington Publishing Corp, 900 Third Ave, 26th fl, New York, NY 10022 *Tel:* 212-407-1500 *Toll Free Tel:* 800-221-2647 *Fax:* 212-935-0699 *Web Site:* www.kensingtonbooks.com, pg 109

Engwall, Emily, Poisoned Pen Press, 4014 N Goldwater Blvd, Suite 201, Scottsdale, AZ 85251 *Tel:* 480-945-3375 *Toll Free Tel:* 800-421-3976 *Fax:* 480-949-1707 *E-mail:* info@poisonedpenpress.com *Web Site:* www.poisonedpenpress.com, pg 161

Enrich, Jordanna, Fulbright Scholar Program, 1400 "K" St NW, Washington, DC 20005 *Tel:* 202-686-4000 *E-mail:* scholars@iie.org *Web Site:* www.cies.org; www.iie.org, pg 605

Enriquez, Alana, The University of Arizona Press, 1510 E University Blvd, Tucson, AZ 85721 *Tel:* 520-621-1441 *Toll Free Tel:* 800-621-2736 (orders) *Fax:* 520-621-8899 *Toll Free Fax:* 800-621-8476 (orders) *E-mail:* uap@uapress.arizona.edu *Web Site:* www.uapress.arizona.edu, pg 214

Ens, Sarah, University of Manitoba Press, University of Manitoba, 301 St Johns College, 92 Dysart Rd, Winnipeg, MB R3T 2M5, Canada *Tel:* 204-474-9495 *Fax:* 204-474-7566 *E-mail:* uofmpress@umanitoba.ca *Web Site:* uofmpress.ca, pg 422

Ensor, Kendra, Rand McNally, 9855 Woods Dr, Skokie, IL 60077 *Tel:* 847-329-8100 *Toll Free Tel:* 877-446-4863 *Toll Free Fax:* 877-469-1298 *E-mail:* mediarelations@randmcnally.com; tndsupport@randmcnally.com *Web Site:* www.randmcnally.com, pg 169

Enss, Chris, Spur Awards, 271 CR 219, Encampment, WY 82325 *Tel:* 307-329-8942 *Web Site:* westernwriters.org/spur-awards, pg 665

Enss, Chris, Western Writers of America Inc (WWA), 271 CR 219, Encampment, WY 82325 *Tel:* 307-329-8942 *Web Site:* westernwriters.org, pg 521

Entrekin, Morgan, Grove Atlantic Inc, 154 W 14 St, 12th fl, New York, NY 10011 *Tel:* 212-614-7850 *Toll Free Tel:* 800-521-0178 *Fax:* 212-614-7886 *E-mail:* info@groveatlantic.com; sales@groveatlantic.com; publicity@groveatlantic.com; rights@groveatlantic.com *Web Site:* www.groveatlantic.com, pg 82

Epler, Barbara, New Directions Publishing Corp, 80 Eighth Ave, 19th fl, New York, NY 10011 *Tel:* 212-255-0230 *E-mail:* editorial@ndbooks.com; publicity@ndbooks.com *Web Site:* ndbooks.com, pg 139

Erb, Sophie, Flamingo Books, c/o Penguin Random House LLC, 1745 Broadway, New York, NY 10019 *Tel:* 212-782-9000 *Web Site:* www.penguin.com/flamingo-overview/, pg 72

Erfer, Jessica, American Academy of Political & Social Science (AAPSS), 220 S 40 St, Suite 201-E, Philadelphia, PA 19104-3543 *Tel:* 215-746-6500 *Fax:* 215-573-2667 *Web Site:* www.aapss.org, pg 494

Erickson, Anna, Creative Editions, 2140 Howard Dr W, North Mankato, MN 56003 *Tel:* 507-388-6273 *Toll Free Tel:* 800-445-6209 *Fax:* 507-388-2746 *E-mail:* info@thecreativecompany.us; orders@thecreativecompany.us *Web Site:* www.thecreativecompany.us, pg 55

Erickson, Chris, Emmaus Road Publishing Inc, 1468 Parkview Circle, Steubenville, OH 43952 *Tel:* 750-264-9535 *Fax:* 740-475-0230 (orders) *E-mail:* questions@emmausroad.org *Web Site:* stpaulcenter.com/emmaus-road-publishing, pg 66

Erickson, Lisa, HarperCollins Publishers LLC, 195 Broadway, New York, NY 10007 *Tel:* 212-207-7000 *Web Site:* www.harpercollins.com, pg 86

Erickson, Stephen, St Martin's Press, LLC, 120 Broadway, New York, NY 10271 *E-mail:* publicity@stmartins.com; trademarketing@stmartins.com; foreignrights@stmartins.com *Web Site:* us.macmillan.com/smp, pg 181

Erickson, Tim, RAND Corp, 1776 Main St, Santa Monica, CA 90407-2138 *Tel:* 310-393-0411 *Fax:* 310-393-4818 *Web Site:* www.rand.org, pg 169

Ernest, James, Wm B Eerdmans Publishing Co, 4035 Park East Ct SE, Grand Rapids, MI 49546 *Tel:* 616-459-4591 *Toll Free Tel:* 800-253-7521 *E-mail:* customerservice@eerdmans.com; sales@eerdmans.com *Web Site:* www.eerdmans.com, pg 64

Ernst, Christopher D, Artech House®, 685 Canton St, Norwood, MA 02062 *Tel:* 781-769-9750 *Toll Free Tel:* 800-225-9977 *Fax:* 781-769-6334 *E-mail:* artech@artechhouse.com *Web Site:* us.artechhouse.com, pg 17

Ernst, Tobin, Society for Advancing Business Editing and Writing (SABEW), Walter Cronkite School of Journalism & Mass Communication, Arizona State University, 555 N Central Ave, Suite 406E, Phoenix, AZ 85004-1248 *Tel:* 602-496-7862 *E-mail:* sabew@sabew.org *Web Site:* sabew.org, pg 519

Ernst, Toby L, Random House Publishing Group, 1745 Broadway, New York, NY 10019 *Toll Free Tel:* 800-200-3552 *Web Site:* www.randomhousebooks.com, pg 171

Erolin, Chantz, Graywolf Press, 212 Third Ave N, Suite 485, Minneapolis, MN 55401 *Tel:* 651-641-0077 *Fax:* 651-641-0036 *E-mail:* wolves@graywolfpress.org (no ms queries, sample chapters or proposals) *Web Site:* www.graywolfpress.org, pg 81

Errera, Jessica, Jane Rotrosen Agency LLC, 318 E 51 St, New York, NY 10022-7803 *Tel:* 212-593-4330 *E-mail:* info@janerotrosen.com *Web Site:* janerotrosen.com, pg 474

Errico, Annalise, Ladderbird Literary Agency, 460 Yellow Brick Rd, Orange, CT 06477 *Tel:* 203-290-1703 *Web Site:* www.ladderbird.com, pg 466

Errico, Kristin, little bee books, 598 Broadway, 7th fl, New York, NY 10012 *Tel:* 212-321-0237 *Toll Free Tel:* 844-321-0237 *E-mail:* info@littlebeebooks.com; sales@littlebeebooks.com; publicity@littlebeebooks.com *Web Site:* littlebeebooks.com, pg 117

Errico, Vincent, Trusted Media Brands Inc, 750 Third Ave, 3rd fl, New York, NY 10017 *Tel:* 646-293-6299 *Toll Free Tel:* 877-732-4438 (cust serv) *Fax:* 646-293-6251 *E-mail:* customercare@trustedmediabrands.com; press@trustedmediabrands.com *Web Site:* www.trustedmediabrands.com; www.rd.com, pg 210

Ertl, Julie, Doubleday, c/o Penguin Random House LLC, 1745 Broadway, New York, NY 10019 *Tel:* 212-751-2600 *Fax:* 212-940-7390 (dom rts); 212-572-2662 (foreign rts) *Web Site:* knopfdoubleday.com/imprint/doubleday/; knopfdoubleday.com, pg 61

Erwin, Lisa, Simon & Schuster, LLC, 1230 Avenue of the Americas, New York, NY 10020 *Tel:* 212-698-7000 *Toll Free Tel:* 800-223-2336 (orders) *Fax:* 212-698-7007 *Toll Free Fax:* 800-943-9831 (orders) *E-mail:* firstname.lastname@simonandschuster.com; purchaseorders@simonandschuster.com (orders) *Web Site:* www.simonandschuster.com, pg 190

Escoto, Allison, The Center for Fiction, 15 Lafayette Ave, Brooklyn, NY 11217 *Tel:* 212-755-6710 *E-mail:* info@centerforfiction.org *Web Site:* centerforfiction.org, pg 503

Esersky, Gareth, Carol Mann Agency, 55 Fifth Ave, 18th fl, New York, NY 10003 *Tel:* 212-206-5635 *Fax:* 212-675-4809 *E-mail:* submissions@carolmannagency.com *Web Site:* www.carolmannagency.com, pg 468

Esner, Melissa, HarperCollins Publishers LLC, 195 Broadway, New York, NY 10007 *Tel:* 212-207-7000 *Web Site:* www.harpercollins.com, pg 86

Espinosa, Maria, Atria Books, 1230 Avenue of the Americas, New York, NY 10020 *Tel:* 212-698-7000 *Fax:* 212-698-7007 *Web Site:* www.simonandschuster.com, pg 86

Espinoza, Ana, Doubleday, c/o Penguin Random House LLC, 1745 Broadway, New York, NY 10019 *Tel:* 212-751-2600 *Fax:* 212-940-7390 (dom rts); 212-572-2662 (foreign rts) *Web Site:* knopfdoubleday.com/imprint/doubleday/; knopfdoubleday.com, pg 61

Esposito, Cathy, University of South Carolina Press, 1600 Hampton St, Suite 544, Columbia, SC 29208 Tel: 803-777-5245 Toll Free Tel: 800-768-2500 (orders) Fax: 803-777-0160 Toll Free Fax: 800-868-0740 (orders) Web Site: uscpress.com, pg 220

Esposito, Valerie, Macmillan, 120 Broadway, 22nd fl, New York, NY 10271 E-mail: press.inquiries@macmillan.com Web Site: us.macmillan.com, pg 122

Essary, Loris, International Titles, 931 E 56 St, Austin, TX 78751-1724 Tel: 512-909-2447 Web Site: www.internationaltitles.com, pg 464

Essex, Laura, Hachette Audio, 1290 Avenue of the Americas, New York, NY 10104 Tel: 212-364-1100 Web Site: www.hachettebookgroup.com/imprint/hachette-audio/, pg 83

Estel, Matt, Zondervan, 3900 Sparks Dr SE, Grand Rapids, MI 49546 Tel: 616-698-6900 Toll Free Tel: 800-226-1122; 800-727-1309 (retail orders) Fax: 616-698-3350 Toll Free Fax: 800-698-3256 (retail orders) E-mail: customercare@harpercollins.com Web Site: www.zondervan.com, pg 237

Ester, Alicia, Beaver's Pond Press Inc, 939 Seventh St W, St Paul, MN 55102 Tel: 952-829-8818 E-mail: submissions@beaverspondpress.com Web Site: www.beaverspondpress.com, pg 26

Esterly, Flora, Farrar, Straus & Giroux, LLC, 120 Broadway, New York, NY 10271 Tel: 212-741-6900 E-mail: fsg.publicity@fsgbooks.com; sales@fsgbooks.com Web Site: us.macmillan.com/fsg, pg 70

Esteves, Patricia, Kids Can Press Ltd, 25 Dockside Dr, Toronto, ON M5A 0B5, Canada Tel: 416-479-7000 Toll Free Tel: 800-265-0884 Fax: 416-960-5437 E-mail: info@kidscan.com; customerservice@kidscan.com Web Site: www.kidscanpress.com; www.kidscanpress.ca, pg 411

Etcheson, Amy, Southern Illinois University Press, 1915 University Press Dr, SIUC Mail Code 6806, Carbondale, IL 62901-4323 Tel: 618-453-2281 Fax: 618-453-1221 E-mail: rights@siu.edu Web Site: www.siupress.com, pg 195

Etcheverry, Gabrielle, Livres Canada Books, One Nicholas, Suite 504, Ottawa, ON K1N 7B7, Canada Tel: 613-562-2324 Fax: 613-562-2329 E-mail: info@livrescanadabooks.com Web Site: www.livrescanadabooks.com, pg 510

Eteng, Jhonson, Kensington Publishing Corp, 900 Third Ave, 26th fl, New York, NY 10022 Tel: 212-407-1500 Toll Free Tel: 800-221-2647 Fax: 212-935-0699 Web Site: www.kensingtonbooks.com, pg 109

Eth, Felicia, Felicia Eth Literary Representation, 555 Bryant St, Suite 350, Palo Alto, CA 94301 Tel: 415-970-9717 E-mail: feliciaeth.literary@gmail.com Web Site: www.ethliterary.com, pg 458

Etling, Brian, Alfred A Knopf, c/o Penguin Random House LLC, 1745 Broadway, New York, NY 10019 Tel: 212-751-2600 Fax: 212-940-7390 (dom rts); 212-572-2662 (foreign rts) Web Site: knopfdoubleday.com/imprint/knopf/; knopfdoubleday.com, pg 110

Etra, Judith, Whittier Publications Inc, 121 Regent Dr, Lido Beach, NY 11561 Tel: 516-432-8120 Toll Free Tel: 800-897-TEXT (897-8398) Fax: 516-889-0341 E-mail: info@whitbooks.com Web Site: www.whitbooks.com, pg 229

Etsell, Christopher, The Guilford Press, 370 Seventh Ave, Suite 1200, New York, NY 10001-1020 Tel: 212-431-9800 Toll Free Tel: 800-365-7006 Fax: 212-966-6708 E-mail: info@guilford.com; orders@guilford.com Web Site: www.guilford.com, pg 82

Ettinger, Kathryn, Running Press, 1290 Avenue of the Americas, New York, NY 10104 Tel: 212-364-1100 Toll Free Tel: 800-759-0190 (cust serv) Fax: 212-364-0933 (intl orders) Toll Free Fax: 800-286-9471 (cust serv) E-mail: customer.service@hbgusa.com; orders@hbgusa.com Web Site: www.hachettebookgroup.com/imprint/running-press/; www.moon.com (Moon Travel Guides), pg 178

Etzkorn, Laura, Tor Publishing Group, 120 Broadway, New York, NY 10271 Toll Free Tel: 800-455-0340 (Macmillan) E-mail: torpublicity@tor.com; forgepublicity@forgebooks.com Web Site: us.macmillan.com/torpublishinggroup, pg 208

Eubanks, Debra, American Psychiatric Association Publishing, 800 Maine Ave SW, Suite 900, Washington, DC 20024 Tel: 202-459-9722 Toll Free Tel: 800-368-5777 Fax: 202-403-3094 E-mail: appi@psych.org Web Site: www.appi.org; www.psychiatryonline.org, pg 11

Eulau, Dennis, Simon & Schuster, LLC, 1230 Avenue of the Americas, New York, NY 10020 Tel: 212-698-7000 Toll Free Tel: 800-223-2336 (orders) Fax: 212-698-7007 Toll Free Fax: 800-943-9831 (orders) E-mail: firstname.lastname@simonandschuster.com; purchaseorders@simonandschuster.com (orders) Web Site: www.simonandschuster.com, pg 189

Evans, Ashten, Ulysses Press, 195 Montague St, 14th fl, Brooklyn, NY 11201 Tel: 510-601-8301 Toll Free Tel: 800-377-2542 Fax: 510-601-8307 E-mail: ulysses@ulyssespress.com Web Site: www.ulyssespress.com, pg 212

Evans, Claire Lewis, University of Alabama Press, 200 Hackberry Lane, 2nd fl, Tuscaloosa, AL 35487 Tel: 205-348-5180 Fax: 205-348-9201 Web Site: www.uapress.ua.edu, pg 214

Evans, Clark, Abraham Lincoln Institute Book Award, c/o ALI Treasurer, 4158 Vernoy Hills Rd, Fairfax, VA 22030 Web Site: www.lincoln-institute.org, pg 625

Evans, Erin, Oak Knoll Press, 310 Delaware St, New Castle, DE 19720 Tel: 302-328-7232 Fax: 302-328-7274 E-mail: oakknoll@oakknoll.com; orders@oakknoll.com; publishing@oakknoll.com Web Site: www.oakknoll.com, pg 144

Evans, Jamie, Holiday House Publishing Inc, 50 Broad St, New York, NY 10004 Tel: 212-688-0085 Fax: 212-421-6134 E-mail: info@holidayhouse.com Web Site: www.holidayhouse.com, pg 94

Evans, Jamie, Peachtree Publishing Co Inc, 1700 Chattahoochee Ave, Atlanta, GA 30318-2112 Tel: 404-876-8761 Toll Free Tel: 800-241-0113 Fax: 404-875-2578 Toll Free Fax: 800-875-8909 E-mail: hello@peachtree-online.com; orders@peachtree-online.com; sales@peachtree-online.com Web Site: www.peachtreebooks.com; www.peachtree-online.com, pg 153

Evans, Janice, University of Toronto Press, Book Publishing Div, 800 Bay St, Mezzanine, Toronto, ON M5S 3A9, Canada Tel: 416-978-2239 Fax: 416-978-4736 E-mail: utpbooks@utorontopress.com (orders) Web Site: utorontopress.com, pg 423

Evans, Jennifer, Springer, One New York Plaza, Suite 4600, New York, NY 10004-1562 Tel: 212-460-1500 Toll Free Tel: 800-SPRINGER (777-4643) Fax: 212-460-1700 E-mail: customerservice@springernature.com Web Site: www.springer.com, pg 196

Evans, John, PAGE International Screenwriting Awards, 7190 W Sunset Blvd, Suite 610, Hollywood, CA 90046 E-mail: info@pageawards.com Web Site: pageawards.com, pg 645

Evans, Lois, Random House Children's Books, c/o Penguin Random House LLC, 1745 Broadway, New York, NY 10019 Tel: 212-782-9000 Web Site: www.rhcbooks.com, pg 170

Evans, Mary, Mary Evans Inc, 242 E Fifth St, New York, NY 10003-8501 Fax: 212-979-5344 E-mail: info@maryevansinc.com Web Site: maryevansinc.com, pg 458

Evans, Megan, Harry N Abrams Inc, 195 Broadway, 9th fl, New York, NY 10007 Tel: 212-206-7715 Toll Free Tel: 800-345-1359 Fax: 212-645-8437 E-mail: abrams@abramsbooks.com; publicity@abramsbooks.com; sales@abramsbooks.com Web Site: www.abramsbooks.com, pg 3

Evans, Mike, Houghton Mifflin Harcourt, 125 High St, Boston, MA 02110 Tel: 617-351-5000 Toll Free Tel: 855-969-4642; 800-225-5425 (K-12 educ materials); 800-323-9540 (assessment materials); 877-219-1537 (SkillsTutor); 888-242-6747 (Innovation in Educ Group); 800-225-3362 (Trade & Ref Div) Toll Free Fax: 800-269-5232 E-mail: myhmhco@hmhco.com Web Site: www.hmhco.com, pg 95

Evans, Stacie, VONA Voices Summer Writing Workshops, 2820 SW 20 St, Miami, FL 33145 E-mail: info@vonavoices.org Web Site: www.vonavoices.org, pg 558

Evans, Tamiko, 4A's (American Association of Advertising Agencies), 25 W 45 St, 16th fl, New York, NY 10036 Tel: 212-682-2500 E-mail: media@4as.org; membership@4as.org Web Site: www.aaaa.org, pg 506

Evans, Tom, World Book Inc, 180 N LaSalle, Suite 900, Chicago, IL 60601 Tel: 312-729-5800 Toll Free Tel: 800-967-5325 (consumer sales, US); 800-975-3250 (school & lib sales, US); 800-837-5365 (school & lib sales, CN) Toll Free Fax: 888-922-3766 E-mail: customerservice@worldbook.com Web Site: www.worldbook.com, pg 233

Evans, Tracy Wareing, American Public Human Services Association (APHSA), 1300 17 St N, Suite 340, Arlington, VA 22209-3801 Tel: 202-682-0100 Fax: 202-289-6555 E-mail: memberservice@aphsa.org Web Site: www.aphsa.org, pg 496

Evans, Will, Dalkey Archive Press, c/o Deep Vellum Publishing, 3000 Commerce St, Dallas, TX 75226 E-mail: admin@deepvellum.org Web Site: www.dalkeyarchive.com, pg 56

Evans-Lombe, Monica, Special Libraries Association (SLA), 7918 Jones Branch Dr, Suite 300, McLean, VA 22102 Tel: 703-647-4900 Fax: 703-506-3266 E-mail: info@sla.org Web Site: www.sla.org, pg 520

Eveleigh, Douglas, Encyclopaedia Britannica Inc, 325 N La Salle St, Suite 200, Chicago, IL 60654 Tel: 312-347-7000 (all other countries) Toll Free Tel: 800-323-1229 (US & CN) Fax: 312-294-2104 E-mail: contact@eb.com Web Site: www.britannica.com, pg 66

Everhart, Deborah L, Andrews University Press, Sutherland House, 8360 W Campus Circle Dr, Berrien Springs, MI 49104-1700 Tel: 269-471-6134 Toll Free Tel: 800-467-6369 (Visa, MC & American Express orders only) Fax: 269-471-6224 E-mail: aupo@andrews.edu; aup@andrews.edu Web Site: www.universitypress.andrews.edu, pg 14

Evert, Kelly, Village Books Literary Citizenship Award, 1200 11 St, Bellingham, WA 98225 Tel: 360-671-2626 E-mail: biblioinfo@villagebooks.com; marketing@villagebooks.com Web Site: www.villagebooks.com/literary-citizenship-award, pg 672

Ewen, Rachel, Bloomsbury Publishing Inc, 1385 Broadway, 5th fl, New York, NY 10018 Tel: 212-419-5300 E-mail: marketingusa@bloomsbury.com; adultpublicityusa@bloomsbury.com; askacademic@bloomsbury.com Web Site: www.bloomsbury.com, pg 31

Ewers, Christy, The CAT Agency Inc, 345 Old Oaks Rd, Fairfield, CT 06825 Tel: 917-434-3141 Web Site: catagencyinc.com, pg 485

Ewing, Linda, Coffee House Press, 79 13 Ave NE, Suite 110, Minneapolis, MN 55413 Tel: 612-338-0125 Fax: 612-338-4004 E-mail: info@coffeehousepress.org Web Site: coffeehousepress.org, pg 50

Ewing, Su, Dog Writers Association of America Inc (DWAA) Annual Writing Competition, PO Box 787, Hughesville, MD 20637 Web Site: dogwriters.org, pg 596

Eyoh, Malaika, Doubleday Canada, 320 Front St W, Suite 1400, Toronto, ON M5V 3B6, Canada Tel: 416-364-4449 Fax: 416-598-7764 Web Site: www.penguinrandomhouse.ca, pg 401

Eyoh, Malaika, Knopf Canada, 320 Front St W, Suite 1400, Toronto, ON M5V 3B6, Canada Tel: 416-364-4449 Toll Free Tel: 888-523-9292 Fax: 416-598-7764 Web Site: www.penguinrandomhouse.ca, pg 411

Eyring, Teresa, Theatre Communications Group, 520 Eighth Ave, 24th fl, New York, NY 10018-4156 Tel: 212-609-5900 Fax: 212-609-5901 E-mail: info@tcg.org Web Site: www.tcg.org, pg 206

Faber, Kathy, HarperCollins Publishers LLC, 195 Broadway, New York, NY 10007 Tel: 212-207-7000 Web Site: www.harpercollins.com, pg 86

Fabian, BrocheAroe, Sourcebooks LLC, 1935 Brookdale Rd, Suite 139, Naperville, IL 60563 Tel: 630-961-3900 Toll Free Tel: 800-432-7444 Fax: 630-961-2168 E-mail: info@sourcebooks.com Web Site: www.sourcebooks.com, pg 194

Fabian, Elizabeth, Random House Publishing Group, 1745 Broadway, New York, NY 10019 Toll Free Tel: 800-200-3552 Web Site: www.randomhousebooks.com, pg 171

Fabricant, David, Abbeville Press, 655 Third Ave, New York, NY 10017 Tel: 212-366-5585 Toll Free Tel: 800-ART-BOOK (278-2665); 800-343-4499 (orders) E-mail: abbeville@abbeville.com; sales@abbeville.com; marketing@abbeville.com; rights@abbeville.com Web Site: www.abbeville.com, pg 1

Fabricant, David, Abbeville Publishing Group, 655 Third Ave, New York, NY 10017 Tel: 646-375-2136 E-mail: abbeville@abbeville.com; rights@abbeville.com Web Site: www.abbeville.com, pg 2

Fabricant, Shannon, Running Press, 1290 Avenue of the Americas, New York, NY 10104 Tel: 212-364-1100 Toll Free Tel: 800-759-0190 (cust serv) Fax: 212-364-0933 (intl orders) Toll Free Fax: 800-286-9471 (cust serv) E-mail: customer.service@hbgusa.com; orders@hbgusa.com Web Site: www.hachettebookgroup.com/imprint/running-press/; www.moon.com (Moon Travel Guides), pg 178

Fabris, Casey, Education Writers Association (EWA), 1825 "K" St NW, Suite 200, Washington, DC 20006 Tel: 202-452-9830 Web Site: ewa.org, pg 505

Fadia, Shreya, Don Belton Fiction Reading Period, Indiana University English Dept, Ballantine Hall 554, 1020 E Kirkwood Ave, Bloomington, IN 47405 Tel: 812-855-3439 E-mail: inreview@indiana.edu Web Site: indianareview.org, pg 578

Fadia, Shreya, Blue Light Books Prize, Indiana University English Dept, Ballantine Hall 554, 1020 E Kirkwood Ave, Bloomington, IN 47405 Tel: 812-855-3439 E-mail: inreview@indiana.edu Web Site: indianareview.org, pg 582

Fadia, Shreya, 1/2 K Prize, Indiana University English Dept, Ballantine Hall 554, 1020 E Kirkwood Ave, Bloomington, IN 47405 Tel: 812-855-3439 E-mail: inreview@indiana.edu Web Site: indianareview.org, pg 610

Fadia, Shreya, Indiana Review Creative Nonfiction Prize, Indiana University English Dept, Ballantine Hall 554, 1020 E Kirkwood Ave, Bloomington, IN 47405 Tel: 812-855-3439 E-mail: inreview@indiana.edu Web Site: indianareview.org, pg 616

Fadia, Shreya, Indiana Review Fiction Prize, Indiana University English Dept, Ballantine Hall 554, 1020 E Kirkwood Ave, Bloomington, IN 47405 Tel: 812-855-3439 E-mail: inreview@indiana.edu Web Site: indianareview.org, pg 616

Fadia, Shreya, Indiana Review Poetry Prize, Indiana University English Dept, Ballantine Hall 554, 1020 E Kirkwood Ave, Bloomington, IN 47405 Tel: 812-855-3439 E-mail: inreview@indiana.edu Web Site: indianareview.org, pg 616

Fafard, Katherine, Association des Libraires du Quebec (ALQ), 483, blvd St Joseph E, Montreal, QC H2J 1J8, Canada Tel: 514-526-3349 Fax: 514-526-3340 E-mail: info@alq.qc.ca Web Site: www.alq.qc.ca, pg 498

Fagan, Alexis, Association of University Presses (AUPresses), 1412 Broadway, Suite 2135, New York, NY 10018 Tel: 212-989-1010 Fax: 212-989-0275 E-mail: info@aupresses.org Web Site: www.aupresses.org, pg 500

Fagan, John, University of Pittsburgh Press, 7500 Thomas Blvd, Pittsburgh, PA 15260 Tel: 412-383-2456 Fax: 412-383-2466 E-mail: info@upress.pitt.edu Web Site: www.upress.pitt.edu, pg 219

Fagan, Lisa, NYSCA/NYFA Artist Fellowships, 20 Jay St, Suite 740, Brooklyn, NY 11201 Tel: 212-366-6900 Fax: 212-366-1778 E-mail: fellowships@nyfa.org Web Site: www.nyfa.org, pg 642

Fagan, Raymond, William H Sadlier Inc, 9 Pine St, New York, NY 10005 Tel: 212-227-2120 Toll Free Tel: 800-221-5175 (cust serv) Fax: 212-312-6080 E-mail: customerservice@sadlier.com Web Site: www.sadlier.com, pg 179

Fahlgren, Erik, W W Norton & Company Inc, 500 Fifth Ave, New York, NY 10110-0017 Tel: 212-354-5500 Toll Free Tel: 800-233-4830 (orders & cust serv) Fax: 212-869-0856 Toll Free Fax: 800-458-6515 E-mail: orders@wwnorton.com Web Site: wwnorton.com, pg 143

Fairchild, Linda, Linda Fairchild & Company LLC, 101 Lucas Valley Rd, Suite 363, San Rafael, CA 94903 Tel: 415-336-6407 Web Site: www.lindafairchild.com, pg 439

Faizi, Asma, Access Copyright, The Canadian Copyright Licensing Agency, 69 Younge St, Suite 1100, Toronto, ON M5E 1K3, Canada Tel: 416-868-1620 Toll Free Tel: 800-893-5777 Fax: 416-868-1621 E-mail: info@accesscopyright.ca Web Site: www.accesscopyright.ca, pg 493

Fakih, Samia, Roaring Brook Press, 120 Broadway, New York, NY 10271 Tel: 646-307-5151 Web Site: us.macmillan.com/publishers/roaring-brook-press, pg 176

Faktorovich, Anna PhD, Anaphora Literary Press, 1108 W Third St, Quanah, TX 79252 Tel: 470-289-6395 Web Site: anaphoraliterary.com, pg 13

Falb, Mark C, Kendall Hunt Publishing Co, 4050 Westmark Dr, Dubuque, IA 52002-2624 Tel: 563-589-1000 Toll Free Tel: 800-228-0810 (orders) Fax: 563-589-1071 Toll Free Fax: 800-772-9165 E-mail: ordernow@kendallhunt.com Web Site: www.kendallhunt.com, pg 108

Falcon, Mary, Safer Society Press, PO Box 340, Brandon, VT 05733-0340 Tel: 802-247-3132 Fax: 802-247-4233 E-mail: info@safersociety.org Web Site: safersocietypress.org, pg 179

Faley, Erin, Academy of Nutrition & Dietetics, 120 S Riverside Plaza, Suite 2190, Chicago, IL 60606-6995 Tel: 312-899-0040 (ext 5000) Toll Free Tel: 800-877-1600 E-mail: publications@eatright.org; sales@eatright.org Web Site: www.eatrightstore.org, pg 3

Falkner, Julia, Viking Penguin, c/o Penguin Random House LLC, 1745 Broadway, New York, NY 10019 Tel: 212-782-9000 Web Site: www.penguin.com/overview-vikingbooks/; www.penguin.com/pamela-dorman-books-overview/; www.penguin.com/penguin-classics-overview/; www.penguin.com/penguin-life-overview/, pg 225

Fallert, Joanne, Liza Dawson Associates, 121 W 27 St, Suite 1201, New York, NY 10001 Tel: 212-465-9071 Web Site: www.lizadawsonassociates.com, pg 455

Fallon, Claire, International Society of Automation (ISA), 3252 S Miami Blvd, Suite 102, Durham, NC 27703 Tel: 919-549-8411 Fax: 919-549-8288 E-mail: info@isa.org Web Site: www.isa.org/standards-and-publications/isa-publications, pg 104

Fallon, Steve, Walter De Gruyter Inc, 121 High St, 3rd fl, Boston, MA 02110 Tel: 857-284-7073; 617-377-4392 Fax: 857-284-7358 E-mail: service@degruyter.com; orders@degruyter.com Web Site: www.degruyter.com, pg 58

Falter, Sarah, HarperCollins Publishers LLC, 195 Broadway, New York, NY 10007 Tel: 212-207-7000 Web Site: www.harpercollins.com, pg 86

Fan, Shenggen, International Food Policy Research Institute, 1201 Eye St NW, Washington, DC 20005-3915 Tel: 202-862-5600 Fax: 202-862-5606 E-mail: ifpri@cgiar.org Web Site: www.ifpri.org, pg 103

Fang-Horvath, Sierra, Gallery Books, 1230 Avenue of the Americas, New York, NY 10020 Toll Free Tel: 800-456-6798 Fax: 212-698-7284 E-mail: consumer.customerservice@simonandschuster.com Web Site: www.simonandschuster.com, pg 76

Fanning, Chris, Gell: A Finger Lakes Creative Retreat, 740 University Ave, Rochester, NY 14607-1259 Tel: 585-473-2590 Fax: 585-442-9333 Web Site: www.wab.org, pg 554

Fanning, Eileen, NRP Direct, 220 College Ave, Suite 618, Athens, GA 30601-9801 Tel: 908-517-0780 Toll Free Tel: 844-592-4197 E-mail: info@nrpdirect.com Web Site: www.nrpdirect.com, pg 144

Farahani, Jay, Sourcebooks LLC, 1935 Brookdale Rd, Suite 139, Naperville, IL 60563 Tel: 630-961-3900 Toll Free Tel: 800-432-7444 Fax: 630-961-2168 E-mail: info@sourcebooks.com Web Site: www.sourcebooks.com, pg 195

Farebrother, Emily, Simon & Schuster, 1230 Avenue of the Americas, New York, NY 10020 Tel: 212-698-7000 Toll Free Tel: 800-223-2348 (cust serv); 800-223-2336 (orders) Toll Free Fax: 800-943-9831 (orders) Web Site: simonandschusterpublishing.com/simonandschuster/, pg 188

Fargis, Alison, Stonesong, 270 W 39 St, Suite 201, New York, NY 10018 Tel: 212-929-4600 E-mail: editors@stonesong.com Web Site: www.stonesong.com, pg 478

Fargnoli, Jayne M, Harvard Education Publishing Group, 8 Story St, 1st fl, Cambridge, MA 02138 Tel: 617-495-3432 Fax: 617-496-3584 Web Site: www.hepg.org, pg 88

Fariello, Melissa, Random House Children's Books, c/o Penguin Random House LLC, 1745 Broadway, New York, NY 10019 Tel: 212-782-9000 Web Site: www.rhcbooks.com, pg 170

Faris, Curran, University of Regina Press, 2 Research Dr, Suite 160, Regina, SK S4S 7H9, Canada Tel: 306-585-4758 Fax: 306-585-4699 E-mail: uofrpress@uregina.ca Web Site: uofrpress.ca, pg 423

Farkas, Sam, Jill Grinberg Literary Management LLC, 392 Vanderbilt Ave, Brooklyn, NY 11238 Tel: 212-620-5883 E-mail: info@jillgrinbergliterary.com Web Site: www.jillgrinbergliterary.com, pg 461

Farkas, Susan, City & Regional Magazine Association (CRMA), 287 Richards Ave, Norwalk, CT 06850 Tel: 203-515-9294 Web Site: citymag.org, pg 504

Farland, David, L Ron Hubbard's Writers of the Future Contest, 7051 Hollywood Blvd, Hollywood, CA 90028 Tel: 323-466-3310 Fax: 323-466-6474 E-mail: contests@authorservicesinc.com Web Site: www.writersofthefuture.com, pg 614

Farley, Rick, HarperCollins Children's Books, 195 Broadway, New York, NY 10007 Tel: 212-207-7000 Web Site: www.harpercollins.com/childrens, pg 85

Farmer, Brad, Gibbs Smith Publisher, 1877 E Gentile St, Layton, UT 84041 Tel: 801-544-9800 Toll Free Tel: 800-748-5439; 800-835-4993 (orders) Fax: 801-544-5582 Toll Free Fax: 800-213-3023 (orders only) E-mail: info@gibbs-smith.com; orders@gibbs-smith.com Web Site: gibbs-smith.com, pg 78

Farmer, Brent Jr, Charlesbridge Publishing Inc, 85 Main St, Watertown, MA 02472 Tel: 617-926-0329 Toll Free Tel: 800-225-3214 Fax: 617-926-5720 Toll Free Fax: 800-926-5775 E-mail: books@charlesbridge.com Web Site: www.charlesbridge.com, pg 45

Farmer, Brent, Charlesbridge Publishing Inc, 85 Main St, Watertown, MA 02472 Tel: 617-926-0329 Toll Free Tel: 800-225-3214 Fax: 617-926-5720 Toll Free Fax: 800-926-5775 E-mail: books@charlesbridge.com Web Site: www.charlesbridge.com, pg 45

Farmer, Chris, University of Texas Press, 3001 Lake Austin Blvd, 2.200, Austin, TX 78703 Tel: 512-471-7233 Fax: 512-232-7178 E-mail: utpress@uts.cc.utexas.edu; info@utpress.utexas.edu Web Site: utpress.utexas.edu, pg 205

Farmer, Susan, DEStech Publications Inc, 439 N Duke St, Lancaster, PA 17602-4967 Tel: 717-290-1660 Toll Free Tel: 877-500-4DES (500-4337) Fax: 717-509-6100 E-mail: info@destechpub.com; orders@destechpub.com Web Site: www.destechpub.com, pg 59

Farnol, Jane, Astor Indexers, 22 S Commons, Kent, CT 06757 Tel: 860-592-0225; 570-534-8951 (cell), pg 436

Farnsworth, David, Casemate | publishers, 1950 Lawrence Rd, Havertown, PA 19083 Tel: 610-853-9131 Fax: 610-853-9146 E-mail: casemate@casematepublishers.com Web Site: www.casematepublishers.com, pg 41

Farnsworth, Will, Casemate | publishers, 1950 Lawrence Rd, Havertown, PA 19083 Tel: 610-853-9131 Fax: 610-853-9146 E-mail: casemate@casematepublishers.com Web Site: www.casematepublishers.com, pg 42

Farranto, Amy, Cornell University Press, Sage House, 512 E State St, Ithaca, NY 14850 Tel: 607-253-2338 E-mail: cupressinfo@cornell.edu; cupress-sales@cornell.edu; cupress-perms@cornell.edu (reprint/class use permissions) Web Site: www.cornellpress.cornell.edu, pg 52

Farranto, Amy, Northern Illinois University Press, Sage House, 512 E State St, Ithaca, NY 14850 Tel: 607-253-2338 Web Site: cornellpress.cornell.edu/imprints/northern-illinois-university-press, pg 143

Farrar, Amy E, Farrar Writing & Editing, 4638 Manchester Rd, Mound, MN 55364 Tel: 952-451-5982 Web Site: www.writeandedit.net, pg 439

Farrell, Dan, Crossway, 1300 Crescent St, Wheaton, IL 60187 Tel: 630-682-4300 Toll Free Tel: 800-635-7993 (orders); 800-543-1659 (cust serv) Fax: 630-682-4785 E-mail: info@crossway.org Web Site: www.crossway.org, pg 56

Farrell, Della, Holiday House Publishing Inc, 50 Broad St, New York, NY 10004 Tel: 212-688-0085 Fax: 212-421-6134 E-mail: info@holidayhouse.com Web Site: www.holidayhouse.com, pg 94

Farrell, James, Curtis Brown, Ltd, 228 E 45 St, Suite 310, New York, NY 10017 Tel: 212-473-5400 Fax: 212-598-0917 E-mail: info@cbltd.com Web Site: www.curtisbrown.com, pg 452

Farrell, Jessica, Society for Technical Communication (STC), 3251 Blenheim Blvd, Suite 406, Fairfax, VA 22030 Tel: 703-522-4114 Fax: 703-522-2075 E-mail: stc@stc.org Web Site: www.stc.org, pg 519

Farrell, Kate, Henry Holt and Company, LLC, 120 Broadway, 23rd fl, New York, NY 10271 Tel: 646-307-5151 Toll Free Tel: 888-330-8477 (orders) Fax: 646-307-5285 Web Site: www.henryholt.com, pg 94

Farrell, Michael, Florida Writers Association Inc, 127 W Fairbanks Ave, No 407, Winter Park, FL 32789 E-mail: contactus@floridawriters.org Web Site: www.floridawriters.org, pg 506

Farrell, Michael, Florida WritersCon, 127 W Fairbanks Ave, No 407, Winter Park, FL 32789 E-mail: contactus@floridawriters.org Web Site: www.floridawriters.org, pg 554

Farrell, Tanya, Publishers' Publicity Association (PPA), PO Box 2437, New York, NY 10017 Tel: 212-790-7259 E-mail: publisherspublicity@gmail.com Web Site: publisherspublicityassociation.square.site, pg 518

Farris, Sienna, Simon & Schuster, LLC, 1230 Avenue of the Americas, New York, NY 10020 Tel: 212-698-7000 Toll Free Tel: 800-223-2336 (orders) Fax: 212-698-7007 Toll Free Fax: 800-943-9831 (orders) E-mail: firstname.lastname@simonandschuster.com; purchaseorders@simonandschuster.com (orders) Web Site: www.simonandschuster.com, pg 190

Fassett, David, InterVarsity Press, 430 Plaza Dr, Westmont, IL 60559-1234 Tel: 630-734-4000 Toll Free Tel: 800-843-9487 Fax: 630-734-4200 E-mail: email@ivpress.com Web Site: www.ivpress.com, pg 104

Fastiggi, Ray, The Rockefeller University Press, 950 Third Ave, 2nd fl, New York, NY 10022 Tel: 212-327-7938 E-mail: rupress@rockefeller.edu Web Site: www.rupress.org, pg 176

Fata, Jillian, Dutton, c/o Penguin Random House LLC, 1745 Broadway, New York, NY 10019 Tel: 212-366-2000 Web Site: www.penguin.com/dutton-overview/; www.penguin.com/plume-books-overview/; www.penguin.com/tiny-reparations-overview/, pg 62

Fata, Jillian, TarcherPerigee, c/o Penguin Random House LLC, 1745 Broadway, New York, NY 10019 Tel: 212-782-9000 Web Site: www.penguin.com/tarcherperigee-overview/; www.facebook.com/TarcherPerigee, pg 202

Fatka, Jacqui, North American Agricultural Journalists (NAAJ), c/o Jacqui Fatka, 6866 County Rd, 183, Fredericktown, OH 43019 Tel: 979-324-4302 E-mail: naajnews@yahoo.com Web Site: www.naaj.net, pg 515

Fattman, Kelly, Harvard Education Publishing Group, 8 Story St, 1st fl, Cambridge, MA 02138 Tel: 617-495-3432 Fax: 617-496-3584 Web Site: www.hepg.org, pg 88

Faughnan, Mary Ann, May Sarton New Hampshire Poetry Prize, 44 Main St, 2nd fl, Peterborough, NH 03458 Tel: 603-567-4430 Web Site: www.bauhanpublishing.com, pg 659

Faulls, Heather, Portfolio, c/o Penguin Random House LLC, 1745 Broadway, New York, NY 10019 Tel: 212-782-9000 Web Site: www.penguin.com/portfolio-overview/; www.penguin.com/sentinel-overview/; www.penguin.com/thesis/, pg 162

Fausset, Katherine, Curtis Brown, Ltd, 228 E 45 St, Suite 310, New York, NY 10017 Tel: 212-473-5400 Fax: 212-598-0917 E-mail: info@cbltd.com Web Site: www.curtisbrown.com, pg 452

Faust, Harmony, Gale, 27555 Executive Dr, Suite 270, Farmington Hills, MI 48331 Toll Free Tel: 800-877-4253 Toll Free Fax: 877-363-4253 E-mail: gale.customerexperience@cengage.com Web Site: www.gale.com, pg 75

Faust, Harmony, Macmillan Reference USA™, 27500 Drake Rd, Farmington Hills, MI 48331-3535 Tel: 248-699-4253 Toll Free Tel: 800-877-4253 Toll Free Fax: 877-363-4253 E-mail: gale.customercare@cengage.com Web Site: www.gale.cengage.com/macmillan, pg 123

Faust, Jessica H, BookEnds Literary Agency, 136 Long Hill Rd, Gillette, NJ 07933 Web Site: www.bookendsliterary.com, pg 450

Favreau, Marc, The New Press, 120 Wall St, 31st fl, New York, NY 10005 Tel: 212-629-8802 Fax: 212-629-8617 E-mail: newpress@thenewpress.com Web Site: thenewpress.com, pg 140

Fay-LeBlanc, Gibson, Maine Writers & Publishers Alliance (MWPA), Glickman Family Library, 314 Forest Ave, Rm 318, Portland, ME 04101 Tel: 207-228-8263 E-mail: info@mainewriters.org Web Site: www.mainewriters.org, pg 510

Fazzalaro, Kristina, Viking Penguin, c/o Penguin Random House LLC, 1745 Broadway, New York, NY 10019 Tel: 212-782-9000 Web Site: www.penguin.com/overview-vikingbooks/; www.penguin.com/pamela-dorman-books-overview/; www.penguin.com/penguin-classics-overview/; www.penguin.com/penguin-life-overview/, pg 225

Fearing, Marion F, Islandport Press, 247 Portland St, Bldg C, Yarmouth, ME 04096 Tel: 207-846-3344 E-mail: info@islandportpress.com; orders@islandportpress.com Web Site: www.islandportpress.com, pg 105

Feather, Kasey, HarperCollins Publishers LLC, 195 Broadway, New York, NY 10007 Tel: 212-207-7000 Web Site: www.harpercollins.com, pg 87

Feathers, Lori, Republic of Consciousness Prize for Small Presses in the USA, c/o Interabang Books, 56 Lovers Lane, No 142, Dallas, TX 75209 E-mail: rofcusa@gmail.com Web Site: www.republicofconsciousnessprize-usa.com, pg 655

Febregat, Eduard, HarperCollins Publishers LLC, 195 Broadway, New York, NY 10007 Tel: 212-207-7000 Web Site: www.harpercollins.com, pg 87

Febus, Fernando, Lectorum Publications Inc, 10 New Maple Ave, Suite 303, Pine Brook, NJ 07058 Tel: 201-559-2200 Toll Free Tel: 800-345-5946 E-mail: lectorum@lectorum.com Web Site: www.lectorum.com, pg 114

Fedewa, Natalie, Brilliance Publishing Inc, 1704 Eaton Dr, Grand Haven, MI 49417 Tel: 616-846-5256 Toll Free Tel: 800-648-2312 (orders only) E-mail: brilliance-publishing@amazon.com; customerservice@brilliancepublishing.com; media@brilliancepublishing.com; publicity@brilliancepublishing.com Web Site: www.brilliancepublishing.com, pg 37

Fedor, Ashley, Christopher Lightfoot Walker Award, 633 W 155 St, New York, NY 10032 Tel: 212-368-5900 E-mail: academy@artsandletters.org Web Site: artsandletters.org/awards, pg 673

Fedor, John, American Water Works Association (AWWA), 6666 W Quincy Ave, Denver, CO 80235-3098 Tel: 303-794-7711 Toll Free Tel: 800-926-7337 E-mail: service@awwa.org (cust serv); aws@awwa.org; books@awwa.org Web Site: www.awwa.org/publications, pg 13

Fee, Alfredo, HarperCollins Publishers LLC, 195 Broadway, New York, NY 10007 Tel: 212-207-7000 Web Site: www.harpercollins.com, pg 87

Feehan, Tara, HarperCollins Publishers LLC, 195 Broadway, New York, NY 10007 Tel: 212-207-7000 Web Site: www.harpercollins.com, pg 86

Feeney, Hannah, Dutton, c/o Penguin Random House LLC, 1745 Broadway, New York, NY 10019 Tel: 212-366-2000 Web Site: www.penguin.com/dutton-overview/; www.penguin.com/plume-books-overview/; www.penguin.com/tiny-reparations-overview/, pg 62

Fegan, Trudy, Penguin Random House Canada, a Penguin Random House company, 320 Front St W, Suite 1400, Toronto, ON M5V 3B6, Canada Tel: 416-364-4449 Toll Free Tel: 888-523-9292 (cust serv) E-mail: canadaweb@penguinrandomhouse.com; customerservicescanada@penguinrandomhouse.com Web Site: www.penguinrandomhouse.ca, pg 416

Fehr, Don, Trident Media Group LLC, 355 Lexington Ave, 12th fl, New York, NY 10017 Tel: 212-333-1511 E-mail: info@tridentmediagroup.com; press@tridentmediagroup.com; foreignrights@tridentmediagroup.com; office.assistant@tridentmediagroup.com Web Site: www.tridentmediagroup.com, pg 480

Feifer, Adam, Simon & Schuster, LLC, 1230 Avenue of the Americas, New York, NY 10020 Tel: 212-698-7000 Toll Free Tel: 800-223-2336 (orders) Fax: 212-698-7007 Toll Free Fax: 800-943-9831 (orders) E-mail: firstname.lastname@simonandschuster.com; purchaseorders@simonandschuster.com (orders) Web Site: www.simonandschuster.com, pg 190

Feigenbaum, Laurie, Feigenbaum Publishing Consultants Inc, 61 Bounty Lane, Jericho, NY 11753 Tel: 516-647-8314 (cell), pg 458

Feigenbaum, Rachael, Advertising Research Foundation (ARF), 432 Park Ave S, 4th fl, New York, NY 10016 Tel: 212-751-5656 Fax: 212-689-1859 E-mail: membership@thearf.org; new-member-info@thearf.org Web Site: thearf.org, pg 493, 525

Feimer, Melissa, Pearson Business Publishing, 221 River St, Hoboken, NJ 07030-4772 Tel: 201-236-7000 Web Site: www.pearsonhighered.com, pg 153

Feinberg, Emily, Roaring Brook Press, 120 Broadway, New York, NY 10271 Tel: 646-307-5151 Web Site: us.macmillan.com/publishers/roaring-brook-press, pg 176

Feinberg, Lili, Random House Children's Books, c/o Penguin Random House LLC, 1745 Broadway, New York, NY 10019 Tel: 212-782-9000 Web Site: www.rhcbooks.com, pg 170

Feinberg, Madeleine, The Experiment, 220 E 23 St, Suite 600, New York, NY 10010-4658 Tel: 212-889-1659 E-mail: info@theexperimentpublishing.com Web Site: www.theexperimentpublishing.com, pg 68

Feist, Betsy, Betsy Feist Resources, 140 E 81 St, Unit 7-E, New York, NY 10028-1875 Tel: 212-861-2014 E-mail: betsyfeist@gmail.com, pg 439

Fekadu, Mesfin, Society for Features Journalism (SFJ), Eugene S Pulliam National Journalism Ctr, 3909 N Meridian St, Indianapolis, IN 46208 E-mail: wearesfj@gmail.com Web Site: featuresjournalism.org, pg 519

Felder, David W PhD, Wellington Press, 3811 Long & Winding Rd, Tallahassee, FL 32309 *E-mail:* peacegames@aol.com *Web Site:* www.peacegames.com, pg 227

Feldheim, Yitzchak, Feldheim Publishers, 208 Airport Executive Park, Nanuet, NY 10954 *Tel:* 845-356-2282 *Toll Free Tel:* 800-237-7149 (orders) *Fax:* 845-425-1908 *E-mail:* sales@feldheim.com *Web Site:* www.feldheim.com, pg 70

Feldman, Ellen, Knopf Doubleday Publishing Group, c/o Penguin Random House LLC, 1745 Broadway, New York, NY 10019 *Tel:* 212-751-2600 *Fax:* 212-940-7390 (dom rts); 212-572-2662 (foreign rts) *Web Site:* knopfdoubleday.com, pg 110

Feldman, Ellen, Penguin Random House LLC, 1745 Broadway, New York, NY 10019 *Tel:* 212-782-9000 *Toll Free Tel:* 800-726-0600 *Web Site:* www.penguinrandomhouse.com, pg 155

Feldman, Gwen, Silman-James Press Inc, 141 N Clark Dr, Unit 1, West Hollywood, CA 90048 *Tel:* 310-205-0665 *E-mail:* info@silmanjamespress.com *Web Site:* www.silmanjamespress.com, pg 188

Feldman, Jennifer, Teachers College Press, 1234 Amsterdam Ave, New York, NY 10027 *Tel:* 212-678-3929 *Fax:* 212-678-4149 *E-mail:* tcpress@tc.edu *Web Site:* www.tcpress.com, pg 203

Feldman, Kait, Houghton Mifflin Harcourt Trade & Reference Division, 125 High St, Boston, MA 02110 *Tel:* 617-351-5000 *Web Site:* www.hmhco.com, pg 96

Feldman, Roxanne, Candied Plums, 7548 Ravenna Ave NE, Seattle, WA 98115 *E-mail:* candiedplums@gmail.com *Web Site:* www.candiedplums.com, pg 39

Feldman, Todd David, American Law Institute, 4025 Chestnut St, Philadelphia, PA 19104-3099 *Tel:* 215-243-1600 *Toll Free Tel:* 800-253-6397 *E-mail:* custserv@ali.org *Web Site:* www.ali.org, pg 10

Feldmann, Sharon, Mel Bay Publications Inc, 16 N Gore Ave, Suite 203, Webster Groves, MO 63119-2315 *Tel:* 636-257-3970 *Toll Free Tel:* 800-863-5229 *E-mail:* email@melbay.com *Web Site:* www.melbay.com, pg 129

Felgar, Cathy, Princeton University Press, 41 William St, Princeton, NJ 08540-5237 *Tel:* 609-258-4900 *Fax:* 609-258-6305 *E-mail:* info@press.princeton.edu *Web Site:* press.princeton.edu, pg 164

Felicelli, Anita, National Book Critics Circle (NBCC), c/o Jacob M Appel, Icahn School of Medicine at Mount Sinai, One Gustave L Levy Place, New York, NY 10029 *E-mail:* info@bookcritics.org; membership@bookcritics.org *Web Site:* www.bookcritics.org, pg 512

Feliciano, Anthony, Sourcebooks LLC, 1935 Brookdale Rd, Suite 139, Naperville, IL 60563 *Tel:* 630-961-3900 *Toll Free Tel:* 800-432-7444 *Fax:* 630-961-2168 *E-mail:* info@sourcebooks.com *Web Site:* www.sourcebooks.com, pg 195

Fell, Sarah, American Psychological Association, 750 First St NE, Washington, DC 20002 *Tel:* 202-336-5510 *Toll Free Tel:* 800-374-2721 *Fax:* 202-336-5502 *E-mail:* order@apa.org; booksales@apa.org *Web Site:* www.apa.org/books, pg 12

Felt, Robert L, Paradigm Publications, 202 Bendix Dr, Taos, NM 87571 *Tel:* 575-758-7758 *Toll Free Tel:* 800-873-3946 (US); 888-873-3947 (CN) *Fax:* 575-758-7768 *E-mail:* info@paradigm-pubs.com *Web Site:* www.paradigm-pubs.com; www.redwingbooks.com, pg 151

Felty, Stephanie, Berkley, c/o Penguin Random House LLC, 1745 Broadway, 19th fl, New York, NY 10019 *Tel:* 212-366-2000 *Web Site:* www.penguin.com/publishers/berkley/; www.penguin.com/ace-overview/, pg 28

Fendrich, Debra, Meriwether Publishing, c/o Pioneer Drama Service, 109 Inverness Dr E, Suite H, Centennial, CO 80112 *Tel:* 303-779-4035 *Toll Free Tel:* 800-333-7262 *Fax:* 303-779-4315 *Web Site:* meriwetherpublishing.com; www.pioneerdrama.com, pg 129

Fendrich, Steven, Meriwether Publishing, c/o Pioneer Drama Service, 109 Inverness Dr E, Suite H, Centennial, CO 80112 *Tel:* 303-779-4035 *Toll Free Tel:* 800-333-7262 *Fax:* 303-779-4315 *Web Site:* meriwetherpublishing.com; www.pioneerdrama.com, pg 129

Feneux, Marion, La Courte Echelle, 4388, rue Saint-Denis, Suite 315, Montreal, QC H2J 2L1, Canada *Tel:* 514-312-6950 *E-mail:* info@courteechelle.com *Web Site:* www.groupecourteechelle.com/la-courte-echelle, pg 400

Feng, Kelly, China Books, 360 Swift Ave, Suite 48, South San Francisco, CA 94080 *Fax:* 650-872-7808 *E-mail:* editor.sinomedia@gmail.com, pg 47

Fennell, Saraciea, Tor Publishing Group, 120 Broadway, New York, NY 10271 *Toll Free Tel:* 800-455-0340 (Macmillan) *E-mail:* torpublicity@tor.com; forgepublicity@forgebooks.com *Web Site:* us.macmillan.com/torpublishinggroup, pg 208

Fenske, Kelsey, Sourcebooks LLC, 1935 Brookdale Rd, Suite 139, Naperville, IL 60563 *Tel:* 630-961-3900 *Toll Free Tel:* 800-432-7444 *Fax:* 630-961-2168 *E-mail:* info@sourcebooks.com *Web Site:* www.sourcebooks.com, pg 194

Fenter, Maya, Random House Publishing Group, 1745 Broadway, New York, NY 10019 *Toll Free Tel:* 800-200-3552 *Web Site:* www.randomhousebooks.com, pg 171

Fenton, Carter, Morton Publishing Co, 925 W Kenyon Ave, Unit 12, Englewood, CO 80110 *Tel:* 303-761-4805 *Fax:* 303-762-9923 *E-mail:* contact@morton-pub.com; returns@morton-pub.com *Web Site:* www.morton-pub.com, pg 134

Fenton, Morgan, Doubleday, c/o Penguin Random House LLC, 1745 Broadway, New York, NY 10019 *Tel:* 212-751-2600 *Fax:* 212-940-7390 (dom rts); 212-572-2662 (foreign rts) *Web Site:* knopfdoubleday.com/imprint/doubleday/; knopfdoubleday.com, pg 61

Fenton, Morgan, Alfred A Knopf, c/o Penguin Random House LLC, 1745 Broadway, New York, NY 10019 *Tel:* 212-751-2600 *Fax:* 212-940-7390 (dom rts); 212-572-2662 (foreign rts) *Web Site:* knopfdoubleday.com/imprint/knopf/; knopfdoubleday.com, pg 110

Fergus, Julie, University of Washington Press, 4333 Brooklyn Ave NE, Seattle, WA 98105-9570 *Toll Free Tel:* 800-537-5487 (orders) *Tel:* 206-543-3932; 410-516-6998 (orders) *E-mail:* uwapress@uw.edu *Web Site:* uwapress.uw.edu, pg 220

Ferguson, David, Morton Publishing Co, 925 W Kenyon Ave, Unit 12, Englewood, CO 80110 *Tel:* 303-761-4805 *Fax:* 303-762-9923 *E-mail:* contact@morton-pub.com; returns@morton-pub.com *Web Site:* www.morton-pub.com, pg 134

Ferguson, Jill, Springer Publishing Co, 11 W 42 St, 15th fl, New York, NY 10036-8002 *Tel:* 212-431-4370 *Toll Free Tel:* 877-687-7476 *E-mail:* marketing@springerpub.com; cs@springerpub.com (orders); textbook@springerpub.com; specialsales@springerpub.com *Web Site:* www.springerpub.com, pg 196

Ferguson, Laura J, Tuttle Publishing, Airport Business Park, 364 Innovation Dr, North Clarendon, VT 05759-9436 *Tel:* 802-773-8930 *Toll Free Tel:* 800-526-2778 *Fax:* 802-773-6993 *Toll Free Fax:* 800-FAX-TUTL (329-8885) *E-mail:* info@tuttlepublishing.com; orders@tuttlepublishing.com *Web Site:* www.tuttlepublishing.com, pg 211

Ferguson, Margaret, Holiday House Publishing Inc, 50 Broad St, New York, NY 10004 *Tel:* 212-688-0085 *Fax:* 212-421-6134 *E-mail:* info@holidayhouse.com *Web Site:* www.holidayhouse.com, pg 94

Ferko, Emily, ECW Press, 665 Gerrard St E, Toronto, ON M4M 1Y2, Canada *Tel:* 416-694-3348 *E-mail:* info@ecwpress.com *Web Site:* www.ecwpress.com, pg 401

Fernald, Tom, Chronicle Books LLC, 680 Second St, San Francisco, CA 94107 *Tel:* 415-537-4200 *Fax:* 415-537-4460 (perms) *E-mail:* hello@chroniclebooks.com; subrights@chroniclebooks.com *Web Site:* www.chroniclebooks.com, pg 47

Fernandes, Darlene, Macmillan, 120 Broadway, 22nd fl, New York, NY 10271 *E-mail:* press.inquiries@macmillan.com *Web Site:* us.macmillan.com, pg 122

Fernandez, Andreina, The University of North Carolina Press, 116 S Boundary St, Chapel Hill, NC 27514-3808 *Tel:* 919-966-3561; 919-966-7449 (orders) *Toll Free Tel:* 800-848-3224 (orders) *Fax:* 919-962-2704 (orders) *Toll Free Fax:* 800-272-6817 (orders) *E-mail:* uncpress@unc.edu *Web Site:* uncpress.org, pg 218

Fernandez, Aurora, Trident Media Group LLC, 355 Lexington Ave, 12th fl, New York, NY 10017 *Tel:* 212-333-1511 *E-mail:* info@tridentmediagroup.com; press@tridentmediagroup.com; foreignrights@tridentmediagroup.com; office.assistant@tridentmediagroup.com *Web Site:* www.tridentmediagroup.com, pg 480

Fernandez, Maya, Beacon Press, 24 Farnsworth St, Boston, MA 02210-1409 *Tel:* 617-742-2110 *Fax:* 617-723-3097 *E-mail:* production@beacon.org *Web Site:* www.beacon.org, pg 25

Fernando, Mark, American Sociological Association (ASA), 1430 "K" St NW, Suite 600, Washington, DC 20005-4701 *Tel:* 202-383-9005 *E-mail:* asa@asanet.org; communications@asanet.org; membership@asanet.org *Web Site:* www.asanet.org, pg 497

Fernando, Mark, Jessie Bernard Award, c/o Governance Off, 1430 "K" St NW, Suite 600, Washington, DC 20005 *Tel:* 202-383-9005 *E-mail:* asa@asanet.org; nominations@asanet.org *Web Site:* www.asanet.org/about/awards, pg 578

Fernando, Mark, Distinguished Scholarly Book Award, c/o Governance Off, 1430 "K" St NW, Suite 600, Washington, DC 20005 *Tel:* 202-383-9005 *E-mail:* asa@asanet.org; nominations@asanet.org *Web Site:* www.asanet.org/about/awards, pg 596

Feron, Carrie, Gallery Books, 1230 Avenue of the Americas, New York, NY 10020 *Toll Free Tel:* 800-456-6798 *Fax:* 212-698-7284 *E-mail:* consumer.customerservice@simonandschuster.com *Web Site:* www.simonandschuster.com, pg 76

Ferraiolo, Teresa, Farrar, Straus & Giroux Books for Young Readers, 120 Broadway, New York, NY 10271 *Tel:* 212-741-6900 *Toll Free Tel:* 888-330-8477 (orders) *E-mail:* childrens.publicity@macmillanusa.com; childrensrights@macmillanusa.com *Web Site:* us.macmillan.com/mackids, pg 70

Ferraiolo, Teresa, Roaring Brook Press, 120 Broadway, New York, NY 10271 *Tel:* 646-307-5151 *Web Site:* us.macmillan.com/publishers/roaring-brook-press, pg 176

Ferrante, Chris, Princeton University Press, 41 William St, Princeton, NJ 08540-5237 *Tel:* 609-258-4900 *Fax:* 609-258-6305 *E-mail:* info@press.princeton.edu *Web Site:* press.princeton.edu, pg 164

Ferrara, Moe, BookEnds Literary Agency, 136 Long Hill Rd, Gillette, NJ 07933 *Web Site:* www.bookendsliterary.com, pg 451

Ferrari-Adler, Jofie, Avid Reader Press, 1230 Avenue of the Americas, New York, NY 10020 *Web Site:* avidreaderpress.com, pg 23

Ferrari-Adler, Jofie, Simon & Schuster, LLC, 1230 Avenue of the Americas, New York, NY 10020 *Tel:* 212-698-7000 *Toll Free Tel:* 800-223-2336 (orders) *Fax:* 212-698-7007 *Toll Free Fax:* 800-943-9831 (orders) *E-mail:* firstname.lastname@simonandschuster.com; purchaseorders@simonandschuster.com (orders) *Web Site:* www.simonandschuster.com, pg 189

Ferre, Helen Aguirre, National Endowment for the Arts, 400 Seventh St SW, Washington, DC 20506-0001 *Tel:* 202-682-5400 *Web Site:* www.arts.gov, pg 526

Ferre, Helen Aguirre, The National Medal of Arts, 400 Seventh St SW, Washington, DC 20506-0001 *Tel:* 202-682-5570 *Web Site:* www.arts.gov/honors/medals, pg 638

Ferrell, Adam, Arcadia Publishing Inc, 210 Wingo Way, Suite 200, Mount Pleasant, SC 29464 *Tel:* 843-853-2070 *E-mail:* retailers@arcadiapublishing.com *Web Site:* www.arcadiapublishing.com, pg 16

Ferreyra, Jane, University of Nebraska Press, 1225 "L" St, Suite 200, Lincoln, NE 68588-0630 *Tel:* 402-472-3581; 919-966-7449 (cust serv & foreign orders) *Toll Free Tel:* 800-848-6224 (cust serv & US orders) *Fax:* 402-472-6214; 919-962-2704 (cust serv & foreign orders) *Toll Free Fax:* 800-272-6817 (cust serv & US orders) *E-mail:* presswebmail@unl.edu *Web Site:* www.nebraskapress.unl.edu, pg 218

Ferri, Sandra Ozzola, Europa Editions, 27 Union Sq W, Suite 302, New York, NY 10003 *Tel:* 212-868-6844 *Fax:* 212-868-6845 *E-mail:* info@europaeditions.com; books@europaeditions.com; publicity@europaeditions.com *Web Site:* www.europaeditions.com, pg 67

Ferri, Sandro, Europa Editions, 27 Union Sq W, Suite 302, New York, NY 10003 *Tel:* 212-868-6844 *Fax:* 212-868-6845 *E-mail:* info@europaeditions.com; books@europaeditions.com; publicity@europaeditions.com *Web Site:* www.europaeditions.com, pg 67

Ferriera, Kayla, Chronicle Books LLC, 680 Second St, San Francisco, CA 94107 *Tel:* 415-537-4200 *Fax:* 415-537-4460 (perms) *E-mail:* hello@chroniclebooks.com; subrights@chroniclebooks.com *Web Site:* www.chroniclebooks.com, pg 48

Ferron, Michel, Les Editions Un Monde Different, 3905 Isabelle, bureau 101, Brossard, QC J4Y 2R2, Canada *Tel:* 450-656-2660 *Toll Free Tel:* 800-443-2582 *Fax:* 450-659-9328 *E-mail:* info@umd.ca *Web Site:* umd.ca, pg 405

Ferrufino, Jasmine, Random House Children's Books, c/o Penguin Random House LLC, 1745 Broadway, New York, NY 10019 *Tel:* 212-782-9000 *Web Site:* www.rhcbooks.com, pg 170

Fershleiser, Rachel, Counterpoint Press LLC, 2560 Ninth St, Suite 318, Berkeley, CA 94710 *Tel:* 510-704-0230 *Fax:* 510-704-0268 *E-mail:* info@counterpointpress.com *Web Site:* counterpointpress.com; softskull.com, pg 54

Fessenden, Molly, Viking Penguin, c/o Penguin Random House LLC, 1745 Broadway, New York, NY 10019 *Tel:* 212-782-9000 *Web Site:* www.penguin.com/overview-vikingbooks/; www.penguin.com/pameladorman-books-overview/; www.penguin.com/penguin-classics-overview/; www.penguin.com/penguin-life-overview/, pg 225

Fessio SJ, Fr Joseph, Ignatius Press, 1348 Tenth Ave, San Francisco, CA 94122-2304 *Toll Free Tel:* 800-651-1531 (orders); 888-615-3186 (cust serv) *Fax:* 415-387-0896 *E-mail:* info@ignatius.com *Web Site:* www.ignatius.com, pg 98

Fessler, Bill, Golden West Cookbooks, 5738 N Central Ave, Phoenix, AZ 85012-1316 *Tel:* 602-234-1574 *Toll Free Tel:* 800-521-9221 *Fax:* 602-234-3062 *E-mail:* info@americantravelerpress.com *Web Site:* www.americantravelerpress.com, pg 79

Festa, Lauren, Penguin Young Readers Group, c/o Penguin Random House LLC, 1745 Broadway, New York, NY 10019 *Tel:* 212-782-9000 *Web Site:* www.penguin.com/penguin-young-readers-overview, pg 156

Fetcho, Brittany, Simon & Schuster Children's Publishing, 1230 Avenue of the Americas, New York, NY 10020 *Tel:* 212-698-7000 *Web Site:* www.simonandschuster.com/kids; www.simonandschuster.com/teen; simonandschuster.net; simonandschuster.biz, pg 189

Fetterman, Bonny, The Editors Circle, 24 Holly Circle, Easthampton, MA 01027 *Tel:* 862-596-9709 *E-mail:* query@theeditorscircle.com *Web Site:* www.theeditorscircle.com, pg 438

Fetters, Viengsamai, Kensington Publishing Corp, 900 Third Ave, 26th fl, New York, NY 10022 *Tel:* 212-407-1500 *Toll Free Tel:* 800-221-2647 *Fax:* 212-935-0699 *Web Site:* www.kensingtonbooks.com, pg 109

Ficarra, Elise, The Academy of American Poets Harold Taylor Prize, 511-512 Humanities Bldg, 1600 Holloway Ave, San Francisco, CA 94132 *Tel:* 415-338-2227 *Fax:* 415-338-0966 *E-mail:* poetry@sfsu.edu *Web Site:* poetry.sfsu.edu, pg 569

Ficarra, Elise, The Audre Lorde Creative Writing Award, 511-512 Humanities Bldg, 1600 Holloway Ave, San Francisco, CA 94132 *Tel:* 415-338-2227 *Fax:* 415-338-0966 *E-mail:* poetry@sfsu.edu *Web Site:* poetry.sfsu.edu, pg 626

Ficarra, Elise, Poetry Center Book Award, 511-512 Humanities Bldg, 1600 Holloway Ave, San Francisco, CA 94132 *Tel:* 415-338-2227 *Fax:* 415-338-0966 *E-mail:* poetry@sfsu.edu *Web Site:* poetry.sfsu.edu, pg 651

Ficarra, Elise, San Francisco Browning Society Award, 511-512 Humanities Bldg, 1600 Holloway Ave, San Francisco, CA 94132 *Tel:* 415-338-2227 *Fax:* 415-338-0966 *E-mail:* poetry@sfsu.edu *Web Site:* poetry.sfsu.edu, pg 658

Ficarra, Elise, The Piri Thomas Poetry Prize, 511-512 Humanities Bldg, 1600 Holloway Ave, San Francisco, CA 94132 *Tel:* 415-338-2227 *Fax:* 415-338-0966 *E-mail:* poetry@sfsu.edu *Web Site:* poetry.sfsu.edu, pg 669

Fichtelberg, Joseph PhD, Hofstra University, Department of English, 204 Mason Hall, Hempstead, NY 11549 *Tel:* 516-463-5454 *E-mail:* english@hofstra.edu *Web Site:* www.hofstra.edu/english, pg 563

Fichter, Jessica Francis, Trustus Playwrights' Festival, 520 Lady St, Columbia, SC 29201 *Tel:* 803-254-9732 *E-mail:* boxoffice@trustus.org *Web Site:* trustus.org/playwrights-festival, pg 670

Fidis, Stephanie, Dover Publications Inc, 1325 Franklin Ave, Suite 250, Garden City, NY 11530 *Tel:* 516-294-7000 *Toll Free Tel:* 800-223-3130 (orders) *Fax:* 516-742-6953 *E-mail:* rights@doverpublications.com *Web Site:* store.doverpublications.com; store.doverdirect.com, pg 61

Fidler, Patricia, Yale University Press, 302 Temple St, New Haven, CT 06511-8909 *Tel:* 203-432-0960; 203-432-0966 (sales); 401-531-2800 (cust serv) *Toll Free Tel:* 800-405-1619 (cust serv) *Fax:* 203-432-0948; 203-432-8485 (sales); 401-531-2801 (cust serv) *Toll Free Fax:* 800-406-9145 (cust serv) *E-mail:* sales.press@yale.edu (sales); customer.care@triliteral.org (cust serv) *Web Site:* www.yalebooks.com; yalepress.yale.edu/yupbooks, pg 235

Fiedelman, David, Bolchazy-Carducci Publishers Inc, 1000 Brown St, Unit 301, Wauconda, IL 60084 *Tel:* 847-526-4344 *Fax:* 847-526-2867 *E-mail:* info@bolchazy.com; orders@bolchazy.com *Web Site:* www.bolchazy.com, pg 33

Fiedler, Jonathan, BISG Industry Awards, 232 Madison Ave, Suite 1200, New York, NY 10016 *Tel:* 646-336-7141 *E-mail:* info@bisg.org *Web Site:* www.bisg.org, pg 581

Fiedler, Jonathan, Book Industry Study Group Inc (BISG), 232 Madison Ave, Suite 1200, New York, NY 10016 *Tel:* 646-336-7141 *E-mail:* info@bisg.org *Web Site:* www.bisg.org, pg 501

Fields, Billy, DK, c/o Penguin Random House LLC, 1745 Broadway, 20th fl, New York, NY 10019 *Tel:* 646-674-4000 *Toll Free Tel:* 800-733-3000 *Fax:* 646-674-4020 *E-mail:* marketing@dk.com (lib servs); publicity@dk.com; csorders@penguinrandomhouse.com; customerservice@penguinrandomhouse.com *Web Site:* www.dk.com, pg 60

Fields, Cedar, American Booksellers Association, 600 Mamaroneck Ave, Suite 400, Harrison, NY 10528 *Tel:* 914-406-7500 *Toll Free Tel:* 800-637-0037 *Fax:* 914-417-4013 *E-mail:* info@bookweb.org *Web Site:* www.bookweb.org, pg 494

Fields, Hannah, American Academy of Political & Social Science (AAPSS), 220 S 40 St, Suite 201-E, Philadelphia, PA 19104-3543 *Tel:* 215-746-6500 *Fax:* 215-573-2667 *Web Site:* www.aapss.org, pg 494

Fields, Matthew Mugo, Houghton Mifflin Harcourt, 125 High St, Boston, MA 02110 *Tel:* 617-351-5000 *Toll Free Tel:* 855-969-4642; 800-225-5425 (K-12 educ materials); 800-323-9540 (assessment materials); 877-219-1537 (SkillsTutor); 888-242-6747 (Innovation in Educ Group); 800-225-3362 (Trade & Ref Div) *Toll Free Fax:* 800-269-5232 *E-mail:* myhmhco@hmhco.com *Web Site:* www.hmhco.com, pg 96

Fields, Monique, Harper Lee Prize for Legal Fiction, 101 Paul Bryant Dr, Tuscaloosa, AL 35487 *Tel:* 205-348-5195 *Web Site:* www.harperleeprize.com, pg 623

Fierman, Stephanie, Association of National Advertisers Inc (ANA), 155 E 44 St, New York, NY 10017 *Tel:* 212-697-5950 *Fax:* 212-687-7310 *E-mail:* info@ana.net *Web Site:* www.ana.net, pg 499

Fierst, Anna Eleanor, Eleanor Roosevelt Award for Bravery in Literature, PO Box 255, Hyde Park, NY 12538 *Tel:* 845-229-5302 *E-mail:* admin@ervk.org *Web Site:* ervk.org/banned-book-awards, pg 657

Figueroa, Michelle, Hachette Audio, 1290 Avenue of the Americas, New York, NY 10104 *Tel:* 212-364-1100 *Web Site:* www.hachettebookgroup.com/imprint/hachette-audio/, pg 83

Files, Erin, Aevitas Creative Management LLC, 19 W 21 St, Suite 501, New York, NY 10010 *Tel:* 212-765-6900 *Web Site:* www.aevitascreative.com, pg 448

Fillon, Barbara, Random House Publishing Group, 1745 Broadway, New York, NY 10019 *Toll Free Tel:* 800-200-3552 *Web Site:* www.randomhousebooks.com, pg 170

Finamore, Rosa, Europa Editions, 27 Union Sq W, Suite 302, New York, NY 10003 *Tel:* 212-868-6844 *Fax:* 212-868-6845 *E-mail:* info@europaeditions.com; books@europaeditions.com; publicity@europaeditions.com *Web Site:* www.europaeditions.com, pg 67

Finan, Bill, The Brookings Institution Press, 1775 Massachusetts Ave NW, Washington, DC 20036-2188 *Tel:* 202-797-6000 *E-mail:* permissions@brookings.edu *Web Site:* www.brookings.edu, pg 37

Finch, Hunter, Princeton University Press, 41 William St, Princeton, NJ 08540-5237 *Tel:* 609-258-4900 *Fax:* 609-258-6305 *E-mail:* info@press.princeton.edu *Web Site:* press.princeton.edu, pg 164

Fine, Antony, Fine Creative Media, Inc, 589 Eighth Ave, 6th fl, New York, NY 10018 *Tel:* 212-595-3500 *Fax:* 212-202-4195 *E-mail:* info@mjfbooks.com, pg 72

Fine, Kaethe, Fine Creative Media, Inc, 589 Eighth Ave, 6th fl, New York, NY 10018 *Tel:* 212-595-3500 *Fax:* 212-202-4195 *E-mail:* info@mjfbooks.com, pg 72

Fine, Michael J, Fine Creative Media, Inc, 589 Eighth Ave, 6th fl, New York, NY 10018 *Tel:* 212-595-3500 *Fax:* 212-202-4195 *E-mail:* info@mjfbooks.com, pg 72

Fine, Steven, Fine Creative Media, Inc, 589 Eighth Ave, 6th fl, New York, NY 10018 *Tel:* 212-595-3500 *Fax:* 212-202-4195 *E-mail:* info@mjfbooks.com, pg 72

Finegan, Annelise, New York University, Center for Publishing & Applied Liberal Arts, 7 E 12 St, New York, NY 10003 *Tel:* 212-998-7200 *E-mail:* sps.info@nyu.edu *Web Site:* www.scps.nyu.edu/professional-pathways/topics.html, pg 563

Finegan, P G, 1765 Productions, 2911 Hunting Hills Ct, Oakton, VA 22124-1752 *Tel:* 202-813-9421 *E-mail:* 1765productions@gmail.com, pg 187

Fingerhut, Benjamin, St Augustine's Press Inc, PO Box 2285, South Bend, IN 46680-2285 *Tel:* 574-291-3500 *Fax:* 574-291-3700 *Web Site:* www.staugustine.net, pg 180

Fingerhut, Bruce, St Augustine's Press Inc, PO Box 2285, South Bend, IN 46680-2285 *Tel:* 574-291-3500 *Fax:* 574-291-3700 *Web Site:* www.staugustine.net, pg 180

Fingleton, Emma, Trident Media Group LLC, 355 Lexington Ave, 12th fl, New York, NY 10017 *Tel:* 212-333-1511 *E-mail:* info@tridentmediagroup.com; press@tridentmediagroup.com; foreignrights@tridentmediagroup.com; office.assistant@tridentmediagroup.com *Web Site:* www.tridentmediagroup.com, pg 480

Finkel, Erica, Harry N Abrams Inc, 195 Broadway, 9th fl, New York, NY 10007 *Tel:* 212-206-7715 *Toll Free Tel:* 800-345-1359 *Fax:* 212-645-8437

E-mail: abrams@abramsbooks.com; publicity@abramsbooks.com; sales@abramsbooks.com *Web Site:* www.abramsbooks.com, pg 3

Finkelman, Jamie, W W Norton & Company Inc, 500 Fifth Ave, New York, NY 10110-0017 *Tel:* 212-354-5500 *Toll Free Tel:* 800-233-4830 (orders & cust serv) *Fax:* 212-869-0856 *Toll Free Fax:* 800-458-6515 *E-mail:* orders@wwnorton.com *Web Site:* wwnorton.com, pg 143

Finkelstein, Roxanne, Harlequin Enterprises Ltd, Bay Adelaide Centre, East Tower, 22 Adelaide St W, 41st fl, Toronto, ON M5H 4E3, Canada *Tel:* 416-445-5860 *Toll Free Tel:* 888-432-4879; 800-370-5838 (ebook inquiries) *E-mail:* customerservice@harlequin.com *Web Site:* www.harlequin.com, pg 409

Finkin, Jordan, Hebrew Union College Press, 3101 Clifton Ave, Cincinnati, OH 45220 *Tel:* 513-221-1875 *Fax:* 513-221-0321 *Web Site:* press.huc.edu, pg 90

Finman, Stephanie, The Martell Agency, 1350 Avenue of the Americas, Suite 1205, New York, NY 10019 *Tel:* 212-317-2672 *Web Site:* www.themartellagency.com, pg 469

Finn, Candace, Houghton Mifflin Harcourt Trade & Reference Division, 125 High St, Boston, MA 02110 *Tel:* 617-351-5000 *Web Site:* www.hmhco.com, pg 96

Finn, Hayley, Jerome Fellowship, 2301 Franklin Ave E, Minneapolis, MN 55406-1099 *Tel:* 612-332-7481 *Fax:* 612-332-6037 *E-mail:* info@pwcenter.org *Web Site:* www.pwcenter.org, pg 618

Finn, Hayley, Many Voices Fellowships & Mentorships, 2301 Franklin Ave E, Minneapolis, MN 55406-1099 *Tel:* 612-332-7481 *Fax:* 612-332-6037 *E-mail:* info@pwcenter.org *Web Site:* www.pwcenter.org, pg 629

Finn, Hayley, McKnight Fellowships in Playwriting, 2301 Franklin Ave E, Minneapolis, MN 55406-1099 *Tel:* 612-332-7481 *Fax:* 612-332-6037 *E-mail:* info@pwcenter.org *Web Site:* www.pwcenter.org, pg 631

Finn, Hayley, McKnight National Residency & Commission, 2301 Franklin Ave E, Minneapolis, MN 55406-1099 *Tel:* 612-332-7481 *Fax:* 612-332-6037 *E-mail:* info@pwcenter.org *Web Site:* www.pwcenter.org, pg 631

Finn, Nettie, St Martin's Press, LLC, 120 Broadway, New York, NY 10271 *E-mail:* publicity@stmartins.com; trademarketing@stmartins.com; foreignrights@stmartins.com *Web Site:* us.macmillan.com/smp, pg 181

Finn, Peter, International Association of Business Communicators (IABC), 330 N Wabash Ave, Suite 2000, Chicago, IL 60611 *Tel:* 312-321-6868 *Toll Free Tel:* 800-218-8097 *Fax:* 312-673-6708 *E-mail:* member_relations@iabc.com *Web Site:* www.iabc.com, pg 508

Finnamore, Kerry, Sourcebooks LLC, 1935 Brookdale Rd, Suite 139, Naperville, IL 60563 *Tel:* 630-961-3900 *Toll Free Tel:* 800-432-7444 *Fax:* 630-961-2168 *E-mail:* info@sourcebooks.com *Web Site:* www.sourcebooks.com, pg 194

Finne, Hannah, Holiday House Publishing Inc, 50 Broad St, New York, NY 10004 *Tel:* 212-688-0085 *Fax:* 212-421-6134 *E-mail:* info@holidayhouse.com *Web Site:* www.holidayhouse.com, pg 94

Finnegan, Danielle, Little, Brown and Company, 1290 Avenue of the Americas, New York, NY 10104 *Tel:* 212-364-1100 *Fax:* 212-364-0952 *E-mail:* firstname.lastname@hbgusa.com *Web Site:* www.hachettebookgroup.com/imprint/little-brown-and-company/, pg 118

Fiorillo, Jessica T, Harvard Education Publishing Group, 8 Story St, 1st fl, Cambridge, MA 02138 *Tel:* 617-495-3432 *Fax:* 617-496-3584 *Web Site:* www.hepg.org, pg 88

Firer, Dmitriy, Macmillan, 120 Broadway, 22nd fl, New York, NY 10271 *E-mail:* press.inquiries@macmillan.com *Web Site:* us.macmillan.com, pg 122

Firger, Jessica, Union Square & Co, 1166 Avenue of the Americas, 17th fl, New York, NY 10036-2715 *Tel:* 212-532-7160 *Toll Free Tel:* 800-367-9692 *Fax:* 212-213-2495 *Toll Free Fax:* 800-542-7567 *E-mail:* custservice@sterlingpublishing.com; customerservice@sterlingpublishing.com; editorial@sterlingpublishing.com; tradesales@sterlingpublishing.com *Web Site:* www.sterlingpublishing.com, pg 212

Firing, Rob, Transatlantic Agency, 2 Bloor St E, Suite 3500, Toronto, ON M4W 1A8, Canada *Tel:* 416-488-9214 *E-mail:* info@transatlanticagency.com; royalties@transatlanticagency.com *Web Site:* www.transatlanticagency.com, pg 479

Firman, Tony, Miniature Book Society Inc, 518 High St, Fall River, MA 02720 *Web Site:* www.mbs.org, pg 511

Fischer, Christie, Manitoba Arts Council (MAC), 525-93 Lombard Ave, Winnipeg, MB R3B 3B1, Canada *Tel:* 204-945-2237 *Toll Free Tel:* 866-994-2787 *Fax:* 204-945-5925 *Web Site:* artscouncil.mb.ca, pg 510

Fischer, Craig, Police Executive Research Forum, 1120 Connecticut Ave NW, Suite 930, Washington, DC 20036 *Tel:* 202-466-7820 *Web Site:* www.policeforum.org, pg 162

Fischer, Grada, The Fischer Ross Group Inc, 2 Greenwich Off Park, Suite 300, Greenwich, CT 06831 *Tel:* 203-622-4950 *Fax:* 203-531-4132 *E-mail:* frgstaff@earthlink.net *Web Site:* frg-speakers.com, pg 487

Fischer, Liz, BMI®, 7 World Trade Center, 250 Greenwich St, New York, NY 10007-0030 *Tel:* 212-220-3000 *Toll Free Tel:* 888-689-5264 (sales) *E-mail:* newyork@bmi.com *Web Site:* www.bmi.com, pg 501

Fischer, Nicole, HarperCollins Publishers LLC, 195 Broadway, New York, NY 10007 *Tel:* 212-207-7000 *Web Site:* www.harpercollins.com, pg 87

Fischer, Skip, HarperCollins Publishers LLC, 195 Broadway, New York, NY 10007 *Tel:* 212-207-7000 *Web Site:* www.harpercollins.com, pg 86

Fischer, Tom, Workman Publishing, 1290 Avenue of the Americas, New York, NY 10104 *Toll Free Tel:* 800-759-0190 *Fax:* 212-364-0950 *E-mail:* workman-inquiry@hbgusa.com *Web Site:* www.hachettebookgroup.com/imprint/workman-publishing-company/, pg 232

Fischer-Harbage, Ryan, The Fischer-Harbage Agency Inc, 237 36 St, Brooklyn, NY 11232 *Tel:* 212-695-7105 *E-mail:* submissions@fischerharbage.com *Web Site:* www.fischerharbage.com, pg 458

Fiscia, Charlie, Macmillan Learning, One New York Plaza, Suite 46, New York, NY 10004 *Tel:* 212-576-9400 *E-mail:* salesoperations@macmillanusa.com *Web Site:* www.macmillanlearning.com/college/us, pg 123

Fisco, Dion, HarperCollins Publishers LLC, 195 Broadway, New York, NY 10007 *Tel:* 212-207-7000 *Web Site:* www.harpercollins.com, pg 86

Fish, Laura, University of Washington Press, 4333 Brooklyn Ave NE, Seattle, WA 98105-9570 *Toll Free Tel:* 800-537-5487 (orders) *Fax:* 206-543-3932; 410-516-6998 (orders) *E-mail:* uwapress@uw.edu *Web Site:* uwapress.uw.edu, pg 221

Fisher, Alison, Tor Publishing Group, 120 Broadway, New York, NY 10271 *Toll Free Tel:* 800-455-0340 (Macmillan) *E-mail:* torpublicity@tor.com; forgepublicity@forgebooks.com *Web Site:* us.macmillan.com/torpublishinggroup, pg 208

Fisher, Cherise, Wendy Sherman Associates Inc, 138 W 25 St, Suite 1018, New York, NY 10001 *Tel:* 212-279-9027 *E-mail:* submissions@wsherman.com *Web Site:* www.wsherman.com, pg 476

Fisher, Emily, HarperCollins Publishers LLC, 195 Broadway, New York, NY 10007 *Tel:* 212-207-7000 *Web Site:* www.harpercollins.com, pg 87

Fisher, Gabby, Harry N Abrams Inc, 195 Broadway, 9th fl, New York, NY 10007 *Tel:* 212-206-7715 *Toll Free Tel:* 800-345-1359 *Fax:* 212-645-8437 *E-mail:* abrams@abramsbooks.com; publicity@abramsbooks.com; sales@abramsbooks.com *Web Site:* www.abramsbooks.com, pg 2

Fisher, Kristen, DK, c/o Penguin Random House LLC, 1745 Broadway, 20th fl, New York, NY 10019 *Tel:* 646-674-4000 *Toll Free Tel:* 800-733-3000 *Fax:* 646-674-4020 *E-mail:* marketing@dk.com (lib servs); publicity@dk.com; csorders@penguinrandomhouse.com; customerservice@penguinrandomhouse.com *Web Site:* www.dk.com, pg 60

Fisher, Paul, Zondervan, 3900 Sparks Dr SE, Grand Rapids, MI 49546 *Tel:* 616-698-6900 *Toll Free Tel:* 800-226-1122; 800-727-1309 (retail orders) *Fax:* 616-698-3350 *Toll Free Fax:* 800-698-3256 (retail orders) *E-mail:* customercare@harpercollins.com *Web Site:* www.zondervan.com, pg 236

Fisher, Stephen, Buchwald, 10 E 44 St, New York, NY 10017 *Tel:* 212-867-1200 *E-mail:* info@buchwald.com *Web Site:* www.buchwald.com, pg 453

Fisher, Vickie, Pennwriters Conference, PO Box 685, Dalton, PA 18414 *E-mail:* conferencecoordinator@pennwriters.org; submissions@pennwriters.org *Web Site:* pennwriters.org, pg 556

Fisher-Tranese, Ashley, Penguin Publishing Group, c/o Penguin Random House LLC, 1745 Broadway, New York, NY 10019 *Tel:* 212-782-9000 *Web Site:* www.penguin.com, pg 154

Fishman, Emily, Bloomsbury Publishing Inc, 1385 Broadway, 5th fl, New York, NY 10018 *Tel:* 212-419-5300 *E-mail:* marketingusa@bloomsbury.com; adultpublicityusa@bloomsbury.com; askacademic@bloomsbury.com *Web Site:* www.bloomsbury.com, pg 32

Fishmann, Megan, Counterpoint Press LLC, 2560 Ninth St, Suite 318, Berkeley, CA 94710 *Tel:* 510-704-0230 *Fax:* 510-704-0268 *E-mail:* info@counterpointpress.com *Web Site:* counterpointpress.com; softskull.com, pg 54

Fisk, Heather, Chronicle Books LLC, 680 Second St, San Francisco, CA 94107 *Tel:* 415-537-4200 *Fax:* 415-537-4460 (perms) *E-mail:* hello@chroniclebooks.com; subrights@chroniclebooks.com *Web Site:* www.chroniclebooks.com, pg 48

Fisk, Raymond G, Down The Shore Publishing, 106 Forge Rd, West Creek, NJ 08092 *Tel:* 609-812-5076 *Fax:* 609-812-5098 *E-mail:* downshore@gmail.com *Web Site:* www.down-the-shore.com, pg 61

Fitch, Katie, Scholastic Trade Publishing, 557 Broadway, New York, NY 10012 *Tel:* 212-343-6100; 212-343-4685 (export sales) *Fax:* 212-343-4714 (export sales) *Web Site:* www.scholastic.com, pg 184

Fitterling, Michael Alan, Lost Classics Book Company LLC, 411 N Wales Dr, Lake Wales, FL 33853-3881 *Tel:* 863-632-1981 (edit off) *E-mail:* mgeditor@lostclassicsbooks.com *Web Site:* www.lostclassicsbooks.com, pg 120

Fitts, Sarah, Henry Holt and Company, LLC, 120 Broadway, 23rd fl, New York, NY 10271 *Tel:* 646-307-5151 *Toll Free Tel:* 888-330-8477 (orders) *Fax:* 646-307-5285 *Web Site:* www.henryholt.com, pg 94

Fitzgerald, Amy, Carolrhoda Books Inc, 241 First Ave N, Minneapolis, MN 55401 *Tel:* 612-332-3344 *Toll Free Tel:* 800-328-4929 *Fax:* 612-332-7615 *Toll Free Fax:* 800-332-1132 *E-mail:* info@lernerbooks.com; custserve@lernerbooks.com *Web Site:* www.lernerbooks.com; www.facebook.com/lernerbooks, pg 41

Fitzgerald, Amy, Carolrhoda Lab™, 241 First Ave N, Minneapolis, MN 55401 *Tel:* 612-332-3344 *Toll Free Tel:* 800-328-4929 *Fax:* 612-332-7615 *Toll Free Fax:* 800-332-1132 *E-mail:* info@lernerbooks.com; custserve@lernerbooks.com *Web Site:* www.lernerbooks.com; www.facebook.com/lernerbooks, pg 41

Fitzgerald, Brenda, University of Virginia Press, PO Box 400318, Charlottesville, VA 22904-4318 *Tel:* 434-924-3469 (cust serv) *Toll Free Tel:* 800-831-3406 *Fax:* 434-982-2655 *Toll Free Fax:* 877-288-6400 *E-mail:* vapress@virginia.edu *Web Site:* www.upress.virginia.edu, pg 220

Fitzgerald, Lance, Penguin Random House Audio Publishing Group, 1745 Broadway, New York, NY 10019 *Toll Free Tel:* 800-793-2665 (cust serv) *E-mail:* audio@penguinrandomhouse.com; ecustomerservice@penguinrandomhouse.com *Web Site:* www.penguinrandomhouseaudio.com, pg 154

Fitzgerald, Laura, DAW Books, 19 W 21 St, No 1201, New York, NY 10010 *E-mail:* info@astrapublishinghouse.com *Web Site:* astrapublishinghouse.com/imprints/daw-books, pg 57

Fitzgibbon, Stuart, Dr Tony Ryan Book Award, 2469 Ironworks Pike, Lexington, KY 40511 *Tel:* 859-455-9222 *Web Site:* www.castletonlyons.com, pg 658

Fitzsimmons, Erin, Sourcebooks LLC, 1935 Brookdale Rd, Suite 139, Naperville, IL 60563 *Tel:* 630-961-3900 *Toll Free Tel:* 800-432-7444 *Fax:* 630-961-2168 *E-mail:* info@sourcebooks.com *Web Site:* www.sourcebooks.com, pg 194

Fiyak-Burkley, Michele, University Press of Florida, 2046 NE Waldo Rd, Suite 2100, Gainesville, FL 32609 *Tel:* 352-392-1351 *Toll Free Tel:* 800-226-3822 (orders only) *Fax:* 352-392-0590 *Toll Free Fax:* 800-680-1955 (orders only) *E-mail:* press@upress.ufl.edu; orders@upress.ufl.edu *Web Site:* www.upf.com, pg 221

Flach, Andrew, Hatherleigh Press Ltd, 62545 State Hwy 10, Hobart, NY 13788 *Toll Free Tel:* 800-528-2550 *E-mail:* info@hatherleighpress.com; publicity@hatherleighpress.com *Web Site:* www.hatherleighpress.com, pg 88

Flachs, David, G Schirmer Inc/Associated Music Publishers Inc, 180 Madison Ave, 24th fl, New York, NY 10016 *Tel:* 212-254-2100 *Fax:* 212-254-2013 *E-mail:* schirmer@schirmer.com *Web Site:* www.musicsalesclassical.com, pg 183

Flahaven, Brian, Council for Advancement & Support of Education (CASE), 1201 Eye St NW, Suite 300, Washington, DC 20005 *Tel:* 202-328-CASE (328-2273) *Fax:* 202-387-4973 *E-mail:* membersupportcenter@case.org *Web Site:* www.case.org, pg 504

Flaherty, Rue, Running Press, 1290 Avenue of the Americas, New York, NY 10104 *Tel:* 212-364-1100 *Toll Free Tel:* 800-759-0190 (cust serv) *Fax:* 212-364-0933 (intl orders) *Toll Free Fax:* 800-286-9471 (cust serv) *E-mail:* customer.service@hbgusa.com; orders@hbgusa.com *Web Site:* www.hachettebookgroup.com/imprint/running-press/; www.moon.com (Moon Travel Guides); pg 178

Flame, Amber, Hedgebrook Radical Craft Retreats, PO Box 1231, Freeland, WA 98249 *Tel:* 360-321-4786 *E-mail:* hedgebrook@hedgebrook.org *Web Site:* www.hedgebrook.org/radical-craft-retreats; www.facebook.com/hedgebrook, pg 554

Flame, Amber, Hedgebrook VorTEXT Intensives Writing Retreat, PO Box 1231, Freeland, WA 98249 *Tel:* 360-321-4786 *E-mail:* hedgebrook@hedgebrook.org; programs@hedgebrook.org *Web Site:* www.hedgebrook.org/vortext; www.facebook.com/hedgebrook, pg 554

Flame, Amber, Hedgebrook Writers in Residence Program, PO Box 1231, Freeland, WA 98249 *Tel:* 360-321-4786 *E-mail:* hedgebrook@hedgebrook.org; programs@hedgebrook.org *Web Site:* www.hedgebrook.org/writers-in-residence; www.facebook.com/hedgebrook, pg 554

Flamini, Michael, St Martin's Press, LLC, 120 Broadway, New York, NY 10271 *E-mail:* publicity@stmartins.com; trademarketing@stmartins.com; foreignrights@stmartins.com *Web Site:* us.macmillan.com/smp, pg 181

Flanagan, Mollie, Artist Fellowships, One Capital Hill, 3rd fl, Providence, RI 02908 *Tel:* 401-222-3880 *Fax:* 401-222-3018 *Web Site:* risca.online/grants/artist-fellowships, pg 574

Flancher, Sonja, Henry Holt and Company, LLC, 120 Broadway, 23rd fl, New York, NY 10271 *Tel:* 646-307-5151 *Toll Free Tel:* 888-330-8477 (orders) *Fax:* 646-307-5285 *Web Site:* www.henryholt.com, pg 94

Flanders, Margaret, Judy Lopez Memorial Award For Children's Literature, 1225 Selby Ave, Los Angeles, CA 90024 *Tel:* 310-474-9917 *Fax:* 310-474-6436 *Web Site:* www.wnba-books.org/la; www.judylopezbookaward.org, pg 626

Flanigan, Elissa, Quirk Books, 215 Church St, Philadelphia, PA 19106 *Tel:* 215-627-3581 *Fax:* 215-627-5220 *E-mail:* general@quirkbooks.com *Web Site:* www.quirkbooks.com, pg 168

Flannery, Carol, Rowman & Littlefield, 4501 Forbes Blvd, Suite 200, Lanham, MD 20706 *Tel:* 301-459-3366 *Toll Free Tel:* 800-462-6420 (ext 3024, cust serv) *Fax:* 301-429-5748 *Web Site:* rowman.com, pg 178

Flannery, Jennifer, Flannery Literary, 1140 Wickfield Ct, Naperville, IL 60563 *E-mail:* jennifer@flanneryliterary.com *Web Site:* flanneryliterary.com, pg 459

Flannery-McCoy, Bridget, Princeton University Press, 41 William St, Princeton, NJ 08540-5237 *Tel:* 609-258-4900 *Fax:* 609-258-6305 *E-mail:* info@press.princeton.edu *Web Site:* press.princeton.edu, pg 164

Flashman, Melissa, Janklow & Nesbit Associates, 285 Madison Ave, 21st fl, New York, NY 10017 *Tel:* 212-421-1700 *Fax:* 212-355-1403 *E-mail:* info@janklow.com; submissions@janklow.com; filmtvrights@janklow.com *Web Site:* www.janklowandnesbit.com, pg 464

Flath, Regina, Random House Publishing Group, 1745 Broadway, New York, NY 10019 *Toll Free Tel:* 800-200-3552 *Web Site:* www.randomhousebooks.com, pg 171

Flavin, Laura, Henry Holt and Company, LLC, 120 Broadway, 23rd fl, New York, NY 10271 *Tel:* 646-307-5151 *Toll Free Tel:* 888-330-8477 (orders) *Fax:* 646-307-5285 *Web Site:* www.henryholt.com, pg 94

Flax, Margery, Lilian Jackson Braun Award, 1140 Broadway, Suite 1507, New York, NY 10001 *Tel:* 212-888-8171 *E-mail:* mwa@mysterywriters.org *Web Site:* mysterywriters.org/edgars/lilian-jackson-braun-award, pg 583

Flax, Margery, The Edgar Awards®, 1140 Broadway, Suite 1507, New York, NY 10001 *Tel:* 212-888-8171 *E-mail:* mwa@mysterywriters.org *Web Site:* theedgars.com; mysterywriters.org, pg 598

Flax, Margery, Minotaur Books/Mystery Writers of America First Crime Novel Competition, 1140 Broadway, Suite 1507, New York, NY 10001 *Tel:* 212-888-8171 *E-mail:* mwa@mysterywriters.org *Web Site:* mysterywriters.org/about-mwa/st-martins; us.macmillan.com/minotaurbooks/submit-manuscript, pg 633

Flax, Margery, Mystery Writers of America (MWA), 1140 Broadway, Suite 1507, New York, NY 10001 *Tel:* 212-888-8171 *E-mail:* mwa@mysterywriters.org *Web Site:* mysterywriters.org, pg 511

Flax, Margery, Barbara Neely Memorial Scholarship Program, 1140 Broadway, Suite 1507, New York, NY 10001 *Tel:* 212-888-8171 *E-mail:* mwa@mysterywriters.org *Web Site:* mysterywriters.org, pg 639

Fleck, Robert III, Oak Knoll Press, 310 Delaware St, New Castle, DE 19720 *Tel:* 302-328-7232 *Fax:* 302-328-7274 *E-mail:* oakknoll@oakknoll.com; orders@oakknoll.com; publishing@oakknoll.com *Web Site:* www.oakknoll.com, pg 144

Fleck-Nisbet, Andrea, IBPA Book Awards, 1020 Manhattan Beach Blvd, Suite 204, Manhattan Beach, CA 90266 *Tel:* 310-546-1818 *E-mail:* info@ibpa-online.org *Web Site:* www.ibpa-online.org, pg 615

Fleck-Nisbet, Andrea, The Independent Book Publishers Association (IBPA), 1020 Manhattan Beach Blvd, Suite 204, Manhattan Beach, CA 90266 *Tel:* 310-546-1818 *E-mail:* info@ibpa-online.org *Web Site:* www.ibpa-online.org, pg 507

Flegal, Diana, Hartline Literary Agency LLC, 123 Queenston Dr, Pittsburgh, PA 15235 *Tel:* 412-829-2483 *Toll Free Fax:* 888-279-6007 *Web Site:* www.hartlineliterary.com, pg 462

Flegg, Caleigh, Simon & Schuster, 1230 Avenue of the Americas, New York, NY 10020 *Tel:* 212-698-7000 *Toll Free Tel:* 800-223-2348 (cust serv); 800-223-2336 (orders) *Toll Free Fax:* 800-943-9831 (orders) *Web Site:* simonandschusterpublishing.com/simonandschuster/, pg 188

Fleischer, Chip, Steerforth Press & Services, 31 Hanover St, Suite 1, Lebanon, NH 03766 *Tel:* 603-643-4787 *Fax:* 603-643-4788 *E-mail:* info@steerforth.com *Web Site:* www.steerforth.com, pg 198

Fleishman, Sam, Literary Artists Representatives, 575 West End Ave, Suite GRC, New York, NY 10024-2711 *Tel:* 212-679-7788 *E-mail:* litartists@aol.com, pg 467

Fleming, Cindy, Savvas Learning Co LLC, 15 E Midland Ave, Suite 502, Paramus, NJ 07652 *Toll Free Tel:* 800-848-9500 *Web Site:* www.savvas.com, pg 183

Fleming, Deena, Harry N Abrams Inc, 195 Broadway, 9th fl, New York, NY 10007 *Tel:* 212-206-7715 *Toll Free Tel:* 800-345-1359 *Fax:* 212-645-8437 *E-mail:* abrams@abramsbooks.com; publicity@abramsbooks.com; sales@abramsbooks.com *Web Site:* www.abramsbooks.com, pg 2

Fleming, James, C D Howe Institute, 67 Yonge St, Suite 300, Toronto, ON M5E 1J8, Canada *Tel:* 416-865-1904 *Fax:* 416-865-1866 *E-mail:* cdhowe@cdhowe.org *Web Site:* www.cdhowe.org, pg 410

Fleming, Liz, Barefoot Books, 23 Bradford St, 2nd fl, Concord, MA 01742 *Tel:* 617-576-0660 *Toll Free Tel:* 866-215-1756 (cust serv); 866-417-2369 (orders) *Fax:* 617-576-0049 *E-mail:* help@barefootbooks.com *Web Site:* www.barefootbooks.com, pg 24

Fleming, Marta, St Martin's Press, LLC, 120 Broadway, New York, NY 10271 *E-mail:* publicity@stmartins.com; trademarketing@stmartins.com; foreignrights@stmartins.com *Web Site:* us.macmillan.com/smp, pg 181

Fleming, Marta, Tor Publishing Group, 120 Broadway, New York, NY 10271 *Toll Free Tel:* 800-455-0340 (Macmillan) *E-mail:* torpublicity@tor.com; forgepublicity@forgebooks.com *Web Site:* us.macmillan.com/torpublishinggroup, pg 208

Fleming, Odette, Penguin Random House LLC, 1745 Broadway, New York, NY 10019 *Tel:* 212-782-9000 *Toll Free Tel:* 800-726-0600 *Web Site:* www.penguinrandomhouse.com, pg 155

Fletcher, Claire, Chronicle Books LLC, 680 Second St, San Francisco, CA 94107 *Tel:* 415-537-4200 *Fax:* 415-537-4460 (perms) *E-mail:* hello@chroniclebooks.com; subrights@chroniclebooks.com *Web Site:* www.chroniclebooks.com, pg 47

Fletcher, Kate, Candlewick Press, 99 Dover St, Somerville, MA 02144-2825 *Tel:* 617-661-3330 *Fax:* 617-661-0565 *E-mail:* bigbear@candlewick.com; salesinfo@candlewick.com *Web Site:* candlewick.com, pg 39

Fletcher, Lesley, Gerald Lampert Memorial Award, 2 Carlton St, Suite 1519, Toronto, ON M5B 1J3, Canada *Tel:* 416-504-1657 *E-mail:* info@poets.ca; admin@poets.ca *Web Site:* poets.ca/awards/lampert, pg 622

Fletcher, Lesley, The League of Canadian Poets, 2 Carlton St, Suite 1519, Toronto, ON M5B 1J3, Canada *Tel:* 416-504-1657 *E-mail:* info@poets.ca *Web Site:* poets.ca, pg 509

Fletcher, Lesley, Pat Lowther Memorial Award, 2 Carlton St, Suite 1519, Toronto, ON M5B 1J3, Canada *Tel:* 416-504-1657 *E-mail:* info@poets.ca *Web Site:* poets.ca/awards/lowther, pg 627

Fletcher, Lesley, Raymond Souster Award, 2 Carlton St, Suite 1519, Toronto, ON M5B 1J3, Canada *Tel:* 416-504-1657 *E-mail:* admin@poets.ca *Web Site:* poets.ca/awards/souster, pg 664

Fletcher, Lesley, Jessamy Stursberg Poetry Prize for Canadian Youth, 2 Carlton St, Suite 1519, Toronto, ON M5B 1J3, Canada *Tel:* 416-504-1657 *E-mail:* info@poets.ca; admin@poets.ca *Web Site:* poets.ca, pg 667

Fletcher, Lesley, Sheri-D Wilson Golden Beret Award, 2 Carlton St, Suite 1519, Toronto, ON M5B 1J3, Canada *Tel:* 416-504-1657 *E-mail:* admin@poets.ca *Web Site:* poets.ca/awards/goldenberet, pg 676

Fletcher, Molly, Albert Whitman & Company, 250 S Northwest Hwy, Suite 320, Park Ridge, IL 60068 *Tel:* 847-232-2800 *Toll Free Tel:* 800-255-7675 (orders) *Fax:* 847-581-0039 *E-mail:* mail@albertwhitman.com; orders@albertwhitman.com *Web Site:* www.albertwhitman.com, pg 6

Fletcher, Paul, Savvas Learning Co LLC, 15 E Midland Ave, Suite 502, Paramus, NJ 07652 *Toll Free Tel:* 800-848-9500 *Web Site:* www.savvas.com, pg 183

Fletcher, Stephanie, HarperCollins Publishers LLC, 195 Broadway, New York, NY 10007 *Tel:* 212-207-7000 *Web Site:* www.harpercollins.com, pg 86

Fletcher, Stephen, Rand McNally, 9855 Woods Dr, Skokie, IL 60077 *Tel:* 847-329-8100 *Toll Free Tel:* 877-446-4863 *Toll Free Fax:* 877-469-1298 *E-mail:* mediarelations@randmcnally.com; tndsupport@randmcnally.com *Web Site:* www.randmcnally.com, pg 169

Flick, Sharon, Great Lakes Graphics Association (GLGA), N27 W23960 Paul Rd, Suite 200, Pewaukee, WI 53072 *Tel:* 262-522-2210 *Toll Free Tel:* 855-522-2210 *Fax:* 262-522-2211 *E-mail:* info@glga.info *Web Site:* glga.info, pg 507

Flis, Nathan, Yale Center for British Art, 1080 Chapel St, New Haven, CT 06510-2302 *Tel:* 203-432-8929 *Fax:* 203-432-1626 *E-mail:* ycba.publications@yale.edu *Web Site:* britishart.yale.edu, pg 235

Florence, Jenny, The Monacelli Press, 65 Bleecker St, 8th fl, New York, NY 10012 *Tel:* 212-652-5400 *E-mail:* contact@monacellipress.com *Web Site:* www.phaidon.com/monacelli, pg 133

Florence, Kyle, J J Keller & Associates, Inc®, 3003 Breezewood Lane, Neenah, WI 54957 *Tel:* 920-722-2848 *Toll Free Tel:* 877-564-2333 *Toll Free Fax:* 800-727-7516 *E-mail:* customerservice@jjkeller.com; sales@jjkeller.com *Web Site:* www.jjkeller.com, pg 108

Flores, Bianca, Riverhead Books, c/o Penguin Random House LLC, 1745 Broadway, New York, NY 10019 *Tel:* 212-782-9000 *Web Site:* www.penguin.com/riverhead-overview/, pg 175

Flores, Feather, Simon & Schuster Children's Publishing, 1230 Avenue of the Americas, New York, NY 10020 *Tel:* 212-698-7000 *Web Site:* www.simonandschuster.com/kids; www.simonandschuster.com/teen; simonandschuster.net; simonandschuster.biz, pg 189

Florian, Meghan, Herald Press, PO Box 866, Harrisonburg, VA 22803 *Toll Free Tel:* 800-245-7894 (orders) *Fax:* 540-242-4476 *Toll Free Fax:* 877-271-0760 *E-mail:* info@mennomedia.org; customerservice@mennomedia.org *Web Site:* www.heraldpress.com; store.mennomedia.org, pg 91

Floridia, Allyson, Farrar, Straus & Giroux Books for Young Readers, 120 Broadway, New York, NY 10271 *Tel:* 212-741-6900 *Toll Free Tel:* 888-330-8477 (orders) *E-mail:* childrens.publicity@macmillanusa.com; childrensrights@macmillanusa.com *Web Site:* us.macmillan.com/mackids, pg 70

Floridia, Allyson, Roaring Brook Press, 120 Broadway, New York, NY 10271 *Tel:* 646-307-5151 *Web Site:* us.macmillan.com/publishers/roaring-brook-press, pg 176

Floyd, Chriscynethia, Our Daily Bread Publishing, 3000 Kraft Ave SE, Grand Rapids, MI 49512 *Toll Free Tel:* 800-653-8333 (cust serv) *E-mail:* customerservice@odb.org *Web Site:* ourdailybreadpublishing.org, pg 148

Floyd, Steve, August House Inc, 3500 Piedmont Rd NE, Suite 310, Atlanta, GA 30305 *Tel:* 404-442-4420 *Toll Free Tel:* 800-284-8784 *Fax:* 404-442-4435 *E-mail:* ahinfo@augusthouse.com *Web Site:* www.augusthouse.com, pg 22

Flucker, Benita, Houghton Mifflin Harcourt Trade & Reference Division, 125 High St, Boston, MA 02110 *Tel:* 617-351-5000 *Web Site:* www.hmhco.com, pg 96

Flum, Caitie, Liza Dawson Associates, 121 W 27 St, Suite 1201, New York, NY 10001 *Tel:* 212-465-9071 *Web Site:* www.lizadawsonassociates.com, pg 455

Flum, David, Rutgers University Press, 106 Somerset St, 3rd fl, New Brunswick, NJ 08901 *Tel:* 848-445-7762; 848-445-7761 (sales) *Fax:* 732-745-4935 *E-mail:* sales@rutgersuniversitypress.org *Web Site:* www.rutgersuniversitypress.org, pg 178

Flute, Matthew, Penguin Random House Canada, a Penguin Random House company, 320 Front St W, Suite 1400, Toronto, ON M5V 3B6, Canada *Tel:* 416-364-4449 *Toll Free Tel:* 888-523-9292 (cust serv) *E-mail:* canadaweb@penguinrandomhouse.com; customerservicescanada@penguinrandomhouse.com *Web Site:* www.penguinrandomhouse.ca, pg 416

Flynn, Amy Thrall, Aevitas Creative Management LLC, 19 W 21 St, Suite 501, New York, NY 10010 *Tel:* 212-765-6900 *Web Site:* www.aevitascreative.com, pg 448

Flynn, Ian, Visual Media Alliance (VMA), 665 Third St, Suite 500, San Francisco, CA 94107-1926 *Tel:* 415-495-8242 *Toll Free Tel:* 800-659-3363 *Fax:* 415-520-1126 *E-mail:* info@vma.bz *Web Site:* main.vma.bz, pg 521

Flynn, Jacqueline, Rowman & Littlefield, 4501 Forbes Blvd, Suite 200, Lanham, MD 20706 *Tel:* 301-459-3366 *Toll Free Tel:* 800-462-6420 (ext 3024, cust serv) *Fax:* 301-429-5748 *Web Site:* rowman.com, pg 178

Flynn, Jay, John Wiley & Sons Inc, 111 River St, Hoboken, NJ 07030-5774 *Tel:* 201-748-6000 *Toll Free Tel:* 800-225-5945 (cust serv) *Fax:* 201-748-6088 *Web Site:* www.wiley.com, pg 230

Flynn, Katherine, Calligraph LLC, 45 Main St, No 850, Brooklyn, NY 11201 *Tel:* 212-253-1074 *E-mail:* mail@calligraphlit.com; rights@calligraphlit.com; submissions@calligraphlit.com *Web Site:* www.calligraphlit.com, pg 453

Flynn, Michael F, Robert A Heinlein Award, PO Box 686, Baltimore, MD 21203-0686 *Tel:* 410-563-2737 *E-mail:* webmeister@bsfs.org *Web Site:* www.bsfs.org/bsfsheinlein.htm, pg 612

Flynn, Tanya, Cedar Fort Inc, 2373 W 700 S, Suite 100, Springville, UT 84663 *Tel:* 801-489-4084 *Toll Free Tel:* 800-SKY-BOOK (759-2665) *E-mail:* marketinginfo@cedarfort.com *Web Site:* cedarfort.com, pg 43

Fodera, Amy, Macmillan, 120 Broadway, 22nd fl, New York, NY 10271 *E-mail:* press.inquiries@macmillan.com *Web Site:* us.macmillan.com, pg 122

Foerster, Maureen, William Holmes McGuffey Longevity Award, PO Box 367, Fountain City, WI 54629 *E-mail:* info@taaonline.net *Web Site:* www.taaonline.net/mcguffey-longevity-award, pg 630

Foerster, Maureen, Most Promising New Textbook Award, PO Box 367, Fountain City, WI 54629 *E-mail:* info@taaonline.net *Web Site:* www.taaonline.net/promising-new-textbook-award, pg 636

Foerster, Maureen, Pynn-Silverman Lifetime Achievement Award, PO Box 367, Fountain City, WI 54629 *E-mail:* info@taaonline.net *Web Site:* www.taaonline.net/council-awards#pynn, pg 654

Foerster, Maureen, TAA Council of Fellows, PO Box 367, Fountain City, WI 54629 *E-mail:* info@taaonline.net *Web Site:* www.taaonline.net/council-of-fellows, pg 668

Foerster, Maureen, Textbook Excellence Award, PO Box 367, Fountain City, WI 54629 *E-mail:* info@taaonline.net *Web Site:* www.taaonline.net/textbook-excellence-award, pg 669

Fogelman, Sheldon, Sheldon Fogelman Agency Inc, 420 E 72 St, New York, NY 10021 *Tel:* 212-532-7250 *Fax:* 212-685-8939 *E-mail:* info@sheldonfogelmanagency.com; submissions@sheldonfogelmanagency.com *Web Site:* sheldonfogelmanagency.com, pg 459

Foggy, Jessalyn, Penguin Random House LLC, 1745 Broadway, New York, NY 10019 *Tel:* 212-782-9000 *Toll Free Tel:* 800-726-0600 *Web Site:* www.penguinrandomhouse.com, pg 155

Folan, Ellen, Penguin Random House Audio Publishing Group, 1745 Broadway, New York, NY 10019 *Toll Free Tel:* 800-793-2665 (cust serv) *E-mail:* audio@penguinrandomhouse.com; ecustomerservice@penguinrandomhouse.com *Web Site:* www.penguinrandomhouseaudio.com, pg 154

Folds, Melissa, Random House Publishing Group, 1745 Broadway, New York, NY 10019 *Toll Free Tel:* 800-200-3552 *Web Site:* www.randomhousebooks.com, pg 171

Foley, Ehren, University of South Carolina Press, 1600 Hampton St, Suite 544, Columbia, SC 29208 *Tel:* 803-777-5245 *Toll Free Tel:* 800-768-2500 (orders) *Fax:* 803-777-0160 *Toll Free Fax:* 800-868-0740 (orders) *Web Site:* uscpress.com, pg 220

Foley, Margaret, Royal Fireworks Press, 41 First Ave, Unionville, NY 10988 *Tel:* 845-726-4444 *E-mail:* mail@rfwp.com *Web Site:* www.rfwp.com, pg 178

Foley, Meaghan, American Diabetes Association, 2451 Crystal Dr, Suite 900, Arlington, VA 22202 *Tel:* 703-549-1500 *Toll Free Tel:* 800-342-2383 *E-mail:* booksales@diabetes.org; ada_pubs@diabetes.org *Web Site:* diabetes.org; diabetesjournals.org/books; www.facebook.com/adapublications, pg 9

Folkedal, Joy, BoardSource, 750 Ninth St NW, Suite 520, Washington, DC 20001-4793 *Tel:* 202-349-2500 *E-mail:* members@boardsource.org; mediarelations@boardsource.org *Web Site:* www.boardsource.org, pg 33

Fonseca, Sarah, American Federation of Arts, 305 E 47 St, 10th fl, New York, NY 10017 *Tel:* 212-988-7700 *Toll Free Tel:* 800-232-0270 *Fax:* 212-861-2487 *E-mail:* pubinfo@amfedarts.org *Web Site:* www.amfedarts.org, pg 9

Fontana, Virginia, University of Nevada Press, c/o University of Nevada, Continuing Educ Bldg, MS 0166, Reno, NV 89557-0166 *Tel:* 775-784-6573 *Fax:* 775-784-6200 *Web Site:* www.unpress.nevada.edu, pg 218

Foo, Bill, Other Press, 267 Fifth Ave, 6th fl, New York, NY 10016 *Tel:* 212-414-0054 *Toll Free Tel:* 877-THEOTHER (843-6843) *Fax:* 212-414-0939 *E-mail:* editor@otherpress.com; marketing@otherpress.com; publicity@otherpress.com *Web Site:* otherpress.com, pg 148

Foran, Charlie, Atwood Gibson Writers' Trust Fiction Prize, 600-460 Richmond St W, Toronto, ON M5V 1Y1, Canada *Tel:* 416-504-8222 *Toll Free Tel:* 877-906-6548 *Fax:* 416-504-9090 *E-mail:* info@writerstrust.com *Web Site:* www.writerstrust.com, pg 575

Foran, Charlie, Balsillie Prize for Public Policy, 600-460 Richmond St W, Toronto, ON M5V 1Y1, Canada *Tel:* 416-504-8222 *Toll Free Tel:* 877-906-6548 *Fax:* 416-504-9090 *E-mail:* info@writerstrust.com *Web Site:* www.writerstrust.com, pg 577

Foran, Charlie, Latner Griffin Writers' Trust Poetry Prize, 600-460 Richmond St W, Toronto, ON M5V 1Y1, Canada *Tel:* 416-504-8222 *Toll Free Tel:* 877-906-6548 *Fax:* 416-504-9090 *E-mail:* info@writerstrust.com *Web Site:* www.writerstrust.com/awards/latner-writers-trust-poetry-prize, pg 622

Foran, Charlie, Matt Cohen Award: In Celebration of a Writing Life, 600-460 Richmond St W, Toronto, ON M5V 1Y1, Canada *Tel:* 416-504-8222 *Toll Free Tel:* 877-906-6548 *Fax:* 416-504-9090 *E-mail:* info@writerstrust.com *Web Site:* www.writerstrust.com, pg 630

Foran, Charlie, Dayne Ogilvie Prize for LGBTQ2S+ Emerging Writers, 600-460 Richmond St W, Toronto, ON M5V 1Y1, Canada *Tel:* 416-504-8222 *Toll Free Tel:* 877-906-6548 *Fax:* 416-504-9090 *E-mail:* info@writerstrust.com *Web Site:* www.writerstrust.com, pg 643

Foran, Charlie, RBC Bronwen Wallace Award for Emerging Writers, 600-460 Richmond St W, Toronto, ON M5V 1Y1, Canada *Tel:* 416-504-8222 *Toll Free*

Foran, Charlie, Shaughnessy Cohen Prize for Political Writing, 600-460 Richmond St W, Toronto, ON M5V 1Y1, Canada *Tel:* 416-504-8222 *Toll Free Tel:* 877-906-6548 *Fax:* 416-504-9090 *E-mail:* info@writerstrust.com *Web Site:* www.writerstrust.com, pg 661

Foran, Charlie, Vicky Metcalf Award for Literature for Young People, 600-460 Richmond St W, Toronto, ON M5V 1Y1, Canada *Tel:* 416-504-8222 *Toll Free Tel:* 877-906-6548 *Fax:* 416-504-9090 *E-mail:* info@writerstrust.com *Web Site:* www.writerstrust.com, pg 672

Foran, Charlie, Hilary Weston Writers' Trust Prize for Nonfiction, 600-460 Richmond St W, Toronto, ON M5V 1Y1, Canada *Tel:* 416-504-8222 *Toll Free Tel:* 877-906-6548 *Fax:* 416-504-9090 *E-mail:* info@writerstrust.com *Web Site:* www.writerstrust.com, pg 674

Foran, Charlie, Weston International Award, 600-460 Richmond St W, Toronto, ON M5V 1Y1, Canada *Tel:* 416-504-8222 *Toll Free Tel:* 877-906-6548 *Fax:* 416-504-9090 *E-mail:* info@westoninternationalaward.com, pg 674

Foran, Charlie, Writers' Trust Engel Findley Award, 600-460 Richmond St W, Toronto, ON M5V 1Y1, Canada *Tel:* 416-504-8222 *Toll Free Tel:* 877-906-6548 *Fax:* 416-504-9090 *E-mail:* info@writerstrust. com *Web Site:* www.writerstrust.com, pg 678

Foran, Charlie, Writers' Trust McClelland & Stewart Journey Prize, 600-460 Richmond St W, Toronto, ON M5V 1Y1, Canada *Tel:* 416-504-8222 *Toll Free Tel:* 877-906-6548 *Fax:* 416-504-9090 *E-mail:* info@writerstrust.com *Web Site:* www.writerstrust.com, pg 678

Forbes, Alyson, Counterpoint Press LLC, 2560 Ninth St, Suite 318, Berkeley, CA 94710 *Tel:* 510-704-0230 *Fax:* 510-704-0268 *E-mail:* info@counterpointpress. com *Web Site:* counterpointpress.com; softskull.com, pg 54

Ford, Chelsey Moler, Sourcebooks LLC, 1935 Brookdale Rd, Suite 139, Naperville, IL 60563 *Tel:* 630-961-3900 *Toll Free Tel:* 800-432-7444 *Fax:* 630-961-2168 *E-mail:* info@sourcebooks.com *Web Site:* www.sourcebooks.com, pg 194

Ford, David, US Government Publishing Office (GPO), Superintendent of Documents, 732 N Capitol St NW, Washington, DC 20401 *Tel:* 202-512-1800 *Toll Free Tel:* 866-512-1800 (orders) *Fax:* 202-512-1998 *E-mail:* contactcenter@gpo.gov *Web Site:* www.gpo.gov; bookstore.gpo.gov (sales), pg 223

Ford, June, JFE Editorial, 190 Ocean Dr, Gun Barrel City, TX 75156 *Tel:* 817-560-7018 *E-mail:* jford@jfe-editorial.com, pg 441

Ford, Sean, Macmillan, 120 Broadway, 22nd fl, New York, NY 10271 *E-mail:* press.inquiries@macmillan.com *Web Site:* us.macmillan.com, pg 122

Ford, Stella, BoardSource, 750 Ninth St NW, Suite 520, Washington, DC 20001-4793 *Tel:* 202-349-2500 *E-mail:* members@boardsource.org; mediarelations@boardsource.org *Web Site:* www.boardsource.org, pg 33

Forde, Carolyn, Transatlantic Agency, 2 Bloor St E, Suite 3500, Toronto, ON M4W 1A8, Canada *Tel:* 416-488-9214 *E-mail:* info@transatlanticagency.com; royalties@transatlanticagency.com *Web Site:* www.transatlanticagency.com, pg 479

Forde, Diamond, Southeast Review's Gearhart Poetry Contest, Florida State University, Dept of English, Tallahassee, FL 32306 *E-mail:* southeastreview@gmail.com *Web Site:* www.southeastreview.org/writing-contests, pg 664

Forde, Diamond, Ned Stuckey-French Nonfiction Contest, Florida State University, Dept of English, Tallahassee, FL 32306 *E-mail:* southeastreview@gmail.com *Web Site:* www.southeastreview.org/writing-contests, pg 667

Forde, Diamond, World's Best Short-Short Story Contest, Florida State University, Dept of English, Tallahassee, FL 32306 *E-mail:* southeastreview@gmail.com *Web Site:* www.southeastreview.org/writing-contests, pg 677

Forder, Reg A, American Christian Writers, 4854 Aster Dr, Nashville, TN 37211 *Tel:* 615-331-8668; 615-498-8630 *E-mail:* acwriters@aol.com *Web Site:* acwriters.com, pg 494

Forland, Emily, Brandt & Hochman Literary Agents Inc, 1501 Broadway, Suite 2310, New York, NY 10036 *Tel:* 212-840-5760 *Fax:* 212-840-5776 *Web Site:* brandthochman.com, pg 452

Formica, Ron, Tantor Media Inc, 6 Business Park, Old Saybrook, CT 06475 *Tel:* 860-395-1155 *Toll Free Tel:* 877-782-6867 *Toll Free Fax:* 888-782-7821 *E-mail:* service@tantor.com; rights@tantor.com *Web Site:* www.tantor.com, pg 202

Forner, Alison, Avid Reader Press, 1230 Avenue of the Americas, New York, NY 10020 *Web Site:* avidreaderpress.com, pg 23

Forner, Alison, Simon & Schuster, 1230 Avenue of the Americas, New York, NY 10020 *Tel:* 212-698-7000 *Toll Free Tel:* 800-223-2348 (cust serv); 800-223-2336 (orders) *Toll Free Fax:* 800-943-9831 (orders) *Web Site:* simonandschusterpublishing.com/simonandschuster/, pg 188

Forney, Emily, BookEnds Literary Agency, 136 Long Hill Rd, Gillette, NJ 07933 *Web Site:* www.bookendsliterary.com, pg 451

Forrer, David, InkWell Management, 521 Fifth Ave, Suite 2600, New York, NY 10175 *Tel:* 212-922-3500 *Fax:* 212-922-0535 *E-mail:* info@inkwellmanagement.com; submissions@inkwellmanagement.com; permissions@inkwellmanagement.com *Web Site:* inkwellmanagement.com, pg 463

Forrest, Julie, Penguin Random House Canada, a Penguin Random House company, 320 Front St W, Suite 1400, Toronto, ON M5V 3B6, Canada *Tel:* 416-364-4449 *Toll Free Tel:* 888-523-9292 (cust serv) *E-mail:* canadaweb@penguinrandomhouse.com; customerservicescanada@penguinrandomhouse.com *Web Site:* www.penguinrandomhouse.ca, pg 416

Forrest, Will, Temple University Press, 1852 N Tenth St, Philadelphia, PA 19122-6099 *Tel:* 215-926-2140 *Toll Free Tel:* 800-621-2736 *Fax:* 215-926-2141 *E-mail:* tempress@temple.edu *Web Site:* tupress.temple.edu, pg 204

Forrister, Brad, M Lee Smith Publishers, 100 Winners Circle, Suite 300, Brentwood, TN 37027 *Tel:* 615-373-7517 *Toll Free Tel:* 800-274-6774; 800-727-5257 *E-mail:* custserv@mleesmith.com; service@blr.com *Web Site:* www.mleesmith.com; www.blr.com, pg 192

Forsa, Bethlam, Savvas Learning Co LLC, 15 E Midland Ave, Suite 502, Paramus, NJ 07652 *Toll Free Tel:* 800-848-9500 *Web Site:* www.savvas.com, pg 183

Forte, Fran, The New Press, 120 Wall St, 31st fl, New York, NY 10005 *Tel:* 212-629-8802 *Fax:* 212-629-8617 *E-mail:* newpress@thenewpress.com *Web Site:* thenewpress.com, pg 140

Fortier, Gary, Cengage Learning, 20 Channel Center St, Boston, MA 02210 *Tel:* 617-289-7700 *Toll Free Tel:* 800-354-9706 *Fax:* 617-289-7844 *E-mail:* esales@cengage.com *Web Site:* www.cengage.com, pg 43

Fortin, Jacques, QA International (QAI), 7240 Rue Saint-Hubert, Montreal, QC H2R 2N1, Canada *Tel:* 514-499-3000 *Fax:* 514-499-3010 *Web Site:* www.qa-international.com, pg 417

Fortin, Ms Josee, Broquet Inc, 97-B, Montee des Bouleaux, St-Constant, QC J5A 1A9, Canada *Tel:* 450-638-3338 *Fax:* 450-638-4338 *E-mail:* info@broquet.qc.ca *Web Site:* www.broquet.qc.ca, pg 397

Fortner, Shannon T, Johns Hopkins University Press, 2715 N Charles St, Baltimore, MD 21218-4363 *Tel:* 410-516-6900; 410-516-6987 *Toll Free Tel:* 800-537-5487 (book orders & cust serv); 800-548-1784 (journal orders) *Fax:* 410-516-6968; 410-516-6998 (orders) *E-mail:* hfscustserv@press.jhu.edu (cust serv); jrnlcirc@jh.edu (journal orders) *Web Site:* www.press.jhu.edu; muse.jhu.edu, pg 106

Fortuna, Nina, American Society of Magazine Editors (ASME), 23 Barnabas Rd, Suite 34, Hawleyville, CT 06440-0034 *Tel:* 212-872-3737 *E-mail:* asme@asme.media *Web Site:* www.asme.media, pg 496

Fortuna, Nina, ASME Award for Fiction, 23 Barnabas Rd, Suite 34, Hawleyville, CT 06440-0034 *Tel:* 212-872-3737 *E-mail:* asme@asme.media *Web Site:* www.asme.media, pg 575

Fortunato, John A, Fordham University, Gabelli School of Business, 140 W 62 St, Rm 440, New York, NY 10023 *Web Site:* www.fordham.edu, pg 603

Fortunato, John A, Gabelli School of Business Communications & Media Management Program, 140 W 62 St, Rm 440, New York, NY 10023 *Tel:* 212-636-6150 *Fax:* 718-817-4999 *Web Site:* www.fordham.edu/gabelli-school-of-business, pg 562

Fortune, John, Math Solutions®, One Harbor Dr, Suite 101, Sausalito, CA 94965 *Tel:* 877-234-7323 *Toll Free Tel:* 800-724-4716 *E-mail:* info@mathsolutions.com; orders@mathsolutions.com *Web Site:* www.mathsolutions.com; store.mathsolutions.com, pg 127

Fosado, Gisela, Duke University Press, 905 W Main St, Suite 18B, Durham, NC 27701 *Tel:* 919-688-5134 *Toll Free Tel:* 888-651-0122 (US) *Fax:* 919-688-2615 *Toll Free Fax:* 888-651-0124 *E-mail:* orders@dukeupress.edu *Web Site:* www.dukeupress.edu, pg 62

Foster, Cynthia, University Press of Mississippi, 3825 Ridgewood Rd, Jackson, MS 39211-6492 *Tel:* 601-432-6205 *Toll Free Tel:* 800-737-7788 (orders & cust serv) *Fax:* 601-432-6217 *E-mail:* press@mississippi.edu *Web Site:* www.upress.state.ms.us, pg 222

Foster, Dianne, Amber Lotus Publishing, PO Box 11329, Portland, OR 97211 *Tel:* 503-284-6400 *Toll Free Tel:* 800-326-2375 (orders only) *Fax:* 503-284-6417 *E-mail:* info@amberlotus.com; neworder@amberlotus.com *Web Site:* www.amberlotus.com, pg 8

Foster, Frank, Medals of America Press, 114 Southchase Blvd, Fountain Inn, SC 29644 *Toll Free Tel:* 800-605-4001 *Toll Free Fax:* 800-407-8640 *Web Site:* moapress.com, pg 128

Foster, Gloria, Global Publishing Solutions LLC, PO Box 2043, Matteson, IL 60443 *Toll Free Tel:* 888-351-2411 *E-mail:* info@globalpublishingsolutions.com *Web Site:* globalpublishingsolutions.com, pg 79

Foster, Laura, United States Holocaust Memorial Museum, 100 Raoul Wallenberg Place SW, Washington, DC 20024-2126 *Tel:* 202-488-0400; 202-488-6144 (orders) *Toll Free Tel:* 800-259-9998 (orders) *E-mail:* academicpublications@ushmm.org *Web Site:* www.ushmm.org, pg 213

Foster, Lee, Foster Travel Publishing, 1623 Martin Luther King Jr Way, Berkeley, CA 94709 *Tel:* 510-549-2202 *Web Site:* www.fostertravel.com, pg 439

Foster, Roz, Frances Goldin Literary Agency, Inc, 214 W 29 St, Suite 410, New York, NY 10001 *Tel:* 212-777-0047 *Fax:* 212-228-1660 *E-mail:* agency@goldinlit.com *Web Site:* www.goldinlit.com, pg 460

Foster, Shawn, Macmillan, 120 Broadway, 22nd fl, New York, NY 10271 *E-mail:* press.inquiries@macmillan.com *Web Site:* us.macmillan.com, pg 122

Foszcz, Timothy, Sourcebooks LLC, 1935 Brookdale Rd, Suite 139, Naperville, IL 60563 *Tel:* 630-961-3900 *Toll Free Tel:* 800-432-7444 *Fax:* 630-961-2168 *E-mail:* info@sourcebooks.com *Web Site:* www.sourcebooks.com, pg 195

Fotinos, Joel, St Martin's Press, LLC, 120 Broadway, New York, NY 10271 *E-mail:* publicity@stmartins.com; trademarketing@stmartins.com; foreignrights@stmartins.com *Web Site:* us.macmillan.com/smp, pg 180

Foulon, Alexandrine, Editions Hurtubise, 1815, ave de Lorimier, Montreal, QC H2K 3W6, Canada *Tel:* 514-523-1523 *Toll Free Tel:* 800-361-1664 *Web Site:* editionshurtubise.com, pg 403

Foulon, Arnaud, Editions Hurtubise, 1815, ave de Lorimier, Montreal, QC H2K 3W6, Canada *Tel:* 514-523-1523 *Toll Free Tel:* 800-361-1664 *Web Site:* editionshurtubise.com, pg 403

Foulon, Herve, Editions Hurtubise, 1815, ave de Lorimier, Montreal, QC H2K 3W6, Canada *Tel:* 514-523-1523 *Toll Free Tel:* 800-361-1664 *Web Site:* editionshurtubise.com, pg 403

Fournier, Mary Davis, Public Library Association (PLA), 225 N Michigan Ave, Suite 1300, Chicago, IL 60601 *Toll Free Tel:* 800-545-2433 (ext 5752) *Fax:* 312-280-5029 *E-mail:* pla@ala.org *Web Site:* www.ala.org/pla/, pg 518

Fowler, Gloria, Chronicle Books LLC, 680 Second St, San Francisco, CA 94107 *Tel:* 415-537-4200 *Fax:* 415-537-4460 (perms) *E-mail:* hello@chroniclebooks.com; subrights@chroniclebooks.com *Web Site:* www.chroniclebooks.com, pg 47

Fowler, J K, San Francisco Foundation/Nomadic Press Literary Awards, 111 Fairmount Ave, Oakland, CA 94611 *Tel:* 510-500-5162 *E-mail:* info@nomadicpress.org *Web Site:* www.nomadicpress.org/sff/nomadicpressliteraryawards; nomadicpress.submittable.com/submit; www.nomadicpress.org, pg 658

Fowler, Karen Joy, The Clarion Science Fiction & Fantasy Writers' Workshop, Arthur C Clarke Ctr for Human Imagination, UC San Diego, 9500 Gilman Dr, MC0445, La Jolla, CA 92093-0445 *Tel:* 858-534-6875 *E-mail:* clarion@ucsd.edu *Web Site:* clarion.ucsd.edu; imagination.ucsd.edu, pg 553

Fowler, Karen Joy, James Tiptree Jr Literary Award, 173 Anderson St, San Francisco, CA 94110 *Tel:* 415-641-4103 *E-mail:* info@tiptree.org *Web Site:* tiptree.org, pg 669

Fox, Anna, ChemTec Publishing, 38 Earswick Dr, Toronto, ON M1E 1C6, Canada *Tel:* 416-265-2603 *E-mail:* orderdesk@chemtec.org *Web Site:* www.chemtec.org, pg 399

Fox, Jim, Silman-James Press Inc, 141 N Clark Dr, Unit 1, West Hollywood, CA 90048 *Tel:* 310-205-0665 *E-mail:* info@silmanjamespress.com *Web Site:* www.silmanjamespress.com, pg 188

Fox, Keith, Phaidon, 65 Bleecker St, 8th fl, New York, NY 10012 *Tel:* 212-652-5400 *Toll Free Tel:* 800-759-0190 (cust serv) *Fax:* 212-652-5410 *Toll Free Fax:* 800-286-9471 (cust serv) *E-mail:* enquiries@phaidon.com *Web Site:* www.phaidon.com, pg 159

Fox, Laurie, Linda Chester Literary Agency, 630 Fifth Ave, Suite 2000, New York, NY 10111 *Tel:* 212-218-3350 *E-mail:* submissions@lindachester.com *Web Site:* www.lindachester.com, pg 453

Fox, Leisette, Wildflower Press, c/o Oakbrook Press, 3301 S Valley Dr, Rapid City, SD 57703 *Tel:* 605-381-6385 *E-mail:* info@wildflowerpress.org *Web Site:* www.wildflowerpress.org, pg 229

Fox, R K, American Press, 75 State St, Suite 100, Boston, MA 02109 *Tel:* 617-247-0022 *E-mail:* americanpress@flash.net *Web Site:* www.americanpresspublishers.com, pg 11

Fox, Robert, Berrett-Koehler Publishers Inc, 1333 Broadway, Suite 1000, Oakland, CA 94612 *Tel:* 510-817-2277 *Fax:* 510-817-2278 *E-mail:* bkpub@bkpub.com *Web Site:* www.bkconnection.com, pg 29

Fox, Sam, HarperCollins Children's Books, 195 Broadway, New York, NY 10007 *Tel:* 212-207-7000 *Web Site:* www.harpercollins.com/childrens, pg 85

Fox, Sam, HarperCollins Publishers LLC, 195 Broadway, New York, NY 10007 *Tel:* 212-207-7000 *Web Site:* www.harpercollins.com, pg 86

Fox, Sophia, Chronicle Books LLC, 680 Second St, San Francisco, CA 94107 *Tel:* 415-537-4200 *Fax:* 415-537-4460 (perms) *E-mail:* hello@chroniclebooks.com; subrights@chroniclebooks.com *Web Site:* www.chroniclebooks.com, pg 48

Foxley, Christina, Random House Publishing Group, 1745 Broadway, New York, NY 10019 *Toll Free Tel:* 800-200-3552 *Web Site:* www.randomhousebooks.com, pg 171

Foxman, Janet, The University of Arkansas Press, McIlroy House, 105 N McIlroy Ave, Fayetteville, AR 72701 *Tel:* 479-575-7544 *E-mail:* info@uapress.com *Web Site:* www.uapress.com, pg 214

Foytek, Michelle, Tor Publishing Group, 120 Broadway, New York, NY 10271 *Toll Free Tel:* 800-455-0340 (Macmillan) *E-mail:* torpublicity@tor.com; forgepublicity@forgebooks.com *Web Site:* us.macmillan.com/torpublishinggroup, pg 208

Fradkoff, Lindsay, Running Press, 1290 Avenue of the Americas, New York, NY 10104 *Tel:* 212-364-1100 *Toll Free Tel:* 800-759-0190 (cust serv) *Fax:* 212-364-0933 (intl orders) *Toll Free Fax:* 800-286-9471 (cust serv) *E-mail:* customer.service@hbgusa.com; orders@hbgusa.com *Web Site:* www.hachettebookgroup.com/imprint/running-press/; www.moon.com (Moon Travel Guides), pg 178

Francavilla, Luisa, Penguin Random House LLC, 1745 Broadway, New York, NY 10019 *Tel:* 212-782-9000 *Toll Free Tel:* 800-726-0600 *Web Site:* www.penguinrandomhouse.com, pg 155

Franceschelli, Christopher, Handprint Books Inc, 413 Sixth Ave, Brooklyn, NY 11215 *Tel:* 718-768-3696 *Toll Free Tel:* 800-759-0190 (orders) *E-mail:* hello@chroniclebooks.com (orders); publicity@chroniclebooks.com *Web Site:* www.handprintbooks.com, pg 84

Francis, Carol, Perfection Learning®, 1000 N Second Ave, Logan, IA 51546-1061 *Tel:* 712-644-2831 *Toll Free Tel:* 800-831-4190 *Toll Free Fax:* 800-543-2745 *E-mail:* orders@perfectionlearning.com *Web Site:* www.perfectionlearning.com, pg 158

Francis, Jason, Signature Books Publishing LLC, 564 W 400 N, Salt Lake City, UT 84116-3411 *Toll Free Tel:* 800-356-5687 *E-mail:* people@signaturebooks.com *Web Site:* www.signaturebooks.com; signaturebookslibrary.org, pg 188

Francis, Mary C, University of Pennsylvania Press, 3905 Spruce St, Philadelphia, PA 19104 *Tel:* 215-898-6261 *Fax:* 215-898-0404 *E-mail:* custserv@pobox.upenn.edu *Web Site:* www.pennpress.org, pg 219

Francis, Saige, Random House Publishing Group, 1745 Broadway, New York, NY 10019 *Toll Free Tel:* 800-200-3552 *Web Site:* www.randomhousebooks.com, pg 171

Francis-Sharma, Lauren, Bread Loaf Fellowships & Scholarships, Middlebury College, 204 College St, Middlebury, VT 05753 *Tel:* 802-443-5286 *Fax:* 802-443-2087 *E-mail:* blwc@middlebury.edu *Web Site:* www.middlebury.edu/blwc, pg 584

Franco, Jimmy, Grand Central Publishing, 1290 Avenue of the Americas, New York, NY 10104 *Tel:* 212-364-1100 *Web Site:* www.hachettebookgroup.com/imprint/grand-central-publishing/, pg 80

Francoeur, Charlotte, Les Editions du Noroit, 4609, rue D'Iberville, espace 202, Montreal, QC H2H 2L9, Canada *Tel:* 514-727-0005 *E-mail:* poesie@lenoroit.com *Web Site:* lenoroit.com, pg 403

Franek, Robert, The Princeton Review, 110 E 42 St, 7th fl, New York, NY 10017 *Toll Free Tel:* 800-273-8439 (orders only) *Web Site:* www.princetonreview.com, pg 164

Frank, Abigail, Sanford J Greenburger Associates Inc, 55 Fifth Ave, New York, NY 10003 *Tel:* 212-206-5600 *Web Site:* greenburger.com, pg 461

Frank, Alexa, HarperCollins Publishers LLC, 195 Broadway, New York, NY 10007 *Tel:* 212-207-7000 *Web Site:* www.harpercollins.com, pg 87

Frank, Carol, Tradewind Books, 202-1807 Maritime Mews, Vancouver, BC V6H 3W7, Canada *Tel:* 604-662-4405 *E-mail:* tradewindbooks@yahoo.com; tradewindbooks@gmail.com *Web Site:* www.tradewindbooks.com, pg 421

Frank, Cynthia, Cypress House, 155 Cypress St, Suite A, Fort Bragg, CA 95437 *Tel:* 707-964-9520 *Toll Free Tel:* 800-773-7782 *Fax:* 707-964-7531 *E-mail:* office@cypresshouse.com *Web Site:* www.cypresshouse.com, pg 56, 437

Frank, Hannah, Random House Publishing Group, 1745 Broadway, New York, NY 10019 *Toll Free Tel:* 800-200-3552 *Web Site:* www.randomhousebooks.com, pg 171

Frank, Jerry, Vandamere Press, 3580 Morris St N, St Petersburg, FL 33713 *Tel:* 727-556-0950 *Toll Free Tel:* 800-551-7776 *Fax:* 727-556-2560 *E-mail:* orders@vandamere.com *Web Site:* www.vandamere.com, pg 224

Frank, Mike, Speakers Unlimited, 7532 Courtyard Place, Cary, NC 27519 *Tel:* 919-466-7676 *E-mail:* prospeak@aol.com *Web Site:* www.speakersunlimited.com, pg 487

Frank, Sandy, Chronicle Books LLC, 680 Second St, San Francisco, CA 94107 *Tel:* 415-537-4200 *Fax:* 415-537-4460 (perms) *E-mail:* hello@chroniclebooks.com; subrights@chroniclebooks.com *Web Site:* www.chroniclebooks.com, pg 48

Frank, Sylvie, Disney-Hyperion Books, 1101 Flower St, Glendale, CA 91201 *Web Site:* books.disney.com/imprint/disney-hyperion, pg 59

Frankel, Valerie, Aevitas Creative Management LLC, 19 W 21 St, Suite 501, New York, NY 10010 *Tel:* 212-765-6900 *Web Site:* www.aevitascreative.com, pg 448

Frankl, Beth, Shambhala Publications Inc, 2129 13 St, Boulder, CO 80302 *Tel:* 978-829-2599 (intl callers) *Toll Free Tel:* 866-424-0030 (off); 888-424-2329 (orders & cust serv) *Fax:* 617-236-1563 *E-mail:* customercare@shambhala.com; royalties@shambhala.com *Web Site:* www.shambhala.com, pg 187

Franklin, Alexandra, Curtis Brown, Ltd, 228 E 45 St, Suite 310, New York, NY 10017 *Tel:* 212-473-5400 *Fax:* 212-598-0917 *E-mail:* info@cbltd *Web Site:* www.curtisbrown.com, pg 452

Franklin, Alison, American Academy of Arts & Sciences (AAAS), 136 Irving St, Cambridge, MA 02138 *Tel:* 617-576-5000 *Fax:* 617-576-5050 *E-mail:* aaas@amacad.org *Web Site:* www.amacad.org, pg 494

Franklin, Jill, No Starch Press, 245 Eighth St, San Francisco, CA 94103 *Tel:* 415-863-9900 *Toll Free Tel:* 800-420-7240 *Fax:* 415-863-9950 *E-mail:* info@nostarch.com; sales@nostarch.com; editors@nostarch.com; marketing@nostarch.com *Web Site:* www.nostarch.com, pg 141

Franklin, Robert, McFarland, 960 NC Hwy 88 W, Jefferson, NC 28640 *Tel:* 336-246-4460 *Toll Free Tel:* 800-253-2187 (orders) *Fax:* 336-246-5018; 336-246-4403 (orders) *E-mail:* info@mcfarlandpub.com *Web Site:* mcfarlandbooks.com, pg 127

Franson, Maya, Random House Publishing Group, 1745 Broadway, New York, NY 10019 *Toll Free Tel:* 800-200-3552 *Web Site:* www.randomhousebooks.com, pg 171

Fransson, Jane Fleming, Words into Print, 208 Java St, 5th fl, Brooklyn, NY 11222 *E-mail:* query@wordsintoprint.org *Web Site:* wordsintoprint.org, pg 445

Frantz, Kristen, Berrett-Koehler Publishers Inc, 1333 Broadway, Suite 1000, Oakland, CA 94612 *Tel:* 510-817-2277 *Fax:* 510-817-2278 *E-mail:* bkpub@bkpub.com *Web Site:* www.bkconnection.com, pg 29

Franze, Anthony, Thriller Awards Competition, PO Box 311, Eureka, CA 95502 *Web Site:* thrillerwriters.org, pg 669

Fraser, Kate, McGill-Queen's University Press, 1010 Sherbrooke W, Suite 1720, Montreal, QC H3A 2R7, Canada *Tel:* 514-398-3750 *Fax:* 514-398-4333 *E-mail:* mqup@mcgill.ca *Web Site:* www.mqup.ca, pg 412

Fraser, Kathleen, The Association of English-Language Publishers of Quebec-AELAQ (Association des Editeurs de Langue Anglaise du Quebec), Atwater Library, 1200 Atwater Ave, Suite 3, Westmount, QC H3Z 1X4, Canada *Tel:* 514-932-5633 *E-mail:* admin@aelaq.org *Web Site:* aelaq.org, pg 499

Fraser, Kathleen, McGill-Queen's University Press, 1010 Sherbrooke W, Suite 1720, Montreal, QC H3A 2R7, Canada *Tel:* 514-398-3750 *Fax:* 514-398-4333 *E-mail:* mqup@mcgill.ca *Web Site:* www.mqup.ca, pg 412

Fraser, Simon, Insight Editions, 800 "A" St, San Rafael, CA 94901 *Tel:* 415-526-1370 *Toll Free Tel:* 800-809-3792 *Toll Free Fax:* 866-509-0515 *E-mail:* info@insighteditions.com; marketing@insighteditions.com *Web Site:* insighteditions.com, pg 101

Fraser, Stephen, The Jennifer DeChiara Literary Agency, 245 Park Ave, 39th fl, New York, NY 10167 *Tel:* 212-372-8989 *Web Site:* www.jdlit.com, pg 455

Fraser, Valerie, Center for the Collaborative Classroom, 1001 Marina Village Pkwy, Suite 110, Alameda, CA 94501-1042 *Tel:* 510-533-0213 *Toll Free Tel:* 800-666-7270 *Fax:* 510-464-3670 *E-mail:* info@collaborativeclassroom.org; clientsupport@collaborativeclassroom.org *Web Site:* www.collaborativeclassroom.org, pg 44

Frasier, Elise, American Psychological Association, 750 First St NE, Washington, DC 20002 *Tel:* 202-336-5510 *Toll Free Tel:* 800-374-2721 *Fax:* 202-336-5502 *E-mail:* order@apa.org; booksales@apa.org *Web Site:* www.apa.org/books, pg 12

Frazer, Rebecca, Chronicle Books LLC, 680 Second St, San Francisco, CA 94107 *Tel:* 415-537-4200 *Fax:* 415-537-4460 (perms) *E-mail:* hello@chroniclebooks.com; subrights@chroniclebooks.com *Web Site:* www.chroniclebooks.com, pg 47

Frazer-Giles, Angelyn, BoardSource, 750 Ninth St NW, Suite 520, Washington, DC 20001-4793 *Tel:* 202-349-2500 *E-mail:* members@boardsource.org; mediarelations@boardsource.org *Web Site:* www.boardsource.org, pg 33

Frazier, Warren, John Hawkins and Associates Inc, 80 Maiden Lane, Suite 1503, New York, NY 10038 *Tel:* 212-807-7040 *E-mail:* jha@jhalit.com *Web Site:* jhalit.com, pg 462

Frechette, Jacques, Saint-Jean Editeur Inc, 4490, rue Garand, Laval, QC H7L 5Z6, Canada *Tel:* 450-663-1777 *E-mail:* info@saint-jeanediteur.com *Web Site:* saint-jeanediteur.com, pg 418

Freda, Kristin, Irma Simonton & James H Black Award, 610 W 112 St, New York, NY 10025 *Tel:* 212-875-4458 *E-mail:* bookcom@bankstreet.edu *Web Site:* www.bankstreet.edu/library/center-for-childrens-literature/irma-black-award, pg 581

Frederick, Holly, Curtis Brown, Ltd, 228 E 45 St, Suite 310, New York, NY 10017 *Tel:* 212-473-5400 *Fax:* 212-598-0917 *E-mail:* info@cbltd.com *Web Site:* www.curtisbrown.com, pg 452

Fredericksen, Gretchen, Macmillan, 120 Broadway, 22nd fl, New York, NY 10271 *Tel:* press.inquiries@macmillan.com *Web Site:* us.macmillan.com, pg 122

Free, Jenna Land, Folio Literary Management, The Film Center Bldg, 630 Ninth Ave, Suite 1101, New York, NY 10036 *Tel:* 212-400-1494 *Fax:* 212-967-0977 *Web Site:* www.foliolit.com, pg 459

Freedman, Mary Ann, The National Business Book Award (NBBA), c/o Freedman & Associates Inc, 10 Delisle Ave, Suite 214, Toronto, ON M4V 3C6, Canada *Tel:* 416-868-1500 *Web Site:* www.nbbaward.com, pg 637

Freedman, Robert A, Robert A Freedman Dramatic Agency Inc, PO Box 3544, New York, NY 10163 *Tel:* 718-897-0950, pg 459

Freeman, Darla, Kensington Publishing Corp, 900 Third Ave, 26th fl, New York, NY 10022 *Tel:* 212-407-1500 *Toll Free Tel:* 800-221-2647 *Fax:* 212-935-0699 *Web Site:* www.kensingtonbooks.com, pg 109

Freeman, Evelyn B, United States Board on Books for Young People (USBBY), National Luis University, Ctr for Teaching through Children's Books, 1000 Capitol Dr, Wheeling, IL 60090 *Tel:* 224-233-2798 *E-mail:* secretariat@usbby.org *Web Site:* www.usbby.org, pg 521

Freeman, John, Alfred A Knopf, c/o Penguin Random House LLC, 1745 Broadway, New York, NY 10019 *Tel:* 212-751-2600 *Fax:* 212-940-7390 (dom rts); 212-572-2662 (foreign rts) *Web Site:* knopfdoubleday.com/imprint/knopf/; knopfdoubleday.com, pg 110

Freeman Lifschutz, Gracie, Dystel, Goderich & Bourret LLC, One Union Sq W, Suite 904, New York, NY 10003 *Tel:* 212-627-9100 *Fax:* 212-627-9313 *Web Site:* www.dystel.com, pg 457

Freeman, Raphael, KTAV Publishing House Inc, 527 Empire Blvd, Brooklyn, NY 11225 *Tel:* 201-963-9524; 718-972-5449 *Fax:* 718-972-6307 *E-mail:* orders@ktav.com *Web Site:* www.ktav.com, pg 111

Freeman, Timothy, Printing Industries Alliance, 636 N French Rd, Suite 1, Amherst, NY 14228 *Tel:* 716-691-3211 *Toll Free Tel:* 800-777-4742 *Fax:* 716-691-4249 *E-mail:* info@pialliance.org *Web Site:* pialliance.org, pg 517

Freeny, Phyllis Jones, Professional Communications Inc, 1223 W Main, Suite 1427, Durant, OK 74702-1427 *Tel:* 580-745-9838 *Toll Free Tel:* 800-337-9838 *Fax:* 580-745-9837 *E-mail:* info@pcibooks.com *Web Site:* www.pcibooks.com, pg 165

Freiler, Ellen, Yale University Press, 302 Temple St, New Haven, CT 06511-8909 *Tel:* 203-432-0960; 203-432-0966 (sales); 401-531-2800 (cust serv) *Toll Free Tel:* 800-405-1619 (cust serv) *Fax:* 203-432-0948; 203-432-8485 (sales); 401-531-2801 (cust serv) *Toll Free Fax:* 800-406-9145 (cust serv) *E-mail:* sales.press@yale.edu (sales); customer.care@triliteral.org (cust serv) *Web Site:* www.yalebooks.com; yalepress.yale.edu/yupbooks, pg 235

Freiss, Susan, Jane Addams Children's Book Award, 276 Fifth Ave, Suite 704, PMB 45, New York, NY 10001 *Tel:* 212-682-8830 *E-mail:* info@janeaddamspeace.org *Web Site:* www.janeaddamspeace.org, pg 570

French, Dan, Simon & Schuster Canada, 166 King St E, Suite 300, Toronto, ON M5A 1J3, Canada *Tel:* 647-427-8882 *Toll Free Tel:* 800-387-0446; 800-268-3216 (orders) *Fax:* 647-430-9446 *Toll Free Fax:* 888-849-8151 (orders) *E-mail:* info@simonandschuster.ca *Web Site:* www.simonandschuster.ca, pg 419

French, Drew, Sourcebooks LLC, 1935 Brookdale Rd, Suite 139, Naperville, IL 60563 *Tel:* 630-961-3900 *Toll Free Tel:* 800-432-7444 *Fax:* 630-961-2168 *E-mail:* info@sourcebooks.com *Web Site:* www.sourcebooks.com, pg 195

French, Kenneth, New York University, Center for Publishing & Applied Liberal Arts, 7 E 12 St, New York, NY 10003 *Tel:* 212-998-7200 *E-mail:* sps.info@nyu.edu *Web Site:* www.scps.nyu.edu/professional-pathways/topics.html, pg 564

French, Pamela, Book Industry Charitable Foundation (BINC), 3135 S State St, Suite 203, Ann Arbor, MI 48108 *Toll Free Tel:* 866-733-9064 *E-mail:* info@bincfoundation.org *Web Site:* www.bincfoundation.org, pg 525

French, Pamela, Denver Publishing Institute Scholarship, 3135 S State St, Suite 203, Ann Arbor, MI 48108 *Toll Free Tel:* 866-733-9064 *E-mail:* info@bincfoundation.org *Web Site:* www.bincfoundation.org/denver-publishing-institute/, pg 595

French, Pamela, Carla Gray Memorial Scholarship, 3135 S State St, Suite 203, Ann Arbor, MI 48108 *Toll Free Tel:* 866-733-9064 *E-mail:* info@bincfoundation.org *Web Site:* www.bincfoundation.org/carla-gray/, pg 609

French, Pamela, Higher Education Scholarship Program, 3135 S State St, Suite 203, Ann Arbor, MI 48108 *Toll Free Tel:* 866-733-9064 *E-mail:* info@bincfoundation.org *Web Site:* www.bincfoundation.org/scholarship, pg 612

French, Pamela, Susan Kamil Scholarship for Emerging Writers, 3135 S State St, Suite 203, Ann Arbor, MI 48108 *Toll Free Tel:* 866-733-9064 *E-mail:* info@bincfoundation.org *Web Site:* bincfoundation.org/susankamil-scholarship, pg 619

French, Pamela, George Markey Keating Memorial Scholarships, 3135 S State St, Suite 203, Ann Arbor, MI 48108 *Toll Free Tel:* 866-733-9064 *E-mail:* info@bincfoundation.org *Web Site:* www.bincfoundation.org, pg 619

French, Pamela, Macmillan Booksellers Professional Development Scholarship, 3135 S State St, Suite 203, Ann Arbor, MI 48108 *Toll Free Tel:* 866-733-9064 *E-mail:* info@bincfoundation.org *Web Site:* www.bincfoundation.org/scholarship, pg 628

French, Pamela, Karl Pohrt Tribute Award, 3135 S State St, Suite 203, Ann Arbor, MI 48108 *Toll Free Tel:* 866-733-9064 *E-mail:* info@bincfoundation.org *Web Site:* www.bincfoundation.org/scholarship, pg 651

Frenes, Gabriella, Chronicle Books LLC, 680 Second St, San Francisco, CA 94107 *Tel:* 415-537-4200 *Fax:* 415-537-4460 (perms) *E-mail:* hello@chroniclebooks.com; subrights@chroniclebooks.com *Web Site:* www.chroniclebooks.com, pg 48

Frerich, Stephanie, Simon & Schuster, 1230 Avenue of the Americas, New York, NY 10020 *Tel:* 212-698-7000 *Toll Free Tel:* 800-223-2348 (cust serv); 800-223-2336 (orders) *Toll Free Fax:* 800-943-9831 (orders) *Web Site:* simonandschusterpublishing.com/simonandschuster/, pg 188

Frerking, Beth, Women's National Book Association Inc, PO Box 237, FDR Sta, New York, NY 10150-0231 *Toll Free Tel:* 866-610-WNBA (610-9622) *E-mail:* info@wnba-books.org *Web Site:* wnba-books.org, pg 522

Freund, Dusty, Boulevard Magazine Short Fiction Contest for Emerging Writers, 3829 Hartford St, St Louis, MO 63116 *E-mail:* editors@boulevardmagazine.org *Web Site:* www.boulevardmagazine.org, pg 583

Frew, Elizabeth, Harry N Abrams Inc, 195 Broadway, 9th fl, New York, NY 10007 *Tel:* 212-206-7715 *Toll Free Tel:* 800-345-1359 *Fax:* 212-645-8437 *E-mail:* abrams@abramsbooks.com; publicity@abramsbooks.com; sales@abramsbooks.com *Web Site:* www.abramsbooks.com, pg 2

Freyer, Emily, Teachers College Press, 1234 Amsterdam Ave, New York, NY 10027 *Tel:* 212-678-3929 *Fax:* 212-678-4149 *E-mail:* tcpress@tc.edu *Web Site:* www.tcpress.com, pg 203

Freymann, Sarah Jane, Sarah Jane Freymann Literary Agency LLC, 59 W 71 St, Suite 9-B, New York, NY 10023 *Tel:* 212-362-9277 *E-mail:* submissions@sarahjanefreymann.com *Web Site:* www.sarahjanefreymann.com, pg 459

Friberg, Matthew, Parallax Press, 2236B Sixth St, Berkeley, CA 94710 *Tel:* 510-325-2945 *Toll Free Tel:* 800-863-5290 (orders) *Web Site:* www.parallax.org, pg 151

Fricas, Katie, New York City Book Awards, 53 E 79 St, New York, NY 10075 *Tel:* 212-288-6900 *Fax:* 212-744-5832 *E-mail:* events@nysoclib.org *Web Site:* www.nysoclib.org, pg 640

Frick, Whitney, Random House Publishing Group, 1745 Broadway, New York, NY 10019 *Toll Free Tel:* 800-200-3552 *Web Site:* www.randomhousebooks.com, pg 171

Fricke, Cate, Eisenbrauns, 820 N University Dr, USB 1, Suite C, University Park, PA 16802-1003 *Tel:* 814-865-1327 *Toll Free Tel:* 800-326-9180 (orders & cust serv) *Fax:* 814-863-1408 *Toll Free Fax:* 877-778-2665 (orders) *E-mail:* orders@psupress.org; customerservice@psupress.org *Web Site:* www.eisenbrauns.org, pg 65

Fricke, Cate, Penn State University Press, University Support Bldg 1, Suite C, 820 N University Dr, University Park, PA 16802-1003 *Tel:* 814-865-1327 *Toll Free Tel:* 800-326-9180 (orders & cust serv) *Fax:* 814-863-1408 *Toll Free Fax:* 877-778-2665 (book orders) *E-mail:* orders@psupress.org; customerservice@psupress.org *Web Site:* www.psupress.org, pg 157

Fried, Gabriel, Persea Books, 90 Broad St, Suite 2100, New York, NY 10004 *Tel:* 212-260-9256 *E-mail:* info@perseabooks.com; poetry@perseabooks.com; publicity@perseabooks.com *Web Site:* www.perseabooks.com, pg 158

Fried, Gabriel, Lexi Rudnitsky First Book Prize in Poetry, 90 Broad St, Suite 2100, New York, NY 10004 Tel: 212-260-9256 E-mail: poetry@ perseabooks.com Web Site: www.perseabooks.com, pg 657

Fried, Jonah, George Braziller Inc, 90 Broad St, Suite 2100, New York, NY 10004 Tel: 212-260-9256 E-mail: editorial@georgebraziller.com Web Site: www. georgebraziller.com, pg 35

Fried, Jonah, Persea Books, 90 Broad St, Suite 2100, New York, NY 10004 Tel: 212-260-9256 E-mail: info@perseabooks.com; poetry@perseabooks. com; publicity@perseabooks.com Web Site: www. perseabooks.com, pg 158

Fried, Jonah, Lexi Rudnitsky First Book Prize in Poetry, 90 Broad St, Suite 2100, New York, NY 10004 Tel: 212-260-9256 E-mail: poetry@perseabooks.com Web Site: www.perseabooks.com, pg 657

Fried, Melanie, Harlequin Enterprises Ltd, 195 Broadway, 24th fl, New York, NY 10007 Tel: 212-207-7000 Toll Free Tel: 888-432-4879; 800-370-5838 (ebooks) E-mail: customerservice@harlequin. com Web Site: www.harlequin.com/shop/index.html; corporate.harlequin.com, pg 85

Friedlander, Nick, One-Act Playwriting Competition, 600 Wolfe St, Alexandria, VA 22314 Tel: 703-683-5778 (ext 2) Fax: 703-683-1378 E-mail: oneactslta@gmail. com Web Site: thelittletheatre.com, pg 644

Friedlander, Samantha, Tor Publishing Group, 120 Broadway, New York, NY 10271 Toll Free Tel: 800-455-0340 (Macmillan) E-mail: torpublicity@tor. com; forgepublicity@forgebooks.com Web Site: us. macmillan.com/torpublishinggroup, pg 208

Friedman, Andy, American Marketing Association, 130 E Randolph St, 22nd fl, Chicago, IL 60601 Tel: 312-542-9000 Toll Free Tel: 800-AMA-1150 (262-1150) Web Site: www.ama.org, pg 495

Friedman, Claire, InkWell Management, 521 Fifth Ave, Suite 2600, New York, NY 10175 Tel: 212-922-3500 Fax: 212-922-0535 E-mail: info@inkwellmanagement. com; submissions@inkwellmanagement. com; permissions@inkwellmanagement.com Web Site: inkwellmanagement.com, pg 463

Friedman, Dina, Accurate Writing & More, 16 Barstow Lane, Hadley, MA 01035 Tel: 413-586-2388 Web Site: www.accuratewriting.com; frugalmarketing. com, pg 435

Friedman, Fredrica S, Fredrica S Friedman & Co Inc, 857 Fifth Ave, New York, NY 10065 Tel: 212-639-9455 E-mail: info@fredricafriedman.com Web Site: www.fredricafriedman.com, pg 459

Friedman, Gail, Macmillan, 120 Broadway, 22nd fl, New York, NY 10271 E-mail: press.inquiries@macmillan. com Web Site: us.macmillan.com, pg 122

Friedman, Jessica, Sterling Lord Literistic Inc, 594 Broadway, Suite 205, New York, NY 10012 Tel: 212-780-6050 Fax: 212-780-6095 E-mail: info@sll.com Web Site: www.sll.com, pg 477

Friedman, Jonathan, PEN America, 120 Broadway, 26th fl N, New York, NY 10271 Tel: 212-334-1660 Fax: 212-334-2181 E-mail: info@pen. org; membership@pen.org; education@pen.org Web Site: pen.org, pg 516

Friedman, Walter, The Alfred & Fay Chandler Book Award, c/o Harvard Business School, Connell House 301A, Boston, MA 02163 Tel: 617-495-1003 Fax: 617-495-2705 E-mail: bhr@hbs.edu Web Site: www.hbs.edu/businesshistory/fellowships, pg 588

Friedman, Wendy, Quarto Publishing Group USA Inc, 100 Cummings Ctr, Suite 265D, Beverly, MA 01915 Tel: 978-282-9590 Toll Free Tel: 800-328-0590 (sales) Fax: 978-283-2742 E-mail: sales@quartous.com Web Site: www.quartoknows.com, pg 168

Friedman, Yali, Logos Press, 3909 Witmer Rd, Suite 416, Niagara Falls, NY 14305 Fax: 815-346-3514 E-mail: info@logos-press.com Web Site: www.logos-press.com, pg 119

Friel, Rose, Maria Carvainis Agency Inc, Rockefeller Center, 1270 Avenue of the Americas, Suite 2915, New York, NY 10020 Tel: 212-245-6365 Fax: 212-245-7196 E-mail: mca@mariacarvainisagency.com Web Site: mariacarvainisagency.com, pg 453

Frieman, Nina, Farrar, Straus & Giroux, LLC, 120 Broadway, New York, NY 10271 Tel: 212-741-6900 E-mail: fsg.publicity@fsgbooks.com; sales@fsgbooks. com Web Site: us.macmillan.com/fsg, pg 70

Fries, Hannah, Workman Publishing, 1290 Avenue of the Americas, New York, NY 10104 Toll Free Tel: 800-759-0190 Fax: 212-364-0950 E-mail: workman-inquiry@hbgusa.com Web Site: www.hachettebookgroup.com/imprint/ workman-publishing-company/, pg 233

Fries, Lauren Ollerhead, Bloomsbury Publishing Inc, 1385 Broadway, 5th fl, New York, NY 10018 Tel: 212-419-5300 E-mail: marketingusa@ bloomsbury.com; adultpublicityusa@bloomsbury. com; askacademic@bloomsbury.com Web Site: www. bloomsbury.com, pg 32

Friesen, Desirae, Tor Publishing Group, 120 Broadway, New York, NY 10271 Toll Free Tel: 800-455-0340 (Macmillan) E-mail: torpublicity@tor.com; forgepublicity@forgebooks.com Web Site: us. macmillan.com/torpublishinggroup, pg 208

Friesen, Rilla, Thistledown Press, 220 20 St W, Unit 222, Saskatoon, SK S7M 0W9, Canada Tel: 306-244-1722 E-mail: tdpress@thistledownpress.com Web Site: www.thistledownpress.com, pg 420

Frisch, Shelley, Markus Wiener Publishers Inc, 231 Nassau St, Princeton, NJ 08542 Tel: 609-921-1141 E-mail: publisher@markuswiener.com Web Site: www. markuswiener.com, pg 229

Froman, Craig, Master Books®, 3142 Hwy 103 N, Green Forest, AR 72638 Tel: 870-438-5288 Toll Free Tel: 800-999-3777 E-mail: sales@masterbooks. com; nlp@nlpg.com; submissions@newleafpress.net Web Site: www.masterbooks.com; www.nlpg.com, pg 126

Froman, Craig, New Leaf Press, 3142 Hwy 103 N, Green Forest, AR 72638-2233 Tel: 870-438-5288 Toll Free Tel: 800-999-3777 Fax: 870-438-5120 E-mail: submissions@nlpg.com Web Site: www.nlpg. com, pg 140

Fromer, Margot J, Fromer, 1606 Noyes Dr, Silver Spring, MD 20910-2224 Tel: 301-585-8827, pg 439

Fruin, Christine, American Counseling Association (ACA), 6101 Stevenson Ave, Suite 600, Alexandria, VA 22304 Tel: 703-823-9800 Toll Free Tel: 800-298-2276 Toll Free Fax: 800-473-2329 E-mail: orders@ counseling.org (book orders) Web Site: www. counseling.org, pg 9

Fry, Douglas, ACP Best of the Best Awards, 104 Westland Dr, Columbia, TN 38401 Toll Free Tel: 877-203-2327 E-mail: info@communitypublishers.com Web Site: www.communitypublishers.com/awards, pg 570

Fry, Douglas, Association of Community Publishers Inc (ACP), 8119 Circuit Rider Path, Cicero, NY 13039 Toll Free Tel: 877-203-2327 Fax: 315-670-3121 (memb registration) E-mail: info@ communitypublishers.com Web Site: www. communitypublishers.com, pg 499

Fry, Sonali, Random House Children's Books, c/o Penguin Random House LLC, 1745 Broadway, New York, NY 10019 Tel: 212-782-9000 Web Site: www. rhcbooks.com, pg 169

Frye, Sebastian, Knopf Canada, 320 Front St W, Suite 1400, Toronto, ON M5V 3B6, Canada Tel: 416-364-4449 Toll Free Tel: 888-523-9292 Fax: 416-598-7764 Web Site: www.penguinrandomhouse.ca, pg 411

Fryman, Alona, Bloomsbury Publishing Inc, 1385 Broadway, 5th fl, New York, NY 10018 Tel: 212-419-5300 E-mail: marketingusa@bloomsbury.com; adultpublicityusa@bloomsbury.com; askacademic@ bloomsbury.com Web Site: www.bloomsbury.com, pg 31

Fu, Sarah Christensen, DAW Books, 19 W 21 St, No 1201, New York, NY 10010 E-mail: info@astrapublishinghouse.com Web Site: astrapublishinghouse.com/imprints/daw-books, pg 57

Fuchs, George, National Association of Printing Ink Manufacturers (NAPIM), National Press Bldg, 529 14 St NW, Suite 1280, Washington, DC 20045 Tel: 410-940-6589 E-mail: info@napim.org Web Site: www. napim.org, pg 512

Fuchs, Robert E, Wildflower Press, c/o Oakbrook Press, 3301 S Valley Dr, Rapid City, SD 57703 Tel: 605-381-6385 E-mail: info@wildflowerpress.org Web Site: www.wildflowerpress.org, pg 229

Fuersich, Larry, Visual Profile Books Inc, 389 Fifth Ave, Suite 1105, New York, NY 10016 Tel: 516-445-0116 Web Site: www.visualprofilebooks.com, pg 225

Fugate, Alice, The Joy Harris Literary Agency Inc, 1501 Broadway, Suite 2310, New York, NY 10036 Tel: 212-924-6269 Fax: 212-840-5776 E-mail: contact@ joyharrisliterary.com Web Site: www.joyharrisliterary. com, pg 462

Fugate, LaShawn, Information Today, Inc, 143 Old Marlton Pike, Medford, NJ 08055-8750 Tel: 609-654-6266 Toll Free Tel: 800-300-9868 (cust serv) Fax: 609-654-4309 E-mail: custserv@infotoday.com Web Site: informationtodayinc.com, pg 100

Fuhrman, Candice, Candice Fuhrman Literary Agency, 10 Cypress Hollow Dr, Tiburon, CA 94920 Tel: 415-383-1014 E-mail: fuhrmancandice@gmail.com, pg 459

Fujii, Saho, Little, Brown Books for Young Readers (LBYR), 1290 Avenue of the Americas, New York, NY 10104 Tel: 212-364-1100 Toll Free Tel: 800-759-0190 (cust serv) E-mail: rights@lbchildrens.com Web Site: www.hachettebookgroup.com/imprint/little-brown-books-for-young-readers/, pg 118

Fujimoto, Grace, Running Press, 1290 Avenue of the Americas, New York, NY 10104 Tel: 212-364-1100 Toll Free Tel: 800-759-0190 (cust serv) Fax: 212-364-0933 (intl orders) Toll Free Fax: 800-286-9471 (cust serv) E-mail: customer.service@hbgusa.com; orders@ hbgusa.com Web Site: www.hachettebookgroup. com/imprint/running-press/; www.moon.com (Moon Travel Guides), pg 178

Fulford, David, Institute of Public Administration of Canada, 1075 Bay St, Suite 401, Toronto, ON M5S 2B1, Canada Tel: 416-924-8787 Fax: 416-924-4992 E-mail: ntl@ipac.ca Web Site: www.ipac.ca, pg 410

Fulkerson, Rachel, Graywolf Press, 212 Third Ave N, Suite 485, Minneapolis, MN 55401 Tel: 651-641-0077 Fax: 651-641-0036 E-mail: wolves@graywolfpress. org (no ms queries, sample chapters or proposals) Web Site: www.graywolfpress.org, pg 81

Fuller, Alfonzo, Andrews McMeel Publishing LLC, 1130 Walnut St, Kansas City, MO 64106-2109 Tel: 816-581-7500 Toll Free Tel: 800-851-8923 Web Site: www. andrewsmcmeel.com; publishing.andrewsmcmeel.com, pg 14

Fuller, Barbara, Editcetera, 2034 Blake St, Suite 5, Berkeley, CA 94704 Tel: 510-849-1110 E-mail: info@ editcetera.com Web Site: www.editcetera.com, pg 438

Fuller, Jessica, Rizzoli International Publications Inc, 300 Park Ave S, 4th fl, New York, NY 10010-5399 Tel: 212-387-3400 Toll Free Tel: 800-522-6657 (orders only) Fax: 212-387-3535 E-mail: publicity@rizzoliusa. com Web Site: www.rizzoliusa.com, pg 175

Fulton, Matt, Writers House, 21 W 26 St, New York, NY 10010 Tel: 212-685-2400 Web Site: www. writershouse.com, pg 482

Funk, Cameon, MAR*CO Products Inc, PO Box 686, Hatfield, PA 19440 Tel: 215-956-0313 Toll Free Tel: 800-448-2197 Fax: 215-956-9041 E-mail: help@ marcoproducts.com; sales@marcoproducts.com Web Site: www.marcoproducts.com, pg 124

Funk, Warren, MAR*CO Products Inc, PO Box 686, Hatfield, PA 19440 Tel: 215-956-0313 Toll Free Tel: 800-448-2197 Fax: 215-956-9041 E-mail: help@ marcoproducts.com; sales@marcoproducts.com Web Site: www.marcoproducts.com, pg 124

Fuqua, Jennifer, University of Alabama Program in Creative Writing, PO Box 870244, Tuscaloosa, AL 35487-0244 Tel: 205-348-5065 Fax: 205-348-1388 E-mail: english@ua.edu Web Site: www.as.ua.edu/english, pg 566

Furnish, Ben, BkMk Press Inc, 5 W Third St, Parkville, MO 64152 Tel: 816-200-7895 E-mail: info@bkmkpress.org Web Site: www.bkmkpress.org, pg 30

Furnish, Ben, G S Sharat Chandra Prize for Short Fiction, 5 W Third St, Parkville, MO 64152 Tel: 816-200-7895 E-mail: info@bkmkpress.org Web Site: www.bkmkpress.org, pg 588

Furnish, Ben, John Ciardi Prize for Poetry, 5 W Third St, Parkville, MO 64152 Tel: 816-200-7895 E-mail: info@bkmkpress.org Web Site: www.bkmkpress.org, pg 589

Furr, Madison, Random House Children's Books, c/o Penguin Random House LLC, 1745 Broadway, New York, NY 10019 Tel: 212-782-9000 Web Site: www.rhcbooks.com, pg 170

Furuta, Evelyn, Chronicle Books LLC, 680 Second St, San Francisco, CA 94107 Tel: 415-537-4200 Fax: 415-537-4460 (perms) E-mail: hello@chroniclebooks.com; subrights@chroniclebooks.com Web Site: www.chroniclebooks.com, pg 48

Fusting, Donald W, Lanahan Publishers Inc, 324 Hawthorne Rd, Baltimore, MD 21210-2303 Tel: 410-366-2434 Toll Free Tel: 866-345-1949 Fax: 410-366-8798 E-mail: lanahan@aol.com Web Site: www.lanahanpublishers.com, pg 112

G'Schwind, Stephanie, Colorado Prize for Poetry, 9105 Campus Delivery, Colorado State University, Fort Collins, CO 80523-9105 Tel: 970-491-5449 E-mail: creview@colostate.edu Web Site: coloradoreview.colostate.edu/colorado-prize-for-poetry, pg 591

G'Schwind, Stephanie, Nelligan Prize for Short Fiction, Colorado State University, Dept of English, Center for Literary Publishing, 9105 Campus Delivery, Fort Collins, CO 80523-9105 Tel: 970-491-5449 E-mail: creview@colostate.edu Web Site: coloradoreview.colostate.edu/nelligan-prize, pg 639

Gabrino, Orlene, Knopf Doubleday Publishing Group, c/o Penguin Random House LLC, 1745 Broadway, New York, NY 10019 Tel: 212-751-2600 Fax: 212-940-7390 (dom rts); 212-572-2662 (foreign rts) Web Site: knopfdoubleday.com, pg 110

Gabrino, Orlene, Penguin Random House LLC, 1745 Broadway, New York, NY 10019 Tel: 212-782-9000 Toll Free Tel: 800-726-0600 Web Site: www.penguinrandomhouse.com, pg 155

Gadney, Alan, One On One Book Publishing/Film-Video Publications, 7944 Capistrano Ave, West Hills, CA 91304 Tel: 818-340-6620; 818-340-0175 Fax: 818-340-6620 E-mail: onebookpro@aol.com, pg 146

Gadney, Nancy, One On One Book Publishing/Film-Video Publications, 7944 Capistrano Ave, West Hills, CA 91304 Tel: 818-340-6620; 818-340-0175 Fax: 818-340-6620 E-mail: onebookpro@aol.com, pg 146

Gadoury, Bill, Macmillan Learning, One New York Plaza, Suite 46, New York, NY 10004 Tel: 212-576-9400 E-mail: salesoperations@macmillanusa.com Web Site: www.macmillanlearning.com/college/us, pg 123

Gadre, Sonia, Viking Penguin, c/o Penguin Random House LLC, 1745 Broadway, New York, NY 10019 Tel: 212-782-9000 Web Site: www.penguin.com/overview-vikingbooks/; www.penguin.com/pamela-dorman-books-overview/; www.penguin.com/penguin-classics-overview/; www.penguin.com/penguin-life-overview/, pg 225

Gafron, Stephanie, Sourcebooks LLC, 1935 Brookdale Rd, Suite 139, Naperville, IL 60563 Tel: 630-961-3900 Toll Free Tel: 800-432-7444 Fax: 630-961-2168 E-mail: info@sourcebooks.com Web Site: www.sourcebooks.com, pg 195

Gagnon, Andre, Editions Hurtubise, 1815, ave de Lorimier, Montreal, QC H2K 3W6, Canada Tel: 514-523-1523 Toll Free Tel: 800-361-1664 Web Site: editionshurtubise.com, pg 403

Gagnon, Manon, La Fondation Emile Nelligan, 100, rue Sherbrooke, Suite 202, Montreal, QC H2X 1C3, Canada Tel: 514-278-4657 E-mail: info@fondation-nelligan.org Web Site: www.fondation-nelligan.org, pg 506

Gagnon, Manon, Prix Emile-Nelligan, 100, rue Sherbrooke, Suite 202, Montreal, QC H2X 1C3, Canada Tel: 514-278-4657 Fax: 514-271-6369 E-mail: info@fondation-nelligan.org Web Site: www.fondation-nelligan.org, pg 653

Gagnon, Matt, BOOM! Studios, 5670 Wilshire Blvd, Suite 400, Los Angeles, CA 90036 E-mail: contact@boom-studios.com; customerservice@boom-studios.com; press@boom-studios.com Web Site: www.boom-studios.com, pg 34

Gaillard, Polly, American Photographic Artists (APA), 5042 Wilshire Blvd, No 321, Los Angeles, CA 90036 E-mail: membershiprep@apanational.org Web Site: apanational.org, pg 496

Gaines, Christian, Western States Arts Federation (WESTAF), 1536 Wynkoop St, Suite 522, Denver, CO 80202 Tel: 303-629-1166 E-mail: staff@westaf.org Web Site: www.westaf.org, pg 526

Galang, M Evelina, VONA Voices Summer Writing Workshops, 2820 SW 20 St, Miami, FL 33145 E-mail: info@vonavoices.org Web Site: www.vonavoices.org, pg 558

Galarrita, Mark, Scribner, 1230 Avenue of the Americas, New York, NY 10020 Web Site: www.simonandschusterpublishing.com/scribner/, pg 185

Galassi, Jonathan, Farrar, Straus & Giroux, LLC, 120 Broadway, New York, NY 10271 Tel: 212-741-6900 E-mail: fsg.publicity@fsgbooks.com; sales@fsgbooks.com Web Site: us.macmillan.com/fsg, pg 70

Galassi, Jonathan, Macmillan, 120 Broadway, 22nd fl, New York, NY 10271 E-mail: press.inquiries@macmillan.com Web Site: us.macmillan.com, pg 122

Galasso, Al, National Association of Book Entrepreneurs (NABE), PO Box 606, Cottage Grove, OR 97424 Tel: 541-942-7455 Fax: 541-942-7455 E-mail: nabe@bookmarketingprofits.com Web Site: www.bookmarketingprofits.com, pg 511

Galasso, Al, Pinnacle Book Achievement Awards, PO Box 606, Cottage Grove, OR 97424 Tel: 541-942-7455 Fax: 541-942-7455 E-mail: nabe@bookmarketingprofits.com Web Site: www.bookmarketingprofits.com/PinnacleBookEntryFormE.html, pg 650

Galde, Phyllis, Galde Press Inc, PO Box 774, Hendersonville, NC 28793 Tel: 828-702-3032 Web Site: www.galdepress.com, pg 75

Gale, Kate, Red Hen Press, PO Box 40820, Pasadena, CA 91114 Tel: 626-356-4760 Fax: 626-356-9974 Web Site: www.redhen.org, pg 172

Gale, Meighan, Zone Books, 633 Vanderbilt St, Brooklyn, NY 11218 Tel: 718-686-0048 E-mail: info@zonebooks.org Web Site: www.zonebooks.org, pg 237

Galen, Russell, Scovil Galen Ghosh Literary Agency Inc, 348 W 57 St, New York, NY 10019 Tel: 212-679-8686 E-mail: info@sgglit.com Web Site: www.sgglit.com, pg 475

Gall, Angela, Friends of American Writers Young People's Literature Awards, c/o 506 Rose Ave, Des Plaines, IL 60016 Tel: 847-827-8339 E-mail: info@fawchicago.org Web Site: www.fawchicago.org, pg 604

Gall, John, Alfred A Knopf, c/o Penguin Random House LLC, 1745 Broadway, New York, NY 10019 Tel: 212-751-2600 Fax: 212-940-7390 (dom rts); 212-572-2662 (foreign rts) Web Site: knopfdoubleday.com/imprint/knopf/; knopfdoubleday.com, pg 110

Gallagher, Amy, North River Press Publishing Corp, 27 Rosseter St, Great Barrington, MA 01230 Tel: 413-528-0034 Toll Free Tel: 800-486-2665 Fax: 413-528-3163 Toll Free Fax: 800-BOOK-FAX (266-5329) E-mail: info@northriverpress.com Web Site: www.northriverpress.com, pg 142

Gallagher, Caitlin, Yale University Press, 302 Temple St, New Haven, CT 06511-8909 Tel: 203-432-0960; 203-432-0966 (sales); 401-531-2800 (cust serv) Toll Free Tel: 800-405-1619 (cust serv) Fax: 203-432-0948; 203-432-8485 (sales); 401-531-2801 (cust serv) Toll Free Fax: 800-406-9145 (cust serv) E-mail: sales.press@yale.edu (sales); customer.care@triliteral.org (cust serv) Web Site: www.yalebooks.com; yalepress.yale.edu/yupbooks, pg 235

Gallagher, Julia, Holiday House Publishing Inc, 50 Broad St, New York, NY 10004 Tel: 212-688-0085 Fax: 212-421-6134 E-mail: info@holidayhouse.com Web Site: www.holidayhouse.com, pg 94

Gallagher, Lisa, DeFiore and Company Literary Management Inc, 47 E 19 St, 3rd fl, New York, NY 10003 Tel: 212-925-7744 Fax: 212-925-9803 E-mail: info@defliterary.com; submissions@defliterary.com Web Site: www.defliterary.com, pg 456

Gallagher, Richard, Annual Reviews, 1875 S Grant St, Suite 700, San Mateo, CA 94402 Tel: 650-493-4400 Toll Free Tel: 800-523-8635 Fax: 650-424-0910; 650-855-9815 E-mail: service@annualreviews.org Web Site: www.annualreviews.org, pg 14

Gallagher, Violetta, Ivey Publishing, Ivey Business School Foundation, Western University, 1255 Western Rd, London, ON N6G 0N1, Canada Tel: 519-661-3206; 519-661-3208 Toll Free Tel: 800-649-6355 Fax: 519-661-3485; 519-661-3882 E-mail: cases@ivey.ca Web Site: www.iveypublishing.ca, pg 411

Gallalee, Erin, Society for Technical Communication (STC), 3251 Blenheim Blvd, Suite 406, Fairfax, VA 22030 Tel: 703-522-4114 Fax: 703-522-2075 E-mail: stc@stc.org Web Site: www.stc.org, pg 519

Gallant, Barry, Doubleday Canada, 320 Front St W, Suite 1400, Toronto, ON M5V 3B6, Canada Tel: 416-364-4449 Fax: 416-598-7764 Web Site: www.penguinrandomhouse.ca, pg 401

Gallant, Barry, Knopf Canada, 320 Front St W, Suite 1400, Toronto, ON M5V 3B6, Canada Tel: 416-364-4449 Toll Free Tel: 888-523-9292 Fax: 416-598-7764 Web Site: www.penguinrandomhouse.ca, pg 411

Gallant, Barry, Penguin Random House Canada, a Penguin Random House company, 320 Front St W, Suite 1400, Toronto, ON M5V 3B6, Canada Tel: 416-364-4449 Toll Free Tel: 888-523-9292 (cust serv) E-mail: canadaweb@penguinrandomhouse.com; customerservicescanada@penguinrandomhouse.com Web Site: www.penguinrandomhouse.ca, pg 415

Gallant, Barry, Seal Books, 320 Front St W, Suite 1400, Toronto, ON M5V 3B6, Canada Tel: 416-364-4449 Toll Free Tel: 888-523-9292 (order desk) Fax: 416-598-7764 Web Site: www.penguinrandomhouse.ca, pg 419

Gallaway, Matthew, Cambridge University Press, One Liberty Plaza, 20th fl, New York, NY 10006 Tel: 212-924-3900; 212-337-5000 Fax: 212-691-3239; 845-353-4141 E-mail: customer_service@cambridge.org; orders@cambridge.org; subscriptions_newyork@cambridge.org Web Site: www.cambridge.org/us, pg 39

Galle, Suzanne, University Press of Kansas, 2502 Westbrooke Circle, Lawrence, KS 66045-4444 Tel: 785-864-4154 Fax: 785-864-4586 E-mail: upress@ku.edu Web Site: www.kansaspress.ku.edu, pg 221

Gallegos, Anna, Museum of New Mexico Press, 725 Camino Lejo, Suite C, Santa Fe, NM 87505 Tel: 505-476-1155; 505-272-7777 (orders) Toll Free Tel: 800-249-7737 (orders) Fax: 505-476-1156 Toll Free Fax: 800-622-8667 (orders) Web Site: www.mnmpress.org, pg 135

Gallent, Janet L, Gabelli School of Business Communications & Media Management Program, 140 W 62 St, Rm 440, New York, NY 10023 Tel: 212-636-6150 Fax: 718-817-4999 Web Site: www.fordham.edu/gabelli-school-of-business, pg 562

Gallo, Vincent, William H Sadlier Inc, 9 Pine St, New York, NY 10005 Tel: 212-227-2120 Toll Free Tel: 800-221-5175 (cust serv) Fax: 212-312-6080 E-mail: customerservice@sadlier.com Web Site: www.sadlier.com, pg 179

Gallof, Katie, Bloomsbury Academic, 1385 Broadway, 5th fl, New York, NY 10018 Tel: 212-419-5300 Web Site: www.bloomsbury.com/us/academic, pg 31

Galloway, Erin, Berkley, c/o Penguin Random House LLC, 1745 Broadway, 19th fl, New York, NY 10019 Tel: 212-366-2000 Web Site: www.penguin.com/publishers/berkley/; www.penguin.com/ace-overview/, pg 28

Galloway, Greg, American Booksellers Association, 600 Mamaroneck Ave, Suite 400, Harrison, NY 10528 Tel: 914-406-7500 Toll Free Tel: 800-637-0037 Fax: 914-417-4013 E-mail: info@bookweb.org Web Site: www.bookweb.org, pg 494

Galloway, Victor, Macmillan, 120 Broadway, 22nd fl, New York, NY 10271 E-mail: press.inquiries@macmillan.com Web Site: us.macmillan.com, pg 122

Galusha, Dale, Pacific Press® Publishing Association, 1350 N Kings Rd, Nampa, ID 83687-3193 Tel: 208-465-2500 Fax: 208-465-2531 E-mail: booksubmissions@pacificpress.com Web Site: www.pacificpress.com, pg 149

Galvin, Lori, Aevitas Creative Management LLC, 19 W 21 St, Suite 501, New York, NY 10010 Tel: 212-765-6900 Web Site: www.aevitascreative.com, pg 448

Galyan, Sheyna, Yotzeret Publishing, PO Box 18662, St Paul, MN 55118-0662 E-mail: info@yotzeretpublishing.com; orders@yotzeretpublishing.com Web Site: yotzeretpublishing.com, pg 236

Gamblin, Janine Pourroy, The Hillary Gravendyk Prize, 4178 Chestnut St, Riverside, CA 92501 E-mail: inlandia@inlandiainstitute.org Web Site: inlandiainstitute.org/books/the-hillary-gravendyk-prize, pg 609

Gamblin, Janine Pourroy, The Eliud Martinez Prize, 4178 Chestnut St, Riverside, CA 92501 E-mail: inlandia@inlandiainstitute.org Web Site: inlandiainstitute.org/books/the-eliud-martinez-prize, pg 630

Gambrell, Gabrielle, Hachette Book Group Inc, 1290 Avenue of the Americas, New York, NY 10104 Tel: 212-364-1100 Toll Free Tel: 800-759-0190 (cust serv) Fax: 212-364-0933 (intl orders) Toll Free Fax: 800-286-9471 (cust serv) E-mail: customer.service@hbgusa.com; orders@hbgusa.com Web Site: www.hachettebookgroup.com, pg 83

Gammello, Alyssa, St Martin's Press, LLC, 120 Broadway, New York, NY 10271 E-mail: publicity@stmartins.com; trademarketing@stmartins.com; foreignrights@stmartins.com Web Site: us.macmillan.com/smp, pg 181

Gammons, Keith, Smyth & Helwys Publishing Inc, 6316 Peake Rd, Macon, GA 31210-3960 Tel: 478-757-0564 Toll Free Tel: 800-747-3016 (orders only) Fax: 478-757-1305 E-mail: information@helwys.com Web Site: www.helwys.com, pg 192

Gande, Rae, HarperCollins Children's Books, 195 Broadway, New York, NY 10007 Tel: 212-207-7000 Web Site: www.harpercollins.com/childrens, pg 85

Gandolfo, Italia, Vesuvian Books, 711 Dolly Parton Pkwy, No 4313, Sevierville, TN 37864 E-mail: info@vesuvianmedia.com Web Site: www.vesuvianmedia.com, pg 224

Gang, Jessie, HarperCollins Children's Books, 195 Broadway, New York, NY 10007 Tel: 212-207-7000 Web Site: www.harpercollins.com/childrens, pg 85

Gannon, Mary, Black Literary Publishing Award, 154 Christopher St, Suite 3C, New York, NY 10014-9110 Tel: 212-741-9110 E-mail: info@clmp.org Web Site: www.clmp.org, pg 581

Gannon, Mary, Community of Literary Magazines & Presses (CLMP), 154 Christopher St, Suite 3C, New York, NY 10014-9110 Tel: 212-741-9110 E-mail: info@clmp.org Web Site: www.clmp.org, pg 504

Gannon, Mary, Firecracker Awards, 154 Christopher St, Suite 3C, New York, NY 10014-9110 Tel: 212-741-9110 E-mail: info@clmp.org Web Site: www.clmp.org/firecracker, pg 602

Gannon, Matt, HarperCollins Publishers LLC, 195 Broadway, New York, NY 10007 Tel: 212-207-7000 Web Site: www.harpercollins.com, pg 86

Gannon, Melissa, Berghahn Books, 20 Jay St, Suite 512, Brooklyn, NY 11201 Tel: 212-233-6004 Fax: 212-233-6007 E-mail: info@berghahnbooks.com; salesus@berghahnbooks.com; editorial@journals.berghahnbooks.com Web Site: www.berghahnbooks.com, pg 28

Gantz, Gabrielle, St Martin's Press, LLC, 120 Broadway, New York, NY 10271 E-mail: publicity@stmartins.com; trademarketing@stmartins.com; foreignrights@stmartins.com Web Site: us.macmillan.com/smp, pg 181

Garbuz, Sulamita, Frances Goldin Literary Agency, Inc, 214 W 29 St, Suite 410, New York, NY 10001 Tel: 212-777-0047 Fax: 212-228-1660 E-mail: agency@goldinlit.com Web Site: www.goldinlit.com, pg 460

Garcia, Alyssa, Sourcebooks LLC, 1935 Brookdale Rd, Suite 139, Naperville, IL 60563 Tel: 630-961-3900 Toll Free Tel: 800-432-7444 Fax: 630-961-2168 E-mail: info@sourcebooks.com Web Site: www.sourcebooks.com, pg 194

Garcia, Brieana, HarperCollins Publishers LLC, 195 Broadway, New York, NY 10007 Tel: 212-207-7000 Web Site: www.harpercollins.com, pg 86

Garcia, Jeneen, Public Relations Society of America Inc, 120 Wall St, 21st fl, New York, NY 10005 Tel: 212-460-1400 E-mail: membership@prsa.org Web Site: www.prsa.org, pg 518

Garcia, Maria Isela, The University of North Carolina Press, 116 S Boundary St, Chapel Hill, NC 27514-3808 Tel: 919-966-3561; 919-966-7449 (orders) Toll Free Tel: 800-848-3224 (orders) Fax: 919-962-2704 (orders) Toll Free Fax: 800-272-6817 (orders) E-mail: uncpress@unc.edu Web Site: uncpress.org, pg 218

Garcia, Rick, HarperCollins Publishers LLC, 195 Broadway, New York, NY 10007 Tel: 212-207-7000 Web Site: www.harpercollins.com, pg 86

Garcia Rivera, Nomaris, Macmillan, 120 Broadway, 22nd fl, New York, NY 10271 E-mail: press.inquiries@macmillan.com Web Site: us.macmillan.com, pg 122

Garcia-Brown, Pilar, Dutton, c/o Penguin Random House LLC, 1745 Broadway, New York, NY 10019 Tel: 212-366-2000 Web Site: www.penguin.com/dutton-overview/; www.penguin.com/plume-books-overview/; www.penguin.com/tiny-reparations-overview/, pg 62

Gardiner, Eileen, Italica Press, 99 Wall St, Suite 650, New York, NY 10005 Tel: 917-371-0563 E-mail: inquiries@italicapress.com Web Site: www.italicapress.com, pg 105

Gardner, Jason, New World Library, 14 Pamaron Way, Novato, CA 94949 Tel: 415-884-2100 Fax: 415-884-2199 E-mail: escort@newworldlibrary.com Web Site: www.newworldlibrary.com, pg 140

Gardner, Joseph, Child's Play® Inc, 250 Minot Ave, Auburn, ME 04210 Tel: 207-784-7252 Toll Free Tel: 800-639-6404 Fax: 207-784-7358 Toll Free Fax: 800-854-6989 E-mail: chpmaine@aol.com Web Site: www.childs-play.com, pg 46

Garfield, Valerie, Simon & Schuster Children's Publishing, 1230 Avenue of the Americas, New York, NY 10020 Tel: 212-698-7000 Web Site: www.simonandschuster.com/kids; www.simonandschuster.com/teen; simonandschuster.net; simonandschuster.biz, pg 189

Garland, Ashley, Riverhead Books, c/o Penguin Random House LLC, 1745 Broadway, New York, NY 10019 Tel: 212-782-9000 Web Site: www.penguin.com/riverhead-overview/, pg 175

Garnett, Callie, Bloomsbury Publishing Inc, 1385 Broadway, 5th fl, New York, NY 10018 Tel: 212-419-5300 E-mail: marketingusa@bloomsbury.com; adultpublicityusa@bloomsbury.com; askacademic@bloomsbury.com Web Site: www.bloomsbury.com, pg 31

Garon, Jessica, American Public Human Services Association (APHSA), 1300 17 St N, Suite 340, Arlington, VA 22209-3801 Tel: 202-682-0100 Fax: 202-289-6555 E-mail: memberservice@aphsa.org Web Site: www.aphsa.org, pg 496

Garonzik, Joe, Clearfield Co Inc, 3600 Clipper Mill Rd, Suite 229, Baltimore, MD 21211 Tel: 410-837-8271 Toll Free Tel: 800-296-6687 (orders & cust serv) Fax: 410-752-8492 E-mail: sales@genealogical.com Web Site: www.genealogical.com, pg 49

Garonzik, Joe, Genealogical Publishing Co, 3600 Clipper Mill Rd, Suite 229, Baltimore, MD 21211 Tel: 410-837-8271 Toll Free Tel: 800-296-6687 Fax: 410-752-8492 Toll Free Fax: 800-599-9561 E-mail: info@genealogical.com; web@genealogical.com Web Site: www.genealogical.com, pg 77

Garrett, Edward, Macmillan, 120 Broadway, 22nd fl, New York, NY 10271 E-mail: press.inquiries@macmillan.com Web Site: us.macmillan.com, pg 122

Garrett, Michael, ManuscriptCritique.com, PO Box 362, Clay, AL 35048 Web Site: manuscriptcritique.com, pg 442

Garrett, Phil, Epicenter Press Inc, 6524 NE 181 St, Suite 2, Kenmore, WA 98028 Tel: 425-485-6822 (edit, mktg, busn off) Fax: 425-481-8253 E-mail: info@epicenterpress.com Web Site: www.epicenterpress.com, pg 67

Garrett, Susan, The University of North Carolina Press, 116 S Boundary St, Chapel Hill, NC 27514-3808 Tel: 919-966-3561; 919-966-7449 (orders) Toll Free Tel: 800-848-3224 (orders) Fax: 919-962-2704 (orders) Toll Free Fax: 800-272-6817 (orders) E-mail: uncpress@unc.edu Web Site: uncpress.org, pg 218

Garrido, Cris, Thomas Nelson, 501 Nelson Place, Nashville, TN 37214 Tel: 615-889-9000 Toll Free Tel: 800-251-4000 Web Site: www.thomasnelson.com, pg 206

Garriga, Elizabeth, Little, Brown and Company, 1290 Avenue of the Americas, New York, NY 10104 Tel: 212-364-1100 Fax: 212-364-0952 E-mail: firstname.lastname@hbgusa.com Web Site: www.hachettebookgroup.com/imprint/little-brown-and-company/, pg 118

Garriga, Natalie, Canadian Scholars, 425 Adelaide St W, Suite 200, Toronto, ON M5V 3C1, Canada Tel: 416-929-2774 Toll Free Tel: 800-463-1998 E-mail: info@canadianscholars.ca; editorial@canadianscholars.ca Web Site: www.canadianscholars.ca; www.womenspress.ca, pg 399

Garrison, Deborah, Alfred A Knopf, c/o Penguin Random House LLC, 1745 Broadway, New York, NY 10019 Tel: 212-751-2600 Fax: 212-940-7390 (dom rts); 212-572-2662 (foreign rts) Web Site: knopfdoubleday.com/imprint/knopf/; knopfdoubleday.com, pg 110

Garrison, Jessica Dandino, Dial Books for Young Readers, c/o Penguin Random House LLC, 1745 Broadway, New York, NY 10019 Tel: 212-782-9000 Web Site: www.penguin.com/dial-overview/, pg 59

Garrison, Mary, Math Solutions®, One Harbor Dr, Suite 101, Sausalito, CA 94965 Toll Free Tel: 877-234-7323 Toll Free Fax: 800-724-4716 E-mail: info@mathsolutions.com; orders@mathsolutions.com Web Site: www.mathsolutions.com; store.mathsolutions.com, pg 127

Garry, Peggy, Harry N Abrams Inc, 195 Broadway, 9th fl, New York, NY 10007 Tel: 212-206-7715 Toll Free Tel: 800-345-1359 Fax: 212-645-8437 E-mail: abrams@abramsbooks.com; publicity@abramsbooks.com; sales@abramsbooks.com Web Site: www.abramsbooks.com, pg 2

Garton, Keith, Red Chair Press, PO Box 333, South Egremont, MA 01258-0333 *Tel:* 413-528-2398 (edit off) *Toll Free Tel:* 800-328-4929 (orders & cust serv) *E-mail:* info@redchairpress.com *Web Site:* www.redchairpress.com, pg 172

Garvey, Brann, Harry N Abrams Inc, 195 Broadway, 9th fl, New York, NY 10007 *Tel:* 212-206-7715 *Toll Free Tel:* 800-345-1359 *Fax:* 212-645-8437 *E-mail:* abrams@abramsbooks.com; publicity@abramsbooks.com; sales@abramsbooks.com *Web Site:* www.abramsbooks.com, pg 3

Gary, Nina, University of Texas at Austin, New Writers Project, Dept of English, 204 W 21 St, B-5000, Austin, TX 78712-1164 *Tel:* 512-471-4991 *Fax:* 512-471-4909 *E-mail:* newwritersproject@utexas.edu *Web Site:* liberalarts.utexas.edu/nwp, pg 567

Garych, Leslie, Scholastic Trade Publishing, 557 Broadway, New York, NY 10012 *Tel:* 212-343-6100; 212-343-4685 (export sales) *Fax:* 212-343-4714 (export sales) *Web Site:* www.scholastic.com, pg 184

Garza, Jennifer, Random House Publishing Group, 1745 Broadway, New York, NY 10019 *Toll Free Tel:* 800-200-3552 *Web Site:* www.randomhousebooks.com, pg 170

Garza, John, Fordham University Press, Joseph A Martino Hall, 45 Columbus Ave, 3rd fl, New York, NY 10023 *Fax:* 347-842-3083 *Web Site:* www.fordhampress.com, pg 73

Gasbarrini, Tiffany, Johns Hopkins University Press, 2715 N Charles St, Baltimore, MD 21218-4363 *Tel:* 410-516-6900; 410-516-6987 *Toll Free Tel:* 800-537-5487 (book orders & cust serv); 800-548-1784 (journal orders) *Fax:* 410-516-6968; 410-516-6998 (orders) *E-mail:* hfscustserv@press.jhu.edu (cust serv); jrnlcirc@jh.edu (journal orders) *Web Site:* www.press.jhu.edu; muse.jhu.edu, pg 106

Gash, Amy, Little, Brown and Company, 1290 Avenue of the Americas, New York, NY 10104 *Tel:* 212-364-1100 *Fax:* 212-364-0952 *E-mail:* firstname.lastname@hbgusa.com *Web Site:* www.hachettebookgroup.com/imprint/little-brown-and-company/, pg 118

Gasior, Eric, Amateur Writing Contest, PO Box 686, Baltimore, MD 21203-0686 *Tel:* 410-563-2737 *E-mail:* bsfs-amc@bsfs.org *Web Site:* www.bsfs.org/bsfsssc.htm, pg 572

Gasior, Eric, BSFS Poetry Contest, PO Box 686, Baltimore, MD 21203-0686 *Tel:* 410-563-2737 *E-mail:* poetry@bsfs.org *Web Site:* www.bsfs.org/bsfspoetry.htm, pg 585

Gasior, Eric, Jack L Chalker Young Writers' Contest, PO Box 686, Baltimore, MD 21203-0686 *Tel:* 410-563-2737 *E-mail:* ywc@balticon.org *Web Site:* www.bsfs.org/bsfsywc.htm, pg 588

Gasior, Eric, Compton Crook Award, PO Box 686, Baltimore, MD 21203-0686 *Tel:* 410-563-2737 *E-mail:* webmeister@bsfs.org *Web Site:* www.bsfs.org/CCA/bsfsccnu2014.htm, pg 593

Gasior, Eric, Writer's Workshop at Balticon, PO Box 686, Baltimore, MD 21203-0686 *Tel:* 410-563-2737 *E-mail:* writersworkshop@bsfs.org *Web Site:* bsfs.org/bsfswriterwork.htm, pg 558

Gaskamp, Hannah, Texas Tech University Press, 1120 Main St, 2nd fl, Lubbock, TX 79401 *Tel:* 806-742-2982 *Toll Free Tel:* 800-832-4042 *E-mail:* ttup@ttu.edu *Web Site:* www.ttupress.org, pg 205

Gassman, Elizabeth, Diversion Books, 11 E 44 St, Suite 1603, New York, NY 10017 *Tel:* 212-961-6390 *E-mail:* info@diversionbooks.com *Web Site:* www.diversionbooks.com, pg 60

Gastonguay, Nicole, Random House Children's Books, c/o Penguin Random House LLC, 1745 Broadway, New York, NY 10019 *Tel:* 212-782-9000 *Web Site:* www.rhcbooks.com, pg 170

Gately, Michael, Biblio Award, PO Box 33020, Santa Fe, NM 87594 *Web Site:* biographersinternational.org/award/biblio-award, pg 580

Gately, Michael, BIO Award, PO Box 33020, Santa Fe, NM 87594 *Web Site:* biographersinternational.org/award/the-bio-award, pg 580

Gately, Michael, Chip Bishop Fellowship, PO Box 33020, Santa Fe, NM 87594 *Web Site:* biographersinternational.org/award/chip-bishop-fellowship, pg 581

Gately, Michael, The Robert & Ina Caro Research/Travel Fellowship, PO Box 33020, Santa Fe, NM 87594 *Web Site:* biographersinternational.org/award/the-robert-and-ina-caro-research-travel-fellowship, pg 587

Gately, Michael, Editorial Excellence Award, PO Box 33020, Santa Fe, NM 87594 *Web Site:* biographersinternational.org/award/editorial-excellence, pg 598

Gately, Michael, Plutarch Award, PO Box 33020, Santa Fe, NM 87594 *Tel:* 505-983-4671 *E-mail:* plutarch@biographersinternational.org *Web Site:* biographersinternational.org/award/the-plutarch, pg 650

Gately, Michael, The Frances "Frank" Rollin Fellowship, PO Box 33020, Santa Fe, NM 87594 *Tel:* 505-983-4671 *Web Site:* biographersinternational.org/award/the-frances-frank-rollin-fellowship, pg 657

Gately, Michael, Hazel Rowley Prize, PO Box 33020, Santa Fe, NM 87594 *Web Site:* biographersinternational.org/award/hazel-rowley-prize, pg 657

Gates, Henry Louis Jr, The Anisfield-Wolf Book Awards, 1422 Euclid Ave, Suite 1300, Cleveland, OH 44115 *Tel:* 216-861-3810 *Fax:* 216-861-1729 *E-mail:* awinfo@clevefdn.org *Web Site:* www.anisfield-wolf.org; www.clevelandfoundation.org, pg 573

Gates, Jennifer, Aevitas Creative Management LLC, 19 W 21 St, Suite 501, New York, NY 10010 *Tel:* 212-765-6900 *Web Site:* www.aevitascreative.com, pg 448

Gates, Rob, The Gaylactic Spectrum Awards, 1425 "S" St NW, Washington, DC 20009 *E-mail:* nominations@spectrumawards.org *Web Site:* www.spectrumawards.org, pg 606

Gatsch, Mary E, Springer Publishing Co, 11 W 42 St, 15th fl, New York, NY 10036-8002 *Tel:* 212-431-4370 *Toll Free Tel:* 877-687-7476 *E-mail:* marketing@springerpub.com; cs@springerpub.com (orders); textbook@springerpub.com; specialsales@springerpub.com *Web Site:* www.springerpub.com, pg 196

Gatt, Michelle, SLACK® Incorporated, A Wyanoke Group Company, 6900 Grove Rd, Thorofare, NJ 08086-9447 *Tel:* 856-848-1000 *Toll Free Tel:* 800-257-8290 *Fax:* 856-848-6091 *E-mail:* sales@slackinc.com; editor@slackinc.com; customerservice@slackinc.com *Web Site:* www.healio.com/books, pg 191

Gaudet, Michael, Hachette Book Group Inc, 1290 Avenue of the Americas, New York, NY 10104 *Tel:* 212-364-1100 *Toll Free Tel:* 800-759-0190 (cust serv) *Fax:* 212-364-0933 (intl orders) *Toll Free Fax:* 800-286-9471 (cust serv) *E-mail:* customer.service@hbgusa.com; orders@hbgusa.com *Web Site:* www.hachettebookgroup.com, pg 83

Gaughan, Jay, Highlights for Children Inc, 815 Church St, Honesdale, PA 18431 *Tel:* 570-253-1164 *Toll Free Tel:* 800-490-5111 *Fax:* 570-253-0179 *E-mail:* salesandmarketing@highlightspress.com *Web Site:* www.highlightspress.com; www.highlights.com; www.facebook.com/HighlightsforChildren, pg 92

Gaughan, Laura Rock, The Literary Press Group of Canada, 234 Eglinton Ave E, Suite 401, Toronto, ON M4P 1K5, Canada *Tel:* 416-483-1321 *Fax:* 416-483-2510 *E-mail:* sales@lpg.ca *Web Site:* www.lpg.ca, pg 509

Gaughan, Maura, Focus, PO Box 390007, Cambridge, MA 02139-0001 *Tel:* 317-635-9250 *Fax:* 317-635-9292 *E-mail:* customer@hackettpublishing.com; editorial@hackettpublishing.com *Web Site:* focusbookstore.com; www.hackettpublishing.com, pg 73

Gaule, Mary, HarperCollins Publishers LLC, 195 Broadway, New York, NY 10007 *Tel:* 212-207-7000 *Web Site:* www.harpercollins.com, pg 87

Gauthier, Daniel J, Gauthier Publications Inc, PO Box 806241, St Clair Shores, MI 48080 *Tel:* 313-458-7141 *Fax:* 586-279-1515 *E-mail:* info@gauthierpublications.com *Web Site:* www.gauthierpublications.com, pg 77

Gauthier, Donna, Bloomsbury Publishing Inc, 1385 Broadway, 5th fl, New York, NY 10018 *Tel:* 212-419-5300 *E-mail:* marketingusa@bloomsbury.com; adultpublicityusa@bloomsbury.com; askacademic@bloomsbury.com *Web Site:* www.bloomsbury.com, pg 31

Gauthier, Elizabeth, Gauthier Publications Inc, PO Box 806241, St Clair Shores, MI 48080 *Tel:* 313-458-7141 *Fax:* 586-279-1515 *E-mail:* info@gauthierpublications.com *Web Site:* www.gauthierpublications.com, pg 77

Gauthier, Helene, Ordre des traducteurs, terminologues et interpretes agrees du quebec (OTTIAQ), 1108-2021 Ave Union, Montreal, QC H3A 2S9, Canada *Tel:* 514-845-4411 *Toll Free Tel:* 800-265-4815 *Fax:* 514-845-9903 *E-mail:* info@ottiaq.org; direction@ottiaq.org; reception@ottiaq.org; communications@ottiaq.org *Web Site:* www.ottiaq.org, pg 515

Gauthier, Jen, Greystone Books Ltd, 343 Railway St, Suite 302, Vancouver, BC V6A 1A4, Canada *Tel:* 604-875-1550 *Fax:* 604-875-1556 *E-mail:* info@greystonebooks.com; rights@greystonebooks.com *Web Site:* www.greystonebooks.com, pg 407

Gauthier, Tammy, Hilton Publishing Co, 5261-A Fountain Dr, Crown Point, IN 46307 *Tel:* 219-922-4868 *Fax:* 219-924-6811 *E-mail:* info@hpcinternationalinc.com *Web Site:* www.hpcinternationalinc.com; www.hpcinternationalinc.com/bookstore (orders), pg 92

Gay, Grace, St Martin's Press, LLC, 120 Broadway, New York, NY 10271 *E-mail:* publicity@stmartins.com; trademarketing@stmartins.com; foreignrights@stmartins.com *Web Site:* us.macmillan.com/smp, pg 181

Gay, Roxane, The Flannery O'Connor Award for Short Fiction, Main Library, 3rd fl, 320 S Jackson St, Athens, GA 30602 *Fax:* 706-542-2558 *Web Site:* www.ugapress.org, pg 642

Gayle, Stephanie, Eleanor Taylor Bland Crime Fiction Writers of Color Award, PO Box 442124, Lawrence, KS 66044 *Tel:* 785-842-1325 *Fax:* 785-856-6314 *E-mail:* admin@sistersincrime.org *Web Site:* www.sistersincrime.org, pg 581

Gaymon, Lee, SLACK® Incorporated, A Wyanoke Group Company, 6900 Grove Rd, Thorofare, NJ 08086-9447 *Tel:* 856-848-1000 *Toll Free Tel:* 800-257-8290 *Fax:* 856-848-6091 *E-mail:* sales@slackinc.com; editor@slackinc.com; customerservice@slackinc.com *Web Site:* www.healio.com/books, pg 191

Gaynor, Rosie, Sourcebooks LLC, 1935 Brookdale Rd, Suite 139, Naperville, IL 60563 *Tel:* 630-961-3900 *Toll Free Tel:* 800-432-7444 *Fax:* 630-961-2168 *E-mail:* info@sourcebooks.com *Web Site:* www.sourcebooks.com, pg 195

Gazlay, Laura, Library of America, 14 E 60 St, New York, NY 10022-1006 *Tel:* 212-308-3360 *Fax:* 212-750-8352 *E-mail:* info@loa.org *Web Site:* www.loa.org, pg 116

Gazzolo, Paul, Gale, 27555 Executive Dr, Suite 270, Farmington Hills, MI 48331 *Toll Free Tel:* 800-877-4253 *Toll Free Fax:* 877-363-4253 *E-mail:* gale.customerexperience@cengage.com *Web Site:* www.gale.com, pg 75

Gazzolo, Paul, Macmillan Reference USA™, 27500 Drake Rd, Farmington Hills, MI 48331-3535 *Tel:* 248-699-4253 *Toll Free Tel:* 800-877-4253 *Toll Free Fax:* 877-363-4253 *E-mail:* gale.customercare@cengage.com *Web Site:* www.gale.cengage.com/macmillan, pg 123

Geary, Christine, Harry N Abrams Inc, 195 Broadway, 9th fl, New York, NY 10007 *Tel:* 212-206-7715 *Toll Free Tel:* 800-345-1359 *Fax:* 212-645-8437 *E-mail:* abrams@abramsbooks.com; publicity@abramsbooks.com; sales@abramsbooks.com *Web Site:* www.abramsbooks.com, pg 3

Geary, Tracy, Boston Authors Club Inc, c/o Prof Julie Dobrow, 103 Conant Rd, Lincoln, MA 01773 *Tel:* 781-259-1220 *E-mail:* bostonauthorsclub2@gmail.com *Web Site:* bostonauthorsclub.org, pg 501

Geary, Tracy, Julia Ward Howe Book Awards, c/o Prof Julie Dobrow, 103 Conant Rd, Lincoln, MA 01773 *Tel:* 781-259-1220 *E-mail:* bostonauthorsclub2@gmail.com *Web Site:* bostonauthorsclub.org, pg 614

Gebhardt, Phyllis, Trusted Media Brands Inc, 750 Third Ave, 3rd fl, New York, NY 10017 *Tel:* 646-293-6299 *Toll Free Tel:* 877-732-4438 (cust serv) *Fax:* 646-293-6251 *E-mail:* customercare@trustedmediabrands.com; press@trustedmediabrands.com *Web Site:* www.trustedmediabrands.com; www.rd.com, pg 210

Gebremedhin, Thomas, Doubleday, c/o Penguin Random House LLC, 1745 Broadway, New York, NY 10019 *Tel:* 212-751-2600 *Fax:* 212-940-7390 (dom rts); 212-572-2662 (foreign rts) *Web Site:* knopfdoubleday.com/imprint/doubleday/; knopfdoubleday.com, pg 61

Geck, Steve, Sourcebooks LLC, 1935 Brookdale Rd, Suite 139, Naperville, IL 60563 *Tel:* 630-961-3900 *Toll Free Tel:* 800-432-7444 *Fax:* 630-961-2168 *E-mail:* info@sourcebooks.com *Web Site:* www.sourcebooks.com, pg 194

Gee, Diana, Macmillan, 120 Broadway, 22nd fl, New York, NY 10271 *E-mail:* press.inquiries@macmillan.com *Web Site:* us.macmillan.com, pg 122

Geer, David, Samuel French, Inc, 250 W 57 St, 6th fl, New York, NY 10107-0102 *Toll Free Tel:* 866-979-0447 *E-mail:* info@concordtheatricals.com *Web Site:* www.concordtheatricals.com/a/4346/samuel-a-french, pg 75

Geer, Kelly, Carson Dellosa Publishing LLC, PO Box 35665, Greensboro, NC 27425-5665 *Tel:* 336-632-0084 *Toll Free Tel:* 800-321-0943 *Fax:* 336-632-0084 *E-mail:* custsvc@carsondellosa.com *Web Site:* www.carsondellosa.com, pg 41

Geffen, Brian, Henry Holt and Company, LLC, 120 Broadway, 23rd fl, New York, NY 10271 *Tel:* 646-307-5151 *Toll Free Tel:* 888-330-8477 (orders) *Fax:* 646-307-5285 *Web Site:* www.henryholt.com, pg 94

Gehy, Farah, Peachtree Publishing Co Inc, 1700 Chattahoochee Ave, Atlanta, GA 30318-2112 *Tel:* 404-876-8761 *Toll Free Tel:* 800-241-0113 *Fax:* 404-875-2578 *Toll Free Fax:* 800-875-8909 *E-mail:* hello@peachtree-online.com; sales@peachtree-online.com *Web Site:* www.peachtreebooks.com; www.peachtree-online.com, pg 153

Geiger, Ellen, Frances Goldin Literary Agency, Inc, 214 W 29 St, Suite 410, New York, NY 10001 *Tel:* 212-777-0047 *Fax:* 212-228-1660 *E-mail:* agency@goldinlit.com *Web Site:* www.goldinlit.com, pg 460

Geiger, Rachel, Chronicle Books LLC, 680 Second St, San Francisco, CA 94107 *Tel:* 415-537-4200 *Fax:* 415-537-4460 (perms) *E-mail:* hello@chroniclebooks.com; subrights@chroniclebooks.com *Web Site:* www.chroniclebooks.com, pg 47

Geissler, Cynara, Arsenal Pulp Press, 211 E Georgia St, No 202, Vancouver, BC V6A 1Z6, Canada *Tel:* 604-687-4233 *Toll Free Tel:* 888-600-PULP (600-7857) *Fax:* 604-687-4283 *E-mail:* info@arsenalpulp.com *Web Site:* www.arsenalpulp.com, pg 395

Geist, Jennifer, Open Books Press, 4719 Holly Hills Ave, St Louis, MO 63116 *Tel:* 314-827-6567 *E-mail:* info@openbookspress.com *Web Site:* openbookspress.com, pg 146

Geist, Jennifer, Pen & Publish LLC, 4719 Holly Hills Ave, St Louis, MO 63116 *Tel:* 314-827-6567 *E-mail:* info@penandpublish.com *Web Site:* penandpublish.com, pg 153

Geist, Ken, Scholastic Trade Publishing, 557 Broadway, New York, NY 10012 *Tel:* 212-343-6100; 212-343-4685 (export sales) *Fax:* 212-343-4714 (export sales) *Web Site:* www.scholastic.com, pg 184

Gelb, Joe, Small Business Advisors Inc, 2005 Park St, Atlantic Beach, NY 11509 *Tel:* 516-374-1387 *Fax:* 516-374-1175 *E-mail:* info@smallbusinessadvice.com *Web Site:* www.smallbusinessadvice.com, pg 191

Gelbard, Erica, Chronicle Books LLC, 680 Second St, San Francisco, CA 94107 *Tel:* 415-537-4200 *Fax:* 415-537-4460 (perms) *E-mail:* hello@chroniclebooks.com; subrights@chroniclebooks.com *Web Site:* www.chroniclebooks.com, pg 47

Gelber, Alice, Little, Brown Books for Young Readers (LBYR), 1290 Avenue of the Americas, New York, NY 10104 *Tel:* 212-364-1100 *Toll Free Tel:* 800-759-0190 (cust serv) *E-mail:* rights@lbchildrens.com *Web Site:* www.hachettebookgroup.com/imprint/little-brown-books-for-young-readers/, pg 118

Gelbman, Leslie, St Martin's Press, LLC, 120 Broadway, New York, NY 10271 *E-mail:* publicity@stmartins.com; trademarketing@stmartins.com; foreignrights@stmartins.com *Web Site:* us.macmillan.com/smp, pg 181

Geldermann, Taylor, Sourcebooks LLC, 1935 Brookdale Rd, Suite 139, Naperville, IL 60563 *Tel:* 630-961-3900 *Toll Free Tel:* 800-432-7444 *Fax:* 630-961-2168 *E-mail:* info@sourcebooks.com *Web Site:* www.sourcebooks.com, pg 194

Gelfand, Dr Sergei, American Mathematical Society (AMS), 201 Charles St, Providence, RI 02904-2213 *Tel:* 401-455-4000 *Toll Free Tel:* 800-321-4267 *Fax:* 401-331-3842; 401-455-4046 (cust serv) *E-mail:* ams@ams.org; cust-serv@ams.org *Web Site:* www.ams.org, pg 11

Gelfman, Jane, Gelfman Schneider Literary Agents Inc, 850 Seventh Ave, Suite 903, New York, NY 10019 *Tel:* 212-245-1993 *E-mail:* mail@gelfmanschneider.com *Web Site:* gelfmanschneider.com, pg 460

Geller, Elizabeth, The Guilford Press, 370 Seventh Ave, Suite 1200, New York, NY 10001-1020 *Tel:* 212-431-9800 *Toll Free Tel:* 800-365-7006 *Fax:* 212-966-6708 *E-mail:* info@guilford.com; orders@guilford.com *Web Site:* www.guilford.com, pg 82

Geller, Nick, Yale University Press, 302 Temple St, New Haven, CT 06511-8909 *Tel:* 203-432-0960; 203-432-0966 (sales); 401-531-2800 (cust serv) *Toll Free Tel:* 800-405-1619 (cust serv) *Fax:* 203-432-0948; 203-432-8485 (sales); 401-531-2801 (cust serv) *Toll Free Fax:* 800-406-9145 (cust serv) *E-mail:* sales.press@yale.edu (sales); customer.care@triliteral.org (cust serv) *Web Site:* www.yalebooks.com; yalepress.yale.edu/yupbooks, pg 235

Gelles-Cole, Sandi, Gelles-Cole Literary Enterprises, 2163 Lima Loop, PMB 01-408, Laredo, TX 78045-9452 *Tel:* 845-810-0029 *Web Site:* www.literaryenterprises.com, pg 440

Gelman, Jaime, little bee books, 598 Broadway, 7th fl, New York, NY 10012 *Tel:* 212-321-0237 *Toll Free Tel:* 844-321-0237 *E-mail:* info@littlebeebooks.com; sales@littlebeebooks.com; publicity@littlebeebooks.com *Web Site:* littlebeebooks.com, pg 117

Genao, Maudee, Atria Books, 1230 Avenue of the Americas, New York, NY 10020 *Tel:* 212-698-7000 *Fax:* 212-698-7007 *Web Site:* www.simonandschuster.com, pg 21

Gendler, Anne, Northwestern University Press, 629 Noyes St, Evanston, IL 60208-4210 *Tel:* 847-491-2046 *Toll Free Tel:* 800-621-2736 (orders only) *Fax:* 847-491-8150 *E-mail:* nupress@northwestern.edu *Web Site:* www.nupress.northwestern.edu, pg 143

Gendreau, Philippe, Les Editions du Boreal, 4447, rue St-Denis, Montreal, QC H2J 2L2, Canada *Tel:* 514-287-7401 *Fax:* 514-287-7664 *E-mail:* info@editionsboreal.qc.ca; boreal@editionsboreal.qc.ca; communications@editionsboreal.qc.ca *Web Site:* www.editionsboreal.qc.ca, pg 402

Gendron, Greg, National Endowment for the Arts, 400 Seventh St SW, Washington, DC 20506-0001 *Tel:* 202-682-5400 *Web Site:* www.arts.gov, pg 526

Genett, Johannah, John Phillip Immroth Memorial Award, 225 Michigan Ave, Suite 1300, Chicago, IL 60601 *Tel:* 312-280-4226 *Toll Free Tel:* 800-545-2433 *E-mail:* ifrt@ala.org *Web Site:* www.ala.org/rt/ifrt/immroth, pg 615

Genett, Johannah, Eli M Oboler Memorial Award, 225 Michigan Ave, Suite 1300, Chicago, IL 60601 *Tel:* 312-280-4226 *Toll Free Tel:* 800-545-2433 *E-mail:* ifrt@ala.org *Web Site:* www.ala.org/rt/ifrt/oboler, pg 642

Gennaro, Tea, National Association of Broadcasters (NAB), One "M" St SE, Washington, DC 20003 *Tel:* 202-429-5300 *E-mail:* nab@nab.org *Web Site:* www.nab.org, pg 136, 511

Gens, Alice, New Jersey Business & Industry Association (NJBIA), 10 W Lafayette St, Trenton, NJ 08608-2002 *Tel:* 609-393-7707 *Web Site:* njbia.org, pg 514

Gentes, Brian, Jeanne Cordova Prize for Lesbian/Queer Nonfiction, PO Box 20186, New York, NY 10014 *Tel:* 213-277-5755 *E-mail:* awards@lambdaliterary.org; admin@lambdaliterary.org *Web Site:* www.lambdaliterary.org/awards/special-awards, pg 592

Gentes, Brian, Jim Duggins PhD Outstanding Mid-Career Novelist Prize, PO Box 20186, New York, NY 10014 *Tel:* 213-277-5755 *E-mail:* awards@lambdaliterary.org; admin@lambdaliterary.org *Web Site:* www.lambdaliterary.org/awards/special-awards, pg 597

Gentes, Brian, Randall Kenan Prize for Black LGBTQ Fiction, PO Box 20186, New York, NY 10014 *Tel:* 213-277-5755 *E-mail:* awards@lambdaliterary.org; admin@lambdaliterary.org *Web Site:* www.lambdaliterary.org/awards/special-awards, pg 620

Gentes, Brian, Lambda Literary Awards (Lammys), PO Box 20186, New York, NY 10014 *Tel:* 213-277-5755 *E-mail:* awards@lambdaliterary.org; admin@lambdaliterary.org *Web Site:* www.lambdaliterary.org, pg 621

Gentes, Brian, Judith A Markowitz Award for Emerging LGBTQ Writers, PO Box 20186, New York, NY 10014 *Tel:* 213-277-5755 *E-mail:* awards@lambdaliterary.org; admin@lambdaliterary.org *Web Site:* www.lambdaliterary.org/awards/special-awards, pg 629

Gentile, Michael, Penguin Random House LLC, 1745 Broadway, New York, NY 10019 *Tel:* 212-782-9000 *Toll Free Tel:* 800-726-0600 *Web Site:* www.penguinrandomhouse.com, pg 155

Gentillo, Eileen, Simon & Schuster, LLC, 1230 Avenue of the Americas, New York, NY 10020 *Tel:* 212-698-7000 *Toll Free Tel:* 800-223-2336 (orders) *Fax:* 212-698-7007 *Toll Free Fax:* 800-943-9831 (orders) *E-mail:* firstname.lastname@simonandschuster.com; purchaseorders@simonandschuster.com (orders) *Web Site:* www.simonandschuster.com, pg 190

Geoffroy, Kyler, Island Press, 2000 "M" St NW, Suite 480-B, Washington, DC 20036 *Tel:* 202-232-7933 *Toll Free Tel:* 800-621-2736 *Fax:* 202-234-1328 *E-mail:* info@islandpress.org *Web Site:* www.islandpress.org, pg 104

George, Kallie, Greystone Books Ltd, 343 Railway St, Suite 302, Vancouver, BC V6A 1A4, Canada *Tel:* 604-875-1550 *Fax:* 604-875-1556 *E-mail:* info@greystonebooks.com; rights@greystonebooks.com *Web Site:* www.greystonebooks.com, pg 407

George, Kayleigh, HarperCollins Publishers LLC, 195 Broadway, New York, NY 10007 *Tel:* 212-207-7000 *Web Site:* www.harpercollins.com, pg 86

George, Kayleigh, Sourcebooks LLC, 1935 Brookdale Rd, Suite 139, Naperville, IL 60563 *Tel:* 630-961-3900 *Toll Free Tel:* 800-432-7444 *Fax:* 630-961-2168 *E-mail:* info@sourcebooks.com *Web Site:* www.sourcebooks.com, pg 194

George, Peter, Houghton Mifflin Harcourt, 125 High St, Boston, MA 02110 *Tel:* 617-351-5000 *Toll Free Tel:* 855-969-4642; 800-225-5425 (K-12 educ materials); 800-323-9540 (assessment materials); 877-219-1537 (SkillsTutor); 888-242-6747 (Innovation in Educ Group); 800-225-3362 (Trade & Ref Div) *Toll Free Fax:* 800-269-5232 *E-mail:* myhmhco@hmhco.com *Web Site:* www.hmhco.com, pg 96

George, Sarah, Sourcebooks LLC, 1935 Brookdale Rd, Suite 139, Naperville, IL 60563 *Tel:* 630-961-3900 *Toll Free Tel:* 800-432-7444 *Fax:* 630-961-2168 *E-mail:* info@sourcebooks.com *Web Site:* www.sourcebooks.com, pg 194

George, Tina, Sourcebooks LLC, 1935 Brookdale Rd, Suite 139, Naperville, IL 60563 *Tel:* 630-961-3900 *Toll Free Tel:* 800-432-7444 *Fax:* 630-961-2168 *E-mail:* info@sourcebooks.com *Web Site:* www.sourcebooks.com, pg 194

Georges, Patrick, Penguin Random House Canada, a Penguin Random House company, 320 Front St W, Suite 1400, Toronto, ON M5V 3B6, Canada *Tel:* 416-364-4449 *Toll Free Tel:* 888-523-9292 (cust serv) *E-mail:* canadaweb@penguinrandomhouse.com; customerservicescanada@penguinrandomhouse.com *Web Site:* www.penguinrandomhouse.ca, pg 416

Georgieva, Antoaneta "Ant", Sourcebooks LLC, 1935 Brookdale Rd, Suite 139, Naperville, IL 60563 *Tel:* 630-961-3900 *Toll Free Tel:* 800-432-7444 *Fax:* 630-961-2168 *E-mail:* info@sourcebooks.com *Web Site:* www.sourcebooks.com, pg 195

Geppert, Brent, Educational Insights®, 152 W Walnut St, Suite 201, Gardena, CA 90248 *Toll Free Tel:* 800-995-4436 *Toll Free Fax:* 888-892-8731 *E-mail:* info@educationalinsights.com; cs@educationalinsights.com *Web Site:* www.educationalinsights.com, pg 64

Geraghty, Kate, Macmillan Learning, One New York Plaza, Suite 46, New York, NY 10004 *Tel:* 212-576-9400 *E-mail:* salesoperations@macmillanusa.com *Web Site:* www.macmillanlearning.com/college/us, pg 123

Gerak, Peggy, Workman Publishing, 1290 Avenue of the Americas, New York, NY 10104 *Toll Free Tel:* 800-759-0190 *Fax:* 212-364-0950 *E-mail:* workman-inquiry@hbgusa.com *Web Site:* www.hachettebookgroup.com/imprint/workman-publishing-company/, pg 232

Gerbasi, Catherine, Portage & Main Press, 318 McDermot Ave, Suite 100, Winnipeg, MB R3A 0A2, Canada *Tel:* 204-987-3500 *Toll Free Tel:* 800-667-9673 *Fax:* 204-947-0080 *Toll Free Fax:* 866-734-8477 *E-mail:* customerservice@portageandmainpress.com *Web Site:* www.portageandmainpress.com, pg 416

Gerber, Marty, Terra Nova Books, 33 Alondra Rd, Santa Fe, NM 87508 *Tel:* 505-670-9319 *Fax:* 509-461-9333 *E-mail:* publisher@terranovabooks.com; marketing@terranovabooks.com *Web Site:* www.terranovabooks.com, pg 204

Gerber, Scott, Terra Nova Books, 33 Alondra Rd, Santa Fe, NM 87508 *Tel:* 505-670-9319 *Fax:* 509-461-9333 *E-mail:* publisher@terranovabooks.com; marketing@terranovabooks.com *Web Site:* www.terranovabooks.com, pg 204

Germain, Bronte, Second Story Press, 20 Maud St, Suite 401, Toronto, ON M5V 2M5, Canada *Tel:* 416-537-7850 *Fax:* 416-537-0588 *E-mail:* info@secondstorypress.ca *Web Site:* secondstorypress.ca, pg 419

German, Donna, Arbordale Publishing, 612 Johnnie Dodds Blvd, Suite A2, Mount Pleasant, SC 29464 *Tel:* 843-971-6722 *Toll Free Tel:* 877-243-3457 *Fax:* 843-216-3804 *E-mail:* info@arbordalepublishing.com *Web Site:* www.arbordalepublishing.com, pg 16

German, Mr Lee, Arbordale Publishing, 612 Johnnie Dodds Blvd, Suite A2, Mount Pleasant, SC 29464 *Tel:* 843-971-6722 *Toll Free Tel:* 877-243-3457 *Fax:* 843-216-3804 *E-mail:* info@arbordalepublishing.com *Web Site:* www.arbordalepublishing.com, pg 16

Gernenz, Heather, University of Illinois Press, 1325 S Oak St, MC-566, Champaign, IL 61820-6903 *Tel:* 217-333-0950 *Fax:* 217-244-8082 *E-mail:* uipress@uillinois.edu; journals@uillinois.edu *Web Site:* www.press.uillinois.edu, pg 216

Gerritse, Danielle, Penguin Random House Canada, a Penguin Random House company, 320 Front St W, Suite 1400, Toronto, ON M5V 3B6, Canada *Tel:* 416-364-4449 *Toll Free Tel:* 888-523-9292 (cust serv) *E-mail:* canadaweb@penguinrandomhouse.com; customerservicescanada@penguinrandomhouse.com *Web Site:* www.penguinrandomhouse.ca, pg 416

Gersch, Chantal, Farrar, Straus & Giroux Books for Young Readers, 120 Broadway, New York, NY 10271 *Tel:* 212-741-6900 *Toll Free Tel:* 888-330-8477 (orders) *E-mail:* childrens.publicity@macmillanusa.com; childrensrights@macmillanusa.com *Web Site:* us.macmillan.com/mackids/, pg 70

Gersch, Chantal, Roaring Brook Press, 120 Broadway, New York, NY 10271 *Tel:* 646-307-5151 *Web Site:* us.macmillan.com/publishers/roaring-brook-press, pg 176

Gershenowitz, Debbie, The University of North Carolina Press, 116 S Boundary St, Chapel Hill, NC 27514-3808 *Tel:* 919-966-3561; 919-966-7449 (orders) *Toll Free Tel:* 800-848-3224 (orders) *Fax:* 919-962-2704 (orders) *Toll Free Fax:* 800-272-6817 (orders) *E-mail:* uncpress@unc.edu *Web Site:* uncpress.org, pg 218

Gershowitz, Elissa, Boston Globe-Horn Book Award, c/o Book Reviews, The Horn Book Inc, Palace Road Bldg, 300 The Fenway, Suite P-311, Boston, MA 02115-5820 *Tel:* 617-278-0225 *Toll Free Tel:* 888-628-0225 *E-mail:* bghb@hbook.com *Web Site:* www.hbook.com, pg 583

Gerstle, Dan, W W Norton & Company Inc, 500 Fifth Ave, New York, NY 10110-0017 *Tel:* 212-354-5500 *Toll Free Tel:* 800-233-4830 (orders & cust serv) *Fax:* 212-869-0856 *Toll Free Fax:* 800-458-6515 *E-mail:* orders@wwnorton.com *Web Site:* wwnorton.com, pg 143

Gervais, Alison, Harry N Abrams Inc, 195 Broadway, 9th fl, New York, NY 10007 *Tel:* 212-206-7715 *Toll Free Tel:* 800-345-1359 *Fax:* 212-645-8437 *E-mail:* abrams@abramsbooks.com; publicity@abramsbooks.com; sales@abramsbooks.com *Web Site:* www.abramsbooks.com, pg 2

Geter, Hafizah, Janklow & Nesbit Associates, 285 Madison Ave, 21st fl, New York, NY 10017 *Tel:* 212-421-1700 *Fax:* 212-355-1403 *E-mail:* info@janklow.com; submissions@janklow.com; filmtvrights@janklow.com *Web Site:* www.janklowandnesbit.com, pg 464

Getzler, Josh, HG Literary, 6 W 18 St, Suite 7R, New York, NY 10011 *E-mail:* foreign@hgliterary.com; rights@hgliterary.com *Web Site:* www.hgliterary.com, pg 463

Ghaffar, Jamie, Candlewick Press, 99 Dover St, Somerville, MA 02144-2825 *Tel:* 617-661-3330 *Fax:* 617-661-0565 *E-mail:* bigbear@candlewick.com; salesinfo@candlewick.com *Web Site:* candlewick.com, pg 39

Gharib, Linda, Wolters Kluwer Law & Business, 76 Ninth Ave, 7th fl, New York, NY 10011-5201 *Tel:* 212-771-0600; 301-698-7100 (cust serv outside US) *Toll Free Tel:* 800-234-1660 (cust serv) *E-mail:* customer.service@wolterskluwer.com; lrusmedia@wolterskluwer.com *Web Site:* lrus.wolterskluwer.com, pg 232

Ghim, Deborah, HarperCollins Publishers LLC, 195 Broadway, New York, NY 10007 *Tel:* 212-207-7000 *Web Site:* www.harpercollins.com, pg 86

Ghione, Yvette, IBBY Canada, c/o The Canadian Children's Book Ctr, 425 Adelaide St W, Suite 200, Toronto, ON M5V 3C1, Canada *Tel:* 416-975-8970 *E-mail:* info@ibby-canada.org *Web Site:* www.ibby-canada.org, pg 507

Ghione, Yvette, Kids Can Press Ltd, 25 Dockside Dr, Toronto, ON M5A 0B5, Canada *Tel:* 416-479-7000 *Toll Free Tel:* 800-265-0884 *Fax:* 416-960-5437 *E-mail:* info@kidscan; customerservice@kidscan.com *Web Site:* www.kidscanpress.com; www.kidscanpress.ca, pg 411

Ghione, Yvette, Elizabeth Mrazik-Cleaver Canadian Picture Book Award, c/o The Canadian Children's Book Ctr, 425 Adelaide St W, Suite 200, Toronto, ON M5V 3C1, Canada *Fax:* 416-975-8970 *E-mail:* cleaver@ibby-canada.org; info@ibby-canada.org *Web Site:* www.ibby-canada.org/awards/elizabeth-mrazik-cleaver-award/, pg 636

Ghosh, Dr Shreelina, Gannon University's High School Poetry Contest, Gannon University, 109 University Sq, Erie, PA 16541 *Tel:* 814-871-5583 *Web Site:* www.gannon.edu/poetrycontest, pg 605

Ghoura, Judy, Fitzhenry & Whiteside Limited, 209 Wicksteed Ave, Unit 51, Markham, ON M4G 0B1, Canada *Tel:* 905-477-9700 *Toll Free Tel:* 800-387-9776 *Fax:* 905-477-2834 *E-mail:* bookinfo@fitzhenry.ca *Web Site:* www.fitzhenry.ca, pg 406

Ghoura, Judy, Red Deer Press Inc, 209 Wicksteed Ave, Unit 51, Toronto, ON M4G 0B1, Canada *Tel:* 905-477-9700 *Toll Free Tel:* 800-387-9776 *E-mail:* bookinfo@fitzhenry.ca *Web Site:* www.reddeerpress.com, pg 418

Giacomini, Cara, Council for Advancement & Support of Education (CASE), 1201 Eye St NW, Suite 300, Washington, DC 20005 *Tel:* 202-328-CASE (328-2273) *Fax:* 202-387-4973 *E-mail:* membersupportcenter@case.org *Web Site:* www.case.org, pg 504

Giagnocavo, Alan, Fox Chapel Publishing Co Inc, 1970 Broad St, East Petersburg, PA 17520 *Tel:* 717-560-4703 *Toll Free Tel:* 800-457-9112 *Fax:* 717-560-4702 *E-mail:* customerservice@foxchapelpublishing.com *Web Site:* www.foxchapelpublishing.com, pg 74

Giampoala, Matthew, American Geophysical Union (AGU), 2000 Florida Ave NW, Washington, DC 20009 *Tel:* 202-462-6900 *Toll Free Tel:* 800-966-2481 (North America) *Fax:* 202-328-0566 *E-mail:* service@agu.org (cust serv) *Web Site:* www.agu.org, pg 10

Giangreco, Karen, The Experiment, 220 E 23 St, Suite 600, New York, NY 10010-4658 *Tel:* 212-889-1659 *E-mail:* info@theexperimentpublishing.com *Web Site:* www.theexperimentpublishing.com, pg 68

Giarratano, Matt, Viking Penguin, c/o Penguin Random House LLC, 1745 Broadway, New York, NY 10019 *Tel:* 212-782-9000 *Web Site:* www.penguin.com/overview-vikingbooks/; www.penguin.com/pamela-dorman-books-overview/; www.penguin.com/penguin-classics-overview/; www.penguin.com/penguin-life-overview/, pg 225

Gibbons, Donna, Society for Industrial & Applied Mathematics, 3600 Market St, 6th fl, Philadelphia, PA 19104-2688 *Tel:* 215-382-9800 *Toll Free Tel:* 800-447-7426 *E-mail:* siam@siam.org *Web Site:* www.siam.org, pg 192

Gibbons, Meg, Sourcebooks LLC, 1935 Brookdale Rd, Suite 139, Naperville, IL 60563 *Tel:* 630-961-3900 *Toll Free Tel:* 800-432-7444 *Fax:* 630-961-2168 *E-mail:* info@sourcebooks.com *Web Site:* www.sourcebooks.com, pg 194

Gibbons, Melissa, William H Sadlier Inc, 9 Pine St, New York, NY 10005 *Tel:* 212-227-2120 *Toll Free Tel:* 800-221-5175 (cust serv) *Fax:* 212-312-6080 *E-mail:* customerservice@sadlier.com *Web Site:* www.sadlier.com, pg 179

Gibbs, David, Community of Literary Magazines & Presses (CLMP), 154 Christopher St, Suite 3C, New York, NY 10014-9110 *Tel:* 212-741-9110 *E-mail:* info@clmp.org *Web Site:* www.clmp.org, pg 504

Gibbs, David, Firecracker Awards, 154 Christopher St, Suite 3C, New York, NY 10014-9110 *Tel:* 212-741-9110 *E-mail:* info@clmp.org *Web Site:* www.clmp.org/firecracker, pg 602

Gibbs, Naomi, Pantheon Books, c/o Penguin Random House LLC, 1745 Broadway, New York, NY 10019 *Tel:* 212-751-2600 *Fax:* 212-940-7390 (dom rts); 212-572-2662 (foreign rts) *Web Site:* knopfdoubleday.com/imprint/pantheon/; knopfdoubleday.com, pg 150

Gibeley, Andrew, Harry N Abrams Inc, 195 Broadway, 9th fl, New York, NY 10007 *Tel:* 212-206-7715 *Toll Free Tel:* 800-345-1359 *Fax:* 212-645-8437 *E-mail:* abrams@abramsbooks.com; publicity@abramsbooks.com; sales@abramsbooks.com *Web Site:* www.abramsbooks.com, pg 3

Gibson, Amanda, Agate Publishing Academy, 1328 Greenleaf St, Evanston, IL 60202 *Tel:* 847-475-4457 *E-mail:* help@agatepublishingacademy.com *Web Site:* agatepublishingacademy.com, pg 561

Gibson, Angela, Modern Language Association (MLA), 85 Broad St, New York, NY 10004 Tel: 646-576-5000 E-mail: help@mla.org Web Site: www.mla.org; x.com/MLAnews; www.facebook.com/modernlanguageassociation; www.linkedin.com/company/modern-language-association, pg 133

Gibson, Angela, Modern Language Association (MLA), 85 Broad St, New York, NY 10004 Tel: 646-576-5000 E-mail: help@mla.org; membership@mla.org Web Site: www.mla.org; x.com/MLAnews; www.facebook.com/modernlanguageassociation; www.linkedin.com/company/modern-language-association, pg 511

Gibson, Bethany, Goose Lane Editions, 500 Beaverbrook Ct, Suite 330, Fredericton, NB E3B 5X4, Canada Tel: 506-450-4251 Toll Free Tel: 888-926-8377 Fax: 506-459-4991 E-mail: orders@gooselane.com Web Site: www.gooselane.com, pg 407

Gibson, Dan, American Political Science Association (APSA), 1527 New Hampshire Ave NW, Washington, DC 20036-1203 Tel: 202-483-2512 Fax: 202-483-2657 E-mail: apsa@apsanet.org; membership@apsanet.org; press@apsanet.org Web Site: www.apsanet.org, pg 496

Gibson, George, Grove Atlantic Inc, 154 W 14 St, 12th fl, New York, NY 10011 Tel: 212-614-7850 Toll Free Tel: 800-521-0178 Fax: 212-614-7886 E-mail: info@groveatlantic.com; sales@groveatlantic.com; publicity@groveatlantic.com; rights@groveatlantic.com Web Site: www.groveatlantic.com, pg 82

Gibson, Jack, International Risk Management Institute Inc, 12222 Merit Dr, Suite 1600, Dallas, TX 75251-2266 Tel: 972-960-7693 Fax: 972-371-5120 E-mail: info27@irmi.com Web Site: www.irmi.com, pg 103

Gibson, Maggie, Random House Children's Books, c/o Penguin Random House LLC, 1745 Broadway, New York, NY 10019 Tel: 212-782-9000 Web Site: www.rhcbooks.com, pg 170

Gibson, Sarah, Simon & Schuster Canada, 166 King St E, Suite 300, Toronto, ON M5A 1J3, Canada Tel: 647-427-8882 Toll Free Tel: 800-387-0446; 800-268-3216 (orders) Fax: 647-430-9446 Toll Free Fax: 888-849-8151 (orders) E-mail: info@simonandschuster.ca Web Site: www.simonandschuster.ca, pg 419

Giddens, Mary, SteinerBooks Inc, 610 Main St, Suite 1, Great Barrington, MA 01230 Tel: 413-528-8233 E-mail: service@steinerbooks.org; friends@steinerbooks.org Web Site: steiner.presswarehouse.com, pg 198

Gier, Lora, Trusted Media Brands Inc, 750 Third Ave, 3rd fl, New York, NY 10017 Tel: 646-293-6299 Toll Free Tel: 877-732-4438 (cust serv) Fax: 646-293-6251 E-mail: customercare@trustedmediabrands.com; press@trustedmediabrands.com Web Site: www.trustedmediabrands.com; www.rd.com, pg 210

Gieseke, Tyler, ABDO, 8000 W 78 St, Suite 310, Edina, MN 55439 Tel: 952-698-2403 Toll Free Tel: 800-800-1312 Fax: 952-831-1632 Toll Free Fax: 800-862-3480 E-mail: customerservice@abdobooks.com; info@abdobooks.com Web Site: abdobooks.com, pg 2

Gifford, James, Fairleigh Dickinson University Press, 842 Cambie St, Vancouver, BC V6B 2P6, Canada Tel: 604-648-4476 Fax: 604-648-4489 E-mail: fdupress@fdu.edu Web Site: www.fdupress.org, pg 405

Gifford, James M PhD, The Jesse Stuart Foundation (JSF), 4440 13 St, Ashland, KY 41102 Tel: 606-326-1667 Fax: 606-325-2519 E-mail: jsf@jsfbooks.com Web Site: www.jsfbooks.com, pg 200

Gifford, Jim, Simon & Schuster Canada, 166 King St E, Suite 300, Toronto, ON M5A 1J3, Canada Tel: 647-427-8882 Toll Free Tel: 800-387-0446; 800-268-3216 (orders) Fax: 647-430-9446 Toll Free Fax: 888-849-8151 (orders) E-mail: info@simonandschuster.ca Web Site: www.simonandschuster.ca, pg 419

Giffuni, Cathe, Research Research, 240 E 27 St, Suite 20-K, New York, NY 10016-9238 Tel: 212-779-9540 Fax: 212-779-9540 E-mail: ehtac@msn.com, pg 444

Gift, Patricia, Hay House LLC, PO Box 5100, Carlsbad, CA 92018-5100 Tel: 760-431-7695 (ext 1, intl) Toll Free Tel: 800-654-5126 (ext 1, US) Toll Free Fax: 800-650-5115 Web Site: www.hayhouse.com, pg 89

Gignilliat-Day, Leslie, Amber Lotus Publishing, PO Box 11329, Portland, OR 97211 Tel: 503-284-6400 Toll Free Tel: 800-326-2375 (orders only) Fax: 503-284-6417 E-mail: info@amberlotus.com; neworder@amberlotus.com Web Site: www.amberlotus.com, pg 8

Giguere, Melanie, Les Editions de Mortagne, CP 116, Boucherville, QC J4B 5E6, Canada Tel: 450-641-2387 E-mail: info@editionsdemortagne.com Web Site: editionsdemortagne.com, pg 402

Gil, Priscilla, National Paper Trade Association (NPTA), 330 N Wabash Ave, Suite 2000, Chicago, IL 60611 Tel: 312-321-4092 Toll Free Tel: 800-355-NPTA (355-6782) Fax: 312-673-6736 Web Site: www.gonpta.com, pg 513

Gil, Samantha, Workman Publishing, 1290 Avenue of the Americas, New York, NY 10104 Toll Free Tel: 800-759-0190 Fax: 212-364-0950 E-mail: workman-inquiry@hbgusa.com Web Site: www.hachettebookgroup.com/imprint/workman-publishing-company/, pg 233

Gilbert, Alexis, Grand Central Publishing, 1290 Avenue of the Americas, New York, NY 10104 Tel: 212-364-1100 Web Site: www.hachettebookgroup.com/imprint/grand-central-publishing/, pg 80

Gilbert, Cristina, Macmillan, 120 Broadway, 22nd fl, New York, NY 10271 E-mail: press.inquiries@macmillan.com Web Site: us.macmillan.com, pg 122

Gilbert, Deborah, Soul Mate Publishing, 3210 Sherwood Dr, Walworth, NY 14568 Web Site: www.soulmatepublishing.com, pg 194

Gilbert, Frances, Random House Children's Books, c/o Penguin Random House LLC, 1745 Broadway, New York, NY 10019 Tel: 212-782-9000 Web Site: www.rhcbooks.com, pg 170

Gilbert, Jon, Seven Stories Press, 140 Watts St, New York, NY 10013 Tel: 212-226-8760 Toll Free Tel: 800-733-3000 (orders) Fax: 212-226-1411 E-mail: sevenstories@sevenstories.com Web Site: www.sevenstories.com, pg 186

Gilbert, Lisa, Public Citizen, 1600 20 St NW, Washington, DC 20009 Tel: 202-588-1000 Web Site: www.citizen.org, pg 167

Gilbride, Tara, Portfolio, c/o Penguin Random House LLC, 1745 Broadway, New York, NY 10019 Tel: 212-782-9000 Web Site: www.penguin.com/portfolio-overview/; www.penguin.com/sentinel-overview/; www.penguin.com/thesis/, pg 162

Gildea, Kelly, Penguin Random House Audio Publishing Group, 1745 Broadway, New York, NY 10019 Toll Free Tel: 800-793-2665 (cust serv) E-mail: audio@penguinrandomhouse.com; ecustomerservice@penguinrandomhouse.com Web Site: www.penguinrandomhouseaudio.com, pg 154

Gildea, Matthew, Arcadia Publishing Inc, 210 Wingo Way, Suite 200, Mount Pleasant, SC 29464 Tel: 843-853-2070 E-mail: retailers@arcadiapublishing.com Web Site: www.arcadiapublishing.com, pg 16

Gilg, Erik, Fair Winds Press, 100 Cummings Ctr, Suite 265-D, Beverly, MA 01915 Tel: 978-282-9590 Fax: 978-282-7765 E-mail: sales@quarto.com Web Site: www.quartoknows.com, pg 69

Gilg, Kerstin, Individual Artist Fellowships, 25 State House Sta, 193 State St, Augusta, ME 04333-0025 Tel: 207-287-2724 Fax: 207-287-2725 E-mail: mainearts.maine.gov, pg 616

Gilhuly, Claire, Chronicle Books LLC, 680 Second St, San Francisco, CA 94107 Tel: 415-537-4200 Fax: 415-537-4460 (perms) E-mail: hello@chroniclebooks.com; subrights@chroniclebooks.com Web Site: www.chroniclebooks.com, pg 47

Gill, Caleb, University of Pittsburgh Press, 7500 Thomas Blvd, Pittsburgh, PA 15260 Tel: 412-383-2456 Fax: 412-383-2466 E-mail: info@upress.pitt.edu Web Site: www.upress.pitt.edu, pg 219

Gill, Craig, University Press of Mississippi, 3825 Ridgewood Rd, Jackson, MS 39211-6492 Tel: 601-432-6205 Toll Free Tel: 800-737-7788 (orders & cust serv) Fax: 601-432-6217 E-mail: press@mississippi.edu Web Site: www.upress.state.ms.us, pg 222

Gillan, Maria Mazziotti, Allen Ginsberg Poetry Award, One College Blvd, Paterson, NJ 07505-1179 Tel: 973-684-6555 Fax: 973-523-6085 Web Site: www.poetrycenterpccc.com, pg 606

Gillan, Maria Mazziotti, The Paterson Poetry Prize, One College Blvd, Paterson, NJ 07505-1179 Tel: 973-684-6555 Fax: 973-523-6085 Web Site: www.poetrycenterpccc.com, pg 646

Gillan, Maria Mazziotti, The Paterson Prize for Books for Young People, One College Blvd, Paterson, NJ 07505-1179 Tel: 973-684-6555 Fax: 973-523-6085 Web Site: www.poetrycenterpccc.com, pg 646

Gilles, Misti, Sagamore Publishing LLC, 3611 N Staley Rd, Suite B, Champaign, IL 61822 Tel: 217-359-5940 Toll Free Tel: 800-327-5557 (orders) Fax: 217-359-5975 E-mail: web@sagamorepub.com Web Site: www.sagamorepub.com, pg 180

Gilligan, Rev Michael PhD, American Catholic Press (ACP), 16565 S State St, South Holland, IL 60473 Tel: 708-331-5485 Fax: 708-331-5484 E-mail: acp@acpress.org Web Site: www.acpress.org, pg 9

Gillingham, Sara, Greystone Books Ltd, 343 Railway St, Suite 302, Vancouver, BC V6A 1A4, Canada Tel: 604-875-1550 Fax: 604-875-1556 E-mail: info@greystonebooks.com; rights@greystonebooks.com Web Site: www.greystonebooks.com, pg 407

Gillis, Claire, Access Copyright, The Canadian Copyright Licensing Agency, 69 Yonge St, Suite 1100, Toronto, ON M5E 1K3, Canada Tel: 416-868-1620 Toll Free Tel: 800-893-5777 Fax: 416-868-1621 E-mail: info@accesscopyright.ca Web Site: www.accesscopyright.ca, pg 493

Gillooly, Diana, Princeton University Press, 41 William St, Princeton, NJ 08540-5237 Tel: 609-258-4900 Fax: 609-258-6305 E-mail: info@press.princeton.edu Web Site: press.princeton.edu, pg 164

Gilly, Holly, Human Kinetics Inc, 1607 N Market St, Champaign, IL 61820 Tel: 217-351-5076 Toll Free Tel: 800-747-4457 Fax: 217-351-1549 (orders/cust serv) E-mail: info@hkusa.com Web Site: us.humankinetics.com, pg 97

Gilman, Dana S, J J Keller & Associates, Inc®, 3003 Breezewood Lane, Neenah, WI 54957 Tel: 920-722-2848 Toll Free Tel: 877-564-2333 Toll Free Fax: 800-727-7516 E-mail: customerservice@jjkeller.com; sales@jjkeller.com Web Site: www.jjkeller.com, pg 108

Gilman, Rachel, The Feminist Press at The City University of New York, 365 Fifth Ave, Suite 5406, New York, NY 10016 Tel: 212-817-7915 Fax: 212-817-1593 E-mail: info@feministpress.org Web Site: www.feministpress.org, pg 71

Gilmer, Rachel, Sourcebooks LLC, 1935 Brookdale Rd, Suite 139, Naperville, IL 60563 Tel: 630-961-3900 Toll Free Tel: 800-432-7444 Fax: 630-961-2168 E-mail: info@sourcebooks.com Web Site: www.sourcebooks.com, pg 194

Gilmore, David, Random House Children's Books, c/o Penguin Random House LLC, 1745 Broadway, New York, NY 10019 Tel: 212-782-9000 Web Site: www.rhcbooks.com, pg 170

Gilmore, David, The Society of Southwestern Authors (SSA), PO Box 30355, Tucson, AZ 85751-0355 Web Site: www.ssa-az.org, pg 520

Gilmore, David, The Society of Southwestern Authors Writing Contest, PO Box 30355, Tucson, AZ 85751-0355 E-mail: contest@ssa-az.org Web Site: www.ssa-az.org/contest.htm, pg 664

Gilo, Jessica, HarperCollins Publishers LLC, 195 Broadway, New York, NY 10007 Tel: 212-207-7000 Web Site: www.harpercollins.com, pg 86

Gilreath, Taylor, Potomac Books, c/o University of Nebraska Press, 1225 "L" St, Suite 200, Lincoln, NE 68588-0630 *Tel:* 402-472-5937 *Web Site:* www.nebraskapress.unl.edu/potomac/, pg 162

Gilson, Kristin, Simon & Schuster Children's Publishing, 1230 Avenue of the Americas, New York, NY 10020 *Tel:* 212-698-7000 *Web Site:* www.simonandschuster.com/kids; www.simonandschuster.com/teen; simonandschuster.net; simonandschuster.biz, pg 189

Gimenez, Carmen, Graywolf Press, 212 Third Ave N, Suite 485, Minneapolis, MN 55401 *Tel:* 651-641-0077 *Fax:* 651-641-0036 *E-mail:* wolves@graywolfpress.org (no ms queries, sample chapters or proposals) *Web Site:* www.graywolfpress.org, pg 81

Gingerich, Amy, Herald Press, PO Box 866, Harrisonburg, VA 22803 *Toll Free Tel:* 800-245-7894 (orders) *Tel:* 540-242-4476 *Toll Free Fax:* 877-271-0760 *E-mail:* info@mennomedia.org; customerservice@mennomedia.org *Web Site:* www.heraldpress.com; store.mennomedia.org, pg 91

Gingerich, Amy, MennoMedia, 841 Mount Clinton Pike, Harrisonburg, VA 22802 *Toll Free Tel:* 800-245-7894 (orders & cust serv US) *Toll Free Fax:* 877-271-0760 *E-mail:* info@mennomedia.org *Web Site:* www.mennomedia.org, pg 129

Gingerich, Jennifer, Thomas Nelson, 501 Nelson Place, Nashville, TN 37214 *Tel:* 615-889-9000 *Toll Free Tel:* 800-251-4000 *Web Site:* www.thomasnelson.com, pg 206

Gingras, Dominique, Les Presses de l'Universite Laval, 2180, Chemin Sainte-Foy, 1st fl, Quebec, QC G1V 0A6, Canada *Tel:* 418-656-2803 *Fax:* 418-656-3305 *E-mail:* presses@pul.ulaval.ca *Web Site:* www.pulaval.com, pg 417

Ginsberg, Daniel, Colorado Authors' League, 700 Colorado Blvd, Denver, CO 80206 *Tel:* 913-369-5040 *Web Site:* coloradoauthors.org, pg 504

Ginsberg, Peter L, Curtis Brown, Ltd, 228 E 45 St, Suite 310, New York, NY 10017 *Tel:* 212-473-5400 *Fax:* 212-598-0917 *E-mail:* info@cbltd.com *Web Site:* www.curtisbrown.com, pg 452

Ginsburg, Susan, Writers House, 21 W 26 St, New York, NY 10010 *Tel:* 212-685-2400 *Web Site:* www.writershouse.com, pg 482

Giovinazzo, Elena, Pippin Properties Inc, 110 W 40 St, Suite 1704, New York, NY 10018 *Tel:* 212-338-9310 *E-mail:* info@pippinproperties.com *Web Site:* www.pippinproperties.com; www.facebook.com/pippinproperties, pg 472

Giovino, Vanessa, Kids Can Press Ltd, 25 Dockside Dr, Toronto, ON M5A 0B5, Canada *Tel:* 416-479-7000 *Toll Free Tel:* 800-265-0884 *Fax:* 416-960-5437 *E-mail:* info@kidscan.com; customerservice@kidscan.com *Web Site:* www.kidscanpress.com; www.kidscanpress.ca, pg 411

Gipson, Scott, Caxton Press, 312 Main St, Caldwell, ID 83605-3299 *Tel:* 208-459-7421 *Toll Free Tel:* 800-657-6465 *Fax:* 208-459-7450 *E-mail:* publish@caxtonpress.com *Web Site:* www.caxtonpress.com, pg 42

Girard, Guylaine, Les Editions XYZ inc, 1815, ave De Lorimier, Montreal, QC H2K 3W6, Canada *Tel:* 514-525-2170 *Fax:* 514-525-7537 *E-mail:* info@editionsxyz.com *Web Site:* editionsxyz.com, pg 405

Girard, Melissa, Emmaus Road Publishing Inc, 1468 Parkview Circle, Steubenville, OH 43952 *Tel:* 750-264-9535 *Fax:* 740-475-0230 (orders) *E-mail:* questions@emmausroad.org *Web Site:* stpaulcenter.com/emmaus-road-publishing, pg 66

Girard, Sara, AIP Publishing LLC, 1305 Walt Whitman Rd, Suite 110, Melville, NY 11747 *Tel:* 516-576-2200 *E-mail:* help@aip.org; press@aip.org; rights@aip.org *Web Site:* www.aip.org; publishing.aip.org, pg 6

Girdy, Bre'Anna, Kensington Publishing Corp, 900 Third Ave, 26th fl, New York, NY 10022 *Tel:* 212-407-1500 *Toll Free Tel:* 800-221-2647 *Fax:* 212-935-0699 *Web Site:* www.kensingtonbooks.com, pg 109

Giron, Robert L, Gival Press Oscar Wilde Award, PO Box 3812, Arlington, VA 22203 *Tel:* 703-351-0079 *Fax:* 703-351-0079 (call first) *E-mail:* givalpress@yahoo.com *Web Site:* www.givalpress.com; givalpress.submittable.com, pg 606

Giron, Robert L, Gival Press Short Story Award, PO Box 3812, Arlington, VA 22203 *Tel:* 703-351-0079 *Fax:* 703-351-0079 (call first) *E-mail:* givalpress@yahoo.com *Web Site:* www.givalpress.com; givalpress.submittable.com, pg 607

Giroux, Steve, Teacher's Discovery®, 2741 Paldan Dr, Auburn Hills, MI 48326 *Toll Free Tel:* 800-TEACHER (832-2437) *Toll Free Fax:* 800-287-4509 *E-mail:* help@teachersdiscovery.com; orders@teachersdiscovery.com *Web Site:* www.teachersdiscovery.com, pg 204

Girsch, Laurie Y, Professional Resource Press, 5864 Elegant Orchid Way, Sarasota, FL 34232 *Tel:* 941-343-9601 *Toll Free Tel:* 800-443-3364 (orders & cust serv) *Fax:* 941-343-9201 *Toll Free Fax:* 866-804-4843 (orders only) *E-mail:* cs@prpress.com *Web Site:* www.prpress.com, pg 165

Gissinger-Rivera, Beth, Adams Media, 100 Technology Center Dr, Suite 501, Stoughton, MA 02072 *Tel:* 508-427-7100 *Web Site:* www.simonandschuster.com, pg 4

Gittis, Brian, Farrar, Straus & Giroux, LLC, 120 Broadway, New York, NY 10271 *Tel:* 212-741-6900 *E-mail:* fsg.publicity@fsgbooks.com; sales@fsgbooks.com *Web Site:* us.macmillan.com/fsg, pg 70

Gittis, Brian, Picador, 120 Broadway, New York, NY 10271 *Tel:* 646-307-5151 *Fax:* 212-253-9627 *E-mail:* publicity@picadorusa.com *Web Site:* us.macmillan.com/picador, pg 159

Giuffrida, Amy, The Jennifer DeChiara Literary Agency, 245 Park Ave, 39th fl, New York, NY 10167 *Tel:* 212-372-8989 *Web Site:* www.jdlit.com, pg 455

Givens, Ivy, HarperCollins Publishers LLC, 195 Broadway, New York, NY 10007 *Tel:* 212-207-7000 *Web Site:* www.harpercollins.com, pg 87

Glaser, Jane, Viking Penguin, c/o Penguin Random House LLC, 1745 Broadway, New York, NY 10019 *Tel:* 212-782-9000 *Web Site:* www.penguin.com/overview-vikingbooks/; www.penguin.com/pamela-dorman-books-overview/; www.penguin.com/penguin-classics-overview/; www.penguin.com/penguin-life-overview/, pg 225

Glaser, Rebecca, Amicus, PO Box 227, Mankato, MN 56002 *Tel:* 507-388-9357 *Toll Free Tel:* 800-445-6209 (cust serv/orders) *E-mail:* info@thecreativecompany.us (gen inquiries); orders@thecreativecompany.us (cust serv) *Web Site:* amicuspublishing.us, pg 13

Glasner, Lynne, Associated Editors, 27 W 96 St, New York, NY 10025 *Tel:* 917-744-3481; 212-662-9703, pg 435

Glass, Jeanne, The Writers' Colony at Dairy Hollow, 515 Spring St, Eureka Springs, AR 72632 *Tel:* 479-253-7444 *E-mail:* director@writerscolony.org *Web Site:* www.writerscolony.org, pg 558

Glass, Joy L, Edgewise Press Inc, 24 Fifth Ave, Suite 224, New York, NY 10011 *Tel:* 212-387-0931 *E-mail:* epinc@mindspring.com *Web Site:* www.edgewisepress.org, pg 63

Glasser, Carla, The Betsy Nolan Literary Agency, 112 E 17 St, Suite 1W, New York, NY 10003 *Tel:* 212-967-8200 *Web Site:* www.nolanlehrgroup.com, pg 471

Glatt, Jane, SF Canada, c/o Jane Glatt, 35 Southshore Crescent, No 103, Hamilton, ON L8E 0J2, Canada *Web Site:* www.sfcanada.org, pg 519

Glave, Thomas, Binghamton University Creative Writing Program, c/o Dept of English, General Literature & Rhetoric, PO Box 6000, Binghamton, NY 13902-6000 *Tel:* 607-777-2168 *Fax:* 607-777-2408 *E-mail:* cwpro@binghamton.edu *Web Site:* www.binghamton.edu/english/creative-writing/index.html, pg 561

Glaz, Linda, Hartline Literary Agency LLC, 123 Queenston Dr, Pittsburgh, PA 15235 *Tel:* 412-829-2483 *Toll Free Fax:* 888-279-6007 *Web Site:* www.hartlineliterary.com, pg 462

Glazer, Lori, Houghton Mifflin Harcourt Trade & Reference Division, 125 High St, Boston, MA 02110 *Tel:* 617-351-5000 *Web Site:* www.hmhco.com, pg 96

Glazner, Steve, APPA - Leadership in Education Facilities, 1643 Prince St, Alexandria, VA 22314-2818 *Tel:* 703-684-1446; 703-542-3837 (bookshop) *E-mail:* webmaster@appa.org *Web Site:* www.appa.org, pg 15

Gleason, Alexander, American Institute for Economic Research (AIER), 250 Division St, Great Barrington, MA 01230 *Tel:* 413-528-1216 *Toll Free Tel:* 888-528-1216 (orders) *Fax:* 413-528-0103 *E-mail:* press@aier.org; submissions@aier.org *Web Site:* www.aier.org, pg 10

Gleason, Ben, Wisdom Publications Inc, 199 Elm St, Somerville, MA 02144 *Tel:* 617-776-7416 *Toll Free Tel:* 800-272-4050 (orders) *Fax:* 617-776-7841 *E-mail:* submission@wisdompubs.org *Web Site:* wisdomexperience.org, pg 231

Gleason, Bill, Society for Mining, Metallurgy & Exploration, 12999 E Adam Aircraft Circle, Englewood, CO 80112 *Tel:* 303-948-4200 *Toll Free Tel:* 800-763-3132 *Fax:* 303-973-3845 *E-mail:* cs@smenet.org; books@smenet.org *Web Site:* www.smenet.org, pg 192

Gleason, Bob, Tor Publishing Group, 120 Broadway, New York, NY 10271 *Toll Free Tel:* 800-455-0340 (Macmillan) *E-mail:* torpublicity@tor.com; forgepublicity@forgebooks.com *Web Site:* us.macmillan.com/torpublishinggroup, pg 208

Gleason, Carrie, James Lorimer & Co Ltd, Publishers, 117 Peter St, Suite 304, Toronto, ON M5V 0M3, Canada *Tel:* 416-362-4762 *Fax:* 416-362-3939 *E-mail:* sales@lorimer.ca; promotion@lorimer.ca; rights@lorimer.ca *Web Site:* www.lorimer.ca, pg 412

Gleason, Cathy, Gelfman Schneider Literary Agents Inc, 850 Seventh Ave, Suite 903, New York, NY 10019 *Tel:* 212-245-1993 *E-mail:* mail@gelfmanschneider.com *Web Site:* gelfmanschneider.com, pg 460

Gleason, Jeff, Reed Environmental Writing Award, 201 W Main St, Suite 14, Charlottesville, VA 22902 *Tel:* 434-977-4090 *Fax:* 434-977-1483 *Web Site:* www.southernenvironment.org, pg 655

Gleaves, Jeff, Academy of American Poets Fellowship, 75 Maiden Lane, Suite 901, New York, NY 10038 *Tel:* 212-274-0343 *E-mail:* awards@poets.org *Web Site:* poets.org/academy-american-poets/prizes/academy-american-poets-fellowship, pg 569

Gleaves, Jeff, Academy of American Poets First Book Award, 75 Maiden Lane, Suite 901, New York, NY 10038 *Tel:* 212-274-0343 *E-mail:* awards@poets.org *Web Site:* poets.org/academy-american-poets/prizes/first-book-award, pg 569

Gleaves, Jeff, The Academy of American Poets Inc, 75 Maiden Lane, Suite 901, New York, NY 10038 *Tel:* 212-274-0343 *E-mail:* academy@poets.org *Web Site:* poets.org, pg 493

Gleaves, Jeff, Ambroggio Prize, 75 Maiden Lane, Suite 901, New York, NY 10038 *Tel:* 212-274-0343 *E-mail:* awards@poets.org *Web Site:* poets.org/academy-american-poets/prizes/ambroggio-prize, pg 572

Gleaves, Jeff, James Laughlin Award, 75 Maiden Lane, Suite 901, New York, NY 10038 *Tel:* 212-274-0343 *E-mail:* awards@poets.org *Web Site:* poets.org/academy-american-poets/prizes/james-laughlin-award, pg 622

Gleaves, Jeff, Lenore Marshall Poetry Prize, 75 Maiden Lane, Suite 901, New York, NY 10038 *Tel:* 212-274-0343 *E-mail:* awards@poets.org *Web Site:* poets.org/academy-american-poets/prizes/lenore-marshall-poetry-prize, pg 629

Gleaves, Jeff, Harold Morton Landon Translation Award, 75 Maiden Lane, Suite 901, New York, NY 10038 *Tel:* 212-274-0343 *E-mail:* awards@poets.org *Web Site:* poets.org/academy-american-poets/prizes/harold-morton-landon-translation-award, pg 635

Gleaves, Jeff, Aliki Perroti & Seth Frank Most Promising Young Poet Award, 75 Maiden Lane, Suite 901, New York, NY 10038 *Tel:* 212-274-0343 *E-mail:* awards@poets.org *Web Site:* poets.org/academy-american-poets/american-poets-prizes, pg 649

Gleaves, Jeff, Raiziss/de Palchi Fellowship, 75 Maiden Lane, Suite 901, New York, NY 10038 *Tel:* 212-274-0343 *E-mail:* awards@poets.org *Web Site:* poets.org/academy-american-poets/american-poets-prizes, pg 654

Gleaves, Jeff, Wallace Stevens Award, 75 Maiden Lane, Suite 901, New York, NY 10038 *Tel:* 212-274-0343 *E-mail:* awards@poets.org *Web Site:* poets.org/academy-american-poets/prizes/wallace-stevens-award, pg 666

Gleaves, Jeff, Treehouse Climate Action Poem Prize, 75 Maiden Lane, Suite 901, New York, NY 10038 *Tel:* 212-274-0343 *E-mail:* awards@poets.org *Web Site:* poets.org, pg 670

Gleick, Betsy, Little, Brown and Company, 1290 Avenue of the Americas, New York, NY 10104 *Tel:* 212-364-1100 *Fax:* 212-364-0952 *E-mail:* firstname.lastname@hbgusa.com *Web Site:* www.hachettebookgroup.com/imprint/little-brown-and-company/, pg 118

Glemot, Suzanne, University of Iowa Press, 119 W Park Rd, 100 Kuhl House, Iowa City, IA 52242-1000 *Tel:* 319-335-2000 *Toll Free Tel:* 800-621-2736 (orders only) *Fax:* 319-335-2055 *Toll Free Fax:* 800-621-8476 (orders only) *E-mail:* uipress@uiowa.edu *Web Site:* www.uipress.uiowa.edu, pg 217

Glenn, Heather, Ave Maria Press Inc, PO Box 428, Notre Dame, IN 46556 *Toll Free Tel:* 800-282-1865 *Toll Free Fax:* 800-282-5681 *E-mail:* avemariapress.1@nd.edu *Web Site:* www.avemariapress.com, pg 22

Glenn, Mary, United Nations Publications, 405 E 42 St, 11th fl, New York, NY 10017 *Tel:* 703-661-1571 *E-mail:* publications@un.org *Web Site:* shop.un.org, pg 213

Glennon, Robin, Abingdon Press, 810 12 Ave S, Nashville, TN 37203 *Toll Free Tel:* 800-251-3320 *E-mail:* orders@abingdonpress.com; permissions@abingdonpress.com *Web Site:* www.abingdonpress.com, pg 2

Glesne, Mark, Zondervan, 3900 Sparks Dr SE, Grand Rapids, MI 49546 *Tel:* 616-698-6900 *Toll Free Tel:* 800-226-1122; 800-727-1309 (retail orders) *Fax:* 616-698-3350 *Toll Free Fax:* 800-698-3256 (retail orders) *E-mail:* customercare@harpercollins.com *Web Site:* www.zondervan.com, pg 236

Glibbery, Jessey, Groundwood Books, 128 Sterling Rd, Lower Level, Toronto, ON M6R 2B7, Canada *Tel:* 416-363-4343 *Fax:* 416-363-1017 *E-mail:* customerservice@houseofanansi.com *Web Site:* www.houseofanansi.com, pg 407

Glibbery, Jessey, House of Anansi Press Inc, 128 Sterling Rd, Lower Level, Toronto, ON M6R 2B7, Canada *Tel:* 416-363-4343 *Fax:* 416-363-1017 *E-mail:* customerservice@houseofanansi.com *Web Site:* houseofanansi.com, pg 409

Glick, Jonathan, Chronicle Books LLC, 680 Second St, San Francisco, CA 94107 *Tel:* 415-537-4200 *Fax:* 415-537-4460 (perms) *E-mail:* hello@chroniclebooks.com; subrights@chroniclebooks.com *Web Site:* www.chroniclebooks.com, pg 48

Glick, Stacey Kendall, Dystel, Goderich & Bourret LLC, One Union Sq W, Suite 904, New York, NY 10003 *Tel:* 212-627-9100 *Fax:* 212-627-9313 *Web Site:* www.dystel.com, pg 449

Glidden, Hanna, Random House Children's Books, c/o Penguin Random House LLC, 1745 Broadway, New York, NY 10019 *Tel:* 212-782-9000 *Web Site:* www.rhcbooks.com, pg 169

Glidden-Lyon, Sophie, Theatre Library Association (TLA), c/o The New York Public Library for the Performing Arts, 40 Lincoln Center Plaza, New York, NY 10023 *E-mail:* theatrelibraryassociation@gmail.com *Web Site:* www.tla-online.org, pg 521

Glider, Kate, Random House Children's Books, c/o Penguin Random House LLC, 1745 Broadway, New York, NY 10019 *Tel:* 212-782-9000 *Web Site:* www.rhcbooks.com, pg 170

Globenfelt, Mike, Florida Outdoor Writers Association Inc (FOWA), 235 Apollo Beach Blvd, Unit 271, Apollo Beach, FL 33572 *Tel:* 813-579-0990 *E-mail:* info@fowa.org *Web Site:* www.fowa.org, pg 506

Glosband, Oliver, Shambhala Publications Inc, 2129 13 St, Boulder, CO 80302 *Tel:* 978-829-2599 (intl callers) *Toll Free Tel:* 866-424-0030 (off); 888-424-2329 (orders & cust serv) *Fax:* 617-236-1563 *E-mail:* customercare@shambhala.com; royalties@shambhala.com *Web Site:* www.shambhala.com, pg 187

Gloude, Carolyn, Ruth & Sylvia Schwartz Children's Book Awards, c/o Ontario Arts Council, 121 Bloor St E, 7th fl, Toronto, ON M4W 3M5, Canada *Tel:* 416-961-1660 *Toll Free Tel:* 800-387-0058 (ON) *Fax:* 416-961-7796 (Ontario Arts Council) *E-mail:* info@oafdn.ca (Ontario Arts Foundation); info@arts.on.ca (Ontario Arts Council) *Web Site:* www.arts.on.ca; www.oafdn.ca/pages/ruth-sylvia-schwartz-awards, pg 661

Glover, Elizabeth, University of Pennsylvania Press, 3905 Spruce St, Philadelphia, PA 19104 *Tel:* 215-898-6261 *Fax:* 215-898-0404 *E-mail:* custserv@pobox.upenn.edu *Web Site:* www.pennpress.org, pg 219

Glover, Kelly, Penguin Random House Canada, a Penguin Random House company, 320 Front St W, Suite 1400, Toronto, ON M5V 3B6, Canada *Tel:* 416-364-4449 *Toll Free Tel:* 888-523-9292 (cust serv) *E-mail:* canadaweb@penguinrandomhouse.com; customerservicescanada@penguinrandomhouse.com *Web Site:* www.penguinrandomhouse.ca, pg 416

Glover, Sally, Lynne Rienner Publishers Inc, 1800 30 St, Suite 314, Boulder, CO 80301 *Tel:* 303-444-6684 *Fax:* 303-444-0824 *E-mail:* questions@rienner.com; cservice@rienner.com *Web Site:* www.rienner.com, pg 174

Glusman, John, W W Norton & Company Inc, 500 Fifth Ave, New York, NY 10110-0017 *Tel:* 212-354-5500 *Toll Free Tel:* 800-233-4830 (orders & cust serv) *Fax:* 212-869-0856 *Toll Free Fax:* 800-458-6515 *E-mail:* orders@wwnorton.com *Web Site:* wwnorton.com, pg 143

Go, Sarah Lin, Chronicle Books LLC, 680 Second St, San Francisco, CA 94107 *Tel:* 415-537-4200 *Fax:* 415-537-4460 (perms) *E-mail:* hello@chroniclebooks.com; subrights@chroniclebooks.com *Web Site:* www.chroniclebooks.com, pg 48

Gobel, Ursula, Social Sciences & Humanities Research Council (SSHRC), 350 Albert St, Ottawa, ON K1P 6G4, Canada *Tel:* 613-995-4273 *Toll Free Tel:* 855-275-2861 *E-mail:* research@sshrc-crsh.gc.ca *Web Site:* www.sshrc-crsh.gc.ca, pg 519

Gocke, Meghan, Houghton Mifflin Harcourt, 125 High St, Boston, MA 02110 *Tel:* 617-351-5000 *Toll Free Tel:* 855-969-4642; 800-225-5425 (K-12 educ materials); 800-323-9540 (assessment materials); 877-219-1537 (SkillsTutor); 888-242-6747 (Innovation in Educ Group); 800-225-3362 (Trade & Ref Div) *Toll Free Fax:* 800-269-5232 *E-mail:* myhmhco@hmhco.com *Web Site:* www.hmhco.com, pg 96

Gocke, Meghan, Houghton Mifflin Harcourt Trade & Reference Division, 125 High St, Boston, MA 02110 *Tel:* 617-351-5000 *Web Site:* www.hmhco.com, pg 96

Goderich, Miriam, Dystel, Goderich & Bourret LLC, One Union Sq W, Suite 904, New York, NY 10003 *Tel:* 212-627-9100 *Fax:* 212-627-9313 *Web Site:* www.dystel.com, pg 457

Godfrey, Katie, St Augustine's Press Inc, PO Box 2285, South Bend, IN 46680-2285 *Tel:* 574-291-3500 *Fax:* 574-291-3700 *Web Site:* www.staugustine.net, pg 180

Godin, Lynda, Ordre des traducteurs, terminologues et interpretes agrees du quebec (OTTIAQ), 1108-2021 Ave Union, Montreal, QC H3A 2S9, Canada *Tel:* 514-845-4411 *Toll Free Tel:* 800-265-4815 *Fax:* 514-845-9903 *E-mail:* info@ottiaq.org; direction@ottiaq.org; reception@ottiaq.org; communications@ottiaq.org *Web Site:* www.ottiaq.org, pg 516

Godlasky, Anne, National Press Foundation, 1211 Connecticut Ave NW, Suite 310, Washington, DC 20036 *Tel:* 202-663-7286 *Web Site:* nationalpress.org, pg 526

Godoff, Ann, Penguin Press, c/o Penguin Random House LLC, 1745 Broadway, New York, NY 10019 *Tel:* 212-782-9000 *E-mail:* penguinpress@penguinrandomhouse.com *Web Site:* www.penguin.com/penguin-press-overview/, pg 154

Godoff, Ann, Penguin Publishing Group, c/o Penguin Random House LLC, 1745 Broadway, New York, NY 10019 *Tel:* 212-782-9000 *Web Site:* www.penguin.com, pg 154

Godwin, Laura, Henry Holt and Company, LLC, 120 Broadway, 23rd fl, New York, NY 10271 *Tel:* 646-307-5151 *Toll Free Tel:* 888-330-8477 (orders) *Fax:* 646-307-5285 *Web Site:* www.henryholt.com, pg 94

Godzieba, Matt, Penguin Random House LLC, 1745 Broadway, New York, NY 10019 *Tel:* 212-782-9000 *Toll Free Tel:* 800-726-0600 *Web Site:* www.penguinrandomhouse.com, pg 155

Goel, Sonali, Macmillan, 120 Broadway, 22nd fl, New York, NY 10271 *E-mail:* press.inquiries@macmillan.com *Web Site:* us.macmillan.com, pg 122

Goeser, Nicholas J PhD, Soil Science Society of America (SSSA), 5585 Guilford Rd, Madison, WI 53711-5801 *Tel:* 608-273-8080 *Fax:* 608-273-2021 *Web Site:* www.soils.org, pg 193

Goetz, Barbara, Small Business Advisors Inc, 2005 Park St, Atlantic Beach, NY 11509 *Tel:* 516-374-1387 *Fax:* 516-374-1175 *E-mail:* info@smallbusinessadvice.com *Web Site:* www.smallbusinessadvice.com, pg 191

Goff, Ellen, HG Literary, 6 W 18 St, Suite 7R, New York, NY 10011 *E-mail:* foreign@hgliterary.com; rights@hgliterary.com *Web Site:* www.hgliterary.com, pg 463

Goff, Gordon, ORO editions, 31 Commercial Blvd, Suite F, Novato, CA 94949 *Tel:* 415-883-3300 *Fax:* 415-883-3309 *E-mail:* info@oroeditions.com *Web Site:* www.oroeditions.com, pg 148

Goff, Jacqui, Insight Editions, 800 "A" St, San Rafael, CA 94901 *Tel:* 415-526-1370 *Toll Free Tel:* 800-809-3792 *Toll Free Fax:* 866-509-0515 *E-mail:* info@insighteditions.com; marketing@insighteditions.com *Web Site:* insighteditions.com, pg 101

Goff, Jacqui, Mandala Earth, 800 "A" St, San Rafael, CA 94901 *Tel:* 415-526-1370 *Toll Free Fax:* 866-509-0515 *E-mail:* info@mandalapublishing.com *Web Site:* www.mandalaeartheditions.com, pg 124

Goff, Michaela, Casemate | publishers, 1950 Lawrence Rd, Havertown, PA 19083 *Tel:* 610-853-9131 *Fax:* 610-853-9146 *E-mail:* casemate@casematepublishers.com *Web Site:* www.casematepublishers.com, pg 41

Goff, Raoul, Insight Editions, 800 "A" St, San Rafael, CA 94901 *Tel:* 415-526-1370 *Toll Free Tel:* 800-809-3792 *Toll Free Fax:* 866-509-0515 *E-mail:* info@insighteditions.com; marketing@insighteditions.com *Web Site:* insighteditions.com, pg 101

Goff, Raoul, Mandala Earth, 800 "A" St, San Rafael, CA 94901 *Tel:* 415-526-1370 *Toll Free Fax:* 866-509-0515 *E-mail:* info@mandalapublishing.com *Web Site:* www.mandalaeartheditions.com, pg 124

Goff, Sam, Chronicle Books LLC, 680 Second St, San Francisco, CA 94107 *Tel:* 415-537-4200 *Fax:* 415-537-4460 (perms) *E-mail:* hello@chroniclebooks.com; subrights@chroniclebooks.com *Web Site:* www.chroniclebooks.com, pg 47

Goggins, Rebecca Miller, The Carle Honors, 125 W Bay Rd, Amherst, MA 01002 *Tel:* 413-559-6300 *E-mail:* info@carlemuseum.org *Web Site:* www.carlemuseum.org/content/carle-honors, pg 586

Goh, Jaymee, Tachyon Publications LLC, 1459 18 St, No 139, San Francisco, CA 94107 Tel: 415-285-5615 E-mail: tachyon@tachyonpublications.com; submissions@tachyonpublications.com Web Site: www.tachyonpublications.com, pg 202

Gold, Heather, Yale University Press, 302 Temple St, New Haven, CT 06511-8909 Tel: 203-432-0960; 203-432-0966 (sales); 401-531-2800 (cust serv) Toll Free Tel: 800-405-1619 (cust serv) Fax: 203-432-0948; 203-432-8485 (sales); 401-531-2801 (cust serv) Toll Free Fax: 800-406-9145 (cust serv) E-mail: sales.press@yale.edu (sales); customer.care@triliteral.org (cust serv) Web Site: www.yalebooks.com; yalepress.yale.edu/yupbooks, pg 235

Gold, Ilana, Workman Publishing, 1290 Avenue of the Americas, New York, NY 10104 Toll Free Tel: 800-759-0190 Fax: 212-364-0950 E-mail: workman-inquiry@hbgusa.com Web Site: www.hachettebookgroup.com/imprint/workman-publishing-company/, pg 232

Gold, Jerry, Black Heron Press, PO Box 614, Anacortes, WA 98221 Tel: 360-899-9335 Web Site: blackheronpress.com, pg 30

Gold, Leslie J, PRB Productions, 963 Peralta Ave, Albany, CA 94706-2144 Tel: 510-526-0722 E-mail: prbprdns@aol.com Web Site: www.prbmusic.com, pg 163

Gold, Maxwell, Horror Writers Association (HWA), PO Box 56687, Sherman Oaks, CA 91413 Tel: 818-220-3965 E-mail: admin@horror.org; membership@horror.org Web Site: horror.org, pg 507

Goldbaum, Milton J, Alan Wofsy Fine Arts, 1109 Geary Blvd, San Francisco, CA 94109 Tel: 415-292-6500 Toll Free Tel: 800-660-6403 Fax: 415-292-6594 (off & cust serv); 510-251-1840 (acctg) E-mail: order@art-books.com (orders); editeur@earthlink.net (edit); beauxarts@earthlink.net (cust serv) Web Site: www.art-books.com, pg 231

Goldberg, David, The MIT Press, One Broadway, 12th fl, Cambridge, MA 02142 Tel: 617-253-5255 Toll Free Tel: 800-405-1619 (orders) Fax: 617-258-6779; 617-577-1545 (orders) Web Site: mitpress.mit.edu, pg 132

Goldberg, David, Steerforth Press & Services, 31 Hanover St, Suite 1, Lebanon, NH 03766 Tel: 603-643-4787 Fax: 603-643-4788 E-mail: info@steerforth.com Web Site: www.steerforth.com, pg 198

Goldberg, Debra, Sami Rohr Prize for Jewish Literature, 452 Fifth Ave, 24th fl, New York, NY 10018 Tel: 516-548-3921 Web Site: www.samirohrprize.org, pg 657

Goldberg, Madeline, DAW Books, 19 W 21 St, No 1201, New York, NY 10010 E-mail: info@astrapublishinghouse.com Web Site: astrapublishinghouse.com/imprints/daw-books, pg 57

Goldberg, Michael, MedMaster Inc, 360 NE 191 St, Miami, FL 33179 Tel: 954-962-8414 E-mail: info@medmaster.net Web Site: www.medmaster.net, pg 129

Goldberg, Stephen, MedMaster Inc, 360 NE 191 St, Miami, FL 33179 Tel: 954-962-8414 E-mail: info@medmaster.net Web Site: www.medmaster.net, pg 129

Goldberg, Sylvan, ASLE Graduate Student Paper Awards, PO Box 502, Keene, NH 03431-0502 Tel: 603-357-7411 Fax: 603-357-7411 Web Site: www.asle.org/research-write/asle-book-paper-awards, pg 575

Goldbetter, Larry, National Writers Union (NWU), 61 Broadway, Suite 1630, New York, NY 10006 Tel: 315-545-5034 E-mail: nwu@nwu.org Web Site: nwu.org, pg 514

Golden, Lori, Health Communications Inc, 301 Crawford Blvd, Suite 200, Boca Raton, FL 33432 Tel: 561-453-0696 Toll Free Tel: 800-441-5569 (cust serv & orders) Fax: 561-453-1009 Toll Free Fax: 800-943-9831 (orders) E-mail: editorial@hcibooks.com Web Site: hcibooks.com, pg 90

Goldenberg, Lauren, Cullman Center Fellowships, New York Public Library, Stephen A Schwarzman Bldg, Fifth Ave & 42 St, Rm 225, New York, NY 10018-2788 Tel: 917-275-6975 E-mail: csw@nypl.org Web Site: www.nypl.org/help/about-nypl/fellowships-institutes, pg 594

Goldfarb, Ronald L, Goldfarb & Associates, 721 Gibbon St, Alexandria, VA 22314 Tel: 202-466-3030 E-mail: rlglawlit@gmail.com Web Site: www.ronaldgoldfarb.com, pg 460

Golding, Jennifer, Macmillan, 120 Broadway, 22nd fl, New York, NY 10271 E-mail: press.inquiries@macmillan.com Web Site: us.macmillan.com, pg 122

Golding, Melissa, Macmillan, 120 Broadway, 22nd fl, New York, NY 10271 E-mail: press.inquiries@macmillan.com Web Site: us.macmillan.com, pg 122

Goldinger, Sharon, PeopleSpeak, 24338 El Toro Rd, No E227, Laguna Woods, CA 92637 Tel: 949-581-6190 Fax: 949-581-4958 E-mail: pplspeak@att.net Web Site: www.peoplespeakservices.com, pg 443

Goldklang, Janice, Other Press, 267 Fifth Ave, 6th fl, New York, NY 10016 Tel: 212-414-0054 Toll Free Tel: 877-THEOTHER (843-6843) Fax: 212-414-0939 E-mail: editor@otherpress.com; marketing@otherpress.com; publicity@otherpress.com Web Site: otherpress.com, pg 148

Goldman, Becca, Pants On Fire Press, 10441 Waterbird Way, Bradenton, FL 34209 Tel: 941-405-3078 E-mail: submission@pantsonfirepress.com Web Site: www.pantsonfirepress.com, pg 150

Goldman, Emily, Tor Publishing Group, 120 Broadway, New York, NY 10271 Toll Free Tel: 800-455-0340 (Macmillan) E-mail: torpublicity@tor.com; forgepublicity@forgebooks.com Web Site: us.macmillan.com/torpublishinggroup, pg 208

Goldman, Erika, Bellevue Literary Press, 90 Broad St, Suite 2100, New York, NY 10004 Tel: 917-732-3603 Web Site: blpress.org, pg 27

Goldman, Gloria, Judaica Press Inc, 123 Ditmas Ave, Brooklyn, NY 11218 Tel: 718-972-6200 Toll Free Tel: 800-972-6201 Fax: 718-972-6204 E-mail: info@judaicapress.com; orders@judaicapress.com; submissions@judaicapress.com Web Site: www.judaicapress.com, pg 107

Goldman, Gloria, Soncino Press Ltd, 123 Ditmas Ave, Brooklyn, NY 11218 Tel: 718-972-6200 Toll Free Tel: 800-972-6201 Fax: 718-972-6204 E-mail: info@soncino.com Web Site: www.soncino.com, pg 193

Goldman, Jeffrey, Santa Monica Press LLC, 249 S Hwy 101, No 301, Solana Beach, CA 92075 Tel: 858-832-7906 Toll Free Tel: 800-784-9553 E-mail: books@santamonicapress.com; acquisitions@santamonicapress.com (edit submissions) Web Site: www.santamonicapress.com, pg 182

Goldman, Lea, IRP editeur, CP 68, succursale St-Dominique, Montreal, QC H2S 3K6, Canada Tel: 514-382-3000 E-mail: info@irpcanada.com Web Site: www.irpcanada.com, pg 410

Goldman, Paul, IRP editeur, CP 68, succursale St-Dominique, Montreal, QC H2S 3K6, Canada Tel: 514-382-3000 E-mail: info@irpcanada.com Web Site: www.irpcanada.com, pg 410

Goldmintz, Benny, Penguin Random House Audio Publishing Group, 1745 Broadway, New York, NY 10019 Toll Free Tel: 800-793-2665 (cust serv) E-mail: audio@penguinrandomhouse.com; ecustomerservice@penguinrandomhouse.com Web Site: www.penguinrandomhouseaudio.com, pg 154

Goldsack, Felicity, Casemate | publishers, 1950 Lawrence Rd, Havertown, PA 19083 Tel: 610-853-9131 Fax: 610-853-9146 E-mail: casemate@casematepublishers.com Web Site: www.casematepublishers.com, pg 42

Goldschein, Joe, St Martin's Press, LLC, 120 Broadway, New York, NY 10271 E-mail: publicity@stmartins.com; trademarketing@stmartins.com; foreignrights@stmartins.com Web Site: us.macmillan.com/smp, pg 180

Goldsmith, Andy, 4A's (American Association of Advertising Agencies), 25 W 45 St, 16th fl, New York, NY 10036 Tel: 212-682-2500 E-mail: media@4as.org; membership@4as.org Web Site: www.aaaa.org, pg 506

Goldsmith, Cathy, Random House Children's Books, c/o Penguin Random House LLC, 1745 Broadway, New York, NY 10019 Tel: 212-782-9000 Web Site: www.rhcbooks.com, pg 169

Goldsmith, Michael, Doubleday, c/o Penguin Random House LLC, 1745 Broadway, New York, NY 10019 Tel: 212-751-2600 Fax: 212-940-7390 (dom rts); 212-572-2662 (foreign rts) Web Site: knopfdoubleday.com/imprint/doubleday/; knopfdoubleday.com, pg 61

Goldstein, Bryn, Macmillan, 120 Broadway, 22nd fl, New York, NY 10271 E-mail: press.inquiries@macmillan.com Web Site: us.macmillan.com, pg 122

Goldstein, Gary, Kensington Publishing Corp, 900 Third Ave, 26th fl, New York, NY 10022 Tel: 212-407-1500 Toll Free Tel: 800-221-2647 Fax: 212-935-0699 Web Site: www.kensingtonbooks.com, pg 109

Goldstein, Jeffry, Trans-Atlantic Publications Inc, 33 Ashley Dr, Schwenksville, PA 19473 Tel: 215-925-2762 Fax: 215-925-1912 Web Site: www.transatlanticpub.com; www.businesstitles.com, pg 209

Goldverg, Maria, W W Norton & Company Inc, 500 Fifth Ave, New York, NY 10110-0017 Tel: 212-354-5500 Toll Free Tel: 800-233-4830 (orders & cust serv) Fax: 212-869-0856 Toll Free Fax: 800-458-6515 E-mail: orders@wwnorton.com Web Site: wwnorton.com, pg 143

Golebiewski, John, Shambhala Publications Inc, 2129 13 St, Boulder, CO 80302 Tel: 978-829-2599 (intl callers) Toll Free Tel: 866-424-0030 (off); 888-424-2329 (orders & cust serv) Fax: 617-236-1563 E-mail: customercare@shambhala.com; royalties@shambhala.com Web Site: www.shambhala.com, pg 187

Golikova, Maria, Doubleday Canada, 320 Front St W, Suite 1400, Toronto, ON M5V 3B6, Canada Tel: 416-364-4449 Fax: 416-598-7764 Web Site: www.penguinrandomhouse.ca, pg 401

Golikova, Maria, Groundwood Books, 128 Sterling Rd, Lower Level, Toronto, ON M6R 2B7, Canada Tel: 416-363-4343 Fax: 416-363-1017 E-mail: customerservice@houseofanansi.com Web Site: www.houseofanansi.com, pg 407

Golikova, Maria, House of Anansi Press Inc, 128 Sterling Rd, Lower Level, Toronto, ON M6R 2B7, Canada Tel: 416-363-4343 Fax: 416-363-1017 E-mail: customerservice@houseofanansi.com Web Site: houseofanansi.com, pg 409

Gollmer, Donna, American Bar Association Publishing, 321 N Clark St, Chicago, IL 60654 Tel: 312-988-5000 Toll Free Tel: 800-285-2221 (orders) Fax: 312-988-5850 (orders) E-mail: service@americanbar.org Web Site: www.americanbar.org/groups/departments_offices/publishing, pg 8

Gollub, Matthew, Tortuga Press, 2777 Yulupa Ave, PMB 181, Santa Rosa, CA 95405 Tel: 707-544-4720 Fax: 707-595-5331 E-mail: info@tortugapress.com Web Site: www.tortugapress.com, pg 208

Goloboy, Jennifer, Donald Maass Literary Agency, 1000 Dean St, Suite 331, Brooklyn, NY 11238 Tel: 212-727-8383 E-mail: info@maassagency.com Web Site: www.maassagency.com, pg 468

Golomb, Susan, Writers House, 21 W 26 St, New York, NY 10010 Tel: 212-685-2400 Web Site: www.writershouse.com, pg 482

Gombis, Sarah, Wm B Eerdmans Publishing Co, 4035 Park East Ct SE, Grand Rapids, MI 49546 Tel: 616-459-4591 Toll Free Tel: 800-253-7521 E-mail: customerservice@eerdmans.com; sales@eerdmans.com Web Site: www.eerdmans.com, pg 64

Gomez, Carolyn, Goodheart-Willcox Publisher, 18604 W Creek Dr, Tinley Park, IL 60477-6243 Tel: 708-687-5000 Toll Free Tel: 800-323-0440 Toll Free Fax: 888-409-3900 E-mail: custserv@g-w.com; orders@g-w.com Web Site: www.g-w.com, pg 79

Gomez, Lauren, Simon & Schuster, 1230 Avenue of the Americas, New York, NY 10020 *Tel:* 212-698-7000 *Toll Free Tel:* 800-223-2348 (cust serv); 800-223-2336 (orders) *Toll Free Fax:* 800-943-9831 (orders) *Web Site:* simonandschusterpublishing.com/simonandschuster/, pg 188

Gomez, Leticia, Kensington Publishing Corp, 900 Third Ave, 26th fl, New York, NY 10022 *Tel:* 212-407-1500 *Toll Free Tel:* 800-221-2647 *Fax:* 212-935-0699 *Web Site:* www.kensingtonbooks.com, pg 109

Goncharenko, Kathy, Scholastic Canada Ltd, 175 Hillmount Rd, Markham, ON L6C 1Z7, Canada *Tel:* 905-887-7323 *Toll Free Tel:* 800-268-3860 (CN) *Toll Free Tel:* 800-387-4944 *E-mail:* custserve@scholastic.ca *Web Site:* www.scholastic.ca, pg 418

Gong-Wong, Kirsten, Locus Awards, 655 13 St, Suite 100, Oakland, CA 94612 *Tel:* 510-339-9196 *Fax:* 510-339-9198 *E-mail:* locus@locusmag.com *Web Site:* www.locusmag.com; lsff.net, pg 625

Gonneville, Michel, La Fondation Emile Nelligan, 100, rue Sherbrooke, Suite 202, Montreal, QC H2X 1C3, Canada *Tel:* 514-278-4657 *E-mail:* info@fondation-nelligan.org *Web Site:* www.fondation-nelligan.org, pg 506

Gonneville, Michel, Prix Emile-Nelligan, 100, rue Sherbrooke, Suite 202, Montreal, QC H2X 1C3, Canada *Tel:* 514-278-4657 *Fax:* 514-271-6369 *E-mail:* info@fondation-nelligan.org *Web Site:* www.fondation-nelligan.org, pg 653

Gonzales, Cassie, Farrar, Straus & Giroux Books for Young Readers, 120 Broadway, New York, NY 10271 *Tel:* 212-741-6900 *Toll Free Tel:* 888-330-8477 (orders) *E-mail:* childrens.publicity@macmillanusa.com; childrensrights@macmillanusa.com *Web Site:* us.macmillan.com/mackids, pg 70

Gonzales, Cassie, Roaring Brook Press, 120 Broadway, New York, NY 10271 *Tel:* 646-307-5151 *Web Site:* us.macmillan.com/publishers/roaring-brook-press, pg 176

Gonzales, Gail, Random House Publishing Group, 1745 Broadway, New York, NY 10019 *Toll Free Tel:* 800-200-3552 *Web Site:* www.randomhousebooks.com, pg 170

Gonzales, Gia, The New Press, 120 Wall St, 31st fl, New York, NY 10005 *Tel:* 212-629-8802 *Fax:* 212-629-8617 *E-mail:* newpress@thenewpress.com *Web Site:* thenewpress.com, pg 140

Gonzalez, Cecilia, The Brookings Institution Press, 1775 Massachusetts Ave NW, Washington, DC 20036-2188 *Tel:* 202-797-6000 *E-mail:* permissions@brookings.edu *Web Site:* www.brookings.edu, pg 37

Gonzalez, Christopher, Macmillan, 120 Broadway, 22nd fl, New York, NY 10271 *E-mail:* press.inquiries@macmillan.com *Web Site:* us.macmillan.com, pg 122

Gonzalez, Diana, Consumer Press, 13326 SW 28 St, Suite 102, Fort Lauderdale, FL 33330-1102 *Tel:* 954-370-9153 *E-mail:* info@consumerpress.com *Web Site:* www.consumerpress.com, pg 52

Gonzalez, Erica, Random House Publishing Group, 1745 Broadway, New York, NY 10019 *Toll Free Tel:* 800-200-3552 *Web Site:* www.randomhousebooks.com, pg 171

Gonzalez, Giselle, Tor Publishing Group, 120 Broadway, New York, NY 10271 *Toll Free Tel:* 800-455-0340 (Macmillan) *E-mail:* torpublicity@tor.com; forgepublicity@forgebooks.com *Web Site:* us.macmillan.com/torpublishinggroup, pg 208

Gonzalez, Jennifer, Sourcebooks LLC, 1935 Brookdale Rd, Suite 139, Naperville, IL 60563 *Tel:* 630-961-3900 *Toll Free Tel:* 800-432-7444 *Fax:* 630-961-2168 *E-mail:* info@sourcebooks.com *Web Site:* www.sourcebooks.com, pg 194

Gonzalez, Laura, HarperCollins Publishers LLC, 195 Broadway, New York, NY 10007 *Tel:* 212-207-7000 *Web Site:* www.harpercollins.com, pg 87

Gonzalez, Miranda, Kurt Brown Prizes, 440 Monticello Ave, Suite 1802, PMB 73708, Norfolk, VA 23510-2670 *Tel:* 240-696-7700 *E-mail:* awp@awpwriter.org *Web Site:* www.awpwriter.org/contests/kurt_brown_prizes_overview, pg 584

Gonzalez, Neil, Greenleaf Book Group LLC, PO Box 91869, Austin, TX 78709 *Tel:* 512-891-6100 *Fax:* 512-891-6150 *E-mail:* contact@greenleafbookgroup.com; orders@greenleafbookgroup.com; foreignrights@greenleafbookgroup.com; media@greenleafbookgroup.com *Web Site:* greenleafbookgroup.com, pg 81

Gonzalez Palacios, Edder, Editorial de la Universidad de Puerto Rico, PO Box 23322, San Juan, PR 00931-3322 *Tel:* 787-525-7654 *Web Site:* www.facebook.com/editorialupr, pg 63

Gonzalez, Paola, Penguin Random House Canada, a Penguin Random House company, 320 Front St W, Suite 1400, Toronto, ON M5V 3B6, Canada *Tel:* 416-364-4449 *Toll Free Tel:* 888-523-9292 (cust serv) *E-mail:* canadaweb@penguinrandomhouse.com; customerservicescanada@penguinrandomhouse.com *Web Site:* www.penguinrandomhouse.ca, pg 416

Gonzalez, Veronica, Macmillan, 120 Broadway, 22nd fl, New York, NY 10271 *E-mail:* press.inquiries@macmillan.com *Web Site:* us.macmillan.com, pg 122

Goodell, Lizzie, Penguin Young Readers Group, c/o Penguin Random House LLC, 1745 Broadway, New York, NY 10019 *Tel:* 212-782-9000 *Web Site:* www.penguin.com/penguin-young-readers-overview, pg 156

Goodline, Lori, Ave Maria Press Inc, PO Box 428, Notre Dame, IN 46556 *Toll Free Tel:* 800-282-1865 *Toll Free Fax:* 800-282-5681 *E-mail:* avemariapress.1@nd.edu *Web Site:* www.avemariapress.com, pg 22

Goodman, Christie, Intercultural Development Research Association (IDRA), 5815 Callaghan Rd, Suite 101, San Antonio, TX 78228 *Tel:* 210-444-1710 *Fax:* 210-444-1714 *E-mail:* contact@idra.org *Web Site:* www.idra.org, pg 102

Goodman, Eleanor, Penn State University Press, University Support Bldg 1, Suite C, 820 N University Dr, University Park, PA 16802-1003 *Tel:* 814-865-1327 *Toll Free Tel:* 800-326-9180 (orders & cust serv) *Fax:* 814-863-1408 *Toll Free Fax:* 877-778-2665 (book orders) *E-mail:* orders@psupress.org; customerservice@psupress.org *Web Site:* www.psupress.org, pg 157

Goodman, Irene, Irene Goodman Literary Agency, 27 W 24 St, Suite 700B, New York, NY 10010 *Tel:* 212-604-0330 *E-mail:* queries@irenegoodman.com *Web Site:* www.irenegoodman.com, pg 460

Goodman, Juliet, Random House Children's Books, c/o Penguin Random House LLC, 1745 Broadway, New York, NY 10019 *Tel:* 212-782-9000 *Web Site:* www.rhcbooks.com, pg 170

Goodman, Offauna, Macmillan, 120 Broadway, 22nd fl, New York, NY 10271 *E-mail:* press.inquiries@macmillan.com *Web Site:* us.macmillan.com, pg 122

Goodman, Peter, Stone Bridge Press Inc, 1393 Solano Ave, Suite C, Albany, CA 94706 *Tel:* 510-524-8732 *E-mail:* sbp@stonebridge.com; sbpedit@stonebridge.com *Web Site:* www.stonebridge.com, pg 199

Goodman, Sara, St Martin's Press, LLC, 120 Broadway, New York, NY 10271 *E-mail:* publicity@stmartins.com; trademarketing@stmartins.com; foreignrights@stmartins.com *Web Site:* us.macmillan.com/smp, pg 180

Goodnough, Doris, Orbis Books, PO Box 302, Maryknoll, NY 10545-0302 *Tel:* 914-941-7636 *Toll Free Tel:* 800-258-5838 (orders, Mon-Fri 8AM-4PM EST) *Fax:* 914-941-7005 *E-mail:* orbisbooks@maryknoll.org *Web Site:* orbisbooks.com, pg 147

Goodrich, David, American Printing History Association, PO Box 4519, Grand Central Sta, New York, NY 10163 *E-mail:* secretary@printinghistory.org *Web Site:* printinghistory.org, pg 496

Goodrich, David, American Printing History Association Award, PO Box 4519, Grand Central Sta, New York, NY 10163 *E-mail:* secretary@printinghistory.org *Web Site:* printinghistory.org/programs/awards, pg 573

Goodspeed, Brianne, Chelsea Green Publishing Co, 85 N Main St, Suite 120, White River Junction, VT 05001 *Tel:* 802-295-6300 *Toll Free Tel:* 800-639-4099 (cust serv & orders) *Fax:* 802-295-6444 *E-mail:* customerservice@chelseagreen.com; editorial@chelseagreen.com; publicity@chelseagreen.com; rights@chelseagreen.com *Web Site:* www.chelseagreen.com, pg 45

Goodwin, Daneen, National Geographic Books, 1145 17 St NW, Washington, DC 20036-4688 *Tel:* 202-857-7000 *Toll Free Tel:* 877-866-6486 *E-mail:* ngbooks@cdsfulfillment.com *Web Site:* www.nationalgeographic.com/books/; ngbooks.buysub.com, pg 138

Goody, Margo, Macmillan Audio, 120 Broadway, 22nd fl, New York, NY 10271 *Tel:* 646-600-7856 *Toll Free Tel:* 888-330-8477 (cust serv) *Toll Free Fax:* 800-672-7703 *E-mail:* macmillan.audio@macmillanusa.com *Web Site:* us.macmillan.com/audio, pg 123

Goolsby, Anna, Dreamscape Media LLC, 1417 Timberwolf Dr, Holland, OH 43528 *Tel:* 419-867-6965 *Toll Free Tel:* 877-983-7326 *E-mail:* info@dreamscapeab.com *Web Site:* www.dreamscapepublishing.com, pg 62

Goossen, Chester, PrairieView Press, 625 Seventh St, Gretna, MB R0G 0V0, Canada *Tel:* 204-327-6543 *Toll Free Tel:* 800-477-7377 *Toll Free Fax:* 866-480-0253 *Web Site:* prairieviewpress.com, pg 417

Goranescu, Elena, McGill-Queen's University Press, 1010 Sherbrooke W, Suite 1720, Montreal, QC H3A 2R7, Canada *Tel:* 514-398-3750 *Fax:* 514-398-4333 *E-mail:* mqup@mcgill.ca *Web Site:* www.mqup.ca, pg 412

Gordon, Annette, Clarity Press Inc, 2625 Piedmont Rd NE, Suite 56, Atlanta, GA 30324 *Tel:* 404-647-6501 *E-mail:* claritypress@usa.net (foreign rts & perms) *Web Site:* www.claritypress.com, pg 49

Gordon, Clayton, Illuminating Engineering Society of North America (IES), 120 Wall St, 17th fl, New York, NY 10005-4001 *Tel:* 212-248-5000 *Fax:* 212-248-5017; 212-248-5018 *E-mail:* ies@ies.org *Web Site:* www.ies.org, pg 99

Gordon, Douglas C, P M Gordon Associates Inc, 2115 Wallace St, Philadelphia, PA 19130 *Tel:* 215-769-2525 *Web Site:* www.pmgordonassociates.com, pg 440

Gordon, Emma, Houghton Mifflin Harcourt Trade & Reference Division, 125 High St, Boston, MA 02110 *Tel:* 617-351-5000 *Web Site:* www.hmhco.com, pg 96

Gordon, Jason, Writers Guild of America, East (WGAE), 250 Hudson St, Suite 700, New York, NY 10013 *Tel:* 212-767-7800 *Fax:* 212-582-1909 *Web Site:* www.wgaeast.org, pg 522

Gordon, Joan, Friends of American Writers (FAW), c/o 506 Rose Ave, Des Plaines, IL 60016 *E-mail:* info@fawchicago.org *Web Site:* www.fawchicago.org, pg 506

Gordon, Kathryn, Grand Central Publishing, 1290 Avenue of the Americas, New York, NY 10104 *Tel:* 212-364-1100 *Web Site:* www.hachettebookgroup.com/imprint/grand-central-publishing/, pg 80

Gordon, Leah, Running Press, 1290 Avenue of the Americas, New York, NY 10104 *Tel:* 212-364-1100 *Toll Free Tel:* 800-759-0190 (cust serv) *Fax:* 212-364-0933 (intl orders) *Toll Free Fax:* 800-286-9471 (cust serv) *E-mail:* customer.service@hbgusa.com; orders@hbgusa.com *Web Site:* www.hachettebookgroup.com/imprint/running-press/; www.moon.com (Moon Travel Guides), pg 178

Gordon, Lindsay, Avery, c/o Penguin Random House LLC, 1745 Broadway, New York, NY 10019 *Tel:* 212-366-2000 *Web Site:* www.penguin.com/avery-overview/, pg 23

Gordon, Lindsay, TarcherPerigee, c/o Penguin Random House LLC, 1745 Broadway, New York, NY 10019 *Tel:* 212-782-9000 *Web Site:* www.penguin.com/tarcherperigee-overview/; www.facebook.com/TarcherPerigee, pg 202

Gordon, Marilyn, Baker Books, 6030 E Fulton Rd, Ada, MI 49301 *Tel:* 616-676-9185 *Toll Free Tel:* 800-877-2665 (orders) *Fax:* 616-676-9573 *Toll Free Fax:* 800-398-3111 (orders) *E-mail:* media@bakerpublishinggroup.com;

orders@bakerpublishinggroup.com; sales@bakerpublishinggroup.com *Web Site:* www.bakerpublishinggroup.com, pg 23

Gordon, Nadia, Society of Professional Journalists (SPJ), PO Box 441748, Indianapolis, IN 46244 *Tel:* 317-927-8000 *Fax:* 317-920-4789 *E-mail:* communications@spj.org *Web Site:* www.spj.org, pg 520

Gordon, Peggy M, P M Gordon Associates Inc, 2115 Wallace St, Philadelphia, PA 19130 *Tel:* 215-769-2525 *Web Site:* www.pmgordonassociates.com, pg 440

Gore, Katie, Macmillan, 120 Broadway, 22nd fl, New York, NY 10271 *E-mail:* press.inquiries@macmillan.com *Web Site:* us.macmillan.com, pg 122

Gore, Molly, Ascend Books LLC, 11722 W 91 St, Overland Park, KS 66214 *Tel:* 913-948-5500 *Web Site:* www.ascendbooks.com, pg 18

Gorecki, Sabine, BrainStorm Poetry Contest for Mental Health Consumers, 36 Elgin St, 2nd fl, Sudbury, ON P3C 5B4, Canada *Tel:* 705-222-6472 (ext 303) *E-mail:* openminds@nisa.on.ca *Web Site:* www.openmindsquarterly.com/poetry-contest, pg 583

Gorg, Brian, Educational Book & Media Association (EBMA), 11 Main St, Suite D, Warrenton, VA 20186 *Tel:* 540-318-7770 *Fax:* 202-962-3939 *E-mail:* info@edupaperback.org; admin@edupaperback.org *Web Site:* www.edupaperback.org, pg 505

Gorg, Brian, Jeremiah Ludington Award, 11 Main St, Suite D, Warrenton, VA 20186 *Tel:* 540-318-7770 *Fax:* 202-962-3939 *E-mail:* info@edupaperback.org; admin@edupaperback.org *Web Site:* www.edupaperback.org, pg 627

Gorman, Don, Rocky Mountain Books Ltd (RMB), 103-1075 Pendergast St, Victoria, BC V8V 0A1, Canada *Tel:* 250-360-0829 *Fax:* 250-386-0829 *Web Site:* rmbooks.com, pg 418

Gorman, Grace, Rocky Mountain Books Ltd (RMB), 103-1075 Pendergast St, Victoria, BC V8V 0A1, Canada *Tel:* 250-360-0829 *Fax:* 250-386-0829 *Web Site:* rmbooks.com, pg 418

Gorman, Roberta, Society of Motion Picture and Television Engineers® (SMPTE®), White Plains Plaza, 445 Hamilton Ave, Suite 601, White Plains, NY 10601-1827 *Tel:* 914-761-1100 *E-mail:* hello@smpte.org (mktg) *Web Site:* www.smpte.org, pg 520

Gosling, Anthony, Crossway, 1300 Crescent St, Wheaton, IL 60187 *Tel:* 630-682-4300 *Toll Free Tel:* 800-635-7993 (orders); 800-543-1659 (cust serv) *Fax:* 630-682-4785 *E-mail:* info@crossway.org *Web Site:* www.crossway.org, pg 56

Gosling, Nicole, Crossway, 1300 Crescent St, Wheaton, IL 60187 *Tel:* 630-682-4300 *Toll Free Tel:* 800-635-7993 (orders); 800-543-1659 (cust serv) *Fax:* 630-682-4785 *E-mail:* info@crossway.org *Web Site:* www.crossway.org, pg 56

Goss, Christine, FinePrint Literary Management, 207 W 106 St, Suite 1D, New York, NY 10025 *Tel:* 212-279-6214 *E-mail:* info@fineprintlit.com; submissions@fineprint.com *Web Site:* www.fineprintlit.com, pg 458

Gosse, Jonathan, American Technical Publishers, 10100 Orland Pkwy, Suite 200, Orland Park, IL 60467-5756 *Toll Free Tel:* 800-323-3471 *Fax:* 708-957-1101 *E-mail:* service@atplearning.com; order@atplearning.com *Web Site:* www.atplearning.com; www.atpcanada.com (CN orders), pg 13

Gosselin, Guy, Corporation of Professional Librarians of Quebec, 2065, rue Parthenais, Bureau 387, Montreal, QC H2K 3T1, Canada *Tel:* 514-845-3327 *E-mail:* info@cbpq.qc.ca *Web Site:* www.cbpq.qc.ca, pg 504

Gosser, Marty, Yale University Press, 302 Temple St, New Haven, CT 06511-8909 *Tel:* 203-432-0960; 203-432-0966 (sales); 401-531-2800 (cust serv) *Toll Free Tel:* 800-405-1619 (cust serv) *Fax:* 203-432-0948; 203-432-8485 (sales); 401-531-2801 (cust serv) *Toll Free Fax:* 800-406-9145 (cust serv) *E-mail:* sales.press@yale.edu (sales); customer.care@triliteral.org (cust serv) *Web Site:* www.yalebooks.com; yalepress.yale.edu/yupbooks, pg 235

Gott, Jennifer, Thomas Nelson, 501 Nelson Place, Nashville, TN 37214 *Tel:* 615-889-9000 *Toll Free Tel:* 800-251-4000 *Web Site:* www.thomasnelson.com, pg 206

Gott, Jennifer, Zondervan, 3900 Sparks Dr SE, Grand Rapids, MI 49546 *Tel:* 616-698-6900 *Toll Free Tel:* 800-226-1122; 800-727-1309 (retail orders) *Fax:* 616-698-3350 *Toll Free Fax:* 800-698-3256 (retail orders) *E-mail:* customercare@harpercollins.com *Web Site:* www.zondervan.com, pg 236

Gottier, Aaron, P & R Publishing Co, 1102 Marble Hill Rd, Phillipsburg, NJ 08865 *Tel:* 908-454-0505 *Toll Free Tel:* 800-631-0094 *E-mail:* sales@prpbooks.com; info@prpbooks.com *Web Site:* www.prpbooks.com, pg 149

Gottlieb, Mark Owen, Trident Media Group LLC, 355 Lexington Ave, 12th fl, New York, NY 10017 *Tel:* 212-333-1511 *E-mail:* info@tridentmediagroup.com; press@tridentmediagroup.com; foreignrights@tridentmediagroup.com; office.assistant@tridentmediagroup.com *Web Site:* www.tridentmediagroup.com, pg 480

Gottlieb, Melanie, American Association of Collegiate Registrars & Admissions Officers (AACRAO), 1108 16 St NW, Washington, DC 20011 *Tel:* 202-293-9161 *Fax:* 202-872-8857 *E-mail:* pubs@aacrao.org *Web Site:* www.aacrao.org, pg 8

Gottlieb, Richard, Grey House Publishing Inc™, 4919 Rte 22, Amenia, NY 12501 *Tel:* 518-789-8700 *Toll Free Tel:* 800-562-2139 *Fax:* 518-789-0556 *E-mail:* books@greyhouse.com; customerservice@greyhouse.com *Web Site:* greyhouse.com, pg 81

Gottlieb, Robert, Trident Media Group LLC, 355 Lexington Ave, 12th fl, New York, NY 10017 *Tel:* 212-333-1511 *E-mail:* info@tridentmediagroup.com; press@tridentmediagroup.com; foreignrights@tridentmediagroup.com; office.assistant@tridentmediagroup.com *Web Site:* www.tridentmediagroup.com, pg 480

Gougeon, Guy, Flammarion Quebec, 3700A, Blvd Saint-Laurent, Montreal, QC H2X 2V4, Canada *Tel:* 514-499-1002 *Fax:* 514-499-1002 *E-mail:* info@flammarion.qc.ca *Web Site:* flammarionquebec.com, pg 406

Gould, Barbara, National Magazine Awards, 2300 Yonge St, Suite 1600, Toronto, ON M4P 1E4, Canada *Tel:* 416-939-6200 *E-mail:* staff@magazine-awards.com *Web Site:* www.magazine-awards.com; x.com/magawards, pg 638

Gould, Morgan, Houghton Mifflin Harcourt, 125 High St, Boston, MA 02110 *Tel:* 617-351-5000 *Toll Free Tel:* 855-969-4642; 800-225-5425 (K-12 educ materials); 800-323-9540 (assessment materials); 877-219-1537 (SkillsTutor); 888-242-6747 (Innovation in Educ Group); 800-225-3362 (Trade & Ref Div) *Toll Free Fax:* 800-269-5232 *E-mail:* myhmhco@hmhco.com *Web Site:* www.hmhco.com, pg 96

Gould, Robert, BiG GUY BOOKS, 6866 Embarcadero Lane, Carlsbad, CA 92011 *Tel:* 760-652-5360 *Toll Free Tel:* 800-536-3030 (booksellers' cust serv) *E-mail:* info@greatbooksforboys.com *Web Site:* www.bigguybooks.com, pg 29

Gourlay, Jonathan, MacDowell Fellowships, 100 High St, Peterborough, NH 03458 *Tel:* 603-924-3886 *E-mail:* info@macdowell.org; admissions@macdowell.org *Web Site:* www.macdowell.org, pg 628

Gouverneur, Mustafa, Fons Vitae, 49 Mockingbird Valley Dr, Louisville, KY 40207-1366 *Tel:* 502-897-3641 *Fax:* 502-893-7373 *E-mail:* fonsvitaeky@aol.com *Web Site:* www.fonsvitae.com, pg 73

Governa, Mark, Running Press, 1290 Avenue of the Americas, New York, NY 10104 *Tel:* 212-364-1100 *Toll Free Tel:* 800-759-0190 (cust serv) *Fax:* 212-364-0933 (intl orders) *Toll Free Fax:* 800-286-9471 (cust serv) *E-mail:* customer.service@hbgusa.com; orders@hbgusa.com *Web Site:* www.hachettebookgroup.com/imprint/running-press/; www.moon.com (Moon Travel Guides), pg 178

Govin, Chad, J J Keller & Associates, Inc®, 3003 Breezewood Lane, Neenah, WI 54957 *Tel:* 920-722-2848 *Toll Free Tel:* 877-564-2333 *Toll Free Fax:* 800-727-7516 *E-mail:* customerservice@jjkeller.com; sales@jjkeller.com *Web Site:* www.jjkeller.com, pg 108

Gow, Val, Penguin Random House Canada, a Penguin Random House company, 320 Front St W, Suite 1400, Toronto, ON M5V 3B6, Canada *Tel:* 416-364-4449 *Toll Free Tel:* 888-523-9292 (cust serv) *E-mail:* canadaweb@penguinrandomhouse.com; customerservicescanada@penguinrandomhouse.com *Web Site:* www.penguinrandomhouse.ca, pg 416

Gowrie, Katie, Harlequin Enterprises Ltd, Bay Adelaide Centre, East Tower, 22 Adelaide St W, 41st fl, Toronto, ON M5H 4E3, Canada *Tel:* 416-445-5860 *Toll Free Tel:* 888-432-4879; 800-370-5838 (ebook inquiries) *E-mail:* customerservice@harlequin.com *Web Site:* www.harlequin.com, pg 409

Grace, Bill, Little, Brown Books for Young Readers (LBYR), 1290 Avenue of the Americas, New York, NY 10104 *Tel:* 212-364-1100 *Toll Free Tel:* 800-759-0190 (cust serv) *E-mail:* rights@lbchildrens.com *Web Site:* www.hachettebookgroup.com/imprint/little-brown-books-for-young-readers/, pg 118

Grace-Petinos, Stephanie, Bloomsbury Academic, 1385 Broadway, 5th fl, New York, NY 10018 *Tel:* 212-419-5300 *Web Site:* www.bloomsbury.com/us/academic, pg 31

Grad, Doug, Doug Grad Literary Agency Inc, 156 Prospect Park W, No 3L, Brooklyn, NY 11215 *Tel:* 718-788-6067 *E-mail:* query@dgliterary.com *Web Site:* www.dgliterary.com, pg 460

Gradel, Melissa Ford, The Amy Award, 90 Broad St, Suite 2100, New York, NY 10004 *Tel:* 212-226-3586 *Fax:* 212-226-3963 *E-mail:* admin@pw.org *Web Site:* www.pw.org, pg 573

Gradel, Melissa Ford, Barnes & Noble Writers for Writers Award, 90 Broad St, Suite 2100, New York, NY 10004 *Tel:* 212-226-3586 *Fax:* 212-226-3963 *E-mail:* admin@pw.org *Web Site:* www.pw.org, pg 577

Gradel, Melissa Ford, Editor's Award, 90 Broad St, Suite 2100, New York, NY 10004 *Tel:* 212-226-3586 *Fax:* 212-226-3963 *E-mail:* admin@pw.org *Web Site:* www.pw.org/about-us/sponsored-prizes, pg 598

Gradel, Melissa Ford, The Jackson Poetry Prize, 90 Broad St, Suite 2100, New York, NY 10004 *Tel:* 212-226-3586 *Fax:* 212-226-3963 *E-mail:* admin@pw.org *Web Site:* www.pw.org, pg 618

Gradel, Melissa Ford, Poets & Writers Inc, 90 Broad St, Suite 2100, New York, NY 10004 *Tel:* 212-226-3586 *Fax:* 212-226-3963 *E-mail:* admin@pw.org *Web Site:* www.pw.org, pg 517

Grady, Lynn, Chronicle Books LLC, 680 Second St, San Francisco, CA 94107 *Tel:* 415-537-4200 *Fax:* 415-537-4460 (perms) *E-mail:* hello@chroniclebooks.com; subrights@chroniclebooks.com *Web Site:* www.chroniclebooks.com, pg 47

Grady, Lynn, PA Press, 202 Warren St, Hudson, NY 12534 *Tel:* 518-671-6100 *Toll Free Tel:* 800-722-6657 (dist); 800-759-0190 (sales) *E-mail:* sales@papress.com *Web Site:* www.papress.com, pg 149

Graff, Emily, Atria Books, 1230 Avenue of the Americas, New York, NY 10020 *Tel:* 212-698-7000 *Fax:* 212-698-7007 *Web Site:* www.simonandschuster.com, pg 21

Graham, Cassidy, St Martin's Press, LLC, 120 Broadway, New York, NY 10271 *E-mail:* publicity@stmartins.com; trademarketing@stmartins.com; foreignrights@stmartins.com *Web Site:* us.macmillan.com/smp, pg 181

Graham, Cassidy, Viking Penguin, c/o Penguin Random House LLC, 1745 Broadway, New York, NY 10019 *Tel:* 212-782-9000 *Web Site:* www.penguin.com/overview-vikingbooks/; www.penguin.com/pamela-dorman-books-overview/; www.penguin.com/penguin-classics-overview/; www.penguin.com/penguin-life-overview/, pg 225

Graham, Jenissa, BookEnds Literary Agency, 136 Long Hill Rd, Gillette, NJ 07933 Web Site: www.bookendsliterary.com, pg 451

Graham, Jon, Bear & Co Inc, One Park St, Rochester, VT 05767 Tel: 802-767-3174 Toll Free Tel: 800-932-3277 Fax: 802-767-3726 E-mail: customerservice@InnerTraditions.com Web Site: InnerTraditions.com, pg 26

Graham, Jon, Inner Traditions International Ltd, One Park St, Rochester, VT 05767 Tel: 802-767-3174 Toll Free Tel: 800-246-8648 Fax: 802-767-3726 E-mail: customerservice@InnerTraditions.com Web Site: www.InnerTraditions.com, pg 101

Graham, Kathleen, Society for Advancing Business Editing and Writing (SABEW), Walter Cronkite School of Journalism & Mass Communication, Arizona State University, 555 N Central Ave, Suite 406E, Phoenix, AZ 85004-1248 Tel: 602-496-7862 E-mail: sabew@sabew.org Web Site: sabew.org, pg 519

Graham, Kimberly Gladfelter, Miles Conrad Award, 3600 Clipper Mill Rd, Suite 302, Baltimore, MD 21211-1948 Tel: 301-654-2512 Fax: 410-685-5278 E-mail: nisohq@niso.org Web Site: www.niso.org, pg 591

Graham, Kimberly Gladfelter, National Information Standards Organization (NISO), 3600 Clipper Mill Rd, Suite 302, Baltimore, MD 21211-1948 Tel: 301-654-2512 Fax: 410-685-5278 E-mail: nisohq@niso.org Web Site: www.niso.org, pg 138, 513

Graham, Nan, Scribner, 1230 Avenue of the Americas, New York, NY 10020 Web Site: www.simonandschusterpublishing.com/scribner/, pg 185

Graham, Nan, Simon & Schuster, LLC, 1230 Avenue of the Americas, New York, NY 10020 Tel: 212-698-7000 Toll Free Tel: 800-223-2336 (orders) Fax: 212-698-7007 Toll Free Fax: 800-943-9831 (orders) E-mail: firstname.lastname@simonandschuster.com; purchaseorders@simonandschuster.com (orders) Web Site: www.simonandschuster.com, pg 189

Graham, Rachel, National Geographic Books, 1145 17 St NW, Washington, DC 20036-4688 Tel: 202-857-7000 Toll Free Tel: 877-866-6486 E-mail: ngbooks@cdsfulfillment.com Web Site: www.nationalgeographic.com/books/; ngbooks.buysub.com, pg 138

Graham, Sara Lacey, American Booksellers Association, 600 Mamaroneck Ave, Suite 400, Harrison, NY 10528 Tel: 914-406-7500 Toll Free Tel: 800-637-0037 Fax: 914-417-4013 E-mail: info@bookweb.org Web Site: www.bookweb.org, pg 494

Graham, Stacey, 3 Seas Literary Agency, PO Box 444, Sun Prairie, WI 53590 Tel: 608-834-9317 E-mail: threeseaslit@aol.com Web Site: threeseasagency.com, pg 479

Grahek, Greg, APS PRESS, 3340 Pilot Knob Rd, St Paul, MN 55121 Tel: 651-454-7250 Toll Free Tel: 800-328-7560 Fax: 651-454-0766 E-mail: aps@scisoc.org Web Site: my.apsnet.org/apsstore, pg 16

Grahek, Greg, Cereals & Grains Association, 3285 Northwood Circle, Suite 100, St Paul, MN 55121 Tel: 651-454-7250 E-mail: info@cerealsgrains.org Web Site: cerealsgrains.org, pg 44

Grainger, Jeremy, Rutgers University Press, 106 Somerset St, 3rd fl, New Brunswick, NJ 08901 Tel: 848-445-7762; 848-445-7761 (sales) Fax: 732-745-4935 E-mail: sales@rutgersuniversitypress.org Web Site: www.rutgersuniversitypress.org, pg 178

Grajkowski, Michelle, 3 Seas Literary Agency, PO Box 444, Sun Prairie, WI 53590 Tel: 608-834-9317 E-mail: threeseaslit@aol.com Web Site: threeseasagency.com, pg 479

Grames, Juliet, Soho Press Inc, 853 Broadway, New York, NY 10003 Tel: 212-260-1900 E-mail: soho@sohopress.com; publicity@sohopress.com Web Site: sohopress.com, pg 193

Granada, Lina, Brandt & Hochman Literary Agents Inc, 1501 Broadway, Suite 2310, New York, NY 10036 Tel: 212-840-5760 Fax: 212-840-5776 Web Site: brandthochman.com, pg 452

Granata, Abby, Farrar, Straus & Giroux Books for Young Readers, 120 Broadway, New York, NY 10271 Tel: 212-741-6900 Toll Free Tel: 888-330-8477 (orders) E-mail: childrens.publicity@macmillanusa.com; childrensrights@macmillanusa.com Web Site: us.macmillan.com/mackids, pg 70

Granata, Abby, Roaring Brook Press, 120 Broadway, New York, NY 10271 Tel: 646-307-5151 Web Site: us.macmillan.com/publishers/roaring-brook-press, pg 176

Grande, Scott, DK, c/o Penguin Random House LLC, 1745 Broadway, 20th fl, New York, NY 10019 Tel: 646-674-4000 Toll Free Tel: 800-733-3000 Fax: 646-674-4020 E-mail: marketing@dk.com (lib servs); publicity@dk.com; csorders@penguinrandomhouse.com; customerservice@penguinrandomhouse.com Web Site: www.dk.com, pg 60

Graner, Daniella, Workman Publishing, 1290 Avenue of the Americas, New York, NY 10104 Toll Free Tel: 800-759-0190 Fax: 212-364-0950 E-mail: workman-inquiry@hbgusa.com Web Site: www.hachettebookgroup.com/imprint/workman-publishing-company/, pg 233

Grange, Laura, Mountaineers Books, 1001 SW Klickitat Way, Suite 201, Seattle, WA 98134 Tel: 206-223-6303 Fax: 206-223-6306 E-mail: mbooks@mountaineersbooks.org; customerservice@mountaineersbooks.org Web Site: www.mountaineers.org/books, pg 135

Granger, David, Aevitas Creative Management LLC, 19 W 21 St, Suite 501, New York, NY 10010 Tel: 212-765-6900 Web Site: www.aevitascreative.com, pg 448

Grant, Emma, Houghton Mifflin Harcourt Trade & Reference Division, 125 High St, Boston, MA 02110 Tel: 617-351-5000 Web Site: www.hmhco.com, pg 96

Grant, Emma, Sourcebooks LLC, 1935 Brookdale Rd, Suite 139, Naperville, IL 60563 Tel: 630-961-3900 Toll Free Tel: 800-432-7444 Fax: 630-961-2168 E-mail: info@sourcebooks.com Web Site: www.sourcebooks.com, pg 195

Grant, Gavin J, Small Beer Press, 150 Pleasant St, No 306, Easthampton, MA 01027 Tel: 413-240-4197 E-mail: info@smallbeerpress.com Web Site: smallbeerpress.com, pg 191

Grant, Janet Kobobel, Books & Such, 2222 Cleveland Ave, No 1005, Santa Rosa, CA 95403 Tel: 707-538-4184 Web Site: booksandsuch.com, pg 451

Grant, Kyrell, Penguin Random House Canada, a Penguin Random House company, 320 Front St W, Suite 1400, Toronto, ON M5V 3B6, Canada Tel: 416-364-4449 Toll Free Tel: 888-523-9292 (cust serv) E-mail: canadaweb@penguinrandomhouse.com; customerservicecanada@penguinrandomhouse.com Web Site: www.penguinrandomhouse.ca, pg 416

Grant, Pamela, Gallery Books, 1230 Avenue of the Americas, New York, NY 10020 Toll Free Tel: 800-456-6798 Fax: 212-698-7284 E-mail: consumer.customerservice@simonandschuster.com Web Site: www.simonandschuster.com, pg 76

Grant, Patricia, VanDam Inc, The VanDam Bldg, 121 W 27 St, New York, NY 10001 Tel: 917-297-5445 E-mail: info@vandam.com Web Site: www.vandam.com, pg 223

Grathwohl, Casper, Oxford University Press USA, 198 Madison Ave, New York, NY 10016 Toll Free Tel: 800-451-7556 (orders); 800-445-9714 (cust serv) Fax: 919-677-1303 E-mail: custserv.us@oup.com Web Site: global.oup.com, pg 149

Gratz, Mike, Olde & Oppenheim Publishers, 3219 N Margate Place, Chandler, AZ 85224 E-mail: olde_oppenheim@hotmail.com, pg 146

Gray, Andrew, University of British Columbia Creative Writing Program, Buchanan Rm E-462, 1866 Main Mall, Vancouver, BC V6T 1Z1, Canada Tel: 604-822-0699 Web Site: creativewriting.ubc.ca, pg 566

Gray, David, Gray & Company Publishers, 1588 E 40 St, Suite 1B, Cleveland, OH 44103 Tel: 216-431-2665 Toll Free Tel: 800-915-3609 E-mail: sales@grayco.com; editorial@grayco.com; publicity@grayco.com Web Site: www.grayco.com, pg 81

Gray, Jason, Association of Writers & Writing Programs (AWP), 440 Monticello Ave, Suite 1802, PMB 73708, Norfolk, VA 23510-2670 Tel: 240-696-7700 E-mail: awp@awpwriter.org; press@awpwriter.org Web Site: www.awpwriter.org, pg 500

Gray, Jason, AWP Award Series, 440 Monticello Ave, Suite 1802, PMB 73708, Norfolk, VA 23510-2670 Tel: 240-696-7700 E-mail: awp@awpwriter.org; press@awpwriter.org Web Site: www.awpwriter.org, pg 576

Gray, Kim, Simon & Schuster, LLC, 1230 Avenue of the Americas, New York, NY 10020 Tel: 212-698-7000 Toll Free Tel: 800-223-2336 (orders) Fax: 212-698-7007 Toll Free Fax: 800-943-9831 (orders) E-mail: firstname.lastname@simonandschuster.com; purchaseorders@simonandschuster.com (orders) Web Site: www.simonandschuster.com, pg 190

Gray, Rebecca B, American Institute of Aeronautics and Astronautics (AIAA), 12700 Sunrise Valley Dr, Suite 200, Reston, VA 20191-5807 Tel: 703-264-7500 Toll Free Tel: 800-639-AIAA (639-2422) Fax: 703-264-7551 E-mail: custserv@aiaa.org Web Site: www.aiaa.org; arc.aiaa.org (orders), pg 10

Gray-Donald, David, Between the Lines, 401 Richmond St W, No 281, Toronto, ON M5V 3A8, Canada Tel: 416-535-9914 Toll Free Tel: 800-718-7201 E-mail: info@btlbooks.com Web Site: btlbooks.com, pg 396

Gray-Winter, Shannon, Kensington Publishing Corp, 900 Third Ave, 26th fl, New York, NY 10022 Tel: 212-407-1500 Toll Free Tel: 800-221-2647 Fax: 212-935-0699 Web Site: www.kensingtonbooks.com, pg 109

Graziani, Mike, SLACK® Incorporated, A Wyanoke Group Company, 6900 Grove Rd, Thorofare, NJ 08086-9447 Tel: 856-848-1000 Toll Free Tel: 800-257-8290 Fax: 856-848-6091 E-mail: sales@slackinc.com; editor@slackinc.com; customerservice@slackinc.com Web Site: www.healio.com/books, pg 191

Grecco, Melissa, Chronicle Books LLC, 680 Second St, San Francisco, CA 94107 Tel: 415-537-4200 Fax: 415-537-4460 (perms) E-mail: hello@chroniclebooks.com; subrights@chroniclebooks.com Web Site: www.chroniclebooks.com, pg 47

Greco, John, American Bible Society, 101 N Independence Mall E, 8th fl, Philadelphia, PA 19106-2112 Tel: 215-309-0900 Toll Free Tel: 800-322-4253 (cust serv); 888-596-6296 E-mail: info@americanbible.org Web Site: www.americanbible.org, pg 8

Greco, Kristin, Psychological Assessment Resources Inc (PAR), 16204 N Florida Ave, Lutz, FL 33549 Tel: 813-449-4065 Toll Free Tel: 800-331-8378 Fax: 813-961-2196 Toll Free Fax: 800-727-9329 Web Site: www.parinc.com, pg 166

Greco, Marilyn, Schoolhouse Network, PO Box 1518, Northampton, MA 01061 Tel: 480-427-4836 E-mail: schoolhousenetwork@gmail.com, pg 444

Greco, Tim, Macmillan, 120 Broadway, 22nd fl, New York, NY 10271 E-mail: press.inquiries@macmillan.com Web Site: us.macmillan.com, pg 122

Greeman, Amy, Workman Publishing, 1290 Avenue of the Americas, New York, NY 10104 Toll Free Tel: 800-759-0190 Fax: 212-364-0950 E-mail: workman-inquiry@hbgusa.com Web Site: www.hachettebookgroup.com/imprint/workman-publishing-company/, pg 232

Green, Allegra, Roaring Brook Press, 120 Broadway, New York, NY 10271 Tel: 646-307-5151 Web Site: us.macmillan.com/publishers/roaring-brook-press, pg 176

Green, Allison, Simon & Schuster, 1230 Avenue of the Americas, New York, NY 10020 Tel: 212-698-7000 Toll Free Tel: 800-223-2348 (cust serv); 800-223-2336 (orders) Toll Free Fax: 800-943-9831 (orders) Web Site: simonandschusterpublishing.com/simonandschuster/, pg 188

Green, Becky, Penguin Young Readers Group, c/o Penguin Random House LLC, 1745 Broadway, New York, NY 10019 Tel: 212-782-9000 Web Site: www.penguin.com/penguin-young-readers-overview, pg 156

Green, Becky, Random House Children's Books, c/o Penguin Random House LLC, 1745 Broadway, New York, NY 10019 Tel: 212-782-9000 Web Site: www.rhcbooks.com, pg 169

Green, Dr Bridgett, Presbyterian Publishing Corp (PPC), 100 Witherspoon St, Louisville, KY 40202 Tel: 502-569-5000 Toll Free Tel: 800-533-4371; 800-523-1631 (US only) Fax: 502-569-5113 E-mail: customerservice@presbypub.com Web Site: www.ppcbooks.com; www.wjkbooks.com, pg 163

Green, Chris, The Weatherford Awards, Loyal Jones Appalachian Ctr, 101 Chestnut St, Berea, KY 40404 Tel: 859-985-3000 Web Site: www.berea.edu/centers/loyal-jones-appalachian-center/awards/weatherford-award, pg 673

Green, Dan, Pom Inc, 18-15 215 St, Bayside, NY 11360, pg 472

Green, Erin, Boys Town Press, 13603 Flanagan Blvd, 2nd fl, Boys Town, NE 68010 Tel: 531-355-1320 Toll Free Tel: 800-282-6657 Fax: 531-355-1310 E-mail: btpress@boystown.org Web Site: www.boystownpress.org, pg 35

Green, Heidi, Upstart Books™, PO Box 7488, Madison, WI 53707 Tel: 608-241-1201 Toll Free Tel: 800-356-1200 (orders); 800-962-4463 (cust serv) Toll Free Fax: 800-245-1329 (orders) E-mail: custserv@demco.com; order@demco.com Web Site: www.demco.com/upstart, pg 223

Green, Jennifer, Casemate | publishers, 1950 Lawrence Rd, Havertown, PA 19083 Tel: 610-853-9131 Fax: 610-853-9146 E-mail: casemate@casematepublishers.com Web Site: www.casematepublishers.com, pg 42

Green, Jessica, Atlantic Center for the Arts Mentoring Artist-in-Residence Program, 1414 Art Center Ave, New Smyrna Beach, FL 32168 Tel: 386-427-6975 E-mail: program@atlanticcenterforthearts.org Web Site: atlanticcenterforthearts.org, pg 553

Green, Joanna, Beacon Press, 24 Farnsworth St, Boston, MA 02210-1409 Tel: 617-742-2110 Fax: 617-723-3097 E-mail: production@beacon.org Web Site: www.beacon.org, pg 25

Green, Karen, Anvil Press Publishers, PO Box 3008, MPO, Vancouver, BC V6B 3X5, Canada Tel: 604-876-8710 E-mail: info@anvilpress.com Web Site: www.anvilpress.com, pg 395

Green, Kathy, Embolden Literary, PO Box 953607, Lake Mary, FL 32795-3607 E-mail: info@emboldenmediagroup.com; submissions@emboldenmediagroup.com Web Site: emboldenmediagroup.com/literary-representation, pg 458

Green, Morgan, Penguin Random House LLC, 1745 Broadway, New York, NY 10019 Tel: 212-782-9000 Toll Free Tel: 800-726-0600 Web Site: www.penguinrandomhouse.com, pg 155

Green, Natalie, National Book Foundation, 90 Broad St, Suite 604, New York, NY 10004 Tel: 212-685-0261 Fax: 212-213-6570 E-mail: nationalbook@nationalbook.org Web Site: www.nationalbook.org, pg 526

Green, Novella, Nursesbooks.org, The Publishing Program of ANA, 8515 Georgia Ave, Suite 400, Silver Spring, MD 20910-3492 Tel: 301-628-5000 Toll Free Tel: 800-274-4262; 800-637-0323 (orders) Fax: 301-628-5342 E-mail: anp@ana.org Web Site: www.Nursesbooks.org; www.NursingWorld.org, pg 144

Green, Simon, Pom Inc, 18-15 215 St, Bayside, NY 11360, pg 472

Greenbaum, Charlotte, Harry N Abrams Inc, 195 Broadway, 9th fl, New York, NY 10007 Tel: 212-206-7715 Toll Free Tel: 800-345-1359 Fax: 212-645-8437 E-mail: abrams@abramsbooks.com; publicity@abramsbooks.com; sales@abramsbooks.com Web Site: www.abramsbooks.com, pg 3

Greenberg, Ben, Random House Publishing Group, 1745 Broadway, New York, NY 10019 Toll Free Tel: 800-200-3552 Web Site: www.randomhousebooks.com, pg 170

Greenberg, Daniel, Levine|Greenberg|Rostan Literary Agency, 307 Seventh Ave, Suite 2407, New York, NY 10001 Tel: 212-337-0934 Fax: 212-337-0948 E-mail: submit@lgrliterary.com Web Site: lgrliterary.com, pg 467

Greenberg, Karen, Penguin Random House LLC, 1745 Broadway, New York, NY 10019 Tel: 212-782-9000 Toll Free Tel: 800-726-0600 Web Site: www.penguinrandomhouse.com, pg 155

Greenberg, Zeke, Alan Wofsy Fine Arts, 1109 Geary Blvd, San Francisco, CA 94109 Tel: 415-292-6500 Toll Free Tel: 800-660-6403 Fax: 415-292-6594 (off & cust serv); 510-251-1840 (acctg) E-mail: order@art-books.com (orders); editeur@earthlink.net (edit); beauxarts@earthlink.net (cust serv) Web Site: www.art-books.com, pg 231

Greene, Beth, BLR®—Business & Legal Resources, 5511 Virginia Way, Suite 150, Brentwood, TN 37027 Tel: 860-510-0100 Toll Free Tel: 800-727-5257 Toll Free Fax: 800-785-9212 E-mail: media@blr.com; sales@blr.com; service@blr.com; techsupport@blr.com Web Site: blr.com, pg 32

Greene, Daniel, The Pattis Family Foundation Book Award, 60 W Walton St, Chicago, IL 60610 Tel: 312-943-9090 E-mail: pattisprize@newberry.org Web Site: www.newberry.org/pattis-family-foundation-chicago-book-award, pg 646

Greene, Jennifer B, Nosy Crow Inc, 145 Lincoln Rd, Lincoln, MA 01773 E-mail: nosycrowinc@nosycrow.com; salesinfo@nosycrow.com; export@nosycrow.com (export sales); rights@nosycrow.com Web Site: nosycrow.us, pg 144

Greene, Julie, Island Press, 2000 "M" St NW, Suite 480-B, Washington, DC 20036 Tel: 202-232-7933 Toll Free Tel: 800-621-2736 Fax: 202-234-1328 E-mail: info@islandpress.org Web Site: www.islandpress.org, pg 104

Greenfield, George M, CreativeWell Inc, PO Box 3130, Memorial Sta, Upper Montclair, NJ 07043 Tel: 973-783-7575 E-mail: info@creativewell.com Web Site: www.creativewell.com, pg 454, 487

Greenfield-Binstock, Nadine, American Jewish Committee (AJC), Mail Code 6760, PO Box 7247, Philadelphia, PA 19170-0001 Tel: 212-751-4000 Fax: 212-891-1450 E-mail: social@ajc.org Web Site: www.ajc.org, pg 495

Greenhut, Carol, Schonfeld & Associates Inc, 1932 Terramar Lane, Virginia Beach, VA 23456 Toll Free Tel: 800-205-0030 E-mail: saiinfo@saibooks.com Web Site: www.saibooks.com, pg 184

Greenland, Paul R, Paul Greenland Communications Inc, 5062 Rockrose Ct, Suite 209, Roscoe, IL 61073 Tel: 815-240-4108 Web Site: www.paulgreenland.com, pg 440

Greenleaf, Clint, Greenleaf Book Group LLC, PO Box 91869, Austin, TX 78709 Tel: 512-891-6100 Fax: 512-891-6150 E-mail: contact@greenleafbookgroup.com; orders@greenleafbookgroup.com; foreignrights@greenleafbookgroup.com; media@greenleafbookgroup.com Web Site: greenleafbookgroup.com, pg 81

Greenlee, Cynthia R, University of Georgia Press, Main Library, 3rd fl, 320 S Jackson St, Athens, GA 30602 Fax: 706-542-2558; 706-542-6770 Web Site: www.ugapress.org, pg 216

Greenman-Schmitz, Fran, Kar-Ben Publishing, 241 First Ave N, Minneapolis, MN 55401 Tel: 612-332-3344 Toll Free Tel: 800-4-KARBEN (452-7236) Fax: 612-332-7615 Toll Free Fax: 800-332-1132 E-mail: custserve@karben.com Web Site: www.karben.com, pg 108

Greenspan, Elizabeth, Society for Industrial & Applied Mathematics, 3600 Market St, 6th fl, Philadelphia, PA 19104-2688 Tel: 215-382-9800 Toll Free Tel: 800-447-7426 E-mail: siam@siam.org Web Site: www.siam.org, pg 192

Greenspan, Shari Dash, Flashlight Press, 527 Empire Blvd, Brooklyn, NY 11225 Tel: 718-288-8300 Fax: 718-972-6307 Web Site: www.flashlightpress.com, pg 72

Greenspon, Joshua, House of Anansi Press Inc, 128 Sterling Rd, Lower Level, Toronto, ON M6R 2B7, Canada Tel: 416-363-4343 Fax: 416-363-1017 E-mail: customerservice@houseofanansi.com Web Site: houseofanansi.com, pg 409

Greenstein, Ruth, Turtle Point Press, 208 Java St, 5th fl, Brooklyn, NY 11222-5748 Tel: 212-741-1393 E-mail: info@turtlepointpress.com Web Site: www.turtlepointpress.com, pg 210

Greenstein, Ruth, Words into Print, 208 Java St, 5th fl, Brooklyn, NY 11222 E-mail: query@wordsintoprint.org Web Site: wordsintoprint.org, pg 445

Greenwald, Zach, Workman Publishing, 1290 Avenue of the Americas, New York, NY 10104 Toll Free Tel: 800-759-0190 Fax: 212-364-0950 E-mail: workman-inquiry@hbgusa.com Web Site: www.hachettebookgroup.com/imprint/workman-publishing-company/, pg 232

Greenway, Brittany, Macmillan, 120 Broadway, 22nd fl, New York, NY 10271 E-mail: press.inquiries@macmillan.com Web Site: us.macmillan.com, pg 122

Greer, Jessica, Other Press, 267 Fifth Ave, 6th fl, New York, NY 10016 Tel: 212-414-0054 Toll Free Tel: 877-THEOTHER (843-6843) Fax: 212-414-0939 E-mail: editor@otherpress; marketing@otherpress.com; publicity@otherpress.com Web Site: otherpress.com, pg 148

Greer, Somer, University of Louisiana at Lafayette Press, PO Box 43558, Lafayette, LA 70504-3558 Tel: 337-482-6027 E-mail: press.submissions@louisiana.edu Web Site: ulpress.org, pg 217

Gregg, Richard, Aperture Books, 548 W 28 St, 4th fl, New York, NY 10001 Tel: 212-505-5555 Toll Free Fax: 888-623-6908 E-mail: customerservice@aperture.org Web Site: aperture.org, pg 15

Gregory, Evan, Ethan Ellenberg Literary Agency, 548 Broadway, Apt 5C, New York, NY 10012 Tel: 212-431-4554 E-mail: agent@ethanellenberg.com Web Site: www.ethanellenberg.com, pg 458

Gregory, Josh, Albert Whitman & Company, 250 S Northwest Hwy, Suite 320, Park Ridge, IL 60068 Tel: 847-232-2800 Toll Free Tel: 800-255-7675 (orders) Fax: 847-581-0039 E-mail: mail@albertwhitman.com; orders@albertwhitman.com Web Site: www.albertwhitman.com, pg 6

Gregory, Michael Steven, Southern California Writers' Conference (SCWC), PO Box 433, Redmond, OR 97756 Tel: 619-303-8185 Fax: 619-906-7462 E-mail: msg@writersconference.com Web Site: www.writersconference.com; www.facebook.com/SouthernCaliforniaWritersConference/, pg 557

Gregory, Molly, Gallery Books, 1230 Avenue of the Americas, New York, NY 10020 Toll Free Tel: 800-456-6798 Fax: 212-698-7284 E-mail: consumer.customerservice@simonandschuster.com Web Site: www.simonandschuster.com, pg 76

Gregovic, Lydia, Random House Children's Books, c/o Penguin Random House LLC, 1745 Broadway, New York, NY 10019 Tel: 212-782-9000 Web Site: www.rhcbooks.com, pg 170

Greku, Borana, Harry N Abrams Inc, 195 Broadway, 9th fl, New York, NY 10007 Tel: 212-206-7715 Toll Free Tel: 800-345-1359 Fax: 212-645-8437 E-mail: abrams@abramsbooks.com; publicity@abramsbooks.com; sales@abramsbooks.com Web Site: www.abramsbooks.com, pg 3

Grenfell, Katy, Editorial Freelancers Association (EFA), 266 W 37 St, 20th fl, New York, NY 10018 Tel: 212-920-4816 Toll Free Tel: 866-929-5425 E-mail: info@the-efa.org; membership@the-efa.org Web Site: www.the-efa.org, pg 505

Grennan, Karen, SDP Publishing Solutions LLC, 36 Captain's Way, East Bridgewater, MA 02333 *Tel:* 617-775-0656 *Web Site:* www.sdppublishingsolutions.com, pg 444

Gress, Priti Chitnis, Hippocrene Books Inc, 171 Madison Ave, Suite 1605, New York, NY 10016 *Tel:* 212-685-4373 *E-mail:* info@hippocrenebooks.com; orderdept@hippocrenebooks.com (orders) *Web Site:* www.hippocrenebooks.com, pg 92

Greuel, Greg, Wayside Publishing, 2 Stonewood Dr, Freeport, ME 04032 *Toll Free Tel:* 888-302-2519 *E-mail:* info@waysidepublishing.com; support@waysidepublishing.com *Web Site:* waysidepublishing.com, pg 227

Gribbin, Dorothy, Simon & Schuster Children's Publishing, 1230 Avenue of the Americas, New York, NY 10020 *Tel:* 212-698-7000 *Web Site:* www.simonandschuster.com/kids; www.simonandschuster.com/teen; simonandschuster.net; simonandschuster.biz, pg 189

Gribble, Jessica, Bloomsbury Academic, 1385 Broadway, 5th fl, New York, NY 10018 *Tel:* 212-419-5300 *Web Site:* www.bloomsbury.com/us/academic, pg 31

Grier, Desirae, Chronicle Books LLC, 680 Second St, San Francisco, CA 94107 *Tel:* 415-537-4200 *Fax:* 415-537-4460 (perms) *E-mail:* hello@chroniclebooks.com; subrights@chroniclebooks.com *Web Site:* www.chroniclebooks.com, pg 48

Griffes, Peter L, ProStar Publications Inc, 226 W Florence Ave, Inglewood, CA 90301 *Toll Free Tel:* 800-481-6277 *E-mail:* editor@prostarpublications.com *Web Site:* www.prostarpublications.com, pg 166

Griffey, Jason, Miles Conrad Award, 3600 Clipper Mill Rd, Suite 302, Baltimore, MD 21211-1948 *Tel:* 301-654-2512 *Fax:* 410-685-5278 *E-mail:* nisohq@niso.org *Web Site:* www.niso.org, pg 591

Griffey, Jason, National Information Standards Organization (NISO), 3600 Clipper Mill Rd, Suite 302, Baltimore, MD 21211-1948 *Tel:* 301-654-2512 *Fax:* 410-685-5278 *E-mail:* nisohq@niso.org *Web Site:* www.niso.org, pg 138, 513

Griffie, LK, Vesuvian Books, 711 Dolly Parton Pkwy, No 4313, Sevierville, TN 37864 *E-mail:* info@vesuvianmedia.com *Web Site:* www.vesuvianmedia.com, pg 224

Griffin, Dakota, Tor Publishing Group, 120 Broadway, New York, NY 10271 *Toll Free Tel:* 800-455-0340 (Macmillan) *E-mail:* torpublicity@tor.com; forgepublicity@forgebooks.com *Web Site:* us.macmillan.com/torpublishinggroup, pg 208

Griffin, Diana, Workman Publishing, 1290 Avenue of the Americas, New York, NY 10104 *Toll Free Tel:* 800-759-0190 *Fax:* 212-364-0950 *E-mail:* workman-inquiry@hbgusa.com *Web Site:* www.hachettebookgroup.com/imprint/workman-publishing-company/, pg 232

Griffin, Emily, Henry Holt and Company, LLC, 120 Broadway, 23rd fl, New York, NY 10271 *Tel:* 646-307-5151 *Toll Free Tel:* 888-330-8477 (orders) *Fax:* 646-307-5285 *Web Site:* www.henryholt.com, pg 94

Griffin, Mary Lynn, Goodheart-Willcox Publisher, 18604 W Creek Dr, Tinley Park, IL 60477-6243 *Tel:* 708-687-5000 *Toll Free Tel:* 800-323-0440 *Toll Free Fax:* 888-409-3900 *E-mail:* custserv@g-w.com; orders@g-w.com *Web Site:* www.g-w.com, pg 79

Griffin, Scott, Canadian First Book Prize, 363 Parkridge Crescent, Oakville, ON L6M 1A8, Canada *Tel:* 905-618-0420 *E-mail:* info@griffinpoetryprize.com; publicity@griffinpoetryprize.com *Web Site:* griffinpoetryprize.com, pg 586

Griffin, Scott, Griffin Poetry Prize, 363 Parkridge Crescent, Oakville, ON L6M 1A8, Canada *Tel:* 905-618-0420 *E-mail:* info@griffinpoetryprize.com; publicity@griffinpoetryprize.com *Web Site:* griffinpoetryprize.com, pg 609

Griffin, Scott, Groundwood Books, 128 Sterling Rd, Lower Level, Toronto, ON M6R 2B7, Canada *Tel:* 416-363-4343 *Fax:* 416-363-1017 *E-mail:* customerservice@houseofanansi.com *Web Site:* www.houseofanansi.com, pg 407

Griffin, Scott, House of Anansi Press Inc, 128 Sterling Rd, Lower Level, Toronto, ON M6R 2B7, Canada *Tel:* 416-363-4343 *Fax:* 416-363-1017 *E-mail:* customerservice@houseofanansi.com *Web Site:* houseofanansi.com, pg 409

Griffith, Drew, University of Missouri Press, 113 Heinkel Bldg, 201 S Seventh St, Columbia, MO 65211 *Tel:* 573-882-7641; 573-882-9672 (publicity & sales enquiries) *Toll Free Tel:* 800-621-2736 (orders) *Fax:* 573-884-4498 *Toll Free Fax:* 800-621-8476 (orders) *E-mail:* upress@missouri.edu; umpmarketing@missouri.edu (publicity & sales enquiries) *Web Site:* upress.missouri.edu, pg 217

Griffith, Glenn, Naval Institute Press, 291 Wood Rd, Annapolis, MD 21402-5034 *Tel:* 410-268-6110 *Toll Free Tel:* 800-233-8764 *Fax:* 410-295-1084 *E-mail:* customer@usni.org (cust inquiries) *Web Site:* www.usni.org/press/books; www.usni.org, pg 139

Griffiths, Harley, 4A's (American Association of Advertising Agencies), 25 W 45 St, 16th fl, New York, NY 10036 *Tel:* 212-682-2500 *E-mail:* media@4as.org; membership@4as.org *Web Site:* www.aaaa.org, pg 506

Griffiths, Kadeen, HarperCollins Children's Books, 195 Broadway, New York, NY 10007 *Tel:* 212-207-7000 *Web Site:* www.harpercollins.com/childrens, pg 86

Griffor, Mariela, Marick Press, 1342 Three Mile Dr, Grosse Pointe Park, MI 48230 *Tel:* 313-407-9236 *E-mail:* orders@marickpress.com; info@marickpress.com *Web Site:* www.marickpress.com, pg 125

Grill, Sarah, Atria Books, 1230 Avenue of the Americas, New York, NY 10020 *Tel:* 212-698-7000 *Fax:* 212-698-7007 *Web Site:* www.simonandschuster.com, pg 21

Grilliot, Bob, JIST Publishing, 4050 Westmark Dr, Dubuque, IA 52002 *Tel:* 563-589-1000 *Toll Free Tel:* 800-328-1452; 800-228-0810 *Fax:* 563-589-1046 *Toll Free Fax:* 800-772-9165 *E-mail:* orders@kendallhunt.com *Web Site:* www.paradigmeducation.com, pg 106

Grillo, Scott, McGraw-Hill Education, 2 Penn Plaza, New York, NY 10121-2298 *Tel:* 212-904-2000 *E-mail:* international_cs@mheducation.com; seg_customerservice@mheducation.com (PreK-12); hep_customerservice@mheducation.com (higher education) *Web Site:* www.mheducation.com, pg 128

Grillo, Scott, McGraw-Hill Professional Publishing Group, 2 Penn Plaza, New York, NY 10121 *Tel:* 646-766-2000 *Web Site:* www.mhprofessional.com; www.mheducation.com, pg 128

Grima, Tony, National Braille Press, 88 Saint Stephen St, Boston, MA 02115-4312 *Tel:* 617-266-6160 *Toll Free Tel:* 800-548-7323 (cust serv); 888-965-8965 *Fax:* 617-437-0456 *E-mail:* contact@nbp.org *Web Site:* www.nbp.org, pg 137

Grimaldi, Dana, Harlequin Enterprises Ltd, Bay Adelaide Centre, East Tower, 22 Adelaide St W, 41st fl, Toronto, ON M5H 4E3, Canada *Tel:* 416-445-5860 *Toll Free Tel:* 888-432-4879; 800-370-5838 (ebook inquiries) *E-mail:* customerservice@harlequin.com *Web Site:* www.harlequin.com, pg 409

Grimbleby, Jennifer, Kids Can Press Ltd, 25 Dockside Dr, Toronto, ON M5A 0B5, Canada *Tel:* 416-479-7000 *Toll Free Tel:* 800-265-0884 *Fax:* 416-960-5437 *E-mail:* info@kidscan.com; customerservice@kidscan.com *Web Site:* www.kidscanpress.com; www.kidscanpress.ca, pg 411

Grimes, Christopher, University of Illinois at Chicago, Program for Writers, College of Liberal Arts & Sciences, 601 S Morgan St, Chicago, IL 60607 *Tel:* 312-413-2200 (Eng dept) *E-mail:* english@uic.edu *Web Site:* engl.uic.edu/graduate-studies/program-for-writers, pg 566

Grimes, Mark, American Academy of Pediatrics, 345 Park Blvd, Itasca, IL 60143 *Toll Free Tel:* 888-227-1770 *Fax:* 847-228-1281 *Web Site:* www.aap.org; shop.aap.org; publishing.aap.org, pg 8

Grimm, Katie, Curtis Brown, Ltd, 228 E 45 St, Suite 310, New York, NY 10017 *Tel:* 212-473-5400 *Fax:* 212-598-0917 *E-mail:* info@cbltd.com *Web Site:* www.curtisbrown.com, pg 452

Grinberg, Jill, Jill Grinberg Literary Management LLC, 392 Vanderbilt Ave, Brooklyn, NY 11238 *Tel:* 212-620-5883 *E-mail:* info@jillgrinbergliterary.com *Web Site:* www.jillgrinbergliterary.com, pg 461

Grindle, David, Society of Motion Picture and Television Engineers® (SMPTE®), White Plains Plaza, 445 Hamilton Ave, Suite 601, White Plains, NY 10601-1827 *Tel:* 914-761-1100 *E-mail:* hello@smpte.org (mktg) *Web Site:* www.smpte.org, pg 520

Grinstead, Georgana (Nina), The Seymour Agency, 475 Miner Street Rd, Canton, NY 13617 *Tel:* 239-398-8209 *Web Site:* www.theseymouragency.com, pg 475

Grisafi, Lora, Harry N Abrams Inc, 195 Broadway, 9th fl, New York, NY 10007 *Tel:* 212-206-7715 *Toll Free Tel:* 800-345-1359 *Fax:* 212-645-8437 *E-mail:* abrams@abramsbooks.com; publicity@abramsbooks.com; sales@abramsbooks.com *Web Site:* www.abramsbooks.com, pg 2

Grobicki, Barbara, American Marketing Association, 130 E Randolph St, 22nd fl, Chicago, IL 60601 *Tel:* 312-542-9000 *Toll Free Tel:* 800-AMA-1150 (262-1150) *Web Site:* www.ama.org, pg 495

Groell, Anne, Random House Publishing Group, 1745 Broadway, New York, NY 10019 *Toll Free Tel:* 800-200-3552 *Web Site:* www.randomhousebooks.com, pg 171

Grogan, David, American Booksellers Association, 600 Mamaroneck Ave, Suite 400, Harrison, NY 10528 *Tel:* 914-406-7500 *Toll Free Tel:* 800-637-0037 *Fax:* 914-417-4013 *E-mail:* info@bookweb.org *Web Site:* www.bookweb.org, pg 494

Grogan, Kayla, Aevitas Creative Management LLC, 19 W 21 St, Suite 501, New York, NY 10010 *Tel:* 212-765-6900 *Web Site:* www.aevitascreative.com, pg 448

Grondahl, Paul, New York State Edith Wharton Citation of Merit for Fiction Writers, University at Albany, Science Library 320, 1400 Washington Ave, Albany, NY 12222 *Tel:* 518-442-5620 *E-mail:* writers@albany.edu *Web Site:* www.nyswritersinstitute.org, pg 640

Grondahl, Paul, New York State Walt Whitman Citation of Merit for Poets, University at Albany, Science Library 320, 1400 Washington Ave, Albany, NY 12222 *Tel:* 518-442-5620 *E-mail:* writers@albany.edu *Web Site:* www.nyswritersinstitute.org, pg 640

Grondahl, Paul, New York State Writers Institute, University at Albany, Science Library 320, 1400 Washington Ave, Albany, NY 12222 *Tel:* 518-442-5620 *Fax:* 518-442-5621 *E-mail:* writers@albany.edu *Web Site:* www.nyswritersinstitute.org, pg 556

Groom, Kelle, Atlantic Center for the Arts Mentoring Artist-in-Residence Program, 1414 Art Center Ave, New Smyrna Beach, FL 32168 *Tel:* 386-427-6975 *E-mail:* program@atlanticcenterforthearts.org *Web Site:* atlanticcenterforthearts.org, pg 553

Grooms, TeMika, Society of Children's Book Writers & Illustrators (SCBWI), 6363 Wilshire Blvd, Suite 425, Los Angeles, CA 90048 *Tel:* 323-782-1010 *E-mail:* membership@scbwi.org *Web Site:* www.scbwi.org, pg 520

Groschup-Black, Maria, Sunbelt Publications Inc, 664 Marsat Ct, Suite A, Chula Vista, CA 91911 *Tel:* 619-258-4911 *Toll Free Tel:* 800-626-6579 (cust serv) *Fax:* 619-258-4916 *E-mail:* info@sunbeltpub.com; service@sunbeltpub.com *Web Site:* sunbeltpublications.com, pg 200

Groschup-Black, Nichole, Sunbelt Publications Inc, 664 Marsat Ct, Suite A, Chula Vista, CA 91911 *Tel:* 619-258-4911 *Toll Free Tel:* 800-626-6579 (cust serv) *Fax:* 619-258-4916 *E-mail:* info@sunbeltpub.com; service@sunbeltpub.com *Web Site:* sunbeltpublications.com, pg 200

Grosjean, Jill, Jill Grosjean Literary Agency, 1390 Millstone Rd, Sag Harbor, NY 11963 Tel: 631-725-7419 Fax: 631-725-8632 E-mail: JillLit310@aol.com, pg 461

Gross, Cassie, Georges Borchardt Inc, 136 E 57 St, New York, NY 10022 Tel: 212-753-5785 E-mail: georges@gbagency.com Web Site: www.gbagency.com, pg 451

Gross, Laura, Laura Gross Literary Agency, PO Box 610326, Newton Highlands, MA 02461 Tel: 617-964-2977 E-mail: query@lg-la.com; rights@lg-la.com Web Site: www.lg-la.com, pg 461

Grossberg, Aileen, Sydney Taylor Manuscript Award, 204 Park St, Montclair, NJ 07042 Tel: 201-371-3255 E-mail: info@jewishlibraries.org Web Site: jewishlibraries.org, pg 668

Grossberg, Michael, Prometheus Awards, 650 Castro St, Suite 120-433, Mountain View, CA 94041 Tel: 650-968-6319 E-mail: bestnovel@lfs.org; specialaward@lfs.org Web Site: www.lfs.org, pg 653

Grossinger, Richard, Inner Traditions International Ltd, One Park St, Rochester, VT 05767 Tel: 802-767-3174 Toll Free Tel: 800-246-8648 Fax: 802-767-3726 E-mail: customerservice@InnerTraditions.com Web Site: www.InnerTraditions.com, pg 101

Grosskopf, Lauren, Pleasure Boat Studio: A Literary Press, 3710 SW Barton St, Seattle, WA 98126 Tel: 206-962-0460 E-mail: pleasboatpublishing@gmail.com Web Site: www.pleasureboatstudio.com, pg 160

Grossman, Jim, American Historical Association (AHA), 400 "A" St SE, Washington, DC 20003 Tel: 202-544-2422 E-mail: info@historians.org; awards@historians.org Web Site: www.historians.org, pg 10

Grossman, Sarah E M, Cornell University Press, Sage House, 512 E State St, Ithaca, NY 14850 Tel: 607-253-2338 E-mail: cupressinfo@cornell.edu; cupress-sales@cornell.edu; cupress-perms@cornell.edu (reprint/class use permissions) Web Site: www.cornellpress.cornell.edu, pg 52

Grossmeyer, Carol, Porchlight Book Co Business Book Awards, 544 S First St, Milwaukee, WI 53204 Toll Free Tel: 800-236-7323 E-mail: info@porchlightbooks.com Web Site: porchlightbooks.com, pg 651

Grotz, Jennifer, Bread Loaf Fellowships & Scholarships, Middlebury College, 204 College St, Middlebury, VT 05753 Tel: 802-443-5286 Fax: 802-443-2087 E-mail: blwc@middlebury.edu Web Site: www.middlebury.edu/blwc, pg 584

Grotz, Jennifer, Bread Loaf Writers' Conference, 204 College St, Middlebury, VT 05753 Tel: 802-443-5286 Fax: 802-443-2087 E-mail: blwc@middlebury.edu Web Site: www.middlebury.edu/blwc, pg 553

Grove, Alyssa Hickman, Utah Original Writing Competition, 617 E South Temple, Salt Lake City, UT 84102 Tel: 801-236-7555 Fax: 801-236-7556 Web Site: arts.utah.gov, pg 672

Groveman, Sara, Miles Conrad Award, 3600 Clipper Mill Rd, Suite 302, Baltimore, MD 21211-1948 Tel: 301-654-2512 Fax: 410-685-5278 E-mail: nisohq@niso.org Web Site: www.niso.org, pg 591

Groveman, Sara, National Information Standards Organization (NISO), 3600 Clipper Mill Rd, Suite 302, Baltimore, MD 21211-1948 Tel: 301-654-2512 Fax: 410-685-5278 E-mail: nisohq@niso.org Web Site: www.niso.org, pg 138, 513

Groves, Colby, Verso Books, 388 Atlantic Ave, Brooklyn, NY 11217 Tel: 718-246-8160 Fax: 718-246-8165 E-mail: verso@versobooks.com Web Site: www.versobooks.com, pg 224

Grubb, Nora, Doubleday, c/o Penguin Random House LLC, 1745 Broadway, New York, NY 10019 Tel: 212-751-2600 Fax: 212-940-7390 (dom rts); 212-572-2662 (foreign rts) Web Site: www.knopfdoubleday.com/imprint/doubleday/; knopfdoubleday.com, pg 61

Grubb, Randell C, Theosophical University Press, PO Box C, Pasadena, CA 91109-7107 Tel: 626-798-3378 E-mail: tupress@theosociety.org Web Site: www.theosociety.org, pg 206

Gruber, Pam, Irene Goodman Literary Agency, 27 W 24 St, Suite 700B, New York, NY 10010 Tel: 212-604-0330 E-mail: queries@irenegoodman.com Web Site: www.irenegoodman.com, pg 460

Gruenberger, Jaclyn, Penguin Random House Canada, a Penguin Random House company, 320 Front St W, Suite 1400, Toronto, ON M5V 3B6, Canada Tel: 416-364-4449 Toll Free Tel: 888-523-9292 (cust serv) E-mail: canadaweb@penguinrandomhouse.com; customerservicescanada@penguinrandomhouse.com Web Site: www.penguinrandomhouse.ca, pg 416

Gruender, Nataly, Dystel, Goderich & Bourret LLC, One Union Sq W, Suite 904, New York, NY 10003 Tel: 212-627-9100 Fax: 212-627-9313 Web Site: www.dystel.com, pg 457

Gruninger, Susanna, Kensington Publishing Corp, 900 Third Ave, 26th fl, New York, NY 10022 Tel: 212-407-1500 Toll Free Tel: 800-221-2647 Fax: 212-935-0699 Web Site: www.kensingtonbooks.com, pg 109

Grupp, Nikolas, George T Bisel Co Inc, 710 S Washington Sq, Philadelphia, PA 19106-3519 Tel: 215-922-5760 Toll Free Tel: 800-247-3526 Fax: 215-922-2235 E-mail: gbisel@bisel.com Web Site: www.bisel.com, pg 29

Grutjen, Wibke, Simon & Schuster, LLC, 1230 Avenue of the Americas, New York, NY 10020 Tel: 212-698-7000 Toll Free Tel: 800-223-2336 (orders) Fax: 212-698-7007 Toll Free Fax: 800-943-9831 (orders) E-mail: firstname.lastname@simonandschuster.com; purchaseorders@simonandschuster.com (orders) Web Site: www.simonandschuster.com, pg 189

Gu, Wendi, Sanford J Greenburger Associates Inc, 55 Fifth Ave, New York, NY 10003 Tel: 212-206-5600 Web Site: greenburger.com, pg 461

Guan, Sarah, Kensington Publishing Corp, 900 Third Ave, 26th fl, New York, NY 10022 Tel: 212-407-1500 Toll Free Tel: 800-221-2647 Fax: 212-935-0699 Web Site: www.kensingtonbooks.com, pg 109

Guare, Sarah, Workman Publishing, 1290 Avenue of the Americas, New York, NY 10104 Toll Free Tel: 800-759-0190 Fax: 212-364-0950 E-mail: workman-inquiry@hbgusa.com Web Site: www.hachettebookgroup.com/imprint/workman-publishing-company/, pg 233

Guarin, Imelda, Marshall Cavendish Education, 99 White Plains Rd, Tarrytown, NY 10591-9001 Tel: 914-332-8888 Toll Free Tel: 800-821-9881 Fax: 914-332-1082 E-mail: mce@marshallcavendish.com; customerservice@marshallcavendish.com Web Site: www.mceducation.us, pg 125

Guay, Amy, Avid Reader Press, 1230 Avenue of the Americas, New York, NY 10020 Web Site: avidreaderpress.com, pg 23

Guay, Kenneth, Princeton University Press, 41 William St, Princeton, NJ 08540-5237 Tel: 609-258-4900 Fax: 609-258-6305 E-mail: info@press.princeton.edu Web Site: press.princeton.edu, pg 164

Guay, Marie-Noelle, Editions Yvon Blais, 75 rue Queen, bureau 4700, Montreal, QC H3C 2N6, Canada Toll Free Tel: 800-363-3047 E-mail: editionsyvonblais.commandes@tr.com (cust serv) Web Site: store.thomsonreuters.ca/fr-ca/nouveautes, pg 405

Guenzi, Carol, Carol Guenzi Agents Inc, 865 Delaware St, Denver, CO 80204 Tel: 303-820-2599 Toll Free Tel: 800-417-5120 E-mail: art@artagent.com Web Site: artagent.com, pg 485

Guerin, Tom, Little, Brown Books for Young Readers (LBYR), 1290 Avenue of the Americas, New York, NY 10104 Tel: 212-364-1100 Toll Free Tel: 800-759-0190 (cust serv) E-mail: rights@lbchildrens.com Web Site: www.hachettebookgroup.com/imprint/little-brown-books-for-young-readers/, pg 118

Guerra, Delin, Bogle Pratt International Library Travel Fund, c/o The American Library Association, 225 N Michigan Ave, Suite 1300, Chicago, IL 60601-7757 Tel: 312-280-3201 Toll Free Tel: 800-545-2433 (ext 3201) Fax: 312-280-4392 E-mail: intl@ala.org Web Site: www.ala.org, pg 582

Guerra, Margie, The Experiment, 220 E 23 St, Suite 600, New York, NY 10010-4658 Tel: 212-889-1659 E-mail: info@theexperimentpublishing.com Web Site: www.theexperimentpublishing.com, pg 68

Guerth, Jan-Erik, BlueBridge, 8 Cottage Place, Katonah, NY 10536 Tel: 914-301-5901 Web Site: www.bluebridgebooks.com, pg 32

Guess, Elizabeth Blue, Basic Books Group, 1290 Avenue of the Americas, New York, NY 10104 Tel: 212-340-8100 Toll Free Tel: 800-343-4499 (cust serv) Fax: 212-340-8105 E-mail: customer.service@hbgusa.com; orders@hbgusa.com Web Site: www.hachettebookgroup.com/imprint/basic-books/, pg 25

Guess, Elizabeth Blue, Grand Central Publishing, 1290 Avenue of the Americas, New York, NY 10104 Tel: 212-364-1100 Web Site: www.hachettebookgroup.com/imprint/grand-central-publishing/, pg 80

Guess, Elizabeth Blue, Hachette Nashville, 6100 Tower Circle, Room 210, Franklin, TN 37067 Tel: 615-221-0996 Fax: 615-221-0962 Web Site: www.hachettebookgroup.com/imprint/hachette-nashville/, pg 83

Guess, Elizabeth Blue, Orbit, 1290 Avenue of the Americas, New York, NY 10104 Tel: 212-364-1100 Toll Free Tel: 800-759-0190 Web Site: www.orbitbooks.net; www.hachettebookgroup.com/imprint/orbit, pg 147

Guevara, Linda L, All About Kids Publishing, PO Box 159, Gilroy, CA 95021 Tel: 408-337-1152 E-mail: info@allaboutkidspub.com Web Site: www.allaboutkidspub.com, pg 7

Guevin, John R, Biographical Publishing Co, 95 Sycamore Dr, Prospect, CT 06712-1011 Tel: 203-758-3661 Fax: 253-793-2618 E-mail: biopub@aol.com Web Site: www.biopub.us, pg 29

Guglielmelli, Rachel, Penguin Random House Canada, a Penguin Random House company, 320 Front St W, Suite 1400, Toronto, ON M5V 3B6, Canada Tel: 416-364-4449 Toll Free Tel: 888-523-9292 (cust serv) E-mail: canadaweb@penguinrandomhouse.com; customerservicescanada@penguinrandomhouse.com Web Site: www.penguinrandomhouse.ca, pg 416

Guibord, Maurice, BCHF Historical Writing Competition, PO Box 448, Fort Langley, BC V1M 2R7, Canada E-mail: info@bchistory.ca Web Site: www.bchistory.ca/awards/historical-writing, pg 578

Guidone, Kimberly, The Jennifer DeChiara Literary Agency, 245 Park Ave, 39th fl, New York, NY 10167 Tel: 212-372-8989 Web Site: www.jdlit.com, pg 455

Guild, Christa, Random House Publishing Group, 1745 Broadway, New York, NY 10019 Toll Free Tel: 800-200-3552 Web Site: www.randomhousebooks.com, pg 171

Guili, Lisa, Educational Insights®, 152 W Walnut St, Suite 201, Gardena, CA 90248 Toll Free Tel: 800-995-4436 Toll Free Fax: 888-892-8731 E-mail: info@educationalinsights.com; cs@educationalinsights.com Web Site: www.educationalinsights.com, pg 64

Guillaume, Daphney, HarperCollins Publishers LLC, 195 Broadway, New York, NY 10007 Tel: 212-207-7000 Web Site: www.harpercollins.com, pg 87

Guimaraes, Sophie, Scribner, 1230 Avenue of the Americas, New York, NY 10020 Web Site: www.simonandschusterpublishing.com/scribner/, pg 185

Guinn, Darby, Holiday House Publishing Inc, 50 Broad St, New York, NY 10004 Tel: 212-688-0085 Fax: 212-421-6134 E-mail: info@holidayhouse.com Web Site: www.holidayhouse.com, pg 94

Guinsler, Robert, Sterling Lord Literistic Inc, 594 Broadway, Suite 205, New York, NY 10012 Tel: 212-780-6050 Fax: 212-780-6095 E-mail: info@sll.com Web Site: www.sll.com, pg 477

Guinta, Kimberly, Rutgers University Press, 106 Somerset St, 3rd fl, New Brunswick, NJ 08901 Tel: 848-445-7762; 848-445-7761 (sales) Fax: 732-745-4935 E-mail: sales@rutgersuniversitypress.org Web Site: www.rutgersuniversitypress.org, pg 178

Guiod, Suzanne, Bucknell University Press, One Dent Dr, Lewisburg, PA 17837 *Tel:* 570-577-1049 *E-mail:* universitypress@bucknell.edu *Web Site:* www.bucknell.edu/universitypress, pg 38

Guiterman, Carina, Simon & Schuster, 1230 Avenue of the Americas, New York, NY 10020 *Tel:* 212-698-7000 *Toll Free Tel:* 800-223-2348 (cust serv); 800-223-2336 (orders) *Toll Free Fax:* 800-943-9831 (orders) *Web Site:* simonandschusterpublishing.com/simonandschuster/, pg 188

Gulick, Lisa, Sunbelt Publications Inc, 664 Marsat Ct, Suite A, Chula Vista, CA 91911 *Tel:* 619-258-4911 *Toll Free Tel:* 800-626-6579 (cust serv) *Fax:* 619-258-4916 *E-mail:* info@sunbeltpub.com; service@sunbeltpub.com *Web Site:* sunbeltpublications.com, pg 200

Gunderson, Shaun, J J Keller & Associates, Inc®, 3003 Breezewood Lane, Neenah, WI 54957 *Tel:* 920-722-2848 *Toll Free Tel:* 877-564-2333 *Toll Free Fax:* 800-727-7516 *E-mail:* customerservice@jjkeller.com; sales@jjkeller.com *Web Site:* www.jjkeller.com, pg 108

Gundry, Stanley N, Zondervan, 3900 Sparks Dr SE, Grand Rapids, MI 49546 *Tel:* 616-698-6900 *Toll Free Tel:* 800-226-1122; 800-727-1309 (retail orders) *Fax:* 616-698-3350 *Toll Free Fax:* 800-698-3256 (retail orders) *E-mail:* customercare@harpercollins.com *Web Site:* www.zondervan.com, pg 236

Gunn, David, Regular Baptist Press, 3715 N Ventura Dr, Arlington Heights, IL 60004 *Tel:* 847-843-1600 *Toll Free Tel:* 800-727-4440 (cust serv) *Fax:* 847-843-3757 *E-mail:* orders@rbpstore.org *Web Site:* regularbaptistpress.org, pg 174

Gunn, Olivia Noble, The Ibsen Society of America (ISA), c/o Indiana University, Global & Intl Studies Bldg 3111, 355 N Jordan Ave, Bloomington, IN 47405-1105 *Web Site:* www.ibsensociety.org, pg 507

Gunnison, Toni, University of Wisconsin Press, 728 State St, Suite 443, Madison, WI 53706-1418 *Tel:* 608-263-1110; 608-263-0668 (journal orders) *Toll Free Tel:* 800-621-2736 (book orders) *Fax:* 608-263-1173 *Toll Free Fax:* 800-621-2736 (book orders) *E-mail:* uwiscpress@uwpress.wisc.edu *Web Site:* uwpress.wisc.edu, pg 221

Guo, Janalyn, The University of Utah Press, J Willard Marriott Library, Suite 5400, 295 S 1500 E, Salt Lake City, UT 84112-0860 *Tel:* 801-585-9786 *Fax:* 801-581-3365 *E-mail:* hannah.new@utah.edu *Web Site:* www.uofupress.com, pg 220

Gupta, Ashis, Bayeux Arts Inc, 2403, 510-Sixth Ave SE, Calgary, AB T2G 1L7, Canada *E-mail:* mail@bayeux.com *Web Site:* bayeux.com, pg 396

Gupta, Jay, The New Press, 120 Wall St, 31st fl, New York, NY 10005 *Tel:* 212-629-8802 *Fax:* 212-629-8617 *E-mail:* newpress@thenewpress.com *Web Site:* thenewpress.com, pg 140

Gupta, Dr Swapna, Bayeux Arts Inc, 2403, 510-Sixth Ave SE, Calgary, AB T2G 1L7, Canada *E-mail:* mail@bayeux.com *Web Site:* bayeux.com, pg 396

Guralnick, June, Sally Buckner Emerging Writers' Fellowship, PO Box 21591, Winston-Salem, NC 27120-1591 *Tel:* 336-293-8844 *E-mail:* mail@ncwriters.org; nclrsubmissions@ecu.edu *Web Site:* www.ncwriters.org, pg 585

Gurdian, Alvaro, National Association of Hispanic Publications Inc (NAHP), National Press Bldg, 529 14 St NW, Suite 923, Washington, DC 20045 *Web Site:* nahp.org, pg 511

Gureli, Nicole, Holiday House Publishing Inc, 50 Broad St, New York, NY 10004 *Tel:* 212-688-0085 *Fax:* 212-421-6134 *E-mail:* info@holidayhouse.com *Web Site:* www.holidayhouse.com, pg 94

Gurewich, Judith, Other Press, 267 Fifth Ave, 6th fl, New York, NY 10016 *Tel:* 212-414-0054 *Toll Free Tel:* 877-THEOTHER (843-6843) *Fax:* 212-414-0939 *E-mail:* editor@otherpress.com; marketing@otherpress.com; publicity@otherpress.com *Web Site:* otherpress.com, pg 148

Gurreri, Wayne, Harry N Abrams Inc, 195 Broadway, 9th fl, New York, NY 10007 *Tel:* 212-206-7715 *Toll Free Tel:* 800-345-1359 *Fax:* 212-645-8437 *E-mail:* abrams@abramsbooks.com; publicity@abramsbooks.com; sales@abramsbooks.com *Web Site:* www.abramsbooks.com, pg 3

Gusinde-Duffy, Mick, University of Georgia Press, Main Library, 3rd fl, 320 S Jackson St, Athens, GA 30602 *Fax:* 706-542-2558; 706-542-6770 *Web Site:* www.ugapress.org, pg 216

Gustafson, Lauraine, Classical Academic Press, 515 S 32 St, Camp Hill, PA 17011 *Tel:* 717-730-0711 *Toll Free Tel:* 866-730-0711 *Fax:* 717-730-0721 *Toll Free Fax:* 866-730-0721 *E-mail:* info@classicalsubjects.com; orders@classicalsubjects.com *Web Site:* classicalacademicpress.com, pg 49

Gustin, Dominique, Annual & Rolling Grants for Artists, 136 State St, Montpelier, VT 05633 *Tel:* 802-828-3291 *E-mail:* info@vermontartscouncil.org *Web Site:* www.vermontartscouncil.org, pg 573

Guthro, Clem, University of Hawaii Press, 2840 Kolowalu St, Honolulu, HI 96822-1888 *Tel:* 808-956-8255 *Toll Free Tel:* 888-UHPRESS (847-7377) *Toll Free Fax:* 800-650-7811 *E-mail:* uhpbooks@hawaii.edu *Web Site:* www.uhpress.hawaii.edu, pg 216

Gutierrez, Amanda, Macmillan, 120 Broadway, 22nd fl, New York, NY 10271 *E-mail:* press.inquiries@macmillan.com *Web Site:* us.macmillan.com, pg 122

Gutierrez, Lizbeth, Penguin Random House Audio Publishing Group, 1745 Broadway, New York, NY 10019 *Toll Free Tel:* 800-793-2665 (cust serv) *E-mail:* audio@penguinrandomhouse.com; ecustomerservice@penguinrandomhouse.com *Web Site:* www.penguinrandomhouseaudio.com, pg 154

Gutierrez, Romi, University Press of Florida, 2046 NE Waldo Rd, Suite 2100, Gainesville, FL 32609 *Tel:* 352-392-1351 *Toll Free Tel:* 800-226-3822 (orders only) *Fax:* 352-392-0590 *Toll Free Fax:* 800-680-1955 (orders only) *E-mail:* press@upress.ufl.edu; orders@upress.ufl.edu *Web Site:* www.upf.com, pg 221

Gutin, Julie, NASW Press, 750 First St NE, Suite 800, Washington, DC 20002 *Tel:* 202-408-8600 *Fax:* 203-336-8312 *E-mail:* press@naswdc.org *Web Site:* www.naswpress.org, pg 136

Gutmajer, Shoshana, Workman Publishing, 1290 Avenue of the Americas, New York, NY 10104 *Toll Free Tel:* 800-759-0190 *Fax:* 212-364-0950 *E-mail:* workman-inquiry@hbgusa.com *Web Site:* www.hachettebookgroup.com/imprint/workman-publishing-company/, pg 233

Gutman, Cassie, Macmillan, 120 Broadway, 22nd fl, New York, NY 10271 *E-mail:* press.inquiries@macmillan.com *Web Site:* us.macmillan.com, pg 122

Guttman, Joseph, University of Pennsylvania Press, 3905 Spruce St, Philadelphia, PA 19104 *Tel:* 215-898-6261 *Fax:* 215-898-0404 *E-mail:* custserv@pobox.upenn.edu *Web Site:* www.pennpress.org, pg 219

Guttman, Naomi, Hamilton College, Literature & Creative Writing, Literature & Creative Writing Dept, 198 College Hill Rd, Clinton, NY 13323 *Tel:* 315-859-4370 *Fax:* 315-859-4390 *Web Site:* www.hamilton.edu, pg 563

Guttman, Rob, Macmillan, 120 Broadway, 22nd fl, New York, NY 10271 *E-mail:* press.inquiries@macmillan.com *Web Site:* us.macmillan.com, pg 122

Guy, Kristin, Random House Children's Books, c/o Penguin Random House LLC, 1745 Broadway, New York, NY 10019 *Tel:* 212-782-9000 *Web Site:* www.rhcbooks.com, pg 170

Guy, Melody, Hay House LLC, PO Box 5100, Carlsbad, CA 92018-5100 *Tel:* 760-431-7695 (ext 1, intl) *Toll Free Tel:* 800-654-5126 (ext 1, US) *Toll Free Fax:* 800-650-5115 *Web Site:* www.hayhouse.com, pg 89

Guy-Haddock, Michael, Simon & Schuster Canada, 166 King St E, Suite 300, Toronto, ON M5A 1J3, Canada *Tel:* 647-427-8882 *Toll Free Tel:* 800-387-0446; 800-268-3216 (orders) *Fax:* 647-430-9446 *Toll Free Fax:* 888-849-8151 (orders) *E-mail:* info@simonandschuster.ca *Web Site:* www.simonandschuster.ca, pg 419

Guzman, Angela, HarperCollins Publishers LLC, 195 Broadway, New York, NY 10007 *Tel:* 212-207-7000 *Web Site:* www.harpercollins.com, pg 86

Guzman, Elena, Macmillan, 120 Broadway, 22nd fl, New York, NY 10271 *E-mail:* press.inquiries@macmillan.com *Web Site:* us.macmillan.com, pg 122

Guzman, Martha, Maria Carvainis Agency Inc, Rockefeller Center, 1270 Avenue of the Americas, Suite 2915, New York, NY 10020 *Tel:* 212-245-6365 *Fax:* 212-245-7196 *E-mail:* mca@mariacarvainisagency.com *Web Site:* mariacarvainisagency.com, pg 453

Guzman, Robert, Penguin Random House Audio Publishing Group, 1745 Broadway, New York, NY 10019 *Toll Free Tel:* 800-793-2665 (cust serv) *E-mail:* audio@penguinrandomhouse.com; ecustomerservice@penguinrandomhouse.com *Web Site:* www.penguinrandomhouseaudio.com, pg 154

Guzzardo, Lindsay, Martin Literary Management, 914 164 St SE, Suite B12, Box 307, Mill Creek, WA 98012 *Tel:* 206-466-1773 (no phone queries) *Web Site:* www.martinliterarymanagement.com, pg 469

Gwinn, Julie, The Seymour Agency, 475 Miner Street Rd, Canton, NY 13617 *Tel:* 239-398-8209 *Web Site:* www.theseymouragency.com, pg 475

Gwizdala, Angela, The American Library Association (ALA), 225 N Michigan Ave, Suite 1300, Chicago, IL 60601 *Tel:* 312-944-6780 *Toll Free Tel:* 800-545-2433; 866-SHOP-ALA (746-7252, orders) *Fax:* 312-280-5275; 312-440-9374; 312-280-5860 (orders) *E-mail:* ala@ala.org; alastore@ala.org *Web Site:* www.alastore.ala.org; www.ala.org, pg 10

Gyllenhaal, Rebecca, Quirk Books, 215 Church St, Philadelphia, PA 19106 *Tel:* 215-627-3581 *Fax:* 215-627-5220 *E-mail:* general@quirkbooks.com *Web Site:* www.quirkbooks.com, pg 168

Ha, Alex, Concordia Publishing House, 3558 S Jefferson Ave, St Louis, MO 63118-3968 *Tel:* 314-268-1000; 314-268-1268 (bookshop) *Toll Free Tel:* 800-325-3040 (cust serv) *Toll Free Fax:* 800-490-9889 (cust serv) *E-mail:* order@cph.org *Web Site:* www.cph.org, pg 51

Ha, Paul C, MIT List Visual Arts Center, MIT E 15-109, 20 Ames St, Cambridge, MA 02139 *Tel:* 617-253-4680 *E-mail:* listinfo@mit.edu *Web Site:* listart.mit.edu, pg 132

Haas, Linda, StarGroup International Inc, 1194 Old Dixie Hwy, Suite 201, West Palm Beach, FL 33413 *Tel:* 561-547-0667 *Fax:* 561-843-8530 *E-mail:* info@stargroupinternational.com *Web Site:* stargroupinternational.com, pg 198

Haas, Maggie, Chronicle Books LLC, 680 Second St, San Francisco, CA 94107 *Tel:* 415-537-4200 *Fax:* 415-537-4460 (perms) *E-mail:* hello@chroniclebooks.com; subrights@chroniclebooks.com *Web Site:* www.chroniclebooks.com, pg 48

Haase, H W, Quintessence Publishing Co Inc, 411 N Raddant Rd, Batavia, IL 60510 *Tel:* 630-736-3600 *Toll Free Tel:* 800-621-0387 *Fax:* 630-736-3633 *E-mail:* contact@quintpub.com; service@quintbook.com *Web Site:* www.quintpub.com, pg 168

Haase, Olivia, Sourcebooks LLC, 1935 Brookdale Rd, Suite 139, Naperville, IL 60563 *Tel:* 630-961-3900 *Toll Free Tel:* 800-432-7444 *Fax:* 630-961-2168 *E-mail:* info@sourcebooks.com *Web Site:* www.sourcebooks.com, pg 195

Haav, Julia, Princeton University Press, 41 William St, Princeton, NJ 08540-5237 *Tel:* 609-258-4900 *Fax:* 609-258-6305 *E-mail:* info@press.princeton.edu *Web Site:* press.princeton.edu, pg 164

Habayeb, Amy, Simon & Schuster Children's Publishing, 1230 Avenue of the Americas, New York, NY 10020 *Tel:* 212-698-7000 *Web Site:* www.simonandschuster.com/kids; www.simonandschuster.com/teen; simonandschuster.net; simonandschuster.biz, pg 189

Habegger, Larry, Travelers' Tales, 2320 Bowdoin St, Palo Alto, CA 94306 Tel: 650-462-2110 E-mail: ttales@travelerstales.com; info@travelerstales.com Web Site: travelerstales.com, pg 209

Haber, Mark, Coffee House Press, 79 13 Ave NE, Suite 110, Minneapolis, MN 55413 Tel: 612-338-0125 Fax: 612-338-4004 E-mail: info@coffeehousepress.org Web Site: coffeehousepress.org, pg 50

Haberstroh, Kelly, HarperCollins Children's Books, 195 Broadway, New York, NY 10007 Tel: 212-207-7000 Web Site: www.harpercollins.com/childrens, pg 86

Hackenberg, Rev Rachel, The Pilgrim Press/United Church Press, 700 Prospect Ave, Cleveland, OH 44115-1100 Tel: 216-736-2100 Toll Free Tel: 800-537-3394 (orders) E-mail: permissions@thepilgrimpress.com; store@ucc.org (orders) Web Site: www.thepilgrimpress.com, pg 160

Hackett, Azriel, Viking Children's Books, c/o Penguin Random House LLC, 1745 Broadway, New York, NY 10019 Tel: 212-782-9000 Web Site: www.penguin.com/viking-childrens-books-overview/, pg 224

Hackinson, Kevin, FJH Music Co Inc, 100 SE Third Ave, Suite 1000, Fort Lauderdale, FL 33394 Tel: 954-382-6061 Fax: 954-382-3073 E-mail: sales@fjhmusic.com Web Site: www.fjhmusic.com, pg 72

Hackinson, Kyle, FJH Music Co Inc, 100 SE Third Ave, Suite 1000, Fort Lauderdale, FL 33394 Tel: 954-382-6061 Fax: 954-382-3073 E-mail: sales@fjhmusic.com Web Site: www.fjhmusic.com, pg 72

Haddrill, Keri, Sourcebooks LLC, 1935 Brookdale Rd, Suite 139, Naperville, IL 60563 Tel: 630-961-3900 Toll Free Tel: 800-432-7444 Fax: 630-961-2168 E-mail: info@sourcebooks.com Web Site: www.sourcebooks.com, pg 195

Hades, Brian, EDGE Science Fiction & Fantasy Publishing Inc, PO Box 1714, Calgary, AB T2P 2L7, Canada Tel: 403-254-0160 Fax: 403-254-0456 E-mail: admin@hadespublications.com Web Site: www.edgewebsite.com, pg 401

Haeckel, Sarah, Farrar, Straus & Giroux, LLC, 120 Broadway, New York, NY 10271 Tel: 212-741-6900 E-mail: fsg.publicity@fsgbooks.com; sales@fsgbooks.com Web Site: us.macmillan.com/fsg, pg 70

Haeckel, Sarah, Picador, 120 Broadway, New York, NY 10271 Tel: 646-307-5151 Fax: 212-253-9627 E-mail: publicity@picadorusa.com Web Site: us.macmillan.com/picador, pg 160

Haffner, Brandon, John Dos Passos Prize for Literature, Dept of English & Modern Languages, 201 High St, Farmville, VA 23909 Tel: 434-395-2155 Web Site: www.longwood.edu/english/dos-passos-prize, pg 597

Hagaman, Jane, Red Wheel/Weiser, 65 Parker St, Suite 7, Newburyport, MA 01950 Tel: 978-465-0504 Toll Free Tel: 800-423-7087 (orders) Fax: 978-465-0243 E-mail: info@rwwbooks.com Web Site: www.redwheelweiser.com, pg 173

Hagan, Lisa, Lisa Hagan Literary, 110 Martin Dr, Bracey, VA 23919 Tel: 434-636-4138 E-mail: Lisa@lisahaganbooks.com Web Site: www.publishersmarketplace.com/members/LisaHagan, pg 462

Hagedorn, Amy, Alfred A Knopf, c/o Penguin Random House LLC, 1745 Broadway, New York, NY 10019 Tel: 212-751-2600 Fax: 212-940-7390 (dom rts); 212-572-2662 (foreign rts) Web Site: knopfdoubleday.com/imprint/knopf/; knopfdoubleday.com, pg 110

Hager, Betsy, Dr Tony Ryan Book Award, 2469 Ironworks Pike, Lexington, KY 40511 Tel: 859-455-9222 Web Site: www.castletonlyons.com, pg 658

Hager, Emma, City Lights Publishers, 261 Columbus Ave, San Francisco, CA 94133 Tel: 415-362-8193 E-mail: staff@citylights.com Web Site: citylights.com, pg 48

Hagerty, Denise M, American Medical Association (AMA), AMA Plaza, 330 N Wabash, Suite 39300, Chicago, IL 60611-5885 Tel: 312-464-5000 Toll Free Tel: 800-621-8335 E-mail: media@ama-assn.org (media & edit) Web Site: www.ama-assn.org; www.jamanetwork.org, pg 495

Haggar, Darren, Penguin Press, c/o Penguin Random House LLC, 1745 Broadway, New York, NY 10019 Tel: 212-782-9000 E-mail: penguinpress@penguinrandomhouse.com Web Site: www.penguin.com/penguin-press-overview/, pg 154

Haggen, Michael, Scholastic Education Solutions, 557 Broadway, New York, NY 10012 Tel: 212-343-6100 Fax: 212-343-6189 Web Site: www.scholastic.com, pg 184

Hagman, Lorri, University of Washington Press, 4333 Brooklyn Ave NE, Seattle, WA 98105-9570 Toll Free Tel: 800-537-5487 (orders) Fax: 206-543-3932; 410-516-6998 (orders) E-mail: uwapress@uw.edu Web Site: uwapress.uw.edu, pg 220

Haines, Stephen, Annie Dillard Award for Creative Nonfiction, Mail Stop 9053, Western Washington University, Bellingham, WA 98225 Tel: 360-650-4863 E-mail: bellingham.review@wwu.edu Web Site: bhreview.org; bhreview.submittable.com, pg 596

Haines, Stephen, 49th Parallel Poetry Award, Mail Stop 9053, Western Washington University, Bellingham, WA 98225 Tel: 360-650-4863 E-mail: bellingham.review@wwu.edu Web Site: bhreview.org; bhreview.submittable.com, pg 603

Haines, Stephen, Tobias Wolff Award for Fiction, Mail Stop 9053, Western Washington University, Bellingham, WA 98225 Tel: 360-650-4863 E-mail: bellingham.review@wwu.edu Web Site: bhreview.org; bhreview.submittable.com, pg 677

Haire, Timothy, Yale University Press, 302 Temple St, New Haven, CT 06511-8909 Tel: 203-432-0960; 203-432-0966 (sales); 401-531-2800 (cust serv) Toll Free Tel: 800-405-1619 (cust serv) Fax: 203-432-0948; 203-432-8485 (sales); 401-531-2801 (cust serv) Toll Free Fax: 800-406-9145 (cust serv) E-mail: sales.press@yale.edu (sales); customer.care@triliteral.org (cust serv) Web Site: www.yalebooks.com; yalepress.yale.edu/yupbooks, pg 235

Hajnoczky, Helen, University of Calgary Press, 2500 University Dr NW, Calgary, AB T2N 1N4, Canada Tel: 403-220-7578 E-mail: ucpbooks@ucalgary.ca Web Site: press.ucalgary.ca, pg 422

Hake, Jesse, Classical Academic Press, 515 S 32 St, Camp Hill, PA 17011 Tel: 717-730-0711 Toll Free Tel: 866-730-0711 Fax: 717-730-0721 Toll Free Fax: 866-730-0721 E-mail: info@classicalsubjects.com; orders@classicalsubjects.com Web Site: classicalacademicpress.com, pg 49

Halata, Katie, Random House Children's Books, c/o Penguin Random House LLC, 1745 Broadway, New York, NY 10019 Tel: 212-782-9000 Web Site: www.rhcbooks.com, pg 169

Haldorson, Sally, Porchlight Book Co Business Book Awards, 544 S First St, Milwaukee, WI 53204 Toll Free Tel: 800-236-7323 E-mail: info@porchlightbooks.com Web Site: porchlightbooks.com, pg 651

Hale, Charles, The MIT Press, One Broadway, 12th fl, Cambridge, MA 02142 Tel: 617-253-5255 Toll Free Tel: 800-405-1619 (orders) Fax: 617-258-6779; 617-577-1545 (orders) Web Site: mitpress.mit.edu, pg 132

Hale, David B, One-Act Playwriting Competition, 600 Wolfe St, Alexandria, VA 22314 Tel: 703-683-5778 (ext 2) Fax: 703-683-1378 E-mail: oneactslta@gmail.com Web Site: thelittletheatre.com, pg 644

Hales, Stuart, Special Libraries Association (SLA), 7918 Jones Branch Dr, Suite 300, McLean, VA 22102 Tel: 703-647-4900 Fax: 703-506-3266 E-mail: info@sla.org Web Site: www.sla.org, pg 520

Haley, Elma, Arbordale Publishing, 612 Johnnie Dodds Blvd, Suite A2, Mount Pleasant, SC 29464 Tel: 843-971-6722 Toll Free Tel: 877-243-3457 Fax: 843-216-3804 E-mail: info@arbordalepublishing.com Web Site: www.arbordalepublishing.com, pg 16

Haley, Rebecca, Radcliffe Institute Fellowship Program, Byerly Hall, 8 Garden St, Cambridge, MA 02138 Tel: 617-495-8212 Fax: 617-495-8136 E-mail: fellowships@radcliffe.harvard.edu Web Site: www.radcliffe.harvard.edu/fellowship-program, pg 654

Halgas, Sarah, Association for Talent Development (ATD) Press, 1640 King St, Box 1443, Alexandria, VA 22314-1443 Tel: 703-683-8100 Toll Free Tel: 800-628-2783 Fax: 703-299-8723; 703-683-1523 (cust care) E-mail: customercare@td.org Web Site: www.td.org, pg 19

Hall, Carrie, New York City College of Technology Professional & Technical Writing Program, Namm Hall 512, 300 Jay St, Brooklyn, NY 11201 Tel: 718-260-5392 E-mail: english@citytech.cuny.edu Web Site: www.citytech.cuny.edu/english/technical-writing-bs.aspx, pg 563

Hall, Chelsea, Society of Children's Book Writers & Illustrators (SCBWI), 6363 Wilshire Blvd, Suite 425, Los Angeles, CA 90048 Tel: 323-782-1010 E-mail: membership@scbwi.org Web Site: www.scbwi.org, pg 520

Hall, Eric, The Rough Notes Co Inc, 11690 Technology Dr, Carmel, IN 46032-5600 Tel: 317-582-1600 Toll Free Tel: 800-428-4384 (cust serv) Fax: 317-816-1000 Toll Free Fax: 800-321-1909 E-mail: rnc@roughnotes.com Web Site: www.roughnotes.com, pg 177

Hall, Gwen PhD, The American College of Financial Services, 630 Allendale Rd, Suite 400, King of Prussia, PA 19406 Tel: 610-526-1000 Toll Free Tel: 866-883-5640 Web Site: www.theamericancollege.edu, pg 9

Hall, Heather, Sourcebooks LLC, 1935 Brookdale Rd, Suite 139, Naperville, IL 60563 Tel: 630-961-3900 Toll Free Tel: 800-432-7444 Fax: 630-961-2168 E-mail: info@sourcebooks.com Web Site: www.sourcebooks.com, pg 194

Hall, Lauren, Folio Literary Management, The Film Center Bldg, 630 Ninth Ave, Suite 1101, New York, NY 10036 Tel: 212-400-1494 Fax: 212-967-0977 Web Site: www.foliolit.com, pg 459

Hall, Laurie, US Government Publishing Office (GPO), Superintendent of Documents, 732 N Capitol St NW, Washington, DC 20401 Tel: 202-512-1800 Toll Free Tel: 866-512-1800 (orders) Fax: 202-512-1998 E-mail: contactcenter@gpo.gov Web Site: www.gpo.gov; bookstore.gpo.gov (sales), pg 223

Hall, Lindsey, Tor Publishing Group, 120 Broadway, New York, NY 10271 Toll Free Tel: 800-455-0340 (Macmillan) E-mail: torpublicity@tor.com; forgepublicity@forgebooks.com Web Site: us.macmillan.com/torpublishinggroup, pg 208

Hall, Marie, Fordham University Press, Joseph A Martino Hall, 45 Columbus Ave, 3rd fl, New York, NY 10023 Fax: 347-842-3083 Web Site: www.fordhampress.com, pg 73

Hall, Megan, Association of Canadian University Presses, 542 King Edward, Ottawa, ON K1N 6N5, Canada Tel: 780-288-2697 Web Site: acup-apuc.ca, pg 499

Hall, Megan, Athabasca University Press, Edmonton Learning Ctr, Peace Hills Trust Tower, 1200, 10011-109 St, Edmonton, AB T5J 3S8, Canada Tel: 780-497-3412 Fax: 780-421-3298 E-mail: aupress@athabascau.ca Web Site: www.aupress.ca, pg 395

Hall, Nancy, American Book Producers Association (ABPA), 7 Peter Cooper Rd, No 7G, New York, NY 10010 E-mail: office@abpaonline.org Web Site: www.abpaonline.org, pg 494

Hall, Tanya, Greenleaf Book Group LLC, PO Box 91869, Austin, TX 78709 Tel: 512-891-6100 Fax: 512-891-6150 E-mail: contact@greenleafbookgroup.com; orders@greenleafbookgroup.com; foreignrights@greenleafbookgroup.com; media@greenleafbookgroup.com Web Site: greenleafbookgroup.com, pg 81

Hallak, Natalie, Random House Publishing Group, 1745 Broadway, New York, NY 10019 *Toll Free Tel:* 800-200-3552 *Web Site:* www.randomhousebooks.com, pg 171

Haller, Rachel, Harlequin Enterprises Ltd, Bay Adelaide Centre, East Tower, 22 Adelaide St W, 41st fl, Toronto, ON M5H 4E3, Canada *Tel:* 416-445-5860 *Toll Free Tel:* 888-432-4879; 800-370-5838 (ebook inquiries) *E-mail:* customerservice@harlequin.com *Web Site:* www.harlequin.com, pg 409

Hallett, Marta, Glitterati Inc, PO Box 3781, New York, NY 10163 *Tel:* 212-810-7519 *E-mail:* info@glitteratiincorporated.com; media@glitteratiincorporated.com; sales@glitteratiincorporated.com; trade@glitteratiincorporated.com *Web Site:* glitteratiinc.com, pg 78

Halley, Brian, University of Massachusetts Press, New Africa House, 180 Infirmary Way, 4th fl, Amherst, MA 01003-9289 *Web Site:* www.umasspress.com, pg 217

Hallick, Estelle, Grand Central Publishing, 1290 Avenue of the Americas, New York, NY 10104 *Tel:* 212-364-1100 *Web Site:* www.hachettebookgroup.com/imprint/grand-central-publishing/, pg 80

Halliday, Dorothea, Yale University Press, 302 Temple St, New Haven, CT 06511-8909 *Tel:* 203-432-0960; 203-432-0966 (sales); 401-531-2800 (cust serv) *Toll Free Tel:* 800-405-1619 (cust serv) *Fax:* 203-432-0948; 203-432-8485 (sales); 401-531-2801 (cust serv) *Toll Free Fax:* 800-406-9145 (cust serv) *E-mail:* sales.press@yale.edu (sales); customer.care@triliteral.org (cust serv) *Web Site:* www.yalebooks.com; yalepress.yale.edu/yupbooks, pg 235

Halliday, Mark, Ohio University, English Department, Creative Writing Program, Ohio University, English Dept, Ellis Hall, Athens, OH 45701 *E-mail:* english.department@ohio.edu *Web Site:* www.ohio.edu/cas/english, pg 564

Hallinger, Linda Herr, Herr's Indexing Service, 76-340 Kealoha St, Kailua Kona, HI 96740-2915 *Tel:* 808-365-4348 *Web Site:* www.herrsindexing.com, pg 440

Hallock, Meghan, Newbury Street Press, 99-101 Newbury St, Boston, MA 02116 *Tel:* 617-226-1206 *Toll Free Tel:* 888-296-3447 (NEHGS membership) *Fax:* 617-536-7307 *E-mail:* thebookstore@nehgs.org *Web Site:* www.americanancestors.org, pg 141

Hallock, Tom, Independent Publishers Caucus (IPC), c/o Seven Stories Press, 140 Watts St, New York, NY 10013 *E-mail:* info@indiepubs.org *Web Site:* www.indiepubs.org, pg 507

Hally, Sarah Masterson, Harry N Abrams Inc, 195 Broadway, 9th fl, New York, NY 10007 *Tel:* 212-206-7715 *Toll Free Tel:* 800-345-1359 *Fax:* 212-645-8437 *E-mail:* abrams@abramsbooks.com; publicity@abramsbooks.com; sales@abramsbooks.com *Web Site:* www.abramsbooks.com, pg 3

Halpenny, Karen, Workman Publishing, 1290 Avenue of the Americas, New York, NY 10104 *Toll Free Tel:* 800-759-0190 *Fax:* 212-341-0950 *E-mail:* workman-inquiry@hbgusa.com *Web Site:* www.hachettebookgroup.com/imprint/workman-publishing-company/, pg 233

Halpern, Daniel, National Poetry Series Open Competition, 57 Mountain Ave, Princeton, NJ 08540 *Tel:* 609-430-0999 *Fax:* 609-430-9933 *E-mail:* npspoetry@gmail.com *Web Site:* nationalpoetryseries.org, pg 638

Halpern, Hugh Nathanial, US Government Publishing Office (GPO), Superintendent of Documents, 732 N Capitol St NW, Washington, DC 20401 *Tel:* 202-512-1800 *Toll Free Tel:* 866-512-1800 (orders) *Fax:* 202-512-1998 *E-mail:* contactcenter@gpo.gov *Web Site:* www.gpo.gov; bookstore.gpo.gov (sales), pg 223

Halpern, Ilsa PhD, LearningExpress, 224 W 29 St, 3rd fl, New York, NY 10001 *Toll Free Tel:* 800-295-9556 (ext 2) *Web Site:* learningexpresshub.com, pg 114

Halsted, Jody, Midwest Travel Journalists Association Inc (MTJA), PO Box 185, Jessup, IA 50648 *Tel:* 319-529-1109 *E-mail:* admin@mtja.us *Web Site:* www.mtja.us, pg 511

Halverson, Pete, University Press of Mississippi, 3825 Ridgewood Rd, Jackson, MS 39211-6492 *Tel:* 601-432-6205 *Toll Free Tel:* 800-737-7788 (orders & cust serv) *Fax:* 601-432-6217 *E-mail:* press@mississippi.edu *Web Site:* www.upress.state.ms.us, pg 222

Hamblen, Carol, Johns Hopkins University Press, 2715 N Charles St, Baltimore, MD 21218-4363 *Tel:* 410-516-6900; 410-516-6987 *Toll Free Tel:* 800-537-5487 (book orders & cust serv); 800-548-1784 (journal orders) *Fax:* 410-516-6968; 410-516-6998 (orders) *E-mail:* hfscustserv@press.jhu.edu (cust serv); jrnlcirc@jh.edu (journal orders) *Web Site:* www.press.jhu.edu; muse.jhu.edu, pg 106

Hambrick, Elizabeth, Chronicle Books LLC, 680 Second St, San Francisco, CA 94107 *Tel:* 415-537-4200 *Fax:* 415-537-4460 (perms) *E-mail:* hello@chroniclebooks.com; subrights@chroniclebooks.com *Web Site:* www.chroniclebooks.com, pg 48

Hambrock, John, National Cartoonists Society (NCS), PO Box 592927, Orlando, FL 32859-2927 *Tel:* 407-994-6703 *E-mail:* info@nationalcartoonists.com; membership@nationalcartoonists.com *Web Site:* www.nationalcartoonists.com, pg 512

Hamedi, Mina, Janklow & Nesbit Associates, 285 Madison Ave, 21st fl, New York, NY 10017 *Tel:* 212-421-1700 *Fax:* 212-355-1403 *E-mail:* info@janklow.com; submissions@janklow.com; filmtvrights@janklow.com *Web Site:* www.janklowandnesbit.com, pg 464

Hamel, Josh, Cambridge University Press, One Liberty Plaza, 20th fl, New York, NY 10006 *Tel:* 212-924-3900; 212-337-5000 *Fax:* 212-691-3239; 845-353-4141 *E-mail:* customer_service@cambridge.org; orders@cambridge.org; subscriptions_newyork@cambridge.org *Web Site:* www.cambridge.org/us, pg 39

Hames, Charles, New York University Press, 838 Broadway, 3rd fl, New York, NY 10003-4812 *Tel:* 212-998-2575 (edit) *Toll Free Tel:* 800-996-6987 (orders) *Fax:* 212-995-4798 (orders) *E-mail:* nyupressinfo@nyu.edu (cust care) *Web Site:* www.nyupress.org, pg 141

Hamilton, Bridget, National Geographic Books, 1145 17 St NW, Washington, DC 20036-4688 *Tel:* 202-857-7000 *Toll Free Tel:* 877-866-6486 *E-mail:* ngbooks@cdsfulfillment.com *Web Site:* www.nationalgeographic.com/books/; ngbooks.buysub.com, pg 138

Hamilton, Carol, AAAI Press, 2275 E Bayshore Rd, Suite 160, Palo Alto, CA 94303 *Tel:* 650-328-3123 *Fax:* 650-321-4457 *E-mail:* publications21@aaai.org *Web Site:* www.aaai.org/Press/press.php, pg 1

Hamilton, Cindy, HarperCollins Children's Books, 195 Broadway, New York, NY 10007 *Tel:* 212-207-7000 *Web Site:* www.harpercollins.com/childrens, pg 85

Hamilton, Clio, W W Norton & Company Inc, 500 Fifth Ave, New York, NY 10110-0017 *Tel:* 212-354-5500 *Toll Free Tel:* 800-233-4830 (orders & cust serv) *Fax:* 212-869-0856 *Toll Free Fax:* 800-458-6515 *E-mail:* orders@wwnorton.com *Web Site:* wwnorton.com, pg 143

Hamilton, Dylan, Macmillan, 120 Broadway, 22nd fl, New York, NY 10271 *E-mail:* press.inquiries@macmillan.com *Web Site:* us.macmillan.com, pg 122

Hamilton, Emily, University of Minnesota Press, 111 Third Ave S, Suite 290, Minneapolis, MN 55401-2520 *Tel:* 612-301-1990 *Fax:* 612-301-1980 *E-mail:* ump@umn.edu *Web Site:* www.upress.umn.edu, pg 217

Hamilton, Jessica, Reed Environmental Writing Award, 201 W Main St, Suite 14, Charlottesville, VA 22902 *Tel:* 434-977-4090 *Fax:* 434-977-1483 *Web Site:* www.southernenvironment.org, pg 655

Hamilton, Julie, Mandala Earth, 800 "A" St, San Rafael, CA 94901 *Tel:* 415-526-1370 *Toll Free Tel:* 866-509-0515 *E-mail:* info@mandalapublishing.com *Web Site:* www.mandalaeartheditions.com, pg 124

Hamilton, Kathryn Renz, Random House Publishing Group, 1745 Broadway, New York, NY 10019 *Toll Free Tel:* 800-200-3552 *Web Site:* www.randomhousebooks.com, pg 171

Hamilton, Liz, Northwestern University Press, 629 Noyes St, Evanston, IL 60208-4210 *Tel:* 847-491-2046 *Toll Free Tel:* 800-621-2736 (orders only) *Fax:* 847-491-8150 *E-mail:* nupress@northwestern.edu *Web Site:* www.nupress.northwestern.edu, pg 143

Hamilton, Michaela, Kensington Publishing Corp, 900 Third Ave, 26th fl, New York, NY 10022 *Tel:* 212-407-1500 *Toll Free Tel:* 800-221-2647 *Fax:* 212-935-0699 *Web Site:* www.kensingtonbooks.com, pg 109

Hamilton, Morgan, Alfred A Knopf, c/o Penguin Random House LLC, 1745 Broadway, New York, NY 10019 *Tel:* 212-751-2600 *Fax:* 212-940-7390 (dom rts); 212-572-2662 (foreign rts) *Web Site:* knopfdoubleday.com/imprint/knopf/; knopfdoubleday.com, pg 110

Hamilton, Neil, Ferguson Publishing, 132 W 31 St, 16 fl, New York, NY 10001 *Tel:* 212-967-8800 *Toll Free Tel:* 800-322-8755 *Toll Free Fax:* 800-678-3633 *E-mail:* custserv@infobase.com *Web Site:* infobasepublishing.com, pg 71

Hamilton, Patricia, Park Place Publications, 410 Central Ave, No 3, Pacific Grove, CA 93950-2836 *Tel:* 831-649-6640 *E-mail:* publishingbiz@sbcglobal.net *Web Site:* www.parkplacepublications.com, pg 152

Hamilton, Richard, XML Press, 458 Dallas St, Denver, CO 80230 *Tel:* 970-231-3624 *E-mail:* publisher@xmlpress.net *Web Site:* xmlpress.net, pg 235

Hamilton, Sarah, Chronicle Books LLC, 680 Second St, San Francisco, CA 94107 *Tel:* 415-537-4200 *Fax:* 415-537-4460 (perms) *E-mail:* hello@chroniclebooks.com; subrights@chroniclebooks.com *Web Site:* www.chroniclebooks.com, pg 48

Hamlin, Faith, Sanford J Greenburger Associates Inc, 55 Fifth Ave, New York, NY 10003 *Tel:* 212-206-5600 *Web Site:* greenburger.com, pg 461

Hamlin, Kairi, Tanglewood Publishing, 1060 N Capitol Ave, Suite E-395, Indianapolis, IN 46204 *Tel:* 812-877-9488 *Toll Free Tel:* 800-788-3123 (orders) *E-mail:* info@tanglewoodbooks.com; orders@tanglewoodbooks.com; submission@tanglewoodbooks.com *Web Site:* www.tanglewoodbooks.com, pg 202

Hamling, Erin, HarperCollins Children's Books, 195 Broadway, New York, NY 10007 *Tel:* 212-207-7000 *Web Site:* www.harpercollins.com/childrens, pg 85

Hamm, Catharine M, SATW Foundation Lowell Thomas Travel Journalism Competition, 306 Summer Hill Dr, Fredericksburg, TX 78624 *Tel:* 281-217-2872 *E-mail:* marylua@satwf.com *Web Site:* www.satwf.org, pg 659

Hammack, Brice, Rutgers University Press, 106 Somerset St, 3rd fl, New Brunswick, NJ 08901 *Tel:* 848-445-7762; 848-445-7761 (sales) *Fax:* 732-745-4935 *E-mail:* sales@rutgersuniversitypress.org *Web Site:* www.rutgersuniversitypress.org, pg 179

Hammer, Daniel, The Historic New Orleans Collection, 533 Royal St, New Orleans, LA 70130 *Tel:* 504-523-4662 *Fax:* 504-598-7108 *E-mail:* wrc@hnoc.org *Web Site:* www.hnoc.org, pg 93

Hammer, Jennifer, New York University Press, 838 Broadway, 3rd fl, New York, NY 10003-4812 *Tel:* 212-998-2575 (edit) *Toll Free Tel:* 800-996-6987 (orders) *Fax:* 212-995-4798 (orders) *E-mail:* nyupressinfo@nyu.edu (cust care) *Web Site:* www.nyupress.org, pg 141

Hammerquist, Gregg, Candlewick Press, 99 Dover St, Somerville, MA 02144-2825 *Tel:* 617-661-3330 *Fax:* 617-661-0565 *E-mail:* bigbear@candlewick.com; salesinfo@candlewick.com *Web Site:* candlewick.com, pg 39

Hammond, Lizzy, Casemate l publishers, 1950 Lawrence Rd, Havertown, PA 19083 *Tel:* 610-853-9131 *Fax:* 610-853-9146 *E-mail:* casemate@casematepublishers.com *Web Site:* www.casematepublishers.com, pg 42

Hammond, Michelle, William Allen White Children's Book Awards, One Kellogg Circle, Emporia, KS 66801-5092 *Tel:* 620-341-5040 *E-mail:* wawbookaward@emporia.edu *Web Site:* wawchildrensbookaward.com, pg 674

Hamrick, Dave, University of Texas Press, 3001 Lake Austin Blvd, 2.200, Austin, TX 78703 *Tel:* 512-471-7233 *Fax:* 512-232-7178 *E-mail:* utpress@uts.cc.utexas.edu; info@utpress.utexas.edu *Web Site:* utpress.utexas.edu, pg 205

Hamstra, Paul, Evergreen Pacific Publishing Ltd, 10114 19 Ave SE, Suite 8, PMB 703, Everett, WA 98208 *Tel:* 425-493-1451 *E-mail:* sales@evergreenpacific.com *Web Site:* www.evergreenpacific.com, pg 68

Hamza, Dr Mohamed H, ACTA Press, 200-4040 Bowness Rd NW, Calgary, AB T3B 3R7, Canada *Tel:* 403-288-1195 *Fax:* 403-247-6851 *E-mail:* journals@actapress.com; publish@actapress.com; sales@actapress.com *Web Site:* www.actapress.com, pg 395

Han, CJ, Random House Children's Books, c/o Penguin Random House LLC, 1745 Broadway, New York, NY 10019 *Tel:* 212-782-9000 *Web Site:* www.rhcbooks.com, pg 170

Han, Hali, Bloomsbury Academic, 1385 Broadway, 5th fl, New York, NY 10018 *Tel:* 212-419-5300 *Web Site:* www.bloomsbury.com/us/academic, pg 31

Han, Vanessa, Klutz®, 557 Broadway, New York, NY 10012 *Tel:* 212-343-6360 *Toll Free Tel:* 800-737-4123 (cust serv) *E-mail:* scholasticmarketing@scholastic.com; scholasticstore@scholastic.com *Web Site:* www.scholastic.com/parents/klutz.html; store.scholastic.com, pg 110

Han, Vanessa, Scholastic Trade Publishing, 557 Broadway, New York, NY 10012 *Tel:* 212-343-6100; 212-343-4685 (export sales) *Fax:* 212-343-4714 (export sales) *Web Site:* www.scholastic.com, pg 184

Hanas, Jim, HarperCollins Publishers LLC, 195 Broadway, New York, NY 10007 *Tel:* 212-207-7000 *Web Site:* www.harpercollins.com, pg 86

Hancock, David, Hancock House Publishers Ltd, 19313 Zero Ave, Surrey, BC V3S 9R9, Canada *Tel:* 604-538-1114 *Toll Free Tel:* 800-938-1114 *Fax:* 604-538-2262 *Toll Free Fax:* 800-983-2262 *E-mail:* sales@hancockhouse.com; info@hancockhouse.com *Web Site:* www.hancockhouse.com, pg 408

Hancock, David L, Morgan James Publishing, 5 Penn Plaza, 23rd fl, New York, NY 10001 *Tel:* 212-655-5470 *Fax:* 516-908-4496 *E-mail:* support@morganjamespublishing.com *Web Site:* www.morganjamespublishing.com, pg 134

Handberg, Ryan, THE Learning Connection®, 4100 Silverstar Rd, Suite D, Orlando, FL 32808 *Toll Free Tel:* 800-218-8489 *Fax:* 407-292-2123 *E-mail:* tlc@tlconnection.com *Web Site:* www.tlconnection.com, pg 113

Handley, Chris J, Maxim Mazumdar New Play Competition, One Curtain Up Alley, Buffalo, NY 14202-1911 *Tel:* 716-852-2600 *E-mail:* newplays@alleyway.com; email@alleyway.com *Web Site:* www.alleyway.com/playwrights/maxim-mazumdar-new-play-competition, pg 630

Hanes, Peter, Flanker Press Ltd, 1243 Kenmount Rd, Unit 1, Paradise, NL A1L 0V8, Canada *Tel:* 709-739-4477 *Toll Free Tel:* 866-739-4420 *Fax:* 709-739-4420 *E-mail:* info@flankerpress.com; sales@flankerpress.com *Web Site:* www.flankerpress.com, pg 406

Hanesalo, Bruce A, Military Info Publishing, PO Box 41211, Plymouth, MN 55442 *Tel:* 763-533-8627 *E-mail:* publisher@military-info.com *Web Site:* www.military-info.com, pg 131

Haney, Scott, Chronicle Books LLC, 680 Second St, San Francisco, CA 94107 *Tel:* 415-537-4200 *Fax:* 415-537-4460 (perms) *E-mail:* hello@chroniclebooks.com; subrights@chroniclebooks.com *Web Site:* www.chroniclebooks.com, pg 47

Hanger, Nancy C, Windhaven®, 466 Rte 10, Orford, NH 03777 *Tel:* 603-512-9251 (cell) *Web Site:* www.windhavenpress.com, pg 445

Hankins, Luke, The Best Spiritual Literature Awards, PO Box 8385, Asheville, NC 28814 *Tel:* 828-713-1755 *E-mail:* editor@orisonbooks.com *Web Site:* www.orisonbooks.com/submissions, pg 579

Hankins, Luke, The Orison Chapbook Prize, PO Box 8385, Asheville, NC 28814 *Tel:* 828-713-1755 *E-mail:* editor@orisonbooks.com *Web Site:* www.orisonbooks.com/submissions, pg 644

Hankins, Luke, The Orison Prizes in Poetry & Fiction, PO Box 8385, Asheville, NC 28814 *Tel:* 828-713-1755 *E-mail:* editor@orisonbooks.com *Web Site:* www.orisonbooks.com/submissions, pg 644

Hanks, Jo, Quarto Publishing Group USA Inc, 100 Cummings Ctr, Suite 265D, Beverly, MA 01915 *Tel:* 978-282-9590 *Toll Free Tel:* 800-328-0590 (sales) *Fax:* 978-283-2742 *E-mail:* sales@quartous.com *Web Site:* www.quartoknows.com, pg 168

Hanley, Jordan, Tor Publishing Group, 120 Broadway, New York, NY 10271 *Toll Free Tel:* 800-455-0340 (Macmillan) *E-mail:* torpublicity@tor.com; forgepublicity@forgebooks.com *Web Site:* us.macmillan.com/torpublishinggroup, pg 208

Hanley, Maryellen, Candlewick Press, 99 Dover St, Somerville, MA 02144-2825 *Tel:* 617-661-3330 *Fax:* 617-661-0565 *E-mail:* bigbear@candlewick.com; salesinfo@candlewick.com *Web Site:* candlewick.com, pg 39

Hanna, Bill, Acacia House Publishing Services Ltd, 687 Oliver St, Oak Bay, BC V8S 4W2, Canada *Tel:* 226-387-4757, pg 448

Hannagan, Kelly, Johns Hopkins University Press, 2715 N Charles St, Baltimore, MD 21218-4363 *Tel:* 410-516-6900; 410-516-6987 *Toll Free Tel:* 800-537-5487 (book orders & cust serv); 800-548-1784 (journal orders) *Fax:* 410-516-6968; 410-516-6998 (orders) *E-mail:* hfscustserv@press.jhu.edu (cust serv); jrnlcirc@jh.edu (journal orders) *Web Site:* www.press.jhu.edu; muse.jhu.edu, pg 106

Hannah, Michele, Yaddo Artists Residency, 312 Union Ave, Saratoga Springs, NY 12866 *Tel:* 518-584-0746 *Fax:* 518-584-1312 *Web Site:* www.yaddo.org, pg 559

Hannigan, Carrie, HG Literary, 6 W 18 St, Suite 7R, New York, NY 10011 *E-mail:* foreign@hgliterary.com; rights@hgliterary.com *Web Site:* www.hgliterary.com, pg 463

Hanover-Pettit, Rebekah, National Academies Press (NAP), 500 Fifth St NW, Washington, DC 20001 *Toll Free Tel:* 800-624-6242 *Fax:* 202-334-2451 (cust serv); 202-334-2793 (mktg dept) *E-mail:* customer_service@nap.edu *Web Site:* www.nap.edu, pg 136

Hansard, Patrick, American Psychiatric Association Publishing, 800 Maine Ave SW, Suite 900, Washington, DC 20024 *Tel:* 202-459-9722 *Toll Free Tel:* 800-368-5777 *Fax:* 202-403-3094 *E-mail:* appi@psych.org *Web Site:* appi.org; www.psychiatryonline.org, pg 11

Hansen, Glenn J, BPA Worldwide, 100 Beard Sawmill Rd, 6th fl, Shelton, CT 06484 *Tel:* 203-447-2800 *Fax:* 203-447-2900 *E-mail:* info@bpaww.com *Web Site:* www.bpaww.com, pg 501

Hansen, Heather, Princeton University Press, 41 William St, Princeton, NJ 08540-5237 *Tel:* 609-258-4900 *Fax:* 609-258-6305 *E-mail:* info@press.princeton.edu *Web Site:* press.princeton.edu, pg 164

Hansen, Jill, ABDO, 8000 W 78 St, Suite 310, Edina, MN 55439 *Tel:* 952-698-2403 *Toll Free Tel:* 800-800-1312 *Fax:* 952-831-1632 *Toll Free Fax:* 800-862-3480 *E-mail:* customerservice@abdobooks.com; info@abdobooks.com *Web Site:* abdobooks.com, pg 2

Hansen, Michael, Cengage Learning, 20 Channel Center St, Boston, MA 02210 *Tel:* 617-289-7700 *Toll Free Tel:* 800-354-9706 *Fax:* 617-289-7844 *E-mail:* esales@cengage.com *Web Site:* www.cengage.com, pg 43

Hansen, Mike, Hal Leonard LLC, 7777 W Bluemound Rd, Milwaukee, WI 53213 *Tel:* 414-774-3630 *E-mail:* info@halleonard.com; sales@halleonard.com *Web Site:* www.halleonard.com, pg 84

Hansen, Stephanie, Metamorphosis Literary Agency, 12410 S Acuff Ct, Olathe, KS 66062 *Tel:* 646-397-1640 *E-mail:* info@metamorphosisliteraryagency.com *Web Site:* www.metamorphosisliteraryagency.com, pg 470

Hansen, Vaughne L, Virginia Kidd Agency Inc, 538 E Harford St, PO Box 278, Milford, PA 18337 *Tel:* 570-296-6205 *Web Site:* vk-agency.com, pg 465

Hanson, Andy, Illinois State Museum Society, 502 S Spring St, Springfield, IL 62706-5000 *Tel:* 217-782-7386 *Fax:* 217-782-1254 *E-mail:* subscriptions@museum.state.il.us *Web Site:* www.illinoisstatemuseum.org, pg 99

Hanson, Eliza, Gallery Books, 1230 Avenue of the Americas, New York, NY 10020 *Toll Free Tel:* 800-456-6798 *Fax:* 212-698-7284 *E-mail:* consumer.customerservice@simonandschuster.com *Web Site:* www.simonandschuster.com, pg 76

Hanson, Jana, D4EO Literary Agency, 13206 Treviso Dr, Lakewood Ranch, FL 34211 *Tel:* 203-545-7180 (cell) *Web Site:* www.d4eoliteraryagency.com; www.publishersmarketplace.com/members/d4eo/; x.com/d4eo, pg 456

Hanson, Martha, Simon & Schuster Children's Publishing, 1230 Avenue of the Americas, New York, NY 10020 *Tel:* 212-698-7000 *Web Site:* www.simonandschuster.com/kids; www.simonandschuster.com/teen; simonandschuster.net; simonandschuster.biz, pg 189

Hanson, Paul, Village Books Literary Citizenship Award, 1200 11 St, Bellingham, WA 98225 *Tel:* 360-671-2626 *E-mail:* biblioinfo@villagebooks.com; marketing@villagebooks.com *Web Site:* www.villagebooks.com/literary-citizenship-award, pg 672

Hanson, Scott, Alliance for Audited Media (AAM), 4513 Lincoln Ave, Suite 105B, Lisle, IL 60532 *Tel:* 224-366-6939 *Toll Free Tel:* 800-285-2220 *E-mail:* corpcomm@auditedmedia.com *Web Site:* auditedmedia.com, pg 493

Hanson, Todd, Medical Physics Publishing Corp (MPP), 4555 Helgesen Dr, Madison, WI 53718 *Tel:* 608-224-4508 (returns) *Toll Free Tel:* 800-442-5778 (cust serv) *Fax:* 608-224-5016 *E-mail:* mpp@medicalphysics.org *Web Site:* www.medicalphysics.org, pg 129

Hanstedt, Constance, California Writers Club (CWC), PO Box 201, Danville, CA 94526 *E-mail:* membership@calwriters.org; advertising-promotion@calwriters.org *Web Site:* calwriters.org, pg 502

Haproff, David, Russell Sage Foundation, 112 E 64 St, New York, NY 10065 *Tel:* 212-750-6000 *Toll Free Tel:* 800-524-6401 *Fax:* 212-371-4761 *E-mail:* info@rsage.org *Web Site:* www.russellsage.org, pg 178

Harbster, Desiree, Florida Outdoor Writers Association Inc (FOWA), 235 Apollo Beach Blvd, Unit 271, Apollo Beach, FL 33572 *Tel:* 813-579-0990 *E-mail:* info@fowa.org *Web Site:* www.fowa.org, pg 506

Harburg, Emily, Random House Children's Books, c/o Penguin Random House LLC, 1745 Broadway, New York, NY 10019 *Tel:* 212-782-9000 *Web Site:* www.rhcbooks.com, pg 170

Harden, Arik, Roaring Brook Press, 120 Broadway, New York, NY 10271 *Tel:* 646-307-5151 *Web Site:* us.macmillan.com/publishers/roaring-brook-press, pg 176

Harden, Asia, Farrar, Straus & Giroux Books for Young Readers, 120 Broadway, New York, NY 10271 *Tel:* 212-741-6900 *Toll Free Tel:* 888-330-8477 (orders) *E-mail:* childrens.publicity@macmillanusa.com; childrensrights@macmillanusa.com *Web Site:* us.macmillan.com/mackids, pg 77

Harding, Elizabeth, Curtis Brown, Ltd, 228 E 45 St, Suite 310, New York, NY 10017 *Tel:* 212-473-5400 *Fax:* 212-598-0917 *E-mail:* info@cbltd.com *Web Site:* www.curtisbrown.com, pg 452

Hare, Robbie Anna, Goldfarb & Associates, 721 Gibbon St, Alexandria, VA 22314 Tel: 202-466-3030 E-mail: rlglawlit@gmail.com Web Site: www.ronaldgoldfarb.com, pg 460

Haring, Sara Beth, St Martin's Press, LLC, 120 Broadway, New York, NY 10271 E-mail: publicity@stmartins.com; trademarketing@stmartins.com; foreignrights@stmartins.com Web Site: us.macmillan.com/smp, pg 181

Harmon, Trent, Sourcebooks LLC, 1935 Brookdale Rd, Suite 139, Naperville, IL 60563 Tel: 630-961-3900 Toll Free Tel: 800-432-7444 Fax: 630-961-2168 E-mail: info@sourcebooks.com Web Site: www.sourcebooks.com, pg 194

Harmsworth, Esmond, Aevitas Creative Management LLC, 19 W 21 St, Suite 501, New York, NY 10010 Tel: 212-765-6900 Web Site: www.aevitascreative.com, pg 448

Harold, Jess, Henry Holt and Company, LLC, 120 Broadway, 23rd fl, New York, NY 10271 Tel: 646-307-5151 Toll Free Tel: 888-330-8477 (orders) Fax: 646-307-5285 Web Site: www.henryholt.com, pg 94

Harowitz, Sara, Westwood Creative Artists Ltd, 386 Huron St, Toronto, ON M5S 2G6, Canada Tel: 416-964-3302 Fax: 416-964-3302 E-mail: wca_office@wcaltd.com Web Site: www.wcaltd.com, pg 481

Harp, Gabe, The MIT Press, One Broadway, 12th fl, Cambridge, MA 02142 Tel: 617-253-5255 Toll Free Tel: 800-405-1619 (orders) Fax: 617-258-6779; 617-577-1545 (orders) Web Site: mitpress.mit.edu, pg 132

Harper, Chuck, Andrews McMeel Publishing LLC, 1130 Walnut St, Kansas City, MO 64106-2109 Tel: 816-581-7500 Toll Free Tel: 800-851-8923 Web Site: www.andrewsmcmeel.com; publishing.andrewsmcmeel.com, pg 14

Harper, Daria, Chronicle Books LLC, 680 Second St, San Francisco, CA 94107 Tel: 415-537-4200 Fax: 415-537-4460 (perms) E-mail: hello@chroniclebooks.com; subrights@chroniclebooks.com Web Site: www.chroniclebooks.com, pg 47

Harper, Logan, Jane Rotrosen Agency LLC, 318 E 51 St, New York, NY 10022-7803 Tel: 212-593-4330 E-mail: info@janerotrosen.com Web Site: janerotrosen.com, pg 474

Harper, Matt, HarperCollins Publishers LLC, 195 Broadway, New York, NY 10007 Tel: 212-207-7000 Web Site: www.harpercollins.com, pg 86

Harper, Michael, The Little Entrepreneur, c/o Harper Arrington Media, 33228 W 12 Mile Rd, Suite 105, Farmington Hills, MI 48334 Toll Free Tel: 888-435-9234 Fax: 248-281-0373 E-mail: support@digitalfashionpro.com, pg 118

Harpster, Kristin, Wayne State University Press, Leonard N Simons Bldg, 4809 Woodward Ave, Detroit, MI 48201-1309 Tel: 313-577-6120 Toll Free Tel: 800-978-7323 Fax: 313-577-6131 E-mail: bookorders@wayne.edu Web Site: www.wsupress.wayne.edu, pg 227

Harrell, Casey, Thomas Nelson, 501 Nelson Place, Nashville, TN 37214 Tel: 615-889-9000 Toll Free Tel: 800-251-4000 Web Site: www.thomasnelson.com, pg 206

Harrell, Rachel, Chronicle Books LLC, 680 Second St, San Francisco, CA 94107 Tel: 415-537-4200 Fax: 415-537-4460 (perms) E-mail: hello@chroniclebooks.com; subrights@chroniclebooks.com Web Site: www.chroniclebooks.com, pg 48

Harri, Kaitlin, HarperCollins Publishers LLC, 195 Broadway, New York, NY 10007 Tel: 212-207-7000 Web Site: www.harpercollins.com, pg 86

Harrigan, Casey, American Political Science Association (APSA), 1527 New Hampshire Ave NW, Washington, DC 20036-1203 Tel: 202-483-2512 Fax: 202-483-2657 E-mail: apsa@apsanet.org; membership@apsanet.org; press@apsanet.org Web Site: www.apsanet.org, pg 496

Harrigan, Kristen, SDP Publishing Solutions LLC, 36 Captain's Way, East Bridgewater, MA 02333 Tel: 617-775-0656 Web Site: www.sdppublishingsolutions.com, pg 444

Harrington, Joyce, Adams & Ambrose Publishing, 1622 Capital Ave, Madison, WI 53705-1228 Tel: 608-572-2471 E-mail: info@adamsambrose.com, pg 4

Harrington, Mark, Harry N Abrams Inc, 195 Broadway, 9th fl, New York, NY 10007 Tel: 212-206-7715 Toll Free Tel: 800-345-1359 Fax: 212-645-8437 E-mail: abrams@abramsbooks.com; publicity@abramsbooks.com; sales@abramsbooks.com Web Site: www.abramsbooks.com, pg 2

Harrington, Meghan, St Martin's Press, LLC, 120 Broadway, New York, NY 10271 E-mail: publicity@stmartins.com; trademarketing@stmartins.com; foreignrights@stmartins.com Web Site: us.macmillan.com/smp, pg 181

Harrington, Neil, Dreamscape Media LLC, 1417 Timberwolf Dr, Holland, OH 43528 Tel: 419-867-6965 Toll Free Tel: 877-983-7326 E-mail: info@dreamscapeab.com Web Site: www.dreamscapepublishing.com, pg 62

Harrington, Paul, Well-Trained Mind Press, 18021 The Glebe Lane, Charles City, VA 23030 Tel: 804-593-0306 Toll Free Tel: 877-322-3445 Fax: 804-829-5704 E-mail: support@welltrainedmind.com Web Site: welltrainedmind.com, pg 227

Harrington, Dr Robert M, American Mathematical Society (AMS), 201 Charles St, Providence, RI 02904-2213 Tel: 401-455-4000 Toll Free Tel: 800-321-4267 Fax: 401-331-3842; 401-455-4046 (cust serv) E-mail: ams@ams.org; cust-serv@ams.org Web Site: www.ams.org, pg 11

Harrington, Roby, W W Norton & Company Inc, 500 Fifth Ave, New York, NY 10110-0017 Tel: 212-354-5500 Toll Free Tel: 800-233-4830 (orders & cust serv) Fax: 212-869-0856 Toll Free Fax: 800-458-6515 E-mail: orders@wwnorton.com Web Site: wwnorton.com, pg 143

Harrington, Tim, Little, Brown and Company, 1290 Avenue of the Americas, New York, NY 10104 Tel: 212-364-1100 Fax: 212-364-0952 E-mail: firstname.lastname@hbgusa.com Web Site: www.hachettebookgroup.com/imprint/little-brown-and-company/, pg 118

Harriot, Michael, Folio Literary Management, The Film Center Bldg, 630 Ninth Ave, Suite 1101, New York, NY 10036 Tel: 212-400-1494 Fax: 212-967-0977 Web Site: www.foliolit.com, pg 459

Harris, Alec, GIA Publications Inc, 7404 S Mason Ave, Chicago, IL 60638 Tel: 708-496-3800 Toll Free Tel: 800-GIA-1358 (442-1358) E-mail: custserv@giamusic.com Web Site: www.giamusic.com, pg 78

Harris, David A, American Jewish Committee (AJC), Mail Code 6760, PO Box 7247, Philadelphia, PA 19170-0001 Tel: 212-751-4000 Fax: 212-891-1450 E-mail: social@ajc.org Web Site: www.ajc.org, pg 495

Harris, Debra, All Things That Matter Press, 79 Jones Rd, Somerville, ME 04348 E-mail: allthingsthatmatterpress@gmail.com Web Site: www.allthingsthatmatterpress.com, pg 7

Harris, Erin, Folio Literary Management, The Film Center Bldg, 630 Ninth Ave, Suite 1101, New York, NY 10036 Tel: 212-400-1494 Fax: 212-967-0977 Web Site: www.foliolit.com, pg 459

Harris, Hadar, PEN America Washington, DC, 1100 13 St NW, Suite 800, Washington, DC 20005 E-mail: info@pen.org Web Site: pen.org/region/washington-dc, pg 516

Harris, Jake, United States Institute of Peace Press, 2301 Constitution Ave NW, Washington, DC 20037 Tel: 703-661-1590 (cust serv) Toll Free Tel: 800-868-8064 (cust serv) E-mail: usipmail@presswarehouse.com (orders) Web Site: bookstore.usip.org, pg 213

Harris, Joy, The Joy Harris Literary Agency Inc, 1501 Broadway, Suite 2310, New York, NY 10036 Tel: 212-924-6269 Fax: 212-840-5776 E-mail: contact@joyharrisliterary.com Web Site: www.joyharrisliterary.com, pg 462

Harris, Judy, Evan-Moor Educational Publishers, 10 Harris Ct, Suite C-3, Monterey, CA 93940 Tel: 831-649-5901 Toll Free Tel: 800-777-4362 (orders) Fax: 831-649-6256 Toll Free Fax: 800-777-4332 (orders) E-mail: sales@evan-moor.com; marketing@evan-moor.com Web Site: www.evan-moor.com, pg 68

Harris, Kathy, Paul H Brookes Publishing Co Inc, PO Box 10624, Baltimore, MD 21285-0624 Tel: 410-337-9580 (outside US & CN) Toll Free Tel: 800-638-3775 (US & CN) Fax: 410-337-8539 E-mail: custserv@brookespublishing.com Web Site: www.brookespublishing.com, pg 37

Harris, Lis, Columbia University School of the Arts Creative Writing Program, 609 Kent Hall, New York, NY 10027 Tel: 212-854-3774 E-mail: writingprogram@columbia.edu Web Site: arts.columbia.edu/writing, pg 562

Harris, Naomi, Education Writers Association (EWA), 1825 "K" St NW, Suite 200, Washington, DC 20006 Tel: 202-452-9830 Web Site: ewa.org, pg 505

Harris, Sonya, Chronicle Books LLC, 680 Second St, San Francisco, CA 94107 Tel: 415-537-4200 Fax: 415-537-4460 (perms) E-mail: hello@chroniclebooks.com; subrights@chroniclebooks.com Web Site: www.chroniclebooks.com, pg 48

Harris-Etheridge, Renee, Software & Information Industry Association (SIIA), 1620 Eye St NW, Washington, DC 20005 Tel: 202-289-7442 Fax: 202-289-7097 E-mail: info@siia.net Web Site: www.siia.net, pg 520

Harrison, Adriane, PRINTING United Alliance, 10015 Main St, Fairfax, VA 22031 Tel: 703-385-1335 Toll Free Tel: 888-385-3588 Fax: 703-273-0456; 703-691-7492 (membership) E-mail: assist@printing.org; info@printing.org Web Site: www.printing.org, pg 517

Harrison, Colin, Scribner, 1230 Avenue of the Americas, New York, NY 10020 Web Site: www.simonandschusterpublishing.com/scribner/, pg 185

Harrison, Joyce, University Press of Kansas, 2502 Westbrooke Circle, Lawrence, KS 66045-4444 Tel: 785-864-4154 Fax: 785-864-4586 E-mail: upress@ku.edu Web Site: www.kansaspress.ku.edu, pg 221

Harrison, Kate, Dial Books for Young Readers, c/o Penguin Random House LLC, 1745 Broadway, New York, NY 10019 Tel: 212-782-9000 Web Site: www.penguin.com/dial-overview/, pg 59

Harrison, Katherine, Random House Children's Books, c/o Penguin Random House LLC, 1745 Broadway, New York, NY 10019 Tel: 212-782-9000 Web Site: www.rhcbooks.com, pg 170

Harrison, Kristen, The Brookings Institution Press, 1775 Massachusetts Ave NW, Washington, DC 20036-2188 Tel: 202-797-6000 E-mail: permissions@brookings.edu Web Site: www.brookings.edu, pg 37

Harrison, Patricia de Stacy, Corporation for Public Broadcasting (CPB), 401 Ninth St NW, Washington, DC 20004-2129 Tel: 202-879-9600 E-mail: press@cpb.org Web Site: cpb.org, pg 504

Harriton, Jess, Alloy Entertainment LLC, 30 Hudson Yards, 22nd fl, New York, NY 10001, pg 7

Harry, Lou, Society of Professional Journalists (SPJ), PO Box 441748, Indianapolis, IN 46244 Tel: 317-927-8000 Fax: 317-920-4789 E-mail: communications@spj.org Web Site: www.spj.org, pg 520

Harshberger, Laura, HarperCollins Children's Books, 195 Broadway, New York, NY 10007 Tel: 212-207-7000 Web Site: www.harpercollins.com/childrens, pg 85

Hart, Becca, Beaver's Pond Press Inc, 939 Seventh St W, St Paul, MN 55102 Tel: 952-829-8818 E-mail: submissions@beaverspondpress.com Web Site: www.beaverspondpress.com, pg 26

Hart, Cate, Harvey Klinger Inc, 300 W 55 St, Suite 11V, New York, NY 10019 Tel: 212-581-7068 Fax: 212-315-3823 E-mail: queries@harveyklinger.com Web Site: www.harveyklinger.com, pg 465

Hart, Chris, Penguin Random House LLC, 1745 Broadway, New York, NY 10019 *Tel:* 212-782-9000 *Toll Free Tel:* 800-726-0600 *Web Site:* www.penguinrandomhouse.com, pg 155

Hart, Jennifer, HarperCollins Publishers LLC, 195 Broadway, New York, NY 10007 *Tel:* 212-207-7000 *Web Site:* www.harpercollins.com, pg 86

Hart, Jim, Hartline Literary Agency LLC, 123 Queenston Dr, Pittsburgh, PA 15235 *Tel:* 412-829-2483 *Toll Free Fax:* 888-279-6007 *Web Site:* www.hartlineliterary.com, pg 462

Hart, Joyce, Hartline Literary Agency LLC, 123 Queenston Dr, Pittsburgh, PA 15235 *Tel:* 412-829-2483 *Toll Free Tel:* 888-279-6007 *Web Site:* www.hartlineliterary.com, pg 462

Hart, Laura, Bellevue Literary Press, 90 Broad St, Suite 2100, New York, NY 10004 *Tel:* 917-732-3603 *Web Site:* blpress.org, pg 27

Hart, Suzy, Florida Writers Association Inc, 127 W Fairbanks Ave, No 407, Winter Park, FL 32789 *E-mail:* contactus@floridawriters.org *Web Site:* www.floridawriters.org, pg 506

Hart, Suzy, Florida WritersCon, 127 W Fairbanks Ave, No 407, Winter Park, FL 32789 *E-mail:* contactus@floridawriters.org *Web Site:* www.floridawriters.org, pg 554

Hart, Tara, Penguin Random House Audio Publishing Group, 1745 Broadway, New York, NY 10019 *Toll Free Tel:* 800-793-2665 (cust serv) *E-mail:* audio@penguinrandomhouse.com; ecustomerservice@penguinrandomhouse.com *Web Site:* www.penguinrandomhouseaudio.com, pg 154

Hart, Terrence, Association of American Publishers (AAP), 455 Massachusetts Ave NW, Suite 700, Washington, DC 20001-2777 *Tel:* 202-347-3375 *Fax:* 202-347-3690 *E-mail:* info@publishers.org *Web Site:* publishers.org, pg 498

Hartland, Julia, Penguin Random House Canada, a Penguin Random House company, 320 Front St W, Suite 1400, Toronto, ON M5V 3B6, Canada *Tel:* 416-364-4449 *Toll Free Tel:* 888-523-9292 (cust serv) *E-mail:* canadaweb@penguinrandomhouse.com; customerservicescanada@penguinrandomhouse.com *Web Site:* www.penguinrandomhouse.ca, pg 416

Hartley, Emily, Random House Publishing Group, 1745 Broadway, New York, NY 10019 *Toll Free Tel:* 800-200-3552 *Web Site:* www.randomhousebooks.com, pg 171

Hartley, Glen, Writers' Representatives LLC, 116 W 14 St, 11th fl, New York, NY 10011-7305 *Tel:* 212-620-9009 *E-mail:* transom@writersreps.com *Web Site:* www.writersreps.com, pg 482

Hartley, John, Peter Pauper Press, Inc, 202 Mamaroneck Ave, Suite 400, White Plains, NY 10601-5376 *Tel:* 914-681-0144 *Fax:* 914-681-0389 *E-mail:* customerservice@peterpauper.com; orders@peterpauper.com; marketing@peterpauper.com *Web Site:* www.peterpauper.com, pg 158

Hartman, Charles, National Council of Teachers of English (NCTE), 340 N Neil St, Suite 104, Champaign, IL 61820 *Tel:* 217-328-3870 *Toll Free Tel:* 877-369-6283 (cust serv) *Fax:* 217-328-9645 *E-mail:* customerservice@ncte.org *Web Site:* ncte.org, pg 137

Hartman, Erinn, Alfred A Knopf, c/o Penguin Random House LLC, 1745 Broadway, New York, NY 10019 *Tel:* 212-751-2600 *Fax:* 212-940-7390 (dom rts); 212-572-2662 (foreign rts) *Web Site:* knopfdoubleday.com/imprint/knopf/; knopfdoubleday.com, pg 110

Hartman, Jan, American Book Producers Association (ABPA), 7 Peter Cooper Rd, No 7G, New York, NY 10010 *E-mail:* office@abpaonline.org *Web Site:* www.abpaonline.org, pg 494

Hartman, Mark, Hartman Publishing Inc, 1313 Iron Ave SW, Albuquerque, NM 87102 *Tel:* 505-291-1274 *Toll Free Tel:* 800-999-9534 *Toll Free Fax:* 800-474-6106 *E-mail:* info@hartmanonline.com *Web Site:* www.hartmanonline.com, pg 87

Hartman, William, Quintessence Publishing Co Inc, 411 N Raddant Rd, Batavia, IL 60510 *Tel:* 630-736-3600 *Toll Free Tel:* 800-621-0387 *Fax:* 630-736-3633 *E-mail:* contact@quintbook.com; service@quintbook.com *Web Site:* www.quintpub.com, pg 168

Hartogh, Frances, Rocky Mountain Mineral Law Foundation, 9191 Sheridan Blvd, Suite 203, Westminster, CO 80031 *Tel:* 303-321-8100 *Fax:* 303-321-7657 *E-mail:* info@rmmlf.org *Web Site:* www.rmmlf.org, pg 176

Harty, Pamela, The Knight Agency Inc, 232 W Washington St, Madison, GA 30650 *E-mail:* admin@knightagency.net *Web Site:* www.knightagency.net, pg 466

Hartz, Kortney, Random House Children's Books, c/o Penguin Random House LLC, 1745 Broadway, New York, NY 10019 *Tel:* 212-782-9000 *Web Site:* www.rhcbooks.com, pg 170

Hartzell, Ken, Island Press, 2000 "M" St NW, Suite 480-B, Washington, DC 20036 *Tel:* 202-232-7933 *Toll Free Tel:* 800-621-2736 *Fax:* 202-234-1328 *E-mail:* info@islandpress.org *Web Site:* www.islandpress.org, pg 104

Harveland, MariLou, Northwest Independent Editors Guild, 7511 Greenwood Ave N, No 307, Seattle, WA 98103 *E-mail:* info@edsguild.org *Web Site:* www.edsguild.org, pg 515

Harveland, MariLou, Red Pencil Conference, 7511 Greenwood Ave N, No 307, Seattle, WA 98103 *E-mail:* conference@edsguild.org *Web Site:* www.edsguild.org/red-pencil-conferences, pg 557

Harvey, Dr Alan, Stanford University Press, 425 Broadway St, Redwood City, CA 94063-3126 *Tel:* 650-723-9434 *Fax:* 650-725-3457 *E-mail:* info@www.sup.org; publicity@www.sup.org; sales@www.sup.org *Web Site:* www.sup.org, pg 197

Harvey, Ghenet, Hachette Audio, 1290 Avenue of the Americas, New York, NY 10104 *Tel:* 212-364-1100 *Web Site:* www.hachettebookgroup.com/imprint/hachette-audio/, pg 83

Harvey, Katherine Alexandra, ReLit Awards, PO Box 250, Burnt Head, Cupids, NL A0A 2B0, Canada *Web Site:* www.relitawards.com, pg 655

Harwell, Andrew, HarperCollins Children's Books, 195 Broadway, New York, NY 10007 *Tel:* 212-207-7000 *Web Site:* www.harpercollins.com/childrens, pg 85

Harwell, Sarah C, Syracuse University Creative Writing Program, 401 Hall of Languages, Syracuse, NY 13244-1170 *Tel:* 315-443-2173 *Fax:* 315-443-3660 *Web Site:* artsandsciences.syracuse.edu/english-department/creative-writing-mf-program; artsandsciences.syracuse.edu/english-department/cw-undergraduate-program, pg 565

Hasegawa, Carter, Candlewick Press, 99 Dover St, Somerville, MA 02144-2825 *Tel:* 617-661-3330 *Fax:* 617-661-0565 *E-mail:* bigbear@candlewick.com; salesinfo@candlewick.com *Web Site:* candlewick.com, pg 40

Hashmi, Bilal, John Glassco Translation Prize, Concordia University, LB 601, 1455 De Maisonneuve W, Montreal, QC H3G 1M8, Canada *Tel:* 514-848-2424 (ext 8702) *E-mail:* info@attlc-ltac.org *Web Site:* www.attlc-ltac.org, pg 607

Hashmi, Bilal, Literary Translators' Association of Canada, Concordia University, LB 601, 1455 De Maisonneuve W, Montreal, QC H3G 1M8, Canada *Tel:* 514-848-2424 (ext 8702) *E-mail:* info@attlc-ltac.org *Web Site:* www.attlc-ltac.org, pg 509

Hashmi, Bilal, Quattro Books Inc, 12 Concord Ave, 2nd fl, Toronto, ON M6H 2P1, Canada *Tel:* 416-893-7979 *E-mail:* info@quattrobooks.ca *Web Site:* www.quattrobooks.ca, pg 417

Haskell, Arlo, Key West Literary Seminar, 717 Love Lane, Key West, FL 33040 *Tel:* 305-293-9291 *E-mail:* mail@kwls.org *Web Site:* www.kwls.org/seminar, pg 555

Haskell, Arlo, Key West Literary Seminar's Writers' Workshop Program, 717 Love Lane, Key West, FL 33040 *Tel:* 305-293-9291 *E-mail:* mail@kwls.org *Web Site:* www.kwls.org, pg 555

Haskell, Sarah Snow, Safer Society Press, PO Box 340, Brandon, VT 05733-0340 *Tel:* 802-247-3132 *Fax:* 802-247-4233 *E-mail:* info@safersociety.org *Web Site:* safersocietypress.org, pg 179

Hassan, Alyssa, Beacon Press, 24 Farnsworth St, Boston, MA 02210-1409 *Tel:* 617-742-2110 *Fax:* 617-723-3097 *E-mail:* production@beacon.org *Web Site:* www.beacon.org, pg 25

Hassan, Shannon, Marsal Lyon Literary Agency LLC, 665 San Rodolfo Dr, Suite 124, PMB 121, Solana Beach, CA 92075 *Tel:* 760-814-8507 *Web Site:* www.marsallyonliteraryagency.com, pg 468

Hassan, Yazmine, Berkley, c/o Penguin Random House LLC, 1745 Broadway, 19th fl, New York, NY 10019 *Tel:* 212-366-2000 *Web Site:* www.penguin.com/publishers/berkley/; www.penguin.com/ace-overview/, pg 28

Hastings, Robert, Pacific Press® Publishing Association, 1350 N Kings Rd, Nampa, ID 83687-3193 *Tel:* 208-465-2500 *Fax:* 208-465-2531 *E-mail:* booksubmissions@pacificpress.com *Web Site:* www.pacificpress.com, pg 149

Hatch, John, Signature Books Publishing LLC, 564 W 400 N, Salt Lake City, UT 84116-3411 *Toll Free Tel:* 800-356-5687 *E-mail:* people@signaturebooks.com *Web Site:* www.signaturebooks.com; www.signaturebookslibrary.org, pg 188

Hathorne, Nancy, Writers Guild of America, East (WGAE), 250 Hudson St, Suite 700, New York, NY 10013 *Tel:* 212-767-7800 *Fax:* 212-582-1909 *Web Site:* www.wgaeast.org, pg 522

Hatton, Kelly, BOA Editions Ltd, 250 N Goodman St, Suite 306, Rochester, NY 14607 *Tel:* 585-546-3410 *Fax:* 585-546-3913 *E-mail:* contact@boaeditions.org *Web Site:* www.boaeditions.org, pg 33

Haubner, Julianna, Avid Reader Press, 1230 Avenue of the Americas, New York, NY 10020 *Web Site:* avidreaderpress.com, pg 23

Haugen, Sarah, HarperCollins Publishers LLC, 195 Broadway, New York, NY 10007 *Tel:* 212-207-7000 *Web Site:* www.harpercollins.com, pg 86

Haughian, Karen, Signature Editions, PO Box 206, RPO Corydon, Winnipeg, MB R3M 3S7, Canada *Tel:* 204-779-7803 *E-mail:* signature@allstream.net; orders@signature-editions.com *Web Site:* www.signature-editions.com, pg 419

Haught, Natassja, Tor Publishing Group, 120 Broadway, New York, NY 10271 *Toll Free Tel:* 800-455-0340 (Macmillan) *E-mail:* torpublicity@tor.com; forgepublicity@forgebooks.com *Web Site:* us.macmillan.com/torpublishinggroup, pg 208

Haughton, Vanessa, Alfred A Knopf, c/o Penguin Random House LLC, 1745 Broadway, New York, NY 10019 *Tel:* 212-751-2600 *Fax:* 212-940-7390 (dom rts); 212-572-2662 (foreign rts) *Web Site:* knopfdoubleday.com/imprint/knopf/; knopfdoubleday.com, pg 110

Haukap, Sara, National Paper Trade Association (NPTA), 330 N Wabash Ave, Suite 2000, Chicago, IL 60611 *Tel:* 312-321-4092 *Toll Free Tel:* 800-355-NPTA (355-6782) *Fax:* 312-673-6736 *Web Site:* www.gonpta.com, pg 513

Haupt, Madeline, St Martin's Press, LLC, 120 Broadway, New York, NY 10271 *E-mail:* publicity@stmartins.com; trademarketing@stmartins.com; foreignrights@stmartins.com *Web Site:* us.macmillan.com/smp, pg 181

Hauser, Robert M, American Philosophical Society Press, 104 S Fifth St, Philadelphia, PA 19106 *Tel:* 215-440-3425 *Fax:* 215-440-3450 *Web Site:* www.amphilsoc.org, pg 11

Haut, Judith, Random House Children's Books, c/o Penguin Random House LLC, 1745 Broadway, New York, NY 10019 *Tel:* 212-782-9000 *Web Site:* www.rhcbooks.com, pg 169

Haw, Kate, National Gallery of Art, Sixth & Constitution Ave NW, Washington, DC 20565 Tel: 202-842-6280 E-mail: thecenter@nga.gov Web Site: www.nga.gov, pg 137

Hawkins, Anne, John Hawkins and Associates Inc, 80 Maiden Lane, Suite 1503, New York, NY 10038 Tel: 212-807-7040 E-mail: jha@jhalit.com Web Site: jhalit.com, pg 462

Hawkins, Bob Jr, Harvest House Publishers Inc, PO Box 41210, Eugene, OR 97404-0322 Tel: 541-343-0123 Toll Free Tel: 888-501-6991 Fax: 541-343-9711 E-mail: admin@harvesthousepublishers.com; permissions@harvesthousepublishers.com Web Site: harvesthousepublishers.com, pg 88

Hawkins, Jaclyn, Sounds True Inc, 413 S Arthur Ave, Louisville, CO 80027 Tel: 303-665-3151 Toll Free Tel: 800-333-9185 (US); 888-303-9185 (US & CN) E-mail: customerservice@soundstrue.com; stpublicity@soundstrue.com Web Site: www.soundstrue.com, pg 194

Hawkins, Jordana, Running Press, 1290 Avenue of the Americas, New York, NY 10104 Tel: 212-364-1100 Toll Free Tel: 800-759-0190 (cust serv) Fax: 212-364-0933 (intl orders) Toll Free Fax: 800-286-9471 (cust serv) E-mail: customer.service@hbgusa.com; orders@hbgusa.com Web Site: www.hachettebookgroup.com/imprint/running-press/; www.moon.com (Moon Travel Guides), pg 178

Hawley, Marcy, Orange Frazer Press Inc, 37 1/2 W Main St, Wilmington, OH 45177 Tel: 937-382-3196 Fax: 937-383-3159 E-mail: ofrazer@erinet.com Web Site: www.orangefrazer.com, pg 147

Hawley, Sarah, Orange Frazer Press Inc, 37 1/2 W Main St, Wilmington, OH 45177 Tel: 937-382-3196 Fax: 937-383-3159 E-mail: ofrazer@erinet.com Web Site: www.orangefrazer.com, pg 147

Hawse, Jen, Island Press, 2000 "M" St NW, Suite 480-B, Washington, DC 20036 Tel: 202-232-7933 Toll Free Tel: 800-621-2736 Fax: 202-234-1328 E-mail: info@islandpress.org Web Site: www.islandpress.org, pg 104

Hayden, Patrick Nielsen, Tor Publishing Group, 120 Broadway, New York, NY 10271 Toll Free Tel: 800-455-0340 (Macmillan) E-mail: torpublicity@tor.com; forgepublicity@forgebooks.com Web Site: us.macmillan.com/torpublishinggroup, pg 208

Hayden, Thomas K, National Notary Association (NNA), 9350 De Soto Ave, Chatsworth, CA 91311-4926 Tel: 818-739-4000 Toll Free Tel: 800-876-6827 Toll Free Fax: 800-833-1211 E-mail: services@nationalnotary.org Web Site: www.nationalnotary.org, pg 138

Hayden, William, The H W Wilson Foundation, 750 Third Ave, 13th fl, New York, NY 10017 Tel: 212-418-8473 Web Site: www.thwwf.org, pg 526

Hayes, Amber, Coretta Scott King - John Steptoe Award for New Talent, 225 N Michigan Ave, Suite 1300, Chicago, IL 60601 Tel: 312-944-6780 Toll Free Tel: 800-545-2433 (ext 4294) Fax: 312-280-3256 E-mail: diversity@ala.org Web Site: www.ala.org/awardsgrants, pg 620

Hayes, Amber, Coretta Scott King - Virginia Hamilton Award for Lifetime Achievement, 225 N Michigan Ave, Suite 1300, Chicago, IL 60601 Toll Free Tel: 800-545-2433 E-mail: diversity@ala.org Web Site: www.ala.org/emiert/virginia-hamilton-award-lifetime-achievement, pg 620

Hayes, Amber, Stonewall Book Awards, 225 N Michigan Ave, Suite 1300, Chicago, IL 60601 Tel: 312-944-6780 Toll Free Tel: 800-545-2433 Fax: 312-440-9374 E-mail: diversity@ala.org Web Site: www.ala.org/rt/rrt/award/stonewall; www.ala.org/rt/rrt; www.ala.org, pg 666

Hayes, Kevin, Omnigraphics Inc, 615 Griswold, Suite 520, Detroit, MI 48226 Tel: 610-461-3548 Toll Free Tel: 800-234-1340 (cust serv) Fax: 610-532-9001 Toll Free Fax: 800-875-1340 (cust serv) E-mail: contact@omnigraphics.com; customerservice@omnigraphics.com Web Site: omnigraphics.com, pg 146

Hayes, Ryan, Chronicle Books LLC, 680 Second St, San Francisco, CA 94107 Tel: 415-537-4200 Fax: 415-537-4460 (perms) E-mail: hello@chroniclebooks.com; subrights@chroniclebooks.com Web Site: www.chroniclebooks.com, pg 48

Hayet, Sara, Doubleday, c/o Penguin Random House LLC, 1745 Broadway, New York, NY 10019 Tel: 212-751-2600 Fax: 212-940-7390 (dom rts); 212-572-2662 (foreign rts) Web Site: knopfdoubleday.com/imprint/doubleday/; knopfdoubleday.com, pg 61

Hays, John, Bear & Co Inc, One Park St, Rochester, VT 05767 Tel: 802-767-3174 Toll Free Tel: 800-932-3277 Fax: 802-767-3726 E-mail: customerservice@InnerTraditions.com Web Site: InnerTraditions.com, pg 26

Hays, John, Red Wheel/Weiser, 65 Parker St, Suite 7, Newburyport, MA 01950 Tel: 978-465-0504 Toll Free Tel: 800-423-7087 (orders) Fax: 978-465-0243 E-mail: info@rwwbooks.com Web Site: www.redwheelweiser.com, pg 173

Hays, Tommy, Thomas Wolfe Fiction Prize, PO Box 21591, Winston-Salem, NC 27120-1591 Tel: 336-293-8844 E-mail: mail@ncwriters.org Web Site: www.ncwriters.org, pg 677

Hayskar, Bonnie, Pangaea Publications, 110183 Friendship Lane S, Chaska, MN 55318 Tel: 651-226-2032 E-mail: info@pangaea.org Web Site: pangaea.org, pg 150

Hayward, Alice, Foundation Press, c/o West Academic, 860 Blue Gentian Rd, Eagan, MN 55121 Toll Free Tel: 877-888-1330 E-mail: support@westacademic.com Web Site: www.westacademic.com, pg 74

Haywood, Samantha, Transatlantic Agency, 2 Bloor St E, Suite 3500, Toronto, ON M4W 1A8, Canada Tel: 416-488-9214 E-mail: info@transatlanticagency.com; royalties@transatlanticagency.com Web Site: www.transatlanticagency.com, pg 479

Hazboun, Alma, Judson Press, 1075 First Ave, King of Prussia, PA 19406 Toll Free Tel: 800-458-3766 Fax: 610-768-2107 E-mail: publisher@judsonpress.com; editor@judsonpress.com; marketing@judsonpress.com Web Site: www.judsonpress.com, pg 107

Hazelwood, Morgan, Amateur Writing Contest, PO Box 686, Baltimore, MD 21203-0686 Tel: 410-563-2737 E-mail: bsfs-amc@bsfs.org Web Site: www.bsfs.org/bsfsssc.htm, pg 572

Hazelwood, Morgan, BSFS Poetry Contest, PO Box 686, Baltimore, MD 21203-0686 Tel: 410-563-2737 E-mail: poetry@bsfs.org Web Site: www.bsfs.org/bsfspoetry.htm, pg 585

Hazelwood, Morgan, Jack L Chalker Young Writers' Contest, PO Box 686, Baltimore, MD 21203-0686 Tel: 410-563-2737 E-mail: ywc@balticon.org Web Site: www.bsfs.org/bsfsywc.htm, pg 588

Hazelwood, Morgan, Compton Crook Award, PO Box 686, Baltimore, MD 21203-0686 Tel: 410-563-2737 E-mail: webmeister@bsfs.org Web Site: www.bsfs.org/CCA/bsfsccnu2014.htm, pg 593

Hazelwood, Morgan, Writer's Workshop at Balticon, PO Box 686, Baltimore, MD 21203-0686 Tel: 410-563-2737 E-mail: writersworkshop@bsfs.org Web Site: bsfs.org/bsfswriterwork.htm, pg 558

Hazelwood, Morgan, Writer's Workshop at BSFS, PO Box 686, Baltimore, MD 21203-0686 Tel: 410-563-2737 E-mail: bsfsevents@bsfs.org Web Site: bsfs.org/bsfswriterwork.htm, pg 558

Heacock, Kait, University of Washington Press, 4333 Brooklyn Ave NE, Seattle, WA 98105-9570 Toll Free Tel: 800-537-5487 (orders) Fax: 206-543-3932; 410-516-6998 (perms) E-mail: uwapress@uw.edu Web Site: uwapress.uw.edu, pg 221

Head, Karen J PhD, International Poetry Competition, 686 Cherry St NW, Suite 333, Atlanta, GA 30332-0161 E-mail: atlantareview@gatech.edu Web Site: www.atlantareview.com, pg 617

Headley, Jennifer, BJU Press, 1430 Wade Hampton Blvd, Greenville, SC 29609-5046 Tel: 864-770-1317; 864-546-4600 Toll Free Tel: 800-845-5731 E-mail: bjupinfo@bju.edu Web Site: www.bjupress.com, pg 30

Headrick, Rebecca, The American Library Association (ALA), 225 N Michigan Ave, Suite 1300, Chicago, IL 60601 Tel: 312-944-6780 Toll Free Tel: 800-545-2433; 866-SHOP-ALA (746-7252, orders) Fax: 312-280-5275; 312-440-9374; 312-280-5860 (orders) E-mail: ala@ala.org; alastore@ala.org Web Site: www.alastore.ala.org; www.ala.org, pg 10

Headrick, Rebecca, The American Library Association (ALA), 225 N Michigan Ave, Suite 1300, Chicago, IL 60601 Tel: 312-944-6780; 312-280-4299 (memb & cust serv) Toll Free Tel: 800-545-2433 Fax: 312-440-9374 E-mail: ala@ala.org; customerservice@ala.org Web Site: www.ala.org, pg 495

Healey-Cunningham, Helen, Portfolio, c/o Penguin Random House LLC, 1745 Broadway, New York, NY 10019 Tel: 212-782-9000 Web Site: www.penguin.com/portfolio-overview/; www.penguin.com/sentinel-overview/; www.penguin.com/thesis/, pg 162

Healy, Chuck, Liguori Publications, One Liguori Dr, Liguori, MO 63057-1000 Tel: 636-464-2500 Toll Free Tel: 800-325-9521 Toll Free Fax: 800-325-9526 (sales) E-mail: liguori@liguori.org (sales & cust serv) Web Site: www.liguori.org, pg 137

Healy, Howard, New York State Bar Association, One Elk St, Albany, NY 12207 Tel: 518-463-3200 Toll Free Tel: 800-582-2452 Fax: 518-463-5993 E-mail: mrc@nysba.org Web Site: nysba.org, pg 141

Heard, Janet, Davies Publishing Inc, 32 S Raymond Ave, Suites 4 & 5, Pasadena, CA 91105-1961 Tel: 626-792-3046 Toll Free Tel: 877-792-0005 Fax: 626-792-5308 E-mail: info@daviespublishing.com Web Site: daviespublishing.com, pg 57

Hearn, Ashley, Peachtree Publishing Co Inc, 1700 Chattahoochee Ave, Atlanta, GA 30318-2112 Tel: 404-876-8761 Toll Free Tel: 800-241-0113 Fax: 404-875-2578 Toll Free Fax: 800-875-8909 E-mail: hello@peachtree-online.com; orders@peachtree-online.com; sales@peachtree-online.com Web Site: www.peachtreebooks.com; www.peachtree-online.com, pg 153

Hearn, Katie, Annick Press Ltd, 388 Carlaw Ave, Suite 200, Toronto, ON M4M 2T4, Canada Tel: 416-221-4802 Fax: 416-221-8400 E-mail: annickpress@annickpress.com Web Site: www.annickpress.com, pg 395

Hearn, Will, Wm B Eerdmans Publishing Co, 4035 Park East Ct SE, Grand Rapids, MI 49546 Tel: 616-459-4591 Toll Free Tel: 800-253-7521 E-mail: customerservice@eerdmans.com; sales@eerdmans.com Web Site: www.eerdmans.com, pg 64

Heaston, John, National Association of Hispanic Publications Inc (NAHP), National Press Bldg, 529 14 St NW, Suite 923, Washington, DC 20045 Web Site: nahp.org, pg 511

Heater, Maria, Nelson Literary Agency LLC, 700 Colorado Blvd, No 352, Denver, CO 80206 Tel: 303-292-2805 E-mail: info@nelsonagency.com Web Site: www.nelsonagency.com, pg 471

Heath, Mary, University Press of Mississippi, 3825 Ridgewood Rd, Jackson, MS 39211-6492 Tel: 601-432-6205 Toll Free Tel: 800-737-7788 (orders & cust serv) Fax: 601-432-6217 E-mail: press@mississippi.edu Web Site: www.upress.state.ms.us, pg 222

Heaton, Ashleigh, Random House Publishing Group, 1745 Broadway, New York, NY 10019 Toll Free Tel: 800-200-3552 Web Site: www.randomhousebooks.com, pg 171

Hebel, Brad, Columbia University Press, 61 W 62 St, New York, NY 10023 Tel: 212-459-0600 Toll Free Tel: 800-944-8648 Fax: 212-459-3678 Web Site: cup.columbia.edu, pg 51

Hebert, Henry, Guild of Book Workers, 521 Fifth Ave, New York, NY 10175 E-mail: communications@guildofbookworkers.org; membership@guildofbookworkers.org Web Site: www.guildofbookworkers.org, pg 507

Hebert, Jean-Francois, Editions du CHU Sainte-Justine, 3175, chemin de la Cote-Sainte-Catherine, Montreal, QC H3T 1C5, Canada *Tel:* 514-345-4671 *Fax:* 514-345-4631 *E-mail:* edition.hsj@ssss.gouv.qc.ca *Web Site:* www.editions-chu-sainte-justine.org, pg 402

Hechler, Kay, Association for Talent Development (ATD) Press, 1640 King St, Box 1443, Alexandria, VA 22314-1443 *Tel:* 703-683-8100 *Toll Free Tel:* 800-628-2783 *Fax:* 703-299-8723; 703-683-1523 (cust care) *E-mail:* customercare@td.org *Web Site:* www.td.org, pg 19

Heckenthorn, Steve, Medals of America Press, 114 Southchase Blvd, Fountain Inn, SC 29644 *Toll Free Tel:* 800-605-4001 *Toll Free Fax:* 800-407-8640 *Web Site:* moapress.com, pg 128

Hecker, J L, Stipes Publishing LLC, 204 W University Ave, Champaign, IL 61820 *Tel:* 217-356-8391 *Fax:* 217-356-5753 *E-mail:* stipes01@sbcglobal.net *Web Site:* www.stipes.com, pg 198

Hecker, Mel, United States Holocaust Memorial Museum, 100 Raoul Wallenberg Place SW, Washington, DC 20024-2126 *Tel:* 202-488-0400; 202-488-6144 (orders) *Toll Free Tel:* 800-259-9998 (orders) *E-mail:* academicpublications@ushmm.org *Web Site:* www.ushmm.org, pg 213

Heckman, Briar, Westwood Creative Artists Ltd, 386 Huron St, Toronto, ON M5S 2G6, Canada *Tel:* 416-964-3302 *Fax:* 416-964-3302 *E-mail:* wca_office@wcaltd.com *Web Site:* www.wcaltd.com, pg 481

Hector, Jade, Random House Children's Books, c/o Penguin Random House LLC, 1745 Broadway, New York, NY 10019 *Tel:* 212-782-9000 *Web Site:* www.rhcbooks.com, pg 170

Heddelson, Emily, Scholastic Trade Publishing, 557 Broadway, New York, NY 10012 *Tel:* 212-343-6100; 212-343-4685 (export sales) *Fax:* 212-343-4714 (export sales) *Web Site:* www.scholastic.com, pg 184

Hedden, Andrew, Scholastic Inc, 557 Broadway, New York, NY 10012 *Tel:* 212-343-6100 *Toll Free Tel:* 800-SCHOLASTIC (724-6527) *Web Site:* www.scholastic.com, pg 184

Heddle, Jennifer, Disney Publishing Worldwide, 1101 Flower St, Glendale, CA 91201 *Web Site:* books.disney.com, pg 60

Hedman, Susan Alvare, Hartman Publishing Inc, 1313 Iron Ave SW, Albuquerque, NM 87102 *Tel:* 505-291-1274 *Toll Free Tel:* 800-999-9534 *Toll Free Fax:* 800-474-6106 *E-mail:* info@hartmanonline.com *Web Site:* www.hartmanonline.com, pg 87

Hedrick, Chris, Scholastic Education Solutions, 557 Broadway, New York, NY 10012 *Tel:* 212-343-6100 *Fax:* 212-343-6189 *Web Site:* www.scholastic.com, pg 184

Hedrick-Armstrong, Cathie, Marsal Lyon Literary Agency LLC, 665 San Rodolfo Dr, Suite 124, PMB 121, Solana Beach, CA 92075 *Tel:* 760-814-8507 *Web Site:* www.marsallyonliteraryagency.com, pg 468

Heffner, Samantha (Sami), Indiana University Press, Off of Scholarly Publg, Herman B Wells Library 350, 1320 E Tenth St, Bloomington, IN 47405-3907 *Tel:* 812-855-8817 *Fax:* 812-855-7931; 812-855-8507 *E-mail:* iupress@indiana.edu *Web Site:* iupress.org, pg 100

Heflin, Mark, American Illustration/American Photography, 225 W 36 St, Suite 602, New York, NY 10018 *Tel:* 646-669-8111 *E-mail:* info@ai-ap.com *Web Site:* www.ai-ap.com, pg 573

Heidhausen, Katerina, University Science Books, 1305 Walt Whitman Rd, Suite 110, Melville, NY 11747 *Tel:* 703-661-1572 (cust serv & orders) *Fax:* 703-661-1501 *E-mail:* usbmail@presswarehouse.com (cust serv, orders) *Web Site:* uscibooks.aip.org, pg 222

Heifetz, Merrilee, Writers House, 21 W 26 St, New York, NY 10010 *Tel:* 212-685-2400 *Web Site:* www.writershouse.com, pg 482

Heilman, Erika, Harvard Business Review Press, 20 Guest St, Suite 700, Brighton, MA 02135 *Tel:* 617-783-7400 *Fax:* 617-783-7489 *E-mail:* custserv@hbsp.harvard.edu *Web Site:* www.harvardbusiness.org, pg 87

Heimbouch, Hollis, HarperCollins Publishers LLC, 195 Broadway, New York, NY 10007 *Tel:* 212-207-7000 *Web Site:* www.harpercollins.com, pg 86

Heimburger, Donald J, Heimburger House Publishing Co, 7236 W Madison St, Forest Park, IL 60130 *Tel:* 708-366-1973 *Fax:* 708-366-1973 *E-mail:* info@heimburgerhouse.com *Web Site:* www.heimburgerhouse.com, pg 90

Heimert, Lara, Basic Books Group, 1290 Avenue of the Americas, New York, NY 10104 *Tel:* 212-340-8100 *Toll Free Tel:* 800-343-4499 (cust serv) *Fax:* 212-340-8105 *E-mail:* customer.service@hbgusa.com; orders@hbgusa.com *Web Site:* www.hachettebookgroup.com/imprint/basic-books/, pg 25

Heimert, Lara, Hachette Book Group Inc, 1290 Avenue of the Americas, New York, NY 10104 *Tel:* 212-364-1100 *Toll Free Tel:* 800-759-0190 (cust serv) *Fax:* 212-364-0933 (intl orders) *Toll Free Fax:* 800-286-9471 (cust serv) *E-mail:* customer.service@hbgusa.com; orders@hbgusa.com *Web Site:* www.hachettebookgroup.com, pg 83

Hein, Kristi, Pictures & Words Editorial Services, 3100 "B" Ave, Anacortes, WA 98221 *Tel:* 360-293-8476 *Web Site:* www.picturesandwords.com/words, pg 443

Hein, William S Jr, William S Hein & Co Inc, 2350 N Forest Rd, Suite 10A, Getzville, NY 14068 *Tel:* 716-882-2600 *Toll Free Tel:* 800-828-7571 *Fax:* 716-883-8100 *E-mail:* mail@wshein.com; marketing@wshein.com; customerservice@wshein.com *Web Site:* home.heinonline.org, pg 90

Heinen, Jonathan, The Crazyhorse Fiction Prize, College of Charleston, Dept of English, 66 George St, Charleston, SC 29424 *Tel:* 843-953-4470 *E-mail:* crazyhorse@cofc.edu *Web Site:* crazyhorse.cofc.edu/prizes, pg 593

Heinen, Jonathan, Lynda Hull Memorial Poetry Prize, College of Charleston, Dept of English, 66 George St, Charleston, SC 29424 *Tel:* 843-953-4470 *E-mail:* crazyhorse@cofc.edu *Web Site:* crazyhorse.cofc.edu/prizes, pg 614

Heinrich, Lucas, Random House Publishing Group, 1745 Broadway, New York, NY 10019 *Toll Free Tel:* 800-200-3552 *Web Site:* www.randomhousebooks.com, pg 171

Heiser, Christopher, University of Chicago Press, 1427 E 60 St, Chicago, IL 60637-2954 *Tel:* 773-702-7700; 773-702-7600 *Toll Free Tel:* 800-621-2736 (orders) *Fax:* 773-702-9756; 773-660-2235 (orders); 773-702-2708 *E-mail:* custserv@press.uchicago.edu; marketing@press.uchicago.edu *Web Site:* www.press.uchicago.edu, pg 215

Heistand, Yakira, Amateur Writing Contest, PO Box 686, Baltimore, MD 21203-0686 *Tel:* 410-563-2737 *E-mail:* bsfs-amc@bsfs.org *Web Site:* www.bsfs.org/bsfsssc.htm, pg 572

Heistand, Yakira, BSFS Poetry Contest, PO Box 686, Baltimore, MD 21203-0686 *Tel:* 410-563-2737 *E-mail:* poetry@bsfs.org *Web Site:* www.bsfs.org/bsfspoetry.htm, pg 585

Heistand, Yakira, Jack L Chalker Young Writers' Contest, PO Box 686, Baltimore, MD 21203-0686 *Tel:* 410-563-2737 *E-mail:* ywc@balticon.org *Web Site:* www.bsfs.org/bsfsywc.htm, pg 588

Heistand, Yakira, Compton Crook Award, PO Box 686, Baltimore, MD 21203-0686 *Tel:* 410-563-2737 *E-mail:* webmeister@bsfs.org *Web Site:* www.bsfs.org/CCA/bsfsccnu2014.htm, pg 593

Heistand, Yakira, Writer's Workshop at Balticon, PO Box 686, Baltimore, MD 21203-0686 *Tel:* 410-563-2737 *E-mail:* writersworkshop@bsfs.org *Web Site:* bsfs.org/bsfswriterwork.htm, pg 558

Heisterkamp, Delaney, Sourcebooks LLC, 1935 Brookdale Rd, Suite 139, Naperville, IL 60563 *Tel:* 630-961-3900 *Toll Free Tel:* 800-432-7444 *Fax:* 630-961-2168 *E-mail:* info@sourcebooks.com *Web Site:* www.sourcebooks.com, pg 195

Heitner, Michael, Advertising Research Foundation (ARF), 432 Park Ave S, 4th fl, New York, NY 10016 *Tel:* 212-751-5656 *Fax:* 212-689-1859 *E-mail:* membership@thearf.org; new-member-info@thearf.org *Web Site:* thearf.org, pg 493, 525

Helaine, Chrissy, DK, c/o Penguin Random House LLC, 1745 Broadway, 20th fl, New York, NY 10019 *Tel:* 646-674-4000 *Toll Free Tel:* 800-733-3000 *Fax:* 646-674-4020 *E-mail:* marketing@dk.com (lib servs); publicity@dk.com; csorders@penguinrandomhouse.com; customerservice@penguinrandomhouse.com *Web Site:* www.dk.com, pg 60

Held, Barb, Television Academy, 5220 Lankershim Blvd, North Hollywood, CA 91601-3109 *Tel:* 818-754-2800 *Web Site:* www.emmys.com, pg 521

Held, Ivan, Berkley, c/o Penguin Random House LLC, 1745 Broadway, 19th fl, New York, NY 10019 *Tel:* 212-366-2000 *Web Site:* www.penguin.com/publishers/berkley/; www.penguin.com/ace-overview/, pg 28

Held, Ivan, Dutton, c/o Penguin Random House LLC, 1745 Broadway, New York, NY 10019 *Tel:* 212-366-2000 *Web Site:* www.penguin.com/dutton-overview/; www.penguin.com/plume-books-overview/; www.penguin.com/tiny-reparations-overview/, pg 62

Held, Ivan, Penguin Publishing Group, c/o Penguin Random House LLC, 1745 Broadway, New York, NY 10019 *Tel:* 212-782-9000 *Web Site:* www.penguin.com, pg 154

Held, Ivan, GP Putnam's Sons, c/o Penguin Random House LLC, 1745 Broadway, New York, NY 10019 *Tel:* 212-782-9000 *Web Site:* www.penguin.com/putnam/, pg 167

Held, Robbie, Fence Books, 36-09 28 Ave, Apt 3R, Astoria, NY 11103-4518 *Tel:* 518-567-7006 *Web Site:* www.fenceportal.org, pg 71

Heleine, Chrissy, Hachette Book Group Inc, 1290 Avenue of the Americas, New York, NY 10104 *Tel:* 212-364-1100 *Toll Free Tel:* 800-759-0190 (cust serv) *Fax:* 212-364-0933 (intl orders) *Toll Free Fax:* 800-286-9471 (cust serv) *E-mail:* customer.service@hbgusa.com; orders@hbgusa.com *Web Site:* www.hachettebookgroup.com, pg 83

Helfand, Debra, Farrar, Straus & Giroux, LLC, 120 Broadway, New York, NY 10271 *Tel:* 212-741-6900 *E-mail:* fsg.publicity@fsgbooks.com; sales@fsgbooks.com *Web Site:* us.macmillan.com/fsg, pg 70

Helke, Katie, Oxford University Press USA, 198 Madison Ave, New York, NY 10016 *Toll Free Tel:* 800-451-7556 (orders); 800-445-9714 (cust serv) *Fax:* 919-677-1303 *E-mail:* custserv.us@oup.com *Web Site:* global.oup.com, pg 149

Helleberg, Tom, Mountaineers Books, 1001 SW Klickitat Way, Suite 201, Seattle, WA 98134 *Tel:* 206-223-6303 *Fax:* 206-223-6306 *E-mail:* mbooks@mountaineersbooks.org; customerservice@mountaineersbooks.org *Web Site:* www.mountaineers.org/books, pg 135

Hellegers, Allison, Stimola Literary Studio Inc, 11 Briarwood Lane, West Tisbury, MA 02575 *Tel:* 201-945-9353 *Fax:* 201-490-5920 *E-mail:* info@stimolaliterarystudio.com *Web Site:* www.stimolaliterarystudio.com, pg 478

Heller, Allyson, Simon & Schuster Children's Publishing, 1230 Avenue of the Americas, New York, NY 10020 *Tel:* 212-698-7000 *Web Site:* www.simonandschuster.com/kids; www.simonandschuster.com/teen; simonandschuster.net; simonandschuster.biz, pg 189

Heller, Andra, American Medical Association (AMA), AMA Plaza, 330 N Wabash, Suite 39300, Chicago, IL 60611-5885 *Tel:* 312-464-5000 *Toll Free Tel:* 800-621-8335 *E-mail:* media@ama-assn.org (media & edit) *Web Site:* www.ama-assn.org; www.jamanetwork.org, pg 495

Heller, Jonah, Peachtree Publishing Co Inc, 1700 Chattahoochee Ave, Atlanta, GA 30318-2112 *Tel:* 404-876-8761 *Toll Free Tel:* 800-241-0113 *Fax:* 404-875-2578 *Toll Free Fax:* 800-875-8909 *E-mail:* hello@

peachtree-online.com; orders@peachtree-online.com; sales@peachtree-online.com *Web Site:* www.peachtreebooks.com; www.peachtree-online.com, pg 153

Heller, Moshe, KTAV Publishing House Inc, 527 Empire Blvd, Brooklyn, NY 11225 *Tel:* 201-963-9524; 718-972-5449 *Fax:* 718-972-6307 *E-mail:* orders@ktav.com *Web Site:* www.ktav.com, pg 111

Helm, Kevin, ASET - The Neurodiagnostic Society, 402 E Bannister Rd, Suite A, Kansas City, MO 64131-3019 *Tel:* 816-931-1120 *Fax:* 816-931-1145 *E-mail:* info@aset.org *Web Site:* www.aset.org, pg 18

Helms, Derek, University Press of Kansas, 2502 Westbrooke Circle, Lawrence, KS 66045-4444 *Tel:* 785-864-4154 *Fax:* 785-864-4586 *E-mail:* upress@ku.edu *Web Site:* www.kansaspress.ku.edu, pg 221

Helmy, Shahenda, Wordsmith, Open Book Bldg, Suite 200, 1011 Washington Ave S, Minneapolis, MN 55415 *Tel:* 612-215-2575 *Fax:* 612-215-2576 *E-mail:* loft@loft.org *Web Site:* loft.org/conference/about-wordsmith, pg 558

Heltzel, Anne, Harry N Abrams Inc, 195 Broadway, 9th fl, New York, NY 10007 *Tel:* 212-206-7715 *Toll Free Tel:* 800-345-1359 *Fax:* 212-645-8437 *E-mail:* abrams@abramsbooks.com; publicity@abramsbooks.com; sales@abramsbooks.com *Web Site:* www.abramsbooks.com, pg 2

Hemmer, Ryan, Augsburg Fortress Publishers, Publishing House of the Evangelical Lutheran Church in America, 411 Washington Ave N, 3rd fl, Minneapolis, MN 55401 *Tel:* 612-330-3300 *Toll Free Tel:* 800-426-0115 (ext 639, subns); 800-328-4648 (orders) *Fax:* 612-330-3455 *E-mail:* info@augsburgfortress.org; copyright@augsburgfortress.org (reprint permission requests); customercare@augsburgfortress.org *Web Site:* www.augsburgfortress.org; www.1517.media, pg 22

Hemperly, Becky S, Candlewick Press, 99 Dover St, Somerville, MA 02144-2825 *Tel:* 617-661-3330 *Fax:* 617-661-0565 *E-mail:* bigbear@candlewick.com; salesinfo@candlewick.com *Web Site:* candlewick.com, pg 39

Hempstead, Andrew, Summerthought Publishing, PO Box 2309, Banff, AB T1L 1C1, Canada *Tel:* 403-762-0535 *E-mail:* info@summerthought.com *Web Site:* summerthought.com, pg 420

Hendee, Laura, American Fisheries Society, 425 Barlow Place, Suite 110, Bethesda, MD 20814-2144 *Tel:* 301-897-8616; 703-661-1570 (book orders) *Fax:* 301-897-8096; 703-996-1010 (book orders) *E-mail:* main@fisheries.org *Web Site:* fisheries.org/books-journals, pg 9

Hendersen, Victoria, Brower Literary & Management Inc, 13720 Old St Augustine Rd, Suite 8-512, Jacksonville, FL 32258 *Tel:* 646-854-6073 *E-mail:* admin@browerliterary.com; foreign@browerliterary.com (foreign publr inquiries); queries@browerliterary.com; subrights@browerliterary.com (busn inquiries) *Web Site:* browerliterary.com, pg 452

Henderson, Alex, Bay Area Women in Publishing (BAWiP), 680 Second St, San Francisco, CA 94107 *E-mail:* bayareawomeninpublishing@gmail.com *Web Site:* www.bayareawomeninpublishing.com, pg 500

Henderson, Bill, Pushcart Press, PO Box 380, Wainscott, NY 11975-0380 *Tel:* 631-324-9300 *Web Site:* www.pushcartprize.com/pushcartpress, pg 167

Henderson, Bill, Pushcart Prize: Best of the Small Presses, PO Box 380, Wainscott, NY 11975-0380 *Tel:* 631-324-9300 *Web Site:* www.pushcartprize.com, pg 654

Henderson, Diane, Homestead Publishing, Box 193, Moose, WY 83012-0193 *Tel:* 307-733-6248 *Fax:* 307-733-6248 *E-mail:* info@homesteadpublishing.com; orders@homesteadpublishing.net *Web Site:* www.homesteadpublishing.net, pg 95

Henderson-Brown, Zakia, The New Press, 120 Wall St, 31st fl, New York, NY 10005 *Tel:* 212-629-8802 *Fax:* 212-629-8617 *E-mail:* newpress@thenewpress.com *Web Site:* thenewpress.com, pg 140

Hendricks, Kent, Zondervan, 3900 Sparks Dr SE, Grand Rapids, MI 49546 *Tel:* 616-698-6900 *Toll Free Tel:* 800-226-1122; 800-727-1309 (retail orders) *Fax:* 616-698-3350 *Toll Free Fax:* 800-698-3256 (retail orders) *E-mail:* customercare@harpercollins.com *Web Site:* www.zondervan.com, pg 236

Hendricksen, Sara, University of Nevada Press, c/o University of Nevada, Continuing Educ Bldg, MS 0166, Reno, NV 89557-0166 *Tel:* 775-784-6573 *Fax:* 775-784-6200 *Web Site:* www.unpress.nevada.edu, pg 218

Hendrickson, Craig, BePuzzled, 2030 Harrison St, San Francisco, CA 94110 *Tel:* 415-934-3705 *Toll Free Tel:* 800-347-4818 *E-mail:* info@ugames.com; consumer@ugames.com *Web Site:* universitygames.com, pg 28

Hendrie, Caroline, Society of Professional Journalists (SPJ), PO Box 441748, Indianapolis, IN 46244 *Tel:* 317-927-8000 *Fax:* 317-920-4789 *E-mail:* communications@spj.org *Web Site:* www.spj.org, pg 520

Henley, Kristin, The Center for Fiction, 15 Lafayette Ave, Brooklyn, NY 11217 *Tel:* 212-755-6710 *E-mail:* info@centerforfiction.org *Web Site:* centerforfiction.org, pg 503

Henn, J Garrett, McGraw-Hill Professional Publishing Group, 2 Penn Plaza, New York, NY 10121 *Tel:* 646-766-2000 *Web Site:* www.mhprofessional.com; www.mheducation.com, pg 128

Hennessey, Shannon, Simon & Schuster, 1230 Avenue of the Americas, New York, NY 10020 *Tel:* 212-698-7000 *Toll Free Tel:* 800-223-2348 (cust serv); 800-223-2336 (orders) *Toll Free Fax:* 800-943-9831 (orders) *Web Site:* simonandschusterpublishing.com/simonandschuster/, pg 188

Henning, Alyssa, Indiana University Press, Off of Scholarly Publg, Herman B Wells Library 350, 1320 E Tenth St, Bloomington, IN 47405-3907 *Tel:* 812-855-8817 *Fax:* 812-855-7931; 812-855-8507 *E-mail:* iupress@indiana.edu *Web Site:* iupress.org, pg 100

Henning-Stout, Sara, Princeton University Press, 41 William St, Princeton, NJ 08540-5237 *Tel:* 609-258-4900 *Fax:* 609-258-6305 *E-mail:* info@press.princeton.edu *Web Site:* press.princeton.edu, pg 164

Henoch, Larissa, Health Communications Inc, 301 Crawford Blvd, Suite 200, Boca Raton, FL 33432 *Tel:* 561-453-0696 *Toll Free Tel:* 800-441-5569 (cust serv & orders) *Fax:* 561-453-1009 *Toll Free Fax:* 800-943-9831 (orders) *E-mail:* editorial@hcibooks.com *Web Site:* hcibooks.com, pg 90

Henriquez, Cristela, Levine|Greenberg|Rostan Literary Agency, 307 Seventh Ave, Suite 2407, New York, NY 10001 *Tel:* 212-337-0934 *Fax:* 212-337-0948 *E-mail:* submit@lgrliterary.com *Web Site:* lgrliterary.com, pg 467

Henry, Christie, Princeton University Press, 41 William St, Princeton, NJ 08540-5237 *Tel:* 609-258-4900 *Fax:* 609-258-6305 *E-mail:* info@press.princeton.edu *Web Site:* press.princeton.edu, pg 164

Henry, Christie, Supporting Diverse Voices: Book Proposal Development Grants, 41 William St, Princeton, NJ 08540-5237 *Tel:* 609-258-4900 *E-mail:* info@press.princeton.edu *Web Site:* press.princeton.edu/book-proposal-development-grants, pg 668

Henry, Drew, HarperCollins Publishers LLC, 195 Broadway, New York, NY 10007 *Tel:* 212-207-7000 *Web Site:* www.harpercollins.com, pg 87

Henry, Georgia, Penguin Random House Canada, a Penguin Random House company, 320 Front St W, Suite 1400, Toronto, ON M5V 3B6, Canada *Tel:* 416-364-4449 *Toll Free Tel:* 888-523-9292 (cust serv) *E-mail:* canadaweb@penguinrandomhouse.com; customerservicescanada@penguinrandomhouse.com *Web Site:* www.penguinrandomhouse.ca, pg 416

Henry, Gray, Fons Vitae, 49 Mockingbird Valley Dr, Louisville, KY 40207-1366 *Tel:* 502-897-3641 *Fax:* 502-893-7373 *E-mail:* fonsvitaeky@aol.com *Web Site:* www.fonsvitae.com, pg 73

Henry, Jack, World Citizens, PO Box 131, Mill Valley, CA 94942-0131 *Tel:* 415-380-8020; 415-233-2822 (direct), pg 233

Henry, Jason, Dial Books for Young Readers, c/o Penguin Random House LLC, 1745 Broadway, New York, NY 10019 *Tel:* 212-782-9000 *Web Site:* www.penguin.com/dial-overview/, pg 59

Henry, Jason, Rocky Pond Books, c/o Penguin Random House LLC, 1745 Broadway, New York, NY 10019 *Tel:* 212-782-9000 *Web Site:* www.penguin.com/rocky-pond-overview/, pg 176

Henry, Kirti, Penguin Random House Canada, a Penguin Random House company, 320 Front St W, Suite 1400, Toronto, ON M5V 3B6, Canada *Tel:* 416-364-4449 *Toll Free Tel:* 888-523-9292 (cust serv) *E-mail:* canadaweb@penguinrandomhouse.com; customerservicescanada@penguinrandomhouse.com *Web Site:* www.penguinrandomhouse.ca, pg 416

Henry, Lorna, Dreamscape Media LLC, 1417 Timberwolf Dr, Holland, OH 43528 *Tel:* 419-867-6965 *Toll Free Tel:* 877-983-7326 *E-mail:* info@dreamscapeab.com *Web Site:* www.dreamscapepublishing.com, pg 62

Henry, Lynn, Knopf Canada, 320 Front St W, Suite 1400, Toronto, ON M5V 3B6, Canada *Tel:* 416-364-4449 *Toll Free Tel:* 888-523-9292 *Fax:* 416-598-7764 *Web Site:* www.penguinrandomhouse.ca, pg 411

Hensley, Kate, Princeton University Press, 41 William St, Princeton, NJ 08540-5237 *Tel:* 609-258-4900 *Fax:* 609-258-6305 *E-mail:* info@press.princeton.edu *Web Site:* press.princeton.edu, pg 164

Hensley, Todd, C&T Publishing Inc, 1651 Challenge Dr, Concord, CA 94520-5206 *Tel:* 925-677-0377 *E-mail:* ctinfo@ctpub.com *Web Site:* www.ctpub.com, pg 40

Hensley, Tony, C&T Publishing Inc, 1651 Challenge Dr, Concord, CA 94520-5206 *Tel:* 925-677-0377 *E-mail:* ctinfo@ctpub.com *Web Site:* www.ctpub.com, pg 40

Henson, Felicity, University Science Books, 1305 Walt Whitman Rd, Suite 110, Melville, NY 11747 *Tel:* 703-661-1572 (cust serv & orders) *Fax:* 703-661-1501 *E-mail:* usbmail@presswarehouse.com (cust serv, orders) *Web Site:* uscibooks.aip.org, pg 222

Henson, Gwen, American Society for Indexing Inc (ASI), 1628 E Southern Ave, Suite 9-223, Tempe, AZ 85282 *Tel:* 480-245-6750 *E-mail:* info@asindexing.org *Web Site:* www.asindexing.org, pg 496

Henson, Gwen, ASI Excellence in Indexing Award, 1628 E Southern Ave, Suite 9-223, Tempe, AZ 85282 *Tel:* 480-245-6750 *E-mail:* info@asindexing.org *Web Site:* www.asindexing.org/about/awards/asi-indexing-award, pg 574

Henson, Gwen, Theodore C Hines Award, 1628 E Southern Ave, Suite 9-223, Tempe, AZ 85282 *Tel:* 480-245-6750 *E-mail:* info@asindexing.org *Web Site:* www.asindexing.org/about/awards/hines-award, pg 613

Henson, Tori, Random House Publishing Group, 1745 Broadway, New York, NY 10019 *Toll Free Tel:* 800-200-3552 *Web Site:* www.randomhousebooks.com, pg 171

Herbert, Kaitlyn, Macmillan, 120 Broadway, 22nd fl, New York, NY 10271 *E-mail:* press.inquiries@macmillan.com *Web Site:* us.macmillan.com, pg 122

Hergenroeder, Jennifer, The Experiment, 220 E 23 St, Suite 600, New York, NY 10010-4658 *Tel:* 212-889-1659 *E-mail:* info@theexperimentpublishing.com *Web Site:* www.theexperimentpublishing.com, pg 68

Herholdt, Cathy, David C Cook, 4050 Lee Vance Dr, Colorado Springs, CO 80918 *Tel:* 719-536-0100 *Toll Free Tel:* 800-323-7543 (orders & cust serv) *Toll Free Fax:* 800-430-0726 (cust serv) *E-mail:* bookstores@davidccook.org; customercare@davidccook.org *Web Site:* www.davidccook.org, pg 52

Herits, Noreen, Random House Children's Books, c/o Penguin Random House LLC, 1745 Broadway, New York, NY 10019 *Tel:* 212-782-9000 *Web Site:* www.rhcbooks.com, pg 169

Herman, Cheryl, Books on Tape™, 1745 Broadway, New York, NY 10019 *Toll Free Tel:* 800-733-3000 (cust serv) *Toll Free Fax:* 800-940-7046 *Web Site:* PenguinRandomHouseLibrary.com, pg 34

Herman, Elizabeth, Simon & Schuster, 1230 Avenue of the Americas, New York, NY 10020 *Tel:* 212-698-7000 *Toll Free Tel:* 800-223-2348 (cust serv); 800-223-2336 (orders) *Toll Free Fax:* 800-943-9831 (orders) *Web Site:* simonandschusterpublishing.com/simonandschuster/, pg 188

Herman, Gilles, Les Editions du Septentrion, 86, Cote de la Montagne, bureau 200, Quebec, QC G1K 4E3, Canada *Tel:* 418-688-3556 *Fax:* 418-527-4978 *E-mail:* info@septentrion.qc.ca *Web Site:* www.septentrion.qc.ca, pg 403

Herman, Heather, Morton Publishing Co, 925 W Kenyon Ave, Unit 12, Englewood, CO 80110 *Tel:* 303-761-4805 *Fax:* 303-762-9923 *E-mail:* contact@morton-pub.com; returns@morton-pub.com *Web Site:* www.morton-pub.com, pg 134

Herman, Jeffrey H, The Jeff Herman Agency LLC, 29 Park St, Stockbridge, MA 01262 *Tel:* 413-298-0077 *Web Site:* www.jeffherman.com, pg 463

Herman, Kate, Chronicle Books LLC, 680 Second St, San Francisco, CA 94107 *Tel:* 415-537-4200 *Fax:* 415-537-4460 (perms) *E-mail:* hello@chroniclebooks.com; subrights@chroniclebooks.com *Web Site:* www.chroniclebooks.com, pg 47

Herman, Liz, STC Technical Communication Summit, 3251 Blenheim Blvd, Suite 406, Fairfax, VA 22030 *Tel:* 703-522-4114 *Fax:* 703-522-2075 *E-mail:* stc@stc.org; summit@stc.org *Web Site:* summit.stc.org; www.stc.org, pg 557

Herman, Rhonda, McFarland, 960 NC Hwy 88 W, Jefferson, NC 28640 *Tel:* 336-246-4460 *Toll Free Tel:* 800-253-2187 (orders) *Fax:* 336-246-5018; 336-246-4403 (orders) *E-mail:* info@mcfarlandpub.com *Web Site:* mcfarlandbooks.com, pg 127

Herman, Ronnie Ann, Herman Agency, 350 Central Park W, Apt 4I, New York, NY 10025 *Tel:* 212-749-4907 *Web Site:* www.hermanagencyinc.com, pg 485

Hermann, Sara, Parmenides Publishing, 3753 Howard Hughes Pkwy, Suite 200, Las Vegas, NV 89169 *Tel:* 702-892-3934 *Fax:* 702-892-3939 *E-mail:* info@parmenides.com; editor@parmenides.com *Web Site:* www.parmenides.com, pg 152

Hermes, Sr Kathryn James, Pauline Books & Media, 50 Saint Paul's Ave, Boston, MA 02130 *Tel:* 617-522-8911 *Toll Free Tel:* 800-876-4463 (orders); 800-836-9723 (cust serv) *Fax:* 617-541-9805 *E-mail:* editorial@paulinemedia.com (ms submissions); orderentry@pauline.org (cust serv) *Web Site:* www.pauline.org/pbmpublishing, pg 152

Hernandez, Alexandra, Grand Central Publishing, 1290 Avenue of the Americas, New York, NY 10104 *Tel:* 212-364-1100 *Web Site:* www.hachettebookgroup.com/imprint/grand-central-publishing/, pg 80

Hernandez, Alexandra, Penguin Random House Audio Publishing Group, 1745 Broadway, New York, NY 10019 *Toll Free Tel:* 800-793-2665 (cust serv) *E-mail:* audio@penguinrandomhouse.com; ecustomerservice@penguinrandomhouse.com *Web Site:* www.penguinrandomhouseaudio.com, pg 154

Hernandez, Christopher, GP Putnam's Sons Books for Young Readers, c/o Penguin Random House LLC, 1745 Broadway, New York, NY 10019 *Tel:* 212-782-9000 *Web Site:* www.penguin.com/putnam-young-readers/, pg 167

Hernandez, Cynthia, Casa Bautista de Publicaciones, 130 Montoya Rd, El Paso, TX 79932 *Tel:* 915-566-9656 *Toll Free Tel:* 800-755-5958 (cust serv & orders) *E-mail:* orders@editorialmh.org *Web Site:* www.editorialmh.org, pg 41

Hernandez, Gabriel, Florida Graphics Alliance (FGA), 10524 Mosspark Rd, Suite 204, PMB 334, Orlando, FL 32832 *Tel:* 407-240-8009 *E-mail:* info@floridagraphics.org *Web Site:* www.floridagraphics.org, pg 506

Hernandez, Ricardo, The Maureen Egen Writers Exchange Award, 90 Broad St, Suite 2100, New York, NY 10004 *Tel:* 212-226-3586 *Fax:* 212-226-3963 *E-mail:* wex@pw.org; admin@pw.org *Web Site:* www.pw.org, pg 598

Hernandez, Tim Z, University of Texas at El Paso, Department of Creative Writing, MFA/Department of Creative Writing, M520, University Towers, Oregon St, El Paso, TX 79968 *E-mail:* creativewriting@utep.edu *Web Site:* www.utep.edu/liberalarts/creative-writing, pg 567

Herr, Maddie, Sourcebooks LLC, 1935 Brookdale Rd, Suite 139, Naperville, IL 60563 *Tel:* 630-961-3900 *Toll Free Tel:* 800-432-7444 *Fax:* 630-961-2168 *E-mail:* info@sourcebooks.com *Web Site:* www.sourcebooks.com, pg 195

Herrera, Aida, BenBella Books Inc, 10440 N Central Expwy, Suite 800, Dallas, TX 75231-2264 *Tel:* 214-750-3600 *Web Site:* www.benbellabooks.com; www.smartpopbooks.com, pg 27

Herrera, Jennifer, David Black Agency, 335 Adams St, 27th fl, Suite 2707, Brooklyn, NY 11201 *Tel:* 718-852-5500 *Fax:* 718-852-5539 *Web Site:* www.davidblackagency.com, pg 450

Herrera, Katia, Sourcebooks LLC, 1935 Brookdale Rd, Suite 139, Naperville, IL 60563 *Tel:* 630-961-3900 *Toll Free Tel:* 800-432-7444 *Fax:* 630-961-2168 *E-mail:* info@sourcebooks.com *Web Site:* www.sourcebooks.com, pg 194

Herrera Mulligan, Michelle, Atria Books, 1230 Avenue of the Americas, New York, NY 10020 *Tel:* 212-698-7000 *Fax:* 212-698-7007 *Web Site:* www.simonandschuster.com, pg 21

Herring, John, HarperCollins Publishers LLC, 195 Broadway, New York, NY 10007 *Tel:* 212-207-7000 *Web Site:* www.harpercollins.com, pg 86

Herrington, Jennifer, Harvey Klinger Inc, 300 W 55 St, Suite 11V, New York, NY 10019 *Tel:* 212-581-7068 *Fax:* 212-315-3823 *E-mail:* queries@harveyklinger.com *Web Site:* www.harveyklinger.com, pg 465

Herrmann, Laurie, Beaver's Pond Press Inc, 939 Seventh St W, St Paul, MN 55102 *Tel:* 952-829-8818 *E-mail:* submissions@beaverspondpress.com *Web Site:* www.beaverspondpress.com, pg 26

Hershey, Elena, Doubleday, c/o Penguin Random House LLC, 1745 Broadway, New York, NY 10019 *Tel:* 212-751-2600 *Fax:* 212-940-7390 (dom rts); 212-572-2662 (foreign rts) *Web Site:* knopfdoubleday.com/imprint/doubleday/; knopfdoubleday.com/, pg 61

Hershey, Jennifer, Penguin Random House LLC, 1745 Broadway, New York, NY 10019 *Tel:* 212-782-9000 *Toll Free Tel:* 800-726-0600 *Web Site:* www.penguinrandomhouse.com, pg 155

Hershey, Jennifer, Random House Publishing Group, 1745 Broadway, New York, NY 10019 *Toll Free Tel:* 800-200-3552 *Web Site:* www.randomhousebooks.com, pg 171

Hershon, Robert, Hanging Loose Press, 231 Wyckoff St, Brooklyn, NY 11217 *Tel:* 347-529-4738 *Fax:* 347-227-8215 *E-mail:* print225@aol.com *Web Site:* www.hangingloosepress.com, pg 85

Hertrick, Jeff, National Press Foundation, 1211 Connecticut Ave NW, Suite 310, Washington, DC 20036 *Tel:* 202-663-7286 *Web Site:* nationalpress.org, pg 526

Herz, Suzanne, Penguin Random House LLC, 1745 Broadway, New York, NY 10019 *Tel:* 212-782-9000 *Toll Free Tel:* 800-726-0600 *Web Site:* www.penguinrandomhouse.com, pg 155

Heschke, Christa, McIntosh and Otis Inc, 235 Main St, Suite 318, White Plains, NY 10601 *Tel:* 212-687-7400 *Fax:* 212-687-6894 *E-mail:* info@mcintoshandotis.com *Web Site:* www.mcintoshandotis.com, pg 470

Hess, Laura, Island Press, 2000 "M" St NW, Suite 480-B, Washington, DC 20036 *Tel:* 202-232-7933 *Toll Free Tel:* 800-621-2736 *Fax:* 202-234-1328 *E-mail:* info@islandpress.org *Web Site:* www.islandpress.org, pg 104

Hess, Stephanie, Orbit, 1290 Avenue of the Americas, New York, NY 10104 *Tel:* 212-364-1100 *Toll Free Tel:* 800-759-0190 *Web Site:* www.orbitbooks.net; www.hachettebookgroup.com/imprint/orbit, pg 147

Hesse, Lauren, Little, Brown and Company, 1290 Avenue of the Americas, New York, NY 10104 *Tel:* 212-364-1100 *Fax:* 212-364-0952 *E-mail:* firstname.lastname@hbgusa.com *Web Site:* www.hachettebookgroup.com/imprint/little-brown-and-company/, pg 118

Hessel, Beth PhD, The Athenaeum Literary Award, 219 S Sixth St, Philadelphia, PA 19106-3794 *Tel:* 215-925-2688 *Web Site:* www.philaathenaeum.org/literary.html, pg 575

Hetrick, J Thomas, Pocol Press, 320 Sutton St, Punxsutawney, PA 15767 *Tel:* 703-870-9611 *E-mail:* chrisandtom@erols.com *Web Site:* www.pocolpress.com, pg 161

Hetzler, Guillian, Bay Area Women in Publishing (BAWiP), 680 Second St, San Francisco, CA 94107 *E-mail:* bayareawomeninpublishing@gmail.com *Web Site:* www.bayareawomeninpublishing.com, pg 500

Heuer, Jennifer, Penguin Publishing Group, c/o Penguin Random House LLC, 1745 Broadway, New York, NY 10019 *Tel:* 212-782-9000 *Web Site:* www.penguin.com, pg 154

Heukerott, Sara Kate, ACM Books, 1601 Broadway, 10th fl, New York, NY 10019-7434 *Tel:* 212-869-7440 *E-mail:* acmbooks-info@acm.org *Web Site:* www.acm.org; books.acm.org, pg 4

Heward-Mills, Leon, Taylor & Francis Inc, 530 Walnut St, Suite 850, Philadelphia, PA 19106 *Tel:* 215-625-8900 *Toll Free Tel:* 800-354-1420 *Fax:* 215-207-0050; 215-207-0046 (cust serv) *E-mail:* support@tandfonline.com *Web Site:* www.taylorandfrancis.com, pg 203

Hewes, Lauren B, American Antiquarian Society (AAS), 185 Salisbury St, Worcester, MA 01609-1634 *Tel:* 508-755-5221 *Fax:* 508-754-9069 *E-mail:* library@mwa.org *Web Site:* www.americanantiquarian.org, pg 494

Hewes, Lauren B, Fellowships for Creative & Performing Artists & Writers, 185 Salisbury St, Worcester, MA 01609-1634 *Tel:* 508-755-5221 *Fax:* 508-754-9069 *E-mail:* library@mwa.org *Web Site:* www.americanantiquarian.org, pg 602

Hewes, Lauren B, Fellowships for Historical Research, 185 Salisbury St, Worcester, MA 01609-1634 *Tel:* 508-755-5221 *Fax:* 508-754-9069 *Web Site:* www.americanantiquarian.org, pg 602

Hewitt, Kristen, Chronicle Books LLC, 680 Second St, San Francisco, CA 94107 *Tel:* 415-537-4200 *Fax:* 415-537-4460 (perms) *E-mail:* hello@chroniclebooks.com; subrights@chroniclebooks.com *Web Site:* www.chroniclebooks.com, pg 47

Hewitt, Ted, Social Sciences & Humanities Research Council (SSHRC), 350 Albert St, Ottawa, ON K1P 6G4, Canada *Tel:* 613-995-4273 *Toll Free Tel:* 855-275-2861 *E-mail:* research@sshrc-crsh.gc.ca *Web Site:* www.sshrc-crsh.gc.ca, pg 519

Hewlett, Ashley, GP Putnam's Sons, c/o Penguin Random House LLC, 1745 Broadway, New York, NY 10019 *Tel:* 212-782-9000 *Web Site:* www.penguin.com/putnam/, pg 167

Hewlett, Moneka, Gibbs Smith Publisher, 1877 E Gentile St, Layton, UT 84041 *Tel:* 801-544-9800 *Toll Free Tel:* 800-748-5439; 800-835-4993 (orders) *Fax:* 801-544-5582 *Toll Free Fax:* 800-213-3023 (orders only) *E-mail:* info@gibbs-smith.com; orders@gibbs-smith.com *Web Site:* gibbs-smith.com, pg 78

Heydt, David, HarperCollins Publishers LLC, 195 Broadway, New York, NY 10007 *Tel:* 212-207-7000 *Web Site:* www.harpercollins.com, pg 86

Heydweiller, Tracy, Random House Children's Books, c/o Penguin Random House LLC, 1745 Broadway, New York, NY 10019 *Tel:* 212-782-9000 *Web Site:* www.rhcbooks.com, pg 170

Heymann, Thomas A, National Notary Association (NNA), 9350 De Soto Ave, Chatsworth, CA 91311-4926 *Tel:* 818-739-4000 *Toll Free Tel:* 800-876-6827 *Toll Free Fax:* 800-833-1211 *E-mail:* services@nationalnotary.org *Web Site:* www.nationalnotary.org, pg 138

Heyward, William, Penguin Press, c/o Penguin Random House LLC, 1745 Broadway, New York, NY 10019 *Tel:* 212-782-9000 *E-mail:* penguinpress@penguinrandomhouse.com *Web Site:* www.penguin.com/penguin-press-overview/, pg 154

Heywood, Leslie, Binghamton University Creative Writing Program, c/o Dept of English, General Literature & Rhetoric, PO Box 6000, Binghamton, NY 13902-6000 *Tel:* 607-777-2168 *Fax:* 607-777-2408 *E-mail:* cwpro@binghamton.edu *Web Site:* www.binghamton.edu/english/creative-writing/index.html, pg 561

Hickey, Mackenzie, Gallery Books, 1230 Avenue of the Americas, New York, NY 10020 *Toll Free Tel:* 800-456-6798 *Fax:* 212-698-7284 *E-mail:* consumer.customerservice@simonandschuster.com *Web Site:* www.simonandschuster.com, pg 76

Hicks, Becky Koh, Workman Publishing, 1290 Avenue of the Americas, New York, NY 10104 *Toll Free Tel:* 800-759-0190 *Fax:* 212-364-0950 *E-mail:* workman-inquiry@hbgusa.com *Web Site:* www.hachettebookgroup.com/imprint/workman-publishing-company/, pg 232

Hicks, Kaylon, Basic Health Publications Inc, 4507 Charlotte Ave, Suite 100, Nashville, TN 37209 *Tel:* 615-255-2665 *E-mail:* marketing@turnerpublishing.com, pg 25

Hicks, Patricia, Peradam Press, PO Box 6, North San Juan, CA 95960-0006 *Tel:* 530-277-9324 *Fax:* 530-559-0754 *E-mail:* peradam@earthlink.net, pg 158

Hicks, Rod, Society of Professional Journalists (SPJ), PO Box 441748, Indianapolis, IN 46244 *Tel:* 317-927-8000 *Fax:* 317-920-4789 *E-mail:* communications@spj.org *Web Site:* www.spj.org, pg 520

Hidalgo, Monica, ASF Translation Awards, Scandinavia House, 58 Park Ave, New York, NY 10016 *Tel:* 212-779-3587 *E-mail:* grants@amscan.org *Web Site:* www.amscan.org, pg 574

Higbee, Alexa, Bloomsbury Publishing Inc, 1385 Broadway, 5th fl, New York, NY 10018 *Tel:* 212-419-5300 *E-mail:* marketingusa@bloomsbury.com; adultpublicityusa@bloomsbury.com; askacademic@bloomsbury.com *Web Site:* www.bloomsbury.com, pg 32

Higdon, Emmy Nordstrom, Westwood Creative Artists Ltd, 386 Huron St, Toronto, ON M5S 2G6, Canada *Tel:* 416-964-3302 *Fax:* 416-964-3302 *E-mail:* wca_office@wcaltd.com *Web Site:* www.wcaltd.com, pg 481

Higgins, Ben, Nelson Education Ltd, 1120 Birchmount Rd, Scarborough, ON M1K 5G4, Canada *Tel:* 416-752-9448 *Toll Free Tel:* 800-268-2222 (cust serv) *Fax:* 416-752-9646 *E-mail:* peopleandengagement@nelson.com *Web Site:* www.nelson.com, pg 413

Higgins, Iain, Constance Rooke Creative Nonfiction Prize, University of Victoria, PO Box 1700, Sta CSC, Victoria, BC V8W 2Y2, Canada *Tel:* 250-721-8524 *E-mail:* malahat@uvic.ca *Web Site:* www.malahatreview.ca/contests/creative_non-fiction_prize/info.html; www.malahatreview.ca, pg 591

Higgins, Iain, Far Horizons Award for Poetry, University of Victoria, PO Box 1700, Sta CSC, Victoria, BC V8W 2Y2, Canada *Tel:* 250-721-8524 *E-mail:* malahat@uvic.ca *Web Site:* www.malahatreview.ca/contests/far_horizons_poetry/info.html; www.malahatreview.ca, pg 601

Higgins, Iain, Far Horizons Award for Short Fiction, University of Victoria, PO Box 1700, Sta CSC, Victoria, BC V8W 2Y2, Canada *Tel:* 250-721-8524 *E-mail:* malahat@uvic.ca *Web Site:* www.malahatreview.ca/contests/far_horizons_fiction/info.html; www.malahatreview.ca, pg 601

Higgins, Iain, Long Poem Prize, University of Victoria, PO Box 1700, Sta CSC, Victoria, BC V8W 2Y2, Canada *Tel:* 250-721-8524 *E-mail:* malahat@uvic.ca *Web Site:* www.malahatreview.ca/contests/long_poem_prize/info.html; www.malahatreview.ca, pg 626

Higgins, Iain, Novella Prize, University of Victoria, PO Box 1700, Sta CSC, Victoria, BC V8W 2Y2, Canada *Tel:* 250-721-8524 *E-mail:* malahat@uvic.ca *Web Site:* www.malahatreview.ca/contests/novella_contest/info.html; www.malahatreview.ca, pg 642

Higgins, Iain, Open Season Awards, University of Victoria, PO Box 1700, Sta CSC, Victoria, BC V8W 2Y2, Canada *Tel:* 250-721-8524 *E-mail:* malahat@uvic.ca *Web Site:* www.malahatreview.ca/contests/open_season/info.html; www.malahatreview.ca, pg 644

Higgins, Leigh Ann, Farrar, Straus & Giroux Books for Young Readers, 120 Broadway, New York, NY 10271 *Tel:* 212-741-6900 *Toll Free Tel:* 888-330-8477 (orders) *E-mail:* childrens.publicity@macmillanusa.com; childrensrights@macmillanusa.com *Web Site:* us.macmillan.com/mackids, pg 70

Higgins, Leigh Ann, Roaring Brook Press, 120 Broadway, New York, NY 10271 *Tel:* 646-307-5151 *Web Site:* us.macmillan.com/publishers/roaring-brook-press, pg 176

High, Holly, DEStech Publications Inc, 439 N Duke St, Lancaster, PA 17602-4967 *Tel:* 717-290-1660 *Toll Free Tel:* 877-500-4DES (500-4337) *Fax:* 717-509-6100 *E-mail:* info@destechpub.com; orders@destechpub.com *Web Site:* www.destechpub.com, pg 59

High, Sara, Hachette Book Group Inc, 1290 Avenue of the Americas, New York, NY 10104 *Tel:* 212-364-1100 *Toll Free Tel:* 800-759-0190 (cust serv) *Fax:* 212-364-0933 (intl orders) *Toll Free Fax:* 800-286-9471 (cust serv) *E-mail:* customer.service@hbgusa.com; orders@hbgusa.com *Web Site:* www.hachettebookgroup.com, pg 83

Higman, Nicole, Workman Publishing, 1290 Avenue of the Americas, New York, NY 10104 *Toll Free Tel:* 800-759-0190 *Fax:* 212-364-0950 *E-mail:* workman-inquiry@hbgusa.com *Web Site:* www.hachettebookgroup.com/imprint/workman-publishing-company/, pg 232

Hilario-Ruiz, Michelle, Workman Publishing, 1290 Avenue of the Americas, New York, NY 10104 *Toll Free Tel:* 800-759-0190 *Fax:* 212-364-0950 *E-mail:* workman-inquiry@hbgusa.com *Web Site:* www.hachettebookgroup.com/imprint/workman-publishing-company/, pg 233

Hilbin, Janet, Michael L Printz Award, 225 N Michigan Ave, Suite 1300, Chicago, IL 60601 *Tel:* 312-280-4390 *Toll Free Tel:* 800-545-2433 *E-mail:* yalsa@ala.org *Web Site:* www.ala.org/yalsa/printz-award, pg 163

Hildebrand, Cole, Jean V Naggar Literary Agency Inc (JVNLA), 216 E 75 St, Suite 1-E, New York, NY 10021 *Tel:* 212-794-1082 *E-mail:* jvnla@jvnla.com *Web Site:* www.jvnla.com, pg 471

Hildebrand, Douglas, University of Alberta Press, Ring House 2, Edmonton, AB T6G 2E1, Canada *Tel:* 780-492-3662 *Fax:* 780-492-0719 *E-mail:* www.uap.ualberta.ca, pg 421

Hildreth, Mary Anne, Tower Publishing Co, 650 Cape Rd, Standish, ME 04084 *Tel:* 207-642-5400 *Toll Free Tel:* 800-969-8693 *E-mail:* info@towerpub.com *Web Site:* www.towerpub.com, pg 208

Hiles, Rachel, Chronicle Books LLC, 680 Second St, San Francisco, CA 94107 *Tel:* 415-537-4200 *Fax:* 415-537-4460 (perms) *E-mail:* hello@chroniclebooks.com; subrights@chroniclebooks.com *Web Site:* www.chroniclebooks.com, pg 47

Hilferty, Dan, Mason Crest Publishers, 450 Parkway Dr, Suite D, Broomall, PA 19008 *Tel:* 610-543-6200 *Toll Free Tel:* 866-MCP-BOOK (627-2665) *Fax:* 610-543-3878 *Web Site:* www.masoncrest.com, pg 126

Hili, Heather, Macmillan, 120 Broadway, 22nd fl, New York, NY 10271 *E-mail:* press.inquiries@macmillan.com *Web Site:* us.macmillan.com, pg 122

Hill, Allison, American Booksellers Association, 600 Mamaroneck Ave, Suite 400, Harrison, NY 10528 *Tel:* 914-406-7500 *Toll Free Tel:* 800-637-0037 *Fax:* 914-417-4013 *E-mail:* info@bookweb.org *Web Site:* www.bookweb.org, pg 494

Hill, Allison Hunter, Nosy Crow Inc, 145 Lincoln Rd, Lincoln, MA 01773 *E-mail:* nosycrowinc@nosycrow.com; salesinfo@nosycrow.com; export@nosycrow.com (export sales); rights@nosycrow.com *Web Site:* nosycrow.us, pg 144

Hill, Brad, HarperCollins Publishers LLC, 195 Broadway, New York, NY 10007 *Tel:* 212-207-7000 *Web Site:* www.harpercollins.com, pg 86

Hill, Brandon, Ludwig von Mises Institute, 518 W Magnolia Ave, Auburn, AL 36832 *Tel:* 334-321-2100 *Fax:* 334-321-2119 *E-mail:* info@mises.org *Web Site:* www.mises.org, pg 225

Hill, David, Kregel Publications, 2450 Oak Industrial Dr NE, Grand Rapids, MI 49505 *Tel:* 616-451-4775 *Toll Free Tel:* 800-733-2607 *Fax:* 616-451-9330 *E-mail:* kregelbooks@kregel.com *Web Site:* www.kregel.com, pg 111

Hill, Emma, Chronicle Books LLC, 680 Second St, San Francisco, CA 94107 *Tel:* 415-537-4200 *Fax:* 415-537-4460 (perms) *E-mail:* hello@chroniclebooks.com; subrights@chroniclebooks.com *Web Site:* www.chroniclebooks.com, pg 48

Hill, Frances, Emerging Playwright Award, 555 Eighth Ave, Suite 1800, New York, NY 10018 *Tel:* 212-421-1380 *Fax:* 212-421-1387 *E-mail:* urbanstage@aol.com *Web Site:* urbanstages.org, pg 599

Hill, Hannah, Random House Children's Books, c/o Penguin Random House LLC, 1745 Broadway, New York, NY 10019 *Tel:* 212-782-9000 *Web Site:* www.rhcbooks.com, pg 170

Hill, James L, RockHill Publishing LLC, PO Box 62523, Virginia Beach, VA 23466-2523 *Tel:* 757-692-2021 *Web Site:* rockhillpublishing.com, pg 176

Hill, Janet Muirhead, Raven Publishing Inc, 125 Cherry Creek Rd, Norris, MT 59745 *Tel:* 406-685-3545 *Toll Free Tel:* 866-685-3545 *E-mail:* info@ravenpublishing.net *Web Site:* www.ravenpublishing.net, pg 172

Hill, Joann, Disney-Hyperion Books, 1101 Flower St, Glendale, CA 91201 *Web Site:* books.disney.com/imprint/disney-hyperion, pg 59

Hill, Joanna V, Terra Nova Books, 33 Alondra Rd, Santa Fe, NM 87508 *Tel:* 505-670-9319 *Fax:* 509-461-9333 *E-mail:* publisher@terranovabooks.com; marketing@terranovabooks.com *Web Site:* www.terranovabooks.com, pg 204

Hill, Katie, Milkweed Editions, 1011 Washington Ave S, Suite 300, Minneapolis, MN 55415-1246 *Tel:* 612-332-3192 *Toll Free Tel:* 800-520-6455 *E-mail:* orders@milkweed.org *Web Site:* milkweed.org, pg 131

Hill, Linda, Bella Books, PO Box 10543, Tallahassee, FL 32302 *Tel:* 850-576-2370 *Toll Free Tel:* 800-729-4992 *E-mail:* info@bellabooks.com; orders@bellabooks.com; ebooks@bellabooks.com *Web Site:* www.bellabooks.com, pg 27

Hill, Mike, Stephen Leacock Memorial Medal for Humour, PO Box 854, Orillia, ON L3V 6K8, Canada *Tel:* 705-326-9286 *E-mail:* info@leacock.ca *Web Site:* www.leacock.ca, pg 622

Hill, Mindy, University of New Mexico Press, One University of New Mexico, Albuquerque, NM 87131-0001 *Tel:* 505-272-7777 *Fax:* 505-277-3343 *E-mail:* custserv@unm.edu (order dept) *Web Site:* unmpress.com, pg 218

Hill, Sandy, Simon & Schuster, 1230 Avenue of the Americas, New York, NY 10020 *Tel:* 212-698-7000 *Toll Free Tel:* 800-223-2348 (cust serv); 800-223-2336 (orders) *Toll Free Fax:* 800-943-9831 (orders) *Web Site:* simonandschusterpublishing.com/simonandschuster/, pg 188

Hill, Stephen W, Kiva Publishing Inc, 10 Bella Loma, Santa Fe, NM 87506 Tel: 909-896-0518 E-mail: kivapub@aol.com Web Site: www.kivapub.com, pg 110

Hilliard, Kathy, Andrews McMeel Publishing LLC, 1130 Walnut St, Kansas City, MO 64106-2109 Tel: 816-581-7500 Toll Free Tel: 800-851-8923 Web Site: www.andrewsmcmeel.com; publishing.andrewsmcmeel.com, pg 14

Hillman, Brenda, Community of Writers Summer Workshops, PO Box 1416, Nevada City, CA 95959 Tel: 530-470-8440 E-mail: info@communityofwriters.org Web Site: www.communityofwriters.org, pg 553

Hillman, Jesse, Zondervan, 3900 Sparks Dr SE, Grand Rapids, MI 49546 Tel: 616-698-6900 Toll Free Tel: 800-226-1122; 800-727-1309 (retail orders) Fax: 616-698-3350 Toll Free Fax: 800-698-3256 (retail orders) E-mail: customercare@harpercollins.com Web Site: www.zondervan.com, pg 236

Hillman, Morgan, Holiday House Publishing Inc, 50 Broad St, New York, NY 10004 Tel: 212-688-0085 Fax: 212-421-6134 E-mail: info@holidayhouse.com Web Site: www.holidayhouse.com, pg 94

Hillstrom, Kevin, Bloomsbury Academic, 1385 Broadway, 5th fl, New York, NY 10018 Tel: 212-419-5300 Web Site: www.bloomsbury.com/us/academic, pg 31

Hils, Abigail, AAAS/Subaru Prize for Excellence in Science Books, 1200 New York Ave NW, Washington, DC 20005 Tel: 202-326-6400 E-mail: sbf@aaas.org Web Site: www.sbfprize.org, pg 569

Himelstein, Abram Shalom, University of New Orleans Press, 2000 Lakeshore Dr, New Orleans, LA 70148 Tel: 504-280-7457 E-mail: unopress@uno.edu Web Site: www.uno.edu/unopress, pg 218

Himmel, Eric, Harry N Abrams Inc, 195 Broadway, 9th fl, New York, NY 10007 Tel: 212-206-7715 Toll Free Tel: 800-345-1359 Fax: 212-645-8437 E-mail: abrams@abramsbooks.com; publicity@abramsbooks.com; sales@abramsbooks.com Web Site: www.abramsbooks.com, pg 3

Hinchliffe, Alison, Atria Books, 1230 Avenue of the Americas, New York, NY 10020 Tel: 212-698-7000 Fax: 212-698-7007 Web Site: www.simonandschuster.com, pg 21

Hinck, Angela, St Martin's Press, LLC, 120 Broadway, New York, NY 10271 E-mail: publicity@stmartins.com; trademarketing@stmartins.com; foreignrights@stmartins.com Web Site: us.macmillan.com/smp, pg 181

Hine, Emma, Black Literary Publishing Award, 154 Christopher St, Suite 3C, New York, NY 10014-9110 Tel: 212-741-9110 E-mail: info@clmp.org Web Site: www.clmp.org, pg 581

Hine, Emma, Community of Literary Magazines & Presses (CLMP), 154 Christopher St, Suite 3C, New York, NY 10014-9110 Tel: 212-741-9110 E-mail: info@clmp.org Web Site: www.clmp.org, pg 504

Hine, Emma, Firecracker Awards, 154 Christopher St, Suite 3C, New York, NY 10014-9110 Tel: 212-741-9110 E-mail: info@clmp.org Web Site: www.clmp.org/firecracker, pg 602

Hine, Sam, Plough Publishing House, 151 Bowne Dr, Walden, NY 12586-2832 Tel: 845-572-3455 Toll Free Tel: 800-521-8011 E-mail: info@plough.com; editor@plough.com Web Site: www.plough.com, pg 161

Hinkelman, Edward G, World Trade Press LLC, 616 E Eighth St, Suite 7, Traverse City, MI 49686 Tel: 707-778-1124 Toll Free Tel: 800-833-8586 Fax: 231-642-5300 Web Site: www.worldtradepress.com, pg 234

Hinkle, Eleanor, Houghton Mifflin Harcourt Trade & Reference Division, 125 High St, Boston, MA 02110 Tel: 617-351-5000 Web Site: www.hmhco.com, pg 96

Hinkle, Paula, The Graphic Artists Guild Inc, 2248 Broadway, Suite 1341, New York, NY 10024 Tel: 212-791-3400 E-mail: admin@graphicartistsguild.org; membership@graphicartistsguild.org Web Site: www.graphicartistsguild.org, pg 507, 563

Hinkley, John, Moody Publishers, 820 N La Salle Blvd, Chicago, IL 60610 Tel: 312-329-2101 Toll Free Tel: 800-678-8812 Fax: 312-329-2144 Toll Free Fax: 800-678-3329 E-mail: mpcustomerservice@moody.edu; mporders@moody.edu; publicity@moody.edu Web Site: www.moodypublishers.com, pg 134

Hinton, Mary Beth, Mandel Vilar Press, 19 Oxford Ct, Simsbury, CT 06070 Tel: 806-790-4731 E-mail: info@mvpress.org Web Site: www.mvpublishers.org, pg 124

Hinton, Will, Tor Publishing Group, 120 Broadway, New York, NY 10271 Toll Free Tel: 800-455-0340 (Macmillan) E-mail: torpublicity@tor.com; forgepublicity@forgebooks.com Web Site: us.macmillan.com/torpublishinggroup, pg 208

Hintzen, Emma, Sourcebooks LLC, 1935 Brookdale Rd, Suite 139, Naperville, IL 60563 Tel: 630-961-3900 Toll Free Tel: 800-432-7444 Fax: 630-961-2168 E-mail: info@sourcebooks.com Web Site: www.sourcebooks.com, pg 194

Hinz, Carol, Carolrhoda Books Inc, 241 First Ave N, Minneapolis, MN 55401 Tel: 612-332-3344 Toll Free Tel: 800-328-4929 Fax: 612-332-7615 Toll Free Fax: 800-332-1132 E-mail: info@lernerbooks.com; custserve@lernerbooks.com Web Site: www.lernerbooks.com; www.facebook.com/lernerbooks, pg 41

Hinz, Carol, Millbrook Press, 241 First Ave N, Minneapolis, MN 55401 Tel: 612-332-3344 Toll Free Tel: 800-328-4929 Fax: 612-332-7615 Toll Free Fax: 800-332-1132 E-mail: info@lernerbooks.com; custserve@lernerbooks.com Web Site: www.lernerbooks.com; www.facebook.com/millbrookpress, pg 131

Hipwell, Kristin, Perfection Learning®, 1000 N Second Ave, Logan, IA 51546-1061 Tel: 712-644-2831 Toll Free Tel: 800-831-4190 Toll Free Fax: 800-543-2745 E-mail: orders@perfectionlearning.com Web Site: www.perfectionlearning.com, pg 158

Hirsch, Edward, John Simon Guggenheim Memorial Foundation, 90 Park Ave, New York, NY 10016 Tel: 212-687-4470 Fax: 212-697-3248 Web Site: www.gf.org, pg 525

Hitchcock, Stephanie, Atria Books, 1230 Avenue of the Americas, New York, NY 10020 Tel: 212-698-7000 Fax: 212-698-7007 Web Site: www.simonandschuster.com, pg 21

Hitchens, Clare, Wilfrid Laurier University Press, 75 University Ave W, Waterloo, ON N2L 3C5, Canada Tel: 519-884-0710 Toll Free Tel: 866-836-5551 (CN & US) Fax: 519-725-1399 E-mail: press@wlu.ca Web Site: www.wlupress.wlu.ca, pg 424

Hittel, Robert A, Florida Antiquarian Booksellers Association (FABA), c/o Lighthouse Books, ABAA, 14046 Fifth St, Dade City, FL 33525 Tel: 727-234-7759 E-mail: floridabooksellers@gmail.com Web Site: floridabooksellers.com, pg 506

Hixson, Karlyn, Atria Books, 1230 Avenue of the Americas, New York, NY 10020 Tel: 212-698-7000 Fax: 212-698-7007 Web Site: www.simonandschuster.com, pg 21

Hlavac, Julia, Sleeping Bear Press™, 2395 S Huron Pkwy, Suite 200, Ann Arbor, MI 48104 Toll Free Tel: 800-487-2323 Fax: 734-794-0004 E-mail: customerservice@sleepingbearpress.com Web Site: www.sleepingbearpress.com, pg 191

Hlavinka, Hal, Penguin Random House LLC, 1745 Broadway, New York, NY 10019 Tel: 212-782-9000 Toll Free Tel: 800-726-0600 Web Site: www.penguinrandomhouse.com, pg 155

Ho, Joey, Random House Children's Books, c/o Penguin Random House LLC, 1745 Broadway, New York, NY 10019 Tel: 212-782-9000 Web Site: www.rhcbooks.com, pg 170

Hoagland, Nancy, Duke University Press, 905 W Main St, Suite 18B, Durham, NC 27701 Tel: 919-688-5134 Toll Free Tel: 888-651-0122 (US) Fax: 919-688-2615 Toll Free Fax: 888-651-0124 E-mail: orders@dukepress.edu Web Site: www.dukeupress.edu, pg 62

Hoak, Michael, Random House Publishing Group, 1745 Broadway, New York, NY 10019 Toll Free Tel: 800-200-3552 Web Site: www.randomhousebooks.com, pg 171

Hoard, Trish, Library of America, 14 E 60 St, New York, NY 10022-1006 Tel: 212-308-3360 Fax: 212-750-8352 E-mail: info@loa.org Web Site: www.loa.org, pg 116

Hoare, Jess, Calligraph LLC, 45 Main St, No 850, Brooklyn, NY 11201 Tel: 212-253-1074 E-mail: mail@calligraphlit.com; rights@calligraphlit.com; submissions@calligraphlit.com Web Site: www.calligraphlit.com, pg 453

Hoare, Steve, Black Dome Press Corp, PO Box 64, Catskill, NY 12414 Tel: 518-577-5238 E-mail: blackdomep@aol.com Web Site: www.blackdomepress.com, pg 30

Hobeika, Joelle, Alloy Entertainment LLC, 30 Hudson Yards, 22nd fl, New York, NY 10001, pg 7

Hochman, Gail, Brandt & Hochman Literary Agents Inc, 1501 Broadway, Suite 2310, New York, NY 10036 Tel: 212-840-5760 Fax: 212-840-5776 Web Site: brandthochman.com, pg 452

Hochman, Paul, St Martin's Press, LLC, 120 Broadway, New York, NY 10271 E-mail: publicity@stmartins.com; trademarketing@stmartins.com; foreignrights@stmartins.com Web Site: us.macmillan.com/smp, pg 180

Hocutt, Steph, Penguin Random House LLC, 1745 Broadway, New York, NY 10019 Tel: 212-782-9000 Toll Free Tel: 800-726-0600 Web Site: www.penguinrandomhouse.com, pg 155

Hodapp, Angie, Nelson Literary Agency LLC, 700 Colorado Blvd, No 352, Denver, CO 80206 Tel: 303-292-2805 E-mail: query@nelsonagency.com Web Site: www.nelsonagency.com, pg 471

Hodell, Courtney, Whiting Awards, 16 Court St, Suite 2308, Brooklyn, NY 11241 Tel: 718-701-5962 E-mail: info@whiting.org Web Site: www.whiting.org, pg 675

Hodell, Courtney, Whiting Creative Nonfiction Grant, 16 Court St, Suite 2308, Brooklyn, NY 11241 Tel: 718-701-5962 E-mail: nonfiction@whiting.org; info@whiting.org Web Site: www.whiting.org, pg 675

Hodell, Courtney, Whiting Literary Magazine Prizes, 16 Court St, Suite 2308, Brooklyn, NY 11241 Tel: 718-701-5962 E-mail: info@whiting.org Web Site: www.whiting.org/writers/whiting-literary-magazine-prizes, pg 675

Hodes, Martha, Allan Nevins Prize, Columbia University, 3009 Broadway MC 802, New York, NY 10027 Tel: 212-854-1919 E-mail: amhistsociety@columbia.edu Web Site: sah.columbia.edu, pg 639

Hodes, Martha, Francis Parkman Prize, Columbia University, 3009 Broadway MC 802, New York, NY 10027 Tel: 212-854-1919 E-mail: amhistsociety@columbia.edu Web Site: sah.columbia.edu, pg 646

Hodes, Martha, SAH Prize for Historical Fiction, Columbia University, 3009 Broadway MC 802, New York, NY 10027 Tel: 212-854-1919 E-mail: amhistsociety@columbia.edu Web Site: sah.columbia.edu, pg 658

Hodge, Jasmine, Random House Children's Books, c/o Penguin Random House LLC, 1745 Broadway, New York, NY 10019 Tel: 212-782-9000 Web Site: www.rhcbooks.com, pg 170

Hodge, Joelle, Classical Academic Press, 515 S 32 St, Camp Hill, PA 17011 Tel: 717-730-0711 Toll Free Tel: 866-730-0711 Fax: 717-730-0721 Toll Free Fax: 866-730-0721 E-mail: info@classicalsubjects.com; orders@classicalsubjects.com Web Site: classicalacademicpress.com, pg 49

Hodnett, Megan, HarperCollins Publishers LLC, 195 Broadway, New York, NY 10007 Tel: 212-207-7000 Web Site: www.harpercollins.com, pg 86

Hodorowicz, Cate, The University of North Carolina Press, 116 S Boundary St, Chapel Hill, NC 27514-3808 *Tel:* 919-966-3561; 919-966-7449 (orders) *Toll Free Tel:* 800-848-3224 (orders) *Fax:* 919-962-2704 (orders) *Toll Free Fax:* 800-272-6817 (orders) *E-mail:* uncpress@unc.edu *Web Site:* uncpress.org, pg 218

Hodson, Brad, Horror Writers Association (HWA), PO Box 56687, Sherman Oaks, CA 91413 *Tel:* 818-220-3965 *E-mail:* admin@horror.org; membership@horror.org *Web Site:* horror.org, pg 507

Hoeler, Tom, Penguin Random House LLC, 1745 Broadway, New York, NY 10019 *Tel:* 212-782-9000 *Toll Free Tel:* 800-726-0600 *Web Site:* www.penguinrandomhouse.com, pg 155

Hoeler, Tom, Random House Publishing Group, 1745 Broadway, New York, NY 10019 *Toll Free Tel:* 800-200-3552 *Web Site:* www.randomhousebooks.com, pg 171

Hofeldt, Sara E, Tapestry Press Ltd, 19 Nashoba Rd, Littleton, MA 01460 *Tel:* 978-486-0200 *Toll Free Tel:* 800-535-2007 *E-mail:* publish@tapestrypress.com *Web Site:* www.tapestrypress.com, pg 202

Hofer, Shari, John Wiley & Sons Inc, 111 River St, Hoboken, NJ 07030-5774 *Tel:* 201-748-6000 *Toll Free Tel:* 800-225-5945 (cust serv) *Fax:* 201-748-6088 *Web Site:* www.wiley.com, pg 230

Hoff, Alexandra, University of New Mexico Press, One University of New Mexico, Albuquerque, NM 87131-0001 *Tel:* 505-272-7777 *Fax:* 505-277-3343 *E-mail:* custserv@unm.edu (order dept) *Web Site:* unmpress.com, pg 218

Hoff, Janine, Northwest Territories Public Library Services, 75 Woodland Dr, Hay River, NT X0E 1G1, Canada *Tel:* 867-874-6531 *Toll Free Tel:* 866-297-0232 (CN) *Fax:* 867-874-3321 *Web Site:* ece.gov.nt.ca/en/services/nwt-public-libraries, pg 515

Hoffman, Emily, Random House Children's Books, c/o Penguin Random House LLC, 1745 Broadway, New York, NY 10019 *Tel:* 212-782-9000 *Web Site:* www.rhcbooks.com, pg 170

Hoffman, Jonathan, School Zone Publishing Co, 1819 Industrial Dr, Grand Haven, MI 49417 *Tel:* 616-846-5030 *Toll Free Tel:* 800-253-0564 *Fax:* 616-846-6181 *Web Site:* www.schoolzone.com, pg 185

Hoffman, Katie, DAW Books, 19 W 21 St, No 1201, New York, NY 10010 *E-mail:* info@astrapublishinghouse.com *Web Site:* astrapublishinghouse.com/imprints/daw-books, pg 57

Hoffman, Lauren, Chronicle Books LLC, 680 Second St, San Francisco, CA 94107 *Tel:* 415-537-4200 *Fax:* 415-537-4460 (perms) *E-mail:* hello@chroniclebooks.com; subrights@chroniclebooks.com *Web Site:* www.chroniclebooks.com, pg 47

Hoffman, Mitch, The Aaron M Priest Literary Agency Inc, 370 Lexington Ave, Suite 1202, New York, NY 10017 *Tel:* 212-818-0344 *Fax:* 212-573-9417 *E-mail:* info@aaronpriest.com *Web Site:* www.aaronpriest.com, pg 472

Hoffman, Philip, Penguin Random House LLC, 1745 Broadway, New York, NY 10019 *Tel:* 212-782-9000 *Toll Free Tel:* 800-726-0600 *Web Site:* www.penguinrandomhouse.com, pg 155

Hoffman, Randy, Captus Press Inc, 1600 Steeles Ave W, Units 14 & 15, Concord, ON L4K 4M2, Canada *Tel:* 905-760-2723 *Fax:* 905-760-7523 *E-mail:* info@captus.com *Web Site:* www.captus.com, pg 399

Hoffman, Stefanie, Little, Brown Books for Young Readers (LBYR), 1290 Avenue of the Americas, New York, NY 10104 *Tel:* 212-364-1100 *Toll Free Tel:* 800-759-0190 (cust serv) *E-mail:* rights@lbchildrens.com *Web Site:* www.hachettebookgroup.com/imprint/little-brown-books-for-young-readers/, pg 118

Hoffman, Stuart A, Star Publishing Co Inc, PO Box 5165, Belmont, CA 94002-5165 *Tel:* 650-591-3505 *E-mail:* starpublishing@gmail.com *Web Site:* www.starpublishing.com, pg 197

Hoffmann, Markus, Regal Hoffmann & Associates LLC, 157 13 St, Brooklyn, NY 11215 *Tel:* 212-684-7900 *E-mail:* info@rhaliterary.com; submissions@rhaliterary.com *Web Site:* www.rhaliterary.com, pg 473

Hoffnagle, Jerry, Rizzoli International Publications Inc, 300 Park Ave S, 4th fl, New York, NY 10010-5399 *Tel:* 212-387-3400 *Toll Free Tel:* 800-522-6657 (orders only) *Fax:* 212-387-3535 *E-mail:* publicity@rizzoliusa.com *Web Site:* www.rizzoliusa.com, pg 175

Hofmann, Ashley, AOTA Press, 6116 Executive Blvd, Suite 200, North Bethesda, MD 20852-4929 *Tel:* 301-652-6611 *Fax:* 770-238-0414 (orders) *E-mail:* aotapress@aota.org; customerservice@aota.org *Web Site:* store.aota.org; www.aota.org, pg 15

Hofmann, Deborah, David Black Agency, 335 Adams St, 27th fl, Suite 2707, Brooklyn, NY 11201 *Tel:* 718-852-5500 *Fax:* 718-852-5539 *Web Site:* www.davidblackagency.com, pg 450

Hogan, Mary S, Plexus Publishing, Inc, 143 Old Marlton Pike, Medford, NJ 08055 *Tel:* 609-654-6500 *Fax:* 609-654-4309 *E-mail:* info@plexuspublishing.com *Web Site:* www.plexuspublishing.com, pg 160

Hogan, Megan, Simon & Schuster, 1230 Avenue of the Americas, New York, NY 10020 *Tel:* 212-698-7000 *Toll Free Tel:* 800-223-2348 (cust serv); 800-223-2336 (orders) *Toll Free Fax:* 800-943-9831 (orders) *Web Site:* simonandschusterpublishing.com/simonandschuster/, pg 188

Hogan, Thomas Jr, Information Today, Inc, 143 Old Marlton Pike, Medford, NJ 08055-8750 *Tel:* 609-654-6266 *Toll Free Tel:* 800-300-9868 (cust serv) *Fax:* 609-654-4309 *E-mail:* custserv@infotoday.com *Web Site:* informationtodayinc.com, pg 100

Hogan, Thomas Jr, Plexus Publishing, Inc, 143 Old Marlton Pike, Medford, NJ 08055 *Tel:* 609-654-6500 *Fax:* 609-654-4309 *E-mail:* info@plexuspublishing.com *Web Site:* www.plexuspublishing.com, pg 160

Hogan, Thomas H, Information Today, Inc, 143 Old Marlton Pike, Medford, NJ 08055-8750 *Tel:* 609-654-6266 *Toll Free Tel:* 800-300-9868 (cust serv) *Fax:* 609-654-4309 *E-mail:* custserv@infotoday.com *Web Site:* informationtodayinc.com, pg 100

Hogan, Thomas H, Plexus Publishing, Inc, 143 Old Marlton Pike, Medford, NJ 08055 *Tel:* 609-654-6500 *Fax:* 609-654-4309 *E-mail:* info@plexuspublishing.com *Web Site:* www.plexuspublishing.com, pg 160

Hoge, Steve, W W Norton & Company Inc, 500 Fifth Ave, New York, NY 10110-0017 *Tel:* 212-354-5500 *Toll Free Tel:* 800-233-4830 (orders & cust serv) *Fax:* 212-869-0856 *Toll Free Fax:* 800-458-6515 *E-mail:* orders@wwnorton.com *Web Site:* wwnorton.com, pg 143

Hogeland, Kim, Oregon State University Press, 121 The Valley Library, Corvallis, OR 97331-4501 *Tel:* 541-737-3166, pg 147

Hogenson, Barbara, The Barbara Hogenson Agency Inc, 165 West End Ave, Suite 19-C, New York, NY 10023 *Tel:* 212-874-8084 *E-mail:* barbarahogenson@gmail.com, pg 463

Hoggutt, Brenda Jo, University of Texas Press, 3001 Lake Austin Blvd, 2.200, Austin, TX 78703 *Tel:* 512-471-7233 *Fax:* 512-232-7178 *E-mail:* utpress@uts.cc.utexas.edu; info@utpress.utexas.edu *Web Site:* utpress.utexas.edu, pg 205

Hogrebe, Christina, Jane Rotrosen Agency LLC, 318 E 51 St, New York, NY 10022-7803 *Tel:* 212-593-4330 *E-mail:* info@janerotrosen.com *Web Site:* janerotrosen.com, pg 474

Hohenboken, Larisa, Skinner House Books, c/o Unitarian Universalist Assn, 24 Farnsworth St, Boston, MA 02210-1409 *Tel:* 617-742-2100 *Fax:* 617-948-6466 *E-mail:* skinnerhouse@uua.org *Web Site:* www.uua.org/publications/skinnerhouse, pg 190

Hohman, Laura, The University Press of Kentucky, 663 S Limestone St, Lexington, KY 40508-4008 *Tel:* 859-257-8400 *Fax:* 859-323-1873 *Web Site:* www.kentuckypress.com, pg 222

Hok, Keang, American Diabetes Association, 2451 Crystal Dr, Suite 900, Arlington, VA 22202 *Tel:* 703-549-1500 *Toll Free Tel:* 800-342-2383 *E-mail:* booksales@diabetes.org; ada_pubs@diabetes.org *Web Site:* diabetes.org; diabetesjournals.org/books; www.facebook.com/adapublications, pg 9

Hokanson, Sarah, Random House Children's Books, c/o Penguin Random House LLC, 1745 Broadway, New York, NY 10019 *Tel:* 212-782-9000 *Web Site:* www.rhcbooks.com, pg 169

Hoke, Dylan, Hachette Book Group Inc, 1290 Avenue of the Americas, New York, NY 10104 *Tel:* 212-364-1100 *Toll Free Tel:* 800-759-0190 (cust serv) *Fax:* 212-364-0933 (intl orders) *Toll Free Fax:* 800-286-9471 (cust serv) *E-mail:* customer.service@hbgusa.com; orders@hbgusa.com *Web Site:* www.hachettebookgroup.com, pg 83

Holahan, Jessica, Yale University Press, 302 Temple St, New Haven, CT 06511-8909 *Tel:* 203-432-0960; 203-432-0966 (sales); 401-531-2800 (cust serv) *Toll Free Tel:* 800-405-1619 (cust serv) *Fax:* 203-432-0948; 203-432-8485 (sales); 401-531-2801 (cust serv) *Toll Free Fax:* 800-406-9145 (cust serv) *E-mail:* sales.press@yale.edu (sales); customer.care@triliteral.org (cust serv) *Web Site:* www.yalebooks.com; yalepress.yale.edu/yupbooks, pg 235

Holbert, Christine, The Idaho Prize for Poetry, 1025 S Garry Rd, Liberty Lake, WA 99019 *Tel:* 208-597-3008 *Fax:* 208-255-1560 *E-mail:* losthorsepress@mindspring.com *Web Site:* www.losthorsepress.org, pg 615

Holbert, Christine, Lost Horse Press, 1025 S Garry Rd, Liberty Lake, WA 99019 *Tel:* 208-597-3008 *Fax:* 208-255-1560 *E-mail:* losthorsepress@mindspring.com *Web Site:* www.losthorsepress.org, pg 120

Holder, Doug, Samuel Washington Allen Prize, c/o Linda Haviland Conte, 18 Hall Ave, Apt 2, Somerville, MA 02144 *E-mail:* info@nepoetryclub.org *Web Site:* nepoetryclub.org, pg 572

Holder, Doug, E E Cummings Prize, c/o Linda Haviland Conte, 18 Hall Ave, Apt 2, Somerville, MA 02144 *E-mail:* info@nepoetryclub.org *Web Site:* nepoetryclub.org, pg 594

Holder, Doug, Der Hovanessian Prize, c/o Linda Haviland Conte, 18 Hall Ave, Apt 2, Somerville, MA 02144 *E-mail:* info@nepoetryclub.org *Web Site:* nepoetryclub.org, pg 595

Holder, Doug, Golden Rose Award, c/o Linda Haviland Conte, 18 Hall Ave, Apt 2, Somerville, MA 02144 *E-mail:* info@nepoetryclub.org *Web Site:* nepoetryclub.org, pg 608

Holder, Doug, Amy Lowell Prize, c/o Linda Haviland Conte, 18 Hall Ave, Apt 2, Somerville, MA 02144 *E-mail:* info@nepoetryclub.org *Web Site:* nepoetryclub.org, pg 627

Holder, Doug, Sheila Margaret Motton Book Prize, c/o Linda Haviland Conte, 18 Hall Ave, Apt 2, Somerville, MA 02144 *E-mail:* info@nepoetryclub.org *Web Site:* nepoetryclub.org, pg 636

Holder, Doug, New England Poetry Club, c/o Linda Haviland Conte, 18 Hall Ave, Apt 2, Somerville, MA 02144 *E-mail:* info@nepoetryclub.org; president@nepoetryclub.org *Web Site:* nepoetryclub.org, pg 514

Holder, Doug, Jean Pedrick Chapbook Prize, c/o Linda Haviland Conte, 18 Hall Ave, Apt 2, Somerville, MA 02144 *E-mail:* info@nepoetryclub.org *Web Site:* nepoetryclub.org, pg 646

Holder, Jakob, William Flanagan Memorial Creative Persons Center, 14 Harrison St, New York, NY 10013 *Tel:* 212-226-2020 *Fax:* 212-226-5551 *E-mail:* info@albeefoundation.org *Web Site:* www.albeefoundation.org, pg 675

Holdridge, Jefferson, Wake Forest University Press, 2518 Reynolda Rd, Winston-Salem, NC 27106 *Tel:* 336-758-5448 *Fax:* 336-842-3853 *E-mail:* wfupress@wfu.edu *Web Site:* wfupress.wfu.edu, pg 225

Holford, Makenna, HarperCollins Publishers LLC, 195 Broadway, New York, NY 10007 *Tel:* 212-207-7000 *Web Site:* www.harpercollins.com, pg 87

Holland, David, Western States Arts Federation (WESTAF), 1536 Wynkoop St, Suite 522, Denver, CO 80202 Tel: 303-629-1166 E-mail: staff@westaf.org Web Site: www.westaf.org, pg 526

Holland, Mark, Rocky Mountain Mineral Law Foundation, 9191 Sheridan Blvd, Suite 203, Westminster, CO 80031 Tel: 303-321-8100 Fax: 303-321-7657 E-mail: info@rmmlf.org Web Site: www.rmmlf.org, pg 176

Hollander, Eli M, Feldheim Publishers, 208 Airport Executive Park, Nanuet, NY 10954 Tel: 845-356-2282 Toll Free Tel: 800-237-7149 (orders) Fax: 845-425-1908 E-mail: sales@feldheim.com Web Site: www.feldheim.com, pg 70

Hollander, Mara, FinePrint Literary Management, 207 W 106 St, Suite 1D, New York, NY 10025 Tel: 212-279-6214 E-mail: info@fineprintlit.com; submissions@fineprint.com Web Site: www.fineprintlit.com, pg 458

Hollein, Max, The Metropolitan Museum of Art, 1000 Fifth Ave, New York, NY 10028 Tel: 212-535-7710 E-mail: editorial@metmuseum.org Web Site: www.metmuseum.org, pg 130

Hollenbeck, Xander, Harry N Abrams Inc, 195 Broadway, 9th fl, New York, NY 10007 Tel: 212-206-7715 Toll Free Tel: 800-345-1359 Fax: 212-645-8437 E-mail: abrams@abramsbooks.com; publicity@abramsbooks.com; sales@abramsbooks.com Web Site: www.abramsbooks.com, pg 3

Holler, Rivka, St Martin's Press, LLC, 120 Broadway, New York, NY 10271 E-mail: publicity@stmartins.com; trademarketing@stmartins.com; foreignrights@stmartins.com Web Site: us.macmillan.com/smp, pg 181

Hollins-Alexander, Sonja EdD, Corwin, 2455 Teller Rd, Thousand Oaks, CA 91320 Tel: 805-499-9734 Toll Free Tel: 800-233-9936 Fax: 805-499-5323 Toll Free Fax: 800-417-2466 E-mail: info@corwin.com; order@corwin.com Web Site: www.corwin.com, pg 53

Hollomon, Dawn, Thomas Nelson, 501 Nelson Place, Nashville, TN 37214 Tel: 615-889-9000 Toll Free Tel: 800-251-4000 Web Site: www.thomasnelson.com, pg 206

Holloway, Kathleen, Catholic Book Awards, 10 S Riverside Plaza, Suite 875, Chicago, IL 60606 Tel: 312-380-6789 E-mail: awards@catholicmediaassociation.org Web Site: www.catholicmediaassociation.org, pg 587

Holloway, Kathleen, Catholic Media Association (CMA), 10 S Riverside Plaza, Suite 875, Chicago, IL 60606 Tel: 312-380-6789 Web Site: www.catholicmediaassociation.org, pg 503

Holloway, Kathleen, Catholic Media Awards, 10 S Riverside Plaza, Suite 875, Chicago, IL 60606 Tel: 312-380-6789 E-mail: awards@catholicmediaassociation.org Web Site: www.catholicmediaassociation.org, pg 587

Hollrah, Amy, Western States Arts Federation (WESTAF), 1536 Wynkoop St, Suite 522, Denver, CO 80202 Tel: 303-629-1166 E-mail: staff@westaf.org Web Site: www.westaf.org, pg 526

Holly, Karen, Women's National Book Association Award, PO Box 237, FDR Sta, New York, NY 10150-0231 Toll Free Tel: 866-610-WNBA (610-9622) Web Site: wnba-books.org/wnba-award, pg 677

Holly, Karen, Women's National Book Association Inc, PO Box 237, FDR Sta, New York, NY 10150-0231 Toll Free Tel: 866-610-WNBA (610-9622) E-mail: info@wnba-books.org Web Site: wnba-books.org, pg 522

Holly, Nathaniel, University of Georgia Press, Main Library, 3rd fl, 320 S Jackson St, Athens, GA 30602 Fax: 706-542-2558; 706-542-6770 Web Site: www.ugapress.org, pg 216

Holman, Tim, Hachette Book Group Inc, 1290 Avenue of the Americas, New York, NY 10104 Tel: 212-364-1100 Toll Free Tel: 800-759-0190 (cust serv) Fax: 212-364-0933 (intl orders) Toll Free Fax: 800-286-9471 (cust serv) E-mail: customer.service@hbgusa.com; orders@hbgusa.com Web Site: www.hachettebookgroup.com, pg 83

Holman, Tim, Orbit, 1290 Avenue of the Americas, New York, NY 10104 Tel: 212-364-1100 Toll Free Tel: 800-759-0190 Web Site: www.orbitbooks.net; www.hachettebookgroup.com/imprint/orbit, pg 147

Holmes, J D, Holmes Publishing Group LLC, PO Box 2370, Sequim, WA 98382 Tel: 360-681-2900 E-mail: holmespub@fastmail.fm Web Site: www.jdholmes.com, pg 94

Holmes, James, ProQuest LLC, part of Clarivate PLC, 789 E Eisenhower Pkwy, Ann Arbor, MI 48108 Tel: 734-761-4700 Toll Free Tel: 800-521-0600; 877-779-6768 (sales) E-mail: sales@proquest.com Web Site: www.proquest.com, pg 166

Holstein, Stephanie, PA Press, 202 Warren St, Hudson, NY 12534 Tel: 518-671-6100 Toll Free Tel: 800-722-6657 (dist); 800-759-0190 (sales) E-mail: sales@papress.com Web Site: www.papress.com, pg 149

Holstrom, Ashley, Sourcebooks LLC, 1935 Brookdale Rd, Suite 139, Naperville, IL 60563 Tel: 630-961-3900 Toll Free Tel: 800-432-7444 Fax: 630-961-2168 E-mail: info@sourcebooks.com Web Site: www.sourcebooks.com, pg 195

Holt, Matt, BenBella Books Inc, 10440 N Central Expwy, Suite 800, Dallas, TX 75231-2264 Tel: 214-750-3600 Web Site: www.benbellabooks.com; www.smartpopbooks.com, pg 27

Holt, Sidney, American Society of Magazine Editors (ASME), 23 Barnabas Rd, Suite 34, Hawleyville, CT 06440-0034 Tel: 212-872-3737 E-mail: asme@asme.media Web Site: www.asme.media, pg 496

Holt, Sidney, ASME Award for Fiction, 23 Barnabas Rd, Suite 34, Hawleyville, CT 06440-0034 Tel: 212-872-3737 E-mail: asme@asme.media Web Site: www.asme.media, pg 575

Holtzer, Mastan, Rand McNally, 9855 Woods Dr, Skokie, IL 60077 Tel: 847-329-8100 Toll Free Tel: 877-446-4863 Toll Free Fax: 877-469-1298 E-mail: mediarelations@randmcnally.com; tndsupport@randmcnally.com Web Site: www.randmcnally.com, pg 169

Holway, Pamela, Athabasca University Press, Edmonton Learning Ctr, Peace Hills Trust Tower, 1200, 10011-109 St, Edmonton, AB T5J 3S8, Canada Tel: 780-497-3412 Fax: 780-421-3298 E-mail: aupress@athabascau.ca Web Site: www.aupress.ca, pg 395

Holzapfel, Cynthia, BPC, 415 Farm Rd, Summertown, TN 38483 Tel: 931-964-3571 Toll Free Tel: 888-260-8458 Fax: 931-964-3518 E-mail: info@bookpubco.com Web Site: www.bookpubco.com, pg 35

Holzapfel, Robert, BPC, 415 Farm Rd, Summertown, TN 38483 Tel: 931-964-3571 Toll Free Tel: 888-260-8458 Fax: 931-964-3518 E-mail: info@bookpubco.com Web Site: www.bookpubco.com, pg 35

Holzman, Sonja, Sourcebooks LLC, 1935 Brookdale Rd, Suite 139, Naperville, IL 60563 Tel: 630-961-3900 Toll Free Tel: 800-432-7444 Fax: 630-961-2168 E-mail: info@sourcebooks.com Web Site: www.sourcebooks.com, pg 195

Homer, Sarah, HarperCollins Children's Books, 195 Broadway, New York, NY 10007 Tel: 212-207-7000 Web Site: www.harpercollins.com/childrens, pg 85

Homler, Michael, St Martin's Press, LLC, 120 Broadway, New York, NY 10271 E-mail: publicity@stmartins.com; trademarketing@stmartins.com; foreignrights@stmartins.com Web Site: us.macmillan.com/smp, pg 181

Honcoop, Marlee, International Association of Business Communicators (IABC), 330 N Wabash Ave, Suite 2000, Chicago, IL 60611 Tel: 312-321-6868 Toll Free Tel: 800-218-8097 Fax: 312-673-6708 E-mail: member_relations@iabc.com Web Site: www.iabc.com, pg 508

Honer, Emily, Tor Publishing Group, 120 Broadway, New York, NY 10271 Toll Free Tel: 800-455-0340 (Macmillan) E-mail: torpublicity@tor.com; forgepublicity@forgebooks.com Web Site: us.macmillan.com/torpublishinggroup, pg 208

Honey, Zach, FinePrint Literary Management, 207 W 106 St, Suite 1D, New York, NY 10025 Tel: 212-279-6214 E-mail: info@fineprintlit.com; submissions@fineprint.com Web Site: www.fineprintlit.com, pg 458

Honeycutt, Will, BLR®—Business & Legal Resources, 5511 Virginia Way, Suite 150, Brentwood, TN 37027 Tel: 860-510-0100 Toll Free Tel: 800-727-5257 Toll Free Fax: 800-785-9212 E-mail: media@blr.com; sales@blr.com; service@blr.com; techsupport@blr.com Web Site: blr.com, pg 32

Honour, Carolyn, Springer, One New York Plaza, Suite 4600, New York, NY 10004-1562 Tel: 212-460-1500 Toll Free Tel: 800-SPRINGER (777-4643) Fax: 212-460-1700 E-mail: customerservice@springernature.com Web Site: www.springer.com, pg 196

Hood, Courtney, Peachtree Publishing Co Inc, 1700 Chattahoochee Ave, Atlanta, GA 30318-2112 Tel: 404-876-8761 Toll Free Tel: 800-241-0113 Fax: 404-875-2578 Toll Free Fax: 800-875-8909 E-mail: hello@peachtree-online.com; orders@peachtree-online.com; sales@peachtree-online.com Web Site: www.peachtreebooks.com; www.peachtree-online.com, pg 153

Hooge, Tim, William S Hein & Co Inc, 2350 N Forest Rd, Suite 10A, Getzville, NY 14068 Tel: 716-882-2600 Toll Free Tel: 800-828-7571 Fax: 716-883-8100 E-mail: mail@wshein.com; marketing@wshein.com; customerservice@wshein.com Web Site: home.heinonline.org, pg 90

Hooker, Lauren, Seven Stories Press, 140 Watts St, New York, NY 10013 Tel: 212-226-8760 Toll Free Tel: 800-733-3000 (orders) Fax: 212-226-1411 E-mail: sevenstories@sevenstories.com Web Site: www.sevenstories.com, pg 186

Hooper, Kartraice, National Music Publishers' Association (NMPA), 1900 "N" St NW, Suite 500, Washington, DC 20036 Tel: 202-393-6672 E-mail: members@nmpa.org Web Site: nmpa.org, pg 513

Hooper, Niels, University of California Press, 155 Grand Ave, Suite 400, Oakland, CA 94612-3758 Tel: 510-883-8232 Fax: 510-836-8910 E-mail: customerservice@ucpress.edu Web Site: www.ucpress.edu, pg 215

Hooper, R Barrett, Chronicle Books LLC, 680 Second St, San Francisco, CA 94107 Tel: 415-537-4200 Fax: 415-537-4460 (perms) E-mail: hello@chroniclebooks.com; subrights@chroniclebooks.com Web Site: www.chroniclebooks.com, pg 48

Hoort, Cat, Hachette Nashville, 6100 Tower Circle, Room 210, Franklin, TN 37067 Tel: 615-221-0996 Fax: 615-221-0962 Web Site: www.hachettebookgroup.com/imprint/hachette-nashville/, pg 83

Hoover, Aliza R, The CAT Agency Inc, 345 Old Oaks Rd, Fairfield, CT 06825 Tel: 917-434-3141 Web Site: catagencyinc.com, pg 485

Hoover, Holly, Wm B Eerdmans Publishing Co, 4035 Park East Ct SE, Grand Rapids, MI 49546 Tel: 616-459-4591 Toll Free Tel: 800-253-7521 E-mail: customerservice@eerdmans.com; sales@eerdmans.com Web Site: www.eerdmans.com, pg 64

Hooyboer, Kim, American Booksellers Association, 600 Mamaroneck Ave, Suite 400, Harrison, NY 10528 Tel: 914-406-7500 Toll Free Tel: 800-637-0037 Fax: 914-417-4013 E-mail: info@bookweb.org Web Site: www.bookweb.org, pg 494

Hop, Kristen, University of Alabama Press, 200 Hackberry Lane, 2nd fl, Tuscaloosa, AL 35487 Tel: 205-348-5180 Fax: 205-348-9201 Web Site: www.uapress.ua.edu, pg 214

Hope, Amy, APS PRESS, 3340 Pilot Knob Rd, St Paul, MN 55121 Tel: 651-454-7250 Toll Free Tel: 800-328-7560 Fax: 651-454-0766 E-mail: aps@scisoc.org Web Site: my.apsnet.org/apsstore, pg 16

Hope, Katie, Princeton University Press, 41 William St, Princeton, NJ 08540-5237 Tel: 609-258-4900 Fax: 609-258-6305 E-mail: info@press.princeton.edu Web Site: press.princeton.edu, pg 164

Hopke, Tom, HarperCollins Publishers LLC, 195 Broadway, New York, NY 10007 Tel: 212-207-7000 Web Site: www.harpercollins.com, pg 86

Hopkins, Alayne, Minnesota Book Awards, 1080 Montreal Ave, Suite 2, St Paul, MN 55116 Tel: 651-222-3242 Fax: 651-222-1988 E-mail: friends@thefriends.org Web Site: thefriends.org/events/mnba, pg 633

Hopkins, Nancy, IACP Cookbook Awards, c/o Marshall Jones, 4625 Alexander Dr, Alpharetta, GA 30022 Toll Free Fax: 866-358-2524 E-mail: awards@iacp.com; info@iacp.org Web Site: www.iacp.com/awards/cookbook-awards, pg 614

Hopkins, Tiffany Annette, Austin Area Translators & Interpreters Association (AATIA), PO Box 92334, Austin, TX 78709-2334 E-mail: info@aatia.org; communications@aatia.org; membership@aatia.org; finance@aatia.org; profdev@aatia.org Web Site: aatia.org, pg 500

Hoppe, Anne, Clarion Books, 195 Broadway, New York, NY 10007 Tel: 212-207-7000 Toll Free Tel: 800-242-7737 E-mail: consumercare@harpercollins.com Web Site: www.harpercollins.com/collections/books-by-clarion-books, pg 49

Horbachevsky, Juliana (Jules), Little, Brown and Company, 1290 Avenue of the Americas, New York, NY 10104 Tel: 212-364-1100 Fax: 212-364-0952 E-mail: firstname.lastname@hbgusa.com Web Site: www.hachettebookgroup.com/imprint/little-brown-and-company/, pg 118

Horgan, Rick, Scribner, 1230 Avenue of the Americas, New York, NY 10020 Web Site: www.simonandschusterpublishing.com/scribner/, pg 185

Horgan, Sarah, Random House Publishing Group, 1745 Broadway, New York, NY 10019 Toll Free Tel: 800-200-3552 Web Site: www.randomhousebooks.com, pg 171

Horler, Fred, Groundwood Books, 128 Sterling Rd, Lower Level, Toronto, ON M6R 2B7, Canada Tel: 416-363-4343 Fax: 416-363-1017 E-mail: customerservice@houseofanansi.com Web Site: houseofanansi.com, pg 407

Horler, Fred, House of Anansi Press Inc, 128 Sterling Rd, Lower Level, Toronto, ON M6R 2B7, Canada Tel: 416-363-4343 Fax: 416-363-1017 E-mail: customerservice@houseofanansi.com Web Site: houseofanansi.com, pg 409

Horn, Katie, Random House Publishing Group, 1745 Broadway, New York, NY 10019 Toll Free Tel: 800-200-3552 Web Site: www.randomhousebooks.com, pg 171

Horn, Leah, Western States Arts Federation (WESTAF), 1536 Wynkoop St, Suite 522, Denver, CO 80202 Tel: 303-629-1166 E-mail: staff@westaf.org Web Site: www.westaf.org, pg 526

Horn, Robyn Lee, Maxim Mazumdar New Play Competition, One Curtain Up Alley, Buffalo, NY 14202-1911 Tel: 716-852-2600 E-mail: newplays@alleyway.com; email@alleyway.com Web Site: www.alleyway.com/playwrights/maxim-mazumdar-new-play-competition, pg 630

Horner, Christine, In the Garden Publishing, 6460 E Grant Rd, No 31944, Tucson, AZ 85715 Tel: 937-317-0859 E-mail: admin@inthegardenpublishing.com Web Site: www.inthegardenpublishing.com, pg 99

Horner, Michael, McNeese State University MFA in Creative Writing Program, PO Box 92655, Lake Charles, LA 70609-0001 Tel: 337-475-5325; 337-475-5327 Web Site: www.mcneese.edu/academics/graduate/creative-writing, pg 563

Hornfischer, Jim, Hornfischer Literary Management LP, PO Box 50544, Austin, TX 78763 Tel: 512-472-0011 E-mail: queries@hornfischerlit.com Web Site: www.hornfischerlit.com, pg 463

Hornick, Betsy, Academy of Nutrition & Dietetics, 120 S Riverside Plaza, Suite 2190, Chicago, IL 60606-6995 Tel: 312-899-0040 (ext 5000) Toll Free Tel: 800-877-1600 E-mail: publications@eatright.org; sales@eatright.org Web Site: www.eatrightstore.org, pg 3

Hornik, Lauri, Penguin Young Readers Group, c/o Penguin Random House LLC, 1745 Broadway, New York, NY 10019 Tel: 212-782-9000 Web Site: www.penguin.com/penguin-young-readers-overview, pg 156

Hornik, Lauri, Rocky Pond Books, c/o Penguin Random House LLC, 1745 Broadway, New York, NY 10019 Tel: 212-782-9000 Web Site: www.penguin.com/rocky-pond-overview/, pg 176

Hornsby, Wendy, International Association of Crime Writers Inc, North American Branch, PO Box 863, Norman, OK 73071 E-mail: crimewritersna@gmail.com Web Site: www.crimewritersna.org, pg 508

Horowitz, David, Media Coalition Inc, 19 Fulton St, Suite 407, New York, NY 10038 Tel: 212-587-4025 E-mail: info@mediacoalition.org Web Site: mediacoalition.org, pg 510

Horowitz, Rachel, HarperCollins Children's Books, 195 Broadway, New York, NY 10007 Tel: 212-207-7000 Web Site: www.harpercollins.com/childrens, pg 85

Horowitz, Shel, Accurate Writing & More, 16 Barstow Lane, Hadley, MA 01035 Tel: 413-586-2388 Web Site: www.accuratewriting.com; frugalmarketing.com, pg 435

Horowitz, Stacy, Random House Publishing Group, 1745 Broadway, New York, NY 10019 Toll Free Tel: 800-200-3552 Web Site: www.randomhousebooks.com, pg 171

Horrer, Simon, Macmillan Learning, One New York Plaza, Suite 46, New York, NY 10004 Tel: 212-576-9400 E-mail: salesoperations@macmillanusa.com Web Site: www.macmillanlearning.com/college/us, pg 123

Horry, Luana Kay, HarperCollins Children's Books, 195 Broadway, New York, NY 10007 Tel: 212-207-7000 Web Site: www.harpercollins.com/childrens, pg 85

Horst, Ines ter, University of Texas Press, 3001 Lake Austin Blvd, 2.200, Austin, TX 78703 Tel: 512-471-7233 Fax: 512-232-7178 E-mail: utpress@uts.cc.utexas.edu; info@utpress.utexas.edu Web Site: utpress.utexas.edu, pg 205

Horton, David, Bethany House Publishers, 11400 Hampshire Ave S, Bloomington, MN 55438 Tel: 952-829-2500 Toll Free Tel: 800-877-2665 (orders) Fax: 952-829-2568 Toll Free Fax: 800-398-3111 (orders) Web Site: www.bethanyhouse.com; www.bakerpublishinggroup.com, pg 29

Horton, Kelsey, Random House Children's Books, c/o Penguin Random House LLC, 1745 Broadway, New York, NY 10019 Tel: 212-782-9000 Web Site: www.rhcbooks.com, pg 170

Horvit, Beverly J PhD, Frank Luther Mott-KTA Journalism & Mass Communication Research Award, University of Missouri, School of Journalism, 203 Neff Hall, Columbia, MO 65211-1200 Tel: 573-882-7685 E-mail: umcjourkta@missouri.edu Web Site: www.kappataualpha.net, pg 636

Hosek, Jim, SFWA Nebula Awards, PO Box 215, San Lorenzo, CA 94580 Tel: 860-698-0536 E-mail: office@sfwa.org; operations@sfwa.org Web Site: www.sfwa.org, pg 661

Hoshijo, Amara, Simon & Schuster, 1230 Avenue of the Americas, New York, NY 10020 Tel: 212-698-7000 Toll Free Tel: 800-223-2348 (cust serv); 800-223-2336 (orders) Toll Free Fax: 800-943-9831 (orders) Web Site: simonandschusterpublishing.com/simonandschuster/, pg 188

Hosier, Erin, Dunow, Carlson & Lerner Literary Agency Inc, 27 W 20 St, Suite 1107, New York, NY 10011 Tel: 212-645-7606 E-mail: mail@dclagency.com Web Site: www.dclagency.com, pg 457

Hosken, Yana, Macmillan, 120 Broadway, 22nd fl, New York, NY 10271 E-mail: press.inquiries@macmillan.com Web Site: us.macmillan.com, pg 122

Hoskin, Christine, Schoolhouse Indexing, 10-B Parade Ground Rd, Etna, NH 03750 Tel: 603-359-5826 Web Site: schoolhouseindexing.com, pg 444

Hostein, Lisa, The Harold U Ribalow Prize, 40 Wall St, 8th fl, New York, NY 10005-1387 Tel: 212-451-6289 E-mail: magazine@hadassah.org Web Site: www.hadassahmagazine.org, pg 655

Hosty, Lizzy, Tor Publishing Group, 120 Broadway, New York, NY 10271 Toll Free Tel: 800-455-0340 (Macmillan) E-mail: torpublicity@tor.com; forgepublicity@forgebooks.com Web Site: us.macmillan.com/torpublishinggroup, pg 208

Hottensen, Judy, Grove Atlantic Inc, 154 W 14 St, 12th fl, New York, NY 10011 Tel: 212-614-7850 Toll Free Tel: 800-521-0178 Fax: 212-614-7886 E-mail: info@groveatlantic.com; sales@groveatlantic.com; publicity@groveatlantic.com; rights@groveatlantic.com Web Site: www.groveatlantic.com, pg 82

Hough, Milly, Individual Artist's Fellowships, 1026 Sumter St, Suite 200, Columbia, SC 29201-3746 Tel: 803-734-8696 Fax: 803-734-8526 E-mail: info@arts.sc.gov Web Site: www.southcarolinaarts.com, pg 616

Houghton, Harmon, Clear Light Publishers, 823 Don Diego Ave, Santa Fe, NM 87505 Tel: 505-989-9590 Toll Free Tel: 800-253-2747 (orders) E-mail: info@clearlightbooks.com Web Site: www.clearlightbooks.com, pg 49

Houghton, Jenn, Viking Penguin, c/o Penguin Random House LLC, 1745 Broadway, New York, NY 10019 Tel: 212-782-9000 Web Site: www.penguin.com/overview-vikingbooks/; www.penguin.com/pamela-dorman-books-overview/; www.penguin.com/penguin-classics-overview/; www.penguin.com/penguin-life-overview/, pg 225

Houghton, Quincy, The Metropolitan Museum of Art, 1000 Fifth Ave, New York, NY 10028 Tel: 212-535-7710 E-mail: editorial@metmuseum.org Web Site: www.metmuseum.org, pg 130

Houot, Elisa, The Seymour Agency, 475 Miner Street Rd, Canton, NY 13617 Tel: 239-398-8209 Web Site: www.theseymouragency.com, pg 475

Houpt, Madeline, St Martin's Press, LLC, 120 Broadway, New York, NY 10271 E-mail: publicity@stmartins.com; trademarketing@stmartins.com; foreignrights@stmartins.com Web Site: us.macmillan.com/smp, pg 181

House, J, Townson Publishing Co Ltd, PO Box 1404, Sta A, Vancouver, BC V6C 2P7, Canada Tel: 604-886-0594 E-mail: gpubinc@gmail.com; translationrights@gmail.com Web Site: www.generalpublishing.com, pg 420

Houser, David, Psychological Assessment Resources Inc (PAR), 16204 N Florida Ave, Lutz, FL 33549 Tel: 813-449-4065 Toll Free Tel: 800-331-8378 Fax: 813-961-2196 Toll Free Fax: 800-727-9329 Web Site: www.parinc.com, pg 166

Housley, Jim, Facts On File, 1000 N West St, Suite 1281-230, Wilmington, DE 19801 Tel: 212-967-8800 Toll Free Tel: 800-322-8755 Toll Free Fax: 800-678-3633 E-mail: custserv@factsonfile.com Web Site: www.infobasepublishing.com, pg 69

Houston, Brant, University of Illinois, Department of Journalism, 119 Gregory Hall, 810 S Wright St, Urbana, IL 61801 Tel: 217-333-0709 E-mail: journ@illinois.edu Web Site: catalog.illinois.edu/graduate/media/journalism-ms; media.illinois.edu/journalism/degrees-programs/masters, pg 567

Houston, Chris, Dundurn Press Ltd, PO Box 19510, RPO Manulife, Toronto, ON M4W 3T9, Canada Tel: 416-214-5544 E-mail: info@dundurn.com; publicity@dundurn.com; sales@dundurn.com Web Site: www.dundurn.com, pg 401

Houston, Lawrence, Guild of Book Workers, 521 Fifth Ave, New York, NY 10175 E-mail: communications@guildofbookworkers.org; membership@guildofbookworkers.org Web Site: www.guildofbookworkers.org, pg 507

Houstoun, Tessa, Phaidon, 65 Bleecker St, 8th fl, New York, NY 10012 Tel: 212-652-5400 Toll Free Tel: 800-759-0190 (cust serv) Fax: 212-652-5410 Toll Free Fax: 800-286-9471 (cust serv) E-mail: enquiries@phaidon.com Web Site: www.phaidon.com, pg 159

Houton, Jackie, Candlewick Press, 99 Dover St, Somerville, MA 02144-2825 Tel: 617-661-3330 Fax: 617-661-0565 E-mail: bigbear@candlewick.com; salesinfo@candlewick.com Web Site: candlewick.com, pg 40

Hovey, Kim, Random House Publishing Group, 1745 Broadway, New York, NY 10019 Toll Free Tel: 800-200-3552 Web Site: www.randomhousebooks.com, pg 170

Howard, Alex, Holiday House Publishing Inc, 50 Broad St, New York, NY 10004 Tel: 212-688-0085 Fax: 212-421-6134 E-mail: info@holidayhouse.com Web Site: www.holidayhouse.com, pg 94

Howard, Assuanta, Asta Publications LLC, 3 E Evergreen Rd, No 1112, New City, NY 10956 Tel: 678-814-1320 Toll Free Tel: 800-482-4190 Fax: 678-814-1370 E-mail: info@astapublications.com Web Site: www.astapublications.com, pg 20

Howard, Elise, DeFiore and Company Literary Management Inc, 47 E 19 St, 3rd fl, New York, NY 10003 Tel: 212-925-7744 Fax: 212-925-9803 E-mail: info@defliterary.com; submissions@defliterary.com Web Site: www.defliterary.com, pg 456

Howard, Glenda, Harlequin Enterprises Ltd, 195 Broadway, 24th fl, New York, NY 10007 Tel: 212-207-7000 Toll Free Tel: 888-432-4879; 800-370-5838 (ebooks) E-mail: customerservice@harlequin.com Web Site: www.harlequin.com/shop/index.html; corporate.harlequin.com, pg 85

Howard, Jackson, Farrar, Straus & Giroux, LLC, 120 Broadway, New York, NY 10271 Tel: 212-741-6900 E-mail: fsg.publicity@fsgbooks.com; sales@fsgbooks.com Web Site: us.macmillan.com/fsg, pg 70

Howard, Jeff, Rand-Smith Publishing, 204 College Ave, Ashland, VA 23005 Tel: 804-874-6012 E-mail: randsmithllc@gmail.com Web Site: www.rand-smith.com, pg 169

Howard, Kait, Johns Hopkins University Press, 2715 N Charles St, Baltimore, MD 21218-4363 Tel: 410-516-6900; 410-516-6987 Toll Free Tel: 800-537-5487 (book orders & cust serv); 800-548-1784 (journal orders) Fax: 410-516-6968; 410-516-6998 (orders) E-mail: hfscustserv@press.jhu.edu (cust serv); jrnlcirc@jh.edu (journal orders) Web Site: www.press.jhu.edu; muse.jhu.edu, pg 106

Howard, MacKenzie, Tommy Nelson®, 501 Nelson Place, Nashville, TN 37214 Tel: 615-889-9000; 615-902-1485 (cust serv) Toll Free Tel: 800-251-4000 Web Site: www.tommynelson.com, pg 207

Howard, Meredith, Columbia University Press, 61 W 62 St, New York, NY 10023 Tel: 212-459-0600 Toll Free Tel: 800-944-8648 Fax: 212-459-3678 Web Site: cup.columbia.edu, pg 51

Howard-Woods, Chris, Doubleday, c/o Penguin Random House LLC, 1745 Broadway, New York, NY 10019 Tel: 212-751-2600 Fax: 212-940-7390 (dom rts); 212-572-2662 (foreign rts) Web Site: knopfdoubleday.com/imprint/doubleday/; knopfdoubleday.com, pg 61

Howe, David, Dutton, c/o Penguin Random House LLC, 1745 Broadway, New York, NY 10019 Tel: 212-366-2000 Web Site: www.penguin.com/dutton-overview/; www.penguin.com/plume-books-overview/; www.penguin.com/tiny-reparations-overview/, pg 62

Howe, Meghan, Marilyn Baillie Picture Book Award, 425 Adelaide St W, Suite 200, Toronto, ON M5V 3C1, Canada Tel: 416-975-0010 E-mail: info@bookcentre.ca Web Site: www.bookcentre.ca, pg 576

Howe, Meghan, The Geoffrey Bilson Award for Historical Fiction for Young People, 425 Adelaide St W, Suite 200, Toronto, ON M5V 3C1, Canada Tel: 416-975-0010 E-mail: info@bookcentre.ca Web Site: www.bookcentre.ca, pg 580

Howe, Meghan, Prix Harry Black, 425 Adelaide St W, Suite 200, Toronto, ON M5V 3C1, Canada Tel: 416-975-0010 E-mail: info@bookcentre.ca Web Site: www.bookcentre.ca, pg 581

Howe, Meghan, The Canadian Children's Book Centre, 425 Adelaide St W, Suite 200, Toronto, ON M5V 3C1, Canada Tel: 416-975-0010 E-mail: info@bookcentre.ca Web Site: www.bookcentre.ca, pg 502

Howe, Meghan, Norma Fleck Award for Canadian Children's Non-Fiction, 425 Adelaide St W, Suite 200, Toronto, ON M5V 3C1, Canada Tel: 416-975-0010 E-mail: info@bookcentre.ca Web Site: www.bookcentre.ca, pg 602

Howe, Meghan, Jean Little First Novel Award, 425 Adelaide St W, Suite 200, Toronto, ON M5V 3C1, Canada Tel: 416-975-0010 E-mail: info@bookcentre.ca Web Site: www.bookcentre.ca, pg 625

Howe, Meghan, Amy Mathers Teen Book Award, 425 Adelaide St W, Suite 200, Toronto, ON M5V 3C1, Canada Tel: 416-975-0010 E-mail: info@bookcentre.ca Web Site: www.bookcentre.ca, pg 630

Howe, Meghan, TD Canadian Children's Literature Award, 425 Adelaide St W, Suite 200, Toronto, ON M5V 3C1, Canada Tel: 416-975-0010 E-mail: info@bookcentre.ca Web Site: www.bookcentre.ca, pg 668

Howe, Sally, Scribner, 1230 Avenue of the Americas, New York, NY 10020 Web Site: www.simonandschusterpublishing.com/scribner/, pg 185

Howell, Christopher, Lynx House Press, 420 W 24 St, Spokane, WA 99203 Tel: 509-624-4894 E-mail: lynxhousepress@gmail.com Web Site: www.lynxhousepress.org, pg 121

Howells, Richard, Harvard University Press, 79 Garden St, Cambridge, MA 02138-1499 Tel: 617-495-2600; 401-531-2800 (intl orders) Toll Free Tel: 800-405-1619 (orders) Fax: 617-495-5898 (gen); 617-496-4677 (edit & rts); 401-531-2801 (intl orders) Toll Free Fax: 800-406-9145 (orders) E-mail: contact_hup@harvard.edu Web Site: www.hup.harvard.edu, pg 88

Howry, Michelle, GP Putnam's Sons, c/o Penguin Random House LLC, 1745 Broadway, New York, NY 10019 Tel: 212-782-9000 Web Site: www.penguin.com/putnam/, pg 167

Howson, Christine, Marick Press, 1342 Three Mile Dr, Grosse Pointe Park, MI 48230 Tel: 313-407-9236 E-mail: orders@marickpress.com; info@marickpress.com Web Site: www.marickpress.com, pg 125

Hoy, Angela, WritersWeekly.com's 24-Hour Short Story Contest, 200 Second Ave S, Unit 526, St Petersburg, FL 33701 Tel: 305-768-0261 Web Site: 24hourshortstorycontest.com, pg 678

Hrab, Naseem, Kids Can Press Ltd, 25 Dockside Dr, Toronto, ON M5A 0B5, Canada Tel: 416-479-7000 Toll Free Tel: 800-265-0884 Fax: 416-960-5437 E-mail: info@kidscan.com; customerservice@kidscan.com Web Site: www.kidscanpress.com; www.kidscanpress.ca, pg 411

Hrappstead, Trevor, PrairieView Press, 625 Seventh St, Gretna, MB R0G 0V0, Canada Tel: 204-327-6543 Toll Free Tel: 800-477-7377 Toll Free Fax: 866-480-0253 Web Site: prairieviewpress.com, pg 417

Hromjak, Jasmine, North Atlantic Books (NAB), 2526 Martin Luther King Jr Way, Berkeley, CA 94704 Tel: 510-549-4270 Web Site: www.northatlanticbooks.com, pg 142

Hruska, Bronwen, Soho Press Inc, 853 Broadway, New York, NY 10003 Tel: 212-260-1900 E-mail: soho@sohopress.com; publicity@sohopress.com Web Site: sohopress.com, pg 193

Hsu, Connie, Roaring Brook Press, 120 Broadway, New York, NY 10271 Tel: 646-307-5151 Web Site: us.macmillan.com/publishers/roaring-brook-press, pg 176

Hsu, Ellen, InterVarsity Press, 430 Plaza Dr, Westmont, IL 60559-1234 Tel: 630-734-4000 Toll Free Tel: 800-843-9487 Fax: 630-734-4200 E-mail: email@ivpress.com Web Site: www.ivpress.com, pg 104

Hsu, Mabel, HarperCollins Children's Books, 195 Broadway, New York, NY 10007 Tel: 212-207-7000 Web Site: www.harpercollins.com/childrens, pg 85

Hsu, Mabel, Sourcebooks LLC, 1935 Brookdale Rd, Suite 139, Naperville, IL 60563 Tel: 630-961-3900 Toll Free Tel: 800-432-7444 Fax: 630-961-2168 E-mail: info@sourcebooks.com Web Site: www.sourcebooks.com, pg 194

Huang, Linda, Pantheon Books, c/o Penguin Random House LLC, 1745 Broadway, New York, NY 10019 Tel: 212-751-2600 Fax: 212-940-7390 (dom rts); 212-572-2662 (foreign rts) Web Site: knopfdoubleday.com/imprint/pantheon/; knopfdoubleday.com, pg 150

Huang, Lisa, Macmillan, 120 Broadway, 22nd fl, New York, NY 10271 E-mail: press.inquiries@macmillan.com Web Site: us.macmillan.com, pg 122

Huard, Ricky S, Ohio University Press, Alden Library, Suite 101, 30 Park Place, Athens, OH 45701-2909 Tel: 740-593-1154 Web Site: www.ohioswallow.com, pg 146

Huard, Ricky S, Swallow Press, Alden Library, Suite 101, 30 Park Place, Athens, OH 45701-2909 Tel: 740-593-1154 Web Site: www.ohioswallow.com, pg 201

Hubbard, Elizabeth, Macmillan, 120 Broadway, 22nd fl, New York, NY 10271 E-mail: press.inquiries@macmillan.com Web Site: us.macmillan.com, pg 122

Hubbard, Peter, HarperCollins Publishers LLC, 195 Broadway, New York, NY 10007 Tel: 212-207-7000 Web Site: www.harpercollins.com, pg 86

Hubbart, Dustin, University of Illinois Press, 1325 S Oak St, MC-566, Champaign, IL 61820-6903 Tel: 217-333-0950 Fax: 217-244-8082 E-mail: uipress@uillinois.edu; journals@uillinois.edu Web Site: www.press.uillinois.edu, pg 216

Hubbell, Drew PhD, Susquehanna University, Department of English & Creative Writing, 514 University Ave, Selinsgrove, PA 17870 Tel: 570-372-4196 Web Site: www.susqu.edu, pg 565

Hubbert, Tyler, Princeton University Press, 41 William St, Princeton, NJ 08540-5237 Tel: 609-258-4900 Fax: 609-258-6305 E-mail: info@press.princeton.edu Web Site: press.princeton.edu, pg 164

Hubenthal, Dayna, Koho Pono LLC, 15024 SE Pinegrove Loop, Clackamas, OR 97015 Tel: 503-723-7392 E-mail: info@kohopono.com; orders@ingrambook.com Web Site: kohopono.com, pg 111

Huber, Jennifer, Florida Outdoor Writers Association Inc (FOWA), 235 Apollo Beach Blvd, Unit 271, Apollo Beach, FL 33572 Tel: 813-579-0990 E-mail: info@fowa.org Web Site: www.fowa.org, pg 506

Huber-Rodriguez, Jacqueline, Macmillan, 120 Broadway, 22nd fl, New York, NY 10271 E-mail: press.inquiries@macmillan.com Web Site: us.macmillan.com, pg 122

Huckaby, Billy, Eakin Press, PO Box 331779, Fort Worth, TX 76163 Tel: 817-344-7036 Toll Free Tel: 888-982-8270 Fax: 817-344-7036 Web Site: www.eakinpress.com, pg 62

Hudder, Cliff, Kay Cattarulla Award for Best Short Story, PO Box 130294, Spring, TX 77393 Web Site: texasinstituteofletters.org, pg 587

Hudder, Cliff, Carr P Collins Award, PO Box 130294, Spring, TX 77393 Web Site: texasinstituteofletters.org, pg 591

Hudder, Cliff, Brigid Erin Flynn Award for Best Picture Book, PO Box 130294, Spring, TX 77393 Web Site: texasinstituteofletters.org, pg 603

Hudder, Cliff, Jean Flynn Award for Best Young Adult Book, PO Box 130294, Spring, TX 77393 Web Site: texasinstituteofletters.org, pg 603

Hudder, Cliff, Deirdre Siobhan FlynnBass Award for Best Middle Grade Book, PO Box 130294, Spring, TX 77393 Web Site: texasinstituteofletters.org, pg 603

Hudder, Cliff, Soeurette Diehl Fraser Translation Award, PO Box 130294, Spring, TX 77393 Web Site: texasinstituteofletters.org, pg 604

Hudder, Cliff, Jesse H Jones Award, PO Box 130294, Spring, TX 77393 Web Site: texasinstituteofletters.org, pg 618

Hudder, Cliff, Ramirez Family Award, PO Box 130294, Spring, TX 77393 Web Site: texasinstituteofletters.org, pg 654

Hudder, Cliff, John A Robertson Award for Best First Book of Poetry, PO Box 130294, Spring, TX 77393 *Web Site:* texasinstituteofletters.org, pg 657

Hudder, Cliff, Edwin "Bud" Shrake Award for Best Short Nonfiction, PO Box 130294, Spring, TX 77393 *Web Site:* texasinstituteofletters.org, pg 662

Hudder, Cliff, Helen C Smith Memorial Award, PO Box 130294, Spring, TX 77393 *Web Site:* texasinstituteofletters.org, pg 663

Hudder, Cliff, Texas Institute of Letters (TIL), PO Box 130294, Spring, TX 77393 *Web Site:* texasinstituteofletters.org, pg 521

Hudder, Cliff, Lon Tinkle Award for Lifetime Achievement, PO Box 130294, Spring, TX 77393 *Web Site:* texasinstituteofletters.org, pg 669

Hudder, Cliff, Sergio Troncoso Award for Best Book of Fiction, PO Box 130294, Spring, TX 77393 *Web Site:* texasinstituteofletters.org, pg 670

Hudder, Cliff, Fred Whitehead Award for Best Design of a Trade Book, PO Box 130294, Spring, TX 77393 *Web Site:* texasinstituteofletters.org, pg 675

Huddleston, Courtney, Penny-Farthing Productions, One Sugar Creek Center Blvd, Suite 820, Sugar Land, TX 77478 *Tel:* 713-780-0300 *Toll Free Tel:* 800-926-2669 *Fax:* 713-780-4004 *E-mail:* corp@pfproductions.com *Web Site:* www.pfproductions.com, pg 157

Hudson, Dawn, Academy of Motion Picture Arts & Sciences (AMPAS), 8949 Wilshire Blvd, Beverly Hills, CA 90211 *Tel:* 310-247-3000 *Fax:* 310-859-9619 *E-mail:* ampas@oscars.org *Web Site:* www.oscars.org, pg 493

Hudson, Jeanne-Marie, Berkley, c/o Penguin Random House LLC, 1745 Broadway, 19th fl, New York, NY 10019 *Tel:* 212-366-2000 *Web Site:* www.penguin.com/publishers/berkley/; www.penguin.com/ace-overview/, pg 28

Hudson, Linda, J M Abraham Poetry Award, 1113 Marginal Rd, Halifax, NS B3H 4P7, Canada *Tel:* 902-423-8116 *Fax:* 902-422-0881 *E-mail:* wits@writers.ns.ca (awards) *Web Site:* writers.ns.ca, pg 569

Hudson, Linda, Ann Conner Brimer Award for Atlantic Canadian Children's Literature, 1113 Marginal Rd, Halifax, NS B3H 4P7, Canada *Tel:* 902-423-8116 *Fax:* 902-422-0881 *E-mail:* wits@writers.ns.ca (awards) *Web Site:* writers.ns.ca, pg 584

Hudson, Linda, Thomas Raddall Atlantic Fiction Award, 1113 Marginal Rd, Halifax, NS B3H 4P7, Canada *Tel:* 902-423-8116 *Fax:* 902-422-0881 *E-mail:* wits@writers.ns.ca (awards) *Web Site:* writers.ns.ca, pg 654

Hudson, Linda, Evelyn Richardson Nonfiction Award, 1113 Marginal Rd, Halifax, NS B3H 4P7, Canada *Tel:* 902-423-8116 *Fax:* 902-422-0881 *E-mail:* wits@writers.ns.ca (awards) *Web Site:* writers.ns.ca, pg 655

Hudson, Linda, Writers' Federation of Nova Scotia (WFNS), 1113 Marginal Rd, Halifax, NS B3H 4P7, Canada *Tel:* 902-423-8116 *Fax:* 902-422-0881 *E-mail:* contact@writers.ns.ca; wits@writers.ns.ca (awards); programs@writers.ns.ca; communications@writers.ns.ca *Web Site:* writers.ns.ca, pg 522

Hudson, Liz, University of British Columbia Press, 2029 West Mall, Vancouver, BC V6T 1Z2, Canada *Tel:* 604-822-5959 *Toll Free Tel:* 877-377-9378 *Fax:* 604-822-6083 *Toll Free Fax:* 800-668-0821 *E-mail:* frontdesk@ubcpress.ca *Web Site:* www.ubcpress.ca, pg 422

Hudson, Matt, Entomological Society of America, 170 Jennifer Rd, Suite 230, Annapolis, MD 21401 *Tel:* 301-731-4535 *Fax:* 301-731-4538 *E-mail:* esa@entsoc.org *Web Site:* www.entsoc.org, pg 67

Huelsing, Kristi, Coaches Choice, PO Box 1828, Monterey, CA 93942 *Toll Free Tel:* 888-229-5745 *E-mail:* info@coacheschoice.com *Web Site:* www.coacheschoice.com, pg 50

Huff, Mickey, The 25 Most "Censored" Stories Annual, PO Box 1177, Fair Oaks, CA 95628 *Tel:* 707-241-4596 *E-mail:* info@projectcensored.org *Web Site:* www.projectcensored.org/censorship/nominate, pg 671

Huff-Roberson, Samantha, University of Alabama Press, 200 Hackberry Lane, 2nd fl, Tuscaloosa, AL 35487 *Tel:* 205-348-5180 *Fax:* 205-348-9201 *Web Site:* www.uapress.ua.edu, pg 214

Huffaker, Dru, Cedar Fort Inc, 2373 W 700 S, Suite 100, Springville, UT 84663 *Tel:* 801-489-4084 *Toll Free Tel:* 800-SKY-BOOK (759-2665) *E-mail:* marketinginfo@cedarfort.com *Web Site:* cedarfort.com, pg 43

Huffman, Brittany, One-Act Playwriting Competition, 600 Wolfe St, Alexandria, VA 22314 *Tel:* 703-683-5778 (ext 2) *Fax:* 703-683-1378 *E-mail:* oneactslta@gmail.com *Web Site:* thelittletheatre.com, pg 644

Hufford, Allison, Jane Rotrosen Agency LLC, 318 E 51 St, New York, NY 10022-7803 *Tel:* 212-593-4330 *E-mail:* info@janerotrosen.com *Web Site:* janerotrosen.com, pg 474

Huggins, Allison, Workman Publishing, 1290 Avenue of the Americas, New York, NY 10104 *Toll Free Tel:* 800-759-0190 *Fax:* 212-364-0950 *E-mail:* workman-inquiry@hbgusa.com *Web Site:* www.hachettebookgroup.com/imprint/workman-publishing-company/, pg 233

Hughes, Brigid, A Public Space Fellowships, 323 Dean St, Brooklyn, NY 11217 *Tel:* 718-858-8067 *E-mail:* general@apublicspace.org *Web Site:* apublicspace.org, pg 569

Hughes, Brigid, Deborah Pease Prize, 323 Dean St, Brooklyn, NY 11217 *Tel:* 718-858-8067 *E-mail:* general@apublicspace.org *Web Site:* apublicspace.org, pg 646

Hughes, Connie, Lippincott Williams & Wilkins, 333 Seventh Ave, New York, NY 10001 *Toll Free Tel:* 800-933-6525 *E-mail:* orders@lww.com *Web Site:* www.lww.com, pg 117

Hughes, Emily Wallis, Fence Books, 36-09 28 Ave, Apt 3R, Astoria, NY 11103-4518 *Tel:* 518-567-7006 *Web Site:* www.fenceportal.org, pg 71

Hughes, Emily Wallis, Fence Modern Poets Series, 36-09 28 Ave, Apt 3R, Astoria, NY 11103-4518 *Tel:* 518-567-7006 *Web Site:* www.fenceportal.org, pg 602

Hughes, Emily Wallis, Ottoline Prize, 36-09 28 Ave, Apt 3R, Astoria, NY 11103-4518 *Tel:* 518-567-7006 *Web Site:* www.fenceportal.org, pg 645

Hughes, Georgia, New World Library, 14 Pamaron Way, Novato, CA 94949 *Tel:* 415-884-2100 *Fax:* 415-884-2199 *E-mail:* escort@newworldlibrary.com *Web Site:* www.newworldlibrary.com, pg 140

Hughes, Heather, Sleeping Bear Press™, 2395 S Huron Pkwy, Suite 200, Ann Arbor, MI 48104 *Toll Free Tel:* 800-487-2323 *Fax:* 734-794-0004 *E-mail:* customerservice@sleepingbearpress.com *Web Site:* www.sleepingbearpress.com, pg 191

Hughes, Jessica, Andrew Carnegie Medals for Excellence in Fiction & Nonfiction, 225 N Michigan Ave, Suite 1300, Chicago, IL 60601 *Tel:* 312-944-6780 *Toll Free Tel:* 800-545-2433 *Fax:* 312-440-9374 *E-mail:* ala@ala.org *Web Site:* www.ala.org/awardsgrants/carnegieadult, pg 587

Hughes, Jodi, Thomas Nelson, 501 Nelson Place, Nashville, TN 37214 *Tel:* 615-889-9000 *Toll Free Tel:* 800-251-4000 *Web Site:* www.thomasnelson.com, pg 206

Hughes, Jodi, Zondervan, 3900 Sparks Dr SE, Grand Rapids, MI 49546 *Tel:* 616-698-6900 *Toll Free Tel:* 800-226-1122; 800-727-1309 (retail orders) *Fax:* 616-698-3350 *Toll Free Fax:* 800-698-3256 (retail orders) *E-mail:* customercare@harpercollins.com *Web Site:* www.zondervan.com, pg 237

Hughes, Larry, Simon & Schuster, 1230 Avenue of the Americas, New York, NY 10020 *Tel:* 212-698-7000 *Toll Free Tel:* 800-223-2348 (cust serv); 800-223-2336 (orders) *Toll Free Fax:* 800-943-9831 (orders) *Web Site:* simonandschusterpublishing.com/simonandschuster/, pg 188

Hughes, LeKeisha, University of California Press, 155 Grand Ave, Suite 400, Oakland, CA 94612-3758 *Tel:* 510-883-8232 *Fax:* 510-836-8910 *E-mail:* customerservice@ucpress.edu *Web Site:* www.ucpress.edu, pg 215

Hughes, Megan Barlog, Random House Children's Books, c/o Penguin Random House LLC, 1745 Broadway, New York, NY 10019 *Tel:* 212-782-9000 *Web Site:* www.rhcbooks.com, pg 170

Hughes, Morgan, FinePrint Literary Management, 207 W 106 St, Suite 1D, New York, NY 10025 *Tel:* 212-279-6214 *E-mail:* info@fineprintlit.com; submissions@fineprint.com *Web Site:* www.fineprintlit.com, pg 458

Hughes, Morgan, Pippin Properties Inc, 110 W 40 St, Suite 1704, New York, NY 10018 *Tel:* 212-338-9310 *E-mail:* info@pippinproperties.com *Web Site:* www.pippinproperties.com; www.facebook.com/pippinproperties, pg 472

Hui, Jade, Atria Books, 1230 Avenue of the Americas, New York, NY 10020 *Tel:* 212-698-7000 *Fax:* 212-698-7007 *Web Site:* www.simonandschuster.com, pg 21

Huizenga, Alan, Tyndale House Publishers Inc, 351 Executive Dr, Carol Stream, IL 60188 *Tel:* 630-668-8300 *Toll Free Tel:* 800-323-9400; 855-277-9400 *Toll Free Fax:* 866-622-9474 *Web Site:* www.tyndale.com, pg 211

Hull, Stephen, University of New Mexico Press, One University of New Mexico, Albuquerque, NM 87131-0001 *Tel:* 505-272-7777 *Fax:* 505-277-3343 *E-mail:* custserv@unm.edu (order dept) *Web Site:* unmpress.com, pg 218

Hulse, Patrick, Little, Brown Books for Young Readers (LBYR), 1290 Avenue of the Americas, New York, NY 10104 *Tel:* 212-364-1100 *Toll Free Tel:* 800-759-0190 (cust serv) *E-mail:* rights@lbchildrens.com *Web Site:* www.hachettebookgroup.com/imprint/little-brown-books-for-young-readers/, pg 118

Hulsebosch, Betsy, Running Press, 1290 Avenue of the Americas, New York, NY 10104 *Tel:* 212-364-1100 *Toll Free Tel:* 800-759-0190 (cust serv) *Fax:* 212-364-0933 (intl orders) *Toll Free Fax:* 800-286-9471 (cust serv) *E-mail:* customer.service@hbgusa.com; orders@hbgusa.com *Web Site:* www.hachettebookgroup.com/imprint/running-press/; www.moon.com (Moon Travel Guides), pg 178

Hulsey, Dave, Indiana University Press, Off of Scholarly Publg, Herman B Wells Library 350, 1320 E Tenth St, Bloomington, IN 47405-3907 *Tel:* 812-855-8817 *Fax:* 812-855-7931; 812-855-8507 *E-mail:* iupress@indiana.edu *Web Site:* iupress.org, pg 100

Hultenschmidt, Leah, Grand Central Publishing, 1290 Avenue of the Americas, New York, NY 10104 *Tel:* 212-364-1100 *Web Site:* www.hachettebookgroup.com/imprint/grand-central-publishing/, pg 80

Humphreys, Lindy, Harry N Abrams Inc, 195 Broadway, 9th fl, New York, NY 10007 *Tel:* 212-206-7715 *Toll Free Tel:* 800-345-1359 *Fax:* 212-645-8437 *E-mail:* abrams@abramsbooks.com; publicity@abramsbooks.com; sales@abramsbooks.com *Web Site:* www.abramsbooks.com, pg 2

Hundley, Amy, Grove Atlantic Inc, 154 W 14 St, 12th fl, New York, NY 10011 *Tel:* 212-614-7850 *Toll Free Tel:* 800-521-0178 *Fax:* 212-614-7886 *E-mail:* info@groveatlantic.com; sales@groveatlantic.com; publicity@groveatlantic.com; rights@groveatlantic.com *Web Site:* www.groveatlantic.com, pg 82

Hunegs, Simon, Phaidon, 65 Bleecker St, 8th fl, New York, NY 10012 *Tel:* 212-652-5400 *Toll Free Tel:* 800-759-0190 (cust serv) *Fax:* 212-652-5410 *Toll Free Fax:* 800-286-9471 (cust serv) *E-mail:* enquiries@phaidon.com *Web Site:* www.phaidon.com, pg 159

Hunnewell, Lindsey, Wilfrid Laurier University Press, 75 University Ave W, Waterloo, ON N2L 3C5, Canada *Tel:* 519-884-0710 *Toll Free Tel:* 866-836-5551 (CN & US) *Fax:* 519-725-1399 *E-mail:* press@wlu.ca *Web Site:* www.wlupress.wlu.ca, pg 424

Hunt, Clynton, Bisk Education, 9417 Princess Palm Ave, Suite 400, Tampa, FL 33619 *Tel:* 813-621-6200 *E-mail:* media@bisk.com *Web Site:* www.bisk.com, pg 29

Hunt, Jenny, Baylor University Press, Baylor University, One Bear Place, Waco, TX 76798-7363 *Tel:* 254-710-3164 *E-mail:* bup_marketing@baylor.edu *Web Site:* www.baylorpress.com, pg 25

Hunt, Lia, PA Press, 202 Warren St, Hudson, NY 12534 *Tel:* 518-671-6100 *Toll Free Tel:* 800-722-6657 (dist); 800-759-0190 (sales) *E-mail:* sales@papress.com *Web Site:* www.papress.com, pg 149

Hunt, Sr Marie James, Pauline Books & Media, 50 Saint Paul's Ave, Boston, MA 02130 *Tel:* 617-522-8911 *Toll Free Tel:* 800-876-4463 (orders); 800-836-9723 (cust serv) *Fax:* 617-541-9805 *E-mail:* editorial@paulinemedia.com (ms submissions); orderentry@pauline.org (cust serv) *Web Site:* www.pauline.org/pbmpublishing, pg 152

Hunt, Richard, AdventureKEEN, 2204 First Ave S, Suite 102, Birmingham, AL 35233 *Tel:* 763-689-9800 *Toll Free Tel:* 800-678-7006 *Fax:* 763-689-9039 *Toll Free Fax:* 877-374-9016 *E-mail:* info@adventurewithkeen.com *Web Site:* adventurewithkeen.com, pg 5

Hunt, Richard, Clerisy Press, 306 Greenup St, Covington, KY 41011 *Tel:* 859-815-7204 *E-mail:* info@clerisypress.com *Web Site:* www.clerisypress.com, pg 49

Hunter, Ann A, AAH Graphics Inc, 9293 Fort Valley Rd, Fort Valley, VA 22652 *Tel:* 540-933-6210 *Fax:* 540-933-6523 *E-mail:* aah@aahgraphics.com *Web Site:* www.aahgraphics.com, pg 435

Hunter, Ann A, Loft Press Inc, 9293 Fort Valley Rd, Fort Valley, VA 22652 *Tel:* 540-933-6210 *Fax:* 540-933-6523 *E-mail:* Books@LoftPress.com *Web Site:* www.loftpress.com, pg 119

Hunter, Chelsea, Holiday House Publishing Inc, 50 Broad St, New York, NY 10004 *Tel:* 212-688-0085 *Fax:* 212-421-6134 *E-mail:* info@holidayhouse.com *Web Site:* www.holidayhouse.com, pg 94

Hunter, Chelsea, Peachtree Publishing Co Inc, 1700 Chattahoochee Ave, Atlanta, GA 30318-2112 *Tel:* 404-876-8761 *Toll Free Tel:* 800-241-0113 *Fax:* 404-875-2578 *Toll Free Fax:* 800-875-8909 *E-mail:* hello@peachtree-online.com; orders@peachtree-online.com; sales@peachtree-online.com *Web Site:* www.peachtreebooks.com; www.peachtree-online.com, pg 153

Hunter, Clint, Cedar Fort Inc, 2373 W 700 S, Suite 100, Springville, UT 84663 *Tel:* 801-489-4084 *Toll Free Tel:* 800-SKY-BOOK (759-2665) *E-mail:* marketinginfo@cedarfort.com *Web Site:* cedarfort.com, pg 43

Hunter, Daniele, McIntosh and Otis Inc, 235 Main St, Suite 318, White Plains, NY 10601 *Tel:* 212-687-7400 *Fax:* 212-687-6894 *E-mail:* info@mcintoshandotis.com *Web Site:* www.mcintoshandotis.com, pg 470

Hunter, Emma, Kids Can Press Ltd, 25 Dockside Dr, Toronto, ON M5A 0B5, Canada *Tel:* 416-479-7000 *Toll Free Tel:* 800-265-0884 *Fax:* 416-960-5437 *E-mail:* info@kidscan.com; customerservice@kidscan.com *Web Site:* www.kidscanpress.com; www.kidscanpress.ca, pg 411

Hunter, Greg, Graphic Universe™, 241 First Ave N, Minneapolis, MN 55401 *Tel:* 612-332-3344 *Toll Free Tel:* 800-328-4929 *Fax:* 612-332-7615 *Toll Free Fax:* 800-332-1132 *E-mail:* info@lernerbooks.com; custserve@lernerbooks.com *Web Site:* www.lernerbooks.com; www.facebook.com/lernerbooks, pg 80

Hunter, Greg, Lerner Publishing Group Inc, 241 First Ave N, Minneapolis, MN 55401 *Tel:* 612-332-3344 *Toll Free Tel:* 800-328-4929 *Fax:* 612-332-7615 *Toll Free Fax:* 800-332-1132 *E-mail:* info@lernerbooks.com; custserve@lernerbooks.com *Web Site:* www.lernerbooks.com; www.facebook.com/lernerbooks, pg 115

Hunter, India, Sourcebooks LLC, 1935 Brookdale Rd, Suite 139, Naperville, IL 60563 *Tel:* 630-961-3900 *Toll Free Tel:* 800-432-7444 *Fax:* 630-961-2168 *E-mail:* info@sourcebooks.com *Web Site:* www.sourcebooks.com, pg 194

Hunter, Kristy, The Knight Agency Inc, 232 W Washington St, Madison, GA 30650 *E-mail:* admin@knightagency.net *Web Site:* www.knightagency.net, pg 466

Hunter, Stephen R, Loft Press Inc, 9293 Fort Valley Rd, Fort Valley, VA 22652 *Tel:* 540-933-6210 *Fax:* 540-933-6523 *E-mail:* Books@LoftPress.com *Web Site:* www.loftpress.com, pg 119

Huntwork, Stephanie, Penguin Random House LLC, 1745 Broadway, New York, NY 10019 *Tel:* 212-782-9000 *Toll Free Tel:* 800-726-0600 *Web Site:* www.penguinrandomhouse.com, pg 155

Hupp, Dennis, Highlights for Children Inc, 815 Church St, Honesdale, PA 18431 *Tel:* 570-253-1164 *Toll Free Tel:* 800-490-5111 *Fax:* 570-253-0179 *E-mail:* salesandmarketing@highlightspress.com *Web Site:* www.highlightspress.com; www.highlights.com; www.facebook.com/HighlightsforChildren, pg 92

Hurley, Alexis, InkWell Management, 521 Fifth Ave, Suite 2600, New York, NY 10175 *Tel:* 212-922-3500 *Fax:* 212-922-0535 *E-mail:* info@inkwellmanagement.com; submissions@inkwellmanagement.com; permissions@inkwellmanagement.com *Web Site:* inkwellmanagement.com, pg 463

Hurley, Kate, Candlewick Press, 99 Dover St, Somerville, MA 02144-2825 *Tel:* 617-661-3330 *Fax:* 617-661-0565 *E-mail:* bigbear@candlewick.com; salesinfo@candlewick.com *Web Site:* candlewick.com, pg 39

Hurst, Caitlin, Columbia University Press, 61 W 62 St, New York, NY 10023 *Tel:* 212-459-0600 *Toll Free Tel:* 800-944-8648 *Fax:* 212-459-3678 *Web Site:* cup.columbia.edu, pg 51

Hurston, Vernita, The Guilford Press, 370 Seventh Ave, Suite 1200, New York, NY 10001-1020 *Tel:* 212-431-9800 *Toll Free Tel:* 800-365-7006 *Fax:* 212-966-6708 *E-mail:* info@guilford; orders@guilford.com *Web Site:* www.guilford.com, pg 82

Hurtado, Ricardo, National Association of Hispanic Publications Inc (NAHP), National Press Bldg, 529 14 St NW, Suite 923, Washington, DC 20045 *Web Site:* nahp.org, pg 511

Husband, Shelley, Association of American Publishers (AAP), 455 Massachusetts Ave NW, Suite 700, Washington, DC 20001-2777 *Tel:* 202-347-3375 *Fax:* 202-347-3690 *E-mail:* info@publishers.org *Web Site:* publishers.org, pg 498

Hussey, Ron, Houghton Mifflin Harcourt, 125 High St, Boston, MA 02110 *Tel:* 617-351-5000 *Toll Free Tel:* 855-969-4642; 800-225-5425 (K-12 educ materials); 800-323-9540 (assessment materials); 877-219-1537 (SkillsTutor); 888-242-6747 (Innovation in Educ Group); 800-225-3362 (Trade & Ref Div) *Toll Free Fax:* 800-269-5232 *E-mail:* myhmhco@hmhco.com *Web Site:* www.hmhco.com, pg 96

Hutchins, Meredith, AdventureKEEN, 2204 First Ave S, Suite 102, Birmingham, AL 35233 *Tel:* 763-689-9800 *Toll Free Tel:* 800-678-7006 *Fax:* 763-689-9039 *Toll Free Fax:* 877-374-9016 *E-mail:* info@adventurewithkeen.com *Web Site:* adventurewithkeen.com, pg 5

Hutchinson, Bailey, Ballard Spahr Prize for Poetry, 1011 Washington Ave S, Suite 300, Minneapolis, MN 55415-1246 *Tel:* 612-332-3192 *Toll Free Tel:* 800-520-6455 *Web Site:* milkweed.org/ballard-spahr-prize-for-poetry, pg 577

Hutchinson, Bailey, Milkweed Editions, 1011 Washington Ave S, Suite 300, Minneapolis, MN 55415-1246 *Tel:* 612-332-3192 *Toll Free Tel:* 800-520-6455 *E-mail:* orders@milkweed.org *Web Site:* milkweed.org, pg 131

Hutchinson, Bailey, Max Ritvo Poetry Prize, 1011 Washington Ave S, Suite 300, Minneapolis, MN 55415-1246 *Tel:* 612-332-3192 *Toll Free Tel:* 800-520-6455 *Web Site:* milkweed.org/max-ritvo-poetry-prize, pg 656

Hutchinson, Ginger, Movable Type Management, 244 Madison Ave, Suite 334, New York, NY 10016 *Web Site:* www.movabletm.com, pg 471

Hutchinson, Jennifer, ABC-CLIO, 147 Castilian Dr, Santa Barbara, CA 93117 *Tel:* 805-968-1911 *Toll Free Tel:* 800-368-6868 *Toll Free Fax:* 866-270-3856 *E-mail:* customerservice@abc-clio.com *Web Site:* www.abc-clio.com, pg 2

Hutchison, Margot Maley, Waterside Productions Inc, 2055 Oxford Ave, Cardiff, CA 92007 *Tel:* 760-632-9190 *Fax:* 760-632-9295 *E-mail:* admin@waterside.com *Web Site:* www.waterside.com, pg 481

Hutnan, Val, The Society of Naval Architects & Marine Engineers (SNAME), 99 Canal Center Plaza, Suite 310, Alexandria, VA 22314 *Tel:* 703-997-6701 *Toll Free Tel:* 800-798-2188 *Fax:* 703-997-6702 *Web Site:* www.sname.org, pg 193

Hutson, Sarah, Penguin Press, c/o Penguin Random House LLC, 1745 Broadway, New York, NY 10019 *Tel:* 212-782-9000 *E-mail:* penguinpress@penguinrandomhouse.com *Web Site:* www.penguin.com/penguin-press-overview/, pg 154

Hutter, Victoria, National Endowment for the Arts, 400 Seventh St SW, Washington, DC 20506-0001 *Tel:* 202-682-5400 *Web Site:* www.arts.gov, pg 526

Hutto, Alicia Chandler, South Carolina Bar, 1501 Park St, Columbia, SC 29201 *Tel:* 803-799-6653 *Toll Free Tel:* 800-768-7787 *E-mail:* scbar-info@scbar.org *Web Site:* www.scbar.org, pg 195

Hutton, Caroline DuBois, Hutton Publishing, 12 Golden Hill St, Norwalk, CT 06854 *Tel:* 203-558-4478 *E-mail:* huttonbooks@hotmail.com, pg 97

Hutton, Caroline DuBois, Jones Hutton Literary Associates, 140D Heritage Village, Southbury, CT 06488 *Tel:* 203-558-4478 *E-mail:* huttonbooks@hotmail.com, pg 465

Hutton, Daisy, Hachette Book Group Inc, 1290 Avenue of the Americas, New York, NY 10104 *Tel:* 212-364-1100 *Toll Free Tel:* 800-759-0190 (cust serv) *Fax:* 212-364-0933 (intl orders) *Toll Free Fax:* 800-286-9471 (cust serv) *E-mail:* customer.service@hbgusa.com; orders@hbgusa.com *Web Site:* www.hachettebookgroup.com, pg 83

Hutton, Daisy, Hachette Nashville, 6100 Tower Circle, Room 210, Franklin, TN 37067 *Tel:* 615-221-0996 *Fax:* 615-221-0962 *Web Site:* www.hachettebookgroup.com/imprint/hachette-nashville/, pg 83

Hutton, Sarah, Village Books Literary Citizenship Award, 1200 11 St, Bellingham, WA 98225 *Tel:* 360-671-2626 *E-mail:* biblioinfo@villagebooks.com; marketing@villagebooks.com *Web Site:* www.villagebooks.com/literary-citizenship-award, pg 672

Hvide, Brit, Orbit, 1290 Avenue of the Americas, New York, NY 10104 *Tel:* 212-364-1100 *Toll Free Tel:* 800-759-0190 *Web Site:* www.orbitbooks.net; www.hachettebookgroup.com/imprint/orbit, pg 147

Hwang, Cindy, Berkley, c/o Penguin Random House LLC, 1745 Broadway, 19th fl, New York, NY 10019 *Tel:* 212-366-2000 *Web Site:* www.penguin.com/publishers/berkley/; www.penguin.com/ace-overview/, pg 28

Hyatt, Ruth, Arkansas Diamond Primary Book Award, Arkansas State Library, Suite 100, 900 W Capitol Ave, Little Rock, AR 72201-3108 *Tel:* 501-682-2860 *Web Site:* www.library.arkansas.gov/programs/book-awards, pg 574

Hyatt, Ruth, Charlie May Simon Children's Book Award, Arkansas State Library, Suite 100, 900 W Capitol Ave, Little Rock, AR 72201-3108 *Tel:* 501-682-2860 *Web Site:* www.library.arkansas.gov/programs/book-awards, pg 663

Hyde, Dara, Hill Nadell Literary Agency, 6442 Santa Monica Blvd, Suite 200A, Los Angeles, CA 90038 *Tel:* 310-860-9605 *E-mail:* queries@hillnadell.com; rights@hillnadell.com (rts & perms) *Web Site:* www.hillnadell.com, pg 463

Hyde, Mallory, BenBella Books Inc, 10440 N Central Expwy, Suite 800, Dallas, TX 75231-2264 *Tel:* 214-750-3600 *Web Site:* www.benbellabooks.com; www.smartpopbooks.com, pg 27

Hyman, Alan, The Picasso Project, 1109 Geary Blvd, San Francisco, CA 94109 *Tel:* 415-292-6500 *Fax:* 415-292-6594 *E-mail:* editeur@earthlink.net (edit); picasso@art-books.com (orders) *Web Site:* www.art-books.com, pg 160

Hyman, Ben, Schocken Books, c/o Penguin Random House LLC, 1745 Broadway, New York, NY 10019 *Tel:* 212-571-2600 *Fax:* 212-940-7390 (dom rts); 212-572-2662 (foreign rts) *Web Site:* knopfdoubleday.com/imprint/schocken/; knopfdoubleday.com, pg 183

Hymer, Bennett, Mutual Publishing LLC, 1215 Center St, Suite 210, Honolulu, HI 96816 *Tel:* 808-732-1709 *Fax:* 808-734-4094 *E-mail:* info@mutualpublishing.com *Web Site:* www.mutualpublishing.com, pg 136

Hyne, Richard, American Jewish Committee (AJC), Mail Code 6760, PO Box 7247, Philadelphia, PA 19170-0001 *Tel:* 212-751-4000 *Fax:* 212-891-1450 *E-mail:* social@ajc.org *Web Site:* www.ajc.org, pg 495

Iannacone, Nicholas, Macmillan, 120 Broadway, 22nd fl, New York, NY 10271 *E-mail:* press.inquiries@macmillan.com *Web Site:* us.macmillan.com, pg 122

Iannone, Carla, Avery, c/o Penguin Random House LLC, 1745 Broadway, New York, NY 10019 *Tel:* 212-366-2000 *Web Site:* www.penguin.com/avery-overview/, pg 23

Iannone, Carla, TarcherPerigee, c/o Penguin Random House LLC, 1745 Broadway, New York, NY 10019 *Tel:* 212-782-9000 *Web Site:* www.penguin.com/tarcherperigee-overview/; www.facebook.com/TarcherPerigee, pg 202

Iaquinta, Gina, W W Norton & Company Inc, 500 Fifth Ave, New York, NY 10110-0017 *Tel:* 212-354-5500 *Toll Free Tel:* 800-233-4830 (orders & cust serv) *Fax:* 212-869-0856 *Toll Free Fax:* 800-458-6515 *E-mail:* orders@wwnorton.com *Web Site:* wwnorton.com, pg 143

Iaria, Carmela, Penguin Young Readers Group, c/o Penguin Random House LLC, 1745 Broadway, New York, NY 10019 *Tel:* 212-782-9000 *Web Site:* www.penguin.com/penguin-young-readers-overview, pg 156

Iarrera, Linda, Penguin Random House Canada, a Penguin Random House company, 320 Front St W, Suite 1400, Toronto, ON M5V 3B6, Canada *Tel:* 416-364-4449 *Toll Free Tel:* 888-523-9292 (cust serv) *E-mail:* canadaweb@penguinrandomhouse.com; customerservicescanada@penguinrandomhouse.com *Web Site:* www.penguinrandomhouse.ca, pg 416

Ibarra, Allan, Groundwood Books, 128 Sterling Rd, Lower Level, Toronto, ON M6R 2B7, Canada *Tel:* 416-363-4343 *Fax:* 416-363-1017 *E-mail:* customerservice@houseofanansi.com *Web Site:* www.houseofanansi.com, pg 407

Ibarra, Allan, House of Anansi Press Inc, 128 Sterling Rd, Lower Level, Toronto, ON M6R 2B7, Canada *Tel:* 416-363-4343 *Fax:* 416-363-1017 *E-mail:* customerservice@houseofanansi.com *Web Site:* houseofanansi.com, pg 409

Ibrahim, Masie, Dystel, Goderich & Bourret LLC, One Union Sq W, Suite 904, New York, NY 10003 *Tel:* 212-627-9100 *Fax:* 212-627-9313 *Web Site:* www.dystel.com, pg 457

Ibur, Edward S, Saint Louis Literary Award, Pius XII Memorial Library, 3650 Lindell Blvd, St Louis, MO 63108 *Tel:* 314-977-3100; 314-977-3087 *Fax:* 314-977-3108 *E-mail:* slula@slu.edu *Web Site:* lib.slu.edu/about/associates/literary-award, pg 658

Idil, Ahmet, Tughra Books, 335 Clifton Ave, Clifton, NJ 07011 *Tel:* 646-415-9331 *Fax:* 646-827-6228 *E-mail:* info@tughrabooks.com *Web Site:* www.tughrabooks.com, pg 210

Igarashi, Yuka, Graywolf Press, 212 Third Ave N, Suite 485, Minneapolis, MN 55401 *Tel:* 651-641-0077 *Fax:* 651-641-0036 *E-mail:* wolves@graywolfpress.org (no ms queries, sample chapters or proposals) *Web Site:* www.graywolfpress.org, pg 81

Iglesias Perez, Melanie, Atria Books, 1230 Avenue of the Americas, New York, NY 10020 *Tel:* 212-698-7000 *Fax:* 212-698-7007 *Web Site:* www.simonandschuster.com, pg 21

Ignatius, Adi, Harvard Business Review Press, 20 Guest St, Suite 700, Brighton, MA 02135 *Tel:* 617-783-7400 *Fax:* 617-783-7489 *E-mail:* custserv@hbsp.harvard.edu *Web Site:* www.harvardbusiness.org, pg 87

Iguchi, Yasuyo, The MIT Press, One Broadway, 12th fl, Cambridge, MA 02142 *Tel:* 617-253-5255 *Toll Free Tel:* 800-405-1619 (orders) *Fax:* 617-258-6779; 617-577-1545 (orders) *Web Site:* mitpress.mit.edu, pg 132

Ikedia, Masako, University of Hawaii Press, 2840 Kolowalu St, Honolulu, HI 96822-1888 *Tel:* 808-956-8255 *Toll Free Tel:* 888-UHPRESS (847-7377) *Toll Free Fax:* 800-650-7811 *E-mail:* uhpbooks@hawaii.edu *Web Site:* www.uhpress.hawaii.edu, pg 216

Ikkanda, Emi, Dutton, c/o Penguin Random House LLC, 1745 Broadway, New York, NY 10019 *Tel:* 212-366-2000 *Web Site:* www.penguin.com/dutton-overview/; www.penguin.com/plume-books-overview/; www.penguin.com/tiny-reparations-overview/, pg 62

Ilgunas, Charlie, little bee books, 598 Broadway, 7th fl, New York, NY 10012 *Tel:* 212-321-0237 *Toll Free Tel:* 844-321-0237 *E-mail:* info@littlebeebooks.com; sales@littlebeebooks.com; publicity@littlebeebooks.com *Web Site:* littlebeebooks.com, pg 117

Illingworth, Jack, Association of Canadian Publishers (ACP), 401 Richmond St W, Studio 257A, Toronto, ON M5V 3A8, Canada *Tel:* 416-487-6116 *E-mail:* admin@canbook.org *Web Site:* publishers.ca, pg 499

Illingworth, Sasha, Little, Brown Books for Young Readers (LBYR), 1290 Avenue of the Americas, New York, NY 10104 *Tel:* 212-364-1100 *Toll Free Tel:* 800-759-0190 (cust serv) *E-mail:* rights@lbchildrens.com *Web Site:* www.hachettebookgroup.com/imprint/little-brown-books-for-young-readers/, pg 118

Ilnitzki, Megan, HarperCollins Children's Books, 195 Broadway, New York, NY 10007 *Tel:* 212-207-7000 *Web Site:* www.harpercollins.com/childrens, pg 85

Imbornone, Carina, Picador, 120 Broadway, New York, NY 10271 *Tel:* 646-307-5151 *Fax:* 212-253-9627 *E-mail:* publicity@picadorusa.com *Web Site:* us.macmillan.com/picador, pg 160

Imfeld, Robert, HarperCollins Children's Books, 195 Broadway, New York, NY 10007 *Tel:* 212-207-7000 *Web Site:* www.harpercollins.com/childrens, pg 85

Imperiale, Danielle, Farrar, Straus & Giroux Books for Young Readers, 120 Broadway, New York, NY 10271 *Tel:* 212-741-6900 *Toll Free Tel:* 888-330-8477 (orders) *E-mail:* childrens.publicity@macmillanusa.com; childrensrights@macmillanusa.com *Web Site:* us.macmillan.com/mackids, pg 70

Imperiale, Danielle, Roaring Brook Press, 120 Broadway, New York, NY 10271 *Tel:* 646-307-5151 *Web Site:* us.macmillan.com/publishers/roaring-brook-press, pg 176

Imranyi, Erika, Harlequin Enterprises Ltd, 195 Broadway, 24th fl, New York, NY 10007 *Tel:* 212-207-7000 *Toll Free Tel:* 888-432-4879; 800-370-5838 (ebooks) *E-mail:* customerservice@harlequin.com *Web Site:* www.harlequin.com/shop/index.html; corporate.harlequin.com, pg 85

Indek, Lizzy, Random House Children's Books, c/o Penguin Random House LLC, 1745 Broadway, New York, NY 10019 *Tel:* 212-782-9000 *Web Site:* www.rhcbooks.com, pg 170

Indrigo, Miranda, Harlequin Enterprises Ltd, Bay Adelaide Centre, East Tower, 22 Adelaide St W, 41st fl, Toronto, ON M5H 4E3, Canada *Tel:* 416-445-5860 *Toll Free Tel:* 888-432-4879; 800-370-5838 (ebook inquiries) *E-mail:* customerservice@harlequin.com *Web Site:* www.harlequin.com, pg 409

Ineson, Beth, New England Book Awards, One Beacon St, 15th fl, Boston, MA 02108 *Tel:* 617-547-3642 *Web Site:* www.newenglandbooks.org/page/book-awards, pg 640

Ineson, Beth, New England Independent Booksellers Association Inc (NEIBA), One Beacon St, 15th fl, Boston, MA 02108 *Tel:* 617-547-3642 *Web Site:* www.newenglandbooks.org, pg 514

Ingalls, Johanna, Akashic Books, 232 Third St, Suite A115, Brooklyn, NY 11215 *Tel:* 718-643-9193 *E-mail:* info@akashicbooks.com *Web Site:* www.akashicbooks.com, pg 6

Ingenito, Kim Thornton, Penguin Random House Speakers Bureau, a Penguin Random House company, 1745 Broadway, Mail Drop 13-1, New York, NY 10019 *Tel:* 212-572-2013 *E-mail:* speakers@penguinrandomhouse.com *Web Site:* www.prhspeakers.com, pg 487

Ingersoll, Tessa, Chronicle Books LLC, 680 Second St, San Francisco, CA 94107 *Tel:* 415-537-4200 *Fax:* 415-537-4460 (perms) *E-mail:* hello@chroniclebooks.com; subrights@chroniclebooks.com *Web Site:* www.chroniclebooks.com, pg 47

Ingerson, Trevor, Penguin Young Readers Group, c/o Penguin Random House LLC, 1745 Broadway, New York, NY 10019 *Tel:* 212-782-9000 *Web Site:* www.penguin.com/penguin-young-readers-overview, pg 156

Ingle, Stephanie, Llewellyn Publications, 2143 Wooddale Dr, Woodbury, MN 55125 *Tel:* 651-291-1970 *Toll Free Tel:* 800-843-6666 *Fax:* 651-291-1908 *E-mail:* publicity@llewellyn.com; customerservice@llewellyn.com *Web Site:* www.llewellyn.com, pg 119

Ingle, Stephen, WordCo Indexing Services Inc, 66 Franklin St, Norwich, CT 06360 *E-mail:* office@wordco.com *Web Site:* www.wordco.com, pg 445

Inglis, John, Cold Spring Harbor Laboratory Press, 500 Sunnyside Blvd, Woodbury, NY 11797-2924 *Tel:* 516-422-4100 *Toll Free Tel:* 800-843-4388 *E-mail:* cshpress@cshl.edu *Web Site:* www.cshlpress.com, pg 50

Inglis, Sharon, Newbury Street Press, 99-101 Newbury St, Boston, MA 02116 *Tel:* 617-226-1206 *Toll Free Tel:* 888-296-3447 (NEHGS membership) *Fax:* 617-536-7307 *E-mail:* thebookstore@nehgs.org *Web Site:* www.americanancestors.org, pg 141

Ingraffea, Sarah, AAAS/Subaru Prize for Excellence in Science Books, 1200 New York Ave NW, Washington, DC 20005 *Tel:* 202-326-6400 *E-mail:* sbf@aaas.org *Web Site:* www.sbfprize.org, pg 569

Ingram, Ashley, Berrett-Koehler Publishers Inc, 1333 Broadway, Suite 1000, Oakland, CA 94612 *Tel:* 510-817-2277 *Fax:* 510-817-2278 *E-mail:* bkpub@bkpub.com *Web Site:* www.bkconnection.com, pg 29

Ingwell, Carmen, The National Humanities Medal, 400 Seventh St SW, Washington, DC 20506 *Tel:* 202-606-8400 *Toll Free Tel:* 800-NEH-1121 (634-1121) *E-mail:* questions@neh.gov *Web Site:* www.neh.gov/about/awards, pg 637

Inkster, Tim, Porcupine's Quill Inc, 68 Main St, Erin, ON N0B 1T0, Canada *Tel:* 519-833-9158 *E-mail:* pql@sentex.net *Web Site:* porcupinesquill.ca; www.facebook.com/theporcupinesquill, pg 416

Inteli, Nancy, Clarion Books, 195 Broadway, New York, NY 10007 *Tel:* 212-207-7000 *Toll Free Tel:* 800-242-7737 *E-mail:* consumercare@harpercollins.com *Web Site:* www.harpercollins.com/collections/books-by-clarion-books, pg 49

Inteli, Nancy, HarperCollins Children's Books, 195 Broadway, New York, NY 10007 *Tel:* 212-207-7000 *Web Site:* www.harpercollins.com/childrens, pg 85

Interdonati, Mary, HarperCollins Publishers LLC, 195 Broadway, New York, NY 10007 *Tel:* 212-207-7000 *Web Site:* www.harpercollins.com, pg 87

Inzetta, Jenn, Random House Children's Books, c/o Penguin Random House LLC, 1745 Broadway, New York, NY 10019 *Tel:* 212-782-9000 *Web Site:* www.rhcbooks.com, pg 170

Ioannidi, Vanessa, Simon & Schuster, 1230 Avenue of the Americas, New York, NY 10020 *Tel:* 212-698-7000 *Toll Free Tel:* 800-223-2348 (cust serv);

800-223-2336 (orders) *Toll Free Fax:* 800-943-9831 (orders) *Web Site:* simonandschusterpublishing.com/simonandschuster/, pg 188

Iossa, Lauren, American Society of Composers, Authors & Publishers (ASCAP), 250 W 57 St, New York, NY 10107 *Tel:* 212-621-6000 *Toll Free Tel:* 800-952-7227 (cust serv) *Fax:* 212-621-6595 *Web Site:* www.ascap.com, pg 496

Ippolito, Marc, Burns Entertainment, 3637 Westfield Lane, Glenview, IL 60026 *Tel:* 847-866-9400 *Web Site:* burnsent.com, pg 487

Iqbal, Sana, Penguin Random House Audio Publishing Group, 1745 Broadway, New York, NY 10019 *Toll Free Tel:* 800-793-2665 (cust serv) *E-mail:* audio@penguinrandomhouse.com; ecustomerservice@penguinrandomhouse.com *Web Site:* www.penguinrandomhouseaudio.com, pg 154

Iravani, Samira, Farrar, Straus & Giroux Books for Young Readers, 120 Broadway, New York, NY 10271 *Tel:* 212-741-6900 *Toll Free Tel:* 888-330-8477 (orders) *E-mail:* childrens.publicity@macmillanusa.com; childrensrights@macmillanusa.com *Web Site:* us.macmillan.com/mackids, pg 70

Irayani, Samira, Henry Holt and Company, LLC, 120 Broadway, 23rd fl, New York, NY 10271 *Tel:* 646-307-5151 *Toll Free Tel:* 888-330-8477 (orders) *Fax:* 646-307-5285 *Web Site:* www.henryholt.com, pg 94

Irayani, Samira, Roaring Brook Press, 120 Broadway, New York, NY 10271 *Tel:* 646-307-5151 *Web Site:* us.macmillan.com/publishers/roaring-brook-press, pg 176

Ireland, Pamela, BelleBooks, PO Box 300921, Memphis, TN 38130 *Tel:* 901-344-9024 *Fax:* 901-344-9068 *E-mail:* bellebooks@bellebooks.com *Web Site:* www.bellebooks.com, pg 27

Irish, Jenny, Arizona State University Creative Writing Program, 1102 S McAllister Ave, Rm 170, Tempe, AZ 85281 *Tel:* 480-965-3168 *Fax:* 480-965-3451 *Web Site:* www.asu.edu/clas/english/creativewriting, pg 561

Irvin, Margo, Stanford University Press, 425 Broadway St, Redwood City, CA 94063-3126 *Tel:* 650-723-9434 *Fax:* 650-725-3457 *E-mail:* info@www.sup.org; publicity@www.sup.org; sales@www.sup.org *Web Site:* www.sup.org, pg 197

Irvine, Dominique, Reference Publications Inc, 5419 Fawn Lake Rd, Shelbyville, MI 49344, pg 173

Irza-Leggatt, Anne, Candlewick Press, 99 Dover St, Somerville, MA 02144-2825 *Tel:* 617-661-3330 *Fax:* 617-661-0565 *E-mail:* bigbear@candlewick.com; salesinfo@candlewick.com *Web Site:* candlewick.com, pg 40

Isaacs, Suzanne Talbot, Ampersand Inc/Professional Publishing Services, 515 Madison St, New Orleans, LA 70116 *Tel:* 312-280-8905 *Fax:* 312-944-1582 *E-mail:* info@ampersandworks.com *Web Site:* www.ampersandworks.com, pg 13

Isayeff, Emily, Random House Publishing Group, 1745 Broadway, New York, NY 10019 *Toll Free Tel:* 800-200-3552 *Web Site:* www.randomhousebooks.com, pg 171

Isbell, Bradley, Iron Stream Media, 100 Missionary Ridge, Birmingham, AL 35242 *E-mail:* info@ironstreammedia.com *Web Site:* ironstreammedia.com, pg 104

Isbill, Bob, California Writers Club (CWC), PO Box 201, Danville, CA 94526 *E-mail:* membership@calwriters.org; advertising-promotion@calwriters.org *Web Site:* calwriters.org, pg 502

Isdahl, Danika, Sarabande Books Inc, 822 E Market St, Louisville, KY 40206 *Tel:* 502-458-4028 *Fax:* 502-458-4065 *E-mail:* info@sarabandebooks.org *Web Site:* www.sarabandebooks.org, pg 182

Isenberg, Scott, Business Expert Press, 222 E 46 St, Suite 203, New York, NY 10017-2906 *Tel:* 212-661-8810 *Fax:* 646-478-8107 *E-mail:* sales@businessexpertpress.com *Web Site:* www.businessexpertpress.com, pg 38

Ishaq, Nic, Doubleday, c/o Penguin Random House LLC, 1745 Broadway, New York, NY 10019 *Tel:* 212-751-2600 *Fax:* 212-940-7390 (dom rts); 212-572-2662 (foreign rts) *Web Site:* knopfdoubleday.com/imprint/doubleday/; knopfdoubleday.com, pg 61

Ishaq, Nic, Alfred A Knopf, c/o Penguin Random House LLC, 1745 Broadway, New York, NY 10019 *Tel:* 212-751-2600 *Fax:* 212-940-7390 (dom rts); 212-572-2662 (foreign rts) *Web Site:* knopfdoubleday.com/imprint/knopf/; knopfdoubleday.com, pg 110

Ishizuka, Tom, Writers House, 21 W 26 St, New York, NY 10010 *Tel:* 212-685-2400 *Web Site:* www.writershouse.com, pg 482

Ismael, Kim, Quirk Books, 215 Church St, Philadelphia, PA 19106 *Tel:* 215-627-3581 *Fax:* 215-627-5220 *E-mail:* general@quirkbooks.com *Web Site:* www.quirkbooks.com, pg 168

Isman, Sami, Sanford J Greenburger Associates Inc, 55 Fifth Ave, New York, NY 10003 *Tel:* 212-206-5600 *Web Site:* greenburger.com, pg 461

Israel, Yahdon, Simon & Schuster, 1230 Avenue of the Americas, New York, NY 10020 *Tel:* 212-698-7000 *Toll Free Tel:* 800-223-2348 (cust serv); 800-223-2336 (orders) *Toll Free Fax:* 800-943-9831 (orders) *Web Site:* simonandschusterpublishing.com/simonandschuster/, pg 188

Israeli, Henry, Saturnalia Books Poetry Prize & Editors Prize, 105 Woodside Rd, Ardmore, PA 19003 *Tel:* 267-278-9541 *Web Site:* saturnaliabooks.com, pg 659

Israelite, David M, National Music Publishers' Association (NMPA), 1900 "N" St NW, Suite 500, Washington, DC 20036 *Tel:* 202-393-6672 *E-mail:* members@nmpa.org *Web Site:* nmpa.org, pg 513

Itkin, Bridget Monro, Workman Publishing, 1290 Avenue of the Americas, New York, NY 10104 *Toll Free Tel:* 800-759-0190 *Fax:* 212-364-0950 *E-mail:* workman-inquiry@hbgusa.com *Web Site:* www.hachettebookgroup.com/imprint/workman-publishing-company/, pg 233

Itterly, Allison, WriteLife Publishing, Wilkinson Pass Lane, Waynesville, NC 28786 *E-mail:* writelife@boutiqueofqualitybooks.com *Web Site:* www.writelife.com; www.facebook.com/writelife, pg 234

Iura, Lesley, Berrett-Koehler Publishers Inc, 1333 Broadway, Suite 1000, Oakland, CA 94612 *Tel:* 510-817-2277 *Fax:* 510-817-2278 *E-mail:* bkpub@bkpub.com *Web Site:* www.bkconnection.com, pg 29

Iverson, Anne, Mountain Press Publishing Co, 1301 S Third W, Missoula, MT 59801 *Tel:* 406-728-1900 *Toll Free Tel:* 800-234-5308 *Fax:* 406-728-1635 *E-mail:* info@mtnpress.com *Web Site:* www.mountain-press.com, pg 135

Ivey, Elisabeth, MennoMedia, 841 Mount Clinton Pike, Harrisonburg, VA 22802 *Toll Free Tel:* 800-245-7894 (orders & cust serv US) *Toll Free Fax:* 877-271-0760 *E-mail:* info@mennomedia.org *Web Site:* www.mennomedia.org, pg 129

Iwashiro, Kristi, Harry N Abrams Inc, 195 Broadway, 9th fl, New York, NY 10007 *Tel:* 212-206-7715 *Toll Free Tel:* 800-345-1359 *Fax:* 212-645-8437 *E-mail:* abrams@abramsbooks.com; publicity@abramsbooks.com; sales@abramsbooks.com *Web Site:* www.abramsbooks.com, pg 3

Iwasutiak, Adria, Penguin Random House Canada, a Penguin Random House company, 320 Front St W, Suite 1400, Toronto, ON M5V 3B6, Canada *Tel:* 416-364-4449 *Toll Free Tel:* 888-523-9292 (cust serv) *E-mail:* canadaweb@penguinrandomhouse.com; customerservicescanada@penguinrandomhouse.com *Web Site:* www.penguinrandomhouse.ca, pg 416

Iyer, Akshaya, Bloomsbury Publishing Inc, 1385 Broadway, 5th fl, New York, NY 10018 *Tel:* 212-419-5300 *E-mail:* marketingusa@bloomsbury.com; adultpublicityusa@bloomsbury.com; askacademic@bloomsbury.com *Web Site:* www.bloomsbury.com, pg 31

Jabbari, Dr A Kamron, Mazda Publishers Inc, PO Box 2603, Costa Mesa, CA 92628 *Tel:* 714-751-5252 *Fax:* 714-751-4805 *E-mail:* mazdapub@aol.com *Web Site:* www.mazdapublishers.com, pg 127

Jabbour, Anthony, Dun & Bradstreet, 103 JFK Pkwy, Short Hills, NJ 07078 *Tel:* 973-921-5500 *Toll Free Tel:* 844-869-8244; 800-234-3867 (cust serv) *Web Site:* www.dnb.com, pg 62

Jacks, Nathaniel, InkWell Management, 521 Fifth Ave, Suite 2600, New York, NY 10175 *Tel:* 212-922-3500 *Fax:* 212-922-0535 *E-mail:* info@inkwellmanagement.com; submissions@inkwellmanagement.com; permissions@inkwellmanagement.com *Web Site:* inkwellmanagement.com, pg 463

Jackson, Amy, Sourcebooks LLC, 1935 Brookdale Rd, Suite 139, Naperville, IL 60563 *Tel:* 630-961-3900 *Toll Free Tel:* 800-432-7444 *Fax:* 630-961-2168 *E-mail:* info@sourcebooks.com *Web Site:* www.sourcebooks.com, pg 195

Jackson, Bobby L, Multicultural Publications Inc, 1939 Manchester Rd, Akron, OH 44314 *Tel:* 330-865-9578 *Fax:* 330-865-9578 *E-mail:* multiculturalpub@prodigy.net *Web Site:* www.multiculturalpub.net, pg 135

Jackson, Christopher, Penguin Random House LLC, 1745 Broadway, New York, NY 10019 *Tel:* 212-782-9000 *Toll Free Tel:* 800-726-0600 *Web Site:* www.penguinrandomhouse.com, pg 155

Jackson, Christopher, Random House Publishing Group, 1745 Broadway, New York, NY 10019 *Toll Free Tel:* 800-200-3552 *Web Site:* www.randomhousebooks.com, pg 170

Jackson, Devon, Atwood Gibson Writers' Trust Fiction Prize, 600-460 Richmond St W, Toronto, ON M5V 1Y1, Canada *Tel:* 416-504-8222 *Toll Free Tel:* 877-906-6548 *Fax:* 416-504-9090 *E-mail:* info@writerstrust.com *Web Site:* www.writerstrust.com, pg 575

Jackson, Devon, Balsillie Prize for Public Policy, 600-460 Richmond St W, Toronto, ON M5V 1Y1, Canada *Tel:* 416-504-8222 *Toll Free Tel:* 877-906-6548 *Fax:* 416-504-9090 *E-mail:* info@writerstrust.com *Web Site:* www.writerstrust.com, pg 577

Jackson, Devon, Latner Griffin Writers' Trust Poetry Prize, 600-460 Richmond St W, Toronto, ON M5V 1Y1, Canada *Tel:* 416-504-8222 *Toll Free Tel:* 877-906-6548 *Fax:* 416-504-9090 *E-mail:* info@writerstrust.com *Web Site:* www.writerstrust.com/awards/latner-writers-trust-poetry-prize, pg 622

Jackson, Devon, Matt Cohen Award: In Celebration of a Writing Life, 600-460 Richmond St W, Toronto, ON M5V 1Y1, Canada *Tel:* 416-504-8222 *Toll Free Tel:* 877-906-6548 *Fax:* 416-504-9090 *E-mail:* info@writerstrust.com *Web Site:* www.writerstrust.com, pg 630

Jackson, Devon, Dayne Ogilvie Prize for LGBTQ2S+ Emerging Writers, 600-460 Richmond St W, Toronto, ON M5V 1Y1, Canada *Tel:* 416-504-8222 *Toll Free Tel:* 877-906-6548 *Fax:* 416-504-9090 *E-mail:* info@writerstrust.com *Web Site:* www.writerstrust.com, pg 643

Jackson, Devon, RBC Bronwen Wallace Award for Emerging Writers, 600-460 Richmond St W, Toronto, ON M5V 1Y1, Canada *Tel:* 416-504-8222 *Toll Free Tel:* 877-906-6548 *Fax:* 416-504-9090 *E-mail:* info@writerstrust.com *Web Site:* www.writerstrust.com, pg 655

Jackson, Devon, Shaughnessy Cohen Prize for Political Writing, 600-460 Richmond St W, Toronto, ON M5V 1Y1, Canada *Tel:* 416-504-8222 *Toll Free Tel:* 877-906-6548 *Fax:* 416-504-9090 *E-mail:* info@writerstrust.com *Web Site:* www.writerstrust.com, pg 661

Jackson, Devon, Vicky Metcalf Award for Literature for Young People, 600-460 Richmond St W, Toronto, ON M5V 1Y1, Canada *Tel:* 416-504-8222 *Toll Free Tel:* 877-906-6548 *Fax:* 416-504-9090 *E-mail:* info@writerstrust.com *Web Site:* www.writerstrust.com, pg 672

Jackson, Devon, Hilary Weston Writers' Trust Prize for Nonfiction, 600-460 Richmond St W, Toronto, ON M5V 1Y1, Canada *Tel:* 416-504-8222 *Toll Free Tel:* 877-906-6548 *Fax:* 416-504-9090 *E-mail:* info@writerstrust.com *Web Site:* www.writerstrust.com, pg 674

Jackson, Devon, Writers' Trust Engel Findley Award, 600-460 Richmond St W, Toronto, ON M5V 1Y1, Canada *Tel:* 416-504-8222 *Toll Free Tel:* 877-906-6548 *Fax:* 416-504-9090 *E-mail:* info@writerstrust.com *Web Site:* www.writerstrust.com, pg 678

Jackson, Devon, Writers' Trust McClelland & Stewart Journey Prize, 600-460 Richmond St W, Toronto, ON M5V 1Y1, Canada *Tel:* 416-504-8222 *Toll Free Tel:* 877-906-6548 *Fax:* 416-504-9090 *E-mail:* info@writerstrust.com *Web Site:* www.writerstrust.com, pg 678

Jackson, Eleanor, Dunow, Carlson & Lerner Literary Agency Inc, 27 W 20 St, Suite 1107, New York, NY 10011 *Tel:* 212-645-7606 *E-mail:* mail@dclagency.com *Web Site:* www.dclagency.com, pg 457

Jackson, Jared, Poets & Writers Inc, 90 Broad St, Suite 2100, New York, NY 10004 *Tel:* 212-226-3586 *Fax:* 212-226-3963 *E-mail:* admin@pw.org *Web Site:* www.pw.org, pg 517

Jackson, Jennifer, Doubleday, c/o Penguin Random House LLC, 1745 Broadway, New York, NY 10019 *Tel:* 212-751-2600 *Fax:* 212-940-7390 (dom rts); 212-572-2662 (foreign rts) *Web Site:* knopfdoubleday.com/imprint/doubleday/; knopfdoubleday.com, pg 61

Jackson, Jennifer, Alfred A Knopf, c/o Penguin Random House LLC, 1745 Broadway, New York, NY 10019 *Tel:* 212-751-2600 *Fax:* 212-940-7390 (dom rts); 212-572-2662 (foreign rts) *Web Site:* knopfdoubleday.com/imprint/knopf/; knopfdoubleday.com, pg 110

Jackson, Jennifer, Donald Maass Literary Agency, 1000 Dean St, Suite 331, Brooklyn, NY 11238 *Tel:* 212-727-8383 *E-mail:* info@maassagency.com *Web Site:* www.maassagency.com, pg 468

Jackson, Joe, Princeton University Press, 41 William St, Princeton, NJ 08540-5237 *Tel:* 609-258-4900 *Fax:* 609-258-6305 *E-mail:* info@press.princeton.edu *Web Site:* press.princeton.edu, pg 164

Jackson, LaTonya, Alliance for Women in Media (AWM), 2365 Harrodsburg Rd, A325, Lexington, KY 40504 *Tel:* 202-750-3664 *Fax:* 202-750-3664 *E-mail:* info@allwomeninmedia.org *Web Site:* allwomeninmedia.org, pg 494

Jackson, LaTonya, The Gracies®, 2365 Harrodsburg Rd, Suite A325, Lexington, KY 40504 *Tel:* 202-750-3664 *Fax:* 202-750-3664 *E-mail:* info@allwomeninmedia.org *Web Site:* allwomeninmedia.org, pg 608

Jackson, Leah, Penguin Random House Audio Publishing Group, 1745 Broadway, New York, NY 10019 *Toll Free Tel:* 800-793-2665 (cust serv) *E-mail:* audio@penguinrandomhouse.com; ecustomerservice@penguinrandomhouse.com *Web Site:* www.penguinrandomhouseaudio.com, pg 154

Jackson, Lindsey, Guild of Book Workers, 521 Fifth Ave, New York, NY 10175 *E-mail:* communications@guildofbookworkers.org; membership@guildofbookworkers.org *Web Site:* www.guildofbookworkers.org, pg 507

Jackson, Lisa, Miles Conrad Award, 3600 Clipper Mill Rd, Suite 302, Baltimore, MD 21211-1948 *Tel:* 301-654-2512 *Fax:* 410-685-5278 *E-mail:* nisohq@niso.org *Web Site:* www.niso.org, pg 591

Jackson, Lisa, National Information Standards Organization (NISO), 3600 Clipper Mill Rd, Suite 302, Baltimore, MD 21211-1948 *Tel:* 301-654-2512 *Fax:* 410-685-5278 *E-mail:* nisohq@niso.org *Web Site:* www.niso.org, pg 138, 513

Jackson, Melanie, Melanie Jackson Agency LLC, 41 W 72 St, Suite 3F, New York, NY 10023 *Web Site:* www.mjalit.com, pg 464

Jackson, Ose, Stegner Fellowship, Stanford University, Dept of English, Stanford, CA 94305-2087 *Tel:* 650-723-0011 *E-mail:* stegnerfellowship@stanford.edu *Web Site:* creativewriting.stanford.edu, pg 666

Jackson, Regina, Warner Press, 2902 Enterprise Dr, Anderson, IN 46013 *Tel:* 765-644-7721 *Toll Free Tel:* 800-741-7721 (orders) *Fax:* 765-640-8005 *E-mail:* wporders@warnerpress.org *Web Site:* www.warnerpress.org, pg 226

Jackson, Sarah, Penguin Random House Canada, a Penguin Random House company, 320 Front St W, Suite 1400, Toronto, ON M5V 3B6, Canada *Tel:* 416-364-4449 *Toll Free Tel:* 888-523-9292 (cust serv) *E-mail:* canadaweb@penguinrandomhouse.com; customerservicescanada@penguinrandomhouse.com *Web Site:* www.penguinrandomhouse.ca, pg 416

Jackson, Tilly, Artist-in-Residence Program, 225 King St, Suite 201, Fredericton, NB E3B 1E1, Canada *Tel:* 506-444-4444 *Toll Free Tel:* 866-460-ARTS (460-2787) *Fax:* 506-444-5543 *E-mail:* prog@artsnb.ca *Web Site:* www.artsnb.ca, pg 574

Jackson, Tilly, Arts Scholarships, 225 King St, Suite 201, Fredericton, NB E3B 1E1, Canada *Tel:* 506-444-4444 *Toll Free Tel:* 866-460-ARTS (460-2787) *Fax:* 506-444-5543 *E-mail:* prog@artsnb.ca *Web Site:* www.artsnb.ca, pg 574

Jackson, Tilly, Career Development Program, 225 King St, Suite 201, Fredericton, NB E3B 1E1, Canada *Tel:* 506-444-4444 *Toll Free Tel:* 866-460-ARTS (460-2787) *Fax:* 506-444-5543 *E-mail:* prog@artsnb.ca *Web Site:* www.artsnb.ca, pg 586

Jackson, Tilly, Creation Grant Program, 225 King St, Suite 201, Fredericton, NB E3B 1E1, Canada *Tel:* 506-444-4444 *Toll Free Tel:* 866-460-ARTS (460-2787) *Fax:* 506-444-5543 *E-mail:* prog@artsnb.ca *Web Site:* www.artsnb.ca, pg 593

Jackson, Tilly, Creative Residencies-Quebec, 225 King St, Suite 201, Fredericton, NB E3B 1E1, Canada *Tel:* 506-444-4444 *Toll Free Tel:* 866-460-ARTS (460-2787) *Fax:* 506-444-5543 *E-mail:* prog@artsnb.ca *Web Site:* www.artsnb.ca, pg 593

Jackson, Tilly, Documentation Grant Program, 225 King St, Suite 201, Fredericton, NB E3B 1E1, Canada *Tel:* 506-444-4444 *Toll Free Tel:* 866-460-ARTS (460-2787) *Fax:* 506-444-5543 *E-mail:* prog@artsnb.ca *Web Site:* www.artsnb.ca, pg 596

Jackson, Tilly, The Lieutenant-Governor's Awards for High Achievement in the Arts, 225 King St, Suite 201, Fredericton, NB E3B 1E1, Canada *Tel:* 506-444-4444 *Toll Free Tel:* 866-460-ARTS (460-2787) *Fax:* 506-444-5543 *E-mail:* prog@artsnb.ca *Web Site:* www.artsnb.ca, pg 624

Jackson, Troix, Tor Publishing Group, 120 Broadway, New York, NY 10271 *Toll Free Tel:* 800-455-0340 (Macmillan) *E-mail:* torpublicity@tor.com; forgepublicity@forgebooks.com *Web Site:* us.macmillan.com/torpublishinggroup, pg 208

Jackson, William, Workman Publishing, 1290 Avenue of the Americas, New York, NY 10104 *Toll Free Tel:* 800-759-0190 *Fax:* 212-364-0950 *E-mail:* workman-inquiry@hbgusa.com *Web Site:* www.hachettebookgroup.com/imprint/workman-publishing-company/, pg 232

Jacob, Mary Ann, Texas A&M University Press, John H Lindsey Bldg, Lewis St, 4354 TAMU, College Station, TX 77843-4354 *Tel:* 979-845-1436 *Toll Free Tel:* 800-826-8911 (orders) *Fax:* 979-847-8752 *Toll Free Fax:* 888-617-2421 (orders) *E-mail:* bookorders@tamu.edu *Web Site:* www.tamupress.com, pg 205

Jacob, Robert, Florida Authors and Publishers Association Inc (FAPA), 6237 Presidential Ct, Suite 140, Fort Myers, FL 33919 *E-mail:* admin@myfapa.org *Web Site:* myfapa.org, pg 506

Jacobs, Andrea, The Globe Pequot Press, 64 S Main St, Essex, CT 06426 *Tel:* 203-458-4500 *Toll Free Tel:* 800-243-0495 (orders only); 888-249-7586 (cust serv) *Fax:* 203-458-4601 *Toll Free Fax:* 800-820-2329 (orders & cust serv) *E-mail:* editorial@globepequot.com; info@rowman.com; orders@rowman.com *Web Site:* www.rowman.com, pg 79

Jacobs, Ben, Bloom's Literary Criticism, 132 W 31 St, 16th fl, New York, NY 10001 *Toll Free Tel:* 800-322-8755 *Toll Free Fax:* 800-678-3633 *E-mail:* custserv@infobase.com *Web Site:* www.infobasepublishing.com; www.infobase.com (online resources), pg 31

Jacobs, Ben, Chelsea House, 132 W 31 St, 16th fl, New York, NY 10001 *Toll Free Tel:* 800-322-8755 *Toll Free Fax:* 800-678-3633 *E-mail:* custserv@infobase.com; info@infobase.com *Web Site:* www.infobasepublishing.com; www.infobase.com (online resources), pg 46

Jacobs, Donald, Georgetown University Press, 3520 Prospect St NW, Suite 140, Washington, DC 20007 *Tel:* 202-687-5889 (busn) *Fax:* 202-687-6340 (edit) *E-mail:* gupress@georgetown.edu *Web Site:* press.georgetown.edu, pg 77

Jacobs, Farrin, Random House Children's Books, c/o Penguin Random House LLC, 1745 Broadway, New York, NY 10019 *Tel:* 212-782-9000 *Web Site:* www.rhcbooks.com, pg 170

Jacobs, Joanna, University of Alabama Press, 200 Hackberry Lane, 2nd fl, Tuscaloosa, AL 35487 *Tel:* 205-348-5180 *Fax:* 205-348-9201 *Web Site:* www.uapress.ua.edu, pg 214

Jacobs, Katherine, Roaring Brook Press, 120 Broadway, New York, NY 10271 *Tel:* 646-307-5151 *Web Site:* us.macmillan.com/publishers/roaring-brook-press, pg 176

Jacobs, Laurence, Craftsman Book Co, 6058 Corte Del Cedro, Carlsbad, CA 92011 *Tel:* 760-438-7828 *Toll Free Tel:* 800-829-8123 *Fax:* 760-438-0398 *Web Site:* www.craftsman-book.com, pg 54

Jacobs, Michael, Harry N Abrams Inc, 195 Broadway, 9th fl, New York, NY 10007 *Tel:* 212-206-7715 *Toll Free Tel:* 800-345-1359 *Fax:* 212-645-8437 *E-mail:* abrams@abramsbooks.com; publicity@abramsbooks.com; sales@abramsbooks.com *Web Site:* www.abramsbooks.com, pg 2

Jacobs, Michael, Stewart, Tabori & Chang, 195 Broadway, 9th fl, New York, NY 10007 *Tel:* 212-206-7715 *Fax:* 212-519-1210 *E-mail:* abrams@abramsbooks.com *Web Site:* www.abramsbooks.com/imprints/stc, pg 198

Jacobs, Robert H, Univelt Inc, 740 Metcalf St, No 13, Escondido, CA 92025 *Tel:* 760-746-4005 *Fax:* 760-746-3139 *E-mail:* sales@univelt.com *Web Site:* www.univelt.com; www.astronautical.org, pg 213

Jacobson, Don, Thomas Nelson, 501 Nelson Place, Nashville, TN 37214 *Tel:* 615-889-9000 *Toll Free Tel:* 800-251-4000 *Web Site:* www.thomasnelson.com, pg 206

Jacobson, John, Harlequin Enterprises Ltd, 195 Broadway, 24th fl, New York, NY 10007 *Tel:* 212-207-7000 *Toll Free Tel:* 888-432-4879; 800-370-5838 (ebooks) *E-mail:* customerservice@harlequin.com *Web Site:* www.harlequin.com/shop/index.html; corporate.harlequin.com, pg 85

Jacoby, Judy, Doubleday, c/o Penguin Random House LLC, 1745 Broadway, New York, NY 10019 *Tel:* 212-751-2600 *Fax:* 212-940-7390 (dom rts); 212-572-2662 (foreign rts) *Web Site:* knopfdoubleday.com/imprint/doubleday/; knopfdoubleday.com, pg 61

Jaconette, Anne, Doubleday, c/o Penguin Random House LLC, 1745 Broadway, New York, NY 10019 *Tel:* 212-751-2600 *Fax:* 212-940-7390 (dom rts); 212-572-2662 (foreign rts) *Web Site:* knopfdoubleday.com/imprint/doubleday/; knopfdoubleday.com, pg 61

Jacques, Kelly Chrisman, University Press of Kansas, 2502 Westbrooke Circle, Lawrence, KS 66045-4444 *Tel:* 785-864-4154 *Fax:* 785-864-4586 *E-mail:* upress@ku.edu *Web Site:* www.kansaspress.ku.edu, pg 221

Jaeger, Christine, Macmillan, 120 Broadway, 22nd fl, New York, NY 10271 *E-mail:* press.inquiries@macmillan.com *Web Site:* us.macmillan.com, pg 122

Jaffe, Sarah, Penguin Random House Audio Publishing Group, 1745 Broadway, New York, NY 10019 *Toll Free Tel:* 800-793-2665 (cust serv) *E-mail:* audio@penguinrandomhouse.com; ecustomerservice@penguinrandomhouse.com *Web Site:* www.penguinrandomhouseaudio.com, pg 154

Jaffee, Marc, Alfred A Knopf, c/o Penguin Random House LLC, 1745 Broadway, New York, NY 10019 *Tel:* 212-751-2600 *Fax:* 212-940-7390 (dom rts); 212-572-2662 (foreign rts) *Web Site:* knopfdoubleday.com/imprint/knopf/; knopfdoubleday.com, pg 110

Jaffee, Pamela, Sourcebooks LLC, 1935 Brookdale Rd, Suite 139, Naperville, IL 60563 *Tel:* 630-961-3900 *Toll Free Tel:* 800-432-7444 *Fax:* 630-961-2168 *E-mail:* info@sourcebooks.com *Web Site:* www.sourcebooks.com, pg 194

Jaffery, Zareen, Kokila, c/o Penguin Random House LLC, 1745 Broadway, New York, NY 10019 *Tel:* 212-782-9000 *Web Site:* www.penguin.com/kokila-books-overview/, pg 111

Jagai, Kat, Alloy Entertainment LLC, 30 Hudson Yards, 22nd fl, New York, NY 10001, pg 7

Jager, Carson, BoardSource, 750 Ninth St NW, Suite 520, Washington, DC 20001-4793 *Tel:* 202-349-2500 *E-mail:* members@boardsource.org; mediarelations@boardsource.org *Web Site:* www.boardsource.org, pg 33

Jaggers, Tara, Sourcebooks LLC, 1935 Brookdale Rd, Suite 139, Naperville, IL 60563 *Tel:* 630-961-3900 *Toll Free Tel:* 800-432-7444 *Fax:* 630-961-2168 *E-mail:* info@sourcebooks.com *Web Site:* www.sourcebooks.com, pg 195

Jahns, Randy, Crossway, 1300 Crescent St, Wheaton, IL 60187 *Tel:* 630-682-4300 *Toll Free Tel:* 800-635-7993 (orders); 800-543-1659 (cust serv) *Fax:* 630-682-4785 *E-mail:* info@crossway.org *Web Site:* www.crossway.org, pg 56

Jain, Amanda, BookEnds Literary Agency, 136 Long Hill Rd, Gillette, NJ 07933 *Web Site:* www.bookendsliterary.com, pg 451

Jain, Aranya, GP Putnam's Sons, c/o Penguin Random House LLC, 1745 Broadway, New York, NY 10019 *Tel:* 212-782-9000 *Web Site:* www.penguin.com/putnam/, pg 167

Jain, Mukesh, Jain Publishing Co, 164 Concho Dr, Fremont, CA 94539 *Tel:* 510-659-8272 *E-mail:* mail@jainpub.com *Web Site:* www.jainpub.com, pg 105

Jain, Prachi, Women Who Write Inc, PO Box 652, Madison, NJ 07940-0652 *Web Site:* www.womenwhowrite.org, pg 522

Jaksha, Joseph, Hazelden Publishing, 15251 Pleasant Valley Rd, Center City, MN 55012-0011 *Tel:* 651-213-4200 *Toll Free Tel:* 800-257-7810; 866-328-9000 *Fax:* 651-213-4793 *Web Site:* www.hazelden.org, pg 89

Jamal, Zakiya, Atria Books, 1230 Avenue of the Americas, New York, NY 10020 *Tel:* 212-698-7000 *Fax:* 212-698-7007 *Web Site:* www.simonandschuster.com, pg 21

James, Carly, Berkley, c/o Penguin Random House LLC, 1745 Broadway, 19th fl, New York, NY 10019 *Tel:* 212-366-2000 *Web Site:* www.penguin.com/publishers/berkley/; www.penguin.com/ace-overview/, pg 28

James, Mark, Perfection Learning®, 1000 N Second Ave, Logan, IA 51546-1061 *Tel:* 712-644-2831 *Toll Free Tel:* 800-831-4190 *Toll Free Fax:* 800-543-2745 *E-mail:* orders@perfectionlearning.com *Web Site:* www.perfectionlearning.com, pg 158

James, Nicole, Quarto Publishing Group USA Inc, 100 Cummings Ctr, Suite 265D, Beverly, MA 01915 *Tel:* 978-282-9590 *Toll Free Tel:* 800-328-0590 (sales) *Fax:* 978-283-2742 *E-mail:* sales@quartous.com *Web Site:* www.quartoknows.com, pg 168

James, Tessa, HarperCollins Publishers LLC, 195 Broadway, New York, NY 10007 *Tel:* 212-207-7000 *Web Site:* www.harpercollins.com, pg 87

James, Thea, Penguin Random House LLC, 1745 Broadway, New York, NY 10019 *Tel:* 212-782-9000 *Toll Free Tel:* 800-726-0600 *Web Site:* www.penguinrandomhouse.com, pg 155

James, Tina, Love Inspired Books, 233 Broadway, Suite 1001, New York, NY 10279 *Tel:* 212-553-4200 *Toll Free Tel:* 888-432-4879 *Fax:* 212-227-8969 *E-mail:* customerservice@harlequin.ca *Web Site:* www.harlequin.com, pg 120

Jamison, Joylanda, Embolden Literary, PO Box 953607, Lake Mary, FL 32795-3607 *E-mail:* info@emboldenmediagroup.com; submissions@emboldenmediagroup.com *Web Site:* emboldenmediagroup.com/literary-representation, pg 458

Janakiram, Emily, The New Press, 120 Wall St, 31st fl, New York, NY 10005 *Tel:* 212-629-8802 *Fax:* 212-629-8617 *E-mail:* newpress@thenewpress.com *Web Site:* thenewpress.com, pg 140

Janas, Kayla, St Martin's Press, LLC, 120 Broadway, New York, NY 10271 *E-mail:* publicity@stmartins.com; trademarketing@stmartins.com; foreignrights@stmartins.com *Web Site:* us.macmillan.com/smp, pg 181

Janecek, C E, Nelligan Prize for Short Fiction, Colorado State University, Dept of English, Center for Literary Publishing, 9105 Campus Delivery, Fort Collins, CO 80523-9105 *Tel:* 970-491-5449 *E-mail:* creview@colostate.edu *Web Site:* coloradoreview.colostate.edu/nelligan-prize, pg 639

Janecek, Kristin, Macmillan, 120 Broadway, 22nd fl, New York, NY 10271 *E-mail:* press.inquiries@macmillan.com *Web Site:* us.macmillan.com, pg 122

Janecke, Roger, Visible Ink Press®, 43311 Joy Rd, Suite 414, Canton, MI 48187-2075 *Tel:* 734-667-3211 *Fax:* 734-667-4311 *E-mail:* info@visibleinkpress.com *Web Site:* www.visibleinkpress.com, pg 225

Janeri, Bill, The American Ceramic Society, 550 Polaris Pkwy, Suite 510, Westerville, OH 43082 *Tel:* 240-646-7054 *Toll Free Tel:* 866-721-3322 *Fax:* 240-396-5637 *E-mail:* customerservice@ceramics.org *Web Site:* ceramics.org, pg 9

Janeway, Brant, St Martin's Press, LLC, 120 Broadway, New York, NY 10271 *E-mail:* publicity@stmartins.com; trademarketing@stmartins.com; foreignrights@stmartins.com *Web Site:* us.macmillan.com/smp, pg 180

Janice, Allison, Hay House LLC, PO Box 5100, Carlsbad, CA 92018-5100 *Tel:* 760-431-7695 (ext 1, intl) *Toll Free Tel:* 800-654-5126 (ext 1, US) *Toll Free Fax:* 800-650-5115 *Web Site:* www.hayhouse.com, pg 89

Janik, Daniel S, Savant Books & Publications LLC, 2630 Kapiolani Blvd, Suite 1601, Honolulu, HI 96826 *Tel:* 808-941-3927 (9AM-noon HST) *E-mail:* savantbooks@gmail.com; savantdistribution@gmail.com *Web Site:* www.savantbooksandpublications.com; www.savantdistribution.com, pg 182

Jankauskas, Monica, Highlights for Children Inc, 815 Church St, Honesdale, PA 18431 *Tel:* 570-253-1164 *Toll Free Tel:* 800-490-5111 *Fax:* 570-253-0179 *E-mail:* salesandmarketing@highlightspress.com *Web Site:* www.highlightspress.com; www.highlights.com; www.facebook.com/HighlightsforChildren, pg 92

Jankiewicz, Adam, Casemate I publishers, 1950 Lawrence Rd, Havertown, PA 19083 *Tel:* 610-853-9131 *Fax:* 610-853-9146 *E-mail:* casemate@casematepublishers.com *Web Site:* www.casematepublishers.com, pg 42

Janklow, Luke, Janklow & Nesbit Associates, 285 Madison Ave, 21st fl, New York, NY 10017 *Tel:* 212-421-1700 *Fax:* 212-355-1403 *E-mail:* info@janklow.com; submissions@janklow.com; filmtvrights@janklow.com *Web Site:* www.janklowandnesbit.com, pg 464

Jankowski, Jenna, Sourcebooks LLC, 1935 Brookdale Rd, Suite 139, Naperville, IL 60563 *Tel:* 630-961-3900 *Toll Free Tel:* 800-432-7444 *Fax:* 630-961-2168 *E-mail:* info@sourcebooks.com *Web Site:* www.sourcebooks.com, pg 194

Jannuzzi, Christopher J, The Electrochemical Society (ECS), 65 S Main St, Bldg D, Pennington, NJ 08534-2839 *Tel:* 609-737-1902 *Fax:* 609-737-0629 *E-mail:* publications@electrochem.org; customerservice@electrochem.org; ecs@ioppublishing.org *Web Site:* www.electrochem.org, pg 65

Janowski, Elizabeth Pham, Viking Penguin, c/o Penguin Random House LLC, 1745 Broadway, New York, NY 10019 *Tel:* 212-782-9000 *Web Site:* www.penguin.com/overview-vikingbooks/; www.penguin.com/pamela-dorman-books-overview/; www.penguin.com/penguin-classics-overview/; www.penguin.com/penguin-life-overview/, pg 225

Jansen, Amy, J J Keller & Associates, Inc®, 3003 Breezewood Lane, Neenah, WI 54957 *Tel:* 920-722-2848 *Toll Free Tel:* 877-564-2333 *Toll Free Fax:* 800-727-7516 *E-mail:* customerservice@jjkeller.com; sales@jjkeller.com *Web Site:* www.jjkeller.com, pg 108

Jansen, Gary, Loyola Press, 8770 W Bryn Mawr Ave, Suite 1125, Chicago, IL 60631 *Tel:* 773-281-1818 *Toll Free Tel:* 800-621-1008 *Fax:* 773-281-0555 (cust serv); 773-281-4129 (edit) *E-mail:* customerservice@loyolapress.com *Web Site:* www.loyolapress.com, pg 121

Janssen, Karl, University Press of Kansas, 2502 Westbrooke Circle, Lawrence, KS 66045-4444 *Tel:* 785-864-4154 *Fax:* 785-864-4586 *E-mail:* upress@ku.edu *Web Site:* www.kansaspress.ku.edu, pg 221

Janssen, Sarah, World Almanac®, 307 W 36 St, 11 fl, New York, NY 10018 *Tel:* 212-643-6816 *Fax:* 212-643-6819 *E-mail:* info@skyhorsepublishing.com *Web Site:* skyhorsepublishing.com, pg 233

Jantzen, Rod, Bethany House Publishers, 11400 Hampshire Ave S, Bloomington, MN 55438 *Tel:* 952-829-2500 *Toll Free Tel:* 800-877-2665 (orders) *Fax:* 952-829-2568 *Toll Free Fax:* 800-398-3111 (orders) *Web Site:* www.bethanyhouse.com; www.bakerpublishinggroup.com, pg 29

Janus, Rev Mark-David PhD, Paulist Press, 997 Macarthur Blvd, Mahwah, NJ 07430-9990 *Tel:* 201-825-7300 *Toll Free Tel:* 800-218-1903 *Fax:* 201-825-6921 *E-mail:* info@paulistpress.com; publicity@paulistpress.com *Web Site:* www.paulistpress.com, pg 152

Jao, Jonathan, Simon & Schuster, 1230 Avenue of the Americas, New York, NY 10020 *Tel:* 212-698-7000 *Toll Free Tel:* 800-223-2348 (cust serv); 800-223-2336 (orders) *Toll Free Fax:* 800-943-9831 (orders) *Web Site:* simonandschusterpublishing.com/simonandschuster/, pg 188

Japikse, Carl, Ariel Press, 2317 Quail Cove Dr, Jasper, GA 30143 *Tel:* 770-894-4226 *E-mail:* lig201@lightariel.com *Web Site:* www.lightariel.com, pg 16

Jaque, Cathy, The Karpfinger Agency, 357 W 20 St, New York, NY 10011-3379 *Tel:* 212-691-2690 *Fax:* 212-691-7129 *E-mail:* info@karpfinger.com (no queries or submissions) *Web Site:* www.karpfinger.com, pg 465

Jarosh, Jon, Midwest Travel Journalists Association Inc (MTJA), PO Box 185, Jessup, IA 50648 *Tel:* 319-529-1109 *E-mail:* admin@mtja.us *Web Site:* www.mtja.us, pg 511

Jarquin, Horacio, IBFD North America Inc (International Bureau of Fiscal Documentation), 8300 Boone Blvd, Suite 380, Vienna, VA 22182 *Tel:* 703-442-7757 *E-mail:* info@ibfd.org *Web Site:* www.ibfd.org, pg 98

Jarrad, Mary Beth, New York University Press, 838 Broadway, 3rd fl, New York, NY 10003-4812 *Tel:* 212-998-2575 (edit) *Toll Free Tel:* 800-996-6987 (orders) *Fax:* 212-995-4798 (orders) *E-mail:* nyupressinfo@nyu.edu (cust care) *Web Site:* www.nyupress.org, pg 141

Jarrell, Cade, Baylor University Press, Baylor University, One Bear Place, Waco, TX 76798-7363 *Tel:* 254-710-3164 *E-mail:* bup_marketing@baylor.edu *Web Site:* www.baylorpress.com, pg 25

Jarrett, Emily, Random House Publishing Group, 1745 Broadway, New York, NY 10019 *Toll Free Tel:* 800-200-3552 *Web Site:* www.randomhousebooks.com, pg 171

Jarvie, Craig, Health Communications Inc, 301 Crawford Blvd, Suite 200, Boca Raton, FL 33432 *Tel:* 561-453-0696 *Toll Free Tel:* 800-441-5569 (cust serv & orders) *Fax:* 561-453-1009 *Toll Free Fax:* 800-943-9831 (orders) *E-mail:* editorial@hcibooks.com *Web Site:* hcibooks.com, pg 90

Jarvis-Miller, Donna, American Public Human Services Association (APHSA), 1300 17 St N, Suite 340, Arlington, VA 22209-3801 *Tel:* 202-682-0100 *Fax:* 202-289-6555 *E-mail:* memberservice@aphsa.org *Web Site:* www.aphsa.org, pg 496

Jarzab, Anna, Simon & Schuster Children's Publishing, 1230 Avenue of the Americas, New York, NY 10020 *Tel:* 212-698-7000 *Web Site:* www.simonandschuster.com/kids; www.simonandschuster.com/teen; simonandschuster.net; simonandschuster.biz, pg 189

Jasmine, Michelle, Random House Publishing Group, 1745 Broadway, New York, NY 10019 *Toll Free Tel:* 800-200-3552 *Web Site:* www.randomhousebooks.com, pg 171

Jason, Beatrice, HarperCollins Publishers LLC, 195 Broadway, New York, NY 10007 *Tel:* 212-207-7000 *Web Site:* www.harpercollins.com, pg 86

Jason, Beatrice, St Martin's Press, LLC, 120 Broadway, New York, NY 10271 *E-mail:* publicity@stmartins.com; trademarketing@stmartins.com; foreignrights@stmartins.com *Web Site:* us.macmillan.com/smp, pg 181

Jatoba, Marcelo, UCLA Latin American Center Publications, UCLA Latin American Institute, 10343 Bunche Hall, Los Angeles, CA 90095 *Tel:* 310-825-4571 *Fax:* 310-206-6859 *E-mail:* latinamctr@international.ucla.edu *Web Site:* www.international.ucla.edu/lai, pg 212

Jattan, Darshanie, ACM Books, 1601 Broadway, 10th fl, New York, NY 10019-7434 *Tel:* 212-869-7440 *E-mail:* acmbooks-info@acm.org *Web Site:* www.acm.org; books.acm.org, pg 4

Javier, Crisandry, Random House Children's Books, c/o Penguin Random House LLC, 1745 Broadway, New York, NY 10019 *Tel:* 212-782-9000 *Web Site:* www.rhcbooks.com, pg 170

Javit, Felice, Simon & Schuster, LLC, 1230 Avenue of the Americas, New York, NY 10020 *Tel:* 212-698-7000 *Toll Free Tel:* 800-223-2336 (orders) *Fax:* 212-698-7007 *Toll Free Fax:* 800-943-9831 (orders) *E-mail:* firstname.lastname@simonandschuster.com; purchaseorders@simonandschuster.com (orders) *Web Site:* www.simonandschuster.com, pg 189

Javsicas, Aaron, Temple University Press, 1852 N Tenth St, Philadelphia, PA 19122-6099 *Tel:* 215-926-2140 *Toll Free Tel:* 800-621-2736 *Fax:* 215-926-2141 *E-mail:* tempress@temple.edu *Web Site:* tupress.temple.edu, pg 204

Jaw, Farina, St Martin's Press, LLC, 120 Broadway, New York, NY 10271 *E-mail:* publicity@stmartins.com; trademarketing@stmartins.com; foreignrights@stmartins.com *Web Site:* us.macmillan.com/smp, pg 181

Jay, Alyssia, South Carolina Bar, 1501 Park St, Columbia, SC 29201 *Tel:* 803-799-6653 *Toll Free Tel:* 800-768-7787 *E-mail:* scbar-info@scbar.org *Web Site:* www.scbar.org, pg 195

Jay, Kate, Mountaineers Books, 1001 SW Klickitat Way, Suite 201, Seattle, WA 98134 *Tel:* 206-223-6303 *Fax:* 206-223-6306 *E-mail:* mbooks@mountaineersbooks.org; customerservice@mountaineersbooks.org *Web Site:* www.mountaineers.org/books, pg 135

Jayo, James, Countryman Press, c/o W W Norton & Company Inc, 500 Fifth Ave, New York, NY 10110 *Tel:* 212-354-5500 *Fax:* 212-869-0856 *E-mail:* countrymanpress@wwnorton.com *Web Site:* wwnorton.com/countryman-press, pg 54

Jean-Francois, Reginald, Penguin Random House Speakers Bureau, a Penguin Random House company, 1745 Broadway, Mail Drop 13-1, New York, NY 10019 *Tel:* 212-572-2013 *E-mail:* speakers@penguinrandomhouse.com *Web Site:* www.prhspeakers.com, pg 487

Jeffrey, Douglas A, Hillsdale College Press, 33 E College St, Hillsdale, MI 49242 *Tel:* 517-437-7341 *Toll Free Tel:* 800-437-2268 *Fax:* 517-607-2658 *E-mail:* pr@hillsdale.edu *Web Site:* www.hillsdale.edu, pg 92

Jeffrey, Robyn, Canadian Museum of History (Musee canadien de l'histoire), 100 Laurier St, Gatineau, QC K1A 0M8, Canada *Tel:* 819-776-7000 *Toll Free Tel:* 800-555-5621 (North American orders only) *Fax:* 819-776-7187 *Web Site:* www.historymuseum.ca, pg 398

Jeffries, Christina, Random House Children's Books, c/o Penguin Random House LLC, 1745 Broadway, New York, NY 10019 *Tel:* 212-782-9000 *Web Site:* www.rhcbooks.com, pg 169

Jeglinski, Melissa, The Knight Agency Inc, 232 W Washington St, Madison, GA 30650 *E-mail:* admin@knightagency.net *Web Site:* www.knightagency.net, pg 466

Jelen, Carole, Waterside Productions Inc, 2055 Oxford Ave, Cardiff, CA 92007 *Tel:* 760-632-9190 *Fax:* 760-632-9295 *E-mail:* admin@waterside.com *Web Site:* www.waterside.com, pg 481

Jelinek, Ginger, Mari Sandoz Award, PO Box 21756, Lincoln, NE 68542-1756 *Web Site:* www.nebraskalibraries.org/mari_sandoz_award, pg 659

Jellinek, Roger, Jellinek & Murray Literary Agency, 47-231 Kamakoi Rd, Kaneohe, HI 96744 *Tel:* 808-239-8451, pg 464

Jemison, Lisa, University of Toronto Press, Book Publishing Div, 800 Bay St, Mezzanine, Toronto, ON M5S 3A9, Canada *Tel:* 416-978-2239 *Fax:* 416-978-4736 *E-mail:* utpbooks@utorontopress.com (orders) *Web Site:* utorontopress.com, pg 423

Jenkins, Daniel, Lutheran Braille Workers Inc, 13471 California St, Yucaipa, CA 92399 *Tel:* 909-795-8977 *Toll Free Tel:* 800-925-6092 *E-mail:* lbw@lbwloveworks.org *Web Site:* www.lbwloveworks.org, pg 121

Jenkins, Jerrold R, Jenkins Group Inc, 1129 Woodmere Ave, Suite B, Traverse City, MI 49686 *Tel:* 231-933-0445; 213-883-5365 *E-mail:* info@jenkinsgroupinc.com *Web Site:* www.jenkinsgroupinc.com, pg 441

Jenkins, John, The MIT Press, One Broadway, 12th fl, Cambridge, MA 02142 *Tel:* 617-253-5255 *Toll Free Tel:* 800-405-1619 (orders) *Fax:* 617-258-6779; 617-577-1545 (orders) *Web Site:* mitpress.mit.edu, pg 132

Jenkins, Joyce, Northern California Book Awards, c/o Poetry Flash, 1450 Fourth St, Suite 4, Berkeley, CA 94710 *Tel:* 510-525-5476 *E-mail:* editor@poetryflash.org; ncbr@poetryflash.org *Web Site:* poetryflash.org, pg 641

Jenkins, Joyce, Poetry Flash Reading Series, 1450 Fourth St, Suite 4, Berkeley, CA 94710 *Tel:* 510-525-5476 *E-mail:* editor@poetryflash.org *Web Site:* poetryflash.org, pg 556

Jenkins, Kate, Arcadia Publishing Inc, 210 Wingo Way, Suite 200, Mount Pleasant, SC 29464 *Tel:* 843-853-2070 *E-mail:* retailers@arcadiapublishing.com *Web Site:* www.arcadiapublishing.com, pg 16

Jenks, Carolyn, Carolyn Jenks Agency, 30 Cambridge Park Dr, Suite 5115, Cambridge, MA 02140 *Tel:* 617-233-9130 *Web Site:* www.carolynjenksagency.com, pg 464

Jennette, Alyssa, Stonesong, 270 W 39 St, Suite 201, New York, NY 10018 *Tel:* 212-929-4600 *E-mail:* editors@stonesong.com *Web Site:* www.stonesong.com, pg 478

Jennings, Abegail, TCU Press, 3000 Sandage Ave, Fort Worth, TX 76109 *Tel:* 817-257-7822 *E-mail:* tcupress@tcu.edu *Web Site:* www.tcupress.com, pg 203

Jennings, Jaime, Island Press, 2000 "M" St NW, Suite 480-B, Washington, DC 20036 *Tel:* 202-232-7933 *Toll Free Tel:* 800-621-2736 *Fax:* 202-234-1328 *E-mail:* info@islandpress.org *Web Site:* www.islandpress.org, pg 104

Jennings, Lanora, Princeton University Press, 41 William St, Princeton, NJ 08540-5237 *Tel:* 609-258-4900 *Fax:* 609-258-6305 *E-mail:* info@press.princeton.edu *Web Site:* press.princeton.edu, pg 164

Jennings, Randy, SDP Publishing Solutions LLC, 36 Captain's Way, East Bridgewater, MA 02333 *Tel:* 617-775-0656 *Web Site:* www.sdppublishingsolutions.com, pg 444

Jennings, Sharon, Canadian Society of Children's Authors, Illustrators & Performers (CANSCAIP), 720 Bathurst St, Suite 503, Toronto, ON M5S 2R4, Canada *Tel:* 416-515-1559 *E-mail:* office@canscaip.org *Web Site:* www.canscaip.org, pg 503

Jensen, Connie, Saint Mary's Press, 702 Terrace Heights, Winona, MN 55987-1320 *Tel:* 507-457-7900 *Toll Free Tel:* 800-533-8095 *Toll Free Fax:* 800-344-9225 *E-mail:* smpress@smp.org *Web Site:* www.smp.org, pg 181

Jensen, Jack, PA Press, 202 Warren St, Hudson, NY 12534 *Tel:* 518-671-6100 *Toll Free Tel:* 800-722-6657 (dist); 800-759-0190 (sales) *E-mail:* sales@papress.com *Web Site:* www.papress.com, pg 149

Jensen, Jana, Technical Association of the Pulp & Paper Industry (TAPPI), 15 Technology Pkwy S, Suite 115, Peachtree Corners, GA 30092 *Tel:* 770-446-1400 *Toll Free Tel:* 800-332-8686 (US); 800-446-9431 (CN) *Fax:* 770-446-6947 *E-mail:* memberconnection@tappi.org *Web Site:* www.tappi.org, pg 521

Jensen, Joseph, The Astronomical Society of the Pacific, 390 Ashton Ave, San Francisco, CA 94112 *Tel:* 415-337-1100; 415-715-1414 (cust serv) *Toll Free Tel:* 800-335-2624 (cust serv) *Fax:* 415-337-5205 *E-mail:* service@astrosociety.org *Web Site:* astrosociety.org, pg 20

Jerald, Mike, Pro Lingua Associates Inc, 74 Cotton Mill Hill, Suite A-315, Brattleboro, VT 05301 *Tel:* 802-257-7779 *Toll Free Tel:* 800-366-4775 *Fax:* 802-257-5117 *E-mail:* info@prolinguaassociates.com *Web Site:* www.prolinguaassociates.com, pg 165

Jerman, Alice, HarperCollins Children's Books, 195 Broadway, New York, NY 10007 *Tel:* 212-207-7000 *Web Site:* www.harpercollins.com/childrens, pg 85

Jernigan, Lauren, Kensington Publishing Corp, 900 Third Ave, 26th fl, New York, NY 10022 *Tel:* 212-407-1500 *Toll Free Tel:* 800-221-2647 *Fax:* 212-935-0699 *Web Site:* www.kensingtonbooks.com, pg 109

Jessen, Eric, Psychological Assessment Resources Inc (PAR), 16204 N Florida Ave, Lutz, FL 33549 *Tel:* 813-449-4065 *Toll Free Tel:* 800-331-8378 *Fax:* 813-961-2196 *Toll Free Fax:* 800-727-9329 *E-mail:* custsup@parinc.com *Web Site:* www.parinc.com, pg 166

Jessup, Martha, Lannan Foundation, 313 Read St, Santa Fe, NM 87501-2628 *Tel:* 505-986-8160 *E-mail:* info@lannan.org *Web Site:* lannan.org, pg 526

Jessup, Martha, Lannan Literary Awards & Fellowships, 313 Read St, Santa Fe, NM 87501-2628 *Tel:* 505-986-8160 *E-mail:* info@lannan.org *Web Site:* lannan.org, pg 622

Jester, Walker, BRAVE Books, 13614 Poplar Circle, Suite 302, Conroe, TX 77304 *Tel:* 932-380-5648 *E-mail:* info@brave.us *Web Site:* bravebooks.us, pg 35

Jett, Rebekah, Scribner, 1230 Avenue of the Americas, New York, NY 10020 *Web Site:* www.simonandschusterpublishing.com/scribner/, pg 185

Jia, Joanna, John Wiley & Sons Inc, 111 River St, Hoboken, NJ 07030-5774 *Tel:* 201-748-6000 *Toll Free Tel:* 800-225-5945 (cust serv) *Fax:* 201-748-6088 *Web Site:* www.wiley.com, pg 230

Jiang, Leying, Astra Books for Young Readers, 19 W 21 St, No 1201, New York, NY 10010 *Tel:* 646-844-3485 *E-mail:* ahinfo@astrahouse.com; permissions@astrapublishinghouse.com *Web Site:* astrapublishinghouse.com, pg 20

Jimenez, Alex, Sudden Fiction Contest, c/o ASUC Publications, Univ of California, 10-B Eshleman Hall, Berkeley, CA 94720-4500 *E-mail:* berkeleyfictionreview@gmail.com *Web Site:* berkeleyfictionreview.org, pg 667

Jimenez, Carmen, Princeton University Press, 41 William St, Princeton, NJ 08540-5237 Tel: 609-258-4900 Fax: 609-258-6305 E-mail: info@press.princeton.edu Web Site: press.princeton.edu, pg 164

Jimenez, Saul, Highlights for Children Inc, 815 Church St, Honesdale, PA 18431 Tel: 570-253-1164 Toll Free Tel: 800-490-5111 Fax: 570-253-0179 E-mail: salesandmarketing@highlightspress.com Web Site: www.highlightspress.com; www.highlights.com; www.facebook.com/HighlightsforChildren, pg 92

Jimenez, Sophia, Simon & Schuster Children's Publishing, 1230 Avenue of the Americas, New York, NY 10020 Tel: 212-698-7000 Web Site: www.simonandschuster.com/kids; www.simonandschuster.com/teen; simonandschuster.net; simonandschuster.biz, pg 189

Jin, Ha, Boston University Creative Writing Program, 236 Bay State Rd, Boston, MA 02215 Tel: 617-353-2510 E-mail: crwr@bu.edu Web Site: www.bu.edu/creativewriting, pg 561

Joakimson, Laura, Omnidawn, 1632 Elm Ave, Richmond, CA 94805 Tel: 510-439-6285 E-mail: manager@omnidawn.com Web Site: www.omnidawn.com, pg 146

Jodoin, Isabelle, Modus Vivendi Publishing Inc, 55, rue Jean-Talon Ouest, Montreal, QC H2R 2W8, Canada Tel: 514-272-0433 Fax: 514-272-7234 E-mail: info@groupemodus.com Web Site: www.groupemodus.com, pg 413

Joell, Tina, Berkley, c/o Penguin Random House LLC, 1745 Broadway, 19th fl, New York, NY 10019 Tel: 212-366-2000 Web Site: www.penguin.com/publishers/berkley/; www.penguin.com/ace-overview/, pg 28

Johannesen, Jeremy, Empire State Award for Excellence in Literature for Young People, 6021 State Farm Rd, Guilderland, NY 12084 Tel: 518-432-6952 Toll Free Tel: 800-252-6952 Fax: 518-427-1697 E-mail: info@nyla.org; marketing@nyla.org Web Site: www.nyla.org, pg 599

Johanson, Molly, Roaring Brook Press, 120 Broadway, New York, NY 10271 Tel: 646-307-5151 Web Site: us.macmillan.com/publishers/roaring-brook-press, pg 176

Johns, Chelcee, Random House Publishing Group, 1745 Broadway, New York, NY 10019 Toll Free Tel: 800-200-3552 Web Site: www.randomhousebooks.com, pg 171

Johns, Jess, Sourcebooks LLC, 1935 Brookdale Rd, Suite 139, Naperville, IL 60563 Tel: 630-961-3900 Toll Free Tel: 800-432-7444 Fax: 630-961-2168 E-mail: info@sourcebooks.com Web Site: www.sourcebooks.com, pg 194

Johns, Jorun, Ariadne Press, 270 Goins Ct, Riverside, CA 92507 Tel: 951-684-9202 E-mail: ariadnepress@aol.com Web Site: www.ariadnebooks.com, pg 16

Johns, Joshua, Little, Brown Books for Young Readers (LBYR), 1290 Avenue of the Americas, New York, NY 10104 Tel: 212-364-1100 Toll Free Tel: 800-759-0190 (cust serv) E-mail: rights@lbchildrens.com Web Site: www.hachettebookgroup.com/imprint/little-brown-books-for-young-readers/, pg 118

Johns, Linda, Washington State Book Awards, c/o The Seattle Public Library, 1000 Fourth Ave, Seattle, WA 98104-1109 Web Site: washingtoncenterforthebook.org, pg 673

Johnson, Abigail, Princeton University Press, 41 William St, Princeton, NJ 08540-5237 Tel: 609-258-4900 Fax: 609-258-6305 E-mail: info@press.princeton.edu Web Site: press.princeton.edu, pg 164

Johnson, Anna, Concordia Publishing House, 3558 S Jefferson Ave, St Louis, MO 63118-3968 Tel: 314-268-1000; 314-268-1268 (bookshop) Toll Free Tel: 800-325-3040 (cust serv) Toll Free Fax: 800-490-9889 (cust serv) E-mail: order@cph.org Web Site: www.cph.org, pg 51

Johnson, Annette R, AllWrite Publishing, PO Box 1071, Atlanta, GA 30301 Tel: 770-284-8983 Fax: 770-284-8986 E-mail: questions@allwritepublishing.com; support@allwritepublishing.com (orders & returns) Web Site: allwritepublishing.com, pg 7

Johnson, Bennett J, Path Press Inc, 708 Washington St, Evanston, IL 60202 Tel: 847-492-0177 E-mail: pathpressinc@aol.com, pg 152

Johnson, Bennie F, AIGA 50 Books | 50 Covers, 228 Park Ave S, Suite 58603, New York, NY 10003 Tel: 212-807-1990 E-mail: competitions@aiga.org Web Site: www.aiga.org, pg 571

Johnson, Bennie F, AIGA, the professional association for design, 228 Park Ave S, Suite 58603, New York, NY 10003 Tel: 212-807-1990 E-mail: general@aiga.org Web Site: www.aiga.org, pg 493

Johnson, Blanche, Wilderness Adventures Press Inc, 45 Buckskin Rd, Belgrade, MT 59714 Tel: 406-388-0112 Toll Free Tel: 866-400-2012 Toll Free Fax: 866-400-2013 E-mail: books@wildadvpress.com Web Site: store.wildadvpress.com, pg 229

Johnson, Bri, HG Literary, 6 W 18 St, Suite 7R, New York, NY 10011 E-mail: foreign@hgliterary.com; rights@hgliterary.com Web Site: www.hgliterary.com, pg 463

Johnson, Caitlin, HarperCollins Children's Books, 195 Broadway, New York, NY 10007 Tel: 212-207-7000 Web Site: www.harpercollins.com/childrens, pg 85

Johnson, Chuck, Wilderness Adventures Press Inc, 45 Buckskin Rd, Belgrade, MT 59714 Tel: 406-388-0112 Toll Free Tel: 866-400-2012 Toll Free Fax: 866-400-2013 E-mail: books@wildadvpress.com Web Site: store.wildadvpress.com, pg 229

Johnson, Connie, Double Play, 303 Hillcrest Rd, Belton, MO 64012-1852 Tel: 816-651-7118, pg 438

Johnson, Corrynn, Princeton University Press, 41 William St, Princeton, NJ 08540-5237 Tel: 609-258-4900 Fax: 609-258-6305 E-mail: info@press.princeton.edu Web Site: press.princeton.edu, pg 164

Johnson, Dayna, Atria Books, 1230 Avenue of the Americas, New York, NY 10020 Tel: 212-698-7000 Fax: 212-698-7007 Web Site: www.simonandschuster.com, pg 21

Johnson, DeAndrea L, Hurston/Wright Award for College Writers, 10 "G" St NE, Suite 600, Washington, DC 20002 E-mail: info@hurstonwright.org Web Site: www.hurstonwright.org/awards/hurston-wright-award-for-college-writers, pg 614

Johnson, DeAndrea L, Hurston/Wright Legacy Awards, 10 "G" St NE, Suite 600, Washington, DC 20002 E-mail: info@hurstonwright.org Web Site: www.hurstonwright.org/awards/legacy-awards, pg 614

Johnson, DeAndrea L, Hurston/Wright Writers Week Workshops, 10 "G" St NE, Suite 600, Washington, DC 20002 E-mail: info@hurstonwright.org Web Site: www.hurstonwright.org/workshops/writers-week-workshops, pg 555

Johnson, DeAndrea L, The Zora Neale Hurston/Richard Wright Foundation, 10 "G" St NE, Suite 600, Washington, DC 20002 E-mail: info@hurstonwright.org Web Site: www.hurstonwright.org, pg 525

Johnson, Desiree, Penguin Random House Audio Publishing Group, 1745 Broadway, New York, NY 10019 Toll Free Tel: 800-793-2665 (cust serv) E-mail: audio@penguinrandomhouse.com; ecustomerservice@penguinrandomhouse.com Web Site: www.penguinrandomhouseaudio.com, pg 154

Johnson, Erin, Island Press, 2000 "M" St NW, Suite 480-B, Washington, DC 20036 Tel: 202-232-7933 Toll Free Tel: 800-621-2736 Fax: 202-234-1328 E-mail: info@islandpress.org Web Site: www.islandpress.org, pg 104

Johnson, Erin-Elizabeth, RAND Corp, 1776 Main St, Santa Monica, CA 90407-2138 Tel: 310-393-0411 Fax: 310-393-4818 Web Site: www.rand.org, pg 169

Johnson, Frankie, Chronicle Books LLC, 680 Second St, San Francisco, CA 94107 Tel: 415-537-4200 Fax: 415-537-4460 (perms) E-mail: hello@chroniclebooks.com; subrights@chroniclebooks.com Web Site: www.chroniclebooks.com, pg 47

Johnson, George F, Information Age Publishing Inc, PO Box 79049, Charlotte, NC 28271-7047 Tel: 704-752-9125 Fax: 704-752-9113 E-mail: infoage@infoagepub.com Web Site: www.infoagepub.com, pg 100

Johnson, Harmony, University of British Columbia Press, 2029 West Mall, Vancouver, BC V6T 1Z2, Canada Tel: 604-822-5959 Toll Free Tel: 877-377-9378 Fax: 604-822-6083 Toll Free Fax: 800-668-0821 E-mail: frontdesk@ubcpress.ca Web Site: www.ubcpress.ca, pg 422

Johnson, Howard Jr, Edgewise Press Inc, 24 Fifth Ave, Suite 224, New York, NY 10011 Tel: 212-387-0931 E-mail: epinc@mindspring.com Web Site: www.edgewisepress.org, pg 63

Johnson, Howard, SDP Publishing Solutions LLC, 36 Captain's Way, East Bridgewater, MA 02333 Tel: 617-775-0656 Web Site: www.sdppublishingsolutions.com, pg 444

Johnson, Jenna, Farrar, Straus & Giroux, LLC, 120 Broadway, New York, NY 10271 Tel: 212-741-6900 E-mail: fsg.publicity@fsgbooks.com; sales@fsgbooks.com Web Site: us.macmillan.com/fsg, pg 70

Johnson, Jennifer, Craftsman Book Co, 6058 Corte Del Cedro, Carlsbad, CA 92011 Tel: 760-438-7828 Toll Free Tel: 800-829-8123 Fax: 760-438-0398 Web Site: www.craftsman-book.com, pg 54

Johnson, Jennifer, Vermont Golden Dome Book Award, 60 Washington St, Suite 2, Barre, VT 05641 Tel: 802-636-0040 Web Site: libraries.vermont.gov/services/children_and_teens/book_awards/vtgdba, pg 672

Johnson, Joy, Centering Corp, 6406 Maple St, Omaha, NE 68104 Tel: 402-553-1200 Toll Free Tel: 866-218-0101 Fax: 402-553-0507 E-mail: orders@centeringcorp.com Web Site: www.centering.org, pg 44

Johnson, Julie, Copper Canyon Press, Fort Worden State Park, Bldg 313, Port Townsend, WA 98368 Tel: 360-385-4925 E-mail: poetry@coppercanyonpress.org; publicity@coppercanyonpress.org; digitalcontent@coppercanyonpress.com Web Site: www.coppercanyonpress.org, pg 52

Johnson, Kait, Kensington Publishing Corp, 900 Third Ave, 26th fl, New York, NY 10022 Tel: 212-407-1500 Toll Free Tel: 800-221-2647 Fax: 212-935-0699 Web Site: www.kensingtonbooks.com, pg 109

Johnson, Kevin, Kendall Hunt Publishing Co, 4050 Westmark Dr, Dubuque, IA 52002-2624 Tel: 563-589-1000 Toll Free Tel: 800-228-0810 (orders) Fax: 563-589-1071 Toll Free Fax: 800-772-9165 E-mail: ordernow@kendallhunt.com Web Site: www.kendallhunt.com, pg 108

Johnson, Kij, Intensive Novel Architects Writing Workshop, 1809 Indiana St, Lawrence, KS 66044 Tel: 785-766-7039 Web Site: adastra-sf.com/Workshop-stuff/Johnson-Webb-Workshops.htm, pg 555

Johnson, Kij, Speculative Fiction Writing Workshop, 1809 Indiana St, Lawrence, KS 66044 Tel: 785-766-7039 Web Site: adastra-sf.com/Workshop-stuff/Spec-Fic-Workshop.htm, pg 557

Johnson, Lars, Christian Liberty Press, 502 W Euclid Ave, Arlington Heights, IL 60004-5402 Toll Free Tel: 800-348-0899 Fax: 847-259-2941 E-mail: custserv@christianlibertypress.com Web Site: www.shopchristianliberty.com, pg 47

Johnson, Lloyd, Double Play, 303 Hillcrest Rd, Belton, MO 64012-1852 Tel: 816-651-7118, pg 438

Johnson, Maren Anderson, The Ibsen Society of America (ISA), c/o Indiana University, Global & Intl Studies Bldg 3111, 355 N Jordan Ave, Bloomington, IN 47405-1105 Web Site: www.ibsensociety.org, pg 507

Johnson, Mark, International Code Council Inc, 3060 Saturn St, Suite 100, Brea, CA 92821 Tel: 562-699-0541 Toll Free Tel: 888-422-7233 Fax: 562-908-5524 Toll Free Fax: 866-891-1695 E-mail: order@icc-es.org Web Site: www.iccsafe.org, pg 102

Johnson, Matt, Kensington Publishing Corp, 900 Third Ave, 26th fl, New York, NY 10022 *Tel:* 212-407-1500 *Toll Free Tel:* 800-221-2647 *Fax:* 212-935-0699 *Web Site:* www.kensingtonbooks.com, pg 109

Johnson, Melinda, Ancient Faith Publishing, PO Box 748, Chesterton, IN 46304 *Tel:* 219-728-2216 *Toll Free Tel:* 800-967-7377 *E-mail:* general@ancientfaith.com; support@ancientfaith.com *Web Site:* www.ancientfaith.com/publishing, pg 13

Johnson, Meredith, Entangled Publishing LLC, 644 Shrewsbury Commons Ave, Suite 181, Shrewsbury, PA 17361 *Toll Free Tel:* 877-677-9451 *E-mail:* publisher@entangledpublishing.com *Web Site:* www.entangledpublishing.com, pg 67

Johnson, Michelle, Neustadt International Prize for Literature, c/o University of Oklahoma, 630 Parrington Oval, Suite 110, Norman, OK 73019-4033 *Tel:* 405-325-4531 *Web Site:* www.worldliteraturetoday.org; www.neustadtprize.org, pg 639

Johnson, Michelle, NSK Neustadt Prize for Children's Literature, c/o University of Oklahoma, 630 Parrington Oval, Suite 110, Norman, OK 73019-4033 *Tel:* 405-325-4531 *Web Site:* www.worldliteraturetoday.org; www.neustadtprize.org, pg 642

Johnson, Rebecca, Sourcebooks LLC, 1935 Brookdale Rd, Suite 139, Naperville, IL 60563 *Tel:* 630-961-3900 *Toll Free Tel:* 800-432-7444 *Fax:* 630-961-2168 *E-mail:* info@sourcebooks.com *Web Site:* www.sourcebooks.com, pg 194

Johnson, Rick, Concordia Publishing House, 3558 S Jefferson Ave, St Louis, MO 63118-3968 *Tel:* 314-268-1000; 314-268-1268 (bookshop) *Toll Free Tel:* 800-325-3040 (cust serv) *Toll Free Fax:* 800-490-9889 (cust serv) *E-mail:* order@cph.org *Web Site:* www.cph.org, pg 51

Johnson, Sharnell, Penguin Random House LLC, 1745 Broadway, New York, NY 10019 *Tel:* 212-782-9000 *Toll Free Tel:* 800-726-0600 *Web Site:* www.penguinrandomhouse.com, pg 155

Johnson, Theresa, PEN Canada, 401 Richmond St W, Suite 244, Toronto, ON M5V 3A8, Canada *Tel:* 416-703-8448 *E-mail:* queries@pencanada.ca *Web Site:* www.pencanada.ca, pg 516

Johnson, Thomas D, Business Research Services Inc, PO Box 42674, Washington, DC 20015 *Tel:* 301-229-5561 *Toll Free Fax:* 877-516-0818 *E-mail:* brspubs@sba8a.com *Web Site:* www.sba8a.com; www.setasidealert.com, pg 39

Johnston, Allyn, Simon & Schuster Children's Publishing, 1230 Avenue of the Americas, New York, NY 10020 *Tel:* 212-698-7000 *Web Site:* www.simonandschuster.com/kids; www.simonandschuster.com/teen; simonandschuster.net; simonandschuster.biz, pg 189

Johnston, Bret Anthony, University of Texas at Austin, New Writers Project, Dept of English, 204 W 21 St, B-5000, Austin, TX 78712-1164 *Tel:* 512-471-4991 *Fax:* 512-471-4909 *E-mail:* newwritersproject@utexas.edu *Web Site:* liberalarts.utexas.edu/nwp, pg 567

Johnston, Charidy, Penguin Random House Canada, a Penguin Random House company, 320 Front St W, Suite 1400, Toronto, ON M5V 3B6, Canada *Tel:* 416-364-4449 *Toll Free Tel:* 888-523-9292 (cust serv) *E-mail:* canadaweb@penguinrandomhouse.com; customerservicescanada@penguinrandomhouse.com *Web Site:* www.penguinrandomhouse.ca, pg 415

Johnston, Christine, Penguin Press, c/o Penguin Random House LLC, 1745 Broadway, New York, NY 10019 *Tel:* 212-782-9000 *E-mail:* penguinpress@penguinrandomhouse.com *Web Site:* www.penguin.com/penguin-press-overview/, pg 154

Johnston, Christine, Random House Publishing Group, 1745 Broadway, New York, NY 10019 *Toll Free Tel:* 800-200-3552 *Web Site:* www.randomhousebooks.com, pg 171

Johnston, Dillon, Wake Forest University Press, 2518 Reynolda Rd, Winston-Salem, NC 27106 *Tel:* 336-758-5448 *Fax:* 336-842-3853 *E-mail:* wfupress@wfu.edu *Web Site:* wfupress.wfu.edu, pg 225

Johnston, MJ, Sourcebooks LLC, 1935 Brookdale Rd, Suite 139, Naperville, IL 60563 *Tel:* 630-961-3900 *Toll Free Tel:* 800-432-7444 *Fax:* 630-961-2168 *E-mail:* info@sourcebooks.com *Web Site:* www.sourcebooks.com, pg 194

Johnston, Pam, Penny-Farthing Productions, One Sugar Creek Center Blvd, Suite 820, Sugar Land, TX 77478 *Tel:* 713-780-0300 *Toll Free Tel:* 800-926-2669 *Fax:* 713-780-4004 *E-mail:* corp@pfproductions.com *Web Site:* www.pfproductions.com, pg 157

Johnston, Rachel, Candlewick Press, 99 Dover St, Somerville, MA 02144-2825 *Tel:* 617-661-3330 *Fax:* 617-661-0565 *E-mail:* bigbear@candlewick.com; salesinfo@candlewick.com *Web Site:* candlewick.com, pg 40

Johnston, Mr Robin, Pentecostal Resources Group, 36 Research Park Ct, Weldon Spring, MO 63304 *Tel:* 636-229-7900 *Toll Free Tel:* 866-819-7667 *Web Site:* www.pentecostalpublishing.com, pg 157

Johnston, Shannon, Farcountry Press, 2750 Broadwater Ave, Helena, MT 59602-9202 *Tel:* 406-422-1263 *Toll Free Tel:* 800-821-3874 (sales off) *Fax:* 406-443-5480 *E-mail:* books@farcountrypress.com; sales@farcountrypress.com *Web Site:* www.farcountrypress.com, pg 69

Johnstone, Jim, Palimpsest Press, 1171 Eastlawn Ave, Windsor, ON N8S 3J1, Canada *Tel:* 519-259-2112 *E-mail:* publicity@palimpsestpress.ca *Web Site:* www.palimpsestpress.ca, pg 415

Jolley, Marc, Mercer University Press, 368 Orange St, Macon, GA 31201 *Tel:* 478-301-2880 *Toll Free Tel:* 866-895-1472 *Fax:* 478-301-2585 *E-mail:* mupressorders@mercer.edu *Web Site:* www.mupress.org, pg 129

Jonaitis, Alice, Random House Children's Books, c/o Penguin Random House LLC, 1745 Broadway, New York, NY 10019 *Tel:* 212-782-9000 *Web Site:* www.rhcbooks.com, pg 170

Jones, Alena, Johns Hopkins University Press, 2715 N Charles St, Baltimore, MD 21218-4363 *Tel:* 410-516-6900; 410-516-6987 *Toll Free Tel:* 800-537-5487 (book orders & cust serv); 800-548-1784 (journal orders) *Fax:* 410-516-6968; 410-516-6998 (orders) *E-mail:* hfscustserv@press.jhu.edu (cust serv); jrnlcirc@jh.edu (journal orders) *Web Site:* www.press.jhu.edu; muse.jhu.edu, pg 106

Jones, Allie, Holiday House Publishing Inc, 50 Broad St, New York, NY 10004 *Tel:* 212-688-0085 *Fax:* 212-421-6134 *E-mail:* info@holidayhouse.com *Web Site:* www.holidayhouse.com, pg 94

Jones, Allie, Peachtree Publishing Co Inc, 1700 Chattahoochee Ave, Atlanta, GA 30318-2112 *Tel:* 404-876-8761 *Toll Free Tel:* 800-241-0113 *Fax:* 404-875-2578 *Toll Free Fax:* 800-875-8909 *E-mail:* hello@peachtree-online.com; orders@peachtree-online.com; sales@peachtree-online.com *Web Site:* www.peachtreebooks.com; www.peachtree-online.com, pg 153

Jones, Amy, Harlequin Enterprises Ltd, Bay Adelaide Centre, East Tower, 22 Adelaide St W, 41st fl, Toronto, ON M5H 4E3, Canada *Tel:* 416-445-5860 *Toll Free Tel:* 888-432-4879; 800-370-5838 (ebook inquiries) *E-mail:* customerservice@harlequin.com *Web Site:* www.harlequin.com, pg 409

Jones, Ashley, National Music Publishers' Association (NMPA), 1900 "N" St NW, Suite 500, Washington, DC 20036 *Tel:* 202-393-6672 *E-mail:* members@nmpa.org *Web Site:* nmpa.org, pg 513

Jones, Barbara, Stuart Krichevsky Literary Agency Inc, 118 E 28 St, Suite 908, New York, NY 10016 *Tel:* 212-725-5288 *Fax:* 212-725-5275 *E-mail:* query@skagency.com *Web Site:* skagency.com, pg 466

Jones, Ms Brett Hall, Community of Writers Summer Workshops, PO Box 1416, Nevada City, CA 95959 *Tel:* 530-470-8440 *E-mail:* info@communityofwriters.org *Web Site:* www.communityofwriters.org, pg 553

Jones, Candide, Wake Forest University Press, 2518 Reynolda Rd, Winston-Salem, NC 27106 *Tel:* 336-758-5448 *Fax:* 336-842-3853 *E-mail:* wfupress@wfu.edu *Web Site:* wfupress.wfu.edu, pg 225

Jones, Caroline, The Monacelli Press, 65 Bleecker St, 8th fl, New York, NY 10012 *Tel:* 212-652-5400 *E-mail:* contact@monacellipress.com *Web Site:* www.phaidon.com/monacelli, pg 133

Jones, Carrie, Greenleaf Book Group LLC, PO Box 91869, Austin, TX 78709 *Tel:* 512-891-6100 *Fax:* 512-891-6150 *E-mail:* contact@greenleafbookgroup.com; orders@greenleafbookgroup.com; foreignrights@greenleafbookgroup.com; media@greenleafbookgroup.com *Web Site:* greenleafbookgroup.com, pg 81

Jones, Cassie, HarperCollins Publishers LLC, 195 Broadway, New York, NY 10007 *Tel:* 212-207-7000 *Web Site:* www.harpercollins.com, pg 86

Jones, Cathy, William B Ruggles Journalism Scholarship, 5211 Port Royal Rd, Suite 510, Springfield, VA 22151 *Tel:* 703-321-9606 *Fax:* 703-327-8101 *Web Site:* www.nilrr.org, pg 657

Jones, Chris Mackenzie, Excellence in Teaching Fellowships, Open Book Bldg, Suite 200, 1011 Washington Ave S, Minneapolis, MN 55415 *Tel:* 612-215-2575 *Fax:* 612-215-2576 *E-mail:* loft@loft.org *Web Site:* loft.org/awards/excellence-teaching-fellowships, pg 601

Jones, Chris Mackenzie, Loft-Mentor Series in Poetry & Creative Prose, Open Book Bldg, Suite 200, 1011 Washington Ave S, Minneapolis, MN 55415 *Tel:* 612-215-2575 *Fax:* 612-215-2576 *E-mail:* loft@loft.org *Web Site:* loft.org, pg 626

Jones, Chris Mackenzie, McKnight Artist Fellowship for Writers, Open Book Bldg, Suite 200, 1011 Washington Ave S, Minneapolis, MN 55415 *Tel:* 612-215-2575 *Fax:* 612-215-2576 *E-mail:* loft@loft.org *Web Site:* loft.org, pg 631

Jones, Chris Mackenzie, Mirrors & Windows Fellowship, Open Book Bldg, Suite 200, 1011 Washington Ave S, Minneapolis, MN 55415 *Tel:* 612-215-2575 *Fax:* 612-215-2576 *E-mail:* loft@loft.org *Web Site:* loft.org/awards/mirrors-windows, pg 633

Jones, Christine, HarperCollins Publishers LLC, 195 Broadway, New York, NY 10007 *Tel:* 212-207-7000 *Web Site:* www.harpercollins.com, pg 86

Jones, Christopher, Toronto Book Awards, c/o Toronto Arts & Culture, City Hall, 9E, 100 Queen St W, Toronto, ON M5H 2N2, Canada *Web Site:* www.toronto.ca/book_awards, pg 669

Jones, Don, Crossway, 1300 Crescent St, Wheaton, IL 60187 *Tel:* 630-682-4300 *Toll Free Tel:* 800-635-7993 (orders); 800-543-1659 (cust serv) *Fax:* 630-682-4785 *E-mail:* info@crossway.org *Web Site:* www.crossway.org, pg 56

Jones, Doug, HarperCollins Publishers LLC, 195 Broadway, New York, NY 10007 *Tel:* 212-207-7000 *Web Site:* www.harpercollins.com, pg 86

Jones, Erin, Odyssey Books, 2421 Redwood Ct, Longmont, CO 80503-8155 *Tel:* 720-494-1473 *Fax:* 720-494-1471 *E-mail:* books@odysseybooks.net, pg 145

Jones, Greg, Signature Books Publishing LLC, 564 W 400 N, Salt Lake City, UT 84116-3411 *Toll Free Tel:* 800-356-5687 *E-mail:* people@signaturebooks.com *Web Site:* www.signaturebooks.com; www.signaturebookslibrary.org, pg 188

Jones, Hannah, St Martin's Press, LLC, 120 Broadway, New York, NY 10271 *E-mail:* publicity@stmartins.com; trademarketing@stmartins.com; foreignrights@stmartins.com *Web Site:* us.macmillan.com/smp, pg 181

Jones, Jennifer, Nilgiri Press, 3600 Tomales Rd, Tomales, CA 94971 *Tel:* 707-878-2369 *E-mail:* info@easwaran.org *Web Site:* www.easwaran.org, pg 141

Jones, Jordan, New Mexico Book Association (NMBA), PO Box 1285, Santa Fe, NM 87504 *E-mail:* libroentry@gmail.com *Web Site:* www.nmbookassociation.org, pg 514

Jones, Josephine, Colorado Book Awards, 7935 E Prentice Ave, Suite 450, Greenwood Village, CO 80111 Tel: 303-894-7951 (ext 19) Fax: 303-864-9361 E-mail: info@coloradohumanities.org Web Site: coloradohumanities.org, pg 591

Jones, Kathryn, Kay Cattarulla Award for Best Short Story, PO Box 130294, Spring, TX 77393 Web Site: texasinstituteofletters.org, pg 587

Jones, Kathryn, Carr P Collins Award, PO Box 130294, Spring, TX 77393 Web Site: texasinstituteofletters.org, pg 591

Jones, Kathryn, Brigid Erin Flynn Award for Best Picture Book, PO Box 130294, Spring, TX 77393 Web Site: texasinstituteofletters.org, pg 603

Jones, Kathryn, Jean Flynn Award for Best Young Adult Book, PO Box 130294, Spring, TX 77393 Web Site: texasinstituteofletters.org, pg 603

Jones, Kathryn, Deirdre Siobhan FlynnBass Award for Best Middle Grade Book, PO Box 130294, Spring, TX 77393 Web Site: texasinstituteofletters.org, pg 603

Jones, Kathryn, Soeurette Diehl Fraser Translation Award, PO Box 130294, Spring, TX 77393 Web Site: texasinstituteofletters.org, pg 604

Jones, Kathryn, Jesse H Jones Award, PO Box 130294, Spring, TX 77393 Web Site: texasinstituteofletters.org, pg 618

Jones, Kathryn, Ramirez Family Award, PO Box 130294, Spring, TX 77393 Web Site: texasinstituteofletters.org, pg 654

Jones, Kathryn, John A Robertson Award for Best First Book of Poetry, PO Box 130294, Spring, TX 77393 Web Site: texasinstituteofletters.org, pg 657

Jones, Kathryn, Edwin "Bud" Shrake Award for Best Short Nonfiction, PO Box 130294, Spring, TX 77393 Web Site: texasinstituteofletters.org, pg 662

Jones, Kathryn, Helen C Smith Memorial Award, PO Box 130294, Spring, TX 77393 Web Site: texasinstituteofletters.org, pg 663

Jones, Kathryn, Texas Institute of Letters (TIL), PO Box 130294, Spring, TX 77393 Web Site: texasinstituteofletters.org, pg 521

Jones, Kathryn, Lon Tinkle Award for Lifetime Achievement, PO Box 130294, Spring, TX 77393 Web Site: texasinstituteofletters.org, pg 669

Jones, Kathryn, Sergio Troncoso Award for Best Book of Fiction, PO Box 130294, Spring, TX 77393 Web Site: texasinstituteofletters.org, pg 670

Jones, Kathryn, Fred Whitehead Award for Best Design of a Trade Book, PO Box 130294, Spring, TX 77393 Web Site: texasinstituteofletters.org, pg 675

Jones, Keiko, Signature Books Publishing LLC, 564 W 400 N, Salt Lake City, UT 84116-3411 Toll Free Tel: 800-356-5687 E-mail: people@signaturebooks.com Web Site: www.signaturebooks.com; www.signaturebookslibrary.org, pg 188

Jones, Lara, Atria Books, 1230 Avenue of the Americas, New York, NY 10020 Tel: 212-698-7000 Fax: 212-698-7007 Web Site: www.simonandschuster.com, pg 21

Jones, Louis B, Community of Writers Summer Workshops, PO Box 1416, Nevada City, CA 95959 Tel: 530-470-8440 E-mail: info@communityofwriters.org Web Site: www.communityofwriters.org, pg 553

Jones, Lucy, Fons Vitae, 49 Mockingbird Valley Dr, Louisville, KY 40207-1366 Tel: 502-897-3641 Fax: 502-893-7373 E-mail: fonsvitaeky@aol.com Web Site: www.fonsvitae.com, pg 73

Jones, Marla F, Doodle and Peck Publishing, 413 Cedarburg Ct, Yukon, OK 73099 Tel: 405-354-7422 E-mail: mjones@doodleandpeck.com Web Site: www.doodleandpeck.com, pg 60

Jones, Mary, Harry N Abrams Inc, 195 Broadway, 9th fl, New York, NY 10007 Tel: 212-206-7715 Toll Free Tel: 800-345-1359 Fax: 212-645-8437 E-mail: abrams@abramsbooks.com; publicity@abramsbooks.com; sales@abramsbooks.com Web Site: www.abramsbooks.com, pg 3

Jones, Megan, Greystone Books Ltd, 343 Railway St, Suite 302, Vancouver, BC V6A 1A4, Canada Tel: 604-875-1550 Fax: 604-875-1556 E-mail: info@greystonebooks.com; rights@greystonebooks.com Web Site: www.greystonebooks.com, pg 407

Jones, Meryl, Craven Design Inc, 229 E 85 St, New York, NY 10028 Tel: 212-288-1022 Fax: 212-249-9910 E-mail: cravendesign@mac.com Web Site: www.cravendesignstudios.com, pg 485

Jones, Michael, Dreamscape Media LLC, 1417 Timberwolf Dr, Holland, OH 43528 Tel: 419-867-6965 Toll Free Tel: 877-983-7326 E-mail: info@dreamscapeab.com Web Site: www.dreamscapepublishing.com, pg 62

Jones, Michael, SK Arts, 1355 Broad St, Regina, SK S4R 7V1, Canada Tel: 306-787-4056 Toll Free Tel: 800-667-7526 (CN) E-mail: info@sk-arts.ca Web Site: sk-arts.ca, pg 519

Jones, Morgan, Bloomsbury Publishing Inc, 1385 Broadway, 5th fl, New York, NY 10018 Tel: 212-419-5300 E-mail: marketingusa@bloomsbury.com; adultpublicityusa@bloomsbury.com; askacademic@bloomsbury.com Web Site: www.bloomsbury.com, pg 32

Jones, Parneshia, Northwestern University Press, 629 Noyes St, Evanston, IL 60208-4210 Tel: 847-491-2046 Toll Free Tel: 800-621-2736 (orders only) Fax: 847-491-8150 E-mail: nupress@northwestern.edu Web Site: www.nupress.northwestern.edu, pg 143

Jones, Parneshia, TriQuarterly Books, 629 Noyes St, Evanston, IL 60208 Tel: 847-491-7420 Toll Free Tel: 800-621-2736 (orders only) Fax: 847-491-8150 E-mail: nupress@northwestern.edu Web Site: www.nupress.northwestern.edu, pg 209

Jones, Patsy S, Hachette Nashville, 6100 Tower Circle, Room 210, Franklin, TN 37067 Tel: 615-221-0996 Fax: 615-221-0962 Web Site: www.hachettebookgroup.com/imprint/hachette-nashville/, pg 83

Jones, Peter, Pinder Lane & Garon-Brooke Associates Ltd, 2136 NE 58 Ct, Fort Lauderdale, FL 33308 Tel: 212-489-0880 Fax: 212-489-7104 Web Site: www.pinderlaneandgaronbrooke.com, pg 472

Jones, Rachel, National Press Foundation, 1211 Connecticut Ave NW, Suite 310, Washington, DC 20036 Tel: 202-663-7286 Web Site: nationalpress.org, pg 526

Jones, Serena, Henry Holt and Company, LLC, 120 Broadway, 23rd fl, New York, NY 10271 Tel: 646-307-5151 Toll Free Tel: 888-330-8477 (orders) Fax: 646-307-5285 Web Site: www.henryholt.com, pg 94

Jones, Tim, Harvard University Press, 79 Garden St, Cambridge, MA 02138-1499 Tel: 617-495-2600; 401-531-2800 (intl orders) Toll Free Tel: 800-405-1619 (orders) Fax: 617-495-5898 (gen); 617-496-4677 (edit & rts); 401-531-2801 (intl orders) Toll Free Fax: 800-406-9145 (orders) E-mail: contact_hup@harvard.edu Web Site: www.hup.harvard.edu, pg 88

Jones, Todd, Highlights for Children Inc, 815 Church St, Honesdale, PA 18431 Tel: 570-253-1164 Toll Free Tel: 800-490-5111 Fax: 570-253-0179 E-mail: salesandmarketing@highlightspress.com Web Site: www.highlightspress.com; www.highlights.com; www.facebook.com/HighlightsforChildren, pg 92

Jones, Valerie, University Press of Mississippi, 3825 Ridgewood Rd, Jackson, MS 39211-6492 Tel: 601-432-6205 Toll Free Tel: 800-737-7788 (orders & cust serv) Fax: 601-432-6217 E-mail: press@mississippi.edu Web Site: www.upress.state.ms.us, pg 222

Jongsma, Jennifer, Annual Reviews, 1875 S Grant St, Suite 700, San Mateo, CA 94402 Tel: 650-493-4400 Toll Free Tel: 800-523-8635 Fax: 650-424-0910; 650-855-9815 E-mail: service@annualreviews.org Web Site: www.annualreviews.org, pg 14

Jonker, Rosie, Ann Rittenberg Literary Agency Inc, 15 Maiden Lane, Suite 206, New York, NY 10038 Tel: 212-684-6936 Fax: 212-684-6929 E-mail: info@rittlit.com Web Site: www.rittlit.com, pg 473

Joran, Aurelina, Macmillan, 120 Broadway, 22nd fl, New York, NY 10271 E-mail: press.inquiries@macmillan.com Web Site: us.macmillan.com, pg 122

Jordan, Jesse, Triumph Books LLC, 814 N Franklin St, Chicago, IL 60610 Tel: 312-337-0747 Toll Free Tel: 800-888-4741 (cust serv) Fax: 312-280-5470; 312-337-5985 Web Site: www.triumphbooks.com, pg 209

Jordan, Renee, Taunton Books, 63 S Main St, Newtown, CT 06470 Tel: 203-426-8171 Toll Free Tel: 866-505-4689 (orders) Fax: 203-270-9373, pg 203

Jordan, Roger, Gulf Energy Information, 2 Greenway Plaza, Suite 1020, Houston, TX 77046 Tel: 713-520-4498; 713-529-4301 E-mail: store@gulfpub.com; customerservice@gulfenergyinfo.com Web Site: www.gulfenergyinfo.com, pg 83

Jordan, Sara, Sara Jordan Publishing, RPO Lakeport Box 28105, St Catharines, ON L2N 7P8, Canada Tel: 905-938-5050 Toll Free Tel: 800-567-7733 Fax: 905-938-9970 Toll Free Fax: 800-229-3855 Web Site: www.sara-jordan.com; www.songsthatteach.com, pg 418

Jordan, Veronica, Simon & Schuster, LLC, 1230 Avenue of the Americas, New York, NY 10020 Tel: 212-698-7000 Toll Free Tel: 800-223-2336 (orders) Fax: 212-698-7007 Toll Free Fax: 800-943-9831 (orders) E-mail: firstname.lastname@simonandschuster.com; purchaseorders@simonandschuster.com (orders) Web Site: www.simonandschuster.com, pg 189

Jorden, Brooke, Familius, PO Box 1249, Reedley, CA 93654 Tel: 559-876-2170 Fax: 559-876-2180 E-mail: orders@familius.com Web Site: www.familius.com, pg 69

Jose, Kathy, Forward Movement, 412 Sycamore St, Cincinnati, OH 45202-4110 Tel: 513-721-6659 Toll Free Tel: 800-543-1813 Fax: 513-721-0729 (orders) E-mail: orders@forwardmovement.org (orders & cust serv) Web Site: www.forwardmovement.org, pg 73

Joseph, Jeff, CODiE Awards, PO Box 34340, Washington, DC 20043 Tel: 202-789-4446 Fax: 202-289-7097 Web Site: www.siia.net, pg 590

Joseph, Jeff, Software & Information Industry Association (SIIA), 1620 Eye St NW, Washington, DC 20005 Tel: 202-289-7442 Fax: 202-289-7097 E-mail: info@siia.net Web Site: www.siia.net, pg 520

Joseph, Jennifer, Manic D Press Inc, 250 Banks St, San Francisco, CA 94110 Tel: 415-648-8288 E-mail: info@manicdpress.com Web Site: www.manicdpress.com, pg 124

Joseph, Kelly, McClelland & Stewart Ltd, 320 Front St W, Suite 1400, Toronto, ON M5V 3B6, Canada Tel: 416-364-4449 Toll Free Tel: 888-523-9292 E-mail: customerservicecanada@penguinrandomhouse.com; mcclellandsubmissions@prh.com Web Site: penguinrandomhouse.ca/imprints/mcclelland-stewart, pg 412

Joseph, Kelly, Penguin Random House Canada, a Penguin Random House company, 320 Front St W, Suite 1400, Toronto, ON M5V 3B6, Canada Tel: 416-364-4449 Toll Free Tel: 888-523-9292 (cust serv) E-mail: canadaweb@penguinrandomhouse.com; customerservicecanada@penguinrandomhouse.com Web Site: www.penguinrandomhouse.ca, pg 416

Jospitre, Sarah, Penguin Young Readers Group, c/o Penguin Random House LLC, 1745 Broadway, New York, NY 10019 Tel: 212-782-9000 Web Site: www.penguin.com/penguin-young-readers-overview, pg 156

Joss, Emma, Doubleday, c/o Penguin Random House LLC, 1745 Broadway, New York, NY 10019 Tel: 212-751-2600 Fax: 212-940-7390 (dom rts); 212-572-2662 (foreign rts) Web Site: knopfdoubleday.com/imprint/doubleday/; knopfdoubleday.com, pg 61

Joy, Michael L, The Seymour Agency, 475 Miner Street Rd, Canton, NY 13617 Tel: 239-398-8209 Web Site: www.theseymouragency.com, pg 475

Joyce, Ashley, National Music Publishers' Association (NMPA), 1900 "N" St NW, Suite 500, Washington, DC 20036 Tel: 202-393-6672 E-mail: members@nmpa.org Web Site: nmpa.org, pg 513

Joyce, Jack, ITMB Publishing Ltd, 12300 Bridgeport Rd, Richmond, BC V6V 1J5, Canada Tel: 604-273-1400 Fax: 604-273-1488 E-mail: itmb@itmb.com Web Site: www.itmb.com, pg 411

Joyce, Robinson, Firefall Editions, 4905 Tunlaw St, Alexandria, VA 22312 Tel: 510-549-2461 E-mail: literary@att.net Web Site: www.firefallmedia.com, pg 72

Joynt, Randy, Manitoba Arts Council (MAC), 525-93 Lombard Ave, Winnipeg, MB R3B 3B1, Canada Tel: 204-945-2237 Toll Free Tel: 866-994-2787 Fax: 204-945-5925 Web Site: artscouncil.mb.ca, pg 510

Jozwiak, Hayley, Roaring Brook Press, 120 Broadway, New York, NY 10271 Tel: 646-307-5151 Web Site: us.macmillan.com/publishers/roaring-brook-press, pg 176

Juarez, Benny, Ross Books, PO Box 4340, Berkeley, CA 94704-0340 Tel: 510-841-2474 Fax: 510-295-2531 E-mail: sales@rossbooks.com Web Site: www.rossbooks.com, pg 177

Juarez, David, University of Notre Dame Press, 310 Flanner Hall, Notre Dame, IN 46556 Tel: 574-631-6346 Fax: 574-631-8148 E-mail: undpress@nd.edu Web Site: www.undpress.nd.edu, pg 219

Juarez, Eucarol, Catholic Book Awards, 10 S Riverside Plaza, Suite 875, Chicago, IL 60606 Tel: 312-380-6789 E-mail: awards@catholicmediaassociation.org Web Site: www.catholicmediaassociation.org, pg 587

Juarez, Eucarol, Catholic Media Association (CMA), 10 S Riverside Plaza, Suite 875, Chicago, IL 60606 Tel: 312-380-6789 Web Site: www.catholicmediaassociation.org, pg 503

Juarez, Eucarol, Catholic Media Awards, 10 S Riverside Plaza, Suite 875, Chicago, IL 60606 Tel: 312-380-6789 E-mail: awards@catholicmediaassociation.org Web Site: www.catholicmediaassociation.org, pg 587

Jud, Brian, Association of Publishers for Special Sales (APSS), PO Box 715, Avon, CT 06001-0715 Tel: 860-675-1344 Web Site: www.bookapss.org, pg 500

Jud, Brian, Book Marketing Works LLC, 50 Lovely St (Rte 177), Avon, CT 06001 Tel: 860-675-1344 Web Site: www.bookmarketingworks.com, pg 33

Jud, Brian, Connecticut Authors & Publishers Association (CAPA), PO Box 715, Avon, CT 06001-0715 Tel: 860-675-1344 Web Site: ctauthorsandpublishers.com, pg 504

Judd, Darrell, Artech House®, 685 Canton St, Norwood, MA 02062 Tel: 781-769-9750 Toll Free Tel: 800-225-9977 Fax: 781-769-6334 E-mail: artech@artechhouse.com Web Site: us.artechhouse.com, pg 17

Judson, Jen, National Press Club (NPC), 529 14 St NW, 13th fl, Washington, DC 20045 Tel: 202-662-7500 Web Site: www.press.org, pg 513

Jueds, Kasey, The Tenth Gate Prize, PO Box 42164, Washington, DC 20015 E-mail: editor@wordworksbooks.org Web Site: www.wordworksbooks.org, pg 668

Juenemann, Brian, Pacific Northwest Book Awards, 520 W 13 Ave, Eugene, OR 97401-3461 Tel: 541-683-4363 Fax: 541-683-3910 E-mail: info@pnba.org; awards@pnba.org Web Site: www.pnba.org/book-awards.html, pg 645

Juenemann, Brian, Pacific Northwest Booksellers Association (PNBA), 520 W 13 Ave, Eugene, OR 97401-3461 Tel: 541-683-4363 Toll Free Tel: 800-353-6764 Fax: 541-683-3910 E-mail: info@pnba.org Web Site: www.pnba.org, pg 516

Juergens, Kathryn, Workman Publishing, 1290 Avenue of the Americas, New York, NY 10104 Toll Free Tel: 800-759-0190 Fax: 212-364-0950 E-mail: workman-inquiry@hbgusa.com Web Site: www.hachettebookgroup.com/imprint/workman-publishing-company/, pg 232

Julavits, Heidi, Columbia University School of the Arts Creative Writing Program, 609 Kent Hall, New York, NY 10027 Tel: 212-854-3774 E-mail: writingprogram@columbia.edu Web Site: arts.columbia.edu/writing, pg 562

Juliar, Troy, Recorded Books Inc, an RBmedia company, 8400 Corporate Dr, Landover, MD 20785 Toll Free Tel: 800-305-3450 Web Site: rbmediaglobal.com/recorded-books, pg 172

Julien, Ria, Frances Goldin Literary Agency, Inc, 214 W 29 St, Suite 410, New York, NY 10001 Tel: 212-777-0047 Fax: 212-228-1660 E-mail: agency@goldinlit.com Web Site: www.goldinlit.com, pg 460

Junior, Melissa, ASM Publishing, 1752 "N" St NW, Washington, DC 20036-2904 Tel: 202-737-3600 E-mail: communications@asmusa.org; service@asmusa.org Web Site: www.asm.org; journals.asm.org, pg 19

Juodaitis, Thomas W, The Trinity Foundation, PO Box 68, Unicoi, TN 37692-0068 Tel: 423-743-0199 Web Site: www.trinityfoundation.org, pg 209

Jusino, John, HarperCollins Publishers LLC, 195 Broadway, New York, NY 10007 Tel: 212-207-7000 Web Site: www.harpercollins.com, pg 86

Jutkowitz, Edward, Camino Books Inc, PO Box 59026, Philadelphia, PA 19102-9026 Tel: 215-413-1917 Fax: 215-413-3255 E-mail: camino@caminobooks.com Web Site: www.caminobooks.com, pg 39

Juvier, Cristina, Scholastic Inc, 557 Broadway, New York, NY 10012 Tel: 212-343-6100 Toll Free Tel: 800-SCHOLASTIC (724-6527) Web Site: www.scholastic.com, pg 184

Kabaker, Brian, HeartMath LLC, 14700 W Park Ave, Boulder Creek, CA 95006 Tel: 831-338-8500 Toll Free Tel: 800-711-6221 Fax: 831-338-8504 E-mail: info@heartmath.org; service@heartmath.org Web Site: www.heartmath.org, pg 90

Kacian, Jim, Red Moon Press, PO Box 2461, Winchester, VA 22604-1661 Tel: 540-722-2156 Web Site: www.redmoonpress.com, pg 172

Kadair, Catherine, Louisiana State University Press, 338 Johnston Hall, Baton Rouge, LA 70803 Tel: 225-578-6294 E-mail: lsupress@lsu.edu Web Site: lsupress.org, pg 120

Kado, Martina PhD, Maryland Center for History & Culture (MCHC), 610 Park Ave, Baltimore, MD 21201 Tel: 410-685-3750; 410-685-3750 ext 377 (orders) Fax: 410-385-2105 E-mail: shop@mdhistory.org Web Site: www.mdhistory.org; shop.mdhistory.org, pg 126

Kaeser, Scott, Tide-mark Press, 207 Oakwood Ave, West Hartford, CT 06119 Tel: 860-310-3370 Toll Free Tel: 800-338-2508 Fax: 860-310-3654 E-mail: customerservice@tide-mark.com, pg 207

Kafoury, Matt, The Center for Fiction, 15 Lafayette Ave, Brooklyn, NY 11217 Tel: 212-755-6710 E-mail: info@centerforfiction.org Web Site: centerforfiction.org, pg 503

Kahan, Rachel, HarperCollins Publishers LLC, 195 Broadway, New York, NY 10007 Tel: 212-207-7000 Web Site: www.harpercollins.com, pg 86

Kahansky, Noah, Penguin Random House Canada, a Penguin Random House company, 320 Front St W, Suite 1400, Toronto, ON M5V 3B6, Canada Tel: 416-364-4449 Toll Free Tel: 888-523-9292 (cust serv) E-mail: canadaweb@penguinrandomhouse.com; customerservicescanada@penguinrandomhouse.com Web Site: www.penguinrandomhouse.ca, pg 416

Kahn, Jody, Brandt & Hochman Literary Agents Inc, 1501 Broadway, Suite 2310, New York, NY 10036 Tel: 212-840-5760 Fax: 212-840-5776 Web Site: brandthochman.com, pg 452

Kahn, Julie, New Harbinger Publications Inc, 5674 Shattuck Ave, Oakland, CA 94609 Tel: 510-652-0215 Toll Free Tel: 800-748-6273 (orders only) Fax: 510-652-5472 Toll Free Fax: 800-652-1613 E-mail: customerservice@newharbinger.com Web Site: www.newharbinger.com, pg 140

Kahn, Kenneth F, LRP Publications, 360 Hiatt Dr, Palm Beach Gardens, FL 33418 Tel: 561-622-6520 Toll Free Tel: 800-341-7874 Fax: 561-622-2423 E-mail: custserve@lrp.com Web Site: www.lrp.com; www.shoplrp.com, pg 121

Kaiman, Ken, Square One Publishers Inc, 115 Herricks Rd, Garden City Park, NY 11040 Tel: 516-535-2010 Toll Free Tel: 877-900-BOOK (900-2665) Fax: 516-535-2014 E-mail: sq1publish@aol.com Web Site: www.squareonepublishers.com, pg 196

Kaiser, Cecily, Penguin Workshop, c/o Penguin Random House LLC, 1745 Broadway, New York, NY 10019 Tel: 212-782-9000 Web Site: www.penguin.com/publishers/penguinworkshop/, pg 156

Kaiser, Jackie, Westwood Creative Artists Ltd, 386 Huron St, Toronto, ON M5S 2G6, Canada Tel: 416-964-3302 Fax: 416-964-3302 E-mail: wca_office@wcaltd.com Web Site: www.wcaltd.com, pg 481

Kaiser, Kathleen, Writers & Publishers Network (WPN), 1129 Maricopa Hwy, No 142, Ojai, CA 93023 Web Site: writersandpublishersnetwork.org, pg 522

Kaiser, Menachem, Fence Books, 36-09 28 Ave, Apt 3R, Astoria, NY 11103-4518 Tel: 518-567-7006 Web Site: www.fenceportal.org, pg 71

Kaita, Melissa, Second Story Press, 20 Maud St, Suite 401, Toronto, ON M5V 2M5, Canada Tel: 416-537-7850 Fax: 416-537-0588 E-mail: info@secondstorypress.ca Web Site: secondstorypress.ca, pg 419

Kaitano, Chiwoniso "Chi", MacDowell Fellowships, 100 High St, Peterborough, NH 03458 Tel: 603-924-3886 E-mail: info@macdowell.org; admissions@macdowell.org Web Site: www.macdowell.org, pg 628

Kakar, Samir, Aptara Inc, 2901 Telestar Ct, Suite 522, Falls Church, VA 22042 Tel: 703-352-0001 E-mail: moreinfo@aptaracorp.com Web Site: www.aptaracorp.com, pg 435

Kakoutis, Katherine, House of Anansi Press Inc, 128 Sterling Rd, Lower Level, Toronto, ON M6R 2B7, Canada Tel: 416-363-4343 Fax: 416-363-1017 E-mail: customerservice@houseofanansi.com Web Site: houseofanansi.com, pg 409

Kalajian, James, Jenkins Group Inc, 1129 Woodmere Ave, Suite B, Traverse City, MI 49686 Tel: 231-933-0445; 213-883-5365 E-mail: info@jenkinsgroupinc.com Web Site: www.jenkinsgroupinc.com, pg 441

Kalchik, Judey, Book Industry Charitable Foundation (BINC), 3135 S State St, Suite 203, Ann Arbor, MI 48108 Toll Free Tel: 866-733-9064 E-mail: info@bincfoundation.org Web Site: www.bincfoundation.org, pg 525

Kalchik, Judey, Denver Publishing Institute Scholarship, 3135 S State St, Suite 203, Ann Arbor, MI 48108 Toll Free Tel: 866-733-9064 E-mail: info@bincfoundation.org Web Site: www.bincfoundation.org/denver-publishing-institute/, pg 595

Kalchik, Judey, Carla Gray Memorial Scholarship, 3135 S State St, Suite 203, Ann Arbor, MI 48108 Toll Free Tel: 866-733-9064 E-mail: info@bincfoundation.org Web Site: www.bincfoundation.org/carla-gray/, pg 609

Kalchik, Judey, Higher Education Scholarship Program, 3135 S State St, Suite 203, Ann Arbor, MI 48108 Toll Free Tel: 866-733-9064 E-mail: info@bincfoundation.org Web Site: www.bincfoundation.org/scholarship, pg 612

Kalchik, Judey, Susan Kamil Scholarship for Emerging Writers, 3135 S State St, Suite 203, Ann Arbor, MI 48108 Toll Free Tel: 866-733-9064 E-mail: info@bincfoundation.org Web Site: bincfoundation.org/susankamil-scholarship, pg 619

Kalchik, Judey, George Markey Keating Memorial Scholarships, 3135 S State St, Suite 203, Ann Arbor, MI 48108 Toll Free Tel: 866-733-9064 E-mail: info@bincfoundation.org Web Site: www.bincfoundation.org, pg 619

Kalchik, Judey, Macmillan Booksellers Professional Development Scholarship, 3135 S State St, Suite 203, Ann Arbor, MI 48108 *Toll Free Tel:* 866-733-9064 *E-mail:* info@bincfoundation.org *Web Site:* www.bincfoundation.org/scholarship, pg 628

Kalchik, Judey, Karl Pohrt Tribute Award, 3135 S State St, Suite 203, Ann Arbor, MI 48108 *Toll Free Tel:* 866-733-9064 *E-mail:* info@bincfoundation.org *Web Site:* www.bincfoundation.org/scholarship, pg 651

Kaler, Michael, Basic Books Group, 1290 Avenue of the Americas, New York, NY 10104 *Tel:* 212-340-8100 *Toll Free Tel:* 800-343-4499 (cust serv) *Fax:* 212-340-8105 *E-mail:* customer.service@hbgusa.com; orders@hbgusa.com *Web Site:* www.hachettebookgroup.com/imprint/basic-books/, pg 25

Kalett, Alison, Princeton University Press, 41 William St, Princeton, NJ 08540-5237 *Tel:* 609-258-4900 *Fax:* 609-258-6305 *E-mail:* info@press.princeton.edu *Web Site:* press.princeton.edu, pg 164

Kalia, Aneeka, Viking Children's Books, c/o Penguin Random House LLC, 1745 Broadway, New York, NY 10019 *Tel:* 212-782-9000 *Web Site:* www.penguin.com/viking-childrens-books-overview/, pg 224

Kalina, Sarah, Kirkus Prize, 1140 Broadway, Suite 802, New York, NY 10001 *Web Site:* www.kirkusreviews.com/prize, pg 620

Kalish, Ilene, New York University Press, 838 Broadway, 3rd fl, New York, NY 10003-4812 *Tel:* 212-998-2575 (edit) *Toll Free Tel:* 800-996-6987 (orders) *Fax:* 212-995-4798 (orders) *E-mail:* nyupressinfo@nyu.edu (cust care) *Web Site:* www.nyupress.org, pg 141

Kallet, Jeff, Ohio University Press, Alden Library, Suite 101, 30 Park Place, Athens, OH 45701-2909 *Tel:* 740-593-1154 *Web Site:* www.ohioswallow.com, pg 146

Kallin, Anne, Stephen Leacock Memorial Medal for Humour, PO Box 854, Orillia, ON L3V 6K8, Canada *Tel:* 705-326-9286 *E-mail:* info@leacock.ca *Web Site:* www.leacock.ca, pg 622

Kalman, Bobbie, Crabtree Publishing Co, 347 Fifth Ave, Suite 1402-145, New York, NY 10016 *Tel:* 212-496-5040 *Toll Free Tel:* 800-387-7650 *Toll Free Fax:* 800-355-7166 *E-mail:* custserv@crabtreebooks.com *Web Site:* www.crabtreebooks.com, pg 54

Kalman, Bobbie, Crabtree Publishing Co Ltd, 616 Welland Ave, St Catharines, ON L2M 5V6, Canada *Tel:* 905-682-5221 *Toll Free Tel:* 800-387-7650 *Fax:* 905-682-7166 *Toll Free Fax:* 800-355-7166 *E-mail:* custserv@crabtreebooks.com; sales@crabtreebooks.com; orders@crabtreebooks.com *Web Site:* www.crabtreebooks.ca, pg 400

Kalman, Jason, Hebrew Union College Press, 3101 Clifton Ave, Cincinnati, OH 45220 *Tel:* 513-221-1875 *Fax:* 513-221-0321 *Web Site:* press.huc.edu, pg 90

Kals, Josefine, Simon & Schuster, 1230 Avenue of the Americas, New York, NY 10020 *Tel:* 212-698-7000 *Toll Free Tel:* 800-223-2348 (cust serv); 800-223-2336 (orders) *Toll Free Fax:* 800-943-9831 (orders) *Web Site:* simonandschusterpublishing.com/simonandschuster/, pg 188

Kalweit, Burk, American Academy of Environmental Engineers & Scientists®, 147 Old Solomons Island Rd, Suite 303, Annapolis, MD 21401 *Tel:* 410-266-3311 *Fax:* 410-266-7653 *E-mail:* info@aaees.org *Web Site:* www.aaees.org, pg 8

Kam, Bridgette, Westwood Creative Artists Ltd, 386 Huron St, Toronto, ON M5S 2G6, Canada *Tel:* 416-964-3302 *Fax:* 416-964-3302 *E-mail:* wca_office@wcaltd.com *Web Site:* www.wcaltd.com, pg 481

Kam, Kristopher, Random House Children's Books, c/o Penguin Random House LLC, 1745 Broadway, New York, NY 10019 *Tel:* 212-782-9000 *Web Site:* rhcbooks.com, pg 170

Kamalhedayat, Neda, Candlewick Press, 99 Dover St, Somerville, MA 02144-2825 *Tel:* 617-661-3330 *Fax:* 617-661-0565 *E-mail:* bigbear@candlewick.com; salesinfo@candlewick.com *Web Site:* candlewick.com, pg 40

Kamalhedayat, Neda, Holiday House Publishing Inc, 50 Broad St, New York, NY 10004 *Tel:* 212-688-0085 *Fax:* 212-421-6134 *E-mail:* info@holidayhouse.com *Web Site:* www.holidayhouse.com, pg 94

Kamalhedayat, Neda, Peachtree Publishing Co Inc, 1700 Chattahoochee Ave, Atlanta, GA 30318-2112 *Tel:* 404-876-8761 *Toll Free Tel:* 800-241-0113 *Fax:* 404-875-2578 *Toll Free Fax:* 800-875-8909 *E-mail:* hello@peachtree-online.com; orders@peachtree-online.com; sales@peachtree-online.com *Web Site:* www.peachtreebooks.com; www.peachtree-online.com, pg 153

Kamaliddin, Hala, Penguin Random House Canada, a Penguin Random House company, 320 Front St W, Suite 1400, Toronto, ON M5V 3B6, Canada *Tel:* 416-364-4449 *Toll Free Tel:* 888-523-9292 (cust serv) *E-mail:* canadaweb@penguinrandomhouse.com; customerservicescanada@penguinrandomhouse.com *Web Site:* www.penguinrandomhouse.ca, pg 416

Kamat, Kaustubh, Macmillan, 120 Broadway, 22nd fl, New York, NY 10271 *E-mail:* press.inquiries@macmillan.com *Web Site:* us.macmillan.com, pg 122

Kamath, Angie, New York University, Center for Publishing & Applied Liberal Arts, 7 E 12 St, New York, NY 10003 *Tel:* 212-998-7200 *E-mail:* sps.info@nyu.edu *Web Site:* www.scps.nyu.edu/professional-pathways/topics.html, pg 563

Kambury, Rachel, HarperCollins Publishers LLC, 195 Broadway, New York, NY 10007 *Tel:* 212-207-7000 *Web Site:* www.harpercollins.com, pg 87

Kamin, Hayley, American Psychological Association, 750 First St NE, Washington, DC 20002 *Tel:* 202-336-5510 *Toll Free Tel:* 800-374-2721 *Fax:* 202-336-5502 *E-mail:* order@apa.org; booksales@apa.org *Web Site:* www.apa.org/books, pg 12

Kamin, Rachel, AJL Jewish Fiction Award, PO Box 1118, Teaneck, NJ 07666 *Tel:* 201-371-3255 *E-mail:* info@jewishlibraries.org *Web Site:* jewishlibraries.org/AJL_Jewish_Fiction_Award, pg 571

Kamin, Sari, Houghton Mifflin Harcourt Trade & Reference Division, 125 High St, Boston, MA 02110 *Tel:* 617-351-5000 *Web Site:* www.hmhco.com, pg 96

Kamir, Taeyana, Math Solutions®, One Harbor Dr, Suite 101, Sausalito, CA 94965 *Toll Free Tel:* 877-234-7323 *Toll Free Fax:* 800-724-4716 *E-mail:* info@mathsolutions.com; orders@mathsolutions.com *Web Site:* www.mathsolutions.com; store.mathsolutions.com, pg 127

Kan, Elianna, Regal Hoffmann & Associates LLC, 157 13 St, Brooklyn, NY 11215 *Tel:* 212-684-7900 *E-mail:* info@rhaliterary.com; submissions@rhaliterary.com *Web Site:* www.rhaliterary.com, pg 473

Kanagy, Dave, Society for Mining, Metallurgy & Exploration, 12999 E Adam Aircraft Circle, Englewood, CO 80112 *Tel:* 303-948-4200 *Toll Free Tel:* 800-763-3132 *Fax:* 303-973-3845 *E-mail:* cs@smenet.org; books@smenet.org *Web Site:* www.smenet.org, pg 192

Kanar, Erin, Simon & Schuster, 1230 Avenue of the Americas, New York, NY 10020 *Tel:* 212-698-7000 *Toll Free Tel:* 800-223-2348 (cust serv); 800-223-2336 (orders) *Toll Free Fax:* 800-943-9831 (orders) *Web Site:* simonandschusterpublishing.com/simonandschuster/, pg 188

Kandel, Rama, Sourcebooks LLC, 1935 Brookdale Rd, Suite 139, Naperville, IL 60563 *Tel:* 630-961-3900 *Toll Free Tel:* 800-432-7444 *Fax:* 630-961-2168 *E-mail:* info@sourcebooks.com *Web Site:* www.sourcebooks.com, pg 195

Kane, Adam, Naval Institute Press, 291 Wood Rd, Annapolis, MD 21402-5034 *Tel:* 410-268-6110 *Toll Free Tel:* 800-233-8764 *Fax:* 410-295-1084 *E-mail:* customer@usni.org (cust inquiries) *Web Site:* www.usni.org/press/books; www.usni.org, pg 139

Kane, Barry, Light-Beams Publishing, 36 Blandings Way, Biddeford, ME 04005 *Tel:* 603-659-1300 *E-mail:* info@light-beams.com *Web Site:* www.light-beams.com, pg 116

Kane, Brenda, American Program Bureau Inc, One Gateway Center, Suite 751, Newton, MA 02458 *Tel:* 617-614-1600 *E-mail:* apb@apbspeakers.com *Web Site:* www.apbspeakers.com, pg 487

Kane, Erin, Random House Publishing Group, 1745 Broadway, New York, NY 10019 *Toll Free Tel:* 800-200-3552 *Web Site:* www.randomhousebooks.com, pg 171

Kane, Morgan, Farrar, Straus & Giroux Books for Young Readers, 120 Broadway, New York, NY 10271 *Tel:* 212-741-6900 *Toll Free Tel:* 888-330-8477 (orders) *E-mail:* childrens.publicity@macmillanusa.com; childrensrights@macmillanusa.com *Web Site:* us.macmillan.com/mackids, pg 70

Kane, Morgan, Roaring Brook Press, 120 Broadway, New York, NY 10271 *Tel:* 646-307-5151 *Web Site:* us.macmillan.com/publishers/roaring-brook-press, pg 176

Kane, Sonia, Boydell & Brewer Inc, 668 Mount Hope Ave, Rochester, NY 14620-2731 *Tel:* 585-275-0419 *Fax:* 585-271-8778 *E-mail:* boydell@boydellusa.net *Web Site:* www.boydellandbrewer.com, pg 35

Kane, Sonia, University of Rochester Press, 668 Mount Hope Ave, Rochester, NY 14620-2731 *Tel:* 585-275-0419 *Fax:* 585-271-8778 *E-mail:* boydell@boydellusa.net *Web Site:* www.urpress.com, pg 220

Kane, Tracey, Liguori Publications, One Liguori Dr, Liguori, MO 63057-1000 *Tel:* 636-464-2500 *Toll Free Tel:* 800-325-9521 *Toll Free Fax:* 800-325-9526 (sales) *E-mail:* liguori@liguori.org (sales & cust serv) *Web Site:* www.liguori.org, pg 117

Kaneko, Amy, Arcadia Publishing Inc, 210 Wingo Way, Suite 200, Mount Pleasant, SC 29464 *Tel:* 843-853-2070 *E-mail:* retailers@arcadiapublishing.com *Web Site:* www.arcadiapublishing.com, pg 16

Kanellos, Dr Nicolas, Arte Publico Press, 4902 Gulf Fwy, Bldg 19, Rm 100, Houston, TX 77204-2004 *Tel:* 713-743-2998 (orders) *E-mail:* appinfo@uh.edu; bkorders@uh.edu *Web Site:* artepublicopress.com, pg 17

Kangas, Matt, Macmillan, 120 Broadway, 22nd fl, New York, NY 10271 *E-mail:* press.inquiries@macmillan.com *Web Site:* us.macmillan.com, pg 122

Kania, Alicia, BenBella Books Inc, 10440 N Central Expwy, Suite 800, Dallas, TX 75231-2264 *Tel:* 214-750-3600 *Web Site:* www.benbellabooks.com; www.smartpopbooks.com, pg 27

Kannath, Preethi, American Booksellers Association, 600 Mamaroneck Ave, Suite 400, Harrison, NY 10528 *Tel:* 914-406-7500 *Toll Free Tel:* 800-637-0037 *Fax:* 914-417-4013 *E-mail:* info@bookweb.org *Web Site:* www.bookweb.org, pg 494

Kantor, Camille, Kimberley Cameron & Associates LLC, 1550 Tiburon Blvd, Suite 704, Tiburon, CA 94920 *E-mail:* info@kimberleycameron.com *Web Site:* www.kimberleycameron.com, pg 453

Kantor, Sylvia, Ev Clark/Seth Payne Award for Young Science Journalists, PO Box 17337, Seattle, WA 98127 *Tel:* 206-880-0177 *E-mail:* info@casw.org *Web Site:* casw.org/casw/evert-clarkseth-payne-award-young-science-journalists; casw.submittable.com/submit, pg 590

Kantor, Sylvia, The Victor Cohn Prize for Excellence in Medical Science Reporting, PO Box 17337, Seattle, WA 98127 *Tel:* 206-880-0177 *E-mail:* info@casw.org *Web Site:* casw.org/casw/victor-cohn-prize-excellence-medical-science-reporting-0, pg 590

Kantor, Sylvia, Council for the Advancement of Science Writing (CASW), PO Box 17337, Seattle, WA 98127 *Tel:* 206-880-0177 *E-mail:* info@casw.org *Web Site:* casw.org, pg 504

Kantor, Sylvia, Taylor/Blakeslee Graduate Fellowships, PO Box 17337, Seattle, WA 98127 *Tel:* 206-880-0177 *E-mail:* info@casw.org *Web Site:* casw.org/casw/graduate-school-fellowships, pg 668

Kanya-Forstner, Martha, Doubleday Canada, 320 Front St W, Suite 1400, Toronto, ON M5V 3B6, Canada *Tel:* 416-364-4449 *Fax:* 416-598-7764 *Web Site:* www.penguinrandomhouse.ca, pg 401

Kanya-Forstner, Martha, Knopf Canada, 320 Front St W, Suite 1400, Toronto, ON M5V 3B6, Canada *Tel:* 416-364-4449 *Toll Free Tel:* 888-523-9292 *Fax:* 416-598-7764 *Web Site:* www.penguinrandomhouse.ca, pg 411

Kaplan, Genevieve, Kate Tufts Discovery Award, Harper East, Unit B-7, 160 E Tenth St, Claremont, CA 91711-6165 *Tel:* 909-621-8974 *E-mail:* tufts@cgu.edu *Web Site:* www.cgu.edu/tufts, pg 671

Kaplan, Genevieve, Kingsley Tufts Poetry Award, Harper East, Unit B-7, 160 E Tenth St, Claremont, CA 91711-6165 *Tel:* 909-621-8974 *E-mail:* tufts@cgu.edu *Web Site:* www.cgu.edu/tufts, pg 671

Kaplan, Joel, Syracuse University, SI Newhouse School of Public Communications, 215 University Place, Syracuse, NY 13244 *Tel:* 315-443-3627 *E-mail:* newhouse@syr.edu *Web Site:* newhouse.syr.edu/academics/programs, pg 565

Kaplan, Joyce, Kensington Publishing Corp, 900 Third Ave, 26th fl, New York, NY 10022 *Tel:* 212-407-1500 *Toll Free Tel:* 800-221-2647 *Fax:* 212-935-0699 *Web Site:* www.kensingtonbooks.com, pg 109

Kaplan, Liat, Picador, 120 Broadway, New York, NY 10271 *Tel:* 646-307-5151 *Fax:* 212-253-9627 *E-mail:* publicity@picadorusa.com *Web Site:* us.macmillan.com/picador, pg 160

Kaplan, Linda, DeFiore and Company Literary Management Inc, 47 E 19 St, 3rd fl, New York, NY 10003 *Tel:* 212-925-7744 *Fax:* 212-925-9803 *E-mail:* info@defliterary.com; submissions@defliterary.com *Web Site:* www.defliterary.com, pg 455

Kaplan, Rebecca, Harry N Abrams Inc, 195 Broadway, 9th fl, New York, NY 10007 *Tel:* 212-206-7715 *Toll Free Tel:* 800-345-1359 *Fax:* 212-645-8437 *E-mail:* abrams@abramsbooks.com; publicity@abramsbooks.com; sales@abramsbooks.com *Web Site:* www.abramsbooks.com, pg 3

Kaplan, Rick, National Association of Broadcasters (NAB), One "M" St SE, Washington, DC 20003 *Tel:* 202-429-5300 *E-mail:* nab@nab.org *Web Site:* www.nab.org, pg 136, 511

Kaplan, Stuart R, US Games Systems Inc, 179 Ludlow St, Stamford, CT 06902 *Tel:* 203-353-8400 *Toll Free Tel:* 800-54-GAMES (544-2637) *Fax:* 203-353-8431 *E-mail:* info@usgamesinc.com *Web Site:* www.usgamesinc.com, pg 223

Kaplow, Margaret, National Catholic Educational Association, 200 N Glebe Rd, Suite 310, Arlington, VA 22203 *Tel:* 571-257-0010 *Toll Free Tel:* 800-711-6232 *Fax:* 703-243-0025 *E-mail:* nceaadmin@ncea.org *Web Site:* www.ncea.org, pg 137

Kaplowitz, Marla, 4A's (American Association of Advertising Agencies), 25 W 45 St, 16th fl, New York, NY 10036 *Tel:* 212-682-2500 *E-mail:* media@4as.org; membership@4as.org *Web Site:* www.aaaa.org, pg 506

Kapoor, Prashant, Aptara Inc, 2901 Telestar Ct, Suite 522, Falls Church, VA 22042 *Tel:* 703-352-0001 *E-mail:* moreinfo@aptaracorp.com *Web Site:* www.aptaracorp.com, pg 435

Karagueuzian, Dikran, CSLI Publications, Stanford University, Cordura Hall, 220 Panama St, Stanford, CA 94305-4115 *Tel:* 650-723-1839 *Fax:* 650-725-2166 *E-mail:* pubs@csli.stanford.edu *Web Site:* cslipublications.stanford.edu, pg 56

Karchmar, Dorian, WME, 11 Madison Ave, New York, NY 10010 *Tel:* 212-586-5100 *Web Site:* www.wmeagency.com, pg 482

Kardon, Julia, HG Literary, 6 W 18 St, Suite 7R, New York, NY 10011 *E-mail:* foreign@hgliterary.com; rights@hgliterary.com *Web Site:* www.hgliterary.com, pg 463

Karl, Laraine, The Rockefeller University Press, 950 Third Ave, 2nd fl, New York, NY 10022 *Tel:* 212-327-7938 *E-mail:* rupress@rockefeller.edu *Web Site:* rupress.org, pg 176

Karle, John, St Martin's Press, LLC, 120 Broadway, New York, NY 10271 *E-mail:* publicity@stmartins.com; trademarketing@stmartins.com; foreignrights@stmartins.com *Web Site:* us.macmillan.com/smp, pg 181

Karnane, Pooja, Penguin Random House LLC, 1745 Broadway, New York, NY 10019 *Tel:* 212-782-9000 *Fax:* 212-726-0600 *Web Site:* www.penguinrandomhouse.com, pg 155

Karnedy, Frankie, Beacon Press, 24 Farnsworth St, Boston, MA 02210-1409 *Tel:* 617-742-2110 *Fax:* 617-723-3097 *E-mail:* production@beacon.org *Web Site:* www.beacon.org, pg 25

Karp, Jonathan, Simon & Schuster, 1230 Avenue of the Americas, New York, NY 10020 *Tel:* 212-698-7000 *Toll Free Tel:* 800-223-2348 (cust serv); 800-223-2336 (orders) *Toll Free Fax:* 800-943-9831 (orders) *Web Site:* simonandschusterpublishing.com/simonandschuster/, pg 188

Karp, Jonathan, Simon & Schuster, LLC, 1230 Avenue of the Americas, New York, NY 10020 *Tel:* 212-698-7000 *Toll Free Tel:* 800-223-2336 (orders) *Fax:* 212-698-7007 *Toll Free Fax:* 800-943-9831 (orders) *E-mail:* firstname.lastname@simonandschuster.com; purchaseorders@simonandschuster.com (orders) *Web Site:* www.simonandschuster.com, pg 189

Karpfinger, Barney M, The Karpfinger Agency, 357 W 20 St, New York, NY 10011-3379 *Tel:* 212-691-2690 *Fax:* 212-691-7129 *E-mail:* info@karpfinger.com (no queries or submissions) *Web Site:* karpfinger.com, pg 465

Karpinski, Lisa, J J Keller & Associates, Inc®, 3003 Breezewood Lane, Neenah, WI 54957 *Tel:* 920-722-2848 *Toll Free Tel:* 877-564-2333 *Toll Free Fax:* 800-727-7516 *E-mail:* customerservice@jjkeller.com; sales@jjkeller.com *Web Site:* www.jjkeller.com, pg 108

Karre, Andrew, Dutton Children's Books, c/o Penguin Random House LLC, 1745 Broadway, New York, NY 10019 *Tel:* 212-782-9000 *Web Site:* www.penguin.com/dutton-childrens-overview/, pg 62

Kartsev, Dr Vladimir, Metropolitan Classics, 26 Arthur Place, Yonkers, NY 10701 *Tel:* 914-375-6448 *Web Site:* www.fortrossinc.com, pg 130

Kartsev, Dr Vladimir P, Fort Ross Inc - International Representation for Artists, 26 Arthur Place, Yonkers, NY 10701 *Tel:* 914-375-6448, pg 459, 485

Kartz, Ellen, R Ross Annett Award for Children's Literature, 11759 Groat Rd NW, Edmonton, AB T5M 3K6, Canada *Tel:* 780-422-8174 *Toll Free Tel:* 800-665-5354 (AB only) *E-mail:* mail@writersguild.ab.ca *Web Site:* writersguild.ca, pg 573

Kartz, Ellen, Georges Bugnet Award for Fiction, 11759 Groat Rd NW, Edmonton, AB T5M 3K6, Canada *Tel:* 780-422-8174 *Toll Free Tel:* 800-665-5354 (AB only) *E-mail:* mail@writersguild.ab.ca *Web Site:* writersguild.ca, pg 585

Kartz, Ellen, The City of Calgary W O Mitchell Book Prize, 11759 Groat Rd NW, Edmonton, AB T5M 3K6, Canada *Tel:* 780-422-8174 *Toll Free Tel:* 800-665-5354 (AB only) *E-mail:* mail@writersguild.ab.ca *Web Site:* writersguild.ca, pg 590

Kartz, Ellen, Wilfrid Eggleston Award for Nonfiction, 11759 Groat Rd NW, Edmonton, AB T5M 3K6, Canada *Tel:* 780-422-8174 *Toll Free Tel:* 800-665-5354 (AB only) *E-mail:* mail@writersguild.ab.ca *Web Site:* writersguild.ca, pg 598

Kartz, Ellen, James H Gray Award for Short Nonfiction, 11759 Groat Rd NW, Edmonton, AB T5M 3K6, Canada *Tel:* 780-422-8174 *Toll Free Tel:* 800-665-5354 (AB only) *E-mail:* mail@writersguild.ab.ca *Web Site:* writersguild.ca, pg 609

Kartz, Ellen, The Robert Kroetsch City of Edmonton Book Prize, 11759 Groat Rd NW, Edmonton, AB T5M 3K6, Canada *Tel:* 780-422-8174 *Toll Free Tel:* 800-665-5354 (AB only) *E-mail:* mail@writersguild.ab.ca *Web Site:* writersguild.ca, pg 621

Kartz, Ellen, Howard O'Hagan Award for Short Story, 11759 Groat Rd NW, Edmonton, AB T5M 3K6, Canada *Tel:* 780-422-8174 *Toll Free Tel:* 800-665-5354 (AB only) *E-mail:* mail@writersguild.ab.ca *Web Site:* writersguild.ca, pg 643

Kartz, Ellen, Gwen Pharis Ringwood Award for Drama, 11759 Groat Rd NW, Edmonton, AB T5M 3K6, Canada *Tel:* 780-422-8174 *Toll Free Tel:* 800-665-5354 (AB only) *E-mail:* mail@writersguild.ab.ca *Web Site:* writersguild.ca, pg 656

Kartz, Ellen, Stephan G Stephansson Award for Poetry, 11759 Groat Rd NW, Edmonton, AB T5M 3K6, Canada *Tel:* 780-422-8174 *Toll Free Tel:* 800-665-5354 (AB only) *E-mail:* mail@writersguild.ab.ca *Web Site:* writersguild.ca, pg 666

Kartz, Ellen, Jon Whyte Memorial Essay Prize, 11759 Groat Rd NW, Edmonton, AB T5M 3K6, Canada *Tel:* 780-422-8174 *Toll Free Tel:* 800-665-5354 (AB only) *E-mail:* mail@writersguild.ab.ca *Web Site:* writersguild.ca, pg 675

Kartz, Ellen, Writers' Guild of Alberta, 11759 Groat Rd NW, Edmonton, AB T5M 3K6, Canada *Tel:* 780-422-8174 *Toll Free Tel:* 800-665-5354 (AB only) *E-mail:* mail@writersguild.ab.ca *Web Site:* writersguild.ca, pg 522

Kasper, Karl, Crabtree Publishing Co, 347 Fifth Ave, Suite 1402-145, New York, NY 10016 *Tel:* 212-496-5040 *Toll Free Tel:* 800-387-7650 *Toll Free Fax:* 800-355-7166 *E-mail:* custserv@crabtreebooks.com *Web Site:* www.crabtreebooks.com, pg 54

Kasper, Karl, Crabtree Publishing Co Ltd, 616 Welland Ave, St Catharines, ON L2M 5V6, Canada *Tel:* 905-682-5221 *Toll Free Tel:* 800-387-7650 *Fax:* 905-682-7166 *Toll Free Fax:* 800-355-7166 *E-mail:* custserv@crabtreebooks.com; sales@crabtreebooks.com; orders@crabtreebooks.com *Web Site:* www.crabtreebooks.ca, pg 400

Kass, David, Avid Reader Press, 1230 Avenue of the Americas, New York, NY 10020 *Web Site:* avidreaderpress.com, pg 23

Kass, Jenna, Random House Publishing Group, 1745 Broadway, New York, NY 10019 *Toll Free Tel:* 800-200-3552 *Web Site:* www.randomhousebooks.com, pg 171

Kass, Mallory, Scholastic Trade Publishing, 557 Broadway, New York, NY 10012 *Tel:* 212-343-6100; 212-343-4685 (export sales) *Fax:* 212-343-4714 (export sales) *Web Site:* www.scholastic.com, pg 184

Kastenmeier, Edward, Doubleday, c/o Penguin Random House LLC, 1745 Broadway, New York, NY 10019 *Tel:* 212-751-2600 *Fax:* 212-940-7390 (dom rts); 212-572-2662 (foreign rts) *Web Site:* knopfdoubleday.com/imprint/doubleday/; knopfdoubleday.com, pg 61

Kastner, Suzanne, GW Inc, 2290 Ball Dr, St Louis, MO 63146 *Tel:* 314-567-9854 *E-mail:* media@gwinc.com *Web Site:* www.gwinc.com, pg 440

Kasuga, Mika, Union Square & Co, 1166 Avenue of the Americas, 17th fl, New York, NY 10036-2715 *Tel:* 212-532-7160 *Toll Free Tel:* 800-387-9692 *Fax:* 212-213-2495 *Toll Free Fax:* 800-542-7567 *E-mail:* custservice@sterlingpublishing.com; customerservice@sterlingpublishing.com; editorial@sterlingpublishing.com; tradesales@sterlingpublishing.com *Web Site:* www.sterlingpublishing.com, pg 212

Katula, Ken, The Rosen Publishing Group Inc, 29 E 21 St, New York, NY 10010 *Toll Free Tel:* 800-237-9932 *Toll Free Fax:* 888-436-4643 *E-mail:* info@rosenpub.com *Web Site:* www.rosenpublishing.com, pg 177

Katz, David, Visual Media Alliance (VMA), 665 Third St, Suite 500, San Francisco, CA 94107-1926 *Tel:* 415-495-8242 *Toll Free Tel:* 800-659-3363 *Fax:* 415-520-1126 *E-mail:* info@vma.bz *Web Site:* main.vma.bz, pg 521

Katz, Elisha, Berkley, c/o Penguin Random House LLC, 1745 Broadway, 19th fl, New York, NY 10019 *Tel:* 212-366-2000 *Web Site:* www.penguin.com/publishers/berkley/; www.penguin.com/ace-overview/, pg 28

Katz, Laurie, Bloom's Literary Criticism, 132 W 31 St, 16th fl, New York, NY 10001 *Toll Free Tel:* 800-322-8755 *Toll Free Fax:* 800-678-3633 *E-mail:* custserv@infobase.com *Web Site:* www.infobasepublishing.com; www.infobase.com (online resources), pg 31

Katz, Laurie, Chelsea House, 132 W 31 St, 16th fl, New York, NY 10001 Toll Free Tel: 800-322-8755 Toll Free Fax: 800-678-3633 E-mail: custserv@infobase.com; info@infobase.com Web Site: www.infobasepublishing.com; www.infobase.com (online resources), pg 46

Katz, Michael, Tradewind Books, 202-1807 Maritime Mews, Vancouver, BC V6H 3W7, Canada Tel: 604-662-4405 E-mail: tradewindbooks@yahoo.com; tradewindbooks@gmail.com Web Site: www.tradewindbooks.com, pg 421

Katz, Tilden, International Association of Business Communicators (IABC), 330 N Wabash Ave, Suite 2000, Chicago, IL 60611 Tel: 312-321-6868 Toll Free Tel: 800-218-8097 Fax: 312-673-6708 E-mail: member_relations@iabc.com Web Site: www.iabc.com, pg 508

Katzenberger, Elaine, City Lights Publishers, 261 Columbus Ave, San Francisco, CA 94133 Tel: 415-362-8193 E-mail: staff@citylights.com Web Site: citylights.com, pg 48

Katzman, Julie T, Inter-American Development Bank, 1300 New York Ave NW, Washington, DC 20577 Tel: 202-623-1000 Fax: 202-623-3096 E-mail: pic@iadb.org Web Site: publications.iadb.org, pg 102

Kauffman, Elisabeth, San Francisco Writers Conference, 1901 Cleveland Ave, Suite D, Santa Rosa, CA 94501 Tel: 415-689-6301 E-mail: registrations@sfwriters.org; director@sfwriters.org; bizdev@sfwriters.org Web Site: www.sfwriters.org, pg 557

Kauffman, Elisabeth, San Francisco Writing Contest (SFWC), 1901 Cleveland Ave, Suite D, Santa Rosa, CA 94501 Tel: 415-689-6301 E-mail: contest@sfwriters.org; director@sfwriters.org Web Site: www.sfwriters.org, pg 658

Kauffman, Lisa, Rational Island Publishers, 719 Second Ave N, Seattle, WA 98109 Tel: 206-284-0311 E-mail: ircc@rc.org Web Site: www.rc.org, pg 171

Kaufman, Anna, Pantheon Books, c/o Penguin Random House LLC, 1745 Broadway, New York, NY 10019 Tel: 212-751-2600 Fax: 212-940-7390 (dom rts); 212-572-2662 (foreign rts) Web Site: knopfdoubleday.com/imprint/pantheon/; knopfdoubleday.com, pg 150

Kaufman, Brian, Anvil Press Publishers, PO Box 3008, MPO, Vancouver, BC V6B 3X5, Canada Tel: 604-876-8710 E-mail: info@anvilpress.com Web Site: www.anvilpress.com, pg 395

Kaufman, Carol, Jewish Book Council, 520 Eighth Ave, 4th fl, New York, NY 10018 Tel: 212-201-2920 Fax: 212-532-4952 E-mail: info@jewishbooks.org Web Site: www.jewishbookcouncil.org, pg 509

Kaufman, Carol, National Jewish Book Award-Children's Picture Book, 520 Eighth Ave, 4th fl, New York, NY 10018 Tel: 212-201-2920 Fax: 212-532-4952 E-mail: njba@jewishbooks.org Web Site: www.jewishbookcouncil.org/awards, pg 637

Kaufman, Carol, National Jewish Book Award-Natan Notable Books, 520 Eighth Ave, 4th fl, New York, NY 10018 Tel: 212-201-2920 Fax: 212-532-4952 E-mail: njba@jewishbooks.org; natannotable@jewishbooks.org Web Site: www.jewishbookcouncil.org/awards, pg 637

Kaufman, Carol, National Jewish Book Award-Young Adult Literature, 520 Eighth Ave, 4th fl, New York, NY 10018 Tel: 212-201-2920 Fax: 212-532-4952 E-mail: njba@jewishbooks.org Web Site: www.jewishbookcouncil.org/awards, pg 637

Kaufman, Carol, National Jewish Book Awards, 520 Eighth Ave, 4th fl, New York, NY 10018 Tel: 212-201-2920 Fax: 212-532-4952 E-mail: njba@jewishbooks.org Web Site: www.jewishbookcouncil.org/awards, pg 637

Kaufman, Celeste, The Center for Fiction, 15 Lafayette Ave, Brooklyn, NY 11217 Tel: 212-755-6710 E-mail: info@centerforfiction.org Web Site: centerforfiction.org, pg 503

Kaufman, Gabe, Jump!, 5357 Penn Ave, Minneapolis, MN 55419 Toll Free Tel: 888-799-1860 Toll Free Fax: 800-675-6679 E-mail: customercare@jumplibrary.com Web Site: www.jumplibrary.com, pg 107

Kaufman, Jason, Doubleday, c/o Penguin Random House LLC, 1745 Broadway, New York, NY 10019 Tel: 212-751-2600 Fax: 212-940-7390 (dom rts); 212-572-2662 (foreign rts) Web Site: knopfdoubleday.com/imprint/doubleday/; knopfdoubleday.com, pg 61

Kaufman, Sophia, HarperCollins Publishers LLC, 195 Broadway, New York, NY 10007 Tel: 212-207-7000 Web Site: www.harpercollins.com, pg 87

Kavaler, Ethan Matt, Centre for Reformation & Renaissance Studies (CRRS), 71 Queen's Park Crescent E, Toronto, ON M5S 1K7, Canada Tel: 416-585-4465 Fax: 416-585-4430 (attn: CRRS) E-mail: crrs.publications@utoronto.ca Web Site: crrs.ca, pg 399

Kawar, Tamara, DeFiore and Company Literary Management Inc, 47 E 19 St, 3rd fl, New York, NY 10003 Tel: 212-925-7744 Fax: 212-925-9803 E-mail: info@defliterary.com; submissions@defliterary.com Web Site: www.defliterary.com, pg 456

Kay, Jeremy, Bartleby Press, 8926 Baltimore St, No 858, Savage, MD 20763 Tel: 301-589-5831 Toll Free Tel: 800-953-9929 E-mail: inquiries@bartlebythepublisher.com Web Site: www.bartlebythepublisher.com, pg 24

Kean, Carla, Penguin Random House Canada, a Penguin Random House company, 320 Front St W, Suite 1400, Toronto, ON M5V 3B6, Canada Tel: 416-364-4449 Toll Free Tel: 888-523-9292 (cust serv) E-mail: canadaweb@penguinrandomhouse.com; customerservicescanada@penguinrandomhouse.com Web Site: www.penguinrandomhouse.ca, pg 415

Kean, Carla, Seal Books, 320 Front St W, Suite 1400, Toronto, ON M5V 3B6, Canada Tel: 416-364-4449 Toll Free Tel: 888-523-9292 (order desk) Fax: 416-598-7764 Web Site: www.penguinrandomhouse.ca, pg 419

Kean, Linda, International Monetary Fund (IMF), Editorial & Publications Division, 700 19 St NW, HQ1-5-355, Washington, DC 20431 Tel: 202-623-7430 E-mail: publications@imf.org Web Site: bookstore.imf.org; elibrary.imf.org (online collection); www.imf.org/publications, pg 103

Kean, Michael, The Baker Street Irregulars (BSI), 3040 Sloat Rd, Pebble Beach, CA 93953 Tel: 831-372-8852 E-mail: service@bakerstreetirregulars.com Web Site: bakerstreetirregulars.com, pg 500

Keane, Christopher, American Geosciences Institute (AGI), 4220 King St, Alexandria, VA 22302-1502 Tel: 703-379-2480 (ext 246) E-mail: agi@americangeosciences.org Web Site: www.americangeosciences.org; www.geosciencestore.org, pg 10

Keane, Stephanie, Harry N Abrams Inc, 195 Broadway, 9th fl, New York, NY 10007 Tel: 212-206-7715 Toll Free Tel: 800-345-1359 Fax: 212-645-8437 E-mail: abrams@abramsbooks.com; publicity@abramsbooks.com; sales@abramsbooks.com Web Site: www.abramsbooks.com, pg 3

Kearn, Vickie, Princeton University Press, 41 William St, Princeton, NJ 08540-5237 Tel: 609-258-4900 Fax: 609-258-6305 E-mail: info@press.princeton.edu Web Site: press.princeton.edu, pg 164

Kearney, Bridget, Random House Publishing Group, 1745 Broadway, New York, NY 10019 Toll Free Tel: 800-200-3552 Web Site: www.randomhousebooks.com, pg 171

Kearney, Ryan, Random House Publishing Group, 1745 Broadway, New York, NY 10019 Toll Free Tel: 800-200-3552 Web Site: www.randomhousebooks.com, pg 171

Keat, David, Abraham Lincoln Institute Book Award, c/o ALI Treasurer, 4158 Vernoy Hills Rd, Fairfax, VA 22030 Web Site: www.lincoln-institute.org, pg 625

Keating, Kat, HarperCollins Children's Books, 195 Broadway, New York, NY 10007 Tel: 212-207-7000 Web Site: www.harpercollins.com/childrens, pg 85

Keating, Kate, Random House Children's Books, c/o Penguin Random House LLC, 1745 Broadway, New York, NY 10019 Tel: 212-782-9000 Web Site: www.rhcbooks.com, pg 169

Keating, Katelyn, Berrett-Koehler Publishers Inc, 1333 Broadway, Suite 1000, Oakland, CA 94612 Tel: 510-817-2277 Fax: 510-817-2278 E-mail: bkpub@bkpub.com Web Site: www.bkconnection.com, pg 29

Keating, Trena, Union Literary, 30 Vandam St, Suite 5A, New York, NY 10013 Tel: 212-255-2112 Web Site: www.unionliterary.com, pg 480

Keay, Rebecca, Perfection Learning®, 1000 N Second Ave, Logan, IA 51546-1061 Tel: 712-644-2831 Toll Free Tel: 800-831-4190 Toll Free Fax: 800-543-2745 E-mail: orders@perfectionlearning.com Web Site: www.perfectionlearning.com, pg 158

Keay, Steve, Perfection Learning®, 1000 N Second Ave, Logan, IA 51546-1061 Tel: 712-644-2831 Toll Free Tel: 800-831-4190 Toll Free Fax: 800-543-2745 E-mail: orders@perfectionlearning.com Web Site: www.perfectionlearning.com, pg 158

Keck, Elle, HarperCollins Publishers LLC, 195 Broadway, New York, NY 10007 Tel: 212-207-7000 Web Site: www.harpercollins.com, pg 87

Kecskemethy, Tom, American Academy of Political & Social Science (AAPSS), 220 S 40 St, Suite 201-E, Philadelphia, PA 19104-3543 Tel: 215-746-6500 Fax: 215-573-2667 Web Site: www.aapss.org, pg 494

Keefe, Alison, Sasquatch Books, 1904 S Third Ave, Suite 710, Seattle, WA 98101 Tel: 206-467-4300 Toll Free Tel: 800-775-0817 Fax: 206-467-4301 E-mail: custserv@sasquatchbooks.com Web Site: sasquatchbooks.com, pg 182

Keefe, Deanna M, Liturgy Training Publications, 3949 S Racine Ave, Chicago, IL 60609-2523 Tel: 773-579-4900 Toll Free Tel: 800-933-1800 (US & CN only orders) Fax: 773-579-4929 E-mail: orders@ltp.org Web Site: www.ltp.org, pg 119

Keefe, Laura, Alfred A Knopf, c/o Penguin Random House LLC, 1745 Broadway, New York, NY 10019 Tel: 212-751-2600 Fax: 212-940-7390 (dom rts); 212-572-2662 (foreign rts) Web Site: knopfdoubleday.com/imprint/knopf/; knopfdoubleday.com, pg 110

Keeler, Laura, The MIT Press, One Broadway, 12th fl, Cambridge, MA 02142 Tel: 617-253-5255 Toll Free Tel: 800-405-1619 (orders) Fax: 617-258-6779; 617-577-1545 (orders) Web Site: mitpress.mit.edu, pg 132

Keenan, Jennifer, Houghton Mifflin Harcourt Trade & Reference Division, 125 High St, Boston, MA 02110 Tel: 617-351-5000 Web Site: www.hmhco.com, pg 96

Keenan, Kathleen, Kids Can Press Ltd, 25 Dockside Dr, Toronto, ON M5A 0B5, Canada Tel: 416-479-7000 Toll Free Tel: 800-265-0884 Fax: 416-960-5437 E-mail: info@kidscan.com; customerservice@kidscan.com Web Site: www.kidscanpress.com; www.kidscanpress.ca, pg 411

Keene, Ann T, Edit Etc, 26 Country Lane, Brunswick, ME 04011 Tel: 914-715-5849 E-mail: atkedit@cs.com Web Site: www.anntkeene.com, pg 438

Keene, Elizabeth, Thames & Hudson, 500 Fifth Ave, New York, NY 10110 Tel: 212-354-3763 Toll Free Tel: 800-233-4830 Fax: 212-398-1252 E-mail: bookinfo@thames.wwnorton.com Web Site: www.thamesandhudsonusa.com, pg 205

Keene, Katie, University Press of Mississippi, 3825 Ridgewood Rd, Jackson, MS 39211-6492 Tel: 601-432-6205 Toll Free Tel: 800-737-7788 (orders & cust serv) Fax: 601-432-6217 E-mail: press@mississippi.edu Web Site: www.upress.state.ms.us, pg 222

Keener, Lamar, Evangelical Press Association (EPA), PO Box 1787, Queen Creek, AZ 85142 Toll Free Tel: 888-311-1731 E-mail: info@evangelicalpress.com Web Site: www.evangelicalpress.com, pg 505

Keesler, Darin, Picador, 120 Broadway, New York, NY 10271 Tel: 646-307-5151 Fax: 212-253-9627 E-mail: publicity@picadorusa.com Web Site: us.macmillan.com/picador, pg 159

Kehoe, Bret, Sourcebooks LLC, 1935 Brookdale Rd, Suite 139, Naperville, IL 60563 *Tel:* 630-961-3900 *Toll Free Tel:* 800-432-7444 *Fax:* 630-961-2168 *E-mail:* info@sourcebooks.com *Web Site:* www.sourcebooks.com, pg 194

Kehoe, Jeff, Harvard Business Review Press, 20 Guest St, Suite 700, Brighton, MA 02135 *Tel:* 617-783-7400 *Fax:* 617-783-7489 *E-mail:* custserv@hbsp.harvard.edu *Web Site:* www.harvardbusiness.org, pg 87

Keim, Betty, Keim Publishing, 66 Main St, Suite 807, Yonkers, NY 10701 *Tel:* 917-655-7190, pg 441

Keiper, Ben, Samuel French, Inc, 250 W 57 St, 6th fl, New York, NY 10107-0102 *Toll Free Tel:* 866-979-0447 *E-mail:* info@concordtheatricals.com *Web Site:* www.concordtheatricals.com/a/4346/samuel-a-french, pg 75

Keir, Danielle, Berkley, c/o Penguin Random House LLC, 1745 Broadway, 19th fl, New York, NY 10019 *Tel:* 212-366-2000 *Web Site:* www.penguin.com/publishers/berkley/; www.penguin.com/ace-overview/, pg 28

Keiser, Alana, Graywolf Press, 212 Third Ave N, Suite 485, Minneapolis, MN 55401 *Tel:* 651-641-0077 *Fax:* 651-641-0036 *E-mail:* wolves@graywolfpress.org (no ms queries, sample chapters or proposals) *Web Site:* www.graywolfpress.org, pg 81

Keith, Amanda, Wake Forest University Press, 2518 Reynolda Rd, Winston-Salem, NC 27106 *Tel:* 336-758-5448 *Fax:* 336-842-3853 *E-mail:* wfupress@wfu.edu *Web Site:* wfupress.wfu.edu, pg 225

Keith, Jeffrey, Linda Fairchild & Company LLC, 101 Lucas Valley Rd, Suite 363, San Rafael, CA 94903 *Tel:* 415-336-6407 *Web Site:* www.lindafairchild.com, pg 439

Kelada, Mike, Aquila Communications Inc, 176 Beacon Hill, Montreal, QC H9W 1T6, Canada *Toll Free Tel:* 800-667-7071 *Web Site:* www.aquilacommunications.com, pg 395

Kelada, Sami, Aquila Communications Inc, 176 Beacon Hill, Montreal, QC H9W 1T6, Canada *Toll Free Tel:* 800-667-7071 *Web Site:* www.aquilacommunications.com, pg 395

Kelaher, Christopher, American Psychological Association, 750 First St NE, Washington, DC 20002 *Tel:* 202-336-5510 *Toll Free Tel:* 800-374-2721 *Fax:* 202-336-5502 *E-mail:* order@apa.org; booksales@apa.org *Web Site:* www.apa.org/books, pg 12

Kelleher, Alex, Simon & Schuster Children's Publishing, 1230 Avenue of the Americas, New York, NY 10020 *Tel:* 212-698-7000 *Web Site:* www.simonandschuster.com/kids; www.simonandschuster.com/teen; simonandschuster.net; simonandschuster.biz, pg 189

Kelleher, Michael, Windham-Campbell Prizes, Beinecke Rare Book & Manuscript Library, 121 Wall St, New Haven, CT 06511 *Fax:* 203-432-9033 *Web Site:* windhamcampbell.org, pg 676

Kelleher, Thomas, Basic Books Group, 1290 Avenue of the Americas, New York, NY 10104 *Tel:* 212-340-8100 *Toll Free Tel:* 800-343-4499 (cust serv) *Fax:* 212-340-8105 *E-mail:* customer.service@hbgusa.com; orders@hbgusa.com *Web Site:* www.hachettebookgroup.com/imprint/basic-books/, pg 25

Keller, Cisa, Redleaf Press®, 10 Yorkton Ct, St Paul, MN 55117 *Tel:* 651-641-0508 *Toll Free Tel:* 800-423-8309 *Fax:* 651-641-0115 *E-mail:* customerservice@redleafpress.org; info@redleafpress.org; marketing@redleafpress.org *Web Site:* www.redleafpress.org, pg 173

Keller, Jim, J J Keller & Associates, Inc®, 3003 Breezewood Lane, Neenah, WI 54957 *Tel:* 920-722-2848 *Toll Free Tel:* 877-564-2333 *Toll Free Fax:* 800-727-7516 *E-mail:* customerservice@jjkeller.com; sales@jjkeller.com *Web Site:* www.jjkeller.com, pg 108

Keller, Phoebe, The AEI Press, 1789 Massachusetts Ave NW, Washington, DC 20036 *Tel:* 202-862-5800 *Fax:* 202-862-7177 *Web Site:* www.aei.org, pg 5

Keller, Robert L, J J Keller & Associates, Inc®, 3003 Breezewood Lane, Neenah, WI 54957 *Tel:* 920-722-2848 *Toll Free Tel:* 877-564-2333 *Toll Free Fax:* 800-727-7516 *E-mail:* customerservice@jjkeller.com; sales@jjkeller.com *Web Site:* www.jjkeller.com, pg 108

Keller, Rustin, J J Keller & Associates, Inc®, 3003 Breezewood Lane, Neenah, WI 54957 *Tel:* 920-722-2848 *Toll Free Tel:* 877-564-2333 *Toll Free Fax:* 800-727-7516 *E-mail:* customerservice@jjkeller.com; sales@jjkeller.com *Web Site:* www.jjkeller.com, pg 108

Keller, Shannon, The New York Public Library Helen Bernstein Book Award for Excellence in Journalism, 445 Fifth Ave, 4th fl, New York, NY 10016 *Tel:* 212-930-9206 *Fax:* 212-930-0983 *E-mail:* bernsteinawards@nypl.org *Web Site:* www.nypl.org, pg 640

Keller, Suzanne, Bloomsbury Publishing Inc, 1385 Broadway, 5th fl, New York, NY 10018 *Tel:* 212-419-5300 *E-mail:* marketingusa@bloomsbury.com; adultpublicityusa@bloomsbury.com; askacademic@bloomsbury.com *Web Site:* www.bloomsbury.com, pg 32

Keller, Wendy, Keller Media Inc, 578 Washington Blvd, No 745, Marina del Rey, CA 90292 *Toll Free Tel:* 800-278-8706 *E-mail:* query@kellermedia.com *Web Site:* kellermedia.com/submission-guidelines, pg 465

Kelley, Annie, Random House Children's Books, c/o Penguin Random House LLC, 1745 Broadway, New York, NY 10019 *Tel:* 212-782-9000 *Web Site:* www.rhcbooks.com, pg 170

Kelley, Brandon, Little, Brown and Company, 1290 Avenue of the Americas, New York, NY 10104 *Tel:* 212-364-1100 *Fax:* 212-364-0952 *E-mail:* firstname.lastname@hbgusa.com *Web Site:* www.hachettebookgroup.com/imprint/little-brown-and-company/, pg 118

Kelley, Bruce, Trusted Media Brands Inc, 750 Third Ave, 3rd fl, New York, NY 10017 *Tel:* 646-293-6299 *Toll Free Tel:* 877-732-4438 (cust serv) *Fax:* 646-293-6251 *E-mail:* customercare@trustedmediabrands.com; press@trustedmediabrands.com *Web Site:* www.trustedmediabrands.com; www.rd.com, pg 210

Kelley, Claire, Seven Stories Press, 140 Watts St, New York, NY 10013 *Tel:* 212-226-8760 *Toll Free Tel:* 800-733-3000 (orders) *Fax:* 212-226-1411 *E-mail:* sevenstories@sevenstories.com *Web Site:* www.sevenstories.com, pg 186

Kelley, Raina, Disney Publishing Worldwide, 1101 Flower St, Glendale, CA 91201 *Web Site:* books.disney.com, pg 60

Kellogg, Camille, Bloomsbury Publishing Inc, 1385 Broadway, 5th fl, New York, NY 10018 *Tel:* 212-419-5300 *E-mail:* marketingusa@bloomsbury.com; adultpublicityusa@bloomsbury.com; askacademic@bloomsbury.com *Web Site:* www.bloomsbury.com, pg 31

Kelly, August, Black Warrior Review Fiction, Nonfiction & Poetry Contest, University of Alabama, Off of Student Media, 414 Campus Dr E, Tuscaloosa, AL 35487 *Tel:* 205-348-4518 *Fax:* 205-348-8036 *E-mail:* blackwarriorreview@gmail.com; bwr@ua.edu *Web Site:* www.bwr.ua.edu, pg 581

Kelly, Barb, Kids Can Press Ltd, 25 Dockside Dr, Toronto, ON M5A 0B5, Canada *Tel:* 416-479-7000 *Toll Free Tel:* 800-265-0884 *Fax:* 416-960-5437 *E-mail:* info@kidscan.com; customerservice@kidscan.com *Web Site:* www.kidscanpress.com; www.kidscanpress.ca, pg 411

Kelly, Carolyn, Avid Reader Press, 1230 Avenue of the Americas, New York, NY 10020 *Web Site:* avidreaderpress.com, pg 23

Kelly, Catherine E, Omohundro Institute of Early American History & Culture, Swem Library, Ground fl, 400 Landrum Dr, Williamsburg, VA 23185 *Tel:* 757-221-1114 *Fax:* 757-221-1047 *E-mail:* ieahc1@wm.edu *Web Site:* oieahc.wm.edu, pg 146

Kelly, Claire, NeWest Press, 8540 109 St, No 201, Edmonton, AB T6G 1E6, Canada *Tel:* 780-432-9427 *Fax:* 780-433-3179 *E-mail:* info@newestpress.com; orders@newestpress.com *Web Site:* www.newestpress.com, pg 414

Kelly, Erin, Penguin Random House Canada, a Penguin Random House company, 320 Front St W, Suite 1400, Toronto, ON M5V 3B6, Canada *Tel:* 416-364-4449 *Toll Free Tel:* 888-523-9292 (cust serv) *E-mail:* canadaweb@penguinrandomhouse.com; customerservicescanada@penguinrandomhouse.com *Web Site:* www.penguinrandomhouse.ca, pg 416

Kelly, Heather, Harry N Abrams Inc, 195 Broadway, 9th fl, New York, NY 10007 *Tel:* 212-206-7715 *Toll Free Tel:* 800-345-1359 *Fax:* 212-645-8437 *E-mail:* abrams@abramsbooks.com; publicity@abramsbooks.com; sales@abramsbooks.com *Web Site:* www.abramsbooks.com, pg 3

Kelly, Jacki, RISING STAR Award, PO Box 190, Jefferson, OR 97352 *E-mail:* risingstar@womenfictionwriters.org *Web Site:* wfwa.memberclicks.net/rising-star-award, pg 656

Kelly, Jacki, STAR Award, PO Box 190, Jefferson, OR 97352 *E-mail:* staraward@womenfictionwriters.org *Web Site:* wfwa.memberclicks.net/star-award, pg 666

Kelly, Jacki, Women's Fiction Writers Association (WFWA), PO Box 190, Jefferson, OR 97352 *E-mail:* communications@womensfictionwriters.org; membership@womensfictionwriters.org; programs@womensfictionwriters.org *Web Site:* www.womensfictionwriters.org, pg 522

Kelly, Jane, University of Toronto Press, Book Publishing Div, 800 Bay St, Mezzanine, Toronto, ON M5S 3A9, Canada *Tel:* 416-978-2239 *Fax:* 416-978-4736 *E-mail:* utpbooks@utorontopress.com (orders) *Web Site:* utorontopress.com, pg 423

Kelly, Jenny, Dial Books for Young Readers, c/o Penguin Random House LLC, 1745 Broadway, New York, NY 10019 *Tel:* 212-782-9000 *Web Site:* www.penguin.com/dial-overview/, pg 59

Kelly, Jenny, Rocky Pond Books, c/o Penguin Random House LLC, 1745 Broadway, New York, NY 10019 *Tel:* 212-782-9000 *Web Site:* www.penguin.com/rocky-pond-overview/, pg 176

Kelly, Jules, Random House Children's Books, c/o Penguin Random House LLC, 1745 Broadway, New York, NY 10019 *Tel:* 212-782-9000 *Web Site:* www.rhcbooks.com, pg 170

Kelly, Margaret, Sourcebooks LLC, 1935 Brookdale Rd, Suite 139, Naperville, IL 60563 *Tel:* 630-961-3900 *Toll Free Tel:* 800-432-7444 *Fax:* 630-961-2168 *E-mail:* info@sourcebooks.com *Web Site:* www.sourcebooks.com, pg 194

Kelly, Michelle, Bloomsbury Publishing Inc, 1385 Broadway, 5th fl, New York, NY 10018 *Tel:* 212-419-5300 *E-mail:* marketingusa@bloomsbury.com; adultpublicityusa@bloomsbury.com; askacademic@bloomsbury.com *Web Site:* www.bloomsbury.com, pg 31

Kelly, Paul, DK, c/o Penguin Random House LLC, 1745 Broadway, 20th fl, New York, NY 10019 *Tel:* 646-674-4000 *Toll Free Tel:* 800-733-3000 *Fax:* 646-674-4020 *E-mail:* marketing@dk.com (lib servs); publicity@dk.com; csorders@penguinrandomhouse.com; customerservice@penguinrandomhouse.com *Web Site:* www.dk.com, pg 60

Kelly, Rachael, Dutton, c/o Penguin Random House LLC, 1745 Broadway, New York, NY 10019 *Tel:* 212-366-2000 *Web Site:* www.penguin.com/dutton-overview/; www.penguin.com/plume-books-overview/; www.penguin.com/tiny-reparations-overview/, pg 62

Kelly, Renee, Penguin Workshop, c/o Penguin Random House LLC, 1745 Broadway, New York, NY 10019 *Tel:* 212-782-9000 *Web Site:* www.penguin.com/publishers/penguinworkshop/, pg 156

Kelly, Shannon, Running Press, 1290 Avenue of the Americas, New York, NY 10104 *Tel:* 212-364-1100 *Toll Free Tel:* 800-759-0190 (cust serv) *Fax:* 212-364-0933 (intl orders) *Toll Free Fax:* 800-286-9471 (cust serv) E-mail: customer.service@hbgusa.com; orders@hbgusa.com Web Site: www.hachettebookgroup.com/imprint/running-press/; www.moon.com (Moon Travel Guides), pg 178

Kelly, Susana J, Ave Maria Press Inc, PO Box 428, Notre Dame, IN 46556 Toll Free Tel: 800-282-1865 Toll Free Fax: 800-282-5681 E-mail: avemariapress.1@nd.edu Web Site: www.avemariapress.com, pg 22

Kelly, Tianna, Gallery Books, 1230 Avenue of the Americas, New York, NY 10020 Toll Free Tel: 800-456-6798 Fax: 212-698-7284 E-mail: consumer.customerservice@simonandschuster.com Web Site: www.simonandschuster.com, pg 76

Kelly, Tianna, Sourcebooks LLC, 1935 Brookdale Rd, Suite 139, Naperville, IL 60563 Tel: 630-961-3900 Toll Free Tel: 800-432-7444 Fax: 630-961-2168 E-mail: info@sourcebooks.com Web Site: www.sourcebooks.com, pg 195

Kelly, William P, John Simon Guggenheim Memorial Foundation, 90 Park Ave, New York, NY 10016 Tel: 212-687-4470 Fax: 212-697-3248 Web Site: www.gf.org, pg 525

Kelly-Pye, Laurie, Red Wheel/Weiser, 65 Parker St, Suite 7, Newburyport, MA 01950 Tel: 978-465-0504 Toll Free Tel: 800-423-7087 (orders) Fax: 978-465-0243 E-mail: info@rwwbooks.com Web Site: www.redwheelweiser.com, pg 173

Kelman, Pat, Simon & Schuster, LLC, 1230 Avenue of the Americas, New York, NY 10020 Tel: 212-698-7000 Toll Free Tel: 800-223-2336 (orders) Fax: 212-698-7007 Toll Free Fax: 800-943-9831 (orders) E-mail: firstname.lastname@simonandschuster.com; purchaseorders@simonandschuster.com (orders) Web Site: www.simonandschuster.com, pg 189

Kelsch, Liz, Sourcebooks LLC, 1935 Brookdale Rd, Suite 139, Naperville, IL 60563 Tel: 630-961-3900 Toll Free Tel: 800-432-7444 Fax: 630-961-2168 E-mail: info@sourcebooks.com Web Site: www.sourcebooks.com, pg 194

Kelsey, Karla Anne PhD, Susquehanna University, Department of English & Creative Writing, 514 University Ave, Selinsgrove, PA 17870 Tel: 570-372-4196 Web Site: www.susqu.edu, pg 565

Kelsey, Micah, Alfred A Knopf, c/o Penguin Random House LLC, 1745 Broadway, New York, NY 10019 Tel: 212-751-2600 Fax: 212-940-7390 (dom rts); 212-572-2662 (foreign rts) Web Site: knopfdoubleday.com/imprint/knopf/; knopfdoubleday.com, pg 110

Kelsey, Zoe, House of Anansi Press Inc, 128 Sterling Rd, Lower Level, Toronto, ON M6R 2B7, Canada Tel: 416-363-4343 Fax: 416-363-1017 E-mail: customerservice@houseofanansi.com Web Site: houseofanansi.com, pg 409

Kemp, Kimberlee, Penguin Random House Canada, a Penguin Random House company, 320 Front St W, Suite 1400, Toronto, ON M5V 3B6, Canada Tel: 416-364-4449 Toll Free Tel: 888-523-9292 (cust serv) E-mail: canadaweb@penguinrandomhouse.com; customerservicescanada@penguinrandomhouse.com Web Site: www.penguinrandomhouse.ca, pg 416

Kemp, Steve, Blue Whale Press, 237 Rainbow Dr, No 13702, Livingston, TX 77399-2037 Toll Free Tel: 800-848-1451 E-mail: info@bluewhalepress.com; sales@bluewhalepress.com Web Site: www.bluewhalepress.com, pg 32

Kendall, George, The American Library Association (ALA), 225 N Michigan Ave, Suite 1300, Chicago, IL 60601 Tel: 312-944-6780 Toll Free Tel: 800-545-2433; 866-SHOP-ALA (746-7252, orders) Fax: 312-280-5275; 312-440-9374; 312-280-5860 (orders) E-mail: ala@ala.org; alastore@ala.org Web Site: www.alastore.ala.org; www.ala.org, pg 10

Kendall, Grace, Farrar, Straus & Giroux Books for Young Readers, 120 Broadway, New York, NY 10271 Tel: 212-741-6900 Toll Free Tel: 888-330-8477 (orders) E-mail: childrens.publicity@macmillanusa.com; childrensrights@macmillanusa.com Web Site: us.macmillan.com/mackids, pg 70

Kendall, Joshua, Little, Brown and Company, 1290 Avenue of the Americas, New York, NY 10104 Tel: 212-364-1100 Fax: 212-364-0952 E-mail: firstname.lastname@hbgusa.com Web Site: www.hachettebookgroup.com/imprint/little-brown-and-company/, pg 118

Keneston, Fran, State University of New York Press, 10 N Pearl St, 4th fl, Albany, NY 12207 Tel: 518-944-2800 Toll Free Tel: 877-204-6073 (orders) Fax: 518-320-1592 Toll Free Fax: 877-204-6074 (orders) E-mail: info@sunypress.edu (edit off); suny@presswarehouse.com (orders) Web Site: www.sunypress.edu, pg 198

Kenmore, Deborah, Chronicle Books LLC, 680 Second St, San Francisco, CA 94107 Tel: 415-537-4200 Fax: 415-537-4460 (perms) E-mail: hello@chroniclebooks.com; subrights@chroniclebooks.com Web Site: www.chroniclebooks.com, pg 48

Kennedy, Clara-Swan, Black Rose Books Ltd, CP 35788, succursale Leo-Pariseau, Montreal, QC H2X 0A4, Canada Tel: 514-844-4076 E-mail: info@blackrosebooks.com Web Site: blackrosebooks.com, pg 396

Kennedy, Deborah, National Coalition for Literacy (NCL), PO Box 2932, Washington, DC 20013-2932 E-mail: ncl@ncladvocacy.org Web Site: www.national-coalition-literacy.org, pg 512

Kennedy, Jeffe, Science Fiction and Fantasy Writers Association, Inc (SFWA), PO Box 215, San Lorenzo, CA 94580 Tel: 860-698-0536 E-mail: office@sfwa.org; operations@sfwa.org Web Site: www.sfwa.org, pg 519

Kennedy, Jeffe, SFWA Nebula Awards, PO Box 215, San Lorenzo, CA 94580 Tel: 860-698-0536 E-mail: office@sfwa.org; operations@sfwa.org Web Site: www.sfwa.org, pg 661

Kennedy, Lesley, National Conference of State Legislatures (NCSL), 7700 E First Place, Denver, CO 80230 Tel: 303-364-7700 E-mail: press-room@ncsl.org Web Site: www.ncsl.org, pg 137

Kennedy, Lindsey, HarperCollins Publishers LLC, 195 Broadway, New York, NY 10007 Tel: 212-207-7000 Web Site: www.harpercollins.com, pg 86

Kennedy, Martha, Candlewick Press, 99 Dover St, Somerville, MA 02144-2825 Tel: 617-661-3330 Fax: 617-661-0565 E-mail: bigbear@candlewick.com; salesinfo@candlewick.com Web Site: candlewick.com, pg 39

Kennedy, Mary, Institute of Intergovernmental Relations, Queen's University, Robert Sutherland Hall, Rm 412, Kingston, ON K7L 3N6, Canada Tel: 613-533-2080 E-mail: iigr@queensu.ca Web Site: www.queensu.ca/iigr, pg 410

Kennedy, Ryan, Hatherleigh Press Ltd, 62545 State Hwy 10, Hobart, NY 13788 Toll Free Tel: 800-528-2550 E-mail: info@hatherleighpress.com; publicity@hatherleighpress.com Web Site: www.hatherleighpress.com, pg 88

Kennedy, Shane, Lone Pine Publishing, 87 E Pender, Vancouver, BC V6A 1S9, Canada Tel: 780-433-9333 Toll Free Tel: 800-661-9017 Fax: 780-433-9646 Toll Free Fax: 800-424-7173 E-mail: info@lonepinepublishing.com Web Site: www.lonepinepublishing.com, pg 412

Kennedy, Stephen, The Mathematical Association of America, 1529 18 St NW, Washington, DC 20036-1358 Tel: 202-387-5200 Toll Free Tel: 800-741-9415 Fax: 202-265-2384 E-mail: maahq@maa.org; advertising@maa.org (pubns) Web Site: www.maa.org, pg 127

Kennedy, Tara, Grand Central Publishing, 1290 Avenue of the Americas, New York, NY 10104 Tel: 212-364-1100 Web Site: www.hachettebookgroup.com/imprint/grand-central-publishing/, pg 80

Kennedy, Terry L, Randall Jarrell Poetry Competition, PO Box 21591, Winston-Salem, NC 27120-1591 Tel: 336-293-8844 E-mail: mail@ncwriters.org; nclrsubmissions@ecu.edu Web Site: www.ncwriters.org, pg 618

Kennedy, Terry L, The Robert Watson Literary Prizes in Fiction & Poetry, MFA Writing Program, The Greensboro Review, UNC-Greensboro, 3302 MHRA Bldg, Greensboro, NC 27402-6170 Tel: 336-334-5459 Web Site: www.greensbororeview.org, pg 673

Kennedy, William, New York State Edith Wharton Citation of Merit for Fiction Writers, University at Albany, Science Library 320, 1400 Washington Ave, Albany, NY 12222 Tel: 518-442-5620 E-mail: writers@albany.edu Web Site: www.nyswritersinstitute.org, pg 640

Kennedy, William, New York State Walt Whitman Citation of Merit for Poets, University at Albany, Science Library 320, 1400 Washington Ave, Albany, NY 12222 Tel: 518-442-5620 E-mail: writers@albany.edu Web Site: www.nyswritersinstitute.org, pg 640

Kennedy, William, New York State Writers Institute, University at Albany, Science Library 320, 1400 Washington Ave, Albany, NY 12222 Tel: 518-442-5620 Fax: 518-442-5621 E-mail: writers@albany.edu Web Site: www.nyswritersinstitute.org, pg 556

Kennelly, Savannah, Little, Brown Books for Young Readers (LBYR), 1290 Avenue of the Americas, New York, NY 10104 Tel: 212-364-1100 Toll Free Tel: 800-759-0190 (cust serv) E-mail: rights@lbchildrens.com Web Site: www.hachettebookgroup.com/imprint/little-brown-books-for-young-readers/, pg 118

Kenney, Deirdre, Bloomsbury Academic, 1385 Broadway, 5th fl, New York, NY 10018 Tel: 212-419-5300 Web Site: www.bloomsbury.com/us/academic, pg 31

Kenney, Madeleine, Random House Publishing Group, 1745 Broadway, New York, NY 10019 Toll Free Tel: 800-200-3552 Web Site: www.randomhousebooks.com, pg 171

Kenniff, Thomas, National Press Photographers Association Inc (NPPA), 120 Hooper St, Athens, GA 30602-3018 Tel: 706-542-2506 E-mail: info@nppa.org; director@nppa.org Web Site: nppa.org, pg 514

Kenny, Joanne, Getty Publications, 1200 Getty Center Dr, Suite 500, Los Angeles, CA 90049-1682 Tel: 310-440-7365 Toll Free Tel: 800-223-3431 (orders) Fax: 310-440-7758 E-mail: pubsinfo@getty.edu Web Site: www.getty.edu/publications, pg 78

Kenny, Julia, Dunow, Carlson & Lerner Literary Agency Inc, 27 W 20 St, Suite 1107, New York, NY 10011 Tel: 212-645-7606 E-mail: mail@dclagency.com Web Site: www.dclagency.com, pg 457

Kenny, Maryanne, The Blackburn Press, PO Box 287, Caldwell, NJ 07006-0287 Tel: 973-228-7077 Fax: 973-228-7276 Web Site: www.blackburnpress.com, pg 30

Kenoun, Sabrina, HarperCollins Children's Books, 195 Broadway, New York, NY 10007 Tel: 212-207-7000 Web Site: www.harpercollins.com/childrens, pg 86

Kenshole, Fiona, Transatlantic Agency, 2 Bloor St E, Suite 3500, Toronto, ON M4W 1A8, Canada Tel: 416-488-9214 E-mail: info@transatlanticagency.com; royalties@transatlanticagency.com Web Site: www.transatlanticagency.com, pg 479

Kent, Amy R, Wm B Eerdmans Publishing Co, 4035 Park East Ct SE, Grand Rapids, MI 49546 Tel: 616-459-4591 Toll Free Tel: 800-253-7521 E-mail: customerservice@eerdmans.com; sales@eerdmans.com Web Site: www.eerdmans.com, pg 64

Kent, Ansley, Macmillan, 120 Broadway, 22nd fl, New York, NY 10271 E-mail: press.inquiries@macmillan.com Web Site: us.macmillan.com, pg 122

Kent, Holly, Ontario Book Publishers Organization (OBPO), 2 Amelia St, Picton, ON K0K 2T0, Canada Tel: 416-536-7584 Web Site: obpo.ca, pg 515

Kent, Jake-Ryan, Llewellyn Publications, 2143 Wooddale Dr, Woodbury, MN 55125 Tel: 651-291-1970 Toll Free Tel: 800-843-6666 Fax: 651-291-1908 E-mail: publicity@llewellyn.com; customerservice@llewellyn.com Web Site: www.llewellyn.com, pg 119

Kent, Julia, HarperCollins Publishers LLC, 195 Broadway, New York, NY 10007 *Tel:* 212-207-7000 *Web Site:* www.harpercollins.com, pg 86

Kent, Kiara, Knopf Canada, 320 Front St W, Suite 1400, Toronto, ON M5V 3B6, Canada *Tel:* 416-364-4449 *Toll Free Tel:* 888-523-9292 *Fax:* 416-598-7764 *Web Site:* www.penguinrandomhouse.ca, pg 411

Kent, Rachel, Books & Such, 2222 Cleveland Ave, No 1005, Santa Rosa, CA 95403 *Tel:* 707-538-4184 *Web Site:* booksandsuch.com, pg 451

Kentowski, Daniel, Norbert Blei/August Derleth Nonfiction Book Award, c/o 4414 W Fillmore Dr, Milwaukee, WI 53219 *E-mail:* wiswriters@gmail.com *Web Site:* wiswriters.org/awards, pg 582

Kentowski, Daniel, Zona Gale Award for Short Fiction, c/o 4414 W Fillmore Dr, Milwaukee, WI 53219 *E-mail:* wiswriters@gmail.com *Web Site:* wiswriters.org/awards, pg 605

Kentwell, Richard, Reedswain Inc, 88 Wells Rd, Spring City, PA 19475 *Tel:* 610-495-9578 *Toll Free Tel:* 800-331-5191 *Fax:* 610-495-6632 *E-mail:* orders@reedswain.com *Web Site:* www.reedswain.com, pg 173

Kenward, Lucy, Greystone Books Ltd, 343 Railway St, Suite 302, Vancouver, BC V6A 1A4, Canada *Tel:* 604-875-1550 *Fax:* 604-875-1556 *E-mail:* info@greystonebooks.com; rights@greystonebooks.com *Web Site:* www.greystonebooks.com, pg 407

Kenyon, John, Paul Engle Prize, 123 S Linn St, Iowa City, IA 52240 *E-mail:* info@iowacityofliterature.org *Web Site:* www.iowacityofliterature.org/paul-engle-prize, pg 600

Kenyon, Todd A, Henry Allen Moe Prize, 5798 State Hwy 80, Cooperstown, NY 13326 *Tel:* 607-547-2586 *E-mail:* publications@fenimoreart.org *Web Site:* fenimoreartmuseum.org/publication-awards, pg 634

Kephart, Sheri, Easy Money Press, 82-5800 Napo'opo'o Rd, Captain Cook, HI 96704 *Tel:* 808-313-2808 *E-mail:* easymoneypress@yahoo.com, pg 63

Keplinger, Kristy, Harry N Abrams Inc, 195 Broadway, 9th fl, New York, NY 10007 *Tel:* 212-206-7715 *Toll Free Tel:* 800-345-1359 *Fax:* 212-645-8437 *E-mail:* abrams@abramsbooks.com; publicity@abramsbooks.com; sales@abramsbooks.com *Web Site:* www.abramsbooks.com, pg 3

Kerber, Michael, Red Wheel/Weiser, 65 Parker St, Suite 7, Newburyport, MA 01950 *Tel:* 978-465-0504 *Toll Free Tel:* 800-423-7087 (orders) *Fax:* 978-465-0243 *E-mail:* info@rwwbooks.com *Web Site:* www.redwheelweiser.com, pg 173

Kercheval, Caleb, The Permanent Press, 4170 Noyac Rd, Sag Harbor, NY 11963 *Tel:* 631-725-1101 *E-mail:* info@thepermanentpress.com *Web Site:* www.thepermanentpress.com, pg 158

Kerman, Anne, Workman Publishing, 1290 Avenue of the Americas, New York, NY 10104 *Toll Free Tel:* 800-759-0190 *Fax:* 212-364-0950 *E-mail:* workman-inquiry@hbgusa.com *Web Site:* www.hachettebookgroup.com/imprint/workman-publishing-company/, pg 232

Kern, Natasha, Natasha Kern Literary Agency Inc, PO Box 1069, White Salmon, WA 98672 *Tel:* 509-493-3803 *Web Site:* www.natashakernliterary.com, pg 465

Kern, Rose, SouthWest Writers Conference Series, 3200 Carlisle Blvd NE, Suite 114, Albuquerque, NM 87110-1663 *Tel:* 505-830-6034 *E-mail:* info@swwriters.com *Web Site:* www.southwestwriters.com, pg 557

Kerner, Diane, Scholastic Canada Ltd, 175 Hillmount Rd, Markham, ON L6C 1Z7, Canada *Tel:* 905-887-7323 *Toll Free Tel:* 800-268-3860 (CN) *Toll Free Fax:* 800-387-4944 *E-mail:* custserve@scholastic.ca *Web Site:* www.scholastic.ca, pg 418

Kerr, Adrienne, Simon & Schuster Canada, 166 King St E, Suite 300, Toronto, ON M5A 1J3, Canada *Tel:* 647-427-8882 *Toll Free Tel:* 800-387-0446; 800-268-3216 (orders) *Fax:* 647-430-9446 *Toll Free Fax:* 888-849-8151 (orders) *E-mail:* info@simonandschuster.ca *Web Site:* www.simonandschuster.ca, pg 419

Kerr, Elisabeth, W W Norton & Company Inc, 500 Fifth Ave, New York, NY 10110-0017 *Tel:* 212-354-5500 *Toll Free Tel:* 800-233-4830 (orders & cust serv) *Fax:* 212-869-0856 *Toll Free Fax:* 800-458-6515 *E-mail:* orders@wwnorton.com *Web Site:* wwnorton.com, pg 143

Kerr, Kat, Donald Maass Literary Agency, 1000 Dean St, Suite 331, Brooklyn, NY 11238 *Tel:* 212-727-8383 *E-mail:* info@maassagency.com *Web Site:* www.maassagency.com, pg 468

Kerr, Kristine Rodriguez, New York University, Center for Publishing & Applied Liberal Arts, 7 E 12 St, New York, NY 10003 *Tel:* 212-998-7200 *E-mail:* sps.info@nyu.edu *Web Site:* www.scps.nyu.edu/professional-pathways/topics.html, pg 563

Kerrigan, Moira, Workman Publishing, 1290 Avenue of the Americas, New York, NY 10104 *Toll Free Tel:* 800-759-0190 *Fax:* 212-364-0950 *E-mail:* workman-inquiry@hbgusa.com *Web Site:* www.hachettebookgroup.com/imprint/workman-publishing-company/, pg 232

Kerstetter, Abby, Colorado Book Awards, 7935 E Prentice Ave, Suite 450, Greenwood Village, CO 80111 *Tel:* 303-894-7951 (ext 19) *Fax:* 303-864-9361 *E-mail:* info@coloradohumanities.org *Web Site:* coloradohumanities.org, pg 591

Kessinger, Lily, Houghton Mifflin Harcourt Trade & Reference Division, 125 High St, Boston, MA 02110 *Tel:* 617-351-5000 *Web Site:* www.hmhco.com, pg 96

Kessinger, Roger A, Kessinger Publishing LLC, PO Box 1404, Whitefish, MT 59937 *Web Site:* www.kessingerpublishing.com, pg 109

Kessler, Joseph I, World Class Speakers & Entertainers, 5158 Clareton Dr, Suite 1034, Agoura Hills, CA 91376 *Tel:* 818-991-5400 *E-mail:* wcse@wcspeakers.com *Web Site:* www.wcspeakers.com, pg 488

Kessler, Kristin, American Political Science Association (APSA), 1527 New Hampshire Ave NW, Washington, DC 20036-1203 *Tel:* 202-483-2512 *Fax:* 202-483-2657 *E-mail:* apsa@apsanet.org; membership@apsanet.org; press@apsanet.org *Web Site:* www.apsanet.org, pg 496

Kessler, Robert J, Pendragon Press, 52 White Hill Rd, Hillsdale, NY 12529-5839 *Tel:* 518-325-6100 *Toll Free Tel:* 877-656-6381 (orders) *E-mail:* editor@pendragonpress.com; orders@pendragonpress.com *Web Site:* www.pendragonpress.com, pg 154

Ketchersid, Sarah, Candlewick Press, 99 Dover St, Somerville, MA 02144-2825 *Tel:* 617-661-3330 *Fax:* 617-661-0565 *E-mail:* bigbear@candlewick.com; salesinfo@candlewick.com *Web Site:* candlewick.com, pg 39

Ketz, Louise B, Louise B Ketz Agency, 414 E 78 St, Suite 1B, New York, NY 10075 *Tel:* 212-249-0668 *E-mail:* ketzagency@aol.com, pg 465

Keusch, Lyssa, Grand Central Publishing, 1290 Avenue of the Americas, New York, NY 10104 *Tel:* 212-364-1100 *Web Site:* www.hachettebookgroup.com/imprint/grand-central-publishing/, pg 80

Key, Anthony, Penguin Random House LLC, 1745 Broadway, New York, NY 10019 *Tel:* 212-782-9000 *Toll Free Tel:* 800-726-0600 *Web Site:* www.penguinrandomhouse.com, pg 155

Key, Curtis, Casemate | publishers, 1950 Lawrence Rd, Havertown, PA 19083 *Tel:* 610-853-9131 *Fax:* 610-853-9146 *E-mail:* casemate@casematepublishers.com *Web Site:* www.casematepublishers.com, pg 41

Key, Jazz, Macmillan, 120 Broadway, 22nd fl, New York, NY 10271 *E-mail:* press.inquiries@macmillan.com *Web Site:* us.macmillan.com, pg 122

Key, Jessica, Anvil Press Publishers, PO Box 3008, MPO, Vancouver, BC V6B 3X5, Canada *Tel:* 604-876-8710 *E-mail:* info@anvilpress.com *Web Site:* www.anvilpress.com, pg 395

Key, John R, Photographic Society of America® (PSA®), 8241 S Walker Ave, Suite 104, Oklahoma City, OK 73139 *Tel:* 405-843-1437 *Toll Free Tel:* 855-PSA-INFO (772-4636) *E-mail:* hq@psa-photo.org *Web Site:* psa-photo.org, pg 516

Keyles, Shayna, North Atlantic Books (NAB), 2526 Martin Luther King Jr Way, Berkeley, CA 94704 *Tel:* 510-549-4270 *Web Site:* www.northatlanticbooks.com, pg 142

Keyton, Nicole-Anne, Beacon Press, 24 Farnsworth St, Boston, MA 02210-1409 *Tel:* 617-742-2110 *Fax:* 617-723-3097 *E-mail:* production@beacon.org *Web Site:* www.beacon.org, pg 25

Khader, Sareer, Berkley, c/o Penguin Random House LLC, 1745 Broadway, 19th fl, New York, NY 10019 *Tel:* 212-366-2000 *Web Site:* www.penguin.com/publishers/berkley/; www.penguin.com/ace-overview/, pg 28

Khalfan, Aun Ali, Tahrike Tarsile Qur'an Inc, 8008 51 Ave, Elmhurst, NY 11373 *Tel:* 718-446-6472 *Fax:* 718-446-4370 *E-mail:* read@koranusa.org *Web Site:* www.koranusa.org, pg 202

Khalil, Maha, Insight Editions, 800 "A" St, San Rafael, CA 94901 *Tel:* 415-526-1370 *Toll Free Tel:* 800-809-3792 *Toll Free Fax:* 866-509-0515 *E-mail:* info@insighteditions.com; marketing@insighteditions.com *Web Site:* insighteditions.com, pg 101

Khalil, Sarah, Calligraph LLC, 45 Main St, No 850, Brooklyn, NY 11201 *Tel:* 212-253-1074 *E-mail:* mail@calligraphlit.com; rights@calligraphlit.com; submissions@calligraphlit.com *Web Site:* www.calligraphlit.com, pg 453

Khan, Erum, Harry N Abrams Inc, 195 Broadway, 9th fl, New York, NY 10007 *Tel:* 212-206-7715 *Toll Free Tel:* 800-345-1359 *Fax:* 212-645-8437 *E-mail:* abrams@abramsbooks.com; publicity@abramsbooks.com; sales@abramsbooks.com *Web Site:* www.abramsbooks.com, pg 3

Khan, Erum, Random House Publishing Group, 1745 Broadway, New York, NY 10019 *Toll Free Tel:* 800-200-3552 *Web Site:* www.randomhousebooks.com, pg 171

Khan, Sabila, Penguin Publishing Group, c/o Penguin Random House LLC, 1745 Broadway, New York, NY 10019 *Tel:* 212-782-9000 *Web Site:* www.penguin.com, pg 154

Khanna, Rachna, The Jewish Publication Society, c/o Gratz College, 7605 Old York Rd, Melrose Park, PA 19027 *Tel:* 215-832-0600 *Web Site:* www.jps.org; www.nebraskapress.unl.edu/jps/, pg 105

Khanna, Vedika, HarperCollins Publishers LLC, 195 Broadway, New York, NY 10007 *Tel:* 212-207-7000 *Web Site:* www.harpercollins.com, pg 87

Khanukaev, Miriam, Random House Publishing Group, 1745 Broadway, New York, NY 10019 *Toll Free Tel:* 800-200-3552 *Web Site:* www.randomhousebooks.com, pg 171

Kharbanda, Sanj, Beacon Press, 24 Farnsworth St, Boston, MA 02210-1409 *Tel:* 617-742-2110 *Fax:* 617-723-3097 *E-mail:* production@beacon.org *Web Site:* www.beacon.org, pg 25

Khawam, Jennifer, Lee & Low Books Inc, 95 Madison Ave, Suite 1205, New York, NY 10016 *Tel:* 212-779-4400 *Toll Free Tel:* 888-320-3190 (ext 28, orders only) *Fax:* 212-683-1894 (orders only); 212-532-6035 *E-mail:* general@leeandlow.com *Web Site:* www.leeandlow.com, pg 114

Khazan, Denis, Teaching Strategies LLC, 4500 East-West Hwy, Suite 300, Bethesda, MD 20814 *Tel:* 301-634-0818 *Toll Free Tel:* 800-637-3652 *E-mail:* info@teachingstrategies.com; support@teachingstrategies.com *Web Site:* teachingstrategies.com, pg 204

Kheradi, Cyrus, Random House Publishing Group, 1745 Broadway, New York, NY 10019 *Toll Free Tel:* 800-200-3552 *Web Site:* www.randomhousebooks.com, pg 170

Kheradi, Irene, Simon & Schuster, 1230 Avenue of the Americas, New York, NY 10020 *Tel:* 212-698-7000 *Toll Free Tel:* 800-223-2348 (cust serv); 800-223-2336 (orders) *Toll Free Fax:* 800-943-9831 (orders) *Web Site:* simonandschusterpublishing.com/simonandschuster/, pg 188

Khmelnik, Sasha, The Iowa Short Fiction Award, 102 Dey House, 507 N Clinton St, Iowa City, IA 52242-1000 *Tel:* 319-335-0416 *Fax:* 319-335-0420 *Web Site:* writersworkshop.uiowa.edu/about/iowa-short-fiction-awards, pg 617

Khmelnik, Sasha, Sonny Mehta Fellowships in Creative Writing, 102 Dey House, 507 N Clinton St, Iowa City, IA 52242-1000 *Tel:* 319-335-0416 *Web Site:* writersworkshop.uiowa.edu/mehta, pg 632

Khmelnik, Sasha, The John Simmons Short Fiction Award, 102 Dey House, 507 N Clinton St, Iowa City, IA 52242-1000 *Tel:* 319-335-0416 *Fax:* 319-335-0420 *Web Site:* writersworkshop.uiowa.edu/about/iowa-short-fiction-awards, pg 663

Kidd, Chip, Alfred A Knopf, c/o Penguin Random House LLC, 1745 Broadway, New York, NY 10019 *Tel:* 212-751-2600 *Fax:* 212-940-7390 (dom rts); 212-572-2662 (foreign rts) *Web Site:* knopfdoubleday.com/imprint/knopf/; knopfdoubleday.com, pg 110

Kidd, Nancy, American Sociological Association (ASA), 1430 "K" St NW, Suite 600, Washington, DC 20005-4701 *Tel:* 202-383-9005 *E-mail:* asa@asanet.org; communications@asanet.org; membership@asanet.org *Web Site:* www.asanet.org, pg 497

Kiddoo, Megan, Macmillan, 120 Broadway, 22nd fl, New York, NY 10271 *E-mail:* press.inquiries@macmillan.com *Web Site:* us.macmillan.com, pg 122

Kidisevic, Olga, Kids Can Press Ltd, 25 Dockside Dr, Toronto, ON M5A 0B5, Canada *Tel:* 416-479-7000 *Toll Free Tel:* 800-265-0884 *Fax:* 416-960-5437 *E-mail:* info@kidscan.com; customerservice@kidscan.com *Web Site:* www.kidscanpress.com; www.kidscanpress.ca, pg 411

Kiefer, Kim, Houghton Mifflin Harcourt Trade & Reference Division, 125 High St, Boston, MA 02110 *Tel:* 617-351-5000 *Web Site:* www.hmhco.com, pg 96

Kiehl, Kimberlee, Ohioana Book Awards, 274 E First Ave, Suite 300, Columbus, OH 43201 *Tel:* 614-466-3831 *Fax:* 614-728-6974 *E-mail:* ohioana@ohioana.org *Web Site:* www.ohioana.org, pg 643

Kiehl, Kimberlee, Ohioana Walter Rumsey Marvin Grant, 274 E First Ave, Suite 300, Columbus, OH 43201 *Tel:* 614-466-3831 *Fax:* 614-728-6974 *E-mail:* ohioana@ohioana.org *Web Site:* www.ohioana.org, pg 643

Kiell, Karen, AIGA, the professional association for design, 228 Park Ave S, Suite 58603, New York, NY 10003 *Tel:* 212-807-1990 *E-mail:* general@aiga.org *Web Site:* www.aiga.org, pg 493

Kiely, Garrett P, University of Chicago Press, 1427 E 60 St, Chicago, IL 60637-2954 *Tel:* 773-702-7700; 773-702-7600 *Toll Free Tel:* 800-621-2736 (orders) *Fax:* 773-702-9756; 773-660-2235 (orders); 773-702-2708 *E-mail:* custserv@press.uchicago.edu; marketing@press.uchicago.edu *Web Site:* www.press.uchicago.edu, pg 215

Kiernan, Laura, Committee on Scholarly Editions, c/o Modern Language Association of America, 85 Broad St, Suite 500, New York, NY 10004-2434 *Tel:* 646-646-5000 *E-mail:* cse@mla.org *Web Site:* www.mla.org, pg 504

Kiernan-najar, Regeen Runes, Philosophical Library Inc, 275 Central Park W, Suite 12D, New York, NY 10024 *Tel:* 212-873-6070 *Fax:* 212-873-6070 *E-mail:* editors@philosophicallibrary.com *Web Site:* philosophicallibrary.com, pg 159

Kietlinski, Teresa, Bookmark Literary, 189 Berdan Ave, No 101, Wayne, NJ 07470 *E-mail:* bookmarkliterary@gmail.com *Web Site:* bookmarkliterary.com, pg 451

Kikut, Tracey, Ucross Foundation Residency Program, 30 Big Red Lane, Clearmont, WY 82835 *Tel:* 307-737-2291 *E-mail:* info@ucross.org *Web Site:* www.ucross.org, pg 672

Kil, Hannah, Sourcebooks LLC, 1935 Brookdale Rd, Suite 139, Naperville, IL 60563 *Tel:* 630-961-3900 *Toll Free Tel:* 800-432-7444 *Fax:* 630-961-2168 *E-mail:* info@sourcebooks.com *Web Site:* sourcebooks.com, pg 195

Kilbourne, Charles, Adirondack Mountain Club (ADK), 4833 Cascade Rd, Lake Placid, NY 12946-4113 *Tel:* 518-837-5047 *Toll Free Tel:* 800-395-8080 *E-mail:* info@adk.org *Web Site:* www.adk.org, pg 5

Kiley, Eileen, Materials Research Society, 506 Keystone Dr, Warrendale, PA 15086-7537 *Tel:* 724-779-3003 *Fax:* 724-779-8313 *E-mail:* info@mrs.org *Web Site:* www.mrs.org, pg 127

Kiley, Jess, Tor Publishing Group, 120 Broadway, New York, NY 10271 *Toll Free Tel:* 800-455-0340 (Macmillan) *E-mail:* torpublicity@tor.com; forgepublicity@forgebooks.com *Web Site:* us.macmillan.com/torpublishinggroup, pg 208

Kilgras, Heidi, Random House Children's Books, c/o Penguin Random House LLC, 1745 Broadway, New York, NY 10019 *Tel:* 212-782-9000 *Web Site:* www.rhcbooks.com, pg 169

Killebrew, Katie, Insight Editions, 800 "A" St, San Rafael, CA 94901 *Tel:* 415-526-1370 *Toll Free Tel:* 800-809-3792 *Toll Free Fax:* 866-509-0515 *E-mail:* info@insighteditions.com; marketing@insighteditions.com *Web Site:* insighteditions.com, pg 101

Killebrew, Katie, Mandala Earth, 800 "A" St, San Rafael, CA 94901 *Tel:* 415-526-1370 *Toll Free Fax:* 866-509-0515 *E-mail:* info@mandalapublishing.com *Web Site:* www.mandalaeartheditions.com, pg 124

Killeen, Valerie, Central Recovery Press (CRP), 3321 N Buffalo Dr, Suite 200, Las Vegas, NV 89129 *Tel:* 702-868-5830 *Fax:* 702-868-5831 *E-mail:* sales@recoverypress.com *Web Site:* centralrecoverypress.com, pg 44

Kilman, Drew, Macmillan Audio, 120 Broadway, 22nd fl, New York, NY 10271 *Tel:* 646-600-7856 *Toll Free Tel:* 888-330-8477 (cust serv) *Toll Free Fax:* 800-672-7703 *E-mail:* macmillan.audio@macmillanusa.com *Web Site:* us.macmillan.com/audio, pg 123

Kilmartin, Kerry, University of British Columbia Press, 2029 West Mall, Vancouver, BC V6T 1Z2, Canada *Tel:* 604-822-5959 *Toll Free Tel:* 877-377-9378 *Fax:* 604-822-6083 *Toll Free Fax:* 800-668-0821 *E-mail:* frontdesk@ubcpress.ca *Web Site:* www.ubcpress.ca, pg 422

Kim, Angela, Berkley, c/o Penguin Random House LLC, 1745 Broadway, 19th fl, New York, NY 10019 *Tel:* 212-366-2000 *Web Site:* www.penguin.com/publishers/berkley/; www.penguin.com/ace-overview/, pg 28

Kim, Bora, Chronicle Books LLC, 680 Second St, San Francisco, CA 94107 *Tel:* 415-537-4200 *Fax:* 415-537-4460 (perms) *E-mail:* hello@chroniclebooks.com; subrights@chroniclebooks.com *Web Site:* www.chroniclebooks.com, pg 48

Kim, Emily Sylvan, Prospect Agency, 551 Valley Rd, PMB 337, Upper Montclair, NJ 07043 *Tel:* 718-788-3217 *Web Site:* www.prospectagency.com, pg 472

Kim, Esther, Macmillan, 120 Broadway, 22nd fl, New York, NY 10271 *E-mail:* press.inquiries@macmillan.com *Web Site:* us.macmillan.com, pg 122

Kim, Gail, Judy Lopez Memorial Award For Children's Literature, 1225 Selby Ave, Los Angeles, CA 90024 *Tel:* 310-474-9917 *Fax:* 310-474-6436 *Web Site:* www.wnba-books.org/la; www.judylopezbookaward.org, pg 626

Kim, Hannah, The Museum of Modern Art (MoMA), Publications Dept, 11 W 53 St, New York, NY 10019 *Tel:* 212-708-9400 *E-mail:* moma_publications@moma.org *Web Site:* www.moma.org, pg 135

Kim, Jennifer, Sandra Dijkstra Literary Agency, 1155 Camino del Mar, PMB 515, Del Mar, CA 92014-2605 *Web Site:* dijkstraagency.com, pg 456

Kim, Kirby, Janklow & Nesbit Associates, 285 Madison Ave, 21st fl, New York, NY 10017 *Tel:* 212-421-1700 *Fax:* 212-355-1403 *E-mail:* info@janklow.com; submissions@janklow.com; filmtvrights@janklow.com *Web Site:* www.janklowandnesbit.com, pg 464

Kim, Kirsten, Sanford J Greenburger Associates Inc, 55 Fifth Ave, New York, NY 10003 *Tel:* 212-206-5600 *Web Site:* greenburger.com, pg 461

Kim, Kristen, Basic Books Group, 1290 Avenue of the Americas, New York, NY 10104 *Tel:* 212-340-8100 *Toll Free Tel:* 800-343-4499 (cust serv) *Fax:* 212-340-8105 *E-mail:* customer.service@hbgusa.com; orders@hbgusa.com *Web Site:* www.hachettebookgroup.com/imprint/basic-books/, pg 25

Kim, Lea, Macmillan, 120 Broadway, 22nd fl, New York, NY 10271 *E-mail:* press.inquiries@macmillan.com *Web Site:* us.macmillan.com, pg 122

Kim, Linette, Chronicle Books LLC, 680 Second St, San Francisco, CA 94107 *Tel:* 415-537-4200 *Fax:* 415-537-4460 (perms) *E-mail:* hello@chroniclebooks.com; subrights@chroniclebooks.com *Web Site:* www.chroniclebooks.com, pg 47

Kim, Michelle, Random House Children's Books, c/o Penguin Random House LLC, 1745 Broadway, New York, NY 10019 *Tel:* 212-782-9000 *Web Site:* www.rhcbooks.com, pg 170

Kim, Na, Farrar, Straus & Giroux, LLC, 120 Broadway, New York, NY 10271 *Tel:* 212-741-6900 *E-mail:* fsg.publicity@fsgbooks.com; sales@fsgbooks.com *Web Site:* us.macmillan.com/fsg, pg 70

Kim, Sally, Hachette Book Group Inc, 1290 Avenue of the Americas, New York, NY 10104 *Tel:* 212-364-1100 *Toll Free Tel:* 800-759-0190 (cust serv) *Fax:* 212-364-0933 (intl orders) *Toll Free Fax:* 800-286-9471 (cust serv) *E-mail:* customer.service@hbgusa.com; orders@hbgusa.com *Web Site:* www.hachettebookgroup.com, pg 83

Kim, Sally, Little, Brown and Company, 1290 Avenue of the Americas, New York, NY 10104 *Tel:* 212-364-1100 *Fax:* 212-364-0952 *E-mail:* firstname.lastname@hbgusa.com *Web Site:* www.hachettebookgroup.com/imprint/little-brown-and-company/, pg 118

Kim, Steve, Chronicle Books LLC, 680 Second St, San Francisco, CA 94107 *Tel:* 415-537-4200 *Fax:* 415-537-4460 (perms) *E-mail:* hello@chroniclebooks.com; subrights@chroniclebooks.com *Web Site:* www.chroniclebooks.com, pg 48

Kimball, Janet, Mountaineers Books, 1001 SW Klickitat Way, Suite 201, Seattle, WA 98134 *Tel:* 206-223-6303 *Fax:* 206-223-6306 *E-mail:* mbooks@mountaineersbooks.org; customerservice@mountaineersbooks.org *Web Site:* www.mountaineers.org/books, pg 135

Kimball, Roger, Encounter Books, 900 Broadway, Suite 601, New York, NY 10003 *Tel:* 212-871-6310 *Toll Free Tel:* 855-203-7220 *E-mail:* publicity@encounterbooks.com *Web Site:* www.encounterbooks.com, pg 66

Kimbel, Travis, Yale University Press, 302 Temple St, New Haven, CT 06511-8909 *Tel:* 203-432-0960; 203-432-0966 (sales); 401-531-2800 (cust serv) *Toll Free Tel:* 800-405-1619 (cust serv) *Fax:* 203-432-0948; 203-432-8485 (sales); 401-531-2801 (cust serv) *Toll Free Fax:* 800-406-9145 (cust serv) *E-mail:* sales.press@yale.edu (sales); customer.care@triliteral.org (cust serv) *Web Site:* www.yalebooks.com; yalepress.yale.edu/yupbooks, pg 235

Kimberling, Andrea, Island Press, 2000 "M" St NW, Suite 480-B, Washington, DC 20036 *Tel:* 202-232-7933 *Toll Free Tel:* 800-621-2736 *Fax:* 202-234-1328 *E-mail:* info@islandpress.org *Web Site:* www.islandpress.org, pg 104

Kimura, Jenny, Little, Brown Books for Young Readers (LBYR), 1290 Avenue of the Americas, New York, NY 10104 *Tel:* 212-364-1100 *Toll Free Tel:* 800-759-0190 (cust serv) *E-mail:* rights@lbchildrens.com *Web Site:* www.hachettebookgroup.com/imprint/little-brown-books-for-young-readers/, pg 118

Kimzey, Anne, Alabama Artists Fellowship Awards, 201 Monroe St, Suite 110, Montgomery, AL 36130-1800 *Tel:* 334-242-4076 *Fax:* 334-240-3269 *Web Site:* arts.alabama.gov/programs/literary_arts/literary_fellowships.aspx, pg 571

Kincaid, Christen, New Women's Voices Chapbook Competition, PO Box 1626, Georgetown, KY 40324 *Tel:* 502-603-0670 *E-mail:* finishingbooks@

aol.com; flpbookstore@aol.com *Web Site:* www.finishinglinepress.com; finishinglinepress.submittable.com/submit, pg 640

Kincaid, Christen, Open Chapbook Competition, PO Box 1626, Georgetown, KY 40324 *Tel:* 502-603-0670 *E-mail:* finishingbooks@aol.com; flpbookstore@aol.com *Web Site:* www.finishinglinepress.com, pg 644

Kincaid, Laura, Holiday House Publishing Inc, 50 Broad St, New York, NY 10004 *Tel:* 212-688-0085 *Fax:* 212-421-6134 *E-mail:* info@holidayhouse.com *Web Site:* www.holidayhouse.com, pg 94

Kind, Rachel, Random House Publishing Group, 1745 Broadway, New York, NY 10019 *Toll Free Tel:* 800-200-3552 *Web Site:* www.randomhousebooks.com, pg 170

Kindelsperger, Rage, Quarto Publishing Group USA Inc, 100 Cummings Ctr, Suite 265D, Beverly, MA 01915 *Tel:* 978-282-9590 *Toll Free Tel:* 800-328-0590 (sales) *Fax:* 978-283-2742 *E-mail:* sales@quartous.com *Web Site:* www.quartoknows.com, pg 168

Kindig, Jessie, Yale University Press, 302 Temple St, New Haven, CT 06511-8909 *Tel:* 203-432-0960; 203-432-0966 (sales); 401-531-2800 (cust serv) *Toll Free Tel:* 800-405-1619 (cust serv) *Fax:* 203-432-0948; 203-432-8485 (sales); 401-531-2801 (cust serv) *Toll Free Fax:* 800-406-9145 (cust serv) *E-mail:* sales.press@yale.edu (sales); customer.care@triliteral.org (cust serv) *Web Site:* www.yalebooks.com; yalepress.yale.edu/yupbooks, pg 235

Kindler, Rachel, University of Notre Dame Press, 310 Flanner Hall, Notre Dame, IN 46556 *Tel:* 574-631-6346 *Fax:* 574-631-8148 *E-mail:* undpress@nd.edu *Web Site:* www.undpress.nd.edu, pg 219

King, Allison, Kids Can Press Ltd, 25 Dockside Dr, Toronto, ON M5A 0B5, Canada *Tel:* 416-479-7000 *Toll Free Tel:* 800-265-0884 *Fax:* 416-960-5437 *E-mail:* info@kidscan.com; customerservice@kidscan.com *Web Site:* www.kidscanpress.com; www.kidscanpress.ca, pg 411

King, Amy, Disney-Hyperion Books, 1101 Flower St, Glendale, CA 91201 *Web Site:* books.disney.com/imprint/disney-hyperion, pg 59

King, Andrew, Tor Publishing Group, 120 Broadway, New York, NY 10271 *Toll Free Tel:* 800-455-0340 (Macmillan) *E-mail:* torpublicity@tor.com; forgepublicity@forgebooks.com *Web Site:* us.macmillan.com/torpublishinggroup, pg 208

King, Brenda, Yale University Press, 302 Temple St, New Haven, CT 06511-8909 *Tel:* 203-432-0960; 203-432-0966 (sales); 401-531-2800 (cust serv) *Toll Free Tel:* 800-405-1619 (cust serv) *Fax:* 203-432-0948; 203-432-8485 (sales); 401-531-2801 (cust serv) *Toll Free Fax:* 800-406-9145 (cust serv) *E-mail:* sales.press@yale.edu (sales); customer.care@triliteral.org (cust serv) *Web Site:* www.yalebooks.com; yalepress.yale.edu/yupbooks, pg 235

King, Donna, BHTG - Julie Harris Playwright Award Competition, PO Box 148, Beverly Hills, CA 90213 *Tel:* 310-765-1605 *E-mail:* submissions@beverlyhillstheatreguild.com *Web Site:* www.beverlyhillstheatreguild.com, pg 580

King, Donna, BHTG - Michael J Libow Youth Theatre Award, PO Box 148, Beverly Hills, CA 90213 *Tel:* 310-765-1605 *E-mail:* submissions@beverlyhillstheatreguild.com *Web Site:* www.beverlyhillstheatreguild.com, pg 580

King, Emily, University of Notre Dame Press, 310 Flanner Hall, Notre Dame, IN 46556 *Tel:* 574-631-6346 *Fax:* 574-631-8148 *E-mail:* undpress@nd.edu *Web Site:* www.undpress.nd.edu, pg 219

King, Eric, Warner Press, 2902 Enterprise Dr, Anderson, IN 46013 *Tel:* 765-644-7721 *Toll Free Tel:* 800-741-7721 (orders) *Fax:* 765-640-8005 *E-mail:* wporders@warnerpress.org *Web Site:* www.warnerpress.org, pg 226

King, Dr Jennifer, Bisk Education, 9417 Princess Palm Ave, Suite 400, Tampa, FL 33619 *Tel:* 813-621-6200 *E-mail:* media@bisk.com *Web Site:* www.bisk.com, pg 29

King, London, Random House Publishing Group, 1745 Broadway, New York, NY 10019 *Toll Free Tel:* 800-200-3552 *Web Site:* www.randomhousebooks.com, pg 171

King, Margaret J PhD, Cultural Studies & Analysis, 1123 Montrose St, Philadelphia, PA 19147-3721 *Tel:* 215-592-8544 *E-mail:* info@culturalanalysis.com *Web Site:* www.culturalanalysis.com, pg 437

King, Margaret Riley, WME, 11 Madison Ave, New York, NY 10010 *Tel:* 212-586-5100 *Web Site:* www.wmeagency.com, pg 482

King, Melissa, The University of Arkansas Press, McIlroy House, 105 N McIlroy Ave, Fayetteville, AR 72701 *Tel:* 479-575-7544 *E-mail:* info@uapress.com *Web Site:* www.uapress.com, pg 214

King, Michael, YES New Play Festival, 205 FA Theatre Dept, Nunn Dr, Highland Heights, KY 41099-1007 *Tel:* 859-572-7622 *Web Site:* www.nku.edu/yesfestival, pg 679

King, Stephen, W W Norton & Company Inc, 500 Fifth Ave, New York, NY 10110-0017 *Tel:* 212-354-5500 *Toll Free Tel:* 800-233-4830 (orders & cust serv) *Fax:* 212-869-0856 *Toll Free Fax:* 800-458-6515 *E-mail:* orders@wwnorton.com *Web Site:* wwnorton.com, pg 143

King, Terry, The Authors Registry Inc, 31 E 32 St, 7th fl, New York, NY 10016 *Tel:* 212-563-6920 *E-mail:* staff@authorsregistry.org *Web Site:* www.authorsregistry.org, pg 500

Kingra, Mr Mahinder S, Cornell University Press, Sage House, 512 E State St, Ithaca, NY 14850 *Tel:* 607-253-2338 *E-mail:* cupressinfo@cornell.edu; cupress-sales@cornell.edu; cupress-perms@cornell.edu (reprint/class use permissions) *Web Site:* www.cornellpress.cornell.edu, pg 52

Kingsberry, Tania, Canada Council for the Arts (Conseil des arts du Canada), 150 Elgin St, 2nd fl, Ottawa, ON K2P 1L4, Canada *Tel:* 613-566-4414 *Toll Free Tel:* 800-263-5588 (CN only) *Fax:* 613-566-4390 *E-mail:* info@canadacouncil.ca; media@canadacouncil.ca *Web Site:* canadacouncil.ca, pg 502

Kingsley, Jessica, Jessica Kingsley Publishers Inc, 123 S Broad St, Suite 2750, Philadelphia, PA 19109 *Tel:* 215-922-1161 *Toll Free Tel:* 866-416-1078 (cust serv) *Fax:* 215-922-1474 *E-mail:* hello.usa@jkp.com *Web Site:* us.jkp.com, pg 110

Kinman, Gay Toltl, Shamus Awards, 3665 S Needles Hwy, 7G, Laughlin, NV 89029 *Web Site:* www.privateeyewriters.com, pg 661

Kinney, Andrew, The MIT Press, One Broadway, 12th fl, Cambridge, MA 02142 *Tel:* 617-253-5255 *Toll Free Tel:* 800-405-1619 (orders) *Fax:* 617-258-6779; 617-577-1545 (orders) *Web Site:* mitpress.mit.edu, pg 132

Kinney, Erika, Paul H Brookes Publishing Co Inc, PO Box 10624, Baltimore, MD 21285-0624 *Tel:* 410-337-9580 (outside US & CN) *Toll Free Tel:* 800-638-3775 (US & CN) *Fax:* 410-337-8539 *E-mail:* custserv@brookespublishing.com *Web Site:* www.brookespublishing.com, pg 37

Kinney, Jim, Baker Books, 6030 E Fulton Rd, Ada, MI 49301 *Tel:* 616-676-9185 *Toll Free Tel:* 800-877-2665 (orders) *Fax:* 616-676-9573 *Toll Free Fax:* 800-398-3111 (orders) *E-mail:* media@bakerpublishinggroup.com; orders@bakerpublishinggroup.com; sales@bakerpublishinggroup.com *Web Site:* www.bakerpublishinggroup.com, pg 23

Kinney, Noreen, Cordon d' Or - Gold Ribbon International Culinary Academy Awards, 7312 Sixth Ave N, St Petersburg, FL 33710 *Tel:* 727-347-2437 *E-mail:* cordonor@aol.com *Web Site:* www.cordondorcuisine.com; www.florida-americasculinaryparadise.com; www.culinaryambassadorofireland.com, pg 592

Kintigh, Cynthia, ANR Publications University of California, 2801 Second St, Davis, CA 95618 *Tel:* 530-400-0725 (cust serv) *Toll Free Tel:* 800-994-8849 *E-mail:* anrcatalog@ucanr.edu *Web Site:* anrcatalog.ucanr.edu, pg 14

Kintzer, Bonnie, Trusted Media Brands Inc, 750 Third Ave, 3rd fl, New York, NY 10017 *Tel:* 646-293-6299 *Toll Free Tel:* 877-732-4438 (cust serv) *Fax:* 646-293-6251 *E-mail:* customercare@trustedmediabrands.com; press@trustedmediabrands.com *Web Site:* www.trustedmediabrands.com; www.rd.com, pg 210

Kiraz, Christine PhD, Gorgias Press LLC, PO Box 6939, Piscataway, NJ 08854-6939 *Tel:* 732-885-8900 *Fax:* 732-885-8908 *E-mail:* helpdesk@gorgiaspress.com *Web Site:* www.gorgiaspress.com, pg 80

Kiraz, George Anton PhD, Gorgias Press LLC, PO Box 6939, Piscataway, NJ 08854-6939 *Tel:* 732-885-8900 *Fax:* 732-885-8908 *E-mail:* helpdesk@gorgiaspress.com *Web Site:* www.gorgiaspress.com, pg 80

Kirby, Falon, Atria Books, 1230 Avenue of the Americas, New York, NY 10020 *Tel:* 212-698-7000 *Fax:* 212-698-7007 *Web Site:* www.simonandschuster.com, pg 21

Kirby, Gwen E, Sewanee Writers' Conference, 735 University Ave, Sewanee, TN 37383 *Tel:* 931-598-1654 *E-mail:* swc@sewanee.edu *Web Site:* www.sewaneewriters.org, pg 557

Kirchoff, Morris A, Kirchoff/Wohlberg Inc, 897 Boston Post Rd, Madison, CT 06443 *Tel:* 203-245-7308 *Fax:* 203-245-3218 *E-mail:* info@kirchoffwohlberg.com *Web Site:* www.kirchoffwohlberg.com, pg 465

Kirilyuk, Olya, St Martin's Press, LLC, 120 Broadway, New York, NY 10271 *E-mail:* publicity@stmartins.com; trademarketing@stmartins.com; foreignrights@stmartins.com *Web Site:* us.macmillan.com/smp, pg 181

Kirk, Christy, Berrett-Koehler Publishers Inc, 1333 Broadway, Suite 1000, Oakland, CA 94612 *Tel:* 510-817-2277 *Fax:* 510-817-2278 *E-mail:* bkpub@bkpub.com *Web Site:* www.bkconnection.com, pg 29

Kirk, Kara, Getty Publications, 1200 Getty Center Dr, Suite 500, Los Angeles, CA 90049-1682 *Tel:* 310-440-7365 *Toll Free Tel:* 800-223-3431 (orders) *Fax:* 310-440-7758 *E-mail:* pubsinfo@getty.edu *Web Site:* www.getty.edu/publications, pg 78

Kirk, Robert, Princeton University Press, 41 William St, Princeton, NJ 08540-5237 *Tel:* 609-258-4900 *Fax:* 609-258-6305 *E-mail:* info@press.princeton.edu *Web Site:* press.princeton.edu, pg 164

Kirkey, Jeffrey E, Institute of Continuing Legal Education, 1020 Greene St, Ann Arbor, MI 48109-1444 *Tel:* 734-764-0533 *Toll Free Tel:* 877-229-4350 *Fax:* 734-763-2412 *Toll Free Fax:* 877-229-4351 *E-mail:* icle@umich.edu *Web Site:* www.icle.org, pg 101

Kirkpatrick, Emily, National Council of Teachers of English (NCTE), 340 N Neil St, Suite 104, Champaign, IL 61820 *Tel:* 217-328-3870 *Toll Free Tel:* 877-369-6283 (cust serv) *Fax:* 217-328-9645 *E-mail:* customerservice@ncte.org *Web Site:* ncte.org, pg 137, 512

Kirkpatrick, Kristin, University Press of Mississippi, 3825 Ridgewood Rd, Jackson, MS 39211-6492 *Tel:* 601-432-6205 *Toll Free Tel:* 800-737-7788 (orders & cust serv) *Fax:* 601-432-6217 *E-mail:* press@mississippi.edu *Web Site:* www.upress.state.ms.us, pg 222

Kirkpatrick, Tonia, Diversion Books, 11 E 44 St, Suite 1603, New York, NY 10017 *Tel:* 212-961-6390 *E-mail:* info@diversionbooks.com *Web Site:* www.diversionbooks.com, pg 60

Kirsch, Julie, Rowman & Littlefield, 4501 Forbes Blvd, Suite 200, Lanham, MD 20706 *Tel:* 301-459-3366 *Toll Free Tel:* 800-462-6420 (ext 3024, cust serv) *Fax:* 301-429-5748 *Web Site:* rowman.com, pg 178

Kirsch, Julie E, Jason Aronson Inc, 4501 Forbes Blvd, Suite 200, Lanham, MD 20706 *Tel:* 301-459-3366 *Toll Free Tel:* 800-462-6420 ext 3024 (cust serv) *Fax:* 301-429-5748 *Toll Free Fax:* 800-338-4550 (cust serv) *E-mail:* orders@rowman.com; customercare@rowman.com *Web Site:* www.rowman.com, pg 17

Kirschbaum, Klaus, Welcome Books, 300 Park Ave S, New York, NY 10010 *Tel:* 212-387-3400 *Fax:* 212-387-3535 *Web Site:* www.rizzoliusa.com/publisher/rizzoli/imprint/wb, pg 227

Kirshbaum, Larry, Waxman Literary Agency, 443 Park Ave S, No 1004, New York, NY 10016 *Tel:* 212-675-5556 *Web Site:* www.waxmanliteraryagency.com, pg 481

Kirtland, Kim-Mei, Howard Morhaim Literary Agency Inc, 30 Pierrepont St, Brooklyn, NY 11201-3371 *Tel:* 718-222-8400 *E-mail:* info@morhaimliterary.com *Web Site:* www.morhaimliterary.com, pg 470

Kiser, Kristin, Hachette Book Group Inc, 1290 Avenue of the Americas, New York, NY 10104 *Tel:* 212-364-1100 *Toll Free Tel:* 800-759-0190 (cust serv) *Fax:* 212-364-0933 (intl orders) *Toll Free Fax:* 800-286-9471 (cust serv) *E-mail:* customer.service@hbgusa.com; orders@hbgusa.com *Web Site:* www.hachettebookgroup.com, pg 83

Kiser, Kristin, Running Press, 1290 Avenue of the Americas, New York, NY 10104 *Tel:* 212-364-1100 *Toll Free Tel:* 800-759-0190 (cust serv) *Fax:* 212-364-0933 (intl orders) *Toll Free Fax:* 800-286-9471 (cust serv) *E-mail:* customer.service@hbgusa.com; orders@hbgusa.com *Web Site:* www.hachettebookgroup.com/imprint/running-press/; www.moon.com (Moon Travel Guides), pg 178

Kish, Rudy, Hachette Nashville, 6100 Tower Circle, Room 210, Franklin, TN 37067 *Tel:* 615-221-0996 *Fax:* 615-221-0962 *Web Site:* www.hachettebookgroup.com/imprint/hachette-nashville/, pg 83

Kisman, Eddy, World Book Inc, 180 N LaSalle, Suite 900, Chicago, IL 60601 *Tel:* 312-729-5800 *Toll Free Tel:* 800-967-5325 (consumer sales, US); 800-975-3250 (school & lib sales, US); 800-837-5365 (school & lib sales, CN) *Toll Free Fax:* 888-922-3766 *E-mail:* customerservice@worldbook.com *Web Site:* www.worldbook.com, pg 233

Kispert, Peter, HarperCollins Publishers LLC, 195 Broadway, New York, NY 10007 *Tel:* 212-207-7000 *Web Site:* www.harpercollins.com, pg 87

Kisray, Philip, John Wiley & Sons Inc, 111 River St, Hoboken, NJ 07030-5774 *Tel:* 201-748-6000 *Toll Free Tel:* 800-225-5945 (cust serv) *Fax:* 201-748-6088 *Web Site:* www.wiley.com, pg 230

Kissler, Helen, Barefoot Books, 23 Bradford St, 2nd fl, Concord, MA 01742 *Tel:* 617-576-0660 *Toll Free Tel:* 866-215-1756 (cust serv); 866-417-2369 (orders) *Fax:* 617-576-0049 *E-mail:* help@barefootbooks.com *Web Site:* www.barefootbooks.com, pg 24

Kissner, Matthew S, John Wiley & Sons Inc, 111 River St, Hoboken, NJ 07030-5774 *Tel:* 201-748-6000 *Toll Free Tel:* 800-225-5945 (cust serv) *Fax:* 201-748-6088 *Web Site:* www.wiley.com, pg 230

Kistler, Steve, RAND Corp, 1776 Main St, Santa Monica, CA 90407-2138 *Tel:* 310-393-0411 *Fax:* 310-393-4818 *Web Site:* www.rand.org, pg 169

Kitman, Taya, The Ridenhour Courage Prize, 116 E 16 St, 8th fl, New York, NY 10003 *Tel:* 212-822-0250 *Fax:* 212-253-5356 *E-mail:* ridenhour@typemediacenter.org; admin@ridenhour.org *Web Site:* www.ridenhour.org, pg 656

Kitson, Richard, Hachette Book Group Inc, 1290 Avenue of the Americas, New York, NY 10104 *Tel:* 212-364-1100 *Toll Free Tel:* 800-759-0190 (cust serv) *Fax:* 212-364-0933 (intl orders) *Toll Free Fax:* 800-286-9471 (cust serv) *E-mail:* customer.service@hbgusa.com; orders@hbgusa.com *Web Site:* www.hachettebookgroup.com, pg 83

Kittelstrom, David, Wisdom Publications Inc, 199 Elm St, Somerville, MA 02144 *Tel:* 617-776-7416 *Toll Free Tel:* 800-272-4050 (orders) *Fax:* 617-776-7841 *E-mail:* submission@wisdompubs.org *Web Site:* wisdomexperience.org, pg 231

Kittrell, Tiara, HarperCollins Children's Books, 195 Broadway, New York, NY 10007 *Tel:* 212-207-7000 *Web Site:* www.harpercollins.com/childrens, pg 85

Kiyan, Juliana, Penguin Press, c/o Penguin Random House LLC, 1745 Broadway, New York, NY 10019 *Tel:* 212-782-9000 *E-mail:* penguinpress@penguinrandomhouse.com *Web Site:* www.penguin.com/penguin-press-overview/, pg 154

Kjoller, Maria, Carolrhoda Books Inc, 241 First Ave N, Minneapolis, MN 55401 *Tel:* 612-332-3344 *Toll Free Tel:* 800-328-4929 *Fax:* 612-332-7615 *Toll Free Fax:* 800-332-1132 *E-mail:* info@lernerbooks.com; custserve@lernerbooks.com *Web Site:* www.lernerbooks.com; www.facebook.com/lernerbooks, pg 41

Kjoller, Maria, Carolrhoda Lab™, 241 First Ave N, Minneapolis, MN 55401 *Tel:* 612-332-3344 *Toll Free Tel:* 800-328-4929 *Fax:* 612-332-7615 *Toll Free Fax:* 800-332-1132 *E-mail:* info@lernerbooks.com; custserve@lernerbooks.com *Web Site:* www.lernerbooks.com; www.facebook.com/lernerbooks, pg 41

Kjoller, Maria, ediciones Lerner, 241 First Ave N, Minneapolis, MN 55401 *Tel:* 612-332-3344 *Toll Free Tel:* 800-328-4929 *Fax:* 612-332-7615 *Toll Free Fax:* 800-332-1132 *E-mail:* info@lernerbooks.com; custserve@lernerbooks.com *Web Site:* www.lernerbooks.com; www.facebook.com/lernerbooks, pg 63

Kjoller, Maria, First Avenue Editions, 241 First Ave N, Minneapolis, MN 55401 *Tel:* 612-332-3344 *Toll Free Tel:* 800-328-4929 *Fax:* 612-332-7615 *Toll Free Fax:* 800-332-1132 *E-mail:* info@lernerbooks.com; custserve@lernerbooks.com *Web Site:* www.lernerbooks.com; www.facebook.com/lernerbooks, pg 72

Kjoller, Maria, Graphic Universe™, 241 First Ave N, Minneapolis, MN 55401 *Tel:* 612-332-3344 *Toll Free Tel:* 800-328-4929 *Fax:* 612-332-7615 *Toll Free Fax:* 800-332-1132 *E-mail:* info@lernerbooks.com; custserve@lernerbooks.com *Web Site:* www.lernerbooks.com; www.facebook.com/lernerbooks, pg 80

Kjoller, Maria, Kar-Ben Publishing, 241 First Ave N, Minneapolis, MN 55401 *Tel:* 612-332-3344 *Toll Free Tel:* 800-4-KARBEN (452-7236) *Fax:* 612-332-7615 *Toll Free Fax:* 800-332-1132 *E-mail:* custserve@karben.com *Web Site:* www.karben.com, pg 108

Kjoller, Maria, Lerner Publications, 241 First Ave N, Minneapolis, MN 55401 *Tel:* 612-332-3344 *Toll Free Tel:* 800-328-4929 *Fax:* 612-332-7615 *Toll Free Fax:* 800-332-1132 *E-mail:* info@lernerbooks.com; custserve@lernerbooks.com *Web Site:* www.lernerbooks.com; www.facebook.com/lernerbooks, pg 115

Kjoller, Maria, Lerner Publishing Group Inc, 241 First Ave N, Minneapolis, MN 55401 *Tel:* 612-332-3344 *Toll Free Tel:* 800-328-4929 *Fax:* 612-332-7615 *Toll Free Fax:* 800-332-1132 *E-mail:* info@lernerbooks.com; custserve@lernerbooks.com *Web Site:* www.lernerbooks.com; www.facebook.com/lernerbooks, pg 115

Kjoller, Maria, LernerClassroom, 241 First Ave N, Minneapolis, MN 55401 *Tel:* 612-332-3344 *Toll Free Tel:* 800-328-4929 *Fax:* 612-332-7615 *Toll Free Fax:* 800-332-1132 *E-mail:* info@lernerbooks.com; custserve@lernerbooks.com *Web Site:* www.lernerbooks.com; www.facebook.com/lernerbooks, pg 115

Kjoller, Maria, Millbrook Press, 241 First Ave N, Minneapolis, MN 55401 *Tel:* 612-332-3344 *Toll Free Tel:* 800-328-4929 *Fax:* 612-332-7615 *Toll Free Fax:* 800-332-1132 *E-mail:* info@lernerbooks.com; custserve@lernerbooks.com *Web Site:* www.lernerbooks.com; www.facebook.com/millbrookpress, pg 131

Kjoller, Maria, Twenty-First Century Books, 241 First Ave N, Minneapolis, MN 55401 *Tel:* 612-332-3344 *Toll Free Tel:* 800-328-4929 *Fax:* 612-332-7615 *Toll Free Fax:* 800-332-1132 *E-mail:* info@lernerbooks.com; custserve@lernerbooks.com *Web Site:* www.lernerbooks.com; www.facebook.com/lernerbooks, pg 211

Kjoller, Maria, Zest Books, 241 First Ave N, Minneapolis, MN 55401 *Tel:* 612-332-3344 *Toll Free Tel:* 800-328-4929 *Toll Free Fax:* 800-332-1132 *E-mail:* info@lernerbooks.com; publicity@lernerbooks.com; custserve@lernerbooks.com (orders) *Web Site:* lernerbooks.com, pg 236

Klancher, Lee, Octane Press, 1211 W Sixth St, Suite 600-144, Austin, TX 78703 *Tel:* 512-334-9441; 512-761-4555 (sales) *E-mail:* info@octanepress.com; sales@octanepress.com *Web Site:* octanepress.com/content/submissions, pg 145

Klapp, Kendall, HarperCollins Children's Books, 195 Broadway, New York, NY 10007 *Tel:* 212-207-7000 *Web Site:* www.harpercollins.com/childrens, pg 85

Klaw, Rick, Tachyon Publications LLC, 1459 18 St, No 139, San Francisco, CA 94107 *Tel:* 415-285-5615 *E-mail:* tachyon@tachyonpublications.com; submissions@tachyonpublications.com *Web Site:* www.tachyonpublications.com, pg 202

Klebanoff, Arthur, Rodin Books, 666 Old Country Rd, Suite 510, Garden City, NY 11530 *Tel:* 917-685-1064 *Web Site:* www.rodinbooks.com, pg 176

Klebanoff, Arthur, RosettaBooks, 1035 Park Ave, No 3A, New York, NY 10028-0912 *Tel:* 917-685-1064 *Web Site:* www.rosettabooks.com; www.rosettaebooks.com, pg 177

Klebanoff, Arthur M, Scott Meredith Literary Agency LP, 1035 Park Ave, Apt 3-A, New York, NY 10028 *Tel:* 917-685-1064 *E-mail:* info@scottmeredith.com *Web Site:* www.scottmeredith.com, pg 470

Klein, Barry, Todd Publications, 15494 Fiorenza Circle, Delray Beach, FL 33446 *Tel:* 561-910-0440 *Fax:* 561-910-0440 *E-mail:* toddpub@yahoo.com, pg 207

Klein, Hannah, Little, Brown Books for Young Readers (LBYR), 1290 Avenue of the Americas, New York, NY 10104 *Tel:* 212-364-1100 *Toll Free Tel:* 800-759-0190 (cust serv) *E-mail:* rights@lbchildrens.com *Web Site:* www.hachettebookgroup.com/imprint/little-brown-books-for-young-readers/, pg 118

Klein, Lauren, Penguin Random House Audio Publishing Group, 1745 Broadway, New York, NY 10019 *Toll Free Tel:* 800-793-2665 (cust serv) *E-mail:* audio@penguinrandomhouse.com; ecustomerservice@penguinrandomhouse.com *Web Site:* www.penguinrandomhouseaudio.com, pg 154

Klein, Russ, American Marketing Association, 130 E Randolph St, 22nd fl, Chicago, IL 60601 *Tel:* 312-542-9000 *Toll Free Tel:* 800-AMA-1150 (262-1150) *Web Site:* www.ama.org, pg 495

Klein, Shmuel Yaakov, Torah Umesorah Publications, 620 Foster Ave, Brooklyn, NY 11230 *Tel:* 718-259-1223 *E-mail:* publications@torahumesorah.org *Web Site:* www.torahumesorah.org/publications, pg 208

Kleinburg, Emily, Macmillan, 120 Broadway, 22nd fl, New York, NY 10271 *E-mail:* press.inquiries@macmillan.com *Web Site:* us.macmillan.com, pg 122

Kleiner, Karen, Clear Concepts, 1329 Federal Ave, Suite 6, Los Angeles, CA 90025 *Tel:* 323-285-0325, pg 437

Kleinman, Jeff, Folio Literary Management, The Film Center Bldg, 630 Ninth Ave, Suite 1101, New York, NY 10036 *Tel:* 212-400-1494 *Fax:* 212-967-0977 *Web Site:* www.foliolit.com, pg 459

Kleit, Micah, Rutgers University Press, 106 Somerset St, 3rd fl, New Brunswick, NJ 08901 *Tel:* 848-445-7762; 848-445-7761 (sales) *Fax:* 732-745-4935 *E-mail:* sales@rutgersuniversitypress.org *Web Site:* www.rutgersuniversitypress.org, pg 178

Klemesrud, Deanna, Print Industries Market Information and Research Organization (PRIMIR), 1899 Preston White Dr, Reston, VA 20191 *Tel:* 703-264-7200 *E-mail:* aptech@aptech.org *Web Site:* www.printtechnologies.org; www.npes.org/primirresearch/primir.aspx, pg 517

Kliegl, Amanda, PRINTING United Alliance, 10015 Main St, Fairfax, VA 22031 *Tel:* 703-385-1335 *Toll Free Tel:* 888-385-3588 *Fax:* 703-273-0456; 703-691-7492 (membership) *E-mail:* assist@printing.org; info@printing.org *Web Site:* www.printing.org, pg 517

Klim, Christopher, Eric Hoffer Award, PO Box 11, Titusville, NJ 08560 E-mail: info@hofferaward.com Web Site: www.hofferaward.com, pg 613

Klimowicz, Katie, Tor Publishing Group, 120 Broadway, New York, NY 10271 Toll Free Tel: 800-455-0340 (Macmillan) E-mail: torpublicity@tor.com; forgepublicity@forgebooks.com Web Site: us.macmillan.com/torpublishinggroup, pg 208

Kling, Larry, Research & Education Association (REA), 258 Prospect Plains Rd, Cranbury, NJ 08512 Toll Free Tel: 833-591-2798 (cust care) Fax: 516-742-5049 (orders) E-mail: info@rea.com Web Site: www.rea.com, pg 174

Kling, Sally, Teachers College Press, 1234 Amsterdam Ave, New York, NY 10027 Tel: 212-678-3929 Fax: 212-678-4149 E-mail: tcpress@tc.edu Web Site: www.tcpress.com, pg 203

Klingborg, Brian, Kumon Publishing North America Inc (KPNA), 301 Rte 17 N, Suite 704, Rutherford, NJ 07070-2581 Tel: 201-836-2105; 201-836-1559; 703-661-1501 (orders) Toll Free Tel: 800-657-7970 (cust serv) Fax: 201-836-1559 E-mail: books@kumon.com; kumon@presswarehouse.com Web Site: kumonbooks.com, pg 112

Klinger, Harvey, Harvey Klinger Inc, 300 W 55 St, Suite 11V, New York, NY 10019 Tel: 212-581-7068 Fax: 212-315-3823 E-mail: queries@harveyklinger.com Web Site: www.harveyklinger.com, pg 465

Klonsky, Jennifer, Dial Books for Young Readers, c/o Penguin Random House LLC, 1745 Broadway, New York, NY 10019 Tel: 212-782-9000 Web Site: www.penguin.com/dial-overview/, pg 59

Klonsky, Jennifer, Penguin Young Readers Group, c/o Penguin Random House LLC, 1745 Broadway, New York, NY 10019 Tel: 212-782-9000 Web Site: www.penguin.com/penguin-young-readers-overview, pg 156

Klonsky, Jennifer, GP Putnam's Sons Books for Young Readers, c/o Penguin Random House LLC, 1745 Broadway, New York, NY 10019 Tel: 212-782-9000 Web Site: www.penguin.com/putnam-young-readers/, pg 167

Klose, Lisa, Johns Hopkins University Press, 2715 N Charles St, Baltimore, MD 21218-4363 Tel: 410-516-6900; 410-516-6987 Toll Free Tel: 800-537-5487 (book orders & cust serv); 800-548-1784 (journal orders) Fax: 410-516-6968; 410-516-6998 (orders) E-mail: hfscustserv@press.jhu.edu (cust serv); jrnlcirc@jh.edu (journal orders) Web Site: www.press.jhu.edu; muse.jhu.edu, pg 106

Kloske, Geoffrey, Penguin Publishing Group, c/o Penguin Random House LLC, 1745 Broadway, New York, NY 10019 Tel: 212-782-9000 Web Site: www.penguin.com, pg 154

Kloske, Geoffrey, Riverhead Books, c/o Penguin Random House LLC, 1745 Broadway, New York, NY 10019 Tel: 212-782-9000 Web Site: www.penguin.com/riverhead-overview/, pg 175

Kloss, Karissa, Shambhala Publications Inc, 2129 13 St, Boulder, CO 80302 Tel: 978-829-2599 (intl callers) Toll Free Tel: 866-424-0030 (off); 888-424-2329 (orders & cust serv) Fax: 617-236-1563 E-mail: customercare@shambhala.com; royalties@shambhala.com Web Site: www.shambhala.com, pg 187

Klosterman, Jeffrey D, Professional Resource Press, 5864 Elegant Orchid Way, Sarasota, FL 34232 Tel: 941-343-9601 Toll Free Tel: 800-443-3364 (orders & cust serv) Fax: 941-343-9201 Toll Free Fax: 866-804-4843 (orders only) E-mail: cs@prpress.com Web Site: www.prpress.com, pg 165

Knapp, Jamie, Dutton, c/o Penguin Random House LLC, 1745 Broadway, New York, NY 10019 Tel: 212-366-2000 Web Site: www.penguin.com/dutton-overview/; www.penguin.com/plume-books-overview/; www.penguin.com/tiny-reparations-overview/, pg 62

Knauff, Carol, The Massachusetts Historical Society, 1154 Boylston St, Boston, MA 02215-3695 Tel: 617-536-1608 Fax: 617-859-0074 E-mail: publications@masshist.org Web Site: www.masshist.org, pg 126

Kneafsey, Kaitlin, Penguin Young Readers Group, c/o Penguin Random House LLC, 1745 Broadway, New York, NY 10019 Tel: 212-782-9000 Web Site: www.penguin.com/penguin-young-readers-overview, pg 156

Knight, Barb, Tiger Tales, 5 River Rd, Suite 128, Wilton, CT 06897-4069 Tel: 920-387-2333 Fax: 920-387-9994 Web Site: www.tigertalesbooks.com, pg 207

Knight, Brennan, Naval Institute Press, 291 Wood Rd, Annapolis, MD 21402-5034 Tel: 410-268-6110 Toll Free Tel: 800-233-8764 Fax: 410-295-1084 E-mail: customer@usni.org (cust inquiries) Web Site: www.usni.org/press/books; www.usni.org, pg 139

Knight, Carol Lynne, Anhinga Press Inc, PO Box 3665, Tallahassee, FL 32315 E-mail: info@anhinga.org Web Site: www.anhingapress.org; www.facebook.com/anhingapress, pg 14

Knight, Carol Lynne, Anhinga Prize for Poetry, PO Box 3665, Tallahassee, FL 32315 E-mail: info@anhinga.org Web Site: www.anhingapress.org, pg 573

Knight, Deidre, The Knight Agency Inc, 232 W Washington St, Madison, GA 30650 E-mail: admin@knightagency.net Web Site: www.knightagency.net, pg 466

Knight, Elliot A PhD, Alabama Artists Fellowship Awards, 201 Monroe St, Suite 110, Montgomery, AL 36130-1800 Tel: 334-242-4076 Fax: 334-240-3269 Web Site: arts.alabama.gov/programs/literary_arts/literary_fellowships.aspx, pg 571

Knight, Judson, The Knight Agency Inc, 232 W Washington St, Madison, GA 30650 E-mail: admin@knightagency.net Web Site: www.knightagency.net, pg 466

Knighton, Anna, Doubleday, c/o Penguin Random House LLC, 1745 Broadway, New York, NY 10019 Tel: 212-751-2600 Fax: 212-940-7390 (dom rts); 212-572-2662 (foreign rts) Web Site: knopfdoubleday.com/imprint/doubleday/; knopfdoubleday.com, pg 61

Knill, Ellen, Bellerophon Books, PO Box 21307, Santa Barbara, CA 93121-1307 Tel: 805-965-7034 Toll Free Tel: 800-253-9943 Fax: 805-965-8286 E-mail: sales.bellerophon@gmail.com Web Site: www.bellerophonbooks.com, pg 27

Knoll, Lori, Canada-Japan Literary Awards, 150 Elgin St, 2nd fl, Ottawa, ON K2P 1L4, Canada Tel: 613-566-4414 Toll Free Tel: 800-263-5588 (CN only) Fax: 613-566-4390 E-mail: canadajapan-prizes@canadacouncil.ca Web Site: canadacouncil.ca/funding/prizes/canada-japan-literary-awards, pg 586

Knoll, Lori, Governor General's Literary Awards, 150 Elgin St, 2nd fl, Ottawa, ON K2P 1L4, Canada Tel: 613-566-4414 Toll Free Tel: 800-263-5588 (CN only) Fax: 613-566-4390 E-mail: ggbooks@canadacouncil.ca Web Site: ggbooks.ca, pg 608

Knoll, Zack, Harry N Abrams Inc, 195 Broadway, 9th fl, New York, NY 10007 Tel: 212-206-7715 Toll Free Tel: 800-345-1359 Fax: 212-645-8437 E-mail: abrams@abramsbooks.com; publicity@abramsbooks.com; sales@abramsbooks.com Web Site: www.abramsbooks.com, pg 3

Knopf, Susan, American Book Producers Association (ABPA), 7 Peter Cooper Rd, No 7G, New York, NY 10010 E-mail: office@abpaonline.org Web Site: www.abpaonline.org, pg 494

Knopf, Susan, WNBA Pannell Award for Excellence in Children's Bookselling, PO Box 237, FDR Sta, New York, NY 10150-0231 Toll Free Tel: 866-610-WNBA (610-9622) E-mail: pannell@wnba-books.org Web Site: wnba-books.org/pannell-award, pg 676

Knott, Ronald, Andrews University Press, Sutherland House, 8360 W Campus Circle Dr, Berrien Springs, MI 49104-1700 Tel: 269-471-6134 Toll Free Tel: 800-467-6369 (Visa, MC & American Express orders only) Fax: 269-471-6224 E-mail: aupo@andrews.edu; aup@andrews.edu Web Site: www.universitypress.andrews.edu, pg 14

Knowles, Alison, Berrett-Koehler Publishers Inc, 1333 Broadway, Suite 1000, Oakland, CA 94612 Tel: 510-817-2277 Fax: 510-817-2278 E-mail: bkpub@bkpub.com Web Site: www.bkconnection.com, pg 29

Knowlton, Ginger, Curtis Brown, Ltd, 228 E 45 St, Suite 310, New York, NY 10017 Tel: 212-473-5400 Fax: 212-598-0917 E-mail: info@cbltd.com Web Site: www.curtisbrown.com, pg 452

Knowlton, Timothy F, Curtis Brown, Ltd, 228 E 45 St, Suite 310, New York, NY 10017 Tel: 212-473-5400 Fax: 212-598-0917 E-mail: info@cbltd.com Web Site: www.curtisbrown.com, pg 452

Knudsen, Celeste, HarperCollins Children's Books, 195 Broadway, New York, NY 10007 Tel: 212-207-7000 Web Site: www.harpercollins.com/childrens, pg 85

Knudson, Celeste, Sourcebooks LLC, 1935 Brookdale Rd, Suite 139, Naperville, IL 60563 Tel: 630-961-3900 Toll Free Tel: 800-432-7444 Fax: 630-961-2168 E-mail: info@sourcebooks.com Web Site: www.sourcebooks.com, pg 194

Knutsen, Trond, University of Hawaii Press, 2840 Kolowalu St, Honolulu, HI 96822-1888 Tel: 808-956-8255 Toll Free Tel: 888-UHPRESS (847-7377) Toll Free Fax: 800-650-7811 E-mail: uhpbooks@hawaii.edu Web Site: www.uhpress.hawaii.edu, pg 216

Ko, Jessica, Penguin Random House LLC, 1745 Broadway, New York, NY 10019 Tel: 212-782-9000 Toll Free Tel: 800-726-0600 Web Site: www.penguinrandomhouse.com, pg 155

Koball, Heather PhD, National Center for Children in Poverty, 722 W 168 St, New York, NY 10032 Tel: 646-284-9600; 212-304-6073 E-mail: info@nccp.org Web Site: www.nccp.org, pg 137

Koch, Bea, The Ripped Bodice Awards for Excellence in Romantic Fiction, 3806 Main St, Culver City, CA 90232 Tel: 424-603-4776 E-mail: therippedbodicela@gmail.com Web Site: www.therippedbodicela.com, pg 656

Koch, Elizabeth R, Counterpoint Press LLC, 2560 Ninth St, Suite 318, Berkeley, CA 94710 Tel: 510-704-0230 Fax: 510-704-0268 E-mail: info@counterpointpress.com Web Site: counterpointpress.com; softskull.com, pg 54

Koch, Leah, The Ripped Bodice Awards for Excellence in Romantic Fiction, 3806 Main St, Culver City, CA 90232 Tel: 424-603-4776 E-mail: therippedbodicela@gmail.com Web Site: www.therippedbodicela.com, pg 656

Koch, Melanie, Penguin Publishing Group, c/o Penguin Random House LLC, 1745 Broadway, New York, NY 10019 Tel: 212-782-9000 Web Site: www.penguin.com, pg 154

Kochan, Susan, GP Putnam's Sons Books for Young Readers, c/o Penguin Random House LLC, 1745 Broadway, New York, NY 10019 Tel: 212-782-9000 Web Site: www.penguin.com/putnam-young-readers/, pg 167

Kochman, Charles, Harry N Abrams Inc, 195 Broadway, 9th fl, New York, NY 10007 Tel: 212-206-7715 Toll Free Tel: 800-345-1359 Fax: 212-645-8437 E-mail: abrams@abramsbooks.com; publicity@abramsbooks.com; sales@abramsbooks.com Web Site: www.abramsbooks.com, pg 3

Koehler, Beth, Penguin Random House LLC, 1745 Broadway, New York, NY 10019 Tel: 212-782-9000 Toll Free Tel: 800-726-0600 Web Site: www.penguinrandomhouse.com, pg 155

Koenig, Renee, Austin Area Translators & Interpreters Association (AATIA), PO Box 92334, Austin, TX 78709-2334 E-mail: info@aatia.org; communications@aatia.org; membership@aatia.org; finance@aatia.org; profdev@aatia.org Web Site: aatia.org, pg 500

Koenigsknecht, Michelle, AIGA 50 Books | 50 Covers, 228 Park Ave S, Suite 58603, New York, NY 10003 Tel: 212-807-1990 E-mail: competitions@aiga.org Web Site: www.aiga.org, pg 571

Koenigsknecht, Michelle, AIGA, the professional association for design, 228 Park Ave S, Suite 58603, New York, NY 10003 Tel: 212-807-1990 E-mail: general@aiga.org Web Site: www.aiga.org, pg 493

Koerner, Darrell, Chelsea Green Publishing Co, 85 N Main St, Suite 120, White River Junction, VT 05001 Tel: 802-295-6300 Toll Free Tel: 800-639-4099 (cust serv & orders) Fax: 802-295-6444 E-mail: customerservice@chelseagreen.com; editorial@chelseagreen.com; publicity@chelseagreen.com; rights@chelseagreen.com Web Site: www.chelseagreen.com, pg 45

Koester, Robert J, dbS Productions, PO Box 94, Charlottesville, VA 22902 Tel: 434-293-5502 Toll Free Tel: 800-745-1581 E-mail: info@dbs-sar.com Web Site: www.dbs-sar.com, pg 58

Koffler, Lionel, Firefly Books Ltd, 50 Staples Ave, Unit 1, Richmond Hill, ON L4B 0A7, Canada Tel: 416-499-8412 Toll Free Tel: 800-387-6192 (CN); 800-387-5085 (US) Fax: 416-499-8313 Toll Free Fax: 800-450-0391 (CN); 800-565-6034 (US) E-mail: service@fireflybooks.com Web Site: www.fireflybooks.com, pg 406

Kohl, Deborah, University of Baltimore - Yale Gordon College of Arts & Sciences, Liberal Arts & Policy Bldg, 10 W Preston St, Rm 107, Baltimore, MD 21201 Web Site: www.ubalt.edu/cas/about-the-college/schools-and-divisions/school-of-communications-design, pg 566

Kohler, Christian S, American Diabetes Association, 2451 Crystal Dr, Suite 900, Arlington, VA 22202 Tel: 703-549-1500 Toll Free Tel: 800-342-2383 E-mail: booksales@diabetes.org; ada_pubs@diabetes.org Web Site: diabetes.org; diabetesjournals.org/books; www.facebook.com/adapublications, pg 9

Kohlmeister, Kayla, Penguin Random House Audio Publishing Group, 1745 Broadway, New York, NY 10019 Toll Free Tel: 800-793-2665 (cust serv) E-mail: audio@penguinrandomhouse.com; ecustomerservice@penguinrandomhouse.com Web Site: www.penguinrandomhouseaudio.com, pg 154

Kok, John H, Dordt Press, 700 Seventh St NE, Sioux Center, IA 51250-1671 Tel: 712-722-6420 Toll Free Tel: 800-343-6738 Fax: 712-722-6035 E-mail: dordtpress@dordt.edu; bookstore@dordt.edu Web Site: www.dordt.edu/about-dordt/publications/dordt-press-catalog, pg 61

Kolani, Alison, Random House Children's Books, c/o Penguin Random House LLC, 1745 Broadway, New York, NY 10019 Tel: 212-782-9000 Web Site: www.rhcbooks.com, pg 169

Kolbe, Kimberly, New Issues Poetry & Prose, c/o Western Michigan University, 1903 W Michigan Ave, Kalamazoo, MI 49008-5463 Tel: 269-387-8185 E-mail: new-issues@wmich.edu Web Site: newissuespress.com, pg 140

Kolby, Jeff, Nova Press, PO Box 692023, West Hollywood, CA 90069 Tel: 310-601-8551 E-mail: novapress@aol.com Web Site: www.novapress.net, pg 144

Kolendo, Kate, Association of University Presses (AUPresses), 1412 Broadway, Suite 2135, New York, NY 10018 Tel: 212-989-1010 Fax: 212-989-0275 E-mail: info@aupresses.org Web Site: www.aupresses.org, pg 500

Kolendo, Kate, AUPresses Book, Jacket & Journal Show, 1412 Broadway, Suite 2135, New York, NY 10018 Tel: 212-989-1010 Fax: 212-989-0275 E-mail: info@aupresses.org Web Site: www.aupresses.org, pg 576

Kolodkin, Danielle, Harry N Abrams Inc, 195 Broadway, 9th fl, New York, NY 10007 Tel: 212-206-7715 Toll Free Tel: 800-345-1359 Fax: 212-645-8437 E-mail: abrams@abramsbooks.com; publicity@abramsbooks.com; sales@abramsbooks.com Web Site: www.abramsbooks.com, pg 3

Kolsrud, Kelli, International Foundation of Employee Benefit Plans, 18700 W Bluemound Rd, Brookfield, WI 53045 Tel: 262-786-6700 Toll Free Tel: 888-334-3327 Fax: 262-786-8780 E-mail: editor@ifebp.org Web Site: www.ifebp.org, pg 103

Kolwitz, Ok Hee, Penguin Random House Audio Publishing Group, 1745 Broadway, New York, NY 10019 Toll Free Tel: 800-793-2665 (cust serv) E-mail: audio@penguinrandomhouse.com; ecustomerservice@penguinrandomhouse.com Web Site: www.penguinrandomhouseaudio.com, pg 154

Komie, Michelle, Princeton University Press, 41 William St, Princeton, NJ 08540-5237 Tel: 609-258-4900 Fax: 609-258-6305 E-mail: info@press.princeton.edu Web Site: press.princeton.edu, pg 164

Kompik, Natalie, Wm B Eerdmans Publishing Co, 4035 Park East Ct SE, Grand Rapids, MI 49546 Tel: 616-459-4591 Toll Free Tel: 800-253-7521 E-mail: customerservice@eerdmans.com; sales@eerdmans.com Web Site: www.eerdmans.com, pg 64

Koncsol, Siena, Sourcebooks LLC, 1935 Brookdale Rd, Suite 139, Naperville, IL 60563 Tel: 630-961-3900 Toll Free Tel: 800-432-7444 Fax: 630-961-2168 E-mail: info@sourcebooks.com Web Site: www.sourcebooks.com, pg 194

Kondrick, Maureen, Marquette University Press, 1415 W Wisconsin Ave, Milwaukee, WI 53233 Tel: 414-288-1564 Web Site: www.marquette.edu/mupress, pg 125

Konecke, Kaitlin, Health Professions Press, 409 Washington Ave, Suite 500, Towson, MD 21204 Tel: 410-337-9585 Toll Free Tel: 888-337-8808 Fax: 410-337-8539 Web Site: www.healthpropress.com, pg 90

Konecky, Sean, Konecky & Konecky LLC, 72 Ayers Point Rd, Old Saybrook, CT 06475 Tel: 860-388-0878 E-mail: sean.konecky@gmail.com Web Site: www.koneckyandkonecky.com, pg 111

Kong, Adriane, Bloomsbury Academic, 1385 Broadway, 5th fl, New York, NY 10018 Tel: 212-419-5300 Web Site: www.bloomsbury.com/us/academic, pg 31

Kong, Ken, Random House Children's Books, c/o Penguin Random House LLC, 1745 Broadway, New York, NY 10019 Tel: 212-782-9000 Web Site: www.rhcbooks.com, pg 170

Kong, Molly, Macmillan, 120 Broadway, 22nd fl, New York, NY 10271 E-mail: press.inquiries@macmillan.com Web Site: us.macmillan.com, pg 122

Konner, Linda, Linda Konner Literary Agency (LKLA), 10 W 15 St, Suite 1918, New York, NY 10011 Web Site: www.lindakonnerliteraryagency.com, pg 466

Konopinski, Natalie, American Anthropological Association (AAA), 2300 Clarendon Blvd, Suite 1301, Arlington, VA 22201 E-mail: pubs@americananthro.org Web Site: www.americananthro.org, pg 8

Konowitch, Paul, Sundance/Newbridge Publishing, 33 Boston Post Rd W, Suite 440, Marlborough, MA 01752 Toll Free Tel: 888-200-2720; 800-343-8204 Toll Free Fax: 800-456-2419 (orders) E-mail: info@sundancenewbridge.com; orders@sundancenewbridge.com Web Site: www.sundancenewbridge.com, pg 200

Konzelman, Megan, Penguin Random House Canada, a Penguin Random House company, 320 Front St W, Suite 1400, Toronto, ON M5V 3B6, Canada Tel: 416-364-4449 Toll Free Tel: 888-523-9292 (cust serv) E-mail: canadaweb@penguinrandomhouse.com; customerservicescanada@penguinrandomhouse.com Web Site: www.penguinrandomhouse.ca, pg 416

Koohi-Kamali, Dr Farideh, Peter Lang Publishing Inc, 80 Broadway, 5th fl, New York, NY 10004 Tel: 703-661-1584 Toll Free Tel: 800-770-5264 (cust serv) Fax: 703-996-1010 E-mail: info@peterlang.com; newyork.editorial@peterlang.com; customerservice@plang.com Web Site: www.peterlang.com, pg 112

Kooij, Nina, Pelican Publishing, 990 N Corporate Dr, Suite 100, New Orleans, LA 70123 Tel: 504-684-8976 Toll Free Tel: 844-868-1798 (orders) E-mail: editorial@pelicanpub.com (submissions) Web Site: www.pelicanpub.com; www.arcadiapublishing.com/imprints/pelican-publishing, pg 153

Kopit, Kat, Farrar, Straus & Giroux Books for Young Readers, 120 Broadway, New York, NY 10271 Tel: 212-741-6900 Toll Free Tel: 888-330-8477 (orders) E-mail: childrens.publicity@macmillanusa.com; childrensrights@macmillanusa.com Web Site: us.macmillan.com/mackids, pg 70

Kopit, Kat, Roaring Brook Press, 120 Broadway, New York, NY 10271 Tel: 646-307-5151 Web Site: us.macmillan.com/publishers/roaring-brook-press, pg 176

Kopley, Beth, American Antiquarian Society (AAS), 185 Salisbury St, Worcester, MA 01609-1634 Tel: 508-755-5221 Fax: 508-754-9069 E-mail: library@mwa.org Web Site: www.americanantiquarian.org, pg 494

Kopley, Beth, Fellowships for Creative & Performing Artists & Writers, 185 Salisbury St, Worcester, MA 01609-1634 Tel: 508-755-5221 Fax: 508-754-9069 E-mail: library@mwa.org Web Site: www.americanantiquarian.org, pg 602

Kopley, Beth, Fellowships for Historical Research, 185 Salisbury St, Worcester, MA 01609-1634 Tel: 508-755-5221 Fax: 508-754-9069 Web Site: www.americanantiquarian.org, pg 602

Koplik, Mark, New York State Edith Wharton Citation of Merit for Fiction Writers, University at Albany, Science Library 320, 1400 Washington Ave, Albany, NY 12222 Tel: 518-442-5620 E-mail: writers@albany.edu Web Site: www.nyswritersinstitute.org, pg 640

Koplik, Mark, New York State Walt Whitman Citation of Merit for Poets, University at Albany, Science Library 320, 1400 Washington Ave, Albany, NY 12222 Tel: 518-442-5620 E-mail: writers@albany.edu Web Site: www.nyswritersinstitute.org, pg 640

Kordic, Lara, Heritage House Publishing Co Ltd, 1075 Pendergast St, No 103, Victoria, BC V8V 0A1, Canada Tel: 250-360-0829 Fax: 250-386-0829 E-mail: heritage@heritagehouse.ca; info@heritagehouse.ca; orders@heritagehouse.ca Web Site: www.heritagehouse.ca, pg 409

Korn, Linda, Penguin Random House Audio Publishing Group, 1745 Broadway, New York, NY 10019 Toll Free Tel: 800-793-2665 (cust serv) E-mail: audio@penguinrandomhouse.com; ecustomerservice@penguinrandomhouse.com Web Site: www.penguinrandomhouseaudio.com, pg 154

Korn, Mirabelle, Chronicle Books LLC, 680 Second St, San Francisco, CA 94107 Tel: 415-537-4200 Fax: 415-537-4460 (perms) E-mail: hello@chroniclebooks.com; subrights@chroniclebooks.com Web Site: www.chroniclebooks.com, pg 47

Korn, Sandra, Duke University Press, 905 W Main St, Suite 18B, Durham, NC 27701 Tel: 919-688-5134 Toll Free Tel: 888-651-0122 (US) Fax: 919-688-2615 Toll Free Fax: 888-651-0124 E-mail: orders@dukeupress.edu Web Site: www.dukeupress.edu, pg 62

Kornbluh, Rena, Hachette Book Group Inc, 1290 Avenue of the Americas, New York, NY 10104 Tel: 212-364-1100 Toll Free Tel: 800-759-0190 (cust serv) Fax: 212-364-0933 (intl orders) Toll Free Fax: 800-286-9471 (cust serv) E-mail: customer.service@hbgusa.com; orders@hbgusa.com Web Site: www.hachettebookgroup.com, pg 83

Korpus, Kristiina, Harry N Abrams Inc, 195 Broadway, 9th fl, New York, NY 10007 Tel: 212-206-7715 Toll Free Tel: 800-345-1359 Fax: 212-645-8437 E-mail: abrams@abramsbooks.com; publicity@abramsbooks.com; sales@abramsbooks.com Web Site: www.abramsbooks.com, pg 3

Koski, Abby, Soho Press Inc, 853 Broadway, New York, NY 10003 Tel: 212-260-1900 E-mail: soho@sohopress.com; publicity@sohopress.com Web Site: sohopress.com, pg 193

Kosko, Susan, HarperCollins Publishers LLC, 195 Broadway, New York, NY 10007 Tel: 212-207-7000 Web Site: www.harpercollins.com, pg 86

Kosmach, Jack, Whole Person Associates Inc, 101 W Second St, Suite 203, Duluth, MN 55802 Tel: 218-727-0500 Toll Free Tel: 800-247-6789 Fax: 218-727-0505 E-mail: books@wholeperson.com Web Site: www.wholeperson.com, pg 229

Kosman, Phoebe, Candlewick Press, 99 Dover St, Somerville, MA 02144-2825 Tel: 617-661-3330 Fax: 617-661-0565 E-mail: bigbear@candlewick.com; salesinfo@candlewick.com Web Site: candlewick.com, pg 39

Kosmoski, Anne, Avery, c/o Penguin Random House LLC, 1745 Broadway, New York, NY 10019 Tel: 212-366-2000 Web Site: www.penguin.com/avery-overview/, pg 23

Kosmoski, Anne, TarcherPerigee, c/o Penguin Random House LLC, 1745 Broadway, New York, NY 10019 Tel: 212-782-9000 Web Site: www.penguin.com/tarcherperigee-overview/; www.facebook.com/TarcherPerigee, pg 202

Kosowski, Mary Beth, Mercer University Press, 368 Orange St, Macon, GA 31201 Tel: 478-301-2880 Toll Free Tel: 866-895-1472 Fax: 478-301-2585 E-mail: mupressorders@mercer.edu Web Site: www.mupress.org, pg 129

Kossakowski, Sophie, Sourcebooks LLC, 1935 Brookdale Rd, Suite 139, Naperville, IL 60563 Tel: 630-961-3900 Toll Free Tel: 800-432-7444 Fax: 630-961-2168 E-mail: info@sourcebooks.com Web Site: www.sourcebooks.com, pg 194

Kost, Jordan, Sourcebooks LLC, 1935 Brookdale Rd, Suite 139, Naperville, IL 60563 Tel: 630-961-3900 Toll Free Tel: 800-432-7444 Fax: 630-961-2168 E-mail: info@sourcebooks.com Web Site: www.sourcebooks.com, pg 194

Koster, Susan, WNBA Pannell Award for Excellence in Children's Bookselling, PO Box 237, FDR Sta, New York, NY 10150-0231 Toll Free Tel: 866-610-WNBA (610-9622) E-mail: pannell@wnba-books.org Web Site: wnba-books.org/pannell-award, pg 676

Kosztolnyik, Karen, Grand Central Publishing, 1290 Avenue of the Americas, New York, NY 10104 Tel: 212-364-1100 Web Site: www.hachettebookgroup.com/imprint/grand-central-publishing/, pg 80

Kotchman, Katie, Don Congdon Associates Inc, 110 William St, Suite 2202, New York, NY 10038-3914 Tel: 212-645-1229 Fax: 212-727-2688 E-mail: dca@doncongdon.com Web Site: www.doncongdon.com, pg 454

Kothiwal, Shruti, Independent Institute, 100 Swan Way, Oakland, CA 94621-1428 Tel: 510-632-1366 Fax: 510-568-6040 Web Site: www.independent.org, pg 99

Kotovets, Gary, Dun & Bradstreet, 103 JFK Pkwy, Short Hills, NJ 07078 Tel: 973-921-5500 Toll Free Tel: 844-869-8244; 800-234-3867 (cust serv) Web Site: www.dnb.com, pg 62

Kotsyuba, Dr Oleh, Harvard Ukrainian Research Institute, 34 Kirkland St, Cambridge, MA 02138 Tel: 617-495-4053 Fax: 617-495-8097 E-mail: huripubs@fas.harvard.edu Web Site: books.huri.harvard.edu, pg 88

Kouma, Cecelia, California Young Playwrights Contest, 3675 Ruffin Rd, Suite 330, San Diego, CA 92123 Tel: 858-384-2970 Fax: 858-384-2974 E-mail: write@playwrightsproject.org Web Site: www.playwrightsproject.org, pg 586

Koundoura, Maria, Emerson College Department of Writing, Literature & Publishing, 180 Tremont St, 10th fl, Boston, MA 02116-4624 Tel: 617-824-8750 Web Site: www.emerson.edu; www.emerson.edu/writing-literature-publishing, pg 562

Kovach, Lynn, Random House Publishing Group, 1745 Broadway, New York, NY 10019 Toll Free Tel: 800-200-3552 Web Site: www.randomhousebooks.com, pg 170

Kowal, Basia, University of Alberta Press, Ring House 2, Edmonton, AB T6G 2E1, Canada Tel: 780-492-3662 Fax: 780-492-0719 Web Site: www.uap.ualberta.ca, pg 421

Kowal, Rachel, Soho Press Inc, 853 Broadway, New York, NY 10003 Tel: 212-260-1900 E-mail: soho@sohopress.com; publicity@sohopress.com Web Site: sohopress.com, pg 193

Kowalchuk, Tavia, HarperCollins Publishers LLC, 195 Broadway, New York, NY 10007 Tel: 212-207-7000 Web Site: www.harpercollins.com, pg 86

Kowalski, Jennifer, New York State Edith Wharton Citation of Merit for Fiction Writers, University at Albany, Science Library 320, 1400 Washington Ave, Albany, NY 12222 Tel: 518-442-5620 E-mail: writers@albany.edu Web Site: www.nyswritersinstitute.org, pg 640

Kowalski, Jennifer, New York State Walt Whitman Citation of Merit for Poets, University at Albany, Science Library 320, 1400 Washington Ave, Albany, NY 12222 Tel: 518-442-5620 E-mail: writers@albany.edu Web Site: www.nyswritersinstitute.org, pg 640

Kowara, Theresia, HarperCollins Children's Books, 195 Broadway, New York, NY 10007 Tel: 212-207-7000 Web Site: www.harpercollins.com/childrens, pg 86

Kozu, Joy, Brower Literary & Management Inc, 13720 Old St Augustine Rd, Suite 8-512, Jacksonville, FL 32258 Tel: 646-854-6073 E-mail: admin@browerliterary.com; foreign@browerliterary.com (foreign publr inquiries); queries@browerliterary.com; subrights@browerliterary.com (busn inquiries) Web Site: browerliterary.com, pg 452

Kracht, Elizabeth, Kimberley Cameron & Associates LLC, 1550 Tiburon Blvd, Suite 704, Tiburon, CA 94920 Tel: 415-789-9191 E-mail: info@kimberleycameron.com Web Site: www.kimberleycameron.com, pg 453

Kracht, Peter W, Drue Heinz Literature Prize, 7500 Thomas Blvd, Pittsburgh, PA 15260 Tel: 412-383-2456 Fax: 412-383-2466 E-mail: info@upress.pitt.edu Web Site: upittpress.org/prize/drue-heinz-literature-prize; www.upress.pitt.edu, pg 612

Kracht, Peter W, Agnes Lynch Starrett Poetry Prize, 7500 Thomas Blvd, Pittsburgh, PA 15260 Tel: 412-383-2456 Fax: 412-383-2466 E-mail: info@upress.pitt.edu Web Site: upittpress.org/prize/agnes-lynch-starrett-poetry-prize/; www.upress.pitt.edu, pg 666

Kracht, Peter W, University of Pittsburgh Press, 7500 Thomas Blvd, Pittsburgh, PA 15260 Tel: 412-383-2456 Fax: 412-383-2466 E-mail: info@upress.pitt.edu Web Site: www.upress.pitt.edu, pg 219

Krainin, Colin, Macmillan, 120 Broadway, 22nd fl, New York, NY 10271 E-mail: press.inquiries@macmillan.com Web Site: us.macmillan.com, pg 122

Kral, Steve, Society for Mining, Metallurgy & Exploration, 12999 E Adam Aircraft Circle, Englewood, CO 80112 Tel: 303-948-4200 Toll Free Tel: 800-763-3132 Fax: 303-973-3845 E-mail: cs@smenet.org; books@smenet.org Web Site: www.smenet.org, pg 192

Kralstein, Samantha, American Psychiatric Association Publishing, 800 Maine Ave SW, Suite 900, Washington, DC 20024 Tel: 202-459-9722 Toll Free Tel: 800-368-5777 Fax: 202-403-3094 E-mail: appi@psych.org Web Site: www.appi.org; www.psychiatryonline.org, pg 11

Kramer, David, United Talent Agency LLC, 9336 Civic Center Dr, Beverly Hills, CA 90210 Tel: 310-273-6700 Web Site: www.unitedtalent.com, pg 481

Kramer, Gary, Temple University Press, 1852 N Tenth St, Philadelphia, PA 19122-6099 Tel: 215-926-2140 Toll Free Tel: 800-621-2736 Fax: 215-926-2141 E-mail: tempress@temple.edu Web Site: tupress.temple.edu, pg 204

Kramer, Jill, Waterside Productions Inc, 2055 Oxford Ave, Cardiff, CA 92007 Tel: 760-632-9190 Fax: 760-632-9295 E-mail: admin@waterside.com Web Site: www.waterside.com, pg 481

Kramer, Kateri, Fulcrum Publishing Inc, 3970 Youngfield St, Wheat Ridge, CO 80033 Tel: 303-277-1623 Toll Free Tel: 800-888-4741 (orders) E-mail: info@fulcrumbooks.com Web Site: www.fulcrumbooks.com, pg 75

Kramp, John, Thomas Nelson, 501 Nelson Place, Nashville, TN 37214 Tel: 615-889-9000 Toll Free Tel: 800-251-4000 Web Site: www.thomasnelson.com, pg 206

Kranz, Deb, Plexus Publishing, Inc, 143 Old Marlton Pike, Medford, NJ 08055 Tel: 609-654-6500 Fax: 609-654-4309 E-mail: info@plexuspublishing.com Web Site: www.plexuspublishing.com, pg 160

Kranz, Patricia, Overseas Press Club of America (OPC), 40 W 45 St, New York, NY 10036 Tel: 212-626-9220 E-mail: info@opcofamerica.org Web Site: opcofamerica.org, pg 516

Kranz, Patricia, The Cornelius Ryan Award, 40 W 45 St, New York, NY 10036 Tel: 212-626-9220 E-mail: info@opcofamerica.org Web Site: opcofamerica.org, pg 658

Kraska, Katie, Macmillan, 120 Broadway, 22nd fl, New York, NY 10271 E-mail: press.inquiries@macmillan.com Web Site: us.macmillan.com, pg 122

Krasner, Emily, Workman Publishing, 1290 Avenue of the Americas, New York, NY 10104 Toll Free Tel: 800-759-0190 Fax: 212-364-0950 E-mail: workman-inquiry@hbgusa.com Web Site: www.hachettebookgroup.com/imprint/workman-publishing-company/, pg 232

Krassner, Kaye, Association of Publishers for Special Sales (APSS), PO Box 715, Avon, CT 06001-0715 Tel: 860-675-1344 Web Site: www.bookapss.org, pg 500

Krattenmaker, Kathleen, Philadelphia Museum of Art, PO Box 7646, Philadelphia, PA 19101-7646 Tel: 215-763-8100 Fax: 215-236-4465 Web Site: www.philamuseum.org, pg 159

Kraus, Eric, Smith & Kraus Publishers Inc, 177 Lyme Rd, Hanover, NH 03755 Tel: 618-783-0519 Toll Free Tel: 877-668-8680 Fax: 618-783-0520 E-mail: editor@smithandkraus.com; customerservice@smithandkraus.com Web Site: www.smithandkraus.com, pg 192

Krause, Amanda, The University of Arizona Press, 1510 E University Blvd, Tucson, AZ 85721 Tel: 520-621-1441 Toll Free Tel: 800-621-2736 (orders) Fax: 520-621-8899 Toll Free Fax: 800-621-8476 (orders) E-mail: uap@uapress.arizona.edu Web Site: www.uapress.arizona.edu, pg 214

Krause, Bill, Llewellyn Publications, 2143 Wooddale Dr, Woodbury, MN 55125 Tel: 651-291-1970 Toll Free Tel: 800-843-6666 Fax: 651-291-1908 E-mail: publicity@llewellyn.com; customerservice@llewellyn.com Web Site: www.llewellyn.com, pg 119

Krause, Thomas, Bloomsbury Academic, 1385 Broadway, 5th fl, New York, NY 10018 Tel: 212-419-5300 Web Site: www.bloomsbury.com/us/academic, pg 31

Krauss, Molly, Chronicle Books LLC, 680 Second St, San Francisco, CA 94107 Tel: 415-537-4200 Fax: 415-537-4460 (perms) E-mail: hello@chroniclebooks.com; subrights@chroniclebooks.com Web Site: www.chroniclebooks.com, pg 48

Kraut, Diane, DK Research Inc, 9 Wicks Dr, Commack, NY 11725-3921 Tel: 631-543-5537 Fax: 631-543-5549 E-mail: dkresearch@optimum.net Web Site: www.dkresearchinc.com, pg 438

Krebs, Paula, Modern Language Association (MLA), 85 Broad St, New York, NY 10004 Tel: 646-576-5000 E-mail: help@mla.org Web Site: www.mla.org; x.com/MLAnews; www.facebook.com/modernlanguageassociation; www.linkedin.com/company/modern-language-association, pg 133

Krebs, Paula, Modern Language Association (MLA), 85 Broad St, New York, NY 10004 Tel: 646-576-5000 E-mail: help@mla.org; membership@mla.org Web Site: www.mla.org; x.com/MLAnews; www.facebook.com/modernlanguageassociation; www.linkedin.com/company/modern-language-association, pg 511

Kregel, Jerold W, Editorial Portavoz, 2450 Oak Industrial Dr NE, Grand Rapids, MI 49505 Toll Free Tel: 877-733-2607 (ext 206) E-mail: kregelbooks@kregel.com Web Site: www.portavoz.com, pg 64

Kregel, Jerold W, Kregel Publications, 2450 Oak Industrial Dr NE, Grand Rapids, MI 49505 *Tel:* 616-451-4775 *Toll Free Tel:* 800-733-2607 *Fax:* 616-451-9330 *E-mail:* kregelbooks@kregel.com *Web Site:* www.kregel.com, pg 111

Krehbiel, Ken, National Council of Teachers of Mathematics (NCTM), 1906 Association Dr, Reston, VA 20191-1502 *Tel:* 703-620-9840 *Toll Free Tel:* 800-235-7566 *Fax:* 703-476-2970 *E-mail:* nctm@nctm.org *Web Site:* www.nctm.org, pg 137

Kreit, Eileen, Pace University Press, Pace University, One Pace Plaza, New York, NY 10038 *Tel:* 212-346-1417 *Fax:* 212-346-1417 *E-mail:* paceupress@gmail.com *Web Site:* www.pace.edu/press, pg 149

Kreiter, Lance, BOOM! Studios, 5670 Wilshire Blvd, Suite 400, Los Angeles, CA 90036 *E-mail:* contact@boom-studios.com; customerservice@boom-studios.com; press@boom-studios.com *Web Site:* www.boom-studios.com, pg 34

Krell, Henry, Springer, One New York Plaza, Suite 4600, New York, NY 10004-1562 *Tel:* 212-460-1500 *Toll Free Tel:* 800-SPRINGER (777-4643) *Fax:* 212-460-1700 *E-mail:* customerservice@springernature.com *Web Site:* www.springer.com, pg 196

Kremer, John, Open Horizons Publishing Co, PO Box 271, Dolan Springs, NM 86441 *Tel:* 575-741-1581 *E-mail:* books@bookmarketingbestsellers.com *Web Site:* bookmarketingbestsellers.com, pg 147

Kresan, Dawn, Palimpsest Press, 1171 Eastlawn Ave, Windsor, ON N8S 3J1, Canada *Tel:* 519-259-2112 *E-mail:* publicity@palimpsestpress.ca *Web Site:* www.palimpsestpress.ca, pg 415

Kreuser, Joe, Bloomsbury Academic, 1385 Broadway, 5th fl, New York, NY 10018 *Tel:* 212-419-5300 *Web Site:* www.bloomsbury.com/us/academic, pg 31

Krichevsky, Stuart, Stuart Krichevsky Literary Agency Inc, 118 E 28 St, Suite 908, New York, NY 10016 *Tel:* 212-725-5288 *Fax:* 212-725-5275 *E-mail:* query@skagency.com *Web Site:* skagency.com, pg 466

Krieger, Ann, Krieger Publishing Co, 1725 Krieger Lane, Malabar, FL 32950 *Tel:* 321-724-9542 *Fax:* 321-951-3671 *E-mail:* info@krieger-publishing.com *Web Site:* www.krieger-publishing.com, pg 111

Krieger, Donald E, Krieger Publishing Co, 1725 Krieger Lane, Malabar, FL 32950 *Tel:* 321-724-9542 *Fax:* 321-951-3671 *E-mail:* info@krieger-publishing.com *Web Site:* www.krieger-publishing.com, pg 111

Krienke, Mary, Sterling Lord Literistic Inc, 594 Broadway, Suite 205, New York, NY 10012 *Tel:* 212-780-6050 *Fax:* 212-780-6095 *E-mail:* info@sll.com *Web Site:* www.sll.com, pg 477

Krinsky, Santosh, Lotus Press, 1100 E Lotus Dr, Silver Lake, WI 53170 *Tel:* 262-889-8561 *Toll Free Tel:* 800-824-6396 (orders) *Fax:* 262-889-2461; 262-889-8591 *E-mail:* lotuspress@lotuspress.com *Web Site:* www.lotuspress.com, pg 120

Krishnan, Priyanka, HarperCollins Publishers LLC, 195 Broadway, New York, NY 10007 *Tel:* 212-207-7000 *Web Site:* www.harpercollins.com, pg 86

Kriss, Miriam, Irene Goodman Literary Agency, 27 W 24 St, Suite 700B, New York, NY 10010 *Tel:* 212-604-0330 *E-mail:* queries@irenegoodman.com *Web Site:* www.irenegoodman.com, pg 460

Krissoff, Derek, West Virginia University Press, West Virginia University, PO Box 6295, Morgantown, WV 26506-6295 *Tel:* 304-293-8400 *Web Site:* www.wvupress.com, pg 228

Kristal, Jennifer, Adams Media, 100 Technology Center Dr, Suite 501, Stoughton, MA 02072 *Tel:* 508-427-7100 *Web Site:* www.simonandschuster.com, pg 4

Kroell, Alicia, Counterpoint Press LLC, 2560 Ninth St, Suite 318, Berkeley, CA 94710 *Tel:* 510-704-0230 *Fax:* 510-704-0268 *E-mail:* info@counterpointpress.com *Web Site:* counterpointpress.com; softskull.com, pg 54

Kroger, Rev Dan OFM, Franciscan Media, 28 W Liberty St, Cincinnati, OH 45202 *Tel:* 513-241-5615 *E-mail:* admin@franciscanmedia.org *Web Site:* www.franciscanmedia.org, pg 74

Krohn, Amanda Chiu, Turner Publishing Co LLC, 4507 Charlotte Ave, Suite 100, Nashville, TN 37209 *Tel:* 615-255-BOOK (255-2665) *Fax:* 615-255-5081 *E-mail:* info@turnerpublishing.com; marketing@turnerpublishing.com; submissions@turnerpublishing.com; editorial@turnerpublishing.com; admin@turnerpublishing.com; orders@turnerpublishing.com *Web Site:* turnerpublishing.com; www.facebook.com/turner.publishing, pg 210

Krohn, Talia, Little, Brown and Company, 1290 Avenue of the Americas, New York, NY 10104 *Tel:* 212-364-1100 *Fax:* 212-364-0952 *E-mail:* firstname.lastname@hbgusa.com *Web Site:* www.hachettebookgroup.com/imprint/little-brown-and-company/, pg 118

Krones, Chris, Clarion Books, 195 Broadway, New York, NY 10007 *Tel:* 212-207-7000 *Toll Free Tel:* 800-242-7737 *E-mail:* consumercare@harpercollins.com *Web Site:* www.harpercollins.com/collections/books-by-clarion-books, pg 49

Krones, Christine, Houghton Mifflin Harcourt Trade & Reference Division, 125 High St, Boston, MA 02110 *Tel:* 617-351-5000 *Web Site:* www.hmhco.com, pg 96

Kronzek, Lynn C, Lynn C Kronzek, Richard A Flom & Robert Flom, 145 S Glenoaks Blvd, Suite 240, Burbank, CA 91502 *Tel:* 818-768-7688, pg 441

Krotov, Mark, n+1 Writers' Fellowship, Cadman Plaza Sta, PO Box 26428, Brooklyn, NY 11202 *E-mail:* editors@nplusonemag.com; subs@nplusonemag.com (submission queries); submissions@nplusonemag.com *Web Site:* www.nplusonemag.com/awards, pg 642

Krotov, Mark, Anthony Veasna So Fiction Prize, Cadman Plaza Sta, PO Box 26428, Brooklyn, NY 11202 *E-mail:* editors@nplusonemag.com; subs@nplusonemag.com (submission queries); submissions@nplusonemag.com *Web Site:* www.nplusonemag.com/awards, pg 664

Krouk, Dean, The Ibsen Society of America (ISA), c/o Indiana University, Global & Intl Studies Bldg 3111, 355 N Jordan Ave, Bloomington, IN 47405-1105 *Web Site:* www.ibsensociety.org, pg 507

Krovitz, Debbie, DeVorss & Co, 1100 Flynn Rd, Unit 104, Camarillo, CA 93012 *Tel:* 805-322-9010 *Toll Free Tel:* 800-843-5743 *Fax:* 805-322-9011 *E-mail:* service@devorss.com *Web Site:* www.devorss.com, pg 59

Krowl, Michelle A, Abraham Lincoln Institute Book Award, c/o ALI Treasurer, 4158 Vernoy Hills Rd, Fairfax, VA 22030 *Web Site:* www.lincoln-institute.org, pg 625

Krueger, Jenny, ediciones Lerner, 241 First Ave N, Minneapolis, MN 55401 *Tel:* 612-332-3344 *Toll Free Tel:* 800-328-4929 *Fax:* 612-332-7615 *Toll Free Fax:* 800-332-1132 *E-mail:* info@lernerbooks.com; custserve@lernerbooks.com *Web Site:* www.lernerbooks.com; www.facebook.com/lernerbooks, pg 63

Krueger, Jenny, First Avenue Editions, 241 First Ave N, Minneapolis, MN 55401 *Tel:* 612-332-3344 *Toll Free Tel:* 800-328-4929 *Fax:* 612-332-7615 *Toll Free Fax:* 800-332-1132 *E-mail:* info@lernerbooks.com; custserve@lernerbooks.com *Web Site:* www.lernerbooks.com; www.facebook.com/lernerbooks, pg 72

Krueger, Jenny, Graphic Universe™, 241 First Ave N, Minneapolis, MN 55401 *Tel:* 612-332-3344 *Toll Free Tel:* 800-328-4929 *Fax:* 612-332-7615 *Toll Free Fax:* 800-332-1132 *E-mail:* info@lernerbooks.com; custserve@lernerbooks.com *Web Site:* www.lernerbooks.com; www.facebook.com/lernerbooks, pg 80

Krueger, Jenny, Lerner Publications, 241 First Ave N, Minneapolis, MN 55401 *Tel:* 612-332-3344 *Toll Free Tel:* 800-328-4929 *Fax:* 612-332-7615 *Toll Free Fax:* 800-332-1132 *E-mail:* info@lernerbooks.com; custserve@lernerbooks.com *Web Site:* www.lernerbooks.com; www.facebook.com/lernerbooks, pg 115

Krueger, Jenny, Lerner Publishing Group Inc, 241 First Ave N, Minneapolis, MN 55401 *Tel:* 612-332-3344 *Toll Free Tel:* 800-328-4929 *Fax:* 612-332-7615 *Toll Free Fax:* 800-332-1132 *E-mail:* info@lernerbooks.com; custserve@lernerbooks.com *Web Site:* www.lernerbooks.com; www.facebook.com/lernerbooks, pg 115

Krueger, Jenny, LernerClassroom, 241 First Ave N, Minneapolis, MN 55401 *Tel:* 612-332-3344 *Toll Free Tel:* 800-328-4929 *Fax:* 612-332-7615 *Toll Free Fax:* 800-332-1132 *E-mail:* info@lernerbooks.com; custserve@lernerbooks.com *Web Site:* www.lernerbooks.com; www.facebook.com/lernerbooks, pg 115

Krueger, Jenny, Millbrook Press, 241 First Ave N, Minneapolis, MN 55401 *Tel:* 612-332-3344 *Toll Free Tel:* 800-328-4929 *Fax:* 612-332-7615 *Toll Free Fax:* 800-332-1132 *E-mail:* info@lernerbooks.com; custserve@lernerbooks.com *Web Site:* www.lernerbooks.com; www.facebook.com/millbrookpress, pg 131

Krueger, Jenny, Twenty-First Century Books, 241 First Ave N, Minneapolis, MN 55401 *Tel:* 612-332-3344 *Toll Free Tel:* 800-328-4929 *Fax:* 612-332-7615 *Toll Free Fax:* 800-332-1132 *E-mail:* info@lernerbooks.com; custserve@lernerbooks.com *Web Site:* www.lernerbooks.com; www.facebook.com/lernerbooks, pg 211

Krueger, Jenny, Zest Books, 241 First Ave N, Minneapolis, MN 55401 *Tel:* 612-332-3344 *Toll Free Tel:* 800-328-4929 *Toll Free Fax:* 800-332-1132 *E-mail:* info@lernerbooks.com; publicity@lernerbooks.com; custserve@lernerbooks.com (orders) *Web Site:* lernerbooks.com, pg 236

Krueger, Jo Ann, The Aaland Agency, PO Box 849, Inyokern, CA 93527-0849 *Tel:* 760-384-3910 *E-mail:* anniejo41@gmail.com *Web Site:* www.the-aaland-agency.com, pg 447

Krug, Susan, American Medical Writers Association (AMWA), 9841 Washingtonian Blvd, Suite 500-26, Gaithersburg, MD 20878 *Tel:* 240-238-0940 *Fax:* 301-294-9006 *E-mail:* amwa@amwa.org *Web Site:* www.amwa.org, pg 496

Krump, Emily, HarperCollins Publishers LLC, 195 Broadway, New York, NY 10007 *Tel:* 212-207-7000 *Web Site:* www.harpercollins.com, pg 86

Krumpfer, Jorie, W W Norton & Company Inc, 500 Fifth Ave, New York, NY 10110-0017 *Tel:* 212-354-5500 *Toll Free Tel:* 800-233-4830 (orders & cust serv) *Fax:* 212-869-0856 *Toll Free Fax:* 800-458-6515 *E-mail:* orders@wwnorton.com *Web Site:* wwnorton.com, pg 143

Krysik, Karol, ABAC/ALAC, c/o 1938 Bloor St W, Toronto, ON M6P 3K8, Canada *E-mail:* info@abac.org *Web Site:* www.abac.org, pg 493

Kubek, Anne, Bay Area Women in Publishing (BAWiP), 680 Second St, San Francisco, CA 94107 *E-mail:* bayareawomeninpublishing@gmail.com *Web Site:* www.bayareawomeninpublishing.com, pg 500

Kubes, Alicia, New York University, Center for Publishing & Applied Liberal Arts, 7 E 12 St, New York, NY 10003 *Tel:* 212-998-7200 *E-mail:* sps.info@nyu.edu *Web Site:* www.scps.nyu.edu/professional-pathways/topics.html, pg 563

Kubie, Greg, Random House Publishing Group, 1745 Broadway, New York, NY 10019 *Toll Free Tel:* 800-200-3552 *Web Site:* www.randomhousebooks.com, pg 171

Kubinec, Jessica, LARB Books, 6671 Sunset Blvd, Suite 1521, Los Angeles, CA 90028 *Tel:* 323-952-3950 *E-mail:* larbbooks@lareviewofbooks.org *Web Site:* larbbooks.org, pg 113

Kubinec, Jessica, LARB/USC Publishing Workshop, 6671 Sunset Blvd, Suite 1521, Los Angeles, CA 90028 *E-mail:* publishingworkshop@lareviewofbooks.org *Web Site:* thepublishingworkshop.com, pg 556

Kuehl, Ashley, Zest Books, 241 First Ave N, Minneapolis, MN 55401 Tel: 612-332-3344 Toll Free Tel: 800-328-4929 Toll Free Fax: 800-332-1132 E-mail: info@lernerbooks.com; publicity@lernerbooks.com; custserve@lernerbooks.com (orders) Web Site: lernerbooks.com, pg 236

Kuehl, Kathy, The Guilford Press, 370 Seventh Ave, Suite 1200, New York, NY 10001-1020 Tel: 212-431-9800 Toll Free Tel: 800-365-7006 Fax: 212-966-6708 E-mail: info@guilford.com; orders@guilford.com Web Site: www.guilford.com, pg 82

Kuehl, Monte, ABDO, 8000 W 78 St, Suite 310, Edina, MN 55439 Tel: 952-698-2403 Toll Free Tel: 800-800-1312 Fax: 952-831-1632 Toll Free Fax: 800-862-3480 E-mail: customerservice@abdobooks.com; info@abdobooks.com Web Site: abdobooks.com, pg 2

Kuehm, Scot, Princeton University Press, 41 William St, Princeton, NJ 08540-5237 Tel: 609-258-4900 Fax: 609-258-6305 E-mail: info@press.princeton.edu Web Site: press.princeton.edu, pg 164

Kuerbis, Lisa, Syracuse University Press, 621 Skytop Rd, Suite 110, Syracuse, NY 13244-5290 Tel: 315-443-5534 Toll Free Tel: 800-365-8929 (cust serv) Fax: 315-443-5545 E-mail: supress@syr.edu Web Site: press.syr.edu, pg 201

Kuhn, David, Aevitas Creative Management LLC, 19 W 21 St, Suite 501, New York, NY 10010 Tel: 212-765-6900 Web Site: www.aevitascreative.com, pg 448

Kuhn, Lynda, Inclusion Press International, 47 Indian Trail, Toronto, ON M6R 1Z8, Canada Tel: 416-658-5363 Fax: 416-658-5067 E-mail: inclusionpress@inclusion.com Web Site: inclusion.com, pg 410

Kuipers, Keetje, Nona Balakian Citation for Excellence in Reviewing, c/o Jacob M Appel, Icahn School of Medicine at Mount Sinai, One Gustave L Levy Place, New York, NY 10029 E-mail: info@bookcritics.org Web Site: www.bookcritics.org/awards/balakian/, pg 576

Kuipers, Keetje, Gregg Barrios Book in Translation Prize, c/o Jacob M Appel, Icahn School of Medicine at Mount Sinai, One Gustave L Levy Place, New York, NY 10029 E-mail: info@bookcritics.org Web Site: www.bookcritics.org/gregg-barrios-book-in-translation-prize/, pg 577

Kuipers, Keetje, Emerging Critics Fellowship, c/o Jacob M Appel, Icahn School of Medicine at Mount Sinai, One Gustave L Levy Place, New York, NY 10029 E-mail: info@bookcritics.org Web Site: www.bookcritics.org/awards, pg 599

Kuipers, Keetje, John Leonard Prize, c/o Jacob M Appel, Icahn School of Medicine at Mount Sinai, One Gustave L Levy Place, New York, NY 10029 E-mail: info@bookcritics.org Web Site: www.bookcritics.org/awards/leonard-prize, pg 623

Kuipers, Keetje, The Toni Morrison Achievement Award, c/o Jacob M Appel, Icahn School of Medicine at Mount Sinai, One Gustave L Levy Place, New York, NY 10029 E-mail: info@bookcritics.org Web Site: www.bookcritics.org/the-toni-morrison-achievement-award, pg 635

Kuipers, Keetje, National Book Critics Circle (NBCC), c/o Jacob M Appel, Icahn School of Medicine at Mount Sinai, One Gustave L Levy Place, New York, NY 10029 E-mail: info@bookcritics.org; membership@bookcritics.org Web Site: www.bookcritics.org, pg 512

Kuipers, Keetje, National Book Critics Circle Award, c/o Jacob M Appel, Icahn School of Medicine at Mount Sinai, One Gustave L Levy Place, New York, NY 10029 E-mail: info@bookcritics.org Web Site: www.bookcritics.org/awards, pg 637

Kuipers, Keetje, Ivan Sandrof Lifetime Achievement Award, c/o Jacob M Appel, Icahn School of Medicine at Mount Sinai, One Gustave L Levy Place, New York, NY 10029 E-mail: info@bookcritics.org Web Site: www.bookcritics.org/awards/sandrof/, pg 659

Kujichagulia, Phavia, Media Alliance, 2830 20 St, Suite 102, San Francisco, CA 94110 Tel: 415-746-9475 E-mail: information@media-alliance.org; info@media-alliance.org Web Site: www.media-alliance.org, pg 510

Kuka, Ronald, Chris O'Malley Fiction Prize, University of Wisconsin, 6193 Helen C White Hall, English Dept, 600 N Park St, Madison, WI 53706 E-mail: madisonrevw@gmail.com Web Site: www.themadisonrevw.com, pg 643

Kuka, Ronald, Phyllis Smart-Young Poetry Prize, University of Wisconsin, 6193 Helen C White Hall, English Dept, 600 N Park St, Madison, WI 53706 E-mail: madisonrevw@gmail.com Web Site: www.themadisonrevw.com, pg 663

Kukkal, Puneet, Hachette Book Group Inc, 1290 Avenue of the Americas, New York, NY 10104 Tel: 212-364-1100 Toll Free Tel: 800-759-0190 (cust serv) Fax: 212-364-0933 (intl orders) Toll Free Fax: 800-286-9471 (cust serv) E-mail: customer.service@hbgusa.com; orders@hbgusa.com Web Site: www.hachettebookgroup.com, pg 83

Kukla, Lauren, Mighty Media Press, 1201 Currie Ave, Minneapolis, MN 55403 Tel: 612-455-0252; 612-399-1969 Fax: 612-338-4817 E-mail: info@mightymedia.com Web Site: www.mightymediapress.com, pg 131

Kulic, Matea, The Association of Book Publishers of British Columbia (ABPBC), 600-402 W Pender St, Vancouver, BC V6B 1T6, Canada Tel: 604-684-0228 E-mail: admin@books.bc.ca Web Site: www.books.bc.ca, pg 499

Kulick, Gregg, Little, Brown and Company, 1290 Avenue of the Americas, New York, NY 10104 Tel: 212-364-1100 Fax: 212-364-0952 E-mail: firstname.lastname@hbgusa.com Web Site: www.hachettebookgroup.com/imprint/little-brown-and-company/, pg 118

Kulka, John, Library of America, 14 E 60 St, New York, NY 10022-1006 Tel: 212-308-3360 Fax: 212-750-8352 E-mail: info@loa.org Web Site: www.loa.org, pg 116

Kull, Irene Imperio, Temple University Press, 1852 N Tenth St, Philadelphia, PA 19122-6099 Tel: 215-926-2140 Toll Free Tel: 800-621-2736 Fax: 215-926-2141 E-mail: tempress@temple.edu Web Site: tupress.temple.edu, pg 204

Kullberg, Adam, Excellence in Graphic Literature Awards, 2760 W Fifth Ave, Denver, CO 80204 Tel: 303-325-1236 E-mail: egl@popcultureclassroom.org Web Site: www.popcultureclassroom.org/events, pg 600

Kulp, Kelsey, Sourcebooks LLC, 1935 Brookdale Rd, Suite 139, Naperville, IL 60563 Tel: 630-961-3900 Toll Free Tel: 800-432-7444 Fax: 630-961-2168 E-mail: info@sourcebooks.com Web Site: www.sourcebooks.com, pg 195

Kundert, Beth, McGraw-Hill Create, 2 Penn Plaza, New York, NY 10121 Toll Free Tel: 800-962-9342 E-mail: mhhe.create@mheducation.com Web Site: create.mheducation.com; shop.mheducation.com, pg 127

Kundert, Samantha, The American Library Association (ALA), 225 N Michigan Ave, Suite 1300, Chicago, IL 60601 Tel: 312-944-6780 Toll Free Tel: 800-545-2433; 866-SHOP-ALA (746-7252, orders) Fax: 312-280-5275; 312-440-9374; 312-280-5860 (orders) E-mail: ala@ala.org; alastore@ala.org Web Site: www.alastore.ala.org; www.ala.org, pg 10

Kunjufu, Dr Jawanza PhD, African American Images Inc (AAI), 3126 E Fruitvale Ct, Gilbert, AZ 85297 Tel: 480-621-8307 Fax: 480-621-7794 E-mail: customersvc@africanamericanimages.com Web Site: africanamericanimages.com, pg 5

Kuny, Greg, American Psychiatric Association Publishing, 800 Maine Ave SW, Suite 900, Washington, DC 20024 Tel: 202-459-9722 Toll Free Tel: 800-368-5777 Fax: 202-403-3094 E-mail: appi@psych.org Web Site: www.appi.org; www.psychiatryonline.org, pg 11

Kunz, Jeannine, SME (Society of Manufacturing Engineers), 1000 Town Ctr, Suite 1910, Southfield, MI 48075 Tel: 313-425-3000 Toll Free Tel: 800-733-4763 (cust serv) Fax: 313-425-3400 E-mail: publications@sme.org Web Site: www.sme.org, pg 191

Kuo, Michelle, The Museum of Modern Art (MoMA), Publications Dept, 11 W 53 St, New York, NY 10019 Tel: 212-708-9400 E-mail: moma_publications@moma.org Web Site: www.moma.org, pg 135

Kuong, Jay, Management Advisory Services & Publications (MASP), PO Box 81151, Wellesley Hills, MA 02481-0001 Tel: 781-235-2895 Fax: 781-235-5446 E-mail: info@masp.com Web Site: www.masp.com, pg 123

Kupihea, Jhanteigh, Quirk Books, 215 Church St, Philadelphia, PA 19106 Tel: 215-627-3581 Fax: 215-627-5220 E-mail: general@quirkbooks.com Web Site: www.quirkbooks.com, pg 168

Kupor, Emma, HarperCollins Publishers LLC, 195 Broadway, New York, NY 10007 Tel: 212-207-7000 Web Site: www.harpercollins.com, pg 87

Kurki, Ella, Dutton, c/o Penguin Random House LLC, 1745 Broadway, New York, NY 10019 Tel: 212-366-2000 Web Site: www.penguin.com/dutton-overview/; www.penguin.com/plume-books-overview/; www.penguin.com/tiny-reparations-overview/, pg 62

Kurtaran, Dilara, Penguin Random House Canada, a Penguin Random House company, 320 Front St W, Suite 1400, Toronto, ON M5V 3B6, Canada Tel: 416-364-4449 Toll Free Tel: 888-523-9292 (cust serv) E-mail: canadaweb@penguinrandomhouse.com; customerservicescanada@penguinrandomhouse.com Web Site: www.penguinrandomhouse.ca, pg 416

Kurtz, Dustin, Counterpoint Press LLC, 2560 Ninth St, Suite 318, Berkeley, CA 94710 Tel: 510-704-0230 Fax: 510-704-0268 E-mail: info@counterpointpress.com Web Site: counterpointpress.com; softskull.com, pg 54

Kurtz, Gretchen, Prometheus Books, 59 John Glenn Dr, Amherst, NY 14228-2119 Fax: 716-691-0137 E-mail: marketing@prometheusbooks.com; editorial@prometheusbooks.com; rights@prometheusbooks.com Web Site: www.prometheusbooks.com, pg 166

Kurtz, Jonathan, Prometheus Books, 59 John Glenn Dr, Amherst, NY 14228-2119 Fax: 716-691-0137 E-mail: marketing@prometheusbooks.com; editorial@prometheusbooks.com; rights@prometheusbooks.com Web Site: www.prometheusbooks.com, pg 166

Kurtzman, Nellie, HarperCollins Children's Books, 195 Broadway, New York, NY 10007 Tel: 212-207-7000 Web Site: www.harpercollins.com/childrens, pg 85

Kurtzman, Nellie, HarperCollins Publishers LLC, 195 Broadway, New York, NY 10007 Tel: 212-207-7000 Web Site: www.harpercollins.com, pg 86

Kurzbach, Colleen, Penguin Publishing Group, c/o Penguin Random House LLC, 1745 Broadway, New York, NY 10019 Tel: 212-782-9000 Web Site: www.penguin.com, pg 154

Kuschner, Sarah, Harvard Art Museums, 32 Quincy St, Cambridge, MA 02138 Tel: 617-495-9400 Web Site: www.harvardartmuseums.org, pg 87

Kushto, Maude, Paul Dry Books, 1700 Sansom St, Suite 700, Philadelphia, PA 19103 Tel: 215-231-9939 E-mail: editor@pauldrybooks.com Web Site: www.pauldrybooks.com, pg 152

Kusler, Jack, Addicus Books Inc, PO Box 45327, Omaha, NE 68145 Tel: 402-330-7493 Fax: 402-330-1707 E-mail: info@addicusbooks.com Web Site: www.addicusbooks.com, pg 5

Kuss, Rebecca, Disney-Hyperion Books, 1101 Flower St, Glendale, CA 91201 Web Site: books.disney.com/imprint/disney-hyperion, pg 59

Kutys, Ronnie, HarperCollins Publishers LLC, 195 Broadway, New York, NY 10007 Tel: 212-207-7000 Web Site: www.harpercollins.com, pg 86

Kuznetcova, Anna, Peter Lampack Agency Inc, 350 Fifth Ave, Suite 5300, New York, NY 10118 Tel: 212-687-9106 Fax: 212-687-9109 Web Site: www.peterlampackagency.com, pg 467

Kwak, Sarah, HarperCollins Publishers LLC, 195 Broadway, New York, NY 10007 Tel: 212-207-7000 Web Site: www.harpercollins.com, pg 86

Kwan, Lisa, Pantheon Books, c/o Penguin Random House LLC, 1745 Broadway, New York, NY 10019 *Tel:* 212-751-2600 *Fax:* 212-940-7390 (dom rts); 212-572-2662 (foreign rts) *Web Site:* knopfdoubleday.com/imprint/pantheon/; knopfdoubleday.com, pg 150

Kwan, Megan, Penguin Random House Canada, a Penguin Random House company, 320 Front St W, Suite 1400, Toronto, ON M5V 3B6, Canada *Tel:* 416-364-4449 *Toll Free Tel:* 888-523-9292 (cust serv) *E-mail:* canadaweb@penguinrandomhouse.com; customerservicescanada@penguinrandomhouse.com *Web Site:* www.penguinrandomhouse.ca, pg 416

Kwasnik, Marlene, Chronicle Books LLC, 680 Second St, San Francisco, CA 94107 *Tel:* 415-537-4200 *Fax:* 415-537-4460 (perms) *E-mail:* hello@chroniclebooks.com; subrights@chroniclebooks.com *Web Site:* www.chroniclebooks.com, pg 48

Kwon, Chris, HarperCollins Children's Books, 195 Broadway, New York, NY 10007 *Tel:* 212-207-7000 *Web Site:* www.harpercollins.com/childrens, pg 85

Kye-Casella, Maura, Don Congdon Associates Inc, 110 William St, Suite 2202, New York, NY 10038-3914 *Tel:* 212-645-1229 *Fax:* 212-727-2688 *E-mail:* dca@doncongdon.com *Web Site:* www.doncongdon.com, pg 454

Kyle, Harold, American Printing History Association, PO Box 4519, Grand Central Sta, New York, NY 10163 *E-mail:* secretary@printinghistory.org *Web Site:* printinghistory.org, pg 496

Kyle, Harold, American Printing History Association Award, PO Box 4519, Grand Central Sta, New York, NY 10163 *E-mail:* secretary@printinghistory.org *Web Site:* printinghistory.org/programs/awards, pg 573

La Marca, Tricia, The Conference Board Inc, 845 Third Ave, New York, NY 10022-6600 *Tel:* 212-759-0900; 212-339-0345 (cust serv) *E-mail:* customer.service@tcb.org *Web Site:* www.conference-board.org/us; www.linkedin.com/company/the-conference-board, pg 51

La Mattina, Elaine, White Pine Press, PO Box 236, Buffalo, NY 14201 *Tel:* 716-573-8202 *E-mail:* wpine@whitepine.org *Web Site:* www.whitepine.org, pg 228

La Rosa, Suzanne, NewSouth Books, 105 S Court St, Montgomery, AL 36104 *Tel:* 334-834-3556 *E-mail:* info@newsouthbooks.com *Web Site:* www.newsouthbooks.com, pg 141

La Rosa, Suzanne, University of Georgia Press, Main Library, 3rd fl, 320 S Jackson St, Athens, GA 30602 *Fax:* 706-542-2558; 706-542-6770 *Web Site:* www.ugapress.org, pg 216

La Salle, Peter, University of Texas at Austin, New Writers Project, Dept of English, 204 W 21 St, B-5000, Austin, TX 78712-1164 *Tel:* 512-471-4991 *Fax:* 512-471-4909 *E-mail:* newwritersproject@utexas.edu *Web Site:* liberalarts.utexas.edu/nwp, pg 567

La Traverse, Valerie, Social Sciences & Humanities Research Council (SSHRC), 350 Albert St, Ottawa, ON K1P 6G4, Canada *Tel:* 613-995-4273 *Toll Free Tel:* 855-275-2861 *E-mail:* research@sshrc-crsh.gc.ca *Web Site:* www.sshrc-crsh.gc.ca, pg 519

Labaqui, Joni, L Ron Hubbard's Writers of the Future Contest, 7051 Hollywood Blvd, Hollywood, CA 90028 *Tel:* 323-466-3310 *Fax:* 323-466-6474 *E-mail:* contests@authorservicesinc.com *Web Site:* www.writersofthefuture.com, pg 614

Labbe, Lise, Les Editions Un Monde Different, 3905 Isabelle, bureau 101, Brossard, QC J4Y 2R2, Canada *Tel:* 450-656-2660 *Toll Free Tel:* 800-443-2582 *Fax:* 450-659-9328 *E-mail:* info@umd.ca *Web Site:* umd.ca, pg 405

Labes, Karolyn, SPIE, 1000 20 St, Bellingham, WA 98225-6705 *Tel:* 360-676-3290 *Toll Free Tel:* 888-504-8171 (orders) *Fax:* 360-647-1445 *E-mail:* help@spie.org; customerservice@spie.org (orders) *Web Site:* www.spie.org, pg 196

Labonte, Melissa, Les Editions du Noroit, 4609, rue D'Iberville, espace 202, Montreal, QC H2H 2L9, Canada *Tel:* 514-727-0005 *E-mail:* poesie@lenoroit.com *Web Site:* lenoroit.com, pg 403

Labov, Christine, Penguin Random House Speakers Bureau, a Penguin Random House company, 1745 Broadway, Mail Drop 13-1, New York, NY 10019 *Tel:* 212-572-2013 *E-mail:* speakers@penguinrandomhouse.com *Web Site:* www.prhspeakers.com, pg 487

Labrecque, Marise, Editions du CHU Sainte-Justine, 3175, chemin de la Cote-Sainte-Catherine, Montreal, QC H3T 1C5, Canada *Tel:* 514-345-4671 *Fax:* 514-345-4631 *E-mail:* edition.hsj@ssss.gouv.qc.ca *Web Site:* www.editions-chu-sainte-justine.org, pg 402

Labrie, Sarah, Kids Can Press Ltd, 25 Dockside Dr, Toronto, ON M5A 0B5, Canada *Tel:* 416-479-7000 *Toll Free Tel:* 800-265-0884 *Fax:* 416-960-5437 *E-mail:* info@kidscan.com; customerservice@kidscan.com *Web Site:* www.kidscanpress.com; www.kidscanpress.ca, pg 411

LaBrie, Sarah, LARB/USC Publishing Workshop, 6671 Sunset Blvd, Suite 1521, Los Angeles, CA 90028 *E-mail:* publishingworkshop@lareviewofbooks.org *Web Site:* thepublishingworkshop.com, pg 556

Lachat, Nicole, Prairie Schooner Annual Strousse Award, 110 Andrews Hall, University of Nebraska-Lincoln, Lincoln, NE 68588-0334 *Tel:* 402-472-0911 *Fax:* 402-472-1817 *E-mail:* psbookprize@unl.edu; prairieschooner@unl.edu *Web Site:* prairieschooner.unl.edu, pg 651

Lachat, Nicole, Prairie Schooner Bernice Slote Award, 110 Andrews Hall, University of Nebraska-Lincoln, Lincoln, NE 68588-0334 *Tel:* 402-472-0911 *Fax:* 402-472-1817 *E-mail:* psbookprize@unl.edu; prairieschooner@unl.edu *Web Site:* prairieschooner.unl.edu, pg 651

Lachat, Nicole, Prairie Schooner Book Prize in Poetry, 110 Andrews Hall, University of Nebraska-Lincoln, Lincoln, NE 68588-0334 *Tel:* 402-472-0911 *Fax:* 402-472-1817 *E-mail:* psbookprize@unl.edu; prairieschooner@unl.edu *Web Site:* prairieschooner.unl.edu, pg 651

Lachat, Nicole, Prairie Schooner Edward Stanley Award, 110 Andrews Hall, University of Nebraska-Lincoln, Lincoln, NE 68588-0334 *Tel:* 402-472-0911 *Fax:* 402-472-1817 *E-mail:* psbookprize@unl.edu; prairieschooner@unl.edu *Web Site:* prairieschooner.unl.edu, pg 652

Lachat, Nicole, Prairie Schooner Glenna Luschei Award, 110 Andrews Hall, University of Nebraska-Lincoln, Lincoln, NE 68588-0334 *Tel:* 402-472-0911 *Fax:* 402-472-1817 *E-mail:* psbookprize@unl.edu; prairieschooner@unl.edu *Web Site:* prairieschooner.unl.edu, pg 652

Lachat, Nicole, Prairie Schooner Hugh J Luke Award, 110 Andrews Hall, University of Nebraska-Lincoln, Lincoln, NE 68588-0334 *Tel:* 402-472-0911 *Fax:* 402-472-1817 *E-mail:* psbookprize@unl.edu; prairieschooner@unl.edu *Web Site:* prairieschooner.unl.edu, pg 652

Lachat, Nicole, Prairie Schooner Jane Geske Award, 110 Andrews Hall, University of Nebraska-Lincoln, Lincoln, NE 68588-0334 *Tel:* 402-472-0911 *Fax:* 402-472-1817 *E-mail:* psbookprize@unl.edu; prairieschooner@unl.edu *Web Site:* prairieschooner.unl.edu, pg 652

Lachat, Nicole, Prairie Schooner Lawrence Foundation Award, 110 Andrews Hall, University of Nebraska-Lincoln, Lincoln, NE 68588-0334 *Tel:* 402-472-0911 *Fax:* 402-472-1817 *E-mail:* psbookprize@unl.edu; prairieschooner@unl.edu *Web Site:* prairieschooner.unl.edu, pg 652

Lachat, Nicole, Prairie Schooner Raz-Shumaker Book Prize Contest, 110 Andrews Hall, University of Nebraska-Lincoln, Lincoln, NE 68588-0334 *Tel:* 402-472-0911 *Fax:* 402-472-1817 *E-mail:* psbookprize@unl.edu; prairieschooner@unl.edu *Web Site:* prairieschooner.unl.edu, pg 652

Lachat, Nicole, Prairie Schooner Virginia Faulkner Award for Excellence in Writing, 110 Andrews Hall, University of Nebraska-Lincoln, Lincoln, NE 68588-0334 *Tel:* 402-472-0911 *Fax:* 402-472-1817 *E-mail:* psbookprize@unl.edu; prairieschooner@unl.edu *Web Site:* prairieschooner.unl.edu, pg 652

Lachat, Rodolphe, Harry N Abrams Inc, 195 Broadway, 9th fl, New York, NY 10007 *Tel:* 212-206-7715 *Toll Free Tel:* 800-345-1359 *Fax:* 212-645-8437 *E-mail:* abrams@abramsbooks.com; publicity@abramsbooks.com; sales@abramsbooks.com *Web Site:* www.abramsbooks.com, pg 2

Lachatanere, Diana, Faith Childs Literary Agency Inc, 915 Broadway, Suite 1009, New York, NY 10010 *Tel:* 212-995-9600 *Web Site:* faithchildsliteraryagency.com, pg 454

Lachina, Jeffrey A, Lachina Creative Inc, 3791 S Green Rd, Cleveland, OH 44122 *Tel:* 216-292-7959 *E-mail:* info@lachina.com *Web Site:* www.lachina.com, pg 441

Lacombe, Joanne, Editions Marie-France, CP 32263 BP Waverly, Montreal, QC H3L 3X1, Canada *Tel:* 514-329-3700 *Toll Free Tel:* 800-563-6644 (CN) *Fax:* 514-329-0630 *E-mail:* editions@marie-france.qc.ca *Web Site:* www.marie-france.qc.ca, pg 404

Lacombe, Leighe, Broadview Press, 280 Perry St, Unit 5, Peterborough, ON K9J 2J4, Canada *Tel:* 705-482-5915 *Fax:* 705-743-8353 *E-mail:* customerservice@broadviewpress.com *Web Site:* www.broadviewpress.com, pg 397

Lacy, Linda M, Carolina Academic Press, 700 Kent St, Durham, NC 27701 *Tel:* 919-489-7486 *Toll Free Tel:* 800-489-7486 *Fax:* 919-493-5668 *E-mail:* cap@cap-press.com *Web Site:* www.cap-press.com; www.caplaw.com, pg 41

Ladewski, Bill, Sophie Brody Medal, 225 N Michigan Ave, Suite 1300, Chicago, IL 60601 *Web Site:* rusaupdate.org/awards/sophie-brody-medal, pg 584

LaDue, Holly, The Monacelli Press, 65 Bleecker St, 8th fl, New York, NY 10012 *Tel:* 212-652-5400 *E-mail:* contact@monacellipress.com *Web Site:* www.phaidon.com/monacelli, pg 133

Lafferty, Bridget, Association of American Publishers (AAP), 455 Massachusetts Ave NW, Suite 700, Washington, DC 20001-2777 *Tel:* 202-347-3375 *Fax:* 202-347-3690 *E-mail:* info@publishers.org *Web Site:* publishers.org, pg 498

Lagace, Genevieve, Editions Hurtubise, 1815, ave de Lorimier, Montreal, QC H2K 3W6, Canada *Tel:* 514-523-1523 *Toll Free Tel:* 800-361-1664 *Web Site:* editionshurtubise.com, pg 404

Lagace, Nettie, Miles Conrad Award, 3600 Clipper Mill Rd, Suite 302, Baltimore, MD 21211-1948 *Tel:* 301-654-2512 *Fax:* 410-685-5278 *E-mail:* nisohq@niso.org *Web Site:* www.niso.org, pg 591

Lagace, Nettie, National Information Standards Organization (NISO), 3600 Clipper Mill Rd, Suite 302, Baltimore, MD 21211-1948 *Tel:* 301-654-2512 *Fax:* 410-685-5278 *E-mail:* nisohq@niso.org *Web Site:* www.niso.org, pg 138, 513

Lago, Bredna, Workman Publishing, 1290 Avenue of the Americas, New York, NY 10104 *Toll Free Tel:* 800-759-0190 *Fax:* 212-364-0950 *E-mail:* workman-inquiry@hbgusa.com *Web Site:* www.hachettebookgroup.com/imprint/workman-publishing-company/, pg 233

Lagunarajan, Ankanee, Penguin Random House Canada, a Penguin Random House company, 320 Front St W, Suite 1400, Toronto, ON M5V 3B6, Canada *Tel:* 416-364-4449 *Toll Free Tel:* 888-523-9292 (cust serv) *E-mail:* canadaweb@penguinrandomhouse.com; customerservicescanada@penguinrandomhouse.com *Web Site:* www.penguinrandomhouse.ca, pg 416

Lagunoff, Liza, Oscar Williams/Gene Derwood Award, 909 Third Ave, New York, NY 10022 *Tel:* 212-686-0010 *Fax:* 212-532-8528 *E-mail:* info@nycommunitytrust.org *Web Site:* www.nycommunitytrust.org, pg 675

Lai, Chin-Yee, Basic Books Group, 1290 Avenue of the Americas, New York, NY 10104 *Tel:* 212-340-8100 *Toll Free Tel:* 800-343-4499 (cust serv) *Fax:* 212-340-

8105 *E-mail:* customer.service@hbgusa.com; orders@hbgusa.com *Web Site:* www.hachettebookgroup.com/imprint/basic-books/, pg 25

Lai, Pauline, Captus Press Inc, 1600 Steeles Ave W, Units 14 & 15, Concord, ON L4K 4M2, Canada *Tel:* 905-760-2723 *Fax:* 905-760-7523 *E-mail:* info@captus.com *Web Site:* www.captus.com, pg 399

Laine, Claire, Graywolf Press, 212 Third Ave N, Suite 485, Minneapolis, MN 55401 *Tel:* 651-641-0077 *Fax:* 651-641-0036 *E-mail:* wolves@graywolfpress.org (no ms queries, sample chapters or proposals) *Web Site:* www.graywolfpress.org, pg 81

Laing, Glenn, American Society of Agricultural & Biological Engineers (ASABE), 2950 Niles Rd, St Joseph, MI 49085-9659 *Tel:* 269-429-0300 *Toll Free Tel:* 800-371-2723 *Fax:* 269-429-3852 *E-mail:* hq@asabe.org *Web Site:* www.asabe.org, pg 12

Laing, Lisa, Adams Media, 100 Technology Center Dr, Suite 501, Stoughton, MA 02072 *Tel:* 508-427-7100 *Web Site:* www.simonandschuster.com, pg 4

Lajeunesse, Danielle, Editions FouLire, 4339, rue des Becassines, Quebec, QC G1G 1V5, Canada *Tel:* 418-628-4029 *Toll Free Tel:* 877-628-4029 (CN & US) *Fax:* 418-628-4801 *E-mail:* edition@foulire.com *Web Site:* www.foulire.com, pg 403

Lakatos, Jessica, Dreamscape Media LLC, 1417 Timberwolf Dr, Holland, OH 43528 *Tel:* 419-867-6965 *Toll Free Tel:* 877-983-7326 *E-mail:* info@dreamscapeab.com *Web Site:* www.dreamscapepublishing.com, pg 62

Lake, Rory, Candlewick Press, 99 Dover St, Somerville, MA 02144-2825 *Tel:* 617-661-3330 *Fax:* 617-661-0565 *E-mail:* bigbear@candlewick.com; salesinfo@candlewick.com *Web Site:* candlewick.com, pg 40

Lakenauth, Gianna, Random House Children's Books, c/o Penguin Random House LLC, 1745 Broadway, New York, NY 10019 *Tel:* 212-782-9000 *Web Site:* www.rhcbooks.com, pg 170

Lakin, Chuck, Zeig, Tucker & Theisen Inc, 2632 E Thomas Rd, Suite 201, Phoenix, AZ 85016 *Tel:* 480-389-4342 *Web Site:* www.zeigtucker.com, pg 236

Lakina, Katie, Penguin Random House Audio Publishing Group, 1745 Broadway, New York, NY 10019 *Toll Free Tel:* 800-793-2665 (cust serv) *E-mail:* audio@penguinrandomhouse.com; ecustomerservice@penguinrandomhouse.com *Web Site:* www.penguinrandomhouseaudio.com, pg 154

Lalli, Sonya, Groundwood Books, 128 Sterling Rd, Lower Level, Toronto, ON M6R 2B7, Canada *Tel:* 416-363-4343 *Fax:* 416-363-1017 *E-mail:* customerservice@houseofanansi.com *Web Site:* www.houseofanansi.com, pg 407

Lalli, Sonya, House of Anansi Press Inc, 128 Sterling Rd, Lower Level, Toronto, ON M6R 2B7, Canada *Tel:* 416-363-4343 *Fax:* 416-363-1017 *E-mail:* customerservice@houseofanansi.com *Web Site:* houseofanansi.com, pg 409

Lalonde, Chantale Gravel, Scholastic Canada Ltd, 175 Hillmount Rd, Markham, ON L6C 1Z7, Canada *Tel:* 905-887-7323 *Toll Free Tel:* 800-268-3860 (CN) *Toll Free Fax:* 800-387-4944 *E-mail:* custserve@scholastic.ca *Web Site:* www.scholastic.ca, pg 418

Lam, Anna, Alex Awards, 225 N Michigan Ave, Suite 1300, Chicago, IL 60601 *Tel:* 312-280-4390 *Toll Free Tel:* 800-545-2433 *E-mail:* yalsa@ala.org *Web Site:* www.ala.org/yalsa/alex-awards, pg 572

Lam, Anna, Margaret A Edwards Award, 225 N Michigan Ave, Suite 1300, Chicago, IL 60601 *Tel:* 312-280-4390 *Toll Free Tel:* 800-545-2433 *E-mail:* yalsa@ala.org *Web Site:* www.ala.org/yalsa/edwards-award, pg 598

Lam, Anna, Excellence in Nonfiction for Young Adults, 225 N Michigan Ave, Suite 1300, Chicago, IL 60601 *Toll Free Tel:* 800-545-2433 (ext 4390) *E-mail:* yalsa@ala.org *Web Site:* www.ala.org/yalsa/nonfiction-award, pg 601

Lam, Anna, Frances Henne/YALSA Research Grant, 225 N Michigan Ave, Suite 1300, Chicago, IL 60601 *Tel:* 312-280-4390 *Toll Free Tel:* 800-545-2433 *E-mail:* yalsa@ala.org *Web Site:* www.ala.org/yalsa/awardsandgrants/franceshenne, pg 604

Lam, Anna, Odyssey Award for Excellence in Audiobook Production, 225 N Michigan Ave, Suite 1300, Chicago, IL 60601 *Toll Free Tel:* 800-545-2433 (ext 4390) *E-mail:* yalsa@ala.org *Web Site:* www.ala.org/yalsa/odyssey, pg 643

Lam, Anna, Michael L Printz Award, 225 N Michigan Ave, Suite 1300, Chicago, IL 60601 *Tel:* 312-280-4390 *Toll Free Tel:* 800-545-2433 *E-mail:* yalsa@ala.org *Web Site:* www.ala.org/yalsa/printz-award, pg 653

Lam, Anna, YALSA Conference Grants, 225 N Michigan Ave, Suite 1300, Chicago, IL 60601 *Tel:* 312-280-4390 *Toll Free Tel:* 800-545-2433 *E-mail:* yalsa@ala.org *Web Site:* www.ala.org/yalsa/awardsandgrants.bakertayloryalsa, pg 679

Lam, Brian, Arsenal Pulp Press, 211 E Georgia St, No 202, Vancouver, BC V6A 1Z6, Canada *Tel:* 604-687-4233 *Toll Free Tel:* 888-600-PULP (600-7857) *Fax:* 604-687-4283 *E-mail:* info@arsenalpulp.com *Web Site:* www.arsenalpulp.com, pg 395

Lam, Lily, New York City College of Technology Professional & Technical Writing Program, Namm Hall 512, 300 Jay St, Brooklyn, NY 11201 *Tel:* 718-260-5392 *E-mail:* english@citytech.cuny.edu *Web Site:* www.citytech.cuny.edu/english/technical-writing-bs.aspx, pg 563

Lamar, Nanci, Upper Room Books, 1908 Grand Ave, Nashville, TN 37212 *Tel:* 615-340-7200 *Toll Free Tel:* 800-972-0433 *Web Site:* books.upperroom.org, pg 223

Lamb, Beth, Vintage Books, c/o Penguin Random House LLC, 1745 Broadway, New York, NY 10019 *Tel:* 212-572-2420 *Fax:* 212-940-7390 (dom rts); 212-572-2662 (foreign rts) *E-mail:* vintageanchorpublicity@randomhouse.com *Web Site:* knopfdoubleday.com/imprint/vintage; knopfdoubleday.com, pg 225

Lamb, Cynthia, Carnegie Mellon University Press, 5032 Forbes Ave, Pittsburgh, PA 15289-1021 *Tel:* 412-268-2861 *E-mail:* cmupress@andrew.cmu.edu *Web Site:* www.cmu.edu/universitypress, pg 41

Lamb, Jason, Bread Loaf Fellowships & Scholarships, Middlebury College, 204 College St, Middlebury, VT 05753 *Tel:* 802-443-5286 *Fax:* 802-443-2087 *E-mail:* blwc@middlebury.edu *Web Site:* www.middlebury.edu/blwc, pg 584

Lamb, Jason, Bread Loaf Writers' Conference, 204 College St, Middlebury, VT 05753 *Tel:* 802-443-5286 *Fax:* 802-443-2087 *E-mail:* blwc@middlebury.edu *Web Site:* www.middlebury.edu/blwc, pg 553

Lamb, John D, Lost Lake Writers Retreat, 627 Lloyd Ave, Royal Oak, MI 48073 *Tel:* 248-589-3913 *E-mail:* info@springfed.org *Web Site:* www.springfed.org, pg 556

Lamba, Cari, The Jennifer DeChiara Literary Agency, 245 Park Ave, 39th fl, New York, NY 10167 *Tel:* 212-372-8989 *Web Site:* www.jdlit.com, pg 455

Lamba, Marie, The Jennifer DeChiara Literary Agency, 245 Park Ave, 39th fl, New York, NY 10167 *Tel:* 212-372-8989 *Web Site:* www.jdlit.com, pg 455

Lambert, Hannah, Simon & Schuster Children's Publishing, 1230 Avenue of the Americas, New York, NY 10020 *Tel:* 212-698-7000 *Web Site:* www.simonandschuster.com/kids; www.simonandschuster.com/teen; simonandschuster.net; simonandschuster.biz, pg 189

Lambert, Julie, Eisenbrauns, 820 N University Dr, USB 1, Suite C, University Park, PA 16802-1003 *Tel:* 814-865-1327 *Toll Free Tel:* 800-326-9180 (orders & cust serv) *Fax:* 814-863-1408 *Toll Free Fax:* 877-778-2665 (orders) *E-mail:* orders@psupress.org; customerservice@psupress.org *Web Site:* www.eisenbrauns.org, pg 65

Lame, Vicki, St Martin's Press, LLC, 120 Broadway, New York, NY 10271 *E-mail:* publicity@stmartins.com; trademarketing@stmartins.com; foreignrights@stmartins.com *Web Site:* us.macmillan.com/smp, pg 181

Lamkins, Tim, SPIE, 1000 20 St, Bellingham, WA 98225-6705 *Tel:* 360-676-3290 *Toll Free Tel:* 888-504-8171 (orders) *Fax:* 360-647-1445 *E-mail:* help@spie.org; customerservice@spie.org (orders) *Web Site:* www.spie.org, pg 196

Lamm, Gigi, University of Pennsylvania Press, 3905 Spruce St, Philadelphia, PA 19104 *Tel:* 215-898-6261 *Fax:* 215-898-0404 *E-mail:* custserv@pobox.upenn.edu *Web Site:* www.pennpress.org, pg 219

Lamolinara, Guy, The Library of Congress Center for the Book, The Library of Congress, 101 Independence Ave SE, Washington, DC 20540-4920 *Tel:* 202-707-5221 *Fax:* 202-707-0269 *E-mail:* cfbook@loc.gov *Web Site:* www.read.gov/cfb, pg 509

Lamolinara, Guy, Library of Congress Prize for American Fiction, 101 Independence Ave SE, Washington, DC 20540-1400 *Tel:* 202-707-5221 (Center for the Book) *Fax:* 202-707-0269 *Web Site:* www.loc.gov, pg 624

Lamont, Myles, Hancock House Publishers, 4550 Birch Bay Lynden Rd, Suite 104, Blaine, WA 98230-9436 *Tel:* 604-538-1114 *Toll Free Tel:* 800-938-1114 *Fax:* 604-538-2262 *Toll Free Fax:* 800-983-2262 *E-mail:* sales@hancockhouse.com *Web Site:* www.hancockhouse.com, pg 84

LaMorte, Gianna, University of Texas Press, 3001 Lake Austin Blvd, 2.200, Austin, TX 78703 *Tel:* 512-471-7233 *Fax:* 512-232-7178 *E-mail:* utpress@uts.cc.utexas.edu; info@utpress.utexas.edu *Web Site:* utpress.utexas.edu, pg 205

Lamoureux, Bruno, Les Editions Fides, 7333 place des Roseraies, bureau 501, Anjou, QC H1M 2X6, Canada *Tel:* 514-745-4290 *Fax:* 514-745-4299 *E-mail:* editions@groupefides.com *Web Site:* www.editionsfides.com, pg 403

Lampack, Andrew, Peter Lampack Agency Inc, 350 Fifth Ave, Suite 5300, New York, NY 10118 *Tel:* 212-687-9106 *Fax:* 212-687-9109 *Web Site:* www.peterlampackagency.com, pg 467

Lampack, Peter A, Peter Lampack Agency Inc, 350 Fifth Ave, Suite 5300, New York, NY 10118 *Tel:* 212-687-9106 *Fax:* 212-687-9109 *Web Site:* www.peterlampackagency.com, pg 467

Lamporte, Richard, Jhpiego, 1615 Thames St, Baltimore, MD 21231-3492 *Tel:* 410-537-1800 *E-mail:* info@jhpiego.org *Web Site:* www.jhpiego.org, pg 106

Lanahan, Cole, The Seymour Agency, 475 Miner Street Rd, Canton, NY 13617 *Tel:* 239-398-8209 *Web Site:* www.theseymouragency.com, pg 475

Lancaster, Terri, Chronicle Books LLC, 680 Second St, San Francisco, CA 94107 *Tel:* 415-537-4200 *Fax:* 415-537-4460 (perms) *E-mail:* hello@chroniclebooks.com; subrights@chroniclebooks.com *Web Site:* www.chroniclebooks.com, pg 48

Lance, James, Cornell University Press, Sage House, 512 E State St, Ithaca, NY 14850 *Tel:* 607-253-2338 *E-mail:* cupressinfo@cornell.edu; cupress-sales@cornell.edu; cupress-perms@cornell.edu (reprint/class use permissions) *Web Site:* www.cornellpress.cornell.edu, pg 52

Lance, Lynne, National Newspaper Association (NNA), PO Box 13323, Pensacola, FL 32591 *Tel:* 850-542-7087 *Web Site:* www.nna.org; nnaweb.org, pg 513

Land, Bob, Land on Demand, 1003 Lakeview Pkwy, Locust Grove, VA 22508 *Tel:* 423-366-0513 *E-mail:* landondemand@gmail.com *Web Site:* boblandedits.blogspot.com, pg 441

Land, Kelley, Mercer University Press, 368 Orange St, Macon, GA 31201 *Tel:* 478-301-2880 *Toll Free Tel:* 866-895-1472 *Fax:* 478-301-2585 *E-mail:* mupressorders@mercer.edu *Web Site:* www.mupress.org, pg 129

Landa, Anne, Walter Foster Publishing, 26391 Crown Valley Pkwy, Suite 220, Mission Viejo, CA 92691 *Tel:* 949-380-7510 *Fax:* 949-380-7575 *E-mail:* walterfoster@quarto.com *Web Site:* www.quartoknows.com/walter-foster, pg 74

Landauer, Jeramy, Landauer Publishing, 903 Square St, Mount Joy, PA 17552 Tel: 717-560-4703 Toll Free Tel: 800-457-9112 Fax: 717-560-4702 E-mail: customerservice@foxchapelpublishing.com Web Site: landauerpub.com, pg 112

Landes, Rachel, Springer Publishing Co, 11 W 42 St, 15th fl, New York, NY 10036-8002 Tel: 212-431-4370 Toll Free Tel: 877-687-7476 E-mail: marketing@springerpub.com; cs@springerpub.com (orders); textbook@springerpub.com; specialsales@springerpub.com Web Site: www.springerpub.com, pg 196

Landgraf, Deirdre, Christian Liberty Press, 502 W Euclid Ave, Arlington Heights, IL 60004-5402 Toll Free Tel: 800-348-0899 Fax: 847-259-2941 E-mail: custserv@christianlibertypress.com Web Site: www.shopchristianliberty.com, pg 47

Landis, Sarah, Sterling Lord Literistic Inc, 594 Broadway, Suite 205, New York, NY 10012 Tel: 212-780-6050 Fax: 212-780-6095 E-mail: info@sll.com Web Site: www.sll.com, pg 477

Landon, Leonard, FineEdge.com LLC, 910 25 St, Unit B, Anacortes, WA 98221 Tel: 360-299-8500 Fax: 360-299-0535 E-mail: orders@fineedge.com; info@waggonerguide.com Web Site: www.waggonerguidebooks.com; waggonerguide.com, pg 72

Landon, Lorena, FineEdge.com LLC, 910 25 St, Unit B, Anacortes, WA 98221 Tel: 360-299-8500 Fax: 360-299-0535 E-mail: orders@fineedge.com; info@waggonerguide.com Web Site: www.waggonerguidebooks.com; waggonerguide.com, pg 72

Landry, Jessica, Bram Stoker Awards®, PO Box 56687, Sherman Oaks, CA 91413 Tel: 818-220-3965 E-mail: stokerchair@horror.org Web Site: www.thebramstokerawards.com; horror.org, pg 666

Landskroener, Marcia, Sophie Kerr Prize, c/o College Relations Off, 300 Washington Ave, Chestertown, MD 21620 Tel: 410-778-2800 Toll Free Tel: 800-422-1782 Fax: 410-810-7150 Web Site: www.washcoll.edu, pg 664

Landwehr, Kathy, Peachtree Publishing Co Inc, 1700 Chattahoochee Ave, Atlanta, GA 30318-2112 Tel: 404-876-8761 Toll Free Tel: 800-241-0113 Fax: 404-875-2578 Toll Free Fax: 800-875-8909 E-mail: hello@peachtree-online.com; orders@peachtree-online.com; sales@peachtree-online.com Web Site: www.peachtreebooks.com; www.peachtree-online.com, pg 153

Lane, Kathryn, Dundurn Press Ltd, PO Box 19510, RPO Manulife, Toronto, ON M4W 3T9, Canada Tel: 416-214-5544 E-mail: info@dundurn.com; publicity@dundurn.com; sales@dundurn.com Web Site: www.dundurn.com, pg 401

Lang, Adrienne, BenBella Books Inc, 10440 N Central Expwy, Suite 800, Dallas, TX 75231-2264 Tel: 214-750-3600 Web Site: www.benbellabooks.com; www.smartpopbooks.com, pg 27

Lang, Amanda, Portfolio, c/o Penguin Random House LLC, 1745 Broadway, New York, NY 10019 Tel: 212-782-9000 Web Site: www.penguin.com/portfolio-overview/; www.penguin.com/sentinel-overview/; www.penguin.com/thesis/, pg 162

Lang, Heather PhD, Susquehanna University, Department of English & Creative Writing, 514 University Ave, Selinsgrove, PA 17870 Tel: 570-372-4196 Web Site: www.susqu.edu, pg 565

Lang, Rebecca, St Martin's Press, LLC, 120 Broadway, New York, NY 10271 E-mail: publicity@stmartins.com; trademarketing@stmartins.com; foreignrights@stmartins.com Web Site: us.macmillan.com/smp, pg 181

Lange, April, W W Norton & Company Inc, 500 Fifth Ave, New York, NY 10110-0017 Tel: 212-354-5500 Toll Free Tel: 800-233-4830 (orders & cust serv) Fax: 212-869-0856 Toll Free Fax: 800-458-6515 E-mail: orders@wwnorton.com Web Site: wwnorton.com, pg 143

Lange, Heide, Sanford J Greenburger Associates Inc, 55 Fifth Ave, New York, NY 10003 Tel: 212-206-5600 Web Site: greenburger.com, pg 461

Lange, Jocelyn, Penguin Random House LLC, 1745 Broadway, New York, NY 10019 Tel: 212-782-9000 Toll Free Tel: 800-726-0600 Web Site: www.penguinrandomhouse.com, pg 155

Lange, Marty, National Geographic Learning, 20 Channel Center St, Boston, MA 02210 Tel: 617-289-7900 E-mail: schoolcustomerservice@cengage.com Web Site: www.ngl.cengage.com/school, pg 138

Langen, Olivia, Penguin Random House Audio Publishing Group, 1745 Broadway, New York, NY 10019 Toll Free Tel: 800-793-2665 (cust serv) E-mail: audio@penguinrandomhouse.com; ecustomerservice@penguinrandomhouse.com Web Site: www.penguinrandomhouseaudio.com, pg 154

Langford, Martha, Simon & Schuster, 1230 Avenue of the Americas, New York, NY 10020 Tel: 212-698-7000 Toll Free Tel: 800-223-2348 (cust serv); 800-223-2336 (orders) Toll Free Fax: 800-943-9831 (orders) Web Site: simonandschusterpublishing.com/simonandschuster/, pg 188

Langille, Donald, Palm Island Press, 2039 Georgia St, Sebring, FL 33870 Tel: 305-296-3102 E-mail: pipress2@gmail.com, pg 150

Langley, Cate, Hannah Beiter Graduate Student Research Grants, 140B Purcellville Gateway Dr, Suite 1200, Purcellville, VA 20132 Tel: 630-571-4520 E-mail: info@childlitassn.org Web Site: www.childlitassn.org, pg 578

Langley, Cate, Children's Literature Association Article Award, 140B Purcellville Gateway Dr, Suite 1200, Purcellville, VA 20132 Tel: 630-571-4520 E-mail: info@childlitassn.org Web Site: www.childlitassn.org, pg 588

Langley, Cate, Children's Literature Association Book Award, 140B Purcellville Gateway Dr, Suite 1200, Purcellville, VA 20132 Tel: 630-571-4520 E-mail: info@childlitassn.org Web Site: www.childlitassn.org, pg 589

Langley, Cate, Children's Literature Association Edited Book Award, 140B Purcellville Gateway Dr, Suite 1200, Purcellville, VA 20132 Tel: 630-571-4520 E-mail: info@childlitassn.org Web Site: www.childlitassn.org, pg 589

Langley, Cate, Children's Literature Association Graduate Student Essay Award, 140B Purcellville Gateway Dr, Suite 1200, Purcellville, VA 20132 Tel: 630-571-4520 E-mail: info@childlitassn.org Web Site: www.childlitassn.org, pg 589

Langley, Cate, Anne Devereaux Jordan Award, 140B Purcellville Gateway Dr, Suite 1200, Purcellville, VA 20132 Tel: 630-571-4520 E-mail: info@childlitassn.org Web Site: www.childlitassn.org, pg 595

Langley, Cate, Carol Gay Award, 140B Purcellville Gateway Dr, Suite 1200, Purcellville, VA 20132 Tel: 630-571-4520 E-mail: info@childlitassn.org Web Site: www.childlitassn.org, pg 606

Langley, Cate, Phoenix Award, 140B Purcellville Gateway Dr, Suite 1200, Purcellville, VA 20132 Tel: 630-571-4520 E-mail: info@childlitassn.org Web Site: www.childlitassn.org, pg 649

Langley, Cate, Phoenix Picture Book Award, 140B Purcellville Gateway Dr, Suite 1200, Purcellville, VA 20132 Tel: 630-571-4520 E-mail: info@childlitassn.org Web Site: www.childlitassn.org, pg 649

Langley, Cate, Judith Plotz Emerging Scholar Award, 140B Purcellville Gateway Dr, Suite 1200, Purcellville, VA 20132 Tel: 630-571-4520 E-mail: info@childlitassn.org Web Site: www.childlitassn.org, pg 650

Langley, Catherine E, National Federation of Press Women Inc (NFPW), 140B Purcellville Gateway Dr, Suite 120, Purcellville, VA 20132 Tel: 571-295-5900 E-mail: info@nfpw.org Web Site: www.nfpw.org, pg 513

Langlois, Dennis, Princeton University Press, 41 William St, Princeton, NJ 08540-5237 Tel: 609-258-4900 Fax: 609-258-6305 E-mail: info@press.princeton.edu Web Site: press.princeton.edu, pg 164

Langlois, Sylvie, Federation des Milieux Documentaires, 2065 rue Parthenais, Bureau 387, Montreal, QC H2K 3T1, Canada Tel: 514-281-5012 E-mail: info@fmdoc.org Web Site: fmdoc.org, pg 505

Langstraat, Brenda, The Carl Sandburg Literary Award, 200 W Madison, 3rd fl, Chicago, IL 60606 Tel: 312-201-9830 E-mail: info@cplfoundation.org Web Site: www.cplfoundation.org, pg 658

Langstraat, Brenda, 21st Century Award, 200 W Madison, 3rd fl, Chicago, IL 60606 Tel: 312-201-9830 E-mail: info@cplfoundation.org Web Site: www.cplfoundation.org, pg 671

Languell, Krystal, Poetry Foundation, 61 W Superior St, Chicago, IL 60654 Tel: 312-787-7070 E-mail: info@poetryfoundation.org Web Site: www.poetryfoundation.org, pg 526

Langum, David J Sr, David J Langum Sr Prize in American Historical Fiction, c/o David J Langum Sr, 2809 Berkeley Dr, Birmingham, AL 35242 Web Site: langumfoundation.org/about-prizes/american-historical-fiction, pg 622

Lanick, Colleen, The MIT Press, One Broadway, 12th fl, Cambridge, MA 02142 Tel: 617-253-5255 Toll Free Tel: 800-405-1619 (orders) Fax: 617-258-6779; 617-577-1545 (orders) Web Site: mitpress.mit.edu, pg 132

Lanman, Nate, HarperCollins Publishers LLC, 195 Broadway, New York, NY 10007 Tel: 212-207-7000 Web Site: www.harpercollins.com, pg 87

Lannan, Lawrence P Jr, Lannan Foundation, 313 Read St, Santa Fe, NM 87501-2628 Tel: 505-986-8160 E-mail: info@lannan.org Web Site: lannan.org, pg 526

Lannan, Lawrence P Jr, Lannan Literary Awards & Fellowships, 313 Read St, Santa Fe, NM 87501-2628 Tel: 505-986-8160 E-mail: info@lannan.org Web Site: lannan.org, pg 622

Lansdale, Kasey, Tachyon Publications LLC, 1459 18 St, No 139, San Francisco, CA 94107 Tel: 415-285-5615 E-mail: tachyon@tachyonpublications.com; submissions@tachyonpublications.com Web Site: www.tachyonpublications.com, pg 202

Lansing, Andrea, The Guilford Press, 370 Seventh Ave, Suite 1200, New York, NY 10001-1020 Tel: 212-431-9800 Toll Free Tel: 800-365-7006 Fax: 212-966-6708 E-mail: info@guilford.com; orders@guilford.com Web Site: www.guilford.com, pg 82

Lansing, Richard, Springer, One New York Plaza, Suite 4600, New York, NY 10004-1562 Tel: 212-460-1500 Toll Free Tel: 800-SPRINGER (777-4643) Fax: 212-460-1700 E-mail: customerservice@springernature.com Web Site: www.springer.com, pg 196

Lanza, Kim, Candlewick Press, 99 Dover St, Somerville, MA 02144-2825 Tel: 617-661-3330 Fax: 617-661-0565 E-mail: bigbear@candlewick.com; salesinfo@candlewick.com Web Site: candlewick.com, pg 39

Lanzi, Gena, Atria Books, 1230 Avenue of the Americas, New York, NY 10020 Tel: 212-698-7000 Fax: 212-698-7007 Web Site: www.simonandschuster.com, pg 21

Lape, Todd, University Press of Mississippi, 3825 Ridgewood Rd, Jackson, MS 39211-6492 Tel: 601-432-6205 Toll Free Tel: 800-737-7788 (orders & cust serv) Fax: 601-432-6217 E-mail: press@mississippi.edu Web Site: www.upress.state.ms.us, pg 222

Lapena, Caitlin, Gerald Lampert Memorial Award, 2 Carlton St, Suite 1519, Toronto, ON M5B 1J3, Canada Tel: 416-504-1657 E-mail: info@poets.ca; admin@poets.ca Web Site: poets.ca/awards/lampert, pg 622

Lapena, Caitlin, The League of Canadian Poets, 2 Carlton St, Suite 1519, Toronto, ON M5B 1J3, Canada Tel: 416-504-1657 E-mail: info@poets.ca Web Site: poets.ca, pg 509

Lapena, Caitlin, Pat Lowther Memorial Award, 2 Carlton St, Suite 1519, Toronto, ON M5B 1J3, Canada Tel: 416-504-1657 E-mail: info@poets.ca Web Site: poets.ca/awards/lowther, pg 627

Lapena, Caitlin, Raymond Souster Award, 2 Carlton St, Suite 1519, Toronto, ON M5B 1J3, Canada *Tel:* 416-504-1657 *E-mail:* admin@poets.ca *Web Site:* poets.ca/awards/souster, pg 664

Lapena, Caitlin, Jessamy Stursberg Poetry Prize for Canadian Youth, 2 Carlton St, Suite 1519, Toronto, ON M5B 1J3, Canada *Tel:* 416-504-1657 *E-mail:* info@poets.ca; admin@poets.ca *Web Site:* poets.ca, pg 667

Lapena, Caitlin, Sheri-D Wilson Golden Beret Award, 2 Carlton St, Suite 1519, Toronto, ON M5B 1J3, Canada *Tel:* 416-504-1657 *E-mail:* admin@poets.ca *Web Site:* poets.ca/awards/goldenberet, pg 676

Lapin, Joseph, Bisk Education, 9417 Princess Palm Ave, Suite 400, Tampa, FL 33619 *Tel:* 813-621-6200 *E-mail:* media@bisk.com *Web Site:* www.bisk.com, pg 29

LaPointe, Erin, Sourcebooks LLC, 1935 Brookdale Rd, Suite 139, Naperville, IL 60563 *Tel:* 630-961-3900 *Toll Free Tel:* 800-432-7444 *Fax:* 630-961-2168 *E-mail:* info@sourcebooks.com *Web Site:* www.sourcebooks.com, pg 195

Laporte, Janine, Doubleday Canada, 320 Front St W, Suite 1400, Toronto, ON M5V 3B6, Canada *Tel:* 416-364-4449 *Fax:* 416-598-7764 *Web Site:* www.penguinrandomhouse.ca, pg 401

Laporte, Janine, Knopf Canada, 320 Front St W, Suite 1400, Toronto, ON M5V 3B6, Canada *Tel:* 416-364-4449 *Toll Free Tel:* 888-523-9292 *Fax:* 416-598-7764 *Web Site:* www.penguinrandomhouse.ca, pg 411

Laporte, Janine, Seal Books, 320 Front St W, Suite 1400, Toronto, ON M5V 3B6, Canada *Tel:* 416-364-4449 *Toll Free Tel:* 888-523-9292 (order desk) *Fax:* 416-598-7764 *Web Site:* www.penguinrandomhouse.ca, pg 419

Lapp, Alison, Kids Can Press Ltd, 25 Dockside Dr, Toronto, ON M5A 0B5, Canada *Tel:* 416-479-7000 *Toll Free Tel:* 800-265-0884 *Fax:* 416-960-5437 *E-mail:* info@kidscan.com; customerservice@kidscan.com *Web Site:* www.kidscanpress.com; www.kidscanpress.ca, pg 411

Laredo, Sam, Laredo Publishing Co, 465 Westview Ave, Englewood, NJ 07631 *Tel:* 201-408-4048 *E-mail:* info@laredopublishing.com *Web Site:* www.laredopublishing.com, pg 113

Laredo, Sam, Renaissance House, 465 Westview Ave, Englewood, NJ 07631 *Tel:* 201-408-4048 *Web Site:* www.renaissancehouse.net, pg 174, 486

Larned, Alex, Penguin Random House LLC, 1745 Broadway, New York, NY 10019 *Tel:* 212-782-9000 *Toll Free Tel:* 800-726-0600 *Web Site:* www.penguinrandomhouse.com, pg 155

Larned, Alex, Random House Publishing Group, 1745 Broadway, New York, NY 10019 *Toll Free Tel:* 800-200-3552 *Web Site:* www.randomhousebooks.com, pg 171

Larochelle, France, Guerin Editeur Ltee, 800, Blvd Industriel, bureau 200, St-Jean-sur-Richelieu, QC J3B 8G4, Canada *Tel:* 514-842-3481 *Toll Free Tel:* 800-398-8337 *Fax:* 514-842-4923 *E-mail:* info@guerin-editeur.qc.ca *Web Site:* www.guerin-editeur.qc.ca, pg 408

Larocque-Poirier, Joanne, Canada Council for the Arts (Conseil des arts du Canada), 150 Elgin St, 2nd fl, Ottawa, ON K2P 1L4, Canada *Tel:* 613-566-4414 *Toll Free Tel:* 800-263-5588 (CN only) *Fax:* 613-566-4390 *E-mail:* info@canadacouncil.ca; media@canadacouncil.ca *Web Site:* canadacouncil.ca, pg 502

Laroya, Colette, Hippocrene Books Inc, 171 Madison Ave, Suite 1605, New York, NY 10016 *Tel:* 212-685-4373 *E-mail:* info@hippocrenebooks.com; orderdept@hippocrenebooks.com (orders) *Web Site:* www.hippocrenebooks.com, pg 92

Larsen, David, University of Manitoba Press, University of Manitoba, 301 St Johns College, 92 Dysart Rd, Winnipeg, MB R3T 2M5, Canada *Tel:* 204-474-9495 *Fax:* 204-474-7566 *E-mail:* uofmpress@umanitoba.ca *Web Site:* uofmpress.ca, pg 422

Larsen Miskin, Elizabeth A, Tapestry Press Ltd, 19 Nashoba Rd, Littleton, MA 01460 *Tel:* 978-486-0200 *Toll Free Tel:* 800-535-2007 *E-mail:* publish@tapestrypress.com *Web Site:* www.tapestrypress.com, pg 202

Larson, John, Cohesion®, 511 W Bay St, Suite 480, Tampa, FL 33606 *Tel:* 813-999-3111 *Toll Free Tel:* 866-727-6800 *Web Site:* www.cohesion.com, pg 437

Larson, Susan, Pinckley Prizes for Crime Fiction, PO Box 13926, New Orleans, LA 70185 *E-mail:* pinckleyprizes@gmail.com *Web Site:* www.pinckleyprizes.org, pg 650

LaRue, Jennifer, Mark Twain American Voice in Literature Award, 351 Farmington Ave, Hartford, CT 06105 *Tel:* 860-247-0998 *E-mail:* info@marktwainhouse.org *Web Site:* marktwainhouse.org, pg 671

LaSala, Jeff, Macmillan, 120 Broadway, 22nd fl, New York, NY 10271 *E-mail:* press.inquiries@macmillan.com *Web Site:* us.macmillan.com, pg 122

Lasher, Eric, The LA Literary Agency, 1264 N Hayworth Ave, Los Angeles, CA 90046 *Tel:* 323-654-5288 *E-mail:* laliteraryagency@mac.com *Web Site:* www.laliteraryagency.com, pg 466

Lasher, Maureen, The LA Literary Agency, 1264 N Hayworth Ave, Los Angeles, CA 90046 *Tel:* 323-654-5288 *E-mail:* laliteraryagency@mac.com *Web Site:* www.laliteraryagency.com, pg 466

Lashinger, Sharon, The Society of Southwestern Authors (SSA), PO Box 30355, Tucson, AZ 85751-0355 *Web Site:* www.ssa-az.org, pg 520

Lashinger, Sharon, The Society of Southwestern Authors Writing Contest, PO Box 30355, Tucson, AZ 85751-0355 *E-mail:* contest@ssa-az.org *Web Site:* www.ssa-az.org/contest.htm, pg 664

Lashof, Dan, World Resources Institute, 10 "G" St NE, Suite 800, Washington, DC 20002 *Tel:* 202-729-7600 *Fax:* 202-729-7610 *Web Site:* www.wri.org, pg 233

Lasky, Cynthia, Random House Publishing Group, 1745 Broadway, New York, NY 10019 *Toll Free Tel:* 800-200-3552 *Web Site:* www.randomhousebooks.com, pg 170

Lasky, Karl, Ravenhawk™ Books, 311 E Drowsey Circle, Payson, AZ 85541 *Tel:* 520-402-9033 *Fax:* 520-402-9033 *Web Site:* www.facebook.com/6DOFRavenhawk, pg 172

Lassiter, Alexis, little bee books, 598 Broadway, 7th fl, New York, NY 10012 *Tel:* 212-321-0237 *Toll Free Tel:* 844-321-0237 *E-mail:* info@littlebeebooks.com; sales@littlebeebooks.com; publicity@littlebeebooks.com *Web Site:* www.littlebeebooks.com, pg 117

Lassiter, Steve, APA Talent & Literary Agency, 405 S Beverly Dr, Beverly Hills, CA 90212 *Tel:* 310-888-4200 *Web Site:* www.apa-agency.com, pg 449

Laster, Stephen, McGraw-Hill Education, 2 Penn Plaza, New York, NY 10121-2298 *Tel:* 212-904-2000 *E-mail:* international_cs@mheducation.com; seg_customerservice@mheducation.com (PreK-12); hep_customerservice@mheducation.com (higher education) *Web Site:* www.mheducation.com, pg 127

Latham, Adam, Sewanee Writers' Conference, 735 University Ave, Sewanee, TN 37383 *Tel:* 931-598-1654 *E-mail:* swc@sewanee.edu *Web Site:* www.sewaneewriters.org, pg 557

Latham, Joyce Eileen, JL Communications, 10205 Green Holly Terr, Silver Spring, MD 20902 *Tel:* 301-593-0640, pg 441

Lathan, Laurie, Thurber Prize for American Humor, 77 Jefferson Ave, Columbus, OH 43215 *Tel:* 614-464-1032 *E-mail:* thurberhouse@thurberhouse.org *Web Site:* www.thurberhouse.org, pg 669

Latko, Raquel, Sourcebooks LLC, 1935 Brookdale Rd, Suite 139, Naperville, IL 60563 *Tel:* 630-961-3900 *Toll Free Tel:* 800-432-7444 *Fax:* 630-961-2168 *E-mail:* info@sourcebooks.com *Web Site:* www.sourcebooks.com, pg 194

Latshaw, Katherine, Folio Literary Management, The Film Center Bldg, 630 Ninth Ave, Suite 1101, New York, NY 10036 *Tel:* 212-400-1494 *Fax:* 212-967-0977 *Web Site:* www.foliolit.com, pg 459

Lau, Ashley, Henry Holt and Company, LLC, 120 Broadway, 23rd fl, New York, NY 10271 *Tel:* 646-307-5151 *Toll Free Tel:* 888-330-8477 (orders) *Fax:* 646-307-5285 *Web Site:* www.henryholt.com, pg 94

Lau, Christine, Macmillan, 120 Broadway, 22nd fl, New York, NY 10271 *E-mail:* press.inquiries@macmillan.com *Web Site:* us.macmillan.com, pg 122

Lau, Eva, Penguin Random House Speakers Bureau, a Penguin Random House company, 1745 Broadway, Mail Drop 13-1, New York, NY 10019 *Tel:* 212-572-2013 *E-mail:* speakers@penguinrandomhouse.com *Web Site:* www.prhspeakers.com, pg 487

Lau, Gigi, Tundra Book Group, 320 Front St W, Suite 1400, Toronto, ON M5V 3B6, Canada *Tel:* 416-364-4449 *Toll Free Tel:* 888-523-9292 (orders); 800-588-1074 *E-mail:* youngreaders@penguinrandomhouse.com *Web Site:* www.tundrabooks.com, pg 421

Lauber, Kim, Harry N Abrams Inc, 195 Broadway, 9th fl, New York, NY 10007 *Tel:* 212-206-7715 *Toll Free Tel:* 800-345-1359 *Fax:* 212-645-8437 *E-mail:* abrams@abramsbooks.com; publicity@abramsbooks.com; sales@abramsbooks.com *Web Site:* www.abramsbooks.com, pg 2

Laudone, Catherine, Simon & Schuster Children's Publishing, 1230 Avenue of the Americas, New York, NY 10020 *Tel:* 212-698-7000 *Web Site:* www.simonandschuster.com/kids; www.simonandschuster.com/teen; simonandschuster.net; simonandschuster.biz, pg 189

Lauer, Brett Fletcher, George Bogin Memorial Award, 119 Smith St, Brooklyn, NY 11201 *Tel:* 212-254-9628 *E-mail:* info@poetrysociety.org *Web Site:* poetrysociety.org/awards, pg 582

Lauer, Brett Fletcher, Alice Fay Di Castagnola Award, 119 Smith St, Brooklyn, NY 11201 *Tel:* 212-254-9628 *E-mail:* info@poetrysociety.org *Web Site:* poetrysociety.org/awards, pg 595

Lauer, Brett Fletcher, Norma Farber First Book Award, 119 Smith St, Brooklyn, NY 11201 *Tel:* 212-254-9628 *E-mail:* info@poetrysociety.org *Web Site:* poetrysociety.org/awards, pg 601

Lauer, Brett Fletcher, Four Quartets Prize, 119 Smith St, Brooklyn, NY 11201 *Tel:* 212-254-9628 *E-mail:* info@poetrysociety.org *Web Site:* poetrysociety.org/awards, pg 603

Lauer, Brett Fletcher, Frost Medal, 119 Smith St, Brooklyn, NY 11201 *Tel:* 212-254-9628 *E-mail:* info@poetrysociety.org *Web Site:* poetrysociety.org/awards, pg 605

Lauer, Brett Fletcher, Cecil Hemley Memorial Award, 119 Smith St, Brooklyn, NY 11201 *Tel:* 212-254-9628 *E-mail:* info@poetrysociety.org *Web Site:* poetrysociety.org/awards, pg 612

Lauer, Brett Fletcher, Louise Louis/Emily F Bourne Student Poetry Award, 119 Smith St, Brooklyn, NY 11201 *Tel:* 212-254-9628 *E-mail:* info@poetrysociety.org *Web Site:* poetrysociety.org/awards, pg 626

Lauer, Brett Fletcher, Lyric Poetry Award, 119 Smith St, Brooklyn, NY 11201 *Tel:* 212-254-9628 *E-mail:* info@poetrysociety.org *Web Site:* poetrysociety.org/awards, pg 627

Lauer, Brett Fletcher, Lucille Medwick Memorial Award, 119 Smith St, Brooklyn, NY 11201 *Tel:* 212-254-9628 *E-mail:* info@poetrysociety.org *Web Site:* poetrysociety.org/awards, pg 632

Lauer, Brett Fletcher, Poetry Society of America (PSA), 119 Smith St, Brooklyn, NY 11201 *Tel:* 212-254-9628 *E-mail:* info@poetrysociety.org *Web Site:* poetrysociety.org, pg 517

Lauer, Brett Fletcher, Shelley Memorial Award, 119 Smith St, Brooklyn, NY 11201 *Tel:* 212-254-9628 *E-mail:* info@poetrysociety.org *Web Site:* poetrysociety.org/awards, pg 662

Lauer, Brett Fletcher, William Carlos Williams Award, 119 Smith St, Brooklyn, NY 11201 *Tel:* 212-254-9628 *E-mail:* info@poetrysociety.org *Web Site:* poetrysociety.org/awards, pg 675

Lauer, Brett Fletcher, The Writer Magazine/Emily Dickinson Award, 119 Smith St, Brooklyn, NY 11201 *Tel:* 212-254-9628 *E-mail:* info@poetrysociety.org *Web Site:* poetrysociety.org/awards, pg 678

Laughlin, Phil, The MIT Press, One Broadway, 12th fl, Cambridge, MA 02142 *Tel:* 617-253-5255 *Toll Free Tel:* 800-405-1619 (orders) *Fax:* 617-258-6779; 617-577-1545 (orders) *Web Site:* mitpress.mit.edu, pg 132

Lauletta, Juliana, Astra Books for Young Readers, 19 W 21 St, No 1201, New York, NY 10010 *Tel:* 646-844-3485 *E-mail:* ahinfo@astrahouse.com; permissions@astrapublishinghouse.com *Web Site:* astrapublishinghouse.com, pg 20

Laur, Mary, University of Chicago Press, 1427 E 60 St, Chicago, IL 60637-2954 *Tel:* 773-702-7700; 773-702-7600 *Toll Free Tel:* 800-621-2736 (orders) *Fax:* 773-702-9756; 773-660-2235 (orders); 773-702-2708 *E-mail:* custserv@press.uchicago.edu; marketing@press.uchicago.edu *Web Site:* www.press.uchicago.edu, pg 215

Laure, Estelle, Folio Literary Management, The Film Center Bldg, 630 Ninth Ave, Suite 1101, New York, NY 10036 *Tel:* 212-400-1494 *Fax:* 212-967-0977 *Web Site:* www.foliolit.com, pg 459

Laurell, David, The Jennifer DeChiara Literary Agency, 245 Park Ave, 39th fl, New York, NY 10167 *Tel:* 212-372-8989 *Web Site:* www.jdlit.com, pg 455

Lauria, Lisa, Simon & Schuster Children's Publishing, 1230 Avenue of the Americas, New York, NY 10020 *Tel:* 212-698-7000 *Web Site:* www.simonandschuster.com/kids; www.simonandschuster.com/teen; simonandschuster.net; simonandschuster.biz, pg 189

Lauriello, Sophia, St Martin's Press, LLC, 120 Broadway, New York, NY 10271 *E-mail:* publicity@stmartins.com; trademarketing@stmartins.com; foreignrights@stmartins.com *Web Site:* us.macmillan.com/smp, pg 181

Laurin, Caroline, Brault & Bouthillier, 700 ave Beaumont, Montreal, QC H3N 1V5, Canada *Tel:* 514-273-9186 *Toll Free Tel:* 800-361-0378 *Fax:* 514-273-8627 *Toll Free Fax:* 800-361-0378 *E-mail:* communicationbb@bb.ca *Web Site:* bb.ca, pg 397

Laurito, Brian, Penguin Random House Audio Publishing Group, 1745 Broadway, New York, NY 10019 *Toll Free Tel:* 800-793-2665 (cust serv) *E-mail:* audio@penguinrandomhouse.com; ecustomerservice@penguinrandomhouse.com *Web Site:* www.penguinrandomhouseaudio.com, pg 154

Lauterbach, Ellen, Marshall Cavendish Education, 99 White Plains Rd, Tarrytown, NY 10591-9001 *Tel:* 914-332-8888 *Toll Free Tel:* 800-821-9881 *Fax:* 914-332-1082 *E-mail:* mce@marshallcavendish.com; customerservice@marshallcavendish.com *Web Site:* www.mceducation.us, pg 126

Lauzon, Lauren, Penguin Press, c/o Penguin Random House LLC, 1745 Broadway, New York, NY 10019 *Tel:* 212-782-9000 *E-mail:* penguinpress@penguinrandomhouse.com *Web Site:* www.penguin.com/penguin-press-overview/, pg 154

Lauzon, Nancy, Les Editions Fides, 7333 place des Roseraies, bureau 501, Anjou, QC H1M 2X6, Canada *Tel:* 514-745-4290 *Fax:* 514-745-4299 *E-mail:* editions@groupefides.com *Web Site:* www.editionsfides.com, pg 403

LaVallee, Donna, Miniature Book Society Inc, 518 High St, Fall River, MA 02720 *Web Site:* www.mbs.org, pg 511

LaVela, Casey, University of Wisconsin Press, 728 State St, Suite 443, Madison, WI 53706-1418 *Tel:* 608-263-1110; 608-263-0668 (journal orders) *Toll Free Tel:* 800-621-2736 (book orders) *Fax:* 608-263-1173 *Toll Free Fax:* 800-621-2736 (book orders) *E-mail:* uwiscpress@uwpress.wisc.edu *Web Site:* uwpress.wisc.edu, pg 221

Laventhall, Don, Folio Literary Management, The Film Center Bldg, 630 Ninth Ave, Suite 1101, New York, NY 10036 *Tel:* 212-400-1494 *Fax:* 212-967-0977 *Web Site:* www.foliolit.com, pg 459

Lavery, Brittany, Simon & Schuster Canada, 166 King St E, Suite 300, Toronto, ON M5A 1J3, Canada *Tel:* 647-427-8882 *Toll Free Tel:* 800-387-0446; 800-268-3216 (orders) *Fax:* 647-430-9446 *Toll Free Fax:* 888-849-8151 (orders) *E-mail:* info@simonandschuster.ca *Web Site:* www.simonandschuster.ca, pg 419

Lavoie, Diane, Harlequin Enterprises Ltd, Bay Adelaide Centre, East Tower, 22 Adelaide St W, 41st fl, Toronto, ON M5H 4E3, Canada *Tel:* 416-445-5860 *Toll Free Tel:* 888-432-4879; 800-370-5838 (ebook inquiries) *E-mail:* customerservice@harlequin.com *Web Site:* www.harlequin.com, pg 409

Law, Elizabeth, Holiday House Publishing Inc, 50 Broad St, New York, NY 10004 *Tel:* 212-688-0085 *Fax:* 212-421-6134 *E-mail:* info@holidayhouse.com *Web Site:* www.holidayhouse.com, pg 94

Law, Larry, Great Lakes Independent Booksellers Association (GLIBA), 3123 Andrea Ct, Woodridge, IL 60517 *Tel:* 630-841-8129 *Web Site:* www.gliba.org, pg 507

Law, Larry, Heartland Booksellers Award, 3123 Andrea Ct, Woodridge, IL 60517 *Tel:* 630-841-8129 *Web Site:* www.gliba.org/heartland-booksellers-award.html, pg 611

Lawler, Caitlin, Sourcebooks LLC, 1935 Brookdale Rd, Suite 139, Naperville, IL 60563 *Tel:* 630-961-3900 *Toll Free Tel:* 800-432-7444 *Fax:* 630-961-2168 *E-mail:* info@sourcebooks.com *Web Site:* www.sourcebooks.com, pg 195

Lawler, Frank C, Lannan Foundation, 313 Read St, Santa Fe, NM 87501-2628 *Tel:* 505-986-8160 *E-mail:* info@lannan.org *Web Site:* lannan.org, pg 526

Lawler, Frank C, Lannan Literary Awards & Fellowships, 313 Read St, Santa Fe, NM 87501-2628 *Tel:* 505-986-8160 *E-mail:* info@lannan.org *Web Site:* lannan.org, pg 622

Lawler, Keegan, Annie Dillard Award for Creative Nonfiction, Mail Stop 9053, Western Washington University, Bellingham, WA 98225 *Tel:* 360-650-4863 *E-mail:* bellingham.review@wwu.edu *Web Site:* bhreview.org; bhreview.submittable.com, pg 596

Lawler, Keegan, 49th Parallel Poetry Award, Mail Stop 9053, Western Washington University, Bellingham, WA 98225 *Tel:* 360-650-4863 *E-mail:* bellingham.review@wwu.edu *Web Site:* bhreview.org; bhreview.submittable.com, pg 603

Lawler, Keegan, Tobias Wolff Award for Fiction, Mail Stop 9053, Western Washington University, Bellingham, WA 98225 *Tel:* 360-650-4863 *E-mail:* bellingham.review@wwu.edu *Web Site:* bhreview.org; bhreview.submittable.com, pg 677

Lawler, Kelly, Sourcebooks LLC, 1935 Brookdale Rd, Suite 139, Naperville, IL 60563 *Tel:* 630-961-3900 *Toll Free Tel:* 800-432-7444 *Fax:* 630-961-2168 *E-mail:* info@sourcebooks.com *Web Site:* www.sourcebooks.com, pg 194

Lawlor, Michaela, Housatonic Book Awards, Dept of Writing, Linguistics & Creative Process, 181 White St, Higgins Hall, Rm 219, Danbury, CT 06810 *Web Site:* housatonicbookawards.wordpress.com, pg 613

Lawrence, Eileen, Tor Publishing Group, 120 Broadway, New York, NY 10271 *Toll Free Tel:* 800-455-0340 (Macmillan) *E-mail:* torpublicity@tor.com; forgepublicity@forgebooks.com *Web Site:* us.macmillan.com/torpublishinggroup, pg 208

Lawrence, Justin Paul, InterVarsity Press, 430 Plaza Dr, Westmont, IL 60559-1234 *Tel:* 630-734-4000 *Toll Free Tel:* 800-843-9487 *Fax:* 630-734-4200 *E-mail:* email@ivpress.com *Web Site:* www.ivpress.com, pg 104

Lawrence, Michael, Orbis Books, PO Box 302, Maryknoll, NY 10545-0302 *Tel:* 914-941-7636 *Toll Free Tel:* 800-258-5838 (orders, Mon-Fri 8AM-4PM EST) *Fax:* 914-941-7005 *E-mail:* orbisbooks@maryknoll.org *Web Site:* orbisbooks.com, pg 147

Lawrence, Mikayla, HarperCollins Children's Books, 195 Broadway, New York, NY 10007 *Tel:* 212-207-7000 *Web Site:* www.harpercollins.com/childrens, pg 85

Lawrence, Rachael, Judson Press, 1075 First Ave, King of Prussia, PA 19406 *Toll Free Tel:* 800-458-3766 *Fax:* 610-768-2107 *E-mail:* publisher@judsonpress.com; editor@judsonpress.com; marketing@judsonpress.com *Web Site:* www.judsonpress.com, pg 107

Lawrence, Richard, Eaton Literary Associates Literary Awards, PO Box 49795, Sarasota, FL 34230-6795 *Tel:* 941-366-6589 *E-mail:* eatonlit@aol.com *Web Site:* www.eatonliterary.com, pg 597

Lawrenson, Sarah, Random House Children's Books, c/o Penguin Random House LLC, 1745 Broadway, New York, NY 10019 *Tel:* 212-782-9000 *Web Site:* www.rhcbooks.com, pg 170

Lawrie, Colleen, Basic Books Group, 1290 Avenue of the Americas, New York, NY 10104 *Tel:* 212-340-8100 *Toll Free Tel:* 800-343-4499 (cust serv) *Fax:* 212-340-8105 *E-mail:* customer.service@hbgusa.com; orders@hbgusa.com *Web Site:* www.hachettebookgroup.com/imprint/basic-books/, pg 25

Laws, Andrea, University Press of Kansas, 2502 Westbrooke Circle, Lawrence, KS 66045-4444 *Tel:* 785-864-4154 *Fax:* 785-864-4586 *E-mail:* upress@ku.edu *Web Site:* www.kansaspress.ku.edu, pg 221

Laws, Kimberly, Gallery Books, 1230 Avenue of the Americas, New York, NY 10020 *Toll Free Tel:* 800-456-6798 *Fax:* 212-698-7284 *E-mail:* consumer.customerservice@simonandschuster.com *Web Site:* www.simonandschuster.com, pg 76

Lawson, Alice, The Gersh Agency (TGA), 41 Madison Ave, 29th fl, New York, NY 10010 *Tel:* 212-997-1818 *Web Site:* gersh.com/books, pg 460

Lawson, Mark, ECS Publishing Group, 1727 Larkin Williams Rd, Fenton, MO 63026 *Tel:* 636-305-0100 *Toll Free Tel:* 800-647-2117 *Web Site:* ecspublishing.com; www.facebook.com/ecspublishing, pg 63

Lawton, Caryn, Washington State University Press, Cooper Publications Bldg, 2300 Grimes Way, Pullman, WA 99164-5910 *Tel:* 509-335-7880 *Toll Free Tel:* 800-354-7360 (orders) *E-mail:* wsupress@wsu.edu *Web Site:* wsupress.wsu.edu, pg 226

Lawton, Wendy, Books & Such, 2222 Cleveland Ave, No 1005, Santa Rosa, CA 95403 *Tel:* 707-538-4184 *Web Site:* booksandsuch.com, pg 451

Lay, Kevin, Scepter Publishers, PO Box 360694, Strongsville, OH 44149 *Tel:* 212-354-0670 *Toll Free Tel:* 800-322-8773 *Fax:* 646-417-7707 *E-mail:* info@scepterpublishers.org *Web Site:* www.scepterpublishers.org, pg 183

Lay, Tom, Fordham University Press, Joseph A Martino Hall, 45 Columbus Ave, 3rd fl, New York, NY 10023 *Fax:* 347-842-3083 *Web Site:* www.fordhampress.com, pg 73

Laycock, Kelly, University of Regina Press, 2 Research Dr, Suite 160, Regina, SK S4S 7H9, Canada *Tel:* 306-585-4758 *Fax:* 306-585-4699 *E-mail:* uofrpress@uregina.ca *Web Site:* uofrpress.ca, pg 423

Layer, Grace, Dutton, c/o Penguin Random House LLC, 1745 Broadway, New York, NY 10019 *Tel:* 212-366-2000 *Web Site:* www.penguin.com/dutton-overview/; www.penguin.com/plume-books-overview/; penguin.com/tiny-reparations-overview/, pg 62

Laytham, Ella, Random House Publishing Group, 1745 Broadway, New York, NY 10019 *Toll Free Tel:* 800-200-3552 *Web Site:* www.randomhousebooks.com, pg 171

Layton, Arthur B, Hutton Publishing, 12 Golden Hill St, Norwalk, CT 06854 *Tel:* 203-558-4478 *E-mail:* huttonbooks@hotmail.com, pg 97

Layton, Arthur B, Jones Hutton Literary Associates, 140D Heritage Village, Southbury, CT 06488 *Tel:* 203-558-4478 *E-mail:* huttonbooks@hotmail.com, pg 465

Lazar, Dan, Writers House, 21 W 26 St, New York, NY 10010 *Tel:* 212-685-2400 *Web Site:* www.writershouse.com, pg 482

Lazer, Jill, Houghton Mifflin Harcourt Trade & Reference Division, 125 High St, Boston, MA 02110 *Tel:* 617-351-5000 *Web Site:* www.hmhco.com, pg 96

Lazin, Sarah, Aevitas Creative Management LLC, 19 W 21 St, Suite 501, New York, NY 10010 *Tel:* 212-765-6900 *Web Site:* www.aevitascreative.com, pg 448

Le Blanc, Ondine E, The Massachusetts Historical Society, 1154 Boylston St, Boston, MA 02215-3695 *Tel:* 617-536-1608 *Fax:* 617-859-0074 *E-mail:* publications@masshist.org *Web Site:* www.masshist.org, pg 126

Le Brun, Paul, Brault & Bouthillier, 700 ave Beaumont, Montreal, QC H3N 1V5, Canada *Tel:* 514-273-9186 *Toll Free Tel:* 800-361-0378 *Fax:* 514-273-8627 *Toll Free Fax:* 800-361-0378 *E-mail:* communicationbb@bb.ca *Web Site:* bb.ca, pg 397

Le Guin, Elisabeth, The Ursula K Le Guin Prize for Fiction, 9450 SW Gemini Dr, PMB 51842, Beaverton, OR 97008-7105 *E-mail:* estateofukl@gmail.com *Web Site:* www.ursulakleguin.com/prize-overview, pg 622

Le, Loan, Atria Books, 1230 Avenue of the Americas, New York, NY 10020 *Tel:* 212-698-7000 *Fax:* 212-698-7007 *Web Site:* www.simonandschuster.com, pg 21

Le May, Konnie, Lake Superior Publishing LLC, 109 W Superior St, Suite 200, Duluth, MN 55802 *Tel:* 218-722-5002 *Toll Free Tel:* 888-BIG-LAKE (244-5253) *Fax:* 218-722-4096 *E-mail:* edit@lakesuperior.com *Web Site:* www.lakesuperior.com, pg 112

Le Ny, Jeanine, little bee books, 598 Broadway, 7th fl, New York, NY 10012 *Tel:* 212-321-0237 *Toll Free Tel:* 844-321-0237 *E-mail:* info@littlebeebooks.com; sales@littlebeebooks.com; publicity@littlebeebooks.com *Web Site:* littlebeebooks.com, pg 117

Le Pan, Don, Broadview Press, 280 Perry St, Unit 5, Peterborough, ON K9J 2J4, Canada *Tel:* 705-482-5915 *Fax:* 705-743-8353 *E-mail:* customerservice@broadviewpress.com *Web Site:* www.broadviewpress.com, pg 397

Le, Thao, Sandra Dijkstra Literary Agency, 1155 Camino del Mar, PMB 515, Del Mar, CA 92014-2605 *Web Site:* dijkstraagency.com, pg 456

Leach, Jeanette, Winterwolf Press, 8635 W Sahara Ave, Suite 425, Las Vegas, NV 89117 *Tel:* 725-222-3442 *E-mail:* info@winterwolfpress.com *Web Site:* winterwolfpress.com, pg 231

Leach, Joan, The Edna Staebler Award for Creative Non-Fiction, Office of the Dean, Faculty of Arts, 75 University Ave W, Waterloo, ON N2L 3C5, Canada *Tel:* 519-884-1970 (ext 3361) *E-mail:* staebleraward@wlu.ca *Web Site:* wlu.ca/staebleraward, pg 665

Leach, Kaitlin, Cambridge University Press, One Liberty Plaza, 20th fl, New York, NY 10006 *Tel:* 212-924-3900; 212-337-5000 *Fax:* 212-691-3239; 845-353-4141 *E-mail:* customer_service@cambridge.org; orders@cambridge.org; subscriptions_newyork@cambridge.org *Web Site:* www.cambridge.org/us, pg 39

Leach, Vicki, University of South Carolina Press, 1600 Hampton St, Suite 544, Columbia, SC 29208 *Tel:* 803-777-5245 *Toll Free Tel:* 800-768-2500 (orders) *Fax:* 803-777-0160 *Toll Free Fax:* 800-868-0740 (orders) *Web Site:* uscpress.com, pg 220

Leader-Picone, Whitney, Houghton Mifflin Harcourt Trade & Reference Division, 125 High St, Boston, MA 02110 *Tel:* 617-351-5000 *Web Site:* www.hmhco.com, pg 96

Leaf, Thalia, Astra Books for Young Readers, 19 W 21 St, No 1201, New York, NY 10010 *Tel:* 646-844-3485 *E-mail:* ahinfo@astrahouse.com; permissions@astrapublishinghouse.com *Web Site:* astrapublishinghouse.com, pg 20

Leaf, Thalia, Princeton University Press, 41 William St, Princeton, NJ 08540-5237 *Tel:* 609-258-4900 *Fax:* 609-258-6305 *E-mail:* info@press.princeton.edu *Web Site:* press.princeton.edu, pg 164

Leahy, Meaghan, Macmillan, 120 Broadway, 22nd fl, New York, NY 10271 *E-mail:* press.inquiries@macmillan.com *Web Site:* us.macmillan.com, pg 122

Leak, Katherine, Random House Publishing Group, 1745 Broadway, New York, NY 10019 *Toll Free Tel:* 800-200-3552 *Web Site:* www.randomhousebooks.com, pg 171

Leaman, George, Philosophy Documentation Center, PO Box 7147, Charlottesville, VA 22906-7147 *Tel:* 434-220-3300 *Toll Free Tel:* 800-444-2419 *Fax:* 434-220-3301 *E-mail:* order@pdcnet.org *Web Site:* www.pdcnet.org, pg 159

Leary, Alaina, WNDB Internship Grants, 10319 Westlake Dr, No 104, Bethesda, MD 20817 *Tel:* 701-404-WNDB (404-9632, voicemail only) *E-mail:* internships@diversebooks.org *Web Site:* diversebooks.org/our-programs/internship-grants, pg 676

Leary, Hillary, Workman Publishing, 1290 Avenue of the Americas, New York, NY 10104 *Toll Free Tel:* 800-759-0190 *Fax:* 212-364-0950 *E-mail:* workman-inquiry@hbgusa.com *Web Site:* www.hachettebookgroup.com/imprint/workman-publishing-company/, pg 233

Leary, Michael, US Government Publishing Office (GPO), Superintendent of Documents, 732 N Capitol St NW, Washington, DC 20401 *Tel:* 202-512-1800 *Toll Free Tel:* 866-512-1800 (orders) *Fax:* 202-512-1998 *E-mail:* contactcenter@gpo.gov *Web Site:* www.gpo.gov; bookstore.gpo.gov (sales), pg 223

Leavitt, Ned, The Ned Leavitt Agency, 752 Creeklocks Rd, Rosendale, NY 12472 *Tel:* 845-658-3333 *Web Site:* www.nedleavittagency.com, pg 467

Leavy, Matt, John Wiley & Sons Inc, 111 River St, Hoboken, NJ 07030-5774 *Tel:* 201-748-6000 *Toll Free Tel:* 800-225-5945 (cust serv) *Fax:* 201-748-6088 *Web Site:* www.wiley.com, pg 230

LeBaron, Susan, Wesleyan Publishing House, 13300 Olio Rd, Fishers, IN 46037 *Tel:* 317-774-3853 *Toll Free Tel:* 800-493-7539 *Fax:* 317-774-3865 *Toll Free Fax:* 800-788-3535 *E-mail:* wph@wesleyan.org *Web Site:* www.wesleyan.org/books, pg 227

LeBlanc, Camille, Viking Penguin, c/o Penguin Random House LLC, 1745 Broadway, New York, NY 10019 *Tel:* 212-782-9000 *Web Site:* www.penguin.com/overview-vikingbooks/; www.penguin.com/pamela-dorman-books-overview/; www.penguin.com/penguin-classics-overview/; www.penguin.com/penguin-life-overview/, pg 225

LeBlanc, Danielle, Canadian Independent Booksellers Association (CIBA), 188 Dublin St N, Guelph, ON N1H 4P2, Canada *E-mail:* info@cibabooks.ca *Web Site:* cibabooks.ca, pg 502

LeBlanc, Hailey, Penguin Random House Canada, a Penguin Random House company, 320 Front St W, Suite 1400, Toronto, ON M5V 3B6, Canada *Tel:* 416-364-4449 *Toll Free Tel:* 888-523-9292 (cust serv) *E-mail:* canadaweb@penguinrandomhouse.com; customerservicescanada@penguinrandomhouse.com *Web Site:* www.penguinrandomhouse.ca, pg 416

Leblanc, Kieran, Alberta Book Publishing Awards, 11759 Groat Rd NW, 2nd fl, Edmonton, AB T5M 3K6, Canada *Tel:* 780-424-5060 *E-mail:* info@bookpublishers.ab.ca *Web Site:* bookpublishers.ab.ca; www.readalberta.ca, pg 571

Leblanc, Kieran, The Book Publishers Association of Alberta (BPAA), 11759 Groat Rd NW, 2nd fl, Edmonton, AB T5M 3K6, Canada *Tel:* 780-424-5060 *E-mail:* info@bookpublishers.ab.ca *Web Site:* bookpublishers.ab.ca; www.readalberta.ca, pg 501

Lecht, Nicole, Sourcebooks LLC, 1935 Brookdale Rd, Suite 139, Naperville, IL 60563 *Tel:* 630-961-3900 *Toll Free Tel:* 800-432-7444 *Fax:* 630-961-2168 *E-mail:* info@sourcebooks.com *Web Site:* www.sourcebooks.com, pg 194

Leckie, Ross, Goose Lane Editions, 500 Beaverbrook Ct, Suite 330, Fredericton, NB E3B 5X4, Canada *Tel:* 506-450-4251 *Toll Free Tel:* 888-926-8377 *Fax:* 506-459-4991 *E-mail:* orders@gooselane.com *Web Site:* www.gooselane.com, pg 407

Leclerc, Dr Richard PhD, Editions du Bois-de-Coulonge, 1142 Ave de Montigny, Quebec, QC G1S 3T7, Canada *Web Site:* www.ebc.qc.ca, pg 396

LeCount, Andy, HarperCollins Publishers LLC, 195 Broadway, New York, NY 10007 *Tel:* 212-207-7000 *Web Site:* www.harpercollins.com, pg 86

Lecumberry, Michelle, Sourcebooks LLC, 1935 Brookdale Rd, Suite 139, Naperville, IL 60563 *Tel:* 630-961-3900 *Toll Free Tel:* 800-432-7444 *Fax:* 630-961-2168 *E-mail:* info@sourcebooks.com *Web Site:* www.sourcebooks.com, pg 195

Leczkowski, Jennifer, Running Press, 1290 Avenue of the Americas, New York, NY 10104 *Tel:* 212-364-1100 *Toll Free Tel:* 800-759-0190 (cust serv) *Fax:* 212-364-0933 (intl orders) *Toll Free Fax:* 800-286-9471 (cust serv) *E-mail:* customer.service@hbgusa.com; orders@hbgusa.com *Web Site:* www.hachettebookgroup.com/imprint/running-press/; www.moon.com (Moon Travel Guides), pg 178

Ledbetter, Jeana, Hachette Nashville, 6100 Tower Circle, Room 210, Franklin, TN 37067 *Tel:* 615-221-0996 *Fax:* 615-221-0962 *Web Site:* www.hachettebookgroup.com/imprint/hachette-nashville/, pg 83

Leder, Meg, Viking Penguin, c/o Penguin Random House LLC, 1745 Broadway, New York, NY 10019 *Tel:* 212-782-9000 *Web Site:* www.penguin.com/overview-vikingbooks/; www.penguin.com/pamela-dorman-books-overview/; www.penguin.com/penguin-classics-overview/; www.penguin.com/penguin-life-overview/, pg 225

Ledges, Tserenchunt, The Mongolia Society Inc, Indiana University, 703 Eigenmann Hall, 1900 E Tenth St, Bloomington, IN 47406-7512 *Tel:* 812-855-4078 *Fax:* 812-855-4078 *E-mail:* monsoc@indiana.edu *Web Site:* mongoliasociety.org, pg 133

Lee, Adam, Lasaria Creative Publishing, 4094 Majestic Lane, Suite 352, Fairfax, VA 22033 *E-mail:* info@lasariacreative.com *Web Site:* www.lasariacreative.com, pg 113

Lee, Allison, PEN America Los Angeles, 1370 N St Andrews Place, Los Angeles, CA 90028 *Tel:* 323-607-1867 *E-mail:* info@pen.org *Web Site:* pen.org, pg 516

Lee, Angela Seowon, Trident Media Group LLC, 355 Lexington Ave, 12th fl, New York, NY 10017 *Tel:* 212-333-1511 *E-mail:* info@tridentmediagroup.com; press@tridentmediagroup.com; foreignrights@tridentmediagroup.com; office.assistant@tridentmediagroup.com *Web Site:* www.tridentmediagroup.com, pg 480

Lee, Benjamin, Fine Creative Media, Inc, 589 Eighth Ave, 6th fl, New York, NY 10018 *Tel:* 212-595-3500 *Fax:* 212-202-4195 *E-mail:* info@mjfbooks.com, pg 72

Lee, Benjamin, Penguin Publishing Group, c/o Penguin Random House LLC, 1745 Broadway, New York, NY 10019 *Tel:* 212-782-9000 *Web Site:* www.penguin.com, pg 154

Lee, Calee, Xist Publishing, 24200 Southwest Fwy, Suite 402, PMB 290, Rosenberg, TX 77471 *Tel:* 949-478-2568 *E-mail:* info@xistpublishing.com *Web Site:* www.xistpublishing.com, pg 234

Lee, Celia, Simon & Schuster Children's Publishing, 1230 Avenue of the Americas, New York, NY 10020 *Tel:* 212-698-7000 *Web Site:* www.simonandschuster.com/kids; www.simonandschuster.com/teen; simonandschuster.net; simonandschuster.biz, pg 189

Lee, Chelsea, American Psychological Association, 750 First St NE, Washington, DC 20002 *Tel:* 202-336-5510 *Toll Free Tel:* 800-374-2721 *Fax:* 202-336-5502 *E-mail:* order@apa.org; booksales@apa.org *Web Site:* www.apa.org/books, pg 12

Lee, Cindy, Workman Publishing, 1290 Avenue of the Americas, New York, NY 10104 *Toll Free Tel:* 800-759-0190 *Fax:* 212-364-0950 *E-mail:* workman-inquiry@hbgusa.com *Web Site:* www.hachettebookgroup.com/imprint/workman-publishing-company/, pg 232

Lee, Denise, Penguin Random House Audio Publishing Group, 1745 Broadway, New York, NY 10019 *Toll Free Tel:* 800-793-2665 (cust serv) *E-mail:* audio@penguinrandomhouse.com; ecustomerservice@penguinrandomhouse.com *Web Site:* www.penguinrandomhouseaudio.com, pg 154

Lee, Elizabeth, Penguin Workshop, c/o Penguin Random House LLC, 1745 Broadway, New York, NY 10019 *Tel:* 212-782-9000 *Web Site:* www.penguin.com/publishers/penguinworkshop/, pg 156

Lee, Ellice, Philomel Books, c/o Penguin Random House LLC, 1745 Broadway, New York, NY 10019 *Tel:* 212-782-9000 *Web Site:* www.penguin.com/philomel/, pg 159

Lee, Helen, InterVarsity Press, 430 Plaza Dr, Westmont, IL 60559-1234 *Tel:* 630-734-4000 *Toll Free Tel:* 800-843-9487 *Fax:* 630-734-4200 *E-mail:* email@ivpress.com *Web Site:* www.ivpress.com, pg 104

Lee, Jacob, Xist Publishing, 24200 Southwest Fwy, Suite 402, PMB 290, Rosenberg, TX 77471 *Tel:* 949-478-2568 *E-mail:* info@xistpublishing.com *Web Site:* www.xistpublishing.com, pg 234

Lee, Jill LeMin, The Athenaeum Literary Award, 219 S Sixth St, Philadelphia, PA 19106-3794 *Tel:* 215-925-2688 *Web Site:* www.philaathenaeum.org/literary.html, pg 575

Lee, Jim, DC Comics Inc, 4000 Warner Blvd, Burbank, CA 91522 *Web Site:* www.dc.com, pg 58

Lee, Joe, McClelland & Stewart Ltd, 320 Front St W, Suite 1400, Toronto, ON M5V 3B6, Canada *Tel:* 416-364-4449 *Toll Free Tel:* 888-523-9292 *E-mail:* customerservicescanada@penguinrandomhouse.com; mcclellandsubmissions@prh.com *Web Site:* penguinrandomhouse.ca/imprints/mcclelland-stewart, pg 412

Lee, Joe, Penguin Random House Canada, a Penguin Random House company, 320 Front St W, Suite 1400, Toronto, ON M5V 3B6, Canada *Tel:* 416-364-4449 *Toll Free Tel:* 888-523-9292 (cust serv) *E-mail:* canadaweb@penguinrandomhouse.com; customerservicescanada@penguinrandomhouse.com *Web Site:* www.penguinrandomhouse.ca, pg 416

Lee, Julianna, Little, Brown and Company, 1290 Avenue of the Americas, New York, NY 10104 *Tel:* 212-364-1100 *Fax:* 212-364-0952 *E-mail:* firstname.lastname@hbgusa.com *Web Site:* www.hachettebookgroup.com/imprint/little-brown-and-company/, pg 118

Lee, Juwon, The Princeton Review, 110 E 42 St, 7th fl, New York, NY 10017 *Toll Free Tel:* 800-273-8439 (orders only) *Web Site:* www.princetonreview.com, pg 164

Lee, Ken, Michael Wiese Productions, 12400 Ventura Blvd, No 1111, Studio City, CA 91604 *Tel:* 818-379-8799 *Toll Free Tel:* 800-833-5738 (orders) *Fax:* 818-986-3408 *E-mail:* mwpsales@earthlink.net; fulfillment@portcity.com *Web Site:* www.mwp.com, pg 229

Lee, Lisa, Candied Plums, 7548 Ravenna Ave NE, Seattle, WA 98115 *E-mail:* candiedplums@gmail.com *Web Site:* www.candiedplums.com, pg 39

Lee, Lisa, Holiday House Publishing Inc, 50 Broad St, New York, NY 10004 *Tel:* 212-688-0085 *Fax:* 212-421-6134 *E-mail:* info@holidayhouse.com *Web Site:* www.holidayhouse.com, pg 94

Lee, Marie, The MIT Press, One Broadway, 12th fl, Cambridge, MA 02142 *Tel:* 617-253-5255 *Toll Free Tel:* 800-405-1619 (orders) *Fax:* 617-258-6779; 617-577-1545 (orders) *Web Site:* mitpress.mit.edu, pg 132

Lee, Mark, Doubleday, c/o Penguin Random House LLC, 1745 Broadway, New York, NY 10019 *Tel:* 212-751-2600 *Fax:* 212-940-7390 (dom rts); 212-572-2662 (foreign rts) *Web Site:* knopfdoubleday.com/imprint/doubleday/; knopfdoubleday.com, pg 61

Lee, Michelle, Dial Books for Young Readers, c/o Penguin Random House LLC, 1745 Broadway, New York, NY 10019 *Tel:* 212-782-9000 *Web Site:* www.penguin.com/dial-overview/, pg 59

Lee, Min, Hachette Book Group Inc, 1290 Avenue of the Americas, New York, NY 10104 *Tel:* 212-364-1100 *Toll Free Tel:* 800-759-0190 (cust serv) *Fax:* 212-364-0933 (intl orders) *Toll Free Fax:* 800-286-9471 (cust serv) *E-mail:* customer.service@hbgusa.com; orders@hbgusa.com *Web Site:* www.hachettebookgroup.com, pg 83

Lee, Nate, Harry N Abrams Inc, 195 Broadway, 9th fl, New York, NY 10007 *Tel:* 212-206-7715 *Toll Free Tel:* 800-345-1359 *Fax:* 212-645-8437 *E-mail:* abrams@abramsbooks.com; publicity@abramsbooks.com; sales@abramsbooks.com *Web Site:* www.abramsbooks.com, pg 3

Lee, Rachel, ANR Publications University of California, 2801 Second St, Davis, CA 95618 *Tel:* 530-400-0725 (cust serv) *Toll Free Tel:* 800-994-8849 *E-mail:* anrcatalog@ucanr.edu *Web Site:* anrcatalog.ucanr.edu, pg 14

Lee, Ray, Master Point Press, 214 Merton St, Suite 205, Toronto, ON M4S 1A6, Canada *Tel:* 647-956-4933 *E-mail:* info@masterpointpress.com *Web Site:* www.masterpointpress.com; www.ebooksbridge.com (ebook sales), pg 412

Lee, Ruby Rose, Henry Holt and Company, LLC, 120 Broadway, 23rd fl, New York, NY 10271 *Tel:* 646-307-5151 *Toll Free Tel:* 888-330-8477 (orders) *Fax:* 646-307-5285 *Web Site:* www.henryholt.com, pg 94

Lee, Sunny, Roaring Brook Press, 120 Broadway, New York, NY 10271 *Tel:* 646-307-5151 *Web Site:* us.macmillan.com/publishers/roaring-brook-press, pg 176

Lee, Suzan, Canadian Bookbinders and Book Artists Guild (CBBAG), 82809-467 Parliament St, Toronto, ON M5A 3Y2, Canada *E-mail:* cbbag@cbbag.ca *Web Site:* www.cbbag.ca, pg 502

Lee, Suzanne, Random House Children's Books, c/o Penguin Random House LLC, 1745 Broadway, New York, NY 10019 *Tel:* 212-782-9000 *Web Site:* www.rhcbooks.com, pg 170

Lee, Tiffany Tran, Asian American Writers' Workshop (AAWW), 112 W 27 St, Suite 600, New York, NY 10001 *Tel:* 212-494-0061 *E-mail:* desk@aaww.org *Web Site:* aaww.org; facebook.com/AsianAmericanWritersWorkshop, pg 497

Lee, Vivian, Little, Brown and Company, 1290 Avenue of the Americas, New York, NY 10104 *Tel:* 212-364-1100 *Fax:* 212-364-0952 *E-mail:* firstname.lastname@hbgusa.com *Web Site:* www.hachettebookgroup.com/imprint/little-brown-and-company/, pg 118

Lee, Young, Berghahn Books, 20 Jay St, Suite 512, Brooklyn, NY 11201 *Tel:* 212-233-6004 *Fax:* 212-233-6007 *E-mail:* info@berghahnbooks.com; salesus@berghahnbooks.com; editorial@journals.berghahnbooks.com *Web Site:* www.berghahnbooks.com, pg 28

Leep, Jennifer, Revell, Publishing Div, 6030 E Fulton Rd, Ada, MI 49301 *Tel:* 616-676-9185 *Toll Free Tel:* 800-877-2665 (orders only) *Fax:* 616-676-9573 *Toll Free Fax:* 800-398-3111 (orders only) *E-mail:* media@bakerpublishinggroup.com; orders@bakerpublishinggroup.com; sales@bakerpublishinggroup.com *Web Site:* www.bakerpublishinggroup.com/revell, pg 174

LeFavour, Harriet, Bloomsbury Publishing Inc, 1385 Broadway, 5th fl, New York, NY 10018 *Tel:* 212-419-5300 *E-mail:* marketingusa@bloomsbury.com; adultpublicityusa@bloomsbury.com; askacademic@bloomsbury.com *Web Site:* www.bloomsbury.com, pg 32

Lefebvre, Marie-Eve, Editions du CHU Sainte-Justine, 3175, chemin de la Cote-Sainte-Catherine, Montreal, QC H3T 1C5, Canada *Tel:* 514-345-4671 *Fax:* 514-345-4631 *E-mail:* edition.hsj@ssss.gouv.qc.ca *Web Site:* www.editions-chu-sainte-justine.org, pg 402

Lefebvre, Sebastian, Les Editions du Boreal, 4447, rue St-Denis, Montreal, QC H2J 2L2, Canada *Tel:* 514-287-7401 *Fax:* 514-287-7664 *E-mail:* info@editionsboreal.qc.ca; boreal@editionsboreal.qc.ca; communications@editionsboreal.qc.ca *Web Site:* www.editionsboreal.qc.ca, pg 402

Leffel, Caitlin, Union Square & Co, 1166 Avenue of the Americas, 17th fl, New York, NY 10036-2715 *Tel:* 212-532-7160 *Toll Free Tel:* 800-367-9692 *Fax:* 212-213-2495 *Toll Free Fax:* 800-542-7567 *E-mail:* custservice@sterlingpublishing.com; customerservice@sterlingpublishing.com; editorial@sterlingpublishing.com; tradesales@sterlingpublishing.com *Web Site:* www.sterlingpublishing.com, pg 212

Leffmann, Laurel, Summertime Publications Inc, 4115 E Palo Verde Dr, Phoenix, AZ 85018 *E-mail:* summertime.publications@gmail.com *Web Site:* www.summertimepublications.com, pg 200

LeGeyt, Curtis, National Association of Broadcasters (NAB), One "M" St SE, Washington, DC 20003 *Tel:* 202-429-5300 *E-mail:* nab@nab.org *Web Site:* www.nab.org, pg 136, 511

Lehman, Michelle, National Association of Broadcasters (NAB), One "M" St SE, Washington, DC 20003 *Tel:* 202-429-5300 *E-mail:* nab@nab.org *Web Site:* www.nab.org, pg 136, 511

Lehman, Sarah, Random House Publishing Group, 1745 Broadway, New York, NY 10019 *Toll Free Tel:* 800-200-3552 *Web Site:* www.randomhousebooks.com, pg 171

Lehmann, Tara, Harry N Abrams Inc, 195 Broadway, 9th fl, New York, NY 10007 *Tel:* 212-206-7715 *Toll Free Tel:* 800-345-1359 *Fax:* 212-645-8437 *E-mail:* abrams@abramsbooks.com; publicity@abramsbooks.com; sales@abramsbooks.com *Web Site:* www.abramsbooks.com, pg 3

Lehr, Donald, The Betsy Nolan Literary Agency, 112 E 17 St, Suite 1W, New York, NY 10003 *Tel:* 212-967-8200 *Web Site:* www.nolanlehrgroup.com, pg 471

Lehr, James, TCU Press, 3000 Sandage Ave, Fort Worth, TX 76109 *Tel:* 817-257-7822 *E-mail:* tcupress@tcu.edu *Web Site:* www.tcupress.com, pg 203

Lehrman, Maggie, Harry N Abrams Inc, 195 Broadway, 9th fl, New York, NY 10007 *Tel:* 212-206-7715 *Toll Free Tel:* 800-345-1359 *Fax:* 212-645-8437 *E-mail:* abrams@abramsbooks.com; publicity@abramsbooks.com; sales@abramsbooks.com *Web Site:* www.abramsbooks.com, pg 2

Leichum, Laura, University of Chicago Press, 1427 E 60 St, Chicago, IL 60637-2954 *Tel:* 773-702-7700; 773-702-7600 *Toll Free Tel:* 800-621-2736 (orders) *Fax:* 773-702-9756; 773-660-2235 (orders); 773-702-2708 *E-mail:* custserv@press.uchicago.edu; marketing@press.uchicago.edu *Web Site:* www.press.uchicago.edu, pg 215

Leidich, Terri, WriteLife Publishing, Wilkinson Pass Lane, Waynesville, NC 28786 *E-mail:* writelife@boutiqueofqualitybooks.com *Web Site:* www.writelife.com; www.facebook.com/writelife, pg 234

Leifso, Brenda, Brick Books, 22 Spencer Ave, Toronto, ON M6K 2J6, Canada *Tel:* 416-455-8385 *Web Site:* www.brickbooks.ca, pg 397

LeJeune, Becky, Bond Literary Agency, 201 Milwaukee St, Suite 200, Denver, CO 80206 *Tel:* 303-781-9305 *Web Site:* bondliteraryagency.com, pg 450

Lellos, Stacy, Workman Publishing, 1290 Avenue of the Americas, New York, NY 10104 *Toll Free Tel:* 800-759-0190 *Fax:* 212-364-0950 *E-mail:* workman-inquiry@hbgusa.com *Web Site:* www.hachettebookgroup.com/imprint/workman-publishing-company/, pg 232

Lema, Evelyn, Harry N Abrams Inc, 195 Broadway, 9th fl, New York, NY 10007 *Tel:* 212-206-7715 *Toll Free Tel:* 800-345-1359 *Fax:* 212-645-8437

E-mail: abrams@abramsbooks.com; publicity@abramsbooks.com; sales@abramsbooks.com *Web Site:* www.abramsbooks.com, pg 3

Lemari, Marion, Austin Area Translators & Interpreters Association (AATIA), PO Box 92334, Austin, TX 78709-2334 *E-mail:* info@aatia.org; communications@aatia.org; membership@aatia.org; finance@aatia.org; profdev@aatia.org *Web Site:* aatia.org, pg 500

Lemay, Dominique, Editions Hurtubise, 1815, ave de Lorimier, Montreal, QC H2K 3W6, Canada *Tel:* 514-523-1523 *Toll Free Tel:* 800-361-1664 *Web Site:* editionshurtubise.com, pg 403

Lemay, Dominique, Editions MultiMondes, 1815, Avenue de Lorimier, Montreal, QC H2K 3W6, Canada *Tel:* 514-523-1523 *Toll Free Tel:* 800-361-1664 *Web Site:* editionsmultimondes.com, pg 404

Lemieux, Raymond, Editions MultiMondes, 1815, Avenue de Lorimier, Montreal, QC H2K 3W6, Canada *Tel:* 514-523-1523 *Toll Free Tel:* 800-361-1664 *Web Site:* editionsmultimondes.com, pg 404

Lemmer, John, Inter-University Consortium for Political & Social Research (ICPSR), 330 Packard St, Ann Arbor, MI 48104 *Tel:* 734-647-5000; 734-647-2200 *Fax:* 734-647-8200 *E-mail:* icpsr-help@umich.edu *Web Site:* www.icpsr.umich.edu, pg 102

Lemmons, Dr Thom, Texas A&M University Press, John H Lindsey Bldg, Lewis St, 4354 TAMU, College Station, TX 77843-4354 *Tel:* 979-845-1436 *Toll Free Tel:* 800-826-8911 (orders) *Fax:* 979-847-8752 *Toll Free Fax:* 888-617-2421 (orders) *E-mail:* bookorders@tamu.edu *Web Site:* www.tamupress.com, pg 205

LeMoal, Lara, Greystone Books Ltd, 343 Railway St, Suite 302, Vancouver, BC V6A 1A4, Canada *Tel:* 604-875-1550 *Fax:* 604-875-1556 *E-mail:* info@greystonebooks.com; rights@greystonebooks.com *Web Site:* www.greystonebooks.com, pg 407

Lemon, Carolyn, Ignatius Press, 1348 Tenth Ave, San Francisco, CA 94122-2304 *Toll Free Tel:* 800-651-1531 (orders); 888-615-3186 (cust serv) *Fax:* 415-387-0896 *E-mail:* info@ignatius.com *Web Site:* www.ignatius.com, pg 98

Lencicki, Alex, Orbit, 1290 Avenue of the Americas, New York, NY 10104 *Tel:* 212-364-1100 *Toll Free Tel:* 800-759-0190 *Web Site:* www.orbitbooks.net; www.hachettebookgroup.com/imprint/orbit, pg 147

Lengronne, Catherine, Berrett-Koehler Publishers Inc, 1333 Broadway, Suite 1000, Oakland, CA 94612 *Tel:* 510-817-2277 *Fax:* 510-817-2278 *E-mail:* bkpub@bkpub.com *Web Site:* www.bkconnection.com, pg 29

Lengyel, Heather, Paul H Brookes Publishing Co Inc, PO Box 10624, Baltimore, MD 21285-0624 *Tel:* 410-337-9580 (outside US & CN) *Toll Free Tel:* 800-638-3775 (US & CN) *Fax:* 410-337-8539 *E-mail:* custserv@brookespublishing.com *Web Site:* www.brookespublishing.com, pg 37

Lennard, Jeff, Brethren Press, 1451 Dundee Ave, Elgin, IL 60120 *Tel:* 847-742-5100 *Toll Free Tel:* 800-441-3712 *Toll Free Fax:* 800-667-8188 *E-mail:* brethrenpress@brethren.org *Web Site:* www.brethrenpress.com, pg 36

Lennertz, Carl, CBC Diversity Outstanding Achievement Awards, 54 W 39 St, 14th fl, New York, NY 10018 *E-mail:* cbc.info@cbcbooks.org *Web Site:* www.cbcbooks.org, pg 587

Lennertz, Carl, The Children's Book Council (CBC), 54 W 39 St, 14th fl, New York, NY 10018 *E-mail:* cbc.info@cbcbooks.org *Web Site:* www.cbcbooks.org, pg 503

Lennertz, Carl, Anna Dewdney Read Together Award, 54 W 39 St, 14th fl, New York, NY 10018 *Web Site:* everychildareader.net/anna, pg 595

Lennon, Margaret, Workman Publishing, 1290 Avenue of the Americas, New York, NY 10104 *Toll Free Tel:* 800-759-0190 *Fax:* 212-364-0950 *E-mail:* workman-inquiry@hbgusa.com *Web Site:* www.hachettebookgroup.com/imprint/workman-publishing-company/, pg 232

Lentz, Dr Cheryl, The Lentz Leadership Institute LLC, 540 Arlington Lane, Grayslake, IL 60030 *Tel:* 702-719-9214 *E-mail:* orders@lentzleadership.com *Web Site:* www.lentzleadership.com; www.refractivethinker.com; www.pensieropress.com; www.narratorepress.com, pg 115

Leo, April, The Geological Society of America Inc (GSA), 3300 Penrose Place, Boulder, CO 80301-1806 *Tel:* 303-357-1000 *Toll Free Tel:* 800-472-1988 *Fax:* 303-357-1070 *E-mail:* pubs@geosociety.org (prodn); editing@geosociety.org (edit); books@geosociety.org; gsaservice@geosociety.org (sales & serv) *Web Site:* www.geosociety.org, pg 77

Leo, Michelle, Simon & Schuster Children's Publishing, 1230 Avenue of the Americas, New York, NY 10020 *Tel:* 212-698-7000 *Web Site:* www.simonandschuster.com/kids; www.simonandschuster.com/teen; simonandschuster.net; simonandschuster.biz, pg 189

Leo, Michelle, Simon & Schuster, LLC, 1230 Avenue of the Americas, New York, NY 10020 *Tel:* 212-698-7000 *Toll Free Tel:* 800-223-2336 (orders) *Fax:* 212-698-7007 *Toll Free Fax:* 800-943-9831 (orders) *E-mail:* firstname.lastname@simonandschuster.com; purchaseorders@simonandschuster.com (orders) *Web Site:* www.simonandschuster.com, pg 189

Leon, Karina, Atria Books, 1230 Avenue of the Americas, New York, NY 10020 *Tel:* 212-698-7000 *Fax:* 212-698-7007 *Web Site:* www.simonandschuster.com, pg 21

Leonard, Alexandria, Princeton University Press, 41 William St, Princeton, NJ 08540-5237 *Tel:* 609-258-4900 *Fax:* 609-258-6305 *E-mail:* info@press.princeton.edu *Web Site:* press.princeton.edu, pg 164

Leonard, Connor, Harry N Abrams Inc, 195 Broadway, 9th fl, New York, NY 10007 *Tel:* 212-206-7715 *Toll Free Tel:* 800-345-1359 *Fax:* 212-645-8437 *E-mail:* abrams@abramsbooks.com; publicity@abramsbooks.com; sales@abramsbooks.com *Web Site:* www.abramsbooks.com, pg 3

Leonard, John-Paul, Progressive Press, 4028 Texas St, No 7, San Diego, CA 92104 *E-mail:* info@progressivepress.com *Web Site:* www.progressivepress.com, pg 165

Leonard, Kristi, RISING STAR Award, PO Box 190, Jefferson, OR 97352 *E-mail:* risingstar@womenfictionwriters.org *Web Site:* wfwa.memberclicks.net/rising-star-award, pg 656

Leonard, Kristi, STAR Award, PO Box 190, Jefferson, OR 97352 *E-mail:* staraward@womenfictionwriters.org *Web Site:* wfwa.memberclicks.net/star-award, pg 666

Leonard, Kristi, Women's Fiction Writers Association (WFWA), PO Box 190, Jefferson, OR 97352 *E-mail:* communications@womensfictionwriters.org; membership@womensfictionwriters.org; programs@womensfictionwriters.org *Web Site:* www.womensfictionwriters.org, pg 522

Leonard, Mark, Association for Intelligent Information Management (AIIM), 8403 Colesville Rd, No 1100, Silver Spring, MD 20910 *Tel:* 301-587-8202 *Toll Free Tel:* 800-477-2446 *Fax:* 301-587-2711 *E-mail:* hello@aiim.org *Web Site:* www.aiim.org, pg 498

Leonard, Sara, Viking Penguin, c/o Penguin Random House LLC, 1745 Broadway, New York, NY 10019 *Tel:* 212-782-9000 *Web Site:* www.penguin.com/overview-vikingbooks/; www.penguin.com/pamela-dorman-books-overview/; www.penguin.com/penguin-classics-overview/; www.penguin.com/penguin-life-overview/, pg 225

Leonards, David, International Entertainment Bureau, 3618 N Washington Blvd, Indianapolis, IN 46205 *Tel:* 317-926-7566 *E-mail:* ieb@prodigy.net, pg 487

Leone, Dan, ReferencePoint Press Inc, 17150 Via del Campo, Suite 205, San Diego, CA 92127 *Tel:* 858-618-1314 *Toll Free Tel:* 888-479-6436 *Fax:* 858-618-1730 *E-mail:* info@referencepointpress.com *Web Site:* www.referencepointpress.com, pg 173

Leopard, Bones, Random House Publishing Group, 1745 Broadway, New York, NY 10019 *Toll Free Tel:* 800-200-3552 *Web Site:* www.randomhousebooks.com, pg 171

Leopard, Whitney, Random House Children's Books, c/o Penguin Random House LLC, 1745 Broadway, New York, NY 10019 *Tel:* 212-782-9000 *Web Site:* www.rhcbooks.com, pg 170

Leporati, Gabrielle, Little, Brown and Company, 1290 Avenue of the Americas, New York, NY 10104 *Tel:* 212-364-1100 *Fax:* 212-364-0952 *E-mail:* firstname.lastname@hbgusa.com *Web Site:* www.hachettebookgroup.com/imprint/little-brown-and-company/, pg 118

Leppig, Angela, Gallaudet University Press, 800 Florida Ave NE, Washington, DC 20002-3695 *Tel:* 202-651-5488 *Fax:* 202-651-5489 *E-mail:* gupress@gallaudet.edu *Web Site:* gupress.gallaudet.edu, pg 76

Leppig, Jason, Island Press, 2000 "M" St NW, Suite 480-B, Washington, DC 20036 *Tel:* 202-232-7933 *Toll Free Tel:* 800-621-2736 *Fax:* 202-234-1328 *E-mail:* info@islandpress.org *Web Site:* www.islandpress.org, pg 104

Lerner, Adam, Carolrhoda Books Inc, 241 First Ave N, Minneapolis, MN 55401 *Tel:* 612-332-3344 *Toll Free Tel:* 800-328-4929 *Fax:* 612-332-7615 *Toll Free Fax:* 800-332-1132 *E-mail:* info@lernerbooks.com; custserve@lernerbooks.com *Web Site:* www.lernerbooks.com; www.facebook.com/lernerbooks, pg 41

Lerner, Adam, Carolrhoda Lab™, 241 First Ave N, Minneapolis, MN 55401 *Tel:* 612-332-3344 *Toll Free Tel:* 800-328-4929 *Fax:* 612-332-7615 *Toll Free Fax:* 800-332-1132 *E-mail:* info@lernerbooks.com; custserve@lernerbooks.com *Web Site:* www.lernerbooks.com; www.facebook.com/lernerbooks, pg 41

Lerner, Adam, ediciones Lerner, 241 First Ave N, Minneapolis, MN 55401 *Tel:* 612-332-3344 *Toll Free Tel:* 800-328-4929 *Fax:* 612-332-7615 *Toll Free Fax:* 800-332-1132 *E-mail:* info@lernerbooks.com; custserve@lernerbooks.com *Web Site:* www.lernerbooks.com; www.facebook.com/lernerbooks, pg 63

Lerner, Adam, First Avenue Editions, 241 First Ave N, Minneapolis, MN 55401 *Tel:* 612-332-3344 *Toll Free Tel:* 800-328-4929 *Fax:* 612-332-7615 *Toll Free Fax:* 800-332-1132 *E-mail:* info@lernerbooks.com; custserve@lernerbooks.com *Web Site:* www.lernerbooks.com; www.facebook.com/lernerbooks, pg 72

Lerner, Adam, Graphic Universe™, 241 First Ave N, Minneapolis, MN 55401 *Tel:* 612-332-3344 *Toll Free Tel:* 800-328-4929 *Fax:* 612-332-7615 *Toll Free Fax:* 800-332-1132 *E-mail:* info@lernerbooks.com; custserve@lernerbooks.com *Web Site:* www.lernerbooks.com; www.facebook.com/lernerbooks, pg 80

Lerner, Adam, Kar-Ben Publishing, 241 First Ave N, Minneapolis, MN 55401 *Tel:* 612-332-3344 *Toll Free Tel:* 800-4-KARBEN (452-7236) *Fax:* 612-332-7615 *Toll Free Fax:* 800-332-1132 *E-mail:* custserve@karben.com *Web Site:* www.karben.com, pg 108

Lerner, Adam, Lerner Publications, 241 First Ave N, Minneapolis, MN 55401 *Tel:* 612-332-3344 *Toll Free Tel:* 800-328-4929 *Fax:* 612-332-7615 *Toll Free Fax:* 800-332-1132 *E-mail:* info@lernerbooks.com; custserve@lernerbooks.com *Web Site:* www.lernerbooks.com; www.facebook.com/lernerbooks, pg 115

Lerner, Adam, Lerner Publishing Group Inc, 241 First Ave N, Minneapolis, MN 55401 *Tel:* 612-332-3344 *Toll Free Tel:* 800-328-4929 *Fax:* 612-332-7615 *Toll Free Fax:* 800-332-1132 *E-mail:* info@lernerbooks.com; custserve@lernerbooks.com *Web Site:* www.lernerbooks.com; www.facebook.com/lernerbooks, pg 115

Lerner, Adam, LernerClassroom, 241 First Ave N, Minneapolis, MN 55401 *Tel:* 612-332-3344 *Toll Free Tel:* 800-328-4929 *Fax:* 612-332-7615 *Toll Free Fax:* 800-332-1132 *E-mail:* info@lernerbooks.

com; custserve@lernerbooks.com *Web Site:* www.lernerbooks.com; www.facebook.com/lernerbooks, pg 115

Lerner, Adam, Millbrook Press, 241 First Ave N, Minneapolis, MN 55401 *Tel:* 612-332-3344 *Toll Free Tel:* 800-328-4929 *Fax:* 612-332-7615 *Toll Free Fax:* 800-332-1132 *E-mail:* info@lernerbooks.com; custserve@lernerbooks.com *Web Site:* www.lernerbooks.com; www.facebook.com/millbrookpress, pg 131

Lerner, Adam, Twenty-First Century Books, 241 First Ave N, Minneapolis, MN 55401 *Tel:* 612-332-3344 *Toll Free Tel:* 800-328-4929 *Fax:* 612-332-7615 *Toll Free Fax:* 800-332-1132 *E-mail:* info@lernerbooks.com; custserve@lernerbooks.com *Web Site:* www.lernerbooks.com; www.facebook.com/lernerbooks, pg 211

Lerner, Adam, Zest Books, 241 First Ave N, Minneapolis, MN 55401 *Tel:* 612-332-3344 *Toll Free Tel:* 800-328-4929 *Toll Free Fax:* 800-332-1132 *E-mail:* info@lernerbooks.com; publicity@lernerbooks.com; custserve@lernerbooks.com (orders) *Web Site:* lernerbooks.com, pg 236

Lerner, Betsy, Dunow, Carlson & Lerner Literary Agency Inc, 27 W 20 St, Suite 1107, New York, NY 10011 *Tel:* 212-645-7606 *E-mail:* mail@dclagency.com *Web Site:* www.dclagency.com, pg 457

Lerner, Harry J, Carolrhoda Books Inc, 241 First Ave N, Minneapolis, MN 55401 *Tel:* 612-332-3344 *Toll Free Tel:* 800-328-4929 *Fax:* 612-332-7615 *Toll Free Fax:* 800-332-1132 *E-mail:* info@lernerbooks.com; custserve@lernerbooks.com *Web Site:* www.lernerbooks.com; www.facebook.com/lernerbooks, pg 41

Lerner, Harry J, Carolrhoda Lab™, 241 First Ave N, Minneapolis, MN 55401 *Tel:* 612-332-3344 *Toll Free Tel:* 800-328-4929 *Fax:* 612-332-7615 *Toll Free Fax:* 800-332-1132 *E-mail:* info@lernerbooks.com; custserve@lernerbooks.com *Web Site:* www.lernerbooks.com; www.facebook.com/lernerbooks, pg 41

Lerner, Harry J, ediciones Lerner, 241 First Ave N, Minneapolis, MN 55401 *Tel:* 612-332-3344 *Toll Free Tel:* 800-328-4929 *Fax:* 612-332-7615 *Toll Free Fax:* 800-332-1132 *E-mail:* info@lernerbooks.com; custserve@lernerbooks.com *Web Site:* www.lernerbooks.com; www.facebook.com/lernerbooks, pg 63

Lerner, Harry J, First Avenue Editions, 241 First Ave N, Minneapolis, MN 55401 *Tel:* 612-332-3344 *Toll Free Tel:* 800-328-4929 *Fax:* 612-332-7615 *Toll Free Fax:* 800-332-1132 *E-mail:* info@lernerbooks.com; custserve@lernerbooks.com *Web Site:* www.lernerbooks.com; www.facebook.com/lernerbooks, pg 72

Lerner, Harry J, Graphic Universe™, 241 First Ave N, Minneapolis, MN 55401 *Tel:* 612-332-3344 *Toll Free Tel:* 800-328-4929 *Fax:* 612-332-7615 *Toll Free Fax:* 800-332-1132 *E-mail:* info@lernerbooks.com; custserve@lernerbooks.com *Web Site:* www.lernerbooks.com; www.facebook.com/lernerbooks, pg 80

Lerner, Harry J, Kar-Ben Publishing, 241 First Ave N, Minneapolis, MN 55401 *Tel:* 612-332-3344 *Toll Free Tel:* 800-4-KARBEN (452-7236) *Fax:* 612-332-7615 *Toll Free Fax:* 800-332-1132 *E-mail:* custserve@karben.com *Web Site:* www.karben.com, pg 108

Lerner, Harry J, Lerner Publications, 241 First Ave N, Minneapolis, MN 55401 *Tel:* 612-332-3344 *Toll Free Tel:* 800-328-4929 *Fax:* 612-332-7615 *Toll Free Fax:* 800-332-1132 *E-mail:* info@lernerbooks.com; custserve@lernerbooks.com *Web Site:* www.lernerbooks.com; www.facebook.com/lernerbooks, pg 115

Lerner, Harry J, Lerner Publishing Group Inc, 241 First Ave N, Minneapolis, MN 55401 *Tel:* 612-332-3344 *Toll Free Tel:* 800-328-4929 *Fax:* 612-332-7615 *Toll Free Fax:* 800-332-1132 *E-mail:* info@lernerbooks.com; custserve@lernerbooks.com *Web Site:* www.lernerbooks.com; www.facebook.com/lernerbooks, pg 115

Lerner, Harry J, LernerClassroom, 241 First Ave N, Minneapolis, MN 55401 *Tel:* 612-332-3344 *Toll Free Tel:* 800-328-4929 *Fax:* 612-332-7615 *Toll Free Fax:* 800-332-1132 *E-mail:* info@lernerbooks.com; custserve@lernerbooks.com *Web Site:* www.lernerbooks.com; www.facebook.com/lernerbooks, pg 115

Lerner, Harry J, Millbrook Press, 241 First Ave N, Minneapolis, MN 55401 *Tel:* 612-332-3344 *Toll Free Tel:* 800-328-4929 *Fax:* 612-332-7615 *Toll Free Fax:* 800-332-1132 *E-mail:* info@lernerbooks.com; custserve@lernerbooks.com *Web Site:* www.lernerbooks.com; www.facebook.com/millbrookpress, pg 131

Lerner, Harry J, Twenty-First Century Books, 241 First Ave N, Minneapolis, MN 55401 *Tel:* 612-332-3344 *Toll Free Tel:* 800-328-4929 *Fax:* 612-332-7615 *Toll Free Fax:* 800-332-1132 *E-mail:* info@lernerbooks.com; custserve@lernerbooks.com *Web Site:* www.lernerbooks.com; www.facebook.com/lernerbooks, pg 211

Lerner, Harry J, Zest Books, 241 First Ave N, Minneapolis, MN 55401 *Tel:* 612-332-3344 *Toll Free Tel:* 800-328-4929 *Toll Free Fax:* 800-332-1132 *E-mail:* info@lernerbooks.com; publicity@lernerbooks.com; custserve@lernerbooks.com (orders) *Web Site:* lernerbooks.com, pg 236

Lerner, Mark, Fordham University Press, Joseph A Martino Hall, 45 Columbus Ave, 3rd fl, New York, NY 10023 *Fax:* 347-842-3083 *Web Site:* www.fordhampress.com, pg 73

LeSage, Danielle, Penguin Random House Canada, a Penguin Random House company, 320 Front St W, Suite 1400, Toronto, ON M5V 3B6, Canada *Tel:* 416-364-4449 *Toll Free Tel:* 888-523-9292 (cust serv) *E-mail:* canadaweb@penguinrandomhouse.com; customerservicescanada@penguinrandomhouse.com *Web Site:* www.penguinrandomhouse.ca, pg 416

Lescaze, Alexandra, Hillman Prizes for Journalism, 330 W 42 St, Suite 900, New York, NY 10036 *Tel:* 646-448-6413 *Web Site:* www.hillmanfoundation.org, pg 613

Lescht, Jamie, Avery, c/o Penguin Random House LLC, 1745 Broadway, New York, NY 10019 *Tel:* 212-366-2000 *Web Site:* www.penguin.com/avery-overview/, pg 23

Lescht, Jamie, TarcherPerigee, c/o Penguin Random House LLC, 1745 Broadway, New York, NY 10019 *Tel:* 212-782-9000 *Web Site:* www.penguin.com/tarcherperigee-overview/; www.facebook.com/TarcherPerigee, pg 203

Leseul, Erwan, Flammarion Quebec, 3700A, Blvd Saint-Laurent, Montreal, QC H2X 2V4, Canada *Tel:* 514-499-1002 *Fax:* 514-499-1002 *E-mail:* info@flammarion.qc.ca *Web Site:* flammarionquebec.com, pg 406

Leslie, Nathan, Hamilton Stone Editions, PO Box 43, Maplewood, NJ 07040 *Tel:* 973-378-8361 *E-mail:* hstone@hamiltonstone.org *Web Site:* www.hamiltonstone.org, pg 84

Lessne, Donald L, Frederick Fell Publishers Inc, 1403 Shoreline Way, Hollywood, FL 33019 *Tel:* 954-925-5242 *E-mail:* fellpub@aol.com (admin only) *Web Site:* www.fellpub.com, pg 74

Lester, Liz, The University of Arkansas Press, McIlroy House, 105 N McIlroy Ave, Fayetteville, AR 72701 *Tel:* 479-575-7544 *E-mail:* info@uapress.com *Web Site:* www.uapress.com, pg 214

Letso, Chris, Macmillan, 120 Broadway, 22nd fl, New York, NY 10271 *E-mail:* press.inquiries@macmillan.com *Web Site:* us.macmillan.com, pg 122

Lett, Ivan, Basic Books Group, 1290 Avenue of the Americas, New York, NY 10104 *Tel:* 212-340-8100 *Toll Free Tel:* 800-343-4499 (cust serv) *Fax:* 212-340-8105 *E-mail:* customer.service@hbgusa.com; orders@hbgusa.com *Web Site:* www.hachettebookgroup.com/imprint/basic-books/, pg 25

Lettice, Jenna, Random House Children's Books, c/o Penguin Random House LLC, 1745 Broadway, New York, NY 10019 *Tel:* 212-782-9000 *Web Site:* www.rhcbooks.com, pg 170

Letz, Renee, Sourcebooks LLC, 1935 Brookdale Rd, Suite 139, Naperville, IL 60563 *Tel:* 630-961-3900 *Toll Free Tel:* 800-432-7444 *Fax:* 630-961-2168 *E-mail:* info@sourcebooks.com *Web Site:* www.sourcebooks.com, pg 194

Leu, Chelsea, National Book Critics Circle (NBCC), c/o Jacob M Appel, Icahn School of Medicine at Mount Sinai, One Gustave L Levy Place, New York, NY 10029 *E-mail:* info@bookcritics.org; membership@bookcritics.org *Web Site:* www.bookcritics.org, pg 512

Leung, Julie, Random House Publishing Group, 1745 Broadway, New York, NY 10019 *Toll Free Tel:* 800-200-3552 *Web Site:* www.randomhousebooks.com, pg 171

Leung, Katrina, James Beard Foundation Book Awards, 167 W 12 St, New York, NY 10011 *Tel:* 212-627-2308 *E-mail:* awards@jamesbeard.org *Web Site:* www.jamesbeard.org/awards, pg 578

Leung, Phil, Penguin Random House LLC, 1745 Broadway, New York, NY 10019 *Tel:* 212-782-9000 *Toll Free Tel:* 800-726-0600 *Web Site:* www.penguinrandomhouse.com, pg 155

Leurpecht, Dr Christian, Institute of Intergovernmental Relations, Queen's University, Robert Sutherland Hall, Rm 412, Kingston, ON K7L 3N6, Canada *Tel:* 613-533-2080 *E-mail:* iigr@queensu.ca *Web Site:* www.queensu.ca/iigr, pg 410

Levasseur, Stephanie, Sourcebooks LLC, 1935 Brookdale Rd, Suite 139, Naperville, IL 60563 *Tel:* 630-961-3900 *Toll Free Tel:* 800-432-7444 *Fax:* 630-961-2168 *E-mail:* info@sourcebooks.com *Web Site:* www.sourcebooks.com, pg 194

Levay, Rachael, Princeton University Press, 41 William St, Princeton, NJ 08540-5237 *Tel:* 609-258-4900 *Fax:* 609-258-6305 *E-mail:* info@press.princeton.edu *Web Site:* press.princeton.edu, pg 164

Levenberg, Rachel, HarperCollins Publishers LLC, 195 Broadway, New York, NY 10007 *Tel:* 212-207-7000 *Web Site:* www.harpercollins.com, pg 86

Levens, Rachel, Annual Off Off Broadway Short Play Festival, 250 W 57 St, 6th fl, New York, NY 10107-0102 *Toll Free Tel:* 866-979-0447 *E-mail:* oobfestival@samuelfrench; info@concordtheatricals.com; oobfestival@concordtheatricals.com; www.concordtheatricals.com, pg 643

Levenson, Roy, AIP Publishing LLC, 1305 Walt Whitman Rd, Suite 110, Melville, NY 11747 *Tel:* 516-576-2200 *E-mail:* help@aip.org; press@aip.org; rights@aip.org *Web Site:* www.aip.org; publishing.aip.org, pg 6

Levenstein, Maggie, Inter-University Consortium for Political & Social Research (ICPSR), 330 Packard St, Ann Arbor, MI 48104 *Tel:* 734-647-5000; 734-647-2200 *Fax:* 734-647-8200 *E-mail:* icpsr-help@umich.edu *Web Site:* www.icpsr.umich.edu, pg 102

Leventhal, Philip, Columbia University Press, 61 W 62 St, New York, NY 10023 *Tel:* 212-459-0600 *Toll Free Tel:* 800-944-8648 *Fax:* 212-459-3678 *Web Site:* cup.columbia.edu, pg 51

Leverton, Yossi, Hachai Publishing, 527 Empire Blvd, Brooklyn, NY 11225 *Tel:* 718-633-0100 *Fax:* 718-633-0103 *E-mail:* info@hachai.com *Web Site:* www.hachai.com, pg 83

Levesque, Brigit, Broquet Inc, 97-B, Montee des Bouleaux, St-Constant, QC J5A 1A9, Canada *Tel:* 450-638-3338 *Fax:* 450-638-4338 *E-mail:* info@broquet.qc.ca *Web Site:* www.broquet.qc.ca, pg 397

Levesque, Jennifer, Disney-Hyperion Books, 1101 Flower St, Glendale, CA 91201 *Web Site:* books.disney.com/imprint/disney-hyperion, pg 59

Levesque, Jennifer, Disney Publishing Worldwide, 1101 Flower St, Glendale, CA 91201 *Web Site:* books.disney.com, pg 60

Levi, Katie, The Art Institute of Chicago, 111 S Michigan Ave, Chicago, IL 60603-6404 *Tel:* 312-443-3600 *Toll Free Tel:* 855-301-9612 *E-mail:* aicshop@artic.edu *Web Site:* www.artic.edu/print-publications; shop.artic.edu, pg 17

Levia, Anna, AJL Judaica Bibliography Award, PO Box 1118, Teaneck, NJ 07666 *Tel:* 201-371-3255 *E-mail:* info@jewishlibraries.org *Web Site:* jewishlibraries.org, pg 571

Levia, Anna, AJL Judaica Reference Award, PO Box 1118, Teaneck, NJ 07666 *Tel:* 201-371-3255 *E-mail:* info@jewishlibraries.org *Web Site:* jewishlibraries.org, pg 571

Levick, Alexandra, Writers House, 21 W 26 St, New York, NY 10010 *Tel:* 212-685-2400 *Web Site:* www.writershouse.com, pg 482

Levin, Kendra, Simon & Schuster Children's Publishing, 1230 Avenue of the Americas, New York, NY 10020 *Tel:* 212-698-7000 *Web Site:* www.simonandschuster.com/kids; www.simonandschuster.com/teen; simonandschuster.net; simonandschuster.biz, pg 189

Levine, Deborah, The Jeff Herman Agency LLC, 29 Park St, Stockbridge, MA 01262 *Tel:* 413-298-0077 *Web Site:* www.jeffherman.com, pg 463

Levine, Ellen, Trident Media Group LLC, 355 Lexington Ave, 12th fl, New York, NY 10017 *Tel:* 212-333-1511 *E-mail:* info@tridentmediagroup.com; press@tridentmediagroup.com; foreignrights@tridentmediagroup.com; office.assistant@tridentmediagroup.com *Web Site:* www.tridentmediagroup.com, pg 480

Levine, Ellie, Phaidon, 65 Bleecker St, 8th fl, New York, NY 10012 *Tel:* 212-652-5400 *Toll Free Tel:* 800-759-0190 (cust serv) *Fax:* 212-652-5410 *Toll Free Fax:* 800-286-9471 (cust serv) *E-mail:* enquiries@phaidon.com *Web Site:* www.phaidon.com, pg 159

Levine, James, Levine|Greenberg|Rostan Literary Agency, 307 Seventh Ave, Suite 2407, New York, NY 10001 *Tel:* 212-337-0934 *Fax:* 212-337-0948 *E-mail:* submit@lgrliterary.com *Web Site:* lgrliterary.com, pg 467

Levine, Jeffrey, Dorset Prize, 60 Roberts Dr, Suite 308, North Adams, MA 01247 *Tel:* 413-664-9611 *Fax:* 413-664-9711 *E-mail:* info@tupelopress.org *Web Site:* www.tupelopress.org, pg 596

Levine, Jeffrey, Tupelo Press Berkshire Prize for a First or Second Book of Poetry, 60 Roberts Dr, Suite 308, North Adams, MA 01247 *Tel:* 413-664-9611 *Fax:* 413-664-9711 *E-mail:* info@tupelopress.org *Web Site:* www.tupelopress.org, pg 671

Levine, Jeffrey, Tupelo Press Inc, 60 Roberts Dr, Suite 308, North Adams, MA 01247 *Tel:* 413-664-9611 *Fax:* 413-664-9711 *E-mail:* info@tupelopress.org *Web Site:* www.tupelopress.org, pg 210

Levine, Jeffrey, Tupelo Press Snowbound Series Chapbook Award, 60 Roberts Dr, Suite 308, North Adams, MA 01247 *Tel:* 413-664-9611 *Fax:* 413-664-9711 *E-mail:* info@tupelopress.org *Web Site:* www.tupelopress.org, pg 671

Levine, Karen, University of Chicago Press, 1427 E 60 St, Chicago, IL 60637-2954 *Tel:* 773-702-7700; 773-702-7600 *Toll Free Tel:* 800-621-2736 (orders) *Fax:* 773-702-9756; 773-660-2235 (orders); 773-702-2708 *E-mail:* custserv@press.uchicago.edu; marketing@press.uchicago.edu *Web Site:* www.press.uchicago.edu, pg 215

Levine, Michael, Westwood Creative Artists Ltd, 386 Huron St, Toronto, ON M5S 2G6, Canada *Tel:* 416-964-3302 *Fax:* 416-964-3302 *E-mail:* wca_office@wcaltd.com *Web Site:* www.wcaltd.com, pg 481

Levine, Nathalie, Princeton University Press, 41 William St, Princeton, NJ 08540-5237 *Tel:* 609-258-4900 *Fax:* 609-258-6305 *E-mail:* info@press.princeton.edu *Web Site:* press.princeton.edu, pg 164

Levine, Ronn, AM&P Network, 1620 "I" St NW, Suite 501, Washington, DC 20005 *Tel:* 202-289-7442 *Fax:* 202-289-7097 *Web Site:* www.siia.net/amp-network, pg 494

Levinson, Diane, Chronicle Books LLC, 680 Second St, San Francisco, CA 94107 *Tel:* 415-537-4200 *Fax:* 415-537-4460 (perms) *E-mail:* hello@chroniclebooks.com; subrights@chroniclebooks.com *Web Site:* www.chroniclebooks.com, pg 47

Levinson, Meagan, Cornell University Press, Sage House, 512 E State St, Ithaca, NY 14850 *Tel:* 607-253-2338 *E-mail:* cupressinfo@cornell.edu; cupress-sales@cornell.edu; cupress-perms@cornell.edu (reprint/class use permissions) *Web Site:* www.cornellpress.cornell.edu, pg 52

Levinson, Wendy, Harvey Klinger Inc, 300 W 55 St, Suite 11V, New York, NY 10019 *Tel:* 212-581-7068 *Fax:* 212-315-3823 *E-mail:* queries@harveyklinger.com *Web Site:* www.harveyklinger.com, pg 465

Levitan, Jeanie, Bear & Co Inc, One Park St, Rochester, VT 05767 *Tel:* 802-767-3174 *Toll Free Tel:* 800-932-3277 *Fax:* 802-767-3726 *E-mail:* customerservice@InnerTraditions.com *Web Site:* InnerTraditions.com, pg 26

Levitan, Jeanie, Inner Traditions International Ltd, One Park St, Rochester, VT 05767 *Tel:* 802-767-3174 *Toll Free Tel:* 800-246-8648 *Fax:* 802-767-3726 *E-mail:* customerservice@InnerTraditions.com *Web Site:* www.InnerTraditions.com, pg 101

Levite, Lauren, HarperCollins Children's Books, 195 Broadway, New York, NY 10007 *Tel:* 212-207-7000 *Web Site:* www.harpercollins.com/childrens, pg 85

Levithan, David, Scholastic Trade Publishing, 557 Broadway, New York, NY 10012 *Tel:* 212-343-6100; 212-343-4685 (export sales) *Fax:* 212-343-4714 (export sales) *Web Site:* www.scholastic.com, pg 184

Levitt, Sarah, Aevitas Creative Management LLC, 19 W 21 St, Suite 501, New York, NY 10010 *Tel:* 212-765-6900 *Web Site:* www.aevitascreative.com, pg 448

Levy, Emma, Soho Press Inc, 853 Broadway, New York, NY 10003 *Tel:* 212-260-1900 *E-mail:* soho@sohopress.com; publicity@sohopress.com *Web Site:* sohopress.com, pg 193

Levy, Jeanette, Bloomsbury Publishing Inc, 1385 Broadway, 5th fl, New York, NY 10018 *Tel:* 212-419-5300 *E-mail:* marketingusa@bloomsbury.com; adultpublicityusa@bloomsbury.com; askacademic@bloomsbury.com *Web Site:* www.bloomsbury.com, pg 31

Levy, Michael, Corporation for Public Broadcasting (CPB), 401 Ninth St NW, Washington, DC 20004-2129 *Tel:* 202-879-9600 *E-mail:* press@cpb.org *Web Site:* cpb.org, pg 504

Levy, Roanie, Access Copyright, The Canadian Copyright Licensing Agency, 69 Younge St, Suite 1100, Toronto, ON M5E 1K3, Canada *Tel:* 416-868-1620 *Toll Free Tel:* 800-893-5777 *Fax:* 416-868-1621 *E-mail:* info@accesscopyright.ca *Web Site:* www.accesscopyright.ca, pg 493

Lew, Cheryl, Little, Brown Books for Young Readers (LBYR), 1290 Avenue of the Americas, New York, NY 10104 *Tel:* 212-364-1100 *Toll Free Tel:* 800-759-0190 (cust serv) *E-mail:* rights@lbchildrens.com *Web Site:* www.hachettebookgroup.com/imprint/little-brown-books-for-young-readers/, pg 118

Lew, Kimberly, Grand Central Publishing, 1290 Avenue of the Americas, New York, NY 10104 *Tel:* 212-364-1100 *Web Site:* www.hachettebookgroup.com/imprint/grand-central-publishing/, pg 80

Lewandoski, Joyce, University of Texas Press, 3001 Lake Austin Blvd, 2.200, Austin, TX 78703 *Tel:* 512-471-7233 *Fax:* 512-232-7178 *E-mail:* utpress@uts.cc.utexas.edu; info@utpress.utexas.edu *Web Site:* utpress.utexas.edu, pg 205

Lewis, Alison, Frances Goldin Literary Agency, Inc, 214 W 29 St, Suite 410, New York, NY 10001 *Tel:* 212-777-0047 *Fax:* 212-228-1660 *E-mail:* agency@goldinlit.com *Web Site:* www.goldinlit.com, pg 460

Lewis, Allison, Sourcebooks LLC, 1935 Brookdale Rd, Suite 139, Naperville, IL 60563 *Tel:* 630-961-3900 *Toll Free Tel:* 800-432-7444 *Fax:* 630-961-2168 *E-mail:* info@sourcebooks.com *Web Site:* www.sourcebooks.com, pg 194

Lewis, Beth, Protestant Church-Owned Publishers Association, 841 Mount Clinton Pike, Suite D, Harrisonburg, VA 22802 *Web Site:* www.pcpaonline.org, pg 518

Lewis, BiBi, Ethan Ellenberg Literary Agency, 548 Broadway, Apt 5C, New York, NY 10012 *Tel:* 212-431-4554 *E-mail:* agent@ethanellenberg.com *Web Site:* www.ethanellenberg.com, pg 458

Lewis, Brent, Harlequin Enterprises Ltd, Bay Adelaide Centre, East Tower, 22 Adelaide St W, 41st fl, Toronto, ON M5H 4E3, Canada *Tel:* 416-445-5860 *Toll Free Tel:* 888-432-4879; 800-370-5838 (ebook inquiries) *E-mail:* customerservice@harlequin.com *Web Site:* www.harlequin.com, pg 409

Lewis, Dave, Baker Books, 6030 E Fulton Rd, Ada, MI 49301 *Tel:* 616-676-9185 *Toll Free Tel:* 800-877-2665 (orders) *Fax:* 616-676-9573 *Toll Free Fax:* 800-398-3111 (orders) *E-mail:* media@bakerpublishinggroup.com; orders@bakerpublishinggroup.com; sales@bakerpublishinggroup.com *Web Site:* www.bakerpublishinggroup.com, pg 23

Lewis, Dave, Bethany House Publishers, 11400 Hampshire Ave S, Bloomington, MN 55438 *Tel:* 952-829-2500 *Toll Free Tel:* 800-877-2665 (orders) *Fax:* 952-829-2568 *Toll Free Fax:* 800-398-3111 (orders) *Web Site:* www.bethanyhouse.com; www.bakerpublishinggroup.com, pg 29

Lewis, David, Association of School Business Officials International, 44790 Maynard Sq, Suite 200, Ashburn, VA 20147 *Tel:* 703-478-0405 *Toll Free Tel:* 866-682-2729 *Fax:* 703-478-0205; 703-708-7060 (membership) *E-mail:* asboreq@asbointl.org; membership@asbointl.org *Web Site:* www.asbointl.org, pg 20

Lewis, David, Buchwald, 10 E 44 St, New York, NY 10017 *Tel:* 212-867-1200 *E-mail:* info@buchwald.com *Web Site:* www.buchwald.com, pg 453

Lewis, Jack, Hewitt Homeschooling Resources, 8117 N Division, Suite D, Spokane, WA 99208 *Toll Free Tel:* 800-348-1750 *Fax:* 360-835-8697 *E-mail:* sales@hewitthomeschooling.com *Web Site:* hewitthomeschooling.com, pg 91

Lewis, Jennifer, Gryphon House Inc, 6848 Leon's Way, Lewisville, NC 27023 *Toll Free Tel:* 800-638-0928 *Toll Free Fax:* 877-638-7576 *E-mail:* info@ghbooks.com *Web Site:* www.gryphonhouse.com, pg 82

Lewis, John, Savvas Learning Co LLC, 15 E Midland Ave, Suite 502, Paramus, NJ 07652 *Toll Free Tel:* 800-848-9500 *Web Site:* www.savvas.com, pg 183

Lewis, Kate, Institute for Immigration Research New American Voices Award, 4400 University Dr, MS 3E4, Fairfax, VA 22030 *Tel:* 703-993-3986 *E-mail:* submissions@fallforthebook.org *Web Site:* fallforthebook.org/aboutnewamericanvoices, pg 617

Lewis, Katie, Princeton University Press, 41 William St, Princeton, NJ 08540-5237 *Tel:* 609-258-4900 *Fax:* 609-258-6305 *E-mail:* info@press.princeton.edu *Web Site:* press.princeton.edu, pg 164

Lewis, Maya, Grand Central Publishing, 1290 Avenue of the Americas, New York, NY 10104 *Tel:* 212-364-1100 *Web Site:* www.hachettebookgroup.com/imprint/grand-central-publishing/, pg 80

Lewis, Nora, College of Liberal & Professional Studies, University of Pennsylvania, 3440 Market St, Suite 100, Philadelphia, PA 19104-3335 *Tel:* 215-898-7326 *Fax:* 215-573-2053 *E-mail:* lps@sas.upenn.edu *Web Site:* www.upenn.edu/lps, pg 561

Lewis, Penelope, AIP Publishing LLC, 1305 Walt Whitman Rd, Suite 110, Melville, NY 11747 *Tel:* 516-576-2200 *E-mail:* help@aip.org; rights@aip.org *Web Site:* www.aip.org; publishing.aip.org, pg 6

Lewis, Rick, Martin Literary Management, 914 164 St SE, Suite B12, Box 307, Mill Creek, WA 98012 *Tel:* 206-466-1773 (no phone queries) *Web Site:* www.martinliterarymanagement.com, pg 469

Lewis, Stacey, City Lights Publishers, 261 Columbus Ave, San Francisco, CA 94133 *Tel:* 415-362-8193 *E-mail:* staff@citylights.com *Web Site:* citylights.com, pg 48

Lewis, Stephanie, Highlights for Children Inc, 815 Church St, Honesdale, PA 18431 *Tel:* 570-253-1164 *Toll Free Tel:* 800-490-5111 *Fax:* 570-253-0179 *E-mail:* salesandmarketing@highlightspress.com *Web Site:* www.highlightspress.com; www.highlights.com; www.facebook.com/HighlightsforChildren, pg 92

Lewis, Tanisha, American Association for the Advancement of Science (AAAS), 1200 New York Ave NW, Washington, DC 20005 *Tel:* 202-326-6400 *E-mail:* membership@aaas.org *Web Site:* www.aaas.org, pg 494

Lewter, Jela, Simon & Schuster, 1230 Avenue of the Americas, New York, NY 10020 *Tel:* 212-698-7000 *Toll Free Tel:* 800-223-2348 (cust serv); 800-223-2336 (orders) *Toll Free Fax:* 800-943-9831 (orders) *Web Site:* simonandschusterpublishing.com/simonandschuster/, pg 188

Leydig, Dana, Viking Children's Books, c/o Penguin Random House LLC, 1745 Broadway, New York, NY 10019 *Tel:* 212-782-9000 *Web Site:* www.penguin.com/viking-childrens-books-overview/, pg 224

Leyendecker, Cassidy, Macmillan, 120 Broadway, 22nd fl, New York, NY 10271 *E-mail:* press.inquiries@macmillan.com *Web Site:* us.macmillan.com, pg 122

Lhotsky, Gregg, B&A, 433 Broadway, Suite 420, New York, NY 10013 *Tel:* 212-682-1490 *E-mail:* info@ba-reps.com *Web Site:* www.ba-reps.com, pg 485

Li, Jen Jie, Random House Children's Books, c/o Penguin Random House LLC, 1745 Broadway, New York, NY 10019 *Tel:* 212-782-9000 *Web Site:* www.rhcbooks.com, pg 170

Li, Johanna, Simon & Schuster, 1230 Avenue of the Americas, New York, NY 10020 *Tel:* 212-698-7000 *Toll Free Tel:* 800-223-2348 (cust serv); 800-223-2336 (orders) *Toll Free Fax:* 800-943-9831 (orders) *Web Site:* simonandschusterpublishing.com/simonandschuster/, pg 188

Li, Karen, Groundwood Books, 128 Sterling Rd, Lower Level, Toronto, ON M6R 2B7, Canada *Tel:* 416-363-4343 *Fax:* 416-363-1017 *E-mail:* customerservice@houseofanansi.com *Web Site:* www.houseofanansi.com, pg 407

Li, Stephanie, National Music Publishers' Association (NMPA), 1900 "N" St NW, Suite 500, Washington, DC 20036 *Tel:* 202-393-6672 *E-mail:* members@nmpa.org *Web Site:* nmpa.org, pg 513

Li, Vivian, Grouse Grind Lit Prize for V Short Form, University of British Columbia, Buch E462, 1866 Main Mall, Vancouver, BC V6T 1Z1, Canada *Tel:* 604-822-2514 *Fax:* 604-822-3616 *E-mail:* promotions@prismmagazine.ca *Web Site:* www.prismmagazine.ca/contests, pg 609

Li, Vivian, The Pacific Spirit Poetry Prize, University of British Columbia, Buch E462, 1866 Main Mall, Vancouver, BC V6T 1Z1, Canada *Tel:* 604-822-2514 *Fax:* 604-822-3616 *E-mail:* promotions@prismmagazine.ca *Web Site:* www.prismmagazine.ca/contests, pg 645

Li, Vivian, PRISM international Creative Nonfiction Contest, University of British Columbia, Buch E462, 1866 Main Mall, Vancouver, BC V6T 1Z1, Canada *Tel:* 604-822-2514 *Fax:* 604-822-3616 *E-mail:* promotions@prismmagazine.ca *Web Site:* www.prismmagazine.ca/contests, pg 653

Li, Vivian, The Jacob Zilber Prize for Short Fiction, University of British Columbia, Buch E462, 1866 Main Mall, Vancouver, BC V6T 1Z1, Canada *Tel:* 604-822-2514 *Fax:* 604-822-3616 *E-mail:* promotions@prismmagazine.ca *Web Site:* www.prismmagazine.ca/contests, pg 680

Liao, Tiffany, Random House Children's Books, c/o Penguin Random House LLC, 1745 Broadway, New York, NY 10019 *Tel:* 212-782-9000 *Web Site:* www.rhcbooks.com, pg 170

Liberati, Maria, Art of Living, PrimaMedia Inc, 1250 Bethlehem Pike, Suite 241, Hatfield, PA 19440 *Tel:* 267-421-7326 *E-mail:* info@artoflivingprimamedia.com *Web Site:* artoflivingprimamedia.com, pg 17

Libertini, Kathryn, Chronicle Books LLC, 680 Second St, San Francisco, CA 94107 *Tel:* 415-537-4200 *Fax:* 415-537-4460 (perms) *E-mail:* hello@chroniclebooks.com; subrights@chroniclebooks.com *Web Site:* www.chroniclebooks.com, pg 48

Licon, Carina, Henry Holt and Company, LLC, 120 Broadway, 23rd fl, New York, NY 10271 *Tel:* 646-307-5151 *Toll Free Tel:* 888-330-8477 (orders) *Fax:* 646-307-5285 *Web Site:* www.henryholt.com, pg 94

Liebenthal, Ellen, National Cartoonists Society (NCS), PO Box 592927, Orlando, FL 32859-2927 *Tel:* 407-994-6703 *E-mail:* info@nationalcartoonists.com; membership@nationalcartoonists.com *Web Site:* www.nationalcartoonists.com, pg 512

Lieberman, Beth, The Editors Circle, 24 Holly Circle, Easthampton, MA 01027 *Tel:* 862-596-9709 *E-mail:* query@theeditorscircle.com *Web Site:* www.theeditorscircle.com, pg 438

Lieberman, Robert H, Robert Lieberman Agency, 475 Nelson Rd, Ithaca, NY 14850 *Tel:* 607-273-8801 *Web Site:* roberthlieberman.com, pg 467

Lieberman, Sarah, Simon & Schuster Audio, 1230 Avenue of the Americas, New York, NY 10020 *Web Site:* audio.simonandschuster.com, pg 189

Lieberman, Stefanie, Janklow & Nesbit Associates, 285 Madison Ave, 21st fl, New York, NY 10017 *Tel:* 212-421-1700 *Fax:* 212-355-1403 *E-mail:* info@janklow.com; submissions@janklow.com; filmtvrights@janklow.com *Web Site:* www.janklowandnesbit.com, pg 464

Liebert, Mary Ann, Mary Ann Liebert Inc, 140 Huguenot St, 3rd fl, New Rochelle, NY 10801-5215 *Tel:* 914-740-2100 *Toll Free Tel:* 800-654-3237 *Fax:* 914-740-2101 *E-mail:* info@liebertpub.com *Web Site:* www.liebertonline.com, pg 116

Liebling, Sara, Disney-Hyperion Books, 1101 Flower St, Glendale, CA 91201 *Web Site:* books.disney.com/imprint/disney-hyperion, pg 59

Liebmann, Nicholas, St Herman Press, 4430 Mushroom Lane, Platina, CA 96076 *Tel:* 530-352-4430 *Fax:* 530-352-4432 *E-mail:* stherman@stherman.com *Web Site:* www.sainthermanmonastery.com, pg 180

Liebmann, Ruth, Penguin Random House LLC, 1745 Broadway, New York, NY 10019 *Tel:* 212-782-9000 *Toll Free Tel:* 800-726-0600 *Web Site:* www.penguinrandomhouse.com, pg 155

Liese, Debra, Princeton University Press, 41 William St, Princeton, NJ 08540-5237 *Tel:* 609-258-4900 *Fax:* 609-258-6305 *E-mail:* info@press.princeton.edu *Web Site:* press.princeton.edu, pg 164

Liese, Donna, Princeton University Press, 41 William St, Princeton, NJ 08540-5237 *Tel:* 609-258-4900 *Fax:* 609-258-6305 *E-mail:* info@press.princeton.edu *Web Site:* press.princeton.edu, pg 164

Light, Tan, The Literary Press Group of Canada, 234 Eglinton Ave E, Suite 401, Toronto, ON M4P 1K5, Canada *Tel:* 416-483-1321 *Fax:* 416-483-2510 *E-mail:* sales@lpg.ca *Web Site:* www.lpg.ca, pg 509

Lightner, Carrie, Sun Valley Writers' Conference (SVWC), Galleria Bldg, 2nd fl, 351 Leadville Ave N, Ketchum, ID 83340 *Tel:* 208-726-5454 *E-mail:* info@svwc.com *Web Site:* svwc.com, pg 558

Likoff, Laurie, Bloom's Literary Criticism, 132 W 31 St, 16th fl, New York, NY 10001 *Tel:* 212-967-8800 *Toll Free Tel:* 800-322-8755 *Toll Free Fax:* 800-678-3633 *E-mail:* custserv@infobase.com *Web Site:* www.infobasepublishing.com; www.infobase.com (online resources), pg 31

Likoff, Laurie, Chelsea House, 132 W 31 St, 16th fl, New York, NY 10001 *Toll Free Tel:* 800-322-8755 *Toll Free Fax:* 800-678-3633 *E-mail:* custserv@infobase.com; info@infobase.com *Web Site:* www.infobasepublishing.com; www.infobase.com (online resources), pg 46

Likoff, Laurie, Facts On File, 1000 N West St, Suite 1281-230, Wilmington, DE 19801 *Tel:* 212-967-8800 *Toll Free Tel:* 800-322-8755 *Toll Free Fax:* 800-678-3633 *E-mail:* custserv@factsonfile.com *Web Site:* infobasepublishing.com, pg 69

Likoff, Laurie, Ferguson Publishing, 132 W 31 St, 16 fl, New York, NY 10001 *Tel:* 212-967-8800 *Toll Free Tel:* 800-322-8755 *Toll Free Fax:* 800-678-3633 *E-mail:* custserv@infobase.com *Web Site:* infobasepublishing.com, pg 71

Lilian, Farnaz, Penguin Random House Canada, a Penguin Random House company, 320 Front St W, Suite 1400, Toronto, ON M5V 3B6, Canada *Tel:* 416-364-4449 *Toll Free Tel:* 888-523-9292 (cust serv) *E-mail:* canadaweb@penguinrandomhouse.com; customerservicescanada@penguinrandomhouse.com *Web Site:* www.penguinrandomhouse.ca, pg 416

Lilley, Gary Copeland, Port Townsend Writers Conference, 223 Battery Way, Port Townsend, WA 98368 *Tel:* 360-385-3102 *Fax:* 360-385-2470 *E-mail:* info@centrum.org *Web Site:* centrum.org, pg 557

Lilly, Aida, Duende-Word BIPOC Bookseller Award, 757 E 20 Ave, Suite 370-335, Denver, CO 80205 *E-mail:* info@thewordfordiversity.org *Web Site:* www.thewordfordiversity.org/booksellerward, pg 597

Lilly, Aida, The Word, A Storytelling Sanctuary Inc, 757 E 20 Ave, Suite 370-335, Denver, CO 80205 *E-mail:* info@thewordfordiversity.org *Web Site:* www.thewordfordiversity.org, pg 522

Lilly, Greg, Writers & Readers Days, PO Box 801, Abingdon, VA 24212 *Tel:* 276-623-5266 *E-mail:* info@vahighlandsfestival.org *Web Site:* www.vahighlandsfestival.com, pg 558

Lilly, Heidi, Random House Publishing Group, 1745 Broadway, New York, NY 10019 *Toll Free Tel:* 800-200-3552 *Web Site:* www.randomhousebooks.com, pg 171

Lim, Alicia, The Feminist Press at The City University of New York, 365 Fifth Ave, Suite 5406, New York, NY 10016 *Tel:* 212-817-7915 *Fax:* 212-817-1593 *E-mail:* info@feministpress.org *Web Site:* www.feministpress.org, pg 71

Lim, Jasmine, Andrews McMeel Publishing LLC, 1130 Walnut St, Kansas City, MO 64106-2109 *Tel:* 816-581-7500 *Toll Free Tel:* 800-851-8923 *Web Site:* www.andrewsmcmeel.com; publishing.andrewsmcmeel.com, pg 14

Lim, Reg, Chronicle Books LLC, 680 Second St, San Francisco, CA 94107 *Tel:* 415-537-4200 *Fax:* 415-537-4460 (perms) *E-mail:* hello@chroniclebooks.com; subrights@chroniclebooks.com *Web Site:* www.chroniclebooks.com, pg 48

Lim, Regina, Sudden Fiction Contest, c/o ASUC Publications, Univ of California, 10-B Eshleman Hall, Berkeley, CA 94720-4500 *E-mail:* berkeleyfictionreview@gmail.com *Web Site:* berkeleyfictionreview.org, pg 667

Lim, Young, St Martin's Press, LLC, 120 Broadway, New York, NY 10271 *E-mail:* publicity@stmartins.com; trademarketing@stmartins.com; foreignrights@stmartins.com *Web Site:* us.macmillan.com/smp, pg 181

Lima, Ricky, House of Anansi Press Inc, 128 Sterling Rd, Lower Level, Toronto, ON M6R 2B7, Canada *Tel:* 416-363-4343 *Fax:* 416-363-1017 *E-mail:* customerservice@houseofanansi.com *Web Site:* houseofanansi.com, pg 409

Liming, Garra, American Society for Nondestructive Testing, 1201 Dublin Rd, Suite G04, Columbus, OH 43215 *Toll Free Tel:* 800-222-2768 *E-mail:* customersupport@asnt.org *Web Site:* www.asnt.org; source.asnt.org (orders); asntmediaplanner.com (ad & sponsored content), pg 12

Lin, Alice, The Arion Press, The Presidio, 1802 Hays St, San Francisco, CA 94129 *Tel:* 415-668-2542 *Fax:* 415-668-2550 *E-mail:* arionpress@arionpress.com *Web Site:* www.arionpress.com, pg 17

Lin, Tricia, Random House Children's Books, c/o Penguin Random House LLC, 1745 Broadway, New York, NY 10019 *Tel:* 212-782-9000 *Web Site:* www.rhcbooks.com, pg 170

Linares, Mariana, House of Anansi Press Inc, 128 Sterling Rd, Lower Level, Toronto, ON M6R 2B7, Canada *Tel:* 416-363-4343 *Fax:* 416-363-1017 *E-mail:* customerservice@houseofanansi.com *Web Site:* houseofanansi.com, pg 409

Linden, Judy, Stonesong, 270 W 39 St, Suite 201, New York, NY 10018 *Tel:* 212-929-4600 *E-mail:* editors@stonesong.com *Web Site:* www.stonesong.com, pg 478

Lindensmith, Chris, Bitingduck Press LLC, 1262 Sunnyoaks Circle, Altadena, CA 91001 *Tel:* 626-507-8033 *E-mail:* notifications@bitingduckpress.com *Web Site:* bitingduckpress.com, pg 30

Lindensmith, Chris, Boson Books™, 1262 Sunnyoaks Circle, Altadena, CA 91001 *Tel:* 626-507-8033 *Fax:* 626-818-1842 *Web Site:* bitingduckpress.com, pg 34

Lindgren, Pat, Lindgren & Smith, 888C Eighth Ave, No 329, New York, NY 10019 *Tel:* 212-397-7330 *E-mail:* info@lindgrensmith.com; hello@lindgrensmith.com *Web Site:* lindgrensmith.com, pg 485

Lindman, Kim, Stonesong, 270 W 39 St, Suite 201, New York, NY 10018 *Tel:* 212-929-4600 *E-mail:* editors@stonesong.com *Web Site:* www.stonesong.com, pg 478

Lindner, Stefanie, HarperCollins Publishers LLC, 195 Broadway, New York, NY 10007 *Tel:* 212-207-7000 *Web Site:* www.harpercollins.com, pg 86

Lindquist, Evert A, Institute of Public Administration of Canada, 1075 Bay St, Suite 401, Toronto, ON M5S 2B1, Canada *Tel:* 416-924-8787 *Fax:* 416-924-4992 *E-mail:* ntl@ipac.ca *Web Site:* www.ipac.ca, pg 410

Lindquist, Gina, American Society of Civil Engineers (ASCE), 1801 Alexander Bell Dr, Reston, VA 20191-4400 *Tel:* 703-295-6300 *Toll Free Tel:* 800-548-ASCE (548-2723) *Toll Free Fax:* 866-913-6085 *E-mail:* ascelibrary@asce.org; pubsful@asce.org *Web Site:* www.asce.org, pg 12

Lindquist, Greta, Stanford University Press, 425 Broadway St, Redwood City, CA 94063-3126 *Tel:* 650-723-9434 *Fax:* 650-725-3457 *E-mail:* info@www.sup.org; publicity@www.sup.org; sales@www.sup.org *Web Site:* www.sup.org, pg 197

Lindsay, Elizabeth, Alfred A Knopf, c/o Penguin Random House LLC, 1745 Broadway, New York, NY 10019 *Tel:* 212-751-2600 *Fax:* 212-940-7390 (dom rts); 212-572-2662 (foreign rts) *Web Site:* knopfdoubleday.com/imprint/knopf/; knopfdoubleday.com, pg 110

Lindsay, James, Coach House Books, 80 bpNichol Lane, Toronto, ON M5S 3J4, Canada *Tel:* 416-979-2217 *Toll Free Tel:* 800-367-6360 (outside Toronto) *Fax:* 416-977-1158 *E-mail:* mail@chbooks.com *Web Site:* www.chbooks.com, pg 400

Lindsay, Matthew, Dayton Playhouse FutureFest, PO Box 3017, Dayton, OH 45401-3017 *Tel:* 937-424-8477 *Fax:* 937-424-0062 *E-mail:* futurefest@daytonplayhouse.com *Web Site:* wordpress.thedaytonplayhouse.com/future-fest-2, pg 595

Lindsay, Nick, The MIT Press, One Broadway, 12th fl, Cambridge, MA 02142 *Tel:* 617-253-5255 *Toll Free Tel:* 800-405-1619 (orders) *Fax:* 617-258-6779; 617-577-1545 (orders) *Web Site:* mitpress.mit.edu, pg 132

Lindsey, Chandler, Gaylord College of Journalism & Mass Communication, Professional Writing Program, c/o University of Oklahoma, 395 W Lindsey St, Rm 3000, Norman, OK 73019-0270 *Tel:* 405-325-2721 *Web Site:* www.ou.edu/gaylord; www.ou.edu/gaylord/undergraduate/professional-writing, pg 563

Lindsey, Joy D, Carter G Woodson Book Awards, 8555 16 St, Suite 500, Silver Spring, MD 20910 *Tel:* 301-588-1800 *E-mail:* ncss@ncss.org *Web Site:* www.socialstudies.org/membership/awards/carter-g-woodson-book-awards, pg 677

Lindstrom, Allen, Simon & Schuster, LLC, 1230 Avenue of the Americas, New York, NY 10020 *Tel:* 212-698-7000 *Toll Free Tel:* 800-223-2336 (orders) *Fax:* 212-698-7007 *Toll Free Fax:* 800-943-9831 (orders) *E-mail:* firstname.lastname@simonandschuster.com; purchaseorders@simonandschuster.com (orders) *Web Site:* www.simonandschuster.com, pg 189

Ling, Alvina, Little, Brown Books for Young Readers (LBYR), 1290 Avenue of the Americas, New York, NY 10104 *Tel:* 212-364-1100 *Toll Free Tel:* 800-759-0190 (cust serv) *Fax:* 212-364-1125 *E-mail:* rights@lbchildrens.com *Web Site:* www.hachettebookgroup.com/imprint/little-brown-books-for-young-readers/, pg 118

Ling, Jessica, Chronicle Books LLC, 680 Second St, San Francisco, CA 94107 *Tel:* 415-537-4200 *Fax:* 415-537-4460 (perms) *E-mail:* hello@chroniclebooks.com; subrights@chroniclebooks.com *Web Site:* www.chroniclebooks.com, pg 47

Ling, Yuyi, Tumblehome Learning Inc, 201 Newbury St, Suite 201, Boston, MA 02116 *E-mail:* info@tumblehomelearning.com *Web Site:* www.tumblehomelearning.com, pg 210

Linge, Zach, Southeast Review's Gearhart Poetry Contest, Florida State University, Dept of English, Tallahassee, FL 32306 *E-mail:* southeastreview@gmail.com *Web Site:* www.southeastreview.org/writing-contests, pg 664

Linge, Zach, Ned Stuckey-French Nonfiction Contest, Florida State University, Dept of English, Tallahassee, FL 32306 *E-mail:* southeastreview@gmail.com *Web Site:* www.southeastreview.org/writing-contests, pg 667

Linge, Zach, World's Best Short-Short Story Contest, Florida State University, Dept of English, Tallahassee, FL 32306 *E-mail:* southeastreview@gmail.com *Web Site:* www.southeastreview.org/writing-contests, pg 677

Linhoff, Clara, Diversion Books, 11 E 44 St, Suite 1603, New York, NY 10017 *Tel:* 212-961-6390 *E-mail:* info@diversionbooks.com *Web Site:* www.diversionbooks.com, pg 60

Link, Kelly, Small Beer Press, 150 Pleasant St, No 306, Easthampton, MA 01027 *Tel:* 413-240-4197 *E-mail:* info@smallbeerpress.com *Web Site:* smallbeerpress.com, pg 191

Link, Maureen, Savvas Learning Co LLC, 15 E Midland Ave, Suite 502, Paramus, NJ 07652 *Toll Free Tel:* 800-848-9500 *Web Site:* www.savvas.com, pg 183

Linker, Dave, HarperCollins Children's Books, 195 Broadway, New York, NY 10007 *Tel:* 212-207-7000 *Web Site:* www.harpercollins.com/childrens, pg 85

Linsmeier, Charles, Macmillan Learning, One New York Plaza, Suite 46, New York, NY 10004 *Tel:* 212-576-9400 *E-mail:* salesoperations@macmillanusa.com *Web Site:* www.macmillanlearning.com/college/us, pg 123

Liodice, Bob, Association of National Advertisers Inc (ANA), 155 E 44 St, New York, NY 10017 *Tel:* 212-697-5950 *Fax:* 212-687-7310 *E-mail:* info@ana.net *Web Site:* www.ana.net, pg 499

Lionetti, Kim, BookEnds Literary Agency, 136 Long Hill Rd, Gillette, NJ 07933 *Web Site:* www.bookendsliterary.com, pg 451

Lior, Noam Tzvi, Centre for Reformation & Renaissance Studies (CRRS), 71 Queen's Park Crescent E, Toronto, ON M5S 1K7, Canada *Tel:* 416-585-4465 *Fax:* 416-585-4430 (attn: CRRS) *E-mail:* crrs.publications@utoronto.ca *Web Site:* crrs.ca, pg 399

Lipinski, Michelle, University of California Press, 155 Grand Ave, Suite 400, Oakland, CA 94612-3758 *Tel:* 510-883-8232 *Fax:* 510-836-8910 *E-mail:* customerservice@ucpress.edu *Web Site:* www.ucpress.edu, pg 215

Lipkin, Suzanne, George Freedley Memorial Award, c/o The New York Public Library for the Performing Arts, 111 Amsterdam Ave, New York, NY 10023 *E-mail:* tlabookawards@gmail.com; theatrelibraryassociation@gmail.com *Web Site:* www.tla-online.org/awards/bookawards, pg 604

Lipkin, Suzanne, Richard Wall Memorial Award, c/o The New York Public Library for the Performing Arts, 111 Amsterdam Ave, New York, NY 10023 *E-mail:* theatrelibraryassociation@gmail.com; tlabookawards@gmail.com *Web Site:* www.tla-online.org/awards/bookawards, pg 673

Lipman, Andrew, Allan Nevins Prize, Columbia University, 3009 Broadway MC 802, New York, NY 10027 *Tel:* 212-854-1919 *E-mail:* amhistsociety@columbia.edu *Web Site:* sah.columbia.edu, pg 639

Lipman, Andrew, Francis Parkman Prize, Columbia University, 3009 Broadway MC 802, New York, NY 10027 *Tel:* 212-854-1919 *E-mail:* amhistsociety@columbia.edu *Web Site:* sah.columbia.edu, pg 646

Lipman, Andrew, SAH Prize for Historical Fiction, Columbia University, 3009 Broadway MC 802, New York, NY 10027 *Tel:* 212-854-1919 *E-mail:* amhistsociety@columbia.edu *Web Site:* sah.columbia.edu, pg 658

Lipp, Marty, Oscar Williams/Gene Derwood Award, 909 Third Ave, New York, NY 10022 *Tel:* 212-686-0010 *Fax:* 212-532-8528 *E-mail:* info@nycommunitytrust.org *Web Site:* www.nycommunitytrust.org, pg 675

Lippe, James, Savvas Learning Co LLC, 15 E Midland Ave, Suite 502, Paramus, NJ 07652 *Toll Free Tel:* 800-848-9500 *Web Site:* www.savvas.com, pg 183

Lippenholz, Michael, Rowman & Littlefield, 4501 Forbes Blvd, Suite 200, Lanham, MD 20706 *Tel:* 301-459-3366 *Toll Free Tel:* 800-462-6420 (ext 3024, cust serv) *Fax:* 301-429-5748 *Web Site:* rowman.com, pg 178

Lippert, Jennifer, PA Press, 202 Warren St, Hudson, NY 12534 *Tel:* 518-671-6100 *Toll Free Tel:* 800-722-6657 (dist); 800-759-0190 (sales) *E-mail:* sales@papress.com *Web Site:* www.papress.com, pg 149

Lippert, Megan, Hilton Publishing Co, 5261-A Fountain Dr, Crown Point, IN 46307 *Tel:* 219-922-4868 *Fax:* 219-924-6811 *E-mail:* info@hpcinternationalinc.com *Web Site:* www.hpcinternationalinc.com; hpcinternationalinc.com/bookstore (orders), pg 92

Lippincott, Will, Aevitas Creative Management LLC, 19 W 21 St, Suite 501, New York, NY 10010 *Tel:* 212-765-6900 *Web Site:* www.aevitascreative.com, pg 448

Lipscombe, Trevor C, The Catholic University of America Press, 240 Leahy Hall, 620 Michigan Ave NE, Washington, DC 20064 *Tel:* 202-319-5052 *Toll Free Tel:* 800-537-5487 (orders only) *Fax:* 202-319-4985 *E-mail:* cua-press@cua.edu *Web Site:* cuapress.org, pg 42

Lipskar, Simon, Writers House, 21 W 26 St, New York, NY 10010 *Tel:* 212-685-2400 *Web Site:* www.writershouse.com, pg 482

Lisanti, Jenna, Harry N Abrams Inc, 195 Broadway, 9th fl, New York, NY 10007 *Tel:* 212-206-7715 *Toll Free Tel:* 800-345-1359 *Fax:* 212-645-8437 *E-mail:* abrams@abramsbooks.com; publicity@abramsbooks.com; sales@abramsbooks.com *Web Site:* www.abramsbooks.com, pg 3

Lisik, L'Amour, Constance Rooke Creative Nonfiction Prize, University of Victoria, PO Box 1700, Sta CSC, Victoria, BC V8W 2Y2, Canada *Tel:* 250-721-8524 *E-mail:* malahat@uvic.ca *Web Site:* www.malahatreview.ca/contests/creative_non-fiction_prize/info.html; www.malahatreview.ca, pg 591

Lisik, L'Amour, Far Horizons Award for Poetry, University of Victoria, PO Box 1700, Sta CSC, Victoria, BC V8W 2Y2, Canada *Tel:* 250-721-8524 *E-mail:* malahat@uvic.ca *Web Site:* www.malahatreview.ca/contests/far_horizons_poetry/info.html; www.malahatreview.ca, pg 601

Lisik, L'Amour, Far Horizons Award for Short Fiction, University of Victoria, PO Box 1700, Sta CSC, Victoria, BC V8W 2Y2, Canada *Tel:* 250-721-8524 *E-mail:* malahat@uvic.ca *Web Site:* www.malahatreview.ca/contests/far_horizons_fiction/info.html; www.malahatreview.ca, pg 601

Lisik, L'Amour, Long Poem Prize, University of Victoria, PO Box 1700, Sta CSC, Victoria, BC V8W 2Y2, Canada *Tel:* 250-721-8524 *E-mail:* malahat@

uvic.ca *Web Site:* www.malahatreview.ca/contests/long_poem_prize/info.html; www.malahatreview.ca, pg 626

Lisik, L'Amour, Novella Prize, University of Victoria, PO Box 1700, Sta CSC, Victoria, BC V8W 2Y2, Canada *Tel:* 250-721-8524 *E-mail:* malahat@uvic.ca *Web Site:* www.malahatreview.ca/contests/novella_contest/info.html; www.malahatreview.ca, pg 642

Lisik, L'Amour, Open Season Awards, University of Victoria, PO Box 1700, Sta CSC, Victoria, BC V8W 2Y2, Canada *Tel:* 250-721-8524 *E-mail:* malahat@uvic.ca *Web Site:* www.malahatreview.ca/contests/open_season/info.html; www.malahatreview.ca, pg 644

Liss, Laurie, Sterling Lord Literistic Inc, 594 Broadway, Suite 205, New York, NY 10012 *Tel:* 212-780-6050 *Fax:* 212-780-6095 *E-mail:* info@sll.com *Web Site:* www.sll.com, pg 477

Litak, Marissa, Mountaineers Books, 1001 SW Klickitat Way, Suite 201, Seattle, WA 98134 *Tel:* 206-223-6303 *Fax:* 206-223-6306 *E-mail:* mbooks@mountaineersbooks.org; customerservice@mountaineersbooks.org *Web Site:* www.mountaineers.org/books, pg 135

Lite, Lori, Stress Free Kids®, 2561 Chimney Springs Dr, Marietta, GA 30062 *Tel:* 678-642-9555 *Toll Free Fax:* 866-302-2759 *E-mail:* media@stressfreekids.com *Web Site:* www.stressfreekids.com, pg 200

Lite, Rick, Stress Free Kids®, 2561 Chimney Springs Dr, Marietta, GA 30062 *Tel:* 678-642-9555 *Toll Free Fax:* 866-302-2759 *E-mail:* media@stressfreekids.com *Web Site:* www.stressfreekids.com, pg 200

Litt, Neil, Princeton University Press, 41 William St, Princeton, NJ 08540-5237 *Tel:* 609-258-4900 *Fax:* 609-258-6305 *E-mail:* info@press.princeton.edu *Web Site:* press.princeton.edu, pg 164

Little, Arleta M, Excellence in Teaching Fellowships, Open Book Bldg, Suite 200, 1011 Washington Ave S, Minneapolis, MN 55415 *Tel:* 612-215-2575 *Fax:* 612-215-2576 *E-mail:* loft@loft.org *Web Site:* loft.org/awards/excellence-teaching-fellowships, pg 601

Little, Arleta M, Loft-Mentor Series in Poetry & Creative Prose, Open Book Bldg, Suite 200, 1011 Washington Ave S, Minneapolis, MN 55415 *Tel:* 612-215-2575 *Fax:* 612-215-2576 *E-mail:* loft@loft.org *Web Site:* loft.org, pg 626

Little, Arleta M, McKnight Artist Fellowship for Writers, Open Book Bldg, Suite 200, 1011 Washington Ave S, Minneapolis, MN 55415 *Tel:* 612-215-2575 *Fax:* 612-215-2576 *E-mail:* loft@loft.org *Web Site:* loft.org, pg 631

Little, Arleta M, Mirrors & Windows Fellowship, Open Book Bldg, Suite 200, 1011 Washington Ave S, Minneapolis, MN 55415 *Tel:* 612-215-2575 *Fax:* 612-215-2576 *E-mail:* loft@loft.org *Web Site:* loft.org/awards/mirrors-windows, pg 633

Little, Kathryn, Roaring Brook Press, 120 Broadway, New York, NY 10271 *Tel:* 646-307-5151 *Web Site:* us.macmillan.com/publishers/roaring-brook-press, pg 176

Little, Lena, Little, Brown and Company, 1290 Avenue of the Americas, New York, NY 10104 *Tel:* 212-364-1100 *Fax:* 212-364-0952 *E-mail:* firstname.lastname@hbgusa.com *Web Site:* www.hachettebookgroup.com/imprint/little-brown-and-company/, pg 118

Little, Timothy, J J Keller & Associates, Inc®, 3003 Breezewood Lane, Neenah, WI 54957 *Tel:* 920-722-2848 *Toll Free Tel:* 877-564-2333 *Toll Free Fax:* 800-727-7516 *E-mail:* customerservice@jjkeller.com; sales@jjkeller.com *Web Site:* www.jjkeller.com, pg 108

Littlefield, Alex, Little, Brown and Company, 1290 Avenue of the Americas, New York, NY 10104 *Tel:* 212-364-1100 *Fax:* 212-364-0952 *E-mail:* firstname.lastname@hbgusa.com *Web Site:* www.hachettebookgroup.com/imprint/little-brown-and-company/, pg 118

Littlefield, Kyle, Texas A&M University Press, John H Lindsey Bldg, Lewis St, 4354 TAMU, College Station, TX 77843-4354 *Tel:* 979-845-1436 *Toll Free Tel:* 800-826-8911 (orders) *Fax:* 979-847-8752 *Toll Free Fax:* 888-617-2421 (orders) *E-mail:* bookorders@tamu.edu *Web Site:* www.tamupress.com, pg 205

Littler, Courtney, St Martin's Press, LLC, 120 Broadway, New York, NY 10271 *E-mail:* publicity@stmartins.com; trademarketing@stmartins.com; foreignrights@stmartins.com *Web Site:* us.macmillan.com/smp, pg 181

Litwack, Lisa, Gallery Books, 1230 Avenue of the Americas, New York, NY 10020 *Toll Free Tel:* 800-456-6798 *Fax:* 212-698-7284 *E-mail:* consumer.customerservice@simonandschuster.com *Web Site:* www.simonandschuster.com, pg 76

Liu, Alyza, Simon & Schuster Children's Publishing, 1230 Avenue of the Americas, New York, NY 10020 *Tel:* 212-698-7000 *Web Site:* www.simonandschuster.com/kids; www.simonandschuster.com/teen; simonandschuster.net; simonandschuster.biz, pg 189

Liu, Anni, Graywolf Press, 212 Third Ave N, Suite 485, Minneapolis, MN 55401 *Tel:* 651-641-0077 *Fax:* 651-641-0036 *E-mail:* wolves@graywolfpress.org (no ms queries, sample chapters or proposals) *Web Site:* www.graywolfpress.org, pg 81

Liu, Doreen, World Scientific Publishing Co Inc, 27 Warren St, Suite 401-402, Hackensack, NJ 07601 *Tel:* 201-487-9655 *Fax:* 201-487-9656 *E-mail:* sales@wspc.com; mkt@wspc.com; editor@wspc.com; customercare@wspc.com *Web Site:* www.worldscientific.com, pg 233

Liu, Ingsu, W W Norton & Company Inc, 500 Fifth Ave, New York, NY 10110-0017 *Tel:* 212-354-5500 *Toll Free Tel:* 800-233-4830 (orders & cust serv) *Fax:* 212-869-0856 *Toll Free Fax:* 800-458-6515 *E-mail:* orders@wwnorton.com *Web Site:* wwnorton.com, pg 143

Liu, Kitty, Cornell University Press, Sage House, 512 E State St, Ithaca, NY 14850 *Tel:* 607-253-2338 *E-mail:* cupressinfo@cornell.edu; cupress-sales@cornell.edu; cupress-perms@cornell.edu (reprint/class use permissions) *Web Site:* www.cornellpress.cornell.edu, pg 52

Liu, Newton, Bridge to Asia, 1505 Juanita Way, Berkeley, CA 94702, pg 525

Livesay, Diana, Histria Books, 7181 N Hualapai Way, Suite 130-86, Las Vegas, NV 89166 *Tel:* 561-299-0802 *E-mail:* info@histriabooks.com; orders@histriabooks.com; rights@histriabooks.com *Web Site:* histriabooks.com, pg 93

Livingston, Susan, Penguin Random House LLC, 1745 Broadway, New York, NY 10019 *Tel:* 212-782-9000 *Toll Free Tel:* 800-726-0600 *Web Site:* www.penguinrandomhouse.com, pg 155

Lizzi, Marian, TarcherPerigee, c/o Penguin Random House LLC, 1745 Broadway, New York, NY 10019 *Tel:* 212-782-9000 *Web Site:* www.penguin.com/tarcherperigee-overview/; www.facebook.com/TarcherPerigee, pg 202

Lkhagvadorj, Soyolmaa, Harry N Abrams Inc, 195 Broadway, 9th fl, New York, NY 10007 *Tel:* 212-206-7715 *Toll Free Tel:* 800-345-1359 *Fax:* 212-645-8437 *E-mail:* abrams@abramsbooks.com; publicity@abramsbooks.com; sales@abramsbooks.com *Web Site:* www.abramsbooks.com, pg 3

Llewellyn, Anna, Brockman Inc, 260 Fifth Ave, 10th fl, New York, NY 10001 *Tel:* 212-935-8900 *E-mail:* rights@brockman.com *Web Site:* www.brockman.com, pg 452

Lliguichuzhca, Cynthia, Random House Children's Books, c/o Penguin Random House LLC, 1745 Broadway, New York, NY 10019 *Tel:* 212-782-9000 *Web Site:* www.rhcbooks.com, pg 170

Lloyd, Dennis, University of Wisconsin Press, 728 State St, Suite 443, Madison, WI 53706-1418 *Tel:* 608-263-1110; 608-263-0668 (journal orders) *Toll Free Tel:* 800-621-2736 (book orders) *Fax:* 608-263-1173 *Toll Free Fax:* 800-621-2736 (book orders) *E-mail:* uwiscpress@uwpress.wisc.edu *Web Site:* uwpress.wisc.edu, pg 221

Lloyd, Kathryn, Texas A&M University Press, John H Lindsey Bldg, Lewis St, 4354 TAMU, College Station, TX 77843-4354 *Tel:* 979-845-1436 *Toll Free Tel:* 800-826-8911 (orders) *Fax:* 979-847-8752 *Toll Free Fax:* 888-617-2421 (orders) *E-mail:* bookorders@tamu.edu *Web Site:* www.tamupress.com, pg 205

Lloyd, Ronane, Editorial Freelancers Association (EFA), 266 W 37 St, 20th fl, New York, NY 10018 *Tel:* 212-920-4816 *Toll Free Tel:* 866-929-5425 *E-mail:* info@the-efa.org; membership@the-efa.org *Web Site:* www.the-efa.org, pg 505

Lloyd-Sidle, Elena, Fons Vitae, 49 Mockingbird Valley Dr, Louisville, KY 40207-1366 *Tel:* 502-897-3641 *Fax:* 502-893-7373 *E-mail:* fonsvitaeky@aol.com *Web Site:* www.fonsvitae.com, pg 73

Lo Brutto, Patrick, Philip K Dick Award, PO Box 3447, Hoboken, NJ 07030 *Tel:* 201-876-2551 *Web Site:* www.philipkdickaward.org, pg 596

Lo, Hilary, Penguin Random House Canada, a Penguin Random House company, 320 Front St W, Suite 1400, Toronto, ON M5V 3B6, Canada *Tel:* 416-364-4449 *Toll Free Tel:* 888-523-9292 (cust serv) *E-mail:* canadaweb@penguinrandomhouse.com; customerservicescanada@penguinrandomhouse.com *Web Site:* www.penguinrandomhouse.ca, pg 416

Lo Ricco, Peter, The Lawbook Exchange, Ltd, 33 Terminal Ave, Clark, NJ 07066-1321 *Tel:* 732-382-1800 *Toll Free Tel:* 800-422-6686 *Fax:* 732-382-1887 *E-mail:* law@lawbookexchange.com *Web Site:* www.lawbookexchange.com, pg 113

Lobdell, Lauren, The Princeton Review, 110 E 42 St, 7th fl, New York, NY 10017 *Toll Free Tel:* 800-273-8439 (orders only) *Web Site:* www.princetonreview.com, pg 164

Loberg, Erica, Soho Press Inc, 853 Broadway, New York, NY 10003 *Tel:* 212-260-1900 *E-mail:* soho@sohopress.com; publicity@sohopress.com *Web Site:* sohopress.com, pg 193

Lochner, Wendy, Columbia University Press, 61 W 62 St, New York, NY 10023 *Tel:* 212-459-0600 *Toll Free Tel:* 800-944-8648 *Fax:* 212-459-3678 *Web Site:* cup.columbia.edu, pg 51

Lockard, Eric, Salina Bookshelf Inc, 1120 W University Ave, Suite 102, Flagstaff, AZ 86001 *Toll Free Tel:* 877-527-0070 *Fax:* 928-526-0386 *Web Site:* www.salinabookshelf.com, pg 181

Locke, Annie, Vintage Books, c/o Penguin Random House LLC, 1745 Broadway, New York, NY 10019 *Tel:* 212-572-2420 *Fax:* 212-940-7390 (dom rts); 212-572-2662 (foreign rts) *E-mail:* vintageanchorpublicity@randomhouse.com *Web Site:* knopfdoubleday.com/imprint/vintage; knopfdoubleday.com, pg 225

Locke, Charlene, Davies Publishing Inc, 32 S Raymond Ave, Suites 4 & 5, Pasadena, CA 91105-1961 *Tel:* 626-792-3046 *Toll Free Tel:* 877-792-0005 *Fax:* 626-792-5308 *E-mail:* info@daviespublishing.com *Web Site:* daviespublishing.com, pg 57

Locke, Christopher, The Independent Book Publishers Association (IBPA), 1020 Manhattan Beach Blvd, Suite 204, Manhattan Beach, CA 90266 *Tel:* 310-546-1818 *E-mail:* info@ibpa-online.org *Web Site:* www.ibpa-online.org, pg 507

Lockhart, Brianna, Penguin Young Readers Group, c/o Penguin Random House LLC, 1745 Broadway, New York, NY 10019 *Tel:* 212-782-9000 *Web Site:* www.penguin.com/penguin-young-readers-overview, pg 156

Lockhart, Doug, Thomas Nelson, 501 Nelson Place, Nashville, TN 37214 *Tel:* 615-889-9000 *Toll Free Tel:* 800-251-4000 *Web Site:* www.thomasnelson.com, pg 206

Lockhart, Doug, Zondervan, 3900 Sparks Dr SE, Grand Rapids, MI 49546 *Tel:* 616-698-6900 *Toll Free Tel:* 800-226-1122; 800-727-1309 (retail orders) *Fax:* 616-698-3350 *Toll Free Fax:* 800-698-3256 (retail orders) *E-mail:* customercare@harpercollins.com *Web Site:* www.zondervan.com, pg 236

Lockhart, Emma, Knopf Canada, 320 Front St W, Suite 1400, Toronto, ON M5V 3B6, Canada *Tel:* 416-364-4449 *Toll Free Tel:* 888-523-9292 *Fax:* 416-598-7764 *Web Site:* www.penguinrandomhouse.ca, pg 411

Lockhart, Robert, University of Pennsylvania Press, 3905 Spruce St, Philadelphia, PA 19104 *Tel:* 215-898-6261 *Fax:* 215-898-0404 *E-mail:* custserv@pobox.upenn.edu *Web Site:* www.pennpress.org, pg 219

Lockley, Beth, Penguin Random House Canada, a Penguin Random House company, 320 Front St W, Suite 1400, Toronto, ON M5V 3B6, Canada *Tel:* 416-364-4449 *Toll Free Tel:* 888-523-9292 (cust serv) *E-mail:* canadaweb@penguinrandomhouse.com; customerservicescanada@penguinrandomhouse.com *Web Site:* www.penguinrandomhouse.ca, pg 415

Locks, Sueyun, Locks Art Publications/Locks Gallery, 600 Washington Sq S, Philadelphia, PA 19106 *Tel:* 215-629-1000 *E-mail:* info@locksgallery.com *Web Site:* www.locksgallery.com, pg 119

Lockwood, Diana Alarid, Northern California Translators Association, 2261 Market St, Suite 160, San Francisco, CA 94114-1600 *Tel:* 510-845-8712 *E-mail:* ncta@ncta.org *Web Site:* ncta.org, pg 515

Lockwood, Karen, Syracuse University Press, 621 Skytop Rd, Suite 110, Syracuse, NY 13244-5290 *Tel:* 315-443-5534 *Toll Free Tel:* 800-365-8929 (cust serv) *Fax:* 315-443-5545 *E-mail:* supress@syr.edu *Web Site:* press.syr.edu, pg 201

Lodato, Mark J, Syracuse University, SI Newhouse School of Public Communications, 215 University Place, Syracuse, NY 13244 *Tel:* 315-443-3627 *E-mail:* newhouse@syr.edu *Web Site:* newhouse.syr.edu/academics/programs, pg 565

Loeb, Sharon, Cengage Learning, 20 Channel Center St, Boston, MA 02210 *Tel:* 617-289-7700 *Toll Free Tel:* 800-354-9706 *Fax:* 617-289-7844 *E-mail:* esales@cengage.com *Web Site:* www.cengage.com, pg 43

Loehnen, Ben, Avid Reader Press, 1230 Avenue of the Americas, New York, NY 10020 *Web Site:* avidreaderpress.com, pg 23

Loehr, Julie L, Michigan State University Press (MSU Press), Manly Miles Bldg, Suite 25, 1405 S Harrison Rd, East Lansing, MI 48823-5245 *Tel:* 517-355-9543 *Fax:* 517-432-2611 *Web Site:* msupress.org, pg 130

Loehr, Mallory, Random House Children's Books, c/o Penguin Random House LLC, 1745 Broadway, New York, NY 10019 *Tel:* 212-782-9000 *Web Site:* www.rhcbooks.com, pg 169

Loertscher, David V, Hi Willow Research & Publishing, 146 S 700 E, Provo, UT 84601 *Tel:* 801-755-1122 *E-mail:* lmcsourceutah@gmail.com *Web Site:* www.lmcsource.com; www.davidvl.org, pg 91

Loewen, Darleen, PrairieView Press, 625 Seventh St, Gretna, MB R0G 0V0, Canada *Tel:* 204-327-6543 *Toll Free Tel:* 800-477-7377 *Toll Free Fax:* 866-480-0253 *Web Site:* prairieviewpress.com, pg 417

Loewen, Isaac, Macmillan, 120 Broadway, 22nd fl, New York, NY 10271 *E-mail:* press.inquiries@macmillan.com *Web Site:* us.macmillan.com, pg 122

Loewen-Young, Anais, Penguin Random House Canada, a Penguin Random House company, 320 Front St W, Suite 1400, Toronto, ON M5V 3B6, Canada *Tel:* 416-364-4449 *Toll Free Tel:* 888-523-9292 (cust serv) *E-mail:* canadaweb@penguinrandomhouse.com; customerservicescanada@penguinrandomhouse.com *Web Site:* www.penguinrandomhouse.ca, pg 416

Loftus, Maria, Bear & Co Inc, One Park St, Rochester, VT 05767 *Tel:* 802-767-3174 *Toll Free Tel:* 800-932-3277 *Fax:* 802-767-3726 *E-mail:* customerservice@InnerTraditions.com *Web Site:* InnerTraditions.com, pg 26

Loftus, Maria, Inner Traditions International Ltd, One Park St, Rochester, VT 05767 *Tel:* 802-767-3174 *Toll Free Tel:* 800-246-8648 *Fax:* 802-767-3726 *E-mail:* customerservice@InnerTraditions.com *Web Site:* www.InnerTraditions.com, pg 101

Logan, Alex, Grand Central Publishing, 1290 Avenue of the Americas, New York, NY 10104 *Tel:* 212-364-1100 *Web Site:* www.hachettebookgroup.com/imprint/grand-central-publishing/, pg 80

Logan, Emily, Houghton Mifflin Harcourt, 125 High St, Boston, MA 02110 *Tel:* 617-351-5000 *Toll Free Tel:* 855-969-4642; 800-225-5425 (K-12 educ materials); 800-323-9540 (assessment materials); 877-219-1537 (SkillsTutor); 888-242-6747 (Innovation in Educ Group); 800-225-3362 (Trade & Ref Div) *Toll Free Fax:* 800-269-5232 *E-mail:* myhmhco@hmhco.com *Web Site:* www.hmhco.com, pg 96

Logan, Megan, Workman Publishing, 1290 Avenue of the Americas, New York, NY 10104 *Toll Free Tel:* 800-759-0190 *Fax:* 212-364-0950 *E-mail:* workman-inquiry@hbgusa.com *Web Site:* www.hachettebookgroup.com/imprint/workman-publishing-company/, pg 233

Loganbill, Alec, University Press of Kansas, 2502 Westbrooke Circle, Lawrence, KS 66045-4444 *Tel:* 785-864-4154 *Fax:* 785-864-4586 *E-mail:* upress@ku.edu *Web Site:* www.kansaspress.ku.edu, pg 221

Logback, Liz, Sourcebooks LLC, 1935 Brookdale Rd, Suite 139, Naperville, IL 60563 *Tel:* 630-961-3900 *Toll Free Tel:* 800-432-7444 *Fax:* 630-961-2168 *E-mail:* info@sourcebooks.com *Web Site:* www.sourcebooks.com, pg 195

Loggia, Wendy, Random House Children's Books, c/o Penguin Random House LLC, 1745 Broadway, New York, NY 10019 *Tel:* 212-782-9000 *Web Site:* www.rhcbooks.com, pg 169

Lohr, Lece, Highlights for Children Inc, 815 Church St, Honesdale, PA 18431 *Tel:* 570-253-1164 *Toll Free Tel:* 800-490-5111 *Fax:* 570-253-0179 *E-mail:* salesandmarketing@highlightspress.com *Web Site:* www.highlightspress.com; www.highlights.com; www.facebook.com/HighlightsforChildren, pg 92

Loja, Jennifer, Penguin Publishing Group, c/o Penguin Random House LLC, 1745 Broadway, New York, NY 10019 *Tel:* 212-782-9000 *Web Site:* www.penguin.com, pg 154

Loja, Jennifer, Penguin Young Readers Group, c/o Penguin Random House LLC, 1745 Broadway, New York, NY 10019 *Tel:* 212-782-9000 *Web Site:* www.penguin.com/penguin-young-readers-overview, pg 156

Lokhandwala, Khadija, Tor Publishing Group, 120 Broadway, New York, NY 10271 *Toll Free Tel:* 800-455-0340 (Macmillan) *E-mail:* torpublicity@tor.com; forgepublicity@forgebooks.com *Web Site:* us.macmillan.com/torpublishinggroup, pg 208

Lombardini, Kim, Philip G Spitzer Literary Agency Inc, 50 Talmage Farm Lane, East Hampton, NY 11937 *Tel:* 631-329-3650 *Fax:* 631-329-3651 *Web Site:* www.spitzeragency.com, pg 477

London, Mark, Papercutz, 8838 SW 129 St, Miami, FL 33176 *Tel:* 786-953-4195 *E-mail:* contact@papercutz.com; snellis@madcavestudios.com *Web Site:* www.papercutz.com, pg 150

Lonesome, Kelly O'Connor, Tor Publishing Group, 120 Broadway, New York, NY 10271 *Toll Free Tel:* 800-455-0340 (Macmillan) *E-mail:* torpublicity@tor.com; forgepublicity@forgebooks.com *Web Site:* us.macmillan.com/torpublishinggroup, pg 208

Long, Ben, Dancing Dakini Press, 2935 NE 77 Ave, Portland, OR 97213 *Tel:* 503-415-0229 *E-mail:* editor@dancingdakinipress.com *Web Site:* www.dancingdakinipress.com, pg 57

Long, Clarissa, Henry Holt and Company, LLC, 120 Broadway, 23rd fl, New York, NY 10271 *Tel:* 646-307-5151 *Toll Free Tel:* 888-330-8477 (orders) *Fax:* 646-307-5285 *Web Site:* www.henryholt.com, pg 94

Long, Jennifer, Gallery Books, 1230 Avenue of the Americas, New York, NY 10020 *Toll Free Tel:* 800-456-6798 *Fax:* 212-698-7284 *E-mail:* consumer.customerservice@simonandschuster.com *Web Site:* www.simonandschuster.com, pg 76

Long, Karen R, The Anisfield-Wolf Book Awards, 1422 Euclid Ave, Suite 1300, Cleveland, OH 44115 *Tel:* 216-861-3810 *Fax:* 216-861-1729 *E-mail:* awinfo@clevefdn.org *Web Site:* www.anisfield-wolf.org; www.clevelandfoundation.org, pg 573

Long, Sandy, The Authors Guild®, 31 E 32 St, Suite 901, New York, NY 10016 *Tel:* 212-563-5904 *Fax:* 212-564-5363 *E-mail:* staff@authorsguild.org *Web Site:* www.authorsguild.org, pg 500

Long, Thayer, Association for PRINT Technologies (APTech), 113 Seaboard Lane, Suite C-250, Franklin, TN 37067 *Tel:* 703-264-7200 *E-mail:* aptech@aptech.org *Web Site:* printtechnologies.org, pg 498

Long, Thayer, Graphic Arts Education & Research Foundation (GAERF), 1899 Preston White Dr, Reston, VA 20191 *Tel:* 703-264-7200 *E-mail:* gaerf@npes.org *Web Site:* www.gaerf.org, pg 525

Longmeyer, Michael, Gallopade International Inc, 611 Hwy 74 S, Suite 2000, Peachtree City, GA 30269 *Tel:* 770-631-4222 *Toll Free Tel:* 800-536-2438 *Fax:* 770-631-4810 *Toll Free Fax:* 800-871-2979 *E-mail:* customerservice@gallopade.com *Web Site:* www.gallopade.com, pg 76

Longo, Edward, Recorded Books Inc, an RBmedia company, 8400 Corporate Dr, Landover, MD 20785 *Toll Free Tel:* 800-305-3450 *Web Site:* rbmediaglobal.com/recorded-books, pg 172

Lonie, Tonia, University Press of Mississippi, 3825 Ridgewood Rd, Jackson, MS 39211-6492 *Tel:* 601-432-6205 *Toll Free Tel:* 800-737-7788 (orders & cust serv) *Fax:* 601-432-6217 *E-mail:* press@mississippi.edu *Web Site:* www.upress.state.ms.us, pg 222

Lonning, Caitlin, HarperCollins Children's Books, 195 Broadway, New York, NY 10007 *Tel:* 212-207-7000 *Web Site:* www.harpercollins.com/childrens, pg 85

Loomis, Gloria, Watkins/Loomis Agency Inc, PO Box 20925, New York, NY 10025 *Tel:* 212-532-0080 *Fax:* 646-383-2449 *E-mail:* assistant@watkinsloomis.com; permissions@watkinsloomis.com *Web Site:* watkins-loomis.squarespace.com, pg 481

Looney, Megan, HarperCollins Publishers LLC, 195 Broadway, New York, NY 10007 *Tel:* 212-207-7000 *Web Site:* www.harpercollins.com, pg 87

Loose, Emily, Words into Print, 208 Java St, 5th fl, Brooklyn, NY 11222 *E-mail:* query@wordsintoprint.org *Web Site:* wordsintoprint.org, pg 445

Loosvelt, Derek, Vault.com Inc, 132 W 31 St, 16th fl, New York, NY 10001 *Tel:* 212-366-4212 *Toll Free Tel:* 800-535-2074 *Fax:* 212-366-6117 *E-mail:* mediainquiries@vault.com; customerservice@vault.com *Web Site:* www.vault.com, pg 224

Lopes, David, Gingko Press Inc, 2332 Fourth St, Suite E, Berkeley, CA 94710 *Tel:* 510-898-1195 *Fax:* 510-898-1196 *E-mail:* books@gingkopress.com *Web Site:* www.gingkopress.com, pg 78

Lopez, Ally, Princeton University Press, 41 William St, Princeton, NJ 08540-5237 *Tel:* 609-258-4900 *Fax:* 609-258-6305 *E-mail:* info@press.princeton.edu *Web Site:* press.princeton.edu, pg 164

Lopez, Christina, St Martin's Press, LLC, 120 Broadway, New York, NY 10271 *E-mail:* publicity@stmartins.com; trademarketing@stmartins.com; foreignrights@stmartins.com *Web Site:* us.macmillan.com/smp, pg 181

Lopez, Dan, Counterpoint Press LLC, 2560 Ninth St, Suite 318, Berkeley, CA 94710 *Tel:* 510-704-0230 *Fax:* 510-704-0268 *E-mail:* info@counterpointpress.com *Web Site:* counterpointpress.com; softskull.com, pg 54

Lopez, Daphne, Macmillan, 120 Broadway, 22nd fl, New York, NY 10271 *E-mail:* press.inquiries@macmillan.com *Web Site:* us.macmillan.com, pg 122

Lopez, Diego, Harry N Abrams Inc, 195 Broadway, 9th fl, New York, NY 10007 *Tel:* 212-206-7715 *Toll Free Tel:* 800-345-1359 *Fax:* 212-645-8437 *E-mail:* abrams@abramsbooks.com; publicity@abramsbooks.com; sales@abramsbooks.com *Web Site:* www.abramsbooks.com, pg 3

Lopez, Jenny, Sourcebooks LLC, 1935 Brookdale Rd, Suite 139, Naperville, IL 60563 *Tel:* 630-961-3900 *Toll Free Tel:* 800-432-7444 *Fax:* 630-961-2168 *E-mail:* info@sourcebooks.com *Web Site:* www.sourcebooks.com, pg 194

Lopez, Lourdes, Simon & Schuster, LLC, 1230 Avenue of the Americas, New York, NY 10020 *Tel:* 212-698-7000 *Toll Free Tel:* 800-223-2336 (orders) *Fax:* 212-698-7007 *Toll Free Fax:* 800-943-9831 (orders) *E-mail:* firstname.lastname@simonandschuster.com; purchaseorders@simonandschuster.com (orders) *Web Site:* www.simonandschuster.com, pg 189

Lopez, Samantha, Public Library Association (PLA), 225 N Michigan Ave, Suite 1300, Chicago, IL 60601 *Toll Free Tel:* 800-545-2433 (ext 5752) *Fax:* 312-280-5029 *E-mail:* pla@ala.org *Web Site:* www.ala.org/pla/, pg 518

Lopez, Summer, PEN America, 120 Broadway, 26th fl N, New York, NY 10271 *Tel:* 212-334-1660 *Fax:* 212-334-2181 *E-mail:* info@pen.org; membership@pen.org; education@pen.org *Web Site:* pen.org, pg 516

Lopez, Vanessa, Insight Editions, 800 "A" St, San Rafael, CA 94901 *Tel:* 415-526-1370 *Toll Free Tel:* 800-809-3792 *Toll Free Fax:* 866-509-0515 *E-mail:* info@insighteditions.com; marketing@insighteditions.com *Web Site:* insighteditions.com, pg 101

Lopezlena, Julie, Great Lakes Graphics Association (GLGA), N27 W23960 Paul Rd, Suite 200, Pewaukee, WI 53072 *Tel:* 262-522-2210 *Toll Free Tel:* 855-522-2210 *Fax:* 262-522-2211 *E-mail:* info@glga.info *Web Site:* glga.info, pg 507

Lorber, Giraud, Teachers College Press, 1234 Amsterdam Ave, New York, NY 10027 *Tel:* 212-678-3929 *Fax:* 212-678-4149 *E-mail:* tcpress@tc.edu *Web Site:* www.tcpress.com, pg 203

Lord, Allyson, Random House Publishing Group, 1745 Broadway, New York, NY 10019 *Toll Free Tel:* 800-200-3552 *Web Site:* www.randomhousebooks.com, pg 171

Lord, Devon, University of Louisiana at Lafayette Press, PO Box 43558, Lafayette, LA 70504-3558 *Tel:* 337-482-6027 *E-mail:* press.submissions@louisiana.edu *Web Site:* ulpress.org, pg 217

Lord, Jacklyn, Society for Scholarly Publishing (SSP), 1120 Rte 73, Suite 200, Mount Laurel, NJ 08054 *Tel:* 856-439-1385 *Fax:* 856-439-0525 *E-mail:* info@sspnet.org *Web Site:* www.sspnet.org, pg 519

Lord, Tayler, Princeton University Press, 41 William St, Princeton, NJ 08540-5237 *Tel:* 609-258-4900 *Fax:* 609-258-6305 *E-mail:* info@press.princeton.edu *Web Site:* press.princeton.edu, pg 164

Lord, Tayler, University of Nebraska Press, 1225 "L" St, Suite 200, Lincoln, NE 68588-0630 *Tel:* 402-472-3581; 919-966-7449 (cust serv & foreign orders) *Toll Free Tel:* 800-848-6224 (cust serv & US orders) *Fax:* 402-472-6214; 919-962-2704 (cust serv & foreign orders) *Toll Free Fax:* 800-272-6817 (cust serv & US orders) *E-mail:* presswebmail@unl.edu *Web Site:* www.nebraskapress.unl.edu, pg 218

Lord, Wendi, David C Cook, 4050 Lee Vance Dr, Colorado Springs, CO 80918 *Tel:* 719-536-0100 *Toll Free Tel:* 800-323-7543 (orders & cust serv) *Toll Free Fax:* 800-430-0726 (cust serv) *E-mail:* bookstores@davidccook.org; customercare@davidccook.org *Web Site:* www.davidccook.org, pg 52

Lore, Matthew, The Experiment, 220 E 23 St, Suite 600, New York, NY 10010-4658 *Tel:* 212-889-1659 *E-mail:* info@theexperimentpublishing.com *Web Site:* www.theexperimentpublishing.com, pg 68

Lore, Tom, Brush Education Inc, 6531-111 St NW, Edmonton, AB T6H 4R5, Canada *Tel:* 780-989-0910 *Toll Free Tel:* 855-283-0900 *Fax:* 780-989-0930 *Toll Free Fax:* 855-283-6947 *E-mail:* contact@brusheducation.ca *Web Site:* www.brusheducation.ca, pg 397

Lorencz, Amy, Atlantic Provinces Library Association (APLA), Dalhouse University, Kenneth C Rowe Management Bldg, 6100 University Ave, Suite 4010, Halifax, NS B3H 4R2, Canada *Web Site:* www.apla.ca, pg 500

Lorentzen, Allison, Viking Penguin, c/o Penguin Random House LLC, 1745 Broadway, New York, NY 10019 *Tel:* 212-782-9000 *Web site:* www.penguin.com/overview-vikingbooks/; www.penguin.com/pamela-dorman-books-overview/; www.penguin.com/penguin-classics-overview/; www.penguin.com/penguin-life-overview/, pg 225

Lorimer, James, James Lorimer & Co Ltd, Publishers, 117 Peter St, Suite 304, Toronto, ON M5V 0M3, Canada *Tel:* 416-362-4762 *Fax:* 416-362-3939 *E-mail:* sales@lorimer.ca; promotion@lorimer.ca; rights@lorimer.ca *Web Site:* www.lorimer.ca, pg 412

Loss, Kaitlin, Farrar, Straus & Giroux Books for Young Readers, 120 Broadway, New York, NY 10271 *Tel:* 212-741-6900 *Toll Free Tel:* 888-330-8477 (orders) *E-mail:* childrens.publicity@macmillanusa.com; childrensrights@macmillanusa.com *Web Site:* us.macmillan.com/mackids, pg 70

Loss, Kaitlin, Roaring Brook Press, 120 Broadway, New York, NY 10271 *Tel:* 646-307-5151 *Web Site:* us.macmillan.com/publishers/roaring-brook-press, pg 176

Lotis, Christopher, Yale Center for British Art, 1080 Chapel St, New Haven, CT 06510-2302 *Tel:* 203-432-8929 *Fax:* 203-432-1626 *E-mail:* ycba.publications@yale.edu *Web Site:* britishart.yale.edu, pg 235

Lotowycz, Randall, Running Press, 1290 Avenue of the Americas, New York, NY 10104 *Tel:* 212-364-1100 *Toll Free Tel:* 800-759-0190 (cust serv) *Fax:* 212-364-0933 (intl orders) *Toll Free Fax:* 800-286-9471 (cust serv) *E-mail:* customer.service@hbgusa.com; orders@hbgusa.com *Web Site:* www.hachettebookgroup.com/imprint/running-press/; www.moon.com (Moon Travel Guides), pg 178

Lott, Peter, Lott Representatives Ltd, PO Box 3607, New York, NY 10163 *Tel:* 212-755-5737 *Web Site:* www.lottreps.com, pg 485

Lotz, Karen, Candlewick Press, 99 Dover St, Somerville, MA 02144-2825 *Tel:* 617-661-3330 *Fax:* 617-661-0565 *E-mail:* bigbear@candlewick.com; salesinfo@candlewick.com *Web Site:* candlewick.com, pg 39

Lotz, Sallie, St Martin's Press, LLC, 120 Broadway, New York, NY 10271 *E-mail:* publicity@stmartins.com; trademarketing@stmartins.com; foreignrights@stmartins.com *Web Site:* us.macmillan.com/smp, pg 181

Lough, Chris, Tor Publishing Group, 120 Broadway, New York, NY 10271 *Toll Free Tel:* 800-455-0340 (Macmillan) *E-mail:* torpublicity@tor.com; forgepublicity@forgebooks.com *Web Site:* us.macmillan.com/torpublishinggroup, pg 208

Loughrey, Mary, Looseleaf Law Publications Inc, 43-08 162 St, Flushing, NY 11358 *Tel:* 718-359-5559 *Toll Free Tel:* 800-647-5547 *Fax:* 718-539-0941 *E-mail:* info@looseleaflaw.com *Web Site:* www.looseleaflaw.com, pg 120

Loughrey, Michael L, Looseleaf Law Publications Inc, 43-08 162 St, Flushing, NY 11358 *Tel:* 718-359-5559 *Toll Free Tel:* 800-647-5547 *Fax:* 718-539-0941 *E-mail:* info@looseleaflaw.com *Web Site:* www.looseleaflaw.com, pg 120

Louie, Jon, Haynes North America Inc, 2801 Townsgate Rd, Suite 340, Westlake Village, CA 91361 *Tel:* 805-498-6703 *Toll Free Tel:* 800-4-HAYNES (442-9637) *Fax:* 805-498-2867 *E-mail:* customerservice.haynes@infopro-digital.com *Web Site:* www.haynes.com, pg 89

Louie, Matthew, Columbia Books & Information Services (CBIS), 1530 Wilson Blvd, Suite 400, Arlington, VA 22209 *Tel:* 202-464-1662 *Fax:* 301-664-9600 *E-mail:* info@columbiabooks.com *Web Site:* www.columbiabooks.com; www.association-insight.com; www.ceoupdate.com; www.thealmanacofamericanpolitics.com; www.thompsongrants.com, pg 51

Lourie, Dick, Hanging Loose Press, 231 Wyckoff St, Brooklyn, NY 11217 *Tel:* 347-529-4738 *Fax:* 347-227-8215 *E-mail:* print225@aol.com *Web Site:* www.hangingloosepress.com, pg 85

Lourie, Mr Iven, Gateways Books & Tapes, PO Box 370, Nevada City, CA 95959-0370 *Tel:* 530-271-2239 *Toll Free Tel:* 800-869-0658 *Web Site:* www.gatewaysbooksandtapes.com, pg 77

Love, Robert, Square One Publishers Inc, 115 Herricks Rd, Garden City Park, NY 11040 *Tel:* 516-535-2010 *Toll Free Tel:* 877-900-BOOK (900-2665) *Fax:* 516-535-2014 *E-mail:* sq1publish@aol.com *Web Site:* www.squareonepublishers.com, pg 196

Lovell, Jake, Sandra Dijkstra Literary Agency, 1155 Camino del Mar, PMB 515, Del Mar, CA 92014-2605 *Web Site:* dijkstraagency.com, pg 456

Lovett, Emily, National Book Foundation, 90 Broad St, Suite 604, New York, NY 10004 *Tel:* 212-685-0261 *Fax:* 212-213-6570 *E-mail:* nationalbook@nationalbook.org *Web Site:* www.nationalbook.org, pg 526

Lovett, Erin Sinesky, W W Norton & Company Inc, 500 Fifth Ave, New York, NY 10110-0017 *Tel:* 212-354-5500 *Toll Free Tel:* 800-233-4830 (orders & cust serv) *Fax:* 212-869-0856 *Toll Free Fax:* 800-458-6515 *E-mail:* orders@wwnorton.com *Web Site:* wwnorton.com, pg 143

Loving, Lindsey, News/Media Alliance, 4401 N Fairfax Dr, Suite 300, Arlington, VA 22203 *Tel:* 571-366-1000 *E-mail:* info@newsmediaalliance.org *Web Site:* www.newsmediaalliance.org, pg 515

Lovitz, Dara, American Law Institute Continuing Legal Education (ALI CLE), 4025 Chestnut St, Philadelphia, PA 19104 *Tel:* 215-243-1600 *Toll Free Tel:* 800-CLE-NEWS (253-6397) *Fax:* 215-243-1664 *E-mail:* custserv@ali-cle.org; press@ali-cle.org *Web Site:* www.ali-cle.org, pg 10

Lovsin, Ian, Canada Council for the Arts (Conseil des arts du Canada), 150 Elgin St, 2nd fl, Ottawa, ON K2P 1L4, Canada *Tel:* 613-566-4414 *Toll Free Tel:* 800-263-5588 (CN only) *Fax:* 613-566-4390 *E-mail:* info@canadacouncil.ca; media@canadacouncil.ca *Web Site:* canadacouncil.ca, pg 502

Low, Craig, Children's Book Press, 95 Madison Ave, Suite 1205, New York, NY 10016 *Tel:* 212-779-4400 *Fax:* 212-683-1894 *E-mail:* editorial@leeandlow.com; orders@leeandlow.com; customer.support@leeandlow.com *Web Site:* www.leeandlow.com/imprints/childrens-book-press, pg 46

Low, Craig, Lee & Low Books Inc, 95 Madison Ave, Suite 1205, New York, NY 10016 *Tel:* 212-779-4400 *Toll Free Tel:* 888-320-3190 (ext 28, orders only) *Fax:* 212-683-1894 (orders only); 212-532-6035 *E-mail:* general@leeandlow.com *Web Site:* www.leeandlow.com, pg 114

Low, Harriet, Houghton Mifflin Harcourt Trade & Reference Division, 125 High St, Boston, MA 02110 *Tel:* 617-351-5000 *Web Site:* www.hmhco.com, pg 96

Low, Jason, Lee & Low Books Inc, 95 Madison Ave, Suite 1205, New York, NY 10016 *Tel:* 212-779-4400 *Toll Free Tel:* 888-320-3190 (ext 28, orders only) *Fax:* 212-683-1894 (orders only); 212-532-6035 *E-mail:* general@leeandlow.com *Web Site:* www.leeandlow.com, pg 114

Lowe, Greg, Classical Academic Press, 515 S 32 St, Camp Hill, PA 17011 *Tel:* 717-730-0711 *Toll Free Tel:* 866-730-0711 *Fax:* 717-730-0721 *Toll Free Fax:* 866-730-0721 *E-mail:* info@classicalsubjects.com; orders@classicalsubjects.com *Web Site:* classicalacademicpress.com, pg 49

Lowe, Sandy, Bold Strokes Books Inc, 648 S Cambridge Rd, Bldg A, Johnsonville, NY 12094 *Tel:* 518-859-8965 *E-mail:* service@boldstrokesbooks.com *Web Site:* www.boldstrokesbooks.com, pg 33

Lowell, Nathan, Science Fiction and Fantasy Writers Association, Inc (SFWA), PO Box 215, San Lorenzo, CA 94580 *Tel:* 860-698-0536 *E-mail:* office@sfwa.org; operations@sfwa.org *Web Site:* www.sfwa.org, pg 519

Lowell, Nathan, SFWA Nebula Awards, PO Box 215, San Lorenzo, CA 94580 *Tel:* 860-698-0536 *E-mail:* office@sfwa.org; operations@sfwa.org *Web Site:* www.sfwa.org, pg 661

Lowenstein, Barbara, Lowenstein Associates Inc, 115 E 23 St, 4th fl, New York, NY 10010 Tel: 212-206-1630 E-mail: assistant@bookhaven.com (queries, no attachments) Web Site: www.lowensteinassociates.com, pg 468

Lowenstein, Elizabeth, The Acheven Book Prize for Young Adult Fiction, c/o Regal House Publishing, 806 Oberlin Rd, No 12094, Raleigh, NC 27605 E-mail: info@regalhousepublishing.com Web Site: regalhousepublishing.com/the-acheven-book-prize-for-young-adult-fiction/, pg 570

Lowenstein, Elizabeth, Fitzroy Books, c/o Regal House Publishing, 806 Oberlin Rd, No 12094, Raleigh, NC 27605 E-mail: info@regalhousepublishing.com Web Site: fitzroybooks.com, pg 72

Lowenstein, Elizabeth, The Kraken Book Prize for Middle-Grade Fiction, c/o Regal House Publishing, 806 Oberlin Rd, No 12094, Raleigh, NC 27605 E-mail: info@regalhousepublishing.com Web Site: regalhousepublishing.com/the-kraken-book-award/, pg 621

Lowery, Andrea Bakewell, Pennsylvania Historical & Museum Commission, State Museum Bldg, 300 North St, Harrisburg, PA 17120-0053 Tel: 717-787-3362; 717-787-5526 (orders) E-mail: ra-shoppaheritage@pa.gov Web Site: www.phmc.pa.gov; www.shoppaheritage.com, pg 157

Lowes, Tara, Broadview Press, 280 Perry St, Unit 5, Peterborough, ON K9J 2J4, Canada Tel: 705-482-5915 Fax: 705-743-8353 E-mail: customerservice@broadviewpress.com Web Site: www.broadviewpress.com, pg 397

Lowman, Sarah, NASW Press, 750 First St NE, Suite 800, Washington, DC 20002 Tel: 202-408-8600 Fax: 203-336-8312 E-mail: press@naswdc.org Web Site: www.naswpress.org, pg 136

Lowry, Marina Padakis, Union Square & Co, 1166 Avenue of the Americas, 17th fl, New York, NY 10036-2715 Tel: 212-532-7160 Toll Free Tel: 800-367-9692 Fax: 212-213-2495 Toll Free Fax: 800-542-7567 E-mail: custservice@sterlingpublishing.com; customerservice@sterlingpublishing.com; editorial@sterlingpublishing.com; tradesales@sterlingpublishing.com Web Site: www.sterlingpublishing.com, pg 212

Lowry, Monica, BenBella Books Inc, 10440 N Central Expwy, Suite 800, Dallas, TX 75231-2264 Tel: 214-750-3600 Web Site: www.benbellabooks.com; www.smartpopbooks.com, pg 27

Lowry, Sadie, Insight Editions, 800 "A" St, San Rafael, CA 94901 Tel: 415-526-1370 Toll Free Tel: 800-809-3792 Toll Free Fax: 866-509-0515 E-mail: info@insighteditions.com; marketing@insighteditions.com Web Site: insighteditions.com, pg 101

Lowry, Dr Samuel, Ambassador International, 411 University Ridge, Suite B14, Greenville, SC 29601 Tel: 864-751-4844 E-mail: info@emeraldhouse.com; publisher@emeraldhouse.com (ms submissions); sales@emeraldhouse.com (orders/order inquiries); media@emeraldhouse.com; design@emeraldhouse.com Web Site: ambassador-international.com; www.facebook.com/AmbassadorIntl; x.com/ambassadorintl, pg 7

Loyd, Mike, In-Plant Printing & Mailing Association (IPMA), 103 N Jefferson St, Kearney, MO 64060 Tel: 816-919-1691 E-mail: ipmainfo@ipma.org Web Site: www.ipma.org, pg 507

Lozar, Paula, New Mexico Book Association (NMBA), PO Box 1285, Santa Fe, NM 87504 E-mail: libroentry@gmail.com Web Site: www.nmbookassociation.org, pg 514

Lu, Alex, Random House Children's Books, c/o Penguin Random House LLC, 1745 Broadway, New York, NY 10019 Tel: 212-782-9000 Web Site: www.rhcbooks.com, pg 170

Lu, Alvin, Kodansha USA Inc, 451 Park Ave S, 7th fl, New York, NY 10016 Tel: 917-322-6200 Fax: 212-935-6929 E-mail: info@kodansha-usa.com Web Site: kodansha.us, pg 111

Lu, Jenny, HarperCollins Children's Books, 195 Broadway, New York, NY 10007 Tel: 212-207-7000 Web Site: www.harpercollins.com/childrens, pg 85

Lu, Ling Ling, Macmillan, 120 Broadway, 22nd fl, New York, NY 10271 E-mail: press.inquiries@macmillan.com Web Site: us.macmillan.com, pg 122

Lubash, Samantha, HarperCollins Publishers LLC, 195 Broadway, New York, NY 10007 Tel: 212-207-7000 Web Site: www.harpercollins.com, pg 87

Lubeck, Roger, California Writers Club (CWC), PO Box 201, Danville, CA 94526 E-mail: membership@calwriters.org; advertising-promotion@calwriters.org Web Site: calwriters.org, pg 502

Lubwama, Julie, Penguin Publishing Group, c/o Penguin Random House LLC, 1745 Broadway, New York, NY 10019 Tel: 212-782-9000 Web Site: www.penguin.com, pg 154

Luby, Kristen, Harry N Abrams Inc, 195 Broadway, 9th fl, New York, NY 10007 Tel: 212-206-7715 Toll Free Tel: 800-345-1359 Fax: 212-645-8437 E-mail: abrams@abramsbooks.com; publicity@abramsbooks.com; sales@abramsbooks.com Web Site: www.abramsbooks.com, pg 3

Lucas, George, InkWell Management, 521 Fifth Ave, Suite 2600, New York, NY 10175 Tel: 212-922-3500 Fax: 212-922-0535 E-mail: info@inkwellmanagement.com; submissions@inkwellmanagement.com; permissions@inkwellmanagement.com Web Site: inkwellmanagement.com, pg 463

Lucas, LaBruce M S, Southern Historical Press Inc, 375 W Broad St, Greenville, SC 29601 Tel: 864-233-2346 E-mail: southernhistoricalpress@gmail.com Web Site: www.southernhistoricalpress.com, pg 195

Lucas, Paul, Janklow & Nesbit Associates, 285 Madison Ave, 21st fl, New York, NY 10017 Tel: 212-421-1700 Fax: 212-355-1403 E-mail: info@janklow.com; submissions@janklow.com; filmtvrights@janklow.com Web Site: www.janklowandnesbit.com, pg 464

Lucchese, Iole, Scholastic Inc, 557 Broadway, New York, NY 10012 Tel: 212-343-6100 Toll Free Tel: 800-SCHOLASTIC (724-6527) Web Site: www.scholastic.com, pg 184

Luchars, Alex, Industrial Press Inc, One Chestnut St, South Norwalk, CT 06854 Tel: 203-956-5593 Toll Free Tel: 888-528-7852 (ext 1, cust serv) E-mail: info@industrialpress.com Web Site: books.industrialpress.com; ebooks.industrialpress.com, pg 100

Luchette, Clair, Binghamton University Creative Writing Program, c/o Dept of English, General Literature & Rhetoric, PO Box 6000, Binghamton, NY 13902-6000 Tel: 607-777-2168 Fax: 607-777-2408 E-mail: cwpro@binghamton.edu Web Site: www.binghamton.edu/english/creative-writing/index.html, pg 561

Luciano, Jeannie, W W Norton & Company Inc, 500 Fifth Ave, New York, NY 10110-0017 Tel: 212-354-5500 Toll Free Tel: 800-233-4830 (orders & cust serv) Fax: 212-869-0856 Toll Free Fax: 800-458-6515 E-mail: orders@wwnorton.com Web Site: wwnorton.com, pg 143

Ludlam, Kim, St Martin's Press, LLC, 120 Broadway, New York, NY 10271 E-mail: publicity@stmartins.com; trademarketing@stmartins.com; foreignrights@stmartins.com Web Site: us.macmillan.com/smp, pg 181

Ludlow, Roberta, Random House Children's Books, c/o Penguin Random House LLC, 1745 Broadway, New York, NY 10019 Tel: 212-782-9000 Web Site: www.rhcbooks.com, pg 169

Ludwin, Corey, Referee Books, 2017 Lathrop Ave, Racine, WI 53405 Tel: 262-632-8855 Toll Free Tel: 800-733-6100 Fax: 262-632-5460 E-mail: customerservice@referee.com Web Site: www.referee.com, pg 173

Luedloff, Emily, Sourcebooks LLC, 1935 Brookdale Rd, Suite 139, Naperville, IL 60563 Tel: 630-961-3900 Toll Free Tel: 800-432-7444 Fax: 630-961-2168 E-mail: info@sourcebooks.com Web Site: www.sourcebooks.com, pg 195

Lui, Adeline, IBPA Book Awards, 1020 Manhattan Beach Blvd, Suite 204, Manhattan Beach, CA 90266 Tel: 310-546-1818 E-mail: info@ibpa-online.org Web Site: www.ibpa-online.org, pg 615

Lui, Adeline, The Independent Book Publishers Association (IBPA), 1020 Manhattan Beach Blvd, Suite 204, Manhattan Beach, CA 90266 Tel: 310-546-1818 E-mail: info@ibpa-online.org Web Site: www.ibpa-online.org, pg 507

Luibl, Chad, Janklow & Nesbit Associates, 285 Madison Ave, 21st fl, New York, NY 10017 Tel: 212-421-1700 Fax: 212-355-1403 E-mail: info@janklow.com; submissions@janklow.com; filmtvrights@janklow.com Web Site: www.janklowandnesbit.com, pg 464

Luke, Michelle, Mason Crest Publishers, 450 Parkway Dr, Suite D, Broomall, PA 19008 Tel: 610-543-6200 Toll Free Tel: 866-MCP-BOOK (627-2665) Fax: 610-543-3878 Web Site: www.masoncrest.com, pg 126

Lum, Robert, PRO-ED Inc, 8700 Shoal Creek Blvd, Austin, TX 78757-6897 Tel: 512-451-3246 Toll Free Tel: 800-897-3202 Fax: 512-451-8542 Toll Free Fax: 800-397-7633 E-mail: info@proedinc.com Web Site: www.proedinc.com, pg 165

Lum, Roxanne, Ignatius Press, 1348 Tenth Ave, San Francisco, CA 94122-2304 Toll Free Tel: 800-651-1531 (orders); 888-615-3186 (cust serv) Fax: 415-387-0896 E-mail: info@ignatius.com Web Site: www.ignatius.com, pg 98

Lumelsky, Irina, United Nations Publications, 405 E 42 St, 11th fl, New York, NY 10017 Tel: 703-661-1571 E-mail: publications@un.org Web Site: shop.un.org, pg 213

Lumenello, Susan, Beacon Press, 24 Farnsworth St, Boston, MA 02210-1409 Tel: 617-742-2110 Fax: 617-723-3097 E-mail: production@beacon.org Web Site: www.beacon.org, pg 25

Lumpris, Maritza, Hachette Book Group Inc, 1290 Avenue of the Americas, New York, NY 10104 Tel: 212-364-1100 Toll Free Tel: 800-759-0190 (cust serv) Fax: 212-364-0933 (intl orders) Toll Free Fax: 800-286-9471 (cust serv) E-mail: customer.service@hbgusa.com; orders@hbgusa.com Web Site: www.hachettebookgroup.com, pg 83

Lumsden, Michal, Workman Publishing, 1290 Avenue of the Americas, New York, NY 10104 Toll Free Tel: 800-759-0190 Fax: 212-364-0950 E-mail: workman-inquiry@hbgusa.com Web Site: www.hachettebookgroup.com/imprint/workman-publishing-company/, pg 233

Luna, Andrea, Police Executive Research Forum, 1120 Connecticut Ave NW, Suite 930, Washington, DC 20036 Tel: 202-466-7820 Web Site: www.policeforum.org, pg 162

Luna, Devin Kirk, Macmillan, 120 Broadway, 22nd fl, New York, NY 10271 E-mail: press.inquiries@macmillan.com Web Site: us.macmillan.com, pg 122

Lund, Kyle, Cedar Fort Inc, 2373 W 700 S, Suite 100, Springville, UT 84663 Tel: 801-489-4084 Toll Free Tel: 800-SKY-BOOK (759-2665) E-mail: marketinginfo@cedarfort.com Web Site: cedarfort.com, pg 43

Lund, Tom, Llewellyn Publications, 2143 Wooddale Dr, Woodbury, MN 55125 Tel: 651-291-1970 Toll Free Tel: 800-843-6666 Fax: 651-291-1908 E-mail: publicity@llewellyn.com; customerservice@llewellyn.com Web Site: www.llewellyn.com, pg 119

Lunghi, Meghan, Merriam-Webster Inc, 47 Federal St, Springfield, MA 01102 Tel: 413-734-3134 Toll Free Tel: 800-828-1880 (orders & cust serv) Fax: 413-731-5979 (sales) E-mail: support@merriam-webster.com Web Site: www.merriam-webster.com, pg 130

Lunn, Jenny, American Geophysical Union (AGU), 2000 Florida Ave NW, Washington, DC 20009 Tel: 202-462-6900 Toll Free Tel: 800-966-2481 (North America) Fax: 202-328-0566 E-mail: service@agu.org (cust serv) Web Site: www.agu.org, pg 10

Lunsford, Alexis, little bee books, 598 Broadway, 7th fl, New York, NY 10012 *Tel:* 212-321-0237 *Toll Free Tel:* 844-321-0237 *E-mail:* info@littlebeebooks.com; sales@littlebeebooks.com; publicity@littlebeebooks.com *Web Site:* littlebeebooks.com, pg 117

Lunt, Dean L, Islandport Press, 247 Portland St, Bldg C, Yarmouth, ME 04096 *Tel:* 207-846-3344 *E-mail:* info@islandportpress.com; orders@islandportpress.com *Web Site:* www.islandportpress.com, pg 105

Lunt, Emily A, Islandport Press, 247 Portland St, Bldg C, Yarmouth, ME 04096 *Tel:* 207-846-3344 *E-mail:* info@islandportpress.com; orders@islandportpress.com *Web Site:* www.islandportpress.com, pg 105

Luongo, Nicole, Harlequin Enterprises Ltd, 195 Broadway, 24th fl, New York, NY 10007 *Tel:* 212-207-7000 *Toll Free Tel:* 888-432-4879; 800-370-5838 (ebooks) *E-mail:* customerservice@harlequin.com *Web Site:* www.harlequin.com/shop/index.html; corporate.harlequin.com, pg 85

Luther, Kay, Ave Maria Press Inc, PO Box 428, Notre Dame, IN 46556 *Toll Free Tel:* 800-282-1865 *Toll Free Fax:* 800-282-5681 *E-mail:* avemariapress.1@nd.edu *Web Site:* www.avemariapress.com, pg 22

Lutjen, Peter, Tor Publishing Group, 120 Broadway, New York, NY 10271 *Toll Free Tel:* 800-455-0340 (Macmillan) *E-mail:* torpublicity@tor.com; forgepublicity@forgebooks.com *Web Site:* us.macmillan.com/torpublishinggroup, pg 208

Luttrell, Marsha, Mercer University Press, 368 Orange St, Macon, GA 31201 *Tel:* 478-301-2880 *Toll Free Tel:* 866-895-1472 *Fax:* 478-301-2585 *E-mail:* mupressorders@mercer.edu *Web Site:* www.mupress.org, pg 129

Lutz, Bryan, University Press of Florida, 2046 NE Waldo Rd, Suite 2100, Gainesville, FL 32609 *Tel:* 352-392-1351 *Toll Free Tel:* 800-226-3822 (orders only) *Fax:* 352-392-0590 *Toll Free Fax:* 800-680-1955 (orders only) *E-mail:* press@upress.ufl.edu; orders@upress.ufl.edu *Web Site:* www.upf.com, pg 221

Lutz, Tom, LARB Books, 6671 Sunset Blvd, Suite 1521, Los Angeles, CA 90028 *Tel:* 323-952-3950 *E-mail:* larbbooks@lareviewofbooks.org *Web Site:* larbbooks.org, pg 113

Lutz, Tom, LARB/USC Publishing Workshop, 6671 Sunset Blvd, Suite 1521, Los Angeles, CA 90028 *E-mail:* publishingworkshop@lareviewofbooks.org *Web Site:* thepublishingworkshop.com, pg 556

Lutz, Zachary, Doubleday, c/o Penguin Random House LLC, 1745 Broadway, New York, NY 10019 *Tel:* 212-751-2600 *Fax:* 212-940-7390 (dom rts); 212-572-2662 (foreign rts) *Web Site:* knopfdoubleday.com/imprint/doubleday/; knopfdoubleday.com, pg 61

Lutz, Zachary, Alfred A Knopf, c/o Penguin Random House LLC, 1745 Broadway, New York, NY 10019 *Tel:* 212-751-2600 *Fax:* 212-940-7390 (dom rts); 212-572-2662 (foreign rts) *Web Site:* knopfdoubleday.com/imprint/knopf/; knopfdoubleday.com, pg 110

Lutzy, Patrick, Cheneliere Education Inc, 5800, rue St Denis, bureau 900, Montreal, QC H2S 3L5, Canada *Tel:* 514-273-1066 *Toll Free Tel:* 800-565-5531 *Fax:* 514-276-0324 *Toll Free Fax:* 800-814-0324 *E-mail:* info@cheneliere.ca *Web Site:* www.cheneliere.ca, pg 399

Lutzy, Patrick, Gaetan Morin Editeur, 5800, rue St-Denis, bureau 900, Montreal, QC H2S 3L5, Canada *Tel:* 514-273-1066 *Toll Free Tel:* 800-565-5531 *Fax:* 514-276-0324 *Toll Free Fax:* 800-814-0324 *E-mail:* info@cheneliere.ca *Web Site:* www.cheneliere.ca, pg 407

Luvaas, William, Rick DeMarinis Short Story Award, PO Box 2414, Durango, CO 81302 *Tel:* 970-903-7914 *E-mail:* cutthroatmag@gmail.com *Web Site:* www.cutthroatmag.com, pg 595

Ly, Carol, Random House Children's Books, c/o Penguin Random House LLC, 1745 Broadway, New York, NY 10019 *Tel:* 212-782-9000 *Web Site:* www.rhcbooks.com, pg 170

Ly, Jenny, HarperCollins Children's Books, 195 Broadway, New York, NY 10007 *Tel:* 212-207-7000 *Web Site:* www.harpercollins.com/childrens, pg 85

Ly, Jenny, Kokila, c/o Penguin Random House LLC, 1745 Broadway, New York, NY 10019 *Tel:* 212-782-9000 *Web Site:* www.penguin.com/kokila-books-overview/, pg 111

Ly, Jenny, Nancy Paulsen Books, c/o Penguin Random House LLC, 1745 Broadway, New York, NY 10019 *Tel:* 212-782-9000 *Web Site:* www.penguin.com/nancy-paulsen-books-overview/, pg 153

Lyke, Jenn, The Catholic Health Association of the United States, 4455 Woodson Rd, St Louis, MO 63134-3797 *Tel:* 314-427-2500 *Fax:* 314-427-0029 *E-mail:* servicecenter@chausa.org *Web Site:* www.chausa.org, pg 42

Lykke, Kristina, Johns Hopkins University Press, 2715 N Charles St, Baltimore, MD 21218-4363 *Tel:* 410-516-6900; 410-516-6987 *Toll Free Tel:* 800-537-5487 (book orders & cust serv); 800-548-1784 (journal orders) *Fax:* 410-516-6968; 410-516-6998 (orders) *E-mail:* hfscustserv@press.jhu.edu (cust serv); jrnlcirc@jh.edu (journal orders) *Web Site:* www.press.jhu.edu; muse.jhu.edu, pg 106

Lyman, Joe, Great Lakes Graphics Association (GLGA), N27 W23960 Paul Rd, Suite 200, Pewaukee, WI 53072 *Tel:* 262-522-2210 *Toll Free Tel:* 855-522-2210 *Fax:* 262-522-2211 *E-mail:* info@glga.info *Web Site:* glga.info, pg 507

Lynch, Besse, The Experiment, 220 E 23 St, Suite 600, New York, NY 10010-4658 *Tel:* 212-889-1659 *E-mail:* info@theexperimentpublishing.com *Web Site:* www.theexperimentpublishing.com, pg 68

Lynch, Catharine, Penguin Random House LLC, 1745 Broadway, New York, NY 10019 *Tel:* 212-782-9000 *Toll Free Tel:* 800-726-0600 *Web Site:* www.penguinrandomhouse.com, pg 155

Lynch, Chris, Simon & Schuster Audio, 1230 Avenue of the Americas, New York, NY 10020 *Web Site:* audio.simonandschuster.com, pg 189

Lynch, Chris, Simon & Schuster, LLC, 1230 Avenue of the Americas, New York, NY 10020 *Tel:* 212-698-7000 *Toll Free Tel:* 800-223-2336 (orders) 212-698-7007 *Toll Free Fax:* 800-943-9831 (orders) *E-mail:* firstname.lastname@simonandschuster.com; purchaseorders@simonandschuster.com (orders) *Web Site:* www.simonandschuster.com, pg 189

Lynch, Danielle, Soil Science Society of America (SSSA), 5585 Guilford Rd, Madison, WI 53711-5801 *Tel:* 608-273-8080 *Fax:* 608-273-2021 *Web Site:* www.soils.org, pg 193

Lynch, Elizabeth, HarperCollins Children's Books, 195 Broadway, New York, NY 10007 *Tel:* 212-207-7000 *Web Site:* www.harpercollins.com/childrens, pg 85

Lynch, Haley, Beacon Press, 24 Farnsworth St, Boston, MA 02210-1409 *Tel:* 617-742-2110 *Fax:* 617-723-3097 *E-mail:* production@beacon.org *Web Site:* www.beacon.org, pg 25

Lynch, Jennifer, Society of Environmental Toxicology & Chemistry (SETAC), 229 S Baylen St, 2nd fl, Pensacola, FL 32502 *Tel:* 850-469-1500 *Toll Free Fax:* 888-296-4136 *E-mail:* setac@setac.org *Web Site:* www.setac.org, pg 192

Lynch, John (Jack) J Jr, Houghton Mifflin Harcourt, 125 High St, Boston, MA 02110 *Tel:* 617-351-5000 *Toll Free Tel:* 855-969-4642; 800-225-5425 (K-12 educ materials); 800-323-9540 (assessment materials); 877-219-1537 (SkillsTutor); 888-242-6747 (Innovation in Educ Group); 800-225-3362 (Trade & Ref Div) *Toll Free Fax:* 800-269-5232 *E-mail:* myhmhco@hmhco.com *Web Site:* www.hmhco.com, pg 95

Lynch, John (Jack) J Jr, Houghton Mifflin Harcourt Trade & Reference Division, 125 High St, Boston, MA 02110 *Tel:* 617-351-5000 *Web Site:* www.hmhco.com, pg 96

Lynch, Kelly, Workman Publishing, 1290 Avenue of the Americas, New York, NY 10104 *Toll Free Tel:* 800-759-0190 *Fax:* 212-364-0950 *E-mail:* workman-inquiry@hbgusa.com *Web Site:* www.hachettebookgroup.com/imprint/workman-publishing-company/, pg 232

Lynch, Nadia, Talcott Notch Literary, 127 Broad St, 2P, Milford, CT 06460 *Tel:* 203-876-4959 *Web Site:* www.talcottnotch.net, pg 479

Lynch, Patrick, Oxford University Press USA, 198 Madison Ave, New York, NY 10016 *Toll Free Tel:* 800-451-7556 (orders); 800-445-9714 (cust serv) *Fax:* 919-677-1303 *E-mail:* custserv.us@oup.com *Web Site:* global.oup.com, pg 149

Lynch, Rosa, American Catholic Press (ACP), 16565 S State St, South Holland, IL 60473 *Tel:* 708-331-5485 *Fax:* 708-331-5484 *E-mail:* acp@acpress.org *Web Site:* www.acpress.org, pg 9

Lynch-Comer, Eva, HarperCollins Children's Books, 195 Broadway, New York, NY 10007 *Tel:* 212-207-7000 *Web Site:* www.harpercollins.com/childrens, pg 85

Lynell, James, Multicultural Publications Inc, 1939 Manchester Rd, Akron, OH 44314 *Tel:* 330-865-9578 *Fax:* 330-865-9578 *E-mail:* multiculturalpub@prodigy.net *Web Site:* www.multiculturalpub.net, pg 135

Lynley, Cason, Duke University Press, 905 W Main St, Suite 18B, Durham, NC 27701 *Tel:* 919-688-5134 *Toll Free Tel:* 888-651-0122 (US) *Fax:* 919-688-2615 *Toll Free Fax:* 888-651-0124 *E-mail:* orders@dukepress.edu *Web Site:* www.dukeupress.edu, pg 62

Lyon, Kevan, Marsal Lyon Literary Agency LLC, 665 San Rodolfo Dr, Suite 124, PMB 121, Solana Beach, CA 92075 *Tel:* 760-814-8507 *Web Site:* www.marsallyonliteraryagency.com, pg 468

Lyons, Allison, Harlequin Enterprises Ltd, 195 Broadway, 24th fl, New York, NY 10007 *Tel:* 212-207-7000 *Toll Free Tel:* 888-432-4879; 800-370-5838 (ebooks) *E-mail:* customerservice@harlequin.com *Web Site:* www.harlequin.com/shop/index.html; corporate.harlequin.com, pg 85

Lyons, Amy, Red Wheel/Weiser, 65 Parker St, Suite 7, Newburyport, MA 01950 *Tel:* 978-465-0504 *Toll Free Tel:* 800-423-7087 (orders) *Fax:* 978-465-0243 *E-mail:* info@rwwbooks.com *Web Site:* www.redwheelweiser.com, pg 173

Lyons, Brad, Chalice Press, 11939 Manchester Rd, No 100, St Louis, MO 63131 *Tel:* 314-231-8500 *Toll Free Tel:* 800-366-3383 *E-mail:* customerservice@chalicepress.com *Web Site:* www.chalicepress.com, pg 44

Lyons, Jed, Rowman & Littlefield, 4501 Forbes Blvd, Suite 200, Lanham, MD 20706 *Tel:* 301-459-3366 *Toll Free Tel:* 800-462-6420 (ext 3024, cust serv) *Fax:* 301-429-5748 *Web Site:* rowman.com, pg 178

Lyons, Jessica, HarperCollins Publishers LLC, 195 Broadway, New York, NY 10007 *Tel:* 212-207-7000 *Web Site:* www.harpercollins.com, pg 87

Lyons, Jonathan, Curtis Brown, Ltd, 228 E 45 St, Suite 310, New York, NY 10017 *Tel:* 212-473-5400 *Fax:* 212-598-0917 *E-mail:* info@cbltd.com *Web Site:* www.curtisbrown.com, pg 452

Lyons, Kim, Jason Aronson Inc, 4501 Forbes Blvd, Suite 200, Lanham, MD 20706 *Tel:* 301-459-3366 *Toll Free Tel:* 800-462-6420 ext 3024 (cust serv) *Fax:* 301-429-5748 *Toll Free Fax:* 800-338-4550 (cust serv) *E-mail:* orders@rowman.com; customercare@rowman.com *Web Site:* www.rowman.com, pg 17

Lyons, Lisbeth A, PRINTING United Alliance, 10015 Main St, Fairfax, VA 22031 *Tel:* 703-385-1335 *Toll Free Tel:* 888-385-3588 *Fax:* 703-273-0456; 703-691-7492 (membership) *E-mail:* assist@printing.org; info@printing.org *Web Site:* www.printing.org, pg 517

Lyons, Michael, Rowman & Littlefield, 4501 Forbes Blvd, Suite 200, Lanham, MD 20706 *Tel:* 301-459-3366 *Toll Free Tel:* 800-462-6420 (ext 3024, cust serv) *Fax:* 301-429-5748 *Web Site:* rowman.com, pg 178

Lyons, Michael, Tower Publishing Co, 650 Cape Rd, Standish, ME 04084 *Tel:* 207-642-5400 *Toll Free Tel:* 800-969-8693 *E-mail:* info@towerpub.com *Web Site:* www.towerpub.com, pg 208

Lyons, Nicole, Wayside Publishing, 2 Stonewood Dr, Freeport, ME 04032 Toll Free Tel: 888-302-2519 E-mail: info@waysidepublishing.com; support@waysidepublishing.com Web Site: waysidepublishing.com, pg 227

Lyons, Tony, Arcade Publishing Inc, 307 W 36 St, 11th fl, New York, NY 10018 Tel: 212-643-6816 Fax: 212-643-6819 E-mail: info@skyhorsepublishing.com (subs & foreign rts) Web Site: www.arcadepub.com, pg 16

Lyons, Tony, Sky Pony Press, 307 W 36 St, 11th fl, New York, NY 10018 Tel: 212-643-6816 Fax: 212-643-6819 E-mail: info@skyhorsepublishing.com; skyponysubmissions@skyhorsepublishing.com Web Site: www.skyhorsepublishing.com/sky-pony-press, pg 191

Ma, Amy, Immedium, 535 Rockdale Dr, San Francisco, CA 94127 Tel: 415-452-8546 Fax: 360-937-6272 E-mail: orders@immedium.com; sales@immedium.com Web Site: www.immedium.com, pg 99

Ma, Karen, Penguin Random House Canada, a Penguin Random House company, 320 Front St W, Suite 1400, Toronto, ON M5V 3B6, Canada Tel: 416-364-4449 Toll Free Tel: 888-523-9292 (cust serv) E-mail: canadaweb@penguinrandomhouse.com; customerservicescanada@penguinrandomhouse.com Web Site: www.penguinrandomhouse.ca, pg 416

Ma, Tiffany, Random House Publishing Group, 1745 Broadway, New York, NY 10019 Toll Free Tel: 800-200-3552 Web Site: www.randomhousebooks.com, pg 171

Maaghul, Johanna, Waterside Productions Inc, 2055 Oxford Ave, Cardiff, CA 92007 Tel: 760-632-9190 Fax: 760-632-9295 E-mail: admin@waterside.com Web Site: www.waterside.com, pg 481

Maass, Donald, Donald Maass Literary Agency, 1000 Dean St, Suite 331, Brooklyn, NY 11238 Tel: 212-727-8383 E-mail: info@maassagency.com Web Site: www.maassagency.com, pg 468

Maassen, Lillian, Alaska Native Language Center (ANLC), PO Box 757680, Fairbanks, AK 99775-7680 Tel: 907-474-7874 E-mail: uaf-anlc@alaska.edu (orders) Web Site: www.uaf.edu/anlc, pg 6

Mabbot, J D, Histria Books, 7181 N Hualapai Way, Suite 130-86, Las Vegas, NV 89166 Tel: 561-299-0802 E-mail: info@histriabooks.com; orders@histriabooks.com; rights@histriabooks.com Web Site: histriabooks.com, pg 93

Mabry, John R, The Apocryphile Press, 1700 Shattuck Ave, Suite 81, Berkeley, CA 94709 Tel: 510-290-4349 E-mail: apocryphile@me.com Web Site: www.apocryphilepress.com, pg 15

MacAleese, Michelle, House of Anansi Press Inc, 128 Sterling Rd, Lower Level, Toronto, ON M6R 2B7, Canada Tel: 416-363-4343 Fax: 416-363-1017 E-mail: customerservice@houseofanansi.com Web Site: houseofanansi.com, pg 409

Macancela, Jennifer, Macmillan, 120 Broadway, 22nd fl, New York, NY 10271 E-mail: press.inquiries@macmillan.com Web Site: us.macmillan.com, pg 122

Macarthur, Lindsey, Candlewick Press, 99 Dover St, Somerville, MA 02144-2825 Tel: 617-661-3330 Fax: 617-661-0565 E-mail: bigbear@candlewick.com; salesinfo@candlewick.com Web Site: candlewick.com, pg 40

Macbrien, Nathan, University of Wisconsin Press, 728 State St, Suite 443, Madison, WI 53706-1418 Tel: 608-263-1110; 608-263-0668 (journal orders) Toll Free Tel: 800-621-2736 (book orders) Fax: 608-263-1173 Toll Free Fax: 800-621-2736 (book orders) E-mail: uwiscpress@uwpress.wisc.edu Web Site: uwpress.wisc.edu, pg 221

Macca, Joe, Scholastic International, 557 Broadway, New York, NY 10012 Tel: 212-343-6100; 646-330-5288 (intl cust serv) Toll Free Tel: 800-SCHOLASTIC (724-6527) Fax: 646-837-7878 E-mail: international@scholastic.com, pg 184

Maccarone, Grace, Holiday House Publishing Inc, 50 Broad St, New York, NY 10004 Tel: 212-688-0085 Fax: 212-421-6134 E-mail: info@holidayhouse.com Web Site: www.holidayhouse.com, pg 94

Maccoby, Gina, Gina Maccoby Literary Agency, PO Box 60, Chappaqua, NY 10514-0060 Tel: 914-238-5630 E-mail: query@maccobylit.com Web Site: www.publishersmarketplace.com/members/GinaMaccoby, pg 468

MacColl, Pamela, Beacon Press, 24 Farnsworth St, Boston, MA 02210-1409 Tel: 617-742-2110 Fax: 617-723-3097 E-mail: production@beacon.org Web Site: www.beacon.org, pg 25

MacDiarmid, Anna, Doubleday Canada, 320 Front St W, Suite 1400, Toronto, ON M5V 3B6, Canada Tel: 416-364-4449 Fax: 416-598-7764 Web Site: www.penguinrandomhouse.ca, pg 401

MacDonald, Alphonse, National Academies Press (NAP), 500 Fifth St NW, Washington, DC 20001 Toll Free Tel: 800-624-6242 Fax: 202-334-2451 (cust serv); 202-334-2793 (mktg dept) E-mail: customer_service@nap.edu Web Site: www.nap.edu, pg 136

MacDonald, Brian A, National Braille Press, 88 Saint Stephen St, Boston, MA 02115-4312 Tel: 617-266-6160 Toll Free Tel: 800-548-7323 (cust serv); 888-965-8965 Fax: 617-437-0456 E-mail: contact@nbp.org Web Site: www.nbp.org, pg 137

MacDonald, Dani, Association of Canadian Publishers (ACP), 401 Richmond St W, Studio 257A, Toronto, ON M5V 3A8, Canada Tel: 416-487-6116 E-mail: admin@canbook.org Web Site: publishers.ca, pg 499

MacDonald, Deb, Wood Lake Publishing Inc, 485 Beaver Lake Rd, Kelowna, BC V4V 1S5, Canada Tel: 250-766-2778 Toll Free Tel: 800-663-2775 (orders & cust serv) Fax: 250-766-2736 Toll Free Fax: 888-841-9991 (orders & cust serv) E-mail: info@woodlake.com; customerservice@woodlake.com Web Site: www.woodlake.com, pg 425

MacDonald, Dougald, American Alpine Club, 710 Tenth St, Suite 100, Golden, CO 80401 Tel: 303-384-0110 Fax: 303-384-0111 E-mail: info@americanalpineclub.org Web Site: americanalpineclub.org, pg 8

MacDonald, Leo, HarperCollins Canada Ltd, 22 Adelaide St W, 41st fl, Toronto, ON M5H 4E3, Canada Tel: 416-975-9334 E-mail: hcorder@harpercollins.com Web Site: www.harpercollins.ca, pg 409

Macdonald, Meghan, Dundurn Press Ltd, PO Box 19510, RPO Manulife, Toronto, ON M4W 3T9, Canada Tel: 416-214-5544 E-mail: info@dundurn.com; publicity@dundurn.com; sales@dundurn.com Web Site: www.dundurn.com, pg 401

MacDonald, Tom, Albert Whitman & Company, 250 S Northwest Hwy, Suite 320, Park Ridge, IL 60068 Tel: 847-232-2800 Toll Free Tel: 800-255-7675 (orders) Fax: 847-581-0039 E-mail: mail@albertwhitman.com; orders@albertwhitman.com Web Site: www.albertwhitman.com, pg 6

MacDonnell, Margo, Rocky Mountain Mineral Law Foundation, 9191 Sheridan Blvd, Suite 203, Westminster, CO 80031 Tel: 303-321-8100 Fax: 303-321-7657 E-mail: info@rmmlf.org Web Site: www.rmmlf.org, pg 176

MacFarlane, Fraser, One Act Play Depot, Box 335, Spiritwood, SK S0J 2M0, Canada E-mail: plays@oneactplays.net; orders@oneactplays.net Web Site: oneactplays.net, pg 414

MacGillivray, Sadie, R Ross Annett Award for Children's Literature, 11759 Groat Rd NW, Edmonton, AB T5M 3K6, Canada Tel: 780-422-8174 Toll Free Tel: 800-665-5354 (AB only) E-mail: mail@writersguild.ab.ca Web Site: writersguild.ca, pg 573

MacGillivray, Sadie, Georges Bugnet Award for Fiction, 11759 Groat Rd NW, Edmonton, AB T5M 3K6, Canada Tel: 780-422-8174 Toll Free Tel: 800-665-5354 (AB only) E-mail: mail@writersguild.ab.ca Web Site: writersguild.ca, pg 585

MacGillivray, Sadie, The City of Calgary W O Mitchell Book Prize, 11759 Groat Rd NW, Edmonton, AB T5M 3K6, Canada Tel: 780-422-8174 Toll Free Tel: 800-665-5354 (AB only) E-mail: mail@writersguild.ab.ca Web Site: writersguild.ca, pg 590

MacGillivray, Sadie, Wilfrid Eggleston Award for Nonfiction, 11759 Groat Rd NW, Edmonton, AB T5M 3K6, Canada Tel: 780-422-8174 Toll Free Tel: 800-665-5354 (AB only) E-mail: mail@writersguild.ab.ca Web Site: writersguild.ca, pg 599

MacGillivray, Sadie, James H Gray Award for Short Nonfiction, 11759 Groat Rd NW, Edmonton, AB T5M 3K6, Canada Tel: 780-422-8174 Toll Free Tel: 800-665-5354 (AB only) E-mail: mail@writersguild.ab.ca Web Site: writersguild.ca, pg 609

MacGillivray, Sadie, The Robert Kroetsch City of Edmonton Book Prize, 11759 Groat Rd NW, Edmonton, AB T5M 3K6, Canada Tel: 780-422-8174 Toll Free Tel: 800-665-5354 (AB only) E-mail: mail@writersguild.ab.ca Web Site: writersguild.ca, pg 621

MacGillivray, Sadie, Howard O'Hagan Award for Short Story, 11759 Groat Rd NW, Edmonton, AB T5M 3K6, Canada Tel: 780-422-8174 Toll Free Tel: 800-665-5354 (AB only) E-mail: mail@writersguild.ab.ca Web Site: writersguild.ca, pg 643

MacGillivray, Sadie, Gwen Pharis Ringwood Award for Drama, 11759 Groat Rd NW, Edmonton, AB T5M 3K6, Canada Tel: 780-422-8174 Toll Free Tel: 800-665-5354 (AB only) E-mail: mail@writersguild.ab.ca Web Site: writersguild.ca, pg 656

MacGillivray, Sadie, Stephan G Stephansson Award for Poetry, 11759 Groat Rd NW, Edmonton, AB T5M 3K6, Canada Tel: 780-422-8174 Toll Free Tel: 800-665-5354 (AB only) E-mail: mail@writersguild.ab.ca Web Site: writersguild.ca, pg 666

MacGillivray, Sadie, Jon Whyte Memorial Essay Prize, 11759 Groat Rd NW, Edmonton, AB T5M 3K6, Canada Tel: 780-422-8174 Toll Free Tel: 800-665-5354 (AB only) E-mail: mail@writersguild.ab.ca Web Site: writersguild.ca, pg 675

MacGillivray, Sadie, Writers' Guild of Alberta, 11759 Groat Rd NW, Edmonton, AB T5M 3K6, Canada Tel: 780-422-8174 Toll Free Tel: 800-665-5354 (AB only) E-mail: mail@writersguild.ab.ca Web Site: writersguild.ca, pg 522

MacGregor, Robert, Crabtree Publishing Co, 347 Fifth Ave, Suite 1402-145, New York, NY 10016 Tel: 212-496-5040 Toll Free Tel: 800-387-7650 Toll Free Fax: 800-355-7166 E-mail: custserv@crabtreebooks.com Web Site: www.crabtreebooks.com, pg 54

MacGregor, Robert, Crabtree Publishing Co Ltd, 616 Welland Ave, St Catharines, ON L2M 5V6, Canada Tel: 905-682-5221 Toll Free Tel: 800-387-7650 Fax: 905-682-7166 Toll Free Fax: 800-355-7166 E-mail: custserv@crabtreebooks.com; sales@crabtreebooks.com; orders@crabtreebooks.com Web Site: www.crabtreebooks.ca, pg 400

Machado, Sierra, Running Press, 1290 Avenue of the Americas, New York, NY 10104 Tel: 212-364-1100 Toll Free Tel: 800-759-0190 (cust serv) Fax: 212-364-0933 (intl orders) Toll Free Fax: 800-286-9471 (cust serv) E-mail: customer.service@hbgusa.com; orders@hbgusa.com Web Site: www.hachettebookgroup.com/imprint/running-press/; www.moon.com (Moon Travel Guides), pg 178

Machicado, Sheila, HarperCollins Children's Books, 195 Broadway, New York, NY 10007 Tel: 212-207-7000 Web Site: www.harpercollins.com/childrens, pg 85

Macias, Stephanie Frescas, Lee & Low Books Inc, 95 Madison Ave, Suite 1205, New York, NY 10016 Tel: 212-779-4400 Toll Free Tel: 888-320-3190 (ext 28, orders only) Fax: 212-683-1894 (orders only); 212-532-6035 E-mail: general@leeandlow.com Web Site: www.leeandlow.com, pg 114

Maciel, Amanda, Scholastic Trade Publishing, 557 Broadway, New York, NY 10012 Tel: 212-343-6100; 212-343-4685 (export sales) Fax: 212-343-4714 (export sales) Web Site: www.scholastic.com, pg 184

Macintosh, Adrienne, Harlequin Enterprises Ltd, Bay Adelaide Centre, East Tower, 22 Adelaide St W, 41st fl, Toronto, ON M5H 4E3, Canada Tel: 416-445-5860

Toll Free Tel: 888-432-4879; 800-370-5838 (ebook inquiries) E-mail: customerservice@harlequin.com Web Site: www.harlequin.com, pg 409

Mack, Amelia, Astra Books for Young Readers, 19 W 21 St, No 1201, New York, NY 10010 Tel: 646-844-3485 E-mail: ahinfo@astrahouse.com; permissions@astrapublishinghouse.com Web Site: astrapublishinghouse.com, pg 20

Mack, Breeyn, Teaching Strategies LLC, 4500 East-West Hwy, Suite 300, Bethesda, MD 20814 Tel: 301-634-0818 Toll Free Tel: 800-637-3652 E-mail: info@teachingstrategies.com; support@teachingstrategies.com Web Site: teachingstrategies.com, pg 204

Mack, Kate, Aevitas Creative Management LLC, 19 W 21 St, Suite 501, New York, NY 10010 Tel: 212-765-6900 Web Site: www.aevitascreative.com, pg 448

Macke, Alison, Macmillan, 120 Broadway, 22nd fl, New York, NY 10271 E-mail: press.inquiries@macmillan.com Web Site: us.macmillan.com, pg 122

MacKeen, Alison, Calligraph LLC, 45 Main St, No 850, Brooklyn, NY 11201 Tel: 212-253-1074 E-mail: mail@calligraphlit.com; rights@calligraphlit.com; submissions@calligraphlit.com Web Site: www.calligraphlit.com, pg 453

MacKenzie, Joanna, Nelson Literary Agency LLC, 700 Colorado Blvd, No 352, Denver, CO 80206 Tel: 303-292-2805 E-mail: info@nelsonagency.com Web Site: www.nelsonagency.com, pg 471

MacKenzie, Julia, American Association for the Advancement of Science (AAAS), 1200 New York Ave NW, Washington, DC 20005 Tel: 202-326-6400 E-mail: membership@aaas.org Web Site: www.aaas.org, pg 494

Mackenzie, Leslie, Grey House Publishing Inc™, 4919 Rte 22, Amenia, NY 12501 Tel: 518-789-8700 Toll Free Tel: 800-562-2139 Fax: 518-789-0556 E-mail: books@greyhouse.com; customerservice@greyhouse.com Web Site: greyhouse.com, pg 81

MacKenzie, Megan, Penguin Random House Canada, a Penguin Random House company, 320 Front St W, Suite 1400, Toronto, ON M5V 3B6, Canada Tel: 416-364-4449 Toll Free Tel: 888-523-9292 (cust serv) E-mail: canadaweb@penguinrandomhouse.com; customerservicescanada@penguinrandomhouse.com Web Site: www.penguinrandomhouse.ca, pg 416

Macklem, Ann, University of British Columbia Press, 2029 West Mall, Vancouver, BC V6T 1Z2, Canada Tel: 604-822-5959 Toll Free Tel: 877-377-9378 Fax: 604-822-6083 Toll Free Fax: 800-668-0821 E-mail: frontdesk@ubcpress.ca Web Site: www.ubcpress.ca, pg 422

Mackwood, Robert, Seventh Avenue Literary Agency, 6318 Rimrock Rd, Sechelt, BC V7Z 0L1, Canada Tel: 604-538-7252 E-mail: info@seventhavenuelit.com Web Site: www.seventhavenuelit.com, pg 475

MacLachlan, Christina, Wildflower Press, c/o Oakbrook Press, 3301 S Valley Dr, Rapid City, SD 57703 Tel: 605-381-6385 E-mail: info@wildflowerpress.org Web Site: www.wildflowerpress.org, pg 229

Maclagan, Maral, Scholastic Canada Ltd, 175 Hillmount Rd, Markham, ON L6C 1Z7, Canada Tel: 905-887-7323 Toll Free Tel: 800-268-3860 (CN) Toll Free Fax: 800-387-4944 E-mail: custserve@scholastic.ca Web Site: www.scholastic.ca, pg 418

MacLeod, Lauren, Aevitas Creative Management LLC, 19 W 21 St, Suite 501, New York, NY 10010 Tel: 212-765-6900 Web Site: www.aevitascreative.com, pg 448

MacLeod, Lorisia, Library Association of Alberta (LAA), c/o The Alberta Library, 7 Sir Winston Churchill Sq NW, No 623, Edmonton, AB T5J 2V5, Canada E-mail: info@laa.ca Web Site: www.laa.ca, pg 509

MacLeod, Sam, HRD Press, PO Box 2600, Amherst, MA 01004 Tel: 413-253-3488 Toll Free Tel: 800-822-2801 E-mail: info@hrdpress.com; customerservice@hrdpress.com Web Site: www.hrdpress.com, pg 97

MacLeod-English, Katie, Avery, c/o Penguin Random House LLC, 1745 Broadway, New York, NY 10019 Tel: 212-366-2000 Web Site: www.penguin.com/avery-overview/, pg 23

MacLeod-English, Katie, TarcherPerigee, c/o Penguin Random House LLC, 1745 Broadway, New York, NY 10019 Tel: 212-782-9000 Web Site: www.penguin.com/tarcherperigee-overview/; www.facebook.com/TarcherPerigee, pg 203

Macnair, Randal, Oolichan Books, PO Box 2278, Fernie, BC V0B 1M0, Canada Tel: 250-423-6113 E-mail: info@oolichan.com Web Site: www.oolichan.com, pg 414

MacNevin, James, University of British Columbia Press, 2029 West Mall, Vancouver, BC V6T 1Z2, Canada Tel: 604-822-5959 Toll Free Tel: 877-377-9378 Fax: 604-822-6083 Toll Free Fax: 800-668-0821 E-mail: frontdesk@ubcpress.ca Web Site: www.ubcpress.ca, pg 422

Maco, Mark Kate, University of Virginia Press, PO Box 400318, Charlottesville, VA 22904-4318 Tel: 434-924-3469 (cust serv) Toll Free Tel: 800-831-3406 Fax: 434-982-2655 Toll Free Fax: 877-288-6400 E-mail: vapress@virginia.edu Web Site: www.upress.virginia.edu, pg 220

Macrides, Kristine, HarperCollins Publishers LLC, 195 Broadway, New York, NY 10007 Tel: 212-207-7000 Web Site: www.harpercollins.com, pg 86

Macris, Natalie, Solano Press Books, PO Box 773, Point Arena, CA 95468 Tel: 707-884-4508 Toll Free Tel: 800-931-9373 E-mail: spbooks@solano.com Web Site: www.solano.com, pg 193

MacSweeney, Eve, Calligraph LLC, 45 Main St, No 850, Brooklyn, NY 11201 Tel: 212-253-1074 E-mail: mail@calligraphlit.com; rights@calligraphlit.com; submissions@calligraphlit.com Web Site: www.calligraphlit.com, pg 453

Macy, Stephanie, HarperCollins Children's Books, 195 Broadway, New York, NY 10007 Tel: 212-207-7000 Web Site: www.harpercollins.com/childrens, pg 85

Madan, Ashish, Aptara Inc, 2901 Telestar Ct, Suite 522, Falls Church, VA 22042 Tel: 703-352-0001 E-mail: moreinfo@aptaracorp.com Web Site: www.aptaracorp.com, pg 435

Madan, Neeti, Sterling Lord Literistic Inc, 594 Broadway, Suite 205, New York, NY 10012 Tel: 212-780-6050 Fax: 212-780-6095 E-mail: info@sll.com Web Site: www.sll.com, pg 477

Madan, Praveen, Berrett-Koehler Publishers Inc, 1333 Broadway, Suite 1000, Oakland, CA 94612 Tel: 510-817-2277 Fax: 510-817-2278 E-mail: bkpub@bkpub.com Web Site: www.bkconnection.com, pg 29

Madara, James L MD, American Medical Association (AMA), AMA Plaza, 330 N Wabash, Suite 39300, Chicago, IL 60611-5885 Tel: 312-464-5000; 312-464-4430 (media & edit) Toll Free Tel: 800-621-8335 E-mail: media@ama-assn.org (media & edit); bookandonlinesales@ama-assn.org (volume book/ebook sales) Web Site: www.ama-assn.org, pg 11

Madara, James L MD, American Medical Association (AMA), AMA Plaza, 330 N Wabash, Suite 39300, Chicago, IL 60611-5885 Tel: 312-464-5000 Toll Free Tel: 800-621-8335 E-mail: media@ama-assn.org (media & edit) Web Site: www.ama-assn.org; www.jamanetwork.org, pg 495

Madden, Kyla, McGill-Queen's University Press, 1010 Sherbrooke W, Suite 1720, Montreal, QC H3A 2R7, Canada Tel: 514-398-3750 Fax: 514-398-4333 E-mail: mqup@mcgill.ca Web Site: www.mqup.ca, pg 412

Maddox, Amy, University of North Texas Press, 941 Precision Dr, Denton, TX 76207 Tel: 940-565-2142 Fax: 940-369-8760 Web Site: untpress.unt.edu, pg 218

Maddrey, Thomas, American Society of Media Photographers Inc, Four Embarcadero Ctr, Suite 1400, San Francisco, CA 94111 Toll Free Tel: 844-762-3386 Web Site: asmp.org, pg 497

Madhubuti, Haki R, Third World Press Foundation, 7822 S Dobson Ave, Chicago, IL 60619 Tel: 773-651-0700 E-mail: twpbooks@thirdworldpressfoundation.org Web Site: thirdworldpressfoundation.org, pg 206

Madigan, Carleen, Workman Publishing, 1290 Avenue of the Americas, New York, NY 10104 Toll Free Tel: 800-759-0190 Fax: 212-364-0950 E-mail: workman-inquiry@hbgusa.com Web Site: www.hachettebookgroup.com/imprint/workman-publishing-company/, pg 232

Madson, Trish, Macmillan, 120 Broadway, 22nd fl, New York, NY 10271 E-mail: press.inquiries@macmillan.com Web Site: us.macmillan.com, pg 122

Maeda Allman, Karen, Wales Literary Agency Inc, 1508 Tenth Ave E, No 401, Seattle, WA 98102 Tel: 206-553-9684 E-mail: waleslit@waleslit.com Web Site: www.waleslit.com, pg 481

Mafchir, James, Sherman Asher Publishing, 126 Candelario St, Santa Fe, NM 87501 Tel: 505-988-7214 E-mail: westernedge@santa-fe.net Web Site: www.shermanasher.com; www.westernedgepress.com, pg 187

Mafchir, James, Western Edge Press, 126 Candelario St, Santa Fe, NM 87501 Tel: 505-988-7214 E-mail: westernedge@santa-fe.net Web Site: www.westernedgepress.com; www.shermanasher.com, pg 228

Maffei, Dorian, Kimberley Cameron & Associates LLC, 1550 Tiburon Blvd, Suite 704, Tiburon, CA 94920 E-mail: info@kimberleycameron.com Web Site: www.kimberleycameron.com, pg 453

Magarino, Zandra, HarperCollins Publishers LLC, 195 Broadway, New York, NY 10007 Tel: 212-207-7000 Web Site: www.harpercollins.com, pg 86

Magee, Lauren, No Starch Press, 245 Eighth St, San Francisco, CA 94103 Tel: 415-863-9900 Toll Free Tel: 800-420-7240 Fax: 415-863-9950 E-mail: info@nostarch.com; sales@nostarch.com; editors@nostarch.com; marketing@nostarch.com Web Site: www.nostarch.com, pg 141

Magin, Michelle, United States Holocaust Memorial Museum, 100 Raoul Wallenberg Place SW, Washington, DC 20024-2126 Tel: 202-488-0400; 202-488-6144 (orders) Toll Free Tel: 800-259-9998 (orders) E-mail: academicpublications@ushmm.org Web Site: www.ushmm.org, pg 213

Magliato, Nick, Penguin Workshop, c/o Penguin Random House LLC, 1745 Broadway, New York, NY 10019 Tel: 212-782-9000 Web Site: www.penguin.com/publishers/penguinworkshop/, pg 156

Magnani, Enrico MA, Scribendi Inc, 405 Riverview Dr, Chatham, ON N7M 0N3, Canada Tel: 519-351-1626 (cust serv) Toll Free Tel: 519-354-0192 E-mail: customerservice@scribendi.com Web Site: www.scribendi.com, pg 444

Magnell, Molly, Workman Publishing, 1290 Avenue of the Americas, New York, NY 10104 Toll Free Tel: 800-759-0190 Fax: 212-364-0950 E-mail: workman-inquiry@hbgusa.com Web Site: www.hachettebookgroup.com/imprint/workman-publishing-company/, pg 233

Magnus, Mary H, Health Professions Press, 409 Washington Ave, Suite 500, Towson, MD 21204 Tel: 410-337-9585 Toll Free Tel: 888-337-8808 Fax: 410-337-8539 Web Site: www.healthpropress.com, pg 90

Magowan, Mark, The Vendome Press, 244 Fifth Ave, Suite 2043, New York, NY 10001 Tel: 212-737-1857 E-mail: info@vendomepress.com Web Site: www.vendomepress.com, pg 224

Magrisso, Mary, Houghton Mifflin Harcourt Trade & Reference Division, 125 High St, Boston, MA 02110 Tel: 617-351-5000 Web Site: www.hmhco.com, pg 96

Maguda, Matt, HarperCollins Children's Books, 195 Broadway, New York, NY 10007 Tel: 212-207-7000 Web Site: www.harpercollins.com/childrens, pg 86

Maguire, Evelyn, New England Independent Booksellers Association Inc (NEIBA), One Beacon St, 15th fl, Boston, MA 02108 Tel: 617-547-3642 Web Site: www.newenglandbooks.org, pg 514

Maguire, Mike, R Ross Annett Award for Children's Literature, 11759 Groat Rd NW, Edmonton, AB T5M 3K6, Canada *Tel:* 780-422-8174 *Toll Free Tel:* 800-665-5354 (AB only) *E-mail:* mail@writersguild.ab.ca *Web Site:* writersguild.ca, pg 573

Maguire, Mike, Georges Bugnet Award for Fiction, 11759 Groat Rd NW, Edmonton, AB T5M 3K6, Canada *Tel:* 780-422-8174 *Toll Free Tel:* 800-665-5354 (AB only) *E-mail:* mail@writersguild.ab.ca *Web Site:* writersguild.ca, pg 585

Maguire, Mike, The City of Calgary W O Mitchell Book Prize, 11759 Groat Rd NW, Edmonton, AB T5M 3K6, Canada *Tel:* 780-422-8174 *Toll Free Tel:* 800-665-5354 (AB only) *E-mail:* mail@writersguild.ab.ca *Web Site:* writersguild.ca, pg 590

Maguire, Mike, Wilfrid Eggleston Award for Nonfiction, 11759 Groat Rd NW, Edmonton, AB T5M 3K6, Canada *Tel:* 780-422-8174 *Toll Free Tel:* 800-665-5354 (AB only) *E-mail:* mail@writersguild.ab.ca *Web Site:* writersguild.ca, pg 599

Maguire, Mike, James H Gray Award for Short Nonfiction, 11759 Groat Rd NW, Edmonton, AB T5M 3K6, Canada *Tel:* 780-422-8174 *Toll Free Tel:* 800-665-5354 (AB only) *E-mail:* mail@writersguild.ab.ca *Web Site:* writersguild.ca, pg 609

Maguire, Mike, The Robert Kroetsch City of Edmonton Book Prize, 11759 Groat Rd NW, Edmonton, AB T5M 3K6, Canada *Tel:* 780-422-8174 *Toll Free Tel:* 800-665-5354 (AB only) *E-mail:* mail@writersguild.ab.ca *Web Site:* writersguild.ca, pg 621

Maguire, Mike, Howard O'Hagan Award for Short Story, 11759 Groat Rd NW, Edmonton, AB T5M 3K6, Canada *Tel:* 780-422-8174 *Toll Free Tel:* 800-665-5354 (AB only) *E-mail:* mail@writersguild.ab.ca *Web Site:* writersguild.ca, pg 643

Maguire, Mike, Gwen Pharis Ringwood Award for Drama, 11759 Groat Rd NW, Edmonton, AB T5M 3K6, Canada *Tel:* 780-422-8174 *Toll Free Tel:* 800-665-5354 (AB only) *E-mail:* mail@writersguild.ab.ca *Web Site:* writersguild.ca, pg 656

Maguire, Mike, Stephan G Stephansson Award for Poetry, 11759 Groat Rd NW, Edmonton, AB T5M 3K6, Canada *Tel:* 780-422-8174 *Toll Free Tel:* 800-665-5354 (AB only) *E-mail:* mail@writersguild.ab.ca *Web Site:* writersguild.ca, pg 666

Maguire, Mike, Jon Whyte Memorial Essay Prize, 11759 Groat Rd NW, Edmonton, AB T5M 3K6, Canada *Tel:* 780-422-8174 *Toll Free Tel:* 800-665-5354 (AB only) *E-mail:* mail@writersguild.ab.ca *Web Site:* writersguild.ca, pg 675

Maguire, Mike, Writers' Guild of Alberta, 11759 Groat Rd NW, Edmonton, AB T5M 3K6, Canada *Tel:* 780-422-8174 *Toll Free Tel:* 800-665-5354 (AB only) *E-mail:* mail@writersguild.ab.ca *Web Site:* writersguild.ca, pg 522

Mahajan, Vinod, Nataraj Books, 7967 Twist Lane, Springfield, VA 22153 *Tel:* 703-455-4996 *E-mail:* orders@natarajbooks.com; natarajbooks@gmail.com *Web Site:* www.natarajbooks.com, pg 136

Mahanian, Seema, Viking Penguin, c/o Penguin Random House LLC, 1745 Broadway, New York, NY 10019 *Tel:* 212-782-9000 *Web Site:* www.penguin.com/overview-vikingbooks/; www.penguin.com/pamela-dorman-books-overview/; www.penguin.com/penguin-classics-overview/; www.penguin.com/penguin-life-overview/, pg 225

Mahar, Emily, Henry Holt and Company, LLC, 120 Broadway, 23rd fl, New York, NY 10271 *Tel:* 646-307-5151 *Toll Free Tel:* 888-330-8477 (orders) *Fax:* 646-307-5285 *Web Site:* www.henryholt.com, pg 94

Maher, Kelsey, Association of American Editorial Cartoonists (AAEC), PO Box 160314, Sacramento, CA 95816 *Tel:* 954-356-4945 *E-mail:* editorialcartoonists@gmail.com *Web Site:* www.editorialcartoonists.com, pg 498

Maher, Sean, Chelsea Green Publishing Co, 85 N Main St, Suite 120, White River Junction, VT 05001 *Tel:* 802-295-6300 *Toll Free Tel:* 800-639-4099 (cust serv & orders) *Fax:* 802-295-6444 *E-mail:* customerservice@chelseagreen.com; editorial@chelseagreen.com; publicity@chelseagreen.com; rights@chelseagreen.com *Web Site:* www.chelseagreen.com, pg 45

Mahler, Cathy, The Edna Staebler Award for Creative Non-Fiction, Office of the Dean, Faculty of Arts, 75 University Ave W, Waterloo, ON N2L 3C5, Canada *Tel:* 519-884-1970 (ext 3361) *E-mail:* staebleraward@wlu.ca *Web Site:* wlu.ca/staebleraward, pg 665

Mahmood, Aima, The New Press, 120 Wall St, 31st fl, New York, NY 10005 *Tel:* 212-629-8802 *Fax:* 212-629-8617 *E-mail:* newpress@thenewpress.com *Web Site:* thenewpress.com, pg 140

Mahon, Emily, Doubleday, c/o Penguin Random House LLC, 1745 Broadway, New York, NY 10019 *Tel:* 212-751-2600 *Fax:* 212-940-7390 (dom rts); 212-572-2662 (foreign rts) *Web Site:* knopfdoubleday.com/imprint/doubleday/; knopfdoubleday.com, pg 61

Mahoney, Natasha, Management Sciences for Health, 200 Rivers Edge Dr, Medford, MA 02155 *Tel:* 617-250-9500 *Fax:* 617-250-9090 *E-mail:* bookstore@msh.org *Web Site:* www.msh.org, pg 123

Mahoney, Tyrrell Hammer, Chronicle Books LLC, 680 Second St, San Francisco, CA 94107 *Tel:* 415-537-4200 *Fax:* 415-537-4460 (perms) *E-mail:* hello@chroniclebooks.com; subrights@chroniclebooks.com *Web Site:* www.chroniclebooks.com, pg 47

Mahorter, Rosie, Bloomsbury Publishing Inc, 1385 Broadway, 5th fl, New York, NY 10018 *Tel:* 212-419-5300 *E-mail:* marketingusa@bloomsbury.com; adultpublicityusa@bloomsbury.com; askacademic@bloomsbury.com *Web Site:* www.bloomsbury.com, pg 32

Maier, Skip, Human Kinetics Inc, 1607 N Market St, Champaign, IL 61820 *Tel:* 217-351-5076 *Toll Free Tel:* 800-747-4457 *Fax:* 217-351-1549 (orders/cust serv) *E-mail:* info@hkusa.com *Web Site:* us.humankinetics.com, pg 97

Maillet, Neal, Berrett-Koehler Publishers Inc, 1333 Broadway, Suite 1000, Oakland, CA 94612 *Tel:* 510-817-2277 *Fax:* 510-817-2278 *E-mail:* bkpub@bkpub.com *Web Site:* www.bkconnection.com, pg 29

Mailloux, Alison, Johns Hopkins University Press, 2715 N Charles St, Baltimore, MD 21218-4363 *Tel:* 410-516-6900; 410-516-6987 *Toll Free Tel:* 800-537-5487 (book orders & cust serv); 800-548-1784 (journal orders) *Fax:* 410-516-6968; 410-516-6998 (orders) *E-mail:* hfscustserv@press.jhu.edu (cust serv); jrnlcirc@jh.edu (journal orders) *Web Site:* www.press.jhu.edu; muse.jhu.edu, pg 106

Maines, Kevin Murphy, New Women's Voices Chapbook Competition, PO Box 1626, Georgetown, KY 40324 *Tel:* 502-603-0670 *E-mail:* finishingbooks@aol.com; flpbookstore@aol.com *Web Site:* www.finishinglinepress.com; finishinglinepress.submittable.com/submit, pg 640

Maines, Kevin Murphy, Open Chapbook Competition, PO Box 1626, Georgetown, KY 40324 *Tel:* 502-603-0670 *E-mail:* finishingbooks@aol.com; flpbookstore@aol.com *Web Site:* www.finishinglinepress.com, pg 644

Maines, Leah, New Women's Voices Chapbook Competition, PO Box 1626, Georgetown, KY 40324 *Tel:* 502-603-0670 *E-mail:* finishingbooks@aol.com; flpbookstore@aol.com *Web Site:* www.finishinglinepress.com; finishinglinepress.submittable.com/submit, pg 640

Maines, Leah, Open Chapbook Competition, PO Box 1626, Georgetown, KY 40324 *Tel:* 502-603-0670 *E-mail:* finishingbooks@aol.com; flpbookstore@aol.com *Web Site:* www.finishinglinepress.com, pg 644

Mainhardt, Ricia, RMA, 47 Tiffany Way, Plattsburgh, NY 12901 *Tel:* 718-434-1893 *Fax:* 518-310-0668 *Web Site:* ricia.com, pg 473

Mainville, Lara MA, University of Ottawa Press (Presses de l'Université d'Ottawa), 542 King Edward Ave, Ottawa, ON K1N 6N5, Canada *Tel:* 613-562-5246 *Fax:* 613-562-5247 *E-mail:* puo-uop@uottawa.ca; acquisitions@uottawa.ca *Web Site:* press.uottawa.ca, pg 422

Maitland, Arnaud, Dharma Publishing, 35788 Hauser Bridge Rd, Cazadero, CA 95421 *Tel:* 707-847-3717 *Fax:* 707-847-3380 *E-mail:* contact@dharmapublishing.com *Web Site:* www.dharmapublishing.com, pg 59

Maitland, LaToya, HarperCollins Children's Books, 195 Broadway, New York, NY 10007 *Tel:* 212-207-7000 *Web Site:* www.harpercollins.com/childrens, pg 85

Majczyk, Amy, RAND Corp, 1776 Main St, Santa Monica, CA 90407-2138 *Tel:* 310-393-0411 *Fax:* 310-393-4818 *Web Site:* www.rand.org, pg 169

Majeed, Yasmin Adele, Asian American Writers' Workshop (AAWW), 112 W 27 St, Suite 600, New York, NY 10001 *Tel:* 212-494-0061 *E-mail:* desk@aaww.org *Web Site:* aaww.org; facebook.com/AsianAmericanWritersWorkshop, pg 497

Majeska, Hannah, Notable Wisconsin Authors, 112 Owen Rd, Unit 6437, Monona, WI 53716 *Tel:* 608-245-3640 *E-mail:* wla@wisconsinlibraries.org *Web Site:* www.wisconsinlibraries.org, pg 642

Majeska, Hannah, WLA Literary Award, 112 Owen Rd, Unit 6437, Monona, WI 53716 *Tel:* 608-245-3640 *E-mail:* wla@wisconsinlibraries.org *Web Site:* www.wisconsinlibraries.org, pg 676

Majumder, Molly, Entangled Publishing LLC, 644 Shrewsbury Commons Ave, Suite 181, Shrewsbury, PA 17361 *Toll Free Tel:* 877-677-9451 *E-mail:* publisher@entangledpublishing.com *Web Site:* www.entangledpublishing.com, pg 67

Makanju, Kay, Harry N Abrams Inc, 195 Broadway, 9th fl, New York, NY 10007 *Tel:* 212-206-7715 *Toll Free Tel:* 800-345-1359 *Fax:* 212-645-8437 *E-mail:* abrams@abramsbooks.com; publicity@abramsbooks.com; sales@abramsbooks.com *Web Site:* www.abramsbooks.com, pg 3

Makholm, Lauren, The Art Institute of Chicago, 111 S Michigan Ave, Chicago, IL 60603-6404 *Tel:* 312-443-3600 *Toll Free Tel:* 855-301-9612 *E-mail:* aicshop@artic.edu *Web Site:* www.artic.edu/print-publications; shop.artic.edu, pg 17

Makras, Penny, HarperCollins Publishers LLC, 195 Broadway, New York, NY 10007 *Tel:* 212-207-7000 *Web Site:* www.harpercollins.com, pg 86

Malak, Stephanie, LARB Books, 6671 Sunset Blvd, Suite 1521, Los Angeles, CA 90028 *Tel:* 323-952-3950 *E-mail:* larbbooks@lareviewofbooks.org *Web Site:* larbbooks.org, pg 113

Malarkey, Sarah, Random House Publishing Group, 1745 Broadway, New York, NY 10019 *Toll Free Tel:* 800-200-3552 *Web Site:* www.randomhousebooks.com, pg 171

Malashewsky, Megan, University of British Columbia Press, 2029 West Mall, Vancouver, BC V6T 1Z2, Canada *Tel:* 604-822-5959 *Toll Free Tel:* 877-377-9378 *Fax:* 604-822-6083 *Toll Free Fax:* 800-668-0821 *E-mail:* frontdesk@ubcpress.ca *Web Site:* www.ubcpress.ca, pg 422

Malaviya, Nihar, Penguin Random House LLC, 1745 Broadway, New York, NY 10019 *Tel:* 212-782-9000 *Toll Free Tel:* 800-726-0600 *Web Site:* www.penguinrandomhouse.com, pg 155

Malcolm, Ian, Harvard University Press, 79 Garden St, Cambridge, MA 02138-1499 *Tel:* 617-495-2600; 401-531-2800 (intl orders) *Toll Free Tel:* 800-405-1619 (orders) *Fax:* 617-495-5898 (gen); 617-496-4677 (edit & rts); 401-531-2801 (intl orders) *Toll Free Fax:* 800-406-9145 (orders) *E-mail:* contact_hup@harvard.edu *Web Site:* www.hup.harvard.edu, pg 88

Malcolm, Reed, University of California Press, 155 Grand Ave, Suite 400, Oakland, CA 94612-3758 *Tel:* 510-883-8232 *Fax:* 510-836-8910 *E-mail:* customerservice@ucpress.edu *Web Site:* www.ucpress.edu, pg 215

Malcom, Lily, Dial Books for Young Readers, c/o Penguin Random House LLC, 1745 Broadway, New York, NY 10019 *Tel:* 212-782-9000 *Web Site:* www.penguin.com/dial-overview/, pg 59

Malcom, Lily, Nancy Paulsen Books, c/o Penguin Random House LLC, 1745 Broadway, New York, NY 10019 Tel: 212-782-9000 Web Site: www.penguin.com/nancy-paulsen-books-overview/, pg 152

Malcom, Lily, GP Putnam's Sons Books for Young Readers, c/o Penguin Random House LLC, 1745 Broadway, New York, NY 10019 Tel: 212-782-9000 Web Site: www.penguin.com/putnam-young-readers/, pg 167

Malcom, Lily, Rocky Pond Books, c/o Penguin Random House LLC, 1745 Broadway, New York, NY 10019 Tel: 212-782-9000 Web Site: www.penguin.com/rocky-pond-overview/, pg 176

Malden, Cheryl M, EBSCO Information Services Library Staff Development Award, 225 N Michigan Ave, Suite 1300, Chicago, IL 60601 Tel: 312-280-3247 Toll Free Tel: 800-545-2433 (ext 3247) Fax: 312-944-3897 E-mail: awards@ala.org Web Site: www.ala.org/awardsgrants, pg 598

Malden, Cheryl M, Joseph W Lippincott Award, 225 N Michigan Ave, Suite 1300, Chicago, IL 60601 Tel: 312-280-3247 Toll Free Tel: 800-545-2433 (ext 3247) Fax: 312-944-3897 E-mail: awards@ala.org Web Site: www.ala.org, pg 625

Malden, Cheryl M, Schneider Family Book Awards, 225 N Michigan Ave, Suite 1300, Chicago, IL 60601 Tel: 312-280-3247 Toll Free Tel: 800-545-2433 Fax: 312-944-3897 E-mail: ala@ala.org Web Site: www.ala.org/awardsgrants/schneider-family-book-award, pg 661

Maldonado, Joaquin, Editorial Unilit, 8167 NW 84 St, Medley, FL 33166 Tel: 305-592-6136; 305-592-6135 Toll Free Tel: 800-767-7726 Fax: 305-592-0087 E-mail: info@editorialunilit.com; ventas@editorialunilit.com (sales) Web Site: www.editorialunilit.com, pg 64

Maldonado, Ricardo Alberto, Academy of American Poets Fellowship, 75 Maiden Lane, Suite 901, New York, NY 10038 Tel: 212-274-0343 E-mail: awards@poets.org Web Site: poets.org/academy-american-poets/prizes/academy-american-poets-fellowship, pg 569

Maldonado, Ricardo Alberto, Academy of American Poets First Book Award, 75 Maiden Lane, Suite 901, New York, NY 10038 Tel: 212-274-0343 E-mail: awards@poets.org Web Site: poets.org/academy-american-poets/prizes/first-book-award, pg 569

Maldonado, Ricardo Alberto, The Academy of American Poets Inc, 75 Maiden Lane, Suite 901, New York, NY 10038 Tel: 212-274-0343 E-mail: academy@poets.org Web Site: poets.org, pg 493

Maldonado, Ricardo Alberto, Ambroggio Prize, 75 Maiden Lane, Suite 901, New York, NY 10038 Tel: 212-274-0343 E-mail: awards@poets.org Web Site: poets.org/academy-american-poets/prizes/ambroggio-prize, pg 572

Maldonado, Ricardo Alberto, James Laughlin Award, 75 Maiden Lane, Suite 901, New York, NY 10038 Tel: 212-274-0343 E-mail: awards@poets.org Web Site: poets.org/academy-american-poets/prizes/james-laughlin-award, pg 622

Maldonado, Ricardo Alberto, Lenore Marshall Poetry Prize, 75 Maiden Lane, Suite 901, New York, NY 10038 Tel: 212-274-0343 E-mail: awards@poets.org Web Site: poets.org/academy-american-poets/prizes/lenore-marshall-poetry-prize, pg 629

Maldonado, Ricardo Alberto, Harold Morton Landon Translation Award, 75 Maiden Lane, Suite 901, New York, NY 10038 Tel: 212-274-0343 E-mail: awards@poets.org Web Site: poets.org/academy-american-poets/prizes/harold-morton-landon-translation-award, pg 635

Maldonado, Ricardo Alberto, Aliki Perroti & Seth Frank Most Promising Young Poet Award, 75 Maiden Lane, Suite 901, New York, NY 10038 Tel: 212-274-0343 E-mail: awards@poets.org Web Site: poets.org/academy-american-poets/american-poets-prizes, pg 649

Maldonado, Ricardo Alberto, Raiziss/de Palchi Fellowship, 75 Maiden Lane, Suite 901, New York, NY 10038 Tel: 212-274-0343 E-mail: awards@poets.org Web Site: poets.org/academy-american-poets/american-poets-prizes, pg 654

Maldonado, Ricardo Alberto, Wallace Stevens Award, 75 Maiden Lane, Suite 901, New York, NY 10038 Tel: 212-274-0343 E-mail: awards@poets.org Web Site: poets.org/academy-american-poets/prizes/wallace-stevens-award, pg 666

Maldonado, Ricardo Alberto, Treehouse Climate Action Poem Prize, 75 Maiden Lane, Suite 901, New York, NY 10038 Tel: 212-274-0343 E-mail: awards@poets.org Web Site: poets.org, pg 670

Malec, Erin, Reed Environmental Writing Award, 201 W Main St, Suite 14, Charlottesville, VA 22902 Tel: 434-977-4090 Fax: 434-977-1483 Web Site: www.southernenvironment.org, pg 655

Malhotra, Aakanksha, Penguin Random House Canada, a Penguin Random House company, 320 Front St W, Suite 1400, Toronto, ON M5V 3B6, Canada Tel: 416-364-4449 Toll Free Tel: 888-523-9292 (cust serv) E-mail: canadaweb@penguinrandomhouse.com; customerservicescanada@penguinrandomhouse.com Web Site: www.penguinrandomhouse.ca, pg 416

Malhotra, Megha, Women Who Write Inc, PO Box 652, Madison, NJ 07940-0652 Web Site: www.womenwhowrite.org, pg 522

Malisch, Susan, American Medical Association (AMA), AMA Plaza, 330 N Wabash, Suite 39300, Chicago, IL 60611-5885 Tel: 312-464-5000 Toll Free Tel: 800-621-8335 E-mail: media@ama-assn.org (media & edit) Web Site: www.ama-assn.org; www.jamanetwork.org, pg 495

Malk, Steven, Writers House, 21 W 26 St, New York, NY 10010 Tel: 212-685-2400 Web Site: www.writershouse.com, pg 482

Mallach, Larry, Penguin Random House LLC, 1745 Broadway, New York, NY 10019 Tel: 212-782-9000 Toll Free Tel: 800-726-0600 Web Site: www.penguinrandomhouse.com, pg 155

Mallardi, Vincent, Printing Brokerage/Buyers Association International (PBBA), 74-5576 Pawai Place, No 599, Kailua Kona, HI 96740 Tel: 808-339-0880 E-mail: contactus@pbba.org Web Site: pbba.org, pg 517

Mallette, Stephanie, Les Editions du Boreal, 4447, rue St-Denis, Montreal, QC H2J 2L2, Canada Tel: 514-287-7401 Fax: 514-287-7664 E-mail: info@editionsboreal.qc.ca; boreal@editionsboreal.qc.ca; communications@editionsboreal.qc.ca Web Site: www.editionsboreal.qc.ca, pg 402

Mallia-Barsati, Jo, Penguin Random House LLC, 1745 Broadway, New York, NY 10019 Tel: 212-782-9000 Toll Free Tel: 800-726-0600 Web Site: www.penguinrandomhouse.com, pg 155

Mallin, Sean, American Anthropological Association (AAA), 2300 Clarendon Blvd, Suite 1301, Arlington, VA 22201 E-mail: pubs@americananthro.org Web Site: www.americananthro.org, pg 8

Malmud, Deborah A, W W Norton & Company Inc, 500 Fifth Ave, New York, NY 10110-0017 Tel: 212-354-5500 Toll Free Tel: 800-233-4830 (orders & cust serv) Fax: 212-869-0856 Toll Free Fax: 800-458-6515 E-mail: orders@wwnorton.com Web Site: wwnorton.com, pg 143

Maloney, Casey, Avery, c/o Penguin Random House LLC, 1745 Broadway, New York, NY 10019 Tel: 212-366-2000 Web Site: www.penguin.com/avery-overview/, pg 23

Maloney, Casey, TarcherPerigee, c/o Penguin Random House LLC, 1745 Broadway, New York, NY 10019 Tel: 212-782-9000 Web Site: www.penguin.com/tarcherperigee-overview/; www.facebook.com/TarcherPerigee, pg 202

Maloney, Dennis, White Pine Press, PO Box 236, Buffalo, NY 14201 Tel: 716-573-8202 E-mail: wpine@whitepine.org Web Site: www.whitepine.org, pg 228

Maloney, Joy, Southern Playwrights Competition, 700 Pelham Rd N, Jacksonville, AL 36265-1602 Tel: 256-782-5412 Web Site: www.jsu.edu/english/southpla.html, pg 665

Malonzo, Michelle, Duende-Word BIPOC Bookseller Award, 757 E 20 Ave, Suite 370-335, Denver, CO 80205 E-mail: info@thewordfordiversity.org Web Site: www.thewordfordiversity.org/booksellerawarad, pg 597

Malonzo, Michelle, The Word, A Storytelling Sanctuary Inc, 757 E 20 Ave, Suite 370-335, Denver, CO 80205 E-mail: info@thewordfordiversity.org Web Site: www.thewordfordiversity.org, pg 522

Malter, Emily, Chronicle Books LLC, 680 Second St, San Francisco, CA 94107 Tel: 415-537-4200 Fax: 415-537-4460 (perms) E-mail: hello@chroniclebooks.com; subrights@chroniclebooks.com Web Site: www.chroniclebooks.com, pg 48

Maluccio, Paul, Blue Note Publications Inc, 721 North Dr, Suite D, Melbourne, FL 32934 Tel: 321-799-2583; 321-622-6289 Toll Free Tel: 800-624-0401 (orders) Fax: 321-799-1942; 321-622-6830 E-mail: bluenotebooks@gmail.com Web Site: bluenotepublications.com, pg 32

Man, Angela, Orbit, 1290 Avenue of the Americas, New York, NY 10104 Tel: 212-364-1100 Toll Free Tel: 800-759-0190 Web Site: www.orbitbooks.net; www.hachettebookgroup.com/imprint/orbit, pg 147

Man-Kong, Mary, Random House Children's Books, c/o Penguin Random House LLC, 1745 Broadway, New York, NY 10019 Tel: 212-782-9000 Web Site: www.rhcbooks.com, pg 170

Manaktala, Gita, The MIT Press, One Broadway, 12th fl, Cambridge, MA 02142 Tel: 617-253-5255 Toll Free Tel: 800-405-1619 (orders) Fax: 617-258-6779; 617-577-1545 (orders) Web Site: mitpress.mit.edu, pg 132

Manalio-Bonaventura, Gia, Adams Media, 100 Technology Center Dr, Suite 501, Stoughton, MA 02072 Tel: 508-427-7100 Web Site: www.simonandschuster.com, pg 4

Manchee, Bill, Top Publications Ltd, 5101 Brouette Ct, Plano, TX 75023 Tel: 972-628-6414 Fax: 972-233-0713 E-mail: bill@topfiction.net (sales & admin) Web Site: toppub.com, pg 207

Mancuso, Leslie D PhD, Jhpiego, 1615 Thames St, Baltimore, MD 21231-3492 Tel: 410-537-1800 E-mail: info@jhpiego.org Web Site: www.jhpiego.org, pg 106

Mandel, Dan, Sanford J Greenburger Associates Inc, 55 Fifth Ave, New York, NY 10003 Tel: 212-206-5600 Web Site: greenburger.com, pg 461

Mandel, David, Arcadia Publishing Inc, 210 Wingo Way, Suite 200, Mount Pleasant, SC 29464 Tel: 843-853-2070 E-mail: retailers@arcadiapublishing.com Web Site: www.arcadiapublishing.com, pg 16

Mandel, David, Pelican Publishing, 990 N Corporate Dr, Suite 100, New Orleans, LA 70123 Tel: 504-684-8976 Toll Free Tel: 844-868-1798 (orders) E-mail: editorial@pelicanpub.com (submissions) Web Site: www.pelicanpub.com; www.arcadiapublishing.com/imprints/pelican-publishing, pg 153

Mandel, Dr Dena, Mandel Vilar Press, 19 Oxford Ct, Simsbury, CT 06070 Tel: 806-790-4731 E-mail: info@mvpress.org Web Site: www.mvpublishers.org, pg 124

Mandel, Jay, WME, 11 Madison Ave, New York, NY 10010 Tel: 212-586-5100 Web Site: www.wmeagency.com, pg 482

Mandel, Lindsay, Doubleday, c/o Penguin Random House LLC, 1745 Broadway, New York, NY 10019 Tel: 212-751-2600 Fax: 212-940-7390 (dom rts); 212-572-2662 (foreign rts) Web Site: knopfdoubleday.com/imprint/doubleday/; knopfdoubleday.com, pg 61

Mandel, Dr Robert A, Mandel Vilar Press, 19 Oxford Ct, Simsbury, CT 06070 Tel: 806-790-4731 E-mail: info@mvpress.org Web Site: www.mvpublishers.org, pg 124

Mangan, Diane, Andrews McMeel Publishing LLC, 1130 Walnut St, Kansas City, MO 64106-2109 *Tel:* 816-581-7500 *Toll Free Tel:* 800-851-8923 *Web Site:* www.andrewsmcmeel.com; publishing.andrewsmcmeel.com, pg 14

Mangicaro, Jessica, Berkley, c/o Penguin Random House LLC, 1745 Broadway, 19th fl, New York, NY 10019 *Tel:* 212-366-2000 *Web Site:* www.penguin.com/publishers/berkley/; www.penguin.com/ace-overview/, pg 28

Mangum, Jeff, The Astronomical Society of the Pacific, 390 Ashton Ave, San Francisco, CA 94112 *Tel:* 415-337-1100; 415-715-1414 (cust serv) *Toll Free Tel:* 800-335-2624 (cust serv) *Fax:* 415-337-5205 *E-mail:* service@astrosociety.org *Web Site:* astrosociety.org, pg 20

Mangum, Lisa, Deseret Book Co, 55 N 300 W, 3rd fl, Salt Lake City, UT 84101-3502 *Tel:* 801-517-3369; 801-534-1515 (corp) *Toll Free Tel:* 800-453-4532 (orders); 888-846-7302 (orders) *Fax:* 801-517-3126 *E-mail:* service@deseretbook.com *Web Site:* www.deseretbook.com, pg 58

Mangum, Lisa, Shadow Mountain Publishing, PO Box 30178, Salt Lake City, UT 84130-0178 *Tel:* 801-534-1515 *Toll Free Tel:* 800-453-3876 *E-mail:* info@shadowmountain.com; submissions@shadowmountain.com *Web Site:* shadowmountain.com, pg 187

Mani, Bhaskaran, Macmillan, 120 Broadway, 22nd fl, New York, NY 10271 *E-mail:* press.inquiries@macmillan.com *Web Site:* us.macmillan.com, pg 122

Manion, Deborah, Syracuse University Press, 621 Skytop Rd, Suite 110, Syracuse, NY 13244-5290 *Tel:* 315-443-5534 *Toll Free Tel:* 800-365-8929 (cust serv) *Fax:* 315-443-5545 *E-mail:* supress@syr.edu *Web Site:* press.syr.edu, pg 201

Manlove, Melissa, Sourcebooks LLC, 1935 Brookdale Rd, Suite 139, Naperville, IL 60563 *Tel:* 630-961-3900 *Toll Free Tel:* 800-432-7444 *Fax:* 630-961-2168 *E-mail:* info@sourcebooks.com *Web Site:* www.sourcebooks.com, pg 194

Mann, Ashley, R Ross Annett Award for Children's Literature, 11759 Groat Rd NW, Edmonton, AB T5M 3K6, Canada *Tel:* 780-422-8174 *Toll Free Tel:* 800-665-5354 (AB only) *E-mail:* mail@writersguild.ab.ca *Web Site:* writersguild.ca, pg 573

Mann, Ashley, Georges Bugnet Award for Fiction, 11759 Groat Rd NW, Edmonton, AB T5M 3K6, Canada *Tel:* 780-422-8174 *Toll Free Tel:* 800-665-5354 (AB only) *E-mail:* mail@writersguild.ab.ca *Web Site:* writersguild.ca, pg 585

Mann, Ashley, The City of Calgary W O Mitchell Book Prize, 11759 Groat Rd NW, Edmonton, AB T5M 3K6, Canada *Tel:* 780-422-8174 *Toll Free Tel:* 800-665-5354 (AB only) *E-mail:* mail@writersguild.ab.ca *Web Site:* writersguild.ca, pg 590

Mann, Ashley, Wilfrid Eggleston Award for Nonfiction, 11759 Groat Rd NW, Edmonton, AB T5M 3K6, Canada *Tel:* 780-422-8174 *Toll Free Tel:* 800-665-5354 (AB only) *E-mail:* mail@writersguild.ab.ca *Web Site:* writersguild.ca, pg 599

Mann, Ashley, James H Gray Award for Short Nonfiction, 11759 Groat Rd NW, Edmonton, AB T5M 3K6, Canada *Tel:* 780-422-8174 *Toll Free Tel:* 800-665-5354 (AB only) *E-mail:* mail@writersguild.ab.ca *Web Site:* writersguild.ca, pg 609

Mann, Ashley, The Robert Kroetsch City of Edmonton Book Prize, 11759 Groat Rd NW, Edmonton, AB T5M 3K6, Canada *Tel:* 780-422-8174 *Toll Free Tel:* 800-665-5354 (AB only) *E-mail:* mail@writersguild.ab.ca *Web Site:* writersguild.ca, pg 621

Mann, Ashley, Howard O'Hagan Award for Short Story, 11759 Groat Rd NW, Edmonton, AB T5M 3K6, Canada *Tel:* 780-422-8174 *Toll Free Tel:* 800-665-5354 (AB only) *E-mail:* mail@writersguild.ab.ca *Web Site:* writersguild.ca, pg 643

Mann, Ashley, Gwen Pharis Ringwood Award for Drama, 11759 Groat Rd NW, Edmonton, AB T5M 3K6, Canada *Tel:* 780-422-8174 *Toll Free Tel:* 800-665-5354 (AB only) *E-mail:* mail@writersguild.ab.ca *Web Site:* writersguild.ca, pg 656

Mann, Ashley, Stephan G Stephansson Award for Poetry, 11759 Groat Rd NW, Edmonton, AB T5M 3K6, Canada *Tel:* 780-422-8174 *Toll Free Tel:* 800-665-5354 (AB only) *E-mail:* mail@writersguild.ab.ca *Web Site:* writersguild.ca, pg 666

Mann, Ashley, Jon Whyte Memorial Essay Prize, 11759 Groat Rd NW, Edmonton, AB T5M 3K6, Canada *Tel:* 780-422-8174 *Toll Free Tel:* 800-665-5354 (AB only) *E-mail:* mail@writersguild.ab.ca *Web Site:* writersguild.ca, pg 675

Mann, Ashley, Writers' Guild of Alberta, 11759 Groat Rd NW, Edmonton, AB T5M 3K6, Canada *Tel:* 780-422-8174 *Toll Free Tel:* 800-665-5354 (AB only) *E-mail:* mail@writersguild.ab.ca *Web Site:* writersguild.ca, pg 522

Mann, Carol, Carol Mann Agency, 55 Fifth Ave, 18th fl, New York, NY 10003 *Tel:* 212-206-5635 *Fax:* 212-675-4809 *E-mail:* submissions@carolmannagency.com *Web Site:* www.carolmannagency.com, pg 468

Mann, Jennifer, WNDB Internship Grants, 10319 Westlake Dr, No 104, Bethesda, MD 20817 *Tel:* 701-404-WNDB (404-9632, voicemail only) *E-mail:* internships@diversebooks.org *Web Site:* diversebooks.org/our-programs/internship-grants, pg 676

Mann, Maria, Atria Books, 1230 Avenue of the Americas, New York, NY 10020 *Tel:* 212-698-7000 *Fax:* 212-698-7007 *Web Site:* www.simonandschuster.com, pg 21

Mann, Sue, Working With Words, 5320 SW Mayfair Ct, Beaverton, OR 97005 *Tel:* 503-626-4998 *E-mail:* editor@zzz.com, pg 445

Manna, Christine, Association of National Advertisers Inc (ANA), 155 E 44 St, New York, NY 10017 *Tel:* 212-697-5950 *Fax:* 212-687-7310 *E-mail:* info@ana.net *Web Site:* www.ana.net, pg 499

Manning, Kelsey, HarperCollins Publishers LLC, 195 Broadway, New York, NY 10007 *Tel:* 212-207-7000 *Web Site:* www.harpercollins.com, pg 86

Manning, Sabrey, Portfolio, c/o Penguin Random House LLC, 1745 Broadway, New York, NY 10019 *Tel:* 212-782-9000 *Web Site:* www.penguin.com/portfolio-overview/; www.penguin.com/sentinel-overview/; www.penguin.com/thesis/, pg 162

Manning, Sean, Simon & Schuster, 1230 Avenue of the Americas, New York, NY 10020 *Tel:* 212-698-7000 *Toll Free Tel:* 800-223-2348 (cust serv); 800-223-2336 (orders) *Toll Free Fax:* 800-943-9831 (orders) *Web Site:* simonandschusterpublishing.com/simonandschuster/, pg 188

Mannon, Emily, HarperCollins Children's Books, 195 Broadway, New York, NY 10007 *Tel:* 212-207-7000 *Web Site:* www.harpercollins.com/childrens, pg 85

Mano, Barry, Referee Books, 2017 Lathrop Ave, Racine, WI 53405 *Tel:* 262-632-8855 *Toll Free Tel:* 800-733-6100 *Fax:* 262-632-5460 *E-mail:* customerservice@referee.com *Web Site:* www.referee.com, pg 173

Manoogian, Daron, Harvard Art Museums, 32 Quincy St, Cambridge, MA 02138 *Tel:* 617-495-9400 *Web Site:* www.harvardartmuseums.org, pg 87

Manos, Wayne, Cold Spring Harbor Laboratory Press, 500 Sunnyside Blvd, Woodbury, NY 11797-2924 *Tel:* 516-422-4100 *Toll Free Tel:* 800-843-4388 *E-mail:* cshpress@cshl.edu *Web Site:* www.cshlpress.com, pg 50

Mansfield, Katherine, IEEE Computer Society, 2001 "L" St NW, Suite 700, Washington, DC 20036-4928 *Tel:* 202-371-0101 *Toll Free Tel:* 800-678-4333 (memb info) *Fax:* 202-728-9614 *E-mail:* help@computer.org *Web Site:* www.computer.org, pg 98

Mansoor, Leah, Encyclopaedia Britannica Inc, 325 N La Salle St, Suite 200, Chicago, IL 60654 *Tel:* 312-347-7000 (all other countries) *Toll Free Tel:* 800-323-1229 (US & CN) *Fax:* 312-294-2104 *E-mail:* contact@eb.com *Web Site:* www.britannica.com, pg 17

Mantele, Katie Qiaoling, Counterpoint Press LLC, 2560 Ninth St, Suite 318, Berkeley, CA 94710 *Tel:* 510-704-0230 *Fax:* 510-704-0268 *E-mail:* info@counterpointpress.com *Web Site:* counterpointpress.com; softskull.com, pg 54

Mantilla, Tito, Editorial Portavoz, 2450 Oak Industrial Dr NE, Grand Rapids, MI 49505 *Toll Free Tel:* 877-733-2607 (ext 206) *E-mail:* kregelbooks@kregel.com *Web Site:* www.portavoz.com, pg 64

Mantz, Erika, Book Industry Charitable Foundation (BINC), 3135 S State St, Suite 203, Ann Arbor, MI 48108 *Toll Free Tel:* 866-733-9064 *E-mail:* info@bincfoundation.org *Web Site:* www.bincfoundation.org, pg 525

Mantz, Erika, Denver Publishing Institute Scholarship, 3135 S State St, Suite 203, Ann Arbor, MI 48108 *Toll Free Tel:* 866-733-9064 *E-mail:* info@bincfoundation.org *Web Site:* www.bincfoundation.org/denver-publishing-institute/, pg 595

Mantz, Erika, Carla Gray Memorial Scholarship, 3135 S State St, Suite 203, Ann Arbor, MI 48108 *Toll Free Tel:* 866-733-9064 *E-mail:* info@bincfoundation.org *Web Site:* www.bincfoundation.org/carla-gray/, pg 609

Mantz, Erika, Higher Education Scholarship Program, 3135 S State St, Suite 203, Ann Arbor, MI 48108 *Toll Free Tel:* 866-733-9064 *E-mail:* info@bincfoundation.org *Web Site:* www.bincfoundation.org/scholarship, pg 612

Mantz, Erika, Susan Kamil Scholarship for Emerging Writers, 3135 S State St, Suite 203, Ann Arbor, MI 48108 *Toll Free Tel:* 866-733-9064 *E-mail:* info@bincfoundation.org *Web Site:* bincfoundation.org/susankamil-scholarship, pg 619

Mantz, Erika, George Markey Keating Memorial Scholarships, 3135 S State St, Suite 203, Ann Arbor, MI 48108 *Toll Free Tel:* 866-733-9064 *E-mail:* info@bincfoundation.org *Web Site:* www.bincfoundation.org, pg 619

Mantz, Erika, Macmillan Booksellers Professional Development Scholarship, 3135 S State St, Suite 203, Ann Arbor, MI 48108 *Toll Free Tel:* 866-733-9064 *E-mail:* info@bincfoundation.org *Web Site:* www.bincfoundation.org/scholarship, pg 628

Mantz, Erika, Karl Pohrt Tribute Award, 3135 S State St, Suite 203, Ann Arbor, MI 48108 *Toll Free Tel:* 866-733-9064 *E-mail:* info@bincfoundation.org *Web Site:* www.bincfoundation.org/scholarship, pg 651

Manus, Ron, Alfred Music, 285 Century Place, Louisville, CO 80027 *Tel:* 818-891-5999 (dealer sales, intl) *Toll Free Tel:* 800-292-6122 (dealer sales, US & CN); 800-628-1528 (cust serv) *Fax:* 818-893-5560 (dealer sales); 818-830-6252 (cust serv) *Toll Free Fax:* 800-632-1928 (dealer sales) *E-mail:* customerservice@alfred.com; sales@alfred.com *Web Site:* www.alfred.com, pg 7

Manzanero, Paula, Penguin Workshop, c/o Penguin Random House LLC, 1745 Broadway, New York, NY 10019 *Tel:* 212-782-9000 *Web Site:* www.penguin.com/publishers/penguinworkshop/, pg 156

Mao, Clare, Sanford J Greenburger Associates Inc, 55 Fifth Ave, New York, NY 10003 *Tel:* 212-206-5600 *Web Site:* greenburger.com, pg 461

Maravelis, Peter, City Lights Publishers, 261 Columbus Ave, San Francisco, CA 94133 *Tel:* 415-362-8193 *E-mail:* staff@citylights.com *Web Site:* citylights.com, pg 48

Marchand, Emily, Candlewick Press, 99 Dover St, Somerville, MA 02144-2825 *Tel:* 617-661-3330 *Fax:* 617-661-0565 *E-mail:* bigbear@candlewick.com; salesinfo@candlewick.com *Web Site:* candlewick.com, pg 39

Marchant, Leigh, Hachette Book Group Inc, 1290 Avenue of the Americas, New York, NY 10104 *Tel:* 212-364-1100 *Toll Free Tel:* 800-759-0190 (cust serv) *Fax:* 212-364-0933 (intl orders) *Toll Free Fax:* 800-286-9471 (cust serv) *E-mail:* customer.service@hbgusa.com; orders@hbgusa.com *Web Site:* www.hachettebookgroup.com, pg 83

Marchese, Shannon, Thomas Nelson, 501 Nelson Place, Nashville, TN 37214 *Tel:* 615-889-9000 *Toll Free Tel:* 800-251-4000 *Web Site:* www.thomasnelson.com, pg 206

Marchese, Shannon, Tommy Nelson®, 501 Nelson Place, Nashville, TN 37214 *Tel:* 615-889-9000; 615-902-1485 (cust serv) *Toll Free Tel:* 800-251-4000 *Web Site:* www.tommynelson.com, pg 207

Marchese, Susan, AIHA (American Industrial Hygiene Association), 3141 Fairview Park Dr, Suite 777, Falls Church, VA 22042 *Tel:* 703-849-8888 *Fax:* 703-207-3561 *E-mail:* infonet@aiha.org *Web Site:* www.aiha.org, pg 6

Marchini, Tracy, BookEnds Literary Agency, 136 Long Hill Rd, Gillette, NJ 07933 *Web Site:* www.bookendsliterary.com, pg 451

Marchman, Stephanie, University of Notre Dame Press, 310 Flanner Hall, Notre Dame, IN 46556 *Tel:* 574-631-6346 *Fax:* 574-631-8148 *E-mail:* undpress@nd.edu *Web Site:* www.undpress.nd.edu, pg 219

Marciano, Michael, The Connecticut Law Tribune, c/o 10 Talcott Ridge Rd, Unit A3, Farmington, CT 06032 *Toll Free Tel:* 877-256-2472 *E-mail:* editorial@alm.com *Web Site:* www.law.com/ctlawtribune/, pg 52

Marcil, Denise, Denise Marcil Literary Agency LLC, 483 Westover Rd, Stamford, CT 06902 *Tel:* 203-327-9970 *Fax:* 203-327-9970 *Web Site:* www.marcilofarrellagency.com, pg 468

Marciniszyn, Alex, Palladium Books Inc, 39074 Webb Ct, Westland, MI 48185 *Tel:* 734-721-2903 (orders) *Web Site:* www.palladiumbooks.com, pg 150

Marcok, Vicki, Vehicule Press, PO Box 42094, CP Roy, Montreal, QC H2W 2T3, Canada *Tel:* 514-844-6073 *E-mail:* vp@vehiculepress.com; admin@vehiculepress.com *Web Site:* www.vehiculepress.com, pg 424

Marcum, Lucy, Sourcebooks LLC, 1935 Brookdale Rd, Suite 139, Naperville, IL 60563 *Tel:* 630-961-3900 *Toll Free Tel:* 800-432-7444 *Fax:* 630-961-2168 *E-mail:* info@sourcebooks.com *Web Site:* www.sourcebooks.com, pg 195

Marcus, Barbara, Penguin Random House LLC, 1745 Broadway, New York, NY 10019 *Tel:* 212-782-9000 *Toll Free Tel:* 800-726-0600 *Web Site:* www.penguinrandomhouse.com, pg 155

Marcus, Barbara, Random House Children's Books, c/o Penguin Random House LLC, 1745 Broadway, New York, NY 10019 *Tel:* 212-782-9000 *Web Site:* www.rhcbooks.com, pg 169

Marcus, Bonnie, The Maureen Egen Writers Exchange Award, 90 Broad St, Suite 2100, New York, NY 10004 *Tel:* 212-226-3586 *Fax:* 212-226-3963 *E-mail:* wex@pw.org; admin@pw.org *Web Site:* www.pw.org, pg 598

Marcus, Karyn, Grand Central Publishing, 1290 Avenue of the Americas, New York, NY 10104 *Tel:* 212-364-1100 *Web Site:* www.hachettebookgroup.com/imprint/grand-central-publishing/, pg 80

Marcus, Kendra, BookStop Literary Agency LLC, 67 Meadow View Rd, Orinda, CA 94563 *E-mail:* info@bookstopliterary.com *Web Site:* www.bookstopliterary.com, pg 451

Marcus, Leonard, Astra Books for Young Readers, 19 W 21 St, No 1201, New York, NY 10010 *Tel:* 646-844-3485 *E-mail:* ahinfo@astrahouse.com; permissions@astrapublishinghouse.com *Web Site:* astrapublishinghouse.com, pg 20

Marcus, Leonard S, Astra International Picture Book Writing Contest, 19 W 21 St, No 1201, New York, NY 10010 *E-mail:* astrawritingcontest@readinglife.com *Web Site:* www.readinglife.com/writingcontest, pg 575

Marcus, Leonard S, The Carle Honors, 125 W Bay Rd, Amherst, MA 01002 *Tel:* 413-559-6300 *E-mail:* info@carlemuseum.org *Web Site:* www.carlemuseum.org/content/carle-honors, pg 586

Marcus, Rachel, National Academies Press (NAP), 500 Fifth St NW, Washington, DC 20001 *Toll Free Tel:* 800-624-6242 *Fax:* 202-334-2451 (cust serv); 202-334-2793 (mktg dept) *E-mail:* customer_service@nap.edu *Web Site:* www.nap.edu, pg 136

Mardon, Austin, Golden Meteorite Press, 11919 82 St NW, Suite 103, Edmonton, AB T5B 2W4, Canada *Tel:* 587-783-0059 *Web Site:* goldenmeteoritepress.com, pg 407

Margolis, Amy, Iowa Summer Writing Festival, 24E Phillips Hall, University of Iowa, Iowa City, IA 52242 *Tel:* 319-335-4160 *E-mail:* iswfestival@uiowa.edu *Web Site:* iowasummerwritingfestival.uiowa.edu, pg 555

Margolis, Michelle, AJL Jewish Fiction Award, PO Box 1118, Teaneck, NJ 07666 *Tel:* 201-371-3255 *E-mail:* info@jewishlibraries.org *Web Site:* jewishlibraries.org/AJL_Jewish_Fiction_Award, pg 571

Margolis, Michelle, AJL Judaica Bibliography Award, PO Box 1118, Teaneck, NJ 07666 *Tel:* 201-371-3255 *E-mail:* info@jewishlibraries.org *Web Site:* jewishlibraries.org, pg 571

Margolis, Michelle, AJL Judaica Reference Award, PO Box 1118, Teaneck, NJ 07666 *Tel:* 201-371-3255 *E-mail:* info@jewishlibraries.org *Web Site:* jewishlibraries.org, pg 571

Margolis, Michelle, AJL Scholarship, PO Box 1118, Teaneck, NJ 07666 *Tel:* 201-371-3255 *E-mail:* scholarship@jewishlibraries.org; info@jewishlibraries.org *Web Site:* jewishlibraries.org/student-scholarship-award, pg 571

Margolis, Michelle, Association of Jewish Libraries Inc (AJL), PO Box 1118, Teaneck, NJ 07666 *Tel:* 201-371-3255 *E-mail:* info@jewishlibraries.org *Web Site:* jewishlibraries.org, pg 499

Margolis, Michelle, Sydney Taylor Book Award, PO Box 1118, Teaneck, NJ 07666 *Tel:* 201-371-3255 *E-mail:* sydneytaylorbookaward@jewishlibraries.org; info@jewishlibraries.org *Web Site:* jewishlibraries.org/sydney_taylor_book_award, pg 668

Margolis, Michelle, Sydney Taylor Manuscript Award, 204 Park St, Montclair, NJ 07042 *Tel:* 201-371-3255 *E-mail:* info@jewishlibraries.org *Web Site:* jewishlibraries.org, pg 668

Marie, Emma, CALIBA Golden Poppy Awards, 100 Black Diamond Rd, Stonyford, CA 95979 *Tel:* 415-561-7686 *E-mail:* info@caliballiance.org *Web Site:* caliballiance.org/golden-poppy-awards.html, pg 585

Marie, Emma, California Independent Booksellers Alliance (CALIBA), 100 Black Diamond Rd, Stonyford, CA 95979 *Tel:* 415-561-7686 *E-mail:* info@caliballiance.org *Web Site:* caliballiance.org, pg 502

Marin, Joe, PRINTING United Alliance, 10015 Main St, Fairfax, VA 22031 *Tel:* 703-385-1335 *Toll Free Tel:* 888-385-3588 *Fax:* 703-273-0456; 703-691-7492 (membership) *E-mail:* assist@printing.org; info@printing.org *Web Site:* www.printing.org, pg 517

Marin, Marcos, National Association of Hispanic Publications Inc (NAHP), National Press Bldg, 529 14 St NW, Suite 923, Washington, DC 20045 *Web Site:* nahp.org, pg 511

Marinacci, Barbara, The Bookmill, 501 Palisades Dr, No 315, Pacific Palisades, CA 90272-2848 *Tel:* 310-459-0190 *E-mail:* thebookmill1@verizon.net *Web Site:* www.thebookmill.us, pg 436

Marinaccio, Fran, Woodbine House, 6510 Bells Mill Rd, Bethesda, MD 20817 *Tel:* 301-897-3570 *Toll Free Tel:* 800-843-7323 *Fax:* 301-897-5838 *E-mail:* info@woodbinehouse.com *Web Site:* www.woodbinehouse.com, pg 232

Marinaccio, Fran M, Woodbine House, 6510 Bells Mill Rd, Bethesda, MD 20817 *Tel:* 301-897-3570 *Toll Free Tel:* 800-843-7323 *Fax:* 301-897-5838 *E-mail:* info@woodbinehouse.com *Web Site:* www.woodbinehouse.com, pg 232

Marini, Victoria, Irene Goodman Literary Agency, 27 W 24 St, Suite 700B, New York, NY 10010 *Tel:* 212-604-0330 *E-mail:* queries@irenegoodman.com *Web Site:* www.irenegoodman.com, pg 460

Marino, Julianna Lee, National Book Foundation, 90 Broad St, Suite 604, New York, NY 10004 *Tel:* 212-685-0261 *Fax:* 212-213-6570 *E-mail:* nationalbook@nationalbook.org *Web Site:* www.nationalbook.org, pg 526

Marino, Krista, Random House Children's Books, c/o Penguin Random House LLC, 1745 Broadway, New York, NY 10019 *Tel:* 212-782-9000 *Web Site:* www.rhcbooks.com, pg 169

Marion, Niki, Lee & Low Books Inc, 95 Madison Ave, Suite 1205, New York, NY 10016 *Tel:* 212-779-4400 *Toll Free Tel:* 888-320-3190 (ext 28, orders only) *Fax:* 212-683-1894 (orders only); 212-532-6035 *E-mail:* general@leeandlow.com *Web Site:* www.leeandlow.com, pg 114

Maripudi, Ragav, Bloomsbury Publishing Inc, 1385 Broadway, 5th fl, New York, NY 10018 *Tel:* 212-419-5300 *E-mail:* marketingusa@bloomsbury.com; adultpublicityusa@bloomsbury.com; askacademic@bloomsbury.com *Web Site:* www.bloomsbury.com, pg 32

Mariucci, Sam, Chronicle Books LLC, 680 Second St, San Francisco, CA 94107 *Tel:* 415-537-4200 *Fax:* 415-537-4460 (perms) *E-mail:* hello@chroniclebooks.com; subrights@chroniclebooks.com *Web Site:* www.chroniclebooks.com, pg 48

Mark, P J, Janklow & Nesbit Associates, 285 Madison Ave, 21st fl, New York, NY 10017 *Tel:* 212-421-1700 *Fax:* 212-355-1403 *E-mail:* info@janklow.com; submissions@janklow.com; filmtvrights@janklow.com *Web Site:* www.janklowandnesbit.com, pg 464

Markell, Rick, Gingko Press Inc, 2332 Fourth St, Suite E, Berkeley, CA 94710 *Tel:* 510-898-1195 *Fax:* 510-898-1196 *E-mail:* books@gingkopress.com *Web Site:* www.gingkopress.com, pg 78

Markfield, Barbara, Association of National Advertisers Inc (ANA), 155 E 44 St, New York, NY 10017 *Tel:* 212-697-5950 *Fax:* 212-687-7310 *E-mail:* info@ana.net *Web Site:* www.ana.net, pg 499

Markham, Jim, Apress Media LLC, One New York Plaza, Suite 4600, New York, NY 10004-1562 *Tel:* 212-460-1500 *E-mail:* editorial@apress.com; customerservice@springernature.com *Web Site:* www.apress.com, pg 16

Markoe, Kaija, Rizzoli International Publications Inc, 300 Park Ave S, 4th fl, New York, NY 10010-5399 *Tel:* 212-387-3400 *Toll Free Tel:* 800-522-6657 (orders only) *Fax:* 212-387-3535 *E-mail:* publicity@rizzoliusa.com *Web Site:* www.rizzoliusa.com, pg 175

Markowitz, Cora, Georges Borchardt Inc, 136 E 57 St, New York, NY 10022 *Tel:* 212-753-5785 *E-mail:* georges@gbagency.com *Web Site:* www.gbagency.com, pg 451

Markowski, Michael Anthony, Markowski International Publishers, One Oakglade Circle, Hummelstown, PA 17036-9525 *Tel:* 717-566-0468 *E-mail:* info@possibilitypress.com *Web Site:* www.possibilitypress.com; www.aeronauticalpublishers.com, pg 125

Marks, Corey PhD, Rilke Prize, Auditorium Bldg, Rm 214, 1155 Union Circle, Denton, TX 76203 *E-mail:* untrilkeprize@unt.edu *Web Site:* english.unt.edu/creative-writing/unt-rilke-prize, pg 656

Marks, Rachael, Beacon Press, 24 Farnsworth St, Boston, MA 02210-1409 *Tel:* 617-742-2110 *Fax:* 617-723-3097 *E-mail:* production@beacon.org *Web Site:* www.beacon.org, pg 25

Marks, Rachael, Chronicle Books LLC, 680 Second St, San Francisco, CA 94107 *Tel:* 415-537-4200 *Fax:* 415-537-4460 (perms) *E-mail:* hello@chroniclebooks.com; subrights@chroniclebooks.com *Web Site:* www.chroniclebooks.com, pg 48

Markson, Todd, Cengage Learning, 20 Channel Center St, Boston, MA 02210 *Tel:* 617-289-7700 *Toll Free Tel:* 800-354-9706 *Fax:* 617-289-7844 *E-mail:* esales@cengage.com *Web Site:* www.cengage.com, pg 43

Markusic, Kirsten, Northwestern University Press, 629 Noyes St, Evanston, IL 60208-4210 Tel: 847-491-2046 Toll Free Tel: 800-621-2736 (orders only) Fax: 847-491-8150 E-mail: nupress@northwestern.edu Web Site: www.nupress.northwestern.edu, pg 143

Marmion, Shane, William S Hein & Co Inc, 2350 N Forest Rd, Suite 10A, Getzville, NY 14068 Tel: 716-882-2600 Toll Free Tel: 800-828-7571 Fax: 716-883-8100 E-mail: mail@wshein.com; marketing@wshein.com; customerservice@wshein.com Web Site: home.heinonline.org, pg 90

Marmur, Mildred, Mildred Marmur Associates Ltd, 2005 Palmer Ave, PMB 127, Larchmont, NY 10538 Tel: 914-843-5582 Fax: 914-833-1175 E-mail: marmur@westnet.com, pg 468

Marohn, Stephanie, Angel Editing Services, PO Box 752, Mountain Ranch, CA 95246 Tel: 209-728-8364 E-mail: info@stephaniemarohn.com Web Site: www.stephaniemarohn.com, pg 435

Marohn, Stephanie, Elite Books, PO Box 222, Petaluma, CA 94953-0222 Tel: 707-525-9292 Toll Free Fax: 800-330-9798 E-mail: support@eftuniverse.com Web Site: www.elitebooksonline.com, pg 65

Marohn, Stephanie, Energy Psychology Press, PO Box 222, Petaluma, CA 94953-0222 Tel: 707-525-9292 Toll Free Fax: 800-330-9798 E-mail: energypsychologypress@gmail.com; support@eftuniverse.com Web Site: www.energypsychologypress.com; www.elitebooksonline.com, pg 66

Marolla, Mary, Harry N Abrams Inc, 195 Broadway, 9th fl, New York, NY 10007 Tel: 212-206-7715 Toll Free Tel: 800-345-1359 Fax: 212-645-8437 E-mail: abrams@abramsbooks.com; publicity@abramsbooks.com; sales@abramsbooks.com Web Site: www.abramsbooks.com, pg 3

Marotta, Mary, Candlewick Press, 99 Dover St, Somerville, MA 02144-2825 Tel: 617-661-3330 Fax: 617-661-0565 E-mail: bigbear@candlewick.com; salesinfo@candlewick.com Web Site: candlewick.com, pg 39

Marotta, Mary, Holiday House Publishing Inc, 50 Broad St, New York, NY 10004 Tel: 212-688-0085 Fax: 212-421-6134 E-mail: info@holidayhouse.com Web Site: www.holidayhouse.com, pg 94

Marotta, Mary, Peachtree Publishing Co Inc, 1700 Chattahoochee Ave, Atlanta, GA 30318-2112 Tel: 404-876-8761 Toll Free Tel: 800-241-0113 Fax: 404-875-2578 Toll Free Fax: 800-875-8909 E-mail: hello@peachtree-online.com; orders@peachtree-online.com; sales@peachtree-online.com Web Site: www.peachtreebooks.com; www.peachtree-online.com, pg 153

Marotte, Liz, Chronicle Books LLC, 680 Second St, San Francisco, CA 94107 Tel: 415-537-4200 Fax: 415-537-4460 (perms) E-mail: hello@chroniclebooks.com; subrights@chroniclebooks.com Web Site: chroniclebooks.com, pg 47

Marques, Mindy, Simon & Schuster, 1230 Avenue of the Americas, New York, NY 10020 Tel: 212-698-7000 Toll Free Tel: 800-223-2348 (cust serv); 800-223-2336 (orders) Toll Free Fax: 800-943-9831 (orders) Web Site: simonandschusterpublishing.com/simonandschuster/, pg 188

Marquet, Tom, Random House Children's Books, c/o Penguin Random House LLC, 1745 Broadway, New York, NY 10019 Tel: 212-782-9000 Web Site: rhcbooks.com, pg 170

Marquis, Emily, Alice James Books, 60 Pineland Dr, Suite 206, New Gloucester, ME 04260 Tel: 207-926-8283 E-mail: info@alicejamesbooks.org Web Site: alicejamesbooks.org, pg 105

Marr, Jill, Sandra Dijkstra Literary Agency, 1155 Camino del Mar, PMB 515, Del Mar, CA 92014-2605 Web Site: dijkstraagency.com, pg 456

Marrelli, Nancy, Vehicule Press, PO Box 42094, CP Roy, Montreal, QC H2W 2T3, Canada Tel: 514-844-6073 E-mail: vp@vehiculepress.com; admin@vehiculepress.com Web Site: www.vehiculepress.com, pg 424

Marrow, Linda, Random House Publishing Group, 1745 Broadway, New York, NY 10019 Toll Free Tel: 800-200-3552 Web Site: www.randomhousebooks.com, pg 170

Marrs, Carrie, Thomas Nelson, 501 Nelson Place, Nashville, TN 37214 Tel: 615-889-9000 Toll Free Tel: 800-251-4000 Web Site: www.thomasnelson.com, pg 206

Marrs, Daniel, Thomas Nelson, 501 Nelson Place, Nashville, TN 37214 Tel: 615-889-9000 Toll Free Tel: 800-251-4000 Web Site: www.thomasnelson.com, pg 206

Marrujo, Kelsey, Farrar, Straus & Giroux Books for Young Readers, 120 Broadway, New York, NY 10271 Tel: 212-741-6900 Toll Free Tel: 888-330-8477 (orders) E-mail: childrens.publicity@macmillanusa.com; childrensrights@macmillanusa.com Web Site: us.macmillan.com/mackids, pg 70

Marrujo, Kelsey, Roaring Brook Press, 120 Broadway, New York, NY 10271 Tel: 646-307-5151 Web Site: us.macmillan.com/publishers/roaring-brook-press, pg 176

Mars, Laura, Grey House Publishing Inc™, 4919 Rte 22, Amenia, NY 12501 Tel: 518-789-8700 Toll Free Tel: 800-562-2139 Fax: 518-789-0556 E-mail: books@greyhouse.com; customerservice@greyhouse.com Web Site: greyhouse.com, pg 81

Marsal, Jill, Marsal Lyon Literary Agency LLC, 665 San Rodolfo Dr, Suite 124, PMB 121, Solana Beach, CA 92075 Tel: 760-814-8507 Web Site: www.marsallyonliteraryagency.com, pg 468

Marsella, Gianna, University of Hawaii Press, 2840 Kolowalu St, Honolulu, HI 96822-1888 Tel: 808-956-8255 Toll Free Tel: 888-UHPRESS (847-7377) Toll Free Fax: 800-650-7811 E-mail: uhpbooks@hawaii.edu Web Site: www.uhpress.hawaii.edu, pg 216

Marsh, Carole, Gallopade International Inc, 611 Hwy 74 S, Suite 2000, Peachtree City, GA 30269 Tel: 770-631-4222 Toll Free Tel: 800-536-2438 Fax: 770-631-4810 Toll Free Fax: 800-871-2979 E-mail: customerservice@gallopade.com Web Site: www.gallopade.com, pg 76

Marsh, Dr Peter, The Mongolia Society Inc, Indiana University, 703 Eigenmann Hall, 1900 E Tenth St, Bloomington, IN 47406-7512 Tel: 812-855-4078 Fax: 812-855-4078 E-mail: monsoc@indiana.edu Web Site: mongoliasociety.org, pg 133

Marsh, Rebecca, Viking Penguin, c/o Penguin Random House LLC, 1745 Broadway, New York, NY 10019 Tel: 212-782-9000 Web Site: www.penguin.com/overview-vikingbooks/; www.penguin.com/pamela-dorman-books-overview/; www.penguin.com/penguin-classics-overview/; www.penguin.com/penguin-life-overview/, pg 225

Marsh, Robert, Rowman & Littlefield, 4501 Forbes Blvd, Suite 200, Lanham, MD 20706 Tel: 301-459-3366 Fax: 800-462-6420 (ext 3024, cust serv) Fax: 301-429-5748 Web Site: rowman.com, pg 178

Marshall, Christine, Simon & Schuster Children's Publishing, 1230 Avenue of the Americas, New York, NY 10020 Tel: 212-698-7000 Web Site: www.simonandschuster.com/kids; www.simonandschuster.com/teen; simonandschuster.net; simonandschuster.biz, pg 189

Marshall, Elyse, Penguin Young Readers Group, c/o Penguin Random House LLC, 1745 Broadway, New York, NY 10019 Tel: 212-782-9000 Web Site: www.penguin.com/penguin-young-readers-overview, pg 156

Marshall, Evan S, The Evan Marshall Agency, One Pacio Ct, Roseland, NJ 07068-1121 Tel: 973-287-6216 Web Site: www.evanmarshallagency.com, pg 469

Marshall, Jen, Aevitas Creative Management LLC, 19 W 21 St, Suite 501, New York, NY 10010 Tel: 212-765-6900 Web Site: www.aevitascreative.com, pg 448

Marshall, Julie, Island Press, 2000 "M" St NW, Suite 480-B, Washington, DC 20036 Tel: 202-232-7933 Toll Free Tel: 800-621-2736 Fax: 202-234-1328 E-mail: info@islandpress.org Web Site: www.islandpress.org, pg 104

Marshall, Kate, University of California Press, 155 Grand Ave, Suite 400, Oakland, CA 94612-3758 Tel: 510-883-8232 Fax: 510-836-8910 E-mail: customerservice@ucpress.edu Web Site: www.ucpress.edu, pg 215

Marshall, Kirk, Harlequin Enterprises Ltd, Bay Adelaide Centre, East Tower, 22 Adelaide St W, 41st fl, Toronto, ON M5H 4E3, Canada Tel: 416-445-5860 Toll Free Tel: 888-432-4879; 800-370-5838 (ebook inquiries) E-mail: customerservice@harlequin.com Web Site: www.harlequin.com, pg 409

Marshall, Kirk, HarperCollins Canada Ltd, 22 Adelaide St W, 41st fl, Toronto, ON M5H 4E3, Canada Tel: 416-975-9334 E-mail: hcorder@harpercollins.com Web Site: www.harpercollins.ca, pg 409

Marshall, Lindsay, BenBella Books Inc, 10440 N Central Expwy, Suite 800, Dallas, TX 75231-2264 Tel: 214-750-3600 Web Site: www.benbellabooks.com; www.smartpopbooks.com, pg 27

Marshea, Beth, Ladderbird Literary Agency, 460 Yellow Brick Rd, Orange, CT 06477 Tel: 203-290-1703 Web Site: www.ladderbird.com, pg 466

Marsiglia, Caroline, Aevitas Creative Management LLC, 19 W 21 St, Suite 501, New York, NY 10010 Tel: 212-765-6900 Web Site: www.aevitascreative.com, pg 448

Marson, Amy, C&T Publishing Inc, 1651 Challenge Dr, Concord, CA 94520-5206 Tel: 925-677-0377 E-mail: ctinfo@ctpub.com Web Site: www.ctpub.com, pg 40

Martel, Manon, Les Editions Un Monde Different, 3905 Isabelle, bureau 101, Brossard, QC J4Y 2R2, Canada Tel: 450-656-2660 Toll Free Tel: 800-443-2582 Fax: 450-659-9328 E-mail: info@umd.ca Web Site: umd.ca, pg 405

Martell, Alice Fried, The Martell Agency, 1350 Avenue of the Americas, Suite 1205, New York, NY 10019 Tel: 212-317-2672 Web Site: www.themartellagency.com, pg 469

Martens, Patricia, Boys Town Press, 13603 Flanagan Blvd, 2nd fl, Boys Town, NE 68010 Tel: 531-355-1320 Toll Free Tel: 800-282-6657 Fax: 531-355-1310 E-mail: btpress@boystown.org Web Site: www.boystownpress.org, pg 35

Martens, Rainer, Human Kinetics Inc, 1607 N Market St, Champaign, IL 61820 Tel: 217-351-5076 Toll Free Tel: 800-747-4457 Fax: 217-351-1549 (orders/cust serv) E-mail: info@hkusa.com Web Site: us.humankinetics.com, pg 97

Martenz, Arden, MAR*CO Products Inc, PO Box 686, Hatfield, PA 19440 Tel: 215-956-0313 Toll Free Tel: 800-448-2197 Fax: 215-956-9041 E-mail: help@marcoproducts.com; sales@marcoproducts.com Web Site: www.marcoproducts.com, pg 124

Martin, Alison, Penguin Random House LLC, 1745 Broadway, New York, NY 10019 Tel: 212-782-9000 Toll Free Tel: 800-726-0600 Web Site: www.penguinrandomhouse.com, pg 155

Martin, Amanda, Research Press, 2612 N Mattis Ave, Champaign, IL 61822 Tel: 217-352-3273 Toll Free Tel: 800-519-2707 Fax: 217-352-1221 E-mail: rp@researchpress.com; orders@researchpress.com Web Site: www.researchpress.com, pg 174

Martin, Amy, Bloomsbury Academic, 1385 Broadway, 5th fl, New York, NY 10018 Tel: 212-419-5300 Web Site: www.bloomsbury.com/us/academic, pg 31

Martin, Andrew, St Martin's Press, LLC, 120 Broadway, New York, NY 10271 E-mail: publicity@stmartins.com; trademarketing@stmartins.com; foreignrights@stmartins.com Web Site: us.macmillan.com/smp, pg 180

Martin, Annie, Wayne State University Press, Leonard N Simons Bldg, 4809 Woodward Ave, Detroit, MI 48201-1309 Tel: 313-577-6120 Toll Free Tel: 800-978-7323 Fax: 313-577-6131 E-mail: bookorders@wayne.edu Web Site: www.wsupress.wayne.edu, pg 226

Martin, Caroline, United States Pharmacopeia (USP), 12601 Twinbrook Pkwy, Rockville, MD 20852-1790 Tel: 301-881-0666 Toll Free Tel: 800-227-8772 E-mail: marketing@usp.org Web Site: www.usp.org, pg 213

Martin, Courtney J, Yale Center for British Art, 1080 Chapel St, New Haven, CT 06510-2302 Tel: 203-432-8929 Fax: 203-432-1626 E-mail: ycba.publications@yale.edu Web Site: britishart.yale.edu, pg 235

Martin, Denny, Piano Press, 1425 Ocean Ave, Suite 5, Del Mar, CA 92014 Tel: 619-884-1401 E-mail: pianopress@pianopress.com Web Site: www.pianopress.com, pg 159

Martin, Dorothea, Ohio Genealogical Society, 611 State Rte 97 W, Bellville, OH 44813-8813 Tel: 419-886-1903 E-mail: ogs@ogs.org Web Site: www.ogs.org, pg 145

Martin, Emily, Harlequin Enterprises Ltd, Bay Adelaide Centre, East Tower, 22 Adelaide St W, 41st fl, Toronto, ON M5H 4E3, Canada Tel: 416-445-5860 Toll Free Tel: 888-432-4879; 800-370-5838 (ebook inquiries) E-mail: customerservice@harlequin.com Web Site: www.harlequin.com, pg 409

Martin, James, PRINTING United Alliance, 10015 Main St, Fairfax, VA 22031 Tel: 703-385-1335 Toll Free Tel: 888-385-3588 Fax: 703-273-0456; 703-691-7492 (membership) E-mail: assist@printing.org; info@printing.org Web Site: www.printing.org, pg 517

Martin, John D, Rod & Staff Publishers Inc, 14193 Hwy 172, Crockett, KY 41413 Tel: 606-522-4348 Fax: 606-522-4896, pg 176

Martin, Jynne Dilling, Riverhead Books, c/o Penguin Random House LLC, 1745 Broadway, New York, NY 10019 Tel: 212-782-9000 Web Site: www.penguin.com/riverhead-overview/, pg 175

Martin, Kelli, Wendy Sherman Associates Inc, 138 W 25 St, Suite 1018, New York, NY 10001 Tel: 212-279-9027 E-mail: submissions@wsherman.com Web Site: www.wsherman.com, pg 476

Martin, Kendra, Dundurn Press Ltd, PO Box 19510, RPO Manulife, Toronto, ON M4W 3T9, Canada Tel: 416-214-5544 E-mail: publicity@dundurn.com; sales@dundurn.com Web Site: www.dundurn.com, pg 401

Martin, Kerry, Holiday House Publishing Inc, 50 Broad St, New York, NY 10004 Tel: 212-688-0085 Fax: 212-421-6134 E-mail: info@holidayhouse.com Web Site: www.holidayhouse.com, pg 94

Martin, Kerry, Peachtree Publishing Co Inc, 1700 Chattahoochee Ave, Atlanta, GA 30318-2112 Tel: 404-876-8761 Toll Free Tel: 800-241-0113 Fax: 404-875-2578 Toll Free Fax: 800-875-8909 E-mail: hello@peachtree-online.com; orders@peachtree-online.com; pr@peachtree-online.com Web Site: www.peachtreebooks.com; www.peachtree-online.com, pg 153

Martin, Lesley, Aperture Books, 548 W 28 St, 4th fl, New York, NY 10001 Tel: 212-505-5555 Toll Free Fax: 888-623-6908 E-mail: customerservice@aperture.org Web Site: aperture.org, pg 15

Martin, Lisa Ann PhD, On the Write Path Publishing, 5023 W 120 Ave, Suite 228, Broomfield, CO 80020 Tel: 303-465-2056 Fax: 303-465-2056, pg 146

Martin, Marianne K, Bywater Books Inc, 3415 Porter Rd, Ann Arbor, MI 48103 Tel: 734-662-8815 Web Site: bywaterbooks.com, pg 39

Martin, Mark, Verso Books, 388 Atlantic Ave, Brooklyn, NY 11217 Tel: 718-246-8160 Fax: 718-246-8165 E-mail: verso@versobooks.com Web Site: www.versobooks.com, pg 224

Martin, Matthew, Penguin Random House LLC, 1745 Broadway, New York, NY 10019 Tel: 212-782-9000 Toll Free Tel: 800-726-0600 Web Site: www.penguinrandomhouse.com, pg 155

Martin, Miranda, Columbia University Press, 61 W 62 St, New York, NY 10023 Tel: 212-459-0600 Toll Free Tel: 800-944-8648 Fax: 212-459-3678 Web Site: cup.columbia.edu, pg 51

Martin, Natasha, Harry N Abrams Inc, 195 Broadway, 9th fl, New York, NY 10007 Tel: 212-206-7715 Toll Free Tel: 800-345-1359 Fax: 212-645-8437 E-mail: abrams@abramsbooks.com; publicity@abramsbooks.com; sales@abramsbooks.com Web Site: www.abramsbooks.com, pg 3

Martin, Patrick, Prometheus Books, 59 John Glenn Dr, Amherst, NY 14228-2119 Fax: 716-691-0137 E-mail: marketing@prometheusbooks.com; editorial@prometheusbooks.com; rights@prometheusbooks.com Web Site: www.prometheusbooks.com, pg 166

Martin, Peter Stanley, G Schirmer Inc/Associated Music Publishers Inc, 180 Madison Ave, 24th fl, New York, NY 10016 Tel: 212-254-2100 Fax: 212-254-2013 E-mail: schirmer@schirmer.com Web Site: www.musicsalesclassical.com, pg 183

Martin, Rux, Houghton Mifflin Harcourt Trade & Reference Division, 125 High St, Boston, MA 02110 Tel: 617-351-5000 Web Site: www.hmhco.com, pg 96

Martin, Sharlene Levin, Martin Literary Management, 914 164 St SE, Suite B12, Box 307, Mill Creek, WA 98012 Tel: 206-466-1773 (no phone queries) Web Site: www.martinliterarymanagement.com, pg 469

Martin, Stephen Hawley, The Oaklea Press Inc, 41 Old Mill Rd, Richmond, VA 23226-3111 Tel: 804-218-2394 Web Site: oakleapress.com, pg 145

Martin, Wayne, North Carolina Arts Council Writers Fellowships, 109 E Jones St, Raleigh, NC 27601 Tel: 919-807-6500 Fax: 919-807-6532 E-mail: ncarts@ncdcr.gov Web Site: www.ncarts.org, pg 641

Martin-Dent, Ron, BOA Editions Ltd, 250 N Goodman St, Suite 306, Rochester, NY 14607 Tel: 585-546-3410 Fax: 585-546-3913 E-mail: contact@boaeditions.org Web Site: www.boaeditions.org, pg 33

Martinelli, Mike, City & Regional Magazine Association (CRMA), 287 Richards Ave, Norwalk, CT 06850 Tel: 203-515-9294 Web Site: citymag.org, pg 504

Martinelli, Theresa, Wayne State University Press, Leonard N Simons Bldg, 4809 Woodward Ave, Detroit, MI 48201-1309 Tel: 313-577-6120 Toll Free Tel: 800-978-7323 Fax: 313-577-6131 E-mail: bookorders@wayne.edu Web Site: www.wsupress.wayne.edu, pg 227

Martinez, Alexandria, Chronicle Books LLC, 680 Second St, San Francisco, CA 94107 Tel: 415-537-4200 Fax: 415-537-4460 (perms) E-mail: hello@chroniclebooks.com; subrights@chroniclebooks.com Web Site: www.chroniclebooks.com, pg 48

Martinez, Aysha, Chronicle Books LLC, 680 Second St, San Francisco, CA 94107 Tel: 415-537-4200 Fax: 415-537-4460 (perms) E-mail: hello@chroniclebooks.com; subrights@chroniclebooks.com Web Site: www.chroniclebooks.com, pg 48

Martinez, Bree, Holiday House Publishing Inc, 50 Broad St, New York, NY 10004 Tel: 212-688-0085 Fax: 212-421-6134 E-mail: info@holidayhouse.com Web Site: www.holidayhouse.com, pg 94

Martinez, Gabriel, Chronicle Books LLC, 680 Second St, San Francisco, CA 94107 Tel: 415-537-4200 Fax: 415-537-4460 (perms) E-mail: hello@chroniclebooks.com; subrights@chroniclebooks.com Web Site: www.chroniclebooks.com, pg 48

Martinez, Lulu, Random House Publishing Group, 1745 Broadway, New York, NY 10019 Toll Free Tel: 800-200-3552 Web Site: www.randomhousebooks.com, pg 171

Martinez, Mae, Random House Publishing Group, 1745 Broadway, New York, NY 10019 Toll Free Tel: 800-200-3552 Web Site: www.randomhousebooks.com, pg 171

Martinez, Michelle, Tiger Tales, 5 River Rd, Suite 128, Wilton, CT 06897-4069 Tel: 920-387-2333 Fax: 920-387-9994 Web Site: www.tigertalesbooks.com, pg 207

Martinez, Rudy, Soho Press Inc, 853 Broadway, New York, NY 10003 Tel: 212-260-1900 E-mail: soho@sohopress.com; publicity@sohopress.com Web Site: sohopress.com, pg 193

Martinez, Vanessa, Macmillan, 120 Broadway, 22nd fl, New York, NY 10271 E-mail: press.inquiries@macmillan.com Web Site: us.macmillan.com, pg 122

Martino, Alfred C, Listen & Live Audio Inc, 803 13 St, Union City, NJ 07087 Tel: 201-558-9000 Web Site: www.listenandlive.com, pg 117

Martino, John B, The Catholic University of America Press, 240 Leahy Hall, 620 Michigan Ave NE, Washington, DC 20064 Tel: 202-319-5052 Toll Free Tel: 800-537-5487 (orders only) Fax: 202-319-4985 E-mail: cua-press@cua.edu Web Site: cuapress.org, pg 42

Martir, Vanessa, Idyllwild Arts Summer Program, 52500 Temecula Rd, No 38, Idyllwild, CA 92549 Tel: 951-659-2171 E-mail: summer@idyllwildarts.org; adultprograms@idyllwildarts.org Web Site: idyllwildarts.org/summer, pg 555

Martirano, Erica, St Martin's Press, LLC, 120 Broadway, New York, NY 10271 E-mail: publicity@stmartins.com; trademarketing@stmartins.com; foreignrights@stmartins.com Web Site: us.macmillan.com/smp, pg 181

Marton, Meghan O'Brien, DK, c/o Penguin Random House LLC, 1745 Broadway, 20th fl, New York, NY 10019 Tel: 646-674-4000 Toll Free Tel: 800-733-3000 Fax: 646-674-4020 E-mail: marketing@dk.com (lib servs); publicity@dk.com; csorders@penguinrandomhouse.com; customerservice@penguinrandomhouse.com Web Site: www.dk.com, pg 60

Martorelli, Nick, Penguin Random House Audio Publishing Group, 1745 Broadway, New York, NY 10019 Toll Free Tel: 800-793-2665 (cust serv) E-mail: audio@penguinrandomhouse.com; ecustomerservice@penguinrandomhouse.com Web Site: www.penguinrandomhouseaudio.com, pg 154

Marts, Mike, Papercutz, 8838 SW 129 St, Miami, FL 33176 Tel: 786-953-4195 E-mail: contact@papercutz.com; snellis@madcavestudios.com Web Site: www.papercutz.com, pg 151

Martschenko, Allegra, Ladderbird Literary Agency, 460 Yellow Brick Rd, Orange, CT 06477 Tel: 203-290-1703 Web Site: www.ladderbird.com, pg 466

Martschenko, Allegra, Princeton University Press, 41 William St, Princeton, NJ 08540-5237 Tel: 609-258-4900 Fax: 609-258-6305 E-mail: info@press.princeton.edu Web Site: press.princeton.edu, pg 164

Martynick, Christine, SLACK® Incorporated, A Wyanoke Group Company, 6900 Grove Rd, Thorofare, NJ 08086-9447 Tel: 856-848-1000 Toll Free Tel: 800-257-8290 Fax: 856-848-6091 E-mail: sales@slackinc.com; editor@slackinc.com; customerservice@slackinc.com Web Site: www.healio.com/books, pg 191

Maruca, Lisa, Society for the History of Authorship, Reading & Publishing Inc (SHARP), c/o Johns Hopkins University Press, Journals Publishing Div, PO Box 19966, Baltimore, MD 21211-0966 Tel: 410-516-6987 Toll Free Tel: 800-548-1784 Fax: 410-516-3866 E-mail: members@sharpweb.org Web Site: www.sharpweb.org, pg 519

Marvel, Julia, Chronicle Books LLC, 680 Second St, San Francisco, CA 94107 Tel: 415-537-4200 Fax: 415-537-4460 (perms) E-mail: hello@chroniclebooks.com; subrights@chroniclebooks.com Web Site: www.chroniclebooks.com, pg 48

Marven, Shannon, Dupree, Miller & Associates Inc, 4311 Oak Lawn Ave, Suite 650, Dallas, TX 75219 Tel: 214-559-2665 E-mail: editorial@dupreemiller.com Web Site: www.dupreemiller.com, pg 457

Marvin, Catherine, Macmillan, 120 Broadway, 22nd fl, New York, NY 10271 E-mail: press.inquiries@macmillan.com Web Site: us.macmillan.com, pg 122

Marvin, Sally, Gallery Books, 1230 Avenue of the Americas, New York, NY 10020 Toll Free Tel: 800-456-6798 Fax: 212-698-7284 E-mail: consumer.customerservice@simonandschuster.com Web Site: www.simonandschuster.com, pg 76

Maschino, Matthew, Independent Institute, 100 Swan Way, Oakland, CA 94621-1428 *Tel:* 510-632-1366 *Fax:* 510-568-6040 *Web Site:* www.independent.org, pg 99

Mascia, Vanisse, Industrial Press Inc, One Chestnut St, South Norwalk, CT 06854 *Tel:* 203-956-5593 *Toll Free Tel:* 888-528-7852 (ext 1, cust serv) *E-mail:* info@industrialpress.com *Web Site:* books.industrialpress.com; ebooks.industrialpress.com, pg 100

Maselli, Elisabeth, Rutgers University Press, 106 Somerset St, 3rd fl, New Brunswick, NJ 08901 *Tel:* 848-445-7762; 848-445-7761 (sales) *Fax:* 732-745-4935 *E-mail:* sales@rutgersuniversitypress.org *Web Site:* www.rutgersuniversitypress.org, pg 178

Maselli, Elisabeth, University of Pennsylvania Press, 3905 Spruce St, Philadelphia, PA 19104 *Tel:* 215-898-6261 *Fax:* 215-898-0404 *E-mail:* custserv@pobox.upenn.edu *Web Site:* www.pennpress.org, pg 219

Mashumba, Kwangu, Penguin Random House Canada, a Penguin Random House company, 320 Front St W, Suite 1400, Toronto, ON M5V 3B6, Canada *Tel:* 416-364-4449 *Toll Free Tel:* 888-523-9292 (cust serv) *E-mail:* canadaweb@penguinrandomhouse.com; customerservicescanada@penguinrandomhouse.com *Web Site:* www.penguinrandomhouse.ca, pg 415

Masi de Casanova, Erynn, American Sociological Association (ASA), 1430 "K" St NW, Suite 600, Washington, DC 20005-4701 *Tel:* 202-383-9005 *E-mail:* asa@asanet.org; communications@asanet.org; membership@asanet.org *Web Site:* www.asanet.org, pg 497

Maslin, Ella, Random House Publishing Group, 1745 Broadway, New York, NY 10019 *Toll Free Tel:* 800-200-3552 *Web Site:* www.randomhousebooks.com, pg 171

Maslow, Zoe, Doubleday Canada, 320 Front St W, Suite 1400, Toronto, ON M5V 3B6, Canada *Tel:* 416-364-4449 *Fax:* 416-598-7764 *Web Site:* www.penguinrandomhouse.ca, pg 401

Masnica, Karen, Sourcebooks LLC, 1935 Brookdale Rd, Suite 139, Naperville, IL 60563 *Tel:* 630-961-3900 *Toll Free Tel:* 800-432-7444 *Fax:* 630-961-2168 *E-mail:* info@sourcebooks.com *Web Site:* www.sourcebooks.com, pg 194

Masnik, Julia, Watkins/Loomis Agency Inc, PO Box 20925, New York, NY 10025 *Tel:* 212-532-0080 *Fax:* 646-383-2449 *E-mail:* assistant@watkinsloomis.com; permissions@watkinsloomis.com *Web Site:* watkins-loomis.squarespace.com, pg 481

Mason, Alane, W W Norton & Company Inc, 500 Fifth Ave, New York, NY 10110-0017 *Tel:* 212-354-5500 *Toll Free Tel:* 800-233-4830 (orders & cust serv) *Fax:* 212-869-0856 *Toll Free Fax:* 800-458-6515 *E-mail:* orders@wwnorton.com *Web Site:* wwnorton.com, pg 143

Mason, Cecilia, Special Libraries Association (SLA), 7918 Jones Branch Dr, Suite 300, McLean, VA 22102 *Tel:* 703-647-4900 *Fax:* 703-506-3266 *E-mail:* info@sla.org *Web Site:* www.sla.org, pg 520

Mason, Jessie, OCP, 340 Oswego Pointe Dr, Lake Oswego, OR 97034 *Tel:* 503-281-1191 *Toll Free Tel:* 800-LITURGY (548-8749) *Fax:* 503-282-3486 *Toll Free Fax:* 800-843-8181 *E-mail:* liturgy@ocp.org *Web Site:* www.ocp.org, pg 145

Mason, Jonathan, Buchwald, 10 E 44 St, New York, NY 10017 *Tel:* 212-867-1200 *E-mail:* info@buchwald.com *Web Site:* www.buchwald.com, pg 453

Mason, Lizzy, Entangled Publishing LLC, 644 Shrewsbury Commons Ave, Suite 181, Shrewsbury, PA 17361 *Toll Free Tel:* 877-677-9451 *E-mail:* publisher@entangledpublishing.com *Web Site:* www.entangledpublishing.com, pg 67

Mason-Swaab, Sally, Hay House LLC, PO Box 5100, Carlsbad, CA 92018-5100 *Tel:* 760-431-7695 (ext 1, intl) *Toll Free Tel:* 800-654-5126 (ext 1, US) *Toll Free Fax:* 800-650-5115 *Web Site:* www.hayhouse.com, pg 89

Massabrook, Jessica, Princeton University Press, 41 William St, Princeton, NJ 08540-5237 *Tel:* 609-258-4900 *Fax:* 609-258-6305 *E-mail:* info@press.princeton.edu *Web Site:* press.princeton.edu, pg 164

Massey, Jeanne, APC Publishing, PO Box 461166, Aurora, CO 80046-1166 *Tel:* 303-660-2158 *Toll Free Tel:* 800-660-5107 (sales & orders) *E-mail:* mail@4wdbooks.com; orders@4wdbooks.com *Web Site:* www.4wdbooks.com, pg 15

Massey, Peter, APC Publishing, PO Box 461166, Aurora, CO 80046-1166 *Tel:* 303-660-2158 *Toll Free Tel:* 800-660-5107 (sales & orders) *E-mail:* mail@4wdbooks.com; orders@4wdbooks.com *Web Site:* www.4wdbooks.com, pg 15

Massey, Robyn, Columbia University Press, 61 W 62 St, New York, NY 10023 *Tel:* 212-459-0600 *Toll Free Tel:* 800-944-8648 *Fax:* 212-459-3678 *Web Site:* cup.columbia.edu, pg 51

Massicotte, Celine, Groupe Sogides Inc, 955 rue Amherst, Montreal, QC H2L 3K4, Canada *Tel:* 514-523-1182 *Fax:* 514-597-0370 *Web Site:* sogides.com, pg 408

Massie, Maria, Massie & McQuilkin, 27 W 20 St, Suite 305, New York, NY 10011 *Tel:* 212-352-2055 *E-mail:* info@mmqlit.com *Web Site:* www.mmqlit.com, pg 469

Massy, Julie, La Courte Echelle, 4388, rue Saint-Denis, Suite 315, Montreal, QC H2J 2L1, Canada *Tel:* 514-312-6950 *E-mail:* info@courteechelle.com *Web Site:* www.groupecourteechelle.com/la-courte-echelle, pg 400

Masterson, Amanda, Bureau of Economic Geology, c/o The University of Texas at Austin, 10100 Burnet Rd, Bldg 130, Austin, TX 78758 *Tel:* 512-471-1534 *Fax:* 512-471-0140 *E-mail:* pubsales@beg.utexas.edu *Web Site:* www.beg.utexas.edu, pg 38

Maswood, Zaina, Sourcebooks LLC, 1935 Brookdale Rd, Suite 139, Naperville, IL 60563 *Tel:* 630-961-3900 *Toll Free Tel:* 800-432-7444 *Fax:* 630-961-2168 *E-mail:* info@sourcebooks.com *Web Site:* www.sourcebooks.com, pg 195

Mateo, Karen, Public Relations Society of America Inc, 120 Wall St, 21st fl, New York, NY 10005 *Tel:* 212-460-1400 *E-mail:* membership@prsa.org *Web Site:* www.prsa.org, pg 518

Mateo Toledo, Jenice, Jane Addams Children's Book Award, 276 Fifth Ave, Suite 704, PMB 45, New York, NY 10001 *Tel:* 212-682-8830 *E-mail:* info@janeaddamspeace.org *Web Site:* www.janeaddamspeace.org, pg 570

Math, Noelle Falcis, Transatlantic Agency, 2 Bloor St E, Suite 3500, Toronto, ON M4W 1A8, Canada *Tel:* 416-488-9214 *E-mail:* info@transatlanticagency.com; royalties@transatlanticagency.com *Web Site:* www.transatlanticagency.com, pg 479

Matheny, Sam, National Association of Broadcasters (NAB), One "M" St SE, Washington, DC 20003 *Tel:* 202-429-5300 *E-mail:* nab@nab.org *Web Site:* www.nab.org, pg 136, 511

Matheson, Ed, Ampersand Group, 1136 Maritime Way, Suite 717, Kanata, ON K2K 0M1, Canada *Tel:* 613-435-5066, pg 435

Matheson, Laurie, University of Illinois Press, 1325 S Oak St, MC-566, Champaign, IL 61820-6903 *Tel:* 217-333-0950 *Fax:* 217-244-8082 *E-mail:* uipress@uillinois.edu; journals@uillinois.edu *Web Site:* www.press.uillinois.edu, pg 216

Matheson, Rebecca, Running Press, 1290 Avenue of the Americas, New York, NY 10104 *Tel:* 212-364-1100 *Toll Free Tel:* 800-759-0190 (cust serv) *Fax:* 212-364-0933 (intl orders) *Toll Free Fax:* 800-286-9471 (cust serv) *E-mail:* customer.service@hbgusa.com; orders@hbgusa.com *Web Site:* www.hachettebookgroup.com/imprint/running-press/; www.moon.com (Moon Travel Guides), pg 178

Mathews, Jeffrey, Scholastic Inc, 557 Broadway, New York, NY 10012 *Tel:* 212-343-6100 *Toll Free Tel:* 800-SCHOLASTIC (724-6527) *Web Site:* www.scholastic.com, pg 184

Mathews, Kaitlyn, The Association of Medical Illustrators (AMI), 201 E Main St, Suite 810, Lexington, KY 40507 *Toll Free Tel:* 866-393-4AMI (393-4264) *E-mail:* hq@ami.org *Web Site:* www.ami.org, pg 499

Mathews, Lisa Vitarisi, Evan-Moor Educational Publishers, 10 Harris Ct, Suite C-3, Monterey, CA 93940 *Tel:* 831-649-5901 *Toll Free Tel:* 800-777-4362 (orders) *Fax:* 831-649-6256 *Toll Free Fax:* 800-777-4332 (orders) *E-mail:* sales@evan-moor.com; marketing@evan-moor.com *Web Site:* www.evan-moor.com, pg 68

Mathews, Richard, The Danahy Fiction Prize, University of Tampa Press, 401 W Kennedy Blvd, Tampa, FL 33606 *Tel:* 813-253-6266 *E-mail:* utpress@ut.edu *Web Site:* tampareview.org/the-danahy-fiction-prize, pg 594

Mathews, Richard, The Tampa Review Prize for Poetry, University of Tampa Press, 401 W Kennedy Blvd, Tampa, FL 33606 *Tel:* 813-253-6266 *E-mail:* utpress@ut.edu *Web Site:* tampareview.org/the-tampa-review-prize-for-poetry, pg 668

Mathias, Ashley, University of South Carolina Press, 1600 Hampton St, Suite 544, Columbia, SC 29208 *Tel:* 803-777-5245 *Toll Free Tel:* 800-768-2500 (orders) *Fax:* 803-777-0160 *Toll Free Fax:* 800-868-0740 (orders) *Web Site:* uscpress.com, pg 220

Mathiesen, Tim, Faith & Fellowship Publishing, 1020 W Alcott Ave, Fergus Falls, MN 56537 *Tel:* 218-736-7357 *Toll Free Tel:* 800-332-9232 *E-mail:* ffpublishing@clba.org *Web Site:* www.clba.org, pg 69

Mathis, Catherine J, McGraw-Hill Education, 2 Penn Plaza, New York, NY 10121-2298 *Tel:* 212-904-2000 *E-mail:* international_cs@mheducation.com; seg_customerservice@mheducation.com (PreK-12); hep_customerservice@mheducation.com (higher education) *Web Site:* www.mheducation.com, pg 127

Matin, Aref, John Wiley & Sons Inc, 111 River St, Hoboken, NJ 07030-5774 *Tel:* 201-748-6000 *Toll Free Tel:* 800-225-5945 (cust serv) *Fax:* 201-748-6088 *Web Site:* www.wiley.com, pg 230

Mativat, Genevieve, Les Editions Pierre Tisseyre, 155, rue Maurice, Rosemere, QC J7A 2S8, Canada *Tel:* 514-335-0777 *Fax:* 514-335-6723 *E-mail:* info@edtisseyre.ca *Web Site:* www.tisseyre.ca, pg 404

Matson, Faith, Oceanview Publishing Inc, PO Box 3168, Sarasota, FL 34230 *Tel:* 941-387-8500 *Web Site:* oceanviewpub.com, pg 145

Matson, Katinka, Brockman Inc, 260 Fifth Ave, 10th fl, New York, NY 10001 *Tel:* 212-935-8900 *E-mail:* rights@brockman.com *Web Site:* www.brockman.com, pg 452

Matson, Peter, Sterling Lord Literistic Inc, 594 Broadway, Suite 205, New York, NY 10012 *Tel:* 212-780-6050 *Fax:* 212-780-6095 *E-mail:* info@sll.com *Web Site:* www.sll.com, pg 477

Matsuda, Hisae, Parallax Press, 2236B Sixth St, Berkeley, CA 94710 *Tel:* 510-325-2945 *Toll Free Tel:* 800-863-5290 (orders) *Web Site:* www.parallax.org, pg 151

Matsui, Victory, Random House Publishing Group, 1745 Broadway, New York, NY 10019 *Toll Free Tel:* 800-200-3552 *Web Site:* www.randomhousebooks.com, pg 171

Matta, Danielle, Robin Straus Agency, Inc, 229 E 79 St, Suite 5A, New York, NY 10075 *Tel:* 212-472-3282 *Fax:* 212-472-3833 *E-mail:* info@robinstrausagency.com *Web Site:* www.robinstrausagency.com, pg 478

Matte, Rebecca, Bradford Literary Agency, 5694 Mission Center Rd, Suite 347, San Diego, CA 92108 *Tel:* 619-521-1201 *E-mail:* hillary@bradfordlit.com *Web Site:* www.bradfordlit.com, pg 451

Matthews, Elizabeth, American Society of Composers, Authors & Publishers (ASCAP), 250 W 57 St, New York, NY 10107 *Tel:* 212-621-6000 *Toll Free Tel:* 800-952-7227 (cust serv) *Fax:* 212-621-6595 *Web Site:* www.ascap.com, pg 496

Matthews, Graham, Dundurn Press Ltd, PO Box 19510, RPO Manulife, Toronto, ON M4W 3T9, Canada *Tel:* 416-214-5544 *E-mail:* info@dundurn.com; publicity@dundurn.com; sales@dundurn.com *Web Site:* www.dundurn.com, pg 401

Matthews, Heath, Alfred Music, 285 Century Place, Louisville, CO 80027 *Tel:* 818-891-5999 (dealer sales, intl) *Toll Free Tel:* 800-292-6122 (dealer sales, US & CN); 800-628-1528 (cust serv) *Fax:* 818-893-5560 (dealer sales); 818-830-6252 (cust serv) *Toll Free Fax:* 800-632-1928 (dealer sales) *E-mail:* customerservice@alfred.com; sales@alfred.com *Web Site:* www.alfred.com, pg 7

Matthews, Jermey, The MIT Press, One Broadway, 12th fl, Cambridge, MA 02142 *Tel:* 617-253-5255 *Toll Free Tel:* 800-405-1619 (orders) *Fax:* 617-258-6779; 617-577-1545 (orders) *Web Site:* mitpress.mit.edu, pg 132

Matthews, Melanie, Piano Press, 1425 Ocean Ave, Suite 5, Del Mar, CA 92014 *Tel:* 619-884-1401 *E-mail:* pianopress@pianopress.com *Web Site:* www.pianopress.com, pg 159

Matthews, Pete, Candlewick Press, 99 Dover St, Somerville, MA 02144-2825 *Tel:* 617-661-3330 *Fax:* 617-661-0565 *E-mail:* bigbear@candlewick.com; salesinfo@candlewick.com *Web Site:* candlewick.com, pg 40

Mattura, Cat, McGraw-Hill Create, 2 Penn Plaza, New York, NY 10121 *Toll Free Tel:* 800-962-9342 *E-mail:* mhhe.create@mheducation.com *Web Site:* create.mheducation.com; shop.mheducation.com, pg 127

Matus, Robyn, Seedling Publications Inc, 520 E Bainbridge St, Elizabethtown, PA 17022 *Toll Free Tel:* 800-233-0759 *Toll Free Fax:* 888-834-1303 *E-mail:* edcsr@continentalpress.com *Web Site:* www.continentalpress.com, pg 186

Matushev, Aline, Arcadia Publishing Inc, 210 Wingo Way, Suite 200, Mount Pleasant, SC 29464 *Tel:* 843-853-2070 *E-mail:* retailers@arcadiapublishing.com *Web Site:* www.arcadiapublishing.com, pg 16

Matuszak, Hannah, The Experiment, 220 E 23 St, Suite 600, New York, NY 10010-4658 *Tel:* 212-889-1659 *E-mail:* info@theexperimentpublishing.com *Web Site:* www.theexperimentpublishing.com, pg 68

Matysik, Julie, Running Press, 1290 Avenue of the Americas, New York, NY 10104 *Tel:* 212-364-1100 *Toll Free Tel:* 800-759-0190 (cust serv) *Fax:* 212-364-0933 (intl orders) *Toll Free Fax:* 800-286-9471 (cust serv) *E-mail:* customer.service@hbgusa.com; orders@hbgusa.com *Web Site:* www.hachettebookgroup.com/imprint/running-press/; www.moon.com (Moon Travel Guides), pg 178

Matysko, Harriet I, Mary Ann Liebert Inc, 140 Huguenot St, 3rd fl, New Rochelle, NY 10801-5215 *Tel:* 914-740-2100 *Toll Free Tel:* 800-654-3237 *Fax:* 914-740-2101 *E-mail:* info@liebertpub.com *Web Site:* www.liebertonline.com, pg 116

Matzie, Bridget Wagner, Aevitas Creative Management LLC, 19 W 21 St, Suite 501, New York, NY 10010 *Tel:* 212-765-6900 *Web Site:* www.aevitascreative.com, pg 448

Mauer, Clare, St Martin's Press, LLC, 120 Broadway, New York, NY 10271 *E-mail:* publicity@stmartins.com; trademarketing@stmartins.com; foreignrights@stmartins.com *Web Site:* us.macmillan.com/smp, pg 181

Mauer, Harry, Flashlight Press, 527 Empire Blvd, Brooklyn, NY 11225 *Tel:* 718-288-8300 *Fax:* 718-972-6307 *Web Site:* www.flashlightpress.com, pg 72

Mauer, Tzvi, KTAV Publishing House Inc, 527 Empire Blvd, Brooklyn, NY 11225 *Tel:* 201-963-9524; 718-972-5449 *Fax:* 718-972-6307 *E-mail:* orders@ktav.com *Web Site:* www.ktav.com, pg 111

Mauer, Tzvi, Urim Publications, 527 Empire Blvd, Brooklyn, NY 11225-3121 *Tel:* 718-972-5449 *Fax:* 718-972-6307 *E-mail:* urimpublisher@gmail.com; orders@urimpublications.com *Web Site:* www.urimpublications.com, pg 223

Maurer, Amanda, Berkley, c/o Penguin Random House LLC, 1745 Broadway, 19th fl, New York, NY 10019 *Tel:* 212-366-2000 *Web Site:* www.penguin.com/publishers/berkley/; www.penguin.com/ace-overview/, pg 28

Maurer, Clare, Atria Books, 1230 Avenue of the Americas, New York, NY 10020 *Tel:* 212-698-7000 *Fax:* 212-698-7007 *Web Site:* www.simonandschuster.com, pg 21

Maurer, Rolf, New Star Books Ltd, 107-3477 Commercial St, Vancouver, BC V5N 4E8, Canada *Tel:* 604-738-9429 *E-mail:* info@newstarbooks.com *Web Site:* www.newstarbooks.com, pg 413

Maurier, Carlee, Farrar, Straus & Giroux Books for Young Readers, 120 Broadway, New York, NY 10271 *Tel:* 212-741-6900 *Toll Free Tel:* 888-330-8477 (orders) *E-mail:* childrens.publicity@macmillanusa.com; childrensrights@macmillanusa.com *Web Site:* us.macmillan.com/mackids, pg 70

Maurier, Carlee, Roaring Brook Press, 120 Broadway, New York, NY 10271 *Tel:* 646-307-5151 *Web Site:* us.macmillan.com/publishers/roaring-brook-press, pg 176

Mavi, Raj, Dreamscape Media LLC, 1417 Timberwolf Dr, Holland, OH 43528 *Tel:* 419-867-6965 *Toll Free Tel:* 877-983-7326 *E-mail:* info@dreamscapeab.com *Web Site:* www.dreamscapepublishing.com, pg 62

Mavjee, Maya, Knopf Doubleday Publishing Group, c/o Penguin Random House LLC, 1745 Broadway, New York, NY 10019 *Tel:* 212-751-2600 *Fax:* 212-940-7390 (dom rts); 212-572-2662 (foreign rts) *Web Site:* knopfdoubleday.com, pg 110

Mavjee, Maya, Penguin Random House LLC, 1745 Broadway, New York, NY 10019 *Tel:* 212-782-9000 *Toll Free Tel:* 800-726-0600 *Web Site:* www.penguinrandomhouse.com, pg 155

Max, P J, Easy Money Press, 82-5800 Napo'opo'o Rd, Captain Cook, HI 96704 *Tel:* 808-313-2808 *E-mail:* easymoneypress@yahoo.com, pg 63

Maxfield, Marcela, Stanford University Press, 425 Broadway St, Redwood City, CA 94063-3126 *Tel:* 650-723-9434 *Fax:* 650-725-3457 *E-mail:* info@www.sup.org; publicity@www.sup.org; sales@www.sup.org *Web Site:* www.sup.org, pg 197

Maxick, Jill, Prometheus Books, 59 John Glenn Dr, Amherst, NY 14228-2119 *Fax:* 716-691-0137 *E-mail:* marketing@prometheusbooks.com; editorial@prometheusbooks.com; rights@prometheusbooks.com *Web Site:* www.prometheusbooks.com, pg 166

Maxwell, Ed, Transatlantic Agency, 2 Bloor St E, Suite 3500, Toronto, ON M4W 1A8, Canada *Tel:* 416-488-9214 *E-mail:* info@transatlanticagency.com; royalties@transatlanticagency.com *Web Site:* www.transatlanticagency.com, pg 479

Maxwell, J Carl, Association of American Publishers (AAP), 455 Massachusetts Ave NW, Suite 700, Washington, DC 20001-2777 *Tel:* 202-347-3375 *Fax:* 202-347-3690 *E-mail:* info@publishers.org *Web Site:* publishers.org, pg 498

Maxwell, Nancy, Ariel Press, 2317 Quail Cove Dr, Jasper, GA 30143 *Tel:* 770-894-4226 *E-mail:* lig201@lightariel.com *Web Site:* www.lightariel.com, pg 16

May, Elizabeth, Kensington Publishing Corp, 900 Third Ave, 26th fl, New York, NY 10022 *Tel:* 212-407-1500 *Toll Free Tel:* 800-221-2647 *Fax:* 212-935-0699 *Web Site:* www.kensingtonbooks.com, pg 109

May, Gergana, The Ibsen Society of America (ISA), c/o Indiana University, Global & Intl Studies Bldg 3111, 355 N Jordan St, Bloomington, IN 47405-1105 *Web Site:* www.ibsensociety.org, pg 507

May, Jonathan, Redleaf Press®, 10 Yorkton Ct, St Paul, MN 55117 *Tel:* 651-641-0508 *Toll Free Tel:* 800-423-8309 *Fax:* 651-641-0115 *E-mail:* customerservice@redleafpress.org; info@redleafpress.org; marketing@redleafpress.org *Web Site:* www.redleafpress.org, pg 173

May, Louise, Lee & Low Books, 95 Madison Ave, Suite 1205, New York, NY 10016 *Tel:* 212-779-4400 *Toll Free Tel:* 888-320-3190 (ext 28, orders only) *Fax:* 212-683-1894 (orders only); 212-532-6035 *E-mail:* general@leeandlow.com *Web Site:* www.leeandlow.com, pg 114

May, Dr Timothy, The Mongolia Society Inc, Indiana University, 703 Eigenmann Hall, 1900 E Tenth St, Bloomington, IN 47406-7512 *Tel:* 812-855-4078 *Fax:* 812-855-4078 *E-mail:* monsoc@indiana.edu *Web Site:* mongoliasociety.org, pg 133

Maybank, Aletha MD, American Medical Association (AMA), AMA Plaza, 330 N Wabash, Suite 39300, Chicago, IL 60611-5885 *Tel:* 312-464-5000 *Toll Free Tel:* 800-621-8335 *E-mail:* media@ama-assn.org (media & edit) *Web Site:* www.ama-assn.org; www.jamanetwork.org, pg 495

Mayer, Dan, Prometheus Books, 59 John Glenn Dr, Amherst, NY 14228-2119 *Fax:* 716-691-0137 *E-mail:* marketing@prometheusbooks.com; editorial@prometheusbooks.com; rights@prometheusbooks.com *Web Site:* www.prometheusbooks.com, pg 166

Mayer, Liese, Little, Brown and Company, 1290 Avenue of the Americas, New York, NY 10104 *Tel:* 212-364-1100 *Fax:* 212-364-0952 *E-mail:* firstname.lastname@hbgusa.com *Web Site:* www.hachettebookgroup.com/imprint/little-brown-and-company/, pg 118

Mayer, Tom, W W Norton & Company Inc, 500 Fifth Ave, New York, NY 10110-0017 *Tel:* 212-354-5500 *Toll Free Tel:* 800-233-4830 (orders & cust serv) *Fax:* 212-869-0856 *Toll Free Fax:* 800-458-6515 *E-mail:* orders@wwnorton.com *Web Site:* wwnorton.com, pg 143

Mayfield, Tyler, Louisville Grawemeyer Award in Religion, 1044 Alta Vista Rd, Louisville, KY 40205-1798 *Tel:* 502-895-3411 *Toll Free Tel:* 800-264-1839 *Fax:* 502-895-1096 *E-mail:* grawemeyer@lpts.edu *Web Site:* www.grawemeyer.org, pg 626

Mayhall, Michelle, Sourcebooks LLC, 1935 Brookdale Rd, Suite 139, Naperville, IL 60563 *Tel:* 630-961-3900 *Toll Free Tel:* 800-432-7444 *Fax:* 630-961-2168 *E-mail:* info@sourcebooks.com *Web Site:* www.sourcebooks.com, pg 194

Mayland, Chris, Encyclopaedia Britannica Inc, 325 N La Salle St, Suite 200, Chicago, IL 60654 *Tel:* 312-347-7000 (all other countries) *Toll Free Tel:* 800-323-1229 (US & CN) *Fax:* 312-294-2104 *E-mail:* contact@eb.com *Web Site:* www.britannica.com, pg 66

Maynard, Gary, The Gary-Paul Agency (GPA), 1549 Main St, Stratford, CT 06615 *Tel:* 203-345-6167 *Web Site:* www.thegarypaulagency.com, pg 439

Mayo, Kierna, Random House Publishing Group, 1745 Broadway, New York, NY 10019 *Toll Free Tel:* 800-200-3552 *Web Site:* www.randomhousebooks.com, pg 170

Mayotte, Alain, Editions Prise de parole, 359-27 rue Larch, Sudbury, ON P3E 1B7, Canada *Tel:* 705-675-6491 *E-mail:* info@prisedeparole.ca *Web Site:* www.prisedeparole.ca, pg 405

Mays, Jessica, Chronicle Books LLC, 680 Second St, San Francisco, CA 94107 *Tel:* 415-537-4200 *Fax:* 415-537-4460 (perms) *E-mail:* hello@chroniclebooks.com; subrights@chroniclebooks.com *Web Site:* www.chroniclebooks.com, pg 47

Mazer, Laura, Wendy Sherman Associates Inc, 138 W 25 St, Suite 1018, New York, NY 10001 *Tel:* 212-279-9027 *E-mail:* submissions@wsherman.com *Web Site:* www.wsherman.com, pg 476

Mazia, Judith, Alan Wofsy Fine Arts, 1109 Geary Blvd, San Francisco, CA 94109 *Tel:* 415-292-6500 *Toll Free Tel:* 800-660-6403 *Fax:* 415-292-6594 (off & cust serv); 510-251-1840 (acctg) *E-mail:* order@art-books.com (orders); editeur@earthlink.net (edit); beauxarts@earthlink.net (cust serv) *Web Site:* www.art-books.com, pg 231

Maziarz, Julia, Trident Media Group LLC, 355 Lexington Ave, 12th fl, New York, NY 10017 *Tel:* 212-333-1511 *E-mail:* info@tridentmediagroup.com; foreignrights@tridentmediagroup.com; office.assistant@tridentmediagroup.com *Web Site:* www.tridentmediagroup.com, pg 480

Mazurak, Walter, Macmillan, 120 Broadway, 22nd fl, New York, NY 10271 E-mail: press.inquiries@macmillan.com Web Site: us.macmillan.com, pg 122

Mazurkiewicz, Orchid, UCLA Latin American Center Publications, UCLA Latin American Institute, 10343 Bunche Hall, Los Angeles, CA 90095 Tel: 310-825-4571 Fax: 310-206-6859 E-mail: latinamctr@international.ucla.edu Web Site: www.international.ucla.edu/lai, pg 212

Mazza, Cris, University of Illinois at Chicago, Program for Writers, College of Liberal Arts & Sciences, 601 S Morgan St, Chicago, IL 60607 Tel: 312-413-2200 (Eng dept) E-mail: english@uic.edu Web Site: engl.uic.edu/graduate-studies/program-for-writers, pg 566

Mazza, Melissa, Bloomsbury Publishing Inc, 1385 Broadway, 5th fl, New York, NY 10018 Tel: 212-419-5300 E-mail: marketingusa@bloomsbury.com; adultpublicityusa@bloomsbury.com; askacademic@bloomsbury.com Web Site: www.bloomsbury.com, pg 32

Mazzone, Devon, Farrar, Straus & Giroux, LLC, 120 Broadway, New York, NY 10271 Tel: 212-741-6900 E-mail: fsg.publicity@fsgbooks.com; sales@fsgbooks.com Web Site: us.macmillan.com/fsg, pg 70

Mbalia, Kwame, Disney Publishing Worldwide, 1101 Flower St, Glendale, CA 91201 Web Site: books.disney.com, pg 60

McAdam, Matthew, Johns Hopkins University Press, 2715 N Charles St, Baltimore, MD 21218-4363 Tel: 410-516-6900; 410-516-6987 Toll Free Tel: 800-537-5487 (book orders & cust serv); 800-548-1784 (journal orders) Fax: 410-516-6968; 410-516-6998 (orders) E-mail: hfscustserv@press.jhu.edu (cust serv); jrnlcirc@jh.edu (journal orders) Web Site: www.press.jhu.edu; muse.jhu.edu, pg 106

McAdoo, Lynne, Andrews McMeel Publishing LLC, 1130 Walnut St, Kansas City, MO 64106-2109 Tel: 816-581-7500 Toll Free Tel: 800-851-8923 Web Site: www.andrewsmcmeel.com; publishing.andrewsmcmeel.com, pg 14

McAdoo, Timothy, American Psychological Association, 750 First St NE, Washington, DC 20002 Tel: 202-336-5510 Toll Free Tel: 800-374-2721 Fax: 202-336-5502 E-mail: order@apa.org; booksales@apa.org Web Site: www.apa.org/books, pg 12

McAllister, Casey, PRINTING United Alliance, 10015 Main St, Fairfax, VA 22031 Tel: 703-385-1335 Toll Free Tel: 888-385-3588 Fax: 703-273-0456; 703-691-7492 (membership) E-mail: assist@printing.org; info@printing.org Web Site: www.printing.org, pg 517

McAnespia, Elena, University of California Press, 155 Grand Ave, Suite 400, Oakland, CA 94612-3758 Tel: 510-883-8232 Fax: 510-836-8910 E-mail: customerservice@ucpress.edu Web Site: www.ucpress.edu, pg 215

McAnespie, Elena, Bloomsbury Publishing Inc, 1385 Broadway, 5th fl, New York, NY 10018 Tel: 212-419-5300 E-mail: marketingusa@bloomsbury.com; adultpublicityusa@bloomsbury.com; askacademic@bloomsbury.com Web Site: www.bloomsbury.com, pg 31

McArdle, Nicole, Penguin Random House Audio Publishing Group, 1745 Broadway, New York, NY 10019 Toll Free Tel: 800-793-2665 (cust serv) E-mail: audio@penguinrandomhouse.com; ecustomerservice@penguinrandomhouse.com Web Site: www.penguinrandomhouseaudio.com, pg 154

McArthur, Stephen, Rootstock Publishing, 27 Main St, Suite 6, Montpelier, VT 05602 Tel: 802-839-0371 E-mail: info@rootstockpublishing.com Web Site: www.rootstockpublishing.com, pg 176

McAuley, Genny, Chronicle Books LLC, 680 Second St, San Francisco, CA 94107 Tel: 415-537-4200 Fax: 415-537-4460 (perms) E-mail: hello@chroniclebooks.com; subrights@chroniclebooks.com Web Site: www.chroniclebooks.com, pg 47

McAuley, Scott, Angel City Press, 2118 Wilshire Blvd, Suite 880, Santa Monica, CA 90403 Tel: 310-395-9982 E-mail: info@angelcitypress.com Web Site: www.angelcitypress.com, pg 14

McAuliffe, Lisa, HarperCollins Publishers LLC, 195 Broadway, New York, NY 10007 Tel: 212-207-7000 Web Site: www.harpercollins.com, pg 87

McAuliffe, Lisa, Houghton Mifflin Harcourt, 125 High St, Boston, MA 02110 Tel: 617-351-5000 Toll Free Tel: 855-969-4642; 800-225-5425 (K-12 educ materials); 800-323-9540 (assessment materials); 877-219-1537 (SkillsTutor); 888-242-6747 (Innovation in Educ Group); 800-225-3362 (Trade & Ref Div) Toll Free Fax: 800-269-5232 E-mail: myhmhco@hmhco.com Web Site: www.hmhco.com, pg 96

McAveney, Mary, Harry N Abrams Inc, 195 Broadway, 9th fl, New York, NY 10007 Tel: 212-206-7715 Toll Free Tel: 800-345-1359 Fax: 212-645-8437 E-mail: abrams@abramsbooks.com; publicity@abramsbooks.com; sales@abramsbooks.com Web Site: www.abramsbooks.com, pg 2

McAweeney, Terry, MFA Publications, 465 Huntington Ave, Boston, MA 02115 Tel: 617-369-4233 E-mail: publications@mfa.org Web Site: www.mfa.org/publications, pg 130

McBride, Andre, Penny-Farthing Productions, One Sugar Creek Center Blvd, Suite 820, Sugar Land, TX 77478 Tel: 713-780-0300 Toll Free Tel: 800-926-2669 Fax: 713-780-4004 E-mail: corp@pfproductions.com Web Site: www.pfproductions.com, pg 157

McBride, David, Oxford University Press USA, 198 Madison Ave, New York, NY 10016 Toll Free Tel: 800-451-7556 (orders); 800-445-9714 (cust serv) Fax: 919-677-1303 E-mail: custserv.us@oup.com Web Site: global.oup.com, pg 149

McBride, Gerilee, University of British Columbia Press, 2029 West Mall, Vancouver, BC V6T 1Z2, Canada Tel: 604-822-5959 Toll Free Tel: 877-377-9378 Fax: 604-822-6083 Toll Free Fax: 800-668-0821 E-mail: frontdesk@ubcpress.ca Web Site: www.ubcpress.ca, pg 422

McBride, Margret, Margret McBride Literary Agency, PO Box 9128, La Jolla, CA 92038 Tel: 858-454-1550 E-mail: staff@mcbridelit.com Web Site: www.mcbrideliterary.com, pg 469

McCabe, Ginny, National Society of Newspaper Columnists (NSNC), 205 Gun Hill St, Milton, MA 02186 Tel: 617-697-6854 Web Site: www.columnists.com, pg 514

McCabe, Ginny, National Society of Newspaper Columnists Annual Conference, 205 Gun Hill St, Milton, MA 02186 Tel: 617-697-6854 Web Site: www.columnists.com, pg 556

McCabe, Sarah, Simon & Schuster Children's Publishing, 1230 Avenue of the Americas, New York, NY 10020 Tel: 212-698-7000 Web Site: www.simonandschuster.com/kids; www.simonandschuster.com/teen; simonandschuster.net; simonandschuster.biz, pg 189

McCaffrey, Roger A, Roman Catholic Books, PO Box 2286, Fort Collins, CO 80522-2286 Tel: 970-490-2735 Fax: 904-493-8781 Web Site: www.booksforcatholics.com, pg 176

McCagg, Mary, Candlewick Press, 99 Dover St, Somerville, MA 02144-2825 Tel: 617-661-3330 Fax: 617-661-0565 E-mail: bigbear@candlewick.com; salesinfo@candlewick.com Web Site: candlewick.com, pg 40

McCaig, JoAnn, Thistledown Press, 220 20 St W, Unit 222, Saskatoon, SK S7M 0W9, Canada Tel: 306-244-1722 E-mail: tdpress@thistledownpress.com Web Site: www.thistledownpress.com, pg 420

McCaig, Michelle, Baylor University Press, Baylor University, One Bear Place, Waco, TX 76798-7363 Tel: 254-710-3164 E-mail: bup_marketing@baylor.edu Web Site: www.baylorpress.com, pg 25

McCain, Shannon, Sourcebooks LLC, 1935 Brookdale Rd, Suite 139, Naperville, IL 60563 Tel: 630-961-3900 Toll Free Tel: 800-432-7444 Fax: 630-961-2168 E-mail: info@sourcebooks.com Web Site: www.sourcebooks.com, pg 194

McCall, Carol, IODE Violet Downey Book Award, 40 Orchard View Blvd, Suite 219, Toronto, ON M4R 1B9, Canada Tel: 416-487-4416 Toll Free Tel: 866-827-7428 Fax: 416-487-4417 E-mail: iodecanada@bellnet.ca Web Site: www.iode.ca, pg 617

McCall, Jeff, Twenty-Third Publications, One Montauk Ave, Suite 200, New London, CT 06320 Tel: 860-437-3012 Toll Free Tel: 800-321-0411 (orders) Toll Free Fax: 800-572-0788 E-mail: resources@twentythirdpublications.com Web Site: www.twentythirdpublications.com, pg 211

McCann, Peg, American Society of Agricultural & Biological Engineers (ASABE), 2950 Niles Rd, St Joseph, MI 49085-9659 Tel: 269-429-0300 Toll Free Tel: 800-371-2723 Fax: 269-429-3852 E-mail: hq@asabe.org Web Site: www.asabe.org, pg 12

McCants, Cassidy, The Pablo Neruda Prize for Poetry, University of Tulsa, Kendall College of Arts & Sciences, 800 S Tucker Dr, Tulsa, OK 74104 Tel: 918-631-3080 E-mail: nimrod@utulsa.edu Web Site: artsandsciences.utulsa.edu/nimrod/nimrod-literary-awards/, pg 639

McCants, Cassidy, Katherine Anne Porter Prize for Fiction, University of Tulsa, Kendall College of Arts & Sciences, 800 S Tucker Dr, Tulsa, OK 74104 Tel: 918-631-3080 E-mail: nimrod@utulsa.edu Web Site: artsandsciences.utulsa.edu/nimrod/nimrod-literary-awards/, pg 651

McCarren, William, National Press Club (NPC), 529 14 St NW, 13th fl, Washington, DC 20045 Tel: 202-662-7500 Web Site: www.press.org, pg 513

McCarthy, Bill, Faithlife Corp, 1313 Commercial St, Bellingham, WA 98225 Tel: 360-527-1700 Toll Free Tel: 888-563-0382 E-mail: support@faithlife.com; customerservice@logos.com Web Site: faithlife.com, pg 69

McCarthy, Brian, Library of America, 14 E 60 St, New York, NY 10022-1006 Tel: 212-308-3360 Fax: 212-750-8352 E-mail: info@loa.org Web Site: www.loa.org, pg 116

McCarthy, E J, E J McCarthy Agency, 405 Maple St, Suite H, Mill Valley, CA 94941 Tel: 415-383-6639 E-mail: ejmagency@gmail.com Web Site: www.publishersmarketplace.com/members/ejmccarthy, pg 470

McCarthy, Isabel, Avery, c/o Penguin Random House LLC, 1745 Broadway, New York, NY 10019 Tel: 212-366-2000 Web Site: www.penguin.com/avery-overview/, pg 23

McCarthy, Isabel, TarcherPerigee, c/o Penguin Random House LLC, 1745 Broadway, New York, NY 10019 Tel: 212-782-9000 Web Site: www.penguin.com/tarcherperigee-overview/; www.facebook.com/TarcherPerigee, pg 202

McCarthy, Jim, Dystel, Goderich & Bourret LLC, One Union Sq W, Suite 904, New York, NY 10003 Tel: 212-627-9100 Fax: 212-627-9313 Web Site: www.dystel.com, pg 457

McCarthy, Julia, Simon & Schuster Children's Publishing, 1230 Avenue of the Americas, New York, NY 10020 Tel: 212-698-7000 Web Site: www.simonandschuster.com/kids; www.simonandschuster.com/teen; simonandschuster.net; simonandschuster.biz, pg 189

McCarthy, Sabrina, Bloomsbury Publishing Inc, 1385 Broadway, 5th fl, New York, NY 10018 Tel: 212-419-5300 E-mail: marketingusa@bloomsbury.com; adultpublicityusa@bloomsbury.com; askacademic@bloomsbury.com Web Site: www.bloomsbury.com, pg 31

McCaslin, Rick, Texas State Historical Association, 3001 Lake Austin Blvd, Suite 3.116, Austin, TX 78703 Tel: 512-471-2600 Fax: 512-473-8691 Web Site: www.tshaonline.org, pg 205

McCauley, Gerard, Gerard McCauley Agency Inc, PO Box 844, Katonah, NY 10536-0844 Tel: 914-232-5700, pg 470

McCauley, Kay, Aurous Inc, PO Box 20490, New York, NY 10017 *Tel:* 212-628-9729 *Fax:* 212-535-7861, pg 449

McCauley, Kirby, Aurous Inc, PO Box 20490, New York, NY 10017 *Tel:* 212-628-9729 *Fax:* 212-535-7861, pg 449

McCauley, Patricia, Quincannon Publishing Group, PO Box 8100, Glen Ridge, NJ 07028-8100 *Tel:* 973-380-9942 *E-mail:* editors@quincannongroup.com (query first via e-mail) *Web Site:* www.quincannongroup.com, pg 168

McCauley, Prilliana, Chronicle Books LLC, 680 Second St, San Francisco, CA 94107 *Tel:* 415-537-4200 *Fax:* 415-537-4460 (perms) *E-mail:* hello@chroniclebooks.com; subrights@chroniclebooks.com *Web Site:* www.chroniclebooks.com, pg 48

McCauslin, Mark, Penguin Random House LLC, 1745 Broadway, New York, NY 10019 *Tel:* 212-782-9000 *Toll Free Tel:* 800-726-0600 *Web Site:* www.penguinrandomhouse.com, pg 155

McClain, J Cameron, Cedar Grove Publishing, 3205 Elmhurst St, Rowlett, TX 75088 *Tel:* 415-364-8292 *E-mail:* queries@cedargrovebooks.com *Web Site:* www.cedargrovebooks.com, pg 43

McClay, Ashley Pattison, GP Putnam's Sons, c/o Penguin Random House LLC, 1745 Broadway, New York, NY 10019 *Tel:* 212-782-9000 *Web Site:* www.penguin.com/putnam/, pg 167

McClearn, Lauren, Sourcebooks LLC, 1935 Brookdale Rd, Suite 139, Naperville, IL 60563 *Tel:* 630-961-3900 *Toll Free Tel:* 800-432-7444 *Fax:* 630-961-2168 *E-mail:* info@sourcebooks.com *Web Site:* www.sourcebooks.com, pg 195

McClelland, Anne, Book & Periodical Council (BPC), 36 Springhurst Ave, Toronto, ON M6K 1B6, Canada *Tel:* 416-975-9366 *E-mail:* info@thebpc.ca *Web Site:* www.thebpc.ca, pg 501

McClelland-Smith, Jennifer, Tor Publishing Group, 120 Broadway, New York, NY 10271 *Toll Free Tel:* 800-455-0340 (Macmillan) *E-mail:* torpublicity@tor.com; forgepublicity@forgebooks.com *Web Site:* us.macmillan.com/torpublishinggroup, pg 208

McCloy-Kelley, Liisa, Penguin Random House LLC, 1745 Broadway, New York, NY 10019 *Tel:* 212-782-9000 *Toll Free Tel:* 800-726-0600 *Web Site:* www.penguinrandomhouse.com, pg 155

McClure, Cameron, Donald Maass Literary Agency, 1000 Dean St, Suite 331, Brooklyn, NY 11238 *Tel:* 212-727-8383 *E-mail:* info@maassagency.com *Web Site:* www.maassagency.com, pg 468

McClure, John, Signalman Publishing, 3700 Commerce Blvd, Kissimmee, FL 34741 *Tel:* 407-504-4103 *Toll Free Tel:* 888-907-4423 *E-mail:* info@signalmanpublishing.com *Web Site:* www.signalmanpublishing.com, pg 187

McClure, Lauren, Michelin Maps & Guides, One Parkway S, Greenville, SC 29615-5022 *E-mail:* michelin.guides@michelin.com *Web Site:* guide.michelin.com; michelinmedia.com, pg 130

McClure, Wendy, Sourcebooks LLC, 1935 Brookdale Rd, Suite 139, Naperville, IL 60563 *Tel:* 630-961-3900 *Toll Free Tel:* 800-432-7444 *Fax:* 630-961-2168 *E-mail:* info@sourcebooks.com *Web Site:* www.sourcebooks.com, pg 194

McCluskey, Deirdre, Harlequin Enterprises Ltd, Bay Adelaide Centre, East Tower, 22 Adelaide St W, 41st fl, Toronto, ON M5H 4E3, Canada *Tel:* 416-445-5860 *Toll Free Tel:* 888-432-4879; 800-370-5838 (ebook inquiries) *E-mail:* customerservice@harlequin.com *Web Site:* www.harlequin.com, pg 409

McColley, Claire, Wm B Eerdmans Publishing Co, 4035 Park East Ct SE, Grand Rapids, MI 49546 *Tel:* 616-459-4591 *Toll Free Tel:* 800-253-7521 *E-mail:* customerservice@eerdmans.com; sales@eerdmans.com *Web Site:* www.eerdmans.com, pg 64

McConkey, Jill, University of Manitoba Press, University of Manitoba, 301 St Johns College, 92 Dysart Rd, Winnipeg, MB R3T 2M5, Canada *Tel:* 204-474-9495 *Fax:* 204-474-7566 *E-mail:* uofmpress@umanitoba.ca *Web Site:* uofmpress.ca, pg 422

McCord, Jennifer, Epicenter Press Inc, 6524 NE 181 St, Suite 2, Kenmore, WA 98028 *Tel:* 425-485-6822 (edit, mktg, busn off) *Fax:* 425-481-8253 *E-mail:* info@epicenterpress.com *Web Site:* www.epicenterpress.com, pg 67

McCord, Luke, Random House Children's Books, c/o Penguin Random House LLC, 1745 Broadway, New York, NY 10019 *Tel:* 212-782-9000 *Web Site:* www.rhcbooks.com, pg 170

McCormack, Megan, Portfolio, c/o Penguin Random House LLC, 1745 Broadway, New York, NY 10019 *Tel:* 212-782-9000 *Web Site:* www.penguin.com/portfolio-overview/; www.penguin.com/sentinel-overview/; www.penguin.com/thesis/, pg 162

McCormack, Sandy, PNWA Writers' Contest, 1420 NW Gilman Blvd, Suite 29, PMB 2717, Issaquah, WA 98027 *Tel:* 425-673-2665 *E-mail:* pnwa@pnwa.org *Web Site:* www.pnwa.org, pg 650

McCormack, Sandy, PNWA - a writer's resource, 1420 NW Gilman Blvd, Suite 29, PMB 2717, Issaquah, WA 98027 *Tel:* 425-673-2665 *E-mail:* pnwa@pnwa.org *Web Site:* www.pnwa.org, pg 517

McCormack, Sandy, PNWA Writers Conference, 1420 NW Gilman Blvd, Suite 29, PMB 2717, Issaquah, WA 98027 *Tel:* 425-673-2665 *E-mail:* pnwa@pnwa.org *Web Site:* www.pnwa.org, pg 557

McCormack, Wendy, National Institute for Trial Advocacy (NITA), 1685 38 St, Suite 200, Boulder, CO 80301-2735 *Tel:* 720-890-4860 *Toll Free Tel:* 877-648-2632; 800-225-6482 (orders & returns) *Fax:* 720-890-7069 *E-mail:* customerservice@nita.org; sales@nita.org *Web Site:* www.nita.org, pg 138

McCormick, Wynona, Texas A&M University Press, John H Lindsey Bldg, Lewis St, 4354 TAMU, College Station, TX 77843-4354 *Tel:* 979-845-1436 *Toll Free Tel:* 800-826-8911 (orders) *Fax:* 979-847-8752 *Toll Free Fax:* 888-617-2421 (orders) *E-mail:* bookorders@tamu.edu *Web Site:* www.tamupress.com, pg 205

McCoy, James, Iowa Poetry Prize, 119 W Park Rd, 100 Kuhl House, Iowa City, IA 52242-1000 *Tel:* 319-335-2000 *Fax:* 319-335-2055 *E-mail:* uipress@uiowa.edu *Web Site:* www.uipress.uiowa.edu, pg 617

McCoy, James, University of Iowa Press, 119 W Park Rd, 100 Kuhl House, Iowa City, IA 52242-1000 *Tel:* 319-335-2000 *Toll Free Tel:* 800-621-2736 (orders only) *Fax:* 319-335-2055 *Toll Free Fax:* 800-621-8476 (orders only) *E-mail:* uipress@uiowa.edu *Web Site:* www.uipress.uiowa.edu, pg 216

McCoy, Margo, Macmillan, 120 Broadway, 22nd fl, New York, NY 10271 *E-mail:* press.inquiries@macmillan.com *Web Site:* us.macmillan.com, pg 122

McCoy, Taj, Rees Literary Agency, One Westinghouse Plaza, Suite A203, Boston, MA 02136 *Tel:* 617-227-9014 *Web Site:* www.reesagency.com, pg 473

McCracken, Elizabeth, University of Texas at Austin, New Writers Project, Dept of English, 204 W 21 St, B-5000, Austin, TX 78712-1164 *Tel:* 512-471-4991 *Fax:* 512-471-4909 *E-mail:* newwritersproject@utexas.edu *Web Site:* liberalarts.utexas.edu/nwp, pg 567

McCracken, Kelly, Franciscan Media, 28 W Liberty St, Cincinnati, OH 45202 *Tel:* 513-241-5615 *E-mail:* admin@franciscanmedia.org *Web Site:* www.franciscanmedia.org, pg 74

McCraty, Rollin PhD, HeartMath LLC, 14700 W Park Ave, Boulder Creek, CA 95006 *Tel:* 831-338-8500 *Toll Free Tel:* 800-711-6221 *Fax:* 831-338-8504 *E-mail:* info@heartmath.org; service@heartmath.org *Web Site:* www.heartmath.org, pg 90

McCreary, Courtney, University Press of Mississippi, 3825 Ridgewood Rd, Jackson, MS 39211-6492 *Tel:* 601-432-6205 *Toll Free Tel:* 800-737-7788 (orders & cust serv) *Fax:* 601-432-6217 *E-mail:* press@mississippi.edu *Web Site:* www.upress.state.ms.us, pg 222

McCrorey, Charles, Hachette Audio, 1290 Avenue of the Americas, New York, NY 10104 *Tel:* 212-364-1100 *Web Site:* www.hachettebookgroup.com/imprint/hachette-audio/, pg 83

McCue, Mary, Little, Brown Books for Young Readers (LBYR), 1290 Avenue of the Americas, New York, NY 10104 *Tel:* 212-364-1100 *Toll Free Tel:* 800-759-0190 (cust serv) *E-mail:* rights@lbchildrens.com *Web Site:* www.hachettebookgroup.com/imprint/little-brown-books-for-young-readers/, pg 118

McCullough, Mark S, Wyndham Hall Press, 10372 W Munro Lake Dr, Levering, MI 49755 *Tel:* 419-648-9124 *E-mail:* orders@wyndhamhallpress.com *Web Site:* www.wyndhamhallpress.com, pg 234

McCullough, Robert, Penguin Random House Canada, a Penguin Random House company, 320 Front St W, Suite 1400, Toronto, ON M5V 3B6, Canada *Tel:* 416-364-4449 *Toll Free Tel:* 888-523-9292 (cust serv) *E-mail:* canadaweb@penguinrandomhouse.com; customerservicescanada@penguinrandomhouse.com *Web Site:* www.penguinrandomhouse.ca, pg 415

McCune, Sara Miller, SAGE Publishing, 2455 Teller Rd, Thousand Oaks, CA 91320 *Toll Free Tel:* 800-818-7243 *Toll Free Fax:* 800-583-2665 *E-mail:* info@sagepub.com; orders@sagepub.com *Web Site:* www.sagepublishing.com, pg 180

McCurdy, Wendy, Kensington Publishing Corp, 900 Third Ave, 26th fl, New York, NY 10022 *Tel:* 212-407-1500 *Toll Free Tel:* 800-221-2647 *Fax:* 212-935-0699 *Web Site:* www.kensingtonbooks.com, pg 109

McCutcheon, Camille, Southern Books Competition, PO Box 30703, Savannah, GA 31410 *Tel:* 912-999-7979 *E-mail:* selaadminservices@selaonline.org *Web Site:* selaonline.org, pg 664

McCutcheon, Kathleen, Macmillan, 120 Broadway, 22nd fl, New York, NY 10271 *E-mail:* press.inquiries@macmillan.com *Web Site:* us.macmillan.com, pg 122

McDermott, Kathleen, Harvard University Press, 79 Garden St, Cambridge, MA 02138-1499 *Tel:* 617-495-2600; 401-531-2800 (intl orders) *Toll Free Tel:* 800-405-1619 (orders) *Fax:* 617-495-5898 (gen); 617-496-4677 (edit & rts); 401-531-2801 (intl orders) *Toll Free Fax:* 800-406-9145 (orders) *E-mail:* contact_hup@harvard.edu *Web Site:* www.hup.harvard.edu, pg 88

McDermott, Susan, Apress Media LLC, One New York Plaza, Suite 4600, New York, NY 10004-1562 *Tel:* 212-460-1500 *E-mail:* editorial@apress.com; customerservice@springernature.com *Web Site:* www.apress.com, pg 16

McDonagh, Sean, Backbeat Books, PO Box 1520, Wayne, NJ 07042-1520 *Tel:* 973-987-5363 *E-mail:* submissions@halleonardbooks.com *Web Site:* www.backbeatbooks.com, pg 23

McDonagh, Sean, The Lyons Press, 64 S Main St, Essex, CT 06426 *Tel:* 203-458-4500 *E-mail:* info@rowman.com *Web Site:* rowman.com/page/lyonspress, pg 121

McDonald, Alison, Gagosian Gallery, 980 Madison Ave, New York, NY 10075 *Tel:* 212-744-2313 *Fax:* 212-772-7962 *E-mail:* newyork@gagosian.com *Web Site:* www.gagosian.com, pg 75

McDonald, Caitlin, Donald Maass Literary Agency, 1000 Dean St, Suite 331, Brooklyn, NY 11238 *Tel:* 212-727-8383 *E-mail:* info@maassagency.com *Web Site:* www.maassagency.com, pg 468

McDonald, Erroll, The Center for Fiction, 15 Lafayette Ave, Brooklyn, NY 11217 *Tel:* 212-755-6710 *E-mail:* info@centerforfiction.org *Web Site:* centerforfiction.org, pg 503

McDonald, Erroll, Alfred A Knopf, c/o Penguin Random House LLC, 1745 Broadway, New York, NY 10019 *Tel:* 212-751-2600 *Fax:* 212-940-7390 (dom rts); 212-572-2662 (foreign rts) *Web Site:* knopfdoubleday.com/imprint/knopf/; knopfdoubleday.com, pg 110

McDonald, Jerry N, The McDonald & Woodward Publishing Co, 695 Tall Oaks Dr, Newark, OH 43055 *Tel:* 740-641-2691 *Toll Free Tel:* 800-233-8787 *Fax:* 740-641-2692 *E-mail:* mwpubco@mwpubco.com *Web Site:* www.mwpubco.com, pg 127

McDonald, Joni, Skinner House Books, c/o Unitarian Universalist Assn, 24 Farnsworth St, Boston, MA 02210-1409 *Tel:* 617-742-2100 *Fax:* 617-948-6466 *E-mail:* skinnerhouse@uua.org *Web Site:* www.uua.org/publications/skinnerhouse, pg 190

McDonald, Kristi M, Ave Maria Press Inc, PO Box 428, Notre Dame, IN 46556 *Toll Free Tel:* 800-282-1865 *Toll Free Fax:* 800-282-5681 *E-mail:* avemariapress.1@nd.edu *Web Site:* www.avemariapress.com, pg 22

McDonald, Leigh, The University of Arizona Press, 1510 E University Blvd, Tucson, AZ 85721 *Tel:* 520-621-1441 *Toll Free Tel:* 800-621-2736 (orders) *Fax:* 520-621-8899 *Toll Free Fax:* 800-621-8476 (orders) *E-mail:* uap@uapress.arizona.edu *Web Site:* www.uapress.arizona.edu, pg 214

McDonald, Megan, Farrar, Straus & Giroux Books for Young Readers, 120 Broadway, New York, NY 10271 *Tel:* 212-741-6900 *Toll Free Fax:* 888-330-8477 (orders) *E-mail:* childrens.publicity@macmillanusa.com; childrensrights@macmillanusa.com *Web Site:* us.macmillan.com/mackids, pg 70

McDonald, Megan, Roaring Brook Press, 120 Broadway, New York, NY 10271 *Tel:* 646-307-5151 *Web Site:* us.macmillan.com/publishers/roaring-brook-press, pg 176

McDonald, Scott PhD, Advertising Research Foundation (ARF), 432 Park Ave S, 4th fl, New York, NY 10016 *Tel:* 212-751-5656 *Fax:* 212-689-1859 *E-mail:* membership@thearf.org; new-member-info@thearf.org *Web Site:* thearf.org, pg 493, 525

McDonald, Sean, Farrar, Straus & Giroux, LLC, 120 Broadway, New York, NY 10271 *Tel:* 212-741-6900 *E-mail:* fsg.publicity@fsgbooks.com; sales@fsgbooks.com *Web Site:* us.macmillan.com/fsg, pg 70

McDonough, Brian, Gale, 27555 Executive Dr, Suite 270, Farmington Hills, MI 48331 *Toll Free Tel:* 800-877-4253 *Toll Free Fax:* 877-363-4253 *E-mail:* gale.customerexperience@cengage.com *Web Site:* www.gale.com, pg 75

McDonough, Brian, Macmillan Reference USA™, 27500 Drake Rd, Farmington Hills, MI 48331-3535 *Tel:* 248-699-4253 *Toll Free Tel:* 800-877-4253 *Toll Free Fax:* 877-363-4253 *E-mail:* gale.customercare@cengage.com *Web Site:* www.gale.cengage.com/macmillan, pg 123

McDonough, Peter, American Council on Education (ACE), One Dupont Circle NW, Washington, DC 20036 *Tel:* 202-939-9300 *Web Site:* www.acenet.edu, pg 9, 495

McDowell, Andy, Gulf Energy Information, 2 Greenway Plaza, Suite 1020, Houston, TX 77046 *Tel:* 713-520-4498; 713-529-4301 *E-mail:* store@gulfpub.com; customerservice@gulfenergyinfo.com *Web Site:* www.gulfenergyinfo.com, pg 83

McDowell, John, Iona & Peter Opie Prize, Indiana University, Classroom-Off Bldg, 800 E Third St, Bloomington, IN 47405 *Tel:* 812-856-2379 *Fax:* 812-856-2483 *E-mail:* americanfolkloresociety@afsnet.org; cf.section@afsnet.org *Web Site:* www.afsnet.org; childrensfolklore.org/opie-prize, pg 644

McEachern, Sarah, Dalkey Archive Press, c/o Deep Vellum Publishing, 3000 Commerce St, Dallas, TX 75226 *E-mail:* admin@deepvellum.org *Web Site:* www.dalkeyarchive.com, pg 56

McElhinney, Sinead, Kobo Emerging Writer Prize, 135 Liberty St, Suite 101, Toronto, ON M6K 1A7, Canada *E-mail:* pr@kobo.com *Web Site:* www.kobo.com/emergingwriterprize, pg 621

McElhinny, Dan, William H Sadlier Inc, 9 Pine St, New York, NY 10005 *Tel:* 212-227-2120 *Toll Free Tel:* 800-221-5175 (cust serv) *Fax:* 212-312-6080 *E-mail:* customerservice@sadlier.com *Web Site:* www.sadlier.com, pg 179

McElroy, Iris, Penguin Random House Audio Publishing Group, 1745 Broadway, New York, NY 10019 *Toll Free Tel:* 800-793-2665 (cust serv) *E-mail:* audio@penguinrandomhouse.com; ecustomerservice@penguinrandomhouse.com *Web Site:* www.penguinrandomhouseaudio.com, pg 154

McEvoy, Nion, Chronicle Books LLC, 680 Second St, San Francisco, CA 94107 *Tel:* 415-537-4200 *Fax:* 415-537-4460 (perms) *E-mail:* hello@chroniclebooks.com; subrights@chroniclebooks.com *Web Site:* www.chroniclebooks.com, pg 47

McFadden, Daniel, Psychological Assessment Resources Inc (PAR), 16204 N Florida Ave, Lutz, FL 33549 *Tel:* 813-449-4065 *Toll Free Tel:* 800-331-8378 *Fax:* 813-961-2196 *Toll Free Fax:* 800-727-9329 *Web Site:* www.parinc.com, pg 166

McFadden, Trinity, Zondervan, 3900 Sparks Dr SE, Grand Rapids, MI 49546 *Tel:* 616-698-6900 *Toll Free Tel:* 800-226-1122; 800-727-1309 (retail orders) *Fax:* 616-698-3350 *Toll Free Fax:* 800-698-3256 (retail orders) *E-mail:* customercare@harpercollins.com *Web Site:* www.zondervan.com, pg 237

McFadden, Wendy, Brethren Press, 1451 Dundee Ave, Elgin, IL 60120 *Tel:* 847-742-5100 *Toll Free Tel:* 800-441-3712 *Toll Free Fax:* 800-667-8188 *E-mail:* brethrenpress@brethren.org *Web Site:* www.brethrenpress.com, pg 36

McFarland, Alan, SAMS Technical Publishing LLC, 9850 E 30 St, Indianapolis, IN 46229 *Toll Free Tel:* 800-428-7267 *E-mail:* customercare@samswebsite.com *Web Site:* www.samswebsite.com, pg 181

McGalagly, John, Penguin Random House Audio Publishing Group, 1745 Broadway, New York, NY 10019 *Toll Free Tel:* 800-793-2665 (cust serv) *E-mail:* audio@penguinrandomhouse.com; ecustomerservice@penguinrandomhouse.com *Web Site:* www.penguinrandomhouseaudio.com, pg 154

McGandy, Michael J, University of South Carolina Press, 1600 Hampton St, Suite 544, Columbia, SC 29208 *Tel:* 803-777-5245 *Toll Free Tel:* 800-768-2500 (orders) *Fax:* 803-777-0160 *Toll Free Fax:* 800-868-0740 (orders) *Web Site:* uscpress.com, pg 220

McGann, Michael, Teachers College Press, 1234 Amsterdam Ave, New York, NY 10027 *Tel:* 212-678-3929 *Fax:* 212-678-4149 *E-mail:* tcpress@tc.edu *Web Site:* www.tcpress.com, pg 203

McGarity, Todd, Hachette Book Group Inc, 1290 Avenue of the Americas, New York, NY 10104 *Tel:* 212-364-1100 *Toll Free Tel:* 800-759-0190 (cust serv) *Fax:* 212-364-0933 (intl orders) *Toll Free Fax:* 800-286-9471 (cust serv) *E-mail:* customer.service@hbgusa.com; orders@hbgusa.com *Web Site:* www.hachettebookgroup.com, pg 83

McGarvey, Joey, Milkweed Editions, 1011 Washington Ave S, Suite 300, Minneapolis, MN 55415-1246 *Tel:* 612-332-3192 *Toll Free Tel:* 800-520-6455 *E-mail:* orders@milkweed.org *Web Site:* milkweed.org, pg 131

McGauley, Kelly, Random House Children's Books, c/o Penguin Random House LLC, 1745 Broadway, New York, NY 10019 *Tel:* 212-782-9000 *Web Site:* www.rhcbooks.com, pg 169

McGee, Heather, Candlewick Press, 99 Dover St, Somerville, MA 02144-2825 *Tel:* 617-661-3330 *Fax:* 617-661-0565 *E-mail:* bigbear@candlewick.com; salesinfo@candlewick.com *Web Site:* candlewick.com, pg 39

McGeehon, Allison, Workman Publishing, 1290 Avenue of the Americas, New York, NY 10104 *Toll Free Tel:* 800-759-0190 *Fax:* 212-364-0950 *E-mail:* workman-inquiry@hbgusa.com *Web Site:* www.hachettebookgroup.com/imprint/workman-publishing-company/, pg 232

McGehee, Elizabeth, The French-American Foundation & Florence Gould Foundation Annual Translation Prize, 28 W 44 St, Suite 812, New York, NY 10036 *Web Site:* www.frenchamerican.org, pg 604

McGehee, Robert J, American Literacy Council, c/o Los Alamos National Laboratory, Los Alamos, NM 87545 *E-mail:* questions@americanliteracy.com *Web Site:* www.americanliteracy.com, pg 495

McGhee, Holly M, Pippin Properties Inc, 110 W 40 St, Suite 1704, New York, NY 10018 *Tel:* 212-338-9310 *E-mail:* info@pippinproperties.com *Web Site:* www.pippinproperties.com; www.facebook.com/pippinproperties, pg 472

McGhee, Matthew, Thomas Nelson, 501 Nelson Place, Nashville, TN 37214 *Tel:* 615-889-9000 *Toll Free Tel:* 800-251-4000 *Web Site:* www.thomasnelson.com, pg 206

McGhee, Molly, Tor Publishing Group, 120 Broadway, New York, NY 10271 *Toll Free Tel:* 800-455-0340 (Macmillan) *E-mail:* torpublicity@tor.com; forgepublicity@forgebooks.com *Web Site:* us.macmillan.com/torpublishinggroup, pg 208

McGinley, Jean, HarperCollins Children's Books, 195 Broadway, New York, NY 10007 *Tel:* 212-207-7000 *Web Site:* www.harpercollins.com/childrens, pg 85

McGinley, Jean, HarperCollins Publishers LLC, 195 Broadway, New York, NY 10007 *Tel:* 212-207-7000 *Web Site:* www.harpercollins.com, pg 86

McGinley, Trish, HarperCollins Publishers LLC, 195 Broadway, New York, NY 10007 *Tel:* 212-207-7000 *Web Site:* www.harpercollins.com, pg 86

McGinnis, Claire, Riverhead Books, c/o Penguin Random House LLC, 1745 Broadway, New York, NY 10019 *Tel:* 212-782-9000 *Web Site:* www.penguin.com/riverhead-overview/, pg 175

McGinnis, Meredith, W W Norton & Company Inc, 500 Fifth Ave, New York, NY 10110-0017 *Tel:* 212-354-5500 *Toll Free Tel:* 800-233-4830 (orders & cust serv) *Fax:* 212-869-0856 *Toll Free Fax:* 800-458-6515 *E-mail:* orders@wwnorton.com *Web Site:* wwnorton.com, pg 143

McGinty, James, Police Executive Research Forum, 1120 Connecticut Ave NW, Suite 930, Washington, DC 20036 *Tel:* 202-466-7820 *Web Site:* www.policeforum.org, pg 162

McGinty, Lindsay, Hay House LLC, PO Box 5100, Carlsbad, CA 92018-5100 *Tel:* 760-431-7695 (ext 1, intl) *Toll Free Tel:* 800-654-5126 (ext 1, US) *Toll Free Fax:* 800-650-5115 *Web Site:* www.hayhouse.com, pg 89

McGlynn, Rebecca, Bloomsbury Publishing Inc, 1385 Broadway, 5th fl, New York, NY 10018 *Tel:* 212-419-5300 *E-mail:* marketingusa@bloomsbury.com; adultpublicityusa@bloomsbury.com; askacademic@bloomsbury.com *Web Site:* www.bloomsbury.com, pg 31

McGowan, James, BookEnds Literary Agency, 136 Long Hill Rd, Gillette, NJ 07933 *Web Site:* www.bookendsliterary.com, pg 451

McGowan, Matt, Frances Goldin Literary Agency, Inc, 214 W 29 St, Suite 410, New York, NY 10001 *Tel:* 212-777-0047 *Fax:* 212-228-1660 *E-mail:* agency@goldinlit.com *Web Site:* www.goldinlit.com, pg 460

McGrath, Anne, Monkfish Book Publishing Co, 22 E Market St, Suite 304, Rhinebeck, NY 12572 *Tel:* 845-876-4861 *Web Site:* www.monkfishpublishing.com, pg 133

McGrath, Sarah, Riverhead Books, c/o Penguin Random House LLC, 1745 Broadway, New York, NY 10019 *Tel:* 212-782-9000 *Web Site:* www.penguin.com/riverhead-overview/, pg 175

McGregor, Natalie, Adams Media, 100 Technology Center Dr, Suite 501, Stoughton, MA 02072 *Tel:* 508-427-7100 *Web Site:* www.simonandschuster.com, pg 4

McGregor, Natalie, Artech House®, 685 Canton St, Norwood, MA 02062 *Tel:* 781-769-9750 *Toll Free Tel:* 800-225-9977 *Fax:* 781-769-6334 *E-mail:* artech@artechhouse.com *Web Site:* us.artechhouse.com, pg 17

McGroarty, Charlie, Sourcebooks LLC, 1935 Brookdale Rd, Suite 139, Naperville, IL 60563 *Tel:* 630-961-3900 *Toll Free Tel:* 800-432-7444 *Fax:* 630-961-2168 *E-mail:* info@sourcebooks.com *Web Site:* www.sourcebooks.com, pg 195

McGrone, Carlton, University Press of Mississippi, 3825 Ridgewood Rd, Jackson, MS 39211-6492 *Tel:* 601-432-6205 *Toll Free Tel:* 800-737-7788 (orders & cust serv) *Fax:* 601-432-6217 *E-mail:* press@mississippi.edu *Web Site:* www.upress.state.ms.us, pg 222

McGuire, Beverly, Coastside Editorial, PO Box 181, Moss Beach, CA 94038 *E-mail:* bevjoe@pacific.net, pg 437

McGuire, Katherine, Quirk Books, 215 Church St, Philadelphia, PA 19106 *Tel:* 215-627-3581 *Fax:* 215-627-5220 *E-mail:* general@quirkbooks.com *Web Site:* www.quirkbooks.com, pg 168

McGuire, Libby, Atria Books, 1230 Avenue of the Americas, New York, NY 10020 *Tel:* 212-698-7000 *Fax:* 212-698-7007 *Web Site:* www.simonandschuster.com, pg 21

McGuire, Libby, Books Like Us First Novel Contest, 1230 Avenue of the Americas, New York, NY 10020 *Tel:* 212-698-7000 *Web Site:* www.simonandschuster.com/p/simon-and-schuster-books-like-us, pg 583

McGuire, Libby, Simon & Schuster, LLC, 1230 Avenue of the Americas, New York, NY 10020 *Tel:* 212-698-7000 *Toll Free Tel:* 800-223-2336 (orders) *Fax:* 212-698-7007 *Toll Free Fax:* 800-943-9831 (orders) *E-mail:* firstname.lastname@simonandschuster.com; purchaseorders@simonandschuster.com (orders) *Web Site:* www.simonandschuster.com, pg 189

McGuire, Tim, W W Norton & Company Inc, 500 Fifth Ave, New York, NY 10110-0017 *Tel:* 212-354-5500 *Toll Free Tel:* 800-233-4830 (orders & cust serv) *Fax:* 212-869-0856 *Toll Free Fax:* 800-458-6515 *E-mail:* orders@wwnorton.com *Web Site:* wwnorton.com, pg 143

McGuirl, Erin, Bibliographical Society of America (BSA), 67 West St, Suite 401, Unit C17, Brooklyn, NY 11222 *E-mail:* bsa@bibsocamer.org *Web Site:* bibsocamer.org, pg 501

McHatton, Ron PhD, Gordon W Dillon/Richard C Peterson Memorial Essay Contest, PO Box 565477, Miami, FL 33156-5477 *Tel:* 305-740-2010 *Fax:* 305-747-7154 *E-mail:* theaos@aos.org *Web Site:* www.aos.org, pg 596

McHugh, Arianne, Saddleback Educational Publishing, 151 Kalmus Dr, Suite J-1, Costa Mesa, CA 92626 *Tel:* 714-640-5200 *Toll Free Tel:* 888-SDLBACK (735-2225); 800-637-8715 *Fax:* 714-640-5297 *Toll Free Fax:* 888-734-4010 *E-mail:* contact@sdlback.com *Web Site:* www.sdlback.com, pg 179

McHugh, Daniel, National Institute for Trial Advocacy (NITA), 1685 38 St, Suite 200, Boulder, CO 80301-2735 *Tel:* 720-890-4860 *Toll Free Tel:* 877-648-2632; 800-225-6482 (orders & returns) *Fax:* 720-890-7069 *E-mail:* customerservice@nita.org; sales@nita.org *Web Site:* www.nita.org, pg 138

McHugh, Elise M, University of New Mexico Press, One University of New Mexico, Albuquerque, NM 87131-0001 *Tel:* 505-272-7777 *Fax:* 505-277-3343 *E-mail:* custserv@unm.edu (order dept) *Web Site:* unmpress.com, pg 218

McInerney, Brittany Hamblin, Chronicle Books LLC, 680 Second St, San Francisco, CA 94107 *Tel:* 415-537-4200 *Fax:* 415-537-4460 (perms) *E-mail:* hello@chroniclebooks.com; subrights@chroniclebooks.com *Web Site:* www.chroniclebooks.com, pg 47

McInnes, Candis, Ivey Publishing, Ivey Business School Foundation, Western University, 1255 Western Rd, London, ON N6G 0N1, Canada *Tel:* 519-661-3206; 519-661-3208 *Toll Free Tel:* 800-649-6355 *Fax:* 519-661-3485; 519-661-3882 *E-mail:* cases@ivey.ca *Web Site:* www.iveypublishing.ca, pg 411

McInnis, Karen, Association of American Publishers (AAP), 455 Massachusetts Ave NW, Suite 700, Washington, DC 20001-2777 *Tel:* 202-347-3375 *Fax:* 202-347-3690 *E-mail:* info@publishers.org *Web Site:* publishers.org, pg 498

McIntosh, Kelly, Barbour Publishing Inc, 1810 Barbour Dr, Uhrichsville, OH 44683 *Tel:* 740-922-6045 *Fax:* 740-922-5948 *E-mail:* info@barbourbooks.com *Web Site:* www.barbourbooks.com, pg 24

McIntosh, Patti, IBBY Canada, c/o The Canadian Children's Book Ctr, 425 Adelaide St W, Suite 200, Toronto, ON M5V 3C1, Canada *Fax:* 416-975-8970 *E-mail:* info@ibby-canada.org *Web Site:* www.ibby-canada.org, pg 507

McIntyre, Amy, ASLE Book Awards, PO Box 502, Keene, NH 03431-0502 *Tel:* 603-357-7411 *Fax:* 603-357-7411 *E-mail:* info@asle.org *Web Site:* www.asle.org/research-write/asle-book-paper-awards, pg 575

McIntyre, Amy, ASLE Graduate Student Paper Awards, PO Box 502, Keene, NH 03431-0502 *Tel:* 603-357-7411 *Fax:* 603-357-7411 *E-mail:* info@asle.org *Web Site:* www.asle.org/research-write/asle-book-paper-awards, pg 575

McIntyre, Amy, Association for the Study of Literature and Environment (ASLE), PO Box 502, Keene, NH 03431-0502 *Tel:* 603-357-7411 *Fax:* 603-357-7411 *E-mail:* info@asle.org *Web Site:* www.asle.org, pg 498

McIntyre, Jack, Jane Rotrosen Agency LLC, 318 E 51 St, New York, NY 10022-7803 *Tel:* 212-593-4330 *E-mail:* info@janerotrosen.com *Web Site:* janerotrosen.com, pg 474

McIntyre, Kheil, LearningExpress, 224 W 29 St, 3rd fl, New York, NY 10001 *Toll Free Tel:* 800-295-9556 (ext 2) *Web Site:* learningexpresshub.com, pg 114

McIntyre, Maury, Television Academy, 5220 Lankershim Blvd, North Hollywood, CA 91601-3109 *Tel:* 818-754-2800 *Web Site:* www.emmys.com, pg 521

McIntyre, Suzanne Ostiguy, Institute for Research on Public Policy (IRPP), 1470 Peel St, No 200, Montreal, QC H3A 1T1, Canada *Tel:* 514-985-2461 *Fax:* 514-985-2559 *E-mail:* irpp@irpp.org *Web Site:* irpp.org, pg 410

McKay, Amy, Avery Color Studios, 511 "D" Ave, Gwinn, MI 49841 *Tel:* 906-346-3908 *Toll Free Tel:* 800-722-9925 *Fax:* 906-346-3015 *E-mail:* averycolor@averycolorstudios.com *Web Site:* www.averycolorstudios.com, pg 23

McKay, Angela, Institute of Environmental Sciences & Technology - IEST, 1827 Walden Office Sq, Suite 400, Schaumburg, IL 60173 *Tel:* 847-981-0100 *Fax:* 847-981-4130 *E-mail:* information@iest.org *Web Site:* www.iest.org, pg 101

McKay, John, Association of American Publishers (AAP), 455 Massachusetts Ave NW, Suite 700, Washington, DC 20001-2777 *Tel:* 202-347-3375 *Fax:* 202-347-3690 *E-mail:* info@publishers.org *Web Site:* publishers.org, pg 498

McKay, Sara, PA Press, 202 Warren St, Hudson, NY 12534 *Tel:* 518-671-6100 *Toll Free Tel:* 800-722-6657 (dist); 800-759-0190 (sales) *E-mail:* sales@papress.com *Web Site:* www.papress.com, pg 149

McKay-Keizer, Laura, Portage & Main Press, 318 McDermot Ave, Suite 100, Winnipeg, MB R3A 0A2, Canada *Tel:* 204-987-3500 *Toll Free Tel:* 800-667-9673 *Fax:* 204-947-0080 *Toll Free Fax:* 866-734-8477 *E-mail:* customerservice@portageandmainpress.com *Web Site:* www.portageandmainpress.com, pg 416

McKean, Kate, Howard Morhaim Literary Agency Inc, 30 Pierrepont St, Brooklyn, NY 11201-3371 *Tel:* 718-222-8400 *E-mail:* info@morhaimliterary.com *Web Site:* www.morhaimliterary.com, pg 470

McKee, Christopher, The PRS Group Inc, 5800 Heritage Landing Dr, Suite E, East Syracuse, NY 13057-9358 *Tel:* 315-431-0511 *Fax:* 315-431-0200 *E-mail:* custserv@prsgroup.com *Web Site:* www.prsgroup.com, pg 166

McKee, Katie, GP Putnam's Sons, c/o Penguin Random House LLC, 1745 Broadway, New York, NY 10019 *Tel:* 212-782-9000 *Web Site:* www.penguin.com/putnam/, pg 167

McKee, Marc, The Jeffrey E Smith Editors' Prize, 357 McReynolds Hall, University of Missouri, Columbia, MO 65211 *Tel:* 573-882-4474 *Toll Free Tel:* 800-949-2505 *Fax:* 573-884-4671 *E-mail:* question@moreview.com; contest_question@moreview.com *Web Site:* www.missourireview.com/contests/jeffrey-e-smith-editors-prize, pg 664

McKee, Tim, North Atlantic Books (NAB), 2526 Martin Luther King Jr Way, Berkeley, CA 94704 *Tel:* 510-549-4270 *Web Site:* www.northatlanticbooks.com, pg 142

McKellar, Elizabeth, Parallax Press, 2236B Sixth St, Berkeley, CA 94710 *Tel:* 510-325-2945 *Toll Free Tel:* 800-863-5290 (orders) *Web Site:* www.parallax.org, pg 151

McKendry, Hannah, Canadian Bookbinders and Book Artists Guild (CBBAG), 82809-467 Parliament St, Toronto, ON M5A 3Y2, Canada *E-mail:* cbbag@cbbag.ca *Web Site:* www.cbbag.ca, pg 502

McKenna, Anne, University of Wisconsin Press, 728 State St, Suite 443, Madison, WI 53706-1418 *Tel:* 608-263-1110; 608-263-0668 (journal orders) *Toll Free Tel:* 800-621-2736 (book orders) *Fax:* 608-263-1173 *Toll Free Fax:* 800-621-2736 (book orders) *E-mail:* uwiscpress@uwpress.wisc.edu *Web Site:* uwpress.wisc.edu, pg 221

McKenna, Caitlin, Random House Publishing Group, 1745 Broadway, New York, NY 10019 *Toll Free Tel:* 800-200-3552 *Web Site:* www.randomhousebooks.com, pg 171

McKenna, Gwen, Mountain Press Publishing Co, 1301 S Third W, Missoula, MT 59801 *Tel:* 406-728-1900 *Toll Free Tel:* 800-234-5308 *Fax:* 406-728-1635 *E-mail:* info@mtnpress.com *Web Site:* www.mountain-press.com, pg 135

McKenna, James, Black Warrior Review Fiction, Nonfiction & Poetry Contest, University of Alabama, Off of Student Media, 414 Campus Dr E, Tuscaloosa, AL 35487 *Tel:* 205-348-4518 *Fax:* 205-348-8036 *E-mail:* blackwarriorreview@gmail.com; bwr@ua.edu *Web Site:* www.bwr.ua.edu, pg 581

McKenna, Kathy, New Hampshire Literary Awards, 2500 N River Rd, Manchester, NH 03106 *Tel:* 603-270-5466 *E-mail:* info@nhwritersproject.org *Web Site:* www.nhwritersproject.org/new-hampshire-literary-awards, pg 640

McKenna, Kathy, New Hampshire Writers' Project (NHWP), 2500 N River Rd, Manchester, NH 03106 *Tel:* 603-270-5466 *E-mail:* info@nhwritersproject.org *Web Site:* www.nhwritersproject.org, pg 514

McKenna, Stephanie, Adams Media, 100 Technology Center Dr, Suite 501, Stoughton, MA 02072 *Tel:* 508-427-7100 *Web Site:* www.simonandschuster.com, pg 4

McKenna, Tom, Taunton Books, 63 S Main St, Newtown, CT 06470 *Tel:* 203-426-8171 *Toll Free Tel:* 866-505-4689 (orders) *Fax:* 203-270-9373, pg 203

McKenzie, Michael, Little, Brown and Company, 1290 Avenue of the Americas, New York, NY 10104 *Tel:* 212-364-1100 *Fax:* 212-364-0952 *E-mail:* firstname.lastname@hbgusa.com *Web Site:* www.hachettebookgroup.com/imprint/little-brown-and-company/, pg 118

McKeon, Hilary, Looseleaf Law Publications Inc, 43-08 162 St, Flushing, NY 11358 *Tel:* 718-359-5559 *Toll Free Tel:* 800-647-5547 *Fax:* 718-539-0941 *E-mail:* info@looseleaflaw.com *Web Site:* www.looseleaflaw.com, pg 120

McKie, Ellen, University of Texas Press, 3001 Lake Austin Blvd, 2.200, Austin, TX 78703 *Tel:* 512-471-7233 *Fax:* 512-232-7178 *E-mail:* utpress@uts.cc.utexas.edu; info@utpress.utexas.edu *Web Site:* utpress.utexas.edu, pg 205

McKiernan, Diane, Penguin Random House Audio Publishing Group, 1745 Broadway, New York, NY 10019 *Toll Free Tel:* 800-793-2665 (cust serv) *E-mail:* audio@penguinrandomhouse.com; ecustomerservice@penguinrandomhouse.com *Web Site:* www.penguinrandomhouseaudio.com, pg 154

McKinney, Charlie, Sophia Institute Press®, 18 Celina Ave, Unit 1, Nashua, NH 03063 *Tel:* 603-641-9344 *Toll Free Tel:* 800-888-9344 *Fax:* 603-641-8108 *Toll Free Fax:* 888-288-2259 *E-mail:* orders@sophiainstitute.com *Web Site:* www.sophiainstitute.com, pg 193

McKinnish, Milly, Sourcebooks LLC, 1935 Brookdale Rd, Suite 139, Naperville, IL 60563 *Tel:* 630-961-3900 *Toll Free Tel:* 800-432-7444 *Fax:* 630-961-2168 *E-mail:* info@sourcebooks.com *Web Site:* www.sourcebooks.com, pg 195

McKitterick, Christopher, "Science into Fiction" Speculative Fiction Writing Workshop Series, 1809 Indiana St, Lawrence, KS 66044 *Tel:* 785-766-7039 *Web Site:* adastra-sf.com/Workshop-stuff/AdAstranauts-workshop.htm, pg 557

McKitterick, Christopher, Speculative Fiction Writing Workshop, 1809 Indiana St, Lawrence, KS 66044 *Tel:* 785-766-7039 *Web Site:* adastra-sf.com/Workshop-stuff/Spec-Fic-Workshop.htm, pg 557

McKusick, Caroline, Stanford University Press, 425 Broadway St, Redwood City, CA 94063-3126 *Tel:* 650-723-9434 *Fax:* 650-725-3457 *E-mail:* info@www.sup.org; publicity@www.sup.org; sales@www.sup.org *Web Site:* www.sup.org, pg 197

McLain, Kevin, Workman Publishing, 1290 Avenue of the Americas, New York, NY 10104 *Toll Free Tel:* 800-759-0190 *Fax:* 212-364-0950 *E-mail:* workman-inquiry@hbgusa.com *Web Site:* www.hachettebookgroup.com/imprint/workman-publishing-company/, pg 232

McLaren, Colleen, Llewellyn Publications, 2143 Wooddale Dr, Woodbury, MN 55125 *Tel:* 651-291-1970 *Toll Free Tel:* 800-843-6666 *Fax:* 651-291-1908 *E-mail:* publicity@llewellyn.com; customerservice@llewellyn.com *Web Site:* www.llewellyn.com, pg 119

McLaughlin, Brenna, Association of University Presses (AUPresses), 1412 Broadway, Suite 2135, New York, NY 10018 *Tel:* 212-989-1010 *Fax:* 212-989-0275 *E-mail:* info@aupresses.org *Web Site:* www.aupresses.org, pg 500

McLaughlin, Kellie, Aperture Books, 548 W 28 St, 4th fl, New York, NY 10001 *Tel:* 212-505-5555 *Toll Free Fax:* 888-623-6908 *E-mail:* customerservice@aperture.org *Web Site:* aperture.org, pg 15

McLaughlin, Kristin, Kensington Publishing Corp, 900 Third Ave, 26th fl, New York, NY 10022 *Tel:* 212-407-1500 *Toll Free Tel:* 800-221-2647 *Fax:* 212-935-0699 *Web Site:* www.kensingtonbooks.com, pg 109

McLaughlin, Larin, University of Washington Press, 4333 Brooklyn Ave NE, Seattle, WA 98105-9570 *Toll Free Tel:* 800-537-5487 (orders) *Fax:* 206-543-3932; 410-516-6998 (orders) *E-mail:* uwapress@uw.edu *Web Site:* uwapress.uw.edu, pg 220

McLaughlin, Maureen, Random House Children's Books, c/o Penguin Random House LLC, 1745 Broadway, New York, NY 10019 *Tel:* 212-782-9000 *Web Site:* www.rhcbooks.com, pg 169

McLaughlin, Tess, Best in Business Book Award, Walter Cronkite School of Journalism & Mass Communication, Arizona State University, 555 N Central Ave, Suite 406E, Phoenix, AZ 85004-1248 *Tel:* 602-496-7862 *E-mail:* sabew@sabew.org *Web Site:* sabew.org/best-in-business-book-awards, pg 578

McLaughlin, Tess, Society for Advancing Business Editing and Writing (SABEW), Walter Cronkite School of Journalism & Mass Communication, Arizona State University, 555 N Central Ave, Suite 406E, Phoenix, AZ 85004-1248 *Tel:* 602-496-7862 *E-mail:* sabew@sabew.org *Web Site:* sabew.org, pg 519

McLean, Christian, Southampton Writers' Conference, 239 Montauk Hwy, Southampton, NY 11968 *Tel:* 631-632-5007 *Web Site:* www.stonybrook.edu/writers, pg 557

McLean, Helen, Donner Canadian Foundation, 8 Prince Arthur Ave, 3rd fl, Toronto, ON M5R 1A9, Canada *Tel:* 416-920-6400 *Fax:* 416-920-5577 *Web Site:* www.donnerfoundation.org, pg 525

McLean, Laurie, San Francisco Writers Conference, 1901 Cleveland Ave, Suite D, Santa Rosa, CA 94501 *Tel:* 415-689-6301 *E-mail:* registrations@sfwriters.org; director@sfwriters.org; bizdev@sfwriters.org *Web Site:* www.sfwriters.org, pg 557

McLean, Laurie, San Francisco Writing Contest (SFWC), 1901 Cleveland Ave, Suite D, Santa Rosa, CA 94501 *Tel:* 415-689-6301 *E-mail:* contest@sfwriters.org; director@sfwriters.org *Web Site:* www.sfwriters.org, pg 658

McLean, Rebecca, Chickadee Prince Books LLC, 1030 Lake Ave, Greenwich, CT 06830 *Tel:* 212-808-5500 *E-mail:* submissions@chickadeeprince.com *Web Site:* chickadeeprince.com, pg 46

McLean, Tom, Simon & Schuster Audio, 1230 Avenue of the Americas, New York, NY 10020 *Web Site:* audio.simonandschuster.com, pg 189

McLemore, Deve, Sourcebooks LLC, 1935 Brookdale Rd, Suite 139, Naperville, IL 60563 *Tel:* 630-961-3900 *Toll Free Tel:* 800-432-7444 *Fax:* 630-961-2168 *E-mail:* info@sourcebooks.com *Web Site:* www.sourcebooks.com, pg 194

McLennan, David, University of Regina Press, 2 Research Dr, Suite 109, Regina, SK S4S 7H9, Canada *Tel:* 306-585-4758 *Fax:* 306-585-4699 *E-mail:* uofrpress@uregina.ca *Web Site:* uofrpress.ca, pg 423

McLeod, Stephen, George Washington Prize, c/o Fred W Smith National Library, 3600 Mount Vernon Memorial Hwy, Mount Vernon, VA 22121 *Tel:* 703-799-8686 *Web Site:* www.mountvernon.org/library/george-washington-prize, pg 673

McMahan, Danielle, John Wiley & Sons Inc, 111 River St, Hoboken, NJ 07030-5774 *Tel:* 201-748-6000 *Toll Free Tel:* 800-225-5945 (cust serv) *Fax:* 201-748-6088 *Web Site:* www.wiley.com, pg 230

McMahon, Hilary, Westwood Creative Artists Ltd, 386 Huron St, Toronto, ON M5S 2G6, Canada *Tel:* 416-964-3302 *Fax:* 416-964-3302 *E-mail:* wca_office@wcaltd.com *Web Site:* www.wcaltd.com, pg 481

McMahon, Meredith, Princeton University Press, 41 William St, Princeton, NJ 08540-5237 *Tel:* 609-258-4900 *Fax:* 609-258-6305 *E-mail:* info@press.princeton.edu *Web Site:* press.princeton.edu, pg 164

McMahon, Paul, Orbis Books, PO Box 302, Maryknoll, NY 10545-0302 *Tel:* 914-941-7636 *Toll Free Tel:* 800-258-5838 (orders, Mon-Fri 8AM-4PM EST) *Fax:* 914-941-7005 *E-mail:* orbisbooks@maryknoll.org *Web Site:* orbisbooks.com, pg 147

McMahon, Siobhan, Association of School Business Officials International, 44790 Maynard Sq, Suite 200, Ashburn, VA 20147 *Tel:* 703-478-0405 *Toll Free Tel:* 866-682-2729 *Fax:* 703-478-0205; 703-708-7060 (membership) *E-mail:* asboreq@asbointl.org; membership@asbointl.org *Web Site:* www.asbointl.org, pg 20

McMan, Ann, Bywater Books Inc, 3415 Porter Rd, Ann Arbor, MI 48103 *Tel:* 734-662-8815 *Web Site:* bywaterbooks.com, pg 39

McManus, Kerry, Astra Books for Young Readers, 19 W 21 St, No 1201, New York, NY 10010 *Tel:* 646-844-3485 *E-mail:* ahinfo@astrahouse.com; permissions@astrapublishinghouse.com *Web Site:* astrapublishinghouse.com, pg 20

McManus, Sean, Dreamscape Media LLC, 1417 Timberwolf Dr, Holland, OH 43528 *Tel:* 419-867-6965 *Toll Free Tel:* 877-983-7326 *E-mail:* info@dreamscapeab.com *Web Site:* www.dreamscapepublishing.com, pg 62

McMaster, Amanda, EXCEL Awards, 1620 "I" St NW, Suite 501, Washington, DC 20005 *Tel:* 202-289-7442 *Fax:* 202-289-7097 *E-mail:* excelawards@siia.net *Web Site:* siia.net/excel, pg 600

McMaster, Amanda, The Jesse H Neal Awards, 1620 Eye St NW, Washington, DC 20005 *Tel:* 202-289-7442 *E-mail:* nealawards@siia.net *Web Site:* siia.net/neals, pg 639

McMaster, Amanda, The SIIA IMPACT Awards, 1620 Eye St NW, Washington, DC 20005 *Tel:* 202-289-7442 *E-mail:* info@siia.net *Web Site:* www.siia.net/impact-award, pg 662

McMenemy, Siobhan, Wilfrid Laurier University Press, 75 University Ave W, Waterloo, ON N2L 3C5, Canada *Tel:* 519-884-0710 *Toll Free Tel:* 866-836-5551 (CN & US) *Fax:* 519-725-1399 *E-mail:* press@wlu.ca *Web Site:* www.wlupress.wlu.ca, pg 424

McMillan, Darin, BLR®—Business & Legal Resources, 5511 Virginia Way, Suite 150, Brentwood, TN 37027 *Tel:* 860-510-0100 *Toll Free Tel:* 800-727-5257 *Toll Free Fax:* 800-785-9212 *E-mail:* media@blr.com; sales@blr.com; service@blr.com; techsupport@blr.com *Web Site:* blr.com, pg 32

McMillen, Wendy, University of Notre Dame Press, 310 Flanner Hall, Notre Dame, IN 46556 *Tel:* 574-631-6346 *Fax:* 574-631-8148 *E-mail:* undpress@nd.edu *Web Site:* www.undpress.nd.edu, pg 219

McMullen, Kate, C Michael Curtis Short Story Book Prize, 186 W Main St, Spartanburg, SC 29306 *Tel:* 864-577-9349 *Fax:* 864-577-0188 *E-mail:* info@hubcity.org; submit@hubcity.org *Web Site:* hubcity.org/press/c-michael-curtis-short-story-book-prize, pg 594

McMullen-Ciotti, Elise, Lee & Low Books Inc, 95 Madison Ave, Suite 1205, New York, NY 10016 *Tel:* 212-779-4400 *Toll Free Tel:* 888-320-3190 (ext 28, orders only) *Fax:* 212-683-1894 (orders only); 212-532-6035 *E-mail:* general@leeandlow.com *Web Site:* www.leeandlow.com, pg 114

McMurray, Debbie, Nilgiri Press, 3600 Tomales Rd, Tomales, CA 94971 *Tel:* 707-878-2369 *E-mail:* info@easwaran.org *Web Site:* www.easwaran.org, pg 141

McMurray, Heather, SBL Press, The Luce Ctr, Suite 350, 825 Houston Mill Rd, Atlanta, GA 30329 *Tel:* 404-727-3100 *Fax:* 404-727-3101 (corp) *E-mail:* sbl@sbl-site.org *Web Site:* www.sbl-site.org, pg 183

McMurtray, Lisa, University Press of Mississippi, 3825 Ridgewood Rd, Jackson, MS 39211-6492 *Tel:* 601-432-6205 *Toll Free Tel:* 800-737-7788 (orders & cust serv) *Fax:* 601-432-6217 *E-mail:* press@mississippi.edu *Web Site:* www.upress.state.ms.us, pg 222

McNair, Christine, Canadian Bookbinders and Book Artists Guild (CBBAG), 82809-467 Parliament St, Toronto, ON M5A 3Y2, Canada *E-mail:* cbbag@cbbag.ca *Web Site:* www.cbbag.ca, pg 502

McNair, Melanie, The Center for Fiction, 15 Lafayette Ave, Brooklyn, NY 11217 *Tel:* 212-755-6710 *E-mail:* info@centerforfiction.org *Web Site:* centerforfiction.org, pg 503

McNair, Shanna, Knightville Poetry Contest, PO Box 472, Brunswick, ME 04011 *E-mail:* info@newguardreview.com; editors@writershotel.com *Web Site:* www.newguardreview.com, pg 621

McNair, Shanna, Machigonne Fiction Contest, PO Box 472, Brunswick, ME 04011 *E-mail:* info@newguardreview.com; editors@writershotel.com *Web Site:* www.newguardreview.com, pg 628

McNamara, Ally, Macmillan, 120 Broadway, 22nd fl, New York, NY 10271 *E-mail:* press.inquiries@macmillan.com *Web Site:* us.macmillan.com, pg 122

McNamara, Christine, Penguin Random House LLC, 1745 Broadway, New York, NY 10019 *Tel:* 212-782-9000 *Toll Free Tel:* 800-726-0600 *Web Site:* www.penguinrandomhouse.com, pg 155

McNamara, Lauren, Macmillan, 120 Broadway, 22nd fl, New York, NY 10271 *E-mail:* press.inquiries@macmillan.com *Web Site:* us.macmillan.com, pg 122

McNamara, Rebecca, Cengage Learning, 20 Channel Center St, Boston, MA 02210 *Tel:* 617-289-7700 *Toll Free Tel:* 800-354-9706 *Fax:* 617-289-7844 *E-mail:* esales@cengage.com *Web Site:* www.cengage.com, pg 43

McNamee, Grace, Bloomsbury Publishing Inc, 1385 Broadway, 5th fl, New York, NY 10018 *Tel:* 212-419-5300 *E-mail:* marketingusa@bloomsbury.com; adultpublicityusa@bloomsbury.com; askacademic@bloomsbury.com *Web Site:* www.bloomsbury.com, pg 31

McNaughton, Danielle, Sourcebooks LLC, 1935 Brookdale Rd, Suite 139, Naperville, IL 60563 *Tel:* 630-961-3900 *Toll Free Tel:* 800-432-7444 *Fax:* 630-961-2168 *E-mail:* info@sourcebooks.com *Web Site:* www.sourcebooks.com, pg 195

McNeill, Timothy J, Wisdom Publications Inc, 199 Elm St, Somerville, MA 02144 *Tel:* 617-776-7416 *Toll Free Tel:* 800-272-4050 (orders) *Fax:* 617-776-7841 *E-mail:* submission@wisdompubs.org *Web Site:* wisdomexperience.org, pg 231

McNicholl, Damian, The Jennifer DeChiara Literary Agency, 245 Park Ave, 39th fl, New York, NY 10167 *Tel:* 212-372-8989 *Web Site:* www.jdlit.com, pg 455

McNicol, Andy, Aevitas Creative Management LLC, 19 W 21 St, Suite 501, New York, NY 10010 *Tel:* 212-765-6900 *Web Site:* www.aevitascreative.com, pg 448

McNiel, Jessie, Atria Books, 1230 Avenue of the Americas, New York, NY 10020 *Tel:* 212-698-7000 *Fax:* 212-698-7007 *Web Site:* www.simonandschuster.com, pg 21

McParland, Connie, Guernica Editions Inc, 287 Templemead Dr, Hamilton, ON L8W 2W4, Canada *Tel:* 905-599-5304 *E-mail:* info@guernicaeditions.com *Web Site:* www.guernicaeditions.com; www.facebook.com/guernicaed, pg 408

McPartland, Pat, Albert Whitman & Company, 250 S Northwest Hwy, Suite 320, Park Ridge, IL 60068 *Tel:* 847-232-2800 *Toll Free Tel:* 800-255-7675 (orders) *Fax:* 847-581-0039 *E-mail:* mail@albertwhitman.com; orders@albertwhitman.com *Web Site:* www.albertwhitman.com, pg 6

McPhee, Jenny, New York University, Center for Publishing & Applied Liberal Arts, 7 E 12 St, New York, NY 10003 *Tel:* 212-998-7200 *E-mail:* sps.info@nyu.edu *Web Site:* www.scps.nyu.edu/professional-pathways/topics.html, pg 563

McPherson, Bruce R, McPherson & Co, 148 Smith Ave, Kingston, NY 12401 *Tel:* 845-331-5807 *E-mail:* bmcphersonco@gmail.com *Web Site:* www.mcphersonco.com, pg 128

McPherson, Susan, David C Cook, 4050 Lee Vance Dr, Colorado Springs, CO 80918 *Tel:* 719-536-0100 *Toll Free Tel:* 800-323-7543 (orders & cust serv) *Toll Free Fax:* 800-430-0726 (cust serv) *E-mail:* bookstores@davidccook.org; customercare@davidccook.org *Web Site:* www.davidccook.org, pg 52

McQuade, Suzanne, Living Language, c/o Penguin Random House LLC, 1745 Broadway, New York, NY 10019 *Tel:* 212-782-9000 *Toll Free Tel:* 800-733-3000 (orders) *E-mail:* support@livinglanguage.com *Web Site:* www.livinglanguage.com, pg 119

McQuagge, Cassie, ARE Press, 215 67 St, Virginia Beach, VA 23451 *Tel:* 757-428-3588 *Toll Free Tel:* 800-333-4499 *Web Site:* www.edgarcayce.org, pg 16

McQuilkin, Rob, Massie & McQuilkin, 27 W 20 St, Suite 305, New York, NY 10011 *Tel:* 212-352-2055 *E-mail:* info@mmqlit.com *Web Site:* www.mmqlit.com, pg 469

McQuillan, Dennis, World Book Inc, 180 N LaSalle, Suite 900, Chicago, IL 60601 *Tel:* 312-729-5800 *Toll Free Tel:* 800-967-5325 (consumer sales, US); 800-975-3250 (school & lib sales, US); 800-837-5365 (school & lib sales, CN) *Toll Free Fax:* 888-922-3766 *E-mail:* customerservice@worldbook.com *Web Site:* www.worldbook.com, pg 233

McQuillen, John T, Bibliographical Society of America (BSA), 67 West St, Suite 401, Unit C17, Brooklyn, NY 11222 *E-mail:* bsa@bibsocamer.org *Web Site:* bibsocamer.org, pg 501

McRae, Cefus, Florida Outdoor Writers Association Inc (FOWA), 235 Apollo Beach Blvd, Unit 271, Apollo Beach, FL 33572 *Tel:* 813-579-0990 *E-mail:* info@fowa.org *Web Site:* www.fowa.org, pg 506

McRaney, Emma, Book of the Year Award, William F Winter Archives & History Bldg, 200 North St, Jackson, MS 39201 *Tel:* 601-576-6936 *Fax:* 601-576-6975 *E-mail:* mhs@mdah.ms.gov *Web Site:* www.mdah.ms.gov, pg 583

McSharry, Brian, Macmillan, 120 Broadway, 22nd fl, New York, NY 10271 *E-mail:* press.inquiries@macmillan.com *Web Site:* us.macmillan.com, pg 122

McSwain, Larsson, Candlewick Press, 99 Dover St, Somerville, MA 02144-2825 *Tel:* 617-661-3330 *Fax:* 617-661-0565 *E-mail:* bigbear@candlewick.com; salesinfo@candlewick.com *Web Site:* candlewick.com, pg 40

McWilliams, Skip, Teacher's Discovery®, 2741 Paldan Dr, Auburn Hills, MI 48326 *Toll Free Tel:* 800-TEACHER (832-2437) *Toll Free Fax:* 800-287-4509 *E-mail:* help@teachersdiscovery.com; orders@teachersdiscovery.com *Web Site:* www.teachersdiscovery.com, pg 204

Mead, Katharine, The Jean Kennedy Smith VSA Playwright Discovery Award, 2700 "F" St NW, Washington, DC 20566 *Tel:* 202-416-8898 *Fax:* 202-416-4840 *E-mail:* vsainfo@kennedy-center.org *Web Site:* www.kennedy-center.org/education/opportunities-for-artists/competitions-and-commissions, pg 663

Meader, James, Picador, 120 Broadway, New York, NY 10271 *Tel:* 646-307-5151 *Fax:* 212-253-9627 *E-mail:* publicity@picadorusa.com *Web Site:* us.macmillan.com/picador, pg 159

Meader, James, Vintage Books, c/o Penguin Random House LLC, 1745 Broadway, New York, NY 10019 *Tel:* 212-572-2420 *Fax:* 212-940-7390 (dom rts); 212-572-2662 (foreign rts) *E-mail:* vintageanchorpublicity@randomhouse.com *Web Site:* knopfdoubleday.com/imprint/vintage; knopfdoubleday.com, pg 225

Meadows, Amanda, Andrews McMeel Publishing LLC, 1130 Walnut St, Kansas City, MO 64106-2109 *Tel:* 816-581-7500 *Toll Free Tel:* 800-851-8923 *Web Site:* www.andrewsmcmeel; publishing.andrewsmcmeel.com, pg 14

Meadows, Rob, Bear & Co Inc, One Park St, Rochester, VT 05767 *Tel:* 802-767-3174 *Toll Free Tel:* 800-932-3277 *Fax:* 802-767-3726 *E-mail:* customerservice@InnerTraditions.com *Web Site:* InnerTraditions.com, pg 26

Means, Allison T, Iowa Poetry Prize, 119 W Park Rd, 100 Kuhl House, Iowa City, IA 52242-1000 *Tel:* 319-335-2000 *Fax:* 319-335-2055 *E-mail:* uipress@uiowa.edu *Web Site:* www.uipress.uiowa.edu, pg 617

Means, Allison T, University of Iowa Press, 119 W Park Rd, 100 Kuhl House, Iowa City, IA 52242-1000 *Tel:* 319-335-2000 *Toll Free Tel:* 800-621-2736 (orders only) *Fax:* 319-335-2055 *Toll Free Fax:* 800-621-8476 (orders only) *E-mail:* uipress@uiowa.edu *Web Site:* www.uipress.uiowa.edu, pg 216

Mechanic, Leslie, Simon & Schuster Children's Publishing, 1230 Avenue of the Americas, New York, NY 10020 *Tel:* 212-698-7000 *Web Site:* www.simonandschuster.com/kids; www.simonandschuster.com/teen; simonandschuster.net; simonandschuster.biz, pg 189

Mecklenborg, Mark, The American Ceramic Society, 550 Polaris Pkwy, Suite 510, Westerville, OH 43082 *Tel:* 240-646-7054 *Toll Free Tel:* 866-721-3322 *Fax:* 240-396-5637 *E-mail:* customerservice@ceramics.org *Web Site:* ceramics.org, pg 9

Medeiros, Maria, Novalis Publishing, One Eglinton Ave E, Suite 800, Toronto, ON M4P 3A1, Canada *Tel:* 416-363-3303 *Toll Free Tel:* 877-702-7773 *Fax:* 416-363-9409 *Toll Free Fax:* 877-702-7775 *E-mail:* books@novalis.ca *Web Site:* www.novalis.ca, pg 414

Medeot, William, Orbis Books, PO Box 302, Maryknoll, NY 10545-0302 *Tel:* 914-941-7636 *Toll Free Tel:* 800-258-5838 (orders, Mon-Fri 8AM-4PM EST) *Fax:* 914-941-7005 *E-mail:* orbisbooks@maryknoll.org *Web Site:* orbisbooks.com, pg 147

Medford, Edna Greene PhD, Abraham Lincoln Institute Book Award, c/o ALI Treasurer, 4158 Vernoy Hills Rd, Fairfax, VA 22030 *Web Site:* www.lincoln-institute.org, pg 625

Medina, Daniela, Grand Central Publishing, 1290 Avenue of the Americas, New York, NY 10104 *Tel:* 212-364-1100 *Web Site:* www.hachettebookgroup.com/imprint/grand-central-publishing/, pg 80

Medina, Darelyanel, HarperCollins Publishers LLC, 195 Broadway, New York, NY 10007 *Tel:* 212-207-7000 *Web Site:* www.harpercollins.com, pg 87

Medina, Kate, Random House Publishing Group, 1745 Broadway, New York, NY 10019 *Toll Free Tel:* 800-200-3552 *Web Site:* www.randomhousebooks.com, pg 170

Medina, Nico, Penguin Young Readers Group, c/o Penguin Random House LLC, 1745 Broadway, New York, NY 10019 *Tel:* 212-782-9000 *Web Site:* www.penguin.com/penguin-young-readers-overview, pg 156

Medlen, Jordan, Bisk Education, 9417 Princess Palm Ave, Suite 400, Tampa, FL 33619 *Tel:* 813-621-6200 *E-mail:* media@bisk.com *Web Site:* www.bisk.com, pg 29

Mednansky, Kristine, Productivity Press, 605 Third Ave, 22nd fl, New York, NY 10158 *Toll Free Tel:* 800-634-7064 (orders); 800-797-3803 *E-mail:* orders@taylorandfrancis.com *Web Site:* www.crcpress.com, pg 165

Medrich, Lucy, Chronicle Books LLC, 680 Second St, San Francisco, CA 94107 *Tel:* 415-537-4200 *Fax:* 415-537-4460 (perms) *E-mail:* hello@chroniclebooks.com; subrights@chroniclebooks.com *Web Site:* www.chroniclebooks.com, pg 47

Meehan, Emily, Union Square & Co, 1166 Avenue of the Americas, 17th fl, New York, NY 10036-2715 *Tel:* 212-532-7160 *Toll Free Tel:* 800-367-9692 *Fax:* 212-213-2495 *Toll Free Fax:* 800-542-7567 *E-mail:* custservice@sterlingpublishing.com; customerservice@sterlingpublishing.com; editorial@sterlingpublishing.com; tradesales@sterlingpublishing.com *Web Site:* www.sterlingpublishing.com, pg 212

Meeropol, Ellen, Chocorua Writing Workshop, PO Box 2280, Conway, NH 03818-2280 *Tel:* 603-447-2280 *E-mail:* office@worldfellowship.org *Web Site:* www.worldfellowship.org; www.facebook.com/World.Fellowship.Center, pg 553

Meese, Ryan, Macmillan, 120 Broadway, 22nd fl, New York, NY 10271 *E-mail:* press.inquiries@macmillan.com *Web Site:* us.macmillan.com, pg 122

Megan, Terry, Remember Point Inc, PO Box 1448, Pacific Palisades, CA 90272 *Tel:* 310-896-8716 *E-mail:* info@rememberpoint.com *Web Site:* www.rememberpoint.com; www.longfellowfindsahome.com, pg 174

Megill, Christie, The CAT Agency Inc, 345 Old Oaks Rd, Fairfield, CT 06825 *Tel:* 917-434-3141 *Web Site:* catagencyinc.com, pg 485

Mehring, Adam, University of Wisconsin Press, 728 State St, Suite 443, Madison, WI 53706-1418 *Tel:* 608-263-1110; 608-263-0668 (journal orders) *Toll Free Tel:* 800-621-2736 (book orders) *Fax:* 608-263-1173 *Toll Free Fax:* 800-621-2736 (book orders) *E-mail:* uwiscpress@uwpress.wisc.edu *Web Site:* uwpress.wisc.edu, pg 221

Meidenbauer, Ed, American Psychological Association, 750 First St NE, Washington, DC 20002 *Tel:* 202-336-5510 *Toll Free Tel:* 800-374-2721 *Fax:* 202-336-5502 *E-mail:* order@apa.org; booksales@apa.org *Web Site:* www.apa.org/books, pg 12

Meier, Rick, Knopf Canada, 320 Front St W, Suite 1400, Toronto, ON M5V 3B6, Canada *Tel:* 416-364-4449 *Toll Free Tel:* 888-523-9292 *Fax:* 416-598-7764 *Web Site:* www.penguinrandomhouse.ca, pg 411

Meigs, Michael, Austin Area Translators & Interpreters Association (AATIA), PO Box 92334, Austin, TX 78709-2334 *E-mail:* info@aatia.org; communications@aatia.org; membership@aatia.org; finance@aatia.org; profdev@aatia.org *Web Site:* aatia.org, pg 500

Meigs, Sonja, Sourcebooks LLC, 1935 Brookdale Rd, Suite 139, Naperville, IL 60563 *Tel:* 630-961-3900 *Toll Free Tel:* 800-432-7444 *Fax:* 630-961-2168 *E-mail:* info@sourcebooks.com *Web Site:* www.sourcebooks.com, pg 195

Meilun, Kimberly, Atria Books, 1230 Avenue of the Americas, New York, NY 10020 Tel: 212-698-7000 Fax: 212-698-7007 Web Site: www.simonandschuster.com, pg 21

Meinichok, Erica, Knopf Doubleday Publishing Group, c/o Penguin Random House LLC, 1745 Broadway, New York, NY 10019 Tel: 212-751-2600 Fax: 212-940-7390 (dom rts); 212-572-2662 (foreign rts) Web Site: knopfdoubleday.com, pg 110

Meints, Rick, Chaosium Inc, 3450 Wooddale Ct, Ann Arbor, MI 48104 Tel: 734-972-9551 E-mail: customerservice@chaosium.com Web Site: www.chaosium.com, pg 45

Meister, Beth, Doubleday, c/o Penguin Random House LLC, 1745 Broadway, New York, NY 10019 Tel: 212-751-2600 Fax: 212-940-7390 (dom rts); 212-572-2662 (foreign rts) Web Site: knopfdoubleday.com/imprint/doubleday/; knopfdoubleday.com, pg 61

Meister, Beth, Alfred A Knopf, c/o Penguin Random House LLC, 1745 Broadway, New York, NY 10019 Tel: 212-751-2600 Fax: 212-940-7390 (dom rts); 212-572-2662 (foreign rts) Web Site: knopfdoubleday.com/imprint/knopf/; knopfdoubleday.com, pg 110

Meister, Beth, Pantheon Books, c/o Penguin Random House LLC, 1745 Broadway, New York, NY 10019 Tel: 212-751-2600 Fax: 212-940-7390 (dom rts); 212-572-2662 (foreign rts) Web Site: knopfdoubleday.com/imprint/pantheon/; knopfdoubleday.com, pg 150

Meister, Beth, Schocken Books, c/o Penguin Random House LLC, 1745 Broadway, New York, NY 10019 Tel: 212-751-2600 Fax: 212-940-7390 (dom rts); 212-572-2662 (foreign rts) Web Site: knopfdoubleday.com/imprint/schocken/; knopfdoubleday.com, pg 183

Meister, Sarah, Aperture Books, 548 W 28 St, 4th fl, New York, NY 10001 Tel: 212-505-5555 Toll Free Fax: 888-623-6908 E-mail: customerservice@aperture.org Web Site: aperture.org, pg 15

Meixelsperger, Wes, Soil Science Society of America (SSSA), 5585 Guilford Rd, Madison, WI 53711-5801 Tel: 608-273-8080 Fax: 608-273-2021 Web Site: www.soils.org, pg 193

Meizlik, Shelby, Viking Penguin, c/o Penguin Random House LLC, 1745 Broadway, New York, NY 10019 Tel: 212-782-9000 Web Site: www.penguin.com/overview-vikingbooks/; www.penguin.com/pamela-dorman-books-overview/; www.penguin.com/penguin-classics-overview/; www.penguin.com/penguin-life-overview/, pg 225

Mekarnom, Mary, Penguin Young Readers Group, c/o Penguin Random House LLC, 1745 Broadway, New York, NY 10019 Tel: 212-782-9000 Web Site: www.penguin.com/penguin-young-readers-overview/, pg 156

Melancon, Barry C, AICPA® & CIMA®, 220 Leigh Farm Rd, Durham, NC 27707 Tel: 919-402-4500 Toll Free Tel: 888-777-7077 (memb serv ctr) Web Site: www.aicpa-cima.com/cpe-learning, pg 5

Melendez, Marisa, Doubleday, c/o Penguin Random House LLC, 1745 Broadway, New York, NY 10019 Tel: 212-751-2600 Fax: 212-940-7390 (dom rts); 212-572-2662 (foreign rts) Web Site: knopfdoubleday.com/imprint/doubleday/; knopfdoubleday.com, pg 61

Melendez, Marisa, Alfred A Knopf, c/o Penguin Random House LLC, 1745 Broadway, New York, NY 10019 Tel: 212-751-2600 Fax: 212-940-7390 (dom rts); 212-572-2662 (foreign rts) Web Site: knopfdoubleday.com/imprint/knopf/; knopfdoubleday.com, pg 110

Melfi, Amanda, Tor Publishing Group, 120 Broadway, New York, NY 10271 Toll Free Tel: 800-455-0340 (Macmillan) E-mail: torpublicity@tor.com; forgepublicity@forgebooks.com Web Site: us.macmillan.com/torpublishinggroup, pg 208

Melia, James, Gallery Books, 1230 Avenue of the Americas, New York, NY 10020 Toll Free Tel: 800-456-6798 Fax: 212-698-7284 E-mail: consumer.customerservice@simonandschuster.com Web Site: www.simonandschuster.com, pg 76

Melnichok, Erica, Penguin Random House LLC, 1745 Broadway, New York, NY 10019 Tel: 212-782-9000 Toll Free Tel: 800-726-0600 Web Site: www.penguinrandomhouse.com, pg 155

Melnyk, Sarah, St Martin's Press, LLC, 120 Broadway, New York, NY 10271 E-mail: publicity@stmartins.com; trademarketing@stmartins.com; foreignrights@stmartins.com Web Site: us.macmillan.com/smp, pg 181

Melo Pienkowski, Larissa, Jill Grinberg Literary Management LLC, 392 Vanderbilt Ave, Brooklyn, NY 11238 Tel: 212-620-5883 E-mail: info@jillgrinbergliterary.com Web Site: www.jillgrinbergliterary.com, pg 461

Meloto, Charisse, Scholastic Trade Publishing, 557 Broadway, New York, NY 10012 Tel: 212-343-6100; 212-343-4685 (export sales) Fax: 212-343-4714 (export sales) Web Site: www.scholastic.com, pg 184

Melton, Dianne, Summerthought Publishing, PO Box 2309, Banff, AB T1L 1C1, Canada Tel: 403-762-0535 E-mail: info@summerthought.com Web Site: summerthought.com, pg 420

Melton, Mark, Hudson Institute, 1201 Pennsylvania Ave NW, 4th fl, Washington, DC 20004 Tel: 202-974-2400 Fax: 202-974-2410 E-mail: info@hudson.org Web Site: www.hudson.org, pg 97

Melton, Taylor, Art In Literature: The Mary Lynn Kotz Award, 800 E Broad St, Richmond, VA 23219 Tel: 804-692-3535 Web Site: www.lva.virginia.gov/public/litawards/kotz.htm; lvafoundation.org/home/literaryawards/, pg 574

Melton, Taylor, Library of Virginia Literary Awards, 800 E Broad St, Richmond, VA 23219 Tel: 804-692-3535 Web Site: www.lva.virginia.gov/public/litawards/, pg 624

Meltzer, Kate, Roaring Brook Press, 120 Broadway, New York, NY 10271 Fax: 646-307-5151 Web Site: us.macmillan.com/publishers/roaring-brook-press, pg 176

Meltzer, Lauren, Charles Press Publishers, 1754 Wylie St, No 4, Philadelphia, PA 19130 Tel: 215-470-5977 E-mail: mail@charlespresspub.com Web Site: charlespresspub.com, pg 45

Meltzer, Max, Gallery Books, 1230 Avenue of the Americas, New York, NY 10020 Toll Free Tel: 800-456-6798 Fax: 212-698-7284 E-mail: consumer.customerservice@simonandschuster.com Web Site: www.simonandschuster.com, pg 76

Melville, Kirsty, Andrews McMeel Publishing LLC, 1130 Walnut St, Kansas City, MO 64106-2109 Tel: 816-581-7500 Toll Free Tel: 800-851-8923 Web Site: www.andrewsmcmeel.com; publishing.andrewsmcmeel.com, pg 14

Melvin, Annette, Random House Publishing Group, 1745 Broadway, New York, NY 10019 Toll Free Tel: 800-200-3552 Web Site: www.randomhousebooks.com, pg 171

Mena, Karolyn, Workman Publishing, 1290 Avenue of the Americas, New York, NY 10104 Toll Free Tel: 800-759-0190 Fax: 212-364-0950 E-mail: workman-inquiry@hbgusa.com Web Site: www.hachettebookgroup.com/imprint/workman-publishing-company/, pg 233

Menaker, Dru, PEN America, 120 Broadway, 26th fl N, New York, NY 10271 Tel: 212-334-1660 Fax: 212-334-2181 E-mail: info@pen.org; membership@pen.org; education@pen.org Web Site: pen.org, pg 516

Mendel, Scott, Mendel Media Group LLC, PO Box 5032, East Hampton, NY 11937 Tel: 646-239-9896 Web Site: www.mendelmedia.com, pg 470

Mendelson, John, Nosy Crow Inc, 145 Lincoln Rd, Lincoln, MA 01773 E-mail: nosycrowinc@nosycrow.com; salesinfo@nosycrow.com; export@nosycrow.com (export sales); rights@nosycrow.com Web Site: nosycrow.us, pg 144

Mendez Berry, Elizabeth, Random House Publishing Group, 1745 Broadway, New York, NY 10019 Toll Free Tel: 800-200-3552 Web Site: www.randomhousebooks.com, pg 170

Mendez, Maria, Simon & Schuster, 1230 Avenue of the Americas, New York, NY 10020 Tel: 212-698-7000 Toll Free Tel: 800-223-2348 (cust serv); 800-223-2336 (orders) Toll Free Fax: 800-943-9831 (orders) Web Site: simonandschusterpublishing.com/simonandschuster, pg 188

Mendola, Tim, Morgan Gaynin, 41 N Main St, Norwalk, CT 06854 Tel: 212-475-0440 E-mail: info@morgangaynin.com Web Site: www.morgangaynin.com, pg 486

Mendola-Hobbie, Jaime, Berkley, c/o Penguin Random House LLC, 1745 Broadway, 19th fl, New York, NY 10019 Tel: 212-366-2000 Web Site: www.penguin.com/publishers/berkley/; www.penguin.com/ace-overview/, pg 28

Mendola-Hobbie, Jaime, Dutton, c/o Penguin Random House LLC, 1745 Broadway, New York, NY 10019 Tel: 212-366-2000 Web Site: www.penguin.com/dutton-overview/; www.penguin.com/plume-books-overview/; www.penguin.com/tiny-reparations-overview/, pg 62

Mendola-Hobbie, Jaime, GP Putnam's Sons, c/o Penguin Random House LLC, 1745 Broadway, New York, NY 10019 Tel: 212-782-9000 Web Site: www.penguin.com/putnam/, pg 167

Mendoza, Deanne, Free Spirit Publishing Inc, 9850 51 Ave N, Suite 100, Minneapolis, MN 55442 Tel: 714-891-2273 Toll Free Tel: 800-858-7339 Fax: 714-230-7070 Toll Free Fax: 888-877-7606 E-mail: customerservice@tcmpub.com Web Site: www.teachercreatedmaterials.com/free-spirit-publishing, pg 74

Menn, Don, Immedium, 535 Rockdale Dr, San Francisco, CA 94127 Tel: 415-452-8546 Fax: 360-937-6272 E-mail: orders@immedium.com; sales@immedium.com Web Site: www.immedium.com, pg 99

Mennel, Timothy, University of Chicago Press, 1427 E 60 St, Chicago, IL 60637-2954 Tel: 773-702-7700; 773-702-7600 Toll Free Tel: 800-621-2736 (orders) Fax: 773-702-9756; 773-660-2235 (orders); 773-702-2708 E-mail: custserv@press.uchicago.edu; marketing@press.uchicago.edu Web Site: www.press.uchicago.edu, pg 215

Menth, Rachel, Macmillan, 120 Broadway, 22nd fl, New York, NY 10271 E-mail: press.inquiries@macmillan.com Web Site: us.macmillan.com, pg 122

Menzie, Karen, Candlewick Press, 99 Dover St, Somerville, MA 02144-2825 Tel: 617-661-3330 Fax: 617-661-0565 E-mail: bigbear@candlewick.com; salesinfo@candlewick.com Web Site: candlewick.com, pg 40

Menzie, Karen, Holiday House Publishing Inc, 50 Broad St, New York, NY 10004 Tel: 212-688-0085 Fax: 212-421-6134 E-mail: info@holidayhouse.com Web Site: www.holidayhouse.com, pg 94

Menzie, Karen, Peachtree Publishing Co Inc, 1700 Chattahoochee Ave, Atlanta, GA 30318-2112 Tel: 404-876-8761 Toll Free Tel: 800-241-0113 Fax: 404-875-2578 Toll Free Fax: 800-875-8909 E-mail: hello@peachtree-online.com; orders@peachtree-online.com; sales@peachtree-online.com Web Site: www.peachtreebooks.com; www.peachtree-online.com, pg 153

Menzies, Tracey, HarperCollins Publishers LLC, 195 Broadway, New York, NY 10007 Tel: 212-207-7000 Web Site: www.harpercollins.com, pg 86

Menzimer, Parker, PA Press, 202 Warren St, Hudson, NY 12534 Tel: 518-671-6100 Toll Free Tel: 800-722-6657 (dist); 800-759-0190 (sales) E-mail: sales@papress.com Web Site: www.papress.com, pg 149

Mercado, Gracie, Macmillan, 120 Broadway, 22nd fl, New York, NY 10271 E-mail: press.inquiries@macmillan.com Web Site: us.macmillan.com, pg 122

Mercado, Jessica, Little, Brown Books for Young Readers (LBYR), 1290 Avenue of the Americas, New York, NY 10104 Tel: 212-364-1100 Toll Free Tel: 800-759-0190 (cust serv) E-mail: rights@lbchildrens.com Web Site: www.hachettebookgroup.com/imprint/little-brown-books-for-young-readers/, pg 118

Mercado, Nancy, GP Putnam's Sons Books for Young Readers, c/o Penguin Random House LLC, 1745 Broadway, New York, NY 10019 Tel: 212-782-9000 Web Site: www.penguin.com/putnam-young-readers/, pg 167

Mercandetti, Susan, Random House Publishing Group, 1745 Broadway, New York, NY 10019 Toll Free Tel: 800-200-3552 Web Site: www.randomhousebooks.com, pg 171

Merced-Zarou, Tatiana, Farrar, Straus & Giroux Books for Young Readers, 120 Broadway, New York, NY 10271 Tel: 212-741-6900 Toll Free Tel: 888-330-8477 (orders) E-mail: childrens.publicity@macmillanusa.com; childrensrights@macmillanusa.com Web Site: us.macmillan.com/mackids, pg 70

Merced-Zarou, Tatiana, Roaring Brook Press, 120 Broadway, New York, NY 10271 Tel: 646-307-5151 Web Site: us.macmillan.com/publishers/roaring-brook-press, pg 176

Mercer, Brian, PNWA Writers' Contest, 1420 NW Gilman Blvd, Suite 29, PMB 2717, Issaquah, WA 98027 Tel: 425-673-2665 E-mail: pnwa@pnwa.org Web Site: www.pnwa.org, pg 650

Mercer, Brian, PNWA - a writer's resource, 1420 NW Gilman Blvd, Suite 29, PMB 2717, Issaquah, WA 98027 Tel: 425-673-2665 E-mail: pnwa@pnwa.org Web Site: www.pnwa.org, pg 517

Mercer, Brian, PNWA Writers Conference, 1420 NW Gilman Blvd, Suite 29, PMB 2717, Issaquah, WA 98027 Tel: 425-673-2665 E-mail: pnwa@pnwa.org Web Site: www.pnwa.org, pg 557

Mercer, Sue, Diversion Books, 11 E 44 St, Suite 1603, New York, NY 10017 Tel: 212-961-6390 E-mail: info@diversionbooks.com Web Site: www.diversionbooks.com, pg 60

Meredith, Leslie, Dystel, Goderich & Bourret LLC, One Union Sq W, Suite 904, New York, NY 10003 Tel: 212-627-9100 Fax: 212-627-9313 Web Site: www.dystel.com, pg 457

Merino, Melinda, Harvard Business Review Press, 20 Guest St, Suite 700, Brighton, MA 02135 Tel: 617-783-7400 Fax: 617-783-7489 E-mail: custserv@hbsp.harvard.edu Web Site: www.harvardbusiness.org, pg 87

Merkle, Molly, AdventureKEEN, 2204 First Ave S, Suite 102, Birmingham, AL 35233 Tel: 763-689-9800 Toll Free Tel: 800-678-7006 Fax: 763-689-9039 Toll Free Fax: 877-374-9016 E-mail: info@adventurewithkeen.com Web Site: adventurewithkeen.com, pg 5

Merkle, Molly, Menasha Ridge Press, 2204 First Ave S, Suite 102, Birmingham, AL 35233 Toll Free Tel: 888-604-4537 Fax: 205-326-1012 E-mail: info@adventurewithkeen.com Web Site: www.menasharidge.com; www.adventurewithkeen.com, pg 129

Merlo, Erin, Doubleday, c/o Penguin Random House LLC, 1745 Broadway, New York, NY 10019 Tel: 212-751-2600 Fax: 212-940-7390 (dom rts); 212-572-2662 (foreign rts) Web Site: knopfdoubleday.com/imprint/doubleday/; knopfdoubleday.com, pg 61

Merola, Allie, Viking Penguin, c/o Penguin Random House LLC, 1745 Broadway, New York, NY 10019 Tel: 212-782-9000 Web Site: www.penguin.com/overview-vikingbooks/; www.penguin.com/pamela-dorman-books-overview/; www.penguin.com/penguin-classics-overview/; www.penguin.com/penguin-life-overview/, pg 225

Merola, Marianne, Brandt & Hochman Literary Agents Inc, 1501 Broadway, Suite 2310, New York, NY 10036 Tel: 212-840-5760 Fax: 212-840-5776 Web Site: brandthochman.com, pg 452

Merritt, Jason, Forward Movement, 412 Sycamore St, Cincinnati, OH 45202-4110 Tel: 513-721-6659 Toll Free Tel: 800-543-1813 Fax: 513-721-0729 (orders) E-mail: orders@forwardmovement.org (orders & cust serv) Web Site: www.forwardmovement.org, pg 73

Merritt, Sara, Zondervan, 3900 Sparks Dr SE, Grand Rapids, MI 49546 Tel: 616-698-6900 Toll Free Tel: 800-226-1122; 800-727-1309 (retail orders) Fax: 616-698-3350 Toll Free Fax: 800-698-3256 (retail orders) E-mail: customercare@harpercollins.com Web Site: www.zondervan.com, pg 236

Merto, Alex, Picador, 120 Broadway, New York, NY 10271 Tel: 646-307-5151 Fax: 212-253-9627 E-mail: publicity@picadorusa.com Web Site: us.macmillan.com/picador, pg 159

Merz, Anneliese, Harry N Abrams Inc, 195 Broadway, 9th fl, New York, NY 10007 Tel: 212-206-7715 Toll Free Tel: 800-345-1359 Fax: 212-645-8437 E-mail: abrams@abramsbooks.com; publicity@abramsbooks.com; sales@abramsbooks.com Web Site: www.abramsbooks.com, pg 3

Merz, Kathleen, Wm B Eerdmans Publishing Co, 4035 Park East Ct SE, Grand Rapids, MI 49546 Tel: 616-459-4591 Toll Free Tel: 800-253-7521 E-mail: customerservice@eerdmans.com; sales@eerdmans.com Web Site: www.eerdmans.com, pg 64

Mesquita, Anne, Bancroft Prizes, 517 Butler Library, Mail Code 1101, 535 W 114 St, New York, NY 10027 Tel: 212-854-3051 E-mail: bancroft-prize@library.columbia.edu Web Site: library.columbia.edu/about/awards/bancroft.html, pg 577

Messenger, Robert, Simon & Schuster, 1230 Avenue of the Americas, New York, NY 10020 Tel: 212-698-7000 Toll Free Tel: 800-223-2348 (cust serv); 800-223-2336 (orders) Toll Free Fax: 800-943-9831 (orders) Web Site: simonandschusterpublishing.com/simonandschuster/, pg 188

Messer, Melissa A, Psychological Assessment Resources Inc (PAR), 16204 N Florida Ave, Lutz, FL 33549 Tel: 813-449-4065 Toll Free Tel: 800-331-8378 Fax: 813-961-2196 Toll Free Fax: 800-727-9329 Web Site: www.parinc.com, pg 166

Messer, Randy, Perfection Learning®, 1000 N Second Ave, Logan, IA 51546-1061 Tel: 712-644-2831 Toll Free Tel: 800-831-4190 Toll Free Fax: 800-543-2745 E-mail: orders@perfectionlearning.com Web Site: www.perfectionlearning.com, pg 158

Messerli, Douglas, Green Integer, 750 S Spaulding Ave, Suite 112, Los Angeles, CA 90036 E-mail: info@greeninteger.com Web Site: www.greeninteger.com, pg 81

Messick, Mary K, Schoolhouse Network, PO Box 1518, Northampton, MA 01061 Tel: 480-427-4836 E-mail: schoolhousenetwork@gmail.com, pg 444

Messina, Angela, Basic Books Group, 1290 Avenue of the Americas, New York, NY 10104 Tel: 212-340-8100 Toll Free Tel: 800-343-4499 (cust serv) Fax: 212-340-8105 E-mail: customer.service@hbgusa.com; orders@hbgusa.com Web Site: www.hachettebookgroup.com/imprint/basic-books/, pg 25

Messina, Tom, Hachette Audio, 1290 Avenue of the Americas, New York, NY 10104 Tel: 212-364-1100 Web Site: www.hachettebookgroup.com/imprint/hachette-audio/, pg 83

Metcho, Jeff, University of California Extension - Writing, Editing & Humanities, 1995 University Ave, Suite 110, Berkeley, CA 94720-7000 Tel: 510-643-8916 Fax: 510-643-0216 E-mail: extension-letters@berkeley.edu Web Site: www.extension.berkeley.edu, pg 566

Meth, David L, Writers' Productions, PO Box 630, Westport, CT 06881-0630 Tel: 203-227-8199, pg 482

Methot, JD, Access Copyright, The Canadian Copyright Licensing Agency, 69 Younge St, Suite 1100, Toronto, ON M5E 1K3, Canada Tel: 416-868-1620 Toll Free Tel: 800-893-5777 Fax: 416-868-1621 E-mail: info@accesscopyright.ca Web Site: www.accesscopyright.ca, pg 493

Methven, Robert, Perfection Learning®, 1000 N Second Ave, Logan, IA 51546-1061 Tel: 712-644-2831 Toll Free Tel: 800-831-4190 Toll Free Fax: 800-543-2745 E-mail: orders@perfectionlearning.com Web Site: www.perfectionlearning.com, pg 158

Metivier, Michael, Chelsea Green Publishing Co, 85 N Main St, Suite 120, White River Junction, VT 05001 Tel: 802-295-6300 Toll Free Tel: 800-639-4099 (cust serv & orders) Fax: 802-295-6444 E-mail: customerservice@chelseagreen.com; editorial@chelseagreen.com; publicity@chelseagreen.com; rights@chelseagreen.com Web Site: www.chelseagreen.com, pg 45

Metoui, Meriam, Viking Children's Books, c/o Penguin Random House LLC, 1745 Broadway, New York, NY 10019 Tel: 212-782-9000 Web Site: www.penguin.com/viking-childrens-books-overview/, pg 224

Metz, Mary, Mountaineers Books, 1001 SW Klickitat Way, Suite 201, Seattle, WA 98134 Tel: 206-223-6303 Fax: 206-223-6306 E-mail: mbooks@mountaineersbooks.org; customerservice@mountaineersbooks.org Web Site: www.mountaineers.org/books, pg 135

Metzger, Greg, New City Press, 202 Comforter Blvd, Hyde Park, NY 12538 Tel: 845-229-0335 Toll Free Tel: 800-462-5980 (orders only) Fax: 845-229-0351 E-mail: info@newcitypress.com; orders@newcitypress.com Web Site: www.newcitypress.com, pg 139

Metzger, Julia, Macmillan, 120 Broadway, 22nd fl, New York, NY 10271 E-mail: press.inquiries@macmillan.com Web Site: us.macmillan.com, pg 122

Metzler, Maria J, Eisenbrauns, 820 N University Dr, USB 1, Suite C, University Park, PA 16802-1003 Tel: 814-865-1327 Toll Free Tel: 800-326-9180 (orders & cust serv) Fax: 814-863-1408 Toll Free Fax: 877-778-2665 (orders) E-mail: orders@psupress.org; customerservice@psupress.org Web Site: www.eisenbrauns.org, pg 64

Metzner, Joerg, Rand McNally, 9855 Woods Dr, Skokie, IL 60077 Tel: 847-329-8100 Toll Free Tel: 877-446-4863 Toll Free Fax: 877-469-1298 E-mail: mediarelations@randmcnally.com; tndsupport@randmcnally.com Web Site: www.randmcnally.com, pg 169

Meuse, Elena, Random House Children's Books, c/o Penguin Random House LLC, 1745 Broadway, New York, NY 10019 Tel: 212-782-9000 Web Site: www.rhcbooks.com, pg 170

Meuser, Caitlin, Random House Publishing Group, 1745 Broadway, New York, NY 10019 Toll Free Tel: 800-200-3552 Web Site: www.randomhousebooks.com, pg 171

Meyer, Astrid, Penn State University Press, University Support Bldg 1, Suite C, 820 N University Dr, University Park, PA 16802-1003 Tel: 814-865-1327 Toll Free Tel: 800-326-9180 (orders & cust serv) Fax: 814-863-1408 Toll Free Fax: 877-778-2665 (book orders) E-mail: orders@psupress.org; customerservice@psupress.org Web Site: www.psupress.org, pg 157

Meyer, Caitlin, Beacon Press, 24 Farnsworth St, Boston, MA 02210-1409 Tel: 617-742-2110 Fax: 617-723-3097 E-mail: production@beacon.org Web Site: www.beacon.org, pg 25

Meyer, Dan, Doubleday, c/o Penguin Random House LLC, 1745 Broadway, New York, NY 10019 Tel: 212-751-2600 Fax: 212-940-7390 (dom rts); 212-572-2662 (foreign rts) Web Site: knopfdoubleday.com/imprint/doubleday/; knopfdoubleday.com, pg 61

Meyer, Dan, Nan A Talese, c/o Penguin Random House LLC, 1745 Broadway, New York, NY 10019 Tel: 212-751-2600 Fax: 212-940-7390 (dom rts); 212-572-2662 (foreign rts) Web Site: knopfdoubleday.com/imprint/nan-a-talese/; knopfdoubleday.com, pg 202

Meyer, Emma, HarperCollins Children's Books, 195 Broadway, New York, NY 10007 Tel: 212-207-7000 Web Site: www.harpercollins.com/childrens, pg 86

Meyer, Steve J, LAMA Books, 2381 Sleepy Hollow Ave, Hayward, CA 94545 Tel: 510-785-1091 Toll Free Tel: 888-452-6244 Fax: 510-785-1099 Web Site: www.lamabooks.com, pg 112

Meyers, Catharine A, New Harbinger Publications Inc, 5674 Shattuck Ave, Oakland, CA 94609 Tel: 510-652-0215 Toll Free Tel: 800-748-6273 (orders only) Fax: 510-652-5472 Toll Free Fax: 800-652-1613 E-mail: customerservice@newharbinger.com Web Site: www.newharbinger.com, pg 140

Meyers, Izzy, Alfred A Knopf, c/o Penguin Random House LLC, 1745 Broadway, New York, NY 10019 *Tel:* 212-751-2600 *Fax:* 212-940-7390 (dom rts); 212-572-2662 (foreign rts) *Web Site:* knopfdoubleday.com/imprint/knopf/; knopfdoubleday.com, pg 110

Meyers, Tona Pearce, New World Library, 14 Pamaron Way, Novato, CA 94949 *Tel:* 415-884-2100 *Fax:* 415-884-2199 *E-mail:* escort@newworldlibrary.com *Web Site:* www.newworldlibrary.com, pg 140

Mezhibovskaya, Katya, Bloomsbury Publishing Inc, 1385 Broadway, 5th fl, New York, NY 10018 *Tel:* 212-419-5300 *E-mail:* marketingusa@bloomsbury.com; adultpublicityusa@bloomsbury.com; askacademic@bloomsbury.com *Web Site:* www.bloomsbury.com, pg 31

Mezrich, Mor, Penguin Random House Audio Publishing Group, 1745 Broadway, New York, NY 10019 *Toll Free Tel:* 800-793-2665 (cust serv) *E-mail:* audio@penguinrandomhouse.com; ecustomerservice@penguinrandomhouse.com *Web Site:* www.penguinrandomhouseaudio.com, pg 154

Miceli, Jaya, Scribner, 1230 Avenue of the Americas, New York, NY 10020 *Web Site:* www.simonandschusterpublishing.com/scribner/, pg 185

Miceli, Lin, Sourcebooks LLC, 1935 Brookdale Rd, Suite 139, Naperville, IL 60563 *Tel:* 630-961-3900 *Toll Free Tel:* 800-432-7444 *Fax:* 630-961-2168 *E-mail:* info@sourcebooks.com *Web Site:* www.sourcebooks.com, pg 194

Mich, Matt, Macmillan, 120 Broadway, 22nd fl, New York, NY 10271 *E-mail:* press.inquiries@macmillan.com *Web Site:* us.macmillan.com, pg 122

Michael, Ann, AIP Publishing LLC, 1305 Walt Whitman Rd, Suite 110, Melville, NY 11747 *Tel:* 516-576-2200 *E-mail:* help@aip.org; press@aip.org; rights@aip.org *Web Site:* www.aip.org; publishing.aip.org, pg 6

Michael, Jonathan, Annual Reviews, 1875 S Grant St, Suite 700, San Mateo, CA 94402 *Tel:* 650-493-4400 *Toll Free Tel:* 800-523-8635 *Fax:* 650-424-0910; 650-855-9815 *E-mail:* service@annualreviews.org *Web Site:* www.annualreviews.org, pg 14

Michaels, Zoe, Harry N Abrams Inc, 195 Broadway, 9th fl, New York, NY 10007 *Tel:* 212-206-7715 *Toll Free Tel:* 800-345-1359 *Fax:* 212-645-8437 *E-mail:* abrams@abramsbooks.com; publicity@abramsbooks.com; sales@abramsbooks.com *Web Site:* www.abramsbooks.com, pg 3

Michailidis, Parisa, Firefly Books Ltd, 50 Staples Ave, Unit 1, Richmond Hill, ON L4B 0A7, Canada *Tel:* 416-499-8412 *Toll Free Tel:* 800-387-5085 (US) *Fax:* 416-499-8313 *Toll Free Fax:* 800-450-0391 (CN); 800-565-6034 (US) *E-mail:* service@fireflybooks.com *Web Site:* www.fireflybooks.com, pg 406

Michalski, Anthony Raymond, International Wealth Success (IWS), 332 Center St, Wilkes-Barre, PA 18702 *Tel:* 570-825-3598 *E-mail:* admin@iwsmoney.com *Web Site:* iwealthsuccess.com, pg 104

Michalski, Anthony Raymond, Kallisti Publishing Inc, 332 Center St, Wilkes-Barre, PA 18702 *Tel:* 570-825-3598 *E-mail:* editor@kallistipublishing.com *Web Site:* www.kallistipublishing.com; arisbooks.com, pg 108

Michaud, Ann, ALSC Baker & Taylor Summer Reading Grant, 225 N Michigan Ave, Suite 1300, Chicago, IL 60601 *Tel:* 312-280-2163 *Toll Free Tel:* 800-545-2433 *Fax:* 312-280-5271 *E-mail:* alsc@ala.org *Web Site:* www.ala.org/alsc/awardsgrants/profawards/bakertaylor, pg 572

Michaud, Ann, The Mildred L Batchelder Award, 225 N Michigan Ave, Suite 1300, Chicago, IL 60601 *Tel:* 312-280-2163 *Toll Free Tel:* 800-545-2433 *Fax:* 312-280-5271 *E-mail:* alsc@ala.org *Web Site:* www.ala.org/alsc/awardsgrants/bookmedia/batchelder, pg 577

Michaud, Ann, The Pura Belpre Award, 225 N Michigan Ave, Suite 1300, Chicago, IL 60601 *Tel:* 312-280-2163 *Toll Free Tel:* 800-545-2433 *Fax:* 312-280-5271 *E-mail:* alsc@ala.org *Web Site:* www.ala.org/alsc/awardsgrants/bookmedia/belpre, pg 578

Michaud, Ann, Bound to Stay Bound Books Scholarship, 225 N Michigan Ave, Suite 1300, Chicago, IL 60601 *Tel:* 312-280-2163 *Toll Free Tel:* 800-545-2433 *Fax:* 312-280-5271 *E-mail:* alsc@ala.org *Web Site:* www.ala.org/alsc/awardsgrants/scholarships; www.btsb.com/about-us/scholarships, pg 583

Michaud, Ann, The Randolph Caldecott Medal, 225 N Michigan Ave, Suite 1300, Chicago, IL 60601 *Tel:* 312-280-2163 *Toll Free Tel:* 800-545-2433 *Fax:* 312-280-5271 *E-mail:* alsc@ala.org *Web Site:* www.ala.org/alsc/awardsgrants/bookmedia/caldecott, pg 585

Michaud, Ann, Children's Literature Lecture Award, 225 N Michigan Ave, Suite 1300, Chicago, IL 60601 *Tel:* 312-280-2163 *Toll Free Tel:* 800-545-2433 *Fax:* 312-280-5271 *E-mail:* alsc@ala.org *Web Site:* www.ala.org/alsc/awardsgrants/profawards/chll, pg 589

Michaud, Ann, Children's Literature Legacy Award, 225 N Michigan Ave, Suite 1300, Chicago, IL 60601 *Tel:* 312-280-2163 *Toll Free Tel:* 800-545-2433 *Fax:* 312-280-5271 *E-mail:* alsc@ala.org *Web Site:* www.ala.org/awardsgrants/childrens-literature-legacy-award; www.ala.org/alsc/awardsgrants/bookmedia/clla, pg 589

Michaud, Ann, Frederic G Melcher Scholarship, 225 N Michigan Ave, Suite 1300, Chicago, IL 60601 *Tel:* 312-280-2163 *Toll Free Tel:* 800-545-2433 *Fax:* 312-280-5271 *E-mail:* alsc@ala.org *Web Site:* www.ala.org/alsc/awardsgrants/scholarships, pg 632

Michaud, Ann, John Newbery Medal, 225 N Michigan Ave, Suite 1300, Chicago, IL 60601 *Tel:* 312-280-2163 *Toll Free Tel:* 800-545-2433 *Fax:* 312-280-5271 *E-mail:* alsc@ala.org *Web Site:* www.ala.org/alsc/awardsgrants/bookmedia/newbery, pg 641

Michaud, Ann, Robert F Sibert Informational Book Award, 225 N Michigan Ave, Suite 1300, Chicago, IL 60601 *Tel:* 312-280-2163 *Toll Free Tel:* 800-545-2433 *Fax:* 312-280-5271 *E-mail:* alsc@ala.org *Web Site:* www.ala.org/alsc/awardsgrants/bookmedia/sibert, pg 662

Michel, Christie, Little, Brown Books for Young Readers (LBYR), 1290 Avenue of the Americas, New York, NY 10104 *Tel:* 212-364-1100 *Toll Free Tel:* 800-759-0190 (cust serv) *E-mail:* rights@lbchildrens.com *Web Site:* www.hachettebookgroup.com/imprint/little-brown-books-for-young-readers/, pg 118

Michels, Anna, Poisoned Pen Press, 4014 N Goldwater Blvd, Suite 201, Scottsdale, AZ 85251 *Tel:* 480-945-3375 *Toll Free Tel:* 800-421-3976 *Fax:* 480-949-1707 *E-mail:* info@poisonedpenpress.com *Web Site:* www.poisonedpenpress.com, pg 161

Michels, Anna, Sourcebooks LLC, 1935 Brookdale Rd, Suite 139, Naperville, IL 60563 *Tel:* 630-961-3900 *Toll Free Tel:* 800-432-7444 *Fax:* 630-961-2168 *E-mail:* info@sourcebooks.com *Web Site:* www.sourcebooks.com, pg 194

Michels, Dia L, Platypus Media LLC, 725 Eighth St SE, Washington, DC 20003 *Tel:* 202-546-1674 *Toll Free Tel:* 877-PLATYPS (752-8977) *Fax:* 202-546-2356 *E-mail:* info@platypusmedia.com *Web Site:* www.platypusmedia.com, pg 160

Michels, Dia L, Science, Naturally, 725 Eighth St SE, Washington, DC 20003 *Tel:* 202-465-4798 *Fax:* 202-558-2132 *E-mail:* info@sciencenaturally.com *Web Site:* www.sciencenaturally.com, pg 185

Michels, Marie, Viking Penguin, c/o Penguin Random House LLC, 1745 Broadway, New York, NY 10019 *Tel:* 212-782-9000 *Web Site:* www.penguin.com/overview-vikingbooks/; www.penguin.com/pamela-dorman-books-overview/; www.penguin.com/penguin-classics-overview/; www.penguin.com/penguin-life-overview/, pg 225

Miciak, Kate, Random House Publishing Group, 1745 Broadway, New York, NY 10019 *Toll Free Tel:* 800-200-3552 *Web Site:* www.randomhousebooks.com, pg 170

Mickulas, Peter, Rutgers University Press, 106 Somerset St, 3rd fl, New Brunswick, NJ 08901 *Tel:* 848-445-7762; 848-445-7761 (sales) *Fax:* 732-745-4935 *E-mail:* sales@rutgersuniversitypress.org *Web Site:* www.rutgersuniversitypress.org, pg 178

Middlebrook, Ron, Centerstream Publishing LLC, PO Box 17878, Anaheim Hills, CA 92817-7878 *Tel:* 714-779-9390 *E-mail:* centerstrm@aol.com *Web Site:* www.centerstream-usa.com, pg 44

Middleton, Kathy, Crabtree Publishing Co, 347 Fifth Ave, Suite 1402-145, New York, NY 10016 *Tel:* 212-496-5040 *Toll Free Tel:* 800-387-7650 *Toll Free Fax:* 800-355-7166 *E-mail:* custserv@crabtreebooks.com *Web Site:* www.crabtreebooks.com, pg 54

Middleton, Kathy, Crabtree Publishing Co Ltd, 616 Welland Ave, St Catharines, ON L2M 5V6, Canada *Tel:* 905-682-5221 *Toll Free Tel:* 800-387-7650 *Fax:* 905-682-7166 *Toll Free Fax:* 800-355-7166 *E-mail:* custserv@crabtreebooks.com; sales@crabtreebooks.com; orders@crabtreebooks.com *Web Site:* www.crabtreebooks.ca, pg 400

Middleton, Lydia, Association for Information Science & Technology (ASIS&T), 673 Potomac Station Dr, Suite 155, Leesburg, VA 20176 *Tel:* 301-495-0900 *Fax:* 301-495-0810 *E-mail:* asist@asist.org *Web Site:* www.asist.org, pg 19

Middleton, Lydia, Association for Information Science & Technology (ASIS&T), 673 Potomac Station Dr, Suite 155, Leesburg, VA 20176 *Tel:* 301-495-0900 *Fax:* 301-495-0810 *E-mail:* asist@asist.org; membership@asist.org *Web Site:* www.asist.org, pg 498

Middleton, Maria, Candlewick Press, 99 Dover St, Somerville, MA 02144-2825 *Tel:* 617-661-3330 *Fax:* 617-661-0565 *E-mail:* bigbear@candlewick.com; salesinfo@candlewick.com *Web Site:* candlewick.com, pg 39

Midgley, Peter, University of Alberta Press, Ring House 2, Edmonton, AB T6G 2E1, Canada *Tel:* 780-492-3662 *Fax:* 780-492-0719 *Web Site:* www.uap.ualberta.ca, pg 421

Miele, Alyssa, HarperCollins Children's Books, 195 Broadway, New York, NY 10007 *Tel:* 212-207-7000 *Web Site:* www.harpercollins.com/childrens, pg 85

Miers, Charles, Rizzoli International Publications Inc, 300 Park Ave S, 4th fl, New York, NY 10010-5399 *Tel:* 212-387-3400 *Toll Free Tel:* 800-522-6657 (orders only) *Fax:* 212-387-3535 *E-mail:* publicity@rizzoliusa.com *Web Site:* www.rizzoliusa.com, pg 175

Mierzejewska, Bozena I, Gabelli School of Business Communications & Media Management Program, 140 W 62 St, Rm 440, New York, NY 10023 *Tel:* 212-636-6150 *Fax:* 718-817-4999 *Web Site:* www.fordham.edu/gabelli-school-of-business, pg 562

Miesionczek, Julie, Words into Print, 208 Java St, 5th fl, Brooklyn, NY 11222 *E-mail:* query@wordsintoprint.org *Web Site:* wordsintoprint.org, pg 445

Migalti, Linda, Susan Schulman Literary Agency LLC, 454 W 44 St, New York, NY 10036 *Tel:* 212-713-1633; 917-488-0906 (direct line) *E-mail:* queries@schulmanagency.com *Web Site:* www.schulmanagency.com, pg 475

Migner-Laurin, Anne, Les Editions du Remue-Menage, 469, Jean-Talon Ouest, bureau 401, Montreal, QC H3N 1R4, Canada *Tel:* 514-876-0097 *E-mail:* info@editions-rm.ca *Web Site:* www.editions-rm.ca, pg 403

Mihlebach, Ashley, HarperCollins Publishers LLC, 195 Broadway, New York, NY 10007 *Tel:* 212-207-7000 *Web Site:* www.harpercollins.com, pg 86

Miholer, Sue, Cascade Christian Writers (CCW), PO Box 22, Gladstone, OR 97027 *Tel:* 503-393-3356 *E-mail:* contact@oregonchristianwriters.org *Web Site:* oregonchristianwriters.org, pg 503

Miholer, Sue, Cascade Christian Writers Conference, PO Box 22, Gladstone, OR 97027 *Tel:* 503-393-3356 *E-mail:* business@cascadechristianwriters.org *Web Site:* cascadechristianwriters.org, pg 553

Miiller, Emily, Macmillan, 120 Broadway, 22nd fl, New York, NY 10271 *E-mail:* press.inquiries@macmillan.com *Web Site:* us.macmillan.com, pg 122

Miiller, Emily, St Martin's Press, LLC, 120 Broadway, New York, NY 10271 *E-mail:* publicity@stmartins.com; trademarketing@stmartins.com; foreignrights@stmartins.com *Web Site:* us.macmillan.com/smp, pg 181

Mike, Jamin, House of Anansi Press Inc, 128 Sterling Rd, Lower Level, Toronto, ON M6R 2B7, Canada *Tel:* 416-363-4343 *Fax:* 416-363-1017 *E-mail:* customerservice@houseofanansi.com *Web Site:* houseofanansi.com, pg 409

Miklos, Lauren, Encounter Books, 900 Broadway, Suite 601, New York, NY 10003 *Tel:* 212-871-6310 *Toll Free Tel:* 855-203-7220 *E-mail:* publicity@encounterbooks.com *Web Site:* www.encounterbooks.com, pg 66

Mikula, Deborah E, Michigan Library Association (MLA), 3410 Belle Chase Way, Lansing, MI 48911 *Tel:* 517-394-2774 *E-mail:* mla@milibraries.org *Web Site:* www.milibraries.org, pg 510

Mila, Juan, HarperCollins Publishers LLC, 195 Broadway, New York, NY 10007 *Tel:* 212-207-7000 *Web Site:* www.harpercollins.com, pg 86

Milano, Gioia, Johns Hopkins University Press, 2715 N Charles St, Baltimore, MD 21218-4363 *Tel:* 410-516-6900; 410-516-6987 *Toll Free Tel:* 800-537-5487 (book orders & cust serv); 800-548-1784 (journal orders) *Fax:* 410-516-6968; 410-516-6998 (orders) *E-mail:* hfscustserv@press.jhu.edu (cust serv); jrnlcirc@jh.edu (journal orders) *Web Site:* www.press.jhu.edu; muse.jhu.edu, pg 106

Milazzo, Richard, Edgewise Press Inc, 24 Fifth Ave, Suite 224, New York, NY 10011 *Tel:* 212-387-0931 *E-mail:* epinc@mindspring.com *Web Site:* www.edgewisepress.org, pg 63

Mileo, Jessica, InkWell Management, 521 Fifth Ave, Suite 2600, New York, NY 10175 *Tel:* 212-922-3500 *Fax:* 212-922-0535 *E-mail:* info@inkwellmanagement.com; submissions@inkwellmanagement.com; permissions@inkwellmanagement.com *Web Site:* inkwellmanagement.com, pg 463

Miles, Jessica, Macmillan, 120 Broadway, 22nd fl, New York, NY 10271 *E-mail:* press.inquiries@macmillan.com *Web Site:* us.macmillan.com, pg 122

Miles-Cohen, Shari PhD, National Communication Association, 1765 "N" St NW, Washington, DC 20036 *Tel:* 202-464-4622 *Fax:* 202-464-4600 *E-mail:* inbox@natcom.org *Web Site:* www.natcom.org, pg 512

Milford, Brian, Abingdon Press, 810 12 Ave S, Nashville, TN 37203 *Toll Free Tel:* 800-251-3320 *E-mail:* orders@abingdonpress.com; permissions@abingdonpress.com *Web Site:* www.abingdonpress.com, pg 2

Milford, Kristen, Harry N Abrams Inc, 195 Broadway, 9th fl, New York, NY 10007 *Tel:* 212-206-7715 *Toll Free Tel:* 800-345-1359 *Fax:* 212-645-8437 *E-mail:* abrams@abramsbooks.com; publicity@abramsbooks.com; sales@abramsbooks.com *Web Site:* www.abramsbooks.com, pg 3

Millard, Dwaine, Scholastic Education Solutions, 557 Broadway, New York, NY 10012 *Tel:* 212-343-6100 *Fax:* 212-343-6189 *Web Site:* www.scholastic.com, pg 184

Millen, Tim, Center for the Collaborative Classroom, 1001 Marina Village Pkwy, Suite 110, Alameda, CA 94501-1042 *Tel:* 510-533-0213 *Toll Free Tel:* 800-666-7270 *Fax:* 510-464-3670 *E-mail:* info@collaborativeclassroom.org; clientsupport@collaborativeclassroom.org *Web Site:* www.collaborativeclassroom.org, pg 44

Miller, Andra, Random House Publishing Group, 1745 Broadway, New York, NY 10019 *Toll Free Tel:* 800-200-3552 *Web Site:* www.randomhousebooks.com, pg 171

Miller, Andrea, Harry N Abrams Inc, 195 Broadway, 9th fl, New York, NY 10007 *Tel:* 212-206-7715 *Toll Free Tel:* 800-345-1359 *Fax:* 212-645-8437 *E-mail:* abrams@abramsbooks.com; publicity@abramsbooks.com; sales@abramsbooks.com *Web Site:* www.abramsbooks.com, pg 3

Miller, Andrew, Henry Holt and Company, LLC, 120 Broadway, 23rd fl, New York, NY 10271 *Tel:* 646-307-5151 *Toll Free Tel:* 888-330-8477 (orders) *Fax:* 646-307-5285 *Web Site:* www.henryholt.com, pg 94

Miller, Anelle, Society of Illustrators (SI), 128 E 63 St, New York, NY 10065 *Tel:* 212-838-2560 *Fax:* 212-838-2561 *E-mail:* info@societyillustrators.org *Web Site:* www.societyillustrators.org, pg 520

Miller, Angela, Folio Literary Management, The Film Center Bldg, 630 Ninth Ave, Suite 1101, New York, NY 10036 *Tel:* 212-400-1494 *Fax:* 212-967-0977 *Web Site:* www.foliolit.com, pg 459

Miller, Austin, Dupree, Miller & Associates Inc, 4311 Oak Lawn Ave, Suite 650, Dallas, TX 75219 *Tel:* 214-559-2665 *E-mail:* editorial@dupreemiller.com *Web Site:* www.dupreemiller.com, pg 457

Miller, Barbara, Transatlantic Agency, 2 Bloor St E, Suite 3500, Toronto, ON M4W 1A8, Canada *Tel:* 416-488-9214 *E-mail:* info@transatlanticagency.com; royalties@transatlanticagency.com *Web Site:* www.transatlanticagency.com, pg 479

Miller, Fr Byron, Liguori Publications, One Liguori Dr, Liguori, MO 63057-1000 *Tel:* 636-464-2500 *Toll Free Tel:* 800-325-9521 *Toll Free Fax:* 800-325-9526 (sales) *E-mail:* liguori@liguori.org (sales & cust serv) *Web Site:* www.liguori.org, pg 117

Miller, Cassidy, HarperCollins Children's Books, 195 Broadway, New York, NY 10007 *Tel:* 212-207-7000 *Web Site:* www.harpercollins.com/childrens, pg 86

Miller, Ceci, CeciBooks Editorial & Publishing Consultation, 7057 26 Ave NW, Seattle, WA 98117 *E-mail:* info@cecibooks.com *Web Site:* www.cecibooks.com, pg 437

Miller, Chadd, David C Cook, 4050 Lee Vance Dr, Colorado Springs, CO 80918 *Tel:* 719-536-0100 *Toll Free Tel:* 800-323-7543 (orders & cust serv) *Toll Free Fax:* 800-430-0726 (cust serv) *E-mail:* bookstores@davidccook.org; customercare@davidccook.org *Web Site:* www.davidccook.org, pg 52

Miller, Christopher, Eisenbrauns, 820 N University Dr, USB 1, Suite C, University Park, PA 16802-1003 *Tel:* 814-865-1327 *Toll Free Tel:* 800-326-9180 (orders & cust serv) *Fax:* 814-863-1408 *Toll Free Fax:* 877-778-2665 (orders) *E-mail:* orders@psupress.org; customerservice@psupress.org *Web Site:* www.eisenbrauns.org, pg 65

Miller, Craig A, Practising Law Institute (PLI), 1177 Avenue of the Americas, 2nd fl, New York, NY 10036 *Tel:* 212-824-5710 (cust serv) *Toll Free Tel:* 800-260-4PLI (260-4754) *Toll Free Fax:* 800-321-0093 (cust serv) *E-mail:* info@pli.edu; membership@pli.edu *Web Site:* www.pli.edu, pg 163

Miller, D Patrick, Linda Chester Literary Agency, 630 Fifth Ave, Suite 2000, New York, NY 10111 *Tel:* 212-218-3350 *E-mail:* submissions@lindachester.com *Web Site:* www.lindachester.com, pg 454

Miller, David, Evan-Moor Educational Publishers, 10 Harris Ct, Suite C-3, Monterey, CA 93940 *Tel:* 831-649-5901 *Toll Free Tel:* 800-777-4362 (orders) *Fax:* 831-649-6256 *Toll Free Fax:* 800-777-4332 (orders) *E-mail:* sales@evan-moor.com; marketing@evan-moor.com *Web Site:* www.evan-moor.com, pg 68

Miller, David, The Garamond Agency Inc, 12 Horton St, Newburyport, MA 01950 *E-mail:* query@garamondagency.com *Web Site:* www.garamondagency.com, pg 459

Miller, David, Island Press, 2000 "M" St NW, Suite 480-B, Washington, DC 20036 *Tel:* 202-232-7933 *Toll Free Tel:* 800-621-2736 *Fax:* 202-234-1328 *E-mail:* info@islandpress.org *Web Site:* www.islandpress.org, pg 104

Miller, David P, New England Poetry Club, c/o Linda Haviland Conte, 18 Hall Ave, Apt 2, Somerville, MA 02144 *E-mail:* info@nepoetryclub.org; president@nepoetryclub.org *Web Site:* nepoetryclub.org, pg 514

Miller, Diana Tejerina, Alfred A Knopf, c/o Penguin Random House LLC, 1745 Broadway, New York, NY 10019 *Tel:* 212-751-2600 *Fax:* 212-940-7390 (dom rts); 212-572-2662 (foreign rts) *Web Site:* knopfdoubleday.com/imprint/knopf/; knopfdoubleday.com, pg 110

Miller, George, Cengage Learning, 20 Channel Center St, Boston, MA 02210 *Tel:* 617-289-7700 *Toll Free Tel:* 800-354-9706 *Fax:* 617-289-7844 *E-mail:* esales@cengage.com *Web Site:* www.cengage.com, pg 43

Miller, Heather, University of British Columbia Creative Writing Program, Buchanan Rm E-462, 1866 Main Mall, Vancouver, BC V6T 1Z1, Canada *Tel:* 604-822-0699 *Web Site:* creativewriting.ubc.ca, pg 566

Miller, Jan, Dupree, Miller & Associates Inc, 4311 Oak Lawn Ave, Suite 650, Dallas, TX 75219 *Tel:* 214-559-2665 *E-mail:* editorial@dupreemiller.com *Web Site:* www.dupreemiller.com, pg 457

Miller, Jeffrey, Irwin Law Inc, 14 Duncan St, Suite 206, Toronto, ON M5H 3G8, Canada *Tel:* 416-862-7690 *Toll Free Tel:* 888-314-9014 *Fax:* 416-862-9236 *E-mail:* info@irwinlaw.com; contact@irwinlaw.com *Web Site:* www.irwinlaw.com, pg 410

Miller, Jennifer, Utah Geological Survey, 1594 W North Temple, Suite 3110, Salt Lake City, UT 84116-3154 *Tel:* 801-537-3300 *Toll Free Tel:* 888-UTAH-MAP (882-4627, bookshop) *Fax:* 801-537-3400 *E-mail:* geostore@utah.gov *Web Site:* geology.utah.gov, pg 223

Miller, Katy, Random House Children's Books, c/o Penguin Random House LLC, 1745 Broadway, New York, NY 10019 *Tel:* 212-782-9000 *Web Site:* www.rhcbooks.com, pg 170

Miller, Kim, Association of University Presses (AUPresses), 1412 Broadway, Suite 2135, New York, NY 10018 *Tel:* 212-989-1010 *Fax:* 212-989-0275 *E-mail:* info@aupresses.org *Web Site:* www.aupresses.org, pg 500

Miller, Kim, AUPresses Book, Jacket & Journal Show, 1412 Broadway, Suite 2135, New York, NY 10018 *Tel:* 212-989-1010 *Fax:* 212-989-0275 *E-mail:* info@aupresses.org *Web Site:* www.aupresses.org, pg 576

Miller, Kristen Renee, Sarabande Books Inc, 822 E Market St, Louisville, KY 40206 *Tel:* 502-458-4028 *Fax:* 502-458-4065 *E-mail:* info@sarabandebooks.org *Web Site:* www.sarabandebooks.org, pg 182

Miller, Laurie, Society of Children's Book Writers & Illustrators (SCBWI), 6363 Wilshire Blvd, Suite 425, Los Angeles, CA 90048 *Tel:* 323-782-1010 *E-mail:* membership@scbwi.org *Web Site:* www.scbwi.org, pg 520

Miller, Lawton, M Lee Smith Publishers, 100 Winners Circle, Suite 300, Brentwood, TN 37027 *Tel:* 615-373-7517 *Toll Free Tel:* 800-274-6774; 800-727-5257 *E-mail:* custserv@mleesmith.com; service@blr.com *Web Site:* www.mleesmith.com; www.blr.com, pg 192

Miller, Linda Sue, Remember Point Inc, PO Box 1448, Pacific Palisades, CA 90272 *Tel:* 310-896-8716 *E-mail:* info@rememberpoint.com *Web Site:* www.rememberpoint.com; www.longfellowfindsahome.com, pg 174

Miller, Matthew, Macmillan, 120 Broadway, 22nd fl, New York, NY 10271 *E-mail:* press.inquiries@macmillan.com *Web Site:* us.macmillan.com, pg 122

Miller, Melissa, American Society of Agricultural & Biological Engineers (ASABE), 2950 Niles Rd, St Joseph, MI 49085-9659 *Tel:* 269-429-0300 *Toll Free Tel:* 800-371-2723 *Fax:* 269-429-3852 *E-mail:* hq@asabe.org *Web Site:* www.asabe.org, pg 12

Miller, Michelle, The International Women's Writing Guild (IWWG), 888 Eighth Ave, No 537, New York, NY 10019 *Tel:* 917-720-6959 *E-mail:* iwwgquestions@iwwg.org *Web Site:* www.iwwg.org, pg 508

Miller, Michelle, IWWG Annual Summer Conference, 888 Eighth Ave, No 537, New York, NY 10019 *Tel:* 917-720-6959 *E-mail:* iwwgquestions@iwwg.org *Web Site:* www.iwwg.org, pg 555

Miller, Michelle, IWWG Annual Writing Conference, 888 Eighth Ave, No 537, New York, NY 10019 *Tel:* 617-792-7272 *E-mail:* iwwgquestions@iwwg.org *Web Site:* www.iwwg.org, pg 555

Miller, Mike, BPA Worldwide, 100 Beard Sawmill Rd, 6th fl, Shelton, CT 06484 *Tel:* 203-447-2800 *Fax:* 203-447-2900 *E-mail:* info@bpaww.com *Web Site:* www.bpaww.com, pg 501

Miller, Miriam, Holiday House Publishing Inc, 50 Broad St, New York, NY 10004 *Tel:* 212-688-0085 *Fax:* 212-421-6134 *E-mail:* info@holidayhouse.com *Web Site:* www.holidayhouse.com, pg 94

Miller, Monica, Heritage House Publishing Co Ltd, 1075 Pendergast St, No 103, Victoria, BC V8V 0A1, Canada *Tel:* 250-360-0829 *Fax:* 250-386-0829 *E-mail:* heritage@heritagehouse.ca; info@heritagehouse.ca; orders@heritagehouse.ca *Web Site:* www.heritagehouse.ca, pg 409

Miller, Nancy, Bloomsbury Publishing Inc, 1385 Broadway, 5th fl, New York, NY 10018 *Tel:* 212-419-5300 *E-mail:* marketingusa@bloomsbury.com; adultpublicityusa@bloomsbury.com; askacademic@bloomsbury.com *Web Site:* www.bloomsbury.com, pg 31

Miller, Nicole, Modern Memoirs Inc, 417 West St, Suite 104, Amherst, MA 01002 *Tel:* 413-253-2353 *Web Site:* www.modernmemoirs.com, pg 133

Miller, Peter, Global Lion Intellectual Property Management Inc, PO Box 669238, Pompano Beach, FL 33066 *Tel:* 754-222-6948 *Fax:* 754-222-6948 *E-mail:* queriesgloballionmgt@gmail.com *Web Site:* www.globallionmanagement.com, pg 460

Miller, Peter, The Institutes™, 720 Providence Rd, Suite 100, Malvern, PA 19355-3433 *Tel:* 610-644-2100 *Toll Free Tel:* 800-644-2101 *Fax:* 610-640-9576 *E-mail:* customerservice@theinstitutes.org *Web Site:* www.theinstitutes.org, pg 102

Miller, Peter, W W Norton & Company Inc, 500 Fifth Ave, New York, NY 10110-0017 *Tel:* 212-354-5500 *Toll Free Tel:* 800-233-4830 (orders & serv) *Fax:* 212-869-0856 *Toll Free Fax:* 800-458-6515 *E-mail:* orders@wwnorton.com *Web Site:* wwnorton.com, pg 143

Miller, Rachel, Johns Hopkins University Press, 2715 N Charles St, Baltimore, MD 21218-4363 *Tel:* 410-516-6900; 410-516-6987 *Toll Free Tel:* 800-537-5487 (book orders & cust serv); 800-548-1784 (journal orders) *Fax:* 410-516-6968; 410-516-6998 (orders) *E-mail:* hfscustserv@press.jhu.edu (cust serv); jrnlcirc@jh.edu (journal orders) *Web Site:* www.press.jhu.edu; muse.jhu.edu, pg 106

Miller, Richard K, Richard K Miller Associates, 2413 Main St, Suite 331, Miramar, FL 33025 *Tel:* 404-276-3376 *Fax:* 404-581-5335 *Web Site:* rkma.com, pg 132

Miller, Robert, Paul H Brookes Publishing Co Inc, PO Box 10624, Baltimore, MD 21285-0624 *Tel:* 410-337-9580 (outside US & CN) *Toll Free Tel:* 800-638-3775 (US & CN) *Fax:* 410-337-8539 *E-mail:* custserv@brookespublishing.com *Web Site:* www.brookespublishing.com, pg 37

Miller, Samantha, Sciendex, 1388 Leisure Dr, Summerville, SC 29486 *Tel:* 843-693-6689 *Web Site:* www.sciendex.com, pg 444

Miller, Sarah, Award for Excellence in Poetry for Children, 340 N Neil St, Suite 104, Champaign, IL 61820 *Tel:* 217-328-3870 *Toll Free Tel:* 877-369-6283 (cust serv) *Fax:* 217-328-9645 *Web Site:* ncte.org/awards/ncte-childrens-book-awards, pg 576

Miller, Sarah, Charlotte Huck Award, 340 N Neil St, Suite 104, Champaign, IL 61820 *Tel:* 217-328-3870 *Toll Free Tel:* 877-369-6283 (cust serv) *Fax:* 217-328-9645 *E-mail:* bookawards@ncte.org *Web Site:* ncte.org/awards/ncte-childrens-book-awards, pg 614

Miller, Sarah, National Council of Teachers of English (NCTE), 340 N Neil St, Suite 104, Champaign, IL 61820 *Tel:* 217-328-3870 *Toll Free Tel:* 877-369-6283 (cust serv) *Fax:* 217-328-9645 *E-mail:* customerservice@ncte.org *Web Site:* ncte.org, pg 512

Miller, Sarah, Orbis Pictus Award, 340 N Neil St, Suite 104, Champaign, IL 61820 *Tel:* 217-328-3870 *Toll Free Tel:* 877-369-6283 (cust serv) *Fax:* 217-328-9645 *E-mail:* bookawards@ncte.org *Web Site:* ncte.org/awards/ncte-childrens-book-awards, pg 644

Miller, Sarah, George Orwell Award, 340 N Neil St, Suite 104, Champaign, IL 61820 *Tel:* 217-328-3870 *Toll Free Tel:* 877-369-6283 (cust serv) *Fax:* 217-328-9645 *E-mail:* publiclangaward@ncte.org *Web Site:* ncte.org/awards/george-orwell-award, pg 645

Miller, Sarah, Yale University Press, 302 Temple St, New Haven, CT 06511-8909 *Tel:* 203-432-0960; 203-432-0966 (sales); 401-531-2800 (cust serv) *Toll Free Tel:* 800-405-1619 (cust serv) *Fax:* 203-432-0948; 203-432-8485 (sales); 401-531-2801 (cust serv) *Toll Free Fax:* 800-406-9145 (cust serv) *E-mail:* sales.press@yale.edu (sales); customer.care@triliteral.org (cust serv) *Web Site:* www.yalebooks.com; yalepress.yale.edu/yupbooks, pg 235

Miller, Scott, Trident Media Group LLC, 355 Lexington Ave, 12th fl, New York, NY 10017 *Tel:* 212-333-1511 *E-mail:* info@tridentmediagroup.com; press@tridentmediagroup.com; foreignrights@tridentmediagroup.com; office.assistant@tridentmediagroup.com *Web Site:* www.tridentmediagroup.com, pg 480

Miller, Shaughnessy, Lee & Low Books Inc, 95 Madison Ave, Suite 1205, New York, NY 10016 *Tel:* 212-779-4400 *Toll Free Tel:* 888-320-3190 (ext 28, orders only) *Fax:* 212-683-1894 (orders only); 212-532-6035 *E-mail:* general@leeandlow.com *Web Site:* www.leeandlow.com, pg 114

Miller, Stephen M, Stephen M Miller Inc, 15727 S Madison Dr, Olathe, KS 66062 *Tel:* 913-945-0200 *Web Site:* www.stephenmillerbooks.com, pg 442

Miller, Suzanne, New York City College of Technology Professional & Technical Writing Program, Namm Hall 512, 300 Jay St, Brooklyn, NY 11201 *Tel:* 718-260-5392 *E-mail:* english@citytech.cuny.edu *Web Site:* www.citytech.cuny.edu/english/technical-writing-bs.aspx, pg 563

Miller, Ted, Human Kinetics Inc, 1607 N Market St, Champaign, IL 61820 *Tel:* 217-351-5076 *Toll Free Tel:* 800-747-4457 *Fax:* 217-351-1549 (orders/cust serv) *E-mail:* info@hkusa.com *Web Site:* us.humankinetics.com, pg 97

Miller, Tom, Liza Dawson Associates, 121 W 27 St, Suite 1201, New York, NY 10001 *Tel:* 212-465-9071 *Web Site:* www.lizadawsonassociates.com, pg 455

Miller, Zoe, St Martin's Press, LLC, 120 Broadway, New York, NY 10271 *E-mail:* publicity@stmartins.com; trademarketing@stmartins.com; foreignrights@stmartins.com *Web Site:* us.macmillan.com/smp, pg 181

Miller-Hunter, Jodi, Lynx House Press, 420 W 24 St, Spokane, WA 99203 *Tel:* 509-624-4894 *E-mail:* lynxhousepress@gmail.com *Web Site:* www.lynxhousepress.org, pg 118

Millett, Maya, Random House Publishing Group, 1745 Broadway, New York, NY 10019 *Toll Free Tel:* 800-200-3552 *Web Site:* www.randomhousebooks.com, pg 171

Milligan, M, Wings Press, PO Box 591176, San Antonio, TX 78259 *E-mail:* wingspresspublishing@gmail.com *Web Site:* www.wingspress.com, pg 231

Milliken, Jean Mellichamp, Lyric Poetry Prizes, PO Box 110, Jericho, VT 05465 *E-mail:* themuse@thelyricmagazine.com *Web Site:* thelyricmagazine.com, pg 627

Milliken, Leif, Potomac Books, c/o University of Nebraska Press, 1225 "L" St, Suite 200, Lincoln, NE 68588-0630 *Tel:* 402-472-5937 *Web Site:* www.nebraskapress.unl.edu/potomac/, pg 162

Milliken, Leif, University of Nebraska Press, 1225 "L" St, Suite 200, Lincoln, NE 68588-0630 *Tel:* 402-472-3581; 919-966-7449 (cust serv & foreign orders) *Toll Free Tel:* 800-848-6224 (cust serv & US orders) *Fax:* 402-472-6214; 919-962-2704 (cust serv & foreign orders) *Toll Free Fax:* 800-272-6817 (cust serv & US orders) *E-mail:* presswebmail@unl.edu *Web Site:* www.nebraskapress.unl.edu, pg 218

Millinger, Jenny, Write Now, 900 S Mitchell Dr, Tempe, AZ 85281 *Tel:* 480-921-5700 *Fax:* 480-921-5777 *E-mail:* info@writenow.co *Web Site:* www.writenow.co, pg 678

Milliron, Kerry, Random House Children's Books, c/o Penguin Random House LLC, 1745 Broadway, New York, NY 10019 *Tel:* 212-782-9000 *Web Site:* www.rhcbooks.com, pg 169

Millman, Michael, University of New Mexico Press, One University of New Mexico, Albuquerque, NM 87131-0001 *Tel:* 505-272-7777 *Fax:* 505-277-3343 *E-mail:* custserv@unm.edu (order dept) *Web Site:* unmpress.com, pg 218

Millner, Denene, Simon & Schuster Children's Publishing, 1230 Avenue of the Americas, New York, NY 10020 *Tel:* 212-698-7000 *Web Site:* www.simonandschuster.com/kids; www.simonandschuster.com/teen; simonandschuster.net; simonandschuster.biz, pg 189

Mills, Elizabeth M, Temporal Mechanical Press, 6760 Hwy 7, Estes Park, CO 80517-6404 *Tel:* 970-586-4706 *E-mail:* info@enosmills.com *Web Site:* www.enosmills.com, pg 204

Mills, Eryn, Temporal Mechanical Press, 6760 Hwy 7, Estes Park, CO 80517-6404 *Tel:* 970-586-4706 *E-mail:* info@enosmills.com *Web Site:* www.enosmills.com, pg 204

Mills, Kathleen, Kathleen Mills Editorial Services, 327 E King St, Chardon, OH 44024 *Tel:* 440-285-4347 *E-mail:* mills_edit@yahoo.com, pg 443

Mills, Kevin, The Tuesday Agency, 404 E College St, Suite 408, Iowa City, IA 52240 *Tel:* 319-338-7080; 319-400-9031 (cell) *E-mail:* info@tuesdayagency.com *Web Site:* tuesdayagency.com, pg 487

Mills, Megan, Books on Tape™, 1745 Broadway, New York, NY 10019 *Toll Free Tel:* 800-733-3000 (cust serv) *Toll Free Fax:* 800-940-7046 *Web Site:* PenguinRandomHouseLibrary.com, pg 34

Mills, Tracey, Casemate | publishers, 1950 Lawrence Rd, Havertown, PA 19083 *Tel:* 610-853-9131 *Fax:* 610-853-9146 *E-mail:* casemate@casematepublishers.com *Web Site:* www.casematepublishers.com, pg 42

Milne, James PhD, ACS Publications, 1155 16 St NW, Washington, DC 20036 *Tel:* 202-872-4600 *Toll Free Tel:* 800-227-5558 (US) *Fax:* 202-872-6067 *E-mail:* help@acs.org *Web Site:* pubs.acs.org; publish.acs.org/publish, pg 4

Mimms, Cory, Pomegranate Communications Inc, 105 SE 18 Ave, Portland, OR 97214 *Tel:* 503-328-6500 *Toll Free Tel:* 800-227-1428 *Fax:* 503-328-9330 *Toll Free Fax:* 800-848-4376 *E-mail:* hello@pomegranate.com *Web Site:* www.pomegranate.com, pg 162

Min, Erica, Random House Publishing Group, 1745 Broadway, New York, NY 10019 *Toll Free Tel:* 800-200-3552 *Web Site:* www.randomhousebooks.com, pg 171

Minar, Scott, Marick Press, 1342 Three Mile Dr, Grosse Pointe Park, MI 48230 *Tel:* 313-407-9236 *E-mail:* orders@marickpress.com; info@marickpress.com *Web Site:* www.marickpress.com, pg 125

Minchew, Laura, Thomas Nelson, 501 Nelson Place, Nashville, TN 37214 *Tel:* 615-889-9000 *Toll Free Tel:* 800-251-4000 *Web Site:* www.thomasnelson.com, pg 206

Minchew, Laura, Zondervan, 3900 Sparks Dr SE, Grand Rapids, MI 49546 *Tel:* 616-698-6900 *Toll Free Tel:* 800-226-1122; 800-727-1309 (retail orders) *Fax:* 616-698-3350 *Toll Free Fax:* 800-698-3256 (retail orders) *E-mail:* customercare@harpercollins.com *Web Site:* www.zondervan.com, pg 236

Minkin, James, The Dawn Horse Press, 12040 N Seigler Rd, Middletown, CA 95461 Tel: 707-928-6590 Toll Free Tel: 877-770-0772 Fax: 707-928-5068 E-mail: dhp@adidam.org Web Site: www.dawnhorsepress.com, pg 57

Mintz, Laura, The Monacelli Press, 65 Bleecker St, 8th fl, New York, NY 10012 Tel: 212-652-5400 E-mail: contact@monacellipress.com Web Site: www.phaidon.com/monacelli, pg 133

Mintzer, Conor, Henry Holt and Company, LLC, 120 Broadway, 23rd fl, New York, NY 10271 Tel: 646-307-5151 Toll Free Tel: 888-330-8477 (orders) Fax: 646-307-5285 Web Site: www.henryholt.com, pg 94

Miracle, Tracy, Candlewick Press, 99 Dover St, Somerville, MA 02144-2825 Tel: 617-661-3330 Fax: 617-661-0565 E-mail: bigbear@candlewick.com; salesinfo@candlewick.com Web Site: candlewick.com, pg 39

Miracle, Tracy, Holiday House Publishing Inc, 50 Broad St, New York, NY 10004 Tel: 212-688-0085 Fax: 212-421-6134 E-mail: info@holidayhouse.com Web Site: www.holidayhouse.com, pg 94

Miracle, Tracy, Peachtree Publishing Co Inc, 1700 Chattahoochee Ave, Atlanta, GA 30318-2112 Tel: 404-876-8761 Toll Free Tel: 800-241-0113 Fax: 404-875-2578 Toll Free Fax: 800-875-8909 E-mail: hello@peachtree-online.com; orders@peachtree-online.com; sales@peachtree-online.com Web Site: www.peachtreebooks.com; www.peachtree-online.com, pg 153

Miranda, Isabella, Farrar, Straus & Giroux, LLC, 120 Broadway, New York, NY 10271 Tel: 212-741-6900 E-mail: fsg.publicity@fsgbooks.com; sales@fsgbooks.com Web Site: us.macmillan.com/fsg, pg 70

Miranda, Joseph, Bloomsbury Academic, 1385 Broadway, 5th fl, New York, NY 10018 Tel: 212-419-5300 Web Site: www.bloomsbury.com/us/academic, pg 31

Miranda, Joseph, Fairchild Books, 1385 Broadway, 5th fl, New York, NY 10018 Tel: 212-419-5300 Toll Free Tel: 800-932-4724; 888-330-8477 (orders) Web Site: www.bloomsbury.com/us/discover/bloomsbury-academic/fairchild-books/, pg 69

Miranda, Lori, Cognizant Communication Corp, PO Box 37, Putnam Valley, NY 10579-0037 Tel: 845-603-6440 Fax: 845-603-6442 E-mail: inquiries@cognizantcommunication.com; sales@cognizantcommunication.com Web Site: www.cognizantcommunication.com, pg 50

Miranda, Robert N, Cognizant Communication Corp, PO Box 37, Putnam Valley, NY 10579-0037 Tel: 845-603-6440 Fax: 845-603-6442 E-mail: inquiries@cognizantcommunication.com; sales@cognizantcommunication.com Web Site: www.cognizantcommunication.com, pg 50

Mireles-Guerrero, Ashley, Familius, PO Box 1249, Reedley, CA 93654 Tel: 559-876-2170 Fax: 559-876-2180 E-mail: orders@familius.com Web Site: www.familius.com, pg 69

Mirolla, Michael, Guernica Editions Inc, 287 Templemead Dr, Hamilton, ON L8W 2W4, Canada Tel: 905-599-5304 E-mail: info@guernicaeditions.com Web Site: www.guernicaeditions.com; www.facebook.com/guernicaed, pg 408

Mirrer, Louise, Children's History Book Prize, 170 Central Park W, New York, NY 10024 Tel: 212-873-3400 Fax: 212-595-5707 E-mail: info@nyhistory.org Web Site: www.nyhistory.org/childrens-museum/connect/book-prize, pg 588

Misarti, Alicia, Adult Writers Workshops, Finn House, 102 W Wiggin St, Gambier, OH 43022-9623 Tel: 740-427-5196 Fax: 740-427-5417 E-mail: writers@kenyonreview.org Web Site: kenyonreview.org/adult-writers, pg 553

Misarti, Alicia, Young Writers Workshops, Finn House, 102 W Wiggin St, Gambier, OH 43022-9623 Tel: 740-427-5391 Fax: 740-427-5417 E-mail: youngwriters@kenyonreview.org Web Site: kenyonreview.org/high-school-workshops, pg 559

Mishagina, Natalia, Institute for Research on Public Policy (IRPP), 1470 Peel St, No 200, Montreal, QC H3A 1T1, Canada Tel: 514-985-2461 Fax: 514-985-2559 E-mail: irpp@irpp.org Web Site: irpp.org, pg 410

Mishra, Pradeep C, Arkansas State University Graphic Communications Program, Dept of Media, PO Box 1930, State University, AR 72467-1930 Tel: 870-972-3114 Fax: 870-972-3321 Web Site: www.astate.edu, pg 561

Miskin, Michael J, Tapestry Press Ltd, 19 Nashoba Rd, Littleton, MA 01460 Tel: 978-486-0200 Toll Free Tel: 800-535-2007 E-mail: publish@tapestrypress.com Web Site: www.tapestrypress.com, pg 202

Mistry, Jaclyn, Penguin Random House Canada, a Penguin Random House company, 320 Front St W, Suite 1400, Toronto, ON M5V 3B6, Canada Tel: 416-364-4449 Toll Free Tel: 888-523-9292 (cust serv) E-mail: canadaweb@penguinrandomhouse.com; customerservicescanada@penguinrandomhouse.com Web Site: www.penguinrandomhouse.ca, pg 416

Mitchell, Ashley, Simon & Schuster Children's Publishing, 1230 Avenue of the Americas, New York, NY 10020 Tel: 212-698-7000 Web Site: www.simonandschuster.com/kids; www.simonandschuster.com/teen; simonandschuster.net; simonandschuster.biz, pg 189

Mitchell, Brittany, Chronicle Books LLC, 680 Second St, San Francisco, CA 94107 Tel: 415-537-4200 Fax: 415-537-4460 (perms) E-mail: hello@chroniclebooks.com; subrights@chroniclebooks.com Web Site: www.chroniclebooks.com, pg 47

Mitchell, Catherine, Claude Aubry Award, c/o The Canadian Children's Book Ctr, 425 Adelaide St W, Suite 200, Toronto, ON M5V 3C1, Canada Fax: 416-975-8970 E-mail: aubry@ibby-canada.org Web Site: www.ibby-canada.org/awards/claude-aubry-award/, pg 575

Mitchell, David, The Guilford Press, 370 Seventh Ave, Suite 1200, New York, NY 10001-1020 Tel: 212-431-9800 Toll Free Tel: 800-365-7006 Fax: 212-966-6708 E-mail: info@guilford.com; orders@guilford.com Web Site: www.guilford.com, pg 82

Mitchell, Elizabeth, HarperCollins Publishers LLC, 195 Broadway, New York, NY 10007 Tel: 212-207-7000 Web Site: www.harpercollins.com, pg 86

Mitchell, Dr Francis, New World Publishing (Canada), PO Box 36075, Halifax, NS B3J 3S9, Canada Tel: 902-576-2055 (inquiries) Toll Free Tel: 877-211-3334 (orders) Fax: 902-576-2095 Web Site: www.newworldpublishing.com, pg 414

Mitchell, Jack, Lumina Datamatics Inc, 600 Cordwainer Dr, Unit 103, Norwell, MA 02061 Tel: 508-746-0300 Fax: 508-746-3233 E-mail: marketing@luminad.com Web Site: www.luminadatamatics.com, pg 442

Mitchell, Krista, Canadian Scholars, 425 Adelaide St W, Suite 200, Toronto, ON M5V 3C1, Canada Tel: 416-929-2774 Toll Free Tel: 800-463-1998 E-mail: info@canadianscholars.ca; editorial@canadianscholars.ca Web Site: www.canadianscholars.ca; www.womenspress.ca, pg 399

Mitchell, Margaret, Sun Valley Writers' Conference (SVWC), Galleria Bldg, 2nd fl, 351 Leadville Ave N, Ketchum, ID 83340 Tel: 208-726-5454 E-mail: info@svwc.com Web Site: svwc.com, pg 558

Mitchell, Megan, Random House Children's Books, c/o Penguin Random House LLC, 1745 Broadway, New York, NY 10019 Tel: 212-782-9000 Web Site: www.rhcbooks.com, pg 170

Mitchell, Morgan, Macmillan, 120 Broadway, 22nd fl, New York, NY 10271 E-mail: press.inquiries@macmillan.com Web Site: us.macmillan.com, pg 122

Mitchell, Nicole F, University of Washington Press, 4333 Brooklyn Ave NE, Seattle, WA 98105-9570 Toll Free Tel: 800-537-5487 (orders) Fax: 206-543-3932; 410-516-6998 (orders) E-mail: uwapress@uw.edu Web Site: uwapress.uw.edu, pg 220

Mitchell, Steven L, Prometheus Books, 59 John Glenn Dr, Amherst, NY 14228-2119 Fax: 716-691-0137 E-mail: marketing@prometheusbooks.com; editorial@prometheusbooks.com; rights@prometheusbooks.com Web Site: www.prometheusbooks.com, pg 166

Mitchell, Suzanne, HarperCollins Publishers LLC, 195 Broadway, New York, NY 10007 Tel: 212-207-7000 Web Site: www.harpercollins.com, pg 86

Mitchell, Ted, American Council on Education (ACE), One Dupont Circle NW, Washington, DC 20036 Tel: 202-939-9300 Web Site: www.acenet.edu, pg 9, 495

Mitchem, Gary, McFarland, 960 NC Hwy 88 W, Jefferson, NC 28640 Tel: 336-246-4460 Toll Free Tel: 800-253-2187 (orders) Fax: 336-246-5018; 336-246-4403 (orders) E-mail: info@mcfarlandpub.com Web Site: mcfarlandbooks.com, pg 127

Miteva, Jodi, Close Up Publishing, 671 N Glebe Rd, Suite 900, Arlington, VA 22203 Tel: 703-706-3300 Toll Free Tel: 800-CLOSE-UP (256-7387) E-mail: info@closeup.org Web Site: www.closeup.org, pg 49

Mitsuda, Kristi, Running Press, 1290 Avenue of the Americas, New York, NY 10104 Tel: 212-364-1100 Toll Free Tel: 800-759-0190 (cust serv) Fax: 212-364-0933 (intl orders) Toll Free Fax: 800-286-9471 (cust serv) E-mail: customer.service@hbgusa.com; orders@hbgusa.com Web Site: www.hachettebookgroup.com/imprint/running-press/; www.moon.com (Moon Travel Guides), pg 178

Miura, Robin, Blair, 905 W Main St, Suite 19 D-1, Durham, NC 27701 Tel: 919-682-0555 E-mail: customersupport@blair.com Web Site: www.blairpub.com, pg 30

Mixon, Jennifer, University Press of Mississippi, 3825 Ridgewood Rd, Jackson, MS 39211-6492 Tel: 601-432-6205 Toll Free Tel: 800-737-7788 (orders & cust serv) Fax: 601-432-6217 E-mail: press@mississippi.edu Web Site: www.upress.state.ms.us, pg 222

Mize, Angelique, American Medical Writers Association (AMWA), 9841 Washingtonian Blvd, Suite 500-26, Gaithersburg, MD 20878 Tel: 240-238-0940 Fax: 301-294-9006 E-mail: amwa@amwa.org Web Site: www.amwa.org, pg 496

Mize, Angelique, Medical Writing & Communication Conference, 9841 Washingtonian Blvd, Suite 500-26, Gaithersburg, MD 20878 Tel: 240-238-0940 Fax: 301-294-9006 E-mail: amwa@amwa.org; conference@amwa.org Web Site: www.amwa.org, pg 556

Mlynek, Emily, Tor Publishing Group, 120 Broadway, New York, NY 10271 Toll Free Tel: 800-455-0340 (Macmillan) E-mail: torpublicity@tor.com; forgepublicity@forgebooks.com Web Site: us.macmillan.com/torpublishinggroup, pg 208

Moberg, Valentina, CALIBA Golden Poppy Awards, 100 Black Diamond Rd, Stonyford, CA 95979 Tel: 415-561-7686 E-mail: info@caliballiance.org Web Site: caliballiance.org/golden-poppy-awards.html, pg 585

Moberg, Valentina, California Independent Booksellers Alliance (CALIBA), 100 Black Diamond Rd, Stonyford, CA 95979 Tel: 415-561-7686 E-mail: info@caliballiance.org Web Site: caliballiance.org, pg 502

Moberly, Laura, Legacy Bound, 5 N Central Ave, Ely, MN 55731 Tel: Legacy Bound Toll Free Tel: 800-909-9698 E-mail: orders@legacybound.net Web Site: www.legacybound.net, pg 114

Mobley, Jen-Scott, Jane Chambers Playwriting Award, Georgetown University, 108 David Performing Arts Ctr, Box 571063, 37 & "O" St, NW, Washington, DC 20057-1063 Web Site: www.athe.org/page/jane_chambers; www.womenandtheatreprogram.com/jane-chambers, pg 588

Mock, Eli, Harry N Abrams Inc, 195 Broadway, 9th fl, New York, NY 10007 Tel: 212-206-7715 Toll Free Tel: 800-345-1359 Fax: 212-645-8437 E-mail: abrams@abramsbooks.com; publicity@abramsbooks.com; sales@abramsbooks.com Web Site: www.abramsbooks.com, pg 2

Mocklow, Courtney, Random House Publishing Group, 1745 Broadway, New York, NY 10019 *Toll Free Tel:* 800-200-3552 *Web Site:* www.randomhousebooks.com, pg 171

Mode-Stavros, Marcia, Sun Valley Writers' Conference (SVWC), Galleria Bldg, 2nd fl, 351 Leadville Ave N, Ketchum, ID 83340 *Tel:* 208-726-5454 *E-mail:* info@svwc.com *Web Site:* svwc.com, pg 558

Modell, Ruby, Phaidon, 65 Bleecker St, 8th fl, New York, NY 10012 *Tel:* 212-652-5400 *Toll Free Tel:* 800-759-0190 (cust serv) *Fax:* 212-652-5410 *Toll Free Fax:* 800-286-9471 (cust serv) *E-mail:* enquiries@phaidon.com *Web Site:* www.phaidon.com, pg 159

Moe, Madeleine, Chronicle Books LLC, 680 Second St, San Francisco, CA 94107 *Tel:* 415-537-4200 *Fax:* 415-537-4460 (perms) *E-mail:* hello@chroniclebooks.com; subrights@chroniclebooks.com *Web Site:* www.chroniclebooks.com, pg 47

Moeckel, Prof Thorpe, Hollins University-Jackson Center for Creative Writing, 7916 Williamson Rd, Roanoke, VA 24020 *Tel:* 540-362-6317 *E-mail:* creative.writing@hollins.edu *Web Site:* www.hollins.edu; www.hollins.edu/jacksoncenter/index.shtml, pg 563

Moeller, Kristen, Waterside Productions Inc, 2055 Oxford Ave, Cardiff, CA 92007 *Tel:* 760-632-9190 *Fax:* 760-632-9295 *E-mail:* admin@waterside.com *Web Site:* www.waterside.com, pg 481

Moen, Jeff, University of Minnesota Press, 111 Third Ave S, Suite 290, Minneapolis, MN 55401-2520 *Tel:* 612-301-1990 *Fax:* 612-301-1980 *E-mail:* ump@umn.edu *Web Site:* www.upress.umn.edu, pg 217

Moench, David, Random House Publishing Group, 1745 Broadway, New York, NY 10019 *Toll Free Tel:* 800-200-3552 *Web Site:* www.randomhousebooks.com, pg 170

Moffet, Jacinthe, Editions Hurtubise, 1815, ave de Lorimier, Montreal, QC H2K 3W6, Canada *Tel:* 514-523-1523 *Toll Free Tel:* 800-361-1664 *Web Site:* editionshurtubise.com, pg 404

Moffett, Sandy, California Writers Club (CWC), PO Box 201, Danville, CA 94526 *E-mail:* membership@calwriters.org; advertising-promotion@calwriters.org *Web Site:* calwriters.org, pg 502

Moggy, Dianne, Harlequin Enterprises Ltd, Bay Adelaide Centre, East Tower, 22 Adelaide St W, 41st fl, Toronto, ON M5H 4E3, Canada *Tel:* 416-445-5860 *Toll Free Tel:* 888-432-4879; 800-370-5838 (ebook inquiries) *E-mail:* customerservice@harlequin.com *Web Site:* www.harlequin.com, pg 409

Mogollon, Abby, The University of Arizona Press, 1510 E University Blvd, Tucson, AZ 85721 *Tel:* 520-621-1441 *Toll Free Tel:* 800-621-2736 (orders) *Fax:* 520-621-8899 *Toll Free Fax:* 800-621-8476 (orders) *E-mail:* uap@uapress.arizona.edu *Web Site:* www.uapress.arizona.edu, pg 214

Mohammed, Zuha, Sourcebooks LLC, 1935 Brookdale Rd, Suite 139, Naperville, IL 60563 *Tel:* 630-961-3900 *Toll Free Tel:* 800-432-7444 *Fax:* 630-961-2168 *E-mail:* info@sourcebooks.com *Web Site:* www.sourcebooks.com, pg 195

Mohan, Joseph, The Art Institute of Chicago, 111 S Michigan Ave, Chicago, IL 60603-6404 *Tel:* 312-443-3600 *Toll Free Tel:* 855-301-9612 *E-mail:* aicshop@artic.edu *Web Site:* www.artic.edu/print-publications; shop.artic.edu, pg 17

Mohan, Joseph, The Museum of Modern Art (MoMA), Publications Dept, 11 W 53 St, New York, NY 10019 *Tel:* 212-708-9400 *E-mail:* moma_publications@moma.org *Web Site:* www.moma.org, pg 135

Mohney, Chris, Zagat Inc, 424 Broadway, 5th fl, New York, NY 10013 *E-mail:* feedback@zagat.com *Web Site:* www.zagat.com, pg 236

Mohr, Abby, Atria Books, 1230 Avenue of the Americas, New York, NY 10020 *Tel:* 212-698-7000 *Fax:* 212-698-7007 *Web Site:* www.simonandschuster.com, pg 21

Mohrfeld, Jenny, Andrews McMeel Publishing LLC, 1130 Walnut St, Kansas City, MO 64106-2109 *Tel:* 816-581-7500 *Toll Free Tel:* 800-851-8923 *Web Site:* www.andrewsmcmeel.com; publishing.andrewsmcmeel.com, pg 14

Mohyde, Colleen, The Doe Coover Agency, PO Box 668, Winchester, MA 01890 *Tel:* 781-721-6000 *Fax:* 781-721-6727 *E-mail:* info@doecooveragency.com *Web Site:* www.doecooveragency.com, pg 454

Moisan, Christopher, Little, Brown and Company, 1290 Avenue of the Americas, New York, NY 10104 *Tel:* 212-364-1100 *Fax:* 212-364-0952 *E-mail:* firstname.lastname@hbgusa.com *Web Site:* www.hachettebookgroup.com/imprint/little-brown-and-company/, pg 118

Mojica, JoAnne, Scholastic Trade Publishing, 557 Broadway, New York, NY 10012 *Tel:* 212-343-6100; 212-343-4685 (export sales) *Fax:* 212-343-4714 (export sales) *Web Site:* www.scholastic.com, pg 184

Mojzes, Erica, House of Anansi Press Inc, 128 Sterling Rd, Lower Level, Toronto, ON M6R 2B7, Canada *Tel:* 416-363-4343 *Fax:* 416-363-1017 *E-mail:* customerservice@houseofanansi.com *Web Site:* houseofanansi.com, pg 409

Mol, Leah, Harlequin Enterprises Ltd, 195 Broadway, 24th fl, New York, NY 10007 *Tel:* 212-207-7000 *Toll Free Tel:* 888-432-4879; 800-370-5838 (ebooks) *E-mail:* customerservice@harlequin.com *Web Site:* www.harlequin.com/shop/index.html; corporate.harlequin.com, pg 85

Molano Rodriguez, Diego, Macmillan, 120 Broadway, 22nd fl, New York, NY 10271 *E-mail:* press.inquiries@macmillan.com *Web Site:* us.macmillan.com, pg 122

Molina, Stefanie, The Jennifer DeChiara Literary Agency, 245 Park Ave, 39th fl, New York, NY 10167 *Tel:* 212-372-8989 *Web Site:* www.jdlit.com, pg 455

Molina, Stefanie, Ladderbird Literary Agency, 460 Yellow Brick Rd, Orange, CT 06477 *Tel:* 203-290-1703 *Web Site:* www.ladderbird.com, pg 466

Molito, Justin, Writers Guild of America, East (WGAE), 250 Hudson St, Suite 700, New York, NY 10013 *Tel:* 212-767-7800 *Fax:* 212-582-1909 *Web Site:* www.wgaeast.org, pg 522

Molland, Rachel, HarperCollins Publishers LLC, 195 Broadway, New York, NY 10007 *Tel:* 212-207-7000 *Web Site:* www.harpercollins.com, pg 87

Moller, Marilyn, W W Norton & Company Inc, 500 Fifth Ave, New York, NY 10110-0017 *Tel:* 212-354-5500 *Toll Free Tel:* 800-233-4830 (orders & cust serv) *Fax:* 212-869-0856 *Toll Free Fax:* 800-458-6515 *E-mail:* orders@wwnorton.com *Web Site:* wwnorton.com, pg 143

Mollica, Greg, Random House Publishing Group, 1745 Broadway, New York, NY 10019 *Toll Free Tel:* 800-200-3552 *Web Site:* www.randomhousebooks.com, pg 170

Molnar, Szilvia, Sterling Lord Literistic Inc, 594 Broadway, Suite 205, New York, NY 10012 *Tel:* 212-780-6050 *Fax:* 212-780-6095 *E-mail:* info@sll.com *Web Site:* www.sll.com, pg 477

Monacelli, Gianfranco, The Monacelli Press, 65 Bleecker St, 8th fl, New York, NY 10012 *Tel:* 212-652-5400 *E-mail:* contact@monacellipress.com *Web Site:* www.phaidon.com/monacelli, pg 133

Monaco, Danielle, Hay House LLC, PO Box 5100, Carlsbad, CA 92018-5100 *Tel:* 760-431-7695 (ext 1, intl) *Toll Free Tel:* 800-654-5126 (ext 1, US) *Toll Free Fax:* 800-650-5115 *Web Site:* www.hayhouse.com, pg 89

Monaco, Kathryn, Penguin Random House LLC, 1745 Broadway, New York, NY 10019 *Tel:* 212-782-9000 *Toll Free Tel:* 800-726-0600 *Web Site:* www.penguinrandomhouse.com, pg 155

Monaco, Kevin, John Wiley & Sons Inc, 111 River St, Hoboken, NJ 07030-5774 *Tel:* 201-748-6000 *Toll Free Tel:* 800-225-5945 (cust serv) *Fax:* 201-748-6088 *Web Site:* www.wiley.com, pg 230

Monaco, Lauren, Hachette Book Group Inc, 1290 Avenue of the Americas, New York, NY 10104 *Tel:* 212-364-1100 *Toll Free Tel:* 800-759-0190 (cust serv) *Fax:* 212-364-0933 (intl orders) *Toll Free Fax:* 800-286-9471 (cust serv) *E-mail:* customer.service@hbgusa.com; orders@hbgusa.com *Web Site:* www.hachettebookgroup.com, pg 83

Monaghan, Katie, Scribner, 1230 Avenue of the Americas, New York, NY 10020 *Web Site:* www.simonandschusterpublishing.com/scribner/, pg 185

Monahan, Math, Simon & Schuster, 1230 Avenue of the Americas, New York, NY 10020 *Tel:* 212-698-7000 *Toll Free Tel:* 800-223-2348 (cust serv); 800-223-2336 (orders) *Toll Free Fax:* 800-943-9831 (orders) *Web Site:* simonandschusterpublishing.com/simonandschuster/, pg 188

Moncy, Alee, Workman Publishing, 1290 Avenue of the Americas, New York, NY 10104 *Toll Free Tel:* 800-759-0190 *Fax:* 212-364-0950 *E-mail:* workman-inquiry@hbgusa.com *Web Site:* www.hachettebookgroup.com/imprint/workman-publishing-company/, pg 232

Monday, Sydnee, Kokila, c/o Penguin Random House LLC, 1745 Broadway, New York, NY 10019 *Tel:* 212-782-9000 *Web Site:* www.penguin.com/kokila-books-overview/, pg 111

Mondesir, Shannon, Random House Publishing Group, 1745 Broadway, New York, NY 10019 *Toll Free Tel:* 800-200-3552 *Web Site:* www.randomhousebooks.com, pg 171

Mondloch, Ben, Sleeping Bear Press™, 2395 S Huron Pkwy, Suite 200, Ann Arbor, MI 48104 *Toll Free Tel:* 800-487-2323 *Fax:* 734-794-0004 *E-mail:* customerservice@sleepingbearpress.com *Web Site:* www.sleepingbearpress.com, pg 191

Monds, Becky, Thomas Nelson, 501 Nelson Place, Nashville, TN 37214 *Tel:* 615-889-9000 *Toll Free Tel:* 800-251-4000 *Web Site:* www.thomasnelson.com, pg 206

Monds, Becky, Zondervan, 3900 Sparks Dr SE, Grand Rapids, MI 49546 *Tel:* 616-698-6900 *Toll Free Tel:* 800-226-1122; 800-727-1309 (retail orders) *Fax:* 616-698-3350 *Toll Free Fax:* 800-698-3256 (retail orders) *E-mail:* customercare@harpercollins.com *Web Site:* www.zondervan.com, pg 236

Mones, Mark, University of Virginia Press, PO Box 400318, Charlottesville, VA 22904-4318 *Tel:* 434-924-3469 (cust serv) *Toll Free Tel:* 800-831-3406 *Fax:* 434-982-2655 *Toll Free Fax:* 877-288-6400 *E-mail:* vapress@virginia.edu *Web Site:* www.upress.virginia.edu, pg 220

Monette, Lindsay, Christian Schools International (CSI), 99 Monroe Ave NW, Suite 200, Grand Rapids, MI 49503 *Tel:* 616-957-1070 *Toll Free Tel:* 800-635-8288 *Web Site:* www.csionline.org, pg 47

Monge, Sr Marlyn Evangelina, Pauline Books & Media, 50 Saint Paul's Ave, Boston, MA 02130 *Tel:* 617-522-8911 *Toll Free Tel:* 800-876-4463 (orders); 800-836-9723 (cust serv) *Fax:* 617-541-9805 *E-mail:* editorial@paulinemedia.com (ms submissions); orderentry@pauline.org (cust serv) *Web Site:* www.pauline.org/pbmpublishing, pg 152

Mongelli, Gabriella, Little, Brown and Company, 1290 Avenue of the Americas, New York, NY 10104 *Tel:* 212-364-1100 *Fax:* 212-364-0952 *E-mail:* firstname.lastname@hbgusa.com *Web Site:* www.hachettebookgroup.com/imprint/little-brown-and-company/, pg 118

Monical, Olivia, Chronicle Books LLC, 680 Second St, San Francisco, CA 94107 *Tel:* 415-537-4200 *Fax:* 415-537-4460 (perms) *E-mail:* hello@chroniclebooks.com; subrights@chroniclebooks.com *Web Site:* www.chroniclebooks.com, pg 48

Monique, Danielle, Crystal Kite Awards, 6363 Wilshire Blvd, Suite 425, Los Angeles, CA 90048 *Tel:* 323-782-1010 *E-mail:* info@scbwi.org *Web Site:* www.scbwi.org/awards/crystal-kite-member-choice-award, pg 593

Monique, Danielle, Karen & Philip Cushman Late Bloomer Award, 6363 Wilshire Blvd, Suite 425, Los Angeles, CA 90048 Tel: 323-782-1010 E-mail: info@scbwi.org Web Site: www.scbwi.org/awards-and-grants-new, pg 594

Monique, Danielle, Golden Kite Awards, 6363 Wilshire Blvd, Suite 425, Los Angeles, CA 90048 Tel: 323-782-1010 E-mail: info@scbwi.org Web Site: www.scbwi.org/awards/golden-kite-award, pg 607

Monique, Danielle, Magazine Merit Awards, 6363 Wilshire Blvd, Suite 425, Los Angeles, CA 90048 Tel: 323-782-1010 E-mail: info@scbwi.org Web Site: www.scbwi.org/awards/magazine-merit-award, pg 628

Monique, Danielle, On-the-Verge Emerging Voices Award, 6363 Wilshire Blvd, Suite 425, Los Angeles, CA 90048 Tel: 323-782-1010 E-mail: info@scbwi.org Web Site: www.scbwi.org/awards/grants/on-the-verge-emerging-voices-grant, pg 644

Monique, Danielle, SCBWI Work-In-Progress Awards, 6363 Wilshire Blvd, Suite 425, Los Angeles, CA 90048 Tel: 323-782-1010 E-mail: info@scbwi.org Web Site: www.scbwi.org/awards/grants/work-in-progress-grants, pg 660

Monique, Danielle, Society of Children's Book Writers & Illustrators (SCBWI), 6363 Wilshire Blvd, Suite 425, Los Angeles, CA 90048 Tel: 323-782-1010 E-mail: membership@scbwi.org Web Site: www.scbwi.org, pg 520

Monique, Danielle, Spark Award, 6363 Wilshire Blvd, Suite 425, Los Angeles, CA 90048 Tel: 323-782-1010 E-mail: grants@scbwi.org; info@scbwi.org Web Site: www.scbwi.org, pg 665

Monroe, Elvira, Wide World Publishing, PO Box 476, San Carlos, CA 94070-0476 Tel: 650-593-2839 E-mail: wwpbl@aol.com Web Site: widewordpublishing.com, pg 229

Monroe, Jen, Berkley, c/o Penguin Random House LLC, 1745 Broadway, 19th fl, New York, NY 10019 Tel: 212-366-2000 Web Site: www.penguin.com/publishers/berkley/; www.penguin.com/ace-overview/, pg 28

Monson, Tyler, Sterling Lord Literistic Inc, 594 Broadway, Suite 205, New York, NY 10012 Tel: 212-780-6050 Fax: 212-780-6095 E-mail: info@sll.com Web Site: www.sll.com, pg 477

Montagne, Joseph, Harry N Abrams Inc, 195 Broadway, 9th fl, New York, NY 10007 Tel: 212-206-7715 Toll Free Tel: 800-345-1359 Fax: 212-645-8437 E-mail: abrams@abramsbooks.com; publicity@abramsbooks.com; sales@abramsbooks.com Web Site: www.abramsbooks.com, pg 2

Montague, Anna, HarperCollins Publishers LLC, 195 Broadway, New York, NY 10007 Tel: 212-207-7000 Web Site: www.harpercollins.com, pg 87

Montague, Kestrel, Wisdom Publications Inc, 199 Elm St, Somerville, MA 02144 Tel: 617-776-7416 Toll Free Tel: 800-272-4050 (orders) Fax: 617-776-7841 E-mail: submission@wisdompubs.org Web Site: wisdomexperience.org, pg 231

Montague, Larry N, Technical Association of the Pulp & Paper Industry (TAPPI), 15 Technology Pkwy S, Suite 115, Peachtree Corners, GA 30092 Tel: 770-446-1400 Toll Free Tel: 800-332-8686 (US); 800-446-9431 (CN) Fax: 770-446-6947 E-mail: memberconnection@tappi.org Web Site: www.tappi.org, pg 521

Montague, Michelle, Candlewick Press, 99 Dover St, Somerville, MA 02144-2825 Tel: 617-661-3330 Fax: 617-661-0565 E-mail: bigbear@candlewick.com; salesinfo@candlewick.com Web Site: candlewick.com, pg 39

Montague, Michelle, Holiday House Publishing Inc, 50 Broad St, New York, NY 10004 Tel: 212-688-0085 Fax: 212-421-6134 E-mail: info@holidayhouse.com Web Site: www.holidayhouse.com, pg 94

Montague, Michelle, Peachtree Publishing Co Inc, 1700 Chattahoochee Ave, Atlanta, GA 30318-2112 Tel: 404-876-8761 Toll Free Tel: 800-241-0113 Fax: 404-875-2578 Toll Free Fax: 800-875-8909 E-mail: hello@peachtree-online.com; orders@peachtree-online.com; sales@peachtree-online.com Web Site: www.peachtreebooks.com; www.peachtree-online.com, pg 153

Montalto-Giannini, Chiara, Writers Guild of America, East (WGAE), 250 Hudson St, Suite 700, New York, NY 10013 Tel: 212-767-7800 Fax: 212-582-1909 Web Site: www.wgaeast.org, pg 522

Montanari, Dylan, University of Chicago Press, 1427 E 60 St, Chicago, IL 60637-2954 Tel: 773-702-7700; 773-702-7600 Toll Free Tel: 800-621-2736 (orders) Fax: 773-702-9756; 773-660-2235 (orders); 773-702-2708 E-mail: custserv@press.uchicago.edu; marketing@press.uchicago.edu Web Site: www.press.uchicago.edu, pg 215

Montebello, Lisa, Alfred A Knopf, c/o Penguin Random House LLC, 1745 Broadway, New York, NY 10019 Tel: 212-751-2600 Fax: 212-940-7390 (dom rts); 212-572-2662 (foreign rts) Web Site: knopfdoubleday.com/imprint/knopf/; knopfdoubleday.com, pg 110

Monteith, Barnas, Tumblehome Learning Inc, 201 Newbury St, Suite 201, Boston, MA 02116 E-mail: info@tumblehomelearning.com Web Site: www.tumblehomelearning.com, pg 210

Montgomery, Brandy, Piano Press, 1425 Ocean Ave, Suite 5, Del Mar, CA 92014 Tel: 619-884-1401 E-mail: pianopress@pianopress.com Web Site: www.pianopress.com, pg 159

Montgomery, Michele, RISING STAR Award, PO Box 190, Jefferson, OR 97352 E-mail: risingstar@womenfictionwriters.org Web Site: wfwa.memberclicks.net/rising-star-award, pg 656

Montgomery, Michele, STAR Award, PO Box 190, Jefferson, OR 97352 E-mail: staraward@womenfictionwriters.org Web Site: wfwa.memberclicks.net/star-award, pg 666

Montgomery, Michele, Women's Fiction Writers Association (WFWA), PO Box 190, Jefferson, OR 97352 E-mail: communications@womensfictionwriters.org; membership@womensfictionwriters.org; programs@womensfictionwriters.org Web Site: www.womensfictionwriters.org, pg 522

Monti, Joe, Simon & Schuster, 1230 Avenue of the Americas, New York, NY 10020 Tel: 212-698-7000 Toll Free Tel: 800-223-2348 (cust serv); 800-223-2336 (orders) Toll Free Fax: 800-943-9831 (orders) Web Site: simonandschusterpublishing.com/simonandschuster/, pg 188

Monturio, Tayla, Harry N Abrams Inc, 195 Broadway, 9th fl, New York, NY 10007 Tel: 212-206-7715 Toll Free Tel: 800-345-1359 Fax: 212-645-8437 E-mail: abrams@abramsbooks.com; publicity@abramsbooks.com; sales@abramsbooks.com Web Site: www.abramsbooks.com, pg 3

Moody, Adam, Chronicle Books LLC, 680 Second St, San Francisco, CA 94107 Tel: 415-537-4200 Fax: 415-537-4460 (perms) E-mail: hello@chroniclebooks.com; subrights@chroniclebooks.com Web Site: www.chroniclebooks.com, pg 48

Moody, Jessica, Grey House Publishing Inc™, 4919 Rte 22, Amenia, NY 12501 Tel: 518-789-8700 Fax: 518-789-0556 E-mail: books@greyhouse.com; customerservice@greyhouse.com Web Site: greyhouse.com, pg 81

Moody, Rodger, Gerald Cable Book Award, PO Box 3541, Eugene, OR 97403 Tel: 541-228-0422 E-mail: sfrpress@gmail.com Web Site: www.silverfishreviewpress.com, pg 585

Moog, Bob, BePuzzled, 2030 Harrison St, San Francisco, CA 94110 Tel: 415-934-3705 Toll Free Tel: 800-347-4818 E-mail: info@ugames.com; consumer@ugames.com Web Site: universitygames.com, pg 28

Moon, Danelle, American Printing History Association, PO Box 4519, Grand Central Sta, New York, NY 10163 E-mail: secretary@printinghistory.org Web Site: printinghistory.org, pg 496

Moon, Danelle, American Printing History Association Award, PO Box 4519, Grand Central Sta, New York, NY 10163 E-mail: secretary@printinghistory.org Web Site: printinghistory.org/programs/awards, pg 573

Moon, Emily, Houghton Mifflin Harcourt Trade & Reference Division, 125 High St, Boston, MA 02110 Tel: 617-351-5000 Web Site: www.hmhco.com, pg 96

Moon, Sierra, Macmillan, 120 Broadway, 22nd fl, New York, NY 10271 E-mail: press.inquiries@macmillan.com Web Site: us.macmillan.com, pg 122

Mooney, Dr Robert, Etruscan Press, Wilkes University, 84 W South St, Wilkes-Barre, PA 18766 Tel: 570-408-4546 Fax: 570-408-3333 E-mail: books@etruscanpress.org Web Site: www.etruscanpress.org, pg 67

Moore, Brian, Houghton Mifflin Harcourt Trade & Reference Division, 125 High St, Boston, MA 02110 Tel: 617-351-5000 Web Site: www.hmhco.com, pg 96

Moore, Bridgette, The Geological Society of America Inc (GSA), 3300 Penrose Place, Boulder, CO 80301-1806 Tel: 303-357-1000 Toll Free Tel: 800-472-1988 Fax: 303-357-1070 E-mail: pubs@geosociety.org (prodn); editing@geosociety.org (edit); books@geosociety.org; gsaservice@geosociety.org (sales & serv) Web Site: www.geosociety.org, pg 77

Moore, Cameron, Candlewick Press, 99 Dover St, Somerville, MA 02144-2825 Tel: 617-661-3330 Fax: 617-661-0565 E-mail: bigbear@candlewick.com; salesinfo@candlewick.com Web Site: candlewick.com, pg 40

Moore, Celia, Bloomsbury Academic, 1385 Broadway, 5th fl, New York, NY 10018 Tel: 212-419-5300 Web Site: www.bloomsbury.com/us/academic, pg 31

Moore, George, Cengage Learning, 20 Channel Center St, Boston, MA 02210 Tel: 617-289-7700 Toll Free Tel: 800-354-9706 Fax: 617-289-7844 E-mail: esales@cengage.com Web Site: www.cengage.com, pg 43

Moore, Heather, Sourcebooks LLC, 1935 Brookdale Rd, Suite 139, Naperville, IL 60563 Tel: 630-961-3900 Toll Free Tel: 800-432-7444 Fax: 630-961-2168 E-mail: info@sourcebooks.com Web Site: www.sourcebooks.com, pg 194

Moore, Joseph, Scarsdale Publishing Ltd, 333 Mamaroneck Ave, White Plains, NY 10607 E-mail: scarsdale@scarsdalepublishing.com Web Site: scarsdalepublishing.com, pg 183

Moore, Karen, Literary Management Group LLC, 1020 San Antonio Lane, Lady Lake, FL 32159 Tel: 615-812-4445 Web Site: www.literarymanagementgroup.com, pg 467

Moore, Kyle, Running Press, 1290 Avenue of the Americas, New York, NY 10104 Tel: 212-364-1100 Toll Free Tel: 800-759-0190 (cust serv) Fax: 212-364-0933 (intl orders) Toll Free Fax: 800-286-9471 (cust serv) E-mail: customer.service@hbgusa.com; orders@hbgusa.com Web Site: www.hachettebookgroup.com/imprint/running-press/; www.moon.com (Moon Travel Guides), pg 178

Moore, Maggie, Harry N Abrams Inc, 195 Broadway, 9th fl, New York, NY 10007 Tel: 212-206-7715 Toll Free Tel: 800-345-1359 Fax: 212-645-8437 E-mail: abrams@abramsbooks.com; publicity@abramsbooks.com; sales@abramsbooks.com Web Site: www.abramsbooks.com, pg 3

Moore, Mary C, Aevitas Creative Management LLC, 19 W 21 St, Suite 501, New York, NY 10010 Tel: 212-765-6900 Web Site: www.aevitascreative.com, pg 448

Moore, Mary-Alice, Highlights for Children Inc, 815 Church St, Honesdale, PA 18431 Tel: 570-253-1164 Toll Free Tel: 800-490-5111 Fax: 570-253-0179 E-mail: salesandmarketing@highlightspress.com Web Site: www.highlightspress.com; www.highlights.com; www.facebook.com/HighlightsforChildren, pg 92

Moore, Michael, Augsburg Fortress Publishers, Publishing House of the Evangelical Lutheran Church in America, 411 Washington Ave N, 3rd fl, Minneapolis, MN 55401 Tel: 612-330-3300 Toll Free Tel: 800-426-0115 (ext 639, subns); 800-328-

4648 (orders) *Fax:* 612-330-3455 *E-mail:* info@augsburgfortress.org; copyright@augsburgfortress.org (reprint permission requests); customercare@augsburgfortress.org *Web Site:* www.augsburgfortress.org; www.1517.media, pg 22

Moore, Nancy, Gerald & Cullen Rapp, 41 N Main St, Suite 103, South Norwalk, CT 06854 *Tel:* 212-889-3337 *E-mail:* info@rappart.com *Web Site:* www.rappart.com, pg 486

Moore, Penny, Aevitas Creative Management LLC, 19 W 21 St, Suite 501, New York, NY 10010 *Tel:* 212-765-6900 *Web Site:* www.aevitascreative.com, pg 448

Moore, Rachel, Bloomsbury Academic, 1385 Broadway, 5th fl, New York, NY 10018 *Tel:* 212-419-5300 *Web Site:* www.bloomsbury.com/us/academic, pg 31

Moore, Randi, Macmillan, 120 Broadway, 22nd fl, New York, NY 10271 *E-mail:* press.inquiries@macmillan.com *Web Site:* us.macmillan.com, pg 122

Moore, Sandra, Macmillan, 120 Broadway, 22nd fl, New York, NY 10271 *E-mail:* press.inquiries@macmillan.com *Web Site:* us.macmillan.com, pg 122

Moore, Stacey, Zeig, Tucker & Theisen Inc, 2632 E Thomas Rd, Suite 201, Phoenix, AZ 85016 *Tel:* 480-389-4342 *Web Site:* www.zeigtucker.com, pg 236

Moore, Susan, Oregon Book Awards, 925 SW Washington St, Portland, OR 97205 *Tel:* 503-227-2583 *Fax:* 503-241-4256 *E-mail:* la@literary-arts.org *Web Site:* literary-arts.org/about/programs/oba/book-awards, pg 644

Moore, Tricia J, Lehigh University Press, B-040 Christmas-Saucon Hall, 14 E Packer Ave, Bethlehem, PA 18015 *Tel:* 610-758-3933 *Fax:* 610-758-6331 *E-mail:* inlup@lehigh.edu *Web Site:* lupress.cas2.lehigh.edu, pg 114

Moose, Christina, Davies Publishing Inc, 32 S Raymond Ave, Suites 4 & 5, Pasadena, CA 91105-1961 *Tel:* 626-792-3046 *Toll Free Tel:* 877-792-0005 *Fax:* 626-792-5308 *E-mail:* info@daviespublishing.com *Web Site:* daviespublishing.com, pg 57

Moraleda, Lisa, Simon & Schuster Children's Publishing, 1230 Avenue of the Americas, New York, NY 10020 *Tel:* 212-698-7000 *Web Site:* www.simonandschuster.com/kids; www.simonandschuster.com/teen; simonandschuster.net; simonandschuster.biz, pg 189

Morales, Angela, Idyllwild Arts Summer Program, 52500 Temecula Rd, No 38, Idyllwild, CA 92549 *Tel:* 951-659-2171 *E-mail:* summer@idyllwildarts.org; adultprograms@idyllwildarts.org *Web Site:* idyllwildarts.org/summer, pg 555

Morales, Juan, Television Academy, 5220 Lankershim Blvd, North Hollywood, CA 91601-3109 *Tel:* 818-754-2800 *Web Site:* www.emmys.com, pg 521

Morales, Macey, National Coalition Against Censorship (NCAC), 19 Fulton St, Suite 407, New York, NY 10038 *Tel:* 212-807-6222 *Fax:* 212-807-6245 *E-mail:* ncac@ncac.org *Web Site:* www.ncac.org, pg 512

Morales, Madeline, Harry N Abrams Inc, 195 Broadway, 9th fl, New York, NY 10007 *Tel:* 212-206-7715 *Toll Free Tel:* 800-345-1359 *Fax:* 212-645-8437 *E-mail:* abrams@abramsbooks.com; publicity@abramsbooks.com; sales@abramsbooks.com *Web Site:* www.abramsbooks.com, pg 3

Morales Soto, Denise, Random House Children's Books, c/o Penguin Random House LLC, 1745 Broadway, New York, NY 10019 *Tel:* 212-782-9000 *Web Site:* www.rhcbooks.com, pg 170

Moran, Bruce, TotalRecall Publications Inc, 1103 Middlecreek, Friendswood, TX 77546 *Tel:* 281-992-3131 *E-mail:* sales@totalrecallpress.com *Web Site:* www.totalrecallpress.com, pg 208

Moran, Kelly, Little, Brown Books for Young Readers (LBYR), 1290 Avenue of the Americas, New York, NY 10104 *Tel:* 212-364-1100 *Toll Free Tel:* 800-759-0190 (cust serv) *E-mail:* rights@lbchildrens.com *Web Site:* www.hachettebookgroup.com/imprint/little-brown-books-for-young-readers/, pg 118

Moran, Mia, Farrar, Straus & Giroux Books for Young Readers, 120 Broadway, New York, NY 10271 *Tel:* 212-741-6900 *Toll Free Tel:* 888-330-8477 (orders) *E-mail:* childrens.publicity@macmillanusa.com; childrensrights@macmillanusa.com *Web Site:* us.macmillan.com/mackids, pg 70

Moran, Mia, Roaring Brook Press, 120 Broadway, New York, NY 10271 *Tel:* 646-307-5151 *Web Site:* us.macmillan.com/publishers/roaring-brook-press, pg 176

Moran, Whitney, Nimbus Publishing Ltd, 3660 Strawberry Hill, Halifax, NS B3K 5A9, Canada *Tel:* 902-455-4286 *Toll Free Tel:* 800-NIMBUS9 (646-2879) *Fax:* 902-455-5440 *Toll Free Fax:* 888-253-3133 *E-mail:* customerservice@nimbus.ca *Web Site:* www.nimbus.ca, pg 414

Morance, Claire Easton, Painted-Words Inc, 310 W 97 St, Suite 24, New York, NY 10025 *Tel:* 212-663-2311 *E-mail:* info@painted-words.com *Web Site:* painted-words.com, pg 486

Morandini, Kathleen, Bloomsbury Publishing Inc, 1385 Broadway, 5th fl, New York, NY 10018 *Tel:* 212-419-5300 *E-mail:* marketingusa@bloomsbury.com; adultpublicityusa@bloomsbury.com; askacademic@bloomsbury.com *Web Site:* www.bloomsbury.com, pg 32

Moreau, Deb, Quarto Publishing Group USA Inc, 100 Cummings Ctr, Suite 265D, Beverly, MA 01915 *Tel:* 978-282-9590 *Toll Free Tel:* 800-328-0590 (sales) *Fax:* 978-283-2742 *E-mail:* sales@quartous.com *Web Site:* www.quartoknows.com, pg 168

Moredock, Rebekah, Hachette Nashville, 6100 Tower Circle, Room 210, Franklin, TN 37067 *Tel:* 615-221-0996 *Fax:* 615-221-0962 *Web Site:* www.hachettebookgroup.com/imprint/hachette-nashville/, pg 83

Morehead, Shawn V, Oscar Williams/Gene Derwood Award, 909 Third Ave, New York, NY 10022 *Tel:* 212-686-0010 *Fax:* 212-532-8528 *E-mail:* info@nycommunitytrust.org *Web Site:* www.nycommunitytrust.org, pg 675

Morehouse, Jim, Paradise Cay Publications Inc, 120 Monda Way, Blue Lake, CA 95525 *Tel:* 707-822-9063 *Toll Free Tel:* 800-736-4509 *Fax:* 707-822-9163 *E-mail:* info@paracay.com; orders@paracay.com *Web Site:* www.paracay.com, pg 151

Morel, Madeleine, 2M Communications Ltd, 263 West End Ave, Suite 21A, New York, NY 10023 *Tel:* 212-741-1509 *Fax:* 212-691-4460 *Web Site:* www.2mcommunications.com, pg 480

Moreno, Celina, Intercultural Development Research Association (IDRA), 5815 Callaghan Rd, Suite 101, San Antonio, TX 78228 *Tel:* 210-444-1710 *Fax:* 210-444-1714 *E-mail:* contact@idra.org *Web Site:* www.idra.org, pg 102

Moreno, Jennifer, Random House Children's Books, c/o Penguin Random House LLC, 1745 Broadway, New York, NY 10019 *Tel:* 212-782-9000 *Web Site:* www.rhcbooks.com, pg 170

Moreno, Luis Alberto, Inter-American Development Bank, 1300 New York Ave NW, Washington, DC 20577 *Tel:* 202-623-1000 *Fax:* 202-623-3096 *E-mail:* pic@iadb.org *Web Site:* publications.iadb.org, pg 102

Moreton, Daniel, Penguin Young Readers Group, c/o Penguin Random House LLC, 1745 Broadway, New York, NY 10019 *Tel:* 212-782-9000 *Web Site:* www.penguin.com/penguin-young-readers-overview, pg 156

Morgan, Emma, Princeton University Press, 41 William St, Princeton, NJ 08540-5237 *Tel:* 609-258-4900 *Fax:* 609-258-6305 *E-mail:* info@press.princeton.edu *Web Site:* press.princeton.edu, pg 164

Morgan, Emmanuelle, Stonesong, 270 W 39 St, Suite 201, New York, NY 10018 *Tel:* 212-929-4600 *E-mail:* editors@stonesong.com *Web Site:* www.stonesong.com, pg 478

Morgan, Genevieve, Islandport Press, 247 Portland St, Bldg C, Yarmouth, ME 04096 *Tel:* 207-846-3344 *E-mail:* info@islandportpress.com; orders@islandportpress.com *Web Site:* www.islandportpress.com, pg 105

Morgan, Jill, Purple House Press, 8100 US Hwy 62 E, Cynthiana, KY 41031 *Tel:* 859-235-9970 *Web Site:* www.purplehousepress.com, pg 167

Morgan, Katharine E, ASTM International, 100 Barr Harbor Dr, West Conshohocken, PA 19428-2959 *Tel:* 610-832-9500; 610-832-9585 (intl) *Toll Free Tel:* 877-909-2786 (sales & cust support) *Fax:* 610-832-9555 *E-mail:* sales@astm.org *Web Site:* www.astm.org, pg 20

Morgan, Kristina, Lynx House Press, 420 W 24 St, Spokane, WA 99203 *Tel:* 509-624-4894 *E-mail:* lynxhousepress@gmail.com *Web Site:* www.lynxhousepress.org, pg 121

Morgan, Linda Cicely, The Center for Fiction, 15 Lafayette Ave, Brooklyn, NY 11217 *Tel:* 212-755-6710 *E-mail:* info@centerforfiction.org *Web Site:* centerforfiction.org, pg 503

Morgan, Lindsay, University of California Institute on Global Conflict & Cooperation, 9500 Gilman Dr, MC 0518, La Jolla, CA 92093-0518 *Tel:* 858-534-6106 *Fax:* 858-534-7655 *E-mail:* igcc-communications@ucsd.edu *Web Site:* igcc.ucsd.edu, pg 215

Morgan, Michelle, Nicholas Brealey Publishing, 53 State St, 9th fl, Boston, MA 02109 *Tel:* 617-523-3801 *E-mail:* sales-us@nicholasbrealey.com *Web Site:* nbuspublishing.com, pg 36

Morgan, Nancy, Playwrights Guild of Canada, 401 Richmond St W, Suite 350, Toronto, ON M5V 3A8, Canada *Tel:* 416-703-0201 *E-mail:* info@playwrightsguild.ca; marketing@playwrightsguild.ca; orders@playwrightsguild.ca; membership@playwrightsguild.ca *Web Site:* playwrightsguild.ca, pg 516

Morgan, Stephen, Simon & Schuster, LLC, 1230 Avenue of the Americas, New York, NY 10020 *Tel:* 212-698-7000 *Toll Free Tel:* 800-223-2336 (orders) *Fax:* 212-698-7007 *Toll Free Fax:* 800-943-9831 (orders) *E-mail:* firstname.lastname@simonandschuster.com; purchaseorders@simonandschuster.com (orders) *Web Site:* www.simonandschuster.com, pg 190

Morgan, Thomas, little bee books, 598 Broadway, 7th fl, New York, NY 10012 *Tel:* 212-321-0237 *Toll Free Tel:* 844-321-0237 *E-mail:* info@littlebeebooks.com; sales@littlebeebooks.com; publicity@littlebeebooks.com *Web Site:* littlebeebooks.com, pg 117

Morgan-Sanders, Hayley, Purple House Press, 8100 US Hwy 62 E, Cynthiana, KY 41031 *Tel:* 859-235-9970 *Web Site:* www.purplehousepress.com, pg 167

Morgenstein, Leslie, Alloy Entertainment LLC, 30 Hudson Yards, 22nd fl, New York, NY 10001, pg 7

Morgridge, Sally, Holiday House Publishing Inc, 50 Broad St, New York, NY 10004 *Tel:* 212-688-0085 *Fax:* 212-421-6134 *E-mail:* info@holidayhouse.com *Web Site:* www.holidayhouse.com, pg 94

Morhaim, Howard, Howard Morhaim Literary Agency Inc, 30 Pierrepont St, Brooklyn, NY 11201-3371 *Tel:* 718-222-8400 *E-mail:* info@morhaimliterary.com *Web Site:* www.morhaimliterary.com, pg 470

Moriarty, Adanna, Writers & Publishers Network (WPN), 1129 Maricopa Hwy, No 142, Ojai, CA 93023 *Web Site:* writersandpublishersnetwork.com, pg 522

Moriarty, Amy, WordCo Indexing Services Inc, 66 Franklin St, Norwich, CT 06360 *E-mail:* office@wordco.com *Web Site:* www.wordco.com, pg 445

Moriarty, Kerry, Twenty-Third Publications, One Montauk Ave, Suite 200, New London, CT 06320 *Tel:* 860-437-3012 *Toll Free Tel:* 800-321-0411 (orders) *Toll Free Fax:* 800-572-0788 *E-mail:* resources@twentythirdpublications.com *Web Site:* www.twentythirdpublications.com, pg 211

Morin, Pascale, Editions Hurtubise, 1815, ave de Lorimier, Montreal, QC H2K 3W6, Canada *Tel:* 514-523-1523 *Toll Free Tel:* 800-361-1664 *Web Site:* editionshurtubise.com, pg 404

Morita, Joe, Springer Publishing Co, 11 W 42 St, 15th fl, New York, NY 10036-8002 *Tel:* 212-431-4370 *Toll Free Tel:* 877-687-7476 *E-mail:* marketing@springerpub.com; cs@springerpub.com (orders); textbook@springerpub.com; specialsales@springerpub.com *Web Site:* www.springerpub.com, pg 196

Morley, Jane, Quirk Books, 215 Church St, Philadelphia, PA 19106 *Tel:* 215-627-3581 *Fax:* 215-627-5220 *E-mail:* general@quirkbooks.com *Web Site:* www.quirkbooks.com, pg 168

Morpheus, Jess, Penguin Publishing Group, c/o Penguin Random House LLC, 1745 Broadway, New York, NY 10019 *Tel:* 212-782-9000 *Web Site:* www.penguin.com, pg 154

Morris, Caressa, American Counseling Association (ACA), 6101 Stevenson Ave, Suite 600, Alexandria, VA 22304 *Tel:* 703-823-9800 *Toll Free Tel:* 800-298-2276 *Toll Free Fax:* 800-473-2329 *E-mail:* orders@counseling.org (book orders) *Web Site:* www.counseling.org, pg 9

Morris, Elizabeth, Bloomsbury Academic, 1385 Broadway, 5th fl, New York, NY 10018 *Tel:* 212-419-5300 *Web Site:* www.bloomsbury.com/us/academic, pg 31

Morris, Gary, David Black Agency, 335 Adams St, 27th fl, Suite 2707, Brooklyn, NY 11201 *Tel:* 718-852-5500 *Fax:* 718-852-5539 *Web Site:* www.davidblackagency.com, pg 450

Morris, Heather, Sourcebooks LLC, 1935 Brookdale Rd, Suite 139, Naperville, IL 60563 *Tel:* 630-961-3900 *Toll Free Tel:* 800-432-7444 *Fax:* 630-961-2168 *E-mail:* info@sourcebooks.com *Web Site:* www.sourcebooks.com, pg 194

Morris, Richard, Janklow & Nesbit Associates, 285 Madison Ave, 21st fl, New York, NY 10017 *Tel:* 212-421-1700 *Fax:* 212-355-1403 *E-mail:* info@janklow.com; submissions@janklow.com; filmtvrights@janklow.com *Web Site:* www.janklowandnesbit.com, pg 464

Morris, Sydney, Gallery Books, 1230 Avenue of the Americas, New York, NY 10020 *Toll Free Tel:* 800-456-6798 *Fax:* 212-698-7284 *E-mail:* consumer.customerservice@simonandschuster.com *Web Site:* www.simonandschuster.com, pg 76

Morris, Taylor, SDP Publishing Solutions LLC, 36 Captain's Way, East Bridgewater, MA 02333 *Tel:* 617-775-0656 *Web Site:* www.sdppublishingsolutions.com, pg 444

Morris, W Travis, William E Colby Award, 158 Harmon Dr, Box 60, Northfield, VT 05663 *Tel:* 802-485-2965 *Web Site:* colby.norwich.edu/award, pg 591

Morrison, Alethea, Workman Publishing, 1290 Avenue of the Americas, New York, NY 10104 *Toll Free Tel:* 800-759-0190 *Fax:* 212-364-0950 *E-mail:* workman-inquiry@hbgusa.com *Web Site:* www.hachettebookgroup.com/imprint/workman-publishing-company/, pg 232

Morrison, Charles, Prometheus Awards, 650 Castro St, Suite 120-433, Mountain View, CA 94041 *Tel:* 650-968-6319 *E-mail:* bestnovel@lfs.org; specialaward@lfs.org *Web Site:* www.lfs.org, pg 653

Morrison, Charlotte, Little, Brown and Company, 1290 Avenue of the Americas, New York, NY 10104 *Tel:* 212-364-1100 *Fax:* 212-364-0952 *E-mail:* firstname.lastname@hbgusa.com *Web Site:* www.hachettebookgroup.com/imprint/little-brown-and-company/, pg 118

Morrison, Heath, McGraw-Hill Education, 2 Penn Plaza, New York, NY 10121-2298 *Tel:* 212-904-2000 *E-mail:* international_cs@mheducation.com; seg_customerservice@mheducation.com (PreK-12); hep_customerservice@mheducation.com (higher education) *Web Site:* www.mheducation.com, pg 128

Morrison, Heath, McGraw-Hill School Education Group, 8787 Orion Place, Columbus, OH 43240 *Tel:* 614-430-4000 *Toll Free Tel:* 800-848-1567 *Web Site:* www.mheducation.com, pg 128

Morrison, Richard W, Fordham University Press, Joseph A Martino Hall, 45 Columbus Ave, 3rd fl, New York, NY 10023 *Fax:* 347-842-3083 *Web Site:* www.fordhampress.com, pg 73

Morrison, Rusty, Omnidawn, 1632 Elm Ave, Richmond, CA 94805 *Tel:* 510-439-6285 *E-mail:* manager@omnidawn.com *Web Site:* www.omnidawn.com, pg 146

Morrissey, Jake, Riverhead Books, c/o Penguin Random House LLC, 1745 Broadway, New York, NY 10019 *Tel:* 212-782-9000 *Web Site:* www.penguin.com/riverhead-overview/, pg 175

Morrow, Caitlin, Simon & Schuster, 1230 Avenue of the Americas, New York, NY 10020 *Tel:* 212-698-7000 *Toll Free Tel:* 800-223-2348 (cust serv); 800-223-2336 (orders) *Toll Free Fax:* 800-943-9831 (orders) *Web Site:* simonandschusterpublishing.com/simonandschuster/, pg 188

Morrow, Lauren, Dutton, c/o Penguin Random House LLC, 1745 Broadway, New York, NY 10019 *Tel:* 212-366-2000 *Web Site:* www.penguin.com/dutton-overview/; www.penguin.com/plume-books-overview/; www.penguin.com/tiny-reparations-overview/, pg 62

Morrow, Stephen, Simon & Schuster, 1230 Avenue of the Americas, New York, NY 10020 *Tel:* 212-698-7000 *Toll Free Tel:* 800-223-2348 (cust serv); 800-223-2336 (orders) *Toll Free Fax:* 800-943-9831 (orders) *Web Site:* simonandschusterpublishing.com/simonandschuster/, pg 188

Morse, Leah, Harlequin Enterprises Ltd, 195 Broadway, 24th fl, New York, NY 10007 *Tel:* 212-207-7000 *Toll Free Tel:* 888-432-4879; 800-370-5838 (ebooks) *E-mail:* customerservice@harlequin.com *Web Site:* www.harlequin.com/shop/index.html; corporate.harlequin.com, pg 85

Morse, Leah, Other Press, 267 Fifth Ave, 6th fl, New York, NY 10016 *Tel:* 212-414-0054 *Toll Free Tel:* 877-THEOTHER (843-6843) *Fax:* 212-414-0939 *E-mail:* editor@otherpress.com; marketing@otherpress.com; publicity@otherpress.com *Web Site:* otherpress.com, pg 148

Morse, Nikki, The Gerald Ensley Developing Writer Award, 116 Honors Way, Suite 314, Tallahassee, FL 32306 *Tel:* 850-644-5211 *E-mail:* floridabookawards@gmail.com *Web Site:* www.floridabookawards.org/index.php/ensley-award, pg 600

Morse, Nikki, The Florida Book Awards, 116 Honors Way, Suite 314, Tallahassee, FL 32306 *Tel:* 850-644-5211 *E-mail:* floridabookawards@gmail.com *Web Site:* www.floridabookawards.org, pg 602

Mortensen, Bryan, Federation of BC Writers, PO Box 3503, Courtenay, BC V9N 6Z9, Canada *E-mail:* hello@bcwriters.ca *Web Site:* bcwriters.ca, pg 505

Mortensen, Vivian, Friends of American Writers (FAW), c/o 506 Rose Ave, Des Plaines, IL 60016 *E-mail:* info@fawchicago.org *Web Site:* www.fawchicago.org, pg 506

Mortimer, Bryce, Cedar Fort Inc, 2373 W 700 S, Suite 100, Springville, UT 84663 *Tel:* 801-489-4084 *Toll Free Tel:* 800-SKY-BOOK (759-2665) *E-mail:* marketinginfo@cedarfort.com *Web Site:* cedarfort.com, pg 43

Mortimer, Michele, Darhansoff & Verrill, 529 11 St, 3rd fl, Brooklyn, NY 11215 *Tel:* 917-305-1300 *E-mail:* permissions@dvagency.com *Web Site:* www.dvagency.com, pg 455

Morton, Larry, Hal Leonard LLC, 7777 W Bluemound Rd, Milwaukee, WI 53213 *Tel:* 414-774-3630 *E-mail:* info@halleonard.com; sales@halleonard.com *Web Site:* www.halleonard.com, pg 84

Mosberg, Stephen R, College Publishing, 12309 Lynwood Dr, Glen Allen, VA 23059 *Tel:* 804-364-8410 *Fax:* 804-364-8408 *E-mail:* collegepub@mindspring.com *Web Site:* www.collegepublishing.us, pg 50

Mosbrook, Bill, Pathfinder Publishing Inc, 120 S Houghton Rd, Suite 138, Tucson, AZ 85748 *Tel:* 520-647-0158 *Web Site:* www.pathfinderpublishing.com, pg 152

Moschovakis, Anna, Ugly Duckling Presse, The Old American Can Factory, 232 Third St, Suite E303, Brooklyn, NY 11215 *Tel:* 347-948-5170 *E-mail:* office@uglyducklingpresse.org; orders@uglyducklingpresse.org; publicity@uglyducklingpresse.org; rights@uglyducklingpresse.org *Web Site:* uglyducklingpresse.org, pg 212

Moscovich, Rotem, Penguin Random House LLC, 1745 Broadway, New York, NY 10019 *Tel:* 212-782-9000 *Toll Free Tel:* 800-726-0600 *Web Site:* www.penguinrandomhouse.com, pg 155

Moseley, Lauren, Bloomsbury Publishing Inc, 1385 Broadway, 5th fl, New York, NY 10018 *Tel:* 212-419-5300 *E-mail:* marketingusa@bloomsbury.com; adultpublicityusa@bloomsbury.com; askacademic@bloomsbury.com *Web Site:* www.bloomsbury.com, pg 31

Moselle, Ben, Craftsman Book Co, 6058 Corte Del Cedro, Carlsbad, CA 92011 *Tel:* 760-438-7828 *Toll Free Tel:* 800-829-8123 *Fax:* 760-438-0398 *Web Site:* www.craftsman-book.com, pg 54

Moselle, Gary, Craftsman Book Co, 6058 Corte Del Cedro, Carlsbad, CA 92011 *Tel:* 760-438-7828 *Toll Free Tel:* 800-829-8123 *Fax:* 760-438-0398 *Web Site:* www.craftsman-book.com, pg 54

Moses, Casey, Random House Children's Books, c/o Penguin Random House LLC, 1745 Broadway, New York, NY 10019 *Tel:* 212-782-9000 *Web Site:* www.rhcbooks.com, pg 170

Moses, James, Primary Research Group Inc, 2585 Broadway, Suite 156, New York, NY 10025 *Tel:* 212-736-2316 *Fax:* 212-412-9097 *E-mail:* primaryresearchgroup@gmail.com *Web Site:* www.primaryresearch.com, pg 163

Moses-Schmitt, Lena, Counterpoint Press LLC, 2560 Ninth St, Suite 318, Berkeley, CA 94710 *Tel:* 510-704-0230 *Fax:* 510-704-0268 *E-mail:* info@counterpointpress.com *Web Site:* counterpointpress.com; softskull.com, pg 54

Mosher, Jessica, Nelson Education Ltd, 1120 Birchmount Rd, Scarborough, ON M1K 5G4, Canada *Tel:* 416-752-9448 *Toll Free Tel:* 800-268-2222 (cust serv) *Fax:* 416-752-9646 *E-mail:* peopleandengagement@nelson.com *Web Site:* www.nelson.com, pg 413

Mosher, Jessica, University of Toronto Press, Book Publishing Div, 800 Bay St, Mezzanine, Toronto, ON M5S 3A9, Canada *Tel:* 416-978-2239 *Fax:* 416-978-4736 *E-mail:* utpbooks@utorontopress.com (orders) *Web Site:* utorontopress.com, pg 423

Moskowitz, Orli, Penguin Random House Audio Publishing Group, 1745 Broadway, New York, NY 10019 *Toll Free Tel:* 800-793-2665 (cust serv) *E-mail:* audio@penguinrandomhouse.com; ecustomerservice@penguinrandomhouse.com *Web Site:* www.penguinrandomhouseaudio.com, pg 154

Mosley, Jody, Chronicle Books LLC, 680 Second St, San Francisco, CA 94107 *Tel:* 415-537-4200 *Fax:* 415-537-4460 (perms) *E-mail:* hello@chroniclebooks.com; subrights@chroniclebooks.com *Web Site:* www.chroniclebooks.com, pg 47

Moss, Marissa, Creston Books, PO Box 9369, Berkeley, CA 94709 *Web Site:* www.crestonbooks.co, pg 55

Moss, Princess R, National Education Association (NEA), 1201 16 St NW, Washington, DC 20036-3290 *Tel:* 202-833-4000 *Fax:* 202-822-7974 *Web Site:* www.nea.org, pg 137

Moss, Princess R, National Education Association (NEA), 1201 16 St NW, Washington, DC 20036-3290 *Tel:* 202-833-4000 *Fax:* 202-822-7974 *E-mail:* media-relations-team@nea.org *Web Site:* www.nea.org, pg 513

Moss, Veronica, Goodreads Choice Awards, 188 Spear St, 3rd fl, San Francisco, CA 94105 *E-mail:* press@goodreads.com *Web Site:* www.goodreads.com/award, pg 608

Mosser, Gianna, Vanderbilt University Press, 2301 Vanderbilt Place, PMB 401813, Nashville, TN 37240-1813 *Tel:* 615-322-3585 *Toll Free Tel:* 800-848-6224 (orders only) *Fax:* 615-343-0308 *E-mail:* vupress@vanderbilt.edu *Web Site:* www.vanderbiltuniversitypress.com, pg 224

Mostel, Aly, HarperCollins Publishers LLC, 195 Broadway, New York, NY 10007 *Tel:* 212-207-7000 *Web Site:* www.harpercollins.com, pg 86

Motin, Adam, Triumph Books LLC, 814 N Franklin St, Chicago, IL 60610 *Tel:* 312-337-0747 *Toll Free Tel:* 800-888-4741 (cust serv) *Fax:* 312-280-5470; 312-337-5985 *Web Site:* www.triumphbooks.com, pg 210

Motley, Eric L, National Gallery of Art, Sixth & Constitution Ave NW, Washington, DC 20565 *Tel:* 202-842-6280 *E-mail:* thecenter@nga.gov *Web Site:* www.nga.gov, pg 137

Mott, Andy, Candlewick Press, 99 Dover St, Somerville, MA 02144-2825 *Tel:* 617-661-3330 *Fax:* 617-661-0565 *E-mail:* bigbear@candlewick.com; salesinfo@candlewick.com *Web Site:* candlewick.com, pg 39

Moulaison, Nicole, HarperCollins Publishers LLC, 195 Broadway, New York, NY 10007 *Tel:* 212-207-7000 *Web Site:* www.harpercollins.com, pg 86

Moulden, Yolanda Y, American Academy of Environmental Engineers & Scientists®, 147 Old Solomons Island Rd, Suite 303, Annapolis, MD 21401 *Tel:* 410-266-3311 *Fax:* 410-266-7653 *E-mail:* info@aaees.org *Web Site:* www.aaees.org, pg 8

Moulton, Candy, Spur Awards, 271 CR 219, Encampment, WY 82325 *Tel:* 307-329-8942 *Web Site:* westernwriters.org/spur-awards, pg 665

Moulton, Candy, Western Writers of America Inc (WWA), 271 CR 219, Encampment, WY 82325 *Tel:* 307-329-8942 *Web Site:* westernwriters.org, pg 521

Moulton, Stephen, Himalayan Institute Press, 952 Bethany Tpke, Honesdale, PA 18431 *Tel:* 570-253-5551 *Toll Free Tel:* 800-822-4547 *E-mail:* trade@himalayaninstitute.org *Web Site:* www.himalayaninstitute.org, pg 92

Moushabeck, Hannah, Interlink Publishing Group Inc, 46 Crosby St, Northampton, MA 01060 *Tel:* 413-582-7054 *Toll Free Tel:* 800-238-LINK (238-5465) *E-mail:* info@interlinkbooks.com; publicity@interlinkbooks.com; sales@interlinkbooks.com *Web Site:* www.interlinkbooks.com, pg 102

Moushabeck, Leyla, Interlink Publishing Group Inc, 46 Crosby St, Northampton, MA 01060 *Tel:* 413-582-7054 *Toll Free Tel:* 800-238-LINK (238-5465) *E-mail:* info@interlinkbooks.com; publicity@interlinkbooks.com; sales@interlinkbooks.com *Web Site:* www.interlinkbooks.com, pg 102

Moushabeck, Maha, Interlink Publishing Group Inc, 46 Crosby St, Northampton, MA 01060 *Tel:* 413-582-7054 *Toll Free Tel:* 800-238-LINK (238-5465) *E-mail:* info@interlinkbooks.com; publicity@interlinkbooks.com; sales@interlinkbooks.com *Web Site:* www.interlinkbooks.com, pg 102

Mousseau, Richard, Moose Hide Books, 684 Walls Rd, Prince Township, ON P6A 6K4, Canada *Tel:* 705-779-3331 *Fax:* 705-779-3331 *E-mail:* mooseenterprises@on.aibn.com *Web Site:* www.moosehidebooks.com, pg 413

Moustaki, Susan, Frederick Fell Publishers Inc, 1403 Shoreline Way, Hollywood, FL 33019 *Tel:* 954-925-5242 *E-mail:* fellpub@aol.com (admin only) *Web Site:* www.fellpub.com, pg 74

Movva, Sunanda, Macmillan, 120 Broadway, 22nd fl, New York, NY 10271 *E-mail:* press.inquiries@macmillan.com *Web Site:* us.macmillan.com, pg 122

Mowry, Bethany, Indiana University Press, Off of Scholarly Publg, Herman B Wells Library 350, 1320 E Tenth St, Bloomington, IN 47405-3907 *Tel:* 812-855-8817 *Fax:* 812-855-7931; 812-855-8507 *E-mail:* iupress@indiana.edu *Web Site:* iupress.org, pg 100

Moye, Lauren, Harry N Abrams Inc, 195 Broadway, 9th fl, New York, NY 10007 *Tel:* 212-206-7715 *Toll Free Tel:* 800-345-1359 *Fax:* 212-645-8437 *E-mail:* abrams@abramsbooks.com; publicity@abramsbooks.com; sales@abramsbooks.com *Web Site:* www.abramsbooks.com, pg 3

Moyers, Scott, Penguin Press, c/o Penguin Random House LLC, 1745 Broadway, New York, NY 10019 *Tel:* 212-782-9000 *E-mail:* penguinpress@penguinrandomhouse.com *Web Site:* www.penguin.com/penguin-press-overview/, pg 154

Moynagh, Kerry, HarperCollins Publishers LLC, 195 Broadway, New York, NY 10007 *Tel:* 212-207-7000 *Web Site:* www.harpercollins.com, pg 86

Mroczkowski, Juliette, InterLicense Ltd, 110 Country Club Dr, Suite A, Mill Valley, CA 94941 *Tel:* 415-381-9780 *Fax:* 415-381-6485 *E-mail:* foreignrights@interlicense.net *Web Site:* interlicense.net, pg 464

Mroczkowski, Manfred, InterLicense Ltd, 110 Country Club Dr, Suite A, Mill Valley, CA 94941 *Tel:* 415-381-9780 *Fax:* 415-381-6485 *E-mail:* foreignrights@interlicense.net *Web Site:* interlicense.net, pg 464

Mubarek, Stephen, Hachette Book Group Inc, 1290 Avenue of the Americas, New York, NY 10104 *Tel:* 212-364-1100 *Toll Free Tel:* 800-759-0190 (cust serv) *Fax:* 212-364-0933 (intl orders) *Toll Free Fax:* 800-286-9471 (cust serv) *E-mail:* customer.service@hbgusa.com; orders@hbgusa.com *Web Site:* www.hachettebookgroup.com, pg 83

Mucciardi, Catherine, Random House Children's Books, c/o Penguin Random House LLC, 1745 Broadway, New York, NY 10019 *Tel:* 212-782-9000 *Web Site:* www.rhcbooks.com, pg 170

Muccie, Mary Rose, Temple University Press, 1852 N Tenth St, Philadelphia, PA 19122-6099 *Tel:* 215-926-2140 *Toll Free Tel:* 800-621-2736 *Fax:* 215-926-2141 *E-mail:* tempress@temple.edu *Web Site:* tupress.temple.edu, pg 204

Muchnick, Asya, Little, Brown and Company, 1290 Avenue of the Americas, New York, NY 10104 *Tel:* 212-364-1100 *Fax:* 212-364-0952 *E-mail:* firstname.lastname@hbgusa.com *Web Site:* www.hachettebookgroup.com/imprint/little-brown-and-company/, pg 118

Mudie, Tim, Houghton Mifflin Harcourt Trade & Reference Division, 125 High St, Boston, MA 02110 *Tel:* 617-351-5000 *Web Site:* www.hmhco.com, pg 96

Mueller, Anton, Bloomsbury Publishing Inc, 1385 Broadway, 5th fl, New York, NY 10018 *Tel:* 212-419-5300 *E-mail:* marketingusa@bloomsbury.com; adultpublicityusa@bloomsbury.com; askacademic@bloomsbury.com *Web Site:* www.bloomsbury.com, pg 31

Mueller, Dawn, Association of College & Research Libraries (ACRL), 225 N Michigan Ave, Suite 1300, Chicago, IL 60601 *Tel:* 312-280-2523; 312-280-2516 *Toll Free Tel:* 800-545-2433 (ext 2523) *Fax:* 312-280-2520 *E-mail:* acrl@ala.org; alastore@ala.org *Web Site:* www.ala.org/acrl; alastore.ala.org, pg 19

Mueller-Grote, Susanne, Philosophy Documentation Center, PO Box 7147, Charlottesville, VA 22906-7147 *Tel:* 434-220-3300 *Toll Free Tel:* 800-444-2419 *Fax:* 434-220-3301 *E-mail:* order@pdcnet.org *Web Site:* www.pdcnet.org, pg 159

Muenchrath, Anna, Society for the History of Authorship, Reading & Publishing Inc (SHARP), c/o Johns Hopkins University Press, Journals Publishing Div, PO Box 19966, Baltimore, MD 21211-0966 *Tel:* 410-516-6987 *Toll Free Tel:* 800-548-1784 *Fax:* 410-516-3866 *E-mail:* members@sharpweb.org *Web Site:* www.sharpweb.org, pg 519

Muhlenkamp, Monique, New World Library, 14 Pamaron Way, Novato, CA 94949 *Tel:* 415-884-2100 *Fax:* 415-884-2199 *E-mail:* escort@newworldlibrary.com *Web Site:* www.newworldlibrary.com, pg 140

Muhlig, Adam, McIntosh and Otis Inc, 235 Main St, Suite 318, White Plains, NY 10601 *Tel:* 212-687-7400 *Fax:* 212-687-6894 *E-mail:* info@mcintoshandotis.com *Web Site:* www.mcintoshandotis.com, pg 470

Muhling, Daniela, Gilder Lehrman Prize for Military History, 49 W 45 St, 2nd fl, New York, NY 10036 *Tel:* 646-366-9666 *E-mail:* info@gilderlehrman.org *Web Site:* www.gilderlehrman.org, pg 606

Muir, Breanna, University of Toronto Press, Book Publishing Div, 800 Bay St, Mezzanine, Toronto, ON M5S 3A9, Canada *Tel:* 416-978-2239 *Fax:* 416-978-4736 *E-mail:* utpbooks@utorontopress.com (orders) *Web Site:* utorontopress.com, pg 423

Muir, Sharona, Bowling Green State University Creative Writing Program, Dept of English, 212 East Hall, Bowling Green, OH 43403-0001 *Tel:* 419-372-6864; 419-372-2576 *Fax:* 419-372-0333 *E-mail:* english@bgsu.edu *Web Site:* www.bgsu.edu/academics/creative-writing, pg 561

Mukalla, Doris, International Book Centre Inc, 2391 Auburn Rd, Shelby Township, MI 48317 *Tel:* 586-254-7230 *Fax:* 586-254-7230 *E-mail:* ibc@ibcbooks.com *Web Site:* www.ibcbooks.com, pg 102

Mukavitz, Maria, SME (Society of Manufacturing Engineers), 1000 Town Ctr, Suite 1910, Southfield, MI 48075 *Tel:* 313-425-3000 *Toll Free Tel:* 800-733-4763 (cust serv) *Fax:* 313-425-3400 *E-mail:* publications@sme.org *Web Site:* www.sme.org, pg 191

Mukherji, Sumita, Harvard Education Publishing Group, 8 Story St, 1st fl, Cambridge, MA 02138 *Tel:* 617-495-3432 *Fax:* 617-496-3584 *Web Site:* www.hepg.org, pg 88

Muldrow, Dana, International Council of Shopping Centers (ICSC), 1251 Avenue of the Americas, 41st fl, New York, NY 10020-1099 *Web Site:* www.icsc.com, pg 102

Mulhern, Colleen, Adams Media, 100 Technology Center Dr, Suite 501, Stoughton, MA 02072 *Tel:* 508-427-7100 *Web Site:* www.simonandschuster.com, pg 4

Mullan, Eileen, Adams Media, 100 Technology Center Dr, Suite 501, Stoughton, MA 02072 *Tel:* 508-427-7100 *Web Site:* www.simonandschuster.com, pg 4

Mullen, Laura, Louisiana State University Creative Writing Program MFA, English Dept, 260 Allen Hall, Baton Rouge, LA 70803 *Tel:* 225-578-4086 *Fax:* 225-578-4129 *E-mail:* lsucrwriting@lsu.edu *Web Site:* www.lsu.edu; www.lsu.edu/hss/english/creative_writing, pg 563

Mullen, Richard, Print Industries Market Information and Research Organization (PRIMIR), 1899 Preston White Dr, Reston, VA 20191 *Tel:* 703-264-7200 *E-mail:* aptech@aptech.org *Web Site:* www.printtechnologies.org; www.npes.org/primirresearch/primir.aspx, pg 517

Mullendore, Nick, Loretta Barrett Books, Inc, Brooklyn, NY 11231 *Tel:* 212-242-3420 *E-mail:* lbbagencymail@gmail.com *Web Site:* www.lorettabarrettbooks.com, pg 449

Muller, Abby, Harry N Abrams Inc, 195 Broadway, 9th fl, New York, NY 10007 *Tel:* 212-206-7715 *Toll Free Tel:* 800-345-1359 *Fax:* 212-645-8437 *E-mail:* abrams@abramsbooks.com; publicity@abramsbooks.com; sales@abramsbooks.com *Web Site:* www.abramsbooks.com, pg 3

Mullick, Farah, Harlequin Enterprises Ltd, Bay Adelaide Centre, East Tower, 22 Adelaide St W, 41st fl, Toronto, ON M5H 4E3, Canada *Tel:* 416-445-5860 *Toll Free Tel:* 888-432-4879; 800-370-5838 (ebook inquiries) *E-mail:* customerservice@harlequin.com *Web Site:* www.harlequin.com, pg 409

Mulligan, Ryan A, Temple University Press, 1852 N Tenth St, Philadelphia, PA 19122-6099 *Tel:* 215-926-2140 *Toll Free Tel:* 800-621-2736 *Fax:* 215-926-2141 *E-mail:* tempress@temple.edu *Web Site:* tupress.temple.edu, pg 204

Mullin, Melinda, HarperCollins Publishers LLC, 195 Broadway, New York, NY 10007 *Tel:* 212-207-7000 *Web Site:* www.harpercollins.com, pg 86

Mullins, Antoinette, Emerging Playwright Award, 555 Eighth Ave, Suite 1800, New York, NY 10018 *Tel:* 212-421-1380 *Fax:* 212-421-1387 *E-mail:* urbanstage@aol.com *Web Site:* urbanstages.org, pg 599

Mullins, Josh, Appalachian Writers' Workshop, 51 Center St, Hindman, KY 41822 Tel: 606-785-5475 E-mail: info@hindman.org Web Site: www.hindman.org, pg 553

Mullins, Molly Alton, National Association of Printing Ink Manufacturers (NAPIM), National Press Bldg, 529 14 St NW, Suite 1280, Washington, DC 20045 Tel: 410-940-6589 E-mail: info@napim.org Web Site: www.napim.org, pg 512

Mulqueen, Katie, Association for Intelligent Information Management (AIIM), 8403 Colesville Rd, No 1100, Silver Spring, MD 20910 Tel: 301-587-8202 Toll Free Tel: 800-477-2446 Fax: 301-587-2711 E-mail: hello@aiim.org Web Site: www.aiim.org, pg 498

Mulroney, Michele, Writers Guild of America Awards, 7000 W Third St, Los Angeles, CA 90048 Tel: 323-951-4000; 323-782-4569 Toll Free Tel: 800-548-4532 Fax: 323-782-4801 Web Site: www.wga.org; awards.wga.org, pg 678

Mulroney, Michele, Writers Guild of America West (WGAW), 7000 W Third St, Los Angeles, CA 90048 Tel: 323-951-4000 Toll Free Tel: 800-548-4532 Fax: 323-782-4801 Web Site: www.wga.org, pg 523

Mulrooney-Lyski, Caitlin, Henry Holt and Company, LLC, 120 Broadway, 23rd fl, New York, NY 10271 Tel: 646-307-5151 Toll Free Tel: 888-330-8477 (orders) Fax: 646-307-5285 Web Site: www.henryholt.com, pg 94

Munce, Alayna, Brick Books, 22 Spencer Ave, Toronto, ON M6K 2J6, Canada Tel: 416-455-8385 Web Site: www.brickbooks.ca, pg 397

Munce, Bob, Christian Retail Association Inc (CRA), 200 West Bay Dr, Largo, FL 33770 Tel: 727-596-7625 Toll Free Tel: 800-868-4388 Fax: 727-593-3523 Toll Free Fax: 855-815-9277 E-mail: service@munce.com Web Site: www.christianretailassociation.org, pg 503

Munce, Marti, Christian Retail Association Inc (CRA), 200 West Bay Dr, Largo, FL 33770 Tel: 727-596-7625 Toll Free Tel: 800-868-4388 Fax: 727-593-3523 Toll Free Fax: 855-815-9277 E-mail: service@munce.com Web Site: www.christianretailassociation.org, pg 503

Munday, Evan, Penguin Random House Canada, a Penguin Random House company, 320 Front St W, Suite 1400, Toronto, ON M5V 3B6, Canada Tel: 416-364-4449 Toll Free Tel: 888-523-9292 (cust serv) E-mail: canadaweb@penguinrandomhouse.com; customerservicescanada@penguinrandomhouse.com Web Site: www.penguinrandomhouse.ca, pg 416

Munday, Oliver, Doubleday, c/o Penguin Random House LLC, 1745 Broadway, New York, NY 10019 Tel: 212-751-2600 Fax: 212-940-7390 (dom rts) 212-572-2662 (foreign rts) Web Site: knopfdoubleday.com/imprint/doubleday/; knopfdoubleday.com, pg 61

Mundorff, Emma, Stanford University Press, 425 Broadway St, Redwood City, CA 94063-3126 Tel: 650-723-9434 Fax: 650-725-3457 E-mail: info@www.sup.org; publicity@www.sup.org; sales@www.sup.org Web Site: www.sup.org, pg 197

Mundt, Letty, Sourcebooks LLC, 1935 Brookdale Rd, Suite 139, Naperville, IL 60563 Tel: 630-961-3900 Toll Free Tel: 800-432-7444 Fax: 630-961-2168 E-mail: info@sourcebooks.com Web Site: www.sourcebooks.com, pg 194

Mundy, Meredith, Harry N Abrams Inc, 195 Broadway, 9th fl, New York, NY 10007 Tel: 212-206-7715 Toll Free Tel: 800-345-1359 Fax: 212-645-8437 E-mail: abrams@abramsbooks.com; publicity@abramsbooks.com; sales@abramsbooks.com Web Site: www.abramsbooks.com, pg 2

Mungiello, Michael, InkWell Management, 521 Fifth Ave, Suite 2600, New York, NY 10175 Tel: 212-922-3500 Fax: 212-922-0535 E-mail: info@inkwellmanagement.com; submissions@inkwellmanagement.com; permissions@inkwellmanagement.com Web Site: inkwellmanagement.com, pg 463

Munich, Becky, Little, Brown Books for Young Readers (LBYR), 1290 Avenue of the Americas, New York, NY 10104 Tel: 212-364-1100 Toll Free Tel: 800-759-0190 (cust serv) E-mail: rights@lbchildrens.com Web Site: www.hachettebookgroup.com/imprint/little-brown-books-for-young-readers/, pg 118

Munier, Paula, Talcott Notch Literary, 127 Broad St, 2P, Milford, CT 06460 Tel: 203-876-4959 Web Site: talcottnotch.net, pg 479

Muniz, Kaiya, Adams Media, 100 Technology Center Dr, Suite 501, Stoughton, MA 02072 Tel: 508-427-7100 Web Site: www.simonandschuster.com, pg 4

Munk, Laurie, Association for the Advancement of Blood & Biotherapies, North Tower, 4550 Montgomery Ave, Suite 700, Bethesda, MD 20814 Tel: 301-907-6977; 301-215-6499 (orders outside US) Toll Free Tel: 866-222-2498 (sales) Fax: 301-907-6895 E-mail: aabb@aabb.org; sales@aabb.org (ordering); publications1@aabb.org (catalog) Web Site: www.aabb.org, pg 19

Munn, Duncan, C D Howe Institute, 67 Yonge St, Suite 300, Toronto, ON M5E 1J8, Canada Tel: 416-865-1904 Fax: 416-865-1866 E-mail: cdhowe@cdhowe.org Web Site: www.cdhowe.org, pg 410

Munoz, Gabriella, Random House Publishing Group, 1745 Broadway, New York, NY 10019 Toll Free Tel: 800-200-3552 Web Site: www.randomhousebooks.com, pg 171

Munro, Bob, Cengage Learning, 20 Channel Center St, Boston, MA 02210 Tel: 617-289-7700 Toll Free Tel: 800-354-9706 Fax: 617-289-7844 E-mail: esales@cengage.com Web Site: www.cengage.com, pg 43

Munro, Eliana, Appraisal Institute, 200 W Madison, Suite 1500, Chicago, IL 60606 Tel: 312-335-4100 Toll Free Tel: 888-756-4624 E-mail: aiservice@appraisalinstitute.org Web Site: www.appraisalinstitute.org, pg 15

Munroe, Sarah, West Virginia University Press, West Virginia University, PO Box 6295, Morgantown, WV 26506-6295 Tel: 304-293-8400 Web Site: www.wvupress.com, pg 228

Munz, Tania, American Academy of Arts & Sciences (AAAS), 136 Irving St, Cambridge, MA 02138 Tel: 617-576-5000 Fax: 617-576-5050 E-mail: aaas@amacad.org Web Site: www.amacad.org, pg 494

Mura, David, VONA Voices Summer Writing Workshops, 2820 SW 20 St, Miami, FL 33145 E-mail: info@vonavoices.org Web Site: www.vonavoices.org, pg 558

Murach, Ben, Mike Murach & Associates Inc, 3730 W Swift, Fresno, CA 93722 Tel: 559-440-9071 Toll Free Tel: 800-221-5528 Fax: 559-440-0963 E-mail: murachbooks@murach.com Web Site: www.murach.com, pg 131

Murcray, Colin, National Council of Teachers of English (NCTE), 340 N Neil St, Suite 104, Champaign, IL 61820 Tel: 217-328-3870 Toll Free Tel: 877-369-6283 (cust serv) Fax: 217-328-9645 E-mail: customerservice@ncte.org Web Site: ncte.org, pg 137

Murgolo, Karen, Aevitas Creative Management LLC, 19 W 21 St, Suite 501, New York, NY 10010 Tel: 212-765-6900 Web Site: www.aevitascreative.com, pg 448

Murguia, Nikte, New City Press, 202 Comforter Blvd, Hyde Park, NY 12538 Tel: 845-229-0335 Toll Free Tel: 800-462-5980 (orders only) Fax: 845-229-0351 E-mail: info@newcitypress.com; orders@newcitypress.com Web Site: www.newcitypress.com, pg 139

Murkette, Julie, Satya House Publications, 22 Turkey St, Hardwick, MA 01037 Web Site: www.satyahouse.com, pg 182

Murphy, Barbara, National Academies Press (NAP), 500 Fifth St NW, Washington, DC 20001 Toll Free Tel: 800-624-6242 Fax: 202-334-2451 (cust serv); 202-334-2793 (mktg dept) E-mail: customer_service@nap.edu Web Site: www.nap.edu, pg 136

Murphy, Bekky, William Holmes McGuffey Longevity Award, PO Box 367, Fountain City, WI 54629 E-mail: info@taaonline.net Web Site: www.taaonline.net/mcguffey-longevity-award, pg 630

Murphy, Bekky, Most Promising New Textbook Award, PO Box 367, Fountain City, WI 54629 E-mail: info@taaonline.net Web Site: www.taaonline.net/promising-new-textbook-award, pg 636

Murphy, Bekky, Pynn-Silverman Lifetime Achievement Award, PO Box 367, Fountain City, WI 54629 E-mail: info@taaonline.net Web Site: www.taaonline.net/council-awards#pynn, pg 654

Murphy, Bekky, TAA Council of Fellows, PO Box 367, Fountain City, WI 54629 E-mail: info@taaonline.net Web Site: www.taaonline.net/council-of-fellows, pg 668

Murphy, Bekky, Textbook Excellence Award, PO Box 367, Fountain City, WI 54629 E-mail: info@taaonline.net Web Site: www.taaonline.net/textbook-excellence-award, pg 669

Murphy, Emily, Alfred A Knopf, c/o Penguin Random House LLC, 1745 Broadway, New York, NY 10019 Tel: 212-751-2600 Fax: 212-940-7390 (dom rts); 212-572-2662 (foreign rts) Web Site: knopfdoubleday.com/imprint/knopf/; knopfdoubleday.com, pg 110

Murphy, Erin, Columbia Books & Information Services (CBIS), 1530 Wilson Blvd, Suite 400, Arlington, VA 22209 Tel: 202-464-1662 Fax: 301-664-9600 E-mail: info@columbiabooks.com Web Site: www.columbiabooks.com; www.association-insight.com; www.ceoupdate.com; www.thealmanacofamericanpolitics.com; www.thompsongrants.com, pg 51

Murphy, Erin, Penguin Random House Audio Publishing Group, 1745 Broadway, New York, NY 10019 Toll Free Tel: 800-793-2665 (cust serv) E-mail: audio@penguinrandomhouse.com; ecustomerservice@penguinrandomhouse.com Web Site: www.penguinrandomhouseaudio.com, pg 154

Murphy, Jacqueline, FinePrint Literary Management, 207 W 106 St, Suite 1D, New York, NY 10025 Tel: 212-279-6214 E-mail: info@fineprintlit.com; submissions@fineprint.com Web Site: www.fineprintlit.com, pg 458

Murphy, Jacqueline, InkWell Management, 521 Fifth Ave, Suite 2600, New York, NY 10175 Tel: 212-922-3500 Fax: 212-922-0535 E-mail: info@inkwellmanagement.com; submissions@inkwellmanagement.com; permissions@inkwellmanagement.com Web Site: inkwellmanagement.com, pg 463

Murphy, Jen, News/Media Alliance, 4401 N Fairfax Dr, Suite 300, Arlington, VA 22203 Tel: 571-366-1000 E-mail: info@newsmediaalliance.org Web Site: www.newsmediaalliance.org, pg 515

Murphy, Kelsey, Philomel Books, c/o Penguin Random House LLC, 1745 Broadway, New York, NY 10019 Tel: 212-782-9000 Web Site: www.penguin.com/philomel/, pg 159

Murphy, Kevin, Soho Press Inc, 853 Broadway, New York, NY 10003 Tel: 212-260-1900 E-mail: soho@sohopress.com; publicity@sohopress.com Web Site: sohopress.com, pg 193

Murphy, Lindsay, American Forest & Paper Association (AF&PA), 1101 "K" St NW, Suite 700, Washington, DC 20005 Tel: 202-463-2700 E-mail: info@afandpa.org; comm@afandpa.org Web Site: www.afandpa.org, pg 495

Murphy, Pat, James Tiptree Jr Literary Award, 173 Anderson St, San Francisco, CA 94110 Tel: 415-641-4103 E-mail: info@tiptree.org Web Site: tiptree.org, pg 669

Murphy, Richard J, BPA Worldwide, 100 Beard Sawmill Rd, 6th fl, Shelton, CT 06484 Tel: 203-447-2800 Fax: 203-447-2900 E-mail: info@bpaww.com Web Site: www.bpaww.com, pg 501

Murphy, Ryan, Viking Penguin, c/o Penguin Random House LLC, 1745 Broadway, New York, NY 10019 Tel: 212-782-9000 Web Site: www.penguin.com/overview-vikingbooks/; www.penguin.com/pamela-dorman-books-overview/; www.penguin.com/penguin-classics-overview/; www.penguin.com/penguin-life-overview/, pg 225

Murphy, Sandra, Writers & Publishers Network (WPN), 1129 Maricopa Hwy, No 142, Ojai, CA 93023 *Web Site:* writersandpublishersnetwork.com, pg 522

Murphy, Sarah, HarperCollins Publishers LLC, 195 Broadway, New York, NY 10007 *Tel:* 212-207-7000 *Web Site:* www.harpercollins.com, pg 86

Murphy, Sean, Schaffner Press, PO Box 41567, Tucson, AZ 85717 *Web Site:* www.schaffnerpress.com, pg 183

Murray, Brian, Association of American Publishers (AAP), 455 Massachusetts Ave NW, Suite 700, Washington, DC 20001-2777 *Tel:* 202-347-3375 *Fax:* 202-347-3690 *E-mail:* info@publishers.org *Web Site:* publishers.org, pg 498

Murray, Brian, HarperCollins Publishers LLC, 195 Broadway, New York, NY 10007 *Tel:* 212-207-7000 *Web Site:* www.harpercollins.com, pg 86

Murray, Cindy, Random House Publishing Group, 1745 Broadway, New York, NY 10019 *Toll Free Tel:* 800-200-3552 *Web Site:* www.randomhousebooks.com, pg 170

Murray, David, Piano Press, 1425 Ocean Ave, Suite 5, Del Mar, CA 92014 *Tel:* 619-884-1401 *E-mail:* pianopress@pianopress.com *Web Site:* www.pianopress.com, pg 159

Murray, Michael, Cricket Cottage Publishing LLC, 275 Medical Dr, No 4773, Carmel, IN 46082 *E-mail:* thecricketpublishing@gmail.com *Web Site:* thecricketpublishing.com; www.facebook.com/CricketCottagePublishing, pg 55

Murray, Nancy, Workman Publishing, 1290 Avenue of the Americas, New York, NY 10104 *Toll Free Tel:* 800-759-0190 *Fax:* 212-364-0950 *E-mail:* workman-inquiry@hbgusa.com *Web Site:* www.hachettebookgroup.com/imprint/workman-publishing-company/, pg 232

Murray, Rachael, Sounds True Inc, 413 S Arthur Ave, Louisville, CO 80027 *Tel:* 303-665-3151 *Toll Free Tel:* 800-333-9185 (US); 888-303-9185 (US & CN) *E-mail:* customerservice@soundstrue.com; stpublicity@soundstrue.com *Web Site:* www.soundstrue.com, pg 194

Murray, Rachel, Henry Holt and Company, LLC, 120 Broadway, 23rd fl, New York, NY 10271 *Tel:* 646-307-5151 *Toll Free Tel:* 888-330-8477 (orders) *Fax:* 646-307-5285 *Web Site:* www.henryholt.com, pg 94

Murray, Sara, The Conference Board Inc, 845 Third Ave, New York, NY 10022-6600 *Tel:* 212-759-0900; 212-339-0345 (cust serv) *E-mail:* customer.service@tcb.org *Web Site:* www.conference-board.org/us; www.linkedin.com/company/the-conference-board, pg 51

Murray, Sean, Sourcebooks LLC, 1935 Brookdale Rd, Suite 139, Naperville, IL 60563 *Tel:* 630-961-3900 *Toll Free Tel:* 800-432-7444 *Fax:* 630-961-2168 *E-mail:* info@sourcebooks.com *Web Site:* www.sourcebooks.com, pg 194

Murray, Steven, J J Keller & Associates, Inc®, 3003 Breezewood Lane, Neenah, WI 54957 *Tel:* 920-722-2848 *Toll Free Tel:* 877-564-2333 *Toll Free Fax:* 800-727-7516 *E-mail:* customerservice@jjkeller.com; sales@jjkeller.com *Web Site:* www.jjkeller.com, pg 108

Musa, Sam, US Government Publishing Office (GPO), Superintendent of Documents, 732 N Capitol St NW, Washington, DC 20401 *Tel:* 202-512-1800 *Toll Free Tel:* 866-512-1800 (orders) *Fax:* 202-512-1998 *E-mail:* contactcenter@gpo.gov *Web Site:* www.gpo.gov; bookstore.gpo.gov (sales), pg 223

Muscato, Nate, Aevitas Creative Management LLC, 19 W 21 St, Suite 501, New York, NY 10010 *Tel:* 212-765-6900 *Web Site:* www.aevitascreative.com, pg 448

Muschett, Jim, Rizzoli International Publications Inc, 300 Park Ave S, 4th fl, New York, NY 10010-5399 *Tel:* 212-387-3400 *Toll Free Tel:* 800-522-6657 (orders only) *Fax:* 212-387-3535 *E-mail:* publicity@rizzoliusa.com *Web Site:* www.rizzoliusa.com, pg 175

Musser, Jacqueline, Adams Media, 100 Technology Center Dr, Suite 501, Stoughton, MA 02072 *Tel:* 508-427-7100 *Web Site:* www.simonandschuster.com, pg 4

Musser, Jane, Running Press, 1290 Avenue of the Americas, New York, NY 10104 *Tel:* 212-364-1100 *Toll Free Tel:* 800-759-0190 (cust serv) *Fax:* 212-364-0933 (intl orders) *Toll Free Fax:* 800-286-9471 (cust serv) *E-mail:* customer.service@hbgusa.com; orders@hbgusa.com *Web Site:* www.hachettebookgroup.com/imprint/running-press/; www.moon.com (Moon Travel Guides), pg 178

Musslewhite, Robert, OptumInsight™, 11000 Optum Circle, Eden Prairie, MN 55344 *Tel:* 952-833-7100 *Toll Free Tel:* 888-445-8745 *Web Site:* www.optum.com, pg 147

Mustico, Kerry, National Music Publishers' Association (NMPA), 1900 "N" St NW, Suite 500, Washington, DC 20036 *Tel:* 202-393-6672 *E-mail:* members@nmpa.org *Web Site:* nmpa.org, pg 513

Musto, Ronald G, Italica Press, 99 Wall St, Suite 650, New York, NY 10005 *Tel:* 917-371-0563 *E-mail:* inquiries@italicapress.com *Web Site:* www.italicapress.com, pg 105

Musyimi, Angel, Gallery Books, 1230 Avenue of the Americas, New York, NY 10020 *Toll Free Tel:* 800-456-6798 *Fax:* 212-698-7284 *E-mail:* consumer.customerservice@simonandschuster.com *Web Site:* www.simonandschuster.com, pg 76

Mutean, Eva, Ignatius Press, 1348 Tenth Ave, San Francisco, CA 94122-2304 *Toll Free Tel:* 800-651-1531 (orders); 888-615-3186 (cust serv) *Fax:* 415-387-0896 *E-mail:* info@ignatius.com *Web Site:* www.ignatius.com, pg 98

Muzinic, Jason, Human Kinetics Inc, 1607 N Market St, Champaign, IL 61820 *Tel:* 217-351-5076 *Toll Free Tel:* 800-747-4457 *Fax:* 217-351-1549 (orders/cust serv) *E-mail:* info@hkusa.com *Web Site:* us.humankinetics.com, pg 97

Muzzarelli, Linda, Consumer Press, 13326 SW 28 St, Suite 102, Fort Lauderdale, FL 33330-1102 *Tel:* 954-370-9153 *E-mail:* info@consumerpress.com *Web Site:* www.consumerpress.com, pg 52

Myatovich, Paul, CN Times Books, 100 Jericho Quadrangle, Suite 337, Jericho, NY 11791 *Tel:* 516-719-0886 *E-mail:* yanliu@cntimesbooks.com *Web Site:* www.cntimesbooks.com, pg 50

Myer, Amy, Penguin Random House LLC, 1745 Broadway, New York, NY 10019 *Tel:* 212-782-9000 *Toll Free Tel:* 800-726-0600 *Web Site:* www.penguinrandomhouse.com, pg 155

Myers, Edward, Montemayor Press, 663 Hyland Hill Rd, Washington, VT 05675 *Tel:* 802-552-0750 *E-mail:* mail@montemayorpress.com *Web Site:* www.montemayorpress.com, pg 133

Myers, Jesse, Chosen Books, 7808 Creekridge Circle, Suite 250, Bloomington, MN 55439 *Tel:* 952-829-2500 *Toll Free Tel:* 800-877-2665 (orders only) *Web Site:* www.chosenbooks.com, pg 47

Myers, Katharine, Little, Brown and Company, 1290 Avenue of the Americas, New York, NY 10104 *Tel:* 212-364-1100 *Fax:* 212-364-0952 *E-mail:* firstname.lastname@hbgusa.com *Web Site:* www.hachettebookgroup.com/imprint/little-brown-and-company/, pg 118

Myers, Kelsey, Joyce Meskis Excellence in Bookselling Scholarship, PO Box 746, Denver, CO 80201 *Toll Free Tel:* 800-752-0249 *E-mail:* info@mountainsplains.org *Web Site:* www.mountainsplains.org/meskis-scholarship, pg 632

Myers, Kelsey, Reading the West Book Awards, PO Box 746, Denver, CO 80201 *Tel:* 970-484-3939 *Toll Free Tel:* 800-752-0249 *Fax:* 970-484-0037 *E-mail:* info@mountainsplains.org *Web Site:* www.mountainsplains.org/reading-the-west-book-awards, pg 655

Myers, Steve, Penguin Random House Speakers Bureau, a Penguin Random House company, 1745 Broadway, Mail Drop 13-1, New York, NY 10019 *Tel:* 212-572-2013 *E-mail:* speakers@penguinrandomhouse.com *Web Site:* www.prhspeakers.com, pg 487

Myles, Mytecia, Embolden Literary, PO Box 953607, Lake Mary, FL 32795-3607 *E-mail:* info@emboldenmediagroup.com; submissions@emboldenmediagroup.com *Web Site:* emboldenmediagroup.com/literary-representation, pg 458

Myrden, Andrew, Penguin Random House Canada, a Penguin Random House company, 320 Front St W, Suite 1400, Toronto, ON M5V 3B6, Canada *Tel:* 416-364-4449 *Toll Free Tel:* 888-523-9292 (cust serv) *E-mail:* canadaweb@penguinrandomhouse.com; customerservicescanada@penguinrandomhouse.com *Web Site:* www.penguinrandomhouse.ca, pg 416

Nachbaur, Fredric, Fordham University Press, Joseph A Martino Hall, 45 Columbus Ave, 3rd fl, New York, NY 10023 *Fax:* 347-842-3083 *Web Site:* www.fordhampress.com, pg 73

Naddaff, Sandra, Harvard Summer School Writing Center, 51 Brattle St, Cambridge, MA 02138 *Tel:* 617-495-4024 *E-mail:* dcewriting@gmail.com; inquiry@summerharvard.edu *Web Site:* summer.harvard.edu, pg 554

Nadeau, Jay, Bitingduck Press LLC, 1262 Sunnyoaks Circle, Altadena, CA 91001 *Tel:* 626-507-8033 *E-mail:* notifications@bitingduckpress.com *Web Site:* bitingduckpress.com, pg 30

Nadeau, Jay, Boson Books™, 1262 Sunnyoaks Circle, Altadena, CA 91001 *Tel:* 626-507-8033 *Fax:* 626-818-1842 *Web Site:* bitingduckpress.com, pg 34

Nadeau, Marie, Bitingduck Press LLC, 1262 Sunnyoaks Circle, Altadena, CA 91001 *Tel:* 626-507-8033 *E-mail:* notifications@bitingduckpress.com *Web Site:* bitingduckpress.com, pg 30

Nadell, Bonnie, Hill Nadell Literary Agency, 6442 Santa Monica Blvd, Suite 200A, Los Angeles, CA 90038 *Tel:* 310-860-9605 *E-mail:* queries@hillnadell.com; rights@hillnadell.com (rts & perms) *Web Site:* www.hillnadell.com, pg 463

Nagel, Karen, Simon & Schuster Children's Publishing, 1230 Avenue of the Americas, New York, NY 10020 *Tel:* 212-698-7000 *Web Site:* www.simonandschuster.com/kids; www.simonandschuster.com/teen; simonandschuster.net; simonandschuster.biz, pg 189

Nagler, Michelle, Random House Children's Books, c/o Penguin Random House LLC, 1745 Broadway, New York, NY 10019 *Tel:* 212-782-9000 *Web Site:* www.rhcbooks.com, pg 169

Naimon, Rebecca, Tor Publishing Group, 120 Broadway, New York, NY 10271 *Toll Free Tel:* 800-455-0340 (Macmillan) *E-mail:* torpublicity@tor.com; forgepublicity@forgebooks.com *Web Site:* us.macmillan.com/torpublishinggroup, pg 208

Nakasone, Marisa, Alfred A Knopf, c/o Penguin Random House LLC, 1745 Broadway, New York, NY 10019 *Tel:* 212-751-2600 *Fax:* 212-940-7390 (dom rts); 212-572-2662 (foreign rts) *Web Site:* knopfdoubleday.com/imprint/knopf/; knopfdoubleday.com, pg 110

Nakatsuka, Kei, Bloomsbury Publishing Inc, 1385 Broadway, 5th fl, New York, NY 10018 *Tel:* 212-419-5300 *E-mail:* marketingusa@bloomsbury.com; adultpublicityusa@bloomsbury.com; askacademic@bloomsbury.com *Web Site:* www.bloomsbury.com, pg 32

Nalen, Lucy, Gallery Books, 1230 Avenue of the Americas, New York, NY 10020 *Toll Free Tel:* 800-456-6798 *Fax:* 212-698-7284 *E-mail:* consumer.customerservice@simonandschuster.com *Web Site:* www.simonandschuster.com, pg 76

Nangle, Leslie, Princeton University Press, 41 William St, Princeton, NJ 08540-5237 *Tel:* 609-258-4900 *Fax:* 609-258-6305 *E-mail:* info@press.princeton.edu *Web Site:* press.princeton.edu, pg 16

Nankervis, Madison, Sourcebooks LLC, 1935 Brookdale Rd, Suite 139, Naperville, IL 60563 *Tel:* 630-961-3900 *Toll Free Tel:* 800-432-7444 *Fax:* 630-961-2168 *E-mail:* info@sourcebooks.com *Web Site:* www.sourcebooks.com, pg 194

Nantier, Terry, NBM Publishing Inc, 300 E 54 St, No 12C, New York, NY 10022-5021 *Tel:* 917-628-6777 *E-mail:* nbmgn@nbmpub.com *Web Site:* www.nbmpub.com, pg 139

Napolitano, Kate, Atria Books, 1230 Avenue of the Americas, New York, NY 10020 *Tel:* 212-698-7000 *Fax:* 212-698-7007 *Web Site:* www.simonandschuster.com, pg 21

Napp, Jessica, Rizzoli International Publications Inc, 300 Park Ave S, 4th fl, New York, NY 10010-5399 *Tel:* 212-387-3400 *Toll Free Tel:* 800-522-6657 (orders only) *Fax:* 212-387-3535 *E-mail:* publicity@rizzoliusa.com *Web Site:* www.rizzoliusa.com, pg 175

Napp, Jessica, Welcome Books, 300 Park Ave S, New York, NY 10010 *Tel:* 212-387-3400 *Fax:* 212-387-3535 *Web Site:* www.rizzoliusa.com/publisher/rizzoli/imprint/wb, pg 227

Naqvi, Haaris, Bloomsbury Academic, 1385 Broadway, 5th fl, New York, NY 10018 *Tel:* 212-419-5300 *Web Site:* www.bloomsbury.com/us/academic, pg 31

Naqvi, Haaris, Bloomsbury Publishing Inc, 1385 Broadway, 5th fl, New York, NY 10018 *Tel:* 212-419-5300 *E-mail:* marketingusa@bloomsbury.com; adultpublicityusa@bloomsbury.com; askacademic@bloomsbury.com *Web Site:* www.bloomsbury.com, pg 31

Naqvi, Haaris, Fairchild Books, 1385 Broadway, 5th fl, New York, NY 10018 *Tel:* 212-419-5300 *Toll Free Tel:* 800-932-4724; 888-330-8477 (orders) *Web Site:* www.bloomsbury.com/us/discover/bloomsbury-academic/fairchild-books/, pg 69

Nara, William, American Society of Civil Engineers (ASCE), 1801 Alexander Bell Dr, Reston, VA 20191-4400 *Tel:* 703-295-6300 *Toll Free Tel:* 800-548-ASCE (548-2723) *Toll Free Fax:* 866-913-6085 *E-mail:* ascelibrary@asce.org; pubsful@asce.org *Web Site:* www.asce.org, pg 12

Narasimhan, Lavanya, Penguin Random House Canada, a Penguin Random House company, 320 Front St W, Suite 1400, Toronto, ON M5V 3B6, Canada *Tel:* 416-364-4449 *Toll Free Tel:* 888-523-9292 (cust serv) *E-mail:* canadaweb@penguinrandomhouse.com; customerservicescanada@penguinrandomhouse.com *Web Site:* www.penguinrandomhouse.ca, pg 416

Nardone, Caelan Ernest, Graywolf Press, 212 Third Ave N, Suite 485, Minneapolis, MN 55401 *Tel:* 651-641-0077 *Fax:* 651-641-0036 *E-mail:* wolves@graywolfpress.org (no ms queries, sample chapters or proposals) *Web Site:* www.graywolfpress.org, pg 81

Nardullo, Mike, Simon & Schuster, 1230 Avenue of the Americas, New York, NY 10020 *Tel:* 212-698-7000 *Toll Free Tel:* 800-223-2348 (cust serv); 800-223-2336 (orders) *Toll Free Fax:* 800-943-9831 (orders) *Web Site:* simonandschusterpublishing.com/simonandschuster/, pg 188

Narramore, Richard, Stanford University Press, 425 Broadway St, Redwood City, CA 94063-3126 *Tel:* 650-723-9434 *Fax:* 650-725-3457 *E-mail:* info@www.sup.org; publicity@www.sup.org; sales@www.sup.org *Web Site:* www.sup.org, pg 197

Narwani, Tricia, Penguin Random House LLC, 1745 Broadway, New York, NY 10019 *Tel:* 212-782-9000 *Toll Free Tel:* 800-726-0600 *Web Site:* www.penguinrandomhouse.com, pg 155

Narwani, Tricia, Random House Publishing Group, 1745 Broadway, New York, NY 10019 *Toll Free Tel:* 800-200-3552 *Web Site:* www.randomhousebooks.com, pg 171

Nash, Alex Cotton, Candlewick Press, 99 Dover St, Somerville, MA 02144-2825 *Tel:* 617-661-3330 *Fax:* 617-661-0565 *E-mail:* bigbear@candlewick.com; salesinfo@candlewick.com *Web Site:* candlewick.com, pg 39

Nash, Cathy L, Association for Information Science & Technology (ASIS&T), 673 Potomac Station Dr, Suite 155, Leesburg, VA 20176 *Tel:* 301-495-0900 *Fax:* 301-495-0810 *E-mail:* asist@asist.org; membership@asist.org *Web Site:* www.asist.org, pg 498

Nash-Weninger, Celeste, American Federation of Astrologers Inc, 6535 S Rural Rd, Tempe, AZ 85283-3746 *Tel:* 480-838-1751 *Toll Free Tel:* 888-301-7630 *E-mail:* info@astrologers.com *Web Site:* www.astrologers.com, pg 9

Nason, Emily, American Booksellers Association, 600 Mamaroneck Ave, Suite 400, Harrison, NY 10528 *Tel:* 914-406-7500 *Toll Free Tel:* 800-637-0037 *Fax:* 914-417-4013 *E-mail:* info@bookweb.org *Web Site:* www.bookweb.org, pg 494

Nasrallah, Dimitri, Vehicule Press, PO Box 42094, CP Roy, Montreal, QC H2W 2T3, Canada *Tel:* 514-844-6073 *E-mail:* vp@vehiculepress.com; admin@vehiculepress.com *Web Site:* www.vehiculepress.com, pg 424

Nasset, Daniel, University of Illinois Press, 1325 S Oak St, MC-566, Champaign, IL 61820-6903 *Tel:* 217-333-0950 *Fax:* 217-244-8082 *E-mail:* uipress@uillinois.edu; journals@uillinois.edu *Web Site:* www.press.uillinois.edu, pg 216

Nasson, Melissa Esq, Beacon Press, 24 Farnsworth St, Boston, MA 02210-1409 *Tel:* 617-742-2110 *Fax:* 617-723-3097 *E-mail:* production@beacon.org *Web Site:* www.beacon.org, pg 25

Nasworthy, Jenica, Simon & Schuster Children's Publishing, 1230 Avenue of the Americas, New York, NY 10020 *Tel:* 212-698-7000 *Web Site:* www.simonandschuster.com/kids; www.simonandschuster.com/teen; simonandschuster.net; simonandschuster.biz, pg 189

Natarajan, Jyothi, Asian American Writers' Workshop (AAWW), 112 W 27 St, Suite 600, New York, NY 10001 *Tel:* 212-494-0061 *E-mail:* desk@aaww.org *Web Site:* aaww.org; facebook.com/AsianAmericanWritersWorkshop, pg 497

Nathan, Geetha, American Booksellers Association, 600 Mamaroneck Ave, Suite 400, Harrison, NY 10528 *Tel:* 914-406-7500 *Toll Free Tel:* 800-637-0037 *Fax:* 914-417-4013 *E-mail:* info@bookweb.org *Web Site:* www.bookweb.org, pg 494

Nathan, Terry, IBPA Book Awards, 1020 Manhattan Beach Blvd, Suite 204, Manhattan Beach, CA 90266 *Tel:* 310-546-1818 *E-mail:* info@ibpa-online.org *Web Site:* www.ibpa-online.org, pg 615

Nathan, Terry, The Independent Book Publishers Association (IBPA), 1020 Manhattan Beach Blvd, Suite 204, Manhattan Beach, CA 90266 *Tel:* 310-546-1818 *E-mail:* info@ibpa-online.org *Web Site:* www.ibpa-online.org, pg 507

Nation, Philip, Thomas Nelson, 501 Nelson Place, Nashville, TN 37214 *Tel:* 615-889-9000 *Toll Free Tel:* 800-251-4000 *Web Site:* www.thomasnelson.com, pg 206

Nauman-Montana, Beth, Salmon Bay Indexing, 26026 Wax Orchard Rd SW, Vashon, WA 98070 *Tel:* 206-612-3993 *Web Site:* salmonbayindexing.com, pg 444

Navarra, Angela, Sourcebooks LLC, 1935 Brookdale Rd, Suite 139, Naperville, IL 60563 *Tel:* 630-961-3900 *Toll Free Tel:* 800-432-7444 *Fax:* 630-961-2168 *E-mail:* info@sourcebooks.com *Web Site:* www.sourcebooks.com, pg 194

Navarre, Randy, Roncorp Music, PO Box 1210, Coatesville, PA 19320 *Tel:* 610-679-5400 *E-mail:* info@nemusicpub.com *Web Site:* www.nemusicpub.com, pg 176

Navarrete, Vanessa, Chronicle Books LLC, 680 Second St, San Francisco, CA 94107 *Tel:* 415-537-4200 *Fax:* 415-537-4460 (perms) *E-mail:* hello@chroniclebooks.com; subrights@chroniclebooks.com *Web Site:* www.chroniclebooks.com, pg 47

Navratil, Chris, American Book Producers Association (ABPA), 7 Peter Cooper Rd, No 7G, New York, NY 10010 *E-mail:* office@abpaonline.org *Web Site:* www.abpaonline.org, pg 494

Nawalinski, Beth, United for Libraries, 225 N Michigan Ave, Suite 1300, Chicago, IL 60601 *Tel:* 312-280-2161 *Toll Free Tel:* 800-545-2433 (ext 2161) *E-mail:* united@ala.org *Web Site:* www.ala.org/united, pg 521

Nawrocki, Sarah, Trinity University Press, One Trinity Place, San Antonio, TX 78212-7200 *Tel:* 210-999-8884 *Fax:* 210-999-8838 *E-mail:* books@trinity.edu *Web Site:* www.tupress.org, pg 209

Nayak, Vaishali, Penguin Young Readers Group, c/o Penguin Random House LLC, 1745 Broadway, New York, NY 10019 *Tel:* 212-782-9000 *Web Site:* www.penguin.com/penguin-young-readers-overview, pg 156

Naylor, Jeffrey, Winterwolf Press, 8635 W Sahara Ave, Suite 425, Las Vegas, NV 89117 *Tel:* 725-222-3442 *E-mail:* info@winterwolfpress.com *Web Site:* winterwolfpress.com, pg 231

Naylor, Sherry, Donner Prize, c/o Naylor and Associates, 23 Empire Ave, Toronto, ON M4M 2L3, Canada *Tel:* 416-368-8253 *E-mail:* donnerprize@naylorandassociates.com *Web Site:* donnerbookprize.com, pg 596

Nazarian, Vera, Norilana Books, PO Box 209, Highgate Center, VT 05459-0209 *E-mail:* service@norilana.com *Web Site:* www.norilana.com, pg 142

Neal, Rae, Multicultural Publications Inc, 1939 Manchester Rd, Akron, OH 44314 *Tel:* 330-865-9578 *Fax:* 330-865-9578 *E-mail:* multiculturalpub@prodigy.net *Web Site:* www.multiculturalpub.net, pg 135

Necarsulmer, Edward IV, Dunow, Carlson & Lerner Literary Agency Inc, 27 W 20 St, Suite 1107, New York, NY 10011 *Tel:* 212-645-7606 *E-mail:* mail@dclagency.com *Web Site:* www.dclagency.com, pg 457

Neff, Hannah, HarperCollins Publishers LLC, 195 Broadway, New York, NY 10007 *Tel:* 212-207-7000 *Web Site:* www.harpercollins.com, pg 87

Neill, Carrie, Random House Publishing Group, 1745 Broadway, New York, NY 10019 *Toll Free Tel:* 800-200-3552 *Web Site:* www.randomhousebooks.com, pg 171

Neimark, Nina, Nina Neimark Editorial Services, 543 Third St, Brooklyn, NY 11215 *Tel:* 718-499-6804 *E-mail:* pneimark@hotmail.com, pg 443

Nellis, Muriel G, Literary & Creative Artists Inc, 3543 Albemarle St NW, Washington, DC 20008-4213 *Tel:* 202-362-4688 *Fax:* 202-362-8875 *E-mail:* lca9643@lcadc.com (queries, no attachments) *Web Site:* www.lcadc.com, pg 467

Nelsen, Brian, Penguin Random House LLC, 1745 Broadway, New York, NY 10019 *Tel:* 212-782-9000 *Toll Free Tel:* 800-726-0600 *Web Site:* www.penguinrandomhouse.com, pg 155

Nelson, Brian, Nelson Literary Agency LLC, 700 Colorado Blvd, No 352, Denver, CO 80206 *Tel:* 303-292-2805 *E-mail:* info@nelsonagency.com *Web Site:* www.nelsonagency.com, pg 471

Nelson, Christina Suzann, Cascade Christian Writers (CCW), PO Box 22, Gladstone, OR 97027 *Tel:* 503-393-3356 *E-mail:* contact@oregonchristianwriters.org *Web Site:* oregonchristianwriters.org, pg 503

Nelson, Connie, New Mexico Book Association (NMBA), PO Box 1285, Santa Fe, NM 87504 *E-mail:* libroentry@gmail.com *Web Site:* www.nmbookassociation.org, pg 514

Nelson, Dr Dave, Baylor University Press, Baylor University, One Bear Place, Waco, TX 76798-7363 *Tel:* 254-710-3164 *E-mail:* bup_marketing@baylor.edu *Web Site:* www.baylorpress.com, pg 25

Nelson, Eric, HarperCollins Publishers LLC, 195 Broadway, New York, NY 10007 *Tel:* 212-207-7000 *Web Site:* www.harpercollins.com, pg 86

Nelson, Kristin, Nelson Literary Agency LLC, 700 Colorado Blvd, No 352, Denver, CO 80206 *Tel:* 303-292-2805 *E-mail:* info@nelsonagency.com *Web Site:* www.nelsonagency.com, pg 471

Nelson, Patricia, Marsal Lyon Literary Agency LLC, 665 San Rodolfo Dr, Suite 124, PMB 121, Solana Beach, CA 92075 *Tel:* 760-814-8507 *Web Site:* www.marsallyonliteraryagency.com, pg 468

Nelson, Priya, Princeton University Press, 41 William St, Princeton, NJ 08540-5237 Tel: 609-258-4900 Fax: 609-258-6305 E-mail: info@press.princeton.edu Web Site: press.princeton.edu, pg 164

Nelson, Sara, HarperCollins Publishers LLC, 195 Broadway, New York, NY 10007 Tel: 212-207-7000 Web Site: www.harpercollins.com, pg 86

Nelson, Sarah, Berrett-Koehler Publishers Inc, 1333 Broadway, Suite 1000, Oakland, CA 94612 Tel: 510-817-2277 Fax: 510-817-2278 E-mail: bkpub@bkpub.com Web Site: www.bkconnection.com, pg 29

Nelson, Sarah, Paul Engle Prize, 123 S Linn St, Iowa City, IA 52240 E-mail: info@iowacityofliterature.org Web Site: www.iowacityofliterature.org/paul-engle-prize, pg 600

Nelson, Tracy, Sourcebooks LLC, 1935 Brookdale Rd, Suite 139, Naperville, IL 60563 Tel: 630-961-3900 Toll Free Tel: 800-432-7444 Fax: 630-961-2168 E-mail: info@sourcebooks.com Web Site: www.sourcebooks.com, pg 194

Nemeth, Terence, Theatre Communications Group, 520 Eighth Ave, 24th fl, New York, NY 10018-4156 Tel: 212-609-5900 Fax: 212-609-5901 E-mail: info@tcg.org Web Site: www.tcg.org, pg 206

Neptune, Alyssa, Alice James Books, 60 Pineland Dr, Suite 206, New Gloucester, ME 04260 Tel: 207-926-8283 E-mail: info@alicejamesbooks.org Web Site: alicejamesbooks.org, pg 105

Nericcio, Dr Bill, San Diego State University Press, Arts & Letters 283/MC 6020, 5500 Campanile Dr, San Diego, CA 92182-6020 Tel: 619-594-6220 (orders); 619-594-1524 (returns) E-mail: memo@sdsu.edu Web Site: sdsupress.sdsu.edu, pg 182

Nesa, Kamrun, Grand Central Publishing, 1290 Avenue of the Americas, New York, NY 10104 Tel: 212-364-1100 Web Site: www.hachettebookgroup.com/imprint/grand-central-publishing/, pg 80

Nesbat, Hannah, St Martin's Press, LLC, 120 Broadway, New York, NY 10271 E-mail: publicity@stmartins.com; trademarketing@stmartins.com; foreignrights@stmartins.com Web Site: us.macmillan.com/smp, pg 181

Nesbit, Lynn, Janklow & Nesbit Associates, 285 Madison Ave, 21st fl, New York, NY 10017 Tel: 212-421-1700 Fax: 212-355-1403 E-mail: info@janklow.com; submissions@janklow.com; filmtvrights@janklow.com Web Site: www.janklowandnesbit.com, pg 464

Netschert, Linda, Farcountry Press, 2750 Broadwater Ave, Helena, MT 59602-9202 Tel: 406-422-1263 Toll Free Tel: 800-821-3874 (sales off) Fax: 406-443-5480 E-mail: books@farcountrypress.com; sales@farcountrypress.com Web Site: www.farcountrypress.com, pg 69

Nettles, Ms Jordan, University Press of Mississippi, 3825 Ridgewood Rd, Jackson, MS 39211-6492 Tel: 601-432-6205 Toll Free Tel: 800-737-7788 (orders & cust serv) Fax: 601-432-6217 E-mail: press@mississippi.edu Web Site: www.upress.state.ms.us, pg 222

Neufeld, Jacque, Safari Press, 15621 Chemical Lane, Bldg B, Huntington Beach, CA 92649 Tel: 714-894-9080 Toll Free Tel: 800-451-4788 Fax: 714-894-4949 E-mail: info@safaripress.com Web Site: www.safaripress.com, pg 179

Neuhaus, Dana, Concordia Publishing House, 3558 S Jefferson Ave, St Louis, MO 63118-3968 Tel: 314-268-1000; 314-268-1268 (bookshop) Toll Free Tel: 800-325-3040 (cust serv) Toll Free Fax: 800-490-9889 (cust serv) E-mail: order@cph.org Web Site: www.cph.org, pg 51

Neuhauser, Alice, The Story Plant, 1270 Caroline St, Suite D120-381, Atlanta, GA 30307 Tel: 203-722-7920 E-mail: thestoryplant@thestoryplant.com Web Site: www.thestoryplant.com, pg 199

Neumann, Aki, Chronicle Books LLC, 680 Second St, San Francisco, CA 94107 Tel: 415-537-4200 Fax: 415-537-4460 (perms) E-mail: hello@chroniclebooks.com; subrights@chroniclebooks.com Web Site: www.chroniclebooks.com, pg 48

Neumann, Grant, Random House Publishing Group, 1745 Broadway, New York, NY 10019 Toll Free Tel: 800-200-3552 Web Site: www.randomhousebooks.com, pg 171

Neusner, Dena, Behrman House Inc, 241B Millburn Ave, Millburn, NJ 07041 Tel: 973-379-7200 Toll Free Tel: 800-221-2755 Fax: 973-379-7280 E-mail: customersupport@behrmanhouse.com Web Site: store.behrmanhouse.com, pg 27

Neuville, Alexis, St Martin's Press, LLC, 120 Broadway, New York, NY 10271 E-mail: publicity@stmartins.com; trademarketing@stmartins.com; foreignrights@stmartins.com Web Site: us.macmillan.com/smp, pg 181

Nevins, Alan, Renaissance Literary & Talent, PO Box 17379, Beverly Hills, CA 90209 Tel: 323-848-8305 E-mail: query@renaissancemgmt.net Web Site: renaissancemgmt.net, pg 473

Nevius, Erin, Association of College & Research Libraries (ACRL), 225 N Michigan Ave, Suite 1300, Chicago, IL 60601 Tel: 312-280-2523; 312-280-2516 Toll Free Tel: 800-545-2433 (ext 2523) Fax: 312-280-2520 E-mail: acrl@ala.org; alastore@ala.org Web Site: www.ala.org/acrl; alastore.ala.org, pg 19

New, Sarah, Alfred A Knopf, c/o Penguin Random House LLC, 1745 Broadway, New York, NY 10019 Tel: 212-751-2600 Fax: 212-940-7390 (dom rts); 212-572-2662 (foreign rts) Web Site: knopfdoubleday.com/imprint/knopf/; knopfdoubleday.com, pg 110

Newcomb, Trish, The McDonald & Woodward Publishing Co, 695 Tall Oaks Dr, Newark, OH 43055 Tel: 740-641-2691 Toll Free Tel: 800-233-8787 Fax: 740-641-2692 E-mail: mwpubco@mwpubco.com Web Site: www.mwpubco.com, pg 127

Newell, Butch, Florida Outdoor Writers Association Inc (FOWA), 235 Apollo Beach Blvd, Unit 271, Apollo Beach, FL 33572 Tel: 813-579-0990 E-mail: info@fowa.org Web Site: www.fowa.org, pg 506

Newell, Patricia, North Country Press, 126 Main St, Unity, ME 04988 Tel: 207-948-2208 E-mail: info@northcountrypress.com Web Site: www.northcountrypress.com, pg 142

Newens, Jen, Martin Literary Management, 914 164 St SE, Suite B12, Box 307, Mill Creek, WA 98012 Tel: 206-466-1773 (no phone queries) Web Site: www.martinliterarymanagement.com, pg 469

Newlin, Judith, McGraw-Hill Professional Publishing Group, 2 Penn Plaza, New York, NY 10121 Tel: 646-766-2000 Web Site: www.mhprofessional.com; www.mheducation.com, pg 128

Newlin, Shanta, Penguin Young Readers Group, c/o Penguin Random House LLC, 1745 Broadway, New York, NY 10019 Tel: 212-782-9000 Web Site: www.penguin.com/penguin-young-readers-overview, pg 156

Newman, Carolyn, River City Publishing, 1719 Mulberry St, Montgomery, AL 36106 Tel: 334-265-6753, pg 175

Newman, Jason, Penguin Random House LLC, 1745 Broadway, New York, NY 10019 Tel: 212-782-9000 Toll Free Tel: 800-726-0600 Web Site: www.penguinrandomhouse.com, pg 155

Newman, Judy, Scholastic Inc, 557 Broadway, New York, NY 10012 Tel: 212-343-6100 Toll Free Tel: 800-SCHOLASTIC (724-6527) Web Site: www.scholastic.com, pg 184

Newman, Miriam, Candlewick Press, 99 Dover St, Somerville, MA 02144-2825 Tel: 617-661-3330 Fax: 617-661-0565 E-mail: bigbear@candlewick.com; salesinfo@candlewick.com Web Site: candlewick.com, pg 40

Newman, Sydney, Scribner, 1230 Avenue of the Americas, New York, NY 10020 Web Site: www.simonandschusterpublishing.com/scribner/, pg 185

Newton, Susan Hill, University of Iowa Press, 119 W Park Rd, 100 Kuhl House, Iowa City, IA 52242-1000 Tel: 319-335-2000 Toll Free Tel: 800-621-2736 (orders only) Fax: 319-335-2055 Toll Free Fax: 800-621-8476 (orders only) E-mail: uipress@uiowa.edu Web Site: www.uipress.uiowa.edu, pg 216

Ney, Alison, Radcliffe Institute Fellowship Program, Byerly Hall, 8 Garden St, Cambridge, MA 02138 Tel: 617-495-8212 Fax: 617-495-8136 E-mail: fellowships@radcliffe.harvard.edu Web Site: www.radcliffe.harvard.edu/fellowship-program, pg 654

Ng, Irene, Penguin Random House LLC, 1745 Broadway, New York, NY 10019 Tel: 212-782-9000 Toll Free Tel: 800-726-0600 Web Site: www.penguinrandomhouse.com, pg 155

Ngo, Rebecca, Andrews McMeel Publishing LLC, 1130 Walnut St, Kansas City, MO 64106-2109 Tel: 816-581-7500 Toll Free Tel: 800-851-8923 Web Site: www.andrewsmcmeel.com; publishing.andrewsmcmeel.com, pg 14

Ngobidi, Nina, Association for Intelligent Information Management (AIIM), 8403 Colesville Rd, No 1100, Silver Spring, MD 20910 Tel: 301-587-8202 Toll Free Tel: 800-477-2446 Fax: 301-587-2711 E-mail: hello@aiim.org Web Site: www.aiim.org, pg 498

Nguyen, Andrew, Bloomsbury Publishing Inc, 1385 Broadway, 5th fl, New York, NY 10018 Tel: 212-419-5300 E-mail: marketingusa@bloomsbury.com; adultpublicityusa@bloomsbury.com; askacademic@bloomsbury.com Web Site: www.bloomsbury.com, pg 32

Nguyen, Kathy, Greystone Books Ltd, 343 Railway St, Suite 302, Vancouver, BC V6A 1A4, Canada Tel: 604-875-1550 Fax: 604-875-1556 E-mail: info@greystonebooks.com; rights@greystonebooks.com Web Site: www.greystonebooks.com, pg 407

Nguyen, Lydia, Harry N Abrams Inc, 195 Broadway, 9th fl, New York, NY 10007 Tel: 212-206-7715 Toll Free Tel: 800-345-1359 Fax: 212-645-8437 E-mail: abrams@abramsbooks.com; publicity@abramsbooks.com; sales@abramsbooks.com Web Site: www.abramsbooks.com, pg 3

Nicholas, Calliope, Millay Colony for the Arts Residency, 454 E Hill Rd, Austerlitz, NY 12017 Tel: 518-392-3103 E-mail: apply@millaycolony.org; residency@millaycolony.org Web Site: www.millaycolony.org, pg 633

Nicholas, Mac, St Martin's Press, LLC, 120 Broadway, New York, NY 10271 E-mail: publicity@stmartins.com; trademarketing@stmartins.com; foreignrights@stmartins.com Web Site: us.macmillan.com/smp, pg 181

Nicholas, Susan, Willie Morris Awards for Southern Writing, Dept of Writing & Rhetoric, PO Box 1848, University, MS 38677 E-mail: wmawards@olemiss.edu Web Site: www.williemorrisawards.org; www.williemorrisawards.org/submissions, pg 635

Nicholls, Hanna, Greystone Books Ltd, 343 Railway St, Suite 302, Vancouver, BC V6A 1A4, Canada Tel: 604-875-1550 Fax: 604-875-1556 E-mail: info@greystonebooks.com; rights@greystonebooks.com Web Site: www.greystonebooks.com, pg 407

Nicholls, Shawn, Other Press, 267 Fifth Ave, 6th fl, New York, NY 10016 Tel: 212-414-0054 Toll Free Tel: 877-THEOTHER (843-6843) Fax: 212-414-0939 E-mail: editor@otherpress.com; marketing@otherpress.com; publicity@otherpress.com Web Site: otherpress.com, pg 148

Nichols, George III, The American College of Financial Services, 630 Allendale Rd, Suite 400, King of Prussia, PA 19406 Tel: 610-526-1000 Toll Free Tel: 866-883-5640 Web Site: www.theamericancollege.edu, pg 9

Nichols, Lee, Gulf Energy Information, 2 Greenway Plaza, Suite 1020, Houston, TX 77046 Tel: 713-520-4498; 713-529-4301 E-mail: store@gulfpub.com; customerservice@gulfenergyinfo.com Web Site: www.gulfenergyinfo.com, pg 83

Nichols, Mariah, D4EO Literary Agency, 13206 Treviso Dr, Lakewood Ranch, FL 34211 Tel: 203-545-7180 (cell) Web Site: www.d4eoliteraryagency.com; www.publishersmarketplace.com/members/d4eo/; x.com/d4eo, pg 456

Nichols, Robby, Covenant Communications Inc, 1226 S 630 E, Suite 4, American Fork, UT 84003 *Tel:* 801-756-1041 *E-mail:* info@covenant-lds.com; covenantorders@covenant-lds.com *Web Site:* www.covenant-lds.com, pg 54

Nichols, Sally, University of Massachusetts Press, New Africa House, 180 Infirmary Way, 4th fl, Amherst, MA 01003-9289 *Web Site:* www.umasspress.com, pg 217

Nichols, Suzanne, Russell Sage Foundation, 112 E 64 St, New York, NY 10065 *Tel:* 212-750-6000 *Toll Free Tel:* 800-524-6401 *Fax:* 212-371-4761 *E-mail:* info@rsage.org *Web Site:* www.russellsage.org, pg 178

Nicholson, Erica, University Press of Kansas, 2502 Westbrooke Circle, Lawrence, KS 66045-4444 *Tel:* 785-864-4154 *Fax:* 785-864-4586 *E-mail:* upress@ku.edu *Web Site:* www.kansaspress.ku.edu, pg 221

Nicholson, Kent, Dramatists Play Service Inc, 440 Park Ave S, New York, NY 10016 *E-mail:* dpsinfo@broadwaylicensing.com; publications@broadwaylicensing.com *Web Site:* www.dramatists.com, pg 61

Nicholson, Leah, Jenkins Group Inc, 1129 Woodmere Ave, Suite B, Traverse City, MI 49686 *Tel:* 231-933-0445; 213-883-5365 *E-mail:* info@jenkinsgroupinc.com *Web Site:* www.jenkinsgroupinc.com, pg 441

Nicholson, Sam, Random House Publishing Group, 1745 Broadway, New York, NY 10019 *Toll Free Tel:* 800-200-3552 *Web Site:* www.randomhousebooks.com, pg 171

Nici, Joanne, Buchwald, 10 E 44 St, New York, NY 10017 *Tel:* 212-867-1200 *E-mail:* info@buchwald.com *Web Site:* www.buchwald.com, pg 453

Nicolajsen, Alex, Kensington Publishing Corp, 900 Third Ave, 26th fl, New York, NY 10022 *Tel:* 212-407-1500 *Toll Free Tel:* 800-221-2647 *Fax:* 212-935-0699 *Web Site:* www.kensingtonbooks.com, pg 109

Nicolay, Megan, Workman Publishing, 1290 Avenue of the Americas, New York, NY 10104 *Toll Free Tel:* 800-759-0190 *Fax:* 212-364-0950 *E-mail:* workman-inquiry@hbgusa.com *Web Site:* www.hachettebookgroup.com/imprint/workman-publishing-company/, pg 232

Nicolls, Katlynn, Workman Publishing, 1290 Avenue of the Americas, New York, NY 10104 *Toll Free Tel:* 800-759-0190 *Fax:* 212-364-0950 *E-mail:* workman-inquiry@hbgusa.com *Web Site:* www.hachettebookgroup.com/imprint/workman-publishing-company/, pg 232

Nicolson, Natalie, Chronicle Books LLC, 680 Second St, San Francisco, CA 94107 *Tel:* 415-537-4200 *Fax:* 415-537-4460 (perms) *E-mail:* hello@chroniclebooks.com; subrights@chroniclebooks.com *Web Site:* www.chroniclebooks.com, pg 47

Nieginski, Elizabeth, Springer Publishing Co, 11 W 42 St, 15th fl, New York, NY 10036-8002 *Tel:* 212-431-4370 *Toll Free Tel:* 877-687-7476 *E-mail:* marketing@springerpub.com; cs@springerpub.com (orders); textbook@springerpub.com; specialsales@springerpub.com *Web Site:* www.springerpub.com, pg 196

Nielsen, Margarete, Hay House LLC, PO Box 5100, Carlsbad, CA 92018-5100 *Tel:* 760-431-7695 (ext 1, intl) *Toll Free Tel:* 800-654-5126 (ext 1, US) *Toll Free Fax:* 800-650-5115 *Web Site:* www.hayhouse.com, pg 89

Nielsen, Mary Beth, ASCD, 2800 Shirlington Rd, Suite 1001, Arlington, VA 22206 *Tel:* 703-578-9600 *Toll Free Tel:* 800-933-2723 *Fax:* 703-575-5400 *E-mail:* member@ascd.org; books@ascd.org *Web Site:* www.ascd.org, pg 18

Nielsen, Rob, Northern California Translators Association, 2261 Market St, Suite 160, San Francisco, CA 94114-1600 *Tel:* 510-845-8712 *E-mail:* ncta@ncta.org *Web Site:* ncta.org, pg 515

Nieves, Xiomara, Random House Children's Books, c/o Penguin Random House LLC, 1745 Broadway, New York, NY 10019 *Tel:* 212-782-9000 *Web Site:* www.rhcbooks.com, pg 170

Nikitina, Elena, Corwin, 2455 Teller Rd, Thousand Oaks, CA 91320 *Tel:* 805-499-9734 *Toll Free Tel:* 800-233-9936 *Fax:* 805-499-5323 *Toll Free Fax:* 800-417-2466 *E-mail:* info@corwin.com; order@corwin.com *Web Site:* www.corwin.com, pg 53

Nikolic, Maja, Writers House, 21 W 26 St, New York, NY 10010 *Tel:* 212-685-2400 *Web Site:* www.writershouse.com, pg 482

Nikolis, Anastasia, Open Letter, University of Rochester, Dewey Hall, 1-219, Box 278968, Rochester, NY 14627 *Tel:* 585-319-0823 *Fax:* 585-273-1097 *E-mail:* contact@openletterbooks.org *Web Site:* www.openletterbooks.org, pg 147

Niles, Tyanni, Simon & Schuster, 1230 Avenue of the Americas, New York, NY 10020 *Tel:* 212-698-7000 *Toll Free Tel:* 800-223-2348 (cust serv); 800-223-2336 (orders) *Toll Free Fax:* 800-943-9831 (orders) *Web Site:* simonandschusterpublishing.com/simonandschuster/, pg 188

Nintzel, Kate, HarperCollins Publishers LLC, 195 Broadway, New York, NY 10007 *Tel:* 212-207-7000 *Web Site:* www.harpercollins.com, pg 86

Nip, Charlotte, Penguin Random House Canada, a Penguin Random House company, 320 Front St W, Suite 1400, Toronto, ON M5V 3B6, Canada *Tel:* 416-364-4449 *Toll Free Tel:* 888-523-9292 (cust serv) *E-mail:* canadaweb@penguinrandomhouse.com; customerservicescanada@penguinrandomhouse.com *Web Site:* www.penguinrandomhouse.ca, pg 416

Nippashi, Ill, Graywolf Press, 212 Third Ave N, Suite 485, Minneapolis, MN 55401 *Tel:* 651-641-0077 *Fax:* 651-641-0036 *E-mail:* wolves@graywolfpress.org (no ms queries, sample chapters or proposals) *Web Site:* www.graywolfpress.org, pg 81

Nisbet, Lynette, Prometheus Books, 59 John Glenn Dr, Amherst, NY 14228-2119 *Fax:* 716-691-0137 *E-mail:* marketing@prometheusbooks.com; editorial@prometheusbooks.com; rights@prometheusbooks.com *Web Site:* www.prometheusbooks.com, pg 166

Nisbet, Sarah, Alfred A Knopf, c/o Penguin Random House LLC, 1745 Broadway, New York, NY 10019 *Tel:* 212-751-2600 *Fax:* 212-940-7390 (dom rts); 212-572-2662 (foreign rts) *Web Site:* knopfdoubleday.com/imprint/knopf/; knopfdoubleday.com, pg 110

Nishan, Rachel, Twin Oaks Indexing, 138 Twin Oaks Rd, Suite W, Louisa, VA 23093 *Tel:* 540-894-5126 *E-mail:* twinoaksindexing@gmail.com *Web Site:* www.twinoakscommunity.org, pg 445

Nishimoto, Katy, Random House Publishing Group, 1745 Broadway, New York, NY 10019 *Toll Free Tel:* 800-200-3552 *Web Site:* www.randomhousebooks.com, pg 171

Niumata, Erin, Folio Literary Management, The Film Center Bldg, 630 Ninth Ave, Suite 1101, New York, NY 10036 *Tel:* 212-400-1494 *Fax:* 212-967-0977 *Web Site:* www.foliolit.com, pg 459

Niver, Heather, Macmillan, 120 Broadway, 22nd fl, New York, NY 10271 *E-mail:* press.inquiries@macmillan.com *Web Site:* us.macmillan.com, pg 122

Nobile, Courtney, HarperCollins Publishers LLC, 195 Broadway, New York, NY 10007 *Tel:* 212-207-7000 *Web Site:* www.harpercollins.com, pg 86

Noble, Claire, Naval Institute Press, 291 Wood Rd, Annapolis, MD 21402-5034 *Tel:* 410-268-6110 *Toll Free Tel:* 800-233-8764 *Fax:* 410-295-1084 *E-mail:* customer@usni.org (cust inquiries) *Web Site:* www.usni.org/press/books; www.usni.org, pg 139

Noble, Katrina, University of Washington Press, 4333 Brooklyn Ave NE, Seattle, WA 98105-9570 *Toll Free Tel:* 800-537-5487 (orders) *Fax:* 206-543-3932; 410-516-6998 (orders) *E-mail:* uwapress@uw.edu *Web Site:* uwapress.uw.edu, pg 220

Noble, Nicole, National Braille Press, 88 Saint Stephen St, Boston, MA 02115-4312 *Tel:* 617-266-6160 *Toll Free Tel:* 800-548-7323 (cust serv); 888-965-8965 *Fax:* 617-437-0456 *E-mail:* contact@nbp.org *Web Site:* www.nbp.org, pg 137

Nocera, Bridget, Houghton Mifflin Harcourt Trade & Reference Division, 125 High St, Boston, MA 02110 *Tel:* 617-351-5000 *Web Site:* www.hmhco.com, pg 96

Noe, Paul, American Forest & Paper Association (AF&PA), 1101 "K" St NW, Suite 700, Washington, DC 20005 *Tel:* 202-463-2700 *E-mail:* info@afandpa.org; comm@afandpa.org *Web Site:* www.afandpa.org, pg 495

Noel, Susannah, Macmillan, 120 Broadway, 22nd fl, New York, NY 10271 *E-mail:* press.inquiries@macmillan.com *Web Site:* us.macmillan.com, pg 122

Noel, Taylor, Random House Publishing Group, 1745 Broadway, New York, NY 10019 *Toll Free Tel:* 800-200-3552 *Web Site:* www.randomhousebooks.com, pg 171

Noem, Josh, Ave Maria Press Inc, PO Box 428, Notre Dame, IN 46556 *Toll Free Tel:* 800-282-1865 *Toll Free Fax:* 800-282-5681 *E-mail:* avemariapress.1@nd.edu *Web Site:* www.avemariapress.com, pg 22

Noes, Megan, Avid Reader Press, 1230 Avenue of the Americas, New York, NY 10020 *Web Site:* avidreaderpress.com, pg 23

Noetzel, Donna, Macmillan, 120 Broadway, 22nd fl, New York, NY 10271 *E-mail:* press.inquiries@macmillan.com *Web Site:* us.macmillan.com, pg 122

Noh, Chrissy, Simon & Schuster Children's Publishing, 1230 Avenue of the Americas, New York, NY 10020 *Tel:* 212-698-7000 *Web Site:* www.simonandschuster.com/kids; www.simonandschuster.com/teen; simonandschuster.net; simonandschuster.biz, pg 189

Nolan, Betsy, The Betsy Nolan Literary Agency, 112 E 17 St, Suite 1W, New York, NY 10003 *Tel:* 212-967-8200 *Web Site:* www.nolanlehrgroup.com, pg 471

Nolan, Christian, New York State Bar Association, One Elk St, Albany, NY 12207 *Tel:* 518-463-3200 *Toll Free Tel:* 800-582-2452 *Fax:* 518-463-5993 *E-mail:* mrc@nysba.org *Web Site:* nysba.org, pg 141

Nolan, Laura, Aevitas Creative Management LLC, 19 W 21 St, Suite 501, New York, NY 10010 *Tel:* 212-765-6900 *Web Site:* www.aevitascreative.com, pg 448

Nolan, Melanie, Penguin Random House LLC, 1745 Broadway, New York, NY 10019 *Tel:* 212-782-9000 *Toll Free Tel:* 800-726-0600 *Web Site:* www.penguinrandomhouse.com, pg 155

Nolan, Melanie, Random House Children's Books, c/o Penguin Random House LLC, 1745 Broadway, New York, NY 10019 *Tel:* 212-782-9000 *Web Site:* www.rhcbooks.com, pg 170

Nolan, Patrick, Viking Penguin, c/o Penguin Random House LLC, 1745 Broadway, New York, NY 10019 *Tel:* 212-782-9000 *Web Site:* www.penguin.com/overview-vikingbooks/; www.penguin.com/pameladorman-books-overview/; www.penguin.com/penguin-classics-overview/; www.penguin.com/penguin-life-overview/, pg 225

Nolet, Maximilien, Les Presses de l'Universite Laval, 2180, Chemin Sainte-Foy, 1st fl, Quebec, QC G1V 0A6, Canada *Tel:* 418-656-2803 *Fax:* 418-656-3305 *E-mail:* presses@pul.ulaval.ca *Web Site:* www.pulaval.com, pg 417

Noonan, Margaret, Fordham University Press, Joseph A Martino Hall, 45 Columbus Ave, 3rd fl, New York, NY 10023 *Fax:* 347-842-3083 *Web Site:* www.fordhampress.com, pg 73

Noonan, Robin, Naval Institute Press, 291 Wood Rd, Annapolis, MD 21402-5034 *Tel:* 410-268-6110 *Toll Free Tel:* 800-233-8764 *Fax:* 410-295-1084 *E-mail:* customer@usni.org (cust inquiries) *Web Site:* www.usni.org/press/books; www.usni.org, pg 139

Noorda, Rachel, ThunderStone Books, 6575 Horse Dr, Las Vegas, NV 89131 *E-mail:* info@thunderstonebooks.com *Web Site:* www.thunderstonebooks.com, pg 207

Noorda, Robert, ThunderStone Books, 6575 Horse Dr, Las Vegas, NV 89131 E-mail: info@thunderstonebooks.com Web Site: www.thunderstonebooks.com, pg 207

Noorlander, Mary, Tanenbaum International Literary Agency Ltd (TILA), 1035 Fifth Ave, Suite 15D, New York, NY 10028 Tel: 212-371-4120 Fax: 212-988-0457 E-mail: hello@tanenbauminternational.com Web Site: tanenbauminternational.com, pg 479

Nora, John, Macmillan, 120 Broadway, 22nd fl, New York, NY 10271 E-mail: press.inquiries@macmillan.com Web Site: us.macmillan.com, pg 122

Norat, Ally, Association for Intelligent Information Management (AIIM), 8403 Colesville Rd, No 1100, Silver Spring, MD 20910 Tel: 301-587-8202 Toll Free Tel: 800-477-2446 Fax: 301-587-2711 E-mail: hello@aiim.org Web Site: www.aiim.org, pg 498

Nordhaus, Vincent, Rutgers University Press, 106 Somerset St, 3rd fl, New Brunswick, NJ 08901 Tel: 848-445-7762; 848-445-7761 (sales) Fax: 732-745-4935 E-mail: sales@rutgersuniversitypress.org Web Site: www.rutgersuniversitypress.org, pg 178

Nordling, Kerry, St Martin's Press, LLC, 120 Broadway, New York, NY 10271 E-mail: publicity@stmartins.com; trademarketing@stmartins.com; foreignrights@stmartins.com Web Site: us.macmillan.com/smp, pg 180

Nordskog, Jessica, Sourcebooks LLC, 1935 Brookdale Rd, Suite 139, Naperville, IL 60563 Tel: 630-961-3900 Toll Free Tel: 800-432-7444 Fax: 630-961-2168 E-mail: info@sourcebooks.com Web Site: www.sourcebooks.com, pg 195

Noreault, Pam, STC Technical Communication Summit, 3251 Blenheim Blvd, Suite 406, Fairfax, VA 22030 Tel: 703-522-4114 Fax: 703-522-2075 E-mail: stc@stc.org; summit@stc.org Web Site: summit.stc.org; www.stc.org, pg 557

Norflus, Debbie, Atria Books, 1230 Avenue of the Americas, New York, NY 10020 Tel: 212-698-7000 Fax: 212-698-7007 Web Site: www.simonandschuster.com, pg 21

Nori, Don, Destiny Image Inc, 167 Walnut Bottom Rd, Shippensburg, PA 17257 Tel: 717-532-3040 Toll Free Tel: 800-722-6774 (orders only) Fax: 717-532-9291 Web Site: www.destinyimage.com, pg 59

Noriega, Christina, Sourcebooks LLC, 1935 Brookdale Rd, Suite 139, Naperville, IL 60563 Tel: 630-961-3900 Toll Free Tel: 800-432-7444 Fax: 630-961-2168 E-mail: info@sourcebooks.com Web Site: www.sourcebooks.com, pg 194

Norman, Anne Cole, Words into Print, 208 Java St, 5th fl, Brooklyn, NY 11222 E-mail: query@wordsintoprint.org Web Site: wordsintoprint.org, pg 445

Norman, Devan, St Martin's Press, LLC, 120 Broadway, New York, NY 10271 E-mail: publicity@stmartins.com; trademarketing@stmartins.com; foreignrights@stmartins.com Web Site: us.macmillan.com/smp, pg 181

Norman, Jason, R Ross Annett Award for Children's Literature, 11759 Groat Rd NW, Edmonton, AB T5M 3K6, Canada Tel: 780-422-8174 Toll Free Tel: 800-665-5354 (AB only) E-mail: mail@writersguild.ab.ca Web Site: writersguild.ca, pg 573

Norman, Jason, Georges Bugnet Award for Fiction, 11759 Groat Rd NW, Edmonton, AB T5M 3K6, Canada Tel: 780-422-8174 Toll Free Tel: 800-665-5354 (AB only) E-mail: mail@writersguild.ab.ca Web Site: writersguild.ca, pg 585

Norman, Jason, The City of Calgary W O Mitchell Book Prize, 11759 Groat Rd NW, Edmonton, AB T5M 3K6, Canada Tel: 780-422-8174 Toll Free Tel: 800-665-5354 (AB only) E-mail: mail@writersguild.ab.ca Web Site: writersguild.ca, pg 590

Norman, Jason, Wilfrid Eggleston Award for Nonfiction, 11759 Groat Rd NW, Edmonton, AB T5M 3K6, Canada Tel: 780-422-8174 Toll Free Tel: 800-665-5354 (AB only) E-mail: mail@writersguild.ab.ca Web Site: writersguild.ca, pg 599

Norman, Jason, James H Gray Award for Short Nonfiction, 11759 Groat Rd NW, Edmonton, AB T5M 3K6, Canada Tel: 780-422-8174 Toll Free Tel: 800-665-5354 (AB only) E-mail: mail@writersguild.ab.ca Web Site: writersguild.ca, pg 609

Norman, Jason, The Robert Kroetsch City of Edmonton Book Prize, 11759 Groat Rd NW, Edmonton, AB T5M 3K6, Canada Tel: 780-422-8174 Toll Free Tel: 800-665-5354 (AB only) E-mail: mail@writersguild.ab.ca Web Site: writersguild.ca, pg 621

Norman, Jason, Howard O'Hagan Award for Short Story, 11759 Groat Rd NW, Edmonton, AB T5M 3K6, Canada Tel: 780-422-8174 Toll Free Tel: 800-665-5354 (AB only) E-mail: mail@writersguild.ab.ca Web Site: writersguild.ca, pg 643

Norman, Jason, Gwen Pharis Ringwood Award for Drama, 11759 Groat Rd NW, Edmonton, AB T5M 3K6, Canada Tel: 780-422-8174 Toll Free Tel: 800-665-5354 (AB only) E-mail: mail@writersguild.ab.ca Web Site: writersguild.ca, pg 656

Norman, Jason, Stephan G Stephansson Award for Poetry, 11759 Groat Rd NW, Edmonton, AB T5M 3K6, Canada Tel: 780-422-8174 Toll Free Tel: 800-665-5354 (AB only) E-mail: mail@writersguild.ab.ca Web Site: writersguild.ca, pg 666

Norman, Jason, Jon Whyte Memorial Essay Prize, 11759 Groat Rd NW, Edmonton, AB T5M 3K6, Canada Tel: 780-422-8174 Toll Free Tel: 800-665-5354 (AB only) E-mail: mail@writersguild.ab.ca Web Site: writersguild.ca, pg 675

Norman, Jason, Writers' Guild of Alberta, 11759 Groat Rd NW, Edmonton, AB T5M 3K6, Canada Tel: 780-422-8174 Toll Free Tel: 800-665-5354 (AB only) E-mail: mail@writersguild.ab.ca Web Site: writersguild.ca, pg 522

Norman, Laura, HarperCollins Publishers LLC, 195 Broadway, New York, NY 10007 Tel: 212-207-7000 Web Site: www.harpercollins.com, pg 87

Norman, Nancy Lowden, Atlantic Center for the Arts Mentoring Artist-in-Residence Program, 1414 Art Center Ave, New Smyrna Beach, FL 32168 Tel: 386-427-6975 E-mail: program@atlanticcenterforthearts.org Web Site: atlanticcenterforthearts.org, pg 553

Norman, Taylor, Holiday House Publishing Inc, 50 Broad St, New York, NY 10004 Tel: 212-688-0085 Fax: 212-421-6134 E-mail: info@holidayhouse.com Web Site: www.holidayhouse.com, pg 94

Norman, Troy, Pauline Books & Media, 50 Saint Paul's Ave, Boston, MA 02130 Tel: 617-522-8911 Toll Free Tel: 800-876-4463 (orders); 800-836-9723 (cust serv) Fax: 617-541-9805 E-mail: editorial@paulinemedia.com (ms submissions); orderentry@pauline.org (cust serv) Web Site: www.pauline.org/pbmpublishing, pg 152

Normil, Jasmine, Simon & Schuster, 1230 Avenue of the Americas, New York, NY 10020 Tel: 212-698-7000 Toll Free Tel: 800-223-2348 (cust serv); 800-223-2336 (orders) Toll Free Fax: 800-943-9831 (orders) Web Site: simonandschusterpublishing.com/simonandschuster/, pg 188

Normil, Sophie, Pantheon Books, c/o Penguin Random House LLC, 1745 Broadway, New York, NY 10019 Tel: 212-751-2600 Fax: 212-940-7390 (dom rts); 212-572-2662 (foreign rts) Web Site: knopfdoubleday.com/imprint/pantheon/; knopfdoubleday.com, pg 150

Normil, Sophie, Vintage Books, c/o Penguin Random House LLC, 1745 Broadway, New York, NY 10019 Tel: 212-572-2420 Fax: 212-940-7390 (dom rts); 212-572-2662 (foreign rts) E-mail: vintageanchorpublicity@randomhouse.com Web Site: knopfdoubleday.com/imprint/vintage; knopfdoubleday.com, pg 225

Norris, Fran, River City Publishing, 1719 Mulberry St, Montgomery, AL 36106 Tel: 334-265-6753, pg 175

Norris, Keenan, Idyllwild Arts Summer Program, 52500 Temecula Rd, No 38, Idyllwild, CA 92549 Tel: 951-659-2171 E-mail: summer@idyllwildarts.org; adultprograms@idyllwildarts.org Web Site: idyllwildarts.org/summer, pg 555

Norris, Ryan, Harry N Abrams Inc, 195 Broadway, 9th fl, New York, NY 10007 Tel: 212-206-7715 Toll Free Tel: 800-345-1359 Fax: 212-645-8437 E-mail: abrams@abramsbooks.com; publicity@abramsbooks.com; sales@abramsbooks.com Web Site: www.abramsbooks.com, pg 3

North, Janice, Eisenbrauns, 820 N University Dr, USB 1, Suite C, University Park, PA 16802-1003 Tel: 814-865-1327 Toll Free Tel: 800-326-9180 (orders & cust serv) Fax: 814-863-1408 Toll Free Fax: 877-778-2665 (orders) E-mail: orders@psupress.org; customerservice@psupress.org Web Site: www.eisenbrauns.org, pg 64

North, Jeremy, Association of American Publishers (AAP), 455 Massachusetts Ave NW, Suite 700, Washington, DC 20001-2777 Tel: 202-347-3375 Fax: 202-347-3690 E-mail: info@publishers.org Web Site: publishers.org, pg 498

North, Jeremy, Taylor & Francis Inc, 530 Walnut St, Suite 850, Philadelphia, PA 19106 Tel: 215-625-8900 Toll Free Tel: 800-354-1420 Fax: 215-207-0050; 215-207-0046 (cust serv) E-mail: support@tandfonline.com Web Site: www.taylorandfrancis.com, pg 203

Norton, Debra, Alice James Books, 60 Pineland Dr, Suite 206, New Gloucester, ME 04260 Tel: 207-926-8283 E-mail: info@alicejamesbooks.org Web Site: alicejamesbooks.org, pg 105

Norton, Jennifer, Eisenbrauns, 820 N University Dr, USB 1, Suite C, University Park, PA 16802-1003 Tel: 814-865-1327 Toll Free Tel: 800-326-9180 (orders & cust serv) Fax: 814-863-1408 Toll Free Fax: 877-778-2665 (orders) E-mail: orders@psupress.org; customerservice@psupress.org Web Site: www.eisenbrauns.org, pg 64

Norton, Jennifer, Penn State University Press, University Support Bldg 1, Suite C, 820 N University Dr, University Park, PA 16802-1003 Tel: 814-865-1327 Toll Free Tel: 800-326-9180 (orders & cust serv) Fax: 814-863-1408 Toll Free Fax: 877-778-2665 (book orders) E-mail: orders@psupress.org; customerservice@psupress.org Web Site: www.psupress.org, pg 157

Norton, Maeve, Scholastic Trade Publishing, 557 Broadway, New York, NY 10012 Tel: 212-343-6100; 212-343-4685 (export sales) Fax: 212-343-4714 (export sales) Web Site: www.scholastic.com, pg 184

Norton, Paul, AMMO Books LLC, 3653 Primavera Ave, Los Angeles, CA 90065 Tel: 323-223-AMMO (223-2666) Fax: 323-978-4200 E-mail: weborders@ammobooks.com; orders@ammobooks.com Web Site: ammobooks.com, pg 13

Nosowsky, Ethan, Graywolf Press, 212 Third Ave N, Suite 485, Minneapolis, MN 55401 Tel: 651-641-0077 Fax: 651-641-0036 E-mail: wolves@graywolfpress.org (no ms queries, sample chapters or proposals) Web Site: www.graywolfpress.org, pg 81

Nossel, Suzanne, PEN America, 120 Broadway, 26th fl N, New York, NY 10271 Tel: 212-334-1660 Fax: 212-334-2181 E-mail: info@pen.org; membership@pen.org; education@pen.org Web Site: pen.org, pg 516

Notarantonio, Pam, Harry N Abrams Inc, 195 Broadway, 9th fl, New York, NY 10007 Tel: 212-206-7715 Toll Free Tel: 800-345-1359 Fax: 212-645-8437 E-mail: abrams@abramsbooks.com; publicity@abramsbooks.com; sales@abramsbooks.com Web Site: www.abramsbooks.com, pg 2

Noudehou, Lisa, Barranca Press, 17 Rockridge Rd, Mount Vernon, NY 10552 Tel: 347-820-2363 E-mail: editor@barrancapress.com Web Site: www.barrancapress.com, pg 24

Novack, Dan, Penguin Random House LLC, 1745 Broadway, New York, NY 10019 Tel: 212-782-9000 Toll Free Tel: 800-726-0600 Web Site: www.penguinrandomhouse.com, pg 155

Novack, Matt, Alan Wofsy Fine Arts, 1109 Geary Blvd, San Francisco, CA 94109 Tel: 415-292-6500 Toll Free Tel: 800-660-6403 Fax: 415-292-6594 (off & cust serv); 510-251-1840 (acctg) E-mail: order@art-books.

com (orders); editeur@earthlink.net (edit); beauxarts@earthlink.net (cust serv) *Web Site:* www.art-books.com, pg 231

Novak, Abigail, Scribner, 1230 Avenue of the Americas, New York, NY 10020 *Web Site:* www.simonandschusterpublishing.com/scribner/, pg 185

Novak, Lynnette, The Seymour Agency, 475 Miner Street Rd, Canton, NY 13617 *Tel:* 239-398-8209 *Web Site:* www.theseymouragency.com, pg 475

Nowak, Emily, Wayne State University Press, Leonard N Simons Bldg, 4809 Woodward Ave, Detroit, MI 48201-1309 *Tel:* 313-577-6120 *Toll Free Tel:* 800-978-7323 *Fax:* 313-577-6131 *E-mail:* bookorders@wayne.edu *Web Site:* www.wsupress.wayne.edu, pg 227

Nowak, Wanda, Wanda Nowak Creative Illustrators Agency, 231 E 76 St, Suite 5-D, New York, NY 10021 *Tel:* 212-535-0438 *E-mail:* wanda@wandanow.com *Web Site:* www.wandanow.com, pg 486

Nowicki, Alexis, DAW Books, 19 W 21 St, No 1201, New York, NY 10010 *E-mail:* info@astrapublishinghouse.com *Web Site:* astrapublishinghouse.com/imprints/daw-books, pg 57

Nowicki, Lori, Painted-Words Inc, 310 W 97 St, Suite 24, New York, NY 10025 *Tel:* 212-663-2311 *E-mail:* info@painted-words.com *Web Site:* painted-words.com, pg 486

Noyce, Penny, Tumblehome Learning Inc, 201 Newbury St, Suite 201, Boston, MA 02116 *E-mail:* info@tumblehomelearning.com *Web Site:* www.tumblehomelearning.com, pg 210

Noyes, Al, Walch Education, 40 Walch Dr, Portland, ME 04103-1286 *Tel:* 207-772-2846 *Toll Free Tel:* 800-558-2846; 800-341-6094 (cust serv) *Fax:* 207-772-3105 *Toll Free Fax:* 888-991-5755 *E-mail:* customerservice@walch.com *Web Site:* www.walch.com, pg 226

Nugent, Gabrielle, W W Norton & Company Inc, 500 Fifth Ave, New York, NY 10110-0017 *Tel:* 212-354-5500 *Toll Free Tel:* 800-233-4830 (orders & cust serv) *Fax:* 212-869-0856 *Toll Free Fax:* 800-458-6515 *E-mail:* orders@wwnorton.com *Web Site:* wwnorton.com, pg 143

Nugent, Lynne, The Iowa Review Awards, 308 EPB, Iowa City, IA 52242-1408 *E-mail:* iowa-review@uiowa.edu *Web Site:* www.iowareview.org, pg 617

Null, Matthew Neill MFA, Susquehanna University, Department of English & Creative Writing, 514 University Ave, Selinsgrove, PA 17870 *Tel:* 570-372-4196 *Web Site:* www.susqu.edu, pg 565

Nunez, Erica, Grove Atlantic Inc, 154 W 14 St, 12th fl, New York, NY 10011 *Tel:* 212-614-7850 *Toll Free Tel:* 800-521-0178 *Fax:* 212-614-7886 *E-mail:* info@groveatlantic.com; sales@groveatlantic.com; publicity@groveatlantic.com; rights@groveatlantic.com *Web Site:* www.groveatlantic.com, pg 82

Nunez, Gisselda, HarperCollins Publishers LLC, 195 Broadway, New York, NY 10007 *Tel:* 212-207-7000 *Web Site:* www.harpercollins.com, pg 86

Nunez, Maria, Bloomsbury Academic, 1385 Broadway, 5th fl, New York, NY 10018 *Tel:* 212-419-5300 *Web Site:* www.bloomsbury.com/us/academic, pg 31

Nunez, Maria, Fairchild Books, 1385 Broadway, 5th fl, New York, NY 10018 *Tel:* 212-419-5300 *Toll Free Tel:* 800-932-4724; 888-330-8477 (orders) *Web Site:* www.bloomsbury.com/us/discover/bloomsbury-academic/fairchild-books/, pg 69

Nurka, Marsida, Ordre des traducteurs, terminologues et interpretes agrees du quebec (OTTIAQ), 1108-2021 Ave Union, Montreal, QC H3A 2S9, Canada *Tel:* 514-845-4411 *Toll Free Tel:* 800-265-4815 *Fax:* 514-845-9903 *E-mail:* info@ottiaq.org; direction@ottiaq.org; reception@ottiaq.org; communications@ottiaq.org *Web Site:* www.ottiaq.org, pg 515

Nurse, Cheryl, Penguin Random House Canada, a Penguin Random House company, 320 Front St W, Suite 1400, Toronto, ON M5V 3B6, Canada *Tel:* 416-364-4449 *Toll Free Tel:* 888-523-9292 (cust serv) *E-mail:* canadaweb@penguinrandomhouse.com; customerservicescanada@penguinrandomhouse.com *Web Site:* www.penguinrandomhouse.ca, pg 416

Nussbaum, Steve, Cold Spring Harbor Laboratory Press, 500 Sunnyside Blvd, Woodbury, NY 11797-2924 *Tel:* 516-422-4100 *Toll Free Tel:* 800-843-4388 *E-mail:* cshpress@cshl.edu *Web Site:* www.cshlpress.com, pg 50

Nuttall, Kelsey, Black Warrior Review Fiction, Nonfiction & Poetry Contest, University of Alabama, Off of Student Media, 414 Campus Dr E, Tuscaloosa, AL 35487 *Tel:* 205-348-4518 *Fax:* 205-348-8036 *E-mail:* blackwarriorreview@gmail.com; bwr@ua.edu *Web Site:* www.bwr.ua.edu, pg 581

Nutter, Abby, Penguin Random House Audio Publishing Group, 1745 Broadway, New York, NY 10019 *Toll Free Tel:* 800-793-2665 (cust serv) *E-mail:* audio@penguinrandomhouse.com; ecustomerservice@penguinrandomhouse.com *Web Site:* www.penguinrandomhouseaudio.com, pg 154

Nutter, Jane, Kensington Publishing Corp, 900 Third Ave, 26th fl, New York, NY 10022 *Tel:* 212-407-1500 *Toll Free Tel:* 800-221-2647 *Fax:* 212-935-0699 *Web Site:* www.kensingtonbooks.com, pg 109

Nwaobia, Kiana, Skinner House Books, c/o Unitarian Universalist Assn, 24 Farnsworth St, Boston, MA 02210-1409 *Tel:* 617-742-2100 *Fax:* 617-948-6466 *E-mail:* skinnerhouse@uua.org *Web Site:* www.uua.org/publications/skinnerhouse, pg 190

Nyborg, Randell, University Publishing House, PO Box 1664, Mannford, OK 74044 *Tel:* 918-865-4726 *E-mail:* upub5@outlook.com *Web Site:* www.universitypublishinghouse.net, pg 222

O'Beirne, Caitlin, Picador, 120 Broadway, New York, NY 10271 *Tel:* 646-307-5151 *Fax:* 212-253-9627 *E-mail:* publicity@picadorusa.com *Web Site:* us.macmillan.com/picador, pg 160

O'Boyle, Jamie, Cultural Studies & Analysis, 1123 Montrose St, Philadelphia, PA 19147-3721 *Tel:* 215-592-8544 *E-mail:* info@culturalanalysis.com *Web Site:* www.culturalanalysis.com, pg 437

O'Brien, Jill, Orbis Books, PO Box 302, Maryknoll, NY 10545-0302 *Tel:* 914-941-7636 *Toll Free Tel:* 800-258-5838 (orders, Mon-Fri 8AM-4PM EST) *Fax:* 914-941-7005 *E-mail:* orbisbooks@maryknoll.org *Web Site:* orbisbooks.com, pg 147

O'Brien, Kara L, Practising Law Institute (PLI), 1177 Avenue of the Americas, 2nd fl, New York, NY 10036 *Tel:* 212-824-5710 (cust serv) *Toll Free Tel:* 800-260-4PLI (260-4754) *Toll Free Fax:* 800-321-0093 (cust serv) *E-mail:* info@pli.edu; membership@pli.edu *Web Site:* www.pli.edu, pg 163

O'Brien, Katherine, A 2 Z Press LLC, 3670 Woodbridge Rd, Deland, FL 32720 *Tel:* 440-241-3126 *E-mail:* sizemore3630@aol.com *Web Site:* www.a2zpress.com; www.bestlittleonlinebookstore.com, pg 1

O'Brien, Kelly, Writers Guild of America, East (WGAE), 250 Hudson St, Suite 700, New York, NY 10013 *Tel:* 212-767-7800 *Fax:* 212-582-1909 *Web Site:* www.wgaeast.org, pg 522

O'Brien, Megan, Sourcebooks LLC, 1935 Brookdale Rd, Suite 139, Naperville, IL 60563 *Tel:* 630-961-3900 *Toll Free Tel:* 800-432-7444 *Fax:* 630-961-2168 *E-mail:* info@sourcebooks.com *Web Site:* www.sourcebooks.com, pg 195

O'Brien-Nicholson, Kathleen, Fordham University Press, Joseph A Martino Hall, 45 Columbus Ave, 3rd fl, New York, NY 10023 *Fax:* 347-842-3083 *Web Site:* www.fordhampress.com, pg 73

O'Callaghan, Katie, HarperCollins Publishers LLC, 195 Broadway, New York, NY 10007 *Tel:* 212-207-7000 *Web Site:* www.harpercollins.com, pg 86

O'Connell, Chris, Macmillan, 120 Broadway, 22nd fl, New York, NY 10271 *E-mail:* press.inquiries@macmillan.com *Web Site:* us.macmillan.com, pg 122

O'Connell, Colleen, HarperCollins Children's Books, 195 Broadway, New York, NY 10007 *Tel:* 212-207-7000 *Web Site:* www.harpercollins.com/childrens, pg 85

O'Connell, Felecia, Alfred A Knopf, c/o Penguin Random House LLC, 1745 Broadway, New York, NY 10019 *Tel:* 212-751-2600 *Fax:* 212-940-7390 (dom rts); 212-572-2662 (foreign rts) *Web Site:* knopfdoubleday.com/imprint/knopf/; knopfdoubleday.com, pg 110

O'Connell, Tim, Simon & Schuster, 1230 Avenue of the Americas, New York, NY 10020 *Tel:* 212-698-7000 *Toll Free Tel:* 800-223-2348 (cust serv); 800-223-2336 (orders) *Toll Free Fax:* 800-943-9831 (orders) *Web Site:* simonandschusterpublishing.com/simonandschuster/, pg 188

O'Connor, Daniel, Bloomsbury Publishing Inc, 1385 Broadway, 5th fl, New York, NY 10018 *Tel:* 212-419-5300 *E-mail:* marketingusa@bloomsbury.com; adultpublicityusa@bloomsbury.com; askacademic@bloomsbury.com *Web Site:* www.bloomsbury.com, pg 32

O'Connor, Emmily, Basic Books Group, 1290 Avenue of the Americas, New York, NY 10104 *Tel:* 212-340-8100 *Toll Free Tel:* 800-343-4499 (cust serv) *Fax:* 212-340-8105 *E-mail:* customer.service@hbgusa.com; orders@hbgusa.com *Web Site:* www.hachettebookgroup.com/imprint/basic-books/, pg 25

O'Connor, John, Eastland Press, 2421 29 Ave W, Seattle, WA 98199 *Tel:* 206-931-6957 (cust serv) *Fax:* 206-283-7084 (orders) *E-mail:* info@eastlandpress.com; orders@eastlandpress.com *Web Site:* www.eastlandpress.com, pg 63

O'Connor, Nichole, Alex Awards, 225 N Michigan Ave, Suite 1300, Chicago, IL 60601 *Tel:* 312-280-4390 *Toll Free Tel:* 800-545-2433 *E-mail:* yalsa@ala.org *Web Site:* www.ala.org/yalsa/alex-awards, pg 572

O'Connor, Nichole, Margaret A Edwards Award, 225 N Michigan Ave, Suite 1300, Chicago, IL 60601 *Tel:* 312-280-4390 *Toll Free Tel:* 800-545-2433 *E-mail:* yalsa@ala.org *Web Site:* www.ala.org/yalsa/edwards-award, pg 598

O'Connor, Nichole, Excellence in Nonfiction for Young Adults, 225 N Michigan Ave, Suite 1300, Chicago, IL 60601 *Toll Free Tel:* 800-545-2433 (ext 4390) *E-mail:* yalsa@ala.org *Web Site:* www.ala.org/yalsa/nonfiction-award, pg 601

O'Connor, Nichole, Frances Henne/YALSA Research Grant, 225 N Michigan Ave, Suite 1300, Chicago, IL 60601 *Tel:* 312-280-4390 *Toll Free Tel:* 800-545-2433 *E-mail:* yalsa@ala.org *Web Site:* www.ala.org/yalsa/awardsandgrants/franceshenne, pg 604

O'Connor, Nichole, Odyssey Award for Excellence in Audiobook Production, 225 N Michigan Ave, Suite 1300, Chicago, IL 60601 *Toll Free Tel:* 800-545-2433 (ext 4390) *E-mail:* yalsa@ala.org *Web Site:* www.ala.org/yalsa/odyssey, pg 643

O'Connor, Nichole, Michael L Printz Award, 225 N Michigan Ave, Suite 1300, Chicago, IL 60601 *Tel:* 312-280-4390 *Toll Free Tel:* 800-545-2433 *E-mail:* yalsa@ala.org *Web Site:* www.ala.org/yalsa/printz-award, pg 653

O'Connor, Nichole, YALSA Conference Grants, 225 N Michigan Ave, Suite 1300, Chicago, IL 60601 *Tel:* 312-280-4390 *Toll Free Tel:* 800-545-2433 *E-mail:* yalsa@ala.org *Web Site:* www.ala.org/yalsa/awardsandgrants.bakertaloryalsa, pg 679

O'Connor, Patricia, Eastland Press, 2421 29 Ave W, Seattle, WA 98199 *Tel:* 206-931-6957 (cust serv) *Fax:* 206-283-7084 (orders) *E-mail:* info@eastlandpress.com; orders@eastlandpress.com *Web Site:* www.eastlandpress.com, pg 63

O'Connor, Rachel Freire, InterVarsity Press, 430 Plaza Dr, Westmont, IL 60559-1234 *Tel:* 630-734-4000 *Toll Free Tel:* 800-843-9487 *Fax:* 630-734-4200 *E-mail:* email@ivpress.com *Web Site:* www.ivpress.com, pg 104

O'Connor, Siobhan, The Danuta Gleed Literary Award, 600-460 Richmond St W, Toronto, ON M5V 1Y1, Canada *Tel:* 416-703-8982 *E-mail:* info@writersunion.ca *Web Site:* www.writersunion.ca, pg 607

O'Connor, Siobhan, Short Prose Competition for Developing Writers, 600-460 Richmond St W, Toronto, ON M5V 1Y1, Canada *Tel:* 416-703-8982 *E-mail:* info@writersunion.ca *Web Site:* www.writersunion.ca, pg 662

O'Connor, Siobhan, The Writers' Union of Canada (TWUC), 600-460 Richmond St W, Toronto, ON M5V 1Y1, Canada *Tel:* 416-703-8982 *E-mail:* info@writersunion.ca *Web Site:* www.writersunion.ca, pg 523

O'Connor, Tara, Berkley, c/o Penguin Random House LLC, 1745 Broadway, 19th fl, New York, NY 10019 *Tel:* 212-366-2000 *Web Site:* www.penguin.com/publishers/berkley/; www.penguin.com/ace-overview/, pg 28

O'Donnell, James III, Evan-Moor Educational Publishers, 10 Harris Ct, Suite C-3, Monterey, CA 93940 *Tel:* 831-649-5901 *Toll Free Tel:* 800-777-4362 (orders) *Fax:* 831-649-6256 *Toll Free Fax:* 800-777-4332 (orders) *E-mail:* sales@evan-moor.com; marketing@evan-moor.com *Web Site:* www.evan-moor.com, pg 68

O'Donnell, Joan, Peabody Museum Press, 11 Divinity Ave, Cambridge, MA 02138 *Tel:* 617-495-4255; 617-495-3938 (edit) *E-mail:* peapub@fas.harvard.edu *Web Site:* www.peabody.harvard.edu/publications, pg 153

O'Donnell, Kevin, William H Sadlier Inc, 9 Pine St, New York, NY 10005 *Tel:* 212-227-2120 *Toll Free Tel:* 800-221-5175 (cust serv) *Fax:* 212-312-6080 *E-mail:* customerservice@sadlier.com *Web Site:* www.sadlier.com, pg 179

O'Donnell, Robert J, The Rockefeller University Press, 950 Third Ave, 2nd fl, New York, NY 10022 *Tel:* 212-327-7938 *E-mail:* rupress@rockefeller.edu *Web Site:* www.rupress.org, pg 176

O'Dowd, Jocelyn Marquez, Macmillan, 120 Broadway, 22nd fl, New York, NY 10271 *E-mail:* press.inquiries@macmillan.com *Web Site:* us.macmillan.com, pg 122

O'Farrell, Anne Marie, Denise Marcil Literary Agency LLC, 483 Westover Rd, Stamford, CT 06902 *Tel:* 203-327-9970 *Fax:* 203-327-9970 *Web Site:* www.marcilofarrellagency.com, pg 468

O'Grady, Hannah, St Martin's Press, LLC, 120 Broadway, New York, NY 10271 *E-mail:* publicity@stmartins.com; trademarketing@stmartins.com; foreignrights@stmartins.com *Web Site:* us.macmillan.com/smp, pg 181

O'Halloran, Jacinta, Random House Publishing Group, 1745 Broadway, New York, NY 10019 *Toll Free Tel:* 800-200-3552 *Web Site:* www.randomhousebooks.com, pg 171

O'Halloran, Paul, Gallery Books, 1230 Avenue of the Americas, New York, NY 10020 *Toll Free Tel:* 800-456-6798 *Fax:* 212-698-7284 *E-mail:* consumer.customerservice@simonandschuster.com *Web Site:* www.simonandschuster.com, pg 76

O'Halloran, Paul, Scribner, 1230 Avenue of the Americas, New York, NY 10020 *Web Site:* www.simonandschusterpublishing.com/scribner/, pg 185

O'Hanlon, Martin, CWA/SCA Canada, 2200 Prince of Wales Dr, Suite 301, Ottawa, ON K2E 6Z9, Canada *Tel:* 613-820-9777 *Toll Free Tel:* 877-486-4292 *Fax:* 613-820-8188 *E-mail:* info@cwacanada.ca *Web Site:* www.cwacanada.ca, pg 504

O'Hara, Mary, Chronicle Books LLC, 680 Second St, San Francisco, CA 94107 *Tel:* 415-537-4200 *Fax:* 415-537-4460 (perms) *E-mail:* hello@chroniclebooks.com; subrights@chroniclebooks.com *Web Site:* www.chroniclebooks.com, pg 47

O'Hare, Helen, Little, Brown and Company, 1290 Avenue of the Americas, New York, NY 10104 *Tel:* 212-364-1100 *Fax:* 212-364-0952 *E-mail:* firstname.lastname@hbgusa.com *Web Site:* www.hachettebookgroup.com/imprint/little-brown-and-company/, pg 118

O'Hare, Siobhan, Penguin Random House Audio Publishing Group, 1745 Broadway, New York, NY 10019 *Toll Free Tel:* 800-793-2665 (cust serv) *E-mail:* audio@penguinrandomhouse.com; ecustomerservice@penguinrandomhouse.com *Web Site:* www.penguinrandomhouseaudio.com, pg 154

O'Hearn, Thom, Quarto Publishing Group USA Inc, 100 Cummings Ctr, Suite 265D, Beverly, MA 01915 *Tel:* 978-282-9590 *Toll Free Tel:* 800-328-0590 (sales) *Fax:* 978-283-2742 *E-mail:* sales@quartous.com *Web Site:* www.quartoknows.com, pg 168

O'Keefe, Carolyn, Henry Holt and Company, LLC, 120 Broadway, 23rd fl, New York, NY 10271 *Tel:* 646-307-5151 *Toll Free Tel:* 888-330-8477 (orders) *Fax:* 646-307-5285 *Web Site:* www.henryholt.com, pg 94

O'Keefe, Chrystal, Society of Professional Journalists (SPJ), PO Box 441748, Indianapolis, IN 46244 *Tel:* 317-927-8000 *Fax:* 317-920-4789 *E-mail:* communications@spj.org *Web Site:* www.spj.org, pg 520

O'koro, Kemdi, Macmillan, 120 Broadway, 22nd fl, New York, NY 10271 *E-mail:* press.inquiries@macmillan.com *Web Site:* us.macmillan.com, pg 122

O'Leary, Brian, BISG Industry Awards, 232 Madison Ave, Suite 1200, New York, NY 10016 *Tel:* 646-336-7141 *E-mail:* info@bisg.org *Web Site:* www.bisg.org, pg 581

O'Leary, Brian, Book Industry Study Group Inc (BISG), 232 Madison Ave, Suite 1200, New York, NY 10016 *Tel:* 646-336-7141 *E-mail:* info@bisg.org *Web Site:* www.bisg.org, pg 501

O'Leary, Joseph, Macmillan, 120 Broadway, 22nd fl, New York, NY 10271 *E-mail:* press.inquiries@macmillan.com *Web Site:* us.macmillan.com, pg 122

O'Leary, Meghan, Random House Publishing Group, 1745 Broadway, New York, NY 10019 *Toll Free Tel:* 800-200-3552 *Web Site:* www.randomhousebooks.com, pg 171

O'Malley, Austin, Doubleday, c/o Penguin Random House LLC, 1745 Broadway, New York, NY 10019 *Tel:* 212-751-2600 *Fax:* 212-940-7390 (dom rts); 212-572-2662 (foreign rts) *Web Site:* knopfdoubleday.com/imprint/doubleday/; knopfdoubleday.com, pg 61

O'Malley, Austin, Alfred A Knopf, c/o Penguin Random House LLC, 1745 Broadway, New York, NY 10019 *Tel:* 212-751-2600 *Fax:* 212-940-7390 (dom rts); 212-572-2662 (foreign rts) *Web Site:* knopfdoubleday.com/imprint/knopf/; knopfdoubleday.com, pg 110

O'Malley, Eileen, Drue Heinz Literature Prize, 7500 Thomas Blvd, Pittsburgh, PA 15260 *Tel:* 412-383-2456 *Fax:* 412-383-2466 *E-mail:* info@upress.pitt.edu *Web Site:* upittpress.org/prize/drue-heinz-literature-prize; www.upress.pitt.edu, pg 612

O'Malley, Eileen, Agnes Lynch Starrett Poetry Prize, 7500 Thomas Blvd, Pittsburgh, PA 15260 *Tel:* 412-383-2456 *Fax:* 412-383-2466 *E-mail:* info@upress.pitt.edu *Web Site:* upittpress.org/prize/agnes-lynch-starrett-poetry-prize/; www.upress.pitt.edu, pg 666

O'Malley, Eileen, University of Pittsburgh Press, 7500 Thomas Blvd, Pittsburgh, PA 15260 *Tel:* 412-383-2456 *Fax:* 412-383-2466 *E-mail:* info@upress.pitt.edu *Web Site:* www.upress.pitt.edu, pg 219

O'Malley, Janine, Farrar, Straus & Giroux Books for Young Readers, 120 Broadway, New York, NY 10271 *Tel:* 212-741-6900 *Toll Free Tel:* 888-330-8477 (orders) *E-mail:* childrens.publicity@macmillanusa.com; childrensrights@macmillanusa.com *Web Site:* us.macmillan.com/mackids, pg 70

O'Mara, Catherine, Random House Children's Books, c/o Penguin Random House LLC, 1745 Broadway, New York, NY 10019 *Tel:* 212-782-9000 *Web Site:* www.rhcbooks.com, pg 170

O'Mara, Mary, Harry N Abrams Inc, 195 Broadway, 9th fl, New York, NY 10007 *Tel:* 212-206-7715 *Toll Free Tel:* 800-345-1359 *Fax:* 212-645-8437 *E-mail:* abrams@abramsbooks.com; publicity@abramsbooks.com; sales@abramsbooks.com *Web Site:* www.abramsbooks.com, pg 2

O'Moore-Klopf, Katharine, KOK Edit, 15 Hare Lane, East Setauket, NY 11733-3606 *Tel:* 631-997-8191 *E-mail:* editor@kokedit.com *Web Site:* www.kokedit.com; x.com/kokedit; www.facebook.com/K.OmooreKlopf; www.linkedin.com/in/kokedit; www.editor-mom.blogspot.com, pg 441

O'Neal, Eilis, The Pablo Neruda Prize for Poetry, University of Tulsa, Kendall College of Arts & Sciences, 800 S Tucker Dr, Tulsa, OK 74104 *Tel:* 918-631-3080 *E-mail:* nimrod@utulsa.edu *Web Site:* artsandsciences.utulsa.edu/nimrod/nimrod-literary-awards/, pg 639

O'Neal, Eilis, Katherine Anne Porter Prize for Fiction, University of Tulsa, Kendall College of Arts & Sciences, 800 S Tucker Dr, Tulsa, OK 74104 *Tel:* 918-631-3080 *E-mail:* nimrod@utulsa.edu *Web Site:* artsandsciences.utulsa.edu/nimrod/nimrod-literary-awards/, pg 651

O'Neal, Lauren, TarcherPerigee, c/o Penguin Random House LLC, 1745 Broadway, New York, NY 10019 *Tel:* 212-782-9000 *Web Site:* www.penguin.com/tarcherperigee-overview/; www.facebook.com/TarcherPerigee, pg 202

O'Neil, Cara, Dark Horse Comics, 10956 SE Main St, Milwaukie, OR 97222 *Tel:* 503-652-8815 *Fax:* 503-654-9440 *E-mail:* dhcomics@darkhorse.com *Web Site:* www.darkhorse.com, pg 57

O'Neil, Casey, Graywolf Press, 212 Third Ave N, Suite 485, Minneapolis, MN 55401 *Tel:* 651-641-0077 *Fax:* 651-641-0036 *E-mail:* wolves@graywolfpress.org (no ms queries, sample chapters or proposals) *Web Site:* www.graywolfpress.org, pg 81

O'Neill, Brendan, Adams Media, 100 Technology Center Dr, Suite 501, Stoughton, MA 02072 *Tel:* 508-427-7100 *Web Site:* www.simonandschuster.com, pg 4

O'Neill, Jim, Houghton Mifflin Harcourt, 125 High St, Boston, MA 02110 *Tel:* 617-351-5000 *Toll Free Tel:* 855-969-4642; 800-225-5425 (K-12 educ materials); 800-323-9540 (assessment materials); 877-219-1537 (SkillsTutor); 888-242-6747 (Innovation in Educ Group); 800-225-3362 (Trade & Ref Div) *Toll Free Fax:* 800-269-5232 *E-mail:* myhmhco@hmhco.com *Web Site:* www.hmhco.com, pg 96

O'Neill, Josh, Beehive Books, 4700 Kingsessing Ave, Suite C, Philadelphia, PA 19143 *E-mail:* beehivebook@gmail.com *Web Site:* www.beehivebooks.net, pg 26

O'Neill, Marie, Highlights for Children Inc, 815 Church St, Honesdale, PA 18431 *Tel:* 570-253-1164 *Toll Free Tel:* 800-490-5111 *Fax:* 570-253-0179 *E-mail:* salesandmarketing@highlightspress.com *Web Site:* www.highlightspress.com; www.highlights.com; www.facebook.com/HighlightsforChildren, pg 92

O'Neill, Michael, BMI®, 7 World Trade Center, 250 Greenwich St, New York, NY 10007-0030 *Tel:* 212-220-3000 *Toll Free Tel:* 888-689-5264 (sales) *E-mail:* newyork@bmi.com *Web Site:* www.bmi.com, pg 501

O'Neill, Suzanne, Grand Central Publishing, 1290 Avenue of the Americas, New York, NY 10104 *Tel:* 212-364-1100 *Web Site:* www.hachettebookgroup.com/imprint/grand-central-publishing/, pg 80

O'Neill, Trish McNamara, Harry N Abrams Inc, 195 Broadway, 9th fl, New York, NY 10007 *Tel:* 212-206-7715 *Toll Free Tel:* 800-345-1359 *Fax:* 212-645-8437 *E-mail:* abrams@abramsbooks.com; publicity@abramsbooks.com; sales@abramsbooks.com *Web Site:* www.abramsbooks.com, pg 3

O'Reilly, Eileen, National Press Club (NPC), 529 14 St NW, 13th fl, Washington, DC 20045 *Tel:* 202-662-7500 *Web Site:* www.press.org, pg 513

O'Reilly, James, Travelers' Tales, 2320 Bowdoin St, Palo Alto, CA 94306 *Tel:* 650-462-2110 *E-mail:* ttales@travelerstales.com; info@travelerstales.com *Web Site:* travelerstales.com, pg 209

O'Reilly, Sean, Travelers' Tales, 2320 Bowdoin St, Palo Alto, CA 94306 *Tel:* 650-462-2110 *E-mail:* ttales@travelerstales.com; info@travelerstales.com *Web Site:* travelerstales.com, pg 209

O'Reilly, Stephan, SteinerBooks Inc, 610 Main St, Suite 1, Great Barrington, MA 01230 *Tel:* 413-528-8233 *E-mail:* service@steinerbooks.org; friends@steinerbooks.org *Web Site:* steiner.presswarehouse.com, pg 198

O'Reilly, Tim, O'Reilly Media Inc, 1005 Gravenstein Hwy N, Sebastopol, CA 95472 *Tel:* 707-827-7000; 707-827-7019 (cust support) *Toll Free Tel:* 800-998-9938; 800-889-8969 *Fax:* 707-829-0104; 707-824-8268 *E-mail:* orders@oreilly.com; support@oreilly.com *Web Site:* www.oreilly.com, pg 148

O'Rourke, Clare, Macmillan, 120 Broadway, 22nd fl, New York, NY 10271 *E-mail:* press.inquiries@macmillan.com *Web Site:* us.macmillan.com, pg 121

O'Shaughnessy, Caitlin, The Book Group (TBG), 20 W 20 St, Suite 601, New York, NY 10011 *E-mail:* info@thebookgroup.com; submissions@thebookgroup.com *Web Site:* www.thebookgroup.com, pg 450

O'Shaughnessy, Meghan, Workman Publishing, 1290 Avenue of the Americas, New York, NY 10104 *Toll Free Tel:* 800-759-0190 *Fax:* 212-364-0950 *E-mail:* workman-inquiry@hbgusa.com *Web Site:* www.hachettebookgroup.com/imprint/workman-publishing-company/, pg 233

O'Shea, Heather, Teaching Strategies LLC, 4500 East-West Hwy, Suite 300, Bethesda, MD 20814 *Tel:* 301-634-0818 *Toll Free Tel:* 800-637-3652 *E-mail:* info@teachingstrategies.com; support@teachingstrategies.com *Web Site:* teachingstrategies.com, pg 204

O'Shea, Patti, University of Chicago Press, 1427 E 60 St, Chicago, IL 60637-2954 *Tel:* 773-702-7700; 773-702-7600 *Toll Free Tel:* 800-621-2736 (orders) *Fax:* 773-702-9756; 773-660-2235 (orders); 773-702-2708 *E-mail:* custserv@press.uchicago.edu; marketing@press.uchicago.edu *Web Site:* www.press.uchicago.edu, pg 215

O'Shea, Sheila, Farrar, Straus & Giroux, LLC, 120 Broadway, New York, NY 10271 *Tel:* 212-741-6900 *E-mail:* fsg.publicity@fsgbooks.com; sales@fsgbooks.com *Web Site:* us.macmillan.com/fsg, pg 70

O'Shea, Sheila, FSG Writer's Fellowship, 120 Broadway, New York, NY 10271 *Tel:* 212-741-6900 *E-mail:* fsg.publicity@fsgbooks.com *Web Site:* fsgfellowship.com, pg 605

O'Sullivan, Kate, Clarion Books, 195 Broadway, New York, NY 10007 *Tel:* 212-207-7000 *Toll Free Tel:* 800-242-7737 *E-mail:* consumercare@harpercollins.com *Web Site:* www.harpercollins.com/collections/books-by-clarion-books, pg 49

O'Sullivan, Kate, Houghton Mifflin Harcourt Trade & Reference Division, 125 High St, Boston, MA 02110 *Tel:* 617-351-5000 *Web Site:* www.hmhco.com, pg 96

O'Tierney, Maris Maeve, Poetry Foundation, 61 W Superior St, Chicago, IL 60654 *Tel:* 312-787-7070 *E-mail:* info@poetryfoundation.org *Web Site:* www.poetryfoundation.org, pg 526

O'Toole, Bridget, Berkley, c/o Penguin Random House LLC, 1745 Broadway, 19th fl, New York, NY 10019 *Tel:* 212-366-2000 *Web Site:* www.penguin.com/publishers/berkley/; www.penguin.com/ace-overview/, pg 28

Oakes, Eva, Transatlantic Agency, 2 Bloor St E, Suite 3500, Toronto, ON M4W 1A8, Canada *Tel:* 416-488-9214 *E-mail:* info@transatlanticagency.com; royalties@transatlanticagency.com *Web Site:* www.transatlanticagency.com, pg 479

Oakes, Roger B, Adams & Ambrose Publishing, 1622 Capital Ave, Madison, WI 53705-1228 *Tel:* 608-572-2471 *E-mail:* info@adamsambrose.com, pg 4

Oakleaf, Kara, Institute for Immigration Research New American Voices Award, 4400 University Dr, MS 3E4, Fairfax, VA 22030 *Tel:* 703-993-3986 *E-mail:* submissions@fallforthebook.org *Web Site:* fallforthebook.org/aboutnewamericanvoices, pg 617

Oates, Richard, Florida Antiquarian Booksellers Association (FABA), c/o Lighthouse Books, ABAA, 14046 Fifth St, Dade City, FL 33525 *Tel:* 727-234-7759 *E-mail:* floridabooksellers@gmail.com *Web Site:* floridabooksellers.com, pg 506

Oates, Steve, Bethany House Publishers, 11400 Hampshire Ave S, Bloomington, MN 55438 *Tel:* 952-829-2500 *Toll Free Tel:* 800-877-2665 (orders) *Fax:* 952-829-2568 *Toll Free Fax:* 800-398-3111 (orders) *Web Site:* www.bethanyhouse.com; www.bakerpublishinggroup.com, pg 29

Obando, Natalie, Ladderbird Literary Agency, 460 Yellow Brick Rd, Orange, CT 06477 *Tel:* 203-290-1703 *Web Site:* www.ladderbird.com, pg 466

Obando-Desai, Natalie, Women's National Book Association Inc, PO Box 237, FDR Sta, New York, NY 10150-0231 *Toll Free Tel:* 866-610-WNBA (610-9622) *E-mail:* info@wnba-books.org *Web Site:* wnba-books.org, pg 522

Obeng, Kristan, Education Writers Association (EWA), 1825 "K" St NW, Suite 200, Washington, DC 20006 *Tel:* 202-452-9830 *Web Site:* ewa.org, pg 505

Oberdorf, Anya, Penguin Random House Canada, a Penguin Random House company, 320 Front St W, Suite 1400, Toronto, ON M5V 3B6, Canada *Tel:* 416-364-4449 *Toll Free Tel:* 888-523-9292 (cust serv) *E-mail:* canadaweb@penguinrandomhouse.com; customerservicescanada@penguinrandomhouse.com *Web Site:* www.penguinrandomhouse.ca, pg 416

Oberlin, Brent, The MIT Press, One Broadway, 12th fl, Cambridge, MA 02142 *Tel:* 617-253-5255 *Toll Free Tel:* 800-405-1619 (orders) *Fax:* 617-258-6779; 617-577-1545 (orders) *Web Site:* mitpress.mit.edu, pg 132

Obondo, Natalie, Judy Lopez Memorial Award For Children's Literature, 1225 Selby Ave, Los Angeles, CA 90024 *Tel:* 310-474-9917 *Fax:* 310-474-6436 *Web Site:* www.wnba-books.org/la; www.judylopezbookaward.org, pg 626

Obry, Carrie, Midwest Bookseller of the Year Award, 939 W Seventh St, St Paul, MN 55102 *Tel:* 612-208-6279 *Web Site:* www.midwestbooksellers.org/bookseller-of-the-year.html, pg 632

Obry, Carrie, Midwest Independent Booksellers Association (MIBA), 939 W Seventh St, St Paul, MN 55102 *Tel:* 612-208-6279 *Web Site:* www.midwestbooksellers.org, pg 510

Ocampo, Patricia, Kids Can Press Ltd, 25 Dockside Dr, Toronto, ON M5A 0B5, Canada *Tel:* 416-479-7000 *Toll Free Tel:* 800-265-0884 *Fax:* 416-960-5437 *E-mail:* info@kidscan.com; customerservice@kidscan.com *Web Site:* www.kidscanpress.com; www.kidscanpress.ca, pg 411

Ochoa, Gladys, Lectorum Publications Inc, 10 New Maple Ave, Suite 303, Pine Brook, NJ 07058 *Tel:* 201-559-2200 *Toll Free Tel:* 800-345-5946 *E-mail:* lectorum@lectorum.com *Web Site:* www.lectorum.com, pg 114

Ochsner, Daniel, University of Minnesota Press, 111 Third Ave S, Suite 290, Minneapolis, MN 55401-2520 *Tel:* 612-301-1990 *Fax:* 612-301-1980 *E-mail:* ump@umn.edu *Web Site:* www.upress.umn.edu, pg 217

Odders, Annelise, Berkley, c/o Penguin Random House LLC, 1745 Broadway, 19th fl, New York, NY 10019 *Tel:* 212-366-2000 *Web Site:* www.penguin.com/publishers/berkley/; www.penguin.com/ace-overview/, pg 28

Oddo-Budinoff, Francesca, Macmillan, 120 Broadway, 22nd fl, New York, NY 10271 *E-mail:* press.inquiries@macmillan.com *Web Site:* us.macmillan.com, pg 122

Odell, Becky, Dutton, c/o Penguin Random House LLC, 1745 Broadway, New York, NY 10019 *Tel:* 212-366-2000 *Web Site:* www.penguin.com/dutton-overview/; www.penguin.com/plume-books-overview/; www.penguin.com/tiny-reparations-overview/, pg 62

Oden, Kelly, Ballinger Publishing, 21 E Garden St, Suite 205, Pensacola, FL 32502 *Tel:* 850-433-1166 *Fax:* 850-435-9174 *E-mail:* info@ballingerpublishing.com *Web Site:* www.ballingerpublishing.com, pg 24

Odiseos, Nikko, Shambhala Publications Inc, 2129 13 St, Boulder, CO 80302 *Tel:* 978-829-2599 (intl callers) *Toll Free Tel:* 866-424-0030 (off); 888-424-2329 (orders & cust serv) *Fax:* 617-236-1563 *E-mail:* customercare@shambhala.com; royalties@shambhala.com *Web Site:* www.shambhala.com, pg 187

Odiseos, Nikko, Snow Lion, 4720 Walnut St, Boulder, CO 80301 *E-mail:* customercare@shambhala.com *Web Site:* www.shambhala.com/snowlion, pg 192

Odland, Steve, The Conference Board Inc, 845 Third Ave, New York, NY 10022-6600 *Tel:* 212-759-0900; 212-339-0345 (cust serv) *E-mail:* customer.service@tcb.org *Web Site:* www.conference-board.org/us; www.linkedin.com/company/the-conference-board, pg 51

Oeltjen, Dr Natalie, Centre for Reformation & Renaissance Studies (CRRS), 71 Queen's Park Crescent E, Toronto, ON M5S 1K7, Canada *Tel:* 416-585-4465 *Fax:* 416-585-4430 (attn: CRRS) *E-mail:* crrs.publications@utoronto.ca *Web Site:* crrs.ca, pg 399

Oestreich, Julia, University of Delaware Press, 200A Morris Library, 181 S College Ave, Newark, DE 19717-5267 *Tel:* 302-831-1149 *Toll Free Tel:* 800-462-6420 (orders) *Fax:* 302-831-6549 *E-mail:* ud-press@udel.edu; orders@rowman.com *Web Site:* library.udel.edu/udpress, pg 215

Oey, Eric, Tuttle Publishing, Airport Business Park, 364 Innovation Dr, North Clarendon, VT 05759-9436 *Tel:* 802-773-8930 *Toll Free Tel:* 800-526-2778 *Fax:* 802-773-6993 *Toll Free Fax:* 800-FAX-TUTL (329-8885) *E-mail:* info@tuttlepublishing.com; orders@tuttlepublishing.com *Web Site:* www.tuttlepublishing.com, pg 211

Ogg, Jessica, Sourcebooks LLC, 1935 Brookdale Rd, Suite 139, Naperville, IL 60563 *Tel:* 630-961-3900 *Toll Free Tel:* 800-432-7444 *Fax:* 630-961-2168 *E-mail:* info@sourcebooks.com *Web Site:* www.sourcebooks.com, pg 194

Ognibene, Peter E, Breakthrough Publications Inc, 3 Iroquois St, Emmaus, PA 18049 *Tel:* 610-928-4062 *E-mail:* dot@booksonhorses.com; ruth@booksonhorses.com *Web Site:* www.booksonhorses.com, pg 36

Ogunji, Kemi, University of South Carolina Press, 1600 Hampton St, Suite 544, Columbia, SC 29208 *Tel:* 803-777-5245 *Toll Free Tel:* 800-768-2500 (orders) *Fax:* 803-777-0160 *Toll Free Fax:* 800-868-0740 (orders) *Web Site:* uscpress.com, pg 220

Oh, Annabelle, Chronicle Books LLC, 680 Second St, San Francisco, CA 94107 *Tel:* 415-537-4200 *Fax:* 415-537-4460 (perms) *E-mail:* hello@chroniclebooks.com; subrights@chroniclebooks.com *Web Site:* www.chroniclebooks.com, pg 47

Oh, Ellen, Walter Dean Myers Grants, 10319 Westlake Dr, No 104, Bethesda, MD 20817 *Tel:* 701-404-WNDB (404-9632, voicemail only) *E-mail:* waltergrant@diversebooks.org *Web Site:* diversebooks.org, pg 636

Ohe, Kevin, Bloomsbury Academic, 1385 Broadway, 5th fl, New York, NY 10018 *Tel:* 212-419-5300 *Web Site:* www.bloomsbury.com/us/academic, pg 31

Ohe, Kevin, Bloomsbury Publishing Inc, 1385 Broadway, 5th fl, New York, NY 10018 *Tel:* 212-419-5300 *E-mail:* marketingusa@bloomsbury.com; adultpublicityusa@bloomsbury.com; askacademic@bloomsbury.com *Web Site:* www.bloomsbury.com, pg 31

Ohioma, Anu, Penguin Workshop, c/o Penguin Random House LLC, 1745 Broadway, New York, NY 10019 *Tel:* 212-782-9000 *Web Site:* www.penguin.com/publishers/penguinworkshop/, pg 156

Ohlin, Alix, University of British Columbia Creative Writing Program, Buchanan Rm E-462, 1866 Main Mall, Vancouver, BC V6T 1Z1, Canada *Tel:* 604-822-0699 *Web Site:* creativewriting.ubc.ca, pg 566

Ohman, Jack, Association of American Editorial Cartoonists (AAEC), PO Box 160314, Sacramento, CA 95816 *Tel:* 954-356-4945 *E-mail:* editorialcartoonists@gmail.com *Web Site:* www.editorialcartoonists.com, pg 498

Ohmart, Ben, BearManor Media, 1317 Edgewater Dr, No 110, Orlando, FL 32804 *Tel:* 760-709-9696 *Web Site:* www.bearmanormedia.com, pg 26

Oishi, Marie, Harry N Abrams Inc, 195 Broadway, 9th fl, New York, NY 10007 *Tel:* 212-206-7715 *Toll Free Tel:* 800-345-1359 *Fax:* 212-645-8437 *E-mail:* abrams@abramsbooks.com; publicity@abramsbooks.com; sales@abramsbooks.com *Web Site:* www.abramsbooks.com, pg 3

Okoye, Anita, Harry N Abrams Inc, 195 Broadway, 9th fl, New York, NY 10007 *Tel:* 212-206-7715 *Toll Free Tel:* 800-345-1359 *Fax:* 212-645-8437 *E-mail:* abrams@abramsbooks.com; publicity@abramsbooks.com; sales@abramsbooks.com *Web Site:* www.abramsbooks.com, pg 3

Oksen, Kate, Workman Publishing, 1290 Avenue of the Americas, New York, NY 10104 *Toll Free Tel:* 800-759-0190 *Fax:* 212-364-0950 *E-mail:* workman-inquiry@hbgusa.com *Web Site:* www.hachettebookgroup.com/imprint/workman-publishing-company/, pg 233

Okumura, Ritsuko, Avery, c/o Penguin Random House LLC, 1745 Broadway, New York, NY 10019 *Tel:* 212-366-2000 *Web Site:* www.penguin.com/avery-overview/, pg 23

Okumura, Ritsuko, Portfolio, c/o Penguin Random House LLC, 1745 Broadway, New York, NY 10019 *Tel:* 212-782-9000 *Web Site:* www.penguin.com/portfolio-overview/; www.penguin.com/sentinel-overview/; www.penguin.com/thesis/, pg 162

Okumura, Ritsuko, GP Putnam's Sons, c/o Penguin Random House LLC, 1745 Broadway, New York, NY 10019 *Tel:* 212-782-9000 *Web Site:* www.penguin.com/putnam/, pg 167

Okun, William, McGraw-Hill Education, 2 Penn Plaza, New York, NY 10121-2298 *Tel:* 212-904-2000 *E-mail:* international_cs@mheducation.com; seg_customerservice@mheducation.com (PreK-12); hep_customerservice@mheducation.com (higher education) *Web Site:* www.mheducation.com, pg 128

Okuniewska, Tricja, GP Putnam's Sons, c/o Penguin Random House LLC, 1745 Broadway, New York, NY 10019 *Tel:* 212-782-9000 *Web Site:* www.penguin.com/putnam/, pg 167

Olah, Michael, Dreamscape Media LLC, 1417 Timberwolf Dr, Holland, OH 43528 *Tel:* 419-867-6965 *Toll Free Tel:* 877-983-7326 *E-mail:* info@dreamscapeab.com *Web Site:* www.dreamscapepublishing.com, pg 62

Olander, Rebecca, Perugia Press Prize, PO Box 60364, Florence, MA 01062 *Web Site:* www.perugiapress.com; perugiapress.org, pg 649

Olanrewaju, Adenike, HarperCollins Publishers LLC, 195 Broadway, New York, NY 10007 *Tel:* 212-207-7000 *Web Site:* www.harpercollins.com, pg 86

Olbinski, Natalia, Simon & Schuster, 1230 Avenue of the Americas, New York, NY 10020 *Tel:* 212-698-7000 *Toll Free Tel:* 800-223-2348 (cust serv); 800-223-2336 (orders) *Toll Free Fax:* 800-943-9831 (orders) *Web Site:* simonandschusterpublishing.com/simonandschuster/, pg 188

Olczak, Gabrielle (Gabby) L, Independent Press Award®, 63 Clinton Rd, Glen Ridge, NJ 07028 *Web Site:* www.independentpressaward.com, pg 615

Olczak, Gabrielle (Gabby) L, NYC Big Book Award®, 63 Clinton Rd, Glen Ridge, NJ 07028 *Tel:* 973-969-1899 *Web Site:* www.nycbigbookaward.com, pg 642

Olczak, Ted, Independent Press Award®, 63 Clinton Rd, Glen Ridge, NJ 07028 *Web Site:* www.independentpressaward.com, pg 615

Olczak, Ted, NYC Big Book Award®, 63 Clinton Rd, Glen Ridge, NJ 07028 *Tel:* 973-969-1899 *Web Site:* www.nycbigbookaward.com, pg 642

Oldfield, Guy, Macmillan Audio, 120 Broadway, 22nd fl, New York, NY 10271 *Tel:* 646-600-7856 *Toll Free Tel:* 888-330-8477 (cust serv) *Toll Free Fax:* 800-672-7703 *E-mail:* macmillan.audio@macmillanusa.com *Web Site:* us.macmillan.com/audio, pg 123

Oldford, Ed, Flanker Press Ltd, 1243 Kenmount Rd, Unit 1, Paradise, NL A1L 0V8, Canada *Tel:* 709-739-4477 *Toll Free Tel:* 866-739-4420 *Fax:* 709-739-4420 *E-mail:* info@flankerpress.com; sales@flankerpress.com *Web Site:* www.flankerpress.com, pg 406

Oleck, Olivia, Roaring Brook Press, 120 Broadway, New York, NY 10271 *Tel:* 646-307-5151 *Web Site:* us.macmillan.com/publishers/roaring-brook-press, pg 176

Olenick, Michelle, Emmaus Road Publishing Inc, 1468 Parkview Circle, Steubenville, OH 43952 *Tel:* 750-264-9535 *Fax:* 740-475-0230 (orders) *E-mail:* questions@emmausroad.org *Web Site:* stpaulcenter.com/emmaus-road-publishing, pg 66

Oles, Alyssa, Penguin Random House LLC, 1745 Broadway, New York, NY 10019 *Tel:* 212-782-9000 *Toll Free Tel:* 800-726-0600 *Web Site:* www.penguinrandomhouse.com, pg 155

Olisko, Lexy, PRINTING United Alliance, 10015 Main St, Fairfax, VA 22031 *Tel:* 703-385-1335 *Toll Free Tel:* 888-385-3588 *Fax:* 703-273-0456; 703-691-7492 (membership) *E-mail:* assist@printing.org; info@printing.org *Web Site:* www.printing.org, pg 517

Oliva, Brianne, Basic Books Group, 1290 Avenue of the Americas, New York, NY 10104 *Tel:* 212-340-8100 *Toll Free Tel:* 800-343-4499 (cust serv) *Fax:* 212-340-8105 *E-mail:* customer.service@hbgusa.com; orders@hbgusa.com *Web Site:* www.hachettebookgroup.com/imprint/basic-books/, pg 25

Oliver, Amber, Bloomsbury Publishing Inc, 1385 Broadway, 5th fl, New York, NY 10018 *Tel:* 212-419-5300 *E-mail:* marketingusa@bloomsbury.com; adultpublicityusa@bloomsbury.com; askacademic@bloomsbury.com *Web Site:* www.bloomsbury.com, pg 31

Oliver, Becka, Writers' League of Texas (WLT), 611 S Congress Ave, Suite 200 A-3, Austin, TX 78704 *Tel:* 512-499-8914 *E-mail:* wlt@writersleague.org *Web Site:* www.writersleague.org, pg 488, 523, 558

Oliver, Becka, Writers' League of Texas Book Awards, 611 S Congress Ave, Suite 200 A-3, Austin, TX 78704 *Tel:* 512-499-8914 *E-mail:* wlt@writersleague.org *Web Site:* www.writersleague.org, pg 678

Oliver, Paul, Soho Press Inc, 853 Broadway, New York, NY 10003 *Tel:* 212-260-1900 *E-mail:* soho@sohopress.com; publicity@sohopress.com *Web Site:* sohopress.com, pg 193

Olivo, Michael, Teachers College Press, 1234 Amsterdam Ave, New York, NY 10027 *Tel:* 212-678-3929 *Fax:* 212-678-4149 *E-mail:* tcpress@tc.edu *Web Site:* www.tcpress.com, pg 203

Olmanson, Shaina, Sourcebooks LLC, 1935 Brookdale Rd, Suite 139, Naperville, IL 60563 *Tel:* 630-961-3900 *Toll Free Tel:* 800-432-7444 *Fax:* 630-961-2168 *E-mail:* info@sourcebooks.com *Web Site:* www.sourcebooks.com, pg 194

Olmo, J Sammi, American Academy of Environmental Engineers & Scientists®, 147 Old Solomons Island Rd, Suite 303, Annapolis, MD 21401 *Tel:* 410-266-3311 *Fax:* 410-266-7653 *E-mail:* info@aaees.org *Web Site:* www.aaees.org, pg 8

Olmos, Jackie, Sourcebooks LLC, 1935 Brookdale Rd, Suite 139, Naperville, IL 60563 *Tel:* 630-961-3900 *Toll Free Tel:* 800-432-7444 *Fax:* 630-961-2168 *E-mail:* info@sourcebooks.com *Web Site:* www.sourcebooks.com, pg 194

Olsen, Bevan, Cedar Fort Inc, 2373 W 700 S, Suite 100, Springville, UT 84663 *Tel:* 801-489-4084 *Toll Free Tel:* 800-SKY-BOOK (759-2665) *E-mail:* marketinginfo@cedarfort.com *Web Site:* cedarfort.com, pg 43

Olsen, Charlie, InkWell Management, 521 Fifth Ave, Suite 2600, New York, NY 10175 *Tel:* 212-922-3500 *Fax:* 212-922-0535 *E-mail:* info@inkwellmanagement.com; submissions@inkwellmanagement.com; permissions@inkwellmanagement.com *Web Site:* inkwellmanagement.com, pg 463

Olsen, David, University of Chicago Press, 1427 E 60 St, Chicago, IL 60637-2954 *Tel:* 773-702-7700; 773-702-7600 *Toll Free Tel:* 800-621-2736 (orders) *Fax:* 773-702-9756; 773-660-2235 (orders); 773-702-2708 *E-mail:* custserv@press.uchicago.edu; marketing@press.uchicago.edu *Web Site:* www.press.uchicago.edu, pg 215

Olsen, Eric, Twilight Times Books, PO Box 3340, Kingsport, TN 37664-0340 *Tel:* 423-390-1111 *Fax:* 423-390-1111 *E-mail:* publisher@twilighttimes.com *Web Site:* www.twilighttimesbooks.com, pg 211

Olsen, John, Teaching Strategies LLC, 4500 East-West Hwy, Suite 300, Bethesda, MD 20814 *Tel:* 301-634-0818 *Toll Free Tel:* 800-637-3652 *E-mail:* info@teachingstrategies.com; support@teachingstrategies.com *Web Site:* teachingstrategies.com, pg 204

Olsen, Kevin, W W Norton & Company Inc, 500 Fifth Ave, New York, NY 10110-0017 *Tel:* 212-354-5500 *Toll Free Tel:* 800-233-4830 (orders & cust serv) *Fax:* 212-869-0856 *Toll Free Fax:* 800-458-6515 *E-mail:* orders@wwnorton.com *Web Site:* wwnorton.com, pg 143

Olsen, Ted, InterVarsity Press, 430 Plaza Dr, Westmont, IL 60559-1234 *Tel:* 630-734-4000 *Toll Free Tel:* 800-843-9487 *Fax:* 630-734-4200 *E-mail:* email@ivpress.com *Web Site:* www.ivpress.com, pg 104

Olshan, Joseph, Delphinium Books, 16350 Ventura Blvd, Suite D, Encino, CA 91436 *Tel:* 917-301-7496 (e-mail first) *Web Site:* www.delphiniumbooks.com, pg 58

Olson, Amanda, Annick Press Ltd, 388 Carlaw Ave, Suite 200, Toronto, ON M4M 2T4, Canada *Tel:* 416-221-4802 *Fax:* 416-221-8400 *E-mail:* annickpress@annickpress.com *Web Site:* www.annickpress.com, pg 395

Olson, Bianca, Houghton Mifflin Harcourt, 125 High St, Boston, MA 02110 *Tel:* 617-351-5000 *Toll Free Tel:* 855-969-4642; 800-225-5425 (K-12 educ materials); 800-323-9540 (assessment materials); 877-219-1537 (SkillsTutor); 888-242-6747 (Innovation in Educ Group); 800-225-3362 (Trade & Ref Div) *Toll Free Fax:* 800-269-5232 *E-mail:* myhmhco@hmhco.com *Web Site:* www.hmhco.com, pg 96

Olson, Elke, Chronicle Books LLC, 680 Second St, San Francisco, CA 94107 *Tel:* 415-537-4200 *Fax:* 415-537-4460 (perms) *E-mail:* hello@chroniclebooks.com; subrights@chroniclebooks.com *Web Site:* www.chroniclebooks.com, pg 47

Olson, Kaitlin, Atria Books, 1230 Avenue of the Americas, New York, NY 10020 *Tel:* 212-698-7000 *Fax:* 212-698-7007 *Web Site:* www.simonandschuster.com, pg 21

Olson-Getty, Dayna, Herald Press, PO Box 866, Harrisonburg, VA 22803 *Toll Free Tel:* 800-245-7894 (orders) *Fax:* 540-242-4476 *Toll Free Fax:* 877-271-0760 *E-mail:* info@mennomedia.org; customerservice@mennomedia.org *Web Site:* www.heraldpress.com; store.mennomedia.org, pg 91

Olstein, Lisa, University of Texas at Austin, New Writers Project, Dept of English, 204 W 21 St, B-5000, Austin, TX 78712-1164 *Tel:* 512-471-4991 *Fax:* 512-471-4909 *E-mail:* newwritersproject@utexas.edu *Web Site:* liberalarts.utexas.edu/nwp, pg 567

Omana, Veronica, University of Ottawa Press (Presses de l'Université d'Ottawa), 542 King Edward Ave, Ottawa, ON K1N 6N5, Canada *Tel:* 613-562-5246 *Fax:* 613-562-5247 *E-mail:* puo-uop@uottawa.ca; acquisitions@uottawa.ca *Web Site:* press.uottawa.ca, pg 422

Omoruyi, Christian, PEN America Washington, DC, 1100 13 St NW, Suite 800, Washington, DC 20005 *E-mail:* info@pen.org *Web Site:* pen.org/region/washington-dc, pg 516

Opsomer, Liliane, AdventureKEEN, 2204 First Ave S, Suite 102, Birmingham, AL 35233 *Tel:* 763-689-9800 *Toll Free Tel:* 800-678-7006 *Fax:* 763-689-9039 *Toll Free Fax:* 877-374-9016 *E-mail:* info@adventurewithkeen.com *Web Site:* adventurewithkeen.com, pg 5

Orange, Darren, Sourcebooks LLC, 1935 Brookdale Rd, Suite 139, Naperville, IL 60563 *Tel:* 630-961-3900 *Toll Free Tel:* 800-432-7444 *Fax:* 630-961-2168 *E-mail:* info@sourcebooks.com *Web Site:* www.sourcebooks.com, pg 195

Ordower, Patti, Liberty Fund Inc, 11301 N Meridian St, Carmel, IN 46032-4564 *Tel:* 317-842-0880 *Toll Free Tel:* 800-955-8335; 800-866-3520 *Fax:* 317-579-6060 (cust serv); 708-534-7803 *E-mail:* books@libertyfund.org; info@libertyfund.org *Web Site:* www.libertyfund.org, pg 116

Ore-Giron, Nicolas, Roaring Brook Press, 120 Broadway, New York, NY 10271 *Tel:* 646-307-5151 *Web Site:* us.macmillan.com/publishers/roaring-brook-press, pg 176

Oren, Tiffany, Foster City International Writers Contest, 650 Shell Blvd, Foster City, CA 94404 *Tel:* 650-286-3380 *E-mail:* fostercity_writers@yahoo.com *Web Site:* www.fostercity.org, pg 603

Orenstein, Carol, The Conference Board Inc, 845 Third Ave, New York, NY 10022-6600 *Tel:* 212-759-0900; 212-339-0345 (cust serv) *E-mail:* customer.service@tcb.org *Web Site:* www.conference-board.org/us; www.linkedin.com/company/the-conference-board, pg 51

Orlandi, Maria, Adams Media, 100 Technology Center Dr, Suite 501, Stoughton, MA 02072 *Tel:* 508-427-7100 *Web Site:* www.simonandschuster.com, pg 4

Ornstein, Michael, IET USA Inc, 379 Thornall St, Edison, NJ 08837 *Tel:* 732-321-5575 *Fax:* 732-321-5702 *E-mail:* ietusa@theiet.org *Web Site:* www.theiet.org, pg 98

Orozco, Amanda, Transatlantic Agency, 2 Bloor St E, Suite 3500, Toronto, ON M4W 1A8, Canada *Tel:* 416-488-9214 *E-mail:* info@transatlanticagency.com; royalties@transatlanticagency.com *Web Site:* www.transatlanticagency.com, pg 479

Orozco, Polo, GP Putnam's Sons Books for Young Readers, c/o Penguin Random House LLC, 1745 Broadway, New York, NY 10019 *Tel:* 212-782-9000 *Web Site:* www.penguin.com/putnam-young-readers/, pg 167

Orr, Rachel, Prospect Agency, 551 Valley Rd, PMB 337, Upper Montclair, NJ 07043 *Tel:* 718-788-3217 *Web Site:* www.prospectagency.com, pg 472

Ortiz, Alex, Public Relations Society of America Inc, 120 Wall St, 21st fl, New York, NY 10005 *Tel:* 212-460-1400 *E-mail:* membership@prsa.org *Web Site:* www.prsa.org, pg 518

Ortiz, Carolina, HarperCollins Children's Books, 195 Broadway, New York, NY 10007 *Tel:* 212-207-7000 *Web Site:* www.harpercollins.com/childrens, pg 85

Ortiz, Kathleen, KO Media Management, 2817 Wetmore Ave, Everett, WA 98201 *E-mail:* info@komediamanagement.com; query@komediamanagement.com *Web Site:* komediamanagement.com, pg 466

Ortiz, Lauren, Little, Brown and Company, 1290 Avenue of the Americas, New York, NY 10104 *Tel:* 212-364-1100 *Fax:* 212-364-0952 *E-mail:* firstname.lastname@hbgusa.com *Web Site:* www.hachettebookgroup.com/imprint/little-brown-and-company/, pg 118

Ortiz, Lukas, Philip G Spitzer Literary Agency Inc, 50 Talmage Farm Lane, East Hampton, NY 11937 *Tel:* 631-329-3650 *Fax:* 631-329-3651 *Web Site:* www.spitzeragency.com, pg 477

Ortiz-Crane, Miguel, New York University, Center for Publishing & Applied Liberal Arts, 7 E 12 St, New York, NY 10003 *Tel:* 212-998-7200 *E-mail:* sps.info@nyu.edu *Web Site:* www.scps.nyu.edu/professional-pathways/topics.html, pg 563

Orton, Jeramie, Viking Penguin, c/o Penguin Random House LLC, 1745 Broadway, New York, NY 10019 *Tel:* 212-782-9000 *Web Site:* www.penguin.com/overview-vikingbooks/; www.penguin.com/pamela-dorman-books-overview/; www.penguin.com/penguin-classics-overview/; www.penguin.com/penguin-life-overview/, pg 225

Ostergaard, Josh, Graywolf Press, 212 Third Ave N, Suite 485, Minneapolis, MN 55401 *Tel:* 651-641-0077 *Fax:* 651-641-0036 *E-mail:* wolves@graywolfpress.org (no ms queries, sample chapters or proposals) *Web Site:* www.graywolfpress.org, pg 81

Osterrath, Dominique, Social Sciences & Humanities Research Council (SSHRC), 350 Albert St, Ottawa, ON K1P 6G4, Canada *Tel:* 613-995-4273 *Toll Free Tel:* 855-275-2861 *E-mail:* research@sshrc-crsh.gc.ca *Web Site:* www.sshrc-crsh.gc.ca, pg 519

Ostertag, Genny, ASCD, 2800 Shirlington Rd, Suite 1001, Arlington, VA 22206 *Tel:* 703-578-9600 *Toll Free Tel:* 800-933-2723 *Fax:* 703-575-5400 *E-mail:* member@ascd.org; books@ascd.org *Web Site:* www.ascd.org, pg 18

Osti, Pamela, Harlequin Enterprises Ltd, Bay Adelaide Centre, East Tower, 22 Adelaide St W, 41st fl, Toronto, ON M5H 4E3, Canada *Tel:* 416-445-5860 *Toll Free Tel:* 888-432-4879; 800-370-5838 (ebook inquiries) *E-mail:* customerservice@harlequin.com *Web Site:* www.harlequin.com, pg 409

Osuszek, Alex, Harlequin Enterprises Ltd, Bay Adelaide Centre, East Tower, 22 Adelaide St W, 41st fl, Toronto, ON M5H 4E3, Canada *Tel:* 416-445-5860 *Toll Free Tel:* 888-432-4879; 800-370-5838 (ebook inquiries) *E-mail:* customerservice@harlequin.com *Web Site:* www.harlequin.com, pg 409

Oswald, Denise, Pantheon Books, c/o Penguin Random House LLC, 1745 Broadway, New York, NY 10019 *Tel:* 212-751-2600 *Fax:* 212-940-7390 (dom rts); 212-572-2662 (foreign rts) *Web Site:* knopfdoubleday.com/imprint/pantheon/; knopfdoubleday.com, pg 150

Ott, Brian L, Texas Tech University Press, 1120 Main St, 2nd fl, Lubbock, TX 79401 *Tel:* 806-742-2982 *Toll Free Tel:* 800-832-4042 *E-mail:* ttup@ttu.edu *Web Site:* www.ttupress.org, pg 205

Ott, Marc A, International City/County Management Association (ICMA), 777 N Capitol St NE, Suite 500, Washington, DC 20002-4201 *Tel:* 202-962-3680 *Toll Free Tel:* 800-745-8780 *Fax:* 202-962-3500 *E-mail:* customerservices@icma.org *Web Site:* icma.org/about-icma-publications, pg 102

Ottaviano, Christy, Little, Brown Books for Young Readers (LBYR), 1290 Avenue of the Americas, New York, NY 10104 *Tel:* 212-364-1100 *Toll Free Tel:* 800-759-0190 (cust serv) *E-mail:* rights@lbchildrens.com *Web Site:* www.hachettebookgroup.com/imprint/little-brown-books-for-young-readers/, pg 118

Otte, Liz, Sourcebooks LLC, 1935 Brookdale Rd, Suite 139, Naperville, IL 60563 *Tel:* 630-961-3900 *Toll Free Tel:* 800-432-7444 *Fax:* 630-961-2168 *E-mail:* info@sourcebooks.com *Web Site:* www.sourcebooks.com, pg 194

Ou, Michelle, Editors Canada (Reviseurs Canada), 1507-180 Dundas St W, Toronto, ON M5G 1Z8, Canada *Tel:* 416-975-1379 *E-mail:* info@editors.ca; info@reviseurs.ca; communications@editors.ca *Web Site:* www.editors.ca; www.reviseurs.ca, pg 505

Ou, Michelle, Equity Fellowship, 1507-180 Dundas St W, Toronto, ON M5G 1Z8, Canada *Tel:* 416-975-1379 *E-mail:* info@editors.ca; info@reviseurs.ca; communications@editors.ca *Web Site:* www.editors.ca/about/awards/equity-fellowship, pg 600

Ou, Michelle, Tom Fairley Award for Editorial Excellence, 1507-180 Dundas St W, Toronto, ON M5G 1Z8, Canada *Tel:* 416-975-1379 *E-mail:* fairley_award@editors.ca; communications@editors.ca *Web Site:* www.editors.ca/about/awards/tom-fairley-award, pg 601

Ou, Michelle, Claudette Upton Scholarship, 1507-180 Dundas St W, Toronto, ON M5G 1Z8, Canada *Tel:* 416-975-1379 *E-mail:* info@editors.ca; info@reviseurs.ca; communications@editors.ca *Web Site:* www.editors.ca/about/awards/claudette-upton-scholarship, pg 672

Ou, Michelle, Karen Virag Award, 1507-180 Dundas St W, Toronto, ON M5G 1Z8, Canada *Tel:* 416-975-1379 *E-mail:* info@editors.ca; info@reviseurs.ca; communications@editors.ca *Web Site:* www.editors.ca/about/awards/karen-virag-award-0, pg 673

Ouellet, Catherine, Editions Hurtubise, 1815, ave de Lorimier, Montreal, QC H2K 3W6, Canada *Tel:* 514-523-1523 *Toll Free Tel:* 800-361-1664 *Web Site:* editionshurtubise.com, pg 404

Ovedovitz, Nancy, Yale University Press, 302 Temple St, New Haven, CT 06511-8909 *Tel:* 203-432-0960; 203-432-0966 (sales); 401-531-2800 (cust serv) *Toll Free Tel:* 800-405-1619 (cust serv) *Fax:* 203-432-0948; 203-432-8485 (sales); 401-531-2801 (cust serv) *Toll Free Fax:* 800-406-9145 (cust serv) *E-mail:* sales.press@yale.edu (sales); customer.care@triliteral.org (cust serv) *Web Site:* www.yalebooks.com; yalepress.yale.edu/yupbooks, pg 235

Overn, Kristin, PAGE International Screenwriting Awards, 7190 W Sunset Blvd, Suite 610, Hollywood, CA 90046 *E-mail:* info@pageawards.com *Web Site:* pageawards.com, pg 645

Owen, Richard C, Richard C Owen Publishers Inc, PO Box 585, Katonah, NY 10536-0585 *Tel:* 914-232-3903 *Toll Free Tel:* 800-336-5588 *Fax:* 914-232-3977 *Web Site:* www.rcowen.com, pg 149

Owens, John, Cohesion®, 511 W Bay St, Suite 480, Tampa, FL 33606 *Tel:* 813-999-3111 *Toll Free Tel:* 866-727-6800 *Web Site:* www.cohesion.com, pg 437

Owens, Mary Ellen, Random House Children's Books, c/o Penguin Random House LLC, 1745 Broadway, New York, NY 10019 *Tel:* 212-782-9000 *Web Site:* www.rhcbooks.com, pg 170

Owles, John Paul, Joshua Tree Publishing, 3 Golf Ctr, Suite 201, Hoffman Estates, IL 60169 *Tel:* 312-893-7525 *E-mail:* info@joshuatreepublishing.com; info@centaurbooks.com *Web Site:* www.joshuatreepublishing.com; www.centaurbooks.com, pg 107

Oxtoby, David W, American Academy of Arts & Sciences (AAAS), 136 Irving St, Cambridge, MA 02138 *Tel:* 617-576-5000 *Fax:* 617-576-5050 *E-mail:* aaas@amacad.org *Web Site:* www.amacad.org, pg 494

Ozer, Shelby, Harry N Abrams Inc, 195 Broadway, 9th fl, New York, NY 10007 *Tel:* 212-206-7715 *Toll Free Tel:* 800-345-1359 *Fax:* 212-645-8437 *E-mail:* abrams@abramsbooks.com; publicity@abramsbooks.com; sales@abramsbooks.com *Web Site:* www.abramsbooks.com, pg 3

Ozturk, Yusuf, Rand McNally, 9855 Woods Dr, Skokie, IL 60077 *Tel:* 847-329-8100 *Toll Free Tel:* 877-446-4863 *Toll Free Fax:* 877-469-1298 *E-mail:* mediarelations@randmcnally.com; tndsupport@randmcnally.com *Web Site:* www.randmcnally.com, pg 169

O'Hayre, Meredith, Adams Media, 100 Technology Center Dr, Suite 501, Stoughton, MA 02072 *Tel:* 508-427-7100 *Web Site:* www.simonandschuster.com, pg 4

Pabarue, Jay, The New Press, 120 Wall St, 31st fl, New York, NY 10005 *Tel:* 212-629-8802 *Fax:* 212-629-8617 *E-mail:* newpress@thenewpress.com *Web Site:* thenewpress.com, pg 140

Pace, Andrew K, Association of Research Libraries (ARL), 21 Dupont Circle NW, Suite 800, Washington, DC 20036 *Tel:* 202-296-2296 *Fax:* 202-872-0884 *E-mail:* webmgr@arl.org *Web Site:* www.arl.org, pg 20

Pace, Jordan, Random House Publishing Group, 1745 Broadway, New York, NY 10019 *Toll Free Tel:* 800-200-3552 *Web Site:* www.randomhousebooks.com, pg 171

Pace, Steven, W W Norton & Company Inc, 500 Fifth Ave, New York, NY 10110-0017 *Tel:* 212-354-5500 *Toll Free Tel:* 800-233-4830 (orders & cust serv) *Fax:* 212-869-0856 *Toll Free Fax:* 800-458-6515 *E-mail:* orders@wwnorton.com *Web Site:* wwnorton.com, pg 143

Pace, Zachary, The Experiment, 220 E 23 St, Suite 600, New York, NY 10010-4658 *Tel:* 212-889-1659 *E-mail:* info@theexperimentpublishing.com *Web Site:* www.theexperimentpublishing.com, pg 68

Pachaco, Lisa, Museum of New Mexico Press, 725 Camino Lejo, Suite C, Santa Fe, NM 87505 Tel: 505-476-1155; 505-272-7777 (orders) Toll Free Tel: 800-249-7737 (orders) Fax: 505-476-1156 Toll Free Fax: 800-622-8667 (orders) Web Site: www.mnmpress.org, pg 135

Pachon, Gabrielle, Berkley, c/o Penguin Random House LLC, 1745 Broadway, 19th fl, New York, NY 10019 Tel: 212-366-2000 Web Site: www.penguin.com/publishers/berkley/; www.penguin.com/ace-overview/, pg 28

Paddick, Christy, Institute of Public Administration of Canada, 1075 Bay St, Suite 401, Toronto, ON M5S 2B1, Canada Tel: 416-924-8787 Fax: 416-924-4992 E-mail: ntl@ipac.ca Web Site: www.ipac.ca, pg 410

Paddio, Martin, Monthly Review Press, 134 W 29 St, Suite 706, New York, NY 10001 Tel: 212-691-2555 E-mail: social@monthlyreview.org Web Site: monthlyreview.org, pg 134

Padgett, Leslie, Macmillan, 120 Broadway, 22nd fl, New York, NY 10271 E-mail: press.inquiries@macmillan.com Web Site: us.macmillan.com, pg 122

Padmore, Dawn, James Beard Foundation Book Awards, 167 W 12 St, New York, NY 10011 Tel: 212-627-2308 E-mail: awards@jamesbeard.org Web Site: www.jamesbeard.org/awards, pg 578

Paganelli, Courtney, Levine|Greenberg|Rostan Literary Agency, 307 Seventh Ave, Suite 2407, New York, NY 10001 Tel: 212-337-0934 Fax: 212-337-0948 E-mail: submit@lgrliterary.com Web Site: lgrliterary.com, pg 467

Pagano, Megan, HarperCollins Children's Books, 195 Broadway, New York, NY 10007 Tel: 212-207-7000 Web Site: www.harpercollins.com/childrens, pg 85

Page, Lisa, Jenny McKean Moore Writer-in-Washington, English Dept, Rome Hall, 801 22 St NW, Suite 643, Washington, DC 20052 Tel: 202-994-6180 E-mail: engldept@gwu.edu Web Site: english.columbian.gwu.edu, pg 635

Page, Marissa, Houghton Mifflin Harcourt Trade & Reference Division, 125 High St, Boston, MA 02110 Tel: 617-351-5000 Web Site: www.hmhco.com, pg 96

Page, Rachel, The Feminist Press at The City University of New York, 365 Fifth Ave, Suite 5406, New York, NY 10016 Tel: 212-817-7915 Fax: 212-817-1593 E-mail: info@feministpress.org Web Site: www.feministpress.org, pg 71

Page, Terra, Penguin Random House Canada, a Penguin Random House company, 320 Front St W, Suite 1400, Toronto, ON M5V 3B6, Canada Tel: 416-364-4449 Toll Free Tel: 888-523-9292 (cust serv) E-mail: canadaweb@penguinrandomhouse.com; customerservicescanada@penguinrandomhouse.com Web Site: www.penguinrandomhouse.ca, pg 416

Page-Fort, Gabriella, HarperCollins Publishers LLC, 195 Broadway, New York, NY 10007 Tel: 212-207-7000 Web Site: www.harpercollins.com, pg 86

Pagel, Caryl, Lighthouse Poetry Series, Rhodes Tower, Rm 1841, 2121 Euclid Ave, Cleveland, OH 44115 Tel: 216-687-3986 E-mail: poetrycenter@csuohio.edu Web Site: www.csupoetrycenter.com/lighthouse-poetry-series; www.csupoetrycenter.com, pg 624

Pagel, Caryl, Translation Series, Rhodes Tower, Rm 1841, 2121 Euclid Ave, Cleveland, OH 44115 Tel: 216-687-3986 E-mail: poetrycenter@csuohio.edu Web Site: www.csupoetrycenter.com/translation-series; www.csupoetrycenter.com, pg 670

Pager, Morgan (Hoit), Atria Books, 1230 Avenue of the Americas, New York, NY 10020 Tel: 212-698-7000 Fax: 212-698-7007 Web Site: www.simonandschuster.com, pg 21

Pagnamenta, Zoe, Calligraph LLC, 45 Main St, No 850, Brooklyn, NY 11201 Tel: 212-253-1074 E-mail: mail@calligraphlit.com; rights@calligraphlit.com; submissions@calligraphlit.com Web Site: www.calligraphlit.com, pg 453

Paige, David, Bloomsbury Academic, 1385 Broadway, 5th fl, New York, NY 10018 Tel: 212-419-5300 Web Site: www.bloomsbury.com/us/academic, pg 31

Paille, Anthony, Association for Intelligent Information Management (AIIM), 8403 Colesville Rd, No 1100, Silver Spring, MD 20910 Tel: 301-587-8202 Toll Free Tel: 800-477-2446 Fax: 301-587-2711 E-mail: hello@aiim.org Web Site: www.aiim.org, pg 498

Paine, John, The Editors Circle, 24 Holly Circle, Easthampton, MA 01027 Tel: 862-596-9709 E-mail: query@theeditorscircle.com Web Site: www.theeditorscircle.com, pg 438

Painter, Benjamin, Schlager Group Inc, 10228 E Northwest Hwy, No 1151, Dallas, TX 75238 Toll Free Tel: 888-416-5727 Fax: 469-325-3700 E-mail: info@schlagergroup.com; sales@schlagergroup.com Web Site: www.schlagergroup.com, pg 183

Painter, Jeannie, Mountain Press Publishing Co, 1301 S Third W, Missoula, MT 59801 Tel: 406-728-1900 Toll Free Tel: 800-234-5308 Fax: 406-728-1635 E-mail: info@mtnpress.com Web Site: www.mountain-press.com, pg 135

Painton, Priscilla, Simon & Schuster, 1230 Avenue of the Americas, New York, NY 10020 Tel: 212-698-7000 Toll Free Tel: 800-223-2348 (cust serv); 800-223-2336 (orders) Toll Free Fax: 800-943-9831 (orders) Web Site: simonandschusterpublishing.com/simonandschuster/, pg 188

Pak, Eunice, Macmillan, 120 Broadway, 22nd fl, New York, NY 10271 E-mail: press.inquiries@macmillan.com Web Site: us.macmillan.com, pg 122

Palacios, Tomas, HarperCollins Children's Books, 195 Broadway, New York, NY 10007 Tel: 212-207-7000 Web Site: www.harpercollins.com/childrens, pg 85

Palana-Shanahan, Brett, Adams Media, 100 Technology Center Dr, Suite 501, Stoughton, MA 02072 Tel: 508-427-7100 Web Site: www.simonandschuster.com, pg 4

Palenzuela, Monica, Sourcebooks LLC, 1935 Brookdale Rd, Suite 139, Naperville, IL 60563 Tel: 630-961-3900 Toll Free Tel: 800-432-7444 Fax: 630-961-2168 E-mail: info@sourcebooks.com Web Site: www.sourcebooks.com, pg 194

Palermo, Laura, Peachtree Publishing Co Inc, 1700 Chattahoochee Ave, Atlanta, GA 30318-2112 Tel: 404-876-8761 Toll Free Tel: 800-241-0113 Fax: 404-875-2578 Toll Free Fax: 800-875-8909 E-mail: hello@peachtree-online.com; orders@peachtree-online.com; sales@peachtree-online.com Web Site: www.peachtreebooks.com; www.peachtree-online.com, pg 153

Paley, Valerie, Barbara & David Zalaznick Book Prize in American History, 170 Central Park W, New York, NY 10024 Tel: 212-873-3400 Fax: 212-595-5707 E-mail: info@nyhistory.org Web Site: www.nyhistory.org/news/book-prize, pg 679

Palin, Tim, American Book Producers Association (ABPA), 7 Peter Cooper Rd, No 7G, New York, NY 10010 E-mail: office@abpaonline.org Web Site: www.abpaonline.org, pg 494

Palisano, John, Horror Writers Association (HWA), PO Box 56687, Sherman Oaks, CA 91413 Tel: 818-220-3965 E-mail: admin@horror.org; membership@horror.org Web Site: horror.org, pg 507

Palladino, Lily, University of Pennsylvania Press, 3905 Spruce St, Philadelphia, PA 19104 Tel: 215-898-6261 Fax: 215-898-0404 E-mail: custserv@pobox.upenn.edu Web Site: www.pennpress.org, pg 219

Pallante, Maria, Association of American Publishers (AAP), 455 Massachusetts Ave NW, Suite 700, Washington, DC 20001-2777 Tel: 202-347-3375 Fax: 202-347-3690 E-mail: info@publishers.org Web Site: publishers.org, pg 498

Pallotta, Caroline, Gallery Books, 1230 Avenue of the Americas, New York, NY 10020 Toll Free Tel: 800-456-6798 Fax: 212-698-7284 E-mail: consumer.customerservice@simonandschuster.com Web Site: www.simonandschuster.com, pg 76

Palmer, Heather, Penguin Random House Audio Publishing Group, 1745 Broadway, New York, NY 10019 Toll Free Tel: 800-793-2665 (cust serv) E-mail: audio@penguinrandomhouse.com; ecustomerservice@penguinrandomhouse.com Web Site: www.penguinrandomhouseaudio.com, pg 154

Palmer, Paula, US Games Systems Inc, 179 Ludlow St, Stamford, CT 06902 Tel: 203-353-8400 Toll Free Tel: 800-54-GAMES (544-2637) Fax: 203-353-8431 E-mail: info@usgamesinc.com Web Site: www.usgamesinc.com, pg 223

Palmitesta, Karina, Between the Lines, 401 Richmond St W, No 281, Toronto, ON M5V 3A8, Canada Tel: 416-535-9914 Toll Free Tel: 800-718-7201 E-mail: info@btlbooks.com Web Site: btlbooks.com, pg 396

Palmquist, Nancy K, W W Norton & Company Inc, 500 Fifth Ave, New York, NY 10110-0017 Tel: 212-354-5500 Toll Free Tel: 800-233-4830 (orders & cust serv) Fax: 212-869-0856 Toll Free Fax: 800-458-6515 E-mail: orders@wwnorton.com Web Site: wwnorton.com, pg 143

Palomino, Christine, Penguin Random House LLC, 1745 Broadway, New York, NY 10019 Tel: 212-782-9000 Toll Free Tel: 800-726-0600 Web Site: www.penguinrandomhouse.com, pg 155

Palumbo, Elizabeth, Pantheon Books, c/o Penguin Random House LLC, 1745 Broadway, New York, NY 10019 Tel: 212-751-2600 Fax: 212-940-7390 (dom rts); 212-572-2662 (foreign rts) Web Site: knopfdoubleday.com/imprint/pantheon/; knopfdoubleday.com, pg 150

Pambid, Ailyn, Chronicle Books LLC, 680 Second St, San Francisco, CA 94107 Tel: 415-537-4200 Fax: 415-537-4460 (perms) E-mail: hello@chroniclebooks.com; subrights@chroniclebooks.com Web Site: www.chroniclebooks.com, pg 48

Pan, Dr Hui, Information Gatekeepers Inc (IGI), PO Box 606, Winchester, MA 01890 Tel: 617-782-5033 Fax: 617-507-8338 E-mail: info@igigroup.com Web Site: www.igigroup.com, pg 100

Pando, Stephanie, Candlewick Press, 99 Dover St, Somerville, MA 02144-2825 Tel: 617-661-3330 Fax: 617-661-0565 E-mail: bigbear@candlewick.com; salesinfo@candlewick.com Web Site: candlewick.com, pg 40

Pandya-Lorch, Rajul, International Food Policy Research Institute, 1201 Eye St NW, Washington, DC 20005-3915 Tel: 202-862-5600 Fax: 202-862-5606 E-mail: ifpri@cgiar.org Web Site: www.ifpri.org, pg 103

Panec, Don, Treasure Bay Inc, PO Box 119, Novato, CA 94948 Tel: 415-884-2888 Fax: 415-884-2840 E-mail: customerservice@treasurebaybooks.com Web Site: www.treasurebaybooks.com, pg 209

Panepinto, Lauren, Orbit, 1290 Avenue of the Americas, New York, NY 10104 Tel: 212-364-1100 Toll Free Tel: 800-759-0190 Web Site: www.orbitbooks.net; www.hachettebookgroup.com/imprint/orbit, pg 147

Panetta, Jackie, University Press of Florida, 2046 NE Waldo Rd, Suite 2100, Gainesville, FL 32609 Tel: 352-392-1351 Toll Free Tel: 800-226-3822 (orders only) Fax: 352-392-0590 Toll Free Fax: 800-680-1955 (orders only) E-mail: press@upress.ufl.edu; orders@upress.ufl.edu Web Site: www.upf.com, pg 221

Panettieri, Gina, Talcott Notch Literary, 127 Broad St, 2P, Milford, CT 06460 Tel: 203-876-4959 Web Site: talcottnotch.net, pg 479

Pangilinan, Noel T, Asian American Writers' Workshop (AAWW), 112 W 27 St, Suite 600, New York, NY 10001 Tel: 212-494-0061 E-mail: desk@aaww.org Web Site: aaww.org; facebook.com/AsianAmericanWritersWorkshop, pg 497

Pannenberg, Sarah, Tor Publishing Group, 120 Broadway, New York, NY 10271 Toll Free Tel: 800-455-0340 (Macmillan) E-mail: torpublicity@tor.com; forgepublicity@forgebooks.com Web Site: us.macmillan.com/torpublishinggroup, pg 208

Panner, Craig, Oxford University Press USA, 198 Madison Ave, New York, NY 10016 Toll Free Tel: 800-451-7556 (orders); 800-445-9714 (cust serv) Fax: 919-677-1303 E-mail: custserv.us@oup.com Web Site: global.oup.com, pg 149

Panning, Jeanette, American Geophysical Union (AGU), 2000 Florida Ave NW, Washington, DC 20009 *Tel:* 202-462-6900 *Toll Free Tel:* 800-966-2481 (North America) *Fax:* 202-328-0566 *E-mail:* service@agu.org (cust serv) *Web Site:* www.agu.org, pg 10

Pantojan, Marie, Random House Publishing Group, 1745 Broadway, New York, NY 10019 *Toll Free Tel:* 800-200-3552 *Web Site:* www.randomhousebooks.com, pg 171

Panzeri, Chiara, Folio Literary Management, The Film Center Bldg, 630 Ninth Ave, Suite 1101, New York, NY 10036 *Tel:* 212-400-1494 *Fax:* 212-967-0977 *Web Site:* www.foliolit.com, pg 459

Panzica, Bri, Farrar, Straus & Giroux, LLC, 120 Broadway, New York, NY 10271 *Tel:* 212-741-6900 *E-mail:* fsg.publicity@fsgbooks.com; sales@fsgbooks.com *Web Site:* us.macmillan.com/fsg, pg 70

Papademetriou, Dean, Somerset Hall Press, 416 Commonwealth Ave, Suite 612, Boston, MA 02215 *Tel:* 617-236-5126 *E-mail:* info@somersethallpress.com *Web Site:* www.somersethallpress.com, pg 193

Papadimitropoulos, Demetri, Pantheon Books, c/o Penguin Random House LLC, 1745 Broadway, New York, NY 10019 *Tel:* 212-751-2600 *Fax:* 212-940-7390 (dom rts); 212-572-2662 (foreign rts) *Web Site:* knopfdoubleday.com/imprint/pantheon/; knopfdoubleday.com, pg 150

Papadopoulos, Niki, Portfolio, c/o Penguin Random House LLC, 1745 Broadway, New York, NY 10019 *Tel:* 212-782-9000 *Web Site:* www.penguin.com/portfolio-overview/; www.penguin.com/sentinel-overview/; www.penguin.com/thesis/, pg 162

Papas, Sabrina, Penguin Random House Canada, a Penguin Random House company, 320 Front St W, Suite 1400, Toronto, ON M5V 3B6, Canada *Tel:* 416-364-4449 *Toll Free Tel:* 888-523-9292 (cust serv) *E-mail:* canadaweb@penguinrandomhouse.com; customerservicescanada@penguinrandomhouse.com *Web Site:* www.penguinrandomhouse.ca, pg 416

Papin, Jessica, Dystel, Goderich & Bourret LLC, One Union Sq W, Suite 904, New York, NY 10003 *Tel:* 212-627-9100 *Fax:* 212-627-9313 *Web Site:* www.dystel.com, pg 457

Pappalardo, Carra, EPS School Specialty, 625 Mount Auburn St, Suite 202, Cambridge, MA 02138-3039 *Toll Free Tel:* 800-225-5750 *Toll Free Fax:* 888-440-2665 *E-mail:* curriculumcare@schoolspecialty.com; curriculumorders@schoolspecialty.com *Web Site:* eps.schoolspecialty.com, pg 67

Pappas, Cheryl, Harvard Art Museums, 32 Quincy St, Cambridge, MA 02138 *Tel:* 617-495-9400 *Web Site:* www.harvardartmuseums.org, pg 87

Pappas, Joseph J, Consumer Press, 13326 SW 28 St, Suite 102, Fort Lauderdale, FL 33330-1102 *Tel:* 954-370-9153 *E-mail:* info@consumerpress.com *Web Site:* www.consumerpress.com, pg 52

Paprocki, Karin, Simon & Schuster Children's Publishing, 1230 Avenue of the Americas, New York, NY 10020 *Tel:* 212-698-7000 *Web Site:* www.simonandschuster.com/kids; www.simonandschuster.com/teen; simonandschuster.net; simonandschuster.biz, pg 189

Paprocki, Ray, City & Regional Magazine Association (CRMA), 287 Richards Ave, Norwalk, CT 06850 *Tel:* 203-515-9294 *Web Site:* citymag.org, pg 504

Paradis, Anne, Les Editions Chouette, 2515, avenue de la Renaissance, Boisbriand, QC J7H 1T9, Canada *Tel:* 514-925-3325 *E-mail:* info@editions-chouette.com; serviceclient@editions-chouette.com; foreignrights@editions-chouette.com *Web Site:* www.editions-chouette.com, pg 402

Paradis, Rich, Candlewick Press, 99 Dover St, Somerville, MA 02144-2825 *Tel:* 617-661-3330 *Fax:* 617-661-0565 *E-mail:* bigbear@candlewick.com; salesinfo@candlewick.com *Web Site:* candlewick.com, pg 39

Pardo, Wendy, Sounds True Inc, 413 S Arthur Ave, Louisville, CO 80027 *Tel:* 303-665-3151 *Toll Free Tel:* 800-333-9185 (US); 888-303-9185 (US & CN) *E-mail:* customerservice@soundstrue.com; stpublicity@soundstrue.com *Web Site:* www.soundstrue.com, pg 194

Pare, Jean, Saint-Jean Editeur Inc, 4490, rue Garand, Laval, QC H7L 5Z6, Canada *Tel:* 450-663-1777 *E-mail:* info@saint-jeanediteur.com *Web Site:* saint-jeanediteur.com, pg 418

Paredes, Nikay, Academy of American Poets Fellowship, 75 Maiden Lane, Suite 901, New York, NY 10038 *Tel:* 212-274-0343 *E-mail:* awards@poets.org *Web Site:* poets.org/academy-american-poets/prizes/academy-american-poets-fellowship, pg 569

Paredes, Nikay, Academy of American Poets First Book Award, 75 Maiden Lane, Suite 901, New York, NY 10038 *Tel:* 212-274-0343 *E-mail:* awards@poets.org *Web Site:* poets.org/academy-american-poets/prizes/first-book-award, pg 569

Paredes, Nikay, The Academy of American Poets Inc, 75 Maiden Lane, Suite 901, New York, NY 10038 *Tel:* 212-274-0343 *E-mail:* academy@poets.org *Web Site:* poets.org, pg 493

Paredes, Nikay, Ambroggio Prize, 75 Maiden Lane, Suite 901, New York, NY 10038 *Tel:* 212-274-0343 *E-mail:* awards@poets.org *Web Site:* poets.org/academy-american-poets/prizes/ambroggio-prize, pg 572

Paredes, Nikay, James Laughlin Award, 75 Maiden Lane, Suite 901, New York, NY 10038 *Tel:* 212-274-0343 *E-mail:* awards@poets.org *Web Site:* poets.org/academy-american-poets/prizes/james-laughlin-award, pg 622

Paredes, Nikay, Lenore Marshall Poetry Prize, 75 Maiden Lane, Suite 901, New York, NY 10038 *Tel:* 212-274-0343 *E-mail:* awards@poets.org *Web Site:* poets.org/academy-american-poets/prizes/lenore-marshall-poetry-prize, pg 629

Paredes, Nikay, Harold Morton Landon Translation Award, 75 Maiden Lane, Suite 901, New York, NY 10038 *Tel:* 212-274-0343 *E-mail:* awards@poets.org *Web Site:* poets.org/academy-american-poets/prizes/harold-morton-landon-translation-award, pg 635

Paredes, Nikay, Aliki Perroti & Seth Frank Most Promising Young Poet Award, 75 Maiden Lane, Suite 901, New York, NY 10038 *Tel:* 212-274-0343 *E-mail:* awards@poets.org *Web Site:* poets.org/academy-american-poets/american-poets-prizes, pg 649

Paredes, Nikay, Raiziss/de Palchi Fellowship, 75 Maiden Lane, Suite 901, New York, NY 10038 *Tel:* 212-274-0343 *E-mail:* awards@poets.org *Web Site:* poets.org/academy-american-poets/american-poets-prizes, pg 654

Paredes, Nikay, Wallace Stevens Award, 75 Maiden Lane, Suite 901, New York, NY 10038 *Tel:* 212-274-0343 *E-mail:* awards@poets.org *Web Site:* poets.org/academy-american-poets/prizes/wallace-stevens-award, pg 666

Paredes, Nikay, Treehouse Climate Action Poem Prize, 75 Maiden Lane, Suite 901, New York, NY 10038 *Tel:* 212-274-0343 *E-mail:* awards@poets.org *Web Site:* poets.org, pg 670

Parfrey, Jessica, Feral House, 1240 W Sims Way, Suite 124, Port Townsend, WA 98368 *Tel:* 323-666-3311 *E-mail:* info@feralhouse.com *Web Site:* feralhouse.com, pg 71

Parikh, Dhara, Random House Publishing Group, 1745 Broadway, New York, NY 10019 *Toll Free Tel:* 800-200-3552 *Web Site:* www.randomhousebooks.com, pg 171

Parikh, Sudip, American Association for the Advancement of Science (AAAS), 1200 New York Ave NW, Washington, DC 20005 *Tel:* 202-326-6400 *E-mail:* membership@aaas.org *Web Site:* www.aaas.org, pg 494

Parisi, Anthony, Tor Publishing Group, 120 Broadway, New York, NY 10271 *Toll Free Tel:* 800-455-0340 (Macmillan) *E-mail:* torpublicity@tor.com; forgepublicity@forgebooks.com *Web Site:* us.macmillan.com/torpublishinggroup, pg 208

Park, Chris, DeFiore and Company Literary Management Inc, 47 E 19 St, 3rd fl, New York, NY 10003 *Tel:* 212-925-7744 *Fax:* 212-925-9803 *E-mail:* info@defliterary.com; submissions@defliterary.com *Web Site:* www.defliterary.com, pg 456

Park, Hana, Simon & Schuster, 1230 Avenue of the Americas, New York, NY 10020 *Tel:* 212-698-7000 *Toll Free Tel:* 800-223-2348 (cust serv); 800-223-2336 (orders) *Toll Free Fax:* 800-943-9831 (orders) *Web Site:* simonandschusterpublishing.com/simonandschuster/, pg 188

Park, Joshua Hyoung-Jun, The Princeton Review, 110 E 42 St, 7th fl, New York, NY 10017 *Toll Free Tel:* 800-273-8439 (orders only) *Web Site:* www.princetonreview.com, pg 164

Parker, Erika, American Psychiatric Association Publishing, 800 Maine Ave SW, Suite 900, Washington, DC 20024 *Tel:* 202-459-9722 *Toll Free Tel:* 800-368-5777 *Fax:* 202-403-3094 *E-mail:* appi@psych.org *Web Site:* www.appi.org; www.psychiatryonline.org, pg 11

Parker, Hayley, Candlewick Press, 99 Dover St, Somerville, MA 02144-2825 *Tel:* 617-661-3330 *Fax:* 617-661-0565 *E-mail:* bigbear@candlewick.com; salesinfo@candlewick.com *Web Site:* candlewick.com, pg 39

Parker, Mel, Mel Parker Books LLC, 215 E 68 St, 10-O, New York, NY 10065 *Tel:* 917-696-6105 *E-mail:* info@melparkerbooks.com *Web Site:* melparkerbooks.com, pg 471

Parker, Miriam, HarperCollins Publishers LLC, 195 Broadway, New York, NY 10007 *Tel:* 212-207-7000 *Web Site:* www.harpercollins.com, pg 86

Parker, Sarah Jonathan, Artist-in-Residence Program, 225 King St, Suite 201, Fredericton, NB E3B 1E1, Canada *Tel:* 506-444-4444 *Toll Free Tel:* 866-460-ARTS (460-2787) *Fax:* 506-444-5543 *E-mail:* prog@artsnb.ca *Web Site:* www.artsnb.ca, pg 574

Parker, Sarah Jonathan, Arts Scholarships, 225 King St, Suite 201, Fredericton, NB E3B 1E1, Canada *Tel:* 506-444-4444 *Toll Free Tel:* 866-460-ARTS (460-2787) *Fax:* 506-444-5543 *E-mail:* prog@artsnb.ca *Web Site:* www.artsnb.ca, pg 574

Parker, Sarah Jonathan, Career Development Program, 225 King St, Suite 201, Fredericton, NB E3B 1E1, Canada *Tel:* 506-444-4444 *Toll Free Tel:* 866-460-ARTS (460-2787) *Fax:* 506-444-5543 *E-mail:* prog@artsnb.ca *Web Site:* www.artsnb.ca, pg 586

Parker, Sarah Jonathan, Creation Grant Program, 225 King St, Suite 201, Fredericton, NB E3B 1E1, Canada *Tel:* 506-444-4444 *Toll Free Tel:* 866-460-ARTS (460-2787) *Fax:* 506-444-5543 *E-mail:* prog@artsnb.ca *Web Site:* www.artsnb.ca, pg 593

Parker, Sarah Jonathan, Creative Residencies-Quebec, 225 King St, Suite 201, Fredericton, NB E3B 1E1, Canada *Tel:* 506-444-4444 *Toll Free Tel:* 866-460-ARTS (460-2787) *Fax:* 506-444-5543 *E-mail:* prog@artsnb.ca *Web Site:* www.artsnb.ca, pg 593

Parker, Sarah Jonathan, Documentation Grant Program, 225 King St, Suite 201, Fredericton, NB E3B 1E1, Canada *Tel:* 506-444-4444 *Toll Free Tel:* 866-460-ARTS (460-2787) *Fax:* 506-444-5543 *E-mail:* prog@artsnb.ca *Web Site:* www.artsnb.ca, pg 596

Parker, Sarah Jonathan, The Lieutenant-Governor's Awards for High Achievement in the Arts, 225 King St, Suite 201, Fredericton, NB E3B 1E1, Canada *Tel:* 506-444-4444 *Toll Free Tel:* 866-460-ARTS (460-2787) *Fax:* 506-444-5543 *E-mail:* prog@artsnb.ca *Web Site:* www.artsnb.ca, pg 624

Parkerson, Ami, New World Library, 14 Pamaron Way, Novato, CA 94949 *Tel:* 415-884-2100 *Fax:* 415-884-2199 *E-mail:* escort@newworldlibrary.com *Web Site:* www.newworldlibrary.com, pg 140

Parkinson, Judy, Research Press, 2612 N Mattis Ave, Champaign, IL 61822 *Tel:* 217-352-3273 *Toll Free Tel:* 800-519-2707 *Fax:* 217-352-1221 *E-mail:* rp@researchpress.com; orders@researchpress.com *Web Site:* www.researchpress.com, pg 174

Parks, J Evan, Writers' League of Texas (WLT), 611 S Congress Ave, Suite 200 A-3, Austin, TX 78704 *Tel:* 512-499-8914 *E-mail:* wlt@writersleague.org *Web Site:* www.writersleague.org, pg 488, 523, 558

Parks, J Evan, Writers' League of Texas Book Awards, 611 S Congress Ave, Suite 200 A-3, Austin, TX 78704 *Tel:* 512-499-8914 *E-mail:* wlt@writersleague.org *Web Site:* www.writersleague.org, pg 678

Parks, Walter, UnKnownTruths.com Publishing Co, 8815 Conroy Windermere Rd, Suite 190, Orlando, FL 32835 *Tel:* 407-929-9207 *E-mail:* info@unknowntruths.com *Web Site:* unknowntruths.com, pg 222

Parlagreco, Aurora, Farrar, Straus & Giroux Books for Young Readers, 120 Broadway, New York, NY 10271 *Tel:* 212-741-6900 *Toll Free Tel:* 888-330-8477 (orders) *E-mail:* childrens.publicity@macmillanusa.com; childrensrights@macmillanusa.com *Web Site:* us.macmillan.com/mackids, pg 70

Parlagreco, Aurora, Roaring Brook Press, 120 Broadway, New York, NY 10271 *Tel:* 646-307-5151 *Web Site:* us.macmillan.com/publishers/roaring-brook-press, pg 175

Parliman, Emily, Books on Tape™, 1745 Broadway, New York, NY 10019 *Toll Free Tel:* 800-733-3000 (cust serv) *Toll Free Fax:* 800-940-7046 *Web Site:* PenguinRandomHouseLibrary.com, pg 34

Parmiter, Katie Sweeney, Fordham University Press, Joseph A Martino Hall, 45 Columbus Ave, 3rd fl, New York, NY 10023 *Fax:* 347-842-3083 *Web Site:* www.fordhampress.com, pg 73

Parrish, Jim, Bethany House Publishers, 11400 Hampshire Ave S, Bloomington, MN 55438 *Tel:* 952-829-2500 *Toll Free Tel:* 800-877-2665 (orders) *Fax:* 952-829-2568 *Toll Free Fax:* 800-398-3111 (orders) *Web Site:* www.bethanyhouse.com; www.bakerpublishinggroup.com, pg 29

Parry, Emma, Janklow & Nesbit Associates, 285 Madison Ave, 21st fl, New York, NY 10017 *Tel:* 212-421-1700 *Fax:* 212-355-1403 *E-mail:* info@janklow.com; submissions@janklow.com; filmtvrights@janklow.com *Web Site:* www.janklowandnesbit.com, pg 464

Parry, Katie, Applewood Books, 210 Wingo Way, Suite 200, Mount Pleasant, SC 29464 *Tel:* 843-853-2070 *E-mail:* retailers@arcadiapublishing.com; publishing@arcadiapublishing.com *Web Site:* www.arcadiapublishing.com, pg 15

Parry, Katie, Arcadia Publishing Inc, 210 Wingo Way, Suite 200, Mount Pleasant, SC 29464 *Tel:* 843-853-2070 *E-mail:* retailers@arcadiapublishing.com *Web Site:* www.arcadiapublishing.com, pg 16

Parry, Katie, Commonwealth Editions, 210 Wingo Way, Suite 200, Mount Pleasant, SC 29464 *Tel:* 843-853-2070 *E-mail:* retailers@arcadiapublishing.com; publishing@arcadiapublishing.com *Web Site:* www.arcadiapublishing.com, pg 51

Parry, Katie, Dutton, c/o Penguin Random House LLC, 1745 Broadway, New York, NY 10019 *Tel:* 212-366-2000 *Web Site:* www.penguin.com/dutton-overview/; www.penguin.com/plume-books-overview/; www.penguin.com/tiny-reparations-overview/, pg 62

Parsley, John, Dutton, c/o Penguin Random House LLC, 1745 Broadway, New York, NY 10019 *Tel:* 212-366-2000 *Web Site:* www.penguin.com/dutton-overview/; www.penguin.com/plume-books-overview/; www.penguin.com/tiny-reparations-overview/, pg 62

Parsons, Brooke, Basic Books Group, 1290 Avenue of the Americas, New York, NY 10104 *Tel:* 212-340-8100 *Toll Free Tel:* 800-343-4499 (cust serv) *Fax:* 212-340-8105 *E-mail:* customer.service@hbgusa.com; orders@hbgusa.com *Web Site:* www.hachettebookgroup.com/imprint/basic-books/, pg 25

Parsons, Tara, HarperCollins Publishers LLC, 195 Broadway, New York, NY 10007 *Tel:* 212-207-7000 *Web Site:* www.harpercollins.com, pg 86

Partington, Heather Scott, Nona Balakian Citation for Excellence in Reviewing, c/o Jacob M Appel, Icahn School of Medicine at Mount Sinai, One Gustave L Levy Place, New York, NY 10029 *E-mail:* info@bookcritics.org *Web Site:* www.bookcritics.org/awards/balakian/, pg 576

Partington, Heather Scott, Gregg Barrios Book in Translation Prize, c/o Jacob M Appel, Icahn School of Medicine at Mount Sinai, One Gustave L Levy Place, New York, NY 10029 *E-mail:* info@bookcritics.org *Web Site:* www.bookcritics.org/awards/gregg-barrios-book-in-translation-prize/, pg 577

Partington, Heather Scott, Emerging Critics Fellowship, c/o Jacob M Appel, Icahn School of Medicine at Mount Sinai, One Gustave L Levy Place, New York, NY 10029 *E-mail:* info@bookcritics.org *Web Site:* www.bookcritics.org/awards, pg 599

Partington, Heather Scott, John Leonard Prize, c/o Jacob M Appel, Icahn School of Medicine at Mount Sinai, One Gustave L Levy Place, New York, NY 10029 *E-mail:* info@bookcritics.org *Web Site:* www.bookcritics.org/awards/leonard-prize/, pg 623

Partington, Heather Scott, The Toni Morrison Achievement Award, c/o Jacob M Appel, Icahn School of Medicine at Mount Sinai, One Gustave L Levy Place, New York, NY 10029 *E-mail:* info@bookcritics.org *Web Site:* www.bookcritics.org/the-toni-morrison-achievement-award/, pg 635

Partington, Heather Scott, National Book Critics Circle (NBCC), c/o Jacob M Appel, Icahn School of Medicine at Mount Sinai, One Gustave L Levy Place, New York, NY 10029 *E-mail:* info@bookcritics.org; membership@bookcritics.org *Web Site:* www.bookcritics.org, pg 512

Partington, Heather Scott, National Book Critics Circle Award, c/o Jacob M Appel, Icahn School of Medicine at Mount Sinai, One Gustave L Levy Place, New York, NY 10029 *E-mail:* info@bookcritics.org *Web Site:* www.bookcritics.org/awards, pg 637

Partington, Heather Scott, Ivan Sandrof Lifetime Achievement Award, c/o Jacob M Appel, Icahn School of Medicine at Mount Sinai, One Gustave L Levy Place, New York, NY 10029 *E-mail:* info@bookcritics.org *Web Site:* www.bookcritics.org/awards/sandrof/, pg 659

Partner, Maddie, Vintage Books, c/o Penguin Random House LLC, 1745 Broadway, New York, NY 10019 *Tel:* 212-572-2420 *Fax:* 212-940-7390 (dom rts); 212-572-2662 (foreign rts) *E-mail:* vintageanchorpublicity@randomhouse.com *Web Site:* knopfdoubleday.com/imprint/vintage; knopfdoubleday.com, pg 225

Paryel, Andrew, eLit Awards, 1129 Woodmere Ave, Suite B, Traverse City, MI 49686 *Tel:* 231-933-0445 *Toll Free Tel:* 800-706-4636 *Fax:* 231-933-0448 *E-mail:* info@elitawards.com *Web Site:* elitawards.com, pg 599

Pascal, Erinn, Andrews McMeel Publishing LLC, 1130 Walnut St, Kansas City, MO 64106-2109 *Tel:* 816-581-7500 *Toll Free Tel:* 800-851-8923 *Web Site:* www.andrewsmcmeel.com; publishing.andrewsmcmeel.com, pg 14

Pasciuto, Marya, Andrews McMeel Publishing LLC, 1130 Walnut St, Kansas City, MO 64106-2109 *Tel:* 816-581-7500 *Toll Free Tel:* 800-851-8923 *Web Site:* www.andrewsmcmeel.com; publishing.andrewsmcmeel.com, pg 14

Pascocello, Rick, Simon & Schuster, LLC, 1230 Avenue of the Americas, New York, NY 10020 *Tel:* 212-698-7000 *Toll Free Tel:* 800-223-2336 (orders) *Fax:* 212-698-7007 *Toll Free Fax:* 800-943-9831 *E-mail:* firstname.lastname@simonandschuster.com; purchaseorders@simonandschuster.com (orders) *Web Site:* www.simonandschuster.com, pg 190

Pascoe, Chelsea, Berkley, c/o Penguin Random House LLC, 1745 Broadway, 19th fl, New York, NY 10019 *Tel:* 212-366-2000 *Web Site:* www.penguin.com/publishers/berkley/; www.penguin.com/ace-overview/, pg 28

Pasic, Maya, Doubleday, c/o Penguin Random House LLC, 1745 Broadway, New York, NY 10019 *Tel:* 212-751-2600 *Fax:* 212-940-7390 (dom rts); 212-572-2662 (foreign rts) *Web Site:* knopfdoubleday.com/imprint/doubleday/; knopfdoubleday.com, pg 61

Paska, Lawrence, Carter G Woodson Book Awards, 8555 16 St, Suite 500, Silver Spring, MD 20910 *Tel:* 301-588-1800 *E-mail:* ncss@ncss.org *Web Site:* www.socialstudies.org/membership/awards/carter-g-woodson-book-awards, pg 677

Passannante, Donna, Penguin Random House Audio Publishing Group, 1745 Broadway, New York, NY 10019 *Toll Free Tel:* 800-793-2665 (cust serv) *E-mail:* audio@penguinrandomhouse.com; ecustomerservice@penguinrandomhouse.com *Web Site:* www.penguinrandomhouseaudio.com, pg 154

Pasternack, Gail, Kay Snow Writing Contest, 5331 SW Macadam Ave, Suite 258, PMB 215, Portland, OR 97239 *Tel:* 971-200-5385 *E-mail:* wilwrite@willamettewriters.org *Web Site:* willamettewriters.org/kay-snow-writing-contest, pg 664

Pasternack, Gail, Willamette Writers, 5331 SW Macadam Ave, Suite 258, PMB 215, Portland, OR 97239 *Tel:* 971-200-5385 *E-mail:* wilwrite@willamettewriters.org *Web Site:* willamettewriters.org, pg 522

Pasternack, Gail, Willamette Writers' Conference, 5331 SW Macadam Ave, Suite 258, PMB 215, Portland, OR 97239 *Tel:* 971-200-5385 *E-mail:* wilwrite@willamettewriters.org *Web Site:* willamettewriters.org, pg 558

Pasternak, Vicki, Scholastic Canada Ltd, 175 Hillmount Rd, Markham, ON L6C 1Z7, Canada *Tel:* 905-887-7323 *Toll Free Tel:* 800-268-3860 (CN) *Toll Free Fax:* 800-387-4944 *E-mail:* custserve@scholastic.ca *Web Site:* www.scholastic.ca, pg 418

Pastor, Alexa, Simon & Schuster Children's Publishing, 1230 Avenue of the Americas, New York, NY 10020 *Tel:* 212-698-7000 *Web Site:* www.simonandschuster.com/kids; www.simonandschuster.com/teen; simonandschuster.net; simonandschuster.biz, pg 189

Pastor, Paul J, Zondervan, 3900 Sparks Dr SE, Grand Rapids, MI 49546 *Tel:* 616-698-6900 *Toll Free Tel:* 800-226-1122; 800-727-1309 (retail orders) *Fax:* 616-698-3350 *Toll Free Fax:* 800-698-3256 (retail orders) *E-mail:* customercare@harpercollins.com *Web Site:* www.zondervan.com, pg 236

Pate, Ginger, Women Who Write Inc, PO Box 652, Madison, NJ 07940-0652 *Web Site:* www.womenwhowrite.org, pg 522

Patel, Archna, University of California Press, 155 Grand Ave, Suite 400, Oakland, CA 94612-3758 *Tel:* 510-883-8232 *Fax:* 510-836-8910 *E-mail:* customerservice@ucpress.edu *Web Site:* www.ucpress.edu, pg 215

Patel, Darshna, Association of University Presses (AUPresses), 1412 Broadway, Suite 2135, New York, NY 10018 *Tel:* 212-989-1010 *Fax:* 212-989-0275 *E-mail:* info@aupresses.org *Web Site:* www.aupresses.org, pg 500

Patel, Hemali, Macmillan, 120 Broadway, 22nd fl, New York, NY 10271 *E-mail:* press.inquiries@macmillan.com *Web Site:* us.macmillan.com, pg 122

Patel, Punam, Harlequin Enterprises Ltd, Bay Adelaide Centre, East Tower, 22 Adelaide St W, 41st fl, Toronto, ON M5H 4E3, Canada *Tel:* 416-445-5860 *Toll Free Tel:* 888-432-4879; 800-370-5838 (ebook inquiries) *E-mail:* customerservice@harlequin.com *Web Site:* www.harlequin.com, pg 409

Patel, Shina, GP Putnam's Sons, c/o Penguin Random House LLC, 1745 Broadway, New York, NY 10019 *Tel:* 212-782-9000 *Web Site:* www.penguin.com/putnam/, pg 167

Patel, Vandana, Harry N Abrams Inc, 195 Broadway, 9th fl, New York, NY 10007 *Tel:* 212-206-7715 *Toll Free Tel:* 800-345-1359 *Fax:* 212-645-8437 *E-mail:* abrams@abramsbooks.com; publicity@abramsbooks.com; sales@abramsbooks.com *Web Site:* www.abramsbooks.com, pg 2

Paternoster, Heather, Atlantic Center for the Arts Mentoring Artist-in-Residence Program, 1414 Art Center Ave, New Smyrna Beach, FL 32168 *Tel:* 386-427-6975 *E-mail:* program@atlanticcenterforthearts.org *Web Site:* atlanticcenterforthearts.org, pg 553

Paterson, Lindsay, Penguin Random House Canada, a Penguin Random House company, 320 Front St W, Suite 1400, Toronto, ON M5V 3B6, Canada *Tel:* 416-364-4449 *Toll Free Tel:* 888-523-9292 (cust serv) *E-mail:* canadaweb@penguinrandomhouse.com; customerservicescanada@penguinrandomhouse.com *Web Site:* www.penguinrandomhouse.ca, pg 416

Paterson, Shelagh, Ontario Library Association (OLA), 2080 Danforth Ave, Toronto, ON M4C 1J9, Canada *Toll Free Tel:* 877-340-1730 *E-mail:* info@accessola.com *Web Site:* accessola.com, pg 515

Patnaik, Gayatri, Beacon Press, 24 Farnsworth St, Boston, MA 02210-1409 *Tel:* 617-742-2110 *Fax:* 617-723-3097 *E-mail:* production@beacon.org *Web Site:* www.beacon.org, pg 25

Paton, Kathi J, Kathi J Paton Literary Agency, Box 2044, Radio City Sta, New York, NY 10101-2044 *Tel:* 212-265-6586 *E-mail:* kjplitbiz@optonline.net *Web Site:* www.patonliterary.com, pg 471

Patota, Anne, The Guilford Press, 370 Seventh Ave, Suite 1200, New York, NY 10001-1020 *Tel:* 212-431-9800 *Toll Free Tel:* 800-365-7006 *Fax:* 212-966-6708 *E-mail:* info@guilford.com; orders@guilford.com *Web Site:* www.guilford.com, pg 82

Patrick, Amy, Sleeping Bear Press™, 2395 S Huron Pkwy, Suite 200, Ann Arbor, MI 48104 *Toll Free Tel:* 800-487-2323 *Fax:* 734-794-0004 *E-mail:* customerservice@sleepingbearpress.com *Web Site:* www.sleepingbearpress.com, pg 191

Patrick, Harley B, Hellgate Press, PO Box 3531, Ashland, OR 97520 *Tel:* 541-973-5154 *E-mail:* sales@hellgatepress.com *Web Site:* www.hellgatepress.com, pg 91

Patrick, Kate, Kids Can Press Ltd, 25 Dockside Dr, Toronto, ON M5A 0B5, Canada *Tel:* 416-479-7000 *Toll Free Tel:* 800-265-0884 *Fax:* 416-960-5437 *E-mail:* info@kidscan.com; customerservice@kidscan.com *Web Site:* www.kidscanpress.com; www.kidscanpress.ca, pg 411

Patrick, Oona, Bloomsbury Publishing Inc, 1385 Broadway, 5th fl, New York, NY 10018 *Tel:* 212-419-5300 *E-mail:* marketingusa@bloomsbury.com; adultpublicityusa@bloomsbury.com; askacademic@bloomsbury.com *Web Site:* www.bloomsbury.com, pg 31

Patt, Avinoam PhD, Edward Lewis Wallant Award, Maurice Greenberg Center for Judaic Studies, 200 Bloomfield Ave, Harry Jack Gray E 300, West Hartford, CT 06117 *Tel:* 860-768-4964 *Fax:* 860-768-5044 *E-mail:* mgcjs@hartford.edu *Web Site:* www.hartford.edu/a_and_s/greenberg/wallant, pg 673

Patterson, Alexis, Penguin Random House Audio Publishing Group, 1745 Broadway, New York, NY 10019 *Toll Free Tel:* 800-793-2665 (cust serv) *E-mail:* audio@penguinrandomhouse.com; ecustomerservice@penguinrandomhouse.com *Web Site:* www.penguinrandomhouseaudio.com, pg 154

Patterson, David, Stuart Krichevsky Literary Agency Inc, 118 E 28 St, Suite 908, New York, NY 10016 *Tel:* 212-725-5288 *Fax:* 212-725-5275 *E-mail:* query@skagency.com *Web Site:* skagency.com, pg 466

Patterson, Emma, Brandt & Hochman Literary Agents Inc, 1501 Broadway, Suite 2310, New York, NY 10036 *Tel:* 212-840-5760 *Fax:* 212-840-5776 *Web Site:* brandthochman.com, pg 452

Patterson, Hallie, Harry N Abrams Inc, 195 Broadway, 9th fl, New York, NY 10007 *Tel:* 212-206-7715 *Toll Free Tel:* 800-345-1359 *Fax:* 212-645-8437 *E-mail:* abrams@abramsbooks.com; publicity@abramsbooks.com; sales@abramsbooks.com *Web Site:* www.abramsbooks.com, pg 2

Patterson, Helen Elaine, Maryland History Press, 6913 Seneca Dr, Snow Hill, MD 21863 *Tel:* 443-397-0912 *Web Site:* www.marylandhistorypress.com, pg 126

Patterson, Monique, St Martin's Press, LLC, 120 Broadway, New York, NY 10271 *E-mail:* publicity@stmartins.com; trademarketing@stmartins.com; foreignrights@stmartins.com *Web Site:* us.macmillan.com/smp, pg 180

Patterson, Monique, Tor Publishing Group, 120 Broadway, New York, NY 10271 *Toll Free Tel:* 800-455-0340 (Macmillan) *E-mail:* torpublicity@tor.com; forgepublicity@forgebooks.com *Web Site:* us.macmillan.com/torpublishinggroup, pg 208

Patterson, Tiffani, Insight Editions, 800 "A" St, San Rafael, CA 94901 *Tel:* 415-526-1370 *Toll Free Tel:* 800-809-3792 *Toll Free Fax:* 866-509-0515 *E-mail:* info@insighteditions.com; marketing@insighteditions.com *Web Site:* insighteditions.com, pg 101

Patti, Mark, Random House Children's Books, c/o Penguin Random House LLC, 1745 Broadway, New York, NY 10019 *Tel:* 212-782-9000 *Web Site:* www.rhcbooks.com, pg 170

Patton, Kimberlin (Kimi), Watermark Publishing, 1000 Bishop St, Suite 806, Honolulu, HI 96813 *Tel:* 808-587-7766 *Toll Free Tel:* 866-900-BOOK (900-2665) *Fax:* 808-521-3461 *E-mail:* info@bookshawaii.net *Web Site:* www.bookshawaii.net, pg 226

Patton, Susan, Society for Scholarly Publishing (SSP), 1120 Rte 73, Suite 200, Mount Laurel, NJ 08054 *Tel:* 856-439-1385 *Fax:* 856-439-0525 *E-mail:* info@sspnet.org *Web Site:* www.sspnet.org, pg 519

Paul, Hannah, Princeton University Press, 41 William St, Princeton, NJ 08540-5237 *Tel:* 609-258-4900 *Fax:* 609-258-6305 *E-mail:* info@press.princeton.edu *Web Site:* press.princeton.edu, pg 164

Paul, Tisha, Random House Children's Books, c/o Penguin Random House LLC, 1745 Broadway, New York, NY 10019 *Tel:* 212-782-9000 *Web Site:* www.rhcbooks.com, pg 170

Paulauski, Julie, HarperCollins Publishers LLC, 195 Broadway, New York, NY 10007 *Tel:* 212-207-7000 *Web Site:* www.harpercollins.com, pg 86

Paull, Michael, Recorded Books Inc, an RBmedia company, 8400 Corporate Dr, Landover, MD 20785 *Toll Free Tel:* 800-305-3450 *Web Site:* rbmediaglobal.com/recorded-books, pg 172

Paulsen, Nancy, Nancy Paulsen Books, c/o Penguin Random House LLC, 1745 Broadway, New York, NY 10019 *Tel:* 212-782-9000 *Web Site:* www.penguin.com/nancy-paulsen-books-overview/, pg 152

Paulsen, Nancy, Penguin Young Readers Group, c/o Penguin Random House LLC, 1745 Broadway, New York, NY 10019 *Tel:* 212-782-9000 *Web Site:* www.penguin.com/penguin-young-readers-overview/, pg 156

Paulson, Jamis, Turnstone Press, Artspace Bldg, 206-100 Arthur St, Winnipeg, MB R3B 1H3, Canada *Tel:* 204-947-1555 *Toll Free Tel:* 888-363-7718 *Fax:* 204-942-1555 *E-mail:* info@turnstonepress.com *Web Site:* www.turnstonepress.com, pg 421

Paulson, Jennifer, Johns Hopkins University Press, 2715 N Charles St, Baltimore, MD 21218-4363 *Tel:* 410-516-6900; 410-516-6987 *Toll Free Tel:* 800-537-5487 (book orders & cust serv); 800-548-1784 (journal orders) *Fax:* 410-516-6968; 410-516-6998 (orders) *E-mail:* hfscustserv@press.jhu.edu (cust serv); jrnlcirc@jh.edu (journal orders) *Web Site:* www.press.jhu.edu; muse.jhu.edu, pg 106

Paulson, Kristi, The Professional Education Group LLC (PEG), 700 Twelve Oaks Center Dr, Suite 104, Wayzata, MN 55391 *Tel:* 952-933-9990 *Toll Free Tel:* 800-229-2531 *E-mail:* orders@proedgroup.com *Web Site:* www.proedgroup.com, pg 165

Paulson, Tim, University Press of Kansas, 2502 Westbrooke Circle, Lawrence, KS 66045-4444 *Tel:* 785-864-4154 *Fax:* 785-864-4586 *E-mail:* upress@ku.edu *Web Site:* www.kansaspress.ku.edu, pg 221

Paulson, Timothy, Thomas Nelson, 501 Nelson Place, Nashville, TN 37214 *Tel:* 615-889-9000 *Toll Free Tel:* 800-251-4000 *Web Site:* www.thomasnelson.com, pg 206

Pautz, Peter Dennis, World Fantasy Awards, 3519 Glen Ave, Palmer Township, PA 18045-5812 *Web Site:* www.worldfantasy.org, pg 677

Pavlin, Jordan, Alfred A Knopf, c/o Penguin Random House LLC, 1745 Broadway, New York, NY 10019 *Tel:* 212-751-2600 (dom rts); 212-940-7390 (dom rts); 212-572-2662 (foreign rts) *Web Site:* knopfdoubleday.com/imprint/knopf/; knopfdoubleday.com, pg 110

Pavri, Farishteh, Penguin Random House Canada, a Penguin Random House company, 320 Front St W, Suite 1400, Toronto, ON M5V 3B6, Canada *Tel:* 416-364-4449 *Toll Free Tel:* 888-523-9292 (cust serv) *E-mail:* canadaweb@penguinrandomhouse.com; customerservicescanada@penguinrandomhouse.com *Web Site:* www.penguinrandomhouse.ca, pg 416

Pawa, Vandana, Margins Fellowship, 112 W 27 St, Suite 600, New York, NY 10001 *Tel:* 212-494-0061 *E-mail:* fellowships@aaww.org *Web Site:* aaww.org/fellowships/margins, pg 629

Pawa, Vandana, Open City Fellowship, 112 W 27 St, Suite 600, New York, NY 10001 *Tel:* 212-494-0061 *E-mail:* fellowships@aaww.org *Web Site:* aaww.org/fellowships/open-city, pg 644

Pawlak, Kim, William Holmes McGuffey Longevity Award, PO Box 367, Fountain City, WI 54629 *E-mail:* info@taaonline.net *Web Site:* www.taaonline.net/mcguffey-longevity-award, pg 630

Pawlak, Kim, Most Promising New Textbook Award, PO Box 367, Fountain City, WI 54629 *E-mail:* info@taaonline.net *Web Site:* www.taaonline.net/promising-new-textbook-award, pg 636

Pawlak, Kim, Pynn-Silverman Lifetime Achievement Award, PO Box 367, Fountain City, WI 54629 *E-mail:* info@taaonline.net *Web Site:* www.taaonline.net/council-awards#pynn, pg 654

Pawlak, Kim, TAA Council of Fellows, PO Box 367, Fountain City, WI 54629 *E-mail:* info@taaonline.net *Web Site:* www.taaonline.net/council-of-fellows, pg 668

Pawlak, Kim, Textbook Excellence Award, PO Box 367, Fountain City, WI 54629 *E-mail:* info@taaonline.net *Web Site:* www.taaonline.net/textbook-excellence-award, pg 669

Pawlak, Mark, Hanging Loose Press, 231 Wyckoff St, Brooklyn, NY 11217 *Tel:* 347-529-4738 *Fax:* 347-227-8215 *E-mail:* print225@aol.com *Web Site:* www.hangingloosepress.com, pg 85

Pawlitz, Mr Loren D, Concordia Publishing House, 3558 S Jefferson Ave, St Louis, MO 63118-3968 *Tel:* 314-268-1000; 314-268-1268 (bookshop) *Toll Free Tel:* 800-325-3040 (cust serv) *Toll Free Fax:* 800-490-9889 (cust serv) *E-mail:* order@cph.org *Web Site:* www.cph.org, pg 51

Pawluk, Justyna, Bloom's Literary Criticism, 132 W 31 St, 16th fl, New York, NY 10001 *Toll Free Tel:* 800-322-8755 *Toll Free Fax:* 800-678-3633 *E-mail:* custserv@infobase.com *Web Site:* www.infobasepublishing.com; www.infobase.com (online resources), pg 31

Pawluk, Justyna, Chelsea House, 132 W 31 St, 16th fl, New York, NY 10001 *Toll Free Tel:* 800-322-8755 *Toll Free Fax:* 800-678-3633 *E-mail:* custserv@infobase.com; info@infobase.com *Web Site:* www.infobase.com (online resources), pg 46

Payette, Sylvie, Les Editions Heritage Inc, 1101, ave Victoria, St-Lambert, QC J4R 1P8, Canada *Tel:* 514-875-0327 *E-mail:* dominiqueetcie@editionsheritage.com; info@editionsheritage.com *Web Site:* www.dominiqueetcompagnie.com, pg 403

Payne, Allison, Association of College & Research Libraries (ACRL), 225 N Michigan Ave, Suite 1300, Chicago, IL 60601 *Tel:* 312-280-2523; 312-280-2516 *Toll Free Tel:* 800-545-2433 (ext 2523) *Fax:* 312-280-2520 *E-mail:* acrl@ala.org; alastore@ala.org *Web Site:* www.ala.org/acrl; alastore.ala.org, pg 19

Payne, Caroline, Dutton, c/o Penguin Random House LLC, 1745 Broadway, New York, NY 10019 *Tel:* 212-366-2000 *Web Site:* www.penguin.com/dutton-overview/; www.penguin.com/plume-books-overview/; www.penguin.com/tiny-reparations-overview/, pg 62

Payne, Courtney, Sourcebooks LLC, 1935 Brookdale Rd, Suite 139, Naperville, IL 60563 Tel: 630-961-3900 Toll Free Tel: 800-432-7444 Fax: 630-961-2168 E-mail: info@sourcebooks.com Web Site: www.sourcebooks.com, pg 194

Payne, Heather, BLR®—Business & Legal Resources, 5511 Virginia Way, Suite 150, Brentwood, TN 37027 Tel: 860-510-0100 Toll Free Tel: 800-727-5257 Toll Free Fax: 800-785-9212 E-mail: media@blr.com; sales@blr.com; service@blr.com; techsupport@blr.com Web Site: blr.com, pg 32

Payne, Joan, BoardSource, 750 Ninth St NW, Suite 520, Washington, DC 20001-4793 Tel: 202-349-2500 E-mail: members@boardsource.org; mediarelations@boardsource.org Web Site: www.boardsource.org, pg 33

Payne, Jordan, Sourcebooks LLC, 1935 Brookdale Rd, Suite 139, Naperville, IL 60563 Tel: 630-961-3900 Toll Free Tel: 800-432-7444 Fax: 630-961-2168 E-mail: info@sourcebooks.com Web Site: www.sourcebooks.com, pg 195

Payne, Maribeth, W W Norton & Company Inc, 500 Fifth Ave, New York, NY 10110-0017 Tel: 212-354-5500 Toll Free Tel: 800-233-4830 (orders & cust serv) Fax: 212-869-0856 Toll Free Fax: 800-458-6515 E-mail: orders@wwnorton.com Web Site: wwnorton.com, pg 143

Payseur, Cecilia, HarperCollins Children's Books, 195 Broadway, New York, NY 10007 Tel: 212-207-7000 Web Site: www.harpercollins.com/childrens, pg 85

Payton, Thomas, Trinity University Press, One Trinity Place, San Antonio, TX 78212-7200 Tel: 210-999-8884 Fax: 210-999-8838 E-mail: books@trinity.edu Web Site: www.tupress.org, pg 209

Paz, Soleil, St Martin's Press, LLC, 120 Broadway, New York, NY 10271 E-mail: publicity@stmartins.com; trademarketing@stmartins.com; foreignrights@stmartins.com Web Site: us.macmillan.com/smp, pg 181

Pazdur, Ryan, Zondervan, 3900 Sparks Dr SE, Grand Rapids, MI 49546 Tel: 616-698-6900 Toll Free Tel: 800-226-1122; 800-727-1309 (retail orders) Fax: 616-698-3350 Toll Free Fax: 800-698-3256 (retail orders) E-mail: customercare@harpercollins.com Web Site: www.zondervan.com, pg 236

Peabody, William, GP Putnam's Sons, c/o Penguin Random House LLC, 1745 Broadway, New York, NY 10019 Tel: 212-782-9000 Web Site: www.penguin.com/putnam/, pg 167

Pearce, Anne Tate, Simon & Schuster, 1230 Avenue of the Americas, New York, NY 10020 Tel: 212-698-7000 Toll Free Tel: 800-223-2348 (cust serv); 800-223-2336 (orders) Toll Free Fax: 800-943-9831 (orders) Web Site: simonandschusterpublishing.com/simonandschuster/, pg 188

Pearce, John, Westwood Creative Artists Ltd, 386 Huron St, Toronto, ON M5S 2G6, Canada Tel: 416-964-3302 Fax: 416-964-3302 E-mail: wca_office@wcaltd.com Web Site: www.wcaltd.com, pg 481

Pearl, Allyson, Random House Publishing Group, 1745 Broadway, New York, NY 10019 Toll Free Tel: 800-200-3552 Web Site: www.randomhousebooks.com, pg 171

Pearlman, Brittany, Sourcebooks LLC, 1935 Brookdale Rd, Suite 139, Naperville, IL 60563 Tel: 630-961-3900 Toll Free Tel: 800-432-7444 Fax: 630-961-2168 E-mail: info@sourcebooks.com Web Site: www.sourcebooks.com, pg 194

Pearpoint, Jack, Inclusion Press International, 47 Indian Trail, Toronto, ON M6R 1Z8, Canada Tel: 416-658-5363 Fax: 416-658-5067 E-mail: inclusionpress@inclusion.com Web Site: inclusion.com, pg 410

Pearson, Jason, Wm B Eerdmans Publishing Co, 4035 Park East Ct SE, Grand Rapids, MI 49546 Tel: 616-459-4591 Toll Free Tel: 800-253-7521 E-mail: customerservice@eerdmans.com Web Site: www.eerdmans.com, pg 64

Pearson, Lisa, Siglio, PO Box 111, Catskill, NY 12414 Tel: 310-857-6935 E-mail: publisher@sigliopress.com Web Site: sigliopress.com, pg 187

Pearson, Michael, The Mathematical Association of America, 1529 18 St NW, Washington, DC 20036-1358 Tel: 202-387-5200 Toll Free Tel: 800-741-9415 Fax: 202-265-2384 E-mail: maahq@maa.org; advertising@maa.org (pubns) Web Site: www.maa.org, pg 127

Pearson, Nancy, Scholastic Canada Ltd, 175 Hillmount Rd, Markham, ON L6C 1Z7, Canada Tel: 905-887-7323 Toll Free Tel: 800-268-3860 (CN) Toll Free Fax: 800-387-4944 E-mail: custserve@scholastic.ca Web Site: www.scholastic.ca, pg 418

Pease, Pamela, Paintbox Press, 275 Madison Ave, Suite 600, New York, NY 10016 Tel: 212-878-6610 E-mail: info@paintboxpress.com Web Site: www.paintboxpress.com, pg 150

Peattie, Dave, Publishing Professionals Network, c/o Postal Annex, 274 Redwood Shores Pkwy, Redwood City, CA 94065-1173 E-mail: operations@pubpronetwork.org Web Site: pubpronetwork.org, pg 518

Peattie, Gary R, DeVorss & Co, 1100 Flynn Rd, Unit 104, Camarillo, CA 93012 Tel: 805-322-9010 Toll Free Tel: 800-843-5743 Fax: 805-322-9011 E-mail: service@devorss.com Web Site: www.devorss.com, pg 59

Peccatori, Stefano, Chelsea Green Publishing Co, 85 N Main St, Suite 120, White River Junction, VT 05001 Tel: 802-295-6300 Toll Free Tel: 800-639-4099 (cust serv & orders) Fax: 802-295-6444 E-mail: customerservice@chelseagreen.com; editorial@chelseagreen.com; publicity@chelseagreen.com; rights@chelseagreen.com Web Site: www.chelseagreen.com, pg 45

Peccatori, Stefano, Rizzoli International Publications Inc, 300 Park Ave S, 4th fl, New York, NY 10010-5399 Tel: 212-387-3400 Toll Free Tel: 800-522-6657 (orders only) Fax: 212-387-3535 E-mail: publicity@rizzoliusa.com Web Site: www.rizzoliusa.com, pg 175

Pecci, Kristen, Macmillan, 120 Broadway, 22nd fl, New York, NY 10271 E-mail: press.inquiries@macmillan.com Web Site: us.macmillan.com, pg 122

Pecinovsky, Tony, International Publishers Co Inc, 235 W 23 St, New York, NY 10011 Tel: 212-366-9816 Fax: 212-366-9820 E-mail: service@intpubnyc.com Web Site: www.intpubnyc.com, pg 103

Pecorale, Christina, Simon & Schuster, LLC, 1230 Avenue of the Americas, New York, NY 10020 Tel: 212-698-7000 Toll Free Tel: 800-223-2336 (orders) Fax: 212-698-7007 Toll Free Fax: 800-943-9831 (orders) E-mail: firstname.lastname@simonandschuster.com; purchaseorders@simonandschuster.com (orders) Web Site: www.simonandschuster.com, pg 190

Pedersen, Nadine, University of British Columbia Press, 2029 West Mall, Vancouver, BC V6T 1Z2, Canada Tel: 604-822-5959 Toll Free Tel: 877-377-9378 Fax: 604-822-6083 Toll Free Fax: 800-668-0821 E-mail: frontdesk@ubcpress.ca Web Site: www.ubcpress.ca, pg 422

Pederson, Leis, Berkley, c/o Penguin Random House LLC, 1745 Broadway, 19th fl, New York, NY 10019 Tel: 212-366-2000 Web Site: www.penguin.com/publishers/berkley/; www.penguin.com/ace-overview/, pg 28

Peed, Sarah, Penguin Random House LLC, 1745 Broadway, New York, NY 10019 Tel: 212-782-9000 Toll Free Tel: 800-726-0600 Web Site: www.penguinrandomhouse.com, pg 155

Peede, Jon Parrish, Public Scholars, 400 Seventh St SW, Washington, DC 20506 Tel: 202-606-8200 E-mail: publicscholar@neh.gov Web Site: www.neh.gov/grants, pg 653

Peel, Tim, The Canadian Circulations Audit Board (CCAB), 111 Queen St E, Suite 450, Toronto, ON M5C 1S2, Canada Toll Free Tel: 877-302-8348 Web Site: www.bpaww.com, pg 502

Peeler, Denise, University of Illinois Press, 1325 S Oak St, MC-566, Champaign, IL 61820-6903 Tel: 217-333-0950 Fax: 217-244-8082 E-mail: uipress@uillinois.edu; journals@uillinois.edu Web Site: www.press.uillinois.edu, pg 216

Peer, Jeffrey, Turtle Point Press, 208 Java St, 5th fl, Brooklyn, NY 11222-5748 Tel: 212-741-1393 E-mail: info@turtlepointpress.com Web Site: www.turtlepointpress.com, pg 210

Peery, Amanda, Princeton University Press, 41 William St, Princeton, NJ 08540-5237 Tel: 609-258-4900 Fax: 609-258-6305 E-mail: info@press.princeton.edu Web Site: press.princeton.edu, pg 164

Peiffer, Mitchell, Higginson Book Company LLC, 219 Mill Rd, Morgantown, PA 19543 Tel: 484-249-0378 Web Site: www.higginsonbooks.com, pg 91

Peiser, Megan, Bibliographical Society of America (BSA), 67 West St, Suite 401, Unit C17, Brooklyn, NY 11222 Tel: 212-452-2710 E-mail: bsa@bibsocamer.org Web Site: bibsocamer.org, pg 501

Pekoll, Kristen, John Phillip Immroth Memorial Award, 225 Michigan Ave, Suite 1300, Chicago, IL 60601 Tel: 312-280-4226 Toll Free Tel: 800-545-2433 E-mail: ifrt@ala.org Web Site: www.ala.org/rt/ifrt/immroth, pg 615

Pekoll, Kristen, Eli M Oboler Memorial Award, 225 Michigan Ave, Suite 1300, Chicago, IL 60601 Tel: 312-280-4226 Toll Free Tel: 800-545-2433 E-mail: ifrt@ala.org Web Site: www.ala.org/rt/ifrt/oboler, pg 642

Pellerin, Sandy, Les Editions de Mortagne, CP 116, Boucherville, QC J4B 5E6, Canada Tel: 450-641-2387 E-mail: info@editionsdemortagne.com Web Site: editionsdemortagne.com, pg 402

Pelletier, James L, Marine Techniques Publishing, 311 W River Rd, Augusta, ME 04330-3991 Tel: 207-622-7984 E-mail: promariner@roadrunner.com, pg 125

Pelletier, Liz, Entangled Publishing LLC, 644 Shrewsbury Commons Ave, Suite 181, Shrewsbury, PA 17361 Toll Free Tel: 877-677-9451 E-mail: publisher@entangledpublishing.com Web Site: www.entangledpublishing.com, pg 67

Pelletier, Sharon, Dystel, Goderich & Bourret LLC, One Union Sq W, Suite 904, New York, NY 10003 Tel: 212-627-9100 Fax: 212-627-9313 Web Site: www.dystel.com, pg 457

Pellien, Jessica, The MIT Press, One Broadway, 12th fl, Cambridge, MA 02142 Tel: 617-253-5255 Toll Free Tel: 800-405-1619 (orders) Fax: 617-258-6779; 617-577-1545 (orders) Web Site: mitpress.mit.edu, pg 132

Pelsue, Kelly, Morgan Gaynin, 41 N Main St, Norwalk, CT 06854 Tel: 212-475-0440 E-mail: info@morgangaynin.com Web Site: www.morgangaynin.com, pg 486

Pelton, Elena, Naval Institute Press, 291 Wood Rd, Annapolis, MD 21402-5034 Tel: 410-268-6110 Toll Free Tel: 800-233-8764 Fax: 410-295-1084 E-mail: customer@usni.org (cust inquiries) Web Site: www.usni.org/press/books; www.usni.org, pg 139

Pelton, Liz, Yale University Press, 302 Temple St, New Haven, CT 06511-8909 Tel: 203-432-0960; 203-432-0966 (sales); 401-531-2800 (cust serv) Toll Free Tel: 800-405-1619 (cust serv) Fax: 203-432-0948; 203-432-8485 (sales); 401-531-2801 (cust serv) Toll Free Fax: 800-406-9145 (cust serv) E-mail: sales.press@yale.edu (sales); customer.care@triliteral.org (cust serv) Web Site: www.yalebooks.com; yalepress.yale.edu/yupbooks, pg 235

Peltz, James, Excelsior Editions, 10 N Pearl St, 4th fl, Albany, NY 12207 Tel: 518-944-2800 Toll Free Tel: 866-430-7869 Fax: 518-320-1592 E-mail: info@sunypress.edu Web Site: www.sunypress.edu, pg 68

Peltz, James, State University of New York Press, 10 N Pearl St, 4th fl, Albany, NY 12207 Tel: 518-944-2800 Toll Free Tel: 877-204-6073 (orders) Fax: 518-320-1592 Toll Free Fax: 877-204-6074 (orders) E-mail: info@sunypress.edu (edit off); suny@presswarehouse.com (orders) Web Site: www.sunypress.edu, pg 198

Pelz, Sarah, HarperCollins Publishers LLC, 195 Broadway, New York, NY 10007 Tel: 212-207-7000 Web Site: www.harpercollins.com, pg 86

Pelzel, Raquel, Little, Brown and Company, 1290 Avenue of the Americas, New York, NY 10104 Tel: 212-364-1100 Fax: 212-364-0952 E-mail: firstname.lastname@hbgusa.com Web Site: www.hachettebookgroup.com/imprint/little-brown-and-company/, pg 118

Pena, J Fernando, American Printing History Association, PO Box 4519, Grand Central Sta, New York, NY 10163 E-mail: secretary@printinghistory.org Web Site: printinghistory.org, pg 496

Pena, J Fernando, American Printing History Association Award, PO Box 4519, Grand Central Sta, New York, NY 10163 E-mail: secretary@printinghistory.org Web Site: printinghistory.org/programs/awards, pg 573

Pena, Zoila, Workman Publishing, 1290 Avenue of the Americas, New York, NY 10104 Toll Free Tel: 800-759-0190 Fax: 212-364-0950 E-mail: workman-inquiry@hbgusa.com Web Site: www.hachettebookgroup.com/imprint/workman-publishing-company/, pg 233

Pencavel, Alice, Teachers & Writers Collaborative (T&W), 20 W 20 St, Suite 801, New York, NY 10011 Tel: 212-691-6590 E-mail: info@twc.org Web Site: www.twc.org, pg 521

Penco, James, Greystone Books Ltd, 343 Railway St, Suite 302, Vancouver, BC V6A 1A4, Canada Tel: 604-875-1550 Fax: 604-875-1556 E-mail: info@greystonebooks.com; rights@greystonebooks.com Web Site: www.greystonebooks.com, pg 407

Pendergast, Kirby, Fairchild Books, 1385 Broadway, 5th fl, New York, NY 10018 Tel: 212-419-5300 Toll Free Tel: 800-932-4724; 888-330-8477 (orders) Web Site: www.bloomsbury.com/us/discover/bloomsbury-academic/fairchild-books/, pg 69

Pennefeather, Shannon M, Minnesota Historical Society Press, 345 Kellogg Blvd W, St Paul, MN 55102-1906 Tel: 651-259-3205 Fax: 651-297-1345 E-mail: info-mnhspress@mnhs.org Web Site: www.mnhs.org/mnhspress, pg 132

Pennell, Kimberly, Pen-L Publishing, 12 W Dickson St, No 4455, Fayetteville, AR 72702 E-mail: info@pen-l.com Web Site: www.pen-l.com, pg 153

Pennington, Travis, The Knight Agency Inc, 232 W Washington St, Madison, GA 30650 E-mail: admin@knightagency.net Web Site: www.knightagency.net, pg 464

Pennock, Laura, Hachette Book Group Inc, 1290 Avenue of the Americas, New York, NY 10104 Tel: 212-364-1100 Toll Free Tel: 800-759-0190 (cust serv) Fax: 212-364-0933 (intl orders) Toll Free Fax: 800-286-9471 (cust serv) E-mail: customer.service@hbgusa.com; orders@hbgusa.com Web Site: www.hachettebookgroup.com, pg 83

Pennoyer, Peter, Whiting Awards, 16 Court St, Suite 2308, Brooklyn, NY 11241 Tel: 718-701-5962 E-mail: info@whiting.org Web Site: www.whiting.org, pg 675

Pennoyer, Peter, Whiting Creative Nonfiction Grant, 16 Court St, Suite 2308, Brooklyn, NY 11241 Tel: 718-701-5962 E-mail: nonfiction@whiting.org; info@whiting.org Web Site: www.whiting.org, pg 675

Pepe, Paolo, Random House Publishing Group, 1745 Broadway, New York, NY 10019 Toll Free Tel: 800-200-3552 Web Site: www.randomhousebooks.com, pg 170

Pepera, Brian, Brilliance Publishing Inc, 1704 Eaton Dr, Grand Haven, MI 49417 Tel: 616-846-5256 Toll Free Tel: 800-648-2312 (orders only) E-mail: brilliance-publishing@amazon.com; customerservice@brilliancepublishing.com; media@brilliancepublishing.com; publicity@brilliancepublishing.com Web Site: www.brilliancepublishing.com, pg 37

Pepper, Alison, 4A's (American Association of Advertising Agencies), 25 W 45 St, 16th fl, New York, NY 10036 Tel: 212-682-2500 E-mail: media@4as.org; membership@4as.org Web Site: www.aaaa.org, pg 506

Pepper, Eric, SPIE, 1000 20 St, Bellingham, WA 98225-6705 Tel: 360-676-3290 Toll Free Tel: 888-504-8171 (orders) Fax: 360-647-1445 E-mail: help@spie.org; customerservice@spie.org (orders) Web Site: www.spie.org, pg 196

Peragine, Dan, Dan Peragine Literary Agency, PO Box 5032, South Hackensack, NJ 07606 Tel: 201-390-0468 E-mail: dannyperagine@aol.com, pg 472

Peralta, Angela, Editorial Unilit, 8167 NW 84 St, Medley, FL 33166 Tel: 305-592-6136; 305-592-6135 Toll Free Tel: 800-767-7726 Fax: 305-592-0087 E-mail: info@editorialunilit.com; ventas@editorialunilit.com (sales) Web Site: www.editorialunilit.com, pg 64

Peranteau, Paul, John Benjamins Publishing Co, 10 Meadowbrook Rd, Brunswick, ME 04011 Toll Free Tel: 800-562-5666 (orders) Web Site: www.benjamins.com, pg 28

Perciasepe, Laura, Simon & Schuster, 1230 Avenue of the Americas, New York, NY 10020 Tel: 212-698-7000 Toll Free Tel: 800-223-2348 (cust serv); 800-223-2336 (orders) Toll Free Fax: 800-943-9831 (orders) Web Site: simonandschusterpublishing.com/simonandschuster/, pg 188

Perdomo, Willie, Idyllwild Arts Summer Program, 52500 Temecula Rd, No 38, Idyllwild, CA 92549 Tel: 951-659-2171 E-mail: summer@idyllwildarts.org; adultprograms@idyllwildarts.org Web Site: idyllwildarts.org/summer, pg 555

Perel, Kim, Irene Goodman Literary Agency, 27 W 24 St, Suite 700B, New York, NY 10010 Tel: 212-604-0330 E-mail: queries@irenegoodman.com Web Site: www.irenegoodman.com, pg 460

Perez, Anthony, Sourcebooks LLC, 1935 Brookdale Rd, Suite 139, Naperville, IL 60563 Tel: 630-961-3900 Toll Free Tel: 800-432-7444 Fax: 630-961-2168 E-mail: info@sourcebooks.com Web Site: www.sourcebooks.com, pg 195

Perez, Avia, Farrar, Straus & Giroux Books for Young Readers, 120 Broadway, New York, NY 10271 Tel: 212-741-6900 Toll Free Tel: 888-330-8477 (orders) E-mail: childrens.publicity@macmillanusa.com; childrensrights@macmillanusa.com Web Site: us.macmillan.com/mackids, pg 70

Perez, Avia, Roaring Brook Press, 120 Broadway, New York, NY 10271 Tel: 646-307-5151 Web Site: us.macmillan.com/publishers/roaring-brook-press, pg 176

Perez, Carlos, Random House Publishing Group, 1745 Broadway, New York, NY 10019 Toll Free Tel: 800-200-3552 Web Site: www.randomhousebooks.com, pg 171

Perez, Cassandra, Simon & Schuster, 1230 Avenue of the Americas, New York, NY 10020 Tel: 212-698-7000 Toll Free Tel: 800-223-2348 (cust serv); 800-223-2336 (orders) Toll Free Fax: 800-943-9831 (orders) Web Site: simonandschusterpublishing.com/simonandschuster/, pg 188

Perez, Jacquiline, Redleaf Press®, 10 Yorkton Ct, St Paul, MN 55117 Tel: 651-641-0508 Toll Free Tel: 800-423-8309 Fax: 651-641-0115 E-mail: customerservice@redleafpress.org; info@redleafpress.org; marketing@redleafpress.org Web Site: www.redleafpress.org, pg 173

Perez, Janine, Grand Central Publishing, 1290 Avenue of the Americas, New York, NY 10104 Tel: 212-364-1100 Web Site: www.hachettebookgroup.com/imprint/grand-central-publishing/, pg 80

Perez, Joe, Random House Publishing Group, 1745 Broadway, New York, NY 10019 Toll Free Tel: 800-200-3552 Web Site: www.randomhousebooks.com, pg 170

Perez, Peter L, The University of North Carolina Press, 116 S Boundary St, Chapel Hill, NC 27514-3808 Tel: 919-966-3561; 919-966-7449 (orders) Toll Free Tel: 800-848-3224 (orders) Fax: 919-962-2704 (orders) Toll Free Fax: 800-272-6817 (orders) E-mail: uncpress@unc.edu Web Site: uncpress.org, pg 218

Perez, Vincent, Random House Children's Books, c/o Penguin Random House LLC, 1745 Broadway, New York, NY 10019 Tel: 212-782-9000 Web Site: www.rhcbooks.com, pg 170

Perez-Hernandez, Norma, Atria Books, 1230 Avenue of the Americas, New York, NY 10020 Tel: 212-698-7000 Fax: 212-698-7007 Web Site: www.simonandschuster.com, pg 21

Perilli, Britny, Running Press, 1290 Avenue of the Americas, New York, NY 10104 Tel: 212-364-1100 Toll Free Tel: 800-759-0190 (cust serv) Fax: 212-364-0933 (intl orders) Toll Free Fax: 800-286-9471 (cust serv) E-mail: customer.service@hbgusa.com; orders@hbgusa.com Web Site: www.hachettebookgroup.com/imprint/running-press/; www.moon.com (Moon Travel Guides), pg 178

Perino, Lori, Simon & Schuster, LLC, 1230 Avenue of the Americas, New York, NY 10020 Tel: 212-698-7000 Toll Free Tel: 800-223-2336 (orders) Fax: 212-698-7007 Toll Free Fax: 800-943-9831 (orders) E-mail: firstname.lastname@simonandschuster.com; purchaseorders@simonandschuster.com (orders) Web Site: www.simonandschuster.com, pg 190

Perkins, Lori, Circlet Press, 5676 Riverdale Ave, Suite 101, Riverdale, NY 10471 Tel: 212-279-6418 E-mail: customerservice@riverdaleavebooks.com; rab@riverdaleavebooks.com; customerservice@riverdaleavebooks.com (orders) Web Site: www.circlet.com; riverdaleavebooks.com (orders & edit), pg 48

Perkins, Lori, Riverdale Avenue Books (RAB), 5676 Riverdale Ave, Bronx, NY 10471 Tel: 212-279-6418 E-mail: customerservice@riverdaleavebooks.com Web Site: www.riverdaleavebooks.com, pg 175

Perlman, Jim, Holy Cow! Press, PO Box 3170, Mount Royal Sta, Duluth, MN 55803 Tel: 218-606-2792 E-mail: holycow@holycowpress.org Web Site: www.holycowpress.org, pg 95

Perlman, Michael, Simon & Schuster, LLC, 1230 Avenue of the Americas, New York, NY 10020 Tel: 212-698-7000 Toll Free Tel: 800-223-2336 (orders) Fax: 212-698-7007 Toll Free Fax: 800-943-9831 (orders) E-mail: firstname.lastname@simonandschuster.com; purchaseorders@simonandschuster.com (orders) Web Site: www.simonandschuster.com, pg 189

Perlmutter, Christie, Texas Tech University Press, 1120 Main St, 2nd fl, Lubbock, TX 79401 Tel: 806-742-2982 Toll Free Tel: 800-832-4042 E-mail: ttup@ttu.edu Web Site: www.ttupress.org, pg 205

Perlstein, Jill, American Booksellers Association, 600 Mamaroneck Ave, Suite 400, Harrison, NY 10528 Tel: 914-406-7500 Toll Free Tel: 800-637-0037 Fax: 914-417-4013 E-mail: info@bookweb.org Web Site: www.bookweb.org, pg 494

Perny, Caro, Tor Publishing Group, 120 Broadway, New York, NY 10271 Toll Free Tel: 800-455-0340 (Macmillan) E-mail: torpublicity@tor.com; forgepublicity@forgebooks.com Web Site: us.macmillan.com/torpublishinggroup, pg 208

Perreault, Audrey, Association nationale des editeurs de livres-ANEL (The National Association of Book Publishers), 2514, blvd Rosemont, Montreal, QC H1Y 1K4, Canada Tel: 514-273-8130 Toll Free Tel: 866-900-ANEL (900-2635) E-mail: info@anel.qc.ca Web Site: www.anel.qc.ca, pg 498

Perreault, Diane, Beliveau Editeur, 567 rue Bienville, Boucherville, QC J4B 2Z5, Canada Tel: 450-679-1933 Web Site: www.beliveauediteur.com, pg 396

Perreault, Michel, Les Editions Fides, 7333 place des Roseraies, bureau 501, Anjou, QC H1M 2X6, Canada Tel: 514-745-4290 Fax: 514-745-4299 E-mail: editions@groupefides.com Web Site: www.editionsfides.com, pg 403

Perri, Trevor, Northwestern University Press, 629 Noyes St, Evanston, IL 60208-4210 Tel: 847-491-2046 Toll Free Tel: 800-621-2736 (orders only) Fax: 847-491-8150 E-mail: nupress@northwestern.edu Web Site: www.nupress.northwestern.edu, pg 143

Perriello, Rachael, Penguin Random House LLC, 1745 Broadway, New York, NY 10019 Tel: 212-782-9000 Toll Free Tel: 800-726-0600 Web Site: www.penguinrandomhouse.com, pg 155

Perrin, Christopher, Classical Academic Press, 515 S 32 St, Camp Hill, PA 17011 Tel: 717-730-0711 Toll Free Tel: 866-730-0711 Fax: 717-730-0721 Toll Free Fax: 866-730-0721 E-mail: info@classicalsubjects.com; orders@classicalsubjects.com Web Site: classicalacademicpress.com, pg 49

Perrin, Christopher, Plum Tree Books, 2151 Market St, Camp Hill, PA 17011 Tel: 717-730-0711 E-mail: info@classicalsubjects.com Web Site: www.plumtreebooks.com, pg 161

Perrin, Sarah, Alfred A Knopf, c/o Penguin Random House LLC, 1745 Broadway, New York, NY 10019 Tel: 212-751-2600 Fax: 212-940-7390 (dom rts); 212-572-2662 (foreign rts) Web Site: knopfdoubleday.com/imprint/knopf/; knopfdoubleday.com, pg 110

Perritt-Jacobson, Megan, Grand Central Publishing, 1290 Avenue of the Americas, New York, NY 10104 Tel: 212-364-1100 Web Site: www.hachettebookgroup.com/imprint/grand-central-publishing/, pg 80

Perruzza, Lauren, The Literary Press Group of Canada, 234 Eglinton Ave E, Suite 401, Toronto, ON M4P 1K5, Canada Tel: 416-483-1321 Fax: 416-483-2510 E-mail: sales@lpg.ca Web Site: www.lpg.ca, pg 509

Perry, Bonnie, Beacon Hill Press of Kansas City, PO Box 419527, Kansas City, MO 64141 Tel: 816-931-1900 Toll Free Tel: 800-877-0700 (cust serv) Fax: 816-531-0923 Toll Free Fax: 800-849-9827 E-mail: orders@thefoundrypublishing.com; customercare@thefoundrypublishing.com Web Site: www.thefoundrypublishing.com, pg 25

Perry, Jack W, Astra Books for Young Readers, 19 W 21 St, No 1201, New York, NY 10010 Tel: 646-844-3485 E-mail: ahinfo@astrahouse.com; permissions@astrapublishinghouse.com Web Site: astrapublishinghouse.com, pg 20

Perry, Mary Joyce, Holiday House Publishing Inc, 50 Broad St, New York, NY 10004 Tel: 212-688-0085 Fax: 212-421-6134 E-mail: info@holidayhouse.com Web Site: www.holidayhouse.com, pg 94

Perry, Mary Joyce, Peachtree Publishing Co Inc, 1700 Chattahoochee Ave, Atlanta, GA 30318-2112 Tel: 404-876-8761 Toll Free Tel: 800-241-0113 Fax: 404-875-2578 Toll Free Fax: 800-875-8909 E-mail: hello@peachtree-online.com; orders@peachtree-online.com; sales@peachtree-online.com Web Site: www.peachtreebooks.com; www.peachtree-online.com, pg 153

Perry, Rochon, Cedar Grove Publishing, 3205 Elmhurst St, Rowlett, TX 75088 Tel: 415-364-8292 E-mail: queries@cedargrovebooks.com Web Site: www.cedargrovebooks.com, pg 43

Perry, Sheila M, Sophia Institute Press®, 18 Celina Ave, Unit 1, Nashua, NH 03063 Tel: 603-641-9344 Toll Free Tel: 800-888-9344 Fax: 603-641-8108 Toll Free Fax: 888-288-2259 E-mail: orders@sophiainstitute.com Web Site: www.sophiainstitute.com, pg 193

Persad, Sonia, Random House Publishing Group, 1745 Broadway, New York, NY 10019 Toll Free Tel: 800-200-3552 Web Site: www.randomhousebooks.com, pg 171

Pershing, John, Hackett Publishing Co Inc, 3333 Massachusetts Ave, Indianapolis, IN 46218 Tel: 317-635-9250 (orders & cust serv); 617-497-6303 (edit off & sales) Fax: 317-635-9292; 617-661-8703 (edit off) Toll Free Fax: 800-783-9213 E-mail: customer@hackettpublishing.com; editorial@hackettpublishing.com Web Site: www.hackettpublishing.com, pg 84

Person, Hara E, Central Conference of American Rabbis/CCAR Press, 355 Lexington Ave, New York, NY 10017 Tel: 212-972-3636 E-mail: info@ccarpress.org; info@ccarnet.org Web Site: www.ccarpress.org, pg 44

Persons, Alyssa, Little, Brown and Company, 1290 Avenue of the Americas, New York, NY 10104 Tel: 212-364-1100 Fax: 212-364-0952 E-mail: firstname.lastname@hbgusa.com Web Site: www.hachettebookgroup.com/imprint/little-brown-and-company/, pg 118

Persons, Marci, Yaddo Artists Residency, 312 Union Ave, Saratoga Springs, NY 12866 Tel: 518-584-0746 Fax: 518-584-1312 Web Site: www.yaddo.org, pg 559

Perzo, Zoe, American Booksellers Association, 600 Mamaroneck Ave, Suite 400, Harrison, NY 10528 Tel: 914-406-7500 Toll Free Tel: 800-637-0037 Fax: 914-417-4013 E-mail: info@bookweb.org Web Site: www.bookweb.org, pg 494

Pesch, Fran, Dayton Playhouse FutureFest, PO Box 3017, Dayton, OH 45401-3017 Tel: 937-424-8477 Fax: 937-424-0062 E-mail: futurefest@daytonplayhouse.com Web Site: wordpress.thedaytonplayhouse.com/future-fest-2, pg 595

Peskin, Joy, Farrar, Straus & Giroux Books for Young Readers, 120 Broadway, New York, NY 10271 Tel: 212-741-6900 Toll Free Tel: 888-330-8477 (orders) E-mail: childrens.publicity@macmillanusa.com; childrensrights@macmillanusa.com Web Site: us.macmillan.com/mackids, pg 69

Petee, Cecilia, Sourcebooks LLC, 1935 Brookdale Rd, Suite 139, Naperville, IL 60563 Tel: 630-961-3900 Toll Free Tel: 800-432-7444 Fax: 630-961-2168 E-mail: info@sourcebooks.com Web Site: www.sourcebooks.com, pg 195

Peters, Asharee, Pantheon Books, c/o Penguin Random House LLC, 1745 Broadway, New York, NY 10019 Tel: 212-751-2600 Fax: 212-940-7390 (dom rts); 212-572-2662 (foreign rts) Web Site: knopfdoubleday.com/imprint/pantheon/; knopfdoubleday.com, pg 150

Peters, Charlotte, Dutton, c/o Penguin Random House LLC, 1745 Broadway, New York, NY 10019 Tel: 212-366-2000 Web Site: www.penguin.com/dutton-overview/; www.penguin.com/plume-books-overview/; www.penguin.com/tiny-reparations-overview/, pg 62

Peters, Emma, Countryman Press, c/o W W Norton & Company Inc, 500 Fifth Ave, New York, NY 10110 Tel: 212-354-5500 Fax: 212-869-0856 E-mail: countrymanpress@wwnorton.com Web Site: wwnorton.com/countryman-press, pg 54

Peters, Michelle, Association of Manitoba Book Publishers (AMBP), 100 Arthur St, Suite 404, Winnipeg, MB R3B 1H3, Canada Tel: 204-947-3335 E-mail: ambp@mymts.net Web Site: ambp.ca, pg 499

Peters, Simone, Tortuga Press, 2777 Yulupa Ave, PMB 181, Santa Rosa, CA 95405 Tel: 707-544-4720 Fax: 707-595-5331 E-mail: info@tortugapress.com Web Site: www.tortugapress.com, pg 208

Petersen, Alison, Chronicle Books LLC, 680 Second St, San Francisco, CA 94107 Tel: 415-537-4200 Fax: 415-537-4460 (perms) E-mail: hello@chroniclebooks.com; subrights@chroniclebooks.com Web Site: www.chroniclebooks.com, pg 47

Petersen, Eric, Pacific Press® Publishing Association, 1350 N Kings Rd, Nampa, ID 83687-3193 Tel: 208-465-2500 Fax: 208-465-2531 E-mail: booksubmissions@pacificpress.com Web Site: www.pacificpress.com, pg 150

Petersen, Mark, American Literacy Council, c/o Los Alamos National Laboratory, Los Alamos, NM 87545 E-mail: questions@americanliteracy.com Web Site: www.americanliteracy.com, pg 495

Peterson, Eric, Bywater Books Inc, 3415 Porter Rd, Ann Arbor, MI 48103 Tel: 734-662-8815 Web Site: bywaterbooks.com, pg 39

Peterson, Gayla, Foil & Specialty Effects Association (FSEA), 2150 SW Westport Dr, Suite 101, Topeka, KS 66614 Tel: 785-271-5816 Fax: 785-271-6404 Web Site: fsea.com, pg 506

Peterson, Hailey, University of British Columbia Press, 2029 West Mall, Vancouver, BC V6T 1Z2, Canada Tel: 604-822-5959 Toll Free Tel: 877-377-9378 Fax: 604-822-6083 Toll Free Fax: 800-668-0821 E-mail: frontdesk@ubcpress.ca Web Site: www.ubcpress.ca, pg 422

Peterson, Heather, Penguin Random House LLC, 1745 Broadway, New York, NY 10019 Tel: 212-782-9000 Toll Free Tel: 800-726-0600 Web Site: www.penguinrandomhouse.com, pg 155

Peterson, James, Coaches Choice, PO Box 1828, Monterey, CA 93942 Toll Free Tel: 888-229-5745 E-mail: info@coacheschoice.com Web Site: www.coacheschoice.com, pg 50

Peterson, Jeff, Foil & Specialty Effects Association (FSEA), 2150 SW Westport Dr, Suite 101, Topeka, KS 66614 Tel: 785-271-5816 Fax: 785-271-6404 Web Site: fsea.com, pg 506

Peterson, Kelly, Rees Literary Agency, One Westinghouse Plaza, Suite A203, Boston, MA 02136 Tel: 617-227-9014 Web Site: www.reesagency.com, pg 473

Peterson, Laura Blake, Curtis Brown, Ltd, 228 E 45 St, Suite 310, New York, NY 10017 Tel: 212-473-5400 Fax: 212-598-0917 E-mail: info@cbltd.com Web Site: www.curtisbrown.com, pg 452

Peterson, Lowell, Writers Guild of America, East (WGAE), 250 Hudson St, Suite 700, New York, NY 10013 Tel: 212-767-7800 Fax: 212-582-1909 Web Site: www.wgaeast.org, pg 522

Peterson, Madelyn, Sudden Fiction Contest, c/o ASUC Publications, Univ of California, 10-B Eshleman Hall, Berkeley, CA 94720-4500 E-mail: berkeleyfictionreview@gmail.com Web Site: berkeleyfictionreview.org, pg 667

Peterson, Melissa, Midwest Bookseller of the Year Award, 939 W Seventh St, St Paul, MN 55102 Tel: 612-208-6279 Web Site: www.midwestbooksellers.org/bookseller-of-the-year.html, pg 632

Peterson, Melissa, Midwest Independent Booksellers Association (MIBA), 939 W Seventh St, St Paul, MN 55102 Tel: 612-208-6279 Web Site: www.midwestbooksellers.org, pg 510

Peterson, Mike, The Child's World Inc, 21735 E Idyllwilde Dr, Parker, CO 80138-8892 Toll Free Tel: 800-599-READ (599-7323) Toll Free Fax: 888-320-2329 E-mail: info@childsworld.com Web Site: www.childsworld.com, pg 46

Peterson, Sarah M, Northwest Independent Editors Guild, 7511 Greenwood Ave N, No 307, Seattle, WA 98103 E-mail: info@edsguild.org Web Site: www.edsguild.org, pg 515

Peterson, Sarah M, Red Pencil Conference, 7511 Greenwood Ave N, No 307, Seattle, WA 98103 E-mail: conference@edsguild.org Web Site: www.edsguild.org/red-pencil-conferences, pg 557

Peterson, Tom, Creative Editions, 2140 Howard Dr W, North Mankato, MN 56003 Tel: 507-388-6273 Toll Free Tel: 800-445-6209 Fax: 507-388-2746 E-mail: info@thecreativecompany.us; orders@thecreativecompany.us Web Site: www.thecreativecompany.us, pg 55

Petilos, Randolph, University of Chicago Press, 1427 E 60 St, Chicago, IL 60637-2954 Tel: 773-702-7700; 773-702-7600 Toll Free Tel: 800-621-2736 (orders) Fax: 773-702-9756; 773-660-2235 (orders); 773-702-2708 E-mail: custserv@press.uchicago.edu; marketing@press.uchicago.edu Web Site: www.press.uchicago.edu, pg 215

Petitt, Tracey, Rizzoli International Publications Inc, 300 Park Ave S, 4th fl, New York, NY 10010-5399 Tel: 212-387-3400 Toll Free Tel: 800-522-6657 (orders only) Fax: 212-387-3535 E-mail: publicity@rizzoliusa.com Web Site: www.rizzoliusa.com, pg 175

Petkovich, Anna, Aevitas Creative Management LLC, 19 W 21 St, Suite 501, New York, NY 10010 Tel: 212-765-6900 Web Site: www.aevitascreative.com, pg 448

Petranek, Michael, Scholastic Trade Publishing, 557 Broadway, New York, NY 10012 Tel: 212-343-6100; 212-343-4685 (export sales) Fax: 212-343-4714 (export sales) Web Site: www.scholastic.com, pg 184

Petrick, Emily, Random House Children's Books, c/o Penguin Random House LLC, 1745 Broadway, New York, NY 10019 Tel: 212-782-9000 Web Site: www.rhcbooks.com, pg 170

Petrie, Jeremy, Willow Creek Press, 9931 Hwy 70 W, Minocqua, WI 54548 *Tel:* 715-358-7010 *Toll Free Tel:* 800-850-9453 *Fax:* 715-358-2807 *E-mail:* info@willowcreekpress.com *Web Site:* www.willowcreekpress.com; www.wcpretail.com, pg 230

Petrie, Tom, Willow Creek Press, 9931 Hwy 70 W, Minocqua, WI 54548 *Tel:* 715-358-7010 *Toll Free Tel:* 800-850-9453 *Fax:* 715-358-2807 *E-mail:* info@willowcreekpress.com *Web Site:* www.willowcreekpress.com; www.wcpretail.com, pg 230

Petrik, Katrina, University of British Columbia Press, 2029 West Mall, Vancouver, BC V6T 1Z2, Canada *Tel:* 604-822-5959 *Toll Free Tel:* 877-377-9378 *Fax:* 604-822-6083 *Toll Free Fax:* 800-668-0821 *E-mail:* frontdesk@ubcpress.ca *Web Site:* www.ubcpress.ca, pg 422

Petrillo, Alan M, Excalibur Publications, 6855 W Ina Rd, Tucson, AZ 85743-9633 *Tel:* 520-575-9057 *E-mail:* excaliburpublications@centurylink.net, pg 68

Petrovich, Aaron, Akashic Books, 232 Third St, Suite A115, Brooklyn, NY 11215 *Tel:* 718-643-9193 *E-mail:* info@akashicbooks.com *Web Site:* www.akashicbooks.com, pg 6

Petrucci, Ashley, Temple University Press, 1852 N Tenth St, Philadelphia, PA 19122-6099 *Tel:* 215-926-2140 *Toll Free Tel:* 800-621-2736 *Fax:* 215-926-2141 *E-mail:* tempress@temple.edu *Web Site:* tupress.temple.edu, pg 204

Petta, Giovanna, Transatlantic Agency, 2 Bloor St E, Suite 3500, Toronto, ON M4W 1A8, Canada *Tel:* 416-488-9214 *E-mail:* info@transatlanticagency.com; royalties@transatlanticagency.com *Web Site:* www.transatlanticagency.com, pg 479

Pettapiece, Lauren, Candlewick Press, 99 Dover St, Somerville, MA 02144-2825 *Tel:* 617-661-3330 *Fax:* 617-661-0565 *E-mail:* bigbear@candlewick.com; salesinfo@candlewick.com *Web Site:* candlewick.com, pg 40

Pettigrew, Jean, Les Editions Alire, 120 cote du Passage, Levis, QC G6V 5S9, Canada *Tel:* 418-835-4441 *Fax:* 418-838-4443 *E-mail:* info@alire.com *Web Site:* www.alire.com, pg 401

Pfeffer, Keith, Humanix Books LLC, 805 Third Ave, New York, NY 10022 *Toll Free Tel:* 855-371-7810 *E-mail:* info@humanixbooks.com *Web Site:* www.humanixbooks.com, pg 97

Pfeifer, Alice, St Martin's Press, LLC, 120 Broadway, New York, NY 10271 *E-mail:* publicity@stmartins.com; trademarketing@stmartins.com; foreignrights@stmartins.com *Web Site:* us.macmillan.com/smp, pg 181

Pfeiffer, Alice Randal, Syracuse University Press, 621 Skytop Rd, Suite 110, Syracuse, NY 13244-5290 *Tel:* 315-443-5534 *Toll Free Tel:* 800-365-8929 (cust serv) *Fax:* 315-443-5545 *E-mail:* supress@syr.edu *Web Site:* press.syr.edu, pg 201

Pfeiffer, Morgan, Sourcebooks LLC, 1935 Brookdale Rd, Suite 139, Naperville, IL 60563 *Tel:* 630-961-3900 *Toll Free Tel:* 800-432-7444 *Fax:* 630-961-2168 *E-mail:* info@sourcebooks.com *Web Site:* www.sourcebooks.com, pg 195

Pfund, Niko, Oxford University Press USA, 198 Madison Ave, New York, NY 10016 *Toll Free Tel:* 800-451-7556 (orders); 800-445-9714 (cust serv) *Fax:* 919-677-1303 *E-mail:* custserv.us@oup.com *Web Site:* global.oup.com, pg 149

Phail, Evan, Diversion Books, 11 E 44 St, Suite 1603, New York, NY 10017 *Tel:* 212-961-6390 *E-mail:* info@diversionbooks.com *Web Site:* www.diversionbooks.com, pg 60

Phair, Sarah, Sanford J Greenburger Associates Inc, 55 Fifth Ave, New York, NY 10003 *Tel:* 212-206-5600 *Web Site:* greenburger.com, pg 461

Phan, Lara, Penguin Random House LLC, 1745 Broadway, New York, NY 10019 *Tel:* 212-782-9000 *Toll Free Tel:* 800-726-0600 *Web Site:* www.penguinrandomhouse.com, pg 155

Pharand, Ginger, Palimpsest Press, 1171 Eastlawn Ave, Windsor, ON N8S 3J1, Canada *Tel:* 519-259-2112 *E-mail:* publicity@palimpsestpress.ca *Web Site:* www.palimpsestpress.ca, pg 415

Phares, Rachel, BenBella Books Inc, 10440 N Central Expwy, Suite 800, Dallas, TX 75231-2264 *Tel:* 214-750-3600 *Web Site:* www.benbellabooks.com; www.smartpopbooks.com, pg 27

Phelan, Sheila, DK, c/o Penguin Random House LLC, 1745 Broadway, 20th fl, New York, NY 10019 *Tel:* 646-674-4000 *Toll Free Tel:* 800-733-3000 *Fax:* 646-674-4020 *E-mail:* marketing@dk.com (lib servs); publicity@dk.com; csorders@penguinrandomhouse.com; customerservice@penguinrandomhouse.com *Web Site:* www.dk.com, pg 60

Phelps, Abbie, Coffee House Press, 79 13 Ave NE, Suite 110, Minneapolis, MN 55413 *Tel:* 612-338-0125 *Fax:* 612-338-4004 *E-mail:* info@coffeehousepress.org *Web Site:* coffeehousepress.org, pg 50

Philipp, Megan, Transatlantic Agency, 2 Bloor St E, Suite 3500, Toronto, ON M4W 1A8, Canada *Tel:* 416-488-9214 *E-mail:* info@transatlanticagency.com; royalties@transatlanticagency.com *Web Site:* www.transatlanticagency.com, pg 479

Philips, Ariana, Jean V Naggar Literary Agency Inc (JVNLA), 216 E 75 St, Suite 1-E, New York, NY 10021 *Tel:* 212-794-1082 *E-mail:* jvnla@jvnla.com *Web Site:* www.jvnla.com, pg 471

Philips, Elizabeth, Thistledown Press, 220 20 St W, Unit 222, Saskatoon, SK S7M 0W9, Canada *Tel:* 306-244-1722 *E-mail:* tdpress@thistledownpress.com *Web Site:* www.thistledownpress.com, pg 420

Phillips, Adam, McFarland, 960 NC Hwy 88 W, Jefferson, NC 28640 *Tel:* 336-246-4460 *Toll Free Tel:* 800-253-2187 (orders) *Fax:* 336-246-5018; 336-246-4403 (orders) *E-mail:* info@mcfarlandpub.com *Web Site:* mcfarlandbooks.com, pg 127

Phillips, Aemilia, Stuart Krichevsky Literary Agency Inc, 118 E 28 St, Suite 908, New York, NY 10016 *Tel:* 212-725-5288 *Fax:* 212-725-5275 *E-mail:* query@skagency.com *Web Site:* skagency.com, pg 466

Phillips, Andrew V, Windhaven®, 466 Rte 10, Orford, NH 03777 *Tel:* 603-512-9251 (cell) *Web Site:* www.windhavenpress.com, pg 445

Phillips, Barb, The Literary Press Group of Canada, 234 Eglinton Ave E, Suite 401, Toronto, ON M4P 1K5, Canada *Tel:* 416-483-1321 *Fax:* 416-483-2510 *E-mail:* sales@lpg.ca *Web Site:* www.lpg.ca, pg 509

Phillips, Betsy, Vanderbilt University Press, 2301 Vanderbilt Place, PMB 401813, Nashville, TN 37240-1813 *Tel:* 615-322-3585 *Toll Free Tel:* 800-848-6224 (orders only) *Fax:* 615-343-0308 *E-mail:* vupress@vanderbilt.edu *Web Site:* www.vanderbiltuniversitypress.com, pg 224

Phillips, Brittain, Arcadia Publishing Inc, 210 Wingo Way, Suite 200, Mount Pleasant, SC 29464 *Tel:* 843-853-2070 *E-mail:* retailers@arcadiapublishing.com *Web Site:* www.arcadiapublishing.com, pg 16

Phillips, Hannah, St Martin's Press, LLC, 120 Broadway, New York, NY 10271 *E-mail:* publicity@stmartins.com; trademarketing@stmartins.com; foreignrights@stmartins.com *Web Site:* us.macmillan.com/smp, pg 181

Phillips, Jenna, Vanderbilt University Press, 2301 Vanderbilt Place, PMB 401813, Nashville, TN 37240-1813 *Tel:* 615-322-3585 *Toll Free Tel:* 800-848-6224 (orders only) *Fax:* 615-343-0308 *E-mail:* vupress@vanderbilt.edu *Web Site:* www.vanderbiltuniversitypress.com, pg 224

Phillips, Kayla, Candlewick Press, 99 Dover St, Somerville, MA 02144-2825 *Tel:* 617-661-3330 *Fax:* 617-661-0565 *E-mail:* bigbear@candlewick.com; salesinfo@candlewick.com *Web Site:* candlewick.com, pg 40

Phillips, Kayla, Holiday House Publishing Inc, 50 Broad St, New York, NY 10004 *Tel:* 212-688-0085 *Fax:* 212-421-6134 *E-mail:* info@holidayhouse.com *Web Site:* www.holidayhouse.com, pg 94

Phillips, Kayla, Peachtree Publishing Co Inc, 1700 Chattahoochee Ave, Atlanta, GA 30318-2112 *Tel:* 404-876-8761 *Toll Free Tel:* 800-241-0113 *Fax:* 404-875-2578 *Toll Free Fax:* 800-875-8909 *E-mail:* hello@peachtree-online.com; orders@peachtree-online.com; sales@peachtree-online.com *Web Site:* www.peachtreebooks.com; www.peachtree-online.com, pg 153

Phillips, Kirsten, Portage & Main Press, 318 McDermot Ave, Suite 100, Winnipeg, MB R3A 0A2, Canada *Tel:* 204-987-3500 *Toll Free Tel:* 800-667-9673 *Fax:* 204-947-0080 *Toll Free Fax:* 866-734-8477 *E-mail:* customerservice@portageandmainpress.com *Web Site:* www.portageandmainpress.com, pg 416

Phillips, Laura, Bloomsbury Publishing Inc, 1385 Broadway, 5th fl, New York, NY 10018 *Tel:* 212-419-5300 *E-mail:* marketingusa@bloomsbury.com; adultpublicityusa@bloomsbury.com; askacademic@bloomsbury.com *Web Site:* www.bloomsbury.com, pg 31

Phillips, Meghan, The Vendome Press, 244 Fifth Ave, Suite 2043, New York, NY 10001 *Tel:* 212-737-1857 *E-mail:* info@vendomepress.com *Web Site:* www.vendomepress.com, pg 224

Phillips, Witt, St Martin's Press, LLC, 120 Broadway, New York, NY 10271 *E-mail:* publicity@stmartins.com; trademarketing@stmartins.com; foreignrights@stmartins.com *Web Site:* us.macmillan.com/smp, pg 181

Phillips, Zach, Pantheon Books, c/o Penguin Random House LLC, 1745 Broadway, New York, NY 10019 *Tel:* 212-751-2600 *Fax:* 212-940-7390 (dom rts); 212-572-2662 (foreign rts) *Web Site:* knopfdoubleday.com/imprint/pantheon/; knopfdoubleday.com, pg 150

Philpott, Lily, Margins Fellowship, 112 W 27 St, Suite 600, New York, NY 10001 *Tel:* 212-494-0061 *E-mail:* fellowships@aaww.org *Web Site:* aaww.org/fellowships/margins, pg 629

Philpott, Lily, Open City Fellowship, 112 W 27 St, Suite 600, New York, NY 10001 *Tel:* 212-494-0061 *E-mail:* fellowships@aaww.org *Web Site:* aaww.org/fellowships/open-city, pg 644

Phinn, Jessica, Nelson Education Ltd, 1120 Birchmount Rd, Scarborough, ON M1K 5G4, Canada *Tel:* 416-752-9448 *Toll Free Tel:* 800-268-2222 (cust serv) *Fax:* 416-752-9646 *E-mail:* peopleandengagement@nelson.com *Web Site:* www.nelson.com, pg 413

Phipps, Matt, GP Putnam's Sons Books for Young Readers, c/o Penguin Random House LLC, 1745 Broadway, New York, NY 10019 *Tel:* 212-782-9000 *Web Site:* www.penguin.com/putnam-young-readers/, pg 167

Phirman, James, HarperCollins Publishers LLC, 195 Broadway, New York, NY 10007 *Tel:* 212-207-7000 *Web Site:* www.harpercollins.com, pg 86

Phua, Max, World Scientific Publishing Co Inc, 27 Warren St, Suite 401-402, Hackensack, NJ 07601 *Tel:* 201-487-9655 *Fax:* 201-487-9656 *E-mail:* sales@wspc.com; mkt@wspc.com; editor@wspc.com; customercare@wspc.com *Web Site:* www.worldscientific.com, pg 233

Phuna, K K, World Scientific Publishing Co Inc, 27 Warren St, Suite 401-402, Hackensack, NJ 07601 *Tel:* 201-487-9655 *Fax:* 201-487-9656 *E-mail:* sales@wspc.com; mkt@wspc.com; editor@wspc.com; customercare@wspc.com *Web Site:* www.worldscientific.com, pg 233

Piasecki, Dr Bruce, The Bruce Piasecki & Andrea Masters Annual Award on Business & Science Writing, 158 Stone Church Rd, Ballston Spa, NY 12020 *Tel:* 518-583-9615 *Fax:* 518-583-9726 *Web Site:* www.ahcgroup.com, pg 649

Picazio, Mr Ryan, Hackett Publishing Co Inc, 3333 Massachusetts Ave, Indianapolis, IN 46218 *Tel:* 317-635-9250 (orders & cust serv); 617-497-6303 (edit off & sales) *Fax:* 317-635-9292; 617-261-8703 (edit off) *Toll Free Fax:* 800-783-9213 *E-mail:* customer@hackettpublishing.com; editorial@hackettpublishing.com *Web Site:* www.hackettpublishing.com, pg 84

Pichardo, Joselin, Holiday House Publishing Inc, 50 Broad St, New York, NY 10004 *Tel:* 212-688-0085 *Fax:* 212-421-6134 *E-mail:* info@holidayhouse.com *Web Site:* www.holidayhouse.com, pg 94

Piche, Mireille, University of Ottawa Press (Presses de l'Université d'Ottawa), 542 King Edward Ave, Ottawa, ON K1N 6N5, Canada *Tel:* 613-562-5246 *Fax:* 613-562-5247 *E-mail:* puo-uop@uottawa.ca; acquisitions@uottawa.ca *Web Site:* press.uottawa.ca, pg 423

Pickus, Abby, Harry N Abrams Inc, 195 Broadway, 9th fl, New York, NY 10007 *Tel:* 212-206-7715 *Toll Free Tel:* 800-345-1359 *Fax:* 212-645-8437 *E-mail:* abrams@abramsbooks.com; publicity@abramsbooks.com; sales@abramsbooks.com *Web Site:* www.abramsbooks.com, pg 3

Pidgeon, Sean, ACM Books, 1601 Broadway, 10th fl, New York, NY 10019-7434 *Tel:* 212-869-7440 *E-mail:* acmbooks-info@acm.org *Web Site:* www.acm.org; books.acm.org, pg 4

Piekarz, Jeffrey, Sourcebooks LLC, 1935 Brookdale Rd, Suite 139, Naperville, IL 60563 *Tel:* 630-961-3900 *Toll Free Tel:* 800-432-7444 *Fax:* 630-961-2168 *E-mail:* info@sourcebooks.com *Web Site:* www.sourcebooks.com, pg 195

Pieper, Molly, GP Putnam's Sons, c/o Penguin Random House LLC, 1745 Broadway, New York, NY 10019 *Tel:* 212-782-9000 *Web Site:* www.penguin.com/putnam/, pg 167

Pierce, Ashley, Penguin Random House LLC, 1745 Broadway, New York, NY 10019 *Tel:* 212-782-9000 *Toll Free Tel:* 800-726-0600 *Web Site:* www.penguinrandomhouse.com, pg 155

Pierce, Charlotte R, Independent Publishers of New England (IPNE), c/o Eddie Vincent, Encircle Publications, Farmington, ME 04955 *Tel:* 339-368-8229 *E-mail:* talktous@ipne.org *Web Site:* www.ipne.org, pg 508

Pierce, Charlotte R, Independent Publishers of New England Book Awards, c/o Eddie Vincent, Encircle Publications, Farmington, ME 04955 *Tel:* 339-368-8229 *E-mail:* bookawards@ipne.org *Web Site:* www.ipne.org/awards, pg 615

Pierce, Mrs Erin, Ave Maria Press Inc, PO Box 428, Notre Dame, IN 46556 *Toll Free Tel:* 800-282-1865 *Toll Free Fax:* 800-282-5681 *E-mail:* avemariapress.1@nd.edu *Web Site:* www.avemariapress.com, pg 22

Pierce, Gregory F A, ACTA Publications, 7135 W Keeney St, Niles, IL 60714 *Toll Free Tel:* 800-397-2282 *E-mail:* actapublications@actapublications.com *Web Site:* www.actapublications.com, pg 4

Pierce, Jennifer Tolo, Chronicle Books LLC, 680 Second St, San Francisco, CA 94107 *Tel:* 415-537-4200 *Fax:* 415-537-4460 (perms) *E-mail:* hello@chroniclebooks.com; subrights@chroniclebooks.com *Web Site:* www.chroniclebooks.com, pg 47

Pierce, Valerie, Sourcebooks LLC, 1935 Brookdale Rd, Suite 139, Naperville, IL 60563 *Tel:* 630-961-3900 *Toll Free Tel:* 800-432-7444 *Fax:* 630-961-2168 *E-mail:* info@sourcebooks.com *Web Site:* www.sourcebooks.com, pg 194

Pierpont, Amy, Grand Central Publishing, 1290 Avenue of the Americas, New York, NY 10104 *Tel:* 212-364-1100 *Web Site:* www.hachettebookgroup.com/imprint/grand-central-publishing/, pg 80

Pierre, Leah, Ladderbird Literary Agency, 460 Yellow Brick Rd, Orange, CT 06477 *Tel:* 203-290-1703 *Web Site:* www.ladderbird.com, pg 466

Piersanti, Steve, Berrett-Koehler Publishers Inc, 1333 Broadway, Suite 1000, Oakland, CA 94612 *Tel:* 510-817-2277 *Fax:* 510-817-2278 *E-mail:* bkpub@bkpub.com *Web Site:* www.bkconnection.com, pg 29

Pierson, Brian, Harry N Abrams Inc, 195 Broadway, 9th fl, New York, NY 10007 *Tel:* 212-206-7715 *Toll Free Tel:* 800-345-1359 *Fax:* 212-645-8437 *E-mail:* abrams@abramsbooks.com; publicity@abramsbooks.com; sales@abramsbooks.com *Web Site:* www.abramsbooks.com, pg 2

Pierson, Caryl K, Math Teachers Press Inc, 4850 Park Glen Rd, Minneapolis, MN 55416 *Tel:* 952-545-6535 *Toll Free Tel:* 800-852-2435 *Fax:* 952-546-7502 *E-mail:* info@movingwithmath.com *Web Site:* www.movingwithmath.com, pg 127

Pierson, Jennifer deForest, Rizzoli International Publications Inc, 300 Park Ave S, 4th fl, New York, NY 10010-5399 *Tel:* 212-387-3400 *Toll Free Tel:* 800-522-6657 (orders only) *Fax:* 212-387-3535 *E-mail:* publicity@rizzoliusa.com *Web Site:* www.rizzoliusa.com, pg 175

Pike, Nadyne, Sterling Lord Literistic Inc, 594 Broadway, Suite 205, New York, NY 10012 *Tel:* 212-780-6050 *Fax:* 212-780-6095 *E-mail:* info@sll.com *Web Site:* www.sll.com, pg 477

Pillai, Devi, Macmillan, 120 Broadway, 22nd fl, New York, NY 10271 *E-mail:* press.inquiries@macmillan.com *Web Site:* us.macmillan.com, pg 122

Pillai, Devi, Tor Publishing Group, 120 Broadway, New York, NY 10271 *Toll Free Tel:* 800-455-0340 (Macmillan) *E-mail:* torpublicity@tor.com; forgepublicity@forgebooks.com *Web Site:* us.macmillan.com/torpublishinggroup, pg 208

Pillari, Maddie, HarperCollins Publishers LLC, 195 Broadway, New York, NY 10007 *Tel:* 212-207-7000 *Web Site:* www.harpercollins.com, pg 87

Pimentel, Sasha, University of Texas at El Paso, Department of Creative Writing, MFA/Department of Creative Writing, M520, University Towers, Oregon St, El Paso, TX 79968 *E-mail:* creativewriting@utep.edu *Web Site:* www.utep.edu/liberalarts/creative-writing, pg 567

Pimentel, Stephanie, Ontario Library Association (OLA), 2080 Danforth Ave, Toronto, ON M4C 1J9, Canada *Toll Free Tel:* 877-340-1730 *E-mail:* info@accessola.com *Web Site:* accessola.com, pg 515

Pina, Ramona, BookEnds Literary Agency, 136 Long Hill Rd, Gillette, NJ 07933 *Web Site:* www.bookendsliterary.com, pg 451

Pincus, Caroline, Caroline Pincus Book Midwife, 101 Wool St, San Francisco, CA 94110 *Tel:* 415-516-6206 *E-mail:* cpincus1958@gmail.com *Web Site:* www.carolinepincus.com, pg 443

Pincus, Caroline, Sounds True Inc, 413 S Arthur Ave, Louisville, CO 80027 *Tel:* 303-665-3151 *Toll Free Tel:* 800-333-9185 (US); 888-303-9185 (US & CN) *E-mail:* customerservice@soundstrue.com; stpublicity@soundstrue.com *Web Site:* www.soundstrue.com, pg 194

Pinder, Garrett, Interlink Publishing Group Inc, 46 Crosby St, Northampton, MA 01060 *Tel:* 413-582-7054 *Toll Free Tel:* 800-238-LINK (238-5465) *E-mail:* info@interlinkbooks.com; publicity@interlinkbooks.com; sales@interlinkbooks.com *Web Site:* www.interlinkbooks.com, pg 102

Pine, Richard S, InkWell Management, 521 Fifth Ave, Suite 2600, New York, NY 10175 *Tel:* 212-922-3500 *Fax:* 212-922-0535 *E-mail:* info@inkwellmanagement.com; submissions@inkwellmanagement.com; permissions@inkwellmanagement.com *Web Site:* inkwellmanagement.com, pg 463

Pineda, Marlene, Idyllwild Arts Summer Program, 52500 Temecula Rd, No 38, Idyllwild, CA 92549 *Tel:* 951-659-2171 *E-mail:* summer@idyllwildarts.org; adultprograms@idyllwildarts.org *Web Site:* idyllwildarts.org/summer, pg 555

Pingelton, Nicole, HarperCollins Publishers LLC, 195 Broadway, New York, NY 10007 *Tel:* 212-207-7000 *Web Site:* www.harpercollins.com, pg 87

Pink, Jeremy, St Martin's Press, LLC, 120 Broadway, New York, NY 10271 *E-mail:* publicity@stmartins.com; trademarketing@stmartins.com; foreignrights@stmartins.com *Web Site:* us.macmillan.com/smp, pg 181

Pinkerton, Candice, Crabtree Publishing Co, 347 Fifth Ave, Suite 1402-145, New York, NY 10016 *Tel:* 212-496-5040 *Toll Free Tel:* 800-387-7650 *Toll Free Fax:* 800-355-7166 *E-mail:* custserv@crabtreebooks.com *Web Site:* www.crabtreebooks.com, pg 54

Pinkerton, Candice, Crabtree Publishing Co Ltd, 616 Welland Ave, St Catharines, ON L2M 5V6, Canada *Tel:* 905-682-5221 *Toll Free Tel:* 800-387-7650 *Fax:* 905-682-7166 *Toll Free Fax:* 800-355-7166 *E-mail:* custserv@crabtreebooks.com; sales@crabtreebooks.com; orders@crabtreebooks.com *Web Site:* www.crabtreebooks.ca, pg 400

Pinkney, Andrea, Scholastic Trade Publishing, 557 Broadway, New York, NY 10012 *Tel:* 212-343-6100; 212-343-4685 (export sales) *Fax:* 212-343-4714 (export sales) *Web Site:* www.scholastic.com, pg 184

Pinn, Naomi, Penguin Random House Canada, a Penguin Random House company, 320 Front St W, Suite 1400, Toronto, ON M5V 3B6, Canada *Tel:* 416-364-4449 *Toll Free Tel:* 888-523-9292 (cust serv) *E-mail:* canadaweb@penguinrandomhouse.com; customerservicescanada@penguinrandomhouse.com *Web Site:* www.penguinrandomhouse.ca, pg 416

Pinsker, Joanna, Atria Books, 1230 Avenue of the Americas, New York, NY 10020 *Tel:* 212-698-7000 *Fax:* 212-698-7007 *Web Site:* www.simonandschuster.com, pg 21

Pintauro, Michael, Trident Media Group LLC, 355 Lexington Ave, 12th fl, New York, NY 10017 *Tel:* 212-333-1511 *E-mail:* info@tridentmediagroup.com; press@tridentmediagroup.com; foreignrights@tridentmediagroup.com; office.assistant@tridentmediagroup.com *Web Site:* www.tridentmediagroup.com, pg 480

Pinter, Jason, Polis Books, 1201 Hudson St, No 211S, Hoboken, NJ 07030 *E-mail:* info@polisbooks.com; submissions@polisbooks.com *Web Site:* www.polisbooks.com; facebook.com/PolisBooks; x.com/PolisBooks, pg 162

Pires, Lauren, Simon & Schuster Audio, 1230 Avenue of the Americas, New York, NY 10020 *Web Site:* audio.simonandschuster.com, pg 189

Pisani, Emilia, Penguin Random House LLC, 1745 Broadway, New York, NY 10019 *Tel:* 212-782-9000 *Toll Free Tel:* 800-726-0600 *Web Site:* www.penguinrandomhouse.com, pg 155

Pitcher, Katherine, US Government Publishing Office (GPO), Superintendent of Documents, 732 N Capitol St NW, Washington, DC 20401 *Tel:* 202-512-1800 *Toll Free Tel:* 866-512-1800 (orders) *Fax:* 202-512-1998 *E-mail:* contactcenter@gpo.gov *Web Site:* www.gpo.gov; bookstore.gpo.gov (sales), pg 223

Pitoniak, Anna, Random House Publishing Group, 1745 Broadway, New York, NY 10019 *Toll Free Tel:* 800-200-3552 *Web Site:* www.randomhousebooks.com, pg 171

Pittman, Elizabeth, Concordia Publishing House, 3558 S Jefferson Ave, St Louis, MO 63118-3968 *Tel:* 314-268-1000; 314-268-1268 (bookshop) *Toll Free Tel:* 800-325-3040 (cust serv) *Toll Free Fax:* 800-490-9889 (cust serv) *E-mail:* order@cph.org *Web Site:* www.cph.org, pg 51

Pittman, Judith (Jude), BWL Publishing Inc, 5030 44 St, Drayton Valley, AB T7A 1B9, Canada *Tel:* 780-833-1215 *E-mail:* bookswelove@telus.net *Web Site:* bookswelove.net; bwlpublishing.ca, pg 398

Pitts, Bryan, UCLA Latin American Center Publications, UCLA Latin American Institute, 10343 Bunche Hall, Los Angeles, CA 90095 *Tel:* 310-825-4571 *Fax:* 310-206-6859 *E-mail:* latinamctr@international.ucla.edu *Web Site:* www.international.ucla.edu/lai, pg 212

Pitts, Melissa, University of British Columbia Press, 2029 West Mall, Vancouver, BC V6T 1Z2, Canada *Tel:* 604-822-5959 *Toll Free Tel:* 877-377-9378 *Fax:* 604-822-6083 *Toll Free Fax:* 800-668-0821 *E-mail:* frontdesk@ubcpress.ca *Web Site:* www.ubcpress.ca, pg 422

Pitts, Naomi, New York State Bar Association, One Elk St, Albany, NY 12207 *Tel:* 518-463-3200 *Toll Free Tel:* 800-582-2452 *Fax:* 518-463-5993 *E-mail:* mrc@nysba.org *Web Site:* nysba.org, pg 141

Pitts, Stephanie, GP Putnam's Sons Books for Young Readers, c/o Penguin Random House LLC, 1745 Broadway, New York, NY 10019 *Tel:* 212-782-9000 *Web Site:* www.penguin.com/putnam-young-readers/, pg 167

Pitts, Taylor, Roaring Brook Press, 120 Broadway, New York, NY 10271 *Tel:* 646-307-5151 *Web Site:* us.macmillan.com/publishers/roaring-brook-press, pg 176

Pizio, Beth, Penguin Random House LLC, 1745 Broadway, New York, NY 10019 *Tel:* 212-782-9000 *Toll Free Tel:* 800-726-0600 *Web Site:* www.penguinrandomhouse.com, pg 155

Plackis, Shannon, HarperCollins Publishers LLC, 195 Broadway, New York, NY 10007 *Tel:* 212-207-7000 *Web Site:* www.harpercollins.com, pg 87

Plafsky, Danielle, Penguin Press, c/o Penguin Random House LLC, 1745 Broadway, New York, NY 10019 *Tel:* 212-782-9000 *E-mail:* penguinpress@penguinrandomhouse.com *Web Site:* www.penguin.com/penguin-press-overview/, pg 154

Plant, Alisa, Louisiana State University Press, 338 Johnston Hall, Baton Rouge, LA 70803 *Tel:* 225-578-6294 *E-mail:* lsupress@lsu.edu *Web Site:* lsupress.org, pg 120

Plantier, Paula, EditAmerica, 115 Jacobs Creek Rd, Ewing, NJ 08628-1014 *Tel:* 609-882-5852 *Web Site:* www.EditAmerica.com; www.linkedin.com/in/PaulaPlantier, pg 438

Platt, Erik, St Martin's Press, LLC, 120 Broadway, New York, NY 10271 *E-mail:* publicity@stmartins.com; trademarketing@stmartins.com; foreignrights@stmartins.com *Web Site:* us.macmillan.com/smp, pg 181

Platter, Clara, New York University Press, 838 Broadway, 3rd fl, New York, NY 10003-4812 *Tel:* 212-998-2575 (edit) *Toll Free Tel:* 800-996-6987 (orders) *Fax:* 212-995-4798 (orders) *E-mail:* nyupressinfo@nyu.edu (cust care) *Web Site:* www.nyupress.org, pg 141

Pleuler, Rose, HarperCollins Children's Books, 195 Broadway, New York, NY 10007 *Tel:* 212-207-7000 *Web Site:* www.harpercollins.com/childrens, pg 85

Ploetz, Michael, DK, c/o Penguin Random House LLC, 1745 Broadway, 20th fl, New York, NY 10019 *Tel:* 646-674-4000 *Toll Free Tel:* 800-733-3000 *Fax:* 646-674-4020 *E-mail:* marketing@dk.com (lib servs); publicity@dk.com; csorders@penguinrandomhouse.com; customerservice@penguinrandomhouse.com *Web Site:* www.dk.com, pg 60

Plose, Matt, OAG Worldwide, 801 Warrenville Rd, Suite 555, Lisle, IL 60532 *Tel:* 630-515-5300 *Toll Free Tel:* 800-342-5624 (cust serv) *E-mail:* contactus@oag.com *Web Site:* www.oag.com, pg 144

Ploss, Patricia, Joshua Tree Publishing, 3 Golf Ctr, Suite 201, Hoffman Estates, IL 60169 *Tel:* 312-893-7525 *E-mail:* info@joshuatreepublishing.com; info@centaurbooks.com *Web Site:* www.joshuatreepublishing.com; www.centaurbooks.com, pg 107

Plotnick, Jerry, Norma Epstein Foundation Awards in Creative Writing, 15 King's College Circle, UC 165, Toronto, ON M5S 3H7, Canada *Tel:* 416-946-0271 *E-mail:* uc.programs@utoronto.ca *Web Site:* www.uc.utoronto.ca/norma-epstein, pg 600

Plum, Hilary, Lighthouse Poetry Series, Rhodes Tower, Rm 1841, 2121 Euclid Ave, Cleveland, OH 44115 *Tel:* 216-687-3986 *E-mail:* poetrycenter@csuohio.edu *Web Site:* www.csupoetrycenter.com/lighthouse-poetry-series; www.csupoetrycenter.com, pg 624

Plum, Hilary, Translation Series, Rhodes Tower, Rm 1841, 2121 Euclid Ave, Cleveland, OH 44115 *Tel:* 216-687-3986 *E-mail:* poetrycenter@csuohio.edu *Web Site:* www.csupoetrycenter.com/translation-series; www.csupoetrycenter.com, pg 670

Plummer, Adrian, The Electrochemical Society (ECS), 65 S Main St, Bldg D, Pennington, NJ 08534-2839 *Tel:* 609-737-1902 *Fax:* 609-737-0629 *E-mail:* publications@electrochem.org; customerservice@electrochem.org; ecs@iopublishing.org *Web Site:* www.electrochem.org, pg 65

Plummer, Jessica, Berkley, c/o Penguin Random House LLC, 1745 Broadway, 19th fl, New York, NY 10019 *Tel:* 212-366-2000 *Web Site:* www.penguin.com/publishers/berkley/; www.penguin.com/ace-overview/, pg 28

Plunkett, Daniela, Macmillan, 120 Broadway, 22nd fl, New York, NY 10271 *E-mail:* press.inquiries@macmillan.com *Web Site:* us.macmillan.com, pg 122

Plunkett, Jack W, Plunkett Research Ltd, PO Drawer 541737, Houston, TX 77254-1737 *Tel:* 713-932-0000 *Fax:* 713-932-7080 *E-mail:* customersupport@plunkettresearch.com *Web Site:* www.plunkettresearch.com, pg 161

Pluta, Christina, Silver Gavel Awards for Media & the Arts, Division for Public Education, 321 N Clark St, MS 17.2, Chicago, IL 60654 *Tel:* 312-988-5719 *Toll Free Tel:* 800-285-2221 *E-mail:* gavelawards@americanbar.org *Web Site:* www.americanbar.org/groups/public_education/programs/silver_gavel, pg 662

Pneuman, Angela, Napa Valley Writers' Conference, 2277 Napa-Vallejo Hwy, Off 1753, Napa, CA 94558 *Tel:* 707-256-7113 *E-mail:* info@napawritersconference.org; fiction@napawritersconference.org; poetry@napawritersconference.org *Web Site:* www.napawritersconference.org, pg 556

Poapst, Heidi, ISBN Canada, Library & Archives Canada, 550, blvd de la Cit, Gatineau, QC J8T 0A7, Canada *Tel:* 819-994-6872 *Toll Free Tel:* 866-578-7777 (CN & US) *Fax:* 819-934-7535 *E-mail:* isbn@bac-lac.gc.ca *Web Site:* www.bac-lac.gc.ca/eng/services/isbn-canada/pages/isbn-canada.aspx, pg 509

Podesta, Mark, Henry Holt and Company, LLC, 120 Broadway, 23rd fl, New York, NY 10271 *Tel:* 646-307-5151 *Toll Free Tel:* 888-330-8477 (orders) *Fax:* 646-307-5285 *Web Site:* www.henryholt.com, pg 94

Podmajersky, Rachel, Gallery Books, 1230 Avenue of the Americas, New York, NY 10020 *Toll Free Tel:* 800-456-6798 *Fax:* 212-698-7284 *E-mail:* consumer.customerservice@simonandschuster.com *Web Site:* www.simonandschuster.com, pg 76

Podolsky, Jolena, Atria Books, 1230 Avenue of the Americas, New York, NY 10020 *Tel:* 212-698-7000 *Fax:* 212-698-7007 *Web Site:* www.simonandschuster.com, pg 21

Podos, Rebecca, Rees Literary Agency, One Westinghouse Plaza, Suite A203, Boston, MA 02136 *Tel:* 617-227-9014 *Web Site:* www.reesagency.com, pg 473

Poelle, Barbara, Irene Goodman Literary Agency, 27 W 24 St, Suite 700B, New York, NY 10010 *Tel:* 212-604-0330 *E-mail:* queries@irenegoodman.com *Web Site:* www.irenegoodman.com, pg 460

Pogodzinski, Mark, NFB Publishing, 119 Dorchester Rd, Buffalo, NY 14213 *Tel:* 716-510-0520 *E-mail:* submissions@nfbpublishing.com *Web Site:* www.nfbpublishing.com, pg 141

Pogrebin, Letty Cottin, The Authors Registry Inc, 31 E 32 St, 7th fl, New York, NY 10016 *Tel:* 212-563-6920 *E-mail:* staff@authorsregistry.org *Web Site:* www.authorsregistry.org, pg 500

Pohl, Michelle, Macmillan, 120 Broadway, 22nd fl, New York, NY 10271 *E-mail:* press.inquiries@macmillan.com *Web Site:* us.macmillan.com, pg 122

Pohland, Liz, Society for Technical Communication (STC), 3251 Blenheim Blvd, Suite 406, Fairfax, VA 22030 *Tel:* 703-522-4114 *Fax:* 703-522-2075 *E-mail:* stc@stc.org *Web Site:* www.stc.org, pg 519

Pohlen, Jerome, Chicago Review Press, 814 N Franklin St, Chicago, IL 60610 *Tel:* 312-337-0747 *Toll Free Tel:* 800-888-4741 *Fax:* 312-337-5110 *E-mail:* frontdesk@chicagoreviewpress.com *Web Site:* www.chicagoreviewpress.com, pg 46

Pohlman, Tina, The Overlook Press, 195 Broadway, 9th fl, New York, NY 10007 *Tel:* 212-206-7715 *E-mail:* abrams@abramsbooks.com; sales@abramsbooks.com (orders) *Web Site:* www.abramsbooks.com/imprints/overlookpress, pg 148

Pohlmann, Marmie, InScribe Christian Writers' Fellowship (ICWF), PO Box 68025, Edmonton, AB T6C 4N6, Canada *Tel:* 780-646-3068 *E-mail:* inscribe.mail@gmail.com *Web Site:* inscribe.org, pg 508

Poirier, Etienne, Ecrits des Forges, 992-A rue Royale, Trois-Rivieres, QC G9A 4H9, Canada *Tel:* 819-840-8492 *E-mail:* ecritsdesforges@gmail.com *Web Site:* www.ecritsdesforges.com, pg 401

Poirier, Noel, Ohio Genealogical Society, 611 State Rte 97 W, Bellville, OH 44813-8813 *Tel:* 419-886-1903 *E-mail:* ogs@ogs.org *Web Site:* www.ogs.org, pg 145

Poirier, Patrick, Les Presses de l'Universite de Montreal, 5450, chemin de la Cote-des-Neiges, bureau 100, Montreal, QC H3T 1Y6, Canada *Tel:* 514-343-6933 *Fax:* 514-343-2232 *E-mail:* pum@umontreal.ca *Web Site:* www.pum.umontreal.ca, pg 417

Poitras, Chloe, Les Editions de Mortagne, CP 116, Boucherville, QC J4B 5E6, Canada *Tel:* 450-641-2387 *E-mail:* info@editionsdemortagne.com *Web Site:* editionsdemortagne.com, pg 402

Pola, Matthew Dela, Piano Press, 1425 Ocean Ave, Suite 5, Del Mar, CA 92014 *Tel:* 619-884-1401 *E-mail:* pianopress@pianopress.com *Web Site:* www.pianopress.com, pg 159

Polanco, Annysa, Penguin Random House LLC, 1745 Broadway, New York, NY 10019 *Tel:* 212-782-9000 *Toll Free Tel:* 800-726-0600 *Web Site:* www.penguinrandomhouse.com, pg 155

Polansky, Debra, Penguin Young Readers Group, c/o Penguin Random House LLC, 1745 Broadway, New York, NY 10019 *Tel:* 212-782-9000 *Web Site:* www.penguin.com/penguin-young-readers-overview, pg 156

Polay, Brandy, Candlewick Press, 99 Dover St, Somerville, MA 02144-2825 *Tel:* 617-661-3330 *Fax:* 617-661-0565 *E-mail:* bigbear@candlewick.com; salesinfo@candlewick.com *Web Site:* candlewick.com, pg 39

Polcari, Beth, Scholastic Education Solutions, 557 Broadway, New York, NY 10012 *Tel:* 212-343-6100 *Fax:* 212-343-6189 *Web Site:* www.scholastic.com, pg 184

Polcari, Beth, Scholastic Inc, 557 Broadway, New York, NY 10012 *Tel:* 212-343-6100 *Toll Free Tel:* 800-SCHOLASTIC (724-6527) *Web Site:* www.scholastic.com, pg 184

Pold, Tom, Alfred A Knopf, c/o Penguin Random House LLC, 1745 Broadway, New York, NY 10019 *Tel:* 212-751-2600 *Fax:* 212-940-7390 (dom rts); 212-572-2662 (foreign rts) *Web Site:* knopfdoubleday.com/imprint/knopf/; knopfdoubleday.com, pg 110

Polefrone, Philomena, American Booksellers Association, 600 Mamaroneck Ave, Suite 400, Harrison, NY 10528 *Tel:* 914-406-7500 *Toll Free Tel:* 800-637-0037 *Fax:* 914-417-4013 *E-mail:* info@bookweb.org *Web Site:* www.bookweb.org, pg 494

Polese, Richard, Ocean Tree Books, 1325 Cerro Gordo Rd, Santa Fe, NM 87501 *Tel:* 505-983-1412 *Fax:* 505-983-0899 *E-mail:* richard@oceantree.com *Web Site:* www.oceantree.com, pg 145

Policarpo, Fatima, Bloomsbury Academic, 1385 Broadway, 5th fl, New York, NY 10018 *Tel:* 212-419-5300 *Web Site:* www.bloomsbury.com/us/academic, pg 31

Polidori, Josiane, IBBY Canada, c/o The Canadian Children's Book Ctr, 425 Adelaide St W, Suite 200, Toronto, ON M5V 3C1, Canada *Fax:* 416-975-8970 *E-mail:* info@ibby-canada.org *Web Site:* www.ibby-canada.org, pg 507

Poling, Jan A, American Forest & Paper Association (AF&PA), 1101 "K" St NW, Suite 700, Washington, DC 20005 *Tel:* 202-463-2700 *E-mail:* info@afandpa.org; comm@afandpa.org *Web Site:* www.afandpa.org, pg 495

Polivka, Raina, University of California Press, 155 Grand Ave, Suite 400, Oakland, CA 94612-3758 *Tel:* 510-883-8232 *Fax:* 510-836-8910 *E-mail:* customerservice@ucpress.edu *Web Site:* www.ucpress.edu, pg 215

Polizzotti, Mark, The Metropolitan Museum of Art, 1000 Fifth Ave, New York, NY 10028 *Tel:* 212-535-7710 *E-mail:* editorial@metmuseum.org *Web Site:* www.metmuseum.org, pg 130

Poll, Michael R, Cornerstone Book Publishers, PO Box 8423, Hot Springs Village, AR 71910 *Tel:* 504-215-6258 *E-mail:* 1cornerstonebooks@gmail.com *Web Site:* cornerstonepublishers.com, pg 53

Pollard, Ivan, The Conference Board Inc, 845 Third Ave, New York, NY 10022-6600 *Tel:* 212-759-0900; 212-339-0345 (cust serv) *E-mail:* customer.service@tcb.org *Web Site:* www.conference-board.org/us; www.linkedin.com/company/the-conference-board, pg 51

Pollock, Iain Haley MFA, Manhattanville College Master of Fine Arts in Creative Writing Program, 2900 Purchase St, Purchase, NY 10577 *Web Site:* www.mville.edu/programs/masters-creative-writing.php, pg 563

Pollock, Matthew, Perfection Learning®, 1000 N Second Ave, Logan, IA 51546-1061 *Tel:* 712-644-2831 *Toll Free Tel:* 800-831-4190 *Toll Free Fax:* 800-543-2745 *E-mail:* customer@perfectionlearning.com *Web Site:* www.perfectionlearning.com, pg 158

Pollock, William, No Starch Press, 245 Eighth St, San Francisco, CA 94103 *Tel:* 415-863-9900 *Toll Free Tel:* 800-420-7240 *Fax:* 415-863-9950 *E-mail:* info@nostarch.com; sales@nostarch.com; editors@nostarch.com; marketing@nostarch.com *Web Site:* www.nostarch.com, pg 141

Polson, Emily, Scribner, 1230 Avenue of the Americas, New York, NY 10020 *Web Site:* www.simonandschusterpublishing.com/scribner/, pg 185

Polster, Emilie, Little, Brown Books for Young Readers (LBYR), 1290 Avenue of the Americas, New York, NY 10104 *Tel:* 212-364-1100 *Toll Free Tel:* 800-759-0190 (cust serv) *E-mail:* rights@lbchildrens.com *Web Site:* www.hachettebookgroup.com/imprint/little-brown-books-for-young-readers/, pg 118

Polvino, Lynne, Clarion Books, 195 Broadway, New York, NY 10007 *Tel:* 212-207-7000 *Toll Free Tel:* 800-242-7737 *E-mail:* consumercare@harpercollins.com *Web Site:* www.harpercollins.com/collections/books-by-clarion-books, pg 49

Pombo, Tom, HarperCollins Children's Books, 195 Broadway, New York, NY 10007 *Tel:* 212-207-7000 *Web Site:* www.harpercollins.com/childrens, pg 85

Pomerance, Ruth, Folio Literary Management, The Film Center Bldg, 630 Ninth Ave, Suite 1101, New York, NY 10036 *Tel:* 212-400-1494 *Fax:* 212-967-0977 *Web Site:* www.foliolit.com, pg 459

Pomerantz, Lisa, Illustration Online LLC, 13 Wingstone Lane, Devon, PA 19333 *Tel:* 215-232-6666 *Web Site:* www.illustrationonline.com, pg 485

Pomerico, David, HarperCollins Publishers LLC, 195 Broadway, New York, NY 10007 *Tel:* 212-207-7000 *Web Site:* www.harpercollins.com, pg 86

Pomes, Anthony, Square One Publishers Inc, 115 Herricks Rd, Garden City Park, NY 11040 *Tel:* 516-535-2010 *Toll Free Tel:* 877-900-BOOK (900-2665) *Fax:* 516-535-2014 *E-mail:* sq1publish@aol.com *Web Site:* www.squareonepublishers.com, pg 196

Pomp, Joseph, Harvard University Press, 79 Garden St, Cambridge, MA 02138-1499 *Tel:* 617-495-2600; 401-531-2800 (intl orders) *Toll Free Tel:* 800-405-1619 (orders) *Fax:* 617-495-5898 (gen); 617-496-4677 (edit & rts); 401-531-2801 (intl orders) *Toll Free Fax:* 800-406-9145 (orders) *E-mail:* contact_hup@harvard.edu *Web Site:* www.hup.harvard.edu, pg 88

Pompilio, Lisa Marie, Orbit, 1290 Avenue of the Americas, New York, NY 10104 *Tel:* 212-364-1100 *Toll Free Tel:* 800-759-0190 *Web Site:* www.orbitbooks.net; www.hachettebookgroup.com/imprint/orbit, pg 147

Ponder, Eileen M, Ave Maria Press Inc, PO Box 428, Notre Dame, IN 46556 *Toll Free Tel:* 800-282-1865 *Toll Free Fax:* 800-282-5681 *E-mail:* avemariapress.1@nd.edu *Web Site:* www.avemariapress.com, pg 22

Ponton, Danielle, Justin Winsor Library History Essay Award, 225 N Michigan Ave, Suite 1300, Chicago, IL 60601 *Tel:* 312-944-6780 *Toll Free Tel:* 800-545-2433 *Fax:* 312-440-9374 *E-mail:* ala@ala.org *Web Site:* www.ala.org/rt/lhrt/awards/windsor-essay-award; www.ala.org/rt/lhrt; www.ala.org, pg 676

Ponturo, Kayla, Young Lions Fiction Award, 445 Fifth Ave, 4th fl, New York, NY 10016 *Tel:* 212-930-0887 *Fax:* 212-930-0983 *E-mail:* younglions@nypl.org *Web Site:* www.nypl.org/ylfa, pg 679

Poole, Hannah, Dutton, c/o Penguin Random House LLC, 1745 Broadway, New York, NY 10019 *Tel:* 212-366-2000 *Web Site:* www.penguin.com/dutton-overview/; www.penguin.com/plume-books-overview/; www.penguin.com/tiny-reparations-overview/, pg 62

Poole, Kirsten, Reporters Committee for Freedom of the Press, 1156 15 St NW, Suite 1020, Washington, DC 20005-1779 *Tel:* 202-795-9300 *Toll Free Tel:* 800-336-4243 (legal hotline for journalists) *E-mail:* info@rcfp.org *Web Site:* www.rcfp.org, pg 518

Poor, Edith, Montemayor Press, 663 Hyland Hill Rd, Washington, VT 05675 *Tel:* 802-552-0750 *E-mail:* mail@montemayorpress.com *Web Site:* www.montemayorpress.com, pg 133

Poor, Hannah, Chronicle Books LLC, 680 Second St, San Francisco, CA 94107 *Tel:* 415-537-4200 *Fax:* 415-537-4460 (perms) *E-mail:* hello@chroniclebooks.com; subrights@chroniclebooks.com *Web Site:* www.chroniclebooks.com, pg 48

Pop, Antonia, University of Toronto Press, Book Publishing Div, 800 Bay St, Mezzanine, Toronto, ON M5S 3A9, Canada *Tel:* 416-978-2239 *Fax:* 416-978-4736 *E-mail:* utpbooks@utorontopress.com (orders) *Web Site:* utorontopress.com, pg 423

Pop, Lou Light, Light Publications, 306 Thayer St, Suite 2462, Providence, RI 02906 *Tel:* 401-484-0228 *E-mail:* info@lightpublications.com; pr@lightpublications.com (media rel) *Web Site:* lightpublications.com, pg 116

Pope, Anna, BPC, 415 Farm Rd, Summertown, TN 38483 *Tel:* 931-964-3571 *Toll Free Tel:* 888-260-8458 *Fax:* 931-964-3518 *E-mail:* info@bookpubco.com *Web Site:* www.bookpubco.com, pg 35

Pope, Barbara Kline, Johns Hopkins University Press, 2715 N Charles St, Baltimore, MD 21218-4363 *Tel:* 410-516-6900; 410-516-6987 *Toll Free Tel:* 800-537-5487 (book orders & cust serv); 800-548-1784 (journal orders) *Fax:* 410-516-6968; 410-516-6998 (orders) *E-mail:* hfscustserv@press.jhu.edu (cust serv); jrnlcirc@jh.edu (journal orders) *Web Site:* www.press.jhu.edu; muse.jhu.edu, pg 106

Pope, Dr Deborah, Ezra Jack Keats Book Award, 450 14 St, Brooklyn, NY 11215-5702 *E-mail:* foundation@ezra-jack-keats.org *Web Site:* www.ezra-jack-keats.org, pg 619

Pope, William, Rochester Institute of Technology, Department of Packaging & Graphic Media Science, 69 Lomb Memorial Dr, Rochester, NY 14623-5603 *Tel:* 585-475-2728; 585-475-5336 *Fax:* 585-475-5336 *E-mail:* spmofc@rit.edu *Web Site:* rit.edu/engineeringtechnology/department-packaging-and-graphic-media-science, pg 565

Popelars, Craig, Milkweed Editions, 1011 Washington Ave S, Suite 300, Minneapolis, MN 55415-1246 *Tel:* 612-332-3192 *Toll Free Tel:* 800-520-6455 *E-mail:* orders@milkweed.org *Web Site:* milkweed.org, pg 131

Popescu, Adina, Yale University Press, 302 Temple St, New Haven, CT 06511-8909 *Tel:* 203-432-0960; 203-432-0966 (sales); 401-531-2800 (cust serv) *Toll Free Tel:* 800-405-1619 (cust serv) *Fax:* 203-432-0948; 203-432-8485 (sales); 401-531-2801 (cust serv) *Toll Free Fax:* 800-406-9145 (cust serv) *E-mail:* sales.press@yale.edu (sales); customer.care@triliteral.org (cust serv) *Web Site:* www.yalebooks.com; yalepress.yale.edu/yupbooks, pg 235

Popova, Jane, Random House Publishing Group, 1745 Broadway, New York, NY 10019 *Toll Free Tel:* 800-200-3552 *Web Site:* www.randomhousebooks.com, pg 171

Popper, Nicholas, Omohundro Institute of Early American History & Culture, Swem Library, Ground fl, 400 Landrum Dr, Williamsburg, VA 23185 *Tel:* 757-221-1114 *Fax:* 757-221-1047 *E-mail:* ieahc1@wm.edu *Web Site:* oieahc.wm.edu, pg 146

Porcelli, Tiffany, Grand Central Publishing, 1290 Avenue of the Americas, New York, NY 10104 *Tel:* 212-364-1100 *Web Site:* www.hachettebookgroup.com/imprint/grand-central-publishing/, pg 80

Poreda, Alexander, Other Press, 267 Fifth Ave, 6th fl, New York, NY 10016 *Tel:* 212-414-0054 *Toll Free Tel:* 877-THEOTHER (843-6843) *Fax:* 212-414-0939 *E-mail:* editor@otherpress.com; marketing@otherpress.com; publicity@otherpress.com *Web Site:* otherpress.com, pg 148

Porteous, Travis, Macmillan, 120 Broadway, 22nd fl, New York, NY 10271 *E-mail:* press.inquiries@macmillan.com *Web Site:* us.macmillan.com, pg 122

Porter, Barb, University of Toronto Press, Book Publishing Div, 800 Bay St, Mezzanine, Toronto, ON M5S 3A9, Canada *Tel:* 416-978-2239 *Fax:* 416-978-4736 *E-mail:* utpbooks@utorontopress.com (orders) *Web Site:* utorontopress.com, pg 423

Porter, Carolyn, One On One Book Publishing/Film-Video Publications, 7944 Capistrano Ave, West Hills, CA 91304 *Tel:* 818-340-6620; 818-340-0175 *Fax:* 818-340-6620 *E-mail:* onebookpro@aol.com, pg 146

Porter, Cati, The Hillary Gravendyk Prize, 4178 Chestnut St, Riverside, CA 92501 *E-mail:* inlandia@inlandiainstitute.org *Web Site:* inlandiainstitute.org/books/the-hillary-gravendyk-prize, pg 609

Porter, Cati, The Eliud Martinez Prize, 4178 Chestnut St, Riverside, CA 92501 *E-mail:* inlandia@inlandiainstitute.org *Web Site:* inlandinstitute.org/books/the-eliud-martinez-prize, pg 630

Porter, Neal, Holiday House Publishing Inc, 50 Broad St, New York, NY 10004 *Tel:* 212-688-0085 *Fax:* 212-421-6134 *E-mail:* info@holidayhouse.com *Web Site:* www.holidayhouse.com, pg 94

Porter, Susanna, Random House Publishing Group, 1745 Broadway, New York, NY 10019 *Toll Free Tel:* 800-200-3552 *Web Site:* www.randomhousebooks.com, pg 171

Portnowitz, Todd, Alfred A Knopf, c/o Penguin Random House LLC, 1745 Broadway, New York, NY 10019 *Tel:* 212-751-2600 *Fax:* 212-940-7390 (dom rts); 212-572-2662 (foreign rts) *Web Site:* knopfdoubleday.com/imprint/knopf/; knopfdoubleday.com, pg 110

Posada, Priscilla, Regal Hoffmann & Associates LLC, 157 13 St, Brooklyn, NY 11215 *Tel:* 212-684-7900 *E-mail:* info@rhaliterary.com; submissions@rhaliterary.com *Web Site:* www.rhaliterary.com, pg 473

Posen, Adam S, Peterson Institute for International Economics (PIIE), 1750 Massachusetts Ave NW, Washington, DC 20036-1903 *Tel:* 202-328-9000 *E-mail:* media@piie.com *Web Site:* piie.com, pg 158

Posner, Marcy, Folio Literary Management, The Film Center Bldg, 630 Ninth Ave, Suite 1101, New York, NY 10036 *Tel:* 212-400-1494 *Fax:* 212-967-0977 *Web Site:* www.foliolit.com, pg 459

Posner, Michele, Chronicle Books LLC, 680 Second St, San Francisco, CA 94107 *Tel:* 415-537-4200 *Fax:* 415-537-4460 (perms) *E-mail:* hello@chroniclebooks.com; subrights@chroniclebooks.com *Web Site:* www.chroniclebooks.com, pg 47

Posner-Greco, Claire, Random House Publishing Group, 1745 Broadway, New York, NY 10019 *Toll Free Tel:* 800-200-3552 *Web Site:* www.randomhousebooks.com, pg 171

Posner-Sanchez, Andrea, Random House Children's Books, c/o Penguin Random House LLC, 1745 Broadway, New York, NY 10019 Tel: 212-782-9000 Web Site: www.rhcbooks.com, pg 169

Poss, Marielle, Columbia University Press, 61 W 62 St, New York, NY 10023 Tel: 212-459-0600 Toll Free Tel: 800-944-8648 Fax: 212-459-3678 Web Site: cup.columbia.edu, pg 51

Post, Chad, Best Translated Book Award, c/o Open Letter, University of Rochester, Dewey Hall 1-219, Box 278968, Rochester, NY 14627 Tel: 585-319-0823 E-mail: contact@openletterbooks.org Web Site: besttranslatedbook.org, pg 579

Post, Chad, Dalkey Archive Press, c/o Deep Vellum Publishing, 3000 Commerce St, Dallas, TX 75226 E-mail: admin@deepvellum.org Web Site: www.dalkeyarchive.com, pg 56

Post, Chad W, Open Letter, University of Rochester, Dewey Hall, 1-219, Box 278968, Rochester, NY 14627 Tel: 585-319-0823 Fax: 585-273-1097 E-mail: contact@openletterbooks.org Web Site: www.openletterbooks.org, pg 147

Post, Marcie Craig, ILA Children's & Young Adults' Book Awards, PO Box 8139, Newark, DE 19714-8139 Tel: 302-731-1600 Toll Free Tel: 800-336-7323 (US & CN) E-mail: ilaawards@reading.org Web Site: www.literacyworldwide.org, pg 615

Post, Marcie Craig, International Literacy Association (ILA), PO Box 8139, Newark, DE 19714-8139 Tel: 302-731-1600 Toll Free Tel: 800-336-7323 (US & CN) E-mail: customerservice@reading.org Web Site: www.literacyworldwide.org; www.reading.org, pg 103, 508

Post, Marsha, SteinerBooks Inc, 610 Main St, Suite 1, Great Barrington, MA 01230 Tel: 413-528-8233 E-mail: service@steinerbooks.org; friends@steinerbooks.org Web Site: steiner.presswarehouse.com, pg 198

Post, Marvin, ABAC/ALAC, c/o 1938 Bloor St W, Toronto, ON M6P 3K8, Canada E-mail: info@abac.org Web Site: www.abac.org, pg 493

Post, Tom, University of Tennessee Press, 323 Hodges Library, 1015 Volunteer Blvd, Knoxville, TN 37996 Tel: 865-974-3321 Toll Free Tel: 800-621-2736 (orders) Toll Free Fax: 800-621-2736 (orders) E-mail: custserv@utpress.org Web Site: www.utpress.org, pg 220

Posternak, Jeffrey, The Wylie Agency LLC, 250 W 57 St, Suite 2114, New York, NY 10107 Tel: 212-246-0069 E-mail: mail@wylieagency.com Web Site: www.wylieagency.com, pg 483

Potash, Dan, Simon & Schuster Children's Publishing, 1230 Avenue of the Americas, New York, NY 10020 Tel: 212-698-7000 Web Site: www.simonandschuster.com/kids; www.simonandschuster.com/teen; simonandschuster.net; simonandschuster.biz, pg 189

Potorti, David, North Carolina Arts Council Writers Fellowships, 109 E Jones St, Raleigh, NC 27601 Tel: 919-807-6500 Fax: 919-807-6532 E-mail: ncarts@ncdcr.gov Web Site: www.ncarts.org, pg 641

Pottebaum, Gerard A, Treehaus Communications Inc, PO Box 249, Loveland, OH 45140-0249 Tel: 513-683-5716 Toll Free Tel: 800-638-4287 (orders) Fax: 513-683-2882 (orders) E-mail: treehaus@treehaus1.com; treehauscommunications@gmail.com Web Site: www.treehaus1.com, pg 209

Potter, Dr Beverly, Ronin Publishing Inc, PO Box 3436, Oakland, CA 94609 Tel: 510-420-3669 Fax: 510-420-3672 E-mail: ronin@roninpub.com Web Site: www.roninpub.com, pg 176

Potter, Dawn, Conference on Poetry & Teaching, 158 Ridge Rd, Franconia, NH 03580 Tel: 603-823-5510 E-mail: frost@frostplace.org Web Site: frostplace.org, pg 554

Potter, Donn King, Elizabeth H Backman, 86 Johnnycake Hollow Rd, Pine Plains, NY 12567 Tel: 518-398-9344 E-mail: bethcountry@gmail.com, pg 449

Potter, Nell, Zagat Inc, 424 Broadway, 5th fl, New York, NY 10013 E-mail: feedback@zagat.com Web Site: www.zagat.com, pg 236

Potts, Jeffrey, Radcliffe Institute Fellowship Program, Byerly Hall, 8 Garden St, Cambridge, MA 02138 Tel: 617-495-8212 Fax: 617-495-8136 E-mail: fellowships@radcliffe.harvard.edu Web Site: www.radcliffe.harvard.edu/fellowship-program, pg 654

Potts, Patricia, BuilderBooks, 1201 15 St NW, Washington, DC 20005 Toll Free Tel: 800-368-5242 E-mail: info@nahb.com Web Site: builderbooks.com, pg 38

Pouliot, Dan, New Hampshire Literary Awards, 2500 N River Rd, Manchester, NH 03106 Tel: 603-270-5466 E-mail: info@nhwritersproject.org Web Site: www.nhwritersproject.org/new-hampshire-literary-awards, pg 640

Pouliot, Dan, New Hampshire Writers' Project (NHWP), 2500 N River Rd, Manchester, NH 03106 Tel: 603-270-5466 E-mail: info@nhwritersproject.org Web Site: www.nhwritersproject.org, pg 514

Poundstone, Haygood, Capstone Publishers™, 1710 Roe Crest Dr, North Mankato, MN 56003 Toll Free Tel: 800-747-4992 (cust serv) Toll Free Fax: 888-262-0705 E-mail: customer.service@capstonepub.com Web Site: www.capstonepub.com, pg 40

Powell, David-Anthony, 4A's (American Association of Advertising Agencies), 25 W 45 St, 16th fl, New York, NY 10036 Tel: 212-682-2500 E-mail: media@4as.org; membership@4as.org Web Site: www.aaaa.org, pg 506

Power, Nancy, Teachers College Press, 1234 Amsterdam Ave, New York, NY 10027 Tel: 212-678-3929 Fax: 212-678-4149 E-mail: tcpress@tc.edu Web Site: www.tcpress.com, pg 203

Powers, David, Pants On Fire Press, 10441 Waterbird Way, Bradenton, FL 34209 Tel: 941-405-3078 E-mail: submission@pantsonfirepress.com Web Site: www.pantsonfirepress.com, pg 150

Powers, Emily, Beacon Press, 24 Farnsworth St, Boston, MA 02210-1409 Tel: 617-742-2110 Fax: 617-723-3097 E-mail: production@beacon.org Web Site: www.beacon.org, pg 25

Powers, Marcia, Wilshire Book Co, 22647 Ventura Blvd, No 314, Woodland Hills, CA 91364-1416 Tel: 818-700-1522 E-mail: sales@mpowers.com Web Site: www.mpowers.com, pg 230

Powers, Melinda, CALIBA Golden Poppy Awards, 100 Black Diamond Rd, Stonyford, CA 95979 Tel: 415-561-7686 E-mail: info@caliballiance.org Web Site: caliballiance.org/golden-poppy-awards.html, pg 585

Powers, Melinda, California Independent Booksellers Alliance (CALIBA), 100 Black Diamond Rd, Stonyford, CA 95979 Tel: 415-561-7686 E-mail: info@caliballiance.org Web Site: caliballiance.org, pg 502

Powers, Retha, Henry Holt and Company, LLC, 120 Broadway, 23rd fl, New York, NY 10271 Tel: 646-307-5151 Toll Free Tel: 888-330-8477 (orders) Fax: 646-307-5285 Web Site: www.henryholt.com, pg 94

Pozier, Bernard, Ecrits des Forges, 992-A rue Royale, Trois-Rivieres, QC G9A 4H9, Canada Tel: 819-840-8492 E-mail: ecritsdesforges@gmail.com Web Site: www.ecritsdesforges.com, pg 401

Pozzuoli, Kristin, DK, c/o Penguin Random House LLC, 1745 Broadway, 20th fl, New York, NY 10019 Tel: 646-674-4000 Toll Free Tel: 800-733-3000 Fax: 646-674-4020 E-mail: marketing@dk.com (lib servs); publicity@dk.com; csorders@penguinrandomhouse.com; customerservice@penguinrandomhouse.com Web Site: www.dk.com, pg 60

Prado, Alyssa, Random House Children's Books, c/o Penguin Random House LLC, 1745 Broadway, New York, NY 10019 Tel: 212-782-9000 Web Site: www.rhcbooks.com, pg 170

Praeger, Marta, Robert A Freedman Dramatic Agency Inc, PO Box 3544, New York, NY 10163 Tel: 718-897-0950, pg 459

Pramik, Wendy, Midwest Travel Journalists Association Inc (MTJA), PO Box 185, Jessup, IA 50648 Tel: 319-529-1109 E-mail: admin@mtja.us Web Site: www.mtja.us, pg 511

Pranter, Matthew, AAPG (American Association of Petroleum Geologists), 1444 S Boulder Ave, Tulsa, OK 74119 Tel: 918-584-2555 Toll Free Tel: 800-364-AAPG (364-2274) Fax: 918-580-2665 E-mail: info@aapg.org Web Site: www.aapg.org, pg 1

Pranzatelli, Robert, Yale University Press, 302 Temple St, New Haven, CT 06511-8909 Tel: 203-432-0960; 203-432-0966 (sales); 401-531-2800 (cust serv) Toll Free Tel: 800-405-1619 (cust serv) Fax: 203-432-0948; 203-432-8485 (sales); 401-531-2801 (cust serv) Toll Free Fax: 800-406-9145 (cust serv) E-mail: sales.press@yale.edu (sales); customer.care@triliteral.org (cust serv) Web Site: www.yalebooks.com; yalepress.yale.edu/yupbooks, pg 235

Prasad, Viniyanka, Duende-Word BIPOC Bookseller Award, 757 E 20 Ave, Suite 370-335, Denver, CO 80205 E-mail: info@thewordfordiversity.org Web Site: www.thewordfordiversity.org/bookselleraward, pg 597

Prasad, Viniyanka, The Word, A Storytelling Sanctuary Inc, 757 E 20 Ave, Suite 370-335, Denver, CO 80205 E-mail: info@thewordfordiversity.org Web Site: www.thewordfordiversity.org, pg 522

Prasanna, Tanusri, DeFiore and Company Literary Management Inc, 47 E 19 St, 3rd fl, New York, NY 10003 Tel: 212-925-7744 Fax: 212-925-9803 E-mail: info@defliterary.com; submissions@defliterary.com Web Site: www.defliterary.com, pg 456

Prasher, Madhu, Running Press, 1290 Avenue of the Americas, New York, NY 10104 Tel: 212-364-1100 Toll Free Tel: 800-759-0190 (cust serv) Fax: 212-364-0933 (intl orders) Toll Free Fax: 800-286-9471 (cust serv) E-mail: customer.service@hbgusa.com; orders@hbgusa.com Web Site: www.hachettebookgroup.com/imprint/running-press/; www.moon.com (Moon Travel Guides), pg 178

Pratt, Anne-Marie, Yaddo Artists Residency, 312 Union Ave, Saratoga Springs, NY 12866 Tel: 518-584-0746 Fax: 518-584-1312 Web Site: www.yaddo.org, pg 559

Pratt, Beth, Ohio University Press, Alden Library, Suite 101, 30 Park Place, Athens, OH 45701-2909 Tel: 740-593-1154 Web Site: www.ohioswallow.com, pg 146

Pratt, Beth, Hollis Summers Poetry Prize, Alden Library, Suite 101, 30 Park Place, Athens, OH 45701-2909 Tel: 740-593-1154 Web Site: www.ohioswallow.com/poetry_prize; ohiouniversitypress.submittable.com/submit (online submissions), pg 667

Pratt, Darrin, University Press of Colorado, 1580 N Logan St, Suite 660, PMB 39883, Denver, CO 80203-1942 Tel: 720-406-8849 Toll Free Tel: 800-621-2736 (orders) Fax: 720-406-3443 Web Site: www.upcolorado.com, pg 221

Pratt, Darrin, Utah State University Press, 3078 Old Main Hill, Logan, UT 84322-3078 Tel: 435-797-1362 Web Site: www.usupress.com, pg 223

Pratt, Jane, Association for PRINT Technologies (APTech), 113 Seaboard Lane, Suite C-250, Franklin, TN 37067 Tel: 703-264-7200 E-mail: aptech@aptech.org Web Site: printtechnologies.org, pg 498

Pratt, Makenzie, Greystone Books Ltd, 343 Railway St, Suite 302, Vancouver, BC V6A 1A4, Canada Tel: 604-875-1550 Fax: 604-875-1556 E-mail: info@greystonebooks.com; rights@greystonebooks.com Web Site: www.greystonebooks.com, pg 407

Pratt, Nekasha, Thomas Nelson, 501 Nelson Place, Nashville, TN 37214 Tel: 615-889-9000 Toll Free Tel: 800-251-4000 Web Site: www.thomasnelson.com, pg 206

Pratt, Nekasha, Zondervan, 3900 Sparks Dr SE, Grand Rapids, MI 49546 Tel: 616-698-6900 Toll Free Tel: 800-226-1122; 800-727-1309 (retail orders) Fax: 616-698-3350 Toll Free Fax: 800-698-3256 (retail orders) E-mail: customercare@harpercollins. com Web Site: www.zondervan.com, pg 236

Pratt, Randy, Master Books®, 3142 Hwy 103 N, Green Forest, AR 72638 Tel: 870-438-5288 Toll Free Tel: 800-999-3777 E-mail: sales@masterbooks. com; nlp@nlpg.com; submissions@newleafpress.net Web Site: www.masterbooks.com; www.nlpg.com, pg 126

Pratt, Randy, New Leaf Press, 3142 Hwy 103 N, Green Forest, AR 72638-2233 Tel: 870-438-5288 Toll Free Tel: 800-999-3777 Fax: 870-438-5120 E-mail: submissions@nlpg.com Web Site: www.nlpg. com, pg 140

Pray, Judy, Workman Publishing, 1290 Avenue of the Americas, New York, NY 10104 Toll Free Tel: 800-759-0190 Fax: 212-364-0950 E-mail: workman-inquiry@hbgusa.com Web Site: www.hachettebookgroup.com/imprint/workman-publishing-company/, pg 232

Preeg, Jessica, Atria Books, 1230 Avenue of the Americas, New York, NY 10020 Tel: 212-698-7000 Fax: 212-698-7007 Web Site: www.simonandschuster. com, pg 21

Prentiss, Winnie, Fair Winds Press, 100 Cummings Ctr, Suite 265-D, Beverly, MA 01915 Tel: 978-282-9590 Fax: 978-282-7765 E-mail: sales@quarto.com Web Site: www.quartoknows.com, pg 69

Prentiss, Winnie, Harvard Common Press, 100 Cummings Ctr, Suite 265-D, Beverly, MA 01915 Tel: 978-282-9590 Fax: 978-282-7765 Web Site: www. quartoknows.com/harvard-common-press, pg 88

Prescott, David, Safer Society Press, PO Box 340, Brandon, VT 05733-0340 Tel: 802-247-3132 Fax: 802-247-4233 E-mail: info@safersociety.org Web Site: safersocietypress.org, pg 179

Presley, Danielle, Penguin Young Readers Group, c/o Penguin Random House LLC, 1745 Broadway, New York, NY 10019 Tel: 212-782-9000 Web Site: www. penguin.com/penguin-young-readers-overview, pg 156

Presley, Eric, BRAVE Books, 13614 Poplar Circle, Suite 302, Conroe, TX 77304 Tel: 932-380-5648 E-mail: info@brave.us Web Site: bravebooks.us, pg 35

Presley, Todd, Chronicle Books LLC, 680 Second St, San Francisco, CA 94107 Tel: 415-537-4200 Fax: 415-537-4460 (perms) E-mail: hello@ chroniclebooks.com; subrights@chroniclebooks.com Web Site: www.chroniclebooks.com, pg 47

Presley, Tracey, Penguin Random House LLC, 1745 Broadway, New York, NY 10019 Tel: 212-782-9000 Toll Free Tel: 800-726-0600 Web Site: www. penguinrandomhouse.com, pg 155

Presley, Whitney, Printing Industry Association of the South (PIAS), 305 Plus Park Blvd, Nashville, TN 37217 Tel: 615-366-1094 Fax: 615-366-4192 Web Site: www.pias.org, pg 517

Presson, Greg, Psychological Assessment Resources Inc (PAR), 16204 N Florida Ave, Lutz, FL 33549 Tel: 813-449-4065 Toll Free Tel: 800-331-8378 Fax: 813-961-2196 Toll Free Fax: 800-727-9329 Web Site: www.parinc.com, pg 166

Prestia, Chris, Jane Rotrosen Agency LLC, 318 E 51 St, New York, NY 10022-7803 Tel: 212-593-4330 E-mail: info@janerotrosen.com Web Site: janerotrosen. com, pg 474

Preston, Afua, New York University, Center for Publishing & Applied Liberal Arts, 7 E 12 St, New York, NY 10003 Tel: 212-998-7200 E-mail: sps.info@ nyu.edu Web Site: www.scps.nyu.edu/professional-pathways/topics.html, pg 563

Preuss, Jeff, Andrews McMeel Publishing LLC, 1130 Walnut St, Kansas City, MO 64106-2109 Tel: 816-581-7500 Toll Free Tel: 800-851-8923 Web Site: www. andrewsmcmeel.com; publishing.andrewsmcmeel.com, pg 14

Preziosi, Alessandra, Houghton Mifflin Harcourt Trade & Reference Division, 125 High St, Boston, MA 02110 Tel: 617-351-5000 Web Site: www.hmhco.com, pg 96

Preziosi, Alex, HarperCollins Children's Books, 195 Broadway, New York, NY 10007 Tel: 212-207-7000 Web Site: www.harpercollins.com/childrens, pg 85

Pricci, Linda, Rizzoli International Publications Inc, 300 Park Ave S, 4th fl, New York, NY 10010-5399 Tel: 212-387-3400 Toll Free Tel: 800-522-6657 (orders only) Fax: 212-387-3535 E-mail: publicity@rizzoliusa. com Web Site: www.rizzoliusa.com, pg 175

Price, Allyssa, Random House Children's Books, c/o Penguin Random House LLC, 1745 Broadway, New York, NY 10019 Tel: 212-782-9000 Web Site: www. rhcbooks.com, pg 170

Price, Bernadette B, Orbis Books, PO Box 302, Maryknoll, NY 10545-0302 Tel: 914-941-7636 Toll Free Tel: 800-258-5838 (orders, Mon-Fri 8AM-4PM EST) Fax: 914-941-7005 E-mail: orbisbooks@ maryknoll.org Web Site: orbisbooks.com, pg 147

Price, Bruce, Marathon Press, 1500 Square Turn Blvd, Norfolk, NE 68701 Tel: 402-371-5040 Toll Free Tel: 800-228-0629 Fax: 402-371-9382 E-mail: info@ marathonpress.net Web Site: www.marathonpress.net, pg 124

Price, Rev Cheryl L, Judson Press, 1075 First Ave, King of Prussia, PA 19406 Toll Free Tel: 800-458-3766 Fax: 610-768-2107 E-mail: publisher@judsonpress. com; editor@judsonpress.com; marketing@ judsonpress.com Web Site: www.judsonpress.com, pg 107

Price, Fred, Mandel Vilar Press, 19 Oxford Ct, Simsbury, CT 06070 Tel: 806-790-4731 E-mail: info@mvpress. org Web Site: www.mvpublishers.org, pg 124

Price, Jodi, Princeton University Press, 41 William St, Princeton, NJ 08540-5237 Tel: 609-258-4900 Fax: 609-258-6305 E-mail: info@press.princeton.edu Web Site: press.princeton.edu, pg 164

Price, Maddy, HarperCollins Children's Books, 195 Broadway, New York, NY 10007 Tel: 212-207-7000 Web Site: www.harpercollins.com/childrens, pg 85

Price, Robert, Gatekeeper Press, 7853 Gunn Hwy, Suite 209, Tampa, FL 33626 Toll Free Tel: 866-535-0913 Fax: 216-803-0350 E-mail: info@gatekeeperpress.com Web Site: www.gatekeeperpress.com, pg 77

Price, Todd Alan, Stanley Drama Award, One Campus Rd, Staten Island, NY 10301 Tel: 718-390-3223 Fax: 718-390-3323 Web Site: wagner.edu/theatre/stanley-drama, pg 665

Priddis, Ronald L, Signature Books Publishing LLC, 564 W 400 N, Salt Lake City, UT 84116-3411 Toll Free Tel: 800-356-5687 E-mail: people@signaturebooks. com Web Site: www.signaturebooks.com; www. signaturebookslibrary.org, pg 188

Priddle, Clive, Basic Books Group, 1290 Avenue of the Americas, New York, NY 10104 Tel: 212-340-8100 Toll Free Tel: 800-343-4499 (cust serv) Fax: 212-340-8105 E-mail: customer.service@hbgusa.com; orders@ hbgusa.com Web Site: www.hachettebookgroup. com/imprint/basic-books/, pg 25

Priddy, Kristine, Southern Illinois University Press, 1915 University Press Dr, SIUC Mail Code 6806, Carbondale, IL 62901-4323 Tel: 618-453-2281 Fax: 618-453-1221 E-mail: rights@siu.edu Web Site: www.siupress.com, pg 195

Prielipp, Danielle, Simon & Schuster, 1230 Avenue of the Americas, New York, NY 10020 Tel: 212-698-7000 Toll Free Tel: 800-223-2348 (cust serv); 800-223-2336 (orders) Toll Free Fax: 800-943-9831 (orders) Web Site: simonandschusterpublishing.com/simonandschuster/, pg 188

Priest, Aaron M, The Aaron M Priest Literary Agency Inc, 370 Lexington Ave, Suite 1202, New York, NY 10017 Tel: 212-818-0344 Fax: 212-573-9417 E-mail: info@aaronpriest.com Web Site: www. aaronpriest.com, pg 472

Primiani, Alexandra, Avid Reader Press, 1230 Avenue of the Americas, New York, NY 10020 Web Site: avidreaderpress.com, pg 23

Prince, Monica MFA, Susquehanna University, Department of English & Creative Writing, 514 University Ave, Selinsgrove, PA 17870 Tel: 570-372-4196 Web Site: www.susqu.edu, pg 565

Prince, William Danforth, Blood Moon Productions Ltd, 75 Saint Marks Place, Staten Island, NY 10301-1606 Tel: 718-556-9410 Web Site: bloodmoonproductions. com, pg 31

Pringle, Becky, National Education Association (NEA), 1201 16 St NW, Washington, DC 20036-3290 Tel: 202-833-4000 Fax: 202-822-7974 Web Site: www. nea.org, pg 137

Pringle, Becky, National Education Association (NEA), 1201 16 St NW, Washington, DC 20036-3290 Tel: 202-833-4000 Fax: 202-822-7974 E-mail: media-relations-team@nea.org Web Site: www.nea.org, pg 513

Prins, Joel, New World Library, 14 Pamaron Way, Novato, CA 94949 Tel: 415-884-2100 Fax: 415-884-2199 E-mail: escort@newworldlibrary.com Web Site: www.newworldlibrary.com, pg 140

Prior, Robert, The MIT Press, One Broadway, 12th fl, Cambridge, MA 02142 Tel: 617-253-5255 Toll Free Tel: 800-405-1619 (orders) Fax: 617-258-6779; 617-577-1545 (orders) Web Site: mitpress.mit.edu, pg 132

Pritchett, Ellie, Vintage Books, c/o Penguin Random House LLC, 1745 Broadway, New York, NY 10019 Tel: 212-572-2420 Fax: 212-940-7390 (dom rts); 212-572-2662 (foreign rts) E-mail: vintageanchorpublicity@randomhouse.com Web Site: knopfdoubleday.com/imprint/vintage; knopfdoubleday.com, pg 225

Pritchett, Jamie, The Knight Agency Inc, 232 W Washington St, Madison, GA 30650 E-mail: admin@ knightagency.net Web Site: www.knightagency.net, pg 466

Pritzker, Amanda, HarperCollins Publishers LLC, 195 Broadway, New York, NY 10007 Tel: 212-207-7000 Web Site: www.harpercollins.com, pg 86

Prives, Leslie, Penguin Random House LLC, 1745 Broadway, New York, NY 10019 Tel: 212-782-9000 Toll Free Tel: 800-726-0600 Web Site: www. penguinrandomhouse.com, pg 155

Proano, Emily, Sourcebooks LLC, 1935 Brookdale Rd, Suite 139, Naperville, IL 60563 Tel: 630-961-3900 Toll Free Tel: 800-432-7444 Fax: 630-961-2168 E-mail: info@sourcebooks.com Web Site: www. sourcebooks.com, pg 194

Proia, Brandon, Basic Books Group, 1290 Avenue of the Americas, New York, NY 10104 Tel: 212-340-8100 Toll Free Tel: 800-343-4499 (cust serv) Fax: 212-340-8105 E-mail: customer.service@hbgusa.com; orders@ hbgusa.com Web Site: www.hachettebookgroup. com/imprint/basic-books/, pg 25

Pronk, Gord, Pronk Media Inc, 16 Glen Davis Crescent, Toronto, ON M4E 1X5, Canada Tel: 416-716-9660 (cell) E-mail: info@pronk.com; hello@pronk.com Web Site: www.pronk.com; www.h5engines.com; www.html5alive.com, pg 443

Prosser, Julia, Simon & Schuster, 1230 Avenue of the Americas, New York, NY 10020 Tel: 212-698-7000 Toll Free Tel: 800-223-2348 (cust serv); 800-223-2336 (orders) Toll Free Fax: 800-943-9831 (orders) Web Site: simonandschusterpublishing.com/simonandschuster/, pg 188

Prosswimmer, Kate, Simon & Schuster Children's Publishing, 1230 Avenue of the Americas, New York, NY 10020 Tel: 212-698-7000 Web Site: www. simonandschuster.com/kids; www.simonandschuster. com/teen; simonandschuster.net; simonandschuster.biz, pg 189

Protano, Generosa Gina, GGP Publishing Inc, Larchmont, NY 10538 Tel: 914-834-8896 Fax: 914-834-7566 Web Site: www.GGPPublishing.com, pg 440, 460

Provost, Cherry, Medal of Honor for Literature, 15 Gramercy Park S, New York, NY 10003 Tel: 212-475-3424 E-mail: literary@thenationalartsclub.org Web Site: www.nationalartsclub.org, pg 631

Provost, Denise, Samuel Washington Allen Prize, c/o Linda Haviland Conte, 18 Hall Ave, Apt 2, Somerville, MA 02144 E-mail: info@nepoetryclub.org Web Site: nepoetryclub.org, pg 572

Provost, Denise, E E Cummings Prize, c/o Linda Haviland Conte, 18 Hall Ave, Apt 2, Somerville, MA 02144 E-mail: info@nepoetryclub.org Web Site: nepoetryclub.org, pg 594

Provost, Denise, Der Hovanessian Prize, c/o Linda Haviland Conte, 18 Hall Ave, Apt 2, Somerville, MA 02144 E-mail: info@nepoetryclub.org Web Site: nepoetryclub.org, pg 595

Provost, Denise, Golden Rose Award, c/o Linda Haviland Conte, 18 Hall Ave, Apt 2, Somerville, MA 02144 E-mail: info@nepoetryclub.org Web Site: nepoetryclub.org, pg 608

Provost, Denise, Amy Lowell Prize, c/o Linda Haviland Conte, 18 Hall Ave, Apt 2, Somerville, MA 02144 E-mail: info@nepoetryclub.org Web Site: nepoetryclub.org, pg 627

Provost, Denise, Sheila Margaret Motton Book Prize, c/o Linda Haviland Conte, 18 Hall Ave, Apt 2, Somerville, MA 02144 E-mail: info@nepoetryclub.org Web Site: nepoetryclub.org, pg 636

Provost, Denise, New England Poetry Club, c/o Linda Haviland Conte, 18 Hall Ave, Apt 2, Somerville, MA 02144 E-mail: info@nepoetryclub.org; president@nepoetryclub.org Web Site: nepoetryclub.org, pg 514

Provost, Denise, Jean Pedrick Chapbook Prize, c/o Linda Haviland Conte, 18 Hall Ave, Apt 2, Somerville, MA 02144 E-mail: info@nepoetryclub.org Web Site: nepoetryclub.org, pg 646

Provost, Lissa, San Francisco Writers Conference, 1901 Cleveland Ave, Suite D, Santa Rosa, CA 94501 Tel: 415-689-6301 E-mail: registrations@sfwriters.org; director@sfwriters.org; bizdev@sfwriters.org Web Site: www.sfwriters.org, pg 557

Provost, Lissa, San Francisco Writing Contest (SFWC), 1901 Cleveland Ave, Suite D, Santa Rosa, CA 94501 Tel: 415-689-6301 E-mail: contest@sfwriters.org; director@sfwriters.org Web Site: www.sfwriters.org, pg 658

Pruett, Robert H, Brandylane Publishers Inc, 5 S First St, Richmond, VA 23219 Tel: 804-644-3090 Web Site: brandylanepublishers.com, pg 35

Prufer, Kevin, University of Houston Creative Writing Program, Dept of English/College of Liberal Arts & Social Science, 3687 Cullen Blvd, Rm 229, Houston, TX 77204-5008 Tel: 713-743-3015 E-mail: cwp@uh.edu Web Site: uh.edu/class/english/programs/graduate-studies/index, pg 566

Pruitt, Zora Squish, Dial Books for Young Readers, c/o Penguin Random House LLC, 1745 Broadway, New York, NY 10019 Tel: 212-782-9000 Web Site: www.penguin.com/dial-overview/, pg 59

Prusiewicz, Chloe, Sounds True Inc, 413 S Arthur Ave, Louisville, CO 80027 Tel: 303-665-3151 Toll Free Tel: 800-333-9185 (US); 888-303-9185 (US & CN) E-mail: customerservice@soundstrue.com; stpublicity@soundstrue.com Web Site: www.soundstrue.com, pg 194

Prussen, Linda, Greystone Books Ltd, 343 Railway St, Suite 302, Vancouver, BC V6A 1A4, Canada Tel: 604-875-1550 Fax: 604-875-1556 E-mail: info@greystonebooks.com; rights@greystonebooks.com Web Site: www.greystonebooks.com, pg 407

Pryor, Ann, Kensington Publishing Corp, 900 Third Ave, 26th fl, New York, NY 10022 Tel: 212-407-1500 Toll Free Tel: 800-221-2647 Fax: 212-935-0699 Web Site: www.kensingtonbooks.com, pg 109

Pryor, Victoria Gould, Arcadia, 159 Lake Place S, Danbury, CT 06810-7261 Tel: 203-797-0993 E-mail: arcadialit@gmail.com, pg 449

Psaltis, Liz, HarperCollins Publishers LLC, 195 Broadway, New York, NY 10007 Tel: 212-207-7000 Web Site: www.harpercollins.com, pg 86

Pucci, Cameron, Institute of Police Technology & Management (IPTM), 12000 Alumni Dr, Jacksonville, FL 32224-2678 Tel: 904-620-4786 Fax: 904-620-2453 E-mail: info@iptm.org Web Site: iptm.unf.edu, pg 102

Pugalia, Nidhi, Viking Penguin, c/o Penguin Random House LLC, 1745 Broadway, New York, NY 10019 Tel: 212-782-9000 Web Site: www.penguin.com/overview-vikingbooks/; www.penguin.com/pamela-dorman-books-overview/; www.penguin.com/penguin-classics-overview/; www.penguin.com/penguin-life-overview/, pg 225

Pugh, Christina, University of Illinois at Chicago, Program for Writers, College of Liberal Arts & Sciences, 601 S Morgan St, Chicago, IL 60607 Tel: 312-413-2200 (Eng dept) E-mail: english@uic.edu Web Site: engl.uic.edu/graduate-studies/program-for-writers, pg 566

Pugh, Marsha, Dog Writers Association of America Inc (DWAA), PO Box 787, Hughesville, MD 20637 Web Site: dogwriters.org, pg 505

Pugh, Marsha, Dog Writers Association of America Inc (DWAA) Annual Writing Competition, PO Box 787, Hughesville, MD 20637 Web Site: dogwriters.org, pg 596

Pulice, Mario, Little, Brown and Company, 1290 Avenue of the Americas, New York, NY 10104 Tel: 212-364-1100 Fax: 212-364-0952 E-mail: firstname.lastname@hbgusa.com Web Site: www.hachettebookgroup.com/imprint/little-brown-and-company/, pg 118

Pullano, Michelle, The MIT Press, One Broadway, 12th fl, Cambridge, MA 02142 Tel: 617-253-5255 Toll Free Tel: 800-405-1619 (orders) Fax: 617-258-6779; 617-577-1545 (orders) Web Site: mitpress.mit.edu, pg 132

Pulver, Karen, Friends of American Writers Literature Awards, c/o 506 Rose Ave, Des Plaines, IL 60016 Tel: 847-827-8339 E-mail: info@fawchicago.org Web Site: www.fawchicago.org, pg 604

Pumphrey, Shelby, Simon & Schuster, 1230 Avenue of the Americas, New York, NY 10020 Tel: 212-698-7000 Toll Free Tel: 800-223-2348 (cust serv); 800-223-2336 (orders) Toll Free Fax: 800-943-9831 (orders) Web Site: simonandschusterpublishing.com/simonandschuster/, pg 188

Punia, Katherine Fleming, Living Language, c/o Penguin Random House LLC, 1745 Broadway, New York, NY 10019 Tel: 212-782-9000 Toll Free Tel: 800-733-3000 (orders) E-mail: support@livinglanguage.com Web Site: www.livinglanguage.com, pg 119

Punia, Katie, Penguin Random House Audio Publishing Group, 1745 Broadway, New York, NY 10019 Toll Free Tel: 800-793-2665 (cust serv) E-mail: audio@penguinrandomhouse.com; ecustomerservice@penguinrandomhouse.com Web Site: www.penguinrandomhouseaudio.com, pg 154

Punja, Athmika, Penguin Random House Canada, a Penguin Random House company, 320 Front St W, Suite 1400, Toronto, ON M5V 3B6, Canada Tel: 416-364-4449 Toll Free Tel: 888-523-9292 (cust serv) E-mail: canadaweb@penguinrandomhouse.com; customerservicecanada@penguinrandomhouse.com Web Site: www.penguinrandomhouse.ca, pg 415

Punzo, Dana Faulkner, Women Who Write Inc, PO Box 652, Madison, NJ 07940-0652 Web Site: www.womenwhowrite.org, pg 522

Puopolo, Kristine, Doubleday, c/o Penguin Random House LLC, 1745 Broadway, New York, NY 10019 Tel: 212-751-2600 Fax: 212-940-7390 (dom rts); 212-572-2662 (foreign rts) Web Site: knopfdoubleday.com/imprint/doubleday/; knopfdoubleday.com, pg 61

Pupo, Indira, Penguin Random House LLC, 1745 Broadway, New York, NY 10019 Tel: 212-782-9000 Toll Free Tel: 800-726-0600 Web Site: www.penguinrandomhouse.com, pg 155

Puppa, Brian, TCP Press, 20200 Marsh Hill Rd, Uxbridge, ON L9P 1R3, Canada Tel: 905-852-3777 Toll Free Tel: 800-772-7765 E-mail: tcp@tcpnow.com Web Site: www.tcppress.com, pg 420

Pura, Andrea, Random House Publishing Group, 1745 Broadway, New York, NY 10019 Toll Free Tel: 800-200-3552 Web Site: www.randomhousebooks.com, pg 171

Purcell, Anita, Canadian Authors Association (CAA), 45 Penetang St, Orillia, ON L3V 3N3, Canada Tel: 705-955-0716 E-mail: office@canadianauthors.org Web Site: www.canadianauthors.org, pg 502

Purcell, Jessica, Alfred A Knopf, c/o Penguin Random House LLC, 1745 Broadway, New York, NY 10019 Tel: 212-751-2600 Fax: 212-940-7390 (dom rts); 212-572-2662 (foreign rts) Web Site: knopfdoubleday.com/imprint/knopf/; knopfdoubleday.com, pg 110

Purelis, Eileen, Springer, One New York Plaza, Suite 4600, New York, NY 10004-1562 Tel: 212-460-1500 Toll Free Tel: 800-SPRINGER (777-4643) Fax: 212-460-1700 E-mail: customerservice@springernature.com Web Site: www.springer.com, pg 196

Purple, Katherine, Purdue University Press, Stewart Ctr 190, 504 W State St, West Lafayette, IN 47907-2058 Tel: 765-494-2038 Fax: 765-496-2442 E-mail: pupress@purdue.edu Web Site: www.thepress.purdue.edu, pg 167

Pursiful, Darrell, Smyth & Helwys Publishing Inc, 6316 Peake Rd, Macon, GA 31210-3960 Tel: 478-757-0564 Toll Free Tel: 800-747-3016 (orders only) Fax: 478-757-1305 E-mail: information@helwys.com Web Site: www.helwys.com, pg 192

Putman, Becca, HarperCollins Publishers LLC, 195 Broadway, New York, NY 10007 Tel: 212-207-7000 Web Site: www.harpercollins.com, pg 86

Putter, Raina, Holiday House Publishing Inc, 50 Broad St, New York, NY 10004 Tel: 212-688-0085 Fax: 212-421-6134 E-mail: info@holidayhouse.com Web Site: www.holidayhouse.com, pg 94

Pye, Michael, Red Wheel/Weiser, 65 Parker St, Suite 7, Newburyport, MA 01950 Tel: 978-465-0504 Toll Free Tel: 800-423-7087 (orders) Fax: 978-465-0243 E-mail: info@rwwbooks.com Web Site: www.redwheelweiser.com, pg 173

Pyland, Mike, Recorded Books Inc, an RBmedia company, 8400 Corporate Dr, Landover, MD 20785 Toll Free Tel: 800-305-3450 Web Site: rbmediaglobal.com/recorded-books, pg 172

Pyles, Barbara, National Coalition Against Censorship (NCAC), 19 Fulton St, Suite 407, New York, NY 10038 Tel: 212-807-6222 Fax: 212-807-6245 E-mail: ncac@ncac.org Web Site: www.ncac.org, pg 512

Pyritz, Nathan, Candlewick Press, 99 Dover St, Somerville, MA 02144-2825 Tel: 617-661-3330 Fax: 617-661-0565 E-mail: bigbear@candlewick.com; salesinfo@candlewick.com Web Site: candlewick.com, pg 40

Pyun, Sabrina, Scribner, 1230 Avenue of the Americas, New York, NY 10020 Web Site: www.simonandschusterpublishing.com/scribner/, pg 185

Quasha, George, Barrytown/Station Hill Press, 120 Station Hill Rd, Barrytown, NY 12507 Tel: 845-758-5293 E-mail: publishers@stationhill.org Web Site: www.stationhill.org, pg 24

Quasha, Susan, Barrytown/Station Hill Press, 120 Station Hill Rd, Barrytown, NY 12507 Tel: 845-758-5293 E-mail: publishers@stationhill.org Web Site: www.stationhill.org, pg 24

Quatraro, Jenna, Sourcebooks LLC, 1935 Brookdale Rd, Suite 139, Naperville, IL 60563 Tel: 630-961-3900 Toll Free Tel: 800-432-7444 Fax: 630-961-2168 E-mail: info@sourcebooks.com Web Site: www.sourcebooks.com, pg 194

Quattrocchi, John, Albert Whitman & Company, 250 S Northwest Hwy, Suite 320, Park Ridge, IL 60068 Tel: 847-232-2800 Toll Free Tel: 800-255-7675 (orders) Fax: 847-581-0039 E-mail: mail@albertwhitman.com; orders@albertwhitman.com Web Site: www.albertwhitman.com, pg 6

Quereau, Jennifer, Cold Spring Harbor Laboratory Press, 500 Sunnyside Blvd, Woodbury, NY 11797-2924 *Tel:* 516-422-4100 *Toll Free Tel:* 800-843-4388 *E-mail:* cshpress@cshl.edu *Web Site:* www.cshlpress.com, pg 50

Querido, Levine, Dreamscape Media LLC, 1417 Timberwolf Dr, Holland, OH 43528 *Tel:* 419-867-6965 *Toll Free Tel:* 877-983-7326 *E-mail:* info@dreamscapeab.com *Web Site:* www.dreamscapepublishing.com, pg 62

Quick, Brianna, Wisdom Publications Inc, 199 Elm St, Somerville, MA 02144 *Tel:* 617-776-7416 *Toll Free Tel:* 800-272-4050 (orders) *Fax:* 617-776-7841 *E-mail:* submission@wisdompubs.org *Web Site:* wisdomexperience.org, pg 231

Quill, Alexandra, Farrar, Straus & Giroux Books for Young Readers, 120 Broadway, New York, NY 10271 *Tel:* 212-741-6900 *Toll Free Tel:* 888-330-8477 (orders) *E-mail:* childrens.publicity@macmillanusa.com; childrensrights@macmillanusa.com *Web Site:* us.macmillan.com/mackids, pg 70

Quill, Alexandra, Roaring Brook Press, 120 Broadway, New York, NY 10271 *Tel:* 646-307-5151 *Web Site:* us.macmillan.com/publishers/roaring-brook-press, pg 176

Quillen, Lida E, Twilight Times Books, PO Box 3340, Kingsport, TN 37664-0340 *Tel:* 423-390-1111 *Fax:* 423-390-1111 *E-mail:* publisher@twilighttimes.com *Web Site:* www.twilighttimesbooks.com, pg 211

Quin, Matt, Ivey Publishing, Ivey Business School Foundation, Western University, 1255 Western Rd, London, ON N6G 0N1, Canada *Tel:* 519-661-3206; 519-661-3208 *Toll Free Tel:* 800-649-6355 *Fax:* 519-661-3485; 519-661-3882 *E-mail:* cases@ivey.ca *Web Site:* www.iveypublishing.ca, pg 411

Quincannon, Alan, Quincannon Publishing Group, PO Box 8100, Glen Ridge, NJ 07028-8100 *Tel:* 973-380-9942 *E-mail:* editors@quincannongroup.com (query first via e-mail) *Web Site:* www.quincannongroup.com, pg 168

Quinlan, Kathleen, Random House Publishing Group, 1745 Broadway, New York, NY 10019 *Toll Free Tel:* 800-200-3552 *Web Site:* www.randomhousebooks.com, pg 171

Quinlin, Margaret, Peachtree Publishing Co Inc, 1700 Chattahoochee Ave, Atlanta, GA 30318-2112 *Tel:* 404-876-8761 *Toll Free Tel:* 800-241-0113 *Fax:* 404-875-2578 *Toll Free Fax:* 800-875-8909 *E-mail:* hello@peachtree-online.com; orders@peachtree-online.com; sales@peachtree-online.com *Web Site:* www.peachtreebooks.com; www.peachtree-online.com, pg 153

Quinn, Dr Angie, Educators Book Award, 1801 E 51 St, Suite 365-163, Austin, TX 78701 *Tel:* 512-478-5748 *Toll Free Tel:* 888-762-4685 *Fax:* 512-478-3961 *Web Site:* www.dkg.org, pg 598

Quinn, Carly, Penguin Random House Audio Publishing Group, 1745 Broadway, New York, NY 10019 *Toll Free Tel:* 800-793-2665 (cust serv) *E-mail:* audio@penguinrandomhouse.com; ecustomerservice@penguinrandomhouse.com *Web Site:* www.penguinrandomhouseaudio.com, pg 154

Quinn, Jean, Random House Publishing Group, 1745 Broadway, New York, NY 10019 *Toll Free Tel:* 800-200-3552 *Web Site:* www.randomhousebooks.com, pg 171

Quinn, John, Harry N Abrams Inc, 195 Broadway, 9th fl, New York, NY 10007 *Tel:* 212-206-7715 *Toll Free Tel:* 800-345-1359 *Fax:* 212-645-8437 *E-mail:* abrams@abramsbooks.com; publicity@abramsbooks.com; sales@abramsbooks.com *Web Site:* www.abramsbooks.com, pg 2

Quinn, Katie, Farrar, Straus & Giroux Books for Young Readers, 120 Broadway, New York, NY 10271 *Tel:* 212-741-6900 *Toll Free Tel:* 888-330-8477 (orders) *E-mail:* childrens.publicity@macmillanusa.com; childrensrights@macmillanusa.com *Web Site:* us.macmillan.com/mackids, pg 70

Quinn, Katie, Roaring Brook Press, 120 Broadway, New York, NY 10271 *Tel:* 646-307-5151 *Web Site:* us.macmillan.com/publishers/roaring-brook-press, pg 176

Quinn, Lisa, Wilfrid Laurier University Press, 75 University Ave W, Waterloo, ON N2L 3C5, Canada *Tel:* 519-884-0710 *Toll Free Tel:* 866-836-5551 (CN & US) *Fax:* 519-725-1399 *E-mail:* press@wlu.ca *Web Site:* www.wlupress.wlu.ca, pg 424

Quinn, Martin, St Martin's Press, LLC, 120 Broadway, New York, NY 10271 *E-mail:* publicity@stmartins.com; trademarketing@stmartins.com; foreignrights@stmartins.com *Web Site:* us.macmillan.com/smp, pg 181

Quinn, Megan Bencivenni, Charlesbridge Publishing Inc, 85 Main St, Watertown, MA 02472 *Tel:* 617-926-0329 *Toll Free Tel:* 800-225-3214 *Fax:* 617-926-5720 *Toll Free Fax:* 800-926-5775 *E-mail:* books@charlesbridge.com *Web Site:* www.charlesbridge.com, pg 45

Quinn, Michele Myatt, University of Alabama Press, 200 Hackberry Lane, 2nd fl, Tuscaloosa, AL 35487 *Tel:* 205-348-5180 *Fax:* 205-348-9201 *Web Site:* www.uapress.ua.edu, pg 214

Quinn, Ryan, American Booksellers Association, 600 Mamaroneck Ave, Suite 400, Harrison, NY 10528 *Tel:* 914-406-7500 *Toll Free Tel:* 800-637-0037 *Fax:* 914-417-4013 *E-mail:* info@bookweb.org *Web Site:* www.bookweb.org, pg 494

Quinn, Tony, Fire Engineering Books & Videos, Clarion Events LLC, 110 S Hartford, Suite 220, Tulsa, OK 74120 *Tel:* 918-831-9421 *Toll Free Tel:* 800-752-9764 *Fax:* 918-831-9555 *E-mail:* info@fireengineeringbooks.com *Web Site:* fireengineeringbooks.com, pg 72

Quinn, Yelba, The Brookings Institution Press, 1775 Massachusetts Ave NW, Washington, DC 20036-2188 *Tel:* 202-797-6000 *E-mail:* permissions@brookings.edu *Web Site:* www.brookings.edu, pg 37

Quinones, Deanna, Chronicle Books LLC, 680 Second St, San Francisco, CA 94107 *Tel:* 415-537-4200 *Fax:* 415-537-4460 (perms) *E-mail:* hello@chroniclebooks.com; subrights@chroniclebooks.com *Web Site:* www.chroniclebooks.com, pg 48

Quintanilla, Joseph, National Braille Press, 88 Saint Stephen St, Boston, MA 02115-4312 *Tel:* 617-266-6160 *Toll Free Tel:* 800-548-7323 (cust serv); 888-965-8965 *Fax:* 617-437-0456 *E-mail:* contact@nbp.org *Web Site:* www.nbp.org, pg 137

Quintin, Michel, Editions Michel Quintin, 2259 Papineau Ave, Suite 104, Montreal, QC H2K 4J5, Canada *Tel:* 514-379-3774 *Fax:* 450-539-4905 *E-mail:* info@editionsmichelquintin.ca; commande@editionsmichelquintin.ca (orders) *Web Site:* www.editionsmichelquintin.ca, pg 404

Quinton, Linda, Tor Publishing Group, 120 Broadway, New York, NY 10271 *Toll Free Tel:* 800-455-0340 (Macmillan) *E-mail:* torpublicity@tor.com; forgepublicity@forgebooks.com *Web Site:* us.macmillan.com/torpublishinggroup, pg 208

Quinton, Sasha, Scholastic Inc, 557 Broadway, New York, NY 10012 *Tel:* 212-343-6100 *Toll Free Tel:* 800-SCHOLASTIC (724-6527) *Web Site:* www.scholastic.com, pg 184

Quraishi, Mariam, Farrar, Straus & Giroux Books for Young Readers, 120 Broadway, New York, NY 10271 *Tel:* 212-741-6900 *Toll Free Tel:* 888-330-8477 (orders) *E-mail:* childrens.publicity@macmillanusa.com; childrensrights@macmillanusa.com *Web Site:* us.macmillan.com/mackids, pg 70

Raab, Jamie, Macmillan, 120 Broadway, 22nd fl, New York, NY 10271 *E-mail:* press.inquiries@macmillan.com *Web Site:* us.macmillan.com, pg 122

Raats, Anna, Ambassador International, 411 University Ridge, Suite B14, Greenville, SC 29601 *Tel:* 864-751-4844 *E-mail:* info@emeraldhouse.com; publisher@emeraldhouse.com (ms submissions); sales@emeraldhouse.com (orders/order inquiries); media@emeraldhouse.com; design@emeraldhouse.com *Web Site:* ambassador-international.com; www.facebook.com/AmbassadorIntl; x.com/ambassadorintl, pg 7

Rab, Sharon, The Ambassador Richard C Holbrooke Distinguished Achievement Award, PO Box 461, Wright Brothers Branch, Dayton, OH 45409-0461 *Tel:* 937-298-5072 *E-mail:* sharon.rab@daytonliterarypeaceprize.org *Web Site:* www.daytonliterarypeaceprize.org, pg 572

Rab, Sharon, Dayton Literary Peace Prize, PO Box 461, Wright Brothers Branch, Dayton, OH 45409-0461 *Tel:* 937-298-5072 *Web Site:* www.daytonliterarypeaceprize.org, pg 595

Rabaut, Brigitte, Marick Press, 1342 Three Mile Dr, Grosse Pointe Park, MI 48230 *Tel:* 313-407-9236 *E-mail:* orders@marickpress.com; info@marickpress.com *Web Site:* www.marickpress.com, pg 125

Rabin, Netta, Klutz®, 557 Broadway, New York, NY 10012 *Tel:* 212-343-6360 *Toll Free Tel:* 800-737-4123 (cust serv) *E-mail:* scholasticmarketing@scholastic.com; scholasticstore@scholastic.com *Web Site:* www.scholastic.com/parents/klutz.html; store.scholastic.com, pg 110

Rabin, Netta, Scholastic Trade Publishing, 557 Broadway, New York, NY 10012 *Tel:* 212-343-6100; 212-343-4685 (export sales) *Fax:* 212-343-4714 (export sales) *Web Site:* www.scholastic.com, pg 184

Rabinovitch, Daphna, Scotiabank Giller Prize, 499 Douglas Ave, Toronto, ON M5M 1H6, Canada *Web Site:* www.scotiabankgillerprize.ca, pg 661

Rabinovitch, Elana, Scotiabank Giller Prize, 499 Douglas Ave, Toronto, ON M5M 1H6, Canada *Web Site:* www.scotiabankgillerprize.ca, pg 661

Raby, Brooke, The University Press of Kentucky, 663 S Limestone St, Lexington, KY 40508-4008 *Tel:* 859-257-8400 *Fax:* 859-323-1873 *Web Site:* www.kentuckypress.com, pg 222

Raccah, Dominique, Sourcebooks LLC, 1935 Brookdale Rd, Suite 139, Naperville, IL 60563 *Tel:* 630-961-3900 *Toll Free Tel:* 800-432-7444 *Fax:* 630-961-2168 *E-mail:* info@sourcebooks.com *Web Site:* www.sourcebooks.com, pg 194

Race, Justin, Purdue University Press, Stewart Ctr 190, 504 W State St, West Lafayette, IN 47907-2058 *Tel:* 765-494-2038 *Fax:* 765-496-2442 *E-mail:* pupress@purdue.edu *Web Site:* www.thepress.purdue.edu, pg 167

Racenis, Peter, Sourcebooks LLC, 1935 Brookdale Rd, Suite 139, Naperville, IL 60563 *Tel:* 630-961-3900 *Toll Free Tel:* 800-432-7444 *Fax:* 630-961-2168 *E-mail:* info@sourcebooks.com *Web Site:* www.sourcebooks.com, pg 195

Racette, Rita, University of Regina Press, 2 Research Dr, Suite 160, Regina, SK S4S 7H9, Canada *Tel:* 306-585-4758 *Fax:* 306-585-4699 *E-mail:* uofrpress@uregina.ca *Web Site:* www.uofrpress.ca, pg 423

Radant, Cyndi, Millbrook Press, 241 First Ave N, Minneapolis, MN 55401 *Tel:* 612-332-3344 *Toll Free Tel:* 800-328-4929 *Fax:* 612-332-7615 *Toll Free Fax:* 800-332-1132 *E-mail:* info@lernerbooks.com; custserve@lernerbooks.com *Web Site:* www.lernerbooks.com; www.facebook.com/millbrookpress, pg 131

Rade, David, Swan Isle Press, c/o Chicago Distribution Ctr, 11030 S Langley Ave, Chicago, IL 60628 *Tel:* 773-636-1818 (edit) *E-mail:* info@swanislepress.com *Web Site:* www.swanislepress.com, pg 201

Rademaker, Kent, Highlights for Children Inc, 815 Church St, Honesdale, PA 18431 *Tel:* 570-253-1164 *Toll Free Tel:* 800-490-5111 *Fax:* 570-253-0179 *E-mail:* salesandmarketing@highlightspress.com *Web Site:* www.highlightspress.com; www.highlights.com; www.facebook.com/HighlightsforChildren, pg 92

Radke, Linda F, Story Monsters Approved! Program, 4696 W Tyson St, Chandler, AZ 85226-2903 *Tel:* 480-940-8182 *Fax:* 480-940-8787 *Web Site:* www.StoryMonstersBookAwards.com/sma-details, pg 666

Radke, Linda F, Story Monsters® Book Awards, 4696 W Tyson St, Chandler, AZ 85226-2903 *Tel:* 480-940-8182 *Fax:* 480-940-8787 *E-mail:* info@StoryMonsters.com *Web Site:* www.StoryMonstersBookAwards.com, pg 667

Radke, Linda F, Story Monsters LLC, 4696 W Tyson St, Chandler, AZ 85226-2903 *Tel:* 480-940-8182 *Fax:* 480-940-8787 *Web Site:* www.StoryMonsters.com; www.StoryMonstersBookAwards.com; www.AuthorBookings.com; www.StoryMonstersBookAwards.com/sma-details; www.StoryMonstersInk.com, pg 199

Radler, Kyle, W W Norton & Company Inc, 500 Fifth Ave, New York, NY 10110-0017 *Tel:* 212-354-5500 *Toll Free Tel:* 800-233-4830 (orders & cust serv) *Fax:* 212-869-0856 *Toll Free Fax:* 800-458-6515 *E-mail:* orders@wwnorton.com *Web Site:* wwnorton.com, pg 143

Raducanu, Teodor, Teora USA LLC, 9443 Rosehill Dr, Bethesda, MD 20817 *Tel:* 301-986-6990 *E-mail:* teorausa@gmail.com *Web Site:* www.teora.com, pg 204

Raeber, Rick, W W Norton & Company Inc, 500 Fifth Ave, New York, NY 10110-0017 *Tel:* 212-354-5500 *Toll Free Tel:* 800-233-4830 (orders & cust serv) *Fax:* 212-869-0856 *Toll Free Fax:* 800-458-6515 *E-mail:* orders@wwnorton.com *Web Site:* wwnorton.com, pg 143

Raessler, Jon, The Geological Society of America Inc (GSA), 3300 Penrose Place, Boulder, CO 80301-1806 *Tel:* 303-357-1000 *Toll Free Tel:* 800-472-1988 *Fax:* 303-357-1070 *E-mail:* pubs@geosociety.org (prodn); editing@geosociety.org (edit); books@geosociety.org; gsaservice@geosociety.org (sales & serv) *Web Site:* www.geosociety.org, pg 77

Rafert, Samara, The Ohio State University Press, 180 Pressey Hall, 1070 Carmack Rd, Columbus, OH 43210-1002 *Tel:* 614-292-6930 *Fax:* 614-292-2065 *Toll Free Fax:* 800-621-8476 *E-mail:* OSUPInfo@osu.edu *Web Site:* ohiostatepress.org, pg 145

Raffa, Angie, Leadership Ministries Worldwide, 1928 Central Ave, Chattanooga, TN 37408 *Tel:* 423-855-2181 *Toll Free Tel:* 800-987-8790 *E-mail:* info@lmw.org *Web Site:* lmw.org; store.lmw.org, pg 113

Raffa, Anthony, Leadership Ministries Worldwide, 1928 Central Ave, Chattanooga, TN 37408 *Tel:* 423-855-2181 *Toll Free Tel:* 800-987-8790 *E-mail:* info@lmw.org *Web Site:* lmw.org; store.lmw.org, pg 113

Raffensperger, Daniel, Seedling Publications Inc, 520 E Bainbridge St, Elizabethtown, PA 17022 *Toll Free Tel:* 800-233-0759 *Toll Free Fax:* 888-834-1303 *E-mail:* edcsr@continentalpress.com *Web Site:* www.continentalpress.com, pg 186

Raffio, Michael, Pflaum Publishing Group, 3055 Kettering Blvd, Suite 100, Dayton, OH 45439 *Toll Free Tel:* 800-523-4625; 800-543-4383 (ext 1136, cust serv) *Toll Free Fax:* 800-370-4450 *E-mail:* service@pflaum.com *Web Site:* www.pflaum.com, pg 159

Rafter, Katherine, Art of Living, PrimaMedia Inc, 1250 Bethlehem Pike, Suite 241, Hatfield, PA 19440 *Tel:* 267-421-7326 *E-mail:* info@artoflivingprimamedia.com *Web Site:* artoflivingprimamedia.com, pg 17

Ragan-Fore, Jennifer, International Society for Technology in Education, 2111 Wilson Blvd, Suite 300, Arlington, VA 22201 *Tel:* 503-342-2848 (intl) *Toll Free Tel:* 800-336-5191 (US & CN) *Fax:* 541-302-3778 *E-mail:* iste@iste.org *Web Site:* www.iste.org, pg 103

Rager, Shari, American Medical Writers Association (AMWA), 9841 Washingtonian Blvd, Suite 500-26, Gaithersburg, MD 20878 *Tel:* 240-238-0940 *Fax:* 301-294-9006 *E-mail:* amwa@amwa.org *Web Site:* www.amwa.org, pg 496

Ragin, Bria, Random House Children's Books, c/o Penguin Random House LLC, 1745 Broadway, New York, NY 10019 *Tel:* 212-782-9000 *Web Site:* www.rhcbooks.com, pg 170

Ragland, Kelley, St Martin's Press, LLC, 120 Broadway, New York, NY 10271 *E-mail:* publicity@stmartins.com; trademarketing@stmartins.com; foreignrights@stmartins.com *Web Site:* us.macmillan.com/smp, pg 180

Rago, Martha, Random House Children's Books, c/o Penguin Random House LLC, 1745 Broadway, New York, NY 10019 *Tel:* 212-782-9000 *Web Site:* www.rhcbooks.com, pg 169

Rahaeuser, Alice, Random House Children's Books, c/o Penguin Random House LLC, 1745 Broadway, New York, NY 10019 *Tel:* 212-782-9000 *Web Site:* www.rhcbooks.com, pg 170

Rahill, Hannah, Random House Publishing Group, 1745 Broadway, New York, NY 10019 *Toll Free Tel:* 800-200-3552 *Web Site:* www.randomhousebooks.com, pg 170

Rahm, Willi, Alan Wofsy Fine Arts, 1109 Geary Blvd, San Francisco, CA 94109 *Tel:* 415-292-6500 *Toll Free Tel:* 800-660-6403 *Fax:* 415-292-6594 (off & cust serv); 510-251-1840 (acctg) *E-mail:* order@art-books.com (orders); editeur@earthlink.net (edit); beauxarts@earthlink.net (cust serv) *Web Site:* www.art-books.com, pg 231

Rahn, Jillian, Sourcebooks LLC, 1935 Brookdale Rd, Suite 139, Naperville, IL 60563 *Tel:* 630-961-3900 *Toll Free Tel:* 800-432-7444 *Fax:* 630-961-2168 *E-mail:* info@sourcebooks.com *Web Site:* www.sourcebooks.com, pg 194

Rahner, Clare, Encounter Books, 900 Broadway, Suite 601, New York, NY 10003 *Tel:* 212-871-6310 *Toll Free Tel:* 855-203-7220 *E-mail:* publicity@encounterbooks.com *Web Site:* www.encounterbooks.com, pg 66

Rahrig, Jana, Industrial Press Inc, One Chestnut St, South Norwalk, CT 06854 *Tel:* 203-956-5593 *Toll Free Tel:* 888-528-7852 (ext 1, cust serv) *E-mail:* info@industrialpress.com *Web Site:* books.industrialpress.com; ebooks.industrialpress.com, pg 100

Raihofer, Susan, David Black Agency, 335 Adams St, 27th fl, Suite 2707, Brooklyn, NY 11201 *Tel:* 718-852-5500 *Fax:* 718-852-5539 *Web Site:* www.davidblackagency.com, pg 450

Railsback, Julie, Andrews McMeel Publishing LLC, 1130 Walnut St, Kansas City, MO 64106-2109 *Tel:* 816-581-7500 *Toll Free Tel:* 800-851-8923 *Web Site:* www.andrewsmcmeel.com; publishing.andrewsmcmeel.com, pg 14

Raines, Nicholas A, The Ambassador Richard C Holbrooke Distinguished Achievement Award, PO Box 461, Wright Brothers Branch, Dayton, OH 45409-0461 *Tel:* 937-298-5072 *E-mail:* sharon.rab@daytonliterarypeaceprize.org *Web Site:* www.daytonliterarypeaceprize.org, pg 572

Raines, Nicholas A, Dayton Literary Peace Prize, PO Box 461, Wright Brothers Branch, Dayton, OH 45409-0461 *Tel:* 937-298-5072 *Web Site:* www.daytonliterarypeaceprize.org, pg 595

Rains, Lesley, University of Pittsburgh Press, 7500 Thomas Blvd, Pittsburgh, PA 15260 *Tel:* 412-383-2456 *Fax:* 412-383-2466 *E-mail:* info@upress.pitt.edu *Web Site:* www.upress.pitt.edu, pg 219

Raissian, Katie, Scribner, 1230 Avenue of the Americas, New York, NY 10020 *Web Site:* www.simonandschusterpublishing.com/scribner/, pg 185

Raja, Gautham, Penguin Random House Canada, a Penguin Random House company, 320 Front St W, Suite 1400, Toronto, ON M5V 3B6, Canada *Tel:* 416-364-4449 *Toll Free Tel:* 888-523-9292 (cust serv) *E-mail:* canadaweb@penguinrandomhouse.com; customerservicescanada@penguinrandomhouse.com *Web Site:* www.penguinrandomhouse.ca, pg 416

Rajagopala, Raaga, Random House Publishing Group, 1745 Broadway, New York, NY 10019 *Toll Free Tel:* 800-200-3552 *Web Site:* www.randomhousebooks.com, pg 171

Rajamani, Madhu, diacriTech Inc, 4 S Market St, 4th fl, Boston, MA 02109 *Tel:* 617-600-3366 *Fax:* 617-848-2938 *Web Site:* www.diacritech.com, pg 438

Rajbanshi, Dr Reema, Bowling Green State University Creative Writing Program, Dept of English, 212 East Hall, Bowling Green, OH 43403-0001 *Tel:* 419-372-6864; 419-372-2576 *Fax:* 419-372-0333 *E-mail:* english@bgsu.edu *Web Site:* www.bgsu.edu/academics/creative-writing, pg 561

Rajendran, Nithya, Penguin Random House Audio Publishing Group, 1745 Broadway, New York, NY 10019 *Toll Free Tel:* 800-793-2665 (cust serv) *E-mail:* audio@penguinrandomhouse.com; ecustomerservice@penguinrandomhouse.com *Web Site:* www.penguinrandomhouseaudio.com, pg 154

Rak, Brian, Focus, PO Box 390007, Cambridge, MA 02139-0001 *Tel:* 317-635-9250 *Fax:* 317-635-9292 *E-mail:* customer@hackettpublishing.com; editorial@hackettpublishing.com *Web Site:* focusbookstore.com; www.hackettpublishing.com, pg 73

Rakunas, Adam, Science Fiction and Fantasy Writers Association, Inc (SFWA), PO Box 215, San Lorenzo, CA 94580 *Tel:* 860-698-0536 *E-mail:* office@sfwa.org; operations@sfwa.org *Web Site:* www.sfwa.org, pg 519

Rakunas, Adam, SFWA Nebula Awards, PO Box 215, San Lorenzo, CA 94580 *Tel:* 860-698-0536 *E-mail:* office@sfwa.org; operations@sfwa.org *Web Site:* www.sfwa.org, pg 661

Ram, Hari, Chronicle Books LLC, 680 Second St, San Francisco, CA 94107 *Tel:* 415-537-4200 *Fax:* 415-537-4460 (perms) *E-mail:* hello@chroniclebooks.com; subrights@chroniclebooks.com *Web Site:* www.chroniclebooks.com, pg 47

Raman, Praveena, San Francisco Writers Conference, 1901 Cleveland Ave, Suite D, Santa Rosa, CA 94501 *Tel:* 415-689-6301 *E-mail:* registrations@sfwriters.org; director@sfwriters.org; bizdev@sfwriters.org *Web Site:* www.sfwriters.org, pg 557

Raman, Praveena, San Francisco Writing Contest (SFWC), 1901 Cleveland Ave, Suite D, Santa Rosa, CA 94501 *Tel:* 415-689-6301 *E-mail:* contest@sfwriters.org; director@sfwriters.org *Web Site:* www.sfwriters.org, pg 658

Rambert-Valaskova, Lisa, Transatlantic Agency, 2 Bloor St E, Suite 3500, Toronto, ON M4W 1A8, Canada *Tel:* 416-488-9214 *E-mail:* info@transatlanticagency.com; royalties@transatlanticagency.com *Web Site:* www.transatlanticagency.com, pg 479

Ramcharan, Brian, Penguin Random House Audio Publishing Group, 1745 Broadway, New York, NY 10019 *Toll Free Tel:* 800-793-2665 (cust serv) *E-mail:* audio@penguinrandomhouse.com; ecustomerservice@penguinrandomhouse.com *Web Site:* www.penguinrandomhouseaudio.com, pg 154

Ramer, Susan, Don Congdon Associates Inc, 110 William St, Suite 2202, New York, NY 10038-3914 *Tel:* 212-645-1229 *Fax:* 212-727-2688 *E-mail:* dca@doncongdon.com *Web Site:* www.doncongdon.com, pg 454

Ramirez, Brittany, Random House Children's Books, c/o Penguin Random House LLC, 1745 Broadway, New York, NY 10019 *Tel:* 212-782-9000 *Web Site:* www.rhcbooks.com, pg 170

Ramirez, Jason, Viking Penguin, c/o Penguin Random House LLC, 1745 Broadway, New York, NY 10019 *Tel:* 212-782-9000 *Web Site:* www.penguin.com/overview-vikingbooks/; www.penguin.com/pamela-dorman-books-overview/; www.penguin.com/penguin-classics-overview/; www.penguin.com/penguin-life-overview/, pg 225

Ramirez, Sofia, Penguin Random House Canada, a Penguin Random House company, 320 Front St W, Suite 1400, Toronto, ON M5V 3B6, Canada *Tel:* 416-364-4449 *Toll Free Tel:* 888-523-9292 (cust serv) *E-mail:* canadaweb@penguinrandomhouse.com; customerservicescanada@penguinrandomhouse.com *Web Site:* www.penguinrandomhouse.ca, pg 416

Ramondo, Anthony, Berkley, c/o Penguin Random House LLC, 1745 Broadway, 19th fl, New York, NY 10019 *Tel:* 212-366-2000 *Web Site:* www.penguin.com/publishers/berkley/; www.penguin.com/ace-overview/, pg 28

Ramondo, Anthony, Dutton, c/o Penguin Random House LLC, 1745 Broadway, New York, NY 10019 Tel: 212-366-2000 Web Site: www.penguin.com/dutton-overview/; www.penguin.com/plume-books-overview/; www.penguin.com/tiny-reparations-overview/, pg 62

Ramondo, Anthony, GP Putnam's Sons, c/o Penguin Random House LLC, 1745 Broadway, New York, NY 10019 Tel: 212-782-9000 Web Site: www.penguin.com/putnam/, pg 167

Ramos, Alex, Eisenbrauns, 820 N University Dr, USB 1, Suite C, University Park, PA 16802-1003 Tel: 814-865-1327 Toll Free Tel: 800-326-9180 (orders & cust serv) Fax: 814-863-1408 Toll Free Fax: 877-778-2665 (orders) E-mail: orders@psupress.org; customerservice@psupress.org Web Site: www.eisenbrauns.org, pg 64

Ramos, Alex, Penn State University Press, University Support Bldg 1, Suite C, 820 N University Dr, University Park, PA 16802-1003 Tel: 814-865-1327 Toll Free Tel: 800-326-9180 (orders & cust serv) Fax: 814-863-1408 Toll Free Fax: 877-778-2665 (book orders) E-mail: orders@psupress.org; customerservice@psupress.org Web Site: www.psupress.org, pg 157

Ramos, Mariana, Random House Children's Books, c/o Penguin Random House LLC, 1745 Broadway, New York, NY 10019 Tel: 212-782-9000 Web Site: www.rhcbooks.com, pg 170

Ramos, Michelle, HarperCollins Publishers LLC, 195 Broadway, New York, NY 10007 Tel: 212-207-7000 Web Site: www.harpercollins.com, pg 87

Ramos, Sophia, Sourcebooks LLC, 1935 Brookdale Rd, Suite 139, Naperville, IL 60563 Tel: 630-961-3900 Toll Free Tel: 800-432-7444 Fax: 630-961-2168 E-mail: info@sourcebooks.com Web Site: www.sourcebooks.com, pg 195

Ramsahai, Sharon, Penguin Random House Canada, a Penguin Random House company, 320 Front St W, Suite 1400, Toronto, ON M5V 3B6, Canada Tel: 416-364-4449 Toll Free Tel: 888-523-9292 (cust serv) E-mail: canadaweb@penguinrandomhouse.com; customerservicescanada@penguinrandomhouse.com Web Site: www.penguinrandomhouse.ca, pg 416

Ramsay, Jo, Transatlantic Agency, 2 Bloor St E, Suite 3500, Toronto, ON M4W 1A8, Canada Tel: 416-488-9214 E-mail: info@transatlanticagency.com; royalties@transatlanticagency.com Web Site: www.transatlanticagency.com, pg 479

Ramsess, Akili, National Press Photographers Association Inc (NPPA), 120 Hooper St, Athens, GA 30602-3018 Tel: 706-542-2506 E-mail: info@nppa.org; director@nppa.org Web Site: nppa.org, pg 514

Ramsey, Becca, Macmillan, 120 Broadway, 22nd fl, New York, NY 10271 E-mail: press.inquiries@macmillan.com Web Site: us.macmillan.com, pg 122

Ramsudh, Sarah, Macmillan, 120 Broadway, 22nd fl, New York, NY 10271 E-mail: press.inquiries@macmillan.com Web Site: us.macmillan.com, pg 122

Rand Silverman, Erica, Stimola Literary Studio Inc, 11 Briarwood Lane, West Tisbury, MA 02575 Tel: 201-945-9353 Fax: 201-490-5920 E-mail: info@stimolaliterarystudio.com Web Site: www.stimolaliterarystudio.com, pg 478

Randall, Deidre C, Peter E Randall Publisher, 5 Greenleaf Woods Dr, Suite 102, Portsmouth, NH 03801 Tel: 603-431-5667 Fax: 603-431-3566 E-mail: media@perpublisher.com Web Site: www.perpublisher.com, pg 169

Randall, Lee, Oceanview Publishing Inc, PO Box 3168, Sarasota, FL 34230 Tel: 941-387-8500 Web Site: oceanviewpub.com, pg 145

Randisi, Robert J, The Private Eye Writers of America (PWA), 3665 S Needles Hwy, 7G, Laughlin, NV 89029 Web Site: www.privateeyewriters.com, pg 518

Randol, Susan, Penguin Random House LLC, 1745 Broadway, New York, NY 10019 Tel: 212-782-9000 Toll Free Tel: 800-726-0600 Web Site: www.penguinrandomhouse.com, pg 155

Randolph, Ladette, Ploughshares, Emerson College, 120 Boylston St, Boston, MA 02116 Tel: 617-824-3757 E-mail: pshares@pshares.org Web Site: www.pshares.org, pg 161

Randolph, Ladette, Ploughshares Emerging Writer's Contest, Emerson College, 120 Boylston St, Boston, MA 02116 Tel: 617-824-3757 E-mail: pshares@pshares.org Web Site: www.pshares.org, pg 650

Randolph, Tony, Regular Baptist Press, 3715 N Ventura Dr, Arlington Heights, IL 60004 Tel: 847-843-1600 Toll Free Tel: 800-727-4440 (cust serv) Fax: 847-843-3757 E-mail: orders@rbpstore.org Web Site: regularbaptistpress.org, pg 174

Ranic, Elena, Dundurn Press Ltd, PO Box 19510, RPO Manulife, Toronto, ON M4W 3T9, Canada Tel: 416-214-5544 E-mail: info@dundurn.com; publicity@dundurn.com; sales@dundurn.com Web Site: www.dundurn.com, pg 401

Rankin, Jenni, Annual Reviews, 1875 S Grant St, Suite 700, San Mateo, CA 94402 Tel: 650-493-4400 Toll Free Tel: 800-523-8635 Fax: 650-424-0910; 650-855-9815 E-mail: service@annualreviews.org Web Site: www.annualreviews.org, pg 14

Rankin, Kelly, Penguin Random House Canada, a Penguin Random House company, 320 Front St W, Suite 1400, Toronto, ON M5V 3B6, Canada Tel: 416-364-4449 Toll Free Tel: 888-523-9292 (cust serv) E-mail: canadaweb@penguinrandomhouse.com; customerservicescanada@penguinrandomhouse.com Web Site: www.penguinrandomhouse.ca, pg 416

Rankin, Mimi, HarperCollins Children's Books, 195 Broadway, New York, NY 10007 Tel: 212-207-7000 Web Site: www.harpercollins.com/childrens, pg 85

Rao, Angie, Tor Publishing Group, 120 Broadway, New York, NY 10271 Toll Free Tel: 800-455-0340 (Macmillan) E-mail: torpublicity@tor.com; forgepublicity@forgebooks.com Web Site: us.macmillan.com/torpublishinggroup, pg 208

Rao, Shan, Kundiman Retreat, Fordham University, English Dept, 113 W 60 St, Rm 924, New York, NY 10023 E-mail: info@kundiman.org Web Site: www.kundiman.org, pg 556

Raoult, Marie-Madeleine, Editions de la Pleine Lune, 223 34 Ave, Lachine, QC H8T 1Z4, Canada Tel: 514-634-7954 E-mail: editpllune@videotron.ca Web Site: www.pleinelune.qc.ca, pg 402

Rapach, Nate, Sourcebooks LLC, 1935 Brookdale Rd, Suite 139, Naperville, IL 60563 Tel: 630-961-3900 Toll Free Tel: 800-432-7444 Fax: 630-961-2168 E-mail: info@sourcebooks.com Web Site: www.sourcebooks.com, pg 195

Raphel, Neil, Brigantine Media, 211 North Ave, St Johnsbury, VT 05819 Tel: 802-751-8802 Fax: 802-751-8804 Web Site: brigantinemedia.com, pg 37

Rapp, Alan, The Monacelli Press, 65 Bleecker St, 8th fl, New York, NY 10012 Tel: 212-652-5400 E-mail: contact@monacellipress.com Web Site: www.phaidon.com/monacelli, pg 133

Raps, Beth, SDP Publishing Solutions LLC, 36 Captain's Way, East Bridgewater, MA 02333 Tel: 617-775-0656 Web Site: www.sdppublishingsolutions.com, pg 444

Rarick, Ethan, Institute of Governmental Studies, 109 Moses Hall, No 2370, Berkeley, CA 94720-2370 Tel: 510-642-1428 E-mail: igspress@berkeley.edu Web Site: www.igs.berkeley.edu, pg 101

Rasanen, John, American Geosciences Institute (AGI), 4220 King St, Alexandria, VA 22302-1502 Tel: 703-379-2480 (ext 246) E-mail: agi@americangeosciences.org Web Site: www.americangeosciences.org; www.geosciencestore.org, pg 10

Rasche, Janet, Penguin Random House LLC, 1745 Broadway, New York, NY 10019 Tel: 212-782-9000 Toll Free Tel: 800-726-0600 Web Site: www.penguinrandomhouse.com, pg 155

Rasenberger, Mary, The Authors Guild®, 31 E 32 St, Suite 901, New York, NY 10016 Tel: 212-563-5904 Fax: 212-564-5363 E-mail: staff@authorsguild.org Web Site: www.authorsguild.org, pg 500

Rasenberger, Mary, The Authors Registry Inc, 31 E 32 St, 7th fl, New York, NY 10016 Tel: 212-563-6920 E-mail: staff@authorsregistry.org Web Site: www.authorsregistry.org, pg 500

Raskin, Rebecca, HarperCollins Publishers LLC, 195 Broadway, New York, NY 10007 Tel: 212-207-7000 Web Site: www.harpercollins.com, pg 87

Rasmussen, Daniel, Bethlehem Books, 10194 Garfield St S, Bathgate, ND 58216 Toll Free Tel: 800-757-6831 Fax: 701-265-3716 E-mail: contact@bethlehembooks.com Web Site: www.bethlehembooks.com, pg 29

Rasmussen, Jim, Bethlehem Books, 10194 Garfield St S, Bathgate, ND 58216 Toll Free Tel: 800-757-6831 Fax: 701-265-3716 E-mail: contact@bethlehembooks.com Web Site: www.bethlehembooks.com, pg 29

Rasmussen, Katie, Vermont College of Fine Arts MFA in Writing for Children & Young Adults Program, 36 College St, Montpelier, VT 05602 Toll Free Tel: 866-934-VCFA (934-8232) Web Site: vcfa.edu/mfa-writing-for-children-and-young-adults, pg 567

Rasmussen, Lydia, Adams Media, 100 Technology Center Dr, Suite 501, Stoughton, MA 02072 Tel: 508-427-7100 Web Site: www.simonandschuster.com, pg 4

Ratcliff, Robert A, Westminster John Knox Press (WJK), 100 Witherspoon St, Louisville, KY 40202-1396 Tel: 502-569-5052 Toll Free Tel: 800-523-1631 (US & CN) Fax: 502-569-8308 Toll Free Fax: 800-541-5113 (US & CN) E-mail: customer_service@wjkbooks.com; orders@wjkbooks.com Web Site: www.wjkbooks.com, pg 228

Rath, Morgan, Farrar, Straus & Giroux Books for Young Readers, 120 Broadway, New York, NY 10271 Tel: 212-741-6900 Toll Free Tel: 888-330-8477 (orders) E-mail: childrens.publicity@macmillanusa.com; childrensrights@macmillanusa.com Web Site: us.macmillan.com/mackids, pg 70

Rath, Morgan, Roaring Brook Press, 120 Broadway, New York, NY 10271 Tel: 646-307-5151 Web Site: us.macmillan.com/publishers/roaring-brook-press, pg 176

Rathbun, Jennifer, The Ashland Poetry Press, Bixler Center for the Humanities, Ashland University, 401 College Ave, Ashland, OH 44805 E-mail: app@ashland.edu Web Site: www.ashlandpoetrypress.com, pg 19

Rathjen, Melinda, Hachette Nashville, 6100 Tower Circle, Room 210, Franklin, TN 37067 Tel: 615-221-0996 Fax: 615-221-0962 Web Site: www.hachettebookgroup.com/imprint/hachette-nashville/, pg 83

Ratliff, Therese, Cistercian Publications, Saint John's Abbey, PO Box 7500, Collegeville, MN 56321 Tel: 320-363-2213 Toll Free Tel: 800-436-8431 Fax: 320-363-3299 Toll Free Fax: 800-445-5899 E-mail: sales@litpress.org Web Site: www.cistercianpublications.org, pg 48

Ratliff, Therese L, Liturgical Press, PO Box 7500, St John's Abbey, Collegeville, MN 56321-7500 Tel: 320-363-2213 Toll Free Tel: 800-858-5450 Fax: 320-363-3299 Toll Free Fax: 800-445-5899 E-mail: sales@litpress.org Web Site: www.litpress.org, pg 118

Ratnam, Rekha, Print Industries Market Information and Research Organization (PRIMIR), 1899 Preston White Dr, Reston, VA 20191 Tel: 703-264-7200 E-mail: aptech@aptech.org Web Site: www.printtechnologies.org; www.npes.org/primirresearch/primir.aspx, pg 517

Rauchbauer, Martin, Djerassi Resident Artists Program, 2325 Bear Gulch Rd, Woodside, CA 94062 Tel: 650-747-0691 E-mail: info@djerassi.org Web Site: www.djerassi.org, pg 554

Rauenhorst, Whitney, Princeton University Press, 41 William St, Princeton, NJ 08540-5237 Tel: 609-258-4900 Fax: 609-258-6305 E-mail: info@press.princeton.edu Web Site: press.princeton.edu, pg 164

Ravenelle, Anna, HarperCollins Children's Books, 195 Broadway, New York, NY 10007 Tel: 212-207-7000 Web Site: www.harpercollins.com/childrens, pg 85

Ravenelle, Anna, Houghton Mifflin Harcourt Trade & Reference Division, 125 High St, Boston, MA 02110 *Tel:* 617-351-5000 *Web Site:* www.hmhco.com, pg 96

Rawitch, Jeremy, RAND Corp, 1776 Main St, Santa Monica, CA 90407-2138 *Tel:* 310-393-0411 *Fax:* 310-393-4818 *Web Site:* www.rand.org, pg 169

Rawlings, Jeremy, HarperCollins Canada Ltd, 22 Adelaide St W, 41st fl, Toronto, ON M5H 4E3, Canada *Tel:* 416-975-9334 *E-mail:* hcorder@harpercollins.com *Web Site:* www.harpercollins.ca, pg 409

Rawlings, Wendy, University of Alabama Program in Creative Writing, PO Box 870244, Tuscaloosa, AL 35487-0244 *Tel:* 205-348-5065 *Fax:* 205-348-1388 *E-mail:* english@ua.edu *Web Site:* www.as.ua.edu/english, pg 566

Rawlins, Dr Brad, Arkansas State University Graphic Communications Program, Dept of Media, PO Box 1930, State University, AR 72467-1930 *Tel:* 870-972-3114 *Fax:* 870-972-3321 *Web Site:* www.astate.edu, pg 561

Rawlins, Melissa, LRS, 6150 Little Willow Rd, Payette, ID 83661 *Toll Free Tel:* 800-255-5002 *E-mail:* largeprint@lrsbooks.com *Web Site:* www.lrsbooks.com, pg 121

Rawls, Sue, Houghton Mifflin Harcourt Assessments, One Pierce Place, Itasca, IL 60143 *Tel:* 630-467-7000 *Toll Free Tel:* 800-323-9540 *Fax:* 630-467-7192 (cust serv) *E-mail:* assessmentsorders@hmhco.com *Web Site:* www.hmhco.com/classroom-solutions/assessment, pg 96

Ray, Carissa, Houghton Mifflin Harcourt, 125 High St, Boston, MA 02110 *Tel:* 617-351-5000 *Toll Free Tel:* 855-969-4642; 800-225-5425 (K-12 educ materials); 800-323-9540 (assessment materials); 877-219-1537 (SkillsTutor); 888-242-6747 (Innovation in Educ Group); 800-225-3362 (Trade & Ref Div) *Toll Free Fax:* 800-269-5232 *E-mail:* myhmhco@hmhco.com *Web Site:* www.hmhco.com, pg 96

Ray, Jo-Anne, Canadian Institute for Studies in Publishing (CISP), Simon Fraser University at Harbour Centre, 515 W Hastings St, Suite 3576, Vancouver, BC V6B 5K3, Canada *Tel:* 778-782-5242 *E-mail:* pub-info@sfu.ca *Web Site:* publishing.sfu.ca/research-2, pg 502

Ray, Priyanka, Beacon Press, 24 Farnsworth St, Boston, MA 02210-1409 *Tel:* 617-742-2110 *Fax:* 617-723-3097 *E-mail:* production@beacon.org *Web Site:* www.beacon.org, pg 25

Ray, Trinity, The Tuesday Agency, 404 E College St, Suite 408, Iowa City, IA 52240 *Tel:* 319-338-7080; 319-400-9031 (cell) *E-mail:* info@tuesdayagency.com *Web Site:* tuesdayagency.com, pg 487

Raycroft, Kristie, Chronicle Books LLC, 680 Second St, San Francisco, CA 94107 *Tel:* 415-537-4200 *Fax:* 415-537-4460 (perms) *E-mail:* hello@chroniclebooks.com; subrights@chroniclebooks.com *Web Site:* www.chroniclebooks.com, pg 47

Raye, Janis, Brigantine Media, 211 North Ave, St Johnsbury, VT 05819 *Tel:* 802-751-8802 *Fax:* 802-751-8804 *Web Site:* brigantinemedia.com, pg 37

Rayess, Dena, Chronicle Books LLC, 680 Second St, San Francisco, CA 94107 *Tel:* 415-537-4200 *Fax:* 415-537-4460 (perms) *E-mail:* hello@chroniclebooks.com; subrights@chroniclebooks.com *Web Site:* www.chroniclebooks.com, pg 47

Raymond, Andrea, Bear & Co Inc, One Park St, Rochester, VT 05767 *Tel:* 802-767-3174 *Toll Free Tel:* 800-932-3277 *Fax:* 802-767-3726 *E-mail:* customerservice@InnerTraditions.com *Web Site:* InnerTraditions.com, pg 26

Raymond, Andrea, Inner Traditions International Ltd, One Park St, Rochester, VT 05767 *Tel:* 802-767-3174 *Toll Free Tel:* 800-246-8648 *Fax:* 802-767-3726 *E-mail:* customerservice@InnerTraditions.com *Web Site:* www.InnerTraditions.com, pg 101

Raymond, Chris, Harry N Abrams Inc, 195 Broadway, 9th fl, New York, NY 10007 *Tel:* 212-206-7715 *Toll Free Tel:* 800-345-1359 *Fax:* 212-645-8437 *E-mail:* abrams@abramsbooks.com; publicity@abramsbooks.com; sales@abramsbooks.com *Web Site:* www.abramsbooks.com, pg 2

Raymond, Midge, Ashland Creek Press, 2305 Ashland St, Suite C417, Ashland, OR 97520 *Tel:* 760-300-3620 *E-mail:* editors@ashlandcreekpress.com *Web Site:* www.ashlandcreekpress.com, pg 18

Raynor, Bruce, Hillman Prizes for Journalism, 330 W 42 St, Suite 900, New York, NY 10036 *Tel:* 646-448-6413 *Web Site:* www.hillmanfoundation.org, pg 613

Razo, Rebecca, Walter Foster Publishing, 26391 Crown Valley Pkwy, Suite 220, Mission Viejo, CA 92691 *Tel:* 949-380-7510 *Fax:* 949-380-7575 *E-mail:* walterfoster@quarto.com *Web Site:* www.quartoknows.com/walter-foster, pg 74

Razzouk, Monique, Random House Children's Books, c/o Penguin Random House LLC, 1745 Broadway, New York, NY 10019 *Tel:* 212-782-9000 *Web Site:* www.rhcbooks.com, pg 170

Reagan, Don, Newbury Street Press, 99-101 Newbury St, Boston, MA 02116 *Tel:* 617-226-1206 *Toll Free Tel:* 888-296-3447 (NEHGS membership) *Fax:* 617-536-7307 *E-mail:* thebookstore@nehgs.org *Web Site:* www.americanancestors.org, pg 141

Reale, Tom, Brown Books Publishing Group (BBPG), 16250 Knoll Trail, Suite 205, Dallas, TX 75248 *Tel:* 972-381-0009 *E-mail:* publishing@brownbooks.com *Web Site:* www.brownbooks.com, pg 38

Reaman, Micki, Oregon State University Press, 121 The Valley Library, Corvallis, OR 97331-4501 *Tel:* 541-737-3166, pg 147

Reamer, Jodi Esq, Writers House, 21 W 26 St, New York, NY 10010 *Tel:* 212-685-2400 *Web Site:* www.writershouse.com, pg 482

Reardon, Emily, Alfred A Knopf, c/o Penguin Random House LLC, 1745 Broadway, New York, NY 10019 *Tel:* 212-751-2600 *Fax:* 212-940-7390 (dom rts); 212-572-2662 (foreign rts) *Web Site:* knopfdoubleday.com/imprint/knopf/; knopfdoubleday.com, pg 110

Reardon, Emily, Pantheon Books, c/o Penguin Random House LLC, 1745 Broadway, New York, NY 10019 *Tel:* 212-751-2600 *Fax:* 212-940-7390 (dom rts); 212-572-2662 (foreign rts) *Web Site:* knopfdoubleday.com/imprint/pantheon/; knopfdoubleday.com, pg 150

Reaume, Julie K, Michigan State University Press (MSU Press), Manly Miles Bldg, Suite 25, 1405 S Harrison Rd, East Lansing, MI 48823-5245 *Tel:* 517-355-9543 *Fax:* 517-432-2611 *Web Site:* msupress.org, pg 130

Reback, Erin, HarperCollins Publishers LLC, 195 Broadway, New York, NY 10007 *Tel:* 212-207-7000 *Web Site:* www.harpercollins.com, pg 87

Rebora, Anthony, ASCD, 2800 Shirlington Rd, Suite 1001, Arlington, VA 22206 *Tel:* 703-578-9600 *Toll Free Tel:* 800-933-2723 *Fax:* 703-575-5400 *E-mail:* member@ascd.org; books@ascd.org *Web Site:* www.ascd.org, pg 18

Reck, Sarah, Random House Children's Books, c/o Penguin Random House LLC, 1745 Broadway, New York, NY 10019 *Tel:* 212-782-9000 *Web Site:* www.rhcbooks.com, pg 170

Reckelhoff, Judy, BoardSource, 750 Ninth St NW, Suite 520, Washington, DC 20001-4793 *Tel:* 202-349-2500 *E-mail:* members@boardsource.org; mediarelations@boardsource.org *Web Site:* www.boardsource.org, pg 33

Recore, Cassey, Association of Community Publishers Inc (ACP), 8119 Circuit Rider Path, Cicero, NY 13039 *Toll Free Tel:* 877-203-2327 *Fax:* 315-670-3121 (memb registration) *E-mail:* info@communitypublishers.com *Web Site:* www.communitypublishers.com, pg 499

Rector, Jade, Harry N Abrams Inc, 195 Broadway, 9th fl, New York, NY 10007 *Tel:* 212-206-7715 *Toll Free Tel:* 800-345-1359 *Fax:* 212-645-8437 *E-mail:* abrams@abramsbooks.com; publicity@abramsbooks.com; sales@abramsbooks.com *Web Site:* www.abramsbooks.com, pg 3

Redd, Kimberly L, David H Clift Scholarship, 225 N Michigan Ave, Suite 1300, Chicago, IL 60601 *Toll Free Tel:* 800-545-2433 (ext 4279) *Fax:* 312-280-4279 *E-mail:* scholarships@ala.org *Web Site:* www.ala.org/scholarships, pg 590

Redkin, Andy, Alan Wofsy Fine Arts, 1109 Geary Blvd, San Francisco, CA 94109 *Tel:* 415-292-6500 *Toll Free Tel:* 800-660-6403 *Fax:* 415-292-6594 (off & cust serv); 510-251-1840 (acctg) *E-mail:* order@art-books.com (orders); editeur@earthlink.net (edit); beauxarts@earthlink.net (cust serv) *Web Site:* www.art-books.com, pg 231

Redlich, Josh, Random House Children's Books, c/o Penguin Random House LLC, 1745 Broadway, New York, NY 10019 *Tel:* 212-782-9000 *Web Site:* www.rhcbooks.com, pg 170

Redmon, Hilary, Random House Publishing Group, 1745 Broadway, New York, NY 10019 *Toll Free Tel:* 800-200-3552 *Web Site:* www.randomhousebooks.com, pg 170

Redmond, Robert, Cold Spring Harbor Laboratory Press, 500 Sunnyside Blvd, Woodbury, NY 11797-2924 *Tel:* 516-422-4100 *Toll Free Tel:* 800-843-4388 *E-mail:* cshpress@cshl.edu *Web Site:* www.cshlpress.com, pg 50

Reed, Adam, The Joy Harris Literary Agency Inc, 1501 Broadway, Suite 2310, New York, NY 10036 *Tel:* 212-924-6269 *Fax:* 212-840-5776 *E-mail:* contact@joyharrisliterary.com *Web Site:* www.joyharrisliterary.com, pg 462

Reed, Adrienne, Wales Literary Agency Inc, 1508 Tenth Ave E, No 401, Seattle, WA 98102 *Tel:* 206-553-9684 *E-mail:* waleslit@waleslit.com *Web Site:* www.waleslit.com, pg 481

Reed, Alyson, Linguistic Society of America (LSA), 522 21 St NW, Suite 120, Washington, DC 20006-5012 *Tel:* 202-835-1714 *Fax:* 202-835-1717 *E-mail:* lsa@lsadc.org; membership@lsadc.org *Web Site:* www.linguisticsociety.org, pg 509

Reed, Chris, University of Toronto Press, Book Publishing Div, 800 Bay St, Mezzanine, Toronto, ON M5S 3A9, Canada *Tel:* 416-978-2239 *Fax:* 416-978-4736 *E-mail:* utpbooks@utorontopress.com (orders) *Web Site:* utorontopress.com, pg 423

Reed, Dakota, Random House Children's Books, c/o Penguin Random House LLC, 1745 Broadway, New York, NY 10019 *Tel:* 212-782-9000 *Web Site:* www.rhcbooks.com, pg 170

Reed, Derek, Penguin Random House LLC, 1745 Broadway, New York, NY 10019 *Tel:* 212-782-9000 *Toll Free Tel:* 800-726-0600 *Web Site:* www.penguinrandomhouse.com, pg 155

Reed, Frances, The Blackburn Press, PO Box 287, Caldwell, NJ 07006-0287 *Tel:* 973-228-7077 *Fax:* 973-228-7276 *Web Site:* www.blackburnpress.com, pg 30

Reed, Griffin, Boulevard Magazine Short Fiction Contest for Emerging Writers, 3829 Hartford St, St Louis, MO 63116 *E-mail:* editors@boulevardmagazine.org *Web Site:* www.boulevardmagazine.org, pg 583

Reed, Ishmael, American Book Awards, The Raymond House, 655 13 St, Suite 302, Oakland, CA 94612 *Tel:* 916-425-7916 *E-mail:* beforecolumbusfoundation@gmail.com *Web Site:* www.beforecolumbusfoundation.com, pg 573

Reed, Ishmael, Before Columbus Foundation, The Raymond House, 655 13 St, Suite 302, Oakland, CA 94612 *Tel:* 916-425-7916 *E-mail:* beforecolumbusfoundation@gmail.com *Web Site:* beforecolumbusfoundation.com, pg 525

Reed, Robert D, Robert D Reed Publishers, PO Box 1992, Bandon, OR 97411-1192 *Tel:* 541-347-9882 *Fax:* 541-347-9883 *E-mail:* 4bobreed@msn.com *Web Site:* rdrpublishers.com, pg 173

Reeder, Lindsey, Harlequin Enterprises Ltd, Bay Adelaide Centre, East Tower, 22 Adelaide St W, 41st fl, Toronto, ON M5H 4E3, Canada *Tel:* 416-445-5860

Toll Free Tel: 888-432-4879; 800-370-5838 (ebook inquiries) *E-mail:* customerservice@harlequin.com *Web Site:* www.harlequin.com, pg 409

Rees, Mr Lorin, Rees Literary Agency, One Westinghouse Plaza, Suite A203, Boston, MA 02136 *Tel:* 617-227-9014 *Web Site:* www.reesagency.com, pg 473

Reese, Julie, Core/Christian Larew Memorial Scholarship in Library & Information Technology, c/o The American Library Association, 225 N Michigan Ave, Suite 1300, Chicago, IL 60601 *Tel:* 312-944-6780 *Toll Free Tel:* 800-545-2433 *Fax:* 312-440-9374 *E-mail:* scholarships@ala.org *Web Site:* www.ala.org/core, pg 592

Reese, Julie, Core/OCLC Spectrum Scholarship in Library & Information Technology, c/o The American Library Association, 225 N Michigan Ave, Suite 1300, Chicago, IL 60601 *Tel:* 312-944-6780 *Toll Free Tel:* 800-545-2433 *Fax:* 312-440-9374 *E-mail:* scholarships@ala.org *Web Site:* www.ala.org/core, pg 592

Reese, Julie, Margaret Mann Citation, c/o The American Library Association, 225 N Michigan Ave, Suite 1300, Chicago, IL 60601 *Tel:* 312-944-6780 *Toll Free Tel:* 800-545-2433 *Fax:* 312-440-9374 *E-mail:* scholarships@ala.org *Web Site:* www.ala.org/core, pg 629

Reeve, William D, Virginia Kidd Agency Inc, 538 E Harford St, PO Box 278, Milford, PA 18337 *Tel:* 570-296-6205 *Web Site:* vk-agency.com, pg 465

Reeves, Bill, David C Cook, 4050 Lee Vance Dr, Colorado Springs, CO 80918 *Tel:* 719-536-0100 *Toll Free Tel:* 800-323-7543 (orders & cust serv) *Toll Free Fax:* 800-430-0726 (cust serv) *E-mail:* bookstores@davidccook.com; customercare@davidccook.org *Web Site:* www.davidccook.org, pg 52

Reeves, Diane Lindsey, American Book Producers Association (ABPA), 7 Peter Cooper Rd, No 7G, New York, NY 10010 *E-mail:* office@abpaonline.org *Web Site:* www.abpaonline.org, pg 494

Reeves, Howard, Harry N Abrams Inc, 195 Broadway, 9th fl, New York, NY 10007 *Tel:* 212-206-7715 *Toll Free Tel:* 800-345-1359 *Fax:* 212-645-8437 *E-mail:* abrams@abramsbooks.com; publicity@abramsbooks.com; sales@abramsbooks.com *Web Site:* www.abramsbooks.com, pg 3

Reeves, Lynn, Jentel Artist Residency, 130 Lower Piney Rd, Banner, WY 82832 *Tel:* 307-737-2311 *Fax:* 307-737-2305 *E-mail:* jentel@jentelarts.org *Web Site:* www.jentelarts.org, pg 555

Reeves, Roger, University of Texas at Austin, New Writers Project, Dept of English, 204 W 21 St, B-5000, Austin, TX 78712-1164 *Tel:* 512-471-4991 *Fax:* 512-471-4909 *E-mail:* newwritersproject@utexas.edu *Web Site:* liberalarts.utexas.edu/nwp, pg 567

Regal, Joseph, Regal Hoffmann & Associates LLC, 157 13 St, Brooklyn, NY 11215 *Tel:* 212-684-7900 *E-mail:* info@rhaliterary.com; submissions@rhaliterary.com *Web Site:* www.rhaliterary.com, pg 473

Regala, Jae, Robert F Kennedy Book Awards, 1300 19 St NW, Suite 750, Washington, DC 20036 *Tel:* 646-553-4750 *Fax:* 202-463-6606 *E-mail:* info@rfkhumanrights.org *Web Site:* rfkhumanrights.org, pg 620

Regan, Ann, Minnesota Historical Society Press, 345 Kellogg Blvd W, St Paul, MN 55102-1906 *Tel:* 651-259-3205 *Fax:* 651-297-1345 *E-mail:* info-mnhspress@mnhs.org *Web Site:* www.mnhs.org/mnhspress, pg 132

Regan, Claire, Deadline Club, c/o Salmagundi Club, 47 Fifth Ave, New York, NY 10003 *Tel:* 646-481-7584 *E-mail:* info@deadlineclub.org *Web Site:* www.deadlineclub.org, pg 505

Regan, Harold, The H W Wilson Foundation, 750 Third Ave, 13th fl, New York, NY 10017 *Tel:* 212-418-8473 *Web Site:* www.thwwf.org, pg 526

Regan, Michael, The H W Wilson Foundation, 750 Third Ave, 13th fl, New York, NY 10017 *Tel:* 212-418-8473 *Web Site:* www.thwwf.org, pg 526

Regenstreif, Jane, Book Industry Charitable Foundation (BINC), 3135 S State St, Suite 203, Ann Arbor, MI 48108 *Toll Free Tel:* 866-733-9064 *E-mail:* info@bincfoundation.org *Web Site:* www.bincfoundation.org, pg 525

Regenstreif, Jane, Denver Publishing Institute Scholarship, 3135 S State St, Suite 203, Ann Arbor, MI 48108 *Toll Free Tel:* 866-733-9064 *E-mail:* info@bincfoundation.org *Web Site:* www.bincfoundation.org/denver-publishing-institute/, pg 595

Regenstreif, Jane, Carla Gray Memorial Scholarship, 3135 S State St, Suite 203, Ann Arbor, MI 48108 *Toll Free Tel:* 866-733-9064 *E-mail:* info@bincfoundation.org *Web Site:* www.bincfoundation.org/carla-gray/, pg 609

Regenstreif, Jane, Higher Education Scholarship Program, 3135 S State St, Suite 203, Ann Arbor, MI 48108 *Toll Free Tel:* 866-733-9064 *E-mail:* info@bincfoundation.org *Web Site:* www.bincfoundation.org/scholarship, pg 612

Regenstreif, Jane, Susan Kamil Scholarship for Emerging Writers, 3135 S State St, Suite 203, Ann Arbor, MI 48108 *Toll Free Tel:* 866-733-9064 *E-mail:* info@bincfoundation.org *Web Site:* bincfoundation.org/susankamil-scholarship, pg 619

Regenstreif, Jane, George Markey Keating Memorial Scholarships, 3135 S State St, Suite 203, Ann Arbor, MI 48108 *Toll Free Tel:* 866-733-9064 *E-mail:* info@bincfoundation.org *Web Site:* www.bincfoundation.org, pg 619

Regenstreif, Jane, Macmillan Booksellers Professional Development Scholarship, 3135 S State St, Suite 203, Ann Arbor, MI 48108 *Toll Free Tel:* 866-733-9064 *E-mail:* info@bincfoundation.org *Web Site:* www.bincfoundation.org/scholarship, pg 628

Regenstreif, Jane, Karl Pohrt Tribute Award, 3135 S State St, Suite 203, Ann Arbor, MI 48108 *Toll Free Tel:* 866-733-9064 *E-mail:* info@bincfoundation.org *Web Site:* www.bincfoundation.org/scholarship, pg 651

Reggio, Chris, Fox Chapel Publishing Co Inc, 1970 Broad St, East Petersburg, PA 17520 *Tel:* 717-560-4703 *Toll Free Tel:* 800-457-9112 *Fax:* 717-560-4702 *E-mail:* customerservice@foxchapelpublishing.com *Web Site:* www.foxchapelpublishing.com, pg 74

Regoli, Michael, Indiana University Press, Off of Scholarly Publg, Herman B Wells Library 350, 1320 E Tenth St, Bloomington, IN 47405-3907 *Tel:* 812-855-8817 *Fax:* 812-855-7931; 812-855-8507 *E-mail:* iupress@indiana.edu *Web Site:* iupress.org, pg 100

Rehl, Dr Beatrice, Cambridge University Press, One Liberty Plaza, 20th fl, New York, NY 10006 *Tel:* 212-924-3900; 212-337-5000 *Fax:* 212-691-3239; 845-353-4141 *E-mail:* customer_service@cambridge.org; orders@cambridge.org; subscriptions_newyork@cambridge.org *Web Site:* www.cambridge.org/us, pg 39

Reich, Stephanie, Vermont College of Fine Arts, MFA in Writing Program, 36 College St, Montpelier, VT 05602 *Tel:* 802-828-8840; 802-828-8839 *Toll Free Tel:* 866-934-VCFA (934-8232) *Fax:* 802-828-8649 *Web Site:* www.vcfa.edu, pg 567

Reichert, Stephen, Beullah Rose Poetry Prize, 2221 Lake Ave, Baltimore, MD 21213 *E-mail:* smartishpace@gmail.com *Web Site:* www.smartishpace.com/poetry-prizes, pg 579

Reichert, Stephen, Erskine J Poetry Prize, 2221 Lake Ave, Baltimore, MD 21213 *E-mail:* smartishpace@gmail.com *Web Site:* www.smartishpace.com/poetry-prizes, pg 600

Reichgott, Stacy, Atria Books, 1230 Avenue of the Americas, New York, NY 10020 *Tel:* 212-698-7000 *Fax:* 212-698-7007 *Web Site:* www.simonandschuster.com, pg 21

Reid, Andie, Quirk Books, 215 Church St, Philadelphia, PA 19106 *Tel:* 215-627-3581 *Fax:* 215-627-5220 *E-mail:* general@quirkbooks.com *Web Site:* www.quirkbooks.com, pg 168

Reid, Daniel, Whiting Awards, 16 Court St, Suite 2308, Brooklyn, NY 11241 *Tel:* 718-701-5962 *E-mail:* info@whiting.org *Web Site:* www.whiting.org, pg 675

Reid, Daniel, Whiting Creative Nonfiction Grant, 16 Court St, Suite 2308, Brooklyn, NY 11241 *Tel:* 718-701-5962 *E-mail:* nonfiction@whiting.org; info@whiting.org *Web Site:* www.whiting.org, pg 675

Reid, Daniel, Whiting Literary Magazine Prizes, 16 Court St, Suite 2308, Brooklyn, NY 11241 *Tel:* 718-701-5962 *E-mail:* info@whiting.org *Web Site:* www.whiting.org/writers/whiting-literary-magazine-prizes, pg 675

Reid, Meg, C Michael Curtis Short Story Book Prize, 186 W Main St, Spartanburg, SC 29306 *Tel:* 864-577-9349 *Fax:* 864-577-0188 *E-mail:* info@hubcity.org; submit@hubcity.org *Web Site:* hubcity.org/press/c-michael-curtis-short-story-book-prize, pg 594

Reid, Meg, Hub City Writing in Place Conference, 186 W Main St, Spartanburg, SC 29306 *Tel:* 864-577-9349 *E-mail:* info@hubcity.org *Web Site:* www.hubcity.org/annual-writing-in-place-conference, pg 554

Reid, Meg, Southern Studies Fellowship in Arts & Letters, 186 W Main St, Spartanburg, SC 29306 *Tel:* 864-577-9349 *E-mail:* info@hubcity.org *Web Site:* southernstudiesfellowship.org, pg 665

Reid, Mollie, Penguin Press, c/o Penguin Random House LLC, 1745 Broadway, New York, NY 10019 *Tel:* 212-782-9000 *E-mail:* penguinpress@penguinrandomhouse.com *Web Site:* www.penguin.com/penguin-press-overview/, pg 154

Reid, Rosalind, Ev Clark/Seth Payne Award for Young Science Journalists, PO Box 17337, Seattle, WA 98127 *Tel:* 206-880-0177 *E-mail:* info@casw.org *Web Site:* casw.org/casw/evert-clarkseth-payne-award-young-science-journalists; casw.submittable.com/submit, pg 590

Reid, Rosalind, The Victor Cohn Prize for Excellence in Medical Science Reporting, PO Box 17337, Seattle, WA 98127 *Tel:* 206-880-0177 *E-mail:* info@casw.org *Web Site:* casw.org/casw/victor-cohn-prize-excellence-medical-science-reporting-0, pg 590

Reid, Rosalind, Council for the Advancement of Science Writing (CASW), PO Box 17337, Seattle, WA 98127 *Tel:* 206-880-0177 *E-mail:* info@casw.org *Web Site:* casw.org, pg 504

Reid, Rosalind, Taylor/Blakeslee Graduate Fellowships, PO Box 17337, Seattle, WA 98127 *Tel:* 206-880-0177 *E-mail:* info@casw.org *Web Site:* casw.org/casw/graduate-school-fellowships, pg 668

Reidhead, Julia A, W W Norton & Company Inc, 500 Fifth Ave, New York, NY 10110-0017 *Tel:* 212-354-5500 *Toll Free Tel:* 800-233-4830 (orders & cust serv) *Fax:* 212-869-0856 *Toll Free Fax:* 800-458-6515 *E-mail:* orders@wwnorton.com *Web Site:* wwnorton.com, pg 143

Reidy, Kiyoko, Phyllis Smart-Young Poetry Prize, University of Wisconsin, 6193 Helen C White Hall, English Dept, 600 N Park St, Madison, WI 53706 *E-mail:* madisonrevw@gmail.com *Web Site:* www.themadisonrevw.com, pg 663

Reidy, Sarah, Tor Publishing Group, 120 Broadway, New York, NY 10271 *Toll Free Tel:* 800-455-0340 (Macmillan) *E-mail:* torpublicity@tor.com; forgepublicity@forgebooks.com *Web Site:* us.macmillan.com/torpublishinggroup, pg 208

Reigal, Jason, Macmillan, 120 Broadway, 22nd fl, New York, NY 10271 *E-mail:* press.inquiries@macmillan.com *Web Site:* us.macmillan.com, pg 122

Reighard, Jessica, Paul H Brookes Publishing Co Inc, PO Box 10624, Baltimore, MD 21285-0624 *Tel:* 410-337-9580 (outside US & CN) *Toll Free Tel:* 800-638-3775 (US & CN) *Fax:* 410-337-8539 *E-mail:* custserv@brookespublishing.com *Web Site:* www.brookespublishing.com, pg 37

Reilly, Amy, Reader's Digest Select Editions, 44 S Broadway, White Plains, NY 10601 *Tel:* 914-238-1000 *Toll Free Tel:* 877-732-4438 (cust serv) *Web Site:* www.rd.com/article/select-editions/; www.facebook.com/selecteditions, pg 172

Reilly, Cara, Doubleday, c/o Penguin Random House LLC, 1745 Broadway, New York, NY 10019 *Tel:* 212-751-2600 *Fax:* 212-940-7390 (dom rts); 212-572-2662 (foreign rts) *Web Site:* knopfdoubleday.com/imprint/doubleday/; knopfdoubleday.com, pg 61

Reilly, Erin, Penguin Random House LLC, 1745 Broadway, New York, NY 10019 *Tel:* 212-782-9000 *Toll Free Tel:* 800-726-0600 *Web Site:* www.penguinrandomhouse.com, pg 155

Reilly, J C, International Poetry Competition, 686 Cherry St NW, Suite 333, Atlanta, GA 30332-0161 *E-mail:* atlantareview@gatech.edu *Web Site:* www.atlantareview.com, pg 617

Reilly, Lena, Random House Children's Books, c/o Penguin Random House LLC, 1745 Broadway, New York, NY 10019 *Tel:* 212-782-9000 *Web Site:* www.rhcbooks.com, pg 170

Reimer, Marleen, Sourcebooks LLC, 1935 Brookdale Rd, Suite 139, Naperville, IL 60563 *Tel:* 630-961-3900 *Toll Free Tel:* 800-432-7444 *Fax:* 630-961-2168 *E-mail:* info@sourcebooks.com *Web Site:* www.sourcebooks.com, pg 194

Reina, Jeanne, HarperCollins Publishers LLC, 195 Broadway, New York, NY 10007 *Tel:* 212-207-7000 *Web Site:* www.harpercollins.com, pg 86

Reinart, Penny, International Society for Technology in Education, 2111 Wilson Blvd, Suite 300, Arlington, VA 22201 *Tel:* 503-342-2848 (intl) *Toll Free Tel:* 800-336-5191 (US & CN) *Fax:* 541-302-3778 *E-mail:* iste@iste.org *Web Site:* www.iste.org, pg 103

Reinhardt, Alysyn, Penguin Random House Speakers Bureau, a Penguin Random House company, 1745 Broadway, Mail Drop 13-1, New York, NY 10019 *Tel:* 212-572-2013 *E-mail:* speakers@penguinrandomhouse.com *Web Site:* www.prhspeakers.com, pg 487

Reino, Jessica, Metamorphosis Literary Agency, 12410 S Acuff Ct, Olathe, KS 66062 *Tel:* 646-397-1640 *E-mail:* info@metamorphosisliteraryagency.com *Web Site:* www.metamorphosisliteraryagency.com, pg 470

Reis, Bethany, Penguin Random House LLC, 1745 Broadway, New York, NY 10019 *Tel:* 212-782-9000 *Toll Free Tel:* 800-726-0600 *Web Site:* www.penguinrandomhouse.com, pg 155

Reisdorff, James J, South Platte Press, PO Box 163, David City, NE 68632-0163 *Tel:* 402-367-3554 *E-mail:* railroads@windstream.net *Web Site:* www.southplattepress.net, pg 195

Reiser, Annie M, Matei Calinescu Prize, 85 Broad St, New York, NY 10004 *Tel:* 646-576-5141; 646-576-5000 *E-mail:* awards@mla.org *Web Site:* www.mla.org, pg 586

Reiser, Annie M, Morton N Cohen Award for a Distinguished Edition of Letters, 85 Broad St, New York, NY 10004 *Tel:* 646-576-5141; 646-576-5000 *E-mail:* awards@mla.org *Web Site:* www.mla.org, pg 590

Reiser, Annie M, Katherine Singer Kovacs Prize, 85 Broad St, New York, NY 10004 *Tel:* 646-576-5141; 646-576-5000 *E-mail:* awards@mla.org *Web Site:* www.mla.org, pg 621

Reiser, Annie M, Fenia & Yaakov Leviant Memorial Prize in Yiddish Studies, 85 Broad St, New York, NY 10004 *Tel:* 646-576-5141; 646-576-5000 *E-mail:* awards@mla.org *Web Site:* www.mla.org, pg 623

Reiser, Annie M, James Russell Lowell Prize, 85 Broad St, New York, NY 10004 *Tel:* 646-576-5141; 646-576-5000 *E-mail:* awards@mla.org *Web Site:* www.mla.org, pg 627

Reiser, Annie M, Howard R Marraro Prize, 85 Broad St, New York, NY 10004 *Tel:* 646-576-5141; 646-576-5000 *E-mail:* awards@mla.org *Web Site:* www.mla.org, pg 629

Reiser, Annie M, Kenneth W Mildenberger Prize, 85 Broad St, New York, NY 10004 *Tel:* 646-576-5141; 646-576-5000 *E-mail:* awards@mla.org *Web Site:* www.mla.org, pg 632

Reiser, Annie M, MLA Prize for a First Book, 85 Broad St, New York, NY 10004 *Tel:* 646-576-5141; 646-576-5000 *E-mail:* awards@mla.org *Web Site:* www.mla.org, pg 634

Reiser, Annie M, MLA Prize for a Scholarly Edition, 85 Broad St, New York, NY 10004 *Tel:* 646-576-5141; 646-576-5000 *E-mail:* awards@mla.org *Web Site:* www.mla.org, pg 634

Reiser, Annie M, MLA Prize for an Edited Collection, 85 Broad St, New York, NY 10004 *Tel:* 646-576-5141; 646-576-5000 *E-mail:* awards@mla.org *Web Site:* www.mla.org, pg 634

Reiser, Annie M, MLA Prize for Bibliographical or Archival Scholarship, 85 Broad St, New York, NY 10004 *Tel:* 646-576-5141; 646-576-5000 *E-mail:* awards@mla.org *Web Site:* www.mla.org, pg 634

Reiser, Annie M, MLA Prize for Independent Scholars, 85 Broad St, New York, NY 10004 *Tel:* 646-576-5141; 646-576-5000 *E-mail:* awards@mla.org *Web Site:* www.mla.org, pg 634

Reiser, Annie M, MLA Prize for Studies in Native American Literatures, Cultures & Languages, 85 Broad St, New York, NY 10004 *Tel:* 646-576-5141; 646-576-5000 *E-mail:* awards@mla.org *Web Site:* www.mla.org, pg 634

Reiser, Annie M, MLA Prize in United States Latina & Latino & Chicana & Chicano Literary & Cultural Studies, 85 Broad St, New York, NY 10004 *Tel:* 646-576-5141; 646-576-5000 *E-mail:* awards@mla.org *Web Site:* www.mla.org, pg 634

Reiser, Annie M, William Riley Parker Prize, 85 Broad St, New York, NY 10004 *Tel:* 646-576-5141; 646-576-5000 *E-mail:* awards@mla.org *Web Site:* www.mla.org, pg 645

Reiser, Annie M, Lois Roth Award, 85 Broad St, New York, NY 10004 *Tel:* 646-576-5141; 646-576-5000 *E-mail:* awards@mla.org *Web Site:* www.mla.org, pg 657

Reiser, Annie M, Aldo & Jeanne Scaglione Prize for a Translation of a Literary Work, 85 Broad St, New York, NY 10004 *Tel:* 646-576-5141; 646-576-5000 *E-mail:* awards@mla.org *Web Site:* www.mla.org, pg 659

Reiser, Annie M, Aldo & Jeanne Scaglione Prize for a Translation of a Scholarly Study of Literature, 85 Broad St, New York, NY 10004 *Tel:* 646-576-5141; 646-576-5000 *E-mail:* awards@mla.org *Web Site:* www.mla.org, pg 659

Reiser, Annie M, Aldo & Jeanne Scaglione Prize for Comparative Literary Studies, 85 Broad St, New York, NY 10004 *Tel:* 646-576-5141; 646-576-5000 *E-mail:* awards@mla.org *Web Site:* www.mla.org, pg 659

Reiser, Annie M, Aldo & Jeanne Scaglione Prize for French & Francophone Studies, 85 Broad St, New York, NY 10004 *Tel:* 646-576-5141; 646-576-5000 *E-mail:* awards@mla.org *Web Site:* www.mla.org, pg 660

Reiser, Annie M, Aldo & Jeanne Scaglione Prize for Italian Studies, 85 Broad St, New York, NY 10004 *Tel:* 646-576-5141; 646-576-5000 *E-mail:* awards@mla.org *Web Site:* www.mla.org, pg 660

Reiser, Annie M, Aldo & Jeanne Scaglione Prize for Studies in Germanic Languages & Literatures, 85 Broad St, New York, NY 10004 *Tel:* 646-576-5141; 646-576-5000 *E-mail:* awards@mla.org *Web Site:* www.mla.org, pg 660

Reiser, Annie M, Aldo & Jeanne Scaglione Prize for Studies in Slavic Languages & Literatures, 85 Broad St, New York, NY 10004 *Tel:* 646-576-5141; 646-576-5000 *E-mail:* awards@mla.org *Web Site:* www.mla.org, pg 660

Reiser, Annie M, Aldo & Jeanne Scaglione Publication Award for a Manuscript in Italian Literary Studies, 85 Broad St, New York, NY 10004 *Tel:* 646-576-5141; 646-576-5000 *E-mail:* awards@mla.org *Web Site:* www.mla.org, pg 660

Reiser, Annie M, William Sanders Scarborough Prize, 85 Broad St, New York, NY 10004 *Tel:* 646-576-5141; 646-576-5000 *E-mail:* awards@mla.org *Web Site:* www.mla.org, pg 660

Reiser, Annie M, Mina P Shaughnessy Prize, 85 Broad St, New York, NY 10004 *Tel:* 646-576-5141; 646-576-5000 *E-mail:* awards@mla.org *Web Site:* www.mla.org, pg 661

Reisinger, Ashley, TriadaUS Literary Agency, PO Box 561, Sewickley, PA 15143 *Tel:* 412-401-3376 *Web Site:* www.triadaus.com, pg 480

Reisner, Rosalind, AJL Jewish Fiction Award, PO Box 1118, Teaneck, NJ 07666 *Tel:* 201-371-3255 *E-mail:* info@jewishlibraries.org *Web Site:* jewishlibraries.org/AJL_Jewish_Fiction_Award, pg 571

Reiss, Damon, Thomas Nelson, 501 Nelson Place, Nashville, TN 37214 *Tel:* 615-889-9000 *Toll Free Tel:* 800-251-4000 *Web Site:* www.thomasnelson.com, pg 206

Reiss, William, John Hawkins and Associates Inc, 80 Maiden Lane, Suite 1503, New York, NY 10038 *Tel:* 212-807-7040 *E-mail:* jha@jhalit.com *Web Site:* jhalit.com, pg 462

Reiter, Jendi, Tom Howard/John H Reid Fiction & Essay Contest, 351 Pleasant St, Suite B, PMB 222, Northampton, MA 01060-3998 *Tel:* 413-320-1847 *Toll Free Tel:* 866-WINWRIT (946-9748) *Fax:* 413-280-0539 *Web Site:* www.winningwriters.com/our-contests/tom-howard-john-h-reid-fiction-essay-contest, pg 614

Reiter, Jendi, Tom Howard/Margaret Reid Poetry Contest, 351 Pleasant St, Suite B, PMB 222, Northampton, MA 01060-3998 *Tel:* 413-320-1847 *Toll Free Tel:* 866-WINWRIT (946-9748) *Fax:* 413-280-0539 *Web Site:* www.winningwriters.com/our-contests/tom-howard-margaret-reid-poetry-contest, pg 614

Reiter, Jendi, North Street Book Prize, 351 Pleasant St, Suite B, PMB 222, Northampton, MA 01060-3998 *Tel:* 413-320-1847 *Toll Free Tel:* 866-WINWRIT (946-9748) *Fax:* 413-280-0539 *Web Site:* www.winningwriters.com/our-contests/north-street-book-prize, pg 641

Reiter, Jendi, Wergle Flomp Humor Poetry Contest, 351 Pleasant St, Suite B, PMB 222, Northampton, MA 01060-3998 *Tel:* 413-320-1847 *Toll Free Tel:* 866-WINWRIT (946-9748) *Fax:* 413-280-0539 *Web Site:* www.winningwriters.com/our-contests/wergle-flomp-humor-poetry-contest-free, pg 674

Remcheck, Allison, Stimola Literary Studio Inc, 11 Briarwood Lane, West Tisbury, MA 02575 *Tel:* 201-945-9353 *Fax:* 201-490-5920 *E-mail:* info@stimolaliterarystudio.com *Web Site:* www.stimolaliterarystudio.com, pg 478

Ren, Tiffani, Random House Publishing Group, 1745 Broadway, New York, NY 10019 *Toll Free Tel:* 800-200-3552 *Web Site:* www.randomhousebooks.com, pg 171

Renaud, Alain-Nicolas, Les Editions de l'Hexagone, 4545, rue Frontenac, 3rd fl, Montreal, QC H2H 2R7, Canada *Tel:* 514-523-1182 *Fax:* 514-521-4434 *Web Site:* editionshexagone.groupelivre.com, pg 402

Renaud, Alain-Nicolas, VLB editeur, 4545, rue Frontenac, 3rd fl, Montreal, QC H2H 2R7, Canada *Tel:* 514-849-5259 *Web Site:* www.edvlb.com, pg 424

Renaud, Marie-Lyne, Innis-Gerin Medal, Walter House, 282 Somerset W, Ottawa, ON K2P 0J6, Canada *Tel:* 613-991-6990 (ext 106) *Fax:* 613-991-6996 *E-mail:* nominations@rsc-src.ca *Web Site:* www.rsc-src.ca, pg 616

Renaud, Marie-Lyne, Lorne Pierce Medal, Walter House, 282 Somerset W, Ottawa, ON K2P 0J6, Canada *Tel:* 613-991-6990 (ext 106) *Fax:* 613-991-6996 *E-mail:* nominations@rsc-src.ca *Web Site:* www.rsc-src.ca, pg 649

Renaud, Monique, Playwrights Guild of Canada, 401 Richmond St W, Suite 350, Toronto, ON M5V 3A8, Canada *Tel:* 416-703-0201 *E-mail:* info@playwrightsguild.ca; marketing@playwrightsguild.ca; orders@playwrightsguild.ca; membership@playwrightsguild.ca *Web Site:* playwrightsguild.ca, pg 516

Renner, Georgene, Society for Mining, Metallurgy & Exploration, 12999 E Adam Aircraft Circle, Englewood, CO 80112 *Tel:* 303-948-4200 *Toll Free Tel:* 800-763-3132 *Fax:* 303-973-3845 *E-mail:* cs@smenet.org; books@smenet.org *Web Site:* www.smenet.org, pg 192

Renner, Kate, Viking Children's Books, c/o Penguin Random House LLC, 1745 Broadway, New York, NY 10019 *Tel:* 212-782-9000 *Web Site:* www.penguin.com/viking-childrens-books-overview/, pg 224

Renner, Rachael, Sourcebooks LLC, 1935 Brookdale Rd, Suite 139, Naperville, IL 60563 *Tel:* 630-961-3900 *Toll Free Tel:* 800-432-7444 *Fax:* 630-961-2168 *E-mail:* info@sourcebooks.com *Web Site:* www.sourcebooks.com, pg 195

Rennert, Amy, The Amy Rennert Agency Inc, 1880 Century Park E, No 1600, Los Angeles, CA 90067 *Tel:* 415-789-8955 *E-mail:* queries@amyrennert.com (no unsol queries), pg 473

Rennie, Kathryn, Penguin Random House Canada, a Penguin Random House company, 320 Front St W, Suite 1400, Toronto, ON M5V 3B6, Canada *Tel:* 416-364-4449 *Toll Free Tel:* 888-523-9292 (cust serv) *E-mail:* canadaweb@penguinrandomhouse.com; customerservicescanada@penguinrandomhouse.com *Web Site:* www.penguinrandomhouse.ca, pg 416

Rennison, Ms Robin, University of Missouri Press, 113 Heinkel Bldg, 201 S Seventh St, Columbia, MO 65211 *Tel:* 573-882-7641; 573-882-9672 (publicity & sales enquiries) *Toll Free Tel:* 800-621-2736 (orders) *Fax:* 573-884-4498 *Toll Free Fax:* 800-621-8476 (orders) *E-mail:* upress@missouri.edu; umpmarketing@missouri.edu (publicity & sales enquiries) *Web Site:* upress.missouri.edu, pg 217

Renwick, Devon, American Psychological Association, 750 First St NE, Washington, DC 20002 *Tel:* 202-336-5510 *Toll Free Tel:* 800-374-2721 *Fax:* 202-336-5502 *E-mail:* order@apa.org; booksales@apa.org *Web Site:* www.apa.org/books, pg 12

Repcheck, Jack, W W Norton & Company Inc, 500 Fifth Ave, New York, NY 10110-0017 *Tel:* 212-354-5500 *Toll Free Tel:* 800-233-4830 (orders & cust serv) *Fax:* 212-869-0856 *Toll Free Fax:* 800-458-6515 *E-mail:* orders@wwnorton.com *Web Site:* wwnorton.com, pg 143

Repetto, David, Cambridge University Press, One Liberty Plaza, 20th fl, New York, NY 10006 *Tel:* 212-924-3900; 212-337-5000 *Fax:* 212-691-3239; 845-353-4141 *E-mail:* customer_service@cambridge.org; orders@cambridge.org; subscriptions_newyork@cambridge.org *Web Site:* www.cambridge.org/us, pg 39

Reschke, Phil, Covenant Communications Inc, 1226 S 630 E, Suite 4, American Fork, UT 84003 *Tel:* 801-756-1041 *E-mail:* info@covenant-lds.com; covenantorders@covenant-lds.com *Web Site:* www.covenant-lds.com, pg 54

Resciniti, Nicole, The Seymour Agency, 475 Miner Street Rd, Canton, NY 13617 *Tel:* 239-398-8209 *Web Site:* www.theseymouragency.com, pg 475

Resek, Theresa, Association for Intelligent Information Management (AIIM), 8403 Colesville Rd, No 1100, Silver Spring, MD 20910 *Tel:* 301-587-8202 *Toll Free Tel:* 800-477-2446 *Fax:* 301-587-2711 *E-mail:* hello@aiim.org *Web Site:* www.aiim.org, pg 498

Resnick, Kerri, St Martin's Press, LLC, 120 Broadway, New York, NY 10271 *E-mail:* publicity@stmartins.com; trademarketing@stmartins.com; foreignrights@stmartins.com *Web Site:* us.macmillan.com/smp, pg 180

Resnick, Marc, St Martin's Press, LLC, 120 Broadway, New York, NY 10271 *E-mail:* publicity@stmartins.com; trademarketing@stmartins.com; foreignrights@stmartins.com *Web Site:* us.macmillan.com/smp, pg 180

Rethy, Sonja, Hebrew Union College Press, 3101 Clifton Ave, Cincinnati, OH 45220 *Tel:* 513-221-1875 *Fax:* 513-221-0321 *Web Site:* press.huc.edu, pg 90

Retief, Glen PhD, Susquehanna University, Department of English & Creative Writing, 514 University Ave, Selinsgrove, PA 17870 *Tel:* 570-372-4196 *Web Site:* www.susqu.edu, pg 565

Rettino, Lucille, Tor Publishing Group, 120 Broadway, New York, NY 10271 *Toll Free Tel:* 800-455-0340 (Macmillan) *E-mail:* torpublicity@tor.com; forgepublicity@forgebooks.com *Web Site:* us.macmillan.com/torpublishinggroup, pg 208

Reubert, Alex, HG Literary, 6 W 18 St, Suite 7R, New York, NY 10011 *E-mail:* foreign@hgliterary.com; rights@hgliterary.com *Web Site:* www.hgliterary.com, pg 463

Reveal, Judith, Just Creative Writing & Indexing Services (JCR), 301 Wood Duck Dr, Greensboro, MD 21639 *Tel:* 443-262-2136 *E-mail:* judy@justcreativewriting.com *Web Site:* www.justcreativewriting.com, pg 441

Reyes, Alejandro, Houghton Mifflin Harcourt, 125 High St, Boston, MA 02110 *Tel:* 617-351-5000 *Toll Free Tel:* 855-969-4642; 800-225-5425 (K-12 educ materials); 800-323-9540 (assessment materials); 877-219-1537 (SkillsTutor); 888-242-6747 (Innovation in Educ Group); 800-225-3362 (Trade & Ref Div) *Toll Free Fax:* 800-269-5232 *E-mail:* myhmhco@hmhco.com *Web Site:* www.hmhco.com, pg 96

Reyes, Jennifer, Random House Publishing Group, 1745 Broadway, New York, NY 10019 *Toll Free Tel:* 800-200-3552 *Web Site:* www.randomhousebooks.com, pg 171

Reyes, Jorge, Penguin Random House Audio Publishing Group, 1745 Broadway, New York, NY 10019 *Toll Free Tel:* 800-793-2665 (cust serv) *E-mail:* audio@penguinrandomhouse.com; ecustomerservice@penguinrandomhouse.com *Web Site:* www.penguinrandomhouseaudio.com, pg 154

Reynics, Mary, Random House Publishing Group, 1745 Broadway, New York, NY 10019 *Toll Free Tel:* 800-200-3552 *Web Site:* www.randomhousebooks.com, pg 171

Reynolds, Cat, Random House Children's Books, c/o Penguin Random House LLC, 1745 Broadway, New York, NY 10019 *Tel:* 212-782-9000 *Web Site:* www.rhcbooks.com, pg 170

Reynolds, Christy, Texas Bluebonnet Award, 3420 Executive Center Dr, Suite 301, Austin, TX 78731 *Tel:* 512-328-1518 *Fax:* 512-328-8852 *E-mail:* tla@txla.org *Web Site:* txla.org/tools-resources/reading-lists/texas-bluebonnet-award/about/; txla.org, pg 669

Reynolds, Christy, Texas Library Association (TLA), 3420 Executive Center Dr, Suite 301, Austin, TX 78731 *Tel:* 512-328-1518 *Fax:* 512-328-8852 *E-mail:* tla@txla.org *Web Site:* txla.org, pg 521

Reynolds, Corina, The Center for Book Arts, 28 W 27 St, 3rd fl, New York, NY 10001 *Tel:* 212-481-0295 *E-mail:* info@centerforbookarts.org *Web Site:* www.centerforbookarts.org, pg 503, 561

Reynolds, Evan B, The Magni Co, 7106 Wellington Point Rd, McKinney, TX 75072 *Tel:* 972-540-2050 *Fax:* 972-540-1057 *E-mail:* sales@magnico.com; info@magnico.com *Web Site:* www.magnico.com, pg 123

Reynolds, Laurie, Child's Play® Inc, 250 Minot Ave, Auburn, ME 04210 *Tel:* 207-784-7252 *Toll Free Tel:* 800-639-6404 *Fax:* 207-784-7358 *Toll Free Fax:* 800-854-6989 *E-mail:* chpmaine@aol.com *Web Site:* www.childs-play.com, pg 46

Reynolds, Mary, The University of Arizona Press, 1510 E University Blvd, Tucson, AZ 85721 *Tel:* 520-621-1441 *Toll Free Tel:* 800-621-2736 (orders) *Fax:* 520-621-8899 *Toll Free Fax:* 800-621-8476 (orders) *E-mail:* uap@uapress.arizona.edu *Web Site:* www.uapress.arizona.edu, pg 214

Reynolds, Megan, National Book Foundation, 90 Broad St, Suite 604, New York, NY 10004 *Tel:* 212-685-0261 *Fax:* 212-213-6570 *E-mail:* nationalbook@nationalbook.org *Web Site:* www.nationalbook.org, pg 526

Reynolds, Michael, Europa Editions, 27 Union Sq W, Suite 302, New York, NY 10003 *Tel:* 212-868-6844 *Fax:* 212-868-6845 *E-mail:* info@europaeditions.com; books@europaeditions.com; publicity@europaeditions.com *Web Site:* www.europaeditions.com, pg 67

Reynolds, Peter, American Booksellers Association, 600 Mamaroneck Ave, Suite 400, Harrison, NY 10528 *Tel:* 914-406-7500 *Toll Free Tel:* 800-637-0037 *Fax:* 914-417-4013 *E-mail:* info@bookweb.org *Web Site:* www.bookweb.org, pg 494

Reynolds, Reagan, Macmillan, 120 Broadway, 22nd fl, New York, NY 10271 *E-mail:* press.inquiries@macmillan.com *Web Site:* us.macmillan.com, pg 122

Reynolds, Victoria, Harry N Abrams Inc, 195 Broadway, 9th fl, New York, NY 10007 *Tel:* 212-206-7715 *Toll Free Tel:* 800-345-1359 *Fax:* 212-645-8437 *E-mail:* abrams@abramsbooks.com; publicity@abramsbooks.com; sales@abramsbooks.com *Web Site:* www.abramsbooks.com, pg 3

Reza, Farah, HarperCollins Children's Books, 195 Broadway, New York, NY 10007 *Tel:* 212-207-7000 *Web Site:* www.harpercollins.com/childrens, pg 85

Rhamey, Ashley, Tundra Book Group, 320 Front St W, Suite 1400, Toronto, ON M5V 3B6, Canada *Tel:* 416-364-4449 *Toll Free Tel:* 888-523-9292 (orders); 800-588-1074 *E-mail:* youngreaders@penguinrandomhouse.com *Web Site:* www.tundrabooks.com, pg 421

Rheault, Marie-Michele, Les Editions du Septentrion, 86, Cote de la Montagne, bureau 200, Quebec, QC G1K 4E3, Canada *Tel:* 418-688-3556 *Fax:* 418-527-4978 *E-mail:* info@septentrion.qc.ca *Web Site:* www.septentrion.qc.ca, pg 403

Rheault, Sonia, University of Ottawa Press (Presses de l'Université d'Ottawa), 542 King Edward Ave, Ottawa, ON K1N 6N5, Canada *Tel:* 613-562-5246 *Fax:* 613-562-5247 *E-mail:* puo-uop@uottawa.ca; acquisitions@uottawa.ca *Web Site:* press.uottawa.ca, pg 423

Rhetts, Paul, LPD Press/Rio Grande Books, 925 Salamanca NW, Los Ranchos de Albuquerque, NM 87107-5647 *Tel:* 505-269-8324 *Web Site:* nmsantos.com, pg 121

Rhie, Gene S, Hollym International Corp, 2647 Gateway Rd, No 105-223, Carlsbad, CA 92009 *Tel:* 760-814-9880 *Fax:* 908-353-0255 *E-mail:* contact@hollym.com *Web Site:* www.hollym.com, pg 94

Rhino, Will, The Experiment, 220 E 23 St, Suite 600, New York, NY 10010-4658 *Tel:* 212-889-1659 *E-mail:* info@theexperimentpublishing.com *Web Site:* www.theexperimentpublishing.com, pg 68

Rhoads, Kassandra, Scribner, 1230 Avenue of the Americas, New York, NY 10020 *Web Site:* www.simonandschusterpublishing.com/scribner/, pg 185

Rhodes, David R, Pyncheon House, 6 University Dr, Suite 105, Amherst, MA 01002, pg 167

Rhodes, Emilia, Atria Books, 1230 Avenue of the Americas, New York, NY 10020 *Tel:* 212-698-7000 *Fax:* 212-698-7007 *Web Site:* www.simonandschuster.com, pg 21

Rhone, Mitzi, The Aaland Agency, PO Box 849, Inyokern, CA 93527-0849 *Tel:* 760-384-3910 *E-mail:* anniejo41@gmail.com *Web Site:* www.the-aaland-agency.com, pg 447

Rhorer, Richard, Atria Books, 1230 Avenue of the Americas, New York, NY 10020 *Tel:* 212-698-7000 *Fax:* 212-698-7007 *Web Site:* www.simonandschuster.com, pg 21

Rhyne, Megan, National Freedom of Information Coalition (NFOIC), PO Box 405, Williamsburg, VA 23187 *Tel:* 757-276-1413 *E-mail:* nfoic@nfoic.org *Web Site:* www.nfoic.org, pg 513

Ribas, Maria, Stonesong, 270 W 39 St, Suite 201, New York, NY 10018 Tel: 212-929-4600 E-mail: editors@stonesong.com Web Site: www.stonesong.com, pg 478

Ribble, Anne G, Bibliographical Society of the University of Virginia, 2014 Hessian Rd, Charlottesville, VA 22903 Tel: 434-996-8663 E-mail: bibsoc@virginia.edu Web Site: bsuva.org, pg 501

Ricci-Thode, Vanessa, Thodestool Fiction Editing, 40 McDougall Rd, Waterloo, ON N2L 2W5, Canada Web Site: www.thodestool.ca, pg 445

Ricciuto, Marianna, Harlequin Enterprises Ltd, Bay Adelaide Centre, East Tower, 22 Adelaide St W, 41st fl, Toronto, ON M5H 4E3, Canada Tel: 416-445-5860 Toll Free Tel: 888-432-4879; 800-370-5838 (ebook inquiries) E-mail: customerservice@harlequin.com Web Site: www.harlequin.com, pg 409

Rice, Marnie, City of Vancouver Book Award, Woodward's Heritage Bldg, Suite 501, 111 W Hastings St, Vancouver, BC V6B 1H4, Canada Tel: 604-871-6634 Fax: 604-871-6005 E-mail: culture@vancouver.ca Web Site: vancouver.ca/bookaward, pg 590

Rice, Patty, Andrews McMeel Publishing LLC, 1130 Walnut St, Kansas City, MO 64106-2109 Tel: 816-581-7500 Toll Free Tel: 800-851-8923 Web Site: www.andrewsmcmeel.com; publishing.andrewsmcmeel.com, pg 14

Rice, Taylor, Penguin Random House Canada, a Penguin Random House company, 320 Front St W, Suite 1400, Toronto, ON M5V 3B6, Canada Tel: 416-364-4449 Toll Free Tel: 888-523-9292 (cust serv) E-mail: canadaweb@penguinrandomhouse.com; customerservicescanada@penguinrandomhouse.com Web Site: www.penguinrandomhouse.ca, pg 416

Rice, Valentina, Bloomsbury Publishing Inc, 1385 Broadway, 5th fl, New York, NY 10018 Tel: 212-419-5300 E-mail: marketingusa@bloomsbury.com; adultpublicityusa@bloomsbury.com; askacademic@bloomsbury.com Web Site: www.bloomsbury.com, pg 31

Rice-Baturin, Holly, Atria Books, 1230 Avenue of the Americas, New York, NY 10020 Tel: 212-698-7000 Fax: 212-698-7007 Web Site: www.simonandschuster.com, pg 21

Rich, Alison, Random House Publishing Group, 1745 Broadway, New York, NY 10019 Toll Free Tel: 800-200-3552 Web Site: www.randomhousebooks.com, pg 170

Rich, Gillian, National Press Club (NPC), 529 14 St NW, 13th fl, Washington, DC 20045 Tel: 202-662-7500 Web Site: www.press.org, pg 513

Rich, Mike, Random House Children's Books, c/o Penguin Random House LLC, 1745 Broadway, New York, NY 10019 Tel: 212-782-9000 Web Site: www.rhcbooks.com, pg 170

Richard, Barbara, Vintage Books, c/o Penguin Random House LLC, 1745 Broadway, New York, NY 10019 Tel: 212-572-2420 Fax: 212-940-7390 (dom rts); 212-572-2662 (foreign rts) E-mail: vintageanchorpublicity@randomhouse.com Web Site: knopfdoubleday.com/imprint/vintage; knopfdoubleday.com, pg 225

Richard, Brent, Penguin Random House Canada, a Penguin Random House company, 320 Front St W, Suite 1400, Toronto, ON M5V 3B6, Canada Tel: 416-364-4449 Toll Free Tel: 888-523-9292 (cust serv) E-mail: canadaweb@penguinrandomhouse.com; customerservicescanada@penguinrandomhouse.com Web Site: www.penguinrandomhouse.ca, pg 416

Richard, Derek, Alfred Music, 285 Century Place, Louisville, CO 80027 Tel: 818-891-5999 (dealer sales, intl) Toll Free Tel: 800-292-6122 (dealer sales, US & CN); 800-628-1528 (cust serv) Fax: 818-893-5560 (dealer sales); 818-830-6252 (cust serv) Toll Free Fax: 800-632-1928 (dealer sales) E-mail: customerservice@alfred.com; sales@alfred.com Web Site: www.alfred.com, pg 7

Richard, Ronald B, The Anisfield-Wolf Book Awards, 1422 Euclid Ave, Suite 1300, Cleveland, OH 44115 Tel: 216-861-3810 Fax: 216-861-1729 E-mail: awinfo@clevefdn.org Web Site: www.anisfield-wolf.org; www.clevelandfoundation.org, pg 573

Richards, Catherine, St Martin's Press, LLC, 120 Broadway, New York, NY 10271 E-mail: publicity@stmartins.com; trademarketing@stmartins.com; foreignrights@stmartins.com Web Site: us.macmillan.com/smp, pg 181

Richards, Christopher, Scribner, 1230 Avenue of the Americas, New York, NY 10020 Web Site: www.simonandschusterpublishing.com/scribner/, pg 185

Richards, Erin, Random House Publishing Group, 1745 Broadway, New York, NY 10019 Toll Free Tel: 800-200-3552 Web Site: www.randomhousebooks.com, pg 171

Richards, Karen Carter, National Newspaper Publishers Association (NNPA), 1816 12 St NW, Washington, DC 20009 Tel: 202-588-8764 E-mail: info@nnpa.org Web Site: nnpa.org; blackpressusa.com, pg 513

Richards, Maggie, Henry Holt and Company, LLC, 120 Broadway, 23rd fl, New York, NY 10271 Tel: 646-307-5151 Toll Free Tel: 888-330-8477 (orders) Fax: 646-307-5285 Web Site: www.henryholt.com, pg 94

Richards, Victor, Bookhaven Press LLC, 302 Scenic Ct, Moon Township, PA 15108 Tel: 412-494-6926 E-mail: info@bookhavenpress.com; orders@bookhavenpress.com Web Site: bookhavenpress.com, pg 34

Richardson, Ariel, Chronicle Books LLC, 680 Second St, San Francisco, CA 94107 Tel: 415-537-4200 Fax: 415-537-4460 (perms) E-mail: hello@chroniclebooks.com; subrights@chroniclebooks.com Web Site: www.chroniclebooks.com, pg 47

Richardson, Elaina, Yaddo Artists Residency, 312 Union Ave, Saratoga Springs, NY 12866 Tel: 518-584-0746 Fax: 518-584-1312 Web Site: www.yaddo.org, pg 559

Richardson, Erik, Major Achievement Award, c/o 3225 N 91 St, Milwaukee, WI 53222 E-mail: wiswriters@gmail.com Web Site: wiswriters.org/awards, pg 628

Richardson, Erik, Lorine Niedecker Poetry Award, c/o 3225 N 91 St, Milwaukee, WI 53222 E-mail: wiswriters@gmail.com Web Site: wiswriters.org/awards, pg 641

Richardson, Erik, Christopher Latham Sholes Award, c/o 3225 N 91 St, Milwaukee, WI 53222 E-mail: wiswriters@gmail.com Web Site: wiswriters.org/awards, pg 662

Richardson, Erik, Arthur Tofte/Betty Ren Wright Children's Literature Award, c/o 3225 N 91 St, Milwaukee, WI 53222 E-mail: wiswriters@gmail.com Web Site: wiswriters.org/awards, pg 669

Richardson, Erik, Young Writers Award, c/o 3225 N 91 St, Milwaukee, WI 53222 E-mail: wiswriters@gmail.com Web Site: wiswriters.org/awards, pg 679

Richardson, Prof Herbert, The Edwin Mellen Press, 450 Ridge St, Lewiston, NY 14092 Tel: 716-754-2266; 716-754-2788 (order fulfillment) E-mail: editor@mellenpress.com; librarian@mellenpress.com Web Site: www.mellenpress.com, pg 129

Richardson, Michael, Dark Horse Comics, 10956 SE Main St, Milwaukie, OR 97222 Tel: 503-652-8815 Fax: 503-654-9440 E-mail: dhcomics@darkhorse.com Web Site: www.darkhorse.com, pg 57

Richardson, Paul E, Storyworkz Inc, PO Box 567, Montpelier, VT 05601 Tel: 802-223-4955 E-mail: orders@storyworkz.com Web Site: www.storyworkz.com, pg 199

Richardson, Robin, Tommy Nelson®, 501 Nelson Place, Nashville, TN 37214 Tel: 615-889-9000; 615-902-1485 (cust serv) Toll Free Tel: 800-251-4000 Web Site: www.tommynelson.com, pg 207

Richardson, Sally, Macmillan, 120 Broadway, 22nd fl, New York, NY 10271 E-mail: press.inquiries@macmillan.com Web Site: us.macmillan.com, pg 122

Richardson, Sally, St Martin's Press, LLC, 120 Broadway, New York, NY 10271 E-mail: publicity@stmartins.com; trademarketing@stmartins.com; foreignrights@stmartins.com Web Site: us.macmillan.com/smp, pg 180

Richason, Brad, Lerner Publishing Group Inc, 241 First Ave N, Minneapolis, MN 55401 Tel: 612-332-3344 Toll Free Tel: 800-328-4929 Fax: 612-332-7615 Toll Free Fax: 800-332-1132 E-mail: info@lernerbooks.com; custserve@lernerbooks.com Web Site: www.lernerbooks.com; www.facebook.com/lernerbooks, pg 115

Richer, Joss, Artist-in-Residence Program, 225 King St, Suite 201, Fredericton, NB E3B 1E1, Canada Tel: 506-444-4444 Toll Free Tel: 866-460-ARTS (460-2787) Fax: 506-444-5543 E-mail: prog@artsnb.ca Web Site: www.artsnb.ca, pg 574

Richer, Joss, Arts Scholarships, 225 King St, Suite 201, Fredericton, NB E3B 1E1, Canada Tel: 506-444-4444 Toll Free Tel: 866-460-ARTS (460-2787) Fax: 506-444-5543 E-mail: prog@artsnb.ca Web Site: www.artsnb.ca, pg 574

Richer, Joss, Career Development Program, 225 King St, Suite 201, Fredericton, NB E3B 1E1, Canada Tel: 506-444-4444 Toll Free Tel: 866-460-ARTS (460-2787) Fax: 506-444-5543 E-mail: prog@artsnb.ca Web Site: www.artsnb.ca, pg 586

Richer, Joss, Creation Grant Program, 225 King St, Suite 201, Fredericton, NB E3B 1E1, Canada Tel: 506-444-4444 Toll Free Tel: 866-460-ARTS (460-2787) Fax: 506-444-5543 E-mail: prog@artsnb.ca Web Site: www.artsnb.ca, pg 593

Richer, Joss, Creative Residencies-Quebec, 225 King St, Suite 201, Fredericton, NB E3B 1E1, Canada Tel: 506-444-4444 Toll Free Tel: 866-460-ARTS (460-2787) Fax: 506-444-5543 E-mail: prog@artsnb.ca Web Site: www.artsnb.ca, pg 593

Richer, Joss, Documentation Grant Program, 225 King St, Suite 201, Fredericton, NB E3B 1E1, Canada Tel: 506-444-4444 Toll Free Tel: 866-460-ARTS (460-2787) Fax: 506-444-5543 E-mail: prog@artsnb.ca Web Site: www.artsnb.ca, pg 596

Richer, Joss, The Lieutenant-Governor's Awards for High Achievement in the Arts, 225 King St, Suite 201, Fredericton, NB E3B 1E1, Canada Tel: 506-444-4444 Toll Free Tel: 866-460-ARTS (460-2787) Fax: 506-444-5543 E-mail: prog@artsnb.ca Web Site: www.artsnb.ca, pg 624

Richert, Scott, Our Sunday Visitor Publishing, 200 Noll Plaza, Huntington, IN 46750 Tel: 260-356-8400 Toll Free Tel: 800-348-2440 (orders) Toll Free Fax: 800-498-6709 E-mail: osvbooks@osv.com (book orders); customerservice@osv.com Web Site: www.osv.com, pg 148

Riches, Jessica, Association of Canadian Publishers (ACP), 401 Richmond St W, Studio 257A, Toronto, ON M5V 3A8, Canada Tel: 416-487-6116 E-mail: admin@canbook.org Web Site: publishers.ca, pg 499

Richesin, Nicki, Dunow, Carlson & Lerner Literary Agency Inc, 27 W 20 St, Suite 1107, New York, NY 10011 Tel: 212-645-7606 E-mail: mail@dclagency.com Web Site: www.dclagency.com, pg 457

Richie, Ross, BOOM! Studios, 5670 Wilshire Blvd, Suite 400, Los Angeles, CA 90036 E-mail: contact@boom-studios.com; customerservice@boom-studios.com; press@boom-studios.com Web Site: www.boom-studios.com, pg 34

Richman, Howard, Sound Feelings Publishing, 18375 Ventura Blvd, No 8000, Tarzana, CA 91356 Tel: 818-757-0600 E-mail: information@soundfeelings.com Web Site: www.soundfeelings.com, pg 194

Richmond, Amanda, Running Press, 1290 Avenue of the Americas, New York, NY 10104 Tel: 212-364-1100 Toll Free Tel: 800-759-0190 (cust serv) Fax: 212-364-0933 (intl orders) Toll Free Fax: 800-286-9471 (cust serv) E-mail: customer.service@hbgusa.com; orders@hbgusa.com Web Site: www.hachettebookgroup.com/imprint/running-press/; www.moon.com (Moon Travel Guides), pg 178

Richmond, Douglas, House of Anansi Press Inc, 128 Sterling Rd, Lower Level, Toronto, ON M6R 2B7, Canada *Tel:* 416-363-4343 *Fax:* 416-363-1017 *E-mail:* customerservice@houseofanansi.com *Web Site:* houseofanansi.com, pg 409

Richter, Heidi, HarperCollins Publishers LLC, 195 Broadway, New York, NY 10007 *Tel:* 212-207-7000 *Web Site:* www.harpercollins.com, pg 86

Richter, Rick, Aevitas Creative Management LLC, 19 W 21 St, Suite 501, New York, NY 10010 *Tel:* 212-765-6900 *Web Site:* www.aevitascreative.com, pg 448

Rickard, Julia, Viking Penguin, c/o Penguin Random House LLC, 1745 Broadway, New York, NY 10019 *Tel:* 212-782-9000 *Web Site:* www.penguin.com/overview-vikingbooks/; www.penguin.com/pameladorman-books-overview/; www.penguin.com/penguin-classics-overview/; www.penguin.com/penguin-life-overview/, pg 225

Rickert, Lynn, Penguin Random House LLC, 1745 Broadway, New York, NY 10019 *Tel:* 212-782-9000 *Toll Free Tel:* 800-726-0600 *Web Site:* www.penguinrandomhouse.com, pg 155

Ricketts, Lucy, Peachtree Publishing Co Inc, 1700 Chattahoochee Ave, Atlanta, GA 30318-2112 *Tel:* 404-876-8761 *Toll Free Tel:* 800-241-0113 *Fax:* 404-875-2578 *Toll Free Fax:* 800-875-8909 *E-mail:* hello@peachtree-online.com; orders@peachtree-online.com; sales@peachtree-online.com *Web Site:* www.peachtreebooks.com; www.peachtree-online.com, pg 153

Rico, Liz, Chronicle Books LLC, 680 Second St, San Francisco, CA 94107 *Tel:* 415-537-4200 *Fax:* 415-537-4460 (perms) *E-mail:* hello@chroniclebooks.com; subrights@chroniclebooks.com *Web Site:* www.chroniclebooks.com, pg 47

Ridder, Brian Jones, Workman Publishing, 1290 Avenue of the Americas, New York, NY 10104 *Toll Free Tel:* 800-759-0190 *Fax:* 212-364-0950 *E-mail:* workman-inquiry@hbgusa.com *Web Site:* www.hachettebookgroup.com/imprint/workman-publishing-company/, pg 232

Ridder, Myles, School Guide Publications, 420 Railroad Way, Mamaroneck, NY 10543 *Tel:* 914-632-1220 *Toll Free Tel:* 800-433-7771 *E-mail:* info@schoolguides.com *Web Site:* www.graduateguide.com; www.schoolguides.com; www.religiousministries.com, pg 185

Ridge, Sam, The University of Arkansas Press, McIlroy House, 105 N McIlroy Ave, Fayetteville, AR 72701 *Tel:* 479-575-7544 *E-mail:* info@uapress.com *Web Site:* www.uapress.com, pg 214

Ridout, Rachel, Harvey Klinger Inc, 300 W 55 St, Suite 11V, New York, NY 10019 *Tel:* 212-581-7068 *Fax:* 212-315-3823 *E-mail:* queries@harveyklinger.com *Web Site:* www.harveyklinger.com, pg 465

Rieck, Jessika, BenBella Books Inc, 10440 N Central Expwy, Suite 800, Dallas, TX 75231-2264 *Tel:* 214-750-3600 *Web Site:* www.benbellabooks.com; www.smartpopbooks.com, pg 27

Riegert, Keith, Ulysses Press, 195 Montague St, 14th fl, Brooklyn, NY 11201 *Tel:* 510-601-8301 *Toll Free Tel:* 800-377-2542 *Fax:* 510-601-8307 *E-mail:* ulysses@ulyssespress.com *Web Site:* www.ulyssespress.com, pg 212

Rienner, Lynne, Kumarian Press, 1800 30 St, Suite 314, Boulder, CO 80301 *Tel:* 303-444-6684 *Fax:* 303-444-0824 *E-mail:* questions@rienner.com *Web Site:* www.rienner.com, pg 112

Rienner, Lynne, Lynne Rienner Publishers Inc, 1800 30 St, Suite 314, Boulder, CO 80301 *Tel:* 303-444-6684 *Fax:* 303-444-0824 *E-mail:* questions@rienner.com; cservice@rienner.com *Web Site:* www.rienner.com, pg 174

Rieselbach, Erik, New Directions Publishing Corp, 80 Eighth Ave, 19th fl, New York, NY 10011 *Tel:* 212-255-0230 *E-mail:* editorial@ndbooks.com; publicity@ndbooks.com *Web Site:* ndbooks.com, pg 139

Riez, Krisztina, Penguin Random House Canada, a Penguin Random House company, 320 Front St W, Suite 1400, Toronto, ON M5V 3B6, Canada *Tel:* 416-364-4449 *Toll Free Tel:* 888-523-9292 (cust serv) *E-mail:* canadaweb@penguinrandomhouse.com; customerservicescanada@penguinrandomhouse.com *Web Site:* www.penguinrandomhouse.ca, pg 416

Rigaud, Emmanuelle, Les Editions du Ble, 340, blvd Provencher, St Boniface, MB R2H 0G7, Canada *Tel:* 204-237-8200 *E-mail:* direction@editionsduble.ca *Web Site:* ble.avoslivres.ca, pg 402

Rigdon, Suzy, Institute for Immigration Research New American Voices Award, 4400 University Dr, MS 3E4, Fairfax, VA 22030 *Tel:* 703-993-3986 *E-mail:* submissions@fallforthebook.org *Web Site:* fallforthebook.org/aboutnewamericanvoices, pg 617

Riggs, Deidra, Embolden Literary, PO Box 953607, Lake Mary, FL 32795-3607 *E-mail:* info@emboldenmediagroup.com; submissions@emboldenmediagroup.com *Web Site:* emboldenmediagroup.com/literary-representation, pg 458

Riillo, Maria, Running Press, 1290 Avenue of the Americas, New York, NY 10104 *Tel:* 212-364-1100 *Toll Free Tel:* 800-759-0190 (cust serv) *Fax:* 212-364-0933 (intl orders) *Toll Free Fax:* 800-286-9471 (cust serv) *E-mail:* customer.service@hbgusa.com; orders@hbgusa.com *Web Site:* www.hachettebookgroup.com/imprint/running-press/; www.moon.com (Moon Travel Guides), pg 178

Riley, Elizabeth, W W Norton & Company Inc, 500 Fifth Ave, New York, NY 10110-0017 *Tel:* 212-354-5500 *Toll Free Tel:* 800-233-4830 (orders & cust serv) *Fax:* 212-869-0856 *Toll Free Fax:* 800-458-6515 *E-mail:* orders@wwnorton.com *Web Site:* wwnorton.com, pg 143

Riley, Jocelyn, Her Own Words LLC, PO Box 5264, Madison, WI 53705-0264 *Tel:* 608-271-7083 *Fax:* 608-271-0209 *Web Site:* www.herownwords.com; www.nontraditionalcareers.com, pg 91

Rimas, Ruta, GP Putnam's Sons Books for Young Readers, c/o Penguin Random House LLC, 1745 Broadway, New York, NY 10019 *Tel:* 212-782-9000 *Web Site:* www.penguin.com/putnam-young-readers/, pg 167

Rimel, John, Mountain Press Publishing Co, 1301 S Third W, Missoula, MT 59801 *Tel:* 406-728-1900 *Toll Free Tel:* 800-234-5308 *Fax:* 406-728-1635 *E-mail:* info@mtnpress.com *Web Site:* www.mountain-press.com, pg 135

Rinaldi, Karen, HarperCollins Publishers LLC, 195 Broadway, New York, NY 10007 *Tel:* 212-207-7000 *Web Site:* www.harpercollins.com, pg 86

Rinehart, Rick, M Evans & Company, c/o Rowman & Littlefield Publishing Group, 4501 Forbes Blvd, Suite 200, Lanham, MD 20706 *Tel:* 301-459-3366 *Fax:* 301-429-5748 *Web Site:* rowman.com, pg 68

Riopel, Patrica, Scribendi Inc, 405 Riverview Dr, Chatham, ON N7M 0N3, Canada *Tel:* 519-351-1626 (cust serv) *Fax:* 519-354-0192 *E-mail:* customerservice@scribendi.com *Web Site:* www.scribendi.com, pg 444

Ripa, Michael, The Experiment, 220 E 23 St, Suite 600, New York, NY 10010-4658 *Tel:* 212-889-1659 *E-mail:* info@theexperimentpublishing.com *Web Site:* www.theexperimentpublishing.com, pg 68

Ripianzi, David, YMAA Publication Center Inc, PO Box 480, Wolfeboro, NH 03894 *Tel:* 603-569-7988 *Toll Free Tel:* 800-669-8892 *Fax:* 603-569-1889 *E-mail:* info@ymaa.com *Web Site:* www.ymaa.com, pg 235

Rishi, Aparna, Random House Publishing Group, 1745 Broadway, New York, NY 10019 *Toll Free Tel:* 800-200-3552 *Web Site:* www.randomhousebooks.com, pg 171

Ristau, Kate, Kay Snow Writing Contest, 5331 SW Macadam Ave, Suite 258, PMB 215, Portland, OR 97239 *Tel:* 971-200-5385 *E-mail:* wilwrite@willamettewriters.org *Web Site:* willamettewriters.org/kay-snow-writing-contest, pg 664

Ristau, Kate, Willamette Writers, 5331 SW Macadam Ave, Suite 258, PMB 215, Portland, OR 97239 *Tel:* 971-200-5385 *E-mail:* wilwrite@willamettewriters.org *Web Site:* willamettewriters.org, pg 522

Ristau, Kate, Willamette Writers' Conference, 5331 SW Macadam Ave, Suite 258, PMB 215, Portland, OR 97239 *Tel:* 971-200-5385 *E-mail:* wilwrite@willamettewriters.org *Web Site:* willamettewriters.org, pg 558

Ritchey, Sharon, RISING STAR Award, PO Box 190, Jefferson, OR 97352 *E-mail:* risingstar@womensfictionwriters.org *Web Site:* wfwa.memberclicks.net/rising-star-award, pg 656

Ritchey, Sharon, STAR Award, PO Box 190, Jefferson, OR 97352 *E-mail:* staraward@womensfictionwriters.org *Web Site:* wfwa.memberclicks.net/star-award, pg 666

Ritchey, Sharon, Women's Fiction Writers Association (WFWA), PO Box 190, Jefferson, OR 97352 *E-mail:* communications@womensfictionwriters.org; membership@womensfictionwriters.org; programs@womensfictionwriters.org *Web Site:* www.womensfictionwriters.org, pg 522

Ritchie, Alex, Rocky Mountain Mineral Law Foundation, 9191 Sheridan Blvd, Suite 203, Westminster, CO 80031 *Tel:* 303-321-8100 *Fax:* 303-321-7657 *E-mail:* info@rmmlf.org *Web Site:* www.rmmlf.org, pg 176

Ritchken, Deborah, Marsal Lyon Literary Agency LLC, 665 San Rodolfo Dr, Suite 124, PMB 121, Solana Beach, CA 92075 *Tel:* 760-814-8507 *Web Site:* www.marsallyonliteraryagency.com, pg 468

Rittenberg, Ann, Ann Rittenberg Literary Agency Inc, 15 Maiden Lane, Suite 206, New York, NY 10038 *Tel:* 212-684-6936 *Fax:* 212-684-6929 *E-mail:* info@rittlit.com *Web Site:* www.rittlit.com, pg 473

Rittenhouse, Nan, Atria Books, 1230 Avenue of the Americas, New York, NY 10020 *Tel:* 212-698-7000 *Fax:* 212-698-7007 *Web Site:* www.simonandschuster.com, pg 21

Riva, Peter, International Transactions Inc, 28 Alope Way, Gila, NM 88038 *Tel:* 845-373-9696 *Fax:* 520-300-7248 *E-mail:* info@internationaltransactions.us *Web Site:* www.intltrans.com, pg 464

Rivas, Laura, Candlewick Press, 99 Dover St, Somerville, MA 02144-2825 *Tel:* 617-661-3330 *Fax:* 617-661-0565 *E-mail:* bigbear@candlewick.com; salesinfo@candlewick.com *Web Site:* candlewick.com, pg 40

Rivas, Mike, Vermont College of Fine Arts, MFA in Writing Program, 36 College St, Montpelier, VT 05602 *Tel:* 802-828-8840; 802-828-8839 *Toll Free Tel:* 866-934-VCFA (934-8232) *Fax:* 802-828-8649 *Web Site:* www.vcfa.edu, pg 567

Rivas-Smith, Alexandra, William H Sadlier Inc, 9 Pine St, New York, NY 10005 *Tel:* 212-227-2120 *Toll Free Tel:* 800-221-5175 (cust serv) *Fax:* 212-312-6080 *E-mail:* customerservice@sadlier.com *Web Site:* www.sadlier.com, pg 179

Riven, Judith, Judith Riven Literary Agent LLC, 250 W 16 St, Suite 4F, New York, NY 10011, pg 444, 473

Rivera, Frank, Adams Media, 100 Technology Center Dr, Suite 501, Stoughton, MA 02072 *Tel:* 508-427-7100 *Web Site:* www.simonandschuster.com, pg 4

Rivera, Hannah, Bloomsbury Publishing Inc, 1385 Broadway, 5th fl, New York, NY 10018 *Tel:* 212-419-5300 *E-mail:* marketingusa@bloomsbury.com; adultpublicityusa@bloomsbury.com; askacademic@bloomsbury.com *Web Site:* www.bloomsbury.com, pg 32

Rivero, Bev, Beacon Press, 24 Farnsworth St, Boston, MA 02210-1409 *Tel:* 617-742-2110 *Fax:* 617-723-3097 *E-mail:* production@beacon.org *Web Site:* www.beacon.org, pg 25

Rivers, Alena, ALSC Baker & Taylor Summer Reading Grant, 225 N Michigan Ave, Suite 1300, Chicago, IL 60601 *Tel:* 312-280-2163 *Toll Free Tel:* 800-

545-2433 *Fax:* 312-280-5271 *E-mail:* alsc@ala.org *Web Site:* www.ala.org/alsc/awardsgrants/profawards/bakertaylor, pg 572

Rivers, Alena, The Mildred L Batchelder Award, 225 N Michigan Ave, Suite 1300, Chicago, IL 60601 *Tel:* 312-280-2163 *Toll Free Tel:* 800-545-2433 *Fax:* 312-280-5271 *E-mail:* alsc@ala.org *Web Site:* www.ala.org/alsc/awardsgrants/bookmedia/batchelder, pg 577

Rivers, Alena, The Pura Belpre Award, 225 N Michigan Ave, Suite 1300, Chicago, IL 60601 *Tel:* 312-280-2163 *Toll Free Tel:* 800-545-2433 *Fax:* 312-280-5271 *E-mail:* alsc@ala.org *Web Site:* www.ala.org/alsc/awardsgrants/bookmedia/belpre, pg 578

Rivers, Alena, Bound to Stay Bound Books Scholarship, 225 N Michigan Ave, Suite 1300, Chicago, IL 60601 *Tel:* 312-280-2163 *Toll Free Tel:* 800-545-2433 *Fax:* 312-280-5271 *E-mail:* alsc@ala.org *Web Site:* www.ala.org/alsc/awardsgrants/scholarships; www.btsb.com/about-us/scholarships, pg 583

Rivers, Alena, The Randolph Caldecott Medal, 225 N Michigan Ave, Suite 1300, Chicago, IL 60601 *Tel:* 312-280-2163 *Toll Free Tel:* 800-545-2433 *Fax:* 312-280-5271 *E-mail:* alsc@ala.org *Web Site:* www.ala.org/alsc/awardsgrants/bookmedia/caldecott, pg 585

Rivers, Alena, Children's Literature Lecture Award, 225 N Michigan Ave, Suite 1300, Chicago, IL 60601 *Tel:* 312-280-2163 *Toll Free Tel:* 800-545-2433 *Fax:* 312-280-5271 *E-mail:* alsc@ala.org *Web Site:* www.ala.org/alsc/awardsgrants/profawards/chll, pg 589

Rivers, Alena, Children's Literature Legacy Award, 225 N Michigan Ave, Suite 1300, Chicago, IL 60601 *Tel:* 312-280-2163 *Toll Free Tel:* 800-545-2433 *Fax:* 312-280-5271 *E-mail:* alsc@ala.org *Web Site:* www.ala.org/awardsgrants/childrens-literature-legacy-award; www.ala.org/alsc/awardsgrants/bookmedia/clla, pg 589

Rivers, Alena, Theodor Seuss Geisel Award, 225 N Michigan Ave, Suite 1300, Chicago, IL 60601 *Toll Free Tel:* 800-545-2433 *E-mail:* alsc@ala.org *Web Site:* www.ala.org/alsc/awardsgrants/bookmedia/geisel, pg 606

Rivers, Alena, Frederic G Melcher Scholarship, 225 N Michigan Ave, Suite 1300, Chicago, IL 60601 *Tel:* 312-280-2163 *Toll Free Tel:* 800-545-2433 *Fax:* 312-280-5271 *E-mail:* alsc@ala.org *Web Site:* www.ala.org/alsc/awardsgrants/scholarships, pg 632

Rivers, Alena, John Newbery Medal, 225 N Michigan Ave, Suite 1300, Chicago, IL 60601 *Tel:* 312-280-2163 *Toll Free Tel:* 800-545-2433 *Fax:* 312-280-5271 *E-mail:* alsc@ala.org *Web Site:* www.ala.org/alsc/awardsgrants/bookmedia/newbery, pg 641

Rivers, Alena, Robert F Sibert Informational Book Award, 225 N Michigan Ave, Suite 1300, Chicago, IL 60601 *Tel:* 312-280-2163 *Toll Free Tel:* 800-545-2433 *Fax:* 312-280-5271 *E-mail:* alsc@ala.org *Web Site:* www.ala.org/alsc/awardsgrants/bookmedia/sibert, pg 662

Rivkin, Claire, Random House Children's Books, c/o Penguin Random House LLC, 1745 Broadway, New York, NY 10019 *Tel:* 212-782-9000 *Web Site:* www.rhcbooks.com, pg 170

Rizzini, Claudia, Radcliffe Institute Fellowship Program, Byerly Hall, 8 Garden St, Cambridge, MA 02138 *Tel:* 617-495-8212 *Fax:* 617-495-8136 *E-mail:* fellowships@radcliffe.harvard.edu *Web Site:* www.radcliffe.harvard.edu/fellowship-program, pg 654

Rizzo, Adriana, Houghton Mifflin Harcourt Trade & Reference Division, 125 High St, Boston, MA 02110 *Tel:* 617-351-5000 *Web Site:* www.hmhco.com, pg 96

Roach, Brian, The Catholic University of America Press, 240 Leahy Hall, 620 Michigan Ave NE, Washington, DC 20064 *Tel:* 202-319-5052 *Toll Free Tel:* 800-537-5487 (orders only) *Fax:* 202-319-4985 *E-mail:* cuapress@cua.edu *Web Site:* cuapress.org, pg 42

Roane, Rick, Cherry Hill Publishing LLC, 24344 Del Amo Rd, Ramona, CA 92065 *Tel:* 858-868-1260 *Toll Free Tel:* 800-407-1072 *Fax:* 760-203-1200 *E-mail:* operations@cherryhillpublishing.com; sales@cherryhillpublishing.com *Web Site:* www.cherryhillpublishing.com, pg 46

Roane, Sharon, Cherry Hill Publishing LLC, 24344 Del Amo Rd, Ramona, CA 92065 *Tel:* 858-868-1260 *Toll Free Tel:* 800-407-1072 *Fax:* 760-203-1200 *E-mail:* operations@cherryhillpublishing.com; sales@cherryhillpublishing.com *Web Site:* www.cherryhillpublishing.com, pg 46

Roback, Bob, United Talent Agency LLC, 9336 Civic Center Dr, Beverly Hills, CA 90210 *Tel:* 310-273-6700 *Web Site:* www.unitedtalent.com, pg 481

Robbins, B J, B J Robbins Literary Agency, 5130 Bellaire Ave, North Hollywood, CA 91607 *E-mail:* robbinsliterary@gmail.com, pg 474

Robbins, Caroline, Trafalgar Square Books, 388 Howe Hill Rd, North Pomfret, VT 05053 *Tel:* 802-457-1911 *Toll Free Tel:* 800-423-4525 *Fax:* 802-457-1913 *E-mail:* contact@trafalgarbooks.com *Web Site:* www.trafalgarbooks.com; www.horseandriderbooks.com, pg 208

Robbins, Christopher, Familius, PO Box 1249, Reedley, CA 93654 *Tel:* 559-876-2170 *Fax:* 559-876-2180 *E-mail:* orders@familius.com *Web Site:* www.familius.com, pg 69

Robbins, Dani, BoardSource, 750 Ninth St NW, Suite 520, Washington, DC 20001-4793 *Tel:* 202-349-2500 *E-mail:* members@boardsource.org; mediarelations@boardsource.org *Web Site:* www.boardsource.org, pg 33

Robbins, Fleetwood, Waxman Literary Agency, 443 Park Ave S, No 1004, New York, NY 10016 *Tel:* 212-675-5556 *Web Site:* www.waxmanliteraryagency.com, pg 481

Robbins, Michele, Familius, PO Box 1249, Reedley, CA 93654 *Tel:* 559-876-2170 *Fax:* 559-876-2180 *E-mail:* orders@familius.com *Web Site:* www.familius.com, pg 69

Robbins, Sandra, See-More's Workshop Arts & Education Workshops, 325 West End Ave, New York, NY 10023 *Tel:* 212-724-0677 *E-mail:* sbt@shadowboxtheatre.org *Web Site:* shadowboxtheatre.org/workshops, pg 557

Robbins, Sarah, Harry N Abrams Inc, 195 Broadway, 9th Fl, New York, NY 10007 *Tel:* 212-206-7715 *Toll Free Tel:* 800-345-1359 *Fax:* 212-645-8437 *E-mail:* abrams@abramsbooks.com; publicity@abramsbooks.com; sales@abramsbooks.com *Web Site:* www.abramsbooks.com, pg 3

Robeck, Edward C, American Geosciences Institute (AGI), 4220 King St, Alexandria, VA 22302-1502 *Tel:* 703-379-2480 (ext 246) *E-mail:* agi@americangeosciences.org *Web Site:* www.americangeosciences.org; www.geosciencestore.org, pg 10

Roberge, Amelie, Kids Can Press Ltd, 25 Dockside Dr, Toronto, ON M5A 0B5, Canada *Tel:* 416-479-7000 *Toll Free Tel:* 800-265-0884 *Fax:* 416-960-5437 *E-mail:* info@kidscan; customerservice@kidscan.com *Web Site:* www.kidscanpress.com; www.kidscanpress.ca, pg 411

Roberson, Jamii, BoardSource, 750 Ninth St NW, Suite 520, Washington, DC 20001-4793 *Tel:* 202-349-2500 *E-mail:* members@boardsource.org; mediarelations@boardsource.org *Web Site:* www.boardsource.org, pg 33

Roberts, Andrew, Penguin Random House Canada, a Penguin Random House company, 320 Front St W, Suite 1400, Toronto, ON M5V 3B6, Canada *Tel:* 416-364-4449 *Toll Free Tel:* 888-523-9292 (cust serv) *E-mail:* canadaweb@penguinrandomhouse.com; customerservicescanada@penguinrandomhouse.com *Web Site:* www.penguinrandomhouse.ca, pg 416

Roberts, April, Chronicle Books LLC, 680 Second St, San Francisco, CA 94107 *Tel:* 415-537-4200 *Fax:* 415-537-4460 (perms) *E-mail:* hello@chroniclebooks.com; subrights@chroniclebooks.com *Web Site:* www.chroniclebooks.com, pg 47

Roberts, Brian, American Society of Composers, Authors & Publishers (ASCAP), 250 W 57 St, New York, NY 10107 *Tel:* 212-621-6000 *Toll Free Tel:* 800-952-7227 (cust serv) *Fax:* 212-621-6595 *Web Site:* www.ascap.com, pg 496

Roberts, Dr Catherine A, American Mathematical Society (AMS), 201 Charles St, Providence, RI 02904-2213 *Tel:* 401-455-4000 *Toll Free Tel:* 800-321-4267 *Fax:* 401-331-3842; 401-455-4046 (cust serv) *E-mail:* ams@ams.org; cust-serv@ams.org *Web Site:* www.ams.org, pg 11

Roberts, Janet, Centering Corp, 6406 Maple St, Omaha, NE 68104 *Tel:* 402-553-1200 *Toll Free Tel:* 866-218-0101 *Fax:* 402-553-0507 *E-mail:* orders@centeringcorp.com *Web Site:* www.centering.org, pg 44

Roberts, Jennifer, Candlewick Press, 99 Dover St, Somerville, MA 02144-2825 *Tel:* 617-661-3330 *Fax:* 617-661-0565 *E-mail:* bigbear@candlewick.com; salesinfo@candlewick.com *Web Site:* candlewick.com, pg 39

Roberts, Jill, Tachyon Publications LLC, 1459 18 St, No 139, San Francisco, CA 94107 *Tel:* 415-285-5615 *E-mail:* tachyon@tachyonpublications.com; submissions@tachyonpublications.com *Web Site:* www.tachyonpublications.com, pg 202

Roberts, Kelly, Harlequin Enterprises Ltd, 195 Broadway, 24th fl, New York, NY 10007 *Tel:* 212-207-7000 *Toll Free Tel:* 888-432-4879; 800-370-5838 (ebooks) *E-mail:* customerservice@harlequin.com *Web Site:* www.harlequin.com/shop/index.html; corporate.harlequin.com, pg 85

Roberts, Kelly, HarperCollins Publishers LLC, 195 Broadway, New York, NY 10007 *Tel:* 212-207-7000 *Web Site:* www.harpercollins.com, pg 86

Roberts, Dr Kevin, The Heritage Foundation, 214 Massachusetts Ave NE, Washington, DC 20002-4999 *Tel:* 202-546-4400 *Toll Free Tel:* 800-546-2843 *Fax:* 202-546-8328 *E-mail:* info@heritage.org *Web Site:* www.heritage.org, pg 91

Roberts, Laura MD, American Psychiatric Association Publishing, 800 Maine Ave SW, Suite 900, Washington, DC 20024 *Tel:* 202-459-9722 *Toll Free Tel:* 800-368-5777 *Fax:* 202-403-3094 *E-mail:* appi@psych.org *Web Site:* www.appi.org; www.psychiatryonline.org, pg 11

Roberts, Lauren, Little, Brown and Company, 1290 Avenue of the Americas, New York, NY 10104 *Tel:* 212-364-1100 *Fax:* 212-364-0952 *E-mail:* firstname.lastname@hbgusa.com *Web Site:* www.hachettebookgroup.com/imprint/little-brown-and-company/, pg 118

Roberts, Marc, Centering Corp, 6406 Maple St, Omaha, NE 68104 *Tel:* 402-553-1200 *Toll Free Tel:* 866-218-0101 *Fax:* 402-553-0507 *E-mail:* orders@centeringcorp.com *Web Site:* www.centering.org, pg 44

Roberts, Marianne, Write Stuff Enterprises LLC, 1001 S Andrews Ave, Suite 200, Fort Lauderdale, FL 33316 *Tel:* 954-462-6657 *Fax:* 954-462-6023 *E-mail:* info@writestuffbooks.com *Web Site:* www.writestuffbooks.com, pg 234

Roberts, Meghan, Basic Books Group, 1290 Avenue of the Americas, New York, NY 10104 *Tel:* 212-340-8100 *Toll Free Tel:* 800-343-4499 (cust serv) *Fax:* 212-340-8105 *E-mail:* customer.service@hbgusa.com; orders@hbgusa.com *Web Site:* www.hachettebookgroup.com/imprint/basic-books/, pg 25

Roberts, Michele, Liberty Fund Inc, 11301 N Meridian St, Carmel, IN 46032-4564 *Tel:* 317-842-0880 *Toll Free Tel:* 800-955-8335; 800-866-3520 *Fax:* 317-579-6060 (cust serv); 708-534-7803 *E-mail:* books@libertyfund.org; info@libertyfund.org *Web Site:* www.libertyfund.org, pg 116

Roberts, Olivia, Chronicle Books LLC, 680 Second St, San Francisco, CA 94107 *Tel:* 415-537-4200 *Fax:* 415-537-4460 (perms) *E-mail:* hello@chroniclebooks.com; subrights@chroniclebooks.com *Web Site:* www.chroniclebooks.com, pg 47

Roberts, Paul, George T Bisel Co Inc, 710 S Washington Sq, Philadelphia, PA 19106-3519 *Tel:* 215-922-5760 *Toll Free Tel:* 800-247-3526 *Fax:* 215-922-2235 *E-mail:* gbisel@bisel.com *Web Site:* www.bisel.com, pg 29

Roberts, Sian, SAS Press, 100 SAS Campus Dr, Cary, NC 27513-2414 *Tel:* 919-677-8000 *Toll Free Tel:* 800-727-0025 *Fax:* 919-677-4444 *E-mail:* saspress@sas.com *Web Site:* support.sas.com/en/books.html, pg 182

Roberts, Soumeya Bendimerad, Association of American Literary Agents Inc (AALA), 302A W 12 St, No 122, New York, NY 10014 *Tel:* 212-840-5770 *E-mail:* info@aalitagents.org *Web Site:* aalitagents.org, pg 498

Roberts, Soumeya Bendimerad, HG Literary, 6 W 18 St, Suite 7R, New York, NY 10011 *E-mail:* foreign@hgliterary.com; rights@hgliterary.com *Web Site:* www.hgliterary.com, pg 463

Roberts, Stuart, HarperCollins Publishers LLC, 195 Broadway, New York, NY 10007 *Tel:* 212-207-7000 *Web Site:* www.harpercollins.com, pg 86

Roberts, Tim, Counterpath Press, 7935 E 14 Ave, Denver, CO 80220 *E-mail:* counterpath@counterpathpress.org *Web Site:* www.counterpathpress.org, pg 54

Roberts, Tony, University of Oklahoma Press, 2800 Venture Dr, Norman, OK 73069-8216 *Tel:* 405-325-2000 *Web Site:* www.oupress.com, pg 219

Roberts, U D, Brentwood Christian Press, PO Box 4773, Columbus, GA 31914-4773 *Toll Free Tel:* 800-334-8861 *E-mail:* brentwood@aol.com *Web Site:* www.brentwoodbooks.com, pg 36

Robertson, Alex, Candlewick Press, 99 Dover St, Somerville, MA 02144-2825 *Tel:* 617-661-3330 *Fax:* 617-661-0565 *E-mail:* bigbear@candlewick.com; salesinfo@candlewick.com *Web Site:* candlewick.com, pg 40

Robertson, Christine, University of Toronto Press, Book Publishing Div, 800 Bay St, Mezzanine, Toronto, ON M5S 3A9, Canada *Tel:* 416-978-2239 *Fax:* 416-978-4736 *E-mail:* utpbooks@utorontopress.com (orders) *Web Site:* utorontopress.com, pg 423

Robertson, David A, Tundra Book Group, 320 Front St W, Suite 1400, Toronto, ON M5V 3B6, Canada *Tel:* 416-364-4449 *Toll Free Tel:* 888-523-9292 (orders); 800-588-1074 *E-mail:* youngreaders@penguinrandomhouse.com *Web Site:* www.tundrabooks.com, pg 421

Robertson, Jocelyn, Literature Fellowship, 9543 W Emerald St, Suite 204, Boise, ID 83704 *Tel:* 208-334-2119 *E-mail:* info@arts.idaho.gov *Web Site:* arts.idaho.gov/grants/fellowships, pg 625

Robertson, Jocelyn, Writer in Residence, 9543 W Emerald St, Suite 204, Boise, ID 83704 *Tel:* 208-334-2119 *E-mail:* info@arts.idaho.gov *Web Site:* arts.idaho.gov/writer-in-residence, pg 678

Robertson, Mia, Gallery Books, 1230 Avenue of the Americas, New York, NY 10020 *Toll Free Tel:* 800-456-6798 *Fax:* 212-698-7284 *E-mail:* consumer.customerservice@simonandschuster.com *Web Site:* www.simonandschuster.com, pg 76

Robertson, Michael, The Joseph R Dunlap Memorial Fellowship, PO Box 53263, Washington, DC 20009 *E-mail:* us@morrissociety.org *Web Site:* www.morrissociety.org, pg 597

Robertson, Randy PhD, Susquehanna University, Department of English & Creative Writing, 514 University Ave, Selinsgrove, PA 17870 *Tel:* 570-372-4196 *Web Site:* www.susqu.edu, pg 565

Robertson, Sarah, Schlager Group Inc, 10228 E Northwest Hwy, No 1151, Dallas, TX 75238 *Toll Free Tel:* 888-416-5727 *Fax:* 469-325-3700 *E-mail:* info@schlagergroup.com; sales@schlagergroup.com *Web Site:* www.schlagergroup.com, pg 183

Robey, Annelise, Jane Rotrosen Agency LLC, 318 E 51 St, New York, NY 10022-7803 *Tel:* 212-593-4330 *E-mail:* info@janerotrosen.com *Web Site:* janerotrosen.com, pg 474

Robinson, Angela Y, National Association of Black Journalists (NABJ), 1100 Knight Hall, Suite 3101, College Park, MD 20742 *Tel:* 301-405-0248 *E-mail:* contact@nabj.org; press@nabj.org *Web Site:* nabjonline.org, pg 511

Robinson, Arianna, HarperCollins Children's Books, 195 Broadway, New York, NY 10007 *Tel:* 212-207-7000 *Web Site:* www.harpercollins.com/childrens, pg 85

Robinson, Brisa, Penguin Random House Audio Publishing Group, 1745 Broadway, New York, NY 10019 *Toll Free Tel:* 800-793-2665 (cust serv) *E-mail:* audio@penguinrandomhouse.com; ecustomerservice@penguinrandomhouse.com *Web Site:* www.penguinrandomhouseaudio.com, pg 154

Robinson, Eileen, Charlesbridge Publishing Inc, 85 Main St, Watertown, MA 02472 *Tel:* 617-926-0329 *Toll Free Tel:* 800-225-3214 *Fax:* 617-926-5720 *Toll Free Fax:* 800-926-5775 *E-mail:* books@charlesbridge.com *Web Site:* www.charlesbridge.com, pg 45

Robinson, Erin, Tor Publishing Group, 120 Broadway, New York, NY 10271 *Toll Free Tel:* 800-455-0340 (Macmillan) *E-mail:* torpublicity@tor.com; forgepublicity@forgebooks.com *Web Site:* us.macmillan.com/torpublishinggroup, pg 208

Robinson, Gene D, Moonshine Cove Publishing LLC, 150 Willow Point, Abbeville, SC 29620 *E-mail:* publisher@moonshinecovepublishing.com *Web Site:* moonshinecovepublishing.com, pg 134

Robinson, Hannah, Grand Central Publishing, 1290 Avenue of the Americas, New York, NY 10104 *Tel:* 212-364-1100 *Web Site:* www.hachettebookgroup.com/imprint/grand-central-publishing/, pg 80

Robinson, James J, The Minerals, Metals & Materials Society (TMS), 5700 Corporate Dr, Suite 750, Pittsburgh, PA 15237 *Tel:* 724-776-9000 *Toll Free Tel:* 800-759-4867 *Fax:* 724-776-3770 *E-mail:* publications@tms.org (orders) *Web Site:* www.tms.org/bookstore (orders); www.tms.org, pg 132

Robinson, Jennifer, Gallery Books, 1230 Avenue of the Americas, New York, NY 10020 *Toll Free Tel:* 800-456-6798 *Fax:* 212-698-7284 *E-mail:* consumer.customerservice@simonandschuster.com *Web Site:* www.simonandschuster.com, pg 76

Robinson, John, Public Relations Society of America Inc, 120 Wall St, 21st fl, New York, NY 10005 *Tel:* 212-460-1400 *E-mail:* membership@prsa.org *Web Site:* www.prsa.org, pg 518

Robinson, Kaitlyn, Penguin Random House Audio Publishing Group, 1745 Broadway, New York, NY 10019 *Toll Free Tel:* 800-793-2665 (cust serv) *E-mail:* audio@penguinrandomhouse.com; ecustomerservice@penguinrandomhouse.com *Web Site:* www.penguinrandomhouseaudio.com, pg 154

Robinson, Kim, University of California Press, 155 Grand Ave, Suite 400, Oakland, CA 94612-3758 *Tel:* 510-883-8232 *Fax:* 510-836-8910 *E-mail:* customerservice@ucpress.edu *Web Site:* www.ucpress.edu, pg 215

Robinson, Kym, Willi Paul Adams Award, 112 N Bryan Ave, Bloomington, IN 47408-4141 *Tel:* 812-855-7311 *E-mail:* oah@oah.org *Web Site:* www.oah.org/awards, pg 570

Robinson, Kym, Ray Allen Billington Prize, 112 N Bryan Ave, Bloomington, IN 47408-4141 *Tel:* 812-855-7311 *E-mail:* oah@oah.org *Web Site:* www.oah.org/awards, pg 580

Robinson, Kym, Binkley-Stephenson Award, 112 N Bryan Ave, Bloomington, IN 47408-4141 *Tel:* 812-855-7311 *E-mail:* oah@oah.org *Web Site:* www.oah.org/awards, pg 580

Robinson, Kym, Civil War and Reconstruction Book Award, 112 N Bryan Ave, Bloomington, IN 47408-4141 *Tel:* 812-855-7311 *E-mail:* oah@oah.org *Web Site:* www.oah.org/awards, pg 590

Robinson, Kym, Merle Curti Intellectual History Award, 112 N Bryan Ave, Bloomington, IN 47408-4141 *Tel:* 812-855-7311 *E-mail:* oah@oah.org *Web Site:* www.oah.org/awards, pg 594

Robinson, Kym, Merle Curti Social History Award, 112 N Bryan Ave, Bloomington, IN 47408-4141 *Tel:* 812-855-7311 *E-mail:* oah@oah.org *Web Site:* www.oah.org/awards, pg 594

Robinson, Kym, Ellis W Hawley Prize, 112 N Bryan Ave, Bloomington, IN 47408-4141 *Tel:* 812-855-7311 *E-mail:* oah@oah.org *Web Site:* www.oah.org/awards, pg 611

Robinson, Kym, Darlene Clark Hine Award, 112 N Bryan Ave, Bloomington, IN 47408-4141 *Tel:* 812-855-7311 *E-mail:* oah@oah.org *Web Site:* www.oah.org/awards, pg 613

Robinson, Kym, Richard W Leopold Prize, 112 N Bryan Ave, Bloomington, IN 47408-4141 *Tel:* 812-855-7311 *E-mail:* oah@oah.org *Web Site:* www.oah.org/awards, pg 623

Robinson, Kym, Lawrence W Levine Award, 112 N Bryan Ave, Bloomington, IN 47408-4141 *Tel:* 812-855-7311 *E-mail:* oah@oah.org *Web Site:* www.oah.org/awards, pg 624

Robinson, Kym, Liberty Legacy Foundation Award, 112 N Bryan Ave, Bloomington, IN 47408-4141 *Tel:* 812-855-7311 *E-mail:* oah@oah.org *Web Site:* www.oah.org/awards, pg 624

Robinson, Kym, David Montgomery Award, 112 N Bryan Ave, Bloomington, IN 47408-4141 *Tel:* 812-855-7311 *E-mail:* oah@oah.org *Web Site:* www.oah.org/awards, pg 634

Robinson, Kym, Mary Nickliss Prize in US Women's and/or Gender History, 112 N Bryan Ave, Bloomington, IN 47408-4141 *Tel:* 812-855-7311 *E-mail:* oah@oah.org *Web Site:* www.oah.org/awards, pg 641

Robinson, Kym, James A Rawley Prize, 112 N Bryan Ave, Bloomington, IN 47408-4141 *Tel:* 812-855-7311 *E-mail:* oah@oah.org *Web Site:* www.oah.org/awards, pg 655

Robinson, Kym, David Thelen Award, 112 N Bryan Ave, Bloomington, IN 47408-4141 *Tel:* 812-855-7311 *E-mail:* oah@oah.org *Web Site:* www.oah.org/awards, pg 669

Robinson, Kym, Frederick Jackson Turner Award, 112 N Bryan Ave, Bloomington, IN 47408-4141 *Tel:* 812-855-7311 *E-mail:* oah@oah.org *Web Site:* www.oah.org/awards, pg 671

Robinson, Mark, American Academy of Arts & Sciences (AAAS), 136 Irving St, Cambridge, MA 02138 *Tel:* 617-576-5000 *Fax:* 617-576-5050 *E-mail:* aaas@amacad.org *Web Site:* www.amacad.org, pg 494

Robinson, Morris (Dino), Northwestern University Press, 629 Noyes St, Evanston, IL 60208-4210 *Tel:* 847-491-2046 *Toll Free Tel:* 800-621-2736 (orders only) *Fax:* 847-491-8150 *E-mail:* nupress@northwestern.edu *Web Site:* www.nupress.northwestern.edu, pg 143

Robinson, Phoebe, Dutton, c/o Penguin Random House LLC, 1745 Broadway, New York, NY 10019 *Tel:* 212-366-2000 *Web Site:* www.penguin.com/dutton-overview/; www.penguin.com/plume-books-overview/; www.penguin.com/tiny-reparations-overview/, pg 62

Robinson, Quressa, Folio Literary Management, The Film Center Bldg, 630 Ninth Ave, Suite 1101, New York, NY 10036 *Tel:* 212-400-1494 *Fax:* 212-967-0977 *Web Site:* www.foliolit.com, pg 459

Robinson, Ramon, The American Library Association (ALA), 225 N Michigan Ave, Suite 1300, Chicago, IL 60601 *Tel:* 312-944-6780 *Toll Free Tel:* 800-545-2433; 866-SHOP-ALA (746-7252, orders) *Fax:* 312-280-5275; 312-440-9374; 312-280-5860 (orders) *E-mail:* ala@ala.org; alastore@ala.org *Web Site:* www.alastore.ala.org; www.ala.org, pg 10

Robinson, Shaina, Graywolf Press, 212 Third Ave N, Suite 485, Minneapolis, MN 55401 *Tel:* 651-641-0077 *Fax:* 651-641-0036 *E-mail:* wolves@graywolfpress.org (no ms queries, sample chapters or proposals) *Web Site:* www.graywolfpress.org, pg 81

Robinson, Shirley, Texas Library Association (TLA), 3420 Executive Center Dr, Suite 301, Austin, TX 78731 Tel: 512-328-1518 Fax: 512-328-8852 E-mail: tla@txla.org Web Site: txla.org, pg 521

Robinson, Terry, Gale, 27555 Executive Dr, Suite 270, Farmington Hills, MI 48331 Toll Free Tel: 800-877-4253 Toll Free Fax: 877-363-4253 E-mail: gale.customerexperience@cengage.com Web Site: www.gale.com, pg 75

Robinson, Terry, Macmillan Reference USA™, 27500 Drake Rd, Farmington Hills, MI 48331-3535 Tel: 248-699-4253 Toll Free Tel: 800-877-4253 Toll Free Fax: 877-363-4253 E-mail: gale.customercare@cengage.com Web Site: www.gale.cengage.com/macmillan, pg 123

Robinson-Smith, Sun, Penguin Random House LLC, 1745 Broadway, New York, NY 10019 Tel: 212-782-9000 Toll Free Tel: 800-726-0600 Web Site: www.penguinrandomhouse.com, pg 155

Robinson-Smith, Sun, Random House Publishing Group, 1745 Broadway, New York, NY 10019 Toll Free Tel: 800-200-3552 Web Site: www.randomhousebooks.com, pg 171

Robson, William B P, C D Howe Institute, 67 Yonge St, Suite 300, Toronto, ON M5E 1J8, Canada Tel: 416-865-1904 Fax: 416-865-1866 E-mail: cdhowe@cdhowe.org Web Site: www.cdhowe.org, pg 410

Robyn, Chris, China Books, 360 Swift Ave, Suite 48, South San Francisco, CA 94080 Fax: 650-872-7808 E-mail: editor.sinomedia@gmail.com, pg 47

Robyn, Chris, Long River Press, 360 Swift Ave, Suite 48, South San Francisco, CA 94080 Tel: 650-872-7718 (ext 312) Fax: 650-872-7808 E-mail: editor@sinomediausa.com, pg 120

Roc, Marco, TCU Press, 3000 Sandage Ave, Fort Worth, TX 76109 Tel: 817-257-7822 E-mail: tcupress@tcu.edu Web Site: www.tcupress.com, pg 203

Rocco, Donna, Random House Children's Books, c/o Penguin Random House LLC, 1745 Broadway, New York, NY 10019 Tel: 212-782-9000 Web Site: www.rhcbooks.com, pg 170

Rocha, Flavia, Rattapallax Press, 532 La Guadia Place, Suite 353, New York, NY 10012 Web Site: www.rattapallax.com, pg 172

Rocha, Stephanie, Sourcebooks LLC, 1935 Brookdale Rd, Suite 139, Naperville, IL 60563 Tel: 630-961-3900 Toll Free Tel: 800-432-7444 Fax: 630-961-2168 E-mail: info@sourcebooks.com Web Site: www.sourcebooks.com, pg 194

Roche, Art, Dubuque Fine Arts Players Annual One Act Play Festival, PO Box 1160, Dubuque, IA 52004-1160 Tel: 563-581-6521 E-mail: contact_dbqoneacts@iowa706.com Web Site: www.dbqoneacts.org, pg 597

Roche, Mary Beth, Macmillan, 120 Broadway, 22nd fl, New York, NY 10271 E-mail: press.inquiries@macmillan.com Web Site: us.macmillan.com, pg 122

Roche, Mary Beth, Macmillan Audio, 120 Broadway, 22nd fl, New York, NY 10271 Tel: 646-600-7856 Toll Free: 888-330-8477 (cust serv) Toll Free Fax: 800-672-7703 E-mail: macmillan.audio@macmillanusa.com Web Site: us.macmillan.com/audio, pg 123

Rock, Victoria, Chronicle Books LLC, 680 Second St, San Francisco, CA 94107 Tel: 415-537-4200 Fax: 415-537-4460 (perms) E-mail: hello@chroniclebooks.com; subrights@chroniclebooks.com Web Site: www.chroniclebooks.com, pg 47

Rockmore, Prof Daniel N, Neukom Institute Literary Arts Award for Playwriting, Dartmouth College, Sudikoff Bldg, Rm 121, 9 Maynard St, Hanover, NH 03755 Web Site: sites.dartmouth.edu/neukominstitutelitawards, pg 639

Rodal, Levi, KTAV Publishing House Inc, 527 Empire Blvd, Brooklyn, NY 11225 Tel: 201-963-9524; 718-972-5449 Fax: 718-972-6307 E-mail: orders@ktav.com Web Site: www.ktav.com, pg 111

Rodd, Rebecca, Levine|Greenberg|Rostan Literary Agency, 307 Seventh Ave, Suite 2407, New York, NY 10001 Tel: 212-337-0934 Fax: 212-337-0948 E-mail: submit@lgrliterary.com Web Site: lgrliterary.com, pg 467

Roddy, Kate, Sourcebooks LLC, 1935 Brookdale Rd, Suite 139, Naperville, IL 60563 Tel: 630-961-3900 Toll Free Tel: 800-432-7444 Fax: 630-961-2168 E-mail: info@sourcebooks.com Web Site: www.sourcebooks.com, pg 194

Rodengen, Jeffrey L, Write Stuff Enterprises LLC, 1001 S Andrews Ave, Suite 200, Fort Lauderdale, FL 33316 Tel: 954-462-6657 Fax: 954-462-6023 E-mail: info@writestuffbooks.com Web Site: www.writestuffbooks.com, pg 234

Roderick, Elka, Alfred A Knopf, c/o Penguin Random House LLC, 1745 Broadway, New York, NY 10019 Tel: 212-751-2600 Fax: 212-940-7390 (dom rts); 212-572-2662 (foreign rts) Web Site: knopfdoubleday.com/imprint/knopf/; knopfdoubleday.com, pg 110

Rodgers, Emma, Second Story Press, 20 Maud St, Suite 401, Toronto, ON M5V 2M5, Canada Tel: 416-537-7850 Fax: 416-537-0588 E-mail: info@secondstorypress.ca Web Site: secondstorypress.ca, pg 419

Rodgers, Loren, National Center For Employee Ownership (NCEO), 440 N Barranca Ave, Suite 3554, Covina, CA 91723 Tel: 510-208-1300 E-mail: customerservice@nceo.org Web Site: www.nceo.org, pg 137

Rodgers, Sara, Harlequin Enterprises Ltd, Bay Adelaide Centre, East Tower, 22 Adelaide St W, 41st fl, Toronto, ON M5H 4E3, Canada Tel: 416-445-5860 Toll Free Tel: 888-432-4879; 800-370-5838 (ebook inquiries) E-mail: customerservice@harlequin.com Web Site: www.harlequin.com, pg 409

Rodgerson, Gillian, Second Story Press, 20 Maud St, Suite 401, Toronto, ON M5V 2M5, Canada Tel: 416-537-7850 Fax: 416-537-0588 E-mail: info@secondstorypress.ca Web Site: secondstorypress.ca, pg 419

Rodgerson, Scott, National Council of Teachers of Mathematics (NCTM), 1906 Association Dr, Reston, VA 20191-1502 Tel: 703-620-9840 Toll Free Tel: 800-235-7566 Fax: 703-476-2970 E-mail: nctm@nctm.org Web Site: www.nctm.org, pg 137

Rodman, Jordan, Alfred A Knopf, c/o Penguin Random House LLC, 1745 Broadway, New York, NY 10019 Tel: 212-751-2600 Fax: 212-940-7390 (dom rts); 212-572-2662 (foreign rts) Web Site: knopfdoubleday.com/imprint/knopf/; knopfdoubleday.com, pg 110

Rodmell, Emily, Love Inspired Books, 233 Broadway, Suite 1001, New York, NY 10279 Tel: 212-553-4200 Toll Free Tel: 888-432-4879 Fax: 212-227-8969 E-mail: customerservice@harlequin.ca Web Site: www.harlequin.com, pg 120

Rodrick, Scott, National Center For Employee Ownership (NCEO), 440 N Barranca Ave, Suite 3554, Covina, CA 91723 Tel: 510-208-1300 E-mail: customerservice@nceo.org Web Site: www.nceo.org, pg 137

Rodrigues, Bianca, Kids Can Press Ltd, 25 Dockside Dr, Toronto, ON M5A 0B5, Canada Tel: 416-479-7000 Toll Free Tel: 800-265-0884 Fax: 416-960-5437 E-mail: info@kidscan.com; customerservice@kidscan.com Web Site: www.kidscanpress.com; www.kidscanpress.ca, pg 411

Rodriguez, Alison, Beacon Press, 24 Farnsworth St, Boston, MA 02210-1409 Tel: 617-742-2110 Fax: 617-723-3097 E-mail: production@beacon.org Web Site: www.beacon.org, pg 25

Rodriguez, Angeline, WME, 11 Madison Ave, New York, NY 10010 Tel: 212-586-5100 Web Site: www.wmeagency.com, pg 482

Rodriguez, Maria, American Booksellers Association, 600 Mamaroneck Ave, Suite 400, Harrison, NY 10528 Tel: 914-406-7500 Toll Free Tel: 800-637-0037 Fax: 914-417-4013 E-mail: info@bookweb.org Web Site: www.bookweb.org, pg 494

Rodriguez, Sharismar, Farrar, Straus & Giroux Books for Young Readers, 120 Broadway, New York, NY 10271 Tel: 212-741-6900 Toll Free Tel: 888-330-8477 (orders) E-mail: childrens.publicity@macmillan.com; childrensrights@macmillanusa.com Web Site: us.macmillan.com/mackids, pg 70

Rodriguez, Sharismar, Henry Holt and Company, LLC, 120 Broadway, 23rd fl, New York, NY 10271 Tel: 646-307-5151 Toll Free Tel: 888-330-8477 (orders) Fax: 646-307-5285 Web Site: www.henryholt.com, pg 94

Rodriguez, Sharismar, Roaring Brook Press, 120 Broadway, New York, NY 10271 Tel: 646-307-5151 Web Site: us.macmillan.com/publishers/roaring-brook-press, pg 175

Rodriguez-Marty, Nina, Viking Penguin, c/o Penguin Random House LLC, 1745 Broadway, New York, NY 10019 Tel: 212-782-9000 Web Site: www.penguin.com/overview-vikingbooks/; www.penguin.com/pamela-dorman-books-overview/; www.penguin.com/penguin-classics-overview/; www.penguin.com/penguin-life-overview/, pg 225

Rodzvilla, John, Emerson College Department of Writing, Literature & Publishing, 180 Tremont St, 10th fl, Boston, MA 02116-4624 Tel: 617-824-8750 Web Site: www.emerson.edu; www.emerson.edu/writing-literature-publishing, pg 562

Roe, Louis, Beacon Press, 24 Farnsworth St, Boston, MA 02210-1409 Tel: 617-742-2110 Fax: 617-723-3097 E-mail: production@beacon.org Web Site: www.beacon.org, pg 25

Roeder, Taryn, Harry N Abrams Inc, 195 Broadway, 9th fl, New York, NY 10007 Tel: 212-206-7715 Toll Free Tel: 800-345-1359 Fax: 212-645-8437 E-mail: abrams@abramsbooks.com; publicity@abramsbooks.com; sales@abramsbooks.com Web Site: www.abramsbooks.com, pg 2

Roelens, Abigail, Palimpsest Press, 1171 Eastlawn Ave, Windsor, ON N8S 3J1, Canada Tel: 519-259-2112 E-mail: publicity@palimpsestpress.ca Web Site: www.palimpsestpress.ca, pg 415

Roessner, Maura, University of California Press, 155 Grand Ave, Suite 400, Oakland, CA 94612-3758 Tel: 510-883-8232 Fax: 510-836-8910 E-mail: customerservice@ucpress.edu Web Site: www.ucpress.edu, pg 215

Rogan, Lynn, Viking Penguin, c/o Penguin Random House LLC, 1745 Broadway, New York, NY 10019 Tel: 212-782-9000 Web Site: www.penguin.com/overview-vikingbooks/; www.penguin.com/pamela-dorman-books-overview/; www.penguin.com/penguin-classics-overview/; www.penguin.com/penguin-life-overview/, pg 225

Rogen, Jessica, Boulevard Magazine Short Fiction Contest for Emerging Writers, 3829 Hartford St, St Louis, MO 63116 E-mail: editors@boulevardmagazine.org Web Site: www.boulevardmagazine.org, pg 583

Rogers, Andy, Zondervan, 3900 Sparks Dr SE, Grand Rapids, MI 49546 Tel: 616-698-6900 Toll Free Tel: 800-226-1122; 800-727-1309 (retail orders) Fax: 616-698-3350 Toll Free Fax: 800-698-3256 (retail orders) E-mail: customercare@harpercollins.com Web Site: www.zondervan.com, pg 237

Rogers, Brother, Book of the Year Award, William F Winter Archives & History Bldg, 200 North St, Jackson, MS 39201 Tel: 601-576-6936 Fax: 601-576-6975 E-mail: mhs@mdah.ms.gov Web Site: www.mdah.ms.gov, pg 583

Rogers, Chris, Dunow, Carlson & Lerner Literary Agency Inc, 27 W 20 St, Suite 1107, New York, NY 10011 Tel: 212-645-7606 E-mail: mail@dclagency.com Web Site: www.dclagency.com, pg 457

Rogers, Dache', Berkley, c/o Penguin Random House LLC, 1745 Broadway, 19th fl, New York, NY 10019 Tel: 212-366-2000 Web Site: www.penguin.com/publishers/berkley/; www.penguin.com/ace-overview/, pg 28

Rogers, Kate, KO Media Management, 2817 Wetmore Ave, Everett, WA 98201 *E-mail:* info@komediamanagement. com; query@komediamanagement.com *Web Site:* komediamanagement.com, pg 466

Rogers, Kate, Mountaineers Books, 1001 SW Klickitat Way, Suite 201, Seattle, WA 98134 *Tel:* 206-223-6303 *Fax:* 206-223-6306 *E-mail:* mbooks@mountaineersbooks.org; customerservice@mountaineersbooks.org *Web Site:* www.mountaineers.org/books, pg 135

Rogers, Kelly, Johns Hopkins University Press, 2715 N Charles St, Baltimore, MD 21218-4363 *Tel:* 410-516-6900; 410-516-6987 *Toll Free Tel:* 800-537-5487 (book orders & cust serv); 800-548-1784 (journal orders) *Fax:* 410-516-6968; 410-516-6998 (orders) *E-mail:* hfscustserv@press.jhu.edu (cust serv); jrnlcirc@jh.edu (journal orders) *Web Site:* www.press.jhu.edu; muse.jhu.edu, pg 106

Rogers, Marian Hartman, BiblioGenesis, 152 Coddington Rd, Ithaca, NY 14850 *Tel:* 607-277-9660 *Web Site:* www.bibliogenesis.com, pg 436

Rogers, Mary Kate, Portfolio, c/o Penguin Random House LLC, 1745 Broadway, New York, NY 10019 *Tel:* 212-782-9000 *Web Site:* www.penguin.com/portfolio-overview/; www.penguin.com/sentinel-overview/; www.penguin.com/thesis/, pg 162

Rogers, Quinne, Random House Publishing Group, 1745 Broadway, New York, NY 10019 *Toll Free Tel:* 800-200-3552 *Web Site:* www.randomhousebooks.com, pg 171

Rogers, Sydney, Rogers & Weil Literary, 530 Divisadero St, No 169, San Francisco, CA 94117 *Web Site:* www.rwliterary.com, pg 474

Roghaar, Linda L, Linda Roghaar Literary Agency LLC, 133 High Point Dr, Amherst, MA 01002 *Tel:* 413-256-1921 *Web Site:* www.lindaroghaar.com, pg 474

Roginsky, Gwen, The Metropolitan Museum of Art, 1000 Fifth Ave, New York, NY 10028 *Tel:* 212-535-7710 *E-mail:* editorial@metmuseum.org *Web Site:* www.metmuseum.org, pg 130

Rohal, Matt, Princeton University Press, 41 William St, Princeton, NJ 08540-5237 *Tel:* 609-258-4900 *Fax:* 609-258-6305 *E-mail:* info@press.princeton.edu *Web Site:* press.princeton.edu, pg 164

Rohatiner, Tova, Macmillan, 120 Broadway, 22nd fl, New York, NY 10271 *E-mail:* press.inquiries@macmillan.com *Web Site:* us.macmillan.com, pg 122

Rohrmann, Meghan, Begell House Inc Publishers, 50 North St, Danbury, CT 06810 *Tel:* 203-456-6161 *Fax:* 203-456-6167 *E-mail:* orders@begellhouse.com *Web Site:* www.begellhouse.com, pg 27

Rohrs, Mike, HarperCollins Publishers LLC, 195 Broadway, New York, NY 10007 *Tel:* 212-207-7000 *Web Site:* www.harpercollins.com, pg 86

Roistacher, Robert E, The Roistacher Literary Agency, 545 W 111 St, Suite 7J, New York, NY 10025-1965 *Tel:* 212-222-1405, pg 474

Rojas, Isaac, Brault & Bouthillier, 700 ave Beaumont, Montreal, QC H3N 1V5, Canada *Tel:* 514-273-9186 *Toll Free Tel:* 800-361-0378 *Fax:* 514-273-8627 *Toll Free Fax:* 800-361-0378 *E-mail:* communicationbb@bb.ca *Web Site:* bb.ca, pg 397

Rojas, Jennifer, Book Industry Charitable Foundation (BINC), 3135 S State St, Suite 203, Ann Arbor, MI 48108 *Toll Free Tel:* 866-733-9064 *E-mail:* info@bincfoundation.org *Web Site:* www.bincfoundation.org, pg 525

Rojas, Jennifer, Denver Publishing Institute Scholarship, 3135 S State St, Suite 203, Ann Arbor, MI 48108 *Toll Free Tel:* 866-733-9064 *E-mail:* info@bincfoundation.org *Web Site:* www.bincfoundation.org/denver-publishing-institute/, pg 595

Rojas, Jennifer, Carla Gray Memorial Scholarship, 3135 S State St, Suite 203, Ann Arbor, MI 48108 *Toll Free Tel:* 866-733-9064 *E-mail:* info@bincfoundation.org *Web Site:* www.bincfoundation.org/carla-gray/, pg 609

Rojas, Jennifer, Higher Education Scholarship Program, 3135 S State St, Suite 203, Ann Arbor, MI 48108 *Toll Free Tel:* 866-733-9064 *E-mail:* info@bincfoundation.org *Web Site:* www.bincfoundation.org/scholarship, pg 612

Rojas, Jennifer, Susan Kamil Scholarship for Emerging Writers, 3135 S State St, Suite 203, Ann Arbor, MI 48108 *Toll Free Tel:* 866-733-9064 *E-mail:* info@bincfoundation.org *Web Site:* bincfoundation.org/susankamil-scholarship, pg 619

Rojas, Jennifer, George Markey Keating Memorial Scholarships, 3135 S State St, Suite 203, Ann Arbor, MI 48108 *Toll Free Tel:* 866-733-9064 *E-mail:* info@bincfoundation.org *Web Site:* www.bincfoundation.org, pg 619

Rojas, Jennifer, Macmillan Booksellers Professional Development Scholarship, 3135 S State St, Suite 203, Ann Arbor, MI 48108 *Toll Free Tel:* 866-733-9064 *E-mail:* info@bincfoundation.org *Web Site:* www.bincfoundation.org/scholarship, pg 628

Rojas, Jennifer, Karl Pohrt Tribute Award, 3135 S State St, Suite 203, Ann Arbor, MI 48108 *Toll Free Tel:* 866-733-9064 *E-mail:* info@bincfoundation.org *Web Site:* www.bincfoundation.org/scholarship, pg 651

Rojas, Stephanie, Princeton University Press, 41 William St, Princeton, NJ 08540-5237 *Tel:* 609-258-4900 *Fax:* 609-258-6305 *E-mail:* info@press.princeton.edu *Web Site:* press.princeton.edu, pg 164

Rokicki, Rachel, Random House Publishing Group, 1745 Broadway, New York, NY 10019 *Toll Free Tel:* 800-200-3552 *Web Site:* www.randomhousebooks.com, pg 170

Rolfe, Colin, Monkfish Book Publishing Co, 22 E Market St, Suite 304, Rhinebeck, NY 12572 *Tel:* 845-876-4861 *Web Site:* www.monkfishpublishing.com, pg 133

Rollans, Glenn, Brush Education Inc, 6531-111 St NW, Edmonton, AB T6H 4R5, Canada *Tel:* 780-989-0910 *Toll Free Tel:* 855-283-0900 *Fax:* 780-989-0930 *Toll Free Fax:* 855-283-6947 *E-mail:* contact@brusheducation.ca *Web Site:* www.brusheducation.ca, pg 397

Rollins, Leslie, Getty Publications, 1200 Getty Center Dr, Suite 500, Los Angeles, CA 90049-1682 *Tel:* 310-440-7365 *Toll Free Tel:* 800-223-3431 (orders) *Fax:* 310-440-7758 *E-mail:* pubsinfo@getty.edu *Web Site:* www.getty.edu/publications, pg 78

Rollins, Onie, Winterthur Museum, Garden & Library, 5105 Kennett Pike, Winterthur, DE 19735 *Tel:* 302-888-4663 *Toll Free Tel:* 800-448-3883 *Fax:* 302-888-4950 *Web Site:* www.winterthur.org, pg 231

Rolph, Stephanie, Book of the Year Award, William F Winter Archives & History Bldg, 200 North St, Jackson, MS 39201 *Tel:* 601-576-6936 *Fax:* 601-576-6975 *E-mail:* mhs@mdah.ms.gov *Web Site:* www.mdah.ms.gov, pg 583

Roman, Steven, The Brookings Institution Press, 1775 Massachusetts Ave NW, Washington, DC 20036-2188 *Tel:* 202-797-6000 *E-mail:* permissions@brookings.edu *Web Site:* www.brookings.edu, pg 37

Romanik, Barbara, University of Manitoba Press, University of Manitoba, 301 St Johns College, 92 Dysart Rd, Winnipeg, MB R3T 2M5, Canada *Tel:* 204-474-9495 *Fax:* 204-474-7566 *E-mail:* uofmpress@umanitoba.ca *Web Site:* uofmpress.ca, pg 422

Romano, Allison, Crystal Clarity Publishers, 14618 Tyler Foote Rd, Nevada City, CA 95959 *Toll Free Tel:* 800-424-1055 *E-mail:* info@crystalclarity.com *Web Site:* www.crystalclarity.com, pg 56

Romano, Philip, Crystal Clarity Publishers, 14618 Tyler Foote Rd, Nevada City, CA 95959 *Toll Free Tel:* 800-424-1055 *E-mail:* info@crystalclarity.com *Web Site:* www.crystalclarity.com, pg 56

Romano, Rich, Random House Children's Books, c/o Penguin Random House LLC, 1745 Broadway, New York, NY 10019 *Tel:* 212-782-9000 *Web Site:* www.rhcbooks.com, pg 169

Romeo, Christina, Empire State Award for Excellence in Literature for Young People, 6021 State Farm Rd, Guilderland, NY 12084 *Tel:* 800-252-6952 *Fax:* 518-427-1697 *E-mail:* info@nyla.org; marketing@nyla.org *Web Site:* www.nyla.org, pg 599

Romero, Ale, 5 Under 35, 90 Broad St, Suite 604, New York, NY 10004 *Tel:* 212-685-0261 *Fax:* 212-213-6570 *E-mail:* nationalbook@nationalbook.org *Web Site:* www.nationalbook.org, pg 602

Romero, Ale, Medal for Distinguished Contribution to American Letters, 90 Broad St, Suite 604, New York, NY 10004 *Tel:* 212-685-0261 *Fax:* 212-213-6570 *E-mail:* nationalbook@nationalbook.org *Web Site:* www.nationalbook.org/amerletters.html, pg 631

Romero, Ale, National Book Awards, 90 Broad St, Suite 604, New York, NY 10004 *Tel:* 212-685-0261 *Fax:* 212-213-6570 *E-mail:* nationalbook@nationalbook.org *Web Site:* www.nationalbook.org, pg 637

Romero, Ale, National Book Foundation, 90 Broad St, Suite 604, New York, NY 10004 *Tel:* 212-685-0261 *Fax:* 212-213-6570 *E-mail:* nationalbook@nationalbook.org *Web Site:* www.nationalbook.org, pg 526

Romero, Ale, Science + Literature Program, 90 Broad St, Suite 604, New York, NY 10004 *Tel:* 212-685-0261 *Fax:* 212-213-6570 *E-mail:* nationalbook@nationalbook.org *Web Site:* www.nationalbook.org/programs/science-literature, pg 661

Romero, Anthony D, American Civil Liberties Union (ACLU), 125 Broad St, 18th fl, New York, NY 10004 *Tel:* 212-549-2500 *E-mail:* media@aclu.org *Web Site:* www.aclu.org, pg 495

Romero, Emily, Penguin Random House LLC, 1745 Broadway, New York, NY 10019 *Tel:* 212-782-9000 *Toll Free Tel:* 800-726-0600 *Web Site:* www.penguinrandomhouse.com, pg 155

Romero, Kim, Chronicle Books LLC, 680 Second St, San Francisco, CA 94107 *Tel:* 415-537-4200 *Fax:* 415-537-4460 (perms) *E-mail:* hello@chroniclebooks.com; subrights@chroniclebooks.com *Web Site:* www.chroniclebooks.com, pg 47

Romig, Alison, Random House Children's Books, c/o Penguin Random House LLC, 1745 Broadway, New York, NY 10019 *Tel:* 212-782-9000 *Web Site:* www.rhcbooks.com, pg 170

Romine, Claire, Trident Media Group LLC, 355 Lexington Ave, 12th fl, New York, NY 10017 *Tel:* 212-333-1511 *E-mail:* info@tridentmediagroup.com; press@tridentmediagroup.com; foreignrights@tridentmediagroup.com; office.assistant@tridentmediagroup.com *Web Site:* www.tridentmediagroup.com, pg 480

Romiti, Ghjulia, Gallery Books, 1230 Avenue of the Americas, New York, NY 10020 *Toll Free Tel:* 800-456-6798 *Fax:* 212-698-7284 *E-mail:* consumer.customerservice@simonandschuster.com *Web Site:* www.simonandschuster.com, pg 76

Rondeau, James, The Art Institute of Chicago, 111 S Michigan Ave, Chicago, IL 60603-6404 *Tel:* 312-443-3600 *Toll Free Tel:* 855-301-9612 *E-mail:* aicshop@artic.edu *Web Site:* www.artic.edu/print-publications; shop.artic.edu, pg 17

Rondestvedt, Taylor, Gallery Books, 1230 Avenue of the Americas, New York, NY 10020 *Toll Free Tel:* 800-456-6798 *Fax:* 212-698-7284 *E-mail:* consumer.customerservice@simonandschuster.com *Web Site:* www.simonandschuster.com, pg 76

Ronnen, Lia, Hachette Book Group Inc, 1290 Avenue of the Americas, New York, NY 10104 *Tel:* 212-364-1100 *Toll Free Tel:* 800-759-0190 (cust serv) *Fax:* 212-364-0933 (intl orders) *Toll Free Fax:* 800-286-9471 (cust serv) *E-mail:* customer.service@hbgusa.com; orders@hbgusa.com *Web Site:* www.hachettebookgroup.com, pg 83

Ronnen, Lia, Workman Publishing, 1290 Avenue of the Americas, New York, NY 10104 *Toll Free Tel:* 800-759-0190 *Fax:* 212-364-

0950 E-mail: workman-inquiry@hbgusa.com Web Site: www.hachettebookgroup.com/imprint/workman-publishing-company/, pg 232

Roode, Laura, Simon & Schuster Children's Publishing, 1230 Avenue of the Americas, New York, NY 10020 Tel: 212-698-7000 Web Site: www.simonandschuster.com/kids; www.simonandschuster.com/teen; simonandschuster.net; simonandschuster.biz, pg 189

Roos, Charlotte, Random House Children's Books, c/o Penguin Random House LLC, 1745 Broadway, New York, NY 10019 Tel: 212-782-9000 Web Site: www.rhcbooks.com, pg 170

Roose, Barb, Books & Such, 2222 Cleveland Ave, No 1005, Santa Rosa, CA 95403 Tel: 707-538-4184 Web Site: booksandsuch.com, pg 451

Rosa-Mendoza, Gladys, me+mi publishing inc, 2600 Beverly Dr, Unit 113, Aurora, IL 60502 Tel: 630-588-9801 Toll Free Tel: 888-251-1444 Web Site: www.memima.com, pg 128

Rosado, Adrienne, Stonesong, 270 W 39 St, Suite 201, New York, NY 10018 Tel: 212-929-4600 E-mail: editors@stonesong.com Web Site: www.stonesong.com, pg 478

Rosales, Dulce, Penguin Random House Canada, a Penguin Random House company, 320 Front St W, Suite 1400, Toronto, ON M5V 3B6, Canada Tel: 416-364-4449 Toll Free Tel: 888-523-9292 (cust serv) E-mail: canadaweb@penguinrandomhouse.com; customerservicescanada@penguinrandomhouse.com Web Site: www.penguinrandomhouse.ca, pg 416

Rosario, Carlos, HarperCollins Children's Books, 195 Broadway, New York, NY 10007 Tel: 212-207-7000 Web Site: www.harpercollins.com/childrens, pg 85

Rosario, Carlos, HarperCollins Publishers LLC, 195 Broadway, New York, NY 10007 Tel: 212-207-7000 Web Site: www.harpercollins.com, pg 86

Rosart, Sharyn, New York University, Center for Publishing & Applied Liberal Arts, 7 E 12 St, New York, NY 10003 Tel: 212-998-7200 E-mail: sps.info@nyu.edu Web Site: www.scps.nyu.edu/professional-pathways/topics.html, pg 563

Rosart, Sharyn, Sasquatch Books, 1904 S Third Ave, Suite 710, Seattle, WA 98101 Tel: 206-467-4300 Toll Free Tel: 800-775-0817 Fax: 206-467-4301 E-mail: custserv@sasquatchbooks.com Web Site: sasquatchbooks.com, pg 182

Rosati, Patty, HarperCollins Children's Books, 195 Broadway, New York, NY 10007 Tel: 212-207-7000 Web Site: www.harpercollins.com/childrens, pg 85

Rosatone, Laurie, The Guilford Press, 370 Seventh Ave, Suite 1200, New York, NY 10001-1020 Tel: 212-431-9800 Toll Free Tel: 800-365-7006 Fax: 212-966-6708 E-mail: info@guilford.com; orders@guilford.com Web Site: www.guilford.com, pg 82

Rosaz Shariyf, Clarisse, PEN/Hemingway Award for Debut Novel, 120 Broadway, 26th fl N, New York, NY 10271 Tel: 212-334-1660 Fax: 212-334-2181 E-mail: awards@pen.org; info@pen.org Web Site: pen.org/pen-hemingway-award, pg 647

Rosborough, Nathan, HarperCollins Publishers LLC, 195 Broadway, New York, NY 10007 Tel: 212-207-7000 Web Site: www.harpercollins.com, pg 86

Rose, Ashley Gilliam, Scribner, 1230 Avenue of the Americas, New York, NY 10020 Web Site: www.simonandschusterpublishing.com/scribner/, pg 185

Rose, LaToya, Macmillan, 120 Broadway, 22nd fl, New York, NY 10271 E-mail: press.inquiries@macmillan.com Web Site: us.macmillan.com, pg 122

Rose, Lindsey, Dutton, c/o Penguin Random House LLC, 1745 Broadway, New York, NY 10019 Tel: 212-366-2000 Web Site: www.penguin.com/dutton-overview/; www.penguin.com/plume-books-overview/; www.penguin.com/tiny-reparations-overview/, pg 62

Rose, Rebecca, Breakwater Books Ltd, One Stamp's Lane, St John's, NL A1C 6E6, Canada Tel: 709-722-6680 Toll Free Tel: 800-563-3333 (orders) Fax: 709-753-0708 E-mail: info@breakwaterbooks.com; orders@breakwaterbooks.com Web Site: www.breakwaterbooks.com, pg 397

Rose, Verena, Agatha Awards, PO Box 8007, Gaithersburg, MD 20898 Tel: 301-730-1675 E-mail: mdregservices@gmail.com Web Site: malicedomestic.org, pg 570

Rose, Wendy, Newfoundland and Labrador Book Awards, Haymarket Sq, 223 Duckworth St, St John's, NL A1C 6N1, Canada Tel: 709-739-5215 Toll Free Tel: 866-739-5215 E-mail: info@wanl.ca; membership@wanl.ca Web Site: wanl.ca, pg 641

Rose, Wendy, Newfoundland and Labrador Credit Union Fresh Fish Award for Emerging Writers, Haymarket Sq, 223 Duckworth St, St John's, NL A1C 6N1, Canada Tel: 709-739-5215 Toll Free Tel: 866-739-5215 E-mail: info@wanl.ca; membership@wanl.ca Web Site: wanl.ca, pg 641

Rose, Wendy, Writers' Alliance of Newfoundland & Labrador, Haymarket Sq, 223 Duckworth St, Suite 202, St John's, NL A1C 6N1, Canada Tel: 709-739-5215 Toll Free Tel: 866-739-5215 E-mail: info@wanl.ca; membership@wanl.ca Web Site: wanl.ca, pg 522

Rose, Zandra, Steerforth Press & Services, 31 Hanover St, Suite 1, Lebanon, NH 03766 Tel: 603-643-4787 Fax: 603-643-4788 E-mail: info@steerforth.com Web Site: www.steerforth.com, pg 198

Roseman, Karl-Heinz, McFarland, 960 NC Hwy 88 W, Jefferson, NC 28640 Tel: 336-246-4460 Toll Free Tel: 800-253-2187 (orders) Fax: 336-246-5018; 336-246-4403 (orders) E-mail: info@mcfarlandpub.com Web Site: mcfarlandbooks.com, pg 127

Rosen, Andrea, Hachette Book Group Inc, 1290 Avenue of the Americas, New York, NY 10104 Tel: 212-364-1100 Toll Free Tel: 800-759-0190 (cust serv) Fax: 212-364-0933 (intl orders) Toll Free Fax: 800-286-9471 (cust serv) E-mail: customer.service@hbgusa.com; orders@hbgusa.com Web Site: www.hachettebookgroup.com, pg 83

Rosen, Jonathan, The Seymour Agency, 475 Miner Street Rd, Canton, NY 13617 Tel: 239-398-8209 Web Site: www.theseymouragency.com, pg 475

Rosen, Lynn, Yard Dog Press, 710 W Redbud Lane, Alma, AR 72921-7247 Tel: 479-632-4693 Fax: 479-632-4693 Web Site: www.yarddogpress.com, pg 235

Rosen, Mollie, 4A's (American Association of Advertising Agencies), 25 W 45 St, 16th fl, New York, NY 10036 Tel: 212-682-2500 E-mail: media@4as.org; membership@4as.org Web Site: www.aaaa.org, pg 506

Rosen, Roger, Enslow Publishing LLC, 101 W 23 St, Suite 240, New York, NY 10011 Toll Free Tel: 800-398-2504 Fax: 908-771-0925 Toll Free Fax: 877-980-4454 E-mail: customerservice@enslow.com Web Site: www.enslow.com, pg 66

Rosen, Roger, The Rosen Publishing Group Inc, 29 E 21 St, New York, NY 10010 Toll Free Tel: 800-237-9932 Toll Free Fax: 888-436-4643 E-mail: info@rosenpub.com Web Site: www.rosenpublishing.com, pg 177

Rosen, Selina, Yard Dog Press, 710 W Redbud Lane, Alma, AR 72921-7247 Tel: 479-632-4693 Fax: 479-632-4693 Web Site: www.yarddogpress.com, pg 235

Rosenbaum, David M, University of Missouri Press, 113 Heinkel Bldg, 201 S Seventh St, Columbia, MO 65211 Tel: 573-882-7641; 573-882-9672 (publicity & sales enquiries) Toll Free Tel: 800-621-2736 (orders) Fax: 573-884-4498 Toll Free Fax: 800-621-8476 (orders) E-mail: upress@missouri.edu; umpmarketing@missouri.edu (publicity & sales enquiries) Web Site: upress.missouri.edu, pg 217

Rosenbaum, Mary, American Medical Writers Association (AMWA), 9841 Washingtonian Blvd, Suite 500-26, Gaithersburg, MD 20878 Tel: 240-238-0940 Fax: 301-294-9006 E-mail: amwa@amwa.org Web Site: www.amwa.org, pg 496

Rosenberg, Alexa, Sourcebooks LLC, 1935 Brookdale Rd, Suite 139, Naperville, IL 60563 Tel: 630-961-3900 Toll Free Tel: 800-432-7444 Fax: 630-961-2168 E-mail: info@sourcebooks.com Web Site: www.sourcebooks.com, pg 195

Rosenberg, Barbara Collins, The Rosenberg Group, 23 Lincoln Ave, Marblehead, MA 01945 E-mail: rosenberglitsubmit@icloud.com Web Site: www.rosenberggroup.com, pg 474

Rosenberg, Dan, Harvard Common Press, 100 Cummings Ctr, Suite 265-D, Beverly, MA 01915 Tel: 978-282-9590 Fax: 978-282-7765 Web Site: www.quartoknows.com/harvard-common-press, pg 88

Rosenberg, Linda, GP Putnam's Sons, c/o Penguin Random House LLC, 1745 Broadway, New York, NY 10019 Tel: 212-782-9000 Web Site: www.penguin.com/putnam/, pg 167

Rosenberg, Liz, Binghamton University Creative Writing Program, c/o Dept of English, General Literature & Rhetoric, PO Box 6000, Binghamton, NY 13902-6000 Tel: 607-777-2168 Fax: 607-777-2408 E-mail: cwpro@binghamton.edu Web Site: www.binghamton.edu/english/creative-writing/index.html, pg 561

Rosenberg, Tracy, Media Alliance, 2830 20 St, Suite 102, San Francisco, CA 94110 Tel: 415-746-9475 E-mail: information@media-alliance.org; info@media-alliance.org Web Site: www.media-alliance.org, pg 510

Rosenberry, Eliza, HarperCollins Publishers LLC, 195 Broadway, New York, NY 10007 Tel: 212-207-7000 Web Site: www.harpercollins.com, pg 86

Rosenbladt, Annie, Holiday House Publishing Inc, 50 Broad St, New York, NY 10004 Tel: 212-688-0085 Fax: 212-421-6134 E-mail: info@holidayhouse.com Web Site: www.holidayhouse.com, pg 94

Rosenblum, Batya, TarcherPerigee, c/o Penguin Random House LLC, 1745 Broadway, New York, NY 10019 Tel: 212-782-9000 Web Site: www.penguin.com/tarcherperigee-overview/; www.facebook.com/TarcherPerigee, pg 202

Rosenfeld, Dina, Hachai Publishing, 527 Empire Blvd, Brooklyn, NY 11225 Tel: 718-633-0100 Fax: 718-633-0103 E-mail: info@hachai.com Web Site: www.hachai.com, pg 83

Rosenfeld, Nancy, AAA Books Unlimited, 3060 Blackthorn Rd, Riverwoods, IL 60015 Tel: 847-444-1220 Fax: 847-607-8335 Web Site: www.aaabooksunlimited.com, pg 447

Rosenkrantz, Mindy, Macmillan, 120 Broadway, 22nd fl, New York, NY 10271 E-mail: press.inquiries@macmillan.com Web Site: us.macmillan.com, pg 122

Rosenkranz, Randi, Penguin Random House LLC, 1745 Broadway, New York, NY 10019 Tel: 212-782-9000 Toll Free Tel: 800-726-0600 Web Site: www.penguinrandomhouse.com, pg 155

Rosenkranz, Rita, Rita Rosenkranz Literary Agency, 440 West End Ave, Suite 15D, New York, NY 10024-5358 Tel: 212-873-6333 Fax: 212-873-5225 Web Site: www.ritarosenkranzliteraryagency.com, pg 474

Rosenstreich, Lilian, Endless Mountains Publishing Co, 72 Glenmaura National Blvd, Suite 104B, Moosic, PA 18507 Tel: 862-251-2296 E-mail: info@endlessmountainspublishing.com Web Site: kalaniotbooks.com, pg 66

Rosenstreich, Lilian, Kalaniot Books, 72 Glenmaura National Blvd, Suite 104B, Moosic, PA 18507 Tel: 862-251-2296; 570-451-6095 E-mail: info@kalaniotbooks.com Web Site: www.kalaniotbooks.com, pg 107

Rosenthal, Alli, Grand Central Publishing, 1290 Avenue of the Americas, New York, NY 10104 Tel: 212-364-1100 Web Site: www.hachettebookgroup.com/imprint/grand-central-publishing/, pg 80

Rosenthal, Ben, Sourcebooks LLC, 1935 Brookdale Rd, Suite 139, Naperville, IL 60563 Tel: 630-961-3900 Toll Free Tel: 800-432-7444 Fax: 630-961-2168 E-mail: info@sourcebooks.com Web Site: www.sourcebooks.com, pg 194

Rosenthal, Carole, Hamilton Stone Editions, PO Box 43, Maplewood, NJ 07040 Tel: 973-378-8361 E-mail: hstone@hamiltonstone.org Web Site: www.hamiltonstone.org, pg 84

Rosenthal, David, Houghton Mifflin Harcourt Trade & Reference Division, 125 High St, Boston, MA 02110 *Tel:* 617-351-5000 *Web Site:* www.hmhco.com, pg 96

Rosenthal, Maggie, Viking Children's Books, c/o Penguin Random House LLC, 1745 Broadway, New York, NY 10019 *Tel:* 212-782-9000 *Web Site:* www.penguin.com/viking-childrens-books-overview/, pg 224

Rosenwald, Robert, Poisoned Pen Press, 4014 N Goldwater Blvd, Suite 201, Scottsdale, AZ 85251 *Tel:* 480-945-3375 *Toll Free Tel:* 800-421-3976 *Fax:* 480-949-1707 *E-mail:* info@poisonedpenpress.com *Web Site:* www.poisonedpenpress.com, pg 161

Rosenwasser, Rena, Kelsey Street Press, 2824 Kelsey St, Berkeley, CA 94705 *E-mail:* info@kelseystreetpress.org *Web Site:* www.kelseystreetpress.org, pg 108

Rosenzweig, Alexis, Farrar, Straus & Giroux, LLC, 120 Broadway, New York, NY 10271 *Tel:* 212-741-6900 *E-mail:* fsg.publicity@fsgbooks.com; sales@fsgbooks.com *Web Site:* us.macmillan.com/fsg, pg 70

Rosewitz, Margaret, Candlewick Press, 99 Dover St, Somerville, MA 02144-2825 *Tel:* 617-661-3330 *Fax:* 617-661-0565 *E-mail:* bigbear@candlewick.com; salesinfo@candlewick.com *Web Site:* candlewick.com, pg 40

Rosinsky, Lisa, Barefoot Books, 23 Bradford St, 2nd fl, Concord, MA 01742 *Tel:* 617-576-0660 *Toll Free Tel:* 866-215-1756 (cust serv); 866-417-2369 (orders) *Fax:* 617-576-0049 *E-mail:* help@barefootbooks.com *Web Site:* www.barefootbooks.com, pg 24

Ross, Alicia, Berkley, c/o Penguin Random House LLC, 1745 Broadway, 19th fl, New York, NY 10019 *Tel:* 212-366-2000 *Web Site:* www.penguin.com/publishers/berkley/; www.penguin.com/ace-overview/, pg 28

Ross, Andy, Andy Ross Literary Agency, 767 Santa Ray Ave, Oakland, CA 94610 *Tel:* 510-238-8965 *E-mail:* andyrossagency@hotmail.com *Web Site:* www.andyrossagency.com, pg 449

Ross, Catherine Barbosa, HarperCollins Publishers LLC, 195 Broadway, New York, NY 10007 *Tel:* 212-207-7000 *Web Site:* www.harpercollins.com, pg 86

Ross, Franz H, Ross Books, PO Box 4340, Berkeley, CA 94704-0340 *Tel:* 510-841-2474 *Fax:* 510-295-2531 *E-mail:* sales@rossbooks.com *Web Site:* www.rossbooks.com, pg 177

Ross, Gail, WME, 11 Madison Ave, New York, NY 10010 *Tel:* 212-586-5100 *Web Site:* www.wmeagency.com, pg 482

Ross, Hedy, American Sociological Association (ASA), 1430 "K" St NW, Suite 600, Washington, DC 20005-4701 *Tel:* 202-383-9005 *E-mail:* asa@asanet.org; communications@asanet.org; membership@asanet.org *Web Site:* www.asanet.org, pg 497

Ross, Jill, American Society for Nondestructive Testing, 1201 Dublin Rd, Suite G04, Columbus, OH 43215 *Toll Free Tel:* 800-222-2768 *E-mail:* customersupport@asnt.org *Web Site:* www.asnt.org; source.asnt.org (orders); asntmediaplanner.com (ad & sponsored content), pg 12

Ross, Katelin, Shambhala Publications Inc, 2129 13 St, Boulder, CO 80302 *Tel:* 978-829-2599 (intl callers) *Toll Free Tel:* 866-424-0030 (off); 888-424-2329 (orders & cust serv) *Fax:* 617-236-1563 *E-mail:* customercare@shambhala.com; royalties@shambhala.com *Web Site:* www.shambhala.com, pg 187

Ross, Maureen, diacriTech Inc, 4 S Market St, 4th fl, Boston, MA 02109 *Tel:* 617-600-3366 *Fax:* 617-848-2938 *Web Site:* www.diacritech.com, pg 438

Ross, Whitney, Irene Goodman Literary Agency, 27 W 24 St, Suite 700B, New York, NY 10010 *Tel:* 212-604-0330 *E-mail:* queries@irenegoodman.com *Web Site:* www.irenegoodman.com, pg 460

Ross, William G, David J Langum Sr Prize in American Legal History or Biography, c/o William G Ross, Cumberland School of Law, 800 Lakeshore Dr, Birmingham, AL 35229 *Web Site:* langumfoundation.org/about-prizes/american-legal-history-or-biography, pg 622

Rossell, Broc, Milkweed Editions, 1011 Washington Ave S, Suite 300, Minneapolis, MN 55415-1246 *Tel:* 612-332-3192 *Toll Free Tel:* 800-520-6455 *E-mail:* orders@milkweed.org *Web Site:* milkweed.org, pg 131

Rossi, Janet, The MIT Press, One Broadway, 12th fl, Cambridge, MA 02142 *Tel:* 617-253-5255 *Toll Free Tel:* 800-405-1619 (orders) *Fax:* 617-258-6779; 617-577-1545 (orders) *Web Site:* mitpress.mit.edu, pg 132

Rossi, Tony, The Christopher Awards, 5 Hanover Sq, 22nd fl, New York, NY 10004-2751 *Tel:* 212-759-4050 *Toll Free Tel:* 888-298-4050 (orders) *Fax:* 212-838-5073 *E-mail:* mail@christophers.org *Web Site:* www.christophers.org, pg 589

Rossi, Wendy, Women's Fiction Writers Association (WFWA), PO Box 190, Jefferson, OR 97352 *E-mail:* communications@womensfictionwriters.org; membership@womensfictionwriters.org; programs@womensfictionwriters.org *Web Site:* www.womensfictionwriters.org, pg 522

Rosso, Don, Waveland Press Inc, 4180 IL Rte 83, Suite 101, Long Grove, IL 60047-9580 *Tel:* 847-634-0081 *Fax:* 847-634-9501 *E-mail:* info@waveland.com *Web Site:* www.waveland.com, pg 226

Rostan, Stephanie, Levine|Greenberg|Rostan Literary Agency, 307 Seventh Ave, Suite 2407, New York, NY 10001 *Tel:* 212-337-0934 *Fax:* 212-337-0948 *E-mail:* submit@lgrliterary.com *Web Site:* lgrliterary.com, pg 467

Rotella, Giuseppe, Cambridge University Press, One Liberty Plaza, 20th fl, New York, NY 10006 *Tel:* 212-924-3900; 212-337-5000 *Fax:* 212-691-3239; 845-353-4141 *E-mail:* customer_service@cambridge.org; orders@cambridge.org; subscriptions_newyork@cambridge.org *Web Site:* www.cambridge.org/us, pg 39

Roth, Andy, CAA Speakers, 2000 Avenue of the Stars, Los Angeles, CA 90067 *Tel:* 424-288-2000 *Fax:* 424-288-2900 *E-mail:* speakers@caa.com *Web Site:* www.caa.com/caaspeakers, pg 487

Roth, Charlotte, Candlewick Press, 99 Dover St, Somerville, MA 02144-2825 *Tel:* 617-661-3330 *Fax:* 617-661-0565 *E-mail:* bigbear@candlewick.com; salesinfo@candlewick.com *Web Site:* candlewick.com, pg 40

Roth, Jessica, Gallery Books, 1230 Avenue of the Americas, New York, NY 10020 *Toll Free Tel:* 800-456-6798 *Fax:* 212-698-7284 *E-mail:* consumer.customerservice@simonandschuster.com *Web Site:* www.simonandschuster.com, pg 76

Roth, Laurence D PhD, Susquehanna University, Department of English & Creative Writing, 514 University Ave, Selinsgrove, PA 17870 *Tel:* 570-372-4196 *Web Site:* www.susqu.edu, pg 565

Roth, Maya E, Jane Chambers Playwriting Award, Georgetown University, 108 David Performing Arts Ctr, Box 571063, 37 & "O" St, NW, Washington, DC 20057-1063 *Web Site:* www.athe.org/page/jane_chambers; www.womenandtheatreprogram.com/jane-chambers, pg 588

Roth, Melanie, Chicago Review Press, 814 N Franklin St, Chicago, IL 60610 *Tel:* 312-337-0747 *Toll Free Tel:* 800-888-4741 *Fax:* 312-337-5110 *E-mail:* frontdesk@chicagoreviewpress.com *Web Site:* www.chicagoreviewpress.com, pg 46

Rother, Marisa, HarperCollins Children's Books, 195 Broadway, New York, NY 10007 *Tel:* 212-207-7000 *Web Site:* www.harpercollins.com/childrens, pg 85

Rothschild, Eileen, St Martin's Press, LLC, 120 Broadway, New York, NY 10271 *E-mail:* publicity@stmartins.com; trademarketing@stmartins.com; foreignrights@stmartins.com *Web Site:* us.macmillan.com/smp, pg 180

Rothschild, Richard, American Book Producers Association (ABPA), 7 Peter Cooper Rd, No 7G, New York, NY 10010 *E-mail:* office@abpaonline.org *Web Site:* www.abpaonline.org, pg 494

Rothstein, Allison, Penguin Random House LLC, 1745 Broadway, New York, NY 10019 *Tel:* 212-782-9000 *Toll Free Tel:* 800-726-0600 *Web Site:* www.penguinrandomhouse.com, pg 155

Rothstein, Eliza, InkWell Management, 521 Fifth Ave, Suite 2600, New York, NY 10175 *Tel:* 212-922-3500 *Fax:* 212-922-0535 *E-mail:* info@inkwellmanagement.com; submissions@inkwellmanagement.com; permissions@inkwellmanagement.com *Web Site:* inkwellmanagement.com, pg 463

Rothstein, Philip Jan, Rothstein Associates Inc, 4 Arapaho Rd, Brookfield, CT 06804-3104 *Tel:* 203-740-7400 *Toll Free Tel:* 888-768-4783 *Fax:* 203-740-7401 *E-mail:* info@rothstein.com *Web Site:* www.rothstein.com; www.rothsteinpublishing.com, pg 177

Rotondo, Michael, Penguin Random House LLC, 1745 Broadway, New York, NY 10019 *Tel:* 212-782-9000 *Toll Free Tel:* 800-726-0600 *Web Site:* www.penguinrandomhouse.com, pg 155

Rotor, Elda, Viking Penguin, c/o Penguin Random House LLC, 1745 Broadway, New York, NY 10019 *Tel:* 212-782-9000 *Web Site:* www.penguin.com/overview-vikingbooks/; www.penguin.com/pamela-dorman-books-overview/; www.penguin.com/penguin-classics-overview/; www.penguin.com/penguin-life-overview/, pg 225

Rotstein, David, St Martin's Press, LLC, 120 Broadway, New York, NY 10271 *E-mail:* publicity@stmartins.com; trademarketing@stmartins.com; foreignrights@stmartins.com *Web Site:* us.macmillan.com/smp, pg 180

Rounds, John, St Martin's Press, LLC, 120 Broadway, New York, NY 10271 *E-mail:* publicity@stmartins.com; trademarketing@stmartins.com; foreignrights@stmartins.com *Web Site:* us.macmillan.com/smp, pg 181

Rouner, Helen, Penguin Press, c/o Penguin Random House LLC, 1745 Broadway, New York, NY 10019 *Tel:* 212-782-9000 *E-mail:* penguinpress@penguinrandomhouse.com *Web Site:* www.penguin.com/penguin-press-overview/, pg 154

Rourke, Kathleen, Candlewick Press, 99 Dover St, Somerville, MA 02144-2825 *Tel:* 617-661-3330 *Fax:* 617-661-0565 *E-mail:* bigbear@candlewick.com; salesinfo@candlewick.com *Web Site:* candlewick.com, pg 39

Rousseau, Christopher, Practising Law Institute (PLI), 1177 Avenue of the Americas, 2nd fl, New York, NY 10036 *Tel:* 212-824-5710 (cust serv) *Toll Free Tel:* 800-260-4PLI (260-4754) *Toll Free Fax:* 800-321-0093 (cust serv) *E-mail:* info@pli.edu; membership@pli.edu *Web Site:* www.pli.edu, pg 163

Roussel, Renaud, Les Editions du Boreal, 4447, rue St-Denis, Montreal, QC H2J 2L2, Canada *Tel:* 514-287-7401 *Fax:* 514-287-7664 *E-mail:* info@editionsboreal.qc.ca; boreal@editionsboreal.qc.ca; communications@editionsboreal.qc.ca *Web Site:* www.editionsboreal.qc.ca, pg 402

Roussopoulos, Dimitrios, Black Rose Books Ltd, CP 35788, succursale Leo-Pariseau, Montreal, QC H2X 0A4, Canada *Tel:* 514-844-4076 *E-mail:* info@blackrosebooks.com *Web Site:* blackrosebooks.com, pg 396

Roux, Michael, University of Illinois Press, 1325 S Oak St, MC-566, Champaign, IL 61820-6903 *Tel:* 217-333-0950 *Fax:* 217-244-8082 *E-mail:* uipress@uillinois.edu; journals@uillinois.edu *Web Site:* www.press.uillinois.edu, pg 216

Rowe, Carol, Waveland Press Inc, 4180 IL Rte 83, Suite 101, Long Grove, IL 60047-9580 *Tel:* 847-634-0081 *Fax:* 847-634-9501 *E-mail:* info@waveland.com *Web Site:* www.waveland.com, pg 226

Rowe, Martin, Lantern Publishing & Media, 128 Second Place, Garden Suite, Brooklyn, NY 11231 *E-mail:* info@lanternpm.org, pg 112

Rowe, Neil, Waveland Press Inc, 4180 IL Rte 83, Suite 101, Long Grove, IL 60047-9580 *Tel:* 847-634-0081 *Fax:* 847-634-9501 *E-mail:* info@waveland.com *Web Site:* www.waveland.com, pg 226

Rowland, Lee, National Coalition Against Censorship (NCAC), 19 Fulton St, Suite 407, New York, NY 10038 Tel: 212-807-6222 Fax: 212-807-6245 E-mail: ncac@ncac.org Web Site: www.ncac.org, pg 512

Rowland, Melissa, Levine|Greenberg|Rostan Literary Agency, 307 Seventh Ave, Suite 2407, New York, NY 10001 Tel: 212-337-0934 Fax: 212-337-0948 E-mail: submit@lgrliterary.com Web Site: lgrliterary.com, pg 467

Roy, Denise, Little, Brown and Company, 1290 Avenue of the Americas, New York, NY 10104 Tel: 212-364-1100 Fax: 212-364-0952 E-mail: firstname.lastname@hbgusa.com Web Site: www.hachettebookgroup.com/imprint/little-brown-and-company/, pg 118

Roy, Mary Lou, University of Alberta Press, Ring House 2, Edmonton, AB T6G 2E1, Canada Tel: 780-492-3662 Fax: 780-492-0719 Web Site: www.uap.ualberta.ca, pg 421

Roy, Michael, American Psychiatric Association Publishing, 800 Maine Ave SW, Suite 900, Washington, DC 20024 Tel: 202-459-9722 Toll Free Tel: 800-368-5777 Fax: 202-403-3094 E-mail: appi@psych.org Web Site: www.appi.org; www.psychiatryonline.org, pg 11

Roy-Chaudhury, Anu, Basic Books Group, 1290 Avenue of the Americas, New York, NY 10104 Tel: 212-340-8100 Toll Free Tel: 800-343-4499 (cust serv) Fax: 212-340-8105 E-mail: customer.service@hbgusa.com; orders@hbgusa.com Web Site: www.hachettebookgroup.com/imprint/basic-books/, pg 25

Royal, Jaynie, The Acheven Book Prize for Young Adult Fiction, c/o Regal House Publishing, 806 Oberlin Rd, No 12094, Raleigh, NC 27605 E-mail: info@regalhousepublishing.com Web Site: regalhousepublishing.com/the-acheven-book-prize-for-young-adult-fiction/, pg 570

Royal, Jaynie, The Terry J Cox Poetry Award, 806 Oberlin Rd, No 12094, Raleigh, NC 27605 E-mail: info@regalhousepublishing.com Web Site: regalhousepublishing.com/the-terry-j-cox-poetry-award/, pg 592

Royal, Jaynie, Fitzroy Books, c/o Regal House Publishing, 806 Oberlin Rd, No 12094, Raleigh, NC 27605 E-mail: info@regalhousepublishing.com Web Site: fitzroybooks.com, pg 72

Royal, Jaynie, The Kraken Book Prize for Middle-Grade Fiction, c/o Regal House Publishing, 806 Oberlin Rd, No 12094, Raleigh, NC 27605 E-mail: info@regalhousepublishing.com Web Site: regalhousepublishing.com/the-kraken-book-award/, pg 621

Royal, Jaynie, The Petrichor Prize for Finely Crafted Fiction, 806 Oberlin Rd, No 12094, Raleigh, NC 27605 E-mail: info@regalhousepublishing.com Web Site: regalhousepublishing.com/the-petrichor-prize-for-finely-crafted-fiction/, pg 649

Royal, Jaynie, Regal House Publishing, 806 Oberlin Rd, No 12094, Raleigh, NC 27605 E-mail: info@regalhousepublishing.com Web Site: regalhousepublishing.com, pg 173

Royall, John T, Gulf Energy Information, 2 Greenway Plaza, Suite 1020, Houston, TX 77046 Tel: 713-520-4498; 713-529-4301 E-mail: store@gulfpub.com; customerservice@gulfenergyinfo.com Web Site: www.gulfenergyinfo.com, pg 83

Royce, Michael L, NYSCA/NYFA Artist Fellowships, 20 Jay St, Suite 740, Brooklyn, NY 11201 Tel: 212-366-6900 Fax: 212-366-1778 E-mail: fellowships@nyfa.org Web Site: www.nyfa.org, pg 642

Rozenberg, Rebecca, Simon & Schuster, 1230 Avenue of the Americas, New York, NY 10020 Tel: 212-698-7000 Toll Free Tel: 800-223-2348 (cust serv); 800-223-2336 (orders) Toll Free Fax: 800-943-9831 (orders) Web Site: simonandschusterpublishing.com/simonandschuster/, pg 188

Ruane, Kate, PEN America, 120 Broadway, 26th fl N, New York, NY 10271 Tel: 212-334-1660 Fax: 212-334-2181 E-mail: info@pen.org; membership@pen.org; education@pen.org Web Site: pen.org, pg 516

Rubenstein, Ellis, New York Academy of Sciences (NYAS), 7 World Trade Center, 40th fl, 250 Greenwich St, New York, NY 10007-2157 Tel: 212-298-8600 Toll Free Tel: 800-843-6927 Fax: 212-298-3650 E-mail: nyas@nyas.org; annals@nyas.org; customerservice@nyas.org Web Site: www.nyas.org, pg 140

Rubero, Jasmin, Kokila, c/o Penguin Random House LLC, 1745 Broadway, New York, NY 10019 Tel: 212-782-9000 Web Site: www.penguin.com/kokila-books-overview/, pg 111

Rubiano, Brittany, Disney-Hyperion Books, 1101 Flower St, Glendale, CA 91201 Web Site: books.disney.com/imprint/disney-hyperion, pg 59

Rubie, Peter, FinePrint Literary Management, 207 W 106 St, Suite 1D, New York, NY 10025 Tel: 212-279-6214 E-mail: info@fineprintlit.com; submissions@fineprint.com Web Site: www.fineprintlit.com, pg 458

Rubin, Barry, Lederer Books, 6120 Day Long Lane, Clarksville, MD 21029 Tel: 410-531-6644 Toll Free Tel: 800-410-7367 (orders) Web Site: www.messianicjewish.net, pg 114

Rubin, Barry, Messianic Jewish Publishers, 6120 Day Long Lane, Clarksville, MD 21029 Tel: 410-531-6644; 616-970-2449 Toll Free Tel: 800-410-7367 (orders) Fax: 410-531-9440; 717-761-7273 (orders) Toll Free Fax: 800-327-0048 (orders) E-mail: editor@messianicjewish.net; customerservice@messianicjewish.net Web Site: messianicjewish.net/publish, pg 130

Rubin, Elyssa, Advertising Research Foundation (ARF), 432 Park Ave S, 4th fl, New York, NY 10016 Tel: 212-751-5656 Fax: 212-689-1859 E-mail: membership@thearf.org; new-member-info@thearf.org Web Site: thearf.org, pg 493, 525

Rubin, Lisa, Lederer Books, 6120 Day Long Lane, Clarksville, MD 21029 Tel: 410-531-6644 Toll Free Tel: 800-410-7367 (orders) Web Site: www.messianicjewish.net, pg 114

Rubin, Reka, Harlequin Enterprises Ltd, 195 Broadway, 24th fl, New York, NY 10007 Tel: 212-207-7000 Toll Free Tel: 888-432-4879; 800-370-5838 (ebooks) E-mail: customerservice@harlequin.com Web Site: www.harlequin.com/shop/index.html; corporate.harlequin.com, pg 85

Rubino, Gabriella, Workman Publishing, 1290 Avenue of the Americas, New York, NY 10104 Toll Free Tel: 800-759-0190 Fax: 212-364-0950 E-mail: workman-inquiry@hbgusa.com Web Site: www.hachettebookgroup.com/imprint/workman-publishing-company/, pg 233

Rubins, Jennifer, Penguin Random House Audio Publishing Group, 1745 Broadway, New York, NY 10019 Toll Free Tel: 800-793-2665 (cust serv) E-mail: audio@penguinrandomhouse.com; ecustomerservice@penguinrandomhouse.com Web Site: www.penguinrandomhouseaudio.com, pg 154

Rubinstein, Elizabeth Winick, McIntosh and Otis Inc, 235 Main St, Suite 318, White Plains, NY 10601 Tel: 212-687-7400 Fax: 212-687-6894 E-mail: info@mcintoshandotis.com Web Site: www.mcintoshandotis.com, pg 470

Rubsam, Jeannie, Tiger Tales, 5 River Rd, Suite 128, Wilton, CT 06897-4069 Tel: 920-387-2333 Fax: 920-387-9994 Web Site: www.tigertalesbooks.com, pg 207

Rucci, Marysue, Atria Books, 1230 Avenue of the Americas, New York, NY 10020 Tel: 212-698-7000 Fax: 212-698-7007 Web Site: www.simonandschuster.com, pg 21

Ruchti, Cynthia, Books & Such, 2222 Cleveland Ave, No 1005, Santa Rosa, CA 95403 Tel: 707-538-4184 Web Site: booksandsuch.com, pg 451

Ruchti, Spencer, Cercador Prize, c/o Third Place Books, 6504 20 Ave NE, Seattle, WA 98115 E-mail: info@cercadorprize.com Web Site: www.cercadorprize.com, pg 588

Rucinski, Beth, National Catholic Educational Association, 200 N Glebe Rd, Suite 310, Arlington, VA 22203 Tel: 571-257-0010 Toll Free Tel: 800-711-6232 Fax: 703-243-0025 E-mail: nceaadmin@ncea.org Web Site: www.ncea.org, pg 137

Ruck, Holly, Macmillan, 120 Broadway, 22nd fl, New York, NY 10271 E-mail: press.inquiries@macmillan.com Web Site: us.macmillan.com, pg 122

Ruckdeschel, Sharon L, American Medical Writers Association (AMWA), 9841 Washingtonian Blvd, Suite 500-26, Gaithersburg, MD 20878 Tel: 240-238-0940 Fax: 301-294-9006 E-mail: amwa@amwa.org Web Site: www.amwa.org, pg 496

Rucker, Karen, Macmillan, 120 Broadway, 22nd fl, New York, NY 10271 E-mail: press.inquiries@macmillan.com Web Site: us.macmillan.com, pg 122

Rucker, Sarah, HarperCollins Publishers LLC, 195 Broadway, New York, NY 10007 Tel: 212-207-7000 Web Site: www.harpercollins.com, pg 86

Rudden, Lisa, Candlewick Press, 99 Dover St, Somerville, MA 02144-2825 Tel: 617-661-3330 Fax: 617-661-0565 E-mail: bigbear@candlewick.com; salesinfo@candlewick.com Web Site: candlewick.com, pg 39

Rudin, Max, Library of America, 14 E 60 St, New York, NY 10022-1006 Tel: 212-308-3360 Fax: 212-750-8352 E-mail: info@loa.org Web Site: www.loa.org, pg 116

Rudloff, Megan, Atria Books, 1230 Avenue of the Americas, New York, NY 10020 Tel: 212-698-7000 Fax: 212-698-7007 Web Site: www.simonandschuster.com, pg 21

Rudman, Michael P, National Learning Corp, 212 Michael Dr, Syosset, NY 11791 Tel: 516-921-8888 Toll Free Tel: 800-632-8888 Fax: 516-921-8743 E-mail: info@passbooks.com Web Site: www.passbooks.com, pg 138

Rudolph, Janet, Macavity Award, 7155 Marlborough Terr, Berkeley, CA 94705 Tel: 510-845-3600 Web Site: www.mysteryreaders.org, pg 628

Rudolph, John, Dystel, Goderich & Bourret LLC, One Union Sq W, Suite 904, New York, NY 10003 Tel: 212-627-9100 Fax: 212-627-9313 Web Site: www.dystel.com, pg 457

Rudolph, Kelly, HarperCollins Children's Books, 195 Broadway, New York, NY 10007 Tel: 212-207-7000 Web Site: www.harpercollins.com/childrens, pg 85

Rudolph, Kelly, HarperCollins Publishers LLC, 195 Broadway, New York, NY 10007 Tel: 212-207-7000 Web Site: www.harpercollins.com, pg 86

Rudy, Caryn Karmatz, DeFiore and Company Literary Management Inc, 47 E 19 St, 3rd fl, New York, NY 10003 Tel: 212-925-7744 Fax: 212-925-9803 E-mail: info@defliterary.com; submissions@defliterary.com Web Site: www.defliterary.com, pg 456

Rue, Robin, Writers House, 21 W 26 St, New York, NY 10010 Tel: 212-685-2400 Web Site: www.writershouse.com, pg 482

Ruffin, Michael L, Smyth & Helwys Publishing Inc, 6316 Peake Rd, Macon, GA 31210-3960 Tel: 478-757-0564 Toll Free Tel: 800-747-3016 (orders only) Fax: 478-757-1305 E-mail: information@helwys.com Web Site: www.helwys.com, pg 192

Ruffino, Dan, Simon & Schuster, LLC, 1230 Avenue of the Americas, New York, NY 10020 Tel: 212-698-7000 Toll Free Tel: 800-223-2336 (orders) Fax: 212-698-7007 Toll Free Fax: 800-943-9831 (orders) E-mail: firstname.lastname@simonandschuster.com; purchaseorders@simonandschuster.com (orders) Web Site: www.simonandschuster.com, pg 189

Ruffino, Terri, Workman Publishing, 1290 Avenue of the Americas, New York, NY 10104 Toll Free Tel: 800-759-0190 Fax: 212-364-0950 E-mail: workman-inquiry@hbgusa.com Web Site: www.hachettebookgroup.com/imprint/workman-publishing-company/, pg 233

Ruffner, Peter E, Omnigraphics Inc, 615 Griswold, Suite 520, Detroit, MI 48226 Tel: 610-461-3548 Toll Free Tel: 800-234-1340 (cust serv) Fax: 610-532-9001 Toll

Free Fax: 800-875-1340 (cust serv) *E-mail:* contact@omnigraphics.com; customerservice@omnigraphics.com *Web Site:* omnigraphics.com, pg 146

Rufus, Molly, Hurston/Wright Award for College Writers, 10 "G" St NE, Suite 600, Washington, DC 20002 *E-mail:* info@hurstonwright.org *Web Site:* www.hurstonwright.org/awards/hurston-wright-award-for-college-writers, pg 614

Rufus, Molly, Hurston/Wright Legacy Awards, 10 "G" St NE, Suite 600, Washington, DC 20002 *E-mail:* info@hurstonwright.org *Web Site:* www.hurstonwright.org/awards/legacy-awards, pg 614

Rufus, Molly, Hurston/Wright Writers Week Workshops, 10 "G" St NE, Suite 600, Washington, DC 20002 *E-mail:* info@hurstonwright.org *Web Site:* www.hurstonwright.org/workshops/writers-week-workshops, pg 555

Rufus, Molly, The Zora Neale Hurston/Richard Wright Foundation, 10 "G" St NE, Suite 600, Washington, DC 20002 *E-mail:* info@hurstonwright.org *Web Site:* www.hurstonwright.org, pg 525

Ruggiero, Anthony, Pauline Books & Media, 50 Saint Paul's Ave, Boston, MA 02130 *Tel:* 617-522-8911 *Toll Free Tel:* 800-876-4463 (orders); 800-836-9723 (cust serv) *Fax:* 617-541-9805 *E-mail:* editorial@paulinemedia.com (ms submissions); orderentry@pauline.org (cust serv) *Web Site:* www.pauline.org/pbmpublishing, pg 152

Ruggiero, Sal, Doubleday, c/o Penguin Random House LLC, 1745 Broadway, New York, NY 10019 *Tel:* 212-751-2600 *Fax:* 212-940-7390 (dom rts); 212-572-2662 (foreign rts) *Web Site:* knopfdoubleday.com/imprint/doubleday/; knopfdoubleday.com, pg 61

Ruggiero, Sal, Alfred A Knopf, c/o Penguin Random House LLC, 1745 Broadway, New York, NY 10019 *Tel:* 212-751-2600 *Fax:* 212-940-7390 (dom rts); 212-572-2662 (foreign rts) *Web Site:* knopfdoubleday.com/imprint/knopf/; knopfdoubleday.com, pg 110

Ruhlig, Steve, Human Kinetics Inc, 1607 N Market St, Champaign, IL 61820 *Tel:* 217-351-5076 *Toll Free Tel:* 800-747-4457 *Fax:* 217-351-1549 (orders/cust serv) *E-mail:* info@hkusa.com *Web Site:* us.humankinetics.com, pg 97

Ruiz, Bea, National Catholic Educational Association, 200 N Glebe Rd, Suite 310, Arlington, VA 22203 *Tel:* 571-257-0010 *Toll Free Tel:* 800-711-6232 *Fax:* 703-243-0025 *E-mail:* nceaadmin@ncea.org *Web Site:* www.ncea.org, pg 137

Ruiz, Jonathan, Velazquez Press, 9682 Telstar Ave, Suite 110, El Monte, CA 91731 *Tel:* 626-448-3448 *Fax:* 626-602-3817 *E-mail:* info@academiclearningcompany.com *Web Site:* www.velazquezpress.com, pg 224

Ruiz, Natalia, Henry Holt and Company, LLC, 120 Broadway, 23rd fl, New York, NY 10271 *Tel:* 646-307-5151 *Toll Free Tel:* 888-330-8477 (orders) *Fax:* 646-307-5285 *Web Site:* www.henryholt.com, pg 94

Ruiz, Paloma, Viking Penguin, c/o Penguin Random House LLC, 1745 Broadway, New York, NY 10019 *Tel:* 212-782-9000 *Web Site:* www.penguin.com/overview-vikingbooks/; www.penguin.com/pamela-dorman-books-overview/; www.penguin.com/penguin-classics-overview/; www.penguin.com/penguin-life-overview/, pg 225

Rukkila, Roy, ACMRS Press, Arizona State University, PO Box 874402, Tempe, AZ 85287-4402 *Tel:* 480-727-6503 *Toll Free Tel:* 800-621-2736 (orders) *Fax:* 480-965-1681 *Toll Free Fax:* 800-621-8476 (orders) *E-mail:* acmrs@asu.edu *Web Site:* acmrspress.com, pg 4

Ruley, Meg, Jane Rotrosen Agency LLC, 318 E 51 St, New York, NY 10022-7803 *Tel:* 212-593-4330 *E-mail:* info@janerotrosen.com *Web Site:* janerotrosen.com, pg 474

Rulfs, Sarah, Cy Twombly Award for Poetry, 820 Greenwich St, New York, NY 10014 *Tel:* 212-807-7077 *E-mail:* info@contemporary-arts.org *Web Site:* www.foundationforcontemporaryarts.org/grants/cy-twombly-award-for-poetry, pg 672

Rummel, Chad, Council for Exceptional Children (CEC), 3100 Clarendon Blvd, Suite 600, Arlington, VA 22201 *Toll Free Tel:* 888-232-7733 *E-mail:* service@exceptionalchildren.org *Web Site:* www.exceptionalchildren.org, pg 53

Rundle, Lisa, HarperCollins Canada Ltd, 22 Adelaide St W, 41st fl, Toronto, ON M5H 4E3, Canada *Tel:* 416-975-9334 *E-mail:* hcorder@harpercollins.com *Web Site:* www.harpercollins.ca, pg 409

Runft, Lindsay Graber, Livestock Publications Council (LPC), 301 Main St, Courtland, KS 66939 *Tel:* 785-614-5371 *Web Site:* livestockpublications.com, pg 510

Runge, Gailen, C&T Publishing Inc, 1651 Challenge Dr, Concord, CA 94520-5206 *Tel:* 925-677-0377 *E-mail:* ctinfo@ctpub.com *Web Site:* www.ctpub.com, pg 40

Runyon, Ashley, The University Press of Kentucky, 663 S Limestone St, Lexington, KY 40508-4008 *Tel:* 859-257-8400 *Fax:* 859-323-1873 *Web Site:* www.kentuckypress.com, pg 222

Rupp, Rebecca, Vermont Golden Dome Book Award, 60 Washington St, Suite 2, Barre, VT 05641 *Tel:* 802-636-0040 *Web Site:* libraries.vermont.gov/services/children_and_teens/book_awards/vtgdba, pg 672

Ruppel, Philip, Phaidon, 65 Bleecker St, 8th fl, New York, NY 10012 *Tel:* 212-652-5400 *Toll Free Tel:* 800-759-0190 (cust serv) *Fax:* 212-652-5410 *Toll Free Fax:* 800-286-9471 (cust serv) *E-mail:* enquiries@phaidon.com *Web Site:* www.phaidon.com, pg 159

Rush, Caitlyn, Macmillan, 120 Broadway, 22nd fl, New York, NY 10271 *E-mail:* press.inquiries@macmillan.com *Web Site:* us.macmillan.com, pg 122

Rusin, Matthew, Tor Publishing Group, 120 Broadway, New York, NY 10271 *Toll Free Tel:* 800-455-0340 (Macmillan) *E-mail:* torpublicity@tor.com; forgepublicity@forgebooks.com *Web Site:* us.macmillan.com/torpublishinggroup, pg 208

Russ, Travis, Gabelli School of Business Communications & Media Management Program, 140 W 62 St, Rm 440, New York, NY 10023 *Tel:* 212-636-6150 *Fax:* 718-817-4999 *Web Site:* www.fordham.edu/gabelli-school-of-business, pg 562

Russell, Ally, Nosy Crow Inc, 145 Lincoln Rd, Lincoln, MA 01773 *E-mail:* nosycrowinc@nosycrow.com; salesinfo@nosycrow.com; export@nosycrow.com (export sales); rights@nosycrow.com *Web Site:* nosycrow.us, pg 144

Russell, Jack, Naval Institute Press, 291 Wood Rd, Annapolis, MD 21402-5034 *Tel:* 410-268-6110 *Toll Free Tel:* 800-233-8764 *Fax:* 410-295-1084 *E-mail:* customer@usni.org (cust inquiries) *Web Site:* www.usni.org/press/books; www.usni.org, pg 139

Russell, Jeannine, Wichita State University Playwriting Contest, 1845 Fairmount St, Box 153, Wichita, KS 67260-0153 *Tel:* 316-978-3360 *Web Site:* www.wichita.edu, pg 675

Russell, Kenn, Henry Holt and Company, LLC, 120 Broadway, 23rd fl, New York, NY 10271 *Tel:* 646-307-5151 *Toll Free Tel:* 888-330-8477 (orders) *Fax:* 646-307-5285 *Web Site:* www.henryholt.com, pg 94

Russell, Kenn, Macmillan, 120 Broadway, 22nd fl, New York, NY 10271 *E-mail:* press.inquiries@macmillan.com *Web Site:* us.macmillan.com, pg 122

Russell, Linda, The Continuing Legal Education Society of British Columbia (CLEBC), 500-1155 W Pender St, Vancouver, BC V6E 2P4, Canada *Tel:* 604-669-3544; 604-893-2121 (cust serv) *Toll Free Tel:* 800-663-0437 (CN) *Fax:* 604-669-9260 *E-mail:* custserv@cle.bc.ca *Web Site:* www.cle.bc.ca, pg 400

Russell, Tom, Random House Children's Books, c/o Penguin Random House LLC, 1745 Broadway, New York, NY 10019 *Tel:* 212-782-9000 *Web Site:* www.rhcbooks.com, pg 169

Russo, Carmine, The Bureau for At-Risk Youth, 40 Aero Rd, Unit 2, Bohemia, NY 11716 *Toll Free Tel:* 800-99YOUTH (999-6884) *Toll Free Fax:* 800-262-1886 *Web Site:* www.at-risk.com, pg 38

Russo, Chris, Holiday House Publishing Inc, 50 Broad St, New York, NY 10004 *Tel:* 212-688-0085 *Fax:* 212-421-6134 *E-mail:* info@holidayhouse.com *Web Site:* www.holidayhouse.com, pg 94

Russo, Maria, Astra Books for Young Readers, 19 W 21 St, No 1201, New York, NY 10010 *Tel:* 646-844-3485 *E-mail:* ahinfo@astrahouse.com; permissions@astrapublishinghouse.com *Web Site:* astrapublishinghouse.com, pg 20

Russo, Molly, Sophia Institute Press®, 18 Celina Ave, Unit 1, Nashua, NH 03063 *Tel:* 603-641-9344 *Toll Free Tel:* 800-888-9344 *Fax:* 603-641-8108 *Toll Free Fax:* 888-288-2259 *E-mail:* orders@sophiainstitute.com *Web Site:* www.sophiainstitute.com, pg 193

Russo, Nicole, Simon & Schuster Children's Publishing, 1230 Avenue of the Americas, New York, NY 10020 *Tel:* 212-698-7000 *Web Site:* www.simonandschuster.com/kids; www.simonandschuster.com/teen; simonandschuster.net; simonandschuster.biz, pg 189

Russo, Olivia, Penguin Young Readers Group, c/o Penguin Random House LLC, 1745 Broadway, New York, NY 10019 *Tel:* 212-782-9000 *Web Site:* www.penguin.com/penguin-young-readers-overview, pg 156

Russolese, Kaitlin Darcy, Random House Publishing Group, 1745 Broadway, New York, NY 10019 *Toll Free Tel:* 800-200-3552 *Web Site:* www.randomhousebooks.com, pg 171

Rust, Ned, Little, Brown and Company, 1290 Avenue of the Americas, New York, NY 10104 *Tel:* 212-364-1100 *Fax:* 212-364-0952 *E-mail:* firstname.lastname@hbgusa.com *Web Site:* www.hachettebookgroup.com/imprint/little-brown-and-company/, pg 118

Rutigliano, Olivia, Grove Atlantic Inc, 154 W 14 St, 12th fl, New York, NY 10011 *Tel:* 212-614-7850 *Toll Free Tel:* 800-521-0178 *Fax:* 212-614-7886 *E-mail:* info@groveatlantic.com; sales@groveatlantic.com; publicity@groveatlantic.com; rights@groveatlantic.com *Web Site:* www.groveatlantic.com, pg 82

Rutland-Starks, Kimberly, The Mathematical Association of America, 1529 18 St NW, Washington, DC 20036-1358 *Tel:* 202-387-5200 *Toll Free Tel:* 800-741-9415 *Fax:* 202-265-2384 *E-mail:* maahq@maa.org; advertising@maa.org (pubns) *Web Site:* www.maa.org, pg 127

Rutman, Jim, Sterling Lord Literistic Inc, 594 Broadway, Suite 205, New York, NY 10012 *Tel:* 212-780-6050 *Fax:* 212-780-6095 *E-mail:* info@sll.com *Web Site:* www.sll.com, pg 477

Rutter-Bowman, Walker, Dalkey Archive Press, c/o Deep Vellum Publishing, 3000 Commerce St, Dallas, TX 75226 *E-mail:* admin@deepvellum.org *Web Site:* www.dalkeyarchive.com, pg 56

Ryan, Amy, HarperCollins Children's Books, 195 Broadway, New York, NY 10007 *Tel:* 212-207-7000 *Web Site:* www.harpercollins.com/childrens, pg 85

Ryan, Anthony J, Ignatius Press, 1348 Tenth Ave, San Francisco, CA 94122-2304 *Toll Free Tel:* 800-651-1531 (orders); 888-615-3186 (cust serv) *Fax:* 415-387-0896 *E-mail:* info@ignatius.com *Web Site:* www.ignatius.com, pg 98

Ryan, Becky, DawnSignPress, 6130 Nancy Ridge Dr, San Diego, CA 92121-3223 *Tel:* 858-625-0600 *Toll Free Tel:* 800-549-5350 *Fax:* 858-625-2336 *E-mail:* contactus@dawnsign.com *Web Site:* www.dawnsign.com, pg 58

Ryan, Lindy, Vesuvian Books, 711 Dolly Parton Pkwy, No 4313, Sevierville, TN 37864 *E-mail:* info@vesuvianmedia.com *Web Site:* www.vesuvianmedia.com, pg 224

Ryan, Liv, Little, Brown and Company, 1290 Avenue of the Americas, New York, NY 10104 *Tel:* 212-364-1100 *Fax:* 212-364-0952 *E-mail:* firstname.lastname@hbgusa.com *Web Site:* www.hachettebookgroup.com/imprint/little-brown-and-company/, pg 118

Ryan, Mary Meghan, Bernan, 4501 Forbes Blvd, Suite 200, Lanham, MD 20706 Tel: 717-794-3800 (cust serv & orders) Toll Free Tel: 800-462-6420 (cust serv & orders) Fax: 717-794-3803 Toll Free Fax: 800-338-4550 E-mail: customercare@rowman. com; orders@rowman.com; publicity@rowman.com Web Site: rowman.com/page/bernan, pg 28

Ryan, Michael, McGraw-Hill Higher Education, 1325 Avenue of the Americas, New York, NY 10019 Toll Free Tel: 800-338-3987 (cust serv) Toll Free Fax: 800-953-8691 (cust serv) Web Site: www.mheducation.com/highered, pg 128

Ryan, Peter K, Stimola Literary Studio Inc, 11 Briarwood Lane, West Tisbury, MA 02575 Tel: 201-945-9353 Fax: 201-490-5920 E-mail: info@stimolaliterarystudio.com Web Site: www.stimolaliterarystudio.com, pg 477

Ryan, Regina, Regina Ryan Books, 251 Central Park W, Suite 7-D, New York, NY 10024 Tel: 212-787-5589 E-mail: queries@reginaryanbooks.com Web Site: www.reginaryanbooks.com, pg 474

Ryan, Regina Sara, Hohm Press, PO Box 4410, Chino Valley, AZ 86323 Tel: 928-636-3331 Toll Free Tel: 800-381-2700 Fax: 928-636-7519 E-mail: publisher@hohmpress.com Web Site: www.hohmpress.com, pg 94

Ryder, Jordan, Second Story Press, 20 Maud St, Suite 401, Toronto, ON M5V 2M5, Canada Tel: 416-537-7850 Fax: 416-537-0588 E-mail: info@secondstorypress.ca Web Site: secondstorypress.ca, pg 419

Ryoo, Catherine, Penguin Random House Canada, a Penguin Random House company, 320 Front St W, Suite 1400, Toronto, ON M5V 3B6, Canada Tel: 416-364-4449 Toll Free Tel: 888-523-9292 (cust serv) E-mail: canadaweb@penguinrandomhouse.com; customerservicescanada@penguinrandomhouse.com Web Site: www.penguinrandomhouse.ca, pg 416

Ryzner, Tricia, Random House Children's Books, c/o Penguin Random House LLC, 1745 Broadway, New York, NY 10019 Tel: 212-782-9000 Web Site: www.rhcbooks.com, pg 170

Saarela, Alexis, Tor Publishing Group, 120 Broadway, New York, NY 10271 Toll Free Tel: 800-455-0340 (Macmillan) E-mail: torpublicity@tor.com; forgepublicity@forgebooks.com Web Site: us.macmillan.com/torpublishinggroup, pg 208

Saari, Annaka, Boston University Creative Writing Program, 236 Bay State Rd, Boston, MA 02215 Tel: 617-353-2510 E-mail: crwr@bu.edu Web Site: www.bu.edu/creativewriting, pg 561

Sabga, Lesley, The Seymour Agency, 475 Miner Street Rd, Canton, NY 13617 Tel: 239-398-8209 Web Site: www.theseymouragency.com, pg 475

Sabia, Mary Ann, Charlesbridge Publishing Inc, 85 Main St, Watertown, MA 02472 Tel: 617-926-0329 Toll Free Tel: 800-225-3214 Fax: 617-926-5720 Toll Free Fax: 800-926-5775 E-mail: books@charlesbridge.com Web Site: www.charlesbridge.com, pg 45

Sablik, Filip, BOOM! Studios, 5670 Wilshire Blvd, Suite 400, Los Angeles, CA 90036 E-mail: contact@boom-studios.com; customerservice@boom-studios.com; press@boom-studios.com Web Site: www.boom-studios.com, pg 34

Sablik, Rachael, Running Press, 1290 Avenue of the Americas, New York, NY 10104 Tel: 212-364-1100 Toll Free Tel: 800-759-0190 (cust serv) Fax: 212-364-0933 (intl orders) Toll Free Fax: 800-286-9471 (cust serv) E-mail: customer.service@hbgusa.com; orders@hbgusa.com Web Site: www.hachettebookgroup.com/imprint/running-press/; www.moon.com (Moon Travel Guides), pg 178

Sablosky, Lindsay, Chronicle Books LLC, 680 Second St, San Francisco, CA 94107 Tel: 415-537-4200 Fax: 415-537-4460 (perms) E-mail: hello@chroniclebooks.com; subrights@chroniclebooks.com Web Site: www.chroniclebooks.com, pg 47

Sabo, Slater MA, South Dakota Historical Society Press, 900 Governors Dr, Pierre, SD 57501 Tel: 605-773-6009 Fax: 605-773-6041 E-mail: info@sdhspress.com; orders@sdhspress.com Web Site: sdhspress.com, pg 195

Sabol, Stephanie, Penguin Young Readers Group, c/o Penguin Random House LLC, 1745 Broadway, New York, NY 10019 Tel: 212-782-9000 Web Site: www.penguin.com/penguin-young-readers-overview, pg 156

Sachdev, Rachana PhD, Susquehanna University, Department of English & Creative Writing, 514 University Ave, Selinsgrove, PA 17870 Tel: 570-372-4196 Web Site: www.susqu.edu, pg 565

Sacher, Jay, Union Square & Co, 1166 Avenue of the Americas, 17th fl, New York, NY 10036-2715 Tel: 212-532-7160 Toll Free Tel: 800-367-9692 Fax: 212-213-2495 Toll Free Fax: 800-542-7567 E-mail: custservice@sterlingpublishing.com; customerservice@sterlingpublishing.com; editorial@sterlingpublishing.com; tradesales@sterlingpublishing.com Web Site: www.sterlingpublishing.com, pg 212

Sachs, Cassidy, Dutton, c/o Penguin Random House LLC, 1745 Broadway, New York, NY 10019 Tel: 212-366-2000 Web Site: www.penguin.com/dutton-overview/; www.penguin.com/plume-books-overview/; www.penguin.com/tiny-reparations-overview/, pg 62

Sacilotto, Loriana, Harlequin Enterprises Ltd, Bay Adelaide Centre, East Tower, 22 Adelaide St W, 41st fl, Toronto, ON M5H 4E3, Canada Tel: 416-445-5860 Toll Free Tel: 888-432-4879; 800-370-5838 (ebook inquiries) E-mail: customerservice@harlequin.com Web Site: www.harlequin.com, pg 409

Sacks, Dr Elias, The Jewish Publication Society, c/o Gratz College, 7605 Old York Rd, Melrose Park, PA 19027 Tel: 215-832-0600 Web Site: www.jps.org; www.nebraskapress.unl.edu/jps/, pg 105

Sacks, Samantha, Farrar, Straus & Giroux Books for Young Readers, 120 Broadway, New York, NY 10271 Tel: 212-741-6900 Toll Free Tel: 888-330-8477 (orders) E-mail: childrens.publicity@macmillanusa.com; childrensrights@macmillanusa.com Web Site: us.macmillan.com/mackids, pg 70

Sacks, Samantha, Roaring Brook Press, 120 Broadway, New York, NY 10271 Tel: 646-307-5151 Web Site: us.macmillan.com/publishers/roaring-brook-press, pg 176

Sadikot, Sasha, Penguin Random House LLC, 1745 Broadway, New York, NY 10019 Tel: 212-782-9000 Toll Free Tel: 800-726-0600 Web Site: www.penguinrandomhouse.com, pg 155

Sadovskaya, Polina, PEN America, 120 Broadway, 26th fl N, New York, NY 10271 Tel: 212-334-1660 Fax: 212-334-2181 E-mail: info@pen.org; membership@pen.org; education@pen.org Web Site: pen.org, pg 516

Sadowski, Br Frank, St Pauls, 2187 Victory Blvd, Staten Island, NY 10314-6603 Tel: 718-761-0047 (edit & prodn); 718-698-2759 (mktg & billing) Toll Free Tel: 800-343-2522 Fax: 718-761-0057 E-mail: sales@stpauls.us; marketing@stpauls.us Web Site: www.stpauls.us, pg 181

Sadowski, Julia, North Atlantic Books (NAB), 2526 Martin Luther King Jr Way, Berkeley, CA 94704 Tel: 510-549-4270 Web Site: www.northatlanticbooks.com, pg 142

Saenz, Octavia, Astra Books for Young Readers, 19 W 21 St, No 1201, New York, NY 10010 Tel: 646-844-3485 E-mail: ahinfo@astrahouse.com; permissions@astrapublishinghouse.com Web Site: astrapublishinghouse.com, pg 20

Saferstein-Hansen, Jacklyn, Renaissance Literary & Talent, PO Box 17379, Beverly Hills, CA 90209 Tel: 323-848-8305 E-mail: query@renaissancemgmt.net Web Site: renaissancemgmt.net, pg 473

Safon, Teresa, Corporation for Public Broadcasting (CPB), 401 Ninth St NW, Washington, DC 20004-2129 Tel: 202-879-9600 E-mail: press@cpb.org Web Site: cpb.org, pg 504

Safronova, Yelena, Bloomsbury Publishing Inc, 1385 Broadway, 5th fl, New York, NY 10018 Tel: 212-419-5300 E-mail: marketingusa@bloomsbury.com; adultpublicityusa@bloomsbury.com; askacademic@bloomsbury.com Web Site: www.bloomsbury.com, pg 32

Sagara, Mike, Stanford University Press, 425 Broadway St, Redwood City, CA 94063-3126 Tel: 650-723-9434 Fax: 650-725-3457 E-mail: info@www.sup.org; publicity@www.sup.org; sales@www.sup.org Web Site: www.sup.org, pg 197

Saggau, Andrea, Penguin Random House LLC, 1745 Broadway, New York, NY 10019 Tel: 212-782-9000 Toll Free Tel: 800-726-0600 Web Site: www.penguinrandomhouse.com, pg 155

Saginario, Jill, Sasquatch Books, 1904 S Third Ave, Suite 710, Seattle, WA 98101 Tel: 206-467-4300 Toll Free Tel: 800-775-0817 Fax: 206-467-4301 E-mail: custserv@sasquatchbooks.com Web Site: sasquatchbooks.com, pg 182

Sagnette, Lindsay, GP Putnam's Sons, c/o Penguin Random House LLC, 1745 Broadway, New York, NY 10019 Tel: 212-782-9000 Web Site: www.penguin.com/putnam/, pg 167

Sahagian, Sarah, Marilyn Baillie Picture Book Award, 425 Adelaide St W, Suite 200, Toronto, ON M5V 3C1, Canada Tel: 416-975-0010 E-mail: info@bookcentre.ca Web Site: www.bookcentre.ca, pg 576

Sahagian, Sarah, The Geoffrey Bilson Award for Historical Fiction for Young People, 425 Adelaide St W, Suite 200, Toronto, ON M5V 3C1, Canada Tel: 416-975-0010 E-mail: info@bookcentre.ca Web Site: www.bookcentre.ca, pg 580

Sahagian, Sarah, Prix Harry Black, 425 Adelaide St W, Suite 200, Toronto, ON M5V 3C1, Canada Tel: 416-975-0010 E-mail: info@bookcentre.ca Web Site: www.bookcentre.ca, pg 581

Sahagian, Sarah, The Canadian Children's Book Centre, 425 Adelaide St W, Suite 200, Toronto, ON M5V 3C1, Canada Tel: 416-975-0010 E-mail: info@bookcentre.ca Web Site: www.bookcentre.ca, pg 502

Sahagian, Sarah, Norma Fleck Award for Canadian Children's Non-Fiction, 425 Adelaide St W, Suite 200, Toronto, ON M5V 3C1, Canada Tel: 416-975-0010 E-mail: info@bookcentre.ca Web Site: www.bookcentre.ca, pg 602

Sahagian, Sarah, Jean Little First Novel Award, 425 Adelaide St W, Suite 200, Toronto, ON M5V 3C1, Canada Tel: 416-975-0010 E-mail: info@bookcentre.ca Web Site: www.bookcentre.ca, pg 625

Sahagian, Sarah, Amy Mathers Teen Book Award, 425 Adelaide St W, Suite 200, Toronto, ON M5V 3C1, Canada Tel: 416-975-0010 E-mail: info@bookcentre.ca Web Site: www.bookcentre.ca, pg 630

Sahagian, Sarah, TD Canadian Children's Literature Award, 425 Adelaide St W, Suite 200, Toronto, ON M5V 3C1, Canada Tel: 416-975-0010 E-mail: info@bookcentre.ca Web Site: www.bookcentre.ca, pg 668

Said, Beter, Macmillan, 120 Broadway, 22nd fl, New York, NY 10271 E-mail: press.inquiries@macmillan.com Web Site: us.macmillan.com, pg 122

Saikia-Wilson, Becky, Houghton Mifflin Harcourt Trade & Reference Division, 125 High St, Boston, MA 02110 Tel: 617-351-5000 Web Site: www.hmhco.com, pg 96

Saint Jean, Jessica, Jill Grinberg Literary Management LLC, 392 Vanderbilt Ave, Brooklyn, NY 11238 Tel: 212-620-5883 E-mail: info@jillgrinbergliterary.com Web Site: www.jillgrinbergliterary.com, pg 461

Saint-Jean, Marie-Claire, Saint-Jean Editeur Inc, 4490, rue Garand, Laval, QC H7L 5Z6, Canada Tel: 450-663-1777 E-mail: info@saint-jeanediteur.com Web Site: saint-jeanediteur.com, pg 418

Saint-Jean, Nicole, Saint-Jean Editeur Inc, 4490, rue Garand, Laval, QC H7L 5Z6, Canada Tel: 450-663-1777 E-mail: info@saint-jeanediteur.com Web Site: saint-jeanediteur.com, pg 418

Sakamoto, Carla, The Monacelli Press, 65 Bleecker St, 8th fl, New York, NY 10012 Tel: 212-652-5400 E-mail: contact@monacellipress.com Web Site: www.phaidon.com/monacelli, pg 133

Sakuda, Takashi, Kodansha USA Inc, 451 Park Ave S, 7th fl, New York, NY 10016 *Tel:* 917-322-6200 *Fax:* 212-935-6929 *E-mail:* wsupress@kodansha-usa.com *Web Site:* kodansha.us, pg 111

Sala, Edward, Washington State University Press, Cooper Publications Bldg, 2300 Grimes Way, Pullman, WA 99164-5910 *Tel:* 509-335-7880 *Toll Free Tel:* 800-354-7360 (orders) *E-mail:* wsupress@wsu.edu *Web Site:* wsupress.wsu.edu, pg 226

Salaman, Marisol, Little, Brown and Company, 1290 Avenue of the Americas, New York, NY 10104 *Tel:* 212-364-1100 *Fax:* 212-364-0952 *E-mail:* firstname.lastname@hbgusa.com *Web Site:* www.hachettebookgroup.com/imprint/little-brown-and-company/, pg 118

Salane, Jeffrey, Simon & Schuster Children's Publishing, 1230 Avenue of the Americas, New York, NY 10020 *Tel:* 212-698-7000 *Web Site:* www.simonandschuster.com/kids; www.simonandschuster.com/teen; simonandschuster.net; simonandschuster.biz, pg 189

Salazar, Manuel, New City Press, 202 Comforter Blvd, Hyde Park, NY 12538 *Tel:* 845-229-0335 *Toll Free Tel:* 800-462-5980 (orders only) *Fax:* 845-229-0351 *E-mail:* info@newcitypress.com; orders@newcitypress.com *Web Site:* www.newcitypress.com, pg 139

Saldana, Shane, Sourcebooks LLC, 1935 Brookdale Rd, Suite 139, Naperville, IL 60563 *Tel:* 630-961-3900 *Toll Free Tel:* 800-432-7444 *Fax:* 630-961-2168 *E-mail:* info@sourcebooks.com *Web Site:* www.sourcebooks.com, pg 195

Salerno, Carey, Alice James Books, 60 Pineland Dr, Suite 206, New Gloucester, ME 04260 *Tel:* 207-926-8283 *E-mail:* info@alicejamesbooks.org *Web Site:* alicejamesbooks.org, pg 105

Saletan, Rebecca, Riverhead Books, c/o Penguin Random House LLC, 1745 Broadway, New York, NY 10019 *Tel:* 212-782-9000 *Web Site:* www.penguin.com/riverhead-overview/, pg 175

Saliman, Aaron, Sudden Fiction Contest, c/o ASUC Publications, Univ of California, 10-B Eshleman Hall, Berkeley, CA 94720-4500 *E-mail:* berkeleyfictionreview@gmail.com *Web Site:* berkeleyfictionreview.org, pg 667

Salina-I, Kim, Berkley, c/o Penguin Random House LLC, 1745 Broadway, 19th fl, New York, NY 10019 *Tel:* 212-366-2000 *Web Site:* www.penguin.com/publishers/berkley/; www.penguin.com/ace-overview/, pg 28

Salko, Maggie, little bee books, 598 Broadway, 7th fl, New York, NY 10012 *Tel:* 212-321-0237 *Toll Free Tel:* 844-321-0237 *E-mail:* info@littlebeebooks.com; sales@littlebeebooks.com; publicity@littlebeebooks.com *Web Site:* littlebeebooks.com, pg 117

Salko, Maggie, Random House Publishing Group, 1745 Broadway, New York, NY 10019 *Toll Free Tel:* 800-200-3552 *Web Site:* www.randomhousebooks.com, pg 171

Salky, Jesseca, Charlotte Sheedy Literary Agency Inc, 928 Broadway, Suite 901, New York, NY 10010 *Tel:* 212-780-9800 *Web Site:* www.sheedylit.com, pg 476

Sallese, Peter, Kensington Publishing Corp, 900 Third Ave, 26th fl, New York, NY 10022 *Tel:* 212-407-1500 *Toll Free Tel:* 800-221-2647 *Fax:* 212-935-0699 *Web Site:* www.kensingtonbooks.com, pg 109

Sallick, Hilary, Samuel Washington Allen Prize, c/o Linda Haviland Conte, 18 Hall Ave, Apt 2, Somerville, MA 02144 *E-mail:* info@nepoetryclub.org *Web Site:* nepoetryclub.org, pg 572

Sallick, Hilary, E E Cummings Prize, c/o Linda Haviland Conte, 18 Hall Ave, Apt 2, Somerville, MA 02144 *E-mail:* info@nepoetryclub.org *Web Site:* nepoetryclub.org, pg 594

Sallick, Hilary, Der Hovanessian Prize, c/o Linda Haviland Conte, 18 Hall Ave, Apt 2, Somerville, MA 02144 *E-mail:* info@nepoetryclub.org *Web Site:* nepoetryclub.org, pg 595

Sallick, Hilary, Golden Rose Award, c/o Linda Haviland Conte, 18 Hall Ave, Apt 2, Somerville, MA 02144 *E-mail:* info@nepoetryclub.org *Web Site:* nepoetryclub.org, pg 608

Sallick, Hilary, Amy Lowell Prize, c/o Linda Haviland Conte, 18 Hall Ave, Apt 2, Somerville, MA 02144 *E-mail:* info@nepoetryclub.org *Web Site:* nepoetryclub.org, pg 627

Sallick, Hilary, Sheila Margaret Motton Book Prize, c/o Linda Haviland Conte, 18 Hall Ave, Apt 2, Somerville, MA 02144 *E-mail:* info@nepoetryclub.org *Web Site:* nepoetryclub.org, pg 636

Sallick, Hilary, New England Poetry Club, c/o Linda Haviland Conte, 18 Hall Ave, Apt 2, Somerville, MA 02144 *E-mail:* info@nepoetryclub.org; president@nepoetryclub.org *Web Site:* nepoetryclub.org, pg 514

Sallick, Hilary, Jean Pedrick Chapbook Prize, c/o Linda Haviland Conte, 18 Hall Ave, Apt 2, Somerville, MA 02144 *E-mail:* info@nepoetryclub.org *Web Site:* nepoetryclub.org, pg 646

Salo, Gay, Piano Press, 1425 Ocean Ave, Suite 5, Del Mar, CA 92014 *Tel:* 619-884-1401 *E-mail:* pianopress@pianopress.com *Web Site:* www.pianopress.com, pg 159

Salois, Katerine, Les Editions de Mortagne, CP 116, Boucherville, QC J4B 5E6, Canada *Tel:* 450-641-2387 *E-mail:* info@editionsdemortagne.com *Web Site:* editionsdemortagne.com, pg 402

Salotti, Ana, Northern California Translators Association, 2261 Market St, Suite 160, San Francisco, CA 94114-1600 *Tel:* 510-845-8712 *E-mail:* ncta@ncta.org *Web Site:* ncta.org, pg 515

Salovaara, Malcolm, Encounter Books, 900 Broadway, Suite 601, New York, NY 10003 *Tel:* 212-871-6310 *Toll Free Tel:* 855-203-7220 *E-mail:* publicity@encounterbooks.com *Web Site:* www.encounterbooks.com, pg 66

Salpeter, Gabriella, Farrar, Straus & Giroux Books for Young Readers, 120 Broadway, New York, NY 10271 *Tel:* 212-741-6900 *Toll Free Tel:* 888-330-8477 (orders) *E-mail:* childrens.publicity@macmillanusa.com; childrensrights@macmillanusa.com *Web Site:* us.macmillan.com/mackids, pg 70

Salpeter, Gabriella, Roaring Brook Press, 120 Broadway, New York, NY 10271 *Tel:* 646-307-5151 *Web Site:* us.macmillan.com/publishers/roaring-brook-press, pg 176

Salser, Mark, National Book Co, PO Box 3428, Hillsboro, OR 97123-1943 *Tel:* 503-245-1500 *Fax:* 810-885-5811 *E-mail:* info@eralearning.com *Web Site:* www.eralearning.com, pg 137

Salton, Jay, Harry N Abrams Inc, 195 Broadway, 9th fl, New York, NY 10007 *Tel:* 212-206-7715 *Toll Free Tel:* 800-345-1359 *Fax:* 212-645-8437 *E-mail:* abrams@abramsbooks.com; publicity@abramsbooks.com; sales@abramsbooks.com *Web Site:* www.abramsbooks.com, pg 3

Saltzman, Allison, HarperCollins Publishers LLC, 195 Broadway, New York, NY 10007 *Tel:* 212-207-7000 *Web Site:* www.harpercollins.com, pg 86

Saltzman, Glenn, Georgetown University Press, 3520 Prospect St NW, Suite 140, Washington, DC 20007 *Tel:* 202-687-5889 (busn) *Fax:* 202-687-6340 (edit) *E-mail:* gupress@georgetown.edu *Web Site:* press.georgetown.edu, pg 77

Salvadore, Maria, Walter Dean Myers Awards for Outstanding Children's Literature, 10319 Westlake Dr, No 104, Bethesda, MD 20817 *Tel:* 701-404-WNDB (404-9632, voicemail only) *E-mail:* walteraward@diversebooks.org *Web Site:* diversebooks.org/our-programs/walter-award, pg 636

Salvati, Taylan, HarperCollins Children's Books, 195 Broadway, New York, NY 10007 *Tel:* 212-207-7000 *Web Site:* www.harpercollins.com/childrens, pg 85

Salvi, Erin, Theatre Communications Group, 520 Eighth Ave, 24th fl, New York, NY 10018-4156 *Tel:* 212-609-5900 *Fax:* 212-609-5901 *E-mail:* info@tcg.org *Web Site:* www.tcg.org, pg 206

Salvo, Katie, Metamorphosis Literary Agency, 12410 S Acuff Ct, Olathe, KS 66062 *Tel:* 646-397-1640 *E-mail:* info@metamorphosisliteraryagency.com *Web Site:* www.metamorphosisliteraryagency.com, pg 470

Salzano, Tammi, Tiger Tales, 5 River Rd, Suite 128, Wilton, CT 06897-4069 *Tel:* 920-387-2333 *Fax:* 920-387-9994 *Web Site:* www.tigertalesbooks.com, pg 207

Salzman, Rachel, W W Norton & Company Inc, 500 Fifth Ave, New York, NY 10110-0017 *Tel:* 212-354-5500 *Toll Free Tel:* 800-233-4830 (orders & cust serv) *Fax:* 212-869-0856 *Toll Free Fax:* 800-458-6515 *E-mail:* orders@wwnorton.com *Web Site:* wwnorton.com, pg 143

Salzman, Richard, Salzman International, 1751 Charles Ave, Arcata, CA 95521 *Tel:* 707-822-5500 *Fax:* 707-825-6600 *Web Site:* salzmanart.com, pg 486

Samakow, Lindsay, CAA Speakers, 2000 Avenue of the Stars, Los Angeles, CA 90067 *Tel:* 424-288-2000 *Fax:* 424-288-2900 *E-mail:* speakers@caa.com *Web Site:* www.caa.com/caaspeakers, pg 487

Samedi, Peggy, Pantheon Books, c/o Penguin Random House LLC, 1745 Broadway, New York, NY 10019 *Tel:* 212-751-2600 *Fax:* 212-940-7390 (dom rts); 212-572-2662 (foreign rts) *Web Site:* knopfdoubleday.com/imprint/pantheon/; knopfdoubleday.com, pg 150

Sammis, Aidan, Vermont College of Fine Arts MFA in Writing for Children & Young Adults Program, 36 College St, Montpelier, VT 05602 *Toll Free Tel:* 866-934-VCFA (934-8232) *Web Site:* vcfa.edu/mfa-writing-for-children-and-young-adults, pg 567

Samms, June, Kids Can Press Ltd, 25 Dockside Dr, Toronto, ON M5A 0B5, Canada *Tel:* 416-479-7000 *Toll Free Tel:* 800-265-0884 *Fax:* 416-960-5437 *E-mail:* info@kidscan.com; customerservice@kidscan.com *Web Site:* www.kidscanpress.com; www.kidscanpress.ca, pg 411

Samper, Marjorie, Lectorum Publications Inc, 10 New Maple Ave, Suite 303, Pine Brook, NJ 07058 *Tel:* 201-559-2200 *Toll Free Tel:* 800-345-5946 *E-mail:* lectorum@lectorum.com *Web Site:* www.lectorum.com, pg 114

Sampson, Bess Schelper, Random House Children's Books, c/o Penguin Random House LLC, 1745 Broadway, New York, NY 10019 *Tel:* 212-782-9000 *Web Site:* www.rhcbooks.com, pg 170

Sampson, Mandy, Quirk Books, 215 Church St, Philadelphia, PA 19106 *Tel:* 215-627-3581 *Fax:* 215-627-5220 *E-mail:* general@quirkbooks.com *Web Site:* www.quirkbooks.com, pg 168

Samual, Curtis, House of Anansi Press Inc, 128 Sterling Rd, Lower Level, Toronto, ON M6R 2B7, Canada *Tel:* 416-363-4343 *Fax:* 416-363-1017 *E-mail:* customerservice@houseofanansi.com *Web Site:* houseofanansi.com, pg 409

Samuel, Patrick, Northwestern University Press, 629 Noyes St, Evanston, IL 60208-4210 *Tel:* 847-491-2046 *Toll Free Tel:* 800-621-2736 (orders only) *Fax:* 847-491-8150 *E-mail:* nupress@northwestern.edu *Web Site:* www.nupress.northwestern.edu, pg 143

Samuels, Alicia, Presbyterian Publishing Corp (PPC), 100 Witherspoon St, Louisville, KY 40202 *Tel:* 502-569-5000 *Toll Free Tel:* 800-533-4371; 800-523-1631 (US only) *Fax:* 502-569-5113 *E-mail:* customerservice@presbypub.com *Web Site:* www.ppcbooks.com; www.wjkbooks.com, pg 163

Samuels, Alicia, Westminster John Knox Press (WJK), 100 Witherspoon St, Louisville, KY 40202-1396 *Tel:* 502-569-5052 *Toll Free Tel:* 800-523-1631 (US & CN) *Fax:* 502-569-8308 *Toll Free Fax:* 800-541-5113 (US & CN) *E-mail:* customer_service@wjkbooks.com; orders@wjkbooks.com *Web Site:* www.wjkbooks.com, pg 228

Samuelson, Beth, Indiana University African Studies Program, Indiana University, 355 N Eagleson Ave, Rm GA 3072, Bloomington, IN 47405-1105 *Tel:* 812-855-8284 *Fax:* 812-855-6734 *E-mail:* afrist@indiana.edu *Web Site:* www.indiana.edu/~afrist; www.go.iu.edu/afrist, pg 100

Samuelson, Paul, Scribner, 1230 Avenue of the Americas, New York, NY 10020 *Web Site:* www.simonandschusterpublishing.com/scribner/, pg 185

Samulski, Emily, Bloomsbury Academic, 1385 Broadway, 5th fl, New York, NY 10018 *Tel:* 212-419-5300 *Web Site:* www.bloomsbury.com/us/academic, pg 31

Samulski, Emily, Fairchild Books, 1385 Broadway, 5th fl, New York, NY 10018 *Tel:* 212-419-5300 *Toll Free Tel:* 800-932-4724; 888-330-8477 (orders) *Web Site:* www.bloomsbury.com/us/discover/bloomsbury-academic/fairchild-books/, pg 69

Sanborn, Kat, Llewellyn Publications, 2143 Wooddale Dr, Woodbury, MN 55125 *Tel:* 651-291-1970 *Toll Free Tel:* 800-843-6666 *Fax:* 651-291-1908 *E-mail:* publicity@llewellyn.com; customerservice@llewellyn.com *Web Site:* www.llewellyn.com, pg 119

Sanchez, Irene, Liturgy Training Publications, 3949 S Racine Ave, Chicago, IL 60609-2523 *Tel:* 773-579-4900 *Toll Free Tel:* 800-933-1800 (US & CN only orders) *Fax:* 773-579-4929 *E-mail:* orders@ltp.org *Web Site:* www.ltp.org, pg 119

Sanchez, Isabella, Beacon Press, 24 Farnsworth St, Boston, MA 02210-1409 *Tel:* 617-742-2110 *Fax:* 617-723-3097 *E-mail:* production@beacon.org *Web Site:* www.beacon.org, pg 25

Sanchez, Kaitlyn, Bradford Literary Agency, 5694 Mission Center Rd, Suite 347, San Diego, CA 92108 *Tel:* 619-521-1201 *E-mail:* hillary@bradfordlit.com *Web Site:* www.bradfordlit.com, pg 451

Sand, Michael, Harry N Abrams Inc, 195 Broadway, 9th fl, New York, NY 10007 *Tel:* 212-206-7715 *Toll Free Tel:* 800-345-1359 *Fax:* 212-645-8437 *E-mail:* abrams@abramsbooks.com; publicity@abramsbooks; sales@abramsbooks.com *Web Site:* www.abramsbooks.com, pg 2

Sand, Michael, Stewart, Tabori & Chang, 195 Broadway, 9th fl, New York, NY 10007 *Tel:* 212-206-7715 *Fax:* 212-519-1210 *E-mail:* abrams@abramsbooks.com *Web Site:* www.abramsbooks.com/imprints/stc, pg 198

Sanders, Gene, The Society of Naval Architects & Marine Engineers (SNAME), 99 Canal Center Plaza, Suite 310, Alexandria, VA 22314 *Tel:* 703-997-6701 *Toll Free Tel:* 800-798-2188 *Fax:* 703-997-6702 *Web Site:* www.sname.org, pg 193

Sanders, Meredith K, Goose River Press, 3400 Friendship Rd, Waldoboro, ME 04572-6337 *Tel:* 207-832-6665 *E-mail:* gooseriverpress@gmail.com *Web Site:* gooseriverpress.com, pg 79

Sanders, Mike, DK, c/o Penguin Random House LLC, 1745 Broadway, 20th fl, New York, NY 10019 *Tel:* 646-674-4000 *Toll Free Tel:* 800-733-3000 *Fax:* 646-674-4020 *E-mail:* marketing@dk.com (lib servs); publicity@dk.com; csorders@penguinrandomhouse.com; customerservice@penguinrandomhouse.com *Web Site:* www.dk.com, pg 60

Sanders, Rachel, Houghton Mifflin Harcourt, 125 High St, Boston, MA 02110 *Tel:* 617-351-5000 *Toll Free Tel:* 855-969-4642; 800-225-5425 (K-12 educ materials); 800-323-9540 (assessment materials); 877-219-1537 (SkillsTutor); 888-242-6747 (Innovation in Educ Group); 800-225-3362 (Trade & Ref Div) *Toll Free Fax:* 800-269-5232 *E-mail:* myhmhco@hmhco.com *Web Site:* www.hmhco.com, pg 96

Sanders, Ray, Purple House Press, 8100 US Hwy 62 E, Cynthiana, KY 41031 *Tel:* 859-235-9970 *Web Site:* www.purplehousepress.com, pg 167

Sanders, Rob, Greystone Books Ltd, 343 Railway St, Suite 302, Vancouver, BC V6A 1A4, Canada *Tel:* 604-875-1550 *Fax:* 604-875-1556 *E-mail:* info@greystonebooks.com; rights@greystonebooks.com *Web Site:* www.greystonebooks.com, pg 407

Sanders, Ruth PhD, Impact Publications/Development Concepts Inc, 7820 Sudley Rd, Suite 100, Manassas, VA 20109 *Tel:* 703-361-7300 *Toll Free Tel:* 800-361-1055 (cust serv) *Fax:* 703-335-9486 *E-mail:* query2@impactpublications.com *Web Site:* www.impactpublications.com, pg 99

Sanders, Victoria, Victoria Sanders & Associates LLC, 440 Buck Rd, Stone Ridge, NY 12484 *Tel:* 212-633-8811 *Web Site:* www.victoriasanders.com, pg 475

Sanderson, Cate, City & Regional Magazine Association (CRMA), 287 Richards Ave, Norwalk, CT 06850 *Tel:* 203-515-9294 *Web Site:* citymag.org, pg 504

Sanderson, Cate, National City & Regional Magazine Awards, 287 Richards Ave, Norwalk, CT 06850 *Tel:* 203-515-9294 *Web Site:* citymag.org/awards, pg 637

Sanderson, Dean, AIP Publishing LLC, 1305 Walt Whitman Rd, Suite 110, Melville, NY 11747 *Tel:* 516-576-2200 *E-mail:* help@aip.org; press@aip.org; rights@aip.org *Web Site:* www.aip.org; publishing.aip.org, pg 6

Sandford, Bria, Portfolio, c/o Penguin Random House LLC, 1745 Broadway, New York, NY 10019 *Tel:* 212-782-9000 *Web Site:* www.penguin.com/portfolio-overview/; www.penguin.com/sentinel-overview/; www.penguin.com/thesis/, pg 162

Sandler, Zoe, Sanford J Greenburger Associates Inc, 55 Fifth Ave, New York, NY 10003 *Tel:* 212-206-5600 *Web Site:* greenburger.com, pg 461

Sandlin, Leila, Portfolio, c/o Penguin Random House LLC, 1745 Broadway, New York, NY 10019 *Tel:* 212-782-9000 *Web Site:* www.penguin.com/portfolio-overview/; www.penguin.com/sentinel-overview/; www.penguin.com/thesis/, pg 162

Sandmeyer, Kirby, HarperCollins Publishers LLC, 195 Broadway, New York, NY 10007 *Tel:* 212-207-7000 *Web Site:* www.harpercollins.com, pg 87

Sands, Katharine, Sarah Jane Freymann Literary Agency LLC, 59 W 71 St, Suite 9-B, New York, NY 10023 *Tel:* 212-362-9277 *E-mail:* submissions@sarahjanefreymann.com *Web Site:* www.sarahjanefreymann.com, pg 459

Sandve, Kerri, Milkweed Editions, 1011 Washington Ave S, Suite 300, Minneapolis, MN 55415-1246 *Tel:* 612-332-3192 *Toll Free Tel:* 800-520-6455 *E-mail:* orders@milkweed.org *Web Site:* milkweed.org, pg 131

Sandweiss, Martha A, Allan Nevins Prize, Columbia University, 3009 Broadway MC 802, New York, NY 10027 *Tel:* 212-854-1919 *E-mail:* amhistsociety@columbia.edu *Web Site:* sah.columbia.edu, pg 639

Sandweiss, Martha A, Francis Parkman Prize, Columbia University, 3009 Broadway MC 802, New York, NY 10027 *Tel:* 212-854-1919 *E-mail:* amhistsociety@columbia.edu *Web Site:* sah.columbia.edu, pg 646

Sandweiss, Martha A, SAH Prize for Historical Fiction, Columbia University, 3009 Broadway MC 802, New York, NY 10027 *Tel:* 212-854-1919 *E-mail:* amhistsociety@columbia.edu *Web Site:* sah.columbia.edu, pg 658

Sanfilippo, Tony, The Ohio State University Press, 180 Pressey Hall, 1070 Carmack Rd, Columbus, OH 43210-1002 *Tel:* 614-292-6930 *Fax:* 614-292-2065 *Toll Free Fax:* 800-621-8476 *E-mail:* OSUPInfo@osu.edu *Web Site:* ohiostatepress.org, pg 145

Sanford, Alyssa, Princeton University Press, 41 William St, Princeton, NJ 08540-5237 *Tel:* 609-258-4900 *Fax:* 609-258-6305 *E-mail:* info@press.princeton.edu *Web Site:* press.princeton.edu, pg 164

Sanford, Melissa, Random House Publishing Group, 1745 Broadway, New York, NY 10019 *Toll Free Tel:* 800-200-3552 *Web Site:* www.randomhousebooks.com, pg 171

Sangiacomo, Marissa, St Martin's Press, LLC, 120 Broadway, New York, NY 10271 *E-mail:* publicity@stmartins.com; trademarketing@stmartins.com; foreignrights@stmartins.com *Web Site:* us.macmillan.com/smp, pg 181

Sangwan, Shivangi, Chronicle Books LLC, 680 Second St, San Francisco, CA 94107 *Tel:* 415-537-4200 *Fax:* 415-537-4460 (perms) *E-mail:* hello@chroniclebooks.com; subrights@chroniclebooks.com *Web Site:* www.chroniclebooks.com, pg 47

Sankaran, Vanitha, Historical Novel Society North American Conference, PO Box 1146, Jacksonville, AL 36265 *E-mail:* hnsnorthamerica@gmail.com *Web Site:* hns-conference.com; historicalnovelsociety.org/event/hns-north-american-conference; historicalnovelsociety.org, pg 554

Sankarin, Raghushri, Scholastic Inc, 557 Broadway, New York, NY 10012 *Tel:* 212-343-6100 *Toll Free Tel:* 800-SCHOLASTIC (724-6527) *Web Site:* www.scholastic.com, pg 184

Sankner, Jane Haas, Random House Publishing Group, 1745 Broadway, New York, NY 10019 *Toll Free Tel:* 800-200-3552 *Web Site:* www.randomhousebooks.com, pg 171

Sanocki, Savannah, Penguin Random House LLC, 1745 Broadway, New York, NY 10019 *Tel:* 212-782-9000 *Toll Free Tel:* 800-726-0600 *Web Site:* www.penguinrandomhouse.com, pg 155

Sansigre, Manuel, Penguin Random House LLC, 1745 Broadway, New York, NY 10019 *Tel:* 212-782-9000 *Toll Free Tel:* 800-726-0600 *Web Site:* www.penguinrandomhouse.com, pg 155

Sansigre, Manuel, Random House Publishing Group, 1745 Broadway, New York, NY 10019 *Toll Free Tel:* 800-200-3552 *Web Site:* www.randomhousebooks.com, pg 170

Santana, Dee, Penguin Random House Audio Publishing Group, 1745 Broadway, New York, NY 10019 *Toll Free Tel:* 800-793-2665 (cust serv) *E-mail:* audio@penguinrandomhouse.com; ecustomerservice@penguinrandomhouse.com *Web Site:* www.penguinrandomhouseaudio.com, pg 154

Santana, Reina, Springer Publishing Co, 11 W 42 St, 15th fl, New York, NY 10036-8002 *Tel:* 212-431-4370 *Toll Free Tel:* 877-687-7476 *E-mail:* marketing@springerpub.com; cs@springerpub.com (orders); textbook@springerpub.com; specialsales@springerpub.com *Web Site:* www.springerpub.com, pg 196

Santella, Mark, Random House Children's Books, c/o Penguin Random House LLC, 1745 Broadway, New York, NY 10019 *Tel:* 212-782-9000 *Web Site:* www.rhcbooks.com, pg 169

Santhouse, Paul, Moody Publishers, 820 N La Salle Blvd, Chicago, IL 60610 *Tel:* 312-329-2101 *Toll Free Tel:* 800-678-8812 *Fax:* 312-329-2144 *Toll Free Fax:* 800-678-3329 *E-mail:* mpcustomerservice@moody.edu; mporders@moody.edu; publicity@moody.edu *Web Site:* www.moodypublishers.com, pg 134

Santiago, Lilly, 5 Under 35, 90 Broad St, Suite 604, New York, NY 10004 *Tel:* 212-685-0261 *Fax:* 212-213-6570 *E-mail:* nationalbook@nationalbook.org *Web Site:* www.nationalbook.org, pg 602

Santiago, Lilly, Medal for Distinguished Contribution to American Letters, 90 Broad St, Suite 604, New York, NY 10004 *Tel:* 212-685-0261 *Fax:* 212-213-6570 *E-mail:* nationalbook@nationalbook.org *Web Site:* www.nationalbook.org/amerletters.html, pg 631

Santiago, Lilly, National Book Awards, 90 Broad St, Suite 604, New York, NY 10004 *Tel:* 212-685-0261 *Fax:* 212-213-6570 *E-mail:* nationalbook@nationalbook.org *Web Site:* www.nationalbook.org, pg 637

Santiago, Lilly, National Book Foundation, 90 Broad St, Suite 604, New York, NY 10004 *Tel:* 212-685-0261 *Fax:* 212-213-6570 *E-mail:* nationalbook@nationalbook.org *Web Site:* www.nationalbook.org, pg 526

Santiago, Lilly, Science + Literature Program, 90 Broad St, Suite 604, New York, NY 10004 *Tel:* 212-685-0261 *Fax:* 212-213-6570 *E-mail:* nationalbook@nationalbook.org *Web Site:* www.nationalbook.org/programs/science-literature, pg 661

Santokhi, Vimi, Doubleday, c/o Penguin Random House LLC, 1745 Broadway, New York, NY 10019 *Tel:* 212-751-2600 *Fax:* 212-940-7390 (dom rts); 212-572-2662 (foreign rts) *Web Site:* knopfdoubleday.com/imprint/doubleday/; knopfdoubleday.com, pg 61

Santokhi, Vimi, Pantheon Books, c/o Penguin Random House LLC, 1745 Broadway, New York, NY 10019 *Tel:* 212-751-2600 *Fax:* 212-940-7390 (dom rts); 212-572-2662 (foreign rts) *Web Site:* knopfdoubleday.com/imprint/pantheon/; knopfdoubleday.com, pg 150

Santopolo, Jill, Philomel Books, c/o Penguin Random House LLC, 1745 Broadway, New York, NY 10019 *Tel:* 212-782-9000 *Web Site:* www.penguin.com/philomel/, pg 159

Santoro, Corina, Milady, 5191 Natorp Blvd, Mason, OH 45040 *Toll Free Tel:* 866-848-5143 *Fax:* 518-373-6309 *E-mail:* info@milady.com *Web Site:* www.milady.com, pg 131

Santoro, Jamie, The American Library Association (ALA), 225 N Michigan Ave, Suite 1300, Chicago, IL 60601 *Tel:* 312-944-6780 *Toll Free Tel:* 800-545-2433; 866-SHOP-ALA (746-7252, orders) *Fax:* 312-280-5275; 312-440-9374; 312-280-5860 (orders) *E-mail:* ala@ala.org; alastore@ala.org *Web Site:* www.alastore.ala.org; www.ala.org, pg 10

Santoro, Jed, Merriam-Webster Inc, 47 Federal St, Springfield, MA 01102 *Tel:* 413-734-3134 *Toll Free Tel:* 800-828-1880 (orders & cust serv) *Fax:* 413-731-5979 (sales) *E-mail:* support@merriam-webster.com *Web Site:* www.merriam-webster.com, pg 130

Santoro, Nadine, The Feminist Press at The City University of New York, 365 Fifth Ave, Suite 5406, New York, NY 10016 *Tel:* 212-817-7915 *Fax:* 212-817-1593 *E-mail:* info@feministpress.org *Web Site:* www.feministpress.org, pg 71

Santucci, Ernest, Agency Chicago, 7000 Phoenix Ave NE, Suite 202, Albuquerque, NM 87110 *E-mail:* agency.chicago@usa.com, pg 448

Saphire-Bernstein, Evie, Jewish Book Council, 520 Eighth Ave, 4th fl, New York, NY 10018 *Tel:* 212-201-2920 *Fax:* 212-532-4952 *E-mail:* info@jewishbooks.org *Web Site:* www.jewishbookcouncil.org, pg 509

Saphire-Bernstein, Evie, National Jewish Book Award-Children's Picture Book, 520 Eighth Ave, 4th fl, New York, NY 10018 *Tel:* 212-201-2920 *Fax:* 212-532-4952 *E-mail:* njba@jewishbooks.org *Web Site:* www.jewishbookcouncil.org/awards, pg 637

Saphire-Bernstein, Evie, National Jewish Book Award-Natan Notable Books, 520 Eighth Ave, 4th fl, New York, NY 10018 *Tel:* 212-201-2920 *Fax:* 212-532-4952 *E-mail:* njba@jewishbooks.org; natannotable@jewishbooks.org *Web Site:* www.jewishbookcouncil.org/awards, pg 637

Saphire-Bernstein, Evie, National Jewish Book Award-Young Adult Literature, 520 Eighth Ave, 4th fl, New York, NY 10018 *Tel:* 212-201-2920 *Fax:* 212-532-4952 *E-mail:* njba@jewishbooks.org *Web Site:* www.jewishbookcouncil.org/awards, pg 637

Saphire-Bernstein, Evie, National Jewish Book Awards, 520 Eighth Ave, 4th fl, New York, NY 10018 *Tel:* 212-201-2920 *Fax:* 212-532-4952 *E-mail:* njba@jewishbooks.org *Web Site:* www.jewishbookcouncil.org/awards, pg 637

Saraydarian, Gita, TSG Publishing Foundation Inc, 8685 E Stagecoach Pass Rd, Scottsdale, AZ 85266 *Tel:* 480-502-1909 *E-mail:* info@tsgfoundation.org *Web Site:* www.tsgfoundation.org, pg 210

Saretsky, Kerry, HarperCollins Children's Books, 195 Broadway, New York, NY 10007 *Tel:* 212-207-7000 *Web Site:* www.harpercollins.com/childrens, pg 85

Sarfraz, Rabeet, Magazines Canada (MC), 555 Richmond St W, Suite 604, Mailbox 201, Toronto, ON M5V 3B1, Canada *Tel:* 416-994-6471 *Toll Free Tel:* 877-238-8354 *Fax:* 416-504-0437 *E-mail:* info@magazinescanada.ca *Web Site:* magazinescanada.ca, pg 510

Sargeant, Anna, Sourcebooks LLC, 1935 Brookdale Rd, Suite 139, Naperville, IL 60563 *Tel:* 630-961-3900 *Toll Free Tel:* 800-432-7444 *Fax:* 630-961-2168 *E-mail:* info@sourcebooks.com *Web Site:* sourcebooks.com, pg 194

Sargent, April, Sounds True Inc, 413 S Arthur Ave, Louisville, CO 80027 *Tel:* 303-665-3151 *Toll Free Tel:* 800-333-9185 (US); 888-303-9185 (US & CN) *E-mail:* customerservice@soundstrue.com; stpublicity@soundstrue.com *Web Site:* www.soundstrue.com, pg 194

Sargent, Kara, Simon & Schuster Children's Publishing, 1230 Avenue of the Americas, New York, NY 10020 *Tel:* 212-698-7000 *Web Site:* www.simonandschuster.com/kids; www.simonandschuster.com/teen; simonandschuster.net; simonandschuster.biz, pg 189

Sargent, Matt, Bisk Education, 9417 Princess Palm Ave, Suite 400, Tampa, FL 33619 *Tel:* 813-621-6200 *E-mail:* media@bisk.com *Web Site:* www.bisk.com, pg 30

Sargent, Michael, Tuttle Publishing, Airport Business Park, 364 Innovation Dr, North Clarendon, VT 05759-9436 *Tel:* 802-773-8930 *Toll Free Tel:* 800-526-2778 *Fax:* 802-773-6993 *Toll Free Fax:* 800-FAX-TUTL (329-8885) *E-mail:* info@tuttlepublishing.com; orders@tuttlepublishing.com *Web Site:* www.tuttlepublishing.com, pg 211

Sargent, Rachel, HarperCollins Publishers LLC, 195 Broadway, New York, NY 10007 *Tel:* 212-207-7000 *Web Site:* www.harpercollins.com, pg 87

Sargent, Sara, Random House Children's Books, c/o Penguin Random House LLC, 1745 Broadway, New York, NY 10019 *Tel:* 212-782-9000 *Web Site:* www.rhcbooks.com, pg 170

Sarles, Shawn, DK, c/o Penguin Random House LLC, 1745 Broadway, 20th fl, New York, NY 10019 *Tel:* 646-674-4000 *Toll Free Tel:* 800-733-3000 *Fax:* 646-674-4020 *E-mail:* marketing@dk.com (lib servs); publicity@dk.com; csorders@penguinrandomhouse.com; customerservice@penguinrandomhouse.com *Web Site:* www.dk.com, pg 60

Sarlo, Frank, Summit University Press, 63 Summit Way, Gardiner, MT 59030 *Tel:* 406-848-9292; 406-848-9500 (retail orders) *Fax:* 406-848-9555 *E-mail:* info@tsl.org; rights@summituniversitypress.com *Web Site:* www.summituniversitypress.com, pg 200

Sarratt, Blanche, University of Alabama Press, 200 Hackberry Lane, 2nd fl, Tuscaloosa, AL 35487 *Tel:* 205-348-5180 *Fax:* 205-348-9201 *Web Site:* www.uapress.ua.edu, pg 214

Sashti, Divya, Brooklyn Public Library Literary Prize, 10 Grand Army Plaza, Brooklyn, NY 11238 *Tel:* 718-230-2100 *E-mail:* brooklyneagles@bklynlibrary.org *Web Site:* www.bklynlibrary.org/support/bpl-literary-prize, pg 584

Sassa, Jackie, Houghton Mifflin Harcourt Trade & Reference Division, 125 High St, Boston, MA 02110 *Tel:* 617-351-5000 *Web Site:* www.hmhco.com, pg 96

Sassa, Jaclyn, Bloomsbury Publishing Inc, 1385 Broadway, 5th fl, New York, NY 10018 *Tel:* 212-419-5300 *E-mail:* marketingusa@bloomsbury.com; adultpublicityusa@bloomsbury.com; askacademic@bloomsbury.com *Web Site:* www.bloomsbury.com, pg 32

Satris, Marthine, Heyday, 1808 San Pablo Ave, Suite A, Berkeley, CA 94702 *Tel:* 510-549-3564 *E-mail:* heyday@heydaybooks.com *Web Site:* heydaybooks.com, pg 91

Satrom, Ellen, University of Virginia Press, PO Box 400318, Charlottesville, VA 22904-4318 *Tel:* 434-924-3469 (cust serv) *Toll Free Tel:* 800-831-3406 *Fax:* 434-982-2655 *Toll Free Fax:* 877-288-6400 *E-mail:* vapress@virginia.edu *Web Site:* www.upress.virginia.edu, pg 220

Sattler, Maggie, University of Minnesota Press, 111 Third Ave S, Suite 290, Minneapolis, MN 55401-2520 *Tel:* 612-301-1990 *Fax:* 612-301-1980 *E-mail:* ump@umn.edu *Web Site:* www.upress.umn.edu, pg 217

Sattler, Shalyn, Barbour Publishing Inc, 1810 Barbour Dr, Uhrichsville, OH 44683 *Tel:* 740-922-6045 *Fax:* 740-922-5948 *E-mail:* info@barbourbooks.com *Web Site:* www.barbourbooks.com, pg 24

Satyal, Rakesh, HarperCollins Publishers LLC, 195 Broadway, New York, NY 10007 *Tel:* 212-207-7000 *Web Site:* www.harpercollins.com, pg 86

Saulsbury, Marlene, Child Welfare League of America (CWLA), 727 15 St NW, Suite 1200, Washington, DC 20005 *Tel:* 202-590-8748 *E-mail:* cwla@cwla.org *Web Site:* www.cwla.org/pubs, pg 46

Saunders, Kat, Kent State University Press, 1118 University Library Bldg, 1125 Risman Dr, Kent, OH 44242 *Tel:* 330-672-7913 *Fax:* 330-672-3104 *E-mail:* ksupress@kent.edu *Web Site:* www.kentstateuniversitypress.com, pg 109

Saurette, Elyse, Manitoba Arts Council (MAC), 525-93 Lombard Ave, Winnipeg, MB R3B 3B1, Canada *Tel:* 204-945-2237 *Toll Free Tel:* 866-994-2787 *Fax:* 204-945-5925 *Web Site:* artscouncil.mb.ca, pg 510

Sauvgeau, Annie, Editions Le Dauphin Blanc Inc, 825, blvd Lebourgneuf, Suite 125, Quebec, QC G2J 0B9, Canada *Tel:* 418-845-4045 *Fax:* 418-845-1933 *E-mail:* info@dauphinblanc.com *Web Site:* dauphinblanc.com, pg 404

Savage, Eileen, Nancy Paulsen Books, c/o Penguin Random House LLC, 1745 Broadway, New York, NY 10019 *Tel:* 212-782-9000 *Web Site:* www.penguin.com/nancy-paulsen-books-overview/, pg 152

Savage, Eileen, GP Putnam's Sons Books for Young Readers, c/o Penguin Random House LLC, 1745 Broadway, New York, NY 10019 *Tel:* 212-782-9000 *Web Site:* www.penguin.com/putnam-young-readers/, pg 167

Savanh, Victoria, John Wiley & Sons Inc, 111 River St, Hoboken, NJ 07030-5774 *Tel:* 201-748-6000 *Toll Free Tel:* 800-225-5945 (cust serv) *Fax:* 201-748-6088 *Web Site:* www.wiley.com, pg 230

Savarese, Anne, Princeton University Press, 41 William St, Princeton, NJ 08540-5237 *Tel:* 609-258-4900 *Fax:* 609-258-6305 *E-mail:* info@press.princeton.edu *Web Site:* press.princeton.edu, pg 164

Savarese, Carolyn, Calligraph LLC, 45 Main St, No 850, Brooklyn, NY 11201 *Tel:* 212-253-1074 *E-mail:* mail@calligraphlit.com; rights@calligraphlit.com; submissions@calligraphlit.com *Web Site:* www.calligraphlit.com, pg 453

Savo, Nancy Mellichamp, Lyric Poetry Prizes, PO Box 110, Jericho, VT 05465 *E-mail:* themuse@thelyricmagazine.com *Web Site:* thelyricmagazine.com, pg 627

Savoy, Gina, W W Norton & Company Inc, 500 Fifth Ave, New York, NY 10110-0017 *Tel:* 212-354-5500 *Toll Free Tel:* 800-233-4830 (orders & cust serv) *Fax:* 212-869-0856 *Toll Free Fax:* 800-458-6515 *E-mail:* orders@wwnorton.com *Web Site:* wwnorton.com, pg 143

Sawhney, Divya, Penguin Random House LLC, 1745 Broadway, New York, NY 10019 *Tel:* 212-782-9000 *Fax:* 800-726-0600 *Web Site:* www.penguinrandomhouse.com, pg 155

Sawyer, Fametta, HarperCollins Publishers LLC, 195 Broadway, New York, NY 10007 *Tel:* 212-207-7000 *Web Site:* www.harpercollins.com, pg 87

Sawyer, Isabel, Center for the Collaborative Classroom, 1001 Marina Village Pkwy, Suite 110, Alameda, CA 94501-1042 *Tel:* 510-533-0213 *Toll Free Tel:* 800-666-7270 *Fax:* 510-464-3670 *E-mail:* info@collaborativeclassroom.org; clientsupport@collaborativeclassroom.org *Web Site:* www.collaborativeclassroom.org, pg 44

Sawyer, Peter, Fifi Oscard Agency Inc, 1140 Avenue of the Americas, 9th fl, New York, NY 10036 *Tel:* 212-764-1100 *E-mail:* agency@fifioscard.com *Web Site:* fifioscard.com, pg 471

Saxe, Dr Karen, American Mathematical Society (AMS), 201 Charles St, Providence, RI 02904-2213 *Tel:* 401-455-4000 *Toll Free Tel:* 800-321-4267 *Fax:* 401-331-3842; 401-455-4046 (cust serv) *E-mail:* ams@ams.org; cust-serv@ams.org *Web Site:* www.ams.org, pg 11

Saxton, Heidi Hess, Ave Maria Press Inc, PO Box 428, Notre Dame, IN 46556 *Toll Free Tel:* 800-282-1865 *Toll Free Fax:* 800-282-5681 *E-mail:* avemariapress.1@nd.edu *Web Site:* www.avemariapress.com, pg 22

Sayers, Frances, Macmillan, 120 Broadway, 22nd fl, New York, NY 10271 *E-mail:* press.inquiries@macmillan.com *Web Site:* us.macmillan.com, pg 122

Sayle, Kim, Hachette Audio, 1290 Avenue of the Americas, New York, NY 10104 *Tel:* 212-364-1100 *Web Site:* www.hachettebookgroup.com/imprint/hachette-audio/, pg 83

Saylor, David, Scholastic Trade Publishing, 557 Broadway, New York, NY 10012 *Tel:* 212-343-6100; 212-343-4685 (export sales) *Fax:* 212-343-4714 (export sales) *Web Site:* www.scholastic.com, pg 184

Scalissi, Linda, 3 Seas Literary Agency, PO Box 444, Sun Prairie, WI 53590 *Tel:* 608-834-9317 *E-mail:* threeseaslit@aol.com *Web Site:* threeseasagency.com, pg 479

Scanlon, Elizabeth, Honickman First Book Prize, 1906 Rittenhouse Sq, Philadelphia, PA 19103 *Tel:* 215-309-3722 *Web Site:* www.aprweb.org, pg 613

Scanlon, Liz Garton, Vermont College of Fine Arts MFA in Writing for Children & Young Adults Program, 36 College St, Montpelier, VT 05602 *Toll Free Tel:* 866-934-VCFA (934-8232) *Web Site:* vcfa.edu/mfa-writing-for-children-and-young-adults, pg 567

Scarbrough, Hillary, Macmillan, 120 Broadway, 22nd fl, New York, NY 10271 *E-mail:* press.inquiries@macmillan.com *Web Site:* us.macmillan.com, pg 122

Scarpulla, Zina, Bloom's Literary Criticism, 132 W 31 St, 16th fl, New York, NY 10001 *Toll Free Tel:* 800-322-8755 *Toll Free Fax:* 800-678-3633 *E-mail:* custserv@infobase.com *Web Site:* www.infobasepublishing.com; www.infobase.com (online resources), pg 31

Scarpulla, Zina, Chelsea House, 132 W 31 St, 16th fl, New York, NY 10001 *Toll Free Tel:* 800-322-8755 *Toll Free Fax:* 800-678-3633 *E-mail:* custserv@infobase.com; info@infobase.com *Web Site:* www.infobasepublishing.com; www.infobase.com (online resources), pg 46

Scarpulla, Zina, Facts On File, 1000 N West St, Suite 1281-230, Wilmington, DE 19801 *Tel:* 212-967-8800 *Toll Free Tel:* 800-322-8755 *Toll Free Fax:* 800-678-3633 *E-mail:* custserv@factsonfile.com *Web Site:* infobasepublishing.com, pg 69

Scarpulla, Zina, Ferguson Publishing, 132 W 31 St, 16 fl, New York, NY 10001 *Tel:* 212-967-8800 *Toll Free Tel:* 800-322-8755 *Toll Free Fax:* 800-678-3633 *E-mail:* custserv@infobase.com *Web Site:* infobasepublishing.com, pg 71

Schaefer, Elizabeth, Random House Publishing Group, 1745 Broadway, New York, NY 10019 *Toll Free Tel:* 800-200-3552 *Web Site:* www.randomhousebooks.com, pg 171

Schaefer, Mark, Linguistic Society of America (LSA), 522 21 St NW, Suite 120, Washington, DC 20006-5012 *Tel:* 202-835-1714 *Fax:* 202-835-1717 *E-mail:* lsa@lsadc.org; membership@lsadc.org *Web Site:* www.linguisticsociety.org, pg 509

Schaefer, Peggy, Hachette Nashville, 6100 Tower Circle, Room 210, Franklin, TN 37067 *Tel:* 615-221-0996 *Fax:* 615-221-0962 *Web Site:* www.hachettebookgroup.com/imprint/hachette-nashville/, pg 83

Schaeffer, Nicole, Farrar, Straus & Giroux Books for Young Readers, 120 Broadway, New York, NY 10271 *Tel:* 212-741-6900 *Toll Free Tel:* 888-330-8477 (orders) *E-mail:* childrens.publicity@macmillanusa.com; childrensrights@macmillanusa.com *Web Site:* us.macmillan.com/mackids, pg 70

Schaeffer, Nicole, Roaring Brook Press, 120 Broadway, New York, NY 10271 *Tel:* 646-307-5151 *Web Site:* us.macmillan.com/publishers/roaring-brook-press, pg 176

Schaffner, Tim, Nicholas Schaffner Award for Music in Literature, PO Box 41567, Tucson, AZ 85717 *Web Site:* www.schaffnerawards.com, pg 660

Schaffner, Tim, Schaffner Press, PO Box 41567, Tucson, AZ 85717 *Web Site:* www.schaffnerpress.com, pg 183

Schair, Julie, American Jewish Committee (AJC), Mail Code 6760, PO Box 7247, Philadelphia, PA 19170-0001 *Tel:* 212-751-4000 *Fax:* 212-891-1450 *E-mail:* social@ajc.org *Web Site:* www.ajc.org, pg 495

Schambach, Tristin, Classical Academic Press, 515 S 32 St, Camp Hill, PA 17011 *Tel:* 717-730-0711 *Toll Free Tel:* 866-730-0711 *Fax:* 717-730-0721 *Toll Free Fax:* 866-730-0721 *E-mail:* info@classicalsubjects.com; orders@classicalsubjects.com *Web Site:* classicalacademicpress.com, pg 49

Schantz, Jennifer, The Carle Honors, 125 W Bay Rd, Amherst, MA 01002 *Tel:* 413-559-6300 *E-mail:* info@carlemuseum.org *Web Site:* www.carlemuseum.org/content/carle-honors, pg 586

Schaper, Jennifer, Duke University Press, 905 W Main St, Suite 18B, Durham, NC 27701 *Tel:* 919-688-5134 *Toll Free Tel:* 888-651-0122 (US) *Fax:* 919-688-2615 *Toll Free Fax:* 888-651-0124 *E-mail:* orders@dukeupress.edu *Web Site:* www.dukeupress.edu, pg 62

Schaps, Eric, Center for the Collaborative Classroom, 1001 Marina Village Pkwy, Suite 110, Alameda, CA 94501-1042 *Tel:* 510-533-0213 *Toll Free Tel:* 800-666-7270 *Fax:* 510-464-3670 *E-mail:* info@collaborativeclassroom.org; clientsupport@collaborativeclassroom.org *Web Site:* www.collaborativeclassroom.org, pg 44

Scharfenberg, Brianna, Picador, 120 Broadway, New York, NY 10271 *Tel:* 646-307-5151 *Fax:* 212-253-9627 *E-mail:* publicity@picadorusa.com *Web Site:* us.macmillan.com/picador, pg 160

Scharfenberg, Brianna, Simon & Schuster, 1230 Avenue of the Americas, New York, NY 10020 *Tel:* 212-698-7000 *Toll Free Tel:* 800-223-2348 (cust serv); 800-223-2336 (orders) *Toll Free Fax:* 800-943-9831 (orders) *Web Site:* simonandschusterpublishing.com/simonandschuster/, pg 188

Scharfstein, Bernie, KTAV Publishing House Inc, 527 Empire Blvd, Brooklyn, NY 11225 *Tel:* 201-963-9524; 718-972-5449 *Fax:* 718-972-6307 *E-mail:* orders@ktav.com *Web Site:* www.ktav.com, pg 111

Scharp, Brian, Thomas Nelson, 501 Nelson Place, Nashville, TN 37214 *Tel:* 615-889-9000 *Toll Free Tel:* 800-251-4000 *Web Site:* www.thomasnelson.com, pg 206

Schear, Adam, DeFiore and Company Literary Management Inc, 47 E 19 St, 3rd fl, New York, NY 10003 *Tel:* 212-925-7744 *Fax:* 212-925-9803 *E-mail:* info@defliterary.com; submissions@defliterary.com *Web Site:* www.defliterary.com, pg 455

Schechner, Jacklyn Wertman, Workman Publishing, 1290 Avenue of the Americas, New York, NY 10104 *Toll Free Tel:* 800-759-0190 *Fax:* 212-364-0950 *E-mail:* workman-inquiry@hbgusa.com *Web Site:* www.hachettebookgroup.com/imprint/workman-publishing-company/, pg 233

Schechter, Pamela, The Experiment, 220 E 23 St, Suite 600, New York, NY 10010-4658 *Tel:* 212-889-1659 *E-mail:* info@theexperimentpublishing.com *Web Site:* www.theexperimentpublishing.com, pg 68

Scheel, Joanne, CWA/SCA Canada, 2200 Prince of Wales Dr, Suite 301, Ottawa, ON K2E 6Z9, Canada *Tel:* 613-820-9777 *Toll Free Tel:* 877-486-4292 *Fax:* 613-820-8188 *E-mail:* info@cwacanada.ca *Web Site:* www.cwacanada.ca, pg 504

Scheffers, Todd, Goodheart-Willcox Publisher, 18604 W Creek Dr, Tinley Park, IL 60477-6243 *Tel:* 708-687-5000 *Toll Free Tel:* 800-323-0440 *Toll Free Fax:* 888-409-3900 *E-mail:* custserv@g-w.com; orders@g-w.com *Web Site:* www.g-w.com, pg 79

Scheibling, Kathleen, Harlequin Enterprises Ltd, Bay Adelaide Centre, East Tower, 22 Adelaide St W, 41st fl, Toronto, ON M5H 4E3, Canada *Tel:* 416-445-5860 *Toll Free Tel:* 888-432-4879; 800-370-5838 (ebook inquiries) *E-mail:* customerservice@harlequin.com *Web Site:* www.harlequin.com, pg 409

Scheina, Chris, St Martin's Press, LLC, 120 Broadway, New York, NY 10271 *E-mail:* publicity@stmartins.com; trademarketing@stmartins.com; foreignrights@stmartins.com *Web Site:* us.macmillan.com/smp, pg 181

Scheiner, C J, C J Scheiner Books, 275 Linden Blvd, Unit B2, Brooklyn, NY 11226 *Tel:* 718-469-1089, pg 444

Schell, Kate, Planners Press, 205 N Michigan Ave, Suite 1200, Chicago, IL 60601 *Tel:* 312-431-9100 *Fax:* 312-786-6700 *E-mail:* customerservice@planning.org *Web Site:* www.planning.org, pg 160

Schell, Lucina, University of Chicago Press, 1427 E 60 St, Chicago, IL 60637-2954 *Tel:* 773-702-7700; 773-702-7600 *Toll Free Tel:* 800-621-2736 (orders) *Fax:* 773-702-9756; 773-660-2235 (orders); 773-702-2708 *E-mail:* custserv@press.uchicago.edu; marketing@press.uchicago.edu *Web Site:* www.press.uchicago.edu, pg 215

Schell, Trecia, Atlantic Provinces Library Association (APLA), Dalhouse University, Kenneth C Rowe Management Bldg, 6100 University Ave, Suite 4010, Halifax, NS B3H 4R2, Canada *Web Site:* www.apla.ca, pg 500

Schelper, Bess, Random House Children's Books, c/o Penguin Random House LLC, 1745 Broadway, New York, NY 10019 *Tel:* 212-782-9000 *Web Site:* www.rhcbooks.com, pg 170

Schenker, Elina, Chronicle Books LLC, 680 Second St, San Francisco, CA 94107 *Tel:* 415-537-4200 *Fax:* 415-537-4460 (perms) *E-mail:* hello@chroniclebooks.com; subrights@chroniclebooks.com *Web Site:* www.chroniclebooks.com, pg 48

Scherer, Rebecca, Jane Rotrosen Agency LLC, 318 E 51 St, New York, NY 10022-7803 *Tel:* 212-593-4330 *E-mail:* info@janerotrosen.com *Web Site:* janerotrosen.com, pg 474

Scherma, Frank, Television Academy, 5220 Lankershim Blvd, North Hollywood, CA 91601-3109 *Tel:* 818-754-2800 *Web Site:* www.emmys.com, pg 521

Scherman, Nosson, Mesorah Publications Ltd, 313 Regina Ave, Rahway, NJ 07065 *Tel:* 718-921-9000 *Toll Free Tel:* 800-637-6724 *Fax:* 718-680-1875 *E-mail:* info@artscroll.com; orders@artscroll.com *Web Site:* www.artscroll.com, pg 130

Scheyd, John, Pelican Publishing, 990 N Corporate Dr, Suite 100, New Orleans, LA 70123 *Tel:* 504-684-8976 *Toll Free Tel:* 844-868-1798 (orders) *E-mail:* editorial@pelicanpub.com (submissions) *Web Site:* www.pelicanpub.com; www.arcadiapublishing.com/imprints/pelican-publishing, pg 153

Schiff, Robbin, Random House Publishing Group, 1745 Broadway, New York, NY 10019 *Toll Free Tel:* 800-200-3552 *Web Site:* www.randomhousebooks.com, pg 171

Schiffer, Pete, Cornell Maritime Press, 4880 Lower Valley Rd, Atglen, PA 19310 *Tel:* 610-593-1777 *Fax:* 610-593-2002 *E-mail:* info@schifferbooks.com *Web Site:* www.schifferbooks.com, pg 52

Schiffer, Pete, Schiffer Publishing Ltd, 4880 Lower Valley Rd, Atglen, PA 19310 *Tel:* 610-593-1777 *Fax:* 610-593-2002 *E-mail:* info@schifferbooks.com; customercare@schifferbooks.com; sales@schifferbooks.com; marketing@schifferbooks.com *Web Site:* www.schifferbooks.com, pg 183

Schiffman, Marina, HarperCollins Publishers LLC, 195 Broadway, New York, NY 10007 *Tel:* 212-207-7000 *Web Site:* www.harpercollins.com, pg 86

Schiller, David, Workman Publishing, 1290 Avenue of the Americas, New York, NY 10104 *Toll Free Tel:* 800-759-0190 *Fax:* 212-364-0950 *E-mail:* workman-inquiry@hbgusa.com *Web Site:* www.hachettebookgroup.com/imprint/workman-publishing-company/, pg 232

Schilling, Tracy, Hospital & Healthcare Compensation Service, 3 Post Rd, Suite 3, Oakland, NJ 07436 *Tel:* 201-405-0075 *Fax:* 201-405-2110 *E-mail:* allinfo@hhcsinc.com *Web Site:* www.hhcsinc.com, pg 95

Schisgal, Zachary, John Wiley & Sons Inc, 111 River St, Hoboken, NJ 07030-5774 Tel: 201-748-6000 Toll Free Tel: 800-225-5945 (cust serv) Fax: 201-748-6088 Web Site: www.wiley.com, pg 230

Schlager, Neil, Schlager Group Inc, 10228 E Northwest Hwy, No 1151, Dallas, TX 75238 Toll Free Tel: 888-416-5727 Fax: 469-325-3700 E-mail: info@schlagergroup.com; sales@schlagergroup.com Web Site: www.schlagergroup.com, pg 183

Schlect, Walter, Gutekunst Prize, 30 Irving Place, New York, NY 10003 Tel: 212-439-8700 Fax: 212-439-8705 E-mail: gutekunst@goethe.de Web Site: www.goethe.de/ins/us/enkul/ser/uef/gut.html, pg 610

Schlect, Walter, Helen & Kurt Wolff Translator's Prize, 30 Irving Place, New York, NY 10003 Tel: 212-439-8700 Fax: 212-439-8705 E-mail: info-newyork@goethe.de Web Site: www.goethe.de/ins/us/enkul/ser/uef/hkw.html, pg 677

Schlegel, Stephen, Johns Hopkins University Press, 2715 N Charles St, Baltimore, MD 21218-4363 Tel: 410-516-6900; 410-516-6987 Toll Free Tel: 800-537-5487 (book orders & cust serv); 800-548-1784 (journal orders) Fax: 410-516-6968; 410-516-6998 (orders) E-mail: hfscustserv@press.jhu.edu (cust serv); jrnlcirc@jh.edu (journal orders) Web Site: www.press.jhu.edu; muse.jhu.edu, pg 106

Schleicher, Ryan, Porchlight Book Co Business Book Awards, 544 S First St, Milwaukee, WI 53204 Toll Free Tel: 800-236-7323 E-mail: info@porchlightbooks.com Web Site: porchlightbooks.com, pg 651

Schlesinger, David, Agate Publishing Academy, 1328 Greenleaf St, Evanston, IL 60202 Tel: 847-475-4457 E-mail: help@agatepublishingacademy.com Web Site: agatepublishingacademy.com, pg 561

Schlesinger, Ed, Gallery Books, 1230 Avenue of the Americas, New York, NY 10020 Toll Free Tel: 800-456-6798 Fax: 212-698-7284 E-mail: consumer.customerservice@simonandschuster.com Web Site: www.simonandschuster.com, pg 76

Schlesinger, Jeff, Barringer Publishing, 16398 Barclay Ct, Naples, FL 34110 Tel: 239-920-1668 E-mail: schlesadv@gmail.com Web Site: www.barringerpublishing.com, pg 24

Schlesinger, Laurie, Princeton University Press, 41 William St, Princeton, NJ 08540-5237 Tel: 609-258-4900 Fax: 609-258-6305 E-mail: info@press.princeton.edu Web Site: press.princeton.edu, pg 164

Schleuss, Jon, The NewsGuild - CWA, 501 Third St NW, 6th fl, Washington, DC 20001-2797 Tel: 202-434-7177 Fax: 202-434-1472 E-mail: guild@cwa-union.org Web Site: www.newsguild.org, pg 515

Schlich, Eric, The Pinch Writing Awards in Fiction, University of Memphis, English Dept, 431 Patterson Hall, Memphis, TN 38152 Tel: 901-678-2651 Fax: 901-678-2226 E-mail: editor@pinchjournal.com Web Site: www.pinchjournal.com, pg 649

Schlich, Eric, The Pinch Writing Awards in Poetry, University of Memphis, English Dept, 431 Patterson Hall, Memphis, TN 38152 Tel: 901-678-2651 Fax: 901-678-2226 E-mail: editor@pinchjournal.com Web Site: www.pinchjournal.com, pg 649

Schlichenmayer, Ed, National Association of College Stores (NACS), 528 E Lorain St, Oberlin, OH 44074 Toll Free Tel: 800-622-7498 Fax: 440-775-4769 E-mail: info@nacs.org Web Site: www.nacs.org, pg 511

Schlick, Sarah, Gallery Books, 1230 Avenue of the Americas, New York, NY 10020 Toll Free Tel: 800-456-6798 Fax: 212-698-7284 E-mail: consumer.customerservice@simonandschuster.com Web Site: www.simonandschuster.com, pg 76

Schliesman, Megan, Charlotte Zolotow Award, 225 N Mills St, Rm 401, Madison, WI 53706 Tel: 608-263-3720 E-mail: ccbcinfo@education.wisc.edu Web Site: ccbs.education.wisc.edu/books/zolotow.asp, pg 680

Schline, John, Writers House, 21 W 26 St, New York, NY 10010 Tel: 212-685-2400 Web Site: www.writershouse.com, pg 482

Schloss, Katie, DK, c/o Penguin Random House LLC, 1745 Broadway, 20th fl, New York, NY 10019 Tel: 646-674-4000 Toll Free Tel: 800-733-3000 Fax: 646-674-4020 E-mail: marketing@dk.com (lib servs); publicity@dk.com; csorders@penguinrandomhouse.com; customerservice@penguinrandomhouse.com Web Site: www.dk.com, pg 60

Schlussel, Farin, Avery, c/o Penguin Random House LLC, 1745 Broadway, New York, NY 10019 Tel: 212-366-2000 Web Site: www.penguin.com/avery-overview/, pg 23

Schlussel, Farin, TarcherPerigee, c/o Penguin Random House LLC, 1745 Broadway, New York, NY 10019 Tel: 212-782-9000 Web Site: www.penguin.com/tarcherperigee-overview/; www.facebook.com/TarcherPerigee, pg 202

Schmelzle, Alexandra, New England Book Awards, One Beacon St, 15th fl, Boston, MA 02108 Tel: 617-547-3642 Web Site: www.newenglandbooks.org/page/book-awards, pg 640

Schmelzle, Alexandra, New England Independent Booksellers Association Inc (NEIBA), One Beacon St, 15th fl, Boston, MA 02108 Tel: 617-547-3642 Web Site: www.newenglandbooks.org, pg 514

Schmid, Gretchen, HarperCollins Publishers LLC, 195 Broadway, New York, NY 10007 Tel: 212-207-7000 Web Site: www.harpercollins.com, pg 87

Schmidt, Alfred, Windsor Books, 260 W Main St, Suite 5, Bayshore, NY 11706 Tel: 631-665-6688 Toll Free Tel: 800-321-5934 E-mail: windsor.books@att.net Web Site: www.windsorpublishing.com, pg 230

Schmidt, Diana, Sourcebooks LLC, 1935 Brookdale Rd, Suite 139, Naperville, IL 60563 Tel: 630-961-3900 Toll Free Tel: 800-432-7444 Fax: 630-961-2168 E-mail: info@sourcebooks.com Web Site: www.sourcebooks.com, pg 195

Schmidt, Eric A, Basic Books Group, 1290 Avenue of the Americas, New York, NY 10104 Tel: 212-340-8100 Toll Free Tel: 800-343-4499 (cust serv) Fax: 212-340-8105 E-mail: customer.service@hbusa.com; orders@hbusa.com Web Site: www.hachettebookgroup.com/imprint/basic-books/, pg 25

Schmidt, Harold D, Harold Schmidt Literary Agency, 415 W 23 St, Suite 6-F, New York, NY 10011 Tel: 212-727-7473, pg 475

Schmidt, Helga, Steerforth Press & Services, 31 Hanover St, Suite 1, Lebanon, NH 03766 Tel: 603-643-4787 Fax: 603-643-4788 E-mail: info@steerforth.com Web Site: www.steerforth.com, pg 198

Schmidt, Jeff, Windsor Books, 260 W Main St, Suite 5, Bayshore, NY 11706 Tel: 631-665-6688 Toll Free Tel: 800-321-5934 E-mail: windsor.books@att.net Web Site: www.windsorpublishing.com, pg 230

Schmidt, Jenny Newton, Green Earth Book Award, 3100 Clarendon Blvd, Suite 400, Arlington, VA 22201 E-mail: info@natgen.org Web Site: www.natgen.org/green-earth-book-awards, pg 609

Schmidt, Jocelyn, Penguin Young Readers Group, c/o Penguin Random House LLC, 1745 Broadway, New York, NY 10019 Tel: 212-782-9000 Web Site: www.penguin.com/penguin-young-readers-overview, pg 156

Schmidt, Linda, Penguin Random House Audio Publishing Group, 1745 Broadway, New York, NY 10019 Toll Free Tel: 800-793-2665 (cust serv) E-mail: audio@penguinrandomhouse.com; ecustomerservice@penguinrandomhouse.com Web Site: www.penguinrandomhouseaudio.com, pg 154

Schmidt, Melissa, American Anthropological Association (AAA), 2300 Clarendon Blvd, Suite 1301, Arlington, VA 22201 E-mail: pubs@americananthro.org Web Site: www.americananthro.org, pg 8

Schmidt, Randy, University of British Columbia Press, 2029 West Mall, Vancouver, BC V6T 1Z2, Canada Tel: 604-822-5959 Toll Free Tel: 877-377-9378 Fax: 604-822-6083 Toll Free Fax: 800-668-0821 E-mail: frontdesk@ubcpress.ca Web Site: www.ubcpress.ca, pg 422

Schmidt, Rebecca, Macmillan, 120 Broadway, 22nd fl, New York, NY 10271 E-mail: press.inquiries@macmillan.com Web Site: us.macmillan.com, pg 122

Schmidt, Sophie, HarperCollins Children's Books, 195 Broadway, New York, NY 10007 Tel: 212-207-7000 Web Site: www.harpercollins.com/childrens, pg 85

Schmieder, Eric, William Holmes McGuffey Longevity Award, PO Box 367, Fountain City, WI 54629 E-mail: info@taaonline.net Web Site: www.taaonline.net/mcguffey-longevity-award, pg 630

Schmieder, Eric, Most Promising New Textbook Award, PO Box 367, Fountain City, WI 54629 E-mail: info@taaonline.net Web Site: www.taaonline.net/promising-new-textbook-award, pg 636

Schmieder, Eric, Pynn-Silverman Lifetime Achievement Award, PO Box 367, Fountain City, WI 54629 E-mail: info@taaonline.net Web Site: www.taaonline.net/council-awards#pynn, pg 654

Schmieder, Eric, TAA Council of Fellows, PO Box 367, Fountain City, WI 54629 E-mail: info@taaonline.net Web Site: www.taaonline.net/council-of-fellows, pg 668

Schmieder, Eric, Textbook Excellence Award, PO Box 367, Fountain City, WI 54629 E-mail: info@taaonline.net Web Site: www.taaonline.net/textbook-excellence-award, pg 669

Schmierer-Lee, Melonie PhD, Gorgias Press LLC, PO Box 6939, Piscataway, NJ 08854-6939 Tel: 732-885-8900 Fax: 732-885-8908 E-mail: helpdesk@gorgiaspress.com Web Site: www.gorgiaspress.com, pg 80

Schmitt, Dave, Sourcebooks LLC, 1935 Brookdale Rd, Suite 139, Naperville, IL 60563 Tel: 630-961-3900 Toll Free Tel: 800-432-7444 Fax: 630-961-2168 E-mail: info@sourcebooks.com Web Site: www.sourcebooks.com, pg 195

Schmitz, Elisabeth, Grove Atlantic Inc, 154 W 14 St, 12th fl, New York, NY 10011 Tel: 212-614-7850 Toll Free Tel: 800-521-0178 Fax: 212-614-7886 E-mail: info@groveatlantic.com; sales@groveatlantic.com; publicity@groveatlantic.com; rights@groveatlantic.com Web Site: www.groveatlantic.com, pg 82

Schmitz, Erin, Midwest Travel Journalists Association Inc (MTJA), PO Box 185, Jessup, IA 50648 Tel: 319-529-1109 E-mail: admin@mtja.us Web Site: www.mtja.us, pg 511

Schmitz, Kate Breiting, Chronicle Books LLC, 680 Second St, San Francisco, CA 94107 Tel: 415-537-4200 Fax: 415-537-4460 (perms) E-mail: hello@chroniclebooks.com; subrights@chroniclebooks.com Web Site: www.chroniclebooks.com, pg 47

Schnaufer, Wendi, University of Alabama Press, 200 Hackberry Lane, 2nd fl, Tuscaloosa, AL 35487 Tel: 205-348-5180 Fax: 205-348-9201 Web Site: www.uapress.ua.edu, pg 214

Schneider, Bill, Etruscan Press, Wilkes University, 84 W South St, Wilkes-Barre, PA 18766 Tel: 570-408-4546 Fax: 570-408-3333 E-mail: books@etruscanpress.org Web Site: www.etruscanpress.org, pg 67

Schneider, Carol, Workman Publishing, 1290 Avenue of the Americas, New York, NY 10104 Toll Free Tel: 800-759-0190 Fax: 212-364-0950 E-mail: workman-inquiry@hbusa.com Web Site: www.hachettebookgroup.com/imprint/workman-publishing-company/, pg 232

Schneider, Christian, Cato Institute, 1000 Massachusetts Ave NW, Washington, DC 20001-5403 Tel: 202-842-0200 Web Site: www.cato.org, pg 42

Schneider, Dan, BPA Worldwide, 100 Beard Sawmill Rd, 6th fl, Shelton, CT 06484 Tel: 203-447-2800 Fax: 203-447-2900 E-mail: info@bpaww.com Web Site: www.bpaww.com, pg 501

Schneider, Deborah, Gelfman Schneider Literary Agents Inc, 850 Seventh Ave, Suite 903, New York, NY 10019 *Tel:* 212-245-1993 *E-mail:* mail@gelfmanschneider.com *Web Site:* gelfmanschneider.com, pg 460

Schneider, James, Princeton University Press, 41 William St, Princeton, NJ 08540-5237 *Tel:* 609-258-4900 *Fax:* 609-258-6305 *E-mail:* info@press.princeton.edu *Web Site:* press.princeton.edu, pg 164

Schneider, Jennifer, National Institute for Trial Advocacy (NITA), 1685 38 St, Suite 200, Boulder, CO 80301-2735 *Tel:* 720-890-4860 *Toll Free Tel:* 877-648-2632; 800-225-6482 (orders & returns) *Fax:* 720-890-7069 *E-mail:* customerservice@nita.org; sales@nita.org *Web Site:* www.nita.org, pg 138

Schneider, Kathy, Jane Rotrosen Agency LLC, 318 E 51 St, New York, NY 10022-7803 *Tel:* 212-593-4330 *E-mail:* info@janerotrosen.com *Web Site:* janerotrosen.com, pg 474

Schneider, Martin, Center for Creative Leadership LLC, One Leadership Place, Greensboro, NC 27410-9427 *Tel:* 336-545-2810; 336-288-7210 *Fax:* 336-282-3284 *E-mail:* info@ccl.org *Web Site:* shop.ccl.org/usa/books, pg 43

Schneider, Melissa, Turner Publishing Co LLC, 4507 Charlotte Ave, Suite 100, Nashville, TN 37209 *Tel:* 615-255-BOOK (255-2665) *Fax:* 615-255-5081 *E-mail:* info@turnerpublishing.com; marketing@turnerpublishing.com; submissions@turnerpublishing.com; editorial@turnerpublishing.com; admin@turnerpublishing.com; orders@turnerpublishing.com *Web Site:* turnerpublishing.com; www.facebook.com/turner.publishing, pg 210

Schneider, Naomi, University of California Press, 155 Grand Ave, Suite 400, Oakland, CA 94612-3758 *Tel:* 510-883-8232 *Fax:* 510-836-8910 *E-mail:* customerservice@ucpress.edu *Web Site:* www.ucpress.edu, pg 215

Schneider, Sam, Encounter Books, 900 Broadway, Suite 601, New York, NY 10003 *Tel:* 212-871-6310 *Toll Free Tel:* 855-203-7220 *E-mail:* publicity@encounterbooks.com *Web Site:* www.encounterbooks.com, pg 66

Schneider, Sara, Chronicle Books LLC, 680 Second St, San Francisco, CA 94107 *Tel:* 415-537-4200 *Fax:* 415-537-4460 (perms) *E-mail:* hello@chroniclebooks.com; subrights@chroniclebooks.com *Web Site:* www.chroniclebooks.com, pg 47

Schneider, Wendy Caruso, New York Academy of Sciences (NYAS), 7 World Trade Center, 40th fl, 250 Greenwich St, New York, NY 10007-2157 *Tel:* 212-298-8600 *Toll Free Tel:* 800-843-6927 *Fax:* 212-298-3650 *E-mail:* nyas@nyas.org; annals@nyas.org; customerservice@nyas.org *Web Site:* www.nyas.org, pg 140

Schnell, Judith, Astragal Press, 31 E Main St, New Kingstown, PA 17072 *Tel:* 717-590-8974 *Web Site:* astragalpress.com, pg 20

Schnell, Judith, Stackpole Books, 31 E Main St, New Kingstown, PA 17072 *Tel:* 717-590-8974 *Web Site:* www.stackpolebooks.com, pg 197

Schnitzer, Adam, Stanford University Press, 425 Broadway St, Redwood City, CA 94063-3126 *Tel:* 650-723-9434 *Fax:* 650-725-3457 *E-mail:* info@www.sup.org; publicity@www.sup.org; sales@www.sup.org *Web Site:* www.sup.org, pg 197

Schoder, Katie, Alfred A Knopf, c/o Penguin Random House LLC, 1745 Broadway, New York, NY 10019 *Tel:* 212-751-2600 *Fax:* 212-940-7390 (dom rts); 212-572-2662 (foreign rts) *Web Site:* knopfdoubleday.com/imprint/knopf/; knopfdoubleday.com, pg 110

Schoen, John, SLACK® Incorporated, A Wyanoke Group Company, 6900 Grove Rd, Thorofare, NJ 08086-9447 *Tel:* 856-848-1000 *Toll Free Tel:* 800-257-8290 *Fax:* 856-848-6091 *E-mail:* sales@slackinc.com; editor@slackinc.com; customerservice@slackinc.com *Web Site:* www.healio.com/books, pg 191

Schoenfeld, Andie, Simon & Schuster, 1230 Avenue of the Americas, New York, NY 10020 *Tel:* 212-698-7000 *Toll Free Tel:* 800-223-2348 (cust serv); 800-223-2336 (orders) *Toll Free Fax:* 800-943-9831 (orders) *Web Site:* simonandschusterpublishing.com/simonandschuster/, pg 188

Schoenfeld, Deena, The Jewish Publication Society, c/o Gratz College, 7605 Old York Rd, Melrose Park, PA 19027 *Tel:* 215-832-0600 *Web Site:* www.jps.org; www.nebraskapress.unl.edu/jps/, pg 105

Schoenwald, Mark, Thomas Nelson, 501 Nelson Place, Nashville, TN 37214 *Tel:* 615-889-9000 *Toll Free Tel:* 800-251-4000 *Web Site:* www.thomasnelson.com, pg 206

Schoenwald, Mark, Tommy Nelson®, 501 Nelson Place, Nashville, TN 37214 *Tel:* 615-889-9000; 615-902-1485 (cust serv) *Toll Free Tel:* 800-251-4000 *Web Site:* www.tommynelson.com, pg 207

Schonfeld, Sara, HarperCollins Children's Books, 195 Broadway, New York, NY 10007 *Tel:* 212-207-7000 *Web Site:* www.harpercollins.com/childrens, pg 85

Schoof, Sarah, HarperCollins Publishers LLC, 195 Broadway, New York, NY 10007 *Tel:* 212-207-7000 *Web Site:* www.harpercollins.com, pg 87

Schoonmaker, Amanda, Macmillan, 120 Broadway, 22nd fl, New York, NY 10271 *E-mail:* press.inquiries@macmillan.com *Web Site:* us.macmillan.com, pg 122

Schor, Lynda, Hamilton Stone Editions, PO Box 43, Maplewood, NJ 07040 *Tel:* 973-378-8361 *E-mail:* hstone@hamiltonstone.org *Web Site:* www.hamiltonstone.org, pg 84

Schorr, Sari, Levy Creative Management LLC, 425 E 58 St, Suite 37F, New York, NY 10022 *Tel:* 212-687-6463 *E-mail:* info@levycreative.com *Web Site:* www.levycreative.com, pg 485

Schotanus, Kiki, Albert Whitman & Company, 250 S Northwest Hwy, Suite 320, Park Ridge, IL 60068 *Tel:* 847-232-2800 *Toll Free Tel:* 800-255-7675 (orders) *Fax:* 847-581-0039 *E-mail:* mail@albertwhitman.com; orders@albertwhitman.com *Web Site:* www.albertwhitman.com, pg 6

Schrager, Marla, Society of American Travel Writers (SATW), 355 Lexington Ave, 15th fl, New York, NY 10017 *E-mail:* info@satw.org *Web Site:* www.satw.org, pg 519

Schrank, Ben, Astra Books for Young Readers, 19 W 21 St, No 1201, New York, NY 10010 *Tel:* 646-844-3485 *E-mail:* ahinfo@astrahouse.com; permissions@astrapublishinghouse.com *Web Site:* astrapublishinghouse.com, pg 20

Schreiber, Laura, HarperCollins Publishers LLC, 195 Broadway, New York, NY 10007 *Tel:* 212-207-7000 *Web Site:* www.harpercollins.com, pg 86

Schreier, Carl, Homestead Publishing, Box 193, Moose, WY 83012-0193 *Tel:* 307-733-6248 *Fax:* 307-733-6248 *E-mail:* info@homesteadpublishing.com; orders@homesteadpublishing.net *Web Site:* www.homesteadpublishing.net, pg 95

Schricker, Judy, Walter Dean Myers Grants, 10319 Westlake Dr, No 104, Bethesda, MD 20817 *Tel:* 701-404-WNDB (404-9632, voicemail only) *E-mail:* waltergrant@diversebooks.org *Web Site:* diversebooks.org, pg 636

Schroeder, Ben, Centering Corp, 6406 Maple St, Omaha, NE 68104 *Tel:* 402-553-1200 *Toll Free Tel:* 866-218-0101 *Fax:* 402-553-0507 *E-mail:* orders@centeringcorp.com *Web Site:* www.centering.org, pg 44

Schroeder, Bill III, American Quilter's Society (AQS), 5801 Kentucky Dam Rd, Paducah, KY 42003-9323 *Tel:* 270-898-7903 *Toll Free Tel:* 800-626-5420 (orders) *Fax:* 270-898-8890 *E-mail:* orders@americanquilter.com; info@aqsquilt.com *Web Site:* www.americanquilter.com, pg 12

Schroeder, Laura, PEN America Washington, DC, 1100 13 St NW, Suite 800, Washington, DC 20005 *E-mail:* info@pen.org *Web Site:* pen.org/region/washington-dc, pg 516

Schroeder, Sandi, Schroeder Indexing Services, 23 Camilla Pink Ct, Bluffton, SC 29909 *Tel:* 843-415-3900 *E-mail:* sanindex@schroederindexing.com *Web Site:* www.schroederindexing.com, pg 444

Schroedl, Jeff, Hal Leonard LLC, 7777 W Bluemound Rd, Milwaukee, WI 53213 *Tel:* 414-774-3630 *E-mail:* info@halleonard.com; sales@halleonard.com *Web Site:* www.halleonard.com, pg 84

Schubert, Lori, Quebec Writers' Federation (QWF), 1200 Atwater Ave, Suite 3, Westmount, QC H3Z 1X4, Canada *Tel:* 514-933-0878 *E-mail:* info@qwf.org *Web Site:* www.qwf.org; www.hireawriter.ca; quebecbooks.qwf.org, pg 518

Schubert, Lori, QWF Literary Awards, 1200 Atwater Ave, Suite 3, Westmount, QC H3Z 1X4, Canada *Tel:* 514-933-0878 *E-mail:* info@qwf.org *Web Site:* quebecbooks.qwf.org/awards; www.qwf.org; qwf.org/awards/awards-overview/, pg 654

Schubert, Michael, Northern California Translators Association, 2261 Market St, Suite 160, San Francisco, CA 94114-1600 *Tel:* 510-845-8712 *E-mail:* ncta@ncta.org *Web Site:* ncta.org, pg 515

Schulman, Susan, Susan Schulman Literary Agency LLC, 454 W 44 St, New York, NY 10036 *Tel:* 212-713-1633; 917-488-0906 (direct line) *E-mail:* queries@schulmanagency.com *Web Site:* www.schulmanagency.com, pg 475

Schulmonds, Natalie, The New Press, 120 Wall St, 31st fl, New York, NY 10005 *Tel:* 212-629-8802 *Fax:* 212-629-8617 *E-mail:* newpress@thenewpress.com *Web Site:* thenewpress.com, pg 140

Schultz, Amy, Northwestern University Press, 629 Noyes St, Evanston, IL 60208-4210 *Tel:* 847-491-2046 *Toll Free Tel:* 800-621-2736 (orders only) *Fax:* 847-491-8150 *E-mail:* nupress@northwestern.edu *Web Site:* www.nupress.northwestern.edu, pg 143

Schultz, Amy, Stanford University Press, 425 Broadway St, Redwood City, CA 94063-3126 *Tel:* 650-723-9434 *Fax:* 650-725-3457 *E-mail:* info@www.sup.org; publicity@www.sup.org; sales@www.sup.org *Web Site:* www.sup.org, pg 197

Schultz, Jonathan D, Concordia Publishing House, 3558 S Jefferson Ave, St Louis, MO 63118-3968 *Tel:* 314-268-1000; 314-268-1268 (bookshop) *Toll Free Tel:* 800-325-3040 (cust serv) *Toll Free Fax:* 800-490-9889 (cust serv) *E-mail:* order@cph.org *Web Site:* www.cph.org, pg 51

Schultz, Julie, High Plains Book Awards, c/o Billings Public Library, 510 N 28 St, Billings, MT 59101 *Tel:* 406-672-6223 *E-mail:* highplainsbookawards@gmail.com *Web Site:* highplainsbookawards.org, pg 612

Schultz, Thom, Group Publishing Inc, 1515 Cascade Ave, Loveland, CO 80538 *Tel:* 970-669-3836 *Toll Free Tel:* 800-447-1070 *E-mail:* puorgbus@group.com (submissions) *Web Site:* www.group.com, pg 82

Schultz, Tiffany, Sourcebooks LLC, 1935 Brookdale Rd, Suite 139, Naperville, IL 60563 *Tel:* 630-961-3900 *Toll Free Tel:* 800-432-7444 *Fax:* 630-961-2168 *E-mail:* info@sourcebooks.com *Web Site:* www.sourcebooks.com, pg 194

Schulz, Andrea, Viking Penguin, c/o Penguin Random House LLC, 1745 Broadway, New York, NY 10019 *Tel:* 212-782-9000 *Web Site:* www.penguin.com/overview-vikingbooks/; www.penguin.com/pameladorman-books-overview/; www.penguin.com/penguin-classics-overview/; www.penguin.com/penguin-life-overview/, pg 225

Schulz, Claire, BenBella Books Inc, 10440 N Central Expwy, Suite 800, Dallas, TX 75231-2264 *Tel:* 214-750-3600 *Web Site:* www.benbellabooks.com; www.smartpopbooks.com, pg 27

Schulze, Jared, PPI, A Kaplan Company, 332 Front St, Suite 501, La Crosse, WI 54601 *Tel:* 650-593-9119 *Fax:* 650-592-4519 *E-mail:* info@ppi2pass.com *Web Site:* ppi2pass.com, pg 163

Schulze, Karin, Curtis Brown, Ltd, 228 E 45 St, Suite 310, New York, NY 10017 *Tel:* 212-473-5400 *Fax:* 212-598-0917 *E-mail:* info@cbltd.com *Web Site:* www.curtisbrown.com, pg 452

Schumacher, Peter, Shambhala Publications Inc, 2129 13 St, Boulder, CO 80302 *Tel:* 978-829-2599 (intl callers) *Toll Free Tel:* 866-424-0030 (off); 888-424-2329 (orders & cust serv) *Fax:* 617-236-1563 *E-mail:* customercare@shambhala.com; royalties@shambhala.com *Web Site:* www.shambhala.com, pg 187

Schumaker, Scott, City & Regional Magazine Association (CRMA), 287 Richards Ave, Norwalk, CT 06850 *Tel:* 203-515-9294 *Web Site:* citymag.org, pg 504

Schumann, Katrin, Key West Literary Seminar, 717 Love Lane, Key West, FL 33040 *Tel:* 305-293-9291 *E-mail:* mail@kwls.org *Web Site:* www.kwls.org/seminar, pg 555

Schumann, Katrin, Key West Literary Seminar's Writers' Workshop Program, 717 Love Lane, Key West, FL 33040 *Tel:* 305-293-9291 *E-mail:* mail@kwls.org *Web Site:* www.kwls.org, pg 555

Schurer, Kelsey, Round Table Companies, PO Box 1603, Deerfield, IL 60015 *Toll Free Tel:* 833-750-5683 *Web Site:* www.roundtablecompanies.com, pg 177

Schurig, Tiia, AIGA, the professional association for design, 228 Park Ave S, Suite 58603, New York, NY 10003 *Tel:* 212-807-1990 *E-mail:* general@aiga.org *Web Site:* www.aiga.org, pg 493

Schuster, Allison, Random House Publishing Group, 1745 Broadway, New York, NY 10019 *Toll Free Tel:* 800-200-3552 *Web Site:* www.randomhousebooks.com, pg 171

Schuster, Darlene S PhD, American Institute of Chemical Engineers (AIChE), 120 Wall St, 23rd fl, New York, NY 10005-4020 *Tel:* 203-702-7660 *Toll Free Tel:* 800-242-4363 *E-mail:* customerservice@aiche.org *Web Site:* www.aiche.org/publications, pg 10

Schutt, David L, SAE (Society of Automotive Engineers International), 400 Commonwealth Dr, Warrendale, PA 15096-0001 *Tel:* 724-776-4841; 724-776-4970 (outside US & CN) *Toll Free Tel:* 877-606-7323 (cust serv) *Fax:* 724-776-0790 (cust serv) *E-mail:* publications@sae.org; customerservice@sae.org *Web Site:* www.sae.org, pg 179

Schutter, Johanna, Candlewick Press, 99 Dover St, Somerville, MA 02144-2825 *Tel:* 617-661-3330 *Fax:* 617-661-0565 *E-mail:* bigbear@candlewick.com; salesinfo@candlewick.com *Web Site:* candlewick.com, pg 40

Schutz, Glenn, BPA Worldwide, 100 Beard Sawmill Rd, 6th fl, Shelton, CT 06484 *Tel:* 203-447-2800 *Fax:* 203-447-2900 *E-mail:* info@bpaww.com *Web Site:* www.bpaww.com, pg 501

Schwacke, Susanna Sharp, Bottom Dog Press, 813 Seneca Ave, Huron, OH 44839 *Tel:* 419-602-1556 *Fax:* 419-616-3966 *Web Site:* smithdocs.net, pg 34

Schwaiger, Elizabeth, University of Ottawa Press (Presses de l'Université d'Ottawa), 542 King Edward Ave, Ottawa, ON K1N 6N5, Canada *Tel:* 613-562-5246 *Fax:* 613-562-5247 *E-mail:* puo-uop@uottawa.ca; acquisitions@uottawa.ca *Web Site:* press.uottawa.ca, pg 423

Schwalb, Jaime, Sounds True Inc, 413 S Arthur Ave, Louisville, CO 80027 *Tel:* 303-665-3151 *Toll Free Tel:* 800-333-9185 (US); 888-303-9185 (US & CN) *E-mail:* customerservice@soundstrue.com; stpublicity@soundstrue.com *Web Site:* www.soundstrue.com, pg 194

Schwalbe, Will, Macmillan, 120 Broadway, 22nd fl, New York, NY 10271 *E-mail:* press.inquiries@macmillan.com *Web Site:* us.macmillan.com, pg 122

Schwartz, Anne, Random House Children's Books, c/o Penguin Random House LLC, 1745 Broadway, New York, NY 10019 *Tel:* 212-782-9000 *Web Site:* www.rhcbooks.com, pg 169

Schwartz, Bernard, The Authors Guild® Foundation, 31 E 32 St, Suite 901, New York, NY 10016 *Tel:* 212-563-5904 *Fax:* 212-564-5363 *E-mail:* staff@authorsguild.org *Web Site:* authorsguild.org/foundation, pg 525

Schwartz, Dan, HarperCollins Publishers LLC, 195 Broadway, New York, NY 10007 *Tel:* 212-207-7000 *Web Site:* www.harpercollins.com, pg 86

Schwartz, Eric I, New York University Press, 838 Broadway, 3rd fl, New York, NY 10003-4812 *Tel:* 212-998-2575 (edit) *Toll Free Tel:* 800-996-6987 (orders) *Fax:* 212-995-4798 (orders) *E-mail:* nyupressinfo@nyu.edu (cust care) *Web Site:* www.nyupress.org, pg 141

Schwartz, Erika, Random House Children's Books, c/o Penguin Random House LLC, 1745 Broadway, New York, NY 10019 *Tel:* 212-782-9000 *Web Site:* www.rhcbooks.com, pg 170

Schwartz, Hannah, Stuart Krichevsky Literary Agency Inc, 118 E 28 St, Suite 908, New York, NY 10016 *Tel:* 212-725-5288 *Fax:* 212-725-5275 *E-mail:* query@skagency.com *Web Site:* skagency.com, pg 466

Schwartz, John Burnham, Penguin Press, c/o Penguin Random House LLC, 1745 Broadway, New York, NY 10019 *Tel:* 212-782-9000 *E-mail:* penguinpress@penguinrandomhouse.com *Web Site:* www.penguin.com/penguin-press-overview/, pg 154

Schwartz, John Burnham, Sun Valley Writers' Conference (SVWC), Galleria Bldg, 2nd fl, 351 Leadville Ave N, Ketchum, ID 83340 *Tel:* 208-726-5454 *E-mail:* info@svwc.com *Web Site:* svwc.com, pg 558

Schwartz, Justin, Atria Books, 1230 Avenue of the Americas, New York, NY 10020 *Tel:* 212-698-7000 *Fax:* 212-698-7007 *Web Site:* www.simonandschuster.com, pg 21

Schwartz, Leslie, Library of America, 14 E 60 St, New York, NY 10022-1006 *Tel:* 212-308-3360 *Fax:* 212-750-8352 *E-mail:* info@loa.org *Web Site:* www.loa.org, pg 116

Schwartz, Matt, Penguin Random House LLC, 1745 Broadway, New York, NY 10019 *Tel:* 212-782-9000 *Toll Free Tel:* 800-726-0600 *Web Site:* www.penguinrandomhouse.com, pg 155

Schwartz, Matt, Random House Publishing Group, 1745 Broadway, New York, NY 10019 *Toll Free Tel:* 800-200-3552 *Web Site:* www.randomhousebooks.com, pg 170

Schwartz, Rebecca, Porchlight Book Co Business Book Awards, 544 S First St, Milwaukee, WI 53204 *Toll Free Tel:* 800-236-7323 *E-mail:* info@porchlightbooks.com *Web Site:* porchlightbooks.com, pg 651

Schwartz, Steven, Sarah Jane Freymann Literary Agency LLC, 59 W 71 St, Suite 9-B, New York, NY 10023 *Tel:* 212-362-9277 *E-mail:* submissions@sarahjanefreymann.com *Web Site:* www.sarahjanefreymann.com, pg 459

Schwartz, Susan, The Editors Circle, 24 Holly Circle, Easthampton, MA 01027 *Tel:* 862-596-9709 *E-mail:* query@theeditorscircle.com *Web Site:* www.theeditorscircle.com, pg 438

Schwartzberg, Noah, Portfolio, c/o Penguin Random House LLC, 1745 Broadway, New York, NY 10019 *Tel:* 212-782-9000 *Web Site:* www.penguin.com/portfolio-overview/; www.penguin.com/sentinel-overview/; www.penguin.com/thesis/, pg 162

Schwartzman, Jill, Dutton, c/o Penguin Random House LLC, 1745 Broadway, New York, NY 10019 *Tel:* 212-366-2000 *Web Site:* www.penguin.com/dutton-overview/; www.penguin.com/plume-books-overview/; www.penguin.com/tiny-reparations-overview/, pg 62

Schweikert, Vincent, New Jersey Business & Industry Association (NJBIA), 10 W Lafayette St, Trenton, NJ 08608-2002 *Tel:* 609-393-7707 *Web Site:* njbia.org, pg 514

Schweitzer, Jon, American Jewish Committee (AJC), Mail Code 6760, PO Box 7247, Philadelphia, PA 19170-0001 *Tel:* 212-751-4000 *Fax:* 212-891-1450 *E-mail:* social@ajc.org *Web Site:* www.ajc.org, pg 495

Schweitzer, Matt, Houghton Mifflin Harcourt, 125 High St, Boston, MA 02110 *Tel:* 617-351-5000 *Toll Free Tel:* 855-969-4642; 800-225-5425 (K-12 educ materials); 800-323-9540 (assessment materials); 877-219-1537 (SkillsTutor); 888-242-6747 (Innovation in Educ Group); 800-225-3362 (Trade & Ref Div) *Toll Free Fax:* 800-269-5232 *E-mail:* myhmhco@hmhco.com *Web Site:* www.hmhco.com, pg 96

Schweitzer, Matt, Houghton Mifflin Harcourt Trade & Reference Division, 125 High St, Boston, MA 02110 *Tel:* 617-351-5000 *Web Site:* www.hmhco.com, pg 96

Schweitzer, Maxine, Scott Meredith Literary Agency LP, 1035 Park Ave, Apt 3-A, New York, NY 10028 *Tel:* 917-685-1064 *E-mail:* info@scottmeredith.com *Web Site:* www.scottmeredith.com, pg 470

Schwoeri, Lindsey, Viking Penguin, c/o Penguin Random House LLC, 1745 Broadway, New York, NY 10019 *Tel:* 212-782-9000 *Web Site:* www.penguin.com/overview-vikingbooks/; www.penguin.com/pamela-dorman-books-overview/; www.penguin.com/penguin-classics-overview/; www.penguin.com/penguin-life-overview/, pg 225

Sciacca, Nick, Simon & Schuster Children's Publishing, 1230 Avenue of the Americas, New York, NY 10020 *Tel:* 212-698-7000 *Web Site:* www.simonandschuster.com/kids; www.simonandschuster.com/teen; simonandschuster.net; simonandschuster.biz, pg 189

Sciambra, Lisa, Atria Books, 1230 Avenue of the Americas, New York, NY 10020 *Tel:* 212-698-7000 *Fax:* 212-698-7007 *Web Site:* www.simonandschuster.com, pg 21

Sciambra, Lisa, Books Like Us First Novel Contest, 1230 Avenue of the Americas, New York, NY 10020 *Tel:* 212-698-7000 *Web Site:* www.simonandschuster.com/p/simon-and-schuster-books-like-us, pg 583

Sciarappa, Matthew, Doubleday, c/o Penguin Random House LLC, 1745 Broadway, New York, NY 10019 *Tel:* 212-751-2600 *Fax:* 212-940-7390 (dom rts); 212-572-2662 (foreign rts) *Web Site:* knopfdoubleday.com/imprint/doubleday/; knopfdoubleday.com, pg 61

Sciarappa, Matthew, Alfred A Knopf, c/o Penguin Random House LLC, 1745 Broadway, New York, NY 10019 *Tel:* 212-751-2600 *Fax:* 212-940-7390 (dom rts); 212-572-2662 (foreign rts) *Web Site:* knopfdoubleday.com/imprint/knopf/; knopfdoubleday.com, pg 110

Scinta, Sam, Fulcrum Publishing Inc, 3970 Youngfield St, Wheat Ridge, CO 80033 *Tel:* 303-277-1623 *Toll Free Tel:* 800-888-4741 (orders) *E-mail:* info@fulcrumbooks.com *Web Site:* www.fulcrumbooks.com, pg 75

Sciortino, Joseph, Editions Mediaspaul, 3965, blvd Henri-Bourassa E, Montreal, QC H1H 1L1, Canada *Tel:* 514-322-7341 *Fax:* 514-322-4281 *E-mail:* mediaspaul@mediaspaul.ca *Web Site:* mediaspaul.ca, pg 404

Scire, Stefanie, Public Relations Society of America Inc, 120 Wall St, 21st fl, New York, NY 10005 *Tel:* 212-460-1400 *E-mail:* membership@prsa.org *Web Site:* www.prsa.org, pg 518

Scivener, Brian, University of Calgary Press, 2500 University Dr NW, Calgary, AB T2N 1N4, Canada *Tel:* 403-220-7578 *E-mail:* ucpbooks@ucalgary.ca *Web Site:* press.ucalgary.ca, pg 422

Sclama, Nicole, Houghton Mifflin Harcourt Trade & Reference Division, 125 High St, Boston, MA 02110 *Tel:* 617-351-5000 *Web Site:* www.hmhco.com, pg 96

Scognamiglio, John, Kensington Publishing Corp, 900 Third Ave, 26th fl, New York, NY 10022 *Tel:* 212-407-1500 *Toll Free Tel:* 800-221-2647 *Fax:* 212-935-0699 *Web Site:* www.kensingtonbooks.com, pg 109

Scolari, Luci, Bookcase Literary Agency, 5062 Lankershim Blvd, PMB 3046, North Hollywood, CA 91601 *Web Site:* www.bookcaseagency.com, pg 450

Scordato, Ellen, Stonesong, 270 W 39 St, Suite 201, New York, NY 10018 *Tel:* 212-929-4600 *E-mail:* editors@stonesong.com *Web Site:* www.stonesong.com, pg 478

Scott, Allison, Teachers College Press, 1234 Amsterdam Ave, New York, NY 10027 Tel: 212-678-3929 Fax: 212-678-4149 E-mail: tcpress@tc.edu Web Site: www.tcpress.com, pg 203

Scott, Anastasia, Chronicle Books LLC, 680 Second St, San Francisco, CA 94107 Tel: 415-537-4200 Fax: 415-537-4460 (perms) E-mail: hello@chroniclebooks.com; subrights@chroniclebooks.com Web Site: www.chroniclebooks.com, pg 47

Scott, Ardy M, Twilight Times Books, PO Box 3340, Kingsport, TN 37664-0340 Tel: 423-390-1111 Fax: 423-390-1111 E-mail: publisher@twilighttimes.com Web Site: www.twilighttimesbooks.com, pg 211

Scott, Craig R, Heritage Books Inc, 5810 Ruatan St, Berwyn Heights, MD 20740 Toll Free Tel: 800-876-6103 Toll Free Fax: 800-876-6103; 800-297-9954 E-mail: orders@heritagebooks.com; submissions@heritagebooks.com Web Site: www.heritagebooks.com, pg 91

Scott, Curtis R, The Museum of Modern Art (MoMA), Publications Dept, 11 W 53 St, New York, NY 10019 Tel: 212-708-9400 E-mail: moma_publications@moma.org Web Site: www.moma.org, pg 135

Scott, Debra Leigh, The Blue Mountain Novel Award, PO Box 63927, Philadelphia, PA 19147 Tel: 610-764-0813 E-mail: hiddenriverarts@gmail.com Web Site: hiddenriverarts.wordpress.com, pg 582

Scott, Debra Leigh, Hidden River Arts Playwriting Award, PO Box 63927, Philadelphia, PA 19147 Tel: 610-764-0813 E-mail: hiddenriverarts@gmail.com Web Site: www.hiddenriverarts.org; www.hiddenriverarts.com, pg 612

Scott, Debra Leigh, Sandy Run Novella Award, PO Box 63927, Philadelphia, PA 19147 Tel: 610-764-0813 E-mail: info@hiddenriverarts.org Web Site: hiddenriverarts.wordpress.com, pg 658

Scott, Debra Leigh, The Tamaqua Award for a Collection of Essays, PO Box 63927, Philadelphia, PA 19147 Tel: 610-764-0813 E-mail: hiddenriverarts@gmail.com Web Site: hiddenriverarts.wordpress.com, pg 668

Scott, Debra Leigh, The Tuscarora Award for Historical Fiction, PO Box 63927, Philadelphia, PA 19147 Tel: 610-764-0813 E-mail: hiddenriverarts@gmail.com Web Site: hiddenriverarts.wordpress.com, pg 671

Scott, Debra Leigh, The William Van Wert Memorial Fiction Award, PO Box 63927, Philadelphia, PA 19147 Tel: 610-764-0813 E-mail: hiddenriverarts@gmail.com Web Site: www.hiddenriverarts.org; www.hiddenriverarts.com, pg 672

Scott, Ellie, Aspen Words Literary Prize, 110 E Hallam St, Suite 116, Aspen, CO 81611 Tel: 970-925-3122 Fax: 970-920-5700 E-mail: literary.prize@aspeninstitute.org Web Site: www.aspenwords.org/programs/literary-prize/; www.aspenwords.org, pg 575

Scott, Ellie, Bloomsbury Academic, 1385 Broadway, 5th fl, New York, NY 10018 Tel: 212-419-5300 Web Site: www.bloomsbury.com/us/academic, pg 31

Scott, Karima D, American Political Science Association (APSA), 1527 New Hampshire Ave NW, Washington, DC 20036-1203 Tel: 202-483-2512 Fax: 202-483-2657 E-mail: apsa@apsanet.org; membership@apsanet.org; press@apsanet.org Web Site: www.apsanet.org, pg 496

Scott, Kate, Midwest Bookseller of the Year Award, 939 W Seventh St, St Paul, MN 55102 Tel: 612-208-6279 Web Site: www.midwestbooksellers.org/bookseller-of-the-year.html, pg 632

Scott, Kate, Midwest Independent Booksellers Association (MIBA), 939 W Seventh St, St Paul, MN 55102 Tel: 612-208-6279 Web Site: www.midwestbooksellers.org, pg 510

Scott, Katie, Kids Can Press Ltd, 25 Dockside Dr, Toronto, ON M5A 0B5, Canada Tel: 416-479-7000 Toll Free Tel: 800-265-0884 Fax: 416-960-5437 E-mail: info@kidscan.com; customerservice@kidscan.com Web Site: www.kidscanpress.com; www.kidscanpress.ca, pg 411

Scott, Marianne, The Canadian Writers' Foundation Inc (La Fondation des Ecrivains Canadiens), PO Box 13281, Kanata Sta, Ottawa, ON K2K 1X4, Canada Tel: 613-978-2723 Fax: 613-900-6393 E-mail: info@canadianwritersfoundation.org Web Site: www.canadianwritersfoundation.org, pg 525

Scott, Michael, Aptara Inc, 2901 Telestar Ct, Suite 522, Falls Church, VA 22042 Tel: 703-352-0001 E-mail: moreinfo@aptaracorp.com Web Site: www.aptaracorp.com, pg 435

Scott, Yolanda, Charlesbridge Publishing Inc, 85 Main St, Watertown, MA 02472 Tel: 617-926-0329 Toll Free Tel: 800-225-3214 Fax: 617-926-5720 Toll Free Fax: 800-926-5775 E-mail: books@charlesbridge.com Web Site: www.charlesbridge.com, pg 45

Scott-Wiley, Dewey, Trustus Playwrights' Festival, 520 Lady St, Columbia, SC 29201 Tel: 803-254-9732 E-mail: boxoffice@trustus.org Web Site: trustus.org/playwrights-festival, pg 670

Scovel, Lauren, Laura Gross Literary Agency, PO Box 610326, Newton Highlands, MA 02461 Tel: 617-964-2977 E-mail: query@lg-la.com; rights@lg-la.com Web Site: www.lg-la.com, pg 461

Scully, John, Albert Whitman & Company, 250 S Northwest Hwy, Suite 320, Park Ridge, IL 60068 Tel: 847-232-2800 Toll Free Tel: 800-255-7675 (orders) Fax: 847-581-0039 E-mail: mail@albertwhitman.com; orders@albertwhitman.com Web Site: www.albertwhitman.com, pg 6

Seachrist, Helen, Farrar, Straus & Giroux Books for Young Readers, 120 Broadway, New York, NY 10271 Tel: 212-741-6900 Toll Free Tel: 888-330-8477 (orders) E-mail: childrens.publicity@macmillanusa.com; childrensrights@macmillanusa.com Web Site: us.macmillan.com/mackids, pg 70

Seachrist, Helen, Roaring Brook Press, 120 Broadway, New York, NY 10271 Tel: 646-307-5151 Web Site: us.macmillan.com/publishers/roaring-brook-press, pg 176

Seager, Deb, Grove Atlantic Inc, 154 W 14 St, 12th fl, New York, NY 10011 Tel: 212-614-7850 Toll Free Tel: 800-521-0178 Fax: 212-614-7886 E-mail: info@groveatlantic.com; sales@groveatlantic.com; publicity@groveatlantic.com; rights@groveatlantic.com Web Site: www.groveatlantic.com, pg 82

Searl, Patricia, University of Virginia Press, PO Box 400318, Charlottesville, VA 22904-4318 Tel: 434-924-3469 (cust serv) Toll Free Tel: 800-831-3406 Fax: 434-982-2655 Toll Free Fax: 877-288-6400 E-mail: vapress@virginia.edu Web Site: www.upress.virginia.edu, pg 220

Sears, Casey, Macmillan, 120 Broadway, 22nd fl, New York, NY 10271 E-mail: press.inquiries@macmillan.com Web Site: us.macmillan.com, pg 122

Sears, Rene, Prometheus Books, 59 John Glenn Dr, Amherst, NY 14228-2119 Fax: 716-691-0137 E-mail: marketing@prometheusbooks.com; editorial@prometheusbooks.com; rights@prometheusbooks.com Web Site: www.prometheusbooks.com, pg 166

Searson, Lauren, PRINTING United Alliance, 10015 Main St, Fairfax, VA 22031 Tel: 703-385-1335 Toll Free Tel: 888-385-3588 Fax: 703-273-0456 E-mail: assist@printing.org; info@printing.org Web Site: www.printing.org, pg 165

Seaver, Kate, Berkley, c/o Penguin Random House LLC, 1745 Broadway, 19th fl, New York, NY 10019 Tel: 212-366-2000 Web Site: www.penguin.com/publishers/berkley/; www.penguin.com/ace-overview/, pg 28

Seavey, Claire, Penguin Random House Speakers Bureau, a Penguin Random House company, 1745 Broadway, Mail Drop 13-1, New York, NY 10019 Tel: 212-572-2013 E-mail: speakers@penguinrandomhouse.com Web Site: www.prhspeakers.com, pg 487

Secara, Andrea, Algora Publishing, 1632 First Ave, No 20330, New York, NY 10028-4305 Tel: 212-678-0232 Fax: 212-202-5488 E-mail: editors@algora.com Web Site: www.algora.com, pg 7

Secara, Claudiu A, Algora Publishing, 1632 First Ave, No 20330, New York, NY 10028-4305 Tel: 212-678-0232 Fax: 212-202-5488 E-mail: editors@algora.com Web Site: www.algora.com, pg 7

Secreto, Marissa, Penguin Random House Audio Publishing Group, 1745 Broadway, New York, NY 10019 Toll Free Tel: 800-793-2665 (cust serv) E-mail: audio@penguinrandomhouse.com; ecustomerservice@penguinrandomhouse.com Web Site: www.penguinrandomhouseaudio.com, pg 154

Secula, Jim, Holiday House Publishing Inc, 50 Broad St, New York, NY 10004 Tel: 212-688-0085 Fax: 212-421-6134 E-mail: info@holidayhouse.com Web Site: www.holidayhouse.com, pg 94

Sederstrom, Kate, Bloomsbury Publishing Inc, 1385 Broadway, 5th fl, New York, NY 10018 Tel: 212-419-5300 E-mail: marketingusa@bloomsbury.com; adultpublicityusa@bloomsbury.com; askacademic@bloomsbury.com Web Site: www.bloomsbury.com, pg 32

Sedgwick, Moira, James Beard Foundation Book Awards, 167 W 12 St, New York, NY 10011 Tel: 212-627-2308 E-mail: awards@jamesbeard.org Web Site: www.jamesbeard.org/awards, pg 578

Sedita, Francesco, Penguin Workshop, c/o Penguin Random House LLC, 1745 Broadway, New York, NY 10019 Tel: 212-782-9000 Web Site: www.penguin.com/publishers/penguinworkshop/, pg 156

Sedita, Francesco, Penguin Young Readers Group, c/o Penguin Random House LLC, 1745 Broadway, New York, NY 10019 Tel: 212-782-9000 Web Site: www.penguin.com/penguin-young-readers-overview, pg 156

See, Melissa, Holiday House Publishing Inc, 50 Broad St, New York, NY 10004 Tel: 212-688-0085 Fax: 212-421-6134 E-mail: info@holidayhouse.com Web Site: www.holidayhouse.com, pg 94

See, Melissa, Peachtree Publishing Co Inc, 1700 Chattahoochee Ave, Atlanta, GA 30318-2112 Tel: 404-876-8761 Toll Free Tel: 800-241-0113 Fax: 404-875-2578 Toll Free Fax: 800-875-8909 E-mail: hello@peachtree-online.com; orders@peachtree-online.com; sales@peachtree-online.com Web Site: www.peachtreebooks.com; www.peachtree-online.com, pg 153

Seeback, Nicolette, Henry Holt and Company, LLC, 120 Broadway, 23rd fl, New York, NY 10271 Tel: 646-307-5151 Toll Free Tel: 888-330-8477 (orders) Fax: 646-307-5285 Web Site: www.henryholt.com, pg 94

Seeman, Marsha, Writers Guild of America, East (WGAE), 250 Hudson St, Suite 700, New York, NY 10013 Tel: 212-767-7800 Fax: 212-582-1909 Web Site: www.wgaeast.org, pg 522

Seeman, Susan, Random House Publishing Group, 1745 Broadway, New York, NY 10019 Toll Free Tel: 800-200-3552 Web Site: www.randomhousebooks.com, pg 171

Sefton, Amy, Tor Publishing Group, 120 Broadway, New York, NY 10271 Toll Free Tel: 800-455-0340 (Macmillan) E-mail: torpublicity@tor.com; forgepublicity@forgebooks.com Web Site: us.macmillan.com/torpublishinggroup, pg 208

Sehlinger, Robert W, AdventureKEEN, 2204 First Ave S, Suite 102, Birmingham, AL 35233 Tel: 763-689-9800 Toll Free Tel: 800-678-7006 Fax: 763-689-9039 Toll Free Fax: 877-374-9016 E-mail: info@adventurewithkeen.com Web Site: adventurewithkeen.com, pg 5

Sehulster, Alexandra, St Martin's Press, LLC, 120 Broadway, New York, NY 10271 E-mail: publicity@stmartins.com; trademarketing@stmartins.com; foreignrights@stmartins.com Web Site: us.macmillan.com/smp, pg 181

Seibold, Doug, Agate Publishing Academy, 1328 Greenleaf St, Evanston, IL 60202 Tel: 847-475-4457 E-mail: help@agatepublishingacademy.com Web Site: agatepublishingacademy.com, pg 561

Seibold, Doug, Surrey Books, 1328 Greenleaf St, Evanston, IL 60202 Tel: 847-475-4457 Toll Free Tel: 800-326-4430 Web Site: agatepublishing.com/surrey, pg 201

Seidlitz, Lauri, Brush Education Inc, 6531-111 St NW, Edmonton, AB T6H 4R5, Canada *Tel:* 780-989-0910 *Toll Free Tel:* 855-283-0900 *Fax:* 780-989-0930 *Toll Free Fax:* 855-283-6947 *E-mail:* contact@brusheducation.ca *Web Site:* www.brusheducation.ca, pg 397

Seidman, Erika, Farrar, Straus & Giroux, LLC, 120 Broadway, New York, NY 10271 *Tel:* 212-741-6900 *E-mail:* fsg.publicity@fsgbooks.com; sales@fsgbooks.com *Web Site:* us.macmillan.com/fsg, pg 70

Seidman, Erika, Hill & Wang, 120 Broadway, New York, NY 10271 *Tel:* 212-741-6900 *E-mail:* fsg.publicity@fsgbooks.com; sales@fsgbooks.com *Web Site:* us.macmillan.com/fsg, pg 92

Seidman, Erika, North Point Press, 120 Broadway, New York, NY 10271 *Tel:* 212-741-6900 *E-mail:* sales@fsgbooks.com *Web Site:* us.macmillan.com/fsg, pg 142

Seidner, Sophia, Jill Grinberg Literary Management LLC, 392 Vanderbilt Ave, Brooklyn, NY 11238 *Tel:* 212-620-5883 *E-mail:* info@jillgrinbergliterary.com *Web Site:* www.jillgrinbergliterary.com, pg 461

Seigart, Steven, Goldfarb & Associates, 721 Gibbon St, Alexandria, VA 22314 *Tel:* 202-466-3030 *E-mail:* rlglawlit@gmail.com *Web Site:* www.ronaldgoldfarb.com, pg 460

Seigler, Carol, The University of North Carolina Press, 116 S Boundary St, Chapel Hill, NC 27514-3808 *Tel:* 919-966-3561; 919-966-7449 (orders) *Toll Free Tel:* 800-848-3224 (orders) *Fax:* 919-962-2704 (orders) *Toll Free Fax:* 800-272-6817 (orders) *E-mail:* uncpress@unc.edu *Web Site:* uncpress.org, pg 218

Seim, Kristin, Candlewick Press, 99 Dover St, Somerville, MA 02144-2825 *Tel:* 617-661-3330 *Fax:* 617-661-0565 *E-mail:* bigbear@candlewick.com; salesinfo@candlewick.com *Web Site:* candlewick.com, pg 40

Seitz, Jessica (Pollett), Outdoor Writers Association of America Annual Conference, 2814 Brooks St, Box 442, Missoula, MT 59801 *Tel:* 406-728-7434 *E-mail:* info@owaa.org *Web Site:* owaa.org, pg 556

Sekora, Rosemary, University of Nebraska Press, 1225 "L" St, Suite 200, Lincoln, NE 68588-0630 *Tel:* 402-472-3581; 919-966-7449 (cust serv & foreign orders) *Toll Free Tel:* 800-848-6224 (cust serv & US orders) *Fax:* 402-472-6214; 919-962-2704 (cust serv & foreign orders) *Toll Free Fax:* 800-272-6817 (cust serv & US orders) *E-mail:* presswebmail@unl.edu *Web Site:* www.nebraskapress.unl.edu, pg 218

Selby, Laura, The Continuing Legal Education Society of British Columbia (CLEBC), 500-1155 W Pender St, Vancouver, BC V6E 2P4, Canada *Tel:* 604-669-3544; 604-893-2121 (cust serv) *Toll Free Tel:* 800-663-0437 (CN) *Fax:* 604-669-9260 *E-mail:* custserv@cle.bc.ca *Web Site:* www.cle.bc.ca, pg 400

Self, Robert, Baby Tattoo Books, 6045 Longridge Ave, Van Nuys, CA 91401 *Tel:* 818-416-5314 *E-mail:* info@babytattoo.com *Web Site:* www.babytattoo.com, pg 23

Self, Ron, Brick Road Poetry Book Contest, 341 Lee Rd 553, Phenix City, AL 36867 *Web Site:* www.brickroadpoetrypress.com/poetry-book-contest, pg 584

Selinsky, Page PhD, University of Pennsylvania Museum of Archaeology & Anthropology, 3260 South St, Philadelphia, PA 19104-6324 *Tel:* 215-898-4119; 215-898-4000 *E-mail:* publications@pennmuseum.org *Web Site:* www.penn.museum, pg 219

Sellers, Liz, Berkley, c/o Penguin Random House LLC, 1745 Broadway, 19th fl, New York, NY 10019 *Tel:* 212-366-2000 *Web Site:* www.penguin.com/publishers/berkley/; www.penguin.com/ace-overview/, pg 28

Sellers, Scott, Seal Books, 320 Front St W, Suite 1400, Toronto, ON M5V 3B6, Canada *Tel:* 416-364-4449 *Toll Free Tel:* 888-523-9292 (order desk) *Fax:* 416-598-7764 *Web Site:* www.penguinrandomhouse.ca, pg 419

Sellmyer, Charlotte, National Music Publishers' Association (NMPA), 1900 "N" St NW, Suite 500, Washington, DC 20036 *Tel:* 202-393-6672 *E-mail:* members@nmpa.org *Web Site:* nmpa.org, pg 513

Sells, Dianna, Texas A&M University Press, John H Lindsey Bldg, Lewis St, 4354 TAMU, College Station, TX 77843-4354 *Tel:* 979-845-1436 *Toll Free Tel:* 800-826-8911 (orders) *Fax:* 979-847-8752 *Toll Free Fax:* 888-617-2421 (orders) *E-mail:* bookorders@tamu.edu *Web Site:* www.tamupress.com, pg 205

Semach, Geffen, Penguin Random House Canada, a Penguin Random House company, 320 Front St W, Suite 1400, Toronto, ON M5V 3B6, Canada *Tel:* 416-364-4449 *Toll Free Tel:* 888-523-9292 (cust serv) *E-mail:* canadaweb@penguinrandomhouse.com; customerservicescanada@penguinrandomhouse.com *Web Site:* www.penguinrandomhouse.ca, pg 416

Semprun, Erika, Dutton, c/o Penguin Random House LLC, 1745 Broadway, New York, NY 10019 *Tel:* 212-366-2000 *Web Site:* www.penguin.com/dutton-overview/; www.penguin.com/plume-books-overview/; www.penguin.com/tiny-reparations-overview/, pg 62

Sen, Sharmila, Harvard University Press, 79 Garden St, Cambridge, MA 02138-1499 *Tel:* 617-495-2600; 401-531-2800 (intl orders) *Toll Free Tel:* 800-405-1619 (orders) *Fax:* 617-495-5898 (gen); 617-496-4677 (edit & rts); 401-531-2801 (intl orders) *Toll Free Fax:* 800-406-9145 (orders) *E-mail:* contact_hup@harvard.edu *Web Site:* www.hup.harvard.edu, pg 88

Senders, Marci, Disney-Hyperion Books, 1101 Flower St, Glendale, CA 91201 *Web Site:* books.disney.com/imprint/disney-hyperion, pg 59

Senechal, David, Les Editions Fides, 7333 place des Roseraies, bureau 501, Anjou, QC H1M 2X6, Canada *Tel:* 514-745-4290 *Fax:* 514-745-4299 *E-mail:* editions@groupefides.com *Web Site:* www.editionsfides.com, pg 403

Seney, Maranda, Sourcebooks LLC, 1935 Brookdale Rd, Suite 139, Naperville, IL 60563 *Tel:* 630-961-3900 *Toll Free Tel:* 800-432-7444 *Fax:* 630-961-2168 *E-mail:* info@sourcebooks.com *Web Site:* www.sourcebooks.com, pg 194

Senturk, Huseyin, Tughra Books, 335 Clifton Ave, Clifton, NJ 07011 *Tel:* 646-415-9331 *Fax:* 646-827-6228 *E-mail:* info@tughrabooks.com *Web Site:* www.tughrabooks.com, pg 210

Seow, Jackie, Simon & Schuster, 1230 Avenue of the Americas, New York, NY 10020 *Tel:* 212-698-7000 *Toll Free Tel:* 800-223-2348 (cust serv); 800-223-2336 (orders) *Toll Free Fax:* 800-943-9831 (orders) *Web Site:* simonandschusterpublishing.com/simonandschuster/, pg 188

Sepehri, Amin, Mage Publishers Inc, 5600 Wisconsin Ave, No 1408, Chevy Chase, MD 20815 *Web Site:* www.mage.com, pg 123

Sequera, Silvio, Histria Books, 7181 N Hualapai Way, Suite 130-86, Las Vegas, NV 89166 *Tel:* 561-299-0802 *E-mail:* info@histriabooks.com; orders@histriabooks.com; rights@histriabooks.com *Web Site:* histriabooks.com, pg 93

Serabian, Charlie, Global Lion Intellectual Property Management Inc, PO Box 669238, Pompano Beach, FL 33066 *Tel:* 754-222-6948 *Fax:* 754-222-6948 *E-mail:* queriesglobalionmgt@gmail.com *Web Site:* www.globallionmanagement.com, pg 460

Serafimidis, Sarah, North Atlantic Books (NAB), 2526 Martin Luther King Jr Way, Berkeley, CA 94704 *Tel:* 510-549-4270 *Web Site:* www.northatlanticbooks.com, pg 142

Seraphim, Clio, Random House Publishing Group, 1745 Broadway, New York, NY 10019 *Toll Free Tel:* 800-200-3552 *Web Site:* www.randomhousebooks.com, pg 171

Sergel, Christopher III, Dramatic Publishing Co, 311 Washington St, Woodstock, IL 60098-3308 *Tel:* 815-338-7170 *Toll Free Tel:* 800-448-7469 *Fax:* 815-338-8981 *Toll Free Fax:* 800-334-5302 *E-mail:* customerservice@dpcplays.com *Web Site:* www.dramaticpublishing.com, pg 61

Sergel, Gayle, Dramatic Publishing Co, 311 Washington St, Woodstock, IL 60098-3308 *Tel:* 815-338-7170 *Toll Free Tel:* 800-448-7469 *Fax:* 815-338-8981 *Toll Free Fax:* 800-334-5302 *E-mail:* customerservice@dpcplays.com *Web Site:* www.dramaticpublishing.com, pg 61

Sergel, Susan, Dramatic Publishing Co, 311 Washington St, Woodstock, IL 60098-3308 *Tel:* 815-338-7170 *Toll Free Tel:* 800-448-7469 *Fax:* 815-338-8981 *Toll Free Fax:* 800-334-5302 *E-mail:* customerservice@dpcplays.com *Web Site:* www.dramaticpublishing.com, pg 61

Sergio, Christopher, Henry Holt and Company, LLC, 120 Broadway, 23rd fl, New York, NY 10271 *Tel:* 646-307-5151 *Toll Free Tel:* 888-330-8477 (orders) *Fax:* 646-307-5285 *Web Site:* www.henryholt.com, pg 94

Serrano, Elizabeth, ALSC Baker & Taylor Summer Reading Grant, 225 N Michigan Ave, Suite 1300, Chicago, IL 60601 *Tel:* 312-280-2163 *Toll Free Tel:* 800-545-2433 *Fax:* 312-280-5271 *E-mail:* alsc@ala.org *Web Site:* www.ala.org/alsc/awardsgrants/profawards/bakertaylor, pg 572

Serrano, Elizabeth, The Mildred L Batchelder Award, 225 N Michigan Ave, Suite 1300, Chicago, IL 60601 *Tel:* 312-280-2163 *Toll Free Tel:* 800-545-2433 *Fax:* 312-280-5271 *E-mail:* alsc@ala.org *Web Site:* www.ala.org/alsc/awardsgrants/bookmedia/batchelder, pg 577

Serrano, Elizabeth, The Pura Belpre Award, 225 N Michigan Ave, Suite 1300, Chicago, IL 60601 *Tel:* 312-280-2163 *Toll Free Tel:* 800-545-2433 *Fax:* 312-280-5271 *E-mail:* alsc@ala.org *Web Site:* www.ala.org/alsc/awardsgrants/bookmedia/belpre, pg 578

Serrano, Elizabeth, Bound to Stay Bound Books Scholarship, 225 N Michigan Ave, Suite 1300, Chicago, IL 60601 *Tel:* 312-280-2163 *Toll Free Tel:* 800-545-2433 *Fax:* 312-280-5271 *E-mail:* alsc@ala.org *Web Site:* www.ala.org/alsc/awardsgrants/scholarships; www.btsb.com/about-us/scholarships, pg 583

Serrano, Elizabeth, The Randolph Caldecott Medal, 225 N Michigan Ave, Suite 1300, Chicago, IL 60601 *Tel:* 312-280-2163 *Toll Free Tel:* 800-545-2433 *Fax:* 312-280-5271 *E-mail:* alsc@ala.org *Web Site:* www.ala.org/alsc/awardsgrants/bookmedia/caldecott, pg 585

Serrano, Elizabeth, Children's Literature Lecture Award, 225 N Michigan Ave, Suite 1300, Chicago, IL 60601 *Tel:* 312-280-2163 *Toll Free Tel:* 800-545-2433 *Fax:* 312-280-5271 *E-mail:* alsc@ala.org *Web Site:* www.ala.org/alsc/awardsgrants/profawards/chll, pg 589

Serrano, Elizabeth, Children's Literature Legacy Award, 225 N Michigan Ave, Suite 1300, Chicago, IL 60601 *Tel:* 312-280-2163 *Toll Free Tel:* 800-545-2433 *Fax:* 312-280-5271 *E-mail:* alsc@ala.org *Web Site:* www.ala.org/alsc/awardsgrants/childrens-literature-legacy-award; www.ala.org/alsc/awardsgrants/bookmedia/clla, pg 589

Serrano, Elizabeth, Frederic G Melcher Scholarship, 225 N Michigan Ave, Suite 1300, Chicago, IL 60601 *Tel:* 312-280-2163 *Toll Free Tel:* 800-545-2433 *Fax:* 312-280-5271 *E-mail:* alsc@ala.org *Web Site:* www.ala.org/alsc/awardsgrants/scholarships, pg 632

Serrano, Elizabeth, John Newbery Medal, 225 N Michigan Ave, Suite 1300, Chicago, IL 60601 *Tel:* 312-280-2163 *Toll Free Tel:* 800-545-2433 *Fax:* 312-280-5271 *E-mail:* alsc@ala.org *Web Site:* www.ala.org/alsc/awardsgrants/bookmedia/newbery, pg 641

Serrano, Elizabeth, Robert F Sibert Informational Book Award, 225 N Michigan Ave, Suite 1300, Chicago, IL 60601 *Tel:* 312-280-2163 *Toll Free Tel:* 800-545-2433 *Fax:* 312-280-5271 *E-mail:* alsc@ala.org *Web Site:* www.ala.org/alsc/awardsgrants/bookmedia/sibert, pg 662

Serrell, Allison, PA Press, 202 Warren St, Hudson, NY 12534 Tel: 518-671-6100 Toll Free Tel: 800-722-6657 (dist); 800-759-0190 (sales) E-mail: sales@papress.com Web Site: www.papress.com, pg 149

Sery, Douglas, The MIT Press, One Broadway, 12th fl, Cambridge, MA 02142 Tel: 617-253-5255 Toll Free Tel: 800-405-1619 (orders) Fax: 617-258-6779; 617-577-1545 (orders) Web Site: mitpress.mit.edu, pg 132

Seto, Sarah, Penguin Random House Canada, a Penguin Random House company, 320 Front St W, Suite 1400, Toronto, ON M5V 3B6, Canada Tel: 416-364-4449 Toll Free Tel: 888-523-9292 (cust serv) E-mail: canadaweb@penguinrandomhouse.com; customerservicescanada@penguinrandomhouse.com Web Site: www.penguinrandomhouse.ca, pg 416

Sever, Richard, Cold Spring Harbor Laboratory Press, 500 Sunnyside Blvd, Woodbury, NY 11797-2924 Tel: 516-422-4100 Toll Free Tel: 800-843-4388 E-mail: cshpress@cshl.edu Web Site: www.cshlpress.com, pg 50

Severini, Giorgia, R Ross Annett Award for Children's Literature, 11759 Groat Rd NW, Edmonton, AB T5M 3K6, Canada Tel: 780-422-8174 Toll Free Tel: 800-665-5354 (AB only) E-mail: mail@writersguild.ab.ca Web Site: writersguild.ca, pg 573

Severini, Giorgia, Georges Bugnet Award for Fiction, 11759 Groat Rd NW, Edmonton, AB T5M 3K6, Canada Tel: 780-422-8174 Toll Free Tel: 800-665-5354 (AB only) E-mail: mail@writersguild.ab.ca Web Site: writersguild.ca, pg 585

Severini, Giorgia, The City of Calgary W O Mitchell Book Prize, 11759 Groat Rd NW, Edmonton, AB T5M 3K6, Canada Tel: 780-422-8174 Toll Free Tel: 800-665-5354 (AB only) E-mail: mail@writersguild.ab.ca Web Site: writersguild.ca, pg 590

Severini, Giorgia, Wilfrid Eggleston Award for Nonfiction, 11759 Groat Rd NW, Edmonton, AB T5M 3K6, Canada Tel: 780-422-8174 Toll Free Tel: 800-665-5354 (AB only) E-mail: mail@writersguild.ab.ca Web Site: writersguild.ca, pg 599

Severini, Giorgia, James H Gray Award for Short Nonfiction, 11759 Groat Rd NW, Edmonton, AB T5M 3K6, Canada Tel: 780-422-8174 Toll Free Tel: 800-665-5354 (AB only) E-mail: mail@writersguild.ab.ca Web Site: writersguild.ca, pg 609

Severini, Giorgia, The Robert Kroetsch City of Edmonton Book Prize, 11759 Groat Rd NW, Edmonton, AB T5M 3K6, Canada Tel: 780-422-8174 Toll Free Tel: 800-665-5354 (AB only) E-mail: mail@writersguild.ab.ca Web Site: writersguild.ca, pg 621

Severini, Giorgia, Howard O'Hagan Award for Short Story, 11759 Groat Rd NW, Edmonton, AB T5M 3K6, Canada Tel: 780-422-8174 Toll Free Tel: 800-665-5354 (AB only) E-mail: mail@writersguild.ab.ca Web Site: writersguild.ca, pg 643

Severini, Giorgia, Gwen Pharis Ringwood Award for Drama, 11759 Groat Rd NW, Edmonton, AB T5M 3K6, Canada Tel: 780-422-8174 Toll Free Tel: 800-665-5354 (AB only) E-mail: mail@writersguild.ab.ca Web Site: writersguild.ca, pg 656

Severini, Giorgia, Stephan G Stephansson Award for Poetry, 11759 Groat Rd NW, Edmonton, AB T5M 3K6, Canada Tel: 780-422-8174 Toll Free Tel: 800-665-5354 (AB only) E-mail: mail@writersguild.ab.ca Web Site: writersguild.ca, pg 666

Severini, Giorgia, Jon Whyte Memorial Essay Prize, 11759 Groat Rd NW, Edmonton, AB T5M 3K6, Canada Tel: 780-422-8174 Toll Free Tel: 800-665-5354 (AB only) E-mail: mail@writersguild.ab.ca Web Site: writersguild.ca, pg 675

Severini, Giorgia, Writers' Guild of Alberta, 11759 Groat Rd NW, Edmonton, AB T5M 3K6, Canada Tel: 780-422-8174 Toll Free Tel: 800-665-5354 (AB only) E-mail: mail@writersguild.ab.ca Web Site: writersguild.ca, pg 522

Severns, Jennifer, American Marketing Association, 130 E Randolph St, 22nd fl, Chicago, IL 60601 Tel: 312-542-9000 Toll Free Tel: 800-AMA-1150 (262-1150) Web Site: www.ama.org, pg 495

Sevick, Kristin, St Martin's Press, LLC, 120 Broadway, New York, NY 10271 E-mail: publicity@stmartins.com; trademarketing@stmartins.com; foreignrights@stmartins.com Web Site: us.macmillan.com/smp, pg 181

Sevier, Ben, Grand Central Publishing, 1290 Avenue of the Americas, New York, NY 10104 Tel: 212-364-1100 Web Site: www.hachettebookgroup.com/imprint/grand-central-publishing/, pg 80

Sevier, Ben, Hachette Book Group Inc, 1290 Avenue of the Americas, New York, NY 10104 Tel: 212-364-1100 Toll Free Tel: 800-759-0190 (cust serv) Fax: 212-364-0933 (intl orders) Toll Free Fax: 800-286-9471 (cust serv) E-mail: customer.service@hbgusa.com; orders@hbgusa.com Web Site: www.hachettebookgroup.com, pg 83

Sewell, Emily, Bull Publishing Co, PO Box 1377, Boulder, CO 80306 Tel: 303-545-6350 Toll Free Tel: 800-676-2855 E-mail: sales@bullpub.com Web Site: www.bullpub.com, pg 38

Sewell, Nancy, James Lorimer & Co Ltd, Publishers, 117 Peter St, Suite 304, Toronto, ON M5V 0M3, Canada Tel: 416-362-4762 Fax: 416-362-3939 E-mail: sales@lorimer.ca; promotion@lorimer.ca; rights@lorimer.ca Web Site: www.lorimer.ca, pg 412

Sewell, Reid, HarperCollins Children's Books, 195 Broadway, New York, NY 10007 Tel: 212-207-7000 Web Site: www.harpercollins.com/childrens, pg 85

Sexton, Kim, SDP Publishing Solutions LLC, 36 Captain's Way, East Bridgewater, MA 02333 Tel: 617-775-0656 Web Site: www.sdppublishingsolutions.com, pg 444

Seymour, Nicole, ASLE Book Awards, PO Box 502, Keene, NH 03431-0502 Tel: 603-357-7411 Fax: 603-357-7411 E-mail: info@asle.org Web Site: www.asle.org/research-write/asle-book-paper-awards, pg 575

Sferratore, Nadine, Harry N Abrams Inc, 195 Broadway, 9th fl, New York, NY 10007 Tel: 212-206-7715 Toll Free Tel: 800-345-1359 Fax: 212-645-8437 E-mail: abrams@abramsbooks.com; publicity@abramsbooks.com; sales@abramsbooks.com Web Site: www.abramsbooks.com, pg 2

Shabelman, Doug, Burns Entertainment, 3637 Westfield Lane, Glenview, IL 60026 Tel: 847-866-9400 Web Site: burnsent.com, pg 487

Shaeffer, Rob, PA Press, 202 Warren St, Hudson, NY 12534 Tel: 518-671-6100 Toll Free Tel: 800-722-6657 (dist); 800-759-0190 (sales) E-mail: sales@papress.com Web Site: www.papress.com, pg 149

Shafeyeva, Yelena, Begell House Inc Publishers, 50 North St, Danbury, CT 06810 Tel: 203-456-6161 Fax: 203-456-6167 E-mail: orders@begellhouse.com Web Site: www.begellhouse.com, pg 27

Shaffer, Bryan, Purdue University Press, Stewart Ctr 190, 504 W State St, West Lafayette, IN 47907-2058 Tel: 765-494-2038 Fax: 765-496-2442 E-mail: pupress@purdue.edu Web Site: www.thepress.purdue.edu, pg 167

Shaffer, Julie, Association for PRINT Technologies (APTech), 113 Seaboard Lane, Suite C-200, Franklin, TN 37067 Tel: 703-264-7200 E-mail: aptech@aptech.org Web Site: printtechnologies.org, pg 498

Shah, Monica, Harry N Abrams Inc, 195 Broadway, 9th fl, New York, NY 10007 Tel: 212-206-7715 Toll Free Tel: 800-345-1359 Fax: 212-645-8437 E-mail: abrams@abramsbooks.com; publicity@abramsbooks.com; sales@abramsbooks.com Web Site: www.abramsbooks.com, pg 2

Shah, Sonali, Visual Media Alliance (VMA), 665 Third St, Suite 500, San Francisco, CA 94107-1926 Tel: 415-495-8242 Toll Free Tel: 800-659-3363 Fax: 415-520-1126 E-mail: info@vma.bz Web Site: main.vma.bz, pg 521

Shah, Stuti, Transatlantic Agency, 2 Bloor St E, Suite 3500, Toronto, ON M4W 1A8, Canada Tel: 416-488-9214 E-mail: info@transatlanticagency.com; royalties@transatlanticagency.com Web Site: www.transatlanticagency.com, pg 479

Shahan, Nick, University of Alabama Press, 200 Hackberry Lane, 2nd fl, Tuscaloosa, AL 35487 Tel: 205-348-5180 Fax: 205-348-9201 Web Site: www.uapress.ua.edu, pg 214

Shahsamand, Naheid, Farrar, Straus & Giroux Books for Young Readers, 120 Broadway, New York, NY 10271 Tel: 212-741-6900 Toll Free Tel: 888-330-8477 (orders) E-mail: childrens.publicity@macmillanusa.com; childrensrights@macmillanusa.com Web Site: us.macmillan.com/mackids, pg 70

Shahsamand, Naheid, Roaring Brook Press, 120 Broadway, New York, NY 10271 Tel: 646-307-5151 Web Site: us.macmillan.com/publishers/roaring-brook-press, pg 176

Shaine, Ilene, Foster City International Writers Contest, 650 Shell Blvd, Foster City, CA 94404 Tel: 650-286-3380 E-mail: fostercity_writers@yahoo.com Web Site: www.fostercity.org, pg 603

Shaloo, Sharon, Massachusetts Book Awards, Old School Commons, No 302, 17 New South St, Northampton, MA 01060 Tel: 617-872-3718 E-mail: bookawards@massbook.org Web Site: www.massbook.org, pg 630

Shamroe, Amy, Axiom Business Book Awards, 1129 Woodmere Ave, Suite B, Traverse City, MI 49686 Tel: 231-933-0445 Toll Free Tel: 800-706-4636 Fax: 231-933-0448 E-mail: info@axiomawards.com Web Site: www.axiomawards.com, pg 576

Shamroe, Amy, Illumination Book Awards, 1129 Woodmere Ave, Suite B, Traverse City, MI 49686 Tel: 231-933-0445 Toll Free Tel: 800-706-4636 Fax: 231-933-0448 Web Site: illuminationawards.com, pg 615

Shamroe, Amy, The Independent Publisher Book Awards, 1129 Woodmere Ave, Suite B, Traverse City, MI 49686 Tel: 231-933-0445 Toll Free Tel: 800-706-4636 Fax: 231-933-0448 E-mail: ippy@jgibookawards.com Web Site: ippyawards.com, pg 615

Shamroe, Amy, Living Now Book Awards, 1129 Woodmere Ave, Suite B, Traverse City, MI 49686 Tel: 231-933-0445 Toll Free Tel: 800-706-4636 Fax: 231-933-0448 Web Site: livingnowawards.com, pg 625

Shamroe, Amy, Moonbeam Children's Book Awards, 1129 Woodmere Ave, Suite B, Traverse City, MI 49686 Tel: 231-933-0445 Toll Free Tel: 800-706-4636 Fax: 231-933-0448 E-mail: moonbeam@jgibookawards.com Web Site: moonbeamawards.com, pg 635

Shanahan, James, McGraw-Hill Professional Publishing Group, 2 Penn Plaza, New York, NY 10121 Tel: 646-766-2000 Web Site: www.mhprofessional.com; www.mheducation.com, pg 128

Shanahan, Tara, Simon & Schuster Children's Publishing, 1230 Avenue of the Americas, New York, NY 10020 Tel: 212-698-7000 Web Site: www.simonandschuster.com/kids; www.simonandschuster.com/teen; simonandschuster.net; simonandschuster.biz, pg 189

Shandler, Sara, Alloy Entertainment LLC, 30 Hudson Yards, 22nd fl, New York, NY 10001, pg 7

Shanholtzer, Joshua, University of Pittsburgh Press, 7500 Thomas Blvd, Pittsburgh, PA 15260 Tel: 412-383-2456 Fax: 412-383-2466 E-mail: info@upress.pitt.edu Web Site: www.upress.pitt.edu, pg 219

Shannon, Chelsey, University of New Orleans Press, 2000 Lakeshore Dr, New Orleans, LA 70148 Tel: 504-280-7457 E-mail: unopress@uno.edu Web Site: www.uno.edu/unopress, pg 218

Shannon, Denise, Denise Shannon Literary Agency Inc, 280 Madison Ave, Suite 308, New York, NY 10016 E-mail: info@deniseshannonagency.com; submissions@deniseshannonagency.com Web Site: deniseshannonagency.com, pg 475

Shannon, Kari, Omnibus Press, 180 Madison Ave, 24th fl, New York, NY 10016 Tel: 212-254-2100 Toll Free Tel: 800-431-7187 Fax: 212-254-2013 Toll Free

Fax: 800-345-6842 *E-mail:* info@omnibuspress.com *Web Site:* www.omnibuspress.com; www.musicsales.com, pg 146

Shannon, Kim, Simon & Schuster, LLC, 1230 Avenue of the Americas, New York, NY 10020 *Tel:* 212-698-7000 *Toll Free Tel:* 800-223-2336 (orders) *Fax:* 212-698-7007 *Toll Free Fax:* 800-943-9831 (orders) *E-mail:* firstname.lastname@simonandschuster.com; purchaseorders@simonandschuster.com (orders) *Web Site:* www.simonandschuster.com, pg 190

Shannon, Scott, Penguin Random House LLC, 1745 Broadway, New York, NY 10019 *Tel:* 212-782-9000 *Toll Free Tel:* 800-726-0600 *Web Site:* www.penguinrandomhouse.com, pg 155

Shannon, Scott, Random House Publishing Group, 1745 Broadway, New York, NY 10019 *Toll Free Tel:* 800-200-3552 *Web Site:* www.randomhousebooks.com, pg 170

Shapiro, Alexis, Avotaynu Books LLC, 10 Sunset Rd, Needham, MA 02494 *Tel:* 781-449-2131 *E-mail:* info@avotaynubooks.com *Web Site:* www.avotaynubooks.com, pg 23

Shapiro, Karen, Sourcebooks LLC, 1935 Brookdale Rd, Suite 139, Naperville, IL 60563 *Tel:* 630-961-3900 *Toll Free Tel:* 800-432-7444 *Fax:* 630-961-2168 *E-mail:* info@sourcebooks.com *Web Site:* www.sourcebooks.com, pg 194

Shapiro, Nachum, Judaica Press Inc, 123 Ditmas Ave, Brooklyn, NY 11218 *Tel:* 718-972-6200 *Toll Free Tel:* 800-972-6201 *Fax:* 718-972-6204 *E-mail:* info@judaicapress.com; orders@judaicapress.com; submissions@judaicapress.com *Web Site:* www.judaicapress.com, pg 107

Shapiro, Noa, Random House Publishing Group, 1745 Broadway, New York, NY 10019 *Toll Free Tel:* 800-200-3552 *Web Site:* www.randomhousebooks.com, pg 171

Shapiro, Norman, Soncino Press Ltd, 123 Ditmas Ave, Brooklyn, NY 11218 *Tel:* 718-972-6200 *Toll Free Tel:* 800-972-6201 *Fax:* 718-972-6204 *E-mail:* info@soncino.com *Web Site:* www.soncino.com, pg 193

Shapiro, Rob, Alfred A Knopf, c/o Penguin Random House LLC, 1745 Broadway, New York, NY 10019 *Tel:* 212-751-2600 *Fax:* 212-940-7390 (dom rts); 212-572-2662 (foreign rts) *Web Site:* knopfdoubleday.com/imprint/knopf/; knopfdoubleday.com, pg 110

Shappel, Ray, Random House Children's Books, c/o Penguin Random House LLC, 1745 Broadway, New York, NY 10019 *Tel:* 212-782-9000 *Web Site:* www.rhcbooks.com, pg 170

Shariff, Kimberly Ayers, Penguin Random House LLC, 1745 Broadway, New York, NY 10019 *Tel:* 212-782-9000 *Toll Free Tel:* 800-726-0600 *Web Site:* www.penguinrandomhouse.com, pg 155

Sharigian, Kenneth J, American Medical Association (AMA), AMA Plaza, 330 N Wabash, Suite 39300, Chicago, IL 60611-5885 *Tel:* 312-464-5000 *Toll Free Tel:* 800-621-8335 *E-mail:* media@ama-assn.org (media & edit) *Web Site:* www.ama-assn.org; www.jamanetwork.org, pg 495

Shariyf, Clarisse Rosaz, PEN America, 120 Broadway, 26th fl N, New York, NY 10271 *Tel:* 212-334-1660 *Fax:* 212-334-2181 *E-mail:* info@pen.org; membership@pen.org; education@pen.org *Web Site:* pen.org, pg 516

Sharkey, Lisa, HarperCollins Publishers LLC, 195 Broadway, New York, NY 10007 *Tel:* 212-207-7000 *Web Site:* www.harpercollins.com, pg 86

Sharma, Tiara, Alfred A Knopf, c/o Penguin Random House LLC, 1745 Broadway, New York, NY 10019 *Tel:* 212-751-2600 *Fax:* 212-940-7390 (dom rts); 212-572-2662 (foreign rts) *Web Site:* knopfdoubleday.com/imprint/knopf/; knopfdoubleday.com, pg 110

Sharp, Fiona, Gallery Books, 1230 Avenue of the Americas, New York, NY 10020 *Toll Free Tel:* 800-456-6798 *Fax:* 212-698-7284 *E-mail:* consumer.customerservice@simonandschuster.com *Web Site:* www.simonandschuster.com, pg 76

Sharp, Fiona, Scribner, 1230 Avenue of the Americas, New York, NY 10020 *Web Site:* www.simonandschusterpublishing.com/scribner/, pg 185

Sharp, Lauren, Aevitas Creative Management LLC, 19 W 21 St, Suite 501, New York, NY 10010 *Tel:* 212-765-6900 *Web Site:* www.aevitascreative.com, pg 448

Sharp, Tori, The Jennifer DeChiara Literary Agency, 245 Park Ave, 39th fl, New York, NY 10167 *Tel:* 212-372-8989 *Web Site:* www.jdlit.com, pg 455

Shaub, Ms Bobbett, Medical Physics Publishing Corp (MPP), 4555 Helgesen Dr, Madison, WI 53718 *Tel:* 608-224-4508 (returns) *Toll Free Tel:* 800-442-5778 (cust serv) *Fax:* 608-224-5016 *E-mail:* mpp@medicalphysics.org *Web Site:* www.medicalphysics.org, pg 129

Shauger, Laura, Mountaineers Books, 1001 SW Klickitat Way, Suite 201, Seattle, WA 98134 *Tel:* 206-223-6303 *Fax:* 206-223-6306 *E-mail:* mbooks@mountaineersbooks.org; customerservice@mountaineersbooks.org *Web Site:* www.mountaineers.org/books, pg 135

Shaughnessy, Sandy, Individual Artist Project Grants, 500 S Bronough St, Tallahassee, FL 32399-0250 *Tel:* 850-245-6470 *Fax:* 850-245-6497 *E-mail:* dcagrants@dos.myflorida.com *Web Site:* dos.myflorida.com/cultural, pg 616

Shaw, Emma, Simon & Schuster, 1230 Avenue of the Americas, New York, NY 10020 *Tel:* 212-698-7000 *Toll Free Tel:* 800-223-2348 (cust serv); 800-223-2336 (orders) *Toll Free Fax:* 800-943-9831 (orders) *Web Site:* simonandschusterpublishing.com/simonandschuster/, pg 189

Shaw, Grace, House of Anansi Press Inc, 128 Sterling Rd, Lower Level, Toronto, ON M6R 2B7, Canada *Tel:* 416-363-4343 *Fax:* 416-363-1017 *E-mail:* customerservice@houseofanansi.com *Web Site:* houseofanansi.com, pg 409

Shaw, Greg, Levine|Greenberg|Rostan Literary Agency, 307 Seventh Ave, Suite 2407, New York, NY 10001 *Tel:* 212-337-0934 *Fax:* 212-337-0948 *E-mail:* submit@lgrliterary.com *Web Site:* lgrliterary.com, pg 467

Shaw, Joe, Cypress House, 155 Cypress St, Suite A, Fort Bragg, CA 95437 *Tel:* 707-964-9520 *Toll Free Tel:* 800-773-7782 *Fax:* 707-964-7531 *E-mail:* office@cypresshouse.com *Web Site:* www.cypresshouse.com, pg 56, 437

Shaw, Kelly, Scholastic Education Solutions, 557 Broadway, New York, NY 10012 *Tel:* 212-343-6100 *Fax:* 212-343-6189 *Web Site:* www.scholastic.com, pg 184

Shaw, Laura, Northwest Independent Editors Guild, 7511 Greenwood Ave N, No 307, Seattle, WA 98103 *E-mail:* info@edsguild.org *Web Site:* www.edsguild.org, pg 515

Shaw, Laura, RAND Corp, 1776 Main St, Santa Monica, CA 90407-2138 *Tel:* 310-393-0411 *Fax:* 310-393-4818 *Web Site:* www.rand.org, pg 169

Shaw, Laura, Red Pencil Conference, 7511 Greenwood Ave N, No 307, Seattle, WA 98103 *E-mail:* conference@edsguild.org *Web Site:* www.edsguild.org/red-pencil-conferences, pg 557

Shaw, Liz, Shambhala Publications Inc, 2129 13 St, Boulder, CO 80302 *Tel:* 978-829-3139 (intl callers) *Toll Free Tel:* 866-424-0030 (off); 888-424-2329 (orders & cust serv) *Fax:* 617-236-1563 *E-mail:* customercare@shambhala.com; royalties@shambhala.com *Web Site:* www.shambhala.com, pg 187

Shaw, Tracy, Little, Brown Books for Young Readers (LBYR), 1290 Avenue of the Americas, New York, NY 10104 *Tel:* 212-364-1100 *Toll Free Tel:* 800-759-0190 (cust serv) *E-mail:* rights@lbchildrens.com *Web Site:* www.hachettebookgroup.com/imprint/little-brown-books-for-young-readers/, pg 118

Shawa, Salma, Candlewick Press, 99 Dover St, Somerville, MA 02144-2825 *Tel:* 617-661-3330 *Fax:* 617-661-0565 *E-mail:* bigbear@candlewick.com; salesinfo@candlewick.com *Web Site:* candlewick.com, pg 40

Shay, Alison, University of Wisconsin Press, 728 State St, Suite 443, Madison, WI 53706-1418 *Tel:* 608-263-1110; 608-263-0668 (journal orders) *Toll Free Tel:* 800-621-2736 (book orders) *Fax:* 608-263-1173 *Toll Free Fax:* 800-621-2736 (book orders) *E-mail:* uwiscpress@uwpress.wisc.edu *Web Site:* uwpress.wisc.edu, pg 221

Shea, John, Recorded Books Inc, an RBmedia company, 8400 Corporate Dr, Landover, MD 20785 *Toll Free Tel:* 800-305-3450 *Web Site:* rbmediaglobal.com/recorded-books, pg 172

Shea, Samantha, Georges Borchardt Inc, 136 E 57 St, New York, NY 10022 *Tel:* 212-753-5785 *E-mail:* georges@gbagency.com *Web Site:* www.gbagency.com, pg 451

Sheanin, Wendy, Simon & Schuster, LLC, 1230 Avenue of the Americas, New York, NY 10020 *Tel:* 212-698-7000 *Toll Free Tel:* 800-223-2336 (orders) *Fax:* 212-698-7007 *Toll Free Fax:* 800-943-9831 (orders) *E-mail:* firstname.lastname@simonandschuster.com; purchaseorders@simonandschuster.com (orders) *Web Site:* www.simonandschuster.com, pg 190

Shear, Hayley, Penguin Random House Speakers Bureau, a Penguin Random House company, 1745 Broadway, Mail Drop 13-1, New York, NY 10019 *Tel:* 212-572-2013 *E-mail:* speakers@penguinrandomhouse.com *Web Site:* www.prhspeakers.com, pg 487

Shearon, Sam, Vesuvian Books, 711 Dolly Parton Pkwy, No 4313, Sevierville, TN 37864 *E-mail:* info@vesuvianmedia.com *Web Site:* www.vesuvianmedia.com, pg 224

Sheedy, Charlotte, Charlotte Sheedy Literary Agency Inc, 928 Broadway, Suite 901, New York, NY 10010 *Tel:* 212-780-9800 *Web Site:* www.sheedylit.com, pg 476

Sheehan, David P, Red Chair Press, PO Box 333, South Egremont, MA 01258-0333 *Tel:* 413-528-2398 (edit off) *Toll Free Tel:* 800-328-4929 (orders & cust serv) *E-mail:* info@redchairpress.com *Web Site:* www.redchairpress.com, pg 172

Sheehan, Katie, Berrett-Koehler Publishers Inc, 1333 Broadway, Suite 1000, Oakland, CA 94612 *Tel:* 510-817-2277 *Fax:* 510-817-2278 *E-mail:* bkpub@bkpub.com *Web Site:* www.bkconnection.com, pg 29

Sheehan, Rose, Farrar, Straus & Giroux, LLC, 120 Broadway, New York, NY 10271 *Tel:* 212-741-6900 *E-mail:* fsg.publicity@fsgbooks.com; sales@fsgbooks.com *Web Site:* us.macmillan.com/fsg, pg 70

Sheere, Dara, Penguin Random House Canada, a Penguin Random House company, 320 Front St W, Suite 1400, Toronto, ON M5V 3B6, Canada *Tel:* 416-364-4449 *Toll Free Tel:* 888-523-9292 (cust serv) *E-mail:* canadaweb@penguinrandomhouse.com; customerservicescanada@penguinrandomhouse.com *Web Site:* www.penguinrandomhouse.ca, pg 416

Sheerin, Amber, Michigan Library Association (MLA), 3410 Belle Chase Way, Lansing, MI 48911 *Tel:* 517-394-2774 *E-mail:* mla@milibraries.org *Web Site:* www.milibraries.org, pg 510

Sheets, Jami, RISING STAR Award, PO Box 190, Jefferson, OR 97352 *E-mail:* risingstar@womenfictionwriters.org *Web Site:* wfwa.memberclicks.net/rising-star-award, pg 656

Sheets, Jami, STAR Award, PO Box 190, Jefferson, OR 97352 *E-mail:* staraward@womenfictionwriters.org *Web Site:* wfwa.memberclicks.net/star-award, pg 666

Sheets, Jami, Women's Fiction Writers Association (WFWA), PO Box 190, Jefferson, OR 97352 *E-mail:* communications@womensfictionwriters.org; membership@womensfictionwriters.org; programs@womensfictionwriters.org *Web Site:* www.womensfictionwriters.org, pg 522

Sheih, Anita, Henry Holt and Company, LLC, 120 Broadway, 23rd fl, New York, NY 10271 *Tel:* 646-307-5151 *Toll Free Tel:* 888-330-8477 (orders) *Fax:* 646-307-5285 *Web Site:* www.henryholt.com, pg 94

Sheinkopf, Barry, The Writing Center, 601 E Palisade Ave, Suite 4, Englewood Cliffs, NJ 07632 Tel: 201-567-4017 Fax: 201-567-7202 E-mail: writingcenter@optonline.net Web Site: www.writingcenternj.com, pg 559

Shekari, Lauren, Other Press, 267 Fifth Ave, 6th fl, New York, NY 10016 Tel: 212-414-0054 Toll Free Tel: 877-THEOTHER (843-6843) Fax: 212-414-0939 E-mail: editor@otherpress.com; marketing@otherpress.com; publicity@otherpress.com Web Site: otherpress.com, pg 148

Shelley, David, Hachette Book Group Inc, 1290 Avenue of the Americas, New York, NY 10104 Tel: 212-364-1100 Toll Free Tel: 800-759-0190 (cust serv) Fax: 212-364-0933 (intl orders) Toll Free Fax: 800-286-9471 (cust serv) E-mail: customer.service@hbgusa.com; orders@hbgusa.com Web Site: www.hachettebookgroup.com, pg 83

Shelton, Madeleine, 5 Under 35, 90 Broad St, Suite 604, New York, NY 10004 Tel: 212-685-0261 Fax: 212-213-6570 E-mail: nationalbook@nationalbook.org Web Site: www.nationalbook.org, pg 602

Shelton, Madeleine, Medal for Distinguished Contribution to American Letters, 90 Broad St, Suite 604, New York, NY 10004 Tel: 212-685-0261 Fax: 212-213-6570 E-mail: nationalbook@nationalbook.org Web Site: www.nationalbook.org/amerletters.html, pg 631

Shelton, Madeleine, National Book Awards, 90 Broad St, Suite 604, New York, NY 10004 Tel: 212-685-0261 Fax: 212-213-6570 E-mail: nationalbook@nationalbook.org Web Site: www.nationalbook.org, pg 637

Shelton, Madeleine, National Book Foundation, 90 Broad St, Suite 604, New York, NY 10004 Tel: 212-685-0261 Fax: 212-213-6570 E-mail: nationalbook@nationalbook.org Web Site: www.nationalbook.org, pg 526

Shelton, Madeleine, Science + Literature Program, 90 Broad St, Suite 604, New York, NY 10004 Tel: 212-685-0261 Fax: 212-213-6570 E-mail: nationalbook@nationalbook.org Web Site: www.nationalbook.org/programs/science-literature, pg 661

Shelton, Tiffany, St Martin's Press, LLC, 120 Broadway, New York, NY 10271 E-mail: publicity@stmartins.com; trademarketing@stmartins.com; foreignrights@stmartins.com Web Site: us.macmillan.com/smp, pg 181

Shen, Sabrina, Random House Publishing Group, 1745 Broadway, New York, NY 10019 Toll Free Tel: 800-200-3552 Web Site: www.randomhousebooks.com, pg 171

Shen, Tina, Prospect Agency, 551 Valley Rd, PMB 337, Upper Montclair, NJ 07043 Tel: 718-788-3217 Web Site: www.prospectagency.com, pg 472

Shepard, Aaron, Shepard Publications, 1117 N Garden St, Apt 302, Bellingham, WA 98225 Web Site: www.shepardpub.com, pg 187

Shepard, Christopher, Aurous Inc, PO Box 20490, New York, NY 10017 Tel: 212-628-9729 Fax: 212-535-7861, pg 449

Shepard, Diane, Bear & Co Inc, One Park St, Rochester, VT 05767 Tel: 802-767-3174 Toll Free Tel: 800-932-3277 Fax: 802-767-3726 E-mail: customerservice@InnerTraditions.com Web Site: InnerTraditions.com, pg 26

Shepard, Diane, Inner Traditions International Ltd, One Park St, Rochester, VT 05767 Tel: 802-767-3174 Toll Free Tel: 800-246-8648 Fax: 802-767-3726 E-mail: customerservice@InnerTraditions.com Web Site: www.InnerTraditions.com, pg 101

Shepard, Judith, The Permanent Press, 4170 Noyac Rd, Sag Harbor, NY 11963 Tel: 631-725-1101 E-mail: shepard@thepermanentpress.com Web Site: thepermanentpress.com, pg 158

Shepherd, Frederick M, Gene E & Adele R Malott Prize for Recording Community Activism, c/o Frederick M Shepherd, 3900 Seventh Ave S, Birmingham, AL 35222 Web Site: langumfoundation.org/about-prizes/recording-community-activism, pg 629

Shepherd, Jackie, Candlewick Press, 99 Dover St, Somerville, MA 02144-2825 Tel: 617-661-3330 Fax: 617-661-0565 E-mail: bigbear@candlewick.com; salesinfo@candlewick.com Web Site: candlewick.com, pg 40

Sheppard, Alan, Goose Lane Editions, 500 Beaverbrook Ct, Suite 330, Fredericton, NB E3B 5X4, Canada Tel: 506-450-4251 Toll Free Tel: 888-926-8377 Fax: 506-459-4991 E-mail: orders@gooselane.com Web Site: www.gooselane.com, pg 407

Sheppard, Emily, Penguin Random House Canada, a Penguin Random House company, 320 Front St W, Suite 1400, Toronto, ON M5V 3B6, Canada Tel: 416-364-4449 Toll Free Tel: 888-523-9292 (cust serv) E-mail: canadaweb@penguinrandomhouse.com; customerservicescanada@penguinrandomhouse.com Web Site: www.penguinrandomhouse.ca, pg 416

Sheppard, Justin, Bisk Education, 9417 Princess Palm Ave, Suite 400, Tampa, FL 33619 Tel: 813-621-6200 E-mail: media@bisk.com Web Site: www.bisk.com, pg 29

Sheppard, Ruth, Casemate | publishers, 1950 Lawrence Rd, Havertown, PA 19083 Tel: 610-853-9131 Fax: 610-853-9146 E-mail: casemate@casematepublishers.com Web Site: www.casematepublishers.com, pg 41

Sheppard, Scott, Quarto Publishing Group USA Inc, 100 Cummings Ctr, Suite 265D, Beverly, MA 01915 Tel: 978-282-9590 Toll Free Tel: 800-328-0590 (sales) Fax: 978-283-2742 E-mail: sales@quartous.com Web Site: www.quartoknows.com, pg 168

Sherer, John, The University of North Carolina Press, 116 S Boundary St, Chapel Hill, NC 27514-3808 Tel: 919-966-3561; 919-966-7449 (orders) Toll Free Tel: 800-848-3224 (orders) Fax: 919-962-2704 (orders) Toll Free Fax: 800-272-6817 (orders) E-mail: uncpress@unc.edu Web Site: uncpress.org, pg 218

Sherer, Talia, Macmillan, 120 Broadway, 22nd fl, New York, NY 10271 E-mail: press.inquiries@macmillan.com Web Site: us.macmillan.com, pg 122

Sheridan, Michael, Educational Insights®, 152 W Walnut St, Suite 201, Gardena, CA 90248 Toll Free Tel: 800-995-4436 Toll Free Fax: 888-892-8731 E-mail: info@educationalinsights.com; cs@educationalinsights.com Web Site: www.educationalinsights.com, pg 64

Sheridan-Witterschein, Jackie, National Braille Press, 88 Saint Stephen St, Boston, MA 02115-4312 Tel: 617-266-6160 Toll Free Tel: 800-548-7323 (cust serv); 888-965-8965 Fax: 617-437-0456 E-mail: contact@nbp.org Web Site: www.nbp.org, pg 137

Sherman, Amy, University of Pittsburgh Press, 7500 Thomas Blvd, Pittsburgh, PA 15260 Tel: 412-383-2456 Fax: 412-383-2466 E-mail: info@upress.pitt.edu Web Site: www.upress.pitt.edu, pg 219

Sherman, Aurora, The Ralph Waldo Emerson Award, 1606 New Hampshire Ave NW, Washington, DC 20009 Tel: 202-265-3808 Fax: 202-986-1601 E-mail: awards@pbk.org Web Site: www.pbk.org/bookawards, pg 599

Sherman, Aurora, The Christian Gauss Award, 1606 New Hampshire Ave NW, Washington, DC 20009 Tel: 202-265-3808 Fax: 202-986-1601 E-mail: awards@pbk.org Web Site: www.pbk.org/bookawards, pg 605

Sherman, Aurora, Phi Beta Kappa Award in Science, 1606 New Hampshire Ave NW, Washington, DC 20009 Tel: 202-265-3808 Fax: 202-986-1601 E-mail: awards@pbk.org Web Site: www.pbk.org/bookawards, pg 649

Sherman, Ken, Ken Sherman & Associates, 8530 Holloway Dr, Suite 220, West Hollywood, CA 90069 Tel: 310-273-8840 E-mail: kenshermanassociates@gmail.com Web Site: www.kenshermanassociates.com, pg 476

Sherman, Rebecca, Writers House, 21 W 26 St, New York, NY 10010 Tel: 212-685-2400 Web Site: www.writershouse.com, pg 482

Sherman, Sarah, Candlewick Press, 99 Dover St, Somerville, MA 02144-2825 Tel: 617-661-3330 Fax: 617-661-0565 E-mail: bigbear@candlewick.com; salesinfo@candlewick.com Web Site: candlewick.com, pg 40

Sherman, Stephen, Radix Press, 11715 Bandlon Dr, Houston, TX 77072 Tel: 281-879-5688 Web Site: www.vvfh.org; www.specialforcesbooks.com; vinabooks.us, pg 169

Sherman, Wendy, Wendy Sherman Associates Inc, 138 W 25 St, Suite 1018, New York, NY 10001 Tel: 212-279-9027 E-mail: submissions@wsherman.com Web Site: www.wsherman.com, pg 476

Sherr, Roger, Genealogical Publishing Co, 3600 Clipper Mill Rd, Suite 229, Baltimore, MD 21211 Tel: 410-837-8271 Toll Free Tel: 800-296-6687 Fax: 410-752-8492 Toll Free Fax: 800-599-9561 E-mail: info@genealogical.com; web@genealogical.com Web Site: www.genealogical.com, pg 77

Sherrard, Benjamin, Sourcebooks LLC, 1935 Brookdale Rd, Suite 139, Naperville, IL 60563 Tel: 630-961-3900 Toll Free Tel: 800-432-7444 Fax: 630-961-2168 E-mail: info@sourcebooks.com Web Site: www.sourcebooks.com, pg 195

Sherry, Cynthia, Academy Chicago Publishers, 814 N Franklin St, Chicago, IL 60610 Tel: 312-337-0747 Toll Free Tel: 800-888-4741 (orders) Fax: 312-337-5110 E-mail: frontdesk@chicagoreviewpress.com Web Site: www.chicagoreviewpress.com, pg 3

Sherry, Cynthia, Chicago Review Press, 814 N Franklin St, Chicago, IL 60610 Tel: 312-337-0747 Toll Free Tel: 800-888-4741 Fax: 312-337-5110 E-mail: frontdesk@chicagoreviewpress.com Web Site: www.chicagoreviewpress.com, pg 46

Sherry, Cynthia, Triumph Books LLC, 814 N Franklin St, Chicago, IL 60610 Tel: 312-337-0747 Toll Free Tel: 800-888-4741 (cust serv) Fax: 312-280-5470; 312-337-5985 Web Site: www.triumphbooks.com, pg 209

Shewchuk, Alysia, House of Anansi Press Inc, 128 Sterling Rd, Lower Level, Toronto, ON M6R 2B7, Canada Tel: 416-363-4343 Fax: 416-363-1017 E-mail: customerservice@houseofanansi.com Web Site: houseofanansi.com, pg 409

Shi, Kelly, HarperCollins Publishers LLC, 195 Broadway, New York, NY 10007 Tel: 212-207-7000 Web Site: www.harpercollins.com, pg 87

Shickmanter, Margo, Avid Reader Press, 1230 Avenue of the Americas, New York, NY 10020 Web Site: avidreaderpress.com, pg 23

Shield, Nina, HarperCollins Publishers LLC, 195 Broadway, New York, NY 10007 Tel: 212-207-7000 Web Site: www.harpercollins.com, pg 86

Shields, Brian, American Medical Association (AMA), AMA Plaza, 330 N Wabash, Suite 39300, Chicago, IL 60611-5885 Tel: 312-464-5000; 312-464-4430 (media & edit) Toll Free Tel: 800-621-8335 E-mail: media@ama-assn.org (media & edit); bookandonlinesales@ama-assn.org (volume book/ebook sales) Web Site: www.ama-assn.org, pg 11

Shields, Brian, American Medical Association (AMA), AMA Plaza, 330 N Wabash, Suite 39300, Chicago, IL 60611-5885 Tel: 312-464-5000 Toll Free Tel: 800-621-8335 E-mail: media@ama-assn.org (media & edit) Web Site: www.ama-assn.org; www.jamanetwork.org, pg 495

Shields, Charlie, The University of Arkansas Press, McIlroy House, 105 N McIlroy Ave, Fayetteville, AR 72701 Tel: 479-575-7544 E-mail: info@uapress.com Web Site: www.uapress.com, pg 214

Shilhanek, Jared, American Public Works Association (APWA), 1200 Main St, Suite 1400, Kansas City, MO 64105-2100 Tel: 816-472-6100 Toll Free Tel: 800-848-APWA (848-2792) Fax: 816-472-1610 Web Site: www.apwa.org, pg 12

Shillingford, Gordon, J Gordon Shillingford Publishing Inc, PO Box 86, RPO Corydon Ave, Winnipeg, MB R3M 3S3, Canada *Tel:* 204-779-6967 *E-mail:* jgshill2@mymts.net *Web Site:* www.jgshillingford.com, pg 419

Shilova, Anna, Macmillan, 120 Broadway, 22nd fl, New York, NY 10271 *E-mail:* press.inquiries@macmillan.com *Web Site:* us.macmillan.com, pg 122

Shimabukuro, Lisa, St Martin's Press, LLC, 120 Broadway, New York, NY 10271 *E-mail:* publicity@stmartins.com; trademarketing@stmartins.com; foreignrights@stmartins.com *Web Site:* us.macmillan.com/smp, pg 181

Shin, Jinna, Random House Children's Books, c/o Penguin Random House LLC, 1745 Broadway, New York, NY 10019 *Tel:* 212-782-9000 *Web Site:* www.rhcbooks.com, pg 170

Shin, Mina, BoardSource, 750 Ninth St NW, Suite 520, Washington, DC 20001-4793 *Tel:* 202-349-2500 *E-mail:* members@boardsource.org; mediarelations@boardsource.org *Web Site:* www.boardsource.org, pg 33

Shindelbower, Chris, Bisk Education, 9417 Princess Palm Ave, Suite 400, Tampa, FL 33619 *Tel:* 813-621-6200 *E-mail:* media@bisk.com *Web Site:* www.bisk.com, pg 29

Shine, Deborah, Star Bright Books Inc, 13 Landsdowne St, Cambridge, MA 02139 *Tel:* 617-354-1300 *Fax:* 617-354-1399 *E-mail:* info@starbrightbooks.com; orders@starbrightbooks.com *Web Site:* www.starbrightbooks.org, pg 197

Shinsato, David, Savant Books & Publications LLC, 2630 Kapiolani Blvd, Suite 1601, Honolulu, HI 96826 *Tel:* 808-941-3927 (9AM-noon HST) *E-mail:* savantbooks@gmail.com; savantdistribution@gmail.com *Web Site:* www.savantbooksandpublications.com; www.savantdistribution.com, pg 182

Shipman, Dawn, Cascade Christian Writers (CCW), PO Box 22, Gladstone, OR 97027 *Tel:* 503-393-3356 *E-mail:* contact@oregonchristianwriters.org *Web Site:* oregonchristianwriters.org, pg 503

Shipman, Dawn, Cascade Christian Writers Conference, PO Box 22, Gladstone, OR 97027 *Tel:* 503-393-3356 *E-mail:* business@cascadechristianwriters.org *Web Site:* cascadechristianwriters.org, pg 553

Shipton, Justin (JD), BWL Publishing Inc, 5030 44 St, Drayton Valley, AB T7A 1B9, Canada *Tel:* 780-833-1215 *E-mail:* bookswelove@telus.net *Web Site:* bookswelove.net; bwlpublishing.ca, pg 398

Shirley, Melissa, Canadian First Book Prize, 363 Parkridge Crescent, Oakville, ON L6M 1A8, Canada *Tel:* 905-618-0420 *E-mail:* info@griffinpoetryprize.com; publicity@griffinpoetryprize.com *Web Site:* griffinpoetryprize.com, pg 586

Shirley, Melissa, Griffin Poetry Prize, 363 Parkridge Crescent, Oakville, ON L6M 1A8, Canada *Tel:* 905-618-0420 *E-mail:* info@griffinpoetryprize.com; publicity@griffinpoetryprize.com *Web Site:* griffinpoetryprize.com, pg 609

Shirota, Sawako, Candlewick Press, 99 Dover St, Somerville, MA 02144-2825 *Tel:* 617-661-3330 *Fax:* 617-661-0565 *E-mail:* bigbear@candlewick.com; salesinfo@candlewick.com *Web Site:* candlewick.com, pg 40

Shirzad, Mr Farhad, Ibex Publishers, PO Box 30087, Bethesda, MD 20824 *Tel:* 301-718-8188 *Toll Free Tel:* 888-718-8188 *Fax:* 301-907-8707 *E-mail:* info@ibexpub.com *Web Site:* ibexpub.com, pg 98

Shivers, Lottchen, Picador, 120 Broadway, New York, NY 10271 *Tel:* 646-307-5151 *Fax:* 212-253-9627 *E-mail:* publicity@picadorusa.com *Web Site:* us.macmillan.com/picador, pg 159

Shoaff, Will Tom, Grand & Archer Publishing, 463 Coyote, Cathedral City, CA 92234 *Tel:* 323-493-2785 *E-mail:* grandarcher@gmail.com, pg 80

Shodin, Stephen, Penguin Random House LLC, 1745 Broadway, New York, NY 10019 *Tel:* 212-782-9000 *Toll Free Tel:* 800-726-0600 *Web Site:* www.penguinrandomhouse.com, pg 155

Shoemaker, Susannah, Princeton University Press, 41 William St, Princeton, NJ 08540-5237 *Tel:* 609-258-4900 *Fax:* 609-258-6305 *E-mail:* info@press.princeton.edu *Web Site:* press.princeton.edu, pg 164

Shokoff, Elisa, Simon & Schuster Audio, 1230 Avenue of the Americas, New York, NY 10020 *Web Site:* audio.simonandschuster.com, pg 189

Shone, Anne, Penguin Random House Canada, a Penguin Random House company, 320 Front St W, Suite 1400, Toronto, ON M5V 3B6, Canada *Tel:* 416-364-4449 *Toll Free Tel:* 888-523-9292 (cust serv) *E-mail:* canadaweb@penguinrandomhouse.com; customerservicescanada@penguinrandomhouse.com *Web Site:* www.penguinrandomhouse.ca, pg 416

Shone, Anne, Tundra Book Group, 320 Front St W, Suite 1400, Toronto, ON M5V 3B6, Canada *Tel:* 416-364-4449 *Toll Free Tel:* 888-523-9292 (orders); 800-588-1074 *E-mail:* youngreaders@penguinrandomhouse.com *Web Site:* www.tundrabooks.com, pg 421

Shook, Sharon, Harvest House Publishers Inc, PO Box 41210, Eugene, OR 97404-0322 *Tel:* 541-343-0123 *Toll Free Tel:* 888-501-6991 *Fax:* 541-343-9711 *E-mail:* admin@harvesthousepublishers.com; permissions@harvesthousepublishers.com *Web Site:* harvesthousepublishers.com, pg 88

Shor, Deborah, Oxford University Press USA, 198 Madison Ave, New York, NY 10016 *Toll Free Tel:* 800-451-7556 (orders); 800-445-9714 (cust serv) *Fax:* 919-677-1303 *E-mail:* custserv.us@oup.com *Web Site:* global.oup.com, pg 149

Shore, Julie, Television Academy, 5220 Lankershim Blvd, North Hollywood, CA 91601-3109 *Tel:* 818-754-2800 *Web Site:* www.emmys.com, pg 521

Shorney, John, Hope Publishing Co, 380 S Main Place, Carol Stream, IL 60188 *Tel:* 630-665-3200 *Toll Free Tel:* 800-323-1049 *E-mail:* hope@hopepublishing.com *Web Site:* www.hopepublishing.com, pg 95

Shorney, Scott A, Hope Publishing Co, 380 S Main Place, Carol Stream, IL 60188 *Tel:* 630-665-3200 *Toll Free Tel:* 800-323-1049 *E-mail:* hope@hopepublishing.com *Web Site:* www.hopepublishing.com, pg 95

Shorney, Steve, Hope Publishing Co, 380 S Main Place, Carol Stream, IL 60188 *Tel:* 630-665-3200 *Toll Free Tel:* 800-323-1049 *E-mail:* hope@hopepublishing.com *Web Site:* www.hopepublishing.com, pg 95

Shortt, Megan, Random House Children's Books, c/o Penguin Random House LLC, 1745 Broadway, New York, NY 10019 *Tel:* 212-782-9000 *Web Site:* www.rhcbooks.com, pg 170

Shotts, Jeffrey, Graywolf Press, 212 Third Ave N, Suite 485, Minneapolis, MN 55401 *Tel:* 651-641-0077 *Fax:* 651-641-0036 *E-mail:* wolves@graywolfpress.org (no ms queries, sample chapters or proposals) *Web Site:* www.graywolfpress.org, pg 81

Shoults, Janice, EDGE Science Fiction & Fantasy Publishing Inc, PO Box 1714, Calgary, AB T2P 2L7, Canada *Tel:* 403-254-0160 *Fax:* 403-254-0456 *E-mail:* admin@hadespublications.com *Web Site:* www.edgewebsite.com, pg 401

Showers, Eric, Howard Morhaim Literary Agency Inc, 30 Pierrepont St, Brooklyn, NY 11201-3371 *Tel:* 718-222-8400 *E-mail:* info@morhaimliterary.com *Web Site:* www.morhaimliterary.com, pg 470

Shows, Dawn, Eric Hoffer Award, PO Box 11, Titusville, NJ 08560 *E-mail:* info@hofferaward.com *Web Site:* www.hofferaward.com, pg 613

Shrader, Cally, Society for Industrial & Applied Mathematics, 3600 Market St, 6th fl, Philadelphia, PA 19104-2688 *Tel:* 215-382-9800 *Toll Free Tel:* 800-447-7426 *E-mail:* siam@siam.org *Web Site:* www.siam.org, pg 192

Shrestha, Heather, Paul H Brookes Publishing Co Inc, PO Box 10624, Baltimore, MD 21285-0624 *Tel:* 410-337-9580 (outside US & CN) *Toll Free Tel:* 800-638-3775 (US & CN) *Fax:* 410-337-8539 *E-mail:* custserv@brookespublishing.com *Web Site:* www.brookespublishing.com, pg 37

Shubert, Michelle, Safer Society Press, PO Box 340, Brandon, VT 05733-0340 *Tel:* 802-247-3132 *Fax:* 802-247-4233 *E-mail:* info@safersociety.org *Web Site:* safersocietypress.org, pg 179

Shultz, Jennifer, Pennsylvania State Data Center, Penn State Harrisburg, 777 W Harrisburg Pike, Middletown, PA 17057-4898 *Tel:* 717-948-6336 *Fax:* 717-948-6754 *E-mail:* pasdc@psu.edu *Web Site:* pasdc.hbg.psu.edu, pg 157

Shultz, Melissa, Jim Donovan Literary, 5635 SMU Blvd, Suite 201, Dallas, TX 75206 *Tel:* 214-696-9411 *E-mail:* jdlqueries@sbcglobal.net, pg 456

Shumaker, Bradley E, Center for Creative Leadership LLC, One Leadership Place, Greensboro, NC 27410-9427 *Tel:* 336-545-2810; 336-288-7210 *Fax:* 336-282-3284 *E-mail:* info@ccl.org *Web Site:* shop.ccl.org/usa/books, pg 43

Shuman, Jesse, Random House Publishing Group, 1745 Broadway, New York, NY 10019 *Toll Free Tel:* 800-200-3552 *Web Site:* www.randomhousebooks.com, pg 171

Shumway, Sarah, Bloomsbury Publishing Inc, 1385 Broadway, 5th fl, New York, NY 10018 *Tel:* 212-419-5300 *E-mail:* marketingusa@bloomsbury.com; adultpublicityusa@bloomsbury.com; askacademic@bloomsbury.com *Web Site:* www.bloomsbury.com, pg 31

Shur, Rudy, Square One Publishers Inc, 115 Herricks Rd, Garden City Park, NY 11040 *Tel:* 516-535-2010 *Toll Free Tel:* 877-900-BOOK (900-2665) *Fax:* 516-535-2014 *E-mail:* sq1publish@aol.com *Web Site:* www.squareonepublishers.com, pg 196

Shurka, Larissa, Princeton University Press, 41 William St, Princeton, NJ 08540-5237 *Tel:* 609-258-4900 *Fax:* 609-258-6305 *E-mail:* info@press.princeton.edu *Web Site:* press.princeton.edu, pg 164

Shurtleff, William, Soyinfo Center, 1021 Dolores Dr, Lafayette, CA 94549-0234 *Tel:* 925-283-2991 *Web Site:* www.soyinfocenter.com, pg 196

Shuster, Todd, Aevitas Creative Management LLC, 19 W 21 St, Suite 501, New York, NY 10010 *Tel:* 212-765-6900 *Web Site:* www.aevitascreative.com, pg 448

Shutts, Frank, One-Act Playwriting Competition, 600 Wolfe St, Alexandria, VA 22314 *Tel:* 703-683-5778 (ext 2) *Fax:* 703-683-1378 *E-mail:* oneactslta@gmail.com *Web Site:* thelittletheatre.com, pg 644

Sibbald, Anne, Janklow & Nesbit Associates, 285 Madison Ave, 21st fl, New York, NY 10017 *Tel:* 212-421-1700 *Fax:* 212-355-1403 *E-mail:* info@janklow.com; submissions@janklow.com; filmtvrights@janklow.com *Web Site:* www.janklowandnesbit.com, pg 464

Sibiga, Matthew, Knopf Canada, 320 Front St W, Suite 1400, Toronto, ON M5V 3B6, Canada *Tel:* 416-364-4449 *Toll Free Tel:* 888-523-9292 *Fax:* 416-598-7764 *Web Site:* www.penguinrandomhouse.ca, pg 411

Siciliano, John, Viking Penguin, c/o Penguin Random House LLC, 1745 Broadway, New York, NY 10019 *Tel:* 212-782-9000 *Web Site:* www.penguin.com/overview-vikingbooks/; www.penguin.com/pamela-dorman-books-overview/; www.penguin.com/penguin-classics-overview/; www.penguin.com/penguin-life-overview/, pg 225

Sicoli, Dan, Slipstream Annual Poetry Chapbook Contest, PO Box 2071, Dept W-1, Niagara Falls, NY 14301 *Web Site:* www.slipstreampress.org/contest.html, pg 663

Siconolfi, Marcie, Cold Spring Harbor Laboratory Press, 500 Sunnyside Blvd, Woodbury, NY 11797-2924 *Tel:* 516-422-4100 *Toll Free Tel:* 800-843-4388 *E-mail:* cshpress@cshl.edu *Web Site:* www.cshlpress.com, pg 50

Siddiqui, Leila, DK, c/o Penguin Random House LLC, 1745 Broadway, 20th fl, New York, NY 10019 *Tel:* 646-674-4000 *Toll Free Tel:* 800-733-3000 *Fax:* 646-674-4020 *E-mail:* marketing@dk.

com (lib servs); publicity@dk.com; csorders@penguinrandomhouse.com; customerservice@penguinrandomhouse.com Web Site: www.dk.com, pg 60

Siddiqui, Saher, Chronicle Books LLC, 680 Second St, San Francisco, CA 94107 Tel: 415-537-4200 Fax: 415-537-4460 (perms) E-mail: hello@chroniclebooks.com; subrights@chroniclebooks.com Web Site: www.chroniclebooks.com, pg 48

Siddiqui, Shereen, Dissertation.com, 200 Spectrum Center Dr, 3rd fl, Irvine, CA 92618 Tel: 561-750-4344 Toll Free Tel: 800-636-8329 Fax: 561-750-6797 Web Site: www.dissertation.com, pg 60

Siddiqui, Shereen PhD, Universal-Publishers Inc, 200 Spectrum Center Dr, Suite 300, Irvine, CA 92618-5004 Tel: 561-750-4344 Toll Free Tel: 800-636-8329 (US only) Fax: 561-750-6797 Web Site: www.universal-publishers.com, pg 213

Sidle, Makenna, Tor Publishing Group, 120 Broadway, New York, NY 10271 Toll Free Tel: 800-455-0340 (Macmillan) E-mail: torpublicity@tor.com; forgepublicity@forgebooks.com Web Site: us.macmillan.com/torpublishinggroup, pg 208

Sieck, Gary, University of Baltimore - Yale Gordon College of Arts & Sciences, Liberal Arts & Policy Bldg, 10 W Preston St, Rm 107, Baltimore, MD 21201 Web Site: www.ubalt.edu/cas/about-the-college/schools-and-divisions/school-of-communications-design, pg 566

Siegel, Jill, Gallery Books, 1230 Avenue of the Americas, New York, NY 10020 Toll Free Tel: 800-456-6798 Fax: 212-698-7284 E-mail: consumer.customerservice@simonandschuster.com Web Site: www.simonandschuster.com, pg 76

Siegel, Marisa, Northwestern University Press, 629 Noyes St, Evanston, IL 60208-4210 Tel: 847-491-2046 Toll Free Tel: 800-621-2736 (orders only) Fax: 847-491-8150 E-mail: nupress@northwestern.edu Web Site: www.nupress.northwestern.edu, pg 143

Siegel, Mark, Roaring Brook Press, 120 Broadway, New York, NY 10271 Tel: 646-307-5151 Web Site: us.macmillan.com/publishers/roaring-brook-press, pg 175

Sieger, Daniel, Cengage Learning, 20 Channel Center St, Boston, MA 02210 Tel: 617-289-7700 Toll Free Tel: 800-354-9706 Fax: 617-289-7844 E-mail: esales@cengage.com Web Site: www.cengage.com, pg 43

Siekerka, Michele, New Jersey Business & Industry Association (NJBIA), 10 W Lafayette St, Trenton, NJ 08608-2002 Tel: 609-393-7707 Web Site: njbia.org, pg 514

Sielaff, Claire, Ulysses Press, 195 Montague St, 14th fl, Brooklyn, NY 11201 Tel: 510-601-8301 Toll Free Tel: 800-377-2542 Fax: 510-601-8307 E-mail: ulysses@ulyssespress.com Web Site: www.ulyssespress.com, pg 212

Siembieda, Kevin, Palladium Books Inc, 39074 Webb Ct, Westland, MI 48185 Tel: 734-721-2903 (orders) Web Site: www.palladiumbooks.com, pg 150

Siemon, Alexis, Cornell University Press, Sage House, 512 E State St, Ithaca, NY 14850 Tel: 607-253-2338 E-mail: cupressinfo@cornell.edu; cupress-sales@cornell.edu; cupress-perms@cornell.edu (reprint/class use permissions) Web Site: www.cornellpress.cornell.edu, pg 52

Sierra, Hector, National Geographic Books, 1145 17 St NW, Washington, DC 20036-4688 Tel: 202-857-7000 Toll Free Tel: 877-866-6486 E-mail: ngbooks@cdsfulfillment.com Web Site: www.nationalgeographic.com/books/; ngbooks.buysub.com, pg 138

Sierra, Rodrigo A, American Medical Association (AMA), AMA Plaza, 330 N Wabash, Suite 39300, Chicago, IL 60611-5885 Tel: 312-464-5000 Toll Free Tel: 800-621-8335 E-mail: media@ama-assn.org (media & edit) Web Site: www.ama-assn.org; www.jamanetwork.com, pg 495

Siess, Danielle, Random House Publishing Group, 1745 Broadway, New York, NY 10019 Toll Free Tel: 800-200-3552 Web Site: www.randomhousebooks.com, pg 171

Sigers, Faye, National Association of Black Journalists (NABJ), 1100 Knight Suite 3101, College Park, MD 20742 Tel: 301-405-0248 E-mail: contact@nabj.org; press@nabj.org Web Site: nabjonline.org, pg 511

Signorelli, Michael, Aevitas Creative Management LLC, 19 W 21 St, Suite 501, New York, NY 10010 Tel: 212-765-6900 Web Site: www.aevitascreative.com, pg 448

Signorino, Kathy, Individual Excellence Awards, 30 E Broad St, 33rd fl, Columbus, OH 43215 Tel: 614-466-2613 Fax: 614-466-4494 Web Site: www.oac.state.oh.us, pg 616

Siklos, Richard, United Talent Agency LLC, 9336 Civic Center Dr, Beverly Hills, CA 90210 Tel: 310-273-6700 Web Site: www.unitedtalent.com, pg 481

Sikma, Crystal, Coach House Books, 80 bpNichol Lane, Toronto, ON M5S 3J4, Canada Tel: 416-979-2217 Toll Free Tel: 800-367-6360 (outside Toronto) Fax: 416-977-1158 E-mail: mail@chbooks.com Web Site: www.chbooks.com, pg 400

Sikora, Lynn, Sourcebooks LLC, 1935 Brookdale Rd, Suite 139, Naperville, IL 60563 Tel: 630-961-3900 Toll Free Tel: 800-432-7444 Fax: 630-961-2168 E-mail: info@sourcebooks.com Web Site: www.sourcebooks.com, pg 194

Silber, Blake, Bridge Publications Inc, 5600 E Olympic Blvd, Commerce, CA 90022 Tel: 323-888-6200 Toll Free Tel: 800-722-1733 Fax: 323-888-6202 E-mail: info@bridgepub.com Web Site: www.bridgepub.com, pg 36

Silberblatt, Cindy, Agatha Awards, PO Box 8007, Gaithersburg, MD 20898 Tel: 301-730-1675 E-mail: mdregservices@gmail.com Web Site: malicedomestic.org, pg 570

Silberfeld, Ms Heath Lynn, Enough Said: Editing, Writing, Research, Project Management, 3959 NW 29 Lane, Gainesville, FL 32606 Tel: 352-262-2971 E-mail: enoughsaid@cox.net, pg 439

Silberg, Richard, Poetry Flash Reading Series, 1450 Fourth St, Suite 4, Berkeley, CA 94710 Tel: 510-525-5476 E-mail: editor@poetryflash.org Web Site: poetryflash.org, pg 556

Silberman, Jeff, Folio Literary Management, The Film Center Bldg, 630 Ninth Ave, Suite 1101, New York, NY 10036 Tel: 212-400-1494 Fax: 212-967-0977 Web Site: www.foliolit.com, pg 459

Silbersack, Catryn, Henry Holt and Company, LLC, 120 Broadway, 23rd fl, New York, NY 10271 Tel: 646-307-5151 Toll Free Tel: 888-330-8477 (orders) Fax: 646-307-5285 Web Site: www.henryholt.com, pg 94

Silbersack, John, Philip K Dick Award, PO Box 3447, Hoboken, NJ 07030 Tel: 201-876-2551 Web Site: www.philipkdickaward.org, pg 596

Silfin, Beth, HarperCollins Publishers LLC, 195 Broadway, New York, NY 10007 Tel: 212-207-7000 Web Site: www.harpercollins.com, pg 86

Silk, Emily, Harvard University Press, 79 Garden St, Cambridge, MA 02138-1499 Tel: 617-495-2600; 401-531-2800 (intl orders) Toll Free Tel: 800-405-1619 (orders) Fax: 617-495-5898 (gen); 617-496-4677 (edit & rts); 401-531-2801 (intl orders) Toll Free Fax: 800-406-9145 (orders) E-mail: contact_hup@harvard.edu Web Site: www.hup.harvard.edu, pg 88

Sills, Dr Adam, Hofstra University, Department of English, 204 Mason Hall, Hempstead, NY 11549 Tel: 516-463-5454 E-mail: english@hofstra.edu Web Site: www.hofstra.edu/english, pg 563

Silva, Mick, Zondervan, 3900 Sparks Dr SE, Grand Rapids, MI 49546 Tel: 616-698-6900 Toll Free Tel: 800-226-1122; 800-727-1309 (retail orders) Fax: 616-698-3350 Toll Free Fax: 800-698-3256 (retail orders) E-mail: customercare@harpercollins.com Web Site: www.zondervan.com, pg 236

Silva, Pete, McGraw-Hill School Education Group, 8787 Orion Place, Columbus, OH 43240 Tel: 614-430-4000 Toll Free Tel: 800-848-1567 Web Site: www.mheducation.com, pg 128

Silva, Rita, Simon & Schuster Canada, 166 King St E, Suite 300, Toronto, ON M5A 1J3, Canada Tel: 647-427-8882 Toll Free Tel: 800-387-0446; 800-268-3216 (orders) Fax: 647-430-9446 Toll Free Fax: 888-849-8151 (orders) E-mail: info@simonandschuster.ca Web Site: www.simonandschuster.ca, pg 419

Silver, David, YMAA Publication Center Inc, PO Box 480, Wolfeboro, NH 03894 Tel: 603-569-7988 Toll Free Tel: 800-669-8892 Fax: 603-569-1889 E-mail: info@ymaa.com Web Site: www.ymaa.com, pg 235

Silver, Deirdre, John Wiley & Sons Inc, 111 River St, Hoboken, NJ 07030-5774 Tel: 201-748-6000 Toll Free Tel: 800-225-5945 (cust serv) Fax: 201-748-6088 Web Site: www.wiley.com, pg 230

Silver, Janet, Aevitas Creative Management LLC, 19 W 21 St, Suite 501, New York, NY 10010 Tel: 212-765-6900 Web Site: www.aevitascreative.com, pg 448

Silver, Noel, Mazda Publishers Inc, PO Box 2603, Costa Mesa, CA 92628 Tel: 714-751-5252 Fax: 714-751-4805 E-mail: mazdapub@aol.com Web Site: www.mazdapublishers.com, pg 127

Silverio, Naomi, Farrar, Straus & Giroux Books for Young Readers, 120 Broadway, New York, NY 10271 Tel: 212-741-6900 Toll Free Tel: 888-330-8477 (orders) E-mail: childrens.publicity@macmillanusa.com; childrensrights@macmillanusa.com Web Site: us.macmillan.com/mackids, pg 70

Silverio, Naomi, Roaring Brook Press, 120 Broadway, New York, NY 10271 Tel: 646-307-5151 Web Site: us.macmillan.com/publishers/roaring-brook-press, pg 176

Silverman, Adam, HarperCollins Publishers LLC, 195 Broadway, New York, NY 10007 Tel: 212-207-7000 Web Site: www.harpercollins.com, pg 86

Silverman, Lisa, Harry N Abrams Inc, 195 Broadway, 9th fl, New York, NY 10007 Tel: 212-206-7715 Toll Free Tel: 800-345-1359 Fax: 212-645-8437 E-mail: abrams@abramsbooks.com; publicity@abramsbooks.com; sales@abramsbooks.com Web Site: www.abramsbooks.com, pg 3

Silvestro, Denise, Kensington Publishing Corp, 900 Third Ave, 26th fl, New York, NY 10022 Tel: 212-407-1500 Toll Free Tel: 800-221-2647 Fax: 212-935-0699 Web Site: www.kensingtonbooks.com, pg 109

Sima, Emilia, Practising Law Institute (PLI), 1177 Avenue of the Americas, 2nd fl, New York, NY 10036 Tel: 212-824-5710 (cust serv) Toll Free Tel: 800-260-4PLI (260-4754) Toll Free Fax: 800-321-0093 (cust serv) E-mail: info@pli.edu; membership@pli.edu Web Site: www.pli.edu, pg 163

Simione, Maria, Running Press, 1290 Avenue of the Americas, New York, NY 10104 Tel: 212-364-1100 Toll Free Tel: 800-759-0190 (cust serv) Fax: 212-364-0933 (intl orders) Toll Free Tel: 800-286-9471 (cust serv) E-mail: customer.service@hbgusa.com; orders@hbgusa.com Web Site: www.hachettebookgroup.com/imprint/running-press/; www.moon.com (Moon Travel Guides), pg 178

Simmons, Judson, Center for Publishing Departmental Scholarships, Midtown Ctr, Rm 429, 11 W 42 St, New York, NY 10036 Tel: 212-992-3232 Fax: 212-992-3233 E-mail: pub.center@nyu.edu Web Site: www.scps.nyu.edu, pg 588

Simmons, Judson, New York University, Center for Publishing & Applied Liberal Arts, 7 E 12 St, New York, NY 10003 Tel: 212-998-7200 E-mail: sps.info@nyu.edu Web Site: www.scps.nyu.edu/professional-pathways/topics.html, pg 564

Simmons, Zoe, PAGE International Screenwriting Awards, 7190 W Sunset Blvd, Suite 610, Hollywood, CA 90046 E-mail: info@pageawards.com Web Site: pageawards.com, pg 645

Simms, Maria K, Starcrafts LLC, 68A Fogg Rd, Epping, NH 03042 Tel: 603-734-4300 Toll Free Tel: 866-953-8458 (24/7 message ctr) Fax: 603-734-4311 E-mail: astrosales@astrocom.com Web Site: www.astrocom.com, pg 197

Simon, Asha, Harry N Abrams Inc, 195 Broadway, 9th fl, New York, NY 10007 *Tel:* 212-206-7715 *Toll Free Tel:* 800-345-1359 *Fax:* 212-645-8437 *E-mail:* abrams@abramsbooks.com; publicity@abramsbooks.com; sales@abramsbooks.com *Web Site:* www.abramsbooks.com, pg 3

Simon, Dan, Independent Publishers Caucus (IPC), c/o Seven Stories Press, 140 Watts St, New York, NY 10013 *E-mail:* info@indiepubs.org *Web Site:* www.indiepubs.org, pg 507

Simon, Daniel, Neustadt International Prize for Literature, c/o University of Oklahoma, 630 Parrington Oval, Suite 110, Norman, OK 73019-4033 *Tel:* 405-325-4531 *Web Site:* www.worldliteraturetoday.org; www.neustadtprize.org, pg 639

Simon, Daniel, NSK Neustadt Prize for Children's Literature, c/o University of Oklahoma, 630 Parrington Oval, Suite 110, Norman, OK 73019-4033 *Tel:* 405-325-4531 *Web Site:* www.worldliteraturetoday.org; www.neustadtprize.org, pg 642

Simon, Daniel, Seven Stories Press, 140 Watts St, New York, NY 10013 *Tel:* 212-226-8760 *Toll Free Tel:* 800-733-3000 (orders) *Fax:* 212-226-1411 *E-mail:* sevenstories@sevenstories.com *Web Site:* www.sevenstories.com, pg 186

Simon, Elizabeth, CSWE Press, 333 John Carlyle St, Suite 400, Alexandria, VA 22314-3457 *Tel:* 703-683-8080 *Fax:* 703-683-8493 *E-mail:* publications@cswe.org; info@cswe.org *Web Site:* www.cswe.org, pg 56

Simon, Peter J, W W Norton & Company Inc, 500 Fifth Ave, New York, NY 10110-0017 *Tel:* 212-354-5500 *Toll Free Tel:* 800-233-4830 (orders & cust serv) *Fax:* 212-869-0856 *Toll Free Fax:* 800-458-6515 *E-mail:* orders@wwnorton.com *Web Site:* wwnorton.com, pg 143

Simon, Robin, Penguin Press, c/o Penguin Random House LLC, 1745 Broadway, New York, NY 10019 *Tel:* 212-782-9000 *E-mail:* penguinpress@penguinrandomhouse.com *Web Site:* www.penguin.com/penguin-press-overview/, pg 154

Simon, Robin, Riverhead Books, c/o Penguin Random House LLC, 1745 Broadway, New York, NY 10019 *Tel:* 212-782-9000 *Web Site:* www.penguin.com/riverhead-overview/, pg 175

Simon, Robin, Viking Penguin, c/o Penguin Random House LLC, 1745 Broadway, New York, NY 10019 *Tel:* 212-782-9000 *Web Site:* www.penguin.com/overview-vikingbooks/; www.penguin.com/pameladorman-books-overview/; www.penguin.com/penguin-classics-overview/; www.penguin.com/penguin-life-overview/, pg 225

Simon, Samantha, Chronicle Books LLC, 680 Second St, San Francisco, CA 94107 *Tel:* 415-537-4200 *Fax:* 415-537-4460 (perms) *E-mail:* hello@chroniclebooks.com; subrights@chroniclebooks.com *Web Site:* www.chroniclebooks.com, pg 47

Simon, Samantha, Houghton Mifflin Harcourt Trade & Reference Division, 125 High St, Boston, MA 02110 *Tel:* 617-351-5000 *Web Site:* www.hmhco.com, pg 96

Simon, Tami, Sounds True Inc, 413 S Arthur Ave, Louisville, CO 80027 *Tel:* 303-665-3151 *Toll Free Tel:* 800-333-9185 (US); 888-303-9185 (US & CN) *E-mail:* customerservice@soundstrue.com; stpublicity@soundstrue.com *Web Site:* www.soundstrue.com, pg 194

Simone, Kyra, Zone Books, 633 Vanderbilt St, Brooklyn, NY 11218 *Tel:* 718-686-0048 *E-mail:* info@zonebooks.org *Web Site:* www.zonebooks.org, pg 237

Simonello, Lorraine, Morehouse Publishing, 19 E 34 St, New York, NY 10016 *Tel:* 212-592-1800 *Toll Free Tel:* 800-242-1918 (retail orders only) *E-mail:* churchpublishingorders@pbd.com *Web Site:* www.churchpublishing.org, pg 134

Simonian, Sharis, Island Press, 2000 "M" St NW, Suite 480-B, Washington, DC 20036 *Tel:* 202-232-7933 *Toll Free Tel:* 800-621-2736 *Fax:* 202-234-1328 *E-mail:* info@islandpress.org *Web Site:* www.islandpress.org, pg 104

Simonoff, Eric, WME, 11 Madison Ave, New York, NY 10010 *Tel:* 212-586-5100 *Web Site:* www.wmeagency.com, pg 482

Simons, Asante, HarperCollins Publishers LLC, 195 Broadway, New York, NY 10007 *Tel:* 212-207-7000 *Web Site:* www.harpercollins.com, pg 87

Simons, D Brenton, Newbury Street Press, 99-101 Newbury St, Boston, MA 02116 *Tel:* 617-226-1206 *Toll Free Tel:* 888-296-3447 (NEHGS membership) *Fax:* 617-536-7307 *E-mail:* thebookstore@nehgs.org *Web Site:* www.americanancestors.org, pg 141

Simons, Jasper, American Psychological Association, 750 First St NE, Washington, DC 20002 *Tel:* 202-336-5510 *Toll Free Tel:* 800-374-2721 *Fax:* 202-336-5502 *E-mail:* order@apa.org; booksales@apa.org *Web Site:* www.apa.org/books, pg 11

Simons, Natasha, Gallery Books, 1230 Avenue of the Americas, New York, NY 10020 *Toll Free Tel:* 800-456-6798 *Fax:* 212-698-7284 *E-mail:* consumer.customerservice@simonandschuster.com *Web Site:* www.simonandschuster.com, pg 76

Simonsen, Reka, Simon & Schuster Children's Publishing, 1230 Avenue of the Americas, New York, NY 10020 *Tel:* 212-698-7000 *Web Site:* www.simonandschuster.com/kids; www.simonandschuster.com/teen; simonandschuster.net; simonandschuster.biz, pg 189

Simonson, Emily, Simon & Schuster, 1230 Avenue of the Americas, New York, NY 10020 *Tel:* 212-698-7000 *Toll Free Tel:* 800-223-2348 (cust serv); 800-223-2336 (orders) *Toll Free Fax:* 800-943-9831 (orders) *Web Site:* simonandschusterpublishing.com/simonandschuster/, pg 188

Simpkins, Adam, The Continuing Legal Education Society of British Columbia (CLEBC), 500-1155 W Pender St, Vancouver, BC V6E 2P4, Canada *Tel:* 604-669-3544; 604-893-2121 (cust serv) *Toll Free Tel:* 800-663-0437 (CN) *Fax:* 604-669-9260 *E-mail:* custserv@cle.bc.ca *Web Site:* www.cle.bc.ca, pg 400

Simpson, M Lui, Association of American Publishers (AAP), 455 Massachusetts Ave NW, Suite 700, Washington, DC 20001-2777 *Tel:* 202-347-3375 *Fax:* 202-347-3690 *E-mail:* info@publishers.org *Web Site:* publishers.org, pg 498

Simpson, Martha, Sydney Taylor Book Award, PO Box 1118, Teaneck, NJ 07666 *Tel:* 201-371-3255 *E-mail:* sydneytaylorbookaward@jewishlibraries.org; info@jewishlibraries.org *Web Site:* jewishlibraries.org/sydney_taylor_book_award, pg 668

Simpson, Michael, Carter G Woodson Book Awards, 8555 16 St, Suite 500, Silver Spring, MD 20910 *Tel:* 301-588-1800 *E-mail:* ncss@ncss.org *Web Site:* www.socialstudies.org/membership/awards/carter-g-woodson-book-awards, pg 677

Simpson, Zachary, Candlewick Press, 99 Dover St, Somerville, MA 02144-2825 *Tel:* 617-661-3330 *Fax:* 617-661-0565 *E-mail:* bigbear@candlewick.com; salesinfo@candlewick.com *Web Site:* candlewick.com, pg 40

Simpson-Vos, Mark, The University of North Carolina Press, 116 S Boundary St, Chapel Hill, NC 27514-3808 *Tel:* 919-966-3561; 919-966-7449 (orders) *Toll Free Tel:* 800-848-3224 (orders) *Fax:* 919-962-2704 (orders) *Toll Free Fax:* 800-272-6817 (orders) *E-mail:* uncpress@unc.edu *Web Site:* uncpress.org, pg 218

Simqu, Blaise R, SAGE Publishing, 2455 Teller Rd, Thousand Oaks, CA 91320 *Toll Free Tel:* 800-818-7243 *Toll Free Fax:* 800-583-2665 *E-mail:* info@sagepub.com; orders@sagepub.com *Web Site:* www.sagepublishing.com, pg 180

Sims, Michael, The MIT Press, One Broadway, 12th fl, Cambridge, MA 02142 *Tel:* 617-253-5255 *Toll Free Tel:* 800-405-1619 (orders) *Fax:* 617-258-6779; 617-577-1545 (orders) *Web Site:* mitpress.mit.edu, pg 132

Sims-Nichols, Rebecca, Cedar Grove Publishing, 3205 Elmhurst St, Rowlett, TX 75088 *Tel:* 415-364-8292 *E-mail:* queries@cedargrovebooks.com *Web Site:* www.cedargrovebooks.com, pg 43

Sinasac, Joseph, Novalis Publishing, One Eglinton Ave E, Suite 800, Toronto, ON M4P 3A1, Canada *Tel:* 416-363-3303 *Toll Free Tel:* 877-702-7773 *Fax:* 416-363-9409 *Toll Free Fax:* 877-702-7775 *E-mail:* books@novalis.ca *Web Site:* www.novalis.ca, pg 414

Sinclair, Ariana, HarperCollins Publishers LLC, 195 Broadway, New York, NY 10007 *Tel:* 212-207-7000 *Web Site:* www.harpercollins.com, pg 87

Sinclair, Stephanie, McClelland & Stewart Ltd, 320 Front St W, Suite 1400, Toronto, ON M5V 3B6, Canada *Tel:* 416-364-4449 *Toll Free Tel:* 888-523-9292 *E-mail:* customerservicescanada@penguinrandomhouse.com; mcclellandsubmissions@prh.com *Web Site:* penguinrandomhouse.ca/imprints/mcclelland-stewart, pg 412

Sindwani, PK, American Booksellers Association, 600 Mamaroneck Ave, Suite 400, Harrison, NY 10528 *Tel:* 914-406-7500 *Toll Free Tel:* 800-637-0037 *Fax:* 914-417-4013 *E-mail:* info@bookweb.org *Web Site:* www.bookweb.org, pg 494

Singer, Jeremy, The College Board, 250 Vesey St, New York, NY 10281 *Tel:* 212-713-8000 *Toll Free Tel:* 866-630-9305 *Web Site:* www.collegeboard.com, pg 50

Singerline, Robert, Scepter Publishers, PO Box 360694, Strongsville, OH 44149 *Tel:* 212-354-0670 *Toll Free Tel:* 800-322-8773 *Fax:* 646-417-7707 *E-mail:* info@scepterpublishers.org *Web Site:* www.scepterpublishers.org, pg 183

Siniscalchi, Viana, Alloy Entertainment LLC, 30 Hudson Yards, 22nd fl, New York, NY 10001, pg 7

Sinnott, Heidi Ottley, Sun Valley Writers' Conference (SVWC), Galleria Bldg, 2nd fl, 351 Leadville Ave N, Ketchum, ID 83340 *Tel:* 208-726-5454 *E-mail:* info@svwc.com *Web Site:* svwc.com, pg 558

Sinocchi, Michael, Productivity Press, 605 Third Ave, 22nd fl, New York, NY 10158 *Toll Free Tel:* 800-634-7064 (orders); 800-797-3803 *E-mail:* orders@taylorandfrancis.com *Web Site:* www.crcpress.com, pg 165

Sinusas, Felicia, Harvard Business Review Press, 20 Guest St, Suite 700, Brighton, MA 02135 *Tel:* 617-783-7400 *Fax:* 617-783-7489 *E-mail:* custserv@hbsp.harvard.edu *Web Site:* www.harvardbusiness.org, pg 87

Sipala, Cindy, Running Press, 1290 Avenue of the Americas, New York, NY 10104 *Tel:* 212-364-1100 *Toll Free Tel:* 800-759-0190 (cust serv) *Fax:* 212-364-0933 (intl orders) *Toll Free Fax:* 800-286-9471 (cust serv) *E-mail:* customer.service@hbgusa.com; orders@hbgusa.com *Web Site:* www.hachettebookgroup.com/imprint/running-press/; www.moon.com (Moon Travel Guides), pg 178

Sipala, Frank, Running Press, 1290 Avenue of the Americas, New York, NY 10104 *Tel:* 212-364-1100 *Toll Free Tel:* 800-759-0190 (cust serv) *Fax:* 212-364-0933 (intl orders) *Toll Free Fax:* 800-286-9471 (cust serv) *E-mail:* customer.service@hbgusa.com; orders@hbgusa.com *Web Site:* www.hachettebookgroup.com/imprint/running-press/; www.moon.com (Moon Travel Guides), pg 178

Sipe, Keith R, Carolina Academic Press, 700 Kent St, Durham, NC 27701 *Tel:* 919-489-7486 *Toll Free Tel:* 800-489-7486 *Fax:* 919-493-5668 *E-mail:* cap@cap-press.com *Web Site:* www.cap-press.com; www.caplaw.com, pg 41

Sipe, Scott, Carolina Academic Press, 700 Kent St, Durham, NC 27701 *Tel:* 919-489-7486 *Toll Free Tel:* 800-489-7486 *Fax:* 919-493-5668 *E-mail:* cap@cap-press.com *Web Site:* www.cap-press.com; www.caplaw.com, pg 41

Sippel, Julia, Paul Dry Books, 1700 Sansom St, Suite 700, Philadelphia, PA 19103 *Tel:* 215-231-9939 *E-mail:* editor@pauldrybooks.com *Web Site:* www.pauldrybooks.com, pg 152

Sirabian, Stephanie, Tor Publishing Group, 120 Broadway, New York, NY 10271 *Toll Free Tel:* 800-455-0340 (Macmillan) *E-mail:* torpublicity@tor.com; forgepublicity@forgebooks.com *Web Site:* us.macmillan.com/torpublishinggroup, pg 208

Sirisena, Hasanthika MFA, Susquehanna University, Department of English & Creative Writing, 514 University Ave, Selinsgrove, PA 17870 Tel: 570-372-4196 Web Site: www.susqu.edu, pg 565

Sirkin, Jeff, University of Texas at El Paso, Department of Creative Writing, MFA/Department of Creative Writing, M520, University Towers, Oregon St, El Paso, TX 79968 E-mail: creativewriting@utep.edu Web Site: www.utep.edu/liberalarts/creative-writing, pg 567

Sirna-Bruder, Anet, Harry N Abrams Inc, 195 Broadway, 9th fl, New York, NY 10007 Tel: 212-206-7715 Toll Free Tel: 800-345-1359 Fax: 212-645-8437 E-mail: abrams@abramsbooks.com; publicity@abramsbooks.com; sales@abramsbooks.com Web Site: www.abramsbooks.com, pg 2

Sirota, Mark, Trusted Media Brands Inc, 750 Third Ave, 3rd fl, New York, NY 10017 Tel: 646-293-6299 Toll Free Tel: 877-732-4438 (cust serv) Fax: 646-293-6251 E-mail: customercare@trustedmediabrands.com; press@trustedmediabrands.com Web Site: www.trustedmediabrands.com; www.rd.com, pg 210

Sisco, Cody, Editorial Freelancers Association (EFA), 266 W 37 St, 20th fl, New York, NY 10018 Tel: 212-920-4816 Toll Free Tel: 866-929-5425 E-mail: info@the-efa.org; membership@the-efa.org Web Site: www.the-efa.org, pg 505

Siscoe, Nancy, Random House Children's Books, c/o Penguin Random House LLC, 1745 Broadway, New York, NY 10019 Tel: 212-782-9000 Web Site: www.rhcbooks.com, pg 170

Sisk, Jonathan, Rowman & Littlefield, 4501 Forbes Blvd, Suite 200, Lanham, MD 20706 Tel: 301-459-3366 Toll Free Tel: 800-462-6420 (ext 3024, cust serv) Fax: 301-429-5748 Web Site: rowman.com, pg 178

Sisoler, Suzie, Penguin Random House LLC, 1745 Broadway, New York, NY 10019 Tel: 212-782-9000 Toll Free Tel: 800-726-0600 Web Site: www.penguinrandomhouse.com, pg 155

Sisson, Amy Beth, Fence Books, 36-09 28 Ave, Apt 3R, Astoria, NY 11103-4518 Tel: 518-567-7006 Web Site: www.fenceportal.org, pg 71

Sisson, Benny, HarperCollins Children's Books, 195 Broadway, New York, NY 10007 Tel: 212-207-7000 Web Site: www.harpercollins.com/childrens, pg 86

Sisson, Benny, Houghton Mifflin Harcourt Trade & Reference Division, 125 High St, Boston, MA 02110 Tel: 617-351-5000 Web Site: www.hmhco.com, pg 96

Sisterson, Sarah, Sourcebooks LLC, 1935 Brookdale Rd, Suite 139, Naperville, IL 60563 Tel: 630-961-3900 Toll Free Tel: 800-432-7444 Fax: 630-961-2168 E-mail: info@sourcebooks.com Web Site: www.sourcebooks.com, pg 194

Sites, Dr Richard, Bisk Education, 9417 Princess Palm Ave, Suite 400, Tampa, FL 33619 Tel: 813-621-6200 E-mail: media@bisk.com Web Site: www.bisk.com, pg 29

Siu, Fiona, Greystone Books Ltd, 343 Railway St, Suite 302, Vancouver, BC V6A 1A4, Canada Tel: 604-875-1550 Fax: 604-875-1556 E-mail: info@greystonebooks.com; rights@greystonebooks.com Web Site: www.greystonebooks.com, pg 407

Sivasubramaniam, Jeevan, Berrett-Koehler Publishers Inc, 1333 Broadway, Suite 1000, Oakland, CA 94612 Tel: 510-817-2277 Fax: 510-817-2278 E-mail: bkpub@bkpub.com Web Site: www.bkconnection.com, pg 29

Sizemore, Terrie, A 2 Z Press LLC, 3670 Woodbridge Rd, Deland, FL 32720 Tel: 440-241-3126 E-mail: sizemore3630@aol.com Web Site: www.a2zpress.com; www.bestlittleonlinebookstore.com, pg 1

Skaj, Paul, ABDO, 8000 W 78 St, Suite 310, Edina, MN 55439 Tel: 952-698-2403 Toll Free Tel: 800-800-1312 Fax: 952-831-1632 Toll Free Fax: 800-862-3480 E-mail: customerservice@abdobooks.com; info@abdobooks.com Web Site: abdobooks.com, pg 2

Skeels, Emma, Macmillan, 120 Broadway, 22nd fl, New York, NY 10271 E-mail: press.inquiries@macmillan.com Web Site: us.macmillan.com, pg 122

Skehan, Mary Kate, Portfolio, c/o Penguin Random House LLC, 1745 Broadway, New York, NY 10019 Tel: 212-782-9000 Web Site: www.penguin.com/portfolio-overview/; www.penguin.com/sentinel-overview/; www.penguin.com/thesis/, pg 162

Skelly, Sofiya, Macmillan, 120 Broadway, 22nd fl, New York, NY 10271 E-mail: press.inquiries@macmillan.com Web Site: us.macmillan.com, pg 122

Skelton, Samantha, The Writers Lifeline Inc, a Story Merchant company, 400 S Burnside Ave, Suite 11B, Los Angeles, CA 90036 Tel: 310-968-1607 Web Site: www.thewriterslifeline.com, pg 446

Skinner, Heather, University of Minnesota Press, 111 Third Ave S, Suite 290, Minneapolis, MN 55401-2520 Tel: 612-301-1990 Fax: 612-301-1980 E-mail: ump@umn.edu Web Site: www.upress.umn.edu, pg 217

Sklar, Madeline, Inside Literary Prize, 2666 State St, Suite 5A, Hamden, CT 06517 E-mail: freedomreads@freedomreads.org Web Site: freedomreads.org/showing-up/inside-literary-prize, pg 616

Sklena, Jennifer, Institute of Environmental Sciences & Technology - IEST, 1827 Walden Office Sq, Suite 400, Schaumburg, IL 60173 Tel: 847-981-0100 Fax: 847-981-4130 E-mail: information@iest.org Web Site: www.iest.org, pg 101

Skolek, Amanda, Sourcebooks LLC, 1935 Brookdale Rd, Suite 139, Naperville, IL 60563 Tel: 630-961-3900 Toll Free Tel: 800-432-7444 Fax: 630-961-2168 E-mail: info@sourcebooks.com Web Site: www.sourcebooks.com, pg 195

Skolkin, David, Museum of New Mexico Press, 725 Camino Lejo, Suite C, Santa Fe, NM 87505 Tel: 505-476-1155; 505-272-7777 (orders) Toll Free Tel: 800-249-7737 (orders) Fax: 505-476-1156 Toll Free Fax: 800-622-8667 (orders) Web Site: www.mnmpress.org, pg 135

Skordilis, Paul, Bloom's Literary Criticism, 132 W 31 St, 16th fl, New York, NY 10001 Toll Free Tel: 800-322-8755 Toll Free Fax: 800-678-3633 E-mail: custserv@infobase.com Web Site: www.infobasepublishing.com; www.infobase.com (online resources), pg 31

Skordilis, Paul, Chelsea House, 132 W 31 St, 16th fl, New York, NY 10001 Toll Free Tel: 800-322-8755 Toll Free Fax: 800-678-3633 E-mail: custserv@infobase.com; information@infobase.com Web Site: www.infobasepublishing.com; www.infobase.com (online resources), pg 46

Skrabacz, Anna, Simon & Schuster, 1230 Avenue of the Americas, New York, NY 10020 Tel: 212-698-7000 Toll Free Tel: 800-223-2348 (cust serv); 800-223-2336 (orders) Toll Free Fax: 800-943-9831 (orders) Web Site: simonandschusterpublishing.com/simonandschuster/, pg 188

Skrabek, Alison, Living Language, c/o Penguin Random House LLC, 1745 Broadway, New York, NY 10019 Tel: 212-782-9000 Toll Free Tel: 800-733-3000 (orders) E-mail: support@livinglanguage.com Web Site: www.livinglanguage.com, pg 119

Skurnick, Victoria, Levine|Greenberg|Rostan Literary Agency, 307 Seventh Ave, Suite 2407, New York, NY 10001 Tel: 212-337-0934 Fax: 212-337-0948 E-mail: submit@lgrliterary.com Web Site: lgrliterary.com, pg 467

Sky-Peck, Kathryn, Red Wheel/Weiser, 65 Parker St, Suite 7, Newburyport, MA 01950 Tel: 978-465-0504 Toll Free Tel: 800-423-7087 (orders) Fax: 978-465-0243 E-mail: info@rwwbooks.com Web Site: www.redwheelweiser.com, pg 173

Skyvara, Suzanne, Goodreads Choice Awards, 188 Spear St, 3rd fl, San Francisco, CA 94105 E-mail: press@goodreads.com Web Site: www.goodreads.com/award, pg 608

Slager, Daniel, Milkweed Editions, 1011 Washington Ave S, Suite 300, Minneapolis, MN 55415-1246 Tel: 612-332-3192 Toll Free Tel: 800-520-6455 E-mail: orders@milkweed.org Web Site: milkweed.org, pg 131

Slager, Daniel, Max Ritvo Poetry Prize, 1011 Washington Ave S, Suite 300, Minneapolis, MN 55415-1246 Tel: 612-332-3192 Toll Free Tel: 800-520-6455 Web Site: milkweed.org/max-ritvo-poetry-prize, pg 656

Slaiman, Rachel, Women's National Book Association Award, PO Box 237, FDR Sta, New York, NY 10150-0231 Toll Free Tel: 866-610-WNBA (610-9622) Web Site: wnba-books.org/wnba-award, pg 677

Slain, Tonia, Facts On File, 1000 N West St, Suite 1281-230, Wilmington, DE 19801 Tel: 212-967-8800 Toll Free Tel: 800-322-8755 Toll Free Fax: 800-678-3633 E-mail: custserv@factsonfile.com Web Site: infobasepublishing.com, pg 69

Slain, Tonia, Ferguson Publishing, 132 W 31 St, 16 fl, New York, NY 10001 Tel: 212-967-8800 Toll Free Tel: 800-322-8755 Toll Free Fax: 800-678-3633 E-mail: custserv@infobase.com Web Site: infobasepublishing.com, pg 71

Slamp, Jim, The Conference Board Inc, 845 Third Ave, New York, NY 10022-6600 Tel: 212-759-0900; 212-339-0345 (cust serv) E-mail: customer.service@tcb.org Web Site: www.conference-board.org/us; www.linkedin.com/company/the-conference-board, pg 51

Slavin, Samantha, Macmillan, 120 Broadway, 22nd fl, New York, NY 10271 E-mail: press.inquiries@macmillan.com Web Site: us.macmillan.com, pg 122

Slayne, Karen, Ambassador International, 411 University Ridge, Suite B14, Greenville, SC 29601 Tel: 864-751-4844 E-mail: info@emeraldhouse.com; publisher@emeraldhouse.com (ms submissions); sales@emeraldhouse.com (orders/order inquiries); media@emeraldhouse.com; design@emeraldhouse.com Web Site: ambassador-international.com; www.facebook.com/AmbassadorIntl; x.com/ambassadorintl, pg 7

Sleater, Dennis, Harry N Abrams Inc, 195 Broadway, 9th fl, New York, NY 10007 Tel: 212-206-7715 Toll Free Tel: 800-345-1359 Fax: 212-645-8437 E-mail: abrams@abramsbooks.com; publicity@abramsbooks.com; sales@abramsbooks.com Web Site: www.abramsbooks.com, pg 2

Slesin, Suzanne, Pointed Leaf Press, 136 Baxter St, New York, NY 10013 Tel: 212-941-1800 Fax: 212-941-1822 E-mail: info@pointedleafpress.com Web Site: www.pointedleafpress.com, pg 161

Sleven, Paul, Macmillan, 120 Broadway, 22nd fl, New York, NY 10271 E-mail: press.inquiries@macmillan.com Web Site: us.macmillan.com, pg 122

Slick, Colleen, HarperCollins Publishers LLC, 195 Broadway, New York, NY 10007 Tel: 212-207-7000 Web Site: www.harpercollins.com, pg 87

Sloan, Lawrence D, AIHA (American Industrial Hygiene Association), 3141 Fairview Park Dr, Suite 777, Falls Church, VA 22042 Tel: 703-849-8888 Fax: 703-207-3561 E-mail: infonet@aiha.org Web Site: www.aiha.org, pg 6

Slopen, Beverley, Beverley Slopen Literary Agency, 131 Bloor St W, Suite 711, Toronto, ON M5S 1S3, Canada Tel: 416-964-9598 Fax: 416-964-9598 Web Site: www.slopenagency.com, pg 476

Slotowski, Jennifer, Waveland Press Inc, 4180 IL Rte 83, Suite 101, Long Grove, IL 60047-9580 Tel: 847-634-0081 Fax: 847-634-9501 E-mail: info@waveland.com Web Site: www.waveland.com, pg 226

Slutsky, Lorie, Oscar Williams/Gene Derwood Award, 909 Third Ave, New York, NY 10022 Tel: 212-686-0010 Fax: 212-532-8528 E-mail: info@nycommunitytrust.org Web Site: www.nycommunitytrust.org, pg 675

Small, Kim, Random House Children's Books, c/o Penguin Random House LLC, 1745 Broadway, New York, NY 10019 Tel: 212-782-9000 Web Site: www.rhcbooks.com, pg 170

Small, Nick, Sounds True Inc, 413 S Arthur Ave, Louisville, CO 80027 Tel: 303-665-3151 Toll Free Tel: 800-333-9185 (US); 888-303-9185 (US &

CN) *E-mail:* customerservice@soundstrue.com; stpublicity@soundstrue.com *Web Site:* www.soundstrue.com, pg 194

Smallfield, Edward, Apogee Press, PO Box 10066, Berkeley, CA 94709 *E-mail:* apogeelibri@gmail.com *Web Site:* www.apogeepress.com, pg 15

Smart, Ashley, Knight Science Journalism Fellowships, 77 Massachusetts Ave, Cambridge, MA 02139 *Tel:* 617-452-3513 *E-mail:* knight-info@mit.edu *Web Site:* ksj.mit.edu/fellowship, pg 620

Smart, Dan, Twenty-Third Publications, One Montauk Ave, Suite 200, New London, CT 06320 *Tel:* 860-437-3012 *Toll Free Tel:* 800-321-0411 (orders) *Toll Free Fax:* 800-572-0788 *E-mail:* resources@twentythirdpublications.com *Web Site:* www.twentythirdpublications.com, pg 211

Smart, Rebecca, Penguin Random House LLC, 1745 Broadway, New York, NY 10019 *Tel:* 212-782-9000 *Toll Free Tel:* 800-726-0600 *Web Site:* www.penguinrandomhouse.com, pg 155

Smeltz, Leslie Tobin, Pennwriters Conference, PO Box 685, Dalton, PA 18414 *E-mail:* conferencecoordinator@pennwriters.org; info@pennwriters.org *Web Site:* pennwriters.org, pg 556

Smetanka, Dan, Counterpoint Press LLC, 2560 Ninth St, Suite 318, Berkeley, CA 94710 *Tel:* 510-704-0230 *Fax:* 510-704-0268 *E-mail:* info@counterpointpress.com *Web Site:* counterpointpress.com; softskull.com, pg 54

Smetzer, Lauren, Dreamscape Media LLC, 1417 Timberwolf Dr, Holland, OH 43528 *Tel:* 419-867-6965 *Toll Free Tel:* 877-983-7326 *E-mail:* info@dreamscapeab.com *Web Site:* www.dreamscapepublishing.com, pg 62

Smid, Theresa, American Society of Plant Taxonomists, c/o Missouri Botanical Garden, 4344 Shaw Blvd, St Louis, MO 63110 *E-mail:* businessoffice@aspt.net *Web Site:* www.aspt.net, pg 13

Smiley, Matt, University of Minnesota Press, 111 Third Ave S, Suite 290, Minneapolis, MN 55401-2520 *Tel:* 612-301-1990 *Fax:* 612-301-1980 *E-mail:* ump@umn.edu *Web Site:* www.upress.umn.edu, pg 217

Smirnova, Marianna, Random House Children's Books, c/o Penguin Random House LLC, 1745 Broadway, New York, NY 10019 *Tel:* 212-782-9000 *Web Site:* www.rhcbooks.com, pg 170

Smist, Erik A, Johns Hopkins University Press, 2715 N Charles St, Baltimore, MD 21218-4363 *Tel:* 410-516-6900; 410-516-6987 *Toll Free Tel:* 800-537-5487 (book orders & cust serv); 800-548-1784 (journal orders) *Fax:* 410-516-6968; 410-516-6998 (orders) *E-mail:* hfscustserv@press.jhu.edu (cust serv); jrnlcirc@jh.edu (journal orders) *Web Site:* www.press.jhu.edu; muse.jhu.edu, pg 106

Smith, Alison, BMI®, 7 World Trade Center, 250 Greenwich St, New York, NY 10007-0030 *Tel:* 212-220-3000 *Toll Free Tel:* 888-689-5264 (sales) *E-mail:* newyork@bmi.com *Web Site:* www.bmi.com, pg 501

Smith, Andrew, Abrams Amplify Award, 195 Broadway, 9th fl, New York, NY 10007 *E-mail:* childrenspublicity@abramsbooks.com *Web Site:* www.abramsbooks.com/abramsamplifyaward, pg 569

Smith, Andrew, Harry N Abrams Inc, 195 Broadway, 9th fl, New York, NY 10007 *Tel:* 212-206-7715 *Toll Free Tel:* 800-345-1359 *Fax:* 212-645-8437 *E-mail:* abrams@abramsbooks.com; publicity@abramsbooks.com; sales@abramsbooks.com *Web Site:* www.abramsbooks.com, pg 2

Smith, Boshia, Association for Intelligent Information Management (AIIM), 8403 Colesville Rd, No 1100, Silver Spring, MD 20910 *Tel:* 301-587-8202 *Toll Free Tel:* 800-477-2446 *Fax:* 301-587-2711 *E-mail:* hello@aiim.org *Web Site:* www.aiim.org, pg 498

Smith, Bryan, Savvas Learning Co LLC, 15 E Midland Ave, Suite 502, Paramus, NJ 07652 *Toll Free Tel:* 800-848-9500 *Web Site:* www.savvas.com, pg 183

Smith, Clay, Simon & Schuster, 1230 Avenue of the Americas, New York, NY 10020 *Tel:* 212-698-7000 *Toll Free Tel:* 800-223-2348 (cust serv); 800-223-2336 (orders) *Toll Free Fax:* 800-943-9831 (orders) *Web Site:* simonandschusterpublishing.com/simonandschuster/, pg 189

Smith, Colleen M, GLCA New Writers Awards, 535 W William St, Suite 301, Ann Arbor, MI 48103 *Tel:* 734-661-2350 *Fax:* 734-661-2349 *Web Site:* www.glca.org, pg 607

Smith, David Cloyce, Library of America, 14 E 60 St, New York, NY 10022-1006 *Tel:* 212-308-3360 *Fax:* 212-750-8352 *E-mail:* info@loa.org *Web Site:* www.loa.org, pg 116

Smith, David Hale, InkWell Management, 521 Fifth Ave, Suite 2600, New York, NY 10175 *Tel:* 212-922-3500 *Fax:* 212-922-0535 *E-mail:* info@inkwellmanagement.com; submissions@inkwellmanagement.com; permissions@inkwellmanagement.com *Web Site:* inkwellmanagement.com, pg 463

Smith, David M, Practising Law Institute (PLI), 1177 Avenue of the Americas, 2nd fl, New York, NY 10036 *Tel:* 212-824-5710 (cust serv) *Toll Free Tel:* 800-260-4PLI (260-4754) *Toll Free Fax:* 800-321-0093 (cust serv) *E-mail:* info@pli.edu; membership@pli.edu *Web Site:* www.pli.edu, pg 163

Smith, Dean, Duke University Press, 905 W Main St, Suite 18B, Durham, NC 27701 *Tel:* 919-688-5134 *Toll Free Tel:* 888-651-0122 (US) *Fax:* 919-688-2615 *Toll Free Fax:* 888-651-0124 *E-mail:* orders@dukeupress.edu *Web Site:* www.dukeupress.edu, pg 62

Smith, Eleanor, Princeton University Press, 41 William St, Princeton, NJ 08540-5237 *Tel:* 609-258-4900 *Fax:* 609-258-6305 *E-mail:* info@press.princeton.edu *Web Site:* press.princeton.edu, pg 164

Smith, Eliza, Sourcebooks LLC, 1935 Brookdale Rd, Suite 139, Naperville, IL 60563 *Tel:* 630-961-3900 *Toll Free Tel:* 800-432-7444 *Fax:* 630-961-2168 *E-mail:* info@sourcebooks.com *Web Site:* www.sourcebooks.com, pg 194

Smith, Ellie, Phaidon, 65 Bleecker St, 8th fl, New York, NY 10012 *Tel:* 212-652-5400 *Toll Free Tel:* 800-759-0190 (cust serv) *Fax:* 212-652-5410 *Toll Free Fax:* 800-286-9471 (cust serv) *E-mail:* enquiries@phaidon.com *Web Site:* www.phaidon.com, pg 159

Smith, George D, Signature Books Publishing Inc, 564 W 400 N, Salt Lake City, UT 84116-3411 *Toll Free Tel:* 800-356-5687 *E-mail:* people@signaturebooks.com *Web Site:* www.signaturebooks.com; www.signaturebookslibrary.org, pg 188

Smith, Icy, East West Discovery Press, PO Box 3585, Manhattan Beach, CA 90266 *Tel:* 310-545-3730 *Fax:* 310-545-3731 *E-mail:* info@eastwestdiscovery.com *Web Site:* www.eastwestdiscovery.com, pg 63

Smith, Ileene, Farrar, Straus & Giroux, LLC, 120 Broadway, New York, NY 10271 *Tel:* 212-741-6900 *E-mail:* fsg.publicity@fsgbooks.com; sales@fsgbooks.com *Web Site:* us.macmillan.com/fsg, pg 70

Smith, James Clois Jr, Sunstone Press, PO Box 2321, Santa Fe, NM 87504-2321 *Tel:* 505-988-4418 *E-mail:* orders@sunstonepress.com *Web Site:* sunstonepress.com, pg 201

Smith, Jan M, Western Reflections Publishing Co, 951B N Hwy 149, Lake City, CO 81235 *Tel:* 970-944-0110 *E-mail:* publisher@westernreflectionspublishing.com; westernreflectionspublishing@gmail.com *Web Site:* www.westernreflectionspublishing.com, pg 228

Smith, Jeffrey, Bridge to Asia, 1505 Juanita Way, Berkeley, CA 94702, pg 525

Smith, Jenna, Penguin Young Readers Group, c/o Penguin Random House LLC, 1745 Broadway, New York, NY 10019 *Tel:* 212-782-9000 *Web Site:* penguin.com/penguin-young-readers-overview, pg 156

Smith, Jennifer, Thomas Nelson, 501 Nelson Place, Nashville, TN 37214 *Tel:* 615-889-9000 *Toll Free Tel:* 800-251-4000 *Web Site:* www.thomasnelson.com, pg 206

Smith, Jessica, Simon & Schuster Children's Publishing, 1230 Avenue of the Americas, New York, NY 10020 *Tel:* 212-698-7000 *Web Site:* www.simonandschuster.com/kids; www.simonandschuster.com/teen; simonandschuster.net; simonandschuster.biz, pg 189

Smith, Jill, Penguin Random House Canada, a Penguin Random House company, 320 Front St W, Suite 1400, Toronto, ON M5V 3B6, Canada *Tel:* 416-364-4449 *Toll Free Tel:* 888-523-9292 (cust serv) *E-mail:* canadaweb@penguinrandomhouse.com; customerservicescanada@penguinrandomhouse.com *Web Site:* www.penguinrandomhouse.ca, pg 416

Smith, Jill, University of Denver Publishing Institute, 2000 E Asbury Ave, Denver, CO 80208 *Tel:* 303-871-2570 *Fax:* 303-871-2501 *E-mail:* pi-info@du.edu *Web Site:* liberalarts.du.edu/publishing, pg 566

Smith, Joshua, Society of Children's Book Writers & Illustrators (SCBWI), 6363 Wilshire Blvd, Suite 425, Los Angeles, CA 90048 *Tel:* 323-782-1010 *E-mail:* membership@scbwi.org *Web Site:* www.scbwi.org, pg 520

Smith, Kaitlin, Doubleday Canada, 320 Front St W, Suite 1400, Toronto, ON M5V 3B6, Canada *Tel:* 416-364-4449 *Fax:* 416-598-7764 *Web Site:* www.penguinrandomhouse.ca, pg 401

Smith, Karen, Workman Publishing, 1290 Avenue of the Americas, New York, NY 10104 *Toll Free Tel:* 800-759-0190 *Fax:* 212-364-0950 *E-mail:* workman-inquiry@hbgusa.com *Web Site:* www.hachettebookgroup.com/imprint/workman-publishing-company/, pg 233

Smith, Kate, Penguin Random House Audio Publishing Group, 1745 Broadway, New York, NY 10019 *Toll Free Tel:* 800-793-2665 (cust serv) *E-mail:* audio@penguinrandomhouse.com; ecustomerservice@penguinrandomhouse.com *Web Site:* www.penguinrandomhouseaudio.com, pg 154

Smith, Katie Cruice, Ambassador International, 411 University Ridge, Suite B14, Greenville, SC 29601 *Tel:* 864-751-4844 *E-mail:* info@emeraldhouse.com; publisher@emeraldhouse.com (ms submissions); sales@emeraldhouse.com (orders/order inquiries); media@emeraldhouse.com; design@emeraldhouse.com *Web Site:* ambassador-international.com; www.facebook.com/AmbassadorIntl; x.com/ambassadorintl, pg 7

Smith, Larry, Bottom Dog Press, 813 Seneca Ave, Huron, OH 44839 *Tel:* 419-602-1556 *Fax:* 419-616-3966 *Web Site:* smithdocs.net, pg 34

Smith, Laura, Bottom Dog Press, 813 Seneca Ave, Huron, OH 44839 *Tel:* 419-602-1556 *Fax:* 419-616-3966 *Web Site:* smithdocs.net, pg 34

Smith, Marisa, Smith & Kraus Publishers Inc, 177 Lyme Rd, Hanover, NH 03755 *Tel:* 618-783-0519 *Toll Free Tel:* 877-668-8680 *Fax:* 618-783-0520 *E-mail:* editor@smithandkraus.com; info@smithandkraus.com; customerservice@smithandkraus.com *Web Site:* www.smithandkraus.com, pg 192

Smith, Mary Dupuy, Teacher Created Resources Inc, 12621 Western Ave, Garden Grove, CA 92481 *Tel:* 714-891-7895 *Toll Free Tel:* 800-662-4321; 888-343-4335 *Toll Free Fax:* 800-525-1254 *E-mail:* custserv@teachercreated.com *Web Site:* www.teachercreated.com, pg 203

Smith, Megan, Dreamscape Media LLC, 1417 Timberwolf Dr, Holland, OH 43528 *Tel:* 419-867-6965 *Toll Free Tel:* 877-983-7326 *E-mail:* info@dreamscapeab.com *Web Site:* www.dreamscapepublishing.com, pg 62

Smith, Michael, East West Discovery Press, PO Box 3585, Manhattan Beach, CA 90266 *Tel:* 310-545-3730 *Fax:* 310-545-3731 *E-mail:* info@eastwestdiscovery.com *Web Site:* www.eastwestdiscovery.com, pg 63

Smith, Olivia Taylor, Simon & Schuster, 1230 Avenue of the Americas, New York, NY 10020 *Tel:* 212-698-7000 *Toll Free Tel:* 800-223-2348 (cust serv); 800-223-2336 (orders) *Toll Free Fax:* 800-943-9831 (orders) *Web Site:* simonandschusterpublishing.com/simonandschuster/, pg 188

Smith, P David, Western Reflections Publishing Co, 951B N Hwy 149, Lake City, CO 81235 Tel: 970-944-0110 E-mail: publisher@westernreflectionspublishing.com; westernreflectionspublishing@gmail.com Web Site: www.westernreflectionspublishing.com, pg 228

Smith, Paige, Penguin Random House LLC, 1745 Broadway, New York, NY 10019 Tel: 212-782-9000 Toll Free Tel: 800-726-0600 Web Site: www.penguinrandomhouse.com, pg 155

Smith, Pat, Oolichan Books, PO Box 2278, Fernie, BC V0B 1M0, Canada Tel: 250-423-6113 E-mail: info@oolichan.com Web Site: www.oolichan.com, pg 414

Smith, Peggy Boulos, Writers House, 21 W 26 St, New York, NY 10010 Tel: 212-685-2400 Web Site: www.writershouse.com, pg 482

Smith, Piper, Lindgren & Smith, 888C Eighth Ave, No 329, New York, NY 10019 Tel: 212-397-7330 E-mail: info@lindgrensmith.com; hello@lindgrensmith.com Web Site: lindgrensmith.com, pg 485

Smith, R Bob III, Psychological Assessment Resources Inc (PAR), 16204 N Florida Ave, Lutz, FL 33549 Tel: 813-449-4065 Toll Free Tel: 800-331-8378 Fax: 813-961-2196 Toll Free Fax: 800-727-9329 Web Site: www.parinc.com, pg 166

Smith, Rachel, Ave Maria Press Inc, PO Box 428, Notre Dame, IN 46556 Toll Free Tel: 800-282-1865 Toll Free Fax: 800-282-5681 E-mail: avemariapress.1@nd.edu Web Site: www.avemariapress.com, pg 22

Smith, Rebekah, Ugly Duckling Presse, The Old American Can Factory, 232 Third St, Suite E303, Brooklyn, NY 11215 Tel: 347-948-5170 E-mail: office@uglyducklingpresse.org; orders@uglyducklingpresse.org; publicity@uglyducklingpresse.org; rights@uglyducklingpresse.org Web Site: uglyducklingpresse.org, pg 212

Smith, Ronald, Oolichan Books, PO Box 2278, Fernie, BC V0B 1M0, Canada Tel: 250-423-6113 E-mail: info@oolichan.com Web Site: www.oolichan.com, pg 414

Smith, Ronnie L, Writer's Relief, Inc, 18766 John J Williams Hwy, Unit 4, Box 335, Rehoboth Beach, DE 19971 Toll Free Tel: 866-405-3003 Fax: 201-641-1253 E-mail: info@writersrelief.com Web Site: www.WritersRelief.com, pg 446

Smith, Ruth, Canadian First Book Prize, 363 Parkridge Crescent, Oakville, ON L6M 1A8, Canada Tel: 905-618-0420 E-mail: info@griffinpoetryprize.com; publicity@griffinpoetryprize.com Web Site: griffinpoetryprize.com, pg 586

Smith, Ruth, Griffin Poetry Prize, 363 Parkridge Crescent, Oakville, ON L6M 1A8, Canada Tel: 905-618-0420 E-mail: info@griffinpoetryprize.com; publicity@griffinpoetryprize.com Web Site: griffinpoetryprize.com, pg 609

Smith, Sarah, David Black Agency, 335 Adams St, 27th fl, Suite 2707, Brooklyn, NY 11201 Tel: 718-852-5500 Fax: 718-852-5539 Web Site: www.davidblackagency.com, pg 450

Smith, Shris, Viking Penguin, c/o Penguin Random House LLC, 1745 Broadway, New York, NY 10019 Tel: 212-782-9000 Web Site: www.penguin.com/overview-vikingbooks/; www.penguin.com/pamela-dorman-books-overview/; www.penguin.com/penguin-classics-overview/; www.penguin.com/penguin-life-overview/, pg 225

Smith, Steph, Education Writers Association (EWA), 1825 "K" St NW, Suite 200, Washington, DC 20006 Tel: 202-452-9830 Web Site: ewa.org, pg 505

Smith, Stephanie Duncan, HarperCollins Publishers LLC, 195 Broadway, New York, NY 10007 Tel: 212-207-7000 Web Site: www.harpercollins.com, pg 86

Smith, Stephen, Thomas Nelson, 501 Nelson Place, Nashville, TN 37214 Tel: 615-889-9000 Toll Free Tel: 800-251-4000 Web Site: www.thomasnelson.com, pg 206

Smith, Stephen F, AAAI Press, 2275 E Bayshore Rd, Suite 160, Palo Alto, CA 94303 Tel: 650-328-3123 Fax: 650-321-4457 E-mail: publications21@aaai.org Web Site: www.aaai.org/Press/press.php, pg 1

Smith, Steven Rathgeb, American Political Science Association (APSA), 1527 New Hampshire Ave NW, Washington, DC 20036-1203 Tel: 202-483-2512 Fax: 202-483-2657 E-mail: apsa@apsanet.org; membership@apsanet.org; press@apsanet.org Web Site: www.apsanet.org, pg 496

Smith, Stu, Scribner, 1230 Avenue of the Americas, New York, NY 10020 Web Site: www.simonandschusterpublishing.com/scribner/, pg 185

Smith, Sue, Boydell & Brewer Inc, 668 Mount Hope Ave, Rochester, NY 14620-2731 Tel: 585-275-0419 Fax: 585-271-8778 E-mail: boydell@boydellusa.net Web Site: www.boydellandbrewer.com, pg 35

Smith, Sue, University of Rochester Press, 668 Mount Hope Ave, Rochester, NY 14620-2731 Tel: 585-275-0419 Fax: 585-271-8778 E-mail: boydell@boydellusa.net Web Site: www.urpress.com, pg 220

Smith, Suzanne, Alfred A Knopf, c/o Penguin Random House LLC, 1745 Broadway, New York, NY 10019 Tel: 212-751-2600 Fax: 212-940-7390 (dom rts); 212-572-2662 (foreign rts) Web Site: knopfdoubleday.com/imprint/knopf/; knopfdoubleday.com, pg 110

Smith, Victoria L PhD, LD & LaVerne Harrell Clark Fiction Prize, Flowers Hall, Rm 365, 601 University Dr, San Marcos, TX 78666 Tel: 512-245-2163 Fax: 512-245-8546 Web Site: www.english.txstate.edu/clarkfictionprize.html, pg 611

Smith, William, The MIT Press, One Broadway, 12th fl, Cambridge, MA 02142 Tel: 617-253-5255 Toll Free Tel: 800-405-1619 (orders) Fax: 617-258-6779; 617-577-1545 (orders) Web Site: mitpress.mit.edu, pg 132

Smither, Banks, Applewood Books, 210 Wingo Way, Suite 200, Mount Pleasant, SC 29464 Tel: 843-853-2070 E-mail: retailers@arcadiapublishing.com; publishing@arcadiapublishing.com Web Site: www.arcadiapublishing.com, pg 15

Smitherman, David, Rand-Smith Publishing, 204 College Ave, Ashland, VA 23005 Tel: 804-874-6012 E-mail: randsmithllc@gmail.com Web Site: www.rand-smith.com, pg 169

Smithers, Westwood Jr, Corporation for Public Broadcasting (CPB), 401 Ninth St NW, Washington, DC 20004-2129 Tel: 202-879-9600 E-mail: press@cpb.org Web Site: cpb.org, pg 504

Smulders, Marilyn, Writers' Federation of Nova Scotia (WFNS), 1113 Marginal Rd, Halifax, NS B3H 4P7, Canada Tel: 902-423-8116 Fax: 902-422-0881 E-mail: contact@writers.ns.ca; wits@writers.ns.ca (awards); programs@writers.ns.ca; communications@writers.ns.ca Web Site: writers.ns.ca, pg 522

Smyk, Dorothy, New Harbinger Publications Inc, 5674 Shattuck Ave, Oakland, CA 94609 Tel: 510-652-0215 Toll Free Tel: 800-748-6273 (orders only) Fax: 510-652-5472 Toll Free Fax: 800-652-1613 E-mail: customerservice@newharbinger.com Web Site: www.newharbinger.com, pg 140

Smyth, Sam, StarGroup International Inc, 1194 Old Dixie Hwy, Suite 201, West Palm Beach, FL 33413 Tel: 561-547-0667 Fax: 561-843-8530 E-mail: info@stargroupinternational.com Web Site: stargroupinternational.com, pg 198

Snavely, Sheri, W W Norton & Company Inc, 500 Fifth Ave, New York, NY 10110-0017 Tel: 212-354-5500 Toll Free Tel: 800-233-4830 (orders & cust serv) Fax: 212-869-0856 Toll Free Fax: 800-458-6515 E-mail: orders@wwnorton.com Web Site: wwnorton.com, pg 143

Snead, Beth, The Flannery O'Connor Award for Short Fiction, Main Library, 3rd fl, 320 S Jackson St, Athens, GA 30602 Fax: 706-542-2558 Web Site: www.ugapress.org, pg 642

Snead, Beth, University of Georgia Press, Main Library, 3rd fl, 320 S Jackson St, Athens, GA 30602 Fax: 706-542-2558; 706-542-6770 Web Site: www.ugapress.org, pg 216

Snell, Michael, Michael Snell Literary Agency, PO Box 1206, Truro, MA 02666-1206 Tel: 508-349-3718 Web Site: www.michaelsnellagency.com, pg 476

Snell, Patricia, Michael Snell Literary Agency, PO Box 1206, Truro, MA 02666-1206 Tel: 508-349-3718 Web Site: www.michaelsnellagency.com, pg 476

Snelling, Maria, Macmillan Audio, 120 Broadway, 22nd fl, New York, NY 10271 Tel: 646-600-7856 Toll Free Tel: 888-330-8477 (cust serv) Toll Free Fax: 800-672-7703 E-mail: macmillan.audio@macmillanusa.com Web Site: us.macmillan.com/audio, pg 123

Snider, Stephen, St Martin's Press, LLC, 120 Broadway, New York, NY 10271 E-mail: publicity@stmartins.com; trademarketing@stmartins.com; foreignrights@stmartins.com Web Site: us.macmillan.com/smp, pg 180

Snitkin, Damon, Gingko Press Inc, 2332 Fourth St, Suite E, Berkeley, CA 94710 Tel: 510-898-1195 Fax: 510-898-1196 E-mail: books@gingkopress.com Web Site: www.gingkopress.com, pg 78

Snodgrass, Kristine, Anhinga Press Inc, PO Box 3665, Tallahassee, FL 32315 E-mail: info@anhinga.org Web Site: www.anhingapress.org; www.facebook.com/anhingapress, pg 14

Snodgrass, Kristine, Anhinga Prize for Poetry, PO Box 3665, Tallahassee, FL 32315 E-mail: info@anhinga.org Web Site: www.anhingapress.org, pg 573

Snodgrass, Robert, Ascend Books LLC, 11722 W 91 St, Overland Park, KS 66214 Tel: 913-948-5500 Web Site: www.ascendbooks.com, pg 18

Snow, David, Simon & Schuster, LLC, 1230 Avenue of the Americas, New York, NY 10020 Tel: 212-698-7000 Toll Free Tel: 800-223-2336 (orders) Fax: 212-698-7007 Toll Free Fax: 800-943-9831 (orders) E-mail: firstname.lastname@simonandschuster.com; purchaseorders@simonandschuster.com (orders) Web Site: www.simonandschuster.com, pg 189

Snow, Todd, Maren Green Publishing Inc, 7900 Excelsior Blvd, Suite 105K, Hopkins, MN 55343 Tel: 651-439-4500 Toll Free Tel: 800-287-1512 Fax: 651-439-4532 E-mail: info@marengreen.com Web Site: www.marengreen.com, pg 125

Snowden, Elizabeth Regina, Alan Wofsy Fine Arts, 1109 Geary Blvd, San Francisco, CA 94109 Tel: 415-292-6500 Toll Free Tel: 800-660-6403 Fax: 415-292-6594 (off & cust serv); 510-251-1840 (acctg) E-mail: order@art-books.com (orders); editeur@earthlink.net (edit); beauxarts@earthlink.net (cust serv) Web Site: www.art-books.com, pg 231

Snyder, Becky, ABC-CLIO, 147 Castilian Dr, Santa Barbara, CA 93117 Tel: 805-968-1911 Toll Free Tel: 800-368-6868 Toll Free Fax: 866-270-3856 E-mail: customerservice@abc-clio.com Web Site: www.abc-clio.com, pg 2

Snyder, Isabelle, Random House Children's Books, c/o Penguin Random House LLC, 1745 Broadway, New York, NY 10019 Tel: 212-782-9000 Web Site: www.rhcbooks.com, pg 170

Snyder, Ruth, InScribe Christian Writers' Fellowship (ICWF), PO Box 68025, Edmonton, AB T6C 4N6, Canada Tel: 780-646-3068 E-mail: inscribe.mail@gmail.com Web Site: inscribe.org, pg 508

Snyder, Travis, Texas Tech University Press, 1120 Main St, 2nd fl, Lubbock, TX 79401 Tel: 806-742-2982 Toll Free Tel: 800-832-4042 E-mail: ttup@ttu.edu Web Site: www.ttupress.org, pg 205

So, Ariel, Riverhead Books, c/o Penguin Random House LLC, 1745 Broadway, New York, NY 10019 Tel: 212-782-9000 Web Site: www.penguin.com/riverhead-overview/, pg 175

So, Mark, Piano Press, 1425 Ocean Ave, Suite 5, Del Mar, CA 92014 Tel: 619-884-1401 E-mail: pianopress@pianopress.com Web Site: www.pianopress.com, pg 159

Soares, Louis, American Council on Education (ACE), One Dupont Circle NW, Washington, DC 20036 Tel: 202-939-9300 Web Site: www.acenet.edu, pg 9, 495

Soares, Manuela, Pace University, Master of Science in Publishing, 163 William St, 18th fl, New York, NY 10038 Tel: 212-346-1431 E-mail: puboffice@pace.edu Web Site: www.pace.edu/program/publishing-ms, pg 564

Soares, Manuela, Pace University Press, Pace University, One Pace Plaza, New York, NY 10038 Tel: 212-346-1417 Fax: 212-346-1417 E-mail: paceupress@gmail.com Web Site: www.pace.edu/press, pg 149

Sobel, Nat, Sobel Weber Associates Inc, 146 E 19 St, New York, NY 10003-2404 Tel: 212-420-8585 E-mail: info@sobelweber.com Web Site: www.sobelweber.com, pg 476

Sochacki, Beth, Sourcebooks LLC, 1935 Brookdale Rd, Suite 139, Naperville, IL 60563 Tel: 630-961-3900 Toll Free Tel: 800-432-7444 Fax: 630-961-2168 E-mail: info@sourcebooks.com Web Site: www.sourcebooks.com, pg 194

Sogah, Esi, Berkley, c/o Penguin Random House LLC, 1745 Broadway, 19th fl, New York, NY 10019 Tel: 212-366-2000 Web Site: www.penguin.com/publishers/berkley/; www.penguin.com/ace-overview/, pg 28

Soha, Yaniv, Atria Books, 1230 Avenue of the Americas, New York, NY 10020 Tel: 212-698-7000 Fax: 212-698-7007 Web Site: www.simonandschuster.com, pg 21

Sokol, Dr Mick, Drury University One-Act Play Competition, 900 N Benton Ave, Springfield, MO 65802-3344 Tel: 417-873-6821 Web Site: www.drury.edu, pg 597

Sokolowski, Ed, Other Press, 267 Fifth Ave, 6th fl, New York, NY 10016 Tel: 212-414-0054 Toll Free Tel: 877-THEOTHER (843-6843) Fax: 212-414-0939 E-mail: editor@otherpress.com; marketing@otherpress.com; publicity@otherpress.com Web Site: otherpress.com, pg 148

Sokolsky, Abigail, Workman Publishing, 1290 Avenue of the Americas, New York, NY 10104 Toll Free Tel: 800-759-0190 Fax: 212-364-0950 E-mail: workman-inquiry@hbgusa.com Web Site: www.hachettebookgroup.com/imprint/workman-publishing-company/, pg 233

Solano, Nicole, Rutgers University Press, 106 Somerset St, 3rd fl, New Brunswick, NJ 08901 Tel: 848-445-7762; 848-445-7761 (sales) Fax: 732-745-4935 E-mail: sales@rutgersuniversitypress.org Web Site: www.rutgersuniversitypress.org, pg 178

Solazzo, Christina, Simon & Schuster Children's Publishing, 1230 Avenue of the Americas, New York, NY 10020 Tel: 212-698-7000 Web Site: www.simonandschuster.com/kids; www.simonandschuster.com/teen; simonandschuster.net; simonandschuster.biz, pg 189

Soler, Shania, Metamorphosis Literary Agency, 12410 S Acuff Ct, Olathe, KS 66062 Tel: 646-397-1640 E-mail: info@metamorphosisliteraryagency.com Web Site: www.metamorphosisliteraryagency.com, pg 470

Solheim, Tara Dawn, Summer Writing Courses, 1831 College Ave, Suite 324, Regina, SK S4P 4V5, Canada Tel: 306-537-7243 E-mail: sage.hill@sasktel.net; info.sagehill@sasktel.net Web Site: www.sagehillwriting.ca, pg 557

Solic, Peggy, Syracuse University Press, 621 Skytop Rd, Suite 110, Syracuse, NY 13244-5290 Tel: 315-443-5534 Toll Free Tel: 800-365-8929 (cust serv) Fax: 315-443-5545 E-mail: supress@syr.edu Web Site: press.syr.edu, pg 201

Solis, Emma, Modern Memoirs Inc, 417 West St, Suite 104, Amherst, MA 01002 Tel: 413-253-2353 Web Site: www.modernmemoirs.com, pg 133

Soliz, Sarah, School for Advanced Research Press, 660 Garcia St, Santa Fe, NM 87505 E-mail: press@sarsf.org Web Site: sarweb.org, pg 185

Sollenberger, Emily, Independent Artist Awards, 175 W Ostend St, Suite E, Baltimore, MD 21230 Tel: 410-767-6555 E-mail: msac.commerce@maryland.gov Web Site: www.msac.org/programs/independent-artist-award, pg 615

Solomon, Emily, Dreamscape Media LLC, 1417 Timberwolf Dr, Holland, OH 43528 Tel: 419-867-6965 Toll Free Tel: 877-983-7326 E-mail: info@dreamscapeab.com Web Site: www.dreamscapepublishing.com, pg 62

Solomon, Jodi F, Jodi F Solomon Speakers Bureau Inc, PO Box 302123, Boston, MA 02130 Tel: 617-266-3450 Fax: 617-266-5660 E-mail: inquiries@jodisolomonspeakers.com Web Site: www.jodisolomonspeakers.com, pg 487

Solorzano, Elsa, Global Training Center, 550 S Mesa Hills Dr, Suite E4, El Paso, TX 79912 Tel: 915-534-7900 Toll Free Tel: 800-860-5030 Fax: 915-534-7903 E-mail: contact@globaltrainingcenter.com Web Site: www.globaltrainingcenter.com, pg 79

Solorzano, Sarah, Workers Compensation Research Institute, 955 Massachusetts Ave, Cambridge, MA 02139 Tel: 617-661-9274 Fax: 617-661-9284 E-mail: wcri@wcrinet.org Web Site: www.wcrinet.org, pg 232

Solov, Amy, Macmillan, 120 Broadway, 22nd fl, New York, NY 10271 E-mail: press.inquiries@macmillan.com Web Site: us.macmillan.com, pg 122

Somberg, Andrea, Harvey Klinger Inc, 300 W 55 St, Suite 11V, New York, NY 10019 Tel: 212-581-7068 Fax: 212-315-3823 E-mail: queries@harveyklinger.com Web Site: www.harveyklinger.com, pg 465

Somerset, Gary, US Government Publishing Office (GPO), Superintendent of Documents, 732 N Capitol St NW, Washington, DC 20401 Tel: 202-512-1800 Toll Free Tel: 866-512-1800 (orders) Fax: 202-512-1998 E-mail: contactcenter@gpo.gov Web Site: www.gpo.gov; bookstore.gpo.gov (sales), pg 223

Sommer, John, Advance Publishing Inc, 6950 Fulton St, Houston, TX 77022 Tel: 713-695-0600 Toll Free Tel: 800-917-9630 Fax: 713-695-8585 E-mail: info@advancepublishing.com Web Site: www.advancepublishing.com, pg 5

Song, Angela, Random House Children's Books, c/o Penguin Random House LLC, 1745 Broadway, New York, NY 10019 Tel: 212-782-9000 Web Site: www.rhcbooks.com, pg 170

Song, DongWon, Howard Morhaim Literary Agency Inc, 30 Pierrepont St, Brooklyn, NY 11201-3371 Tel: 718-222-8400 E-mail: info@morhaimliterary.com Web Site: www.morhaimliterary.com, pg 470

Sonin Schlesinger, Tara, Houghton Mifflin Harcourt Trade & Reference Division, 125 High St, Boston, MA 02110 Tel: 617-351-5000 Web Site: www.hmhco.com, pg 96

Sonnack, Kelly, Association of American Literary Agents Inc (AALA), 302A W 12 St, No 122, New York, NY 10014 Tel: 212-840-5700 E-mail: info@aalitagents.org Web Site: aalitagents.org, pg 498

Sonnenberg, Liz, Modern Memoirs Inc, 417 West St, Suite 104, Amherst, MA 01002 Tel: 413-253-2353 Web Site: www.modernmemoirs.com, pg 133

Soo Ping Chow, Frances, Running Press, 1290 Avenue of the Americas, New York, NY 10104 Tel: 212-364-1100 Toll Free Tel: 800-759-0190 (cust serv) Fax: 212-364-0933 (intl orders) Toll Free Fax: 800-286-9471 (cust serv) E-mail: customer.service@hbgusa.com; orders@hbgusa.com Web Site: www.hachettebookgroup.com/imprint/running-press/; www.moon.com (Moon Travel Guides), pg 178

Sood, Tej PS, Newgen North America Inc, 2714 Bee Cave Rd, Suite 201, Austin, TX 78746 Tel: 512-478-5341 Fax: 512-476-4756 E-mail: sales@newgen.co Web Site: www.newgen.co, pg 443

Sorensen, Eric, National Institute for Trial Advocacy (NITA), 1685 38 St, Suite 200, Boulder, CO 80301-2735 Tel: 720-890-4860 Toll Free Tel: 877-648-2632; 800-225-6482 (orders & returns) Fax: 720-890-7069 E-mail: customerservice@nita.org; sales@nita.org Web Site: www.nita.org, pg 138

Sorenson, Shannon, National Music Publishers' Association (NMPA), 1900 "N" St NW, Suite 500, Washington, DC 20036 Tel: 202-393-6672 E-mail: members@nmpa.org Web Site: nmpa.org, pg 513

Sorentino, Jessica, Macmillan, 120 Broadway, 22nd fl, New York, NY 10271 E-mail: press.inquiries@macmillan.com Web Site: us.macmillan.com, pg 122

Soriano, Claudette, Sourcebooks LLC, 1935 Brookdale Rd, Suite 139, Naperville, IL 60563 Tel: 630-961-3900 Toll Free Tel: 800-432-7444 Fax: 630-961-2168 E-mail: info@sourcebooks.com Web Site: www.sourcebooks.com, pg 195

Sorrell, Kim, HarperCollins Publishers LLC, 195 Broadway, New York, NY 10007 Tel: 212-207-7000 Web Site: www.harpercollins.com, pg 86

Sorsky, Richard, Linden Publishing Co Inc, 2006 S Mary St, Fresno, CA 93721 Tel: 559-233-6633 Toll Free Tel: 800-345-4447 (orders) Fax: 559-233-6933 Web Site: lindenpub.com; quilldriverbooks.com, pg 117

Sotirovic, Mira, University of Illinois, Department of Journalism, 119 Gregory Hall, 810 S Wright St, Urbana, IL 61801 Tel: 217-333-0709 E-mail: journ@illinois.edu Web Site: catalog.illinois.edu/graduate/media/journalism-ms; media.illinois.edu/journalism/degrees-programs/masters, pg 567

Soto, David, The Princeton Review, 110 E 42 St, 7th fl, New York, NY 10017 Toll Free Tel: 800-273-8439 (orders only) Web Site: www.princetonreview.com, pg 164

Soto, Sabrina, Association of School Business Officials International, 44790 Maynard St, Suite 200, Ashburn, VA 20147 Tel: 703-478-0405 Toll Free Tel: 866-682-2729 Fax: 703-478-0205; 703-708-7060 (membership) E-mail: asboreq@asbointl.org; membership@asbointl.org Web Site: www.asbointl.org, pg 20

Soule, Susan, Cambridge University Press, One Liberty Plaza, 20th fl, New York, NY 10006 Tel: 212-924-3900; 212-337-5000 Fax: 212-691-3239; 845-353-4141 E-mail: customer_service@cambridge.org; orders@cambridge.org; subscriptions_newyork@cambridge.org Web Site: www.cambridge.org/us, pg 39

Soussan, Lionel, Les Editions Phidal Inc, 5740 Ferrier St, Montreal, QC H4P 1M7, Canada Tel: 514-738-0202 Toll Free Tel: 800-738-7349 Fax: 514-738-5102 E-mail: info@phidal.com; orders@phidal.com (sales & export) Web Site: phidal.com, pg 404

South, Joseph, International Society for Technology in Education, 2111 Wilson Blvd, Suite 300, Arlington, VA 22201 Tel: 503-342-2848 (intl) Toll Free Tel: 800-336-5191 (US & CN) Fax: 541-302-3778 E-mail: iste@iste.org Web Site: www.iste.org, pg 103

Southard, Margaret, Simon & Schuster, 1230 Avenue of the Americas, New York, NY 10020 Tel: 212-698-7000 Toll Free Tel: 800-223-2348 (cust serv); 800-223-2336 (orders) Fax: 800-943-9831 (orders) Web Site: simonandschusterpublishing.com/simonandschuster/, pg 188

Southern, Ed, Doris Betts Fiction Prize, PO Box 21591, Winston-Salem, NC 27120-1591 Tel: 336-293-8844 E-mail: mail@ncwriters.org; nclrsubmissions@ecu.edu Web Site: www.ncwriters.org, pg 579

Southern, Ed, Sally Buckner Emerging Writers' Fellowship, PO Box 21591, Winston-Salem, NC 27120-1591 Tel: 336-293-8844 E-mail: mail@ncwriters.org; nclrsubmissions@ecu.edu Web Site: www.ncwriters.org, pg 585

Southern, Ed, Jacobs/Jones African-American Literary Prize, PO Box 21591, Winston-Salem, NC 27120-1591 Tel: 336-293-8844 E-mail: mail@ncwriters.org; nclrsubmissions@ecu.edu Web Site: www.ncwriters.org, pg 618

Southern, Ed, Randall Jarrell Poetry Competition, PO Box 21591, Winston-Salem, NC 27120-1591 Tel: 336-293-8844 E-mail: mail@ncwriters.org; nclrsubmissions@ecu.edu Web Site: www.ncwriters.org, pg 618

Southern, Ed, North Carolina Writers' Network, PO Box 21591, Winston-Salem, NC 27120-1591 Tel: 336-293-8844 E-mail: mail@ncwriters.org Web Site: www.ncwriters.org, pg 515

Southern, Ed, North Carolina Writers' Network Annual Fall Conference, PO Box 21591, Winston-Salem, NC 27120-1591 Tel: 336-293-8844 E-mail: mail@ncwriters.org Web Site: www.ncwriters.org, pg 556

Southern, Ed, Rose Post Creative Nonfiction Competition, PO Box 21591, Winston-Salem, NC 27120-1591 Tel: 336-293-8844 E-mail: mail@ncwriters.org; nclrsubmissions@ecu.edu Web Site: www.ncwriters.org, pg 651

Southern, Ed, Thomas Wolfe Fiction Prize, PO Box 21591, Winston-Salem, NC 27120-1591 Tel: 336-293-8844 E-mail: mail@ncwriters.org Web Site: www.ncwriters.org, pg 677

Sova, Kathy, Theatre Communications Group, 520 Eighth Ave, 24th fl, New York, NY 10018-4156 Tel: 212-609-5900 Fax: 212-609-5901 E-mail: info@tcg.org Web Site: www.tcg.org, pg 206

Sowards, Anne, Berkley, c/o Penguin Random House LLC, 1745 Broadway, 19th fl, New York, NY 10019 Tel: 212-366-2000 Web Site: www.penguin.com/publishers/berkley/; www.penguin.com/ace-overview/, pg 28

Sowersby, Emilia, Roaring Brook Press, 120 Broadway, New York, NY 10271 Tel: 646-307-5151 Web Site: us.macmillan.com/publishers/roaring-brook-press, pg 176

Spade, Ed, HarperCollins Publishers LLC, 195 Broadway, New York, NY 10007 Tel: 212-207-7000 Web Site: www.harpercollins.com, pg 86

Spahr, John Febiger Jr, Teton NewMedia Inc, 5286 Dunewood Dr, Florence, OR 97439 Tel: 541-991-3342 E-mail: lodgepole@tetonnm.com Web Site: www.tetonnm.com, pg 205

Spahr, Welmoed, Apress Media LLC, One New York Plaza, Suite 4600, New York, NY 10004-1562 Tel: 212-460-1500 E-mail: editorial@apress.com; customerservice@springernature.com Web Site: www.apress.com, pg 16

Spain, John, Baton Rouge Area Foundation, 100 North St, Suite 900, Baton Rouge, LA 70802 Tel: 225-387-6126 Web Site: www.braf.org, pg 525

Spain, Mahaylie, Trident Media Group LLC, 355 Lexington Ave, 12th fl, New York, NY 10017 Tel: 212-333-1511 E-mail: info@tridentmediagroup.com; press@tridentmediagroup.com; foreignrights@tridentmediagroup.com; office.assistant@tridentmediagroup.com Web Site: www.tridentmediagroup.com, pg 480

Spain, Tom, Simon & Schuster Audio, 1230 Avenue of the Americas, New York, NY 10020 Web Site: audio.simonandschuster.com, pg 189

Spaisman, Ben, The Mathematical Association of America, 1529 18 St NW, Washington, DC 20036-1358 Tel: 202-387-5200 Toll Free Tel: 800-741-9415 Fax: 202-265-2384 E-mail: maahq@maa.org; advertising@maa.org (pubns) Web Site: www.maa.org, pg 127

Spangler, Emily, Teachers College Press, 1234 Amsterdam Ave, New York, NY 10027 Tel: 212-678-3929 Fax: 212-678-4149 E-mail: tcpress@tc.edu Web Site: www.tcpress.com, pg 203

Spangler, Stephen, DEStech Publications Inc, 439 N Duke St, Lancaster, PA 17602-4967 Tel: 717-290-1660 Toll Free Tel: 877-500-4DES (500-4337) Fax: 717-509-6100 E-mail: info@destechpub; orders@destechpub.com Web Site: www.destechpub.com, pg 59

Spano, Maria, Insight Editions, 800 "A" St, San Rafael, CA 94901 Tel: 415-526-1370 Toll Free Tel: 800-809-3792 Toll Free Fax: 866-509-0515 E-mail: info@insighteditions.com; marketing@insighteditions.com Web Site: insighteditions.com, pg 101

Spanos, Christos, Candlewick Press, 99 Dover St, Somerville, MA 02144-2825 Tel: 617-661-3330 Fax: 617-661-0565 E-mail: bigbear@candlewick.com; salesinfo@candlewick.com Web Site: candlewick.com, pg 40

Sparkes, Kathy, Dumbarton Oaks, 1703 32 St NW, Washington, DC 20007 Tel: 202-339-6400 Fax: 202-339-6401; 202-298-8407 E-mail: doaksbooks@doaks.org; press@doaks.org Web Site: www.doaks.org, pg 62

Sparks, Kerry, Levine|Greenberg|Rostan Literary Agency, 307 Seventh Ave, Suite 2407, New York, NY 10001 Tel: 212-337-0934 Fax: 212-337-0948 E-mail: submit@lgrliterary.com Web Site: lgrliterary.com, pg 467

Sparks, Lee Ann, Trinity University Press, One Trinity Place, San Antonio, TX 78212-7200 Tel: 210-999-8884 Fax: 210-999-8838 E-mail: books@trinity.edu Web Site: www.tupress.org, pg 209

Spatara, Christine, Friends of American Writers (FAW), c/o 506 Rose Ave, Des Plaines, IL 60016 E-mail: info@fawchicago.org Web Site: www.fawchicago.org, pg 506

Speaker, Mary Austin, Milkweed Fellowship, 1011 Washington Ave S, Suite 300, Minneapolis, MN 55415-1246 Tel: 612-332-3192 Toll Free Tel: 800-520-6455 E-mail: fellowship@milkweed.org Web Site: milkweed.org/milkweed-fellowship, pg 633

Spear, Jody, Aaron-Spear, PO Box 42, Brooksville, ME 04617 Tel: 207-326-8764, pg 435

Spector, Alla, North Atlantic Books (NAB), 2526 Martin Luther King Jr Way, Berkeley, CA 94704 Tel: 510-549-4270 Web Site: www.northatlanticbooks.com, pg 142

Spector, Katelin, Ladderbird Literary Agency, 460 Yellow Brick Rd, Orange, CT 06477 Tel: 203-290-1703 Web Site: www.ladderbird.com, pg 466

Spellman-Silverman, Erica, Trident Media Group LLC, 355 Lexington Ave, 12th fl, New York, NY 10017 Tel: 212-333-1511 E-mail: info@tridentmediagroup.com; press@tridentmediagroup.com; foreignrights@tridentmediagroup.com; office.assistant@tridentmediagroup.com Web Site: www.tridentmediagroup.com, pg 480

Spence, Bianca, Trillium Book Award/Prix Trillium, South Tower, Suite 501, 175 Bloor St E, Toronto, ON M4W 3R8, Canada Tel: 416-314-6858 E-mail: programs2@ontariocreates.ca Web Site: ontariocreates.ca, pg 670

Spence, Bill, Information Today, Inc, 143 Old Marlton Pike, Medford, NJ 08055-8750 Tel: 609-654-6266 Toll Free Tel: 800-300-9868 (cust serv) Fax: 609-654-4309 E-mail: custserv@infotoday.com Web Site: informationtodayinc.com, pg 100

Spence, Heather, APH Press, 1839 Frankfort Ave, Louisville, KY 40206 Tel: 502-895-2405 Toll Free Tel: 800-223-1839 E-mail: press@aph.org Web Site: aph.org/shop, pg 15

Spence, Marya, Janklow & Nesbit Associates, 285 Madison Ave, 21st fl, New York, NY 10017 Tel: 212-421-1700 Fax: 212-355-1403 E-mail: info@janklow.com; submissions@janklow.com; filmtvrights@janklow.com Web Site: www.janklowandnesbit.com, pg 464

Spence, Melissa Weinberg, American Jewish Committee (AJC), Mail Code 6760, PO Box 7247, Philadelphia, PA 19170-0001 Tel: 212-751-4000 Fax: 212-891-1450 E-mail: social@ajc.org Web Site: www.ajc.org, pg 495

Spencer, Elaine, The Knight Agency Inc, 232 W Washington St, Madison, GA 30650 E-mail: admin@knightagency.net Web Site: www.knightagency.net, pg 466

Spencer, Susan, Television Academy, 5220 Lankershim Blvd, North Hollywood, CA 91601-3109 Tel: 818-754-2800 Web Site: www.emmys.com, pg 521

Spendley, Alana, Grand Central Publishing, 1290 Avenue of the Americas, New York, NY 10104 Tel: 212-364-1100 Web Site: www.hachettebookgroup.com/imprint/grand-central-publishing/, pg 80

Sperling, Ehud C, Bear & Co Inc, One Park St, Rochester, VT 05767 Tel: 802-767-3174 Toll Free Tel: 800-932-3277 Fax: 802-767-3726 E-mail: customerservice@InnerTraditions.com Web Site: InnerTraditions.com, pg 26

Sperling, Ehud C, Inner Traditions International Ltd, One Park St, Rochester, VT 05767 Tel: 802-767-3174 Toll Free Tel: 800-246-8648 Fax: 802-767-3726 E-mail: customerservice@InnerTraditions.com Web Site: www.InnerTraditions.com, pg 101

Sperling, Mahar, Bear & Co Inc, One Park St, Rochester, VT 05767 Tel: 802-767-3174 Toll Free Tel: 800-932-3277 Fax: 802-767-3726 E-mail: customerservice@InnerTraditions.com Web Site: InnerTraditions.com, pg 26

Sperling, Mahar, Inner Traditions International Ltd, One Park St, Rochester, VT 05767 Tel: 802-767-3174 Toll Free Tel: 800-246-8648 Fax: 802-767-3726 E-mail: customerservice@InnerTraditions.com Web Site: www.InnerTraditions.com, pg 101

Speyer, Anne, Atria Books, 1230 Avenue of the Americas, New York, NY 10020 Tel: 212-698-7000 Fax: 212-698-7007 Web Site: www.simonandschuster.com, pg 21

Spicer, Andrew, Willow Creek Press, 9931 Hwy 70 W, Minocqua, WI 54548 Tel: 715-358-7010 Toll Free Tel: 800-850-9453 Fax: 715-358-2807 E-mail: info@willowcreekpress.com Web Site: www.willowcreekpress.com; www.wcpretail.com, pg 230

Spicer, Charles, St Martin's Press, LLC, 120 Broadway, New York, NY 10271 E-mail: publicity@stmartins.com; trademarketing@stmartins.com; foreignrights@stmartins.com Web Site: us.macmillan.com/smp, pg 180

Spicer, Ed, Eisenbrauns, 820 N University Dr, USB 1, Suite C, University Park, PA 16802-1003 Tel: 814-865-1327 Toll Free Tel: 800-326-9180 (orders & cust serv) Fax: 814-863-1408 Toll Free Fax: 877-778-2665 (orders) E-mail: orders@psupress.org; customerservice@psupress.org Web Site: www.eisenbrauns.org, pg 65

Spicer, Emily, Society for Features Journalism (SFJ), Eugene S Pulliam National Journalism Ctr, 3909 N Meridian St, Indianapolis, IN 46208 E-mail: wearesfj@gmail.com Web Site: featuresjournalism.org, pg 519

Spiegel, Lauren, Gallery Books, 1230 Avenue of the Americas, New York, NY 10020 Toll Free Tel: 800-456-6798 Fax: 212-698-7284 E-mail: consumer.customerservice@simonandschuster.com Web Site: www.simonandschuster.com, pg 76

Spieler, Joseph, The Spieler Agency, 75 Broad St, Suite 304, New York, NY 10004 Tel: 212-757-4439 E-mail: thespieleragency@gmail.com Web Site: thespieleragency.com, pg 477

Spieller, Lauren, Folio Literary Management, The Film Center Bldg, 630 Ninth Ave, Suite 1101, New York, NY 10036 Tel: 212-400-1494 Fax: 212-967-0977 Web Site: www.foliolit.com, pg 459

Spikener, February, Great Lakes Independent Booksellers Association (GLIBA), 3123 Andrea Ct, Woodridge, IL 60517 Tel: 630-841-8129 Web Site: www.gliba.org, pg 507

Spikener, February, Heartland Booksellers Award, 3123 Andrea Ct, Woodridge, IL 60517 Tel: 630-841-8129 Web Site: www.gliba.org/heartland-booksellers-award.html, pg 611

Spinella, Michael, William Holmes McGuffey Longevity Award, PO Box 367, Fountain City, WI 54629 E-mail: info@taaonline.net Web Site: www.taaonline.net/mcguffey-longevity-award, pg 630

Spinella, Michael, Most Promising New Textbook Award, PO Box 367, Fountain City, WI 54629 E-mail: info@taaonline.net Web Site: www.taaonline.net/promising-new-textbook-award, pg 636

Spinella, Michael, Pynn-Silverman Lifetime Achievement Award, PO Box 367, Fountain City, WI 54629 E-mail: info@taaonline.net Web Site: www.taaonline.net/council-awards#pynn, pg 654

Spinella, Michael, TAA Council of Fellows, PO Box 367, Fountain City, WI 54629 E-mail: info@taaonline.net Web Site: www.taaonline.net/council-of-fellows, pg 668

Spinella, Michael, Textbook Excellence Award, PO Box 367, Fountain City, WI 54629 E-mail: info@taaonline.net Web Site: www.taaonline.net/textbook-excellence-award, pg 669

Spinelli, Kathleen, Harry N Abrams Inc, 195 Broadway, 9th fl, New York, NY 10007 Tel: 212-206-7715 Toll Free Tel: 800-345-1359 Fax: 212-645-8437 E-mail: abrams@abramsbooks.com; publicity@abramsbooks.com; sales@abramsbooks.com Web Site: www.abramsbooks.com, pg 2

Spinner, Dianna, The PRS Group Inc, 5800 Heritage Landing Dr, Suite E, East Syracuse, NY 13057-9358 Tel: 315-431-0511 Fax: 315-431-0200 E-mail: custserv@prsgroup.com Web Site: www.prsgroup.com, pg 166

Spitz, Jessica, Janklow & Nesbit Associates, 285 Madison Ave, 21st fl, New York, NY 10017 Tel: 212-421-1700 Fax: 212-355-1403 E-mail: info@janklow.com; submissions@janklow.com; filmtvrights@janklow.com Web Site: www.janklowandnesbit.com, pg 464

Spitzer, Anne-Lise, Philip G Spitzer Literary Agency Inc, 50 Talmage Farm Lane, East Hampton, NY 11937 Tel: 631-329-3650 Fax: 631-329-3651 Web Site: www.spitzeragency.com, pg 477

Spivey, Jim, The Vendome Press, 244 Fifth Ave, Suite 2043, New York, NY 10001 Tel: 212-737-1857 E-mail: info@vendomepress.com Web Site: www.vendomepress.com, pg 224

Spizzirri, Linda, Spizzirri Publishing Inc, PO Box 9397, Rapid City, SD 57709-9397 Tel: 605-348-2749 Toll Free Tel: 800-325-9819 Fax: 605-348-6251 Toll Free Fax: 800-322-9819 E-mail: spizzpub@aol.com Web Site: www.spizzirri.com, pg 196

Spooner, Andrea, Little, Brown Books for Young Readers (LBYR), 1290 Avenue of the Americas, New York, NY 10104 Tel: 212-364-1100 Toll Free Tel: 800-759-0190 (cust serv) E-mail: rights@lbchildrens.com Web Site: www.hachettebookgroup.com/imprint/little-brown-books-for-young-readers/, pg 118

Sprague, Alex, Diversion Books, 11 E 44 St, Suite 1603, New York, NY 10017 Tel: 212-961-6390 E-mail: info@diversionbooks.com Web Site: www.diversionbooks.com, pg 60

Sprague, Donald, Bolchazy-Carducci Publishers Inc, 1000 Brown St, Unit 301, Wauconda, IL 60084 Tel: 847-526-4344 Fax: 847-526-2867 E-mail: info@bolchazy.com; orders@bolchazy.com Web Site: www.bolchazy.com, pg 33

Sprague, Peter, Piano Press, 1425 Ocean Ave, Suite 5, Del Mar, CA 92014 Tel: 619-884-1401 E-mail: pianopress@pianopress.com Web Site: www.pianopress.com, pg 159

Spratley, Naomi, Macmillan, 120 Broadway, 22nd fl, New York, NY 10271 E-mail: press.inquiries@macmillan.com Web Site: us.macmillan.com, pg 122

Spring, Declan, New Directions Publishing Corp, 80 Eighth Ave, 19th fl, New York, NY 10011 Tel: 212-255-0230 E-mail: editorial@ndbooks.com; publicity@ndbooks.com Web Site: ndbooks.com, pg 139

Springer, Jane, Hamilton College, Literature & Creative Writing, Literature & Creative Writing Dept, 198 College Hill Rd, Clinton, NY 13323 Tel: 315-859-4370 Fax: 315-859-4390 Web Site: www.hamilton.edu, pg 563

Springer, Rebecca, Chelsea Green Publishing Co, 85 N Main St, Suite 120, White River Junction, VT 05001 Tel: 802-295-6300 Toll Free Tel: 800-639-4099 (cust serv & orders) Fax: 802-295-6444 E-mail: customerservice@chelseagreen.com; editorial@chelseagreen.com; publicity@chelseagreen.com; rights@chelseagreen.com Web Site: www.chelseagreen.com, pg 45

Springer, Rebecca, Houghton Mifflin Harcourt Trade & Reference Division, 125 High St, Boston, MA 02110 Tel: 617-351-5000 Web Site: www.hmhco.com, pg 96

Springmeyer, Kathy, Farcountry Press, 2750 Broadwater Ave, Helena, MT 59602-9202 Tel: 406-422-1263 Toll Free Tel: 800-821-3874 (sales off) Fax: 406-443-5480 E-mail: books@farcountrypress.com; sales@farcountrypress.com Web Site: www.farcountrypress.com, pg 69

Sprinkle, Nicole, Sasquatch Books, 1904 S Third Ave, Suite 710, Seattle, WA 98101 Tel: 206-467-4300 Toll Free Tel: 800-775-0817 Fax: 206-467-4301 E-mail: custserv@sasquatchbooks.com Web Site: sasquatchbooks.com, pg 182

Sproull, Sara, Harry N Abrams Inc, 195 Broadway, 9th fl, New York, NY 10007 Tel: 212-206-7715 Toll Free Tel: 800-345-1359 Fax: 212-645-8437 E-mail: abrams@abramsbooks.com; publicity@abramsbooks.com; sales@abramsbooks.com Web Site: www.abramsbooks.com, pg 3

Srivastava, Rahul, Simon & Schuster, LLC, 1230 Avenue of the Americas, New York, NY 10020 Tel: 212-698-7000 Toll Free Tel: 800-223-2336 (orders) Fax: 212-698-7007 Toll Free Fax: 800-943-9831 (orders) E-mail: firstname.lastname@simonandschuster.com; purchaseorders@simonandschuster.com (orders) Web Site: www.simonandschuster.com, pg 189

St John, Asia, Elderberry Press Inc, 1393 Old Homestead Dr, Oakland, OR 97462-9690 Tel: 541-459-6043 E-mail: editor@elderberrypress.com Web Site: www.elderberrypress.com, pg 65

St John, Valerie, Elderberry Press Inc, 1393 Old Homestead Dr, Oakland, OR 97462-9690 Tel: 541-459-6043 E-mail: editor@elderberrypress.com Web Site: www.elderberrypress.com, pg 65

St Marie, Megan, Modern Memoirs Inc, 417 West St, Suite 104, Amherst, MA 01002 Tel: 413-253-2353 Web Site: www.modernmemoirs.com, pg 133

St Marie, Sean, Modern Memoirs Inc, 417 West St, Suite 104, Amherst, MA 01002 Tel: 413-253-2353 Web Site: www.modernmemoirs.com, pg 133

St Pierre, Samela, SDP Publishing Solutions LLC, 36 Captain's Way, East Bridgewater, MA 02333 Tel: 617-775-0656 Web Site: www.sdppublishingsolutions.com, pg 444

St Pierre, Sarah, Penguin Random House Canada, a Penguin Random House company, 320 Front St W, Suite 1400, Toronto, ON M5V 3B6, Canada Tel: 416-364-4449 Toll Free Tel: 888-523-9292 (cust serv) E-mail: canadaweb@penguinrandomhouse.com; customerservicescanada@penguinrandomhouse.com Web Site: www.penguinrandomhouse.ca, pg 416

St-Hilaire, France, Institute for Research on Public Policy (IRPP), 1470 Peel St, No 200, Montreal, QC H3A 1T1, Canada Tel: 514-985-2461 Fax: 514-985-2559 E-mail: irpp@irpp.org Web Site: irpp.org, pg 410

Stabel, Meredith, University of Iowa Press, 119 W Park Rd, 100 Kuhl House, Iowa City, IA 52242-1000 Tel: 319-335-2000 Toll Free Tel: 800-621-2736 (orders only) Fax: 319-335-2055 Toll Free Fax: 800-621-8476 (orders only) E-mail: uipress@uiowa.edu Web Site: www.uipress.uiowa.edu, pg 216

Stackler, Ed, Stackler Editorial, 200 Woodland Ave, Summit, NJ 07901 Tel: 510-912-9187 E-mail: ed.stackler@gmail.com Web Site: www.fictioneditor.com, pg 445

Stadnyk, Greg, Simon & Schuster Children's Publishing, 1230 Avenue of the Americas, New York, NY 10020 Tel: 212-698-7000 Web Site: www.simonandschuster.com/kids; www.simonandschuster.com/teen; simonandschuster.net; simonandschuster.biz, pg 189

Stafford, David, McGraw-Hill Education, 2 Penn Plaza, New York, NY 10121-2298 Tel: 212-904-2000 E-mail: international_cs@mheducation.com; seg_customerservice@mheducation.com (PreK-12); hep_customerservice@mheducation.com (higher education) Web Site: www.mheducation.com, pg 128

Stafford-Hill, Jamie, Tor Publishing Group, 120 Broadway, New York, NY 10271 Toll Free Tel: 800-455-0340 (Macmillan) E-mail: torpublicity@tor.com; forgepublicity@forgebooks.com Web Site: us.macmillan.com/torpublishinggroup, pg 208

Stahl, Levi, University of Chicago Press, 1427 E 60 St, Chicago, IL 60637-2954 Tel: 773-702-7700; 773-702-7600 Toll Free Tel: 800-621-2736 (orders); 773-702-9756; 773-660-2235 (orders); 773-702-2708 E-mail: custserv@press.uchicago.edu; marketing@press.uchicago.edu Web Site: www.press.uchicago.edu, pg 215

Stahlman, Abigail, Houghton Mifflin Harcourt Trade & Reference Division, 125 High St, Boston, MA 02110 Tel: 617-351-5000 Web Site: www.hmhco.com, pg 96

Staib, Erich, Duke University Press, 905 W Main St, Suite 18B, Durham, NC 27701 Tel: 919-688-5134 Toll Free Tel: 888-651-0122 (US) Fax: 919-688-2615 Toll Free Fax: 888-651-0124 E-mail: orders@dukepress.edu Web Site: www.dukeupress.edu, pg 62

Stakes, Robert, Texas Western Press, c/o University of Texas at El Paso, 500 W University Ave, El Paso, TX 79968-0633 Tel: 915-747-5688 Toll Free Tel: 800-488-3798 (orders only) Fax: 915-747-5345 E-mail: twpress@utep.edu Web Site: twp.utep.edu, pg 205

Stallings, Luke, Close Up Publishing, 671 N Glebe Rd, Suite 900, Arlington, VA 22203 Tel: 703-706-3300 Toll Free Tel: 800-CLOSE-UP (256-7387) E-mail: info@closeup.org Web Site: www.closeup.org, pg 49

Stamas, Margot, Portfolio, c/o Penguin Random House LLC, 1745 Broadway, New York, NY 10019 Tel: 212-782-9000 Web Site: www.penguin.com/portfolio-overview/; www.penguin.com/sentinel-overview/; www.penguin.com/thesis/, pg 162

Stamathis, George S, Paul H Brookes Publishing Co Inc, PO Box 10624, Baltimore, MD 21285-0624 Tel: 410-337-9580 (outside US & CN) Toll Free Tel: 800-638-3775 (US & CN) Fax: 410-337-8539 E-mail: custserv@brookespublishing.com Web Site: www.brookespublishing.com, pg 37

Stamatkin, Susan, Institute of Environmental Sciences & Technology - IEST, 1827 Walden Office Sq, Suite 400, Schaumburg, IL 60173 Tel: 847-981-0100 Fax: 847-981-4130 E-mail: information@iest.org Web Site: www.iest.org, pg 101

Stambaugh, Doug, Simon & Schuster, LLC, 1230 Avenue of the Americas, New York, NY 10020 Tel: 212-698-7000 Toll Free Tel: 800-223-2336 (orders) Fax: 212-698-7007 Toll Free Fax: 800-943-9831 (orders) E-mail: firstname.lastname@simonandschuster.com; purchaseorders@simonandschuster.com (orders) Web Site: www.simonandschuster.com, pg 189

Stamos, James, Houghton Mifflin Harcourt, 125 High St, Boston, MA 02110 Tel: 617-351-5000 Toll Free Tel: 855-969-4642; 800-225-5425 (K-12 educ materials); 800-323-9540 (assessment materials); 877-219-1537 (SkillsTutor); 888-242-6747 (Innovation in Educ Group); 800-225-3362 (Trade & Ref Div) Toll Free Fax: 800-269-5232 E-mail: myhmco@hmhco.com Web Site: www.hmhco.com, pg 96

Stamper-Halpin, Phil, Penguin Random House LLC, 1745 Broadway, New York, NY 10019 Tel: 212-782-9000 Toll Free Tel: 800-726-0600 Web Site: www.penguinrandomhouse.com, pg 155

Standridge, Jordan, Charlesbridge Publishing Inc, 85 Main St, Watertown, MA 02472 Tel: 617-926-0329 Toll Free Tel: 800-225-3214 Fax: 617-926-5720 Toll Free Fax: 800-926-5775 E-mail: books@charlesbridge.com Web Site: www.charlesbridge.com, pg 45

Stanford, Elisa, Edit Resource LLC, 19265 Lincoln Green Lane, Monument, CO 80132 Tel: 719-290-0757 E-mail: info@editresource.com Web Site: www.editresource.com, pg 438

Stanford, Eric, Edit Resource LLC, 19265 Lincoln Green Lane, Monument, CO 80132 Tel: 719-290-0757 E-mail: info@editresource.com Web Site: www.editresource.com, pg 438

Stange, Karen, Wm B Eerdmans Publishing Co, 4035 Park East Ct SE, Grand Rapids, MI 49546 *Tel:* 616-459-4591 *Toll Free Tel:* 800-253-7521 *E-mail:* customerservice@eerdmans.com; sales@eerdmans.com *Web Site:* www.eerdmans.com, pg 64

Stanley, Lindsay, Cengage Learning, 20 Channel Center St, Boston, MA 02210 *Tel:* 617-289-7700 *Toll Free Tel:* 800-354-9706 *Fax:* 617-289-7844 *E-mail:* esales@cengage.com *Web Site:* www.cengage.com, pg 43

Stanley, Vincent, Macmillan, 120 Broadway, 22nd fl, New York, NY 10271 *E-mail:* press.inquiries@macmillan.com *Web Site:* us.macmillan.com, pg 122

Stansfield, Gwyneth, Random House Publishing Group, 1745 Broadway, New York, NY 10019 *Toll Free Tel:* 800-200-3552 *Web Site:* www.randomhousebooks.com, pg 171

Stanton, Brandi, Island Press, 2000 "M" St NW, Suite 480-B, Washington, DC 20036 *Tel:* 202-232-7933 *Toll Free Tel:* 800-621-2736 *Fax:* 202-234-1328 *E-mail:* info@islandpress.org *Web Site:* www.islandpress.org, pg 104

Stanton, Sarah, Sounds True Inc, 413 S Arthur Ave, Louisville, CO 80027 *Tel:* 303-665-3151 *Toll Free Tel:* 800-333-9185 (US); 888-303-9185 (US & CN) *E-mail:* customerservice@soundstrue.com; stpublicity@soundstrue.com *Web Site:* www.soundstrue.com, pg 194

Stanton, Sierra, Andrews McMeel Publishing LLC, 1130 Walnut St, Kansas City, MO 64106-2109 *Tel:* 816-581-7500 *Toll Free Tel:* 800-851-8923 *Web Site:* www.andrewsmcmeel.com; publishing.andrewsmcmeel.com, pg 14

Stanton, William, The H W Wilson Foundation, 750 Third Ave, 13th fl, New York, NY 10017 *Tel:* 212-418-8473 *Web Site:* www.thwwf.org, pg 526

Stanulis, Roxanne, Delaware Division of the Arts Individual Artist Fellowships, Carvel State Off Bldg, 4th fl, 820 N French St, Wilmington, DE 19801 *Tel:* 302-577-8278 *Fax:* 302-577-6561 *E-mail:* delarts@delaware.gov *Web Site:* arts.delaware.gov/grants-for-artists, pg 595

Stanwood, Karen G, SLACK® Incorporated, A Wyanoke Group Company, 6900 Grove Rd, Thorofare, NJ 08086-9447 *Tel:* 856-848-1000 *Toll Free Tel:* 800-257-8290 *Fax:* 856-848-6091 *E-mail:* sales@slackinc.com; editor@slackinc.com; customerservice@slackinc.com *Web Site:* www.healio.com/books, pg 191

Stapleton, Victoria, Little, Brown Books for Young Readers (LBYR), 1290 Avenue of the Americas, New York, NY 10104 *Tel:* 212-364-1100 *Toll Free Tel:* 800-759-0190 (cust serv) *E-mail:* rights@lbchildrens.com *Web Site:* www.hachettebookgroup.com/imprint/little-brown-books-for-young-readers/, pg 118

Star, Alex, Farrar, Straus & Giroux, LLC, 120 Broadway, New York, NY 10271 *Tel:* 212-741-6900 *E-mail:* fsg.publicity@fsgbooks.com; sales@fsgbooks.com *Web Site:* us.macmillan.com/fsg, pg 70

Star, Brenda, StarGroup International Inc, 1194 Old Dixie Hwy, Suite 201, West Palm Beach, FL 33413 *Tel:* 561-547-0667 *Fax:* 561-843-8530 *E-mail:* info@stargroupinternational.com *Web Site:* stargroupinternational.com, pg 197

Starace, Regina, Penn State University Press, University Support Bldg 1, Suite C, 820 N University Dr, University Park, PA 16802-1003 *Tel:* 814-865-1327 *Toll Free Tel:* 800-326-9180 (orders & cust serv) *Fax:* 814-863-1408 *Toll Free Fax:* 877-778-2665 (book orders) *E-mail:* orders@psupress.org; customerservice@psupress.org *Web Site:* www.psupress.org, pg 157

Starczewski, Kathryn, Yaddo Artists Residency, 312 Union Ave, Saratoga Springs, NY 12866 *Tel:* 518-584-0746 *Fax:* 518-584-1312 *Web Site:* www.yaddo.org, pg 559

Stark, Alexa, Writers House, 21 W 26 St, New York, NY 10010 *Tel:* 212-685-2400 *Web Site:* www.writershouse.com, pg 482

Stark, Kate, Viking Penguin, c/o Penguin Random House LLC, 1745 Broadway, New York, NY 10019 *Tel:* 212-782-9000 *Web Site:* www.penguin.com/overview-vikingbooks/; www.penguin.com/pamela-dorman-books-overview/; www.penguin.com/penguin-classics-overview/; www.penguin.com/penguin-life-overview/, pg 225

Stark, Katherine, Center for Strategic & International Studies (CSIS), 1616 Rhode Island Ave NW, Washington, DC 20036 *Tel:* 202-887-0200 *Fax:* 202-775-3199 *Web Site:* www.csis.org, pg 44

Stark, Stacy Tenenbaum, Cy Twombly Award for Poetry, 820 Greenwich St, New York, NY 10014 *Tel:* 212-807-7077 *E-mail:* info@contemporary-arts.org *Web Site:* www.foundationforcontemporaryarts.org/grants/cy-twombly-award-for-poetry, pg 672

Starke, Alexis, History Publishing Co LLC, PO Box 700, Palisades, NY 10964 *Tel:* 845-359-1765 *Fax:* 845-818-3730 (sales) *E-mail:* info@historypublishingco.com *Web Site:* www.historypublishingco.com, pg 93

Starnino, Carmine, Vehicule Press, PO Box 42094, CP Roy, Montreal, QC H2W 2T3, Canada *Tel:* 514-844-6073 *E-mail:* vp@vehiculepress.com; admin@vehiculepress.com *Web Site:* www.vehiculepress.com, pg 424

Starr, Abigail, Macmillan Audio, 120 Broadway, 22nd fl, New York, NY 10271 *Tel:* 646-600-7856 *Toll Free Tel:* 888-330-8477 (cust serv) *Toll Free Fax:* 800-672-7703 *E-mail:* macmillan.audio@macmillanusa.com *Web Site:* us.macmillan.com/audio, pg 123

Starr, Brent, Indiana University Press, Off of Scholarly Publg, Herman B Wells Library 350, 1320 E Tenth St, Bloomington, IN 47405-3907 *Tel:* 812-855-8817 *Fax:* 812-855-7931; 812-855-8507 *E-mail:* iupress@indiana.edu *Web Site:* iupress.org, pg 100

Starr, Jay, Public Relations Society of America Inc, 120 Wall St, 21st fl, New York, NY 10005 *Tel:* 212-460-1400 *E-mail:* membership@prsa.org *Web Site:* www.prsa.org, pg 518

Starr, Joshua, DAW Books, 19 W 21 St, No 1201, New York, NY 10010 *E-mail:* info@astrapublishinghouse.com *Web Site:* astrapublishinghouse.com/imprints/daw-books, pg 57

Starr, Lindsay, The University of North Carolina Press, 116 S Boundary St, Chapel Hill, NC 27514-3808 *Tel:* 919-966-3561; 919-966-7449 (orders) *Toll Free Tel:* 800-848-3224 (orders) *Fax:* 919-962-2704 (orders) *Toll Free Fax:* 800-272-6817 (orders) *E-mail:* uncpress@unc.edu *Web Site:* uncpress.org, pg 218

Starry, Alexa, The Tuesday Agency, 404 E College St, Suite 408, Iowa City, IA 52240 *Tel:* 319-338-7080; 319-400-9031 (cell) *E-mail:* info@tuesdayagency.com *Web Site:* tuesdayagency.com, pg 487

Staszak-Silva, Suzanne, Johns Hopkins University Press, 2715 N Charles St, Baltimore, MD 21218-4363 *Tel:* 410-516-6900; 410-516-6987 *Toll Free Tel:* 800-537-5487 (book orders & cust serv); 800-548-1784 (journal orders) *Fax:* 410-516-6968; 410-516-6998 (orders) *E-mail:* hfscustserv@press.jhu.edu (cust serv); jrnlcirc@jh.edu (journal orders) *Web Site:* www.press.jhu.edu; muse.jhu.edu, pg 106

Staton, Cecil P Jr, Smyth & Helwys Publishing Inc, 6316 Peake Rd, Macon, GA 31210-3960 *Tel:* 478-757-0564 *Toll Free Tel:* 800-747-3016 (orders only) *Fax:* 478-757-1305 *E-mail:* information@helwys.com *Web Site:* www.helwys.com, pg 192

Staub, Wayne, New Jersey Business & Industry Association (NJBIA), 10 W Lafayette St, Trenton, NJ 08608-2002 *Tel:* 609-393-7707 *Web Site:* njbia.org, pg 514

Stauffer, Jessica, American Booksellers Association, 600 Mamaroneck Ave, Suite 400, Harrison, NY 10528 *Tel:* 914-406-7500 *Toll Free Tel:* 800-637-0037 *Fax:* 914-417-4013 *E-mail:* info@bookweb.org *Web Site:* www.bookweb.org, pg 494

Stavans, Ilan, The Restless Books Prize for New Immigrant Writing, 232 Third St, Suite A101, Brooklyn, NY 11215 *E-mail:* publisher@restlessbooks.com *Web Site:* www.restlessbooks.org/prize-for-new-immigrant-writing, pg 655

Stead, Lauren, Casemate | publishers, 1950 Lawrence Rd, Havertown, PA 19083 *Tel:* 610-853-9131 *Fax:* 610-853-9146 *E-mail:* casemate@casematepublishers.com *Web Site:* www.casematepublishers.com, pg 42

Stearns, Leah, University of Virginia Press, PO Box 400318, Charlottesville, VA 22904-4318 *Tel:* 434-924-3469 (cust serv) *Toll Free Tel:* 800-831-3406 *Fax:* 434-982-2655 *Toll Free Fax:* 877-288-6400 *E-mail:* vapress@virginia.edu *Web Site:* www.upress.virginia.edu, pg 220

Stearns, Rondi, Appalachian Mountain Club Books, 10 City Sq, Boston, MA 02129 *Tel:* 617-523-0655 *E-mail:* amcbooks@outdoors.org; amcpublications@outdoors.org *Web Site:* www.outdoors.org, pg 15

Stebbins, Dr Chad, Eugene Cervi Award, Missouri Southern State University, 3950 E Newman Rd, Joplin, MO 64801-1595 *Web Site:* www.iswne.org/contests, pg 588

Stebbins, Dr Chad, Golden Quill Award, Missouri Southern State University, 3950 E Newman Rd, Joplin, MO 64801-1595 *Web Site:* www.iswne.org/contests, pg 607

Stebbins, Dr Chad, International Society of Weekly Newspaper Editors (ISWNE), Missouri Southern State University, 3950 E Newman Rd, Joplin, MO 64801-1595 *Web Site:* www.iswne.org, pg 508

Stebbins, Hallie, Princeton University Press, 41 William St, Princeton, NJ 08540-5237 *Tel:* 609-258-4900 *Fax:* 609-258-6305 *E-mail:* info@press.princeton.edu *Web Site:* press.princeton.edu, pg 164

Stebbins, Kerri, BenBella Books Inc, 10440 N Central Expwy, Suite 800, Dallas, TX 75231-2264 *Tel:* 214-750-3600 *Web Site:* www.benbellabooks.com; www.smartpopbooks.com, pg 27

Stech, Marko R, Canadian Institute of Ukrainian Studies Press, University of Toronto, 47 Queen's Park Crescent E, Suite B-12, Toronto, ON M5S 2C3, Canada *Tel:* 416-946-7326 *E-mail:* cius@ualberta.ca *Web Site:* www.ciuspress.com, pg 398

Steckley, Ed, National Cartoonists Society (NCS), PO Box 592927, Orlando, FL 32859-2927 *Tel:* 407-994-6703 *E-mail:* info@nationalcartoonists.com; membership@nationalcartoonists.com *Web Site:* www.nationalcartoonists.com, pg 512

Steed, Tobias, Leapfrog Global Fiction Prize, PO Box 505, Fredonia, NY 14063 *E-mail:* leapfrog@leapfrogpress.com *Web Site:* leapfrogpress.com/the-leapfrog-global-fiction-prize-contest, pg 623

Steeds, Harriet, Chronicle Books LLC, 680 Second St, San Francisco, CA 94107 *Tel:* 415-537-4200 *Fax:* 415-537-4460 (perms) *E-mail:* hello@chroniclebooks.com; subrights@chroniclebooks.com *Web Site:* www.chroniclebooks.com, pg 48

Steele, Alex, Gotham Writers' Workshop, 555 Eighth Ave, Suite 1402, New York, NY 10018-4358 *Tel:* 212-974-8377 *E-mail:* contact@gothamwriters.com *Web Site:* www.gothamwriters.com, pg 554

Steele, Harlow, HarperCollins Children's Books, 195 Broadway, New York, NY 10007 *Tel:* 212-207-7000 *Web Site:* www.harpercollins.com/childrens, pg 86

Steele, Lily, Peachtree Publishing Co Inc, 1700 Chattahoochee Ave, Atlanta, GA 30318-2112 *Tel:* 404-876-8761 *Toll Free Tel:* 800-241-0113 *Fax:* 404-875-2578 *Toll Free Fax:* 800-875-8909 *E-mail:* hello@peachtree-online.com; orders@peachtree-online.com; sales@peachtree-online.com *Web Site:* www.peachtreebooks.com; www.peachtree-online.com, pg 153

Steele, Rick, Leadership Ministries Worldwide, 1928 Central Ave, Chattanooga, TN 37408 *Tel:* 423-855-2181 *Toll Free Tel:* 800-987-8790 *E-mail:* info@lmw.org *Web Site:* lmw.org; store.lmw.org, pg 113

Steep, Jamie, Penguin Random House Canada, a Penguin Random House company, 320 Front St W, Suite 1400, Toronto, ON M5V 3B6, Canada *Tel:* 416-

364-4449 *Toll Free Tel:* 888-523-9292 (cust serv) *E-mail:* canadaweb@penguinrandomhouse.com; customerservicescanada@penguinrandomhouse.com *Web Site:* www.penguinrandomhouse.ca, pg 416

Steer, Pamela, Chartered Professional Accountants of Canada (CPA Canada), 277 Wellington St W, Toronto, ON M5V 3H2, Canada *Tel:* 416-977-3222 *Toll Free Tel:* 800-268-3793 *Fax:* 416-977-8585 *E-mail:* member.services@cpacanada.ca; customerservice@cpacanada.ca *Web Site:* www.cpacanada.ca; www.facebook.com/cpacanada; cpastore.ca, pg 399

Steere, Michael, Down East Books, 4501 Forbes Blvd, Suite 200, Lanham, MD 20706 *Web Site:* rowman.com/page/downeastbooks, pg 61

Steeve, Lesley, Irwin Law Inc, 14 Duncan St, Suite 206, Toronto, ON M5H 3G8, Canada *Tel:* 416-862-7690 *Toll Free Tel:* 888-314-9014 *Fax:* 416-862-9236 *E-mail:* info@irwinlaw.com; contact@irwinlaw.com *Web Site:* www.irwinlaw.com, pg 410

Stefanchik, Mary Grace, American Society of Mechanical Engineers (ASME), 2 Park Ave, New York, NY 10016-5990 *Tel:* 646-616-3100 *Toll Free Tel:* 800-843-2763 (cust serv-CN, Mexico & US) *Fax:* 973-882-1717 (orders & inquiries) *E-mail:* customercare@asme.org *Web Site:* www.asme.org, pg 13

Steffy, Julia, Sourcebooks LLC, 1935 Brookdale Rd, Suite 139, Naperville, IL 60563 *Tel:* 630-961-3900 *Toll Free Tel:* 800-432-7444 *Fax:* 630-961-2168 *E-mail:* info@sourcebooks.com *Web Site:* www.sourcebooks.com, pg 194

Stehlik, Liate, HarperCollins Children's Books, 195 Broadway, New York, NY 10007 *Tel:* 212-207-7000 *Web Site:* www.harpercollins.com/childrens, pg 85

Stehlik, Liate, HarperCollins Publishers LLC, 195 Broadway, New York, NY 10007 *Tel:* 212-207-7000 *Web Site:* www.harpercollins.com, pg 86

Steigmeyer, Hannah, Avery, c/o Penguin Random House LLC, 1745 Broadway, New York, NY 10019 *Tel:* 212-366-2000 *Web Site:* www.penguin.com/avery-overview/, pg 23

Steigmeyer, Hannah, TarcherPerigee, c/o Penguin Random House LLC, 1745 Broadway, New York, NY 10019 *Tel:* 212-782-9000 *Web Site:* www.penguin.com/tarcherperigee-overview/; www.facebook.com/TarcherPerigee, pg 202

Steiker, Stephanie, Regal Hoffmann & Associates LLC, 157 13 St, Brooklyn, NY 11215 *Tel:* 212-684-7900 *E-mail:* info@rhaliterary.com; submissions@rhaliterary.com *Web Site:* www.rhaliterary.com, pg 473

Stein, Faith Wilson, Northwestern University Press, 629 Noyes St, Evanston, IL 60208-4210 *Tel:* 847-491-2046 *Toll Free Tel:* 800-621-2736 (orders only) *Fax:* 847-491-8150 *E-mail:* nupress@northwestern.edu *Web Site:* www.nupress.northwestern.edu, pg 143

Stein, Kate, Casemate | publishers, 1950 Lawrence Rd, Havertown, PA 19083 *Tel:* 610-853-9131 *Fax:* 610-853-9146 *E-mail:* casemate@casematepublishers.com *Web Site:* www.casematepublishers.com, pg 41

Stein, Liz, HarperCollins Publishers LLC, 195 Broadway, New York, NY 10007 *Tel:* 212-207-7000 *Web Site:* www.harpercollins.com, pg 86

Stein, Sarah, HarperCollins Publishers LLC, 195 Broadway, New York, NY 10007 *Tel:* 212-207-7000 *Web Site:* www.harpercollins.com, pg 86

Stein, Stacey, Random House Publishing Group, 1745 Broadway, New York, NY 10019 *Toll Free Tel:* 800-200-3552 *Web Site:* www.randomhousebooks.com, pg 171

Stein, Stephanie, Tor Publishing Group, 120 Broadway, New York, NY 10271 *Toll Free Tel:* 800-455-0340 (Macmillan) *E-mail:* torpublicity@tor.com; forgepublicity@forgebooks.com *Web Site:* us.macmillan.com/torpublishinggroup, pg 208

Steinbach, Joe, AuthorHouse, 1663 Liberty Dr, Bloomington, IN 47403 *Toll Free Tel:* 833-262-8899; 888-519-5121 *E-mail:* sales@authorhouse.com; vip@authorhouse.com *Web Site:* www.authorhouse.com, pg 22

Steinbach, Joe, Xlibris Corp, 1663 Liberty Dr, Suite 200, Bloomington, IN 47403 *Toll Free Tel:* 844-714-8691; 888-795-4274 *Fax:* 610-915-0294 *E-mail:* info@xlibris.com; media@xlibris.com *Web Site:* www.xlibris.com; www.authorsolutions.com/our-imprints/xlibris, pg 234

Steinberg, Benjamin, HarperCollins Publishers LLC, 195 Broadway, New York, NY 10007 *Tel:* 212-207-7000 *Web Site:* www.harpercollins.com, pg 86

Steinberg, Michael, Michael Steinberg Literary Agent, PO Box 274, Glencoe, IL 60022-0274 *Tel:* 847-626-1000 *E-mail:* michael14steinberg@comcast.net, pg 477

Steinberger, David, National Book Foundation, 90 Broad St, Suite 604, New York, NY 10004 *Tel:* 212-685-0261 *Fax:* 212-213-6570 *E-mail:* nationalbook@nationalbook.org *Web Site:* www.nationalbook.org, pg 526

Steinbock, Steven, International Association of Crime Writers Inc, North American Branch, PO Box 863, Norman, OK 73071 *E-mail:* crimewritersna@gmail.com *Web Site:* www.crimewritersna.org, pg 508

Steinecke, Anke, Penguin Random House LLC, 1745 Broadway, New York, NY 10019 *Tel:* 212-782-9000 *Toll Free Tel:* 800-726-0600 *Web Site:* www.penguinrandomhouse.com, pg 155

Steiner, Eric, American Forest & Paper Association (AF&PA), 1101 "K" St NW, Suite 700, Washington, DC 20005 *Tel:* 202-463-2700 *E-mail:* info@afandpa.org; comm@afandpa.org *Web Site:* www.afandpa.org, pg 495

Steiner, Kevin, AIP Publishing LLC, 1305 Walt Whitman Rd, Suite 110, Melville, NY 11747 *Tel:* 516-576-2200 *E-mail:* help@aip.org; press@aip.org; rights@aip.org *Web Site:* www.aip.org; publishing.aip.org, pg 6

Steinmetz, Kay, Syracuse University Press, 621 Skytop Rd, Suite 110, Syracuse, NY 13244-5290 *Tel:* 315-443-5534 *Toll Free Tel:* 800-365-8929 (cust serv) *Fax:* 315-443-5545 *E-mail:* supress@syr.edu *Web Site:* press.syr.edu, pg 201

Stelter, Gretchen, Sourcebooks LLC, 1935 Brookdale Rd, Suite 139, Naperville, IL 60563 *Tel:* 630-961-3900 *Toll Free Tel:* 800-432-7444 *Fax:* 630-961-2168 *E-mail:* info@sourcebooks.com *Web Site:* www.sourcebooks.com, pg 194

Stelzig, Chris, Entomological Society of America, 170 Jennifer Rd, Suite 230, Annapolis, MD 21401 *Tel:* 301-731-4535 *Fax:* 301-731-4538 *E-mail:* esa@entsoc.org *Web Site:* www.entsoc.org, pg 67

Stempel-Lobell, Jenna, HarperCollins Children's Books, 195 Broadway, New York, NY 10007 *Tel:* 212-207-7000 *Web Site:* www.harpercollins.com/childrens, pg 85

Stender, Dr Uwe, TriadaUS Literary Agency, PO Box 561, Sewickley, PA 15143 *Tel:* 412-401-3376 *Web Site:* www.triadaus.com, pg 480

Stephen, Michaela, Second Story Press, 20 Maud St, Suite 401, Toronto, ON M5V 2M5, Canada *Tel:* 416-537-7850 *Fax:* 416-537-0588 *E-mail:* info@secondstorypress.ca *Web Site:* secondstorypress.ca, pg 419

Stephens, Bre, The Jennifer DeChiara Literary Agency, 245 Park Ave, 39th fl, New York, NY 10167 *Tel:* 212-372-8989 *Web Site:* www.jdlit.com, pg 455

Stephens, Jenny, Sterling Lord Literistic Inc, 594 Broadway, Suite 205, New York, NY 10012 *Tel:* 212-780-6050 *Fax:* 212-780-6095 *E-mail:* info@sll.com *Web Site:* www.sll.com, pg 477

Stephens, Lily, University of South Carolina Press, 1600 Hampton St, Suite 544, Columbia, SC 29208 *Tel:* 803-777-5245 *Toll Free Tel:* 800-768-2500 (orders) *Fax:* 803-777-0160 *Toll Free Tel:* 800-868-0740 (orders) *Web Site:* uscpress.com, pg 220

Stephens, Michael, Fresh Air Books, 1908 Grand Ave, Nashville, TN 37212 *Tel:* 615-340-7200 *Toll Free Tel:* 800-972-0433 (orders) *Web Site:* books.upperroom.org, pg 75

Stephens, Michael, Manning Publications Co, 20 Baldwin Rd, PO Box 761, Shelter Island, NY 11964 *Tel:* 203-626-1510 *E-mail:* sales@manning.com; support@manning.com (cust serv) *Web Site:* www.manning.com, pg 124

Stephens, Michael, Upper Room Books, 1908 Grand Ave, Nashville, TN 37212 *Tel:* 615-340-7200 *Toll Free Tel:* 800-972-0433 *Web Site:* books.upperroom.org, pg 223

Stephenson, Dave, National Notary Association (NNA), 9350 De Soto Ave, Chatsworth, CA 91311-4926 *Tel:* 818-739-4000 *Toll Free Tel:* 800-876-6827 *Toll Free Fax:* 800-833-1211 *E-mail:* services@nationalnotary.org *Web Site:* www.nationalnotary.org, pg 138

Stephenson, Lisa, Alliance for Women in Media (AWM), 2365 Harrodsburg Rd, A325, Lexington, KY 40504 *Tel:* 202-750-3664 *Fax:* 202-750-3664 *E-mail:* info@allwomeninmedia.org *Web Site:* allwomeninmedia.org, pg 494

Stephenson, Lisa, The Gracies®, 2365 Harrodsburg Rd, Suite A325, Lexington, KY 40504 *Tel:* 202-750-3664 *Fax:* 202-750-3664 *E-mail:* info@allwomeninmedia.org *Web Site:* allwomeninmedia.org, pg 608

Stephenson, Taylor, Association for Intelligent Information Management (AIIM), 8403 Colesville Rd, No 1100, Silver Spring, MD 20910 *Tel:* 301-587-8202 *Toll Free Tel:* 800-477-2446 *Fax:* 301-587-2711 *E-mail:* hello@aiim.org *Web Site:* www.aiim.org, pg 498

Stephney, Karlee, HarperCollins Publishers LLC, 195 Broadway, New York, NY 10007 *Tel:* 212-207-7000 *Web Site:* www.harpercollins.com, pg 87

Sterkowitz, Jennifer, Sourcebooks LLC, 1935 Brookdale Rd, Suite 139, Naperville, IL 60563 *Tel:* 630-961-3900 *Toll Free Tel:* 800-432-7444 *Fax:* 630-961-2168 *E-mail:* info@sourcebooks.com *Web Site:* www.sourcebooks.com, pg 195

Sterling, Meghan, Maine Literary Awards, Glickman Family Library, 314 Forest Ave, Rm 318, Portland, ME 04101 *Tel:* 207-228-8263 *E-mail:* info@mainewriters.org *Web Site:* www.mainewriters.org/programs/maine-literary-awards, pg 628

Sterling, Meghan, Maine Writers & Publishers Alliance (MWPA), Glickman Family Library, 314 Forest Ave, Rm 318, Portland, ME 04101 *Tel:* 207-228-8263 *E-mail:* info@mainewriters.org *Web Site:* www.mainewriters.org, pg 510

Stern, Amy, Sheldon Fogelman Agency Inc, 420 E 72 St, New York, NY 10021 *Tel:* 212-532-7250 *Fax:* 212-685-8939 *E-mail:* info@sheldonfogelmanagency.com; submissions@sheldonfogelmanagency.com *Web Site:* sheldonfogelmanagency.com, pg 459

Sternberg, Joan D, Practising Law Institute (PLI), 1177 Avenue of the Americas, 2nd fl, New York, NY 10036 *Tel:* 212-824-5710 (cust serv) *Toll Free Tel:* 800-260-4PLI (260-4754) *Toll Free Fax:* 800-321-0093 (cust serv) *E-mail:* info@pli.edu; membership@pli.edu *Web Site:* www.pli.edu, pg 163

Stetzer, Claire, Harry N Abrams Inc, 195 Broadway, 9th fl, New York, NY 10007 *Tel:* 212-206-7715 *Toll Free Tel:* 800-345-1359 *Fax:* 212-645-8437 *E-mail:* abrams@abramsbooks.com; publicity@abramsbooks.com; sales@abramsbooks.com *Web Site:* www.abramsbooks.com, pg 3

Steuerwald, Audrey, HarperCollins Children's Books, 195 Broadway, New York, NY 10007 *Tel:* 212-207-7000 *Web Site:* www.harpercollins.com/childrens, pg 85

Steve, Betsy, New York University Press, 838 Broadway, 3rd fl, New York, NY 10003-4812 *Tel:* 212-998-2575 (edit) *Toll Free Tel:* 800-996-6987 (orders) *Fax:* 212-995-4798 (orders) *E-mail:* nyupressinfo@nyu.edu (cust care) *Web Site:* www.nyupress.org, pg 141

Stevens, Demi, Pennwriters Conference, PO Box 685, Dalton, PA 18414 E-mail: conferencecoordinator@pennwriters.org; info@pennwriters.org Web Site: pennwriters.org, pg 556

Stevens, Drew, The Feminist Press at The City University of New York, 365 Fifth Ave, Suite 5406, New York, NY 10016 Tel: 212-817-7915 Fax: 212-817-1593 E-mail: info@feministpress.org Web Site: www.feministpress.org, pg 71

Stevens, Iisha, Other Press, 267 Fifth Ave, 6th fl, New York, NY 10016 Tel: 212-414-0054 Toll Free Tel: 877-THEOTHER (843-6843) Fax: 212-414-0939 E-mail: editor@otherpress.com; marketing@otherpress.com; publicity@otherpress.com Web Site: otherpress.com, pg 148

Stevens, Jacob, Verso Books, 388 Atlantic Ave, Brooklyn, NY 11217 Tel: 718-246-8160 Fax: 718-246-8165 E-mail: verso@versobooks.com Web Site: www.versobooks.com, pg 224

Stevens, Kathryn, Princeton University Press, 41 William St, Princeton, NJ 08540-5237 Tel: 609-258-4900 Fax: 609-258-6305 E-mail: info@press.princeton.edu Web Site: press.princeton.edu, pg 164

Stevens, Martin, Forum Publishing Co, 383 E Main St, Centerport, NY 11721 Tel: 631-754-5000 Toll Free Tel: 800-635-7654 Fax: 631-754-0630 E-mail: forumpublishing@aol.com Web Site: www.forum123.com, pg 73

Stevens, Steffanie Mortis, Trinity University Press, One Trinity Place, San Antonio, TX 78212-7200 Tel: 210-999-8884 Fax: 210-999-8838 E-mail: books@trinity.edu Web Site: www.tupress.org, pg 209

Stevenson, Alice, Children's History Book Prize, 170 Central Park W, New York, NY 10024 Tel: 212-873-3400 Fax: 212-595-5707 E-mail: info@nyhistory.org Web Site: www.nyhistory.org/childrens-museum/connect/book-prize, pg 588

Stevenson, Courtney, HarperCollins Children's Books, 195 Broadway, New York, NY 10007 Tel: 212-207-7000 Web Site: www.harpercollins.com/childrens, pg 85

Stevenson, Deborah, Scott O'Dell Award for Historical Fiction, c/o Horn Book Inc, 300 The Fenway, Suite P-311, Palace Road Bldg, Boston, MA 02215 Tel: 617-278-0225 Toll Free Tel: 888-628-0225 E-mail: scottodellfanpage@gmail.com Web Site: scottodell.com/the-scott-odell-award, pg 643

Steward, Carlos, Black Mountain Press, PO Box 9907, Asheville, NC 28815 Tel: 828-273-3332 Web Site: www.theblackmountainpress.com, pg 30

Steward, Scott C, Newbury Street Press, 99-101 Newbury St, Boston, MA 02116 Tel: 617-226-1206 Toll Free Tel: 888-296-3447 (NEHGS membership) Fax: 617-536-7307 E-mail: thebookstore@nehgs.org Web Site: www.americanancestors.org, pg 141

Stewart, Becki, Mason Crest Publishers, 450 Parkway Dr, Suite D, Broomall, PA 19008 Tel: 610-543-6200 Toll Free Tel: 866-MCP-BOOK (627-2665) Fax: 610-543-3878 Web Site: www.masoncrest.com, pg 126

Stewart, Caitlin, Editors Canada (Reviseurs Canada), 1507-180 Dundas St W, Toronto, ON M5G 1Z8, Canada Tel: 416-975-1379 E-mail: info@editors.ca; info@reviseurs.ca; communications@editors.ca Web Site: www.editors.ca; www.reviseurs.ca, pg 505

Stewart, Caitlin, Equity Fellowship, 1507-180 Dundas St W, Toronto, ON M5G 1Z8, Canada Tel: 416-975-1379 E-mail: info@editors.ca; info@reviseurs.ca; communications@editors.ca Web Site: www.editors.ca/about/awards/equity-fellowship, pg 600

Stewart, Caitlin, Tom Fairley Award for Editorial Excellence, 1507-180 Dundas St W, Toronto, ON M5G 1Z8, Canada Tel: 416-975-1379 E-mail: fairley_award@editors.ca; info@editors.ca; communications@editors.ca Web Site: www.editors.ca/about/awards/tom-fairley-award, pg 601

Stewart, Caitlin, Claudette Upton Scholarship, 1507-180 Dundas St W, Toronto, ON M5G 1Z8, Canada Tel: 416-975-1379 E-mail: info@editors.ca; info@reviseurs.ca; communications@editors.ca Web Site: www.editors.ca/about/awards/claudette-upton-scholarship, pg 672

Stewart, Caitlin, Karen Virag Award, 1507-180 Dundas St W, Toronto, ON M5G 1Z8, Canada Tel: 416-975-1379 E-mail: info@editors.ca; info@reviseurs.ca; communications@editors.ca Web Site: www.editors.ca/about/awards/karen-virag-award-0, pg 673

Stewart, Douglas, Sterling Lord Literistic Inc, 594 Broadway, Suite 205, New York, NY 10012 Tel: 212-780-6050 Fax: 212-780-6095 E-mail: info@sll.com Web Site: www.sll.com, pg 477

Stewart, Jenna Dimmick, Chelsea Green Publishing Co, 85 N Main St, Suite 120, White River Junction, VT 05001 Tel: 802-295-6300 Toll Free Tel: 800-639-4099 (cust serv & orders) Fax: 802-295-6444 E-mail: customerservice@chelseagreen.com; editorial@chelseagreen.com; publicity@chelseagreen.com; rights@chelseagreen.com Web Site: www.chelseagreen.com, pg 45

Stewart, Kanya, National Association of Black Journalists (NABJ), 1100 Knight Hall, Suite 3101, College Park, MD 20742 Tel: 301-405-0248 E-mail: contact@nabj.org; press@nabj.org Web Site: nabjonline.org, pg 511

Stewart, Leah, Sewanee Writers' Conference, 735 University Ave, Sewanee, TN 37383 Tel: 931-598-1654 E-mail: swc@sewanee.edu Web Site: www.sewaneewriters.org, pg 557

Stewart, Melissa, Western Heritage Awards (Wrangler Award), 1700 NE 63 St, Oklahoma City, OK 73111 Tel: 405-478-2250 Fax: 405-478-4714 E-mail: info@nationalcowboymuseum.org Web Site: nationalcowboymuseum.org, pg 674

Stewart, Nick, Grove Atlantic Inc, 154 W 14 St, 12th fl, New York, NY 10011 Tel: 212-614-7850 Toll Free Tel: 800-521-0178 Fax: 212-614-7886 E-mail: info@groveatlantic.com; sales@groveatlantic.com; publicity@groveatlantic.com; rights@groveatlantic.com Web Site: www.groveatlantic.com, pg 82

Stewart, Nick, Picador, 120 Broadway, New York, NY 10271 Tel: 646-307-5151 Fax: 212-253-9627 E-mail: publicity@picadorusa.com Web Site: us.macmillan.com/picador, pg 159

Stewart, Philippa, Human Rights Watch, 350 Fifth Ave, 34th fl, New York, NY 10118-3299 Tel: 212-290-4700 Fax: 212-736-1300 E-mail: hrwpress@hrw.org Web Site: www.hrw.org, pg 97

Stewart, Mrs Shane Gong, University Press of Mississippi, 3825 Ridgewood Rd, Jackson, MS 39211-6492 Tel: 601-432-6205 Toll Free Tel: 800-737-7788 (orders & cust serv) Fax: 601-432-6217 E-mail: press@mississippi.edu Web Site: www.upress.state.ms.us, pg 222

Stiehm, Meredith, Writers Guild of America Awards, 7000 W Third St, Los Angeles, CA 90048 Tel: 323-951-4000; 323-782-4569 Toll Free Tel: 800-548-4532 Fax: 323-782-4801 Web Site: www.wga.org; awards.wga.org, pg 678

Stiehm, Meredith, Writers Guild of America West (WGAW), 7000 W Third St, Los Angeles, CA 90048 Tel: 323-951-4000 Toll Free Tel: 800-548-4532 Fax: 323-782-4801 Web Site: www.wga.org, pg 523

Stillman, Steve, Princeton University Press, 41 William St, Princeton, NJ 08540-5237 Tel: 609-258-4900 Fax: 609-258-6305 E-mail: info@press.princeton.edu Web Site: press.princeton.edu, pg 164

Stimola, Adriana, Stimola Literary Studio Inc, 11 Briarwood Lane, West Tisbury, MA 02575 Tel: 201-945-9353 Fax: 201-490-5920 E-mail: info@stimolaliterarystudio.com Web Site: www.stimolaliterarystudio.com, pg 478

Stimola, Rosemary B, Stimola Literary Studio Inc, 11 Briarwood Lane, West Tisbury, MA 02575 Tel: 201-945-9353 Fax: 201-490-5920 E-mail: info@stimolaliterarystudio.com Web Site: www.stimolaliterarystudio.com, pg 477

Stinchcomb, Dale, Theatre Library Association (TLA), c/o The New York Public Library for the Performing Arts, 40 Lincoln Center Plaza, New York, NY 10023 E-mail: theatrelibraryassociation@gmail.com Web Site: www.tla-online.org, pg 521

Stinchfield, Brandon, PEN/Phyllis Naylor Grant for Children's & Young Adult Novelists, 120 Broadway, 26th fl N, New York, NY 10271 Tel: 212-334-1660 Fax: 212-334-2181 E-mail: awards@pen.org; info@pen.org Web Site: pen.org/literary-awards/grants-fellowships, pg 648

Stinchfield, Brandon, PEN Writers' Emergency Fund, 120 Broadway, 26th fl N, New York, NY 10271 Tel: 212-334-1660 Fax: 212-334-2181 E-mail: writersfund@pen.org; info@pen.org Web Site: pen.org/writers-emergency-fund, pg 648

Stocke, Todd, Sourcebooks LLC, 1935 Brookdale Rd, Suite 139, Naperville, IL 60563 Tel: 630-961-3900 Toll Free Tel: 800-432-7444 Fax: 630-961-2168 E-mail: info@sourcebooks.com Web Site: www.sourcebooks.com, pg 194

Stockton, Hope, MFA Publications, 465 Huntington Ave, Boston, MA 02115 Tel: 617-369-4233 E-mail: publications@mfa.org Web Site: www.mfa.org/publications, pg 130

Stockwell, Diane, Globo Libros Literary Management, 450 E 63 St, New York, NY 10065 Web Site: www.globo-libros.com; www.publishersmarketplace.com/members/dstockwell, pg 460

Stoddard, Andrew, Thomas Nelson, 501 Nelson Place, Nashville, TN 37214 Tel: 615-889-9000 Toll Free Tel: 800-251-4000 Web Site: www.thomasnelson.com, pg 206

Stoddard, Bill, Prometheus Awards, 650 Castro St, Suite 120-433, Mountain View, CA 94041 Tel: 650-968-6319 E-mail: bestnovel@lfs.org; specialaward@lfs.org Web Site: www.lfs.org, pg 653

Stoeger, Lea, Penguin Random House LLC, 1745 Broadway, New York, NY 10019 Tel: 212-782-9000 Toll Free Tel: 800-726-0600 Web Site: www.penguinrandomhouse.com, pg 155

Stokarski, Katlyn, Candlewick Press, 99 Dover St, Somerville, MA 02144-2825 Tel: 617-661-3330 Fax: 617-661-0565 E-mail: bigbear@candlewick.com; salesinfo@candlewick.com Web Site: candlewick.com, pg 40

Stokes, Celia, Teaching Strategies LLC, 4500 East-West Hwy, Suite 300, Bethesda, MD 20814 Tel: 301-634-0818 Toll Free Tel: 800-637-3652 E-mail: info@teachingstrategies.com; support@teachingstrategies.com Web Site: teachingstrategies.com, pg 204

Stokes, Jennifer, Owlkids Books Inc, 10 Lower Spadina Ave, Suite 400, Toronto, ON M5V 2Z2, Canada Tel: 416-340-2700 Fax: 416-340-9769 E-mail: owlkids@owlkids.com Web Site: www.owlkidsbooks.com, pg 415

Stokes, Susan S, Woodbine House, 6510 Bells Mill Rd, Bethesda, MD 20817 Tel: 301-897-3570 Toll Free Tel: 800-843-7323 Fax: 301-897-5838 E-mail: info@woodbinehouse.com Web Site: www.woodbinehouse.com, pg 232

Stokes, Thatcher, Bridge Publications Inc, 5600 E Olympic Blvd, Commerce, CA 90022 Tel: 323-888-6200 Toll Free Tel: 800-722-1733 Fax: 323-888-6202 E-mail: info@bridgepub.com Web Site: bridgepub.com, pg 36

Stokes-Peters, Natalie, Black Classic Press, 3921 Vero Rd, Suite F, Baltimore, MD 21203-3414 Tel: 410-242-6954 Toll Free Tel: 800-476-8870 E-mail: email@blackclassicbooks.com; blackclassicpress@yahoo.com Web Site: www.blackclassicbooks.com; www.agooddaytoprint.com, pg 30

Stokke, Carol, DK, c/o Penguin Random House LLC, 1745 Broadway, 20th fl, New York, NY 10019 Tel: 646-674-4000 Toll Free Tel: 800-733-3000 Fax: 646-674-4020 E-mail: marketing@dk.com (lib servs); publicity@dk.com; csorders@penguinrandomhouse.com; customerservice@penguinrandomhouse.com Web Site: www.dk.com, pg 60

Stolf, Lina, LexisNexis® Canada Inc, 111 Gordon Baker Rd, Suite 900, Toronto, ON M2H 3R1, Canada *Tel:* 905-479-2665 *Toll Free Tel:* 800-668-6481; 800-387-0899 (cust care); 800-255-5174 (sales) *E-mail:* service@lexisnexis.ca (cust serv); sales@lexisnexis.ca *Web Site:* www.lexisnexis.ca, pg 411

Stolls, Amy, National Endowment for the Arts, 400 Seventh St SW, Washington, DC 20506-0001 *Tel:* 202-682-5400 *Web Site:* www.arts.gov, pg 526

Stoloff, Sam, Association of American Literary Agents Inc (AALA), 302A W 12 St, No 122, New York, NY 10014 *Tel:* 212-840-5770 *E-mail:* info@aalitagents.org *Web Site:* aalitagents.org, pg 498

Stoloff, Sam, Frances Goldin Literary Agency, Inc, 214 W 29 St, Suite 410, New York, NY 10001 *Tel:* 212-777-0047 *Fax:* 212-228-1660 *E-mail:* agency@goldinlit.com *Web Site:* www.goldinlit.com, pg 460

Stoltz, Jamison, Harry N Abrams Inc, 195 Broadway, 9th fl, New York, NY 10007 *Tel:* 212-206-7715 *Toll Free Tel:* 800-345-1359 *Fax:* 212-645-8437 *E-mail:* abrams@abramsbooks.com; publicity@abramsbooks.com; sales@abramsbooks.com *Web Site:* www.abramsbooks.com, pg 2

Stoltz, Jamison, The Overlook Press, 195 Broadway, 9th fl, New York, NY 10007 *Tel:* 212-206-7715 *E-mail:* abrams@abramsbooks.com; sales@abramsbooks.com (orders) *Web Site:* www.abramsbooks.com/imprints/overlookpress, pg 148

Stoltzfus, Alison, Random House Children's Books, c/o Penguin Random House LLC, 1745 Broadway, New York, NY 10019 *Tel:* 212-782-9000 *Web Site:* www.rhcbooks.com, pg 169

Stone, Cara, Sun Valley Writers' Conference (SVWC), Galleria Bldg, 2nd fl, 351 Leadville Ave N, Ketchum, ID 83340 *Tel:* 208-726-5454 *E-mail:* info@svwc.com *Web Site:* svwc.com, pg 558

Stone, Erica, Random House Children's Books, c/o Penguin Random House LLC, 1745 Broadway, New York, NY 10019 *Tel:* 212-782-9000 *Web Site:* www.rhcbooks.com, pg 170

Stone, Jennifer, ASJA Freelance Writer Search, 355 Lexington Ave, 15th fl, New York, NY 10017-6603 *Tel:* 212-997-0947 *E-mail:* asjaoffice@asja.org *Web Site:* www.asja.org/finder, pg 435

Stone, Jo Ann, Writers & Readers Days, PO Box 801, Abingdon, VA 24212 *Tel:* 276-623-5266 *E-mail:* info@vahighlandsfestival.org *Web Site:* www.vahighlandsfestival.com, pg 558

Stone, Judi, Artech House®, 685 Canton St, Norwood, MA 02062 *Tel:* 781-769-9750 *Toll Free Tel:* 800-225-9977 *Fax:* 781-769-6334 *E-mail:* artech@artechhouse.com *Web Site:* us.artechhouse.com, pg 17

Stone, Kelly, St Martin's Press, LLC, 120 Broadway, New York, NY 10271 *E-mail:* publicity@stmartins.com; trademarketing@stmartins.com; foreignrights@stmartins.com *Web Site:* us.macmillan.com/smp, pg 181

Stone, Kevin, Cengage Learning, 20 Channel Center St, Boston, MA 02210 *Tel:* 617-289-7700 *Toll Free Tel:* 800-354-9706 *Fax:* 617-289-7844 *E-mail:* esales@cengage.com *Web Site:* www.cengage.com, pg 43

Stone, Kris, Piano Press, 1425 Ocean Ave, Suite 5, Del Mar, CA 92014 *Tel:* 619-884-1401 *E-mail:* pianopress@pianopress.com *Web Site:* www.pianopress.com, pg 159

Stone, Laura, Avant-Guide, 244 Fifth Ave, Suite 2053, New York, NY 10001-7604 *Tel:* 917-512-3881 *Fax:* 212-202-7757 *E-mail:* info@avantguide.com; communications@avantguide.com; editor@avantguide.com *Web Site:* www.avantguide.com, pg 22

Stone, Madelyn, Society for Scholarly Publishing (SSP), 1120 Rte 73, Suite 200, Mount Laurel, NJ 08054 *Tel:* 856-439-1385 *Fax:* 856-439-0525 *E-mail:* info@sspnet.org *Web Site:* www.sspnet.org, pg 519

Stone, Mary, Viking Penguin, c/o Penguin Random House LLC, 1745 Broadway, New York, NY 10019 *Tel:* 212-782-9000 *Web Site:* www.penguin.com/overview-vikingbooks/; www.penguin.com/pamela-dorman-books-overview/; www.penguin.com/penguin-classics-overview/; www.penguin.com/penguin-life-overview/, pg 225

Stone, Patricia, Chelsea Green Publishing Co, 85 N Main St, Suite 120, White River Junction, VT 05001 *Tel:* 802-295-6300 *Toll Free Tel:* 800-639-4099 (cust serv & orders) *Fax:* 802-295-6444 *E-mail:* customerservice@chelseagreen.com; editorial@chelseagreen.com; publicity@chelseagreen.com; rights@chelseagreen.com *Web Site:* www.chelseagreen.com, pg 45

Stone, Sheryl, Gulf Energy Information, 2 Greenway Plaza, Suite 1020, Houston, TX 77046 *Tel:* 713-520-4498; 713-529-4301 *E-mail:* store@gulfpub.com; customerservice@gulfenergyinfo.com *Web Site:* www.gulfenergyinfo.com, pg 83

Stookesberry, Tim, The Guilford Press, 370 Seventh Ave, Suite 1200, New York, NY 10001-1020 *Tel:* 212-431-9800 *Toll Free Tel:* 800-365-7006 *Fax:* 212-966-6708 *E-mail:* info@guilford.com; orders@guilford.com *Web Site:* www.guilford.com, pg 82

Storch, Abigail, Yale University Press, 302 Temple St, New Haven, CT 06511-8909 *Tel:* 203-432-0960; 203-432-0966 (sales); 401-531-2800 (cust serv) *Toll Free Tel:* 800-405-1619 (cust serv) *Fax:* 203-432-0948; 203-432-8485 (sales); 401-531-2801 (cust serv) *Toll Free Fax:* 800-406-9145 (cust serv) *E-mail:* sales.press@yale.edu (sales); customer.care@triliteral.org (cust serv) *Web Site:* www.yalebooks.com; yalepress.yale.edu/yupbooks, pg 235

Stordahl, Derek, Candlewick Press, 99 Dover St, Somerville, MA 02144-2825 *Tel:* 617-661-3330 *Fax:* 617-661-0565 *E-mail:* bigbear@candlewick.com; salesinfo@candlewick.com *Web Site:* candlewick.com, pg 39

Stordahl, Derek, Holiday House Publishing Inc, 50 Broad St, New York, NY 10004 *Tel:* 212-688-0085 *Fax:* 212-421-6134 *E-mail:* info@holidayhouse.com *Web Site:* www.holidayhouse.com, pg 94

Stordahl, Derek, Peachtree Publishing Co Inc, 1700 Chattahoochee Ave, Atlanta, GA 30318-2112 *Tel:* 404-876-8761 *Toll Free Tel:* 800-241-0113 *Fax:* 404-875-2578 *Toll Free Fax:* 800-875-8909 *E-mail:* hello@peachtree-online.com; orders@peachtree-online.com; sales@peachtree-online.com *Web Site:* www.peachtreebooks.com; www.peachtree-online.com, pg 153

Storey, Kendall, Counterpoint Press LLC, 2560 Ninth St, Suite 318, Berkeley, CA 94710 *Tel:* 510-704-0230 *Fax:* 510-704-0268 *E-mail:* info@counterpointpress.com *Web Site:* counterpointpress.com; softskull.com, pg 54

Storey, Tim, National Conference of State Legislatures (NCSL), 7700 E First Place, Denver, CO 80230 *Tel:* 303-364-7700 *E-mail:* press-room@ncsl.org *Web Site:* www.ncsl.org, pg 137

Storrings, Michael, St Martin's Press, LLC, 120 Broadway, New York, NY 10271 *E-mail:* publicity@stmartins.com; trademarketing@stmartins.com; foreignrights@stmartins.com *Web Site:* us.macmillan.com/smp, pg 180

Story, Elizabeth, Tachyon Publications LLC, 1459 18 St, No 139, San Francisco, CA 94107 *Tel:* 415-285-5615 *E-mail:* tachyon@tachyonpublications.com; submissions@tachyonpublications.com *Web Site:* www.tachyonpublications.com, pg 202

Stossel, Cassie, New Harbinger Publications Inc, 5674 Shattuck Ave, Oakland, CA 94609 *Tel:* 510-652-0215 *Toll Free Tel:* 800-748-6273 (orders only) *Fax:* 510-652-5472 *Toll Free Fax:* 800-652-1613 *E-mail:* customerservice@newharbinger.com *Web Site:* www.newharbinger.com, pg 140

Stott, Ann, Candlewick Press, 99 Dover St, Somerville, MA 02144-2825 *Tel:* 617-661-3330 *Fax:* 617-661-0565 *E-mail:* bigbear@candlewick.com; salesinfo@candlewick.com *Web Site:* candlewick.com, pg 39

Stouras, Tom, Macmillan, 120 Broadway, 22nd fl, New York, NY 10271 *E-mail:* press.inquiries@macmillan.com *Web Site:* us.macmillan.com, pg 122

Strachan, Glenn R MA, Jhpiego, 1615 Thames St, Baltimore, MD 21231-3492 *Tel:* 410-537-1800 *E-mail:* info@jhpiego.org *Web Site:* www.jhpiego.org, pg 106

Stramenga, Silvia, Seven Stories Press, 140 Watts St, New York, NY 10013 *Tel:* 212-226-8760 *Toll Free Tel:* 800-733-3000 (orders) *Fax:* 212-226-1411 *E-mail:* sevenstories@sevenstories.com *Web Site:* www.sevenstories.com, pg 186

Stranahan, Elizabeth, Random House Children's Books, c/o Penguin Random House LLC, 1745 Broadway, New York, NY 10019 *Tel:* 212-782-9000 *Web Site:* www.rhcbooks.com, pg 170

Strang, Stephen, Charisma Media, 1150 Greenwood Blvd, Lake Mary, FL 32746 *Tel:* 407-333-0600 (all imprints) *Fax:* 407-333-7100 (all imprints) *E-mail:* info@charismamedia.com; customerservice@charismamedia.com *Web Site:* www.charismamedia.com, pg 45

Strassburger, Hannah, Sourcebooks LLC, 1935 Brookdale Rd, Suite 139, Naperville, IL 60563 *Tel:* 630-961-3900 *Toll Free Tel:* 800-432-7444 *Fax:* 630-961-2168 *E-mail:* info@sourcebooks.com *Web Site:* www.sourcebooks.com, pg 195

Strate, Jonathan, Ascension Press, PO Box 1990, West Chester, PA 19380 *Tel:* 484-875-4550 (admin) *Toll Free Tel:* 800-376-0520 (sales & cust serv) *Fax:* 484-875-4555 *E-mail:* orders@ascensionpress.com; newsroom@ascensionpress.com; sales@ascensionpress.com *Web Site:* ascensionpress.com, pg 18

Stratman, Liv, Simon & Schuster, 1230 Avenue of the Americas, New York, NY 10020 *Tel:* 212-698-7000 *Toll Free Tel:* 800-223-2348 (cust serv); 800-223-2336 (orders) *Toll Free Fax:* 800-943-9831 (orders) *Web Site:* simonandschusterpublishing.com/simonandschuster/, pg 188

Stratton, Matthew, Association of American Publishers (AAP), 455 Massachusetts Ave NW, Suite 700, Washington, DC 20001-2777 *Tel:* 202-347-3375 *Fax:* 202-347-3690 *E-mail:* info@publishers.org *Web Site:* publishers.org, pg 498

Straub, Jill, American Society of Agricultural & Biological Engineers (ASABE), 2950 Niles Rd, St Joseph, MI 49085-9659 *Tel:* 269-429-0300 *Toll Free Tel:* 800-371-2723 *Fax:* 269-429-3852 *E-mail:* hq@asabe.org *Web Site:* www.asabe.org, pg 12

Straumanis, Kaija, Open Letter, University of Rochester, Dewey Hall, 1-219, Box 278968, Rochester, NY 14627 *Tel:* 585-319-0823 *Fax:* 585-273-1097 *E-mail:* contact@openletterbooks.org *Web Site:* www.openletterbooks.org, pg 147

Straus, Ian, Simon & Schuster, 1230 Avenue of the Americas, New York, NY 10020 *Tel:* 212-698-7000 *Toll Free Tel:* 800-223-2348 (cust serv); 800-223-2336 (orders) *Toll Free Fax:* 800-943-9831 (orders) *Web Site:* simonandschusterpublishing.com/simonandschuster/, pg 188

Straus, Jonah, Straus Literary, 77 Van Ness Ave, Suite 101, San Francisco, CA 94102 *Tel:* 646-843-9950 *Web Site:* www.strausliterary.com, pg 478

Straus, Robin, Robin Straus Agency, Inc, 229 E 79 St, Suite 5A, New York, NY 10075 *Tel:* 212-472-3282 *Fax:* 212-472-3833 *E-mail:* info@robinstrausagency.com *Web Site:* www.robinstrausagency.com, pg 478

Strauss, Dave, Teachers College Press, 1234 Amsterdam Ave, New York, NY 10027 *Tel:* 212-678-3929 *Fax:* 212-678-4149 *E-mail:* tcpress@tc.edu *Web Site:* www.tcpress.com, pg 203

Strauss, Leslie R, Housing Assistance Council, 1025 Vermont Ave NW, Suite 606, Washington, DC 20005 *Tel:* 202-842-8600 *Fax:* 202-347-3441 *E-mail:* hac@ruralhome.org *Web Site:* www.ruralhome.org, pg 97

Strauss, Rebecca, DeFiore and Company Literary Management Inc, 47 E 19 St, 3rd fl, New York, NY 10003 *Tel:* 212-925-7744 *Fax:* 212-925-9803 *E-mail:* info@defliterary.com; submissions@defliterary.com *Web Site:* www.defliterary.com, pg 456

Strauss-Gabel, Julie, Dutton Children's Books, c/o Penguin Random House LLC, 1745 Broadway, New York, NY 10019 *Tel:* 212-782-9000 *Web Site:* www.penguin.com/dutton-childrens-overview/, pg 62

Strauss-Gabel, Julie, Penguin Young Readers Group, c/o Penguin Random House LLC, 1745 Broadway, New York, NY 10019 *Tel:* 212-782-9000 *Web Site:* www.penguin.com/penguin-young-readers-overview, pg 156

Strecker, Susan, SDP Publishing Solutions LLC, 36 Captain's Way, East Bridgewater, MA 02333 *Tel:* 617-775-0656 *Web Site:* www.sdppublishingsolutions.com, pg 444

Street, Laura-Gray, ASLE Book Awards, PO Box 502, Keene, NH 03431-0502 *Tel:* 603-357-7411 *Fax:* 603-357-7411 *E-mail:* info@asle.org *Web Site:* www.asle.org/research-write/asle-book-paper-awards, pg 575

Streeter, Jordin, Farrar, Straus & Giroux Books for Young Readers, 120 Broadway, New York, NY 10271 *Tel:* 212-741-6900 *Toll Free Tel:* 888-330-8477 (orders) *E-mail:* childrens.publicity@macmillanusa.com; childrensrights@macmillanusa.com *Web Site:* us.macmillan.com/mackids, pg 70

Streeter, Jordin, Roaring Brook Press, 120 Broadway, New York, NY 10271 *Tel:* 646-307-5151 *Web Site:* us.macmillan.com/publishers/roaring-brook-press, pg 176

Streetman, Ms Burgin, Trinity University Press, One Trinity Place, San Antonio, TX 78212-7200 *Tel:* 210-999-8884 *Fax:* 210-999-8838 *E-mail:* books@trinity.edu *Web Site:* www.tupress.org, pg 209

Strelecki, Heather, AIGA 50 Books | 50 Covers, 228 Park Ave S, Suite 58603, New York, NY 10003 *Tel:* 212-807-1990 *E-mail:* competitions@aiga.org *Web Site:* www.aiga.org, pg 571

Strickland, Jonathan, Black Rabbit Books, 2140 Howard Dr W, North Mankato, MN 56003 *Tel:* 507-388-1609 *Fax:* 507-388-2746 *E-mail:* info@blackrabbitbooks.com; orders@blackrabbitbooks.com *Web Site:* www.blackrabbitbooks.com, pg 30

Strickland, Shelly, Association for Intelligent Information Management (AIIM), 8403 Colesville Rd, No 1100, Silver Spring, MD 20910 *Tel:* 301-587-8202 *Toll Free Tel:* 800-477-2446 *Fax:* 301-587-2711 *E-mail:* hello@aiim.org *Web Site:* www.aiim.org, pg 498

Strickland-Bargh, Carla, Pace University, Master of Science in Publishing, 163 William St, 18th fl, New York, NY 10038 *Tel:* 212-346-1431 *E-mail:* puboffice@pace.edu *Web Site:* www.pace.edu/program/publishing-ms, pg 564

Stringfellow, Kari, ASJA Freelance Writer Search, 355 Lexington Ave, 15th fl, New York, NY 10017-6603 *Tel:* 212-997-0947 *E-mail:* asjaoffice@asja.org *Web Site:* www.asja.org/finder, pg 435

Strobel, Rebecca, Gallery Books, 1230 Avenue of the Americas, New York, NY 10020 *Toll Free Tel:* 800-456-6798 *Fax:* 212-698-7284 *E-mail:* consumer.customerservice@simonandschuster.com *Web Site:* www.simonandschuster.com, pg 76

Strone, Daniel, Trident Media Group LLC, 355 Lexington Ave, 12th fl, New York, NY 10017 *Tel:* 212-333-1511 *E-mail:* info@tridentmediagroup.com; press@tridentmediagroup.com; foreignrights@tridentmediagroup.com; office.assistant@tridentmediagroup.com *Web Site:* www.tridentmediagroup.com, pg 480

Strong, Laura, University Press of Mississippi, 3825 Ridgewood Rd, Jackson, MS 39211-6492 *Tel:* 601-432-6205 *Toll Free Tel:* 800-737-7788 (orders & cust serv) *Fax:* 601-432-6217 *E-mail:* press@mississippi.edu *Web Site:* www.upress.state.ms.us, pg 222

Strong, Neil, Macmillan, 120 Broadway, 22nd fl, New York, NY 10271 *E-mail:* press.inquiries@macmillan.com *Web Site:* us.macmillan.com, pg 121

Strothers, Ruth, Leadership Ministries Worldwide, 1928 Central Ave, Chattanooga, TN 37408 *Tel:* 423-855-2181 *Toll Free Tel:* 800-987-8790 *E-mail:* info@lmw.org *Web Site:* lmw.org; store.lmw.org, pg 113

Strothman, Wendy, Aevitas Creative Management LLC, 19 W 21 St, Suite 501, New York, NY 10010 *Tel:* 212-765-6900 *Web Site:* www.aevitascreative.com, pg 448

Stroud, Christine, Autumn House Poetry, Fiction & Nonfiction Prizes, 5530 Penn Ave, Pittsburgh, PA 15206 *Tel:* 412-362-2665 *E-mail:* info@autumnhouse.org *Web Site:* www.autumnhouse.org; autumnhousepress.submittable.com/submit, pg 576

Stroud, Christine, Autumn House Press, 5530 Penn Ave, Pittsburgh, PA 15206 *Tel:* 412-362-2665 *E-mail:* info@autumnhouse.org *Web Site:* www.autumnhouse.org, pg 22

Strouth, Hannah, Sanford J Greenburger Associates Inc, 55 Fifth Ave, New York, NY 10003 *Tel:* 212-206-5600 *Web Site:* greenburger.com, pg 461

Struna, Barbara, Cape Cod Writers Center Conference, 919 Main St, Osterville, MA 02655 *Tel:* 508-420-0200 *E-mail:* writers@capecodwriterscenter.org *Web Site:* capecodwriterscenter.org, pg 553

Struna, Barbara, Young Writers' Workshop, 919 Main St, Osterville, MA 02655 *Tel:* 508-420-0200 *E-mail:* writers@capecodwriterscenter.org *Web Site:* capecodwriterscenter.org, pg 559

Stuart, Andrew, The Stuart Agency, 450 North End Ave, 25C, New York, NY 10282 *Tel:* 917-842-7589 *Web Site:* www.stuartagency.com, pg 479

Stuart, Kathryn, Writers House, 21 W 26 St, New York, NY 10010 *Tel:* 212-685-2400 *Web Site:* www.writershouse.com, pg 482

Stuart, Kelly, Center for the Collaborative Classroom, 1001 Marina Village Pkwy, Suite 110, Alameda, CA 94501-1042 *Tel:* 510-533-0213 *Toll Free Tel:* 800-666-7270 *Fax:* 510-464-3670 *E-mail:* info@collaborativeclassroom.org; clientsupport@collaborativeclassroom.org *Web Site:* www.collaborativeclassroom.org, pg 44

Stuart, Nancy Rubin, Cape Cod Writers Center Conference, 919 Main St, Osterville, MA 02655 *Tel:* 508-420-0200 *E-mail:* writers@capecodwriterscenter.org *Web Site:* capecodwriterscenter.org, pg 553

Stuart, Nancy Rubin, Young Writers' Workshop, 919 Main St, Osterville, MA 02655 *Tel:* 508-420-0200 *E-mail:* writers@capecodwriterscenter.org *Web Site:* capecodwriterscenter.org, pg 559

Stuart, Spencer, Alcuin Society, PO Box 3216, Sta Terminal, Vancouver, BC V6B 3X8, Canada *Tel:* 604-732-5403 *E-mail:* info@alcuinsociety.com; awards@alcuinsociety.com *Web Site:* alcuinsociety.com, pg 493

Stuart, Spencer, Alcuin Society Awards for Excellence in Book Design in Canada, PO Box 3216, Sta Terminal, Vancouver, BC V6B 3X8, Canada *Tel:* 604-732-5403 *E-mail:* awards@alcuinsociety.com *Web Site:* alcuinsociety.com, pg 571

Stubblefield, Terri, Neustadt International Prize for Literature, c/o University of Oklahoma, 630 Parrington Oval, Suite 110, Norman, OK 73019-4033 *Tel:* 405-325-4531 *Web Site:* www.worldliteraturetoday.org; www.neustadtprize.org, pg 639

Stubblefield, Terri, NSK Neustadt Prize for Children's Literature, c/o University of Oklahoma, 630 Parrington Oval, Suite 110, Norman, OK 73019-4033 *Tel:* 405-325-4531 *Web Site:* www.worldliteraturetoday.org; www.neustadtprize.org, pg 642

Stufflebean, Nathan, The Donning Company Publishers, 731 S Brunswick St, Brookfield, MO 64628 *Toll Free Tel:* 800-369-2646 (ext 3377) *Web Site:* www.donning.com, pg 60

Stumpf, Becca, Penguin Random House Audio Publishing Group, 1745 Broadway, New York, NY 10019 *Toll Free Tel:* 800-793-2665 (cust serv) *E-mail:* audio@penguinrandomhouse.com; ecustomerservice@penguinrandomhouse.com *Web Site:* www.penguinrandomhouseaudio.com, pg 154

Sturdivant, Chris, National Notary Association (NNA), 9350 De Soto Ave, Chatsworth, CA 91311-4926 *Tel:* 818-739-4000 *Toll Free Tel:* 800-876-6827 *Toll Free Fax:* 800-833-1211 *E-mail:* services@nationalnotary.org *Web Site:* www.nationalnotary.org, pg 138

Sturman, Ms Gerrie Lipson, Goldfarb & Associates, 721 Gibbon St, Alexandria, VA 22314 *Tel:* 202-466-3030 *E-mail:* rlglawlit@gmail.com *Web Site:* www.ronaldgoldfarb.com, pg 460

Sturmer, Alan, Edward Elgar Publishing Inc, The William Pratt House, 9 Dewey Ct, Northampton, MA 01060-3815 *Tel:* 413-584-5551 *Toll Free Tel:* 800-390-3149 (orders) *Fax:* 413-584-9933 *E-mail:* elgarinfo@e-elgar.com; elgarsales@e-elgar.com; elgarsubmissions@e-elgar.com (edit) *Web Site:* www.e-elgar.com; www.elgaronline.com (ebooks & journals), pg 65

Stutz, Katie, Sourcebooks LLC, 1935 Brookdale Rd, Suite 139, Naperville, IL 60563 *Tel:* 630-961-3900 *Toll Free Tel:* 800-432-7444 *Fax:* 630-961-2168 *E-mail:* info@sourcebooks.com *Web Site:* www.sourcebooks.com, pg 194

Stvan, Beck, Random House Publishing Group, 1745 Broadway, New York, NY 10019 *Toll Free Tel:* 800-200-3552 *Web Site:* www.randomhousebooks.com, pg 171

Styler, Lori, The Barbara Hogenson Agency Inc, 165 West End Ave, Suite 19-C, New York, NY 10023 *Tel:* 212-874-8084 *E-mail:* barbarahogenson@gmail.com, pg 463

Suarez, Juan Carlos, 4A's (American Association of Advertising Agencies), 25 W 45 St, 16th fl, New York, NY 10036 *Tel:* 212-682-2500 *E-mail:* media@4as.org; membership@4as.org *Web Site:* www.aaaa.org, pg 506

Suarez, Kim, Penguin Random House LLC, 1745 Broadway, New York, NY 10019 *Tel:* 212-782-9000 *Toll Free Tel:* 800-726-0600 *Web Site:* www.penguinrandomhouse.com, pg 155

Subberwal, Kaeli, Random House Publishing Group, 1745 Broadway, New York, NY 10019 *Toll Free Tel:* 800-200-3552 *Web Site:* www.randomhousebooks.com, pg 171

Suber, Danielle, National Music Publishers' Association (NMPA), 1900 "N" St NW, Suite 500, Washington, DC 20036 *Tel:* 202-393-6672 *E-mail:* members@nmpa.org *Web Site:* nmpa.org, pg 513

Suchomel-Casey, Michele, Sourcebooks LLC, 1935 Brookdale Rd, Suite 139, Naperville, IL 60563 *Tel:* 630-961-3900 *Toll Free Tel:* 800-432-7444 *Fax:* 630-961-2168 *E-mail:* info@sourcebooks.com *Web Site:* www.sourcebooks.com, pg 194

Suciu, Ioan, Georgetown University Press, 3520 Prospect St NW, Suite 140, Washington, DC 20007 *Tel:* 202-687-5889 (busn) *Fax:* 202-687-6340 (edit) *E-mail:* gupress@georgetown.edu *Web Site:* press.georgetown.edu, pg 77

Sudusky, Julia, St Martin's Press, LLC, 120 Broadway, New York, NY 10271 *E-mail:* publicity@stmartins.com; trademarketing@stmartins.com; foreignrights@stmartins.com *Web Site:* us.macmillan.com/smp, pg 181

Sugihara, Kenichi, SelectBooks Inc, 325 W 38 St, Suite 306, New York, NY 10018 *Tel:* 212-206-1997 *Fax:* 212-206-3815 *E-mail:* info@selectbooks.com *Web Site:* www.selectbooks.com, pg 186

Sugihara, Kenzi, SelectBooks Inc, 325 W 38 St, Suite 306, New York, NY 10018 *Tel:* 212-206-1997 *Fax:* 212-206-3815 *E-mail:* info@selectbooks.com *Web Site:* www.selectbooks.com, pg 186

Suilebhan, Gwydion, PEN/Bernard & Ann Malamud Award for Excellence in the Short Story, 6218 Georgia Ave NW, Unit 1062, Washington, DC 20011 *Tel:* 202-898-9063 *Fax:* 202-675-0360 *E-mail:* awards@penfaulkner.org; info@penfaulkner.org *Web Site:* www.penfaulkner.org/our-awards/the-pen-malamud-award, pg 647

Suilebhan, Gwydion, PEN/Faulkner Award for Fiction, 6218 Georgia Ave NW, Unit 1062, Washington, DC 20011 *Tel:* 202-898-9063 *E-mail:* awards@penfaulkner.org *Web Site:* www.penfaulkner.org/our-awards/pen-faulkner-award, pg 647

Suitt, Charles M, Gallery Books, 1230 Avenue of the Americas, New York, NY 10020 Toll Free Tel: 800-456-6798 Fax: 212-698-7284 E-mail: consumer.customerservice@simonandschuster.com Web Site: www.simonandschuster.com, pg 76

Sukhram, Hema, Harry N Abrams Inc, 195 Broadway, 9th fl, New York, NY 10007 Tel: 212-206-7715 Toll Free Tel: 800-345-1359 Fax: 212-645-8437 E-mail: abrams@abramsbooks.com; publicity@abramsbooks.com; sales@abramsbooks.com Web Site: www.abramsbooks.com, pg 3

Sulaiman, Saba, Talcott Notch Literary, 127 Broad St, 2P, Milford, CT 06460 Tel: 203-876-4959 Web Site: talcottnotch.net, pg 479

Suljic, Colleen, Princeton University Press, 41 William St, Princeton, NJ 08540-5237 Tel: 609-258-4900 Fax: 609-258-6305 E-mail: info@press.princeton.edu Web Site: press.princeton.edu, pg 164

Sullivan, Derek, Hazy Dell Press, 1001 SE Water Ave, Suite 132, Portland, OR 97214 Tel: 971-279-5779 E-mail: info@hazydellpress.com Web Site: www.hazydellpress.com, pg 89

Sullivan, Drew, American Program Bureau Inc, One Gateway Center, Suite 751, Newton, MA 02458 Tel: 617-614-1600 E-mail: apb@apbspeakers.com Web Site: www.apbspeakers.com, pg 487

Sullivan, Elora, Chronicle Books LLC, 680 Second St, San Francisco, CA 94107 Tel: 415-537-4200 Fax: 415-537-4460 (perms) E-mail: hello@chroniclebooks.com; subrights@chroniclebooks.com Web Site: www.chroniclebooks.com, pg 47

Sullivan, Jessica, Greystone Books Ltd, 343 Railway St, Suite 302, Vancouver, BC V6A 1A4, Canada Tel: 604-875-1550 Fax: 604-875-1556 E-mail: info@greystonebooks.com; rights@greystonebooks.com Web Site: www.greystonebooks.com, pg 407

Sullivan, Kelsey, Disney-Hyperion Books, 1101 Flower St, Glendale, CA 91201 Web Site: books.disney.com/imprint/disney-hyperion, pg 59

Sullivan, Kyle, Hazy Dell Press, 1001 SE Water Ave, Suite 132, Portland, OR 97214 Tel: 971-279-5779 E-mail: info@hazydellpress.com Web Site: www.hazydellpress.com, pg 89

Sullivan, Lisa, Harry S Truman Book Award, 5151 Troost Ave, Suite 300, Kansas City, MO 64110 Tel: 816-400-1212 Toll Free Tel: 844-358-5400 Web Site: www.trumanlibraryinstitute.org/research-grants/bookaward/; trumanlibraryinstitute.org, pg 670

Sullivan, Margaret, University of Washington Press, 4333 Brooklyn Ave NE, Seattle, WA 98105-9570 Toll Free Tel: 800-537-5487 (orders) Fax: 206-543-3932; 410-516-6998 (orders) E-mail: uwapress@uw.edu Web Site: uwapress.uw.edu, pg 221

Sullivan, Mark, Franciscan Media, 28 W Liberty St, Cincinnati, OH 45202 Tel: 513-241-5615 E-mail: admin@franciscanmedia.org Web Site: www.franciscanmedia.org, pg 74

Sullivan, Michaela, Houghton Mifflin Harcourt Trade & Reference Division, 125 High St, Boston, MA 02110 Tel: 617-351-5000 Web Site: www.hmhco.com, pg 96

Sullivan, Tawanna, Penguin Random House LLC, 1745 Broadway, New York, NY 10019 Tel: 212-782-9000 Toll Free Tel: 800-726-0600 Web Site: penguinrandomhouse.com, pg 155

Sullivan, Tim, University of California Press, 155 Grand Ave, Suite 400, Oakland, CA 94612-3758 Tel: 510-883-8232 Fax: 510-836-8910 E-mail: customerservice@ucpress.edu Web Site: www.ucpress.edu, pg 215

Sumereau, Taylor, Princeton University Press, 41 William St, Princeton, NJ 08540-5237 Tel: 609-258-4900 Fax: 609-258-6305 E-mail: info@press.princeton.edu Web Site: press.princeton.edu, pg 164

Summ, Felix, Princeton University Press, 41 William St, Princeton, NJ 08540-5237 Tel: 609-258-4900 Fax: 609-258-6305 E-mail: info@press.princeton.edu Web Site: press.princeton.edu, pg 164

Summerfield, Mary, SPIE, 1000 20 St, Bellingham, WA 98225-6705 Tel: 360-676-3290 Toll Free Tel: 888-504-8171 (orders) Fax: 360-647-1445 E-mail: help@spie.org; customerservice@spie.org (orders) Web Site: www.spie.org, pg 196

Summerhays, Stephanie, Smithsonian Institution Scholarly Press, Aerospace Bldg, 704-A, MRC 957, Washington, DC 20013 Tel: 202-633-3017 Fax: 202-633-6877 E-mail: schol_press@si.edu Web Site: scholarlypress.si.edu, pg 192

Summers, Eric, STARbooks Press, PO Box 711612, Herndon, VA 20171 E-mail: publish@starbookspress.com; contact@starbookspress.com Web Site: www.starbooksnow.com, pg 197

Summers, Shauna, Random House Publishing Group, 1745 Broadway, New York, NY 10019 Toll Free Tel: 800-200-3552 Web Site: www.randomhousebooks.com, pg 171

Sumner, Tom, Franklin, Beedle & Associates Inc, 10350 N Vancouver Way, No 5012, Portland, OR 97217 Tel: 503-284-6348 Toll Free Tel: 800-322-2665 Fax: 503-625-4434 Web Site: www.fbeedle.com, pg 74

Sun, Amy, Viking Penguin, c/o Penguin Random House LLC, 1745 Broadway, New York, NY 10019 Tel: 212-782-9000 Web Site: www.penguin.com/overview-vikingbooks/; www.penguin.com/pamela-dorman-books-overview/; www.penguin.com/penguin-classics-overview/; www.penguin.com/penguin-life-overview/, pg 225

Sun, Celina, Penguin Workshop, c/o Penguin Random House LLC, 1745 Broadway, New York, NY 10019 Tel: 212-782-9000 Web Site: www.penguin.com/publishers/penguinworkshop/, pg 156

Sun de la Cruz, Deborah, Penguin Random House Canada, a Penguin Random House company, 320 Front St W, Suite 1400, Toronto, ON M5V 3B6, Canada Tel: 416-364-4449 Toll Free Tel: 888-523-9292 (cust serv) E-mail: canadaweb@penguinrandomhouse.com; customerservicescanada@penguinrandomhouse.com Web Site: www.penguinrandomhouse.ca, pg 416

Sun, Merry, W W Norton & Company Inc, 500 Fifth Ave, New York, NY 10110-0017 Tel: 212-354-5500 Toll Free Tel: 800-233-4830 (orders & cust serv) Fax: 212-869-0856 Toll Free Fax: 800-458-6515 E-mail: orders@wwnorton.com Web Site: wwnorton.com, pg 143

Sundar, Stacey, Random House Children's Books, c/o Penguin Random House LLC, 1745 Broadway, New York, NY 10019 Tel: 212-782-9000 Web Site: rhcbooks.com, pg 170

Sundaram, Friederike, Stanford University Press, 425 Broadway St, Redwood City, CA 94063-3126 Tel: 650-723-9434 Fax: 650-725-3457 E-mail: info@www.sup.org; publicity@www.sup.org; sales@www.sup.org Web Site: www.sup.org, pg 197

Sundstrom, Allison, Sourcebooks LLC, 1935 Brookdale Rd, Suite 139, Naperville, IL 60563 Tel: 630-961-3900 Toll Free Tel: 800-432-7444 Fax: 630-961-2168 E-mail: info@sourcebooks.com Web Site: www.sourcebooks.com, pg 194

Sung, Jonathan, Penguin Random House LLC, 1745 Broadway, New York, NY 10019 Tel: 212-782-9000 Toll Free Tel: 800-726-0600 Web Site: www.penguinrandomhouse.com, pg 155

Sunshine, Alex Hoopes, Kensington Publishing Corp, 900 Third Ave, 26th fl, New York, NY 10022 Tel: 212-407-1500 Toll Free Tel: 800-221-2647 Fax: 212-935-0699 Web Site: www.kensingtonbooks.com, pg 109

Supovitz, Elise, Candlewick Press, 99 Dover St, Somerville, MA 02144-2825 Tel: 617-661-3330 Fax: 617-661-0565 E-mail: bigbear@candlewick.com; salesinfo@candlewick.com Web Site: candlewick.com, pg 39

Sures, Jay, United Talent Agency LLC, 9336 Civic Center Dr, Beverly Hills, CA 90210 Tel: 310-273-6700 Web Site: www.unitedtalent.com, pg 481

Suresh, Kaushika, Black Warrior Review Fiction, Nonfiction & Poetry Contest, University of Alabama, Off of Student Media, 414 Campus Dr E, Tuscaloosa, AL 35487 Tel: 205-348-4518 Fax: 205-348-8036 E-mail: blackwarriorreview@gmail.com; bwr@ua.edu Web Site: www.bwr.ua.edu, pg 581

Surpin, Jacob, Avery, c/o Penguin Random House LLC, 1745 Broadway, New York, NY 10019 Tel: 212-366-2000 Web Site: www.penguin.com/avery-overview/, pg 23

Sussman, Erica, HarperCollins Children's Books, 195 Broadway, New York, NY 10007 Tel: 212-207-7000 Web Site: www.harpercollins.com/childrens, pg 85

Suter, Michelle, Macmillan, 120 Broadway, 22nd fl, New York, NY 10271 E-mail: press.inquiries@macmillan.com Web Site: us.macmillan.com, pg 122

Sutherland, Victoria, Foreword's INDIES Awards, 12935 W Bay Shore Rd, Suite 380, Traverse City, MI 49684 Tel: 231-933-3699 Web Site: www.forewordreviews.com, pg 603

Sutphin, Heather, The Geological Society of America Inc (GSA), 3300 Penrose Place, Boulder, CO 80301-1806 Tel: 303-357-1000 Toll Free Tel: 800-472-1988 Fax: 303-357-1070 E-mail: pubs@geosociety.org (prodn); editing@geosociety.org (edit); books@geosociety.org; gsaservice@geosociety.org (sales & serv) Web Site: www.geosociety.org, pg 77

Sutton, Caroline, Avid Reader Press, 1230 Avenue of the Americas, New York, NY 10020 Web Site: avidreaderpress.com, pg 23

Sutton, Liz, Random House Children's Books, c/o Penguin Random House LLC, 1745 Broadway, New York, NY 10019 Tel: 212-782-9000 Web Site: www.rhcbooks.com, pg 170

Sutton, Madelene, AIP Publishing LLC, 1305 Walt Whitman Rd, Suite 110, Melville, NY 11747 Tel: 516-576-2200 E-mail: help@aip.org; press@aip.org; rights@aip.org Web Site: www.aip.org; publishing.aip.org, pg 6

Suvikapakornkul, Shane, Serindia Publications, PO Box 10335, Chicago, IL 60610-0335 E-mail: info@serindia.com Web Site: www.serindia.com, pg 186

Suzanne, Claudia, Wambtac Communications LLC, 1512 E Santa Clara Ave, Santa Ana, CA 92705 Tel: 714-954-0580 Toll Free Tel: 800-641-3936 E-mail: wambtac@wambtac.com Web Site: www.wambtac.com; claudiasuzanne.com (prof servs), pg 445

Svehla, Gary, Midnight Marquee Press Inc, 9721 Britinay Lane, Baltimore, MD 21234 Tel: 410-665-1198 E-mail: mmarquee@aol.com Web Site: www.midmar.com, pg 130

Svehla, Susan, Midnight Marquee Press Inc, 9721 Britinay Lane, Baltimore, MD 21234 Tel: 410-665-1198 E-mail: mmarquee@aol.com Web Site: www.midmar.com, pg 130

Svetcov, Danielle, Levine|Greenberg|Rostan Literary Agency, 307 Seventh Ave, Suite 2407, New York, NY 10001 Tel: 212-337-0934 Fax: 212-337-0948 E-mail: submit@lgrliterary.com Web Site: lgrliterary.com, pg 467

Svoboda, Bonnie, Sourcebooks LLC, 1935 Brookdale Rd, Suite 139, Naperville, IL 60563 Tel: 630-961-3900 Toll Free Tel: 800-432-7444 Fax: 630-961-2168 E-mail: info@sourcebooks.com Web Site: www.sourcebooks.com, pg 194

Swados, Sharon, The New Press, 120 Wall St, 31st fl, New York, NY 10005 Tel: 212-629-8802 Fax: 212-629-8617 E-mail: newpress@thenewpress.com Web Site: thenewpress.com, pg 140

Swail, David, Canadian Publishers' Council (CPC), 3080 Yonge St, Suite 6060, Toronto, ON M4N 3N1, Canada Tel: 647-255-8880 Web Site: pubcouncil.ca, pg 502

Swaim, Dennis, Viking Penguin, c/o Penguin Random House LLC, 1745 Broadway, New York, NY 10019 Tel: 212-782-9000 Web Site: www.penguin.com/overview-vikingbooks/; www.penguin.com/pamela-

Swain, Linda, Television Academy, 5220 Lankershim Blvd, North Hollywood, CA 91601-3109 *Tel:* 818-754-2800 *Web Site:* www.emmys.com, pg 521

Swann, Syreeta N, Association of American Publishers (AAP), 455 Massachusetts Ave NW, Suite 700, Washington, DC 20001-2777 *Tel:* 202-347-3375 *Fax:* 202-347-3690 *E-mail:* info@publishers.org *Web Site:* publishers.org, pg 498

Swann, Syreeta N, PROSE Awards, 455 Massachusetts Ave NW, Suite 700, Washington, DC 20001-2777 *Tel:* 202-347-3375 *Fax:* 202-347-3690 *E-mail:* proseawards@publishers.org *Web Site:* proseawards.com; publishers.org, pg 653

Swanson, Bonnie, FinePrint Literary Management, 207 W 106 St, Suite 1D, New York, NY 10025 *Tel:* 212-279-6214 *E-mail:* info@fineprintlit.com; submissions@fineprint.com *Web Site:* www.fineprintlit.com, pg 458

Swanson, Haley, HarperCollins Publishers LLC, 195 Broadway, New York, NY 10007 *Tel:* 212-207-7000 *Web Site:* www.harpercollins.com, pg 87

Swanson, Hilary, HarperCollins Publishers LLC, 195 Broadway, New York, NY 10007 *Tel:* 212-207-7000 *Web Site:* www.harpercollins.com, pg 86

Swanson, O'Ryin, Light Technology Publishing LLC, 4030 E Huntington Dr, Flagstaff, AZ 86004 *Tel:* 928-526-1345 *Toll Free Tel:* 800-450-0985 *Fax:* 928-714-1132 *E-mail:* publishing@lighttechnology.com *Web Site:* www.lighttechnology.com, pg 117

Swanson, Sierra, Atria Books, 1230 Avenue of the Americas, New York, NY 10020 *Tel:* 212-698-7000 *Fax:* 212-698-7007 *Web Site:* www.simonandschuster.com, pg 21

Swartz, Kristine, Berkley, c/o Penguin Random House LLC, 1745 Broadway, 19th fl, New York, NY 10019 *Tel:* 212-366-2000 *Web Site:* www.penguin.com/publishers/berkley/; www.penguin.com/ace-overview/, pg 28

Sweeney, David, little bee books, 598 Broadway, 7th fl, New York, NY 10012 *Tel:* 212-321-0237 *Toll Free Tel:* 844-321-0237 *E-mail:* info@littlebeebooks.com; sales@littlebeebooks.com; publicity@littlebeebooks.com *Web Site:* littlebeebooks.com, pg 117

Sweeney, Jillian, The Ned Leavitt Agency, 752 Creeklocks Rd, Rosendale, NY 12472 *Tel:* 845-658-3333 *Web Site:* www.nedleavittagency.com, pg 467

Sweeney, Jon M, Monkfish Book Publishing Co, 22 E Market St, Suite 304, Rhinebeck, NY 12572 *Tel:* 845-876-4861 *Web Site:* www.monkfishpublishing.com, pg 133

Sweeney, Joyce, The Seymour Agency, 475 Miner Street Rd, Canton, NY 13617 *Tel:* 239-398-8209 *Web Site:* www.theseymouragency.com, pg 475

Sweeney, Margaret, Macmillan, 120 Broadway, 22nd fl, New York, NY 10271 *E-mail:* press.inquiries@macmillan.com *Web Site:* us.macmillan.com, pg 122

Sweeney, Nicholas, Sourcebooks LLC, 1935 Brookdale Rd, Suite 139, Naperville, IL 60563 *Tel:* 630-961-3900 *Toll Free Tel:* 800-432-7444 *Fax:* 630-961-2168 *E-mail:* info@sourcebooks.com *Web Site:* www.sourcebooks.com, pg 194

Sweeney, Renata, Tor Publishing Group, 120 Broadway, New York, NY 10271 *Toll Free Tel:* 800-455-0340 (Macmillan) *E-mail:* torpublicity@tor.com; forgepublicity@forgebooks.com *Web Site:* us.macmillan.com/torpublishinggroup, pg 208

Sweeny, Caitlin, Simon & Schuster Children's Publishing, 1230 Avenue of the Americas, New York, NY 10020 *Tel:* 212-698-7000 *Web Site:* www.simonandschuster.com/kids; www.simonandschuster.com/teen; simonandschuster.net; simonandschuster.biz, pg 189

Sweet, Veronique, Random House Children's Books, c/o Penguin Random House LLC, 1745 Broadway, New York, NY 10019 *Tel:* 212-782-9000 *Web Site:* www.rhcbooks.com, pg 169

Sweet, Dr Willaim, Council for Research in Values & Philosophy, The Catholic University of America, Gibbons Hall, B-20, 620 Michigan Ave NE, Washington, DC 20064 *Tel:* 202-319-6089 *E-mail:* cua-rvp@cua.edu *Web Site:* www.crvp.org, pg 53

Sweetman, Marie, Wayne State University Press, Leonard N Simons Bldg, 4809 Woodward Ave, Detroit, MI 48201-1309 *Tel:* 313-577-6120 *Toll Free Tel:* 800-978-7323 *Fax:* 313-577-6131 *E-mail:* bookorders@wayne.edu *Web Site:* www.wsupress.wayne.edu, pg 227

Swenar, Karen, Dreamscape Media LLC, 1417 Timberwolf Dr, Holland, OH 43528 *Tel:* 419-867-6965 *Toll Free Tel:* 877-983-7326 *E-mail:* info@dreamscapeab.com *Web Site:* www.dreamscapepublishing.com, pg 62

Swensen, Evan, Publication Consultants, 8370 Eleusis Dr, Anchorage, AK 99502 *Tel:* 907-349-2424 *Fax:* 907-349-2426 *E-mail:* books@publicationconsultants.com *Web Site:* www.publicationconsultants.com, pg 167

Swenson, Janine Y, LearningExpress, 224 W 29 St, 3rd fl, New York, NY 10001 *Toll Free Tel:* 800-295-9556 (ext 2) *Web Site:* learningexpresshub.com, pg 114

Sweren, Becky, Aevitas Creative Management LLC, 19 W 21 St, Suite 501, New York, NY 10010 *Tel:* 212-765-6900 *Web Site:* www.aevitascreative.com, pg 448

Swetonic, Carrie, Penguin Publishing Group, c/o Penguin Random House LLC, 1745 Broadway, New York, NY 10019 *Tel:* 212-782-9000 *Web Site:* www.penguin.com, pg 154

Swink, Heather, Institute of Environmental Sciences & Technology - IEST, 1827 Walden Office Sq, Suite 400, Schaumburg, IL 60173 *Tel:* 847-981-0100 *Fax:* 847-981-4130 *E-mail:* information@iest.org *Web Site:* www.iest.org, pg 101

Swinkels, Pieter, Transatlantic Agency, 2 Bloor St E, Suite 3500, Toronto, ON M4W 1A8, Canada *Tel:* 416-488-9214 *E-mail:* info@transatlanticagency.com; royalties@transatlanticagency.com *Web Site:* www.transatlanticagency.com, pg 479

Swinwood, Craig, Harlequin Enterprises Ltd, Bay Adelaide Centre, East Tower, 22 Adelaide St W, 41st fl, Toronto, ON M5H 4E3, Canada *Tel:* 416-445-5860 *Toll Free Tel:* 888-432-4879; 800-370-5838 (ebook inquiries) *E-mail:* customerservice@harlequin.com *Web Site:* www.harlequin.com, pg 409

Swinwood, Craig, HarperCollins Canada Ltd, 22 Adelaide St W, 41st fl, Toronto, ON M5H 4E3, Canada *Tel:* 416-975-9334 *E-mail:* hcorder@harpercollins.com *Web Site:* www.harpercollins.ca, pg 409

Swinwood, Craig, Love Inspired Books, 233 Broadway, Suite 1001, New York, NY 10279 *Tel:* 212-553-4200 *Toll Free Tel:* 888-432-4879 *Fax:* 212-227-8969 *E-mail:* customerservice@harlequin.ca *Web Site:* www.harlequin.com, pg 120

Swinwood, Susan, Harlequin Enterprises Ltd, Bay Adelaide Centre, East Tower, 22 Adelaide St W, 41st fl, Toronto, ON M5H 4E3, Canada *Tel:* 416-445-5860 *Toll Free Tel:* 888-432-4879; 800-370-5838 (ebook inquiries) *E-mail:* customerservice@harlequin.com *Web Site:* www.harlequin.com, pg 409

Switzer, Kristi, Brewers Publications, 1327 Spruce St, Boulder, CO 80302 *Tel:* 303-447-0816 *Toll Free Tel:* 888-822-6273 (CN & US) *Fax:* 303-447-2825 *E-mail:* info@brewersassociation.org *Web Site:* www.brewersassociation.org, pg 36

Swomley, Olivia, Candlewick Press, 99 Dover St, Somerville, MA 02144-2825 *Tel:* 617-661-3330 *Fax:* 617-661-0565 *E-mail:* bigbear@candlewick.com; salesinfo@candlewick.com *Web Site:* candlewick.com, pg 40

Swope, Pamela K, Philosophy Documentation Center, PO Box 7147, Charlottesville, VA 22906-7147 *Tel:* 434-220-3300 *Toll Free Tel:* 800-444-2419 *Fax:* 434-220-3301 *E-mail:* order@pdcnet.org *Web Site:* www.pdcnet.org, pg 159

Sybert, Michelle, University of Notre Dame Press, 310 Flanner Hall, Notre Dame, IN 46556 *Tel:* 574-631-6346 *Fax:* 574-631-8148 *E-mail:* undpress@nd.edu *Web Site:* www.undpress.nd.edu, pg 219

Sydney, Caroline, Penguin Press, c/o Penguin Random House LLC, 1745 Broadway, New York, NY 10019 *Tel:* 212-782-9000 *E-mail:* penguinpress@penguinrandomhouse.com *Web Site:* www.penguin.com/penguin-press-overview/, pg 154

Sykes, Shuntai, Sophie Brody Medal, 225 N Michigan Ave, Suite 1300, Chicago, IL 60601 *Web Site:* rusaupdate.org/awards/sophie-brody-medal, pg 584

Sylve, Elvira C, Clotilde's Secretarial & Management Services, PO Box 871926, New Orleans, LA 70187 *Tel:* 504-242-2912 *E-mail:* elcsy58@att.net, pg 437

Symanoskie, Chris, Houghton Mifflin Harcourt, 125 High St, Boston, MA 02110 *Tel:* 617-351-5000 *Toll Free Tel:* 855-969-4642; 800-225-5425 (K-12 educ materials); 800-323-9540 (assessment materials); 877-219-1537 (SkillsTutor); 888-242-6747 (Innovation in Educ Group); 800-225-3362 (Trade & Ref Div) *Toll Free Fax:* 800-269-5232 *E-mail:* myhmhco@hmhco.com *Web Site:* www.hmhco.com, pg 96

Symons, Alan, SAMS Technical Publishing LLC, 9850 E 30 St, Indianapolis, IN 46229 *Toll Free Tel:* 800-428-7267 *E-mail:* customercare@samswebsite.com *Web Site:* www.samswebsite.com, pg 181

Synatschk, Kathy, PRO-ED Inc, 8700 Shoal Creek Blvd, Austin, TX 78757-6897 *Tel:* 512-451-3246 *Toll Free Tel:* 800-897-3202 *Fax:* 512-451-8542 *Toll Free Fax:* 800-397-7633 *E-mail:* info@proedinc.com *Web Site:* www.proedinc.com, pg 165

Syracuse, Rebecca, Simon & Schuster Children's Publishing, 1230 Avenue of the Americas, New York, NY 10020 *Tel:* 212-698-7000 *Web Site:* www.simonandschuster.com/kids; www.simonandschuster.com/teen; simonandschuster.net; simonandschuster.biz, pg 189

Szczerban, Michael, Little, Brown and Company, 1290 Avenue of the Americas, New York, NY 10104 *Tel:* 212-364-1100 *Fax:* 212-364-0952 *E-mail:* firstname.lastname@hbgusa.com *Web Site:* www.hachettebookgroup.com/imprint/little-brown-and-company/, pg 118

Szporluk, Larissa, Bowling Green State University Creative Writing Program, Dept of English, 212 East Hall, Bowling Green, OH 43403-0001 *Tel:* 419-372-6864; 419-372-2576 *Fax:* 419-372-0333 *E-mail:* english@bgsu.edu *Web Site:* www.bgsu.edu/academics/creative-writing, pg 561

Taber, Emily, Basic Books Group, 1290 Avenue of the Americas, New York, NY 10104 *Tel:* 212-340-8100 *Toll Free Tel:* 800-343-4499 (cust serv) *Fax:* 212-340-8105 *E-mail:* customer.service@hbgusa.com; orders@hbgusa.com *Web Site:* www.hachettebookgroup.com/imprint/basic-books/, pg 25

Tacit, Melody, Penguin Random House Canada, a Penguin Random House company, 320 Front St W, Suite 1400, Toronto, ON M5V 3B6, Canada *Tel:* 416-364-4449 *Toll Free Tel:* 888-523-9292 (cust serv) *E-mail:* canadaweb@penguinrandomhouse.com; customerservicescanada@penguinrandomhouse.com *Web Site:* www.penguinrandomhouse.ca, pg 416

Tackett, Jessica, Chronicle Books LLC, 680 Second St, San Francisco, CA 94107 *Tel:* 415-537-4200 *Fax:* 415-537-4460 (perms) *E-mail:* hello@chroniclebooks.com; subrights@chroniclebooks.com *Web Site:* www.chroniclebooks.com, pg 47

Tackett, Jessica, PA Press, 202 Warren St, Hudson, NY 12534 *Tel:* 518-671-6100 *Toll Free Tel:* 800-722-6657 (dist); 800-759-0190 (sales) *E-mail:* sales@papress.com *Web Site:* www.papress.com, pg 149

Tacuri, Hillary, Berkley, c/o Penguin Random House LLC, 1745 Broadway, 19th fl, New York, NY 10019 *Tel:* 212-366-2000 *Web Site:* www.penguin.com/publishers/berkley/; www.penguin.com/ace-overview/, pg 28

Taets, Andrew, Penguin Publishing Group, c/o Penguin Random House LLC, 1745 Broadway, New York, NY 10019 *Tel:* 212-782-9000 *Web Site:* www.penguin.com, pg 154

Tafura, Mariana, Editorial Unilit, 8167 NW 84 St, Medley, FL 33166 *Tel:* 305-592-6136; 305-592-6135 *Toll Free Tel:* 800-767-7726 *Fax:* 305-592-0087 *E-mail:* info@editorialunilit.com; ventas@editorialunilit.com (sales) *Web Site:* www.editorialunilit.com, pg 64

Tager, Steve, Harry N Abrams Inc, 195 Broadway, 9th fl, New York, NY 10007 *Tel:* 212-206-7715 *Toll Free Tel:* 800-345-1359 *Fax:* 212-645-8437 *E-mail:* abrams@abramsbooks.com; publicity@abramsbooks.com; sales@abramsbooks.com *Web Site:* www.abramsbooks.com, pg 2

Taglienti, Lauren, Random House Children's Books, c/o Penguin Random House LLC, 1745 Broadway, New York, NY 10019 *Tel:* 212-782-9000 *Web Site:* www.rhcbooks.com, pg 170

Tahan, Rosy, HarperCollins Publishers LLC, 195 Broadway, New York, NY 10007 *Tel:* 212-207-7000 *Web Site:* www.harpercollins.com, pg 87

Tai, Sean, Marick Press, 1342 Three Mile Dr, Grosse Pointe Park, MI 48230 *Tel:* 313-407-9236 *E-mail:* orders@marickpress.com; info@marickpress.com *Web Site:* www.marickpress.com, pg 125

Taiwo, Ayomikun, Penguin Random House Canada, a Penguin Random House company, 320 Front St W, Suite 1400, Toronto, ON M5V 3B6, Canada *Tel:* 416-364-4449 *Toll Free Tel:* 888-523-9292 (cust serv) *E-mail:* canadaweb@penguinrandomhouse.com; customerservicescanada@penguinrandomhouse.com *Web Site:* www.penguinrandomhouse.ca, pg 416

Takes, Bill, Penguin Random House LLC, 1745 Broadway, New York, NY 10019 *Tel:* 212-782-9000 *Toll Free Tel:* 800-726-0600 *Web Site:* www.penguinrandomhouse.com, pg 155

Takes, Bill, Random House Publishing Group, 1745 Broadway, New York, NY 10019 *Toll Free Tel:* 800-200-3552 *Web Site:* www.randomhousebooks.com, pg 170

Takoudes, Emily, Phaidon, 65 Bleecker St, 8th fl, New York, NY 10012 *Tel:* 212-652-5400 *Toll Free Tel:* 800-759-0190 (cust serv) *Fax:* 212-652-5410 *Toll Free Fax:* 800-286-9471 (cust serv) *E-mail:* enquiries@phaidon.com *Web Site:* www.phaidon.com, pg 159

Talbert, Janet Hill, Thomas Nelson, 501 Nelson Place, Nashville, TN 37214 *Tel:* 615-889-9000 *Toll Free Tel:* 800-251-4000 *Web Site:* www.thomasnelson.com, pg 206

Talbot, Gregory F, The Lawbook Exchange, Ltd, 33 Terminal Ave, Clark, NJ 07066-1321 *Tel:* 732-382-1800 *Toll Free Tel:* 800-422-6686 *Fax:* 732-382-1887 *E-mail:* law@lawbookexchange.com *Web Site:* www.lawbookexchange.com, pg 113

Talbot, Marieve, La Courte Echelle, 4388, rue Saint-Denis, Suite 315, Montreal, QC H2J 2L1, Canada *Tel:* 514-312-6950 *E-mail:* info@courteechelle.com *Web Site:* www.groupecourteechelle.com/la-courte-echelle, pg 400

Talbot, Trent, BRAVE Books, 13614 Poplar Circle, Suite 302, Conroe, TX 77304 *Tel:* 932-380-5648 *E-mail:* info@brave.us *Web Site:* bravebooks.us, pg 35

Tallberg, Anne Marie, St Martin's Press, LLC, 120 Broadway, New York, NY 10271 *E-mail:* publicity@stmartins.com; trademarketing@stmartins.com; foreignrights@stmartins.com *Web Site:* us.macmillan.com/smp, pg 180

Tallent, Joshua, Book Industry Study Group Inc (BISG), 232 Madison Ave, Suite 1200, New York, NY 10016 *Tel:* 646-336-7141 *E-mail:* info@bisg.org *Web Site:* www.bisg.org, pg 501

Talley, Melanie, Aggiornamento Award, 8550 United Plaza Blvd, Suite 1001, Baton Rouge, LA 70809 *Tel:* 225-408-4417 *E-mail:* cla2@cathla.org *Web Site:* cathla.org, pg 570

Talley, Melanie, John Brubaker Award, 8550 United Plaza Blvd, Suite 1001, Baton Rouge, LA 70809 *Tel:* 225-408-4417 *E-mail:* cla2@cathla.org *Web Site:* cathla.org, pg 584

Talley, Melanie, Catholic Library Association, 8550 United Plaza Blvd, Suite 1001, Baton Rouge, LA 70809 *Tel:* 225-408-4417 *E-mail:* cla2@cathla.org *Web Site:* cathla.org, pg 503

Talley, Melanie, Saint Katharine Drexel Award, 8550 United Plaza Blvd, Suite 1001, Baton Rouge, LA 70809 *Tel:* 225-408-4417 *E-mail:* cla2@cathla.org *Web Site:* cathla.org, pg 597

Talley, Melanie, Jerome Award, 8550 United Plaza Blvd, Suite 1001, Baton Rouge, LA 70809 *Tel:* 225-408-4417 *E-mail:* cla2@cathla.org *Web Site:* cathla.org, pg 618

Talley, Melanie, Regina Medal Award, 8550 United Plaza Blvd, Suite 1001, Baton Rouge, LA 70809 *Tel:* 225-408-4417 *E-mail:* cla2@cathla.org *Web Site:* cathla.org, pg 655

Tallie, Ekere, Chocorua Writing Workshop, PO Box 2280, Conway, NH 03818-2280 *Tel:* 603-447-2280 *E-mail:* office@worldfellowship.org *Web Site:* www.worldfellowship.org; www.facebook.com/World.Fellowship.Center, pg 553

Tamar, Rima, Dharma Publishing, 35788 Hauser Bridge Rd, Cazadero, CA 95421 *Tel:* 707-847-3717 *Fax:* 707-847-3380 *E-mail:* contact@dharmapublishing.com *Web Site:* www.dharmapublishing.com, pg 59

Tamberino, Claire McCabe, Johns Hopkins University Press, 2715 N Charles St, Baltimore, MD 21218-4363 *Tel:* 410-516-6900; 410-516-6987 *Toll Free Tel:* 800-537-5487 (book orders & cust serv); 800-548-1784 (journal orders) *Fax:* 410-516-6968; 410-516-6998 (orders) *E-mail:* hfscustserv@press.jhu.edu (cust serv); jrnlcirc@jh.edu (journal orders) *Web Site:* www.press.jhu.edu; muse.jhu.edu, pg 106

Tambini, Lauren, HarperCollins Children's Books, 195 Broadway, New York, NY 10007 *Tel:* 212-207-7000 *Web Site:* www.harpercollins.com/childrens, pg 85

Tamminen, Suzanna L, Wesleyan University Press, 215 Long Lane, Middletown, CT 06459-0433 *Tel:* 860-685-7712 *Fax:* 860-685-7712 *Web Site:* www.wesleyan.edu/wespress, pg 227

Tamura, Marikka, Nancy Paulsen Books, c/o Penguin Random House LLC, 1745 Broadway, New York, NY 10019 *Tel:* 212-782-9000 *Web Site:* www.penguin.com/nancy-paulsen-books-overview/, pg 152

Tamura, Marikka, GP Putnam's Sons Books for Young Readers, c/o Penguin Random House LLC, 1745 Broadway, New York, NY 10019 *Tel:* 212-782-9000 *Web Site:* www.penguin.com/putnam-young-readers/, pg 167

Tan, Alicia, HarperCollins Publishers LLC, 195 Broadway, New York, NY 10007 *Tel:* 212-207-7000 *Web Site:* www.harpercollins.com, pg 87

Tan, Jamie, Candlewick Press, 99 Dover St, Somerville, MA 02144-2825 *Tel:* 617-661-3330 *Fax:* 617-661-0565 *E-mail:* bigbear@candlewick.com; salesinfo@candlewick.com *Web Site:* candlewick.com, pg 40

Tan, Jenny, University of Pennsylvania Press, 3905 Spruce St, Philadelphia, PA 19104 *Tel:* 215-898-6261 *Fax:* 215-898-0404 *E-mail:* custserv@pobox.upenn.edu *Web Site:* www.pennpress.org, pg 219

Tan, Michael, Amadeus Press, 4501 Forbes Blvd, Suite 200, Lanham, MD 20706 *Tel:* 212-529-3888 *Fax:* 212-529-4223 *Web Site:* www.rowman.com, pg 7

Tanenbaum, Ann, Tanenbaum International Literary Agency Ltd (TILA), 1035 Fifth Ave, Suite 15D, New York, NY 10028 *Tel:* 212-371-4120 *Fax:* 212-988-0457 *E-mail:* hello@tanenbauminternational.com *Web Site:* tanenbauminternational.com, pg 479

Tang, Adrienne, Penguin Random House Canada, a Penguin Random House company, 320 Front St W, Suite 1400, Toronto, ON M5V 3B6, Canada *Tel:* 416-364-4449 *Toll Free Tel:* 888-523-9292 (cust serv) *E-mail:* canadaweb@penguinrandomhouse.com; customerservicescanada@penguinrandomhouse.com *Web Site:* www.penguinrandomhouse.ca, pg 415

Tang, Albert, Grand Central Publishing, 1290 Avenue of the Americas, New York, NY 10104 *Tel:* 212-364-1100 *Web Site:* www.hachettebookgroup.com/imprint/grand-central-publishing/, pg 80

Tang, Andy Jiaming, Atria Books, 1230 Avenue of the Americas, New York, NY 10020 *Tel:* 212-698-7000 *Fax:* 212-698-7007 *Web Site:* www.simonandschuster.com, pg 21

Tank, David, Planert Creek Press, E4843 395 Ave, Menomonie, WI 54751 *Tel:* 715-235-4110 *E-mail:* publisher@planertcreekpress.com *Web Site:* www.planertcreekpress.com, pg 160

Tann, April, NRP Direct, 220 College Ave, Suite 618, Athens, GA 30601-9801 *Tel:* 908-517-0780 *Toll Free Tel:* 844-592-4197 *E-mail:* info@nrpdirect.com *Web Site:* www.nrpdirect.com, pg 144

Tannenbaum, Amy, Jane Rotrosen Agency LLC, 318 E 51 St, New York, NY 10022-7803 *Tel:* 212-593-4330 *E-mail:* info@janerotrosen.com *Web Site:* janerotrosen.com, pg 474

Tanner, Annette K, Michigan State University Press (MSU Press), Manly Miles Bldg, Suite 25, 1405 S Harrison Rd, East Lansing, MI 48823-5245 *Tel:* 517-355-9543 *Fax:* 517-432-2611 *Web Site:* msupress.org, pg 130

Tanselle, G Thomas, Bibliographical Society of the University of Virginia, 2014 Hessian Rd, Charlottesville, VA 22903 *Tel:* 434-996-8663 *E-mail:* bibsoc@virginia.edu *Web Site:* bsuva.org, pg 501

Tansey, Meg, National Book Foundation, 90 Broad St, Suite 604, New York, NY 10004 *Tel:* 212-685-0261 *Fax:* 212-213-6570 *E-mail:* nationalbook@nationalbook.org *Web Site:* www.nationalbook.org, pg 526

Tardiff, Elizabeth, Random House Children's Books, c/o Penguin Random House LLC, 1745 Broadway, New York, NY 10019 *Tel:* 212-782-9000 *Web Site:* www.rhcbooks.com, pg 170

Tarlow, Jennifer, The Conference Board Inc, 845 Third Ave, New York, NY 10022-6600 *Tel:* 212-759-0900; 212-339-0345 (cust serv) *E-mail:* customer.service@tcb.org *Web Site:* www.conference-board.org/us; www.linkedin.com/company/the-conference-board, pg 51

Tarnofsky, Alison, Holiday House Publishing Inc, 50 Broad St, New York, NY 10004 *Tel:* 212-688-0085 *Fax:* 212-421-6134 *E-mail:* info@holidayhouse.com *Web Site:* www.holidayhouse.com, pg 94

Tarshis, Lauren, Scholastic Education Solutions, 557 Broadway, New York, NY 10012 *Tel:* 212-343-6100 *Fax:* 212-343-6189 *Web Site:* www.scholastic.com, pg 184

Tarsky, Sue, Albert Whitman & Company, 250 S Northwest Hwy, Suite 320, Park Ridge, IL 60068 *Tel:* 847-232-2800 *Toll Free Tel:* 800-255-7675 (orders) *Fax:* 847-581-0039 *E-mail:* mail@albertwhitman.com; orders@albertwhitman.com *Web Site:* www.albertwhitman.com, pg 6

Tart, Brian, Penguin Publishing Group, c/o Penguin Random House LLC, 1745 Broadway, New York, NY 10019 *Tel:* 212-782-9000 *Web Site:* www.penguin.com, pg 154

Tart, Brian, Viking Penguin, c/o Penguin Random House LLC, 1745 Broadway, New York, NY 10019 *Tel:* 212-782-9000 *Web Site:* www.penguin.com/overview-vikingbooks/; www.penguin.com/pamela-dorman-books-overview/; www.penguin.com/penguin-classics-overview/; www.penguin.com/penguin-life-overview/, pg 225

Tart, David, Kendall Hunt Publishing Co, 4050 Westmark Dr, Dubuque, IA 52002-2624 *Tel:* 563-589-1000 *Toll Free Tel:* 800-228-0810 (orders)

Fax: 563-589-1071 *Toll Free Fax:* 800-772-9165 *E-mail:* ordernow@kendallhunt.com *Web Site:* www.kendallhunt.com, pg 108

Tasman, Alice, Jean V Naggar Literary Agency Inc (JVNLA), 216 E 75 St, Suite 1-E, New York, NY 10021 *Tel:* 212-794-1082 *E-mail:* jvnla@jvnla.com *Web Site:* www.jvnla.com, pg 471

Tasse, Nathalie, Les Editions XYZ inc, 1815, ave De Lorimier, Montreal, QC H2K 3W6, Canada *Tel:* 514-525-2170 *Fax:* 514-525-7537 *E-mail:* info@editionsxyz.com *Web Site:* editionsxyz.com, pg 405

Tate, Ben, Princeton University Press, 41 William St, Princeton, NJ 08540-5237 *Tel:* 609-258-4900 *Fax:* 609-258-6305 *E-mail:* info@press.princeton.edu *Web Site:* press.princeton.edu, pg 164

Tatsukawa, Maya, Candlewick Press, 99 Dover St, Somerville, MA 02144-2825 *Tel:* 617-661-3330 *Fax:* 617-661-0565 *E-mail:* bigbear@candlewick.com; salesinfo@candlewick.com *Web Site:* candlewick.com, pg 40

Tattersfield, Claire, Flamingo Books, c/o Penguin Random House LLC, 1745 Broadway, New York, NY 10019 *Tel:* 212-782-9000 *Web Site:* www.penguin.com/flamingo-overview/, pg 72

Tattersfield, Claire, Viking Children's Books, c/o Penguin Random House LLC, 1745 Broadway, New York, NY 10019 *Tel:* 212-782-9000 *Web Site:* www.penguin.com/viking-childrens-books-overview/, pg 224

Tattersfield, George, W W Norton & Company Inc, 500 Fifth Ave, New York, NY 10110-0017 *Tel:* 212-354-5500 *Toll Free Tel:* 800-233-4830 (orders & cust serv) *Fax:* 212-869-0856 *Toll Free Fax:* 800-458-6515 *E-mail:* orders@wwnorton.com *Web Site:* wwnorton.com, pg 143

Tatulli, Christina, Quirk Books, 215 Church St, Philadelphia, PA 19106 *Tel:* 215-627-3581 *Fax:* 215-627-5220 *E-mail:* general@quirkbooks.com *Web Site:* www.quirkbooks.com, pg 168

Taurino, Giuseppe, University of Houston Creative Writing Program, Dept of English/College of Liberal Arts & Social Science, 3687 Cullen Blvd, Rm 229, Houston, TX 77204-5008 *Tel:* 713-743-3015 *E-mail:* cwp@uh.edu *Web Site:* uh.edu/class/english/programs/graduate-studies/index, pg 566

Taurisano, Ivan, Harry N Abrams Inc, 195 Broadway, 9th fl, New York, NY 10007 *Tel:* 212-206-7715 *Toll Free Tel:* 800-345-1359 *Fax:* 212-645-8437 *E-mail:* abrams@abramsbooks.com; publicity@abramsbooks.com; sales@abramsbooks.com *Web Site:* www.abramsbooks.com, pg 3

Taussig, Emma, Atria Books, 1230 Avenue of the Americas, New York, NY 10020 *Tel:* 212-698-7000 *Fax:* 212-698-7007 *Web Site:* www.simonandschuster.com, pg 21

Tavani, Mark, David Black Agency, 335 Adams St, 27th fl, Suite 2707, Brooklyn, NY 11201 *Tel:* 718-852-5500 *Fax:* 718-852-5539 *Web Site:* www.davidblackagency.com, pg 450

Taveras, Mabel Marte, Simon & Schuster, 1230 Avenue of the Americas, New York, NY 10020 *Tel:* 212-698-7000 *Toll Free Tel:* 800-223-2348 (cust serv); 800-223-2336 (orders) *Toll Free Fax:* 800-943-9831 (orders) *Web Site:* simonandschusterpublishing.com/simonandschuster/, pg 188

Taveras, Rafael, Simon & Schuster, 1230 Avenue of the Americas, New York, NY 10020 *Tel:* 212-698-7000 *Toll Free Tel:* 800-223-2348 (cust serv); 800-223-2336 (orders) *Toll Free Fax:* 800-943-9831 (orders) *Web Site:* simonandschusterpublishing.com/simonandschuster/, pg 188

Taylor, Autumn, Teaching Strategies LLC, 4500 East-West Hwy, Suite 300, Bethesda, MD 20814 *Tel:* 301-634-0818 *Toll Free Tel:* 800-637-3652 *E-mail:* info@teachingstrategies.com; support@teachingstrategies.com *Web Site:* teachingstrategies.com, pg 204

Taylor, Brent, TriadaUS Literary Agency, PO Box 561, Sewickley, PA 15143 *Tel:* 412-401-3376 *Web Site:* www.triadaus.com, pg 480

Taylor, Brian, Shubert Fendrich Memorial Playwriting Contest, PO Box 4267, Englewood, CO 80155-4267 *Tel:* 303-779-4035 *Toll Free Tel:* 800-333-7262 *Fax:* 303-779-4315 *Web Site:* www.pioneerdrama.com/playwrights/contest.asp, pg 602

Taylor, Carolyn Stanford, Wisconsin Department of Public Instruction, 125 S Webster St, Madison, WI 53703 *Tel:* 608-266-2188 *Toll Free Tel:* 800-441-4563 (US only); 800-243-8782 (US only) *E-mail:* pubsales@dpi.wi.gov *Web Site:* pubsales.dpi.wi.gov, pg 231

Taylor, Joe, Livingston Press, University of West Alabama, Sta 22, Livingston, AL 35470 *Tel:* 205-652-3470 *Web Site:* livingstonpress.uwa.edu, pg 119

Taylor, Justin, Crossway, 1300 Crescent St, Wheaton, IL 60187 *Tel:* 630-682-4300 *Toll Free Tel:* 800-635-7993 (orders); 800-543-1659 (cust serv) *Fax:* 630-682-4785 *E-mail:* info@crossway.org *Web Site:* www.crossway.org, pg 56

Taylor, Marci, American Press, 75 State St, Suite 100, Boston, MA 02109 *Tel:* 617-247-0022 *E-mail:* americanpress@flash.net *Web Site:* www.americanpresspublishers.com, pg 11

Taylor, Mark, Tyndale House Publishers Inc, 351 Executive Dr, Carol Stream, IL 60188 *Tel:* 630-668-8300 *Toll Free Tel:* 800-323-9400; 855-277-9400 *Toll Free Fax:* 866-622-9474 *Web Site:* www.tyndale.com, pg 211

Taylor, Matt, Princeton University Press, 41 William St, Princeton, NJ 08540-5237 *Tel:* 609-258-4900 *Fax:* 609-258-6305 *E-mail:* info@press.princeton.edu *Web Site:* press.princeton.edu, pg 164

Taylor, Matthew, Database Directories Inc, 96-320 Westminster Ave, London, ON N6C 5H5, Canada *Tel:* 519-433-1666 *E-mail:* mail@databasedirectory.com *Web Site:* www.databasedirectory.com, pg 400

Taylor, Maxine, Bloomsbury Academic, 1385 Broadway, 5th fl, New York, NY 10018 *Tel:* 212-419-5300 *Web Site:* www.bloomsbury.com/us/academic, pg 31

Taylor, Natasha, Macmillan, 120 Broadway, 22nd fl, New York, NY 10271 *E-mail:* press.inquiries@macmillan.com *Web Site:* us.macmillan.com, pg 122

Taylor, Rachel, Tor Publishing Group, 120 Broadway, New York, NY 10271 *Toll Free Tel:* 800-455-0340 (Macmillan) *E-mail:* torpublicity@tor.com; forgepublicity@forgebooks.com *Web Site:* us.macmillan.com/torpublishinggroup, pg 208

Taylor, Rebecca "Tay", Penguin Random House LLC, 1745 Broadway, New York, NY 10019 *Tel:* 212-782-9000 *Toll Free Tel:* 800-726-0600 *Web Site:* www.penguinrandomhouse.com, pg 155

Taylor, Sara, Dumbarton Oaks, 1703 32 St NW, Washington, DC 20007 *Tel:* 202-339-6400 *Fax:* 202-339-6401; 202-298-8407 *E-mail:* doaksbooks@doaks.org; press@doaks.org *Web Site:* www.doaks.org, pg 62

Taylor, Simone PhD, American Psychiatric Association Publishing, 800 Maine Ave SW, Suite 900, Washington, DC 20024 *Tel:* 202-459-9722 *Toll Free Tel:* 800-368-5777 *Fax:* 202-403-3094 *E-mail:* appi@psych.org *Web Site:* www.appi.org; www.psychiatryonline.org, pg 11

Taylor, Suzanne Gibbs, Gibbs Smith Publisher, 1877 E Gentile St, Layton, UT 84041 *Tel:* 801-544-9800 *Toll Free Tel:* 800-748-5439; 800-835-4993 (orders) *Fax:* 801-544-5582 *Toll Free Fax:* 800-213-3023 (orders only) *E-mail:* info@gibbs-smith.com; orders@gibbs-smith.com *Web Site:* gibbs-smith.com, pg 78

Taylor, Wendy, Jhpiego, 1615 Thames St, Baltimore, MD 21231-3492 *Tel:* 410-537-1800 *E-mail:* info@jhpiego.org *Web Site:* www.jhpiego.org, pg 106

Tayman, William P Jr, Corporation for Public Broadcasting (CPB), 401 Ninth St NW, Washington, DC 20004-2129 *Tel:* 202-879-9600 *E-mail:* press@cpb.org *Web Site:* cpb.org, pg 504

Teeman, Hilary, Random House Publishing Group, 1745 Broadway, New York, NY 10019 *Toll Free Tel:* 800-200-3552 *Web Site:* www.randomhousebooks.com, pg 171

Tehan, Isabel, Beacon Press, 24 Farnsworth St, Boston, MA 02210-1409 *Tel:* 617-742-2110 *Fax:* 617-723-3097 *E-mail:* production@beacon.org *Web Site:* www.beacon.org, pg 25

Teleb, Hadi, Highlights for Children Inc, 815 Church St, Honesdale, PA 18431 *Tel:* 570-253-1164 *Toll Free Tel:* 800-490-5111 *Fax:* 570-253-0179 *E-mail:* salesandmarketing@highlightspress.com *Web Site:* www.highlightspress.com; www.highlights.com; www.facebook.com/HighlightsforChildren, pg 92

Telesca, Carolyn, Macmillan, 120 Broadway, 22nd fl, New York, NY 10271 *E-mail:* press.inquiries@macmillan.com *Web Site:* us.macmillan.com, pg 122

Telfer, Mekisha, Roaring Brook Press, 120 Broadway, New York, NY 10271 *Tel:* 646-307-5151 *Web Site:* us.macmillan.com/publishers/roaring-brook-press, pg 176

Tellez, Priscilla, Sourcebooks LLC, 1935 Brookdale Rd, Suite 139, Naperville, IL 60563 *Tel:* 630-961-3900 *Toll Free Tel:* 800-432-7444 *Fax:* 630-961-2168 *E-mail:* info@sourcebooks.com *Web Site:* www.sourcebooks.com, pg 195

Telligman, Megan, Eugene & Marilyn Glick Indiana Authors Awards, 1500 N Delaware St, Indianapolis, IN 46202 *Tel:* 317-638-1500 *Toll Free Tel:* 800-675-8897 *E-mail:* info@indianaauthorsawards.org *Web Site:* www.indianaauthorsawards.org, pg 607

Tempe, Kristin, Tor Publishing Group, 120 Broadway, New York, NY 10271 *Toll Free Tel:* 800-455-0340 (Macmillan) *E-mail:* torpublicity@tor.com; forgepublicity@forgebooks.com *Web Site:* us.macmillan.com/torpublishinggroup, pg 208

Tempest, Nephele, The Knight Agency Inc, 232 W Washington St, Madison, GA 30650 *E-mail:* admin@knightagency.net *Web Site:* www.knightagency.net, pg 466

Tempio, Robert, Princeton University Press, 41 William St, Princeton, NJ 08540-5237 *Tel:* 609-258-4900 *Fax:* 609-258-6305 *E-mail:* info@press.princeton.edu *Web Site:* press.princeton.edu, pg 164

Templar, Kate, Stanford University Press, 425 Broadway St, Redwood City, CA 94063-3126 *Tel:* 650-723-9434 *Fax:* 650-725-3457 *E-mail:* info@www.sup.org; publicity@www.sup.org; sales@www.sup.org *Web Site:* www.sup.org, pg 197

Temple, John F III, Guideposts Book & Inspirational Media, 100 Reserve Rd, Suite E200, Danbury, CT 06810 *Tel:* 203-749-0200 *Toll Free Tel:* 800-932-2145 (cust serv) *E-mail:* gpsprod@cdsfulfillment.com; gdpcustserv@cdsfulfillment.com *Web Site:* guideposts.org, pg 82

Temple, Johnny, Akashic Books, 232 Third St, Suite A115, Brooklyn, NY 11215 *Tel:* 718-643-9193 *E-mail:* info@akashicbooks.com *Web Site:* www.akashicbooks.com, pg 6

Temple, Sam, North Star Editions Inc, 2297 Waters Dr, Mendota Heights, MN 55120 *Toll Free Tel:* 888-417-0195 *Fax:* 952-582-1000 *E-mail:* sales@northstareditions.com; publicity@northstareditions.com *Web Site:* www.northstareditions.com, pg 142

Temple, Travis, Penguin Random House LLC, 1745 Broadway, New York, NY 10019 *Tel:* 212-782-9000 *Toll Free Tel:* 800-726-0600 *Web Site:* www.penguinrandomhouse.com, pg 155

Tenaglia, Lisa, Workman Publishing, 1290 Avenue of the Americas, New York, NY 10104 *Toll Free Tel:* 800-759-0190 *Fax:* 212-364-0950 *E-mail:* workman-inquiry@hbgusa.com *Web Site:* www.hachettebookgroup.com/imprint/workman-publishing-company/, pg 233

Tenney, Sara, ACS Publications, 1155 16 St NW, Washington, DC 20036 *Tel:* 202-872-4600 *Toll Free Tel:* 800-227-5558 (US) *Fax:* 202-872-6067 *E-mail:* help@acs.org *Web Site:* pubs.acs.org; publish.acs.org/publish, pg 4

Teoh, Jackie, Cornell University Press, Sage House, 512 E State St, Ithaca, NY 14850 *Tel:* 607-253-2338 *E-mail:* cupressinfo@cornell.edu; cupress-sales@

cornell.edu; cupress-perms@cornell.edu (reprint/class use permissions) *Web Site:* www.cornellpress.cornell. edu, pg 52

Tepper, Michael, Genealogical Publishing Co, 3600 Clipper Mill Rd, Suite 229, Baltimore, MD 21211 *Tel:* 410-837-8271 *Toll Free Tel:* 800-296-6687 *Fax:* 410-752-8492 *Toll Free Fax:* 800-599-9561 *E-mail:* info@genealogical.com; web@genealogical. com *Web Site:* www.genealogical.com, pg 77

Terfloth, Caitlin, Summer Writing Courses, 1831 College Ave, Suite 324, Regina, SK S4P 4V5, Canada *Tel:* 306-537-7243 *E-mail:* sage.hill@sasktel.net; info. sagehill@sasktel.net *Web Site:* www.sagehillwriting.ca, pg 557

Terhune, Nisha Panchal, Little, Brown Books for Young Readers (LBYR), 1290 Avenue of the Americas, New York, NY 10104 *Tel:* 212-364-1100 *Toll Free Tel:* 800-759-0190 (cust serv) *E-mail:* rights@ lbchildrens.com *Web Site:* www.hachettebookgroup. com/imprint/little-brown-books-for-young-readers/, pg 118

Terraciano, Kevin, UCLA Latin American Center Publications, UCLA Latin American Institute, 10343 Bunche Hall, Los Angeles, CA 90095 *Tel:* 310-825-4571 *Fax:* 310-206-6859 *E-mail:* latinamctr@ international.ucla.edu *Web Site:* www.international. ucla.edu/lai, pg 212

Terragni, Emilia, Phaidon, 65 Bleecker St, 8th fl, New York, NY 10012 *Tel:* 212-652-5400 *Toll Free Tel:* 800-759-0190 (cust serv) *Fax:* 212-652-5410 *Toll Free Fax:* 800-286-9471 (cust serv) *E-mail:* enquiries@phaidon.com *Web Site:* www. phaidon.com, pg 159

Terrette, Kristen, Martin Literary Management, 914 164 St SE, Suite B12, Box 307, Mill Creek, WA 98012 *Tel:* 206-466-1773 (no phone queries) *Web Site:* www. martinliterarymanagement.com, pg 469

Terry, Barbara, Waldorf Publishing LLC, 2140 Hall Johnson Rd, No 102-345, Grapevine, TX 76051 *Tel:* 972-674-3131 *E-mail:* info@waldorfpublishing. com *Web Site:* www.waldorfpublishing.com, pg 226

Tesdell, Diana Secker, Vintage Books, c/o Penguin Random House LLC, 1745 Broadway, New York, NY 10019 *Tel:* 212-572-2420 *Fax:* 212-940-7390 (dom rts); 212-572-2662 (foreign rts) *E-mail:* vintageanchorpublicity@randomhouse.com *Web Site:* knopfdoubleday.com/imprint/vintage; knopfdoubleday.com, pg 225

Tesoro, Marisa, PA Press, 202 Warren St, Hudson, NY 12534 *Tel:* 518-671-6100 *Toll Free Tel:* 800-722-6657 (dist); 800-759-0190 (sales) *E-mail:* sales@papress. com *Web Site:* www.papress.com, pg 149

Tessler, Michelle, Tessler Literary Agency LLC, 155 W 68 St, No 27F, New York, NY 10023 *Tel:* 212-242-0466 *Web Site:* www.tessleragency.com, pg 479

Thackara, Will, Theosophical University Press, PO Box C, Pasadena, CA 91109-7107 *Tel:* 626-798-3378 *E-mail:* tupress@theosociety.org *Web Site:* www. theosociety.org, pg 206

Thacker, Erin, Chronicle Books LLC, 680 Second St, San Francisco, CA 94107 *Tel:* 415-537-4200 *Fax:* 415-537-4460 (perms) *E-mail:* hello@ chroniclebooks.com; subrights@chroniclebooks.com *Web Site:* www.chroniclebooks.com, pg 47

Thaker, Nandini, Heritage House Publishing Co Ltd, 1075 Pendergast St, No 103, Victoria, BC V8V 0A1, Canada *Tel:* 250-360-0829 *Fax:* 250-386-0829 *E-mail:* heritage@heritagehouse.ca; info@heritagehouse.ca; orders@heritagehouse.ca *Web Site:* www.heritagehouse.ca, pg 409

Thalheimer, Kylie, Macmillan, 120 Broadway, 22nd fl, New York, NY 10271 *E-mail:* press.inquiries@ macmillan.com *Web Site:* us.macmillan.com, pg 122

Than, Madison, Scribner, 1230 Avenue of the Americas, New York, NY 10020 *Web Site:* www. simonandschusterpublishing.com/scribner/, pg 185

Tharcher, Nicholas, The Original Falcon Press, 1753 E Broadway Rd, No 101-277, Tempe, AZ 85282 *Tel:* 602-708-1409 *E-mail:* info@originalfalcon. com *Web Site:* www.originalfalcon.com, pg 148

Tharp, Brent D, Atlas Publishing, 16050 Circa de Lindo, Rancho Santa Fe, CA 92091 *Tel:* 858-790-1944 *E-mail:* permissions@atlaspublishing.biz *Web Site:* www.atlaspublishing.biz, pg 21

Thaw, Deborah M, National Notary Association (NNA), 9350 De Soto Ave, Chatsworth, CA 91311-4926 *Tel:* 818-739-4000 *Toll Free Tel:* 800-876-6827 *Toll Free Fax:* 800-833-1211 *E-mail:* services@ nationalnotary.org *Web Site:* www.nationalnotary.org, pg 138

Thaxton, Sara, The University of Arizona Press, 1510 E University Blvd, Tucson, AZ 85721 *Tel:* 520-621-1441 *Toll Free Tel:* 800-621-2736 (orders) *Fax:* 520-621-8899 *Toll Free Fax:* 800-621-8476 (orders) *E-mail:* uap@uapress.arizona.edu *Web Site:* www. uapress.arizona.edu, pg 214

Thayer, Henry, Brandt & Hochman Literary Agents Inc, 1501 Broadway, Suite 2310, New York, NY 10036 *Tel:* 212-840-5760 *Fax:* 212-840-5776 *Web Site:* brandthochman.com, pg 452

Thedorff, Jonah, Chronicle Books LLC, 680 Second St, San Francisco, CA 94107 *Tel:* 415-537-4200 *Fax:* 415-537-4460 (perms) *E-mail:* hello@ chroniclebooks.com; subrights@chroniclebooks.com *Web Site:* www.chroniclebooks.com, pg 48

Thegeby, Sarah, Dutton, c/o Penguin Random House LLC, 1745 Broadway, New York, NY 10019 *Tel:* 212-366-2000 *Web Site:* www.penguin.com/dutton-overview/; www.penguin.com/plume-books-overview/; www.penguin.com/tiny-reparations-overview/, pg 62

Thelander, Jessica, Sourcebooks LLC, 1935 Brookdale Rd, Suite 139, Naperville, IL 60563 *Tel:* 630-961-3900 *Toll Free Tel:* 800-432-7444 *Fax:* 630-961-2168 *E-mail:* info@sourcebooks.com *Web Site:* www. sourcebooks.com, pg 194

Thelertis, Dina, IBBY Canada, c/o The Canadian Children's Book Ctr, 425 Adelaide St W, Suite 200, Toronto, ON M5V 3C1, Canada *Fax:* 416-975-8970 *E-mail:* info@ibby-canada.org *Web Site:* www.ibby-canada.org, pg 507

Theophilus, Gayna, Annick Press Ltd, 388 Carlaw Ave, Suite 200, Toronto, ON M4M 2T4, Canada *Tel:* 416-221-4802 *Fax:* 416-221-8400 *E-mail:* annickpress@ annickpress.com *Web Site:* www.annickpress.com, pg 395

Theroux, Mary L G, Independent Institute, 100 Swan Way, Oakland, CA 94621-1428 *Tel:* 510-632-1366 *Fax:* 510-568-6040 *Web Site:* www.independent.org, pg 99

Therrien, Diane, Les Editions Fides, 7333 place des Roseraies, bureau 501, Anjou, QC H1M 2X6, Canada *Tel:* 514-745-4290 *Fax:* 514-745-4299 *E-mail:* editions@groupefides.com *Web Site:* www. editionsfides.com, pg 403

Thibault, Simon, Goose Lane Editions, 500 Beaverbrook Ct, Suite 330, Fredericton, NB E3B 5X4, Canada *Tel:* 506-450-4251 *Toll Free Tel:* 888-926-8377 *Fax:* 506-459-4991 *E-mail:* editions@gooselane.com *Web Site:* www.gooselane.com, pg 407

Thickstun, Margaret, Hamilton College, Literature & Creative Writing, Literature & Creative Writing Dept, 198 College Hill Rd, Clinton, NY 13323 *Tel:* 315-859-4370 *Fax:* 315-859-4390 *Web Site:* www.hamilton.edu, pg 563

Thirsk, Melissa Harris, Law School Admission Council (LSAC), 662 Penn St, Newtown, PA 18940 *Tel:* 215-968-1101 *Toll Free Tel:* 800-336-3982 *E-mail:* lsacinfo@lsac.org *Web Site:* www.lsac.org, pg 113

Thixton, Robert, Pinder Lane & Garon-Brooke Associates Ltd, 2136 NE 58 Ct, Fort Lauderdale, FL 33308 *Tel:* 212-489-0880 *Fax:* 212-489-7104 *Web Site:* www.pinderlaneandgaronbrooke.com, pg 472

Thobani, Monika, The New Press, 120 Wall St, 31st fl, New York, NY 10005 *Tel:* 212-629-8802 *Fax:* 212-629-8617 *E-mail:* newpress@thenewpress.com *Web Site:* thenewpress.com, pg 140

Thomaides, Helen, Random House Publishing Group, 1745 Broadway, New York, NY 10019 *Toll Free Tel:* 800-200-3552 *Web Site:* www.randomhousebooks. com, pg 171

Thomas, Alan G, University of Chicago Press, 1427 E 60 St, Chicago, IL 60637-2954 *Tel:* 773-702-7700; 773-702-7600 *Toll Free Tel:* 800-621-2736 (orders) *Fax:* 773-702-9756; 773-660-2235 (orders); 773-702-2708 *E-mail:* custserv@press.uchicago.edu; marketing@press.uchicago.edu *Web Site:* www.press. uchicago.edu, pg 215

Thomas, Betsy, Writers Guild of America Awards, 7000 W Third St, Los Angeles, CA 90048 *Tel:* 323-951-4000; 323-782-4569 *Toll Free Tel:* 800-548-4532 *Fax:* 323-782-4801 *Web Site:* www.wga.org; awards. wga.org, pg 678

Thomas, Betsy, Writers Guild of America West (WGAW), 7000 W Third St, Los Angeles, CA 90048 *Tel:* 323-951-4000 *Toll Free Tel:* 800-548-4532 *Fax:* 323-782-4801 *Web Site:* www.wga.org, pg 523

Thomas, Christy, Highlights for Children Inc, 815 Church St, Honesdale, PA 18431 *Tel:* 570-253-1164 *Toll Free Tel:* 800-490-5111 *Fax:* 570-253-0179 *E-mail:* salesandmarketing@highlightspress.com *Web Site:* www.highlightspress.com; www.highlights. com; www.facebook.com/HighlightsforChildren, pg 92

Thomas, Elisa, American Booksellers Association, 600 Mamaroneck Ave, Suite 400, Harrison, NY 10528 *Tel:* 914-406-7500 *Toll Free Tel:* 800-637-0037 *Fax:* 914-417-4013 *E-mail:* info@bookweb.org *Web Site:* www.bookweb.org, pg 494

Thomas, Janis, Southern California Writers' Conference (SCWC), PO Box 433, Redmond, OR 97756 *Tel:* 619-303-8185 *Fax:* 619-906-7462 *E-mail:* msg@writersconference.com *Web Site:* www. writersconference.com; www.facebook.com/ SouthernCaliforniaWritersConference/, pg 557

Thomas, John, The Little Entrepreneur, c/o Harper Arrington Media, 33228 W 12 Mile Rd, Suite 105, Farmington Hills, MI 48334 *Tel:* 888-435-9234 *Fax:* 248-281-0373 *E-mail:* support@ digitalfashionpro.com, pg 118

Thomas, Kelly, Society for Industrial & Applied Mathematics, 3600 Market St, 6th fl, Philadelphia, PA 19104-2688 *Tel:* 215-382-9800 *Toll Free Tel:* 800-447-7426 *E-mail:* siam@siam.org *Web Site:* www.siam.org, pg 192

Thomas, Kelly, University of Pittsburgh Press, 7500 Thomas Blvd, Pittsburgh, PA 15260 *Tel:* 412-383-2456 *Fax:* 412-383-2466 *E-mail:* info@upress.pitt.edu *Web Site:* www.upress.pitt.edu, pg 219

Thomas, Kevin, Macmillan, 120 Broadway, 22nd fl, New York, NY 10271 *E-mail:* press.inquiries@macmillan. com *Web Site:* us.macmillan.com, pg 122

Thomas, Lisa, National Geographic Books, 1145 17 St NW, Washington, DC 20036-4688 *Tel:* 202-857-7000 *Toll Free Tel:* 877-866-6486 *E-mail:* ngbooks@ cdsfulfillment.com *Web Site:* www.nationalgeographic. com/books/; ngbooks.buysub.com, pg 138

Thomas, Margaret, Carolrhoda Books Inc, 241 First Ave N, Minneapolis, MN 55401 *Tel:* 612-332-3344 *Toll Free Tel:* 800-328-4929 *Fax:* 612-332-7615 *Toll Free Fax:* 800-332-1132 *E-mail:* info@lernerbooks. com; custserve@lernerbooks.com *Web Site:* www. lernerbooks.com; www.facebook.com/lernerbooks, pg 41

Thomas, Margaret, Carolrhoda Lab™, 241 First Ave N, Minneapolis, MN 55401 *Tel:* 612-332-3344 *Toll Free Tel:* 800-328-4929 *Fax:* 612-332-7615 *Toll Free Fax:* 800-332-1132 *E-mail:* info@lernerbooks. com; custserve@lernerbooks.com *Web Site:* www. lernerbooks.com; www.facebook.com/lernerbooks, pg 41

Thomas, Margaret, ediciones Lerner, 241 First Ave N, Minneapolis, MN 55401 *Tel:* 612-332-3344 *Toll Free Tel:* 800-328-4929 *Fax:* 612-332-7615 *Toll Free Fax:* 800-332-1132 *E-mail:* info@lernerbooks.

com; custserve@lernerbooks.com *Web Site:* www.lernerbooks.com; www.facebook.com/lernerbooks, pg 63

Thomas, Margaret, First Avenue Editions, 241 First Ave N, Minneapolis, MN 55401 *Tel:* 612-332-3344 *Toll Free Tel:* 800-328-4929 *Fax:* 612-332-7615 *Toll Free Fax:* 800-332-1132 *E-mail:* info@lernerbooks.com; custserve@lernerbooks.com *Web Site:* www.lernerbooks.com; www.facebook.com/lernerbooks, pg 72

Thomas, Margaret, Graphic Universe™, 241 First Ave N, Minneapolis, MN 55401 *Tel:* 612-332-3344 *Toll Free Tel:* 800-328-4929 *Fax:* 612-332-7615 *Toll Free Fax:* 800-332-1132 *E-mail:* info@lernerbooks.com; custserve@lernerbooks.com *Web Site:* www.lernerbooks.com; www.facebook.com/lernerbooks, pg 80

Thomas, Margaret, Lerner Publications, 241 First Ave N, Minneapolis, MN 55401 *Tel:* 612-332-3344 *Toll Free Tel:* 800-328-4929 *Fax:* 612-332-7615 *Toll Free Fax:* 800-332-1132 *E-mail:* info@lernerbooks.com; custserve@lernerbooks.com *Web Site:* www.lernerbooks.com; www.facebook.com/lernerbooks, pg 115

Thomas, Margaret, Lerner Publishing Group Inc, 241 First Ave N, Minneapolis, MN 55401 *Tel:* 612-332-3344 *Toll Free Tel:* 800-328-4929 *Fax:* 612-332-7615 *Toll Free Fax:* 800-332-1132 *E-mail:* info@lernerbooks.com; custserve@lernerbooks.com *Web Site:* www.lernerbooks.com; www.facebook.com/lernerbooks, pg 115

Thomas, Margaret, LernerClassroom, 241 First Ave N, Minneapolis, MN 55401 *Tel:* 612-332-3344 *Toll Free Tel:* 800-328-4929 *Fax:* 612-332-7615 *Toll Free Fax:* 800-332-1132 *E-mail:* info@lernerbooks.com; custserve@lernerbooks.com *Web Site:* www.lernerbooks.com; www.facebook.com/lernerbooks, pg 115

Thomas, Margaret, Millbrook Press, 241 First Ave N, Minneapolis, MN 55401 *Tel:* 612-332-3344 *Toll Free Tel:* 800-328-4929 *Fax:* 612-332-7615 *Toll Free Fax:* 800-332-1132 *E-mail:* info@lernerbooks.com; custserve@lernerbooks.com *Web Site:* www.lernerbooks.com; www.facebook.com/millbrookpress, pg 131

Thomas, Margaret, Twenty-First Century Books, 241 First Ave N, Minneapolis, MN 55401 *Tel:* 612-332-3344 *Toll Free Tel:* 800-328-4929 *Fax:* 612-332-7615 *Toll Free Fax:* 800-332-1132 *E-mail:* info@lernerbooks.com; custserve@lernerbooks.com *Web Site:* www.lernerbooks.com; www.facebook.com/lernerbooks, pg 211

Thomas, Margaret, Zest Books, 241 First Ave N, Minneapolis, MN 55401 *Tel:* 612-332-3344 *Toll Free Tel:* 800-328-4929 *Toll Free Fax:* 800-332-1132 *E-mail:* info@lernerbooks.com; publicity@lernerbooks.com; custserve@lernerbooks.com (orders) *Web Site:* lernerbooks.com, pg 236

Thomas, Mary Beth, HarperCollins Publishers LLC, 195 Broadway, New York, NY 10007 *Tel:* 212-207-7000 *Web Site:* www.harpercollins.com, pg 86

Thomas, Michael Payne, Charles C Thomas Publisher Ltd, 2600 S First St, Springfield, IL 62704 *Tel:* 217-789-8980 *Toll Free Tel:* 800-258-8980 *Fax:* 217-789-9130 *E-mail:* books@ccthomas.com *Web Site:* www.ccthomas.com, pg 206

Thomas, Paul, Crossway, 1300 Crescent St, Wheaton, IL 60187 *Tel:* 630-682-4300 *Toll Free Tel:* 800-635-7993 (orders); 800-543-1659 (cust serv) *Fax:* 630-682-4785 *E-mail:* info@crossway.org *Web Site:* www.crossway.org, pg 56

Thomas, Randolph, Louisiana State University Creative Writing Program MFA, English Dept, 260 Allen Hall, Baton Rouge, LA 70803 *Tel:* 225-578-4086 *Fax:* 225-578-4129 *E-mail:* lsucrwriting@lsu.edu *Web Site:* www.lsu.edu; www.lsu.edu/hss/english/creative_writing, pg 563

Thomas, Rebecca Tarr, Adams Media, 100 Technology Center Dr, Suite 501, Stoughton, MA 02072 *Tel:* 508-427-7100 *Web Site:* www.simonandschuster.com, pg 4

Thomas, Rich, HarperCollins Children's Books, 195 Broadway, New York, NY 10007 *Tel:* 212-207-7000 *Web Site:* www.harpercollins.com/childrens, pg 85

Thomas, Sheila, Quail Ridge Press (QRP), 2451 Atrium Way, Nashville, TN 37214 *Toll Free Tel:* 800-358-0560 *Fax:* 615-391-2815 *Web Site:* www.swphbooks.com/quail-ridge-press.html, pg 168

Thomas, Stephanie, BuilderBooks, 1201 15 St NW, Washington, DC 20005 *Toll Free Tel:* 800-368-5242 *E-mail:* info@nahb.com *Web Site:* builderbooks.com, pg 38

Thomas, Sue Timmons, Art of Living, PrimaMedia Inc, 1250 Bethlehem Pike, Suite 241, Hatfield, PA 19440 *Tel:* 267-421-7326 *E-mail:* info@artoflivingprimamedia.com *Web Site:* artoflivingprimamedia.com, pg 17

Thomas, Tim, Verso Books, 388 Atlantic Ave, Brooklyn, NY 11217 *Tel:* 718-246-8160 *Fax:* 718-246-8165 *E-mail:* verso@versobooks.com *Web Site:* www.versobooks.com, pg 224

Thomas, William, Doubleday, c/o Penguin Random House LLC, 1745 Broadway, New York, NY 10019 *Tel:* 212-751-2600 *Fax:* 212-940-7390 (dom rts); 212-572-2662 (foreign rts) *Web Site:* knopfdoubleday.com/imprint/doubleday/; knopfdoubleday.com, pg 61

Thomas-Menter, Keely, Chronicle Books LLC, 680 Second St, San Francisco, CA 94107 *Tel:* 415-537-4200 *Fax:* 415-537-4460 (perms) *E-mail:* hello@chroniclebooks.com; subrights@chroniclebooks.com *Web Site:* www.chroniclebooks.com, pg 47

Thomasch, Emma, Random House Publishing Group, 1745 Broadway, New York, NY 10019 *Toll Free Tel:* 800-200-3552 *Web Site:* www.randomhousebooks.com, pg 171

Thomason, Kevin, McNeese State University MFA in Creative Writing Program, PO Box 92655, Lake Charles, LA 70609-0001 *Tel:* 337-475-5325; 337-475-5327 *Web Site:* www.mcneese.edu/academics/graduate/creative-writing, pg 563

Thompson, Ahmir "Questlove", Farrar, Straus & Giroux, LLC, 120 Broadway, New York, NY 10271 *Tel:* 212-741-6900 *E-mail:* fsg.publicity@fsgbooks.com; sales@fsgbooks.com *Web Site:* us.macmillan.com/fsg, pg 70

Thompson, Alexander, Cy Twombly Award for Poetry, 820 Greenwich St, New York, NY 10014 *Tel:* 212-807-7077 *E-mail:* info@contemporary-arts.org *Web Site:* www.foundationforcontemporaryarts.org/grants/cy-twombly-award-for-poetry, pg 672

Thompson, Barbara, Bitingduck Press LLC, 1262 Sunnyoaks Circle, Altadena, CA 91001 *Tel:* 626-507-8033 *E-mail:* notifications@bitingduckpress.com *Web Site:* bitingduckpress.com, pg 30

Thompson, Faye, Thompson Educational Publishing Inc, 20 Ripley Ave, Toronto, ON M6S 3N9, Canada *Tel:* 416-766-2763 (admin & orders) *Toll Free Tel:* 877-366-2763 *Fax:* 416-766-0398 (admin & orders) *E-mail:* info@thompsonbooks.com; support@thompsonbooks.com *Web Site:* www.thompsonbooks.com, pg 420

Thompson, Jamie, Insight Editions, 800 "A" St, San Rafael, CA 94901 *Tel:* 415-526-1370 *Toll Free Tel:* 800-809-3792 *Toll Free Fax:* 866-509-0515 *E-mail:* info@insighteditions.com; marketing@insighteditions.com *Web Site:* insighteditions.com, pg 101

Thompson, Judy, The Briar Cliff Review Fiction, Poetry & Creative Nonfiction Contest, 3303 Rebecca St, Sioux City, IA 51104-2100 *Tel:* 712-279-1651 *Fax:* 712-279-5486 *Web Site:* www.bcreview.org, pg 584

Thompson, Keith, Thompson Educational Publishing Inc, 20 Ripley Ave, Toronto, ON M6S 3N9, Canada *Tel:* 416-766-2763 (admin & orders) *Toll Free Tel:* 877-366-2763 *Fax:* 416-766-0398 (admin & orders) *E-mail:* info@thompsonbooks.com; support@thompsonbooks.com *Web Site:* www.thompsonbooks.com, pg 420

Thompson, Lance, Perfection Learning®, 1000 N Second Ave, Logan, IA 51546-1061 *Tel:* 712-644-2831 *Toll Free Tel:* 800-831-4190 *Toll Free Fax:* 800-543-2745 *E-mail:* orders@perfectionlearning.com *Web Site:* www.perfectionlearning.com, pg 158

Thompson, Myles, Columbia University Press, 61 W 62 St, New York, NY 10023 *Tel:* 212-459-0600 *Toll Free Tel:* 800-944-8648 *Fax:* 212-459-3678 *Web Site:* cup.columbia.edu, pg 51

Thompson, Richelle, Forward Movement, 412 Sycamore St, Cincinnati, OH 45202-4110 *Tel:* 513-721-6659 *Toll Free Tel:* 800-543-1813 *Fax:* 513-721-0729 (orders) *E-mail:* orders@forwardmovement.org (orders & cust serv) *Web Site:* www.forwardmovement.org, pg 73

Thompson, Robert, G Schirmer Inc/Associated Music Publishers Inc, 180 Madison Ave, 24th fl, New York, NY 10016 *Tel:* 212-254-2100 *Fax:* 212-254-2013 *E-mail:* schirmer@schirmer.com *Web Site:* www.musicsalesclassical.com, pg 183

Thompson, Rowan, Thompson Educational Publishing Inc, 20 Ripley Ave, Toronto, ON M6S 3N9, Canada *Tel:* 416-766-2763 (admin & orders) *Toll Free Tel:* 877-366-2763 *Fax:* 416-766-0398 (admin & orders) *E-mail:* info@thompsonbooks.com; support@thompsonbooks.com *Web Site:* www.thompsonbooks.com, pg 420

Thompson, Sophy, Thames & Hudson, 500 Fifth Ave, New York, NY 10110 *Tel:* 212-354-3763 *Toll Free Tel:* 800-233-4830 *Fax:* 212-398-1252 *E-mail:* bookinfo@thames.wwnorton.com *Web Site:* www.thamesandhudsonusa.com, pg 205

Thompson, Tom, St Martin's Press, LLC, 120 Broadway, New York, NY 10271 *E-mail:* publicity@stmartins.com; trademarketing@stmartins.com; foreignrights@stmartins.com *Web Site:* us.macmillan.com/smp, pg 180

Thomson Black, Jean E, Yale University Press, 302 Temple St, New Haven, CT 06511-8909 *Tel:* 203-432-0960; 203-432-0966 (sales); 401-531-2800 (cust serv) *Toll Free Tel:* 800-405-1619 (cust serv) *Fax:* 203-432-0948; 203-432-8485 (sales); 401-531-2801 (cust serv) *Toll Free Fax:* 800-406-9145 (cust serv) *E-mail:* sales.press@yale.edu (sales); customer.care@triliteral.org (cust serv) *Web Site:* www.yalebooks.com; yalepress.yale.edu/yupbooks, pg 235

Thomson, Ryan J, Captain Fiddle Music & Publications, 94 Wiswall Rd, Lee, NH 03861 *Tel:* 603-659-2658 *E-mail:* cfiddle@tiac.net *Web Site:* captainfiddle.com, pg 40

Thomson, Sue, Art of Living, PrimaMedia Inc, 1250 Bethlehem Pike, Suite 241, Hatfield, PA 19440 *Tel:* 267-421-7326 *E-mail:* info@artoflivingprimamedia.com *Web Site:* artoflivingprimamedia.com, pg 17

Thoreson, Bridget, Ulysses Press, 195 Montague St, 14th fl, Brooklyn, NY 11201 *Tel:* 510-601-8301 *Toll Free Tel:* 800-377-2542 *Fax:* 510-601-8307 *E-mail:* ulysses@ulyssespress.com *Web Site:* www.ulyssespress.com, pg 212

Thorn, Anna, Independent Publishers Caucus (IPC), c/o Seven Stories Press, 140 Watts St, New York, NY 10013 *E-mail:* info@indiepubs.org *Web Site:* www.indiepubs.org, pg 507

Thornton, Carrie, HarperCollins Publishers LLC, 195 Broadway, New York, NY 10007 *Tel:* 212-207-7000 *Web Site:* www.harpercollins.com, pg 86

Thornton, Kara, Running Press, 1290 Avenue of the Americas, New York, NY 10104 *Tel:* 212-364-1100 *Toll Free Tel:* 800-759-0190 (cust serv) *Fax:* 212-364-0933 (intl orders) *Toll Free Fax:* 800-286-9471 (cust serv) *E-mail:* customer.service@hbgusa.com; orders@hbgusa.com *Web Site:* www.hachettebookgroup.com/imprint/running-press/; www.moon.com (Moon Travel Guides), pg 178

Thornton, Marianne, Les Editions du Boreal, 4447, rue St-Denis, Montreal, QC H2J 2L2, Canada *Tel:* 514-287-7401 *Fax:* 514-287-7664 *E-mail:* info@editionsboreal.qc.ca; boreal@editionsboreal.qc.ca; communications@editionsboreal.qc.ca *Web Site:* www.editionsboreal.qc.ca, pg 402

Thorpe, Andrea, Sarah Josepha Hale Award, 58 N Main St, Newport, NH 03773 *Tel:* 603-863-3430 *E-mail:* rfl@newport.lib.nh.us *Web Site:* www.newport.lib.nh.us, pg 610

Thorpe, Wendy, Chronicle Books LLC, 680 Second St, San Francisco, CA 94107 *Tel:* 415-537-4200 *Fax:* 415-537-4460 (perms) *E-mail:* hello@chroniclebooks.com; subrights@chroniclebooks.com *Web Site:* www.chroniclebooks.com, pg 47

Thorsted, Jessie, InkWell Management, 521 Fifth Ave, Suite 2600, New York, NY 10175 *Tel:* 212-922-3500 *Fax:* 212-922-0535 *E-mail:* info@inkwellmanagement.com; submissions@inkwellmanagement.com; permissions@inkwellmanagement.com *Web Site:* inkwellmanagement.com, pg 463

Thurston, Suzanne, AAAS/Subaru Prize for Excellence in Science Books, 1200 New York Ave NW, Washington, DC 20005 *Tel:* 202-326-6400 *E-mail:* sbf@aaas.org *Web Site:* www.sbfprize.org, pg 569

Tiampo, Carmen, University of British Columbia Press, 2029 West Mall, Vancouver, BC V6T 1Z2, Canada *Tel:* 604-822-5959 *Toll Free Tel:* 877-377-9378 *Fax:* 604-822-6083 *Toll Free Fax:* 800-668-0821 *E-mail:* frontdesk@ubcpress.ca *Web Site:* www.ubcpress.ca, pg 422

Tiburcio, Chastery, Lectorum Publications Inc, 10 New Maple Ave, Suite 303, Pine Brook, NJ 07058 *Tel:* 201-559-2200 *Toll Free Tel:* 800-345-5946 *E-mail:* lectorum@lectorum.com *Web Site:* www.lectorum.com, pg 114

Tichnor, Michael L, American Jewish Committee (AJC), Mail Code 6760, PO Box 7247, Philadelphia, PA 19170-0001 *Tel:* 212-751-4000 *Fax:* 212-891-1450 *E-mail:* social@ajc.org *Web Site:* www.ajc.org, pg 495

Tiemens, Ellie, Sourcebooks LLC, 1935 Brookdale Rd, Suite 139, Naperville, IL 60563 *Tel:* 630-961-3900 *Toll Free Tel:* 800-432-7444 *Fax:* 630-961-2168 *E-mail:* info@sourcebooks.com *Web Site:* www.sourcebooks.com, pg 194

Tiernan, Bridget Kinsella, Stanford University Press, 425 Broadway St, Redwood City, CA 94063-3126 *Tel:* 650-723-9434 *Fax:* 650-725-3457 *E-mail:* info@www.sup.org; publicity@www.sup.org; sales@www.sup.org *Web Site:* www.sup.org, pg 197

Tierney, Peggy, Tanglewood Publishing, 1060 N Capitol Ave, Suite E-395, Indianapolis, IN 46204 *Tel:* 812-877-9488 *Toll Free Tel:* 800-788-3123 (orders) *E-mail:* info@tanglewoodbooks.com; orders@tanglewoodbooks.com; submission@tanglewoodbooks.com *Web Site:* www.tanglewoodbooks.com, pg 202

Tiffey, Kesley, Random House Publishing Group, 1745 Broadway, New York, NY 10019 *Toll Free Tel:* 800-200-3552 *Web Site:* www.randomhousebooks.com, pg 171

Tigunait, Pandit Rajmani PhD, Himalayan Institute Press, 952 Bethany Tpke, Honesdale, PA 18431 *Tel:* 570-253-5551 *Toll Free Tel:* 800-822-4547 *E-mail:* trade@himalayaninstitute.org *Web Site:* www.himalayaninstitute.org, pg 92

Tiktinsky, Katrina, Little, Brown and Company, 1290 Avenue of the Americas, New York, NY 10104 *Tel:* 212-364-1100 *Fax:* 212-364-0952 *E-mail:* firstname.lastname@hbgusa.com *Web Site:* www.hachettebookgroup.com/imprint/little-brown-and-company/, pg 118

Tilford, Nicole, SBL Press, The Luce Ctr, Suite 350, 825 Houston Mill Rd, Atlanta, GA 30329 *Tel:* 404-727-3100 *Fax:* 404-727-3101 (corp) *E-mail:* sbl@sbl-site.org *Web Site:* www.sbl-site.org, pg 183

Tiller, Jerome, ArtWrite Productions, 1555 Gardena Ave NE, Minneapolis, MN 55432-5848 *Tel:* 612-803-0436 *Web Site:* artwriteproductions; adaptedclassics.com, pg 18

Tiller, Jocelyn, HarperCollins Publishers LLC, 195 Broadway, New York, NY 10007 *Tel:* 212-207-7000 *Web Site:* www.harpercollins.com, pg 86

Tillman, Lillian Gail, Clotilde's Secretarial & Management Services, PO Box 871926, New Orleans, LA 70187 *Tel:* 504-242-2912 *E-mail:* elcsy58@att.net, pg 437

Timmings, Caroline, Harlequin Enterprises Ltd, 195 Broadway, 24th fl, New York, NY 10007 *Tel:* 212-207-7000 *Toll Free Tel:* 888-432-4879; 800-370-5838 (ebooks) *E-mail:* customerservice@harlequin.com *Web Site:* www.harlequin.com/shop/index.html; corporate.harlequin.com, pg 85

Timmins, Michelle, Macmillan, 120 Broadway, 22nd fl, New York, NY 10271 *E-mail:* press.inquiries@macmillan.com *Web Site:* us.macmillan.com, pg 122

Timmons, Barbara K, Management Sciences for Health, 200 Rivers Edge Dr, Medford, MA 02155 *Tel:* 617-250-9500 *Fax:* 617-250-9090 *E-mail:* bookstore@msh.org *Web Site:* www.msh.org, pg 123

Timmons, Kelly, Atlantic Center for the Arts Mentoring Artist-in-Residence Program, 1414 Art Center Ave, New Smyrna Beach, FL 32168 *Tel:* 386-427-6975 *E-mail:* program@atlanticcenterforthearts.org *Web Site:* atlanticcenterforthearts.org, pg 553

Tinari, Julianne, Jane Rotrosen Agency LLC, 318 E 51 St, New York, NY 10022-7803 *Tel:* 212-593-4330 *E-mail:* info@janerotrosen.com *Web Site:* janerotrosen.com, pg 474

Tingley, Megan, Hachette Book Group Inc, 1290 Avenue of the Americas, New York, NY 10104 *Tel:* 212-364-1100 *Toll Free Tel:* 800-759-0190 (cust serv) *Fax:* 212-364-0933 (intl orders) *Toll Free Fax:* 800-286-9471 (cust serv) *E-mail:* customer.service@hbgusa.com; orders@hbgusa.com *Web Site:* www.hachettebookgroup.com, pg 83

Tingley, Megan, Little, Brown Books for Young Readers (LBYR), 1290 Avenue of the Americas, New York, NY 10104 *Tel:* 212-364-1100 *Toll Free Tel:* 800-759-0190 (cust serv) *E-mail:* rights@lbchildrens.com *Web Site:* www.hachettebookgroup.com/imprint/little-brown-books-for-young-readers/, pg 118

Tinker, Scott W, Bureau of Economic Geology, c/o The University of Texas at Austin, 10100 Burnet Rd, Bldg 130, Austin, TX 78758 *Tel:* 512-471-1534 *Fax:* 512-471-0140 *E-mail:* pubsales@beg.utexas.edu *Web Site:* www.beg.utexas.edu, pg 38

Tinnie, Sung, Business Expert Press, 222 E 46 St, Suite 203, New York, NY 10017-2906 *Tel:* 212-661-8810 *Fax:* 646-478-8107 *E-mail:* sales@businessexpertpress.com *Web Site:* www.businessexpertpress.com, pg 38

Tisch, Vicki, Scholastic Trade Publishing, 557 Broadway, New York, NY 10012 *Tel:* 212-343-6100; 212-343-4685 (export sales) *Fax:* 212-343-4714 (export sales) *Web Site:* www.scholastic.com, pg 184

Tisdel, Laura, Viking Penguin, c/o Penguin Random House LLC, 1745 Broadway, New York, NY 10019 *Tel:* 212-782-9000 *Web Site:* www.penguin.com/overview-vikingbooks/; www.penguin.com/pameladorman-books-overview/; www.penguin.com/penguin-classics-overview/; www.penguin.com/penguin-life-overview/, pg 225

Tisman, Hillary, Farrar, Straus & Giroux, LLC, 120 Broadway, New York, NY 10271 *Tel:* 212-741-6900 *E-mail:* fsg.publicity@fsgbooks.com; sales@fsgbooks.com *Web Site:* us.macmillan.com/fsg, pg 70

Tisman, Hillary, Picador, 120 Broadway, New York, NY 10271 *Tel:* 646-307-5151 *Fax:* 212-253-9627 *E-mail:* publicity@picadorusa.com *Web Site:* us.macmillan.com/picador, pg 159

Tisseyre, Charles, Les Editions Pierre Tisseyre, 155, rue Maurice, Rosemere, QC J7A 2S8, Canada *Tel:* 514-335-0777 *Fax:* 514-335-6723 *E-mail:* info@edtisseyre.ca *Web Site:* www.tisseyre.ca, pg 404

Tisseyre, Michelle, Les Editions Pierre Tisseyre, 155, rue Maurice, Rosemere, QC J7A 2S8, Canada *Tel:* 514-335-0777 *Fax:* 514-335-6723 *E-mail:* info@edtisseyre.ca *Web Site:* www.tisseyre.ca, pg 404

Titta, John, American Society of Composers, Authors & Publishers (ASCAP), 250 W 57 St, New York, NY 10107 *Tel:* 212-621-6000 *Toll Free Tel:* 800-952-7227 (cust serv) *Fax:* 212-621-6595 *Web Site:* www.ascap.com, pg 496

Tizzano, Michael, Alfred A Knopf, c/o Penguin Random House LLC, 1745 Broadway, New York, NY 10019 *Tel:* 212-751-2600 *Fax:* 212-940-7390 (dom rts); 212-572-2662 (foreign rts) *Web Site:* knopfdoubleday.com/imprint/knopf/; knopfdoubleday.com, pg 110

Tjan, AiLing, Chronicle Books LLC, 680 Second St, San Francisco, CA 94107 *Tel:* 415-537-4200 *Fax:* 415-537-4460 (perms) *E-mail:* hello@chroniclebooks.com; subrights@chroniclebooks.com *Web Site:* www.chroniclebooks.com, pg 48

Tjandra, Lia, University of California Press, 155 Grand Ave, Suite 400, Oakland, CA 94612-3758 *Tel:* 510-883-8232 *Fax:* 510-836-8910 *E-mail:* customerservice@ucpress.edu *Web Site:* www.ucpress.edu, pg 215

Tkaczyk, Karen, Lewis Galantiere Translation Award, 211 N Union St, Suite 100, Alexandria, VA 22314 *Tel:* 703-683-6100 *Fax:* 703-778-7222 *E-mail:* honors_awards@atanet.org *Web Site:* www.atanet.org, pg 605

Tobaben, Sarah, Andrews McMeel Publishing LLC, 1130 Walnut St, Kansas City, MO 64106-2109 *Tel:* 816-581-7500 *Toll Free Tel:* 800-851-8923 *Web Site:* www.andrewsmcmeel.com; publishing.andrewsmcmeel.com, pg 14

Tobias, Conan, Doug Wright Awards, PO Box 611, Sta P, Toronto, ON M5S 2Y4, Canada *E-mail:* dougwrightawards@gmail.com *Web Site:* dougwrightawards.com, pg 678

Tobin, Ana, Artech House®, 685 Canton St, Norwood, MA 02062 *Tel:* 781-769-9750 *Toll Free Tel:* 800-225-9977 *Fax:* 781-769-6334 *E-mail:* artech@artechhouse.com *Web Site:* us.artechhouse.com, pg 17

Tobin, Claire, Farrar, Straus & Giroux, LLC, 120 Broadway, New York, NY 10271 *Tel:* 212-741-6900 *E-mail:* fsg.publicity@fsgbooks.com; sales@fsgbooks.com *Web Site:* us.macmillan.com/fsg, pg 70

Todd, Charles, Collier Associates, 309 Kelsey Park Circle, Palm Beach Gardens, FL 33410 *Tel:* 561-514-6548 *E-mail:* dmccabooks@gmail.com, pg 454

Todd, Raymond, See-More's Workshop Arts & Education Workshops, 325 West End Ave, New York, NY 10023 *Tel:* 212-724-0677 *E-mail:* sbt@shadowboxtheatre.org *Web Site:* shadowboxtheatre.org/workshops, pg 557

Toennis, Autumn, Europa Editions, 27 Union Sq W, Suite 302, New York, NY 10003 *Tel:* 212-868-6844 *Fax:* 212-868-6845 *E-mail:* info@europaeditions.com; books@europaeditions.com; publicity@europaeditions.com *Web Site:* www.europaeditions.com, pg 67

Toke, Arun N, Skipping Stones Honor Awards, 166 W 12 Ave, Eugene, OR 97401 *Tel:* 541-342-4956 *E-mail:* info@skippingstones.org *Web Site:* www.skippingstones.org, pg 663

Toke, Arun N, The Skipping Stones Youth Honor Awards, 166 W 12 Ave, Eugene, OR 97401 *Tel:* 541-342-4956 *E-mail:* info@skippingstones.org *Web Site:* www.skippingstones.org, pg 663

Tokunaga, Ruiko, Hachette Book Group Inc, 1290 Avenue of the Americas, New York, NY 10104 *Tel:* 212-364-1100 *Toll Free Tel:* 800-759-0190 (cust serv) *Fax:* 212-364-0933 (intl orders) *Toll Free Fax:* 800-286-9471 (cust serv) *E-mail:* customer.service@hbgusa.com; orders@hbgusa.com *Web Site:* www.hachettebookgroup.com, pg 83

Tolan, Kerri, University of South Carolina Press, 1600 Hampton St, Suite 544, Columbia, SC 29208 *Tel:* 803-777-5245 *Toll Free Tel:* 800-768-2500 (orders) *Fax:* 803-777-0160 *Toll Free Fax:* 800-868-0740 (orders) *Web Site:* uscpress.com, pg 220

Tolentino, Blaine, University of Hawaii Press, 2840 Kolowalu St, Honolulu, HI 96822-1888 *Tel:* 808-956-8255 *Toll Free Tel:* 888-UHPRESS (847-7377) *Toll Free Fax:* 800-650-7811 *E-mail:* uhpbooks@hawaii.edu *Web Site:* www.uhpress.hawaii.edu, pg 216

Toler, Elinor, Roaring Brook Press, 120 Broadway, New York, NY 10271 *Tel:* 646-307-5151 *Web Site:* us.macmillan.com/publishers/roaring-brook-press, pg 176

Tolia, Shimul, little bee books, 598 Broadway, 7th fl, New York, NY 10012 *Tel:* 212-321-0237 *Toll Free Tel:* 844-321-0237 *E-mail:* info@littlebeebooks.com; sales@littlebeebooks.com; publicity@littlebeebooks.com *Web Site:* littlebeebooks.com, pg 117

Toller, Erin, Simon & Schuster Children's Publishing, 1230 Avenue of the Americas, New York, NY 10020 *Tel:* 212-698-7000 *Web Site:* www.simonandschuster.com/kids; www.simonandschuster.com/teen; simonandschuster.net; simonandschuster.biz, pg 189

Tolpin, Ethan, Macmillan, 120 Broadway, 22nd fl, New York, NY 10271 *E-mail:* press.inquiries@macmillan.com *Web Site:* us.macmillan.com, pg 122

Tomasulo, Christina, HarperCollins Publishers LLC, 195 Broadway, New York, NY 10007 *Tel:* 212-207-7000 *Web Site:* www.harpercollins.com, pg 86

Tombul, Angela, Association of School Business Officials International, 44790 Maynard Sq, Suite 200, Ashburn, VA 20147 *Tel:* 703-478-0405 *Toll Free Tel:* 866-682-2729 *Fax:* 703-478-0205; 703-708-7060 (membership) *E-mail:* asboreq@asbointl.org; membership@asbointl.org *Web Site:* www.asbointl.org, pg 20

Tomczak, Melissa, Trident Media Group LLC, 355 Lexington Ave, 12th fl, New York, NY 10017 *Tel:* 212-333-1511 *E-mail:* info@tridentmediagroup.com; press@tridentmediagroup.com; foreignrights@tridentmediagroup.com; office.assistant@tridentmediagroup.com *Web Site:* www.tridentmediagroup.com, pg 480

Tomkiw, Beth, Trusted Media Brands Inc, 750 Third Ave, 3rd fl, New York, NY 10017 *Tel:* 646-293-6299 *Toll Free Tel:* 877-732-4438 (cust serv) *Fax:* 646-293-6251 *E-mail:* customercare@trustedmediabrands.com; press@trustedmediabrands.com *Web Site:* www.trustedmediabrands.com; www.rd.com, pg 210

Tomko, Emma, HarperCollins Publishers LLC, 195 Broadway, New York, NY 10007 *Tel:* 212-207-7000 *Web Site:* www.harpercollins.com, pg 87

Tomlin, Tiffany, Penguin Random House Speakers Bureau, a Penguin Random House company, 1745 Broadway, Mail Drop 13-1, New York, NY 10019 *Tel:* 212-572-2013 *E-mail:* speakers@penguinrandomhouse.com *Web Site:* www.prhspeakers.com, pg 487

Tomlinson, Ciara, Pantheon Books, c/o Penguin Random House LLC, 1745 Broadway, New York, NY 10019 *Tel:* 212-751-2600 *Fax:* 212-940-7390 (dom rts); 212-572-2662 (foreign rts) *Web Site:* knopfdoubleday.com/imprint/pantheon/; knopfdoubleday.com, pg 150

Tompa, Andrea, Candlewick Press, 99 Dover St, Somerville, MA 02144-2825 *Tel:* 617-661-3330 *Fax:* 617-661-0565 *E-mail:* bigbear@candlewick.com; salesinfo@candlewick.com *Web Site:* candlewick.com, pg 39

Tompkins, Amy, Transatlantic Agency, 2 Bloor St E, Suite 3500, Toronto, ON M4W 1A8, Canada *Tel:* 416-488-9214 *E-mail:* info@transatlanticagency.com; royalties@transatlanticagency.com *Web Site:* www.transatlanticagency.com, pg 479

Ton-Aime, Sony, Chautauqua Writers' Workshop, One Ames Ave, Chautauqua, NY 14722 *Tel:* 716-357-6255 *Web Site:* www.chq.org, pg 553

Tonegutti, Marta, University of Chicago Press, 1427 E 60 St, Chicago, IL 60637-2954 *Tel:* 773-702-7700; 773-702-7600 *Toll Free Tel:* 800-621-2736 (orders) *Fax:* 773-702-9756; 773-660-2235 (orders); 773-702-2708 *E-mail:* custserv@press.uchicago.edu; marketing@press.uchicago.edu *Web Site:* www.press.uchicago.edu, pg 215

Tonetti, Barbara, Princeton University Press, 41 William St, Princeton, NJ 08540-5237 *Tel:* 609-258-4900 *Fax:* 609-258-6305 *E-mail:* info@press.princeton.edu *Web Site:* press.princeton.edu, pg 164

Tong, Murray, Wilfrid Laurier University Press, 75 University Ave W, Waterloo, ON N2L 3C5, Canada *Tel:* 519-884-0710 *Toll Free Tel:* 866-836-5551 (CN & US) *Fax:* 519-725-1399 *E-mail:* press@wlu.ca *Web Site:* www.wlupress.wlu.ca, pg 424

Tonuzi, Flamur, Grand Central Publishing, 1290 Avenue of the Americas, New York, NY 10104 *Tel:* 212-364-1100 *Web Site:* www.hachettebookgroup.com/imprint/grand-central-publishing/, pg 80

Toole, Jenny, Mercer University Press, 368 Orange St, Macon, GA 31201 *Tel:* 478-301-2880 *Toll Free Tel:* 866-895-1472 *Fax:* 478-301-2585 *E-mail:* mupressorders@mercer.edu *Web Site:* www.mupress.org, pg 129

Topper, Jenn, Reporters Committee for Freedom of the Press, 1156 15 St NW, Suite 1020, Washington, DC 20005-1779 *Tel:* 202-795-9300 *Toll Free Tel:* 800-336-4243 (legal hotline for journalists) *E-mail:* info@rcfp.org *Web Site:* www.rcfp.org, pg 518

Toppy, Suzanne, Springer Publishing Co, 11 W 42 St, 15th fl, New York, NY 10036-8002 *Tel:* 212-431-4370 *Toll Free Tel:* 877-687-7476 *E-mail:* marketing@springerpub.com; cs@springerpub.com (orders); textbook@springerpub.com; specialsales@springerpub.com *Web Site:* www.springerpub.com, pg 196

Torres, Hector, Penguin Random House LLC, 1745 Broadway, New York, NY 10019 *Tel:* 212-782-9000 *Toll Free Tel:* 800-726-0600 *Web Site:* www.penguinrandomhouse.com, pg 155

Tortorici, Dayna, n+1 Writers' Fellowship, Cadman Plaza Sta, PO Box 26428, Brooklyn, NY 11202 *E-mail:* editors@nplusonemag.com; subs@nplusonemag.com (submission queries); submissions@nplusonemag.com *Web Site:* www.nplusonemag.com/awards, pg 642

Tortorici, Dayna, Anthony Veasna So Fiction Prize, Cadman Plaza Sta, PO Box 26428, Brooklyn, NY 11202 *E-mail:* editors@nplusonemag.com; subs@nplusonemag.com (submission queries); submissions@nplusonemag.com *Web Site:* www.nplusonemag.com/awards, pg 664

Tortoroli, Melanie, W W Norton & Company Inc, 500 Fifth Ave, New York, NY 10110-0017 *Tel:* 212-354-5500 *Toll Free Tel:* 800-233-4830 (orders & cust serv) *Fax:* 212-869-0856 *Toll Free Fax:* 800-458-6515 *E-mail:* orders@wwnorton.com *Web Site:* wwnorton.com, pg 143

Tory, Caroline, Aspen Words, 110 E Hallam St, Suite 116, Aspen, CO 81611 *Tel:* 970-925-3122 *Fax:* 970-920-5700 *E-mail:* aspenwords@aspeninstitute.org *Web Site:* www.aspenwords.org, pg 497

Tory, Caroline, Aspen Words Literary Prize, 110 E Hallam St, Suite 116, Aspen, CO 81611 *Tel:* 970-925-3122 *Fax:* 970-920-5700 *E-mail:* literary.prize@aspeninstitute.org *Web Site:* www.aspenwords.org/programs/literary-prize/; www.aspenwords.org, pg 575

Tory, Caroline, Summer Words Writing Conference & Literary Festival, 110 E Hallam St, Suite 116, Aspen, CO 81611 *Tel:* 970-925-3122 *Fax:* 970-920-5700 *E-mail:* aspenwords@aspeninstitute.org *Web Site:* www.aspenwords.org, pg 557

Tory, Caroline, Winter Words Author Series, 110 E Hallam St, Suite 116, Aspen, CO 81611 *Tel:* 970-925-3122 *Fax:* 970-920-5700 *E-mail:* aspenwords@aspeninstitute.org *Web Site:* www.aspenwords.org, pg 558

Toth, Dani, Pantheon Books, c/o Penguin Random House LLC, 1745 Broadway, New York, NY 10019 *Tel:* 212-751-2600 *Fax:* 212-940-7390 (dom rts); 212-572-2662 (foreign rts) *Web Site:* knopfdoubleday.com/imprint/pantheon/; knopfdoubleday.com, pg 150

Toth, Dani, Schocken Books, c/o Penguin Random House LLC, 1745 Broadway, New York, NY 10019 *Tel:* 212-751-2600 *Fax:* 212-940-7390 (dom rts); 212-572-2662 (foreign rts) *Web Site:* knopfdoubleday.com/imprint/schocken/; knopfdoubleday.com, pg 183

Toth, Sara, The Chautauqua Prize, One Ames Ave, Chautauqua, NY 14722 *Toll Free Tel:* 800-836-ARTS (836-2787) *Web Site:* www.chq.org/prize, pg 588

Totten, Clara, Kent State University Press, 1118 University Library Bldg, 1125 Risman Dr, Kent, OH 44242 *Tel:* 330-672-7913 *Fax:* 330-672-3104 *E-mail:* ksupress@kent.edu *Web Site:* www.kentstateuniversitypress.com, pg 109

Touchie, Rodger, Heritage House Publishing Co Ltd, 1075 Pendergast St, No 103, Victoria, BC V8V 0A1, Canada *Tel:* 250-360-0829 *Fax:* 250-386-0829 *E-mail:* heritage@heritagehouse.ca; info@heritagehouse.ca; orders@heritagehouse.ca *Web Site:* www.heritagehouse.ca, pg 409

Touvell, Anne, Thurber Prize for American Humor, 77 Jefferson Ave, Columbus, OH 43215 *Tel:* 614-464-1032 *E-mail:* thurberhouse@thurberhouse.org *Web Site:* www.thurberhouse.org, pg 669

Tovbis, Grigory, Harvard University Press, 79 Garden St, Cambridge, MA 02138-1499 *Tel:* 617-495-2600; 401-531-2800 (intl orders) *Toll Free Tel:* 800-405-1619 (orders) *Fax:* 617-495-5898 (gen); 617-496-4677 (edit & rts); 401-531-2801 (intl orders) *Toll Free Fax:* 800-406-9145 (orders) *E-mail:* contact_hup@harvard.edu *Web Site:* www.hup.harvard.edu, pg 88

Tower, Carol, SME (Society of Manufacturing Engineers), 1000 Town Ctr, Suite 1910, Southfield, MI 48075 *Tel:* 313-425-3000 *Toll Free Tel:* 800-733-4763 (cust serv) *Fax:* 313-425-3400 *E-mail:* publications@sme.org *Web Site:* www.sme.org, pg 191

Towne, Ashley, University of Chicago Press, 1427 E 60 St, Chicago, IL 60637-2954 *Tel:* 773-702-7700; 773-702-7600 *Toll Free Tel:* 800-621-2736 (orders) *Fax:* 773-702-9756; 773-660-2235 (orders); 773-702-2708 *E-mail:* custserv@press.uchicago.edu; marketing@press.uchicago.edu *Web Site:* www.press.uchicago.edu, pg 215

Townsend, Katie, Reporters Committee for Freedom of the Press, 1156 15 St NW, Suite 1020, Washington, DC 20005-1779 *Tel:* 202-795-9300 *Toll Free Tel:* 800-336-4243 (legal hotline for journalists) *E-mail:* info@rcfp.org *Web Site:* www.rcfp.org, pg 518

Townson, W, Townson Publishing Co Ltd, PO Box 1404, Sta A, Vancouver, BC V6C 2P7, Canada *Tel:* 604-886-0594 *E-mail:* gpubinc@gmail.com; translationrights@gmail.com *Web Site:* generalpublishing.com, pg 420

Tracten, Mark, Crown House Publishing Co LLC, 81 Brook Hills Circle, White Plains, NY 10605 *Tel:* 914-946-3517 *Toll Free Tel:* 877-925-1213 (cust serv) *Fax:* 914-946-1160 *E-mail:* info@chpus.com *Web Site:* www.crownhousepublishing.com, pg 56

Tracy, Kathleen A, SDP Publishing Solutions LLC, 36 Captain's Way, East Bridgewater, MA 02333 *Tel:* 617-775-0656 *Web Site:* www.sdppublishingsolutions.com, pg 444

Tracy, Reid, Hay House LLC, PO Box 5100, Carlsbad, CA 92018-5100 *Tel:* 760-431-7695 (ext 1, intl) *Toll Free Tel:* 800-654-5126 (ext 1, US) *Toll Free Fax:* 800-650-5115 *Web Site:* www.hayhouse.com, pg 89

Tramble, Madrid, ASM International, 9639 Kinsman Rd, Materials Park, OH 44073-0002 *Tel:* 440-338-5151 *Toll Free Tel:* 800-336-5152; 800-368-9800 (Europe) *Fax:* 440-338-4634 *E-mail:* memberservicecenter@asminternational.org *Web Site:* www.asminternational.org, pg 19

Tran, Steven, Soho Press Inc, 853 Broadway, New York, NY 10003 *Tel:* 212-260-1900 *E-mail:* soho@sohopress.com; publicity@sohopress.com *Web Site:* sohopress.com, pg 193

Tranen, Joshua Gutterman, Duke University Press, 905 W Main St, Suite 18B, Durham, NC 27701 *Tel:* 919-688-5134 *Toll Free Tel:* 888-651-0122 (US) *Fax:* 919-688-2615 *Toll Free Fax:* 888-651-0124 *E-mail:* orders@dukeupress.edu *Web Site:* www.dukeupress.edu, pg 62

Trapunski, Edward, The Canadian Jewish Literary Awards, Koschitzy Centre for Jewish Studies, 763 Kaneff Tower, York University, 4700 Keele St, Toronto, ON M3J 1P3, Canada *E-mail:* info@cjlawards.ca; cjs@yorku.ca (digital submissions) *Web Site:* www.cjlawards.ca, pg 586

Traub, Kevin, Zondervan, 3900 Sparks Dr SE, Grand Rapids, MI 49546 *Tel:* 616-698-6900 *Toll Free Tel:* 800-226-1122; 800-727-1309 (retail orders)

PERSONNEL INDEX

Fax: 616-698-3350 Toll Free Fax: 800-698-3256 (retail orders) E-mail: customercare@harpercollins.com Web Site: www.zondervan.com, pg 236

Trautmann, Amanda, Workman Publishing, 1290 Avenue of the Americas, New York, NY 10104 Toll Free Tel: 800-759-0190 Fax: 212-364-0950 E-mail: workman-inquiry@hbgusa.com Web Site: www.hachettebookgroup.com/imprint/workman-publishing-company/, pg 233

Travaglini, Timothy, Transatlantic Agency, 2 Bloor St E, Suite 3500, Toronto, ON M4W 1A8, Canada Tel: 416-488-9214 E-mail: info@transatlanticagency.com; royalties@transatlanticagency.com Web Site: www.transatlanticagency.com, pg 479

Traversy, Nancy, Barefoot Books, 23 Bradford St, 2nd fl, Concord, MA 01742 Tel: 617-576-0660 Toll Free Tel: 866-215-1756 (cust serv); 866-417-2369 (orders) Fax: 617-576-0049 E-mail: help@barefootbooks.com Web Site: www.barefootbooks.com, pg 24

Travis, Jennifer, Workman Publishing, 1290 Avenue of the Americas, New York, NY 10104 Toll Free Tel: 800-759-0190 Fax: 212-364-0950 E-mail: workman-inquiry@hbgusa.com Web Site: www.hachettebookgroup.com/imprint/workman-publishing-company/, pg 232

Travis, Jocelyn, Sourcebooks LLC, 1935 Brookdale Rd, Suite 139, Naperville, IL 60563 Tel: 630-961-3900 Toll Free Tel: 800-432-7444 Fax: 630-961-2168 E-mail: info@sourcebooks.com Web Site: www.sourcebooks.com, pg 194

Traylor, Amanda Clay, San Francisco Writers Conference, 1901 Cleveland Ave, Suite D, Santa Rosa, CA 94501 Tel: 415-689-6301 E-mail: registrations@sfwriters.org; director@sfwriters.org; bizdev@sfwriters.org Web Site: www.sfwriters.org, pg 557

Traylor, Amanda Clay, San Francisco Writing Contest (SFWC), 1901 Cleveland Ave, Suite D, Santa Rosa, CA 94501 Tel: 415-689-6301 E-mail: contest@sfwriters.org; director@sfwriters.org Web Site: www.sfwriters.org, pg 658

Treat, Karen, Bloomsbury Academic, 1385 Broadway, 5th fl, New York, NY 10018 Tel: 212-419-5300 Web Site: www.bloomsbury.com/us/academic, pg 31

Treimel, Scott, S©ott Treimel NY, 434 Lafayette St, New York, NY 10003-6943 Tel: 212-505-8353 E-mail: general@scotttreimelny.com Web Site: scotttreimelny.com; www.linkedin.com/in/scott-treimel-46658727/, pg 475

Treistman, Ann, Countryman Press, c/o W W Norton & Company Inc, 500 Fifth Ave, New York, NY 10110 Tel: 212-354-5500 Fax: 212-869-0856 E-mail: countrymanpress@wwnorton.com Web Site: wwnorton.com/countryman-press, pg 54

Treitl, Berta, Renaissance Literary & Talent, PO Box 17379, Beverly Hills, CA 90209 Tel: 323-848-8305 E-mail: query@renaissancemgmt.net Web Site: renaissancemgmt.net, pg 473

Tremblay, Amelie, Editions Hurtubise, 1815, ave de Lorimier, Montreal, QC H2K 3W6, Canada Tel: 514-523-1523 Toll Free Tel: 800-361-1664 Web Site: editionshurtubise.com, pg 403

Tremblay, Carole, La Courte Echelle, 4388, rue Saint-Denis, Suite 315, Montreal, QC H2J 2L1, Canada Tel: 514-312-6950 E-mail: info@courteechelle.com Web Site: www.groupecourteechelle.com/la-courte-echelle, pg 400

Tremblay, Emilie, Institut de cooperation pour l'education des adultes-ICEA (The Institute for Cooperation on Adult Education), 5000 D'Iberville, Suite 304, Montreal, QC H2H 2S6, Canada Tel: 514-948-2044 E-mail: icae@icea.qc.ca Web Site: www.icea.qc.ca, pg 508

Tremblay-Lamarche, Alex, Les Editions du Septentrion, 86, Cote de la Montagne, bureau 200, Quebec, QC G1K 4E3, Canada Tel: 418-688-3556 Fax: 418-527-4978 E-mail: sep@septentrion.qc.ca Web Site: www.septentrion.qc.ca, pg 403

Tresner, Stephanie, Thomas Nelson, 501 Nelson Place, Nashville, TN 37214 Tel: 615-889-9000 Toll Free Tel: 800-251-4000 Web Site: www.thomasnelson.com, pg 206

Treuer, David, Pantheon Books, c/o Penguin Random House LLC, 1745 Broadway, New York, NY 10019 Tel: 212-751-2600 Fax: 212-940-7390 (dom rts); 212-572-2662 (foreign rts) Web Site: knopfdoubleday.com/imprint/pantheon/; knopfdoubleday.com, pg 150

Triant, Michelle Bonanno, Chronicle Books LLC, 680 Second St, San Francisco, CA 94107 Tel: 415-537-4200 Fax: 415-537-4460 (perms) E-mail: hello@chroniclebooks.com; subrights@chroniclebooks.com Web Site: www.chroniclebooks.com, pg 47

Tribble, Miriam, Harry N Abrams Inc, 195 Broadway, 9th fl, New York, NY 10007 Tel: 212-206-7715 Toll Free Tel: 800-345-1359 Fax: 212-645-8437 E-mail: abrams@abramsbooks.com; publicity@abramsbooks.com; sales@abramsbooks.com Web Site: www.abramsbooks.com, pg 2

Tricarico, Joy Elton, Carol Bancroft & Friends, PO Box 2030, Danbury, CT 06813 Tel: 203-730-8270 Fax: 203-730-8275 E-mail: cbfriends@sbcglobal.net; artists@carolbancroft.com Web Site: www.carolbancroft.com, pg 485

Triebel, Lindsey, Health Communications Inc, 301 Crawford Blvd, Suite 200, Boca Raton, FL 33432 Tel: 561-453-0696 Toll Free Tel: 800-441-5569 (cust serv & orders) Fax: 561-453-1009 Toll Free Fax: 800-943-9831 (orders) E-mail: editorial@hcibooks.com Web Site: hcibooks.com, pg 90

Trigo, Catalina, Riverhead Books, c/o Penguin Random House LLC, 1745 Broadway, New York, NY 10019 Tel: 212-782-9000 Web Site: www.penguin.com/riverhead-overview/, pg 175

Trine, Kate, Random House Publishing Group, 1745 Broadway, New York, NY 10019 Toll Free Tel: 800-200-3552 Web Site: www.randomhousebooks.com, pg 171

Tripathi, Namrata, Kokila, c/o Penguin Random House LLC, 1745 Broadway, New York, NY 10019 Tel: 212-782-9000 Web Site: www.penguin.com/kokila-books-overview/, pg 111

Tripathi, Namrata, Penguin Young Readers Group, c/o Penguin Random House LLC, 1745 Broadway, New York, NY 10019 Tel: 212-782-9000 Web Site: www.penguin.com/penguin-young-readers-overview, pg 156

Tripp, Megan, Random House Publishing Group, 1745 Broadway, New York, NY 10019 Toll Free Tel: 800-200-3552 Web Site: www.randomhousebooks.com, pg 171

Tritschler, Tracy, University of Missouri Press, 113 Heinkel Bldg, 201 S Seventh St, Columbia, MO 65211 Tel: 573-882-7641; 573-882-9672 (publicity & sales enquiries) Toll Free Tel: 800-621-2736 (orders) Fax: 573-884-4498 Toll Free Fax: 800-621-8476 (orders) E-mail: upress@missouri.edu; umpmarketing@missouri.edu (publicity & sales enquiries) Web Site: upress.missouri.edu, pg 217

Trocker, Dana, Atria Books, 1230 Avenue of the Americas, New York, NY 10020 Tel: 212-698-7000 Fax: 212-698-7007 Web Site: www.simonandschuster.com, pg 21

Troha, Steve, Folio Literary Management, The Film Center Bldg, 630 Ninth Ave, Suite 1101, New York, NY 10036 Tel: 212-400-1494 Fax: 212-967-0977 Web Site: www.foliolit.com, pg 459

Troiano, Patty, Lynne Rienner Publishers Inc, 1800 30 St, Suite 314, Boulder, CO 80301 Tel: 303-444-6684 Fax: 303-444-0824 E-mail: questions@rienner.com; cservice@rienner.com Web Site: www.rienner.com, pg 174

Trombetta, Sadie, Little, Brown Books for Young Readers (LBYR), 1290 Avenue of the Americas, New York, NY 10104 Tel: 212-364-1100 Toll Free Tel: 800-759-0190 (cust serv) E-mail: rights@lbchildrens.com Web Site: www.hachettebookgroup.com/imprint/little-brown-books-for-young-readers/, pg 118

Trombi, Liza Groen, Locus Awards, 655 13 St, Suite 100, Oakland, CA 94612 Tel: 510-339-9196 Fax: 510-339-9198 E-mail: locus@locusmag.com Web Site: www.locusmag.com; lsff.net, pg 625

Tromp, Alison, Macmillan, 120 Broadway, 22nd fl, New York, NY 10271 E-mail: press.inquiries@macmillan.com Web Site: us.macmillan.com, pg 122

Trotman, Krishan, Grand Central Publishing, 1290 Avenue of the Americas, New York, NY 10104 Tel: 212-364-1100 Web Site: www.hachettebookgroup.com/imprint/grand-central-publishing/, pg 80

Trotti, Ricardo, Inter American Press Association (IAPA), PO Box 226606, Doral, FL 33222 Tel: 305-987-3363 Fax: 305-860-4264 E-mail: info@sipiapa.org Web Site: www.sipiapa.org, pg 508

Trout, Elizabeth, Kensington Publishing Corp, 900 Third Ave, 26th fl, New York, NY 10022 Tel: 212-407-1500 Toll Free Tel: 800-221-2647 Fax: 212-935-0699 Web Site: www.kensingtonbooks.com, pg 109

Trouwborst, Leah, Portfolio, c/o Penguin Random House LLC, 1745 Broadway, New York, NY 10019 Tel: 212-782-9000 Web Site: www.penguin.com/portfolio-overview/; www.penguin.com/sentinel-overview/; www.penguin.com/thesis/, pg 162

Truax, Denise, Editions Prise de parole, 359-27 rue Larch, Sudbury, ON P3E 1B7, Canada Tel: 705-675-6491 E-mail: info@prisedeparole.ca Web Site: www.prisedeparole.ca, pg 405

Trudel, Joanne, Ordre des traducteurs, terminologues et interpretes agrees du quebec (OTTIAQ), 1108-2021 Ave Union, Montreal, QC H3A 2S9, Canada Tel: 514-845-4411 Toll Free Tel: 800-265-4815 Fax: 514-845-9903 E-mail: info@ottiaq.org; direction@ottiaq.org; reception@ottiaq.org; communications@ottiaq.org Web Site: www.ottiaq.org, pg 516

True, Nathan, Greenleaf Book Group LLC, PO Box 91869, Austin, TX 78709 Tel: 512-891-6100 Fax: 512-891-6150 E-mail: contact@greenleafbookgroup.com; orders@greenleafbookgroup.com; foreignrights@greenleafbookgroup.com; media@greenleafbookgroup.com Web Site: greenleafbookgroup.com, pg 81

Truitt, Sam, Barrytown/Station Hill Press, 120 Station Hill Rd, Barrytown, NY 12507 Tel: 845-758-5293 E-mail: publishers@stationhill.org Web Site: www.stationhill.org, pg 24

Trujillo, Kelli, InterVarsity Press, 430 Plaza Dr, Westmont, IL 60559-1234 Tel: 630-734-4000 Toll Free Tel: 800-843-9487 Fax: 630-734-4200 E-mail: email@ivpress.com Web Site: www.ivpress.com, pg 104

Trujillo, Nereida, Kundiman Retreat, Fordham University, English Dept, 113 W 60 St, Rm 924, New York, NY 10023 E-mail: info@kundiman.org Web Site: www.kundiman.org, pg 556

Truong, Phuong, Second Story Press, 20 Maud St, Suite 401, Toronto, ON M5V 2M5, Canada Tel: 416-537-7850 Fax: 416-537-0588 E-mail: info@secondstorypress.ca Web Site: secondstorypress.ca, pg 419

Trupin, Jim, JET Literary Associates Inc, 941 Calle Mejia, Suite 507, Santa Fe, NM 87501 Tel: 505-780-0721 E-mail: jetliterary@gmail.com Web Site: www.jetliterary.wordpress.com, pg 464

Trupin-Pulli, Elizabeth, JET Literary Associates Inc, 941 Calle Mejia, Suite 507, Santa Fe, NM 87501 Tel: 505-780-0721 E-mail: jetliterary@gmail.com Web Site: www.jetliterary.wordpress.com, pg 464

Trussell, Caroline, Metamorphosis Literary Agency, 12410 S Acuff Ct, Olathe, KS 66062 Tel: 646-397-1640 E-mail: info@metamorphosisliteraryagency.com Web Site: www.metamorphosisliteraryagency.com, pg 470

Trzaska, Jennifer, Little, Brown and Company, 1290 Avenue of the Americas, New York, NY 10104 Tel: 212-364-1100 Fax: 212-364-0952 E-mail: firstname.lastname@hbgusa.com Web Site: www.hachettebookgroup.com/imprint/little-brown-and-company/, pg 118

Trzaska, Jennifer, Running Press, 1290 Avenue of the Americas, New York, NY 10104 Tel: 212-364-1100 Toll Free Tel: 800-759-0190 (cust serv) Fax: 212-364-0933 (intl orders) Toll Free Fax: 800-286-9471 (cust serv) E-mail: customer.service@hbgusa.com; orders@hbgusa.com Web Site: www.hachettebookgroup.com/imprint/running-press/; www.moon.com (Moon Travel Guides), pg 178

Trzaska, Jennifer, Workman Publishing, 1290 Avenue of the Americas, New York, NY 10104 Toll Free Tel: 800-759-0190 Fax: 212-364-0950 E-mail: workman-inquiry@hbgusa.com Web Site: www.hachettebookgroup.com/imprint/workman-publishing-company/, pg 233

Tsakiris, Natasha, Penguin Random House Canada, a Penguin Random House company, 320 Front St W, Suite 1400, Toronto, ON M5V 3B6, Canada Tel: 416-364-4449 Toll Free Tel: 888-523-9292 (cust serv) E-mail: canadaweb@penguinrandomhouse.com; customerservicescanada@penguinrandomhouse.com Web Site: www.penguinrandomhouse.ca, pg 416

Tsang, Erika, Tor Publishing Group, 120 Broadway, New York, NY 10271 Toll Free Tel: 800-455-0340 (Macmillan) E-mail: torpublicity@tor.com; forgepublicity@forgebooks.com Web Site: us.macmillan.com/torpublishinggroup, pg 208

Tsewang, Pema, Wisdom Publications Inc, 199 Elm St, Somerville, MA 02144 Tel: 617-776-7416 Toll Free Tel: 800-272-4050 (orders) Fax: 617-776-7841 E-mail: submission@wisdompubs.org Web Site: wisdomexperience.org, pg 231

Tsuyuki, Kimberly, Society of Professional Journalists (SPJ), PO Box 441748, Indianapolis, IN 46244 Tel: 317-927-8000 Fax: 317-920-4789 E-mail: communications@spj.org Web Site: www.spj.org, pg 520

Tubach, Greg, Houghton Mifflin Harcourt Trade & Reference Division, 125 High St, Boston, MA 02110 Tel: 617-351-5000 Web Site: www.hmhco.com, pg 96

Tuck, Elisabeth, California Writers Club (CWC), PO Box 201, Danville, CA 94526 E-mail: membership@calwriters.org; advertising-promotion@calwriters.org Web Site: calwriters.org, pg 502

Tucker, Angela, Kensington Publishing Corp, 900 Third Ave, 26th fl, New York, NY 10022 Tel: 212-407-1500 Toll Free Tel: 800-221-2647 Fax: 212-935-0699 Web Site: www.kensingtonbooks.com, pg 109

Tucker, Elizabeth, Iona & Peter Opie Prize, Indiana University, Classroom-Off Bldg, 800 E Third St, Bloomington, IN 47405 Tel: 812-856-2379 Fax: 812-856-2483 E-mail: americanfolkloresociety@afsnet.org; cf.section@afsnet.org Web Site: www.afsnet.org; childrensfolklore.org/opie-prize, pg 644

Tucker, Suzi, Zeig, Tucker & Theisen Inc, 2632 E Thomas Rd, Suite 201, Phoenix, AZ 85016 Tel: 480-389-4342 Web Site: www.zeigtucker.com, pg 236

Tudor, Jeannie, Square One Publishers Inc, 115 Herricks Rd, Garden City Park, NY 11040 Tel: 516-535-2010 Toll Free Tel: 877-900-BOOK (900-2665) Fax: 516-535-2014 E-mail: sq1publish@aol.com Web Site: www.squareonepublishers.com, pg 196

Tufariello, Frank, Data Trace Publishing Co (DTP), 110 West Rd, Suite 227, Towson, MD 21204-2316 Tel: 410-494-4994 Toll Free Tel: 800-342-0454 Fax: 410-494-0515 E-mail: help@datatrace.com; customerservice@datatrace.com; salesandmarketing@datatrace.com; editorial@datatrace.com Web Site: www.datatrace.com, pg 57

Tugeau, Nicole, Tugeau 2 Inc, 2231 Grandview Ave, Cleveland Heights, OH 44106 Tel: 216-513-4047 Web Site: www.tugeau2.com, pg 486

Tull, Katie, HarperCollins Publishers LLC, 195 Broadway, New York, NY 10007 Tel: 212-207-7000 Web Site: www.harpercollins.com, pg 86

Tully, Nola, Encounter Books, 900 Broadway, Suite 601, New York, NY 10003 Tel: 212-871-6310 Toll Free Tel: 855-203-7220 E-mail: publicity@encounterbooks.com Web Site: www.encounterbooks.com, pg 66

Tumambing, Ryan, Hatherleigh Press Ltd, 62545 State Hwy 10, Hobart, NY 13788 Toll Free Tel: 800-528-2550 E-mail: info@hatherleighpress.com; publicity@hatherleighpress.com Web Site: www.hatherleighpress.com, pg 88

Tuminelly, Nancy, Mighty Media Press, 1201 Currie Ave, Minneapolis, MN 55403 Tel: 612-455-0252; 612-399-1969 Fax: 612-338-4817 E-mail: info@mightymedia.com Web Site: www.mightymediapress.com, pg 131

Tung, Catherine, Beacon Press, 24 Farnsworth St, Boston, MA 02210-1409 Tel: 617-742-2110 Fax: 617-723-3097 E-mail: production@beacon.org Web Site: www.beacon.org, pg 25

Tupholme, Iris, HarperCollins Canada Ltd, 22 Adelaide St W, 41st fl, Toronto, ON M5H 4E3, Canada Tel: 416-975-9334 E-mail: hcorder@harpercollins.com Web Site: www.harpercollins.ca, pg 409

Tupper Ling, Nancy, Boston Authors Club Inc, c/o Prof Julie Dobrow, 103 Conant Rd, Lincoln, MA 01773 Tel: 781-259-1220 E-mail: bostonauthorsclub2@gmail.com Web Site: bostonauthorsclub.org, pg 501

Turk, Melissa, Melissa Turk & the Artist Network, 9 Babbling Brook Lane, Suffern, NY 10901 Tel: 845-368-8606 E-mail: melissa@melissaturk.com Web Site: www.melissaturk.com, pg 486

Turkington, Taylor, HarperCollins Publishers LLC, 195 Broadway, New York, NY 10007 Tel: 212-207-7000 Web Site: www.harpercollins.com, pg 87

Turner, Emily, Island Press, 2000 "M" St NW, Suite 480-B, Washington, DC 20036 Tel: 202-232-7933 Toll Free Tel: 800-621-2736 Fax: 202-234-1328 E-mail: info@islandpress.org Web Site: www.islandpress.org, pg 104

Turner, Erin, The Globe Pequot Press, 64 S Main St, Essex, CT 06426 Tel: 203-458-4500 Toll Free Tel: 800-243-0495 (orders only); 888-249-7586 (cust serv) Fax: 203-458-4601 Toll Free Fax: 800-820-2329 (orders & cust serv) E-mail: editorial@globepequot.com; info@rowman.com; orders@rowman.com Web Site: rowman.com, pg 79

Turner, Jessica, Entangled Publishing LLC, 644 Shrewsbury Commons Ave, Suite 181, Shrewsbury, PA 17361 Toll Free Tel: 877-677-9451 E-mail: publisher@entangledpublishing.com Web Site: www.entangledpublishing.com, pg 67

Turner, Jessica A, Iona & Peter Opie Prize, Indiana University, Classroom-Off Bldg, 800 E Third St, Bloomington, IN 47405 Tel: 812-856-2379 Fax: 812-856-2483 E-mail: americanfolkloresociety@afsnet.org; cf.section@afsnet.org Web Site: www.afsnet.org; childrensfolklore.org/opie-prize, pg 644

Turner, Katelyn, The Geological Society of America Inc (GSA), 3300 Penrose Place, Boulder, CO 80301-1806 Tel: 303-357-1000 Toll Free Tel: 800-472-1988 Fax: 303-357-1070 E-mail: pubs@geosociety.org (prodn); editing@geosociety.org (edit); books@geosociety.org; gsaservice@geosociety.org (sales & serv) Web Site: www.geosociety.org, pg 77

Turner, Katrina "Katy", Sourcebooks LLC, 1935 Brookdale Rd, Suite 139, Naperville, IL 60563 Tel: 630-961-3900 Toll Free Tel: 800-432-7444 Fax: 630-961-2168 E-mail: info@sourcebooks.com Web Site: www.sourcebooks.com, pg 194

Turner, Liv, Sourcebooks LLC, 1935 Brookdale Rd, Suite 139, Naperville, IL 60563 Tel: 630-961-3900 Toll Free Tel: 800-432-7444 Fax: 630-961-2168 E-mail: info@sourcebooks.com Web Site: www.sourcebooks.com, pg 194

Turpin, Molly, Random House Publishing Group, 1745 Broadway, New York, NY 10019 Toll Free Tel: 800-200-3552 Web Site: www.randomhousebooks.com, pg 171

Turrisi, Kim, Society of Children's Book Writers & Illustrators (SCBWI), 6363 Wilshire Blvd, Suite 425, Los Angeles, CA 90048 Tel: 323-782-1010 E-mail: membership@scbwi.org Web Site: www.scbwi.org, pg 520

Tusk, Bradley, Gotham Book Prize, 251 Park Ave S, New York, NY 10010 Web Site: www.gothambookprize.org, pg 608

Tutela, Joy, David Black Agency, 335 Adams St, 27th fl, Suite 2707, Brooklyn, NY 11201 Tel: 718-852-5500 Fax: 718-852-5539 Web Site: www.davidblackagency.com, pg 450

Tutino, Melanie, Doubleday Canada, 320 Front St W, Suite 1400, Toronto, ON M5V 3B6, Canada Tel: 416-364-4449 Fax: 416-598-7764 Web Site: www.penguinrandomhouse.ca, pg 401

Tutterow, Caitlin, Nancy Paulsen Books, c/o Penguin Random House LLC, 1745 Broadway, New York, NY 10019 Tel: 212-782-9000 Web Site: www.penguin.com/nancy-paulsen-books-overview/, pg 152

Tuttle, Ann Leslie, Dystel, Goderich & Bourret LLC, One Union Sq W, Suite 904, New York, NY 10003 Tel: 212-627-9100 Fax: 212-627-9313 Web Site: www.dystel.com, pg 457

Tutty, Sarah, Penguin Random House Canada, a Penguin Random House company, 320 Front St W, Suite 1400, Toronto, ON M5V 3B6, Canada Tel: 416-364-4449 Toll Free Tel: 888-523-9292 (cust serv) E-mail: canadaweb@penguinrandomhouse.com; customerservicescanada@penguinrandomhouse.com Web Site: www.penguinrandomhouse.ca, pg 415

Tuzzo, Kimberly, Printing Industries Alliance, 636 N French Rd, Suite 1, Amherst, NY 14228 Tel: 716-691-3211 Toll Free Tel: 800-777-4742 Fax: 716-691-4249 E-mail: info@pialliance.org Web Site: pialliance.org, pg 517

Tweed, Thomas P, Plowshare Media, 405 Vincente Way, La Jolla, CA 92037 Tel: 858-454-5446 E-mail: sales@plowsharemedia.com Web Site: plowsharemedia.com, pg 161

Twilley, Stephen, University of Chicago Press, 1427 E 60 St, Chicago, IL 60637-2954 Tel: 773-702-7700; 773-702-7600 Toll Free Tel: 800-621-2736 (orders) Fax: 773-702-9756; 773-660-2235 (orders); 773-702-2708 E-mail: custserv@press.uchicago.edu; marketing@press.uchicago.edu Web Site: www.press.uchicago.edu, pg 215

Twitchell, Betsy, W W Norton & Company Inc, 500 Fifth Ave, New York, NY 10110-0017 Tel: 212-354-5500 Toll Free Tel: 800-233-4830 (orders & cust serv) Fax: 212-869-0856 Toll Free Fax: 800-458-6515 E-mail: orders@wwnorton.com Web Site: wwnorton.com, pg 143

Twombly, Rachel, Jason Aronson Inc, 4501 Forbes Blvd, Suite 200, Lanham, MD 20706 Tel: 301-459-3366 Toll Free Tel: 800-462-6420 ext 3024 (cust serv) Fax: 301-429-5748 Toll Free Fax: 800-338-4550 (cust serv) E-mail: orders@rowman.com; customercare@rowman.com Web Site: www.rowman.com, pg 17

Twumasi, Nana, Grand Central Publishing, 1290 Avenue of the Americas, New York, NY 10104 Tel: 212-364-1100 Web Site: www.hachettebookgroup.com/imprint/grand-central-publishing/, pg 80

Tyillian, Jon, VanDam Inc, The VanDam Bldg, 121 W 27 St, New York, NY 10001 Tel: 917-297-5445 E-mail: info@vandam.com Web Site: www.vandam.com, pg 223

Tyler, Julia, HarperCollins Children's Books, 195 Broadway, New York, NY 10007 Tel: 212-207-7000 Web Site: www.harpercollins.com/childrens, pg 85

Tyrrell, Bob, Orca Book Publishers, 1016 Balmoral Rd, Victoria, BC V8T 1A8, Canada Toll Free Tel: 800-210-5277 Toll Free Fax: 877-408-1551 E-mail: orca@orcabook.com Web Site: www.orcabook.com, pg 415

Tyrrell, Jen, Trusted Media Brands Inc, 750 Third Ave, 3rd fl, New York, NY 10017 Tel: 646-293-6299 Toll Free Tel: 877-732-4438 (cust serv) Fax: 646-293-6251 E-mail: customercare@trustedmediabrands.com; press@trustedmediabrands.com Web Site: www.trustedmediabrands.com; www.rd.com, pg 210

Tyson, Marie, The Pilgrim Press/United Church Press, 700 Prospect Ave, Cleveland, OH 44115-1100 Tel: 216-736-2100 Toll Free Tel: 800-537-3394 (orders) *E-mail:* permissions@thepilgrimpress.com; store@ucc.org (orders) *Web Site:* www.thepilgrimpress.com, pg 160

Tzetzo, Liz, Macmillan, 120 Broadway, 22nd fl, New York, NY 10271 *E-mail:* press.inquiries@macmillan.com *Web Site:* us.macmillan.com, pg 122

Tzou, Hana, Farrar, Straus & Giroux Books for Young Readers, 120 Broadway, New York, NY 10271 *Tel:* 212-741-6900 *Toll Free Tel:* 888-330-8477 (orders) *E-mail:* childrens.publicity@macmillanusa.com; childrensrights@macmillanusa.com *Web Site:* us.macmillan.com/mackids, pg 70

Tzou, Hana, Roaring Brook Press. 120 Broadway, New York, NY 10271 *Tel:* 646-307-5151 *Web Site:* us.macmillan.com/publishers/roaring-brook-press, pg 176

Ucar, Yasemin, Kids Can Press Ltd, 25 Dockside Dr, Toronto, ON M5A 0B5, Canada *Tel:* 416-479-7000 *Toll Free Tel:* 800-265-0884 *Fax:* 416-960-5437 *E-mail:* info@kidscan.com; customerservice@kidscan.com *Web Site:* www.kidscanpress.com; www.kidscanpress.ca, pg 411

Udalova, Polina, Macmillan, 120 Broadway, 22nd fl, New York, NY 10271 *E-mail:* press.inquiries@macmillan.com *Web Site:* us.macmillan.com, pg 122

Uddin, Jafreen, Asian American Writers' Workshop (AAWW), 112 W 27 St, Suite 600, New York, NY 10001 *Tel:* 212-494-0061 *E-mail:* desk@aaww.org *Web Site:* aaww.org; facebook.com/AsianAmericanWritersWorkshop, pg 497

Ude, Wayne, Blue & Ude Writers' Services, 4249 Nuthatch Way, Clinton, WA 98236 *Tel:* 360-341-1630 *E-mail:* blue@whidbey.com *Web Site:* www.sunbreakpress.com, pg 436

Ugalde, Zuleima, Alfred A Knopf, c/o Penguin Random House LLC, 1745 Broadway, New York, NY 10019 *Tel:* 212-751-2600 *Fax:* 212-940-7390 (dom rts); 212-572-2662 (foreign rts) *Web Site:* knopfdoubleday.com/imprint/knopf/; knopfdoubleday.com, pg 110

Uhle, Amanda, McSweeney's Publishing, 849 Valencia St, San Francisco, CA 94110 *E-mail:* custserv@mcsweeneys.net *Web Site:* www.mcsweeneys.net, pg 128

Umbaugh, Brad, Macmillan, 120 Broadway, 22nd fl, New York, NY 10271 *E-mail:* press.inquiries@macmillan.com *Web Site:* us.macmillan.com, pg 122

Umogbai, Kemi, Macmillan, 120 Broadway, 22nd fl, New York, NY 10271 *E-mail:* press.inquiries@macmillan.com *Web Site:* us.macmillan.com, pg 122

Underdown, Harold, Astra Books for Young Readers, 19 W 21 St, No 1201, New York, NY 10010 *Tel:* 646-844-3485 *E-mail:* ahinfo@astrahouse.com; permissions@astrapublishinghouse.com *Web Site:* astrapublishinghouse.com, pg 20

Underweiser, Shara, Penguin Random House LLC, 1745 Broadway, New York, NY 10019 *Tel:* 212-782-9000 *Toll Free Tel:* 800-726-0600 *Web Site:* www.penguinrandomhouse.com, pg 155

Underwood, April, SLACK® Incorporated, A Wyanoke Group Company, 6900 Grove Rd, Thorofare, NJ 08086-9447 *Tel:* 856-848-1000 *Toll Free Tel:* 800-257-8290 *Fax:* 856-848-6091 *E-mail:* sales@slackinc.com; editor@slackinc.com; customerservice@slackinc.com *Web Site:* www.healio.com/books, pg 191

Unferth, Deb Olin, University of Texas at Austin, New Writers Project, Dept of English, 204 W 21 St, B-5000, Austin, TX 78712-1164 *Tel:* 512-471-4991 *Fax:* 512-471-4909 *E-mail:* newwritersproject@utexas.edu *Web Site:* liberalarts.utexas.edu/nwp, pg 567

Ung, Jennifer, HarperCollins Children's Books, 195 Broadway, New York, NY 10007 *Tel:* 212-207-7000 *Web Site:* www.harpercollins.com/childrens, pg 85

Unger, Andrew, Doubleday, c/o Penguin Random House LLC, 1745 Broadway, New York, NY 10019 *Tel:* 212-751-2600 *Fax:* 212-940-7390 (dom rts); 212-572-2662 (foreign rts) *Web Site:* knopfdoubleday.com/imprint/doubleday/; knopfdoubleday.com, pg 61

Unger, Andrew, Alfred A Knopf, c/o Penguin Random House LLC, 1745 Broadway, New York, NY 10019 *Tel:* 212-751-2600 *Fax:* 212-940-7390 (dom rts); 212-572-2662 (foreign rts) *Web Site:* knopfdoubleday.com/imprint/knopf/; knopfdoubleday.com, pg 110

Unger, David, Publishing Certificate Program at City College of New York, Division of Humanities NAC 5225, City College of New York, New York, NY 10031 *Tel:* 212-650-7925 *Fax:* 212-650-7912 *E-mail:* ccnypub@aol.com *Web Site:* english.ccny.cuny.edu/publishing-program, pg 565

Unger, Todd, American Medical Association (AMA), AMA Plaza, 330 N Wabash, Suite 39300, Chicago, IL 60611-5885 *Tel:* 312-464-5000 *Toll Free Tel:* 800-621-8335 *E-mail:* media@ama-assn.org (media & edit) *Web Site:* www.ama-assn.org; www.jamanetwork.org, pg 495

Ungureanu, Dana, Histria Books, 7181 N Hualapai Way, Suite 130-86, Las Vegas, NV 89166 *Tel:* 561-299-0802 *E-mail:* info@histriabooks.com; orders@histriabooks.com; rights@histriabooks.com *Web Site:* histriabooks.com, pg 93

Unwalla, Fred R, Pontifical Institute of Mediaeval Studies, Department of Publications, 59 Queen's Park Crescent E, Toronto, ON M5S 2C4, Canada *Tel:* 416-926-7142 *Fax:* 416-926-7292 *Web Site:* www.pims.ca, pg 416

Updike, David, Philadelphia Museum of Art, PO Box 7646, Philadelphia, PA 19101-7646 *Tel:* 215-763-8100 *Fax:* 215-236-4465 *Web Site:* www.philamuseum.org, pg 159

Updike, Jaci, Penguin Random House LLC, 1745 Broadway, New York, NY 10019 *Tel:* 212-782-9000 *Toll Free Tel:* 800-726-0600 *Web Site:* www.penguinrandomhouse.com, pg 155

Upton, Cody, Arts & Letters Awards in Literature, 633 W 155 St, New York, NY 10032 *Tel:* 212-368-5900 *E-mail:* academy@artsandletters.org *Web Site:* artsandletters.org/awards, pg 574

Upton, Cody, Award of Merit Medal, 633 W 155 St, New York, NY 10032 *Tel:* 212-368-5900 *E-mail:* academy@artsandletters.org *Web Site:* artsandletters.org/awards, pg 576

Upton, Cody, Blake-Dodd Prize, 633 W 155 St, New York, NY 10032 *Tel:* 212-368-5900 *E-mail:* academy@artsandletters.org *Web Site:* artsandletters.org/awards, pg 581

Upton, Cody, Michael Braude Award, 633 W 155 St, New York, NY 10032 *Tel:* 212-368-5900 *E-mail:* academy@artsandletters.org *Web Site:* artsandletters.org/awards, pg 583

Upton, Cody, Benjamin H Danks Award, 633 W 155 St, New York, NY 10032 *Tel:* 212-368-5900 *E-mail:* academy@artsandletters.org *Web Site:* artsandletters.org/awards, pg 594

Upton, Cody, E M Forster Award, 633 W 155 St, New York, NY 10032 *Tel:* 212-368-5900 *E-mail:* academy@artsandletters.org *Web Site:* artsandletters.org/awards, pg 603

Upton, Cody, Gold Medal, 633 W 155 St, New York, NY 10032 *Tel:* 212-368-5900 *E-mail:* academy@artsandletters.org *Web Site:* artsandletters.org/awards, pg 607

Upton, Cody, The William Dean Howells Medal, 633 W 155 St, New York, NY 10032 *Tel:* 212-368-5900 *E-mail:* academy@artsandletters.org *Web Site:* artsandletters.org/awards, pg 614

Upton, Cody, Sue Kaufman Prize for First Fiction, 633 W 155 St, New York, NY 10032 *Tel:* 212-368-5900 *E-mail:* academy@artsandletters.org *Web Site:* artsandletters.org/awards, pg 619

Upton, Cody, Addison M Metcalf Award in Literature, 633 W 155 St, New York, NY 10032 *Tel:* 212-368-5900 *E-mail:* academy@artsandletters.org *Web Site:* artsandletters.org/awards, pg 632

Upton, Cody, Katherine Anne Porter Award, 633 W 155 St, New York, NY 10032 *Tel:* 212-368-5900 *E-mail:* academy@artsandletters.org *Web Site:* artsandletters.org/awards, pg 651

Upton, Cody, Arthur Rense Prize, 633 W 155 St, New York, NY 10032 *Tel:* 212-368-5900 *E-mail:* academy@artsandletters.org *Web Site:* artsandletters.org/awards, pg 655

Upton, Cody, Rosenthal Family Foundation Award for Literature, 633 W 155 St, New York, NY 10032 *Tel:* 212-368-5900 *E-mail:* academy@artsandletters.org *Web Site:* artsandletters.org/awards, pg 657

Upton, Cody, John Updike Award, 633 W 155 St, New York, NY 10032 *Tel:* 212-368-5900 *E-mail:* academy@artsandletters.org *Web Site:* artsandletters.org/awards, pg 672

Upton, Cody, Harold D Vursell Memorial Award, 633 W 155 St, New York, NY 10032 *Tel:* 212-368-5900 *E-mail:* academy@artsandletters.org *Web Site:* artsandletters.org/awards, pg 673

Upton, Cody, E B White Award, 633 W 155 St, New York, NY 10032 *Tel:* 212-368-5900 *E-mail:* academy@artsandletters.org *Web Site:* artsandletters.org/awards, pg 674

Upton, Cody, Thornton Wilder Prize for Translation, 633 W 155 St, New York, NY 10032 *Tel:* 212-368-5900 *E-mail:* academy@artsandletters.org *Web Site:* artsandletters.org/awards, pg 675

Upton, Cody, Morton Dauwen Zabel Award, 633 W 155 St, New York, NY 10032 *Tel:* 212-368-5900 *E-mail:* academy@artsandletters.org *Web Site:* artsandletters.org/awards, pg 679

Urban, Christopher, Macmillan, 120 Broadway, 22nd fl, New York, NY 10271 *E-mail:* press.inquiries@macmillan.com *Web Site:* us.macmillan.com, pg 122

Urban-Brown, Daniel, Shambhala Publications Inc, 2129 13 St, Boulder, CO 80302 *Tel:* 978-829-2599 (intl callers) *Toll Free Tel:* 866-424-0030 (off); 888-424-2329 (orders & cust serv) *Fax:* 617-236-1563 *E-mail:* customercare@shambhala.com; royalties@shambhala.com *Web Site:* www.shambhala.com, pg 187

Urmston, Craig, Kaeden Publishing, 24700 Center Ridge Rd, Suite 240, Westlake, OH 44145 *Tel:* 440-617-1400 *Toll Free Tel:* 800-890-7323 *Fax:* 440-617-1403 *E-mail:* sales@kaeden.com *Web Site:* www.kaeden.com, pg 107

Urmy, Deanne, Houghton Mifflin Harcourt Trade & Reference Division, 125 High St, Boston, MA 02110 *Tel:* 617-351-5000 *Web Site:* www.hmhco.com, pg 96

Urnov, Taz, Soho Press Inc, 853 Broadway, New York, NY 10003 *Tel:* 212-260-1900 *E-mail:* soho@sohopress.com; publicity@sohopress.com *Web Site:* sohopress.com, pg 193

Urrea, Luis, University of Illinois at Chicago, Program for Writers, College of Liberal Arts & Sciences, 601 S Morgan St, Chicago, IL 60607 *Tel:* 312-413-2200 (Eng dept) *E-mail:* english@uic.edu *Web Site:* engl.uic.edu/graduate-studies/program-for-writers, pg 566

Uschuk, Pamela, Rick DeMarinis Short Story Award, PO Box 2414, Durango, CO 81302 *Tel:* 970-903-7914 *E-mail:* cutthroatmag@gmail.com *Web Site:* www.cutthroatmag.com, pg 595

Uschuk, Pamela, Joy Harjo Poetry Award, PO Box 2414, Durango, CO 81302 *Tel:* 970-903-7914 *E-mail:* cutthroatmag@gmail.com *Web Site:* www.cutthroatmag.com, pg 611

Uschuk, Pamela, Barry Lopez Nonfiction Award, PO Box 2414, Durango, CO 81302 *Tel:* 970-903-7914 *E-mail:* cutthroatmag@gmail.com *Web Site:* www.cutthroatmag.com, pg 626

Usselman, Laura, Stuart Krichevsky Literary Agency Inc, 118 E 28 St, Suite 908, New York, NY 10016 *Tel:* 212-725-5288 *Fax:* 212-725-5275 *E-mail:* query@skagency.com *Web Site:* skagency.com, pg 466

Ussenov, Rinat, Macmillan, 120 Broadway, 22nd fl, New York, NY 10271 *E-mail:* press.inquiries@macmillan.com *Web Site:* us.macmillan.com, pg 122

Usuriello, Liz, Disney-Hyperion Books, 1101 Flower St, Glendale, CA 91201 *Web Site:* books.disney.com/imprint/disney-hyperion, pg 59

Utomo, Ricky, Penguin Random House Canada, a Penguin Random House company, 320 Front St W, Suite 1400, Toronto, ON M5V 3B6, Canada *Tel:* 416-364-4449 *Toll Free Tel:* 888-523-9292 (cust serv) *E-mail:* canadaweb@penguinrandomhouse.com; customerservicescanada@penguinrandomhouse.com *Web Site:* www.penguinrandomhouse.ca, pg 416

Vaccaro, Claire, Penguin Publishing Group, c/o Penguin Random House LLC, 1745 Broadway, New York, NY 10019 *Tel:* 212-782-9000 *Web Site:* www.penguin.com, pg 154

Vachon, Karine, Association nationale des editeurs de livres-ANEL (The National Association of Book Publishers), 2514, blvd Rosemont, Montreal, QC H1Y 1K4, Canada *Tel:* 514-273-8130 *Toll Free Tel:* 866-900-ANEL (900-2635) *E-mail:* info@anel.qc.ca *Web Site:* www.anel.qc.ca, pg 498

Vagnetti, Michael, The Monacelli Press, 65 Bleecker St, 8th fl, New York, NY 10012 *Tel:* 212-652-5400 *E-mail:* contact@monacellipress.com *Web Site:* www.phaidon.com/monacelli, pg 133

Vagstad, Marit, Palgrave Macmillan, One New York Plaza, Suite 4500, New York, NY 10004-1562 *Tel:* 212-726-9200 *E-mail:* sales-ny@springernature.com *Web Site:* www.palgrave.com; www.springernature.com, pg 150

Vaillancourt, Claude, Brault & Bouthillier, 700 ave Beaumont, Montreal, QC H3N 1V5, Canada *Tel:* 514-273-9186 *Toll Free Tel:* 800-361-0378 *Fax:* 514-273-8627 *Toll Free Fax:* 800-361-0378 *E-mail:* communicationbb@bb.ca *Web Site:* bb.ca, pg 397

Vairo, John, Gallery Books, 1230 Avenue of the Americas, New York, NY 10020 *Toll Free Tel:* 800-456-6798 *Fax:* 212-698-7284 *E-mail:* consumer.customerservice@simonandschuster.com *Web Site:* www.simonandschuster.com, pg 76

Valcarcel, Juan Mila, HarperCollins Publishers LLC, 195 Broadway, New York, NY 10007 *Tel:* 212-207-7000 *Web Site:* www.harpercollins.com, pg 86

Valcius, Leonicka, Transatlantic Agency, 2 Bloor St E, Suite 3500, Toronto, ON M4W 1A8, Canada *Tel:* 416-488-9214 *E-mail:* info@transatlanticagency.com; royalties@transatlanticagency.com *Web Site:* www.transatlanticagency.com, pg 479

Valdez, Catherine, Bloomsbury Publishing Inc, 1385 Broadway, 5th fl, New York, NY 10018 *Tel:* 212-419-5300 *E-mail:* marketingusa@bloomsbury.com; adultpublicityusa@bloomsbury.com; askacademic@bloomsbury.com *Web Site:* www.bloomsbury.com, pg 32

Valdez, Kiara, Roaring Brook Press, 120 Broadway, New York, NY 10271 *Tel:* 646-307-5151 *Web Site:* us.macmillan.com/publishers/roaring-brook-press, pg 176

Valdez, Nicole, Harry N Abrams Inc, 195 Broadway, 9th fl, New York, NY 10007 *Tel:* 212-206-7715 *Toll Free Tel:* 800-345-1359 *Fax:* 212-645-8437 *E-mail:* abrams@abramsbooks.com; publicity@abramsbooks.com; sales@abramsbooks.com *Web Site:* www.abramsbooks.com, pg 2

Valdivia, Miguel, Pacific Press® Publishing Association, 1350 N Kings Rd, Nampa, ID 83687-3193 *Tel:* 208-465-2500 *Fax:* 208-465-2531 *E-mail:* booksubmissions@pacificpress.com *Web Site:* www.pacificpress.com, pg 150

Valente, Anne, Hamilton College, Literature & Creative Writing, Literature & Creative Writing Dept, 198 College Hill Rd, Clinton, NY 13323 *Tel:* 315-859-4370 *Fax:* 315-859-4390 *Web Site:* www.hamilton.edu, pg 563

Valente, Tara, Herbert Warren Wind Book Award, 77 Liberty Corner Rd, Liberty Corner, NJ 07931-0708 *Tel:* 908-326-1207 *Web Site:* www.usga.org, pg 676

Valenti, Erika, Penn State University Press, University Support Bldg 1, Suite C, 820 N University Dr, University Park, PA 16802-1003 *Tel:* 814-865-1327 *Toll Free Tel:* 800-326-9180 (orders & cust serv) *Fax:* 814-863-1408 *Toll Free Fax:* 877-778-2665 (book orders) *E-mail:* orders@psupress.org; customerservice@psupress.org *Web Site:* www.psupress.org, pg 157

Valentine, Ashley, Pippin Properties Inc, 110 W 40 St, Suite 1704, New York, NY 10018 *Tel:* 212-338-9310 *E-mail:* info@pippinproperties.com *Web Site:* www.pippinproperties.com; www.facebook.com/pippinproperties, pg 472

Valentine, Melissa, Sounds True Inc, 413 S Arthur Ave, Louisville, CO 80027 *Tel:* 303-665-3151 *Toll Free Tel:* 800-333-9185 (US); 888-303-9185 (US & CN) *E-mail:* customerservice@soundstrue.com; stpublicity@soundstrue.com *Web Site:* www.soundstrue.com, pg 194

Valerius, Dr Karyn M, Hofstra University, Department of English, 204 Mason Hall, Hempstead, NY 11549 *Tel:* 516-463-5454 *E-mail:* english@hofstra.edu *Web Site:* www.hofstra.edu/english, pg 563

Valero, Jen, Random House Children's Books, c/o Penguin Random House LLC, 1745 Broadway, New York, NY 10019 *Tel:* 212-782-9000 *Web Site:* www.rhcbooks.com, pg 170

Valetin, David T, Riverdale Avenue Books (RAB), 5676 Riverdale Ave, Bronx, NY 10471 *Tel:* 212-279-6418 *E-mail:* customerservice@riverdaleavebooks.com *Web Site:* www.riverdaleavebooks.com, pg 175

Valko-Warner, Mary Jo Anne, Scott Meredith Literary Agency LP, 1035 Park Ave, Apt 3-A, New York, NY 10028 *Tel:* 917-685-1064 *E-mail:* info@scottmeredith.com *Web Site:* www.scottmeredith.com, pg 470

Vallese, Ray, Human Kinetics Inc, 1607 N Market St, Champaign, IL 61820 *Tel:* 217-351-5076 *Toll Free Tel:* 800-747-4457 *Fax:* 217-351-1549 (orders/cust serv) *E-mail:* info@hkusa.com *Web Site:* us.humankinetics.com, pg 97

Vallina, Joe, Nursesbooks.org, The Publishing Program of ANA, 8515 Georgia Ave, Suite 400, Silver Spring, MD 20910-3492 *Tel:* 301-628-5000 *Toll Free Tel:* 800-274-4262; 800-637-0323 (orders) *Fax:* 301-628-5342 *E-mail:* anp@ana.org *Web Site:* www.Nursesbooks.org; www.NursingWorld.org, pg 144

Valois, Rob, Penguin Workshop, c/o Penguin Random House LLC, 1745 Broadway, New York, NY 10019 *Tel:* 212-782-9000 *Web Site:* www.penguin.com/publishers/penguinworkshop/, pg 156

Van Akin, Mary, Farrar, Straus & Giroux Books for Young Readers, 120 Broadway, New York, NY 10271 *Tel:* 212-741-6900 *Toll Free Tel:* 888-330-8477 (orders) *E-mail:* childrens.publicity@macmillanusa.com; childrensrights@macmillanusa.com *Web Site:* us.macmillan.com/mackids, pg 72

Van Akin, Mary, Roaring Brook Press, 120 Broadway, New York, NY 10271 *Tel:* 646-307-5151 *Web Site:* us.macmillan.com/publishers/roaring-brook-press, pg 176

van Alfen, Dr Peter, American Numismatic Society, 75 Varick St, 11th fl, New York, NY 10013 *Tel:* 212-571-4470 *Fax:* 212-571-4479 *E-mail:* ans@numismatics.org *Web Site:* www.numismatics.org, pg 11

van Beek, Emily, Folio Literary Management, The Film Center Bldg, 630 Ninth Ave, Suite 1101, New York, NY 10036 *Tel:* 212-400-1494 *Fax:* 212-967-0977 *Web Site:* www.foliolit.com, pg 459

Van Beuren, Victor, American Diabetes Association, 2451 Crystal Dr, Suite 900, Arlington, VA 22202 *Tel:* 703-549-1500 *Toll Free Tel:* 800-342-2383 *E-mail:* booksales@diabetes.org; ada_pubs@diabetes.org *Web Site:* diabetes.org; diabetesjournals.org/books; www.facebook.com/adapublications, pg 9

Van Dam, Stephan, VanDam Inc, The VanDam Bldg, 121 W 27 St, New York, NY 10001 *Tel:* 917-297-5445 *E-mail:* info@vandam.com *Web Site:* www.vandam.com, pg 223

van der Geest, Jillian, Rocky Mountain Books Ltd (RMB), 103-1075 Pendergast St, Victoria, BC V8V 0A1, Canada *Tel:* 250-360-0829 *Fax:* 250-386-0829 *Web Site:* rmbooks.com, pg 418

van der Merwe, Michelle, University of British Columbia Press, 2029 West Mall, Vancouver, BC V6T 1Z2, Canada *Tel:* 604-822-5959 *Toll Free Tel:* 877-377-9378 *Fax:* 604-822-6083 *Toll Free Fax:* 800-668-0821 *E-mail:* frontdesk@ubcpress.ca *Web Site:* www.ubcpress.ca, pg 422

Van Derwater, Peter, Fulbright Scholar Program, 1400 "K" St NW, Washington, DC 20005 *Tel:* 202-686-4000 *E-mail:* scholars@iie.org *Web Site:* www.cies.org; www.iie.org, pg 605

Van Dusen, Hilary, Candlewick Press, 99 Dover St, Somerville, MA 02144-2825 *Tel:* 617-661-3330 *Fax:* 617-661-0565 *E-mail:* bigbear@candlewick.com; salesinfo@candlewick.com *Web Site:* candlewick.com, pg 39

Van Dyk, Pam, The Acheven Book Prize for Young Adult Fiction, c/o Regal House Publishing, 806 Oberlin Rd, No 12094, Raleigh, NC 27605 *E-mail:* info@regalhousepublishing.com *Web Site:* regalhousepublishing.com/the-acheven-book-prize-for-young-adult-fiction/, pg 570

Van Dyk, Pam, The Terry J Cox Poetry Award, 806 Oberlin Rd, No 12094, Raleigh, NC 27605 *E-mail:* info@regalhousepublishing.com *Web Site:* regalhousepublishing.com/the-terry-j-cox-poetry-award/, pg 592

Van Dyk, Pam, Fitzroy Books, c/o Regal House Publishing, 806 Oberlin Rd, No 12094, Raleigh, NC 27605 *E-mail:* info@regalhousepublishing.com *Web Site:* fitzroybooks.com, pg 72

Van Dyk, Pam, The Kraken Book Prize for Middle-Grade Fiction, c/o Regal House Publishing, 806 Oberlin Rd, No 12094, Raleigh, NC 27605 *E-mail:* info@regalhousepublishing.com *Web Site:* regalhousepublishing.com/the-kraken-book-award/, pg 621

Van Dyk, Pam, The Petrichor Prize for Finely Crafted Fiction, 806 Oberlin Rd, No 12094, Raleigh, NC 27605 *E-mail:* info@regalhousepublishing.com *Web Site:* regalhousepublishing.com/the-petrichor-prize-for-finely-crafted-fiction/, pg 649

Van Dyk, Pam, Regal House Publishing, 806 Oberlin Rd, No 12094, Raleigh, NC 27605 *E-mail:* info@regalhousepublishing.com *Web Site:* regalhousepublishing.com, pg 173

Van Ek, Jeremy, American Marketing Association, 130 E Randolph St, 22nd fl, Chicago, IL 60601 *Tel:* 312-542-9000 *Toll Free Tel:* 800-AMA-1150 (262-1150) *Web Site:* www.ama.org, pg 495

Van Etten, Grace, Macmillan, 120 Broadway, 22nd fl, New York, NY 10271 *E-mail:* press.inquiries@macmillan.com *Web Site:* us.macmillan.com, pg 122

Van Gelder, Gordon, Philip K Dick Award, PO Box 3447, Hoboken, NJ 07030 *Tel:* 201-876-2551 *Web Site:* www.philipkdickaward.org, pg 596

Van Ginkel, Alison, Kids Can Press Ltd, 25 Dockside Dr, Toronto, ON M5A 0B5, Canada *Tel:* 416-479-7000 *Toll Free Tel:* 800-265-0884 *Fax:* 416-960-5437 *E-mail:* info@kidscan.com; customerservice@kidscan.com *Web Site:* www.kidscanpress.com; www.kidscanpress.ca, pg 411

Van Gorder, Karen, American Law Institute, 4025 Chestnut St, Philadelphia, PA 19104-3099 *Tel:* 215-243-1600 *Toll Free Tel:* 800-253-6397 *E-mail:* custserv@ali.org *Web Site:* www.ali.org, pg 10

Van Gorp, Dan, Thomas Nelson, 501 Nelson Place, Nashville, TN 37214 *Tel:* 615-889-9000 *Toll Free Tel:* 800-251-4000 *Web Site:* www.thomasnelson.com, pg 206

Van Gorp, Dan, Zondervan, 3900 Sparks Dr SE, Grand Rapids, MI 49546 *Tel:* 616-698-6900 *Toll Free Tel:* 800-226-1122; 800-727-1309 (retail orders) *Fax:* 616-698-3350 *Toll Free Fax:* 800-698-3256 (retail orders) *E-mail:* customercare@harpercollins.com *Web Site:* www.zondervan.com, pg 236

Van Horn, Susan, Running Press, 1290 Avenue of the Americas, New York, NY 10104 *Tel:* 212-364-1100 *Toll Free Tel:* 800-759-0190 (cust serv) *Fax:* 212-364-

0933 (intl orders) *Toll Free Fax:* 800-286-9471 (cust serv) *E-mail:* customer.service@hbgusa.com; orders@hbgusa.com *Web Site:* www.hachettebookgroup.com/imprint/running-press/; www.moon.com (Moon Travel Guides), pg 178

Van Keuren, Carol, Theatre Communications Group, 520 Eighth Ave, 24th fl, New York, NY 10018-4156 *Tel:* 212-609-5900 *Fax:* 212-609-5901 *E-mail:* info@tcg.org *Web Site:* www.tcg.org, pg 206

Van Metre, Susan, Candlewick Press, 99 Dover St, Somerville, MA 02144-2825 *Tel:* 617-661-3330 *Fax:* 617-661-0565 *E-mail:* bigbear@candlewick.com; salesinfo@candlewick.com *Web Site:* candlewick.com, pg 39

Van Natten, Lauren, Aperture Books, 548 W 28 St, 4th fl, New York, NY 10001 *Tel:* 212-505-5555 *Toll Free Fax:* 888-623-6908 *E-mail:* customerservice@aperture.org *Web Site:* aperture.org, pg 15

van Ogtrop, Kristin, InkWell Management, 521 Fifth Ave, Suite 2600, New York, NY 10175 *Tel:* 212-922-3500 *Fax:* 212-922-0535 *E-mail:* info@inkwellmanagement.com; submissions@inkwellmanagement.com; permissions@inkwellmanagement.com *Web Site:* inkwellmanagement.com, pg 463

Van Orden, Nick, Sandra Dijkstra Literary Agency, 1155 Camino del Mar, PMB 515, Del Mar, CA 92014-2605 *Web Site:* dijkstraagency.com, pg 456

Van Pelt, Julie, University of Washington Press, 4333 Brooklyn Ave NE, Seattle, WA 98105-9570 *Toll Free Tel:* 800-537-5487 (orders) *Fax:* 206-543-3932; 410-516-6998 (orders) *E-mail:* uwapress@uw.edu *Web Site:* uwapress.uw.edu, pg 220

Van, Quynh, Coffee House Press, 79 13 Ave NE, Suite 110, Minneapolis, MN 55413 *Tel:* 612-338-0125 *Fax:* 612-338-4004 *E-mail:* info@coffeehousepress.org *Web Site:* coffeehousepress.org, pg 50

Van Rheenen, Jessie, The Robert Watson Literary Prizes in Fiction & Poetry, MFA Writing Program, The Greensboro Review, UNC-Greensboro, 3302 MHRA Bldg, Greensboro, NC 27402-6170 *Tel:* 336-334-5459 *Web Site:* www.greensbororeview.org, pg 673

van Rheinberg, Brigitta, Princeton University Press, 41 William St, Princeton, NJ 08540-5237 *Tel:* 609-258-4900 *Fax:* 609-258-6305 *E-mail:* info@press.princeton.edu *Web Site:* press.princeton.edu, pg 164

van Rijn, Erich, University of California Press, 155 Grand Ave, Suite 400, Oakland, CA 94612-3758 *Tel:* 510-883-8232 *Fax:* 510-836-8910 *E-mail:* customerservice@ucpress.edu *Web Site:* www.ucpress.edu, pg 215

van Roessel, Annemarie, George Freedley Memorial Award, c/o The New York Public Library for the Performing Arts, 111 Amsterdam Ave, New York, NY 10023 *E-mail:* tlabookawards@gmail.com; theatrelibraryassociation@gmail.com *Web Site:* www.tla-online.org/awards/bookawards, pg 604

van Roessel, Annemarie, Richard Wall Memorial Award, c/o The New York Public Library for the Performing Arts, 111 Amsterdam Ave, New York, NY 10023 *E-mail:* theatrelibraryassociation@gmail.com; tlabookawards@gmail.com *Web Site:* www.tla-online.org/awards/bookawards, pg 673

Van Tassel, Gabrielle, Penguin Random House LLC, 1745 Broadway, New York, NY 10019 *Tel:* 212-782-9000 *Toll Free Tel:* 800-726-0600 *Web Site:* www.penguinrandomhouse.com, pg 155

Van Tassell, Christina, John Wiley & Sons Inc, 111 River St, Hoboken, NJ 07030-5774 *Tel:* 201-748-6000 *Toll Free Tel:* 800-225-5945 (cust serv) *Fax:* 201-748-6088 *Web Site:* www.wiley.com, pg 230

van Valkenburg, Anna, Guernica Editions Inc, 287 Templemead Dr, Hamilton, ON L8W 2W4, Canada *Tel:* 905-599-5304 *E-mail:* info@guernicaeditions.com *Web Site:* www.guernicaeditions.com; www.facebook.com/guernicaed, pg 408

Van Wye, Ian, Farrar, Straus & Giroux, LLC, 120 Broadway, New York, NY 10271 *Tel:* 212-741-6900 *E-mail:* fsg.publicity@fsgbooks.com; sales@fsgbooks.com *Web Site:* us.macmillan.com/fsg, pg 70

Van Zandt, Christine, Write for Success Editing Services, PO Box 292153, Los Angeles, CA 90029-8653 *Tel:* 323-356-8833 *E-mail:* writeforsuccessediting@gmail.com *Web Site:* www.writeforsuccessediting.com, pg 445

Vanacore, Gabby, Chronicle Books LLC, 680 Second St, San Francisco, CA 94107 *Tel:* 415-537-4200 *Fax:* 415-537-4460 (perms) *E-mail:* hello@chroniclebooks.com; subrights@chroniclebooks.com *Web Site:* www.chroniclebooks.com, pg 47

Vanada, Kelsi, American Literary Translators Association (ALTA), University of Arizona, Esquire Bldg, No 205, 1230 N Park Ave, Tucson, AZ 85721 *Tel:* 520-621-1757 *E-mail:* info@literarytranslators.org *Web Site:* www.literarytranslators.org, pg 495

Vanada, Kelsi, Italian Prose in Translation Award (IPTA), University of Arizona, Esquire Bldg, No 205, 1230 N Park Ave, Tucson, AZ 85721 *Tel:* 520-621-1757 *E-mail:* info@literarytranslators.org *Web Site:* literarytranslators.org/awards/ipta, pg 617

Vanada, Kelsi, National Translation Award, University of Arizona, Esquire Bldg, No 205, 1230 N Park Ave, Tucson, AZ 85721 *Tel:* 520-621-1757 *E-mail:* info@literarytranslators.org *Web Site:* www.literarytranslators.org/awards/national-translation-award, pg 638

Vanada, Kelsi, Spain-USA Foundation Translation Award, University of Arizona, Esquire Bldg, No 205, 1230 N Park Ave, Tucson, AZ 85721 *Tel:* 520-621-1757 *E-mail:* info@literarytranslators.org *Web Site:* literarytranslators.org/awards/spain-usa-award, pg 665

Vanada, Kelsi, Lucien Stryk Asian Translation Prize, University of Arizona, Esquire Bldg, No 205, 1230 N Park Ave, Tucson, AZ 85721 *Tel:* 520-621-1757 *E-mail:* info@literarytranslators.org *Web Site:* literarytranslators.org/awards/lucien-stryk-prize, pg 667

Vance, Alexandra (Alix), AIP Publishing LLC, 1305 Walt Whitman Rd, Suite 110, Melville, NY 11747 *Tel:* 516-576-2200 *E-mail:* help@aip.org; press@aip.org; rights@aip.org *Web Site:* www.aip.org; publishing.aip.org, pg 6

Vance, Ellis, United States Board on Books for Young People (USBBY), National Luis University, Ctr for Teaching through Children's Books, 1000 Capitol Dr, Wheeling, IL 60090 *Tel:* 224-233-2798 *E-mail:* secretariat@usbby.org *Web Site:* www.usbby.org, pg 521

Vance, Kim, Perfection Learning®, 1000 N Second Ave, Logan, IA 51546-1061 *Tel:* 712-644-2831 *Toll Free Tel:* 800-831-4190 *Toll Free Fax:* 800-543-2745 *E-mail:* orders@perfectionlearning.com *Web Site:* www.perfectionlearning.com, pg 158

Vance, Lisa Erbach, The Aaron M Priest Literary Agency Inc, 370 Lexington Ave, Suite 1202, New York, NY 10017 *Tel:* 212-818-0344 *Fax:* 212-573-9417 *E-mail:* info@aaronpriest.com *Web Site:* www.aaronpriest.com, pg 472

Vance, Miriam, Counterpoint Press LLC, 2560 Ninth St, Suite 318, Berkeley, CA 94710 *Tel:* 510-704-0230 *Fax:* 510-704-0268 *E-mail:* info@counterpointpress.com *Web Site:* counterpointpress.com; softskull.com, pg 54

Vandall, Jillian, Random House Children's Books, c/o Penguin Random House LLC, 1745 Broadway, New York, NY 10019 *Tel:* 212-782-9000 *Web Site:* www.rhcbooks.com, pg 169

VanDam, Arthur, Small Business Advisors Inc, 2005 Park St, Atlantic Beach, NY 11509 *Tel:* 516-374-1387 *Fax:* 516-374-1175 *E-mail:* info@smallbusinessadvice.com *Web Site:* www.smallbusinessadvice.com, pg 191

Vandersarl, Elizabeth, American Forest & Paper Association (AF&PA), 1101 "K" St NW, Suite 700, Washington, DC 20005 *Tel:* 202-463-2700 *E-mail:* info@afandpa.org; comm@afandpa.org *Web Site:* www.afandpa.org, pg 495

VanderSchans, Arielle, Canadian Bookbinders and Book Artists Guild (CBBAG), 82809-467 Parliament St, Toronto, ON M5A 3Y2, Canada *E-mail:* cbbag@cbbag.ca *Web Site:* www.cbbag.ca, pg 502

Vanderslice, Stephanie, Phillip H McMath Post Publication Book Award, Dept of Writing, University of Central Arkansas, 201 Donaghey Ave, Thompson Hall 303, Conway, AR 72035 *Web Site:* arkansaswriters.wordpress.com, pg 631

VanDuker, Drue, St Martin's Press, LLC, 120 Broadway, New York, NY 10271 *E-mail:* publicity@stmartins.com; trademarketing@stmartins.com; foreignrights@stmartins.com *Web Site:* us.macmillan.com/smp, pg 181

Vanyek, Melissa, Sophie Brody Medal, 225 N Michigan Ave, Suite 1300, Chicago, IL 60601 *Web Site:* rusaupdate.org/awards/sophie-brody-medal, pg 584

Varga, Anne-Marie, Random House Children's Books, c/o Penguin Random House LLC, 1745 Broadway, New York, NY 10019 *Tel:* 212-782-9000 *Web Site:* www.rhcbooks.com, pg 170

Varga, Lisa R, Jefferson Cup Award, c/o Virginia Library Association (VLA), PO Box 56312, Virginia Beach, VA 23456 *Tel:* 757-689-0594 *Fax:* 757-447-3478 *Web Site:* www.vla.org, pg 618

Vargas, Allison Astor, The Miranda Family Voces Latinx National Playwriting Competition, 138 E 27 St, New York, NY 10016 *Tel:* 212-225-9950 *Fax:* 212-225-9085 *Web Site:* www.repertorio.org, pg 633

Varma, Monika Kalra, BoardSource, 750 Ninth St NW, Suite 520, Washington, DC 20001-4793 *Tel:* 202-349-2500 *E-mail:* members@boardsource.org; mediarelations@boardsource.org *Web Site:* www.boardsource.org, pg 33

Varma, Sarita, Farrar, Straus & Giroux, LLC, 120 Broadway, New York, NY 10271 *Tel:* 212-741-6900 *E-mail:* fsg.publicity@fsgbooks.com; sales@fsgbooks.com *Web Site:* us.macmillan.com/fsg, pg 70

Varma, Sarita, Hill & Wang, 120 Broadway, New York, NY 10271 *Tel:* 212-741-6900 *E-mail:* fsg.publicity@fsgbooks.com; sales@fsgbooks.com *Web Site:* us.macmillan.com/fsg, pg 92

Varma, Sarita, North Point Press, 120 Broadway, New York, NY 10271 *Tel:* 212-741-6900 *E-mail:* sales@fsgbooks.com *Web Site:* us.macmillan.com/fsg, pg 142

Varma, Sarita, Picador, 120 Broadway, New York, NY 10271 *Tel:* 646-307-5151 *Fax:* 212-253-9627 *E-mail:* publicity@picadorusa.com *Web Site:* us.macmillan.com/picador, pg 159

Varno, David, National Book Critics Circle (NBCC), c/o Jacob M Appel, Icahn School of Medicine at Mount Sinai, One Gustave L Levy Place, New York, NY 10029 *E-mail:* info@bookcritics.org; membership@bookcritics.org *Web Site:* www.bookcritics.org, pg 512

Vasishtha, Preeti, American Sociological Association (ASA), 1430 "K" St NW, Suite 600, Washington, DC 20005-4701 *Tel:* 202-383-9005 *E-mail:* asa@asanet.org; communications@asanet.org; membership@asanet.org *Web Site:* www.asanet.org, pg 497

Vasquez, Claribel, Random House Children's Books, c/o Penguin Random House LLC, 1745 Broadway, New York, NY 10019 *Tel:* 212-782-9000 *Web Site:* www.rhcbooks.com, pg 170

Vasquez-Perez, Carmen, Chain Store Guide (CSG), 3710 Corporex Park Dr, Suite 310, Tampa, FL 33619 *Toll Free Tel:* 800-927-9292 (orders) *Fax:* 813-627-6888 *E-mail:* webmaster@chainstoreguide.com *Web Site:* www.chainstoreguide.com, pg 44

Vassallo, Caroline, Westwood Creative Artists Ltd, 386 Huron St, Toronto, ON M5S 2G6, Canada *Tel:* 416-964-3302 *Fax:* 416-964-3302 *E-mail:* wca_office@wcaltd.com *Web Site:* www.wcaltd.com, pg 481

Vaugeois, Denis, Les Editions du Septentrion, 86, Cote de la Montagne, bureau 200, Quebec, QC G1K 4E3, Canada *Tel:* 418-688-3556 *Fax:* 418-527-4978 *E-mail:* info@septentrion.qc.ca *Web Site:* www.septentrion.qc.ca, pg 403

Vaughan, Brendan, Random House Publishing Group, 1745 Broadway, New York, NY 10019 *Toll Free Tel:* 800-200-3552 *Web Site:* www.randomhousebooks.com, pg 171

Vaughan, Elizabeth Montoya, Penguin Young Readers Group, c/o Penguin Random House LLC, 1745 Broadway, New York, NY 10019 *Tel:* 212-782-9000 *Web Site:* www.penguin.com/penguin-young-readers-overview, pg 156

Vaughan, Jerrod, New Leaf Press, 3142 Hwy 103 N, Green Forest, AR 72638-2233 *Tel:* 870-438-5288 *Toll Free Tel:* 800-999-3777 *Fax:* 870-438-5120 *E-mail:* submissions@nlpg.com *Web Site:* www.nlpg.com, pg 140

Vaughan, Lizzie, Chronicle Books LLC, 680 Second St, San Francisco, CA 94107 *Tel:* 415-537-4200 *Fax:* 415-537-4460 (perms) *E-mail:* hello@chroniclebooks.com; subrights@chroniclebooks.com *Web Site:* www.chroniclebooks.com, pg 47

Vaughn, Clare, HarperCollins Children's Books, 195 Broadway, New York, NY 10007 *Tel:* 212-207-7000 *Web Site:* www.harpercollins.com/childrens, pg 85

Vaughn, Hannah, The Gersh Agency (TGA), 41 Madison Ave, 29th fl, New York, NY 10010 *Tel:* 212-997-1818 *Web Site:* gersh.com/books, pg 460

Vaughn, Katie, Bloomsbury Publishing Inc, 1385 Broadway, 5th fl, New York, NY 10018 *Tel:* 212-419-5300 *E-mail:* marketingusa@bloomsbury.com; adultpublicityusa@bloomsbury.com; askacademic@bloomsbury.com *Web Site:* www.bloomsbury.com, pg 32

Vazquez, Nicole, The Authors Guild®, 31 E 32 St, Suite 901, New York, NY 10016 *Tel:* 212-563-5904 *Fax:* 212-564-5363 *E-mail:* staff@authorsguild.org *Web Site:* www.authorsguild.org, pg 500

Vazquez, Shannon Jamieson, Little, Brown and Company, 1290 Avenue of the Americas, New York, NY 10104 *Tel:* 212-364-1100 *Fax:* 212-364-0952 *E-mail:* firstname.lastname@hbgusa.com *Web Site:* www.hachettebookgroup.com/imprint/little-brown-and-company/, pg 118

Vega, Dianna, Tor Publishing Group, 120 Broadway, New York, NY 10271 *Toll Free Tel:* 800-455-0340 (Macmillan) *E-mail:* torpublicity@tor.com; forgepublicity@forgebooks.com *Web Site:* us.macmillan.com/torpublishinggroup, pg 208

Vega, Kristen, Kensington Publishing Corp, 900 Third Ave, 26th fl, New York, NY 10022 *Tel:* 212-407-1500 *Toll Free Tel:* 800-221-2647 *Fax:* 212-935-0699 *Web Site:* www.kensingtonbooks.com, pg 109

Vega, Michelle, Berkley, c/o Penguin Random House LLC, 1745 Broadway, 19th fl, New York, NY 10019 *Tel:* 212-366-2000 *Web Site:* www.penguin.com/publishers/berkley/; www.penguin.com/ace-overview/, pg 28

Vega, Tracey, Chronicle Books LLC, 680 Second St, San Francisco, CA 94107 *Tel:* 415-537-4200 *Fax:* 415-537-4460 (perms) *E-mail:* hello@chroniclebooks.com; subrights@chroniclebooks.com *Web Site:* www.chroniclebooks.com, pg 47

Vega-DeCesario, Rachel, The New Press, 120 Wall St, 31st fl, New York, NY 10005 *Tel:* 212-629-8802 *Fax:* 212-629-8617 *E-mail:* newpress@thenewpress.com *Web Site:* thenewpress.com, pg 140

Vegso, Peter, Health Communications Inc, 301 Crawford Blvd, Suite 200, Boca Raton, FL 33432 *Tel:* 561-453-0696 *Toll Free Tel:* 800-441-5569 (cust serv & orders) *Fax:* 561-453-1009 *Toll Free Fax:* 800-943-9831 (orders) *E-mail:* editorial@hcibooks.com *Web Site:* hcibooks.com, pg 90

Veith, Richard, Cengage Learning, 20 Channel Center St, Boston, MA 02210 *Tel:* 617-289-7700 *Toll Free Tel:* 800-354-9706 *Fax:* 617-289-7844 *E-mail:* esales@cengage.com *Web Site:* www.cengage.com, pg 43

Vela, Mr Rene, Bolchazy-Carducci Publishers Inc, 1000 Brown St, Unit 301, Wauconda, IL 60084 *Tel:* 847-526-4344 *Fax:* 847-526-2867 *E-mail:* info@bolchazy.com; orders@bolchazy.com *Web Site:* www.bolchazy.com, pg 33

Velasco, Abby, Atria Books, 1230 Avenue of the Americas, New York, NY 10020 *Tel:* 212-698-7000 *Fax:* 212-698-7007 *Web Site:* www.simonandschuster.com, pg 21

Velazquez de Leon, Mauricio, Sourcebooks LLC, 1935 Brookdale Rd, Suite 139, Naperville, IL 60563 *Tel:* 630-961-3900 *Toll Free Tel:* 800-432-7444 *Fax:* 630-961-2168 *E-mail:* info@sourcebooks.com *Web Site:* www.sourcebooks.com, pg 194

Veldran, Richard H, Dun & Bradstreet, 103 JFK Pkwy, Short Hills, NJ 07078 *Tel:* 973-921-5500 *Toll Free Tel:* 844-869-8244; 800-234-3867 (cust serv) *Web Site:* www.dnb.com, pg 62

Veldstra, Patricia, Alberta Book Publishing Awards, 11759 Groat Rd NW, 2nd fl, Edmonton, AB T5M 3K6, Canada *Tel:* 780-424-5060 *E-mail:* info@bookpublishers.ab.ca *Web Site:* bookpublishers.ab.ca; www.readalberta.ca, pg 571

Veldstra, Patricia, The Book Publishers Association of Alberta (BPAA), 11759 Groat Rd NW, 2nd fl, Edmonton, AB T5M 3K6, Canada *Tel:* 780-424-5060 *E-mail:* info@bookpublishers.ab.ca *Web Site:* bookpublishers.ab.ca; www.readalberta.ca, pg 501

Velez, Liz, HarperCollins Publishers LLC, 195 Broadway, New York, NY 10007 *Tel:* 212-207-7000 *Web Site:* www.harpercollins.com, pg 87

Velez, Mishell, Hachette Audio, 1290 Avenue of the Americas, New York, NY 10104 *Tel:* 212-364-1100 *Web Site:* www.hachettebookgroup.com/imprint/hachette-audio/, pg 83

Velez, Roberto, Harry N Abrams Inc, 195 Broadway, 9th fl, New York, NY 10007 *Tel:* 212-206-7715 *Toll Free Tel:* 800-345-1359 *Fax:* 212-645-8437 *E-mail:* abrams@abramsbooks.com; publicity@abramsbooks.com; sales@abramsbooks.com *Web Site:* www.abramsbooks.com, pg 2

Veltre, J Joseph III, The Gersh Agency (TGA), 41 Madison Ave, 29th fl, New York, NY 10010 *Tel:* 212-997-1818 *Web Site:* gersh.com/books, pg 460

Venckus, Anna, Sourcebooks LLC, 1935 Brookdale Rd, Suite 139, Naperville, IL 60563 *Tel:* 630-961-3900 *Toll Free Tel:* 800-432-7444 *Fax:* 630-961-2168 *E-mail:* info@sourcebooks.com *Web Site:* www.sourcebooks.com, pg 195

Venecia, Yezanira, Atria Books, 1230 Avenue of the Americas, New York, NY 10020 *Tel:* 212-698-7000 *Fax:* 212-698-7007 *Web Site:* www.simonandschuster.com, pg 21

Venere, Elizabeth, Simon & Schuster, 1230 Avenue of the Americas, New York, NY 10020 *Tel:* 212-698-7000 *Toll Free Tel:* 800-223-2348 (cust serv); 800-223-2336 (orders) *Toll Free Fax:* 800-943-9831 (orders) *Web Site:* simonandschusterpublishing.com/simonandschuster/, pg 188

Venezia, Angie, Vintage Books, c/o Penguin Random House LLC, 1745 Broadway, New York, NY 10019 *Tel:* 212-572-2420 *Fax:* 212-940-7390 (dom rts); 212-572-2662 (foreign rts) *E-mail:* vintageanchorpublicity@randomhouse.com *Web Site:* knopfdoubleday.com/imprint/vintage; knopfdoubleday.com, pg 225

VenHuizen, Heather, Sourcebooks LLC, 1935 Brookdale Rd, Suite 139, Naperville, IL 60563 *Tel:* 630-961-3900 *Toll Free Tel:* 800-432-7444 *Fax:* 630-961-2168 *E-mail:* info@sourcebooks.com *Web Site:* www.sourcebooks.com, pg 194

Venkatesh, Chris, Macmillan, 120 Broadway, 22nd fl, New York, NY 10271 *E-mail:* press.inquiries@macmillan.com *Web Site:* us.macmillan.com, pg 122

Ventimiglia, Diana, Grand Central Publishing, 1290 Avenue of the Americas, New York, NY 10104 *Tel:* 212-364-1100 *Web Site:* www.hachettebookgroup.com/imprint/grand-central-publishing/, pg 80

Verboom, Andy, Writers' Federation of Nova Scotia (WFNS), 1113 Marginal Rd, Halifax, NS B3H 4P7, Canada *Tel:* 902-423-8116 *Fax:* 902-422-0881 *E-mail:* contact@writers.ns.ca; wits@writers.ns.ca (awards); programs@writers.ns.ca; communications@writers.ns.ca *Web Site:* writers.ns.ca, pg 522

Verge, Lauren, Penguin Random House Speakers Bureau, a Penguin Random House company, 1745 Broadway, Mail Drop 13-1, New York, NY 10019 *Tel:* 212-572-2013 *E-mail:* speakers@penguinrandomhouse.com *Web Site:* www.prhspeakers.com, pg 487

Verhoeven, Betsy PhD, Susquehanna University, Department of English & Creative Writing, 514 University Ave, Selinsgrove, PA 17870 *Tel:* 570-372-4196 *Web Site:* www.susqu.edu, pg 565

Verlin, Nicole Vines, Simon & Schuster, LLC, 1230 Avenue of the Americas, New York, NY 10020 *Tel:* 212-698-7000 *Toll Free Tel:* 800-223-2336 (orders) *Fax:* 212-698-7007 *Toll Free Fax:* 800-943-9831 (orders) *E-mail:* firstname.lastname@simonandschuster.com; purchaseorders@simonandschuster.com (orders) *Web Site:* www.simonandschuster.com, pg 190

Verma, Monika, Levine|Greenberg|Rostan Literary Agency, 307 Seventh Ave, Suite 2407, New York, NY 10001 *Tel:* 212-337-0934 *Fax:* 212-337-0948 *E-mail:* submit@lgrliterary.com *Web Site:* lgrliterary.com, pg 467

Verma, Mukul, Baton Rouge Area Foundation, 100 North St, Suite 900, Baton Rouge, LA 70802 *Tel:* 225-387-6126 *Web Site:* www.braf.org, pg 525

Verma, Mukul, Ernest J Gaines Award for Literary Excellence, 100 North St, Suite 900, Baton Rouge, LA 70802 *Tel:* 225-387-6126 *E-mail:* gainesaward@braf.org *Web Site:* www.ernestjgainesaward.org, pg 605

Vermette, Katherena, Simon & Schuster Canada, 166 King St E, Suite 300, Toronto, ON M5A 1J3, Canada *Tel:* 647-427-8882 *Toll Free Tel:* 800-387-0446; 800-268-3216 (orders) *Fax:* 647-430-9446 *Toll Free Fax:* 888-849-8151 (orders) *E-mail:* info@simonandschuster.ca *Web Site:* www.simonandschuster.ca, pg 419

Vernon, Nancy, Ozark Mountain Publishing Inc, PO Box 754, Huntsville, AR 72740-0754 *Tel:* 479-738-2348 *Toll Free Tel:* 800-935-0045 *Fax:* 479-738-2448 *E-mail:* info@ozarkmt.com *Web Site:* www.ozarkmt.com, pg 149

Verold, Annar, Host Publications, 3408 West Ave, Austin, TX 78705 *E-mail:* editors@hostpublications.com *Web Site:* www.hostpublications.com, pg 95

Verost, Allison, Farrar, Straus & Giroux Books for Young Readers, 120 Broadway, New York, NY 10271 *Tel:* 212-741-6900 *Toll Free Tel:* 888-330-8477 (orders) *E-mail:* childrens.publicity@macmillanusa.com; childrensrights@macmillanusa.com *Web Site:* us.macmillan.com/mackids, pg 69

Verost, Allison, Roaring Brook Press, 120 Broadway, New York, NY 10271 *Tel:* 646-307-5151 *Web Site:* us.macmillan.com/publishers/roaring-brook-press, pg 175

Verrat, Aimee, Les Editions de Mortagne, CP 116, Boucherville, QC J4B 5E6, Canada *Tel:* 450-641-2387 *E-mail:* info@editionsdemortagne.com *Web Site:* editionsdemortagne.com, pg 402

Vershbow, Sophie, Random House Publishing Group, 1745 Broadway, New York, NY 10019 *Toll Free Tel:* 800-200-3552 *Web Site:* www.randomhousebooks.com, pg 171

Vertlib, Nadia, Random House Children's Books, c/o Penguin Random House LLC, 1745 Broadway, New York, NY 10019 *Tel:* 212-782-9000 *Web Site:* www.rhcbooks.com, pg 170

Vestuto, Jessica, HarperCollins Publishers LLC, 195 Broadway, New York, NY 10007 *Tel:* 212-207-7000 *Web Site:* www.harpercollins.com, pg 87

Veto, Dori, Perfection Learning®, 1000 N Second Ave, Logan, IA 51546-1061 *Tel:* 712-644-2831 *Toll Free Tel:* 800-831-4190 *Toll Free Fax:* 800-543-2745 *E-mail:* orders@perfectionlearning.com *Web Site:* www.perfectionlearning.com, pg 158

Vibbert, Brittany, Sourcebooks LLC, 1935 Brookdale Rd, Suite 139, Naperville, IL 60563 Tel: 630-961-3900 Toll Free Tel: 800-432-7444 Fax: 630-961-2168 E-mail: info@sourcebooks.com Web Site: www.sourcebooks.com, pg 194

Victor, Nomi, W W Norton & Company Inc, 500 Fifth Ave, New York, NY 10110-0017 Tel: 212-354-5500 Toll Free Tel: 800-233-4830 (orders & cust serv) Fax: 212-869-0856 Toll Free Fax: 800-458-6515 E-mail: orders@wwnorton.com Web Site: wwnorton.com, pg 143

Vigil, Shaun, Temple University Press, 1852 N Tenth St, Philadelphia, PA 19122-6099 Tel: 215-926-2140 Toll Free Tel: 800-621-2736 Fax: 215-926-2141 E-mail: tempress@temple.edu Web Site: tupress.temple.edu, pg 204

Vigilante, Marisa, Hay House LLC, PO Box 5100, Carlsbad, CA 92018-5100 Tel: 760-431-7695 (ext 1, intl) Toll Free Tel: 800-654-5126 (ext 1, US) Toll Free Fax: 800-650-5115 Web Site: www.hayhouse.com, pg 89

Vigliano, David, Vigliano Associates Ltd, 575 Madison Ave, Suite 1006, New York, NY 10022 Tel: 212-888-8525 E-mail: info@viglianoassociates.com Web Site: viglianoassociates.com, pg 481

Viktorin, Brian, Greenleaf Book Group LLC, PO Box 91869, Austin, TX 78709 Tel: 512-891-6100 Fax: 512-891-6150 E-mail: contact@greenleafbookgroup.com; orders@greenleafbookgroup.com; foreignrights@greenleafbookgroup.com; media@greenleafbookgroup.com Web Site: greenleafbookgroup.com, pg 81

Vilar, Irene, Mandel Vilar Press, 19 Oxford Ct, Simsbury, CT 06070 Tel: 806-790-4731 E-mail: info@mvpress.org Web Site: www.mvpublishers.org, pg 124

Vilarello, Meredith, Avid Reader Press, 1230 Avenue of the Americas, New York, NY 10020 Web Site: avidreaderpress.com, pg 23

Villa, Anais, HarperCollins Children's Books, 195 Broadway, New York, NY 10007 Tel: 212-207-7000 Web Site: www.harpercollins.com/childrens, pg 86

Villalobos, Elysse, Farrar, Straus & Giroux Books for Young Readers, 120 Broadway, New York, NY 10271 Tel: 212-741-6900 Toll Free Tel: 888-330-8477 (orders) E-mail: childrens.publicity@macmillanusa.com; childrensrights@macmillanusa.com Web Site: us.macmillan.com/mackids, pg 70

Villalobos, Elysse, Roaring Brook Press, 120 Broadway, New York, NY 10271 Tel: 646-307-5151 Web Site: us.macmillan.com/publishers/roaring-brook-press, pg 176

Villanueva, David, Chronicle Books LLC, 680 Second St, San Francisco, CA 94107 Tel: 415-537-4200 Fax: 415-537-4460 (perms) E-mail: hello@chroniclebooks.com; subrights@chroniclebooks.com Web Site: www.chroniclebooks.com, pg 48

Villanueva, Kristy, Printing Industries Association Inc of Southern California (PIASC), 5800 S Eastern Ave, Suite 400, Los Angeles, CA 90040 Tel: 323-728-9500 E-mail: info@piasc.org Web Site: www.piasc.org, pg 517

Villanueva, Vera, Candlewick Press, 99 Dover St, Somerville, MA 02144-2825 Tel: 617-661-3330 Fax: 617-661-0565 E-mail: bigbear@candlewick.com; salesinfo@candlewick.com Web Site: candlewick.com, pg 40

Villar, Stephania, Random House Children's Books, c/o Penguin Random House LLC, 1745 Broadway, New York, NY 10019 Tel: 212-782-9000 Web Site: www.rhcbooks.com, pg 170

Viloria, Junessa, Grand Central Publishing, 1290 Avenue of the Americas, New York, NY 10104 Tel: 212-364-1100 Web Site: www.hachettebookgroup.com/imprint/grand-central-publishing/, pg 80

Vinarub, Vanessa, Harvard University Press, 79 Garden St, Cambridge, MA 02138-1499 Tel: 617-495-2600; 401-531-2800 (intl orders) Toll Free Tel: 800-405-1619 (orders) Fax: 617-495-5898 (gen); 617-496-4677 (edit & rts); 401-531-2801 (intl orders) Toll Free Fax: 800-406-9145 (orders) E-mail: contact_hup@harvard.edu Web Site: www.hup.harvard.edu, pg 88

Vincent, Dorothy, Sanford J Greenburger Associates Inc, 55 Fifth Ave, New York, NY 10003 Tel: 212-206-5600 Web Site: greenburger.com, pg 461

Vincent, Eddie, Independent Publishers of New England (IPNE), c/o Eddie Vincent, Encircle Publications, Farmington, ME 04955 Tel: 339-368-8229 E-mail: talktous@ipne.org Web Site: www.ipne.org, pg 508

Vincent, Eddie, Independent Publishers of New England Book Awards, c/o Eddie Vincent, Encircle Publications, Farmington, ME 04955 Tel: 339-368-8229 E-mail: bookawards@ipne.org Web Site: www.ipne.org/awards, pg 615

Vincent, Heidi M, Johns Hopkins University Press, 2715 N Charles St, Baltimore, MD 21218-4363 Tel: 410-516-6900; 410-516-6987 Toll Free Tel: 800-537-5487 (book orders & cust serv); 800-548-1784 (journal orders) Fax: 410-516-6968; 410-516-6998 (orders) E-mail: hfscustserv@press.jhu.edu (cust serv); jrnlcirc@jh.edu (journal orders) Web Site: www.press.jhu.edu; muse.jhu.edu, pg 106

Vincenty, Elyse, Holiday House Publishing Inc, 50 Broad St, New York, NY 10004 Tel: 212-688-0085 Fax: 212-421-6134 E-mail: info@holidayhouse.com Web Site: www.holidayhouse.com, pg 94

Vincenty, Elyse, Peachtree Publishing Co Inc, 1700 Chattahoochee Ave, Atlanta, GA 30318-2112 Tel: 404-876-8761 Toll Free Tel: 800-241-0113 Fax: 404-875-2578 Toll Free Fax: 800-875-8909 E-mail: hello@peachtree-online.com; orders@peachtree-online.com; sales@peachtree-online.com Web Site: www.peachtreebooks.com; www.peachtree-online.com, pg 153

Vinciguerra, Megan, Penguin Random House LLC, 1745 Broadway, New York, NY 10019 Tel: 212-782-9000 Toll Free Tel: 800-726-0600 Web Site: www.penguinrandomhouse.com, pg 155

Vinhateiro, Bethany, HarperCollins Children's Books, 195 Broadway, New York, NY 10007 Tel: 212-207-7000 Web Site: www.harpercollins.com/childrens, pg 85

Vinson, Arriel, Henry Holt and Company, LLC, 120 Broadway, 23rd fl, New York, NY 10271 Tel: 646-307-5151 Toll Free Tel: 888-330-8477 (orders) Fax: 646-307-5285 Web Site: www.henryholt.com, pg 94

Viola, Kieran, Disney-Hyperion Books, 1101 Flower St, Glendale, CA 91201 Web Site: books.disney.com/imprint/disney-hyperion, pg 59

Viotti, Flavia, Bookcase Literary Agency, 5062 Lankershim Blvd, PMB 3046, North Hollywood, CA 91601 Web Site: www.bookcaseagency.com, pg 450

Virtucio, Cydel, Chronicle Books LLC, 680 Second St, San Francisco, CA 94107 Tel: 415-537-4200 Fax: 415-537-4460 (perms) E-mail: hello@chroniclebooks.com; subrights@chroniclebooks.com Web Site: www.chroniclebooks.com, pg 48

Visconti, Max, Grand & Archer Publishing, 463 Coyote, Cathedral City, CA 92234 Tel: 323-493-2785 E-mail: grandandarcher@gmail.com, pg 80

Viskovic, Hilda, Lectorum Publications Inc, 10 New Maple Ave, Suite 303, Pine Brook, NJ 07058 Tel: 201-559-2200 Toll Free Tel: 800-345-5946 E-mail: lectorum@lectorum.com Web Site: www.lectorum.com, pg 122

Visser, Kristi, Insight Editions, 800 "A" St, San Rafael, CA 94901 Tel: 415-526-1370 Toll Free Tel: 800-809-3792 Toll Free Fax: 866-509-0515 E-mail: info@insighteditions.com; marketing@insighteditions.com Web Site: insighteditions.com, pg 101

Vitale, Julie, Bloomsbury Academic, 1385 Broadway, 5th fl, New York, NY 10018 Tel: 212-419-5300 Web Site: www.bloomsbury.com/us/academic, pg 31

Vitek, John M, Saint Mary's Press, 702 Terrace Heights, Winona, MN 55987-1320 Tel: 507-457-7900 Toll Free Tel: 800-533-8095 Toll Free Fax: 800-344-9225 E-mail: smpress@smp.org Web Site: www.smp.org, pg 181

Vitelli, Lisa, Penguin Random House LLC, 1745 Broadway, New York, NY 10019 Tel: 212-782-9000 Toll Free Tel: 800-726-0600 Web Site: www.penguinrandomhouse.com, pg 155

Viti, Lynne, New England Poetry Club, c/o Linda Haviland Conte, 18 Hall Ave, Apt 2, Somerville, MA 02144 E-mail: info@nepoetryclub.org; president@nepoetryclub.org Web Site: nepoetryclub.org, pg 514

Vitkus, Rebecca, Random House Children's Books, c/o Penguin Random House LLC, 1745 Broadway, New York, NY 10019 Tel: 212-782-9000 Web Site: www.rhcbooks.com, pg 170

Vito, Marisa, Copper Canyon Press, Fort Worden State Park, Bldg 313, Port Townsend, WA 98368 Tel: 360-385-4925 E-mail: poetry@coppercanyonpress.org; publicity@coppercanyonpress.org; digitalcontent@coppercanyonpress.com Web Site: www.coppercanyonpress.org, pg 52

Vitola, Krista, Simon & Schuster Children's Publishing, 1230 Avenue of the Americas, New York, NY 10020 Tel: 212-698-7000 Web Site: www.simonandschuster.com/kids; www.simonandschuster.com/teen; simonandschuster.net; simonandschuster.biz, pg 189

Vittal, Veena, Macmillan, 120 Broadway, 22nd fl, New York, NY 10271 E-mail: press.inquiries@macmillan.com Web Site: us.macmillan.com, pg 122

Vitucci, Nancy, Health Administration Press, 300 S Riverside Plaza, Suite 1900, Chicago, IL 60606 Tel: 312-424-2800 Fax: 312-424-0014 E-mail: hapbooks@ache.org Web Site: www.ache.org/hap (orders), pg 89

Vitullo, Margaret Weigers, American Sociological Association (ASA), 1430 "K" St NW, Suite 600, Washington, DC 20005-4701 Tel: 202-383-9005 E-mail: asa@asanet.org; communications@asanet.org; membership@asanet.org Web Site: www.asanet.org, pg 497

Vlahov, Alex, Cornell University Press, Sage House, 512 E State St, Ithaca, NY 14850 Tel: 607-253-2338 E-mail: cupressinfo@cornell.edu; cupress-sales@cornell.edu; cupress-perms@cornell.edu (reprint/class use permissions) Web Site: www.cornellpress.cornell.edu, pg 52

Voegele, Oriel, Hachette Audio, 1290 Avenue of the Americas, New York, NY 10104 Tel: 212-364-1100 Web Site: www.hachettebookgroup.com/imprint/hachette-audio/, pg 83

Vogel, Casie, Ulysses Press, 195 Montague St, 14th fl, Brooklyn, NY 11201 Tel: 510-601-8301 Toll Free Tel: 800-377-2542 Fax: 510-601-8307 E-mail: ulysses@ulyssespress.com Web Site: www.ulyssespress.com, pg 212

Vogel, James, Angelus Press, 522 W Bertrand St, St Marys, KS 66536 Tel: 816-753-3150 Toll Free Tel: 800-966-7337 E-mail: support@angeluspress.org Web Site: www.angeluspress.org, pg 14

Vogel, Rachel, Dunow, Carlson & Lerner Literary Agency Inc, 27 W 20 St, Suite 1107, New York, NY 10011 Tel: 212-645-7606 E-mail: mail@dclagency.com Web Site: www.dclagency.com, pg 457

Vogt, Elizabeth, Viking Penguin, c/o Penguin Random House LLC, 1745 Broadway, New York, NY 10019 Tel: 212-782-9000 Web Site: www.penguin.com/overview-vikingbooks/; www.penguin.com/pamela-dorman-books-overview/; www.penguin.com/penguin-classics-overview/; www.penguin.com/penguin-life-overview/, pg 225

Vogt, Morgan, Sourcebooks LLC, 1935 Brookdale Rd, Suite 139, Naperville, IL 60563 Tel: 630-961-3900 Toll Free Tel: 800-432-7444 Fax: 630-961-2168 E-mail: info@sourcebooks.com Web Site: www.sourcebooks.com, pg 194

Volinsky, Slavik, Milady, 5191 Natorp Blvd, Mason, OH 45040 Toll Free Tel: 866-848-5143 Fax: 518-373-6309 E-mail: info@milady.com Web Site: www.milady.com, pg 131

Volkman, Prof Victor R, Loving Healing Press Inc, 5145 Pontiac Trail, Ann Arbor, MI 48105 *Tel:* 734-417-4266 *Toll Free Tel:* 888-761-6268 (US & CN) *Fax:* 734-663-6861 *E-mail:* info@lovinghealing.com; info@lhpress.com *Web Site:* www.lovinghealing.com; www.modernhistorypress.com (imprint), pg 121

Vollmar, Robert, Neustadt International Prize for Literature, c/o University of Oklahoma, 630 Parrington Oval, Suite 110, Norman, OK 73019-4033 *Tel:* 405-325-4531 *Web Site:* www.worldliteraturetoday.org; www.neustadtprize.org, pg 639

Vollmar, Robert, NSK Neustadt Prize for Children's Literature, c/o University of Oklahoma, 630 Parrington Oval, Suite 110, Norman, OK 73019-4033 *Tel:* 405-325-4531 *Web Site:* www.worldliteraturetoday.org; www.neustadtprize.org, pg 642

Von Drasek, Lisa, Ezra Jack Keats/Kerlan Memorial Fellowship, University of Minnesota, 113 Andersen Library, 222 21 Ave S, Minneapolis, MN 55455 *Tel:* 612-624-4576 *E-mail:* asc-clrc@umn.edu *Web Site:* www.lib.umn.edu/clrc, pg 619

Von Hertsenberg, Kurt, National Wildlife Federation, 11100 Wildlife Center Dr, Reston, VA 20190-5362 *Toll Free Tel:* 800-477-5034 *Web Site:* www.zoobooks.com, pg 139

Von Hoelscher, Russ, National Association of Book Entrepreneurs (NABE), PO Box 606, Cottage Grove, OR 97424 *Tel:* 541-942-7455 *Fax:* 541-942-7455 *E-mail:* nabe@bookmarketingprofits.com *Web Site:* www.bookmarketingprofits.com, pg 511

von Knorring, John, Stylus Publishing LLC, 22883 Quicksilver Dr, Sterling, VA 20166-2019 *Tel:* 703-661-1504 (edit & sales) *Toll Free Tel:* 800-232-0223 (orders & cust serv) *Fax:* 703-661-1547 *E-mail:* stylusmail@styluspub.com (orders & cust serv); stylusinfo@styluspub.com *Web Site:* styluspub.com, pg 200

Von Lintel, Rebekah, Embolden Literary, PO Box 953607, Lake Mary, FL 32795-3607 *E-mail:* info@emboldenmediagroup.com; submissions@emboldenmediagroup.com *Web Site:* emboldenmediagroup.com/literary-representation, pg 458

von Mehren, Jane, Aevitas Creative Management LLC, 19 W 21 St, Suite 501, New York, NY 10010 *Tel:* 212-765-6900 *Web Site:* www.aevitascreative.com, pg 448

von Platen, Millie, Astra Books for Young Readers, 19 W 21 St, No 1201, New York, NY 10010 *Tel:* 646-844-3485 *E-mail:* ahinfo@astrahouse.com; permissions@astrapublishinghouse.com *Web Site:* astrapublishinghouse.com, pg 20

von Schilling, Claire, Penguin Random House LLC, 1745 Broadway, New York, NY 10019 *Tel:* 212-782-9000 *Toll Free Tel:* 800-726-0600 *Web Site:* www.penguinrandomhouse.com, pg 155

von Schilling, Claire, Random House Publishing Group, 1745 Broadway, New York, NY 10019 *Toll Free Tel:* 800-200-3552 *Web Site:* www.randomhousebooks.com, pg 170

Vonada, Damaine, Midwest Travel Journalists Association Inc (MTJA), PO Box 185, Jessup, IA 50648 *Tel:* 319-529-1109 *E-mail:* admin@mtja.us *Web Site:* www.mtja.us, pg 511

Voorhees, Madeleine (Maddy), Gallery Books, 1230 Avenue of the Americas, New York, NY 10020 *Toll Free Tel:* 800-456-6798 *Fax:* 212-698-7284 *E-mail:* consumer.customerservice@simonandschuster.com *Web Site:* www.simonandschuster.com, pg 76

Vorenberg, Bonnie L, ArtAge Publications, PO Box 19955, Portland, OR 97280 *Tel:* 503-246-3000 *Toll Free Tel:* 800-858-4998 *Web Site:* www.seniortheatre.com, pg 17

Voros, Stephanie, Simon & Schuster Children's Publishing, 1230 Avenue of the Americas, New York, NY 10020 *Tel:* 212-698-7000 *Web Site:* www.simonandschuster.com/kids; www.simonandschuster.com/teen; simonandschuster.net; simonandschuster.biz, pg 189

Vos, Brian, Baker Books, 6030 E Fulton Rd, Ada, MI 49301 *Tel:* 616-676-9185 *Toll Free Tel:* 800-877-2665 (orders) *Fax:* 616-676-9573 *Toll Free Fax:* 800-398-3111 (orders) *E-mail:* media@bakerpublishinggroup.com; orders@bakerpublishinggroup.com; sales@bakerpublishinggroup.com *Web Site:* www.bakerpublishinggroup.com, pg 23

Vosburgh, Andy, GW Inc, 2290 Ball Dr, St Louis, MO 63146 *Tel:* 314-567-9854 *E-mail:* media@gwinc.com *Web Site:* www.gwinc.com, pg 440

Vrame, Rev Anton, Holy Cross Orthodox Press, 50 Goddard Ave, Brookline, MA 02445 *Tel:* 617-731-3500; 617-850-1303 *E-mail:* press@hchc.edu *Web Site:* www.hchc.edu, pg 95

Vreven, Ms Line, Optometric Extension Program Foundation (OEPF), 2300 York Rd, Suite 113, Timonium, MD 21093 *Tel:* 410-561-3791 *Fax:* 410-252-1719 *Web Site:* www.oepf.org, pg 147

Vroegop, Allison, Houghton Mifflin Harcourt Trade & Reference Division, 125 High St, Boston, MA 02110 *Tel:* 617-351-5000 *Web Site:* www.hmhco.com, pg 96

Vyce, Stephanie, Harvard University Press, 79 Garden St, Cambridge, MA 02138-1499 *Tel:* 617-495-2600; 401-531-2800 (intl orders) *Toll Free Tel:* 800-405-1619 (orders) *Fax:* 617-495-5898 (gen); 617-496-4677 (edit & rts); 401-531-2801 (intl orders) *Toll Free Fax:* 800-406-9145 (orders) *E-mail:* contact_hup@harvard.edu *Web Site:* www.hup.harvard.edu, pg 88

Wachowicz, Mark, Alliance for Audited Media (AAM), 4513 Lincoln Ave, Suite 105B, Lisle, IL 60532 *Tel:* 224-366-6939 *Toll Free Tel:* 800-285-2220 *E-mail:* corpcomm@auditedmedia.com *Web Site:* auditedmedia.com, pg 493

Wachtel, Claire, Union Square & Co, 1166 Avenue of the Americas, 17th fl, New York, NY 10036-2715 *Tel:* 212-532-7160 *Toll Free Tel:* 800-367-9692 *Fax:* 212-213-2495 *Toll Free Fax:* 800-542-7567 *E-mail:* custservice@sterlingpublishing.com; customerservice@sterlingpublishing.com; editorial@sterlingpublishing.com; tradesales@sterlingpublishing.com *Web Site:* www.sterlingpublishing.com, pg 212

Wachtel, Gina, Penguin Random House LLC, 1745 Broadway, New York, NY 10019 *Tel:* 212-782-9000 *Toll Free Tel:* 800-726-0600 *Web Site:* www.penguinrandomhouse.com, pg 155

Wachtel, Gina, Random House Publishing Group, 1745 Broadway, New York, NY 10019 *Toll Free Tel:* 800-200-3552 *Web Site:* www.randomhousebooks.com, pg 170

Wachtell, Diane, The New Press, 120 Wall St, 31st fl, New York, NY 10005 *Tel:* 212-629-8802 *Fax:* 212-629-8617 *E-mail:* newpress@thenewpress.com *Web Site:* thenewpress.com, pg 140

Wackrow, Dan, Harvard University Press, 79 Garden St, Cambridge, MA 02138-1499 *Tel:* 617-495-2600; 401-531-2800 (intl orders) *Toll Free Tel:* 800-405-1619 (orders) *Fax:* 617-495-5898 (gen); 617-496-4677 (edit & rts); 401-531-2801 (intl orders) *Toll Free Fax:* 800-406-9145 (orders) *E-mail:* contact_hup@harvard.edu *Web Site:* www.hup.harvard.edu, pg 88

Wade, Bernardo, Don Belton Fiction Reading Period, Indiana University English Dept, Ballantine Hall 554, 1020 E Kirkwood Ave, Bloomington, IN 47405 *Tel:* 812-855-3439 *E-mail:* inreview@indiana.edu *Web Site:* indianareview.org, pg 578

Wade, Bernardo, Blue Light Books Prize, Indiana University English Dept, Ballantine Hall 554, 1020 E Kirkwood Ave, Bloomington, IN 47405 *Tel:* 812-855-3439 *E-mail:* inreview@indiana.edu *Web Site:* indianareview.org, pg 582

Wade, Bernardo, 1/2 K Prize, Indiana University English Dept, Ballantine Hall 554, 1020 E Kirkwood Ave, Bloomington, IN 47405 *Tel:* 812-855-3439 *E-mail:* inreview@indiana.edu *Web Site:* indianareview.org, pg 610

Wade, Bernardo, Indiana Review Creative Nonfiction Prize, Indiana University English Dept, Ballantine Hall 554, 1020 E Kirkwood Ave, Bloomington, IN 47405 *Tel:* 812-855-3439 *E-mail:* inreview@indiana.edu *Web Site:* indianareview.org, pg 616

Wade, Bernardo, Indiana Review Fiction Prize, Indiana University English Dept, Ballantine Hall 554, 1020 E Kirkwood Ave, Bloomington, IN 47405 *Tel:* 812-855-3439 *E-mail:* inreview@indiana.edu *Web Site:* indianareview.org, pg 616

Wade, Bernardo, Indiana Review Poetry Prize, Indiana University English Dept, Ballantine Hall 554, 1020 E Kirkwood Ave, Bloomington, IN 47405 *Tel:* 812-855-3439 *E-mail:* inreview@indiana.edu *Web Site:* indianareview.org, pg 616

Wade, Cally, Christian Schools International (CSI), 99 Monroe Ave NW, Suite 200, Grand Rapids, MI 49503 *Tel:* 616-957-1070 *Toll Free Tel:* 800-635-8288 *Web Site:* www.csionline.org, pg 47

Wade, Edward, Berrett-Koehler Publishers Inc, 1333 Broadway, Suite 1000, Oakland, CA 94612 *Tel:* 510-817-2277 *Fax:* 510-817-2278 *E-mail:* bkpub@bkpub.com *Web Site:* www.bkconnection.com, pg 29

Wade, Jessica, Berkley, c/o Penguin Random House LLC, 1745 Broadway, 19th fl, New York, NY 10019 *Tel:* 212-366-2000 *Web Site:* www.penguin.com/publishers/berkley/; www.penguin.com/ace-overview/, pg 28

Wade, Lee, Random House Children's Books, c/o Penguin Random House LLC, 1745 Broadway, New York, NY 10019 *Tel:* 212-782-9000 *Web Site:* www.rhcbooks.com, pg 169

Wadsworth, Dr Sarah, Marquette University Press, 1415 W Wisconsin Ave, Milwaukee, WI 53233 *Tel:* 414-288-1564 *Web Site:* www.marquette.edu/mupress, pg 125

Wadsworth-Booth, Susan, Kent State University Press, 1118 University Library Bldg, 1125 Risman Dr, Kent, OH 44242 *Tel:* 330-672-7913 *Fax:* 330-672-3104 *E-mail:* ksupress@kent.edu *Web Site:* www.kentstateuniversitypress.com, pg 109

Waggner, Jackie, Macmillan, 120 Broadway, 22nd fl, New York, NY 10271 *E-mail:* press.inquiries@macmillan.com *Web Site:* us.macmillan.com, pg 122

Waggoner, Lynn, Disney Press, 1101 Flower St, Glendale, CA 91201 *Web Site:* books.disney.com, pg 59

Waggoner, Lynn, Disney Publishing Worldwide, 1101 Flower St, Glendale, CA 91201 *Web Site:* books.disney.com, pg 60

Wagner, Kyle, University of Chicago Press, 1427 E 60 St, Chicago, IL 60637-2954 *Tel:* 773-702-7700; 773-702-7600 *Toll Free Tel:* 800-621-2736 (orders) *Fax:* 773-702-9756; 773-660-2235 (orders); 773-702-2708 *E-mail:* custserv@press.uchicago.edu; marketing@press.uchicago.edu *Web Site:* www.press.uchicago.edu, pg 215

Wagner, Meredith, Random House Children's Books, c/o Penguin Random House LLC, 1745 Broadway, New York, NY 10019 *Tel:* 212-782-9000 *Web Site:* www.rhcbooks.com, pg 170

Wagner, Paul, PA Press, 202 Warren St, Hudson, NY 12534 *Tel:* 518-671-6100 *Toll Free Tel:* 800-722-6657 (dist); 800-759-0190 (sales) *E-mail:* sales@papress.com *Web Site:* www.papress.com, pg 149

Wahl, Kate, Stanford University Press, 425 Broadway St, Redwood City, CA 94063-3126 *Tel:* 650-723-9434 *Fax:* 650-725-3457 *E-mail:* info@www.sup.org; publicity@www.sup.org; sales@www.sup.org *Web Site:* www.sup.org, pg 197

Wainscott, Tina, The Seymour Agency, 475 Miner Street Rd, Canton, NY 13617 *Tel:* 239-398-8209 *Web Site:* www.theseymouragency.com, pg 475

Waintraub, Adrienne, Random House Children's Books, c/o Penguin Random House LLC, 1745 Broadway, New York, NY 10019 *Tel:* 212-782-9000 *Web Site:* www.rhcbooks.com, pg 169

Wainz, Rachel, Viking Penguin, c/o Penguin Random House LLC, 1745 Broadway, New York, NY 10019 *Tel:* 212-782-9000 *Web Site:* www.penguin.com/overview-vikingbooks/; www.penguin.com/pamela-dorman-books-overview/; www.penguin.com/penguin-classics-overview/; www.penguin.com/penguin-life-overview/, pg 225

Wakefield, Julie, Mel Bay Publications Inc, 16 N Gore Ave, Suite 203, Webster Groves, MO 63119-2315 *Tel:* 636-257-3970 *Toll Free Tel:* 800-863-5229 *E-mail:* email@melbay.com *Web Site:* www.melbay.com, pg 129

Walcher, Hannah, CALIBA Golden Poppy Awards, 100 Black Diamond Rd, Stonyford, CA 95979 *Tel:* 415-561-7686 *E-mail:* info@caliballiance.org *Web Site:* caliballiance.org/golden-poppy-awards.html, pg 585

Walcher, Hannah, California Independent Booksellers Alliance (CALIBA), 100 Black Diamond Rd, Stonyford, CA 95979 *Tel:* 415-561-7686 *E-mail:* info@caliballiance.org *Web Site:* caliballiance.org, pg 502

Walden, Angela, Leadership Ministries Worldwide, 1928 Central Ave, Chattanooga, TN 37408 *Tel:* 423-855-2181 *Toll Free Tel:* 800-987-8790 *E-mail:* info@lmw.org *Web Site:* lmw.org; store.lmw.org, pg 113

Walden, Robert, News/Media Alliance, 4401 N Fairfax Dr, Suite 300, Arlington, VA 22203 *Tel:* 571-366-1000 *E-mail:* info@newsmediaalliance.org *Web Site:* www.newsmediaalliance.org, pg 514

Waldman, Brett, TRISTAN Publishing, 2355 Louisiana Ave N, Minneapolis, MN 55427 *Tel:* 763-545-1383 *Toll Free Tel:* 866-545-1383 *Fax:* 763-545-1387 *E-mail:* info@tristanpublishing.com *Web Site:* www.tristanpublishing.com, pg 209

Waldman, Sheila, TRISTAN Publishing, 2355 Louisiana Ave N, Minneapolis, MN 55427 *Tel:* 763-545-1383 *Toll Free Tel:* 866-545-1383 *Fax:* 763-545-1387 *E-mail:* info@tristanpublishing.com *Web Site:* www.tristanpublishing.com, pg 209

Waldmann, Genevieve, Simon & Schuster, LLC, 1230 Avenue of the Americas, New York, NY 10020 *Tel:* 212-698-7000 *Toll Free Tel:* 800-223-2336 (orders) *Fax:* 212-698-7007 *Toll Free Fax:* 800-943-9831 (orders) *E-mail:* firstname.lastname@simonandschuster.com; purchaseorders@simonandschuster.com (orders) *Web Site:* www.simonandschuster.com, pg 189

Waldron, Laura, University of Chicago Press, 1427 E 60 St, Chicago, IL 60637-2954 *Tel:* 773-702-7700; 773-702-7600 *Toll Free Tel:* 800-621-2736 (orders) *Fax:* 773-702-9756; 773-660-2235 (orders); 773-702-2708 *E-mail:* custserv@press.uchicago.edu; marketing@press.uchicago.edu *Web Site:* www.press.uchicago.edu, pg 215

Wales, Elizabeth, Wales Literary Agency Inc, 1508 Tenth Ave E, No 401, Seattle, WA 98102 *Tel:* 206-553-9684 *E-mail:* waleslit@waleslit.com *Web Site:* www.waleslit.com, pg 481

Walker, Alan F, Ruth & Sylvia Schwartz Children's Book Awards, c/o Ontario Arts Council, 121 Bloor St E, 7th fl, Toronto, ON M4W 3M5, Canada *Tel:* 416-961-1660 *Toll Free Tel:* 800-387-0058 (ON) *Fax:* 416-961-7796 (Ontario Arts Council) *E-mail:* info@oafdn.ca (Ontario Arts Foundation); info@arts.on.ca (Ontario Arts Council) *Web Site:* www.arts.on.ca; www.oafdn.ca/pages/ruth-sylvia-schwartz-awards, pg 661

Walker, Amanda, Dutton, c/o Penguin Random House LLC, 1745 Broadway, New York, NY 10019 *Tel:* 212-366-2000 *Web Site:* www.penguin.com/dutton-overview/; www.penguin.com/plume-books-overview/; www.penguin.com/tiny-reparations-overview/, pg 62

Walker, Andrea, Random House Publishing Group, 1745 Broadway, New York, NY 10019 *Toll Free Tel:* 800-200-3552 *Web Site:* www.randomhousebooks.com, pg 170

Walker, Bette, Stephen Leacock Memorial Medal for Humour, PO Box 854, Orillia, ON L3V 6K8, Canada *Tel:* 705-326-9286 *E-mail:* info@leacock.ca *Web Site:* www.leacock.ca, pg 622

Walker, Brian, Charlesbridge Publishing Inc, 85 Main St, Watertown, MA 02472 *Tel:* 617-926-0329 *Toll Free Tel:* 800-225-3214 *Fax:* 617-926-5720 *Toll Free Fax:* 800-926-5775 *E-mail:* books@charlesbridge.com *Web Site:* www.charlesbridge.com, pg 45

Walker, Carl, Software & Information Industry Association (SIIA), 1620 Eye St NW, Washington, DC 20005 *Tel:* 202-289-7442 *Fax:* 202-289-7097 *E-mail:* info@siia.net *Web Site:* www.siia.net, pg 520

Walker, David, HarperCollins Children's Books, 195 Broadway, New York, NY 10007 *Tel:* 212-207-7000 *Web Site:* www.harpercollins.com/childrens, pg 85

Walker, David, HarperCollins Publishers LLC, 195 Broadway, New York, NY 10007 *Tel:* 212-207-7000 *Web Site:* www.harpercollins.com, pg 86

Walker, Graham H, Independent Institute, 100 Swan Way, Oakland, CA 94621-1428 *Tel:* 510-632-1366 *Fax:* 510-568-6040 *Web Site:* www.independent.org, pg 99

Walker, Dr Jenny McCormack, Literacy Texas, PO Box 111, Texarkana, TX 75504-0111 *Tel:* 903-392-9802 *E-mail:* info@literacytexas.org *Web Site:* literacytexas.org; www.facebook.com/LiteracyTX, pg 509

Walker, Joe, American Society of Agricultural & Biological Engineers (ASABE), 2950 Niles Rd, St Joseph, MI 49085-9659 *Tel:* 269-429-0300 *Toll Free Tel:* 800-371-2723 *Fax:* 269-429-3852 *E-mail:* hq@asabe.org *Web Site:* www.asabe.org, pg 12

Walker, Jonathan M, Association of American Publishers (AAP), 455 Massachusetts Ave NW, Suite 700, Washington, DC 20001-2777 *Tel:* 202-347-3375 *Fax:* 202-347-3690 *E-mail:* info@publishers.org *Web Site:* publishers.org, pg 498

Walker, Kirsty, Hobblebush Books, PO Box 1285, Concord, NH 03302 *Tel:* 603-715-9615 *E-mail:* info@hobblebush.com *Web Site:* www.hobblebush.com, pg 93

Walker, Laura, Apogee Press, PO Box 10066, Berkeley, CA 94709 *E-mail:* apogeelibri@gmail.com *Web Site:* www.apogeepress.com, pg 15

Walker, Laura, University of Alaska Press, Elmer E Rasmuson Library, 1732 Tanana Loop, Suite 402, Fairbanks, AK 99775 *Tel:* 907-474-5831 *Toll Free Tel:* 888-252-6657 (US only) *Fax:* 907-474-5502 *Web Site:* www.alaska.edu/uapress, pg 214

Walker, Richard, United States Institute of Peace Press, 2301 Constitution Ave NW, Washington, DC 20037 *Tel:* 703-661-1590 (cust serv) *Toll Free Tel:* 800-868-8064 (cust serv) *E-mail:* usipmail@presswarehouse.com (orders) *Web Site:* bookstore.usip.org, pg 213

Walker, Robert P, American Program Bureau Inc, One Gateway Center, Suite 751, Newton, MA 02458 *Tel:* 617-614-1600 *E-mail:* apb@apbspeakers.com *Web Site:* www.apbspeakers.com, pg 487

Walker, Tara, Tundra Book Group, 320 Front St W, Suite 1400, Toronto, ON M5V 3B6, Canada *Tel:* 416-364-4449 *Toll Free Tel:* 888-523-9292 (orders); 800-588-1074 *E-mail:* youngreaders@penguinrandomhouse.com *Web Site:* www.tundrabooks.com, pg 421

Walker, Theresa, The Catholic University of America Press, 240 Leahy Hall, 620 Michigan Ave NE, Washington, DC 20064 *Tel:* 202-319-5052 *Toll Free Tel:* 800-537-5487 (orders only) *Fax:* 202-319-4985 *E-mail:* cua-press@cua.edu *Web Site:* cuapress.org, pg 42

Wall, Patrick, A-R Editions Inc, 1600 Aspen Commons, Suite 100, Middleton, WI 53562 *Tel:* 608-836-9000 *Toll Free Tel:* 800-736-0070 (North America book orders only) *Fax:* 608-831-8200 *E-mail:* info@areditions.com; orders@areditions.com *Web Site:* www.areditions.com, pg 1

Wall, Rob, little bee books, 598 Broadway, 7th fl, New York, NY 10012 *Tel:* 212-321-0237 *Toll Free Tel:* 844-321-0237 *E-mail:* info@littlebeebooks.com; sales@littlebeebooks.com; publicity@littlebeebooks.com *Web Site:* littlebeebooks.com, pg 117

Wallace, Amelia, Bolchazy-Carducci Publishers Inc, 1000 Brown St, Unit 301, Wauconda, IL 60084 *Tel:* 847-526-4344 *Fax:* 847-526-2867 *E-mail:* info@bolchazy.com; orders@bolchazy.com *Web Site:* www.bolchazy.com, pg 33

Wallace, Courtney, American Booksellers Association, 600 Mamaroneck Ave, Suite 400, Harrison, NY 10528 *Tel:* 914-406-7500 *Toll Free Tel:* 800-637-0037 *Fax:* 914-417-4013 *E-mail:* info@bookweb.org *Web Site:* www.bookweb.org, pg 494

Wallace, Ronald, Brittingham & Pollak Prizes in Poetry, Dept of English, 600 N Park St, Madison, WI 53706 *Web Site:* creativewriting.wisc.edu/submit.html, pg 584

Wallace, Steven, University of Georgia Press, Main Library, 3rd fl, 320 S Jackson St, Athens, GA 30602 *Fax:* 706-542-2558; 706-542-6770 *Web Site:* www.ugapress.org, pg 216

Wallach, Harlan, Poetry Foundation, 61 W Superior St, Chicago, IL 60654 *Tel:* 312-787-7070 *E-mail:* info@poetryfoundation.org *Web Site:* www.poetryfoundation.org, pg 526

Wallenstein, Jackie, Association of School Business Officials International, 44790 Maynard Sq, Suite 200, Ashburn, VA 20147 *Tel:* 703-478-0405 *Toll Free Tel:* 866-682-2729 *Fax:* 703-478-0205; 703-708-7060 (membership) *E-mail:* asboreq@asbointl.org; membership@asbointl.org *Web Site:* www.asbointl.org, pg 20

Wallentine, Lois, Carolrhoda Lab™, 241 First Ave N, Minneapolis, MN 55401 *Tel:* 612-332-3344 *Toll Free Tel:* 800-328-4929 *Fax:* 612-332-7615 *Toll Free Fax:* 800-332-1132 *E-mail:* info@lernerbooks.com; custserve@lernerbooks.com *Web Site:* www.lernerbooks.com; www.facebook.com/lernerbooks, pg 41

Wallentine, Lois, ediciones Lerner, 241 First Ave N, Minneapolis, MN 55401 *Tel:* 612-332-3344 *Toll Free Tel:* 800-328-4929 *Fax:* 612-332-7615 *Toll Free Fax:* 800-332-1132 *E-mail:* info@lernerbooks.com; custserve@lernerbooks.com *Web Site:* www.lernerbooks.com; www.facebook.com/lernerbooks, pg 63

Wallentine, Lois, First Avenue Editions, 241 First Ave N, Minneapolis, MN 55401 *Tel:* 612-332-3344 *Toll Free Tel:* 800-328-4929 *Fax:* 612-332-7615 *Toll Free Fax:* 800-332-1132 *E-mail:* info@lernerbooks.com; custserve@lernerbooks.com *Web Site:* www.lernerbooks.com; www.facebook.com/lernerbooks, pg 72

Wallentine, Lois, Graphic Universe™, 241 First Ave N, Minneapolis, MN 55401 *Tel:* 612-332-3344 *Toll Free Tel:* 800-328-4929 *Fax:* 612-332-7615 *Toll Free Fax:* 800-332-1132 *E-mail:* info@lernerbooks.com; custserve@lernerbooks.com *Web Site:* www.lernerbooks.com; www.facebook.com/lernerbooks, pg 80

Wallentine, Lois, Lerner Publications, 241 First Ave N, Minneapolis, MN 55401 *Tel:* 612-332-3344 *Toll Free Tel:* 800-328-4929 *Fax:* 612-332-7615 *Toll Free Fax:* 800-332-1132 *E-mail:* info@lernerbooks.com; custserve@lernerbooks.com *Web Site:* www.lernerbooks.com; www.facebook.com/lernerbooks, pg 115

Wallentine, Lois, Lerner Publishing Group Inc, 241 First Ave N, Minneapolis, MN 55401 *Tel:* 612-332-3344 *Toll Free Tel:* 800-328-4929 *Fax:* 612-332-7615 *Toll Free Fax:* 800-332-1132 *E-mail:* info@lernerbooks.com; custserve@lernerbooks.com *Web Site:* www.lernerbooks.com; www.facebook.com/lernerbooks, pg 115

Wallentine, Lois, LernerClassroom, 241 First Ave N, Minneapolis, MN 55401 *Tel:* 612-332-3344 *Toll Free Tel:* 800-328-4929 *Fax:* 612-332-7615 *Toll Free Fax:* 800-332-1132 *E-mail:* info@lernerbooks.com; custserve@lernerbooks.com *Web Site:* www.lernerbooks.com; www.facebook.com/lernerbooks, pg 115

Wallentine, Lois, Millbrook Press, 241 First Ave N, Minneapolis, MN 55401 *Tel:* 612-332-3344 *Toll Free Tel:* 800-328-4929 *Fax:* 612-332-7615 *Toll Free Fax:* 800-332-1132 *E-mail:* info@lernerbooks.com; custserve@lernerbooks.com *Web Site:* www.lernerbooks.com; www.facebook.com/millbrookpress, pg 131

Wallentine, Lois, Twenty-First Century Books, 241 First Ave N, Minneapolis, MN 55401 *Tel:* 612-332-3344 *Toll Free Tel:* 800-328-4929 *Fax:* 612-332-7615 *Toll Free Fax:* 800-332-1132 *E-mail:* info@lernerbooks.com; custserve@lernerbooks.com *Web Site:* www.lernerbooks.com; www.facebook.com/lernerbooks, pg 211

Wallentine, Lois, Zest Books, 241 First Ave N, Minneapolis, MN 55401 *Tel:* 612-332-3344 *Toll Free Tel:* 800-328-4929 *Toll Free Fax:* 800-332-1132 *E-mail:* info@lernerbooks.com; publicity@lernerbooks.com; custserve@lernerbooks.com (orders) *Web Site:* lernerbooks.com, pg 236

Waller, Cameron, Penguin Random House Canada, a Penguin Random House company, 320 Front St W, Suite 1400, Toronto, ON M5V 3B6, Canada *Tel:* 416-364-4449 *Toll Free Tel:* 888-523-9292 (cust serv) *E-mail:* canadaweb@penguinrandomhouse.com; customerservicescanada@penguinrandomhouse.com *Web Site:* www.penguinrandomhouse.ca, pg 416

Wallman, Keith, Diversion Books, 11 E 44 St, Suite 1603, New York, NY 10017 *Tel:* 212-961-6390 *E-mail:* info@diversionbooks.com *Web Site:* www.diversionbooks.com, pg 60

Walls, Kathleen, Global Authors Publications (GAP), 38 Bluegrass, Middleberg, FL 32068 *Tel:* 904-425-1608 *E-mail:* gapbook@yahoo.com *Web Site:* www.globalauthorspublications.com, pg 78

Walls, Milo, Farrar, Straus & Giroux, LLC, 120 Broadway, New York, NY 10271 *Tel:* 212-741-6900 *E-mail:* fsg.publicity@fsgbooks.com; sales@fsgbooks.com *Web Site:* us.macmillan.com/fsg, pg 70

Walpole, Erin, Nursesbooks.org, The Publishing Program of ANA, 8515 Georgia Ave, Suite 400, Silver Spring, MD 20910-3492 *Tel:* 301-628-5000 *Toll Free Tel:* 800-274-4262; 800-637-0323 (orders) *Fax:* 301-628-5342 *E-mail:* anp@ana.org *Web Site:* www.Nursesbooks.org; www.NursingWorld.org, pg 144

Walsh, Karen, Candlewick Press, 99 Dover St, Somerville, MA 02144-2825 *Tel:* 617-661-3330 *Fax:* 617-661-0565 *E-mail:* bigbear@candlewick.com; salesinfo@candlewick.com *Web Site:* candlewick.com, pg 39

Walsh, Karen, Holiday House Publishing Inc, 50 Broad St, New York, NY 10004 *Tel:* 212-688-0085 *Fax:* 212-421-6134 *E-mail:* info@holidayhouse.com *Web Site:* www.holidayhouse.com, pg 94

Walsh, Karen, Peachtree Publishing Co Inc, 1700 Chattahoochee Ave, Atlanta, GA 30318-2112 *Tel:* 404-876-8761 *Toll Free Tel:* 800-241-0113 *Fax:* 404-875-2578 *Toll Free Fax:* 800-875-8909 *E-mail:* hello@peachtree-online.com; orders@peachtree-online.com; sales@peachtree-online.com *Web Site:* www.peachtreebooks.com; www.peachtree-online.com, pg 153

Walsh, Maureen, Public Relations Society of America Inc, 120 Wall St, 21st fl, New York, NY 10005 *Tel:* 212-460-1400 *E-mail:* membership@prsa.org *Web Site:* www.prsa.org, pg 518

Walsh, Mike, LexisNexis®, 230 Park Ave, Suite 7, New York, NY 10169 *Tel:* 212-309-8100 *Toll Free Fax:* 800-437-8674 *Web Site:* www.lexisnexis.com, pg 116

Walsh, Molly, Academy of American Poets Fellowship, 75 Maiden Lane, Suite 901, New York, NY 10038 *Tel:* 212-274-0343 *E-mail:* awards@poets.org *Web Site:* poets.org/academy-american-poets/prizes/academy-american-poets-fellowship, pg 569

Walsh, Molly, Academy of American Poets First Book Award, 75 Maiden Lane, Suite 901, New York, NY 10038 *Tel:* 212-274-0343 *E-mail:* awards@poets.org *Web Site:* poets.org/academy-american-poets/prizes/first-book-award, pg 569

Walsh, Molly, The Academy of American Poets Inc, 75 Maiden Lane, Suite 901, New York, NY 10038 *Tel:* 212-274-0343 *E-mail:* academy@poets.org *Web Site:* poets.org, pg 493

Walsh, Molly, Ambroggio Prize, 75 Maiden Lane, Suite 901, New York, NY 10038 *Tel:* 212-274-0343 *E-mail:* awards@poets.org *Web Site:* poets.org/academy-american-poets/prizes/ambroggio-prize, pg 572

Walsh, Molly, James Laughlin Award, 75 Maiden Lane, Suite 901, New York, NY 10038 *Tel:* 212-274-0343 *E-mail:* awards@poets.org *Web Site:* poets.org/academy-american-poets/prizes/james-laughlin-award, pg 622

Walsh, Molly, Lenore Marshall Poetry Prize, 75 Maiden Lane, Suite 901, New York, NY 10038 *Tel:* 212-274-0343 *E-mail:* awards@poets.org *Web Site:* poets.org/academy-american-poets/prizes/lenore-marshall-poetry-prize, pg 629

Walsh, Molly, Harold Morton Landon Translation Award, 75 Maiden Lane, Suite 901, New York, NY 10038 *Tel:* 212-274-0343 *E-mail:* awards@poets.org *Web Site:* poets.org/academy-american-poets/prizes/harold-morton-landon-translation-award, pg 635

Walsh, Molly, Aliki Perroti & Seth Frank Most Promising Young Poet Award, 75 Maiden Lane, Suite 901, New York, NY 10038 *Tel:* 212-274-0343 *E-mail:* awards@poets.org *Web Site:* poets.org/academy-american-poets/american-poets-prizes, pg 649

Walsh, Molly, Raiziss/de Palchi Fellowship, 75 Maiden Lane, Suite 901, New York, NY 10038 *Tel:* 212-274-0343 *E-mail:* awards@poets.org *Web Site:* poets.org/academy-american-poets/american-poets-prizes, pg 654

Walsh, Molly, Wallace Stevens Award, 75 Maiden Lane, Suite 901, New York, NY 10038 *Tel:* 212-274-0343 *E-mail:* awards@poets.org *Web Site:* poets.org/academy-american-poets/prizes/wallace-stevens-award, pg 666

Walsh, Molly, Treehouse Climate Action Poem Prize, 75 Maiden Lane, Suite 901, New York, NY 10038 *Tel:* 212-274-0343 *E-mail:* awards@poets.org *Web Site:* poets.org, pg 670

Walter, Bill, The Center for Learning, PO Box 802, Culver City, CA 90232 *Tel:* 310-839-2436 *Toll Free Tel:* 800-421-4246 *Fax:* 310-839-2249 *Toll Free Fax:* 800-944-5432 *E-mail:* access@socialstudies.com; customerservice@socialstudies.com; submissions@socialstudies.com *Web Site:* www.centerforlearning.org, pg 43

Walters, Craig, South Dakota Historical Society Press, 900 Governors Dr, Pierre, SD 57501 *Tel:* 605-773-6009 *Fax:* 605-773-6041 *E-mail:* info@sdhspress.com; orders@sdhspress.com *Web Site:* sdhspress.com, pg 195

Walters, Emily, Macmillan, 120 Broadway, 22nd fl, New York, NY 10271 *E-mail:* press.inquiries@macmillan.com *Web Site:* us.macmillan.com, pg 122

Walters, Marthe, University Press of Florida, 2046 NE Waldo Rd, Suite 2100, Gainesville, FL 32609 *Tel:* 352-392-1351 *Toll Free Tel:* 800-226-3822 (orders only) *Fax:* 352-392-0590 *Toll Free Fax:* 800-680-1955 (orders only) *E-mail:* press@upress.ufl.edu; orders@upress.ufl.edu *Web Site:* www.upf.com, pg 221

Waltman, Fran, Edward Lewis Wallant Award, Maurice Greenberg Center for Judaic Studies, 200 Bloomfield Ave, Harry Jack Gray E 300, West Hartford, CT 06117 *Tel:* 860-768-4964 *Fax:* 860-768-5044 *E-mail:* mgcjs@hartford.edu *Web Site:* www.hartford.edu/a_and_s/greenberg/wallant, pg 673

Waltman, Irving, Edward Lewis Wallant Award, Maurice Greenberg Center for Judaic Studies, 200 Bloomfield Ave, Harry Jack Gray E 300, West Hartford, CT 06117 *Tel:* 860-768-4964 *Fax:* 860-768-5044 *E-mail:* mgcjs@hartford.edu *Web Site:* www.hartford.edu/a_and_s/greenberg/wallant, pg 673

Walton, Laura Moran, University of Notre Dame Press, 310 Flanner Hall, Notre Dame, IN 46556 *Tel:* 574-631-6346 *Fax:* 574-631-8148 *E-mail:* undpress@nd.edu *Web Site:* www.undpress.nd.edu, pg 219

Wang, Alice, Houghton Mifflin Harcourt Trade & Reference Division, 125 High St, Boston, MA 02110 *Tel:* 617-351-5000 *Web Site:* www.hmhco.com, pg 96

Wanner, Anja, Chris O'Malley Fiction Prize, University of Wisconsin, 6193 Helen C White Hall, English Dept, 600 N Park St, Madison, WI 53706 *E-mail:* madisonrevw@gmail.com *Web Site:* www.themadisonrevw.com, pg 643

Wanner, Anja, Phyllis Smart-Young Poetry Prize, University of Wisconsin, 6193 Helen C White Hall, English Dept, 600 N Park St, Madison, WI 53706 *E-mail:* madisonrevw@gmail.com *Web Site:* www.themadisonrevw.com, pg 663

Wantland, Clydette, University of Illinois Press, 1325 S Oak St, MC-566, Champaign, IL 61820-6903 *Tel:* 217-333-0950 *Fax:* 217-244-8082 *E-mail:* uipress@uillinois.edu; journals@uillinois.edu *Web Site:* www.press.uillinois.edu, pg 216

Ward, Andy, Random House Publishing Group, 1745 Broadway, New York, NY 10019 *Toll Free Tel:* 800-200-3552 *Web Site:* www.randomhousebooks.com, pg 171

Ward, Anne, High Tide Press, 101 Hempstead Place, Suite 1A, Joliet, IL 60433 *Tel:* 779-702-5540 *E-mail:* orders@hightidepress.org; award@hightidepress.org *Web Site:* hightidepress.org, pg 92

Ward, April, Random House Children's Books, c/o Penguin Random House LLC, 1745 Broadway, New York, NY 10019 *Tel:* 212-782-9000 *Web Site:* www.rhcbooks.com, pg 169

Ward, Courtney, Pauline Books & Media, 50 Saint Paul's Ave, Boston, MA 02130 *Tel:* 617-522-8911 *Toll Free Tel:* 800-876-4463 (orders); 800-836-9723 (cust serv) *Fax:* 617-541-9805 *E-mail:* editorial@paulinemedia.com (ms submissions); orderentry@pauline.org (cust serv) *Web Site:* www.pauline.org/pbmpublishing, pg 152

Ward, Elizabeth, Random House Children's Books, c/o Penguin Random House LLC, 1745 Broadway, New York, NY 10019 *Tel:* 212-782-9000 *Web Site:* www.rhcbooks.com, pg 169

Wardeell, Beth, The Astronomical Society of the Pacific, 390 Ashton Ave, San Francisco, CA 94112 *Tel:* 415-337-1100; 415-715-1414 (cust serv) *Toll Free Tel:* 800-335-2624 (cust serv) *Fax:* 415-337-5205 *E-mail:* service@astrosociety.org *Web Site:* astrosociety.org, pg 20

Warden, Yorke, Living Stream Ministry (LSM), 2431 W La Palma Ave, Anaheim, CA 92801 *Tel:* 714-236-6050 *Toll Free Tel:* 800-549-5164 *Fax:* 714-236-6054 *E-mail:* books@lsm.org *Web Site:* www.lsm.org, pg 119

Wardlaw, Andreia, Pantheon Books, c/o Penguin Random House LLC, 1745 Broadway, New York, NY 10019 *Tel:* 212-751-2600 *Fax:* 212-940-7390 (dom rts); 212-572-2662 (foreign rts) *Web Site:* knopfdoubleday.com/imprint/pantheon/; knopfdoubleday.com, pg 150

Warfield, Marshall, Rosemont College, Graduate Publg Prog, 1400 Montgomery Ave, Rosemont, PA 19010 *Tel:* 610-527-0200 (ext 2431) *Web Site:* www.rosemont.edu, pg 565

Waricha, Joan, Parachute Publishing LLC, PO Box 320249, Fairfield, CT 06825 *Tel:* 203-255-1303, pg 151

Warker, Derek, The New Press, 120 Wall St, 31st fl, New York, NY 10005 *Tel:* 212-629-8802 *Fax:* 212-629-8617 *E-mail:* newpress@thenewpress.com *Web Site:* thenewpress.com, pg 140

Warner, Debra, Great Lakes Graphics Association (GLGA), N27 W23960 Paul Rd, Suite 200, Pewaukee, WI 53072 *Tel:* 262-522-2210 *Toll Free Tel:* 855-522-2210 *Fax:* 262-522-2211 *E-mail:* info@glga.info *Web Site:* glga.info, pg 507

Warner, Stephanie, Quarto Publishing Group USA Inc, 100 Cummings Ctr, Suite 265D, Beverly, MA 01915 *Tel:* 978-282-9590 *Toll Free Tel:* 800-328-0590 (sales) *Fax:* 978-283-2742 *E-mail:* sales@quartous.com *Web Site:* www.quartoknows.com, pg 168

Warnock, Mariel, EPS School Specialty, 625 Mount Auburn St, Suite 202, Cambridge, MA 02138-3039 *Toll Free Tel:* 800-225-5750 *Toll Free Fax:* 888-440-

2665 E-mail: curriculumcare@schoolspecialty.com; curriculumorders@schoolspecialty.com Web Site: eps.schoolspecialty.com, pg 67

Warren, Allison, Aevitas Creative Management LLC, 19 W 21 St, Suite 501, New York, NY 10010 Tel: 212-765-6900 Web Site: www.aevitascreative.com, pg 448

Warren, Carolyn, Canada Council for the Arts (Conseil des arts du Canada), 150 Elgin St, 2nd fl, Ottawa, ON K2P 1L4, Canada Tel: 613-566-4414 Toll Free Tel: 800-263-5588 (CN only) Fax: 613-566-4390 E-mail: info@canadacouncil.ca; media@canadacouncil.ca Web Site: canadacouncil.ca, pg 502

Warren, Mark, Random House Publishing Group, 1745 Broadway, New York, NY 10019 Toll Free Tel: 800-200-3552 Web Site: www.randomhousebooks.com, pg 170

Warren, Miriam, Publishers Association of the West Inc (PubWest), 12727 Highland Ct, Auburn, CA 95603-3634 Tel: 720-443-3637 E-mail: executivedirector@pubwest.org Web Site: pubwest.org, pg 518

Warren, Miriam, PubWest Book Design Awards, 12727 Highland Ct, Auburn, CA 95603-3634 Tel: 720-443-3637 E-mail: executivedirector@pubwest.org Web Site: pubwest.org, pg 653

Warren, Miriam, Jack D Rittenhouse Award, 12727 Highland Ct, Auburn, CA 95603-3634 Tel: 720-443-3637 E-mail: executivedirector@pubwest.org Web Site: pubwest.org, pg 656

Warren, Wenche, YWAM Publishing, PO Box 55787, Seattle, WA 98155-0787 Tel: 425-771-1153 Toll Free Tel: 800-922-2143 E-mail: books@ywampublishing.com; marketing@ywampublishing.com Web Site: www.ywampublishing.com, pg 236

Warschausky, Kara, Macmillan, 120 Broadway, 22nd fl, New York, NY 10271 E-mail: press.inquiries@macmillan.com Web Site: us.macmillan.com, pg 122

Warwick, Peter, Scholastic Inc, 557 Broadway, New York, NY 10012 Tel: 212-343-6100 Toll Free Tel: 800-SCHOLASTIC (724-6527) Web Site: www.scholastic.com, pg 184

Warwick-Smith, Simon, Warwick Associates, 18340 Sonoma Hwy, Sonoma, CA 95476 Tel: 707-939-9212 Fax: 707-938-3515 E-mail: warwick@vom.com Web Site: www.warwickassociates.com, pg 481

Wascavage, Matt, American Society of Agronomy (ASA), 5585 Guilford Rd, Madison, WI 53711-5801 Tel: 608-273-8080 E-mail: books@sciencesocieties.org Web Site: www.agronomy.org, pg 12

Wascavage, Matt, Soil Science Society of America (SSSA), 5585 Guilford Rd, Madison, WI 53711-5801 Tel: 608-273-8080 Fax: 608-273-2021 Web Site: www.soils.org, pg 193

Washington, Katrina, Macmillan, 120 Broadway, 22nd fl, New York, NY 10271 E-mail: press.inquiries@macmillan.com Web Site: us.macmillan.com, pg 122

Washington, Paul, The Conference Board Inc, 845 Third Ave, New York, NY 10022-6600 Tel: 212-759-0900; 212-339-0345 (cust serv) E-mail: customer.service@tcb.org Web Site: www.conference-board.org/us; www.linkedin.com/company/the-conference-board, pg 51

Wasielewski, Leah, HarperCollins Publishers LLC, 195 Broadway, New York, NY 10007 Tel: 212-207-7000 Web Site: www.harpercollins.com, pg 86

Wasik, Bethany, Cornell University Press, Sage House, 512 E State St, Ithaca, NY 14850 Tel: 607-253-2338 E-mail: cupressinfo@cornell.edu; cupress-sales@cornell.edu; cupress-perms@cornell.edu (reprint/class use permissions) Web Site: www.cornellpress.cornell.edu, pg 52

Wasko, Jim, OCP, 340 Oswego Pointe Dr, Lake Oswego, OR 97034 Tel: 503-281-1191 Toll Free Tel: 800-LITURGY (548-8749) Fax: 503-282-3486 Toll Free Fax: 800-843-8181 E-mail: liturgy@ocp.org Web Site: www.ocp.org, pg 145

Wasmund, Laurie Marr, Colorado Authors' League, 700 Colorado Blvd, Denver, CO 80206 Tel: 913-369-5040 Web Site: coloradoauthors.org, pg 504

Wasserman, Steve, Heyday, 1808 San Pablo Ave, Suite A, Berkeley, CA 94702 Tel: 510-549-3564 E-mail: heyday@heydaybooks.com Web Site: heydaybooks.com, pg 91

Wasserman, Veronica, Houghton Mifflin Harcourt Trade & Reference Division, 125 High St, Boston, MA 02110 Tel: 617-351-5000 Web Site: www.hmhco.com, pg 96

Wasson, Beth, Eleanor Taylor Bland Crime Fiction Writers of Color Award, PO Box 442124, Lawrence, KS 66044 Tel: 785-842-1325 Fax: 785-856-6314 E-mail: admin@sistersincrime.org Web Site: www.sistersincrime.org, pg 581

Waterman, Daniel, University of Alabama Press, 200 Hackberry Lane, 2nd fl, Tuscaloosa, AL 35487 Tel: 205-348-5180 Fax: 205-348-9201 Web Site: www.uapress.ua.edu, pg 214

Waterman, Marisa, American Academy of Environmental Engineers & Scientists®, 147 Old Solomons Island Rd, Suite 303, Annapolis, MD 21401 Tel: 410-266-3311 Fax: 410-266-7653 E-mail: info@aaees.org Web Site: www.aaees.org, pg 8

Waters, Michele, New Harbinger Publications Inc, 5674 Shattuck Ave, Oakland, CA 94609 Tel: 510-652-0215 Toll Free Tel: 800-748-6273 (orders only) Fax: 510-652-5472 Toll Free Fax: 800-652-1613 E-mail: customerservice@newharbinger.com Web Site: www.newharbinger.com, pg 140

Waters, Michelle, Riverhead Books, c/o Penguin Random House LLC, 1745 Broadway, New York, NY 10019 Tel: 212-782-9000 Web Site: www.penguin.com/riverhead-overview/, pg 175

Waters, Mitchell, Brandt & Hochman Literary Agents Inc, 1501 Broadway, Suite 2310, New York, NY 10036 Tel: 212-840-5760 Fax: 212-840-5776 Web Site: brandthochman.com, pg 452

Watkins, Catherine, Gulf Energy Information, 2 Greenway Plaza, Suite 1020, Houston, TX 77046 Tel: 713-520-4498; 713-529-4301 E-mail: store@gulfpub.com; customerservice@gulfenergyinfo.com Web Site: www.gulfenergyinfo.com, pg 83

Watkins, Kelly, SLACK® Incorporated, A Wyanoke Group Company, 6900 Grove Rd, Thorofare, NJ 08086-9447 Tel: 856-848-1000 Toll Free Tel: 800-257-8290 Fax: 856-848-6091 E-mail: sales@slackinc.com; editor@slackinc.com; customerservice@slackinc.com Web Site: www.healio.com/books, pg 191

Watkinson, Charles, University of Michigan Press, 839 Greene St, Ann Arbor, MI 48104-3209 Tel: 734-764-4388 Fax: 734-615-1540 E-mail: um.press@umich.edu Web Site: www.press.umich.edu, pg 217

Watson, Ben, Chelsea Green Publishing Co, 85 N Main St, Suite 120, White River Junction, VT 05001 Tel: 802-295-6300 Toll Free Tel: 800-639-4099 (cust serv & orders) Fax: 802-295-6444 E-mail: customerservice@chelseagreen.com; editorial@chelseagreen.com; publicity@chelseagreen.com; rights@chelseagreen.com Web Site: www.chelseagreen.com, pg 45

Watson, Courtney, Association of College & University Printers, 2006 E Marlboro Ave, Suite 104, Hyattsville, MD 20785 Tel: 571-409-3533 Web Site: www.acup-edu.org, pg 499

Watson, Cristin, Association of School Business Officials International, 44790 Maynard Sq, Suite 200, Ashburn, VA 20147 Tel: 703-478-0405 Toll Free Tel: 866-682-2729 Fax: 703-478-0205; 703-708-7060 (membership) E-mail: asboreq@asbointl.org; membership@asbointl.org Web Site: www.asbointl.org, pg 20

Watson, David R, Institute of Continuing Legal Education, 1020 Greene St, Ann Arbor, MI 48109-1444 Tel: 734-764-0533 Toll Free Tel: 877-229-4350 Fax: 734-763-2412 Toll Free Fax: 877-229-4351 E-mail: icle@umich.edu Web Site: www.icle.org, pg 101

Watson, Kara, Scribner, 1230 Avenue of the Americas, New York, NY 10020 Web Site: www.simonandschusterpublishing.com/scribner/, pg 185

Watson, Kate, Nimbus Publishing Ltd, 3660 Strawberry Hill, Halifax, NS B3K 5A9, Canada Tel: 902-455-4286 Toll Free Tel: 800-NIMBUS9 (646-2879) Fax: 902-455-5440 Toll Free Fax: 888-253-3133 E-mail: customerservice@nimbus.ca Web Site: www.nimbus.ca, pg 414

Watson, Lucia, Avery, c/o Penguin Random House LLC, 1745 Broadway, New York, NY 10019 Tel: 212-366-2000 Web Site: www.penguin.com/avery-overview/, pg 23

Watson, Mackenzie Brady, Stuart Krichevsky Literary Agency Inc, 118 E 28 St, Suite 908, New York, NY 10016 Tel: 212-725-5288 Fax: 212-725-5275 E-mail: query@skagency.com Web Site: skagency.com, pg 466

Watson, Renee, Books on Tape™, 1745 Broadway, New York, NY 10019 Toll Free Tel: 800-733-3000 (cust serv) Toll Free Fax: 800-940-7046 Web Site: PenguinRandomHouseLibrary.com, pg 34

Wattawa, Gayle, Heyday, 1808 San Pablo Ave, Suite A, Berkeley, CA 94702 Tel: 510-549-3564 E-mail: heyday@heydaybooks.com Web Site: heydaybooks.com, pg 91

Watters, Ron, National Outdoor Book Awards (NOBA), 921 S Eighth Ave, Stop 8128, Pocatello, ID 83209-8128 Tel: 208-282-3912 Fax: 208-282-2127 Web Site: www.noba-web.org, pg 638

Watterson, Jessica, Sandra Dijkstra Literary Agency, 1155 Camino del Mar, PMB A, Del Mar, CA 92014-2605 Web Site: dijkstraagency.com, pg 456

Wawrzyniec, Caroline, Printing Industries Alliance, 636 N French Rd, Suite 1, Amherst, NY 14228 Tel: 716-691-3211 Toll Free Tel: 800-777-4742 Fax: 716-691-4249 E-mail: info@pialliance.org Web Site: pialliance.org, pg 517

Waxman, Molly, Poisoned Pen Press, 4014 N Goldwater Blvd, Suite 201, Scottsdale, AZ 85251 Tel: 480-945-3375 Toll Free Tel: 800-421-3976 Fax: 480-949-1707 E-mail: info@poisonedpenpress.com Web Site: www.poisonedpenpress.com, pg 161

Waxman, Molly, Sourcebooks LLC, 1935 Brookdale Rd, Suite 139, Naperville, IL 60563 Tel: 630-961-3900 Toll Free Tel: 800-432-7444 Fax: 630-961-2168 E-mail: info@sourcebooks.com Web Site: www.sourcebooks.com, pg 194

Waxman, Scott, Diversion Books, 11 E 44 St, Suite 1603, New York, NY 10017 Tel: 212-961-6390 E-mail: info@diversionbooks.com Web Site: www.diversionbooks.com, pg 60

Waxman, Scott, Waxman Literary Agency, 443 Park Ave S, No 1004, New York, NY 10016 Tel: 212-675-5556 Web Site: www.waxmanliteraryagency.com, pg 481

Wayne, Andrew, Canadian Scholars, 425 Adelaide St W, Suite 200, Toronto, ON M5V 3C1, Canada Tel: 416-929-2774 Toll Free Tel: 800-463-1998 E-mail: info@canadianscholars.ca; editorial@canadianscholars.ca Web Site: www.canadianscholars.ca; www.womenspress.ca, pg 398

Weatherhead, Michael, Square One Publishers Inc, 115 Herricks Rd, Garden City Park, NY 11040 Tel: 516-535-2010 Toll Free Tel: 877-900-BOOK (900-2665) Fax: 516-535-2014 E-mail: sq1publish@aol.com Web Site: www.squareonepublishers.com, pg 196

Weaver, Thomas, The MIT Press, One Broadway, 12th fl, Cambridge, MA 02142 Tel: 617-253-5255 Toll Free Tel: 800-405-1619 (orders) Fax: 617-258-6779; 617-577-1545 (orders) Web Site: mitpress.mit.edu, pg 132

Webb, Barbara, Intensive Novel Architects Writing Workshop, 1809 Indiana St, Lawrence, KS 66044 Tel: 785-766-7039 Web Site: adastra-sf.com/Workshop-stuff/Johnson-Webb-Workshops.htm, pg 555

Webb, Dorothy, Write Now, 900 S Mitchell Dr, Tempe, AZ 85281 Tel: 480-921-5700 Fax: 480-921-5777 E-mail: info@writenow.co Web Site: www.writenow.co, pg 678

Webb, Janine G, Highlights for Children Inc, 815 Church St, Honesdale, PA 18431 Tel: 570-253-1164 Toll Free Tel: 800-490-5111 Fax: 570-253-0179

E-mail: salesandmarketing@highlightspress.com Web Site: www.highlightspress.com; www.highlights.com; www.facebook.com/HighlightsforChildren, pg 92

Webb, Kari, Random House Children's Books, c/o Penguin Random House LLC, 1745 Broadway, New York, NY 10019 Tel: 212-782-9000 Web Site: www.rhcbooks.com, pg 170

Webb, Steven, Summit University Press, 63 Summit Way, Gardiner, MT 59030 Tel: 406-848-9292; 406-848-9500 (retail orders) Fax: 406-848-9555 E-mail: info@tsl.org; rights@summituniversitypress.com Web Site: www.summituniversitypress.com, pg 200

Webber, Terry, American Forest & Paper Association (AF&PA), 1101 "K" St NW, Suite 700, Washington, DC 20005 Tel: 202-463-2700 E-mail: info@afandpa.org; comm@afandpa.org Web Site: www.afandpa.org, pg 495

Weber, Andrew, John Wiley & Sons Inc, 111 River St, Hoboken, NJ 07030-5774 Tel: 201-748-6000 Toll Free Tel: 800-225-5945 (cust serv) Fax: 201-748-6088 Web Site: www.wiley.com, pg 230

Weber, Beth, Chronicle Books LLC, 680 Second St, San Francisco, CA 94107 Tel: 415-537-4200 Fax: 415-537-4460 (perms) E-mail: hello@chroniclebooks.com; subrights@chroniclebooks.com Web Site: www.chroniclebooks.com, pg 47

Weber, Jeff, Penguin Random House LLC, 1745 Broadway, New York, NY 10019 Tel: 212-782-9000 Toll Free Tel: 800-726-0600 Web Site: www.penguinrandomhouse.com, pg 155

Weber, John, Welcome Rain Publishers LLC, 217 Thompson St, Suite 473, New York, NY 10012 Tel: 212-686-1909 Web Site: welcomerain.com, pg 227

Weber, Judith, Sobel Weber Associates Inc, 146 E 19 St, New York, NY 10003-2404 Tel: 212-420-8585 E-mail: info@sobelweber.com Web Site: www.sobelweber.com, pg 476

Weber, Lauren, Alfred A Knopf, c/o Penguin Random House LLC, 1745 Broadway, New York, NY 10019 Tel: 212-751-2600 Fax: 212-940-7390 (dom rts); 212-572-2662 (foreign rts) Web Site: knopfdoubleday.com/imprint/knopf/; knopfdoubleday.com, pg 110

Weber, Lauren, Penguin Random House LLC, 1745 Broadway, New York, NY 10019 Tel: 212-782-9000 Toll Free Tel: 800-726-0600 Web Site: www.penguinrandomhouse.com, pg 155

Weber, Louis, Publications International Ltd (PIL), 8140 N Lehigh Ave, Morton Grove, IL 60053 Tel: 847-676-3470 Fax: 847-676-3671 E-mail: customer_service@pubint.com Web Site: pilbooks.com, pg 167

Weber, Nancy L, Teachers & Writers Collaborative (T&W), 20 W 20 St, Suite 801, New York, NY 10011 Tel: 212-691-6590 E-mail: info@twc.org Web Site: www.twc.org, pg 521

Weber, Shelley, The Canadian Writers' Foundation Inc (La Fondation des Ecrivains Canadiens), PO Box 13281, Kanata Sta, Ottawa, ON K2K 1X4, Canada Tel: 613-978-2723 Fax: 613-900-6393 E-mail: info@canadianwritersfoundation.org Web Site: www.canadianwritersfoundation.org, pg 525

Weber, Tory, Young Writers Workshops, Finn House, 102 W Wiggin St, Gambier, OH 43022-9623 Tel: 740-427-5391 Fax: 740-427-5417 E-mail: youngwriters@kenyonreview.org Web Site: kenyonreview.org/high-school-workshops, pg 559

Weber, Vicki, Behrman House Inc, 241B Millburn Ave, Millburn, NJ 07041 Tel: 973-379-7200 Toll Free Tel: 800-221-2755 Fax: 973-379-7280 E-mail: customersupport@behrmanhouse.com Web Site: store.behrmanhouse.com, pg 27

Weberman, Alisa, Listen & Live Audio Inc, 803 13 St, Union City, NJ 07087 Tel: 201-558-9000 Web Site: www.listenandlive.com, pg 117

Webster, Bernadette, Peterson's, 8740 Lucent Blvd, Suite 400, Highlands Ranch, CO 80129 Tel: 609-896-1800 Toll Free Tel: 800-338-3282 E-mail: pubmarketing@petersons.com Web Site: www.petersons.com, pg 158

Webster, Sheila, InScribe Christian Writers' Fellowship (ICWF), PO Box 68025, Edmonton, AB T6C 4N6, Canada Tel: 780-646-3068 E-mail: inscribe.mail@gmail.com Web Site: inscribe.org, pg 508

Weed, Elisabeth, The Book Group (TBG), 20 W 20 St, Suite 601, New York, NY 10011 E-mail: info@thebookgroup.com; submissions@thebookgroup.com Web Site: www.thebookgroup.com, pg 450

Weed, Susun, Ash Tree Publishing, PO Box 64, Woodstock, NY 12498 Tel: 845-246-8081 Fax: 845-246-8081 Web Site: www.ashtreepublishing.com, pg 18

Weeks, Heather, Educational Insights®, 152 W Walnut St, Suite 201, Gardena, CA 90248 Toll Free Tel: 800-995-4436 Toll Free Fax: 888-892-8731 E-mail: info@educationalinsights.com; cs@educationalinsights.com Web Site: www.educationalinsights.com, pg 64

Weeks, Suzanne L, Society for Industrial & Applied Mathematics, 3600 Market St, 6th fl, Philadelphia, PA 19104-2688 Tel: 215-382-9800 Toll Free Tel: 800-447-7426 E-mail: siam@siam.org Web Site: www.siam.org, pg 192

Weening, Catherine, Workman Publishing, 1290 Avenue of the Americas, New York, NY 10104 Toll Free Tel: 800-759-0190 Fax: 212-364-0950 E-mail: workman-inquiry@hbgusa.com Web Site: www.hachettebookgroup.com/imprint/workman-publishing-company/, pg 233

Weerasooriya, Supipi, Penguin Random House Canada, a Penguin Random House company, 320 Front St W, Suite 1400, Toronto, ON M5V 3B6, Canada Tel: 416-364-4449 Toll Free Tel: 888-523-9292 (cust serv) Fax: canadaweb@penguinrandomhouse.com; customerservicescanada@penguinrandomhouse.com Web Site: www.penguinrandomhouse.ca, pg 416

Wegendt, Sr Christina, Pauline Books & Media, 50 Saint Paul's Ave, Boston, MA 02130 Tel: 617-522-8911 Toll Free Tel: 800-876-4463 (orders); 800-836-9723 (cust serv) Fax: 617-541-9805 E-mail: editorial@paulinemedia.com (ms submissions); orderentry@pauline.org (cust serv) Web Site: www.pauline.org/pbmpublishing, pg 152

Wegner, Gregory R, GLCA New Writers Awards, 535 W William St, Suite 301, Ann Arbor, MI 48103 Tel: 734-661-2350 Fax: 734-661-2349 Web Site: www.glca.org, pg 607

Wehner, Oliver, Orbit, 1290 Avenue of the Americas, New York, NY 10104 Tel: 212-364-1100 Toll Free Tel: 800-759-0190 Web Site: www.orbitbooks.net; www.hachettebookgroup.com/imprint/orbit, pg 147

Weidemann, Jason, University of Minnesota Press, 111 Third Ave S, Suite 290, Minneapolis, MN 55401-2520 Tel: 612-301-1990 Fax: 612-301-1980 E-mail: ump@umn.edu Web Site: www.upress.umn.edu, pg 217

Weidman, Pamela, Princeton University Press, 41 William St, Princeton, NJ 08540-5237 Tel: 609-258-4900 Fax: 609-258-6305 E-mail: info@press.princeton.edu Web Site: press.princeton.edu, pg 164

Weigl, Linda, Weigl Educational Publishers Ltd, 6325 Tenth St SE, Calgary, AB T2H 2Z9, Canada Tel: 403-233-7747 Toll Free Tel: 800-668-0766 Fax: 403-233-7769 E-mail: orders@weigl.com Web Site: www.weigl.ca, pg 424

Weikart, Jim, International Association of Crime Writers Inc, North American Branch, PO Box 863, Norman, OK 73071 E-mail: crimewritersna@gmail.com Web Site: www.crimewritersna.org, pg 508

Weikersheimer, Joshua R, ASCP Press, 33 W Monroe St, Suite 1600, Chicago, IL 60603 Tel: 312-541-4999 Toll Free Tel: 800-267-2727 Fax: 312-541-4998 Web Site: www.ascp.org, pg 18

Weikum, Tara, HarperCollins Children's Books, 195 Broadway, New York, NY 10007 Tel: 212-207-7000 Web Site: www.harpercollins.com/childrens, pg 85

Weil, Gideon, HarperCollins Publishers LLC, 195 Broadway, New York, NY 10007 Tel: 212-207-7000 Web Site: www.harpercollins.com, pg 86

Weil, Gideon, Rogers & Weil Literary, 530 Divisadero St, No 169, San Francisco, CA 94117 Web Site: www.rwliterary.com, pg 474

Weil, Joe, Binghamton University Creative Writing Program, c/o Dept of English, General Literature & Rhetoric, PO Box 6000, Binghamton, NY 13902-6000 Tel: 607-777-2168 Fax: 607-777-2408 E-mail: cwpro@binghamton.edu Web Site: www.binghamton.edu/english/creative-writing/index.html, pg 561

Weil, NC, Women's National Book Association Award, PO Box 237, FDR Sta, New York, NY 10150-0231 Toll Free Tel: 866-610-WNBA (610-9622) Web Site: wnba-books.org/wnba-award, pg 677

Weil, NC, Women's National Book Association Inc, PO Box 237, FDR Sta, New York, NY 10150-0231 Toll Free Tel: 866-610-WNBA (610-9622) E-mail: info@wnba-books.org Web Site: wnba-books.org, pg 522

Weil, Robert, W W Norton & Company Inc, 500 Fifth Ave, New York, NY 10110-0017 Tel: 212-354-5500 Toll Free Tel: 800-233-4830 (orders & cust serv) Fax: 212-869-0856 Toll Free Fax: 800-458-6515 E-mail: orders@wwnorton.com Web Site: wwnorton.com, pg 143

Weil, Steve, Farrar, Straus & Giroux, LLC, 120 Broadway, New York, NY 10271 Tel: 212-741-6900 E-mail: fsg.publicity@fsgbooks.com; sales@fsgbooks.com Web Site: us.macmillan.com/fsg, pg 70

Weil, Steve, FSG Writer's Fellowship, 120 Broadway, New York, NY 10271 Tel: 212-741-6900 E-mail: fsg.publicity@fsgbooks.com Web Site: fsgfellowship.com, pg 605

Weil, Steve, Picador, 120 Broadway, New York, NY 10271 Tel: 646-307-5151 Fax: 212-253-9627 E-mail: publicity@picadorusa.com Web Site: us.macmillan.com/picador, pg 159

Weiland, Matt, W W Norton & Company Inc, 500 Fifth Ave, New York, NY 10110-0017 Tel: 212-354-5500 Toll Free Tel: 800-233-4830 (orders & cust serv) Fax: 212-869-0856 Toll Free Fax: 800-458-6515 E-mail: orders@wwnorton.com Web Site: wwnorton.com, pg 143

Weill, Cynthia, The Cook Prize, 610 W 112 St, New York, NY 10025 Web Site: www.bankstreet.edu/library/center-for-childrens-literature/the-cook-prize, pg 591

Weiman, Mark, Regent Press Printers & Publishers, 2747 Regent St, Berkeley, CA 94705 Tel: 510-845-1196 E-mail: regentpress@mindspring.com Web Site: www.regentpress.net, pg 174

Weimann, Frank, Folio Literary Management, The Film Center Bldg, 630 Ninth Ave, Suite 1101, New York, NY 10036 Tel: 212-400-1494 Fax: 212-967-0977 Web Site: www.foliolit.com, pg 459

Wein, Lauren, Avid Reader Press, 1230 Avenue of the Americas, New York, NY 10020 Web Site: avidreaderpress.com, pg 23

Weinberg, Alyssa, Henry Holt and Company, LLC, 120 Broadway, 23rd fl, New York, NY 10271 Tel: 646-307-5151 Toll Free Tel: 888-330-8477 (orders) Fax: 646-307-5285 Web Site: www.henryholt.com, pg 94

Weinberg, Edie, Bloomsbury Academic, 1385 Broadway, 5th fl, New York, NY 10018 Tel: 212-419-5300 Web Site: www.bloomsbury.com/us/academic, pg 31

Weinberg, Joy, The Jewish Publication Society, c/o Gratz College, 7605 Old York Rd, Melrose Park, PA 19027 Tel: 215-832-0600 Web Site: www.jps.org; www.nebraskapress.unl.edu/jps/, pg 105

Weinberg, Kathie, Walter Dean Myers Awards for Outstanding Children's Literature, 10319 Westlake Dr, No 104, Bethesda, MD 20817 Tel: 701-404-WNDB (404-9632, voicemail only) E-mail: walteraward@diversebooks.org Web Site: diversebooks.org/our-programs/walter-award, pg 636

Weinberg, Miriam, Tor Publishing Group, 120 Broadway, New York, NY 10271 *Toll Free Tel:* 800-455-0340 (Macmillan) *E-mail:* torpublicity@tor.com; forgepublicity@forgebooks.com *Web Site:* us.macmillan.com/torpublishinggroup, pg 208

Weinberger, Russell, Brockman Inc, 260 Fifth Ave, 10th fl, New York, NY 10001 *Tel:* 212-935-8900 *E-mail:* rights@brockman.com *Web Site:* www.brockman.com, pg 452

Weiner, Allison, Chronicle Books LLC, 680 Second St, San Francisco, CA 94107 *Tel:* 415-537-4200 *Fax:* 415-537-4460 (perms) *E-mail:* hello@chroniclebooks.com; subrights@chroniclebooks.com *Web Site:* www.chroniclebooks.com, pg 48

Weiner, Andy, Harry N Abrams Inc, 195 Broadway, 9th fl, New York, NY 10007 *Tel:* 212-206-7715 *Toll Free Tel:* 800-345-1359 *Fax:* 212-645-8437 *E-mail:* abrams@abramsbooks.com; publicity@abramsbooks.com; sales@abramsbooks.com *Web Site:* www.abramsbooks.com, pg 2

Weiner, Cherry, Cherry Weiner Literary Agency, 925 Oak Bluff Ct, Dacula, GA 30019-6660 *Tel:* 732-446-2096 *E-mail:* cwliteraryagency@gmail.com, pg 481

Weiner, Ruth, Seven Stories Press, 140 Watts St, New York, NY 10013 *Tel:* 212-226-8760 *Toll Free Tel:* 800-733-3000 (orders) *Fax:* 212-226-1411 *E-mail:* sevenstories@sevenstories.com *Web Site:* www.sevenstories.com, pg 186

Weiner, Samantha, Atria Books, 1230 Avenue of the Americas, New York, NY 10020 *Tel:* 212-698-7000 *Fax:* 212-698-7007 *Web Site:* www.simonandschuster.com, pg 21

Weinfield, Madeline, George Bogin Memorial Award, 119 Smith St, Brooklyn, NY 11201 *Tel:* 212-254-9628 *E-mail:* info@poetrysociety.org *Web Site:* poetrysociety.org/awards, pg 582

Weinfield, Madeline, Alice Fay Di Castagnola Award, 119 Smith St, Brooklyn, NY 11201 *Tel:* 212-254-9628 *E-mail:* info@poetrysociety.org *Web Site:* poetrysociety.org/awards, pg 595

Weinfield, Madeline, Norma Farber First Book Award, 119 Smith St, Brooklyn, NY 11201 *Tel:* 212-254-9628 *E-mail:* info@poetrysociety.org *Web Site:* poetrysociety.org/awards, pg 601

Weinfield, Madeline, Four Quartets Prize, 119 Smith St, Brooklyn, NY 11201 *Tel:* 212-254-9628 *E-mail:* info@poetrysociety.org *Web Site:* poetrysociety.org/awards, pg 603

Weinfield, Madeline, Frost Medal, 119 Smith St, Brooklyn, NY 11201 *Tel:* 212-254-9628 *E-mail:* info@poetrysociety.org *Web Site:* poetrysociety.org/awards, pg 605

Weinfield, Madeline, Cecil Hemley Memorial Award, 119 Smith St, Brooklyn, NY 11201 *Tel:* 212-254-9628 *E-mail:* info@poetrysociety.org *Web Site:* poetrysociety.org/awards, pg 612

Weinfield, Madeline, Louise Louis/Emily F Bourne Student Poetry Award, 119 Smith St, Brooklyn, NY 11201 *Tel:* 212-254-9628 *E-mail:* info@poetrysociety.org *Web Site:* poetrysociety.org/awards, pg 626

Weinfield, Madeline, Lyric Poetry Award, 119 Smith St, Brooklyn, NY 11201 *Tel:* 212-254-9628 *E-mail:* info@poetrysociety.org *Web Site:* poetrysociety.org/awards, pg 627

Weinfield, Madeline, Lucille Medwick Memorial Award, 119 Smith St, Brooklyn, NY 11201 *Tel:* 212-254-9628 *E-mail:* info@poetrysociety.org *Web Site:* poetrysociety.org/awards, pg 632

Weinfield, Madeline, Poetry Society of America (PSA), 119 Smith St, Brooklyn, NY 11201 *Tel:* 212-254-9628 *E-mail:* info@poetrysociety.org *Web Site:* poetrysociety.org, pg 517

Weinfield, Madeline, Shelley Memorial Award, 119 Smith St, Brooklyn, NY 11201 *Tel:* 212-254-9628 *E-mail:* info@poetrysociety.org *Web Site:* poetrysociety.org/awards, pg 662

Weinfield, Madeline, William Carlos Williams Award, 119 Smith St, Brooklyn, NY 11201 *Tel:* 212-254-9628 *E-mail:* info@poetrysociety.org *Web Site:* poetrysociety.org/awards, pg 676

Weinfield, Madeline, The Writer Magazine/Emily Dickinson Award, 119 Smith St, Brooklyn, NY 11201 *Tel:* 212-254-9628 *E-mail:* info@poetrysociety.org *Web Site:* poetrysociety.org/awards, pg 678

Weingarden, Matt, American Marketing Association, 130 E Randolph St, 22nd fl, Chicago, IL 60601 *Tel:* 312-542-9000 *Toll Free Tel:* 800-AMA-1150 (262-1150) *Web Site:* www.ama.org, pg 495

Weingarten, Simone, Harvard Square Editions, Beachwood Terr, Hollywood, CA 90068 *Tel:* 323-203-0233 *E-mail:* submissions@harvardsquareeditions.org *Web Site:* harvardsquareeditions.org, pg 88

Weingel-Fidel, Loretta, The Weingel-Fidel Agency, 310 E 46 St, Suite 21-E, New York, NY 10017 *Tel:* 212-599-2959, pg 481

Weinreb, Jenya, Yale University Press, 302 Temple St, New Haven, CT 06511-8909 *Tel:* 203-432-0960; 203-432-0966 (sales); 401-531-2800 (cust serv) *Toll Free Tel:* 800-405-1619 (cust serv) *Fax:* 203-432-0948; 203-432-8485 (sales); 401-531-2801 (cust serv) *Toll Free Fax:* 800-406-9145 (cust serv) *E-mail:* sales.press@yale.edu (sales); customer.care@triliteral.org (cust serv) *Web Site:* www.yalebooks.com; yalepress.yale.edu/yupbooks, pg 235

Weinrich, Curtis, North Star Press of Saint Cloud Inc, 19485 Estes Rd, Clearwater, MN 55320 *Tel:* 320-558-9062 *E-mail:* info@northstarpress.com *Web Site:* www.northstarpress.com, pg 143

Weinstein, Alexander, Summer Writing Seminar, 7 E Pasture Rd, Aquinnah, MA 02535 *Tel:* 954-242-2903 *Web Site:* mvicw.com, pg 558

Weinstein, Dr Cathrin, Thieme Medical Publishers Inc, 333 Seventh Ave, 18th fl, New York, NY 10001 *Tel:* 212-760-0888 *Toll Free Tel:* 800-782-3488 *Fax:* 212-947-1112 *E-mail:* customerservice@thieme.com *Web Site:* www.thieme.com, pg 206

Weintraub, Allison, HarperCollins Children's Books, 195 Broadway, New York, NY 10007 *Tel:* 212-207-7000 *Web Site:* www.harpercollins.com/childrens, pg 85

Weintraub, Dori, St Martin's Press, LLC, 120 Broadway, New York, NY 10271 *E-mail:* publicity@stmartins.com; trademarketing@stmartins.com; foreignrights@stmartins.com *Web Site:* us.macmillan.com/smp, pg 180

Weintraub, Steve, Lawyers & Judges Publishing Co Inc, 917 N Swan Rd, Suite 300, Tucson, AZ 85711 *Tel:* 520-323-1500 *Fax:* 520-323-0055 *E-mail:* sales@lawyersandjudges.com *Web Site:* www.lawyersandjudges.com, pg 113

Weinzimer, Andrea, Hachette Book Group Inc, 1290 Avenue of the Americas, New York, NY 10104 *Tel:* 212-364-1100 *Toll Free Tel:* 800-759-0190 (cust serv) *Fax:* 212-364-0933 (intl orders) *Toll Free Fax:* 800-286-9471 (cust serv) *E-mail:* customer.service@hbgusa.com; orders@hbgusa.com *Web Site:* www.hachettebookgroup.com, pg 83

Weir, Ivy, Quirk Books, 215 Church St, Philadelphia, PA 19106 *Tel:* 215-627-3581 *Fax:* 215-627-5220 *E-mail:* general@quirkbooks.com *Web Site:* www.quirkbooks.com, pg 168

Weisfeld, Jarred, Objective Entertainment, 609 Greenwich St, 6th fl, New York, NY 10014 *Tel:* 212-431-5454 *Web Site:* www.objectiveent.com, pg 471

Weishuhn, Caroline, HarperCollins Publishers LLC, 195 Broadway, New York, NY 10007 *Tel:* 212-207-7000 *Web Site:* www.harpercollins.com, pg 87

Weisman, Jacob, Tachyon Publications LLC, 1459 18 St, No 139, San Francisco, CA 94107 *Tel:* 415-285-5615 *E-mail:* tachyon@tachyonpublications.com; submissions@tachyonpublications.com *Web Site:* www.tachyonpublications.com, pg 202

Weisman, Steven R, Peterson Institute for International Economics (PIIE), 1750 Massachusetts Ave NW, Washington, DC 20036-1903 *Tel:* 202-328-9000 *E-mail:* media@piie.com *Web Site:* piie.com, pg 158

Weiss, Daniel, The Metropolitan Museum of Art, 1000 Fifth Ave, New York, NY 10028 *Tel:* 212-535-7710 *E-mail:* editorial@metmuseum.org *Web Site:* www.metmuseum.org, pg 130

Weiss, Denise, Cold Spring Harbor Laboratory Press, 500 Sunnyside Blvd, Woodbury, NY 11797-2924 *Tel:* 516-422-4100 *Toll Free Tel:* 800-843-4388 *E-mail:* cshpress@cshl.edu *Web Site:* www.cshlpress.com, pg 50

Weiss, Josh, Harry N Abrams Inc, 195 Broadway, 9th fl, New York, NY 10007 *Tel:* 212-206-7715 *Toll Free Tel:* 800-345-1359 *Fax:* 212-645-8437 *E-mail:* abrams@abramsbooks.com; publicity@abramsbooks.com; sales@abramsbooks.com *Web Site:* www.abramsbooks.com, pg 2

Weiss, Kate, Book Industry Charitable Foundation (BINC), 3135 S State St, Suite 203, Ann Arbor, MI 48108 *Toll Free Tel:* 866-733-9064 *E-mail:* info@bincfoundation.org *Web Site:* www.bincfoundation.org, pg 525

Weiss, Kate, Denver Publishing Institute Scholarship, 3135 S State St, Suite 203, Ann Arbor, MI 48108 *Toll Free Tel:* 866-733-9064 *E-mail:* info@bincfoundation.org *Web Site:* www.bincfoundation.org/denver-publishing-institute/, pg 595

Weiss, Kate, Carla Gray Memorial Scholarship, 3135 S State St, Suite 203, Ann Arbor, MI 48108 *Toll Free Tel:* 866-733-9064 *E-mail:* info@bincfoundation.org *Web Site:* www.bincfoundation.org/carla-gray/, pg 609

Weiss, Kate, Higher Education Scholarship Program, 3135 S State St, Suite 203, Ann Arbor, MI 48108 *Toll Free Tel:* 866-733-9064 *E-mail:* info@bincfoundation.org *Web Site:* www.bincfoundation.org/scholarship, pg 612

Weiss, Kate, Susan Kamil Scholarship for Emerging Writers, 3135 S State St, Suite 203, Ann Arbor, MI 48108 *Toll Free Tel:* 866-733-9064 *E-mail:* info@bincfoundation.org *Web Site:* bincfoundation.org/susankamil-scholarship, pg 619

Weiss, Kate, George Markey Keating Memorial Scholarships, 3135 S State St, Suite 203, Ann Arbor, MI 48108 *Toll Free Tel:* 866-733-9064 *E-mail:* info@bincfoundation.org *Web Site:* www.bincfoundation.org, pg 619

Weiss, Kate, Macmillan Booksellers Professional Development Scholarship, 3135 S State St, Suite 203, Ann Arbor, MI 48108 *Toll Free Tel:* 866-733-9064 *E-mail:* info@bincfoundation.org *Web Site:* www.bincfoundation.org/scholarship, pg 628

Weiss, Kate, Karl Pohrt Tribute Award, 3135 S State St, Suite 203, Ann Arbor, MI 48108 *Toll Free Tel:* 866-733-9064 *E-mail:* info@bincfoundation.org *Web Site:* www.bincfoundation.org/scholarship, pg 651

Weiss, Laura, Independent Artist Awards, 175 W Ostend St, Suite E, Baltimore, MD 21230 *Tel:* 410-767-6555 *E-mail:* msac.commerce@maryland.gov *Web Site:* www.msac.org/programs/independent-artist-award, pg 615

Weiss, Mitchel, Endless Mountains Publishing Co, 72 Glenmaura National Blvd, Suite 104B, Moosic, PA 18507 *Tel:* 862-251-2296 *E-mail:* info@endlessmountainspublishing.com *Web Site:* kalaniotbooks.com, pg 66

Weiss, Mitchel, Kalaniot Books, 72 Glenmaura National Blvd, Suite 104B, Moosic, PA 18507 *Tel:* 862-251-2296; 570-451-6095 *E-mail:* info@kalaniotbooks.com *Web Site:* www.kalaniotbooks.com, pg 107

Weiss, Sara, Random House Publishing Group, 1745 Broadway, New York, NY 10019 *Toll Free Tel:* 800-200-3552 *Web Site:* www.randomhousebooks.com, pg 171

Weiss, Steven, Transcontinental Music Publications (TMP), 1375 Remington Rd, Suite M, Schaumburg, IL 60173-4844 *Tel:* 847-781-7800 *Fax:* 847-781-7801 *E-mail:* tmp@accantors.org *Web Site:* www.transcontinentalmusic.com, pg 209

Weisser, Deborah, Sentient Publications LLC, PO Box 1851, Boulder, CO 80306 Tel: 303-443-2188 E-mail: contact@sentientpublications.com Web Site: www.sentientpublications.com, pg 186

Weisskopf, Toni, Baen Books, PO Box 1188, Wake Forest, NC 27588 Tel: 919-570-1640 Fax: 919-570-1644 E-mail: info@baen.com Web Site: www.baen.com, pg 23

Weissman, Dana, Writers Guild of America, East (WGAE), 250 Hudson St, Suite 700, New York, NY 10013 Tel: 212-767-7800 Fax: 212-582-1909 Web Site: www.wgaeast.org, pg 522

Weissman, Molly, Simon & Schuster, LLC, 1230 Avenue of the Americas, New York, NY 10020 Tel: 212-698-7000 Toll Free Tel: 800-223-2336 (orders) Fax: 212-698-7007 Toll Free Fax: 800-943-9831 (orders) E-mail: firstname.lastname@simonandschuster.com; purchaseorders@simonandschuster.com (orders) Web Site: www.simonandschuster.com, pg 190

Weissman, Robert, Public Citizen, 1600 20 St NW, Washington, DC 20009 Tel: 202-588-1000 Web Site: www.citizen.org, pg 167

Weissner, Pat, Women Who Write Inc, PO Box 652, Madison, NJ 07940-0652 Web Site: www.womenwhowrite.org, pg 522

Weitzner, Tess, Frances Goldin Literary Agency, Inc, 214 W 29 St, Suite 410, New York, NY 10001 Tel: 212-777-0047 Fax: 212-228-1660 E-mail: agency@goldinlit.com Web Site: www.goldinlit.com, pg 460

Wejko, Alexa, Soho Press Inc, 853 Broadway, New York, NY 10003 Tel: 212-260-1900 E-mail: soho@sohopress.com; publicity@sohopress.com Web Site: sohopress.com, pg 193

Welby, Alexis, GP Putnam's Sons, c/o Penguin Random House LLC, 1745 Broadway, New York, NY 10019 Tel: 212-782-9000 Web Site: www.penguin.com/putnam/, pg 167

Welch, Andrea, Simon & Schuster Children's Publishing, 1230 Avenue of the Americas, New York, NY 10020 Tel: 212-698-7000 Web Site: www.simonandschuster.com/kids; www.simonandschuster.com/teen; simonandschuster.net; simonandschuster.biz, pg 189

Welch, Jazmin, Arsenal Pulp Press, 211 E Georgia St, No 202, Vancouver, BC V6A 1Z6, Canada Tel: 604-687-4233 Toll Free Tel: 888-600-PULP (600-7857) Fax: 604-687-4283 E-mail: info@arsenalpulp.com Web Site: www.arsenalpulp.com, pg 395

Welch, Laura, Master Books®, 3142 Hwy 103 N, Green Forest, AR 72638 Tel: 870-438-5288 Toll Free Tel: 800-999-3777 E-mail: sales@masterbooks.com; nlp@nlpg.com; submissions@newleafpress.net Web Site: www.masterbooks.com; www.nlpg.com, pg 126

Welch, Laura, New Leaf Press, 3142 Hwy 103 N, Green Forest, AR 72638-2233 Tel: 870-438-5288 Toll Free Tel: 800-999-3777 Fax: 870-438-5120 E-mail: submissions@nlpg.com Web Site: www.nlpg.com, pg 140

Welch, Sally R, Ohio University Press, Alden Library, Suite 101, 30 Park Place, Athens, OH 45701-2909 Tel: 740-593-1154 Web Site: www.ohioswallow.com, pg 146

Welch, Sally R, Swallow Press, Alden Library, Suite 101, 30 Park Place, Athens, OH 45701-2909 Tel: 740-593-1154 Web Site: www.ohioswallow.com, pg 201

Welch, Shannon, Avid Reader Press, 1230 Avenue of the Americas, New York, NY 10020 Web Site: avidreaderpress.com, pg 23

Weller, Lesley, Ferguson Publishing, 132 W 31 St, 16 fl, New York, NY 10001 Tel: 212-967-8800 Toll Free Tel: 800-322-8755 Toll Free Fax: 800-678-3633 E-mail: custserv@infobase.com Web Site: infobasepublishing.com, pg 71

Weller, Lisa, Eisenbrauns, 820 N University Dr, USB 1, Suite C, University Park, PA 16802-1003 Tel: 814-865-1327 Toll Free Tel: 800-326-9180 (orders & cust serv) Fax: 814-863-1408 Toll Free Fax: 877-778-2665 (orders) E-mail: orders@psupress.org; customerservice@psupress.org Web Site: www.eisenbrauns.org, pg 64

Welling, Brent, Center for the Collaborative Classroom, 1001 Marina Village Pkwy, Suite 110, Alameda, CA 94501-1042 Tel: 510-533-0213 Toll Free Tel: 800-666-7270 Fax: 510-464-3670 E-mail: info@collaborativeclassroom.org; clientsupport@collaborativeclassroom.org Web Site: www.collaborativeclassroom.org, pg 44

Wellnitz, Clare, University of California Press, 155 Grand Ave, Suite 400, Oakland, CA 94612-3758 Tel: 510-883-8232 Fax: 510-836-8910 E-mail: customerservice@ucpress.edu Web Site: www.ucpress.edu, pg 215

Wells, Jason M, American Psychological Association, 750 First St NE, Washington, DC 20002 Tel: 202-336-5510 Toll Free Tel: 800-374-2721 Fax: 202-336-5502 E-mail: order@apa.org; booksales@apa.org Web Site: www.apa.org/books, pg 12

Wells, Jessica, Penguin Random House LLC, 1745 Broadway, New York, NY 10019 Tel: 212-782-9000 Toll Free Tel: 800-726-0600 Web Site: www.penguinrandomhouse.com, pg 155

Wells, Katrina Altersitz, SLACK® Incorporated, A Wyanoke Group Company, 6900 Grove Rd, Thorofare, NJ 08086-9447 Tel: 856-848-1000 Toll Free Tel: 800-257-8290 Fax: 856-848-6091 E-mail: sales@slackinc.com; editor@slackinc.com; customerservice@slackinc.com Web Site: www.healio.com/books, pg 191

Wells, Phyllis, University of Georgia Press, Main Library, 3rd fl, 320 S Jackson St, Athens, GA 30602 Fax: 706-542-2558; 706-542-6770 Web Site: www.ugapress.org, pg 216

Wells, Thomas, University of Tennessee Press, 323 Hodges Library, 1015 Volunteer Blvd, Knoxville, TN 37996 Tel: 865-974-3321 Toll Free Tel: 800-621-2736 (orders) Toll Free Fax: 800-621-2736 (orders) E-mail: custserv@utpress.org Web Site: www.utpress.org, pg 220

Wells-Arms, Victoria, HG Literary, 6 W 18 St, Suite 7R, New York, NY 10011 E-mail: foreign@hgliterary.com; rights@hgliterary.com Web Site: www.hgliterary.com, pg 463

Welsh, Kara, Penguin Random House LLC, 1745 Broadway, New York, NY 10019 Tel: 212-782-9000 Toll Free Tel: 800-726-0600 Web Site: www.penguinrandomhouse.com, pg 155

Welsh, Kara, Random House Publishing Group, 1745 Broadway, New York, NY 10019 Toll Free Tel: 800-200-3552 Web Site: www.randomhousebooks.com, pg 170

Welty, Tara, Scholastic Education Solutions, 557 Broadway, New York, NY 10012 Tel: 212-343-6100 Fax: 212-343-6189 Web Site: www.scholastic.com, pg 184

Weltz, Jennifer, Jean V Naggar Literary Agency Inc (JVNLA), 216 E 75 St, Suite 1-E, New York, NY 10021 Tel: 212-794-1082 E-mail: jvnla@jvnla.com Web Site: www.jvnla.com, pg 471

Wendrich, Willeke, Cotsen Institute of Archaeology Press, 308 Charles E Young Dr N, Fowler A210, Box 951510, Los Angeles, CA 90095 Tel: 310-206-9384 Fax: 310-206-4723 E-mail: cioapress@ioa.ucla.edu Web Site: www.ioa.ucla.edu, pg 53

Wenerstrom, Megan, Portfolio, c/o Penguin Random House LLC, 1745 Broadway, New York, NY 10019 Tel: 212-782-9000 Web Site: www.penguin.com/portfolio-overview/; www.penguin.com/sentinel-overview/; www.penguin.com/thesis/, pg 162

Wenger, Charlotte, Prospect Agency, 551 Valley Rd, PMB 337, Upper Montclair, NJ 07043 Tel: 718-788-3217 Web Site: www.prospectagency.com, pg 472

Wengerd, Marvin, Carlisle Press - Walnut Creek, 2593 Township Rd 421, Sugarcreek, OH 44681 Tel: 330-852-1900 Toll Free Tel: 800-852-4482 Fax: 330-852-3285 E-mail: cpress@cprinting.com, pg 40

Wentworth, Jillian, United for Libraries, 225 N Michigan Ave, Suite 1300, Chicago, IL 60601 Tel: 312-280-2161 Toll Free Tel: 800-545-2433 (ext 2161) E-mail: united@ala.org Web Site: www.ala.org/united, pg 521

Wentworth, Sara, Macmillan, 120 Broadway, 22nd fl, New York, NY 10271 E-mail: press.inquiries@macmillan.com Web Site: us.macmillan.com, pg 122

Wenzel, Kelly Atkinson, Penguin Random House Audio Publishing Group, 1745 Broadway, New York, NY 10019 Toll Free Tel: 800-793-2665 (cust serv) E-mail: audio@penguinrandomhouse.com; ecustomerservice@penguinrandomhouse.com Web Site: www.penguinrandomhouseaudio.com, pg 154

Werden, Barbara, Mandel Vilar Press, 19 Oxford Ct, Simsbury, CT 06070 Tel: 806-790-4731 E-mail: info@mvpress.org Web Site: www.mvpublishers.org, pg 124

Werksman, Deb, Sourcebooks LLC, 1935 Brookdale Rd, Suite 139, Naperville, IL 60563 Tel: 630-961-3900 Toll Free Tel: 800-432-7444 Fax: 630-961-2168 E-mail: info@sourcebooks.com Web Site: www.sourcebooks.com, pg 194

Werner, Doug, Tracks Publishing, 458 Dorothy Ave, Ventura, CA 93003 Tel: 805-754-0248 E-mail: tracks@cox.net Web Site: www.startupsports.com, pg 208

Werner, Rebecca, PEN America, 120 Broadway, 26th fl N, New York, NY 10271 Tel: 212-334-1660 Fax: 212-334-2181 E-mail: info@pen.org; membership@pen.org; education@pen.org Web Site: pen.org, pg 516

Wertz, Chloe, University of Pittsburgh Press, 7500 Thomas Blvd, Pittsburgh, PA 15260 Tel: 412-383-2456 Fax: 412-383-2466 E-mail: info@upress.pitt.edu Web Site: www.upress.pitt.edu, pg 219

Wescott, T C, New York Academy of Sciences (NYAS), 7 World Trade Center, 40th fl, 250 Greenwich St, New York, NY 10007-2157 Tel: 212-298-8600 Toll Free Tel: 800-843-6927 Fax: 212-298-3650 E-mail: nyas@nyas.org; annals@nyas.org; customerservice@nyas.org Web Site: www.nyas.org, pg 140

Wesley, Mark, me+mi publishing inc, 2600 Beverly Dr, Unit 113, Aurora, IL 60502 Tel: 630-588-9801 Toll Free Tel: 888-251-1444 Web Site: www.memima.com, pg 128

Wesley, Stephen, Columbia University Press, 61 W 62 St, New York, NY 10023 Tel: 212-459-0600 Toll Free Tel: 800-944-8648 Fax: 212-459-3678 Web Site: cup.columbia.edu, pg 51

Wessell, Todd, Midwest Travel Journalists Association Inc (MTJA), PO Box 185, Jessup, IA 50648 Tel: 319-529-1109 E-mail: admin@mtja.us Web Site: www.mtja.us, pg 511

West, Abby, HarperCollins Publishers LLC, 195 Broadway, New York, NY 10007 Tel: 212-207-7000 Web Site: www.harpercollins.com, pg 86

West, Alexandra, HarperCollins Children's Books, 195 Broadway, New York, NY 10007 Tel: 212-207-7000 Web Site: www.harpercollins.com/childrens, pg 85

West, Ann, Mazda Publishers Inc, PO Box 2603, Costa Mesa, CA 92628 Tel: 714-751-5252 Fax: 714-751-4805 E-mail: mazdapub@aol.com Web Site: www.mazdapublishers.com, pg 127

West, Deb, Iowa Writers' Workshop, Graduate Program in Creative Writing, 102 Dey House, Iowa City, IA 52242-1000 Tel: 319-335-0416 Web Site: writersworkshop.uiowa.edu, pg 555

West, Krista, University of Alaska Press, Elmer E Rasmuson Library, 1732 Tanana Loop, Suite 402, Fairbanks, AK 99775 Tel: 907-474-5831 Toll Free Tel: 888-252-6657 (US only) Fax: 907-474-5502 Web Site: www.alaska.edu/uapress, pg 214

West, Rebecca, The Association of English-Language Publishers of Quebec-AELAQ (Association des Editeurs de Langue Anglaise du Quebec), Atwater Library, 1200 Atwater Ave, Suite 3, Westmount, QC H3Z 1X4, Canada Tel: 514-932-5633 E-mail: admin@aelaq.org Web Site: aelaq.org, pg 499

West, Salem, Bywater Books Inc, 3415 Porter Rd, Ann Arbor, MI 48103 Tel: 734-662-8815 Web Site: bywaterbooks.com, pg 39

Westermann, Christian, Harry N Abrams Inc, 195 Broadway, 9th fl, New York, NY 10007 Tel: 212-206-7715 Toll Free Tel: 800-345-1359 Fax: 212-645-8437 E-mail: abrams@abramsbooks.com; publicity@abramsbooks.com; sales@abramsbooks.com Web Site: www.abramsbooks.com, pg 3

Westervelt, Brianna, Andrews McMeel Publishing LLC, 1130 Walnut St, Kansas City, MO 64106-2109 Tel: 816-581-7500 Toll Free Tel: 800-851-8923 Web Site: www.andrewsmcmeel.com; publishing.andrewsmcmeel.com, pg 14

Westfall, William, Barbour Publishing Inc, 1810 Barbour Dr, Uhrichsville, OH 44683 Tel: 740-922-6045 Fax: 740-922-5948 E-mail: info@barbourbooks.com Web Site: www.barbourbooks.com, pg 24

Westlund, Laura, University of Minnesota Press, 111 Third Ave S, Suite 290, Minneapolis, MN 55401-2520 Tel: 612-301-1990 Fax: 612-301-1980 E-mail: ump@umn.edu Web Site: www.upress.umn.edu, pg 217

Weston, Pamela, Research & Education Association (REA), 258 Prospect Plains Rd, Cranbury, NJ 08512 Toll Free Tel: 833-591-2798 (cust care) Fax: 516-742-5049 (orders) E-mail: info@rea.com Web Site: www.rea.com, pg 174

Westra, Jessica, Zondervan, 3900 Sparks Dr SE, Grand Rapids, MI 49546 Tel: 616-698-6900 Toll Free Tel: 800-226-1122; 800-727-1309 (retail orders) Fax: 616-698-3350 Toll Free Fax: 800-698-3256 (retail orders) E-mail: customercare@harpercollins.com Web Site: www.zondervan.com, pg 236

Wetter, Erica, Stanford University Press, 425 Broadway St, Redwood City, CA 94063-3126 Tel: 650-723-9434 Fax: 650-725-3457 E-mail: info@www.sup.org; publicity@www.sup.org; sales@www.sup.org Web Site: www.sup.org, pg 197

Wetzel, Liz, Basic Books Group, 1290 Avenue of the Americas, New York, NY 10104 Tel: 212-340-8100 Toll Free Tel: 800-343-4499 (cust serv) Fax: 212-340-8105 E-mail: customer.service@hbgusa.com; orders@hbgusa.com Web Site: www.hachettebookgroup.com/imprint/basic-books/, pg 25

Wetzel, Lucas, Andrews McMeel Publishing LLC, 1130 Walnut St, Kansas City, MO 64106-2109 Tel: 816-581-7500 Toll Free Tel: 800-851-8923 Web Site: www.andrewsmcmeel.com; publishing.andrewsmcmeel.com, pg 14

Wetzler, Sam, Random House Publishing Group, 1745 Broadway, New York, NY 10019 Toll Free Tel: 800-200-3552 Web Site: www.randomhousebooks.com, pg 171

Wexler, Chuck, Police Executive Research Forum, 1120 Connecticut Ave NW, Suite 930, Washington, DC 20036 Tel: 202-466-7820 Web Site: www.policeforum.org, pg 162

Wexler, Daniella, HarperCollins Publishers LLC, 195 Broadway, New York, NY 10007 Tel: 212-207-7000 Web Site: www.harpercollins.com, pg 86

Wexler, David, Carolrhoda Books Inc, 241 First Ave N, Minneapolis, MN 55401 Tel: 612-332-3344 Toll Free Tel: 800-328-4929 Fax: 612-332-7615 Toll Free Fax: 800-332-1132 E-mail: info@lernerbooks.com; custserve@lernerbooks.com Web Site: www.lernerbooks.com; www.facebook.com/lernerbooks, pg 41

Wexler, David, Carolrhoda Lab™, 241 First Ave N, Minneapolis, MN 55401 Tel: 612-332-3344 Toll Free Tel: 800-328-4929 Fax: 612-332-7615 Toll Free Fax: 800-332-1132 E-mail: info@lernerbooks.com; custserve@lernerbooks.com Web Site: www.lernerbooks.com; www.facebook.com/lernerbooks, pg 41

Wexler, David, ediciones Lerner, 241 First Ave N, Minneapolis, MN 55401 Tel: 612-332-3344 Toll Free Tel: 800-328-4929 Fax: 612-332-7615 Toll Free Fax: 800-332-1132 E-mail: info@lernerbooks.com; custserve@lernerbooks.com Web Site: www.lernerbooks.com; www.facebook.com/lernerbooks, pg 63

Wexler, David, First Avenue Editions, 241 First Ave N, Minneapolis, MN 55401 Tel: 612-332-3344 Toll Free Tel: 800-328-4929 Fax: 612-332-7615 Toll Free Fax: 800-332-1132 E-mail: info@lernerbooks.com; custserve@lernerbooks.com Web Site: www.lernerbooks.com; www.facebook.com/lernerbooks, pg 72

Wexler, David, Graphic Universe™, 241 First Ave N, Minneapolis, MN 55401 Tel: 612-332-3344 Toll Free Tel: 800-328-4929 Fax: 612-332-7615 Toll Free Fax: 800-332-1132 E-mail: info@lernerbooks.com; custserve@lernerbooks.com Web Site: www.lernerbooks.com; www.facebook.com/lernerbooks, pg 80

Wexler, David, Lerner Publications, 241 First Ave N, Minneapolis, MN 55401 Tel: 612-332-3344 Toll Free Tel: 800-328-4929 Fax: 612-332-7615 Toll Free Fax: 800-332-1132 E-mail: info@lernerbooks.com; custserve@lernerbooks.com Web Site: www.lernerbooks.com; www.facebook.com/lernerbooks, pg 115

Wexler, David, Lerner Publishing Group Inc, 241 First Ave N, Minneapolis, MN 55401 Tel: 612-332-3344 Toll Free Tel: 800-328-4929 Fax: 612-332-7615 Toll Free Fax: 800-332-1132 E-mail: info@lernerbooks.com; custserve@lernerbooks.com Web Site: www.lernerbooks.com; www.facebook.com/lernerbooks, pg 115

Wexler, David, LernerClassroom, 241 First Ave N, Minneapolis, MN 55401 Tel: 612-332-3344 Toll Free Tel: 800-328-4929 Fax: 612-332-7615 Toll Free Fax: 800-332-1132 E-mail: info@lernerbooks.com; custserve@lernerbooks.com Web Site: www.lernerbooks.com; www.facebook.com/lernerbooks, pg 115

Wexler, David, Millbrook Press, 241 First Ave N, Minneapolis, MN 55401 Tel: 612-332-3344 Toll Free Tel: 800-328-4929 Fax: 612-332-7615 Toll Free Fax: 800-332-1132 E-mail: info@lernerbooks.com; custserve@lernerbooks.com Web Site: www.lernerbooks.com; www.facebook.com/millbrookpress, pg 131

Wexler, David, Twenty-First Century Books, 241 First Ave N, Minneapolis, MN 55401 Tel: 612-332-3344 Toll Free Tel: 800-328-4929 Fax: 612-332-7615 Toll Free Fax: 800-332-1132 E-mail: info@lernerbooks.com; custserve@lernerbooks.com Web Site: www.lernerbooks.com; www.facebook.com/lernerbooks, pg 211

Wexler, David, Zest Books, 241 First Ave N, Minneapolis, MN 55401 Tel: 612-332-3344 Toll Free Tel: 800-328-4929 Toll Free Fax: 800-332-1132 E-mail: info@lernerbooks.com; publicity@lernerbooks.com; custserve@lernerbooks.com (orders) Web Site: lernerbooks.com, pg 236

Wexler, Pearl, The Kohner Agency, 9300 Wilshire Blvd, Suite 300, Beverly Hills, CA 90212 Tel: 310-550-1060 Web Site: kohneragency.com, pg 466

Weyl, Debbie, World Resources Institute, 10 "G" St NE, Suite 800, Washington, DC 20002 Tel: 202-729-7600 Fax: 202-729-7610 Web Site: www.wri.org, pg 233

Whalen, Anastasia, Penguin Random House Speakers Bureau, a Penguin Random House company, 1745 Broadway, Mail Drop 13-1, New York, NY 10019 Tel: 212-572-2013 E-mail: speakers@penguinrandomhouse.com Web Site: www.prhspeakers.com, pg 487

Whalen, John III, Cider Mill Press Book Publishers LLC, 501 Nelson Place, Nashville, TN 37214 Toll Free Tel: 800-250-5308 E-mail: focuscc@harpercollins.com Web Site: www.cidermillpress.com, pg 48

Whalen, Megan, Random House Publishing Group, 1745 Broadway, New York, NY 10019 Toll Free Tel: 800-200-3552 Web Site: www.randomhousebooks.com, pg 171

Whaley, Glenn, STM Learning Inc, 1220 Paddock Dr, Florissant, MO 63033 Tel: 314-434-2424 E-mail: info@stmlearning.com; orders@stmlearning.com Web Site: www.stmlearning.com, pg 199

Whaley, Marianne, STM Learning Inc, 1220 Paddock Dr, Florissant, MO 63033 Tel: 314-434-2424 E-mail: info@stmlearning.com; orders@stmlearning.com Web Site: www.stmlearning.com, pg 199

Whatley, Stacy Brooks, American Counseling Association (ACA), 6101 Stevenson Ave, Suite 600, Alexandria, VA 22304 Tel: 703-823-9800 Toll Free Tel: 800-298-2276 Toll Free Fax: 800-473-2329 E-mail: orders@counseling.org (book orders) Web Site: www.counseling.org, pg 9

Whatnall, Michaela, Dystel, Goderich & Bourret LLC, One Union Sq W, Suite 904, New York, NY 10003 Tel: 212-627-9100 Fax: 212-627-9313 Web Site: www.dystel.com, pg 457

Wheaton, Robert, Doubleday Canada, 320 Front St W, Suite 1400, Toronto, ON M5V 3B6, Canada Tel: 416-364-4449 Toll Free Tel: 416-598-7764 Web Site: www.penguinrandomhouse.ca, pg 401

Wheaton, Robert, Knopf Canada, 320 Front St W, Suite 1400, Toronto, ON M5V 3B6, Canada Tel: 416-364-4449 Toll Free Tel: 888-523-9292 Fax: 416-598-7764 Web Site: www.penguinrandomhouse.ca, pg 411

Wheaton, Robert, Penguin Random House Canada, a Penguin Random House company, 320 Front St W, Suite 1400, Toronto, ON M5V 3B6, Canada Tel: 416-364-4449 Toll Free Tel: 888-523-9292 (cust serv) E-mail: canadaweb@penguinrandomhouse.com; customerservicescanada@penguinrandomhouse.com Web Site: www.penguinrandomhouse.ca, pg 415

Wheaton, Robert, Seal Books, 320 Front St W, Suite 1400, Toronto, ON M5V 3B6, Canada Tel: 416-364-4449 Toll Free Tel: 888-523-9292 (order desk) Fax: 416-598-7764 Web Site: www.penguinrandomhouse.ca, pg 428

Wheeler, Betsy, Juniper Summer Writing Institute, c/o University Conference Services, 810 Campus Center, One Campus Center Way, Amherst, MA 01003 Tel: 413-545-5503 E-mail: juniperinstitute@hfa.umass.edu Web Site: www.umass.edu/juniperinstitute, pg 555

Wheeler, Laura, Thomas Nelson, 501 Nelson Place, Nashville, TN 37214 Tel: 615-889-9000 Toll Free Tel: 800-251-4000 Web Site: www.thomasnelson.com, pg 206

Wheeler, Laura, Zondervan, 3900 Sparks Dr SE, Grand Rapids, MI 49546 Tel: 616-698-6900 Toll Free Tel: 800-226-1122; 800-727-1309 (retail orders) Fax: 616-698-3350 Toll Free Fax: 800-698-3256 (retail orders) E-mail: customercare@harpercollins.com Web Site: www.zondervan.com, pg 237

Wheeler, Meg, Westwood Creative Artists Ltd, 386 Huron St, Toronto, ON M5S 2G6, Canada Tel: 416-964-3302 Fax: 416-964-3302 E-mail: wca_office@wcaltd.com Web Site: www.wcaltd.com, pg 481

Wheeler, Noa, Bloomsbury Publishing Inc, 1385 Broadway, 5th fl, New York, NY 10018 Tel: 212-419-5300 E-mail: marketingusa@bloomsbury.com; adultpublicityusa@bloomsbury.com; askacademic@bloomsbury.com Web Site: www.bloomsbury.com, pg 31

Whelan, Maria, Princeton University Press, 41 William St, Princeton, NJ 08540-5237 Tel: 609-258-4900 Fax: 609-258-6305 E-mail: info@press.princeton.edu Web Site: press.princeton.edu, pg 164

Whelchel, Sandy, National Writers Association, 10940 S Parker Rd, Suite 508, Parker, CO 80134 Tel: 303-656-7235 E-mail: natlwritersassn@hotmail.com Web Site: www.nationalwriters.com, pg 514

Whelchel, Sandy, National Writers Association Novel Contest, 10940 S Parker Rd, Suite 508, Parker, CO 80134 Tel: 303-656-7235 E-mail: natlwritersassn@hotmail.com Web Site: www.nationalwriters.com, pg 638

Whisler, Kirk, International Latino Book Awards, 624 Hillcrest Lane, Fallbrook, CA 92028 Tel: 760-689-2317 E-mail: awards@empoweringlatinofutures.org Web Site: www.latinobookawards.org; www.empoweringlatinofutures.org, pg 617

Whisler, Kirk, International Society of Latino Authors (ISLA), c/o Empowering Latino Futures, 624 Hillcrest Lane, Fallbrook, CA 92084 *Tel:* 760-689-2317 *Fax:* 760-434-7476 *Web Site:* isla.news, pg 508

Whisler, Kirk, Latino Books Into Movies Awards, 624 Hillcrest Lane, Fallbrook, CA 92028 *Tel:* 760 645-3455 (submission info); 760-689-2317 *E-mail:* awards@empoweringlatinofutures.org *Web Site:* www.latinobookawards.org, pg 622

Whitaker, Theresa M, Medieval Institute Publications (MIP), Western Michigan University, Walwood Hall, 1903 W Michigan Ave, Mail Stop 5432, Kalamazoo, MI 49008-5432 *Tel:* 269-387-8755 *Web Site:* wmich.edu/medievalpublications, pg 129

Whitcher, Sarah, Poetry Foundation, 61 W Superior St, Chicago, IL 60654 *Tel:* 312-787-7070 *E-mail:* info@poetryfoundation.org *Web Site:* www.poetryfoundation.org, pg 526

Whitcomb, Laurel, Television Academy, 5220 Lankershim Blvd, North Hollywood, CA 91601-3109 *Tel:* 818-754-2800 *Web Site:* www.emmys.com, pg 521

White, Craig M, EDC Publishing, 5402 S 122 E Ave, Tulsa, OK 74146 *Tel:* 918-622-4522 *Toll Free Tel:* 800-475-4522 *Fax:* 918-663-2525 *Toll Free Fax:* 800-743-5660 *E-mail:* orders@edcpub.com *Web Site:* www.edcpub.com, pg 63

White, Deryck, The Society of Naval Architects & Marine Engineers (SNAME), 99 Canal Center Plaza, Suite 310, Alexandria, VA 22314 *Tel:* 703-997-6701 *Toll Free Tel:* 800-798-2188 *Fax:* 703-997-6702 *Web Site:* www.sname.org, pg 193

White, Elizabeth, The Monacelli Press, 65 Bleecker St, 8th fl, New York, NY 10012 *Tel:* 212-652-5400 *E-mail:* contact@monacellipress.com *Web Site:* www.phaidon.com/monacelli, pg 133

White, Emily, Mountaineers Books, 1001 SW Klickitat Way, Suite 201, Seattle, WA 98134 *Tel:* 206-223-6303 *Fax:* 206-223-6306 *E-mail:* mbooks@mountaineersbooks.org; customerservice@mountaineersbooks.org *Web Site:* www.mountaineers.org/books, pg 135

White, Enola-Riann, Jackie White Memorial National Children's Playwriting Contest, 1800 Nelwood Dr, Columbia, MO 65202 *Web Site:* www.cectheatre.org, pg 617

White, Eric, Kalmbach Media Co, 21027 Crossroads Circle, Waukesha, WI 53186 *Tel:* 262-796-8776 *Web Site:* www.kalmbach.com, pg 108

White, Howard, Harbour Publishing Co Ltd, 4437 Rondeview Rd, Madeira Park, BC V0N 2H0, Canada *Tel:* 604-883-2730 *Toll Free Tel:* 800-667-2988 *Fax:* 604-883-9451 *Toll Free Fax:* 877-604-9449 *E-mail:* info@harbourpublishing.com; orders@harbourpublishing.com *Web Site:* harbourpublishing.com, pg 408

White, Hudson, Ocean Tree Books, 1325 Cerro Gordo Rd, Santa Fe, NM 87501 *Tel:* 505-983-1412 *Fax:* 505-983-0899 *E-mail:* richard@oceantree.com *Web Site:* www.oceantree.com, pg 145

White, Katherine, University of New Mexico Press, One University of New Mexico, Albuquerque, NM 87131-0001 *Tel:* 505-272-7777 *Fax:* 505-277-3343 *E-mail:* custserv@unm.edu (order dept) *Web Site:* unmpress.com, pg 218

White, Ken, Book Industry Charitable Foundation (BINC), 3135 S State St, Suite 203, Ann Arbor, MI 48108 *Toll Free Tel:* 866-733-9064 *E-mail:* info@bincfoundation.org *Web Site:* www.bincfoundation.org, pg 525

White, Ken, Denver Publishing Institute Scholarship, 3135 S State St, Suite 203, Ann Arbor, MI 48108 *Toll Free Tel:* 866-733-9064 *E-mail:* info@bincfoundation.org *Web Site:* www.bincfoundation.org/denver-publishing-institute/, pg 595

White, Ken, Carla Gray Memorial Scholarship, 3135 S State St, Suite 203, Ann Arbor, MI 48108 *Toll Free Tel:* 866-733-9064 *E-mail:* info@bincfoundation.org *Web Site:* www.bincfoundation.org/carla-gray/, pg 609

White, Ken, Higher Education Scholarship Program, 3135 S State St, Suite 203, Ann Arbor, MI 48108 *Toll Free Tel:* 866-733-9064 *E-mail:* info@bincfoundation.org *Web Site:* www.bincfoundation.org/scholarship, pg 612

White, Ken, Susan Kamil Scholarship for Emerging Writers, 3135 S State St, Suite 203, Ann Arbor, MI 48108 *Toll Free Tel:* 866-733-9064 *E-mail:* info@bincfoundation.org *Web Site:* bincfoundation.org/susankamil-scholarship, pg 619

White, Ken, George Markey Keating Memorial Scholarships, 3135 S State St, Suite 203, Ann Arbor, MI 48108 *Toll Free Tel:* 866-733-9064 *E-mail:* info@bincfoundation.org *Web Site:* www.bincfoundation.org, pg 619

White, Ken, Macmillan Booksellers Professional Development Scholarship, 3135 S State St, Suite 203, Ann Arbor, MI 48108 *Toll Free Tel:* 866-733-9064 *E-mail:* info@bincfoundation.org *Web Site:* www.bincfoundation.org/scholarship, pg 628

White, Ken, Karl Pohrt Tribute Award, 3135 S State St, Suite 203, Ann Arbor, MI 48108 *Toll Free Tel:* 866-733-9064 *E-mail:* info@bincfoundation.org *Web Site:* www.bincfoundation.org/scholarship, pg 651

White, Melissa, Folio Literary Management, The Film Center Bldg, 630 Ninth Ave, Suite 1101, New York, NY 10036 *Tel:* 212-400-1494 *Fax:* 212-967-0977 *Web Site:* www.folioIit.com, pg 459

White, Nancy, The Tenth Gate Prize, PO Box 42164, Washington, DC 20015 *E-mail:* editor@wordworksbooks.org *Web Site:* www.wordworksbooks.org, pg 668

White, Nancy, Word Works Washington Prize, PO Box 42164, Washington, DC 20015 *E-mail:* editor@wordworksbooks.org *Web Site:* www.wordworksbooks.org, pg 677

White, Pippa, Harry N Abrams Inc, 195 Broadway, 9th fl, New York, NY 10007 *Tel:* 212-206-7715 *Toll Free Tel:* 800-345-1359 *Fax:* 212-645-8437 *E-mail:* abrams@abramsbooks.com; publicity@abramsbooks.com; sales@abramsbooks.com *Web Site:* www.abramsbooks.com, pg 2

White, Shane, Wm B Eerdmans Publishing Co, 4035 Park East Ct SE, Grand Rapids, MI 49546 *Tel:* 616-459-4591 *Toll Free Tel:* 800-253-7521 *E-mail:* customerservice@eerdmans.com; sales@eerdmans.com *Web Site:* www.eerdmans.com, pg 64

White, Travis, Psychological Assessment Resources Inc (PAR), 16204 N Florida Ave, Lutz, FL 33549 *Tel:* 813-449-4065 *Toll Free Tel:* 800-331-8378 *Fax:* 813-961-2196 *Toll Free Fax:* 800-727-9329 *Web Site:* www.parinc.com, pg 166

White, Wendell, Willow Creek Press, 9931 Hwy 70 W, Minocqua, WI 54548 *Tel:* 715-358-7010 *Toll Free Tel:* 800-850-9453 *Fax:* 715-358-2807 *E-mail:* info@willowcreekpress.com *Web Site:* www.willowcreekpress.com; www.wcpretail.com, pg 230

Whiteway, Doug, Signature Editions, PO Box 206, RPO Corydon, Winnipeg, MB R3M 3S7, Canada *Tel:* 204-779-7803 *E-mail:* signature@allstream.net; orders@signature-editions.com *Web Site:* www.signature-editions.com, pg 419

Whiting, Elizabeth, Scholastic Trade Publishing, 557 Broadway, New York, NY 10012 *Tel:* 212-343-6100; 212-343-4685 (export sales) *Fax:* 212-343-4714 (export sales) *Web Site:* www.scholastic.com, pg 184

Whitman, Mara, The Graduate Group/Booksellers, 86 Norwood Rd, West Hartford, CT 06117-2236 *Tel:* 860-233-2330 *E-mail:* graduategroup@hotmail.com *Web Site:* www.graduategroup.com, pg 80

Whitman, Robert, The Graduate Group/Booksellers, 86 Norwood Rd, West Hartford, CT 06117-2236 *Tel:* 860-233-2330 *E-mail:* graduategroup@hotmail.com *Web Site:* www.graduategroup.com, pg 80

Whitney, April, Chronicle Books LLC, 680 Second St, San Francisco, CA 94107 *Tel:* 415-537-4200 *Fax:* 415-537-4460 (perms) *E-mail:* hello@chroniclebooks.com; subrights@chroniclebooks.com *Web Site:* www.chroniclebooks.com, pg 47

Whitney, Nick, Soho Press Inc, 853 Broadway, New York, NY 10003 *Tel:* 212-260-1900 *E-mail:* soho@sohopress.com; publicity@sohopress.com *Web Site:* sohopress.com, pg 193

Whitson, Skip, Sun Publishing Company, PO Box 5588, Santa Fe, NM 87502-5588 *Tel:* 505-471-5177; 505-660-0704 *Toll Free Tel:* 877-849-0051 *E-mail:* info@sunbooks.com *Web Site:* www.sunbooks.com; abooksource.com, pg 200

Whitt, Lindsey, Farrar, Straus & Giroux Books for Young Readers, 120 Broadway, New York, NY 10271 *Tel:* 212-741-6900 *Toll Free Tel:* 888-330-8477 (orders) *E-mail:* childrens.publicity@macmillanusa.com; childrensrights@macmillanusa.com *Web Site:* us.macmillan.com/mackids, pg 70

Whitt, Lindsey, Roaring Brook Press, 120 Broadway, New York, NY 10271 *Tel:* 646-307-5151 *Web Site:* us.macmillan.com/publishers/roaring-brook-press, pg 176

Wickers, Chandler, Stuart Krichevsky Literary Agency Inc, 118 E 28 St, Suite 908, New York, NY 10016 *Tel:* 212-725-5288 *Fax:* 212-725-5275 *E-mail:* query@skagency.com *Web Site:* skagency.com, pg 466

Widdicombe, Elizabeth, Macmillan Learning, One New York Plaza, Suite 46, New York, NY 10004 *Tel:* 212-576-9400 *E-mail:* salesoperations@macmillanusa.com *Web Site:* www.macmillanlearning.com/college/us, pg 123

Wieckowski, Ania, Harvard Business Review Press, 20 Guest St, Suite 700, Brighton, MA 02135 *Tel:* 617-783-7400 *Fax:* 617-783-7489 *E-mail:* custserv@hbsp.harvard.edu *Web Site:* www.harvardbusiness.org, pg 87

Wiegers, Michael, Copper Canyon Press, Fort Worden State Park, Bldg 313, Port Townsend, WA 98368 *Tel:* 360-385-4925 *E-mail:* poetry@coppercanyonpress.org; publicity@coppercanyonpress.org; digitalcontent@coppercanyonpress.com *Web Site:* www.coppercanyonpress.org, pg 52

Wielgosz, Kathy, Farrar, Straus & Giroux Books for Young Readers, 120 Broadway, New York, NY 10271 *Tel:* 212-741-6900 *Toll Free Tel:* 888-330-8477 (orders) *E-mail:* childrens.publicity@macmillanusa.com; childrensrights@macmillanusa.com *Web Site:* us.macmillan.com/mackids, pg 70

Wielgosz, Kathy, Roaring Brook Press, 120 Broadway, New York, NY 10271 *Tel:* 646-307-5151 *Web Site:* us.macmillan.com/publishers/roaring-brook-press, pg 176

Wiener, Jessica, Harry N Abrams Inc, 195 Broadway, 9th fl, New York, NY 10007 *Tel:* 212-206-7715 *Toll Free Tel:* 800-345-1359 *Fax:* 212-645-8437 *E-mail:* abrams@abramsbooks.com; publicity@abramsbooks.com; sales@abramsbooks.com *Web Site:* www.abramsbooks.com, pg 2

Wiener, M Markus, Markus Wiener Publishers Inc, 231 Nassau St, Princeton, NJ 08542 *Tel:* 609-921-1141 *E-mail:* publisher@markuswiener.com *Web Site:* www.markuswiener.com, pg 229

Wiener, Robert K, Donald M Grant Publisher Inc, 19 Surrey Lane, Hampton Falls, NH 03844 *Tel:* 603-778-7191 *Fax:* 603-778-7191 *Web Site:* secure.grantbooks.com, pg 80

Wier, Mark, American Civil Liberties Union (ACLU), 125 Broad St, 18th fl, New York, NY 10004 *Tel:* 212-549-2500 *E-mail:* media@aclu.org *Web Site:* www.aclu.org, pg 495

Wiese, Michael, Michael Wiese Productions, 12400 Ventura Blvd, No 1111, Studio City, CA 91604 *Tel:* 818-379-8799 *Toll Free Tel:* 800-833-5738 (orders) *Fax:* 818-986-3408 *E-mail:* mwpsales@earthlink.net; fulfillment@portcity.com *Web Site:* www.mwp.com, pg 229

Wiese, Nancy, Hachette Book Group Inc, 1290 Avenue of the Americas, New York, NY 10104 *Tel:* 212-364-1100 *Toll Free Tel:* 800-759-0190 (cust serv) *Fax:* 212-364-0933 (intl orders) *Toll Free Fax:* 800-286-9471 (cust serv) *E-mail:* customer.service@hbgusa.com; orders@hbgusa.com *Web Site:* www.hachettebookgroup.com, pg 83

Wiesenberg, Julia, Kent State University Press, 1118 University Library Bldg, 1125 Risman Dr, Kent, OH 44242 Tel: 330-672-7913 Fax: 330-672-3104 E-mail: ksupress@kent.edu Web Site: www.kentstateuniversitypress.com, pg 109

Wiess, Kathy, Europa Editions, 27 Union Sq W, Suite 302, New York, NY 10003 Tel: 212-868-6844 Fax: 212-868-6845 E-mail: info@europaeditions.com; books@europaeditions.com; publicity@europaeditions.com Web Site: www.europaeditions.com, pg 67

Wigdor, Julia, Knopf Canada, 320 Front St W, Suite 1400, Toronto, ON M5V 3B6, Canada Tel: 416-364-4449 Toll Free Tel: 888-523-9292 Fax: 416-598-7764 Web Site: www.penguinrandomhouse.ca, pg 411

Wiggins, Leonard, Penguin Random House Audio Publishing Group, 1745 Broadway, New York, NY 10019 Toll Free Tel: 800-793-2665 (cust serv) E-mail: audio@penguinrandomhouse.com; ecustomerservice@penguinrandomhouse.com Web Site: www.penguinrandomhouseaudio.com, pg 154

Wight, Katy, Edward Elgar Publishing Inc, The William Pratt House, 9 Dewey Ct, Northampton, MA 01060-3815 Tel: 413-584-5551 Toll Free Tel: 800-390-3149 (orders) Fax: 413-584-9933 E-mail: elgarinfo@e-elgar.com; elgarsales@e-elgar.com; elgarsubmissions@e-elgar.com (edit) Web Site: www.e-elgar.com; www.elgaronline.com (ebooks & journals), pg 65

Wikey, Daniel, Random House Publishing Group, 1745 Broadway, New York, NY 10019 Toll Free Tel: 800-200-3552 Web Site: www.randomhousebooks.com, pg 171

Wilcox, Alana, Coach House Books, 80 bpNichol Lane, Toronto, ON M5S 3J4, Canada Tel: 416-979-2217 Toll Free Tel: 800-367-6360 (outside Toronto) Fax: 416-977-1158 E-mail: mail@chbooks.com Web Site: www.chbooks.com, pg 400

Wilcox, Diane L, Mazda Publishers Inc, PO Box 2603, Costa Mesa, CA 92628 Tel: 714-751-5252 Fax: 714-751-4805 E-mail: mazdapub@aol.com Web Site: www.mazdapublishers.com, pg 127

Wilcox, Jeanne, Quincannon Publishing Group, PO Box 8100, Glen Ridge, NJ 07028-8100 Tel: 973-380-9942 E-mail: editors@quincannongroup.com (query first via e-mail) Web Site: www.quincannongroup.com, pg 168

Wilcox, Lynn, Syracuse University Press, 621 Skytop Rd, Suite 110, Syracuse, NY 13244-5290 Tel: 315-443-5534 Toll Free Tel: 800-365-8929 (cust serv) Fax: 315-443-5545 E-mail: supress@syr.edu Web Site: press.syr.edu, pg 201

Wilder, Elizabeth, The University of Arizona Press, 1510 E University Blvd, Tucson, AZ 85721 Tel: 520-621-1441 Toll Free Tel: 800-621-2736 (orders) Fax: 520-621-8899 Toll Free Fax: 800-621-8476 (orders) E-mail: uap@uapress.arizona.edu Web Site: www.uapress.arizona.edu, pg 214

Wilderson, Joe, Rocky Mountain Books Ltd (RMB), 103-1075 Pendergast St, Victoria, BC V8V 0A1, Canada Tel: 250-360-0829 Fax: 250-386-0829 Web Site: rmbooks.com, pg 418

Wiles, Patricia, Society of Children's Book Writers & Illustrators (SCBWI), 6363 Wilshire Blvd, Suite 425, Los Angeles, CA 90048 Tel: 323-782-1010 E-mail: membership@scbwi.org Web Site: www.scbwi.org, pg 520

Wiley, Jesse C, John Wiley & Sons Inc, 111 River St, Hoboken, NJ 07030-5774 Tel: 201-748-6000 Toll Free Tel: 800-225-5945 (cust serv) Fax: 201-748-6088 Web Site: www.wiley.com, pg 230

Wilhelm, Sharona, Scarsdale Publishing Ltd, 333 Mamaroneck Ave, White Plains, NY 10607 E-mail: scarsdale@scarsdalepublishing.com Web Site: scarsdalepublishing.com, pg 183

Wilhite, Sue, COVR Visionary Awards, PO Box 1397, Palmer Lake, CO 80133 Tel: 719-487-0424 E-mail: info@covr.org Web Site: covr.org/awards, pg 592

Wilke, Crissy, One-Act Playwriting Competition, 600 Wolfe St, Alexandria, VA 22314 Tel: 703-683-5778 (ext 2) Fax: 703-683-1378 E-mail: oneactslta@gmail.com Web Site: thelittletheatre.com, pg 644

Wilkes, Deborah, Focus, PO Box 390007, Cambridge, MA 02139-0001 Tel: 317-635-9250 Fax: 317-635-9292 E-mail: customer@hackettpublishing.com; editorial@hackettpublishing.com Web Site: focusbookstore.com; www.hackettpublishing.com, pg 73

Wilkes, Deborah, Hackett Publishing Co Inc, 3333 Massachusetts Ave, Indianapolis, IN 46218 Tel: 317-635-9250 (orders & cust serv); 617-497-6303 (edit off & sales) Fax: 317-635-9292; 617-661-8703 (edit off) Toll Free Fax: 800-783-9213 E-mail: customer@hackettpublishing.com; editorial@hackettpublishing.com Web Site: www.hackettpublishing.com, pg 84

Wilkie, Devin, Steerforth Press & Services, 31 Hanover St, Suite 1, Lebanon, NH 03766 Tel: 603-643-4787 Fax: 603-643-4788 E-mail: info@steerforth.com Web Site: www.steerforth.com, pg 198

Wilkins, Timothy, Princeton University Press, 41 William St, Princeton, NJ 08540-5237 Tel: 609-258-4900 Fax: 609-258-6305 E-mail: info@press.princeton.edu Web Site: press.princeton.edu, pg 164

Wilkinson, Crystal, The University Press of Kentucky, 663 S Limestone St, Lexington, KY 40508-4008 Tel: 859-257-8400 Fax: 859-323-1873 Web Site: www.kentuckypress.com, pg 222

Wilks, Rick, Annick Press Ltd, 388 Carlaw Ave, Suite 200, Toronto, ON M4M 2T4, Canada Tel: 416-221-4802 Fax: 416-221-8400 E-mail: annickpress@annickpress.com Web Site: www.annickpress.com, pg 395

Will-Thapa, Jen, Hedgebrook Radical Craft Retreats, PO Box 1231, Freeland, WA 98249 Tel: 360-321-4786 E-mail: hedgebrook@hedgebrook.org Web Site: www.hedgebrook.org/radical-craft-retreats; www.facebook.com/hedgebrook, pg 554

Will-Thapa, Jen, Hedgebrook VorTEXT Intensives Writing Retreat, PO Box 1231, Freeland, WA 98249 Tel: 360-321-4786 E-mail: hedgebrook@hedgebrook.org; programs@hedgebrook.org Web Site: www.hedgebrook.org/vortext; www.facebook.com/hedgebrook, pg 554

Will-Thapa, Jen, Hedgebrook Writers in Residence Program, PO Box 1231, Freeland, WA 98249 Tel: 360-321-4786 E-mail: hedgebrook@hedgebrook.org; programs@hedgebrook.org Web Site: www.hedgebrook.org/writers-in-residence; www.facebook.com/hedgebrook, pg 554

Willett, Susan, Dog Writers Association of America Inc (DWAA), PO Box 787, Hughesville, MD 20637 Web Site: dogwriters.org, pg 505

Willett, Susan, Dog Writers Association of America Inc (DWAA) Annual Writing Competition, PO Box 787, Hughesville, MD 20637 Web Site: dogwriters.org, pg 596

Willey, Paul, The Book Tree, 3316 Adams Ave, Suite A, San Diego, CA 92116 Tel: 619-280-1263 Toll Free Tel: 800-700-8733 (orders) Fax: 619-280-1285 E-mail: orders@thebooktree.com; info@thebooktree.com Web Site: thebooktree.com, pg 34

Willey, Susan, New Readers Press, 104 Marcellus, Syracuse, NY 13204 Tel: 315-422-9121 Toll Free Tel: 800-448-8878 Toll Free Fax: 866-894-2100 E-mail: nrp@proliteracy.org Web Site: www.newreaderspress.com, pg 140

Williams, Alexis, New Millennium Awards for Fiction, Poetry & Nonfiction, 821 Indian Gap Rd, Sevierville, TN 37876 Tel: 865-254-4880 E-mail: hello@newmillenniumwritings.org Web Site: newmillenniumwritings.org, pg 640

Williams, Amber, Picador, 120 Broadway, New York, NY 10271 Tel: 646-307-5151 Fax: 212-253-9627 E-mail: publicity@picadorusa.com Web Site: us.macmillan.com/picador, pg 159

Williams, Angela, Goose Lane Editions, 500 Beaverbrook Ct, Suite 330, Fredericton, NB E3B 5X4, Canada Tel: 506-450-4251 Toll Free Tel: 888-926-8377 Fax: 506-459-4991 E-mail: orders@gooselane.com Web Site: www.gooselane.com, pg 407

Williams, Belinda, News Leaders Association (NLA), 209 Reynolds Journalism Institute, Missouri School of Journalism, Columbia, MO 65211 Tel: 202-964-0912 E-mail: contact@newsleaders.org Web Site: www.newsleaders.org, pg 514

Williams, Briana, Bloomsbury Publishing Inc, 1385 Broadway, 5th fl, New York, NY 10018 Tel: 212-419-5300 E-mail: marketingusa@bloomsbury.com; adultpublicityusa@bloomsbury.com; askacademic@bloomsbury.com Web Site: www.bloomsbury.com, pg 32

Williams, Carolyn, Doubleday, c/o Penguin Random House LLC, 1745 Broadway, New York, NY 10019 Tel: 212-751-2600 Fax: 212-940-7390 (dom rts); 212-572-2662 (foreign rts) Web Site: knopfdoubleday.com/imprint/doubleday/; knopfdoubleday.com, pg 61

Williams, Christin, Yaddo Artists Residency, 312 Union Ave, Saratoga Springs, NY 12866 Tel: 518-584-0746 Fax: 518-584-1312 Web Site: www.yaddo.org, pg 559

Williams, Claude, Harry N Abrams Inc, 195 Broadway, 9th fl, New York, NY 10007 Tel: 212-206-7715 Toll Free Tel: 800-345-1359 Fax: 212-645-8437 E-mail: abrams@abramsbooks.com; publicity@abramsbooks.com; sales@abramsbooks.com Web Site: www.abramsbooks.com, pg 3

Williams, Dan, TCU Press, 3000 Sandage Ave, Fort Worth, TX 76109 Tel: 817-257-7822 E-mail: tcupress@tcu.edu Web Site: www.tcupress.com, pg 203

Williams, Emily, Little, Brown and Company, 1290 Avenue of the Americas, New York, NY 10104 Tel: 212-364-1100 Fax: 212-364-0952 E-mail: firstname.lastname@hbgusa.com Web Site: www.hachettebookgroup.com/imprint/little-brown-and-company/, pg 118

Williams, Faith, Samuel French, Inc, 250 W 57 St, 6th fl, New York, NY 10107-0102 Toll Free Tel: 866-979-0447 E-mail: info@concordtheatricals.com Web Site: www.concordtheatricals.com/a/4346/samuel-a-french, pg 75

Williams, Harrison, Interlink Publishing Group Inc, 46 Crosby St, Northampton, MA 01060 Tel: 413-582-7054 Toll Free Tel: 800-238-LINK (238-5465) E-mail: info@interlinkbooks.com; publicity@interlinkbooks.com; sales@interlinkbooks.com Web Site: www.interlinkbooks.com, pg 102

Williams, Jackie, The Knight Agency Inc, 232 W Washington St, Madison, GA 30650 E-mail: admin@knightagency.net Web Site: www.knightagency.net, pg 466

Williams, Jane A, Bluestocking Press, 3045 Sacramento St, No 1014, Placerville, CA 95667-1014 Tel: 530-622-8586 Toll Free Tel: 800-959-8586 Fax: 530-642-9222 E-mail: customerservice@bluestockingpress.com; orders@bluestockingpress.com Web Site: www.bluestockingpress.com, pg 33

Williams, Jasper, Stellar Publishing, 2114 S Live Oak Pkwy, Wilmington, NC 28403 Tel: 910-269-7444 Web Site: www.stellar-publishing.com, pg 198

Williams, Jessica, HarperCollins Publishers LLC, 195 Broadway, New York, NY 10007 Tel: 212-207-7000 Web Site: www.harpercollins.com, pg 86

Williams, John Taylor "Ike", Calligraph LLC, 45 Main St, No 850, Brooklyn, NY 11201 Tel: 212-253-1074 E-mail: mail@calligraphlit.com; rights@calligraphlit.com; submissions@calligraphlit.com Web Site: www.calligraphlit.com, pg 453

Williams, Josh, Triumph Books LLC, 814 N Franklin St, Chicago, IL 60610 Tel: 312-337-0747 Toll Free Tel: 800-888-4741 (cust serv) Fax: 312-280-5470; 312-337-5985 Web Site: www.triumphbooks.com, pg 210

Williams, Kaiulani, Penguin Random House LLC, 1745 Broadway, New York, NY 10019 Tel: 212-782-9000 Toll Free Tel: 800-726-0600 Web Site: www.penguinrandomhouse.com, pg 155

Williams, Kim, Princeton University Press, 41 William St, Princeton, NJ 08540-5237 *Tel:* 609-258-4900 *Fax:* 609-258-6305 *E-mail:* info@press.princeton.edu *Web Site:* press.princeton.edu, pg 164

Williams, Kyle, WendyLynn & Co, 2705 Willow Hill Rd, Annapolis, MD 21403 *Tel:* 410-533-5766 *Web Site:* wendylynn.com, pg 486

Williams, Leita, Penguin Random House LLC, 1745 Broadway, New York, NY 10019 *Tel:* 212-782-9000 *Toll Free Tel:* 800-726-0600 *Web Site:* www.penguinrandomhouse.com, pg 155

Williams, Lisa, US Government Publishing Office (GPO), Superintendent of Documents, 732 N Capitol St NW, Washington, DC 20401 *Tel:* 202-512-1800 *Toll Free Tel:* 866-512-1800 (orders) *Fax:* 202-512-1998 *E-mail:* contactcenter@gpo.gov *Web Site:* www.gpo.gov; bookstore.gpo.gov (sales), pg 223

Williams, Matt, House of Anansi Press Inc, 128 Sterling Rd, Lower Level, Toronto, ON M6R 2B7, Canada *Tel:* 416-363-4343 *Fax:* 416-363-1017 *E-mail:* customerservice@houseofanansi.com *Web Site:* houseofanansi.com, pg 409

Williams, Megan, Penguin Random House LLC, 1745 Broadway, New York, NY 10019 *Tel:* 212-782-9000 *Toll Free Tel:* 800-726-0600 *Web Site:* www.penguinrandomhouse.com, pg 155

Williams, Michelle, Chicago Review Press, 814 N Franklin St, Chicago, IL 60610 *Tel:* 312-337-0747 *Toll Free Tel:* 800-888-4741 *Fax:* 312-337-5110 *E-mail:* frontdesk@chicagoreviewpress.com *Web Site:* www.chicagoreviewpress.com, pg 46

Williams, Paul, American Society of Composers, Authors & Publishers (ASCAP), 250 W 57 St, New York, NY 10107 *Tel:* 212-621-6000 *Toll Free Tel:* 800-952-7227 (cust serv) *Fax:* 212-621-6595 *Web Site:* www.ascap.com, pg 496

Williams, Randall, NewSouth Books, 105 S Court St, Montgomery, AL 36104 *Tel:* 334-834-3556 *E-mail:* info@newsouthbooks.com *Web Site:* www.newsouthbooks.com, pg 141

Williams, Rob, Mountain Press Publishing Co, 1301 S Third W, Missoula, MT 59801 *Tel:* 406-728-1900 *Toll Free Tel:* 800-234-5308 *Fax:* 406-728-1635 *E-mail:* info@mtnpress.com *Web Site:* www.mountain-press.com, pg 135

Williams, Roger S, Roger Williams Agency, 17 Paddock Dr, Lawrence Twp, NJ 08648 *Tel:* 860-973-2439 *E-mail:* roger@rogerwilliamsagency.com *Web Site:* www.rogerwilliamsagency.com, pg 482

Williams, Roslynn, Dun & Bradstreet, 103 JFK Pkwy, Short Hills, NJ 07078 *Tel:* 973-921-5500 *Toll Free Tel:* 844-869-8244; 800-234-3867 (cust serv) *Web Site:* www.dnb.com, pg 62

Williams, Sarah, Penguin Random House LLC, 1745 Broadway, New York, NY 10019 *Tel:* 212-782-9000 *Toll Free Tel:* 800-726-0600 *Web Site:* www.penguinrandomhouse.com, pg 155

Williams, Stephanie, Wayne State University Press, Leonard N Simons Bldg, 4809 Woodward Ave, Detroit, MI 48201-1309 *Tel:* 313-577-6120 *Toll Free Tel:* 800-978-7323 *Fax:* 313-577-6131 *E-mail:* bookorders@wayne.edu *Web Site:* www.wsupress.wayne.edu, pg 226

Williams, Stephen, Indiana University Press, Off of Scholarly Publg, Herman B Wells Library 350, 1320 E Tenth St, Bloomington, IN 47405-3907 *Tel:* 812-855-8817 *Fax:* 812-855-7931; 812-855-8507 *E-mail:* iupress@indiana.edu *Web Site:* iupress.org, pg 100

Williams, Taylor, Portfolio, c/o Penguin Random House LLC, 1745 Broadway, New York, NY 10019 *Tel:* 212-782-9000 *Web Site:* www.penguin.com/portfolio-overview/; www.penguin.com/sentinel-overview/; www.penguin.com/thesis/, pg 162

Williams, Thomas A PhD, Williams & Company Book Publishers, 1317 Pine Ridge Dr, Savannah, GA 31406 *Tel:* 912-352-0404 *E-mail:* bookpub@comcast.net, pg 230

Williams, Tia, Poets & Writers Inc, 90 Broad St, Suite 2100, New York, NY 10004 *Tel:* 212-226-3586 *Fax:* 212-226-3963 *E-mail:* admin@pw.org *Web Site:* www.pw.org, pg 517

Williams, Tishana, Simon & Schuster Children's Publishing, 1230 Avenue of the Americas, New York, NY 10020 *Tel:* 212-698-7000 *Web Site:* www.simonandschuster.com/kids; www.simonandschuster.com/teen; simonandschuster.net; simonandschuster.biz, pg 189

Williams, Wendy, Workman Publishing, 1290 Avenue of the Americas, New York, NY 10104 *Toll Free Tel:* 800-759-0190 *Fax:* 212-364-0950 *E-mail:* workman-inquiry@hbgusa.com *Web Site:* www.hachettebookgroup.com/imprint/workman-publishing-company/, pg 232

Williams-Sullivan, Jessica, Graywolf Press, 212 Third Ave N, Suite 485, Minneapolis, MN 55401 *Tel:* 651-641-0077 *Fax:* 651-641-0036 *E-mail:* wolves@graywolfpress.org (no ms queries, sample chapters or proposals) *Web Site:* www.graywolfpress.org, pg 81

Williamson, Alain, Editions Le Dauphin Blanc Inc, 825, blvd Lebourgneuf, Suite 125, Quebec, QC G2J 0B9, Canada *Tel:* 418-845-4045 *Fax:* 418-845-1933 *E-mail:* info@dauphinblanc.com *Web Site:* dauphinblanc.com, pg 404

Williamson, Heather, Penguin Random House LLC, 1745 Broadway, New York, NY 10019 *Tel:* 212-782-9000 *Toll Free Tel:* 800-726-0600 *Web Site:* www.penguinrandomhouse.com, pg 155

Williamson, Iain, OECD Washington Center, 1776 "I" St NW, Suite 450, Washington, DC 20006 *Tel:* 202-785-6323 *Toll Free Tel:* 800-456-6323 (dist ctr/pubns orders) *Fax:* 202-785-0350 *E-mail:* washington.contact@oecd.org; oecdilibrary@oecd.org (sales) *Web Site:* www.oecd-ilibrary.org, pg 145

Williamson, Iain, Productive Publications, 380 Brooke Ave, Lower Level, North York, ON M5M 2L6, Canada *Tel:* 416-483-0634 *Toll Free Tel:* 877-879-2669 (orders) *Fax:* 416-322-7434 *E-mail:* productivepublications@rogers.com *Web Site:* www.productivepublications.ca, pg 417

Williamson, Jeff, World Book Inc, 180 N LaSalle, Suite 900, Chicago, IL 60601 *Tel:* 312-729-5800 *Toll Free Tel:* 800-967-5325 (consumer sales, US); 800-975-3250 (school & lib sales, US); 800-837-5365 (school & lib sales, CN) *Toll Free Fax:* 888-922-3766 *E-mail:* customerservice@worldbook.com *Web Site:* www.worldbook.com, pg 233

Williamson, Lesley, Artists & Writers Summer Fellowships, 435 Ellis Hollow Creek Rd, Ithaca, NY 14850 *Tel:* 607-539-3146 *E-mail:* artscolony@saltonstall.org *Web Site:* www.saltonstall.org, pg 553

Williford, Lex, University of Texas at El Paso, Department of Creative Writing, MFA/Department of Creative Writing, M520, University Towers, Oregon St, El Paso, TX 79968 *E-mail:* creativewriting@utep.edu *Web Site:* www.utep.edu/liberalarts/creative-writing, pg 567

Willig, Robert, SME (Society of Manufacturing Engineers), 1000 Town Ctr, Suite 1910, Southfield, MI 48075 *Tel:* 313-425-3000 *Toll Free Tel:* 800-733-4763 (cust serv) *Fax:* 313-425-3400 *E-mail:* publications@sme.org *Web Site:* www.sme.org, pg 191

Willinger, James L, Wide World of Maps Inc, 2133 E Indian School Rd, Phoenix, AZ 85016 *Tel:* 602-279-2323 *Toll Free Tel:* 800-279-7654 *Web Site:* www.maps4u.com, pg 229

Willis, Clarissa, Ozark Creative Writers Inc Annual Conference, c/o 900 W Dixson St, Rogers, AR 72758 *E-mail:* ozarkcreativewriters@ozarkcreativewriters.com *Web Site:* www.ozarkcreativewriters.com, pg 556

Willis, Lisa, Cave Canem Foundation Inc, 20 Jay St, Suite 310-A, Brooklyn, NY 11201-8301 *Tel:* 718-858-0000 *Fax:* 718-858-0002 *E-mail:* info@ccpoets.org *Web Site:* cavecanempoets.org, pg 525

Willis, Lisa, Cave Canem Northwestern University Press Poetry Prize, 20 Jay St, Suite 310-A, Brooklyn, NY 11201-8301 *Tel:* 718-858-0000 *Fax:* 718-858-0002 *E-mail:* info@ccpoets.org *Web Site:* cavecanempoets.org/prizes/cave-canem-northwestern-university-press-poetry-prize/, pg 587

Willis, Lisa, Cave Canem Poetry Prize, 20 Jay St, Suite 310-A, Brooklyn, NY 11201-8301 *Tel:* 718-858-0000 *Fax:* 718-858-0002 *E-mail:* info@ccpoets.org *Web Site:* cavecanempoets.org/prizes/cave-canem-poetry-prize/, pg 587

Willis, Meredith Sue, Hamilton Stone Editions, PO Box 43, Maplewood, NJ 07040 *Tel:* 973-378-8361 *E-mail:* hstone@hamiltonstone.org *Web Site:* www.hamiltonstone.org, pg 84

Willis, Wayne, University of Chicago Press, 1427 E 60 St, Chicago, IL 60637-2954 *Tel:* 773-702-7700; 773-702-7600 *Toll Free Tel:* 800-621-2736 (orders) *Fax:* 773-702-9756; 773-660-2235 (orders); 773-702-2708 *E-mail:* custserv@press.uchicago.edu; marketing@press.uchicago.edu *Web Site:* www.press.uchicago.edu, pg 215

Wills, April, Sourcebooks LLC, 1935 Brookdale Rd, Suite 139, Naperville, IL 60563 *Tel:* 630-961-3900 *Toll Free Tel:* 800-432-7444 *Fax:* 630-961-2168 *E-mail:* info@sourcebooks.com *Web Site:* www.sourcebooks.com, pg 194

Wills, Jennifer, The Seymour Agency, 475 Miner Street Rd, Canton, NY 13617 *Tel:* 239-398-8209 *Web Site:* www.theseymouragency.com, pg 475

Wills, Juliet, Galaxy Press Inc, 7051 Hollywood Blvd, Los Angeles, CA 90028 *Tel:* 323-466-3310 *Toll Free Tel:* 877-8GALAXY (842-5299) *E-mail:* info@galaxypress.com; customers@galaxypress.com *Web Site:* www.galaxypress.com, pg 75

Wills, Lydia, Lydia Wills LLC, 5344 N Paulina, 3F, Chicago, IL 60660 *Tel:* 917-292-8314 *E-mail:* lydiawills@gmail.com *Web Site:* www.lydiawills.com, pg 482

Wills, Nicole, HarperCollins Children's Books, 195 Broadway, New York, NY 10007 *Tel:* 212-207-7000 *Web Site:* www.harpercollins.com/childrens, pg 86

Willshire, Tom, Cambridge University Press, One Liberty Plaza, 20th fl, New York, NY 10006 *Tel:* 212-924-3900; 212-337-5000 *Fax:* 212-691-3239; 845-353-4141 *E-mail:* customer_service@cambridge.org; orders@cambridge.org; subscriptions_newyork@cambridge.org *Web Site:* www.cambridge.org/us, pg 39

Willson, Donna, Macmillan, 120 Broadway, 22nd fl, New York, NY 10271 *E-mail:* press.inquiries@macmillan.com *Web Site:* us.macmillan.com, pg 122

Wilson, Adam, Disney-Hyperion Books, 1101 Flower St, Glendale, CA 91201 *Web Site:* books.disney.com/imprint/disney-hyperion, pg 59

Wilson, Amy E, Trafalgar Square Books, 388 Howe Hill Rd, North Pomfret, VT 05053 *Tel:* 802-457-1911 *Toll Free Tel:* 800-423-4525 *Fax:* 802-457-1913 *E-mail:* contact@trafalgarbooks.com *Web Site:* www.trafalgarbooks.com; www.horseandriderbooks.com, pg 208

Wilson, Bev, Information Gatekeepers Inc (IGI), PO Box 606, Winchester, MA 01890 *Tel:* 617-782-5033 *Fax:* 617-507-8338 *E-mail:* info@igigroup.com *Web Site:* www.igigroup.com, pg 100

Wilson, Bob, Sunrise River Press, 838 Lake St S, Forrest Lake, MN 55025 *Tel:* 651-277-1400 *Toll Free Tel:* 800-895-4585 *E-mail:* info@sunriseriverpress.com; sales@sunriseriverpress.com *Web Site:* www.sunriseriverpress.com, pg 201

Wilson, Cristina, Sourcebooks LLC, 1935 Brookdale Rd, Suite 139, Naperville, IL 60563 *Tel:* 630-961-3900 *Toll Free Tel:* 800-432-7444 *Fax:* 630-961-2168 *E-mail:* info@sourcebooks.com *Web Site:* www.sourcebooks.com, pg 195

Wilson, Deborah, The Authors Guild® Foundation, 31 E 32 St, Suite 901, New York, NY 10016 *Tel:* 212-563-5904 *Fax:* 212-564-5363 *E-mail:* staff@authorsguild.org *Web Site:* authorsguild.org/foundation, pg 525

Wilson, Gary, Green Dragon Books, 2275 Ibis Isle Rd W, Palm Beach, FL 33480 Tel: 561-533-6231 Toll Free Tel: 800-874-8844 Fax: 561-533-6233 Toll Free Fax: 888-874-8844 E-mail: info@greendragonbooks.com Web Site: greendragonbooks.com, pg 81

Wilson, Jaclyn, Wesleyan University Press, 215 Long Lane, Middletown, CT 06459-0433 Tel: 860-685-7712 Fax: 860-685-7712 Web Site: www.wesleyan.edu/wespress, pg 227

Wilson, Jamia, Random House Publishing Group, 1745 Broadway, New York, NY 10019 Toll Free Tel: 800-200-3552 Web Site: www.randomhousebooks.com, pg 170

Wilson, JD, University of Alabama Press, 200 Hackberry Lane, 2nd fl, Tuscaloosa, AL 35487 Tel: 205-348-5180 Fax: 205-348-9201 Web Site: www.uapress.ua.edu, pg 214

Wilson, Jennifer, Green Dragon Books, 2275 Ibis Isle Rd W, Palm Beach, FL 33480 Tel: 561-533-6231 Toll Free Tel: 800-874-8844 Fax: 561-533-6233 Toll Free Fax: 888-874-8844 E-mail: info@greendragonbooks.com Web Site: greendragonbooks.com, pg 81

Wilson, Jocie, Pacific Northwest Young Reader's Choice Award, c/o Jocie Wilson, Yellowhead Regional Library, 433 King St, Spruce Grove, AB T7X 2C6, Canada E-mail: yrcachair@gmail.com Web Site: www.pnla.org/yrca, pg 645

Wilson, Julie, Penguin Random House Audio Publishing Group, 1745 Broadway, New York, NY 10019 Toll Free Tel: 800-793-2665 (cust serv) E-mail: audio@penguinrandomhouse.com; ecustomerservice@penguinrandomhouse.com Web Site: www.penguinrandomhouseaudio.com, pg 154

Wilson, Kate Silverman, Grant Program for Diverse Voices, One Broadway, 12th fl, Cambridge, MA 02142 Web Site: mitpress.mit.edu/grant-program-diverse-voices, pg 608

Wilson, Laura, Penguin Random House Audio Publishing Group, 1745 Broadway, New York, NY 10019 Toll Free Tel: 800-793-2665 (cust serv) E-mail: audio@penguinrandomhouse.com; ecustomerservice@penguinrandomhouse.com Web Site: www.penguinrandomhouseaudio.com, pg 154

Wilson, Lauren, Bloomsbury Publishing Inc, 1385 Broadway, 5th fl, New York, NY 10018 Tel: 212-419-5300 E-mail: marketingusa@bloomsbury.com; adultpublicityusa@bloomsbury.com; askacademic@bloomsbury.com Web Site: www.bloomsbury.com, pg 32

Wilson, Leah, BenBella Books Inc, 10440 N Central Expwy, Suite 800, Dallas, TX 75231-2264 Tel: 214-750-3600 Web Site: www.benbellabooks.com; www.smartpopbooks.com, pg 27

Wilson, Martin, HarperCollins Publishers LLC, 195 Broadway, New York, NY 10007 Tel: 212-207-7000 Web Site: www.harpercollins.com, pg 87

Wilson, Sr Mary Leonora, Pauline Books & Media, 50 Saint Paul's Ave, Boston, MA 02130 Tel: 617-522-8911 Toll Free Tel: 800-876-4463 (orders); 800-836-9723 (cust serv) Fax: 617-541-9805 E-mail: editorial@paulinemedia.com (ms submissions); orderentry@pauline.org (cust serv) Web Site: www.pauline.org/pbmpublishing, pg 152

Wilson, Olivia, Houghton Mifflin Harcourt Trade & Reference Division, 125 High St, Boston, MA 02110 Tel: 617-351-5000 Web Site: www.hmhco.com, pg 96

Wilson, Robert, Louisiana Writer Award, 701 N Fourth St, Baton Rouge, LA 70802 Tel: 225-342-4913 Fax: 225-219-4804 E-mail: admin@state.lib.la.us Web Site: louisianabookfestival.org/louisiana_writer_award.html; www.state.lib.la.us/literacy-and-reading/louisiana-writer-award, pg 626

Wilson, Steve, McFarland, 960 NC Hwy 88 W, Jefferson, NC 28640 Tel: 336-246-4460 Toll Free Tel: 800-253-2187 (orders) Fax: 336-246-5018; 336-246-4403 (orders) E-mail: info@mcfarlandpub.com Web Site: mcfarlandbooks.com, pg 127

Wilson, Tatum, Workman Publishing, 1290 Avenue of the Americas, New York, NY 10104 Toll Free Tel: 800-759-0190 Fax: 212-364-0950 E-mail: workman-inquiry@hbgusa.com Web Site: www.hachettebookgroup.com/imprint/workman-publishing-company/, pg 233

Winch, Jordan, Farrar, Straus & Giroux Books for Young Readers, 120 Broadway, New York, NY 10271 Tel: 212-741-6900 Toll Free Tel: 888-330-8477 (orders) E-mail: childrens.publicity@macmillanusa.com; childrensrights@macmillanusa.com Web Site: us.macmillan.com/mackids, pg 70

Winch, Jordan, Roaring Brook Press, 120 Broadway, New York, NY 10271 Tel: 646-307-5151 Web Site: us.macmillan.com/publishers/roaring-brook-press, pg 176

Wind, Lee, IBPA Book Awards, 1020 Manhattan Beach Blvd, Suite 204, Manhattan Beach, CA 90266 Tel: 310-546-1818 E-mail: info@ibpa-online.org Web Site: www.ibpa-online.org, pg 615

Wind, Lee, The Independent Book Publishers Association (IBPA), 1020 Manhattan Beach Blvd, Suite 204, Manhattan Beach, CA 90266 Tel: 310-546-1818 E-mail: info@ibpa-online.org Web Site: www.ibpa-online.org, pg 507

Windhorn, Annette, Association of University Presses (AUPresses), 1412 Broadway, Suite 2135, New York, NY 10018 Tel: 212-989-1010 Fax: 212-989-0275 E-mail: info@aupresses.org Web Site: www.aupresses.org, pg 500

Winke, Mara, Coffee House Press, 79 13 Ave NE, Suite 110, Minneapolis, MN 55413 Tel: 612-338-0125 Fax: 612-338-4004 E-mail: info@coffeehousepress.org Web Site: coffeehousepress.org, pg 50

Winn, Lisa, American Booksellers Association, 600 Mamaroneck Ave, Suite 400, Harrison, NY 10528 Tel: 914-406-7500 Toll Free Tel: 800-637-0037 Fax: 914-417-4013 E-mail: info@bookweb.org Web Site: www.bookweb.org, pg 494

Winningham, Sharon, School Zone Publishing Co, 1819 Industrial Dr, Grand Haven, MI 49417 Tel: 616-846-5030 Toll Free Tel: 800-253-0564 Fax: 616-846-6181 Web Site: www.schoolzone.com, pg 185

Winns, Nadine, Abbeville Press, 655 Third Ave, New York, NY 10017 Tel: 212-366-5585 Toll Free Tel: 800-ART-BOOK (278-2665); 800-343-4499 (orders) E-mail: abbeville@abbeville.com; sales@abbeville.com; marketing@abbeville.com; rights@abbeville.com Web Site: www.abbeville.com, pg 1

Winns, Nadine, Abbeville Publishing Group, 655 Third Ave, New York, NY 10017 Tel: 646-375-2136 E-mail: abbeville@abbeville.com; rights@abbeville.com Web Site: www.abbeville.com, pg 2

Winslow, Susan, Macmillan Learning, One New York Plaza, Suite 46, New York, NY 10004 Tel: 212-576-9400 E-mail: salesoperations@macmillanusa.com Web Site: www.macmillanlearning.com/college/us, pg 123

Winsor, Jen, Newfoundland and Labrador Book Awards, Haymarket Sq, 223 Duckworth St, St John's, NL A1C 6N1, Canada Tel: 709-739-5215 Toll Free Tel: 866-739-5215 E-mail: info@wanl.ca; membership@wanl.ca Web Site: wanl.ca, pg 641

Winsor, Jen, Newfoundland and Labrador Credit Union Fresh Fish Award for Emerging Writers, Haymarket Sq, 223 Duckworth St, St John's, NL A1C 6N1, Canada Tel: 709-739-5215 Toll Free Tel: 866-739-5215 E-mail: info@wanl.ca; membership@wanl.ca Web Site: wanl.ca, pg 641

Winsor, Jen, Writers' Alliance of Newfoundland & Labrador, Haymarket Sq, 223 Duckworth St, Suite 202, St John's, NL A1C 6N1, Canada Tel: 709-739-5215 Toll Free Tel: 866-739-5215 E-mail: info@wanl.ca; membership@wanl.ca Web Site: wanl.ca, pg 522

Winsor, Reg, BMO Winterset Award, Newman Bldg, 2nd fl, One Springdale St, St John's, NL A1C 5H5, Canada Tel: 709-726-2212 Toll Free Tel: 866-726-2212 (NL only) Fax: 709-726-0619 Web Site: www.nlac.ca/awards/winterset.htm, pg 582

Winstanley, Nicole, Simon & Schuster Canada, 166 King St E, Suite 300, Toronto, ON M5A 1J3, Canada Tel: 647-427-8882 Toll Free Tel: 800-387-0446; 800-268-3216 (orders) Fax: 647-430-9446 Toll Free Fax: 888-849-8151 (orders) E-mail: info@simonandschuster.ca Web Site: www.simonandschuster.ca, pg 419

Winstanley, Nicole, Simon & Schuster, LLC, 1230 Avenue of the Americas, New York, NY 10020 Tel: 212-698-7000 Toll Free Tel: 800-223-2336 (orders) Fax: 212-698-7007 Toll Free Fax: 800-943-9831 (orders) E-mail: firstname.lastname@simonandschuster.com; purchaseorders@simonandschuster.com (orders) Web Site: www.simonandschuster.com, pg 189

Winston, Randy, The Center for Fiction, 15 Lafayette Ave, Brooklyn, NY 11217 Tel: 212-755-6710 E-mail: info@centerforfiction.org Web Site: centerforfiction.org, pg 503

Winston, Randy, The Center for Fiction First Novel Prize, 15 Lafayette Ave, Brooklyn, NY 11217 Tel: 212-755-6710 E-mail: info@centerforfiction.org Web Site: www.centerforfiction.org/awards/the-first-novel-prize, pg 587

Winston, Randy, Susan Kamil Award for Emerging Writers, 15 Lafayette Ave, Brooklyn, NY 11217 Tel: 212-755-6710 E-mail: info@centerforfiction.org Web Site: centerforfiction.org, pg 619

Winston, Randy, Medal for Editorial Excellence, 15 Lafayette Ave, Brooklyn, NY 11217 Tel: 212-755-6710 E-mail: info@centerforfiction.org Web Site: www.centerforfiction.org/grants-awards/maxwell-e-perkins-award, pg 631

Winter, Madeline, Macmillan, 120 Broadway, 22nd fl, New York, NY 10271 E-mail: press.inquiries@macmillan.com Web Site: us.macmillan.com, pg 122

Winter, Maureen, Getty Publications, 1200 Getty Center Dr, Suite 500, Los Angeles, CA 90049-1682 Tel: 310-440-7365 Toll Free Tel: 800-223-3431 (orders) Fax: 310-440-7758 E-mail: pubsinfo@getty.edu Web Site: www.getty.edu/publications, pg 78

Winter, Regan, Disney-Hyperion Books, 1101 Flower St, Glendale, CA 91201 Web Site: books.disney.com/imprint/disney-hyperion, pg 59

Winter, Stephanie, KO Media Management, 2817 Wetmore Ave, Everett, WA 98201 E-mail: info@komediamanagement.com; query@komediamanagement.com Web Site: komediamanagement.com, pg 466

Winters, Andrew, The University of North Carolina Press, 116 S Boundary St, Chapel Hill, NC 27514-3808 Tel: 919-966-3561; 919-966-7449 (orders) Toll Free Tel: 800-848-3224 (orders) Fax: 919-962-2704 (orders) Toll Free Fax: 800-272-6817 (orders) E-mail: uncpress@unc.edu Web Site: uncpress.org, pg 218

Winters, Keli, Evan-Moor Educational Publishers, 10 Harris Ct, Suite C-3, Monterey, CA 93940 Tel: 831-649-5901 Toll Free Tel: 800-777-4362 (orders) Fax: 831-649-6256 Toll Free Fax: 800-777-4332 (orders) E-mail: sales@evan-moor.com; marketing@evan-moor.com Web Site: www.evan-moor.com, pg 68

Winters, Mr Tracy, Winters Publishing, 705 E Washington St, Greensburg, IN 47240 Tel: 812-663-4948 Toll Free Tel: 800-457-3230 Fax: 812-663-4948 E-mail: winterspublishing@gmail.com Web Site: www.winterspublishing.com, pg 231

Wischmeyer, Emma, AAAI Press, 2275 E Bayshore Rd, Suite 160, Palo Alto, CA 94303 Tel: 650-328-3123 Fax: 650-321-4457 E-mail: publications21@aaai.org Web Site: www.aaai.org/Press/press.php, pg 1

Wise, Dennis, Mythopoeic Awards, c/o University of Arizona, Dept of English, Rm 445, Tucson, AZ 85721 E-mail: awards@mythsoc.org Web Site: www.mythsoc.org, pg 636

Wise, Gillian, HarperCollins Publishers LLC, 195 Broadway, New York, NY 10007 Tel: 212-207-7000 Web Site: www.harpercollins.com, pg 86

Wise, Tomas, G Schirmer Inc/Associated Music Publishers Inc, 180 Madison Ave, 24th fl, New York, NY 10016 *Tel:* 212-254-2100 *Fax:* 212-254-2013 *E-mail:* schirmer@schirmer.com *Web Site:* www.musicsalesclassical.com, pg 183

Wishard, Tammy, Anson Jones MD Awards, 401 W 15 St, Austin, TX 78701 *Tel:* 512-370-1300 *Toll Free Tel:* 800-880-7955 *E-mail:* ansonjones@texmed.org *Web Site:* www.texmed.org/ansonjones, pg 618

Wisler, Wade, OCP, 340 Oswego Pointe Dr, Lake Oswego, OR 97034 *Tel:* 503-281-1191 *Toll Free Tel:* 800-LITURGY (548-8749) *Fax:* 503-282-3486 *Toll Free Fax:* 800-843-8181 *E-mail:* liturgy@ocp.org *Web Site:* www.ocp.org, pg 145

Wissoker, Ken, Duke University Press, 905 W Main St, Suite 18B, Durham, NC 27701 *Tel:* 919-688-5134 *Toll Free Tel:* 888-651-0122 (US) *Fax:* 919-688-2615 *Toll Free Fax:* 888-651-0124 *E-mail:* orders@dukeupress.edu *Web Site:* www.dukepress.edu, pg 62

Witcraft, Stacey, Random House Publishing Group, 1745 Broadway, New York, NY 10019 *Toll Free Tel:* 800-200-3552 *Web Site:* www.randomhousebooks.com, pg 170

Withers, Jaclyn, Candlewick Press, 99 Dover St, Somerville, MA 02144-2825 *Tel:* 617-661-3330 *Fax:* 617-661-0565 *E-mail:* bigbear@candlewick.com; salesinfo@candlewick.com *Web Site:* candlewick.com, pg 40

Witherspoon, Kimberly, InkWell Management, 521 Fifth Ave, Suite 2600, New York, NY 10175 *Tel:* 212-922-3500 *Fax:* 212-922-0535 *E-mail:* info@inkwellmanagement.com; submissions@inkwellmanagement.com; permissions@inkwellmanagement.com *Web Site:* inkwellmanagement.com, pg 463

Witt, Diana, Theodore C Hines Award, 1628 E Southern Ave, Suite 9-223, Tempe, AZ 85282 *Tel:* 480-245-6750 *E-mail:* info@asindexing.org *Web Site:* www.asindexing.org/about/awards/hines-award, pg 613

Witte, George, St Martin's Press, LLC, 120 Broadway, New York, NY 10271 *E-mail:* publicity@stmartins.com; trademarketing@stmartins.com; foreignrights@stmartins.com *Web Site:* us.macmillan.com/smp, pg 180

Wittmann, Lucas, Discovery Poetry Contest, 1395 Lexington Ave, New York, NY 10128 *Tel:* 212-415-5760 *E-mail:* unterberg@92y.org *Web Site:* www.92y.org/discovery, pg 596

Wix, Angela, Sounds True Inc, 413 S Arthur Ave, Louisville, CO 80027 *Tel:* 303-665-3151 *Toll Free Tel:* 800-333-9185 (US); 888-303-9185 (US & CN) *E-mail:* customerservice@soundstrue.com; stpublicity@soundstrue.com *Web Site:* www.soundstrue.com, pg 194

Wofford, Evelyn B, The Shirley Holden Helberg Grants for Mature Women, The Pen Arts Bldg & Arts Museum, 1300 17 St NW, Washington, DC 20036-1973 *Tel:* 202-785-1997 *Fax:* 202-452-6868 *E-mail:* contact@nlapw.org *Web Site:* www.nlapw.org, pg 612

Wofford, Evelyn B, National League of American Pen Women Inc, The Pen Arts Bldg & Arts Museum, 1300 17 St NW, Washington, DC 20036-1973 *Tel:* 202-785-1997 *Fax:* 202-452-6868 *E-mail:* contact@nlapw.org *Web Site:* www.nlapw.org, pg 513

Wofford-Girand, Sally, Union Literary, 30 Vandam St, Suite 5A, New York, NY 10013 *Tel:* 212-255-2112 *Web Site:* www.unionliterary.com, pg 480

Wofsy, Alan, Alan Wofsy Fine Arts, 1109 Geary Blvd, San Francisco, CA 94109 *Tel:* 415-292-6500 *Toll Free Tel:* 800-660-6403 *Fax:* 415-292-6594 (off & cust serv); 510-251-1840 (acctg) *E-mail:* order@art-books.com (orders); editeur@earthlink.net (edit); beauxarts@earthlink.net (cust serv) *Web Site:* www.art-books.com, pg 231

Wojciechowski, Robert, Knopf Doubleday Publishing Group, c/o Penguin Random House LLC, 1745 Broadway, New York, NY 10019 *Tel:* 212-751-2600 *Fax:* 212-940-7390 (dom rts); 212-572-2662 (foreign rts) *Web Site:* knopfdoubleday.com, pg 110

Wojciechowski, Robert, Penguin Publishing Group, c/o Penguin Random House LLC, 1745 Broadway, New York, NY 10019 *Tel:* 212-782-9000 *Web Site:* www.penguin.com, pg 154

Wojciechowski, Robert, Penguin Random House LLC, 1745 Broadway, New York, NY 10019 *Tel:* 212-782-9000 *Toll Free Tel:* 800-726-0600 *Web Site:* www.penguinrandomhouse.com, pg 155

Wojcik, Tim, Levine|Greenberg|Rostan Literary Agency, 307 Seventh Ave, Suite 2407, New York, NY 10001 *Tel:* 212-337-0934 *Fax:* 212-337-0948 *E-mail:* submit@lgrliterary.com *Web Site:* lgrliterary.com, pg 467

Wojtyla, Karen, Simon & Schuster Children's Publishing, 1230 Avenue of the Americas, New York, NY 10020 *Tel:* 212-698-7000 *Web Site:* www.simonandschuster.com/kids; www.simonandschuster.com/teen; simonandschuster.net; simonandschuster.biz, pg 189

Woktcheu, C Ngako, CPSA Prize in Comparative Politics, 260 Dalhousie St, Suite 204, Ottawa, ON K1N 7E4, Canada *Tel:* 613-562-1202 *Fax:* 613-241-0019 *E-mail:* cpsaprizes@cpsa-acsp.ca; cpsa-acsp@cpsa-acsp.ca *Web Site:* www.cpsa-acsp.ca, pg 592

Woktcheu, C Ngako, CPSA Prize in International Relations, 260 Dalhousie St, Suite 204, Ottawa, ON K1N 7E4, Canada *Tel:* 613-562-1202 *Fax:* 613-241-0019 *E-mail:* cpsaprizes@cpsa-acsp.ca; cpsa-acsp@cpsa-acsp.ca *Web Site:* www.cpsa-acsp.ca, pg 592

Woktcheu, C Ngako, Prix Francophone de l'ACSP, 260 Dalhousie St, Suite 204, Ottawa, ON K1N 7E4, Canada *Tel:* 613-562-1202 *Fax:* 613-241-0019 *E-mail:* cpsaprizes@cpsa-acsp.ca; cpsa-acsp@cpsa-acsp.ca *Web Site:* www.cpsa-acsp.ca, pg 604

Woktcheu, C Ngako, Vincent Lemieux Prize, 260 Dalhousie St, Suite 204, Ottawa, ON K1N 7E4, Canada *Tel:* 613-562-1202 *Fax:* 613-241-0019 *E-mail:* cpsa-acsp@cpsa-acsp.ca; cpsaprizes@cpsa-acsp.ca *Web Site:* www.cpsa-acsp.ca, pg 623

Woktcheu, C Ngako, C B MacPherson Prize, 260 Dalhousie St, Suite 204, Ottawa, ON K1N 7E4, Canada *Tel:* 613-562-1202 *Fax:* 613-241-0019 *E-mail:* cpsa-acsp@cpsa-acsp.ca; cpsaprizes@cpsa-acsp.ca *Web Site:* www.cpsa-acsp.ca, pg 628

Woktcheu, C Ngako, John McMenemy Prize, 260 Dalhousie St, Suite 204, Ottawa, ON K1N 7E4, Canada *Tel:* 613-562-1202 *Fax:* 613-241-0019 *E-mail:* cpsaprizes@cpsa-acsp.ca; cpsa-acsp@cpsa-acsp.ca *Web Site:* www.cpsa-acsp.ca, pg 631

Woktcheu, C Ngako, Donald Smiley Prize, 260 Dalhousie St, Suite 204, Ottawa, ON K1N 7E4, Canada *Tel:* 613-562-1202 *Fax:* 613-241-0019 *E-mail:* cpsaprizes@cpsa-acsp.ca; cpsa-acsp@cpsa-acsp.ca *Web Site:* www.cpsa-acsp.ca, pg 663

Woktcheu, C Ngako, Jill Vickers Prize, 260 Dalhousie St, Suite 204, Ottawa, ON K1N 7E4, Canada *Tel:* 613-562-1202 *Fax:* 613-241-0019 *E-mail:* cpsaprizes@cpsa-acsp.ca; cpsa-acsp@cpsa-acsp.ca *Web Site:* www.cpsa-acsp.ca, pg 672

Wolf, Ingrid, Wm B Eerdmans Publishing Co, 4035 Park East Ct SE, Grand Rapids, MI 49546 *Tel:* 616-459-4591 *Toll Free Tel:* 800-253-7521 *E-mail:* customerservice@eerdmans.com; sales@eerdmans.com *Web Site:* www.eerdmans.com, pg 64

Wolf, Maria, Institute of Governmental Studies, 109 Moses Hall, No 2370, Berkeley, CA 94720-2370 *Tel:* 510-642-1428 *E-mail:* igspress@berkeley.edu *Web Site:* www.igs.berkeley.edu, pg 101

Wolf, Ray, Leisure Arts Inc, 104 Champs Blvd, Suite 100, Maumelle, AR 72113 *Tel:* 501-868-8800 *Toll Free Tel:* 800-643-8030 *Toll Free Fax:* 877-710-5603 (catalog) *E-mail:* customer_service@leisurearts.com *Web Site:* www.leisurearts.com, pg 114

Wolf, Shena, KO Media Management, 2817 Wetmore Ave, Everett, WA 98201 *E-mail:* info@komediamanagement.com; query@komediamanagement.com *Web Site:* komediamanagement.com, pg 466

Wolf, Terrie, AKA Literary Management, 11445 Dallas Rd, Peyton, CO 80831 *Tel:* 646-846-2478 *E-mail:* hello@akaliterary.com *Web Site:* akalm.net, pg 448

Wolf, Wendy, Harvard University Press, 79 Garden St, Cambridge, MA 02138-1499 *Tel:* 617-495-2600; 401-531-2800 (intl orders) *Toll Free Tel:* 800-405-1619 (orders) *Fax:* 617-495-5898 (gen); 617-496-4677 (edit & rts); 401-531-2801 (intl orders) *Toll Free Fax:* 800-406-9145 (orders) *E-mail:* contact_hup@harvard.edu *Web Site:* www.hup.harvard.edu, pg 88

Wolf-Robin, Juliette, American Photographic Artists (APA), 5042 Wilshire Blvd, No 321, Los Angeles, CA 90036 *E-mail:* membershiprep@apanational.org *Web Site:* apanational.org, pg 496

Wolfe, Alex, Penguin Workshop, c/o Penguin Random House LLC, 1745 Broadway, New York, NY 10019 *Tel:* 212-782-9000 *Web Site:* www.penguin.com/publishers/penguinworkshop/, pg 156

Wolfe, Alexander, University of Pittsburgh Press, 7500 Thomas Blvd, Pittsburgh, PA 15260 *Tel:* 412-383-2456 *Fax:* 412-383-2466 *E-mail:* info@upress.pitt.edu *Web Site:* www.upress.pitt.edu, pg 219

Wolfe, Gary, New Author Publishing, 4 E Fulford Place, Brockville, ON K6V 2Z8, Canada *Tel:* 613-865-7471 *Web Site:* www.newauthorpublishing.com, pg 413

Wolfe, John, Association of National Advertisers Inc (ANA), 155 E 44 St, New York, NY 10017 *Tel:* 212-697-5950 *Fax:* 212-687-7310 *E-mail:* info@ana.net *Web Site:* www.ana.net, pg 499

Wolfe, Margie, Second Story Press, 20 Maud St, Suite 401, Toronto, ON M5V 2M5, Canada *Tel:* 416-537-7850 *Fax:* 416-537-0588 *E-mail:* info@secondstorypress.ca *Web Site:* secondstorypress.ca, pg 419

Wolfe, Navah, DAW Books, 19 W 21 St, No 1201, New York, NY 10010 *E-mail:* info@astrapublishinghouse.com *Web Site:* astrapublishinghouse.com/imprints/daw-books, pg 57

Wolff, Anne, New York University, Center for Publishing & Applied Liberal Arts, 7 E 12 St, New York, NY 10003 *Tel:* 212-998-7200 *E-mail:* sps.info@nyu.edu *Web Site:* www.scps.nyu.edu/professional-pathways/topics.html, pg 564

Wolff, Denise, Aperture Books, 548 W 28 St, 4th fl, New York, NY 10001 *Tel:* 212-505-5555 *Toll Free Fax:* 888-623-6908 *E-mail:* customerservice@aperture.org *Web Site:* aperture.org, pg 15

Wolff, Harvey, Haynes North America Inc, 2801 Townsgate Rd, Suite 340, Westlake Village, CA 91361 *Tel:* 805-498-6703 *Toll Free Tel:* 800-4-HAYNES (442-9637) *Fax:* 805-498-2867 *E-mail:* customerservice.haynes@infopro-digital.com *Web Site:* www.haynes.com, pg 89

Wolfinger, Cydni, Transportation Research Board (TRB), 500 Fifth St NW, Washington, DC 20001 *Tel:* 202-334-2934; 202-334-3213 (bookshop) *E-mail:* trbsales@nas.edu; mytrb@nas.edu *Web Site:* www.nationalacademies.org/trb/transportation-research-board, pg 209

Wolford, Henry, Easy Money Press, 82-5800 Napo'opo'o Rd, Captain Cook, HI 96704 *Tel:* 808-313-2808 *E-mail:* easymoneypress@yahoo.com, pg 63

Wolford, Mary, Holiday House Publishing Inc, 50 Broad St, New York, NY 10004 *Tel:* 212-688-0085 *Fax:* 212-421-6134 *E-mail:* info@holidayhouse.com *Web Site:* www.holidayhouse.com, pg 94

Wolford, Shannon, Visual Media Alliance (VMA), 665 Third St, Suite 500, San Francisco, CA 94107-1926 *Tel:* 415-495-8242 *Toll Free Tel:* 800-659-3363 *Fax:* 415-520-1126 *E-mail:* info@vma.bz *Web Site:* main.vma.bz, pg 521

Wolfson, Howard, Gotham Book Prize, 251 Park Ave S, New York, NY 10010 *Web Site:* www.gothambookprize.org, pg 608

Wolfson, Maggie, Carolrhoda Books Inc, 241 First Ave N, Minneapolis, MN 55401 *Tel:* 612-332-3344 *Toll Free Tel:* 800-328-4929 *Fax:* 612-332-7615 *Toll*

Free Fax: 800-332-1132 E-mail: info@lernerbooks. com; custserve@lernerbooks.com Web Site: www. lernerbooks.com; www.facebook.com/lernerbooks, pg 41

Wolfson, Maggie, Lerner Publications, 241 First Ave N, Minneapolis, MN 55401 Tel: 612-332-3344 Toll Free Tel: 800-328-4929 Fax: 612-332-7615 Toll Free Fax: 800-332-1132 E-mail: info@lernerbooks. com; custserve@lernerbooks.com Web Site: www. lernerbooks.com; www.facebook.com/lernerbooks, pg 115

Wolfson, Maggie, Twenty-First Century Books, 241 First Ave N, Minneapolis, MN 55401 Tel: 612-332-3344 Toll Free Tel: 800-328-4929 Fax: 612-332-7615 Toll Free Fax: 800-332-1132 E-mail: info@lernerbooks. com; custserve@lernerbooks.com Web Site: www. lernerbooks.com; www.facebook.com/lernerbooks, pg 211

Wolfson, Margaret, Carolrhoda Lab™, 241 First Ave N, Minneapolis, MN 55401 Tel: 612-332-3344 Toll Free Tel: 800-328-4929 Fax: 612-332-7615 Toll Free Fax: 800-332-1132 E-mail: info@lernerbooks. com; custserve@lernerbooks.com Web Site: www. lernerbooks.com; www.facebook.com/lernerbooks, pg 41

Wolfson, Margaret, ediciones Lerner, 241 First Ave N, Minneapolis, MN 55401 Tel: 612-332-3344 Toll Free Tel: 800-328-4929 Fax: 612-332-7615 Toll Free Fax: 800-332-1132 E-mail: info@lernerbooks. com; custserve@lernerbooks.com Web Site: www. lernerbooks.com; www.facebook.com/lernerbooks, pg 63

Wolfson, Margaret, First Avenue Editions, 241 First Ave N, Minneapolis, MN 55401 Tel: 612-332-3344 Toll Free Tel: 800-328-4929 Fax: 612-332-7615 Toll Free Fax: 800-332-1132 E-mail: info@lernerbooks. com; custserve@lernerbooks.com Web Site: www. lernerbooks.com; www.facebook.com/lernerbooks, pg 72

Wolfson, Margaret, Graphic Universe™, 241 First Ave N, Minneapolis, MN 55401 Tel: 612-332-3344 Toll Free Tel: 800-328-4929 Fax: 612-332-7615 Toll Free Fax: 800-332-1132 E-mail: info@lernerbooks. com; custserve@lernerbooks.com Web Site: www. lernerbooks.com; www.facebook.com/lernerbooks, pg 80

Wolfson, Margaret, Lerner Publishing Group Inc, 241 First Ave N, Minneapolis, MN 55401 Tel: 612-332-3344 Toll Free Tel: 800-328-4929 Fax: 612-332-7615 Toll Free Fax: 800-332-1132 E-mail: info@ lernerbooks.com; custserve@lernerbooks.com Web Site: www.lernerbooks.com; www.facebook. com/lernerbooks, pg 115

Wolfson, Margaret, LernerClassroom, 241 First Ave N, Minneapolis, MN 55401 Tel: 612-332-3344 Toll Free Tel: 800-328-4929 Fax: 612-332-7615 Toll Free Fax: 800-332-1132 E-mail: info@lernerbooks. com; custserve@lernerbooks.com Web Site: www. lernerbooks.com; www.facebook.com/lernerbooks, pg 115

Wolin, Chava, Simon & Schuster Children's Publishing, 1230 Avenue of the Americas, New York, NY 10020 Tel: 212-698-7000 Web Site: www.simonandschuster. com/kids; www.simonandschuster.com/teen; simonandschuster.net; simonandschuster.biz, pg 189

Wolin, Rachel, Education Writers Association (EWA), 1825 "K" St NW, Suite 200, Washington, DC 20006 Tel: 202-452-9830 Web Site: ewa.org, pg 505

Woliner, Tal, American Association for the Advancement of Science (AAAS), 1200 New York Ave NW, Washington, DC 20005 Tel: 202-326-6400 E-mail: membership@aaas.org Web Site: www.aaas. org, pg 494

Wollheim, Elizabeth R, DAW Books, 19 W 21 St, No 1201, New York, NY 10010 E-mail: info@astrapublishinghouse.com Web Site: astrapublishinghouse.com/imprints/daw-books, pg 57

Wollman, Jessica, Scholastic Education Solutions, 557 Broadway, New York, NY 10012 Tel: 212-343-6100 Fax: 212-343-6189 Web Site: www.scholastic.com, pg 184

Wolverton, Nan, American Antiquarian Society (AAS), 185 Salisbury St, Worcester, MA 01609-1634 Tel: 508-755-5221 Fax: 508-754-9069 E-mail: library@mwa.org Web Site: www. americanantiquarian.org, pg 494

Wolverton, Nan, Fellowships for Creative & Performing Artists & Writers, 185 Salisbury St, Worcester, MA 01609-1634 Tel: 508-755-5221 Fax: 508-754-9069 E-mail: library@mwa.org Web Site: www. americanantiquarian.org, pg 602

Wolverton, Nan, Fellowships for Historical Research, 185 Salisbury St, Worcester, MA 01609-1634 Tel: 508-755-5221 Fax: 508-754-9069 Web Site: www. americanantiquarian.org, pg 602

Wolverton, Peter, St Martin's Press, LLC, 120 Broadway, New York, NY 10271 E-mail: publicity@stmartins. com; trademarketing@stmartins.com; foreignrights@ stmartins.com Web Site: us.macmillan.com/smp, pg 180

Wolverton, Susan, Coe College Playwriting Festival, 1220 First Ave NE, Cedar Rapids, IA 52402 Tel: 319-399-8624 Fax: 319-399-8557 Web Site: www. theatre.coe.edu; www.coe.edu/academics/theatrearts/ theatrearts_playwritingfestival, pg 590

Wong, Ann Marie, Henry Holt and Company, LLC, 120 Broadway, 23rd fl, New York, NY 10271 Tel: 646-307-5151 Toll Free Tel: 888-330-8477 (orders) Fax: 646-307-5285 Web Site: www.henryholt.com, pg 94

Wong, Betty, Andrews McMeel Publishing LLC, 1130 Walnut St, Kansas City, MO 64106-2109 Tel: 816-581-7500 Toll Free Tel: 800-851-8923 Web Site: www. andrewsmcmeel.com; publishing.andrewsmcmeel.com, pg 14

Wong, Collin, University of Hawaii Press, 2840 Kolowalu St, Honolulu, HI 96822-1888 Tel: 808-956-8255 Toll Free Tel: 888-UHPRESS (847-7377) Toll Free Fax: 800-650-7811 E-mail: uhpbooks@hawaii. edu Web Site: www.uhpress.hawaii.edu, pg 216

Wong, Harry L III, Kumu Kahua/UHM Theatre & Dance Department Playwriting Contest, 46 Merchant St, Honolulu, HI 96813 Tel: 808-536-4441 (box off); 808-536-4222 (off admin) Fax: 808-536-4226 E-mail: officemanager@kumukahua.org Web Site: www.kumukahua.org, pg 621

Wong, Maddy, Chronicle Books LLC, 680 Second St, San Francisco, CA 94107 Tel: 415-537-4200 Fax: 415-537-4460 (perms) E-mail: hello@ chroniclebooks.com; subrights@chroniclebooks.com Web Site: www.chroniclebooks.com, pg 47

Wong, Wendy, Random House Publishing Group, 1745 Broadway, New York, NY 10019 Toll Free Tel: 800-200-3552 Web Site: www.randomhousebooks.com, pg 171

Wong-Baxter, Jade, Frances Goldin Literary Agency, Inc, 214 W 29 St, Suite 410, New York, NY 10001 Tel: 212-777-0047 Fax: 212-228-1660 E-mail: agency@goldinlit.com Web Site: www. goldinlit.com, pg 460

Wood, Amelia, HarperCollins Publishers LLC, 195 Broadway, New York, NY 10007 Tel: 212-207-7000 Web Site: www.harpercollins.com, pg 87

Wood, Brad, Macmillan, 120 Broadway, 22nd fl, New York, NY 10271 E-mail: press.inquiries@macmillan. com Web Site: us.macmillan.com, pg 122

Wood, Deb, Harry N Abrams Inc, 195 Broadway, 9th fl, New York, NY 10007 Tel: 212-206-7715 Toll Free Tel: 800-345-1359 Fax: 212-645-8437 E-mail: abrams@abramsbooks.com; publicity@ abramsbooks.com; sales@abramsbooks.com Web Site: www.abramsbooks.com, pg 2

Wood, Eleanor, Spectrum Literary Agency, 320 Central Park W, Suite 1-D, New York, NY 10025 Tel: 212-362-4323 Fax: 212-362-4562 Web Site: www. spectrumliteraryagency.com, pg 477

Wood, Laura, FinePrint Literary Management, 207 W 106 St, Suite 1D, New York, NY 10025 Tel: 212-279-6214 E-mail: info@fineprintlit.com; submissions@ fineprint.com Web Site: www.fineprintlit.com, pg 458

Wood, Leighann, Andrew Carnegie Medals for Excellence in Fiction & Nonfiction, 225 N Michigan Ave, Suite 1300, Chicago, IL 60601 Tel: 312-944-6780 Toll Free Tel: 800-545-2433 Fax: 312-440-9374 E-mail: ala@ala.org Web Site: www.ala.org/awardsgrants/carnegieadult, pg 587

Wood, Michael, Anna Zornio Memorial Children's Theatre Playwriting Award, D22 Paul Creative Arts Center, 30 Academic Way, Durham, NH 03824 Tel: 603-862-2919 Fax: 603-862-0298 E-mail: theatre. dance@unh.edu Web Site: cola.unh.edu/theatre-dance/opportunities/competitions, pg 680

Wood, Rachel, Candlewick Press, 99 Dover St, Somerville, MA 02144-2825 Tel: 617-661-3330 Fax: 617-661-0565 E-mail: bigbear@candlewick.com; salesinfo@candlewick.com Web Site: candlewick.com, pg 39

Wood, Sara, HarperCollins Publishers LLC, 195 Broadway, New York, NY 10007 Tel: 212-207-7000 Web Site: www.harpercollins.com, pg 86

Woodard, David, Chalice Press, 11939 Manchester Rd, No 100, St Louis, MO 63131 Tel: 314-231-8500 Toll Free Tel: 800-366-3383 E-mail: customerservice@ chalicepress.com Web Site: www.chalicepress.com, pg 44

Wooden, Heather, Institute of Environmental Sciences & Technology - IEST, 1827 Walden Office Sq, Suite 400, Schaumburg, IL 60173 Tel: 847-981-0100 Fax: 847-981-4130 E-mail: information@iest.org Web Site: www.iest.org, pg 101

Woodford, Charles H, Princeton Book Co Publishers, 15 W Front St, Trenton, NJ 08608 Tel: 609-426-0602 Toll Free Tel: 800-220-7149 Fax: 609-426-1344 E-mail: pbc@dancehorizons.com Web Site: www. dancehorizons.com, pg 163

Woodford, Connie, Princeton Book Co Publishers, 15 W Front St, Trenton, NJ 08608 Tel: 609-426-0602 Toll Free Tel: 800-220-7149 Fax: 609-426-1344 E-mail: pbc@dancehorizons.com Web Site: www. dancehorizons.com, pg 163

Woodhouse, Sharon, Everything Goes Media LLC, PO Box 1524, Milwaukee, WI 53201 Tel: 312-226-8400 E-mail: info@everythinggoesmedia.com Web Site: www.everythinggoesmedia.com, pg 68

Woodland, Wendy, Texas Library Association (TLA), 3420 Executive Center Dr, Suite 301, Austin, TX 78731 Tel: 512-328-1518 Fax: 512-328-8852 E-mail: tla@txla.org Web Site: txla.org, pg 521

Woodley, Trish, Educators Book Award, 1801 E 51 St, Suite 365-163, Austin, TX 78701 Tel: 512-478-5748 Toll Free Tel: 888-762-4685 Fax: 512-478-3961 Web Site: www.dkg.org, pg 598

Woods, Amanda, Zondervan, 3900 Sparks Dr SE, Grand Rapids, MI 49546 Tel: 616-698-6900 Toll Free Tel: 800-226-1122; 800-727-1309 (retail orders) Fax: 616-698-3350 Toll Free Fax: 800-698-3256 (retail orders) E-mail: customercare@harpercollins. com Web Site: www.zondervan.com, pg 236

Woods, Austin, University of Missouri Press, 113 Heinkel Bldg, 201 S Seventh St, Columbia, MO 65211 Tel: 573-882-7641; 573-882-9672 (publicity & sales enquiries) Toll Free Tel: 800-621-2736 (orders) Fax: 573-884-4498 Toll Free Fax: 800-621-8476 (orders) E-mail: upress@missouri.edu; umpmarketing@missouri.edu (publicity & sales enquiries) Web Site: upress.missouri.edu, pg 217

Woods, Brian, Cistercian Publications, Saint John's Abbey, PO Box 7500, Collegeville, MN 56321 Tel: 320-363-2213 Toll Free Tel: 800-436-8431 Fax: 320-363-3299 Toll Free Fax: 800-445-5899 E-mail: sales@litpress.org Web Site: www. cistercianpublications.org, pg 48

Woods, Brian, Liturgical Press, PO Box 7500, St John's Abbey, Collegeville, MN 56321-7500 Tel: 320-363-2213 Toll Free Tel: 800-858-5450 Fax: 320-363-3299 Toll Free Fax: 800-445-5899 E-mail: sales@litpress. org Web Site: www.litpress.org, pg 119

Woods, Catherine, The MIT Press, One Broadway, 12th fl, Cambridge, MA 02142 *Tel:* 617-253-5255 *Toll Free Tel:* 800-405-1619 (orders) *Fax:* 617-258-6779; 617-577-1545 (orders) *Web Site:* mitpress.mit.edu, pg 132

Woods, Eileen McEleney, National Association of Real Estate Editors (NAREE), 1003 NW Sixth Terr, Boca Raton, FL 33486-3455 *Tel:* 561-391-3599 *Web Site:* www.naree.org, pg 512

Woods, Kimberly, Penguin Random House LLC, 1745 Broadway, New York, NY 10019 *Tel:* 212-782-9000 *Toll Free Tel:* 800-726-0600 *Web Site:* www.penguinrandomhouse.com, pg 155

Woods, Ryan, Newbury Street Press, 99-101 Newbury St, Boston, MA 02116 *Tel:* 617-226-1206 *Toll Free Tel:* 888-296-3447 (NEHGS membership) *Fax:* 617-536-7307 *E-mail:* thebookstore@nehgs.org *Web Site:* www.americanancestors.org, pg 141

Woods, Sadie, Atlantic Center for the Arts Mentoring Artist-in-Residence Program, 1414 Art Center Ave, New Smyrna Beach, FL 32168 *Tel:* 386-427-6975 *E-mail:* program@atlanticcenterforthearts.org *Web Site:* atlanticcenterforthearts.org, pg 553

Woodward, Ben, The New Press, 120 Wall St, 31st fl, New York, NY 10005 *Tel:* 212-629-8802 *Fax:* 212-629-8617 *E-mail:* newpress@thenewpress.com *Web Site:* thenewpress.com, pg 140

Woodward, Benjamin, The New Press, 120 Wall St, 31st fl, New York, NY 10005 *Tel:* 212-629-8802 *Fax:* 212-629-8617 *E-mail:* newpress@thenewpress.com *Web Site:* thenewpress.com, pg 140

Woodward, Charlene, Dogwise Publishing, 403 S Mission St, Wenatchee, WA 98801 *Tel:* 509-663-9115 *Toll Free Tel:* 800-776-2665 *E-mail:* mail@dogwise.com *Web Site:* www.dogwise.com, pg 60

Woodward, Larry, Dogwise Publishing, 403 S Mission St, Wenatchee, WA 98801 *Tel:* 509-663-9115 *Toll Free Tel:* 800-776-2665 *E-mail:* mail@dogwise.com *Web Site:* www.dogwise.com, pg 60

Woodward, Tessa, HarperCollins Publishers LLC, 195 Broadway, New York, NY 10007 *Tel:* 212-207-7000 *Web Site:* www.harpercollins.com, pg 86

Woodworth, Bob, Flanker Press Ltd, 1243 Kenmount Rd, Unit 1, Paradise, NL A1L 0V8, Canada *Tel:* 709-739-4477 *Toll Free Tel:* 866-739-4420 *Fax:* 709-739-4420 *E-mail:* info@flankerpress; sales@flankerpress.com *Web Site:* www.flankerpress.com, pg 406

Woolbright, Molly, Sasquatch Books, 1904 S Third Ave, Suite 710, Seattle, WA 98101 *Tel:* 206-467-4300 *Toll Free Tel:* 800-775-0817 *Fax:* 206-467-4301 *E-mail:* custserv@sasquatchbooks.com *Web Site:* sasquatchbooks.com, pg 182

Wooldridge, Andrew, Orca Book Publishers, 1016 Balmoral Rd, Victoria, BC V8T 1A8, Canada *Toll Free Tel:* 800-210-5277 *Toll Free Fax:* 877-408-1551 *E-mail:* orca@orcabook.com *Web Site:* www.orcabook.com, pg 415

Wooldridge, Suzi, Bridge Logos Inc, 14260 W Newberry Rd, Newberry, FL 32669-2765 *E-mail:* info@bridgelogos.com *Web Site:* www.bridgelogos.com, pg 36

Woollen, Jonathan, Farrar, Straus & Giroux, LLC, 120 Broadway, New York, NY 10271 *Tel:* 212-741-6900 *E-mail:* fsg.publicity@fsgbooks.com; sales@fsgbooks.com *Web Site:* us.macmillan.com/fsg, pg 70

Woollen, Jonathan, Picador, 120 Broadway, New York, NY 10271 *Tel:* 646-307-5151 *Fax:* 212-253-9627 *E-mail:* publicity@picadorusa.com *Web Site:* us.macmillan.com/picador, pg 160

Worick, Jennifer, Sasquatch Books, 1904 S Third Ave, Suite 710, Seattle, WA 98101 *Tel:* 206-467-4300 *Toll Free Tel:* 800-775-0817 *Fax:* 206-467-4301 *E-mail:* custserv@sasquatchbooks.com *Web Site:* sasquatchbooks.com, pg 182

Worrell, Ilana, Farrar, Straus & Giroux Books for Young Readers, 120 Broadway, New York, NY 10271 *Tel:* 212-741-6900 *Toll Free Tel:* 888-330-8477 (orders) *E-mail:* childrens.publicity@macmillanusa.com; childrensrights@macmillanusa.com *Web Site:* us.macmillan.com/mackids, pg 70

Worrell, Ilana, Roaring Brook Press, 120 Broadway, New York, NY 10271 *Tel:* 646-307-5151 *Web Site:* us.macmillan.com/publishers/roaring-brook-press, pg 176

Worrell, Lesley, Tor Publishing Group, 120 Broadway, New York, NY 10271 *Toll Free Tel:* 800-455-0340 (Macmillan) *E-mail:* torpublicity@tor.com; forgepublicity@forgebooks.com *Web Site:* us.macmillan.com/torpublishinggroup, pg 208

Wos, Joe, National Cartoonists Society (NCS), PO Box 592927, Orlando, FL 32859-2927 *Tel:* 407-994-6703 *E-mail:* info@nationalcartoonists.com; membership@nationalcartoonists.com *Web Site:* www.nationalcartoonists.com, pg 512

Wren, Jill Robinson, Adams & Ambrose Publishing, 1622 Capital Ave, Madison, WI 53705-1228 *Tel:* 608-572-2471 *E-mail:* info@adamsambrose.com, pg 4

Wright, Abbe, Penguin Random House LLC, 1745 Broadway, New York, NY 10019 *Tel:* 212-782-9000 *Toll Free Tel:* 800-726-0600 *Web Site:* www.penguinrandomhouse.com, pg 155

Wright, Abi, J Anthony Lukas Book Prize, 2950 Broadway, New York, NY 10027 *Tel:* 212-854-6468 *E-mail:* cjsprizes@gmail.com *Web Site:* www.journalism.columbia.edu, pg 627

Wright, Abi, J Anthony Lukas Work-in-Progress Award, 2950 Broadway, New York, NY 10027 *Tel:* 212-854-6468 *E-mail:* cjsprizes@gmail.com *Web Site:* www.journalism.columbia.edu, pg 627

Wright, Abi, Mark Lynton History Prize, 2950 Broadway, New York, NY 10027 *Tel:* 212-854-6468 *E-mail:* cjsprizes@gmail.com *Web Site:* www.journalism.columbia.edu, pg 627

Wright, Ellen, Orbit, 1290 Avenue of the Americas, New York, NY 10104 *Tel:* 212-364-1100 *Toll Free Tel:* 800-759-0190 *Web Site:* www.orbitbooks.net; www.hachettebookgroup.com/imprint/orbit, pg 147

Wright, Eric, LexisNexis® Canada Inc, 111 Gordon Baker Rd, Suite 900, Toronto, ON M2H 3R1, Canada *Tel:* 905-479-2665 *Toll Free Tel:* 800-668-6481; 800-387-0899 (cust care); 800-255-5174 (sales) *E-mail:* service@lexisnexis.ca (cust serv); sales@lexisnexis.ca *Web Site:* www.lexisnexis.ca, pg 411

Wright, J'Nel, Sourced Media Books, 15 Via Picato, San Clemente, CA 92673 *Tel:* 949-813-0182 *E-mail:* editor@sourcedmediabooks.com *Web Site:* sourcedmediabooks.com, pg 195

Wright, Jan C, Wright Information Indexing Services, Sandia Park, NM 87047 *Web Site:* www.wrightinformation.com, pg 445

Wright, Jim, Salem Press, 2 University Plaza, Suite 310, Hackensack, NJ 07601 *Tel:* 201-968-0500 *Toll Free Tel:* 800-221-1592 *Fax:* 201-968-0511 *E-mail:* csr@salempress.com *Web Site:* salempress.com, pg 181

Wright, Kavita, Sourcebooks LLC, 1935 Brookdale Rd, Suite 139, Naperville, IL 60563 *Tel:* 630-961-3900 *Toll Free Tel:* 800-432-7444 *Fax:* 630-961-2168 *E-mail:* info@sourcebooks.com *Web Site:* www.sourcebooks.com, pg 194

Wright, Matthew, SAGE Publishing, 2455 Teller Rd, Thousand Oaks, CA 91320 *Toll Free Tel:* 800-818-7243 *Toll Free Fax:* 800-583-2665 *E-mail:* info@sagepub.com; orders@sagepub.com *Web Site:* www.sagepublishing.com, pg 180

Wright, Michael, W W Norton & Company Inc, 500 Fifth Ave, New York, NY 10110-0017 *Tel:* 212-354-5500 *Toll Free Tel:* 800-233-4830 (orders & cust serv) *Fax:* 212-869-0856 *Toll Free Fax:* 800-458-6515 *E-mail:* orders@wwnorton.com *Web Site:* wwnorton.com, pg 143

Wright, Robert, ABAC/ALAC, c/o 1938 Bloor St W, Toronto, ON M6P 3K8, Canada *E-mail:* info@abac.org *Web Site:* www.abac.org, pg 493

Wrinn, Stephen, Ernest Sandeen Prize in Poetry & Richard Sullivan Prize in Short Fiction, 310 Flanner Hall, Notre Dame, IN 46556 *Tel:* 574-631-6346 *Fax:* 574-631-8148 *E-mail:* undpress@nd.edu; creativewriting@nd.edu *Web Site:* english.nd.edu/creative-writing/awards-and-prizes/; undpress.nd.edu, pg 600

Wrinn, Stephen, University of Notre Dame Press, 310 Flanner Hall, Notre Dame, IN 46556 *Tel:* 574-631-6346 *Fax:* 574-631-8148 *E-mail:* undpress@nd.edu *Web Site:* www.undpress.nd.edu, pg 219

Wrobel, Aleks, Penguin Random House Canada, a Penguin Random House company, 320 Front St W, Suite 1400, Toronto, ON M5V 3B6, Canada *Tel:* 416-364-4449 *Toll Free Tel:* 888-523-9292 (cust serv) *E-mail:* canadaweb@penguinrandomhouse.com; customerservicescanada@penguinrandomhouse.com *Web Site:* www.penguinrandomhouse.ca, pg 416

Wrubel, Jeremy, Penguin Random House LLC, 1745 Broadway, New York, NY 10019 *Tel:* 212-782-9000 *Toll Free Tel:* 800-726-0600 *Web Site:* www.penguinrandomhouse.com, pg 155

Wrubel, Kim, Random House Children's Books, c/o Penguin Random House LLC, 1745 Broadway, New York, NY 10019 *Tel:* 212-782-9000 *Web Site:* www.rhcbooks.com, pg 169

Wrzesinski, Julie, Michigan State University Press (MSU Press), Manly Miles Bldg, Suite 25, 1405 S Harrison Rd, East Lansing, MI 48823-5245 *Tel:* 517-355-9543 *Fax:* 517-432-2611 *Web Site:* msupress.org, pg 130

Wu, Kyle Lucia, Kundiman Retreat, Fordham University, English Dept, 113 W 60 St, Rm 924, New York, NY 10023 *E-mail:* info@kundiman.org *Web Site:* www.kundiman.org, pg 556

Wu, Melissa, HarperCollins Children's Books, 195 Broadway, New York, NY 10007 *Tel:* 212-207-7000 *Web Site:* www.harpercollins.com/childrens, pg 86

Wu, Morgan, Little, Brown and Company, 1290 Avenue of the Americas, New York, NY 10104 *Tel:* 212-364-1100 *Fax:* 212-364-0952 *E-mail:* firstname.lastname@hbgusa.com *Web Site:* www.hachettebookgroup.com/imprint/little-brown-and-company/, pg 118

Wucher, Lisa, Annual Reviews, 1875 S Grant St, Suite 700, San Mateo, CA 94402 *Tel:* 650-493-4400 *Toll Free Tel:* 800-523-8635 *Fax:* 650-424-0910; 650-855-9815 *E-mail:* service@annualreviews.org *Web Site:* www.annualreviews.org, pg 14

Wudurski, Timothy, Chronicle Books LLC, 680 Second St, San Francisco, CA 94107 *Tel:* 415-537-4200 *Fax:* 415-537-4460 (perms) *E-mail:* hello@chroniclebooks.com; subrights@chroniclebooks.com *Web Site:* www.chroniclebooks.com, pg 47

Wuertz von Holt, Mary, Liguori Publications, One Liguori Dr, Liguori, MO 63057-1000 *Tel:* 636-464-2500 *Toll Free Tel:* 800-325-9521 *Toll Free Fax:* 800-325-9526 (sales) *E-mail:* liguori@liguori.org (sales & cust serv) *Web Site:* www.liguori.org, pg 117

Wuest, Dawn, APS PRESS, 3340 Pilot Knob Rd, St Paul, MN 55121 *Tel:* 651-454-7250 *Toll Free Tel:* 800-328-7560 *Fax:* 651-454-0766 *E-mail:* aps@scisoc.org *Web Site:* my.apsnet.org/apsstore, pg 16

Wuest, Dawn, Cereals & Grains Association, 3285 Northwood Circle, Suite 100, St Paul, MN 55121 *Tel:* 651-454-7250 *E-mail:* info@cerealsgrains.org *Web Site:* cerealsgrains.org, pg 44

Wunderlich, Emily, Viking Penguin, c/o Penguin Random House LLC, 1745 Broadway, New York, NY 10019 *Tel:* 212-782-9000 *Web Site:* www.penguin.com/overview-vikingbooks/; www.penguin.com/pamela-dorman-books-overview/; www.penguin.com/penguin-classics-overview/; www.penguin.com/penguin-life-overview/, pg 225

Wurfbain, Ludo J, Safari Press, 15621 Chemical Lane, Bldg B, Huntington Beach, CA 92649 *Tel:* 714-894-9080 *Toll Free Tel:* 800-451-4788 *Fax:* 714-894-4949 *E-mail:* info@safaripress.com *Web Site:* www.safaripress.com, pg 179

Wuthrich, Belle, Greystone Books Ltd, 343 Railway St, Suite 302, Vancouver, BC V6A 1A4, Canada *Tel:* 604-875-1550 *Fax:* 604-875-1556 *E-mail:* info@greystonebooks.com; rights@greystonebooks.com *Web Site:* www.greystonebooks.com, pg 407

Wyatt, Charlotte, Napa Valley Writers' Conference, 2277 Napa-Vallejo Hwy, Off 1753, Napa, CA 94558 *Tel:* 707-256-7113 *E-mail:* info@napawritersconference.org; fiction@napawritersconference.org; poetry@napawritersconference.org *Web Site:* www.napawritersconference.org, pg 556

Wybraniec, Barbara, Oscar Williams/Gene Derwood Award, 909 Third Ave, New York, NY 10022 *Tel:* 212-686-0010 *Fax:* 212-532-8528 *E-mail:* info@nycommunitytrust.org *Web Site:* www.nycommunitytrust.org, pg 675

Wyckoff, Joanne, Carol Mann Agency, 55 Fifth Ave, 18th fl, New York, NY 10003 *Tel:* 212-206-5635 *Fax:* 212-675-4809 *E-mail:* submissions@carolmannagency.com *Web Site:* www.carolmannagency.com, pg 468

Wydysh, Martha, Trident Media Group LLC, 355 Lexington Ave, 12th fl, New York, NY 10017 *Tel:* 212-333-1511 *E-mail:* info@tridentmediagroup.com; press@tridentmediagroup.com; foreignrights@tridentmediagroup.com; office.assistant@tridentmediagroup.com *Web Site:* www.tridentmediagroup.com, pg 480

Wyffels, John, Random House Children's Books, c/o Penguin Random House LLC, 1745 Broadway, New York, NY 10019 *Tel:* 212-782-9000 *Web Site:* www.rhcbooks.com, pg 170

Wygand, Jen, HarperCollins Children's Books, 195 Broadway, New York, NY 10007 *Tel:* 212-207-7000 *Web Site:* www.harpercollins.com/childrens, pg 85

Wygand, Jen, HarperCollins Publishers LLC, 195 Broadway, New York, NY 10007 *Tel:* 212-207-7000 *Web Site:* www.harpercollins.com, pg 86

Wylie, Andrew, The Wylie Agency LLC, 250 W 57 St, Suite 2114, New York, NY 10107 *Tel:* 212-246-0069 *E-mail:* mail@wylieagency.com *Web Site:* www.wylieagency.com, pg 483

Wyman, Pilar, Wyman Indexing, 1311 Delaware Ave SW, Suite S332, Washington, DC 20024 *Tel:* 443-336-5497 *Web Site:* www.wymanindexing.com, pg 446

Wyndham, Lee, Canadian Museum of History (Musee canadien de l'histoire), 100 Laurier St, Gatineau, QC K1A 0M8, Canada *Tel:* 819-776-7000 *Toll Free Tel:* 800-555-5621 (North American orders only) *Fax:* 819-776-7187 *Web Site:* www.historymuseum.ca, pg 398

Wynn, Denise, William Carey Publishing, 10 W Dry Creek Circle, Littleton, CO 80120 *Tel:* 720-372-7036 *E-mail:* publishing@wclbooks.com *Web Site:* www.missionbooks.org, pg 230

Wynn, Gina, Hachette Nashville, 6100 Tower Circle, Room 210, Franklin, TN 37067 *Tel:* 615-221-0996 *Fax:* 615-221-0962 *Web Site:* www.hachettebookgroup.com/imprint/hachette-nashville/, pg 83

Wynn, Mychal, Rising Sun Publishing, PO Box 70906, Marietta, GA 30007-0906 *Tel:* 770-518-0369 *Fax:* 770-587-0862 *E-mail:* info@rspublishing.com *Web Site:* www.rspublishing.com, pg 175

Wynter, Ashley, Copper Canyon Press, Fort Worden State Park, Bldg 313, Port Townsend, WA 98368 *Tel:* 360-385-4925 *E-mail:* poetry@coppercanyonpress.org; publicity@coppercanyonpress.org; digitalcontent@coppercanyonpress.com *Web Site:* www.coppercanyonpress.org, pg 52

Wypych, Anna, ChemTec Publishing, 38 Earswick Dr, Toronto, ON M1E 1C6, Canada *Tel:* 416-265-2603 *E-mail:* orderdesk@chemtec.org *Web Site:* www.chemtec.org, pg 399

Xu, Jenny, Atria Books, 1230 Avenue of the Americas, New York, NY 10020 *Tel:* 212-698-7000 *Fax:* 212-698-7007 *Web Site:* www.simonandschuster.com, pg 21

Yackira, Andrew, HarperCollins Publishers LLC, 195 Broadway, New York, NY 10007 *Tel:* 212-207-7000 *Web Site:* www.harpercollins.com, pg 87

Yadi, Lydia, Portfolio, c/o Penguin Random House LLC, 1745 Broadway, New York, NY 10019 *Tel:* 212-782-9000 *Web Site:* www.penguin.com/portfolio-overview/; www.penguin.com/sentinel-overview/; www.penguin.com/thesis/, pg 162

Yaged, Jon, Macmillan, 120 Broadway, 22nd fl, New York, NY 10271 *E-mail:* press.inquiries@macmillan.com *Web Site:* us.macmillan.com, pg 121

Yaged, Jon, Macmillan Audio, 120 Broadway, 22nd fl, New York, NY 10271 *Tel:* 646-600-7856 *Toll Free Tel:* 888-330-8477 (cust serv) *Toll Free Fax:* 800-672-7703 *E-mail:* macmillan.audio@macmillanusa.com *Web Site:* us.macmillan.com/audio, pg 123

Yager, Dr Jan, Hannacroix Creek Books Inc, 1127 High Ridge Rd, PMB 110, Stamford, CT 06905 *Tel:* 203-968-8098 *E-mail:* hannacroix@aol.com, pg 85

Yahr, Andrea, Round Table Companies, PO Box 1603, Deerfield, IL 60015 *Toll Free Tel:* 833-750-5683 *Web Site:* www.roundtablecompanies.com, pg 177

Yama, Renee, Hazy Dell Press, 1001 SE Water Ave, Suite 132, Portland, OR 97214 *Tel:* 971-279-5779 *E-mail:* info@hazydellpress.com *Web Site:* www.hazydellpress.com, pg 89

Yamaguchi, Ryo, Copper Canyon Press, Fort Worden State Park, Bldg 313, Port Townsend, WA 98368 *Tel:* 360-385-4925 *E-mail:* poetry@coppercanyonpress.org; publicity@coppercanyonpress.org; digitalcontent@coppercanyonpress.com *Web Site:* www.coppercanyonpress.org, pg 52

Yamamoto, Ken, Scholastic Trade Publishing, 557 Broadway, New York, NY 10012 *Tel:* 212-343-6100; 212-343-4685 (export sales) *Fax:* 212-343-4714 (export sales) *Web Site:* www.scholastic.com, pg 184

Yamashita, Brianna, Scribner, 1230 Avenue of the Americas, New York, NY 10020 *Web Site:* www.simonandschusterpublishing.com/scribner/, pg 185

Yang, Caren, Saint Mary's Press, 702 Terrace Heights, Winona, MN 55987-1320 *Tel:* 507-457-7900 *Toll Free Tel:* 800-533-8095 *Toll Free Fax:* 800-344-9225 *E-mail:* smpress@smp.org *Web Site:* www.smp.org, pg 181

Yang, Cecilia, Penguin Random House Canada, a Penguin Random House company, 320 Front St W, Suite 1400, Toronto, ON M5V 3B6, Canada *Tel:* 416-364-4449 *Toll Free Tel:* 888-523-9292 (cust serv) *E-mail:* canadaweb@penguinrandomhouse.com; customerservicescanada@penguinrandomhouse.com *Web Site:* www.penguinrandomhouse.ca, pg 416

Yang, Jessica, Quirk Books, 215 Church St, Philadelphia, PA 19106 *Tel:* 215-627-3581 *Fax:* 215-627-5220 *E-mail:* general@quirkbooks.com *Web Site:* www.quirkbooks.com, pg 168

Yankech, Andrew, Loyola Press, 8770 W Bryn Mawr Ave, Suite 1125, Chicago, IL 60631 *Tel:* 773-281-1818 *Toll Free Tel:* 800-621-1008 *Fax:* 773-281-0555 (cust serv); 773-281-4129 (edit) *E-mail:* customerservice@loyolapress.com *Web Site:* www.loyolapress.com, pg 121

Yanosey, Robert J, Morning Sun Books Inc, 1200 County Rd 523, Flemington, NJ 08822 *Tel:* 908-806-6216 *Fax:* 908-237-2407 *E-mail:* sales@morningsunbooks.com *Web Site:* morningsunbooks.com, pg 134

Yao, Jessica, W W Norton & Company Inc, 500 Fifth Ave, New York, NY 10110-0017 *Tel:* 212-354-5500 *Toll Free Tel:* 800-233-4830 (orders & cust serv) *Fax:* 212-869-0856 *Toll Free Fax:* 800-458-6515 *E-mail:* orders@wwnorton.com *Web Site:* wwnorton.com, pg 143

Yao, Mei C, The Yao Enterprises (Literary Agents) LLC, 67 Banksville Rd, Armonk, NY 10504 *Tel:* 914-765-0296 *E-mail:* yaollc@gmail.com, pg 483

Yarbrough, Cappy, Chronicle Books LLC, 680 Second St, San Francisco, CA 94107 *Tel:* 415-537-4200 *Fax:* 415-537-4460 (perms) *E-mail:* hello@chroniclebooks.com; subrights@chroniclebooks.com *Web Site:* www.chroniclebooks.com, pg 48

Yates, Barbara, Redleaf Press®, 10 Yorkton Ct, St Paul, MN 55117 *Tel:* 651-641-0508 *Toll Free Tel:* 800-423-8309 *Fax:* 651-641-0115 *E-mail:* customerservice@redleafpress.org; info@redleafpress.org; marketing@redleafpress.org *Web Site:* www.redleafpress.org, pg 173

Yates, Candace, Redleaf Press®, 10 Yorkton Ct, St Paul, MN 55117 *Tel:* 651-641-0508 *Toll Free Tel:* 800-423-8309 *Fax:* 651-641-0115 *E-mail:* customerservice@redleafpress.org; info@redleafpress.org; marketing@redleafpress.org *Web Site:* www.redleafpress.org, pg 173

Yates, Michael D, Monthly Review Press, 134 W 29 St, Suite 706, New York, NY 10001 *Tel:* 212-691-2555 *E-mail:* social@monthlyreview.org *Web Site:* monthlyreview.org, pg 134

Yates, Steve, University Press of Mississippi, 3825 Ridgewood Rd, Jackson, MS 39211-6492 *Tel:* 601-432-6205 *Toll Free Tel:* 800-737-7788 (orders & cust serv) *Fax:* 601-432-6217 *E-mail:* press@mississippi.edu *Web Site:* www.upress.state.ms.us, pg 222

Ye, Shawn Xian, Homa & Sekey Books, Mack-Cali Ctr II, N Tower, 3rd fl, 140 E Ridgewood Ave, Paramus, NJ 07652 *Tel:* 201-261-8810 *Fax:* 201-261-8890 *E-mail:* info@homabooks.com *Web Site:* www.homabooks.com, pg 95

Ye, Yvonne, Tor Publishing Group, 120 Broadway, New York, NY 10271 *Tel:* 212-782-9000 *Toll Free Tel:* 800-455-0340 (Macmillan) *E-mail:* torpublicity@tor.com; forgepublicity@forgebooks.com *Web Site:* us.macmillan.com/torpublishinggroup, pg 208

Yeager, Cynthia, Vanderbilt University Press, 2301 Vanderbilt Place, PMB 401813, Nashville, TN 37240-1813 *Tel:* 615-322-3585 *Toll Free Tel:* 800-848-6224 (orders only) *Fax:* 615-343-0308 *E-mail:* vupress@vanderbilt.edu *Web Site:* www.vanderbiltuniversitypress.com, pg 224

Yeager, Rebecca, Tor Publishing Group, 120 Broadway, New York, NY 10271 *Toll Free Tel:* 800-455-0340 (Macmillan) *E-mail:* torpublicity@tor.com; forgepublicity@forgebooks.com *Web Site:* us.macmillan.com/torpublishinggroup, pg 208

Yeamans, Lynne, Random House Publishing Group, 1745 Broadway, New York, NY 10019 *Toll Free Tel:* 800-200-3552 *Web Site:* www.randomhousebooks.com, pg 171

Yeater, Julie, Houghton Mifflin Harcourt Trade & Reference Division, 125 High St, Boston, MA 02110 *Tel:* 617-351-5000 *Web Site:* www.hmhco.com, pg 96

Yee, Amanda, Penguin Random House LLC, 1745 Broadway, New York, NY 10019 *Tel:* 212-782-9000 *Toll Free Tel:* 800-726-0600 *Web Site:* www.penguinrandomhouse.com, pg 155

Yee, Jamie, Random House Children's Books, c/o Penguin Random House LLC, 1745 Broadway, New York, NY 10019 *Tel:* 212-782-9000 *Web Site:* www.rhcbooks.com, pg 170

Yee, Roger, Visual Profile Books Inc, 389 Fifth Ave, Suite 1105, New York, NY 10016 *Tel:* 516-445-0116 *Web Site:* www.visualprofilebooks.com, pg 225

Yeffeth, Glenn, BenBella Books Inc, 10440 N Central Expwy, Suite 800, Dallas, TX 75231-2264 *Tel:* 214-750-3600 *Web Site:* www.benbellabooks.com; www.smartpopbooks.com, pg 27

Yeh, Phoebe, Random House Children's Books, c/o Penguin Random House LLC, 1745 Broadway, New York, NY 10019 *Tel:* 212-782-9000 *Web Site:* www.rhcbooks.com, pg 169

Yehudiel, Jordan, Macmillan, 120 Broadway, 22nd fl, New York, NY 10271 *E-mail:* press.inquiries@macmillan.com *Web Site:* us.macmillan.com, pg 122

Yengle, Lily, Bloomsbury Publishing Inc, 1385 Broadway, 5th fl, New York, NY 10018 *Tel:* 212-419-5300 *E-mail:* marketingusa@bloomsbury.com; adultpublicityusa@bloomsbury.com; askacademic@bloomsbury.com *Web Site:* www.bloomsbury.com, pg 31

Yentus, Helen, Riverhead Books, c/o Penguin Random House LLC, 1745 Broadway, New York, NY 10019 *Tel:* 212-782-9000 *Web Site:* www.penguin.com/riverhead-overview/, pg 175

Yeping, Hu, Council for Research in Values & Philosophy, The Catholic University of America, Gibbons Hall, B-20, 620 Michigan Ave NE, Washington, DC 20064 Tel: 202-319-6089 E-mail: cua-rvp@cua.edu Web Site: www.crvp.org, pg 53

Yepsen, Ashley, HarperCollins Publishers LLC, 195 Broadway, New York, NY 10007 Tel: 212-207-7000 Web Site: www.harpercollins.com, pg 86

Yesilonis, Daniel, Casemate | publishers, 1950 Lawrence Rd, Havertown, PA 19083 Tel: 610-853-9131 Fax: 610-853-9146 E-mail: casemate@casematepublishers.com Web Site: www.casematepublishers.com, pg 41

Yesilova, Hakan, Tughra Books, 335 Clifton Ave, Clifton, NJ 07011 Tel: 646-415-9331 Fax: 646-827-6228 E-mail: info@tughrabooks.com Web Site: www.tughrabooks.com, pg 210

Yi, Janice, Chronicle Books LLC, 680 Second St, San Francisco, CA 94107 Tel: 415-537-4200 Fax: 415-537-4460 (perms) E-mail: hello@chroniclebooks.com; subrights@chroniclebooks.com Web Site: www.chroniclebooks.com, pg 48

Yoder, Carolyn P, Astra Books for Young Readers, 19 W 21 St, No 1201, New York, NY 10010 Tel: 646-844-3485 E-mail: ahinfo@astrahouse.com; permissions@astrapublishinghouse.com Web Site: astrapublishinghouse.com, pg 20

Yoelin, Adam, BOOM! Studios, 5670 Wilshire Blvd, Suite 400, Los Angeles, CA 90036 E-mail: contact@boom-studios.com; customerservice@boom-studios.com; press@boom-studios.com Web Site: www.boom-studios.com, pg 34

Yoh, Eugenia, Chronicle Books LLC, 680 Second St, San Francisco, CA 94107 Tel: 415-537-4200 Fax: 415-537-4460 (perms) E-mail: hello@chroniclebooks.com; subrights@chroniclebooks.com Web Site: www.chroniclebooks.com, pg 48

Yokell, Colby, Adams Media, 100 Technology Center Dr, Suite 501, Stoughton, MA 02072 Tel: 508-427-7100 Web Site: www.simonandschuster.com, pg 4

Yokota, Ms Junko, United States Board on Books for Young People (USBBY), National Luis University, Ctr for Teaching through Children's Books, 1000 Capitol Dr, Wheeling, IL 60090 Tel: 224-233-2798 E-mail: secretariat@usbby.org Web Site: www.usbby.org, pg 521

Yonker, Pamela A, Association for Information Science & Technology (ASIS&T), 673 Potomac Station Dr, Suite 155, Leesburg, VA 20176 Tel: 301-495-0900 Fax: 301-495-0810 E-mail: asist@asist.org; membership@asist.org Web Site: www.asist.org, pg 498

Yoo, Andy, Savvas Learning Co LLC, 15 E Midland Ave, Suite 502, Paramus, NJ 07652 Toll Free Tel: 800-848-9500 Web Site: www.savvas.com, pg 183

Yoon, Howard, WME, 11 Madison Ave, New York, NY 10010 Tel: 212-586-5100 Web Site: www.wmeagency.com, pg 482

Yoon, Irene, LARB/USC Publishing Workshop, 6671 Sunset Blvd, Suite 1521, Los Angeles, CA 90028 E-mail: publishingworkshop@lareviewofbooks.org Web Site: thepublishingworkshop.com, pg 556

Yoon, Janie, Doubleday Canada, 320 Front St W, Suite 1400, Toronto, ON M5V 3B6, Canada Tel: 416-364-4449 Fax: 416-598-7764 Web Site: www.penguinrandomhouse.ca, pg 401

Yoon, Janie, House of Anansi Press Inc, 128 Sterling Rd, Lower Level, Toronto, ON M6R 2B7, Canada Tel: 416-363-4343 Fax: 416-363-1017 E-mail: customerservice@houseofanansi.com Web Site: houseofanansi.com, pg 409

York, Lynn, Blair, 905 W Main St, Suite 19 D-1, Durham, NC 27701 Tel: 919-682-0555 E-mail: customersupport@blair.com Web Site: www.blairpub.com, pg 30

Yoskowitz, Lisa, Little, Brown Books for Young Readers (LBYR), 1290 Avenue of the Americas, New York, NY 10104 Tel: 212-364-1100 Toll Free Tel: 800-759-0190 (cust serv) E-mail: rights@lbchildrens.com Web Site: www.hachettebookgroup.com/imprint/little-brown-books-for-young-readers/, pg 118

Yost, JT, NBM Publishing Inc, 300 E 54 St, No 12C, New York, NY 10022-5021 Tel: 917-628-6777 E-mail: nbmgn@nbmpub.com Web Site: www.nbmpub.com, pg 139

Yother, Michele, Gallopade International Inc, 611 Hwy 74 S, Suite 2000, Peachtree City, GA 30269 Tel: 770-631-4222 Toll Free Tel: 800-536-2438 Fax: 770-631-4810 Toll Free Fax: 800-871-2979 E-mail: customerservice@gallopade.com Web Site: www.gallopade.com, pg 76

Younce, Virginia Smith, Penguin Press, c/o Penguin Random House LLC, 1745 Broadway, New York, NY 10019 Tel: 212-782-9000 E-mail: penguinpress@penguinrandomhouse.com Web Site: www.penguin.com/penguin-press-overview/, pg 154

Younce, Webster, Zondervan, 3900 Sparks Dr SE, Grand Rapids, MI 49546 Tel: 616-698-6900 Toll Free Tel: 800-226-1122; 800-727-1309 (retail orders) Fax: 616-698-3350 Toll Free Fax: 800-698-3256 (retail orders) E-mail: customercare@harpercollins.com Web Site: www.zondervan.com, pg 236

Young, Chelsey, Association of Manitoba Book Publishers (AMBP), 100 Arthur St, Suite 404, Winnipeg, MB R3B 1H3, Canada Tel: 204-947-3335 E-mail: ambp@mymts.net Web Site: ambp.ca, pg 499

Young, Clarissa, Triumph Books LLC, 814 N Franklin St, Chicago, IL 60610 Tel: 312-337-0747 Toll Free Tel: 800-888-4741 (cust serv) Fax: 312-280-5470; 312-337-5985 Web Site: www.triumphbooks.com, pg 210

Young, Courtney, Riverhead Books, c/o Penguin Random House LLC, 1745 Broadway, New York, NY 10019 Tel: 212-782-9000 Web Site: www.penguin.com/riverhead-overview/, pg 175

Young, Cyle, Hartline Literary Agency LLC, 123 Queenston Dr, Pittsburgh, PA 15235 Tel: 412-829-2483 Toll Free Fax: 888-279-6007 Web Site: www.hartlineliterary.com, pg 462

Young, Debi, Sunbelt Publications Inc, 664 Marsat Ct, Suite A, Chula Vista, CA 91911 Tel: 619-258-4911 Toll Free Tel: 800-626-6579 (cust serv) Fax: 619-258-4916 E-mail: info@sunbeltpub.com; service@sunbeltpub.com Web Site: sunbeltpublications.com, pg 200

Young, Hallie, Macmillan, 120 Broadway, 22nd fl, New York, NY 10271 E-mail: press.inquiries@macmillan.com Web Site: us.macmillan.com, pg 122

Young, Jazmia, Curtis Brown, Ltd, 228 E 45 St, Suite 310, New York, NY 10017 Tel: 212-473-5400 Fax: 212-598-0917 E-mail: info@cbltd.com Web Site: www.curtisbrown.com, pg 452

Young, Dr Jeffrey, Dissertation.com, 200 Spectrum Center Dr, 3rd fl, Irvine, CA 92618 Tel: 561-750-4344 Toll Free Tel: 800-636-8329 Fax: 561-750-6797 Web Site: www.dissertation.com, pg 60

Young, Jeffrey R, Universal-Publishers Inc, 200 Spectrum Center Dr, Suite 300, Irvine, CA 92618-5004 Tel: 561-750-4344 Toll Free Tel: 800-636-8329 (US only) Fax: 561-750-6797 Web Site: www.universal-publishers.com, pg 213

Young, Kenli, Bloomsbury Publishing Inc, 1385 Broadway, 5th fl, New York, NY 10018 Tel: 212-419-5300 E-mail: marketingusa@bloomsbury.com; adultpublicityusa@bloomsbury.com; askacademic@bloomsbury.com Web Site: www.bloomsbury.com, pg 32

Young, Marian, The Young Agency, 213 Bennett Ave, No 3H, New York, NY 10040 Tel: 212-229-2612, pg 483

Young, Mary D, Kent State University Press, 1118 University Library Bldg, 1125 Risman Dr, Kent, OH 44242 Tel: 330-672-7913 Fax: 330-672-3104 E-mail: ksupress@kent.edu Web Site: www.kentstateuniversitypress.com, pg 109

Young, Stephen, Poetry Foundation, 61 W Superior St, Chicago, IL 60654 Tel: 312-787-7070 E-mail: info@poetryfoundation.org Web Site: www.poetryfoundation.org, pg 526

Young, Tyler, Pieces of Learning Inc, 1112 N Carbon St, Suite A, Marion, IL 62959-8976 Tel: 618-964-9426 Toll Free Tel: 800-729-5137 Toll Free Fax: 800-844-0455 E-mail: info@piecesoflearning.com Web Site: piecesoflearning.com, pg 160

Younger, Carol, Smyth & Helwys Publishing Inc, 6316 Peake Rd, Macon, GA 31210-3960 Tel: 478-757-0564 Toll Free Tel: 800-747-3016 (orders only) Fax: 478-757-1305 E-mail: information@helwys.com Web Site: www.helwys.com, pg 192

Younger, Natalie, BoardSource, 750 Ninth St NW, Suite 520, Washington, DC 20001-4793 Tel: 202-349-2500 E-mail: members@boardsource.org; mediarelations@boardsource.org Web Site: www.boardsource.org, pg 33

Younging, Greg, Theytus Books Ltd, 154 Enowkin Trail, RR 2, Site 50, Comp 8, Penticton, BC V2A 6J7, Canada Tel: 250-493-7181 Fax: 250-493-5302 E-mail: order@theytus.com; marketing@theytus.com Web Site: www.theytus.com, pg 420

Youngstrom, Cassie, American Booksellers Association, 600 Mamaroneck Ave, Suite 400, Harrison, NY 10528 Tel: 914-406-7500 Toll Free Tel: 800-637-0037 Fax: 914-417-4013 E-mail: info@bookweb.org Web Site: www.bookweb.org, pg 494

Yu, Jin, Berkley, c/o Penguin Random House LLC, 1745 Broadway, 19th fl, New York, NY 10019 Tel: 212-366-2000 Web Site: www.penguin.com/publishers/berkley/; www.penguin.com/ace-overview/, pg 28

Yu, Victoria, Lyndon B Johnson School of Public Affairs, University of Texas at Austin, 2300 Red River St, Stop E2700, Austin, TX 78712-1536 Tel: 512-471-3200 E-mail: lbjdeansoffice@austin.utexas.edu Web Site: lbj.utexas.edu, pg 106

Yudelson, Larry, Ben Yehuda Press, 122 Ayers Ct, No 1B, Teaneck, NJ 07666 E-mail: orders@benyehudapress.com; yudel@benyehudapress.com Web Site: www.benyehudapress.com, pg 27

Yuhas, Thomas, Random House Publishing Group, 1745 Broadway, New York, NY 10019 Toll Free Tel: 800-200-3552 Web Site: www.randomhousebooks.com, pg 171

Yule, Sean, Alfred A Knopf, c/o Penguin Random House LLC, 1745 Broadway, New York, NY 10019 Tel: 212-751-2600 Fax: 212-940-7390 (dom rts); 212-572-2662 (foreign rts) Web Site: knopfdoubleday.com/imprint/knopf/; knopfdoubleday.com, pg 110

Yunker, John, Ashland Creek Press, 2305 Ashland St, Suite C417, Ashland, OR 97520 Tel: 760-300-3620 E-mail: editors@ashlandcreekpress.com Web Site: www.ashlandcreekpress.com, pg 18

Zabka, Rosanne, Hospital & Healthcare Compensation Service, 3 Post Rd, Suite 3, Oakland, NJ 07436 Tel: 201-405-0075 Fax: 201-405-2110 E-mail: allinfo@hhcsinc.com Web Site: www.hhcsinc.com, pg 95

Zaborsky, Katie, Dutton, c/o Penguin Random House LLC, 1745 Broadway, New York, NY 10019 Tel: 212-366-2000 Web Site: www.penguin.com/dutton-overview/; www.penguin.com/plume-books-overview/; www.penguin.com/tiny-reparations-overview/, pg 62

Zaccaria, Marcina, Editorial Freelancers Association (EFA), 266 W 37 St, 20th fl, New York, NY 10018 Tel: 212-920-4816 Toll Free Tel: 866-929-5425 E-mail: info@the-efa.org; membership@the-efa.org Web Site: www.the-efa.org, pg 505

Zacharius, Adam, Kensington Publishing Corp, 900 Third Ave, 26th fl, New York, NY 10022 Tel: 212-407-1500 Toll Free Tel: 800-221-2647 Fax: 212-935-0699 Web Site: www.kensingtonbooks.com, pg 109

Zacharius, Steven, Kensington Publishing Corp, 900 Third Ave, 26th fl, New York, NY 10022 Tel: 212-407-1500 Toll Free Tel: 800-221-2647 Fax: 212-935-0699 Web Site: www.kensingtonbooks.com, pg 109

Zachman, Jana, David C Cook, 4050 Lee Vance Dr, Colorado Springs, CO 80918 Tel: 719-536-0100 Toll Free Tel: 800-323-7543 (orders & cust serv) Toll Free Fax: 800-430-0726 (cust serv) E-mail: bookstores@davidccook.org; customercare@davidccook.org Web Site: www.davidccook.org, pg 52

Zack, Elizabeth, BookCrafters LLC Editing, 24 Old Glen Rd, Morristown, NJ 07960 Tel: 973-984-3868 Web Site: bookcraftersllc.com, pg 436

Zackheim, Adrian, Penguin Publishing Group, c/o Penguin Random House LLC, 1745 Broadway, New York, NY 10019 Tel: 212-782-9000 Web Site: www.penguin.com, pg 154

Zackheim, Adrian, Portfolio, c/o Penguin Random House LLC, 1745 Broadway, New York, NY 10019 Tel: 212-782-9000 Web Site: www.penguin.com/portfolio-overview/; www.penguin.com/sentinel-overview/; www.penguin.com/thesis/, pg 162

Zadrozny, Mark, Cambridge University Press, One Liberty Plaza, 20th fl, New York, NY 10006 Tel: 212-924-3900; 212-337-5000 Fax: 212-691-3239; 845-353-4141 E-mail: customer_service@cambridge.org; orders@cambridge.org; subscriptions_newyork@cambridge.org Web Site: www.cambridge.org/us, pg 39

Zafian, Anne, Simon & Schuster Children's Publishing, 1230 Avenue of the Americas, New York, NY 10020 Tel: 212-698-7000 Web Site: www.simonandschuster.com/kids; www.simonandschuster.com/teen; simonandschuster.net; simonandschuster.biz, pg 189

Zagaceta, Rosana, Macmillan, 120 Broadway, 22nd fl, New York, NY 10271 E-mail: press.inquiries@macmillan.com Web Site: us.macmillan.com, pg 122

Zahorsky, Melissa Rhodes, Andrews McMeel Publishing LLC, 1130 Walnut St, Kansas City, MO 64106-2109 Tel: 816-581-7500 Toll Free Tel: 800-851-8923 Web Site: www.andrewsmcmeel; publishing.andrewsmcmeel.com, pg 14

Zaidi, Jamil, Chronicle Books LLC, 680 Second St, San Francisco, CA 94107 Tel: 415-537-4200 Fax: 415-537-4460 (perms) E-mail: hello@chroniclebooks.com; subrights@chroniclebooks.com Web Site: www.chroniclebooks.com, pg 47

Zajdman, Josh, The New Press, 120 Wall St, 31st fl, New York, NY 10005 Tel: 212-629-8802 Fax: 212-629-8617 E-mail: newpress@thenewpress.com Web Site: thenewpress.com, pg 140

Zalewski, Ellen, University of Chicago Press, 1427 E 60 St, Chicago, IL 60637-2954 Tel: 773-702-7700; 773-702-7600 Toll Free Tel: 800-621-2736 (orders) Fax: 773-702-9756; 773-660-2235 (orders); 773-702-2708 E-mail: custserv@press.uchicago.edu; marketing@press.uchicago.edu Web Site: www.press.uchicago.edu, pg 215

Zamajtuk, Jason, Random House Children's Books, c/o Penguin Random House LLC, 1745 Broadway, New York, NY 10019 Tel: 212-782-9000 Web Site: www.rhcbooks.com, pg 169

Zamani, Fay, Mazda Publishers Inc, PO Box 2603, Costa Mesa, CA 92628 Tel: 714-751-5252 Fax: 714-751-4805 E-mail: mazdapub@aol.com Web Site: www.mazdapublishers.com, pg 127

Zamiar, Jeanine, American Catholic Press (ACP), 16565 S State St, South Holland, IL 60473 Tel: 708-331-5485 Fax: 708-331-5484 E-mail: acp@acpress.org Web Site: www.acpress.org, pg 9

Zampetti, Leslie, Association of American Literary Agents Inc (AALA), 302A W 12 St, No 122, New York, NY 10014 Tel: 212-840-5770 E-mail: info@aalitagents.org Web Site: aalitagents.org, pg 498

Zampetti, Leslie, Open Book Literary, 1500 Chestnut St, Suite 2, No 1436, Philadelphia, PA 19102 E-mail: info@openbooklit.com Web Site: www.openbooklit.com, pg 471

Zancan, Caroline, Henry Holt and Company, LLC, 120 Broadway, 23rd fl, New York, NY 10271 Tel: 646-307-5151 Toll Free Tel: 888-330-8477 (orders) Fax: 646-307-5285 Web Site: www.henryholt.com, pg 94

Zanzucchi, Kate, Yale University Press, 302 Temple St, New Haven, CT 06511-8909 Tel: 203-432-0960; 203-432-0966 (sales); 401-531-2800 (cust serv) Toll Free Tel: 800-405-1619 (cust serv) Fax: 203-432-0948; 203-432-8485 (sales); 401-531-2801 (cust serv) Toll Free Fax: 800-406-9145 (cust serv) E-mail: sales.press@yale.edu (sales); customer.care@triliteral.org (cust serv) Web Site: www.yalebooks.com; yalepress.yale.edu/yupbooks, pg 235

Zappola, John, HarperCollins Publishers LLC, 195 Broadway, New York, NY 10007 Tel: 212-207-7000 Web Site: www.harpercollins.com, pg 86

Zar, Melissa, Farrar, Straus & Giroux Books for Young Readers, 120 Broadway, New York, NY 10271 Tel: 212-741-6900 Toll Free Tel: 888-330-8477 (orders) E-mail: childrens.publicity@macmillanusa.com; childrensrights@macmillanusa.com Web Site: us.macmillan.com/mackids, pg 70

Zar, Melissa, Roaring Brook Press, 120 Broadway, New York, NY 10271 Tel: 646-307-5151 Web Site: us.macmillan.com/publishers/roaring-brook-press, pg 176

Zaragoza, Jason, National Press Foundation, 1211 Connecticut Ave NW, Suite 310, Washington, DC 20036 Tel: 202-663-7286 Web Site: nationalpress.org, pg 526

Zargarpur, Deeba, Simon & Schuster Children's Publishing, 1230 Avenue of the Americas, New York, NY 10020 Tel: 212-698-7000 Web Site: www.simonandschuster.com/kids; www.simonandschuster.com/teen; simonandschuster.net; simonandschuster.biz, pg 189

Zarley, Michael, Sourcebooks LLC, 1935 Brookdale Rd, Suite 139, Naperville, IL 60563 Tel: 630-961-3900 Toll Free Tel: 800-432-7444 Fax: 630-961-2168 E-mail: info@sourcebooks.com Web Site: www.sourcebooks.com, pg 194

Zarro, Alissa, Rutgers University Press, 106 Somerset St, 3rd fl, New Brunswick, NJ 08901 Tel: 848-445-7762; 848-445-7761 (sales) Fax: 732-745-4935 E-mail: sales@rutgersuniversitypress.org Web Site: www.rutgersuniversitypress.org, pg 179

Zatopek, Sara, The Experiment, 220 E 23 St, Suite 600, New York, NY 10010-4658 Tel: 212-889-1659 E-mail: info@theexperimentpublishing.com Web Site: www.theexperimentpublishing.com, pg 68

Zaval, Shara, Sourcebooks LLC, 1935 Brookdale Rd, Suite 139, Naperville, IL 60563 Tel: 630-961-3900 Toll Free Tel: 800-432-7444 Fax: 630-961-2168 E-mail: info@sourcebooks.com Web Site: www.sourcebooks.com, pg 194

Zawistowska, Natalie, Safer Society Press, PO Box 340, Brandon, VT 05733-0340 Tel: 802-247-3132 Fax: 802-247-4233 E-mail: info@safersociety.org Web Site: safersocietypress.org, pg 179

Zeig, Jeffrey K PhD, Zeig, Tucker & Theisen Inc, 2632 E Thomas Rd, Suite 201, Phoenix, AZ 85016 Tel: 480-389-4342 Web Site: www.zeigtucker.com, pg 236

Zeigler, Zach, University Press of Kansas, 2502 Westbrooke Circle, Lawrence, KS 66045-4444 Tel: 785-864-4154 Fax: 785-864-4586 E-mail: upress@ku.edu Web Site: www.kansaspress.ku.edu, pg 221

Zelazko, Kristin, Candlewick Press, 99 Dover St, Somerville, MA 02144-2825 Tel: 617-661-3330 Fax: 617-661-0565 E-mail: bigbear@candlewick.com; salesinfo@candlewick.com Web Site: candlewick.com, pg 40

Zenebework, Bessa, Random House Children's Books, c/o Penguin Random House LLC, 1745 Broadway, New York, NY 10019 Tel: 212-782-9000 Web Site: www.rhcbooks.com, pg 170

Zeng, Cady, Penguin Random House Audio Publishing Group, 1745 Broadway, New York, NY 10019 Toll Free Tel: 800-793-2665 (cust serv) E-mail: audio@penguinrandomhouse.com; ecustomerservice@penguinrandomhouse.com Web Site: www.penguinrandomhouseaudio.com, pg 154

Zengierski, Sophia, Princeton University Press, 41 William St, Princeton, NJ 08540-5237 Tel: 609-258-4900 Fax: 609-258-6305 E-mail: info@press.princeton.edu Web Site: press.princeton.edu, pg 164

Zentner, Alexi, Binghamton University Creative Writing Program, c/o Dept of English, General Literature & Rhetoric, PO Box 6000, Binghamton, NY 13902-6000 Tel: 607-777-2168 Fax: 607-777-2408 E-mail: cwpro@binghamton.edu Web Site: www.binghamton.edu/english/creative-writing/index.html, pg 561

Zeoli, Steve, Safer Society Press, PO Box 340, Brandon, VT 05733-0340 Tel: 802-247-3132 Fax: 802-247-4233 E-mail: info@safersociety.org Web Site: safersocietypress.org, pg 179

Zeolla, David, Dorrance Publishing Co Inc, 585 Alpha Dr, Suite 103, Pittsburgh, PA 15238 Toll Free Tel: 800-695-9599; 800-788-7654 (gen cust orders) Fax: 412-387-1319 E-mail: dorrinfo@dorrancepublishing.com Web Site: www.dorrancepublishing.com, pg 61

Zguta, Stephan, Arcade Publishing Inc, 307 W 36 St, 11th fl, New York, NY 10018 Tel: 212-643-6816 Fax: 212-643-6819 E-mail: info@skyhorsepublishing.com (subs & foreign rts) Web Site: www.arcadepub.com, pg 16

Zhang, Ellen, Penguin Random House Canada, a Penguin Random House company, 320 Front St W, Suite 1400, Toronto, ON M5V 3B6, Canada Tel: 416-364-4449 Toll Free Tel: 888-523-9292 (cust serv) E-mail: canadaweb@penguinrandomhouse.com; customerservicescanada@penguinrandomhouse.com Web Site: www.penguinrandomhouse.ca, pg 416

Zhang, Han, Riverhead Books, c/o Penguin Random House LLC, 1745 Broadway, New York, NY 10019 Tel: 212-782-9000 Web Site: www.penguin.com/riverhead-overview/, pg 175

Zhang, Nancy, Candied Plums, 7548 Ravenna Ave NE, Seattle, WA 98115 E-mail: candiedplums@gmail.com Web Site: www.candiedplums.com, pg 39

Zhou, Jessie Stratton, Penguin Press, c/o Penguin Random House LLC, 1745 Broadway, New York, NY 10019 Tel: 212-782-9000 E-mail: penguinpress@penguinrandomhouse.com Web Site: www.penguin.com/penguin-press-overview/, pg 154

Zhu, Emily, HarperCollins Children's Books, 195 Broadway, New York, NY 10007 Tel: 212-207-7000 Web Site: www.harpercollins.com/childrens, pg 86

Zhu, Fei, Macmillan, 120 Broadway, 22nd fl, New York, NY 10271 E-mail: press.inquiries@macmillan.com Web Site: us.macmillan.com, pg 122

Zhu, George, CN Times Books, 100 Jericho Quadrangle, Suite 337, Jericho, NY 11791 Tel: 516-719-0886 E-mail: yanliu@cntimesbooks.com Web Site: www.cntimesbooks.com, pg 50

Zidle, Abby, Gallery Books, 1230 Avenue of the Americas, New York, NY 10020 Toll Free Tel: 800-456-6798 Fax: 212-698-7284 E-mail: consumer.customerservice@simonandschuster.com Web Site: www.simonandschuster.com, pg 76

Ziegler, Allison, St Martin's Press, LLC, 120 Broadway, New York, NY 10271 E-mail: publicity@stmartins.com; trademarketing@stmartins.com; foreignrights@stmartins.com Web Site: us.macmillan.com/smp, pg 181

Ziegler, Jennifer, Vermont College of Fine Arts MFA in Writing for Children & Young Adults Program, 36 College St, Montpelier, VT 05602 Toll Free Tel: 866-934-VCFA (934-8232) Web Site: vcfa.edu/mfa-writing-for-children-and-young-adults, pg 567

Zielinski, Mark, Facts On File, 1000 N West St, Suite 1281-230, Wilmington, DE 19801 Tel: 212-967-8800 Toll Free Tel: 800-322-8755 Toll Free Fax: 800-678-3633 E-mail: custserv@factsonfile.com Web Site: infobasepublishing.com, pg 69

Zielonka, David, Stanford University Press, 425 Broadway St, Redwood City, CA 94063-3126 Tel: 650-723-9434 Fax: 650-725-3457 E-mail: info@www.sup.org; publicity@www.sup.org; sales@www.sup.org Web Site: www.sup.org, pg 197

Ziff, Dorothy, Melissa Turk & the Artist Network, 9 Babbling Brook Lane, Suffern, NY 10901 Tel: 845-368-8606 E-mail: melissa@melissaturk.com Web Site: www.melissaturk.com, pg 486

Zimar, Heather, American Association of Collegiate Registrars & Admissions Officers (AACRAO), 1108 16 St NW, Washington, DC 20011 Tel: 202-293-9161 Fax: 202-872-8857 E-mail: pubs@aacrao.org Web Site: www.aacrao.org, pg 8

Zimlich, Megan, Kensington Publishing Corp, 900 Third Ave, 26th fl, New York, NY 10022 Tel: 212-407-1500 Toll Free Tel: 800-221-2647 Fax: 212-935-0699 Web Site: www.kensingtonbooks.com, pg 109

Zimmer, Jeremy, United Talent Agency LLC, 9336 Civic Center Dr, Beverly Hills, CA 90210 Tel: 310-273-6700 Web Site: www.unitedtalent.com, pg 481

Zimmer, Jeremy, UTA Speakers, 888 Seventh Ave, Suite 922, New York, NY 10106 Tel: 212-659-2600; 212-645-4200 E-mail: utaspeakers@unitedtalent.com Web Site: www.utaspeakers.com, pg 487

Zimmerli, Nadine, University of Virginia Press, PO Box 400318, Charlottesville, VA 22904-4318 Tel: 434-924-3469 (cust serv) Toll Free Tel: 800-831-3406 Fax: 434-982-2655 Toll Free Fax: 877-288-6400 E-mail: vapress@virginia.edu Web Site: www.upress.virginia.edu, pg 220

Zimmerman, Barbara, BZ/Rights & Permissions Inc, 145 W 86 St, New York, NY 10024 Tel: 212-924-3000 Fax: 212-924-2525 E-mail: info@bzrights.com Web Site: www.bzrights.com, pg 436

Zimmerman, Chad, University of Chicago Press, 1427 E 60 St, Chicago, IL 60637-2954 Tel: 773-702-7700; 773-702-7600 Toll Free Tel: 800-621-2736 (orders) Fax: 773-702-9756; 773-660-2235 (orders); 773-702-2708 E-mail: custserv@press.uchicago.edu; marketing@press.uchicago.edu Web Site: www.press.uchicago.edu, pg 215

Zimmerman, Jess, Quirk Books, 215 Church St, Philadelphia, PA 19106 Tel: 215-627-3581 Fax: 215-627-5220 E-mail: general@quirkbooks.com Web Site: www.quirkbooks.com, pg 168

Zimmerman, Jessica, St Martin's Press, LLC, 120 Broadway, New York, NY 10271 E-mail: publicity@stmartins.com; trademarketing@stmartins.com; foreignrights@stmartins.com Web Site: us.macmillan.com/smp, pg 181

Zimmerman, Jill, HarperCollins Publishers LLC, 195 Broadway, New York, NY 10007 Tel: 212-207-7000 Web Site: www.harpercollins.com, pg 87

Zimmermann, Kate, Union Square & Co, 1166 Avenue of the Americas, 17th fl, New York, NY 10036-2715 Tel: 212-532-7160 Toll Free Tel: 800-367-9692 Fax: 212-213-2495 Toll Free Fax: 800-542-7567 E-mail: custservice@sterlingpublishing.com; customerservice@sterlingpublishing.com; editorial@sterlingpublishing.com; tradesales@sterlingpublishing.com Web Site: www.sterlingpublishing.com, pg 212

Zink, Seta Bedrosian, Running Press, 1290 Avenue of the Americas, New York, NY 10104 Tel: 212-364-1100 Toll Free Tel: 800-759-0190 (cust serv) Fax: 212-364-0933 (intl orders) Toll Free Fax: 800-286-9471 (cust serv) E-mail: customer.service@hbgusa.com; orders@hbgusa.com Web Site: www.hachettebookgroup.com/imprint/running-press/; www.moon.com (Moon Travel Guides), pg 178

Zinner, Eric, New York University Press, 838 Broadway, 3rd fl, New York, NY 10003-4812 Tel: 212-998-2575 (edit) Toll Free Tel: 800-996-6987 (orders) Fax: 212-995-4798 (orders) E-mail: nyupressinfo@nyu.edu (cust care) Web Site: www.nyupress.org, pg 141

Ziolkowski, Thad, Biography Fellowships, 365 Fifth Ave, Rm 6200, New York, NY 10016 Tel: 212-817-2025 E-mail: biography@gc.cuny.edu Web Site: llcb.ws.gc.cuny.edu/fellowships, pg 580

Zion, Claire, Berkley, c/o Penguin Random House LLC, 1745 Broadway, 19th fl, New York, NY 10019 Tel: 212-366-2000 Web Site: www.penguin.com/publishers/berkley/; www.penguin.com/ace-overview/, pg 28

Zipper, Todd, John Wiley & Sons Inc, 111 River St, Hoboken, NJ 07030-5774 Tel: 201-748-6000 Toll Free Tel: 800-225-5945 (cust serv) Fax: 201-748-6088 Web Site: www.wiley.com, pg 230

Zitt, Dan, Living Language, c/o Penguin Random House LLC, 1745 Broadway, New York, NY 10019 Tel: 212-782-9000 Toll Free Tel: 800-733-3000 (orders) E-mail: support@livinglanguage.com Web Site: www.livinglanguage.com, pg 119

Zitt, Dan, Penguin Random House Audio Publishing Group, 1745 Broadway, New York, NY 10019 Toll Free Tel: 800-793-2665 (cust serv) E-mail: audio@penguinrandomhouse.com; ecustomerservice@penguinrandomhouse.com Web Site: www.penguinrandomhouseaudio.com, pg 154

Zitwer, Barbara J, Barbara J Zitwer Agency, 525 West End Ave, Unit 11-H, New York, NY 10024 Tel: 212-501-8423 E-mail: zitwer@gmail.com Web Site: www.barbarajzitweragency.com, pg 483

Ziv, Maya, Dutton, c/o Penguin Random House LLC, 1745 Broadway, New York, NY 10019 Tel: 212-366-2000 Web Site: www.penguin.com/dutton-overview/; www.penguin.com/plume-books-overview/; www.penguin.com/tiny-reparations-overview/, pg 62

Zobal, Silas Dent, Susquehanna University, Department of English & Creative Writing, 514 University Ave, Selinsgrove, PA 17870 Tel: 570-372-4196 Web Site: www.susqu.edu, pg 565

Zodrow, Kristin, Princeton University Press, 41 William St, Princeton, NJ 08540-5237 Tel: 609-258-4900 Fax: 609-258-6305 E-mail: info@press.princeton.edu Web Site: press.princeton.edu, pg 164

Zollshan, Ronald P, Kirchoff/Wohlberg Inc, 897 Boston Post Rd, Madison, CT 06443 Tel: 203-245-7308 Fax: 203-245-3218 E-mail: info@kirchoffwohlberg.com Web Site: www.kirchoffwohlberg.com, pg 465

Zoni, Matthew, American Booksellers Association, 600 Mamaroneck Ave, Suite 400, Harrison, NY 10528 Tel: 914-406-7500 Toll Free Tel: 800-637-0037 Fax: 914-417-4013 E-mail: info@bookweb.org Web Site: www.bookweb.org, pg 494

Zonnefeld, Courtney, Wm B Eerdmans Publishing Co, 4035 Park East Ct SE, Grand Rapids, MI 49546 Tel: 616-459-4591 Toll Free Fax: 800-253-7521 E-mail: customerservice@eerdmans.com; sales@eerdmans.com Web Site: www.eerdmans.com, pg 64

Zorian, Lora, Shambhala Publications Inc, 2129 13 St, Boulder, CO 80302 Tel: 978-829-2599 (intl callers) Toll Free Tel: 866-424-0030 (off); 888-424-2329 (orders & cust serv) Fax: 617-236-1563 E-mail: customercare@shambhala.com; royalties@shambhala.com Web Site: www.shambhala.com, pg 187

Zoro, Theresa, Random House Publishing Group, 1745 Broadway, New York, NY 10019 Toll Free Tel: 800-200-3552 Web Site: www.randomhousebooks.com, pg 170

Zschock, Heather, Peter Pauper Press, Inc, 202 Mamaroneck Ave, Suite 400, White Plains, NY 10601-5376 Tel: 914-681-0144 Fax: 914-681-0389 E-mail: customerservice@peterpauper.com; orders@peterpauper.com; marketing@peterpauper.com Web Site: www.peterpauper.com, pg 158

Zucca, Damon, Oxford University Press USA, 198 Madison Ave, New York, NY 10016 Toll Free Tel: 800-451-7556 (orders); 800-445-9714 (cust serv) Fax: 919-677-1303 E-mail: custserv.us@oup.com Web Site: global.oup.com, pg 179

Zuccarello, Dasya Anthony, Hohm Press, PO Box 4410, Chino Valley, AZ 86323 Tel: 928-636-3331 Toll Free Tel: 800-381-2700 Fax: 928-636-7519 E-mail: publisher@hohmpress.com Web Site: www.hohmpress.com, pg 94

Zuccarello, Joe Bala, Hohm Press, PO Box 4410, Chino Valley, AZ 86323 Tel: 928-636-3331 Toll Free Tel: 800-381-2700 Fax: 928-636-7519 E-mail: publisher@hohmpress.com Web Site: www.hohmpress.com, pg 94

Zuccaro, Jennifer, Princeton University Press, 41 William St, Princeton, NJ 08540-5237 Tel: 609-258-4900 Fax: 609-258-6305 E-mail: info@press.princeton.edu Web Site: press.princeton.edu, pg 164

Zuccato, Mike, Sourcebooks LLC, 1935 Brookdale Rd, Suite 139, Naperville, IL 60563 Tel: 630-961-3900 Toll Free Tel: 800-432-7444 Fax: 630-961-2168 E-mail: info@sourcebooks.com Web Site: www.sourcebooks.com, pg 194

Zuch, Franklin Jon, George T Bisel Co Inc, 710 S Washington Sq, Philadelphia, PA 19106-3519 Tel: 215-922-5760 Toll Free Tel: 800-247-3526 Fax: 215-922-2235 E-mail: gbisel@bisel.com Web Site: www.bisel.com, pg 29

Zucker, Alisha, Workman Publishing, 1290 Avenue of the Americas, New York, NY 10104 Toll Free Tel: 800-759-0190 Fax: 212-364-0950 E-mail: workman-inquiry@hbgusa.com Web Site: www.hachettebookgroup.com/imprint/workman-publishing-company/, pg 232

Zuckerman, Kathy, Alfred A Knopf, c/o Penguin Random House LLC, 1745 Broadway, New York, NY 10019 Tel: 212-751-2600 Fax: 212-940-7390 (dom rts); 212-572-2662 (foreign rts) Web Site: knopfdoubleday.com/imprint/knopf/; knopfdoubleday.com, pg 110

Zuckerman, Kathy, Pantheon Books, c/o Penguin Random House LLC, 1745 Broadway, New York, NY 10019 Tel: 212-751-2600 Fax: 212-940-7390 (dom rts); 212-572-2662 (foreign rts) Web Site: knopfdoubleday.com/imprint/pantheon/; knopfdoubleday.com, pg 150

Zugschwert, Rachel, Carolrhoda Books Inc, 241 First Ave N, Minneapolis, MN 55401 Tel: 612-332-3344 Toll Free Tel: 800-328-4929 Fax: 612-332-7615 Toll Free Fax: 800-332-1132 E-mail: info@lernerbooks.com; custserve@lernerbooks.com Web Site: www.lernerbooks.com; www.facebook.com/lernerbooks, pg 41

Zugschwert, Rachel, Carolrhoda Lab™, 241 First Ave N, Minneapolis, MN 55401 Tel: 612-332-3344 Toll Free Tel: 800-328-4929 Fax: 612-332-7615 Toll Free Fax: 800-332-1132 E-mail: info@lernerbooks.com; custserve@lernerbooks.com Web Site: www.lernerbooks.com; www.facebook.com/lernerbooks, pg 41

Zugschwert, Rachel, ediciones Lerner, 241 First Ave N, Minneapolis, MN 55401 Tel: 612-332-3344 Toll Free Tel: 800-328-4929 Fax: 612-332-7615 Toll Free Fax: 800-332-1132 E-mail: info@lernerbooks.com; custserve@lernerbooks.com Web Site: www.lernerbooks.com; www.facebook.com/lernerbooks, pg 63

Zugschwert, Rachel, First Avenue Editions, 241 First Ave N, Minneapolis, MN 55401 Tel: 612-332-3344 Toll Free Tel: 800-328-4929 Fax: 612-332-7615 Toll Free Fax: 800-332-1132 E-mail: info@lernerbooks.com; custserve@lernerbooks.com Web Site: www.lernerbooks.com; www.facebook.com/lernerbooks, pg 72

Zugschwert, Rachel, Graphic Universe™, 241 First Ave N, Minneapolis, MN 55401 Tel: 612-332-3344 Toll Free Tel: 800-328-4929 Fax: 612-332-7615 Toll Free Fax: 800-332-1132 E-mail: info@lernerbooks.com; custserve@lernerbooks.com Web Site: www.lernerbooks.com; www.facebook.com/lernerbooks, pg 80

Zugschwert, Rachel, Lerner Publications, 241 First Ave N, Minneapolis, MN 55401 Tel: 612-332-3344 Toll Free Tel: 800-328-4929 Fax: 612-332-7615 Toll Free Fax: 800-332-1132 E-mail: info@lernerbooks.com; custserve@lernerbooks.com Web Site: www.lernerbooks.com; www.facebook.com/lernerbooks, pg 115

Zugschwert, Rachel, Lerner Publishing Group Inc, 241 First Ave N, Minneapolis, MN 55401 Tel: 612-332-3344 Toll Free Tel: 800-328-4929 Fax: 612-332-7615 Toll Free Fax: 800-332-1132 E-mail: info@lernerbooks.com; custserve@lernerbooks.com Web Site: www.lernerbooks.com; www.facebook.com/lernerbooks, pg 115

Zugschwert, Rachel, LernerClassroom, 241 First Ave N, Minneapolis, MN 55401 *Tel:* 612-332-3344 *Toll Free Tel:* 800-328-4929 *Fax:* 612-332-7615 *Toll Free Fax:* 800-332-1132 *E-mail:* info@lernerbooks.com; custserve@lernerbooks.com *Web Site:* www.lernerbooks.com; www.facebook.com/lernerbooks, pg 115

Zugschwert, Rachel, Millbrook Press, 241 First Ave N, Minneapolis, MN 55401 *Tel:* 612-332-3344 *Toll Free Tel:* 800-328-4929 *Fax:* 612-332-7615 *Toll Free Fax:* 800-332-1132 *E-mail:* info@lernerbooks.com; custserve@lernerbooks.com *Web Site:* www.lernerbooks.com; www.facebook.com/millbrookpress, pg 131

Zugschwert, Rachel, Twenty-First Century Books, 241 First Ave N, Minneapolis, MN 55401 *Tel:* 612-332-3344 *Toll Free Tel:* 800-328-4929 *Fax:* 612-332-7615 *Toll Free Fax:* 800-332-1132 *E-mail:* info@lernerbooks.com; custserve@lernerbooks.com *Web Site:* www.lernerbooks.com; www.facebook.com/lernerbooks, pg 211

Zugschwert, Rachel, Zest Books, 241 First Ave N, Minneapolis, MN 55401 *Tel:* 612-332-3344 *Toll Free Tel:* 800-328-4929 *Toll Free Fax:* 800-332-1132 *E-mail:* info@lernerbooks.com; publicity@lernerbooks.com; custserve@lernerbooks.com (orders) *Web Site:* lernerbooks.com, pg 236

Zukergood, Samantha, Random House Publishing Group, 1745 Broadway, New York, NY 10019 *Toll Free Tel:* 800-200-3552 *Web Site:* www.randomhousebooks.com, pg 171

Zulli, Jessica, Sourcebooks LLC, 1935 Brookdale Rd, Suite 139, Naperville, IL 60563 *Tel:* 630-961-3900 *Toll Free Tel:* 800-432-7444 *Fax:* 630-961-2168 *E-mail:* info@sourcebooks.com *Web Site:* www.sourcebooks.com, pg 195

Zullo, Julia, Jessica Kingsley Publishers Inc, 123 S Broad St, Suite 2750, Philadelphia, PA 19109 *Tel:* 215-922-1161 *Toll Free Tel:* 866-416-1078 (cust serv) *Fax:* 215-922-1474 *E-mail:* hello.usa@jkp.com *Web Site:* us.jkp.com, pg 110

Zuraw-Friedland, Ayla, Frances Goldin Literary Agency, Inc, 214 W 29 St, Suite 410, New York, NY 10001 *Tel:* 212-777-0047 *Fax:* 212-228-1660 *E-mail:* agency@goldinlit.com *Web Site:* www.goldinlit.com, pg 460

Zuzga, Jason, Fence Books, 36-09 28 Ave, Apt 3R, Astoria, NY 11103-4518 *Tel:* 518-567-7006 *Web Site:* www.fenceportal.org, pg 71

Zuzga, Jason, Fence Modern Poets Series, 36-09 28 Ave, Apt 3R, Astoria, NY 11103-4518 *Tel:* 518-567-7006 *Web Site:* www.fenceportal.org, pg 602

Zuzga, Jason, Ottoline Prize, 36-09 28 Ave, Apt 3R, Astoria, NY 11103-4518 *Tel:* 518-567-7006 *Web Site:* www.fenceportal.org, pg 645

Zwart, Jeanette, Macmillan, 120 Broadway, 22nd fl, New York, NY 10271 *E-mail:* press.inquiries@macmillan.com *Web Site:* us.macmillan.com, pg 122

Zwirner, Johanna, Doubleday, c/o Penguin Random House LLC, 1745 Broadway, New York, NY 10019 *Tel:* 212-751-2600 *Fax:* 212-940-7390 (dom rts); 212-572-2662 (foreign rts) *Web Site:* knopfdoubleday.com/imprint/doubleday/; knopfdoubleday.com, pg 61

Zwolinski, Cari, Sourcebooks LLC, 1935 Brookdale Rd, Suite 139, Naperville, IL 60563 *Tel:* 630-961-3900 *Toll Free Tel:* 800-432-7444 *Fax:* 630-961-2168 *E-mail:* info@sourcebooks.com *Web Site:* www.sourcebooks.com, pg 194

Zychowicz, James, A-R Editions Inc, 1600 Aspen Commons, Suite 100, Middleton, WI 53562 *Tel:* 608-836-9000 *Toll Free Tel:* 800-736-0070 (North America book orders only) *Fax:* 608-831-8200 *E-mail:* info@areditions.com; orders@areditions.com *Web Site:* www.areditions.com, pg 1

Publishers Toll Free Directory

A-R Editions Inc, Middleton, WI *Toll Free Tel:* 800-736-0070 (North America book orders only), pg 1

AAPG (American Association of Petroleum Geologists), Tulsa, OK *Toll Free Tel:* 800-364-AAPG (364-2274), pg 1

Abbeville Press, New York, NY *Toll Free Tel:* 800-ART-BOOK (278-2665); 800-343-4499 (orders), pg 1

ABC-CLIO, Santa Barbara, CA *Toll Free Tel:* 800-368-6868 *Toll Free Fax:* 866-270-3856, pg 2

ABDO, Edina, MN *Toll Free Tel:* 800-800-1312 *Toll Free Fax:* 800-862-3480, pg 2

Abingdon Press, Nashville, TN *Toll Free Tel:* 800-251-3320, pg 2

Harry N Abrams Inc, New York, NY *Toll Free Tel:* 800-345-1359, pg 2

Academy Chicago Publishers, Chicago, IL *Toll Free Tel:* 800-888-4741 (orders), pg 3

Academy of Nutrition & Dietetics, Chicago, IL *Toll Free Tel:* 800-877-1600, pg 3

ACC Art Books, New York, NY *Toll Free Tel:* 800-252-5231, pg 3

ACMRS Press, Tempe, AZ *Toll Free Tel:* 800-621-2736 (orders) *Toll Free Fax:* 800-621-8476 (orders), pg 4

Acres USA, Greeley, CO *Toll Free Tel:* 800-355-5313, pg 4

ACS Publications, Washington, DC *Toll Free Tel:* 800-227-5558 (US), pg 4

ACTA Publications, Niles, IL *Toll Free Tel:* 800-397-2282, pg 4

ACU Press, Abilene, TX *Toll Free Tel:* 877-816-4455, pg 4

Adirondack Mountain Club (ADK), Lake Placid, NY *Toll Free Tel:* 800-395-8080, pg 5

Advance Publishing Inc, Houston, TX *Toll Free Tel:* 800-917-9630, pg 5

AdventureKEEN, Birmingham, AL *Toll Free Tel:* 800-678-7006 *Toll Free Fax:* 877-374-9016, pg 5

AICPA® & CIMA®, Durham, NC *Toll Free Tel:* 888-777-7077 (memb serv ctr), pg 5

ALA Neal-Schuman, Chicago, IL *Toll Free Tel:* 800-545-2433, pg 6

Albert Whitman & Company, Park Ridge, IL *Toll Free Tel:* 800-255-7675 (orders), pg 6

Alexander Street, part of Clarivate PLC, Ann Arbor, MI *Toll Free Tel:* 800-521-0600; 888-963-2071 (sales), pg 6

Alfred Music, Louisville, CO *Toll Free Tel:* 800-292-6122 (dealer sales, US & CN); 800-628-1528 (cust serv) *Toll Free Fax:* 800-632-1928 (dealer sales), pg 6

Amber Lotus Publishing, Portland, OR *Toll Free Tel:* 800-326-2375 (orders only), pg 8

American Academy of Pediatrics, Itasca, IL *Toll Free Tel:* 888-227-1770, pg 8

American Bar Association Publishing, Chicago, IL *Toll Free Tel:* 800-285-2221 (orders), pg 8

American Bible Society, Philadelphia, PA *Toll Free Tel:* 800-322-4253 (cust serv); 888-596-6296, pg 8

American Carriage House Publishing (ACHP), Pen Valley, CA *Toll Free Tel:* 866-986-2665, pg 8

The American Ceramic Society, Westerville, OH *Toll Free Tel:* 866-721-3322, pg 9

The American College of Financial Services, King of Prussia, PA *Toll Free Tel:* 866-883-5640, pg 9

American Correctional Association, Alexandria, VA *Toll Free Tel:* 800-222-5646, pg 9

American Counseling Association (ACA), Alexandria, VA *Toll Free Tel:* 800-298-2276 *Toll Free Fax:* 800-473-2329, pg 9

American Diabetes Association, Arlington, VA *Toll Free Tel:* 800-342-2383, pg 9

American Federation of Arts, New York, NY *Toll Free Tel:* 800-232-0270, pg 9

American Federation of Astrologers Inc, Tempe, AZ *Toll Free Tel:* 888-301-7630, pg 9

American Geophysical Union (AGU), Washington, DC *Toll Free Tel:* 800-966-2481 (North America), pg 10

American Girl Publishing, Middleton, WI *Toll Free Tel:* 800-845-0005 (US & CN), pg 10

American Institute for Economic Research (AIER), Great Barrington, MA *Toll Free Tel:* 888-528-1216 (orders), pg 10

American Institute of Aeronautics and Astronautics (AIAA), Reston, VA *Toll Free Tel:* 800-639-AIAA (639-2422), pg 10

American Institute of Chemical Engineers (AIChE), New York, NY *Toll Free Tel:* 800-242-4363, pg 10

American Law Institute, Philadelphia, PA *Toll Free Tel:* 800-253-6397, pg 10

American Law Institute Continuing Legal Education (ALI CLE), Philadelphia, PA *Toll Free Tel:* 800-CLE-NEWS (253-6397), pg 10

The American Library Association (ALA), Chicago, IL *Toll Free Tel:* 800-545-2433; 866-SHOP-ALA (746-7252, orders), pg 10

American Mathematical Society (AMS), Providence, RI *Toll Free Tel:* 800-321-4267, pg 11

American Medical Association (AMA), Chicago, IL *Toll Free Tel:* 800-621-8335, pg 11

American Psychiatric Association Publishing, Washington, DC *Toll Free Tel:* 800-368-5777, pg 11

American Psychological Association, Washington, DC *Toll Free Tel:* 800-374-2721, pg 11

American Public Works Association (APWA), Kansas City, MO *Toll Free Tel:* 800-848-APWA (848-2792), pg 12

American Quilter's Society (AQS), Paducah, KY *Toll Free Tel:* 800-626-5420 (orders), pg 12

American Society for Nondestructive Testing, Columbus, OH *Toll Free Tel:* 800-222-2768, pg 12

American Society for Quality (ASQ), Milwaukee, WI *Toll Free Tel:* 800-248-1946 (US & CN); 800-514-1564 (Mexico), pg 12

American Society of Agricultural & Biological Engineers (ASABE), St Joseph, MI *Toll Free Tel:* 800-371-2723, pg 12

American Society of Civil Engineers (ASCE), Reston, VA *Toll Free Tel:* 800-548-ASCE (548-2723) *Toll Free Fax:* 866-913-6085, pg 12

American Society of Mechanical Engineers (ASME), New York, NY *Toll Free Tel:* 800-843-2763 (cust serv-CN, Mexico & US), pg 12

American Technical Publishers, Orland Park, IL *Toll Free Tel:* 800-323-3471, pg 13

American Water Works Association (AWWA), Denver, CO *Toll Free Tel:* 800-926-7337, pg 13

Amicus, Mankato, MN *Toll Free Tel:* 800-445-6209 (cust serv/orders), pg 13

Ancient Faith Publishing, Chesterton, IN *Toll Free Tel:* 800-967-7377, pg 13

Andrews McMeel Publishing LLC, Kansas City, MO *Toll Free Tel:* 800-851-8923, pg 14

Andrews University Press, Berrien Springs, MI *Toll Free Tel:* 800-467-6369 (Visa, MC & American Express orders only), pg 14

Angelus Press, St Marys, KS *Toll Free Tel:* 800-966-7337, pg 14

Annual Reviews, San Mateo, CA *Toll Free Tel:* 800-523-8635, pg 14

ANR Publications University of California, Davis, CA *Toll Free Tel:* 800-994-8849, pg 14

APC Publishing, Aurora, CO *Toll Free Tel:* 800-660-5107 (sales & orders), pg 15

Aperture Books, New York, NY *Toll Free Fax:* 888-623-6908, pg 15

APH Press, Louisville, KY *Toll Free Tel:* 800-223-1839, pg 15

Appraisal Institute, Chicago, IL *Toll Free Tel:* 888-756-4624, pg 15

APS PRESS, St Paul, MN *Toll Free Tel:* 800-328-7560, pg 16

Aquila Communications Inc, Montreal, QC Canada *Toll Free Tel:* 800-667-7071, pg 395

Arbordale Publishing, Mount Pleasant, SC *Toll Free Tel:* 877-243-3457, pg 16

ARE Press, Virginia Beach, VA *Toll Free Tel:* 800-333-4499, pg 16

Jason Aronson Inc, Lanham, MD *Toll Free Tel:* 800-462-6420 ext 3024 (cust serv) *Toll Free Fax:* 800-338-4550 (cust serv), pg 17

Arsenal Pulp Press, Vancouver, BC Canada *Toll Free Tel:* 888-600-PULP (600-7857), pg 395

Art Image Publications, Derby Line, VT *Toll Free Tel:* 800-361-2598 *Toll Free Fax:* 800-559-2598, pg 17

The Art Institute of Chicago, Chicago, IL *Toll Free Tel:* 855-301-9612, pg 17

ArtAge Publications, Portland, OR *Toll Free Tel:* 800-858-4998, pg 17

Artech House®, Norwood, MA *Toll Free Tel:* 800-225-9977, pg 17

ASCD, Arlington, VA *Toll Free Tel:* 800-933-2723, pg 18

Ascension Press, West Chester, PA *Toll Free Tel:* 800-376-0520 (sales & cust serv), pg 18

ASCP Press, Chicago, IL *Toll Free Tel:* 800-267-2727, pg 18

ASM International, Materials Park, OH *Toll Free Tel:* 800-336-5152; 800-368-9800 (Europe), pg 19

Aspatore Books, Eagan, MN *Toll Free Tel:* 844-209-1086, pg 19

Association for Talent Development (ATD) Press, Alexandria, VA *Toll Free Tel:* 800-628-2783, pg 19

Association for the Advancement of Blood & Biotherapies, Bethesda, MD *Toll Free Tel:* 866-222-2498 (sales), pg 19

ASSOCIATION OF COLLEGE & RESEARCH LIBRARIES (ACRL)

Association of College & Research Libraries (ACRL), Chicago, IL *Toll Free Tel:* 800-545-2433 (ext 2523), pg 19

Association of School Business Officials International, Ashburn, VA *Toll Free Tel:* 866-682-2729, pg 20

Asta Publications LLC, New City, NY *Toll Free Tel:* 800-482-4190, pg 20

ASTM International, West Conshohocken, PA *Toll Free Tel:* 877-909-2786 (sales & cust support), pg 20

The Astronomical Society of the Pacific, San Francisco, CA *Toll Free Tel:* 800-335-2624 (cust serv), pg 20

Augsburg Fortress Publishers, Publishing House of the Evangelical Lutheran Church in America, Minneapolis, MN *Toll Free Tel:* 800-426-0115 (ext 639, subns); 800-328-4648 (orders), pg 22

August House Inc, Atlanta, GA *Toll Free Tel:* 800-284-8784, pg 22

AuthorHouse, Bloomington, IN *Toll Free Tel:* 833-262-8899; 888-519-5121, pg 22

Ave Maria Press Inc, Notre Dame, IN *Toll Free Tel:* 800-282-1865 *Toll Free Fax:* 800-282-5681, pg 22

Avery Color Studios, Gwinn, MI *Toll Free Tel:* 800-722-9925, pg 23

Baha'i Publishing Trust, Evanston, IL *Toll Free Tel:* 800-999-9019 (orders), pg 23

Baker Books, Ada, MI *Toll Free Tel:* 800-877-2665 (orders) *Toll Free Fax:* 800-398-3111 (orders), pg 23

B&H Publishing Group, Brentwood, TN *Toll Free Tel:* 800-251-3225 (retailers); 800-448-8032 (consumers); 800-458-2772 (churches) *Toll Free Fax:* 800-296-4036 (retailers), pg 24

Barefoot Books, Concord, MA *Toll Free Tel:* 866-215-1756 (cust serv); 866-417-2369 (orders), pg 24

Bartleby Press, Savage, MD *Toll Free Tel:* 800-953-9929, pg 24

Basic Books Group, New York, NY *Toll Free Tel:* 800-343-4499 (cust serv), pg 25

Beacon Hill Press of Kansas City, Kansas City, MO *Toll Free Tel:* 800-877-0700 (cust serv) *Toll Free Fax:* 800-849-9827, pg 25

Bear & Bobcat Books, Los Angeles, CA *Toll Free Tel:* 866-918-6173, pg 26

Bear & Co Inc, Rochester, VT *Toll Free Tel:* 800-932-3277, pg 26

Bearport Publishing, Minneapolis, MN *Toll Free Tel:* 877-337-8577 *Toll Free Fax:* 866-337-8557, pg 26

Behrman House Inc, Millburn, NJ *Toll Free Tel:* 800-221-2755, pg 27

Bella Books, Tallahassee, FL *Toll Free Tel:* 800-729-4992, pg 27

Bellerophon Books, Santa Barbara, CA *Toll Free Tel:* 800-253-9943, pg 27

John Benjamins Publishing Co, Brunswick, ME *Toll Free Tel:* 800-562-5666 (orders), pg 28

BePuzzled, San Francisco, CA *Toll Free Tel:* 800-347-4818, pg 28

Bernan, Lanham, MD *Toll Free Tel:* 800-462-6420 (cust serv & orders) *Toll Free Fax:* 800-338-4550, pg 28

Bethany House Publishers, Bloomington, MN *Toll Free Tel:* 800-877-2665 (orders) *Toll Free Fax:* 800-398-3111 (orders), pg 29

Bethlehem Books, Bathgate, ND *Toll Free Tel:* 800-757-6831, pg 29

Between the Lines, Toronto, ON Canada *Toll Free Tel:* 800-718-7201, pg 396

Bhaktivedanta Book Trust (BBT), Los Angeles, CA *Toll Free Tel:* 800-927-4152, pg 29

BiG GUY BOOKS, Carlsbad, CA *Toll Free Tel:* 800-536-3030 (booksellers' cust serv), pg 29

George T Bisel Co Inc, Philadelphia, PA *Toll Free Tel:* 800-247-3526, pg 29

BJU Press, Greenville, SC *Toll Free Tel:* 800-845-5731, pg 30

Black Classic Press, Baltimore, MD *Toll Free Tel:* 800-476-8870, pg 30

Bloom's Literary Criticism, New York, NY *Toll Free Tel:* 800-322-8755 *Toll Free Fax:* 800-678-3633, pg 31

BLR®—Business & Legal Resources, Brentwood, TN *Toll Free Tel:* 800-727-5257 *Toll Free Fax:* 800-785-9212, pg 32

Blue Book Publications Inc, Eva, AL *Toll Free Tel:* 800-877-4867, pg 32

Blue Mountain Arts Inc, Boulder, CO *Toll Free Tel:* 800-525-0642 *Toll Free Fax:* 800-545-8573, pg 32

Blue Note Publications Inc, Melbourne, FL *Toll Free Tel:* 800-624-0401 (orders), pg 32

Blue Poppy Press, Portland, OR *Toll Free Tel:* 800-487-9296, pg 32

Blue Whale Press, Livingston, TX *Toll Free Tel:* 800-848-1631, pg 32

Bluestocking Press, Placerville, CA *Toll Free Tel:* 800-959-8586, pg 33

BNi Building News, Vista, CA *Toll Free Tel:* 888-BNI-BOOK (264-2665), pg 33

The Book Tree, San Diego, CA *Toll Free Tel:* 800-700-8733 (orders), pg 34

Books In Motion, Spokane Valley, WA *Toll Free Tel:* 800-752-3199, pg 34

Books on Tape™, New York, NY *Toll Free Tel:* 800-733-3000 (cust serv) *Toll Free Fax:* 800-940-7046, pg 34

Borealis Press Ltd, Nepean, ON Canada *Toll Free Tel:* 877-696-2585, pg 396

The Boston Mills Press, Richmond Hill, ON Canada *Toll Free Tel:* 800-387-6192 *Toll Free Fax:* 800-450-0391, pg 397

R R Bowker LLC, Chatham, NJ *Toll Free Tel:* 888-269-5372 (edit & cust serv); 800-521-0600 *Toll Free Fax:* 877-337-7015 (US & CN), pg 34

Boys Town Press, Boys Town, NE *Toll Free Tel:* 800-282-6657, pg 35

BPC, Summertown, TN *Toll Free Tel:* 888-260-8458, pg 35

Brault & Bouthillier, Montreal, QC Canada *Toll Free Tel:* 800-361-0378 *Toll Free Fax:* 800-361-0378, pg 397

Breakwater Books Ltd, St John's, NL Canada *Toll Free Tel:* 800-563-3333 (orders), pg 397

Brentwood Christian Press, Columbus, GA *Toll Free Tel:* 800-334-8861, pg 36

Brethren Press, Elgin, IL *Toll Free Tel:* 800-441-3712 *Toll Free Fax:* 800-667-8188, pg 36

Brewers Publications, Boulder, CO *Toll Free Tel:* 888-822-6273 (CN & US), pg 36

Brick Tower Press, Shelter Island Heights, NY *Toll Free Tel:* 800-68-BRICK (682-7425), pg 36

Bridge Publications Inc, Commerce, CA *Toll Free Tel:* 800-722-1733, pg 36

Brilliance Publishing Inc, Grand Haven, MI *Toll Free Tel:* 800-648-2312 (orders only), pg 37

Paul H Brookes Publishing Co Inc, Baltimore, MD *Toll Free Tel:* 800-638-3775 (US & CN), pg 37

Brooklyn Publishers LLC, Cedar Rapids, IA *Toll Free Tel:* 888-473-8521, pg 37

PUBLISHERS TOLL

Brush Education Inc, Edmonton, AB Canada *Toll Free Tel:* 855-283-0900 *Toll Free Fax:* 855-283-6947, pg 397

BuilderBooks, Washington, DC *Toll Free Tel:* 800-368-5242, pg 38

Bull Publishing Co, Boulder, CO *Toll Free Tel:* 800-676-2855, pg 38

The Bureau for At-Risk Youth, Bohemia, NY *Toll Free Tel:* 800-99YOUTH (999-6884) *Toll Free Fax:* 800-262-1886, pg 38

Burford Books, Ithaca, NY *Toll Free Fax:* 866-212-7750, pg 38

Business Research Services Inc, Washington, DC *Toll Free Fax:* 877-516-0818, pg 38

Campfield & Campfield Publishing LLC, Philadelphia, PA *Toll Free Tel:* 888-518-2440, pg 39

Canadian Bible Society, Toronto, ON Canada *Toll Free Tel:* 800-465-2425, pg 398

Canadian Museum of History (Musee canadien de l'histoire), Gatineau, QC Canada *Toll Free Tel:* 800-555-5621 (North American orders only), pg 398

Canadian Scholars, Toronto, ON Canada *Toll Free Tel:* 800-463-1998, pg 398

Candid, New York, NY *Toll Free Tel:* 800-424-9836, pg 39

Capen Publishing Co Inc, San Diego, CA *Toll Free Tel:* 800-358-0560, pg 40

Capitol Enquiry Inc, South Lake Tahoe, CA *Toll Free Tel:* 800-922-7486, pg 40

Capstone Publishers™, North Mankato, MN *Toll Free Tel:* 800-747-4992 (cust serv) *Toll Free Fax:* 888-262-0705, pg 40

Carlisle Press - Walnut Creek, Sugarcreek, OH *Toll Free Tel:* 800-852-4482, pg 40

Carolina Academic Press, Durham, NC *Toll Free Tel:* 800-489-7486, pg 41

Carolrhoda Books Inc, Minneapolis, MN *Toll Free Tel:* 800-328-4929 *Toll Free Fax:* 800-332-1132, pg 41

Carolrhoda Lab™, Minneapolis, MN *Toll Free Tel:* 800-328-4929 *Toll Free Fax:* 800-332-1132, pg 41

Carson Dellosa Publishing LLC, Greensboro, NC *Toll Free Tel:* 800-321-0943, pg 41

Carswell, Toronto, ON Canada *Toll Free Tel:* 800-387-5164 (CN & US) *Toll Free Fax:* 877-750-9041 (CN only), pg 399

CarTech Inc, North Branch, MN *Toll Free Tel:* 800-551-4754, pg 41

Casa Bautista de Publicaciones, El Paso, TX *Toll Free Tel:* 800-755-5958 (cust serv & orders), pg 41

Catholic Book Publishing Corp, Totowa, NJ *Toll Free Tel:* 877-228-2665, pg 42

The Catholic University of America Press, Washington, DC *Toll Free Tel:* 800-537-5487 (orders only), pg 42

Caxton Press, Caldwell, ID *Toll Free Tel:* 800-657-6465, pg 42

Cedar Fort Inc, Springville, UT *Toll Free Tel:* 800-SKY-BOOK (759-2665), pg 43

CEF Press, Warrenton, MO *Toll Free Tel:* 800-748-7710 (cust serv), pg 43

Cengage Learning, Boston, MA *Toll Free Tel:* 800-354-9706, pg 43

The Center for Learning, Culver City, CA *Toll Free Tel:* 800-421-4246 *Toll Free Fax:* 800-944-5432, pg 43

Center for the Collaborative Classroom, Alameda, CA *Toll Free Tel:* 800-666-7270, pg 44

Centering Corp, Omaha, NE *Toll Free Tel:* 866-218-0101, pg 44

Centre Franco-Ontarien de Ressources en Alphabetisation (Centre FORA), Hanmer, ON Canada *Toll Free Tel:* 888-814-4422 (orders, CN only), pg 399

Chain Store Guide (CSG), Tampa, FL *Toll Free Tel:* 800-927-9292 (orders), pg 44

Chalice Press, St Louis, MO *Toll Free Tel:* 800-366-3383, pg 44

Charlesbridge Publishing Inc, Watertown, MA *Toll Free Tel:* 800-225-3214 *Toll Free Fax:* 800-926-5775, pg 45

The Charlton Press Corp, Dorval, QC Canada *Toll Free Tel:* 866-663-8827, pg 399

Chartered Professional Accountants of Canada (CPA Canada), Toronto, ON Canada *Toll Free Tel:* 800-268-3793, pg 399

Chelsea Green Publishing Co, White River Junction, VT *Toll Free Tel:* 800-639-4099 (cust serv & orders), pg 45

Chelsea House, New York, NY *Toll Free Tel:* 800-322-8755 *Toll Free Fax:* 800-678-3633, pg 45

Cheneliere Education Inc, Montreal, QC Canada *Toll Free Tel:* 800-565-5531 *Toll Free Fax:* 800-814-0324, pg 399

Cheng & Tsui Co Inc, Boston, MA *Toll Free Tel:* 800-554-1963, pg 46

Cherry Hill Publishing LLC, Ramona, CA *Toll Free Tel:* 800-407-1072, pg 46

Chicago Review Press, Chicago, IL *Toll Free Tel:* 800-888-4741, pg 46

Child's Play® Inc, Auburn, ME *Toll Free Tel:* 800-639-6404 *Toll Free Fax:* 800-854-6989, pg 46

The Child's World Inc, Parker, CO *Toll Free Tel:* 800-599-READ (599-7323) *Toll Free Fax:* 888-320-2329, pg 46

Chosen Books, Bloomington, MN *Toll Free Tel:* 800-877-2665 (orders only), pg 47

Christian Liberty Press, Arlington Heights, IL *Toll Free Tel:* 800-348-0899, pg 47

Christian Light Publications Inc, Harrisonburg, VA *Toll Free Tel:* 800-776-0478, pg 47

Christian Schools International (CSI), Grand Rapids, MI *Toll Free Tel:* 800-635-8288, pg 47

Cider Mill Press Book Publishers LLC, Nashville, TN *Toll Free Tel:* 800-250-5308, pg 48

Cistercian Publications, Collegeville, MN *Toll Free Tel:* 800-436-8431 *Toll Free Fax:* 800-445-5899, pg 48

Clarion Books, New York, NY *Toll Free Tel:* 800-242-7737, pg 48

Classical Academic Press, Camp Hill, PA *Toll Free Tel:* 866-730-0711 *Toll Free Fax:* 866-730-0721, pg 49

Clear Light Publishers, Santa Fe, NM *Toll Free Tel:* 800-253-2747 (orders), pg 49

Clearfield Co Inc, Baltimore, MD *Toll Free Tel:* 800-296-6687 (orders & cust serv), pg 49

Clinical and Laboratory Standards Institute (CLSI), Berwyn, PA *Toll Free Tel:* 877-447-1888 (orders), pg 49

Close Up Publishing, Arlington, VA *Toll Free Tel:* 800-CLOSE-UP (256-7387), pg 49

Coach House Books, Toronto, ON Canada *Toll Free Tel:* 800-367-6360 (outside Toronto), pg 399

Coaches Choice, Monterey, CA *Toll Free Tel:* 888-229-5745, pg 50

Cold Spring Harbor Laboratory Press, Woodbury, NY *Toll Free Tel:* 800-843-4388, pg 50

The College Board, New York, NY *Toll Free Tel:* 866-630-9305, pg 50

Columbia University Press, New York, NY *Toll Free Tel:* 800-944-8648, pg 51

Company's Coming Publishing Ltd, Edmonton, AB Canada *Toll Free Tel:* 800-661-9017 (CN) *Toll Free Fax:* 800-424-7133, pg 400

Concordia Publishing House, St Louis, MO *Toll Free Tel:* 800-325-3040 (cust serv) *Toll Free Fax:* 800-490-9889 (cust serv), pg 51

The Connecticut Law Tribune, Farmington, CT *Toll Free Tel:* 877-256-2472, pg 52

The Continuing Legal Education Society of British Columbia (CLEBC), Vancouver, BC Canada *Toll Free Tel:* 800-663-0437 (CN), pg 400

David C Cook, Colorado Springs, CO *Toll Free Tel:* 800-323-7543 (orders & cust serv) *Toll Free Fax:* 800-430-0726 (cust serv), pg 52

Corwin, Thousand Oaks, CA *Toll Free Tel:* 800-233-9936 *Toll Free Fax:* 800-417-2466, pg 53

Council for Exceptional Children (CEC), Arlington, VA *Toll Free Tel:* 888-232-7733, pg 53

CQ Press, Washington, DC *Toll Free Tel:* 866-4CQ-PRESS (427-7737), pg 54

Crabtree Publishing Co, New York, NY *Toll Free Tel:* 800-387-7650 *Toll Free Fax:* 800-355-7166, pg 54

Crabtree Publishing Co Ltd, St Catharines, ON Canada *Toll Free Tel:* 800-387-7650 *Toll Free Fax:* 800-355-7166, pg 400

Craftsman Book Co, Carlsbad, CA *Toll Free Tel:* 800-829-8123, pg 54

CRC Press, Boca Raton, FL *Toll Free Tel:* 800-354-1420; 800-634-7064 (orders), pg 55

Creative Editions, North Mankato, MN *Toll Free Tel:* 800-445-6209, pg 55

Creative Homeowner, Mount Joy, PA *Toll Free Tel:* 844-307-3677 *Toll Free Fax:* 888-369-2885, pg 55

Crossway, Wheaton, IL *Toll Free Tel:* 800-635-7993 (orders); 800-543-1659 (cust serv), pg 56

Crown House Publishing Co LLC, White Plains, NY *Toll Free Tel:* 877-925-1213 (cust serv), pg 56

Crown Publishing Group, New York, NY *Toll Free Tel:* 888-264-1745, pg 56

Crystal Clarity Publishers, Nevada City, CA *Toll Free Tel:* 800-424-1055, pg 56

Cypress House, Fort Bragg, CA *Toll Free Tel:* 800-773-7782, pg 56

D&B Hoovers™, Austin, TX *Toll Free Tel:* 855-858-5974, pg 57

Data Trace Publishing Co (DTP), Towson, MD *Toll Free Tel:* 800-342-0454, pg 57

Davies Publishing Inc, Pasadena, CA *Toll Free Tel:* 877-792-0005, pg 57

F A Davis Co, Philadelphia, PA *Toll Free Tel:* 800-523-4049, pg 57

The Dawn Horse Press, Middletown, CA *Toll Free Tel:* 877-770-0772, pg 57

DawnSignPress, San Diego, CA *Toll Free Tel:* 800-549-5350, pg 58

dbS Productions, Charlottesville, VA *Toll Free Tel:* 800-745-1581, pg 58

DC Canada Education Publishing (DCCED), Ottawa, ON Canada *Toll Free Tel:* 888-565-0262, pg 400

Deseret Book Co, Salt Lake City, UT *Toll Free Tel:* 800-453-4532 (orders); 888-846-7302 (orders), pg 58

DEStech Publications Inc, Lancaster, PA *Toll Free Tel:* 877-500-4DES (500-4337), pg 59

Destiny Image Inc, Shippensburg, PA *Toll Free Tel:* 800-722-6774 (orders only), pg 59

DeVorss & Co, Camarillo, CA *Toll Free Tel:* 800-843-5743, pg 59

Dissertation.com, Irvine, CA *Toll Free Tel:* 800-636-8329, pg 60

DK, New York, NY *Toll Free Tel:* 800-733-3000, pg 60

Dogwise Publishing, Wenatchee, WA *Toll Free Tel:* 800-776-2665, pg 60

The Donning Company Publishers, Brookfield, MO *Toll Free Tel:* 800-369-2646 (ext 3377), pg 60

Dordt Press, Sioux Center, IA *Toll Free Tel:* 800-343-6738, pg 60

Dorrance Publishing Co Inc, Pittsburgh, PA *Toll Free Tel:* 800-695-9599; 800-788-7654 (gen cust orders), pg 61

Dover Publications Inc, Garden City, NY *Toll Free Tel:* 800-223-3130 (orders), pg 61

Dramatic Publishing Co, Woodstock, IL *Toll Free Tel:* 800-448-7469 *Toll Free Fax:* 800-334-5302, pg 61

Dreamscape Media LLC, Holland, OH *Toll Free Tel:* 877-983-7326, pg 62

Duke University Press, Durham, NC *Toll Free Tel:* 888-651-0122 (US) *Toll Free Fax:* 888-651-0124, pg 62

Dun & Bradstreet, Short Hills, NJ *Toll Free Tel:* 844-869-8244; 800-234-3867 (cust serv), pg 62

Eakin Press, Fort Worth, TX *Toll Free Tel:* 888-982-8270, pg 62

ECS Publishing Group, Fenton, MO *Toll Free Tel:* 800-647-2117, pg 63

EDC Publishing, Tulsa, OK *Toll Free Tel:* 800-475-4522 *Toll Free Fax:* 800-743-5660, pg 63

ediciones Lerner, Minneapolis, MN *Toll Free Tel:* 800-328-4929 *Toll Free Fax:* 800-332-1132, pg 63

Les Editions Caractere, Montreal, QC Canada *Toll Free Tel:* 855-861-2782, pg 401

Editions FouLire, Quebec, QC Canada *Toll Free Tel:* 877-628-4029 (CN & US), pg 403

Les Editions Goelette et Coup d-oeil Inc, St-Bruno-de-Montarville, QC Canada *Toll Free Tel:* 800-463-4961, pg 403

Editions Hurtubise, Montreal, QC Canada *Toll Free Tel:* 800-361-1664, pg 403

Editions Marie-France, Montreal, QC Canada *Toll Free Tel:* 800-563-6644 (CN), pg 404

Editions MultiMondes, Montreal, QC Canada *Toll Free Tel:* 800-361-1664, pg 404

Les Editions Phidal Inc, Montreal, QC Canada *Toll Free Tel:* 800-738-7349, pg 404

Les Editions Un Monde Different, Brossard, QC Canada *Toll Free Tel:* 800-443-2582, pg 405

Editions Yvon Blais, Montreal, QC Canada *Toll Free Tel:* 800-363-3047, pg 405

Editorial Bautista Independiente, Sebring, FL *Toll Free Tel:* 800-398-7187 (US), pg 63

Editorial Portavoz, Grand Rapids, MI *Toll Free Tel:* 877-733-2607 (ext 206), pg 64

Editorial Unilit, Medley, FL *Toll Free Tel:* 800-767-7726, pg 64

Educational Insights®, Gardena, CA *Toll Free Tel:* 800-995-4436 *Toll Free Fax:* 888-892-8731, pg 64

Educator's International Press Inc (EIP), Kingston, NY *Toll Free Tel:* 800-758-3756, pg 64

Edupress Inc, Garden Grove, CA *Toll Free Tel:* 800-662-4321 *Toll Free Fax:* 800-525-1254, pg 64

Wm B Eerdmans Publishing Co, Grand Rapids, MI *Toll Free Tel:* 800-253-7521, pg 64

Eisenbrauns, University Park, PA *Toll Free Tel:* 800-326-9180 (orders & cust serv) *Toll Free Fax:* 877-778-2665 (orders), pg 64

Edward Elgar Publishing Inc, Northampton, MA *Toll Free Tel:* 800-390-3149 (orders), pg 65

Elite Books, Petaluma, CA *Toll Free Fax:* 800-330-9798, pg 65

Elsevier Health Sciences, Philadelphia, PA *Toll Free Tel:* 800-523-1649, pg 65

Emerald Books, Seattle, WA *Toll Free Tel:* 800-922-2143, pg 66

Emond Montgomery Publications Ltd, Toronto, ON Canada *Toll Free Tel:* 888-837-0815, pg 405

Encounter Books, New York, NY *Toll Free Tel:* 855-203-7220, pg 66

Encyclopaedia Britannica Inc, Chicago, IL *Toll Free Tel:* 800-323-1229 (US & CN), pg 66

Energy Psychology Press, Petaluma, CA *Toll Free Fax:* 800-330-9798, pg 66

Enslow Publishing LLC, New York, NY *Toll Free Tel:* 800-398-2504 *Toll Free Fax:* 877-980-4454, pg 66

Entangled Publishing LLC, Shrewsbury, PA *Toll Free Tel:* 877-677-9451, pg 67

Environmental Law Institute, Washington, DC *Toll Free Tel:* 800-433-5120, pg 67

EPS School Specialty, Cambridge, MA *Toll Free Tel:* 800-225-5750 *Toll Free Fax:* 888-440-2665, pg 67

ERPI, Montreal, QC Canada *Toll Free Tel:* 800-263-3678 *Toll Free Fax:* 800-643-4720, pg 405

Evan-Moor Educational Publishers, Monterey, CA *Toll Free Tel:* 800-777-4362 (orders) *Toll Free Fax:* 800-777-4332 (orders), pg 68

Excelsior Editions, Albany, NY *Toll Free Tel:* 866-430-7869, pg 68

Facts On File, Wilmington, DE *Toll Free Tel:* 800-322-8755 *Toll Free Fax:* 800-678-3633, pg 69

Fairchild Books, New York, NY *Toll Free Tel:* 800-932-4724; 888-330-8477 (orders), pg 69

Faith & Fellowship Publishing, Fergus Falls, MN *Toll Free Tel:* 800-332-9232, pg 69

Faith Library Publications, Tulsa, OK *Toll Free Tel:* 888-258-0999 (orders), pg 69

Faithlife Corp, Bellingham, WA *Toll Free Tel:* 888-563-0382, pg 69

Farcountry Press, Helena, MT *Toll Free Tel:* 800-821-3874 (sales off), pg 69

Farrar, Straus & Giroux Books for Young Readers, New York, NY *Toll Free Tel:* 888-330-8477 (orders), pg 69

Father & Son Publishing Inc, Tallahassee, FL *Toll Free Tel:* 800-741-2712 (orders only), pg 70

FC&A Publishing, Peachtree City, GA *Toll Free Tel:* 800-226-8024, pg 70

Federal Street Press, Springfield, MA *Toll Free Tel:* 800-828-1880, pg 70

Feldheim Publishers, Nanuet, NY *Toll Free Tel:* 800-237-7149 (orders), pg 70

Ferguson Publishing, New York, NY *Toll Free Tel:* 800-322-8755 *Toll Free Fax:* 800-678-3633, pg 71

Fifth House Publishers, Toronto, ON Canada *Toll Free Tel:* 800-387-9776, pg 406

Filter Press LLC, Palmer Lake, CO *Toll Free Tel:* 888-570-2663, pg 71

Fire Engineering Books & Videos, Tulsa, OK *Toll Free Tel:* 800-752-9764, pg 72

Firefly Books Ltd, Richmond Hill, ON Canada *Toll Free Tel:* 800-387-6192 (CN); 800-387-5085 (US) *Toll Free Fax:* 800-450-0391 (CN); 800-565-6034 (US), pg 406

First Avenue Editions, Minneapolis, MN *Toll Free Tel:* 800-328-4929 *Toll Free Fax:* 800-332-1132, pg 72

Fitzhenry & Whiteside Limited, Markham, ON Canada *Toll Free Tel:* 800-387-9776, pg 406

Flanker Press Ltd, Paradise, NL Canada *Toll Free Tel:* 866-739-4420, pg 406

Flowerpot Press, Oakville, ON Canada *Toll Free Tel:* 866-927-5001, pg 406

Focus on the Family, Colorado Springs, CO *Toll Free Tel:* 800-A-FAMILY (232-6459), pg 73

Forum Publishing Co, Centerport, NY *Toll Free Tel:* 800-635-7654, pg 73

Forward Movement, Cincinnati, OH *Toll Free Tel:* 800-543-1813, pg 73

Foundation Press, Eagan, MN *Toll Free Tel:* 877-888-1330, pg 74

Fox Chapel Publishing Co Inc, East Petersburg, PA *Toll Free Tel:* 800-457-9112, pg 74

Franklin, Beedle & Associates Inc, Portland, OR *Toll Free Tel:* 800-322-2665, pg 74

Free Spirit Publishing Inc, Minneapolis, MN *Toll Free Tel:* 800-858-7339 *Toll Free Fax:* 888-877-7606, pg 74

Samuel French, Inc, New York, NY *Toll Free Tel:* 866-979-0447, pg 75

Fresh Air Books, Nashville, TN *Toll Free Tel:* 800-972-0433 (orders), pg 75

Fulcrum Publishing Inc, Wheat Ridge, CO *Toll Free Tel:* 800-888-4741 (orders), pg 75

Future Horizons Inc, Arlington, TX *Toll Free Tel:* 800-489-0727, pg 75

Gaetan Morin Editeur, Montreal, QC Canada *Toll Free Tel:* 800-565-5531 *Toll Free Fax:* 800-814-0324, pg 407

Galaxy Press Inc, Los Angeles, CA *Toll Free Tel:* 877-8GALAXY (842-5299), pg 75

Gale, Farmington Hills, MI *Toll Free Tel:* 800-877-4253 *Toll Free Fax:* 877-363-4253, pg 75

Gallery Books, New York, NY *Toll Free Tel:* 800-456-6798, pg 76

Gallopade International Inc, Peachtree City, GA *Toll Free Tel:* 800-536-2438 *Toll Free Fax:* 800-871-2979, pg 76

Gareth Stevens Publishing, New York, NY *Toll Free Tel:* 800-542-2595 *Toll Free Fax:* 877-542-2596, pg 76

Gatekeeper Press, Tampa, FL *Toll Free Tel:* 866-535-0913, pg 77

Gateways Books & Tapes, Nevada City, CA *Toll Free Tel:* 800-869-0658, pg 77

Genealogical Publishing Co, Baltimore, MD *Toll Free Tel:* 800-296-6687 *Toll Free Fax:* 800-599-9561, pg 77

The Geological Society of America Inc (GSA), Boulder, CO *Toll Free Tel:* 800-472-1988, pg 77

GeoLytics Inc, Branchburg, NJ *Toll Free Tel:* 800-577-6717, pg 77

Getty Publications, Los Angeles, CA *Toll Free Tel:* 800-223-3431 (orders), pg 78

GIA Publications Inc, Chicago, IL *Toll Free Tel:* 800-GIA-1358 (442-1358), pg 78

Gibbs Smith Publisher, Layton, UT *Toll Free Tel:* 800-748-5439; 800-835-4993 (orders) *Toll Free Fax:* 800-213-3023 (orders only), pg 78

Global Publishing Solutions LLC, Matteson, IL *Toll Free Tel:* 888-351-2411, pg 79

Global Training Center, El Paso, TX *Toll Free Tel:* 800-860-5030, pg 79

The Globe Pequot Press, Essex, CT *Toll Free Tel:* 800-243-0495 (orders only); 888-249-7586 (cust serv) *Toll Free Fax:* 800-820-2329 (orders & cust serv), pg 79

Golden West Cookbooks, Phoenix, AZ *Toll Free Tel:* 800-521-9221, pg 79

Goodheart-Willcox Publisher, Tinley Park, IL *Toll Free Tel:* 800-323-0440 *Toll Free Fax:* 888-409-3900, pg 79

Goose Lane Editions, Fredericton, NB Canada *Toll Free Tel:* 888-926-8377, pg 407

Gospel Publishing House, Springfield, MO *Toll Free Tel:* 855-642-2011 *Toll Free Fax:* 877-840-5100, pg 80

Graphic Universe™, Minneapolis, MN *Toll Free Tel:* 800-328-4929 *Toll Free Fax:* 800-332-1132, pg 80

Gray & Company Publishers, Cleveland, OH *Toll Free Tel:* 800-915-3609, pg 80

Green Dragon Books, Palm Beach, FL *Toll Free Tel:* 800-874-8844 *Toll Free Fax:* 888-874-8844, pg 81

Greenhaven Publishing, Buffalo, NY *Toll Free Tel:* 844-317-7404 *Toll Free Fax:* 844-317-7405, pg 81

Grey House Publishing Inc™, Amenia, NY *Toll Free Tel:* 800-562-2139, pg 81

Group Publishing Inc, Loveland, CO *Toll Free Tel:* 800-447-1070, pg 82

Groupe Educalivres Inc, Laval, QC Canada *Toll Free Tel:* 800-567-3671 (info serv) *Toll Free Fax:* 800-267-4387, pg 408

Groupe Modulo Inc, Montreal, QC Canada *Toll Free Tel:* 800-565-5531 *Toll Free Fax:* 800-814-0324, pg 408

Grove Atlantic Inc, New York, NY *Toll Free Tel:* 800-521-0178, pg 82

Gryphon Editions, Omaha, NE *Toll Free Tel:* 888-655-0134 (US & CN), pg 82

Gryphon House Inc, Lewisville, NC *Toll Free Tel:* 800-638-0928 *Toll Free Fax:* 877-638-7576, pg 82

Guerin Editeur Ltee, St-Jean-sur-Richelieu, QC Canada *Toll Free Tel:* 800-398-8337, pg 408

Guideposts Book & Inspirational Media, Danbury, CT *Toll Free Tel:* 800-932-2145 (cust serv), pg 82

The Guilford Press, New York, NY *Toll Free Tel:* 800-365-7006, pg 82

Hachette Book Group Inc, New York, NY *Toll Free Tel:* 800-759-0190 (cust serv) *Toll Free Fax:* 800-286-9471 (cust serv), pg 83

Hackett Publishing Co Inc, Indianapolis, IN *Toll Free Fax:* 800-783-9213, pg 83

Hameray Publishing Group Inc, Los Angeles, CA *Toll Free Tel:* 866-918-6173, pg 84

Hamilton Books, Lanham, MD *Toll Free Tel:* 800-462-6420 (cust serv) *Toll Free Fax:* 800-388-4550 (cust serv), pg 84

Hampton Roads Publishing, Newburyport, MA *Toll Free Tel:* 800-423-7087 (orders) *Toll Free Fax:* 877-337-3309, pg 84

Hancock House Publishers, Blaine, WA *Toll Free Tel:* 800-938-1114 *Toll Free Fax:* 800-983-2262, pg 84

Hancock House Publishers Ltd, Surrey, BC Canada *Toll Free Tel:* 800-938-1114 *Toll Free Fax:* 800-983-2262, pg 408

Handprint Books Inc, Brooklyn, NY *Toll Free Tel:* 800-759-0190 (orders), pg 84

Hanser Publications LLC, Liberty Township, OH *Toll Free Tel:* 800-950-8977; 888-558-2632 (orders), pg 85

Harbour Publishing Co Ltd, Madeira Park, BC Canada *Toll Free Tel:* 800-667-2988 *Toll Free Fax:* 877-604-9449, pg 408

Harlequin Enterprises Ltd, New York, NY *Toll Free Tel:* 888-432-4879; 800-370-5838 (ebooks), pg 85

Harlequin Enterprises Ltd, Toronto, ON Canada *Toll Free Tel:* 888-432-4879; 800-370-5838 (ebook inquiries), pg 409

Hartman Publishing Inc, Albuquerque, NM *Toll Free Tel:* 800-999-9534 *Toll Free Fax:* 800-474-6106, pg 87

FREE DIRECTORY

Harvard University Press, Cambridge, MA *Toll Free Tel:* 800-405-1619 (orders) *Toll Free Fax:* 800-406-9145 (orders), pg 88

Harvest House Publishers Inc, Eugene, OR *Toll Free Tel:* 888-501-6991, pg 88

Hatherleigh Press Ltd, Hobart, NY *Toll Free Tel:* 800-528-2550, pg 88

Hay House LLC, Carlsbad, CA *Toll Free Tel:* 800-654-5126 (ext 1, US) *Toll Free Fax:* 800-650-5115, pg 89

Haynes North America Inc, Westlake Village, CA *Toll Free Tel:* 800-4-HAYNES (442-9637), pg 89

Hazelden Publishing, Center City, MN *Toll Free Tel:* 800-257-7810; 866-328-9000, pg 89

HCPro/DecisionHealth, Brentwood, TN *Toll Free Tel:* 800-650-6787 *Toll Free Fax:* 800-785-9212, pg 89

Health Communications Inc, Boca Raton, FL *Toll Free Tel:* 800-441-5569 (cust serv & orders) *Toll Free Fax:* 800-943-9831 (orders), pg 89

Health Forum Inc, Chicago, IL *Toll Free Tel:* 800-242-2626, pg 90

Health Professions Press, Towson, MD *Toll Free Tel:* 888-337-8808, pg 90

HeartMath LLC, Boulder Creek, CA *Toll Free Tel:* 800-711-6221, pg 90

Hearts 'n Tummies Cookbook Co, Wever, IA *Toll Free Tel:* 800-571-2665, pg 90

William S Hein & Co Inc, Getzville, NY *Toll Free Tel:* 800-828-7571, pg 90

Heinemann, Portsmouth, NH *Toll Free Tel:* 800-225-5800 (US), pg 90

Hendrickson Publishers Inc, Carol Stream, IL *Toll Free Tel:* 855-277-9400 *Toll Free Fax:* 866-622-9474, pg 91

Herald Press, Harrisonburg, VA *Toll Free Tel:* 800-245-7894 (orders) *Toll Free Fax:* 877-271-0760, pg 91

Heritage Books Inc, Berwyn Heights, MD *Toll Free Tel:* 800-876-6103 *Toll Free Fax:* 800-876-6103; 800-297-9954, pg 91

The Heritage Foundation, Washington, DC *Toll Free Tel:* 800-546-2843, pg 91

Heuer Publishing LLC, Cedar Rapids, IA *Toll Free Tel:* 800-950-7529, pg 91

Hewitt Homeschooling Resources, Spokane, WA *Toll Free Tel:* 800-348-1750, pg 91

High Plains Press, Glendo, WY *Toll Free Tel:* 800-552-7819, pg 91

Highlights for Children Inc, Honesdale, PA *Toll Free Tel:* 800-490-5111, pg 92

Hillsdale College Press, Hillsdale, MI *Toll Free Tel:* 800-437-2268, pg 92

Himalayan Institute Press, Honesdale, PA *Toll Free Tel:* 800-822-4547, pg 92

Hohm Press, Chino Valley, AZ *Toll Free Tel:* 800-381-2700, pg 93

Henry Holt and Company, LLC, New York, NY *Toll Free Tel:* 888-330-8477 (orders), pg 94

Hoover Institution Press, Stanford, CA *Toll Free Tel:* 800-935-2882 (US only); 877-466-8374 (US only), pg 95

Hope Publishing Co, Carol Stream, IL *Toll Free Tel:* 800-323-1049, pg 95

Houghton Mifflin Harcourt, Boston, MA *Toll Free Tel:* 855-969-4642; 800-225-5425 (K-12 educ materials); 800-323-9540 (assessment materials); 877-219-1537 (SkillsTutor); 888-242-6747 (Innovation in Educ Group); 800-225-3362 (Trade & Ref Div) *Toll Free Fax:* 800-269-5232, pg 95

Houghton Mifflin Harcourt Assessments, Itasca, IL *Toll Free Tel:* 800-323-9540, pg 96

House to House Publications, Lititz, PA *Toll Free Tel:* 800-848-5892, pg 97

HRD Press, Amherst, MA *Toll Free Tel:* 800-822-2801, pg 97

Human Kinetics Inc, Champaign, IL *Toll Free Tel:* 800-747-4457, pg 97

Humanix Books LLC, New York, NY *Toll Free Tel:* 855-371-7810, pg 97

Huntington Press Publishing, Las Vegas, NV *Toll Free Tel:* 800-244-2224, pg 97

Ibex Publishers, Bethesda, MD *Toll Free Tel:* 888-718-8188, pg 98

IEEE Computer Society, Washington, DC *Toll Free Tel:* 800-678-4333 (memb info), pg 98

Ignatius Press, San Francisco, CA *Toll Free Tel:* 800-651-1531 (orders); 888-615-3186 (cust serv), pg 98

IHS Press, Norfolk, VA *Toll Free Tel:* 877-447-7737 *Toll Free Fax:* 877-447-7737, pg 98

Impact Publications/Development Concepts Inc, Manassas, VA *Toll Free Tel:* 800-361-1055 (cust serv), pg 99

Incentive Publications by World Book, Chicago, IL *Toll Free Tel:* 800-967-5325; 800-975-3250; 888-482-9764 (trade dept) *Toll Free Fax:* 888-922-3766, pg 99

Indiana Historical Society Press, Indianapolis, IN *Toll Free Tel:* 800-447-1830 (orders), pg 99

Industrial Press Inc, South Norwalk, CT *Toll Free Tel:* 888-528-7852 (ext 1, cust serv), pg 100

Information Today, Inc, Medford, NJ *Toll Free Tel:* 800-300-9868 (cust serv), pg 100

Inner Traditions International Ltd, Rochester, VT *Toll Free Tel:* 800-246-8648, pg 101

Insight Editions, San Rafael, CA *Toll Free Tel:* 800-809-3792 *Toll Free Fax:* 866-509-0515, pg 101

Institute of Continuing Legal Education, Ann Arbor, MI *Toll Free Tel:* 877-229-4350 *Toll Free Fax:* 877-229-4351, pg 101

The Institutes™, Malvern, PA *Toll Free Tel:* 800-644-2101, pg 102

Interlink Publishing Group Inc, Northampton, MA *Toll Free Tel:* 800-238-LINK (238-5465), pg 102

International City/County Management Association (ICMA), Washington, DC *Toll Free Tel:* 800-745-8780, pg 102

International Code Council Inc, Brea, CA *Toll Free Tel:* 888-422-7233 *Toll Free Fax:* 866-891-1695, pg 102

International Foundation of Employee Benefit Plans, Brookfield, WI *Toll Free Tel:* 888-334-3327, pg 103

International Linguistics Corp, Kansas City, MO *Toll Free Tel:* 800-237-1830 (orders), pg 103

International Literacy Association (ILA), Newark, DE *Toll Free Tel:* 800-336-7323 (US & CN), pg 103

International Self-Counsel Press Ltd, North Vancouver, BC Canada *Toll Free Tel:* 800-663-3007, pg 410

International Society for Technology in Education, Arlington, VA *Toll Free Tel:* 800-336-5191 (US & CN), pg 103

InterVarsity Press, Westmont, IL *Toll Free Tel:* 800-843-9487, pg 104

Irwin Law Inc, Toronto, ON Canada *Toll Free Tel:* 888-314-9014, pg 410

Island Press, Washington, DC *Toll Free Tel:* 800-621-2736, pg 104

iUniverse, Bloomington, IN *Toll Free Tel:* 800-AUTHORS (288-4677); 844-349-9409, pg 105

Ivey Publishing, London, ON Canada *Toll Free Tel:* 800-649-6355, pg 411

JIST Publishing, Dubuque, IA *Toll Free Tel:* 800-328-1452; 800-228-0810 *Toll Free Fax:* 800-772-9165, pg 106

Johns Hopkins University Press, Baltimore, MD *Toll Free Tel:* 800-537-5487 (book orders & cust serv); 800-548-1784 (journal orders), pg 106

Jones & Bartlett Learning LLC, Burlington, MA *Toll Free Tel:* 800-832-0034, pg 107

Judaica Press Inc, Brooklyn, NY *Toll Free Tel:* 800-972-6201, pg 107

Judson Press, King of Prussia, PA *Toll Free Tel:* 800-458-3766, pg 107

Jump!, Minneapolis, MN *Toll Free Tel:* 888-799-1860 *Toll Free Fax:* 800-675-6679, pg 107

Just World Books LLC, Washington, DC *Toll Free Tel:* 888-506-3769, pg 107

Kaeden Publishing, Westlake, OH *Toll Free Tel:* 800-890-7323, pg 107

Kar-Ben Publishing, Minneapolis, MN *Toll Free Tel:* 800-4-KARBEN (452-7236) *Toll Free Fax:* 800-332-1132, pg 108

J J Keller & Associates, Inc®, Neenah, WI *Toll Free Tel:* 877-564-2333 *Toll Free Fax:* 800-727-7516, pg 108

Kendall Hunt Publishing Co, Dubuque, IA *Toll Free Tel:* 800-228-0810 (orders) *Toll Free Fax:* 800-772-9165, pg 108

Kennedy Information LLC, Keene, NH *Toll Free Tel:* 800-531-0140, pg 108

Kensington Publishing Corp, New York, NY *Toll Free Tel:* 800-221-2647, pg 109

Kids Can Press Ltd, Toronto, ON Canada *Toll Free Tel:* 800-265-0884, pg 411

Kindred Productions, Winnipeg, MB Canada *Toll Free Tel:* 800-545-7322, pg 411

Kinesis Education Inc, Westmount, QC Canada *Toll Free Tel:* 866-750-9466, pg 411

Jessica Kingsley Publishers Inc, Philadelphia, PA *Toll Free Tel:* 866-416-1078 (cust serv), pg 110

Klutz®, New York, NY *Toll Free Tel:* 800-737-4123 (cust serv), pg 110

Knopf Canada, Toronto, ON Canada *Toll Free Tel:* 888-523-9292, pg 411

Kregel Publications, Grand Rapids, MI *Toll Free Tel:* 800-733-2607, pg 111

Kumon Publishing North America Inc (KPNA), Rutherford, NJ *Toll Free Tel:* 800-657-7970 (cust serv), pg 112

Lake Superior Publishing LLC, Duluth, MN *Toll Free Tel:* 888-BIG-LAKE (244-5253), pg 112

LAMA Books, Hayward, CA *Toll Free Tel:* 888-452-6244, pg 112

Lanahan Publishers Inc, Baltimore, MD *Toll Free Tel:* 866-345-1949, pg 112

Landauer Publishing, Mount Joy, PA *Toll Free Tel:* 800-457-9112, pg 112

Peter Lang Publishing Inc, New York, NY *Toll Free Tel:* 800-770-5264 (cust serv), pg 112

Larson Publications, Burdett, NY *Toll Free Tel:* 800-828-2197, pg 113

Laughing Elephant Books, Seattle, WA *Toll Free Tel:* 800-354-0400, pg 113

Law School Admission Council (LSAC), Newtown, PA *Toll Free Tel:* 800-336-3982, pg 113

The Lawbook Exchange, Ltd, Clark, NJ *Toll Free Tel:* 800-422-6686, pg 113

Leadership Ministries Worldwide, Chattanooga, TN *Toll Free Tel:* 800-987-8790, pg 113

THE Learning Connection®, Orlando, FL *Toll Free Tel:* 800-218-8489, pg 113

Learning Links-USA Inc, Cranbury, NJ *Toll Free Tel:* 800-724-2616, pg 114

LearningExpress, New York, NY *Toll Free Tel:* 800-295-9556 (ext 2), pg 114

Lectorum Publications Inc, Pine Brook, NJ *Toll Free Tel:* 800-345-5946, pg 114

Lederer Books, Clarksville, MD *Toll Free Tel:* 800-410-7367 (orders), pg 114

Lee & Low Books Inc, New York, NY *Toll Free Tel:* 888-320-3190 (ext 28, orders only), pg 114

Legacy Bound, Ely, MN *Toll Free Tel:* 800-909-9698, pg 114

Leisure Arts Inc, Maumelle, AR *Toll Free Tel:* 800-643-8030 *Toll Free Fax:* 877-710-5603 (catalog), pg 114

Lerner Publications, Minneapolis, MN *Toll Free Tel:* 800-328-4929 *Toll Free Fax:* 800-332-1132, pg 115

Lerner Publishing Group Inc, Minneapolis, MN *Toll Free Tel:* 800-328-4929 *Toll Free Fax:* 800-332-1132, pg 115

LernerClassroom, Minneapolis, MN *Toll Free Tel:* 800-328-4929 *Toll Free Fax:* 800-332-1132, pg 115

LexisNexis®, New York, NY *Toll Free Fax:* 800-437-8674, pg 116

LexisNexis® Canada Inc, Toronto, ON Canada *Toll Free Tel:* 800-668-6481; 800-387-0899 (cust care); 800-255-5174 (sales), pg 411

LexisNexis® Matthew Bender®, Charlottesville, VA *Toll Free Tel:* 800-223-1940 (sales), pg 116

Liberty Fund Inc, Carmel, IN *Toll Free Tel:* 800-955-8335; 800-866-3520, pg 116

Lidec Inc, St-Jean-sur-Richlieu, QC Canada *Toll Free Tel:* 800-350-5991 (CN only), pg 411

Mary Ann Liebert Inc, New Rochelle, NY *Toll Free Tel:* 800-654-3237, pg 116

Life Cycle Books, Fort Collins, CO *Toll Free Tel:* 800-214-5849, pg 116

Light Technology Publishing LLC, Flagstaff, AZ *Toll Free Tel:* 800-450-0985, pg 116

Liguori Publications, Liguori, MO *Toll Free Tel:* 800-325-9521 *Toll Free Fax:* 800-325-9526 (sales), pg 117

Linden Publishing Co Inc, Fresno, CA *Toll Free Tel:* 800-345-4447 (orders), pg 117

Lippincott Williams & Wilkins, New York, NY *Toll Free Tel:* 800-933-6525, pg 117

little bee books, New York, NY *Toll Free Tel:* 844-321-0237, pg 117

Little, Brown Books for Young Readers (LBYR), New York, NY *Toll Free Tel:* 800-759-0190 (cust serv), pg 118

The Little Entrepreneur, Farmington Hills, MI *Toll Free Tel:* 888-435-9234, pg 118

Liturgical Press, Collegeville, MN *Toll Free Tel:* 800-858-5450 *Toll Free Fax:* 800-445-5899, pg 118

Liturgy Training Publications, Chicago, IL *Toll Free Tel:* 800-933-1800 (US & CN only orders), pg 119

Living Language, New York, NY *Toll Free Tel:* 800-733-3000 (orders), pg 119

Living Stream Ministry (LSM), Anaheim, CA *Toll Free Tel:* 800-549-5164, pg 119

Llewellyn Publications, Woodbury, MN *Toll Free Tel:* 800-843-6666, pg 119

The Local History Co, Pittsburgh, PA *Toll Free Tel:* 866-362-0789 (orders), pg 119

Lone Pine Publishing, Vancouver, BC Canada *Toll Free Tel:* 800-661-9017 *Toll Free Fax:* 800-424-7173, pg 412

Lonely Planet Publications Inc, Oakland, CA *Toll Free Tel:* 800-275-8555 (orders), pg 120

Looseleaf Law Publications Inc, Flushing, NY *Toll Free Tel:* 800-647-5547, pg 120

Lorenz Educational Press, Dayton, OH *Toll Free Tel:* 800-444-1144, pg 120

Lotus Press, Silver Lake, WI *Toll Free Tel:* 800-824-6396 (orders), pg 120

Love Inspired Books, New York, NY *Toll Free Tel:* 888-432-4879, pg 120

Loving Healing Press Inc, Ann Arbor, MI *Toll Free Tel:* 888-761-6268 (US & CN), pg 121

Loyola Press, Chicago, IL *Toll Free Tel:* 800-621-1008, pg 121

LRP Publications, Palm Beach Gardens, FL *Toll Free Tel:* 800-341-7874, pg 121

LRS, Payette, ID *Toll Free Tel:* 800-255-5002, pg 121

Lucent Press, Buffalo, NY *Toll Free Tel:* 844-317-7404 *Toll Free Fax:* 844-317-7405, pg 121

Lutheran Braille Workers Inc, Yucaipa, CA *Toll Free Tel:* 800-925-6092, pg 121

Macmillan Audio, New York, NY *Toll Free Tel:* 888-330-8477 (cust serv) *Toll Free Fax:* 800-672-7703, pg 123

Macmillan Reference USA™, Farmington Hills, MI *Toll Free Tel:* 800-877-4253 *Toll Free Fax:* 877-363-4253, pg 123

Madonna House Publications, Combermere, ON Canada *Toll Free Tel:* 888-703-7110, pg 412

Maharishi International University Press, Fairfield, IA *Toll Free Tel:* 800-831-6523, pg 123

Mandala Earth, San Rafael, CA *Toll Free Fax:* 866-509-0515, pg 124

MAR*CO Products Inc, Hatfield, PA *Toll Free Tel:* 800-448-2197, pg 124

Marathon Press, Norfolk, NE *Toll Free Tel:* 800-228-0629, pg 124

Maren Green Publishing Inc, Hopkins, MN *Toll Free Tel:* 800-287-1512, pg 125

Marquis Who's Who, Uniondale, NY *Toll Free Tel:* 844-394-6946, pg 125

Marshall Cavendish Education, Tarrytown, NY *Toll Free Tel:* 800-821-9881, pg 125

Martindale LLC, New Providence, NJ *Toll Free Tel:* 800-526-4902, pg 126

Mason Crest Publishers, Broomall, PA *Toll Free Tel:* 866-MCP-BOOK (627-2665), pg 126

Master Books®, Green Forest, AR *Toll Free Tel:* 800-999-3777, pg 126

Mastery Education, Montvale, NJ *Toll Free Tel:* 800-822-1080, pg 126

Math Solutions®, Sausalito, CA *Toll Free Tel:* 877-234-7323 *Toll Free Fax:* 800-724-4716, pg 127

Math Teachers Press Inc, Minneapolis, MN *Toll Free Tel:* 800-852-2435, pg 127

The Mathematical Association of America, Washington, DC *Toll Free Tel:* 800-741-9415, pg 127

McClelland & Stewart Ltd, Toronto, ON Canada *Toll Free Tel:* 888-523-9292, pg 412

The McDonald & Woodward Publishing Co, Newark, OH *Toll Free Tel:* 800-233-8787, pg 127

McFarland, Jefferson, NC *Toll Free Tel:* 800-253-2187 (orders), pg 127

McGraw-Hill Create, New York, NY *Toll Free Tel:* 800-962-9342, pg 127

McGraw-Hill Higher Education, New York, NY *Toll Free Tel:* 800-338-3987 (cust serv) *Toll Free Fax:* 800-953-8691 (cust serv), pg 128

McGraw-Hill Ryerson, Whitby, ON Canada *Toll Free Tel:* 800-565-5758 (cust serv) *Toll Free Fax:* 800-463-5885, pg 413

McGraw-Hill School Education Group, Columbus, OH *Toll Free Tel:* 800-848-1567, pg 128

me+mi publishing inc, Aurora, IL *Toll Free Tel:* 888-251-1444, pg 128

R S Means from The Gordian Group, Rockland, MA *Toll Free Tel:* 800-448-8182 (cust serv); 800-334-3509 (sales) *Toll Free Fax:* 800-632-6732, pg 128

Medals of America Press, Fountain Inn, SC *Toll Free Tel:* 800-605-4001 *Toll Free Fax:* 800-407-8640, pg 128

Medical Group Management Association (MGMA), Englewood, CO *Toll Free Tel:* 877-275-6462, pg 128

Medical Physics Publishing Corp (MPP), Madison, WI *Toll Free Tel:* 800-442-5778 (cust serv), pg 129

Mel Bay Publications Inc, Webster Groves, MO *Toll Free Tel:* 800-863-5229, pg 129

Menasha Ridge Press, Birmingham, AL *Toll Free Tel:* 888-604-4537, pg 129

MennoMedia, Harrisonburg, VA *Toll Free Tel:* 800-245-7894 (orders & cust serv US) *Toll Free Fax:* 877-271-0760, pg 129

Mercer University Press, Macon, GA *Toll Free Tel:* 866-895-1472, pg 129

Meriwether Publishing, Centennial, CO *Toll Free Tel:* 800-333-7262, pg 129

Merriam-Webster Inc, Springfield, MA *Toll Free Tel:* 800-828-1880 (orders & cust serv), pg 129

Mesorah Publications Ltd, Rahway, NJ *Toll Free Tel:* 800-637-6724, pg 130

Messianic Jewish Publishers, Clarksville, MD *Toll Free Tel:* 800-410-7367 (orders) *Toll Free Fax:* 800-327-0048 (orders), pg 130

Mike Murach & Associates Inc, Fresno, CA *Toll Free Tel:* 800-221-5528, pg 131

Milady, Mason, OH *Toll Free Tel:* 866-848-5143, pg 131

Milkweed Editions, Minneapolis, MN *Toll Free Tel:* 800-520-6455, pg 131

Millbrook Press, Minneapolis, MN *Toll Free Tel:* 800-328-4929 *Toll Free Fax:* 800-332-1132, pg 131

Milliken Publishing Co, Dayton, OH *Toll Free Tel:* 800-444-1144, pg 132

The Minerals, Metals & Materials Society (TMS), Pittsburgh, PA *Toll Free Tel:* 800-759-4867, pg 132

The MIT Press, Cambridge, MA *Toll Free Tel:* 800-405-1619 (orders), pg 132

Mitchell Lane Publishers Inc, Hallandale, FL *Toll Free Tel:* 800-223-3251, pg 133

Moody Publishers, Chicago, IL *Toll Free Tel:* 800-678-8812 *Toll Free Fax:* 800-678-3329, pg 134

Morehouse Publishing, New York, NY *Toll Free Tel:* 800-242-1918 (retail orders only), pg 134

Mountain Press Publishing Co, Missoula, MT *Toll Free Tel:* 800-234-5308, pg 135

Multnomah, Colorado Springs, CO *Toll Free Tel:* 800-603-7051 (orders), pg 135

Museum of New Mexico Press, Santa Fe, NM *Toll Free Tel:* 800-249-7737 (orders) *Toll Free Fax:* 800-622-8667 (orders), pg 135

NACE International, Houston, TX *Toll Free Tel:* 800-797-NACE (797-6223), pg 136

National Academies Press (NAP), Washington, DC *Toll Free Tel:* 800-624-6242, pg 136

National Braille Press, Boston, MA *Toll Free Tel:* 800-548-7323 (cust serv); 888-965-8965, pg 137

National Catholic Educational Association, Arlington, VA *Toll Free Tel:* 800-711-6232, pg 137

National Council of Teachers of English (NCTE), Champaign, IL *Toll Free Tel:* 877-369-6283 (cust serv), pg 137

National Council of Teachers of Mathematics (NCTM), Reston, VA *Toll Free Tel:* 800-235-7566, pg 137

National Geographic Books, Washington, DC *Toll Free Tel:* 877-866-6486, pg 137

National Golf Foundation, Jupiter, FL *Toll Free Tel:* 888-275-4643, pg 138

National Institute for Trial Advocacy (NITA), Boulder, CO *Toll Free Tel:* 877-648-2632; 800-225-6482 (orders & returns), pg 138

National Learning Corp, Syosset, NY *Toll Free Tel:* 800-632-8888, pg 138

National Notary Association (NNA), Chatsworth, CA *Toll Free Tel:* 800-876-6827 *Toll Free Fax:* 800-833-1211, pg 138

National Resource Center for Youth Services, Tulsa, OK *Toll Free Tel:* 800-274-2687, pg 138

National Science Teachers Association (NSTA), Arlington, VA *Toll Free Tel:* 800-277-5300 (orders) *Toll Free Fax:* 888-433-0526 (orders), pg 138

The National Underwriter Co, Erlanger, KY *Toll Free Tel:* 800-543-0874, pg 138

National Wildlife Federation, Reston, VA *Toll Free Tel:* 800-477-5034, pg 139

Naval Institute Press, Annapolis, MD *Toll Free Tel:* 800-233-8764, pg 139

Nelson Education Ltd, Scarborough, ON Canada *Toll Free Tel:* 800-268-2222 (cust serv), pg 413

New City Press, Hyde Park, NY *Toll Free Tel:* 800-462-5980 (orders only), pg 139

New Forums Press Inc, Stillwater, OK *Toll Free Tel:* 800-606-3766, pg 139

New Harbinger Publications Inc, Oakland, CA *Toll Free Tel:* 800-748-6273 (orders only) *Toll Free Fax:* 800-652-1613, pg 140

New Leaf Press, Green Forest, AR *Toll Free Tel:* 800-999-3777, pg 140

New Readers Press, Syracuse, NY *Toll Free Tel:* 800-448-8878 *Toll Free Fax:* 866-894-2100, pg 140

New World Publishing (Canada), Halifax, NS Canada *Toll Free Tel:* 877-211-3334 (orders), pg 414

New York Academy of Sciences (NYAS), New York, NY *Toll Free Tel:* 800-843-6927, pg 140

New York State Bar Association, Albany, NY *Toll Free Tel:* 800-582-2452, pg 141

New York University Press, New York, NY *Toll Free Tel:* 800-996-6987 (orders), pg 141

Newbury Street Press, Boston, MA *Toll Free Tel:* 888-296-3447 (NEHGS membership), pg 141

Nimbus Publishing Ltd, Halifax, NS Canada *Toll Free Tel:* 800-NIMBUS9 (646-2879) *Toll Free Fax:* 888-253-3133, pg 414

No Starch Press, San Francisco, CA *Toll Free Tel:* 800-420-7240, pg 141

North River Press Publishing Corp, Great Barrington, MA *Toll Free Tel:* 800-486-2665 *Toll Free Fax:* 800-BOOK-FAX (266-5329), pg 142

North Star Editions Inc, Mendota Heights, MN *Toll Free Tel:* 888-417-0195, pg 142

Northwestern University Press, Evanston, IL *Toll Free Tel:* 800-621-2736 (orders only), pg 143

W W Norton & Company Inc, New York, NY *Toll Free Tel:* 800-233-4830 (orders & cust serv) *Toll Free Fax:* 800-458-6515, pg 143

Norwood House Press, Fairport, NY *Toll Free Tel:* 866-565-2900 *Toll Free Fax:* 866-565-2901, pg 143

Novalis Publishing, Toronto, ON Canada *Toll Free Tel:* 877-702-7773 *Toll Free Fax:* 877-702-7775, pg 414

NRP Direct, Athens, GA *Toll Free Tel:* 844-592-4197, pg 144

Nursesbooks.org, The Publishing Program of ANA, Silver Spring, MD *Toll Free Tel:* 800-274-4262; 800-637-0323 (orders), pg 144

Nystrom Education, Culver City, CA *Toll Free Tel:* 800-421-4246 *Toll Free Fax:* 800-944-5432, pg 144

OAG Worldwide, Lisle, IL *Toll Free Tel:* 800-342-5624 (cust serv), pg 144

OCP, Lake Oswego, OR *Toll Free Tel:* 800-LITURGY (548-8749) *Toll Free Fax:* 800-843-8181, pg 145

OECD Washington Center, Washington, DC *Toll Free Tel:* 800-456-6323 (dist ctr/pubns orders), pg 145

The Ohio State University Press, Columbus, OH *Toll Free Fax:* 800-621-8476, pg 145

Omnibus Press, New York, NY *Toll Free Tel:* 800-431-7187 *Toll Free Fax:* 800-345-6842, pg 146

Omnigraphics Inc, Detroit, MI *Toll Free Tel:* 800-234-1340 (cust serv) *Toll Free Fax:* 800-875-1340 (cust serv), pg 146

OptumInsight™, Eden Prairie, MN *Toll Free Tel:* 888-445-8745, pg 147

Orbis Books, Maryknoll, NY *Toll Free Tel:* 800-258-5838 (orders, Mon-Fri 8AM-4PM EST), pg 147

Orbit, New York, NY *Toll Free Tel:* 800-759-0190, pg 147

Orca Book Publishers, Victoria, BC Canada *Toll Free Tel:* 800-210-5277 *Toll Free Fax:* 877-408-1551, pg 415

O'Reilly Media Inc, Sebastopol, CA *Toll Free Tel:* 800-998-9938; 800-889-8969, pg 147

Other Press, New York, NY *Toll Free Tel:* 877-THEOTHER (843-6843), pg 148

Our Daily Bread Publishing, Grand Rapids, MI *Toll Free Tel:* 800-653-8333 (cust serv), pg 148

Our Sunday Visitor Publishing, Huntington, IN *Toll Free Tel:* 800-348-2440 (orders) *Toll Free Fax:* 800-498-6709, pg 148

Richard C Owen Publishers Inc, Katonah, NY *Toll Free Tel:* 800-336-5588, pg 149

Oxford University Press USA, New York, NY *Toll Free Tel:* 800-451-7556 (orders); 800-445-9714 (cust serv), pg 149

Ozark Mountain Publishing Inc, Huntsville, AR *Toll Free Tel:* 800-935-0045, pg 149

P & R Publishing Co, Phillipsburg, NJ *Toll Free Tel:* 800-631-0094, pg 149

PA Press, Hudson, NY *Toll Free Tel:* 800-722-6657 (dist); 800-759-0190 (sales), pg 149

Pacific Educational Press, Vancouver, BC Canada *Toll Free Tel:* 877-377-9378, pg 415

Paraclete Press Inc, Brewster, MA *Toll Free Tel:* 800-451-5006, pg 151

Paradigm Publications, Taos, NM *Toll Free Tel:* 800-873-3946 (US); 888-873-3947 (CN), pg 151

Paradise Cay Publications Inc, Blue Lake, CA *Toll Free Tel:* 800-736-4509, pg 151

Paragon House, St Paul, MN *Toll Free Tel:* 800-447-3709, pg 151

Parallax Press, Berkeley, CA *Toll Free Tel:* 800-863-5290 (orders), pg 151

Parenting Press, Seattle, WA *Toll Free Tel:* 800-99-BOOKS (992-6657), pg 151

Pauline Books & Media, Boston, MA *Toll Free Tel:* 800-876-4463 (orders); 800-836-9723 (cust serv), pg 152

Paulist Press, Mahwah, NJ *Toll Free Tel:* 800-218-1903, pg 152

Peachpit Press, San Francisco, CA *Toll Free Tel:* 800-283-9444, pg 153

Peachtree Publishing Co Inc, Atlanta, GA *Toll Free Tel:* 800-241-0113 *Toll Free Fax:* 800-875-8909, pg 153

Pearson Education Canada, North York, ON Canada *Toll Free Tel:* 800-567-3800 *Toll Free Fax:* 800-263-7733, pg 415

Pearson Learning Solutions, Boston, MA *Toll Free Tel:* 800-428-4466 (orders); 800-635-1579, pg 153

Pelican Publishing, New Orleans, LA *Toll Free Tel:* 844-868-1798 (orders), pg 153

Pembroke Publishers Ltd, Markham, ON Canada *Toll Free Tel:* 800-997-9807 *Toll Free Fax:* 800-339-5568, pg 415

Pendragon Press, Hillsdale, NY *Toll Free Tel:* 877-656-6381 (orders), pg 154

Penfield Books, Iowa City, IA *Toll Free Tel:* 800-728-9998, pg 154

Penguin Random House Audio Publishing Group, New York, NY *Toll Free Tel:* 800-793-2665 (cust serv), pg 154

Penguin Random House Canada, a Penguin Random House company, Toronto, ON Canada *Toll Free Tel:* 888-523-9292 (cust serv), pg 415

Penguin Random House LLC, New York, NY *Toll Free Tel:* 800-726-0600, pg 155

Penn State University Press, University Park, PA *Toll Free Tel:* 800-326-9180 (orders & cust serv) *Toll Free Fax:* 877-778-2665 (book orders), pg 157

PennWell Books, Tulsa, OK *Toll Free Tel:* 866-777-1814, pg 157

Penny-Farthing Productions, Sugar Land, TX *Toll Free Tel:* 800-926-2669, pg 157

Pentecostal Resources Group, Weldon Spring, MO *Toll Free Tel:* 866-819-7667, pg 157

Perfection Learning®, Logan, IA *Toll Free Tel:* 800-831-4190 *Toll Free Fax:* 800-543-2745, pg 158

Peterson's, Highlands Ranch, CO *Toll Free Tel:* 800-338-3282, pg 158

Petroleum Extension Service (PETEX), Austin, TX *Toll Free Tel:* 800-687-4132 *Toll Free Fax:* 800-687-7839, pg 159

Pflaum Publishing Group, Dayton, OH *Toll Free Tel:* 800-523-4625; 800-543-4383 (ext 1136, cust serv) *Toll Free Fax:* 800-370-4450, pg 159

Phaidon, New York, NY *Toll Free Tel:* 800-759-0190 (cust serv) *Toll Free Fax:* 800-286-9471 (cust serv), pg 159

Philosophy Documentation Center, Charlottesville, VA *Toll Free Tel:* 800-444-2419, pg 159

Pieces of Learning Inc, Marion, IL *Toll Free Tel:* 800-729-5137 *Toll Free Fax:* 800-844-0455, pg 160

The Pilgrim Press/United Church Press, Cleveland, OH *Toll Free Tel:* 800-537-3394 (orders), pg 160

Platypus Media LLC, Washington, DC *Toll Free Tel:* 877-PLATYPS (752-8977), pg 160

Plough Publishing House, Walden, NY *Toll Free Tel:* 800-521-8011, pg 161

Pocket Press Inc, Portland, OR *Toll Free Tel:* 888-237-2110 *Toll Free Fax:* 877-643-3732, pg 161

Poisoned Pen Press, Scottsdale, AZ *Toll Free Tel:* 800-421-3976, pg 161

Pomegranate Communications Inc, Portland, OR *Toll Free Tel:* 800-227-1428 *Toll Free Fax:* 800-848-4376, pg 162

Portage & Main Press, Winnipeg, MB Canada *Toll Free Tel:* 800-667-9673 *Toll Free Fax:* 866-734-8477, pg 416

Pottersfield Press, East Lawrencetown, NS Canada *Toll Free Tel:* 800-646-2879 (orders only), pg 416

Practising Law Institute (PLI), New York, NY *Toll Free Tel:* 800-260-4PLI (260-4754) *Toll Free Fax:* 800-321-0093 (cust serv), pg 163

PrairieView Press, Gretna, MB Canada *Toll Free Tel:* 800-477-7377 *Toll Free Fax:* 866-480-0253, pg 417

Presbyterian Publishing Corp (PPC), Louisville, KY *Toll Free Tel:* 800-533-4371; 800-523-1631 (US only), pg 163

Princeton Book Co Publishers, Trenton, NJ *Toll Free Tel:* 800-220-7149, pg 163

The Princeton Review, New York, NY *Toll Free Tel:* 800-273-8439 (orders only), pg 164

PRINTING United Alliance, Fairfax, VA *Toll Free Tel:* 888-385-3588, pg 165

PRO-ED Inc, Austin, TX *Toll Free Tel:* 800-897-3202 *Toll Free Fax:* 800-397-7633, pg 165

Pro Lingua Associates Inc, Brattleboro, VT *Toll Free Tel:* 800-366-4775, pg 165

Productive Publications, North York, ON Canada *Toll Free Tel:* 877-879-2669 (orders), pg 417

Productivity Press, New York, NY *Toll Free Tel:* 800-634-7064 (orders); 800-797-3803, pg 165

Professional Communications Inc, Durant, OK *Toll Free Tel:* 800-337-9838, pg 165

The Professional Education Group LLC (PEG), Wayzata, MN *Toll Free Tel:* 800-229-2531, pg 165

Professional Resource Press, Sarasota, FL *Toll Free Tel:* 800-443-3364 (orders & cust serv) *Toll Free Fax:* 866-804-4843 (orders only), pg 165

ProQuest LLC, part of Clarivate PLC, Ann Arbor, MI *Toll Free Tel:* 800-521-0600; 877-779-6768 (sales), pg 166

ProStar Publications Inc, Inglewood, CA *Toll Free Tel:* 800-481-6277, pg 166

PSMJ Resources Inc, Newton, MA *Toll Free Tel:* 800-537-PSMJ (537-7765), pg 166

Psychological Assessment Resources Inc (PAR), Lutz, FL *Toll Free Tel:* 800-331-8378 *Toll Free Fax:* 800-727-9329, pg 166

Les Publications du Quebec, Quebec, QC Canada *Toll Free Tel:* 800-463-2100 (Quebec province only) *Toll Free Fax:* 800-561-3479, pg 417

Quail Ridge Press (QRP), Nashville, TN *Toll Free Tel:* 800-358-0560, pg 168

Quarto Publishing Group USA Inc, Beverly, MA *Toll Free Tel:* 800-328-0590 (sales), pg 168

Quintessence Publishing Co Inc, Batavia, IL *Toll Free Tel:* 800-621-0387, pg 168

Quixote Press, Wever, IA *Toll Free Tel:* 800-571-2665, pg 169

Rand McNally, Skokie, IL *Toll Free Tel:* 877-446-4863 *Toll Free Fax:* 877-469-1298, pg 169

Random House Publishing Group, New York, NY *Toll Free Tel:* 800-200-3552, pg 170

Raven Publishing Inc, Norris, MT *Toll Free Tel:* 866-685-3545, pg 172

Reader's Digest Select Editions, White Plains, NY *Toll Free Tel:* 877-732-4438 (cust serv), pg 172

Recorded Books Inc, an RBmedia company, Landover, MD *Toll Free Tel:* 800-305-3450, pg 172

Red Chair Press, South Egremont, MA *Toll Free Tel:* 800-328-4929 (orders & cust serv), pg 172

Red Deer Press Inc, Toronto, ON Canada *Toll Free Tel:* 800-387-9776, pg 417

Red Wheel/Weiser, Newburyport, MA *Toll Free Tel:* 800-423-7087 (orders), pg 173

Redleaf Press®, St Paul, MN *Toll Free Tel:* 800-423-8309, pg 173

Reedswain Inc, Spring City, PA *Toll Free Tel:* 800-331-5191, pg 173

Referee Books, Racine, WI *Toll Free Tel:* 800-733-6100, pg 173

ReferencePoint Press Inc, San Diego, CA *Toll Free Tel:* 888-479-6436, pg 173

Regular Baptist Press, Arlington Heights, IL *Toll Free Tel:* 800-727-4440 (cust serv), pg 174

Research & Education Association (REA), Cranbury, NJ *Toll Free Tel:* 833-591-2798 (cust care), pg 174

Research Press, Champaign, IL *Toll Free Tel:* 800-519-2707, pg 174

Revell, Ada, MI *Toll Free Tel:* 800-877-2665 (orders only) *Toll Free Fax:* 800-398-3111 (orders only), pg 174

Rio Nuevo Publishers, Tucson, AZ *Toll Free Tel:* 800-969-9558 *Toll Free Fax:* 800-715-5888, pg 175

Rizzoli International Publications Inc, New York, NY *Toll Free Tel:* 800-522-6657 (orders only), pg 175

The Rosen Publishing Group Inc, New York, NY *Toll Free Tel:* 800-237-9932 *Toll Free Fax:* 888-436-4643, pg 177

Rothstein Associates Inc, Brookfield, CT *Toll Free Tel:* 888-768-4783, pg 177

The Rough Notes Co Inc, Carmel, IN *Toll Free Tel:* 800-428-4384 (cust serv) *Toll Free Fax:* 800-321-1909, pg 177

Round Table Companies, Deerfield, IL *Toll Free Tel:* 833-750-5683, pg 177

Routledge, New York, NY *Toll Free Tel:* 800-634-7064 (order enquiries, cust serv), pg 177

Rowman & Littlefield, Lanham, MD *Toll Free Tel:* 800-462-6420 (ext 3024, cust serv), pg 178

Running Press, New York, NY *Toll Free Tel:* 800-759-0190 (cust serv) *Toll Free Fax:* 800-286-9471 (cust serv), pg 178

Russell Sage Foundation, New York, NY *Toll Free Tel:* 800-524-6401, pg 178

Saddleback Educational Publishing, Costa Mesa, CA *Toll Free Tel:* 888-SDLBACK (735-2225); 800-637-8715 *Toll Free Fax:* 888-734-4010, pg 179

William H Sadlier Inc, New York, NY *Toll Free Tel:* 800-221-5175 (cust serv), pg 179

SAE (Society of Automotive Engineers International), Warrendale, PA *Toll Free Tel:* 877-606-7323 (cust serv), pg 179

Safari Press, Huntington Beach, CA *Toll Free Tel:* 800-451-4788, pg 179

Sagamore Publishing LLC, Champaign, IL *Toll Free Tel:* 800-327-5557 (orders), pg 179

SAGE Publishing, Thousand Oaks, CA *Toll Free Tel:* 800-818-7243 *Toll Free Fax:* 800-583-2665, pg 180

St James Press®, Farmington Hills, MI *Toll Free Tel:* 800-877-4253 (orders) *Toll Free Fax:* 877-363-4253, pg 180

Saint Mary's Press, Winona, MN *Toll Free Tel:* 800-533-8095 *Toll Free Fax:* 800-344-9225, pg 181

St Nectarios Press, Seattle, WA *Toll Free Tel:* 800-643-4233, pg 181

St Pauls, Staten Island, NY *Toll Free Tel:* 800-343-2522, pg 181

Salem Press, Hackensack, NJ *Toll Free Tel:* 800-221-1592, pg 181

Salina Bookshelf Inc, Flagstaff, AZ *Toll Free Tel:* 877-527-0070, pg 181

SAMS Technical Publishing LLC, Indianapolis, IN *Toll Free Tel:* 800-428-7267, pg 181

Santa Monica Press LLC, Solana Beach, CA *Toll Free Tel:* 800-784-9553, pg 182

Sara Jordan Publishing, St Catharines, ON Canada *Toll Free Tel:* 800-567-7733 *Toll Free Fax:* 800-229-3855, pg 418

SAS Press, Cary, NC *Toll Free Tel:* 800-727-0025, pg 182

Sasquatch Books, Seattle, WA *Toll Free Tel:* 800-775-0817, pg 182

Savvas Learning Co LLC, Paramus, NJ *Toll Free Tel:* 800-848-9500, pg 183

Scepter Publishers, Strongsville, OH *Toll Free Tel:* 800-322-8773, pg 183

Schlager Group Inc, Dallas, TX *Toll Free Tel:* 888-416-5727, pg 183

Scholastic Canada Ltd, Markham, ON Canada *Toll Free Tel:* 800-268-3860 (CN) *Toll Free Fax:* 800-387-4944, pg 418

Scholastic Inc, New York, NY *Toll Free Tel:* 800-SCHOLASTIC (724-6527), pg 184

Scholastic International, New York, NY *Toll Free Tel:* 800-SCHOLASTIC (724-6527), pg 184

Schonfeld & Associates Inc, Virginia Beach, VA *Toll Free Tel:* 800-205-0030, pg 184

School Guide Publications, Mamaroneck, NY *Toll Free Tel:* 800-433-7771, pg 185

School Zone Publishing Co, Grand Haven, MI *Toll Free Tel:* 800-253-0564, pg 185

Schreiber Publishing, Savage, MD *Toll Free Tel:* 800-296-1961 (sales), pg 185

Seal Books, Toronto, ON Canada *Toll Free Tel:* 888-523-9292 (order desk), pg 419

Seedling Publications Inc, Elizabethtown, PA *Toll Free Tel:* 800-233-0759 *Toll Free Fax:* 888-834-1303, pg 186

Self-Realization Fellowship Publishers, Los Angeles, CA *Toll Free Tel:* 888-773-8680, pg 186

Seven Stories Press, New York, NY *Toll Free Tel:* 800-733-3000 (orders), pg 186

Shadow Mountain Publishing, Salt Lake City, UT *Toll Free Tel:* 800-453-3876, pg 186

Shambhala Publications Inc, Boulder, CO *Toll Free Tel:* 866-424-0030 (off); 888-424-2329 (orders & cust serv), pg 187

Signalman Publishing, Kissimmee, FL *Toll Free Tel:* 888-907-4423, pg 187

Signature Books Publishing LLC, Salt Lake City, UT *Toll Free Tel:* 800-356-5687, pg 187

Simon & Schuster, New York, NY *Toll Free Tel:* 800-223-2348 (cust serv); 800-223-2336 (orders) *Toll Free Fax:* 800-943-9831 (orders), pg 188

FREE DIRECTORY

Simon & Schuster Canada, Toronto, ON Canada *Toll Free Tel:* 800-387-0446; 800-268-3216 (orders) *Toll Free Fax:* 888-849-8151 (orders), pg 419

Simon & Schuster, LLC, New York, NY *Toll Free Tel:* 800-223-2336 (orders) *Toll Free Fax:* 800-943-9831 (orders), pg 189

Sinauer Associates, Cary, NC *Toll Free Tel:* 800-280-0280, pg 190

SkillPath Publications, Mission, KS *Toll Free Tel:* 800-873-7545, pg 190

SLACK® Incorporated, A Wyanoke Group Company, Thorofare, NJ *Toll Free Tel:* 800-257-8290, pg 191

Sleeping Bear Press™, Ann Arbor, MI *Toll Free Tel:* 800-487-2323, pg 191

SME (Society of Manufacturing Engineers), Southfield, MI *Toll Free Tel:* 800-733-4763 (cust serv), pg 191

Smith & Kraus Publishers Inc, Hanover, NH *Toll Free Tel:* 877-668-8680, pg 192

M Lee Smith Publishers, Brentwood, TN *Toll Free Tel:* 800-274-6774; 800-727-5257, pg 192

Smyth & Helwys Publishing Inc, Macon, GA *Toll Free Tel:* 800-747-3016 (orders only), pg 192

Society for Human Resource Management (SHRM), Alexandria, VA *Toll Free Tel:* 800-283-7476 (orders), pg 192

Society for Industrial & Applied Mathematics, Philadelphia, PA *Toll Free Tel:* 800-447-7426, pg 192

Society for Mining, Metallurgy & Exploration, Englewood, CO *Toll Free Tel:* 800-763-3132, pg 192

Society of American Archivists, Chicago, IL *Toll Free Tel:* 866-722-7858, pg 192

Society of Environmental Toxicology & Chemistry (SETAC), Pensacola, FL *Toll Free Fax:* 888-296-4136, pg 192

The Society of Naval Architects & Marine Engineers (SNAME), Alexandria, VA *Toll Free Tel:* 800-798-2188, pg 193

Solano Press Books, Point Arena, CA *Toll Free Tel:* 800-931-9373, pg 193

Solution Tree, Bloomington, IN *Toll Free Tel:* 800-733-6786, pg 193

Soncino Press Ltd, Brooklyn, NY *Toll Free Tel:* 800-972-6201, pg 193

Sophia Institute Press®, Nashua, NH *Toll Free Tel:* 800-888-9344 *Toll Free Fax:* 888-288-2259, pg 193

Sounds True Inc, Louisville, CO *Toll Free Tel:* 800-333-9185 (US); 888-303-9185 (US & CN), pg 194

Sourcebooks LLC, Naperville, IL *Toll Free Tel:* 800-432-7444, pg 194

South Carolina Bar, Columbia, SC *Toll Free Tel:* 800-768-7787, pg 195

SPIE, Bellingham, WA *Toll Free Tel:* 888-504-8171 (orders), pg 196

Spizzirri Publishing Inc, Rapid City, SD *Toll Free Tel:* 800-325-9819 *Toll Free Fax:* 800-322-9819, pg 196

Springer, New York, NY *Toll Free Tel:* 800-SPRINGER (777-4643), pg 196

Springer Publishing Co, New York, NY *Toll Free Tel:* 877-687-7476, pg 196

Square One Publishers Inc, Garden City Park, NY *Toll Free Tel:* 877-900-BOOK (900-2665), pg 196

Standard Publishing, Colorado Springs, CO *Toll Free Tel:* 800-323-7543 (orders & cust serv) *Toll Free Fax:* 800-430-0726 (cust serv), pg 197

Standard Publishing Corp, Boston, MA *Toll Free Tel:* 800-682-5759, pg 197

Starcrafts LLC, Epping, NH *Toll Free Tel:* 866-953-8458 (24/7 message ctr), pg 197

State University of New York Press, Albany, NY *Toll Free Tel:* 877-204-6073 (orders) *Toll Free Fax:* 877-204-6074 (orders), pg 198

Stenhouse Publishers, Grandview Heights, OH *Toll Free Tel:* 800-988-9812 *Toll Free Fax:* 800-992-6087, pg 198

Stoneydale Press Publishing Co, Stevensville, MT *Toll Free Tel:* 800-735-7006, pg 199

Stress Free Kids®, Marietta, GA *Toll Free Fax:* 866-302-2759, pg 200

Stylus Publishing LLC, Sterling, VA *Toll Free Tel:* 800-232-0223 (orders & cust serv), pg 200

Sun Publishing Company, Santa Fe, NM *Toll Free Tel:* 877-849-0051, pg 200

Sunbelt Publications Inc, Chula Vista, CA *Toll Free Tel:* 800-626-6579 (cust serv), pg 200

Sundance/Newbridge Publishing, Marlborough, MA *Toll Free Tel:* 888-200-2720; 800-343-8204 *Toll Free Fax:* 800-456-2419 (orders), pg 200

Sunrise River Press, Forrest Lake, MN *Toll Free Tel:* 800-895-4585, pg 201

Surrey Books, Evanston, IL *Toll Free Tel:* 800-326-4430, pg 201

Swedenborg Foundation, West Chester, PA *Toll Free Tel:* 800-355-3222 (cust serv), pg 201

SYBEX, Hoboken, NJ *Toll Free Fax:* 800-565-6802, pg 201

Syracuse University Press, Syracuse, NY *Toll Free Tel:* 800-365-8929 (cust serv), pg 201

TAN Books, Gastonia, NC *Toll Free Tel:* 800-437-5876, pg 202

Tanglewood Publishing, Indianapolis, IN *Toll Free Tel:* 800-788-3123 (orders), pg 202

Tantor Media Inc, Old Saybrook, CT *Toll Free Tel:* 877-782-6867 *Toll Free Fax:* 888-782-7821, pg 202

Tapestry Press Ltd, Littleton, MA *Toll Free Tel:* 800-535-2007, pg 202

Taschen America, Los Angeles, CA *Toll Free Tel:* 888-TASCHEN (827-2436), pg 203

Taunton Books, Newtown, CT *Toll Free Tel:* 866-505-4689 (orders), pg 203

Taylor & Francis Inc, Philadelphia, PA *Toll Free Tel:* 800-354-1420, pg 203

TCP Press, Uxbridge, ON Canada *Toll Free Tel:* 800-772-7765, pg 420

Teacher Created Resources Inc, Garden Grove, CA *Toll Free Tel:* 800-662-4321; 888-343-4335 *Toll Free Fax:* 800-525-1254, pg 203

Teacher's Discovery®, Auburn Hills, MI *Toll Free Tel:* 800-TEACHER (832-2437) *Toll Free Fax:* 800-287-4509, pg 203

Teaching & Learning Co, Dayton, OH *Toll Free Tel:* 800-444-1144, pg 204

Teaching Strategies LLC, Bethesda, MD *Toll Free Tel:* 800-637-3652, pg 204

Temple University Press, Philadelphia, PA *Toll Free Tel:* 800-621-2736, pg 204

Ten Speed Press, Emeryville, CA *Toll Free Tel:* 800-841-BOOK (841-2665), pg 204

TESOL Press, Alexandria, VA *Toll Free Tel:* 888-891-0041 (cust serv), pg 204

Texas A&M University Press, College Station, TX *Toll Free Tel:* 800-826-8911 (orders) *Toll Free Fax:* 888-617-2421 (orders), pg 205

Texas Tech University Press, Lubbock, TX *Toll Free Tel:* 800-832-4042, pg 205

Texas Western Press, El Paso, TX *Toll Free Tel:* 800-488-3798 (orders only), pg 205

Thames & Hudson, New York, NY *Toll Free Tel:* 800-233-4830, pg 205

Thieme Medical Publishers Inc, New York, NY *Toll Free Tel:* 800-782-3488, pg 206

Charles C Thomas Publisher Ltd, Springfield, IL *Toll Free Tel:* 800-258-8980, pg 206

Thomas Nelson, Nashville, TN *Toll Free Tel:* 800-251-4000, pg 206

Thompson Educational Publishing Inc, Toronto, ON Canada *Toll Free Tel:* 877-366-2763, pg 420

Thomson West, Eagan, MN *Toll Free Tel:* 888-728-7677 (cust serv), pg 206

Thorndike Press®, Waterville, ME *Toll Free Tel:* 800-877-4253 (option 1) *Toll Free Fax:* 800-558-4676 (orders), pg 206

Tide-mark Press, West Hartford, CT *Toll Free Tel:* 800-338-2508, pg 207

Tilbury House Publishers, Thomaston, ME *Toll Free Tel:* 800-582-1899 (orders), pg 207

Tommy Nelson®, Nashville, TN *Toll Free Tel:* 800-251-4000, pg 207

Tor Publishing Group, New York, NY *Toll Free Tel:* 800-455-0340 (Macmillan), pg 207

Tower Publishing Co, Standish, ME *Toll Free Tel:* 800-969-8693, pg 208

Trafalgar Square Books, North Pomfret, VT *Toll Free Tel:* 800-423-4525, pg 208

Trafford Publishing, Bloomington, IN *Toll Free Tel:* 844-688-6899, pg 208

Treehaus Communications Inc, Loveland, OH *Toll Free Tel:* 800-638-4287 (orders), pg 209

TriQuarterly Books, Evanston, IL *Toll Free Tel:* 800-621-2736 (orders only), pg 209

TRISTAN Publishing, Minneapolis, MN *Toll Free Tel:* 866-545-1383, pg 209

Triumph Books LLC, Chicago, IL *Toll Free Tel:* 800-888-4741 (cust serv), pg 209

Trusted Media Brands Inc, New York, NY *Toll Free Tel:* 877-732-4438 (cust serv), pg 210

Tundra Book Group, Toronto, ON Canada *Toll Free Tel:* 888-523-9292 (orders); 800-588-1074, pg 421

Turnstone Press, Winnipeg, MB Canada *Toll Free Tel:* 888-363-7718, pg 421

Tuttle Publishing, North Clarendon, VT *Toll Free Tel:* 800-526-2778 *Toll Free Fax:* 800-FAX-TUTL (329-8885), pg 211

Twenty-First Century Books, Minneapolis, MN *Toll Free Tel:* 800-328-4929 *Toll Free Fax:* 800-332-1132, pg 211

Twenty-Third Publications, New London, CT *Toll Free Tel:* 800-321-0411 (orders) *Toll Free Fax:* 800-572-0788, pg 211

Tyndale House Publishers Inc, Carol Stream, IL *Toll Free Tel:* 800-323-9400; 855-277-9400 *Toll Free Fax:* 866-622-9474, pg 211

Ulysses Press, Brooklyn, NY *Toll Free Tel:* 800-377-2542, pg 212

Unarius Academy of Science Publications, El Cajon, CA *Toll Free Tel:* 800-475-7062, pg 212

Union Square & Co, New York, NY *Toll Free Tel:* 800-367-9692 *Toll Free Fax:* 800-542-7567, pg 212

United States Holocaust Memorial Museum, Washington, DC *Toll Free Tel:* 800-259-9998 (orders), pg 213

United States Institute of Peace Press, Washington, DC *Toll Free Tel:* 800-868-8064 (cust serv), pg 213

UNITED STATES PHARMACOPEIA (USP)

United States Pharmacopeia (USP), Rockville, MD *Toll Free Tel:* 800-227-8772, pg 213

Universal-Publishers Inc, Irvine, CA *Toll Free Tel:* 800-636-8329 (US only), pg 213

University of Alaska Press, Fairbanks, AK *Toll Free Tel:* 888-252-6657 (US only), pg 214

The University of Arizona Press, Tucson, AZ *Toll Free Tel:* 800-621-2736 (orders) *Toll Free Fax:* 800-621-8476 (orders), pg 214

University of British Columbia Press, Vancouver, BC Canada *Toll Free Tel:* 877-377-9378 *Toll Free Fax:* 800-668-0821, pg 422

University of Chicago Press, Chicago, IL *Toll Free Tel:* 800-621-2736 (orders), pg 215

University of Delaware Press, Newark, DE *Toll Free Tel:* 800-462-6420 (orders), pg 215

University of Hawaii Press, Honolulu, HI *Toll Free Tel:* 888-UHPRESS (847-7377) *Toll Free Fax:* 800-650-7811, pg 216

University of Iowa Press, Iowa City, IA *Toll Free Tel:* 800-621-2736 (orders only) *Toll Free Fax:* 800-621-8476 (orders only), pg 216

University of Missouri Press, Columbia, MO *Toll Free Tel:* 800-621-2736 (orders) *Toll Free Fax:* 800-621-8476 (orders), pg 217

University of Nebraska Press, Lincoln, NE *Toll Free Tel:* 800-848-6224 (cust serv & US orders) *Toll Free Fax:* 800-272-6817 (cust serv & US orders), pg 217

The University of North Carolina Press, Chapel Hill, NC *Toll Free Tel:* 800-848-3224 (orders) *Toll Free Fax:* 800-272-6817 (orders), pg 218

University of South Carolina Press, Columbia, SC *Toll Free Tel:* 800-768-2500 (orders) *Toll Free Fax:* 800-868-0740 (orders), pg 220

University of Tennessee Press, Knoxville, TN *Toll Free Tel:* 800-621-2736 (orders) *Toll Free Fax:* 800-621-2736 (orders), pg 220

University of Virginia Press, Charlottesville, VA *Toll Free Tel:* 800-831-3406 *Toll Free Fax:* 877-288-6400, pg 220

University of Washington Press, Seattle, WA *Toll Free Tel:* 800-537-5487 (orders), pg 220

University of Wisconsin Press, Madison, WI *Toll Free Tel:* 800-621-2736 (book orders) *Toll Free Fax:* 800-621-2736 (book orders), pg 221

University Press of America Inc, Lanham, MD *Toll Free Tel:* 800-462-6420, pg 221

University Press of Colorado, Denver, CO *Toll Free Tel:* 800-621-2736 (orders), pg 221

University Press of Florida, Gainesville, FL *Toll Free Tel:* 800-226-3822 (orders only) *Toll Free Fax:* 800-680-1955 (orders only), pg 221

University Press of Mississippi, Jackson, MS *Toll Free Tel:* 800-737-7788 (orders & cust serv), pg 222

Upper Room Books, Nashville, TN *Toll Free Tel:* 800-972-0433, pg 223

Upstart Books™, Madison, WI *Toll Free Tel:* 800-356-1200 (orders); 800-962-4463 (cust serv) *Toll Free Fax:* 800-245-1329 (orders), pg 223

US Conference of Catholic Bishops, Washington, DC *Toll Free Tel:* 800-235-8722, pg 223

US Games Systems Inc, Stamford, CT *Toll Free Tel:* 800-54-GAMES (544-2637), pg 223

US Government Publishing Office (GPO), Washington, DC *Toll Free Tel:* 866-512-1800 (orders), pg 223

Utah Geological Survey, Salt Lake City, UT *Toll Free Tel:* 888-UTAH-MAP (882-4627, bookshop), pg 223

Vandamere Press, St Petersburg, FL *Toll Free Tel:* 800-551-7776, pg 223

Vanderbilt University Press, Nashville, TN *Toll Free Tel:* 800-848-6224 (orders only), pg 224

Vault.com Inc, New York, NY *Toll Free Tel:* 800-535-2074, pg 224

Voyager Sopris Learning Inc, Dallas, TX *Toll Free Tel:* 800-547-6747 *Toll Free Fax:* 888-819-7767, pg 225

Walch Education, Portland, ME *Toll Free Tel:* 800-558-2846; 800-341-6094 (cust serv) *Toll Free Fax:* 888-991-5755, pg 225

Warner Press, Anderson, IN *Toll Free Tel:* 800-741-7721 (orders), pg 226

Washington State University Press, Pullman, WA *Toll Free Tel:* 800-354-7360 (orders), pg 226

Water Environment Federation, Alexandria, VA *Toll Free Tel:* 800-666-0206 (cust serv), pg 226

Water Resources Publications LLC, Highlands Ranch, CO *Toll Free Tel:* 800-736-2405 *Toll Free Fax:* 800-616-1971, pg 226

WaterBrook, Colorado Springs, CO *Toll Free Tel:* 800-603-7051 (orders), pg 226

Watermark Publishing, Honolulu, HI *Toll Free Tel:* 866-900-BOOK (900-2665), pg 226

Wayne State University Press, Detroit, MI *Toll Free Tel:* 800-978-7323, pg 226

Wayside Publishing, Freeport, ME *Toll Free Tel:* 888-302-2519, pg 227

Weigl Educational Publishers Ltd, Calgary, AB Canada *Toll Free Tel:* 800-668-0766, pg 424

Well-Trained Mind Press, Charles City, VA *Toll Free Tel:* 877-322-3445, pg 227

Wesleyan Publishing House, Fishers, IN *Toll Free Tel:* 800-493-7539 *Toll Free Fax:* 800-788-3535, pg 227

West Academic, St Paul, MN *Toll Free Tel:* 877-888-1330, pg 227

Westminster John Knox Press (WJK), Louisville, KY *Toll Free Tel:* 800-523-1631 (US & CN) *Toll Free Fax:* 800-541-5113 (US & CN), pg 228

Whitaker House, New Kensington, PA *Toll Free Tel:* 800-444-4484 (sales), pg 228

Whittier Publications Inc, Lido Beach, NY *Toll Free Tel:* 800-897-TEXT (897-8398), pg 229

Whole Person Associates Inc, Duluth, MN *Toll Free Tel:* 800-247-6789, pg 229

Wide World of Maps Inc, Phoenix, AZ *Toll Free Tel:* 800-279-7654, pg 229

Michael Wiese Productions, Studio City, CA *Toll Free Tel:* 800-833-5738 (orders), pg 229

Wilderness Adventures Press Inc, Belgrade, MT *Toll Free Tel:* 866-400-2012 *Toll Free Fax:* 866-400-2013, pg 229

Wiley-Blackwell, Hoboken, NJ *Toll Free Tel:* 800-567-4797 *Toll Free Fax:* 800-565-6802, pg 229

John Wiley & Sons Canada Ltd, Toronto, ON Canada *Toll Free Tel:* 800-567-4797 *Toll Free Fax:* 800-565-6802 (orders), pg 424

John Wiley & Sons Inc, Hoboken, NJ *Toll Free Tel:* 800-225-5945 (cust serv), pg 230

John Wiley & Sons Inc Global Education, Hoboken, NJ *Toll Free Tel:* 800-567-4797 *Toll Free Fax:* 800-565-6802, pg 230

John Wiley & Sons Inc Professional Development, Hoboken, NJ *Toll Free Tel:* 800-567-4797 *Toll Free Fax:* 800-565-6802, pg 230

Wilfrid Laurier University Press, Waterloo, ON Canada *Toll Free Tel:* 866-836-5551 (CN & US), pg 424

Willow Creek Press, Minocqua, WI *Toll Free Tel:* 800-850-9453, pg 230

Windsor Books, Bayshore, NY *Toll Free Tel:* 800-321-5934, pg 230

Winters Publishing, Greensburg, IN *Toll Free Tel:* 800-457-3230, pg 231

Winterthur Museum, Garden & Library, Winterthur, DE *Toll Free Tel:* 800-448-3883, pg 231

Wisconsin Department of Public Instruction, Madison, WI *Toll Free Tel:* 800-441-4563 (US only); 800-243-8782 (US only), pg 231

Wisdom Publications Inc, Somerville, MA *Toll Free Tel:* 800-272-4050 (orders), pg 231

Wizards of the Coast LLC, Renton, WA *Toll Free Tel:* 800-324-6496, pg 231

Alan Wofsy Fine Arts, San Francisco, CA *Toll Free Tel:* 800-660-6403, pg 231

Wolters Kluwer Law & Business, New York, NY *Toll Free Tel:* 800-234-1660 (cust serv), pg 232

Wood Lake Publishing Inc, Kelowna, BC Canada *Toll Free Tel:* 800-663-2775 (orders & cust serv) *Toll Free Fax:* 888-841-9991 (orders & cust serv), pg 425

Woodbine House, Bethesda, MD *Toll Free Tel:* 800-843-7323, pg 232

Workman Publishing, New York, NY *Toll Free Tel:* 800-759-0190, pg 232

World Bank Publications, Washington, DC *Toll Free Tel:* 800-645-7247 (cust serv), pg 233

World Book Inc, Chicago, IL *Toll Free Tel:* 800-967-5325 (consumer sales, US); 800-975-3250 (school & lib sales, US); 800-837-5365 (school & lib sales, CN) *Toll Free Fax:* 888-922-3766, pg 233

World Trade Press LLC, Traverse City, MI *Toll Free Tel:* 800-833-8586, pg 234

Worldwide Library, Toronto, ON Canada *Toll Free Tel:* 888-432-4879, pg 425

Xlibris Corp, Bloomington, IN *Toll Free Tel:* 844-714-8691; 888-795-4274, pg 234

Yale University Press, New Haven, CT *Toll Free Tel:* 800-405-1619 (cust serv) *Toll Free Fax:* 800-406-9145 (cust serv), pg 235

YMAA Publication Center Inc, Wolfeboro, NH *Toll Free Tel:* 800-669-8892, pg 235

YWAM Publishing, Seattle, WA *Toll Free Tel:* 800-922-2143, pg 236

Zaner-Bloser Inc, Grandview Heights, OH *Toll Free Tel:* 800-421-3018 (cust serv) *Toll Free Fax:* 800-992-6087 (orders), pg 236

Zest Books, Minneapolis, MN *Toll Free Tel:* 800-328-4929 *Toll Free Fax:* 800-332-1132, pg 236

Zondervan, Grand Rapids, MI *Toll Free Tel:* 800-226-1122; 800-727-1309 (retail orders) *Toll Free Fax:* 800-698-3256 (retail orders), pg 236

Index to Sections

A

Abstracting	429
Accounts - Bookstores—Wholesalers	1305
Accounts - Libraries—Wholesalers	1305
Accounts - Schools—Wholesalers	1305
Ad Placement – Software	1359
Adaptations, Novelizations	429
Adhesive Binding - Hard	1235
Adhesive Binding - Soft	1235
Advertising & Promotion Copywriting	429
Advertising - Promotional Associations	489
Advertising Agencies	1099
Advertising, Promotion Consultants	1339
App Development – Software	1359
Approval Plans—Wholesalers	1306
Art & Design	1217
Art Editing	1407
Artists & Art Services	1411
Artists & Art Services — Activity Index	1407
Art Editing	1407
Book Design	1407
Calligraphy	1407
Cartoons	1407
Cover Design	1407
Electronic Layout	1407
Film Animation	1407
Icon Design	1407
Illustration	1408
Jacket Design	1408
Layout	1408
Letterheads	1408
Lettering	1408
Logos & Corporate Identity	1409
Map Design	1409
Paste-up	1409
Pictorial Statistics	1409
Poster Design	1409
Prototyping	1409
Retouching	1409
Silk Screen	1409
Spot Drawings	1409
Technical Illustration	1409
Templating	1409
Trademarks	1410
Typesetting	1410
Audiobook Production – Services	1361
AV Materials—Wholesalers	1306
Awards, Prize Contests, Fellowships & Grants	569

B

Bibliographies	429
Binders	1101
Binding Supplies	1263
Binding	1101
Book Clubs	1141
Book Clubs Consultants	1339
Book Covers	1263
Book Design	1407
Book Distributors & Sales Representatives	1285
Book Exhibits	1139
Book Exporters & Importers	1327
Book Jackets	1263
Book Lists & Catalogs	1145
Book Manufacturing Associations	489
Book Manufacturing Equipment	1275
Book Printing - Hardbound	1235
Book Printing - Mass Market	1236
Book Printing - Professional	1236
Book Printing - Softbound	1236
Book Producers	1353
Book Review & Index Journals & Services	1129
Book Review Syndicates	1127
Book Trade & Allied Associations	493
Book Trade & Allied Associations — Index	489
Advertising - Promotional	489
Book Manufacturing	489
Book Trade Suppliers	489
Bookselling	489
Editorial	489
Library	489
Literacy	490
Literary	490
Magazine & Press	490
Media - Communications	490
Publishing	490
Publishing Services	491
Writers	491
Book Trade Suppliers Associations	489
Booklets	1101
Bookselling Associations	489
Bound Galleys	1236
Brochures, Pamphlets	1101
Broker for Manufacturing	429
Burst Binding	1237
Business, Finance Consultants	1339

C

Calendar of Book Trade & Promotional Events	535
Alphabetical Index of Events	531
Alphabetical Index of Sponsors	527
Calendar Printing	1237
Calligraphy	1407
Canadian Publishers	395
Cartoons	1407
Casebinding	1237
Catalog Cards & Kits—Wholesalers	1306
Catalog Printing	1237
Cataloging & Processing—Wholesalers	1306
CD-ROM – Services	1362
CD-ROM Authoring – Software	1359

INDEX TO SECTIONS

CD-ROM Mastering – Hardware 1359
Chart & Graph – Software 1360
Clip Art – Software 1360
Clipping Bureaus 1383
Color Separation – Software 1360
Color Separations 1217
Columnists & Commentators 1125
    Columnists & Commentators — Subject Index 1123
        Animals, Pets 1123
        Art, Antiques 1123
        Automotive 1123
        Books 1123
        Business, Finance 1123
        Consumer Education 1123
        Fashion 1123
        Film, Radio, TV, Video 1123
        Food, Wine 1123
        Gardening, Plants 1123
        General Commentary 1123
        Health, Nutrition 1123
        House & Home 1123
        Humor 1123
        Inspirational 1123
        Music, Dance, Theater 1123
        National & World Affairs 1123
        Personal Advice, Counseling 1123
        Personalities 1123
        Photography 1123
        Politics 1123
        Science, Technology 1123
        Sports, Recreation 1123
        Travel, Resorts 1123
Comic Book Printing 1238
Company Index 709, 1433
Complete Book Manufacturing 1207
Composition – Systems 1361
Computer Software—Wholesalers 1306
Computer Technology Consultants 1339
Computerized Typesetting 1217
Condensations 429
Consultants 1343
    Consultants — Activity Index 1339
        Advertising, Promotion 1339
        Book Clubs 1339
        Business, Finance 1339
        Computer Technology 1339
        Electronic Publishing 1339
        Legal Services 1339
        Libraries 1339
        Literary Scout 1339
        Management 1340
        Manufacturing, Production 1340
        Marketing 1340
        Mergers, Acquisitions 1340
        Paper, Paper Products 1340
        Printing 1340
        Publishing 1340
        Recruiter 1341
        Rights, Permissions 1341
Conversion – Systems 1361
Copy-Editing 429

Courses for the Book Trade 561
Cover Design 1407

D

Data Processing Services 1218
Desktop Publishing – Services 1362
Desktop Publishing – Systems 1361
Dictionaries & Reference Books—Wholesalers 1306
Die-Cutting 1101, 1238
Digital Printing 1238
Direct Mail Specialists 1115
Display Devices – Hardware 1359
Displays 1101
Distribution & Mailing 1275
Draw & Paint – Software 1360
Drop Shipping—Wholesalers 1306

E

Ebook Conversion – Services 1362
Editing – Systems 1361
Edition (Hardcover) Binding 1238
Editorial Associations 489
Editorial Services 435
    Editorial Services — Activity Index 429
        Abstracting 429
        Adaptations, Novelizations 429
        Advertising & Promotion Copywriting 429
        Bibliographies 429
        Broker for Manufacturing 429
        Condensations 429
        Copy-Editing 429
        Fact Checking 430
        Ghostwriting 430
        Indexing 430
        Interviewing 430
        Line Editing 431
        Manuscript Analysis 431
        Permissions 431
        Photo Research 431
        Proofreading 432
        Research 432
        Rewriting 432
        Special Assignment Writing 433
        Statistics 433
        Technical Writing 433
        Transcription Editing 433
        Typemarking 433
Educational Kits 1101
Electronic Layout 1407
Electronic Publishing Consultants 1339
Embossing 1238
Employment Agencies 1381
Engraving 1101, 1239
EP Utility – Software 1360
Export Representatives 1331

F

Fact Checking 430
File Conversion – Software 1360
Film Animation 1407
Film Laminating 1239

INDEX TO SECTIONS

Foiling 1239
Folders 1101
Font Editors – Software 1360
Font Editors – Systems 1361
Fonts & Faces – Software 1360
Foreign Language & Bilingual Materials—
    Wholesalers 1306
Foreign Language Composition 1218
Foundations 525
Front End Systems – Systems 1361

G

General Trade Books - Hardcover—Wholesalers 1307
Ghostwriting 430
Gilding 1239
Glue or Paste Binding 1239
Government Publications—Wholesalers ... 1307
Graphic Systems – Systems 1361
Gravure 1240

H

Hand Bookbinding 1240
Hardware 1359
Holograms 1240

I

Icon Design 1407
Illustration Agents 485
Illustration 1408
Imports—Wholesalers 1307
Imprinting 1101
Imprints, Subsidiaries & Distributors 333
Index to Sections 1089, 1541
Indexing 430, 1218
Input Devices – Hardware 1359
Interfaces – Hardware 1359
Interviewing 430

J

Jacket Design 1408
Journal Printing 1240
Juvenile & Young Adult Books—Wholesalers ... 1307

L

Large Print & Braille Materials—Wholesalers ... 1307
Layout 1408
Lecture Agents 487
Legal Services Consultants 1339
Letterheads 1408
Lettering 1408
Letterpress 1240
Libraries Consultants 1339
Library Associations 489
Line Editing 431
Literacy Associations 490
Literary Agents 447
Literary Associations 490
Literary Scout Consultants 1339
Litho Printing 1240

Logos & Corporate Identity 1409
Looseleaf Binding 1240

M

Magazine & Press Associations 490
Magazines for the Trade 699
Mailing List Brokers & Services 1119
Mailing, Duplicating & Fax Services 1117
Management Consultants 1340
Manual Printing 1240
Manufacturing Brokers or Brokering 1275
Manufacturing Materials 1265
    Manufacturing Materials Index 1263
        Binding Supplies 1263
        Book Covers 1263
        Book Jackets 1263
        Paper Merchants 1263
        Paper Mills 1263
        Printing Ink 1263
Manufacturing Services & Equipment 1277
    Manufacturing Services & Equipment Index ... 1275
        Book Manufacturing Equipment 1275
        Distribution & Mailing 1275
        Manufacturing Brokers or Brokering ... 1275
Manufacturing, Production Consultants ... 1340
Manuscript Analysis 431
Map Design 1409
Map Printing 1241
Maps & Atlases—Wholesalers 1308
Marketing Consultants 1340
Mathematics & Chemistry Composition ... 1218
McCain Sewn Binding 1241
Media - Communications Associations 490
Mergers, Acquisitions Consultants 1340
Metal Composition 1241
Microforms—Wholesalers 1308
Modems – Hardware 1359
Mounting & Finishing 1101
Music Composition 1218

N

News Services & Feature Syndicates 1189
Non-Roman Alphabets 1218
Notch Binding 1241

O

OCR – Hardware 1359
Offset Printing - Sheetfed 1241
Offset Printing - Web 1242
On Demand Printing 1242
Online Ordering—Wholesalers 1308
OP Search—Wholesalers 1308
Other – Hardware 1359
Other – Services 1362
Other – Software 1361
Other – Systems 1361

P

Page Composition – Software 1360
Paper Merchants 1263
Paper Mills 1263

INDEX TO SECTIONS

Paper, Paper Products Consultants 1340
Paperback Books - Mass Market—Wholesalers 1308
Paperback Books - Trade—Wholesalers 1308
Paste-up 1409
Perfect (Adhesive) Binding 1242
Periodicals—Wholesalers 1309
Permissions 431
Personnel Index 785, 1465
Photo Research 431
Photocomposition 1243
Photographers 1419
Photography 1101
Phototypesetters – Hardware 1359
Pictorial Statistics 1409
Plastic Comb Binding 1243
Platforms – Hardware 1359
Poster Design 1409
Posters 1101
Prebinders to Schools & Libraries 1325
Prebinding—Wholesalers 1309
Prepress Services 1221
    Prepress Services Index 1217
        Art & Design 1217
        Color Separations 1217
        Computerized Typesetting 1217
        Data Processing Services 1218
        Foreign Language Composition 1218
        Indexing 1218
        Mathematics & Chemistry Composition 1218
        Music Composition 1218
        Non-Roman Alphabets 1218
        Production Services 1218
        Proofing 1219
        Scientific Composition 1219
        UPC & Bar Code Services 1219
        Word Processing Interface 1219
Printers (Laser & Non-Impact) – Hardware 1359
Printing Consultants 1340
Printing Ink 1263
Printing, Binding & Book Finishing 1247
    Printing, Binding & Book Finishing Index 1235
        Adhesive Binding - Hard 1235
        Adhesive Binding - Soft 1235
        Book Printing - Hardbound 1235
        Book Printing - Mass Market 1236
        Book Printing - Professional 1236
        Book Printing - Softbound 1236
        Bound Galleys 1236
        Burst Binding 1237
        Calendar Printing 1237
        Casebinding 1237
        Catalog Printing 1237
        Comic Book Printing 1238
        Die-Cutting 1238
        Digital Printing 1238
        Edition (Hardcover) Binding 1238
        Embossing 1238
        Engraving 1239
        Film Laminating 1239
        Foiling 1239
        Gilding 1239
        Glue or Paste Binding 1239
        Gravure 1240
        Hand Bookbinding 1240
        Holograms 1240
        Journal Printing 1240
        Letterpress 1240
        Litho Printing 1240
        Looseleaf Binding 1240
        Manual Printing 1240
        Map Printing 1241
        McCain Sewn Binding 1241
        Metal Composition 1241
        Notch Binding 1241
        Offset Printing - Sheetfed 1241
        Offset Printing - Web 1242
        On Demand Printing 1242
        Perfect (Adhesive) Binding 1242
        Photocomposition 1243
        Plastic Comb Binding 1243
        Saddle Stitch Binding 1243
        Short Run Printing 1244
        Side Stitch Binding 1244
        Smyth-type Sewn Binding 1245
        Specialty Binding 1245
        Spiral Binding 1245
        Struck-Image Composition 1245
        Textbook Printing - College 1245
        Textbook Printing - El-Hi 1245
        Wire-O Binding 1246
        Workbook Printing 1246
Printing 1101
Production Services 1218
Promotional Boxes 1101
Promotional Printing & Allied Services 1103
    Promotional Printing & Allied Services — Activity Index 1101
        Binders 1101
        Binding 1101
        Booklets 1101
        Brochures, Pamphlets 1101
        Die-Cutting 1101
        Displays 1101
        Educational Kits 1101
        Engraving 1101
        Folders 1101
        Imprinting 1101
        Mounting & Finishing 1101
        Photography 1101
        Posters 1101
        Printing 1101
        Promotional Boxes 1101
        Silk Screen 1101
        Slip Cases 1102
        Typography 1102
        Varnishing 1102
Proofing 1219
Proofreading 432
Prototyping 1409
Public Relations Services 1107
Publishing Associations 490
Publishing Consultants 1340

INDEX TO SECTIONS

Publishing Services Associations ... 491
Publishing Systems, Services & Technology ... 1363
   Publishing Systems, Services & Technology Index ... 1359
      Hardware ... 1359
         CD-ROM Mastering ... 1359
         Display Devices ... 1359
         Input Devices ... 1359
         Interfaces ... 1359
         Modems ... 1359
         OCR ... 1359
         Other ... 1359
         Phototypesetters ... 1359
         Platforms ... 1359
         Printers (Laser & Non-Impact) ... 1359
         Scanners & Digitizers ... 1359
      Services ... 1361
         Audiobook Production ... 1361
         CD-ROM ... 1362
         Desktop Publishing ... 1362
         Ebook Conversion ... 1362
         Other ... 1362
         SGML ... 1362
         Web Development ... 1362
      Software ... 1359
         Ad Placement ... 1359
         App Development ... 1359
         CD-ROM Authoring ... 1359
         Chart & Graph ... 1360
         Clip Art ... 1360
         Color Separation ... 1360
         Draw & Paint ... 1360
         EP Utility ... 1360
         File Conversion ... 1360
         Font Editors ... 1360
         Fonts & Faces ... 1360
         Other ... 1361
         Page Composition ... 1360
         SGML Programs ... 1360
         Text Formatters ... 1360
         Tracking ... 1360
         Word Processing & Text Editing ... 1360
      Systems ... 1361
         Composition ... 1361
         Conversion ... 1361
         Desktop Publishing ... 1361
         Editing ... 1361
         Font Editors ... 1361
         Front End Systems ... 1361
         Graphic Systems ... 1361
         Other ... 1361

R

Radio Programs Featuring Books ... 1197
Radio, TV & Cable Networks ... 1193
Recruiter Consultants ... 1341
Reference Books for the Trade ... 681
Remainders & Overstock—Wholesalers ... 1309
Research ... 432
Retouching ... 1409
Rewriting ... 432
Rights, Permissions Consultants ... 1341

S

Saddle Stitch Binding ... 1243
Scanners & Digitizers – Hardware ... 1359
Scholarly Books—Wholesalers ... 1309
Sci-Tech & Medicine—Wholesalers ... 1309
Scientific Composition ... 1219
Serials Featuring Books ... 1147
Services ... 1361
SGML – Services ... 1362
SGML Programs – Software ... 1360
Shipping Services ... 1333
Shipping Suppliers ... 1337
Short Run Printing ... 1244
Side Stitch Binding ... 1244
Silk Screen ... 1101, 1409
Slip Cases ... 1102
Smyth-type Sewn Binding ... 1245
Software ... 1359
Special Assignment Writing ... 433
Specialty Binding ... 1245
Spiral Binding ... 1245
Spot Drawings ... 1409
Standing Orders & Continuations—Wholesalers ... 1309
Statistics ... 433
Stock Photo Agencies ... 1427
Struck-Image Composition ... 1245
Systems ... 1361

T

Technical Illustration ... 1409
Technical Writing ... 433
Templating ... 1409
Text Formatters – Software ... 1360
Textbook Printing - College ... 1245
Textbook Printing - El-Hi ... 1245
Textbooks - College—Wholesalers ... 1310
Textbooks - Elementary—Wholesalers ... 1309
Textbooks - Secondary—Wholesalers ... 1309
Toll Free Directory, Publishers ... 1079
Tracking – Software ... 1360
Trademarks ... 1410
Transcription Editing ... 433
Translators & Interpreters ... 1399
   Translators & Interpreters — Source Language
      Index ... 1387
      Afrikaans ... 1387
      Albanian ... 1387
      Arabic ... 1387
      Armenian ... 1387
      Belarussian ... 1387
      Bengali ... 1387
      Bulgarian ... 1387
      Burmese ... 1387
      Catalan ... 1387
      Chinese ... 1387
      Czech ... 1387
      Danish ... 1387
      Dutch ... 1387
      English ... 1387

INDEX TO SECTIONS

Esperanto 1388
Estonian 1388
Finnish 1388
Flemish 1388
French 1388
Gaelic 1388
Georgian 1388
German 1388
Greek 1388
Hebrew 1389
Hindi 1389
Hungarian 1389
Icelandic 1389
Indonesian 1389
Italian 1389
Japanese 1389
Javanese 1389
Khmer 1389
Korean 1389
Kurdish 1389
Latin 1389
Latvian 1389
Lithuanian 1389
Macedonian 1390
Malagasy 1390
Malayalam 1390
Malaysian 1390
Nepali 1390
Norwegian 1390
Persian 1390
Polish 1390
Portuguese 1390
Provencal 1390
Punjabi 1390
Romanian 1390
Russian 1390
Serbo-Croatian 1390
Sinhalese 1390
Slovak 1390
Slovene 1391
Spanish 1391
Swahili 1391
Swedish 1391
Tagalog 1391
Tamil 1391
Telugu 1391
Thai 1391
Turkish 1391
Ukrainian 1391
Urdu 1391
Vietnamese 1391
Welsh 1391
Yiddish 1391
Translators & Interpreters — Target Language
  Index 1393
  Afrikaans 1393
  Albanian 1393
  Arabic 1393
  Armenian 1393
  Belarussian 1393
  Bengali 1393

Bulgarian 1393
Burmese 1393
Catalan 1393
Chinese 1393
Czech 1393
Danish 1393
Dutch 1393
English 1393
Esperanto 1394
Estonian 1394
Finnish 1394
Flemish 1394
French 1394
Gaelic 1394
Georgian 1394
German 1394
Greek 1394
Hebrew 1394
Hindi 1395
Hungarian 1395
Icelandic 1395
Indonesian 1395
Italian 1395
Japanese 1395
Javanese 1395
Khmer 1395
Korean 1395
Kurdish 1395
Latin 1395
Latvian 1395
Lithuanian 1395
Macedonian 1395
Malagasy 1395
Malayalam 1396
Malaysian 1396
Nepali 1396
Norwegian 1396
Persian 1396
Polish 1396
Portuguese 1396
Provencal 1396
Punjabi 1396
Romanian 1396
Russian 1396
Serbo-Croatian 1396
Sinhalese 1396
Slovak 1396
Slovene 1396
Spanish 1396
Swahili 1397
Swedish 1397
Tagalog 1397
Tamil 1397
Telugu 1397
Thai 1397
Turkish 1397
Ukrainian 1397
Urdu 1397
Vietnamese 1397
Welsh 1397
Yiddish 1397

INDEX TO SECTIONS

TV Programs Featuring Books 1201
Typemarking 433
Typesetting 1410
Typing & Word Processing Services 1385
Typography 1102

U

U.S. Publishers 1
   U.S. Publishers — Geographic Index 239
   U.S. Publishers — Subject Index 277
      Accounting 277
      Advertising 277
      Aeronautics, Aviation 277
      African American Studies 277
      Agriculture 278
      Alternative 278
      Americana, Regional 278
      Animals, Pets 279
      Anthropology 279
      Antiques 280
      Archaeology 280
      Architecture & Interior Design 280
      Art 281
      Asian Studies 282
      Astrology, Occult 282
      Astronomy 282
      Automotive 282
      Behavioral Sciences 283
      Biblical Studies 283
      Biography, Memoirs 284
      Biological Sciences 285
      Business 285
      Career Development 287
      Chemistry, Chemical Engineering 287
      Child Care & Development 287
      Civil Engineering 288
      Communications 288
      Computer Science 288
      Computers 288
      Cookery 289
      Crafts, Games, Hobbies 289
      Criminology 290
      Developing Countries 290
      Disability, Special Needs 290
      Drama, Theater 291
      Earth Sciences 291
      Economics 291
      Education 292
      Electronics, Electrical Engineering 293
      Energy 294
      Engineering (General) 294
      English as a Second Language 294
      Environmental Studies 294
      Erotica 295
      Ethnicity 295
      Fashion 296
      Fiction 296
      Film, Video 298
      Finance 298
      Foreign Countries 299
      Gardening, Plants 299
      Genealogy 299
      Geography, Geology 299
      Government, Political Science 300
      Health, Nutrition 301
      History 302
      House & Home 304
      How-to 304
      Human Relations 305
      Humor 305
      Inspirational, Spirituality 306
      Journalism 306
      Labor, Industrial Relations 306
      Language Arts, Linguistics 307
      Law 307
      LGBTQ+ 308
      Library & Information Sciences 308
      Literature, Literary Criticism, Essays 308
      Management 310
      Maritime 310
      Marketing 310
      Mathematics 311
      Mechanical Engineering 311
      Medicine, Nursing, Dentistry 311
      Military Science 312
      Music, Dance 312
      Mysteries, Suspense 313
      Native American Studies 313
      Natural History 314
      Nonfiction (General) 314
      Outdoor Recreation 316
      Parapsychology 316
      Philosophy 317
      Photography 317
      Physical Sciences 318
      Physics 318
      Poetry 318
      Pop Culture 319
      Psychology, Psychiatry 320
      Public Administration 320
      Publishing & Book Trade Reference 320
      Radio, TV 321
      Real Estate 321
      Regional Interests 321
      Religion - Buddhist 321
      Religion - Catholic 322
      Religion - Hindu 322
      Religion - Islamic 322
      Religion - Jewish 322
      Religion - Other 323
      Religion - Protestant 323
      Romance 324
      Science (General) 324
      Science Fiction, Fantasy 325
      Securities 326
      Self-Help 326
      Social Sciences, Sociology 327
      Sports, Athletics 328
      Technology 328
      Theology 329
      Transportation 329
      Travel & Tourism 330

INDEX TO SECTIONS

- Veterinary Science 330
- Western Fiction 330
- Wine & Spirits 331
- Women's Studies 331
- U.S. Publishers — Type of Publication Index 247
  - Association Presses 247
  - Audiobooks 247
  - AV Materials 248
  - Belles Lettres 248
  - Bibles 248
  - Bibliographies 248
  - Braille Books 249
  - Children's Books 249
  - Computer Software 250
  - Databases 250
  - Dictionaries, Encyclopedias 251
  - Directories, Reference Books 251
  - Ebooks or CD-ROMs 252
  - Fine Editions, Illustrated Books 255
  - Foreign Language & Bilingual Books 255
  - General Trade Books - Hardcover 256
  - Juvenile & Young Adult Books 258
  - Large Print Books 260
  - Maps, Atlases 260
  - Paperback Books - Mass Market 260
  - Paperback Books - Trade 261
  - Periodicals, Journals 264
  - Professional Books 266
  - Reprints 268
  - Scholarly Books 269
  - Sidelines 271
  - Subscription & Mail Order Books 271
  - Textbooks - College 272
  - Textbooks - Elementary 271
  - Textbooks - Secondary 272
  - Translations 273
  - University Presses 274
  - Videos, DVDs 275
- University Press Books—Wholesalers 1310
- UPC & Bar Code Services 1219

V

- Varnishing 1102

W

- Web Development – Services 1362
- Wholesalers 1311
  - Wholesalers — Activity Index 1305
    - Accounts - Bookstores 1305
    - Accounts - Libraries 1305
    - Accounts - Schools 1305
    - Approval Plans 1306
    - AV Materials 1306
    - Catalog Cards & Kits 1306
    - Cataloging & Processing 1306
    - Computer Software 1306
    - Dictionaries & Reference Books 1306
    - Drop Shipping 1306
    - Foreign Language & Bilingual Materials 1306
    - General Trade Books - Hardcover 1307
    - Government Publications 1307
    - Imports 1307
    - Juvenile & Young Adult Books 1307
    - Large Print & Braille Materials 1307
    - Maps & Atlases 1308
    - Microforms 1308
    - Online Ordering 1308
    - OP Search 1308
    - Paperback Books - Mass Market 1308
    - Paperback Books - Trade 1308
    - Periodicals 1309
    - Prebinding 1309
    - Remainders & Overstock 1309
    - Scholarly Books 1309
    - Sci-Tech & Medicine 1309
    - Standing Orders & Continuations 1309
    - Textbooks - College 1310
    - Textbooks - Elementary 1309
    - Textbooks - Secondary 1309
    - University Press Books 1310
- Wire-O Binding 1246
- Word Processing & Text Editing – Software 1360
- Word Processing Interface 1219
- Workbook Printing 1246
- Writers Associations 491
- Writers' Conferences & Workshops 553

Essential Resources

for the library, publishing, research, and business professional

www.infotoday.com

For pricing and information, contact:
The ITI Subscription Service Team
Phone: 609-654-6266 x128
Email: jwelsh@infotoday.com

143 Old Marlton Pike, Medford, NJ 08055

American Library Directory™
The Literary Map to U.S. and Canadian Libraries

This is only guide that gives you fast, fingertip access to comparative data, additional resources, and sales prospects for the entire U.S. and Canada. Find full profiles on public, academic, government, and special libraries organized by state and city. Each profile includes everything from official library name and address to key personnel, holdings, collections, budget, expenditures, and special services. Two extensive volumes cover more than 31,000 libraries. Also available online.

American Book Trade Directory™
Your Complete Guide to the Book Trade Industry

This comprehensive directory brings together nearly 18,000 retail and antiquarian book dealers; 1,000 software, paperback, and remainder wholesalers; 100 national and regional book trade associations; and hundreds of book trade service providers and resources from across the U.S. and Canada. No public or academic library should be without this thorough and well-organized research tool. It's simply the most comprehensive and definitive guide available. No other resource does more to keep tabs on the enormous bookselling and distribution industry.

Library and Book Trade Almanac™
The Preeminent Handbook for Librarians and the Book Trade

Get the latest facts and insights into developments and trends within the library and book trade worlds, including the annual best-sellers lists, literary award winners, salary, materials acquisition, and other cost figures. This almanac contains contact information for state, regional, national, and international library associations. Put a wealth of industry data and insight at your immediate disposal. (Formerly published as *The Bowker Annual*.)

ALSO AVAILABLE

Annual Register of Grant Support™

Corporate Giving Directory

Literary Market Place™

Fulltext Sources Online